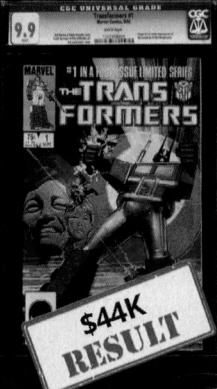

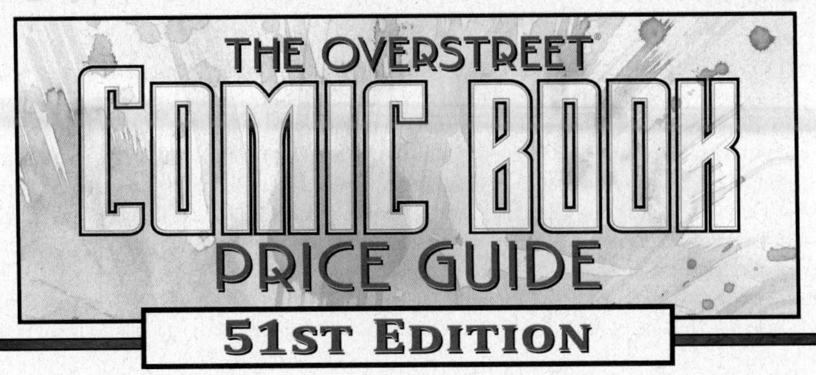

51ST EDITION

COMICS FROM THE 1500s–PRESENT INCLUDED
FULLY ILLUSTRATED CATALOGUE
& EVALUATION GUIDE

by ROBERT M. OVERSTREET

GEMSTONE PUBLISHING

Stephen A. Geppi, President & Chief Executive Officer
J.C. Vaughn, Vice-President of Publishing
Mark Huesman, Creative Director
Amanda Sheriff, Associate Editor
Mike Wilbur, Warehouse Operations
Tom Garey, Kathy Weaver, Brett Canby, Angela Phillips-Mills, Accounting Services

SPECIAL CONTRIBUTORS TO THIS EDITION

Yolanda Ramirez, Senior Research Analyst and Advisor to Robert M. Overstreet

Ed Catto • Brendon & Brian Fraim • Mark Huesman
Howie Noel • Richard Olson • Amanda Sheriff • J.C. Vaughn • Carrie Wood

SPECIAL ADVISORS TO THIS EDITION

Darren Adams • Grant Adey • Bill Alexander • David T. Alexander • Tyler Alexander • Lon Allen • Dave Anderson
David J. Anderson, DDS • Matt Ballesteros • L.E. Becker • Jim Berry • Peter Bilelis, Esq. • Steve Borock • Russ Bright
Richard M. Brown • Shawn Caffrey • Brett Carreras • Charles Cerrito • Jeff Cerrito • John Chruscinski • Paul Clairmont
Art Cloos • Bill Cole • Tim Collins • Jack Copley • Ashley Cotter-Cairns • Jesse James Criscione • Brock Dickinson
Gary Dolgoff • John Dolmayan • Walter Durajlija • Ken Dyber • Daniel Ertle • D'Arcy Farrell • Bill Fidyk • Paul M. Figura
Joseph Fiore • Stephen Fishler • Dan Fogel • Dan Gallo • James Gallo • Stephen Gentner • Josh Geppi
Steve Geppi • Douglas Gillock • Sean Goodrich • Tom Gordon III • Andy Greenham • Eric J. Groves • Jay Halstead
Terry Hoknes • Greg Holland • Steven Houston • Robert Isaac • Jeff Itkin • Dr. Steven Kahn • Nick Katradis
Ivan Kocmarek • Robert Krause • Timothy Kupin • Ben Labonog • Ben Lichtenstein • Morgan Liebman • Stephen Lipson
Paul Litch • Doug Mabry • Brian Marcus • Jim McCallum • Jon McClure • Todd McDevitt • Brent Moeshlin • Steve Mortensen
Marc Nathan • Josh Nathanson • Tom Nelson • Jamie Newbold • Karen O'Brien • Terry O'Neill • Michael Pavlic
Bill Ponseti • Mick Rabin • Alex Reece • Rob Reynolds • Stephen Ritter • Barry Sandoval • Buddy Saunders
Conan Saunders • Matt Schiffman • Alika Seki • Todd Sheffer • Frank Simmons • Marc Sims • Lauren Sisselman
Tony Starks • West Stephan • Al Stoltz • Doug Sulipa • Maggie Thompson • Michael Tierney • Ted VanLiew
Frank Verzyl • John Verzyl II • Rose Verzyl-Shukla • Lon Webb • Mike Wilbur • Harley Yee • Vincent Zurzolo, Jr.

See a full list of Overstreet Advisors on pages 1201-1205

NOTICE: Values for items listed or pictured in this book are based on author's experience, consultations with a network of advisors including collectors specializing in various categories, and actual prices realized for specific items sold through private sales and auctions. The values offered in this book are approximations influenced by many factors including condition, rarity and demand, and they should serve as only guidelines, presenting an average range of what one might expect to pay for the items. In the marketplace, knowledge and opinions held by both sellers and buyers determine prices asked and prices paid. This is not a price list of items for sale or items wanted by the author or publisher. The author and the publisher shall not be held responsible for losses that may occur in the purchase, sale or other transaction of property because of information contained herein. Efforts have been made to present accurate information, but the possibility of error exists. Readers who believe that have discovered an error are invited to mail corrective information to the author, Robert M. Overstreet, at Gemstone Publishing, 10150 York Rd., Suite 300, Hunt Valley, MD 21030. Verified corrections will be incorporated into future editions of this book.

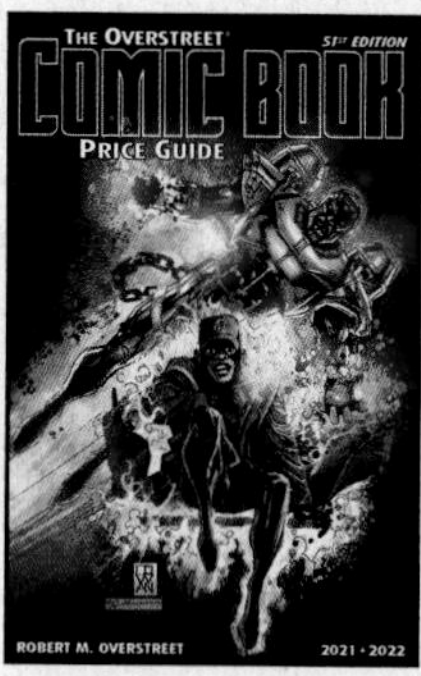

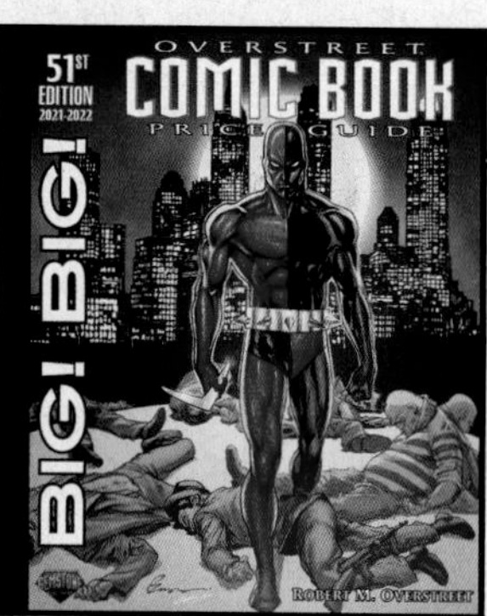

Daredevil and Echo: Art by David Mack. Daredevil and Echo ©2021 MARVEL. All Rights Reserved.

Milestone: Art by Denys Cowan, inks by Bill Sienkiewicz, colors by Christopher Sotomayor. Static and Hardware ©2021 DC Comics. Used by permission. All rights reserved.

Hero Initiative: Art by Joseph Michael Linsner. Dawn ©2021 Joseph Michael Linsner.

Big, Big Edition: Golden Age Daredevil: Art by Buzz, colors by Dash Martin.

Overstreet® is a Registered Trademark of Gemstone Publishing, Inc.

Daredevil and Echo Hardcover Edition ISBN: 978-1-60360-274-7
Daredevil and Echo Soft Cover Edition ISBN: 978-1-60360-275-4

Milestone Hardcover Edition ISBN: 978-1-60360-276-1
Milestone Soft Cover Edition ISBN: 978-1-60360-277-8

Dawn - Hero Initiative Hardcover Edition ISBN: 978-1-60360-280-8

Golden Age Daredevil - Big, Big Edition ISBN: 978-1-60360-282-2

Printed in Canada.

10 9 8 7 6 5 4 3 2 1

Fifty-first Edition: July 2021

TABLE OF CONTENTS

ACKNOWLEDGEMENTS

Kicking off our sixth decade in earnest, artist David Mack brought his beautiful take on Daredevil and Echo, the latter of which he created for Marvel. An original co-founder of Milestone Media, Denys Cowan returned to Static Shock (a.k.a. Static) and Hardware for our cover with his frequent collaborator Bill Sienkiewicz on inks and Christopher Sotomayor on colors. Joseph Michael Linsner unleashed his own creation, Dawn, on the cover of the Hero Initiative Edition, and Buzz and colorist Dash Martin delivered some two-fisted magic with the Golden Age Daredevil.

Special thanks to Gemstone's own Mark Huesman, J.C. Vaughn, Amanda Sheriff and Mike Wilbur.

Special Thanks to the Overstreet Advisors who contributed to this edition, including Darren Adams, Grant Adey, Bill Alexander, David T. Alexander, Tyler Alexander, Lon Allen, Dave Anderson, David J. Anderson, DDS, Matt Ballesteros, L.E. Becker, Jim Berry, Peter Bilelis, Esq., Steve Borock, Russ Bright, Richard M. Brown, Shawn Caffrey, Brent Carreras, Jeff & Charles Cerrito, John Chruscinski, Paul Clairmont, Art Cloos, Bill Cole, Tim Collins, Jack Copley, Ashley Cotter-Cairns, Jesse James Criscione, Brock Dickinson, Gary Dolgoff, John Dolmayan, Walter Durajlija, Ken Dyber, Jon Engel, Daniel Ertle, D'Arcy Farrell, Bill Fidyk, Paul M. Figura, Joseph Fiore, Stephen Fishler, Dan Fogel, Eric Fournier, Dan Gallo, James Gallo, Stephen Gentner, Josh Geppi, Steve Geppi, Douglas Gillock, Sean Goodrich, Tom Gordon III, Andy Greenham, Eric J. Groves, Jim Halperin, Jay Halstead, Rick Hirsch, Terry Hoknes, Greg Holland, Steven Houston, Neville Howard, Robert Isaac, Jeff Itkin, Dr. Steven Kahn, Nick Katradis, Ivan Kocmarek, Robert Krause, Timothy Kupin, Ben Labonog, Morgan Liebman, Stephen Lipson, Paul Litch, Ben Lichtenstein, Doug Mabry, Brian Marcus, Jim McCallum, Jon McClure, Todd McDevitt, Brent Moeshlin, Steve Mortensen, Marc Nathan, Josh Nathanson, Tom Nelson, Jamie Newbold, Karen O'Brien, Terry O'Neill, Michael Pavlic, Bill Ponseti, Mick Rabin, Yolanda Ramirez, Alex Reece, Rob Reynolds, Stephen & Sharon Ritter, Barry Sandoval, Buddy Saunders, Conan Saunders, Matt Schiffman, Alika Seki, Todd Sheffer, Frank Simmons, Marc Sims, Lauren Sisselman, Tony Starks, West Stephan, Al Stoltz, Doug Sulipa, Maggie Thompson, Michael Tierney, Anthony Tincini, Tom Tunnicliff, Ted VanLiew, Frank Verzyl, John Verzyl II, Rose Verzyl-Shukla, Jeff Walker, Lon Webb, Eddie Wendt, Mike Wilbur, Harley Yee, Ryan Yingling and Vincent Zurzolo, Jr., as well as to our additional contributors, including Stephen Baer, Ron Ballard, Dr. Jonathan Calure, Dawn Guzzo, and Kevin Poling. Without their active participation, this project would not have been possible.

Additionally, I would like to personally extend my thanks to all of those who encouraged and supported first the creation of and then subsequently the expansion of the Guide over the past four decades. While it's impossible in this brief space to individually acknowledge every individual, mention is certainly due to Lon Allen (Golden Age data), Mark Arnold (Harvey data), Larry Bigman (Frazetta-Williamson data), Bill Blackbeard (Platinum Age cover photos), Steve Borock and Mark Haspel (Grading), Glenn Bray (Kurtzman data), Gary M. Carter (DC data), J. B. Clifford Jr. (EC data), Gary Coddington (Superman data), Gary Colabuono (Golden Age ashcan data), Wilt Conine (Fawcett data), Chris Cormier (Miracleman data), Dr. S. M. Davidson (Cupples & Leon data), Al Dellinges (Kubert data), Stephen Fishler (10-Point Grading system), Chris Friesen (Glossary additions), David Gerstein (Walt Disney Comics data), Kevin Hancer (Tarzan data), Charles Heffelfinger and Jim Ivey (March of Comics listing), R. C. Holland and Ron Pussell (*Seduction* and *Parade of Pleasure* data), Grant Irwin (Quality data), Richard Kravitz (Kelly data), Phil Levine (giveaway data), Paul Litch (Copper & Modern Age data), Dan Malan & Charles Heffelfinger (Classic Comics data), Jon McClure (Whitman data), Fred Nardelli (Frazetta data), Michelle Nolan (Love comics), Mike Nolan (MLJ, Timely, Nedor data), George Olshevsky (Timely data), Dr. Richard Olson (Grading and Yellow Kid info), Chris Pedrin (DC War data), Scott Pell ('50s data), Greg Robertson (National data), Don Rosa (Late 1940s to 1950s data), Matt Schiffman (Bronze Age data), Frank Scigliano (Little Lulu data), Gene Seger (Buck Rogers data), Rick Sloane (Archie data), David R. Smith, Archivist, Walt Disney Productions (Disney data), Bill Spicer and Zetta DeVoe (Western Publishing Co. data), Tony Starks (Silver and Bronze Age data), Al Stoltz (Golden Age & Promo data), Doug Sulipa (Bronze Age data), Don and Maggie Thompson (Four Color listing), Mike Tiefenbacher & Jerry Sinkovec (Atlas and National data), Raymond True & Philip J. Gaudino (Classic Comics data), Jim Vadeboncoeur Jr. (Williamson and Atlas data), Richard Samuel West (Victorian Age and Platinum Age data), Kim Weston (Disney and Barks data), Cat Yronwode (Spirit data), Andrew Zerbe and Gary Behymer (M. E. data).

A special thanks, as always, to my wife Caroline, for her encouragement and support on such a tremendous project, and to all who placed ads in this edition.

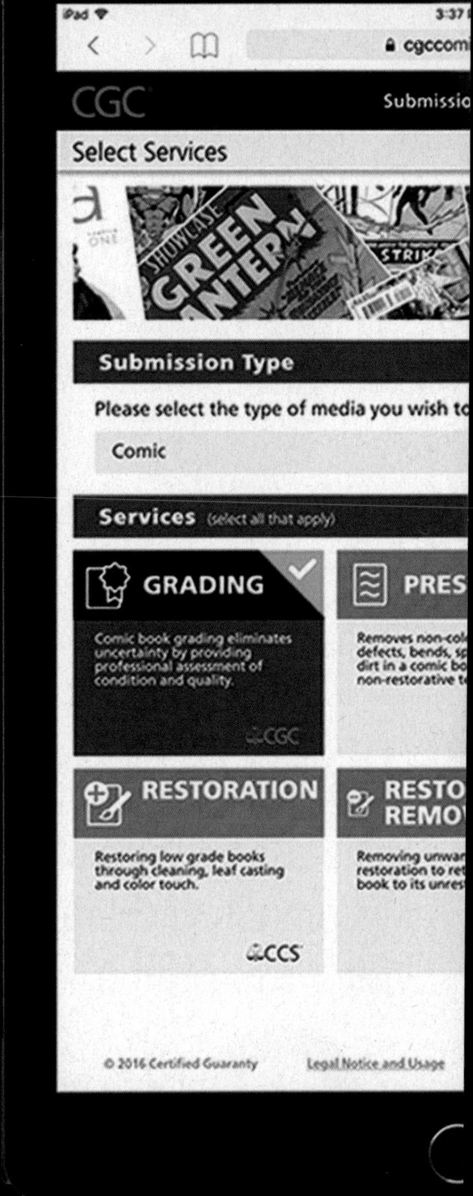

MYCOMICSHOP HAS 8% AUCTIONS!!!

BOB MONTANA

Other comic auctions charge 10%+ in fees to sell your comics.
Some take over 30% of the sale from combined buyer and seller fees.
MyComicShop charges 8% (minimums apply).
Visit mycomicshop.com/overstreet

MY COMIC SHOP

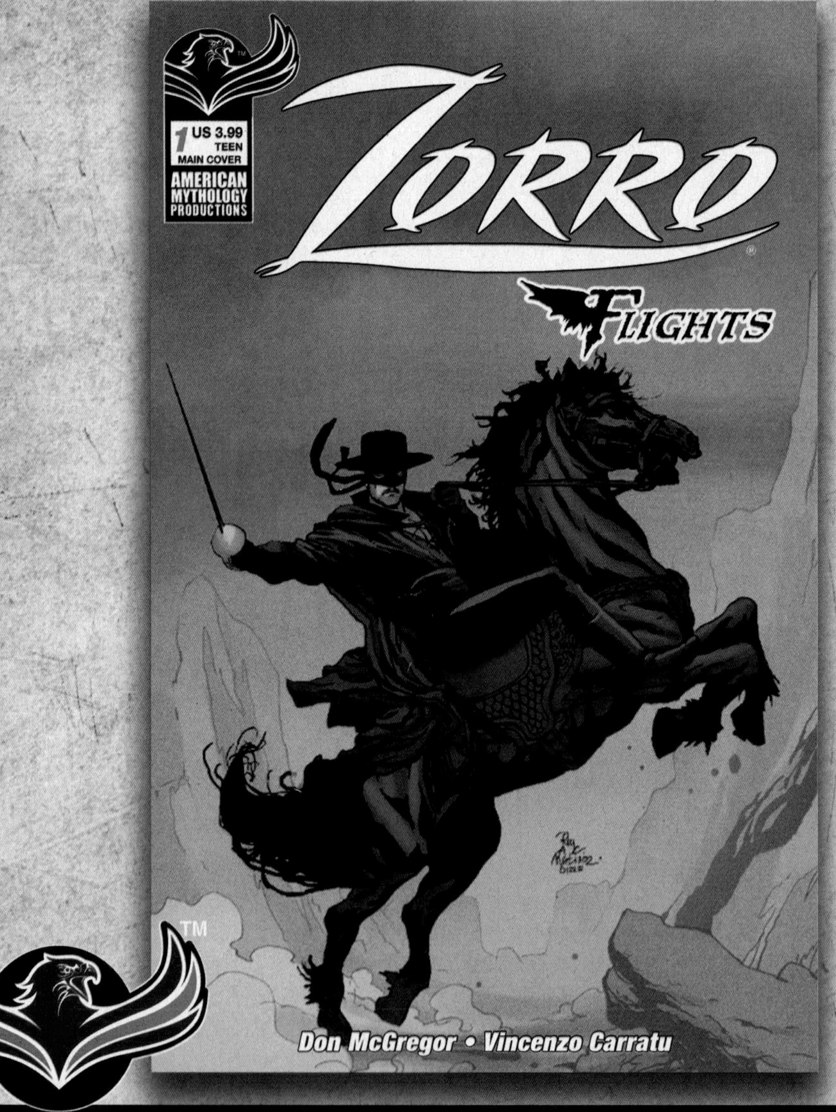
1 US 3.99
TEEN
MAIN COVER
AMERICAN MYTHOLOGY PRODUCTIONS
ZORRO®
FLIGHTS
Don McGregor • Vincenzo Carratu

WORLD COLOR
THE INCREDIBLE HULK
15¢
143
SEPT
MARVEL COMICS GROUP
AT LAST! DOCTOR DOOM!
YELLOW T S
BLACK T S
RED T S
BLUE T S
SPARTA
BRAVE + BOLD
BATMAN
TEEN TITANS
NO ONE LAYS A HAND ON MY SON WHILE I LIVE!
PUNISH NOT MY EVIL SON!

I USED TO BUY OLD COMICS
I STILL DO!
BUYING OLD COMIC BOOKS FOR OVER 50 YEARS!
FIND US ONLINE!
HEROESONLINE.COM
@HEROESONLINE
#HEROESCON
#CLTMINICON
#UNDERTHEWATERTOWER
HEROES
Aren't Hard To Find
AMERICA'S COMIC SOURCE SINCE 1980
SINCE 1977
CHARLOTTE MINI•CON
STOP BY, CALL OR EMAIL US:
HEROESARENTHARDTOFIND@GMAIL.COM
417 PECAN AVENUE · CHARLOTTE, NC 28204 · 704-375-7462
HOST OF AMERICA'S FAVORITE COMIC CONVENTION
HEROES CONVENTION
SINCE 1982
COMICS' GREATEST CREATORS & VENDORS!
CELEBRATING 40 YEARS IN 2022!
WWW.HEROESONLINE.COM

FIRST
COMICS NEWS
COMICS • GAMES • MOVIES • WRESTLING
FIRST COMICS NEWS
COLUMNISTS
Alex Wright
Ben Herman
Bill Black
Bob Almond
Borgy
Braedan Hafichuk
Christopher Watts
Dærick Gröss Sr.
Michael Dunne
Matthew Pulido
Miguel Ortiz
Paul Carberry
Tanya Tate
Tim Chizmar
CONTRIBUTORS
Buzz Dixon
Holly Golightly
Howard Chaykin
J. C. Vaughn
Mark Haney
Marwan El Nashar
Maria Taylor
Mike Bullock
Naif Al-Mutawa
Scott McDaniel
PODCASTERS
Art Sippo
Jamie Coville
Jeff Burton
Sammy J. Maynard II
Steven Butler
REPORTERS
Chris Squires
Eric N. Bennett
Francis Sky
Grant Offenberger
Jez Ibelle
Jim Burrows
Joeseph Simon
Martin Boruta
Peter Breau
Phil Latter
REVIEWERS
Calvin Daniels
David Markowski
Francis Garbut
Giovanni Aria
Harry Sully
Joshua Pantalleresco
Paco X González Muñoz
Ric Croxton
Thomas Bottoms
Wayne Hall
EDITORIAL STAFF
Matthew Szewczyk ♦ MANAGING EDITOR
Richard Vasseur ♦ BUREAU CHIEF CANADA
Rik Offenberger ♦ EDITOR-IN-CHIEF
CLASSIC HEROES
TRADEMARK™ & COPYRIGHT© DC COMICS
INDIE HEROES
TRADEMARK™ & COPYRIGHT© G-MAN COMICS
MOVIE HEROES
TRADEMARK™ & COPYRIGHT© MARVEL COMICS
TV HEROES
TRADEMARK™ & COPYRIGHT© THE WALT DISNEY COMPANY

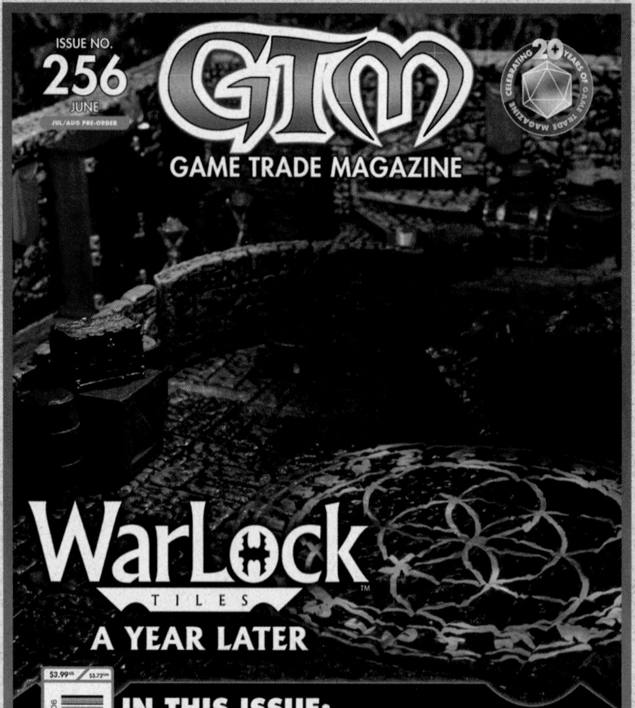

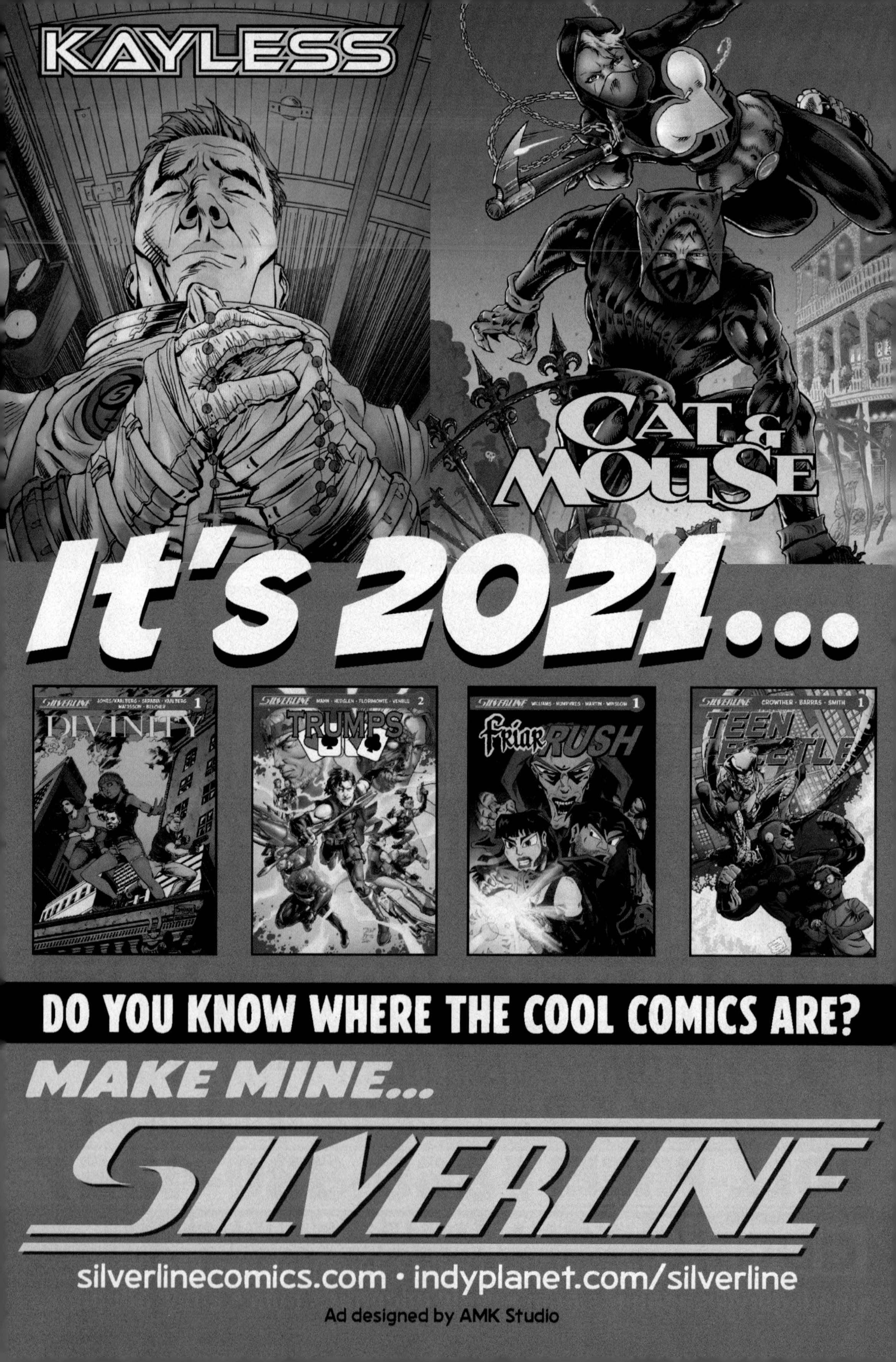

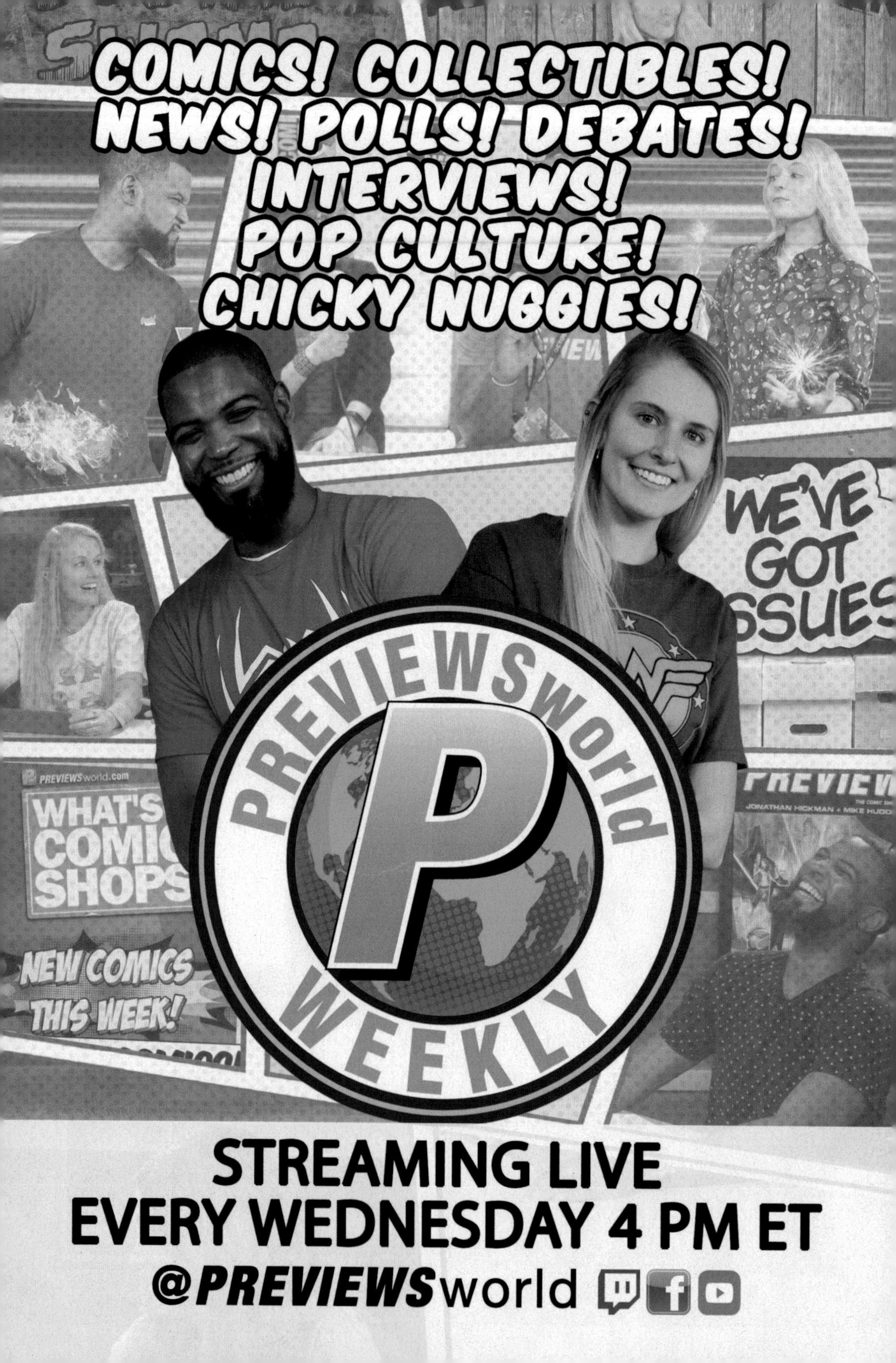

THE OVERSTREET HALL OF FAME

The Overstreet Hall of Fame was conceived to single out individuals who have made great contributions to the comic book arts.

This includes writers, artists, editors, publishers and others who have plied their craft in insightful and meaningful ways.

While such evaluations are inherently subjective, they also serve to aid in reflecting upon those who shaped the experience of reading comic books over the years.

This year's class of inductees begins on this next page.

THE PREVIOUS INDUCTEES

Class of 2006
Murphy Anderson
Jim Aparo
Jim Lee
Mac Raboy

Class of 2007
Dave Cockrum
Steve Ditko
Bruce Hamilton
Martin Nodell
George Pérez
Jim Shooter
Dave Stevens
Alex Toth
Michael Turner

Class of 2008
Carl Barks
Will Eisner
Al Feldstein
Harvey Kurtzman
Stan Lee
Marshall Rogers
John Romita, Sr.
John Romita, Jr.
Julius Schwartz
Mike Wieringo

Class of 2009
Neal Adams
Matt Baker
Chris Claremont
Palmer Cox
Bill Everett
Frank Frazetta
Neil Gaiman
William M. Gaines
Carmine Infantino
Jack Kirby
Joe Kubert
Paul Levitz
Russ Manning
Todd McFarlane
Don Rosa
John Severin
Joe Simon
Al Williamson

Class of 2010
Sergio Aragonés
M.C. Gaines
Archie Goodwin
Winsor McCay
Mike Mignola
Frank Miller
Robert M. Overstreet
Mike Richardson
Jerry Robinson
Joe Shuster
Jerry Siegel
Jim Steranko
Wally Wood

Class of 2011
Jack Davis
Martin Goodman
Dean Mullaney
Marie Severin
Walt Simonson
Major Malcolm Wheeler-Nicholson

Class of 2012
John Buscema
Dan DeCarlo
Jean Giraud (Moebius)
Larry Hama
Kurt Schaffenberger
Bill Sienkiewicz
Curt Swan
Roy Thomas

Class of 2013
Mark Chiarello
Mike Deodato, Jr.
Bill Finger
Jack Kamen
Bob Kane
Andy Kubert

Class of 2014
George Evans
Lou Fine
Gardner Fox
Terry Moore
Dave Sim
Jeff Smith

Class of 2015
Paul Gulacy
Don McGregor
Alex Schomburg
Mark Waid

Class of 2016
Darwyn Cooke
Russ Heath
Rob Liefeld
R.F. Outcault
Tim Truman

Class of 2017
Mike Grell
Osamu Tezuka
Jim Valentino
Mark Wheatley
Bernie Wrightson

Class of 2018
C.C. Beck
Howard Chaykin
Denny O'Neil
Katsuhiro Otomo
Marc Silvestri
Len Wein

Class of 2019
Sal Buscema
José Luis García-López
Michael Wm. Kaluta
Rumiko Takahashi

Class of 2020
Kevin Eastman
Louise Simonson
Dick Sprang

HALL OF FAME

Denys Cowan is a comic artist, TV producer, and co-founder of Milestone Media. His first job in comics was artist Rich Buckler's assistant and his work debuted in *Weird War Tales* #93 (Nov. 1980). In the '80s, Cowan penciled *Power Man and the Iron Fist* and was the main artist on *The Question*. He penciled *Black Panther* Vol. 2 and worked on the *Detective Comics* "Blind Justice" story, which introduced Henri Ducard. He worked with writer Dwayne McDuffie as the penciller on *Deathlok*. Cowan, McDuffie, Michael Davis, and Derek Dingle co-founded Milestone Media in 1993. There he co-created characters like Hardware and Static, and he provided the art on *Hardware*. In television, he was the producer on the *Static Shock* animated series and was the Senior Vice President of Animation at BET, which included the development of *The Boondocks*. Cowan's comic book work has also appeared in *Black Panther/Captain America: Flags of Our Fathers*, *Dominique Laveau: Voodoo Child*, *The Question: The Deaths of Vic Sage*, and the relaunch of Milestone.

– Amanda Sheriff

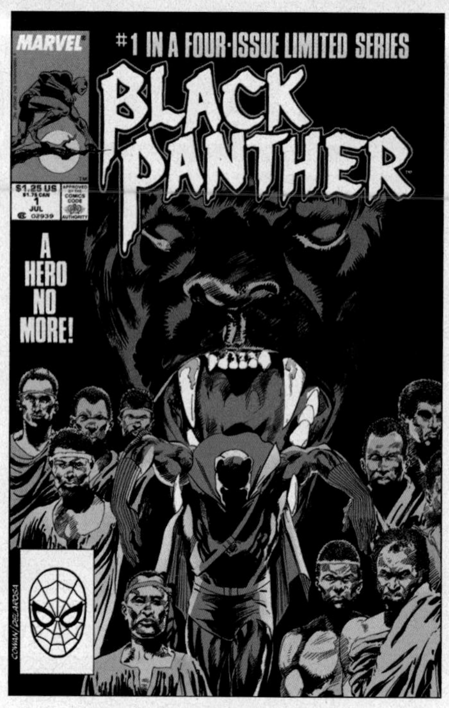

BLACK PANTHER #1
July 1988. © MAR

DEATHLOK #9
March 1992. © MAR

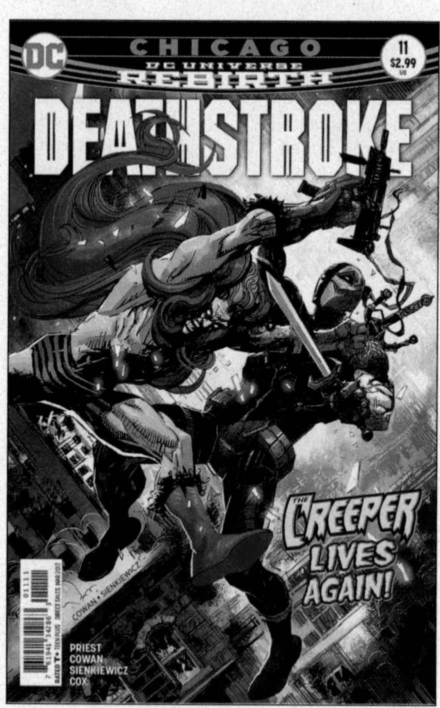

DEATHSTROKE #11
March 2017. © DC

DAVID MACK

JUSTICE LEAGUE OF AMERICA #52
February 2011. © DC

KABUKI: MASKS OF THE NOH #2
June 1996. © David Mack

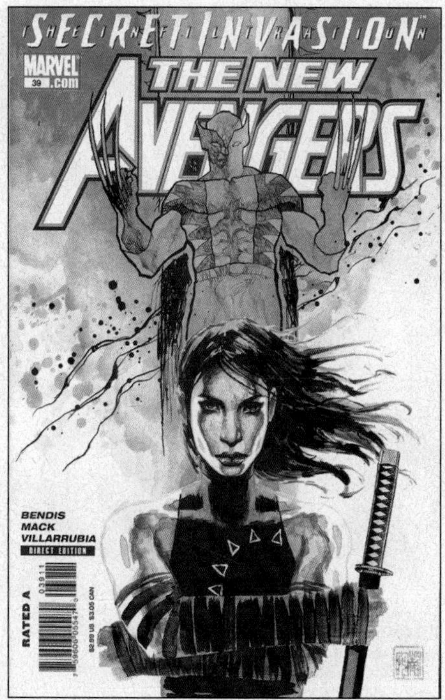

NEW AVENGERS #39
May 2008. © MAR

SWAMP THING #13
May 2001. © DC

HALL OF FAME

William Moulton Marston has a legacy in comics that is quite different from most other creators. Primarily a psychologist and self-help author, he is known in comics for creating Wonder Woman. Marston earned a PhD in psychology from Harvard in 1921. In an interview he discussed the educational potential of comics, gaining the attention of comic publisher Max Gaines, who hired him to be an educational consultant for All-American Publications. In the early 1940s, superheroes were almost exclusively male, with DC dominated by Superman, Batman, and Green Lantern. Noting that most superheroes used aggression to stop villains, Marston suggested creating a new hero who could fight with love. With Gaines' approval he developed Wonder Woman to be like then-modern liberated women. As a new kind of hero, Wonder Woman attracted both male and female readers who were intrigued by the concept of a heroic female character.

- Amanda Sheriff

ALL STAR COMICS #12
August - September 1942. © DC

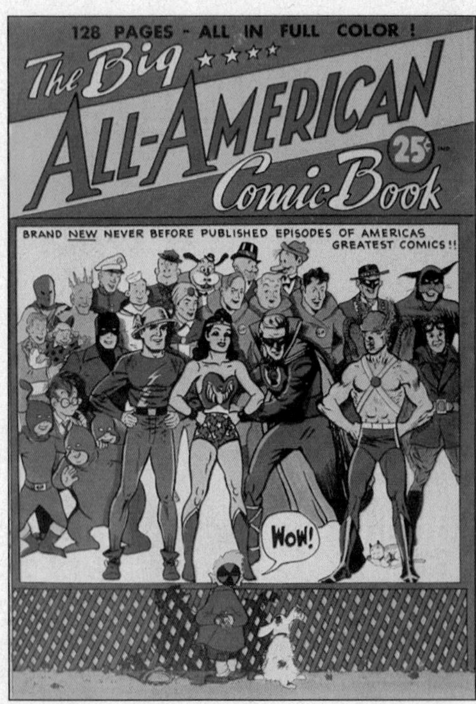

THE BIG ALL-AMERICAN COMIC BOOK #1
1944. © DC

COMIC CAVALCADE #7
Summer 1944. © DC

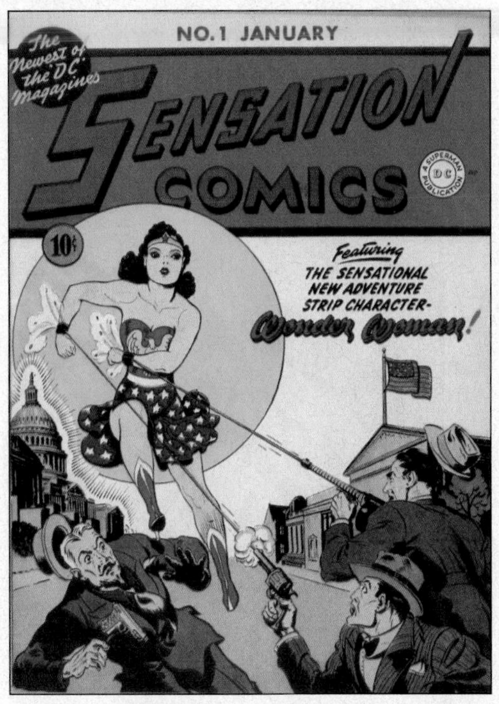

SENSATION COMICS #1
January 1942. © DC

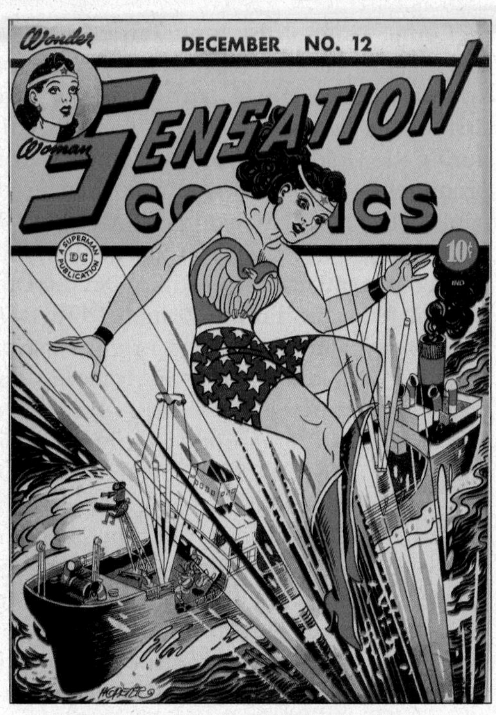

SENSATION COMICS #12
December 1942. © DC

WONDER WOMAN #6
Fall 1943. © DC

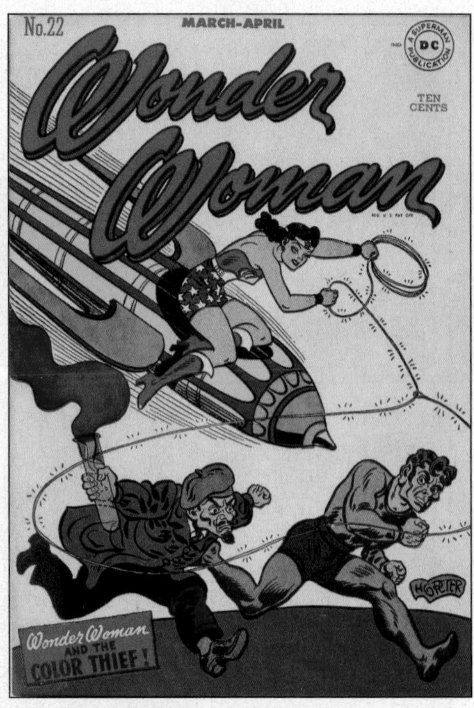

WONDER WOMAN #22
March - April 1947. © DC

Comic writer-artist June Tarpé Mills was one of the earliest female comic creators, known for her comic strip *Miss Fury*, the first female hero created by a woman. Active during the Golden Age when women weren't prominently employed, she used her middle name Tarpé so that her work wouldn't be judged negatively based on her gender. Mills created several characters like Devil's Dust, the Cat Man, the Purple Zombie, and Daredevil Barry Finn. She wrote original scripts, penciled, and inked stories in *Amazing Mystery Funnies*, *Target Comics*, *Funny Pages*, *Masked Marvel*, *Star Comics*, and *Amazing Man Comics*. In 1941, Mills created Miss Fury, the superheroine identity of wealthy socialite Marla Drake. The character became a favored symbol during World War II with her images painted on the noses of American warplanes. The strip ran in Sunday comics until 1952 when she retired. Mills returned for a brief period in 1971 with *Our Love Story* at Marvel and later in '79 for a *Miss Fury* graphic novel, though it was not finished.

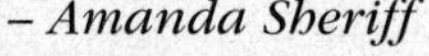

– Amanda Sheriff

MISS FURY #7
Fall 1945. © MAR

MISS FURY NEWSPAPER STRIP

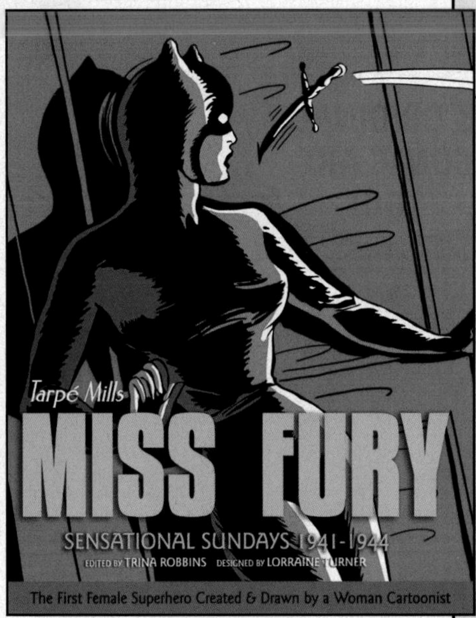

MISS FURY
SENSATIONAL SUNDAYS: 1941-1944
2013 Hardcover archive from IDW

MISS FURY COLOR PRINT

MISS FURY NEWSPAPER STRIPS

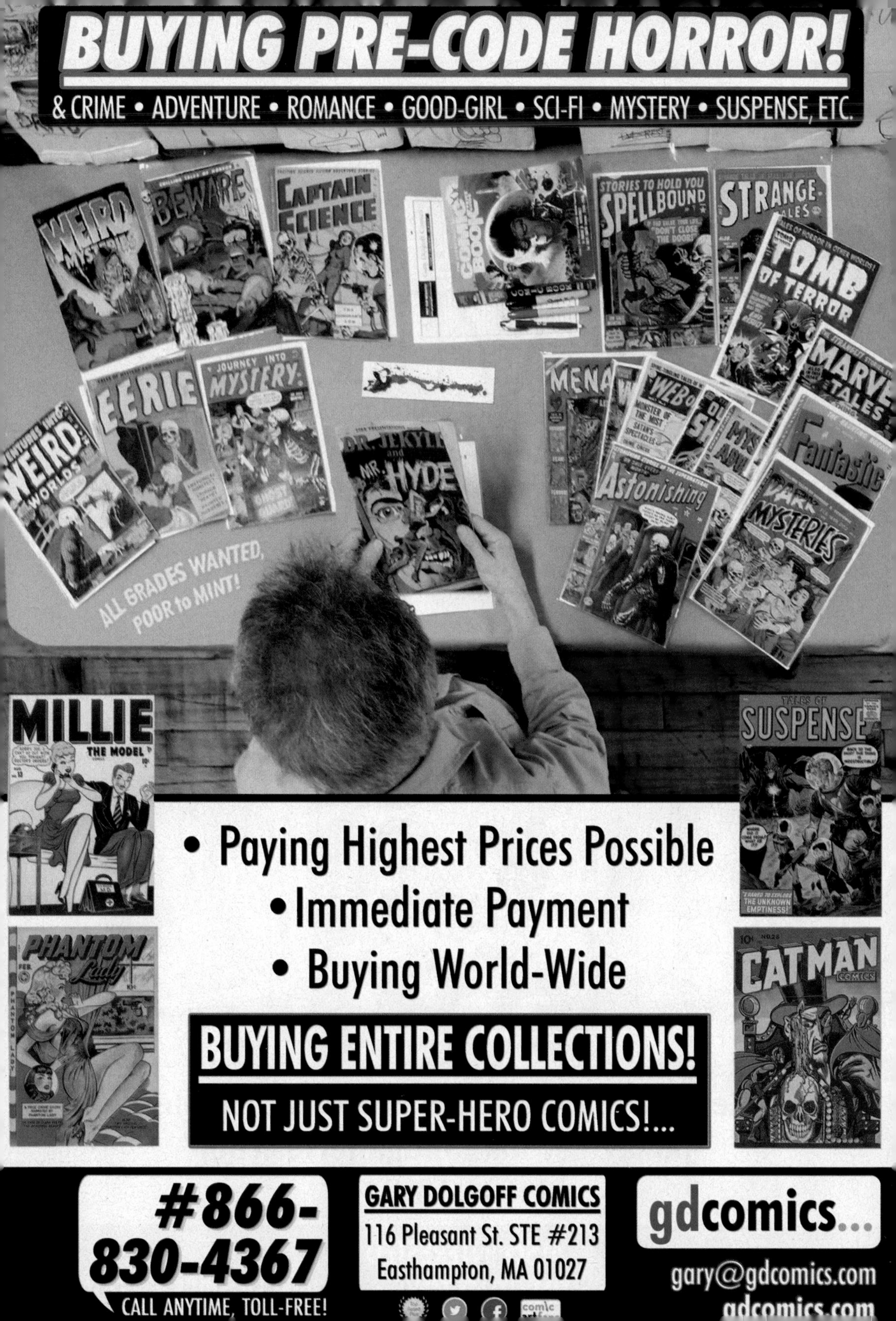

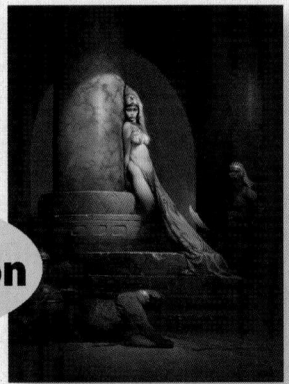

MYCOMICSHOP HAS 8% AUCTIONS!!!

BOB MONTANA

Other comic auctions charge 10%+ in fees to sell your comics.
Some take over 30% of the sale from combined buyer and seller fees.
MyComicShop charges 8% (minimums apply).
Visit mycomicshop.com/overstreet

MY COMIC SHOP

ABOUT THIS
BOOK
AFTER STERANKO
HEY THERE!
THERE'S NEVER BEEN A BETTER TIME TO BE A COMIC BOOK FAN!
EVEN WITH ALL THE INCREDIBLE MOVIES AND RECORD PRICES PAID FOR KEY ISSUES, THERE'S STILL AN IMPRESSIVE AMOUNT OF AFFORDABLE COMICS OUT THERE!
8.5
ACTION COMICS
CAPTAIN AMERICA
WE HOPE YOU'LL FIND THIS BOOK TO BE A SUPERB REFERENCE, NO MATTER WHAT TYPE OF COMICS YOU ENJOY.
OUR MARKET REPORTS START ON PAGE 89 WITH BOB OVERSTREET'S OVERVIEW AND THEN WE'LL HEAR FROM THE OVERSTREET ADVISORS.
THE OVERSTREET
51ST EDITION
COMIC BOOK
PRICE GUIDE
ROBERT M. OVERSTREET
2021 - 2022

THE GUIDE HAS ALWAYS BEEN THE PLACE TO KEEP UP WITH RECORD PRICES, TRENDS, AND MORE...

WE ALWAYS START AND END WITH A SIMPLE PHRASE: *COLLECT WHAT YOU* LOVE, AND YOU'LL NEVER GO WRONG.

NO MATTER HOW MUCH YOU KNOW ABOUT COMICS, THERE'S ALWAYS ***MORE*** TO ***LEARN.***

OVERSTREET'S
SUPER OUTFITTERS

ONE OF THE COOL THINGS ABOUT COMIC BOOKS IS THAT THERE ARE LOTS OF NEW ONES TO DISCOVER.
AND THERE ARE LITERALLY HUNDREDS OF THOUSANDS OF ***BACK ISSUES,*** TOO.

BACK ISSUE COMICS RANGE FROM LESS THAN COVER PRICE TO $3.25 MILLION!

CAN YOU BELIEVE THAT? PERHAPS I SHOULD STEAL ONE OF THEM...
HAHA HAHA!

JUST KIDDING, OF COURSE.
THE FIRST COMIC TO HIT $1 MILLION WAS ACTION COMICS #1, THE FIRST APPEARANCE OF SUPERMAN, BY THE WAY.

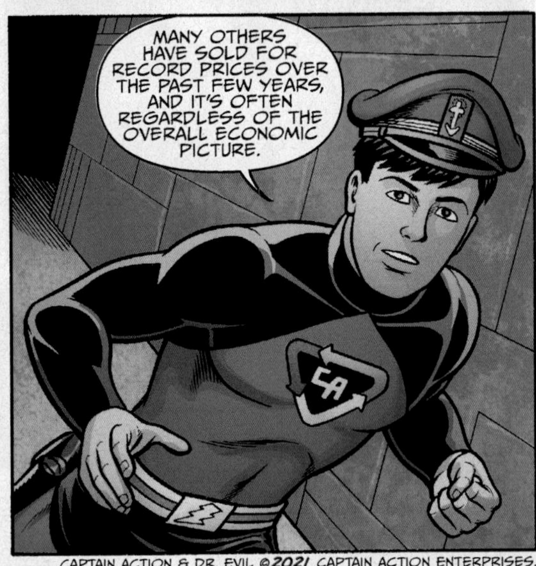
MANY OTHERS HAVE SOLD FOR RECORD PRICES OVER THE PAST FEW YEARS, AND IT'S OFTEN REGARDLESS OF THE OVERALL ECONOMIC PICTURE.

THE GRADE AND SCARCITY OF THE ISSUES HAVE A LOT TO DO WITH THAT AS WELL. WE'LL GET INTO THAT IN JUST A BIT...

BUT OUR ADVICE IS ALWAYS "COLLECT WHAT YOU LOVE AND YOU'LL NEVER BE DISAPPOINTED."

SINCE WE'RE TOUTING OUR 50TH ANNIVERSARY, YOU CAN GUESS THAT THE GUIDE STARTED IN 1970...
THE COMIC BOOK PRICE GUIDE

OVERSTREET PRICING AND GRADING STANDARDS ARE THE ACCEPTED *FOUNDATION* OF THE COMIC BOOK MARKET-PLACE.

COMICS ARE LISTED ALPHABETICALLY BY TITLE, REGARDLESS OF PUBLISHER. THE MAIN SECTION LISTS COMICS FROM 1934 TO THE PRESENT.

THIS BOOK ALSO INCLUDES...

BIG LITTLE BOOKS
PROMOTIONAL COMICS
PIONEER AGE COMICS
VICTORIAN AGE COMICS
PLATINUM AGE COMICS

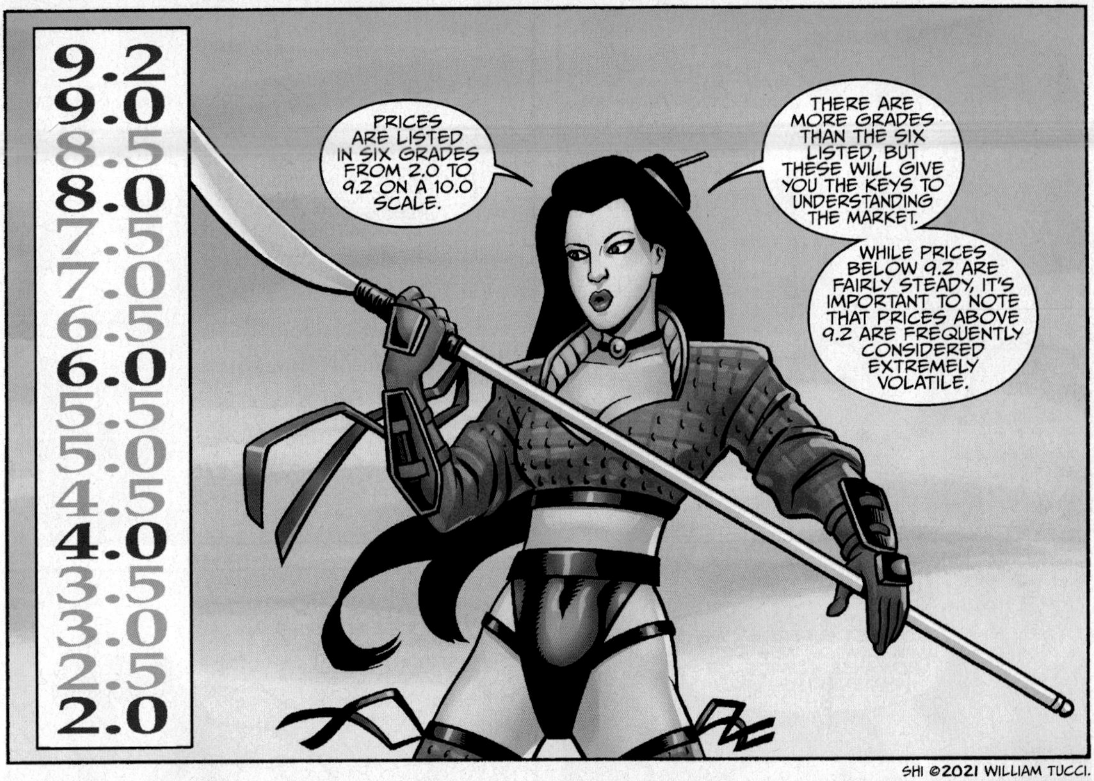

9.2
9.0
8.5
8.0
7.5
7.0
6.5
6.0
5.5
5.0
4.5
4.0
3.5
3.0
2.5
2.0

PRICES ARE LISTED IN SIX GRADES FROM 2.0 TO 9.2 ON A 10.0 SCALE.

THERE ARE MORE GRADES THAN THE SIX LISTED, BUT THESE WILL GIVE YOU THE KEYS TO UNDERSTANDING THE MARKET.

WHILE PRICES BELOW 9.2 ARE FAIRLY STEADY, IT'S IMPORTANT TO NOTE THAT PRICES ABOVE 9.2 ARE FREQUENTLY CONSIDERED EXTREMELY VOLATILE.

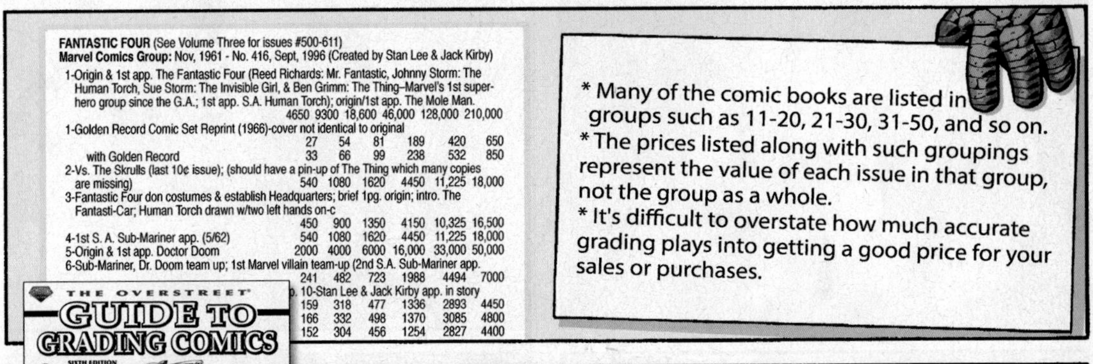

FANTASTIC FOUR (See Volume Three for issues #500-611)
Marvel Comics Group: Nov, 1961 - No. 416, Sept, 1996 (Created by Stan Lee & Jack Kirby)

Issue						
1-Origin & 1st app. The Fantastic Four (Reed Richards: Mr. Fantastic, Johnny Storm: The Human Torch, Sue Storm: The Invisible Girl, & Ben Grimm: The Thing–Marvel's 1st super-hero group since the G.A.; 1st app. S.A. Human Torch); origin/1st app. The Mole Man.	4650	9300	18,600	46,000	128,000	210,000
1-Golden Record Comic Set Reprint (1966)-cover not identical to original	27	54	81	189	420	650
with Golden Record	33	66	99	238	532	850
2-Vs. The Skrulls (last 10¢ issue); (should have a pin-up of The Thing which many copies are missing)	540	1080	1620	4450	11,225	18,000
3-Fantastic Four don costumes & establish Headquarters; brief 1pg. origin; intro. The Fantasti-Car; Human Torch drawn w/two left hands on-c	450	900	1350	4150	10,325	16,500
4-1st S. A. Sub-Mariner app. (5/62)	540	1080	1620	4450	11,225	18,000
5-Origin & 1st app. Doctor Doom	2000	4000	6000	16,000	33,000	50,000
6-Sub-Mariner, Dr. Doom team up; 1st Marvel villain team-up (2nd S.A. Sub-Mariner app.	241	482	723	1988	4494	7000
...p. 10-Stan Lee & Jack Kirby app. in story	159	318	477	1336	2893	4450
	166	332	498	1370	3085	4800
	152	304	456	1254	2827	4400

* Many of the comic books are listed in groups such as 11-20, 21-30, 31-50, and so on.
* The prices listed along with such groupings represent the value of each issue in that group, not the group as a whole.
* It's difficult to overstate how much accurate grading plays into getting a good price for your sales or purchases.

ISN'T THE BEST PART OF COLLECTING THAT THERE ARE SO MANY DIFFERENT WAYS TO COLLECT?

YOU BET! YOU CAN CHOOSE TO FOLLOW INDIVIDUAL WRITERS, ARTISTS, PUBLISHERS OR CHARACTERS...

YOU CAN COLLECT SUPERHEROES, WAR COMICS, WESTERNS, ROMANCE COMICS, OR WHATEVER YOU LIKE!

YOU CAN CHOOSE #1 ISSUES, FIRST APPEARANCES, CROSSOVERS, OR MANY OTHER VARIATIONS.

SO YOU'RE SAYING IT'S REALLY ABOUT COLLECTING WHAT YOU LIKE, NOT WHAT SOMEONE ELSE LIKES?

WHETHER IT'S SPIDER-MAN OR EVERY COMIC BOOK APPEARANCE OF JAMES BOND, MAKE YOUR OWN PLAN AND THEN GO TO IT!

THE BEST WAY TO HAVE A GOOD PLAN IS TO GET INFORMED.
THE BEST WAY TO GET INFORMED IS TO GO TO THE EXPERTS.
LEARN THE INS AND OUTS OF COLLECTING, INCLUDING HOW TO TAKE CARE OF YOUR COLLECTION!
LEARN HOW TO GRADE YOUR COMICS AND WHY THE GRADES MAKE SUCH A DIFFERENCE!
LEARN WHAT TO EXPECT AT CONVENTIONS OR WHEN BUYING AND SELLING COMICS ELSEWHERE.
IT'S ALSO IMPORTANT TO REMEMBER THAT THIS BOOK IS A GUIDE, NOT A DEALER'S PRICE LIST. THE MARKET SETS THE PRICES.
GETTING THAT ISSUE YOU'VE BEEN AFTER IS A GREAT FEELING...
BUT DON'T BE IN SUCH A HURRY THAT YOU DON'T CHECK THINGS OUT THOROUGHLY.
AFTER DAVID MACK

THERE'S ACTUALLY *NO SECRET* TO IT.
THE GUIDE GETS INPUT FROM EXPERIENCED ADVISORS, INCLUDING WELL-ESTABLISHED *COLLECTORS, DEALERS* AND *HISTORIANS.*
WE HAVE UNDERTAKEN *SIGNIFICANT EFFORT* TO ASSEMBLE THIS PRICING INFORMATION.

THE RESULTING LISTINGS COME THROUGH THE OBSERVATION AND DOCUMENTATION OF PRICES REALIZED THROUGH HOBBY AND TRADE SHOWS, CATALOG SALES, RETAIL SALES, AND INTERNET, LIVE AND MAIL-IN AUCTIONS.
DOCUMENTED PERSONAL SALES MAY ALSO BE INCLUDED.

WE HAVE EARNED OUR REPUTATION FOR OUR CAUTIOUS, CONSERVATIVE APPROACH TO PRICING.
WE ACTIVELY ENCOURAGE READERS WHO BELIEVE THEY HAVE DISCOVERED AN ERROR TO MAIL RELATED INFORMATION TO THE AUTHOR.

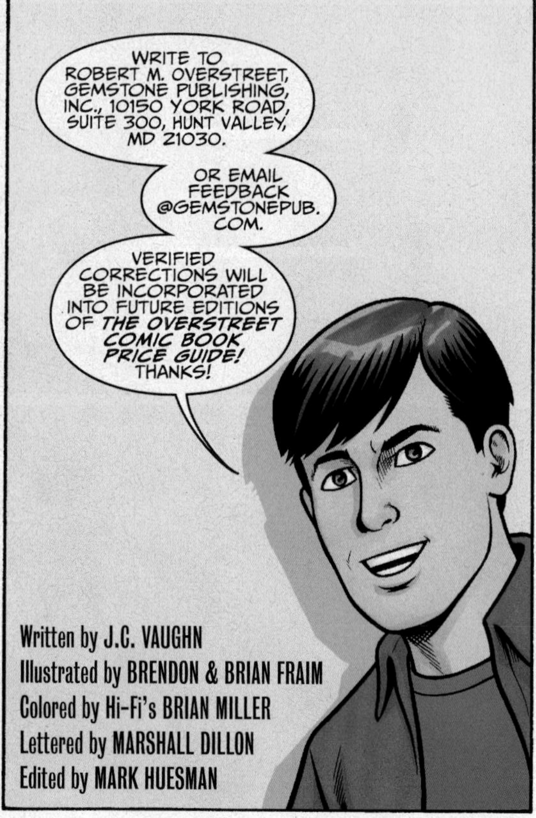
WRITE TO ROBERT M. OVERSTREET, GEMSTONE PUBLISHING, INC., 10150 YORK ROAD, SUITE 300, HUNT VALLEY, MD 21030.
OR EMAIL FEEDBACK @GEMSTONEPUB.COM.
VERIFIED CORRECTIONS WILL BE INCORPORATED INTO FUTURE EDITIONS OF *THE OVERSTREET COMIC BOOK PRICE GUIDE!* THANKS!
Written by J.C. VAUGHN
Illustrated by BRENDON & BRIAN FRAIM
Colored by Hi-Fi's BRIAN MILLER
Lettered by MARSHALL DILLON
Edited by MARK HUESMAN

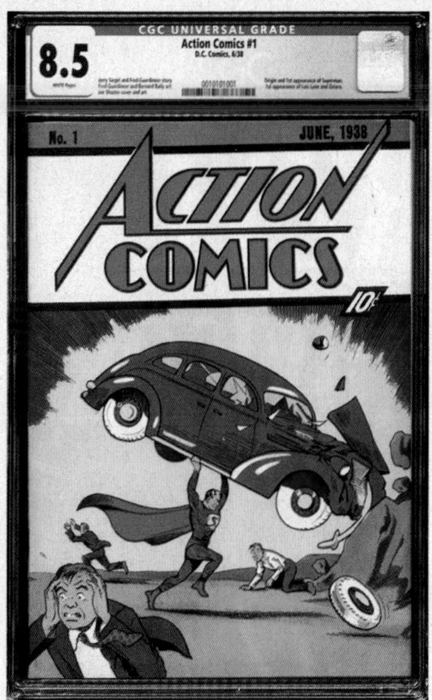

Action Comics #1 CGC 8.5
$3,250,000
by ComicConnect
in April 2021

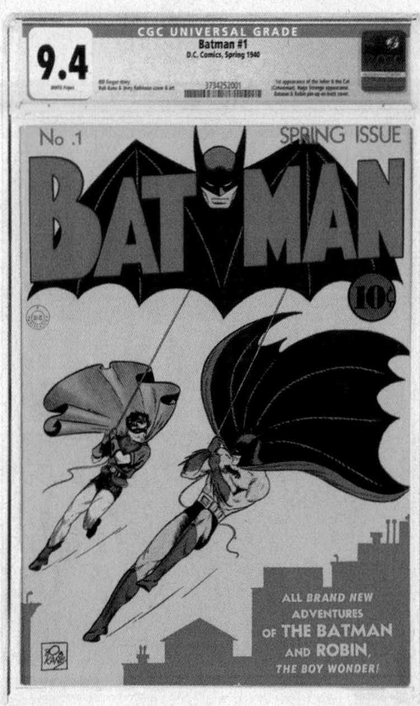

Batman #1 CGC 9.4
$2,220,000
by Heritage Auctions
on January 14, 2021

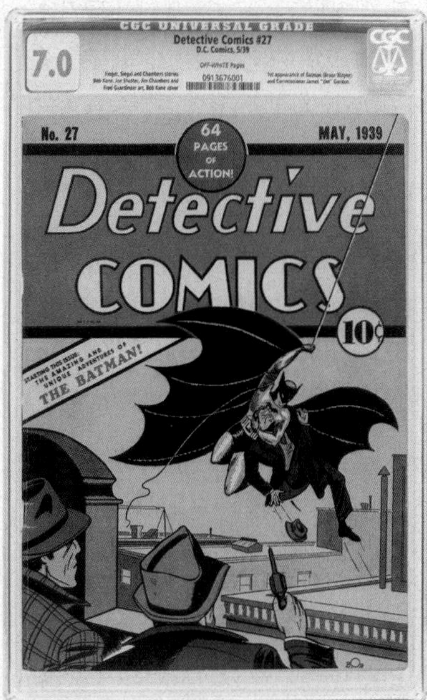

Detective Comics #27 CGC 7.0
$1,500,000
by Heritage Auctions
on November 19, 2020

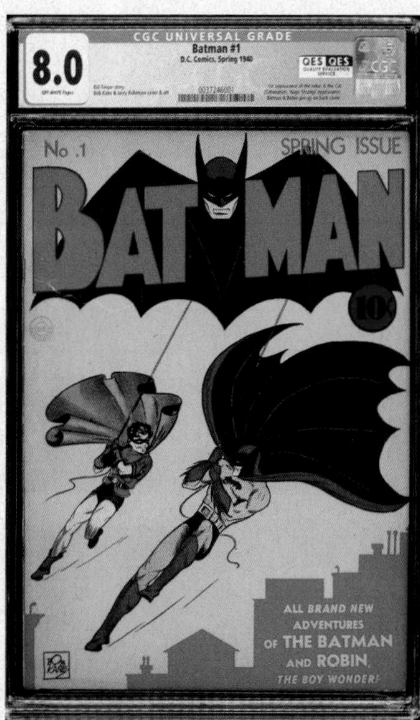

Batman #1 CGC 8.0
$1,207,500
by ComicConnect
in April 2021

THE JOHN VERZYL OVERSTREET® ADVISOR AWARD

The John Verzyl Overstreet Advisor Award, named in honor of our friend and longtime contributor John Verzyl, is presented annually to an Advisor or Advisors whose knowledge, contributions, ethics and reputation are held in the highest esteem by his or her peers.

Nominations may be made by any Overstreet Advisor in good standing by sending the nominee's name and description of why he or she represents the positive attributes that John embodied for our hobby. To make a nomination, email Gemstone Publishing's Mark Huesman at humark@gemstonepub.com. Nominations for our next edition must be received by March 11, 2022.

Covid-19 impact update:

As alluded to in last year's Market Reports, the impact of COVID-19 on the national economy in general and on our industry in specific would have been impossible to predict at the outset of the pandemic. Faced with businesses shutdown by government mandates, things initially seemed bleak at best. And to be sure, there have been devastating hardships resulting from the disease, and it would be insensitive to suggest otherwise. However, there have also been some unexpected upsides, including a thriving back-issue market that one would be hard-pressed not to call "robust." During the closures, many people turned to comics, including people who had not done so in recent times. As you will see, the opinions offered by our Overstreet Advisors span the gamut of experiences in this very odd time. I urge you to consider them through the lenses of both your own personal experience and theirs.

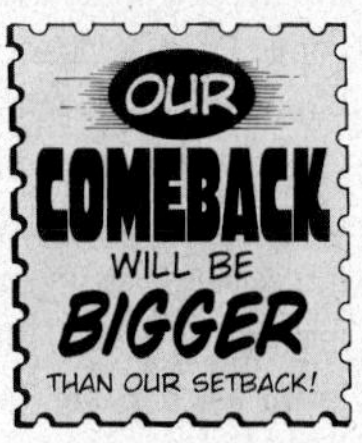

- RMO

Darren Adams and Jeff Walker
Pristine Comics

This was the year 2020: COVID-19, a world turned upside down, and an 11-year-old baseball card selling for more than an 80-year-old comic book - the finest known copy of *Action Comics* #1 from 1938.

Greetings comic aficionados! To say it's been a strange year is a vast understatement, and really doesn't begin to describe 2020. COVID-19 has had its own unique effect on everyone and has permanently altered the path of the entire collectables industry, now, and for years to come. Washington state, initially declared as the epicenter, was one of the very first to order a complete shutdown of most businesses. Initially, we closed our retail, reduced our staffing and kept mail order open, essentially closing ourselves to the public. We reopened to the public approximately five weeks later with reduced days and hours. Today, we continue marking the sidewalk outside with an X spaced six feet apart and limit store capacity to 25% which is the current regulatory limits of Washington state as of this writing.

As COVID initially took its toll in casting an ugly cloud of fear and uncertainty, prices for collectibles initially took an understandable price correction. Surprisingly, and totally unexpected was the quickness in which the market rebounded, as well as a newfound demand resulting in the flourishing of mail order, and rapid escalation of secondary prices.

Mail order demand yielded sales for items that previously had little or any interest and magnified prices of sectors such as *Pokémon* and sports cards by as much as 10 times or more!!

These are surreal times as COVID ironically created a recipe ripe for success fueled by Uncle Sam handing out slices of government cheese to nearly everyone in the form of stimulus checks, and unemployment check bonuses of $600 per week, in addition to regular unemployment benefits everyone on the system received, and retro checks for those getting approved. Imagine that. Being paid to stay at home. Over 20 million Americans collected unemployment in April with many making more money than they had been while working, while at the same time, having fewer expenses like eating out, gas, parking, clothing, Starbucks, etc.

Meanwhile fewer options to spend this newfound money presented itself as more businesses were forced to close and jurisdictional lockdowns began. With newfound money, along with boredom, and in many cases, depression, led to internet sales skyrocketing, as active and former collectors took the opportunity and ran with it. Adding to their collections and rekindling their passions in a world far better than the 24/7 world of masks, riots, empty stadiums, racial injustice, masks, ugly elections, daily death tolls, more masks, and COVID. Collectables provided a much needed and welcome relief. It provided time to reconnect with family and introduce them to your passions of the past, time to catch up on storylines of favorite titles, and yes, time to find and fill in those missing issues.

For the busybody and the bored, this also became an opportunity to finally attend to home repairs and other projects placed on the back burner. For many, this included cleaning the garage, storage units, closets, sheds, etc. only to rediscover old collections or new treasures and refuel their passions of the past.

As our store slowly re-opened our staff discovered many faces of new collectors and "ex" collectors "getting back into it". Under the circumstances I had expected to find more sellers than new buyers yet just the opposite occurred. Sales for trading cards, *Magic the Gathering*, and *Pokémon* exploded. However, the impact COVID-19 has had on comic books, in my humble opinion, has been significantly tapered as compared to the aforementioned. I believe that this was due in part to theater closures, thus demonstrating the impact that Marvel/Disney Studios has on the industry as a whole. The lull in the afterglow of the *Avengers: Endgame* movie had begun and excitement, anticipation, focus and interest were already diminishing in between MCU chapters.

Emerald City Comic Con in Seattle was one of the first conventions to be cancelled, and to many, initial thoughts of over-exaggeration turned to shock, denial, anger and eventually, acceptance as this was only a prelude of what was to come when the granddaddy of them all, San Diego Comic-Con fell victim as well. Movies and TV shows quit filming; shooting schedules were hazy and the hype machine virtually at a standstill. While mail order continued to thrive, the industry was nearly on its own for the first time in two decades leaving only existing TV shows and completed movies available to watch, with little on the horizon to look forward to. Without the Silver Screen, the support and buzz just wasn't there.

The value Hollywood contributes to this industry cannot be understated. Fortunately, the machine began to churn again on December 10, 2020 during the highly-publicized, Disney Investor Day meeting. More character and comic relevant news was released on this day than any single month in the past. The buzz and excitement in the air is back with new announcements, details and somewhat firm dates again. A new innovative redo on HBO MAX - What if Zack Snyder had completed directing *Justice League* - is in the works. *Wonder Woman 1984* is finally getting released. Fantastic Four, now a Disney property has potential again and more to come.

Prior to these announcements, books of all eras had been picking up steam and setting records as comic books of all eras firmly commanded higher prices. Post-1990 books that once only boasted a handful of issues capable of cracking $500, or $1000 an issue now boast more than twice as many as the year before. This sector is growing as the demand and significance of new characters from this era grows and further potential is identified. Once overlooked characters (like Darkhawk, X-Force, and Batman Beyond) are also becoming significant.

Bronze Age books, now approaching 50 years old, are appreciating with terrific financial returns and key Silvers are skyrocketing yet again. Golden Age books are as solid as ever.

With Fantastic Four news on the horizon, there are rumors of one of the last "Marvel Majors" yet to hit the Silver Screen. It's not a matter of if, but simply a matter of when, and investors and collectors alike have been focusing in on the Sub-Mariner. This has resulted in his books of all eras drying up. Books such as *Sub-Mariner Comics* 1941 #1 (well overdue), #11 (classic cover), #32 (origin Issue), *Fantastic Four* #4 (1st SA app.) *Sub-Mariner* #1 1968, *Tales To Astonish* #70, along with many early 1960s Sub-Mariner crossovers and splash covers, have seen solid price appreciation.

I believe a new breed of investor similar to those that have pushed sports card prices into the stratosphere will turn toward key comic book issues of all eras, as investment class "trophies." Someone once asked what the difference was between Batman & Superman. That's a fairly broad question, but to cut to the chase, his answer was "The Villains!" How right he was. Batman Villain keys continue to rise and continue providing an excellent return on investment year after year. First appearances and origins from the pages of *Batman* and *Detective* continue to set records. *Batman* #1 prices are not simply based on it being the first issue of the title run, a tremendous amount of this issue's value can be attributed to the fact it boasts the first ever appearances of the Joker AND Catwoman. In 2020 demand continued to grow and record prices were set for villain covers such as Penguin (*Detective* #58), Two-Face (*Detective* #66), Scarecrow (1st app. in *World's Finest* #3, 1st cover on *Detective Comics* #73), The Riddler (*Detective* #140), Poison Ivy (*Batman* #181), Ra's al Ghul (*Batman* #232) and of course, Harley Quinn (*Batman Adventures* #12). In terms of back issue demand, the Rodney Dangerfield of Batman villains has been the Penguin. Unlike Joker covers, Penguin covers lack the sadistic coolness. Every artist worth their salt wants to draw Joker covers, and some of these very artists have achieved their best or most recognized work in doing so. Any hands raised out there for a Penguin cover? I, for one, would love to see some vintage bad-ass covers of this character. The material is there to be had. The significance of this character cannot be denied, and interest in early Penguin keys has been heating up. Oswald Cobblepot's early appearances and covers have remained undervalued and are only beginning to get their due, as plenty of upside remains ahead for the fowl felon who once shot a man with his umbrella for referring to him as an "Ugly Mary Poppins".

All in all, 2020 has kicked complacency in the teeth as many had to "adapt and thrive" as they say. This industry has been extremely fortunate, as it did indeed thrive during COVID-19, while other industries sadly died. However, it is not all doom and gloom as the future looks to be bright again. Disney's announcements have painted a picture of what's to come, and as of this writing COVID-19 vaccine shots are being released and more people are being inoculated.

Another noteworthy mention in our business is the increase in demand for raw comic books, specifically Marvel Silver Age. If it's a key book, it will sell pretty close to the CGC price even when ungraded.

A Silver Age surprise to some, but not to others, has been the rise in value of *Daredevil* #1. Whether it's because the character rights have reverted from Netflix to the MCU, or a previously underrated character is finally getting his due, this book is now in the limelight with steady gains.

Bronze Age: Every year new issues from this era surface: *Eternals* #1 (who would have thought?), *Marvel Spotlight* #28, *Giant-Size Creatures* #1 (1st Tigra), *Defenders* #4 (1st Valkyrie) and on the DC side, *Strange Adventures* #205, (1st Deadman,) and *Shazam!* #28 (2nd appearance Black Adam.) Many cast members have been added to the *Black Adam* movie with Dwayne (The Rock) Johnson leading the pack. Also, unexpected demand for *Star Wars* by Marvel Comics from 1977-1986. *Star Wars* #42, Boba Fett's first appearance exceeding $2500 for a 9.8??

Also getting some renewed love is *The Teenage Mutant*

Ninja Turtles and anything with a cover by Alex Ross. Usagi Yojimbo and his first app. in *Albedo* #2 has skyrocketed, and with a print run of only 2000 and no second printing, this book has no signs of slowing down.

Golden Age: The aforementioned appearances of the Bat Villains, as well as historic firsts like *All Star Comics*, #7 (1st meeting of Superman and Batman) and #36 (1st meeting of Superman, Batman and Wonder Woman), as well as one shot issues like *Special Edition Comics* #1 featuring the original Captain Marvel (1st solo issue that predates *Captain Marvel Adventures* #1). Early *World's Finest* issues are also heating up. And let's not forget pre-Code Horror books, which always seem to be more expensive every year.

With Rob Liefeld taking over Archie Comics WWII heroes in *The Mighty Crusaders*, look for Shield, Jaguar, The Fly, and The Comet to perhaps spike in value.

An overlooked piece of news was CGC's entry into the market of grading sports, gaming and entertainment cards. The backlog is so long with PSA and BGS that a better entry time into this market could not be had. Using the same plastic material as their new comic slabs, CGC has come out with arguably the clearest and cleanest looking holder on the market. Word on the street is early, but indications are that the card grading is consistent and strict with subgrades offered on the labels.

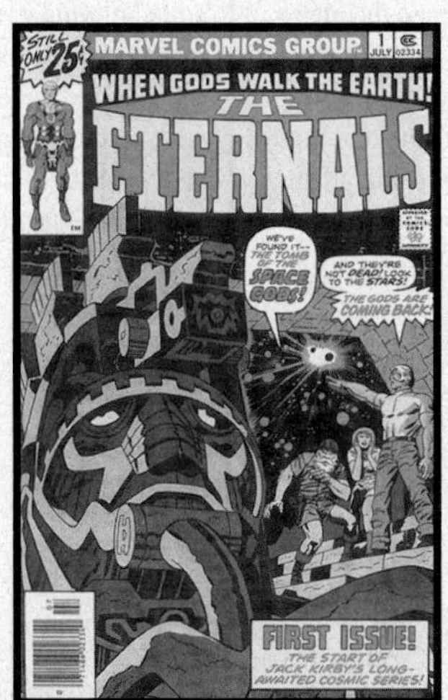

Despite a year's delay in their movie debut, the Eternals are still in the spotlight.

As mentioned, sports cards have taken off to unfathomable levels. Case in point, I will end with yet another strange yet surreal chapter that occurred during the bizarro year of 2020. Only in the year 2020 does any of this make any sense, but apparently it has happened. A sports card has retaken the lead over comics as the most expensive ever sold, and it was not a card that first comes to mind. Our record sale of *Action Comics* #1 for $3.2 million was not eclipsed by a Honus Wagner, Babe Ruth, nor any card from those eras. No, the card that eclipsed the finest known, 80+ year old copy of the 1st ever appearance of Superman resides in the form of an 11-year-old baseball card. A 2 ½" x 3 ½" double sided cardboard square produced in 2011.

Keep in mind, we have been in the 2 ½ " x 3 ½ "double-sided cardboard square cutout business for 30+ years and I thought I had pretty much seen everything, but the sale of this particular card is hard to fathom. A Graded 2009 Mike Trout 1 of 1 signed card sold for .... are you ready for this ...? $3.82 million. That is more than the record-breaking price we achieved when I sold *Action Comics* #1 for 3.2 million dollars (still a record price for a comic book!) Which would you rather hold onto for the next 20 years with blinders on? Sports cards, like comics are historic in nature and very serious business, as a collector of both, I joke about "double-sided cardboard cutouts" but the sale of a 2009 Mike Trout 1 of 1 rookie card for $3.8 million is no joke.

Grant Adey and Neville Howard Halo Certification Pty Ltd. - Australia

The Great Reset: Moving with the times, on the back of an absolutely fantastic year, Halo is on the move. Plummeting rent prices have opened a great opportunity in new premises. Office space at a fraction of the previous years' lease rates. A 5th floor office with city and river views 4 miles from the central business distinct. Brand new amenities: gym, pool, security, parking, and ground floor restaurants for only $1600 a month. This is nice. Halo's office is not open to the public, but we do have the convenience of booking the conference room for customer meetings. The attrition rate on retail shops has been heavy to say the least. Shop rents will have to move down or move out, as it costs a truck load of money to service the walk in general public. I'm positive many employers are now embracing the new work from home. They're asking themselves, "Why am I paying out on rent, insurance, electricity, office furniture so on so on. The employee's brain is snapped after a hour battle in traffic, then looking forward to an hour torture to get home." The days of 9 to 5 are over for most industries. I try to encourage staff and friends to spend the saved time on personal pursuits, education, health, intelligent conversation. Myself I'm studying papyrology, so I've bought some nice Egyptian fragments for the office. The great reset is here and we're in it.

2020 was a pivotal year in the Comic Industry: After 20 years of digital comics threatening to replace printed books, resulting in the end of an era of the humble comic shop, COVID-19 came like a thief in the night and forced the hand of many. Brick and mortar shops were forced to close down by the dozens, and those left standing were in strife as result of the lack of Wednesday comics and consistency in shipments, not to mention titles cancelled by the bundle on a monthly basis. Diamond Distribution shut up shop for months and DC established their own distribution supply chain meaning the shop fronts were waiting on pre-orders, while at the same time wondering when the staged restrictions will ease so customers can return. In Australia we saw many shops go under, while some embraced change and moved to Paypal payments and mail orders to fulfill their regular customer needs and keep money coming in.

Unprecedented is indeed the word for 2020 but instead of dwelling on that, let's instead focus on the positives that the year brought us. Across platforms great quality products have resulted in steady sales and despite all the above, the units of sales have not been as affected as one would have expected from the craziness.

For the readers: quality 'Events' across publishers have kept readers coming back and collectors quickly moved to online shopping to ensure they get the books they wanted. The highlight of the year must be *The Last Ronin* celebrating the return of Peter Laird in collaboration with Kevin Eastman for the first time in years. DC's 80th anniversary books continued month after month, and both *Dark Knights: Death Metal* (paving the way for Future State) and *DCeased* remain best sellers for fans. Similar to Marvel's *King In Black*, *Venom*, *Thor* the proof is in the pudding – quality writing will attract and retain fans, but amazing covers and great art will ensure they will buy multiple copies!

For the collectors: Disney and the MCU's avalanche of TV and movie announcements continue to pique the interest of hobbyists, speculators, and investors alike. With the diversification of the Marvel brand under Disney it means more projects and characters to get excited about, and those collectors chasing 'keys' can whet their appetite and procure books relatively risk free considering many of the Marvel and DC projects are still years away.

The result of this is that we have seen Modern Era comics find their feet in a big way, with some of the biggest movers in comic sales in Australia hailing from books published in the 21st century. Let's look at the top 5 modern 21st century books traded in Australia:

Ultimate Fallout #4: Increased fivefold as Miles Morales establishes himself as a long-term character in the Spider-verse, and with games, movies on the horizon, it's a safe bet that Marvel is investing big in making sure his audience stays engaged and the character stays relevant.

***Ultimate Fallout* #4**
debuted Miles Morales as Spider-Man.

Venom #3: It has been hot for months, and Knull is King, so to say. Donny Cates is introducing readers to a new era of Symbiotes, and with hints in TV and movie teasers pointing the way, Knull collectors are grabbing up as many copies as they can.

Young Avengers #1: It's another fine example of the Disney and the MCU creating a feeding frenzy, with the book being hailed as the next *Giant-Size X-Men* due to the many great characters making their first appearance, including Kate Bishop soon to star in *Hawkeye.*

Thor God of Thunder #2: Gorr The God Butcher is confirmed for the next Thor movie, and it sent the marketplace into a spin resulting in the book rocketing in value overnight. With the movie still 18 months off, there is still room for the book to climb, and where there is potential, there is demand.

Black Panther #2: Chadwick Boseman's passing was a sad day for the comic and movie industry, and with that came an announcement that the Black Panther will not be re-cast. This opened the door to Shuri becoming Black Panther resulting in all the early Shuri books, including her first appearance becoming hotter than a blue tongue lizard on a rock in the outback.

It is worth noting that all five above "modern grails" have variant and ratio covers, and those are prime real estate for any collector.

Australian Price Variant books also enjoyed a renaissance, with the demand and value increasing to that beyond their American peers on general sales platforms, and the international market is waking up to its rarity, meaning many of these are crossing boarders. Big Australia Price Variant Keys include first appearances of Deadpool, Carnage, Spider-Man 2099, War Machine, Bishop and many more – but more on this later.

For the investors: Silver and Bronze Age remain the go-to but unlike yesteryear where investors targeted mid to high grades, any grade will do as the average collectors are squeezed out of the keys market. This is evident for two reasons; much higher volumes being traded in lower grades, and the delta between GD and VG is closing in like never before. The Australian dollar was weak for most of the year (losing 20% against USD) and as result many of the larger keys were simply unaffordable, but with the recovery, the trading of larger books is picking up momentum again, despite the market being very strong.

Grail Hunters Exclusives and Initiatives: The distinct lack of conventions this year led to Grail Hunters Australia moving to private signings in collaboration with Halo Certification and Grading, and some of the amazing talent partaking in private signings included Kevin Eastman, Tom Taylor, Camillo Di Pietrantonio, Ash Madi, and James O'Barr – and the creator focused labels are more popular than ever before!

Grail Hunters also launched an Australian Price Variant Label for graded books in 2020, featuring indigenous artist and member of Wiradjuri Nation, Yaingayaingarra, also known to fellow collectors as Rebecca Beetson! All the funds from the labels were donated to a local Koala sanctuary and we'll continue our initiative for as long as the books come in.

In closing, it was a year many of us would want to forget, but big things happened. Good things also happened and we look forward to next year!

From the furthermost outpost this is Slim & Nev signing off.

Bill Alexander
Collector

Greetings from central California. It's another year over and hopefully at the present time we're headed back to a life of normalcy in regards to COVID-19. The comic market appears to be doing well in general with comics from all ages continuing to set record sales.

I can still remember many years back in the mid 1990s once believing that '80s and '90s comic books would never become valuable in the hobby, but I could not have been more wrong about that. Certain late Bronze Age and Copper Age books are starting to escalate in price, especially in certified 9.8 grade with white pages.

It also appears that newsstand edition comics 1979 on up are starting to sell for a growing premium versus their direct edition counterparts, especially in high grade. I also am starting to see more and more comic listings with "newsstand edition" being highlighted in their listings especially on eBay.

Archie's *TMNT Adventures* series from the late '80s is on the move. and certain issues have become hot and are being sought out by collectors, especially *TMNT Adventures* #1 mini series(1988) and *TMNT Adventures* #1 regular series(1989). *TMNT Adventures* #23 is the 1st appearance of Slash and *TMNT Adventures* #28 is the 1st appearance of Ninjara, both are key books. Also, note that Archie's *TMNT Adventures* regular series issues 1-11 all have 5th printings.

A few high end newsstand edition sales I noticed were *X-Men* #266 CGC 9.8 $1,306, *Swamp Thing* #37 CGC 9.8 $2,095, Marvel's *G.I Joe* #21 CGC 9.8 $4,999, *Amazing Spider-Man* #300 CGC 9.6 $2,245 and *New Mutants* #98 CGC 9.8 $1,550.

Modern era newsstand premiums are also growing quite noteworthy, for example a CGC 9.8 newsstand copy of *Ultimate Fallout* #4 selling for auction at $8,100, and multiple *Batman Adventures* #12 CGC 9.8 newsstand copies selling at auction for above $4,600. Multiple sales of *Spawn* #1 newsstand CGC 9.8 copies set highs this year above $1,000.

Collector interest in both Type 1 and Type 1A comics continues to grow in the hobby at an accelerated pace. Over in the world of Canadian price variants (aka CPVs) an Amazing Spider-Man #238 CGC 9.8 sold for a record high sale of $7,800.00 in November 2020. Some other high end CPV sales observed were *Amazing Spider-Man* #238 CGC 9.8 $4,650.00, *Batman* #386 CGC 9.8 $1,352.00, Archie's *TMNT Adventures* #1 CGC 9.8 mini series (newsstand edition CPV) $2,299.95, *Transformers* #1 CGC 9.8 $2,425.00, *Archie's Girls Betty and Veronica* #320 CGC 9.4 $1,465.00, and *Archie's Pals 'N' Gals* #23 CGC 1.8 $412.00.

I am one of nine collaborators on the 2021 price guide for Type 1A Canadian price variants of the 1980s and 1990s, an annual guide which a group of Overstreet Advisors puts together because, as of now, the *Overstreet Guide* itself still does not yet include separate CPV values. We hope that will one day change, but in the meantime we contribute our guide to the hobby as a freely available resource. This year you can find it at cpvpriceguide.com. Reader interest in our guide continues to grow each year, with the 2020 edition of our guide having received well over 1,000,000 page hits in the past year. Here is our latest top 20 CPV list and the corresponding 9.2 variant values:

1) *Archie's Girls Betty and Veronica* #320 (Archie, 10/1982), 75¢ variant 9.2 = $650
2) *G.I. Joe, a Real American Hero* #21 (Marvel, 3/1984), 75¢ variant 9.2 = $525
3) *Amazing Spider-Man* #238 (Marvel 3/1983), 75¢ variant 9.2 = $510
4) *Saga of the Swamp Thing* #37 (DC, 6/1985), 9¢ variant 9.2 = $375
5) *Batman* #357 (DC, 3/1983), 75¢ variant 9.2 = $315
6) *Transformers* #1 (Marvel, 9/1984), $1.00 variant 9.2 = $300
7) *Jughead* #325 (Archie, 10/1982), 75¢ variant 9.2 = $275
8) *Marvel Graphic Novel* #4 (Marvel, 1982), $5.95 variant 9.2 = $220
9) *Marvel Super Heroes Secret Wars* #8 (Marvel, 12/1984), $1.00 variant 9.2 = $205
10) *Amazing Spider-Man* #252 (Marvel, 5/1984), 75¢ variant 9.2 = $204
11) *Batman* #423 (DC, 9/1988), $1.00 variant 9.2 = $202
12) *Teenage Mutant Ninja Turtles Advs.* (mini) #1 (Archie, 8/1988), $1.25 var. 9.2 = $200
13) *Batman* #386 (DC, 8/1985), 95¢ variant 9.2 = $185
14) *Archie's Girls Betty and Veronica* #322 (Archie, 2/1983), 75¢ variant 9.2 = $170
15) *Punisher* #1 (Marvel, 1/1986), $1.50 variant 9.2 = $162
16) *Star Wars* #68 (Marvel, 2/1983), 75¢ variant 9.2 = $160
17) *Archie's Girls Betty and Veronica* #321 (Archie, 12/1982), 75¢ variant 9.2 = $155
18) *Thor* #337 (Marvel, 11/1983), 75¢ variant 9.2 = $152
19) *Marvel Team-Up* #141 (Marvel, 5/1984), 75¢ variant 9.2 = $150
20) *X-Factor* #6 (Marvel, 7/1986), 95¢ variant 9.2 = $148.

DAVID T. ALEXANDER, TYLER ALEXANDER AND EDDIE WENDT
DTACOLLECTIBLES.COM
CULTUREANDTHRILLS.COM

TERROR and TREASURE were the prevailing themes of 2020 and continue into early 2021. Things came to a standstill when the virus hit our country. All comic stores, conventions, swap meets, flea markets and fan get-togethers came to a halt. I do commend all the show promoters who tried to postpone and reschedule events. In many cases the venue or the government required cancellation. Comic stores took a real beating having to contend with government restrictions and product distribution disruption. New comics were not printed for quite a while.

On top of the virus fears we have had to contend with massive political disruption. Americans have been at each other's throats over their political views. Riots, protests, bombings, looting, murder and fighting have become commonplace, unlike anything we have seen in our country during our lifetimes. Our existence mirrors the fiction you would read in the pages of a *Spider* or *Operator #5* pulp from the 1930s. I know of at least two comic stores that were victims of looting in the early days of the protests. Additionly I have heard of a couple stores that were burned during the mostly peaceful protests. One store that got looted was probably the victim of an inside job because the robbers overlooked all the material in the front sales area and only stole the Silver Age and Golden Age books from the back office. Doesn't it seem strange that looters would restrict themselves to only expensive comic books? This has truly been a time of TERROR.

And what was the TREASURE of 2020? There are two aspects to this. The first being the incredible comic books that we bought and sold during 2020 which will be detailed shortly. The second and more important aspect is being a member of a great hobby that all participants embrace and cherish and love. The hobby means so much to so many people who share their enthusiasm with others. This is a unifying force that gives common ground to many people who would otherwise never know each other. Such a wide range of people are involved from many backgrounds, cultures and creeds. All ages are involved, kids love comics as early as 4 or 5 years old and there are collectors in their 80s who are still sending wantlists to dealers. When we are talking about comics we are not concerned about political or cultural differences. This hobby is truly a TREASURE.

What did we buy and sell in 2020? When the pandemic hit it looked like doom for comic dealers. That was not the case. With retail locations and conventions shut down collectors flocked to internet and mail order dealers. Collecting is important and fans did not let the pandemic or politics slow down enthusiasm in 2020. A majority of dealers have had record sales during the year.

What is really hot this year? The biggest increase in demand has been for pulp magazines. These are often considered the forerunners of comic books. There are so many great titles in this format it is hard to list them all in the space I am allotted but I will provide a few highlights. *Marvel Science Stories* #1 with a cover by Norman Saunders came out in 1938 many months before the first issue of *Marvel Comics* #1 and sells for a fraction of the price of the famous comic. The logo from the pulp was used on all *Marvel Mystery Comics* from #2 on. It is in the early days of a gigantic price increase. All the titles published by Red Circle, which was Timely's pulp division, are poised for huge price jumps. The hero pulps have always been popular and are experiencing increased demand as many comic collectors have entered the hunt. The first issue of *Doc Savage* recently sold for a five figure amount. *Shadow*, *Spider*, *Captain Future*, *G-8 and His Battle Aces*, *Phantom Detective*, *Black Hood*, *Buck Jones*, *Masked Rider*, *Lone Ranger*, *Lone Eagle* and *Dusty Ayers and His Battle Birds* are among titles that are in high demand. Other popular genres are Aviation and Air War titles. These began in the late 1920s and were popular thru World War II. Get them if you can. *Planet Stories* and *Amazing Stories* are among the best Science Fiction titles. *Black Mask*, *Dime Detective* and *Detective Fiction Weekly* along with *Detective Story* are big movers in the mystery field. *Weird Menace* and *Spicy* titles are some of the most popular high value pulps. Never pass up a chance to get *Spicy Mystery*, *Terror Tales* or *Horror Stories* when they become available. Soon you will no longer have a chance to own them.

Comic sales and purchases were massive in 2020. We moved a lot of big books like *Superman* #1, *Detective* #38, early *Captain America*, *More Fun*, *Marvel Mystery* and Silver Age Marvel and DC keys. Western comics are making a strong come back. They were slow sellers for a few years but are now being rediscovered. Movie and TV photo cover titles are popular only being surpassed by Atlas pre-Code westerns. When is the Kid Colt movie coming out? Golden Age books of all types have seen increased demand in 2020. Even low grade copies have been quick to sell. I think many collectors wanted to read some of the older issues while confined to their homes.

War comics of all ages are still steadily gaining in popularity and value. Another lesser collected genre, Romance, is also selling briskly with notable interest increasing in Charlton Romance. Some of the more unique and psychedelic covers go for multiples of *Guide* in any grade. Archie comics, especially suggestive or risqué covers from the 1960s through the 2000s, are picking up steam as collectors search out affordable ways to put together a niche, focused collection.

In the coming year we expect to see more record breaking prices for blue chip Gold and Silver keys, especially in high grade. As institutional money creeps into the hobby as a way to invest and more deep pocketed investors turn their attention to collectibles, expect to see more and more auctions bringing bids that would have seemed unthinkable just a decade ago. There is some hope that the United States could be able to safely allow large gatherings by mid-2021, in which case we expect to see conventions large and small welcome back attendees and dealers alike. I know we have missed treasure hunting through rows and rows of long boxes and I am sure many of you have as well. Anyone who has comments or thoughts on this is welcome to reach out to us at any time. You can find our contact info on our ad page in this book.

Dave Anderson, DDS
Collector

As another year winds down, we find ourselves reflecting on things that have occurred throughtout the year. Foremost in most of our minds is COVID-19 and the effect it had on us. Not surprisingly, it seemed to have little if any negative impact on the online comic market. Prices realized by the major auction houses were stronger than ever and demand for comics in all grades and value ranges surged to near all time highs. Although many collectors were undoubtedly affected financially by the virus, it didn't seem to stop most from finding a way to continue to buy and sell comics and fuel the market. Perhaps with restrictions and closures in place, comic collectors focused on their collections and sold items if necessary and bought more if appropriate. Whatever the reasons, the comic market, at least the online and auction aspect of it, never missed a beat. Of course with many comic stores closed and very few conventions taking place, it naturally drove attention to online activity. I will be interested in hearing how comic store owners, distributors, and convention promoters modified their operations due to COVID in market reports by other Overstreet advisors.

Lauren Becker
Comic*Pop Collectibles

Well...what can be said about 2020?

Whenever there is a large economic downturn, you can almost always depend on one thing. The collectibles market takes a huge upswing. Sports cards (and also non-sports cards), classic cars, and of course...comic books. This played out similarly through previous decades. When Black Monday/October happened in 1987, the Silver Age market began to explode. When the economy was experiencing its 1st economic recession during the Bush years, you saw collectibles being looked at as more "stable" an investment (compared to other stocks and money market accounts).

2020? This was the year that shattered all other records. Not only did Gold, Silver and Bronze reach staggering heights of price increases, but so also did Copper and Modern. *Amazing Spider-Man* #300 CGC 9.8 reached an astonishing high of $5750 (with a current average price of $4500...compared to ONE year ago when the average price for a 9.8 was $2000). *Ultimate Fallout* #4 1:75 variant CGC 9.8 cleared $8500 (one year ago, a "paltry" $2200 average)! Prices once reserved for Gold and Silver pieces, now setting records in the Copper and Modern era of comics! Why? A few theories.

1) As stated above, in times of hard economic downturn (and what could be more of a downturn than a global pandemic, forcing people to stay quarantined in their homes), people/investors rather put their assets into tangible items that can net them more money in the long run. Sounds silly? When the 1st appearance of Spider-Man is going for $5520 December 1, 2019 CGC graded 0.5 and then sells again April 15, 2020 (a 4-1/2 month turn around) for $8265, an almost $3000 profit, during a recession/depression, you better believe people are taking an interest in that and dumping cash from their paper investments to put into...well...*tangible* paper investments.

2) When the pandemic started, shops had to shut down for a few months. The more savvy ones had either started curbside shopping or had an internet presence. I can tell you that our online sales tripled during this time. Before the shutdown, we would ship out an average of 40 packages per week. During the height of the shutdown, we were shipping out almost 40 packages PER DAY. Many of our high end items (and by high end, I mean items over $500) began to move at a rapid rate. It became very difficult to keep certain lower tier product in stock as items that we had multiples of, began to disappear. For example, we had 75 copies of *Justice League* #50 in stock (1st mention of "The Three Jokers" and 1st Jessica Cruz as Green Lantern) that we sold at $15.00 each. Now, due to upcoming news and speculation, we are now sold out as we sold our last copy at $50.00!!!

3) Besides the shops having to basically shut down, so too did the major publishers. With no new product coming out for the foreseeable future, collectors who needed their "fix", and were lucky enough to have disposable income, went towards the back issue market. Again, comics that were plentiful and an average $25 price became 3-7 times more each month. Things slowed down slightly when new comics came back out (and don't get me started on the DC debacle... or as I like to call it, DC&T), but even recent weekly issues became instant collectibles as many stores played cautiously with their orders and cut back to bare bones with economic uncertainty in the air. Best example was *Dark Nights: Death Metal Legend of the Dark Knight* #1 with the 1st appearance of The Robin King. A throw away story at best, many shops had ordered in the single digits with many not even qualifying for the 1:25 variant. The WEEK it came out, regular copies were selling at $25.00+ while the 1:25 sold RAW at $400-600 a pop! Outrageous!

Here are some of our CGC sales from this year. The "*", shows where we sold the item online. As expected, many of our sales were online as opposed to in person....

Amazing Spider-Man #361 (newsstand) 9.6...$200.00*
Amazing Spider-Man #361 (newsstand) 9.4...$150.00*
Amazing Spider-Man #361 (newsstand) 9.8...$600.00*
Thor #337 (newsstand) 9.6...$280.00*
Incredible Hulk #340 9.8...$425.00*i
Incredible Hulk #340 9.8...$430.00*
Power Man & Iron Fist #50 9.6...$130.00*
Amazing Spider-Man #300 9.6...$700.00*
Astonishing Tales #25 9.6...$550.00*
Tomb of Dracula #10 9.2...$1700.00
Tomb of Dracula #10 9.4...$2500.00
Iron Fist #14 9.4...$500.00
Mister Miracle #4 9.0...$350.00*
Swamp Thing #37 9.8...$600.00*
Joker #1 8.0...$110.00*
Ms. Marvel (1977) #1 9.4 (qualified)...$70.00*
X-Men #101 7.0...$270.00*
Captain America #117 6.5...$260.00*
Daredevil #168 9.0...$185.00
Astonishing Tales #25 9.8...$1900.00*
Marvel Spotlight #12 9.4...$250.00*
Marvel Spotlight #32 9.0...$200.00*
Man O'Mars #1 4.0...$550.00
Strange Tales #169 9.6...$1900.00
Frankenstein #32 5.0...$250.00*
Strange Tales #178 9.2...$180.00*
Incredible Hulk #141 8.0...$180.00*
Avengers Annual #10 9.2...$150.00*
Amazing Spider-Man #238 (with tattooz AND Mark Jewelers insert) 6.5...$250.00*
Avengers #57 5.0...$200.00*
Green Lantern #87 8.5...$400.00*
Amazing Spider-Man #301 9.6...$125.00*
Detective Comics #359 5.5...$700.00*

Jimmy Olsen #134 8.0...$400.00*
Amazing Spider-Man #300 9.0...$350.00*
Amazing Spider-Man #194 9.4...$300.00*
Amazing Spider-Man #50 5.0...$450.00*
Moon Knight #55 9.8...$200.00*
Showcase #17 2.0...$350.00*
X-Men #266 9.6...$200.00*
Spawn #300 NYCC gold variant 9.8...$850.00*
Independent Comic Book Sampler #2 SS with
Kevin Eastman sketch 8.5 (CBCS)...$250.00*
Mister Miracle #1 9.4...$600.00*
Nova #1 9.0...$150.00*
Avengers #4 5.5...$1800.00
Amazing Spider-Man #252 9.6...$200.00*
Sandman #8 9.6...$225.00
Green Lantern #59 4.0...$150.00*
Venus #9 3.0...$400.00*
Marvel Team-Up #141 9.6...$150.00*
Fear #20 9.4...$225.00*
Invincible Iron Man #9 (2 copies) 9.8...$250.00@*
Human Torch #4 3.5...$1450.00*
Strange Tales #126 5.0...$200.00*
Savage She-Hulk #1 9.8...$450.00*
Marvel Spotlight #5 8.0...$1500.00*
Marvel Spotlight #5 6.0...$800.00*
Doom Patrol #99 7.0...$350.00
Darth Vader #3 9.8...$250.00*
DC Comics Presents #26...$300.00*
Tales of Teen Titans #44 9.6...$150.00*
Edge of the Spiderverse #2 3rd print 9.8...$250.00*
Batman #92 (2020 1:25 variant) 9.8...$160.00*
Wynd #1 1:25 Momoko variant cover 9.8...$150.00*
Werewolf by Night #33 9.0...$300.00*
Vampire Tales #2 6.0...$200.00*
Showcase #6 1.8...$500.00*
Deadly Hands of Kung-fu #19 9.2...$360.00*
Flash #110 3.5 (qualified)...$230.00*
Spider-Men #1 1:100 variant cover 9.8...$300.00*
Static #1 Platinum Variant 9.2...$170.00*
Batman Adventures #12 7.0...$500.00*
Spider-Man #1 Platinum Variant 9.4...$425.00
Batman #423 9.6...$325.00*
Amazing Spider-Man #33 7.5...$350.00*
The Boys #1 9.8...$350.00*
Aliens #1 9.4...$200.00*
Green Lantern #16 6.5...$400.00*
Tales of Suspense #39 NG...$1500.00*
Werewolf by Night #32 8.0...$2000.00*
Mad #1 5.0...$1500.00*
Giant-Size X-Men #1 7.0...$2400.00
Incredible Hulk #180 8.0...$1000.00*
Sgt. Fury #1 2.5...$600.00*
X-Men #101 8.0...$500.00*
Ultimate Spider-Man #1 white variant 9.8...$500.00*

We had to change our strategy, not only to sell more online (listing an extra 3000 pieces that we normally wouldn't as they would normally sell better in person at conventions), but to do more one day comic/toy shows. This worked out splendidly as we were able to use the shows as a buying tool to keep our warehouse stocked. It didn't hurt that even the one day shows we attended were also selling bonanzas. Being cooped up in the house for months on end made people empty their wallets more. Our last large show we attended was C2E2 in Feburary. We did abnormally well (up by almost 25% from the year before), but didn't have another show, a one day toy/comic show, until June. The main purpose of going was to restock (which we did in abundance), but the sales rivaled, if not surpassed, dealer set up day from C2E2 (which is where many dealers make the bulk of their sales to other dealers).

So 2020 is a year I would like to surpass just from the sheer horribleness of all the events (or lack thereof) that happened, but I would be remiss if I didn't take away some form of lesson that this donkey of a year has taught. I won't tell you what it is...you'll have to figure that one out all by yourself.

Jim Berry
Collector

I am a collector and part-time dealer based in Portland, Oregon and Seattle with a small store on eBay (jb233). I started collecting seriously as a young California kid in the middle 1970s and started purchasing collections in the 1980s as time and money allowed. Now, I'm a photographer and filmmaker by trade (jimberryphotography.com) and I'm proud to say that I'm the only working photographer I know of who takes old comics in exchange for work. (On two occasions I photographed weddings in exchange for comics) My main interest is Golden Age books, particularly WW II era and pre-Code Horror, but I'm interested in comics of all stripes.

Like many folks, most of my work was cancelled in 2020 so my comic budget was significantly reduced. I haven't gotten out much and, obviously, there haven't been any in-person shows. So much of this year has been about navigating a new way of doing things.

That said, it seems as if the comic market is largely progressing as if there were no pandemic. With everything closed and cancelled, the marketplace on eBay is booming. Also, Facebook (private sales), Heritage, ComicLink and the rest consistently do record-breaking online business. It makes sense. In a time when our lives have been so radically reduced, the value of our hobbies and entertainment have become more significant. I can only speak for myself but, this year, I've dug through boxes, sorted, re-organized, and re-read stories more than I ever have.

One of the sectors that I have been focusing on more is War comics from the Golden Age, particularly, the early 1950s. They are relatively cheap – and tough to find in high grade. With prices of WWII stuff and pre-Code Horror both going through the roof, the War comics have become a personal outlet to sate my desire to collect cool old stuff without crashing my budget.

There are so many dealers in Portland and Seattle. It's changed so much in the past 10-20 years – really, since the movies turned the hobby mainstream, and eBay turned everyone into a dealer. Craigslist in my area, was, for a few short years, an absolute treasure trove of old comics. Out of the hundreds of collections I've purchased or traded for over the years, my best were found on Craigslist back in the early-middle 2000s. Now it's almost exclusively a place where dealers advertise for collections and snipe at each other in their posts.

I was lucky to land a few collections this year. There was a little collection (75 books) of Bronze Age Marvels that all featured Mark Jeweler's inserts. One of the books was a high-grade *Amazing Spider-Man* #129. I also picked up a nice collection of late 1950s books at an estate sale right before COVID that had a small stack of beautiful Atlas monster books. That was a fun day . . .

I recently had an interesting conversation with my old friend, John Hill, who owns and operates Hills of Comics in Auburn, Washington. Like myself, John started collecting and trading comics back in the 1970s and when we get to talking we often discuss the old times. One of the tangents we got off on dealt with the difference between collecting back then versus now. John mentioned that the biggest change he's noticed as a store owner is that collectors today seem to focus solely on key books and speculation where as, when we were kids, it was all about completing a run. I recalled the feeling of immense pleasure and satisfaction when I first completed my run of *Silver Surfer*. As a thirteen-year old kid, I knew it was doable because there were only 18 books but I had to wheel and deal to make it happen. When that final book on my list became available, the classic #4, with the awesome cover of Thor versus The Surfer on The Rainbow Bridge, I nabbed it. For me, that euphoric feeling of completion came to define what it meant to collect comics. I asked John when the last time someone came in with a want list looking to fill in their collection. He replied, "It's been years."

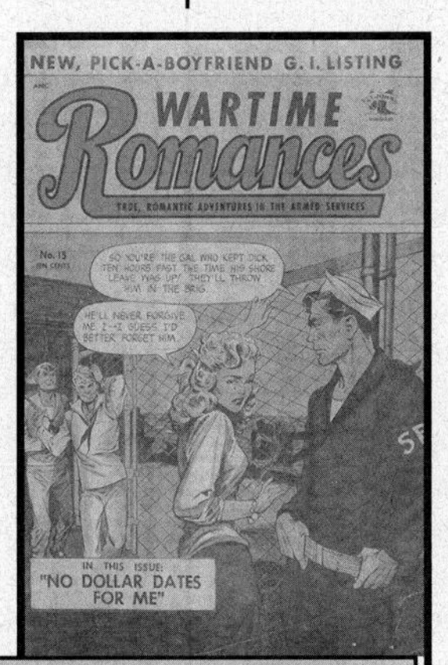

Comics with Matt Baker cover art were popular at auctions this year. ***Wartime Romances*** *#15 shown.*

My best comic book moments this year have been with my daughter, Willa, 12. She enjoys comics but isn't so interested in her old man's collection. Still, she enjoys reading comics from Avatar, the animated series which I highly recommend. We've also watched and read *Runaways*, *Cloak and Dagger*, and *The Mandolorian* (Mando!). Sharing my interest in comic, fantasy, and sci-fi stories with my kid is one of my life's finest pleasures.

As I write this, in early December of 2020, it seems that life has become an exercise in staying positive – as much as possible. It's important that we remember to be patient with one another – this won't last forever. People want to hold close those things they use to remind themselves of better times. For most of the people reading this piece, comics are a touchstone to those better times. We comic collectors are the lucky ones. Keep your chin up and remember that those better times will soon return. With any luck, you're reading this from a convention floor somewhere, surrounded by fellow comic lovers and those times are already back. I hope so.

A hearty Thank You to Bob Overstreet and the entire crew at Gemstone.

Until next time... I wish you good fortune in the comic wars to come.

Peter Bilelis, Esq.
Collector

It's now a week before Christmas 2020. Globally, the COVID-19 pandemic has claimed almost 1.7M lives, four of those souls were people in my circle. Two consequences of the necessary actions taken to curb the pandemic's spread were: a re-imagined work model, with many office workers now working virtually from home; and a weaker economy, with many companies instituting significant workforce reductions and small businesses suffering or disappearing. In a COVID world where "normal" gave way to the surreal, the good news is there is hope and a light at the end of the tunnel ... thanks to a merciful God who gave us science and the intelligence to discover a vaccine.

The effects of this "new normal" have been funky. Unemployment rose. Yet those with jobs had more disposable income due to COVID-related quarantine circumstances, and were using this surplus to mitigate the quarantine blues by increasing their spending on in-home entertainment, and things like comic books. For the Golden Age (GA) and Silver Age (SA) market, these dynamics resulted in a lot of amazing material coming to market and sale prices all over the map.

Auction Sales: Price aside, the selection of choice material this year felt like a 2007 time-warp. Haven't seen two *Police Comics* #1 in any single auction in years, but 2 copies were auctioned in one recent auction. *Detective Comics* #27 in nice shape came to auction. *All Star* #3 & 8 and GA *Green Lantern* #1 surfaced on a couple occasions, as did (Fox) *Wonder Comics* #1, *Detective* #187 (in CGC 6.0), a handful of *Batman* #52s, three copies each of *Detectives* #71 and 73, and several scarce Matt Baker cover art books in higher grade. Pre-Code Crime/Horror genre books, such as *True Crime* #1 and 2; *Punch* #12, two copies of *Fight Against Crime* #20; and two CGC 7.0 copies of *Lawbreakers Suspense Stories* #11 to name a few all came up for sale. It's a rarity for a higher grade copy of *Action* #17 to come up for sale; however, 2 such copies were auctioned this year. *All Winners* #4, three nice copies of *Crime Suspenstories* #22 and *Mask* #1, as well as *Pep* #20 and #34 all came up for sale. And, several SA Marvel keys not seen in the marketplace in CGC 9.2 and 9.4 in a few years were also available. Recorded sale prices confirmed the extreme interest in this top-shelf material.

In terms of prices, the larger on-line comic book auction sites saw choice material that generally tracked to the usual logarithmic premiums, with non-choice material reported sales confirming a slower and flatter market. Not surprisingly, some collectors were forced to part with their treasures due to the economic downturn. In some cases, material typically seen in the high-end quarterly auctions held by one auction house started surfacing in their weekly "pedestrian" auctions, suggesting collectors needed to liquidate urgently. Books like *Avengers* #4 in CGC 8.5 white, some key Mac Raboy WWII classic *Master Comics*, a host of nicely graded L.B. Cole classic cover books, "hot" SA books in grade, and many other such books were all seen in the weekly auctions. In these auctions, and in this auction house's quarterly high-end auctions, many reported sale prices seemed to defy logic. This included many "hot" GA and SA classic covers, first appearances, and in other cases ho-hum books, with reported sales at inexplicably astronomical prices; and even many GA and SA run books, in 7.0 - 8.0, reportedly being sold at new high watermarks. Other reported sale prices more closely correlated with other recent sales data. In the "run book" category, if you're looking for a hidden Batman gem that's still available at a reasonable price, consider *Detective* #60. While it has a nondescript cover, it has one of the best Joker splash pages, with a giant-sized Clown Prince of Crime decked out in a Napoleonesque uniform. And, once cracked out of the slab, it can be thoroughly enjoyed.

Traditional Dealer Sites: In perusing my favorite 12-15 dealer websites, which is a good barometer of market commerce, it was clear the market slowed. It's important to recognize the pandemic has put a halt to most comic book conventions, so dealers are generally relegated to online selling, or selling through large established auctioneers. This had a significant impact on buying, selling, and carrying inventory cost. In many cases where, in the past, certain books would be sold as soon as listed (or soon after), they now sit unsold. Many dealers now advertise price cuts on even choice material; and they are willing to bargain on price even further.

eBay: This auction site remains both a great source for buying and selling comic books and, in a sense, is still the "land of the dreamers." Many really good deals can still be found, especially when buying via auction style listings. Among other nice GA books, a *Captain Marvel Jr.* #10 in VG/FN sold for ~$400. I haven't seen this book being sold by any dealer at even triple this *Overstreet* percentage in years. Similarly, several early GA *Batman*, *Captain America*, *Punch*, *WDCS*, and L.B. Cole classic cover books in 6.0-8.0 were auctioned for ~70-80% of the lowest prices I've seen in any other venue. Many sellers; however, continue to list books under the buy-it-now option with prices that are often 1.5 - 3x the highest prices seen anywhere else; and these books usually sit unsold ... in perpetuity.

Hollywood Effect: The pandemic has also taken a toll on Hollywood's impact on the comic book market. Pay-per-view film releases aren't garnering the same market enthusiasm and pop culture interest as do theater releases. Consequently, pay-per-view film releases are not causing the related comic books to explode in demand and price.

The first obvious example was the release of the *Bloodshot* film. Its trailer generated a lot of hobby interest and, although it was intended for release in theaters, the pandemic caused it to be released via pay-per-view. The result: reported sale prices of Bloodshot's first comic book appearance barely moved. I think a theater release would have moved Bloodshot into the mainstream, given (to me) he very loosely equates to a 21st century technology-enhanced cross between Jason Bourne and the Punisher. Another example is Wonder Woman. Despite this character's enormous and increasing popularity, the second trailer dropped for the film sequel and, while reported sales of *All Star* #8 and *Sensation* #1 remained very strong, they did not catapult to new record high sale prices. I think this will definitely change once theater releases restart.

Interpreting the Data: It's clear the hobby remains strong and continues to grow. And, the increasing amount of quality material coming to market continues to draw greater and greater interest. In terms of the erratic reported sale prices, it's hard to pinpoint any one cause. Certainly, one factor is some hobbyists have more disposable income and are funneling it into the hobby. Another might be caused by the non-hobbyists with relatively unlimited funds (by which I mean anyone from a Hollywood personality's personal shopper/wealth manager to a fine art collector) that are purchasing books like *Action* #1, *Detective* #27, 31, *Batman* #1, *All Star* #8, *Superman* #1, and *Captain America* #1 (and similar) in high grade for investment diversity. In 2020, these types of recorded sales both invigorated the hobby and had a foreseeable but unintended negative ripple effect. The record sales signaled hobby stability and growth. When a top tier book in the same grade reportedly sold in 2020 at a lower price than in the past; however, many saw this as a harbinger of a softening hobby. Those willing to risk say $5k in today's down economy will still bid aggressively on a sought after book and often overpay to get it; whereas, many others will look at these dynamics and decide not to put the money into the hobby, resulting in the slower sales seen in 2020. Yet another factor is larger, more stable dealers (and hobbyists) taking advantage of the panic selling (think Mr. Potter in the film *It's a Wonderful Life*). They are making the calculated assumption that this material will continue to appreciate and, because so much of it is currently available, they are purchasing it to better position themselves for the future. My approach has been to prioritize books on my want list that are rarely seen in the marketplace and then buy with my head, not over it. Using this approach, I've been able to add several classic covers and first appearances to my collection this past year ... at prices that made sense.

Good luck hunting in 2021...

Steve Borock
CBCS
President and Primary Grader

The arrival of the 51st edition of *The Overstreet Comic Book Price Guide* means another year has passed, and what a tumultuous year it has been. For some in our hobby, it's been a devastating time, while for others it has seen tremendous increases in business. Those of us who have thrived during this period should never forget for a moment those who have not weathered it as well, or worse, those who have lost their lives during the pandemic.

Those of us who have enjoyed the overall long-term stability of the field have, of course, to thank Bob Overstreet for that. As I've mentioned previously in my market reports, for so many years – now more than five decades – my personal hero has worked tirelessly and so hard to keep our great hobby afloat. Each year when the *Guide* arrives, I still feel like a kid, reading through it like there is no tomorrow. So, thanks, again, Bob! You really are my personal hero!

And since Bob would be the first to tell you that the *Guide* doesn't happen in a vacuum, the team at Gemstone Publishing deserves a shout out as well: J.C. Vaughn, Mark Huesman, and Amanda Sheriff do a ton of hard work for the *Guide* every year. And last, but definitely not least, a big thanks to Steve Geppi, who has put the *Guide* out for more than half of its existence now.

Best Comics' Tommy Maletta is greatly missed by the hobby.

If you've read my market reports the past few years, you already know that I will not talk about pricing as I need to stay impartial as a grader. Likewise, because of that need to stay impartial, my approach is to treat each and every comic with respect and a serious approach. In other words, I must treat a modern comic with the same care and grading as, say, an *Action Comics* #1. That is without consideration for the final value that the market will set for the issue; I just get the grade correct, check for restoration, and get it to encapsulation.

I can, though, tell you what has been submitted for grading that seems to us at CBCS to be "hot" for submitters: Golden Age and early Silver Age of all genres and grades, Silver Age and Bronze Age keys, Modern keys, and signed issues.

As I am sure this will also be mentioned in many of the market reports you will read here, every time a TV show or movie about a character or team gets mentioned, we see a flood of books with those characters for speculation resale. Our two-day modern turnaround tier has been quite a success with these types of books (I said this last year, and it continues to be true).

Also continuing the trend from last year, our Verified Signature Program (VSP), which verifies signatures that have not been witnessed, has seen so many cool vintage books with creator signatures ranging from Frank Frazetta, Bob Kane, Jack Kirby, Stan Lee, Alex Schomburg, Al Feldstein and many others, as well as Modern Age books signed by creators such as J. Scott Campbell, Adam Hughes, Mark Brooks, and Todd McFarlane, among others. An additional superstar name has popped into this mix, and that's Steve Ditko.

Certifying and authenticating unwitnessed signatures took off previously and has yet to come down!

2020-2021 has been another fantastic year for CBCS, all thanks to the collecting community. So, a big thank-you very much to all of you.

I would like to congratulate my friend and a great force for good in our business, Buddy Saunders, and my late friend Tommy Maletta, for being selected as this year's recipients of The John Verzyl Overstreet Advisor Award.

They have both done so much for our hobby and are truly deserving of this acknowledgment of their respective characters and contributions. Tommy, even though he passed away a year ago, is still missed by the hobby, and I still miss my friend.

This honor is well deserved by these two fantastic gentlemen, both of whom have shared their love for comics with so many.

As I alluded to earlier, this has been another fantastic year for CBCS. Saying that we've been flooded with books this past year would be an understatement of epic proportions. Last year we launched our census (population report), as well as our new archival, tamper-evident case. Based on the reactions we've received since then, the collecting community continues to be very happy with both!

We are enthusiastically looking forward to the year ahead, whatever crazy changes it brings our way.

As I do each year, I want to give a shout out to our hobby's greatest charity, The Hero Initiative. This 501(c)(3) charity is something everyone can get behind. Hero gives back to comic creators – the people who have brought us so much joy over the years – when they are in need, offering assistance with food, medical, housing and other help that is needed. Please check them out at www.heroinitiative.org.

If you weren't already aware of this, this marks the 12th year of the Hero Initiative limited edition of *The Overstreet Comic Book Price Guide*. They're limited to only 500 hardcover copies, and the full proceeds go directly to the charity.

This year's cover is by Joseph Michael Linsner, and it's a standout. I hope this is the copy you are reading right now!

I will end my market report the same way I do every year: This is for the newer collectors in our great hobby, as I would hope that the more seasoned collectors already know this information. Even though I really believe in this hobby, this market and its future, and have so since I was a kid (I am 56), there is no such thing as a free lunch. If you are going to invest in comic books, you had better love what you buy. If the economy ever goes really bad, just like stocks, precious metals, real estate, or anything else considered an investment, you will not be able to sell them for a really high price very quickly and you can certainly not use comic books to feed, house, or take care of your family.

The best advice I can give you is this: Buy what you like and can afford. It's really that simple. It has also been my war cry for so many years. Just enjoy collecting and reading comic books, enjoy the amazing friendships we make in this wonderful hobby, look around and enjoy all the cool stuff this hobby has to offer from original comic art and comic books, to the movies and TV shows based on the characters we all love so much, to comic memorabilia, going to the conventions and it will all seem worth it in the end.

Normally at this point I say, "I hope to see and talk with many of you at the conventions that I, and CBCS, will be attending this coming year!" I certainly hope that will be true again soon and that we'll all be seeing each other again soon. Thank you for taking the time to read this, be kind to each other and, as always, happy collecting!

Russ Bright
Mill Geek Comics

In an industry infatuated with zombies, it's appropriate to have people declare the death of comic collecting, only to have it come back stronger than ever before!

The fragile comic book industry is like constantly walking on thin ice. It does not take much for a shop to fail and close. Most stores must juggle many things to stay in business. If a store ONLY does new comics, they are at a much higher risk if new comics aren't selling, (or WORSE, aren't RELEASED!). If a store sells vintage comics and does not do conventions or sell online, they won't last long. Most shop owners have to supplement their comic business with board or card games to survive. Even if you have a healthy online business, you must diversify to be successful.

2020 has been a roller coaster. Nobody guessed that this year would have Diamond stopping distribution for a few months, conventions being canceled for the foreseeable future, and shops closing left and right. Everyone has been working on getting used to the new normal and finding ways to adapt and overcome. Unfortunately, not every store has been able to come out unscathed. We will not know the full extent of the damage to the industry for years, but, it's been substantial.

This is why it's even more impressive to have the outpouring of support from customers both locally and online. The number of new collectors is staggering. The number of people buying, collecting, and reading is going up substantially.

A couple of years ago it seemed that people were collecting cover art that they liked. Last year, the majority were finding things they wanted to read. This year, we are seeing increased sales for everything. People like the cover art. People like the writers and stories with substance. People are looking to invest. People are looking to escape. People are looking to find things to do with their kids. The benefit of a pandemic is that since people are trying to stay at home more often, comics are a great way to pass the time while doing things they enjoy.

We are selling vintage comics faster than ever before, and variants and new comics are flying off the shelves. Everything seems to be selling and selling well. We are having trouble keeping our cheap bins stocked. In the past, customers stopped by the shop and grabbed their comics quickly. Now we are seeing people take hours browsing for more things to bring home and read.

It's not all good news, though.

The loss of conventions has been a major blow to brick and mortar stores, artists and comic creators. After talking to some stores that depend on revenue from conventions, it's very apparent that the lack of convention income is going to kill more stores. In the Seattle area alone, we have lost over 5 stores this past year. And it's not just older comics that have taken a major blow. DC's distribution transition has caused major ripples in the market for new comics. When they changed distributors, 9 out of the 10 shops I talked to did not transition with them. Even now, we have half as many customers ordering DC. The stories are popular, people are collecting them, but I can only imagine how many more NEW DC comics would be ordered if it was easier for shops and customers alike to order them.

Adapting is tough, and it's difficult to make quick decisions in this industry. Shops have a 2-month delay between orders and arrival for new comics. When you have to keep track of multiple distributors, final order cutoffs, due dates and accounts, it DOUBLES a workload. For many shops that only have 1 or 2 people holding everything together, it become overwhelming. Owning a comic bookstore is a labor of love for most of us. We do this because we LOVE comics. Is it worth the extra work for little to no extra pay? Only time will tell.

How can we combat this? What can shops do to remain relevant? A lot of stores have been moving sales online. eBay, ComicLink and Heritage have been great ways to sell, and even more people than ever before are selling on Instagram and in Facebook groups. Will this be able to replace conventions for the next year or so? What if conventions never return in the same capacity?

Since sellers are favoring online selling, we have customers following suit. We have seen record setting prices for all eras of comics. Modern books are selling for premiums that are astounding. We are seeing instances of comics selling for 5-10 times cover price less than ONE WEEK after release. The print runs of some of these new comics and the demand are driven by speculators and collectors alike. The prices realized in auctions are high, and people seem willing to keep chasing the grails for their personal collections.

When the smoke clears and the dust settles, the industry will be stronger than before. The shops, dealers and collectors that survive will have built a new foundation that we can rely on for many years to come. There will always be small issues and roadblocks, but with as many sales and renewed interest from customers, comic book dealers are more prepared for the uncertainty that lies ahead.

For everyone who has spent years telling us that we work in an industry that is not viable – that comic books are for children – that we work in an industry that will get killed by digital – that we work in an industry that is dying: To them I say: comic collecting is dead! Long live COMIC COLLECTING!!!

Richard M. Brown Collector

Quite obviously, COVID-19 cancelled key conventions, but many felt a new appreciation for reading.

Prices Going Up: Early Black Panther appearances in *Fantastic Four* #52 & #53 and early *Avengers* appearances as well. *Avengers Special* #1 & #2. Early *Fantastic Four.* The first appearance of Bat-Mite in *Detective Comics* #267. *Captain Marvel* #1 (1968). *Brave and the Bold* #38 with Suicide Squad. *Justice League of America* #9 (JLA origin).

Prices Going Down: Not a landslide, just a correction. X-Men has had so many versions, it is even too complicated for us longtime collectors. Green Lantern doesn't have the "old time feel" we grew up with. *Whiz Comics* (for now!)

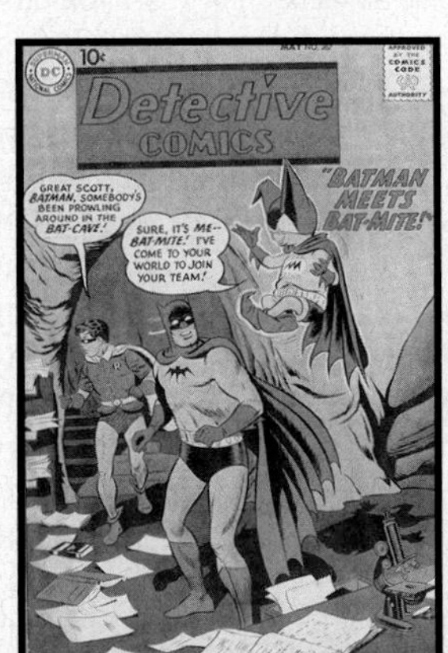

*The first appearance of Bat-Mite in **Detective Comics #267** is charming new fans.*

Brett Carreras Brett's Comic Pile

I'll start off by saying it has been WAAAY too long since I've made a market report, but I've been working in other corners of the industry as show promoter of the Virginia ComiCon, and the newly formed Alaska ComiCon (with Awesome Con founder Ben Penrod). Not surprising to many, the pandemic has forced me to shift my directions back to vintage comics this year, as what I discovered is a FASCINATING new world of selling comics I had stepped away from for too long.

About four and a half years ago, I moved from San Francisco back to Richmond, VA, and not long after I was invited to help my friend, David Leubke of Dave's Comics shut down his store as he was in failing health. Sadly he passed not long afterwards, and we were left trying to make sense of 26 years or retailing, along with warehousing. See...Dave's Comics has two main, but physically separate components. One was his retail store, and the other was a warehouse where he bought the SAME amount of comics for himself as he did for his store, and stored them in a climate controlled warehouse for the entire time...NEVER to be seen or touched by the public. Readers of 1990s Marvel comics will remember his huge ½ page ad in magenta with "Missed an Issue?" and a lightning bolt in big letters.

After many hard years in retail, David's widow was ready to be DONE with comics. She shut down the retail store not long after David's passing, and granted ownership (and all accompanying bills) to me, then she happily retired to the beach. For the next 2 years, I had to cover their storage bills (approximately $1,000 a week) as I began the hunt for a place to put all of this stuff. It certainly wasn't going to fit in my own warehouse... that is already stuffed with almost 700,000 comics … and here I had literally just DOUBLED that inventory, with nowhere to put it, No plan, no long-term employees and crushing debt. Goodness!

Fast forward 2 years, and our lease was about to expire. Thankfully my friend Travis tipped me off to a church for sale about 30 minutes out in the county. It wasn't right for me...but the high school across the street from it was for sale too! After more than a year of negotiating, I secured ownership of a 40,000 square foot school building, and FINALLY had enough space for all of my product... PLUS room to host itty-bitty 30-50 table mini-cons at my own place..yesss…we at least got Dave's stuff moved over, and now I can actually run MY OWN SHOW with my OWN STUFF at my OWN PLACE...it's every show promoter's dream...and it can all begin in the middle of 2020! (Yeah...we'll get to that later).

So...after almost 3 entire years of owning the Dave's Comics inventory, I finally had a chance to look at the Dave's Comics inventory…and what an inventory it was! Other than some best-sellers missing (most of the McFarlane *Amazing Spider-Man* run, and the *New Mutants* #98s) it was just about COMPLETE, and EXACTLY the condition Dave had often boasted about. If you shopped with him, you expected to pay *Guide* and a half. I knew I was looking at the world's largest uncirculated inventory of 1980s and 1990s comics on the planet...and they sure looked like it...but I had to know for sure...so I contacted my friend Steve Borock (founder of CGC and President of CBCS), and asked him to fly out to look at this collection and tell me I wasn't (too) crazy.

So we grabbed a random box of 1980s *Batman* and *Amazing Spider-Man*, and Steve went through them, making stacks of natural 9.8s, natural 9.6s and everything else. About 50% were natural 9.8s, about 25% were 9.6s (MANY pressable) and about 20% were 9.6s or lower (not pressable to a 9.8). My jaw hit the floor. We pulled a modest amount (approximately 3,000 units), and sent them off to CBCS to be pre-screened and graded. While I had no idea what would come of the books, I definitely knew what my next job for the year was: Help run the Alaska ComiCon with my buddy Ben!

It was an honor running the "World's Northern-most Comic-Con" in frigid Fairbanks, Alaska on Feb 22-23, 2020! In addition to fantastic comic talent such as Dan Parent, Aubrey Sitterson and Mike McKone, we had world-class academics such as Dr. N. Scott Robinson and Dr. Herb Fondevilla on hand to discuss comics and culture with folks just a few hours' drive from the Arctic Circle! We had OVER 3,000 fans come out, and it was a blast! I had freighted 30 long boxes up, and my friends Christopher Lloyd (Painted Visions in Woodbridge, VA) and Timothy Kupin (a fellow Overstreet Advisor) made the long flight...both selling some awesome comics!

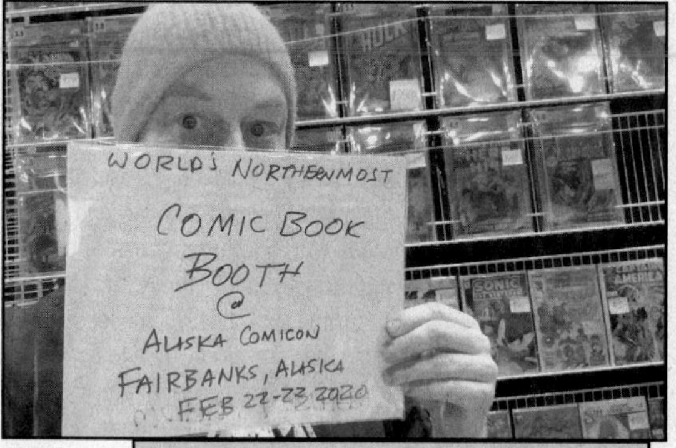

Brett Carreras at the world's northern-most comic booth at the Alaska Comicon.

Coming back from Alaska (which was INSANELY successful), I was filled with excitement for the upcoming year, and then BAM!....Covid struck the world.

I won't lie...I was in a daze for about 2 months trying to make sense of my career, my future, what I was going to do with this new building, and then "CRUNCH!"..insane rains made the roof collapse on the back 20,000 square feet of my new building. Yes...20,000. Square. Feet.

I only mention this, because it was around this time that I realized I better become a comic book dealer again to pay for that broken roof...and pretty *$&#*% FAST!

I began directing ALL of my upcoming shipments to be sent directly to the top auction houses, eager to see how many of the 3,000 books passed muster, and how these 1980s books would hold up in the new economy. Well...let me tell you…They absolutely KILLED it.

The 1980s and '90s comics renaissance is now in full swing, with 9.8 graded examples hitting absolutely record highs, with (not surprisingly) the greatest attention going to cartoon properties (thanks Netflix documentary *Toys That Made Us*)!

Below I will list (alphabetically) our 50 best selling Cartoon property comics (sorry, I don't have any *G.I. Joe* #21s or *Transformers* #1s), almost ALL sales taking place in the second half of 2020. I have noted the date of sale, as I expect many of these may go up another 50-100% by time you read this article. Keep in mind, ALL of these are CBCS 9.8 copies:

Care Bears (1985 Marvel/Star Comics) #1 CBCS 9.8 $97, 10/28/2020 MyComicShop

Care Bears (1985 Marvel/Star Comics) #7 CBCS 9.8 $160, 7/8/2020 (MyCS)

Chuck Norris Karate Kommandos (1987 Marvel/Star Comics) #1 $110, 8/19/2020 MCS

Ewoks (1985 Marvel/Star Comics) #4 $100, 1/23/2020 (MyCS)

Ewoks (1985 Marvel/Star Comics) #5 $125, 1/23/2020 (MyCS)

Ewoks (1985 Marvel/Star Comics) #7 $100, 1/23/2020 (MyCS)

Ewoks (1985 Marvel/Star Comics) #10 $100, 1/23/2020 (MyCS)

Fraggle Rock (1985 Marvel/Star Comics) #1 $104, 5/16/2020 (MyCS)

G.I. Joe (1982 Marvel) #7 $116, 12/16/2020 (MyCS)

G.I. Joe (1982 Marvel) #9 $108, 10/21/2020 (MyCS)

G.I. Joe (1982 Marvel) #12 $140, 9/30/2020 (MyCS)

G.I. Joe (1982 Marvel) #13 $100, 9/30/2020 (MyCS)

G.I. Joe (1982 Marvel) #16 $130, 7/1/2020 (MyCS)

G.I. Joe (1982 Marvel) #22 $180, 7/22/2020 (MyCS)

G.I. Joe (1982 Marvel) #23 $170, 9/30/2020 (MyCS)

G.I. Joe (1982 Marvel) #26 $680, 11/18/2020 (MyCS)

G.I. Joe (1982 Marvel) #27 $306, 11/4/2020 (MyCS)

G.I. Joe (1982 Marvel) #35 $90, 9/30/2020 (MyCS)

G.I. Joe (1982 Marvel) #37 $90, 7/1/2020 (MyCS)

G.I. Joe (1982 Marvel) #38 $122, 10/21/2020 (MyCS)

G.I. Joe and the Transformers (1987) #1 $90, 10/21/2020 (MyCS)

Heathcliff (1985-1991 Marvel/Star Comics) #12 $200, 1/23/2020 (MyCS)

Marvel Tails (1983 Marvel) #1 $243, 8/5/2020 (MyCS)

Masters of the Universe (1986 Marvel/Star Comics) #2 $89, 4/17/2020 (MyCS)

Masters of the Universe (1986 Marvel/Star Comics) #4 $99, 9/30/2020 ComicLink

Masters of the Universe (1986 Marvel/Star Comics) #5 $166, 5/18/2020 (MyCS)

Masters of the Universe (1986 Marvel/Star Comics) #6 $249, 3/9/2020 (MyCS)

Masters of the Universe (1986 Marvel/Star Comics) #7 $148, 5/18/2020 (MyCS)

Masters of the Universe (1986 Marvel/Star Comics) #8 $159, 5/6/2020 (MyCS)

Masters of the Universe (1986 Marvel/Star Comics) #9 $159, 5/6/2020 (MyCS)

Masters of the Universe (1986 Marvel/Star Comics) #10 $159, 5/6/2020 (MyCS)

Muppet Babies (1985-1989 Marvel/Star Comics) #10 $131, 9/16/2020 (MyCS)

Peter Porker #3 $90, 10/26/2020 ComicLink

Peter Porker #6 $85, 10/26/2020 ComicLink

Peter Porker #12 $250, 9/2/2020 (MyCS)

Silverhawks (1987 Marvel/Star Comics) #1 $170, 8/19/2020 (MyCS)

Teenage Mutant Ninja Turtles Adventures (1988) #1 $170, 6/8/2020 (MyCS)

Teenage Mutant Ninja Turtles Adventures (1989) #2 $86, 12/9/2020 (MyCS)

Thundercats (1985 1st Series Marvel) #1 CBCS 9.8 $380, 11/4/2020 (MyCS)

Thundercats (1985 1st Series Marvel) #15 CBCS 9.8 $100, 8/19/2020 (MyCS)

Transformers (1984 Marvel) 1st Printing 4 $125, 3/4/2020 (MyCS)

Transformers (1984 Marvel) 1st Printing #8 $108, 5/26/2020 (MyCS)

Transformers (1984 Marvel) 1st Printing #10 $110, 1/21/2020 (MyCS)

Transformers (1984 Marvel) 1st Printing #16 $96, 6/13/2020 (MyCS)

Transformers (1984 Marvel) 1st Printing #24 $180, 12/9/2020 (MyCS)

Transformers (1984 Marvel) 1st Printing #25 $135, 7/15/2020 (MyCS)

Transformers (1984 Marvel) 1st Printing #30 $100, 9/16/2020 (MyCS)

Voltron (1985 Modern) #1 $180, 10/28/2020 (MyCS)

Voltron (1985 Modern) #2 $100, 9/30/2020 (MyCS)

Voltron (1985 Modern) #3 $92, 9/23/2020 (MyCS)

I think it is very easy to see that *G.I. Joe* is leading the pack from this time period ($680 for #26), but *Thundercats* isn't far behind ($380 for #1). Even Modern's *Voltron* series rarely dips below $100 for any issue. *Heathcliff* #12 and *Peter Porker* #12 still command top-of-market with their 25th Anniversary covers at $200 and $250 respectively.

In between pressing and counting high-grade comics, I managed to (with face-coverings, santizing stations, and 6' social distancing) host two private mini-cons, consisting of friends, fellow dealers and some high-rollers, limited to only 50 people. Even though they weren't huge, it was nice to see my comic friends, even if we couldn't shake hands.

I am so very proud of all of my friends who had to "pivot" this year...especially Ben who is working in high-end real-estate, my buddy Patrick who is ALSO pressing and auctioning off books, after being forced "off the road" by the con circuit closing down, and most especially to my friend Jason, who bit the bullet and opened up a pop-up retail store (Cerebral Vortex here in Richmond, VA) in a mall during the holiday season in order to get comics out to fans!

Today is December 21st. We are 4 days away from our first ever "Pandemic Christmas" and the world is bonkers, but I am excited for comics. I am excited for fans everywhere, and I am excited to be working on my current project. Wanna know what it is? Remember when I said G.I. Joe books were screaming hot, and "*The Toys that Made Us*" was a big driving point? If you re-watch the Joe episode, you will see my friend Larry Hama being interviewed (the "Godfather" of G.I. Joe). Well, last week, I was invited into Mr. Hama's New York apartment to pick up his personal collection of File Copy G.I. Joe comics. I am busy pressing them at the moment, and will be sending them off to CBCS for grading shortly. If you are a "kid of the 1980s" be on the lookout for the "Larry Hama File Copy" books when they enter the market. It's gonna be a total blast.

What a crazy year 2020 has been. I made it to Alaska, Death Valley (I recommend everyone go camping in the desert the weekend before an election) and New York. I am finally just a few months away from having that roof paid off and it's all thanks to comics. What a great industry. Thanks to all of the leaders who came before me, thanks to all of my friends who have got me to this point, and thanks to all of those amazing creators like Mr. Hama who bring joy to the world.

Jeff & Charles Cerrito
Hotflips.com

Whoa!! Well this was some year!! Not for the reasons we all hoped but different for sure. First off, I just want to say I hope everyone and your families are safe and healthy during these crazy times. We all went through a lot and I hope everyone comes back better personally and financially next year.

This year a lot of us had to adapt to a new normal. We here at Hotflips usually do about 20-30 conventions a year and are traveling just about every other weekend. We had one show this year, C2E2, and it was better than last year and gave me high hopes for conventions this year.

We saw a surge in wholesale orders for a while, almost entirely of comic book supplies. Bags, boards, boxes, etc. While stores were closed in the beginning, we were getting a lot of straight to consumer sales. People used their free time to organize and reevaluate their collections. A lot of the new customers we had could definitely be attributed to the conventions that we have set up at for the past 20 years. There were a lot of calls with people saying, "Hey, I met you at Emerald City Comic Con, Chicago, or Fan Expo Dallas or MegaCon." It's always nice to hear from our customers. A lot of these people are those I meet once a year, and yet during the pandemic, we would chat on the phone for a half hour or so talking about these crazy times.

We started buying up comic book collections again and have seen a real uptick in sales in our comic department. I find it amazing that comics that were in the dollar bins 10 years ago now sell for $50-$100 or more!! All a TV show has to do is tease a new character and the book shoots up.

All in all, this year has tested all of us. I assume sometime in 2021 things will start to get back to a sense of normalcy and we will have conventions again. I know at the forefront Reed, along with MCM (UK), Fan Expo, San Diego, Baltimore and countless others will be back. There will be a pent up demand in my opinion. I am certainly looking forward to it and hope to see all of you sooner than later.

John Chruscinski
Tropic Comics

To say 2020 was an unusual year for the comic book industry is an understatement. It went from totally normal at the beginning of the year to crazy when COVID-19 hit. Comic stores were forced to close, and comic shows were postponed or right out cancelled. They even stopped distributing new comics for a while!!! 2020 was absolutely nuts for fandom and the whole world at large.

We found out about COVID in mid-January by accident on Twitter when I ran across a lady pleading to the President for help. I clicked on her page and into the rabbit hole I went. She was an American in Wuhan China under lockdown at the beginning of it all with videos that looked like a Hollywood horror film. To say it affected me is a true understatement. In early February we shut down our warehouse to the public and dealers alike which took a big toll on our bottom line. We deal in a lot more than comics, like board games, Original Art, paper collectibles, historical items, Pop Culture, old books, arcade games, pinball machines, records, rock and roll collectibles, vintage toys, antiques, old advertising, old films, cameras and film projectors, movie posters and other collectibles.

At the beginning of the shutdown our internet sales took off as people were stuck at home with nothing to do. When the 1st stimulus plan was launched, it almost seemed that we couldn't list and ship fast enough but that soon passed as the virus dragged on and the unemployment went up while the economy slowed down.

Now as I sit and write this report, the sales have picked up for Christmas but not at the pace it was at the beginning of the year or in past Christmas seasons, but now with the vaccine being shipped in the USA there is once again hope that we may get back to normal, whatever that new normal will be. I'm ready.

In February we bought the remaining catalog of work from long time comic artist Alex Sanchez, almost 700 published pages and covers that he had done throughout his 20+ year career for companies like DC, Marvel, Valiant, IDW, Dark Horse. On such titles as *X-Men*, *Hulk*, *Star Wars*, *Battlestar Galactica*, *Mulan*, *G.I. Joe*, *Pandemica*, *30 Days of Night*, *Batman*, *JSA*, *Katana*, *Max Ride*, *Time Grunts*, *Fathom*, and *Grimm* stories.

As for comic sales, we still sell Key issues the fastest no matter what the grade as long as they are priced right, but it looks like the collector that is completing runs maybe making a comeback as we are selling a lot more Silver and Bronze Age non-key filler run issues at a faster pace than before. This field of collecting is still holding its own with not many falling prices except on speculative TV or movie appearance issues which tend to go high before the media appearance and then down to a price higher than when it started going up, but lower than afterwards.

I believe that the market is still a safe place for investment as well as a place for the joy of collecting, and it will be for many years. I'm sure we will see a big change in what and how comics are collected in the next few years due to everything we have all been through as a hobby.

God Bless to you and your loved ones and stay safe.

Paul Clairmont
PNJ Comics

2020 was uncharted territory for obvious reasons. I recall in early March of 2020 wondering what the future will hold for my family, friends and my business. All those years of saving to prepare against the unknown and there I was faced with the actual reality playing out as I wondered if my family, neighborhood and community would be safe and if my business would be able to weather any challenges. I became laser-focused on short and mid-term goals for the business. I quickly realized that people were adapting to the new world and the new economics. I could see that people needed an outlet to spend as options became limited on what to do with their money. I am humbled and grateful that my online business model suited these new spending patterns and that I deal with collectibles which seemed to be one area that continued to flourish.

With the success of ***The Mandalorian*** *TV show, previously obscure Star Wars characters are in the spotlight.*

Those who were fortunate enough to still have a steady income started spending money in the hobby like I have never witnessed in my nine years of business. The new money started pushing prices higher on what seemed like any and every book we had in stock. People were also using stimulus payments for shop therapy instead of its intended purpose and all of this created soaring prices or "Pandemic Prices." This touched every collectible market and not only comics. We saw prices with comics, sports cards and non-sports cards such as Pokémon go to unprecedented levels. This adaptation into diversifying our collectibles to hedge against a pandemic gave us our best business year ever and for that I am thankful as I know this year would be one that we would all like to erase for a multitude of other reasons.

In the comic market, we saw the largest increase of interest with:

#1 – *Star Wars* comics

#2 – *Teenage Mutant Ninja Turtles* comics

#3 – The need to collect subsequent printings of modern books, 2nd, 3rd, 4th printing and so on.

#4 – Newsstand Editions and Canadian Price Variants

Any *Star Wars* comic with the hint of a first appearance of any character was easily going from the dollar bin to triple digit numbers in a matter of weeks. Unfortunately, the amount of misinformation that can quickly spread with the internet is going to leave many people holding the hot potato when the dust settles. The prices that *Star Wars* #42 is bringing lately is insane for a reprint book. I'm not going to go down the path of explaining it all but just a little research and you'll see the reality. Collectors need to really take a moment before diving in and getting swept up with the "FOMO – Fear of Missing Out". Nonetheless, we believe *Star Wars* comics will continue in high demand for years to come as Disney mines that material like gold for its new shows with its streaming service. The galaxy is the limit when it comes to the potential and I'm sure we'll see many more books from the Marvel and Dark Horse series pop as time goes on.

The Teenage Mutant Ninja Turtle craze really started ramping up this year. I'm not sure what started that craze as there was nothing new to generate and spike so I'm leaning towards the fact that the pandemic spending encouraged people to go after what they were familiar with when deciding what to overspend on. The Mirage Studios books exploded so fast that it caused other series such as the Archie Publications *Teenage Mutant Ninja Turtles Adventures* to jump exponentially as well. Newsstand and Canadian Price Variants of these books also spiked and are in high demand due to being condition sensitive compared to the direct editions. As 1st prints of these *TMNT* books became too expensive the spotlight quickly turned to higher prices being paid for 2nd to 5th printings of the issues in the Mirage Studios title. The late issues of the *TMNT Adventures* books are also difficult to find in high grade and the demand on these scarce issues is driving prices to new records as well.

The trend I'm not sold on is buying up these Modern era 2nd, 3rd and 4th printings of books that are a month or two old. People want them because the belief is that these books have lower production numbers in circulation and will therefore be more scarce and hence more valuable. That can happen and it has some success in the past when there was a time not every speculator was doing it. Now, everyone is trying to scoop up the books but with so many people doing the same thing you will end up seeing the same effect of the Byrne/Claremont run of *X-Men* from the late '70s and '80s. Everyone has high grade copies because everyone was chasing it. In the long term, sticking with the original 1st printing will be the true 1st appearance but I do realize the fascination of trying to catch the unicorn and everyone hopes that particular 2nd or subsequent printing of the book with a different cover or some other gimmick that resonates with fellow speculators will be their book and increase in value.

Newsstand copies of books seemed to really take off this year. Suddenly it was the *en vogue* thing as a selling feature. I do feel these types of books were certainly overlooked during the '80s, '90s and 2000s and the distribution of these books to certain outlets such as grocery and convenience stores led to conditions that weren't ideal for keeping them in high grade. The amount distributed were also much lower than direct edition books especially as we got into the later period of the 1990s and 2000s. You can now see this pricing effect and I'll use *Ultimate Fallout* #4 as an example. The book is very common but when you look for the Newsstand Edition it is virtually non-existent. The market has spoken and we cannot deny what realized prices are bringing for that book. The same can be said with Canadian Price Variants and I won't go into too much detail as I've written extensively about CPVs for many years in my previous reports and of course with the privilege of being a participant with the Canadian Price Variant Price Guide each year so please check out that free online tool put together by some very passionate people in the hobby.

In closing, I want to thank my wonderful family for their constant support. Nicole, Jack and Hazel, you are the greatest heroes in my life. This year, I would also like to thank the biggest super-heroes behind the real masks and that is all the folks that sacrifice their lives and selflessly give to protect and help us during this pandemic. All the brave doctors, nurses, paramedics and anyone in the health care field along with people like my son, Jack who is considered a frontline worker as he works at a grocery store after school and weekends and is in close contact with the public to ensure that he is there to serve others and never complains about what he does. Stay well and healthy!

ART CLOOS
COLLECTOR

Well I started writing this in mid November 2020, in a year that has repeatedly been called "like no other". The virus has made this year a nightmare in many ways. We know people, one I have known since he was 10 years old, who caught it and was in quarantine for 21 days and one, my wife's co-worker in her school, who wound up in the hospital for 10 days. My better half is a teacher when she does not do the pictures for show reviews for Scoop and I am a retired one. We know multiple people who have lost their battle with it, one who caught it twice but lost the battle a second time. I have no idea when the *Guide* this will appear in will be out and I have been thinking for the last couple of months about just what I was going to say about a year when most of the convention circuit has been wiped out and most comic book stores closed. But the Advisors have been asked to address just how the virus has affected us in terms of our business so I am going to start with that.

First let me say I am one of those Advisors who is a collector, not a dealer, and my focus in the comic world is what both my wife and I collect which covers a wide area. But my business is writing for *Scoop* onine. In a normal year my better half and I average attending between 30 and 40 shows and of them we (my wife does the pictures, I do the writing) review some 10 to 12 of the major ones for *Scoop*, with a schedule we set in early January. Well this year our entire show schedule basically was wiped out. The last show we went to before the virus hit was in early Feb of 2020. By August we had only gone to 3 all year and those were during January and February and we reviewed none. At that time we were climbing the walls wanting to get out of the house but living in NYC we were within a 20 minute drive from ground zero for the virus at that time at Elmhurst Hospital and it just was not a good idea to go anywhere outside unless we absolutely had to. In the meantime show after show was being either postponed or later cancelled or cancelled outright.

Finally in that month of August as the virus was brought under reasonable control in our tri-state area, a few of the local monthly shows in that NY, NJ and Connecticut zone began to open with both a limited set of dealers and the number of attendees allowed in at any one time also limited. We went to three of the shows, all in September. Two of these were not shows we would normally cover but we wound up reviewing all of them to highlight how they were handling the virus protocols as per our editor's request. One of them was a major comic book art show normally held twice a year that wound up holding only one and that was in September and we especially wanted to see how that one was going to be handled. All 3 passed the test but one more so than the other two. Some major comic cons such as NYCC held virtual shows with line ups of artists, panels and things to buy. Even the famed Brimfield antique and toy show went online and was done quite well too.

What will 2021 hold in terms of the show circuit? Well as I type this part of this report on December 1, I have no idea but multiple vaccines are on the way while at the same time a second wave of the virus is exploding across the country and infection rates are climbing quickly here in NY where the state government had done a good job in containing it earlier in the year. As such I suspect that at least early on in the first half of the year there will be few if any major shows held with large numbers of fans attending. I really have no idea what 2021 will be overall for the convention and comic store scene as the year goes on but I hope there will be some normalcy for fandom by the end of 2021.

It goes without saying that both show promoters and comic book stores were hit hard by the virus in 2020. Many comic book stores barely hung on and some closed. A lot of dealers who only did comic shows vented their frustration with the virus on line as did many who ran comic book stores but comic fandom has always had people in it to help those in fandom who needed it. Ed Catto, a long time member of comic fandom who teaches at Ithaca College in upstate NY, is one of them. In his Countdown to Comic Con Course his class, led by one of his students, Kayli DePinto, was involved in helping spread the word about the Give Comics Hope initiative which is a charitable initiative that called on all members of the comic fandom community (and beyond) to rally together to provide vital aid to comic book shops during the pandemic describing those shops as, "the heart and roots of our vibrant comic book community". This was done by accepting donated items to be auctioned off, monetary donations, and by spreading the word about the needs of the stores on social media. I suspect its work will continue in 2021 and if so I hope people reading this will contribute to it. I did an interview with Kayli for *Scoop* where she outlined the efforts of the initiative.

In terms of comics it was a frustrating year with no shows to go to. My better half has a list of books she wanted to add to her collection and she loves the hunt at shows. Well that did not happen. I had some books I wanted to look for and I too love the hunt at shows, much more than I do looking online. Again that was not going to happen. So we turned to our PCs and searched the usual online places for what we wanted. Indeed while the internet has long been an important place for collectors to network and to find pieces for their collections this year showed just how true that is. What I found was that more than ever sellers were finding ways to make money online and those who in the past resisted and whose sales were based on doing shows and as such were hurting, some badly now. They began using the internet and I was glad to see that but it was not unexpected. People adapt to survive. Books I would bookmark as potential buys would be sold quickly and then reappear later in other places. Now I always get a lot of email requests to both sell and buy but COVID took it to a new level. Not a day went by once things started shutting things down that my inbox did not get emails advertising auctions not only from the large auction houses but dealers, collectors liquidating their collections and comic book stores as well. I received lists of books for sale every day from one time sellers and some sellers who sent new lists every week. Auction houses sent repeated requests for items we might want to sell in their next event. Almost every day when I signed into Facebook I got notifications that so and so is hosting a live event selling books on Facebook or would be later in the day or evening. Live video sales were held at set times each week and in fact I will be checking one out tonight that I have been following with a friend and we spend Sunday evenings checking out the offerings (it goes on for hours) and that seller in particular has a nice selection of books each week, some of which came off of eBay I strongly suspect. One thing I noticed was Golden Age was hot this year. Sales were strong in the auction houses (explaining the email requests for sale items) and online auctions and various Facebook groups were full of recent buys and complaints about how expensive books were getting. The virus did not seem to stop a lot of people from buying. This is especially true of Golden Age where I noticed titles that I follow such as *All-American*, *All Star*, *Sensation*, *Wonder Woman*, *Captain Marvel* (Fawcett), *Batman* and *Detective* were being offered at quite robust prices. *All Star* issues in particular were being offered at way over *Guide* and GPA and while slow, the books did sell eventually with Allie doing her share in that regard. The same was true for Silver and Bronze. The Sunday night seller had no problem getting very respectable and often over-*Guide* prices for the Gold he offered each week. That reflected how strong the market was overall, people wanted to buy. Even his low level Silver and Bronze went for prices that quite frankly surprised me. In September, at the one live comic book show (run by Pug Production's John Paul) we went to since the virus hit, the pent up desire to get out and buy was very strong and was felt in the air. Attendees were very very happy to be there and meet up with fellow collectors and dealers, and the money spent proved it as did the animated conversations going on around the room (mostly while following the guide lines of course). We saw more than one large package carried out of the dealer room with happy smiles on the attendees' faces during the day.

My reported sales for 2020 are: *All Star* #30 4.5 $400, #31 CBCS FN/VF 7.0 $610, (#31 6.5 $575) #51 VG+ $325, #53 CGC 7.0 $680, *All American Comics* # 45 FN+ $220, # 91 4.5 $125.00, *Brave And The Bold* #38 7.0 $55, *Fantastic Four* #30 VG+ $48, *Green Lantern* Silver Age #12 (7.0) $80, *Ms. Marvel* #1 VF/NM $60.00, Sensation Comics #27 $450. #86 (3.5) $32, #71 (7.0) $21, Showcase #23 3.5 $160, Tales of Suspense #52 (6.5) $1,200, # 68 f+ $55, Tales To Astonish # 43 F $90.00 Underworld Unleashed #3 NM+ $5.43 Wonder Woman 100-Page Giant Walmart #1 VF/NM $6.50. World

Adventure Library Batman #3 F $50, # 9 F $50, World's Finest #126 VF $220. Hopefully we can expand the list in 2021.

Although beyond the *Guide* focus on comics I do want to mention a few other areas we collect in. I will say that original comic art sales were very strong (scalding hot actually) and Lord knows Allie and I spent our fair share in that area of collecting (Batman and Wonder Woman art only of course). Vintage and rare Batman and Wonder Woman toys also were hot and sale prices for the seriously high end pieces were really up there, and several 2020 first time seen discoveries went for some of the highest sales of the year. Foreign comic sales continue to do quite well and is an area for US collectors to keep an eye on long term.

So there you have it. It is going to be very interesting to see how the new year goes for comic fandom and the world beyond comics. Will the vaccines work and get the virus under control? Will there be a return to big time shows by at least the fall of 2021? Will comic stores recover? Will the move to the internet continue for dealers and sellers? Especially for vintage high end items or when shows begin again will they go back to them? Will my inbox continue to overflow with sales lists, and auction house requests? Will online auction and sales events continue? Well I suspect that next year's Market report will discuss the answers to those questions and more. I hope the new year goes a heck of a lot better for all of us than this one has. Take care and be safe.

Tim Collins
RTS Unlimited

To say 2020 was a record year would be an understatement! The COVID-19 lockdowns and restrictions in Colorado cancelled all the comic cons we had planned to exhibit at. However, our eBay sales and direct mail order improved over the year – especially when the federal stimulus checks went out. We see continued and strong demand across most genres and grades. *Classics Illustrated* continue to lag but, interest in Silver Age Marvel continues to be exceptionally strong. Collectors seem to be scrambling to anticipate TV and movie appearances by chasing storylines and first appearances. Interest in World War II related covers (particularly Hitler covers), L.B. Cole, Horror, Bondage and Good Girl covers remains particularly high.

From an economic perspective, with a volatile stock market coupled with low interest rates, investors seem to be looking towards comic books and other collectibles for diversification. As the Federal deficit continues to grow faster than tax revenue, many people seem to be anticipating higher inflation in the future. Consequently, there is the desire to hold hard assets like key and high-grade comic books. With the rise in values of the top books over the last couple of decades, gone are the days where the average collector could assemble complete runs of long running titles like *Amazing Spider-Man*, *Fantastic Four* let alone *Batman* or *Detective Comics*. For those long-time collectors that managed to assemble runs over the years, they should have a nice nest egg for retirement when they choose to sell their collection.

We look for 2021 to continue the strong momentum of the hobby!

Jack Copley
Coliseum of Comics

Despite the crazy of 2020, back issues seem to remain strong! Any Marvel Key just flies out of our stores! *Amazing Spider-Man*, *X-Men*, *Avengers* lead the way.

Over the last few months, I've noticed even the 1980s keys have steadily grown in value. It's gotten so I can't just trust the price guide value of any 1980s key, we have to research what its latest price is! But there are still a lot of 1980s comics out there in collections. Often collections come in and all of the keys are missing and they want you to buy the left overs at top dollar and are disappointed with what they learn. I throw many 1980s books in the bargain bins. Have we lost the collector that completes runs?

It has become more focused on what's the next movie or TV show on the pipeline. Speculators are coming out of the woodwork! I thought it was high when I drove all over the area buying *Crisis on Infinite Earths* #1 while it was on the newsstands and bringing them back to my store and asking $3 each (4X cover). Now we can have books bringing ten to twenty times cover price before they arrive!

Some of the current crazy we've noticed: *TMNT* #1 - Book is hotter than ever, and prices are skyrocketing. *Star Wars* books (a ton) - Most notably: *The Clone Wars* #1 (and variant), *Heir to the Empire* #1, *Defenders of the Lost Temple*, *Knights of the Old Republic* #9, and *Star Wars: Jedi - Mace Windu*. The popular recent Marvels *Ultimate Fallout* #4, *Edge of Spider-Verse* #2, and *NYX* #3.

***NYX** #3 is among the hottest Marvels on the market.*

Bone #1, *Crow* #1, and *Invincible* #1 have all gone way up based on show/movie deals. *Fightin Five* #40 and *Peacemaker* #1 with John Cena playing Peacemaker in the *Suicide Squad* sequel. *Sandman* #1, 4, 8, 10, 69, 75 are the key issues going up prior to TV show.

Hero Trade #1 (Bad Idea Comics) was an unannounced preview book for the new publisher. Prices continue to climb.

Newsstand copies of hot/key books continue to outpace direct editions by a large margin.

Some of our more notable *Amazing Spider-Man* sales in 2020: #3 CGC 6.0 $3,000, #2 CGC 6.0 $2,500, #33 9.2 $1,000, #41 9.0 $1,000 #300 newsstand 9.0 $1,000, #15 5.5 $900, #6 5.0 $750, #13 3.5 $625, #300 9.4 $600, #129 4.5

$600, #10 5.0 $500, #50 4.5 $450, #46 8.0 $450, #238 9.2 $400, #96 9.2 $350, #25 8.0 $325, #28 5.0 $300, and #100 8.5 $300.

Some of our other cool notable sales: *Avengers* #1 0.5 (panel cut) $1,800, *Showcase* #22 3.0 $1,650, *Action* #252, 3.0 $1,650, *Batman* #121 3.0 $1,200, *X-Men* #12 7.0 $1,000, *Edge of Spider-Verse* #2 9.2 -$800, *Fantastic Four* #52 5.0 $800, *Underworld Crime* #7 3.5 $600, *Ultimate Fall-Out* #4 9.4 $600, *Star Wars: The Clone Wars* #1 9.2 $600, *New Mutants* #98 9.4 $600, *X-23* #3 9.2 $500, *Fantastic Four* #49 6.5 $500, *Brave and Bold* #1 3.0 $500, *Superman* #66 6.5 $450, *Showcase* #37 5.0 $325, *Brave and the Bold* #34 4.5 $400, *Detective* #211 4.5 $350, *Superman* #70 5.0 $325, *Brave and the Bold* #29 2.0 $300, *Daredevil* #7 4.5 $300, *Justice League of America* #4 6.0 $300, #9 6.5 $300, *Journey Into Mystery* #86 4.5 $300, #100 8.5 $300, *New Mutants* #87 9.4 $300, *Flash* #108 3.0 $300, *Wolverine* LS #1 CGC 9.4 $300, and *Detective* #411 6.5 $300.

Ashley Cotter-Cairns & Sean Goodrich SellMyComicBooks.com

What a surprising year, the year that made us question everything we take for granted.

I want to start by saying thank you to our wonderful staff. In a time of great fear for all concerned, they helped us to keep the lights on and books moving. We did our bit to make them feel as secure as possible, and did not have to let anybody go. In fact we hired again in the summer.

Once it was apparent that the pandemic wasn't perhaps the worst-case scenario but a version of it, then questions naturally turned to, "How will our business come out of this, if at all?" That's where the surprise kicked in. This was one of our best years ever, from a selling perspective at least. I tried to predict what would happen to Sell My Comic Books. I figured, people would be desperate for cash, and we'd be flooded with collections, but selling would slow down and we'd suffer a cash crunch.

For the first half of the year, the reverse seemed to be true. We saw a big slowdown in collections coming to the office. For a while, I guess people were anxious about handling cardboard boxes, going to shipping offices and even stepping out of their homes.

Selling was brisk. If you have nowhere to go and nothing to do when you get there, then your disposable income may as well be disposed of on collectibles.

Our customer profile tends to be Boomers retiring and downsizing who want to sell their collections. Boomers sheltered in place. So where did our buying opportunities come from? We picked up more than the usual number of Bronze and Copper Age collections and focused on re-arranging our shifts at the office, to keep our staff socially distanced. The comic book store, DotCom Comics and Collectibles in Freeport, ME, had to close temporarily while Maine had a non-essential closure order, but it's open again now.

That's not to say that it was a bad year from a buying perspective. The second half of the year made up for the first, and we are about the same as last year for purchasing.

We bought two huge collections this year. By far the most interesting and fun was a huge accumulation located in New Jersey. Sean and I travelled down with Ethan, and between us we spent half a day checking over 30 long boxes full of Golden Age through Silver Age horror and suspense titles.

There were also deep runs of Silver Age Marvel superheroes in this collection. But most impressive were the Atlas horror titles. The owner's uncle had bought multiple copies of his favourite books, and even some duplicated horror titles from pretty rare off-beat publishers. There were easily 12 long boxes of Atlas alone, including near-full runs of all the horror series, many of them duplicated.

At the time of writing, we're still selling raw singles from this massive collection, and still waiting for CGC to ship value tier books from the New Jersey purchase.

Let's talk CGC! For a while during the Spring, it felt like CGC was our personal theme park with no other visitors. Value tier was coming back within five working days! Now the opposite is true, and books sent in August are still only marked received.

Perhaps, CGC, you could stop promoting all these special signings that seemingly happen on a weekly basis, and actually work on clearing the backlog of dealer-submitted books? Maybe a good plan moving forward, guys.

Key Moves: Some blue-chip Silver Age keys have softened this year. Most notably, *Amazing Fantasy* #15 has come off the boil. A few others have done better. *X-Men* #1 is red-hot in any grade. *Incredible Hulk* #1 has slowly gained in VG and lower. *Fantastic Four* #1 has consolidated recent gains ahead of the homecoming to the MCU.

X-Men #1 is one of the current blue-chip Silver Age keys.

Marvel is still WAY stronger than DC in the back issue market. I can only think of a few DC keys that are not falling in value. I also find that collections containing both publishers from the Silver Age show that DC issues don't hold up as well, making them much scarcer in high grade than Marvel.

The Bronze Age has seen a weird rollercoaster this year. Early in the pandemic, prices were lower than expected. Since then, books like *Giant-Size X-Men* #1 and *Incredible Hulk* #181 have rebounded and are once more marching upwards in price.

Second-string Copper Age keys are doing very well. On my to-do list is to own one copy each of CGC 9.8s for *Albedo* #2, *Crow* #1, *Aliens* v1 #1, *Comico Primer* #2, *Love and Rockets* #1, *Vampirella* #113, *Bone* #1, *TMNT* #1-3 and *Caliber Presents* #1.

McFarlane books are ridiculous this year. *Spawn* back issues move briskly and at record prices. Venom issues are on fire still. High grade *Amazing Spider-Man* #300s are setting new records again, despite being among the most common books of the period.

Five Books to Watch This Year

Batman #171: Riddler's Silver Age return happens to have a bright pink cover that is impossible to find in high grade. This one has a long way to run.

Black Panther v.4 #2: Shuri will most likely be the latest female version of a mainstream superhero, after the sad death of Chadwick Boseman leaves a vacuum in Wakanda.

Thor #165: Adam Warlock's debut in the MCU has been delayed along with all the other movies this year, so there is plenty more time for this one to appreciate in value.

Ultimate Fallout #4: Already stupidly expensive, but Miles Morales is a big hit and I can see this one doubling in price again.

G.I. Joe, a Real American Hero #21: I am shocked at the prices this book is fetching. The most recent sale of a 9.8 was $3,000! This book is never in nice shape, but it's far from rare.

Thank You and Stay Safe - Sean and I would like to thank everybody who helps to make this industry great. Keep well, take the vaccine, and here's to 2021 being a banner year for us all.

Jesse James Criscione
Jesse James Comics

The year most will try to forget. However, for some it was the best year they had ever had. This year we saw many LCS shut their doors forever. Some would say that it was going to happen to most of them, regardless of COVID. Most that closed may not have listened to how the business was pivoting to online and live shows.

We had our greatest year in sales. Times the previous best by two and we still did better. As I have written over the years, live shows, such as Comic Book Shopping Network CBSN, will continue to grab a hold of the market and expand even more with the current events that have arisen. More customers are searching out live shows that have both entertainment and comics books for sale.

Kickstarter continues to grow a major part of the indie business. As we have seen publishers now hold their main events through Kickstarter. This has allowed expansion and hiring of new staff. This includes a vast number of creators taking ownership of how they keep their customer base fed with new projects.

Virtual cons are now the big thing coming to a computer near you. Live conventions are now the hotbed for thousands of creators to get their product to a live audience without having to do all the back end work. These are almost becoming a monthly event and will control a big portion of convention volume.

However, in 2021 be prepared for comics and pop culture entertainment. Expect to see many publishers and companies take control of their audiences and provide daily entertainment to sell their goods. Be prepared for companies to provide a network that will combine selling with entertaining. With a news cycle of daily events and other webcast info shows. Comic book media will be the largest new "NOW" of 2021.

Comics are selling extremely well at a high volume and there is no limit to value, plus 50% on any book at any time. The Back Issues market has really taken over the market with no telling what new back issue is going to take the market by storm. As movies and shows are announced, so does the back issue market expand and explode.

I do predict though, that DC comics and Marvel will eventually ween themself away from comic books stores and pursue larger profitability strategies over the next couple of years. The smart stores won't care and will continue to sell back issues, expand their live presences, and grow their online stores.

We are now in a world where we control our destiny as sellers and entertainers. We can choose to wait for things to get better or we can do better than we are already doing. The comic book business is going to continue to grow at its fastest pace ever. There might be fewer of us. However, those who survived are the best we have leading the charge.

Brock Dickinson
Collector

What a long, strange trip it's been. The year 2020 is definitely one for the history books, and I hope that by the time you're reading this report, things are returning to normal. It's been a year of highs and lows – from the tragic virulence of the worst pandemic in generations to the triumphant success of a global scientific community reaching for a vaccine, and from the chaos of job loss and economic contraction, to what may the single strongest year of market growth in the comics hobby.

At the outset, 2020 looked bleak for comic collectors – publishers suspended operations, distributors closed their doors, and conventions – long the lifeblood of our hobby – ground to a halt. The first part of the year was difficult for many comic shops, with no product, no supply chain, and no customers. But then something strange happened… Buoyed by government payments, the market for back issue comics caught fire.

To be fair, there was an odd convergence of market forces. The absence of conventions (and – to some extent – of new comics) forced buyers to shift to other marketplaces, and online sales boomed. E-commerce exploded, growing by more in the 8 weeks of March and April than it has in the past ten years. In the 2nd and 3rd quarters of the year, eBay's merchandise sales jumped by a larger margin than at any other time in history. Uncertainty in the equity markets (such as the NYSE) drove money into the traditional havens of gold and precious metals, but also into collectibles. Government handouts flowed to consumers, who – in a lockdown – had nowhere to spend their money except online. That massive government largesse prompted fears of inflation, which also tends to drive money into the collectibles market.

This perfect storm created a monster of a bull market in the comics field, one that shows no signs of abating as 2020 rolls into 2021. Key issues of Gold and Silver Age comics saw truly breathtaking prices recorded, but my market report focuses on the Bronze, Copper and Modern periods, where I would point to six key trends in 2020:

1. First Appearances – First appearances of popular characters have always been a driver of back issue prices, but in an era where run collectors are scarce, these appearances have taken on an energy all their own. Publishers such as Marvel and DC certainly understood this dynamic, and dramatically ramped up the introduction of new characters. Meanwhile, collectors were snatching up introductory appearances of characters, especially those from the last ten years. Leading the way on this front is Miles (Spider-Man) Morales, whose first appearance in *Ultimate Fallout* #4 (from August 2011) is a $300 book, while the 1:25 variant of this book is approaching $2,000. Even Morales' first "appearance" in a catalogue (*Marvel Previews* #95) attracted prices approaching $10,000 for CGC 9.8 copies. This is one example of a broad trend that shaped 2020.

2. Disney+ and the MCU – For years, the market has been driven by film development and production, and 2020 was no exception. However, with movies on hiatus during the pandemic, the focus shifted to the efforts of streaming service Disney+ as it seeks to expand the Marvel Cinematic Universe (MCU) into ongoing television programming. Characters such as She-Hulk, Moon Knight, Ms. Marvel, Scarlet Witch and Hawkeye saw substantial increases in both interest and price, and classic series like What If?, Secret Invasion and Marvel Zombies were pulled into the mix. Recently, television has played second fiddle to movies in its market impact, but 2020 reverses this trend.

3. Star Wars – Disney+ also had a breakout hit with its Star Wars spinoff *The Mandalorian*. Although many Star Wars fans felt let down by recent movies, *The Mandalorian* has reignited ferocious levels of interest, which have spilled into the comic marketplace. Prices on dozens of *Star Wars* issues – each important in the complex history of the Star Wars universe – have skyrocketed, with some of these books now regularly commanding $1,000 or more in high grade. The surprise appearance of Ahsoka Tano in an episode of *The Mandalorian* drove her first comic appearance (*Star Wars: The Clone Wars* #1, 2008) to $1,000, while the simplest mention of the character Admiral Thrawn drove his first appearance (*Star Wars: Heir to the Empire* #1, 1995) to $100. At the end of the year, Disney+ announced the development of 10 additional Star Wars series, which all but guarantees that the explosion in prices will continue.

4. 20th Century Fox – the MCU and Star Wars have collided under Disney, with profound effects on the comic market, but in March of 2019, Disney also acquired 20th Century Fox. Over the course of 2020, this led to speculation that Fox-controlled Marvel properties (including the Fantastic Four and X-Men franchises) could be slated to rejoin the MCU, leading to small but steady increases in corresponding comic prices. By the end of 2020, the market realized that other key media properties – including Aliens and Predator – were also now owned by Disney, raising the possibility that they could be seen in Marvel Comics or Marvel movies. An early beneficiary of this realization was *Uncanny X-Men* #155 (which spiked to $30), featuring the first appearance of the Alien-like extraterrestrial race known as the Brood. By the end of the year, many *Predator* and *Aliens* books were rising in price, and Marvel announced a series of *Aliens* variant covers for its January 2021 books. Then, in late December, Marvel announced that the Fantastic Four was scheduled for a motion picture reboot, setting the Fox properties up to be the hot books of 2021.

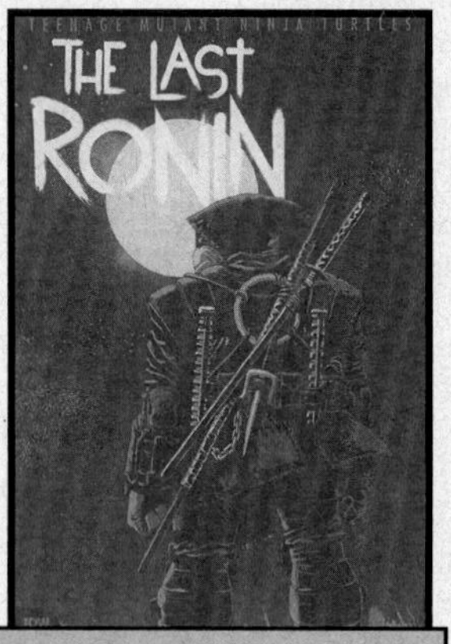

***TMNT: The Last Ronin* #1**
jumped to $30 within days of release.

5. Batman – Though Star Wars and Marvel dominated much of the year, DC's Batman also played a key role in the market. New characters such as Punchline and the Robin King attracted massive attention and drove sharp price increases in the back issue market. Batman sales continued to lead the new release market, but the efforts of current writers to link new characters such as Punchline, existing multimedia characters such as Batman Beyond, and classic favorites like the Joker continued to drive interest in key issues from the Silver through to Modern Ages. Expect the trend to continue in 2021 as the new *The Batman* movie nears release.

6. Teenage Mutant Ninja Turtles and "Blue Chip" Independent Books – The combination of record-breaking prices for 1984's *Teenage Mutant Ninja Turtles* #1 (in one case, breaking $100,000) and the surprise hit of new TMNT release *The Last Ronin* (which jumped to $30 within days of release) created a frenzy around TMNT back issues in general, as collectors began to realize how scarce some of these issues are, and how culturally significant they have become. All issues from the original Mirage *TMNT* series sold well, and the first Archie-produced issue (*Teenage Mutant Ninja Turtles Adventures* #1 from 1988) soared to $250. This trend fed interest in other culturally important key independent issues including *Cerebus* #1, *Bone* #1, *The Crow* #1, and *Albedo* #2 (1st appearance of Usagi Yojimbo). With limited supply in this portion of the market, one should expect price increases to continue.

It will be hard for the 2021 market to top the dizzying heights of 2020, but many of the key forces that drove this year's market remain in place. The market will likely continue to surprise us with its strength, but there will eventually be an inevitable consolidation of gains, and possibly even a retreat. Many are referring to this market as "frothy", suggesting a bit of a bubble. The market is also driven in part by FOMO, the "Fear of Missing Out". While that can be a powerful force, it can also be a fickle one. All in all, the market looks well-positioned for 2021, though some caution may be warranted.

Gary Dolgoff
Gary Dolgoff Comics

A Serious Time For Funny Books…Buying & Selling Comic Books in Troubled Times

I have seen the comics industry survive several 'world or country' downturns, jolts, and recessions first-hand, through my many years as a dealer and collector. For generations, the "Seas of Commerce" have swallowed mighty ships to the ocean floor along with all their treasures - no matter how advanced their technology, or how powerful their artillery. Meanwhile, the comic marketplace has largely drifted safely atop flotsam at the surface. In a world where little if anything is certain, I feel truly fortunate to be part of an industry that not only has been growing for many years, but also has been relatively stable throughout.

In the past, whenever the marketplace would approach choppy waters, whether blinded by passion, blessed with insight, or as a soldier of stubbornness, I have bet on comics! Year after year, it has always been this way for me. This goes back to my teenage years when I bought my first comic collection towards the end of the Silver Age in hometown Manhattan. In the past I was able to keep on truckin' in the comic biz during tough times and never really had to look back. Then, in March of 2020, something happened in the world that was different. The unfolding events and state of the world - like a successful limb re-attachment surgery given to an amputee tiger "gave me paws." Unfortunately, unlike the bad pun in the last sentence, this was quite serious. A world catastrophe, was unfolding.

While the world began dealing with unprecedented problems, and countless people started struggling to have their basic needs met, comic books were not a primary concern for most folks – and rightly so. However, for myself and many of you reading this, our livelihood was inevitably intertwined with comic books – whether building blocks of our income or otherwise. So after the dust began to settle, I couldn't help but wonder, "will our beloved World of Comics survive this one?" Well, I'm happy to report, that - YES, it has! In fact, our sales (including, some formerly weaker titles), have been overall, strong - ever since we got back into selling our funnybooks after lockdown!

Buying & Selling Comic Books - Spring/Summer 2020: Our warehouse was either under lockdown or operating with minimal folks for most of this time, so our insight from that time is accordingly limited. One noteworthy observation from that time was that even though there were exponentially fewer sales in the comic marketplace then, the comics that did sell seemed to do so within range of their typical values. As for buying, at first we could not get around as much as we did in "freer to move about" times. However, shortly after, we were right back to purchasing comics like crazy!

Fortress of Solitude vs. "Warehouse of Solid-Dudes": If you've typically invested in comics and happen to be thinking about evolving from a pure-collector to a dealer/collector, then it is worth considering working with others, moving forward. For me, I still enjoy traveling around the country looking at comic collections, but these days I have a lot of help from my staff. I have a steady and steadfast crew, most of whom have worked for me 10+ years. I've mentored them more and more the last few years in all aspects of the biz. For example, our guy Patrick not only capably grades 50K+ comics per year at our gdcomics warehouse, but also has been traveling and buying collections for us. This setup for one allows me to have more leisure time (when I'm not at the warehouse – I'm often hiking.) Aside from the potential lifestyle & leisure benefits, I've found having trustworthy and knowledgeable folks around is essential for keeping your own skills honed, grading and investments in-check, and provides good company to share the joys of funny books with!

Collections Purchased: Yes, we've been "steamrolling," buying up those collections with many sellers quite happy with our paying prices.

One Silver Age Marvel collection from Queens, New York was noteworthy because of the distinctive condition of the comics. It had some nice books, including early *ASM*s and the like. The thing was that many of the outer wraps had brown border-areas and many of the earlier 1960s comics had downright brittle spines, which were ready to split. Buying a collection like this isn't advisable for everyone. My crew is particularly diligent when appraising/handling these kinds of comics, having lots of experience working with low-mid grade or potentially delicate comic books. Investing in a collection like this without the experience or personnel would likely be not worth it at any fair-price (we weren't surprised when the seller mentioned that another interested party offered less than 60% of what we paid). As a general rule, good time-tested comics are typically worth investing in (for resale) in ALL conditions if they are a good fit for the buyer. As a seller, you can expect high variability in appraisals if the collection has comics with unique flaws, restoration, or "qualifier-books" – trimmed, faded, mis-cut, delicate, etc.

Another collection we purchased consisted of 4 pallets of comics, including some comic magazines. It contained a goodly amount of Silver Age and Bronze Age, plus around 10,000 1980s through 2000s comics. We have always gravitated towards comics from the 1940s-1970s but are always happy to buy Copper/Modern Age books as well – even in volume occasionally. We find ourselves spending more and more time each year appraising and analyzing these post-

1983 comics. Many of these are still waiting for their time in the sun, but increasingly, there are plenty of newer titles and issues that are worth proper consideration. Until recently, a lot of buyers have minimized (or entirely forgone) their assessments of these post Bronze Age comics when tallying their offers on collections that also included a sufficient amount of 1970s & back copies therein – many still do. As time goes on, we find that we can buy collections with more confidence and really maximize our offer when we are allowed the time to really go through the modern component of collections that span multiple ages, and pay good money for those later comics that are better books - and overall, take into account all the comics from the more recent decades.

Overall, despite everything going on in the world, we were able to purchase a number of solid and diverse comic collections, as well as a good amount of Original Comic Art, Comic Magazines, and some collections of comic toys and other comic related memorabilia. The good news is, the market is holding-up really well! We don't know what tomorrow may bring more than anyone else, but for what it is worth, we have good faith in investing confidently in both comics for resale and for collecting moving forward. In the past year, we've seen that most comic collections offered by reasonable sellers can be had for a fair to strong paying price. There are also plenty of options for resale if needed considering the stable and active buyers' market fueled by an ever-widening comic book fanbase and appreciation of comics!

Golden Age Timelys/Marvels: Some of the best sellers of all! Most go for over *Guide*, and I pay aggressive prices for them. I myself collect Timelys, as I love 'em, especially those World War 2 issues, with those fantastic covers!

Golden Age DC: They are the "Brick & Mortar" of Golden Age comics, with a wide variety of titles. Almost all go for at least *Guide*, with a number of them that are worth more than *Guide*, such as *Action Comics* #1, 7, 10, 13 (which are the first four issues of that title with Superman was on the cover!), *Batman* #1, *Detective* #27, #31 (classic cover), #33 (origin The Batman), *All-American* #16 (1st app. Golden Age Green Lantern); #61 (1st app Solomon Grundy), *All Star Comics* #8 (1st app. Wonder Woman), *Flash Comics* #1 (1940), *More Fun* #52 (1st Spectre) and #73 (1st app Aquaman and Green Arrow), *Superman* #1, *Wonder Woman* #1, 7 (WW for President!) and many, many others.

Golden Age Fawcett: They go for *Guide*, or a bit below *Guide*, for the most part. Mac Raboy's *Captain Marvel Jr.* issues #20 thru 39, with those spectacular WW2 covers, can sometimes go for over *Guide*.

Other Golden Age: MLJ was the company that over the years became Archie Publications. They have some really cool, super nostalgic superhero covers (*Pep*, *Shield-Wizard*, *Blue Ribbon*, *Black Hood*, etc.) The "King book" of these comics is *Pep* #22, the 1st appearance of Archie! I bought a copy for my collection a year and change ago. The book is hard to get!

Centaur are mostly scarce, and worth over *Guide*.

Quality was one of the longer-running non DC/Timely groups, with *Crack*, *Hit*, *Smash*, *Military*, *Police*, *Plastic Man*, *Doll Man*, *Feature*, and much more. The early 1940s issues had a blockbuster plethora of various, very well-drawn, colorful and interesting, various superheroes. The later 1940s entries were ok, but did not have the coolness of those 68-page early issues. Most Quality Comics from the early 1940s are instant sellers. Later 1940s are slower to move in general.

Dell Comics, with some exceptions, sell less and less well, in general, as time goes on, but I'm still happy to purchase them, just to have "some of everything."

Pre-Code Horror often sell over *Guide*. I love to buy these books, they're always fun to get, and the covers are wild!

ECs, I really dig 'em! The Horrors sell for over *Guide*. Sci-Fi, *Mad* comics, etc. sell for around *Guide*, sometimes over *Guide*.

Pre-Code Romance, War, etc. - Many of these go for *Guide* or more, with Matt Baker and L.B. Cole covers mostly fetching a premium over *Guide*.

Silver Age Marvel: They are perennial, reliable sellers, and have been for decades. These are the books that primarily launched a world of Baby Boomers, into becoming lifetime comic book aficionados! We read those, gloried in the storylines, the characters with all of those personal problems and neuroses, and we could relate!

The 1st issues from the earlier 1960s have sold well forever, and seem to go up in value, year after year, etc. Consequently, I pay a high percentage of value for these, as they are guaranteed sellers, right away! I do well with all of the S.A. Marvel titles, some better than ever. *Amazing Spider-Man* continues to be the "King of sellers." I keep running out of these, no matter how many collections I purchase!

Silver Age DC: They have been slow sellers for a real long time (with the notable exception of *Batman* - that sells so well that I term the title, an "Honorary Marvel.") They are, at long last, enjoying their day in the sun. Lately, to my surprise and delight, titles such as *The Atom* (I sold two sets of that title lately) have been moving!

I've always enjoyed the S.A. DCs myself, on a personal basis, ever since I was a kid! In the 1960s, I used to get subscriptions to *Justice League* and to *Adventure* (with The Legion of Super Heroes.) They used to come in the mail, tightly folded in half, snug in their paper housing.

Other Silver Age: It's good to have this variety as well, so that folks who (like I did), indulge in enjoying these various companies' comics, can keep on collecting these.

Bronze Age Marvel: Many of them sell well, and I enjoy buying collections that include a good representation of 1970s comics. There are a number of Bronze Age keys, which go for over *Guide*, including (but not limited to) *Amazing Spider-Man* #101 (1st Morbius), #129 (1st Punisher), *Giant-Size X-Men* #1 (1st 'New' X-Men), *Incredible Hulk* #181 (1st full app Wolverine), *Werewolf By Night* #32 (1st Moon Knight), *Tomb Of Dracula* #1, 10 (1st Blade), *Marvel Premiere* #15 (1st Iron Fist), *Special Marvel Edition* #15 (1st Master Of Kung Fu), X-Men #94 (1st New X-Men), #101 (1st Phoenix), #129 (1st Kitty Pryde) and much, much, more. For those I pay an extra premium, and I'm happy to see any or all of them included with a collection I'm offered. Regular Bronze Age Marvels are also always good to get in most grades.

Bronze Age DC: They sell ok, some real good. Everyone loves the 1970s Kirby comics (*Forever People*, *New Gods*, *Mr. Miracle*, especially those three Kirby titles), and of course Batman comics. Bronze Age comics drawn by Neal Adams, especially *Batman* #251 (that fantastic Joker cover!) and the other *Batman* and *Detective* comics by Adams, for the most part, fetch a premium over *Guide*. *Green Lantern* #76 thru 87, and 89, memorable comics drawn by Neal Adams, are perennial great sellers, and deservedly so!

Modern Age Comics: (1980s to The Present): They are mostly under-respected by Silver Age aficionados, so consequently, many comic dealers undervalue these or count comics from this era as "throw-ins" when buying larger collections. At gdcomics, we are willing to pay for these as well, especially for Keys, and for "rank 'n file" issues that are in runs of a title. I list a lot of these as sets, for like 50¢ to a dollar. Some sell more quickly and some are real slow. Of course, I get and pay much more than that for those '80s-and-up keys, and special issues.

We keep track of the values of a number of the special issues from this era, comics like *Amazing Spider-Man* #194 (1st Black Cat), #238 (1st Hobgoblin), #300, and also *NYX* #3, *Edge of Spider-Verse* #2, *Spider-Man Noir* #1, *Avenging Spider-Man* #9, and of course *Walking Dead* #1. We get a premium for many of these, so of course we are willing to pay a premium for them as well. There are a lot of good comics with compelling stories in the Modern Age. However, along with many title expansions etc. at the time, there is a fair bit of "chonk & bloat" as well. Whether key or otherwise, we always take every Modern comic into account when buying a collection.

Original Art: To me, it is an honor' to obtain Original Comic Art. The pages are, by their nature, unique, one of a kind pieces. The variety of value of them is enormous, and we take great pains to keep up with current values, to make a fair offer. Some pieces I pay extra for, as I slowly but surely, add art pieces, to my personal collection (everything from Krazy Kat to Frazetta drawings to *Howard The Duck* covers, to a 1960s *Justice League* cover.)

Pulps: I love the look of these, and those cool spines, with the titles therein. Many of them have very little value (non-special romance, sci-fi, western, etc.) but there are also a number of compelling, cool, pulps that have real good value, titles such as *Horror Stories*, *Terror Tales*, *Strange Tales*, *Spicy Mystery*, *Operator 5*, *G-8 And His Battle Aces*, 1920s & 1930s *Weird Tales*, early 1930s *Astounding*, *Spider*, *Shadow*, *Doc Savage*, *Zeppelin Stories* and many more have real good value (you might be very happily surprised!) Contrary to popular belief, many Pulps are NOT brittle!

Notes on Comic Encapsulation: To CGC, or Not to CGC. There are comics that are worth encapsulating, and CGC is the leading company that does it. However, many comics have too low a value to be worth the expense of encapsulating.

Oddly enough, a number of comics (even more expensive books) actually go for less than *Guide*, once the grading fees are added. If you're not sure whether to certify some of your comics, you could always ask your friendly neighborhood comic book dealer. We at gdcomics pay the seller according to how their books will 'play out' with CGC grading & encapsulating, and their subsequent values, with applicable books for that.

Also, CBCS is a newer third party company that offers a similar service for competitive prices. Their product doesn't always have the same gravitas in the marketplace as CGC's does, but perhaps they will close the gap in time. The head honcho Steve Borock over there is as legit as they come and they've been growing in recent years.

So, that's about it for now. As I'm now in my humble comic book warehouse, where most of my waking hours for the last number of decades have been spent. Here I am surrounded by seemingly endless rows of two-story tall shelves, full of many beloved, back-issue comic books. The ends of thousands of long-boxes each with a comic peeking out of a facing handle-hole create the lines and limits of my sanctum. As I look up and around I can't help but think, "Good ol' comics!" Anyways, I hope you have a good day, and a great comic book year! Comics forever, I say...

Walter Durajlija and Jay Halstead Big B Comics/International Comic Exchange (ICE)

Walter Durajlija, Big B Comics, Hamilton Ontario and Niagara Falls Ontario

A quick congratulations to Bob Overstreet, Mark Huesman, J.C. Vaughn and the whole *Price Guide* team on another fine looking *Guide*. We all appreciate and benefit from the hard work you all put in, thank you.

Well, nobody saw that coming. The onset of the pandemic really did throw everything into disarray, had us all feeling uncertain about the future. At Big B Comics we closed our doors for about 10 weeks, opening back up in late May 2020. As we entered the summer months a few things became clear, traffic and sales at our shops (Hamilton and Niagara Falls, Ontario) were surprisingly strong and online sales through eBay and our icomicexchange.com site were going through the roof. In our shops we were adjusting to the new realities, we ordered the big clear plastic stand up dividers at the check out counters, we provided hand sanitizer and paper towels near the front door and we always had boxes of face masks on the ready in case customer forgot theirs. We posted safe social distancing reminders and we were just more vigilant on all things involving crowds and cleanliness. Things went well.

Of course we were only one half of the equation, I cannot begin to tell you how impressed I am of all the Big B Comics customers that continue to frequent our shops, everyone was doing their part, staying positive, always responsive to customers that may have been the most nervous and cautious. We formed a partnership with our customers, we did our part, and they did theirs and it only worked because there was mutual trust. Easily the biggest takeaway from the uncertainty of last year was the way our customers and our staff at Big B Comics conducted themselves, with courage, dignity, compassion. For me personally all of it was humbling. I'd like to thank all the Big B staff and all the Big B customers for turning something truly scary and challenging into something truly inspiring.

As I mentioned above, sales were strong coming right out of lockdown, some of it was pent up demand but some of it was good stuff coming from the publishers. All the Batman and all the Joker stuff DC was doing was fire and the big Ninja Turtles comics in the Fall were just what the shop needed. The Wednesday that the Ninja Turtles comic came out was a super exciting day, it reminded me of the old days when a big new book came out, there was tons of energy and excitement in the shop all that week, it was good to see.

DC Comics going to a new distributor and scaling back their line were not good news for neither comic shops nor fans. I think it is short sighted for such a big publisher to count pennies and to add hurdles to the marketplace that has led to much of their success.

As a comic book shop we continue to order extra copies for the shelves, we are trying to stock to levels where we can support titles and creative teams, we are trying to grow readership. It is a tough balancing act as nobody likes to be sitting on dead stock but I think trying to sell out by the 2nd day could be even more damaging long term. Decisions, decisions…

Back issues do well at our shops especially raw ungraded comics at the $10 to $200 price points. What sells the quickest are the Copper Age minor keys, comics like *Amazing Spider-Man* #210, 212, *Moon Knight* #1, *Marvel Team-Up* #95, *Hulk* #234 all move very quickly because people can buy these key 1st appearance issues in high grade and at very affordable prices. Comic collecting is extremely fun in this zone. *Spawn* was hot all year, any issue, and some of the lower print run stuff was selling in the $50 range. Even the 1991 Jim Lee *X-Men* books were in demand, I remember when I could not get $2 for the first issues, now they fly out at $5. Back issues are a big part of our business and I want to remind everyone that keeping well stocked back issue bins consistently and over long periods of time takes a lot of work, it takes aggressive buying and hard work at processing and stocking, but the rewards are there if you are willing to put the work in, people love collecting comics.

Jay Halstead - icomicexchange.com

Hello gang and thanks for checking out my report. Because COVID-19 will be discussed at length by all the other advisors, including Walt above, I'm going to try to stick strictly to comic talk.

Amazing Spider-Man my friends, I mean what really needs to be said about this guy? There have been many years where he is the top of the heap as far as it comes to back issues, but this is the year he hammered all other Marvel Super Heroes. Yes, there were hot books strung along other lines of comics, however Spidey is, and continues to be, the man! From his earliest issues that are always on every want list (esp #1-7, #1 is just on fire and we sold a few beauties), and of course all the keys (#14 and #15 continue to hum along), but now we get to discuss the marketplace regarding his modern books that go for big scratch (some of his variant covers, like #667 and #678 come to mind), but also the never-ending demand for issue #300 (and right now as I write this, #299 with the cameo). Like most of you, I didn't think there would ever be a day where #300 would break $2500 in 9.8. But then it broke 3k, then 4k. When will this end? This is truly one of those cross-over books, where old guys like me (I'm 47 and clearly remember this book new), and the young guys who love the anti-hero that Venom is the best representative of in comics, meet. We sold copies to young and old, everybody loves the bad Spider-Man (I know I'm over-simplifying it but that's what my friends and I used to refer to him as when we were teen-agers). When and where will this book end up, nobody knows for sure, but if anything produced in the last 35 years can be considered blue chip I'd have to say this book certainly is it!

And I'd be especially remiss as an advisor in the field of Canadian Price Variants (check out cpvpriceguide.com), to not mention the record sales of one of my favorite characters from my youth, the 1st appearance of the Hobgoblin in *Amazing Spider-Man* #238. This book has always been in very high demand since I started chasing CPV's a good decade + ago, however now, in high grade, it's become the king of the hill. We first had a sale on eBay of $4650 (from a seller that did not ship Internationally believe it or not, only opening up the bidding to Americans), followed only a few months later by the sale of sales, $7600 for a blistering hot CGC 9.8 copy! Not only is this book a juggernaut in 9.8 though, 9.4 and 9.6 copies are not too bad either!

Speaking of Canadian Price Variants, another year goes by, and still no CGC 9.8 copy of *Swamp Thing* #37 exists. It's mind-boggling how elusive this is in grade and I would guess that if one came up in a no reserve auction it would come close or surpass the *ASM* #238 record sale! And don't forget there is still only one copy of *Batman* #404 and incredibly, only one copy of *GI Joe* #21! Speaking of *Joe*, man, can this book get any hotter? It seems that even rough copies are selling for insane money. Everybody wants a copy (CPV or not), and there are just not enough copies to satiate the incredible demand! Don't you dare sleep on #26 and #27 either, with the origins of Snake Eyes and Storm Shadow, these are sure to be hot books in the upcoming years!

The last newer book I'm going to talk about, and that might be the hottest (or biggest value gain), over the last 16 months or so, you know I'm talking about Todd McFarlane's *Spawn*! Man this book has gone to the moon and not come back down, it's incredible! I remember picking up piles of these books say 3 years ago or so for $2 each, and now most of them (between issues #180-250), are $20 copies, with many of them much higher than that! Within those 70 or so issues you've got multiple first appearances, but the big winners are issues #220 to #231 which feature McFarlane homage covers—and the prices have gone bonkers on these! I don't know if this is pent up movie demand or just a long time coming, but either way if you're sitting on *Spawn* collections you might want to investigate those old boxes!

Time to slip back into the wild and wacky world of Silver Age Marvels! Compared to 2019, I haven't seen a lot of massive gains this year, I mean it's still as safe a place to plunk your money as any, however recently we've started to see some titles come out of the cold a bit. The first would be *Silver Surfer*, who I feel has always been a bit of a 2nd tier character, but *Fantastic Four* #48 (earlier this year), followed closely by *Silver Surfer* #1 & #4 (and now #3), are really making strides. And all I can say is, it's about time! I can see the Marvel movies starting to feature this guy over the next decade or so, he's just such a cool character on film.

After many years dormant, we finally get to talk the Man Without Fear, *Daredevil*. Again, one of those books so overlooked for so long, finally getting his due. With word Matt Murdoch may be in the new Spider-Man movie, things have gone nuts, however this book started moving earlier this year. Not that the first Elektra and other early appearances weren't also hot, but now issue #1 is off the charts.

Daredevil *#1 is starting to heat up again.*

Lastly I gotta give props to early Iron Man. *Tales of Suspense* #40 & 41, even issue #1 and the late Silver, early Bronze stuff we can't keep in stock. However *TOS* #39 is a dud right now, flat as a pancake. I'm sure that has to do with Robert Downey Jr. no longer being involved in the Marvel movies but why are these so hot? It's got to have to do with how cheap they've always been, that's my take anyway. But right now if we get anything relatively early and the pages aren't brittle, it sells!

Lastly there are some big things happening at ICE for 2021 that we should let everyone know about. We're still going to continue offering some of the best graded comic books on the market at very competitive prices. However now we've added some things that are more in line with some of our appraiser's expertise.

First will be vintage (and new) action figures, playsets and ships, the majority of which will be AFA graded. The reason we love selling graded comics is because it takes the guesswork and frankly, the debate, out of what that comic is graded. We are looking forward to offering graded toys. We have also added Graded Cards, Sports Cards, Magic, Pokémon etc. ICE is offering a fine selection of graded cards. And finally, we've added Original Art to our product mix. We have some fine pages available right now and we have new stuff always coming in.

We hope you check out the new and improved icomicexchange.com offering a great selection of Comics, Toys, Cards and Original Art! If you are looking to consign any of these collectibles contact Jay or Walt at mailbox@icomicexchange.com.

Ken Dyber
Cloud 9 Comics

Hello comic friends, I own Cloud 9 Comics, which has a brick & mortar store in Portland, OR that has been open for 6 years now. I've also been selling online and at conventions around the country for many years as well. You can shop online via my website: www.cloudninecomics.com or Ebay store (cloudninecomics). I have also started selling on Instagram (dyberken). You can also contact me directly at: ken@cloudninecomics.com.

This is basically a market report about 2020 (even though this guide comes out in July), as we have to submit our reports in December. Wow… I mean, does 2020 suck or what!?! This year was the worst for so many reasons. Selling comics has been a struggle, sure, I get it, there's a pandemic happening with not only mandatory government shutdowns, but also all distribution of new comics shut down for 2 months this spring, and DC leaving Diamond too. Heck, as retailers, we couldn't even *reorder* anything for 2 months, so all the comic stores in Portland started selling comics/trades to one another during these 2 months because we couldn't get anything from Diamond. Additionally, as a retailer, people do not want, or are not able to leave their homes, or they are unemployed, and you have no one from out of town visiting cause no one is traveling. Any advisor in here who says it was a "Banner Year" can just go suck it as far as I'm concerned. Even if you have had a really great year, just keep it to yourself, as 99% of us (or at least us selling new comics and owning a comic book store) have struggled like never before. Some of us will not make it, and for others it may take years to economically return to where we once were.

Also, it appears many people's brains have simply stopped working. Metaphorically speaking, why does half the country think the world is now flat? Having half our population just all together not believe in science makes being a retailer where people walk in/out of your store INCREDIBLY CHALLENGING. I've had more people go 0 to 10 this year than all other years combined. Customers arguing about the most absurd things, like COVID isn't real. Ebay customers leaving the most outlandish feedback I couldn't even conceive of for like $7 comics. COVID is so real, it put one comic store in Portland out of business (and this is comic city USA here), and most likely I believe another 1 or 2 will also not make it due to so many people being out of work, or no tourism happening. Heck I lost 25% of my sales simply because no comic conventions happened this year. Then I also lost another 33% of my box customers, and probably will lose more in the next few months. Things sales wise are abysmal here. Sorry friends, no sugar coating anything. I cannot wait for 2021 and the changes it will bring, because things simply can't be any worse than they currently are. You will read of some good sales I can report about below, but those are collectible back issues, and this is not what keeps comic stores going on a week to week/monthly basis. Also, many of these sales (like my *Invincible* #1) are books from my personal collection that I've had to sell in order to keep the business moving forward. If I was only selling new comics/trades like many stores in America, I would have not survived, and would now be out of business.

Conventions: The only convention I set up at this year was Terry O'Neill's 1 day show in southern CA. With COVID cancelling almost all conventions this year, I have really gotten to thinking about cons moving forward, and will say right now, I will no longer be exhibiting at San Diego Comic-Con, which deeply saddens me as I love this con, but it just doesn't pencil out anymore. In 2021 I plan at setting up at 3 cons: Rose City (Portland), Baltimore & Emerald City (Seattle). I will continue with Rose City as I have a brick & mortar store here so it's good for promoting the shop. As for Baltimore and Seattle, both promotors rolled over my payment, so I will see how those cons go in 2021, but I will most likely stop exhibiting at Emerald City as Reed (the promotor) shows are a pain in the ass to do. They continue to raise prices, make their shows longer, give exhibitors less (NYCC we don't even get chairs or tables) and their load in/out is horrible. Baltimore I love, and hopefully will continue to do this show, but it will depend on if the buyers return as it's a long way for me to travel. I feel COVID may be the tipping point for other mid-size dealers like myself, as large weekend cons have become quite expensive to exhibit at, and year after year, less comic book buyers show up. I believe more parts of the country will return to the inexpensive 1 day show focused just on comic books. Portland currently has one called the Frankenstein Comic Book Swap which is popular here for locals.

Golden Age: Sales have been good this year once again. I've noticed a price correction for pre-Code Horror books in VG or lower unless the cover is great or has excellent eye appeal for the grade (ie: a 3.5 with great front-c eye appeal, but a 2 inch back-c tear will still sell quickly). The same price corrections are happening with Baker & L.B. Cole books, as well as many Good Girl Art books. If they are in Fine or better, then they are still selling quite strong or even breaking previous prices, but low grade ones still sell, just not at such aggressive prices as we saw in 2017-2019.

One specific book I can't believe there is nothing in the *Guide* about is *TV Teens* #5, a Chic Stone cover that is just ridiculous. It features Ozzie and Babs and on the cover, with Ozzie groping Babs breasts with two kids behind a fence looking on. There is no line listing for this book in the *Guide* with just a generic spread of $8 in Good to $60 in NM-. A VG'ish raw copy sold on eBay for $349. I suggest a $200/$400/$600 Good to Fine spread with NM- pricing around $1500. Yes, this is a bit aggressive, but once everyone reads this the "GGA" community will be full on in-the-know and that will drive prices a bit.

There are still good deals to be had in Crime, Romance, cooler Western covers, and other odd ball books. In general though, most Golden Age is getting to be fairly expensive just to get into a copy. One publisher that is starting to look quite affordable compared with others is Standard/Nedor. Great Fine copies of *Fighting Yank* and *Black Terror* can be had for $250-$400, same is true with Fawcett's (Fine Captain Marvel books tend to go for $125-$175). Fiction House books are all getting quite expensive, with *Planet*, *Ghost* and *Fight* leading the way, although I am seeing more interest in *Jumbo/Jungle* and *Wings* than previous years. Also, is it just me, or are Timelys starting to look more and more affordable? Not talking about 9.0s or better, but VG/FN copies of *Marvel Mystery* and *Captain America* (not classic covers or very early issues) seem pretty reasonable lately. Namora is a character to keep an eye on with all the Sub-Mariner hype these days. Who knows if Sun Girl could be the next Groot? What about Mighty Mouse!? Yeah, he's a Timely character. Wouldn't it be amazing to have Mighty Mouse, Groot & Rocket in the Guardians on the big screen!!

Silver Age: Very much in demand, although some blue chips have cooled. NOW is a great time to buy an *Amazing Fantasy* #15 in 3.0-5.5. They are pretty pricey in 1.0-2.5 & 6.0 or better, but this range has dipped in value, so pick one up now if you can afford it and send me a birthday card in March if you do thanking me for all the money you will make in a few years! *X-Men* and *Fantastic Four* issues are all selling quite well (all issues below #50) in any condition as people get excited for their Marvel movies to come. Now is probably a good time to pick up an *Iron Man* #1 or *TOS* #39 as this character will not be used much or at all for some time. *Strange Tales* #110 should be set for a jump at any point, as this is seeming like a steal these days having not shown many gains for years now, and is quite affordable comparably to the other early keys. Also, *Doctor Strange* #169 needs to double in *Guide*! $27 for Good & $81 for Fine is pretty ridiculous. The other Silver Age issues from his series also should go up at least 50%. Another book taking a huge jump is *Batman* #181 (1st Poison Ivy.) Some very strong sales this year.

Overall, I don't really enjoy talking about Silver Age too much, as this is the period that really seems to drive the market, and most collectors seem to be already pretty knowledgeable here, so it's hard to find things to tell people that most don't already know.

Bronze Age: New key issues appear all the time here. Too many to list. *Batman* #313 (1st Tim Fox) has gotten quite hot with DC announcing he'll be the new Batman in Future State. We'll see how long he is actually Batman or if this book is a flash in the pan type, or a new longer standing key issue.

X-Men #135 (killer Dark Phoenix cover) needs its own line listing in guide, maybe with verbiage "Classic Dark Phoenix cover." This book consistently sells for considerably more than #'s 131-134 which it's lumped together with in *Guide*, and it also sells much faster. It should double in *Guide* in Good – Fine and go up 50% in VF – NM-. Another X book that needs to go up in *Guide* (by a TON) is *Giant-Size X-Men* #1! I mean, come on $190 in Good!? It's impossible to get into a complete unrestored copy for under $600 now. Graded 9.2's are going for around $4500, but trending upward a lot (*Guide* is $1900 for NM-! Laughable). I suggest $500 (or more) for GD and $5000 for NM-.

Conan The Barbarian keys are hot again. 9.2s of #1 are now going for around $800 (*Guide* is currently $625 so this needs to go up). #23 & #24 in 9.2 are going for $260 & $225 respectively (with *Guide* values of $145 & $125 respectively). Also, other than these big 3 books in the run, the 1st appearance of Elric (#14) is now going consistently for a good bit to compete with Red Sonja as a major key in this run. 9.2s are going for around $140 currently with not even a mention in *Guide* that #14 is his 1st appearance (*Guide* says 'Elric appearance for #14 & #15). So far the only CGC 9.2 for 2020 that has posted to GPA went for a whopping $400! Also, #15 Elric's 2nd appearance is a fantastic Barry Windsor Smith cover (possibly my favorite in the entire run). Both these 2 books are quite hard to find in high grade at present.

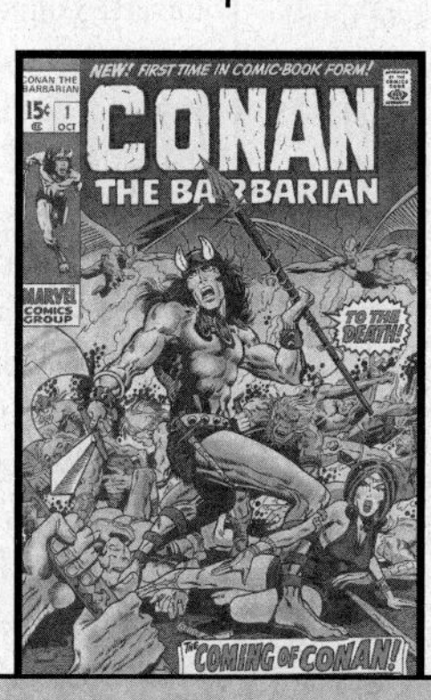

Conan the Barbarian #1 and other Conan keys are going up in price.

Copper Age: TMNT across the board is selling for ridiculous prices!?! All issues, all printings of the Mirage series. *Gobblygooks* are also now selling strong as CGC has started grading them finally if one of the two creators can verify in person that it is an original. NOW is the time to buy these two if you can find them, as they are so rare (50 copies versus 3000) compared with 1st print #1s.

John Byrne's Next Men #14 has one panel with Hellboy partly in it (a movie poster that is partially obscured). This predates #23 by a year. Look for this one to start going up in value. *Guide* needs to add this info, and I suggest a $20 NM- price listing to start with as we can re-evaluate as needed based on sales.

Batman #353 (a Joker cover) that is dated Nov. 1982 contains a 16 page Masters of the Universe preview, the same month as *DC Comics Presents* #51 which the *Guide* currently says is the 2nd appearance of He-Man. This *Batman* issue should have the same notation, and, in all likelihood, is the exact same 16 page preview. I am unsure if one came out on a different week, but they are both the 2nd appearance of He-Man. The *Batman* book currently has a NM- price of $28 (mostly due to the Joker cover). I suggest a separate line listing for this book as it's lumped with #321 & 359 at present, and I also suggest a higher price for *DC Comics Presents* #51, which is currently $15, here I suggest $25, and also a price increase to $150 for #47 He-Man's 1st appearance which regularly sells above *Guide*.

OK, HUGE news… wait for it… Venom's HOT! I know right, none of you knew this or have ever heard of this character before. OK, enough comedy. How many of you knew his first solo story is *Amazing Spider-Man Annual* #25? A very affordable spec book maybe, 'cause you know, Venom's hot! *Amazing* #300s are have basically doubled in all grades.

Another book that the *Guide* is way off on (I know, broken record here) is *Bloodstone* #1 from 2001 on Marvel. This is the 1st appearance of Elsa Bloodstone. I don't know much about the character, and not sure if this is a spec book, or low print run or what, but high grade raw copies seem to be going for around $100 pretty consistently, with 9.8 slabs around $450. It's a cool cover, but really not sure what's driving this book. I have literally never once had someone ask me for this book. In any case, has it at $4.00!? I suggest a starting price of $75 for NM- & we go from there.

OK, everyone who collects knows about *Iron Man* #128 (Bronze Age book), the classic "Demon in a Bottle" Tony Stark cover. The story itself is very tame, and nothing really about his alcohol problem until the last page or two. There are other issues in the series with quite a bit more story wise with Tony being drunk and belligerent, and either on the sidewalk appearing like he's homeless, or drunk and even just yelling at people. One issue that I think is undervalued in this regard is #178, which has him with his dress shirt untucked, his hair messed up and a long beard looking very disheveled. The story is him just being on the street and almost begging for money, and people throwing coins at him. Also this issue as the cool DC 1960's banner on top with a circular Marvel logo with a "MC" in the circle instead of DC. *Guide* should give this book a separate line listing stating Tony Stark alcoholic story and cover. With a suggested NM- price of $20 to start. I sold a raw 9.4 on my site for $25 in 2 days.

Modern Age: *Spawn* across the board has been heating up with a new movie in the works. All issues are selling for me (not for much, but selling). #1 is now a legitimate $40/$50 book in NM. Crazy I know, I'm actually excited when someone calls/comes in with *Spawns*, especially #100-200, as I mostly get offered the early and recent issues. Valiant books just continue to not sell for me at all. *Harbinger* #1, *Rai* #0 and a few other key issues, but run books, forget it. Zero interest.

Renaissance Age: This is what most people still call Modern comics but for me, I fully believe we are in a new time period, and have been since *Walking Dead* #1 came out. To me, this is the beginning of the Renaissance Age of comics. This parallels the 1970s to me when other genre books evolved and the market grew larger because of non-superhero comics. These early years were led by Image Comics, however, AfterShock, BOOM!, Vault, Black Mask and a few other publishers are really pushing Image with good quality books coming out. Also, Image has dramatically slowed for me in sales the last year or two with many of their blue chip titles ending or being on hold forever (ie: *Saga*, *Bitch Planet*!!).

The new hot series for my store this year are *Ice Cream Man*, *Something Is Killing The Children* and *Once & Future*. The first two are selling quite strong, the later has cooled off a bit. *Ice Cream Man* #1 is selling like crazy (really the whole series). Raw 9.2s are going for around $200 at present. *Something Is Killing The Children* is also selling very well with #1s in the $150 range. I've read both, and *Ice Cream Man* for me just does absolutely nothing. I love the concept, but beyond that I just don't get it. Nothing seems to happen in it. *Something Is Killing The Children* though is great, fun, and scary. Kind of reminds me a little of the JJ Abrams *Super 8* movie. *Invincible* has also taking off with Kirkman announcing a show. CGC 9.8s are now going for around $1600 (I had one and it sold in a few weeks).

1st appearance of Corona in *Spectacular Spider-Man* (yeah, a virus character in NYCC, crazy huh) and *Spider-Man* #20 (Bendis's 1st series) has shot up to around $40 as the cover has Miles Morales pinned down on the ground by a police officer.

With COVID, my biggest drop off has been new comic sales. I've lost about 33% of my box customers, and could probably cancel another 15% of them easily. Back issue sales for collectors have been steady if not strong (especially with no cons happening), but new comic sales have fallen off a cliff for me. New trade and Manga sales have held fairly steady compared with last year. I'm thankful to be a comic store selling collectible comics, as the ones in the country that only sell new stuff… wow, I have no idea how you're still in business especially with Diamond shutting down for 2 months this spring, and the ongoing DC fiasco of firings, doom and gloom and switching distributors.

Thanks to everyone who continues to support my small store (literally 680 feet of retail), and buying stuff online with me either via eBay, my website, Instagram or wherever. I am so grateful to everyone this year more than any other who has bought something, so THANK YOU, I hope you will continue to support the business moving forward. !

Daniel Ertle
CBCS - Modern Expert

What a weird year this has been. It started off pretty uncertain for the comic industry with the majority of conventions being canceled, shops being closed or doing live-steam sales only, and the uncertainty of employment for many people. Despite those facts I think 2020 has shown that comic collecting as a hobby is fairly robust and resilient. Books continue to get hot, collectors continue to get books graded and books continue to sell on the secondary market. This year we did see fewer books blow up out of nowhere, modern submissions seemed to be much more influenced by variant covers than anything else. Even to the point that books with nothing impactful or important in the story will get sent in just because they have several variants. Marvel and DC seemed to have made up a bigger portion of submissions compared to other years but with more focus on certain storylines or characters. Indie books outside of Image also have had a strong showing and, surprisingly, even more so with licensed properties. Self published books revolving around a few titles and creators have remained as strong this year as with previous years.

Marvel and DC submissions have seemed to really focus on key storylines. For Marvel this would be anything Venom or Symbiote or adjacent to the character. Books like *Venom* #25 and #27 were huge and are still being submitted at great frequency. *Venom* #25 had a very strange and serendipitous rise to popularity. Virus' first appearance was meant to be the Free Comic Book Day Spider-Man/Venom. However, since FCBD was canceled, the book was actually distributed after *Venom* #25. This has lead us to label *Venom* #25 as the first appearance of Virus. A few more Marvel books that were popular this year were *Strange Academy* #1, *Rise of Kylo Ren* #1 and the *Thor* series by Donny Cates, especially issues 2,5, and 6. DC Comics had a very heavy focus on Batman and Batman related books. *Batman* #89 being the 1st Punchline in cameo remains to be popular as well as *Punchline* #1 and *Harley Quinn* #75. *Detective Comics* #1027 is a recent one that we have seen with a bunch of submissions. Arguably the most popular has been *Dark Nights: Death Metal Legends of the Dark Knights* #1 and *Dark Nights: Death Metal* #2 with both focusing around The Robin King's 1st appearance. And to round it out the title *3 Jokers* has been a pretty big hit for DC as well.

It has been an interesting year for indie books in my opinion. While there have been a ton of really great Image books this year there are only a few that I can think of that have made that big of a splash, two of them from some of the titans in the industry right now. Scott Snyder's *Undiscovered Country* has been very popular but only for the first few issues. Donny Cates *Crossover*, even though as of writing this only 2 issues have come out it, seems like it will have some staying power with all of its great covers. *Walking Dead* usually makes the list for submissions and this year was no different with *Negan Lives*. Also, maybe not surprisingly, *Spawn* has had a huge year for submissions and especially *Spawn* #309 mostly because of Gunslinger Spawn it seems. And who knows, if the movie gets made it could be a super hot series again.

A few indie books that saw overnight popularity for us have been *Something is Killing the Children*, *We Only Find Them When They're Dead*, and *WYND*. *Usagi Yojimbo* is another one that saw a resurgence of popularity with its relaunch at IDW along with the entire series getting reprinted. IDW has had a very good year with their licensed titles. Teenage Mutant Ninja Turtles continues to enjoy a huge portion of submissions. Especially with the recent hit *Last Ronin* finally coming out it seems like they will continue to dominate. Power Rangers also remains very relevant to collectors it seems. People can't get enough of those helmet variants and when they had the *TMNT/Power Rangers* crossover it seemed like a no-brainer to re-do them with the turtles holding them. One book that got big practically overnight was *Star Wars: The Clone Wars* #1 from Dark Horse. This book features Ahsoka Tano's first appearance in comics and with more and more Star Wars properties calling on characters from old I can imagine the speculation machine will be trying to find the next Star Wars book to latch onto.

And finally as far as indie books go there seems to be a certain category of self-published books that remain popular and I can't see any slowing down. This is the *Do You Pooh*s and *Hardlee Thinn*s of the world. I would now include *White Widow* in this category as well. These are books that usually contain the same interiors, maybe a new story every now and then, with a myriad of new covers. No one does it as well as Marat Mychaels with what has been hundreds of covers, most of them being cover swipes. Dan Menoza's books have also remained relatively popular but less so than previous years.

As I had mentioned before variants seemed to have driven much of the modern market this year. With publishers fully embracing this random books are being bought and sold solely for the variants. And I would be remiss to not mention the mostly popular cover artist of the year. None other than the new "Stormbreaker" Peach Momoko. Peach has been doing covers for a while now but this year she seemed to have really blown up. Almost every submission we get has at least one Peach cover. I understand why, as her art style and design sense are incredible and I personally hope she continues to remain just as popular.

I hope all who read this had a somewhat happy and healthy 2020 and I look forward to commenting on the state of CBCS modern submissions in 2021.

D'Arcy Farrell
Pendragon Comics

A Review Of The Industry For 2020: COVID ruined many things in 2020. Small businesses, restaurants, travel and tourism and even comics were severely impacted by the pandemic. Hopefully, by the time this is printed, the world has learned a lesson and we have mostly moved on.

For us this year has been a mixed blessing on the whole. After 30+ years in the same location, we moved into a larger store in a mall. Five weeks later we experienced the first shut-down of the year. We were thankfully in a position where we could use that time to further renovate the new location, including expanding our bins of back issues, adding showcases for a larger selection of Magic Cards as well as Sports Cards and we even started carrying Pop! Vinyl figures. We were allowed to re-open in June and that is when the interruptions to supply chains became apparent – difficulties in getting various bags and boards not only for ourselves but also our customers as well as numerous cancellations and re-solicits from Marvel. DC's decision to ship direct, bypassing Diamond, ran into issues as well, with our first order arriving 3 weeks late.

Our second closure in the Fall of 2020 saw us finally moving to an online presence utilizing Shopify. It was the only way to truly keep funds coming in. Having established a presence a year prior using Instagram, Facebook and Twitter did help, but with many other people out of work, spending on entertainment products like ours will naturally decrease, so being able to provide alternate means for people to buy is necessary for our survival.

The impact on cinemas has also affected comic sales, with many blockbusters severely delayed, or in some cases premiering on streaming services in an attempt to recoup costs. *Black Widow*, *Wonder Woman* and other titles that would normally have driven ancillary sales are still eagerly awaited.

Even with the lack of films, though, DC had a huge sales year for us. Dark Metal, Joker War and more lead the way. But even those sales were not enough to save most of the secondary titles, as evidenced by the number of cancellations and lay-offs at DC. Marvel's sales were flat, with the exception of Venom/King in Black. *Spawn* has seen a huge resurgence in interest this year, but we've also lost many of the smaller independents.

Vintage Book Sales In 2020: Everything key, small or big, was on fire. I have never seen such action for DC and Marvel back issues. First appearances of villains and heroes were the most requested items, followed by particular artists. On the Marvel side, *Amazing Spider-Man* #50, 101, 129, 194, 300 and 361, *Avengers* #8, *X-Men* #12, 109, 120, 121 and *Giant-Size X-Men* #1. For DC, *Batman* #313 in particular, but really any back issue of *Batman* or *Detective Comics*.

As far as artists are concerned, anything by Jack Kirby or Neal Adams were the most sought after. *Eternals*, *Black Panther*, *Fantastic Fou*r, *Green Lantern*, 4th World – anything in those lines by those artists are hard to keep.

New Releases In 2020 - DC: COVID did not seem to slow down DC's pace as they lead the industry in art and story lines. These are all highly recommended: *Joker: Criminal Sanity*, Joker War, anything Black Label, *Death Metal/Dark Universe*, *DCeased* and the various Anniversary specials. First appearance of Punchline, as well as the *Punchline* Special were on fire. The card stock variant covers of most titles were the preferred choice, especially Middleton's *Wonder Woman*, Bermejo's *Batma*n and Inhyuk's *Flash* covers. It was the best year ever for DC in our store.

New Releases - Marvel: Marvel was hit hard with COVID. Many titles were canceled or re-solicited and from March to August, and we saw the impact with very little or no product. Marvel finally rebounded near September.

Biggest title sellers were *Thor* by Donny Cates, *Venom*, *Wolverine*, *Star Wars* and *Empyre*. The Knull story-line looks to be huge for the year. The Alex Ross Timeless covers as well as the Indigenous covers were popular. Rounding out the good were *Immortal Hulk* and *Daredevil*.

What was really bad for Marvel? *Ravencroft*, *Star* and *Tarot* lead the way. *Marvels/Marvels X* showed promise. After

House/Powers of X in 2019 the entire run of X-titles has been a drag. Worst of all is the poor writing on *Amazing Spider-Man*.

New Releases - Image Comics: *Department of Truth* was a huge sell at our store. Conspiracy stuff and cool art. *Criminal* by Brubaker is always good.

New Releases - IDW: *TMNT: The Last Ronin* is a great story and art. A surprise hit for many.

New Releases - BOOM!: The reboot of various Power Ranger titles has seen huge interest in our store. *Something is Killing the Children* is a great read so get the trades.

New Releases - Valiant: Well written and decent art, good value, but they need something better than a failed movie to attract new customers. Too much resetting of main titles does not help.

New Releases - Zenescope: Art can be quite good, but like Valiant, it needs something more to lift it for new fans. Simply re-purposing folk lore heroes won't work without great story lines.

New Releases - Dynamite: Artists Parrillo, Suydam, and Lisner create beautiful covers on many titles at this company. *Red Sonja*, *Secret Six*, *Vampirella* and the new *DIENAMITE!* have seen increased sales.

Other Independents: Titan's *Blade Runner* titles were good, but all the others suffered greatly during the pandemic.

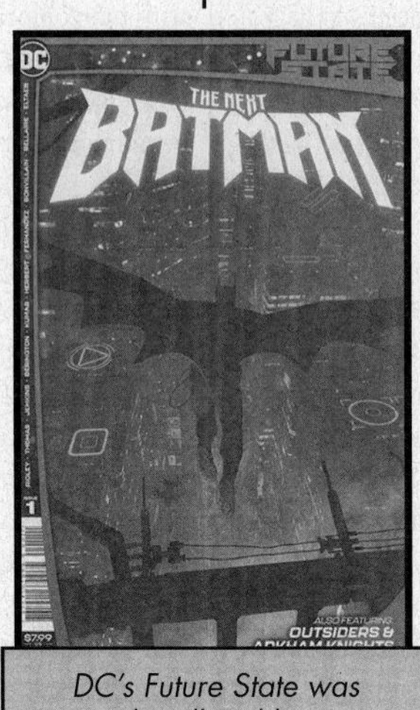

DC's Future State was headlined by **The Next Batman #1**.

2021 New Releases: Future State by DC. Spinning out of Dark Knights Metal series, different timelines and characters appear in short series. Nubia? Immortal Wonder Woman? A new Batman (see *Batman* #313!) this looks good.

Daredevil by Marvel, and Elektra, by writer Chip Zdarsky, looks very promising. I'm not sure how the whole King in Black with Knull will play out, but I am sure sales will be good. Will the return of Phoenix help or hinder the X-Titles?

What To Invest In Vintage Back Issues?: There seems to be no slowdown for Silver Age Marvel especially *Amazing Spider-Man*. But why not go after a run of *Batman* starting around issue 300? Many issues may seem to have little importance but some, like #313, suddenly go from $15 to $100's instantly. Going after keys is fine, but you miss the potential of huge gains doing what many real collectors do. Collect and reading runs of a favourite hero or villain. DC in particular are lower value and print run from 1975-1985.

Older titles like *Flash*, *Wonder Woman*, *JLA*, that ended in the mid-1980s are very affordable.

Also, think of this. What was hot in the past, usually due to amazing art, a solid story, or a key event such as first appearance tend to come back in the future. Can we foresee another *Kingdom Come* sequel? *Watchmen*? Doomsday? Valiant? Frank Miller *Daredevil* runs? Sequels or re-imaging are hard to resist. Movies or TV can make an instant hot series or book too. The 1990s have now turned 30 years old. Think of what was hot then? Neil Gaiman's *Sandman*, Alan Moore's *Swamp Thing*, Death of Superman, *Spawn*, *Savage Dragon* and many more. *Infinity Gauntlet* was a throw-away mini-series.

Bill Fidyk
Collector

It was a stellar year for sales for the comic book back issue market. It seemed as if the pandemic did not have a very large impact on the collecting world in general. The magazine back issue market was no exception and saw tremendous interest from collectors in 2020. High grade keys saw record prices. Being that magazine collectors are primarily run collectors and completists, the term "key" refers to not only first appearances but also to issues that had low print runs or are scarce in high grade.

The following were the top five key issues that were in demand and had climbing price increases in sales figures throughout 2020:

1. *Famous Monsters* #1: A mega key for Warren completists and always in demand for magazine collectors. All grades (low, mid, and high) sell quickly.
2. *Vampirella* #1: A true key that appeals to Frazetta collectors for the cover and the first appearance of Vampirella. High grade copies with white pages above 9.0 sell for multiples of guide prices. This is a book that just keeps getting hotter and hotter.
3. *Savage Tales* #1: The first appearance of Man-Thing and Conan in magazine format. A true collector's item that always disappears as quicky as it shows up for sale.
4. *Eerie* #1: Although it is truly impossible to tell a real from a counterfeit copy, even known counterfeit copies that are second prints are going for strong prices. Again, this is an issue that Warren completists must have.
5. *Eerie* #23: This is an iconic Frazetta cover that is constantly climbing in price.

The following were the top five magazine key issues that were in demand due to scarcity. High grade examples realized multiples of *Guide* and mid-grade copies saw healthy prices as well. Prices for high grade copies of these magazines are erratic due to the lack of copies that surface to market:

1. *Eerie* #39
2. *Eerie* #35
3. *Vampire Tales Annual* #1
4. *Creepy Annual* 1972
5. *Vampirella Annual* #1

Honorable mentions: High grade copies of any Skywald title are always in demand and will realize high prices since these books rarely come to market. The same is true for high grade Eerie Publication titles.

Paul Figura
CBCS - Modern and Vintage Grader

To say that this past year has been a long strange trip would be an understatement. The comic industry was hit hard by the quarantine. Dealers, suppliers and customers had no idea what was going to happen and when it would be over. We saw some books go at auctions for new record prices, and some books go for extremely low and reasonable prices. Why? Because we had a front row seat and got to watch as the world changed before our eyes, and how we do business. Books selling for lower than normal pricing was due, I believe, to people having to clear out a few favorites to survive. This is nothing new, this happens all the time, just never on a worldwide scale. The results were getting comics now into the hands of people that thought they would never own a copy of certain books. Which in turn creates a bit of chatter and excitement in the collecting community. I always felt that dealers and distributors needed to have some support. Whether it was between themselves or some group or committee of like minded individuals to act as a buffer between them and the powers that be. Working together to make the business of comics fun again for everyone. The movies and television shows are doing their part to lure a new audience to our familiar heroes, but without the support of the print media can they survive? I guess we will have to wait and see in the coming years.

Work here at CBCS has been really hectic as some collectors took the quarantine time off to go through their collections and send in comics for pressing and grading. I want to thank everyone for their faith in our product! Our receiving department has been flooded with new submissions. We tip our hats to their professionalism and work ethic in getting these submission to us in such a timely fashion! With no major conventions happening, there were many smaller creator signings happening, where people could send in their comics and get their favorite artist or writers autographs, much like at a convention. We are seeing a steady stream of books from signings, which is a good sight. At least there is some good activity happening around the country! Hard work is bringing the community back together and the hard work done here will help in getting things done and back into everyone's eager hands to view their treasures in a new light! Until next year...Thanks again to everyone who reads our input, and happy collecting!

Joseph Fiore
ComicWiz.com

Rereading my report from last year, the opening two paragraphs could easily have been the opening for this year's report. 2020 will go down as the year we'd all like to put behind us. My year began like any other. We had planned a family trip, were abroad, and due to the nature of my work, I knew what had been happening in Wuhan as early as late January because a client of mine had shut down their operations in the city due to the aggressive spread of this virus. My wife had pre-planned our trip, and I didn't want to be the party-pooper, although I did consider cancelling the trip more than a handful of times out of concern we would not be able to return back into Canada. The trip itself went without any issue, we had travelled to a destination which did not have any reported case until the day we arrived back home, and it was on a resort property far removed from where we were visiting. We still quarantined upon our return as a precaution, even though at that point, it was still early times and such public directives requiring international travelers to do so had not yet been firmly established.

Within that week of returning home, everything changed. We were receiving daily announcements about the virus shoring-up in Canada, and we began seeing public health directives which began putting restrictions on our daily living. These directives were heralded as our only chance of staying alive, and keeping hospital ICU's from being overwhelmed. And for the most part, we were able to transition to the "stay at home" orders when lockdown measures were put in place, thankfully without any incident or issue. In March I had to repatriate my Dad from abroad, and had fought hard to get him on the last flight back home. I was pulled over early Sunday morning on the way to pick him up from the airport, and even though I knew restrictions had tightened up by that point, it was surreal to be told I was not allowed to leave my home and that he needed to make arrangements to shuttle back home.

My Mom's nursing home had managed to stay outbreak free up until around the month of June. Sadly, since that time, there has been at least one reported case every week, but they have otherwise been doing very well in managing their outbreaks, especially when compared to how other homes across the world have not fared as well. At the time of editing this report, I just received word from my Mom's nursing home that they are 48 hours away from receiving the Moderna vaccine, and I'm incredibly thankful for their care, dedication and attention to residents during these challenging times. Hearing that the pandemic would cause the comic industry to shutter was hard to hear at first, but certainly understandable given what I was watching unfold in my own daily life, and the looming predicament of a seeming economic collapse caused by a virus with an aggressive manner of spreading. Despite all this, what was most surprising were the amount of people contacting me, wanting to buy back-issue comics, particularly during the months of April through to June.

Listings which lingered for months, some even nearing a full year without any interest, were suddenly getting significant attention. How could this be, I wondered. How is it that in a moment in global history, where people are being ordered to stay home to save lives, with millions having lost their jobs, their incomes, and would have to start possibly burning through their life savings to survive this pandemic, could people be thinking of buying comics? I suddenly found myself not having much time to think about the 'why', because people were requesting pick-up at our residence, and the term "curbside" pick-up" became the defacto way to ease concerns that the transaction would be carried out with precaution and with public health safety in mind. An example of one such book that suddenly, and inexplicably got hot, was *Raphael: Teenage Mutant Ninja Turtle* #1 (one-shot) from 1985, with an original print run of 60,000. I couldn't figure out what had been causing my online listing to suddenly garner that much interest. With Hollywood being pretty much shut down, and no TMNT movie or script announcement in sight, it seemed an odd occurrence to the type of signals we normally look to which might explain why a book is heating up. I did however notice that NECA released a Raphael and Casey Jones action figure 2-pack, and in most TMNT Facebook groups, there was discussion on its lacking availability. I didn't question the rationale, I just did what I could to satisfy the requests for it. One person drove 2 hours one-way to pick up the comic, and I was glad I was able to provide him with a nice high grade copy to reward his efforts.

Sales of key issues such as *Amazing Spider-Man* #300, and two pre-Code ECs (*Tales From the Crypt* #41 and *Weird Fantasy* #6) represented some of my fastest sales. Sold within hours of listing them. And one of the other surprising listings related to the runaway success of Disney's *Mandalorian* series. I had always seen potential in Marvel *Star Wars* #68 as the first time we would see Boba Fett as being one of a number of super-commandos protecting the planet Mandalore. I had several copies, which had a marker strikethrough on the issue number '68', marked this way as part of a system retailers relied on to return unsold comics during the heyday of affidavit returns. The comics I had in my inventory were assumed over twenty years ago as part of a substantial back-issue inventory that came through Andromeda, which was basically one of a handful of secondary resellers that operated as part of a pseudo distribution network during the days of affidavit returns.

Months prior, I had listed a nice high grade example (albeit with the marker line, that didn't really detract from the eye appeal of the book) and the listing languished with an asking price of $65. Then on December 18th, the second season finale of *The Mandalorian* aired, and it's like that episode shook something loose. The only predicament was shipping due to holiday season delays and the added downside of a pandemic, which seemingly brought shipping to a crawl. Packages that would normally take no more than a week using priority services were taking anywhere from several weeks to well over a month to arrive. I limited the sales of the remaining issues I had to local pick-up, and by Dec 19th, I sold them all to one person locally. I also saw ungraded copies selling consistently at nearly three times my original asking price from months prior.

Other than comic sales, I did quite well selling a wide-range of toys and collectible items through a Facebook group utilizing an interesting "deal-or-no-deal" selling format, whereby sellers are not handcuffed by the predominant FB group policies requiring an asking price be included with the listing. In this group, you simply include photos, a description, and wait for members to make offers on your item. As each offer is made, you reply to the comment whether it's a deal, or no deal. In the case where you begin to receive multiple offers, it begins to take on the appearance of an auction, however the seller is not bound to accept based on the highest offer received. Many times, sellers accept the offer they are most happy with, which only really creates a bit of controversy when someone seemingly puts in a higher offer, but it is declined due to the seller accepting a previous offer. The group works well with items that sell infrequently, are in high demand, or have little to no comparables to base a value on, and I was able to sell several only example prototypes, as well as making some surprising sales on items I had no idea would command the value and interest they did.

Rather unfortunately however, the appraisal side of my activities was impacted by COVID. I had decided to take several months off to concentrate on the simple things like grocery shopping and keeping my family safe. Public health restrictions were limiting one person from each household to go out and do once mundane things like shopping, and I was more than willing to be the one in my household if it meant keeping my family safe. I also had to shop for my Dad, who is at an advanced age and has underlying health issues. As such, I exercised an abundance of precaution with everything I did, and still do. And this also meant I had to decline multiple assignments due to public health orders and circumstances where the risk was too great.

Several of the assignments I declined were willing to wait until I was able to perform them. One such assignment which I was initially cleared to perform had a rather unexpected turn of events where the site I was expected to attend had closed due to a presumptive COVID case. Several attempts to reschedule ended-up being for naught as that location had a string of outbreaks, and between the risks of working in an enclosed area and outbreaks seemingly taking too long to resolve, I decided to suspend the assignment until a later time. One estate I was able to appraise was kept in a storage locker, and I had been assured that the contents had been kept in storage for two years, without anyone visiting the locker during the pandemic. I took all the necessary precautions, wore full PPE, and while wearing gloves, a mask and face shield made it sometimes more difficult to examine items, I was glad I did because we found mail postmarked from April 2020 which meant someone had been in the locker well after lockdown restrictions were in effect. It is unfortunate when you don't have the cooperation of others when taking risks to assist them, but this year was about keeping myself and my family safe, and it's still my number one priority.

In previous reports, I'd conclude by providing recommendations on pitfalls to avoid, and how to better navigate our hobby to avoid disappointment and frustration. This year however, we've all experienced (some, perhaps in greater degrees than others) a sense of danger and fear associated with this pandemic. And while this is often associated with negative experiences because we've had to modify our lives so much to get through these unprecedented times, there is also opportunity and possibility to nurture our sense of belonging and to slow down in ways that can enhance our personal wellbeing. There is an opportunity to strengthen our ties to family and community. 2020 will be the year we began to take notice of everyday essential heroes who weren't born from the panels of comic books or some memorable sporting event. Those calls from people that are downsizing due to them experiencing a terrible financial year, or who feel overwhelmed dealing with the loss of someone to this horrible virus, and are stricken with anxiety on how to properly deal with their collections, are reaching out for our help.

This is the year to take notice. See it as an opportunity to not only look through their collections, but to become that every day hero by checking on them, especially if they are elderly, and maybe even offer to help with shopping. Many of them are experiencing a level of social isolation that leaves them vulnerable and at risk of not being able to properly nourish themselves or to receive life saving medical attention. Hopefully, with the announcements of high efficacy vaccines and preventive treatments, we will be able to return to some level of normalcy soon. Let's keep things simple and turn the corner on this pandemic together. May the year ahead be better than the last, and let's hope this decade continues to usher in a better understanding of what's necessary to maintain our health, our personal wellbeing, and much greater appreciation for the things we sentimentalize about - those same ideals that draw us into the visual storytelling of comics, should inspire us to become real life heroes in our communities. It can be the common thread that unites us as collectors. Please stay well and safe everyone!

Dan Fogel
Hippy Comix

Great Krypton. what a year! I'll leave it to my retailing cohorts to delve deeply into what otherwise would've been the top story of 2020: AT&T/DC vs. Diamond and the Direct Market. My personal Pandemic story has been stressful but not as bad as my many friends who mainly sell at conventions or store fronts and had to quickly ramp up their online game. I will say that from what I've heard across the board, back issue sales were extremely robust online and via mail order!

2020 was the first year before 1975 that I haven't so much as attended, retailed at or run a convention. My previously unbroken string since 1986 selling at San Diego Comic Con being interrupted especially hit my pocket book, although it was extremely nice reducing that overhead. Fortunately I've cultivated repeat mail order retail and wholesale customers over the decades, augmented by an online presence and word of mouth resulting in frequent new leads. Also, a main part of my business has always been wholesaling to other retailers, but this year conventions were replaced with video conferences virtually flipping through short boxes followed by trips to the Post Office. One big in-person sale to an out of state repeat buyer was delayed from March until September, and helped replace con revenues. I expect more of the same until 2022.

I made two large buys, alongside my invaluable retailing partner and running buddy Patrick Sullivan. The first was over several months, local to me in the Cleveland area. Our main effort was in mid-March, when we had already scheduled moving the bulk of tens of thousands of comics, books, toys, posters, DVDs etc., from a 3-story house to a new storage unit. During the course of that week COVID-19 started hitting hard and we watched local businesses gradually close or limit hours as masks and social distancing were mandated. The second collection was in December in Chicago, and by then we were so stir crazy we rolled the dice, hit the road with masks and sanitizer, and survived.

Thanks as always to "Unca" Bob Overstreet and Steve Geppi, J.C. Vaughn, Mark Huesman, Amanda Sheriff, Mike Wilbur, and all the fine folks at Gemstone Publishing for their tireless and consistently high-quality work, and for letting me be a small part of the fun since 1987!

Dan Gallo
Dealer

This time last year I started off my market report writing about eBay's collection of sales tax and how it was taking a bite out of auction prices. I opined that in the short-term things would bottom out, level off, and creep back up again as people get used to the tax component. But what I didn't see was how fast that would occur. The concern for the deflation I saw on Bronze Age keys and commonly traded Silver Age books in lower and middle grades turned out to be nothing more than a hiccup.

The COVID effect on the hobby was twofold. One, on the down side, was the cancelation of almost all conventions and two, on the plus side, hobbyists were forced online which resulted in very strong sales both in volume and in prices realized. Although I am not a "show dealer" necessarily and derive only a tiny fraction of my revenue from show sales I too was affected by the lack of shows indirectly because guys I buy from were. There were out of the trenches and their ability to acquire new material was severely hampered. We now had collectors who could no longer spend at shows and dealers who needed inventory all forced online, some perhaps for the first time while others having to increase their online presence, which in turn jacked up all the prices. Which, by the way, probably helped alleviate the sales tax deflation I mentioned earlier.

It is December 2020 as I write this. We have been locked down for much of the year, there have been no major conventions and we haven't had a new Marvel movie in more than 18 months and yet the prices are higher than ever and no one can keep prime material in stock. And this was supposed to be the bad time? What exactly will the good time look like? I'll get to that later but for now…let's talk books. I will try not to overstate the obvious and will assume that this is not your first day in the hobby. Here we go:

Golden Age: "Big Gold," which I define as the top 20 or so best GA books to have as derived from a combination of both value and desirability, has been at a plateau for the last couple of years but this is going to change. It's like when you smell the rain before the first rain drop hits the ground. You know it's going to happen...and soon!

I still love *More Fun* #73, the first appearances of both Aquaman and Green Arrow. This book is grossly undervalued. I like *Wonder Woman* #6, the first appearance of Cheetah. Relatively speaking it is an inexpensive GA key. Of course, any *Batman* and *Detective* with classic villains on the cover should be on your radar as well. And as always, if you can, try to stay away from problems. I know with GA books we sometimes don't have a choice but the cleaner the book the easier the resale.

Silver Age: DCs are still cold for all the reasons I mentioned in my last year's report. Nothing really has changed on that front. You would think that even with the overall increased sales volume things would have picked up for DCs but they haven't; people still don't want them. There are exceptions like *Batman* #181, *Detective* #359 and *Showcase* #22, but bottom line, if you like DCs or are thinking about getting in, this is the time because they may never be cheaper.

Marvels are seemingly bulletproof. Big movers this past year have been *X-Men* #1, *Daredevil* #1, and *Fantastic Four* #5 with many grades seeing a 50% increase since the beginning of the year. New on my radar is *Strange Tales* #89, the first Fin Fang Foom. It's scarce, it's cheap, and it's worth looking into. Other books to keep an eye on are *Amazing Spider-Man* #3, 14 & 15, *Silver Surfer* #1, 3 & 4, *FF* #4, 48 & 49, and *Journey Into Mystery* #85.

If you're getting an ***Amazing Spider-Man #300,*** *stick with the CGC 9.8s with white pages.*

Bronze Age: BA is heating up. Prices for the top books are increasing even in middle grades. I still believe it is very important to get the highest grade possible even if you have to buy fewer books to do so, (I mean BA is not exactly scarce). If you are more an investor than a collector, I would stick to the big four: *Hulk* #181, *Giant-Size X-Men* #1, *ASM* #129, and *Marvel Spotlight* #5. Already have them? Get more. And if you want to speculate a bit, *Marvel Spotlight* #32.

Copper Age: Stick to 9.8's with white pages. I spent this past summer loading up on a bunch of CA keys, all in 9.8. My hit list included no-brainers like *ASM* #300, *New Mutants* #98, & *Batman Adventures* #12; solid picks like *ASM* #252, *ASM* #316, *Hulk* #340, *Punisher* Limited #1, *NM* #87 & *Thor* #337; and sleeper picks like *ASM* #265, *Cap Annual* #8, *Marvel Tails* #1, *Spider-Man & His Amazing Friends* #1, & *Silver Surfer* #44. And remember, stick to 9.8's with white pages!

Sales Data: Sales data does not necessarily indicate demand. Of course, it would depend on the book and or how you read the data but generally speaking one sale, somewhere by someone, doesn't mean the entire price spread instantly changes like an event in a time travel movie. Just because the last sale was "X" doesn't mean there will be demand for another at the same price. Sometimes a single high sale is a one off and doesn't mean much more until there is a another one, or two. Just like a very low sale is commonly dismissed be cautious of making a purchase based on a lone high one.

Original Art: Original comic art value is not always about consensus "worth" but what it's worth to you. The prices are often abstract and rarely follows any logic whatsoever. When trying to buy a piece from a fellow collector you may have a ballpark idea of "worth" but they are asking considerably more than that. I consider that "the vig"; the amount it will take over the "worth" to pry it away from someone who often time does not want to part with it all. Art prices are often less about "worth" and more about what it will take to get it so don't let your perception of value handcuff you or else you may never get anything. And remember, when it is time for you to sell you will do the same thing!

Conclusion: The hobby is strong but that's not the headline. I believe that our hobby hasn't even scratched the surface of where it is going. Not even scratched the surface. Maybe it will take a few years but this hobby will look vastly different from how it looks today. Things like fractional ownership, six figure sales becoming commonplace, regular seven figure transactions and eventually a breakthrough to an eye popping eight figure transaction will all attract even more money into high end material which will pull everything up with it, (the meat, not the potatoes). Just take a look at the sports card market. As strong as our hobby is, compared to what's going on there we are practically standing still.

We have all used the word "crazy" and "insane" to describe the hobby at times but I think a more accurate term is "normal." What we see regularly is indeed "normal." Things go up, prices spike, we see big sales, and exceptionally nice items get exceptionally nice prices...all "normal." So, what does true crazy or true insanity look like? Just watch because it's coming...

James Gallo
Toy & Comic Heaven

As we come to the end of 2020 most people will be happy to put this year behind them for numerous reasons. It was certainly a crazy year but ironically from a hobby standpoint rather strong. With the stoppage in movie production, we have seen a drop off in movie speculation books which has helped natural growth as opposed to books popping and dropping. Shortly after the shut down ended in early April there was a massive up swing in sales and demand for books all around. I saw an upswing in sales online and in store as people were looking for a distraction from the things happening in the world around them and went to comics and collectibles to help get them through. Although this massive upswing slowed in the last few months of the year, the market was still up from where the year started. I think this year showed true growth, which was a direct result of the drop off in the speculation market. The lack of shows for most of the year certainly dramatically hurt sales, but it did enable me to get more inventory online which boosted sales in that venue.

The Golden Age market remains stable as always. Superheroes still lead the way but we have seen a massive upswing in pre-Code Horror as well. There seems to have been a massive upswing in Batman issues, especially Catwoman and Penguin covers. With additional Batman films down the road, I expect this to continue. However, when it comes to post Avengers films, we have seen some slowing in Captain America books, not that they won't sell per say, just that they aren't flying off the shelf quite as fast, not to mention the prices have softened a tad. This seems to be true with most super-hero Timely books. On the other hand, the Romance books have seen an upswing as have secondary Golden Age super-hero books. Disney has rebounded some but Westerns are still very weak, even when discounted.

Silver Age is very strong with near immediate sales of major keys. *Spider-Man* still leads the way which I expect to continue as his popularity continues to grow with younger audiences. The *Into the Spider-verse* movie was a big help, but more on that later. There has been a huge upswing in the secondary Spider-Man characters which have pushed issues like #25, 31 and 41 up dramatically.

There has been some growth in early *Fantastic Four* and *X-Men* books with the major keys like *Fantastic Four* #4, 5, 48 and 52 remaining super strong. *X-Men* #1 and 12 have gone through the roof and interest in issue #4 remains strong. Run of the mill mid-grade Marvel still sells at or around *Guide*, and there are still some run builders here that are filling in holes.

DC is still lagging here with much of the interest centered around a handful of key Batman books. There just aren't quite as many key Silver Age DC books and the movies haven't done nearly as well which have kept many of the prices down. One exception to this however, is *Showcase* #22 which has found much renewed interest. There is starting to be an upswing on the new generation of classic covers with certain books starting to stick out like *Batman* #169 and #190 (Penguin covers), #197 and #210 (Catwoman covers) gathering a lot of increased attention. These are all tough books in high grade and you should expect to see continued growth on them. Unlike Marvel, the mid-grade DC market isn't quite as strong with non-main titles having to be discounted slightly or selling much slower than the Marvel books.

With Bronze Age being so very strong in recent years, it certainly seems this period has cooled off more than others. Although the softening of the major keys like *Incredible Hulk* #181 and *Amazing Spider-Man* #129 have rebounded, many of the other secondary keys have continued to drop off a bit. There have been a few exceptions with books like *Giant-Size X-Men* #1, *Marvel Spotlight* #5, #28 and *Werewolf by Night* #32 continuing to rise with a demand that far exceeds the supply. Not accounting for the price variants, I think *Giant-Size X-Men* #1, *Marvel Spotlight* #5 and *Werewolf by Night* #32 are now easily in the top 5 Bronze Age books. Much like the Silver Age, there has been an upswing in secondary character demand as people look for the underpriced gems. Books like *X-Men* #130, *Marvel Spotlight* #32, *She-Hulk* #1, and *Amazing Spider-Man* #194 have led the way.

On the DC side, the Horror market has seen a massive upswing as we see classic covers from Neal Adams, Bernie Wrightson and Jack Kirby exploding. These books tend to be very hard to find in high grade. Both because of the dark covers and because they tended not to have been cared for as much as the Super-hero titles. Beyond that it is a very Batman dominated market with Superman and Wonder Woman coming in behind. Much like a running theme, it seems the secondary books have seen massive increases. *Detective* #410 and *Batman* #232 are a couple of examples as well as all the Superman/Flash race books.

Copper Age books are very slow except for a handful of major key issues. It's apparent that the *Guide* does need to be adjusted down on these non-key books since the supply far outweighs the demand. On the other hand, I have seen some books rise massively in price, including *Transformers* #1, *G.I. Joe* #1, and *Marvel Tails* #1. There has also been an upswing in Newsstand edition values and the keys should be pulled out with a newsstand value about 10-20% higher than the direct version. Late run books from various titles have also seen solid growth including the previous mentioned titles along with *Star Wars* among others. The key book from this era is by far *Amazing Spider-Man* #300 which has had massive gains in all grades.

Modern books have seen a massive upswing. This is largely due to books popping. As previously mentioned, the *Into the Spider-verse* film blew up several dollar books into massive keys. *Ultimate Fallout* #4, *Edge of Spider-Verse* #2 and #5, as well as the upcoming movie related *Thor* #2 and *Venom* #3 are books that have exploded. This market is still highly based on speculation so the lack of movies has tamed it some.

On a whole, it's a bit surprising to me that the bottom never fell out of the market which I did expect to happen in March or April. Instead, the market has become stronger with constant sales and key books being extremely hard to replace even when paying 80-90% of market. As a result, the price on keys keep getting pushed up higher. It's unsure when this all may end but for now this has to be the strongest collectible market we have ever seen. Some sales include:

Big Shot #43 CGC 3.5 $325, *Big Shot* #24 CGC 3.0 $400, *Blue Beetle* #32 CGC 2.5 $400, *Detective Comics* #29 CGC 3.0 $75,000, *Superman* #4 CGC 4.0 $2300, *Terry Toons* #7 CGC 1.8 $800, *Whiz Comics* #10 CGC 7.0 Conserved $1200, *Wings* #21 CGC 2.5 $375, *Amazing Spider-Man* #1 CGC 1.8 SS Stan Lee $5500, *Amazing Spider-Man* #14 CGC 4.0 $1200, *Amazing Spider-Man* #20 CGC 7.5 $1200, *Fantastic Four* #5 4.0 $4200, *Hulk* #141 CGC 9.0 $250, *Tales to Astonish*

#27 CGC 3.5 $2000, *Thor* #134 CGC 9.4 $1000, *Thor* #151 9.4 $225, *Tales of Suspense* #80 CGC 9.2 $325, and *Tales to Astonish* #93 CGC 9.2 $800.

Stephen Gentner
Golden Age Specialist

Greetings to All! I hope everyone is safe weathering the COVID-19 pandemic . I want to thank all the editors and staff that work so hard each year to produce this *Guide*! It has served me so well as a source of information in my collecting comics over the years. Dare I say it's indispensable!? It is an honor and a privilege to again write my comic machinations to you all! I pulled my horns in this past year due to the pandemic. COVID, and lack of contact with comic dealers and buddies has diminished my exposure to the material which I pursue. That said, I have watched very healthy sales and appreciation in all three eras of where I collect; that is Golden Age, Silver Age, and Bronze Age. Besides our *Guide*, all the Census and sales data available online makes tracking and watching trends in my favorite eras very accessible. I have enjoyed sharing and receiving great pictures and stories of comic books on Instagram. (My handle is: collecto6) Both buying and selling, and gleaning heretofore unknown comics while staying home so much has been a Godsend! I continue to enjoy all the great acquaintances I have made on Instagram all over the world with collectors who share the love of comic books! There is no language barrier to sharing a cool comic with a "Brother Collector!"

Outstanding artist Frank Brunner had his personal collection of books slabbed by CBCS and sold this past year. In the ensuing frenzy, I replaced my long since sold copy of *Human Torch* #13 in 4.5, and also bought *Marvel Mystery* #51 in 6.0. It is great to add these two Alex Schomburg WWII Propaganda covers to my PC, especially as they were owned by one of my favorite artists!! I also stepped up to two very important books to me this past year. *Archie Comics* #50 in CGC 8.0, and also *Junior Comics* #15, my FAVORITE issue in that short, spectacular run, in CGC 3.0. I decided to utilize CGC to slab one important book I bought, and to have Matt Nelson remove the restoration for the only Restored Book I had in my collection. The book I had slabbed was *Miss Fury* #1. She came back a 7.0, and is tied for the 2nd highest graded copy. Miss Fury is currently coming back in an Indiegogo project by Billy Tucci and Maria Sanapo. The graphic novel looks just great in process, and will pick up the threads to Tarpe Mills' canon so many years ago. Most all the original characters will return. Miss Fury is a favorite of mine, so this will be fun! The Restored book that went in was my *Captain America Comics Annual* nn from 1942. It went in a Purple Label Restored 4.5, and came back a beautiful Blue Label 3.0! Even at that, my Universal Grade 3.0 is the 2nd highest graded copy. The cover colors came up noticeably from the light cleaning that occurred during the restoration removal process. I researched quite awhile before learning that Matt Nelson was the best man for this process….which was great because I have known Matt Nelson since 1995 when we both became Advisors to the *Guide* together! I was very happy with the outcome on this special book in my collection! Matt has weathered the last 25 years a hell of a lot better than ME!! In any event, these were the highlights for this past year for me. I hope you all found SOME success in this bizarre year we have just lived through! Good luck and health to us all in the upcoming year!

Tom Gordon III
Monumental Holdings LLC

This past year has been a wild ride for everyone and life in general, yet all the while the comic book and collectibles markets have been on fire. One would have initially believed that a global pandemic would have caused a potential hard pause to the marketplace, but it did just the opposite. For those of us who attended C2E2 in Chicago which was held over the last weekend in February 2020 it seemed like business as usual. A healthy convention with large attendance and solid buying and selling sent the year off to a good start.

Within weeks of C2E2 we saw major changes on a global level from borders into countries closed to lockdowns and even the shutdown of a wide array of businesses. This past year saw countless conventions cancelled or rescheduled and then postponed until 2021. Some smaller regional shows were able to be held on a limited basis, but the major shows of the year including San Diego, Heroes, New York, Baltimore, and others were cancelled.

2020 has been a strange year on many levels, from "murder hornets" being discovered in the United States to mysterious monoliths appearing. We almost would need to question if we would be truly shocked if one was to witness the coming of Thanos or even Galactus in real life at this point.

The collectibles markets were incredibly hot with numerous record sales of comic books, original comic art, vintage action figures, movie props, Pokémon cards, and many other categories. We witnessed more individuals outside the collecting field taking notice than ever before.

The collectibles industry and related companies also made significant headlines in the mainstream media. The publicly traded company Collectors Universe was sold to an investor group for $700 million dollars. The chairman of Certified Collectibles Group (CCG) Mark Salzberg publicly stated in an open letter that "spurred by the COVID economy, collectibles have emerged as an asset class, with certification providing the confidence, transparency and security that are necessary for a vibrant market." Those with the knowledge of the past of the comic market can recall a time roughly 25 years ago when the idea of a major auction of comics and comic art totaling more than a million dollars would have been a struggle without question. We have watched the marketplace grow due to technology, third party certification, and significant successful comic book and character driven movies and television shows. We are truly living in a Renaissance period for comics and collectibles.

The Golden Age market is a strong consistent seller

with key issues and classic covers leading the pack as usual. We recently acquired an original owner collection of lower grade books as well as a large selection of coverless issues. The Centaur issues in this collection easily sold for multiples of *Guide*. We even had incomplete and coverless books selling fast to collectors looking to just fill in a spot in their collection. We saw *Archie* and related titles sell easily for well over *Guide* as collectors were just happy to find issues they needed. Fawcett key issues and classic covers are seeing stronger demand as collectors are paying more attention to these noteworthy covers. DC and Timely are easy sellers with the only resistance to prices being some of the lesser DC titles like *Boy Commandos*, *Star Spangled Comics*, and the like.

Pre-Code Horror is an area that we are still seeing strong demand and prices even after some have felt this area of the market has possibly slowed. Key issues like *Horrific* #1, *Mister Mystery* #6, *Mask Comics* and classic covers are always a consistent request.

*Centaur issues like **Amazing-Man Comics** #5 sold for multiples of Guide, even when coverless.*

Silver Age comics continue to be one of the hottest areas with Marvel running leaps and bounds ahead of DC comics. A significant part of this is without question Disney's ability to successfully produce movies and television shows versus Warner Bros. who has had some missteps along the way. Requests for Marvel keys far out strips availability in all grades and is an area in the market that is truly a blue chip area for collectors and investors alike. DCs in many cases are harder to find in decent condition than their Marvel counterparts and even non-key issues can be a challenge to find at times. Silver Age DCs might be an area for future growth and interest if DC is able to dramatically improve their future films.

Bronze Age keys are a constant seller with buyers speculating to find the next possible hot book that is undervalued. Books like *Giant-Size X-Men* #1, *Incredible Hulk* #181, *Werewolf By Night* #32, and others continue to lead requests by collectors. Some are also looking for hard to find books in grade like *Werewolf By Night* #33 which is exceptionally difficult in 9.8 due to the dark colors on the cover.

The comic book market has seen some truly interesting areas of note this past year. One area of record sales is that of Canadian Price Variant editions or CPVs. These books are much more difficult to find than their US counterparts. For example a recent US edition of *Star Wars* #68 CGC 9.8 sold for $1,650 and a *Star Wars* #68 CGC 9.8 Canadian Price Variant edition recently realized $3,000 privately. When looking at the available populations of this book on the CGC Census we see 117 copies graded in 9.8 of the US edition and only 9 copies of the Canadian Price Variant edition graded 9.8. Another area that has had significant demand this past year is that of newsstand edition copies versus the direct market copies. An example of this would be *Amazing Spider-Man* #300 CGC 9.4 as a direct market edition that sold for $817 and a newsstand edition in the same grade selling for $1,347.

The pandemic has heavily affected the entertainment industry this year with cast and crew sidelined as productions were shut down due to the pandemic. For Marvel fans this has been the lengthiest wait for a film from Marvel Studios since the gap between *Incredible Hulk* in June, 2008 and the release of *Iron Man 2* in May, 2010. Some speculate that perhaps the break this past year will be a benefit as it left a hunger for fans who anxiously await Marvel's upcoming film releases and Disney+ programming in 2021. The second season of *The Mandalorian* has heavily influenced the sales of *Star Wars* related comics this past year. We have seen major jumps in sales prices and many clamoring for books that are now tied to the series. Warner Bros. announced that they will be releasing *Wonder Woman 1984* in theaters and on their streaming service HBO Max on Christmas day.

With 2021 just around the corner I am hopeful that we will see a healthier year ahead of us with major conventions returning later in the year. I also believe we will continue to see strong interest and growth in the hobby overall.

ERIC J. GROVES
THE COMIC ART FOUNDATION

Greetings from Oklahoma City! Herewith, our outlook on the comic book marketplace for 2020, the year of our discontent.

The Impact of Covid 19: The most severe impact of the pandemic on comic trading is the loss of conventions. Much of our buying and selling occurs at small conventions, chiefly OAFCon, the annual fall gathering of fans from Oklahoma and elsewhere. As a result, our transactions are conducted by internet and by courier, not in person. We had fewer in 2020.

Big auction houses continued selling, albeit without the colorful catalogs from Comic Connect and Heritage. Hake's produced one recently, and in bidding, we observed no significant drop in comic values. We understand that dealers with large inventories continue doing brisk internet business, but we are unaware of price trends in their sales. We cannot say the COVID pandemic has dampened comic sales but it certainly did away with conventions and the camaraderie attendant to them.

The Golden Age: Judging from our auction bidding, and prices realized in those auctions, it appears that comic books have retained their values in 2020. We observe a pervasive characteristic in the Golden Age market: scarcity. For example, with respect to DCs, although hot books turn up, runs of other titles can be difficult to assemble. This applies to *All Star*, *Flash*, *Green Lantern*, *Leading*, *More Fun* and similar titles. This is true with Timelys as well. *Captain America* #1 appears with greater frequency than regular issues of *All Winners*, *Daring*, *Sub-Mariner*, *Marvel Mystery*, *Young Allies*, *Miss Fury* and the like. Nedor and MLJ titles are tough. Attic collections are not surfacing as they once did. When the heirs of a deceased original collector unearth them, they wind up at the auction houses.

Issues from other Golden Age imprints remain relatively available, but are not fast sellers or big earners. Fawcetts, we think, are under-collected and undervalued, except for the *Captain Marvel Jr.* and *Master* issues with Raboy covers and art. Most Fiction House titles can be found except for early issues of *Jumbo*, especially oversized ones. Quality comics like *Plastic Man*, *Police* and *Military* are undervalued.

We recommend some underappreciated titles which are worth owning, not merely as investments, but because of their inherent value as comic art. First, consider the principal Lev Gleason titles. Early issues of *Boy* and *Daredevil*, with WWII covers and monstrous villains like Iron Jaw and the Claw have always been in demand and can bring a hefty price. Later issues, not so much, but they feature very good stories, often with social justice themes. We also recommend the new biography of Lev Gleason, written by his grand-nephew Brett Dakin, titled *American Daredevil*.

Second, the category of "reprint comics" has much to offer. They reprinted previously published comic strips such as the Phantom, Prince Valiant, Tarzan and others. But several included original stories with characters never reprinted elsewhere, as in *Big Shot* (Skyman, the Face, the Cloak and Capt. Yank), *Famous Funnies* (Fearless Flint, the Phantom Magician), *Popular* (the Masked Pilot, Martan the Marvel Man, the Voice, the Owl), *Super* (Magic Morro, Lightning Jim) and *Sparkler* (Sparkman). See also *Ace*, *King*, *Magic* and *Tip Top*. These books are bargains,

Third, every serious collector should own original copies of the *Donald Duck* Four Colors written and drawn by the great Carl Barks. They are available and reasonably priced, although their values have gradually risen in recent years. In particular, consider FC #108 (Terror of the River), FC #159 (Ghost of the Grotto) FC #189 (The Old Castle's Secret) FC #199 (Sheriff of Bullet Valley), and FC #223 (Lost in the Andes). These comics are a thrill to hold and read.

The Atomic Age: We have long touted books from this era. This post-war time of incredible creativity gave birth to the Crime, Horror, War and Romance titles more widely collected than ever. There is more to this period than big books like *Phantom Lady* #17. Of all imprints, the most sought after are Atlas titles. Pre-Code Horror titles lead the way, but we sell Atlas Crime, Romance and War comics as well. The most triumphant publisher of this time was EC. Notwithstanding numerous reprints, some collectors still want original copies, especially *Vault of Horror* and *Tales From the Crypt*. The War, Crime and Science Fiction titles are slower. *Mad* original comics deserve more respect with their splendid covers, marvelous artwork and brilliant satires. Other than *Mad* #1 and #5, they can be hard to sell.

Super-heroes did not fare well in the Atomic Age. Certain DC comics were not well constructed in the first place and finding them in high grade is challenging. This especially applies to *Batman*, *Detective*, *Superman* and *World's Finest*. Condition and scarcity drive their values. Non-superhero DC titles from this era are of some interest, representing a departure from the standard, such as *Danger Trail*, *Miss Beverly Hills*, and *Ozzie and Harriet*. DC crime titles *Gangbusters* and *Mr. District Attorney* are moribund.

Silver Age: Marvel is dominant as always. Collectors seek Marvel keys as usual. *Amazing Fantasy* #15, once a little hard to sell, tops the desirability list. It is an important book and has withstood the test of time. Unlike the Golden Age, scarcity is not so much a factor in assessing Silver Age values. It is more about demand, given the ever-widening Marvel fan base. This expansion in part may be a function of Marvel's exploitation of its characters in movies. The most sought-after titles remain *Amazing Spider Man*, *Avengers*, *Fantastic Four* and *X-Men*. Early superhero issues of *Tales of Suspense*, *Tales to Astonish,* and *Journey Into Mystery* are enduring classics with their splendid covers. We do not advocate comics as investments, but Marvel titles are a good bet.

With some exceptions, DC Silver Age trails Marvel in desirability and value. Collectors continue to assemble runs of *Batman*, maybe the most iconic character in comics. There is increased demand for *Wonder Woman* and scarcity is not as great a factor as it is for Golden Age copies. Regrettably, we do not see fans striving to put together runs of second tier titles like *Rip Hunter*, *Hawkman*, *Metal Men* and *Challengers of the Unknown*. Early key issues of *Showcase* and *Brave and the Bold* hold their own.

One Other Thing: The Oklahoma Alliance of Fandom, known as OAF, was organized around 1967. It put on the MultiCon conventions in the early 1970s, but they faded. In 2007, Bart Bush reinvigorated the convention as OAFCon. It became an annual weekend affair devoted to vintage material only, including comics, pulps, BLBs and movie material. Collectors and dealers from both coasts set up to trade and talk with old friends. The 2020 OAFCon was cancelled due to COVID. Then we lost Bart Bush. He was larger than life, as much curator as collector. He accumulated the most comprehensive Dick Tracy collection known to fandom. Bart had an enormous knowledge of comics. I can see him at my table, cheerfully picking through my books and talking comics. If you have lost a comrade in comics you know how I feel. I hate it. I really hate it.

Terry Hoknes
Pulse Comics and Cards

2020 was a crazy year around the world, but it was an exciting year for comic sales. Almost every modern key book increased in price. Likely as people were not allowed to shop locally, they all went to online shopping and bought up the most popular books. Many key issues had renewed interest and doubled or tripled during the summer. June and July were exceptionally hot months for price jumps across the board.

Some of the major modern keys that kept selling higher and higher during the entire year included first appearances of Miles Morales (*Ultimate Fallout* #4), Silk (*Amazing Spider-Man* #4), Riri Williams (*Invincible Iron Man* #7 and #9).

A major trend continuing to grow in sales was 2nd, 3rd and other later printings of key books. In some cases the later printings were selling higher and more easily than the more common 1st printings. *Edge Of Spider-Verse* #2, *Silk* #1, *Spider-Gwen* #1, *Strange Academy* #1 were some examples.

The hottest comics released in 2020 included: *Outlawed* #1 ratio 1:50 variant reaching $500.00, the *Incapable Trump* hitting a high of $400.00, *Strange Academy* #1 ratio 1:25 variant up to $200.00, *Star Wars: Doctor Aphra* #6 ratio 1:25 variant hit $180.00.

DC Comics split away from Diamond but did not hurt their sales at all. DC had most of the hyped up books of the summer particularly *Dark Nights: Death Metal Legends of the Dark Knight* #1 featuring the new Robin King character which had super high demand even before it was released in August. Sales of the regular cover hit a high of $30.00 and the 1:25 ratio variant hit $300.00.

Greg Holland
Slabdata.com

Certified and encapsulated comic books ("slabs") are only a small percentage of all comic books in existence, but the slabbed comic market represents a much larger percentage of total dollars spent annually. Certified Guaranty Company (CGC) opened to the public in 2000. As this edition is printed, it is now 2021 and with CGC's permission, I have been compiling the CGC census into a searchable database online for almost the entire time. 5,734,747 comic books were reported as professionally graded and encapsulated according to the official CGC census in the first 21 years of CGC (as of mid-December 2020) for 218,968 different comic issues and variants. At this point a small number of CGC graded issues are actually non-comic titles such as *Sports Illustrated* or *Playboy* (around 1% of issues and less than 1% of the CGC totals). Most comic books submitted to CGC have been graded fewer than ten times. More than 60,000 comics have been CGC graded only once. Nearly 110,000 comics have been CGC graded no more than three times. At the other end of the list, 13 comic books have been graded at least 10,000 times each, up from just 10 this time last year. *Amazing Spider-Man* #300 is still the only comic to pass 20,000 CGC graded copies, now at 23,600, but *New Mutants* #98 will be at 20,000 CGC graded copies by the time this report is printed. *Amazing Spider-Man* #361 moved into 3rd place after being 5th this time last year. *Wolverine* Limited Series #1 and *Marvel Super Heroes Secret Wars* #8 are 4th and 5th this year. *Spawn* #1 has moved to 6th, ahead of *Uncanny X-Men* #266 and *Incredible Hulk* #181. *Amazing Spider-Man* #252 and *Amazing Spider-Man* #129 swapped positions for 9th and 10th place this year. Nine of these ten most submitted books are from Marvel along with *Spawn* #1 from Image Comics. The most submitted comic from DC Comics, *Batman: The Killing Joke,* was 18th place last year with 6,615 copies on the CGC census and is now in 20th place with 7,582 copies. The Top 100 most-submitted comics have 99 comics from Marvel (87), DC Comics (8), or Image (4). The only Top 100 book by another publisher is *Rai* #0 (1992) from Valiant Comics in 65th place (4,693 copies graded). The Top 100 most-submitted books to CGC represent 647,845 copies on the CGC census, or 11.3% of all slabs. This 11.3% means that one in nine slabs comes from a short list of just 100 comics (see cgcdata.com for the full list).

CGC Census Counts by Comic Decade (as of mid-December 2020):

1930s = 9,689 (0.2%) –
1940s = 166,882 (2.9%) –
1950s = 175,399 (3.1%) –
1960s = 811,191 (14.1%) –
1970s = 882,078 (15.4%) –
1980s = 867,437 (15.1%) –
1990s = 675,015 (11.8%) –
2000s = 600,916 (10.5%) –
2010s = 1,397,441 (24.4%) –
2020 = 145,246 (2.5%) –
Others = 3,453 (0.1%) – (Includes undated books)
Total = 5,734,747.

Variants abound!: There are currently 1,383,067 books identified as variants in the CGC census. Only 3% of these variants are from dates up to 1989. 6% of graded variants are from the decade of the 1990s. 15% of graded variants are from the decade of the 2000s, leaving 76% of all CGC graded variants are books printed from 2010 to 2020. In the industry today, a regular edition (non-variant) with significant resale value seems to be more like a needle in a variant haystack. CGC counts, totals, and averages are not a random sample of the whole comic book market. Comics which are sent to CGC have often been selected by the submitter for exceptional qualities of high grade condition, high market value, or both. By definition, the average raw comic is unlikely to be exceptional. Another important note is that comics which have few copies on the CGC census are not necessarily rare. When a comic book has little market value, even if it is very old, there is little reason to pay for third-party professional grading and encapsulation. Comics which appear uncommon on the CGC census may be extremely common and of little value in the market. Since most comic books in existence are worth much less than the cost of CGC grading, we should not expect to find many low-valued comics in the CGC census. The opposite is also true, the higher the value of a comic book, we should expect that more of the existing copies will be graded. There will be copies of every valuable comic book which are never sent to CGC, particularly when the owners have no desire to sell the books, but the number of $10,000+ comic books changing hands (publicly) without first being

CGC graded is rapidly decreasing. A review of more than 2,500 sales for $10,000+ comic books at Heritage Auctions shows 99% are "already slabbed" comics. Understanding that the market for $10,000+ comic books has overwhelmingly become slabbed comics; it becomes important to recognize that the CGC census for the highest valued comics now provides significant data points about the existing copies remaining. Expert estimates for the number of surviving copies of *Action Comics* #1 (1938) and *Detective Comics* #27 (1939) generally suggest 100 to 200 copies exist. With more than one-third (and perhaps more than half) of those top two key issue estimates already appearing on the CGC Census, it may be possible to estimate the remaining copies of other $10,000+ comic books as well. With all conditions of *Amazing Fantasy* #15 now worth $10,000+ and the CGC census showing 3,386 copies graded, perhaps an estimate of 6,500 to 10,000 copies is accurate if about one-third to half are already graded. Estimates for surviving copies of books of lower values are certainly not reflected as clearly by the CGC census, however, it may be possible to understand the relative surviving copy estimates between books of similar value. For example, if any two books have been approximately the same value for the past 20 years of CGC grading, and one book has twice the number of CGC graded copies on the CGC census, then it may be fair to estimate that twice as many copies exist. Using simple supply-and-demand logic, when the demand values (prices) are identical then the different counts of CGC graded copies are most likely related to supply. More research is available at slabdata.com and more detailed CGC census analysis can be performed at cgcdata.com.

Marvel Special Edition* #15 *is currently a hot book with a Shang Chi movie on the way

Steven Houston & John Dolmayan Torpedo Comics

Steven Houston

Hello from Las Vegas, I am happy to report that Torpedo Comics has managed to thrive during these tough times and is in fact pushing forward with new business plans. Of course, when I mention tough times, I'm referencing the COVID pandemic which has swept across the entire USA (and the world) since March, which in turn lead to lockdowns and massive job losses and business closures.

I am proud to say, that while others panicked and let employees go, here at Torpedo, we girded ourselves and quickly came up with a plan to keep the money coming into the business at the same rate as pre-COVID days. Basically, we launched Torpedo to a wider audience, using Instagram to promote online sales and mystery box offers. This way, we were able to keep the doors open here at Torpedo and have in fact moved into a larger warehouse, to facilitate in a more efficient manner, the operation of a daily online sales agenda.

As for the industry as a whole, the biggest news is obviously the break away from Diamond Comics by DC Comics. This was a massive sea change within the comic book industry and as I type this report, the full effects of this rather bold move by DC has yet to be fully realized.

As for the comic book industry and collectors and readers alike, the pandemic of 2020 has not stopped the continued expansion of comic collecting and speculating. In fact, the industry seems to have moved towards a more speculator driven model, with variant editions ruling modern comic collecting, while thousands of collectors avidly research the past, hoping to get lucky and find the next key issue. What are they researching I hear you ask? Well, one look online at the various YouTube or Instagram sites where comic fans and retailers gather, you can hear various "experts" pouring over the latest news coming out of the major movie companies latest announcements. Each announcement leads to another spike in speculator activity, as characters who are revealed to be appearing in a given movie are fully researched, with their first appearances exploding in demand and prices. The current hot books being *Werewolf by Night* #32 (1st Moon Knight), *Eternals* #1 and *Marvel Special Edition* #15 (1st Master of Kung Fu).

The current collecting market is the same as its been for the last few years, if one can say something, the market is heating up in regards to lesser known characters and their first appearances, as Disney Plus pushes out series after series, with lower budgets that allow for more experimentation with certain characters.

As to the future, in terms of the actual comic book industry itself, the lack of shows has not had that much of an impact on Torpedo Comics to date, but this retailer is ever hopeful that in 2021, the show season can begin again and we can have more fan interaction, instead of "live feeds" and "zoom".

Robert Isaac Red Hood Comics

As I exhale thinking of all the events of 2020 and the rollercoaster life has been throughout it, I realize truly what a crazy, CRAZY year for collectibles it has been, and continues pushing to be. From comic books to video games, sports cards, Pokemón cards and more, certification companies have been slammed with submissions including CGC, CBCS, WATA, PSA and Beckett which has caused some of these companies major delays in turnaround times. This is mainly a result of the COVID-19 outbreak which has kept people in their homes most of the year with government stimulus checks showing up weekly, comic stores closed or opened with rules and no conventions to look forward to. We are also in an era where the definition of "Modern" comics (consisting mainly of the 1980s, '90s and through the 2000s to Current) should probably be re-thought as we're well into 2-3 decades past that time which really isn't "modern' anymore. Titles from Dark Horse such as *Star Wars* have seen a significant increase in value with the introduction of *The Mandalorian* show streaming on Disney+ and a skyrocketing of value in Teenage Mutant Ninja Turtles comic books and video games. We are also in the rise of a new icon in comics as Miles Morales is quickly taking over the Spider-Man mantle in our hobby, with a meteoric rise in value and popularity of the character. From a market that seemed to be going slightly downhill after *Avengers: Endgame* concluded 12 years of films serving as a catalyst of the industry for buying and selling vintage books, we have created a rising modern market leaving the vintage books further in the past.

I took a large part of the year away from comics while working with WATA Games as a grader and in the operations of the company, concluding nearly a year that I planned on devoting my work habits to its overwhelming growth and during that time, there were major spikes in the comic market that I almost felt estranged to the industry when I returned to it.

The Virus: Let's start by addressing the elephant in the room, as the outbreak of COVID-19 held much responsibility in some of the major changes we all witnessed and experienced this year. With most of the population confined to their homes, and the pouring of government money in the form of weekly checks (in many cases being more than what an individual earned weekly while working), many found themselves with an abundance of funds and a lot of that money found its way into our industry. Comic stores were closed or allowed little shopping opportunities with a common retail practice of "curbside pickups" and the conventions that once harbored thousands of comic fans, collectors and dealers were simply cancelled, sometimes just weeks of their scheduled dates. This forced buyers online, itching to get their addictive comic fix either through eBay, retail web sites and auction houses, or through social media, creating the popular, live "Claim sales" that you're still able to catch daily, given you're following the sellers that offer the service. Sales of both popular books and cheap, modern "filler" books you would have simply skimmed past even just a year ago saw damn near a vertical rise in sales, with multiple transactions supporting most of them.

In a Galaxy Right Under Our Noses…: Some of the insane increases we saw involved the modern *Star Wars* books from Dark Horse Comics. This of course was motivated by the end of the Skywalker saga in films to the debut of *The Mandalorian*, which is the first cinematic release centering around the "Knights of the Old Republic" era of *Star Wars* comics and it makes PERFECT sense: Think of this from a Disney executive's mind, and see it through their eyes; You literally have nearly two decades worth of characters, from Jedi to Sith Lords to dozens of original characters from the Star Wars galaxy originated, drawn out and based out of the Dark Horse era of *Star Wars* comics and they all carry storylines along with them. Why waste company time and money starting from scratch creating new characters and story arcs when you have hundreds of issues worth of them just waiting to be adapted to screen? And they're AMAZING characters, several of them enough that it's just been a shame it took this long to see them come to visual life. There are dozens of key issues, notably first appearances in the Dark Horse series of *Star Wars* comics, from "Knights of the Old Republic" to "Legacy," and even in "The Clone Wars" and various mini-series and one-shots as well. So many of these books were in my dollar boxes just two years ago. I'm pretty sure I gave away a Lamborghini's worth of them at that price so while we're here, let me just speak to some of my customers from Los Angeles to Chicago that pulled many of these expensive books out of my dollar boxes: YOU BETTER REMEMBER WHO YOU GOT THOSE FROM!!

Price Shellshock: Another overdue rise in comics is the *Teenage Mutant Ninja Turtles*, with issue #1's first printing from Mirage Studios serving as the *Action Comics* #1 or the *Amazing Fantasy* #15 of the Copper Age with its 3,000-print run, with 9.6s being offered for the previous 9.8 prices, and 7.0-8.0s selling close to $20K mark. Its second and third printings are hitting five and four figures each in high grade, respectively. First printings of issues #2-4 from Mirage Studios saw a rise in value, but not as surprising as *Raphael* #1, which went from a $200-$300 raw book in high grade, to well over $2,000 if graded. Even as a I type this, the book increases in demand and value as with the previous *TMNT* issues of #1-4, this oversized 1980s gem is a tough find in NM or better condition. Following the Mirage series, the *Teenage Mutant Ninja Turtles Adventures* run by Archie Publications recently saw a huge spike in sales, from its three-issue mini-series to the full seventy-two book run, the series held many key issues in first appearances of familiar TMNT characters such as Slash and Mondo Gecko. While the Turtles have cemented their position as a valuable asset in comics, their demand seems to be greater than Silver and Bronze Age keys lately.

Isn't it crazy? Thirty-six years ago, comic shops shunned two guys away on multiple occasions over a book about four turtles, that were teenagers, and ninjas, taught by a rat, and loved pizza.

Miles Morales, SPIDER-MAN: All my friends with young children, when they think of Spider-Man, they barely seem to reference Peter Parker anymore. Aside from the two recent MCU movies, the animated film, *Into the Spider-Verse* appealed more to them with Miles Morales being the leading man and Peter Parker depicted as an older, seasoned super-hero with a belly. What's happening here is my theory of "The Crossover" that I've spoken to many people about lately. For example, my generation grew up with Hal Jordan as our Green Lantern, Barry Allen as our Flash, etc. We didn't know the Golden Age Green Lantern and the Golden Age

Flash without purposely digging back to them, we know Hal and Barry. Spider-Man seems to be the first major Marvel character transitioning identity recognition from Peter Parker to Miles Morales and I can explain why: I'm older! That's it, I'm gettin' old! And don't worry, you are too. Sure you are! Put this book down, go to the mirror, look at your face. You're around 40-50 years old now. Peter Parker doesn't make sense as a teenager or young adult anymore. They can't keep re-doing his origin through movies and animated TV shows because there's too many versions of them now, it'll get boring if it hasn't already for a rolling twenty years' worth of fans that'll view it.

Miles Morales Is The Future Leading Man Of Marvel Comics: And I love the character. I think he relates to the growing generation; I think his family life speaks to more American households than Peter Parker's did, and I think toning down the sarcasm a bit and increasing the sincerity of Spider-Man is a great thing. And I think these attributes in a Spider-Man can develop a stronger connection to the title hero when reading.

Jeff Itkin
GoldenAgeGuru

With this year's article I want to stay focused on the exceptionally strong comic book market and stay away from some of the more serious global issues that everyone faced in 2020 and possibly still in 2021. This is extremely important to do, as the powerful comic market deserves to be discussed without distraction. Every time frame continues to thrive, from the amazing Golden Age to Modern books. If you are interested in hearing up to date info weekly, please check out our YouTube channel and Podcast at ComicTom101 or follow me on Instagram @goldenageguru. Thank you, Overstreet, for putting together another year of Price Guides and working so diligently to get the community important information with articles, pricing, and advertising.

Why Social Media Saved Comics: This is the biggest and most important discussion that must be had for comic collectors, investors, vendors/dealers and store owners. Conventions vanished last year, and I do not expect them to be here for 2021. There is always the possibility of a limited capacity con, but nowhere near where it was just 2 years ago. Social Media has become the saving grace for the comic industry, whether you like it or not. Every platform has become a potential site to buy and sell comics, and for many last year the only place.

As a collector and seller, I was accustomed to the standard comic convention scene. It is where I sold and bought inventory, picked up personal grails, and socialized with other enthusiasts and peers. It was also where we spent huge dollar amounts for booth spaces, hotel rental, travel, food, entry fees and countless hours on our feet walking con floors, battling crowds and/or operating our booths. These were the standards, the rules, the facts, the guidelines, the trends that we all followed, and it was understood by everyone.

When it all disappeared in 2020 in a blink of an eye it was scary at first. There was a massive amount of uncertainty in the pillars of the comic industry. Specifically stores, dealers, and collectors of the trade, but where one door shuts another will open. Those doors were Facebook and Instagram. They became the new con floor from your living room floor. What was a year of uncertainty became one of the best years for selling comics I have ever witnessed. The amount of interest in back issues was unbelievable and the number of new collectors into the hobby was equally astonishing.

Being a strong user of Instagram for a few years I have developed a decent number of followers and know the strong community and passion that IG contains for comic collectors and fans. This platform and Facebook are so powerful that they are supporting almost the entire industry. Through the streaming of live sales, we see the smallest to some of the largest store fronts, dealers and collectors sell their merchandise. The atmosphere for these sales is positive, interactive, and fun, it also provides extremely good financial returns for the sellers. Without these platforms an already struggling store front would have failed in last year's climate as well as many online vendors. This is not a temporary trend and will continue for at least the next few years.

Movies and TV did not matter: Every year there is a discussion of how this hobby will collapse due to variant covers like the '90s or over hype from movies and TV. I have heard this argument ad nauseum. Last year was a catastrophe of epic proportions and all Film and TV were placed on hold indefinitely. Yet despite everything that happened and how it should have decimated a hobby it instead showed its resilience and strength. Comics are not going anywhere and if you want to sit on the sidelines year after year complaining about it until that one year where maybe something corrects itself and you can say "aha, I was right." then more power to you. Until then I and many others are going to enjoy it responsibly. Which means that we understand a comic can go up in price when there is buzz behind it and go back down when that interest has lessened. Like a sports team that is winning every week, those stadium tickets go up in price and cost more, but when your team consistently loses and interest wains, then those tickets become less expensive and easier to obtain.

Comics in 2021: Should be another wonderful year for my favorite of time frames, the Golden Age, and probably all time frames to be fair. It is nice to see comics collected again without the belief that a movie or TV show influenced it that year. Instead, we are seeing interest in them for their collectability, artwork and storytelling. We will continue to see new collectors entering the hobby and old ones continuing to enjoy the many books they have and the ones they plan to pursue. Social Media platforms will continue to thrive and become the day-to-day norm of purchasing comic books for a large generation that finds the ease and comfort of a digital format and the sense of a community. The more traditional outlets for comics i.e., auction houses, eBay, dealer web sites, and you Local Comic Shop are still excellent resources for comics and will continue to be no matter the state of Social Media sales.

Everyone stay safe, stay healthy and Geek Responsibly. If you ever have a question about a book feel free to reach out on Instagram, @goldenageguru.

Dr. Steven Kahn
Inner Child Comics and Collectibles

Life is so unpredictable. Writing this report finds me in a strange and unfamiliar position. My store, The Inner Child, in Kenosha, Wisconsin, "temporarily" closed its doors on March 15, 2020 due to the propagation of the novel COVID-19 virus. Yet at year's end it remains closed with barely a glimmer of hope of reopening before the spring of 2021, if then.

Just as the virus was ebbing in early summer and stores began to reopen, a local policeman emptied his gun into an unarmed man as he entered his car, riddling his body with seven bullets, one severing his spinal cord. It was all caught on video and spread around the world like a virus. What followed were days of the terror of civil unrest, all of it focused in and around our location. Virtually all of the violence, looting, burning of stores to the ground, killings and associated mayhem occurred within several blocks of us. How the store survived is remarkable as politicians allowed the rioters free reign. The police and fire departments offered neither deterrence or resistance and allowed everything to burn, leaving store owners helpless against the onrushing mob.

Our store was boarded up and remains boarded up today and all of our signs have been removed as well. The instigators, recruited from out of state, didn't know Kenosha, and the only hope of being spared was to not be identified as a business

What sustained me through these many months was my ongoing passion for collecting and the welcome distraction it provided. I remained connected to the collecting community, never taking my finger off the pulse of the hobby.

How Covid Changed the Collecting Universe: Although many jobs were lost, over 75 percent of the country remained employed. Most wage earners had the unique problem of trying to find a place to spend their disposable income. No restaurants, movie theaters, bars, entertainment, travel and the list goes on. Comic stores closed and conventions disappeared as well.

People had time on their hands and soon gravitated to collecting. Collecting pop culture exploded as the shutdown continued. Online resources blossomed and tracking current sale prices of comics became simple and available to anyone with a cellphone, tablet, or computer. This epidemic will eventually pass and people will redirect their resources and spending patterns, but massive investment has and continues to flow into collectibles.

It's been a remarkable year not only for comics, but for a broad range of other collectibles. A couple of weeks ago it was announced that Collector's Universe (the sports card certification company) was to be purchased for 700 million dollars and would be taken private. The purchaser committed to pay a 30 percent premium to the stockholders to own the business. It appears that billionaires have discovered that collectibles are legitimate alternative assets and will remain a part of our cultural landscape for many years to come. They are prepared to invest heavily in these markets, and I believe this transaction was merely the first step.

And yet many experts within the collecting industry itself seem to be missing key points. A highly respected authority on collectibles recently wrote an article on whether video games were a legitimate investable collectible. He ultimately put them in the same category as Beany Babies. Beany Babies was a phenomenon created by Ty Warner, who developed a market and demand that never existed largely by creating artificial rarity. There was nothing innately there to create lasting value. Further, I believe Funko is putting itself in a similar position as its massive overproduction will soon drain pocketbooks and quelch demand.

Video games on the other hand, have been the glue that has bonded generations culturally and emotionally, and as a collectible represent so much more. It appealed to anyone who could move a mouse, joystick, or controller from its primitive beginnings in the 1970s until today. They created deep, warm, and lasting memories to cherish from discovering and entering the world of video games. This market is only just beginning; I guarantee it. While there may be some bubbles burst along the way, its trajectory is steeper than any other collectible in the marketplace today and will have long-term sustainability.

Stick with the Blue Chips: Returning to comics, I continue to remain bullish in the specific areas of comics that are consistent with all of my previous reports, namely pressed and graded key books, which continue to drive demand in the market and draw headlines. And that's where nearly all the action is. All the early Marvel keys remain solid as Marvel continues to dominate the collectible comic market, being responsible for at least 85 percent of comic commerce.

Yet as bullish as I am with the keys, I remain bearish on just about everything else. I've always used *Iron Man* as my go-to example. I ask dealers constantly what they do with the other 600 or so issues of that title once #1 and #55 are gone, and they just shrug their shoulders. The good news for buyers is that prices on common issues across the board continue to drop and should follow that pattern for some time to come. It's a great time to fill in missing holes of common books in your collections.

When Do the Numbers Count?: Following the collapse of the collectible markets in the 1990s, many comic titles were left on life support. Many series and publishers folded as people abandoned collecting. Print runs shrank to the low 5 figures and even 4 figures for many titles, including mainstream DC and Marvel. There was and is a genuine scarcity of product across the board from that period and this is finally being recognized. Demand is spiking for issues, especially those with first appearances and final issues as well. The marketplace will ultimately determine which of these are collectible and caution is advised in choosing where to invest as rarity is only one of the factors determining value.

What Is Hot Right Now: Since last year's report, several books and series picked up steam, including *G.I. Joe*, *Masters of the Universe*, *Transformers*, *Thundercats*, and most importantly, *Teenage Mutant Ninja Turtles*. *TMNT* #1 is on fire and a real standout. Second and third prints are exploding as well and demand at the time of this writing is nearly insatiable. Turtle fans are everywhere, and the numbers tell the story. The first print of issue 1 was a miniscule 3,000 and with less than 1,000 certified copies, its census is dwarfed by Silver keys and literally crushed by the Bronze. The Marvel keys (*Amazing Fantasy* #15, *Tales of Suspense* #39, *Incredible Hulk* #1, *Fantastic Four* #1, etc.) have from double to five times the number of copies in the CGC census. In addition, Turtle collectors cross boundaries and non-comic collectors are interested in this book and broaden its appeal.

Other Independents from the '60s and '70s, like Charlton, have shown recent strength as rumors of TV or movie development have caused first appearance values to move sharply (*Peacemaker* #1, *Captain Atom* #83 and *The Fightin' Five* #40 as examples).

That 800 Pound Gorilla is Actually a Mouse: Every one of my reports has shined a spotlight on Disney and this year is no exception. Disney just closed its purchase of Fox at an unheard of $71 billion. Granted, Fox contains more than the Marvel properties, but the Marvel value cannot be denied. When compared to the fact that Disney bought everything else Marvel for a "mere" $4 billion in 2009, the mind boggles. In 10 short years Marvel has enriched Disney by a whopping $18 billion and they have literally only scratched the surface of content that Marvel can provide.

Now that Disney has closed the circle and owns the Fantastic Four and X-Men, collectors should be prepared for broad growth of specific issues when they reveal plans for those franchises. X-Men may offer a greater potential with its characters and storylines, but remember there has never been a good Fantastic Four production of any sort and the title is rich with content and characters. Its run of bad fortune is about to end.

What remains unclear is the fate of the other Marvel titles that had been operating on Netflix. Disney has rarely shown any inclination to share profits in anything they own and what happens to *Daredevil* and *Punisher* is murky at best. Recasting those series would be unfortunate, as they shined with great performances from Charlie Cox, Jon Bernthal and Vincent D'Onofrio (Kingpin).

Presentation Counts: Many of us collect and prize our books based on the cover art, so how that cover reveals itself is critical. Not all books with the same grade are equal. Anyone who has placed certified books with identical grades side by side can identify inconsistencies, especially in pre-1980 books. Eye appeal has become much more important, with richness and depth of color saturation becoming critical as well. This is especially evident in books with red backgrounds (*Hulk* #181 and *Silver Surfer* #3 as examples), and color richness and gloss can be found on even the earliest Silver Age Marvels as well.

I own about 15 copies of *Amazing Spider-Man* #300 and the background color varies significantly, yet it hasn't appeared to impact grading to date. I have several 9.8 copies, and the background can just as likely be orange as red. If it hasn't already been revisited and factored in at CGC, I believe we will soon see a premium placed on dramatic color impact moving forward.

Variants, Cameos, and Previews: This year collectors were looking for different and different sold very well as interest and demand expanded beyond price variants. Mark Jeweler inserts, later prints, and cover variations showed growth as never before, but there were caveats. For a reprint to be valuable, it first needed to be a direct continuation of the original press run, not a revisit at a much later date, and of course not all reprints were created equal. At this time, the highest values seem to be settling on the last print run, especially if it is a short print. The jury is out concerning the sustainability of these values unless there was an accidental error or a recalled issue. Finally, the real value will likely be isolated to super high graded copies as the lower grades do not get much love.

Newsstand variants, on the other hand, appeared to have the strongest potential for affecting the broader market. Since there are so many bar code variants, it will take some time for prices to settle and become standardized as this market is just beginning to develop. Nonetheless, if I had my druthers, I'd almost invariably prefer to own that special book with the bar code *if* I ever intended on selling it.

*Although not a comic, the very hot **Marvel Previews** #95 had the first peek at Miles Morales*

As collectors are moving towards the next big thing, interest in previews is increasing. Previews have historically been a source of speculation with the Spawn preview in *Malibu Sun* #13 being one and the *Incredible Hulk* #181 preview (*Daredevil* #115, *Marvel Premiere* #19, and *Thor* #229) being another. Full page previews of important Marvel keys (*X-Men* #1, *Avengers* #1, etc.) appeared in many early Marvel titles as well. All of these are fun books to own, and the added bonus is that there is little, if any, premium today to pay above the value of the book itself to own a copy.

However, madness seemed to appear recently when copies of *Marvel Previews* #95 (first Miles Morales), which is not even a comic book, began selling for four figures at 9.8. To put that into perspective, it meant that particular "book(?)" was selling for more than virtually any *Superman* issue (1939-1941) from #5-30 in low-to-mid grade. When you realize that the CGC census on those beautiful classics books is less than 200 for each issue, something just doesn't just add up.

Cameos and brief first appearances, on the other hand, have shown steady growth for a longer time (note *Incredible Hulk* #180) and appear to be where I'd place my bets. In addition, because cameos are tied to the story, the continuity that they provide appears to be the right place to invest in the long run.

For the past three years, I've been the primary collection advisor for the largest online comic tracking service in the world. I help anyone who wants to evaluate or sell their collections, regardless of size. It is a voluntary service without any fee or obligation and I've now advised close to 15,000 collectors. It's been a genuine pleasure to connect with fellow collectors and swap stories and assist in any way I can. Please know that if you ever have a question or want an unbiased opinion on a book or collection, or just want to talk and say hello, don't ever hesitate to call. I'm available 18 hours a day, 7 days a week at (847) 971-1223 and email (Stevenkahn47@GMail.com)and I always look forward to meeting a fellow traveler.

We continue to move closer to our dream of opening our Pop Culture Museum so we can share a lifetime of collectibles. Folding into that will be my son Deniz's Nintendo museum collection, which may be the finest in the country. Currently, Deniz has remained focused on growing WATA Games, the premiere certification company for video games, but I know he yearns to return to his passion of collecting and documenting the evolution and growth of that industry as well.

We continue to purchase as much as we can so we can share our joy of collecting with others and are always looking to provide a home for another set of collectibles. Don't hesitate to contact us if you have anything for sale. Our interests are very broad, and we always offer generous finder's fees as well.

Remember that one of our greatest joys is to treat our Inner Child with the love that he or she deserves. The COVID pandemic acted as a catalyst for people who suddenly had a lot of time on their hands and were searching for something that felt good. Happiness took on a different meaning and chasing returns on stock market investments became less important than something else. Whether it was a Bulls fan finally owning that Michael Jordan rookie card, a millennial finding a long cherished Pokémon card, a gamer snaring that sealed Mike Tyson Punch Out or a Turtle fanatic buying a first print of issue 1, this year people wanted to find something that felt good. We all need that. It goes back to what I've said at the end of every report I have filed. If you collect what you love, you can never go wrong. That sentiment has never been more important than it is right now.

Nick Katradis
Collector

As I sit behind my computer this 2020 Christmas Eve morning, I see that Heritage auctions is currently selling the highest graded copy of *Batman* #1, in CGC 9.4, in their January 2021 signature auction. And only a few months prior, Heritage sold the cover to *Uncanny X-Men* #268 for $300k, a *Killing Joke* panel page for $156k, and a *Peanuts* Daily for $192k. Let those prices sink in for a minute (or two).

The theme of my 2019 and 2020 market reports has been about how so much vintage and historically significant comic art has been coming to market the past few years. It seems now that not only is that trend continuing but it's actually accelerating. There are auctions every other month from each of the major auction houses, as well as weekly Heritage auctions that are showcasing better and better art with each passing week.

I have been collecting comic art since 2002, and I have never seen the kind of quality and the quantity of art coming to market as has surfaced the past few years. For collectors you would think that this is terrific news, but most collectors, except for a very few with deep pockets, are shut out of this game of musical chairs. I think a lot of the new blood that came into the hobby is from the "investor" class, or more appropriately from the "speculator class". And that does not bode well for the hobby.

In general, when the speculators get into any asset class, it's the presage of doom and a potential crash in prices. Why? Because they are not buying at these nose bleed prices, because they love the art, whether because of nostalgia or historical significance. They are buying it because they were led to believe that the art will be worth more in the future. However, the "greater fool theory" may not apply here. Because if speculators get burned, and they realize they can't make money, they all tend to exit at the same time. And that can be a problem as our small hobby cannot absorb a glut of art, without a massive price plunge. And if you subscribe to the notion that "this time, it's different", well, let me just say, "it never is".

Let's just use the common term, "the smart money is cashing out", and see if it's true or not. First, let me clarify. By "the smart money", I certainly do not mean the speculators and/or the new blood in the hobby that sees fit or wise to pay $50k for a modern art complete story. By smart money, I mean the collectors that bought and held on to this great art for decades, and now at these price points, they smartly are selling it hand over fist. The "dumb money" today are the buyers of this overpriced commodity that was presented to them as "one of a kind" and "rare". Yes, its one of a kind, but there are tens of thousands of great examples of great art. And it's not rare, as we know that most of the art published since 1965, all exists and it's all out there. And it's now coming to market.

Let me be clear, I have been more passionate about my comic art collecting recently, than I have ever been in the past. I am a lifetime bull of comic art. I am now seeing grail type pieces that I was looking for since I started collecting, almost on a daily basis. I could never find these pieces in the past but now it seems that every major auction has a few items that I was searching for all those years. But at today's price points, most collectors can barely afford to buy one piece. It's sad for true collectors to get shut out of buying the art they love, and to see these "investors/speculators" get it instead.

But we have to accept the fact that comic art is now more popular now that the Marvel Cinematic Universe has taken over the big screen, and most movie goers are now familiar with the comic characters we grew up reading.

These days, every collector has to develop a strategy on obtaining his share of some comic art for their collections. They should refrain from buying what I call "eye candy" art. I personally have decided to back off from buying any art that I "want", and concentrate on obtaining just some of the comic art I "need". I have developed over the years a discipline of waiting for a piece of art that I need to have in my collection, rather than just buying every piece I see that I would like to own. This strategy has allowed me to still buy some coveted comic art without breaking the bank.

I collect mostly Bronze Age art from 1968-1976, with some more modern art from time to time. I consider myself one of the foremost collectors of Bronze Age art, and my collection is reflective of that. My favorite Marvel characters are: Captain America by far, the mighty Sub-Mariner, Warlock, Thor, Hulk, Black Panther, and Ka-Zar. My favorite DC characters are Superman, Batman, Metamorpho, and Rose & Thorn. And my favorite artists are: John Buscema, Gil Kane, Sal Buscema, Jim Aparo, Irv Novick, Rich Buckler, Nick Cardy, Dick Giordano, Herb Trimpe, George Tuska, Don Heck, and Curt Swan. The few modern artists I collect are Steve Epting and Lee Weeks.

I try to buy art mostly from my favorite artists and art of my favorite superheroes. This limits my collecting focus and prevents the straining of my finances. This allows me to concentrate my purchases to art that I plan to keep forever, and to help me save my bullets for the art I need in my collection.

I believe that comic art collecting is only in the 3rd inning as a hobby, so we should have many years left of happy collecting. The smart collectors are the ones that show the discipline that is required today to navigate the mass supply of endless comic art that seems to be out there. By buying only art they love, with an eye out for value and future appreciation, most true collectors will do just fine over the long term. What I would recommend to younger collectors is to try not to chase the "hot" or the current "popular art", as it probably won't stand the test of time. Buying with your heart is fine, but if you have limited resources, I would recommend you combine artistic merit, the quality of the artist/inker, as well as your personal nostalgia in your purchasing quests. It's very easy today for a younger collector to get carried away by over spending on some art that you won't care for a short time later. If you make a list of what you feel is great art, by a great artist, and from a significant storyline, you will be rewarded down the road if you chose to sell something, in order to buy something you want more.

It's never a bad time to collect original art from a favorite artist. ***Incredible Hulk*** *#156 cover by Herb Trimpe*

Ivan Kocmarek
Collector

I'm glad 2020 is in the rearview mirror now but there's a lot of carnage left stretching down the highway behind us. I hope that by the time you're reading this you've been vaccinated and cons are being scheduled again. 2021 is, in fact, the 80th Anniversary of the first Canadian comic book, *Better Comics* Vol. 1 No. 1 which had a cover date of March 1941. A bunch of us has formed a group called The Society for the Promotion of Canadian Comics (SPCC), put that into your browser to find out about initiatives we've come up with to celebrate this.

Though the commerce in comics was probably dented a little in 2020 by the lack of cons and inaccessibility to brick-and-mortar comic shops at times, the market in Canadian comics still produced some healthy results.

Just to refresh everybody's memory, the Canadian Golden Age is divided into two periods. The war-time or WECA period (1941-46) which was created because the Canadian government wanted to shore up the Canadian dollar during the war and banned a lot of 'unessential' American products, including comics and pulps, from coming into Canada and sucking Canadian dollars out. Canadian publishers stepped up and created our own original comics which were mainly printed in black and white and collectors during the '60s began calling "The Canadian Whites."

After this, the reprint or FECA period (1947-53) followed a brief year or so when American comics were allowed back into Canada. Again, the post war economy and Canadian dollar needed shoring up and the government produced a second ban on American comics, but this time with a difference. Though American comics couldn't be on our shelves, American publishers could send mattes up and Canadian publishers could put out reprints of American comics. However, the reprints that came out were a jumble. The Canadian reprint books were mostly 36 pages and dropped a feature or more from the American original. The Canadian publishers had inferior printing presses and processes so that it wasn't uncommon that the colour register was off. Many of the Canadian books were 'hybrids' so that contents of the guts of a comic didn't match the cover, or sometimes the original American cover wasn't used at all and instead a variant cover was created from an internal splash page or even from a splash page not in the book. Occasionally, a new, original cover was created. Invariably, the American ads in these comics were blanked out (a lot of reprints have blank inside covers) or replaced by Canadian ads. The print runs of these Canadian reprints were far lower than that of their American counterparts because our population was, and still is, about 10% of our neighbour to the south.

My ability to review this year's sales of Canadian books from these two periods comes from collector Jim Finlay's generous sharing of his meticulous data concerning recorded sales of these books. Overall, it looks like the big movement in values this year occurred in books from the latter of the two periods (that is the reprint period) I just described.

First of all, let's review some of the recorded sales of Canadian comics from the war-time period. Here is a list of the top fifteen sales recorded for Canadian war-time comics this past year, with columns for Comic/CGC or Raw Condition/Price Attained in US dollars:

Comic	CGC or Raw Condition	Price Attained
Dime Comics #1	VG	$3,305
Better Comics V1 #2	3.0	$2,499
Dime Comics #3	4.0	$1,620
Super Comics V2 3N	4.0	$1,375
Black Hood Comics nn	4.0	$1,366
Triumph Comics #26	4.0	$1,195
Spy Smasher V2 #9	NM	$1,081
Dime Comics #20	6.0	$1,080
Dime Comics #8	5.5	$927
Commando Comics #2	7.0	$865
Three Ring Comics #3	4.0	$810
Active Comics #1	8.5	$742
Three Aces Comics V1 #7	7.0	$709
Active Comics #23	6.0	$700
Better Comics V5 #9	GD	$685

Remember that, less than ten years ago very few people knew what these comics were and the prices they would fetch would have been about a quarter of these prices at best, often far less. Of these top 15, just over half of them are Toronto publisher Bell Features titles. The rest are a mixture of a couple of comics each from Vancouver's Maple Leaf Publications, Toronto's Anglo-American Publications and F. E. Howard Publications, and peculiar comic, *Three Ring Comics* #3 from Toronto's Century Publications. I cannot understand the value in *Three Ring Comics* #3. Its contents are funny animal reprints taken from the only issue of American *Three Ring Comics* put out about a year earlier by The Spotlight Publications. These contents had already been reprinted in the previous issue of Canadian *Three Ring Comics* as well as in *Dime Comics* #29. However, what I guess does make it stand out for some collectors is the cover. This is a variant of the cover used on American *Pep Comics* #22 that changes The Shield's stars and stripes costume to one bearing the Union Jack which was Canada's flag at the time. It seems to come up only with a British price marker on it, meaning that it was probably printed in Canada solely for British distribution.

There was also a trend at the lower end of the Canadian war-time comics collecting spectrum last year that I should also mention. Market values in low to mid-grade Anglo-American colour titles such as *Freelance Comics*, *Grand Slam Comics*, and *Three Aces Comics* that came out from late 1944 to 1946 seem to have been cut just about in half because more of them appear to be showing up for sale. There seem to be a lot more of them popping up in the UK which means that they were probably aggressively distributed there. We also forget that a good number of the last few issues of these were printed in Cleveland, Ohio (check the indicia in your books to see which you have—CGC doesn't recognize this difference yet) and may have received better US distribution than we originally thought.

Here is the list of the top 20 recorded sales of Canadian books from the reprint (1947-53) period (again the breakdown is Comic/CGC or Raw Condition/US price attained):

Comic	CGC or Raw Condition	US Price Attained
Manhunt #12	5.5	$10,500
Manhunt #12	1.0	$7,525
Manhunt #12	2.5	$7,200
Superman #52	9.8	$4,080
Marvel Mystery #92	8.5	$3,999
Manhunt #12	VG	$3,351
Phantom Lady #14	9.0	$2,760
Captain America #68	8.0	$1,680
Batman #47	6.0	$1,339
Startling #52	5.0	$1,320
My Love Memoires #12	9.4	$1,320
Batman #59	5.0	$1,299
Mysteries #8	8.5	$1,150
Detective Comics #137	7.0	$1,111
Astonishing #27	9.0	$1,100
Captain America #70	VG+	$1,080
Captain America #66	6.5	$1,050
Torchy #6	9.0	$1,049
My Story #11	8.0	$1,020
Journey into Fear #19	5.0	$1,000

The standout, of course, is *Manhunt* #12, which accounts for four of the top six sales results. The magic of this issue is that it apparently fills a gap in an American run for a book that was thought to have never been printed. The original American run of *Manhunt* stopped at 11 in Aug./Sept. 1948 and then began again with #13 in 1952 and #14 in 1953. A #12 was unknown and there was only a blank placeholder in *Gerber's Photo Journal* for it. This Canadian printed #12 had a previously unknown Ogden Whitney cover, but its guts were reprinted from *Trail Colt Comics* #1 and contained Frazetta and L. B. Cole artwork. The first copy to appear on the scene was the 1.0, which actually showed up in early December on Comiclink and caused quite a stir. The raw VG copy showed up on eBay in early January of this year and then the 2.5 in July and the 5.5 in mid November both on Heritage. This issue seems to be the only issue of *Manhunt* reprinted in Canada and gets its value from its American context. Let's see if more copies come out of the weeds.

In previous years, Canadian reprints have generally been frowned upon by collectors, but this year there seems to have been an uptick in demand for them and a corresponding rise in their value. Perhaps it's a function of recent collector interest in Canadian variant price editions and of covers firmly becoming a general driving force in the hobby.

The list above reflects strong interest in Canadian reprints of Superman and Batman titles as well as Marvel hero titles, and any reprint that has a good girl art cover. I wonder if this increase in interest is mainly coming from Canadian collectors who want to complete runs of the Canadian reprints or, as I suspect, it is American collectors who want to have the Canadian reprints fill holes in their American runs or who are completists and want the Canadian reprint variants as well as the American original. Let's see if this trend continues. What it is beginning to show is that the hobby needs a checklist/price guide for these Canadian reprint era books.

Robert Krause
Primo Comics

Greetings to all from Primo Comics. 2020 has been an unprecedented year in the comic book market with record prices for comics and a perceived relative scarcity of comics in the marketplace for all eras. The global pandemic changed the landscape of many industries, this includes the comic book market. As a result of the pandemic, the Federal Reserve has cut interest rates to zero and has pumped trillions of dollars into the economy to keep it afloat. The Federal Government has provided stimulus checks to every American as well as introduced many programs to continue to stimulate the economy. As a result of these "easy money" government programs, the country in awash in cash or access to cash. Much of this money is going into the stock market, housing and alternative investments such as comic books. This has the inevitable effect of pushing up prices for all of the aforementioned respective categories.

People have been under full or partial quarantine for most of 2020. As a result, they have had restrictive or no access to movie theaters, dining out, theme parks and like entertainment and leisure activities. This has created a pent up demand for a pop culture outlet to feed their entertainment and collecting needs. They have strongly engaged streaming services, video games and comic books to satisfy this need. They also have excess disposable income to spend as a result of their having restrictive access to entertainment outlets. Comic books historically perform quite well as an asset class during times of domestic or global strife. There is a flight to real (hard) assets which comic books satisfy. We have seen such a flight to comic books as described above as well as strong prices increases as a result of the demand.

The scarcity of comics cannot be accurately described unless one is out in the marketplace seeking to purchase collections. 2020 was a marked year in terms of the lack of collections we had the opportunity to purchase. Once comics were relatively easy to find at garage sales, flea markets and antique stores. This is no longer the case. Comics are quite a fragile and ever diminishing collectable. Comics and collections are lost everyday due to extreme weather, natural disasters and home fires. One must look at historic print runs for titles to realize, with some exceptions, the relative small quantity of books that were being printed each month. The 1980s print runs of titles were more robust than subsequent years but still not large numbers as the average book back then was between 200,000 to 300,00 copies a month. The 1990s and 2000s saw drastic declines in these print runs. Comics printed within the past ten years have seen print runs as low as 7,000 copies! So, given the huge surge in demand for comics and the ever declining numbers of books that still exist, prices continue to go up.

As of this writing, Disney has presented their Investor Day to the public. They presented a rich catalog of movies and TV shows based upon *Star Wars* and comic book characters. This had an instant impact of dramatically increasing demand and thus prices for the respective properties. There is a strong appetite for anything and all pop culture properties with the public. These pop culture properties have deeply ingrained themselves in the daily lives of people. These people are always seeking to get closer to the characters and stories they so love and they, in large part, do this through the purchase and possession of comic books. Once they purchase comics, it is very likely that these books will remain off the market for quite a long time as their individual identities are tied to the books and characters.

Silver Age Marvel and DC comics are the sweet-spot of the marketplace, particularly in high grade. As the prices of these books continue to increase, collectors have moved down the grade scale and are now quite content to purchase a mid to lower grade copy of early Marvel and DC books. As a result, we are seeing prices increase for mid to lower grade comics from this era. There has been a mantra created with these collectors that any example of a desired issue, even at mid to low grade, is better than not owning one at all. This is most true for the superhero genre but also can be seen with Horror and War books from the same era. Some of the best and legendary creators worked on all different genres during this era and the quality of the storytelling is outstanding.

The Copper Age of comics (the 1980s) has historically been an under-appreciated era. As time has progressed, collectors are starting to see the sheer quality of these books and the fantastic creative teams that produced them. The Copper Age of comics has become the new vintage era. Prices are still relatively affordable for most comics produced during this time. Continue to keep a watchful eye on this era as collectors new and old have begun their accumulation.

Until next time, happy hunting!!

Timothy Kupin
Koops Comics

Once again, I'm honored to be given an opportunity to contribute to the *Overstreet Comic Book Price Guide* Market report. And once again I don't have news of any incredible record setting sales to share with you.

During 2020, Koops Comics was setup at six different Comic Cons in three different states: Arizona, California, and Alaska. That is not a typographical error. You read it correctly. Koops Comics was setup at the Alaska Comic Con in Fairbanks, Alaska in late February 2020.

The show was held in a small hockey arena. I remember standing outside the front doors of the arena the day before the show and looking at the empty snow covered parking lot in sub-zero temperatures and trying to imagine the parking lot being full of vehicles (all plugged into the plugs provided at pretty much every parking lot in Fairbanks). I just saw an empty parking lot and snow. I was having a hard time imagining it being full of vehicles and people.

I'm happy to report that just because I couldn't manage to visualize it, doesn't mean it wouldn't come true. Saturday morning arrived and before long the arena was full of very happy folks many of whom had travelled from as far away as Anchorage (500 miles away) to attend. The parking lot was overflowing. Since we flew in, I only brought 10 magazine boxes (or five suitcases) of comics from Arizona to the land of the midnight sun. I hadn't been on an airplane in 15 years. As you may have heard, I like to drive. Only an opportunity to visit my 49th state AND setup at a comic con in my 29th different state could get me on an airplane. Driving was out of the question.

The show was a huge success and we had a blast. The attendees loved it. Even the panels were packed. My good friend N. Scott Robinson was wondering if anyone would even show up for his panels and he was treated with a captivated standing room only audience.

Everything in Fairbanks is the Northernmost location of anything. We ate at the world's Northernmost Denny's and also the world's Northernmost Southern Bar-B-Q joint.

Alaska Comic Con was the world's Northernmost Comic Con and we were the world's Northernmost comic dealers for the weekend. Big thanks to Brett Carraras, Ben Penrod, Jim Madison, and Dan Nokes for the outstanding job they did with the show and big thanks to Jorge Rico and N. Scott (Doc) Robinson for their help toting suitcases of comics and helping at the booth.

We sold a *Marvel Premiere* # 15 CBCS 7.5 for $250 to the world's Northernmost cloud cosplayer, a raw *Hulk* #142 to the world's Northernmost Tiny Hulk cosplayer and also sold comics to the world's Northernmost Hunter S. Thompson and Dr. Gonzo cosplayers.

***Marvel Premiere** #15 sold at the Northernmost convention in the world.*

The big Northernmost bonus treat was getting to spend time with my old friends Christopher and Adrianna Lloyd of Painted Visions Comics and Games who also braved the trip.

Except for a very small show at Cochise College in Sierra Vista, Arizona the other shows that I exhibited in were all in Southern California.

In a year where shows have been fewer and further between, one happy 2020 memory that comes to mind was getting some of my foreign edition comics from my personal collection signed by the great Jim Steranko at the Cal Comic Con in late January 2020. He was jovial and gregarious as usual and is always interested in seeing his covers on the foreign editions.

In 2020 we managed to sell a little bit of everything. Silver and Bronze Age Marvels were the best sellers with DCs, Dells, Charltons, Archies, Harveys , UGs, Warren and Marvel magazines also continue to do well. Romance comics seem to be picking up steam as we sold a number of them in 2020 primarily at the San Diego Comic Fest in early March 2020.

I rarely sell online and I have a feeling that will change in 2021. I do buy a lot online, primarily foreign comics for my personal collection. Just in the last 2 months I've received shipments of comics from Norway, Denmark, Italy and Brazil.

In addition to being a part-time comic dealer I am a lifelong fan and collector. As rough as 2020 has been, my love for comic books and comic collecting remains undiminished.

I'm looking forward to many more years enjoying this wonderful hobby.

Ben Labonog
Primetime Comics

The fear of COVID-19 shut down jobs, the economy, schools, churches, and comic conventions, but it did not shut down the exchange of comic books and comic art. The initial shock of the pandemic slowed down trading as comic shows were cancelled off the calendar. The rise in online buying and selling from major comic auctions, eBay, dealer websites, and social media virtual cons resulted in a healthy spike in mail orders. USPS, FedEx, and UPS all experienced severe backups since everyone was locked down and ordering all necessities for home delivery. One collector said it took six weeks for a $3500 art page to arrive from Spain to the USA, and the tracking disappeared after one day. Other nerve-racking experiences include 2-3 weeks delivery time for USPS priority parcels shipped within the USA.

With everyone working and studying from home, many collectors had time to access and examine their collections. Runs were filled and new covers added as a result of boredom and ample time to shop online. These purchases would help keep full time dealers in business with the absence of conventions. On eBay, common CGC Silver Age semi/non keys were found with pumped up Buy-It-Nows to offset CGC grading and eBay fees. Thus, causing an over inflation of prices. With patience, one can find suitable raw copies graded strictly and offered by several trusted dealer websites or through private social media contacts.

The absence of movies/trailers released during the pandemic created a clearer separation between speculators and collectors. The pure speculator would not have as much patience to speculate on a book with theaters closed. Collectors still took the investment risk especially if they liked the character. As I type this in December 2020, MCU speculation is rising sharply with keys like *Avengers* #8, *FFs*

1,4,5,48, and *X-Men* #1. The sudden passing of Black Panther actor Chadwick Boseman led to a quick revival of *FF* #52 as demand and price points increased the last quarter of 2020. It's a great time to pick up early Silver Age DCs at bargain prices. DC Silver Age offers goofy story lines, simpler art, and less creative villains, but there is a special charm with 1950s DCs.

Local collectors found themselves upgrading their Bronze *X-Men* run, filling in '50s *Detective/Batman/* Villain covers & Silver Age *FF/Spider-Man* keys, dabbling in pre-hero & funny animal, and acquiring original art. When possible, in person deals were welcomed to give collectors a chance to interact with each other while avoiding the dreaded eBay or auction sales tax. Smaller gatherings of 40 or less started coming around in hotels and rented storage units. The most fun was completing a deal in person involving an *Action Comics* #7 in a McDonald's parking lot ("I'm lovin' it"). All the major conventions were canceled and it is still unknown what the status may be for 2021. Virtual cons were happening daily on all social media platforms - Superworld hosted Treasure Chest Tuesdays on IG and Harley Yee rejuvenated his website and created a Facebook account for networking.

Observation of the original art market in 2020 was a unique experience. Original art is one of a kind material that had little to no market pre 1990. Even Jack Kirby had trouble peddling his pages for $20 in the 1980s, and now any '60s Kirby superhero pages bring big money. Some collectors can't look at black and white inks and pencils all day long, but looking at large panels in hand, without color drowning out detail, is a fantastic experience. All Steve Ditko art is in high demand but low in supply. Everyone wants Ditko Spider-Man and Dr. Strange followed by pre-hero monster pages or his work from Charlton. The torch appears to have been passed from (Kirby to Romita) to (John Buscema to Byrne) to (McFarlane to Jim Lee) with plenty of great artists in between. I have enjoyed watching Comic Art LIVE on YouTube organized by Bill Cox (CAF owner). Weekly market reports and talk show guests provided good information and entertainment throughout the year. As with comics, original art should be visually enjoyed, either in a portfolio, or framed and displayed. With prices strong, finding "an" example from your favorite artist, character, or genre will be most satisfying.

Many collectors have debated when the Golden Age ends and when the Silver Age begins. Since there was a variety of mixed genres (GGA, PCH, Superhero, Sci-fi, Funny Animal, Westerns, etc.) published in this Atomic/post WWII era (1945 to 1955), I have pegged the dawn of the Silver Age when the comics code authority (CCA) stamp was printed on all comics starting in January 1955. Prime Golden Age is designated from 1937-1945, late Gold from 1946-1949, and transitional Gold from 1950-1955. I submit that this is the purest and simplest form of organizing the post WWII era for comic book collecting.

Let's make a plug here for *Detective Comics* #241 (1st app. Rainbow Batman, March 1957) which needs to be broken out separately in the *Guide*. Low grade copies are selling around $150-$175 a point. This was certainly a discovery book for me this past year. Apparently, the 2010 *Brave and the Bold* Batman cartoon re-booted the Rainbow Batman resulting in a revived interest. *Detective* #241 isn't the scarcest in the run, but is not easily stocked by dealers anymore due to the increased demand.

Two books that are semi-sleepers are *ASM* #17 (2nd app Green Goblin) and *FF* #6 (1st Marvel villain team up, 2nd Doom, 2nd SA Subby). With the price points that *ASM* #14 is realizing, the #17 is a bargain. Yes, everyone wants the 1st app, but as the increase in demand and price point (eliminating potential buyers as they are priced out of the market) for *ASM* #14 goes up, the next earliest Goblin appearance should be valued appropriately. The same could be said of *ASM* #11 (2nd Doc Ock app), but prices seem to have jumped more on that one the past year. While everyone is chasing *FF* #1,4,5,48 – the #6 is often the forgotten key. I actually think the #6 has the superior cover over #5, while issue #4 has always been my favorite of the early run. I would love to own an original art page from *FF* #4 or 6. It's doubtful the pages from issue #4 exist today, but I'm told a full-page set of issue #6 does exist but has been locked up for years.

It's great to see more Timely collectors appreciate *All-Select Comics* #2 (Winter 1943-44). While *All-Select* #1 has a beautiful jet black cover by Alex Schomburg, the #2 has always been alluring to me with it's unique green cover, Cap's big 'ole Browning WWII machine gun, Red Skull story, and higher scarcity. A higher grade copy sold privately at close to $2k a point, while low to mid grade copies are now trading at $1000-$1500 per point. I have always considered issue #1 and #2 as bookends similar to *Detective* #29 and #31.

***All Select Comics #2** is getting lots of appreciation from Timely collectors.*

I'll give a final plug to Gene and BJ, who are the fantastic creators and developers of the Shortboxed app that can be downloaded for free via Android and iPhone. This user-friendly app can be used to sell third party graded comic books with a simple registration and upload of pictures. Once inside the app, there are many articles written by collectors from the comic book community. I was honored when Gene asked me if I wished to submit an article. Of course, I accepted his invitation, and I wrote about the "Greatest Comic Book Ever Published: *Marvel Comics* #1." The article provides many historic photos which detail the controversies that surfaced about the book, its publication problems, and the uniqueness of its front cover and popular characters that would help establish the Marvel universe.

2020 has been a year matched by no other. Let's continue to live by faith over fear and appreciate every blessing in our precious lives. May God Bless America, land of the free, and big comic book deals in McDonald's parking lots.

Ben Lichtenstein
Zapp Comics

Greetings from New Jersey! The year 2020 has been an historic one for the planet, for the U.S. and for the comic book industry. The COVID-19 pandemic, social unrest and political turmoil have all made for a stressful 12 months.

We finished up 2019 very strong and the first 2 months of 2020 were gangbusters, so things looked sunny for a great 2020. Then COVID-19 lockdowns hit us in mid-March, and we were forced to pivot hard and go into survival mode. Not only did our brick and mortar stores' business have to shut down, but the comic conventions were all canceled as well. My convention sales are a small, but important area of our business. In fact, our own event, Zappcon, was canceled, as was Free Comic book Day and our own Annual Sale in November.So, this was concerning to say the least.

After laying off my staff, my partner Corry and I went into turbo mode fulfilling online and curbside sales. With so much uncertainty, we made the decision to hustle and grind like crazy, filling orders any way we could. There was no visibility as to how hard this lockdown would hurt spending and hurt the comic book market. Tens of millions of jobs were lost and hundreds of thousands of businesses affected, not good. Then, demand for all types of collectables just exploded!

I can only surmise that, although many have been hurt by the lockdowns, there is still a majority of people who are employed and now have disposable income that is not directed toward travel, dining, concerts and other in-person leisure. Coupled with a tidal wave of stimulus money and unemployment money, large sums of money entered the collectables market. Comics, sports cards, Pokémon, Star Wars, Wrestling, videogames, etc. all experienced an explosion in price increase and volume. Just breathtaking price jumps and volume occurred.

Friends of mine that are pure online sellers reported record sales, as spending shifted on line from in-person sales. As I write this in late December, this trend continues. While some of these price jumps, particularly in trading cards feels "bubbly", I'm feeling good about the comic book market in general going into 2021.

Essentially, if you've been hoarding collectables for a while, 2020 is the year that your inventory or personal collection has exploded in value. While I focus on continually turning my inventory, I've almost managed to accumulate a few thousand long boxes of comics! It's a lot of work to sift through them, but well worth it.

On the new issue front, DC Comics decided to dramatically shake up the new comic world right in the middle of a pandemic. Talk about poor timing! As if the small retailer wasn't already under stress, DC Comics decided to complicate our lives further.

Switching from Diamond to UCS (Midtown Comics) and Lunar (DCBS), DC's decision meant increased shipping cost and administrative hours spent on ordering, while also forcing me to purchase from my on-line competitor. The conflict of interest is obvious. We had no choice but to go along with it and make the best of a strange situation. I have to supply my customers reliably with new comics or they will go elsewhere.

Once we became acclimated to the new world order things actually were OK. UCS did a great job of getting us our books efficiently and with reasonable service and shipping costs. Even better, we started getting our DC books a few days earlier than normal, which reduced stress levels for us. Sales on new books have actually rose since the change, with lots of new faces coming in for their new comics. I'd still far prefer to purchase all of new comics from one source, for simplicity and scale.

Overall, DC has suffered from a lack of strong movie and streaming content while also being under the umbrella of AT&T, which is a laden with debt due to a series of questionable acquisitions. It remains to be seen what the future holds for DC print comics, as its parent company has shown little to no interest in that business and is also under pressure to cut costs.

Marvel and *Star Wars* continue to chug along, getting hotter and hotter, while DC needs help. At this time, Disney has announced an incredible slate of upcoming Marvel and Star Wars projects, which bodes well for the next couple years. Imagine if DC can do the same…wow would I be busy!

Back Issues sales overall are incredibly strong. While there's more competition, there is also a much bigger pool of buyers. It is clear that there's more money than ever in our hobby. Beyond the obvious keys, it seems almost daily there's some new property announced for streaming and movies, resulting in price bumps for 1st appearances. *Star Wars* back issues, both Marvel and Dark Horse, have just exploded. Many of those Dark Horse *Star Wars* comics that used to collect dust now command high prices. The print runs on some of these books, particularly *Clone Wars*, were low. So, small supply + giant demand = big prices jumps.

Overall, Marvel is king of the back issues, with *Amazing Spider-Man* leading the pack. I won't bore you with repeating the list of keys that sell. Suffice to say, sales are brisk on all major Marvel titles.

Another trend we're happy to see is increased sales in '90s comics. Yes, those glut titles are finally moving well, especially the Jim Lee *X-Men*, McFarlane's *Spawn* and *Spider-Man*, and lots more.

Spawn overall is an incredible back issues seller. Reaching the milestone #300 just made the back issues even hotter, in particular the low print run issues after $50 or so. The homage cover issues, from #221 to #233 are becoming quite expensive.

Happily, we are selling a really broad range of back issues from all publishers. I've even seen very strong sales on Charltons, Archies and Gold Keys. Most of these sales are under *Guide* unless it's a key issue, which will go over *Guide*.

Teenage Mutant Ninja Turtles, which have always had a strong loyal fan base exploded this year. Values have doubled, tripled or even more on most *Turtles* back issues. Truly amazing, the Archie series, #1, which sold slowly for $4 or $5, now sells easily for $60 to $80!

Silver Age and Bronze Age Magazines have seen strong interest. We've done really well with Warrens, Marvels, Skywald, miscellaneous horror, etc. This trend, which began last year, has continued, with more and more buyers recognizing how beautiful these books are. Depending on artist and storyline, they are selling well at close to *Guide* for non-keys and multiples of *Guide* for key issues.

We bought much fewer collections, as sellers have resisted in-person transactions. In response, we've taken this time to scour our warehouse for hidden gems and books that recently broke out. This has been a lot of fun as there are a plethora of back issues that were formerly 50 cents and $1 books that are now $5, $10, even $50! A good example is *Static* #1. When news broke this book went from a slow $5 book, to a fast $50 sale. There are hundreds if not thousands of similar examples.

Buying and selling back issues is a bit more complicated, but more profitable as there are so many more breakout mini-keys. The days where I could breeze through a group of comics and price most of them similarly are long gone. My brain simply can't keep track of all these darn first appearances!

As this very strange year closes, I wish to thank my customers, who supported through the lockdown by buying gift cards and dealing with the inconvenience of life during COVID-19. I also have been lucky to have a great team to work with, which makes my job a lot easier. I remain optimistic about 2021, as the new vaccines roll out and there remains a very healthy interest in all types of collectables. Lastly, please contact me if you have a collection of comics and related stuff to sell – we are always buying!

I hope everyone in the comic community and the rest of the world has a healthy and safe 2021!

Stephen Lipson
Collector

The year 2020 had ushered in the COVID-19 pandemic, which had an impact on the hobby in terms of store closures and how proprietors are revisiting their business models and strategies. However, irrespective of the aforementioned, the market remains robust. For example, sales on both eBay and the big auction houses year-to-date illustrate that there is no slow down in sight and vintage comic books are conversely trending upward, particularly with respect to Good Girl Art, Pre-Code Horror and the superhero genre. This may be attributable to the fact that with restrictions on travel, dining, etc. collectors have been relegated to staying at home and this may be the impetus to the strong surge in online sales of vintage comic books accordingly.

My area of collecting and focus is the Canadian Golden Age era. I have sold several books this year to collectors and I see an upswing in prices realized:

2020 Personal Sales of Note:

Golden Arrow nn Canadian miniature giveaway comic CGC 6.0 $600.00

Super Duper Comics #3 Uncertified $1500.00

Active Comics # 16 Uncertified $950.00

Spy Smasher Comics Vol. 1 #10 Uncertified $950.00

Canadian Heroes Vol. 3 #2 Uncertified $800.00

Lucy Comics Vol. 2 #7 Uncertified $1500.00

Smasher Comics #7 Uncertified $595.00

There still appears to be a dearth of availability of the Canadian Golden Age World War II era books from 1941-1946, and I have only been successful in adding a small number to my personal collection accordingly. Due to low print runs and the fact that comics were meant to be read and thrown away, one is hard pressed to find more examples of these vestiges of Canadian pop culture. Hopefully 2021 will bring relief to the hobby once the COVID-19 vaccine is distributed.

Doug Mabry
The Great Escape

Greetings from Tennessee and Kentucky! To quote the Grateful Dead, "What a long, strange trip it's been!" 2020 has thrown lots of curveballs everyone's way this year. So, what's new? DC changed its distribution twice on us. We were shut down for several months. Conventions were all canceled. But we keep plugging along.

We began to notice a big trend starting in March or so. Golden Age superhero and pre-Code Horror books began to make dramatic spikes upward in prices online. One can only assume that since new comics weren't available and conventions were canceled that the money earmarked for those went into purchasing highly desired comics for people that had to remain stuck at home. When we were able to open back up in May, the pent up demand initially overwhelmed us. Unfortunately, economics and the lack of acquisition for a couple of months slowed things down after a bit.

Golden Age: So in Golden Age the hot keeps getting hotter and the cold keeps getting colder. Classic covers, especially anything World War II, keep breaking records. The funny animal, crime, *Classics*, etc., can be had for pennies on the dollar. In particular, L.B. Cole covers seem to be going through one of their periodic spikes in prices. *Captain Marvel Adventures* #10 VG/FN $328, *Donald Duck* (1935) GD $206, *Zip Comics* #32 GD $277, *Kid Komics* #3 Fair $100, *Adventure Comics* #141 VG- $122, *Warrior Comics* #1 FN $108, *Planet Comics* #53 VG $178, *Planet Comics* #39 GD/VG $159, *Web Of Evil* #4 VG+ $125, *Sherry The Showgirl* #1 VG $415.

Silver Age: This is the hardest part of the market for us to acquire. Key books, major or minor, fly off the shelves usually at over *Guide* as soon as you get them. On the other hand, our stock of Silver Age books like *Fantastic Four*, *Daredevil*, *Avengers*, and almost all of the DC Silver Age books except *Batman* and *Flash* seem to sit for quite awhile. In particular, the Superman family of titles and the Gold Key adventure books across the board are really in need of price decreases. We routinely mark these at half *Guide* and they still hang around. Does anyone get anywhere near *Guide* for middle of the run *Superboy*, *Jimmy Olsen*, *Lois Lane*, or *World's Finest*? Maybe in the highest grades, but they're certainly readily available cheaply in mid and low grades. Some sales: *Green Lantern* #76 CGC 6.5 $400, and *Marvel Super-Heroes* #13 VG $200

Modern Age: *Wolverine* vol. 1 #1 CGC 9.4 $125, and *Amazing Spider-Man* #300 CGC 9.0 $550. There are definitely some things that seem to need adjustments this time around. The Spider-Man Maximum Carnage storyline issues are too low at the moment, with the exception of part 1. The regular issues should probably be six or seven dollars each. *Amazing Spider-Man* vol. 2 needs to go up a bit, also. Maybe around five dollars for an average issue.

Happy hunting!

Brian Marcus
Cavalier Comics

Greetings from Southwest Virginia! To say this has been a trying year would be an understatement. The virus put a clamp down on sales for March and April but they rebounded after that and things have been steady. It really hurt with most of the convention season canceled. That will continue into the early part of 2021 but maybe with the vaccine arriving, there's a chance for summer or fall to have a few. The public still wants entertainment products so we had to adapt with online sales, curbside service and limit the amount of people in the store. Don't even get me started with DC Comics breaking from Diamond, I'll just let the other dealers talk about that mess.

New comic sales have been lackluster but the highlights for me were *The Last Ronin*, *Wolverine*, and *Batman*. Once again, way too many variants! Just stop already, if you have to depend on that to sell books, then you're telling me that you're not confident in the quality of the material and need a sales gimmick. Back issues once again have been strong. People are building runs of about everything and all grades are moving. Unfortunately, I haven't picked up any good collections this past year so my stock is running low. Hopefully when we can start getting out more, that might change.

Here are the more notable sales for me this past year: *Amazing Spider-Man* #15 CGC 4.5 $501, *Fantastic Four* $48 CGC 6.5 $1477, *Incredible Hulk* CGC 3.5, $1203, *Werewolf by Night* #32 CGC 8.5 $1200, *Marvel Premiere* #15 CGC 9.6 $656, *Adventure Comics* #235 CGC 8.0 $355, *Uncanny X-Men* #99 CGC 9.6 $456 and *Batman* #139 CGC 5.5 $477.

Jim McCallum
with Eric Fournier
Guardian Comics

Twenty Twenty...the year none of us will ever forget and the year the vintage comic book market exploded!!!

Although it makes absolutely zero sense, the Guardian Comics inventory has been decimated in 2020. People being put on lockdown, losing their jobs, caring for sick family members, began grasping for any sense of normalcy and actively sought out their favourite form of escapism: superheroes and comic book collecting.

In March of 2020 we had over 500 long boxes for our customers perusal of $1.00 books, and as of this writing (December 5th, 2020) we are down to just 81 long boxes. With dollar books providing some of the cheapest forms of entertainment available, our customers continued shopping with us in droves, searching for anything to take their minds off of everything that was happening around them.

Another way to take their minds off of the worldwide chaos was treating themselves to something special, something they have always wanted and keys began flying off the shelves this summer as we have never seen at Guardian in our history. We sold an *Amazing Fantasy* #15 CGC 4.0 for $31,000. We sold a *Fantastic Four* #1, 4, 5 and *Hulk* #1 to a first time customer who has been a loyal customer ever since. We got a *Turtles* #1 CGC 8.5 at the beginning of the summer and in one day it was sold to a customer in Austriailia. The demand has been insatiable.

To meet that demand, we have definitely changed the way we do business. We've been driving all over to hand deliver books to our customers, meeting them in their driveways, in their apartment building parking lots, to make sure they have the opportunity to get their hands on the books they want, and letting them know that we will do whatever it takes to fill that need. That also means a lot of mail orders, and as much as I hate packing up books and the anonymity of it all, and prefer face to face (more personal transactions) we have gained a much bigger customer base and have truly gone "international".

With that surge in demand though, we have had an incredibly tough time restocking our inventory. Normally we'd go on many buying trips throughout the year to be able to restock our inventory at will. With no shows, we just don't have that same opportunity. The part I find most baffling is that nobody is even really bringing collections in for sale, nor have they all year. One would think that as much doom and gloom you hear, that people would be coming in constantly looking to sell books to help make ends meet. We actually had less collections walk through our doors for sale in 2020 than any year ever.

I think that the hardest part of the year has been the loss of convention season, from the local one day show, to the big mega events like a Wizard World Chicago or New York City Comic Con, some of the best networking and buying opportunities have been put on hold. Not getting away to see old friends and bring new and fresh inventory that our customer base has gotten used to, home with us, forces us to look at new avenues and different collectibles to broaden our clientele.

That being said, we were able to pick up three very nice slabbed collections this past year. One in the middle of summer with a very nice *Amazing Spider-Man* collection consisting of #4-30 graded mostly between 7.0-8.5. It didn't take long for our customers to gobble most of those issues up. Desperate for inventory we also took a chance on a 150 book slabbed collection that ranged from Silver to Moderns, and although Moderns have never been our main focus, we couldn't believe how quickly they got snatched up. Our customers were passing over tried and true keys like *FF* #52, *ASM* #121 and *Batman* #232 in favour of *Young Avengers* #1 in CGC 9.8 and *Star Wars: Heir to the Empire* #1 CGC 9.8.

Our favourite collection of the year just came in the middle of Novemeber. It was a small (20 books) but beautiful collection of Spider-Man and Batman books, with three quarters of them being the old CGC label that has become the gold standard of this hobby. Being viewed as unpressed and unmanipulated, they always sell for record prices. The hightlights of this collection were an *ASM* #1 CGC 4.5, *ASM* #3 6.5, *Batman* #5 7.0, *Detective Comics* #45 7.0, *Detective Comics* #71 5.0, *Detective Comics* #73 5.5 amongst others. With all the books showing incredible eye appeal for the grade, it took less than a week to sell half of the collection. That's also one other virtue in this hobby we truly believe in: Buy the book and not the grade. Don't become blinded by whatever the number on the slab says in the left hand corner, because not all 9.6s or 9.4s or even 5.0s are created equal.

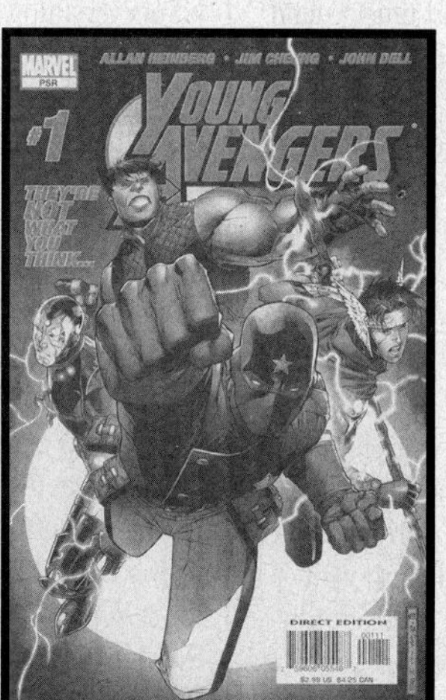

Customers are gravitating to ***Young Avengers #1*** *instead of the tried and true keys.*

With all this being said, nothing in 2020 has really made any sense but of course with housing prices up, the stock market on fire, gold on fire, heck even Pokémon cards have quadrupled or higher since March 2020, does anything even make sense anymore???

So where are we headed? Everyone is always asking for our opinion and why wouldn't you seek advice from those who do it day in and day out?

So here come our 2021 predictions:

1. Major Cons will start to pop back up a bit more, they won't be as big and there will be some hiccups but we are getting there.

2. Don't hesitate on the "good books". With the market run-ups not as strong in comics expect it to happen so don't wait on a deal, find that book you want and make it yours.

3. Books you didn't know you needed will become books you now need. From Disney's slate of new *Star Wars* related stuff, to Marvel's new announcements of all the new heroes ready for the spotlight.

4. DC does something! Like seriously I know this one is a stretch but it has to happen right.

We hope to see everyone in 2021 and hopefully that won't be a prediction we are wrong on?!

Jon McClure
Collector

Greetings from Astoria Oregon! Here's a notable sale from 2020: a complete classic set of *Hand Of Fate*(12/51-12/54), average VG-/VG for $1495. Comics sell in person that won't move online, but when COVID-19 hit and closed the antique malls I usually sell in, the pandemic took its toll. The books that did sell were mostly Marvels. People don't have the expendable income to buy what they were buying. My normal sales dropped by a staggering 75%. Online sales were almost normal but have slowed since June. Overall it has been a tough year, one that I'll never forget, and not just financially. I know I am far from alone in this mess. I have one friend that went out of business, others that were forced to close their stores for extended periods.

The best definition I know for a "Variant" comic book is (1) any non-standard edition created for distribution with a unique purpose, (2) anything reprinted for distribution under the same title with some changes to the cover and/or contents, and (3) any non-standard edition created for distribution in an unplanned or imperfect way. The primary characteristic of a Variant is a strong similarity to the "regular" or standard edition.

Here's a list of the five unique types of Type 1 variants that exist:

Type 1: Test Market Cover Price Variants (US Cents Priced)

Type 1A: Foreign Distribution Variants (UK Pence, Canadian $, Australian $, L Miller Indicias)

Type 1B: Reverse Cover Price Variants (US Cents Priced)

Type 1C: Variant Covers

Type 1D: US Cents Price Font Variants

Type 1: Test Market Cover Price Variants (US Cents Priced): Cover Price Test Market Variants with regional or otherwise limited distribution, published simultaneously with standard or "regular" editions. Such Variants exist because publishers want to test the market prior to raising prices. The indicia and all aspects of the book, except for the cover price, are identical to regular editions.

Type 1A: U.S. Published Foreign Distribution Variants (UK Pence, Canadian $, Australian $, L Miller Indicias): Cover Price Variants intended for foreign distribution with limited regional distribution, published simultaneously with standard or "regular" editions. In the majority of cases, the indicia and all aspects of the book are identical to regular U.S. editions except for the cover price. In some instances other alterations may be present. These may include missing or different cover dates, regional indicia details and variant company logos. Other minor alterations may also be present. Note: The definition of Type 1A has been expanded from my article in *OPG* #40 in 2010 for clarification purposes to accommodate new variant discoveries.

Type 1B: Reverse Cover Price Variants (US Cents Priced): Cover Price Reverse Variants with regional or otherwise limited distribution, published simultaneously with standard or "regular" editions. Reverse Variants exist because material is accidentally printed with a lower price than intended, a mistake not always sufficient for the publisher to destroy otherwise salable goods. The indicia and all aspects of the book are identical to regular editions, regardless of whether it is intended for U.S. or foreign distribution, and the primary characteristic is that there is another version with the same cover logo and markings and the correct cover price. The Gold Key 30 cent and Whitman 40 cent Price Variants are perfect examples.

Type 1C: Variant Covers: Cover Variants with limited or standard distribution, published simultaneously with standard or "regular" editions. This type of Variant exists because publishers choose to experiment with the market without making widespread appearance changes to their logos or regular editions, or to capitalize on current popularity. The indicia and all aspects of the book are identical to regular editions except for the front, inside, and/or back cover deviations, with Variant covers sometimes noted inside. If one book has two different covers, it may be impossible to identify a "regular" edition beyond "cover 1a, 1b," etc. DC's *Fury of Firestorm* #61 and *Justice League* #3 Superman Logos Variant are good examples. A good multiple cover example is DC's *Batman: Legends of the Dark Knight* #1; *The Walking Dead* #100 is another solid example. Many contemporary publishers produce multiple different covers for their titles, and Type 1C is the most commonly employed.

Type 1D: US Cents Price Font Variants: As of 2018, a new Type of variant surfaced, brought to my attention by UK based researcher Steve Cranch. Type 1D is defined as "Cover price variants with a unique price font. All aspects of the book are identical to regular editions but with a unique style of cover price." There are 14 such variants currently proven to exist; they are Marvel U.S. Ten Cent Price Font Variants. Because no copy can be yet said to be the primary copy, all are variants in their own right, and can be catalogued as cover 1a, 1b, etc. Thirteen of fourteen known examples have two unique 10 cent fonts, and the 14th is a key issue, *Rawhide Kid* #17(8/60), which contains an origin story with Jack Kirby art, and which has three different ten cent fonts, not to mention a Type 1A 9d price variant! I know many of you may be thinking I'm splitting hairs, but we're talking about original copies of the same books with different and identifiable characteristics on the covers.

There are three unique cents fonts known: 10 cents in bold with a slashed c, a 'slim font' 10 cents with a small c next to the 10, and a slim font 10 cents with a big C next to the 10. In most cases, the slim font mirrors that of the Type 1A 9d copies raising the possibility of a link between the two. The cents font variations begin when the UK 9d prices are introduced; up until that point, all Marvels had the standard bold 10 / slashed c cents font.

Why do these variants exist and which copy was printed first? Might they have played with the appearance of a few books as an experiment of sorts, just for eye appeal, or on a whim, or due to some error? Or, given the timeline link to the 9d UK copies, could the additional cents fonts indicate some other purpose like foreign distribution - Canada perhaps - especially because of the example of *Rawhide Kid* #17? I believe such variants should be valued equally until data of scarcity difference is determined and further interest develops.

The 14 known Type 1D variants were published from June 1960 to February 1961 inclusive, and more variant examples may exist within the 91 eligible issues across 20 titles, and although most issues have likely been discovered by now, I'm always pleased to confirm new variants. Issues with font variants include *Battle* #70(6/60), with Kirby and Ditko art, *Journey Into Mystery* #60(9/60), 64-65(1-2/61), with Kirby art in #60 and #64, *Kid Colt Outlaw* #91(7/60), *Rawhide Kid* #17 (origin by Kirby), *Strange Tales* #75-77(6, 8, 10/60), 81(2/61), with Ditko art, *Tales To Astonish* #14(12/60), 16(2/61), with Kirby and Ditko art, and *Two-Gun Kid* #54-55(6, 8/60), with Kirby art.

Marvel Type 1 test market cover price variants continue to break record sales results. Publisher experiments in the 20th century repeatedly birthed Type 1 cover price variants immediately before universal price hikes, such as the shift from 10 to 12 cents per copy that occurred in January 1962 from Marvel and DC, and the 25 cent to 30 cent shift famously embodied by the Marvel variants cover dated 4-8/1976 and from 30 to 35 cents for variants cover dated 6-10/1977. Archie and Charlton also played with 15 cent variants in the beginning of the 12 cent era. Despite much heckling back in the day from fellow advisors and critics, when I discovered and publicized the existence of the Marvel cover price variants in *Comic Book Marketplace* #51(8/97), such comics have soared in popularity and value. For a history of comic book variants from the Golden Age to the present, as well as a list of known variants and a detailed lexicon of variant types, with examples that continue to evolve and expand, refer to my article from 2010 in the *Overstreet Comic Book Price Guide* #40, "A History of Publisher Experimentation and Variant Comic Books," pages #1010-1038. An updated version is in progress for a future edition of the Annual *OPG*. All variant types and publishers are historically represented until the 1990s when variants become commonplace.

Todd McDevitt
New Dimension Comics

Greetings from the Pittsburgh region of PA! And St. Clairsville, OH too! I always think it's helpful for readers here to know about where these insights derive. We have five store locations in the Pittsburgh region and one in Ohio. Two are in malls, 2 on main streets, and 2 are in a shopping centers, including our newest store relocation in 35,000 square feet! 2021 celebrates my 35th year in business! I've seen lots of trends and things threaten the comic business over those years, but the COVID-19 pandemic tested the comic industry more than ever.

In addition to the 6 stores, I travel and attend conventions and host one in Pittsburgh, 3 Rivers Comicon. But, COVID. So, all of that got forced to be on pause. We also sell online, primarily eBay as seller ID newdimensioncomics. So, many insights come from these experiences too.

OK, let's hit the elephant in the room. I think every store owner in the country could write a book about experiences during the pandemic and lockdown of our economy. This report is supposed to be about the prices of comics, so I'll try to get to that quickly, but the background of that landscape is important to understand. Pennsylvania has been criticized for having stricter guidelines than many states, so this has been extra fun for me! Quite honestly, it's the worst thing I have ever endured. All 5 of my Pennsylvania stores were shut down completely for about two months. Slightly less time with the Ohio store. During this time, almost my entire staff was laid off. We scrambled to garner some sales online, but this has not been a focus of my business model, only a side project. We did all we could quickly and managed to keep the business on low life support. In opening back up, everything shrunk. Hours, staff, sales, product availability, expectations.

The shut down kicked in with no warning. One of the problems was we now had to shut down buildings and had no way to receive product. Worse, product was in the pipeline from distributors to make its way to us. With no way to sell it, I was not interested in receiving any of it. I said from the beginning that there would be a lot of rare comics coming out of this situation. At the very least, many stores were also shut down and unable to receive. Even if mail order companies were able to keep up, the amount produced was definitely on the low side. I have no examples to offer as of this writing, but keep an eye out. Plus, in the middle of all this, DC Comics decided to completely derail their distribution system. Great timing, thanks guys! As if we didn't have enough to stress about, let's do this with little warning too. During this shift, many stores short sightedly gave up on DC Comics, so releases from that window will have very low print runs. Golden Age, Silver Age... COVID AGE!

Then in early May, we started opening back up. Being closed for Free Comic Book Day, our single biggest day of business all year, was a painful blow. Plus, we paid for all those free books and then had no great use for them. Efforts made by organizers to salvage the event were difficult. Different areas of the country were at different stages of shutdown.

So here's the silver lining. Everyone, in every industry and business, was forced to get really smart really quickly. One of the first things I did was make a list of ways we could manage to make money given these heavy restrictions. We did many of those things, and that's what kept us afloat. Then, as we started to peek out of the shadows, every move we made was with a keen eye on being streamlined and efficient. Things that we used to do that seemed helpful and maybe even important were no longer considered that way if they weren't a top-tier thing that was going to make us a lot of money very quickly. Currently, as things are creeping in the direction of normal, we maintain that mission. And, it has worked. We clawed our way out of the tremendous hole we were in as a result of the lockdown. Currently, things look good. They look different. But stronger and better. I think they will look different for a very long time.

As much as I'm sure you are enjoying reading my rant, I like to involve my awesome staff to share some better opinions from the front lines. I spend much of my time tucked away processing comic books, but these folks hear from customers the most. So, here's the snapshot of what they are witnessing.

Tom Tunnicliff, New Dimension Comics Ellwood City, PA

COVID-19, sounds a bit like the name of the latest team of super heroes from an independent publisher, but it's more like a legion of evil led by a Doctor Doom wannabe. Though the virus has changed many things in many ways this year, especially the way people get their books, the hunt remains the same but how you score your quarry has shifted. With no one coming into stores during the shut-downs, our non-traditional orders (online, email, phone and even a few mail orders) have picked up. We were also fortunate in the fact that we were in the process of adding an online service to our stores when the shut-downs started happening and were able to launch our online services, albeit a little ahead of schedule. During the shut-down our shipping of books quadrupled and our ability to double the size of our shipping department was key to getting us through the year and providing more people with the books they needed, giving joy, hope or even a little bit of escapism. Keep up the hunt, stay safe, be well, mask up (like a hero (or villain) trying to keep a secret identity) and read more comics.

Anthony Tincani, New Dimension Comics Butler, PA

New Dimension Comics in Butler, PA has seen a large increase of people hunting through our back issue and display books. With our wide customer base, we see all sorts of books sold, from ever endearing titles like *Thor* and *Batman*, to modern classics such as *Spawn* and *New Mutants*.

Display books have seen a wide variety in what gets picked through. In the past, most of our sales for display books have been mostly Silver Age Marvel books. Now, we are seeing Silver Age comics from all sorts of publishers, more Golden Age books, and Bronze Age books that were not much of a draw before. Key issues of course, but often just people trying to round out holes in their collections as well. People love collecting, and comics offer something for everyone, so comics are the perfect thing to collect.

Ryan Yingling, New Dimension Comics Tarentum, PA

New Dimension Comics at the Pittsburgh Mills Mall has been doing great with back issue sales! The lead up into this Holiday season has seen back issue sales increase from the previous year. The COVID pandemic unfortunately hit the comic market hard with the shutdown orders across the nation at the beginning of the year. However, this seems to have caused an explosion in people buying issues upon the reopening. After shutdown we saw tons of people coming in looking for back issues and Silver Age books of all kinds. It feels like people used that time to get caught up on reading and it has reinvigorated their interest to find new stories to read and collect. It also helps that over the last few years so many comics are getting adapted into movies and TV shows that it's hard to keep up! All the shows and movies have made the speculator market run wild! I never thought I would see *X-Men* #4 first Omega Red from 1992 go for $30! The comic industry saw a set back this year but just like Diamond said "Our Comeback will be bigger than our setback".

Jon Engel, General Manager of New Dimension Comics

Over the last decade of being in this industry, at least on this side of the counter, I have witnessed some crazy market shifts. While the traditional market of Silver and Golden Age books are on a slight upswing as the world adjusts to the price of living, the modern and key issue market is a trainwreck. In this modern age of technology and comics being adapted to TV/Movie properties left and right, a book can rise and fall on the market in a matter of days. Sometimes even before the customer who picks it off the shelf has time to get it. However, we are now in a great time where people are collecting again, and due to the nationwide shut down, readers are catching up with things so that is a good thing. All of that said, for longer term investments, I really just tell people to bite the bullet and get the evergreen key. As someone who collects full runs, that is also something that is a little crazy to think about and put into practice. If you want to take a chance, then buy every book every week. Just do it. If you don't want to miss the issue and you are a reader, find a store that uses ComicHub as its POS. It has been the best thing we can offer customers so they can get what they need every week. If not, you will have to turn to online and have to pay up for all those books that you should be able to get for cover, or close to that. And those are my thoughts for comic collecting in this age.

Until next year! Collect what you love. Love what you collect.

Brent Moeshlin
Quality Comix

2020 started like other years at Quality Comix. We were busy improving our website and acquiring comic collections to better serve our customers. Then the COVID pandemic hit, and we were forced to temporarily close our brick and mortar store. Everyone was sitting at home buying online, which turned out to be a great opportunity for our company and other online comic companies to take advantage of the additional interest. I think it also provided a measure of escape because they were locked down at home. Comic companies like ours were able to provide some small measure of happiness and comfort in delivering comics right to customers' doorsteps. After a small dip in sales in March and April, our sales numbers significantly increased throughout the rest of 2020 culminating in a record breaking December 2020 for our company.

Regarding specific sales, as the year went on, it became more and more difficult to price our comics for sale. For instance, an *Amazing Spider-Man* #252 CGC NM/MT 9.8 at the beginning of 2020, we would have priced at around $400. By the end of 2020, we were pricing the same book at $1,000. And as I write this market report in March 2021, the price has doubled to $2,000. Another comic that has skyrocketed in recent months is *X-Men* #4. This is the first appearance of the Scarlet Witch so it's no surprise that it has moved up in price since *WandaVision* has proven to be so popular. What is surprising is that it has gone from $450 in GD/VG 3.0 all the way back in September 2020 and is now selling routinely for $2,500 as of this writing! So many sellers, including ourselves, are having to future price key comics so we don't run out of inventory too quickly. It's a tough balance between pricing the book to market and also keeping enough inventory on hand for the next month. I don't believe in my 25 years in the hobby, the industry has ever experienced a sales year like 2020. And, in my opinion, 2021 is shaping up to be like 2020 on steroids.

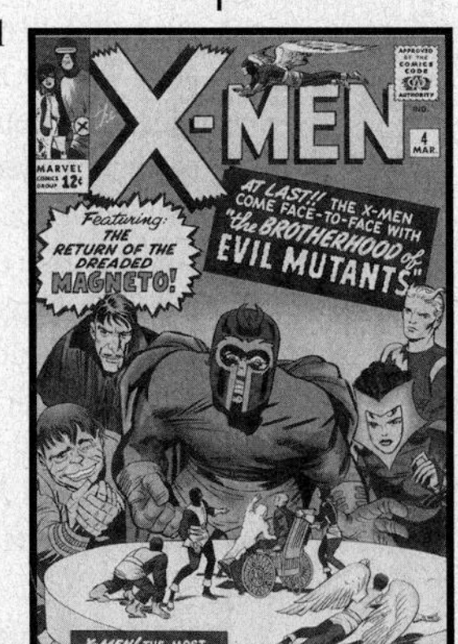

X-Men #4 is perfect for those who Want a Maximum payoff.

My concern is how long can books increase in value by 10% month over month? My guess is that as long as the stimulus money is flowing from our government, the increases will continue. The increases in value will bring even more investors and speculators into the hobby which will further drive the prices up. Basically, all major keys from the Golden, Silver, Bronze and Copper Age of comics are being snapped up in the hopes that in 6 months or 1 year, the investor can double their money. And in many cases, they can! In addition, Disney is continuing to produce quality content for the small screen. The first season of *WandaVision* has been a huge success. *The Falcon and the Winter Soldier* is next, followed by *Black Widow* and then *Loki*. And then there are four more Marvel movies scheduled for the big screen in 2021. All of this content coming out of Disney/Marvel studios is providing massive upticks in prices achieved for speculators, investors and collectors looking to acquire first appearances of characters referenced in these movies / TV shows.

In 2021, since most of the focus in comics is on the Marvel keys, it might be prudent for a long term investor / collector to pick up Silver and Bronze Age DC keys while they are still priced reasonably. Some good books to pick up include *Batman* #181 (first Poison Ivy), *Detective Comics* #359 (first Batgirl), *Batman* #232 (first Ra's al Ghul), *Brave and the Bold* #28 (first Justice League of America), *Strange Adventures* #205 (first Deadman), *Detective Comics* #400 (first Man-Bat), *Jimmy Olsen* #134 (first Darkseid), *House of Secrets* #92 (first Swamp Thing), *New Teen Titans* #2 (first Deathstroke), *Superboy* #68 (first Bizarro), *Showcase* #22 (first appearance of Hal Jordan) and *All Star Comics* #58 (first Power Girl). Although some of these characters have already appeared in film, there is the potential for them to be rebooted in the coming years. It will take some patience for collectors, but there could be a big payday down the road. The other opportunity for investors is to keep a close eye on where the Marvel Universe is heading and pick up keys that haven't moved up in price yet. Books like *Avengers* #186 (First Chthon) fit the bill here. Later on in the year, this book could double or triple in price before the Doctor Strange movie arrives. All in all, most any Marvel and DC key will move up in price if you are a bit patient in your outlook.

Here are some specific highlights (that now look reasonably priced) that we had on QualityComix.com in 2020:

3-D Tales From the Crypt of Terror #2 CGC VF 8.0 $3,500
Amazing Fantasy #15 CGC GD 2.0 $13,000
Amazing Spider-Man #14 CGC VF- 7.5 $3,600
Amazing Spider-Man #41 CGC VF/NM 9.0 $1,700
Avengers #1 CGC VF- 7.5 $10,700
Crime Patrol #15 CGC VF/NM 9.0 $9,000
Daredevil #1 CGC NM 9.4 $33,000
Detective Comics #359 CBCS VF/NM 9.0 $3,600
Fantastic Four #1 CGC GD 2.0 $10,000
Fantastic Four #48 CGC FN 6.0 $1,950
Fantastic Four #48 CGC NM+ 9.6 $19,500
House of Secrets #92 CGC VF+ 8.5 Signature Series by Wein and Wrightson $3,500
Incredible Hulk #1 CGC Fair 1.0 $5,000
Lawbreakers Suspense Stories #11 CGC FN+ 6.5 $4,400
Mad #1 CGC VF/NM 9.0 $6,250
Showcase #22 CBCS VG 4.0 $3,300
Tales of Suspense #39 CGC FN- 5.5 Signature Series by Stan Lee $12,500
Tales of Suspense #52 CGC VF- 7.5 $2,100
Tales of Suspense #57 CGC VF 8.0 $2,000
Tales of Suspense #59 CGC NM 9.4 $2,350
Weird Mysteries #5 GD 2.0 $3,000
Weird Tales of the Future #8 GD/VG 3.0 $1,200
X-Men #1 CGC VG- 3.5 $7,700
X-Men #3 CGC VF+ 8.5 $3,500
X-Men #4 CGC FN- 5.5 $3,300
X-Men #12 CGC VF/NM 9.0 $4,000
X-Men #16 CGC NM 9.4 $1,700

Overall, the outlook for the comic market is very bright. Unless the economy has another major downturn, I expect that demand will continue to outstrip supply for the foreseeable future. Stay healthy and be kind to each other!

Steve Mortensen
Miracle Comics

COVID-19 changed what was 2020. With so much grim news, many people flocked to the collectibles market to pick up their spirits and to invest in tangible assets. We saw record-breaking prices in all genres of collecting. From my view, 2020 may have been the best year ever for the back issue comic market. With shelter-in-place, collectors found joy following auctions and building up their collections. At Miracle Comics, I saw how the demand for high-grade comics from the Bronze Age to Modern surged. In years past, it was hard to sell a graded 9.4 or a graded 9.6 Copper Age back issue -- collectors only wanted graded 9.8s. Then in 2020, more collectors came into the market and the demand for all high grades was lifted. It was truly a banner year in collecting, despite the tragedies of the virus.

Sales of Golden Age comics were solid and grew exponentially in 2020. I saw especially high prices for Timely Comics, as well as many WWII covers from all publishers during the 1940s. In auction, the *Guide* value is the starting point, but it is a race until the end of the auction to see who wins. These comics usually hit multiples of *Guide* in all conditions. Even the obscure titles are doing extraordinarily well. As an example, *Air Ace* v3 #7 (1947) had a *Guide* value of $54 in Fine condition but it sold in 2020 for $432 in Fine condition (ungraded) at auction. It has a great Bob Powell cover and is ultra-rare. The mere fact that a copy surfaced is reason enough to command a high price. This is an example of the demand in the low-mid grade Golden Age market. At prices around $300-500 for an average super-hero book, they are still attainable for collectors willing to pay beyond *Guide*. Early *Captain America* titles in low grade are fetching a premium (above $500). *USA Comics* #7 sold as coverless for more than the value of a Good condition copy. *Wonderworld Comics* #7, which Gerber rates as "scarce," commanded triple the Good value in *Guide* in Poor condition (CGC 0.5). On one occasion, I was bidding on a Fine copy of *Fantastic Worlds* #7. The *Guide* value was $72, but I really wanted this book and the demand was high, so I decided to put in a bid at five times *Guide*. I lost. This shows what a stretch collectors were willing to take in 2020.

Also interesting in 2020 was the greater demand for restored comics from the Golden Age. Golden Age superhero books that have been restored commanded non-restored *Guide* values. It used to be that restored books would sell for a fraction of *Guide*. For many comics, the fact that they exist at all brings value to them. WWII covers show great demand in all levels of restored grades.

The Federal Reserve announced during the summer of 2020 that they would allow for some level of inflation as a way of stimulating the economy. This could be one reason for the large jump in prices. Other factors include scarcity, high demand and a culture with some abundance of comic book spending money, since many of the stores were shut down for some period of time due to COVID-19.

I suggest to the collector community that we officially break up the many years of classification of Modern Age comics into two classifications: Millennial Age (1992-2002) and Modern Age (2003-present). The Golden Age ran for about 20 years (1939-1959); the Silver Age about 12 years (1959-1971); the Bronze Age lasted approximately 12 years (1971-1982); the Copper Age ran for about 10 years (1982-1992). The current "Modern Age" classification has been running for 28 years. There are some significant runs of comics during the Millennial Age including Valiant titles, the 1st appearances of Deadpool, and many Jim Lee titles including *X-Men* and the Death of Superman. The term Millennial age gives a nod to the change in millennia as well as the change in demographic of people born during this era -- many of whom are now purchasing back their collectibles from this time. Millennial also represents a time when a large amount of product was entering the marketplace – print runs were extremely high in many cases. The modern age would then officially begin in 2003, with the dawn of *The Walking Dead*. Print runs decreased at this time with the digital age. Other significant modern titles of this era would include: *Saga*, *Ultimate Fallout* #4 (1st Miles Morales), *Ultimate Comics Spider-Man*, *Batman* Hush and *Star Wars: The Clone Wars* #1, with partial thanks to the ever-growing popularity of *The Mandalorian*.

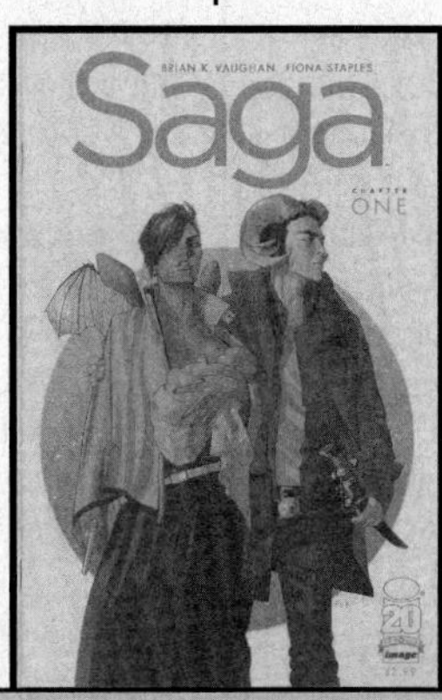

***Saga* #1 would be a prominent part of a re-imagined Modern Age of (2003-present).**

Marc Nathan
Cards, Comics, and Collectibles/ Baltimore Comic-Con

Retailing: I have been in our spacious Reisterstown, Maryland store for three years now, and even with the pandemic, it is a destination for those wanting to buy comics and pop culture-related items. At the same time, the whole year wasn't really a year for us. It was pieces of a year because of the lockdown. With that said, though, I'm a firm believer that retailers who didn't invest in back issues for the last decade and are not buying collections when given the chance must be regretting their decisions now – especially with the incredible increase in eBay traffic due to consumers' limited exposure to comics stores because of their fear of catching COVID-19.

Conventions: We attended a handful of conventions in January and February, but none after that. Some examples are the ones we did in Frederick, Maryland early in the year, following that up with one in Roanoke, Virginia. I remember that books sold okay at both of those shows, but then the lockdown happened and we shifted to selling online.

Online and In-Store Sales: Selling online works fine – even today – but during the lockdown, that was the only outlet we had at the time because of the stay-at-home order. Once we opened up casually at the beginning of spring of 2020, things did sell. Jumping ahead to right now selling in the holiday season we are finding that any good book is selling immediately. As we get new books with first appearances or fan appeal, they sell right away. Important back issues are even more important today. I'm talking about right now. Back issues are selling out without us attending shows; I can't keep them in the store. As a market report for *The Overstreet Comic Book Price Guide*, I want to say that it is a very healthy time for comic book sales – just not real life.

As far as buying books, I am purchasing just a little bit. I bought a collection that had a handful of key issues. I bought a collection of 15 comics, and except for an *X-Men* #5, they are all gone. I sold them within a week. They are selling. They were very good books mind you, but I have had very good books sit around for a long time. Not now. I suspect once people feel more comfortable coming to the store, they will bring their collections to sell because people have had to stay home and look through their collections and clean up their homes. At the same time, anything collectible that has always been collectible – be they comics or sports cards – are super-hot right now.

This year has been about quickly learning how to sell comics and collectibles during the time of plague. Thankfully, we and our customers have survived to see the coming of a vaccine . . . and the hope that 2021 will bring.

Josh Nathanson, Douglas Gillock & Rick Hirsch
ComicLink

ComicLink is proud to be celebrating its 25th Anniversary this year. It was in 1996 that we started the first internet browser-based consignment firm focusing on comic books and related artwork. Through our high profile online auctions and The Comic Book Exchange® we've facilitated hundreds of thousands of sales of just about every valuable vintage comic book that exists, many in a multitude of conditions. Despite the many challenges of 2020, the market for vintage comic books and related artwork grew at an unprecedented rate, and prices have actually increased across the board. Our auctions resulted in many hundreds of record prices for many of the most collected comic books in the hobby, and this was true across all eras and most genres. It was also true of the millions of dollars worth of original artwork sold on ComicLink.com in 2020, and we saw similar growth for other categories of collectibles on our CertifiedLink.com site, which focuses on areas like certified video games, trading cards (sports and non-sports), coins and memorabilia.

Note that all sample sales are CGC graded unless indicated. Many more results can be found on ComicLink.com.

Golden Age (1933-1955): The Golden Age market remained extremely healthy throughout 2020, with many of the trends from previous years continuing. The long-term outlook looks positive as younger collectors in their 20s and 30s are discovering the joys of the era from L.B. Cole, to Baker to Schomburg. Movies and TV have kept Superman and Batman relevant, while fellow Golden Age legends Wonder Woman, Captain America, Aquaman and Captain Marvel ('Shazam') have enjoyed an unprecedented level of global exposure through their films, and Golden Age Green Lantern Alan Scott will be at the center of a new HBO Max series. Drivers include first appearance and origin issues, early appearances, classic covers, World War II themes, lurid Pre-Code Horror/Crime/Sci Fi covers and 'Good Girl' art.

2020 Golden Age sales on ComicLink included:

Action Comics #2 5.0 $39,222, #5 7.0 $15,250 and #12 4.0 $24,000

All Star Comics #8 7.5 $150,000, 6.0 $85,000 and 5.0 CVA $51,000

All Winners Comics #1 8.0 $15,101 and #6 8.0 San Francisco Pedigree $14,950

All-American Comics #16 4.0 $80,750

Amazing-Man Comics #22 2.0 $22,750

Batman #1 3.0 $133,550 and #49 9.6 NM+ $48,000

Black Cat Mystery #50 8.5 $20,727

Captain America Comics #1 5.5 $182,501 & 6.0 $225,000, #2 6.0 $15,237, #3 5.0 $32,003 and 4.0 $26,750, #46 7.5 $25,000 and #74 7.0 $18,341

Captain Marvel Adventures #1 2.5 $14,250

Chamber of Chills #23 9.2 Northford Pedigree $31,000

Crime SuspenStories #22 9.0 $23,583 and 8.5 $19,250

Detective Comics #29 3.5 Conserved $22,500, #38 2.5 $27,775, #69 5.5 $17,703 and #73 7.5 CVA $21,300

Marvel Comics #1 6.0 $280,500

Mask Comics #2 4.0 $16,250

Phantom Lady #16 9.4 Mile High Pedigree $16,277

Sub-Mariner Comics #1 8.0 $55,333

Superman #5 9.6 $60,001, #7 9.2 $16,530, #14 9.0 CVA $31,000, #23 9.4 $17,250, #24 9.2 $27,250, #40 9.8 $14,805 and #76 9.4 $27,805

Wonder Woman #1 6.5 CVA $96,513

World's Best Comics #1 7.5 $15,540

Silver Age (1956-1969): The Silver Age continues to be one of the most popular segments of the hobby, with the super-hero genre dominating. A never-ending flood of movies and shows over the past two decades have exposed most of the heroes of the Silver Age to untold millions of fans across the globe, creating a solid long-term market for the era that gave birth to now iconic characters like Spider-Man, the Hulk, the Fantastic Four, the Avengers and the X-Men. *Amazing Fantasy* #15 remains the "Holy Grail" of the era and the *Amazing Spider-Man* title is the most popular run for collectors. All mainline Marvel titles are popular, however, with DC coming in second. Anticipation for seeing such fan-favorites as the Silver Surfer, Doctor Doom and Sub-Mariner as part of the MCU has driven demand for the key Silver Age appearances of these characters through the stratosphere.

2020 Silver Age sales on ComicLink included:

Amazing Fantasy #15 7.5 CVA $152,500

Amazing Spider-Man #1 6.0 $18,003, #3 9.8 $115,000, #11 9.2 $23,161, #14 9.6 $32,000 and 9.4 $18,750, #19 9.8 $16,750, #21 9.8 $15,500, #28 9.4 $21,801, Annual #1 9.8 $60,500 and 9.0 $14,361

Avengers #2 9.8 $29,390

Batman #171 9.6 $41,000

Brave and the Bold #54 9.8 $52,500

Detective Comics #267 9.4 $14,907

Fantastic Four #1 6.5 $38,000, #4 8.5SS (Stan Lee) $14,500, #5 7.5 $15,500, #26 9.8 $20,000, #48 9.8 $49,000, Annual #1 9.8 $31,277 and #6 9.8 $19,250

Hawkman #4 9.8 $34,505

Incredible Hulk #1 8.5 $122,001, 7.0 $46,000 and 5.0SS (Stan Lee) $20,750, #3 9.6 $22,359, #4 9.6 $22,898, #5 9.4 $22,250 and #6 9.6 $19,510

Journey Into Mystery #83 8.0 $36,887 and 6.5 $15,275, #85 9.6 $53,300, #89 $29,650 and #112 9.8 $20,249

Justice League of America #1 8.0 $14,252

My Greatest Adventure #80 9.6 $26,105

Showcase #19 9.8 $21,361 and #23 9.4 $31,000

Tales of Suspense #42 9.8 $21,408

Tales to Astonish #13 9.2 $33,000

X-Men #1 8.5 $52,500

Bronze Age (1970-1979): We have now passed the 50th Anniversary of the dawn of the Bronze Age, an era that saw the evolution of comic books away from the innocence of the Silver Age, operating as a bridge to the Modern Era. This year saw many record prices achieved for Bronze Age keys sold on ComicLink

This market is driven primarily by first appearances, and major shifts in direction for established characters and classic storylines.

2020 Bronze Age sales on ComicLink included:

Amazing Spider-Man #101 9.6 $5,500

Detective Comics #411 9.8 $20.250

Hero For Hire #1 9.8 $25,800

Incredible Hulk #180 9.8 $14,250 and #181 9.6 $27,577

Marvel Premiere #1 9.8 $6,125

Marvel Spotlight #5 9.6 $22,012

Superman #233 9.8 $14,950

Tomb of Dracula #10 9.8 $14,250
Werewolf By Night #1 9.8 $11,750
X-Men #94 9.8 SS (Stan Lee) $20,250 and 9.8 $17,250

Modern Age (1980-Present): The Modern Age covers the past 40 years during which approximately 150,000 different comic books have been published. Most of these have been carefully saved by collectors, keeping values low. However, there are many thousands of books that have value from this era, with a handful generating the types of prices typically associated with Golden Age or Silver Age keys. Driving this market are first appearances of break-out characters combined with factors like small print runs, popular artists, variant covers, error editions and grading anomalies. Some of these books have been increasing at a fast clip, and will likely be significantly higher in price when this market report is published.

2020 Modern Age sales on ComicLink included:
Albedo #2 9.8 $22,750 and 9.4 $9,850
Amazing Spider-Man #300 9.9 $25,250
Gobbledygook #1 8.5SS (Eastman) $25,002
Marvel Super Heroes: Secret Wars #8 10.0 $32,225
Teenage Mutant Ninja Turtles #1 6.5 $11,350
Ultimate Fallout #4 Variant 9.6 $3,100
Venom: Lethal Protector #1 9.8 CVA Black Cover Error Edition $4,900

If you have valuable comic books or related original artwork to sell, or other valuable collectibles, we invite you to visit ComicLink.com as well as CertifiedLink.com, view our auction schedules, and give us a call at (617) 517-0062. We'll work with you to optimize the value of your collection! We can help with everything including evaluating your collection for certification, processing, pricing, marketing and selling your material. We do all this work, and offer upfront cash advances, for a minimal commission rate.

Tom Nelson
Top Notch Comics

Greetings to everyone again here at the end of 2020. I'm not going to go over the obvious economic challenges during 2020 so I will move in quickly on my market report. The beginning of the year was a continuation of the slowdown that occurred in 2019, things started to pick up around May 2020 and by June going forward the second half of the year we saw an increased demand for almost all eras of books, with the Modern era gaining the most attraction with newly found keys and characters throughout the past 40 years. There has also been a strong movement with CGC graded newsstand editions of popular titles. During the Copper era of the 1980s most books are more available in newsstand 9.8 grade, but as you go through the 1990s and up until the 2013 era when they ended, scarcity drives demand. This will be an interesting market to follow as there likely will be many swings higher and lower as books work their way from dealer inventories into the hands of collectors. Some of the other major market character movers have been *X-Men* and *Fantastic Four* of the Silver Age, *Spawn* and *Star Wars* in the Modern Age with many of the previous commons now with spikes of first appearances and collectible variant covers.

I will give my top ten again by era this year, 1970-2009 broken up into four eras, by decade. They will include comics with normal distribution to the United States. That means I'm excluding price variants, errors, recalled, prepacks, convention exclusive, and mail aways. Tracking sales on some of those books can be difficult due to scarcity, and they do not make up the meat and potatoes of comic collecting.

Here is the list with 1970-1979 listing at 9.2 value:
#1 *Incredible Hulk* #181 $7,500
#2 *Scooby Doo* #1 $6,000
#3 *Cerebus* #1 $5,000
#4 *House of Secrets* #92 $4,750
#5 *Marvel Spotlight* #5 $4,500
#6 *Giant-Size X-Men* #1 $4,500
#7 *Werewolf By Night* #32 $3,000
#8 *Amazing Spider-Man* #129 $2,500
#9 *Tomb of Dracula* #10 $2,200
#10 *Green Lantern* #76 $2,000

The list is similar to last years except there were price increases for most of the books. *Hulk* #181 with the first appearance of Wolverine is still at the top of the charts. The next two books are scarce in 9.2 and higher grade which adds the the value, #2 *Scooby Doo* #1 and *Cerebus* #1. The first DC book on the list is the first appearance of Swamp Thing in *House of Secrets* #92. *Marvel Spotlight* #5 the first appearance of Ghost Rider is in fifth. First appearance of the New X-Men in *Giant-Size X-Men* #1 is in 6th. *Werewolf by Night* #32 with the first Moon Knight is in 7th. The ever popular Punisher *Amazing Spider-Man* #129 is in 8th. *Tomb of Dracula* #10 with the first Blade has moved into 9th place. The final top ten is *Green Lantern* #76 which is the first Neal Adams Green Arrow series. Some books that are close to making the top ten are *Hulk* #180, *Hero for Hire* #1, *X-Men* #94, *Amazing Spider-Man* #101 and *Batman* #227.

Here is the list with 1980-1989 listing at 9.2 value:
#1 *Teenage Mutant Ninja Turtles* #1 $15,000
#2 *Albedo* #2 $8,000
#3 *Teenage Mutant Ninja Turtles* #1 2nd print $3,500
#4 *Teenage Mutant Ninja Turtles* #1 3rd print $1,000
#5 *Raphael* #1 $1,000
#6 *Crow* #1 $800
#7 *Amazing Spider-Man* #300 $750
#8 *Primer* #2 $500
#9 *Teenage Mutant Ninja Turtles* #2 $500
#10 *Archie's Girls, Betty and Veronica* #320 $500

The list has sure changed this past year from the 1980s, as the dominating series is *Teenage Mutant Ninja Turtles* with five of the top ten, and *Raphael* is a Turtles comic also. *Albedo* #2 is a very strong independent with a low print run, the first Usagi Yojimbo. #6 is *Crow* #1 being the first edition of his series. A dominating book all year from Marvel at #7, the first Venom in *Amazing Spider-Man* #300 and has seen price increases in all grades. *Primer* #2 is the first Grendel and is in 8th position. *Betty and Veronica* is holding the final spot this year at #10. Some books knocking on the door of the top ten are *Star Wars* #42, *Caliber Presents* #1, *Swamp Thing* #37, *Amazing Spider-Man* #238, *Tick Special* #1 and *G.I. Joe* #21.

Here is the list with 1990-1999 listing at 9.2 value:

#1 *Bone* #1 $2500
#2 *Batman Adventures* #12 $600
#3 *Goon* #1 $500
#4 *Marvel Collectible Classics* #1 $500
#5 *Spawn* #1 Black and White $450
#6 *Spider-Man* #1 Platinum $400
#7 *Malibu Sun* #13 $400
#8 *New Mutants* #98 $350
#9 *Batman Beyond* #1 $300
#10 *Evil Ernie* #1 $300

First place again this year is *Bone* #1. Second place goes to a DC character with the first Harley Quinn in *Batman Adventures* #12. Third this year is *Goon* #1, fourth is *Marvel Collectible Classics* #1 which is a chrome version of *Amazing Spider-Man* #300. Spawn is a hot property and this keeps *Spawn* #1 Black and White edition at #5. The one per store *Spider-Man* #1 Platinum edition is at #6. #7 *Malibu Sun* #13 is a Spawn preview comic book. The popular first appearance of Deadpool with *New Mutants* #98. We have a new addition this year with *Batman Beyond* #1 in 9th place. The final spot goes to *Evil Ernie* #1 which also has the first Lady Death. Some books on the edge of the top ten are *Tank Girl* #1, *Hulk* #377 3rd print, *Strangers in Paradise* #1, and *Bone* #2.

Here is the list with 2000-2009 listing at 9.2 value:

#1 *Walking Dead* #1 $1000
#2 *Star Wars: The Clone Wars* #1 $750
#3 *NYX* #3 $400
#4 *Invincible* #1 $400
#5 *Walking Dead* #2 $350
#6 *Y the Last Man* #1 $250
#7 *Adam: The Legend of the Blue Marvel* #1 $225
#8 *Star Wars: Knights of the Old Republic* #9 $200
#9 *Walking Dead* #19 $200
#10 *Amazing Fantasy* (2006) #15 $200

There are also a lot of first appearances and hot books on the move from the past twenty years, some of them are *Ultimate Fallout* #4 first Miles Morales, *Edge of Spider-Verse* #2 first Spider-Gwen, *Vengeance* #1 America Chavez, *Detective* #880 Joker cover, *Rick and Morty* #1, *Teen Titans* #12 Batman Who Laughs, *Venom* #3 first Knull, *The Boys* #1, *Chew* #1, *Spider-Man Noir* #1, *Young Avengers* #1, *Black Panther* #2 first Shuri, *Spawn* #174 1st Gunslinger Spawn.

My conclusion this year is that sales have been up across most level of keys from the Golden Age through Modern Age, there are many new found keys in the Modern Age and Newsstand editions have been on the move with many popular titles.

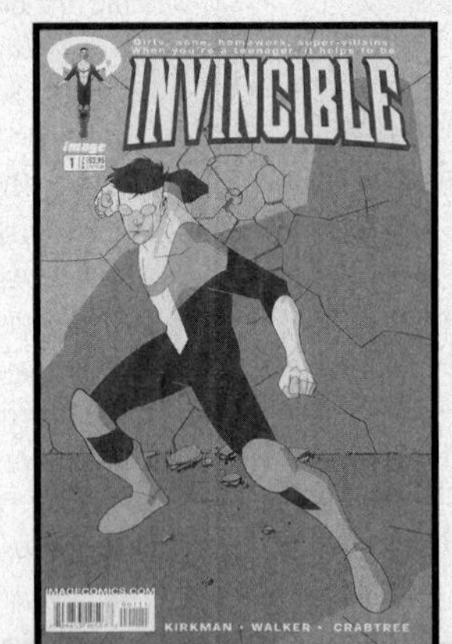

***Invincible** #1 benefitted from a solid TV premiere season.*

Jamie Newbold
Southern California Comics

Yuck. Need I say more? Although, we'd seen record sales numbers in a short period of time, the likes of which we usually worked harder for at SDCC. That Con religiously produced equitable profits against the seven 14-hour days in a row. 'Course, cons seem like a thing of the past so dealers like me had to engage back-up plans against the inevitable ruination of retail outlets.

Our switch was flipped. We expected lockdown and that happened. Then, we saw an enormous eBay/web site ramp-up in sales. Packages had to be mailed when no one really wanted to approach any post office. Our postal carrier became more amicable to daily pick-ups at our store. We had to be present to make those package exchanges which brought me and a token number of employees back to business. Money rolled in and inventory flew out. That was the upside. The downside was the lack of inventory coming in. We'd stalled our Diamond account and dealt with the Lunar Distribution surprise, but we wanted, no, needed back issues. That ever-present market stalled as well. Sellers were reluctant to bring their collections to us, and we were dutifully wary of going to them. This dilemma shrank our back-issue supply which was worrisome because those comics are what we staked our reputation on.

Three local comic book stores closed, probably because of COVID. Maybe they wanted out and needed the right trigger. COVID certainly provided the fear factor to make that tough decision. The rest of us shop-owners tinkered around with the idea of drive-up buyers and even delivery. We skipped the latter as impractical. We succeeded with customer pick-up, especially our regular customers. All went well.

San Diego finally gave us the go-ahead to open up for walk-in buyers. People were counted until we reached a new, lower-than-usual capacity. People wore masks and even the mask-less die-hards were "urged" into compliance with maybe one caving in after I gave him the 'felony cop stare.' Everybody had to disinfect their hands at the door. The capacity was ordered down to 25% of the norm. We had no norm so we guesstimated until someone made the call to hold a line at the door. There was little grief when we provided outdoor shade, chairs and free stuff. We did have to stop two groups of two from entrance. The fallout was anger, frustration and choice obscenities from those pairs of adoring fans. I knew the first pair and I thought they overreacted when we balked at letting them inside. The second pair flat-out made me angry, especially when I went outside to balance the numbers so we had room for them. They were the last customers to almost take the confrontation to a fight.

Picture this: passive employee Caitlin and I hurling challenges at a male/female couple corrupted by lost emotional control. We stood our ground surrounded by comic book people caught up in an abrupt battle of mouths. Our side won as our unworthy opponents fled in a truck with one last, drive-by insult. Caitlin adopted a more vocal, aggressive attitude toward rotten customers.

I'm used to 'key' buyers who scout for the ever-popular comics. The atrocious pressure from the pandemic seemed to encourage panic-buying, instead of the evaporation of business. We got hammered by speculators we normally would have rebuffed for being cheap and indecisive. Not this year. Instead of panic-selling we met the demands of pandemic-buyers. Every key from the Sixties to the present was fair game among multiple buyers who tried to beat out the 'other guy.'

We watched our inventory dwindle in copies. We studied price increases and watched stuff we owned in 9.6 and 9.4 crawl past 9.8 prices. Copies of books from a 2017 warehouse find that didn't qualify by grade and value for CGC, suddenly did.

I asked a few of the buyers about their motivations. Most of them wanted some 'feel good' time and got that from owning the right comics. Others acted as though the end of the world as we knew it was at hand. Conventions were absent for the most part. Cities that permitted gatherings for such shows made sure the size and low-attendance created almost pointless shows. My buyers wanted their comics and bought them as the runner-up opportunity to absent shows.

We energized our Diamond account when we figured we'd get support from our customers. We assumed we'd lose a few regulars, even subscribers, and we did. Conversely, we enjoyed an increase from new customers. Some came from the shut-down stores while others jumped ship from existing stores. The back-issue market never slowed down and was only interrupted by COVID. An outgoing stream of sold back-issues dried up some of our stock once our doors opened to walk-ins. We spent the second half of 2020 purchasing the same stuff that went out the door the weeks before. The beast must be fed constantly.

The fall school semester was a benchmark for the slight dulling of business. That's always the way, but school as we knew it didn't impact students as in the past. Many college-age men and women remained in town since campuses were restricted or still closed. Still, business slowed as though comic book buyers stop distilling comic book spending from every other bill or debt. We returned to a semblance of normalcy.

Our hottest sellers were a cornucopia of Marvel Silver and Bronze keys. Rather than list the numerous sales you can visit socalcomics.com for the highlights. The prices met or exceeded GPA numbers, so I'm comfortable with that site's numbers. Really some of that stuff, *Hulk* #181s, *ASM* #129s, *ASM* #1s and the like were pushing boundaries, according to friends and speculators alike. Maybe before COVID, but I saw price chaos all spring and summer. Things got so bad, tried and trusted dealers I'd relied on in the past to deal keys to me for slight discounts had resisted, thanks to 2020. They got their sales numbers and didn't need my money. Truly, I behaved no differently.

As November rains upon us our store has become an enclave for comic fans who were starved for attention and human conversation during the first lockdown and all the restrictive movement since. San Diego County teeters on the precipice of another lockdown. If we re-enter the more dreadful 'Purple' tier, retail outlets like So Cal Comics faces forcibly reduced shopper 'body-counts' and that could kill us. Sales weren't the only income in the spring/summer of 2020. We were granted the Fed's PPP money. The grant kept five of my employees employed and took care of several months of rent and utilities. Any bailout package the government downloads to small businesses like mine, again, will keep us afloat. I don't believe for a minute we will thrive without that second helping. Reduced walk-in traffic would be a blow that could counter all the previous success.

Department of Mundane Matters: DC splits from Diamond's distribution arm during COVID. Diamond attempts to upgrade its customer service. The normally two to three week wait for replacement copies is accelerated to a reduced waiting time. We get roughly three different shipping dates per week, rather than the all-fits-in-one week's delivery. There's additional tracking paperwork on our behalf, but I appreciate the gesture. Lunar Distribution's dates are all over the map. Friday becomes Monday, or even Thursday. Who ever heard of new comics coming in the day before they're supposed to? Outrageous! We await the future turmoil that might come from Lunar Distribution now that the company has taken on the all of DC's East Coast customers. I have yet to actually speak to a Lunar representative.

The Variant Craze: Sells copies but leak value like sieves. *Gwenpool* #1, so hot two years ago stalls to the level of obsolescence. The ultimate ratio variants are too few to track in 9.8 for repetitive worth. On the other hand, when Marvel sneezed and let Miles Morales' name blow through the Kleenex, *Ultimate Fallout* #4 exploded. The variants are as hot as fire can be. This one diverse character seems destined to be played in live action. The video games are already recording some acclaim. I wish my *Star Wars* 2015 #1 variants had remained sky-high. So does the speculator world.

I released a new book: *In the Company of Cops*, over the summer. COVID lockdown left me with a load of dead-time to scribe a sequel. As of December, San Diego looks to be also headed towards a sequel to the March lockdown. Our red tier has returned to the ungainly purple and businesses are warned to reduce to 25% capacity, work solely outside again, or shut the doors. The upside, COVID means more time to work on my second cop book. The downside is the potential for my employees to suffer an outrageous loss of work for the second time. Lunar and Diamond accounts would have to be put on hold again which will throw our weekly sales into chaos, or kill us altogether. You readers will have the opportunity to learn if we recovered or not when this *OPG* goes up for sale at the 2021 SDCCon. That is, if there's a 2021 Con.

Karen O'Brien
Comics Journalist

What a year! As a comics journalist and lifelong collector, I've witnessed collectors and their local comics shops facing unprecedented challenges courtesy of the COVID-19 pandemic. Lockdowns and stay-at-home orders closed businesses and grounded collectors. Printers also halted the production of comics, forcing the rescheduling of all new releases to summer after restrictions eased.

Shops and collectors responded to the situation by looking inward. Shop owners organized back issue bins, re-evaluated and enhanced their social media presence, and turned to online selling/auction venues to generate income. Collectors embarked on the productive journey of organizing long-neglected collections, causing a demand spike for archival supplies including comic bags, boards, and boxes. As collectors discovered holes in their collections while still deprived of new releases, comics budgets were refocused on obtaining back issues, upgrading to higher-condition books, and employing collection management apps and software.

Although restrictions were eventually eased, allowing shops to reopen, many communities still limited or prohibited in-store shopping. Owners then navigated the challenges of providing comics to pull-list veterans and new customers alike via curbside pickup and mail-order options. And because comics conventions large and small were canceled, many shop owners were also dealing with the loss of typically strong convention sales. And while the upending of the economy led some collectors to seek to liquidate portions of their collections, beleaguered shop owners were hesitant to make offers.

The pandemic has also altered how collectors obtain comics, especially back issues. I'm working on a complete run of a Modern comic and a long run of a Bronze Age comic. These projects give me a fun excuse to spend hours at conventions rooting through back-issue bins. And when traveling, I also budget time to stop in at the local comics shop to sift through its bins. I had picked up a few issues online here and there before the pandemic, but I've never been in a hurry to complete these "wish list" projects, so studying eBay auctions was never a big priority. After about four weeks in lockdown, however, I had a whole list of "saved searches" on eBay and a couple of packages arriving each week. I patronized the eBay stores of brick-and-mortar businesses whenever I could and encouraged others to do the same. I also utilized well-known auction houses for some of the slabbed comics on my wish list. Those packages became my lifeline to the hobby—a function that my local comics shop and conventions usually served—and even though the "thrill of the hunt" was executed with a computer screen rather than working my way through a long box, the pandemic has definitely taught me to appreciate the ability to participate in this hobby through all its diverse avenues.

My observations on the comics marketplace for 2020: Typical collecting advice is to buy the best-condition copy you can afford and don't pass it up when you stumble across it. I think this holds true for most comics in most buying situations, but if you're collecting slabbed books, I'd advise you to do some homework and some online comparison shopping before you buy. The high desirability of CGC and CBCS books in high grades means premium pricing, and it's worth checking the census data to see just how many other copies exist in a particular grade to determine rarity. If you're collecting key issues (keys), the census data may well reveal that the book isn't all that rare in a given grade, which would affect the timing/urgency of a purchase. I bought a CGC copy of *DC Super-Stars* #17 (origin stories for The Huntress and Green Arrow) but not before passing up a lot of auction offerings over a four-month period in favor of getting a better price. (By mid-December 2020, there were 341 slabbed issues of this book in 9.0 or higher condition, according to the CGC census, and of those 133 were either 9.6 or 9.8, so it's not exactly rare in high-grade condition.) Pandemic-born patience can be a collecting virtue.

I noticed a lot of auction activity regarding 1950s space and Atomic Age titles—everything from *Mystery in Space* to *Fightin' Marines*—so that trend is still going strong.

It seems that the high prices and desirability of Silver Age comics brought out a glut of eBay listings for lesser-grade Silver titles, especially Marvel books. And even those aren't cheap, so some homework before purchase is a good idea here.

Bronze Age comics are (mostly) affordable and hot. While the sword & sorcery and adventure books seem to follow predictable pricing patterns, super-hero keys and horror/supernatural titles are moving the needle. *Star Wars* is evergreen, and I noticed more listings this year for higher numbers in the run.

Modern Age collecting remains centered on first issues, specific writers/artists, and major events. Variant issues are a larger discussion because collectors are either addicted to or indifferent regarding them, and stores either move enough issues to qualify for the most desirable variations or they don't and receive variants they are less likely to move off the shelf.

Regarding smaller publishers, it seems worthwhile to keep an investor's eye on releases from BOOM! Studios. With hits like *Once & Future*, *Something Is Killing the Children*, *Wynd*, and *Seven Secrets*, BOOM! is turning out quality material. Since the departure of the *Star Wars* titles, Dark Horse has cast a wider sci-fi net and scored a hit in 2019 with the Eisner Award-winning *Invisible Kingdom*. As of this writing, Image Comics hasn't announced the return date of *Saga* (which has been off the shelves since issue #54 in July 2018), but its back issues are still highly desirable.

"Collect what you enjoy." A cliché, yes, but it's still solid collecting advice as I ride out the pandemic making brief, protocol-adhering visits to my reopened local comics shop, surfing online for "wish list" comics after doing a little pricing research, and waiting for those lifeline packages to hit the porch.

Terry O'Neill
Terry's Comics/CalComicCon/ Nationwide Comics

This report focuses on convention and mail order aspects of vintage comic collecting. Sales from 2019 to 2020 have been down because all but six comic shows had been cancelled. We were fortunate to have our 2020 CalComicCon in January 2020 before the beginning of the lockdowns on comic conventions. Catalog orders have increased, and internet sales have increased enough to help us pay the bills. Despite the lockdown from COVID we have been able to purchase collections with quality material. As always, we pay higher percentages on Marvel keys and most Golden age and Atomic age comics in order to maintain an excellent selection.

Golden Age (1938-1945): Golden Age sales have been particularly good for all the Super-hero titles. We purchased comics by all publishing houses and many esoteric publishers. Most scarce and high-grade super-heroes sell well at and above *Guide*. We purchased a large group of Golden Age comics that were in bound volumes with many exceedingly rare titles in this group. Because they were in bound volumes, they are mostly trimmed with partial spine loss, pin holes and glue from bindings. The strong points are they have beautiful color and paper quality. Some sales of note: *Amazing Man Comics* #24 GD/VG $723, *Superman* #4 CGG 6.5 $3600, #23 FN $1350, *Planet Comics* #33 FR/GD $350, *Blue Ribbon* #9 FR Bv $855, *Tough Kid Squad* #1 CGC 3.5 $1,000, *Mystery Men* #2 GD $1200, *Batman* #16 VG $1,500, *Walt Disney's Comics & Stories* #2 $1,000, *Marvel Mystery* #26 CGC 8.0 $5,000, and *Champion* #2 CGC 8.0 $828.

Golden Age super-hero issues like **Superman** #4 sold well last year.

Atom Age (1946-1955): We were able to purchase some great Teen Humor comics, especially rare Archie titles like *Suzie*, *Laugh*, *Wilbur* and *Pep*. All EC titles are still selling at or above *Guide,* even the war titles like *Frontline Combat* and *Two-Fisted Tales*. Most pre-Code Horror titles that do not have classic covers or great artwork are slow sellers and may have hit a price plateau. This is still my favorite era to collect, the prices are reasonable, and the scarcity is always a challenge. Some sales of note: *Wild Western* #46 CBCS 8.0 $350, *Mister Mystery* #7 GD/VG $900, *Tales from the Crypt* #22 VG/FN $1080, *Journey into Mystery* #1 CGC 0.5 $4400, *Crime SuspenStories* (#1)#15 GD/VG $1530, *Detective Comics* #118 FN/VF $1500, *Sub-Mariner Comics* #36 VG- $350, *Two-Fisted Tales* #25 VF- $220, and *Frontline Combat* #7 FN+ $130.

Silver Age (1956-1970): Higher grade Super-hero titles are selling quite well through mail order and online. *X-Men* from the Silver Age has made a strong comeback from slow sales. Marvel is still out-selling DC but only slightly better in 2020. All main Silver Age titles are selling well even in the middle and lower grades. Early Silver Age keys are in high demand and are increasingly hard to acquire. Even common non-keys from *Adventure*, *Strange Tales*, *Thor*, *Tales to Astonish*, *Worlds' Finest* and *Tales of Suspense* are selling. Most any 1st appearances and or special story lines are being bought up in hopes for price spikes as interest increases demand. Some sales of note: *Amazing Spider-Man* #31 VF+ $1200, *Avengers* #1 CGC 6.0 $5800, *Fantastic Four* #48 VG+ $1200, *Action Comics* #252 CGC 7.0 $4,050, *Batman* #181 CGC 9.0 $3,750, *Showcase* #4 CBCS 2.5 $8350, *Tales of Suspense* #1 CGC 5.5 $1625, *Justice League of America* #1 FN+ $1620, *X-Men* #2 CGC 9.0 $950, #50 CGC 7.0 $200, and *Silver Surfer* #2 CGC 8.5 $250.

Bronze Age (1971-1985): *Conan the Barbarian* #1 is in high demand and short supply, DC mystery titles like *House of Secrets*, *House of Mystery*, *Witches Tales* and *Tales of the Unexpected* are selling well due to excellent artist and amazing covers. Almost all titles from the early part of this era (15¢-20¢ cover priced) selling exceedingly well after many years of languishing in bargain boxes. It is probably just a short matter of time before later Bronze Age (25¢-40¢ cover priced) comics get hot. A few titles to watch are *Champions*, *Howard the Duck*, *Ghost Rider* and *Warlord*. Some sales of note: *Amazing Spider-Man* #194 CGC 9.4 $250, *Shazam* #1 CGC 9.8 $475, *Iron Man* #55 CGC 4.0 $#420, *Strange Tales* #180 CGC 9.6 $401, *Giant-Size Spider-Man* #2 CGC 9.8, $400, *New Gods* #2 CGC 9.6 $245, and *Werewolf by Night* #32 CGC 9.4 $4125.

Magazines: Magazine titles have been steady sellers all year long, especially 1st issues of long running titles like *Deadly Hands of Kung Fu*, *Vampirella*, *Creepy* and *Savage Sword of Conan*. Most of the black & white Horror monster titles are also selling very well. Marvel titles sell best but Warren titles are also doing well followed by Skywald titles like *Nightmare* and Eerie Pubs titles like *Terror Tales*. Some sales of note: *Vampirella* #1 VG $225, *Savage Tales* #1 FN/

VF $225, *Famous Monsters of Filmland* #1 3.0 $550, *Savage Sword of Conan* #1 CGC 9.0 $160, *Blazing Combat* #1 VG- $135, and *Epic Illustrated* #1 CGC 9.6 $120.

Copper Age & Independents(1981-Now): The amount of money spent on these comics has steadily increased over the years. DC has way more requested material in this era. Batman titles such as *Batman Adventures* and *Harley Quinn*, also X-Men titles are selling well. For Indy titles, *Spawn* is a good seller. Sales of note: *Micronauts* #5 PGX 9.8 $55, *Thor* #337 VF/NM $128, *G.I. Joe* #155 CGC 9.4 $107, *Swamp Thing* #37 VF/NM $150, *Amazing Spider-Man* #262 PGX 9.8 $44, *Incredible Hulk* #271 VF/NM $200, and *X-Men* #129 NM- $150, #266 NM $150.

Graded books: We generally offer third party graded comics as the condition is extremely high and/or the value is over $1000. The exception is when we buy collections that already have a few lower or mid-grade third party graded books in them. We have advised customers over the years to third party encapsulate high grade and high value comics to maximize the selling potential. Keep in mind the grading fee and the time out of your control are unavoidable issues using a grading company.

Internet Sales: Due to the COVID convention cancellations we have needed to offer a much larger part of our inventory online through eBay, chat boards and Facebook groups. We also sell comics from our website by phone or e-mail request as we have always done. With over 60,000 comics in inventory, we have no way to scan everything but when we get a request for scans, we try to accommodate all reasonable requests and continue to offer a 30-day unconditional return on all sales. As we also don't re-price all our inventory every year, we often have quite a few bargains in our older inventory as year after year our old friends go unsold. Most of our entire inventory is at www.terryscomics.com It is updated three or four times a year.

In summary, despite a lack of comic conventions in 2020 there was no shortage of demand for the comic books. As always in uncertain times it is good to own tangible investments. Comic books and comic art are great affordable ways to invest and keep up with inflation. Some collectors still buy comics to read them, but most newer collectors are trying to use them for profit. That being the case, buy the comics you like, so if they don't increase in value at least you will have something you like.

Michael Pavlic
Purple Gorilla Comics

I am one of the fortunate ones. As of this writing (mid December 2020), I still have a business. I am still able to pay my bills on time. I have very loyal customers who supported me during the dark times. I have a landlord who went above and beyond to make sure I had a fighting chance to survive after the first lockdown. Most importantly, I have a real good friend who talked me through my anxieties and fears. As I said, I'm one of the fortunate ones and I thank each and everyone of you who have been there for me. I wouldn't be writing this report without you. I wouldn't be in business without you. And while I'm about to begin the second lockdown, although I can remain open this time at a very reduced capacity, there is hope on the horizon. Perhaps by the time you are reading this, the vaccines will be rolled out and the end of this awful experience will be in sight.

Coming out of the (first!) lockdown, I had no idea what to expect. Would people be comfortable coming back? Did they find online shopping a better option than my brick and mortar store? While the first couple of weeks were rather tentative in terms of sales, all it took was two big collections of some fun '60s and '70s stuff for people to come flocking in. Summer 2020 was much better in terms of sales than Summer 2019! So, what are people buying? Read on!

*For indy titles, **Spawn** is a good seller. (#8 shown)*

Of course "key" books sell. They always do. They are the easiest comics to sell. You need no salesmanship, no skills to sell them. I, however, do not go chasing after them, I will not overpay for a key just to have one in the shop. Comics are more than "keys" and "slabs" and "high grade". It's an art form and there are many great comics to read and collect. And what is a "key" anyway? Anyone want to pay full *Guide* for a 1st Apocalypse now? Or a 1st Bloodshot? No? Unless you got in on the ground floor, speculating on these "keys" might leave a sour taste in your mouth! Buy what you like. If it happens to go up in value, great, if not, well you still have comics that you like. Speculation destroyed the card and comic markets in the 1990s. Do we want to go down that road again?

Anyhoo, here are some specifics on what's happening at PGC. Titles that I almost never have any copies: big War titles (*Sgt. Rock*, *Sgt. Fury*, *Unknown Soldier*, *G.I. Combat*), Westerns (*Kid Colt*, *Two Gun Kid*, *Rawhide Kid*, any Charlton titles), kids comics (Archie, Simpsons, Spongebob, Casper, Richie Rich, Disney, Warner Bros.). Hardly ever see any Romance, from any publisher. For superheroes it's Lobo, TMNT, Deadpool, Venom, Preacher, Black Panther, *Star Wars* (1st series).

Titles that supplies are shrinking at an alarming rate: *Amazing Spider-Man*, *Spider-Man* (1990s), *Spectacular Spider-Man* (below #150), *Spawn*, *Uncanny X-Men* (below #213), *Captain America* (1st Silver Age series), *Thor* (1st series), *Iron Man* (1st series), *Hulk* (1st series), *Batman* (below #400), *Robocop* (Dark Horse), *Terminator*, *Aliens*, *Predator*, *AvP*, *Star Wars* (Dark Horse), *Maxx* and *Harley Quinn*. I sell a ton of *Spider-Man* #1 (McFarlane), *X-Men* #1

(Jim Lee), *Maximum Carnage* and Death/Funeral/Return of Superman. Nice to see the *Guide* is catching up to my prices on these, although I get $30 for *Maximum Carnage* Parts 1 and 14 and $20 each for the rest.

I picked up two collections of Horror comics, a nice run of *House of Mystery*, *House of Secrets* and other DC titles from the mid 1960s to pretty much the end of the titles (and no, there was no *House of Secrets* #92). Also got in some of the Marvel Horror books. They were quickly devoured by my customers, and why not? Some of the best 1970s covers are on these books, hard to beat Neal Adams, Bernie Wrightson, and Mike Kaluta in their prime. Even the Charlton and Gold Key horror books get some love, especially the Ditko Charltons. When I get them, the Warren mags, especially *Vampirella* sell quick.

Although I mentioned them briefly before, I cannot stress enough how hard it is to find kids comics. They sell. We need these kids to keep the industry going into the future. So how about some more kid titles from Marvel and DC and less Batman-nudity comics. I will give props to DC who FINALLY put out cheap reprints of the *Batman Adventures* title. About time.

On the opposite end of the spectrum, Underground comix sell well for me too and are also hard to find. Anything by Robert Crumb moves well about the *Fogel Guide* as do *Freak Brothers*, *Zap*, *American Splendor*, *Weirdo* and any other old school underground. Gotta mention *Ralph Snart*. Although not an Underground (it was approved by the Comics Code!), it had the vibe of one. Way more people read it than I thought possible. They're fun and they sell. Haven't seen an issue of *Eightball* in two years. I respectfully ask Overstreet to add Underground Comix to the *Guide* as *Fogel's Guide* comes out too infrequently to be of any use.

I think the most "pure" comic fans are those that love Archie Digests and *Savage Sword of Conan* (1st series). These folks READ these comics. And re-read them. They don't care about condition, in fact *SSOC* fans prefer them a little beat up so they can get more bang for their buck! They love their comics and really, ain't that what this is all about?

I'd like to thank Ben and Martin from Phoenix Comics in Calgary for the help and support. I cannot properly express my gratitude to my friend Dave from Amazing Fantasy in Red Deer. He was there for me when I needed him the most, even though he was dealing with issues that made mine seem stupid. And thanks Doyle, it's still your fault.

This article is dedicated to Diane and Kelly. You are missed.

Bill Ponseti
Fantastic Worlds Comics

Well...wow...what a year 2020 has been! In many ways it has been equal parts bad and good for the comic industry. We've seen all sorts of changes in the way people collect, speculate, sell, and buy. As it relates to new comics, we took a poll of many retail shop owners asking the question of what effect the pandemic had on their overall new comic sales in 2020. For those in states, like our shop is, where lockdowns forced temporary closures of their shops, most reported that the new comic market did not return to pre-lockdown sales levels. However, back issue sales increased for almost everyone.

It seems to be an almost weekly event that when something is leaked, or announced by a film studio or television streaming service, there is a mad scramble by collectors/speculators to scoop up all the comics that tie into the leak or announcement. We've seen prices on those newly minted key issues, or formally dormant key issues, escalate so rapidly in price, that you could sell on a Monday at an all-time high, and by Friday you found you left a considerable amount of money on the table. It is a fast moving and volatile back issue market these days.

Another trend we noticed in 2020 back issues sales, is that almost everything from the early '70s back to the '30s are in higher demand than we have seen in many years. Not just the keys, although those certainly have seen the largest spike in prices. Any back issue collections from these periods that come into the shop are purchased whenever possible, and eager collectors and speculators are primed to pounce on them.

In previous years, our DC Silver Age inventory would just collect dust, now there is much more interest and sales for those comics. Marvel Silver Age still leads the way by a large margin though. Marvel Bronze Age would be the next best selling back issue category.

Just take a look at how prices have spiked for all of the Marvel Silver and Bronze keys this past year. It's astonishing actually. Who would have pegged *Amazing Spider-Man* #300 as a $5000 book in 9.8 last year? *X-Men* #1 and *Hulk* #1 have seen large gains in 2020 as well. Demand outstrips supply for *Hulk* #1, but we were able to sell the three copies we obtained during the year within days of acquiring them.

Golden Age comics have just gotten so expensive in ALL grades, that it is very difficult to buy any to sell to our customers. The few that did come in with collections sold very quickly. Timelys exist, and have for quite some time, in their own universe. They just keep going up and up and up in value. However, MLJs, Fox, Quality and Nedors have also seen significant price increases. An issue you could buy for $500 in 6.0 a couple of years ago, is now $500 for a 1.8. This is driving many Golden Age collectors we encounter to try and fill those gaps in their collections now before they become unattainable. Interest in Fawcett, Dell, and other Golden Age titles has remained flat for the most part.

The Original Comic Art market is strong as ever. Great material has been coming to market, and each month multiple records are set for panel pages, splashes, and covers. But there are still plenty of areas in this market to dive into and enjoy. It is very much artist and character driven, to the degree that even a popular artist on a character they are not known for will sell for many times less than if it is one they are more closely associated with. McFarlane is a great example: Spider-Man page or cover? Big money. Infinity Inc.? Not so much. My recommendation to you is that if a page from a key issue comes to market, and you can afford to buy it, do it. Those rarely come out, and once purchased will probably be off the market again for a long time.

I'm not sure what 2021 will bring for the market as a whole, and I am hesitant to make any predictions. Many comic shops closed during the pandemic and continue to do so. Some of those brick and mortar shops are shifting to an online model for sales now exclusively. However, I've also seen retailers expanding and opening new locations in their areas. The continuing new comic distribution changes have been a bumpy road, but things seem to be settling in, for now.

If forced to make one prediction, I would say the end of the process flow of leak/announcement to rabid interest in the comics related to the leak/announcement and the subsequent massive price increases are likely to continue.

I'm sure like most of you, I have mixed emotions about this. It is certainly good for the grading companies as the speculative market will submit and hope for the 9.6 – 9.8 results. The variance between that small grade deviation can be ten times as much believe it or not. The auction houses probably love it as their consignments sell for more as speculators rush to cash in on the new prices. But the collector suffers, and it gets harder for small shops to compete for collections that contain some of the new and hot comics.

So, it is with equal measures of excitement and trepidation that I look towards 2021. Keep the hobby fun, and it will always reward you. But what you like and you never lose.

Alex Reece
Reece's Rare Comics

Hello to all in the comic collecting community. 2020 was a vastly different year than any that have come before it, but you don't need me to tell you that! I will try not to focus too much on the COVID-19 crisis, as everyone has lived through it and I'm sure other reports will detail it in depth. I'll begin as always with our convention circuit highlights below, albeit in an abridged form!

As hard as it is to believe, Austin and I did start the year off with our annual trip down to Wizard World New Orleans. While it's generally among our weaker shows, this year it was decent, thanks to a surge in spending on Sunday. We also were able to buy some quality material on the way down and at the show, and thank goodness for that as buying was about to become a whole lot more difficult. Overall, it was a fine show.

Following New Orleans was C2E2 in late February. It had not been held that early in the year for at least a few years, so initially we were concerned about people wanting to come out in the cold weather, and we had to dodge a snowstorm or two to make it to the show. That was also right around the time that COVID-19 was believed to be spreading, so we were worried that might affect attendance as well. Our fears were quickly allayed, as people came to the show and they came to buy, sell, and trade. Austin and I were busy literally nonstop, from a few hours before the show opened each day up until the closing bell. We sold a ton of slabs and raw books, and we left the show with about five short boxes of slabs that we purchased at the show. CGC also provided on-site grading which provided an extra boost to show floor activity. Overall, it was our best C2E2 of all time, and it could not have happened at a better time, as we were merely weeks, if not days, away from the beginning of the COVID-19 pandemic.

By the time we arrived back in Maryland, cases had made landfall in the United States, and where else did they begin but in Seattle, the site of the very next show we were supposed to attend. We talked as a business and a family and made the difficult decision to pull out of Emerald City, and Reed cancelled the event a few days later. Looking back, it seems like it would have been an easy decision, but at the time it was gut wrenching knowing we would be potentially disappointing our customer base out there, but ultimately, we decided to put safety first. The cancellation of ECCC was the beginning of the end as far as trade shows in 2020, as shows kept getting cancelled between 4-8 weeks from their scheduled date. I know this was probably frustrating for some attendees, but from a dealer perspective it was a logistical nightmare. Keeping up with all the different promoters was a task, as certain booths were refunded, certain booths were pushed forward to 2021, and hotels, flights, and rentals all had to be cancelled, sometimes on short notice. I know it created a lot of extra work for a lot of people, and I am grateful for all of those who worked with our company in being as flexible as possible. All in all, we ended up doing only two trade shows for the entire calendar year, when we normally do between 10-12.

With a shortened show season, we needed to change gears on the fly as far as the outlook of our year was concerned. Even though shows were beginning their rolling cancellations, we were pretty convinced from early on that we would not be doing any more shows that year. To that end, we focused all our efforts on acquiring, processing, and listing new material on www.reececomics.com. As almost any national dealer will probably tell you, we had accumulated a vast overstock from our years in the hobby. In attempting to make the best out of a bad situation, I began culling through boxes to pick out books that were good for filling raw runs we were missing on the website, and for sending to CGC. In a normal year we would have been too busy travelling to get through that much material, but because of our increased time in the office we were able to add almost 8,500 new listings to the website in 2020, compared to about 6,000 in 2019, or about a 40% increase. This led to a greater number of customers, both returning and new, that checked back in to see what was newly listed more often.

While there was certainly a lot to be disappointed in with 2020, I do not believe comic sales was one of them. Unfortunately shows still make up a large part of our revenue, so we are going to have a down year overall. That said, the increase in online sales and the explosion of prices on books in general have helped mitigate this to a great degree.

Many industries are staggering under unprecedented stress, so to have a year with two trade shows come anywhere near a fantastic 2019 is amazing. When the pandemic initially began, things slowed to a crawl as people were more conservative with their money, not knowing what the future would hold. Once April hit, however, all bets were off, and we saw an explosion in demand for comic books. This is both from first-hand experience, such as seeing our online sales grow during those months, and watching insane auction results week after week, and colloquially talking to other dealers who have across the board said they saw a boom time during the pandemic months. This ranged from small dealers to national brands. I believe this can be attributed to less money being spent on the usual entertainment of restaurants and retail shopping, a pent-up demand for material since buying at shows was no longer an option, and I think a relaxed monetary policy by the Federal Reserve did not hurt. I know some people were borrowing cheap money to put into comic books in the hopes that they would keep rising and they could quickly make a profit. So far in 2020, they have been right!

It will be interesting to see what the year 2021 holds. With a vaccine on the horizon at the time of my writing, the potential for shows to come back seems relatively high. When that happens, I am sure that online sales will level back off to earlier levels to some extent, but how much they do is beyond the scope of my knowledge. While some buyers will revert to going to in person shows, I am sure that more than one person has made a permanent switch to predominately online buying. While I usually reserve my closing paragraph for my next year's "hot book" picks, this year more than ever I have to stick to our tried-and-true wisdom: buy what you like and buy the best grade that you can afford. I have seen this work for collectors time and time again, so if you follow those two rules you will always be happy with your collection. Thanks as always for all of those who supported us throughout 2020, and I look forward to (hopefully) seeing you in 2021!

The shutdown gave dealers a chance to dig out long lost gems from their inventories.

Stephen & Sharon Ritter WorldWide Comics

What can you say about 2020? The year of COVID will not be forgotten by anyone who lived through it, and like the world markets, it had a unique impact on the comic market. With the shutdown of every comic convention throughout the country from March-on (a few small one-day cons did open before the pandemic's second wave hit) and the loss of millions of jobs world-wide, no one was sure what was going to happen to the comic market. Surprisingly, the market adapted and even exceled. Because people were shut in at home for a good portion of 2020, collectors who still had jobs or income had more time than ever to shop online, so comic companies that had an online presence saw a huge upswing in site sales. This branched to the major comic auctions which saw greater activity to include both buyers and consignors (unfortunately there were many people needing funds and had to tap into their comic collections to make ends meet). Record sales of quality and quantity were made by these auction houses, and material not often seen began to surface regularly.

For us at WorldWide Comics, we survived 2020 unexpectedly well due to those collectors confined to their homes. For those not familiar with us, WorldWide Comics is primarily an internet site selling vintage comics catering to both high and low end collectors. We offer comics from the Golden to the Copper Age. We currently have over 10,000 Third Party (CGC & CBCS) graded comics on our website and about 50,000 non-Third party graded comics. We also set up at most major comic conventions and participate in all major auction houses around the country. Although we generally only set up at no more than five conventions a year, conventions have always been a large portion of our total sales. In 2020, we set up at only one convention which greatly hurt our business, but with the time saved from not having to prep and attend these conventions we were able to process a record level of comics from our back-stock (over 250,000 comics strong). It was great going through boxes untouched by us for years, even decades. The jewels we found were surprising. But more importantly, it gave us the time to achieve our ultimate goal in our business model: to have multiple copies in varying grades of every Silver Age and Bronze Age comic and as many as we can for Golden Age titles. It is great to see runs like *Avengers*, *Batman*, *Ghost Rider*, *Richie Rich*, etc. on our site for the first time in our 15 year existence.

Internet Sales: Even though the pandemic limited our ability to travel much of the year, we still managed to be on the road enough to acquire great numbers of Silver Age keys, hot issues, high grade Silver Age runs and a large variety of Golden Age comics to keep supplying our site with auction-quality and lower graded material every month. Pinned in collectors came through with sales for us that almost doubled what we had done in any previous year on our site and even introducing a record number of new collectors to our site.

Convention Sells: As we mentioned before, we managed to attend one convention (C2E2 in February) before the shut-down, and though we did well at it, the lack of conventions for this year greatly hurt our overall sales. The huge increase of our onsite sales almost made up for this deficit, but "almost." The question convention dealers have for 2021 is how and when will they return.

Auction Sells: To make up for the lack of sales from conventions, we went to the auctions. I remember having a talk with some of the Heritage guys early in the pandemic to see if their first Sunday Auction after the country shut down and then their first Signature Auction was going to be impacted by the national crisis. They, like me, were not sure what to expect and were very pleased to see solid numbers early. Little did we expect, solid numbers turned into fantastic numbers as the year went on. We at WorldWide therefore sent a good number of comics to the auction houses as they were seeing some of the best prices witnessed in a decade.

2020 Market Trends: We kind of find it uncomfortable to say that when so many people were having to wait in food lines and out of jobs due to the pandemic, we found the comic market in 2020 to be exceptional. That appears to be the way things can fall in times of crisis. Here is a breakout of particular parts of the comic market that we saw for 2020.

Marvel Silver Age Keys – Hot – Still the best investments in comics. *Amazing Fantasy* #15 slowed a bit after a tremendous surge a few years ago, *Amazing Spider-Man* #1 rose, *Fantastic Four* #1 climbed back up from a low a few years ago, *Hulk* #1 stayed steady.

Timely Golden Age Superhero – Moderate – War time covers remained hot, but later '40s issues slowed. Timelys have lost a bit of the esteem they possessed over the past couple of decades , but they are still consistently selling better than any other Golden Age publisher. However, many smaller companies (Fox, MLJ, Nedor) have made strides to catch them.

DC Golden Age Superhero – Slow/Moderate – Stayed mostly steady but only key issues or exciting covers (like Batman with Joker) sold super well.

Fiction House – Moderate – Mostly cover-dependent on what sells well, but because Fiction House often involved women on most of their covers, there seems to be more interest in them. Their lack of colors on many copies does not seem to dampen their collectability.

Marvel Silver/Bronze Age Superhero – Hot – The best selling comic runs still remains to be Marvel titles from the '60s and '70s. Marvel collectors seem to outnumber DC by at least 1 to 3.

Strong sales on **Avengers #48** can still be tied to the upcoming movie debut of the Black Knight.

DC Silver/Bronze Age Superhero – Moderate/Slow – With the exception of a few titles like *Batman* and *Detective*, DC titles do not fly out the door and seem to lack more semi-keys in the runs.

Pre-Code Horror – Hot/Moderate – Not as hot as they were 2 years ago, but Horror comics still sell consistently above *Guide* with truly sick covers reaching new highs regularly.

Golden Age Romance – Hot – We are still surprised how well even Romance comics with no known artist can still sell. *Guide* is way behind on these books as they are so difficult to find, especially in grade. The only Romance comics not selling well are photo covers and Harvey titles (likely due to the plentiful number of file copies in circulation).

War – Moderate/Slow – War books from the '40s and '50s have been on the upswing for quite some time. DC War has slowed, but other companies *Guide* at a fraction of DC comics and are even scarcer to find in grade, therefore, they sell fast at even well above *Guide* values. DC produced the absolute best War comics in the '60s, but they have remained slow for a few years now as there appears to be few new collectors in this area stagnating this part of the market.

Western – Moderate – Golden Age Western comics have seen a solid increase lately except Dell and Fawcett photo covers which still remain slow. Atlas Westerns seem to be the best sellers as they are truly scarce in grade and do not *Guide* for near the value other comics from that era can. Marvel Western titles dominate the '60s and '70s (no other company competes with them in this timeline) but their sells are still a bit slow except for the earliest issues.

Science Fiction – Moderate – By far, the best selling Sci-Fi comics are the *Planet Comics* run from Fiction House. Fantastic art, good stories and exciting covers make this title hot and highly sought after. DC produced the best Sci-Fi in the later '50s and '60s, but except for high grade scarcer era issues ('50s) they are not fast sellers. Other company's Sci-Fi comics depend upon what is on the cover and what great artist is inside to make them sell well.

Humor – Slow – Except for early Ducks, most humor titles still sell very slow with few exceptions. However, we did see a sizeable increase in Harvey humor comics sells in 2020, hopefully this can continue. Unfortunately, the large number of File Copy issues for Harvey, Dell & Gold Key comics still seems to over-saturate the market on these comics.

Golden Age Teen & Career Girl Humor – Moderate – This genre was the hottest a couple of years ago, and though they still generally sell for above *Guide* prices, they do not possess the demand they did before.

Golden Age Crime – Moderate – Crime comics seem to trend along with Horror comics, but not as fast a pace. They tend to lack the number of horrific type covers, so therefore take a second seat to Horror. Still, they have been selling better in the past year than they have in quite some time.

TV/Movie – Slow/Moderate – TV photo cover comics are still generally slow sellers with the exception of those shows and movies that generate a buzz (*Star Trek*, *Brady Bunch*). *Star Wars* took off again in 2020, two years after the end of the big surge that occurred when the newest run of movies were coming to the theater.

2020 will go down in history due to the pandemic, but we found its impact to the comic market to be minimal. It will take time to see if it retains any long term effects to the market, particularly with comic conventions. It is good to see 2020 go and we have high hopes the world recovers quickly in 2021 and things can return to normal. We are looking forward to that and hope the comic market continues with strong results. Good hunting!!

Conan Saunders & Buddy Saunders Lone Star Comics/ MyComicShop.com

Conan Saunders

In my comments last year I wrote about buyer interest in key first appearance comics, and the growth of that segment relative to non-key "run" issues. How did key comics as a broad category fare in 2020? For us, keys made up a slightly higher percentage of our sales dollars in 2020 than 2018-2019, while representing a slightly lower percentage in terms of quantity sold. Sales were up across all categories in 2020, but by quantity we saw a larger increase in sales of non-key books this year than we did in key books.

What conclusions do I draw from that? 1) Interest in the broader, non-key comic market was very healthy this year, with sales growth outpacing keys in terms of quantity sold. 2) Keys increased in value as buyers redirected more of their discretionary spending to collecting as a result of the pandemic. After a brief period of wariness through March and April, prices were generally strong and rising moderately through the summer and fall.

The big story in comics for 2020 is the resilience and strength of collectible comics during the pandemic, the same resilience we saw during the 2008 era financial crisis. Our sales will be ending the year up strongly over 2019 despite a weaker than usual year for new comic releases including a complete halt to new comic distribution for several weeks in April and May. I've heard reports from other sellers that they have experienced similarly strong growth on eBay and other online channels. We recognize how fortunate we are to be an online business. I know the year has been considerably harder for brick and mortar retailers and dealers who primarily focus on convention sales, and look forward to a better year for them in 2021.

My last topic is newsstand comics, primarily comics from the 1980s and 1990s that were released in both newsstand and direct market editions. Our long-standing approach to these issues has been to list both versions under a single issue listing when the only difference between the two is a minor difference in the barcode area. If the direct edition has a significantly different cover than the newsstand, or if market demand shows a clear difference in value between the two versions, then we'll list the newsstand and direct editions in separate listings in our catalog.

Over the past few months we've seen signs of increased interest in newsstand editions and correspondingly higher sale prices. The interest is focused primarily at the top end of the grade scale, the range of CGC and CBCS 9.8 and 9.6; newsstand editions in fine and very fine generally aren't seeing the same separation in value from their direct edition siblings. Similarly, and unsurprisingly, the interest in newsstand variants is concentrated among higher value key issues and issues of more popular titles like *Amazing Spider-Man*.

Is this increased interest in newsstand variants part of a long term trend, or is this a collecting fad that will recede? Time will tell.

Buddy Saunders

Last year was our best year yet. Despite the coronavirus, 2020 has been an even better year for MyComicShop. That is likely true for most any internet retailer. But for brick-and-mortar, the opposite is true. Texas shut down in April, but has been mostly open for business since then, so businesses in Texas have been spared much of the closure pain many others have endured. Judy, Conan, and I and all of our amazing 100-plus employees have thus far weathered the storm. We followed the best medical advice and it paid off. We haven't lost a moment's sleep over the virus. You do your best to avoid it, and then it either gets you or it doesn't.

But I have lost sleep over what the government is doing to our economy. At this point in the pandemic, 30% of businesses in this country have closed and will not reopen. That includes many comic shops at a time when we need more comic shops, not fewer. The coronavirus didn't do that. We, through our government, did. As a consequence, God only knows what 2021 will bring, and in this case, the worry isn't just about the future of the comic book industry, the concern extends to all corners of our now fragile economy. The quicker we return to normal business operations, the greater the chance of survival for everyone. COVID or no COVID, America needs to get 100% back to work.

So, on to what Lone Star Comics and MyComicShop has seen in 2020 and what we plan for the new year.

In 2020 our comic business increased as never before, but we can't take full credit. COVID has been good to internet retail. In response to the virus, our government virtually obliterated competition, both within the comic book world and beyond. Comic stores closed or were crippled by often foolish restrictions. Movie theaters closed. Sports shut down. Concerts, church attendance, eating in restaurants, all manner of activities were forbidden.

In the environment just described, our low dollar comic sales have exploded. Very affordable and fun to read, such comics fill many a comic store's back room, basement, or mini-storage unit. In order to help us have the inventory to satisfy all those buyers, we purchase several large store lots each year—a quarter-million to a half-million comics each, sometimes more. And we continually buy through our website, 24 hours a day, every day of the year, where we purchase well over 50,000 comics a month, new and old, from fans and stores looking to sell or trade.

Our comic buying has played a significant role in helping some stores through these difficult times. The comic book industry needed more brick-and-mortar stores even before the pandemic. If brick-and-mortar doesn't survive, none of us will in the future prosper as we might otherwise.

While comics will always be at the core of our business, 2021 will see Lone Star Comics branching out into an area where we see growing interest: Vintage Paper, including pulps, SF digests, Big Little Books, paperbacks, and pre-1970 magazines. We're also expanding our offerings of pre-1960 toys and collectibles – pretty much anything that catches fandom's fancy. We have virtually every pulp and BLB listed on our website with stock posted for sale. We also have a comprehensive online buying list for Vintage Paper, so sellers can sell to us by individual item via our want list or contact us to sell a collection or larger group.

Let's all cross our fingers as we head into 2021, prepared for the worst, but hoping for the best. Let's continue to thoroughly enjoy this hobby that gives us so much happiness and pleasure, and new friends along the way!

Matt Schiffman
Collector

The level of market expertise I've witnessed over the past nine months has been really quite impressive. I collect over a wide range of hobbies, and none has done a better job of getting up to speed than ours. Instagram Claim-Fest, direct dealer emails, communication from the top five hobby auctioneers have improved and are really quite impressive. Sellers and artists were completely robbed on conventions, local stores, travel and even those late night furtive hotel room deals. Stepping up their game benefitted us all and it really was fun to couch-surf and find some incredible books and artwork by those sellers that had to find us collectors, out of sheer necessity. Even love those dealers willing to load up a dozen long boxes and meet in an open parking lot under an awning. As the world was often dismantled around us, the comic hobby went from strength to strength.

Pulps: A few nice collections have popped up this year and have done really well at auction. It's nice to see a re-focus on them and their place in our hobby. Some of the great Margaret Brundage covers and Spicy books surpass anything done in comics and many early Timely lineage can be found in some of these rare Marvel titles. Records were set in the Heritage December auction and it was good to see a growing fanbase.

Golden Age: One of the biggest shifts happened in our hobby in the last nine months and it has redefined how the GA is viewed. Over the past 30 years, there has been a growing spread and most non-keys in VG/FN and less have been on the losing end. Prices have continued to erode, interest diminished and dealers have a growing backlog of these issues. No longer. Interest has increased, prices are rising across the board, and these books are starting to find a well deserved home. Fox, Timely and DC keys continue to lead the way, but Fawcett, Fiction House and standard DCs are increasing in price.

Atomic Age: As with the Golden Age, titles and genres that had been neglected over the past twenty years are starting to find collector interest and even excitement. Records set for Matt Baker, Fox good girl, *Phantom Lady* and high grade horror were all set this year, yet it has been the interest in War books, especially the Atlas atrocity issues, that has been the great surprise of the year. Low grade pre-code Horror had been languishing and a real revival has occurred over the past nine months. It was shocking to see the high prices paid for VG and under, yet also nice to see a new spark to this segment of the market. Fiction House, late '50s DC hero and even non-photo cover Westerns are finding new homes.

Silver Age: Nothing particularly new to report about high grade Marvel keys, except they've gone even higher in price. The one thing that did really change was that segment of our hobby in which buyers minutely scrutinized 8.5 to 9.4 graded books to see if there was the ability to re-submit for a higher grade. That in-person transaction dried up completely. One seller even laughingly told me that the buyer asked him outright if he thought the book could get a higher grade. Nothing ventured… DC keys continue to show life and a wider breadth of collectors is starting to recognize that there is a low number of available books from 1958 to 1962. Marvel and DC in VG and below remains plentiful and prices are stagnant, but this is also a great entry point for collectors new to the hobby due to recognizable characters, 50+ years old and single digit purchase prices.

Bronze Age: 9.4 or better. Very strong. Anything lower, not so much. Keys continue to drive this entire market and there is very strong interest in the early to mid '70s magazines. After the tremendous run up of the Guardians of the Galaxy appearances, collectors have been snapping up entire runs looking for the next hit. *Ghost Rider* continues to show a strength that baffles, but no one is complaining. High grade late Bronze books from Marvel and DC that are not yet keys, are doing quite well too.

Copper Age: Do the math. These books are now old, and stumbling on them in high grade out in the wild is increasingly rare. Bargain bins and sloughing long box storage over the past 45+ years has created attrition and that is the word our hobby loves to hear. *TMNT* leads the way with the independents, with early *Cerebus*, indie-publishers and newly anointed keys growing in demand also. Matt Wagner, Dave Stevens, and Brian Bolland books are back in demand and that is great to see.

Modern Age: This is the year of the dilemma. Warehouses upon warehouses of this stuff are sitting out there. Most actually being taken care of as lessons were harshly learned from the Bronze Age through Copper. Tens of thousands are traded for pennies on the dollar, if not outright pennies. Storage costs are high and inventory management is expensive, yet when a key book pops, it really pays off. Yet, what does a dealer do with all those Image and Valiant books from the early '90s? Nobody really thought that a Dark Horse key could bring real money. Until it did. Nobody saw *The Mandalorian* coming and the reignited love it brought to a tired *Star Wars* family. What next? Warehouse fees are being placed on the next big thing.

Alika Seki, P.E.
Maui Comics & Collectibles

Aloha from the absolute hell-scape that has been 2020, price guide reader! We all went through it. No need to go into detail, save to frame the state of the economy. There were tons of comic store closures prior to the pandemic, but now local businesses of all types are closing permanently. Two comic stores on Oahu (both in Kaimuki), Collector Maniacs and Gecko Books & Comics have closed. Gecko Books having been a 30-year fixture in the local community. Ted Mays, the owner of Gecko Books provided us with a lot of help prior to our opening and we wish him the best of luck on his future. The other comic store on Maui, Game Over Comics also closed this year leaving my store, Maui Comics as the only brick-and-mortar shop on our island. Maui Comics has been technically closed since March 2020, but since our new location is inside another business, (Request Music - one of the last of its kind in Hawaii) and the staff of that store makes cash sales for us, we are able to keep our bills paid and new comics coming in for our remaining subscriber base. For the remaining comic shops that have managed to hang on this long I hope for the best.

Collectibles of all kinds have seen a surge in value and interest throughout the pandemic, most noticeably during the spring and summer months. While new comic sales dropped hard at the beginning of the pandemic, and did not recover yet to pre-pandemic levels, back issue sales are as healthy as they've ever been.

Most key and collectible issues are rising across the board. But of note is the major jump in price currently being experienced by the original first volume Mirage Studios *Teenage Mutant Ninja Turtles* comics. Within the last 2 months (October and November 2020) the first 5 printings of issue #1 have at least tripled in value. The first printing in higher grade is now a 5-figure book, whereas in prior years a 5-figure sale would happen intermittently. The second printing that in past years was easy to find for under $500 is now selling for 4-figures even in mid-grade, and not far behind the second is the third print. What was most surprising that the fourth and fifth printings of issue #1 (the first comic-sized printings of issue #1), which would typically sell in the $20-40 range for even high grade copies, are now selling for $100-200 each.

I, like all TMNT collectors, feel so vindicated right now. The TMNT collecting community is a massive and dedicated fandom and well served in all mediums to this day, including; toys, movies, cartoons and (thanks to IDW) comics. Honorable mention to *The Last Ronin* issue #1 for selling out the minute it was released. TMNT was always one of my favorite things to collect because the price point was low and the value was high. No matter what you could sell a TMNT book for, it was worth the fun just to keep it anyways. With prices rising it would be wise for all TMNT collectors to finish up their runs while it's still affordable.

The first volume of **Teenage Mutant Ninja Turtles** is making a major jump in price.

Since the federal unemployment supplement ran out a few months ago I have seen a lot of collections come in to my store for appraisal and sale. Since my store is in kind of a limbo state, I've taken this time to accrue and organize new collections in preparation for the day when in-person retail comes back to strength. I've purchased quite a few complete sets of the first year of *Heavy Metal* magazine, which in previous years was a rare find. It's cool to see how many people have been hoarding these gems. If I were to teach an introductory class to comics and sequential art, the first decade of *Heavy Metal* would be required reading. My mentor in comics, Bruce Ellsworth III (which he hated being called by the way) taught me all about the most important artists and creators via his absolute love of *Heavy Metal* magazine. I remember before his passing in 2013 he had been lobbying for *Heavy Metal* magazine to be included in the *Guide*. I know there are reasons it is not, but inclusion of *Heavy Metal* might do a lot to normalize prices for the series. Values for *Heavy Metal* are generally agreed upon by its fans, but outside of those circles familiar with the series the values are rarely accepted or respected. People tend to only want to pay for the reading material as if it were any other magazine. Prices for *Heavy Metal* have not really increased at a rate commensurate with their popularity and cultural value. I trust that will change soon.

While I am on the subject of my old mentor Brucey-boy (which he preferred to be called) one of his last reports that I helped him write was about the "UPC variant" as we called it at the time, but which has since been labeled more accurately as the "news stand" versus "direct market" copies. While at the time we had posited that the direct editions would be more sought after since UPC codes were not visually attractive it has been widely accepted that the news stand versions with the UPC codes are usually the scarcer version and in some instances just plain rare making them the more valuable version. I wish Bruce were still around to talk story about things like this. Being isolated like this makes one reminisce especially when trapped with collections and ephemera of times gone by.

Moving from the old and nostalgic to the new and hopeful, Bad Idea Comics shocked the comic world this year by dropping its first official book *The Hero Trade* written by Matt Kindt and with art by David Lapham. The comic is entirely in black and white cover-to-cover, and only has 8 pages of story, but it has made a major impact. Bad Idea Comics "snuck" the book into retail shops by sending just a single copy to each of its 100 flagship destination stores with a small, unspectacular sliver of paper with details on how to order more copies before a strict deadline. The comic was not marked to indicate the actual creators or publisher so most people ignored it completely or ordered minimal amounts as they might for any other small-time indy book that solicited itself that way. About 3 days after the order deadline a Bleeding Cool article dropped and Bad Idea destination shops (mine included) scrambled to find their copy of *The Hero Trade*. What ensued was an absolute firestorm of speculation and controversy, from customers getting angry at not being able to read the book (I took pictures of the interior of my copy and sent it to anyone who had subscribed to Bad Idea) to copies of the book starting out selling for $300-500 until rising further to settling on a stable price currently of $1,000 a copy (we still have ours). With only 250 copies confirmed to be in existence by the publisher it is still incredibly hot.

The Hero Trade has also served to prove a few good points about the comic industry, most importantly as a lesson to indy creators soliciting comic shops to carry their wares. What Bad Idea did in sneaking their book into comic stores was basically show how to have your comic ignored. If you are trying to sell a book, or get a shop's attention, you need to do more than just mail a copy with a simple piece of paper to the shop and hope for a response....you're gonna want a world famous creative team and a bombshell news article to go with it!

I also can't bring up Bad Idea Comics without also thanking them for helping my store at the beginning of the pandemic when we needed it most. Bad Idea Comics sent actual money to each of their destination stores before any of us had ever ordered a single comic or paid them a single dime. What Bad Idea Comics is doing for comic shops and the industry in general is amazing. I look forward to the first official releases from Bad Idea in March 2021, and you should too!

Our store was also helped at the beginning of the pandemic with financial support from the Book Industry Charitable Foundation (BINC), which saw creators from all corners of the industry rally to raise funds to save comic shops. Without their help we would be much worse off than we are now and we cannot begin to state how grateful we are for all of the support that the fans, creators and comic-related groups have given comic stores in general. Comic stores are such an integral part of any community, and it is very heartening to see the community show such aloha.

Mahalo for checking out our report! We look forward to the day when it is safer to travel and have visitors. If you plan on visiting let us know via social media (IG: @maui_comics, FB: Maui Comics & Collectibles).

Todd Sheffer
Hake's Auctions

2020 was definitely a year that will not be forgotten, although most people would like to. Beyond the turmoil, the collectibles market, unlike the stock market, hardly had a hiccup. Sales and prices were at all time highs for comics, art and collectibles. A welcome distraction for collectors stuck in their homes for the majority of the year. Let's look forward to a much better 2021 on all fronts.

The original art market keeps getting attention as record breaking prices are paid at auction for covers and key pages from legends and hot new artists. Look for original art to continue to have more interest as newer artists transition to digital formatting.

Vintage Star Wars action figures continue to bring record breaking prices with the success of the movie franchise and now with Disney+ making series like the critically acclaimed *The Mandalorian* and many others slated to hit the streaming service soon. We look for this interest to continue and more collections to come to market thanks to record prices. Classic toys and collectibles have been getting much attention with the 1970s and 1980s now coming into demand. The generations that played with He-Man, G.I. Joe and TMNT are now hitting the age where they realize the investment potential of their childhood toys. No signs of slowing on this front.

Comic book sales are brisk and values keep rising on the key books from the Golden, Silver & Bronze Age but Modern age comics and variants have skyrocketed with interest in finding the next key investment grade books. Interest in certified comics show no slowing down as collectors try to build high graded runs of series.

Golden Age: Early DC and Timely superhero titles have a continued following with movie theater features attracting new collectors and driving the already avid collectors to seek out the early appearances of key characters. Pedigree books such as Mile High copies and others bring top dollar when they come to market. Uncertified issues also command high prices with scarce titles and issues getting scooped up by savvy collectors when they come up for sale.

Silver Age: Marvel continues to be the desired choice in Silver Age. *Amazing Fantasy* #15 shows no signs of slowing down by increasing in value in all grades. Spider-Man leads the pack as the hottest character with early issues being highly sought after by collectors, especially those with first appearances of key villains. Movie and TV involvement also drives prices up on 1960s books, look for more of this as the movie industry ramps production back up.

Bronze/Copper/Modern Age: TV and movies continue to drive these newer issues forward as well with

Disney+, Amazon Prime, Netflix, AMC, the CW and other networks pulling material from comics. *The Walking Dead*, *Watchmen*, *The Boys*, *Titans* and more are getting the attention of viewers weekly with big ratings for most. First appearances of modern characters such as Harley Quinn, Deadpool, Cable, Rocket Raccoon, Miles Morales Spider-Man and others keep increasing with each new film project that is announced.

Notable 2020 Comic Sales at Hakes.com: *Showcase* #4 CGC 8.0 $75,284, *Superman* #1 CGC 6.0 Restored $42,992, *Batman* #1 CGC 6.0 Restored $33,634, *Incredible Hulk* #1 CGC 5.5 $19,275, *Fantastic Four* #1 CGC 6.0 $17,700, *Star Spangled Comics* #7 CGC 9.4 Mile High $21,417, *All Star Comics* #8 CGC 6.0 Restored $13,111, *Tales Of Suspense* #39 CGC 8.0 $26,609, *Human Torch* #2(#1) CGC 7.5 $17,523, *Incredible Hulk* #181 CGC 9.4 $9,482, *Ultimate Fallout* #4 CGC 9.8 $9,937, *Journey Into Mystery* #83 CGC 5.0 $9,261, *Star Wars* #1 (35¢ cover) CGC 8.5 $7,788, and *Sensation Comics* #1 CGC 4.5 Restored $9,281.

Notable 2020 Art Sales at Hakes.com: *Jungle Imps* 1903 Sunday page by Winsor McCay $49,973, *Star Wars* #2 page art by Howard Chaykin $24,273, *Tarzan* #139 cover art by George Wilson $10,689, *Amazing Adventures* Vol. 2 #17 page art by Jim Starlin $12,980, *Buster Brown* 1912 Sunday page by R. F. Outcault $11,033, *Phantom* #8 cover art by George Wilson $8,614, *Where Monsters Dwell* #18 cover art by Jim Starlin $5,458, *Superboy* #197 cover art by Nick Cardy $14,747, and *Gertie The Dinosaur* Animation art by Winsor McCay $13,110.

Notable 2020 Pop Culture Collectible Sales at Hake's: *Star Wars* Boba Fett (Rocket-Firing L-Slot Prototype) AFA 80+ $62,239, *Star Wars* Vlix AFA 40 $19,470, 1916 Boston Red Sox "American League/World's Champions" w/Babe Ruth Advertising Button $62,980 (World Record Price), Beatles Signed 1962 Parlophone Photocard $11,498, James Bond 007 Action Puppet on Card $7,496, Mego Shipping Box w/WGSH Store Display Box $8,555, *Lost In Space* Switch N Go Set $6,490, and Super Queens Mera $9,518.

Frank Simmons
Coast to Coast Comics

Greetings & salutations, Comicdom, Comic Universe and all you "Rock Star" collectors.

The year 2020, also the year of Covid-19, was a very strong buying market! There seemed to be a fair balance between it being a buyers market and a sellers market. If there was a leader or winner, it was "sellers by a nose" as it's said in horse racing. What an exciting year it was for comics as material not seen in decades became available for purchase! CTC thinks that because prices were so strong, especially regarding keys and 1st appearances, this fueled the selling market which in hand created great purchase opportunities.

CTC sales were strong this year, most notably in selling Timely comic titles like *Captain America Comics*, *Daring Comics*, *Human Torch*, *Sub-Mariner Comics*, *Mystic Comics*, and the list goes on and on. We didn't acknowledge or hear of any "record breaking sales" for *Action Comics* #1 or *Detective Comics* #27 type monster keys, however having said this, there were many books that sold for extremely strong or inflated prices. Our Golden Age Specialist Mr. K. Turski in the great state of Texas purchased a great number of great War comics, most with cover art by the late great comic artist Alex Schomburg. Kevin said "I rarely see a Timely I don't like!" Although almost every Timely acquired by us sold and changed hands almost immediately, it was great to see so many incredible Golden Age comics this year going into new homes and collections!

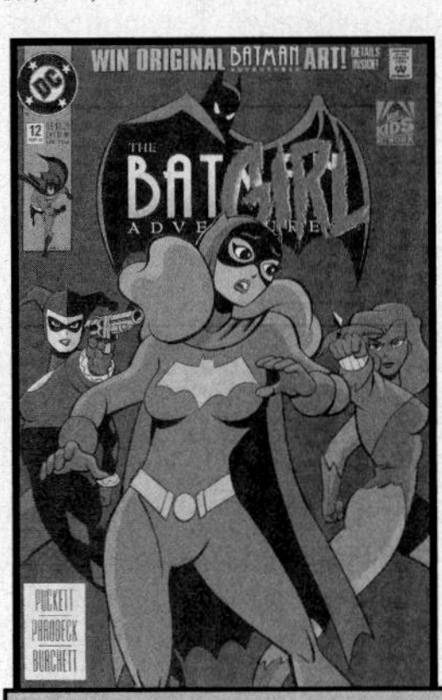

Harley Quinn's debut in ***Batman Adventures*** *#12 is still on fire.*

Current, Copper, Bronze, Silver Age: All keys in all areas were and continue to be hot,hot, hot!!! Comic collecting has been and always will be a great place to expand our imaginations or "escape from reality." A great deal of 2020 was spent by many of us in alternative universes created by talented story tellers and artists from all over the world in this fascinating hobby we all enjoy so much! Coast To Coast Comics wishes everyone a healthy and strong 2021, we pray your new year is filled with comics, fun, health and a great head of momentum for a successful year. Our condolences to all that have lost so much during this pandemic in 2020. COVID-19 was tough, is tough, and to anyone reading this that had an especially difficult year, please have an incredible 2021! Thank you to all of our Customers this year, without you we would not have made it through 2020! Best, Frank!

Marc Sims
Big B Comics - Barrie

2020 was a year of challenges the world over. There was almost no segment of our lives that the global pandemic didn't touch, and the comics market certainly was not immune. My store in Barrie, Ontario, Canada saw an 88% drop in sales between March and May of 2020 as we were forced to close during the first wave of COVID-19 lockdowns. I was fortunate in that the entire comic book industry shut down at the exact same time we were closed under a government order, so I did not have piles of new comics coming in which would have been difficult to sell. With my focus on vintage material and a wide selection of quality stuff already in stock, I was able to weather the storm by selling existing inventory online or through curbside pickup. I was incredibly touched by the outpouring of support from my customer base. So many people went out of their way to make even a small purchase, just to make sure that my shop would still be around when we were able to open to the public again. Robust support from the Canadian government was also key in making sure that businesses and ordinary people had the resources to get through a lockdown. Here in Canada at least, I believe we truly did our best to come together for the good of everyone.

Many months in now, things are largely back to normal even as the pandemic rages worse than ever before. Sales are excellent. The 4th quarter of 2020 is shaping up to be the best in my store's history. Interest in quality back issues is as strong as it has ever been. I price new acquisitions every week and the turnover is nearly immediate on anything remotely in demand. It's remarkable. Demand is especially high on Copper and Modern Age because these are largely still affordable. Besides that, the usual suspects rule the day. Golden Age heroes, Pre-Code Horror, Good Girl, Silver Age Marvels – all the stuff you will read about in just about every report in this *Guide*. Teenage Mutant Ninja Turtles is one title that deserves special mention. I sold a CGC 9.0 1st print *TMNT* #1 a couple years ago for $10k CAD. I don't think you can buy a 6.0 now for that price. For a book with only 3000 copies printed, it still trades fairly regularly and has high census numbers. But Turtles fans are the perfect age to be buying back their childhood and the book is absolutely on fire as a result.

I never thought I'd say this, but I miss setting up at comic conventions! Do anything for long enough, and it can start to feel a whole lot like work, especially when lifting many heavy boxes is involved. But absence really does make the heart grow fonder. I haven't set up at a comic con since February 16th, 2020 and due to COVID I don't anticipate I will be doing so anytime soon. I think it may be another year yet until large conventions can be held safely, and even then there remains the question of just how many people will feel comfortable attending a space with hundreds or thousands of people jammed into a tight space together. I've made so many good friends and forged many more great relationships with customers over 25 years of doing comic cons. It will be nice to get back to it once COVID is in the rearview mirror.

New comics remain a core element of my business so I will touch on this segment of the market a bit. Speculation on new books is rampant. As I always have, I choose not to participate, selling all new comics (other than incentive variants) at cover price for as long as they are on the shelves. My goal has always been to build readership and that is what we continue to do. If people can have some fun along the way flipping books they've bought from me, all the better. I'm happy when everyone is happy. That being said, the flip is the key. I still strongly recommend against anyone who wants to buy and hold modern comics solely for their long term investment potential. We saw in the mid '90s what happened the last time speculation is what drove the market. I'm fearful of the whole industry repeating those mistakes. Buy and read what you love and you will not go wrong.

From a retailer standpoint, the biggest news of the year comics wise was certainly DC abruptly severing ties with Diamond and turning two mail order retailers into their new distributors. Under normal circumstances, this would be frustrating. In the middle of a pandemic, this was infuriating. First, as a Canadian, it was evident from the outset that DC made this decision without any thought whatsoever to the international market, which is larger than any single state in the US. Imagine DC saying they basically don't care about selling comics to California anymore. That would be crazy, right?

To illustrate: I asked a simple question of one of these new distributors regarding sales tax collection and was met with the email equivalent of a blank stare. Shipping went from roughly 3% of wholesale with Diamond to 10-20% with the new guys. Internal systems we all use to track series and individual issues in our databases have been broken for no reason whatsoever (this last one is not specific to international stores – they broke it for everyone!). It's a big mess.

Now, given the choice between doing a whole lot of unnecessary extra work just to sell comics at worse margin and not stocking *Batman* ever again, I decided this was really no choice at all. My customers want *Batman* so I am going to stock *Batman*, even if I have to grit my teeth every day while doing it. I just hope other publishers take note and don't go down the same path.

New collections have been coming in at a steady clip all year and I am buying as much as ever. Copper and Modern continue to be the majority of what I am offered but I don't mind buying these at all. There is plenty of gold buried in those long boxes. One of my bigger purchases was 30 long boxes comprising one customer's collection from the last 20 years. I was as excited to buy a complete run of *Spawn* as I was last year to buy a complete run of *Amazing Spider-Man*! In actual fact I think the *Spawn*s will end up selling faster. Of course any time I am offered quality comics I buy them all. I pride myself on having one of the best selections of any store in Canada of comics Golden Age to present. Even with the pandemic, this was another year in which I spent 6 figures buying comic collections and I don't plan on stopping anytime soon!

While 2020 was certainly a year of challenges for so many of us, it has shown me that there are lots of opportunities to do things differently if we just refuse to accept that something has to be a certain way because it always has been. COVID forced me to re-evaluate what really works and is important to my business and my own life, and because of that 2021 is shaping up to be a year of great possibility. Excelsior!

Lauren Sisselman
Comics Journalist

The Eternal 80-year-old Teenager: Can you believe that it's been 80 whole years since Archie Andrews made his debut in MLJ's *Pep Comics* #22? Neither can I — he looks great for 80! In all seriousness, the eternal teenagers that live within the pages of Archie Comics have seen reboots, horror versions of themselves, and a few -- mostly popular -- live-action adaptations! But what about the collectability of Archie Comics?

With this big milestone birthday on the horizon, it's time to go back to where my comic obsession began. With the mirth of a nation. Archie made his debut in *Pep Comics* #22. This key issue has been a hot ticket item for many, many years. This rare Golden Age key is still easier to come by and is more affordable than its counterparts; *Detective* #27, *Action* #1, and so on. But is now a good time to invest in key Archie books?

A restored *Pep Comics* #22 sold in September of 2020 for $19,200. Two years prior in November of 2018, a universal label 2.5 sold for $36,000, while a universal 5.0 sold for $91,000 a month later. This is still a good key to invest in regardless if you go for restored or unrestored. Its easier to find counterpart -- *Archie Comics* #1 -- has seen better days. Prices for mid-grade copies have dropped slightly. In November of 2020 a universal 4.0 sold for $30,000. Two years prior a similar book sold for $35,500. That same month a universal blue 3.5 sold for $16,200, while in 2012 a similar book sold for $20,315. While 8 years is a long amount of time between sales, it's not a good sign if you're looking to sell *Archie Comics* #1s right now. In fact, other *Archie* #1s that sold this year dropped in value. While I do predict this book to go up in value, it may not be for a while. If you're looking to get an easy to find Golden Age key for a steal, now is the time to buy.

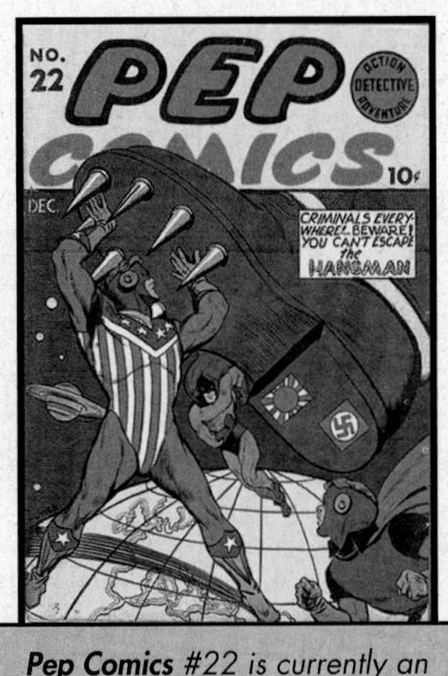

Pep Comics #22 is currently an excellent investment.

Archie's girls have also gone down in value. *Archie's Girls Betty and Veronica* #1 has decreased in value between 2019 and 2020. A universal 7.5 sold in September of 2020 for $2520 -- a similar book sold a year prior for $3840. *Pep Comics* #26 (the first appearance of Veronica) seems to be retaining its value, but only because there were no sales of the book in 2020 per GPA. Sorry girls, better luck next time.

Even the devious redhead Cheryl Blossom's first appearance, *Betty and Veronica* #320, has decreased in value. A universal 9.0 sold in November of 2020 for $183, while mere months prior to that a similar book sold for $525. If you're looking to invest in Cheryl, now is the time. Lower grades of the same book can be had for under $150, but frankly, if you're looking to invest in this book you should be buying a high grade of it. Buying a low grade to complete your set is fine and dandy, but don't expect a high return on the book.

Archie's infamous burger eating pal Jughead has also decreased in value. *Archie's Pal Jughead* #1 can be found fairly easily for under $1500 for a high grade, while lower graded books can be had for under $800. It's fair to say that across the board, Archie Comics have taken a hit. If you were investing in Archie thinking you would make money off of the books, you should hold on to them a little longer. Unfortunately, the success of *Riverdale* only translated into a bump in sales prior to the show's release 5 seasons ago. Their counterparts, Sabrina and Katy Keene (both of which have been canceled) didn't help their comic collectability either.

But what is down will eventually go up. Hang on to your Archie keys. Now is not the time to sell them. I do believe that one day, everything will be Archie once again!

Tony Starks Comics Ina Flash!

OMG - what to say in this year's Market Report?....

We have been buying and selling comic books and related material since 1978. During that time, there have been five recessions in the USA – with the COVID recession being the sixth. The five previous recessions have been times that sales were weak but opportunities to purchase nice collections for resale later presented themselves. This recession is nothing like previous ones.

Sales of collectible comic books have been really, really good since March of 2020. What is selling? Expensive key issues or books out of the dollar bins and all price points in-between. The short version is just about everything is selling well.

Stuck at home or working from home or receiving unemployment benefits equal to working had many collectors buying "comfort" items like comic books for their collection. Not selling to make sure they had reserve cash for daily living expenses as in previous recessions. What were they buying? Well trends from years past continue. Is there upcoming movies or TV shows? Or rumors of movies/TV shows? Collectors want it. One current example is *Fantastic Four* #94. This book is the 1st app. of Agatha Harkness, a main character in the *WandaVision* Disney+ series.

But COVID-19 has even affected the movie/TV collectors, given theaters were closed, movies already made were pushed back and new production largely stopped. Still, characters on the big and small screens continue to draw collector's interest.

Now some representative sales: About one half of our inventory of books priced $3 or less sold out. It was not a huge amount of money, but it was a lot of books. One woman called and bought every issue we had in the dollar boxes for half a dozen characters (Captain America, Fantastic Four, X-Factor, X-Men and more) for her son for Christmas. She was also a real sweetheart and loved talking to her!

A few better sales: *Amazing Spider-Man* #126 CBCS 9.6 @ $150, *Spidey Super Stories* #1 CGC 9.8 @ $275, *Batman* #227 CBCS 8.0 @ $750, *Champions* #1 CGC 9.8 #@ $550,

Lobo #1 (Dell) CGC 6.0 @ $555, *Tales of Suspense* #48 CGC 9.0 @ $1150, *Avengers* #71 CGC 9.4 @ $475, *Conan the Barbarian* #1 CGC 9.4 @ $720 *Incredible Hulk* #102 CGC 9.4 @ $900, and *Hero for Hire* #1 CBCS 8.0 @ $375.

Nice keys are always fun to sell, but we sell a lot of run type books in average condition. They add up: *Adventure Comics* #352 VG+ @ $8.00, *Avengers* #158 NM @ $30.00, *Batman* #321 NM- @ $11.00, *Detective Comics* #469 NM @ $40.00, *Four Color* #1106 FN- @ $12.00, *Movie Classics The Creature* GD (2nd print) @ $10, *Superboy* #59 GD @ $22.00 and *World's Finest* #199 VG @ $10.00.

Adding to the crazy, a lot of the key books sold in March-May now look like bargains just half a year later. Go figure.

As 2020 winds to a close (we write this report mid-December) COVID-19 continues to affect the comic collecting world. As of early December 2020, USPS deliveries have ground to a standstill. Tracking just stops dead in many areas. So as we write this, we have thousands of dollars worth of books in USPS limbo and have shifted all package deliveries to UPS.

2020 has been a wild year. While it has been a good year – even a GREAT year – for comic book sales, we are glad to see the year end.

West Stephan
CBCS Vice President

Last year marked *The Overstreet Comic Book Price Guide*'s 50th Anniversary! It was a momentous occasion and a milestone few publishers ever attain. Thank you, Bob, for all you have done for our hobby. It's very likely most of us would not be where we are at in our collecting endeavors or professionally if not for you. Here's to 50 more years!

I'm sure just about every market report this year will talk about COVID-19 and the effects it has had on them personally and as a business. Early 2020 was tough on everyone. The only silver lining was towards the middle and the end of the year when collectors and dealers realized they still needed to get their comics graded to sell them for a premium. CBCS was flooded with submissions starting in May and luckily, we were able to keep up with that tidal wave of books! Our pressing department was moved from Florida to Dallas in May. This was a very necessary move on our part as turnaround times were sliding due to the high demand. We are now on track and with added staff, things are quickly turning around.

We lost many greats in our industry this year: Richard Corben, Joe Sinnott, Mort Drucker and Allen Bellman, just to name a few. A real shock to the comic book world was the loss of actor Chadwick Boseman. His portrayal of the Black Panther was spot on! He will be sorely missed.

Submissions at CBCS have been pretty consistent. Spider-Man, Batman & Walking Dead titles lead the way. The abrupt stopping of *The Walking Dead* title caught many by surprise! IMO, it was a great ending to a long series.

Once again, a great shout out to Bob Overstreet, Mark Huesman, J.C. Vaughn & the rest of the staff who always pour their hearts and souls into *THE GUIDE*!

Al Stoltz
Basement Comics / Basement Comics Pressing

Far from a typical year of chasing comics to buy and sell either at major shows we do attend or sell online on eBay or Etsy, this year was one that forced adaptations and limited possibilities of buying new inventory greatly. I was amazingly lucky that when the world went bonkers right after my return from the C2E2 comic show in Chicago we would still be able to generate our normal income due to our established twenty-two years selling online. eBay actually is now fantastic again !!

What's funny is that both myself and my ever faithful C2E2 helper Mike Decarl talked about the growing news of COVID and estimates of the pending disaster all the way up and back from the show. We knew something was going to happen and perhaps hit the economy or day-to-day life, but we had no idea of what would actually happen as it played out. What was amazing was the energy at the show was huge and people poured into the building and were not shy about spending their money on vintage comics at my booth or others booths at the show. It was as if they knew it was now or never for a long while before they had the chance to mill around a major show packed with people and dealers and made the most of it. So here we are nearly ten months later and the typical grind of the yearly big shows has not started up again and I have heard of a few regular dealers that were show dependent for income struggling to stay above water for now. With this and the DC Comics shift in print and who distributes their product, those pressures surely will doom a decent amount of local comic shops by the end of this event.

Again, like many in the comic industry I thought about a mail order only business approach that may be needed in the future when driving around the country or age or that model slowing and would make a stay at home selling platform easier and more profitable. So after two decades of building that model we were able to reap the rewards and sell it seems like a little of everything we offer online nowadays during the stranglehold put on shows. People were not going on vacations or going out regularly to blow money and were instead buying lots of stuff from their computers and having fun waiting for it at home. Comics, magazines, graded comics, LPs, posters, art, and vintage toys just started moving out of our packing room daily.

The other part of our business model is Basement Comics Pressing, which has now celebrated our fifth year and took off like crazy this year after the lock downs as well. Other than the administrative side of this part of the business I still do all the work on books and pressing myself. It required a massive amount of time and more equipment but our turnaround times have pretty much stayed at 2-4 weeks. At only $10.00 a press and $15.00 for one week turnaround speed, our lost time and income provided by shows on the road was erased quickly. We have surely added to a fraction of the backlog that CGC has been experiencing as of this report in December and we ourselves have pressed and graded more of our own inventory that we ever have this time of the year. Free shameless plug, visit basementcomicspressing.com if you want to contribute to my daily workload.

Prices being paid for both raw and graded comics have been at insane levels since the lock downs and I am sure that they will stay strong as long as people are being held back from going to shops or to major comic cons. The question is will they taper off? Or hold at present levels ? Or do they do a major roll back after speculative money withdraws? I have talked to a few people recently that want to invest in comics and wanted to know what books I could sell them to invest in long term. The consistent thing with all of the potential future investors was that they had no idea about the history of comics, artists, trends, characters or stories. They didn't even read comics but had seen that they could pay off as a serious investment. So huge outside money is really coming into our once laughed at hobby and all the books we once cherished are nothing more than commodities to be bought and sold by emotionally detached investors. Things change and times change and I guess it was inevitable with comics reaching into the millions of dollars in recent times.

Hopefully one of the investors that wanders into my shop or sees me at a future show may even know who Jack Kirby or Carl Barks are.....it is 2020 and stranger things have happened!

Doug Sulipa
Doug Sulipa's Comic World

The Ancient Apocryphal Saying (commonly known as a Curse) "May you Live in Interesting Times" seems to be prophetic. Beyond the very young, virtually everyone alive today will remember enduring the Coronavirus Crisis for the rest of their cognitive lifetime. Add to that the U.S. election, as even we Canadians were mesmerized by the events as they unfolded.

In March 2020, our Province of Manitoba went into a near complete shutdown. My first instincts were panic, with thoughts of closing for the first time in 50 years and laying off staff. Imagine my shock when the exact opposite happened, and SALES EXPLODED. We have been selling by internet only since 1996, on my own inventory site, eBay, AbeBooks and other sites. With millions around the world stuck at home, people went in droves to buy things online. Buying comfort items filled a void felt around the world by many. The Canada-USA border has been closed for 10 months so far, but luckily Canada Post is an essential service, so we were prepared to "go Gangbusters." We went from our typical 60 hour weeks, to 80-90 hour work weeks, with non-stop buying for ten solid months, and still no end in sight.

It is a good thing we had many thousands of items already listed on multiple websites, as anything and everything seems to be selling. 2020 was my all-time greatest year for sales, in my 50 year history as a seller, with total dollar sales up over 25%, and volume of items shipped at nearly double. My circa 1982 record for quantity of items by mail order is yet unbroken. At that time, I printed a ¼ page ad in all Marvel Comics, with multiple runs of overstocked comics, over 2000 comics to pick from, all at $1.00 each, we sold over 50,000 comics from that little ad (add my store sales, other mail order sales, and wholesale new-comic sales, it was a blockbuster year.)

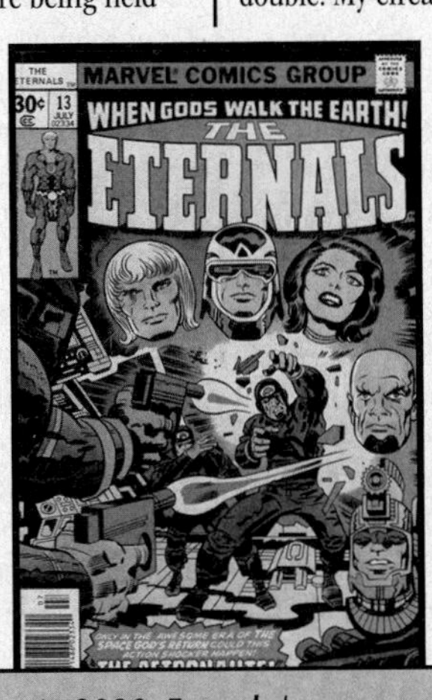

In 2020, ***Eternals*** *bacame a best-selling CGC title.*

We sold about 2000 CGC graded comics in 2020, which is above average. We also got in about 3000 more comics from CGC, but have been so very busy, we really only had time to do relists of items we had duplicates. *Eternals* (1976-78) #1-19 and Annual #1 has now become our #1 best-seller CGC title of all time, with well over 1000 CGC copies sold since the initial 2019 Comic-Con announcement. All the hyped movie, TV and other media related comics continued to be top sellers. There was a notable boom in sales for other cool CGC comics, not related to current media, likely related to the void of new movies and TV shows in 2020. Collectors have been sitting at home, having some extra time, and they seem to doing a bit more reflecting on buying CGC graded copies of under-valued and overlooked key issues, while they are low priced and affordable. These are one of my specialties, as we have thousands of these lower minor keys with big potential in stock, thus this was the our biggest growth area in CGC comic sales, at over double a typical year. To me, this is smarter buying, getting in low, and you can still resell at cost or more if it never pans out. Too many collectors, flippers and dealers, jump on the freight train of buying up overnight hot keys at top prices after they have already skyrocketed to 300-1000% of the price just a few months before. Many of these hot keys cool to lower levels. I have learned to sell these keys when they want them, when they are red hot, while most of the marketplace is buying them at top dollar instead. Yes, occasionally I lose out by selling too early (I sold 12 copies of *Special Marvel Edition* #15 in CGC 9.8 in the $1000 each range, before the Shang-Chi movie announcement), but more often than not, I did much better selling at the peak.

The true volume increase was in raw less expensive comics, magazine and books, sold as both single items and lots. Our sales of 10-20 consecutive issue lots of 1970s to 1990s clearance comics more than doubled. Our vintage 1940s-1990s paperback sales also doubled. Want lists from collectors, through our inventory list site, have tripled, and unfortunately we have a near impossible time keeping up (instead of 1-2 days to fulfill requests, it has become 5-10 days). Once again everyone is mostly buying items from our older listings, as we have been too busy to make many new listings.

On December 10, 2020 Disney announced Star Wars TV shows in the works. earlier CBSI published a hot 100 *Star Wars* comics list and companion list of all known first appearances in the *Star Wars* comics universe. Prices and demand for the 100-200 top keys issues have exploded. *Star Wars* #42 hit the stratosphere (in spite of being a reprint, printed over 6 months later than the undervalued *Marvel Super Special* #16.) Back issues of Dark Horse *Star Wars* have never sold better with dozens of raw keys bringing $25 to $200 (and CGC copies in the $200 to $2000+ range.)

Teenage Mutant Ninja Turtles key back issues are also exploding in demand and price. *TMNT* (Mirage) #1-4 are up 50%-100% in price, with 2nd and later printings of #1-7 bringing $20 to $100 each, as many are scarcer than the originals. *TMNT* #46-62 are bringing 400-1000% *Guide*. All notable first issues, one-shots, and first appearances in the TMNT universe are in huge demand, leaving old *Guide* prices behind in the dust. In particular, all keys related to Space Usagi and Usagi Yojimbo are red hot. *TMNT Adventures* #1(10/88) are bringing $60-400 Raw, with CGC copies $200-$1000 and Canadian variants MUCH higher.

Demand for licensed character comics is a big trend, as they are so very undervalued, many need to see price increases in the two to ten-fold range. This includes: video game related, TV, movie (*Back to the Future*, *Willow*, *Dune*), animated cartoons, Manga, book series, author related (REH, HPL, ERB, etc.), and many more. CPV (Canadian Price Variants) are now routinely bringing 150-600% *Guide*, with record breaking prices for the top keys.

Noteable high demand comics (bringing 150 to 400% of *Guide* #50 prices): comics that inspired Roy Lichtenstein paintings, role-playing comics, *Adam: Legend of The Blue Marvel* #1, *All-Star Squadron* #23, *Aliens* #1, Archie (#1s, key issues, swimsuit covers, Cheryl Blossom, GGA, Josie, Sabrina, suggestive), artists (Neal Adams, Matt Baker, Byrne, Corben, Adam Hughes, Pérez, Wrightson), Black Panther & Shuri, Atlas Seaboard Comics, *Back To The Future*, *Beetlejuice*, *Black Widow*, *Bloodstone* #1, Boba Fett, *Captain Britain*, *Captain Canuck*, Charlton Super-Heroes (who later became DC characters), Crime comics (Pre-Code), *Darkwing Duck*, DC Milestone comics (Dakotaverse, especially *Static*), Dr. Doom, *Eightball*, *FOOM*, Freddy Krueger, Friday Foster, Galactus, GGA covers, *Ghost Rider* (1967 Marvel Western), Gold Key (#1s and key issues), Hanna-Barbara keys, Heralds of Galactus, Horror Comics (all), Jason, *Josie*, *Journey Into Mystery Annual* #1, Kirby 4th World keys, Lilith, *Lobo* (Dell), Love comics, *Love And Rockets*, *Magnus* #1(GK), *Marvel Spotlight* V2#9, *Marvel Super-Heroes* #17, 20, *Marville* (Greg Horn GGA), Masters of The Universe, *Moon Knight*, Nationality-related comics (Asian, Black, Hispanic, etc.), Marvel & DC Limited Series, Promo and try-out comics, *Peacemaker*, *Predator* #1, Red Sonja, Reprints (affordable Bronze Age reprints of SA key issues; affordable Modern reprints of Bronze key issues), Shang-Chi, Satana, Shanna, *Sonic The Hedgehog*, *Space Usagi*, Stan Lee personality related comics, *Star Wars* (all keys & most first appearances), Sub-Mariner key issues, Tigra, TMNT, *Terminator* #1, *Twilight Zone* #1(GK), Universal Monsters Movie Classics, *Usagi Yojimbo*, all Video Game related, Venom & Carnage, *What If* (Many key issues In V1 and V2), White Tiger, Zatanna, TV comics, War comics (Pre-Code), and *Warrior* magazine (UK).

Maggie Thompson
Collector

With COVID-19 putting a stop to nearly all in-person convention activity, online and mail-order sales have helped scratch at least some of the collecting itch during most of 2020. That itch got more persistent, as the pandemic raged on and collectors used the many "stay at home/safer at home" requirements to spend extra time with their collections, appreciating what they have and, more importantly for our purposes, what they need.

We've seen an increase in buying, as collectors fill holes in series' runs or pick up titles that they had previously overlooked, waiting for that "rainy day" when they'd have time to read and enjoy a new-to-them series. The thrill of the hunt had to go virtual rather than in-person, but it was still there throughout the year and led to increased traffic at many online auctions and store fronts.

Binge-watching of comics-related TV series and movies had some effect on back-issue sales, but few predictable trends emerged. The shutdown of comics distribution for a few months and ongoing uncertainty about the economy may have affected new-comics sales, but, as has been the case in past economic downturns, back issues continue to be sound investments. Brainstorming with a bunch of friends in several collecting fields (including the savvy Brent Frankenhoff, a comics expert with whom I've consulted for decades), I'm hearing 2020 may have wrapped up with purchasing opportunities, as shops and collectors look for funds. In addition, there are those among back-issue buyers who actually have more disposable funds—especially in a year in which budgets did not include travel, hotel, and other convention expenses. So super-high-end keys could bring record prices, as some buyers now will outdo each other to get their respective most-wanteds. In those limited cases, the sales won't be as investments, because that's not what the buyer has in mind.

Gazing into the pop-culture crystal ball: If more movie studios release their comics-related blockbusters on streaming services at the same time as they open in movie theaters, expect additional exposure to the casual fan, which could lead to additional sales for the savvy pop-culture dealer.

Michael Tierney
Collector's Edition & The Comic Book Store

To say that 2020 was an unprecedented year in the comic book industry would be an understatement. For the first time ever, the entire industry shut down--something that no previous global event like World War II could even do. DC came back to publishing far quicker than did Marvel, and made a profound shift in the way comics are sold by switching to a new distribution model. But this was just one of the many changes that were brought about by the global pandemic known as COVID-19.

As a publicly elected official, I was aware of and watching details about COVID-19 before it even had a name or was recognized as being a problem in China. A series of YouTube videos made by bio-chemists there raised the alarm about this pandemic very early on, and proved to be prophetic in everything they warned about. When the panic buying hit in America, I was already stocked up and had warned everyone I knew to do the same. They all thought I was crazy. So did other public officials when I tried to clue them in. So, when the comic industry was hit, I knew this was no short-term problem and started making long-term changes.

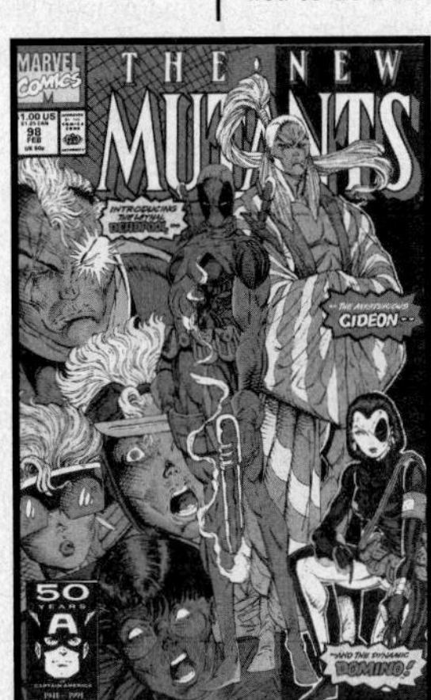

New Mutants **#98 continues to sell notably well.**

Another problem that the pandemic created for me was the loss of my workforce. When the Unemployment Department was offering people a bonus to stay home, it became problematic finding people willing to work, and other employers hired my workforce away with offers I could come nowhere close to matching. Thinking that I was about to have more time away from the stores to work on special projects, I'd contracted with multiple publishers to create two new *Wild Stars* novels and a new four-book art chronology in the next year--and immediately afterwards found myself with two stores to run and no help.

As a retailer for nearly 40 years, one of the things I've always done is quickly adjust to changes in the market, and in 2020 there was a paradigm shift in the way people shopped. My store traffic plummeted, while my online sales exploded. I have always had a catastrophy plan should the comics industry ever collapse, and decided it was time to implement that plan, with some refinements. I converted from multiple brick-and-mortar locations--because the traffic and the selection of new comic releases were no longer there to support 5500 square feet of retail space--to strictly mail order sales. The timing was good for me in that my lease for one location was expiring, and the other I owned. My North Little Rock store was in a premium location, and when I tested the real estate market--two serious offers were made on the very first day.

The next thing was to liquidate the majority of my inventory, which meant I was about to take a beating by letting go of stock that I no longer had a place to store--for pennies on the dollar. But it turned out to be a good move by not hesitating, as the person I sold the stock to later informed me that if we had made the deal a month later, he would have only paid half that price--because by that time so many other stores had started closing around the country. It was painful to do, but not as painful as it would have been if I had procrastinated.

While I closed both retail locations, both stores continued to do business from home. Collector's Edition became my online store, for which I kept the inventory that had already been allotted to that endeavor. Meanwhile, The Comic Book Store became my subscription service store, with the majority of my pull-and-hold customers staying with me. While I did lose my, "don't know if I want it until I see it on the shelves" customers, I gained many new customers online. Plus, shelf sales have always been a game of Russian roulette, having to predict what people will want before they have any idea, a process that has been made far more difficult in recent years because of misleading solicitations coming from the publishers. The bottom line is, with the elimination of unsold shelf stock, retail rent and utilities, and the majority of my employee expenses, my stores are actually more profitable than they were before--even though neither DC nor Marvel have returned to a full publishing schedule as of the time of this writing.

As I said earlier--it's been a paradigm shift.

Here are some examples for my more notable sales made during this tumultuous year.

Amazing Spider-Man #17 sold in VG- for $112.50, #25 in VG+ for $95, #34 in FN for $55, #136 in VG for $50, #194 in NM for $150.

Daredevil #111 (1st Silver Samurai) sold in VF for $50.

G.I. Joe #1 (Marvel) sold in NM for $75.

Klaws of the Panther #1 (the 1:10 Shuri variant) sold in NM for $125.

New Mutants #87 (1st Cable) sold in VG for $75, and #98 (1st Deadpool) sold in VF+ for $175.00 for a direct market copy, and a newsstand version sold in GD- for $275.

Special Marvel Edition #15 (1st Shang Chi) sold in VG+ for $80.

Spider-Gwen #1, the 3rd print green variant, sold in NM for $125.

Star Wars: Jedi of the Republic--Mace Windu #4, the 1:25 Shalvey variant sold in NM for $50.

A Poor copy of *X-Men* #9 (v1) sold for $40, and the 1st appearance of Hope in #205 sold in NM/MT for $90.

While Marvel was the top selling line before the pandemic, after Marvel was slow to rebound, DC moved into the top seller spot in both new comics and vintage.

From independent publishers *Big Top Comics* #1, a 1951 Golden Age comic from Toby Press sold in VG for $40. *Teenage Mutant Ninja Turtles* #1 2009 FCBD edition sold in NM for $75.

Overall I did not see a lot of high dollar sales this year when compared to previous, and the majority of what is shown came before the pandemic struck--with the exceptions being the newsstand edition of *New Mutants* #98 and the variant of *Klaws of the Panther*. But online activity was brisk in the range of comics under $25. This is where DC dominated Marvel during the latter part of the year. Both publishers continued to release variants during this time, and DC's variants drew sales along the ratio of $1 per copy of limitation (i.e.: a 1:25 sells for $25) or better, while Marvel's variants performed far less, drawing sales averaging as much as 75% below that of their DC counterparts.

Ted VanLiew
Superworld Comics

Hoo Boy! 2020, we hardly knew ye. The year started off fantastically, with business percolating along. We travelled to California and set up at the Berkeley Comicon, and then Terry O'Neill's Cal Comic Con the following week in late January.

Both shows were tremendous, especially considering they're just one day affairs. Reed Exhibitions had scheduled their C2E2 show for the end of February, and we thought they were crazy to do a major show in Winter in Chicago. Turned out to be a blessing though, as it was a great show.

Then. . . everything changed. Lisa asked me in early March to start working from home. At first, I was resistant, but she's almost always alert to more practical matters than I am, so I decided to heed. Once it became clear what was happening with the Coronavirus, I was glad I'm in the habit of listening to her wisdom. Once we realized that there wouldn't be any shows for the foreseeable future, we were nervous that half our income would evaporate.

We were also concerned that folks would stop spending. Just didn't really know what to expect! So, we brainstormed ways to ramp up our online presence, from the website, to Instagram Live, to other videos, eBay, Facebook, and so forth. Turns out that folks were restless and bored, with sheltering in place, working from home, social distancing, etc., and went to town buying stuff online! We've been selling books and art very consistently, which has been great to see. Comic fans are undaunted, and gotta have their goodies. Of course, we can relate. We still miss the shows terribly though! Really miss seeing all the other malcontents and miscreants who are our friends, and love buying and selling on location, and seeing everybody in person. We're hoping that by the time this report appears that shows will have started at least tentatively resuming. We figure it'll take some time for folks to reacquire full confidence to congregate in large groups, but we're confident it will happen before long!

So anyways, it seems that demand for Marvel first issues and key first appearances has only intensified. I'm always amazed how the prices for these books steadily increase. Also, most non-obscure Silver and Bronze Age books in high grades are in stead demand as well. We try to stick to carrying the nicer quality issues, and sell all but the scarcer and most significant issues that are in average or lower condition for enticing discounts, as much as 50% off.

DCs are a funny animal. Key issues are still always gonna fly, and Batman's always great. Issues that are hard to find in high grade do well too. Unfortunately, DC as a company has been mismanaged, in my opinion. They've been making various decisions that have dismayed their fandom, readers, and store owners. Some examples are yanking their distribution from Diamond, cancelling the Swamp Thing show before it appeared (it's good, by the way), going exclusively digital, and struggling with their movie making. We're hoping they get their act together, as we love 'em and their characters!

A big surprise area from our point of view, is the '80's to Modern books. We always thought these would forever have limited value. To our surprise and delight, many issues are continually accruing good value and demand. Some of it is related to movies and tv shows related to certain characters and storylines, but also what current books and storylines are being produced new. The first several *Teenage Mutant Ninja Turtles* have been a revelation. The #1 is continually setting records, for first print and also subsequent printings, as have the #2 through 4 as well. I figure the folks who came of age in the 'Turtles Era' have income to toss at 'em now.

Golden Age is always the most fun era to deal with, just because we don't see the books nearly as often, and even are still discovering books we didn't even know existed! Plus, the books are a larger package, and have many more pages than Silver Age and later books. Man, you got your money's worth for a dime!

Here are some examples of sales from 2020: *Action Comics* #54 FN+ $1650; *Action Comics* #116 CGC 9.0 Hawkeye $43,600; *Adventure Comics* #247 VG/FN $3600; *All Select Comics* #11 VF $3500; *Amazing Spider-Man* #1 CGC 5.0 $9750; *ASM* #1 CBCS 4.0 $8000; *ASM* #2 VG/FN $2100; *ASM* #9 VF+ $3100; *ASM* #14 VF- $3300; *ASM* #121 CBCS 9.6 $1250; *ASM* #129 CBCS 9.6 $5200; *ASM* #300 CGC 9.6 $1200; *Aquaman* #1 VF $1500; *Archie Comics* #32 CGC 8.5 $1100; *Batman* #36 NM- $3900; *Batman* #37 FN/VF $2900; *Captain America Comics* #47 CGC 8.0 $4400; *Comic Cavalcade* #4 CGC 9.0 $1950; *Daredevil* #1 VF- $4900; *Detective Comics* #71 VG- $2500; *Detective Comics* #108 VF $1800; *Exciting*

Comics #58 NM- $1400; *Famous Funnies* #215 VF+ $3450; *Fantastic Four* #1 GD+ $9000; *Fantastic Four* #4 FN $4250; *Fantastic Four* #48 VF/NM $5200; *Flash Comics* #15 CGC 9.0 $5700; *Giant-Size X-Men* #1 VF/NM $2800; *Haunted Thrills* #9 FN/VF $1350; *House of Secrets* #92 NM- $4200; *Incredible Hulk* #181 CGC 9.6 $18,000; *Incredible Hulk* #181 CGC 9.2 $6400; *Journey into Mystery* #83 VG/F $9500; *Journey into Mystery* #85 VG/F $1500; *Journey into Mystery Annual* #1 VF/NM $2200; *Mad* #1 VG/FN $1200; *Marvel Mystery* #33 CGC 6.0 $3000; *Out of the Shadows* #11 FN/VF $1500; *Planet Comics* #20 CGC 5.5 $2000; *Real Life* #3 FN/VF $6000; *Sensation Comics* #13 FN/VF $4500; *Showcase* #8 FN- $3000; *Silver Surfer* #3 CGC 9.2 $1600; *Silver Surfer* #4 CGC 9.4 $3500; *Star Wars* #1 35¢ CGC 7.0 $5000; *Startling Comics* #50 CGC 9.0 $3000; *Sunny* #11 VF- $2700; *Superboy* #68 FN+ $2000; *Superman* #14 VG $4,000; *Superman* #17 VG/FN $3800; *Tales of Suspense* #52 VF+ $4200; *Tales of Suspense* #57 CGC 8.5 $2500; *Thrilling Comics* #41 VG+ $2100; *Tomb of Terror* #15 VG/F $4500; *V Comics* #1 VF $2500; *Venus* #1 VF $3200; *Victory Comics* #1 VF $2500; *Whiz Comics* #2 PR $11,500; *X-Men* #1 F $10,500; *X-Men* #4 VF/NM $5200; and *Zip Comics* #8 CGC 6.0 $2700.

Well, that's it for this time around! Hope 2021 is finding you all safe and sound, and we look forward to seeing or talking to you soon!

Frank Verzyl
Long Island Comics

There are many reasons why people say the current comic book market fails to attract many new, younger readers these days. While operating Long Island Comics continually since 1977, I've seen the hobby change so drastically over the decades. Today's customers don't seem to collect back issues the way they used to, say, even 20 years ago.

Even in the 1990s, most store owners (and mail order dealers) felt it necessary to maintain near-complete runs of almost every Marvel and DC title in their stocks, even the relatively inexpensive series like *Micronauts* or *Ka-Zar.* It was just as important then to be able to instantly produce any issue for a customer upon demand, whether it be issue #36 of *Rom* or #1. This was because the collectors were on a quest to complete their runs of each specific title, not for what they could resell them for on eBay, but just to have the entire set in their hands and to be able to read and enjoy the stories. (In other words, they were Comic Collectors.)

Running a comics store has become so much less interesting these days. When the phone rings, the dealer knows the caller is going to ask "Do you have a *Hulk* #181?" or "Do you have *Giant-Size X-Men* #1?". They never ask for *Hulk* #330 or *John Carter* #12, or any of the thousands of other (less valuable) back issues that can be found in a typical comic shop. And when you ask them why those issues, they proudly exclaim "I collect keys!", as if they are the only ones wise enough to be on the lookout for those fabulously expensive eBay books. How monotonous that all of them are looking for the same exact items???

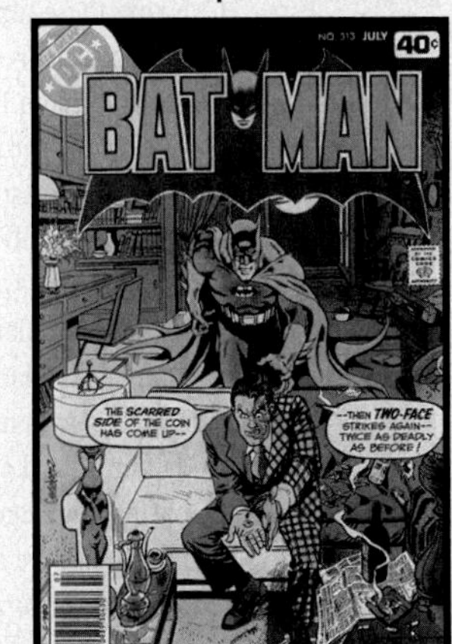

2020 was a great year to have **Batman** #313 in stock.

The other day, I was shocked when an apparently youthful caller asked me "Do you have *Batman* #313 in stock?". I thought "Oh my god, someone who's actually trying to fill in a Batman run!" Then I punched a few keys and the eBay screen showed that that particular comic had only yesterday skyrocketed from its perennial $20.00 NM *Guide* price to like $ 800.00 in CGC 9.8 !!!! My faith in humanity was instantly dashed.

I wonder how much longer retailers will continue to feel the need to pay exorbitant, ever-increasing overheads in order to maintain physical brick-and-mortar stores when all they really need is to stock the 200 or so top-selling "keys" in a short box and sell them right out of their car. The predictability becomes unbearable when the only requests you get for back issues are the same tired titles over and over again. I cringe when a phone call begins with the words, "Do you have any "keys" for sale?". (I'm a comics store, not a locksmith!)

Another big change in collecting that has stealthily wormed its way into the hobby over the last couple of decades is the jaw-dropping disparity in asking prices for "raw" vs "graded" Near Mints. When comics grading first appeared, it seemed to be for the purpose of having a neutral third party resolve grading disputes, initially on very valuable comics where the difference in value between a Fine or a Fine+ could result in a sizeable difference in the selling price of the item.

For example, the *Guide* states that *Avengers* #9 in VF 8.0 grade is worth $450.00, while a VF+ 8.5 copy should sell for over $750.00. One can certainly understand why a person interested in buying the book would desire the neutral opinion of a third party. Who would want to pay $750.00 for a $450.00 book? The problem is, when the book comes back actually graded 8.5, the buyer is offered the item for a multiple of *Guide* in that grade, maybe in the $1,000 to $1,500.00 range!

So now the buyer is certain that he's getting an 8.5 instead of an 8.0, but at a ridiculously inflated price! If the purpose of grading comics is to insure buyers that the book they are purchasing is graded accurately, why is the price then increased to a multiple of what the *Guide* states is the value of that grade? I could see if the seller added the cost of grading the book to the transaction, but why add on hundreds of dollars to the price just because a third party validated its condition? (Imagine the rate of inflation on really rare comics, such as *All Star Comics* #3 or *Batman* #1 ??) It seems to me that the buyer is being punished for daring to ask that the book he is interested in buying gets accurately graded! Does the value of a book double or triple just because someone in authority preferred his or her expert opinion about the item?

Yet people who deal every day in graded books think this process is perfectly normal; they're too close to the industry to see the massive unfairness of the whole thing. To my way of thinking, the purpose of a seller trying to document the grade of an item should be so that when he offers the book for sale at the *Guide* price for that grade, he can feel confident that he's not overcharging on the deal. But the way it now stands, if a collector buys a graded comic, he expects to pay way over *Guide*, which totally defeats the whole purpose of his trying to insure that he is not being taken advantage of!

I'll end here, just briefly noting a few other problems with the industry....the ridiculously inflated cover prices on today's new comics (if the Big Two can sell us 32-page titles for 25 cents on Free Comic Book Day, why are they charging $4.00, or even $5.00, apiece for the same product?); the insane proliferation of variant covers that in most cases feature characters that don't even appear in the pages of the stories themselves (a Ms. Marvel variant for the latest *Iron Man* issue, for example, or the almost risible existence of close to 40 different covers on *Eternals* #1!!); the suicidal marketing ploy of forcing an interested reader to buy 120 crossovers to read a single story that years ago would have been told in one artfully-crafted issue; not to mention the incredibly irritating habit of restarting every superhero title over at #1 again whenever the sales dip a couple of points, making it impossible at this point for fans to put their collection in number order without an open *Overstreet* in front of them and a magnifying glass to decipher the microscopic newsstand dates inside each book (now I'm really showing my age!).

The whole point of my diatribe is not to disparage the hobby, but rather to save it. Collectors work hard for their money, and no one likes to be taken advantage of by sleazy, or lazy, marketing strategies. Stop gouging the back issue collectors with grossly inflated prices just because a book has been professionally graded. Everything in this world has its breaking point (just look at what happened to baseball cards!). Let's keep this wonderful hobby alive and thriving for future generations, and not allow greed or ineptitude to destroy it.

John Verzyl II & Rose Verzyl-Shukla Comic Heaven

To start off, I wanted to congratulate all the comic stores and dealers whose businesses managed to stay open during these tumultuous times. Besides the long reach of economic depression known as COVID-19, questionable decisions from DC Comics has sent small yet noticeable shockwaves throughout the entire market.

The biggest change that has truly affected us is the lack of cons, all shut down in hopes of stunting the virus' increasing growth. The excitement of the yearly trip to San Diego Comic Con has been ingrained in me since I was baby, but the lack of lifting boxes and driving cross-country this year gives me the odd feeling of missing something. My family and I miss the electricity in the air as cosplaying masters and comic enthusiasts wander the convention hall. I miss the ability to communicate face to face with a customer, or to shake the hand of a friendly comic dealer. I miss the conventions so much that I am currently writing this from a Dallas hotel room because I have been going a tiny bit stir crazy. I doubt that the big conventions will return in 2021, but I remain hopeful.

This year has also made me realize how important the internet is to comic collecting as a whole. The largest auction houses in the industry all operate pretty much exclusively on the web. Individual dealers and comic book shops have found refuge on eBay and GoDaddy to sell their precious books while others have decided to wait out the storm. Even all the prices for the books in our inventory are heavily influenced by sales on GPAnalysis, a website where you can view the most current sales from almost every comic selling platform.

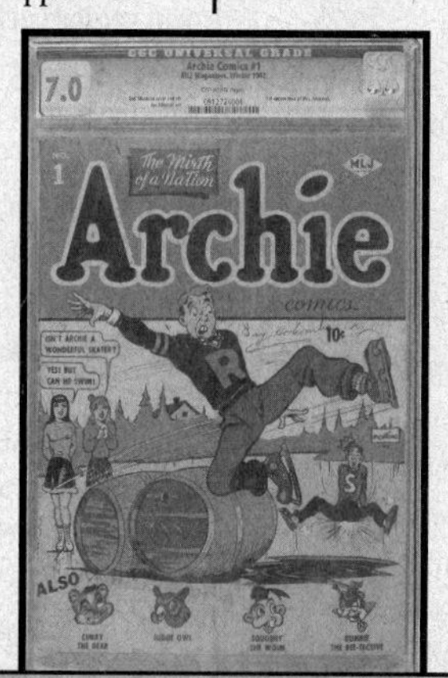

Archie Comics #1 has been rising drastically and keeping its value.

Amidst all the despair during this year, I'm delighted to report how well the market is doing. Anyone that knows me well might remember me saying, "Watch out for 2020! Some big shifts are going to happen!" When it comes to any economy, things tend to follow a pattern and are quite certain to repeat themselves. The Great Depression was over 90 years ago, and the last time there was a significant lull in comics was in the mid '90s. The economy generally has a depression every 75 to 100 years, so my thought process was that we were going to go into a recession and the books that were rising drastically like *Archie Comics* #1 were going to pop, hurting other Golden Age titles. To illustrate my point, a 4.0 (VG) copy of *Archie* #1 sold in 2012 for $23,200 and then in 2015 for $33,111. The 30% increase as well as the fact that a low-grade book is going for well over *Guide* is quite alarming at first glance. I figured that books like this and some Silver Age titles dramatic raises would be signaling the end for the industry.

Instead, they are holding strong as ever. This year, business owners could have folded to the virtual end of physical stores, but many decided to pull up their bootstraps and continue to sell products. An *Archie* #1 sold for $30,000 this year, and this is more realistic now with VG *Guide* at $25,800 rather than whatever lower number it was in the 2015 *Guide*. Comics across the board have been able to hold and, in some cases, go up a little bit in value during these difficult times. Around the time of writing this, a *Detective Comics* #27 in 7.0 (FN/VF) sold for $1.5 million! With a little bit of number crunching, *Guide* is $988,750, meaning that this book went about 1.5 times over *Guide*. Further, this is a great sale considering how rare *Detective Comics* #27 is above FN and the fact that early *Detectives* featuring Batman always go above *Guide*.

I am so pleased with everyone's perseverance and love for comics as collectors, investors, and fans continue to buy, sell, and trade their treasured books. It is everyone's deep love of comics that continues to keep the industry sailing along, no matter how stormy the weather. I would also like to thank everyone that has bought from our new internet store. Our comicheaven.net store is up and running but is still under development. I am enjoying the challenge of adding new books to the website so make sure to check in every now and again. Remember to stay safe and happy hunting!

Lon Webb
Dark Adventure Comics

This year has been a ride to remember – somewhat like new comics in 1992 or Golden Age in 1995. Unless 2020's cumulative market is in itself a massive speculative bubble or a huge roller-coaster of money laundering by reactive white and dark hats (ha!), many seem to have happily thrown everything but their un-leveraged kitchen sinks into it. So, let's dissect this.

The year began as a clean continuation of the previous year's bounty of healthy market activity. Surfing on the nice, long wave of steadily increasing sales across the board, I was watching and waiting for signs of a plateau...which never really fully happened. That was unusual, as waves in this business eventually play out, except on the perennials everyone are always after which just build in value like deserts expand – slow and sure, but with more rapidity in hotter years. When COVID-19 washed in, I figured we were about to enter a World's Series of Comic Poker with antes and cash-outs countering one another until a hurricane or sandstorm of sorts would reconfigure the game.

There was a definite hold 'em pattern that at first swept the basic collector base as stores temporarily closed, conventions went on hiatus, and face-to-face sales tanked. The average player sat out some hands while the up-front costs of living became priority. The industry went into a weird flux from total shut-down to an overwhelmed business-as-unusual event, while eBay, auction house, and online sales continued and spiked. However, the investor end not only forged ahead, but upped their stakes.

My operation got serious early on and not only isolated and COVID-proofed our inventory and shipping process, but radically added to it. Our internet sales rose by a third almost overnight, and increasingly bigger-ticket items moved briskly as people kept themselves fixed online. With stay-at-home constraints, many also searched out reading material and our book and trade sales soared as expected, but surprisingly, once the federal stimulus checks started arriving, scores of basic collectors poured much of that cash into not only readers, but also vintage material.

Our summer was phenomenal – all categories of collectibles moving at rates I haven't collectively seen in years. Then, as with a finger-snap, the average buyer began withdrawing from the scene in late August as nationwide, budgets tightened. As of this mid-December writing, sales from this group have stayed that way, with Black Friday hitting gray while Christmas spending (usually at this group's yearly highest) rolled out at a level less than any previous year. This tells me all I need to know about the state of the average buyer's personal economy, regardless of the stock market figures. It should also throw a red flag at anyone in this business thinking that all of this gravy is a train running with no station stops ahead (as it has been for almost three years). As I'll get into shortly, it's best to understand that in real life, national prosperity tends to flow from the bottom out, not the top down.

Happening simultaneously, better financially-positioned collectors and mid-to high-end investors had an orgiastic spending spree that is still ongoing. Even the last wave of flush newbies that entered the market in the past handful of years that are generally speculators (and mainly in the 9.8 newer/variant comic and movie-related first appearances niche) have been on a wild ride. They've been heat-pressed fueling all of the specially-made creator closed-signings at CGC and playing auction roulette on eBay, betting black every time, while carefully packaging their 9.8 pre-screens for shipping.

Meanwhile, keys of all ages and grades, especially Silver, are changing hands like nitrile gloves on first responders. Books that were hot as the Sahara last year (Horror, Good Girl/bondage/Nazi/American flag/looney-eyed-deformed-sadists-with needles-pokers-claws-and-bloody-murder/atomic bomb covers with hot artists-like Baker/Cole, Cole & Baker, et al) are selling at multiples that should make this *Guide* heavy with the sweat of final averaged sales. What the hell isn't selling? Westerns? No, even the slowest are being packaged for sale as we speak. Low-to mid-grade Silver and Bronze, existing in the thousands upon thousands? Nope-they are individually selling *Guide* and above in nice lots by the major auction houses with buyer's premiums attached. Gold Key/Harvey/Dell files? They're being bought raw and "cha-ching," slabbed and "ka-ching." Everything has been "cha-cha-ka-chinging." Records set weekly, daily, hourly? How? Why? Who? By everyone, apparently...except-as of current – the average buyer. Yes, I've now gotten to it.

What does this mean? I think the obvious reason is buyer/collector/investor faith in the market. I've been in this game since before that first *Guide* gave validity to what we comic geeks all suspected to be true. I have faith in this market as long as people my age (give or take a decade) and the average buyer are still in it. This market finances babies, first and third houses, businesses, addictions and pleasures of all sorts when it's a bull...otherwise, all those things begin to get leveraged into the reality of survival for the average buyer. You can't eat paper and staples, but they can keep one warm in the fireplace or be fire-sold. Even so, overall, collectible comics (not ALL comics, just the thinned-out herd) hold and exceed their value (better than stocks). It's been proven for 50 years among my peers and maybe will for another 20, until they mostly become an over-priced oddity to the young. Until then, I've got faith in those key wonders, my brethren...and the average buyer.

What I don't have any faith in is speculators and investors. Sure, there are many actual deep-pocketed collectors who are both. After all, they made this hobby into the viable market it is – along with the average to mid-level collector – because they bought comics and because they loved them...still do. Speculators and investors alone? They love money, with returns as sole anchor. More than once, I've watched them wreck every collectible field they touch (even this one). They get in all adrenalized, acquire the best of the best, then the best of the rest, and when they have wrung the market out over time by overspending and overselling even the chafe to and from collectors, they cool and do the same to each other, cash out, and bail, monetized to strike again. And when they bail, that hobby is left in free-fall onto salted and scorched ground.

Neal Adams **Batman** books (#232 shown) are best sellers.

It could be happening now and we're in the beginning-to-mid-stage of high-rollers playing with high-end, driving prices to end-sale points. It can look a lot like bubbles and laundry. Or it could simply be market faith writ large by peers and investors in uncertain times. Only currently, there isn't a monetized "average buyer" lower base in the market for recovery, which puts either scenario at approaching critical mass. There are three economies at play in our country and this business' health is measured by all three being active together. COVID has accelerated financial collapse in many business sectors while temporarily boosting others, and futures are arguably uncertain. Our sector has one hand recovering while the other is booming with one foot dancing while the other is lame. That's not surety, just faith. The market is roaring and I'm still buying, but with caution – from the average buyer who's not purchasing or holding, but selling...just to survive indefinitely. That's fact.

Sales Of Note: *Astonishing* #30 CGC 5.5 $4200; *Captain America Comics* #23 CGC 5.5 $2500; *Captain America Comics* #78 CGC 4.0 $1262; *Human Torch* #34 CGC 4.0 $490; *Terrific Comics* #4 CGC 6.0 $3100; *Meteor Comics* #1 CGC 8.0 $495; *Sad Sack Comics* #1 CGC 7.0 $1000 and *Pep Comics* #24 CGC 4.0 $2725.

HARLEY YEE
HARLEY YEE COMICS

First, I hope that everyone has been safe and healthy in these strange times we live in. I also hope that everyone has a great and wonderful 2021.

The market is definitely healthy with record prices in most areas. Bronze and Copper keys, Atlas, pre-Code Horror, Silver Age Marvels, Golden Age and Silver Age DC and Romance have been particularly strong.

Without many of the conventions for 2020 happening, I have been grading more books from the Golden Age to the Copper Age. This has allowed me to put more books online and give the buyers more confidence.

In the Golden Age (besides the keys), pre-Code Horror, Atlas/Timely, Romance, Good Girl art, and Archies are leading the way. Frazetta books have also been heating up in the later half of 2020. Wonder Woman books are also heading up with the new movie generating more interest.

In the Silver Age, Marvels as always lead the way with *Spider-Man* and *X-Men* the strongest. In DC, *Batman* and related titles are the top sellers. Among those books, Neal Adams books, and Jim Steranko books are the best sellers.

In the Bronze Age, there are too many to list but *Teenage Mutant Ninja Turtles* books and *Star Wars* books have been extremely hot.

In the Copper to Modern Ages, Harley Quinn books are doing well along with anything Spider-Man.

In summary, with the conventions probably on hold until the later half of 2021, graded books will represent a greater percentage of the market than ever.

Vincent Zurzolo, Morgan Liebman & Rob Reynolds Metropolis Collectibles ComicConnect.com

Vincent Zurzolo - Metropolis Collectibles and ComicConnect.com

Over the course of my now 35-year career in comics, I have faced many challenges, but I can't think of anything more alarming than what happened in NYC in March 2020. The pandemic lockdown created an anxious period filled with so many unknowns. My partner and entire staff worked from home while I kept the business going. It was daunting at first, buying, selling, taking consignments, helping with the bookkeeping, pulling orders, shipping packages, running to the bank, and everything in between. Once I got into a rhythm, things started coming together, and believe it or not, once April rolled around sales were up for that month by 20% from April 2019. I want to thank my entire team, especially Josh Conley, for their efforts and thank all of you for supporting us throughout 2020.

During the beginning of the Covid-Zombie Apocalypse, things were getting scarier every day. When I left my home, I was literally one of the only non-military or police officers on the streets of what had arguably been the busiest city in the world. It was surreal. At first, things slowed down, but then something amazing happened. All the collectors locked in their homes around the country, around the world, had the time to look through their collections, see what they were missing, what they wanted to buy and sell, and the market exploded! It was sensational. Without traditional conventions, virtual ones popped up, as well as internet claim sales and live sales on social media. I believe in many ways the pandemic reinvigorated the collectibles market. A wise man once told me every dark cloud has a silver lining (thanks Mike Carbonaro via his dad Tony Carbonaro - RIP) and this terrifying chapter filled with so much tragedy and loss did have some positives. Of course, I wish the pandemic never happened, but it did, and the remarkable thing I noticed was collectors were coming together with a reignited passion for collecting. The camaraderie in collectibles increased and an overall desire to adhere to things that make us happy took over. Whether we are collectors, dealers, flippers, investors, or whatever, we share a love for comics, and it is something that makes us happy, otherwise, we wouldn't be in it. Comics make us happy. We now had more time as we didn't have pesky things like commuting to work and going out shopping to distract us from what was important. We were able to focus on what we love, comics!

Hopefully, by the time this book is in your hands, the vaccine will be in place and we will be moving past this pandemic. To review the market over the last year, there continued to be an increased demand for classic and obvious choices in vintage comics. However, just as apparent was the growth and demand for comics in varying grades that you'd normally find in discount boxes being scooped up by collectors everywhere wanting something fun with upside potential. '80s-'90s comics are soaring in demand. This is fun to see, as it shows the diversity of interests in time periods, genres, and conditions of comics, both raw and CGC graded. This also shows a lot of future promise as the collectors buying $10 comics today are the ones who will be buying $100 to $1 million comics in the future.

The big Golden Age comics we moved over the last year include *Detective* #27 CGC 6.0 Rockford copy for $850,000, *Batman* #1 CGC 4.0 $137,888, *Action Comics* #13 CGC 9.2 $166,000, *Detective Comics* #28 CGC 8.5 $80,000, *All Star Comics* #8 CGC 5.5 $75,500, *Superman* #14 CGC 9.4 $120,000, and *Captain America Comics* #1 CGC 8.0 (manufactured without the red ink) $140,000.

Although we saw some cooling off on *Amazing Fantasy* toward the end of 2019 and through the early months of the pandemic, the book is coming back, as it always does. Here are several *AF* #15 sales: CGC 8.0 $177,000, CGC 8.0 $189,000, CGC 8.0 $192,000, CGC 7.0 $110,000, CGC 4.0 $22,000, CGC 4.0 $19,700, CGC 3.0 Stan Lee sig. $19,700, CGC 3.5 $16,900, CGC 3.5 $16,866, CGC 2.0 Stan Lee sig. $16,300, 3.5 tape $15,232, 3.0 $15,000, 2.5 tape $14,000, CGC 1.5 Stan Lee sig. $12,667, CGC 3.5 restored $12,500, CGC 1.8 Stan Lee sig. $12,400, and a 2.0 $10,000. *AF* #15 is my all-time favorite comic. This is the *Action* #1 of the '60s and I believe the book will continue to soar into the stratosphere.

Silver Age sales include: *Avengers* #1 CGC 9.6 $250,000, *Avengers* #1 CGC 9.4 $95,000, *X-Men* #1 CGC 9.4 $215,000, *X-Men* #1 CGC 9.2 $134,000, *Justice League* #1 CGC 9.6 $190,000, *Amazing Spider-Man* #1 CGC 9.4 $165,000, *Fantastic Four* #1 CGC 8.5 $100,000, *Showcase* #4 CGC 8.5 $100,000, *Daredevil* #1 CGC 9.6 $50,000, and *Tales of Suspense* #39 CGC 9.4 $135,000.

A special note about a beautiful collection of Golden and Silver Age keys I picked up from a great guy named Matt. He and I have known one another for a long time. Finally getting to meet him at his home and to be introduced to his family was a special moment. The collection was filled with so many great comics including *Superman* #1, *AF* #15, three copies of *FF* #1, *Showcase* #4, four copies of *Tales of Suspense* #39, three copies of *Journey into Mystery* #83, three copies of *X-Men* #1, two *Avengers* #1, four *Avengers* #4, and the list goes on and on. Sufficed to say it was an amazing collection and both parties walked away with smiles on their faces. As it should be in the world of comics.

Pre-Code Horror comic sales include: *Tales of Terror Annual* #1 CGC 4.0 $13,300, *Weird Mysteries* #5 CGC 6.5 $11,979, *Black Cat Mystery* #50 CGC 9.0 $18,400, and CGC 8.5 $14,800, *Crime SuspenStories* #22 CGC 8.5 Gaines $13,300, and *Tales from the Crypt* #20 CGC 9.8 $11,000. Horror is one of my favorite genres in comics. As they continue to appreciate, I see the lower-priced copies continue to pick up in demand and price.

Bronze to Copper Age sales include: *Star Wars* #1 CGC 9.0 35 cent variant $10,000, *Marvel Spotlight* #5 CGC 9.8 $75,000, *Werewolf by Night* #32 CGC 9.8 $37,000, *Teenage Mutant Ninja Turtles* #1 CGC 9.8 $59,000, *Cerebus* #1 CGC 9.6 $24,000, and *Giant-Size X-Men* #1 CGC 9.8 $15,000. Growing up in the '70s and '80s I have a soft spot for these comics, and I am happy to see others also cherishing them as much.

Original art highlight sales include: *Batman* #184 cover by Carmine Infantino $42,663, *Batman* #50 5-variant covers by J. Scott Campbell $50,000, *Lone Wolf & Cub* #3 by Frank Miller $40,000, *Captain America* #189 cover by Gil Kane $29,000, *Giant-Size Super-Villain Team-Up* by Gil Kane $25,000, *Swamp Thing* #64 double-page spread by Stephen Bissette $11,400, *Daredevil* #4 page 8 by Joe Orlando $10,000, and a *2000 A.D.* 1961 painting by Simon Bisley $12,000. The art market is on fire. Every year I say the same thing, I can't believe the prices have gone this high and then the next year, they push higher.

Over the last year, we've increased our presence in the video game market. There is a tremendous cross-over between comic collectors and video games. We've also expanded into several other categories like graded concert posters, Pokémon cards, sports cards, pulps, action figures, statues, and movie props. Major sales include a Captain America helmet $18,200, Wonder Woman lasso $16,600, a *Stadium Event Family Fun Fitness* WATA graded 6.0 $55,000, *Shantae* WATA 9.8 $28,000, *Metroid* WATA 6.5 $16,000, and a *Kid Icarus* WATA 8.0 $12,977.

My forecast for the future? I dusted off my crystal ball and what it showed me was the following: There will be increased growth in almost every area of comics in 2021. I saw a slight slowdown at the end of 2019 after I wrote my last market report, but the pandemic kicked the collectibles market into overdrive. There is so much renewed interest from older collectors and a burgeoning passion and increased earning potential amongst a newer generation that will fuel continued growth in the market.

As always, I thank you all for your love of comics, patronage, and friendship. I hope we get to meet in person in the near future.

Morgan Liebman - Metropolis Collectibles

Last year, when I stepped into the formidably large shoes of Frank Cwiklik to take over the grading department at Metropolis Collectibles, I was excited and a little intimidated to shoulder all the responsibilities that had previously been the burden of my predecessor. Little did I know that 2020 would have quite a few more surprises in store beyond the scope of learning some of the minutiae of my new position, and the daily ins and outs of meeting the demands of the vintage comics business.

The first challenge that was presented to the staff here at Metropolis was the launch of a brand-new website, which revamped our long-standing, and well-known online presence, updated our look, and overhauled our back-end database. Needless to say, there were wrinkles to iron out when we launched, but nothing could have prepared us for what was to come next. It seemed like one day there was an announcement that COVID-19 had reached the U.S. but there were only a few small incidences across the country, fast forward a few weeks, and New York City's hospitals were being overrun with patients exposed to the virus, there were empty shelves in every store, and it was impossible to find hand sanitizer, face masks, and even staples like toilet paper and groceries. Shortly thereafter NYC shut down completely, all our employees were working remotely from home, doing whatever we could to keep the company functioning, and keeping in touch with our thousands of customers worldwide to let them know what was going on. Plenty of our regulars reached out from as of yet unaffected areas to inquire about our well-being and our plans.

I personally set up shop at a coffee table in my living room on the couch, where I would continue to work for the following three months, enduring the eerie experience of the Big Apple becoming a silent ghost town at night, where the only sounds to be heard were sirens, and even experiencing my first ever curfew. The silver lining to this very difficult and unpredictable moment in history? Business never let up, there was absolutely zero decrease in volume of orders and sales, in fact, we saw an increase in business before we were cleared to resume work and return from our homes back into the world. One can only theorize what led to the upswing in commerce, was it the dearth of free time people suddenly had that led them to sit in front of their computers looking for something to keep themselves occupied? Did reluctant customers finally decide to take the plunge and invest in some vintage comics, which have been proving to be one of the more stable and tangible assets around? Whatever the reason, what began as guarded trepidation soon changed into optimism, providing one of the few positive glimmers of hope through what was a very dark time, especially for New Yorkers. Once we achieved a semblance of normalcy after coming back to work, we were again pleasantly surprised to see our Event Auctions perform as though nothing had happened, bids were through the roof, and prices on almost every key book were still climbing unabated.

Our excursions into other collectible fields also showed growth, our video game inventory has become a center of bustling activity daily, as the relatively new marketplace continues to expand in earnest, bringing a new generation of collectors into our orbit thanks to Jeff Maza, head of the department. The hire of art expert Micah Spivak has helped build our original comic art department into a formidable force in the industry, bringing in new clients and amazing pieces of original art by some of the biggest names in the business. We have also made inroads into other fields, jumping into the extremely hot Pokémon card trade, which has blown up beyond anyone's possible expectations, with sealed boxes going for hundreds of thousands of dollars. Movie and TV props, concert posters, collectible toys, action figures, and more have really helped make 2020 a year filled with a myriad of surprises. The challenges we've encountered over the past twelve months have made us a stronger, and a more tightly knit group, and have reaffirmed the timeworn stereotype about the resilience of New Yorkers. The leadership shown by Director of Consignments, Rob Reynolds, CEO Stephen Fishler, and COO Vincent Zurzolo throughout this crisis has kept everyone on an even keel and helped the ship of Metropolis Collectibles navigate the choppy waters of running a successful business during times of a pandemic. At least I didn't have to work too hard to think about how I would frame this year's Overstreet Market Report, the story basically wrote itself.

Looking toward the future I can't say that we here at Metropolis have cause to feel anything but enthusiasm about 2021, kicking off with *Wonder Woman 1984* and *Zack Snyder's Justice League* the DCEU is poised to infuse some new energy into their silver-screen franchise, while a slate of MCU films await release, beginning with *Black Widow* and followed by *Shang-Chi and the Legend of the Ten Rings* there is plenty of reason to believe the comic market's fortunes will continue to improve thanks to the exposure enjoyed by the blockbuster success of superhero movies. We expect our inroads with video games, original art, Pokémon cards, and other avenues to continue to expand and reap benefits. Younger collectors are aging up into the investment market, and are seeking collectibles beyond comics, as being raised in the digital age has created new fields to explore and new collections to uncover.

From the gang here at Metropolis Collectibles, we wish all our friends, families, and customers a healthy, happy, and successful new year as we live and learn from the hard lessons taught to us in 2020. Thanks for reading!

Rob Reynolds - ComicConnect.com

Dinah Washington sang a song that went "What a difference a day made, twenty-four little hours, brought the sun and the flowers, where there used to be rain." For many, this past year turned in to a solitary day of unending rain and the sun or the flowers never appeared. Then, the lyrics went "there's a rainbow before me, skies above can't be stormy." Undoubtedly, the ballad is about discovering a new love, but that is beside the point. The lesson here is brighter days are ahead. At this stage, we have nowhere to go but up; the detestably endless cloudy day we have all slogged through will be behind us. Sunny skies are ahead - in the meantime, investment collectors are stashing and stockpiling, and at record prices, as stay at home workers have turned to collectibles as a haven for their investments and an escape into nostalgic pleasure.

Carmine Infantino's original art for the cover of **Batman** #184 sold for $42,663.

With launching the new website in January, to the pandemic going viral in March, ComicConnect held the first auction of the year in May featuring Gold and Silver Age comic book keys, a selection of original comic art, and the first hundred WATA-certified video game lots we have ever offered. This year more than ever, our clientele is seeking to both expand and diversify their portfolios and ComicConnect responded by adding more than a half dozen investment categories including video games, movie props, sports cards, Pokémon cards, toys, CGC-certified concert posters, and pulps. We have experts for every department to ensure our clients have everything they need to make the most informed choices.

Event Auction #42 kicked off ComicConnect's 2020 auction season with an exclamation point. With rare pre-Code horror, high grade keys, and long runs of popular titles, the most elite investment collectors in the hobby placed tens of thousands of bids in the millions of dollars. Original art auction highlights include an unused *Amazing Spider-Man* #40 cover by John Romita $9,200, a *Batman* #184 cover by Carmine Infantino $42,663, and a Kobra concept illustration by Jack Kirby $7,900.

Event Auction #42 Comic Book Highlights:

Action Comics #10 CGC 3.0 $76,000
All Star Comics #8 CGC 2.0 $22,500
Amazing Fantasy #15 CGC 8.0 $177,000
Amazing Spider-Man #1 CGC 7.5 $28,888
Amazing Spider-Man #1 CGC 7.0 Stan Lee SS $27,501
Amazing Spider-Man #14 CGC 9.6 $25,001
Batman #1 CGC 3.5 $83,000
Detective Comics #38 CGC 8.5 Restored $38,123
Detective Comics #168 CGC 6.5 $24,000
Fantastic Four #1 CGC 7.0 $34,005
Rawhide Kid #17 CGC 9.4 $20,600
Wonder Woman #2 CGC 9.6 $27,633
Wonder Woman #6 CBCS 9.2 $24,750
X-Men #1 CGC 9.2 $134,000

Bidding in Event Auction #43 started in the middle of

the dog days of August and never cooled by the time the hammer struck a few weeks later. Over 3,000 lots sold, our largest auction to date. The DC Premiere Collection was the headline offering a DC collection packed with firsts, origin and first appearances. When dropping off the consignment, the owner explained, "For investing, DC first appearances were rare and in high enough demand to ensure strong returns in the future, and, when I started buying, they were also undervalued, which gave me a great advantage."

We also added television and movie props including several items from the fan favorite Marvel Cinematic Universe. A battle-distressed combat helmet from *Captain America: The First Avenger* $20,930 and USO Shield $20,930 while a DC fan picked up Wonder Woman's lasso from *Batman V Superman* $19,090. Our original art auctions have grown steadily and the sale of page 6 from *Swamp Thing* #6 by Stephen Bissette $11,400 and a Joe Orlando page from *Daredevil* #4 hit $10,000.

Event Auction #43 Comic Book Highlights:

All American Comics #61 CGC 7.0 $30,500
All Star Comics #8 CGC 4.0 $29,000
Amazing Fantasy #15 CGC 4.0 $22,000
Amazing Spider-Man #1 CGC 7.5 $31,501
Detective Comics #35 CGC 3.0 $26,000
Fantastic Comics #3 CBCS 9.2 R $20,000
Fantastic Four #5 CGC 9.4 $84,667
Green Lantern #1 CGC 9.2 $19,000
Incredible Hulk #1 CGC 8.5 Restored $21,550
More Fun Comics #73 CGC 5.5 $61,000
Sensation Comics #1 CGC 5.5 $45,000
Startling Comics #49 CGC 8.5 $23,500
Superman #3 CGC 8.5 $22,011
Tales of Suspense #39 CBCS 9.2 $41,700
Wonder Woman #6 CGC 9.4 Double Cover $32,833
Wonderworld Comics #3 CGC 9.4 $64,111

By the third and final auction of the year, ComicConnect offered nine separate investment categories. From the beginning, our ComicConnect team has provided our clientele with prospects and opportunities to expand their investment portfolios.

Original Comic Art sales were topped by the cover to *Amazing Spider-Man* #162 by Ross Andru and John Romita $124,200, Frank Miller and Klaus Janson's cover to *Daredevil* #166 $100,050, Gene Colan's cover to *Daredevil* #40 $65,000, *X-Men* #105 double page spread by Dave Cockrum $46,000, *Amazing Spider-Man* #313 page by Todd McFarlane $24,888, Gil Kane's *Doctor Strange* #8 cover $23,575, Frank Miller's *Detective Comics* #27 variant cover $20,000, Howard Chaykin's *American Flagg!* portfolio plate $17,700, the *Star*Reach* #1 cover by Jim Starlin $15,300, Bob Oksner's *Lois Lane* #122 cover $14,644 and a page from Neil Gaiman's *Sandman* #67 by Marc Hempel $13,700.

ComicConnect offered over 100 rare and high-grade video games to choose from with highlights: *Final Fantasy 2* WATA 8.0 $10,000 (S NES); *The Legend of Zelda* WATA 8.5 $8,800 (NES); *Michael Jackson's Moonwalker* WATA 8.0 $6,850 (SMS). As the retro video game market grows by leaps and bounds, expect to see more classics from ComicConnect in 2021.

We did not hesitate to add Pokémon booster boxes to our auctions when the opportunity presented itself. This is one of the most exciting and dynamic new investments ComicConnect is excited to offer to our investment clientele. Event Auction #44 hammer prices: *Neo Genesis* $31,560, *Unlimited Base* $22,000, *Gym Challenge* $15,500, *Gym Heroes* $15,400, *Team Rocket* $15,000, *Fossil* $13,500, *Jungle* (open) $14,600, and an original 1995 Pokémon Japanese box $30,000. Our selection of props was headlined by a screen used Comedians Smiley Badge from 2009's *Watchmen* which realized $2702. This was followed by the Stunt Rifle and Case of Explosive Charges featured in Marvel and Netflix's *Luke Cage* series from 2018 which ended at $1998.

Event Auction #44 comic book highlights:

Action Comics #13 CGC 9.0 Restored $24,500
All Flash Quarterly #1 CGC 9.2 $20,125
All Select Comics #1 CGC 8.5 $47,833
Amazing Fantasy #15 CGC 9.8 Restored $42,222
Amazing Fantasy #15 CGC 5.5 $40,500
Amazing Spider-Man #6 CGC 9.6 $15,000
Avengers #1 CGC 9.0 $36,500
Batman #1 CGC 6.5 Restored $37,007
Captain America Comics #1 CGC 5.0 Restored $32,350
Detective Comics #37 CGC 8.0 $35,000
Fantastic Comics #8 CGC 9.6 $19,000
Fantastic Four #1 CGC 7.0 $56,000
Fantastic Four #5 CGC 9.2 $65,000
Flash #105 CGC 9.4 $58,000
Incredible Hulk #181 CGC 9.8 $47,500
More Fun Comics #54 CGC 9.0 $41,611
More Fun Comics #55 CGC 9.4 $88,000
Pep Comics #34 CGC 5.5 $23,199
Strange Tales #110 CGC 9.4 $47,944
Superman #1 CGC 3.0 $310,111
X-Men #1 CGC 8.5 $51,000

ComicConnect's mission is to grow and develop a following beyond expectations. Our hobby has innumerable facets and sub-genres that all fall under the pop culture umbrella. These collectibles all have a place at the table, under the auction hammer, and with investors and collectors alike diversifying their collections, we make every effort to meet client demands.

Once upon a time, Dinah Washington also sang "And this bitter earth may not be so bitter after all." Because sunnier days lie right around the corner and we know this because a thousand-year-old phrase goes "This too shall pass." Someday all this pandemic nonsense will be squarely in our rearview mirror. It's been one a heck of a year; what a difference 365 days makes. 2021 is going to be glorious. Email me at robr@comicconnect.com or call 888-779-7377 for assistance in selling or with adding to your investment portfolio.

THE WAR REPORT

by Matt Ballesteros & the War Correspondents
(Andy Greenham and Mick Rabin)

We are proud to present the 13th edition of the War Report, an independent assessment of the war comic market segment researched and developed by avid enthusiasts of the niche. This reoccurring dispatch has covered the war segment of the comic book hobby for more than a decade now. It was originally created and is currently maintained for our own edification and, hopefully, for your enjoyment.

Thanks to all our returning readers and supporters, your comments and encouragement have been tank fuel for us.

A HISTORY OF WAR

While we created this report to do open discovery of the war comic segment, we hesitated a bit at first. There was an obvious advantage to anonymity, in that my cohorts and I could gain from astute purchases on issues that no one had intel on. But ultimately, we strongly felt it was better for the hobby, and certainly for the growth of our segment, to openly share our knowledge and findings about the genre.

Thus, in 2007-08 we embarked on a quest to produce a comprehensive detailing of war comics, their creators, the characters, the art, the stories, and the market. This was spurred on by a few factors: momentum originally created by Chris Pedrin's *Big Five* compendium, the creation of the Big Five War Summit, the onset of a frenzy in the war comic after-market not seen prior to 2007, and, finally, the invitation by J.C. Vaughn and the fine crew at Overstreet to develop a comprehensive list of the top war comics in the hobby.

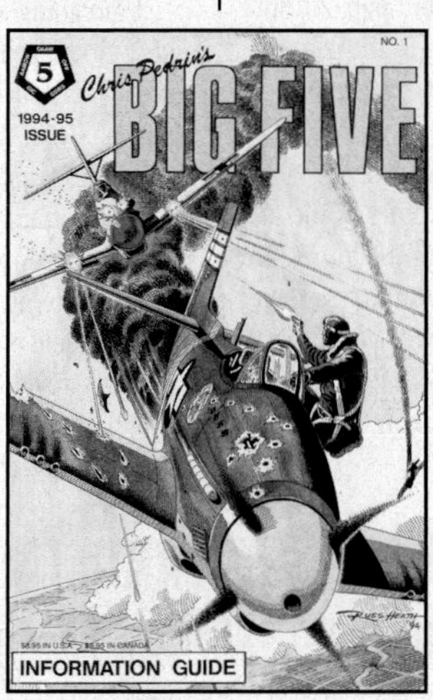

It was obvious to me that I needed to enlist the help of expert enthusiasts. I therefore assembled a team of war comic hobbyists from the US and Canada that I not only hold in the highest esteem, but whom I also consider to be better versed in the matter of war comic specifics, lore, and history. I have since referred to them fondly as The War Correspondents and they contribute in various capacities throughout each yearly report.

I hope you enjoy this year's rendition.

Title Abbreviations of the Big Five
AAMOW – All American Men of War
GIC – G.I. Combat
OAAW – Our Army at War
OFF – Our Fighting Forces
SSWS – Star Spangled War Stories

STOCKING THE WAR CHEST

War Comics to Target in this Bullish Market
(by Matt Ballesteros)

Apparently while the war comic genre has been quietly holding the line on its own front, everyone back at home has been engaged in an optimistic comic book buying frenzy. Particularly so with anything Marvel and/or comics in publishing lines that have had, or will have, movie tie-ins or general pop culture exposure. Granted, I am not telling anyone reading this anything that they do not already know. But in 2021 alone we have watched countless value upswings of a meaningful nature on first appearances, key issues, and even entire comic books runs.

As an admitted *Star Wars* fan (it is a war adventure tale in other galaxies, after all), I have been taken aback by the wild price growth on any *Star Wars* comic book just this year. This is especially true for the original 107-issue Marvel series hailing from 1977. OK, I was not that surprised. With Disney's acquisition of both the Marvel and Star Wars franchises, I certainly expected for strong continued growth in those areas. Disney, as we all know, is one of the greatest marketing entities in existence today. After spending billions acquiring the aforementioned intellectual property rights (IPs), you can be assured that they were going to double down on their investments. Through that, we have been getting quality content and paralleled messaging pumped into our very homes on a daily basis. As a result, the comic book marketplace is now truly experiencing the effects of that. As a completist, it is wreaking havoc on my pursuits of finishing a high grade run of that series.

Consider these two points. First, for today's youth, having pop culture and Disney-managed content served up daily and in real time has been the norm for their entire lives. This is a far cry from those of us who had to actively seek out and buy comics off spinner racks. It would thus seem to make sense that (thanks to that content pipeline coupled with recent technological advancements) as this new generation of pop culture fans acquires disposable income, they have not had to look far to find collectibles that remind them of their youth. Second, it is of no surprise to me that meaningful investment dollars are now being pumped into the comic industry as a variant investment option by shrewd investors. Certainly, the recent need for alternative investment channels and the birth of cryptocurrency have helped diminish the stigma of investing in collectibles, but also the comic book hobby itself has done a good job of establishing itself as a warranted option. I recently read a comment on a comic thread that attributed credit to Bob Overstreet for responsibly managing price increases for the last 50 years (obviously in an attempt to elude unstable runaway markets), and also to long time comic book hobbyists themselves for establishing an investment avenue that historically has been generally very reliable. I largely agree with that assertion, and we are seeing the results of that now.

How does this relate to war comics you may ask? I will tell you.

Using my above ramblings as context, what do we know? The comic book market is hot, there is new incoming money and values growing in robust fashion, specifically in Marvel related titles. But what else is doing well? Well, unsurprisingly, key issues in various publishing lines from the Golden to the Modern Age have been impacted. We are witnessing stellar pricing being adhered to in everything from *Whiz Comics* to *Teenage Mutant Ninja Turtles*, to scores of Modern variants. And the connective tissue? In most cases they are either tied to a superhero narrative, a popular IP, a movie or TV series, or anything attached to the current pop culture zeitgeist. So, what is *not* currently smoldering in the center of the investment bullseye? … Crime, romance, westerns, and yep, you guessed it, war comics.

I purposely left out genres like horror and funny animal, because although they are not dead center of the investment bullseye either, they are closer than the four I just mentioned. This may be because Disney characters keep funny animal runs in a spotlight, and the horror genre has maintained continued popularity resulting from new comic lines, the 21st century horror movie phenomenon, as well as other factors.

Crime, romance, westerns, and war are, however, not slipping. Far from it, they are growing too, each in their own way. It is just that with all the current attention on Marvel, superheroes, and *Star Wars*, these smaller genres are managing to remain within reason from a cost perspective. Consequently, this an opportune time to get into one of these categories, not just for the long-term investment aspect of it, but to discover the amazing art, characters, and stories that you didn't even know about (there is some seriously great storytelling in there). Therefore, in this report, I would love to shed light on some underrated and underestimated issues of the war comic genre, that in some cases, even war fans may have overlooked. Incidentally, as much as I would like to go into specifics on crime, romance and western, I am no expert in those arenas. I know which issues I want from those categories, but leave it to the purists to speak to what matters there. Hopefully, one day we can get a market report from those cats too (nudge-nudge). Either way, whether your interest is for the love of the medium or purely for the excitement of the catch and release, following are specific war comics that you may currently (2021) want to consider acquiring.

TARGET ACQUISITION

I am going to break this into two parts: exposed targets and camouflaged assets. Exposed targets will simply point out obvious issues within the war genre that anyone should already have in their line of sight. New recruits may want to look at these first. Camouflaged assets, on the other hand, are those comics that may be underestimated as a whole and should garner strong consideration for acquisition from newcomer or veteran alike. For those of you who would like to see the entire field of battle, simply refer to the end of this report where we provide our annual ranking of the top war comics in the hobby. We have been carefully curating this list since 2008 and tally what we consider the best issues of the genre.

EXPOSED TARGETS

War comics you probably know about but should take another look at.

Wings Comics #1 (Fiction House, 1940)

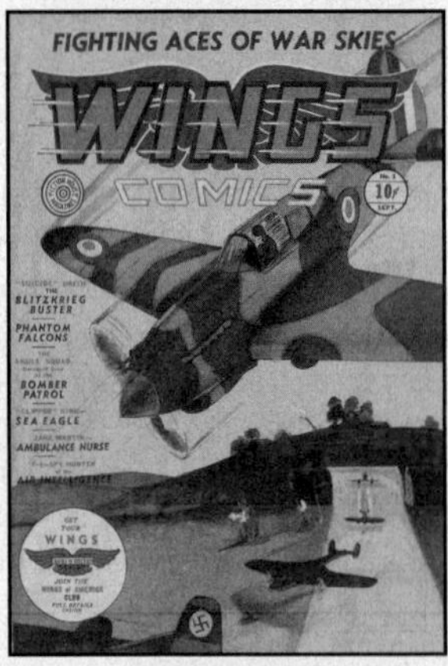

Determinant: First issue of a long running war and adventure series

Basis: A Golden Age war adventure classic with a washtone cover

Stats: Approx. 53 on census, only in 9.8 and two in 9.4

Disclosures: This book is coveted by war comic fans, Golden Age collectors, but mostly by Fiction House completists.

Potentiality: 81 years later, this comic is a pedigree. Although we do not expect wild climbs in value, we do not see it sliding.

Attainability: Moderate (in any grade)

Achievement: $28,680 for CGC 9.8 Edgar Church Mile High in May 2018

Performance: $1,920 for a CGC 8.5 in Sept. 2020

Sgt. Fury #1 (Marvel, 1963)

Determinant: First appearance of Sgt. Fury
Basis: Marvel's best known war comic character
Stats: Approx. 1,050 on census, seven in 9.4 and two in 9.2
Disclosures: Collected by both war hobbyists and Marvel fans.
Potentiality: Disney now owns this character. 'Nuff said.
Attainability: Easy (in any grade)
Achievement: $28,680 for a CGC 9.4 in November 2011
Performance: $2,300 for a CGC 6.5 in Feb. 2021

Sgt Fury #13 (Marvel, 1964)

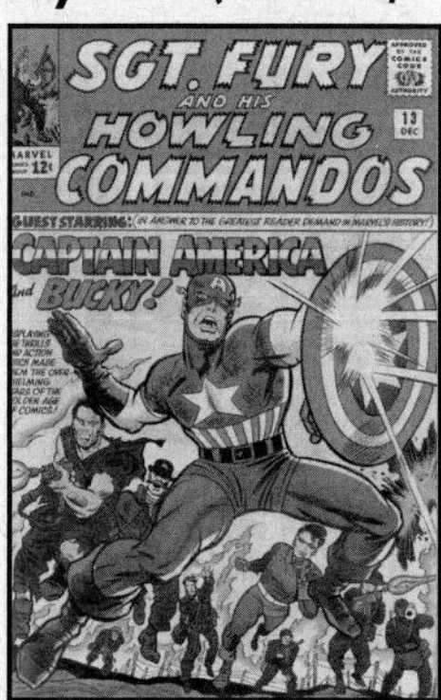

Determinant: First meeting of Nick Fury and Captain America
Basis: Very early Silver Age appearance of Capt. America and Bucky.
Stats: Approx. 1159 on census, four in 9.8 and 16 in 9.6
Disclosures: Although technically a "fantasy story," with Cap's appearance you cannot deny the importance of this book and its popularity amongst Marvel fans in particular.
Potentiality: With this being a Marvel property and a key issue, we see nothing but growth.
Attainability: Easy (in any grade)
Achievement: $11,353 for CGC 9.8 in Feb. 2018
Performance: $1,395 for a CGC 9.2 in Mar. 2021

Our Army at War #83 (DC, 1959)

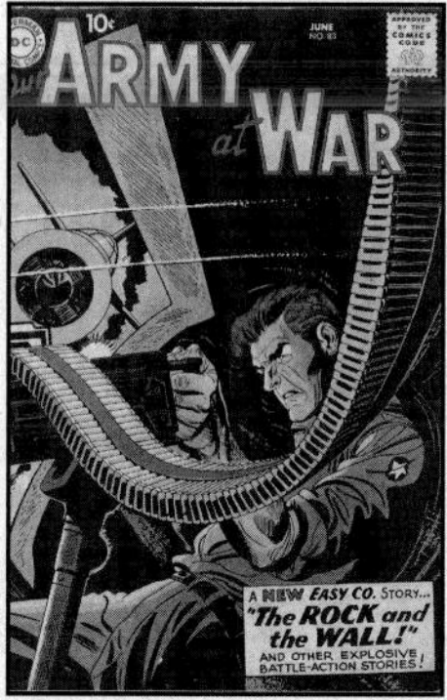

Determinant: First true appearance of Sgt. Rock
Basis: One of the most well-known and regarded war comic characters to date.
Stats: Approx. 200 on census, only one 9.0 and three in 8.0
Disclosures: The black cover makes it tough in grade, considered the grail of war comics.
Potentiality: Strong growth year over year, especially should Warner Bros. develop a feature film.
Attainability: Moderate (in any grade)
Achievement: $16,730 for a CGC 8.0 in Aug. 2015
Performance: $14,400 for a CGC 7.0 in Jan. 2021

Two-Fisted Tales #18 (EC, 1950)

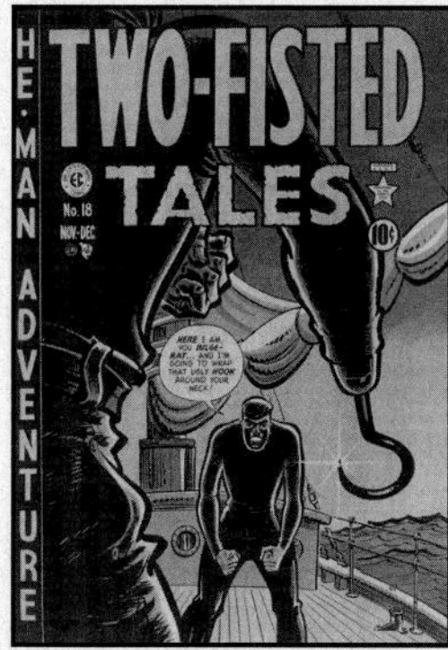

Determinant: First EC War comic
Basis: Begins classic war comic series
Stats: Approx. 42 on census, four in 9.8 and three in 9.6
Disclosures: Highly regarded for its art and potent storytelling.
Potentiality: With less than 50 graded copies of what is considered a seminal war comic, this will surely fuel its financial appreciation.
Attainability: Hard (in any grade)
Achievement: $4,800 for a CGC 9.8 in May 2019
Performance: $450 for a CGC 7.0 in Oct. 2020

Star Spangled War Stories #90 (DC, 1960)

Determinant: First Dinosaur "War That Time Forgot" issue
Basis: Dino's vs. Soldiers motif became popular with the general comic buying populace.
Stats: Approx. 81 on census, only one 8.5 and six in 8.0
Disclosures: Its popularity in the 1960s and beyond makes it impossible to find an unread (and unloved) copy. That, plus its dark purple cover, makes it a tough comic to find in grade.
Potentiality: Although also technically a fantasy comic, it is still a favorite among war collectors. This comic gained value a couple decades ago and has never slipped back. In today's market we believe it will continue to grow.
Attainability: Hard (in any grade)
Achievement: $4,200 for a CGC 8.5 in Dec. 2014
Performance: $504 for a CGC 6.5 in Oct. 2020

Blazing Combat (Warren, 1965)

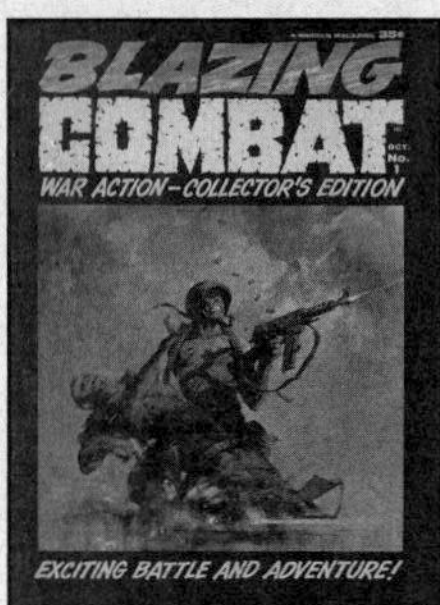

Determinant: First Warren Magazine issue devoted to war
Basis: Classic Frank Frazetta cover and contributions from multiple war genre creative teams.
Stats: Approx. 71 on census, only one 9.4 and three in 9.0
Disclosures: Its popularity through the '60s and '70s make it tough to find in grade.
Potentiality: Although magazine format, its strong storylines and celebrated cover art make this a standout amongst its war comic peers.
Attainability: Moderate (in any grade)
Achievement: $2,000 for a CGC 9.0 in Aug. 2016
Performance: $399 for a CGC 5.5 in Mar. 2021

Star Spangled War Stories #151 (DC, 1970)

Determinant: First solo appearance of the Unknown Soldier
Basis: This is the first issue in a series of classic Unknown Soldier stories.
Stats: Approx. 187 on census, only two in 9.8 and 12 in 9.6
Disclosures: The classic Joe Kubert cover and the beginning of an Unknown Soldier story run in *SSWS* makes this a must have for war comic collectors. Many ardent collectors believe this to be The Unknown Soldier's first appearance. We will explore that further in future editions of the War Report.
Potentiality: This key Bronze Age beauty is highly coveted, and we do not see it losing traction.
Attainability: Easy (in any grade)
Achievement: $2,629 for a CGC 9.8 in May 2009
Performance: $1,320 for a CGC 9.6 in Jan. 2021

Our Army at War #151 (DC, 1965)

Determinant: First appearance of Enemy Ace
Basis: Introduces new WWI character and storyline.
Stats: Approx. 161 on census, only one 9.4 and three in 9.2
Disclosures: With Robert Kanigher and Joe Kubert at the helm (the creative team behind Sgt. Rock), rich and stark storytelling make this a war comic favorite.
Potentiality: A key book and IP that has potential to pop out unto its own rich path due to the nature of its "flying aces" WWI setting.
Attainability: Easy (in any grade)
Achievement: $1,812 for a CGC 9.2 in Dec. 2012
Performance: $151 for a CGC 5.5 in Oct. 2021

Star Spangled War Stories #84 (DC, 1959)

Determinant: First app. of Mademoiselle Marie
Basis: War comics' best-known female character
Stats: Approx. 96 on census, only one 9.0 and four in 8.0
Disclosures: Unique in that the protagonist is a female character from the early DC war universe, and that she is potentially based on real life French Resistance fighters.
Potentiality: This comic and other early issues with her appearance have seen continuous growth over the last few years, and we do not see that waning.
Attainability: Moderate (in any grade)
Achievement: $1,560 for a CGC 7.5 in Sept. 2020
Performance: $408 for a CGC 5.0 in Mar. 2021

Combat #1 (Atlas Comics, 1952)

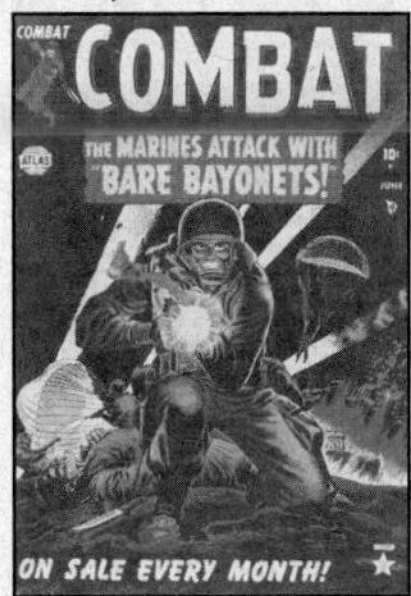

Determinant: first issue of classic '50s war comic
Basis: Considered a classic by collectors alike, especially because of its Russ Heath cover.
Stats: ~20 on census, only one 9.2 and one 8.5
Disclosures: Its classic cover makes this a sought-after comic, but its black cover makes it almost impossible to find in grade. There are only five known copies in a 7.5 grade or better.
Attainability: Hard (in any grade)
Potentiality: Its scarcity keeps it in quiet growth.
Achievement: $1,263 for CGC 9.2 River City in April 2012
Performance: $336 for a CGC 6.5 in Feb. 2020

CAMOUFLAGED ASSETS – War comics that have hidden potential.

Don Winslow of the Navy #1 (Fawcett, 1943)

Determinant: First issue of Don Winslow's own title
Basis: Don Winslow was a popular war adventure character of the 1930s and 1940s.
Stats: Approx. 25 on census, only two in 9.2 and one in 9.0
Disclosures: After appearing in various titles and mediums through the '30s and early '40s Don Winslow gets his own title.
Potentiality: Being a regarded title by Golden Age collectors and also introduced by Captain Marvel himself on the cover of this first issue have helped it have steady growth.
Attainability: Moderate (in any grade)
Achievement: $4,320 for a CGC 9.2 Edgar Church Mile High in August 2019
Performance: $660 for a CGC 6.0 in Apr. 2021

Our Army at War #112 (DC, 1961)

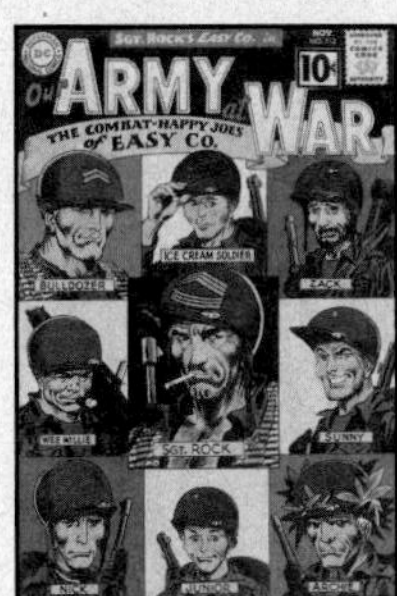

Determinant: Classic roster *Brady Bunch* cover
Basis: Classic Joe Kubert 12¢ war comic
Stats: Approx. 76 on census, only one 9.2 and one 9.0
Disclosures: Cements archetypes within Easy Company as key characters moving forward.
Potentiality: If you are Sgt. Rock fan, this is a must own. Its dark colors make this a tough book to find in grade and drives value even for lower grades.
Attainability: Easy (in any grade)
Achievement: $3,107 for a CGC 8.5 in Nov. 2011
Performance: $250 for a CGC 5.5 in Mar. 2021

Our Army at War #168 (DC, 1966)

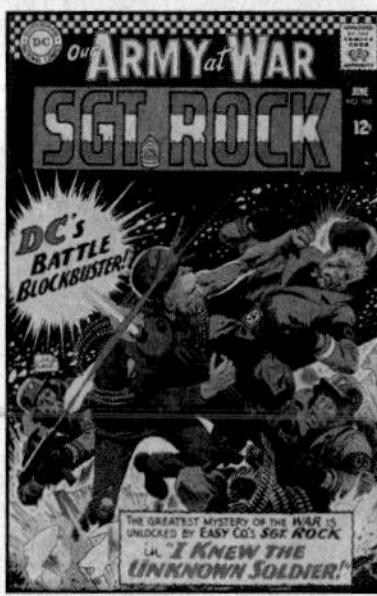

Determinant: First app. of The Unknown Soldier
Basis: The issue that introduces another well-known and revered war comic character.
Stats: Approx. 96 on census, only one in 9.8 and one in 9.6
Disclosures: There is market conflict between this and *Star-Spangled War Stories* #151 (1970), which has been referred to as his first appearance as well. They are both especially important comic books for this enigmatic character; thus, war comic collectors have both. We will be digging deeper and reporting our findings in future War Reports.
Potentiality: Like Sgt. Rock and Enemy Ace, this character has enormous potential. And although people have been buying *SSWS* #151 (as they well should), they may have inadvertently overlooked this important issue as well.
Attainability: Easy (in any grade)
Achievement: $2,175 for a CGC 9.8 in Apr. 2012
Performance: $290 for a CGC 6.5 in Dec. 2020

Our Army at War #109 (DC, 1961)

Determinant: Early and pertinent Sgt. Rock
Basis: Tells the story of Sgt. Rock's very first battle engagement.
Stats: Approx. 15 on census, only one in 9.2 and one in 9.0
Disclosures: It is not openly known that this is a foundational issue.
Potentiality: Eventual gains over time, sharply as collectors discover it is a key.
Attainability: Easy (in any grade)
Achievement: $1,673 for a CGC 9.2 Savannah Pedigree in February 2011
Performance: $360 for a CGC 9.0 in July 2019

War Comics #1 (Dell, 1940)

Determinant: First comic completely devoted to war content
Basis: The first true war comic
Stats: Approx. 20 on census, only two in 9.0 and one in 8.0
Disclosures: Collects a series of war stories and predates the large number of war dedicated titles that came 10 years later.
Potentiality: This is beginning to gain a bit more prominence due to its standing amongst classic war comics.
Attainability: Moderate (in any grade)
Achievement: $1,912 for a CGC 9.0 Edgar Church Mile High in July 2012
Performance: $900 for a CGC 6.0 in Mar. 2021

Our Army at War #82 (DC, 1959)

Determinant: First appearance of a character named Sgt. Rock
Basis: The last prototype issue of Sgt. Rock
Stats: Approx. 86 on census, only one 9.0 and one 8.5
Disclosures: This is the *Incredible Hulk* #180 of war comics, but Sgt. Rock does more than a cameo, thus arguably it's a particularly important comic.
Potentiality: Considered a must have amongst Sgt Rock purists, this book is sealed for growth along with its counterpart *OAAW* #83.
Attainability: Moderate (in any grade)
Achievement: $1,434 for a CGC 8.5 in Nov. 2011
Performance: $360 for a CGC 3.5 in Mar. 2021

Our Army at War #196 (DC, 1968)

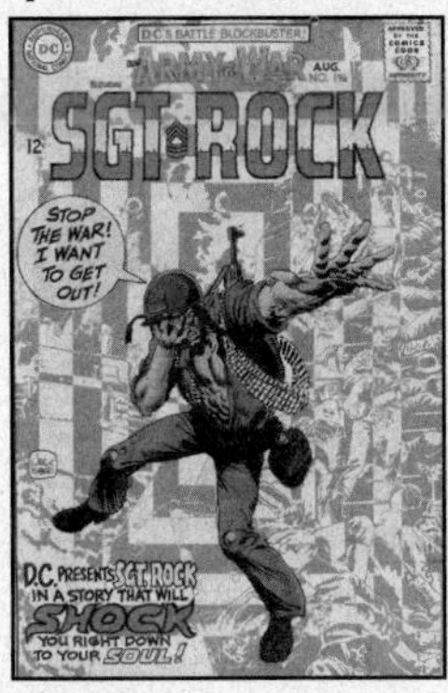

Determinant: Important comic, not just in the war genre
Basis: Classic Joe Kubert cover and fundamental storyline.
Stats: Approx. 30 on census, only two in 9.8 and five in 9.6
Disclosures: Aside from being one of the most universally recognized Sgt. Rock covers from the 1960s, there is editorial intel on the background of this comic that could make it a key issue in the broader hobby.
Potentiality: The War Correspondents are working on securing interview data that speaks to the pivotal importance of this issue. If we are right, its growth in value is more than secured (details in future reports).
Attainability: Easy (in any grade)
Achievement: $1,413 for a CGC 9.8 in August 2009
Performance: $140 for a CGC 9.4 in Sept. 2020

Sgt. Rock #302 (DC, 1977)

Determinant: First issue of seminal war comic title
Basis: After 200+ appearances of Sgt. Rock in *Our Army at War*, its title transforms with this issue.
Stats: Approx. 46 on census, only six in 9.8 and 11 in 9.6
Disclosures: A classic Joe Kubert cover kicks off Sgt. Rock in his own dedicated title.
Potentiality: This is issue 1 of this inherent Bronze Age war comic featuring one of the most recognizable war comic characters. We expect this to grow over time, and sharply should Rock be featured in other mediums.
Attainability: Easy (in any grade)
Achievement: $500 for a CGC 9.8 in March 2015
Performance: $60 for a CGC 9.0 in February 2021

All-American Men of War #89 (DC, 1962)

Determinant: Historic issue that influenced several Lichtenstein paintings
Basis: Key issue amongst (primarily) several war and romance comics that influenced a Roy Lichtenstein art period.
Stats: ~18 on census, only two in 9.2 and two in 8.0
Disclosures: Classic Jerry Grandenetti paneled war cover, Russ Heath, Irv Novick, and Grandenetti interior art, which (some consider controversial) was used by Lichtenstein as *direct* influences on his art
Potentiality: Whaam, Tex, Blam, Brattata are all worth millions now and whether you agree or not, are highly regarded and significant pop art pieces. How this comic with the *original* influencing art is not worth more is beyond us... (psst, check out issues 90-93, some were also utilized or potentially influential).
Attainability: Hard (in any grade)
Achievement: $263 for a CGC 9.2 in September 2010
Performance: $50 for a CGC 7.0 in July 2018

Battle #1 (Atlas, 1951)

Determinant: First issue of this classic 1950s Atlas war title
Basis: This popular Atlas series (which became Marvel Comics) ran for 70 issues
Stats: Approx. 7 on census, only one in 7.5 and one in 7.0
Disclosures: A favorite and beloved title amongst war comic collectors.
Potentiality: Look at the census numbers. This is just about finding a copy in grade. If you do, buy it!
Attainability: Hard (in any grade)
Achievement: $618 for a CGC 7.5 in Dec. 2013
Performance: $310 for a CGC 5.0 in Dec. 2020

The 'Nam #1 (Marvel, 1986)

Determinant: First issue of significant Copper Age war comic
Basis: Marvel digs into war-based storytelling
Stats: Approx. 351 on census, 157 in 9.8 and 80 in 9.6
Disclosures: Popular war comic that also features Vietnam era Punisher stories (in a few issues).
Potentiality: Has gained some cult status in the last few years, we expect it to continue to grow.
Attainability: Easy (in any grade)
Achievement: $125 for a CGC 9.8 in April 2021
Performance: Multiple copies graded at 9.8 are selling at $125 each

---

STRENGTH IN NUMBERS

Comparing Census Data Between Genres
(by Mick Rabin)

This year marks my 32nd year seriously collecting DC war comics. I'd been reading them for much longer, but I started going after back issues of Big Five titles back in 1989. It's been a fun journey. As a teenager, young adult, and then as a teacher, I've never had the cash to drop on seriously expensive keys. It wasn't that I didn't covet them. The only way I could hope to afford them would have been to buy beat copies and I preferred getting higher grade stuff – something about getting comics that looked closer to the way they originally appeared on the stands.

So back in the day, I started buying Silver Age that was affordable, but I was all over the place. A *Spider-Man* here, a *Strange Tales* there, *Tales of Suspense*, Neal Adams' *Detective Comics*, *Green Lantern*, *Daredevil*, *Showcase*, *Fantastic Four*, *Swamp Thing*, *Strange Tales*, *Brave and the Bold*, etc. And though I loved these comics, it was apparent that I couldn't afford most of these runs in grade. I wanted to try and complete some runs, but just didn't settle on something that was relatively affordable in grade but truly compelling. And then I started buying old Big Five titles. At first, anything with Enemy Ace, then Sgt. Rock, Haunted Tank, and then it just made sense to go after all of them.

But they were always just tough to get (at best) and some turned out to be hen's teeth no matter how long I searched. Yes, there are still a lot of issues I need. With all the movies, TV shows, and the staggering surge in comics' values over the course of the pandemic, it's impossible to dismiss the demand for Marvel issues. With no end in sight, the runs and especially the keys just seem to garner interest regardless of grade and sometimes price. Not difficult to argue that there's *always* been greater demand – across the board – for Marvel than for DC over these past 3+ decades. And it would seem that the demand is outpacing supply more than ever for Marvel, especially the keys. So, I just want to acknowledge the basic mechanisms of supply and demand here. There's a *tidal wave* of demand for Marvel books of virtually every stripe compared to the knee-high waves you'd want for a good day of kayaking.

All that said, though, in separate conversations, I've had a few friends speculate about which genres seem to be due for a spike. I don't have a crystal ball, and nor do I have a penchant for reading tea leaves, but I truly think DC war is relatively cheap in the general scheme of things. No whispers of a movie, video game, or TV show on the horizon, so *Our Army at War* and *GI Combat* have a following purely outside the realm of cross-media speculation – so far. For a good stretch there between roughly 2007-2012, there were a good number of competitive collectors in Big Five titles; but for the past nearly 10 years, much of the fervor has flattened out and some of the truly exorbitant prices have come back down to planet Earth. It's partly for that reason that I think that most all of the Big Five titles are a good deal in most grades right now. But the other reason is just pure rarity.

It's been little more than anecdotal conjecture that could explain the relative scarcity of DC books. I've always said that you could find 20 nice Marvel issues in high grade for just about any single nice DC in grade. But with DC war comics, I've always thought that the ratio increases to more like 30 high grade Marvel copies for any one DC war issue. This perception was never much more than speculation, though. Of course, there's no exact science to this, but it would seem that with more than 20 years for the CGC Census to collect data, we could examine some trends that might speak a bit to this dynamic.

I decided to take a look at this with only *Our Army at War* #81-153. A few factors should be considered, but a big one is that I feel that it's harder to approach a trend in data when the motivation to submit comics to CGC tends to drop as a comic's value drops below $200. So going strictly by Overstreet pricing for high book values, *OAAW* hovers above the $200 value until we get to *OAAW* #154. With #153 and earlier issues, the high book value hovers around $250 and up. When the value is $200 or less, the recoup on investment for slabbing the comics is definitely questionable at best, so there's really more of a disincentive to slab when their high grade value gets much cheaper than that. For this reason, I feel that the #81-153 bring us a little closer to a trend that we could generalize about relative scarcity.

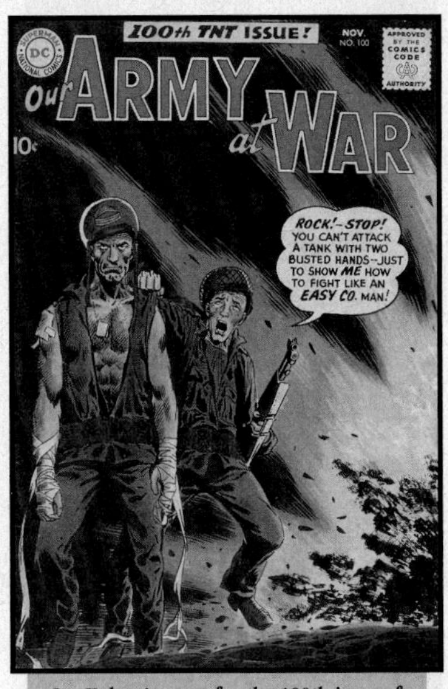

Joe Kubert's cover for the 100th issue of *Our Army at War.*

First, I'll try to draw comparisons of *OAAW* with other (mostly Marvel) issues with comparable price spreads. For example if the 2.0 to 9.2 price spread for *OAAW* #102-120 (excluding keys) is $24-$575, I tried to find a price spread from a Marvel run with a comparable range like *Fantastic Four* #31-40 (excluding keys) that runs $22-$525. And then examine the number of copies of individual issues within these price ranges to compare relative scarcity. I know that this can't be an exact science because there's just so much more popular demand for *FF* than *OAAW* and there are many more surviving issues of *FF* since there's about a four-year difference in publishing dates (generally speaking, the older, the scarcer)

So, let's take two comics to compare from the middle of those runs – *FF* and *OAAW* (I chose two non-keys to compare). *Fantastic Four* #35 (price range of $22-$525) is relatively similar in price to an *OAAW* #110 (price range $24-$575). So, let's look at the current census data on those. Census data for the *FF* #35 shows 292 copies in CGC 8.0 or better out of a total of 552 blue labels (Universals) slabbed for the issue. In comparison, the *OAAW* #110 census data (as of this writing) shows that there are 15 copies total slabbed and eight that are in the CGC 8.0 and above range. The ratio of total copies slabbed of *FF* to *OAAW* is 552:15 which means the *FF* is roughly 37 times more common in any grade. And the ratio on CGC 8.0 and above copies for the *FF* to the *OAAW* is 292:8. Nearly the same ratio showing the *FF* to be roughly 37 times more common than the *OAAW*.

If eight copies in 8.0 range seems like a puny quantity, you should know that eight is actually at the high end of slabbed quantities in the 8.0+ range for that run of *OAAW* between #102-120. The average number of 8.0+ copies for that run between 102-120 is about 6 copies. And the keys don't appear to have revealed any trends in spiking the prevalence of slabbed copies. The beloved *OAAW* #112 *Brady Bunch* cover is broken out a bit, but there are only seven copies in 8.0 or better.

Don't even get me started on representation of issues that are 9.0 or better. The contrast is even more stark. I'm not arguing that those early Rock comics are any better than the *FF* issues. I love those early *FF* books as much as anybody. But I digress, just in terms of relative scarcity in 9.2 and above, there's a staggering dichotomy between that range of early *Sgt. Rock* #83-#120 and the *FF* books. For *FF* #5-42 (same spread of 37 issues), there are 1,833 issues that have received a Universal CGC 9.2 or better. For the 37 issue spread of *OAAW* #83-120, the total number of issues in 9.2 or better is 28. That means there are 65 times more *FF* issues in CGC 9.2 or better than there are for the classic era of *OAAW*.

A few more comparisons: *Amazing Spider-Man* #39 (semi-key) price spread is $46-$1,300. *OAAW* #100 (semi-key – it's a hundred issues – and that Joe Kubert cover is not of this world) price spread is $46-$1,250. Total of 2,189 copies in Universal slabs and 624 in Universal CGC 8.0 or better for that *Spidey* #39. The *OAAW* #100 has 28 total copies and three in Universal CGC 8.0 or better. Highest graded is a solitary 8.5.

Strange Tales #114 and *OAAW* #86 both have similar price spreads from Good to NM-. There are a total of 629 slabbed copies of the *Strange Tales* #114 with 168 of those in CGC 8.0 or better. The *OAAW* #86 (third Kubert Rock), by contrast, has a total of 24 copies on the census and only four copies in 8.0 or better.

Again, drawing comparisons is a bit problematic on a couple different levels. When I try to compare scarcity of similarly priced runs, it's dodgy because the *FF* are from a later time period – roughly three years after the similarly priced *OAAW*. So, the difference in scarcity would most certainly be, at least, partially attributed to the earlier publishing period of *OAAW*. It's also worth mentioning that the attrition rate on *OAAW* is undoubtedly greater simply because war comics were considered birdcage liner for a much longer time in collector consciousness against the nearly immediate recognition inspired by nostalgia for superhero comics. So, let's try a comparison of issues from a similar time period (instead of price range). Ignore the price and focus more on the approximate period that they were hitting the stands.

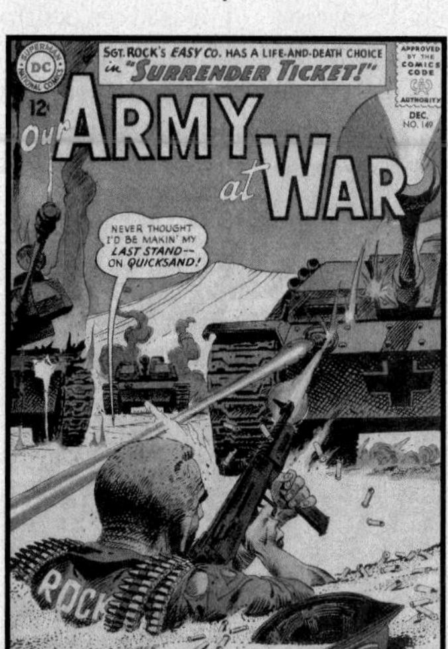

Our Army at War #149.

For mid-1960s Marvel, I thought I'd try other titles. Let's go with *Daredevil*. And I purposefully tried to align a newsstand date for a non-key *DD* with an *OAAW* from the same period that's also a non-key. December 1964 is a good date as *DD* #6 and *OAAW* #149 came out that same month and are non-keys. The *DD* #6 price spread, incidentally, is roughly double the *OAAW* #149 in all grades.

The CGC Census reveals 15 total graded copies for the *OAAW* #149 and nine copies in 8.0 or above. There are 755 total copies of *DD* #6 with 85 slabs in the CGC 8.0 and above range. In the lower grades, the cost of slabbing these negates the return on investment (at least in the short term) and this is especially true for the *OAAW* #149, so this likely is a significant factor in the difference between total numbers of slabs for each copy.

Our Army at War #136.

The final comparison I chose was again for non-keys. In November 1963, *Tales of Suspense* #47 and *OAAW* #136 were both out on the stands. The CGC Census reveals that there are 423 total copies for the *TOS* #47 and 107 of them are in 8.0 or above. By comparison, the *OAAW* #136 has nine copies on the census with four breaking into the CGC 8.0 or above range. I recognize how much more popular Iron Man is than Sgt. Rock and likely always will be. But that differential in availability is massive.

Collectors and investors who've been making purchases that continue to propel Marvel demand clearly know what they're doing. I've kicked myself numerous times for the Marvel books I flipped over the decades for what are comparative pennies against the jaw-dropping prices they're getting now, so I'll be the first to tell you not to follow my model. But I wanted to take a bit of time, once and for all, to examine relative scarcity across a couple indices. Obviously, it's important to consider other factors other than rarity including popularity of the title, genre, or character as well as the art and storyline. Another thing to consider is how many completist collectors there are for non-keys from Marvel vs. non-keys for DC. With all the interest generated by the movie franchises, there's a widening chasm between the values of non-keys vs. minor keys vs. major keys in titles across the board. But as the broken record goes, people should buy what they like.

Our Army at War is probably the most popular of the Big Five titles simply because it features the flagship character of DC war and really the most ubiquitous across all genres and publishers (I'm sure there are Sgt. Fury fans who'd take me to task for this). If we were to dig a bit into the weeds with the other Big Five titles' relative scarcity, I think you'd be even more amazed at just how tough these books are. Some might try to dismiss that scarcity as ambivalence on the part of sellers or collectors because they're not as popular, but CGC's been around the block for a number of years now and I can tell you that when issues from those other titles appear in slabs new to the market, they sell pretty swiftly because the hardcore collectors who have been collecting them know that they simply won't have another chance to get them.

In the case of most Marvel comics, it's usually just a matter of how much a person's willing to spend to get the issue. If you're looking for an issue of Marvel, you can pretty much find it within a month if you check auction sites and are connected to national vendors. This is just not the case for the Big Five titles and even less so for Marvel's own war predecessors, the Atlas war titles. So, with all that in mind, given the significant cooling down of collector fervor for DC war against the veracity of Marvel superhero sales over the past 10 years, and especially over the course of 2020, I'm reiterating what I've said to a number of friends who want to know about sleepers: war comics are looking like pretty affordable right about now. By all means, ignore my advice and keep driving up the Marvel prices, though, because I still have a bunch of Big Five and war titles from other publishers that I need. So, nothing to see here.

GAINING RANK

Here is the 13th edition of the war comic ranking. Each comic book's position in the ranks was based on criteria such as who was on the creative team, key storylines, art, first appearances, popularity, market value, scarcity, etc. For new readers, here's how we developed our ranking system:

The Campaign to Rank War Comics

The first thing we did was go through *The Overstreet Comic Book Price Guide* and record every instance of a title or issue that was either a war comic, or that had war subject matter, or that contained the appearance of a war-related character, etc. We also used resource material outside the *Guide* to fill in holes or corroborate specific findings. But, after we reached well beyond our 1,000th line listing of different war comic titles, with no end in sight, we truly realized what a laborious campaign we had embarked on.

After developing our massive master list, our second task was to determine what truly constituted a war comic. So, we set parameters that narrowed the field by characterizing war comics as stories centered on the military, which is involved in armed conflicts and, as such, needed to be relegated to those wars categorized as a major conflict. We were able to easily eliminate a good deal of candidates by employing the notion that any war story blended with a superhero is, by definition, a fantasy story and would not be a war story.

We also needed to create a sub-classification within the genre to fine tune the report. This classification consisted of defining what type of war themes existed. For instance, war battle tales, war adventure, cold war, war propaganda, etc. We quickly ascertained that we needed to put our focus on stories that were predominantly centered on characters engulfed in battle. Thus, **War Battle Tales** has become our category of choice – a refined list that, still boasts over 700 listings.

Since most of war comics both began and flourished in earlier comic ages, our focus on reporting has been primarily on two of our own comic age classifications: the Golden Age and then the Atom/Silver/Bronze Age. However, we do pay heed to what we refer to as the Modern Age of War, as a good number of incredible war comics have been published from the '80s to present. They just do not typically get as much attention outside our genre.

With all this data in place, each year the War Correspondents and I would vote anonymously on the ranking of the top 50 war comics in existence. Factors on criteria included elements such as: significance of book, character appearances, art and storyline, rarity, value, etc. From this we have not only been able to present and maintain a current ranking on key war titles, but to share reasoning for market fluctuations on interest and value. Through this process, the first War Comic Ranking system was created.

For 13 years now we have judiciously updated this ranking on a yearly basis by watching the market, talking to fellow collectors and dealers, chatting up publishing professionals and discussing variances amongst ourselves. We are careful not to make any brash changes, but we carefully look at which comics need to get more attention, or conversely, which may have had too much stock put into them. Although, the movement year to year has been slight, some adjustments over the cumulative years have been marked, bringing underappreciated issues into the spotlight! We hope this has been a valuable tool for fellow War Comic collectors.

TOP 50 ATOM / SILVER / BRONZE AGE WAR COMICS OF 2021

ISSUE	2021 RANK	2020 RANK	CHANGE	MERIT
Our Army at War #83	1	1		1st true app. of Sgt. Rock (Kanigher/Kubert Master Sgt.)
Sgt. Fury #1	2	2		1st app. of Sgt. Fury
G.I. Combat #87	3	3		1st app. of Haunted Tank
Our Army at War #82	4	4		Sgt. Rock prototype (Non Kanigher/Kubert 4th grade rate Sgt.)
Our Army at War #81	5	5-t		Sgt. Rock prototype (Non Kanigher/Kubert "Sgt. Rocky")
Star Spangled War Stories #84	6	7	+1	1st app. of Mademoiselle Marie
Two-Fisted Tales #18	7	5-t	-1	1st issue to start EC War run
G.I. Combat #68	8	8		Sgt. Rock prototype (Kanigher/Kubert "The Rock" story)
Our Army at War #1	9	9		1st issue of Big Five war title
Our Army at War #90	10	10		How Sgt. Rock got his stripes
Frontline Combat #1	11	11		1st issue of EC all war title
G.I. Combat #44	12	12		1st DC issue of Big Five war Title, early washtone
Our Army at War #84	13	13		2nd app. of Sgt Rock
Star Spangled War Stories #90	13-t	14	+1	1st Dinosaur "War That Time Forgot" ish
Our Fighting Forces #1	15	15		1st issue of Big Five war title
Our Army at War #88	16	16		1st Sgt. Rock cover (Kubert)
Our Army at War #85	17	17		1st app. of Ice Cream Soldier and 2nd Kubert Sgt. Rock
Star Spangled War Stories #131	18	18		1st issue of Big Five war title
All American Men of War #127	19	19		1st issue of Big Five war title
Our Army at War #112	20	20		Classic roster ("Brady Bunch") cover

Our Army at War #151	21	22	+1	1st app. of Enemy Ace
Our Fighting Forces #45	22	21	-1	Gunner & Sarge run begins (predates OAAW #83)
All American Men of War #67	23	23		1st app. of Gunner & Sarge (predates OAAW #83)
G.I. Combat #1	24	24		1st issue of Quality Comics title
Our Army at War #91	25	25		1st all Sgt. Rock issue
Blazing Combat #1	26	27	+1	1st issue of Warren war Magazine
Battle #1	27	26	-1	1st issue of Atlas war title
G.I. Combat #91	28	28		1st Haunted Tank Cover (washtone)
Our Army at War #196	29	30	+1	Key transitional comic (classic Kubert cover)
Star Spangled War Stories #151	30	31	+1	1st solo app. of Unknown Soldier
Combat #1	31	29	-2	1st issue of Atlas War title (black cover)
Our Army at War #100	32	32		Scarce Kubert (black cover)
G.I. Combat #75	33	33		1st in "Perty Thirty" washtone run
Foxhole #1	34	35	+1	1st ish Mainline title (classic Kirby cover)
Our Army at War #168	35	36	+1	1st app. of the Unknown Soldier
All American Men of War #28	36	34	-2	1st Sgt. Rock prototype (Kubert art)
Two-Fisted Tales Annual #1	37	37		Early 132 pg. EC war annual
G.I. Combat #80	38	39	+1	Classic washtone cover
All American Men of War #89	39	40	+1	Historic issue influenced several Lichtenstein paintings
Fightin' Marines 15 (#1)	40	38	-2	1st issue of St. John war title (Baker art)
War Comics #11	41	42	+1	Classic flamethrower cover
Sgt. Fury #13	42	44	+2	2nd Silver Age solo app. of Captain America
Our Army at War #128	43	41	-2	Training & origin of Sgt. Rock
Our Army at War #95	44	46	+2	1st app. of Bulldozer
G.I. Combat #69	45	43	-2	1st in Grandenetti washtone trifecta
Our Army at War #86	46	45	-1	Early Sgt. Rock
Sgt Rock #302	47	48	+1	1st issue of seminal Bronze Age war title
All American Men of War #82	48	49	+1	1st app. of Johnny Cloud
Our Fighting Forces #49	49	47	-2	1st app. of Pooch
G.I. Combat #83	50	50		1st Big Al, Little Al & Charlie (2nd cover of washtone trifecta)
All American Men of War #90	Honorable Mention			2nd historic issue influenced several Lichtenstein paintings

Highlights of the Top 50 Atom /Silver / Bronze Age:

- Very minor changes in the top 20.
- *SSWS* #84 and Mlle. Marie's first appearance gain further footing in the top 10.
- *SSWS* #151 and the Unknown Soldier rightfully cracks the top 30.
- Although rooted with Fantasy storytelling, *Sgt. Fury* #13 continues to climb.
- *OAAW* #95 with Bulldozer's first appearance also gains traction.

TOP 15 GOLDEN AGE WAR COMICS OF 2021

ISSUE	2021 RANK	2020 RANK	CHANGE	MERIT
Wings #1	1	1		1st issue in long running air war title
Real Life #3	2	2		Hitler Cover (early 1942 WWII)
War Comics #1	3	3		1st comic completely devoted to war content
Don Winslow #1 (1937)	4	4		Very early war adventure title
Contact Comics #1	5	5		1st issue of air battles title
Don Winslow #1 (1939)	6	6		Rare Four Color issue (#2)
Real Life Comics #1	7	7		1st issue of adventure title
Rangers Comics #8	8	8		US Rangers begin
US Marines #2	9	9		Classic Cover (Bailey art)
Rangers Comics #26	10	10		Classic cover

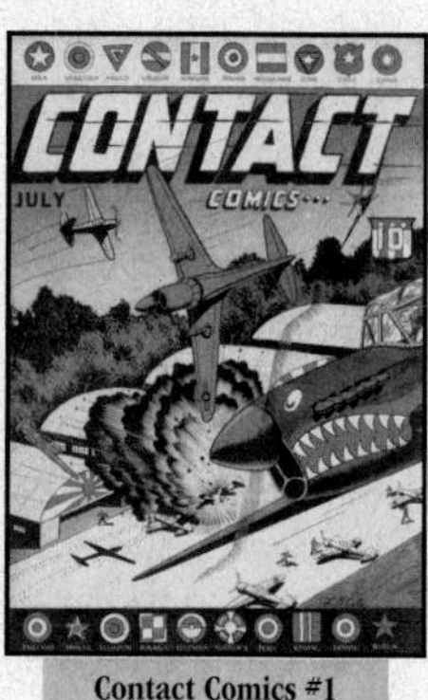

Contact Comics #1

Don Winslow of the Navy #1 ('43)	11	12	+1	1st comic of 73 issue series (Captain Marvel on cover)
Wings Comics #2	12	11	-1	2nd issue of key air war title
Bill Barnes Comics #1	13	13		1st issue of Air Ace title
Remember Pearl Harbor (nn)	14	14		1942 illustrated story of the battle
American Library nn (#1)	15	15		"Thirty Seconds Over Tokyo" (movie)

Highlights of the Top 15 Golden Age: Virtually no movement since last year.

TOP 15 ATLAS WAR COMICS OF 2021

ISSUE	2021 RANK	2020 RANK	MERIT
Battle #1	1	1	1st issue of Atlas war title
Combat #1	2	2	1st issue of Atlas War title (black cover)
War Comics #11	3	3	Classic flamethrower cover
War Adventures #12	4	7	Classic cover
Battlefront #15	5	8	Violent Heath cover
War Action #1	6	5	1st issue of Atlas War title
Battlefront #26	7	9	Classic Heath minesweeper cover
War Comics #1	8	4	1st issue of Atlas War title
Battlefield #6	9	6	Heath flamethrower cover
War Comics #26	10	11	Classic Heath cover
Navy Combat #8	11	10	Classic Everett cover
Navy Action #2	12	15	Heath cover
Battle #37	13	13	Heath cover
Navy Action #1	14	12	Russ Heath cover kicks off series
Battle #38	15	14	Heath cover

War Adventures #12

Highlights of the Top 15 Atlas War: As this is only the second year of listing the top 15 Atlas War comics, were seeing some meaningful adjustments.

• Big climbs by *War Adventures* #12, *Battlefront* #15 and *Navy Action* #2.

• Big drops by *War Comics* #1 and *Battlefield* #6.

• *Battle* #1, *Combat* #1 and *War Comics* #11 continue to dominate the top three slots.

TOP 5 CHARLTON WAR COMICS OF 2021

ISSUE	2021 RANK	2020 RANK	MERIT
Fightin' Marines #15 (#1)	1	1	1st issue in St. John war title (Baker art)
Attack #54	2	2	1st issue in short war title (100 pgs)
Soldier and Marine #11	3	3	1st ish in short war title (Bob Powell art)
US Air Force #1	4	4	1st issue of Charlton war title
Fightin' Navy #74	5	5	1st issue of Charlton war title (formerly Don Winslow)

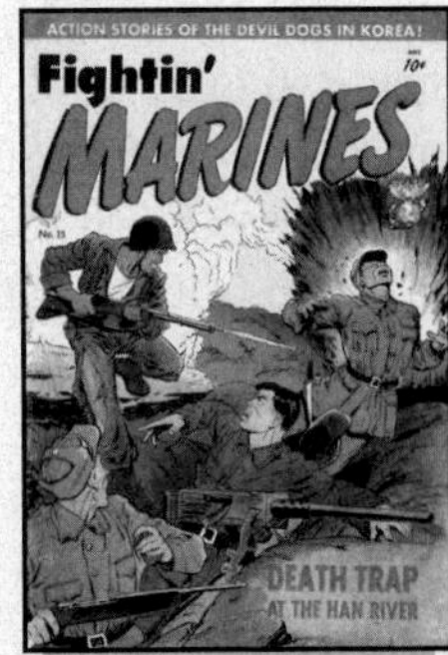

Fightin' Marines #15 (#1)

Highlights of the Top 5 Charlton War: Charlton War remains entrenched in its foxhole with no changes.

Over and Out

Thanks for reading the War Report. A big thank you to those supporters who have stuck by our side and shared excellent thoughts and comments over the years. We so appreciate you. We also salute the men behind this publication: Bob Overstreet, J.C. Vaughn, and Mark Huesman.

Thanks to the troops

As always, I am grateful and humbled by the contributions and sacrifices made by the War Correspondents. Big thanks this year goes to Andy Greenham and Mick Rabin, I appreciate all you do boys!

KEY SALES FROM 2020-2021

The following lists of sales were reported to Gemstone during the year and represent only a small portion of the total amount of important books that have sold. For other sales information, please see the Overstreet Market Report starting on page 89.

GOLDEN AGE - SALES OF CERTIFIED COMICS

Action Comics #1 CGC 8.5 $3,250,000
Action Comics #1 ashcan CGC 9.2 $204,000
Action Comics #12 CGC 3.5 $14,400
Action Comics #18 CGC 4.0 $2,005
Action Comics #23 CBCS 7.0 $10,250
Adventure Comics #40 CGC 7.5 $81,000
All Star Comics #8 CGC 1.5 $18,000
All Star Comics #30 CGC 4.5 $400.00
All Star Comics #31 CBCS 7.0 $610
All Star Comics #31 CGC 6.5 $575
All Star Comics #53 CGC 7.0 $680
All Winners Comics #12 CGC 7.0 $4,200
All-American Comics #61 CGC 7.5 $42,278
All-American Comics #91 CGC 4.5 $125
All-American Comics #92 CGC 7.5 $851
Archie Comics #1 CGC 1.8 $12,600
Batman #1 CGC 8.0 $1,207,500
Batman #1 CGC 5.0 $360,000
Batman #1 CGC 3.0 $192,000
Batman #15 CGC 9.0 $15,600
(Billy Wright pedigree)
Batman #37 CGC 7.0 $3,600
Batman #40 CGC 7.5 $2,015
Batman #62 CGC 9.4 $24,000
Batman #63 CGC 6.0 $825
Batman #66 CGC 9.4 $26,400
Captain America Comics #1 CGC 8.5 $384,000
Captain America Comics #1 CGC 8.0 $395,000
Captain America Comics #1 CGC 5.5 $182,500
Captain America Comics #2 CGC 8.0 $26,400
Captain America Comics #13 CGC 8.5 $26,400
Captain America Comics #41 CGC 5.5 $2,040
Captain America Comics #46 CGC 3.5 $8,602
Cat-Man Comics #7 CGC 6.0 $1,816
Cat-Man Comics #7 CGC 4.5 $947
Cat-Man Comics #25 CGC 9.2 $21,600
(Mile High pedigree)
Daring Mystery Comics #1 CGC 7.0 $31,200
Detective Comics #33 CGC 7.0 $26,400
Detective Comics #38 CGC 7.5 $180,000
Detective Comics #73 CGC 8.0 $26,400
Detective Comics #122 CGC 7.5 $7,000
Detective Comics #124 CGC 7.0 $1,080
Detective Comics #128 CGC 6.5 $1,200
Detective Comics #140 CGC 7.5 $40,800
Detective Comics #180 CGC 6.5 $1,400
Detective Comics #225 CGC 9.4 $138,000
Donald Duck Four Color #4 CGC 7.0 $21,600
Fantastic Comics #3 CGC 0.5 $20,400
Fight Comics #31 CGC 9.4 $36,000
(Mile High pedigree)
Flame #4 CGC 5.5 $735
Hit Comics #5 CGC 7.5 $16,200
Katy Keene #1 CGC 9.4 $21,000
(Mile High pedigree)
Keen Detective Funnies V2 #7 CGC 6.0 $1,755
Mad #1 CGC 9.8 $87,000
Marvel Comics #1 CGC 6.0 $280,500
Marvel Mystery Comics #27 CGC 7.0 $232
More Fun Comics #73 CGC 7.5 $111,000
Mystery in Space #1 CGC 9.0 $10,800
Pep Comics #1 CGC 8.5 $27,600
Phantom Lady #17 CGC 3.5 $11,400
Planet Comics #34 CGC 6.5 $1,110
Planet Comics #34 CGC 3.0 $420
Planet Comics #37 CGC 4.5 $575
Red Raven Comics #1 CGC 9.0 $57,600
(Billy Wright pedigree)
Sensation Comics #1 CGC 8.5 $160,000
Sensation Comics #71 CGC 7.0 $215
Sensation Comics #86 CGC 3.5 $32
Sheena #4 CGC 8.5 $504
Speed Comics #29 CGC 9.4 $21,600
(Mile High pedigree)
Startling Comics #49 CGC 8.5 $16,800
Superboy #17 CGC 9.8 $16,800

Superman #2 CGC 4.5 $16,800
Superman #5 CGC 9.6 $60,000
Superman #11 CGC 9.2 $18,600
Superman #24 CGC 9.0 $14,400
Superman #47 CGC 7.0 $500
Superman #53 CGC 5.5 $1300
Tomb of Terror #15 CGC 8.5 $16,800 (Gaines File)
Top Notch Comics #13 CGC 3.5 $62
USA Comics #1 CGC 9.0 $20,400
Weird Comics #1 CGC 7.0 $21,600
Weird Comics #3 CGC 5.0 $2520
Whiz Comics #2 (#1) CGC 3.5 $72,000
Wonder Woman #1 CGC 6.5 $58,800
Wonder Woman #1 CGC 4.5 $40,000
Wonder Woman #6 CGC 9.2 $28,800
Wonderworld Comics #16 CGC 6.0 $850
World's Best Comics #1 CGC 7.0 $13,200

SILVER AGE - SALES OF CERTIFIED COMICS

Adventure Comics #311 CGC 9.2 $1,440
Amazing Fantasy #15 CGC 9.0 $566,000
Amazing Fantasy #15 CGC 7.5 $156,000
Amazing Fantasy #15 CGC 6.0 $96,000
Amazing Spider-Man #1 CGC 9.2 $150,000
Amazing Spider-Man #1 CGC 8.5 $50,400
Amazing Spider-Man #1 CGC 7.0 $38,400
Amazing Spider-Man #1 CGC 6.0 $27,600
Amazing Spider-Man #3 CGC 9.4 $39,600 (Twin Cities pedigree)
Amazing Spider-Man #7 CGC 9.6 $21,600
Amazing Spider-Man #50 CGC 9.6 $21,600
Avengers #1 CGC 9.2 $63,000
Avengers #1 CGC 8.5 $28,800
Avengers #1 CGC 8.5 $21,600
Avengers #1 CGC 6.0 $5,000
Avengers #4 CGC 9.2 $9,000
Avengers #48 CGC 9.6 $3,600
Batman #121 CGC 9.0 $22,200
Batman #181 CGC 9.2 $6,000 (Pacific Coast pedigree)
Batman #181 CGC 4.5 $715
Batman #189 CGC 9.8 $21,600 (Boston pedigree)
Batman #194 CGC 9.8 $6,000 (Boston pedigree)
Brave and the Bold #28 CGC 7.5 $15,600
Brave and the Bold #38 CGC 7.0 $55
Captain America #100 CGC 9.9 $78,000
Daredevil #1 CGC 9.6 $150,000
Daredevil #1 CGC 9.6 $102,000
Daredevil #2 CGC 9.8 $48,666
Daredevil #7 CGC 9.6 $43,000
Daredevil #21 CGC 9.8 $12,000
Detective Comics #327 CGC 9.8 $5,760
Detective Comics #359 CGC 9.8 $132,000
Detective Comics #371 CGC 9.8 $15,600
Fantastic Four #1 CGC 9.0 $264,000
Fantastic Four #1 CGC 8.5 $132,000
Fantastic Four #1 CGC 7.0 $64,711
Fantastic Four #3 CGC 9.4 $53,000
Fantastic Four #5 CGC 9.4 $138,000
Fantastic Four #5 CGC 9.2 $72,000
Fantastic Four #5 CGC 8.5 $54,000
Fantastic Four #12 CGC 9.4 $31,200
Fantastic Four #36 CGC 9.6 $20,400
Fantastic Four #48 CGC 9.2 $19,200
Fantastic Four #50 CGC 9.6 $28,800
Fantastic Four #52 CGC 9.6 $50,400
Flash #105 CGC 8.0 $12,000
Green Lantern #12 CGC 7.0 $80.00
Green Lantern #23 CGC 3.5 $160.00
Incredible Hulk #1 CGC 7.0 $54,781
Incredible Hulk #1 CGC 7.0 $52,800
Incredible Hulk #1 CGC 6.5 $51,600
Incredible Hulk #1 CGC 5.5 $30,000
Incredible Hulk #2 CGC 9.2 $21,000
Journey Into Mystery #83 CGC 9.0 $87,000
Journey Into Mystery #83 CGC 8.5 $75,000
Journey Into Mystery #83 CGC 6.5 $21,000
Journey Into Mystery #92 CGC 9.4 $3,000
Journey Into Mystery Annual #1 CGC 9.8 $73,000
Our Army at War #83 CGC 7.0 $14,400
Showcase #4 CGC 8.0 $78,000 (Ohio-Fairborn pedigree)
Showcase #22 CGC 7.0 $17,400
Showcase #23 CGC 3.5 $160

Showcase #40 CGC 9.4 $1,320
Showgirls #1 CGC 9.0 $9,600
Silver Surfer #9 CGC 9.8 $42,000
Strange Tales #150 CGC 9.8 $9,600
Strange Tales Annual #2 CGC 9.6 $16,800
Sub-Mariner #1 CGC 9.8 $9,000
Superman #110 CGC 9.0 $2,160
Tales of Suspense #39 CBCS 9.4 $132,000
Tales of Suspense #39 CGC 9.4 $125,000
Tales of Suspense #39 CGC 8.5 $48,000
Tales of Suspense #39 CGC 8.5 $33,600
Tales of Suspense #52 CGC 6.5 $1,200
Tales of Suspense #57 CGC 9.2 $5,760
Tales to Astonish #35 CGC 9.2 $26,400
Teen Titans #1 CGC 9.8 $31,200
Thor #136 CGC 9.8 $7,800
World's Finest Comics #90 CGC 9.6 $15,600
X-Men #1 CGC 9.0 $78,000
X-Men #1 CGC 8.0 $55,000
X-Men #4 CGC 9.6 $59,777

BRONZE - MODERN AGES SALES OF CERTIFIED COMICS

All-Star Western #10 CGC 9.8 $9,000
Amazing Spider-Man #101 CGC 9.6 $9,000 (Twin Cities pedigree)
Amazing Spider-Man #121 CGC 9.8 $6,900
Amazing Spider-Man #194 CGC 9.8 $3,600 (Twin Cities pedigree)
Amazing Spider-Man #300 CGC 9.4 $1,680
Avengers #93 CGC 9.6 $2,520 (Suscha News pedigree)
Batman #227 CGC 9.8 $33,600 (Oakland pedigree)
Batman #227 CGC 9.8 $31,200
Batman #232 CGC 9.8 $9,000
Batman #251 CGC 9.8 $11,100
Batman Adventures #12 CGC 9.8 $3,500
Batman Adventures #12 CGC 9.8 $2,640
Captain America #180 CGC 9.8 $1,800
Chili Annual #1 CGC 9.8 $432
Daredevil #168 CGC 9.0 $312
DC Comics Presents #47 CGC 9.6 $660
Detective Comics #400 CGC 9.6 $3,840
Detective Comics #405 CGC 9.8 $9,000
Detective Comics #411 CGC 9.6 $10,200 (John G. Fantucchio pedigree)
Detective Comics #422 CGC 9.8 $3,480
Eternals #1 CGC 9.4 $720
Fear #1 CGC 9.8 $2,280
Fantastic Four #100 CGC 9.8 $930
Giant-Size X-Men #1 CGC 9.8 $67,900
Giant-Size X-Men #1 CGC 9.8 $40,500
Giant-Size X-Men #1 CGC 9.6 $26,400
The Goon #1 CGC 9.8 $1,680
Green Lantern #87 CGC 9.4 $2,040
Hero For Hire #1 CGC 8.5 $900
Incredible Hulk #181 CGC 9.8 $60,000
Incredible Hulk #181 CGC 9.6 $31,200
Incredible Hulk #181 CGC 9.4 $15,600
Iron Man #55 CGC 8.5 $1,260
Marvel Premiere #15 CGC 9.8 $14,400
Marvel Spotlight 15 CGC 8.0 $5,280
Moon Knight #1 CGC 9.8 $900
New Mutants #98 CGC 9.9 $42,000
Night Nurse #1 CGC 9.8 $21,600
Shazam! #1 CGC 9.8 $780
Special Marvel Edition #15 CGC 9.0 $1,920
Star Wars #42 CGC 9.6 $1,140
Strange Tales #169 CGC 9.8 $21,600
Transformers #1 CGC 9.9 $44,000
Teenage Mutant Ninja Turtles #1 CGC 9.6 $66,000
Teenage Mutant Ninja Turtles #1 CGC 9.4 $38,888
Teenage Mutant Ninja Turtles #1 CGC 9.2 $32,400
Teenage Mutant Ninja Turtles #1 CGC 9.0 $26,400
Tomb of Dracula #1 CGC 8.5 $720
Tomb of Dracula #10 CGC 9.9 $106,350
Warlock #1 CGC 9.8 $15,600
Werewolf By Night #32 CGC 8.5 $4,560
Wolverine #1 (1982) CGC 9.8 $1,050
X-Force #2 CGC 9.8 $264
X-Men #94 CGC 9.8 $63,000
X-Men #94 CGC 9.2 $4,560
X-Men #101 CGC 9.2 $1,260
X-Men #141 CGC 9.8 $1,560

GOLDEN AGE - ATOM AGE SALES

Action Comics #40 GD $799.99
Action Comics #56 VG+ $631
Adventure Comics #103 GD $810
All-American Comics #45 FN+ $220
All Select Comics #10 FN+ $1,300
All Star Comics #24 VG+ $409.55
All Star Comics #51 VG+ $325
Batman #73 GD $272
Captain America Comics #21 VG $2,225.09
Comic Cavalcade #3 GD+ $249.99
Crime SuspenStories #7 FN+ $478
Crime SuspenStories #20 VF- $1,525
Fantastic Comics #15 VG/FN $1,081
Flash Comics #70 FN $300
Haunt of Fear #16 VF $1,450
Shock SuspenStories #6 VG $1,275
Superboy #10 FN- $760
Tales From the Crypt #23 VG+ $496
Tales From the Crypt #46 FN $899
USA Comics #17 VG $560
Whiz Comics #23 VG/FN $284.99
Whiz Comics #125 FN- $202.49

SILVER AGE SALES

Amazing Spider-Man #8 VF/NM $1,800
Amazing Spider-Man #9 NM- $5,500
Amazing Spider-Man #7 GD $215
Amazing Spider-Man #40 VF $360
Avengers #4 GD $1,926
Avengers #57 VF $715
Batman #155 GD $217.50
Batman #181 VG $350
Fantastic Four #5 VG/FN $10,100
Fantastic Four #30 VG+ $48
Fantastic Four #48 GD $2,482.67
Flash #123 VG $600
Flash #129 FN $99.99
Incredible Hulk #3 GD- $475
Incredible Hulk #5 GD $584
Incredible Hulk Annual #1 FN/VF $405
Tales of Suspense #68 FN+ $55
Tales to Astonish #43 FN+ $90
Wonder Woman #178 NM $382
World's Finest Comics #126 VF/NM $220.00

BRONZE AGE TO MODERN AGE SALES

Batman #227 FN $234.50
Batman #251 NM $1463
Captain Marvel (2012) #14 NM $208.50
Daredevil #168 NM $455
Edge of Spider-Verse #2 VF/NM $525
Edge of Spider-Verse #5 NM $39.95
Green Lantern #59 FN $222.50
Green Lantern #87 VG/FN $457
Marvel Super Special #16 NM $325
Ms. Marvel #1 (1977) VF/NM $60
Something Is Killing the Children #1 NM $660
Spawn #174 NM $499.99
Spawn #174 NM- $456
Spawn #175 NM $260
Spawn #175 VF- $330
Star Wars (1977) #2 VF $149.95
Star Wars (1977) #42 VF/NM $399.99
Star Wars: The Clone Wars #1 NM/MT $1,739.26
Star Wars: The Clone Wars #1 NM $1,356.80
Static #1 VF $97.49
Static #1 (Platinum) NM $202.50
Superman's Pal Jimmy Olsen #134 NM $75
Sweet Tooth #1 NM $229.99
Sweet Tooth #1 NM $199.99
Teenage Mutant Ninja Turtles #1 (3rd printing) VF/NM $2,500
Teenage Mutant Ninja Turtles Adventures #1 NM $89.99
Truth: Red, White & Black #1 NM $199.99
Ultimate Fallout #4 NM $1,184
West Coast Avengers #45 NM $530.09

TOP COMICS

The following tables denote the rate of appreciation of the top Golden Age, Platinum Age, Silver Age and Bronze Age comics, as well as selected genres over the past year. The retail value for a Near Mint- copy of each comic (or VF where a Near Mint- copy is not known to exist) in 2021 is compared to its Near Mint- value in 2020. The rate of return for 2021 over 2020 is given. The place in rank is given for each comic by year, with its corresponding value in highest known grade. These tables can be very useful in forecasting trends in the market place. For instance, the investor might want to know which book is yielding the best dividend from one year to the next, or one might just be interested in seeing how the popularity of books changes from year to year. For instance, *Action Comics* #23 was in 42nd place in 2020 and has increased to 40th place in 2021. Premium books are also included in these tables and are denoted with an asterisk(*).

The following tables are meant as a guide to the investor. However, it should be pointed out that trends may change at anytime and that some books can meet market resistance with a slowdown in price increases, while others can develop into real comers from a presently dormant state. In the long run, if the investor sticks to the books that are appreciating steadily each year, he shouldn't go very far wrong.

TOP 100 GOLDEN AGE COMICS

TITLE/ISSUE#	2021 RANK	2021 NM- PRICE	2020 RANK	2020 NM- PRICE	$ INCR.	% INCR.
Action Comics #1	1	$5,000,000	1	$4,600,000	$400,000	9%
Detective Comics #27	2	$3,600,000	2	$3,000,000	$600,000	20%
Superman #1	3	$1,900,000	3	$1,700,000	$200,000	12%
All-American Comics #16	4	$925,000	4	$880,000	$45,000	5%
Batman #1	4	$925,000	5	$860,000	$65,000	8%
Marvel Comics #1	6	$775,000	6	$750,000	$25,000	3%
Captain America Comics #1	7	$600,000	7	$550,000	$50,000	9%
Action Comics #7	8	$575,000	7	$550,000	$25,000	5%
Pep Comics #22	9	$410,000	9	$385,000	$25,000	6%
Detective Comics #31	10	$400,000	10	$350,000	$50,000	14%
Action Comics #10	11	$385,000	10	$350,000	$35,000	10%
All Star Comics #8	12	$375,000	10	$350,000	$25,000	7%
Whiz Comics #2 (#1)	12	$375,000	13	$330,000	$45,000	14%
Detective Comics #29	14	$325,000	14	$300,000	$25,000	8%
Flash Comics #1	15	$300,000	15	$275,000	$25,000	9%
Detective Comics #33	16	$250,000	16	$240,000	$10,000	4%
Action Comics #2	17	$240,000	17	$220,000	$20,000	9%
Detective Comics #35	18	$225,000	17	$220,000	$5,000	2%
More Fun Comics #52	19	$220,000	19	$210,000	$10,000	5%
Wonder Woman #1	19	$220,000	20	$205,000	$15,000	7%
Archie Comics #1	21	$205,000	21	$200,000	$5,000	3%
Action Comics #13	22	$200,000	21	$200,000	$0	0%
Detective Comics #38	23	$190,000	24	$170,000	$20,000	12%
Adventure Comics #40	24	$185,000	23	$180,000	$5,000	3%
Sensation Comics #1	25	$175,000	25	$165,000	$10,000	6%
Action Comics #3	26	$160,000	26	$155,000	$5,000	3%
More Fun Comics #73	27	$145,000	28	$140,000	$5,000	4%
All Star Comics #3	28	$143,000	27	$142,000	$1,000	1%
Suspense Comics #3	29	$140,000	29	$130,000	$10,000	8%
Detective Comics #1	30	VF $130,000	30	VF $120,000	$10,000	8%
Detective Comics #36	31	$118,000	33	$110,000	$8,000	7%
Detective Comics #28	32	$116,000	31	$114,000	$2,000	2%
Marvel Mystery Comics #9	33	$114,000	32	$113,000	$1,000	1%
Captain Marvel Adventures #1	34	$110,000	34	$105,000	$5,000	5%
Sub-Mariner Comics #1	34	$110,000	36	$100,000	$10,000	10%
Marvel Mystery Comics #2	36	$105,000	35	$104,000	$1,000	1%
Marvel Mystery Comics #5	37	$92,000	37	$90,000	$2,000	2%
More Fun Comics #53	38	$88,000	38	$87,000	$1,000	1%
Superman #2	39	$85,000	39	$80,000	$5,000	6%
Action Comics #23	40	$80,000	42	$75,000	$5,000	7%

TITLE/ISSUE#	2021 RANK	2021 NM- PRICE	2020 RANK	2020 NM- PRICE	$ INCR.	% INCR.
Detective Comics #37	41	$78,000	40	$78,000	$0	0%
Green Lantern #1	42	$77,000	41	$76,000	$1,000	1%
Human Torch #2 (#1) #1	43	$73,000	43	$73,000	$0	0%
Action Comics #6	44	$72,000	44	$72,000	$0	0%
Marvel Mystery Comics #4	44	$72,000	45	$70,000	$2,000	3%
Action Comics #4	46	$70,000	45	$70,000	$0	0%
Action Comics #5	46	$70,000	45	$70,000	$0	0%
Captain America Comics #2	46	$70,000	49	$66,000	$4,000	6%
All-American Comics #19	49	$67,000	48	$67,000	$0	0%
Adventure Comics #48	50	$66,000	50	$65,000	$1,000	2%
Captain America Comics #3	51	$65,000	52	$62,000	$3,000	5%
Marvel Mystery Comics #3	51	$65,000	51	$63,000	$2,000	3%
Batman #2	53	$62,000	54	$60,000	$2,000	3%
Motion Picture Funnies Weekly #1	54	$61,000	53	$60,500	$500	1%
New Fun Comics #1	55	VF $60,000	55	VF $59,700	$300	1%
Action Comics #12	56	$58,000	57	$54,000	$4,000	7%
Action Comics #15	57	$57,000	56	$56,000	$1,000	2%
Action Comics #8	58	$56,000	57	$54,000	$2,000	4%
Action Comics #9	58	$56,000	57	$54,000	$2,000	4%
Daring Mystery Comics #1	60	$54,000	60	$53,000	$1,000	2%
Walt Disney's Comics & Stories #1	61	$53,000	60	$53,000	$0	0%
Fantastic Comics #3	62	$50,000	62	$47,000	$3,000	6%
Wonder Comics #1	62	$50,000	63	$46,000	$4,000	9%
Detective Comics #168	64	$48,000	67	$44,000	$4,000	9%
Silver Streak Comics #6	64	$48,000	67	$44,000	$4,000	9%
Captain America Comics #74	66	$47,000	64	$45,000	$2,000	4%
Marvel Mystery Comics 132 pg.	67	VF $45,500	64	VF $45,000	$500	1%
Detective Comics #140	68	$45,000	73	$42,000	$3,000	7%
Four Color Series 1 #4 (Donald Duck)	68	$45,000	64	$45,000	$0	0%
Red Raven Comics #1	68	$45,000	70	$43,000	$2,000	5%
Famous Funnies-Series 1 #1	71	VF $44,500	67	VF $44,000	$500	1%
All-American Comics #61	72	$44,000	73	$42,000	$2,000	5%
All-Select Comics #1	72	$44,000	73	$42,000	$2,000	5%
Amazing Man Comics #5	72	$44,000	70	$43,000	$1,000	2%
More Fun Comics #54	72	$44,000	70	$43,000	$1,000	2%
More Fun Comics #55	72	$44,000	73	$42,000	$2,000	5%
Detective Comics #2	77	VF $42,000	73	VF $42,000	$0	0%
Detective Comics #30	77	$42,000	79	$40,000	$2,000	5%
Detective Comics #40	77	$42,000	79	$40,000	$2,000	5%
Mystic Comics #1	77	$42,000	78	$41,000	$1,000	2%
Phantom Lady #17	77	$42,000	79	$40,000	$2,000	5%
Captain America Comics 132 pg.	82	VF $41,000	79	VF $40,000	$1,000	3%
Detective Comics #225	83	$40,000	83	$39,000	$1,000	3%
Double Action Comics #2	83	$40,000	85	$38,000	$2,000	5%
Superman #3	83	$40,000	83	$39,000	$1,000	3%
Terrific Comics #5	83	$40,000	85	$38,000	$2,000	5%
All Winners Comics #1	87	$38,000	85	$38,000	$0	0%
Punch Comics #12	87	$38,000	89	$36,000	$2,000	6%
Marvel Mystery Comics #8	89	$37,500	88	$37,500	$0	0%
Detective Comics #32	90	$36,000	91	$34,000	$2,000	6%
Jackpot Comics #4	90	$36,000	89	$36,000	$0	0%
Action Comics #17	92	$34,000	91	$34,000	$0	0%
Jumbo Comics #1	92	VF $34,000	93	VF $33,500	$500	1%
Mystery Men Comics #1	92	$34,000	95	$32,000	$2,000	6%
All-American Comics #17	95	$33,000	95	$32,000	$1,000	3%
Archie Comics #2	95	$33,000	95	$32,000	$1,000	3%
Green Giant Comics #1	95	$33,000	95	$32,000	$1,000	3%
Marvel Mystery Comics #10	95	$33,000	94	$32,500	$500	2%
Pep Comics #34	95	$33,000	95	$32,000	$1,000	3%
Action Comics #19	100	$32,000	95	$32,000	$0	0%
Planet Comics #1	100	$32,000	110	$30,000	$2,000	7%

TOP 50 SILVER AGE COMICS

TITLE/ISSUE#	2021 RANK	2021 NM- PRICE	2020 RANK	2020 NM- PRICE	$ INCR.	% INCR.
Amazing Fantasy #15	1	$450,000	1	$425,000	$25,000	6%
Incredible Hulk #1	2	$310,000	2	$295,000	$15,000	5%
Fantastic Four #1	3	$210,000	3	$190,000	$20,000	11%
Showcase #4	4	$175,000	4	$165,000	$10,000	6%
Journey Into Mystery #83	5	$95,000	6	$86,000	$9,000	10%
Brave and the Bold #28	6	$92,000	5	$92,000	$0	0%
Amazing Spider-Man #1	7	$88,000	7	$84,000	$4,000	5%
X-Men #1	8	$70,000	8	$62,000	$8,000	13%
Showcase #22	9	$58,000	10	$55,000	$3,000	5%
Tales of Suspense #39	9	$58,000	9	$56,000	$2,000	4%
Tales to Astonish #27	11	$54,000	11	$52,000	$2,000	4%
Fantastic Four #5	12	$50,000	18	$28,000	$22,000	79%
Avengers #1	13	$46,000	12	$45,000	$1,000	2%
Flash #105	14	$34,000	13	$33,000	$1,000	3%
Action Comics #242	15	$33,000	14	$32,000	$1,000	3%
Adventure Comics #247	16	$31,000	15	$30,000	$1,000	3%
Action Comics #252	17	$30,000	16	$29,000	$1,000	3%
Justice League of America #1	17	$30,000	17	$28,500	$1,500	5%
Our Army at War #83	19	$28,000	19	$27,000	$1,000	4%
Showcase #8	20	$23,500	20	$23,000	$500	2%
Strange Tales #110	21	$21,000	21	$20,000	$1,000	5%
Fantastic Four #2	22	$18,000	23	$17,000	$1,000	6%
Fantastic Four #4	22	$18,000	23	$17,000	$1,000	6%
Green Lantern #1	22	$18,000	22	$18,000	$0	0%
Fantastic Four #3	25	$16,500	25	$16,000	$500	3%
Amazing Spider-Man #2	26	$16,000	26	$15,000	$1,000	7%
Incredible Hulk #2	27	$15,000	27	$14,000	$1,000	7%
Showcase #17	27	$15,000	37	$11,300	$3,700	33%
Batman #121	29	$14,500	32	$13,000	$1,500	12%
Fantastic Four #12	29	$14,500	27	$14,000	$500	4%
Sgt. Fury #1	29	$14,500	27	$14,000	$500	4%
Showcase #9	29	$14,500	27	$14,000	$500	4%
Superman's G.F. Lois Lane #1	29	$14,500	27	$14,000	$500	4%
Daredevil #1	34	$13,000	33	$12,500	$500	4%
Tales to Astonish #13	34	$13,000	36	$11,500	$1,500	13%
Tales to Astonish #35	34	$13,000	34	$12,300	$700	6%
Amazing Spider-Man #3	37	$12,500	35	$12,000	$500	4%
Showcase #6	38	$11,500	37	$11,300	$200	2%
Showcase #13	38	$11,500	37	$11,300	$200	2%
Showcase #14	40	$11,000	40	$11,000	$0	0%
Our Army at War #81	41	$10,500	41	$10,500	$0	0%
Richie Rich #1	41	$10,500	42	$10,000	$500	5%
Amazing Spider-Man #4	43	$10,000	44	$9,000	$1,000	11%
Flash #106	44	$9,800	43	$9,700	$100	1%
Brave and the Bold #25	45	$8,900	45	$8,800	$100	1%
Avengers #4	46	$8,600	47	$8,500	$100	1%
Flash #123	46	$8,600	46	$8,600	$0	0%
Journey Into Mystery #84	46	$8,600	47	$8,500	$100	1%
Journey Into Mystery #85	46	$8,600	49	$8,400	$200	2%
Strange Tales #89	46	$8,600	49	$8,400	$200	2%

TOP 25 BRONZE AGE COMICS

TITLE/ISSUE#	2021 RANK	2021 NM- PRICE	2020 RANK	2020 NM- PRICE	$ INCR.	% INCR.
Star Wars #1 (35¢ price variant)	1	$12,500	1	$12,000	$500	4%
Incredible Hulk #181	2	$8,000	2	$5,500	$2,500	45%
Giant-Size X-Men #1	3	$5,000	9	$2,300	$2,700	117%
Iron Fist #14 (35¢ price variant)	4	$4,600	3	$4,400	$200	5%
House of Secrets #92	5	$4,500	4	$3,350	$1,150	34%
Cerebus #1	6	$4,000	5	$3,200	$800	25%
Marvel Spotlight #5	6	$4,000	7	$2,800	$1,200	43%
Scooby Doo (1970) #1	8	$3,500	6	$3,000	$500	17%
Green Lantern #76	9	$2,700	8	$2,700	$0	0%
Werewolf By Night #32	10	$2,600	10	$2,000	$600	30%
Amazing Spider-Man #129	11	$2,500	11	$1,900	$600	32%
X-Men #94	12	$2,000	16	$1,425	$575	40%
Star Wars #2 (35¢ price variant)	13	$1,850	12	$1,800	$50	3%
Star Wars #3 (35¢ price variant)	13	$1,850	12	$1,800	$50	3%
Star Wars #4 (35¢ price variant)	13	$1,850	12	$1,800	$50	3%
Tomb of Dracula #10	16	$1,650	19	$1,200	$450	38%
Hero For Hire #1	17	$1,600	17	$1,375	$225	16%
Iron Man #55	17	$1,600	15	$1,600	$0	0%
Amazing Spider-Man #101	19	$1,400	19	$1,200	$200	17%
DC 100 Page Sup. Spec. #5	19	$1,400	17	$1,375	$25	2%
Incredible Hulk #180	19	$1,400	22	$1,000	$400	40%
Batman #227	22	$1,300	21	$1,100	$200	18%
Batman #251	23	$1,100	22	$1,000	$100	10%
Batman #232	24	$1,000	25	$900	$100	11%
Uncle Scrooge #179 (Whitman)	25	$950	24	$950	$0	0%

TOP 25 COPPER AGE COMICS

TITLE/ISSUE#	2021 RANK	2021 NM- PRICE	2020 RANK	2020 NM- PRICE	$ INCR.	% INCR.
Teenage Mutant Ninja Turtles #1	1	$16,500	1	$8,000	$8,500	106%
Gobbledygook #1	2	$10,000	2	$6,600	$3,400	52%
Albedo #2	3	$6,000	3	$3,200	$2,800	88%
Gobbledygook #2	4	$4,000	4	$2,600	$1,400	54%
Miracleman Gold #1	5	$1,500	5	$1,500	$0	0%
Miracleman Blue #1	6	$850	6	$850	$0	0%
Vampirella #113	7	$575	7	$550	$25	5%
Crow, The #1	8	$550	14	$230	$320	139%
Sandman #8	8	$550	8	$485	$65	13%
Amazing Spider-Man #300	10	$500	9	$375	$125	33%
Teenage Mutant Ninja Turtles #2	10	$500	12	$270	$230	85%
Primer #2	12	$360	10	$340	$20	6%
New Mutants #98	13	$325	11	$315	$10	3%
Evil Ernie #1	14	$300	14	$230	$70	30%
Spider-Man Platinum #1	14	$300	16	$225	$75	33%
Caliber Presents #1	16	$275	17	$215	$60	28%
Spider-Man #1 (Gold 2nd UPC)	17	$270	13	$260	$10	4%
Swamp Thing #37	18	$250	23	$165	$85	52%
Amazing Spider-Man #238	19	$225	21	$180	$45	25%
Eightball #1	20	$215	17	$215	$0	0%
Cry For Dawn HorrorCon Ed. #3	21	$200	19	$200	$0	0%
Teenage Mutant Ninja Turtles #3	21	$200	23	$165	$35	21%
Grendel #1	23	$190	20	$190	$0	0%
New Mutants #87	24	$175	22	$175	$0	0%
Batman #357	25	$160	25	$140	$20	14%

TOP 20 MODERN AGE COMICS

TITLE/ISSUE#	2021 RANK	2021 NM- PRICE	2020 RANK	2020 NM- PRICE	$ INCR.	% INCR.
Bone #1	1	$1,500	2	$950	$550	58%
Walking Dead #1	2	$1,225	1	$1,225	$0	0%
Venom: Lethal Protector #1 (black-c)	3	$1,200	3	$800	$400	50%
Star Wars: The Clone Wars #1	4	$700	-	$3	$697	23,233%
Marvel Collectible Classics: Spider-Man #1	5	$650	4	$600	$50	8%
Invincible #1	6	$600	10	$270	$330	122%
Batman Adventures #12	7	$500	5	$485	$15	3%
Captain Marvel #17 (2012, 2nd printing)	7	$500	9	$325	$175	54%
Spawn #174	7	$500	-	$3	$497	16,567%
Adam: Legend of the Blue Marvel #1	10	$400	-	$4	$396	9,900%
The Goon #1	10	$400	6	$385	$15	4%
Walking Dead #2	12	$380	7	$370	$10	3%
Spawn #1 (B&W edition)	13	$375	8	$350	$25	7%
Ultimate Fallout #4	14	$350	-	$90	$260	289%
Star Wars: Knights of the Old Republic #9	14	$350	-	$3	$347	11,567%
Spawn #175	16	$300	-	$3	$297	9,900%
Ult. Spider-Man (3rd series) #1 var-c (city)	16	$300	-	$95	$205	216%
Ult. Spider-Man (3rd) #1 var-c (unmasked)	16	$300	-	$70	$230	329%
Incredible Hulk #377 (3rd printing)	19	$275	11	$250	$25	10%
Marvel Collectible Classics: Spider-Man #2	20	$250	13	$225	$25	11%
Something Is Killing the Children #1	20	$250	-	$4	$246	6,150%
Walking Dead #19	20	$250	11	$250	$0	0%

TOP 10 PLATINUM AGE COMICS

TITLE/ISSUE#	2021 RANK	2021 PRICE	2020 RANK	2020 PRICE	$ INCR.	% INCR.
Yellow Kid in McFadden Flats	1	FN $15,000	1	FN $15,000	$0	0%
Little Sammy Sneeze	2	FN $8,500	2	FN $8,500	$0	6%
Mickey Mouse Book (2nd printing)-variant	3	FN $8,000	3	FN $8,000	$0	0%
Little Nemo 1906	4	FN $5,200	4	FN $5,200	$0	0%
Mickey Mouse Book (1st printing)	5	VF $5,100	5	VF $5,100	$0	0%
Pore Li'l Mose	6	FN $4,100	6	FN $4,100	$0	0%
Little Nemo 1909	7	FN $4,000	7	FN $4,000	$0	0%
Yellow Kid #1	7	FN $4,000	7	FN $4,000	$0	0%
Buster Brown and His Resolutions 1903	9	VF $3,400	11	VF $3,300	$100	3%
Happy Hooligan Book 1	9	VF $3,400	9	VF $3,400	$0	0%
Mickey Mouse Book (2nd printing)	9	VF $3,400	9	VF $3,400	$0	0%

TOP 10 CRIME COMICS

TITLE/ISSUE#	2021 RANK	2021 NM- PRICE	2020 RANK	2020 NM- PRICE	$ INCR.	% INCR.
Crime Does Not Pay #24	1	$16,000	1	$15,000	$1,000	7%
Crime Does Not Pay #22	2	$14,000	2	$13,500	$500	4%
Crime Does Not Pay #23	3	$5,600	3	$5,600	$0	0%
Crime Does Not Pay #33	4	$5,000	4	$4,200	$800	19%
Crime Reporter #2	5	$4,000	8	$2,250	$1,750	78%
True Crime Comics #2	6	$3,950	5	$3,900	$50	1%
True Crime Comics #3	7	$2,900	6	$2,800	$100	4%
The Killers #1	8	$2,600	7	$2,500	$100	4%
Crimes By Women #1	9	$2,100	9	$2,050	$50	2%
Crimes By Women #6	9	$2,100	9	$2,050	$50	2%
The Killers #2	9	$2,100	7	$2,000	$100	5%

TOP 10 HORROR COMICS

TITLE/ISSUE#	2021 RANK	2021 NM- PRICE	2020 RANK	2020 NM- PRICE	$ INCR.	% INCR.
Journey into Mystery #1	1	$19,000	1	$18,000	$1,000	6%
Eerie #1	2	$15,500	2	$15,000	$500	3%
Tales to Astonish #1	3	$14,500	3	$14,000	$500	4%
Strange Tales #1	4	$14,000	4	$13,000	$1,000	8%
Tales of Terror Annual #1	5	VF $13,000	5	VF $11,500	$1,500	13%
Vault of Horror #12	5	$12,000	5	$11,500	$500	4%
Crime Patrol #15	7	$6,800	9	$5,400	$1,400	26%
Crypt of Terror #17	7	$6,800	7	$6,500	$300	5%
Haunt of Fear #15	9	$6,000	8	$5,900	$100	2%
House of Mystery #1	10	$4,650	10	$4,600	$50	1%

TOP 10 ROMANCE COMICS

TITLE/ISSUE#	2021 RANK	2021 NM- PRICE	2020 RANK	2020 NM- PRICE	$ INCR.	% INCR.
Giant Comics Edition #12	1	$17,000	1	$16,000	$1,000	6%
Daring Love #1	2	$6,200	2	$6,000	$200	3%
Negro Romance #1	3	$3,800	3	$3,600	$200	6%
Giant Comics Edition #15	4	$3,600	4	$3,300	$300	9%
Intimate Confessions #1	5	$3,400	4	$3,300	$100	3%
Negro Romance #2	6	$3,200	6	$3,000	$200	7%
Negro Romance #3	6	$3,200	6	$3,000	$200	7%
Giant Comics Edition #13	8	$2,900	8	$2,700	$200	7%
Giant Comics Edition #9	9	$2,700	8	$2,700	$0	0%
Forbidden Love #1	10	$2,200	10	$2,150	$50	2%

TOP 10 SCI-FI COMICS

TITLE/ISSUE#	2021 RANK	2021 NM- PRICE	2020 RANK	2020 NM- PRICE	$ INCR.	% INCR.
Showcase #17 (Adam Strange)	1	$15,000	1	$11,300	$3,700	33%
Mystery In Space #1	2	$7,800	2	$7,500	$300	4%
Weird Science #12 (#1)	3	$5,400	3	$5,300	$100	2%
Strange Adventures #1	4	$5,250	4	$5,250	$0	0%
Weird Science-Fantasy Annual 1952	5	$5,200	5	$5,000	$200	4%
Showcase #15 (Space Ranger)	6	$5,000	6	$4,900	$100	2%
Journey Into Unknown Worlds #36	7	$4,800	7	$4,800	$0	0%
Mystery in Space #53	8	$4,550	8	$4,500	$50	1%
Weird Fantasy #13 (#1)	9	$4,000	9	$4,000	$0	0%
Fawcett Movie #15 (Man From Planet X)	10	$3,900	10	$3,800	$100	3%

TOP 10 WESTERN COMICS

TITLE/ISSUE#	2021 RANK	2021 NM- PRICE	2020 RANK	2020 NM- PRICE	$ INCR.	% INCR.
Gene Autry Comics #1	1	$7,500	1	$7,500	$0	0%
*Lone Ranger Ice Cream 1939 2nd	2	VF $4,500	2	VF $4,500	$0	0%
Roy Rogers Four Color #38	2	$4,500	2	$4,500	$0	0%
Red Ryder Comics #1	4	$4,100	4	$4,100	$0	0%
*Lone Ranger Ice Cream 1939	5	VF $4,000	5	VF $4,000	$0	0%
John Wayne Adventure Comics #1	5	$4,000	5	$4,000	$0	0%
Western Picture Stories #1	5	$4,000	7	$3,900	$100	3%
*Tom Mix Ralston #1	8	$3,350	8	$3,350	$0	0%
Hopalong Cassidy #1	9	$3,000	9	$3,000	$0	0%
*Red Ryder Victory Patrol '42	10	$1,350	10	$1,350	$0	0%

GRADING DEFINITIONS

When grading a comic book, common sense must be employed. The overall eye appeal and beauty of the comic book must be taken into account along with its technical flaws to arrive at the appropriate grade.

10.0 GEM MINT (GM): This is an exceptional example of a given book - the best ever seen. The slightest bindery defects and/or printing flaws may be seen only upon very close inspection. The overall look is "as if it has never been handled or released for purchase." Only the slightest bindery or printing defects are allowed, and these would be imperceptible on first viewing. No bindery tears. Cover is flat with no surface wear. Inks are bright with high reflectivity. Well centered and firmly secured to interior pages. Corners are cut square and sharp. No creases. No dates or stamped markings allowed. No soiling, staining or other discoloration. Spine is tight and flat. No spine roll or split allowed. Staples must be original, centered and clean with no rust. No staple tears or stress lines. Paper is white, supple and fresh. No hint of acidity in the odor of the newsprint. No interior autographs or owner signatures. Centerfold is firmly secure. No interior tears.

9.9 MINT (MT): Near perfect in every way. Only subtle bindery or printing defects are allowed. No bindery tears. Cover is flat with no surface wear. Inks are bright with high reflectivity. Generally well centered and firmly secured to interior pages. Corners are cut square and sharp. No creases. Small, inconspicuous, lightly penciled, stamped or inked arrival dates are acceptable as long as they are in an unobtrusive location. No soiling, staining or other discoloration. Spine is tight and flat. No spine roll or split allowed. Staples must be original, generally centered and clean with no rust. No staple tears or stress lines. Paper is white, supple and fresh. No hint of acidity in the odor of the newsprint. Centerfold is firmly secure. No interior tears.

9.8 NEAR MINT/MINT (NM/MT): Nearly perfect in every way with only minor imperfections that keep it from the next higher grade. Only subtle bindery or printing defects are allowed. No bindery tears. Cover is flat with no surface wear. Inks are bright with high reflectivity. Generally well centered and firmly secured to interior pages. Corners are cut square and sharp. No creases. Small, inconspicuous, lightly penciled, stamped or inked arrival dates are acceptable as long as they are in an unobtrusive location. No soiling, staining or other discoloration. Spine is tight and flat. No spine roll or split allowed. Staples must be original, generally centered and clean with no rust. No staple tears or stress lines. Paper is off-white to white, supple and fresh. No hint of acidity in the odor of the newsprint. Centerfold is firmly secure. Only the slightest interior tears are allowed.

9.6 NEAR MINT+ (NM+): Nearly perfect with a minor additional virtue or virtues that raise it from Near Mint. The overall look is "as if it was just purchased and read once or twice." Only subtle bindery or printing defects are allowed. No bindery tears are allowed, although on Golden Age books bindery tears of up to 1/8" have been noted. Cover is flat with no surface wear. Inks are bright with high reflectivity. Well centered and firmly secured to interior pages. One corner may be almost imperceptibly blunted, but still almost sharp and cut square. Almost imperceptible indentations are permissible, but no creases, bends, or color break. Small, inconspicuous, lightly penciled, stamped or inked arrival dates are acceptable as long as they are in an unobtrusive location. No soiling, staining or other discoloration. Spine is tight and flat. No spine roll or split allowed. Staples must be original, generally centered, with only the slightest discoloration. No staple tears, stress lines, or rust migration. Paper is off-white, supple and fresh. No hint of acidity in the odor of the newsprint. Centerfold is firmly secure. Only the slightest interior tears are allowed.

9.4 NEAR MINT (NM): Nearly perfect with only minor imperfections that keep it from the next higher grade. Minor feathering that does not distract from the overall beauty of an otherwise higher grade copy is acceptable for this grade. The overall look is "as if it was just purchased and read once or twice." Subtle bindery defects are allowed. Bindery tears must be less than 1/16" on Silver Age and later books, although on Golden Age books bindery tears of up to 1/4" have been noted. Cover is flat with no surface wear. Inks are bright with high reflectivity. Generally well centered and secured to interior pages. Corners are cut square and sharp with ever-so-slight blunting permitted. A 1/16" bend is permitted with no color break. No creases. Small, inconspicuous, lightly penciled, stamped or inked arrival dates are acceptable as long as they are in an unobtrusive location. No soiling, staining or other discoloration apart from slight foxing. Spine is tight and flat. No spine roll or split allowed. Staples are generally centered; may have slight discoloration. No staple tears are allowed; almost no stress lines. No rust migration. In rare cases, a comic was not stapled at the bindery and therefore has a missing staple; this is not considered a defect. Any staple can be replaced on books up to Fine, but only vintage staples can be used on books from Very Fine to Near Mint. Mint books must have original staples. Paper is cream to off-white, supple and fresh. No hint of acidity in the odor of the newsprint. Centerfold is secure. Slight interior tears are allowed.

9.2 NEAR MINT– (NM–): Nearly perfect with only

a minor additional defect or defects that keep it from Near Mint. A limited number of minor bindery defects are allowed. A light, barely noticeable water stain or minor foxing that does not distract from the beauty of the book is acceptable for this grade. Cover is flat with no surface wear. Inks are bright with only the slightest dimming of reflectivity. Generally well centered and secured to interior pages. Corners are cut square and sharp with ever-so-slight blunting permitted. A 1/16"-1/8" bend is permitted with no color break. No creases. Small, inconspicuous, lightly penciled, stamped or inked arrival dates are acceptable as long as they are in an unobtrusive location. No soiling, staining or other discoloration apart from slight foxing. Spine is tight and flat. No spine roll or split allowed. Staples may show some discoloration. No staple tears are allowed; almost no stress lines. No rust migration. In rare cases, a comic was not stapled at the bindery and therefore has a missing staple; this is not considered a defect. Any staple can be replaced on books up to Fine, but only vintage staples can be used on books from Very Fine to Near Mint. Mint books must have original staples. Paper is cream to off-white, supple and fresh. No hint of acidity in the odor of the newsprint. Centerfold is secure. Slight interior tears are allowed.

9.0 VERY FINE/NEAR MINT (VF/NM): Nearly perfect with outstanding eye appeal. A limited number of bindery defects are allowed. Almost flat cover with almost imperceptible wear. Inks are bright with slightly diminished reflectivity. An 1/8" bend is allowed if color is not broken. Corners are cut square and sharp with ever-so-slight blunting permitted but no creases. Several lightly penciled, stamped or inked arrival dates are acceptable. No obvious soiling, staining or other discoloration, except for very minor foxing. Spine is tight and flat. No spine roll or split allowed. Staples may show some discoloration. Only the slightest staple tears are allowed. A very minor accumulation of stress lines may be present if they are nearly imperceptible. No rust migration. In rare cases, a comic was not stapled at the bindery and therefore has a missing staple; this is not considered a defect. Any staple can be replaced on books up to Fine, but only vintage staples can be used on books from Very Fine to Near Mint. Mint books must have original staples. Paper is cream to off-white and supple. No hint of acidity in the odor of the newsprint. Centerfold is secure. Very minor interior tears may be present.

8.5 VERY FINE+ (VF+): Fits the criteria for Very Fine but with an additional virtue or small accumulation of virtues that improves the book's appearance by a perceptible amount.

8.0 VERY FINE (VF): An excellent copy with outstanding eye appeal. Sharp, bright and clean with supple pages. A comic book in this grade has the appearance of having been carefully handled. A limited accumulation of minor bindery defects is allowed. Cover is relatively flat with minimal surface wear beginning to show, possibly including some minute wear at corners. Inks are generally bright with moderate to high reflectivity. A 1/4" crease is acceptable if color is not broken. Stamped or inked arrival dates may be present. No obvious soiling, staining or other discoloration, except for minor foxing. Spine is almost flat with no roll. Possible minor color break allowed. Staples may show some discoloration. Very slight staple tears and a few almost very minor to minor stress lines may be present. No rust migration. In rare cases, a comic was not stapled at the bindery and therefore has a missing staple; this is not considered a defect. Any staple can be replaced on books up to Fine, but only vintage staples can be used on books from Very Fine to Near Mint. Mint books must have original staples. Paper is tan to cream and supple. No hint of acidity in the odor of the newsprint. Centerfold is mostly secure. Minor interior tears at the margin may be present.

7.5 VERY FINE– (VF–): Fits the criteria for Very Fine but with an additional defect or small accumulation of defects that detracts from the book's appearance by a perceptible amount.

7.0 FINE/VERY FINE (FN/VF): An above-average copy that shows minor wear but is still relatively flat and clean with outstanding eye appeal. A small accumulation of minor bindery defects is allowed. Minor cover wear beginning to show with interior yellowing or tanning allowed, possibly including minor creases. Corners may be blunted or abraded. Inks are generally bright with a moderate reduction in reflectivity. Stamped or inked arrival dates may be present. No obvious soiling, staining or other discoloration, except for minor foxing. The slightest spine roll may be present, as well as a possible moderate color break. Staples may show some discoloration. Slight staple tears and a slight accumulation of light stress lines may be present. Slight rust migration. In rare cases, a comic was not stapled at the bindery and therefore has a missing staple; this is not considered a defect. Any staple can be replaced on books up to Fine, but only vintage staples can be used on books from Very Fine to Near Mint. Mint books must have original staples. Paper is tan to cream, but not brown. No hint of acidity in the odor of the newsprint. Centerfold is mostly secure. Minor interior tears at the margin may be present.

6.5 FINE+ (FN+): Fits the criteria for Fine but with an additional virtue or small accumulation of virtues that improves the book's appearance by a perceptible amount.

6.0 FINE (FN): An above-average copy that shows minor wear but is still relatively flat and clean with no significant creasing or other serious defects. Eye appeal is somewhat reduced because of slight surface wear and the accumulation of small defects, especially on the spine and edges. A FINE condition comic book appears to have been read a few times and has been handled with moderate care. Some accumulation of minor bindery defects is allowed. Minor cover wear apparent, with minor to moderate creases. Inks show a major reduction in reflectivity. Blunted or abraded corners are more common, as is minor staining, soiling, discoloration, and/or foxing. Stamped or inked arrival dates may be present. A minor spine roll is allowed. There can also be a 1/4" spine split or severe color break. Staples show minor discoloration. Minor staple tears and an accumulation of stress lines may be present, as well as minor rust migration. In rare cases, a comic was not stapled at the bindery and therefore has a missing staple; this is not considered a defect. Any staple can be replaced on books up to Fine, but only vintage staples can be used on books from Very Fine to Near Mint. Mint books must have original staples. Paper is brown to tan and fairly supple with no signs of brittleness. No hint of acidity in the odor of the newsprint. Minor interior tears at the margin may be present. Centerfold may be loose but not detached.

5.5 FINE– (FN–): Fits the criteria for Fine but with an additional defect or small accumulation of defects that detracts from the book's appearance by a perceptible amount.

5.0 VERY GOOD/FINE (VG/FN): An above-average but well-used comic book. A comic in this grade shows some moderate wear; eye appeal is somewhat reduced because of the accumulation of defects. Still a desirable copy that has been handled with some care. An accumulation of bindery defects is allowed. Minor to moderate cover wear apparent, with minor to moderate creases and/or dimples. Inks have major to extreme reduction in reflectivity. Blunted or abraded corners are increasingly common, as is minor to moderate staining, discoloration, and/or foxing. Stamped or inked arrival dates may be present. A minor to moderate spine roll is allowed. A spine split of up to 1/2" may be present. Staples show minor discoloration. A slight accumulation of minor staple tears and an accumulation of minor stress lines may also be present, as well as minor rust migration. In rare cases, a comic was not stapled at the bindery and therefore has a missing staple; this is not considered a defect. Any staple can be replaced on books up to Fine, but only vintage staples can be used on books from Very Fine to Near Mint. Mint books must have original staples. Paper is brown to tan with no signs of brittleness. May have the faintest trace of an acidic odor. Centerfold may be loose but not detached. Minor tears may also be present.

4.5 VERY GOOD+ (VG+): Fits the criteria for Very Good but with an additional virtue or small accumulation of virtues that improves the book's appearance by a perceptible amount.

4.0 VERY GOOD (VG): The average used comic book. A comic in this grade shows some significant moderate wear, but still has not accumulated enough total defects to reduce eye appeal to the point that it is not a desirable copy. Cover shows moderate to significant wear, and may be loose but not completely detached. Moderate to extreme reduction in reflectivity. Can have an accumulation of creases or dimples. Corners may be blunted or abraded. Store stamps, name stamps, arrival dates, initials, etc. have no effect on this grade. Some discoloration, fading, foxing, and even minor soiling is allowed. As much as a 1/4" triangle can be missing out of the corner or edge; a missing 1/8" square is also acceptable. Only minor unobtrusive tape and other amateur repair allowed on otherwise high grade copies. Moderate spine roll may be present and/or a 1" spine split. Staples discolored. Minor to moderate staple tears and stress lines may be present, as well as some rust migration. Paper is brown but not brittle. A minor acidic odor can be detectable. Minor to moderate tears may be present. Centerfold may be loose or detached at one staple.

3.5 VERY GOOD– (VG–): Fits the criteria for Very Good but with an additional defect or small accumulation of defects that detracts from the book's appearance by a perceptible amount.

3.0 GOOD/VERY GOOD (GD/VG): A used comic book showing some substantial wear. Cover shows significant wear, and may be loose or even detached at one staple. Cover reflectivity is very low. Can have a book-length crease and/or dimples. Corners may be blunted or even rounded. Discoloration, fading, foxing, and even minor to moderate soiling is allowed. A triangle from 1/4" to 1/2" can be missing out of the corner or edge; a missing 1/8" to 1/4" square is also acceptable. Tape and other amateur repair may be present. Moderate spine roll likely. May have a spine split of anywhere from 1" to 1-1/2". Staples may be rusted or replaced. Minor to moderate staple tears and moderate stress lines may be present, as well as some rust migration. Paper is brown but not brittle. Centerfold may be loose or detached at one staple. Minor to moderate interior tears may be present.

2.5 GOOD+ (GD+): Fits the criteria for Good but with an additional virtue or small accumulation of virtues that improves the book's appearance by a perceptible amount.

2.0 GOOD (GD): Shows substantial wear; often considered a "reading copy." Cover shows significant wear and may even be detached. Cover reflectivity is low and in some cases completely absent. Book-length creases and dimples may be present. Rounded corners are more common. Moderate soiling, staining, discoloration and foxing may be present. The largest piece allowed missing from the front or back cover is usually a 1/2" triangle or a 1/4" square, although some Silver Age books such as 1960s Marvels have had the price corner box clipped from the top left front cover and may be considered Good if they would otherwise have graded higher. Tape and other forms of amateur repair are common in Silver Age and older books. Spine roll is likely. May have up to a 2" spine split. Staples may be degraded, replaced or missing. Moderate staple tears and stress lines may be present, as well as rust migration. Paper is brown but not brittle. Centerfold may be loose or detached. Moderate interior tears may be present.

1.8 GOOD– (GD–): Fits the criteria for Good but with an

additional defect or small accumulation of defects that detracts from the book's appearance by a perceptible amount.

1.5 FAIR/GOOD (FR/GD): A comic showing substantial to heavy wear. A copy in this grade still has all pages and covers, although there may be pieces missing up to and including missing coupons and/or Marvel Value Stamps that do not impact the story. Books in this grade are commonly creased, scuffed, abraded, soiled, and possibly unattractive, but still generally readable. Cover shows considerable wear and may be detached. Nearly no reflectivity to no reflectivity remaining. Store stamp, name stamp, arrival date and initials are permitted. Book-length creases, tears and folds may be present. Rounded corners are increasingly common. Soiling, staining, discoloration and foxing is generally present. Up to 1/10 of the back cover may be missing. Tape and other forms of amateur repair are increasingly common in Silver Age and older books. Spine roll is common. May have a spine split between 2" and 2/3 the length of the book. Staples may be degraded, replaced or missing. Staple tears and stress lines are common, as well as rust migration. Paper is brown and may show brittleness around the edges. Acidic odor may be present. Centerfold may be loose or detached. Interior tears are common.

1.0 FAIR (FR): A copy in this grade shows heavy wear. Some collectors consider this the lowest collectible grade because comic books in lesser condition are usually incomplete and/or brittle. Comics in this grade are usually soiled, faded, ragged and possibly unattractive. This is the last grade in which a comic remains generally readable. Cover may be detached, and inks have lost all reflectivity. Creases, tears and/or folds are prevalent. Corners are commonly rounded or absent. Soiling and staining is present. Books in this condition generally have all pages and most of the covers, although there may be up to 1/4 of the front cover missing or no back cover, but not both. Tape and other forms of amateur repair are more common. Spine roll is more common; spine split can extend up to 2/3 the length of the book. Staples may be missing or show rust and discoloration. An accumulation of staple tears and stress lines may be present, as well as rust migration. Paper is brown and may show brittleness around the edges but not in the central portion of the pages. Acidic odor may be present. Accumulation of interior tears. Chunks may be missing. The centerfold may be missing if readability is generally preserved (although there may be difficulty). Coupons may be cut.

0.5 POOR (PR): Most comic books in this grade have been sufficiently degraded to the point where there is little or no collector value; they are easily identified by a complete absence of eye appeal. Comics in this grade are brittle almost to the point of turning to dust with a touch, and are usually incomplete. Extreme cover fading may render the cover almost indiscernible. May have extremely severe stains, mildew or heavy cover abrasion to the point that some cover inks are indistinct/absent. Covers may be detached with large chunks missing. Can have extremely ragged edges and extensive creasing. Corners are rounded or virtually absent. Covers may have been defaced with paints, varnishes, glues, oil, indelible markers or dyes, and may have suffered heavy water damage. Can also have extensive amateur repairs such as laminated covers. Extreme spine roll present; can have extremely ragged spines or a complete, book-length split. Staples can be missing or show extreme rust and discoloration. Extensive staple tears and stress lines may be present, as well as extreme rust migration. Paper exhibits moderate to severe brittleness (where the comic book literally falls apart when examined). Extreme acidic odor may be present. Extensive interior tears. Multiple pages, including the centerfold, may be missing that affect readability. Coupons may be cut.

0.3 INCOMPLETE (INC): Books that are coverless, but are otherwise complete, or covers missing their interiors.

0.1 INCOMPLETE (INC): Coverless copies that have incomplete interiors, wraps or single pages will receive a grade of .1 as will just front covers or just back covers.

PUBLISHERS' CODES

The following abbreviations are used with cover reproductions throughout the book for copyright purposes:

ABC-America's Best Comics
AC-AC Comics
ACE-Ace Periodicals
ACG-American Comics Group
AJAX-Ajax-Farrell
ACP-Archie Comic Publications
BP-Better Publications
C & L-Cupples & Leon
CC-Charlton Comics
CEN-Centaur Publications
CCG-Columbia Comics Group
CG-Catechetical Guild
CHES-Harry 'A' Chesler
CM-Comics Magazine
CN-Cartoon Network
CPI-Conan Properties Inc.
DC-DC Comics, Inc.
DELL-Dell Publishing Co.
DH-Dark Horse
DIS-Disney Enterprises, Inc.
DMP-David McKay Publishing
DYN-Dynamite Entertainment
DS-D. S. Publishing Co.
EAS-Eastern Color Printing Co.
EC-E. C. Comics
ECL-Eclipse Comics
ENWIL-Enwil Associates
EP-Elliott Publications
ERB-Edgar Rice Burroughs
FAW-Fawcett Publications
FC-First Comics
FF-Famous Funnies
FH-Fiction House Magazines
FOX-Fox Feature Syndicate
GIL-Gilberton
GK-Gold Key
GP-Great Publications
HARV-Harvey Publications
H-B-Hanna-Barbera
HILL-Hillman Periodicals
HOKE-Holyoke Publishing Co.
IM-Image Comics
KING-King Features Syndicate
LEV-Lev Gleason Publications
MAL-Malibu Comics
MAR-Marvel Characters, Inc.
ME-Magazine Enterprises
MLJ-MLJ Magazines
MS-Mirage Studios
NOVP-Novelty Press
NYNS-New York News Syndicate
PG-Premier Group
PINE-Pines
PMI-Parents' Magazine Institute
PRIZE-Prize Publications
QUA-Quality Comics Group
REAL-Realistic Comics
RH-Rural Home
S & S-Street and Smith Publishers
SKY-Skywald Publications
STAR-Star Publications
STD-Standard Comics
STJ-St. John Publishing Co.
SUPR-Superior Comics
TC-Tower Comics
TM-Trojan Magazines
TMP-Todd McFarlane Prods.
TOBY-Toby Press
TOPS-Tops Comics
UFS-United Features Syndicate
VAL-Valiant
VITL-Vital Publications
WB-Warner Brothers.
WEST-Western Publishing Co.
WHIT-Whitman Publishing Co.
WHW-William H. Wise
WMG-William M. Gaines (E. C.)
WP-Warren Publishing Co.
YM-Youthful Magazines
Z-D-Ziff-Davis Publishing Co.

OVERSTREET ADVISORS

Even before the first edition of *The Overstreet Comic Book Price Guide* was printed, author Robert M. Overstreet solicited pricing data, historical notations, and general information from a variety of sources. What was initially an informal group offering input quickly became an organized field of comic book collectors, dealers and historians whose opinions are actively solicited in advance of each edition of this book. Some of these Overstreet Advisors are specialists who deal in particular niches within the comic book world, while others are generalists who are interested in commenting on the broader marketplace. Each advisor provides information from their respective areas of interest and expertise, spanning the history of American comics.

While some choose to offer pricing and historical information in the form of annotated sales catalogs, auction catalogs, or documented private sales, assistance from others comes in the form of the market reports such as those beginning on page 97 in this book. In addition to those who have served as Overstreet Advisors almost since *The Guide*'s inception, each year new contributors are sought.

With that in mind, we are pleased to present our newest Overstreet Advisors:

THE CLASS OF 2021

JAIME ADRIANO DAEZ
Collector/Dealer
Metro Manilla,
Philippines

ERIC FOURNIER
Guardian Comics
Pickering, ON,
Canada

KAREN O'BRIEN
Comics Journalist
Dyer, IN

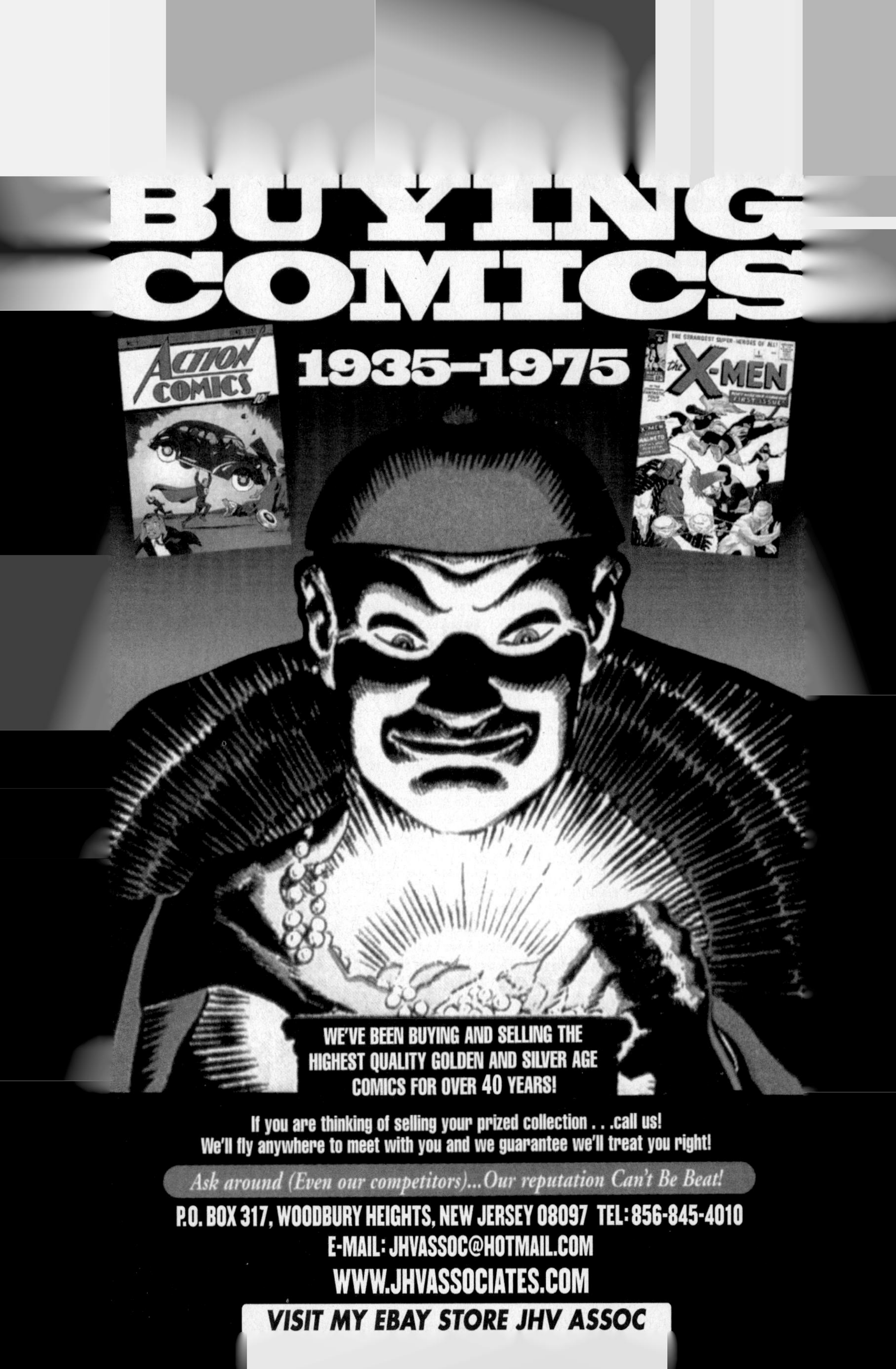
BUYING COMICS
ACTION COMICS
1935–1975
the X-MEN
WE'VE BEEN BUYING AND SELLING THE HIGHEST QUALITY GOLDEN AND SILVER AGE COMICS FOR OVER 40 YEARS!
If you are thinking of selling your prized collection . . .call us!
We'll fly anywhere to meet with you and we guarantee we'll treat you right!
Ask around (Even our competitors)...Our reputation Can't Be Beat!
P.O. BOX 317, WOODBURY HEIGHTS, NEW JERSEY 08097 TEL: 856-845-4010
E-MAIL: JHVASSOC@HOTMAIL.COM
WWW.JHVASSOCIATES.COM
VISIT MY EBAY STORE JHV ASSOC

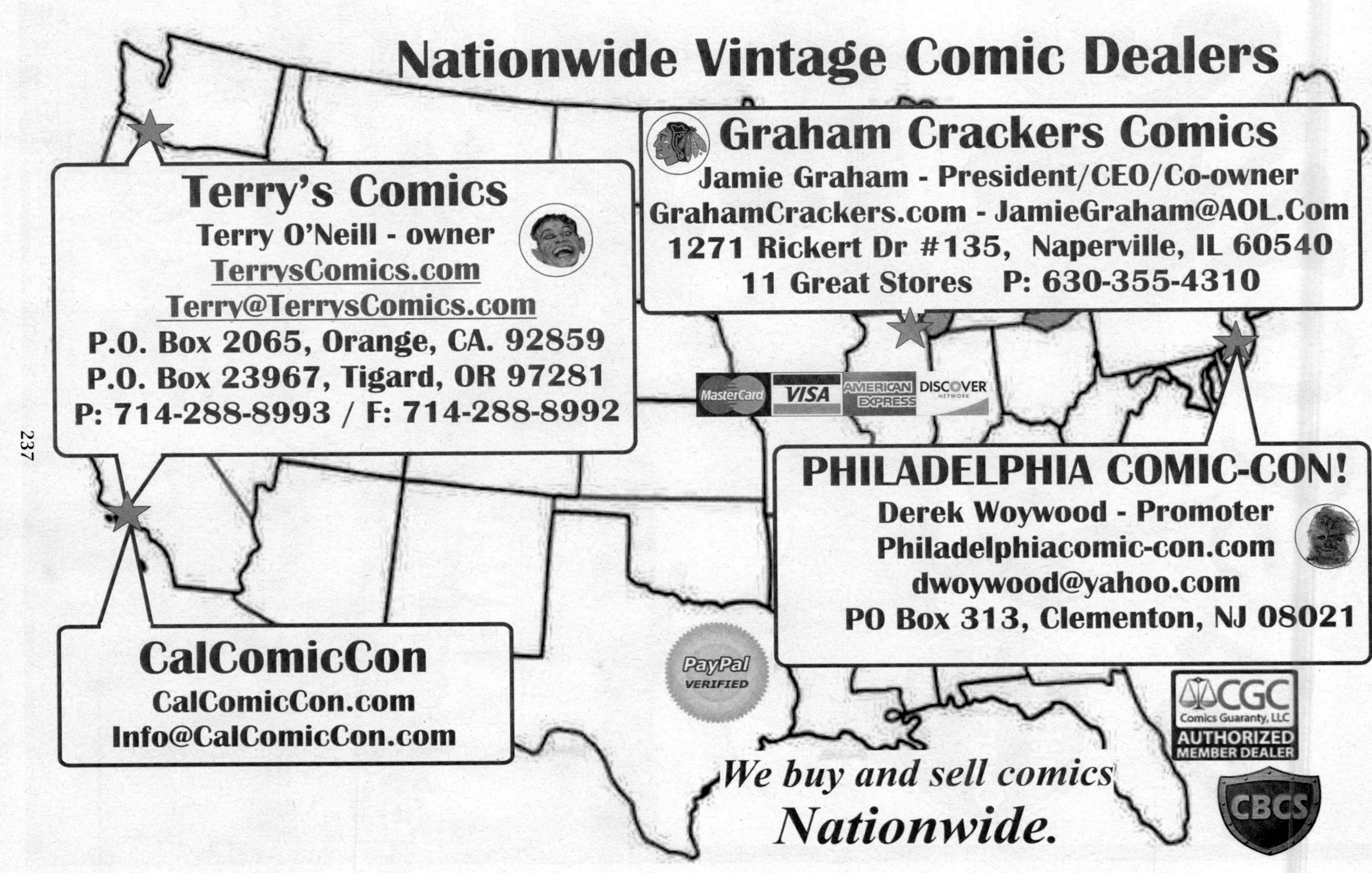
Nationwide Vintage Comic Dealers
Graham Crackers Comics
Jamie Graham - President/CEO/Co-owner
GrahamCrackers.com - JamieGraham@AOL.Com
1271 Rickert Dr #135, Naperville, IL 60540
11 Great Stores P: 630-355-4310
Terry's Comics
Terry O'Neill - owner
TerrysComics.com
Terry@TerrysComics.com
P.O. Box 2065, Orange, CA. 92859
P.O. Box 23967, Tigard, OR 97281
P: 714-288-8993 / F: 714-288-8992
MasterCard
VISA
AMERICAN EXPRESS
DISCOVER NETWORK
PHILADELPHIA COMIC-CON!
Derek Woywood - Promoter
Philadelphiacomic-con.com
dwoywood@yahoo.com
PO Box 313, Clementon, NJ 08021
CalComicCon
CalComicCon.com
Info@CalComicCon.com
PayPal VERIFIED
CGC Comics Guaranty, LLC AUTHORIZED MEMBER DEALER
We buy and sell comics
Nationwide.
CBCS

YEEEEEEEE
Even the Mighty Subby knows that when it comes to Rare Comic Books, No One carries a Finer or more Vast Selection than Harley Yee.
Bill Everett
Senior Advisor to Overstreet Price Guide
© Atlas/Marvel
HARLEY YEE
P.O. Box #51758 • Livonia, MI 48151-5758 USA
(800) 731-1029 or (734) 421-7921
(734) 421-7928 Fax
COMICS GUARANTY, LLC Charter Member Dealer
When dealing with Yee, you will Soar with Glee! His Selection is Second-to-None.
• Golden Age, Silver Age and Bronze Age Comics
• Hard-to-Find and Super High-Grade, Investment Books
• Lower to Mid-Grade, "Collector copy" Books
• Accurate Grading and Competitive Pricing
• Prompt and Professional Service
• Over 25 Years of "Hands On" Experience
• Want-List Service
• Setting Up at 30 or more Comic Conventions Every Year
HarleyYeeComics.com • HarleyComx@aol.com
eBay store: Harleycomics

We are paying 65% of Guide for the following:

Action 16-200
Adventure 32–100
All American
All Flash
All Top 8–18
Blonde Phantom
Blue Beetle 47–57
Brenda Starr 1–12
Crash
Daring Mystery
Fantastic
Flash (1st)
Hit 1–20
John Wayne
JO-JO 7–29
Kid Komics
Miss Fury
More Fun 52–107
Mysterious Adventure
Mystic (1st)
National 1–23
New Book of Comics
Pep 1–21
Phantom Lady
Phantom Stranger
Rangers 1-20
Rulah
Science (Fox)
Sensation
Silver Streak 1-17
Smash
Speed 1-20
Strange Tales 1–100
U.S.A. 1-5
Weird Comics
Zoot 7–16

We are paying 60% of Guide for the following:

Adventure 101–200
Adv. of Bob Hope 1–50
Adv. of Jerry Lewis 1-50
Adv. of Ozzie & Harriet
Air Fighters
All Star
Amazing Spiderman 3–10
America's Greatest
Batman 2-100
Blue Ribbon 2-20
Brave & the Bold 1–20
Bulletman
Captain Marvel
Captain Marvel Jr.
Captain Midnight
Challengers 1–10
Comic Cavalcade 1–29
Daredevil 1st 1–20
Detective 28-100
Dollman
Fantastic Four 3–10
Fight 1–30
Frontier Fighters
Green Hornet 1–20
Green Lantern (1st)
House of Mystery 1–50
House of Secrets 1–25
Ibis
Journey Into Mystery 1–115
Jumbo 11–50
Jungle 1–50
Lash Larue 1–46
Leading 1–14
Legend of D. Boone
Marvel Family
Mary Marvel
Master
Military
Modern
Movie Comics (D.C.)
My Greatest Adv. 1–50
Mystery in Space 1–50
Nickel
Planet
Police 1–20
Red Ryder 1-100
Saint
Shadow (1st)
Showcase 1–3, 5-20
Shield Wizard
Spy Smasher
Star Spangled
Superman 2–125
Superman's Pal 2–30
Strange Adventure 1–120
Superboy 1–50
Top-Notch
W.D. Comics & Stories 1–40
Whiz
World's Finest 1–110
Zip 1–39

We are also paying 50-100% of Guide for many other titles. Comics must be properly graded and complete. Please send your listing of comics for sale or a list of comics you wish to purchase. We are dealing in Marvels, D.C.'s, Timelys, Nedors, Western, Funny Material and much more! Please check our web site or send for our 100-page catalog. We will travel for large collections or, if you're passing through the area, call for an appointment.

JAMES PAYETTE
Rare Books & Comics

P.O. Box 750 • Bethlehem, NH 03574
Tel (603) 869-2097 • Fax (603) 869-3475
www.jamespayettecomics.com
jimpayette@msn.com

CREDENTIALS

Special Advisor to Overstreet Guide	1985–present
Member AACBC	1990–present
Sotheby's Authenticating, Certification, and Grading committee	1991–2002
Experience as a Dealer/Collector	since 1975
CBG Customer Service Award Winner for many years	

PLEASE SEE OUR OTHER ADS FOR FURTHER REFERENCE

I BUY OLD COMICS 1930 to 1975

Any Title
Any Condition
Any Size Collection

Can Easily Travel to:
Atlanta
Chicago
Cincinnati
Dallas
Little Rock
Louisvillle
Memphis
St. Louis

I want your comics:
Superhero
Western
Horror
Humor
Romance

Leroy Harper
PO BOX 212
WEST PADUCAH, KY 42086

PHONE 270-748-9364
EMAIL LHCOMICS@hotmail.com

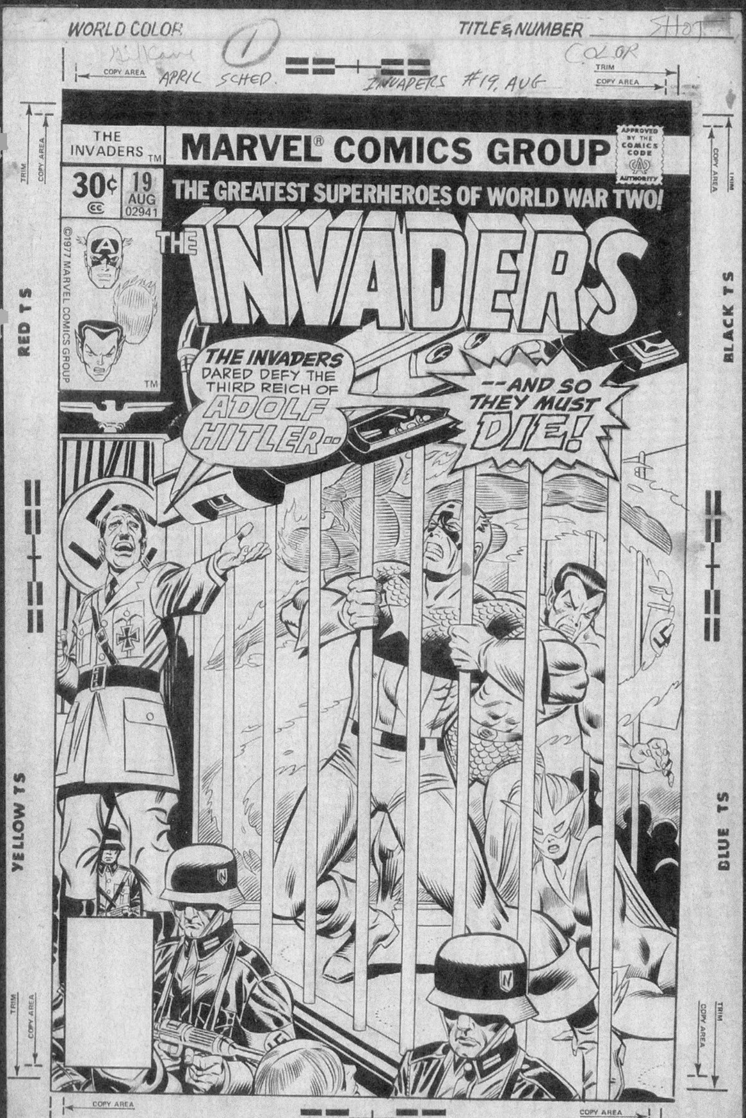

HOUSE OF COMICS

CHECK IN WITH US NOW!

info@houseofcomics.com

510-847-3376

1950s to 1970s SPECIALIST
HOUSE OF COMICS IS KNOWN FOR...
-STRICT GRADING!
-REASONABLE PRICES!
-PERSONAL SERVICE!
-A SURPRISING HOARD OF COMICS!
-HAPPY TO WORK WITH YOU ON WANT LISTS!
SPECIALTIES INCLUDE...
BATMAN, WAR COMICS, DC 1950s & 1960s,
KATY KEENE, and AFFORDABLE MARVELS

DON'T FORGET OUR QUARTERLY OLD SCHOOL COMICS-ONLY SHOW !
www.berkeleycomicshow.com

TURN THOSE VERY FINE COMICS
TO NEAR MINT!

ABC COMIC BOOK PRESSING

All the regular comic book pressing
and dry clean services you need

12 years of experience
Very competitive pricing and turn around time
Call Scott Rice at 916-585-0111

visit the website www.abccomicbookpressing.com

Art by Jason Ulrich capamerica3971@yahoo.com

COMIC HEAVEN

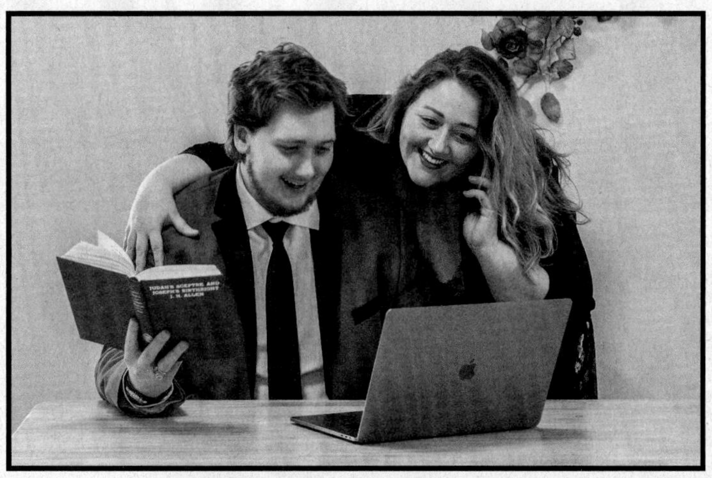

JOHN VERZYL II AND SISTER ROSE "HARD AT WORK"

In 1979, John Verzyl Sr., with his wife Nanette, opened "COMIC HEAVEN", a retail store devoted entirely to the buying and selling of rare comic books. John had started collecting comics in 1965, and within ten years, he had amassed thousands of Golden and Silver Age collectibles. Over the years, he had come to be recognized as an authority in the field of comic books, and served as a special advisor to *The Overstreet Comic Book Price Guide* for 30 years. Thousands of his "near mint" pedigree comics were photographed for Ernst Gerber's *Photo-Journal Guide to Comic Books*. The first annual **Comic Heaven Auction** was held in 1987 and ran continuously for 24 years.

Sadly, John Verzyl passed away in 2018. His untimely death was a shock and a great loss to everyone who knew him. But his children, John II and Rose, having had a love of the hobby instilled in them since childhood by their dad, will continue to operate the business. We will continue to set up our huge retail displays at the annual San Diego Comic-Con, the August Chicago Comic Con, and the New York City Comic Con in October, and will continue to wow our wonderful customers with super-rare collectibles. We will also be updating and using our website, **ComicHeaven.net**, in new and exciting ways, with periodic updates of newly acquired stock items and news about our upcoming convention appearances.

Comic Heaven LLC
John II, Rose & Nanette Verzyl
P.O. Box 900, Big Sandy, TX 75755
www.ComicHeaven.net
(903) 539-8875

THESE DIDN'T HAPPEN WITHOUT YOUR HELP.

The Overstreet Comic Book Price Guide doesn't happen by magic. A network of advisors – made up of experienced dealers, collectors and comics historians – gives us input for every edition we publish. If you spot an error or omission in this edition or any of our publications, let us know!

Write to us at
Gemstone Publishing Inc.,
10150 York Rd., Suite 300,
Hunt Valley, MD 21030.
Or e-mail **feedback@gemstonepub.com**.

We want your help!

BIG LITTLE BOOKS

INTRODUCTION

In 1932, at the depths of the Great Depression, comic books were not selling despite their successes in the previous two decades. Desperate publishers had already reduced prices to 25¢, but this was still too much for many people to spend on entertainment.

Comic books quickly evolved into two newer formats, the comics magazine and the Big Little Book. Both types retailed for 10¢.

Big Little Books began by reprinting the art (and adapting the stories) from newspaper comics. As their success grew and publishers began commissioning original material, movie adaptations and other entertainment-derived stories became commonplace.

GRADING

Before a Big Little Book's value can be assessed, its condition or state of preservation must be determined. A book in **Near Mint** condition will bring many times the price of the same book in **Poor** condition. Many variables influence the grading of a Big Little Book and all must be considered in the final evaluation. Due to the way they are constructed, damage occurs with very little use - usually to the spine, book edges and binding. More important defects that affect grading are: Split spines, pages missing, page browning or brittleness, writing, crayoning, loose pages, color fading, chunks missing, and rolling or out of square. The following grading guide is given to aid the novice:

9.4 Near Mint: The overall look is as if it was just purchased and maybe opened once; only subtle defects are allowed; paper is cream to off-white, supple and fresh; cover is flat with no surface wear or creases; inks and colors are bright; small penciled or inked arrival dates are acceptable; very slight blunting of corners at top and bottom of spine are common; outside corners are cut square and sharp. Books in this grade could bring prices of guide and a half or more.

9.0 Very Fine/Near Mint: Limited number of defects; full cover gloss with only very slight wear on book corners and edges; very minor foxing; very minor tears allowed, binding still square and tight with no pages missing; paper quality still fresh from cream to off-white. Dates, stamps or initials allowed on cover or inside.

8.0 Very Fine: Most of the cover gloss retained with minor wear appearing at corners and around edges; spine tight with no pages missing; cream/tan paper allowed if still supple; up to 1/4" bend allowed on covers with no color break; cover relatively flat; minor tears allowed.

6.0 Fine: Slight wear beginning to show; cover gloss reduced but still clean, pages tan/brown but still supple (not brittle); up to 1/4" split or color break allowed; minor discoloration and/or foxing allowed.

4.0 Very Good: Obviously a read copy with original printing luster almost gone; some fading and discoloration, but not soiled; some signs of wear such as corner splits and spine rolling; paper can be brown but not brittle; a few pages can be loose but not missing; no chunks missing; blunted corners acceptable.

2.0 Good: An average used copy complete with only minor pieces missing from the spine, which may be partially split; slightly soiled or marked with spine rolling; color flaking and wear around edges, but perfectly sound and legible; could have minor tape repairs but otherwise complete.

1.0 Fair: Very heavily read and soiled with small chunks missing from cover; most or all of spine could be missing; multiple splits in spine and loose pages, but still sound and legible, bringing 50 to 70 percent of good price.

0.5 Poor: Damaged, heavily weathered, soiled or otherwise unsuited for collecting purposes.

IMPORTANT

Most BLBs on the market today will fall in the **Good** to **Fine** grade category. When **Very Fine** to **Near Mint** BLBs are offered for sale, they usually bring premium prices.

A WORD ON PRICING

The prices are given for **Good**, **Fine** and **Very Fine/ Near Mint** condition. A book in **Fair** would be 50-70% of the **Good** price. **Very Good** would be halfway between the **Good** and **Fine** price, and **Very Fine** would be halfway between the **Fine** and **Very Fine/ Near Mint** price. The prices listed were averaged from convention sales, dealers' lists, adzines, auctions, and by special contact with dealers and collectors from coast to coast. The prices and the spreads were determined from sales of copies in available condition or the highest grade known. Since most available copies are in the **Good** to **Fine** range, neither dealers nor collectors should let the **Very Fine/Near Mint** column influence the prices they are willing to charge or pay for books in less than near perfect condition.

The prices listed reflect a six times spread from **Good** to **Very Fine/ Near Mint** (1 - 3 - 6). We feel this spread accurately reflects the current market, especially when you consider the scarcity of books in **Very Fine/Near Mint** condition. When one or both end sheets are missing, the book's value would drop about a half grade.

Books with movie scenes are of double importance due to the high crossover demand by movie collectors.

Abbreviations: a-art; c-cover; nn-no number; p-pages; r-reprint.

Publisher Codes: BRP-Blue Ribbon Press; **ERB**-Edgar Rice Burroughs; **EVW**-Engel van Wiseman; **FAW**-Fawcett Publishing Co.; **Gold**-Goldsmith Publishing Co.; **Lynn**-Lynn Publishing Co.; **McKay**-David McKay Co.; **Whit**-Whitman Publishing Co.; **World**-World Syndicate Publishing Co.

Terminology: *All Pictures Comics*-no text, all drawings; *Fast-Action*-A special series of Dell books highly collected; *Flip Pictures*-upper right corner of interior pages contain drawings that are put into motion when rifled; *Movie Scenes*-book illustrated with scenes from the movie. *Soft Cover*-A thin single sheet of cardboard used in binding most of the giveaway versions.

"Big Little Book" and "Better Little Book" are registered trademarks of Whitman Publishing Co. "Little Big Book" is a registered trademark of the Saalfield Publishing Co.

"Pop-Up" is a registered trademark of Blue Ribbon Press. "Little Big Book" is a registered trademark of the Saalfield Co.

Top 20 Big Little Books and related size books*

Issue#	Rank	Title	Price
731	1	Mickey Mouse the Mail Pilot (variant version of Mickey Mouse #717) (A VG copy sold at auction for $7,170)	
nn	2	Mickey Mouse and Minnie Mouse at Macy's	$2,800
nn	3	Mickey Mouse and Minnie March to Macy's	$2,300
717	4	Mickey Mouse (skinny Mickey on-c)	$2,000
W-707	5	Dick Tracy The Detective	$1,600
725	6	Big Little Mother Goose HC	$1,350
717	7	Mickey Mouse (reg. Mickey on-c)	$1,200
nn	8	Mickey Mouse Silly Symphonies	$1,100
721	9	Big Little Paint Book (336 pg.)	$1,050
nn	10	Mickey Mouse Mail Pilot (Great Big Midget Book)	$975
nn	11	Mickey Mouse and the Magic Carpet	$925
725	12	Big Little Mother Goose SC	$900
nn	12	Mickey Mouse (Great Big Midget Book)	$900
721	14	Big Little Paint Book (320 pg.)	$825
nn	14	Mickey Mouse Sails For Treasure Island (Great Big Midget Book)	$825
4063	16	Popeye Thimble Theater Starring... (2nd printing)	$700
1126	17	Laughing Dragon of Oz	$625
nn	17	Buck Rogers	$625
nn	17	Buck Rogers in the City of Floating Globes	$625
4063	20	Popeye Thimble Theater Starring... (1st printing)	$600

*Includes only the various sized BLBs; no premiums, giveaways or other divergent forms are included.

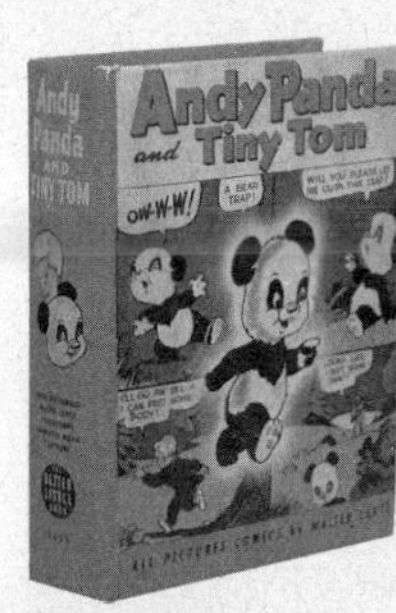

1425 - Andy Panda and Tiny Tom © WHIT

1138 - Bandits at Bay © Saalfield

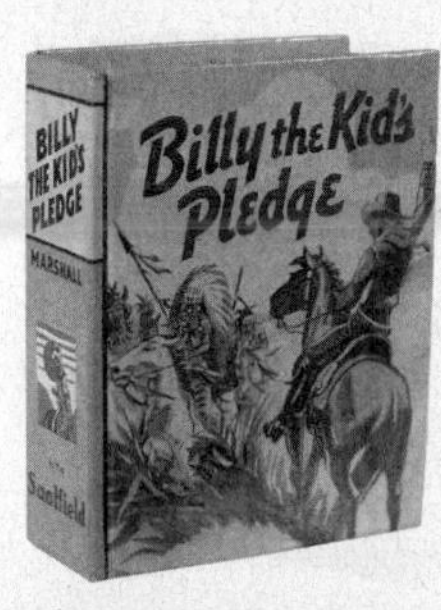

1174 - Billy the Kid's Pledge © Saalfield

	GD	FN	VF/NM
1175-0- **Abbie an' Slats**, 1940, Saalfield, 400 pgs.	12.00	30.00	75.00
1182- **Abbie an' Slats-and Becky**, 1940, Saalfield, 400 pgs.	12.00	30.00	75.00
nn- **ABC's To Draw and Color, The**, 1930s, Whitman, 4" x 5 1/4" x 1 1/12" deep, cardboard box contains 320 double-sided sheets to color and a box of crayons	30.00	75.00	210.00
1177- **Ace Drummond**, 1935, Whitman, 432 pgs.	11.00	27.50	70.00
Admiral Byrd (See Paramount Newsreel ...)			
nn- **Adventures of Charlie McCarthy and Edgar Bergen, The**, 1938, Dell, 194 pgs., Fast-Action Story, soft-c	21.00	52.50	150.00
1422- **Adventures of Huckleberry Finn, The**, 1939, Whitman, 432 pgs., Henry E. Vallely-a	10.00	25.00	65.00
1648- **Adventures of Jim Bowie** (TV Series), 1958, Whitman, 280 pgs.	4.00	10.00	26.00
1056- **Adventures of Krazy Kat and Ignatz Mouse in Koko Land**, 1934, Saalfield, 160 pgs., oblong size, hard-c, Herriman-c/a	61.00	153.00	425.00
1306- **Adventures of Krazy Kat and Ignatz Mouse in Koko Land**, 1934, Saalfield, 164 pgs., oblong size, soft-c, Herriman-c/a	68.00	170.00	475.00
1082- **Adventures of Pete the Tramp, The**, 1935, Saalfield, hard-c, by C. D. Russell	10.00	25.00	65.00
1312- **Adventures of Pete the Tramp, The**, 1935, Saalfield, soft-c, by C. D. Russell	10.00	25.00	65.00
1053- **Adventures of Tim Tyler**, 1934, Saalfield, hard-c, oblong size, by Lyman Young	20.00	50.00	140.00
1303- **Adventures of Tim Tyler**, 1934, Saalfield, soft-c, oblong size, by Lyman Young	20.00	50.00	140.00
1058- **Adventures of Tom Sawyer, The**, 1934, Saalfield, 160 pgs., hard-c, Park Sumner-a	10.00	25.00	65.00
1308- **Adventures of Tom Sawyer, The**, 1934, Saalfield, 160 pgs., soft-c, Park Sumner-a	10.00	25.00	65.00
1448- **Air Fighters of America**, 1941, Whitman, 432 pgs., flip picture	11.00	27.50	70.00
Alexander Smart, ESQ. (See Top Line Comics)			
759- **Alice in Wonderland**, 1933, Whitman, 160 pgs., hard-c, photo-c, movie scenes	39.00	98.00	275.00
1481- **Allen Pike of the Parachute Squad U.S.A.**, 1941, Whitman, 432 pgs.	12.00	30.00	75.00
763- **Alley Oop and Dinny**, 1935, Whitman, 384 pgs., V. T. Hamlin-a	17.00	42.50	120.00
1473- **Alley Oop and Dinny in the Jungles of Moo**, 1938, Whitman, 432 pgs., V. T. Hamlin-a	17.00	42.50	120.00
nn- **Alley Oop and the Missing King of Moo**, 1938, Whitman, 36 pgs., 2 1/2" x 3 1/2", Penny Book	10.00	25.00	60.00
nn- **Alley Oop in the Kingdom of Foo**, 1938, Whitman, 68 pgs., 3 1/4" x 3 1/2", Pan-Am premium	23.00	57.50	160.00
nn- **Alley Oop Taming a Dinosaur**, 1938, Whitman, 68 pgs., 3 1/2" x 3 3/4", Pan-Am premium	23.00	57.50	160.00
nn- **"Alley Oop the Invasion of Moo,"** 1935, Whitman, 260 pgs., Cocomalt premium, soft-c; V. T. Hamlin-a	18.00	45.00	125.00
Andy Burnette (See Walt Disney's...)			
Andy Panda (Also see Walter Lantz ...)			
531- **Andy Panda**, 1943, Whitman, 3 3/4x8 3/4", Tall Comic Book, All Pictures Comics	16.00	40.00	110.00
1425- **Andy Panda and Tiny Tom**, 1944, Whitman, All Pictures Comics	11.00	27.50	70.00
1431- **Andy Panda and the Mad Dog Mystery**, 1947, Whitman, 288 pgs., by Walter Lantz	11.00	27.50	70.00
1441- **Andy Panda in the City of Ice**, 1948, Whitman, All Picture Comics, by Walter Lantz	11.00	27.50	70.00
1459- **Andy Panda and the Pirate Ghosts**, 1949, Whitman, 88 pgs., by Walter Lantz	11.00	27.50	70.00
1485- **Andy Panda's Vacation**, 1946, Whitman, All Pictures Comics, by Walter Lantz	11.00	27.50	70.00
15- **Andy Panda (The Adventures of)**, 1942, Dell, Fast-Action Story	16.00	40.00	110.00
707-10- **Andy Panda and Presto the Pup**, 1949, Whitman	11.00	27.50	70.00
1130- **Apple Mary and Dennie Foil the Swindlers**, 1936, Whitman, 432 pgs. (Forerunner to Mary Worth)	10.00	25.00	65.00

	GD	FN	VF/NM
1403- **Apple Mary and Dennie's Lucky Apples**, 1939, Whitman, 432 pgs.	10.00	25.00	65.00
2017- **(#17)-Aquaman-Scourge of the Sea**, 1968, Whitman, 260 pgs., 39 cents, hard-c, color illos	5.00	12.50	30.00
1192- **Arizona Kid on the Bandit Trail, The**, 1936, Whitman, 432 pgs.	10.00	25.00	60.00
1469- **Bambi** (Walt Disney's), 1942, Whitman, 432 pgs.	19.00	47.50	135.00
1497- **Bambi's Children** (Disney), 1943, Whitman, 432 pgs., Disney Studios-a	19.00	47.50	135.00
1138- **Bandits at Bay**, 1938, Saalfield, 400 pgs.	9.00	22.50	55.00
1459- **Barney Baxter in the Air with the Eagle Squadron**, 1938, Whitman, 432 pgs.	10.00	25.00	65.00
1083- **Barney Google**, 1935, Saalfield, hard-c	17.00	42.50	120.00
1313- **Barney Google**, 1935, Saalfield, soft-c	17.00	42.50	120.00
2031-(#31)- **Batman and Robin in the Cheetah Caper**, 1969, Whitman, 258 pgs.	5.00	12.50	30.00
5771- **Batman and Robin in the Cheetah Caper**, 1974, Whitman, 258 pgs., 49 cents	2.00	5.00	12.00
5771-1- **Batman and Robin in the Cheetah Caper**, 1974, Whitman, 258 pgs., 69 cents	2.00	5.00	12.00
5771-2- **Batman and Robin in the Cheetah Caper**, 1975?, Whitman, 258 pgs.	2.00	5.00	12.00
nn- **Beauty and the Beast**, nd (1930s), np (Whitman), 36 pgs., 3" x 3 1/2" Penny Book	4.00	10.00	25.00
Beep Beep The Road Runner (See Road Runner)			
760- **Believe It or Not!**, 1933, Whitman, 160 pgs., by Ripley (c. 1931)	10.00	25.00	60.00
Betty Bear's Lesson (See Wee Little Books)			
1119- **Betty Boop in Snow White**, 1934, Whitman, 240 pgs., hard-c; adapted from Max Fleischer Paramount Talkartoon	48.00	120.00	340.00
1119- **Betty Boop in Snow White**, 1934, Whitman, 240 pgs., soft-c; same contents as hard-c (Rare)	68.00	170.00	475.00
1158- **Betty Boop in "Miss Gullivers Travels,"** 1935, Whitman, 288 pgs., hard-c (Scarce)	61.00	153.00	425.00
2070- **Big Big Paint Book**, 1936, Whitman, 432 pgs., 8 1/2" x 11 3/8", B&W pages to color	21.00	52.50	150.00
1432- **Big Chief Wahoo and the Lost Pioneers**, 1942, Whitman, 432 pgs., Elmer Woggon-a	11.00	27.50	70.00
1443- **Big Chief Wahoo and the Great Gusto**, 1938, Whitman, 432 pgs., Elmer Woggon-a	11.00	27.50	70.00
1483- **Big Chief Wahoo and the Magic Lamp**, 1940, Whitman, 432 pgs., flip pictures, Woggon-c/a	11.00	27.50	70.00
725- **Big Little Mother Goose, The**, 1934, Whitman, 580 pgs. (Rare) Hardcover	168.00	420.00	1350.00
725- **Big Little Mother Goose, The**, 1934, Whitman, 580 pgs. (Rare) Softcover	123.00	308.00	900.00
1005- **Big Little Nickel Book**, 1935, Whitman, 144 pgs., Blackie Bear stories and Donna the Donkey	8.00	20.00	50.00
1006- **Big Little Nickel Book**, 1935, Whitman, 144 pgs., Blackie Bear stories, folk tales in primer style	8.00	20.00	50.00
1007- **Big Little Nickel Book**, 1935, Whitman, 144 pgs., Peter Rabbit, etc.	8.00	20.00	50.00
1008- **Big Little Nickel Book**, 1935, Whitman, 144 pgs., Wee Wee Woman, etc.	8.00	20.00	50.00
721- **Big Little Paint Book**, The, 1933, Whitman, 320 pgs., 3 3/4" x 8 1/2", for crayoning; first printing has green page ends; second printing has purple page ends (both are rare)	118.00	295.00	825.00
721- **Big Little Paint Book**, The, 1933, Whitman, 336 pgs., 3 3/4" x 8 1/2", for crayoning; first printing has green page ends; second printing has purple page ends (both are rare)	131.00	328.00	1050.00
1178- **Billy of Bar-Zero**, 1940, Saalfield, 400 pgs.	10.00	25.00	60.00
773- **Billy the Kid**, 1935, Whitman, 432 pgs., Hal Arbo-a	10.00	25.00	65.00
1159- **Billy the Kid on Tall Butte**, 1939, Saalfield, 400 pgs.	9.00	22.50	60.00
1174- **Billy the Kid's Pledge**, 1940, Saalfield, 400 pgs.	9.00	22.50	60.00
nn- **Billy the Kid, Western Outlaw**, 1935, Whitman, 260 pgs., Cocomalt premium, Hal Arbo-a, soft-c	12.00	30.00	85.00
1057- **Black Beauty**, 1934, Saalfield, hard-c	8.00	20.00	50.00

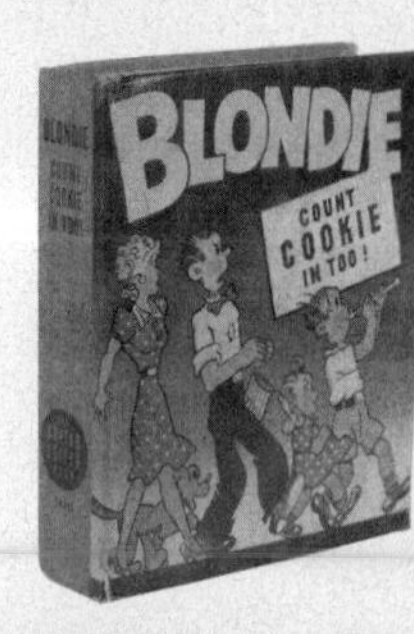

1430 - Blondie Count Cookie in Too! © WHIT

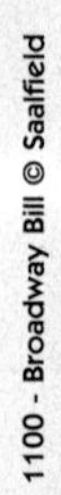
1100 - Broadway Bill © Saalfield

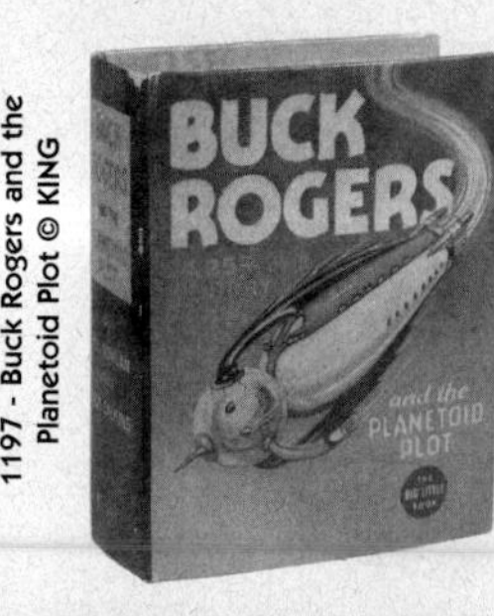

1197 - Buck Rogers and the Planetoid Plot © KING

	GD	FN	VF/NM
1307- **Black Beauty**, 1934, Saalfield, soft-c	8.00	20.00	50.00
1414- **Black Silver and His Pirate Crew**, 1937, Whitman, 300 pgs.	10.00	25.00	65.00
1447- **Blaze Brandon with the Foreign Legion**, 1938, Whitman, 432 pgs.	10.00	25.00	65.00
1410- **Blondie and Dagwood in Hot Water**, 1946, Whitman, 352 pgs., by Chic Young	10.00	25.00	60.00
1415- **Blondie and Baby Dumpling**, 1937, Whitman, 432 pgs., by Chic Young	10.00	25.00	65.00
1419- **Oh, Blondie the Bumsteads Carry On**, 1941, Whitman, 432 pgs., flip pictures, by Chic Young	10.00	25.00	65.00
1423- **Blondie Who's Boss?**, 1942, Whitman, 432 pgs., flip pictures, by Chic Young	10.00	25.00	65.00
1429- **Blondie with Baby Dumpling and Daisy**, 1939, Whitman, 432 pgs., by Chic Young	10.00	25.00	65.00
1430- **Blondie Count Cookie in Too!**, 1947, Whitman, 288 pgs., by Chic Young	10.00	25.00	60.00
1438- **Blondie and Dagwood Everybody's Happy**, 1948, Whitman, 288 pgs., by Chic Young	10.00	25.00	60.00
1450- **Blondie No Dull Moments**, 1948, Whitman, 288 pgs., by Chic Young	10.00	25.00	60.00
1463- **Blondie Fun For All**, 1949, Whitman, 288 pgs., by Chic Young	10.00	25.00	60.00
1466- **Blondie or Life Among the Bumsteads**, 1944, Whitman, 352 pgs., by Chic Young	10.00	25.00	65.00
1476- **Blondie and Bouncing Baby Dumpling**, 1940, Whitman, 432 pgs., by Chic Young	10.00	25.00	65.00
1487- **Blondie Baby Dumpling and All!**, 1941, Whitman, 432 pgs. flip pictures, by Chic Young	10.00	25.00	65.00
1490- **Blondie Papa Knows Best**, 1945, Whitman, 352 pgs., by Chic Young	10.00	25.00	60.00
1491- **Blondie-Cookie and Daisy's Pups**, 1943, Whitman, 1st printing, 432 pgs.	10.00	25.00	65.00
1491- **Blondie-Cookie and Daisy's Pups**, 1943, Whitman,. 2nd printing with different back-c & 352 pgs.	9.00	22.50	55.00
703-10- **Blondie and Dagwood Some Fun!**, 1949, Whitman, by Chic Young	8.00	20.00	48.00
21- **Blondie and Dagwood**, 1936, Lynn, by Chic Young	16.00	40.00	115.00
1108- **Bobby Benson on the H-Bar-O Ranch**, 1934, Whitman, 300 pgs., based on radio serial	12.00	30.00	75.00
Bobby Thatcher and the Samarang Emerald (See Top-Line Comics)			
1432- **Bob Stone the Young Detective**, 1937, Whitman, 240 pgs., movie scenes	11.00	27.50	70.00
2002- **(#2)-Bonanza-The Bubble Gum Kid**, 1967, Whitman, 260 pgs., 39 cents, hard-c, color illos	4.00	10.00	27.00
1139- **Border Eagle, The**, 1938, Saalfield, 400 pgs.	8.00	20.00	50.00
1153- **Boss of the Chisholm Trail**, 1939, Saalfield, 400 pgs.	8.00	20.00	50.00
1425- **Brad Turner in Transatlantic Flight**, 1939, Whitman, 432 pgs.	10.00	25.00	60.00
1058- **Brave Little Tailor, The** (Disney), 1939, Whitman, 5" x 5 1/2", 68 pgs., hard-c (Mickey Mouse)	12.00	30.00	85.00
1427- **Brenda Starr and the Masked Impostor**, 1943, Whitman, 352 pgs., Dale Messick-a	12.00	30.00	80.00
1426- **Brer Rabbit** (Walt Disney's ...), 1947, Whitman, All Picture Comics, from "Song Of The South" movie	19.00	47.50	135.00
704-10- **Brer Rabbit**, 1949, Whitman	16.00	40.00	110.00
1059- **Brick Bradford in the City Beneath the Sea**, 1934, Saalfield, hard-c, by William Ritt & Clarence Gray	14.00	35.00	95.00
1309- **Brick Bradford in the City Beneath the Sea**, 1934, Saalfield, soft-c, by Ritt & Gray	14.00	35.00	95.00
1468- **Brick Bradford with Brocco the Modern Buccaneer**, 1938, Whitman, 432 pgs., by Wm. Ritt & Clarence Gray	10.00	25.00	60.00
1133- **Bringing Up Father**, 1936, Whitman, 432 pgs., by George McManus	12.00	30.00	85.00
1100- **Broadway Bill**, 1935, Saalfield, photo-c, 4 1/2" x 5 1/4", movie scenes (Columbia Pictures, horse racing)	11.00	27.50	70.00
1580- **Broadway Bill**, 1935, Saalfield, soft-c, photo-c, movie scenes	11.00	27.50	70.00
1181- **Broncho Bill**, 1940, Saalfield, 400 pgs.	10.00	25.00	60.00
nn- **Broncho Bill**, 1935, Whitman, 148 pgs., 3 1/2" x 4", Tarzan Ice Cream cup lid premium	25.00	62.50	175.00
nn- **Broncho Bill in Suicide Canyon** (See Top-Line Comics)			
1417- **Bronc Peeler the Lone Cowboy**, 1937, Whitman, 432 pgs., by Fred Harman, forerunner of Red Ryder (also see Red Death on the Range)	10.00	25.00	60.00
nn- **Brownies' Merry Adventures, The**, 1993, Barefoot Books, 202 pgs., reprints from Palmer Cox's late 1800s books	3.00	7.50	18.00
1470- **Buccaneer, The**, 1938, Whitman, 240 pgs., photo-c, movie scenes	12.00	30.00	80.00
1646- **Buccaneers, The** (TV Series), 1958, Whitman, 4 1/2" x 5 1/4", 280 pgs., Russ Manning-a	4.00	10.00	25.00
1104- **Buck Jones in the Fighting Code**, 1934, Whitman, 160 pgs., hard-c, movie scenes	14.00	35.00	95.00
1116- **Buck Jones in Ride 'Em Cowboy** (Universal Presents), 1935, Whitman, 240 pgs., photo-c, movie scenes	14.00	35.00	95.00
1174- **Buck Jones in the Roaring West** (Universal Presents), 1935, Whitman, 240 pgs., movie scenes	14.00	35.00	95.00
1188- **Buck Jones in the Fighting Rangers** (Universal Presents), 1936, Whitman, 240 pgs., photo-c, movie scenes	14.00	35.00	95.00
1404- **Buck Jones and the Two-Gun Kid**, 1937, Whitman, 432 pgs.	10.00	25.00	65.00
1451- **Buck Jones and the Killers of Crooked Butte**, 1940, Whitman, 432 pgs.	10.00	25.00	65.00
1461- **Buck Jones and the Rock Creek Cattle War**, 1938, Whitman, 432 pgs.	10.00	25.00	65.00
1486- **Buck Jones and the Rough Riders in Forbidden Trails**, 1943, Whitman, flip pictures, based on movie; Tim McCoy app.	12.00	30.00	80.00
3- **Buck Jones in the Red Rider**, 1934, EVW, 160 pgs., movie scenes	21.00	52.50	150.00
8- **Buck Jones Cowboy Masquerade**, 1938, Whitman, 132 pgs., soft-c, 3 3/4" x 3 1/2", Buddy Book premium	24.00	60.00	170.00
15- **Buck Jones in Rocky Rhodes**, 1935, EVW, 160 pgs., photo-c, movie scenes	29.00	73.00	200.00
4069- **Buck Jones and the Night Riders**, 1937, Whitman, 7" x 9", 320 pgs., Big Big Book	39.00	98.00	275.00
nn- **Buck Jones on the Six-Gun Trail**, 1939, Whitman, 36 pgs., 2 1/2" x 3 1/2", Penny Book	10.00	25.00	60.00
nn- **Buck Jones Big Thrill Chewing Gum**, 1934, Whitman, 8 pgs., 2 1/2" x 3 1/2" (6 diff.) each...	14.00	35.00	100.00
742- **Buck Rogers in the 25th Century A.D.**, 1933, Whitman, 320 pgs., Dick Calkins-a	45.00	113.00	315.00
nn- **Buck Rogers in the 25th Century A.D.**, 1933, Whitman, 204 pgs.,Cocomalt premium, Calkins-a	30.00	75.00	210.00
765- **Buck Rogers in the City Below the Sea**, 1934, Whitman, 320 pgs., Dick Calkins-a	34.00	85.00	235.00
765- **Buck Rogers in the City Below the Sea**, 1934, Whitman, 324 pgs., soft-c, Dick Calkins-c/a (Rare)	60.00	150.00	420.00
1143- **Buck Rogers on the Moons of Saturn**, 1934, Whitman, 320 pgs., Dick Calkins-a	34.00	85.00	235.00
nn- **Buck Rogers on the Moons of Saturn**, 1934, Whitman, 324 pgs., premium w/no ads, soft 3-color-c, Dick Calkins-a	51.00	128.00	360.00
1169- **Buck Rogers and the Depth Men of Jupiter**, 1935, Whitman, 432 pgs., Calkins-a	36.00	90.00	250.00
1178- **Buck Rogers and the Doom Comet**, 1935, Whitman, 432 pgs., Calkins-a	33.00	83.00	230.00
1197- **Buck Rogers and the Planetoid Plot**, 1936, Whitman, 432 pgs., Calkins-a	33.00	83.00	230.00
1409- **Buck Rogers Vs. the Fiend of Space**, 1940, Whitman, 432 pgs., Calkins-a	41.00	103.00	290.00
1437- **Buck Rogers in the War with the Planet Venus**, 1938, Whitman, 432 pgs., Calkins-a	33.00	83.00	230.00
1474- **Buck Rogers and the Overturned World**, 1941, Whitman, 432 pgs., flip pictures, Calkins-a	34.00	85.00	240.00
1490- **Buck Rogers and the Super-Dwarf of Space**, 1943, Whitman, 11 Pictures Comics, Calkins-a	33.00	83.00	230.00
4057- **Buck Rogers, The Adventures of**, 1934, Whitman, 7" x 9 1/2", 320 pgs., Big Big Book, "The Story of Buck Rogers on the Planet Eros,"			

Bulletman and the Return of Mr. Murder © FAW

L20 - Ceiling Zero © WB

1323 - Chandu the Magician © Saalfield

GD FN VF/NM

Calkins-c/a 75.00 188.00 525.00
nn- Buck Rogers, 1935, Whitman, 4" x 3 1/2", Tarzan Ice Cream cup premium (Rare) 89.00 223.00 625.00
nn- Buck Rogers in the City of Floating Globes, 1935, Whitman, 258 pgs., Cocomalt premium, soft-c, Dick Calkins-a 89.00 230.00 625.00
nn- Buck Rogers Big Thrill Chewing Gum, 1934, Whitman, 8 pgs., 2 1/2" x 3 " (6 diff.) each... 21.00 52.50 150.00
1135- Buckskin and Bullets, 1938, Saalfield, 400 pgs. 8.00 20.00 50.00
Buffalo Bill (See Wild West Adventures of ...)
nn- Buffalo Bill, 1934, World Syndicate, All pictures, by J. Carroll Mansfield 10.00 25.00 60.00
713- Buffalo Bill and the Pony Express, 1934, Whitman, hard-c, 384 pgs., Hal Arbo-a 11.00 27.50 70.00
nn- Buffalo Bill and the Pony Express, 1934, Whitman, soft-c, 384 pgs., Hal Arbo-a; three-color premium (Rare) 43.00 108.00 300.00
1194- Buffalo Bill Plays a Lone Hand, 1936, Whitman, 432 pgs., Hal Arbo-a 10.00 25.00 60.00
530- Bugs Bunny, 1943, Whitman, All Pictures Comics, Tall Comic Book, 3 1/4" x 8 1/4", reprints/Looney Tunes 1 & 5 19.00 47.50 130.00
1403- Bugs Bunny and the Pirate Loot, 1947, Whitman, All Pictures Comics 11.00 27.50 70.00
1435- Bugs Bunny, 1944, Whitman, All Pictures Comics 12.00 30.00 75.00
1440- Bugs Bunny in Risky Business, 1948, Whitman, All Pictures & Comics 11.00 27.50 70.00
1455- Bugs Bunny and Klondike Gold, 1948, Whitman, 288 pgs. 11.00 27.50 70.00
1465- Bugs Bunny The Masked Marvel, 1949, Whitman, 288 pgs. 11.00 27.50 70.00
1496- Bugs Bunny and His Pals, 1945, Whitman, All Pictures Comics; r/Four Color Comics #33 11.00 27.50 70.00
13- Bugs Bunny and the Secret of Storm Island, 1942, Dell,194 pgs., Fast-Action Story 29.00 73.00 200.00
706-10- Bugs Bunny and the Giant Brothers, 1949, Whitman 10.00 25.00 60.00
2007- (#7)-Bugs Bunny-Double Trouble on Diamond Island, 1967, Whitman, 260 pgs., 39 cents, hard-c, color illos 5.00 12.50 33.00
2029-(#29)- Bugs Bunny, Accidental Adventure, 1969, Whitman, 256 pgs., hard-c, color illos. 4.00 10.00 22.00
2952- Bugs Bunny's Mistake, 1949, Whitman, 3 1/4" x 4", 24 pgs., Tiny Tales, full color (5 cents) (1030-5 on back-c) 10.00 25.00 60.00
5757-2- Bugs Bunny in Double Trouble on Diamond Island,1967, (1980-reprints #2007), Whitman, 260 pgs., soft-c, 79 cents, B&W 2.00 5.00 14.00
5758- Bugs Bunny, Accidental Adventure, 1973, Whitman, 256 pgs., soft-c, B&W illos. 2.00 5.00 14.00
5758-1- Bugs Bunny, Accidental Adventure, 1973, Whitman, 256 pgs., soft-c, B&W illos. 2.00 5.00 14.00
5772- Bugs Bunny the Last Crusader, 1975, Whitman, 49 cents, flip-it book 2.00 5.00 14.00
5772-2- Bugs Bunny the Last Crusader, 1975, Whitman, $1.50, flip-it book 1.00 2.50 6.00
1169- Bullet Benton, 1939, Saalfield, 400 pgs. 10.00 25.00 60.00
nn- Bulletman and the Return of Mr. Murder, 1941, Fawcett, 196 pgs., Dime Action Book 41.00 103.00 285.00
1142- Bullets Across the Border (A Billy The Kid story), 1938, Saalfield, 400 pgs. 10.00 25.00 60.00
Bunky (See Top-Line Comics)
837- Bunty (Punch and Judy), 1935, Whitman, 28 pgs., Magic-Action with 3 pop-ups 13.00 32.50 90.00
1091- Burn 'Em Up Barnes, 1935, Saalfield, hard-c, movie scenes 10.00 25.00 60.00
1321- Burn 'Em Up Barnes, 1935, Saalfield, soft-c, movie scenes 10.00 25.00 60.00
1415- Buz Sawyer and Bomber 13,1946, Whitman, 352 pgs., Roy Crane-a 10.00 25.00 60.00
1412- Calling W-1-X-Y-Z, Jimmy Kean and the Radio Spies, 1939, Whitman, 300 pgs. 11.00 27.50 70.00

GD FN VF/NM

Call of the Wild (See Jack London's...)
1107- Camels are Coming, 1935, Saalfield, movie scenes 10.00 25.00 60.00
1587- Camels are Coming, 1935, Saalfield, movie scenes 10.00 25.00 60.00
nn- Captain and the Kids, Boys Vill Be Boys, The, 1938, 68 pgs., Pan-Am Oil premium, soft-c 12.00 30.00 85.00
1128- Captain Easy Soldier of Fortune, 1934, Whitman, 432 pgs., Roy Crane-a 11.00 27.50 70.00
nn- Captain Easy Soldier of Fortune, 1934, Whitman, 436 pgs., Premium, no ads, soft 3-color-c, Roy Crane-a 21.00 52.50 150.00
1474- Captain Easy Behind Enemy Lines, 1943, Whitman, 352 pgs., Roy Crane-a 11.00 27.50 70.00
nn- Captain Easy and Wash Tubbs, 1935, 260 pgs., Cocomalt premium, Roy Crane-a 11.00 27.50 70.00
1444- Captain Frank Hawks Air Ace and the League of Twelve, 1938, Whitman, 432 pgs. 11.00 27.50 70.00
nn- Captain Marvel, 1941, Fawcett, 196 pgs., Dime Action Book 51.00 128.00 360.00
1402- Captain Midnight and Sheik Jomak Khan, 1946, Whitman, 352 pgs. 16.00 40.00 115.00
1452- Captain Midnight and the Moon Woman, 1943, Whitman, 352 pgs. 19.00 47.50 135.00
1458- Captain Midnight Vs. The Terror of the Orient, 1942, Whitman, 432 pgs., flip pictures, Hess-a 19.00 47.50 135.00
1488- Captain Midnight and the Secret Squadron, 1941, Whitman, 432 pgs. 19.00 47.50 135.00
Captain Robb of.. (See Dirigible ZR90 ...)
nn- Cauliflower Catnip Pearls of Peril, 1981, Teacup Tales, 290 pgs., Joe Wehrle Jr.-s/a; deliberately printed on aged-looking paper to look like an old BLB 4.00 10.00 27.00
20- Ceiling Zero, 1936, Lynn, 128 pgs., 7 1/2" x 5", hard-c, James Cagney, Pat O'Brien photos on-c, movie scenes, Warner Bros. Pictures 11.00 27.50 70.00
1093- Chandu the Magician, 1935, Saalfield, 5" x 5 1/4", 160 pgs., hard-c, Bela Lugosi photo-c, movie scenes 14.00 35.00 100.00
1323- Chandu the Magician, 1935, Saalfield, 5" x 5 1/4", 160 pgs., soft-c, Bela Lugosi photo-c 16.00 40.00 110.00
Charlie Chan (See Inspector ...)
1459- Charlie Chan Solves a New Mystery (See Inspector..), 1940, Whitman, 432 pgs., Alfred Andriola-a 12.00 30.00 85.00
1478- Charlie Chan of the Honolulu Police, Inspector, 1939, Whitman, 432 pgs., Andriola-a 12.00 30.00 85.00
Charlie McCarthy (See Story Of ...)
734- Chester Gump at Silver Creek Ranch, 1933, Whitman, 320 pgs., Sidney Smith-a 13.00 32.50 90.00
nn- Chester Gump at Silver Creek Ranch, 1933, Whitman, 204 pgs., Cocomalt premium, soft-c, Sidney Smith-a 14.00 35.00 100.00
nn- Chester Gump at Silver Creek Ranch, 1933, Whitman, 52 pgs., 4" x 5 1/2", premium-no ads, soft-c, Sidney Smith-a 21.00 52.50 150.00
766- Chester Gump Finds the Hidden Treasure, 1934, Whitman, 320 pgs., Sidney Smith-a 12.00 30.00 85.00
nn- Chester Gump Finds the Hidden Treasure, 1934, Whitman, 52 pgs., 3 1/2" x 5 3/4", premium-no ads, soft-c, Sidney Smith-a 21.00 52.50 150.00
nn- Chester Gump Finds the Hidden Treasure, 1934, Whitman, 52 pgs., 4" x 5 1/2", premium-no ads, Sidney Smith-a 21.00 52.50 150.00
1146- Chester Gump in the City Of Gold, 1935, Whitman, 432 pgs., Sidney Smith-a 12.00 30.00 85.00
nn- Chester Gump in the City Of Gold, 1935, Whitman, 436 pgs., premium-no ads, 3-color, soft-c, Sidney Smith-a 24.00 60.00 165.00
1402- Chester Gump in the Pole to Pole Flight, 1937, Whitman, 432 pgs. 12.00 30.00 75.00
5- Chester Gump and His Friends, 1934, Whitman, 132 pgs., 3 1/2" x 3 1/2", soft-c, Tarzan Ice Cream cup lid premium 23.00 57.50 160.00
nn- Chester Gump at the North Pole, 1938, Whitman, 68 pgs. soft-c, 3 3/4" x 3 1/2", Pan-Am giveaway 23.00 57.50 160.00

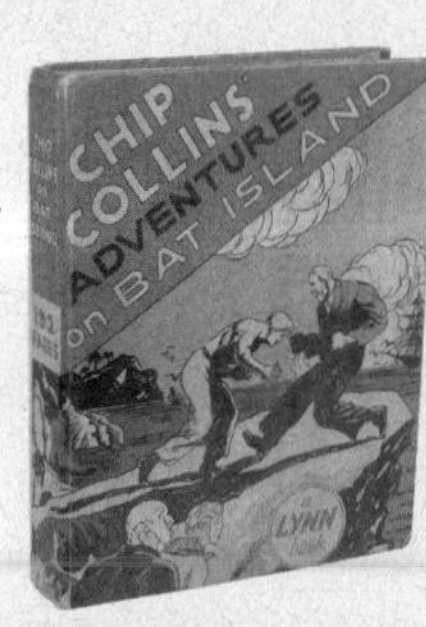

L14 - Chip Collins' Adventures on Bat Island © Lynn

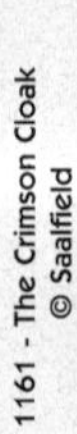

1161 - The Crimson Cloak © Saalfield

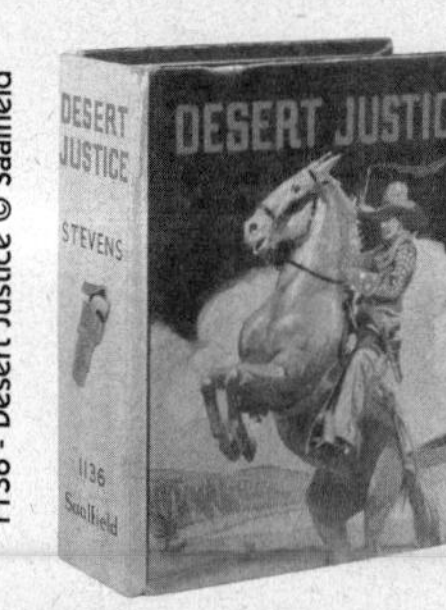

1136 - Desert Justice © Saalfield

	GD	FN	VF/NM
nn- Chicken Greedy, nd(1930s), np (Whitman), 36 pgs., 3" x 2 1/2", Penny Book	4.00	10.00	22.00
nn- Chicken Licken, nd (1930s), np (Whitman), 36 pgs., 3" x 2 1/2", Penny Book	4.00	10.00	22.00
1101- Chief of the Rangers, 1935, Saalfield, hard-c, Tom Mix photo-c, movie scenes from "The Miracle Rider"	13.00	32.50	90.00
1581- Chief of the Rangers, 1935, Saalfield, soft-c, Tom Mix photo-c, movie scenes	13.00	32.50	90.00
Child's Garden of Verses (See Wee Little Books)			
L14- Chip Collins' Adventures on Bat Island, 1935, Lynn, 192 pgs.	11.00	27.50	70.00
2025- Chitty Chitty Bang Bang, 1968, Whitman, movie photos	4.00	10.00	27.00
Chubby Little Books, 1935, Whitman, 3" x 2 1/2", 200 pgs.			
W803- Golden Hours Story Book, The	5.00	12.50	30.00
W803- Story Hours Story Book, The	5.00	12.50	30.00
W804- Gay Book of Little Stories, The	5.00	12.50	30.00
W804- Glad Book of Little Stories, The	5.00	12.50	30.00
W804- Joy Book of Little Stories, The	5.00	12.50	30.00
W804- Sunny Book of Little Stories, The	5.00	12.50	30.00
1453- Chuck Malloy Railroad Detective on the Streamliner, 1938, Whitman, 300 pgs.	8.00	20.00	50.00
Cinderella (See Walt Disney's...)			
Clyde Beatty (See The Steel Arena)			
1410- Clyde Beatty Daredevil Lion and Tiger Tamer, 1939, Whitman, 300 pgs.	12.00	30.00	80.00
1480- Coach Bernie Bierman's Brick Barton and the Winning Eleven, 1938, 300 pgs.	10.00	25.00	60.00
1446- Convoy Patrol (A Thrilling U.S. Navy Story), 1942, Whitman, 432 pgs., flip pictures	10.00	25.00	60.00
1127- Corley of the Wilderness Trail, 1937, Saalfield, hard-c	10.00	25.00	60.00
1607- Corley of the Wilderness Trail, 1937, Saalfield, soft-c	10.00	25.00	60.00
1- Count of Monte Cristo, 1934, EVW, 160 pgs., (Five Star Library), movie scenes, hard-c (Rare)	20.00	50.00	140.00
1457- Cowboy Lingo Boys' Book of Western Facts, 1938, Whitman, 300 pgs., Fred Harman-a	8.00	20.00	50.00
1171- Cowboy Malloy, 1940, Saalfield, 400 pgs.	7.00	17.50	40.00
1106- Cowboy Millionaire, 1935, Saalfield, movie scenes with George O'Brien, photo-c, hard-c	12.00	30.00	80.00
1586- Cowboy Millionaire, 1935, Saalfield, movie scenes with George O'Brien, photo-c, soft-c	12.00	30.00	80.00
724- Cowboy Stories, 1933, Whitman, 300 pgs., Hal Arbo-a	10.00	25.00	65.00
nn- Cowboy Stories, 1933, Whitman, 52 pgs., soft-c, premium-no ads, 4" x 5 1/2" Hal Arbo-a	12.00	30.00	80.00
1161- Crimson Cloak, The, 1939, Saalfield, 400 pgs.	10.00	25.00	60.00
L19- Curley Harper at Lakespur, 1935, Lynn, 192 pgs.	10.00	25.00	60.00
5785-2- Daffy Duck in Twice the Trouble, 1980, Whitman, 260 pgs., 79 cents soft-c	1.00	2.50	6.00
2018-(#18)-Daktari-Night of Terror, 1968, Whitman, 260 pgs., 39 cents, hard-c, color illos	4.00	10.00	27.00
1010- Dan Dunn And The Gangsters' Frame-Up, 1937, Whitman, 7 1/4" x 5 1/2", 64 pgs., Nickel Book	29.00	73.00	200.00
1116- Dan Dunn "Crime Never Pays," 1934, Whitman, 320 pgs., by Norman Marsh	8.00	20.00	50.00
1125- Dan Dunn on the Trail of the Counterfeiters, 1936, Whitman, 432 pgs., by Norman Marsh	8.00	20.00	50.00
1171- Dan Dunn and the Crime Master, 1937, Whitman, 432 pgs., by Norman Marsh	8.00	20.00	50.00
1417- Dan Dunn and the Underworld Gorillas, 1941, Whitman, All Pictures Comics, flip pictures, by Norman Marsh	8.00	20.00	50.00
1454- Dan Dunn on the Trail of Wu Fang, 1938, Whitman, 432 pgs., by Norman Marsh	10.00	25.00	65.00
1481- Dan Dunn and the Border Smugglers, 1938, Whitman, 432 pgs., by Norman Marsh	7.00	17.50	45.00
1492- Dan Dunn and the Dope Ring, 1940, Whitman, 432 pgs., by Norman Marsh	7.00	17.50	45.00
nn- Dan Dunn and the Bank Hold-Up, 1938, Whitman, 36 pgs., 2 1/2" x 3 1/2", Penny Book	8.00	20.00	50.00
nn- Dan Dunn and the Zeppelin Of Doom, 1938, Dell, 196 pgs., Fast-Action Story, soft-c	18.00	45.00	125.00
nn- Dan Dunn Meets Chang Loo, 1938, Whitman, 66 pgs., Pan-Am premium, by Norman Marsh	23.00	57.50	160.00
nn- Dan Dunn Plays a Lone Hand, 1938, Whitman, 36 pgs., 2 1/2" x 3 1/2", Penny Book	8.00	20.00	50.00
3 3/4" x 3 1/2", Buddy book	24.00	60.00	170.00
6- Dan Dunn Secret Operative 48 and the Counterfeiter Ring, 1938, Whitman, 132 pgs., soft-c, 3 3/4" x 3 1/2", Buddy Book premium	24.00	60.00	170.00
9- Dan Dunn's Mysterious Ruse, 1936, Whitman, 132 pgs., soft-c, 3 1/2" x 3 1/2", Tarzan Ice Cream cup lid premium	24.00	60.00	170.00
1177- Danger Trail North, 1940, Saalfield, 400 pgs.	10.00	25.00	60.00
1151- Danger Trails in Africa, 1935, Whitman, 432 pgs.	12.00	30.00	80.00
nn- Daniel Boone, 1934, World Syndicate, High Lights of History Series, hard-c, All in Pictures	10.00	25.00	60.00
1160- Dan of the Lazy L, 1939, Saalfield, 400 pgs.	10.00	25.00	60.00
1148- David Copperfield, 1934, Whitman, hard-c, 160 pgs., photo-c, movie scenes (W. C. Fields)	12.00	30.00	80.00
nn- David Copperfield, 1934, Whitman, soft-c, 164 pgs., movie scenes	12.00	30.00	80.00
1151- Death by Short Wave, 1938, Saalfield	10.00	25.00	65.00
1156- Denny the Ace Detective, 1938, Saalfield, 400 pgs.	10.00	25.00	60.00
1431- Desert Eagle and the Hidden Fortress, The, 1941, Whitman, 432 pgs., flip pictures	10.00	25.00	65.00
1458- Desert Eagle Rides Again, The, 1939, Whitman, 300 pgs.	10.00	25.00	65.00
1136- Desert Justice, 1938, Saalfield, 400 pgs.	10.00	25.00	60.00
1484- Detective Higgins of the Racket Squad, 1938, Whitman, 432 pgs.	10.00	25.00	65.00
1124- Dickie Moore in the Little Red School House, 1936, Whitman, 240 pgs., photo-c, movie scenes (Chesterfield Motion Picts. Corp)	12.00	30.00	80.00
W-707- Dick Tracy the Detective, The Adventures of, 1933, Whitman, 320 pgs. (The 1st Big Little Book), by Chester Gould (Scarce)	200.00	500.00	1600.00
nn- Dick Tracy Detective, The Adventures of, 1933, Whitman, 52 pgs., 4" x 5 1/2", premium-no ads, soft-c, by Chester Gould	82.00	205.00	575.00
nn- Dick Tracy Detective, The Adventures of, 1933, Whitman, 52 pgs., 4" x 5 1/2", inside back-c & back-c ads for Sundial Shoes, soft-c, by Chester Gould	86.00	215.00	600.00
710- Dick Tracy and Dick Tracy, Jr. (The Advs. of ...), 1933, Whitman, 320 pgs., by Chester Gould	61.00	153.00	425.00
nn- Dick Tracy and Dick Tracy, Jr. (The Advs. of ...), 1933, Whitman, 52 pgs., premium-no ads, soft-c, 4" x 5 1/2", by Chester Gould	61.00	153.00	425.00
nn- Dick Tracy the Detective and Dick Tracy, Jr., 1933, Whitman, 52 pgs., premium-no ads, 3 1/2"x 5 1/4", soft-c, by Chester Gould	61.00	153.00	425.00
723- Dick Tracy Out West, 1933, Whitman, 300 pgs., by Chester Gould	36.00	90.00	250.00
749- Dick Tracy from Colorado to Nova Scotia, 1933, Whitman, 320 pgs., by Chester Gould	26.00	65.00	180.00
nn- Dick Tracy from Colorado to Nova Scotia, 1933, Whitman, 204 pgs., premium-no ads, soft-c, by Chester Gould	28.00	70.00	195.00
1105- Dick Tracy and the Stolen Bonds, 1934, Whitman, 320 pgs., by Chester Gould	16.00	40.00	110.00
1112- Dick Tracy and the Racketeer Gang, 1936, Whitman, 432 pgs., by Chester Gould	14.00	35.00	95.00
1137- Dick Tracy Solves the Penfield Mystery, 1934, Whitman, 320 pgs., by Chester Gould	16.00	40.00	110.00
nn- Dick Tracy Solves the Penfield Mystery, 1934, Whitman, 324 pgs., premium-no ads, 3-color, soft-c, by Chester Gould	37.00	93.00	260.00
1163- Dick Tracy and the Boris Arson Gang, 1935, Whitman,			

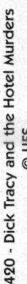

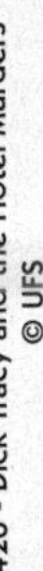
1420 - Dick Tracy and the Hotel Murders © UFS

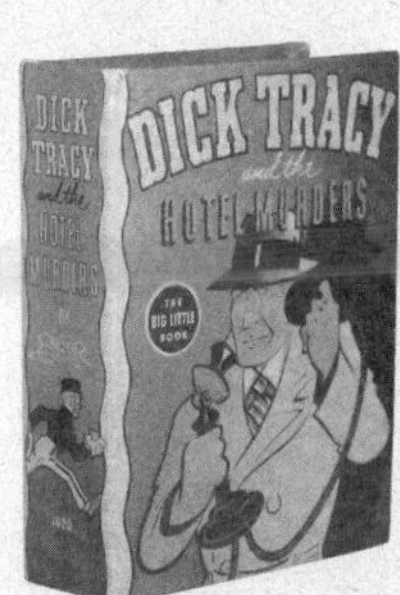

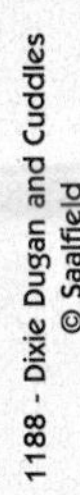
1188 - Dixie Dugan and Cuddles © Saalfield

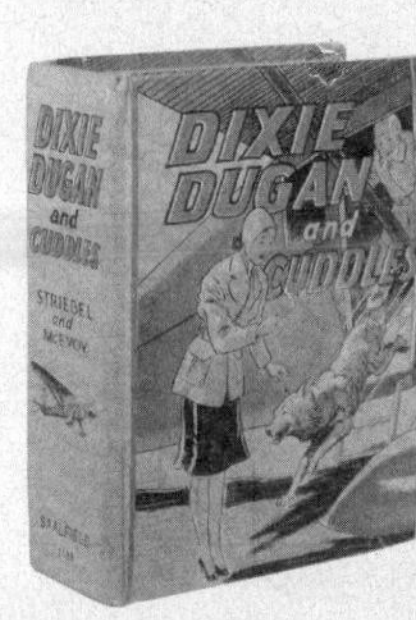

1484 - Donald Duck is Here Again! © DIS

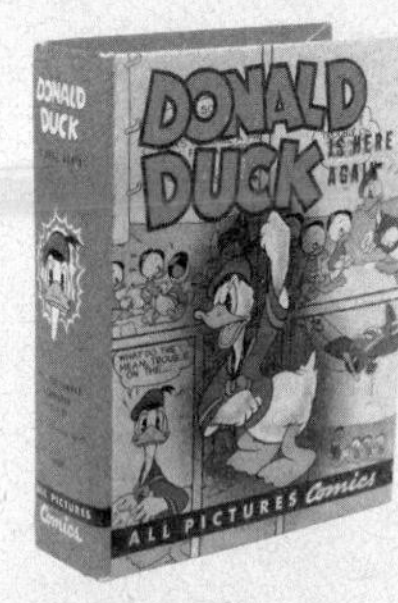

	GD	FN	VF/NM
432 pgs., by Chester Gould	15.00	37.50	105.00
1170- Dick Tracy on the Trail of Larceny Lu, 1935, Whitman, 432 pgs., by Chester Gould	14.00	35.00	95.00
1185- Dick Tracy in Chains of Crime, 1936, Whitman, 432 pgs., by Chester Gould	15.00	37.50	105.00
1412- Dick Tracy and Yogee Yamma, 1946, Whitman, 352 pgs., by Chester Gould	14.00	35.00	95.00
1420- Dick Tracy and the Hotel Murders, 1937, Whitman, 432 pgs., by Chester Gould	15.00	37.50	105.00
1434- Dick Tracy and the Phantom Ship, 1940, Whitman, 432 pgs., by Chester Gould	15.00	37.50	105.00
1436- Dick Tracy and the Mad Killer, 1947, Whitman, 288 pgs., by Chester Gould	13.00	32.50	90.00
1439- Dick Tracy and His G-Men, 1941, Whitman, 432 pgs., flip pictures, by Chester Gould	15.00	37.50	105.00
1445- Dick Tracy and the Bicycle Gang, 1948, Whitman, 288 pgs., by Chester Gould	13.00	32.50	90.00
1446- Detective Dick Tracy and the Spider Gang, 1937, Whitman, 240 pgs., scenes from "Adventures of Dick Tracy" serial	19.00	47.50	130.00
1449- Dick Tracy Special F.B.I. Operative, 1943, Whitman, 432 pgs. by Chester Gould	15.00	37.50	105.00
1454- Dick Tracy on the High Seas, 1939, Whitman, 432 pgs., by Chester Gould	15.00	37.50	105.00
1460- Dick Tracy and the Tiger Lilly Gang, 1949, Whitman, 288 pgs., by Chester Gould	13.00	32.50	90.00
1478- Dick Tracy on Voodoo Island, 1944, Whitman, 352 pgs., by Chester Gould	13.00	32.50	90.00
1479- Detective Dick Tracy Vs. Crooks in Disguise, 1939, Whitman, 432 pgs., flip pictures, by Chester Gould	15.00	37.50	105.00
1482- Dick Tracy and the Wreath Kidnapping Case, 1945, Whitman, 352 pgs.	14.00	35.00	95.00
1488- Dick Tracy the Super-Detective, 1939, Whitman, 432 pgs., by Chester Gould	15.00	37.50	105.00
1491- Dick Tracy the Man with No Face, 1938, Whitman, 432 pgs.	15.00	37.50	105.00
1495- Dick Tracy Returns, 1939, Whitman, 432 pgs., based on Republic Motion Picture serial, Chester Gould-a	15.00	37.50	105.00
2001- (#1)-Dick Tracy-Encounters Facey, 1967, Whitman, 260 pgs., 39 cents, hard-c, color illos	4.00	10.00	27.00
3912- Dick Tracy Big Little Book Picture Puzzles, 1938, Whitman, 7 1/2" x 10 1/4" box with 2 jigsaw puzzles	50.00	125.00	350.00
Variant set, same cover w/2 puzzles showing Dick Tracy & Jr. in crime lab & Dick Tracy patting down a gangster	50.00	125.00	350.00
4055- Dick Tracy, The Adventures of, 1934, Whitman, 7" x 9 1/2", 320 pgs., Big Big Book, by Chester Gould	57.00	143.00	400.00
4071- Dick Tracy and the Mystery of the Purple Cross, 1938, 7" x 9 1/2", 320 pgs., Big Big Book, by Chester Gould (Scarce)	50.00	125.00	350.00
nn- Dick Tracy and the Invisible Man, 1939, Whitman, 3 1/4" x 3 3/4", 132 pgs., stapled, soft-c, Quaker Oats premium; NBC radio play script, Chester Gould-a	39.00	98.00	270.00
Vol. 2- Dick Tracy's Ghost Ship, 1939, Whitman, 3 1/2" x 3 1/2", 132 pgs., soft-c, stapled, Quaker Oats premium; NBC radio play script episode from actual radio show; Gould-a	37.00	93.00	260.00
3- Dick Tracy Meets a New Gang, 1934, Whitman, 3" x 3 1/2", 132 pgs., soft-c, Tarzan Ice Cream cup lid premium	36.00	90.00	250.00
11- Dick Tracy in Smashing the Famon Racket, 1938, Whitman, 3 3/4" x 3 1/2", Buddy Book-ice cream premium, by Chester Gould	36.00	90.00	250.00
nn- Dick Tracy Gets His Man, 1938, Whitman, 36 pgs., 2 1/2" x 3 1/2", Penny Book	8.00	20.00	50.00
nn- Dick Tracy the Detective, 1938, Whitman, 36 pgs., 2 1/2" x 3 1/2", Penny Book	8.00	20.00	50.00
9- Dick Tracy and the Frozen Bullet Murders, 1941, Dell, 196 pgs., Fast-Action Story, soft-c, by Gould	37.00	93.00	260.00
6833- Dick Tracy Detective and Federal Agent, 1936, Dell, 244 pgs., Cartoon Story Books, hard-c, by Gould	39.00	98.00	275.00
nn- Dick Tracy Detective and Federal Agent, 1936, Dell, 244 pgs., Fast-Action Story, soft-c, by Gould	34.00	85.00	240.00
nn- Dick Tracy and the Blackmailers, 1939, Dell, 196 pgs., Fast-Action Story, soft-c, by Gould	34.00	85.00	240.00

	GD	FN	VF/NM
nn- Dick Tracy and the Chain of Evidence, Detective, 1938, Dell, 196 pgs., Fast-Action Story, soft-c, by Chester Gould	34.00	85.00	240.00
nn- Dick Tracy and the Crook Without a Face, 1938, Whitman, 68 pgs., 3 1/4" x 3 1/2", Pan-Am giveaway, Gould-c/a	29.00	73.00	200.00
nn- Dick Tracy and the Maroon Mask Gang, 1938, Dell, 196 pgs., Fast-Action Story, soft-c, by Gould	34.00	85.00	240.00
nn- Dick Tracy Cross-Country Race, 1934, Whitman, 8 pgs., 2 1/2" x 3", Big Thrill chewing gum premium (6 diff.)	12.00	30.00	85.00
nn- Dick Whittington and his Cat, nd(1930s), np(Whitman), 36 pgs., Penny Book	3.00	7.50	20.00
Dinglehoofer und His Dog Adolph (See Top-Line Comics)			
Dinky (See Jackie Cooper in ...)			
1464- Dirigible ZR90 and the Disappearing Zeppelin (Captain Robb of ...), 1941, Whitman, 300 pgs., Al Lewin-a	14.00	35.00	100.00
1167- Dixie Dugan Among the Cowboys, 1939, Saalfield, 400 pgs.	10.00	25.00	65.00
1188- Dixie Dugan and Cuddles, 1940, Saalfield, 400 pgs., by Striebel & McEvoy	10.00	25.00	65.00
Doctor Doom (See Foreign Spies... & International Spy...)			
Dog of Flanders, A (See Frankie Thomas in ...)			
1114- Dog Stars of Hollywood, 1936, Saalfield, photo-c, photo-illos	12.00	30.00	75.00
1594- Dog Stars of Hollywood, 1936, Saalfield, photo-c, soft-c, photo-illos	12.00	30.00	75.00
nn- Dolls and Dresses Big Little Set, 1930s, Whitman, box contains 20 dolls on paper, 128 sheets of clothing to color & cut out, includes crayons	36.00	90.00	250.00
Donald Duck (See Silly Symphony... & Walt Disney's ...)			
800- Donald Duck in Bringing Up the Boys, 1948, Whitman, hard-c, Story Hour series	10.00	25.00	65.00
1404- Donald Duck (Says Such a Life) (Disney), 1939, Whitman, 432 pgs., Taliaferro-a	19.00	47.50	130.00
1411- Donald Duck and Ghost Morgan's Treasure (Disney), 1946, Whitman, All Pictures Comics, Barks-a; reprints FC #9	24.00	60.00	165.00
1422- Donald Duck Sees Stars (Disney), 1941, Whitman, 432 pgs., flip pictures, Taliaferro-a	18.00	45.00	125.00
1424- Donald Duck Says Such Luck (Disney), 1941, Whitman, 432 pgs., flip pictures, Taliaferro-a	18.00	45.00	125.00
1430- Donald Duck Headed For Trouble (Disney), 1942, Whitman, 432 pgs., flip pictures, Taliaferro-a	18.00	45.00	125.00
1432- Donald Duck and the Green Serpent (Disney), 1947, Whitman, All Pictures Comics, Barks-a; reprints FC #108	20.00	50.00	140.00
1434- Donald Duck Forgets To Duck (Disney), 1939, Whitman, 432 pgs., Taliaferro-a	18.00	45.00	125.00
1438- Donald Duck Off the Beam (Disney), 1943, Whitman, 352 pgs., flip pictures, Taliaferro-a	18.00	45.00	125.00
1438- Donald Duck Off the Beam (Disney), 1943, Whitman, 432 pgs., flip pictures, Taliaferro-a	18.00	45.00	125.00
1449- Donald Duck Lays Down the Law, 1948, Whitman, 288 pgs., Barks-a	18.00	45.00	125.00
1457- Donald Duck in Volcano Valley (Disney), 1949, Whitman, 288 pgs., Barks-a	18.00	45.00	125.00
1462- Donald Duck Gets Fed Up (Disney), 1940, Whitman, 432 pgs.,Taliaferro-a	18.00	45.00	125.00
1478- Donald Duck-Hunting For Trouble (Disney), 1938, Whitman, 432 pgs., Taliaferro-a	18.00	45.00	125.00
1484- Donald Duck is Here Again!, 1944, Whitman, All Pictures Comics, Taliaferro-a	18.00	45.00	125.00
1486- Donald Duck Up in the Air (Disney), 1945, Whitman, 352 pgs., Barks-a	20.00	50.00	140.00
705-10- Donald Duck and the Mystery of the Double X, (Disney), 1949, Whitman, Barks-a	12.00	30.00	80.00
2033-(#33)- Donald Duck, Luck of the Ducks, 1969, Whitman, 256 pgs., hard-c, 39 cents, color illos.	4.00	10.00	22.00
2009-(#9)-Donald Duck-The Fabulous Diamond Fountain, (Walt Disney), 1967, Whitman, 260 pgs., 39 cents, hard-c, color illos	4.00	10.00	27.00
5756- Donald Duck-The Fabulous Diamond Fountain, (Walt Disney), 1973, Whitman, 260 pgs., 79 cents, soft-c, color illos	3.00	7.50	20.00
5756-1- Donald Duck-The Fabulous Diamond Fountain,			

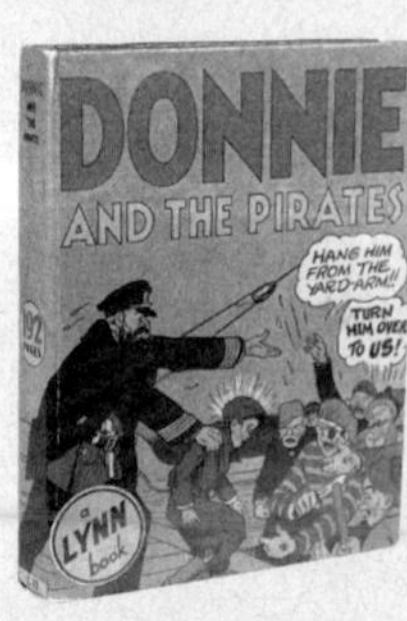

L13 - Donnie and the Pirates © Lynn

1129 - Felix the Cat © WHIT

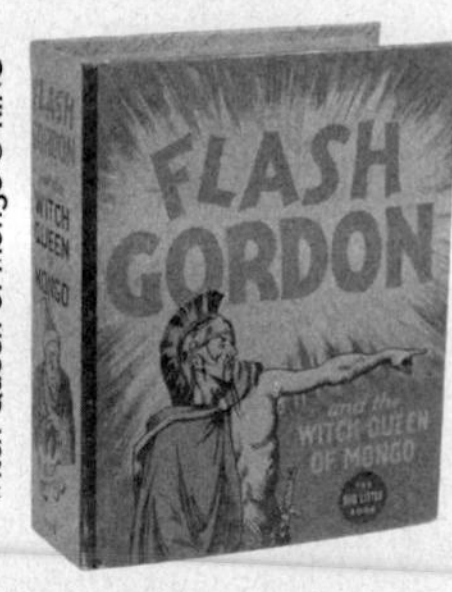

1190 - Flash Gordon and the Witch Queen of Mongo © KING

	GD	FN	VF/NM
(Walt Disney), 1973, Whitman, 260 pgs., 79 cents, soft-c, color illos	3.00	7.50	20.00
5756-2- Donald Duck-The Fabulous Diamond Fountain, (Walt Disney), 1973, Whitman, 260 pgs., 79 cents, soft-c, color illos	3.00	7.50	20.00
5760- Donald Duck in Volcano Valley (Disney), 1973, Whitman, 39 cents, flip-it book	3.00	7.50	20.00
5760-2- Donald Duck in Volcano Valley (Disney), 1973, Whitman, 79 cents, flip-it book	2.00	5.00	14.00
5764- Donald Duck, Luck of the Ducks, 1969, Whitman, 256 pgs., soft-c, 49 cents, color illos.	3.00	7.50	20.00
5773- Donald Duck - The Lost Jungle City, 1975, Whitman, 49 cents, flip-it book; 6 printings through 1980	2.00	5.00	14.00
nn- Donald Duck and the Ducklings, 1938, Dell, 194 pgs., Fast-Action Story, soft-c, Taliaferro-a	36.00	90.00	250.00
nn- Donald Duck Out of Luck (Disney), 1940, Dell, 196 pgs., Fast-Action Story, has Four Color #4 on back-c, Taliaferro-a	36.00	90.00	250.00
8- Donald Duck Takes It on the Chin (Disney), 1941, Dell, 196 pgs., Fast-Action Story, soft-c, Taliaferro-a	36.00	90.00	250.00
L13- Donnie and the Pirates, 1935, Lynn, 192 pgs.	10.00	25.00	60.00
1438- Don O'Dare Finds War, 1940, Whitman, 432 pgs.	10.00	25.00	60.00
1107- Don Winslow, U.S.N., 1935, Whitman, 432 pgs.	16.00	40.00	110.00
nn- Don Winslow, U.S.N., 1935, Whitman, 436 pgs., premium-no ads, 3-color, soft-c	19.00	47.50	130.00
1408- Don Winslow and the Giant Girl Spy, 1946, Whitman, 352 pgs.	12.00	30.00	75.00
1418- Don Winslow Navy Intelligence Ace, 1942, Whitman, 432 pgs., flip pictures	14.00	35.00	100.00
1419- Don Winslow of the Navy Vs. the Scorpion Gang, 1938, Whitman, 432 pgs.	14.00	35.00	100.00
1453- Don Winslow of the Navy and the Secret Enemy Base, 1943, Whitman, 352 pgs.	14.00	35.00	100.00
1489- Don Winslow of the Navy and the Great War Plot, 1940, Whitman, 432 pgs.	14.00	35.00	100.00
nn- Don Winslow U.S. Navy and the Missing Admiral, 1938, Whitman, 36 pgs., 2 1/2" x 3 1/2", Penny Book	7.00	17.50	40.00
1137- Doomed To Die, 1938, Saalfield, 400 pgs.	10.00	25.00	60.00
1140- Down Cartridge Creek, 1938, Saalfield, 400 pgs.	10.00	25.00	60.00
1416- Draftie of the U.S. Army, 1943, Whitman, All Pictures Comics	10.00	25.00	65.00
1100B- Dreams (Your dreams & what they mean), 1938, Whitman, 36 pgs., 2 1/2" x 3 1/2", Penny Book	3.00	7.50	20.00
24- Dumb Dora and Bing Brown, 1936, Lynn	11.00	27.50	70.00
1400- Dumbo, of the Circus - Only His Ears Grew! (Disney), 1941, Whitman, 432 pgs., based on Disney movie	19.00	47.50	135.00
10- Dumbo the Flying Elephant (Disney), 1944, Dell, 194 pgs., Fast-Action Story, soft-c	30.00	75.00	210.00
nn- East O' the Sun and West O' the Moon, nd (1930s), np (Whitman), 36 pgs., 3" x 2 1/2", Penny Book	3.00	7.50	20.00
774- Eddie Cantor in An Hour with You, 1934, Whitman, 154 pgs., 4 1/4" x 5 1/4", photo-c, movie scenes	12.00	30.00	85.00
nn- Eddie Cantor in Laughland, 1934, Goldsmith, 132 pgs., soft-c, photo-c, Vallely-a	12.00	30.00	85.00
1106- Ella Cinders and the Mysterious House, 1934, Whitman, 432 pgs.	12.00	30.00	75.00
nn- Ella Cinders and the Mysterious House, 1934, Whitman, 52 pgs., premium-no ads, soft-c, 3 1/2" x 5 3/4"	14.00	35.00	100.00
nn- Ella Cinders and the Mysterious House, 1934, Whitman, 52 pgs., Lemix Korlix desserts ad by Perkins Products Co. on back-c, soft-c, 3 1/2" x 5 3/4"	18.00	45.00	125.00
nn- Ella Cinders, 1935, Whitman, 148 pgs., 3 1/4" x 4", Tarzan Ice Cream cup lid premium	24.00	60.00	165.00
nn- Ella Cinders Plays Duchess, 1938, Whitman, 68 pgs., 3 3/4" x 3 1/2", Pan-Am Oil premium	16.00	40.00	115.00
nn- Ella Cinders Solves a Mystery, 1938, Whitman, 68 pgs., Pan-Am Oil premium, soft-c	16.00	40.00	115.00

	GD	FN	VF/NM
11- Ella Cinders' Exciting Experience, 1934, Whitman, 3 1/2" x 3 1/2", 132 pgs., Tarzan Ice Cream cup lid giveaway	24.00	60.00	165.00
1406- Ellery Queen the Adventure of the Last Man Club, 1940, Whitman, 432 pgs.	12.00	30.00	80.00
1472- Ellery Queen the Master Detective, 1942, Whitman, 432 pgs., flip pictures	12.00	30.00	80.00
1081- Elmer and his Dog Spot, 1935, Saalfield, hard-c	8.00	20.00	50.00
1311- Elmer and his Dog Spot, 1935, Saalfield, soft-c	8.00	20.00	50.00
722- Erik Noble and the Forty-Niners, 1934, Whitman, 384 pgs.	8.00	20.00	50.00
nn- Erik Noble and the Forty-Niners, 1934, Whitman, 386 pgs., 3-color, soft-c (Rare)	36.00	90.00	250.00
684- Famous Comics (in open box), 1934, Whitman, 48 pgs., 3 3/4" x 8 1/2", (3 books in set): Book 1 - Katzenjammer Kids, Barney Google, & Little Jimmy; Book 2 - Polly and Her Pals, Little Jimmy, & Katzenjammer Kids; Book 3 - Little Annie Rooney, Katzenjammer Kids, & Polly and Her Pals; Complete set	51.00	128.00	360.00
2019-(#19)- Fantastic Four in the House of Horrors, 1968, Whitman, 256 pgs., hard-c, color illos.	4.00	10.00	27.00
5775- Fantastic Four in the House of Horrors, 1976, Whitman, 256 pgs., soft-c, B&W illos.	3.00	7.50	20.00
5775-1- Fantastic Four in the House of Horrors, 1976, Whitman, 256 pgs., soft-c, B&W illos.	3.00	7.50	20.00
1058- Farmyard Symphony, The (Disney), 1939, 5" X 5 1/2", 68 pgs., hard-c	11.00	27.50	70.00
1129- Felix the Cat, 1936, Whitman, 432 pgs., Messmer-a	24.00	60.00	170.00
1439- Felix the Cat, 1943, Whitman, All Pictures Comics, Messmer-a	21.00	52.50	150.00
1465- Felix the Cat, 1945, Whitman, All Pictures Comics, Messmer-a	18.00	45.00	125.00
nn- Felix (Flip book), 1967, World Retrospective of Animation Cinema, 188 pgs., 2 1/2" x 4" by Otto Messmer	4.00	10.00	27.00
nn- Fighting Cowboy of Nugget Gulch, The, 1939, Whitman, 2 1/2" x 3 1/2", Penny Book	4.00	10.00	25.00
1401- Fighting Heroes Battle for Freedom, 1943, Whitman, All Pictures Comics, from "Heroes of Democracy" strip, by Stookie Allen	8.00	20.00	50.00
6- Fighting President, The, 1934, EVW (Five Star Library), 160 pgs., photo-c, photo ill., F. D. Roosevelt	10.00	25.00	60.00
nn- Fire Chief Ed Wynn and "His Old Fire Horse," 1934, Goldsmith, 132 pgs., H. Vallely-a, photo, soft-c	10.00	25.00	60.00
1464- Flame Boy and the Indians' Secret, 1938, Whitman, 300 pgs., Sekakuku-a (Hopi Indian)	8.00	20.00	50.00
22- Flaming Guns, 1935, EVW, with Tom Mix, movie scenes — Hardcover	43.00	108.00	300.00
(Scarce) — Softcover	50.00	125.00	350.00
1110- Flash Gordon on the Planet Mongo, 1934, Whitman, 320 pgs., by Alex Raymond	41.00	103.00	285.00
1166- Flash Gordon and the Monsters of Mongo, 1935, Whitman, 432 pgs., by Alex Raymond	39.00	98.00	270.00
nn- Flash Gordon and the Monsters of Mongo, 1935, Whitman, 436 pgs., premium-no ads, 3-color, soft-c, by Raymond	62.00	155.00	440.00
1171- Flash Gordon and the Tournaments of Mongo, 1935, Whitman, 432 pgs., by Alex Raymond	37.00	93.00	260.00
1190- Flash Gordon and the Witch Queen of Mongo, 1936, Whitman, 432 pgs., by Alex Raymond	37.00	93.00	260.00
1407- Flash Gordon in the Water World of Mongo, 1937, Whitman, 432 pgs., by Alex Raymond	32.00	80.00	225.00
1423- Flash Gordon and the Perils of Mongo, 1940, Whitman, 432 pgs., by Alex Raymond	30.00	75.00	210.00
1424- Flash Gordon in the Jungles of Mongo, 1947, Whitman, 352 pgs., by Alex Raymond	23.00	57.50	160.00
1443- Flash Gordon in the Ice World of Mongo, 1942, Whitman, 432 pgs., flip pictures, by Alex Raymond	31.00	78.00	215.00
1447- Flash Gordon and the Fiery Desert of Mongo, 1948, Whitman, 288 pgs., Raymond-a	23.00	57.50	160.00
1469- Flash Gordon and the Power Men of Mongo, 1943, Whitman, 352 pgs., by Alex Raymond	31.00	78.00	220.00

Flintstones: A Friend From the Past © H-B

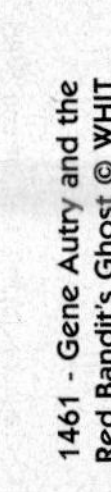

1461 - Gene Autry and the Red Bandit's Ghost © WHIT

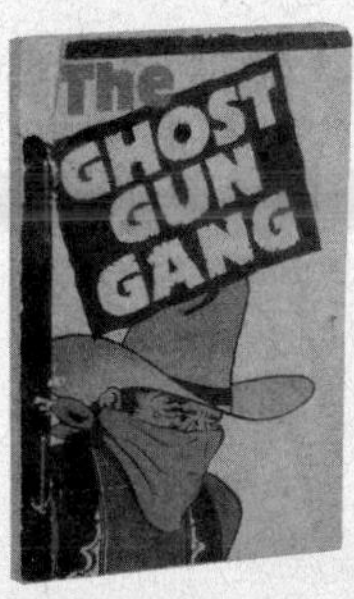

The Ghost Gun Gang Meet Their Match © WHIT

	GD	FN	VF/NM
1479- Flash Gordon and the Red Sword Invaders, 1945, Whitman, 352 pgs., by Alex Raymond	29.00	73.00	200.00
1484- Flash Gordon and the Tyrant of Mongo, 1941, Whitman, 432 pgs., flip pictures, by Alex Raymond	31.00	78.00	220.00
1492- Flash Gordon in the Forest Kingdom of Mongo, 1938, Whitman, 432 pgs., by Alex Raymond	40.00	100.00	280.00
12- Flash Gordon and the Ape Men of Mor, 1942, Dell, 196 pgs., Fast-Action Story, by Alex Raymond	37.00	93.00	260.00
6833- Flash Gordon Vs. the Emperor of Mongo, 1936, Dell, 244 pgs., Cartoon Story Books, hard-c, Raymond-c/a	44.00	110.00	310.00
nn- Flash Gordon Vs. the Emperor of Mongo, 1936, Dell, 244 pgs., Fast-Action Story, soft-c, Alex Raymond-c/a	37.00	93.00	260.00
1467- Flint Roper and the Six-Gun Showdown, 1941, Whitman, 300 pgs.	10.00	25.00	60.00
2014-(#14)- Flintstones-The Case of the Many Missing Things, 1968, Whitman, 260 pgs., 39 cents, hard-c, color illos	4.00	10.00	27.00
nn- Flintstones: A Friend From the Past, 1977, Modern Promotions, 244 pgs., 49 cents, soft-c, flip pictures	2.00	5.00	11.00
nn- Flintstones: It's About Time, 1977, Modern Promotions, 244 pgs., 49 cents, soft-c, flip pictures	2.00	5.00	11.00
nn- Flintstones: Pebbles & Bamm-Bamm Meet Santa Claus, 1977, Modern Promotions, 244 pgs., 49 cents, soft-c, flip pictures	2.00	5.00	11.00
nn- Flintstones: The Great Balloon Race, 1977, Modern Promotions, 244 pgs., 49 cents, soft-c, flip pictures	2.00	5.00	11.00
nn- Flintstones: The Mystery of the Many Missing Things, 1977, Modern Promotions, 244 pgs., 49 cents, soft-c, flip pictures	2.00	5.00	11.00
2003-(#3)- Flipper-Killer Whale Trouble, 1967, Whitman, 260 pgs., hard-c, 39 cents, color illos	3.00	7.50	20.00
2032-(#32)- Flipper, Deep-Sea Photographer, 1969, Whitman, 256 pgs., hard-c, color illos.	3.00	7.50	20.00
1108- Flying the Sky Clipper with Winsie Atkins, 1936, Whitman, 432 pgs.	10.00	25.00	60.00
1460- Foreign Spies Doctor Doom and the Ghost Submarine, 1939, Whitman, 432 pgs., Al McWilliams-a	12.00	30.00	75.00
1100B- Fortune Teller, 1938, Whitman, 36 pgs., 2 1/2" x 3 1/2", Penny Book	3.00	7.50	20.00
1175- Frank Buck Presents Ted Towers Animal Master, 1935, Whitman, 432 pgs.	11.00	27.50	70.00
2015-(#15)-Frankenstein, Jr. - The Menace of the Heartless Monster, 1968, Whitman, 260 pgs., 39 cents, hard-c, color illos.	4.00	10.00	27.00
16- Frankie Thomas in A Dog of Flanders, 1935, EVW, movie scenes	12.00	30.00	75.00
1121- Frank Merriwell at Yale, 1935, 432 pgs.	10.00	25.00	60.00
Freckles and His Friends in the North Woods (See Top-Line Comics)			
nn- Freckles and His Friends Stage a Play, 1938, Whitman, 36 pgs., 2 1/2" x 3 1/2", Penny Book	10.00	25.00	60.00
1164- Freckles and the Lost Diamond Mine, 1937, Whitman, 432 pgs., Merrill Blosser-a	11.00	27.50	70.00
nn- Freckles and the Mystery Ship, 1935, Whitman, 66 pgs., Pan-Am premium	12.00	30.00	75.00
1100B- Fun, Puzzles, Riddles, 1938, Whitman, 36 pgs., 2 1/2" x 3 1/2", Penny Book	3.00	7.50	20.00
1433- Gang Busters Step In, 1939, Whitman, 432 pgs., Henry E. Vallely-a	11.00	27.50	70.00
1437- Gang Busters Smash Through, 1942, Whitman, 432 pgs.	11.00	27.50	70.00
1451- Gang Busters in Action!, 1938, Whitman, 432 pgs.	11.00	27.50	70.00
nn- Gang Busters and Guns of the Law, 1940, Dell, 4" x 5", 194 pgs., Fast-Action Story, soft-c	29.00	73.00	200.00
nn- Gang Busters and the Radio Clues, 1938, Whitman, 36 pgs., 2 1/2" x 3 1/2", Penny Book	8.00	20.00	50.00
1409- Gene Autry and Raiders of the Range, 1946, Whitman, 352 pgs.	12.00	30.00	80.00
1425- Gene Autry and the Mystery of Paint Rock Canyon, 1947, Whitman, 288 pgs.	12.00	30.00	80.00
1428- Gene Autry Special Ranger, 1941, Whitman, 432 pgs., Erwin Hess-a	16.00	40.00	115.00
1433- Gene Autry in Public Cowboy No. 1, 1938, Whitman, 240 pgs., photo-c, movie scenes (1st Autry BLB)	29.00	73.00	200.00
1434- Gene Autry and the Gun-Smoke Reckoning, 1943, Whitman, 352 pgs.	16.00	40.00	110.00
1439- Gene Autry and the Land Grab Mystery, 1948, Whitman, 290 pgs.	12.00	30.00	75.00
1456- Gene Autry in Special Ranger Rule, 1945, Whitman, 352 pgs., Henry E. Vallely-a	16.00	40.00	110.00
1461- Gene Autry and the Red Bandit's Ghost, 1949, Whitman, 288 pgs.	11.00	27.50	70.00
1483- Gene Autry in Law of the Range, 1939, Whitman, 432 pgs.	16.00	40.00	110.00
1493- Gene Autry and the Hawk of the Hills, 1942, Whitman, 428 pgs., flip pictures, Vallely-a	16.00	40.00	110.00
1494- Gene Autry Cowboy Detective, 1940, Whitman, 432 pgs., Erwin Hess-a	16.00	40.00	110.00
700-10- Gene Autry and the Bandits of Silver Tip, 1949, Whitman	11.00	27.50	70.00
714-10- Gene Autry and the Range War, 1950, Whitman	11.00	27.50	70.00
nn- Gene Autry in Gun-Smoke, 1938, Dell, 196 pgs., Fast-Action story, soft-c	27.00	68.00	190.00
2035-(#35)- Gentle Ben, Mystery of the Everglades, 1969, Whitman, 256 pgs., hard-c, color illos.	3.00	7.50	20.00
1176- Gentleman Joe Palooka, 1940, Saalfield, 400 pgs.	10.00	25.00	60.00
George O'Brien (See The Cowboy Millionaire)			
1101- George O'Brien and the Arizona Badman, 1936?, Whitman	10.00	25.00	60.00
1418- George O'Brien in Gun Law, 1938, Whitman, 240 pgs., photo-c, movie scenes, RKO Radio Pictures	10.00	25.00	60.00
1457- George O'Brien and the Hooded Riders, 1940, Whitman, 432 pgs., Erwin Hess-a	8.00	20.00	50.00
nn- George O'Brien and the Arizona Bad Man, 1939, Whitman, 36 pgs., 2 1/2" x 3 1/2", Penny Book	8.00	20.00	50.00
1462- Ghost Avenger, 1943, Whitman, 432 pgs., flip pictures, Henry Vallely-a	10.00	25.00	60.00
nn- Ghost Gun Gang Meet Their Match, The, 1939. Whitman, 2 1/2" x 3 1/2", Penny Book	8.00	20.00	50.00
nn- Gingerbread Boy, The, nd(1930s), np(Whitman), 36 pgs., Penny Book	2.00	5.00	15.00
1118- G-Man on the Crime Trail, 1936, Whitman, 432 pgs.	11.00	27.50	70.00
1147- G-Man Vs. the Red X, 1936, Whitman, 432 pgs.	12.00	30.00	80.00
1162- G-Man Allen, 1939, Saalfield, 400 pgs.	11.00	27.50	70.00
1173- G-Man in Action, A, 1940, Saalfield, 400 pgs., J.R. White-a	11.00	27.50	70.00
1434- G-Man and the Radio Bank Robberies, 1937, Whitman, 432 pgs.	12.00	30.00	80.00
1469- G-Man and the Gun Runners, The, 1940, Whitman, 432 pgs.	12.00	30.00	80.00
1470- G-Man vs. the Fifth Column, 1941, Whitman, 432 pgs., flip pictures	12.00	30.00	80.00
1493- G-Man Breaking the Gambling Ring, 1938, Whitman, 432 pgs., James Gary-a	12.00	30.00	80.00
nn- G-Man on Lightning Island, 1936, Dell, 244 pgs., Fast-Action Story, soft-c, Henry E. Vallely-a	24.00	60.00	170.00
nn- G-Man, Underworld Chief, 1938, Whitman, Buddy Book premium,	29.00	73.00	200.00
6833- G-Man on Lightning Island, 1936, Dell, 244 pgs., Cartoon Story Book, hard-c, Henry E. Vallely-a	18.00	45.00	125.00
4- G-Men Foil the Kidnappers, 1936, Whitman, 132 pgs., 3 1/2" x 3 1/2", soft-c, Tarzan Ice Cream cup lid premium	24.00	60.00	165.00
1157- G-Men on the Trail, 1938, Saalfield, 400 pgs.	10.00	25.00	60.00
1168- G Men on the Job, 1935, Whitman, 432 pgs.	12.00	30.00	75.00
nn- G-Men on the Job Again, 1938, Whitman, 36 pgs., 2 1/2" x 3 1/2", Penny Book	10.00	25.00	60.00
nn- G-Men and Kidnap Justice, 1938, Whitman, 68 pgs., Pan-Am premium, soft-c	12.00	30.00	75.00
nn- G-Men and the Missing Clues, 1938, Whitman, 36 pgs., 2 1/2"x 3 1/2", Penny Book	10.00	25.00	60.00

1159 - Hall of Fame of the Air © WHIT

1403 - Invisible Scarlet O'Neil © WHIT

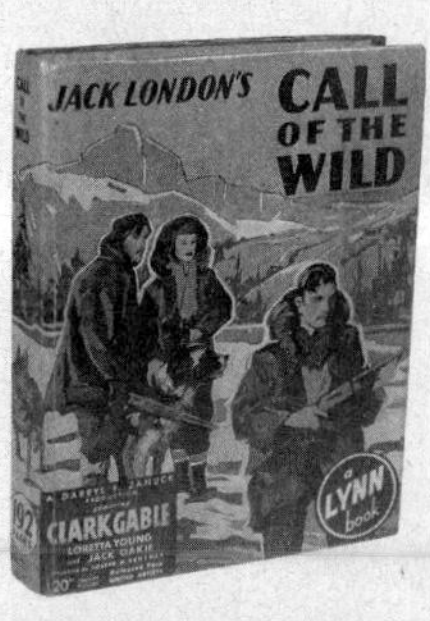

L11 - Jack London's Call of the Wild © Lynn

	GD	FN	VF/NM
1097- Go Into Your Dance, 1935, Saalfield, 160 pgs.. photo-c, movie scenes with Al Jolson & Ruby Keeler	13.00	32.50	90.00
1577- Go Into Your Dance, 1935, Saalfield, 160 pgs., photo-c, movie scenes, soft-c	13.00	32.50	90.00
2021- Goofy in Giant Trouble (Walt Disney's ...), 1968, Whitman, hard-c, 260 pgs., 39 cents, color illos.	3.00	7.50	20.00
5751- Goofy in Giant Trouble (Walt Disney's ...), 1968, Whitman, soft-c, 260 pgs., 39 cents, color illos.	3.00	7.50	20.00
5751-2- Goofy in Giant Trouble, 1968 (1980-reprint of '67 version), Whitman, soft-c, 260 pgs., 79 cents, B&W	1.00	2.50	8.00
8- Great Expectations, 1934, EVW, (Five Star Library), 160 pgs., photo-c, movie scenes	14.00	35.00	100.00
1453- Green Hornet Strikes!, The, 1940, Whitman, 432 pgs., Robert Weisman-a	36.00	90.00	250.00
1480- Green Hornet Cracks Down, The, 1942, Whitman, 432 pgs., flip pictures, Henry Vallely-a	33.00	83.00	230.00
1496- Green Hornet Returns, The, 1941, Whitman, 432 pgs., flip pictures	36.00	90.00	250.00
5778- Grimm's Ghost Stories, 1976, Whitman, 256 pgs., Laura French-s adapted from fairy tales; blue spine & back-c	2.00	5.00	13.00
5778-1- Grimm's Ghost Stories, 1976, Whitman, 256 pgs., reprint of #5778; yellow spine & back-c	2.00	5.00	13.00
1172- Gullivers' Travels, 1939, Saalfield, 320 pgs., adapted from Paramount Pict. Cartoons (Rare) Hardcover	26.00	65.00	180.00
(Scarce) Softcover	29.00	73.00	205.00
nn- Gumps In Radio Land, The (Andy Gump and the Chest of Gold), 1937, Lehn & Fink Prod. Corp., 100 pgs., 3 1/4" x 5 1/2", Pebeco Tooth Paste giveaway, by Gus Edson	20.00	50.00	140.00
nn- Gunmen of Rustlers' Gulch, The, 1939, Whitman, 36 pgs., 2 1/2" x 3 1/2", Penny Book	7.00	17.50	40.00
1426- Guns in the Roaring West, 1937, Whitman, 300 pgs.	7.00	17.50	40.00
1647- Gunsmoke (TV Series), 1958, Whitman, 280 pgs., 4 1/2" x 5 3/4"	5.00	12.50	30.00
1101- Hairbreath Harry in Department QT, 1935, Whitman, 384 pgs., by J. M. Alexander	10.00	25.00	65.00
1413- Hal Hardy in the Lost Land of Giants, 1938, Whitman, 300 pgs., "The World 1,000,000 Years Ago"	10.00	25.00	65.00
1159- Hall of Fame of the Air, 1936, Whitman, 432 pgs., by Capt. Eddie Rickenbacker	8.00	20.00	50.00
nn- Hansel and Grethel, The Story of, nd (1930s), no publ., 36 pgs., Penny Book	3.00	7.50	18.00
1145- Hap Lee's Selection of Movie Gags, 1935, Whitman, 160 pgs., photos of stars	13.00	32.50	90.00
Happy Prince, The (See Wee Little Books)			
1111- Hard Rock Harrigan-A Story of Boulder Dam, 1935, Saalfield, hard-c, photo-c, photo illos.	10.00	25.00	60.00
1591- Hard Rock Harrigan-A Story of Boulder Dam, 1935, Saalfield, soft-c, photo-c, photo illos.	10.00	25.00	60.00
1418- Harold Teen Swinging at the Sugar Bowl, 1939, Whitman, 432 pgs., by Carl Ed	10.00	25.00	60.00
nn- Hercules - The Legendary Journeys, 1998, Chronicle Books, 310 pgs., based on TV series, 1-color (brown) illos	1.00	2.50	9.00
1100B- Hobbies, 1938, Whitman, 36 pgs., 2 1/2" x 3 1/2", Penny Book	2.00	5.00	15.00
1125- Hockey Spare, The, 1937, Saalfield, sports book	7.00	17.50	40.00
1605- Hockey Spare, The, 1937, Saalfield, soft-c	7.00	17.50	40.00
728- Homeless Homer, 1934, Whitman, by Dee Dobbin, for young kids	4.00	10.00	25.00
17- Hoosier Schoolmaster, The, 1935, EVW, movie scenes	13.00	32.50	90.00
715- Houdini's Big Little Book of Magic, 1927 (1933), 300 pgs.	14.00	35.00	100.00
nn- Houdini's Big Little Book of Magic, 1927 (1933), 196 pgs., American Oil Co. premium, soft-c	14.00	35.00	100.00
nn- Houdini's Big Little Book of Magic, 1927 (1933), 204 pgs., Cocomalt premium, soft-c	14.00	35.00	100.00
Huckleberry Finn (See The Adventures of...)			
nn- Huckleberry Hound Newspaper Reporter, 1977, Modern Promotions, 244 pgs., 49 cents, soft-c, flip pictures	2.00	5.00	13.00

	GD	FN	VF/NM
1644- Hugh O'Brian TV's Wyatt Earp (TV Series), 1958, Whitman, 280 pgs.	5.00	12.50	30.00
5782-2- Incredible Hulk Lost in Time, 1980, 260 pgs., 79¢-c, soft-c, B&W	2.00	5.00	10.00
1424- Inspector Charlie Chan Villainy on the High Seas, 1942, Whitman, 432 pgs., flip pictures	14.00	35.00	95.00
1186- Inspector Wade of Scotland Yard, 1940, Saalfield, 400 pgs.	10.00	25.00	60.00
1194- Inspector Wade and The Feathered Serpent, 1939, Saalfield, 400 pgs.	10.00	25.00	60.00
1448- Inspector Wade Solves the Mystery of the Red Aces, 1937, Whitman, 432 pgs.	10.00	25.00	60.00
1148- International Spy Doctor Doom Faces Death at Dawn, 1937, Whitman, 432 pgs., Arbo-a	12.00	30.00	75.00
1155- In the Name of the Law, 1937, Whitman, 432 pgs., Henry E. Vallely-a	10.00	25.00	60.00
2012-(#12)-Invaders, The-Alien Missile Threat (TV Series), 1967, Whitman, 260 pgs., hard-c, 39 cents, color illos.	4.00	10.00	27.00
1403- Invisible Scarlet O'Neil, 1942, Whitman, All Pictures Comics, flip pictures	12.00	30.00	80.00
1406- Invisible Scarlet O'Neil Versus the King of the Slums, 1946, Whitman, 352 pgs.	10.00	25.00	65.00
1098- It Happened One Night, 1935, Saalfield, 160 pgs., Little Big Book, Clark Gable, Claudette Colbert photo-c, movie scenes from Academy Award winner	14.00	35.00	100.00
1578- It Happened One Night, 1935, Saalfield, 160 pgs., soft-c	14.00	35.00	100.00
Jack and Jill (See Wee Little Books)			
1432- Jack Armstrong and the Mystery of the Iron Key, 1939, Whitman, 432 pgs., Henry E. Vallely-a	12.00	30.00	85.00
1435- Jack Armstrong and the Ivory Treasure, 1937, Whitman, 432 pgs., Henry Vallely-a	12.00	30.00	85.00
Jackie Cooper (See Story Of..)			
1084- Jackie Cooper in Peck's Bad Boy, 1934, Saalfield, 160 pgs., hard, photo-c, movie scenes	15.00	37.50	105.00
1314- Jackie Cooper in Peck's Bad Boy, 1934, Saalfield, 160 pgs., soft, photo-c, movie scenes	15.00	37.50	105.00
1402- Jackie Cooper in "Gangster's Boy," 1939, Whitman, 240 pgs., photo-c, movie scenes	15.00	37.50	105.00
13- Jackie Cooper in Dinky, 1935, EVW, 160 pgs., movie scenes	15.00	37.50	105.00
nn- Jack King of the Secret Service and the Counterfeiters, 1939, Whitman, 36 pgs., 2 1/2" x 3 1/2", Penny Book, by John G. Gray	10.00	25.00	60.00
L11- Jack London's Call of the Wild, 1935, Lynn, 20th Cent. Pic., movie scenes with Clark Gable	12.00	30.00	80.00
nn- Jack Pearl as Detective Baron Munchausen, 1934, Goldsmith, 132 pgs., soft-c	12.00	30.00	85.00
1102- Jack Swift and His Rocket Ship, 1934, Whitman, 320 pgs.	16.00	40.00	110.00
1498- Jane Arden the Vanished Princess, Whitman, 300 pgs.	10.00	25.00	60.00
1179- Jane Withers in This is the Life (20th Century-Fox Presents...), 1935, Whitman, 240 pgs., photo-c, movie scenes	12.00	30.00	80.00
1463- Jane Withers in Keep Smiling, 1938, Whitman, 240 pgs., photo-c, movie scenes	12.00	30.00	80.00
Jaragu of the Jungle (See Rex Beach's ...)			
1447- Jerry Parker Police Reporter and the Candid Camera Clue, 1941, Whitman, 300 pgs.	10.00	25.00	60.00
Jim Bowie (See Adventures of ...)			
nn- J im Brant of the Highway Patrol and the Mysterious Accident, 1939, Whitman, 36 pgs., 2 1/2" x 3 1/2", Penny Book	9.00	22.50	55.00
1466- Jim Craig State Trooper and the Kidnapped Governor, 1938, Whitman, 432 pgs.	10.00	25.00	60.00
nn- Jim Doyle Private Detective and the Train Hold-Up, 1939, Whitman, 36 pgs., 2 1/2" x 3 1/2", Penny Book	10.00	25.00	65.00
1180- Jim Hardy Ace Reporter, 1940, Saalfield, 400 pgs., Dick Moores-a	10.00	25.00	65.00
1143- Jimmy Allen in the Air Mail Robbery, 1936, Whitman, 432 pgs.	10.00	25.00	65.00

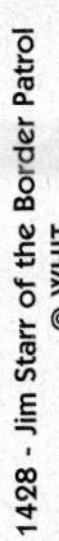
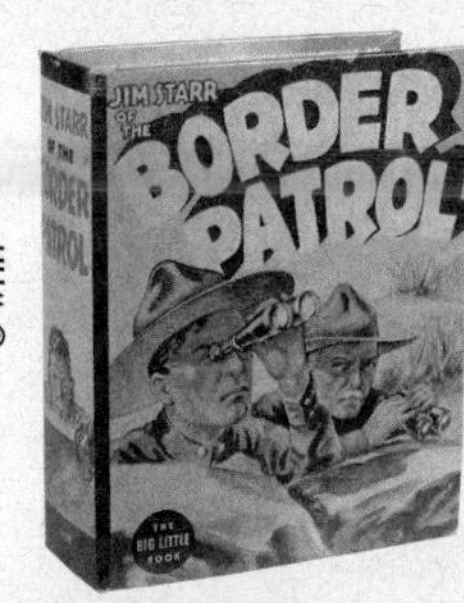

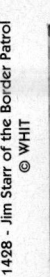

1428 - Jim Starr of the Border Patrol © WHIT

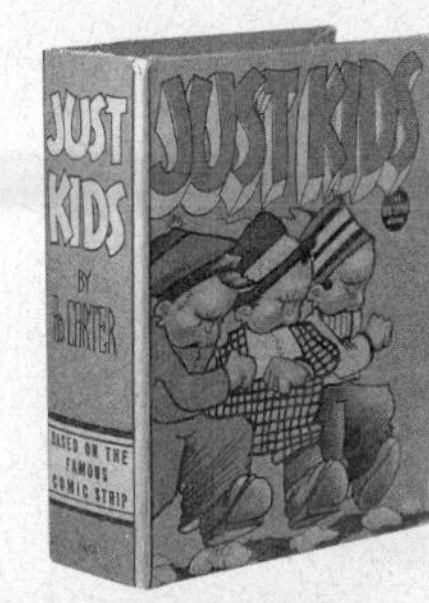

1401 - Just Kids © WHIT

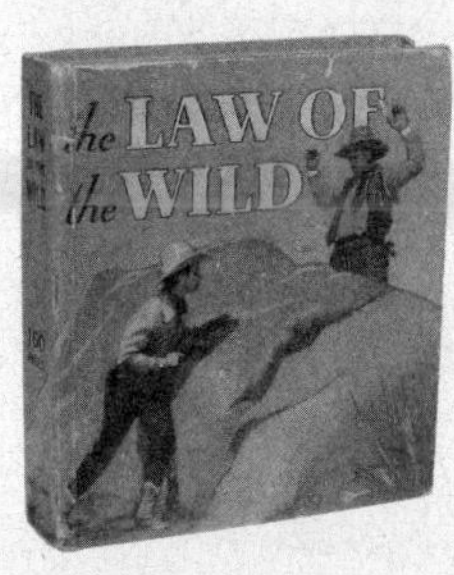

1322 - The Law of the Wild © Saalfield

	GD	FN	VF/NM
27- Jimmy Allen in The Sky Parade, 1936, Lynn, 130 pgs., 5 x 7 1/2", Paramount Pictures, movie scenes	12.00	30.00	75.00
L15- Jimmy and the Tiger, 1935, Lynn, 192 pgs.	10.00	25.00	65.00
1428- Jim Starr of the Border Patrol, 1937, Whitman, 432 pgs.	10.00	25.00	65.00
Joan of Arc (See Wee Little Books)			
1105- Joe Louis the Brown Bomber, 1936, Whitman, 240 pgs., photo-c, photo-illos.	21.00	52.50	150.00
Joe Palooka (See Gentleman ...)			
1123- Joe Palooka the Heavyweight Boxing Champ, 1934, Whitman, 320 pgs., Ham Fisher-a	18.00	45.00	125.00
1168- Joe Palooka's Great Adventure, 1939, Saalfield	14.00	35.00	100.00
nn- Joe Penner's Duck Farm, 1935, Goldsmith, Henry Vallely-a	11.00	27.50	70.00
1402- John Carter of Mars, 1940, Whitman, 432 pgs., John Coleman Burroughs-a	51.00	128.00	360.00
nn- John Carter of Mars, 1940, Dell, 194 pgs., Fast-Action Story, soft-c	65.00	163.00	460.00
1164- Johnny Forty Five, 1938, Saalfield, 400 pgs.	10.00	25.00	60.00
John Wayne (See Westward Ho!)			
1100B- Jokes (A book of laughs galore), 1938, Whitman, 36 pgs., 2 1/2" x 3 1/2", Penny Book, laughing guy-c	2.00	5.00	15.00
1100B- Jokes (A book of side-splitting funny stories), 1938, Whitman, 36 pgs., 2 1/2" x 3 1/2", Penny Book, clowns on-c	2.00	5.00	15.00
2026-(#26)- Journey to the Center of the Earth, The Fiery Foe, 1968, Whitman	4.00	10.00	27.00
Jungle Jim (See Top-Line Comics)			
1138- Jungle Jim, 1936, Whitman, 432 pgs., Alex Raymond-a	21.00	52.50	150.00
1139- Jungle Jim and the Vampire Woman, 1937, Whitman, 432 pgs., Alex Raymond-a	21.00	52.50	150.00
1442- Junior G-Men, 1937, Whitman, 432 pgs., Henry E. Vallely-a	11.00	27.50	70.00
nn- Junior G-Men Solve a Crime, 1939, Whitman, 36 pgs., 2 1/2" x 3 1/2", Penny Book	11.00	27.50	70.00
1422- Junior Nebb on the Diamond Bar Ranch, 1938, Whitman, 300 pgs., by Sol Hess	11.00	27.50	70.00
1470- Junior Nebb Joins the Circus, 1939, Whitman, 300 pgs. by Sol Hess	11.00	27.50	70.00
nn- Junior Nebb Elephant Trainer, 1939, Whitman, 68 pgs., Pan-Am Oil premium, soft-c	13.00	32.50	90.00
1052- "Just Kids" (Adventures of ...), 1934, Saalfield, oblong size, by Ad Carter	18.00	45.00	125.00
1094- Just Kids and the Mysterious Stranger, 1935, Saalfield, 160 pgs., by Ad Carter	13.00	32.50	90.00
1184- Just Kids and Deep-Sea Dan, 1940, Saalfield, 400 pgs., by Ad Carter	12.00	30.00	75.00
1302- Just Kids, The Adventures of, 1934, Saalfield, oblong size, soft-c, by Ad Carter	20.00	50.00	140.00
1324- Just Kids and the Mysterious Stranger, 1935, Saalfield, 160 pgs., soft-c, by Ad Carter ,	13.00	32.50	90.00
1401- Just Kids, 1937, Whitman, 432 pgs., by Ad Carter	13.00	32.50	90.00
1055- Katzenjammer Kids in the Mountains, 1934, Saalfield, hard-c, oblong, H. H. Knerr-a	16.00	40.00	115.00
1305- Katzenjammer Kids in the Mountains, 1934, Saalfield, soft-c, oblong, H. H. Knerr-a	16.00	40.00	115.00
14- Katzenjammer Kids, The, 1942, Dell, 194 pgs., Fast-Action Story, H. H. Knerr-a	18.00	45.00	125.00
1411- Kay Darcy and the Mystery Hideout, 1937, Whitman, 300 pgs., Charles Mueller-a	12.00	30.00	80.00
1180- Kayo in the Land of Sunshine (With Moon Mullins), 1937, Whitman, 432 pgs., by Willard	13.00	32.50	90.00
1415- Kayo and Moon Mullins and the One Man Gang, 1939, Whitman, 432 pgs., by Frank Willard	11.00	27.50	70.00
7- Kayo and Moon Mullins 'Way Down South, 1938, Whitman, 132 pgs., 3 1/2" x 3 1/2", Buddy Book	21.00	52.50	150.00
1105- Kazan in Revenge of the North (James Oliver Curwood's...), 1937, Whitman, 432 pgs., Henry E. Vallely-a	11.00	25.00	60.00
1471- Kazan, King of the Pack (James Oliver Curwood's...), 1940, Whitman, 432 pgs.	9.00	22.50	55.00
1420- Keep 'Em Flying! U.S.A. for America's Defense, 1943, Whitman, 432 pgs., Henry E. Vallely-a, flip pictures	10.00	25.00	60.00
1133- Kelly King at Yale Hall, 1937, Saalfield	9.00	22.50	55.00
Ken Maynard (See Strawberry Roan & Western Frontier)			
5- Ken Maynard in "Wheels of Destiny," 1934, EVW, 160 pgs., movie scenes (scarce)	20.00	50.00	140.00
776- Ken Maynard in "Gun Justice," 1934, Whitman, 160 pgs., hard-c, movie scenes (Universal Pic.)	14.00	35.00	95.00
776- Ken Maynard in "Gun Justice," 1934, Whitman, 160 pgs., soft-c, movie scenes (Universal Pic.)	14.00	35.00	95.00
1430- Ken Maynard in Western Justice, 1938, Whitman, 432 pgs., Irwin Myers-a	11.00	27.50	70.00
1442- Ken Maynard and the Gun Wolves of the Gila, 1939, Whitman, 432 pgs.	11.00	27.50	70.00
nn- Ken Maynard in Six-Gun Law, 1938, Whitman, 36 pgs., 2 1/2" x 3 1/2", Penny Book	9.00	22.50	55.00
1134- King of Crime, 1938, Saalfield, 400 pgs.	10.00	25.00	60.00
King of the Royal Mounted (See Zane Grey)			
nn- Kit Carson, 1933, World Syndicate, by J. Carroll Mansfield, High Lights Of History Series, hard-c	10.00	25.00	60.00
nn- Kit Carson, 1933, World Syndicate, same as hard-c above but with a black cloth-c	10.00	25.00	60.00
1105- Kit Carson and the Mystery Riders, 1935, Saalfield, hard-c, Johnny Mack Brown photo-c, movie scenes	13.00	32.50	90.00
1585- Kit Carson and the Mystery Riders, 1935, Saalfield, soft-c, Johnny Mack Brown photo-c, movie scenes	13.00	32.50	90.00
Krazy Kat (See Adventures of...)			
2004- (#4)-Lassie-Adventure in Alaska (TV Series), 1967, Whitman, hard-c, 260 pgs., 39 cents, color illos	4.00	10.00	27.00
5754- Lassie-Adventure in Alaska (TV Series), 1973, Whitman, soft-c, 260 pgs., 49 cents, color illos	2.00	5.00	15.00
2027- Lassie and the Shabby Sheik (TV Series), 1968, Whitman, hard-c, 260 pgs., 39 cents	4.00	10.00	25.00
5762- Lassie and the Shabby Sheik (TV Series), 1972, Whitman, soft-c, 260 pgs., 39 cents	2.00	5.00	15.00
5769- Lassie, Old One-Eye (TV Series), 1975, Whitman, soft-c, 260 pgs., 49 cents, three printings	2.00	5.00	15.00
1132- Last Days of Pompeii, The, 1935, Whitman, 5 1/4" x 6 1/4", 260 pgs., photo-c, movie scenes	13.00	32.50	90.00
1128- Last Man Out (Baseball), 1937, Saalfield, hard-c	10.00	25.00	60.00
L30- Last of the Mohicans, The, 1936, Lynn, 192 pgs., movie scenes with Randolph Scott, United Artists Pictures	12.00	30.00	80.00
1126- Laughing Dragon of Oz, The, 1934, Whitman 432 pgs., by Frank Baum (scarce)	89.00	223.00	625.00
1086- Laurel and Hardy, 1934, Saalfield, 160 pgs., hard-c, photo-c, movie scenes	21.00	52.50	145.00
1316- Laurel and Hardy, 1934, Saalfield, 160 pgs. soft-c, photo-c, movie scenes	21.00	52.50	145.00
1092- Law of the Wild, The, 1935, Saalfield, 160 pgs., photo-c, movie scenes of Rex, The Wild Horse & Rin-Tin-Tin Jr.	11.00	27.50	70.00
1322- Law of the Wild, The, 1935, Saalfield, 160 pgs., photo-c, movie scenes, soft-c	11.00	27.50	70.00
1100B- Learn to be a Ventriloquist, 1938, Whitman, 36 pgs. 2 1/2" x 3 1/2", Penny Book	2.00	5.00	15.00
1149- Lee Brady Range Detective, 1938, Saalfield, 400 pgs.	9.00	22.50	55.00
L10- Les Miserables (Victor Hugo's ...), 1935, Lynn, 192 pgs., movie scenes	12.00	30.00	85.00
1441- Lightning Jim U.S. Marshal Brings Law to the West, 1940, Whitman, 432 pgs., based on radio program	10.00	25.00	65.00
nn- Lightning Jim Whipple U.S. Marshal in Indian Territory, 1939, Whitman, 36 pgs., 2 1/2" x 3 1/2", Penny Book	8.00	20.00	50.00
653- Lions and Tigers (With Clyde Beatty), 1934, Whitman, 160 pgs., photo-c movie scenes	12.00	30.00	85.00
1187- Li'l Abner and the Ratfields, 1940, Saalfield, 400 pgs., by Al Capp	14.00	35.00	95.00
1193- Li'l Abner and Sadie Hawkins Day, 1940, Saalfield, 400 pgs., by Al Capp	14.00	35.00	95.00
1198- Li'l Abner in New York, 1936, Whitman, 432 pgs., by Al Capp			

1148 - The Little Green Door © Saalfield

1150 - Little Men © WHIT

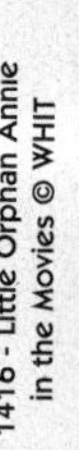
1416 - Little Orphan Annie in the Movies © WHIT

GD FN VF/NM

15.00 37.50 105.00

1401- Li'l Abner Among the Millionaires, 1939, Whitman, 432 pgs., by Al Capp 15.00 37.50 105.00

1054- Little Annie Rooney, 1934, Saalfield, oblong - 4" x 8", All Pictures Comics, hard-c 14.00 35.00 100.00

1304- Little Annie Rooney, 1934, Saalfield, oblong - 4" x 8", All Pictures, soft-c 14.00 35.00 100.00

1117- Little Annie Rooney and the Orphan House, 1936, Whitman, 432 pgs. 11.00 27.50 70.00

1406- Little Annie Rooney on the Highway to Adventure, 1938, Whitman, 432 pgs. 11.00 27.50 70.00

1149- Little Big Shot (With Sybil Jason), 1935, Whitman, 240 pgs., photo-c, movie scenes 12.00 30.00 85.00

nn- Little Black Sambo, nd (1930s), np (Whitman), 36 pgs., 3" x 2 1/2", Penny Book 12.00 30.00 80.00

Little Bo-Peep (See Wee Little Books)

Little Colonel, The (See Shirley Temple)

1148- Little Green Door, The, 1938, Saalfield, 400 pgs. 10.00 25.00 60.00

1112- Little Hollywood Stars, 1935, Saalfield, movie scenes (Little Rascals, etc.), hard-c 12.00 30.00 85.00

1592- Little Hollywood Stars, 1935, Saalfield, movie scenes, soft-c 12.00 30.00 85.00

1087- Little Jimmy's Gold Hunt, 1935, Saalfield, 160 pgs., hard-c, Little Big Book, by Swinnerton 16.00 40.00 110.00

1317- Little Jimmy's Gold Hunt, 1935, Saalfield, 160 pgs., 4 1/4" x 5 3/4", soft-c, by Swinnerton 16.00 40.00 110.00

Little Joe and the City Gangsters (See Top-Line Comics)

Little Joe Otter's Slide (See Wee Little Books)

1118- Little Lord Fauntleroy, 1936, Saalfield, movie scenes, photo-c, 4 1/2" x 5 1/4", starring Mickey Rooney & Freddie Bartholomew, hard-c 10.00 25.00 60.00

1598- Little Lord Fauntleroy, 1936, Saalfield, photo-c, movie scenes, soft-c 10.00 25.00 60.00

1192- Little Mary Mixup and the Grocery Robberies, 1940, Saalfield 10.00 25.00 60.00

8- Little Mary Mixup Wins A Prize, 1936, Whitman, 132 pgs., 3 1/2" x 3 1/2", soft-c, Tarzan Ice Cream cup lid premium 24.00 60.00 165.00

1150- Little Men, 1934, Whitman, 4 3/4" x 5 1/4", movie scenes (Mascot Prod.), photo-c, hard-c 10.00 25.00 65.00

9- Little Minister, The,-Katharine Hepburn, 1935, 160 pgs., 4 1/4" x 5 1/2", EVW (Five Star Library), movie scenes (RKO) 14.00 35.00 100.00

1120- Little Miss Muffet, 1936, Whitman, 432 pgs., by Fanny Y. Cory 11.00 27.50 70.00

708- Little Orphan Annie, 1933, Whitman, 320 pgs., by Harold Gray, the 2nd Big Little Book 43.00 108.00 300.00

nn- Little Orphan Annie, 1928('33), Whitman, 52 pgs., 4" x 5 1/2", premium-no ads, soft-c, by Harold Gray 29.00 73.00 200.00

716- Little Orphan Annie and Sandy, 1933, Whitman, 320 pgs., by Harold Gray 24.00 60.00 170.00

716- Little Orphan Annie and Sandy, 1933, Whitman, 300 pgs., by Harold Gray 20.00 50.00 140.00

nn- Little Orphan Annie and Sandy, 1933, Whitman, 52 pgs., premium, no ads, 4" x 5 1/2", soft-c by Harold Gray 29.00 73.00 200.00

748- Little Orphan Annie and Chizzler, 1933, Whitman, 320 pgs., by Harold Gray 14.00 35.00 100.00

1010- Little Orphan Annie and the Big Town Gunmen, 1937, 7 1/4" x 5 1/2", 64 pgs., Nickel Book 12.00 30.00 85.00

nn- Little Orphan Annie with the Circus, 1934, Whitman, 320 pgs., same cover as L.O.A. 708 but with blue background, Ovaltine giveaway stamp inside front-c, by Harold Gray 36.00 90.00 250.00

1103- Little Orphan Annie with the Circus, 1934, Whitman, 320 pgs. 14.00 35.00 100.00

1140- Little Orphan Annie and the Big Train Robbery, 1934, Whitman, 300 pgs., by Gray 14.00 35.00 100.00

1140- Little Orphan Annie and the Big Train Robbery, 1934, Whitman, 300 pgs., premium-no ads, soft-c, by Harold Gray 26.00 65.00 180.00

1154- Little Orphan Annie and the Ghost Gang, 1935, Whitman, 432 pgs. by Harold Gray 14.00 35.00 100.00

nn- Little Orphan Annie and the Ghost Gang, 1935, Whitman, 436 pgs., premium-no ads, 3-color, soft-c, by Harold Gray 26.00 65.00 180.00

1162- Little Orphan Annie and Punjab the Wizard, 1935, Whitman, 432 pgs., by Harold Gray 14.00 35.00 100.00

1186- Little Orphan Annie and the $1,000,000 Formula, 1936, Whitman, 432 pgs., by Gray 13.00 32.50 90.00

1414- Little Orphan Annie and the Ancient Treasure of Am, 1939, Whitman, 432 pgs., by Gray 12.00 30.00 80.00

1416- Little Orphan Annie in the Movies, 1937, Whitman, 432 pgs., by Harold Gray 12.00 30.00 80.00

1417- Little Orphan Annie and the Secret of the Well, 1947, Whitman, 352 pgs., by Gray 11.00 27.50 70.00

1435- Little Orphan Annie and the Gooneyville Mystery, 1947, Whitman, 288 pgs., by Gray 12.00 30.00 75.00

1446- Little Orphan Annie in the Thieves' Den, 1949, Whitman, 288 pgs., by Harold Gray 12.00 30.00 75.00

1449- Little Orphan Annie and the Mysterious Shoemaker, 1938, Whitman, 432 pgs., by Harold Gray 12.00 30.00 85.00

1457- Little Orphan Annie and Her Junior Commandos, 1943, Whitman, 352 pgs., by H. Gray 10.00 25.00 60.00

1461- Little Orphan Annie and the Underground Hide-Out, 1945, Whitman, 352 pgs., by Gray 10.00 25.00 60.00

1468- Little Orphan Annie and the Ancient Treasure of Am, 1949 (Misdated 1939), 288 pgs., by Gray 10.00 25.00 60.00

1482- Little Orphan Annie and the Haunted Mansion, 1941, Whitman, 432 pgs., flip pictures, by Harold Gray 12.00 30.00 80.00

3048- Little Orphan Annie and Her Big Little Kit, 1937, Whitman, 384 pgs., 4 1/2" x 6 1/2" box, includes miniature box of 4 crayons-red, yellow, blue and green 64.00 160.00 450.00

4054- Little Orphan Annie, The Story of, 1934, Whitman, 7" x 9 1/2", 320 pgs., Big Big Book, Harold Gray-c/a 30.00 75.00 210.00

nn- Little Orphan Annie Gets into Trouble, 1938, Whitman, 36 pgs., 2 1/2" x 3 1/2", Penny Book 9.00 22.50 55.00

nn- Little Orphan Annie in Hollywood, 1937, Whitman, 3 1/2" x 3 1/4", Pan-Am premium, soft-c 23.00 57.50 160.00

nn- Little Orphan Annie in Rags to Riches, 1939, Dell, 194 pgs., Fast-Action Story, soft-c 26.00 65.00 180.00

nn- Little Orphan Annie Saves Sandy, 1938, Whitman, 36 pgs., 2 1/2" x 3 1/2", Penny Book 10.00 25.00 60.00

nn- Little Orphan Annie Under the Big Top, 1938, Dell, 194 pgs., Fast-Action Story, soft-c 25.00 62.50 175.00

nn- Little Orphan Annie Wee Little Books (In open box) nn, 1934, Whitman, 44 pgs., by H. Gray

L.O.A. And Daddy Warbucks 9.00 22.50 55.00
L.O.A. And Her Dog Sandy 9.00 22.50 55.00
L.O.A. And The Lucky Knife 9.00 22.50 55.00
L.O.A. And The Pinch-Pennys 9.00 22.50 55.00
L.O.A. At Happy Home 9.00 22.50 55.00
L.O.A. Finds Mickey 9.00 22.50 55.00
Complete set with box 57.00 143.00 400.00

nn- Little Polly Flinders, The Story of, nd (1930s), no publ., 36 pgs., 2 1/2" x 3", Penny Book 2.00 5.00 15.00

nn- Little Red Hen, The, nd(1930s), np(Whitman), 36 pgs., Penny Book 2.00 5.00 15.00

nn- Little Red Riding Hood, nd(1930s), np(Whitman), 36 pgs., 3" x 2 1/2", Penny Book 2.00 5.00 15.00

nn- Little Red Riding Hood and the Big Bad Wolf (Disney), 1934, McKay, 36 pgs., stiff-c, Disney Studio-a
Sized (7 3/4" x 10") 24.00 60.00 170.00
Different version (6 1/4" x 8 1/2") blue spine 16.00 40.00 115.00

757- Little Women, 1934, Whitman, 4 3/4" x 5 1/4", 160 pgs., photo-c, movie scenes, starring Katharine Hepburn 14.00 35.00 100.00

Littlest Rebel, The (See Shirley Temple)

1181- Lone Ranger and his Horse Silver, 1935, Whitman, 432 pgs., Hal Arbo-a 20.00 50.00 140.00

1196- Lone Ranger and the Vanishing Herd, 1936, Whitman, 432 pgs. 16.00 40.00 110.00

1407- Lone Ranger and Dead Men's Mine, The, 1939, Whitman, 432 pgs. 14.00 35.00 100.00

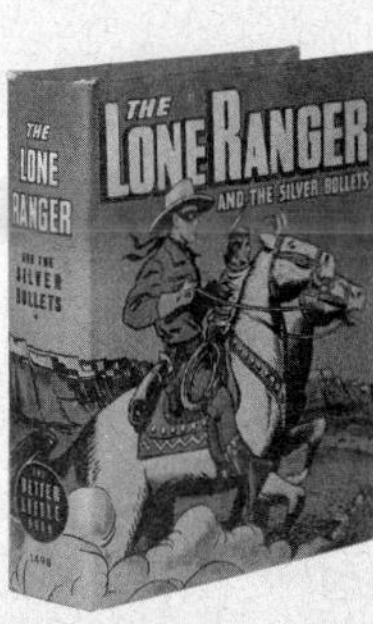

1498 - Lone Ranger and the Silver Bullets © Lone Ranger Inc.

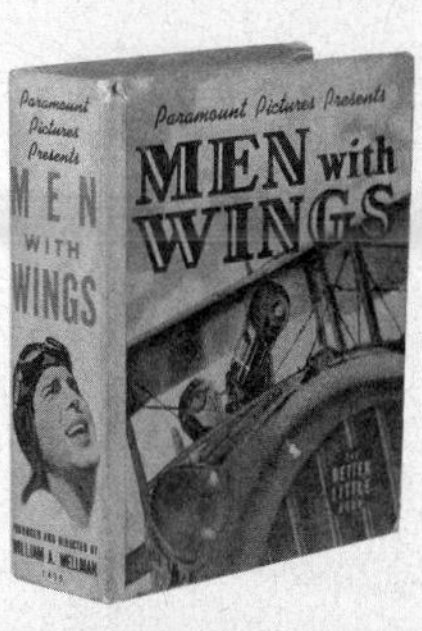

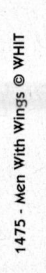

1475 - Men With Wings © WHIT

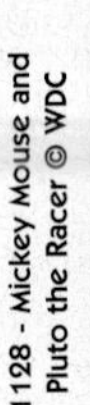
1128 - Mickey Mouse and Pluto the Racer © WDC

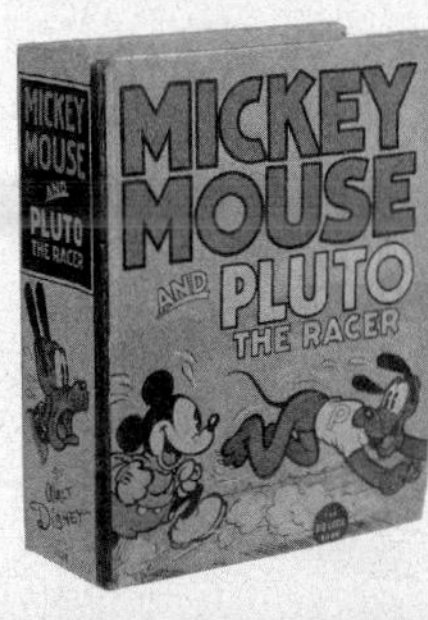

	GD	FN	VF/NM
1421- **Lone Ranger on the Barbary Coast, The**, 1944, Whitman, 352 pgs., Henry Vallely-a	12.00	30.00	80.00
1428- **Lone Ranger and the Secret Weapon, The**, 1943, Whitman,	12.00	30.00	80.00
1431- **Lone Ranger and the Secret Killer, The**, 1937, Whitman 432 pgs., H. Anderson-a	16.00	40.00	110.00
1450- **Lone Ranger and the Black Shirt Highwayman, The**, 1939, Whitman, 432 pgs.	14.00	35.00	100.00
1465- **Lone Ranger and the Menace of Murder Valley, The**, 1938, Whitman, 432 pgs., Robert Wiseman-a	13.00	32.50	90.00
1468- **Lone Ranger Follows Through, The**, 1941, Whitman, 432 pgs., H.E. Vallely-a	13.00	32.50	90.00
1477- **Lone Ranger and the Great Western Span, The**, 1942, Whitman, 424 pgs., H. E. Vallely-a	12.00	30.00	80.00
1489- **Lone Ranger and the Red Renegades, The**, 1939, Whitman, 432 pgs.	16.00	40.00	110.00
1498- **Lone Ranger and the Silver Bullets**, 1946, Whitman, 352 pgs., Henry E. Vallely-a	12.00	30.00	80.00
712-10- **Lone Ranger and the Secret of Somber Cavern, The**, 1950, Whitman	10.00	25.00	65.00
2013- **(#13)-Lone Ranger Outwits Crazy Cougar, The**, 1968, Whitman, 260 pgs., 39 cents, hard-c, color illos	4.00	10.00	27.00
5774- **Lone Ranger Outwits Crazy Cougar, The**, 1976, Whitman, 260 pgs., 49 cents, soft-c, color illos	4.00	10.00	22.00
5774-1- **Lone Ranger Outwits Crazy Cougar, The**, 1979, Whitman, 260 pgs., 69 cents, soft-c, color illos	4.00	10.00	22.00
nn- **Lone Ranger and the Lost Valley, The**, 1938, Dell, 196 pgs., Fast-Action Story, soft-c	26.00	65.00	180.00
1405- **Lone Star Martin of the Texas Rangers**, 1939, Whitman, 432 pgs.	12.00	30.00	85.00
19- **Lost City, The**, 1935, EVW, movie scenes	12.00	30.00	80.00
1103- **Lost Jungle, The** (With Clyde Beatty), 1936, Saalfield, movie scenes, hard-c	12.00	30.00	80.00
1583- **Lost Jungle, The** (With Clyde Beatty), 1936, Saalfield, movie scenes, soft -c	11.00	27.50	70.00
753- **Lost Patrol, The**, 1934, Whitman, 160 pgs., photo-c, movie scenes with Boris Karloff	12.00	30.00	75.00
nn- **Lost World, The - Jurassic Park 2**, 1997, Chronicle Books, 312 pgs., adapts movie, 1-color (green) illos	3.00	7.50	20.00
1189- **Mac of the Marines in Africa**, 1936, Whitman, 432 pgs.	10.00	25.00	60.00
1400- **Mac of the Marines in China**, 1938, Whitman, 432 pgs.	10.00	25.00	60.00
1100B- **Magic Tricks** (With explanations), 1938, Whitman, 36 pgs., 2 1/2" x 3 1/2", Penny Book, rabbit in hat-c	2.00	5.00	15.00
1100B- **Magic Tricks** (How to do them), 1938, Whitman, 36 pgs., 2 1/2" x 3 1/2", Penny Book, genie-c	2.00	5.00	15.00
Major Hoople (See Our Boarding House)			
2022-(#22)- **Major Matt Mason, Moon Mission**, 1968, Whitman, 256 pgs., hard-c, color illos.	4.00	10.00	27.00
1167- **Mandrake the Magician**, 1935, Whitman, 432 pgs., by Lee Falk & Phil Davis	16.00	40.00	115.00
1418- **Mandrake the Magician and the Flame Pearls**, 1946, Whitman, 352 pgs., by Lee Falk & Phil Davis	12.00	30.00	85.00
1431- **Mandrake the Magician and the Midnight Monster**, 1939, Whitman, 432 pgs., by Lee Falk & Phil Davis	14.00	35.00	100.00
1454- **Mandrake the Magician Mighty Solver of Mysteries**, 1941, Whitman, 432 pgs., by Lee Falk & Phil Davis, flip pictures	14.00	35.00	100.00
2011-(#11)-**Man From U.N.C.L.E., The**-The Calcutta Affair (TV Series), 1967, Whitman, 260 pgs., 39¢, hard-c, color illos	4.00	10.00	27.00
1429- **Marge's Little Lulu Alvin and Tubby**, 1947, Whitman, All Pictures Comics, Stanley-a	27.00	68.00	190.00
1438- **Mary Lee and the Mystery of the Indian Beads**, 1937, Whitman, 300 pgs.	10.00	25.00	60.00
1165- **Masked Man of the Mesa, The**, 1939, Saalfield, 400 pgs.	9.00	22.50	55.00
nn- **Mask of Zorro, The**, 1998, Chronicle Books, 312 pgs., adapts movie, 1-color (yellow-green) illos	1.00	2.50	9.00
1436- **Maximo the Amazing Superman**, 1940, Whitman, 432 pgs., Henry E. Vallely-a	12.00	30.00	85.00

	GD	FN	VF/NM
1444- **Maximo the Amazing Superman and the Crystals of Doom**, 1941, Whitman,432 pgs., Henry E. Vallely-a	12.00	30.00	85.00
1445- **Maximo the Amazing Superman and the Supermachine**, 1941, Whitman, 432 pgs.	12.00	30.00	85.00
755- **Men of the Mounted**, 1934, Whitman, 320 pgs.	12.00	30.00	80.00
nn- **Men of the Mounted**, 1933, Whitman, 52 pgs., 3 1/2" x 5 3/4", premium-no ads; other versions with Poll Parrot & Perkins ad; soft-c	14.00	35.00	100.00
nn- **Men of the Mounted**, 1934, Whitman, Cocomalt premium, soft-c, by Ted McCall	10.00	25.00	60.00
1475- **Men With Wings**, 1938, Whitman, 240 pgs., photo-c, movie scenes (Paramount Pics.)	12.00	30.00	85.00
1170- **Mickey Finn**, 1940, Saalfield, 400 pgs., by Frank Leonard	10.00	25.00	865.00
717- **Mickey Mouse** (Disney), (1st printing) 1933, Whitman, 320 pgs., Gottfredson-a, skinny Mickey on cover	235.00	588.00	2000.00
717- **Mickey Mouse** (Disney), (2nd printing)1933, Whitman, 320 pgs., Gottfredson-a, regular Mickey on cover	150.00	375.00	1200.00
nn- **Mickey Mouse** (Disney), 1933, Dean & Son, Great Big Midget Book, 320 pgs.	123.00	308.00	900.00
731- **Mickey Mouse the Mail Pilot** (Disney), 1933, Whitman, (This is the same book as the 1st Mickey Mouse BLB #717(2nd printing) but with "The Mail Pilot" printed on the front. Lower left of back cover has a small box printed over the existing "No. 717." "No. 731" is printed next to it.) (Sold at auction in 2014 in VG+ condition for $7170, and in FR/GD condition for $2,500)			
726- **Mickey Mouse in Blaggard Castle** (Disney), 1934, Whitman, 320 pgs., Gottfredson-a	30.00	75.00	210.00
731- **Mickey Mouse the Mail Pilot** (Disney), 1933, Whitman, 300 pgs., Gottfredson-a	30.00	75.00	210.00
731- **Mickey Mouse the Mail Pilot** (Disney), 1933, Whitman, 300 pgs., soft cover; Gottfredson-a (Rare)	68.00	170.00	475.00
nn- **Mickey Mouse the Mail Pilot** (Disney), 1933, Whitman, 292 pgs., American Oil Co. premium, soft-c, Gottfredson-a; another version 3 1/2" x 4 3/4"	30.00	75.00	210.00
nn- **Mickey Mouse the Mail Pilot** (Disney), 1933, Dean & Son, Great Big Midget Book (Rare)	124.00	311.00	975.00
750- **Mickey Mouse Sails for Treasure Island** (Disney), 1933, Whitman, 320 pgs., Gottfredson-a	30.00	75.00	210.00
nn- **Mickey Mouse Sails for Treasure Island** (Disney), 1935, Whitman, 196 pgs., premium-no ads, soft-c, Gottfredson-a (Scarce)	36.00	90.00	250.00
nn- **Mickey Mouse Sails for Treasure Island** (Disney), 1935, Whitman, 196 pgs., Kolynos Dental Cream premium (Scarce)	36.00	90.00	250.00
nn- **Mickey Mouse Sails for Treasure Island** (Disney), 1933, Dean & Son, Great Big Midget Book, 320 pgs.	118.00	295.00	825.00
756- **Mickey Mouse Presents a Walt Disney Silly Symphony** (Disney), 1934, Whitman, 240 pgs., Bucky Bug app.	29.00	73.00	200.00
801- **Mickey Mouse's Summer Vacation**, 1948, Whitman, hard-c, Story Hour series	12.00	30.00	85.00
1058- **Mickey Mouse Box, The** (Disney), 1939, Whitman, 10" x 11 1/2" x 1", (set includes 6 books from the 1058 series, all 5" x 5 1/2", 68 pgs. Lid features Mickey & Minnie, Donald Duck, Goofy and Clarabelle Cow. The six books are: The Brave Little Tailor, Mother Pluto, The Ugly Ducklings, The Practical Pig, Timid Elmer, and The Farmyard Symphony (a VF set sold for $5175 in Nov, 2014)			
1111- **Mickey Mouse Presents Walt Disney's Silly Symphonies Stories**, 1936, Whitman, 432 pgs., Donald Duck app.	29.00	73.00	200.00
1128- **Mickey Mouse and Pluto the Racer** (Disney), 1936, Whitman, 432 pgs., Gottfredson-a	24.00	60.00	170.00
1139- **Mickey Mouse the Detective** (Disney), 1934, Whitman, 300 pgs., Gottfredson-a	29.00	73.00	200.00
1139- **Mickey Mouse the Detective** (Disney), 1934, Whitman, 304 pgs., premium-no ads, soft-c, Gottfredson-a (Scarce)	46.00	115.00	325.00
1153- **Mickey Mouse and the Bat Bandit** (Disney), 1935, Whitman, 432 pgs., Gottfredson-a	26.00	65.00	180.00
nn- **Mickey Mouse and the Bat Bandit** (Disney), 1935, Whitman, 436 pgs., premium-no ads, 3-color, soft-c, Gottfredson-a (Scarce)	46.00	115.00	325.00

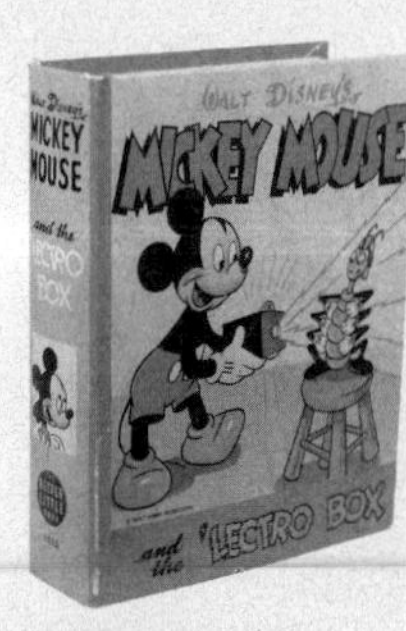

1413 - Mickey Mouse and the 'Lectro Box © DIS

21 - Midsummer Night's Dream © EVW

1400 - Nancy and Sluggo © WHIT

	GD	FN	VF/NM
1160- **Mickey Mouse and Bobo the Elephant** (Disney), 1935, Whitman, 432 pgs., Gottfredson-a	26.00	65.00	180.00
1187- **Mickey Mouse and the Sacred Jewel** (Disney), 1936, Whitman, 432 pgs., Gottfredson-a	24.00	60.00	170.00
1401- **Mickey Mouse in the Treasure Hunt** (Disney), 1941, Whitman, 430 pgs., flip pictures of Pluto, Gottfredson-a	22.00	52.50	155.00
1409- **Mickey Mouse Runs His Own Newspaper** (Disney), 1937, Whitman, 432 pgs., Gottfredson-a	22.00	52.50	155.00
1413- **Mickey Mouse and the 'Lectro Box** (Disney), 1946, Whitman, 352 pgs., Gottfredson-a	16.00	40.00	115.00
1417- **Mickey Mouse on Sky Island** (Disney), 1941, Whitman, 432 pgs., flip pictures, Gottfredson-a; considered by Gottfredson to be his best Mickey story	22.00	52.50	155.00
1428- **Mickey Mouse in the Foreign Legion** (Disney), 1940, Whitman, 432 pgs., Gottfredson-a	22.00	52.50	155.00
1429- **Mickey Mouse and the Magic Lamp** (Disney), 1942, Whitman, 432 pgs., flip pictures	22.00	52.50	155.00
1433- **Mickey Mouse and the Lazy Daisy Mystery** (Disney), 1947, Whitman, 288 pgs.	16.00	40.00	115.00
1444- **Mickey Mouse in the World of Tomorrow** (Disney), 1948, Whitman, 288 pgs., Gottfredson-a	24.00	60.00	170.00
1451- **Mickey Mouse and the Desert Palace** (Disney), 1948, Whitman, 288 pgs.	16.00	40.00	115.00
1463- **Mickey Mouse and the Pirate Submarine** (Disney), 1939, Whitman, 432 pgs., Gottfredson-a	22.00	52.50	155.00
1464- **Mickey Mouse and the Stolen Jewels** (Disney), 1949, Whitman, 288 pgs.	21.00	52.50	145.00
1471- **Mickey Mouse and the Dude Ranch Bandit** (Disney), 1943, Whitman, 432 pgs., flip pictures	22.00	52.50	155.00
1475- **Mickey Mouse and the 7 Ghosts** (Disney), 1940, Whitman, 432 pgs., Gottfredson-a	22.00	52.50	155.00
1476- **Mickey Mouse in the Race for Riches** (Disney), 1938, Whitman, 432 pgs., Gottfredson-a	22.00	52.50	155.00
1483- **Mickey Mouse Bell Boy Detective** (Disney), 1945, Whitman, 352 pgs.	21.00	52.50	145.00
1499- **Mickey Mouse on the Cave-Man Island** (Disney), 1944, Whitman, 352 pgs.	21.00	52.50	145.00
2004- **Mickey Mouse With This Big Big Color Set, Here Comes** (Disney), 1936, Whitman, (Very Rare), 224 pgs., 12" x 8 1/4" box, with red, yellow and blue crayons, contains 224 loose pages to color, reprinted from early Mickey Mouse related movie and strip reprints. Attached to center of lid is a 5" tall separate die-cut cardboard Mickey Mouse figure (a VF/NM set sold for $1701 in July 2014)	235.00	588.00	2000.00
2020-(#20)- **Mickey Mouse, Adventure in Outer Space,** 1968, Whitman, 256 pgs.,hard-c, color illos.	4.00	10.00	27.00
3059- **Mickey Mouse Big Little Set** (Disney), 1936, Whitman, 8 1/4" x 8 1/2", with crayons, box contains a 4" x 5 1/4" soft-c book with 160 pgs. of Mickey to color, reprinted from early Mickey Mouse BLBs, (Rare) (a copy in NM sold for $1897 in Nov, 2011, a VF copy sold for $1147 in 2013)			
5750- **Mickey Mouse, Adventure in Outer Space,** 1973, Whitman, 256 pgs.,soft-c, 39 cents, color illos.	2.00	5.00	15.00
3049- **Mickey Mouse and His Big Little Kit** (Disney), 1937, Whitman, 384 pgs., 4 1/2" x 6 1/2" box, includes miniature box of 4 crayons-red, yellow, blue and green (a copy in VF/NM sold for $335 in 2015)			
3061- **Mickey Mouse to Draw and Color** (The Big Little Set), nd (early 1930s), Whitman, with crayons; box contains 320 loose pages to color, reprinted from early Mickey Mouse BLBs	123.00	308.00	880.00
4062- **Mickey Mouse, The Story Of,** 1935, Whitman, 7" x 9 1/2", 320 pgs., Big Big Book, Gottfredson-a	84.00	210.00	585.00
4062- **Mickey Mouse and the Smugglers, The Story Of,** 1935, Whitman, (Scarce), 7" x 9 1/2", 320 pgs., Big Big Book, same contents as above version; Gottfredson-a	84.00	210.00	585.00
708-10- **Mickey Mouse on the Haunted Island** (Disney), 1950, Whitman, Gottfredson-a	12.00	30.00	80.00
nn- **Mickey Mouse and Minnie at Macy's,** 1934 Whitman, 148 pgs., 3 1/4" x 3 1/2", soft-c, R. H. Macy & Co. Christmas giveaway (Rare, less than 20 known copies)	311.00	778.00	2800.00
nn- **Mickey Mouse and Minnie March to Macy's,** 1935, Whitman, 148 pgs., 3 1/2" x 3 1/2", soft-c, R. H. Macy & Co. Christmas giveaway (scarce)	271.00	678.00	2300.00

	GD	FN	VF/NM
nn- **Mickey Mouse and the Magic Carpet,** 1935, Whitman, 148 pgs., 3 1/2"x 4", soft-c, giveaway, Gottfredson-a, Donald Duck app.	124.00	310.00	925.00
nn- **Mickey Mouse Silly Symphonies,** 1934, Dean & Son, Ltd (England), 48 pgs., with 4 pop-ups, Babes In The Woods, King Neptune			
With dust jacket	138.00	345.00	1100.00
Without dust jacket	100.00	250.00	700.00
nn- **Mickey Mouse the Sheriff of Nugget Gulch** (Disney) 1938, Dell, 196 pgs., Fast-Action Story, soft-c, Gottfredson-a	36.00	90.00	250.00
nn- **Mickey Mouse Waddle Book,** 1934, BRP, 20 pgs., 7 1/2" x 10", forerunner of the Blue Ribbon Pop-Up books; with 4 removable articulated cardboard characters Book Only	100.00	200.00	525.00
(A complete copy in VG/FN w/VF dustjacket sold for $5676 in 2010)			
(A complete copy in VF with dustjacket ramp & band sold for $573 in 2014)			
nn- **Mickey Mouse with Goofy and Mickey's Nephews,** 1938, Dell, Fast-Action Story, Gottfredson-a	36.00	90.00	250.00
16- **Mickey Mouse and Pluto** (Disney), 1942, Dell, 196 pgs., Fast-Action story	36.00	90.00	250.00
512- **Mickey Mouse Wee Little Books** (In open box), nn, 1934, Whitman, 44 pgs., small size, soft-c			
Mickey Mouse and Tanglefoot	13.00	32.50	90.00
Mickey Mouse at the Carnival	13.00	32.50	90.00
Mickey Mouse Will Not Quit!	13.00	32.50	90.00
Mickey Mouse Wins the Race!	13.00	32.50	90.00
Mickey Mouse's Misfortune	13.00	32.50	90.00
Mickey Mouse's Uphill Fight	13.00	32.50	90.00
Complete set with box	96.00	240.00	675.00
1493- **Mickey Rooney and Judy Garland and How They Got into the Movies,** 1941, Whitman, 432 pgs., photo-c	12.00	30.00	75.00
1427- **Mickey Rooney Himself,** 1939, Whitman, 240 pgs., photo-c, movie scenes, life story	12.00	30.00	75.00
532- **Mickey's Dog Pluto** (Disney), 1943, Whitman, All Picture Comics, A Tall Comic Book , 3 3/4" x 8 3/4"	20.00	50.00	140.00
284- **Midget Jumbo Coloring Book,** 1935, Saalfield	43.00	108.00	300.00
2113- **Midget Jumbo Coloring Book,** 1935, Saalfield, 240 pgs.	43.00	108.00	300.00
21- **Midsummer Night's Dream,** 1935, EVW, movie scenes	12.00	30.00	85.00
nn- **Minute-Man** (Mystery of the Spy Ring), 1941, Fawcett, Dime Action Book	36.00	90.00	250.00
710- **Moby Dick the Great White Whale, The Story of,** 1934, Whitman, 160 pgs., photo-c, movie scenes from "The Sea Beast"	12.00	30.00	85.00
746- **Moon Mullins and Kayo** (Kayo and Moon Mullins-inside), 1933, Whitman, 320 pgs., Frank Willard-c/a	12.00	30.00	75.00
nn- **Moon Mullins and Kayo,** 1933, Whitman, Cocomalt premium, soft-c, by Willard	12.00	30.00	75.00
1134- **Moon Mullins and the Plushbottom Twins,** 1935, Whitman, 432 pgs., Willard-c/a	12.00	30.00	75.00
nn- **Moon Mullins and the Plushbottom Twins,** 1935, Whitman, 436 pgs., premium-no ads, 3-color, soft-c, by Willard	18.00	45.00	125.00
1058- **Mother Pluto** (Disney), 1939, Whitman, 68 pgs., hard-c	11.00	27.50	70.00
1100B- **Movie Jokes** (From the talkies), 1938, Whitman, 36 pgs., 2 1/2" x 3 1/2", Penny Book	2.00	5.00	15.00
1408- **Mr. District Attorney on the Job,** 1941, Whitman, 432 pgs., flip pictures	10.00	25.00	65.00
nn- **Musicians of Bremen, The,** nd (1930s), np (Whitman), 36 pgs., 3" x 2 1/2", Penny Book	2.00	5.00	15.00
1113- **Mutt and Jeff,** 1936, Whitman, 300 pgs., by Bud Fisher	26.00	65.00	180.00
1116- **My Life and Times** (By Shirley Temple), 1936, Saalfield, Little Big Book, hard-c, photo-c/illos	12.00	30.00	85.00
1596- **My Life and Times** (By Shirley Temple), 1936, Saalfield, Little Big Book, soft-c, photo-c/illos	12.00	30.00	85.00
1497- **Myra North Special Nurse and Foreign Spies,** 1938, Whitman, 432 pgs.	11.00	27.50	70.00
1400- **Nancy and Sluggo,** 1946, Whitman, All Pictures Comics, Ernie Bushmiller-a	12.00	30.00	75.00

1109 - Oswald the Lucky Rabbit © DIS

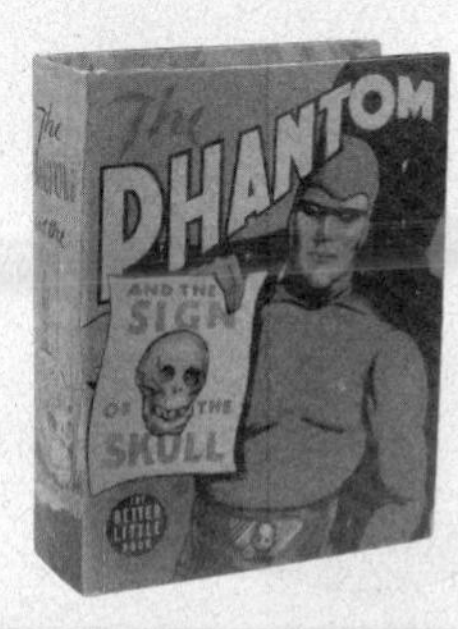

1474 - The Phantom and the Sign of the Skull © KING

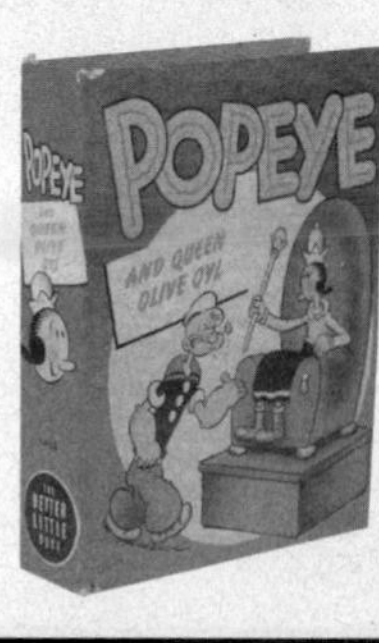

1458 - Popeye and Queen Olive Oyl © KING

	GD	FN	VF/NM
1487- **Nancy Has Fun**, 1946, Whitman, All Pictures Comics	12.00	30.00	75.00
1150- **Napoleon and Uncle Elby**, 1938, Saalfield, 400 pgs., by Clifford McBride	11.00	27.50	70.00
1166- **Napoleon Uncle Elby And Little Mary**, 1939, Saalfield, 400 pgs., by Clifford McBride	11.00	27.50	70.00
1179- **Ned Brant Adventure Bound**, 1940, Saalfield, 400 pgs.	10.00	25.00	60.00
1146- **Nevada Rides The Danger Trail**, 1938, Saalfield, 400 pgs., J.R. White-a	10.00	25.00	60.00
1147- **Nevada Whalen, Avenger**, 1938, Saalfield, 400 pgs.	10.00	25.00	60.00
Nicodemus O'Malley (See Top-Line Comics)			
1115- **Og Son of Fire**, 1936, Whitman, 432 pgs.	12.00	30.00	85.00
1419- **Oh, Blondie the Bumsteads** (See Blondie)			
11- **Oliver Twist**, 1935, EVW (Five Star Library), movie scenes, starring Dickie Moore (Monogram Pictures)	12.00	30.00	80.00
718- **Once Upon a Time**, 1933, Whitman, 364 pgs., soft-c	12.00	30.00	80.00
712- **100 Fairy Tales for Children, The**, 1933, Whitman, 288 pgs., Circle Library	10.00	25.00	60.00
1099- **One Night of Love**, 1935, Saalfield, 160 pgs., hard-c, photo-c, movie scenes, Columbia Pictures, starring Grace Moore	12.00	30.00	85.00
1579- **One Night of Love**, 1935, Sat, 160 pgs., soft-c, photo-c, movie scenes, Columbia Pictures, starring Grace Moore	12.00	30.00	85.00
1155- **$1000 Reward**, 1938, Saalfield, 400 pgs.	10.00	25.00	60.00
Orphan Annie (See Little Orphan ...)			
L17- **O'Shaughnessy's Boy**, 1935, Lynn, 192 pgs., movie scenes, w/Wallace Beery & Jackie Cooper (Metro-Goldwyn-Mayer)	11.00	27.50	70.00
1109- **Oswald the Lucky Rabbit**, 1934, Whitman, 288 pgs.	16.00	40.00	115.00
1403- **Oswald Rabbit Plays G-Man**, 1937, Whitman, 240 pgs., movie scenes by Walter Lantz	18.00	45.00	125.00
1190- **Our Boarding House, Major Hoople and his Horse**, 1940, Saalfield, 400 pgs.	11.00	27.50	70.00
1085- **Our Gang**, 1934, Saalfield, 160 pgs., photo-c, movie scenes, hard-c	15.00	37.50	105.00
1315- **Our Gang**, 1934, Saalfield, 160 pgs., photo-c, movie scenes, soft-c	15.00	37.50	105.00
1451- **"Our Gang" on the March**, 1942, Whitman, 432 pgs., flip pictures, Vallely-a	15.00	37.50	105.00
1456- **Our Gang Adventures**, 1948, Whitman, 288 pgs.	12.00	30.00	85.00
nn- **Paramount Newsreel Men with Admiral Byrd in Little America**, 1934, Whitman, 96 pgs., 6 1/4" x 6 1/4", photo-c, photo ill.	14.00	35.00	100.00
nn- **Patch**, nd (1930s), np (Whitman), 36 pgs., 3" x 2 1/2", Penny Book	2.00	5.00	15.00
1445- **Pat Nelson Ace of Test Pilots**, 1937, Whitman, 432 pgs.	10.00	25.00	60.00
1411- **Peggy Brown and the Mystery Basket**, 1941, Whitman, 432 pgs., flip pictures, Henry E. Vallely-a	10.00	25.00	65.00
1423- **Peggy Brown and the Secret Treasure**, 1947, Whitman, 288 pgs., Henry E. Vallely-a	10.00	25.00	65.00
1427- **Peggy Brown and the Runaway Auto Trailer**, 1937, Whitman, 300 pgs., Henry E. Vallely-a	10.00	25.00	65.00
1463- **Peggy Brown and the Jewel of Fire**, 1943, Whitman, 352 pgs., Henry E. Vallely-a	10.00	25.00	65.00
1491- **Peggy Brown in the Big Haunted House**, 1940, Whitman, 432 pgs., Vallely-a	10.00	25.00	65.00
1143- **Peril Afloat**, 1938, Saalfield, 400 pgs.	10.00	25.00	60.00
1199- **Perry Winkle and the Rinkeydinks**, 1937, Whitman, 432 pgs., by Martin Branner	14.00	35.00	95.00
1487- **Perry Winkle and the Rinkeydinks get a Horse**, 1938, Whitman, 432 pgs., by Martin Branner	14.00	35.00	95.00
Peter Pan (See Wee Little Books)			
nn- **Peter Rabbit**, nd(1930s), np(Whitman), 36 pgs., Penny Book, 3" x 2 1/2"	5.00	12.50	33.00
Peter Rabbit's Carrots (See Wee Little Books)			
1100- **Phantom, The**, 1936, Whitman, 432 pgs., by Lee Falk & Ray Moore	29.00	73.00	200.00
1416- **Phantom and the Girl of Mystery, The**, 1947, Whitman, 352 pgs. by Falk & Moore	12.00	30.00	80.00
1421- **Phantom and Desert Justice, The**, 1941, Whitman, 432 pgs., flip pictures, by Falk & Moore	14.00	35.00	100.00
1468- **Phantom and the Sky Pirates, The**, 1945, Whitman, 352 pgs., by Falk & Moore	13.00	32.50	90.00
1474- **Phantom and the Sign of the Skull, The**, 1939, Whitman, 432 pgs., by Falk & Moore	16.00	40.00	110.00
1489- **Phantom, Return of the...**, 1942, Whitman, 432 pgs., flip pictures, by Falk & Moore	14.00	35.00	100.00
1130- **Phil Burton, Sleuth** (Scout Book), 1937, Saalfield, hard-c	7.00	17.50	40.00
Pied Piper of Hamlin (See Wee Little Books)			
1466- **Pilot Pete Dive Bomber**, 1941, Whitman, 432 pgs., flip pictures	10.00	25.00	60.00
5776- **Pink Panther Adventures in Z-Land, The**, 1976, Whitman, 260 pgs., soft-c, 49 cents, B&W	1.00	2.50	8.00
5776-2- **Pink Panther Adventures in Z-Land, The**, 1980, Whitman, 260 pgs., soft-c, 79 cents, B&W	1.00	2.50	8.00
5783-2- **Pink Panther at Castle Kreep, The**, 1980, Whitman, 260 pgs., soft-c, 79 cents, B&W	1.00	2.50	8.00
Pinocchio and Jiminy Cricket (See Walt Disney's ...)			
nn- **Pioneers of the Wild West** (Blue-c), 1933, World Syndicate, High Lights of History Series	7.00	17.50	40.00
With dustjacket	29.00	73.00	200.00
nn- **Pioneers of the Wild West** (Red-c), 1933, World Syndicate, High Lights of History Series	7.00	17.50	40.00
1123- **Plainsman, The**, 1936, Whitman, 240 pgs., photo-c, movie scenes with Gary Cooper (Paramount Pics.)	14.00	35.00	100.00
Pluto (See Mickey's Dog ... & Walt Disney's ...)			
2114- **Pocket Coloring Book**, 1935, Saalfield	27.00	68.00	190.00
1060- **Polly and Her Pals on the Farm**, 1934, Saalfield, 164 pgs., hard-c, by Cliff Sterrett	12.00	30.00	80.00
1310- **Polly and Her Pals on the Farm**, 1934, Saalfield, soft-c	12.00	30.00	80.00
1051- **Popeye, Adventures of...**, 1934, Saalfield, oblong-size, E.C. Segar-a, hard-c	45.00	113.00	315.00
1088- **Popeye in Puddleburg**, 1934, Saalfield, 160 pgs., hard-c, E. C. Segar-a	19.00	47.50	135.00
1113- **Popeye Starring in Choose Your Weppins**, 1936, Saalfield, 160 pgs., hard-c, Segar-a	37.00	93.00	260.00
1117- **Popeye's Ark**, 1936, Saalfield, 4 1/2" x 5 1/2", hard-c, Segar-a	19.00	47.50	135.00
1163- **Popeye Sees the Sea**, 1936, Whitman, 432 pgs., Segar-a	20.00	50.00	140.00
1301- **Popeye, Adventures of...**, 1934, Saalfield, oblong-size, Segar-a	45.00	113.00	315.00
1318- **Popeye in Puddleburg**, 1934, Saalfield, 160 pgs., soft-c, Segar-a	19.00	47.50	135.00
1405- **Popeye and the Jeep**, 1937, Whitman, 432 pgs., Segar-a	20.00	50.00	140.00
1406- **Popeye the Super-Fighter**, 1939, Whitman, All Pictures Comics, flip pictures, Segar-a	19.00	47.50	135.00
1422- **Popeye the Sailor Man**, 1947, Whitman, All Pictures Comics	12.00	30.00	85.00
1450- **Popeye in Quest of His Poopdeck Pappy**, 1937, Whitman, 432 pgs., Segar-c/a	14.00	35.00	100.00
1458- **Popeye and Queen Olive Oyl**, 1949, Whitman, 288 pgs., Sagendorf-a	12.00	30.00	85.00
1459- **Popeye and the Quest for the Rainbird**, 1943, Whitman, Winner & Zaboly-a	14.00	35.00	95.00
1480- **Popeye the Spinach Eater**, 1945, Whitman, All Pictures Comics	12.00	30.00	85.00
1485- **Popeye in a Sock for Susan's Sake**, 1940, Whitman, 432 pgs., flip pictures	14.00	35.00	95.00
1497- **Popeye and Caster Oyl the Detective**, 1941, Whitman, 432 pgs. flip pictures, Segar-a	16.00	40.00	115.00

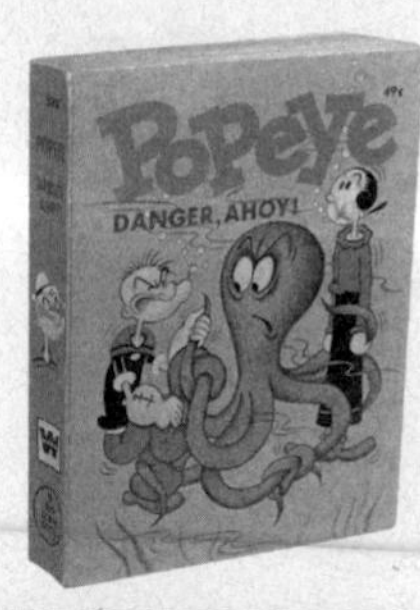

5768 - Popeye, Danger Ahoy! © KING

1176 - Powder Smoke Range © WHIT

1441 - The Range Busters © WHIT

	GD	FN	VF/NM
1499- **Popeye and the Deep Sea Mystery**, 1939, Whitman, 432 pgs., Segar-c/a	16.00	40.00	115.00
1593- **Popeye Starring in Choose Your Weppins**, 1936, Saalfield, 160 pgs., soft-c, Segar-a	16.00	40.00	115.00
1597- **Popeye's Ark**, 1936, Saalfield, 4 1/2" x 5 1/2", soft-c, Segar-a	16.00	40.00	115.00
2008-(#8)- **Popeye-Ghost Ship to Treasure Island**, 1967, Whitman, 260 pgs., 39 cents, hard-c, color illos	4.00	10.00	27.00
5755- **Popeye-Ghost Ship to Treasure Island**, 1973, Whitman, 260 pgs., soft-c, color illos	2.00	5.00	15.00
2034-(#34)- **Popeye, Danger Ahoy!**, 1969, Whitman, 256 pgs., hard-c, color illos.	4.00	10.00	25.00
5768- **Popeye, Danger Ahoy!**, 1975, Whitman, 256 pgs., soft-c, color illos.	2.00	5.00	15.00
4063- **Popeye, Thimble Theatre Starring**, 1935, Whitman, 7" x 9 1/2", 320 pgs., Big Big Book, Segar-c/a; (Cactus cover w/yellow logo)	86.00	215.00	600.00
4063- **Popeye, Thimble Theatre Starring**, 1935, Whitman, 7" x 9 1/2", 320 pgs., Big Big Book, Segar-c/a; (Big Balloon-c with red logo), (2nd printing w/same contents as above)	100.00	250.00	700.00
5761- **Popeye and Queen Olive Oyl**, 1973, 260 pgs., B&W, soft-c	4.00	10.00	27.00
5761-2- **Popeye and Queen Olive Oyl**, 1973 (1980-reprint of 1973 version), 260 pgs., 79 cents, B&W, soft-c	2.00	5.00	15.00
103- **"Pop-Up" Buck Rogers in the Dangerous Mission** (with Pop-Up picture), 1934, BRP, 62 pgs., The Midget Pop-Up Book w/Pop-Up in center of book, Calkins-a	122.00	305.00	875.00
206- **"Pop-Up" Buck Rogers - Strange Adventures in the Spider Ship, The**, 1935, BRP, 24 pgs., 8" x 9", 3 Pop-Ups, hard-c, by Dick Calkins	122.00	305.00	875.00
nn- **"Pop-Up" Cinderella**, 1933, BRP, 7 1/2" x 9 3/4", 4 Pop-Ups, hard-c			
With dustjacket ($2.00)	69.00	173.00	485.00
Without dustjacket	58.00	145.00	410.00
207- **"Pop-Up" Dick Tracy-Capture of Boris Arson**, 1935, BRP, 24 pgs., 8" x 9", 3 Pop-Ups, hard-c, by Gould	69.00	173.00	485.00
210- **"Pop-Up" Flash Gordon Tournament of Death, The**, 1935, BRP, 24 pgs., 8" x 9", 3 Pop-Ups, hard-c, by Alex Raymond	118.00	295.00	825.00
202- **"Pop-Up" Goldilocks and the Three Bears, The**, 1934, BRP, 24 pgs., 8" x 9", 3 Pop-Ups, hard-c	36.00	90.00	250.00
nn- **"Pop-Up" Jack and the Beanstalk**, 1933, BRP, hard-c (50 cents), 1 Pop-Up	36.00	90.00	250.00
nn- **"Pop-Up" Jack the Giant Killer**, 1933, BRP, hard-c (50 cents), 1 Pop-Up	36.00	90.00	250.00
nn- **"Pop-Up" Jack the Giant Killer**, 1933, BRP, 4 Pop-Ups, hard-c			
With dustjacket ($2.00)	69.00	173.00	485.00
Without dust jacket	58.00	145.00	410.00
105- **"Pop-Up" Little Black Sambo**, (with Pop-Up picture), 1934, BRP, 62 pgs., The Midget Pop-Up Book, one Pop-Up in center of book	48.00	120.00	335.00
208- **"Pop-Up" Little Orphan Annie and Jumbo the Circus Elephant**, 1935, BRP, 24 pgs., 8" x 9 1/2", 3 Pop-Ups, hard-c, by H. Gray	68.00	170.00	475.00
nn- **"Pop-Up" Little Red Ridinghood**, 1933, BRP, hard-c (50 cents), 1 Pop-Up	43.00	108.00	300.00
nn- **"Pop-Up" Mickey Mouse, The**, 1933, BRP, 34 pgs., 6 1/2" x 9", 3 Pop-Ups, hard-c, Gottfredson-a (75 cents)	55.00	137.00	385.00
nn- **"Pop-Up" Mickey Mouse in King Arthur's Court, The**,1933, BRP, 56 pgs., 7 1/2" x 9 1/4", 4 Pop-Ups, hard-c, Gottfredson-a			
With dust jacket ($2.00)	124.00	310.00	925.00
Without dustjacket	96.00	240.00	675.00
101- **"Pop-Up" Mickey Mouse in "Ye Olden Days"** (with Pop-Up picture), 1934, 62 pgs., BRP, The Midget Pop-Up Book, one Pop-Up in center of book, Gottfredson-a	110.00	274.00	775.00
nn- **"Pop-Up" Minnie Mouse, The**, 1933, BRP, 36 pgs., 6 1/2" x 9", 3 Pop-Ups, hard-c (75 cents), Gottfredson-a	51.00	128.00	360.00
203- **"Pop-Up" Mother Goose, The**, 1934, BRP, 24 pgs., 8" x 9 1/4", 3 Pop-Ups, hard-c	43.00	108.00	300.00
nn- **"Pop-Up" Mother Goose Rhymes, The**, 1933, BRP, 96 pgs., 7 1/2" x 9 1/4", 4 Pop-Ups, hard-c			
With dustjacket ($2.00)	46.00	115.00	325.00
Without dustjacket	43.00	108.00	300.00
209- **"Pop-Up" New Adventures of Tarzan**, 1935, BRP, 24 pgs., 8" x 9", 3 Pop-Ups, hard-c	110.00	274.00	775.00
104- **"Pop-Up" Peter Rabbit, The** (with Pop-Up picture), 1934, BRP, 62 pgs., The Midget Pop-Up Book, one Pop-Up in center of book	51.00	128.00	360.00
nn- **"Pop-Up" Pinocchio**, 1933, BRP, 7 1/2" x 9 3/4", 4 Pop-Ups, hard-c			
With dustjacket ($2.00)	62.00	154.00	435.00
Without dust jacket	55.00	137.00	385.00
102- **"Pop-Up" Popeye among the White Savages** (with Pop-Up picture), 1934, BRP, 62 pgs., The Midget Pop-Up Book, one Pop-Up in center of book, E. C. Segar-a	61.00	153.00	425.00
205- **"Pop-Up" Popeye with the Hag of the Seven Seas, The**, 1935, BRP, 24 pgs., 8" x 9", 3 Pop-Ups, hard-c, Segar-a	68.00	170.00	475.00
201- **"Pop-Up" Puss In Boots, The**, 1934, BRP, 24 pgs., 3 Pop-Ups, hard-c	37.00	93.00	260.00
nn- **"Pop-Up" Silly Symphonies, The** (Mickey Mouse Presents His ...), 1933, BRP, 56 pgs., 9 3/4" x 7 1/2", 4 Pop-Ups, hard-c			
With dust jacket ($2.00)	107.00	268.00	750.00
Without dust jacket	71.00	178.00	500.00
nn- **"Pop-Up" Sleeping Beauty**, 1933, BRP, hard-c, (50 cents), 1 Pop-up	43.00	108.00	300.00
212- **"Pop-Up" Terry and the Pirates in Shipwrecked, The**, 1935, BRP, 24 pgs., 8" x 9", 3 Pop-Ups, hard-c	7500	188.00	525.00
211- **"Pop-Up" Tim Tyler in the Jungle, The**, 1935, BRP, 24 pgs., 8" x 9", 3 Pop-Ups, hard-c	46.00	115.00	325.00
1404- **Porky Pig and His Gang**, 1946, Whitman, All Pictures Comics, Barks-a, reprints Four Color #48	20.00	50.00	140.00
1408- **Porky Pig and Petunia**, 1942, Whitman, All Pictures Comics, flip pictures, reprints Four Color #16 & Famous Gang Book of Comics	12.00	30.00	85.00
1176- **Powder Smoke Range**, 1935, Whitman, 240 pgs., photo-c, movie scenes, Hoot Gibson, Harey Carey app. (RKO Radio Pict.)	11.00	27.50	70.00
1058- **Practical Pig!, The** (Disney), 1939, Whitman, 68 pgs., 5" x 5 1/2", hard-c	11.00	27.50	70.00
758- **Prairie Bill and the Covered Wagon**, 1934, Whitman, 384 pgs., Hal Arbo-a	10.00	25.00	60.00
nn- **Prairie Bill and the Covered Wagon**, 1934, Whitman, 390 pgs., premium-no ads, 3-color, soft-c, Hal Arbo-a	12.00	30.00	85.00
1440- **Punch Davis of the U.S. Aircraft Carrier**, 1945, Whitman, 352 pgs.	9.00	22.50	55.00
nn- **Puss in Boots**, nd(1930s), np(Whitman), 36 pgs., Penny Book	2.00	5.00	15.00
1100B- **Puzzle Book**, 1938, Whitman, 36 pgs., 2 1/2" x 3 1/2", Penny Book	3.00	7.50	20.00
1100B- **Puzzles**, 1938, Whitman, 36 pgs., 2 1/2" x 3 1/2", Penny Book	3.00	7.50	20.00
1100B- **Quiz Book, The**, 1938, Whitman, 36 pgs., 2 1/2" x 3 1/2", Penny Book	3.00	7.50	20.00
1142- **Radio Patrol**, 1935, Whitman, 432 pgs., by Eddie Sullivan & Charlie Schmidt (#1)	12.00	30.00	75.00
1173- **Radio Patrol Trailing the Safeblowers**, 1937, Whitman, 432 pgs.	10.00	25.00	60.00
1496- **Radio Patrol Outwitting the Gang Chief**, 1939, Whitman, 432 pgs.	10.00	25.00	60.00
1498- **Radio Patrol and Big Dan's Mobsters**, 1937, Whitman, 432 pgs.	10.00	25.00	60.00
nn- **Raiders of the Lost Ark**, 1998, Chronicle Books, 304 pgs., adapts movie, 1-color (green) illos	4.00	10,00	22.00
1441- **Range Busters, The**, 1942, Whitman, 432 pgs., Henry E. Vallely-a	10.00	25.00	60.00
1163- **Ranger and the Cowboy, The**, 1939, Saalfield, 400 pgs.	10.00	25.00	60.00
1154- **Rangers on the Rio Grande**, 1938, Saalfield, 400 pgs.	10.00	25.00	60.00
1447- **Ray Land of the Tank Corps, U.S.A.**, 1942, Whitman, 432 pgs., flip pictures, Hess-a	10.00	25.00	60.00
1157- **Red Barry Ace-Detective**, 1935, Whitman, 432 pgs., by Will Gould	12.00	30.00	85.00
1426- **Red Barry Undercover Man**, 1939, Whitman, 432 pgs.,			

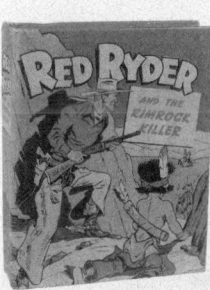

1443 - Red Ryder and the Rimrock Killer © WHIT

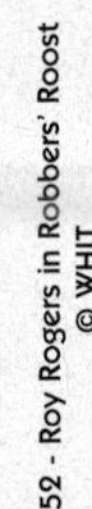

1452 - Roy Rogers in Robbers' Roost © WHIT

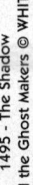

1495 - The Shadow and the Ghost Makers © WHIT

	GD	FN	VF/NM
by Will Gould	12.00	30.00	75.00
20- **Red Davis**, 1935, EVW, 160 pgs.	11.00	27.50	70.00
1449- **Red Death on the Range, The**, 1940, Whitman, 432 pgs., Fred Harman-a (Bronc Peeler)	11.00	27.50	70.00
nn- **Red Falcon Adventures, The**, 1937, Seal Right Ice Cream, 8 pgs., set of 50 books, circular in shape			
Issue #1	64.00	160.00	450.00
Issue #2-5	43.00	108.00	300.00
Issue #6-10	36.00	90.00	250.00
Issue #11-50	21.00	52.50	150.00
nn- **Red Hen and the Fox, The**, nd(1930s), np(Whitman), 36 pgs., 3" x 2 1/2", Penny Book	3.00	7.50	18.00
1145- **Red-Hot Holsters**, 1938, Saalfield, 400 pgs.	10.00	25.00	60.00
1400- **Red Ryder and Little Beaver on Hoofs of Thunder**, 1939, Whitman, 432 pgs., Harman-c/a	13.00	32.50	90.00
1414- **Red Ryder and the Squaw-Tooth Rustlers**, 1946, Whitman, 352 pgs., Fred Harman-a	12.00	30.00	75.00
1427- **Red Ryder and the Code of the West**, 1941, Whitman, 432 pgs., flip pictures, by Harman	12.00	30.00	80.00
1440- **Red Ryder the Fighting Westerner**, 1940, Whitman, Harman-a	12.00	30.00	80.00
1443- **Red Ryder and the Rimrock Killer**, 1948, Whitman, 288 pgs., Harman-a	11.00	27.50	70.00
1450- **Red Ryder and Western Border Guns**, 1942, Whitman, 432 pgs., flip pictures, by Harman	12.00	30.00	80.00
1454- **Red Ryder and the Secret Canyon**, 1948, Whitman, 288 pgs., Harman-a	11.00	27.50	70.00
1466- **Red Ryder and Circus Luck**, 1947, Whitman, 288 pgs., by Fred Harman	11.00	27.50	70.00
1473- **Red Ryder in War on the Range**, 1945, Whitman, 352 pgs., by Fred Harman	12.00	30.00	75.00
1475- **Red Ryder and the Outlaw of Painted Valley**, 1943, Whitman, 352 pgs., by Harman	11.00	27.50	70.00
702-10- **Red Ryder Acting Sheriff**, 1949, Whitman, by Fred Hannan	10.00	25.00	65.00
nn- **Red Ryder Brings Law to Devil's Hole**, 1939, Dell, 196 pgs., Fast-Action Story, Harman-c/a	29.00	73.00	200.00
nn- **Red Ryder and the Highway Robbers**, 1938, Whitman, 36 pgs., 2 1/2" x 3 1/2", Penny Book	10.00	25.00	65.00
754- **Reg'lar Fellers**, 1933, Whitman, 320 pgs., by Gene Byrnes	11.00	27.50	70.00
nn- **Reg'lar Fellers**, 1933, Whitman, 202 pgs., Cocomalt premium, by Gene Byrnes	11.00	27.50	70.00
1424- **Rex Beach's Jaragu of the Jungle**, 1937, Whitman, 432 pgs.	9.00	22.50	55.00
12- **Rex, King of Wild Horses in "Stampede,"** 1935, EVW, 160 pgs., movie scenes, Columbia Pictures	10.00	25.00	60.00
1100B- **Riddles for Fun**, 1938, Whitman, 36 pgs., 2 1/2" x 3 1/2", Penny Book	3.00	7.50	20.00
1100B- **Riddles to Guess**, 1938, Whitman, 36 pgs., 2 1/2" x 3 1/2", Penny Book	3.00	7.50	20.00
1425- **Riders of Lone Trails**, 1937, Whitman, 300 pgs.	10.00	25.00	65.00
1141- **Rio Raiders** (A Billy The Kid Story), 1938, Saalfield, 400 pgs.	10.00	25.00	65.00
2023-(#23)- **The Road Runner, The Super Beep Catcher,** 1968, Whitman, 256 pgs., hard-c, color illos.	1.00	2.50	9.00
5759- **The Road Runner, The Super Beep Catcher,** 1973, Whitman, 256 pgs., soft-c, 39 cents, B&W illos., and flip pictures	2.00	5.00	12.00
5767-2- **Road Runner, The Lost Road Runner Mine, The**, 1974 (1980), 260 pgs., 79 cents, B&W, soft-c	2.00	5.00	12.00
5784- **The Road Runner and the Unidentified Coyote**, 1974, Whitman, 260 pgs., soft-c, flip pictures	2.00	5.00	12.00
5784-2- **The Road Runner and the Unidentified Coyote**, 1980, Whitman, 260 pgs., soft-c, flip pictures	2.00	5.00	12.00
nn- **Road To Perdition**, 2002, Dreamworks, screenplay from movie, hard-c (Dreamworks and 20th Century Fox)	1.00	2.50	9.00
Robin Hood (See Wee Little Books)			
10- **Robin Hood**, 1935, EVW, 160 pgs., movie scenes w/Douglas Fairbanks (United Artists), hard-c	14.00	35.00	100.00
719- **Robinson Crusoe** (The Story of...), nd (1933), Whitman, 364 pgs., soft-c	12.00	30.00	75.00
1421- **Roy Rogers and the Dwarf-Cattle Ranch**, 1947, Whitman, 352 pgs., Henry E. Vallely-a	12.00	30.00	75.00
1437- **Roy Rogers and the Deadly Treasure**, 1947, Whitman, 288 pgs.	12.00	30.00	75.00
1448- **Roy Rogers and the Mystery of the Howling Mesa**, 1948, Whitman, 288 pgs.	12.00	30.00	75.00
1452- **Roy Rogers in Robbers' Roost**, 1948, Whitman, 288 pgs.	12.00	30.00	75.00
1460- **Roy Rogers Robinhood of the Range**, 1942, Whitman, 432 pgs., Hess-a (1st)	14.00	35.00	100.00
1462- **Roy Rogers and the Mystery of the Lazy M**, 1949, Whitman	10.00	25.00	65.00
1476- **Roy Rogers King of the Cowboys**, 1943, Whitman, 352 pgs., Irwin Myers-a, based on movie	16.00	40.00	110.00
1494- **Roy Rogers at Crossed Feathers Ranch**, 1945, Whitman, 320 pgs., Erwin Hess-a , 3 1/4" x 5 1/2"	12.00	30.00	75.00
701-10- **Roy Rogers and the Snowbound Outlaws**, 1949, 3 1/4" x 5 1/2"	10.00	25.00	60.00
715-10- **Roy Rogers Range Detective**, 1950, Whitman, 2 1/2" x 5"	10.00	25.00	60.00
nn- **Sandy Gregg Federal Agent on Special Assignment**, 1939, Whitman, 36 pgs., 2 1/2" x 3 1/2", Penny Book	9.00	22.50	55.00
Sappo (See Top-Line Comics)			
1122- **Scrappy**, 1934, Whitman, 288 pgs.	12.00	30.00	75.00
L12- **Scrappy** (The Adventures of...), 1935, Lynn, 192 pgs., movie scenes	12.00	30.00	75.00
1191- **Secret Agent K-7**,1940, Saalfield, 400 pgs., based on radio show	9.00	22.50	55.00
1144- **Secret Agent X-9**, 1936, Whitman, 432 pgs., Charles Flanders-a	15.00	37.50	105.00
1472- **Secret Agent X-9 and the Mad Assassin**, 1938, Whitman, 432 pgs., Charles Flanders-a	15.00	37.50	105.00
1161- **Sequoia**, 1935, Whitman, 160 pgs., photo-c, movie scenes	12.00	30.00	75.00
1430- **Shadow and the Living Death, The**, 1940, Whitman, 432 pgs., Erwin Hess-a	41.00	103.00	285.00
1443- **Shadow and the Master of Evil, The**, 1941, Whitman, 432 pgs., flip pictures, Hess-a	41.00	103.00	285.00
1495- **Shadow and the Ghost Makers, The**, 1942, Whitman, 432 pgs., John Coleman Burroughs-c	41.00	103.00	285.00
2024- **Shazzan, The Glass Princess**, 1968, Whitman, Hanna-Barbera	3.00	7.50	20.00
Shirley Temple (See My Life and Times & Story of..)			
1095- **Shirley Temple and Lionel Barrymore Starring In "The Little Colonel,"** 1935, Saalfield, photo hard-c, movie scenes	18.00	45.00	125.00
1115- **Shirley Temple in "The Littlest Rebel,"** 1935, Saalfield, photo-c, movie scenes, hard-c	18.00	45.00	125.00
1575- **Shirley Temple and Lionel Barrymore Starring In "The Little Colonel,"** 1935, Saalfield, photo soft-c, movie scenes	18.00	45.00	125.00
1595- **Shirley Temple in "The Littlest Rebel,"** 1935, Saalfield, photo-c, movie scenes, soft-c	18.00	45.00	125.00
1195- **Shooting Sheriffs of the Wild West**, 1936, Whitman, 432 pgs.	8.00	20.00	50.00
1169- **Silly Symphony Featuring Donald Duck** (Disney), 1937, Whitman, 432 pgs., Taliaferro-a	26.00	65.00	185.00
1441- **Silly Symphony Featuring Donald Duck and His (MIS) Adventures** (Disney), 1937, Whitman, 432 pgs., Taliaferro-a	26.00	65.00	185.00
1155- **Silver Streak, The**, 1935, Whitman, 160 pgs., photo-c, movie scenes (RKO Radio Pict.)	11.00	27.50	70.00
Simple Simon (See Wee Little Books)			
1649- **Sir Lancelot** (TV Series), 1958, Whitman, 280 pgs.	6.00	18.00	35.00
1112- **Skeezix in Africa**, 1934, Whitman, 300 pgs., Frank King-a	8.00	20.00	50.00
1408- **Skeezix at the Military Academy**, 1938, Whitman, 432 pgs., Frank King-a	8.00	20.00	50.00
1414- **Skeezix Goes to War**, 1944, Whitman, 352 pgs., Frank King-a	8.00	20.00	50.00
1419- **Skeezix on His Own in the Big City**, 1941, Whitman, All Pictures Comics, flip pictures, Frank King-a	8.00	20.00	50.00

1419 - Skeezix on His Own in the Big City © WHIT

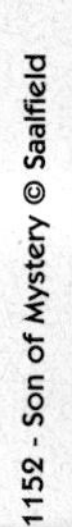
1152 - Son of Mystery © Saalfield

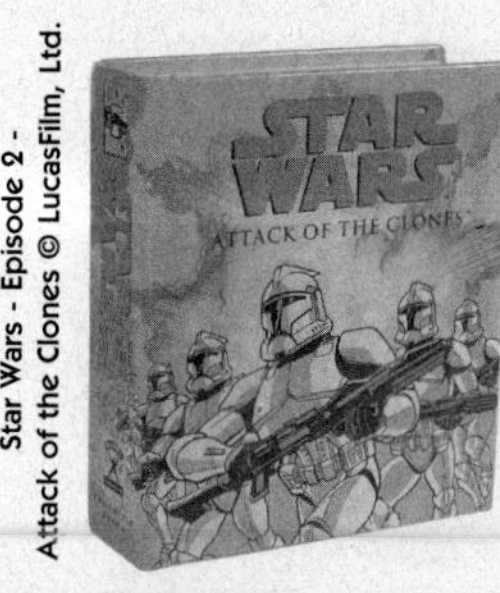

Star Wars - Episode 2 - Attack of the Clones © LucasFilm, Ltd.

	GD	FN	VF/NM
761- Skippy, 1934, Whitman, 320 pgs., by Percy Crosby	8.00	20.00	50.00
4056- Skippy, The Story of, 1934, Whitman, 320 pgs., 7" x 9 1/2", Big Big Book, Percy Crosby-a	23.00	57.50	160.00
nn- Skippy, The Story of, 1934, Whitman, Phillips Dental Magnesia premium, soft-c, by Percy Crosby	8.00	20.00	50.00
1127- Skyroads (Hurricane Hawk's name not on cover), 1936, Whitman, 432 pgs., by Lt. Dick Calkins, Russell Keaton-a	11.00	27.50	70.00
1439- Skyroads with Clipper Williams of the Flying Legion, 1938, Whitman, 432 pgs., by Lt. Dick Calkins, Keaton-a	11.00	27.50	70.00
1127- Skyroads with Hurricane Hawk, 1936, Whitman, 432 pgs., by Lt. Dick Calkins, Russell Keaton-a	10.00	25.00	65.00
Smilin' Jack and his Flivver Plane (See Top-Line Comics)			
1152- Smilin' Jack and the Stratosphere Ascent, 1937, Whitman, 432 pgs., Zack Mosley-a	12.00	30.00	85.00
1412- Smilin' Jack Flying High with "Downwind," 1942, Whitman, 432 pgs., Zack Mosley-a	12.00	30.00	80.00
1416- Smilin' Jack in Wings over the Pacific, 1939, Whitman, 432 pgs., Zack Mosley-a	12.00	30.00	80.00
1419- Smilin' Jack and the Jungle Pipe Line, 1947, Whitman, 352 pgs., Zack Mosley-a	12.00	30.00	75.00
1445- Smilin' Jack and the Escape from Death Rock, 1943, Whitman, 352 pgs., Mosley-a	12.00	30.00	75.00
1464- Smilin' Jack and the Coral Princess, 1945, Whitman, 352 pgs., Zack Mosley-a	12.00	30.00	75.00
1473- Smilin' Jack Speed Pilot, 1941, Whitman, 432 pgs., Zack Mosley-a	12.00	30.00	80.00
2- Smilin' Jack and his Stratosphere Plane, 1938, Whitman, 132 pgs., Buddy Book, soft-c, Zack Mosley-a	27.00	68.00	190.00
nn- Smilin' Jack Grounded on a Tropical Shore, 1938, Whitman, 36 pgs., 2 1/2" x 3 1/2", Penny Book	1000	25.00	60.00
11- Smilin' Jack and the Border Bandits, 1941, Dell, 196 pgs., Fast-Action Story, soft-c, Zack Mosley-a	24.00	60.00	170.00
745- Smitty Golden Gloves Tournament, 1934, Whitman, 320 pgs., Walter Berndt-a	12.00	30.00	75.00
nn- Smitty Golden Gloves Tournament, 1934, Whitman, 204 pgs., Cocomalt premium, soft-c, Walter Berndt-a	12.00	30.00	85.00
1404- Smitty and Herby Lost Among the Indians, 1941, Whitman, All Pictures Comics	10.00	25.00	60.00
1477- Smitty in Going Native, 1938, Whitman, 300 pgs., Walter Berndt-a	10.00	25.00	60.00
2- Smitty and Herby, 1936, Whitman, 132 pgs., 3 1/2" x 3 1/2", soft-c, Tarzan Ice Cream cup lid premium	24.00	60.00	170.00
9- Smitty's Brother Herby and the Police Horse, 1938, Whitman, 132 pgs., 3 1/4" x 3 1/2", Buddy Book-ice cream premium, by Walter Berndt	24.00	60.00	170.00
1010- Smokey Stover Firefighter of Foo, 1937, Whitman, 7 1/4" x 5 1/2", 64 pgs., Nickel Book, Bill Holman-a	12.00	30.00	85.00
1413- Smokey Stover, 1942, Whitman, All Pictures Comics, flip pictures, Bill Holman-a	12.00	30.00	85.00
1421- Smokey Stover the Foo Fighter, 1938, Whitman, 432 pgs., Bill Holman-a	12.00	30.00	85.00
1481- Smokey Stover the Foolish Foo Fighter, 1942, Whitman, All Pictures Comics	12.00	30.00	85.00
1- Smokey Stover the Fireman of Foo, 1938, Whitman, 3 3/4" x 3 1/2", 132 pgs., Buddy Book-ice cream premium, by Bill Holman	27.00	68.00	190.00
1100A- Smokey Stover, 1938, Whitman, 36 pgs., 2 1/2" x 3 1/2", Penny Book	10.00	25.00	65.00
nn- Smokey Stover and the Fire Chief of Foo, 1938, Whitman, 36 pgs., 2 1/2" x 3 1/2", Penny Book, yellow shirt on-c	10.00	25.00	65.00
nn- Smokey Stover and the Fire Chief of Foo, 1938, Whitman, 36 pgs., Penny Book, green shirt on-c	10.00	25.00	65.00
1460- Snow White and the Seven Dwarfs (The Story of Walt Disney's ...), 1938, Whitman, 288 pgs.	18.00	45.00	125.00
1136- Sombrero Pete, 1936, Whitman, 432 pgs.	10.00	25.00	60.00
1152- Son of Mystery, 1939, Saalfield, 400 pgs.	10.00	25.00	60.00
1191- SOS Coast Guard, 1936, Whitman, 432 pgs., Henry E. Vallely-a	10.00	25.00	65.00
2016-(#16)-Space Ghost-The Sorceress of Cyba-3 (TV Cartoon), 1968, Whitman, 260 pgs., 39¢-c, hard-c, color illos	10.00	25.00	60.00

	GD	FN	VF/NM
1455- Speed Douglas and the Mole Gang-The Great Sabotage Plot, 1941, Whitman, 432 pgs., flip pictures	10.00	25.00	60.00
5779- Spider-Man Zaps Mr. Zodiac, 1976, 260 pgs., soft-c, B&W	1.00	2.50	9.00
5779-2- Spider-Man Zaps Mr. Zodiac, 1980, 260 pgs., 79¢-c, soft-c, B&W	1.00	2.50	6.00
1467- Spike Kelly of the Commandos, 1943, Whitman, 352 pgs.	10.00	25.00	60.00
1144- Spook Riders on the Overland, 1938, Saalfield, 400 pgs.	10.00	25.00	60.00
768- Spy, The, 1936, Whitman, 300 pgs.	12.00	30.00	75.00
nn- Spy Smasher and the Red Death, 1941, Fawcett, 4" x 5 1/2", Dime Action Book	46.00	115.00	325.00
1120- Stan Kent Freshman Fullback, 1936, Saalfield, 148 pgs., hard-c	8.00	20.00	50.00
1132- Stan Kent, Captain, 1937, Saalfield	8.00	20.00	50.00
1600- Stan Kent Freshman Fullback, 1936, Saalfield, 148 pgs., soft-c	8.00	20.00	50.00
1123- Stan Kent Varsity Man, 1936, Saalfield, 160 pgs., hard-c	8.00	20.00	50.00
1603- Stan Kent Varsity Man, 1936, Saalfield, 160 pgs., soft-c	8.00	20.00	50.00
nn- Star Wars - A New Hope, 1997, Chronicle Books, 320 pgs., adapts movie, 1-color (blue) illos	3.00	7.50	20.00
nn- Star Wars - Empire Strikes Back, The, 1997, Chronicle Books, 296 pgs., adapts movie, 1-color (blue) illos	3.00	7.50	20.00
nn- Star Wars - Episode 1 - The Phantom Menace, 1999, Chronicle Books, 344 pgs., adapts movie, 1-color (blue) illos	1.00	2.50	9.00
nn- Star Wars - Episode 2 - Attack of the Clones, 2002, Chronicle Books, 340 pgs., adapts movie, 1-color (blue) illos	1.00	2.50	9.00
nn- Star Wars - Return of the Jedi, 1997, Chronicle Books, 312 pgs., adapts movie, 1-color (blue) illos	3.00	7.50	20.00
1104- Steel Arena, The (With Clyde Beatty), 1936, Saalfield, hard-c, movie scenes adapted from "The Lost Jungle"	12.00	30.00	75.00
1584- Steel Arena, The (With Clyde Beatty), 1936, Saalfield, soft-c, movie scenes	12.00	30.00	75.00
1426- Steve Hunter of the U.S. Coast Guard Under Secret Orders, 1942, Whitman, 432 pgs.	10.00	25.00	60.00
1456- Story of Charlie McCarthy and Edgar Bergen, The, 1938, Whitman, 288 pgs.	10.00	25.00	60.00
Story of Daniel, The (See Wee Little Books)			
Story of David, The (See Wee Little Books)			
1110- Story of Freddie Bartholomew, The, 1935, Saalfield, 4 1/2" x 5 1/4", hard-c, movie scenes (MGM)	10.00	25.00	60.00
1590- Story of Freddie Bartholomew, The, 1935, Saalfield, 4 1/2" x 5 1/4", soft-c, movie scenes (MGM)	10.00	25.00	60.00
Story of Gideon, The (See Wee Little Books)			
W714- Story of Jackie Cooper, The, 1933, Whitman, 240 pgs., photo-c, movie scenes, "Skippy" & "Sooky" movie	12.00	30.00	80.00
Story of Joseph, The (See Wee Little Books)			
Story of Moses, The (See Wee Little Books)			
Story of Ruth and Naomi (See Wee Little Books)			
1089- Story of Shirley Temple, The, 1934, Saalfield, 160 pgs., hard-c, photo-c, movie scenes	11.00	27.50	70.00
1319- Story of Shirley Temple, The, 1934, Saalfield, 160 pgs., soft-c, photo-c, movie scenes	11.00	27.50	70.00
1090- Strawberry-Roan, 1934, Saalfield, 160 pgs., hard-c, Ken Maynard photo-c, movie scenes	11.00	27.50	70.00
1320- Strawberry-Roan, 1934, Saalfield, 160 pgs., soft-c, Ken Maynard photo-c, movie scenes	11.00	27.50	70.00
Streaky and the Football Signals (See Top-Line Comics)			
5780-2- Superman in the Phantom Zone Connection, 1980, 260 pgs., 79¢-c, soft-c, B&W	1.00	2.50	9.00
582- "Swap It" Book, The, 1949, Samuel Lowe Co., 260 pgs., 3 1/2" x 4 1/2"			
1. Little Tex in the Midst of Trouble	5.00	12.50	30.00
2. Little Tex's Escape	5.00	12.50	30.00
3. Little Tex Comes to the XY Ranch	5.00	12.50	30.00
4. Get Them Cowboy	5.00	12.50	30.00
5. The Mail Must Go Through! A Story of the Pony Express	5.00	12.50	30.00
6. Nevada Jones, Trouble Shooter	5.00	12.50	30.00

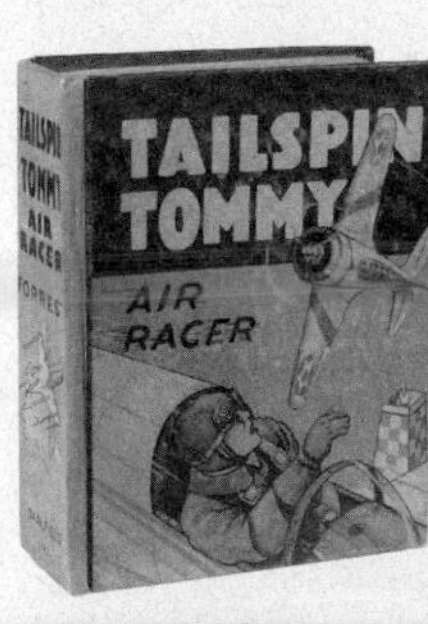

1183 - Tailspin Tommy Air Racer © WHIT

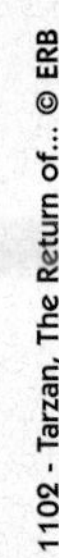
1102 - Tarzan, The Return of... © ERB

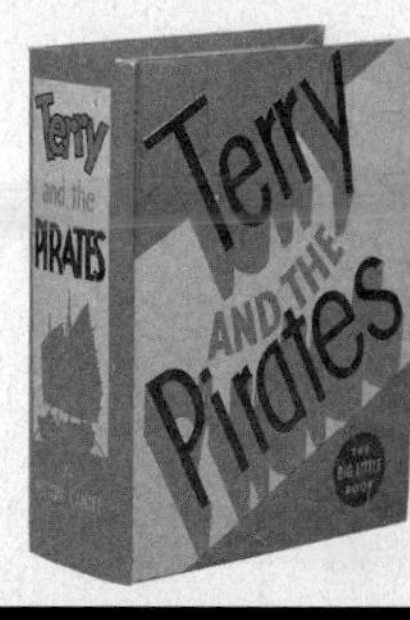

1156 - Terry and the Pirates © WHIT

	GD	FN	VF/NM
7. Danny Meets the Cowboys	5.00	12.50	30.00
8. Flint Adams and the Stage Coach	5.00	12.50	30.00
9. Bud Shinners and the Oregon Trail	5.00	12.50	30.00
10. The Outlaws' Last Ride	5.00	12.50	30.00
Sybil Jason (See Little Big Shot)			
747- **Tailspin Tommy in the Famous Pay-Roll Mystery**, 1933, Whitman, hard-c, 320 pgs., Hal Forrest-a (# 1)	12.00	30.00	85.00
747- **Tailspin Tommy in the Famous Pay-Roll Mystery**, 1933, Whitman, soft-c, 320 pgs., Hal Forrest-a (# 1)	12.00	30.00	85.00
nn- **Tailspin Tommy the Pay-Roll Mystery**, 1934, Whitman, 52 pgs., 3 1/2" x 5 1/4", premium-no ads, soft-c; another version with Perkins ad, Hal Forrest-a	18.00	45.00	125.00
1110- **Tailspin Tommy and the Island in the Sky**, 1936, Whitman, 432 pgs., Hal Forrest-a	11.00	27.50	70.00
1124- **Tailspin Tommy the Dirigible Flight to the North Pole**, 1934, Whitman, 432 pgs., H. Forrest-a	12.00	30.00	85.00
nn- **Tailspin Tommy the Dirigible Flight to the North Pole**, 1934, Whitman, 436 pgs., 3-color, soft-c, premium-no ads, Hal Forrest-a	29.00	73.00	200.00
1172- **Tailspin Tommy Hunting for Pirate Gold**, 1935, Whitman, 432 pgs., Hal Forrest-a	11.00	27.50	70.00
1183- **Tailspin Tommy Air Racer**, 1940, Saalfield, 400 pgs., hard-c	11.00	27.50	70.00
1184- **Tailspin Tommy in the Great Air Mystery**, 1936, Whitman, 240 pgs., photo-c, movie scenes	12.00	30.00	85.00
1410- **Tailspin Tommy the Weasel and His "Skywaymen,"** 1941, Whitman, All Pictures Comics, flip pictures	10.00	25.00	65.00
1413- **Tailspin Tommy and the Lost Transport**, 1940, Whitman, 432 pgs., Hal Forrest-a	10.00	25.00	65.00
1423- **Tailspin Tommy and the Hooded Flyer**, 1937, Whitman, 432 pgs., Hal Forrest-a	11.00	27.50	70.00
1494- **Tailspin Tommy and the Sky Bandits**, 1938, Whitman 432 pgs., Hal Forrest-a	11.00	27.50	70.00
nn- **Tailspin Tommy and the Airliner Mystery**, 1938, Dell, 196 pgs., Fast-Action Story, soft-c, Hal Forrest-a	43.00	108.00	300.00
nn- **Tailspin Tommy in Flying Aces**, 1938, Dell, 196 pgs., Fast-Action Story, soft-c, Hal Forrest-a	43.00	108.00	300.00
nn- **Tailspin Tommy in Wings Over the Arctic**, 1934, Whitman, Cocomalt premium, Forrest-a	14.00	35.00	100.00
nn- **Tailspin Tommy Big Thrill Chewing Gum**, 1934, Whitman, 8 pgs., 2 1/2" x 3 " (6 diff.) each..	11.00	27.50	70.00
3- **Tailspin Tommy on the Mountain of Human Sacrifice**, 1938, Whitman, soft-c, Buddy Book	30.00	75.00	210.00
7- **Tailspin Tommy's Perilous Adventure**, 1934, Whitman, 132 pgs., 3 1/2" x 3 1/2" soft-c, Tarzan Ice Cream cup premium	30.00	75.00	210.00
nn- **Tailspin Tommy**, 1935, Whitman, 148 pgs., 3 1/2" x 4", Tarzan Ice Cream cup premium	32.00	80.00	225.00
L16- **Tale of Two Cities, A**, 1935, Lynn, movie scenes	12.00	30.00	85.00
744- **Tarzan of the Apes**, 1933, Whitman, 320 pgs., by Edgar Rice Burroughs (1st)	43.00	108.00	300.00
nn- **Tarzan of the Apes**, 1935, Whitman, 52 pgs., 3 1/2" x 5 1/4", soft-c, stapled, premium, no ad; another version with a Perkins ad; reprints panels from Hal Foster's newspaper adaptation	54.00	135.00	375.00
769- **Tarzan the Fearless**, 1934, Whitman, 240 pgs., Buster Crabbe photo-c, movie scenes, ERB	29.00	73.00	200.00
770- **Tarzan Twins, The**, 1934, Whitman, 432 pgs., ERB	82.00	205.00	575.00
770- **Tarzan Twins, The**, 1935, Whitman, 432 pgs., ERB	54.00	135.00	375.00
nn- **Tarzan Twins, The**, 1935, Whitman, 52 pgs., 3 1/2" x 5 3/4", premium-with & without ads, soft-c, ERB	68.00	170.00	475.00
nn- **Tarzan Twins, The**, 1935, Whitman, 436 pgs., 3-color, soft-c, premium-no ads, ERB	71.00	178.00	500.00
778- **Tarzan of the Screen** (The Story of Johnny Weissmuller), 1934, Whitman, 240 pgs., photo-c, movie scenes, ERB	29.00	73.00	200.00
1102- **Tarzan, The Return of**, 1936, Whitman, 432 pgs., Edgar Rice Burroughs	21.00	52.50	150.00
1180- **Tarzan, The New Adventures of**, 1935, Whitman, 160 pgs., Herman Brix photo-c, movie scenes, ERB	24.00	60.00	165.00
1182- **Tarzan Escapes**, 1936, Whitman, 240 pgs., Johnny Weissmuller photo-c, movie scenes, ERB	29.00	73.00	200.00
1407- **Tarzan Lord of the Jungle**, 1946, Whitman, 352 pgs., ERB	14.00	35.00	100.00
1410- **Tarzan, The Beasts of**, 1937, Whitman, 432 pgs., Edgar Rice Burroughs	21.00	52.50	145.00
1442- **Tarzan and the Lost Empire**, 1948, Whitman, 288 pgs., ERB	14.00	35.00	100.00
1444- **Tarzan and the Ant Men**, 1945, Whitman, 352 pgs., ERB	14.00	35.00	100.00
1448- **Tarzan and the Golden Lion**, 1943, Whitman, 432 pgs., ERB	20.00	50.00	140.00
1452- **Tarzan the Untamed**, 1941, Whitman, 432 pgs., flip pictures, ERB	20.00	50.00	140.00
1453- **Tarzan the Terrible**, 1942, Whitman, 432 pgs., flip pictures, ERB	20.00	50.00	140.00
1467- **Tarzan in the Land of the Giant Apes**, 1949, Whitman, ERB	14.00	35.00	100.00
1477- **Tarzan, The Son of**, 1939, Whitman, 432 pgs., ERB	20.00	50.00	140.00
1488- **Tarzan's Revenge**, 1938, Whitman, 432 pgs., ERB	20.00	50.00	140.00
1495- **Tarzan and the Jewels of Opar**, 1940, Whitman, 432 pgs.	20.00	50.00	140.00
4056- **Tarzan and the Tarzan Twins with Jad-Bal-Ja the Golden Lion**, 1936, Whitman, 7" x 9 1/2", 320 pgs., Big Big Book	60.00	150.00	470.00
709-10- **Tarzan and the Journey of Terror**, 1950, Whitman, 2 1/2" x 5", ERB, Marsh-a	10.00	25.00	65.00
2005- **(#5)-Tarzan: The Mark of the Red Hyena**, 1967, Whitman, 260 pgs., 39 cents, hard-c, color illos	4.00	10.00	27.00
nn- **Tarzan**, 1935, Whitman, 148 pgs., soft-c, 3 1/2" x 4", Tarzan Ice Cream cup premium, ERB (scarce)	86.00	215.00	600.00
nn- **Tarzan and a Daring Rescue**, 1938, Whitman, 68 pgs., Pan-Am premium, soft-c, ERB (blank back-c version also exists)	50.00	125.00	350.00
nn- **Tarzan and his Jungle Friends**, 1936, Whitman, 132 pgs., soft-c, 3 1/2" x 3 1/2", Tarzan Ice Cream cup premium, ERB (scarce)	86.00	215.00	600.00
nn- **Tarzan in the Golden City**, 1938, Whitman, 68 pgs., Pan-Am premium, soft-c, 3 1/2" x 3 3/4", ERB	50.00	125.00	350.00
nn- **Tarzan The Avenger**, 1939, Dell, 194 pgs., Fast-Action Story, ERB, soft-c	36.00	90.00	250.00
nn- **Tarzan with the Tarzan Twins in the Jungle**, 1938, Dell, 194 pgs., Fast-Action Story, ERB	36.00	90.00	250.00
1100B- **Tell Your Fortune**, 1938, Whitman, 36 pgs., 2 1/2" x 3 1/2", Penny Book	4.00	10.00	24.00
nn- **Terminator 2: Judgment Day**, 1998, Chronicle Books, 310 pgs., adapts movie, 1-color (blue-gray) illos	1.00	2.50	9.00
1156- **Terry and the Pirates**, 1935, Whitman, 432 pgs., Milton Caniff-a (#1)	14.00	35.00	100.00
nn- **Terry and the Pirates**, 1935, Whitman, 52 pgs., 3 1/2" x 5 1/4", soft-c, premium, Milton Caniff-a; 3 versions: No ad, Sears ad & Perkins ad	29.00	73.00	200.00
1412- **Terry and the Pirates Shipwrecked on a Desert Island**, 1938, Whitman, 432 pgs., Milton Caniff-a	12.00	30.00	85.00
1420- **Terry and War in the Jungle**, 1946, Whitman, 352 pgs., Milton Caniff-a	12.00	30.00	80.00
1436- **Terry and the Pirates The Plantation Mystery**, 1942, Whitman, 432 pgs., flip pictures, Milton Caniff-a	12.00	30.00	85.00
1446- **Terry and the Pirates and the Giant's Vengeance**, 1939, Whitman, 432 pgs., Caniff-a	12.00	30.00	85.00
1499- **Terry and the Pirates in the Mountain Stronghold**, 1941, Whitman, 432 pgs., Caniff-a	12.00	30.00	85.00
4073- **Terry and the Pirates, The Adventures of**, 1938, Whitman, 7" x 9 1/2", 320 pgs., Big Big Book, Milton Caniff-a	39.00	98.00	275.00
4- **Terry and the Pirates Ashore in Singapore**, 1938, Whitman, 132 pgs., 3 1/2" x 3 3/4", soft-c, Buddy Book premium	27.00	68.00	190.00
10- **Terry and the Pirates Meet Again**, 1936, Whitman, 132 pgs., 3 1/2" x 3 1/2", soft-c, Tarzan Ice Cream cup lid premium			

The Texas Ranger in the West © WHIT

1409 - Thumper and the Seven Dwarfs © DIS

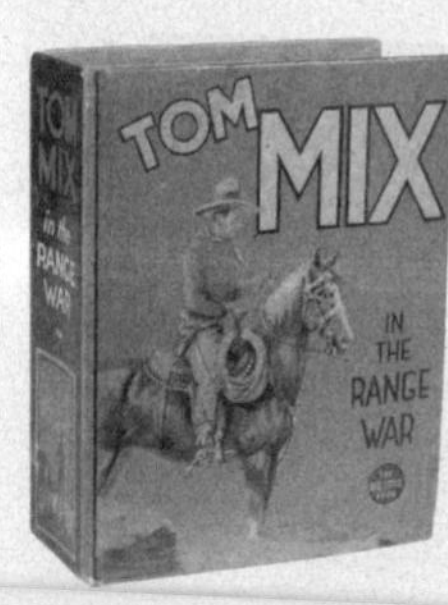

1166 - Tom Mix in the Range War © WHIT

	GD	FN	VF/NM
	39.00	98.00	275.00
nn- Terry and the Pirates, Adventures of, 1938, 36 pgs., 2 1/2" x 3 1/2", Penny Book, Caniff-a	10.00	25.00	60.00
nn- Terry and the Pirates and the Island Rescue, 1938, Whitman, 68 pgs., 3 1/4" x 3 1/2", Pan-Am premium	21.00	52.50	150.00
nn- Terry and the Pirates on Their Travels, 1938, 36 pgs., 2 1/2" x 3 1/2", Penny Book, Caniff-a	10.00	25.00	60.00
nn- Terry and the Pirates and the Mystery Ship, 1938, Dell, 194 pgs., Fast-Action Story, soft-c	29.00	73.00	200.00
1492- Terry Lee Flight Officer U.S.A., 1944, Whitman, 352 pgs., Milton Caniff-a	12.00	30.00	75.00
7- Texas Bad Man, The (Tom Mix), 1934, EVW, 160 pgs., (Five Star Library), movie scenes	18.00	45.00	125.00
1429- Texas Kid, The, 1937, Whitman, 432 pgs.	8.00	20.00	50.00
1135- Texas Ranger, The, 1936, Whitman, 432 pgs., Hal Arbo-a	8.00	20.00	50.00
nn- Texas Ranger, The, 1935, Whitman, 260 pgs., Cocomalt premium, soft-c, Hal Arbo-a	12.00	30.00	75.00
nn- Texas Ranger and the Rustler Gang, The, 1936, Whitman, Pan-Am giveaway	21.00	52.50	150.00
nn- Texas Ranger in the West, The, 1938, Whitman, 36 pgs., 2 1/2" x 3 1/2", Penny Book	8.00	20.00	50.00
nn- Texas Ranger to the Rescue, The, 1938, Whitman, 36 pgs., 2 1/2" x 3 1/2", Penny Book	8.00	20.00	50.00
12- Texas Ranger in Rustler Strategy, The, 1936, Whitman, 132 pgs., 3 1/2" x 3 1/2", soft-c, Tarzan Ice Cream cup lid premium	26.00	65.00	180.00
Tex Thorne (See Zane Grey)			
Thimble Theatre (See Popeye)			
26- 13 Hours By Air, 1936, Lynn, 128 pgs., 5" x 7 1/2", photo-c, movie scenes (Paramount Pictures)	12.00	30.00	75.00
nn- Three Bears, The, nd (1930s), np (Whitman), 36 pgs., 3" x 2 1/2", Penny Book	3.00	7.50	20.00
1129- Three Finger Joe (Baseball), 1937, Saalfield, Robert A. Graef-a	8.00	20.00	50.00
nn- Three Little Pigs, The, nd (1930s), np (Whitman), 36 pgs., 3" x 2 1/2", Penny Book	3.00	7.50	20.00
1131- Three Musketeers, 1935, Whitman, 182 pgs., 5 1/4" x 6 1/4", photo-c, movie scenes	14.00	35.00	100.00
1409- Thumper and the Seven Dwarfs (Disney), 1944, Whitman, All Pictures Comics	23.00	57.50	160.00
1108- Tiger Lady, The (The life of Mabel Stark, animal trainer), 1935, Saalfield, photo-c, movie scenes, hard-c	10.00	25.00	60.00
1588- Tiger Lady, The, 1935, Saalfield, photo-c, movie scenes, soft-c	10.00	25.00	60.00
1442- Tillie the Toiler and the Wild Man of Desert Island, 1941, Whitman, 432 pgs., Russ Westover-a	11.00	27.50	70.00
1058- "Timid Elmer" (Disney), 1939, Whitman, 5" x 5 1/2", 68 pgs., hard-c	11.00	27.50	70.00
1152- Tim McCoy in the Prescott Kid, 1935, Whitman, 160 pgs., hard-c, photo-c, movie scenes	18.00	45.00	125.00
1193- Tim McCoy in the Westerner, 1936, Whitman, 240 pgs., photo-c, movie scenes	1400	35.00	100.00
1436- Tim McCoy on the Tomahawk Trail, 1937, Whitman, 432 pgs., Robert Weisman-a	12.00	30.00	75.00
1490- Tim McCoy and the Sandy Gulch Stampede, 1939, Whitman, 424 pgs.	10.00	25.00	65.00
2- Tim McCoy in Beyond the Law, 1934, EVW, Five Star Library, photo-c, movie scenes (Columbia Pict.) Hardcover	14.00	35.00	100.00
(Rare) Softcover	36.00	90.00	250.00
10- Tim McCoy in Fighting the Redskins, 1938, Whitman, 130 pgs., Buddy Book, soft-c	27.00	68.00	190.00
14- Tim McCoy in Speedwings, 1935, EVW, Five Star Library, 160 pgs., photo-c, movie scenes (Columbia Pictures)	1900	47.50	135.00
nn- Tim the Builder, nd (1930s), np (Whitman), 36 pgs., 3" x 2 1/2", Penny Book	3.00	7.50	20.00
Tim Tyler (Also see Adventures of ...)			
1140- Tim Tyler's Luck Adventures in the Ivory Patrol, 1937, Whitman, 432 pgs., by Lyman Young	10.00	25.00	65.00
1479- Tim Tyler's Luck and the Plot of the Exiled King, 1939, Whitman, 432 pgs., by Lyman Young	10.00	25.00	60.00

	GD	FN	VF/NM
767- Tiny Tim, The Adventures of, 1935, Whitman, 384 pgs., by Stanley Link	12.00	30.00	85.00
1172- Tiny Tim and the Mechanical Men, 1937, Whitman, 432 pgs., by Stanley Link	12.00	30.00	75.00
1472- Tiny Tim in the Big, Big World, 1945, Whitman, 352 pgs., by Stanley Link	12.00	30.00	75.00
2006- (#6)-Tom and Jerry Meet Mr. Fingers, 1967, Whitman, 39¢-c 260 pgs., hard-c, color illos.	4.00	10.00	27.00
5752- Tom and Jerry Meet Mr. Fingers, 1973, Whitman, 39¢-c 260 pgs., soft-c, color illos., 5 printings	2.00	5.00	15.00
2030-(#30)- Tom and Jerry, The Astro-Nots, 1969, Whitman, 256 pgs., hard-c, color illos.	3.00	7.50	20.00
5765- Tom and Jerry, The Astro-Nots, 1974, Whitman, 256 pgs., soft-c, color illos.	2.00	5.00	15.00
5787-2- Tom and Jerry Under the Big Top, 1980, Whitman, 79¢-c, 260 pgs., soft-c, B&W	2.00	5.00	15.00
723- Tom Beatty Ace of the Service, 1934, Whitman, 256 pgs., George Taylor-a	12.00	30.00	75.00
nn- Tom Beatty Ace of the Service, 1934, Whitman, 260 pgs., soft-c	12.00	30.00	75.00
1165- Tom Beatty Ace of the Service Scores Again, 1937, Whitman, 432 pgs., Weisman-a	11.00	27.50	70.00
1420- Tom Beatty Ace of the Service and the Big Brain Gang, 1939, Whitman, 432 pgs.	11.00	27.50	70.00
nn- Tom Beatty Ace Detective and the Gorgon Gang, 1938?, Whitman, 36 pgs., 2 1/2" x 3 1/2", Penny Book	10.00	25.00	60.00
nn- Tom Beatty Ace of the Service and the Kidnapers, 1938?, Whitman, 36 pgs., 2 1/2" x 3 1/2", Penny Book	10.00	25.00	60.00
1102- Tom Mason on Top, 1935, Saalfield, 160 pgs., Tom Mix photo-c, from Mascot serial "The Miracle Rider," movie scenes, hard-c	18.00	45.00	125.00
1582- Tom Mason on Top, 1935, Saalfield, 160 pgs., Tom Mix photo-c, movie scenes, soft-c	18.00	45.00	125.00
Tom Mix (See Chief of the Rangers, Flaming Guns & Texas Bad Man)			
762- Tom Mix and Tony Jr. in "Terror Trail," 1934, Whitman, 160 pgs., movie scenes	18.00	45.00	125.00
1144- Tom Mix in the Fighting Cowboy, 1935, Whitman, 432 pgs., Hal Arbo-a	12.00	30.00	85.00
nn- Tom Mix in the Fighting Cowboy, 1935, Whitman, 436 pgs., premium-no ads, 3 color, soft-c, Hal Arbo-a	21.00	52.50	150.00
1166- Tom Mix in the Range War, 1937, Whitman, 432 pgs., Hal Arbo-a	10.00	25.00	65.00
1173- Tom Mix Plays a Lone Hand, 1935, Whitman, 288 pgs., hard-c, Hal Arbo-a	10.00	25.00	65.00
1183- Tom Mix and the Stranger from the South, 1936, Whitman, 432 pgs.	10.00	25.00	65.00
1462- Tom Mix and the Hoard of Montezuma, 1937, Whitman, H. E. Vallely-a	10.00	25.00	65.00
1482- Tom Mix and His Circus on the Barbary Coast, 1940, Whitman, 432 pgs., James Gary-a	10.00	25.00	65.00
3047- Tom Mix and His Big Little Kit, 1937, Whitman, 384 pgs., 4 1/2" x 6 1/2" box, includes miniature box of 4 crayons-red, yellow, blue and green	71.00	178.00	500.00
4068- Tom Mix and the Scourge of Paradise Valley, 1937, Whitman, 7" x 9 1/2", 320 pgs., Big Big Book, Vallely-a	29.00	73.00	200.00
6833- Tom Mix in the Riding Avenger, 1936, Dell, 244 pgs., Cartoon Story Book, hard-c	19.00	47.50	130.00
nn- Tom Mix Rides to the Rescue, 1939, 36 pgs., 2 1/2" x 3", Penny Book	10.00	25.00	60.00
nn- Tom Mix Avenges the Dry Gulched Range King, 1939, Dell, 196 pgs., Fast-Action Story, soft-c	20.00	50.00	140.00
nn- Tom Mix in the Riding Avenger, 1936, Dell, 244 pgs., Fast-Action Story	20.00	50.00	140.00
nn- Tom Mix the Trail of the Terrible 6, 1935, Ralston Purina Co., 84 pgs., 3" x 3 1/2", premium	18.00	45.00	125.00
4- Tom Mix and Tony in the Rider of Death Valley, 1934, EVW, Five Star Library, 160 pgs., movie scenes (Universal Pictures), hard-c	17.00	42.50	120.00
4- Tom Mix and Tony in the Rider of Death Valley, 1934, EVW, Five Star Library, 160 pgs., movie scenes (Universal Pictures), soft-c (Rare)	36.00	90.00	250.00

1158 - Tracked by a G-Man © Saalfield

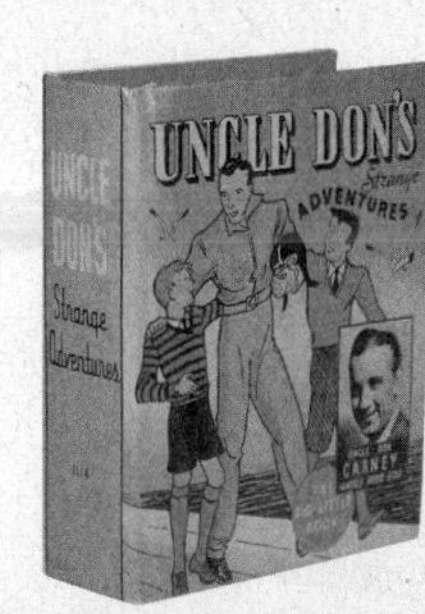
1114 - Uncle Don's Strange Adventures © WHIT

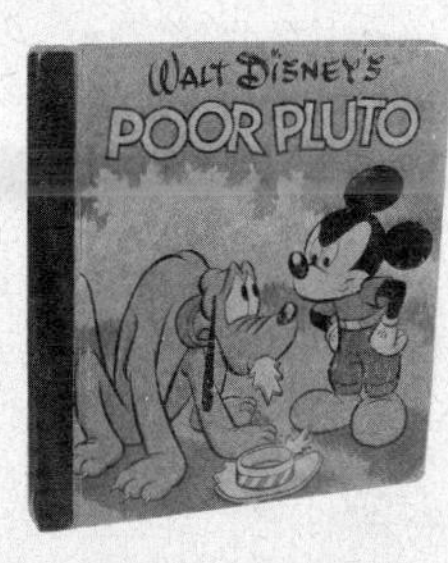
845 - Walt Disney's Poor Pluto © DIS

GD FN VF/NM

7- **Tom Mix in the Texas Bad Man**, 1934, EVW, Five Star Library, 160 pgs., movie scenes, hard-c 18.00 45.00 125.00

7- **Tom Mix in the Texas Bad Man**, 1934, EVW, Five Star Library, 160 pgs., movie scenes; soft-c (Rare) 36.00 90.00 250.00

10- **Tom Mix in the Tepee Ranch Mystery**, 1938, Whitman, 132 pgs., Buddy Book, soft-c 21.00 52.50 150.00

1126- **Tommy of Troop Six** (Scout Book), 1937, Saalfield, hard-c 9.00 22.50 55.00

1606- **Tommy of Troop Six** (Scout Book), 1937, Saalfield, soft-c 9.00 22.50 55.00

Tom Sawyer (See Adventures of ...)

1437- **Tom Swift and His Magnetic Silencer**, 1941, Whitman, 432 pgs., flip pictures 29.00 73.00 200.00

1485- **Tom Swift and His Giant Telescope**, 1939, Whitman, 432 pgs., James Gary-a 21.00 52.50 150.00

540- **Top-Line Comics** (In Open Box), 1935, Whitman, 164 pgs., 3 1/2" x 3 1/2", 3 books in set, all soft-c:
Bobby Thatcher and the Samarang Emerald 16.00 40.00 110.00
Broncho Bill in Suicide Canyon 16.00 40.00 110.00
Freckles and His Friends in the North Woods 16.00 40.00 110.00
Complete set with box 50.00 125.00 350.00

541- **Top-Line Comics** (In Open Box), 1935, Whitman, 164 pgs., 3 1/2" x 3 1/2", 3 books in set; all soft-c:
Little Joe and the City Gangsters 16.00 40.00 110.00
Smilin' Jack and His Flivver Plane 16.00 40.00 110.00
Streaky and the Football Signals 16.00 40.00 110.00
Complete set with box 50.00 125.00 350.00

542- **Top-Line Comics** (In Open Box), 1935, Whitman, 164 pgs., 3 1/2" x 3 1/2", 3 books in set; all soft-c:
Dinglehoofer Und His Dog Adolph by Knerr 16.00 40.00 110.00
Jungle Jim by Alex Raymond 18.00 45.00 125.00
Sappo by Segar 18.00 45.00 125.00
Complete set with box 64.00 160.00 450.00

543- **Top-Line Comics** (In Open Box), 1935, Whitman, 164 pgs., 3 1/2" x 3 1/2", 3 books in set; all soft-c:
Alexander Smart, ESQ by Winner 16.00 40.00 110.00
Bunky by Billy de Beck 16.00 40.00 110.00
Nicodemus O'Malley by Carter 16.00 40.00 110.00
Complete set with box 50.00 125.00 350.00

1158- **Tracked by a G-Man**, 1939, Saalfield, 400 pgs. 9.00 22.50 55.00

25- **Trail of the Lonesome Pine, The**, 1936, Lynn, movie scenes 12.00 30.00 85.00

nn- **Trail of the Terrible 6** (See Tom Mix ...)

1185- **Trail to Squaw Gulch, The**, 1940, Saalfield, 400 pgs. 10.00 25.00 60.00

720- **Treasure Island**, 1933, Whitman, 362 pgs. 12.00 30.00 85.00

1141- **Treasure Island**, 1934, Whitman, 164 pgs., hard-c, 4 1/4" x 5 1/4", Jackie Cooper photo-c, movie scenes 12.00 30.00 85.00

1141- **Treasure Island**, 1934, Whitman, 164 pgs., soft-c, 4 1/4" x 5 1/4", Jackie Cooper photo-c, movie scenes 12.00 30.00 85.00

1018- **Trick and Puzzle Book**, 1939, Whitman, 100 pgs., soft-c 3.00 7.50 20.00

1100B- **Tricks Easy to Do** (Slight of hand & magic), 1938, Whitman, 36 pgs., 2 1/2" x 3 1/2", Penny Book 3.00 7.50 20.00

1100B- **Tricks You Can Do**, 1938, Whitman, 36 pgs., 2 1/2" x 3 1/2", Penny Book 3.00 7.50 20.00

5777- **Tweety and Sylvester, The Magic Voice**, 1976, Whitman, 260 pgs., soft-c, flip-it feature; 5 printings 2.00 5.00 11.00

1104- **Two-Gun Montana**, 1936, Whitman, 432 pgs., Henry E. Vallely-a 10.00 25.00 60.00

nn- **Two-Gun Montana Shoots it Out**, 1939, Whitman, 36 pgs., 2 1/2" x 3 1/2", Penny Book 10.00 25.00 60.00

1058- **Ugly Duckling, The** (Disney), 1939, Whitman, 68 pgs., 5" x 5 1/2", hard-c 14.00 35.00 95.00

nn- **Ugly Duckling, The**, nd (1930s), np (Whitman), 36 pgs., 3" x 2 1/2", Penny Book 4.00 10.00 22.00

Unc' Billy Gets Even (See Wee Little Books)

1114- **Uncle Don's Strange Adventures**, 1935, Whitman, 300 pgs., radio star-Uncle Don Carney 10.00 25.00 65.00

722- **Uncle Ray's Story of the United States**, 1934, Whitman, 300 pgs. 10.00 25.00 65.00

1461- **Uncle Sam's Sky Defenders**, 1941, Whitman, 432 pgs., flip pictures 10.00 25.00 60.00

1405- **Uncle Wiggily's Adventures**, 1946, Whitman, All Pictures Comics 12.00 30.00 85.00

1411- **Union Pacific**, 1939, Whitman, 240 pgs., photo-c, movie scenes 11.00 27.50 70.00
With Union Pacific letter 36.00 90.00 250.00

1189- **Up Dead Horse Canyon**, 1940, Saalfield, 400 pgs. 9.00 22.50 55.00

1455- **Vic Sands of the U.S. Flying Fortress Bomber Squadron**, 1944, Whitman, 352 pgs. 11.00 27.50 70.00

nn- **Visit to Santa Claus**, 1938?, Whitman, Pan Am premium by Snow Plane; soft-c (Rare) 29.00 73.00 200.00

1645- **Walt Disney's Andy Burnett on the Trail** (TV Series), 1958, Whitman, 280 pgs. 4.00 10.00 27.00

803- **Walt Disney's Bongo**, 1948, Whitman, hard-c, Story Hour Series 12.00 30.00 75.00

711-10- **Walt Disney's Cinderella and the Magic Wand**, 1950, Whitman, 2 1/2" x 5", based on Disney movie 10.00 25.00 65.00

845- **Walt Disney's Donald Duck and his Cat Troubles** (Disney), 1948, Whitman, 100 pgs., 5" x 5 1/2", hard-c 12.00 30.00 75.00

845- **Walt Disney's Donald Duck and the Boys**, 1948, Whitman, 100 pgs., 5" x 5 1/2", hard-c, Barks-a 21.00 52.50 150.00

2952- **Walt Disney's Donald Duck in the Great Kite Maker**, 1949, Whitman, 24 pgs., 3 1/4" x 4", Tiny Tales, full color (5 cents) 10.00 25.00 60.00

804- **Walt Disney's Mickey and the Beanstalk**, 1948, Whitman, hard-c, Story Hour Series 12.00 30.00 75.00

845- **Walt Disney's Mickey Mouse and the Boy Thursday**, 194 pgs., Whitman, 5" x 5 1/2", 100 pgs. 12.00 30.00 75.00

845- **Walt Disney's Mickey Mouse the Miracle Maker**, 1948, Whitman, 5" x 5 1/2", 100 pgs. 12.00 30.00 75.00

2952- **Walt Disney's Mickey Mouse and the Night Prowlers**, Whitman, 1949, 24 pgs., 3 1/4" x 4", Tiny Tales, full color (5 ¢) 10.00 25.00 60.00

5770- **Walt Disney's Mickey Mouse - Mystery at Disneyland**, Whitman, 1975, 260 pgs., four printings 2.00 5.00 13.00

5781-2- **Walt Disney's Mickey Mouse - Mystery at Dead Man's Cove**, Whitman, 1980, 260 pgs., two printings 2.00 5.00 11.00

845- **Walt Disney's Minnie Mouse and the Antique Chair**, 1948, Whitman, 5" x 5 1/2", 100 pgs. 12.00 30.00 75.00

1435- **Walt Disney's Pinocchio and Jiminy Cricket**, 1940, Whitman, 432 pgs. 26.00 65.00 185.00

nn- **Walt Disney's Pinocchio and Jiminy Cricket**, Fast Action Story, 1940, Dell, 432 pgs. 37.00 93.00 260.00

845- **Walt Disney's Poor Pluto**, 1948, Whitman, 5" x 5 1/2", 100 pgs., hard-c 12.00 30.00 75.00

1467- **Walt Disney's Pluto the Pup** (Disney), 1938, Whitman, 432 pgs., Gottfredson-a 16.00 40.00 115.00

1066- **Walt Disney's Story of Clarabelle Cow** (Disney), 1938, Whitman, 100 pgs. 12.00 30.00 75.00

66- **Walt Disney's Story of Dippy the Goof** (Disney), 1938, Whitman, 100 pgs. 12.00 30.00 75.00

1066- **Walt Disney's Story of Donald Duck** (Disney), 1938, Whitman, 100 pgs., hard-c, Taliaferro-a 12.00 30.00 75.00

1066- **Walt Disney's Story of Goofy** (Disney), 1938, Whitman, 100 pgs., hard-c 12.00 30.00 75.00

1066- **Walt Disney's Story of Mickey Mouse** (Disney), 1938, Whitman, 100 pgs., hard-c, Gottfredson-a, Donald Duck app. 12.00 30.00 75.00

1066- **Walt Disney's Story of Minnie Mouse** (Disney), 1938, Whitman, 100 pgs., hard-c 12.00 30.00 75.00

1066- **Walt Disney's Story of Pluto the Pup**, (Disney), 1938, Whitman, 100 pgs., hard-c 12.00 30.00 75.00

2952- **Walter Lantz Presents Andy Panda's Rescue**, 1949, Whitman, Tiny Tales, full color (5 cents) (1030-5 on back-c) 10.00 25.00 60.00

751- **Wash Tubbs in Pandemonia**, 1934, Whitman, 320 pgs., Roy Crane-a 12.00 30.00 75.00

nn- **Wash Tubbs in Pandemonia**, 1934, Whitman, 52 pgs., 4" x 5 1/2", premium-no ads, soft-c, Roy Crane-a 20.00 50.00 140.00

1455- **Wash Tubbs and Captain Easy Hunting For Whales**, 1938, Whitman, 432 pgs., Roy Crane-a 12.00 30.00 75.00

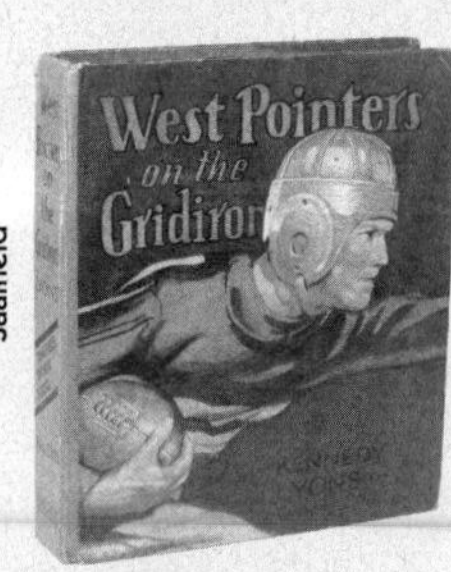

1121 - West Pointers on the Gridiron © Saalfield

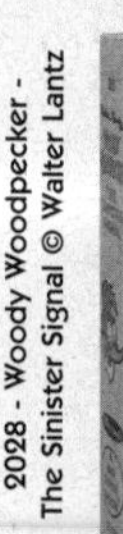
2028 - Woody Woodpecker - The Sinister Signal © Walter Lantz

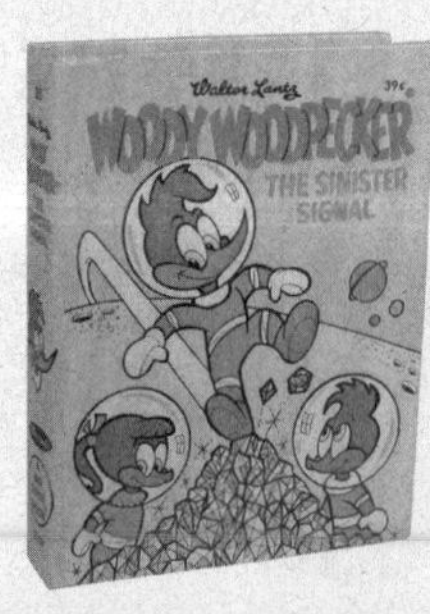

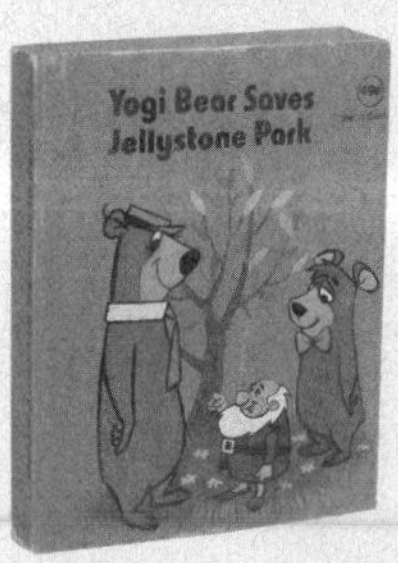

Yogi Bear Saves Jellystone Park © H-B

	GD	FN	VF/NM
6- Wash Tubbs in Foreign Travel, 1934, Whitman, soft-c, 3 1/2" x 3 1/2", Tarzan Ice Cream cup premium	29.00	73.00	200.00
513- Wee Little Books (In Open Box), 1934, Whitman, 44 pgs., small size, 6 books in set (children's classics) (Both Red box and Green box editions exist)			
Child's Garden of Verses	5.00	12.50	30.00
The Happy Prince (The Story of)	5.00	12.50	30.00
Joan of Arc (The Story of)	5.00	12.50	30.00
Peter Pan (The Story of)	5.00	12.50	30.00
Pied Piper Of Hamlin	5.00	12.50	30.00
Robin Hood (A Story of...)	5.00	12.50	30.00
Complete set with box	31.00	78.00	220.00
514- Wee Little Books (In Open Box), 1934, Whitman, 44 pgs., small size, 6 books in set			
Jack And Jill	5.00	12.50	30.00
Little Bo-Peep	5.00	12.50	30.00
Little Tommy Tucker	5.00	12.50	30.00
Mother Goose	5.00	12.50	30.00
Old King Cole	5.00	12.50	30.00
Simple Simon	5.00	12.50	30.00
Complete set with box	33.00	83.00	230.00
518- Wee Little Books (In Open Box), 1933, Whitman, 44 pgs., small size, 6 books in set, written by Thornton Burgess			
Betty Bear's Lesson-1930	5.00	12.50	30.00
Jimmy Skunk's Justice-1933	5.00	12.50	30.00
Little Joe Otter's Slide-1929	5.00	12.50	30.00
Peter Rabbit's Carrots-1933	5.00	12.50	30.00
Unc' Billy Gets Even-1930	5.00	12.50	30.00
Whitefoot's Secret-1933	5.00	12.50	30.00
Complete set with box	33.00	83.00	230.00
519- Wee Little Books (In Open Box) (Bible Stories), 1934, Whitman, 44 pgs., small size, 6 books in set, Helen Janes-a			
The Story of David	5.00	12.50	30.00
The Story of Gideon	5.00	12.50	30.00
The Story of Daniel	5.00	12.50	30.00
The Story of Joseph	5.00	12.50	30.00
The Story of Ruth and Naomi	5.00	12.50	30.00
The Story of Moses	5.00	12.50	30.00
Complete set with box	33.00	83.00	230.00
1471- Wells Fargo, 1938, Whitman, 240 pgs., photo-c, movie scenes	12.00	30.00	80.00
L18- Western Frontier, 1935, Lynn, 192 pgs., starring Ken Maynard, movie scenes	14.00	35.00	100.00
1121- West Pointers on the Gridiron, 1936, Saalfield, 148 pgs., hard-c, sports book	7.00	17.50	45.00
1601- West Pointers on the Gridiron, 1936, Saalfield, 148 pgs., soft-c, sports book	7.00	17.50	45.00
1124- West Point Five, The, 1937, Saalfield, 4 3/4" x 5 1/4", sports book, hard-c	7.00	17.50	45.00
1604- West Point Five, The, 1937, Saalfield, 4 1/4" x 5 1/4", sports book, soft-c	7.00	17.50	45.00
1164- West Point of the Air, 1935, Whitman, 160 pgs., photo-c, movie scenes	12.00	30.00	75.00
18- Westward Ho!, 1935, EVW, 160 pgs., movie scenes, starring John Wayne (Scarce)	57.00	143.00	400.00
1109- We Three, 1935, Saalfield, 160 pgs., photo-c, movie scenes, by John Barrymore, hard-c	10.00	25.00	60.00
1589- We Three, 1935, Saalfield, 160 pgs., photo-c, movie scenes, by John Barrymore, soft-c	10.00	25.00	60.00
Whitefoot's Secret (See Wee Little Books)			
nn- Who's Afraid of the Big Bad Wolf, "Three Little Pigs" (Disney), 1933, McKay, 36 pgs., 6" x 8 1/2", stiff-c, Disney studio-a	27.00	68.00	190.00
nn- Wild West Adventures of Buffalo Bill, 1935, Whitman, 260 pgs., Cocomalt premium, soft-c, Hal Arbo-a	12.00	30.00	80.00
1096- Will Rogers, The Story of, 1935, Saalfield, photo-hard-c	8.00	20.00	50.00
1576- Will Rogers, The Story of, 1935, Saalfield, photo-soft-c	8.00	20.00	50.00

	GD	FN	VF/NM
1458- Wimpy the Hamburger Eater, 1938, Whitman, 432 pgs., E.C. Segar-a	14.00	35.00	100.00
1433- Windy Wayne and His Flying Wing, 1942, Whitman, 432 pgs., flip pictures	10.00	25.00	60.00
1131- Winged Four, The, 1937, Saalfield, sports book, hard-c	10.00	25.00	60.00
1407- Wings of the U.S.A., 1940, Whitman, 432 pgs., Thomas Hickey-a	10.00	25.00	60.00
nn- Winning of the Old Northwest, The, 1934, World Syndicate, High Lights of History Series, full color-c	10.00	25.00	60.00
nn- Winning of the Old Northwest, The, 1934, World Syndicate, High Lights of History Series; red & silver-c	10.00	25.00	60.00
1122- Winning Point, The, 1936, Saalfield, (Football), hard-c	7.00	17.50	40.00
1602- Winning Point, The, 1936, Saalfield, soft-c	7.00	17.50	40.00
nn- Wizard of Oz Waddle Book, 1934, BRP, 20 pgs., 7 1/2" x 10", forerunner of the Blue Ribbon Pop-Up books; with 6 removable articulated cardboard characters. Book only	55.00	137.00	385.00
Dust jacket only	61.00	153.00	500.00
Near Mint Complete - $12,500			
710-10-Woody Woodpecker Big Game Hunter, 1950, Whitman, by Walter Lantz	9.00	22.50	55.00
2010-(#10)-Woody Woodpecker-The Meteor Menace, 1967, Whitman, 260 pgs., 39¢-c, hard-c, color illos.	4.00	10.00	27.00
5753- Woody Woodpecker-The Meteor Menace, 1973, Whitman, 260 pgs., no price, soft-c, color illos.	1.00	2.50	6.00
2028- Woody Woodpecker-The Sinister Signal, 1969, Whitman	4.00	10.00	22.00
5763- Woody Woodpecker-The Sinister Signal, 1974, Whitman, 1st printing-no price; 2nd printing-39¢-c	1.00	2.50	6.00
23- World of Monsters, The, 1935, EVW, Five Star Library, movie scenes	14.00	35.00	95.00
779- World War in Photographs, The, 1934, Whitman, photo-c, photo illus.	9.00	22.50	55.00
Wyatt Earp (See Hugh O'Brian ...)			
nn- Xena - Warrior Princess, 1998, Chronicle Books, 310 pgs., based on TV series, 1-color (purple) illos	1.00	2.50	9.00
nn- Yogi Bear Goes Country & Western, 1977, Modern Promotions, 244 pgs., 49 cents, soft-c, flip pictures	2.00	5.00	13.00
nn- Yogi Bear Saves Jellystone Park, 1977, Modern Promotions, 244 pgs., 49 cents, soft-c, flip pictures	2.00	5.00	13.00
nn- Zane Grey's Cowboys of the West, 1935, Whitman, 148 pgs., 3 3/4" x 4", Tarzan Ice Cream Cup premium, soft-c, Arbo-a	29.00	73.00	200.00
Zane Grey's King of the Royal Mounted (See Men of the Mounted)			
1010- Zane Grey's King of the Royal Mounted in Arctic Law, 1937, Whitman, 7 1/4" x 5 1/2", 64 pgs., Nickel Book	12.00	30.00	75.00
1103- Zane Grey's King of the Royal Mounted, 1936, Whitman, 432 pgs.	10.00	25.00	65.00
nn- Zane Grey's King of the Royal Mounted, 1935, Whitman, 260 pgs., Cocomalt premium, soft-c	12.00	30.00	85.00
1179- Zane Grey's King of the Royal Mounted and the Northern Treasure, 1937, Whitman, 432 pgs.	10.00	25.00	60.00
1405- Zane Grey's King of the Royal Mounted the Long Arm of the Law, 1942, Whitman, All Pictures Comics	10.00	25.00	60.00
1452- Zane Grey's King of the Royal Mounted Gets His Man, 1938, Whitman, 432 pgs.	10.00	25.00	60.00
1486- Zane Grey's King of the Royal Mounted and the Great Jewel Mystery, 1939, Whitman, 432 pgs.	10.00	25.00	60.00
5- Zane Grey's King of the Royal Mounted in the Far North, 1938, Whitman, 132 pgs., Buddy Book, soft-c (Rare)	36.00	90.00	250.00
nn- Zane Grey's King of the Royal Mounted in Law of the North, 1939, Whitman, 36 pgs., 2 1/2" x 3 1/2", Penny Book	7.00	17.50	45.00
nn- Zane Grey's King of the Royal Mounted Policing the Frozen North, 1938, Dell, 196 pgs., Fast-Action Story, soft-c	18.00	45.00	125.00
1440- Zane Grey's Tex Thorne Comes Out of the West, 1937, Whitman, 432 pgs.	10.00	25.00	60.00
1465- Zip Saunders King of the Speedway, 1939, 432 pgs., Weisman-a	10.00	25.00	60.00

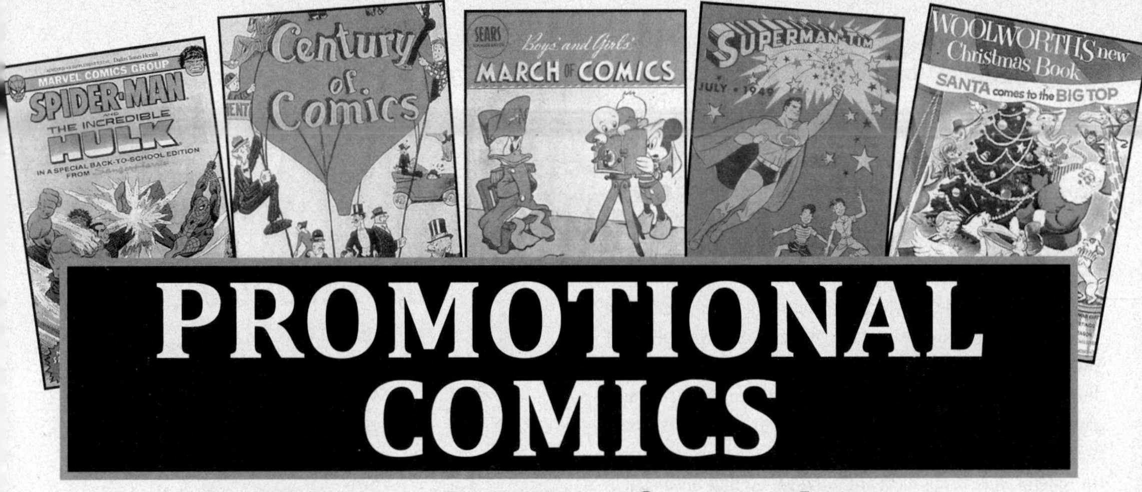

PROMOTIONAL COMICS

The Marketing of a Medium

By Carrie Wood

When it comes to four-letter words, most people probably rank "free" among some of their favorites. But of course, just because you didn't pay for something doesn't mean that there isn't a catch involved. Comic books have hardly been immune to this – a free comic usually meant that someone was trying to sell the reader something additional. And this practice of hiding a sales pitch behind some fun, colorful characters has been around in comics since the very beginning of the medium.

Even as early as the Platinum and Victorian Ages of comics, companies had realized the value of comic strips as promotional material. By the 1850s, free almanacs such as Hostetter's and Wright's were using comics as a way to help sell everything from shoe polish to patent medicine. These books are remarkably rare today, and it's difficult to compile an accurate or complete history (though you can read more about them in the Victorian Comics essay elsewhere in this book). By the end of the 1800s, the popularity of characters like the Yellow Kid and The Brownies heralded in a new age of comics-as-promos.

Some of the earliest characters that were used as successful tools in promotional comics were Palmer Cox's creation "The Brownies." The illustration shown here showcases them drinking and endorsing Seal Brand Coffee.

The very idea of funny pages within newspapers were, essentially, using comics as promotions to help sell more papers. The news publishers of the time started adding supplements to Sunday papers, and soon after, thanks to the key arrival of Buster Brown as a wildly popular character, comics were being nationally licensed for newspapers. And the sales-minded goal of using free comic strip pages to help driver readership? That worked remarkably well. The Yellow Kid, The Brownies, Buster Brown and others helped increase newspaper sales nationwide.

We can even attribute the debut of the comic book itself to promotions: in 1933, Harry Wildenberg managed to convince Procter & Gamble to sponsor the very first comic book, Funnies on Parade, as a premium item. Funnies on Parade was just a few pages long and contained reprints of various comic strips, and it was sent out for free to customers who mailed in coupons clipped from Procter & Gamble products. That book was such a success that it led to the creation of Famous Funnies, the first true "comic book" as we know it today.

A 1933 article in Fortune magazine recognized the incredible marketing power of the comic book, seemingly right away – but it wasn't such a fan of the idea, suggesting that businesses that engaged in such a thing were going against classic decorum and that using comics to sell products was somehow bringing those products "down to the level" of comics. In spite of that, it was clear from the get-go that businessfolk recognized what kind of promotional power comics held.

By the 1950s, promotional comics were being given away for more than just the sake of selling something inside; they were now being used to help educate children on a huge number of topics, from banking and mathematics to great moments in history. A few years later in the '70s, promotional comics were being included as a premium in just about everything, with major characters from DC and Marvel showing up to help save various company mascots in their time of need. By the '80s, comics were being included as premiums with action figures and video games – Atari especially took a liking to comics, leading to a regular newsstand comic series with the company's popular game characters.

In 2002, a whole holiday was created based around free promotional comics: Free Comic Book Day. Facilitated by Diamond Comic Distributors, the day (the first Saturday each May) features dozens of books given away at no charge to the customer, from some of the most popular publishers in the business. These books are often used to promote upcoming or current releases from these publishers, and by giving readers a taste of the story, they hope that the customer will then come back and spend their money on the rest of the series. For the comic shops that host it, these promo books serve the purpose of simply getting people in the door – at which point they'll hopefully find something to spend some money on, thanks to the typical big FCBD sales weekends that shop owners host to play up the event. It's comics-as-advertising in its purest form: giving free comics away for the sake of selling more comics.

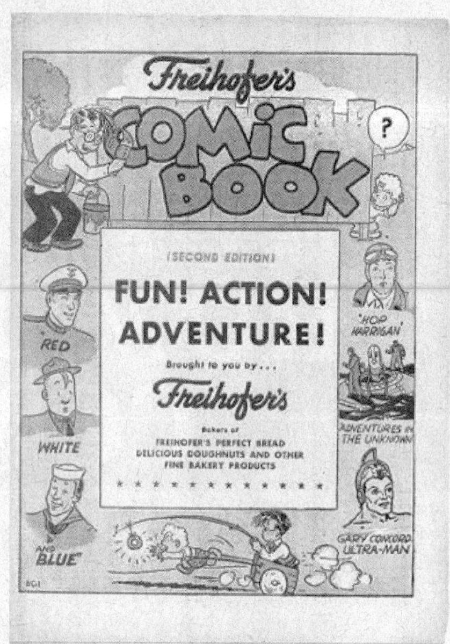

*Every market and product has been on the promotional comic book bandwagon. Freihofer's Baking Company distributed a comic in the 1940s that featured reprinted pages from **All-American Comics**.*

So much as a simple skim through this section will highlight the numerous purposes for which promotional comics have been created: from telling kids not to smoke (Captain America Meets the Asthma Monster), to trying to sway elections (The Story of Harry Truman), to showing the importance of environmentalism (Our Spaceship Earth), to explaining history (Louisiana Purchase), to recruiting for the armed forced (Li'l Abner Joins the Navy) and much more. There's also been the occasional oddball branded team-up that simply served to promote the brand, such as The Craftsman Bolt-On System Saves the Justice League, The KFC Colonel Meets the DC Multiverse, and The X-Men at the Texas State Fair.

Whether being used to educate, entertain or endorse, comics have proven themselves a powerful promotional tool. And as long as people still love the word "free," they'll keep picking them up – meaning that the industry will continue to produce promos.

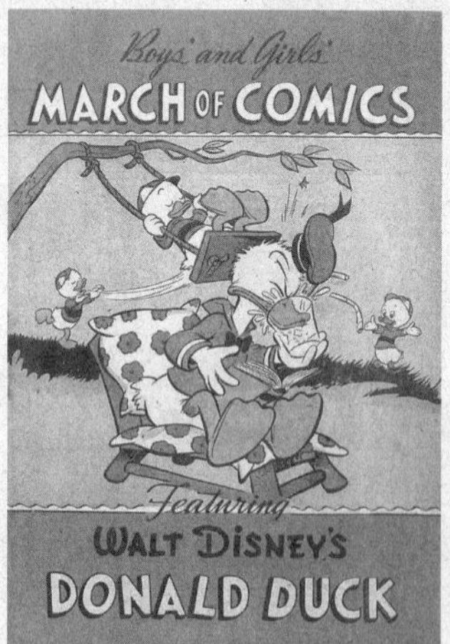

*The promotional title **March of Comics** was a prolific comic that ran for 36 years and 488 issues featuring a variety of subjects and characters. (#20 shown)*

Action Comics #1 (USPS) © DC

Adventures of Big Boy #8 © Timely

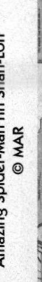

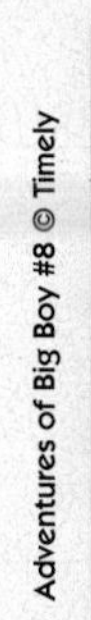

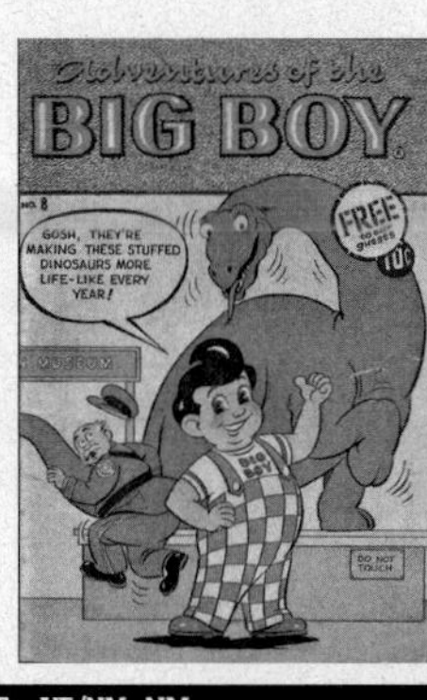

Amazing Spider-Man nn Shan-Lon © MAR

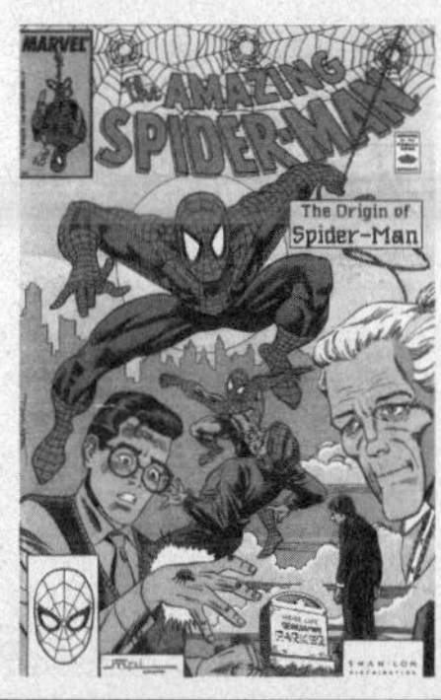

	GD 2.0	VG 4.0	FN 6.0	VF 8.0	VF/NM 9.0	NM- 9.2

ACTION COMICS
DC Comics: 1947 - 1998 (Giveaway)

	GD 2.0	VG 4.0	FN 6.0	VF 8.0	VF/NM 9.0	NM- 9.2
1 (1976) paper cover w/10¢ price, 16 pgs. in color; reprints complete Superman story from #1 ('38)	4	8	12	27	44	60
1 (1976) Safeguard Giveaway; paper cover w/"free", 16 pgs. in color; reprints complete Superman story from #1 ('38)	4	8	12	27	44	60
1 (1983) paper cover w/10¢ price, 16 pgs. in color; reprints complete Superman story from #1 ('38)	3	6	9	15	22	28
1 (1987 Nestle Quik; 1988, 50¢)	2	4	6	8	10	12
1 (1992)-Came w/Reign of Superman packs						4.00
1 (1998 U.S. Postal Service, $7.95) Reprints entire issue; extra outer half-cover contains First Day Issuance of 32¢ Superman stamp with Sept. 10, 1998 Cleveland, OH postmark	1	2	3	5	6	8
Theater (1947, 32 pgs., 5" x 7", nn)-Vigilante story based on Columbia Vigilante serial; no Superman-c or story	76	152	228	486	831	1175

ACTION ZONE
CBS Television: 1994 (Promotes CBS Saturday morning cartoons)

	GD 2.0	VG 4.0	FN 6.0	VF 8.0	VF/NM 9.0	NM- 9.2
1-WildC.A.T.s, T.M.N.Turtles, Skeleton Warriors stories; Jim Lee-c						4.00

ADVENTURE COMICS
IGA: No date (early 1940s) (Paper-c, 32 pgs.)

	GD 2.0	VG 4.0	FN 6.0	VF 8.0	VF/NM 9.0	NM- 9.2
Two diff. issues; Super-Mystery V2 #3-r from 1941; Jim Mooney-c	22	44	66	130	213	295

ADVENTURE IN DISNEYLAND
Walt Disney Productions (Dist. by Richfield Oil): May, 1955 (Giveaway, soft-c., 16 pgs)

	GD 2.0	VG 4.0	FN 6.0	VF 8.0	VF/NM 9.0	NM- 9.2
nn	13	26	39	74	105	135

ADVENTURES @ EBAY
eBay: 2000 (6 3/4" x 4 1/2", 16 pgs.)

	GD 2.0	VG 4.0	FN 6.0	VF 8.0	VF/NM 9.0	NM- 9.2
1-Judd Winick-a/Rucka & Van Meter-s; intro to eBay comic buying						3.00

ADVENTURES IN JET POWER
General Electric: 1950

	GD 2.0	VG 4.0	FN 6.0	VF 8.0	VF/NM 9.0	NM- 9.2
nn	8	16	24	40	50	60

ADVENTURES OF BIG BOY (Also titled Adventures of the Big Boy)
Timely Comics/Webs Adv. Corp./Illus. Features: 1956 - Present
(Giveaway) (East & West editions of early issues)

	GD 2.0	VG 4.0	FN 6.0	VF 8.0	VF/NM 9.0	NM- 9.2
1-Everett-c/a	121	242	363	768	1322	1875
2-Everett-c/a	50	100	150	315	533	750
3-5: 4-Robot-c	21	42	63	126	206	285
6-10: 6-Sci/fic issue	10	20	30	67	141	215
11-20: 11,13-DeCarlo-a	6	12	18	41	76	110
21-30	4	8	12	27	44	60
31-50	3	6	9	17	26	35
51-100	2	4	6	9	13	16
101-150	2	4	6	8	10	12
151-240: 239-Wizard of Oz parody-c	1	2	3	5	7	9
241-265,267-269,271-300:						6.00
266-Superman x-over	3	6	9	17	26	35
270-TV's Buck Rogers-c/s	3	6	9	14	20	25
301-400						4.00
401-500						3.00
1-(2nd series - '76-'84,Paragon Prod.) (...Shoney's Big Boy)	1	3	4	6	8	10
2-20						5.00
21-50						3.00
Summer, 1959 issue, large size	7	14	21	46	86	125

ADVENTURES OF G. I. JOE
1969 (3-1/4x7") (20 & 16 pgs.)

First Series: 1-Danger of the Depths. 2-Perilous Rescue. 3-Secret Mission to Spy Island. 4-Mysterious Explosion. 5-Fantastic Free Fall. 6-Eight Ropes of Danger. 7-Mouth of Doom. 8-Hidden Missile Discovery. 9-Space Walk Mystery. 10-Fight for Survival. 11-The Shark's Surprise.
Second Series: 2-Flying Space Adventure. 4-White Tiger Hunt. 7-Capture of the Pygmy Gorilla. 12-Secret of the Mummy's Tomb.
Third Series: Reprinted surviving titles of First Series. Fourth Series: 13-Adventure Team Headquarters. 14-Search For the Stolen Idol.

	GD 2.0	VG 4.0	FN 6.0	VF 8.0	VF/NM 9.0	NM- 9.2
each....	3	6	9	17	26	35

ADVENTURES OF JELL-O MAN AND WOBBLY, THE
Welsh Publishing Group: 1991 ($1.25)

	GD 2.0	VG 4.0	FN 6.0	VF 8.0	VF/NM 9.0	NM- 9.2
1						4.00

ADVENTURES OF KOOL-AID MAN
Marvel Comics: 1983 - No. 3, 1985 (Mail order giveaway)
Archie Comics: No. 4, 1987 - No. 9, 1989

	GD 2.0	VG 4.0	FN 6.0	VF 8.0	VF/NM 9.0	NM- 9.2
1-9: 4-9-Dan DeCarlo-a/c	1	2	3	5	7	9

ADVENTURES OF MARGARET O'BRIEN, THE
Bambury Fashions (Clothes): 1947 (20 pgs. in color, slick-c, regular size) (Premium)

	GD 2.0	VG 4.0	FN 6.0	VF 8.0	VF/NM 9.0	NM- 9.2
In "The Big City" movie adaptation (scarce)	21	42	63	124	206	280

ADVENTURES OF QUIK BUNNY
Nestle's Quik: 1984 (Giveaway, 32 pgs.)

	GD 2.0	VG 4.0	FN 6.0	VF 8.0	VF/NM 9.0	NM- 9.2
nn-Spider-Man app.	2	4	6	9	13	16

ADVENTURES OF STUBBY, SANTA'S SMALLEST REINDEER, THE
W. T. Grant Co.: nd (early 1940s) (Giveaway, 12 pgs.)

	GD 2.0	VG 4.0	FN 6.0	VF 8.0	VF/NM 9.0	NM- 9.2
nn	9	18	27	52	69	85

ADVENTURES OF VOTEMAN, THE
Foundation For Citizen Education Inc.: 1968

	GD 2.0	VG 4.0	FN 6.0	VF 8.0	VF/NM 9.0	NM- 9.2
nn	4	8	12	27	44	60

ADVENTURES WITH SANTA CLAUS
Promotional Publ. Co. (Murphy's Store): No date (early 50's)
(9-3/4x 6-3/4", 24 pgs., giveaway, paper-c)

	GD 2.0	VG 4.0	FN 6.0	VF 8.0	VF/NM 9.0	NM- 9.2
nn-Contains 8 pgs. ads	7	14	21	37	46	55
16 pg. version	8	16	24	40	50	60

AIR POWER (CBS TV & the U.S. Air Force Presents)
Prudential Insurance Co.: 1956 (5-1/4x7-1/4", 32 pgs., giveaway, soft-c)

	GD 2.0	VG 4.0	FN 6.0	VF 8.0	VF/NM 9.0	NM- 9.2
nn-Toth-a? Based on 'You Are There' TV program by Walter Cronkite	10	20	30	58	79	100

ALASKA BUSH PILOT
Jan Enterprises: 1959 (Paper cover, 10¢)

1-Promotes Bush Pilot Club (A 9.0 copy sold for $75 in Aug. 2020)
NOTE: *A CGC certified 9.9 Mint sold for $632.50 in 2005.*

ALICE IN BLUNDERLAND
Industrial Services: 1952 (Paper cover, 16 pgs. in color)

	GD 2.0	VG 4.0	FN 6.0	VF 8.0	VF/NM 9.0	NM- 9.2
nn-Facts about government waste and inefficiency	16	32	48	92	144	195

ALICE IN WONDERLAND
Western Printing Company/Whitman Publ. Co.: 1965; 1969; 1982

	GD 2.0	VG 4.0	FN 6.0	VF 8.0	VF/NM 9.0	NM- 9.2
Meets Santa Claus(1950s), nd, 16 pgs.	8	16	24	40	50	60
Rexall Giveaway(1965, 16 pgs., 5x7-1/4) Western Printing (TV, Hanna-Barbera)	3	6	9	19	30	40
Wonder Bakery Giveaway(1969, 16 pgs, color, nn, nd) (Continental Baking Company)	3	6	9	17	26	35

ALICE IN WONDERLAND MEETS SANTA
No publisher: nd (6-5/8x9-11/16", 16 pgs., giveaway, paper-c)

	GD 2.0	VG 4.0	FN 6.0	VF 8.0	VF/NM 9.0	NM- 9.2
nn	9	18	27	52	69	85

ALL ABOARD, MR. LINCOLN
Assoc. of American Railroads: Jan, 1959 (16 pgs.)

	GD 2.0	VG 4.0	FN 6.0	VF 8.0	VF/NM 9.0	NM- 9.2
nn-Abraham Lincoln and the Railroads	6	12	18	31	38	45

ALL NEW COMICS
Harvey Comics: Oct, 1993 (Giveaway, no cover price, 16 pgs.)(Hanna-Barbera)

	GD 2.0	VG 4.0	FN 6.0	VF 8.0	VF/NM 9.0	NM- 9.2
1-Flintstones, Scooby Doo, Jetsons, Yogi Bear & Wacky Races previews for upcoming Harvey's new Hanna-Barbera line-up	1	2	3	5	7	9

NOTE: *Material previewed in Harvey giveaway was eventually published by Archie.*

AMAZING SPIDER-MAN, THE
Marvel Comics Group

	GD 2.0	VG 4.0	FN 6.0	VF 8.0	VF/NM 9.0	NM- 9.2
Acme & Dingo Children's Boots (1980)-Spider-Woman app.	3	6	9	15	22	28
Adventures in Reading Starring... (1990,1991) Bogdanove & Romita-c/a						5.00
Aim Toothpaste Giveaway (36 pgs., reg. size)-1 pg. origin recap; Green Goblin-c/story	2	4	6	13	18	22
Aim Toothpaste Giveaway (16 pgs., reg. size)-Dr. Octopus app.	2	4	6	11	16	20
All Detergent Giveaway (1979, 36 pgs.), nn-Origin-r	3	6	9	14	19	24
Amazing Fantasy #15 (8/02) reprint included in Spider-Man DVD Collector's Gift Set	1	2	3	5	6	8
Amazing Fantasy #15 (2006) News America Marketing newspaper giveaway						4.00
Amazing Spider-Man nn (1990, 6-1/8x9", 28 pgs.)-Shan-Lon giveaway; retells origin of Spider-Man; Bagley-a/Saviuk-c	2	4	6	8	10	12
Amazing Spider-Man nn (1990, 6-1/8x9", 28 pgs.)-Shan-Lon giveaway; reprints Amazing Spider-Man #303 w/McFarlane-c/a	2	4	6	8	10	12
Amazing Spider-Man #1 Reprint (1990, 4-1/4x6-1/4", 28 pgs.)-Packaged with the book "Start Collecting Comic Books" from Running Press						4.00

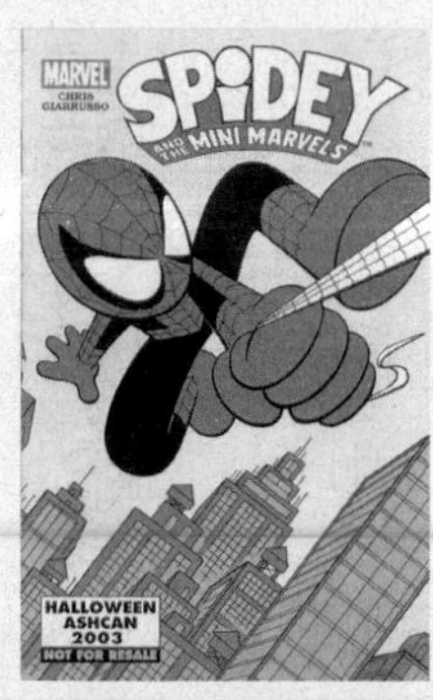

Spidey and the Mini-Marvels © MAR

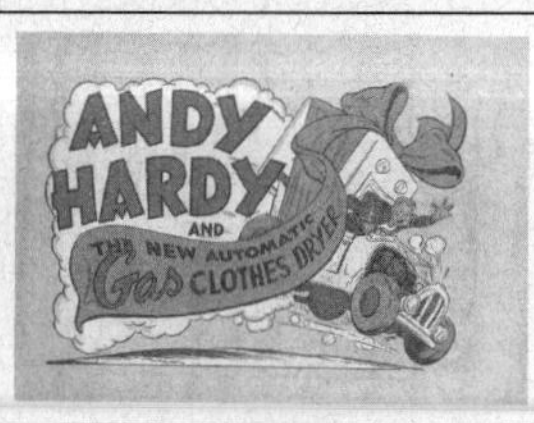

Andy Hardy Comics © WEST

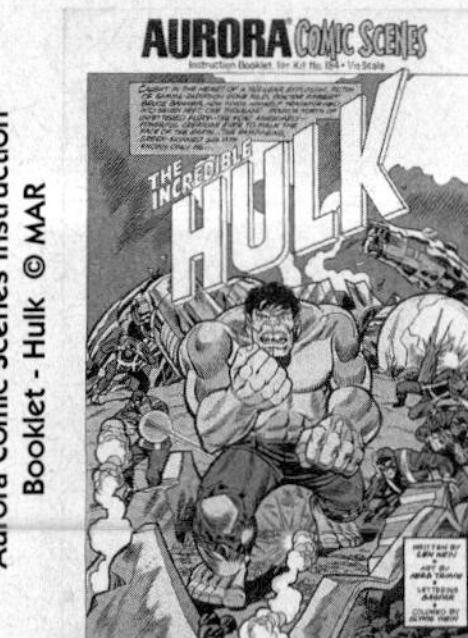

Aurora Comic Scenes Instruction Booklet - Hulk © MAR

GD VG FN VF VF/NM NM-
2.0 4.0 6.0 8.0 9.0 9.2

Amazing Spider-Man #3 Reprint (2004)-Best Buy/Sony giveaway 3.00
Amazing Spider-Man #50 (Sony Pictures Edition) (8/04)-mini-comic included in Spider-Man 2 movie DVD Collector's Gift Set; r/#50 & various ASM covers with Dr. Octopus 3.00
Amazing Spider-Man #129 (Lion Gate Films) (6/04)-promotional comic given away at movie theaters on opening night for The Punisher 3.00
...& Power Pack (1984, nn)(Nat'l Committee for Prevention of Child Abuse) (two versions, mail offer & store giveaway)-Mooney-a; Byrne-c
Mail offer 2 4 6 9 11 14
Store giveaway 5.00
...& The Hulk (Special Edition)(6/8/80; 20 pgs.)-Supplement to Chicago Tribune
2 4 6 11 16 20
...& The Incredible Hulk (1981, 1982; 36 pgs.)-Sanger Harris or May D&F supplement to Dallas Times, Dallas Herald, Denver Post, Kansas City Star, Tulsa World; Foley's supplement to Houston Chronicle (1982, 16 pgs.)- "Great Rodeo Robbery"; The Jones Store-giveaway (1983, 16 pgs.) 3 6 9 14 19 24
...and the New Mutants Featuring Skids nn (1990, National Committee for Prevention of Child Abuse/K-Mart giveaway)-Williams-c(i) 1 2 3 5 6 8
... Battles Ignorance (1992)(Sylvan Learning Systems) giveaway; Mad Thinker app. Kupperberg-a 1 3 4 6 8 10
...Captain America, The Incredible Hulk, & Spider-Woman (1981) (7-11 Stores giveaway; 36 pgs.) 2 4 6 11 16 20
...: Christmas in Dallas (1983) (Supplement to Dallas Times Herald) giveaway 2 4 6 11 16 20
...: Danger in Dallas (1983) (Supplement to Dallas Times Herald) giveaway 2 4 6 11 16 20
...: Danger in Denver (1983) (Supplement to Denver Post) giveaway for May D&F stores 2 4 6 11 16 20
..., Fire-Star, And Ice-Man at the Dallas Ballet Nutcracker (1983; supplement to Dallas Times Herald)-Mooney-p 2 4 6 11 16 20
Giveaway-Esquire Magazine (2/69)-Miniature-Still attached (scarce)
14 28 42 93 204 315
Giveaway-Eye Magazine (2/69)-Miniature-Still attached
9 18 27 63 129 195
...: Riot at Robotworld (1991; 16 pgs.)(National Action Council for Minorities in Engineering, Inc.) giveaway; Saviuk-c 1 2 3 5 6 8
..., Storm & Powerman (1982; 20 pgs.)(American Cancer Society) giveaway; also a 1991 2nd printing and a 1994 printing 1 3 4 6 8 10
...Vs. The Hulk (Special Edition; 1979, 20 pgs.)(Supplement to Columbus Dispatch)
2 4 6 13 18 22
...Vs. The Prodigy (Giveaway, 16 pgs. in color (1976, 5x6-1/2")-Sex education; (1 million printed; 35-50¢) 2 4 6 8 10 12
Spidey & The Mini-Marvels Halloween 2003 Ashcan (12/03, 8 1/2"x 5 1/2") Giarusso-s/a; Venom and Green Goblin app. 2.00

AMERICA MENACED!
Vital Publications: 1950 (Paper-c)
nn-Anti-communism 40 80 120 246 411 575

AMERICAN COMICS
Theatre Giveaways (Liberty Theatre, Grand Rapids, Mich. known): 1940's
Many possible combinations. "Golden Age" superhero comics with new cover added and given away at theaters. Following known: Superman #59, Capt. Marvel #20, 21, Capt. Marvel Jr. #5, Action #33, Classics Comics #8, Whiz #39. Value would vary with book and should be 70-80 percent of the original.

AMERICA UNDER SOCIALISM
National Research Bureau: 1950 (Paper-c)
nn-Anti-communism; 16 pages (a CGC 9.2 copy sold for $2520 in Nov. 2020)

ANDY HARDY COMICS
Western Printing Co.:
...& the New Automatic Gas Clothes Dryer (1952, 5x7-1/4", 16 pgs.) Bendix Giveaway (soft-c) 6 12 18 31 38 45

ANIMANIACS EMERGENCY WORLD
DC Comics: 1995
nn-American Red Cross 5.00

APACHE HUNTER
Creative Pictorials: 1954 (18 pgs. in color) (promo copy) (saddle stitched)
nn-Severin, Heath stories 15 30 45 85 130 175

AQUATEERS MEET THE SUPER FRIENDS
DC Comics: 1979
nn 2 4 6 11 16 20

ARCHIE AND HIS GANG (Zeta Beta Tau Presents...)
Archie Publications: Dec. 1950 (St. Louis National Convention giveaway)
nn-Contains new cover stapled over Archie Comics #47 (11-12/50) on inside; produced for Zeta Beta Tau 29 58 87 170 278 385

GD VG FN VF VF/NM NM-
2.0 4.0 6.0 8.0 9.0 9.2

ARCHIE COMICS (Also see Sabrina)
Archie Publications
... And Friends and the Shield (10/02, 8 1/2"x 5 1/2") Diamond Comic Dist. 4.00
... And Friends - A Halloween Tale (10/98, 8 1/2"x 5 1/2") Diamond Comic Dist.; Sabrina and Sonic app.; Dan DeCarlo-a 4.00
... And Friends - A Timely Tale (10/01, 8 1/2"x 5 1/2") Diamond Comic Dist. 4.00
... And Friends Monster Bash 2003 (8 1/2"x 5 1/2") Diamond Comic Dist. Halloween 4.00
...And His Friends Help Raise Literacy Awareness In Mississippi nn (3/94)
1 2 3 5 6 8
...And His Friends Vs. The Household Toxic Wastes nn (1993, 16 pgs.) produced for the San Diego Regional Household Hazardous Materials Program
1 2 3 5 6 8
...And His Pals in the Peer Helping Program nn (2/91, 7"x4 1/2") produced by the FBI
1 2 3 5 6 8
...And the History of Electronics nn (5/90, 36 pgs.)-Radio Shack giveaway; Bender-c/a
1 2 3 5 6 8
Fairmont Potato Chips Giveaway-Mini comics 1970 (6 issues-nn's.,6 7/8" x 2 1/4", 8 pgs. each)
3 6 9 18 28 38
Fairmont Potato Chips Giveaway-Mini comics 1971 (4 issues-nn's.,6 7/8" x 5", 8 pgs. each)
3 6 9 18 28 38
Little Archie, The House That Wouldn't Move ('07, 8-1/2" x 5-3/8" Halloween mini-comic) 3.00
...'s Ham Radio Adventure (1997) Morse code instruction; Goldberg-a 6.00
...'s Weird Mysteries (9/99, 8 1/2"x 5 1/2") Diamond Comic Dist. Halloween giveaway 3.00
Tales From Riverdale (2006, 8 1/2"x 5 1/2") Diamond Comic Dist. Halloween giveaway 3.00
...: The Dawn of Time ('10, 8-1/2" x 5-3/8" Halloween mini-comic) 3.00
...: The Mystery of the Museum Sleep-In ('08, 8-1/2" x 5-3/8" Halloween mini-comic) 3.00
... Your Official Store Club Magazine nn (10/48, 9-1/2x6-1/2, 16 pgs.)- "Wolf Whistle" Archie on front-c; B. R. Baker Co. ad on back-c (a CGC 7.5 copy sold for $1912 in Feb. 2013)

ARCHIE SHOE-STORE GIVEAWAY
Archie Publications: 1944-50 (12-15 pgs. of games, puzzles, stories like Superman-Tim books, No nos. - came out monthly)
(1944-47)-issues 26 52 78 154 252 350
2/48-Peggy Lee photo-c 26 52 78 154 252 350
3/48-Marylee Robb photo-c 20 40 60 120 195 270
4/48-Gloria De Haven photo-c 26 52 78 154 252 350
5/48, 6/48, 7/48, 10/48 20 40 60 120 195 270
8/48-Story on Shirley Temple 26 52 78 152 249 345
5/49-Kathleen Hughes photo-c 20 40 60 117 189 260
6/49, 7/49, 9/49 18 36 54 107 169 230
8/49-Archie photo-c from radio show 30 60 90 177 289 400
10/49-Gloria Mann photo-c from radio show 22 44 66 128 209 290
11/49, 12/49, 2/50, 3/50 20 40 60 117 189 260

ARCHIE'S JOKE BOOK MAGAZINE (See Joke Book ...)
Archie Publications
Drug Store Giveaway (No. 39 w/new-c) 9 18 27 47 61 75

ARCHIE'S TEN ISSUE COLLECTOR'S SET (Title inside of cover only)
Archie Publications: June, 1997 - No. 10, June, 1997 ($1.50, 20 pgs.)
1-10: 1,7-Archie. 2,8-Betty & Veronica. 3,9-Veronica. 4-Betty. 5-World of Archie. 6-Jughead. 10-Archie and Friends each... 5.00

ASTRO COMICS
American Airlines (Harvey): 1968 - 1979 (Giveaway)(Reprints of Harvey comics)
1968-Richie Rich, Hot Stuff, Casper, Wendy on-c only; Spooky and Nightmare app. inside
3 6 9 19 30 40
1970-Casper, Spooky, Hot Stuff; Stumbo the Giant, Little Audrey, Little Lotta, & Richie Rich reprints. Five different versions 3 6 9 16 23 30
1973,1975,1976: 1973-Three different versions 2 4 6 9 12 15
1977-r/Richie Rich & Casper #20. 1978-r/Richie Rich & Casper #25. 1979-r/Richie Rich & Casper #30 (scarce) 2 4 6 8 10 12

ATARI FORCE (Given away with Atari games)
DC Comics: 1982 - No. 5, 1983
1-3 (1982, 5X7", 52 pgs.) 2 4 6 8 10 12
4,5 (1982-1983, 52 pgs.)(scarcer) 2 4 6 11 16 20

AURORA COMIC SCENES INSTRUCTION BOOKLET (Included with superhero model kits)
Aurora Plastics Co.: 1974 (6-1/4x9-3/4," 8 pgs., slick paper)
181-140-Tarzan; Neal Adams-a 3 6 9 18 27 38
182-140-Spider-Man. 4 8 12 23 37 50
183-140-Tonto(Gil Kane art). 184-140-Hulk. 185-140-Superman. 186-140-Superboy. 187-140-Batman. 188-140-The Lone Ranger(1974-by Gil Kane). 192-140-Captain America(1975). 193-140-Robin 3 6 9 16 23 30

BACK TO THE FUTURE

Batman Onstar edition © DC

Beetle Bailey Bold Detergent © CC

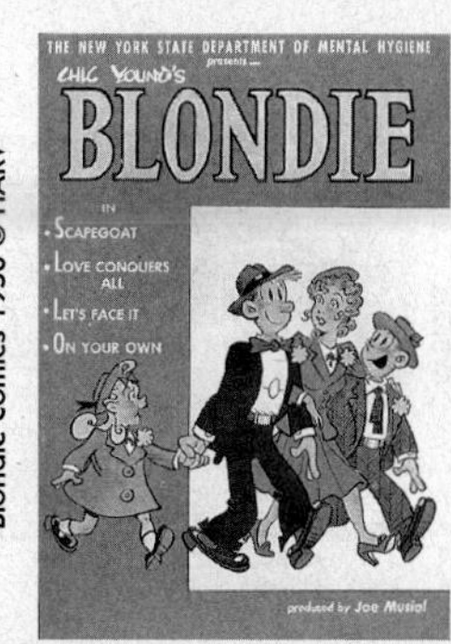

Blondie Comics 1950 © HARV

	GD 2.0	VG 4.0	FN 6.0	VF 8.0	VF/NM 9.0	NM- 9.2

Harvey Comics
Special nn (1991, 20 pgs.)-Brunner-c; given away at Universal Studios in Florida — 2 4 6 8 10 12

BALTIMORE COLTS
American Visuals Corp.: 1950 (Giveaway)
nn-Eisner-c — 45 90 135 284 480 675

BAMBI (Disney)
K. K. Publications (Giveaways): 1941, 1942
1941-Horlick's Malted Milk & various toy stores; text & pictures; most copies mailed out with store stickers on-c — 43 86 129 271 461 650
1942-Same as 4-Color #12, but no price (Same as '41 issue?) (Scarce) — 97 194 291 621 1061 1500

BATMAN
DC Comics: 1966 - Present
Act II Popcorn mini-comic(1998) — 6.00
Batman #121 Toys R Us edition (1997) r/1st Mr. Freeze — 2 4 6 9 12 15
Batman #279 Mini-comic with Monogram Model kit (1995) — 1 2 3 5 6 8
Batman #362 Mervyn's edition (1989) — 6.00
Batman #608 New York Post edition (2002) — 1 3 4 6 8 10
Batman Adventures #25 Best Western edition (1997) — 5.00
Batman and Other DC Classics 1 (1989, giveaway)-DC Comics/Diamond Comic Distributors; Batman origin-r/Batman #47, Camelot 3000-r, Justice League-r('87), New Teen Titans-r — 5.00
Batman and Robin movie preview (1997, 8 pgs.) Kellogg's Cereal promo — 4.00
Batman Beyond Six Flags edition — 1 2 3 5 6 8
Batman: Canadian Multiculturalism Custom (1992) — 5.00
Batman Claritan edition (1999) — 4.00
Kellogg's Poptarts comics (1966, Set of 6, 16 pgs.); All were folded and placed in Poptarts boxes. Infantino art on Catwoman and Joker issues.
"The Man in the Iron Mask", "The Penguin's Fowl Play", "The Joker's Happy Victims", "The Catwoman's Catnapping Caper", "The Mad Hatter's Hat Crimes", "The Case of the Batman II"
each.... — 5 10 15 33 57 80
Mask of the Phantasm (1993) Mini-comic released w/video — 1 3 4 6 8 10
Onstar - Auto Show Special Edition (OnStar Corp., 2001, 8 pgs.) Riddler app. — 3.00
Pizza Hut giveaway (12/77)-exact-r of #122,123; Joker app. — 2 4 6 10 14 18
Prell Shampoo giveaway (1966, 16 pgs.)- "The Joker's Practical Jokes" (6-7/8x3-3/8") — 10 20 30 69 147 225
Revell in pack (1995) — 4.00
...: The 10-Cent Adventure (3/02, 10¢) intro. to the "Bruce Wayne: Murderer" x-over; Rucka-s/Burchett & Janson-a/Dave Johnson-c; these are alternate copies with special outer half-covers (at least 10 different) promoting comics, toys and games shops — 3.00

BATMAN RECORD COMIC
National Periodical Publications: 1966 (one-shot)
1-With record (still sealed) — 13 26 39 87 191 295
Comic only — 9 18 27 58 114 170

BEETLE BAILEY
Charlton Comics: 1969-1970 (Giveaways)
Armed Forces ('69)-same as regular issue (#68) — 2 4 6 10 14 18
Armed Forces ('70) — 2 4 6 10 14 18
Bold Detergent ('69)-same as regular issue (#67) — 2 4 6 10 14 18
Cerebral Palsy Assn. V2#71('69) - V2#73(#1,1/70) — 3.00
Red Cross (1969, 5x7", 16 pgs., paper-c) — 2 4 6 10 14 18

BELLAIRE BICYCLE CO.
Bellaire Bicycle Co.: 1940 (promotional comic)(64 pgs.)
nn-Contains Wonderworld #12 w/new-c. Contents can vary w/diff. 1940's books — 52 104 156 328 552 775

BEST WESTERN GIVEAWAY
DC Comics: 1999
nn-Best Western hotels — 3.00

BETTER LIFE FOR YOU, A
Harvey Publications Inc.: (16 pgs., paper cover)
nn-Better living through higher productivity — 3 6 9 15 22 28

BEWARE THE BOOBY TRAP
Malcolm Alter: 1970 (5" x 7")
nn-Deals with drug abuse — 4 8 12 23 37 50

B-FORCE (Milwaukee Brewers and Wisconsin Dental Asso.)
Dark Horse Comics: 2001 (School and stadium giveaway)
nn-Brewers players combat the evils of smokeless tobacco — 3.00

BIG BOY (see Adventures of...)

BIG JIM'S P.A.C.K.
Mattel, Inc. (Marvel Comics): No date (1975) (16 pgs.)
nn-Giveaway with Big Jim doll; Buscema/Sinnott-c/a — 4 8 12 25 40 55

"BILL AND TED'S EXCELLENT ADVENTURE" MOVIE ADAPTATION
DC Comics: 1989 (No cover price)
nn-Torres-a — 6.00

BIONICLE (LEGO robot toys)
DC Comics: Jun, 2001 - No. 27, Nov, 2005 ($2.25/$3.25, 16 pgs, available to LEGO club members)
1 — 1 3 4 6 8 10
2-5 — 6.00
6-13 — 4.00
14-27 — 3.00
The Legend of Bionicle (McDonald's Mini-comic, 4-1/4 x 7") — 4.00
Special Edition #0 (Six Heroes...One Destiny) '03 San Diego Comic Con; Ashley Wood-c — 6.00

BLACK GOLD
Esso Service Station (Giveaway): 1945? (8 pgs. in color)
nn-Reprints from True Comics — 6 12 18 31 38 45

BLADE SINS OF THE FATHER
Marvel Comics: Aug, 1996 (24 pgs. with paper cover)
1-Theatrical preview; possibly limited to 2000 copies — (Value will be based on sale)

BLAZING FOREST, THE (See Forest Fire and Smokey Bear)
Western Printing: 1962 (20 pgs., 5x7", slick-c)
nn-Smokey The Bear fire prevention — 3 6 9 14 20 26

BLESSED PIUS X
Catechetical Guild (Giveaway): No date (Text/comics, 32 pgs., paper-c)
nn — 9 18 27 47 61 75

BLIND JUSTICE (Also see Batman: Blind Justice)
DC Comics/Diamond Comic Distributors: 1989 (Giveaway, squarebound)
nn-Contains Detective #598-600 by Batman movie writer Sam Hamm, w/covers; published same time as originals? — 6.00

BLONDIE COMICS
Harvey Publications: 1950-1964
1950 Giveaway — 9 18 27 47 61 75
1962,1964 Giveaway — 3 6 9 17 26 35
N. Y. State Dept. of Mental Hygiene Giveaway-(1950) Regular size; 16 pgs.; no # — 4 8 12 27 44 60
N. Y. State Dept. of Mental Hygiene Giveaway-(1956) Regular size; 16 pgs.; no # — 3 6 9 18 27 36
N. Y. State Dept. of Mental Hygiene Giveaway-(1961) Regular size; 16 pgs.; no # — 3 6 9 16 23 30

BLOOD IS THE HARVEST
Catechetical Guild: 1950 (32 pgs., paper-c)
(Scarce)-Anti-communism (35 known copies) — 255 310 765 1619 2785 3950
Black & white version (5 known copies), saddle stitched — 111 222 333 705 1215 1725
Untrimmed version (only one known copy); estimated value - $4500
NOTE: *In 1979 nine copies of the color version surfaced from the old Guild's files plus the five black & white copies.*

BLUE BIRD CHILDREN'S MAGAZINE, THE
Graphic Information Service: V1#2, 1957 - No. 10 1958 (16 pgs., soft-c, regular size)
V1#2-10: Pat, Pete & Blue Bird app. — 2 4 6 9 13 16

BLUE BIRD COMICS
Various Shoe Stores: 1947 - 1950 (Giveaway, 36 pgs.)
Charlton Comics: 1959 - 1964 (Giveaway)
nn-(1947-50, not Charlton)(36 pgs.)-Several issues; Human Torch, Sub-Mariner app. in some — 20 40 60 118 192 265
1959-(Charlton) Lil Genius, Wild Bill Hickok, Black Fury, Masked Raider, Timmy The Timid Ghost, Freddy (All #1) — 3 6 9 14 20 26
1959-(Charlton, same 6 titles; all #2-5) except (#5) Masked Raider #21 — 3 6 9 14 20 25
1959-(#5) Masked Raider #21 — 3 6 9 15 22 28
1960-(6 titles, all #6-9) Black Fury, Masked Raider, Freddy, Timmy the Timid Ghost, Li'l Genius, Six Gun Heroes — 3 6 9 14 19 24
1961-(All #10's) Black Fury, Masked Raider, Freddy, Timmy the Timid Ghost, Li'l Genius, Six Gun Heroes (Charlton) — 2 4 6 13 18 22

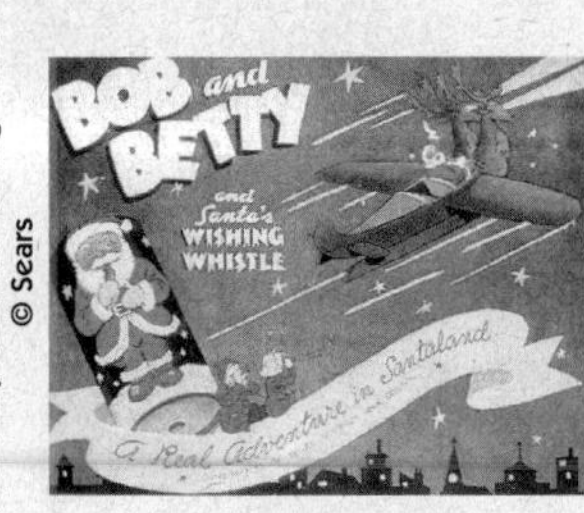

Bob & Betty & Santa's Wishing Whistle © Sears

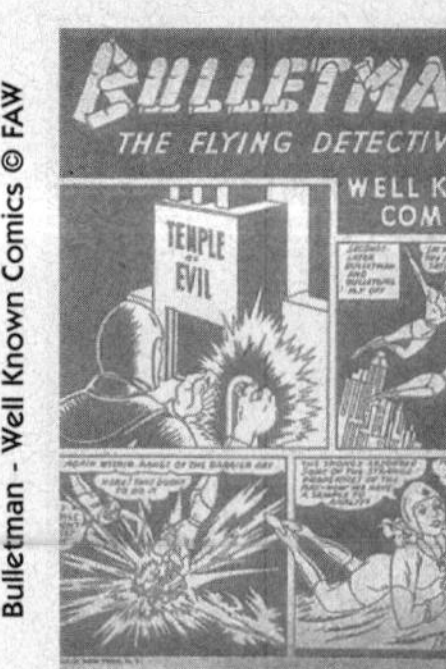

Bulletman - Well Known Comics © FAW

Captain America - Return of the Asthma Monster #2 © MAR

	GD	VG	FN	VF	VF/NM	NM-
	2.0	4.0	6.0	8.0	9.0	9.2

1961-(All #11-13) Lil Genius, Wyatt Earp, Black Fury, Timmy the Timid Ghost, Atomic Mouse, Freddy 2 4 6 13 18 22
1962-(All #14) Lil Genius, Wyatt Earp, Black Fury, Timmy the Timid Ghost, Atomic Mouse, Freddy 2 4 6 13 18 22
1962-(6 titles, all #15) Lil Genius, Six Gun Heroes, Black Fury, Timmy the Timid Ghost, Texas Rangers, Freddy 2 4 6 13 18 22
1962-(7 titles, all #16) Lil Genius, Six Gun Heroes, Black Fury, Timmy the Timid Ghost, Texas Rangers, Wyatt Earp, Atomic Mouse 2 4 6 13 18 22
1963-(All #17) My Little Margie, Lil Genius, Timmy the Timid Ghost, Texas Rangers (Charlton) 2 4 6 9 13 16
1964-(All #18) Mysteries of Unexplored Worlds, Teenage Hotrodders, War Heroes, Wyatt Earp (Charlton) 2 4 6 9 13 16

NOTE: *Reprints comics of regular issue, with Blue Bird shoe promo on back cover, with upper front cover imprint of various shoe retailers. Printed from 1959 to 1962, with issues 1 thru 16. The 8 different front cover imprints for issues 1 thru 16 are, 1) Blue Bird Shoes, 2) Schiff's Shoes, 3) Big Shoe Store, 4) E.D. Edwards Shoe Store, 5) R & S Shoe store, 6) Federal Shoe Store, 7) Kirby's Shoes, 8) Gallenkamps.*

BOB & BETTY & SANTA'S WISHING WHISTLE (Also see A Christmas Carol, Merry Christmas From Sears Toyland, and Santa's Christmas Comic Variety Show)
Sears Roebuck & Co.: 1941 (Christmas giveaway, 12 pgs., oblong)

nn 23 46 69 136 223 310

BOBBY BENSON'S B-BAR-B RIDERS (Radio)
Magazine Enterprises/AC Comics

...in the Tunnel of Gold-(1936, 5-1/4x8"; 100 pgs.) Radio giveaway by Hecker-H.O. Company (H.O. Oats); contains 22 color pgs. of comics, rest in novel form 12 24 36 67 94 120
...And The Lost Herd-same as above 12 24 36 67 94 120

BOBBY GETS HEP
Bell Telephone: 1946

nn-Bell Telephone Systems giveaway 7 14 21 37 46 55

BOBBY SHELBY COMICS
Shelby Cycle Co./Harvey Publications: 1949

nn 6 12 18 28 34 40

BOY SCOUT ADVENTURE
Boy Scouts of America: 1954 (16 pgs., paper cover)

nn 5 10 15 22 26 30

BOYS' RANCH
Harvey Publications: 1951

Shoe Store Giveaway #5,6 (Identical to regular issues except Simon & Kirby centerfold replaced with ad) 14 28 42 76 108 140

BOZO THE CLOWN (TV)
Dell Publishing Co.: 1961

Giveaway-1961, 16 pgs., 3-1/2x7-1/4", Apsco Products 5 10 15 31 53 75

BRER RABBIT IN "ICE CREAM FOR THE PARTY"
American Dairy Association: 1955 (5x7-1/4", 16 pgs., soft-c) (Walt Disney) (Premium)

nn-(Scarce) 39 78 117 236 388 540

BUCK ROGERS (In the 25th Century)
Kelloggs Corn Flakes Giveaway: 1933 (6x8", 36 pgs)

370A-By Phil Nowlan & Dick Calkins; 1st Buck Rogers radio premium & 1st app. in comics (tells origin) (Reissued in 1995) 68 136 204 500 - -
with envelope 90 180 270 675 - -

BUGS BUNNY (Puffed Rice Giveaway)
Quaker Cereals: 1949 (32 pgs. each, 3-1/8x6-7/8")

A1-Traps the Counterfeiters, A2-Aboard Mystery Submarine, A3- Rocket to the Moon, A4-Lion Tamer, A5-Rescues the Beautiful Princess, B1-Buried Treasure, B2-Outwits the Smugglers, B3-Joins the Marines, B4-Meets the Dwarf Ghost, B5-Finds Aladdin's Lamp, C1-Lost in the Frozen North, C2-Secret Agent, C3-Captured by Cannibals, C4-Fights the Man from Mars, C5-And the Haunted Cave
each.... 8 16 24 40 50 60
Mailing Envelope (has illo of Bugs on front)(Each envelope designates what set it contains, A,B or C on front) 8 16 24 40 50 60

BUGS BUNNY (3-D)
Cheerios Giveaway: 1953 (Pocket size) (15 titles)

each.... 10 20 30 56 76 95
Mailing Envelope (has Bugs drawn on front) 10 20 30 56 76 95

BUGS BUNNY
DC Comics: May, 1997 ($4.95, 24 pgs., comic-sized)

1-Numbered ed. of 100,000; "1st Day of Issue" stamp cancellation on-c 6.00

BUGS BUNNY POSTAL COMIC
DC Comics: 1997 (64 pgs., 7.5" x 5")

nn -Mail Fan; Daffy Duck app. 4.50

BULLETMAN
Fawcett Publications

Well Known Comics (1942)-Paper-c, glued binding; printed in red (Bestmaid/Samuel Lowe giveaway) 15 30 45 90 140 190

BULLS-EYE (Cody of The Pony Express No. 8 on)
Charlton: 1955 (Great Scott Shoe Store giveaway)

Reprints #2 with new cover 19 38 57 112 179 240

BUSTER BROWN COMICS (Radio)(Also see My Dog Tige in Promotional sec.)
Brown Shoe Co.: 1945 - No. 43, 1959 (No. 5: paper-c)

nn, nd (#1,scarce)-Featuring Smilin' Ed McConnell & the Buster Brown gang "Midnight" the cat, "Squeaky" the mouse & "Froggy" the Gremlin; covers mention diff. shoe stores. Contains adventure stories 66 132 198 419 722 1025
2 20 40 60 120 195 270
3,5-10 14 28 42 76 108 140
4 (Rare)-Low print run due to paper shortage 19 38 57 112 179 245
11-20 9 18 27 50 65 80
21-24,26-28 7 14 21 35 43 50
25,33-37,40,41-Crandall-a in all 10 20 30 58 79 100
29-32-"Interplanetary Police Vs. the Space Siren" by Crandall (pencils only #29) 11 22 33 60 83 105
38,39,42,43 7 14 21 35 43 50

BUSTER BROWN COMICS (Radio)
Brown Shoe Co: 1950s

...Goes to Mars (2/58-Western Printing), slick-c, 20 pgs., reg. size 14 28 42 81 118 155
...In "Buster Makes the Team!" (1959-Custom Comics) 9 18 27 47 61 75
...In The Jet Age ('50s), slick-c, 20 pgs., 5x7-1/4" 11 22 33 60 83 105
...Of the Safety Patrol ('60-Custom Comics) 3 6 9 19 30 40
...Out of This World ('59-Custom Comics) 7 14 21 37 46 55
...Safety Coloring Book ('58, 16 pgs.)-Slick paper 7 14 21 37 46 55

CALL FROM CHRIST
Catechetical Educational Society: 1952 (Giveaway, 36 pgs.)

nn 7 14 21 35 43 50

CANCELLED COMIC CAVALCADE
DC Comics, Inc.: Summer, 1978 - No. 2, Fall, 1978 (8-1/2x11", B&W)
(Xeroxed pgs. on one side only w/blue cover and taped spine)(Only 35 sets produced)

1-(412 pgs.) Contains xeroxed copies of art for: Black Lightning #12, cover to #13; Claw #13,14; The Deserter #1; Doorway to Nightmare #6; Firestorm #6; The Green Team #2,3.
2-(532 pgs.) Contains xeroxed copies of art for: Kamandi #60 (including Omac), #61; Prez #5; Shade #9 (including The Odd Man); Showcase #105 (Deadman), 106 (The Creeper); Secret Society of Super Villains #16 & 17; The Vixen #1; and covers to Army at War #2, Battle Classics #3, Demand Classics #1 & 2, Dynamic Classics #3, Mr. Miracle #26, Ragman #6, Weird Mystery #25 & 26, & Western Classics #1 & 2.
(A FN set of Number 1 & 2 was sold in 2005 for $3680; a VG set sold in 2007 for $2629)

NOTE: *In June, 1978, DC cancelled several of their titles. For copyright purposes, the unpublished original art for these titles was xeroxed, bound in the above books, published and distributed. Only 35 copies were made. Beware of bootleg copies.*

CAP'N CRUNCH COMICS (See Quaker Oats)
Quaker Oats Co.: 1963; 1965 (16 pgs.; miniature giveaways; 2-1/2x6-1/2")

(1963 titles)- "The Picture Pirates", "The Fountain of Youth", "I'm Dreaming of a Wide Isthmus". (1965 titles)- "Bewitched, Betwitched, & Betweaked", "Seadog Meets the Witch Doctor", "A Witch in Time" 5 10 15 31 53 75

CAPTAIN ACTION (Toy)
National Periodical Publications

...& Action Boy('67)-Ideal Toy Co. giveaway (1st app. Captain Action) 10 20 30 70 150 230

CAPTAIN AMERICA
Marvel Comics Group

...& The Campbell Kids (1980, 36pg. giveaway, Campbell's Soup/U.S. Dept. of Energy) 2 4 6 10 14 18
...Goes To War Against Drugs(1990, no #, giveaway)-Distributed to direct sales shops; 2nd printing exists 1 3 4 6 8 10
...Meets The Asthma Monster (1987, no #, giveaway, Your Physician and Glaxo, Inc.) 1 3 4 6 8 10
Return of The Asthma Monster Vol. 1 #2 (1992, giveaway, Your Physician & Allen & Hanbury's) 1 3 4 6 8 10

Captain Marvel Adventures (Wheaties) © FAW

Carvel Comics #3 © Carvel Corp.

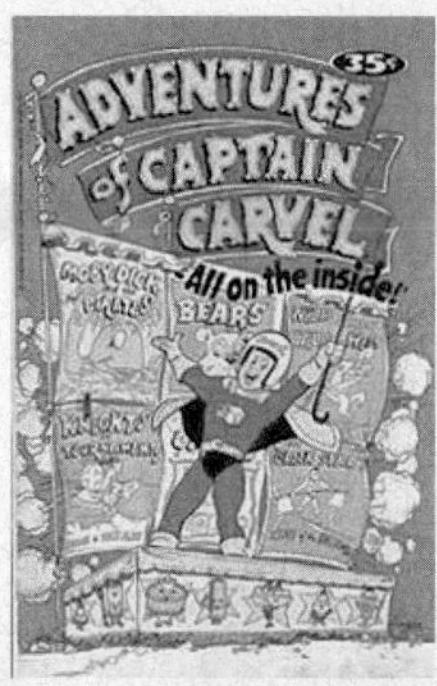

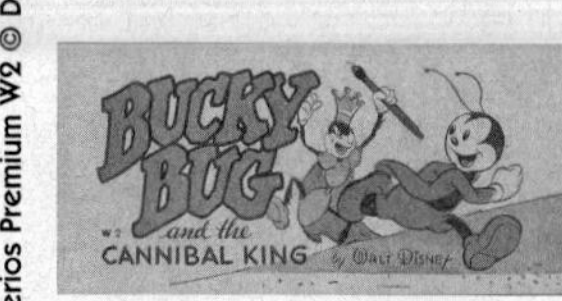

Cheerios Premium W2 © DIS

	GD 2.0	VG 4.0	FN 6.0	VF 8.0	VF/NM 9.0	NM- 9.2
...Vs. Asthma Monster (1990, no #, giveaway, Your Physician & Allen & Hanbury's)	1	3	4	6	8	10

CAPTAIN AMERICA COMICS
Timely/Marvel Comics: 1954

	GD	VG	FN	VF	VF/NM	NM-
Shoestore Giveaway #77	187	374	561	1197	2049	2900

CAPTAIN ATOM
Nationwide Publishers

	GD	VG	FN	VF	VF/NM	NM-
...- Secret of the Columbian Jungle (16 pgs. in color, paper-c, 3-3/4x5-1/8")-Fireside Marshmallow giveaway	6	12	18	31	38	45

CAPTAIN BEN DIX
Bendix Aviation Corporation: 1943 (Small size)

	GD	VG	FN	VF	VF/NM	NM-
nn	9	18	27	50	65	80

CAPTAIN BEN DIX IN ACTION WITH THE INVISIBLE CREW
Bendix Aviation Corp.: 1940s (nd), (20 pgs, 8-1/4"x11", heavy paper)

	GD	VG	FN	VF	VF/NM	NM-
nn-WWII bomber-c; Japanese app.	8	16	24	42	54	65

CAPTAIN BEN DIX IN SECRETS OF THE INVISIBLE CREW
Bendix Aviation Corp.: 1940s (nd), (32 pgs, soft-c)

	GD	VG	FN	VF	VF/NM	NM-
nn	8	16	24	42	54	65

CAPTAIN FORTUNE PRESENTS
Vital Publications: 1955 - 1959 (Giveaway, 3-1/4x6-7/8", 16 pgs.)

	GD	VG	FN	VF	VF/NM	NM-
"Davy Crockett in Episodes of the Creek War", "Davy Crockett at the Alamo", "In Sherwood Forest Tells Strange Tales of Robin Hood" ('57), "Meets Bolivar the Liberator" ('59), "Tells How Buffalo Bill Fights the Dog Soldiers" ('57), "Young Davy Crockett"	4	7	9	14	17	20

CAPTAIN GALLANT (...of the Foreign Legion) (TV)
Charlton Comics

	GD	VG	FN	VF	VF/NM	NM-
Heinz Foods Premium (#1?)(1955; regular size)-U.S. Pictorial; contains Buster Crabbe photos; Don Heck-a	1	3	4	6	8	10
Mailing Envelope						20.00

CAPTAIN JOLLY ADVENTURES
Johnston and Cushing: 1950's, nd (Post Corn Fetti cereal giveaway) (5-1/4" x 4-1/2")

	GD	VG	FN	VF	VF/NM	NM-
1-3: 1-Captain Jolly Advs. 2-Captain Jolly and His Pirate Crew in Off To Treasure Island. 3-C.J. & His Pirate Crew in The Terror Of The Deep	2	4	6	8	10	12

CAPTAIN MARVEL ADVENTURES
Fawcett Publications

	GD	VG	FN	VF	VF/NM	NM-
Bond Bread Giveaways-(24 pgs.; pocket size-7-1/4x3-1/2"; paper cover): "...& the Stolen City" ('48), "The Boy Who Never Heard of Capt. Marvel", "Meets the Weatherman" (1950) (reprint) each....	23	46	69	136	223	310
...Well Known Comics (1944; 12 pgs.; 8-1/2x10-1/2")-printed in red & in blue; soft-c; glued binding - (Bestmaid/Samuel Lowe Co. giveaway)	18	36	54	103	162	220

CAPTAIN MARVEL ADVENTURES (Also see Flash and Funny Stuff)
Fawcett Publications (Wheaties Giveaway): 1945 (6x8", full color, paper-c)

	GD	VG	FN	VF	VF/NM	NM-
nn- "Captain Marvel & the Threads of Life" plus 2 other stories (32 pgs.)	55	110	275	550	-	-

NOTE: *All copies were taped at each corner to a box of Wheaties and are never found in Fine or Mint condition. Prices listed for each grade include tape. File copy stamped "June 21, 1947".*

CAPTAIN MARVEL AND THE LTS. OF SAFETY
Ebasco Services/Fawcett Publications: 1950 - 1951 (3 issues - no No.'s)

	GD	VG	FN	VF	VF/NM	NM-
nn (#1) "Danger Flies a Kite" ('50, scarce),	39	78	117	240	395	550
nn (#2)"Danger Takes to Climbing" ('50),	26	52	78	154	252	350
nn (#3)"Danger Smashes Street Lights" ('51)	26	52	78	154	252	350

CAPTAIN MARVEL, JR.
Fawcett Publications: (1944; 12 pgs.; 8-1/2x10-1/2")

	GD	VG	FN	VF	VF/NM	NM-
...Well Known Comics (Printed in blue; paper-c, glued binding)-Bestmaid/Samuel Lowe Co. giveaway	14	28	42	80	115	150

CARDINAL MINDSZENTY (The Truth Behind the Trial of...)
Catechetical Guild Education Society: 1949 (24 pgs., paper cover)

	GD	VG	FN	VF	VF/NM	NM-
nn-Anti-communism	14	28	42	80	115	150
Press Proof-(Very Rare)-(Full color, 7-1/2x11-3/4", untrimmed) Only two known copies						425.00
Preview Copy (B&W, stapled), 18 pgs.; contains first 13 pgs. of Cardinal Mindszenty and was sent out as an advance promotion. Only one known copy						350.00 - 450.00

NOTE: *Regular edition also printed in French. There was also a movie released in 1949 called "Guilty of Treason" which is a fact-based account of the trial and imprisonment of Cardinal Mindszenty by the Communist regime in Hungary.*

CARNIVAL OF COMICS
Fleet-Air Shoes: 1954 (Giveaway)

	GD	VG	FN	VF	VF/NM	NM-
nn-Contains a comic bound with new cover; several combinations possible; Charlton's Eh! known	5	10	15	24	30	35

CARTOON NETWORK
DC Comics: 1997 (Giveaway)

	GD	VG	FN	VF	VF/NM	NM-
nn-reprints Cow and Chicken, Scooby-Doo, & Flintstones stories						4.00

CARVEL COMICS (Amazing Advs. of Capt. Carvel)
Carvel Corp. (Ice Cream): 1975 - No. 5, 1976 (25¢; #3-5: 35¢) (#4,5: 3-1/4x5")

	GD	VG	FN	VF	VF/NM	NM-
1-3	1	2	3	5	6	8
4,5(1976)-Baseball theme	2	4	6	8	10	12

CASE OF THE WASTED WATER, THE
Rheem Water Heating: 1972? (Giveaway)

	GD	VG	FN	VF	VF/NM	NM-
nn-Neal Adams-a	4	8	12	27	44	60

CASPER SPECIAL
Target Stores (Harvey): nd (Dec, 1990) (Giveaway with $1.00 cover)

	GD	VG	FN	VF	VF/NM	NM-
Three issues-Given away with Casper video						6.00

CASPER, THE FRIENDLY GHOST (Paramount Picture Star...)(2nd Series)
Harvey Publications

American Dental Association (Giveaways):

	GD	VG	FN	VF	VF/NM	NM-
...'s Dental Health Activity Book-1977	2	4	6	8	11	14
...Presents Space Age Dentistry-1972	2	4	6	9	13	16
..., His Den, & Their Dentist Fight the Tooth Demons-1974	2	4	6	9	13	16
Casper Rides the School Bus (1960, 7x3.5", 16 pgs.)	2	4	6	9	13	16

CELEBRATE THE CENTURY SUPERHEROES STAMP ALBUM
DC Comics: 1998 - No. 5, 2000 (32 pgs.)

	GD	VG	FN	VF	VF/NM	NM-
1-5: Historical stories hosted by DC heroes						4.00

CENTIPEDE
DC Comics: 1983

	GD	VG	FN	VF	VF/NM	NM-
1-Based on Atari video game	2	4	6	10	14	18

CENTURY OF COMICS
Eastern Color Printing Co.: 1933 (100 pgs.)
Bought by Wheatena, Malt-O-Milk, John Wanamaker, Kinney Shoe Stores, & others to be used as premiums and radio giveaways. No publisher listed.

	GD	VG	FN	VF	VF/NM	NM-
nn-Mutt & Jeff, Joe Palooka, etc. reprints	1867	3734	5601	14,000	-	-

CHEERIOS PREMIUMS (Disney)
Walt Disney Productions: 1947 (16 titles, pocket size, 32 pgs.)

	GD	VG	FN	VF	VF/NM	NM-
Mailing Envelope for each set "W,X,Y & Z" (has Mickey illo on front)(each envelope designates the set it contains on the front)	9	18	27	47	61	75
Set "W"						
W1-Donald Duck & the Pirates	9	18	27	47	61	75
W2-Bucky Bug & the Cannibal King	5	10	15	24	29	34
W3-Pluto Joins the F.B.I.	5	10	15	24	29	34
W4-Mickey Mouse & the Haunted House	6	12	18	27	33	38
Set "X"						
X1-Donald Duck, Counter Spy	9	18	27	47	61	75
X2-Goofy Lost in the Desert	5	10	15	24	29	34
X3-Br'er Rabbit Outwits Br'er Fox	5	10	15	24	29	34
X4-Mickey Mouse at the Rodeo	6	12	18	28	34	40
Set "Y"						
Y1-Donald Duck's Atom Bomb by Carl Barks. Disney has banned reprinting this book	68	136	204	435	743	1050
Y2-Br'er Rabbit's Secret	5	10	15	24	29	34
Y3-Dumbo & the Circus Mystery	5	10	15	24	29	34
Y4-Mickey Mouse Meets the Wizard	6	12	18	29	36	42
Set "Z"						
Z1-Donald Duck Pilots a Jet Plane (not by Barks)	8	16	24	44	57	70
Z2-Pluto Turns Sleuth Hound	5	10	15	24	29	34
Z3-The Seven Dwarfs & the Enchanted Mtn.	6	12	18	29	36	42
Z4-Mickey Mouse's Secret Room	6	12	18	29	36	42

CHEERIOS 3-D GIVEAWAYS (Disney)
Walt Disney Productions: 1954 (24 titles, pocket size) (Glasses came in envelopes)

	GD	VG	FN	VF	VF/NM	NM-
Glasses only...	4	7	10	14	17	20
Mailing Envelope (no art on front)	6	12	18	27	33	38
(Set 1)						
1-Donald Duck & Uncle Scrooge, the Firefighters	6	12	18	31	38	45
2-Mickey Mouse & Goofy, Pirate Plunder	6	12	18	31	38	45
3-Donald Duck's Nephews, the Fabulous Inventors	7	14	21	35	43	50
4-Mickey Mouse, Secret of the Ming Vase	6	12	18	27	33	38

Cinderella in "Fairest of the Fair" © DIS

Cinema Comics Herald - Bedtime Story

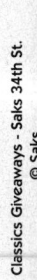

Classics Giveaways - Saks 34th St. © Saks

	GD 2.0	VG 4.0	FN 6.0	VF 8.0	VF/NM 9.0	NM- 9.2
5-Donald Duck with Huey, Dewey, & Louie; ...the Seafarers (title on 2nd page)	6	12	18	31	38	45
6-Mickey Mouse, Moaning Mountain	6	12	18	27	33	38
7-Donald Duck, Apache Gold	6	12	18	31	38	45
8-Mickey Mouse, Flight to Nowhere	6	12	18	27	33	38
(Set 2)						
1-Donald Duck, Treasure of Timbuktu	6	12	18	31	38	45
2-Mickey Mouse & Pluto, Operation China	6	12	18	27	33	38
3-Donald Duck and the Magic Cows	6	12	18	31	38	45
4-Mickey Mouse & Goofy, Kid Kokonut	6	12	18	27	33	38
5-Donald Duck, Mystery Ship	6	12	18	31	38	45
6-Mickey Mouse, Phantom Sheriff	6	12	18	27	33	38
7-Donald Duck, Circus Adventures	6	12	18	31	38	45
8-Mickey Mouse, Arctic Explorers	6	12	18	27	33	38
(Set 3)						
1-Donald Duck & Witch Hazel	6	12	18	31	38	45
2-Mickey Mouse in Darkest Africa	6	12	18	27	33	38
3-Donald Duck & Uncle Scrooge, Timber Trouble	6	12	18	31	38	45
4-Mickey Mouse, Rajah's Rescue	6	12	18	27	33	38
5-Donald Duck in Robot Reporter	6	12	18	31	38	45
6-Mickey Mouse, Slumbering Sleuth	6	12	18	27	33	38
7-Donald Duck in the Foreign Legion	6	12	18	31	38	45
8-Mickey Mouse, Airwalking Wonder	6	12	18	27	33	38
CHESTY AND COPTIE (Disney)						
Los Angeles Community Chest: 1946 (Giveaway, 4pgs.)						
nn-(One known copy) by Floyd Gottfredson	(a GD copy sold for $371.65 on 2/12/17)					
CHESTY AND HIS HELPERS (Disney)						
Los Angeles War Chest: 1943 (Giveaway, 12 pgs., 5-1/2x7-1/4")						
nn-Chesty & Coptie	52	104	156	328	552	775
CHOCOLATE THE FLAVOR OF FRIENDSHIP AROUND THE WORLD						
The Nestle Company: 1955						
nn	6	12	18	31	38	45
CHRISTMAS ADVENTURE, THE						
S. Rose (H. L. Green Giveaway): 1963 (16 pgs.)						
nn	2	4	6	11	16	20
CHRISTMAS ADVENTURES WITH ELMER THE ELF						
1949 (paper-c)						
nn	4	9	13	18	22	26
CHRISTMAS AT THE ROTUNDA (Titled Ford Rotunda Christmas Book 1957 on) (Regular size)						
Ford Motor Co. (Western Printing): 1954 - 1961 (Given away every Christmas at one location)						
1954-56 issues (nn's)	9	18	27	47	61	75
1957-61 issues (nn's)	8	16	24	42	54	65
CHRISTMAS CAROL, A						
Sears Roebuck & Co.: No date (1942-43) (Giveaway, 32 pgs., 8-1/4x10-3/4", paper cover)						
nn-Comics & coloring book	23	46	69	136	223	310
CHRISTMAS CAROL, A (Also see Bob & Santa's Wishing Whistle, Merry Christmas From Sears Toyland, and Santa's Christmas Comic Variety Show)						
Sears Roebuck & Co.: 1940s? (Christmas giveaway, 20 pgs.)						
nn-Comic book & animated coloring book	21	42	63	126	206	285
CHRISTMAS CAROLS						
Hot Shoppes Giveaway: 1959? (16 pgs.)						
nn	4	8	12	18	22	25
CHRISTMAS COLORING FUN						
H. Burnside: 1964 (20 pgs., slick-c, B&W)						
nn	2	4	6	11	16	20
CHRISTMAS DREAM, A						
Promotional Publishing Co.: 1950 (Kinney Shoe Store Giveaway, 16 pgs.)						
nn	5	10	15	24	29	34
CHRISTMAS DREAM, A						
J. J. Newberry Co.: 1952? (Giveaway, paper cover, 16 pgs.)						
nn	5	10	14	20	24	28
CHRISTMAS DREAM, A						
Promotional Publ. Co.: 1952 (Giveaway, 16 pgs., paper cover)						
nn	5	10	14	20	24	28
CHRISTMAS FUN AROUND THE WORLD						
No publisher: No date (early 50's) (16 pgs., paper cover)						
nn	5	10	15	23	28	32
CHRISTMAS FUN BOOK						
G. C. Murphy Co.: 1950 (Giveaway, paper cover)						
nn-Contains paper dolls	6	12	18	31	38	45
CHRISTMAS IS COMING!						
No publisher: No date (early 50's?) (Store giveaway, 16 pgs.)						
nn-Santa cover	6	12	18	29	36	42
CHRISTMAS JOURNEY THROUGH SPACE						
Promotional Publishing Co.: 1960						
nn-Reprints 1954 issue Jolly Christmas Book with new slick cover	3	6	9	16	23	30
CHRISTMAS ON THE MOON						
W. T. Grant Co.: 1958 (Giveaway, 20 pgs., slick cover)						
nn	9	18	27	50	65	80
CHRISTMAS PLAY BOOK						
Gould-Stoner Co.: 1946 (Giveaway, 16 pgs., paper cover)						
nn	10	20	30	54	72	90
CHRISTMAS ROUNDUP						
Promotional Publishing Co.: 1960						
nn-Marv Levy-c/a	2	4	6	9	13	16
CHRISTMAS STORY CUT-OUT BOOK, THE						
Catechetical Guild: No. 393, 1951 (15¢, 36 pgs.)						
393-Half text & half comics	8	16	24	42	54	65
CHRISTMAS USA (Through 300 Years) (Also see Uncle Sam's...)						
Promotional Publ. Co.: 1956 (Giveaway)						
nn-Marv Levy-c/a	4	7	9	14	16	18
CHRISTMAS WITH SNOW WHITE AND THE SEVEN DWARFS						
Kobackers Giftstore of Buffalo, N.Y.: 1953 (16 pgs., paper-c)						
nn	8	16	24	44	57	70
CHRISTOPHERS, THE						
Catechetical Guild: 1951 (Giveaway, 36 pgs.) (Some copies have 15¢ sticker)						
nn-Stalin as Satan in Hell; Hitler & Lincoln app.	26	52	78	154	252	350
CHUCKY JACK'S A-COMIN'						
Great Smoky Mountains Historical Assn., Gatlinburg, TN: 1956 (Reg. size)						
nn-Life of John Sevier, founder of Tennessee	8	16	24	42	54	65
CINDERELLA IN "FAIREST OF THE FAIR" (Walt Disney)						
American Dairy Association (Premium): 1955 (5x7-1/4", 16 pgs., soft-c)						
nn	10	20	30	58	79	100
CINEMA COMICS HERALD						
Paramount Pictures/Universal/RKO/20th Century Fox/Republic: 1941 - 1943 (4-pg. movie "trailers", paper-c, 7-1/2x10-1/2")(Giveaway)						
"Mr. Bug Goes to Town" (1941)	17	34	51	98	154	210
"Bedtime Story"	12	24	36	69	97	125
"Lady For A Night", John Wayne, Joan Blondell ('42)	20	40	60	117	189	260
"Reap The Wild Wind" (1942)	14	28	42	76	108	140
"Thunder Birds" (1942)	12	24	36	69	97	125
"They All Kissed the Bride"	12	24	36	69	97	125
"Arabian Nights" (nd)	14	28	42	76	108	140
"Bombardie" (1943)	12	24	36	69	97	125
"Crash Dive" (1943)-Tyrone Power	14	28	42	76	108	140

NOTE: *The 1941-42 issues contain line art with color photos. 1943 issues are line art.*

	GD 2.0	VG 4.0	FN 6.0	VF 8.0	VF/NM 9.0	NM- 9.2
CLASSICS GIVEAWAYS (Classic Comics reprints)						
12/41–Walter Theatre Enterprises (Huntington, WV) giveaway containing #2 (orig.) w/new generic-c (only 1 known copy)	97	194	291	621	1061	1500
1942–Double Comics containing CC#1 (orig.) (diff. cover) (not actually a giveaway) (very rare) (also see Double Comics) (only one known copy)	168	336	504	1075	1838	2600
12/42–Saks 34th St. Giveaway containing CC#7 (orig.) (diff. cover) (very rare; only 6 known copies)	343	686	1029	2400	4200	6000
2/43–American Comics containing CC#8 (orig.) (Liberty Theatre giveaway) (different cover) (only one known copy) (see American Comics)	123	246	369	787	1344	1900
12/44–Robin Hood Flour Co. Giveaway - #7-CC(R) (diff. cover) (rare) (edition probably 5 [22])	206	412	618	1318	2259	3200

NOTE: How are above editions determined without CC covers? 1942 is dated 1942, and CC#1-first reprint did not come out until 5/43. 12/42 and 2/43 are determined by blue note at bottom of first text page only in original edition. 12/44 is estimated from page width each reprint edition had progressively slightly smaller page width.

1951–Shelter Thru the Ages (C.I. Educational Series) (actually Giveaway by the Ruberoid Co.)

Clear the Track! © AAR

C-M-O Comics #2 © CEN

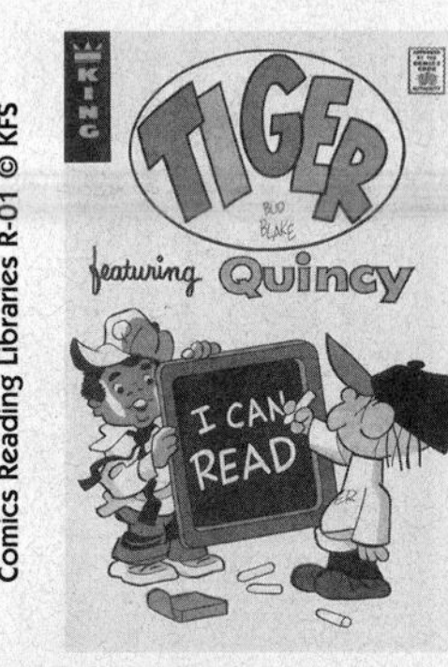

Comics Reading Libraries R-01 © KFS

	GD 2.0	VG 4.0	FN 6.0	VF 8.0	VF/NM 9.0	NM- 9.2

(16 pgs.) (contains original artwork by H. C. Kiefer) (there are 5 diff. back cover ad variations: "Ranch" house ad, "Igloo" ad, "Doll House" ad, "Tree House" ad & blank) (scarce) 68 136 204 435 743 1050

1952–George Daynor Biography Giveaway (CC logo) (partly comic book/pictures/newspaper articles) (story of man who built Palace Depression out of junkyard swamp in NJ) (64 pgs.) (very rare; only 3 known copies, one missing back-c) 377 754 1131 2639 4620 6600

1953–Westinghouse/Dreams of a Man (C.I. Educational Series) (Westinghousebio./Westinghouse Co. giveaway) (contains original artwork by H. C. Kiefer) (16 pgs.) (also French/Spanish/Italian versions) (scarce) 52 104 156 328 552 775

NOTE: Reproductions of 1951, 1952, and 1953 exist with color photocopy covers and black & white photocopy interior ("W.C.N. Reprint") 2 4 5 7 8 10

1951-53–Coward Shoe Giveaways (all editions very rare); 2 variations of back-c ad exist:
With back-c photo ad: 5 (87), 12 (89), 22 (85), 32 (85), 49 (85), 69 (87), 72 (no HRN), 80 (0), 91 (0), 92 (0), 96 (0), 98 (0), 100 (0), 101 (0), 103-105 (all Os) 30 60 90 177 289 400
With back-c cartoon ad: 106-109 (all 0s), 110 (111), 112 (0) 31 62 93 186 303 420

1956–Ben Franklin 5-10 Store Giveaway (#65-PC with back cover ad) (scarce) 24 48 72 142 234 325

1956–Ben Franklin Insurance Co. Giveaway (#65-PC with diff. back cover ad) (very rare) 48 96 144 302 514 725

11/56–Sealtest Co. Edition - #4 (135) (identical to regular edition except for Sealtest logo printed, not stamped, on front cover) (only two copies known to exist) 28 56 84 165 270 375

1958–Get-Well Giveaway containing #15-CI (new cartoon-type cover) (Pressman Pharmacy) (only one copy known to exist) 28 56 84 165 270 375

1967-68–Twin Circle Giveaway Editions - all HRN 166, with back cover ad for National Catholic Press.

	GD	VG	FN	VF	VF/NM	NM-
2(R68), 4(R67), 10(R68), 13(R68)	3	6	9	21	32	42
48(R67), 128(R68), 535(576-R68)	4	8	12	22	34	45
16(R68), 68(R67)	5	10	15	30	48	65

12/69–Christmas Giveaway ("A Christmas Adventure") (reprints Picture Parade #4-1953, new cover) (4 ad variations)

	GD	VG	FN	VF	VF/NM	NM-
Stacey's Dept. Store	4	8	12	23	37	50
Anne & Hope Store	5	10	15	31	53	75
Gibson's Dept. Store (rare)	5	10	15	31	53	75
"Merry Christmas" & blank ad space	4	8	12	23	37	50

CLEAR THE TRACK!
Association of American Railroads: 1954 (paper-c, 16 pgs.)

nn 5 10 15 24 30 35

CLIFF MERRITT SETS THE RECORD STRAIGHT
Brotherhood of Railroad Trainsmen: Giveaway (2 different issues)

...and the Very Candid Candidate by Al Williamson 4 8 12 27 44 60
...Sets the Record Straight by Al Williamson (2 different-c: one by Williamson, the other by McWilliams) 4 8 12 27 44 60

CLYDE BEATTY COMICS (Also see Crackajack Funnies)
Commodore Productions & Artists, Inc.

...African Jungle Book('56)-Richfield Oil Co. 16 pg. giveaway, soft-c 11 22 33 64 90 115

C-M-O COMICS
Chicago Mail Order Co.(Centaur): 1942 - No. 2, 1942 (68 pgs., full color)

1-Invisible Terror, Super Ann, & Plymo the Rubber Man app. (all Centaur costume heroes) 161 322 483 1030 1765 2500
2-Invisible Terror, Super Ann app. 97 194 291 621 1061 1500

COCOMALT BIG BOOK OF COMICS
Harry 'A' Chesler (Cocomalt Premium): 1938 (Reg. size, full color, 52 pgs.)

1-(Scarce)-Biro-c/a; Little Nemo by Winsor McCay Jr., Dan Hastings; Jack Cole, Guardineer, Gustavson, Bob Wood-a 229 458 687 1454 2502 3550

COLONEL OF TWO WORLDS, THE
DC Comics: 2015 (Kentucky Fried Chicken promotion, no price)

1-Flash, Green Lantern and Colonel Sanders vs. the evil Colonel of Earth-3; Derenick-a 3.00

COMIC BOOK (Also see Comics From Weatherbird)
American Juniors Shoe: 1954 (Giveaway)

Contains a comic rebound with new cover. Several combinations possible. Contents determine price.

COMIC BOOK CONFIDENTIAL
Sphinx Productions: 1988 (Givewaway, 16 pgs.)

1-Tie-in to a documentary about comic creators; creator biographies; Chester Brown-c 5.00

COMIC BOOK MAGAZINE
Chicago Tribune & other newspapers: 1940 - 1943 (Similar to Spirit sections) (7-3/4x10-3/4"; full color; 16-24 pgs. ea.)

	GD	VG	FN	VF	VF/NM	NM-
1940 issues	8	16	24	42	54	65
1941, 1942 issues	7	14	21	35	43	50
1943 issues	6	12	18	31	38	45

NOTE: *Published weekly. Texas Slim, Kit Carson, Spooky, Josie, Nuts & Jolts, Lew Loyal, Brenda Starr, Daniel Boone, Captain Storm, Rocky, Smokey Stover, Tiny Tim, Little Joe, Fu Manchu appear among others. Early issues had photo stories with pictures from the movies; later issues had comic art.*

COMIC BOOKS (Series 1)
Metropolitan Printing Co. (Giveaway): 1950 (16 pgs.; 5-1/4x8-1/2"; full color; bound at top; paper cover)

	GD	VG	FN	VF	VF/NM	NM-
1-Boots and Saddles; intro The Masked Marshal	7	14	21	35	43	50
1-The Green Jet; Green Lama by Raboy	21	42	63	124	202	280
1-My Pal Dizzy (Teen-age)	5	10	15	24	30	35
1-New World; origin Atomaster (costumed hero)	10	20	30	56	76	95
1-Talullah (Teen-age)	5	10	15	24	30	35

COMIC CAVALCADE
All-American/National Periodical Publications

Giveaway (1944, 8 pgs., paper-c, in color)-One Hundred Years of Co-operation-r/Comic Cavalcade #9 43 86 129 271 461 650
Giveaway (1945, 16 pgs., paper-c, in color)-Movie "Tomorrow The World" (Nazi theme); r/Comic Cavalcade #10 60 120 180 381 653 925
Giveaway (c. 1944-45; 8 pgs, paper-c, in color)-The Twain Shall Meet-r/Comic Cavalcade #8 43 86 129 271 461 650

COMIC SELECTIONS (Shoe store giveaway)
Parents' Magazine Press: 1944-46 (Reprints from Calling All Girls, True Comics, True Aviation, & Real Heroes) (All contain WWII-c/s)

	GD	VG	FN	VF	VF/NM	NM-
1	6	12	18	27	33	38
2-6	4	9	13	18	22	26

COMICS FROM WEATHER BIRD (Also see Comic Book, Edward's Shoes, Free Comics to You & Weather Bird)
Weather Bird Shoes: 1954 - 1957 (Giveaway)

Contains a comic bound with new cover. Many combinations possible. Contents would determine price. Some issues do not contain complete comics, but only parts of comics. Value equals 40 to 60 percent of contents.

COMICS READING LIBRARIES (Educational Series)
King Features (Charlton Publ.): 1973, 1977, 1979 (36 pgs. in color) (Giveaways)

	GD	VG	FN	VF	VF/NM	NM-
R-01-Tiger, Quincy	2	4	6	9	13	16
R-02-Beetle Bailey, Blondie & Popeye	2	4	6	11	16	20
R-03-Blondie, Beetle Bailey	2	4	6	8	11	14
R-04-Tim Tyler's Luck, Felix the Cat	3	6	9	16	23	30
R-05-Quincy, Henry	2	4	6	8	11	14
R-06-The Phantom, Mandrake	3	6	9	16	24	32
1977 reprint(R-04)	2	4	6	9	13	16
R-07-Popeye, Little King	2	4	6	13	18	22
R-08-Prince Valiant (Foster), Flash Gordon	3	6	9	18	27	36
1977 reprint	2	4	6	11	16	20
R-09-Hagar the Horrible, Boner's Ark	2	4	6	10	14	18
R-10-Redeye, Tiger	2	4	6	8	11	14
R-11-Blondie, Hi & Lois	2	4	6	8	11	14
R-12-Popeye-Swee'pea, Brutus	2	4	6	13	18	22
R-13-Beetle Bailey, Little King	2	4	6	8	11	14
R-14-Quincy-Hamlet	2	4	6	8	11	14
R-15-The Phantom, The Genius	2	4	6	13	18	22
R-16-Flash Gordon, Mandrake	3	6	9	18	28	38
1977 reprint	2	4	6	10	14	18
Other 1977 editions....	2	4	6	8	10	12
1979 editions (68 pgs.)	2	4	6	8	10	12

NOTE: *Above giveaways available with purchase of $45.00 in merchandise. Used as a reading skills aid for small children.*

COMMANDMENTS OF GOD
Catechetical Guild: 1954, 1958

300-Same contents in both editions; diff-c 5 10 15 24 29 34

COMPLIMENTARY COMICS
Sales Promotion Publ.: No date (1950's) (Giveaway)

1-Strongman by Powell, 3 stories 8 16 24 40 50 60

COPPER - THE OLDEST AND NEWEST METAL
Commercial Comics: 1959

nn 3 6 9 14 20 25

CRACKAJACK FUNNIES (Giveaway)
Malto-Meal: 1937 (Full size, soft-c, full color, 32 pgs.)(Before No. 1?)

nn-Features Dan Dunn, G-Man, Speed Bolton, Buck Jones, The Nebbs, Clyde Beatty, Freckles, Major Hoople, Wash Tubbs 95 190 285 603 1039 1475

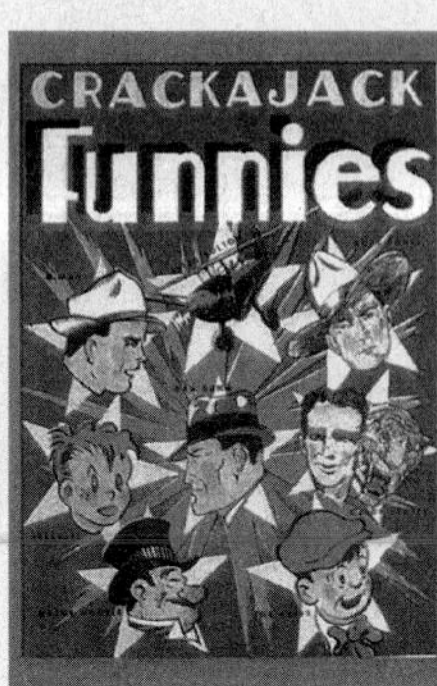

Crackajack Funnies © DELL

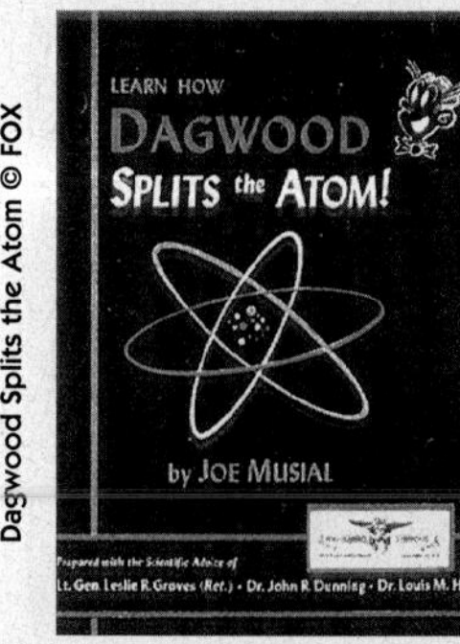

Dagwood Splits the Atom © FOX

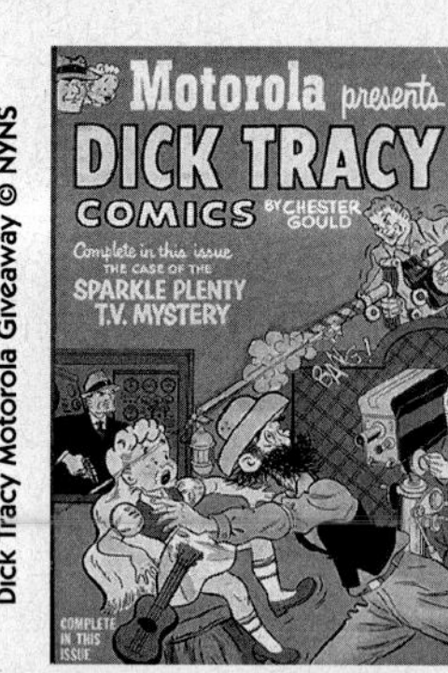

Dick Tracy Motorola Giveaway © NYNS

	GD	VG	FN	VF	VF/NM	NM-
	2.0	4.0	6.0	8.0	9.0	9.2

GD VG FN VF VF/NM NM-
2.0 4.0 6.0 8.0 9.0 9.2

CRAFTSMAN BOLT-ON SYSTEMS SAVE THE JUSTICE LEAGUE
DC Comics: 2012 (Giveaway promo for Craftsman Bolt-On Tool System)
1-Christian Duce-a/c; New-52 Justice League, The Key and Royal Flush Gang app. 4.00

CRISIS AT THE CARSONS
Pictorial Media: 1958 (Reg. size)
nn 6 12 18 27 33 38

CROSLEY'S HOUSE OF FUN (Also see Tee and Vee Crosley...)
Crosley Div. AVCO Mfg. Corp.: 1950 (Giveaway, paper cover, 32 pgs.)
nn-Strips revolve around Crosley appliances 5 10 15 22 26 30

DAGWOOD SPLITS THE ATOM (Also see Topix V8#4)
King Features Syndicate: 1949 (Science comic with King Features characters) (Giveaway)
nn-Half comic, half text; Popeye, Olive Oyl, Henry, Mandrake, Little King, Katzenjammer Kids app. 7 14 21 37 46 55

DAISY COMICS (Daisy Air Rifles)
Eastern Color Printing Co.: Dec, 1936 (5-1/4x7-1/2")
nn-Joe Palooka, Buck Rogers (2 pgs. from Famous Funnies No. 18, 1st full cover app.), Napoleon Flying to Fame, Butty & Fally 39 78 117 240 395 550

DAISY LOW OF THE GIRL SCOUTS
Girl Scouts of America: 1954, 1965 (16 pgs., paper-c)
1954-Story of Juliette Gordon Low 5 10 15 23 28 32
1965 2 4 6 9 13 16

DAN CURTIS GIVEAWAYS
Western Publishing Co.:1974 (3x6", 24 pgs., reprints)
1-Dark Shadows 2 4 6 9 13 16
2,6-Star Trek 2 4 6 9 13 16
3,4,7-9: 3-The Twilight Zone. 4-Ripley's Believe It or Not! 7-The Occult Files of Dr. Spektor. 8-Dagar the Invincible. 9-Grimm's Ghost Stories 2 4 6 8 10 12
5-Turok, Son of Stone (partial-r/Turok #78) 2 4 6 9 13 16

DANNY AND THE DEMOXICYCLE
Virginia Highway Safety Division: 1970s (Reg. size, slick-c)
nn 3 6 9 19 30 40

DANNY KAYE'S BAND FUN BOOK
H & A Selmer: 1959 (Giveaway)
nn 7 14 21 35 43 50

DAREDEVIL
Marvel Comics Group: 1993
...Vs. Vapora 1 (Engineering Show Giveaway, 16 pg.) - Intro Vapora 6.00

DAVY CROCKETT (TV)
Dell Publishing Co.
...Christmas Book (no date, 16 pgs., paper-c)-Sears giveaway 6 12 18 31 38 45
...Safety Trails (1955, 16pgs, 3-1/4x7")-Cities Service giveaway 8 16 24 40 50 60

DAVY CROCKETT
Charlton Comics
Hunting With... nn ('55, 16 pgs.)-Ben Franklin Store giveaway (Publ.-S. Rose) 5 10 15 24 30 35

DAVY CROCKETT
Walt Disney Prod.: (1955, 16 pgs., 5x7-1/4", slick, photo-c)
...In the Raid at Piney Creek-American Motors giveaway 8 16 24 40 50 60

DC SAMPLER
DC Comics: nn (#1) 1983 - No. 3, 1984 (36 pgs.; 6 1/2" x 10", giveaway)
nn(#1) -3: nn-Wraparound-c, previews upcoming issues. 3-Kirby-a 1 2 3 4 5 7

DC SPOTLIGHT
DC Comics: 1985 (50th anniversary special) (giveaway)
1-Includes profiles on Batman: The Dark Knight & Watchmen 6.00

DENNIS THE MENACE
Hallden (Fawcett)
...& Dirt ('59)-Soil Conservation giveaway; r-# 36; Wiseman-c/a 3 6 9 14 20 26
...& Dirt ('68)-reprints '59 edition 2 4 6 8 11 14
...Away We Go('70)-Caladryl giveaway 2 4 6 8 10 12
...Coping with Family Stress-giveaway 2 4 6 8 10 12
...Takes a Poke at Poison('61)-Food & Drug Admin. giveaway; Wiseman-c/a 2 4 6 8 10 12
...Takes a Poke at Poison-Revised 1/66, 11/70 1 2 3 5 6 8
...Takes a Poke at Poison-Revised 1972, 1974, 1977, 1981 1 2 3 4 5 7

DESERT DAWN
E.C./American Museum of Natural History: 1935 (paper-c)
nn-Johnny Jackrabbit stars. Three known copies: A CGC 2.5 copy (brittle) sold for $1320 in 2019. A Fair copy (brittle) sold for $657 in 2007. Another Fair copy (brittle) sold for $690 in 2004.

DETECTIVE COMICS (Also see other Batman titles)
National Periodical Publications/DC Comics
27 (1984)-Oreo Cookies giveaway (32 pgs., paper-c) r-/Det. #27,#38 & Batman #1 (1st Joker) 5 10 15 34 60 85
38 (1995) Blockbuster Video edition; reprints 1st Robin app. 1 2 3 5 6 8
38 (1997) Toys R Us edition 1 2 3 5 6 8
359 (1997) Toys R Us edition; reprints 1st Batgirl app. 1 2 3 5 6 8
373 (1997, 6 1/4" x 4") Warner Brothers Home Video 1 2 3 5 6 8

DICK TRACY GIVEAWAYS
1939 - 1958; 1990
Buster Brown Shoes Giveaway (1940s?, 36 pgs. in color); 1938-39-r by Gould 23 46 69 136 223 310
Gillmore Giveaway (See Superbook)
...Hatful of Fun (No date, 1950-52, 32pgs.; 8-1/2x10")-Dick Tracy hat promotion; Dick Tracy games, magic tricks. Miller Bros. premium 16 32 48 94 147 200
Motorola Giveaway (1953)-Reprints Harvey Comics Library #2; "The Case of the Sparkle Plenty TV Mystery" 6 12 18 31 38 45
Original Dick Tracy by Chester Gould, The (Aug, 1990, 16 pgs., 5-1/2x8-1/2")-Gladstone Publ.; Bread Giveaway 1 3 4 6 8 10
Popped Wheat Giveaway (1947, 16 pgs. in color)-1940-r; Sig Feuchtwanger Publ.; Gould-a 5 10 15 22 26 30
...Presents the Family Fun Book; Tip Top Bread Giveaway, no date or number (1940, Fawcett Publ., 16 pgs. in color)-Spy Smasher, Ibis, Lance O'Casey app. 31 62 93 186 303 420
Same as above but without app. of heroes & Dick Tracy on cover only 15 30 45 84 127 170
Service Station Giveaway (1958, 16 pgs. in color)(regular size, slick cover)-Harvey Info. Press 5 10 15 24 30 35
Shoe Store Giveaway (Weatherbird and Triangle Stores)(1939, 16 pgs.)-Gould-a 14 28 42 82 121 160

DICK TRACY SHEDS LIGHT ON THE MOLE
Western Printing Co.: 1949 (16 pgs.) (Ray-O-Vac Flashlights giveaway)
nn-Not by Gould 9 18 27 50 65 80

DICK WINGATE OF THE U.S. NAVY
Superior Publ./Toby Press: 1951; 1953 (no month)
nn-U.S. Navy giveaway 6 12 18 31 38 45
1(1953, Toby)-Reprints nn issue? (same-c) 5 10 15 24 30 35

DIG 'EM
Kellogg's Sugar Smacks Giveaway: 1973 (2-3/8x6", 16 pgs.)
nn-4 different issues 1 3 4 6 8 10

DISNEY MAGAZINE
Procter and Gamble giveaway: nn (#1), Sept, 1976 - nn (#4), Jan, 1977
nn-All have an original Mickey story in color, 12-13 pgs. ea. and info/articles on Disney movies, cartoons. All have partial photo covers of a movie star with 1-2 pg. story. Covers: 1-Bob Hope, 2-Debbie Reynolds, 3-Groucho Marx, 4-Rock Hudson. 2 4 6 10 14 18

DOC CARTER VD COMICS
Health Publications Institute, Raleigh, N. C. (Giveaway): 1949 (16 pgs. in color) (Paper-c)
nn 30 60 90 177 289 400

DONALD AND MICKEY MERRY CHRISTMAS (Formerly Famous Gang Book Of Comics)
K. K. Publ./Firestone Tire & Rubber Co.: 1943 - 1949 (Giveaway, 20 pgs.)
Put out each Christmas; 1943 issue titled "Firestone Presents Comics" (Disney)
1943-Donald Duck-r/WDC&S #32 by Carl Barks 94 188 282 597 1024 1450
1944-Donald Duck-r/WDC&S #35 by Barks 89 178 267 565 970 1375
1945- "Donald Duck's Best Christmas", 8 pgs. Carl Barks; intro. & 1st app. Grandma Duck in comic books 118 236 354 749 1287 1825
1946-Donald Duck in "Santa's Stormy Visit", 8 pgs. Carl Barks 73 146 219 467 796 1125
1947-Donald Duck in "Three Good Little Ducks", 8 pgs. Carl Barks 73 146 219 467 796 1125
1948-Donald Duck in "Toyland", 8 pgs. Carl Barks 73 146 219 467 796 1125

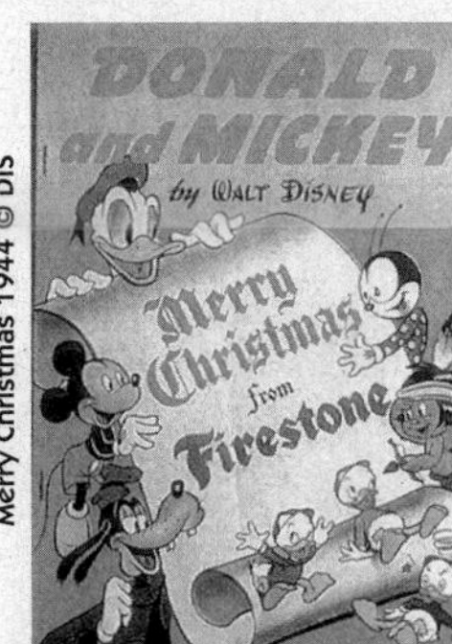
Donald and Mickey Merry Christmas 1944 © DIS

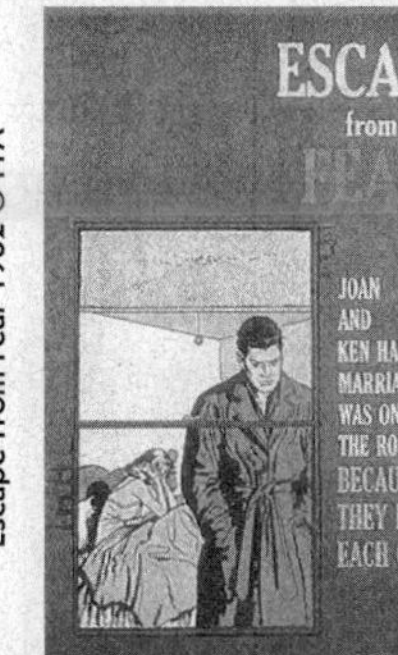
Escape From Fear 1962 © PPA

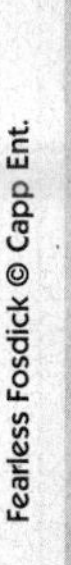
Fearless Fosdick © Capp Ent.

	GD 2.0	VG 4.0	FN 6.0	VF 8.0	VF/NM 9.0	NM- 9.2
1949-Donald Duck in "New Toys", 8 pgs. Barks	66	132	198	419	722	1025

DONALD DUCK
K. K. Publications: 1944 (Christmas giveaway, paper-c, 16 pgs.)(2 versions)
nn-Kelly cover reprint 123 246 369 787 1344 1900

DONALD DUCK AND THE RED FEATHER
Red Feather Giveaway: 1948 (8-1/2x11", 4 pgs., B&W)
nn 22 44 66 128 209 290

DONALD DUCK IN "THE LITTERBUG"
Keep America Beautiful: 1963 (5x7-1/4", 16 pgs., soft-c) (Disney giveaway)
nn 5 10 15 33 57 80

DONALD DUCK "PLOTTING PICNICKERS" (See Frito-Lay Giveaway)

DONALD DUCK'S SURPRISE PARTY
Walt Disney Productions: 1948 (16 pgs.) (Giveaway for Icy Frost Twins Ice Cream Bars)
nn-(Rare)-Kelly-c/a 229 458 687 1454 2502 3550

DON FORTUNE MAGAZINE
Fawcett Publications: 1940s (Mini-comic)
1-3 (Rare) (A set of 3 in 9.0 sold for $116 in 2016)

DOT AND DASH AND THE LUCKY JINGLE PIGGIE
Sears Roebuck Co.: 1942 (Christmas giveaway, 12 pgs.)
nn-Contains a war stamp album and a punch out Jingle Piggie bank
13 26 39 72 101 130

DOUBLE TALK (Also see Two-Faces)
Feature Publications: No date (1961) (32 pgs., full color, slick-c)
Christian Anti-Communism Crusade (Giveaway)
nn-Sickle with blood-c 20 40 60 120 195 270

DRUMMER BOY AT GETTYSBURG
Eastern National Park & Monument Association: 1976
nn-Fred Ray-a 3 6 9 15 22 28

DUMBO (Walt Disney's..., The Flying Elephant)
Weatherbird Shoes/Ernest Kern Co.(Detroit)/ Wieboldt's (Chicago): 1941
(K.K. Publ. Giveaway)
nn-16 pgs., 9x10" (Rare) 45 90 135 284 480 675
nn-52 pgs., 5-1/2x8-1/2", slick cover in color; B&W interior; half text, half reprints 4-Color No. 17 (Dept. store) 23 46 69 136 223 310

DUMBO WEEKLY
Walt Disney Prod.: 1942 (Premium supplied by Diamond D-X Gas Stations)(4 pgs. each)
1 32 64 96 188 307 425
2-16 13 26 39 72 101 130
Binder only (linen-like stock) 160
NOTE: *A cover and binder came separate at gas stations. Came with membership card.*

EAT RIGHT TO WORK AND WIN
Swift & Company: 1942 (16 pgs.) (Giveaway)
Blondie, Henry, Flash Gordon by Alex Raymond, Toots & Casper, Thimble Theatre(Popeye), Tillie the Toiler, The Phantom, The Little King, & Bringing up Father - original strips just for this book -(in daily strip form which shows what foods we should eat and why)
30 60 90 177 289 400

EDWARD'S SHOES GIVEAWAY
Edward's Shoe Store: 1954 (Has clown on cover)
Contains comic with new cover. Many combinations possible. Contents determines price, 50-60 percent of original. (Similar to Comics From Weatherbird & Free Comics to You)

EE-YI-EE-YI-OH!
Consumer Power Co.: 1972 (Paper-c)
nn - A barnyard fable about ecology 1 3 4 6 8 10

ELSIE THE COW
D. S. Publishing Co.
Borden's cheese comic picture bk ("40, giveaway) 21 42 63 124 202 280
Borden Milk Giveaway-(16 pgs., nn) (3 ishs, "A Trip Through Space" and 2 others, 1957)
15 30 45 85 130 175
Elsie's Fun Book(1950; Borden Milk) 15 30 45 85 130 175
Everyday Birthday Fun With... (1957; 20 pgs.)(100th Anniversary); Kubert-a
15 30 45 85 130 175

ESCAPE FROM FEAR
Planned Parenthood of America: 1956, 1962, 1969 (Giveaway, 8 pgs., color) (On birth control)
1956 edition 12 24 36 69 97 125
1962 edition 4 8 12 28 47 65
1969 edition 3 6 9 19 30 40

EVEL KNIEVEL
Marvel Comics Group (Ideal Toy Corp.): 1974 (Giveaway, 20 pgs.)
nn-Contains photo on inside back-c 5 10 15 33 57 80

FAIR PLAY
Anti-Defamation League, NY: 1950s (soft-c, regular size)
nn-Anti-racism/anti-discrimination (A copy sold for $480 in Aug. 2018)

FAMOUS COMICS (Also see Favorite Comics)
Zain-Eppy/United Features Syndicate: No date; Mid 1930's (24 pgs., paper-c)
nn-Reprinted from 1933 & 1934 newspaper strips in color; Joe Palooka, Hairbreadth Harry, Napoleon, The Nebbs, etc. (Many different versions known)
89 178 267 565 970 1375

FAMOUS FAIRY TALES
K. K. Publ. Co.: 1942; 1943 (32 pgs.); 1944 (16 pgs.) (Giveaway, soft-c)
1942-Kelly-a 40 80 120 244 402 560
1943-r-/Fairy Tale Parade No. 2,3; Kelly-a 27 54 81 158 259 360
1944-Kelly-a 24 48 72 140 230 320

FAMOUS FUNNIES - A CARNIVAL OF COMICS
Eastern Color: 1933
36 pgs., no date given, no publisher, no number; contains strip reprints of The Bungle Family, Dixie Dugan, Hairbreadth Harry, Joe Palooka, Keeping Up With the Jones, Mutt & Jeff, Reg'lar Fellers, S'Matter Pop, Strange As It Seems, and others. This book was sold by M. C. Gaines to Wheatena, Malt-O-Milk, John Wanamaker, Kinney Shoe Stores, & others to be given away as premiums and radio giveaways (1933). Originally came with a mailing envelope.
568 1136 1704 4146 7323 10,500

FAMOUS GANG BOOK OF COMICS (Becomes Donald & Mickey Merry Christmas 1943 on)
Firestone Tire & Rubber Co.: Dec, 1942 (Christmas giveaway, 32 pgs., paper-c)
nn-(Rare)-Porky Pig, Bugs Bunny, Mary Jane & Sniffles, Elmer Fudd; r/Looney Tunes
89 178 267 565 970 1375

FANTASTIC FOUR
Marvel Comics
nn (1981, 32 pgs.) Young Model Builders Club 2 4 6 9 13 16
Vol. 3 #60 Baltimore Comic Book Show (10/02, newspaper supplement) 200,000 copies were distributed to Baltimore Sun home subscribers to promote Baltimore Comic Con 4.00

FATHER OF CHARITY
Catechetical Guild Giveaway: No date (32 pgs.; paper cover)
nn 6 12 18 27 33 38

FAVORITE COMICS (Also see Famous Comics)
Grocery Store Giveaway (Diff. Corp.) (detergent): 1934 (36 pgs.)
Book 1-The Nebbs, Strange As It Seems, Napoleon, Joe Palooka, Dixie Dugan, S'Matter Pop, Hairbreadth Harry, etc. reprints 310 620 930 1400 - -
Book 2,3 210 420 630 950 - -

FAWCETT MINIATURES (See Mighty Midget)
Fawcett Publications: 1946 (3-3/4x5", 12-24 pgs.) (Wheaties giveaways)
Captain Marvel "And the Horn of Plenty"; Bulletman story
14 28 42 76 108 140
Captain Marvel "& the Raiders From Space"; Golden Arrow story
14 28 42 76 108 140
Captain Marvel Jr. "The Case of the Poison Press!" Bulletman story
14 28 42 76 108 140
Delecta of the Planets; C. C. Beck art; B&W inside; 12 pgs.; 3 printing variations (coloring) exist 20 40 60 114 182 250

FEARLESS FOSDICK
Capp Enterprises Inc.: 1951
...& The Case of The Red Feather 7 14 21 35 43 50

FIFTY WHO MADE DC GREAT
DC Comics: 1985 (Reg. size, slick-c)
nn 1 3 4 6 8 10

FIGHT FOR FREEDOM
National Assoc. of Mfgrs./General Comics: 1949, 1951 (Giveaway, 16 pgs.)
nn-Dan Barry-c/a; used in **POP**, pg. 102 7 14 21 35 43 50

FIRE AND BLAST
National Fire Protection Assoc.: 1952 (Giveaway, 16 pgs., paper-c)
nn-Mart Baily A-Bomb-c; about fire prevention 18 36 54 103 162 220

FIRE CHIEF AND THE SAFE OL' FIREFLY, THE
National Board of Fire Underwriters: 1952 (16 pgs.) (Safety brochure given away at schools) (produced by American Visuals Corp.)(Eisner)
nn-(Rare) Eisner-c/a 41 82 123 263 442 620

Flash Gordon Bread #1 © KING

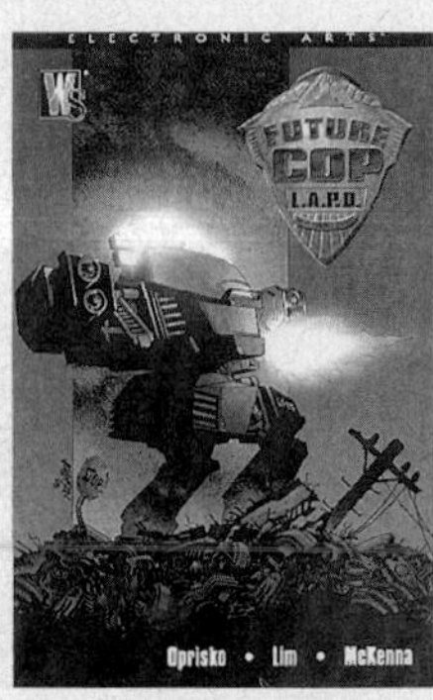

Future Cop: L.A.P.D. © EA

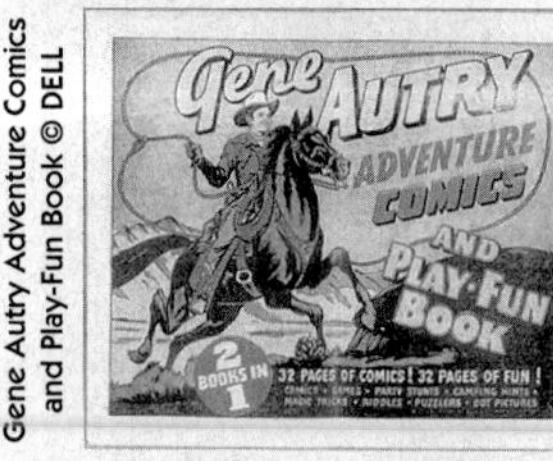

Gene Autry Adventure Comics and Play-Fun Book © DELL

	GD	VG	FN	VF	VF/NM	NM-
	2.0	4.0	6.0	8.0	9.0	9.2

FLASH, THE
DC Comics

nn-(1990) Brochure for CBS TV series 5.00
The Flash Comes to a Standstill (1981, General Foods giveaway, 8 pages, 3-1/2 x 6-3/4", oblong) 2 4 6 11 16 20

FLASH COMICS (Also see Captain Marvel and Funny Stuff)
National Periodical Publications: 1946 (6-1/2x8-1/4", 32 pgs.)(Wheaties Giveaway)

nn-Johnny Thunder, Ghost Patrol, The Flash & Kubert Hawkman app.; Irwin Hasen-c/a 100 200 700 1000 – –
NOTE: *All known copies were taped to Wheaties boxes and are never found in mint condition. Copies with light tape residue bring the listed prices in all grades*

FLASH GORDON
Dell Publishing Co.: 1943 (20 pgs.)

Macy's Giveaway-(Rare); not by Raymond 60 120 180 381 653 925

FLASH GORDON
Harvey Comics: 1951 (16 pgs. in color, regular size, paper-c) (Gordon Bread giveaway)

1,2: 1-r/strips 10/24/37 - 2/6/38. 2-r/strips 7/14/40 - 10/6/40; Reprints by Raymond each.... 3 6 9 14 19 24
NOTE: *Most copies have brittle edges.*

FLINTSTONES FUN BOOK, THE
Denny's giveaway: 1990

1-20 1 3 4 6 8 10

FLOOD RELIEF
Malibu Comics (Ultraverse): Jan, 1994 (36 pgs.)(Ordered thru mail w/$5.00 to Red Cross)

1-Hardcase, Prime & Prototype app. 6.00

FOREST FIRE (Also see The Blazing Forest and Smokey Bear)
American Forestry Assn.(Commerical Comics): 1949 (dated-1950) (16 pgs., paper-c)

nn-Intro/1st app. Smokey The Forest Fire Preventing Bear; created by Rudy Wendelein; Wendelein/Sparling-a; 'Carter Oil Co.' on back-c of original 20 40 60 120 195 270

FOREST RANGER HANDBOOK
Wrather Corp.: 1967 (5x7", 20 pgs., slick-c)

nn-WIth Corey Stuart & Lassie photo-c 2 4 6 13 18 22

FORGOTTEN STORY BEHIND NORTH BEACH, THE
Catechetical Guild: No date (8 pgs., paper-c)

nn 6 12 18 27 33 38

FORK IN THE ROAD
U.S. Army Recruiting Service: 1961 (16 pgs., paper-c)

nn 2 4 6 11 16 20

48 FAMOUS AMERICANS
J. C. Penney Co. (Cpr. Edwin H. Stroh): 1947 (Giveaway) (Half-size in color)

nn - Simon & Kirby-a; war cover 14 28 42 76 108 140

FOXHOLE ON YOUR LAWN
No Publisher: No date

nn-Charles Biro art 4 8 12 17 21 24

FRANKIE LUER'S SPACE ADVENTURES
Luer Packing Co.: 1955 (5x7", 36 pgs., slick-c)

nn - With Davey Rocket 4 9 13 18 22 26

FREDDY
Charlton Comics

Schiff's Shoes Presents... #1 (1959)-Giveaway 4 8 11 16 19 22

FREE COMIC BOOK DAY EDITIONS (Now listed in the regular section)

FREE COMICS TO YOU FROM... (name of shoe store) (Has clown on cover & another with a rabbit) (Like comics from Weather Bird & Edward's Shoes)
Shoe Store Giveaway: Circa 1956, 1960-61

Contains a comic bound with new cover - several combinations possible; some Harvey titles known. Contents determine price.

FREEDOM TRAIN
Street & Smith Publications: 1948 (Giveaway)

nn-Powell-c w/mailer; patriotic cover 18 36 54 107 169 230

FREIHOFER'S COMIC BOOK
All-American Comics: 1940s (7 1/2 x 10 1/4")(Freihofer's Donuts promotional)

2nd edition-(Scarce) Cover features All-American Comics characters Ultra-Man, Hop Harrigan, Red, White and Blue, Scribbly and others (A CGC 3.0 copy sold for $1200 in 2018)

	GD	VG	FN	VF	VF/NM	NM-
	2.0	4.0	6.0	8.0	9.0	9.2

FRIENDLY GHOST, CASPER, THE
Harvey Publications: 1967 (16 pgs.)

American Dental Assoc. giveaway-Small size 3 6 9 17 25 32

FRITO-LAY GIVEAWAY
Frito-Lay: 1962 (3-1/4x7", soft-c, 16 pgs.) (Disney)

nn-Donald Duck "Plotting Picnickers" 5 10 15 30 50 70
nn-Ludwig Von Drake "Fish Stampede" 3 6 9 19 30 40
nn- Mickey Mouse & Goofy "Bicep Bungle" 3 6 9 21 33 45

FROM GOODWILL INDUSTRIES, A GOOD LIFE
Goodwill Industries: 1950s (regular size)

1 8 16 24 40 50 60

FRONTIER DAYS
Robin Hood Shoe Store (Brown Shoe): 1956 (Giveaway)

1 4 7 10 14 17 20

FRONTIERS OF FREEDOM
Institute of Life Insurance: 1950 (Giveaway, paper cover)

nn-Dan Barry-a 9 18 27 47 61 75

FUNNIES ON PARADE (Premium)(See Toy World Funnies)
Eastern Color Printing Co.: 1933 (36 pgs., slick cover)
No date or publisher listed

nn-Contains Sunday page reprints of Mutt & Jeff, Joe Palooka, Hairbreadth Harry, Reg'lar Fellers, Skippy, & others (10,000 print run). This book was printed for Proctor & Gamble to be given away & came out before Famous Funnies or Century of Comics. 1150 2300 3450 8750 15,875 23,000

FUNNY PICTURE STORIES
Comics Magazine Co./Centaur Publications: 1930s (Giveaway, 16-20 pgs., slick-c)

Promotes diff. laundries; has box on cover where "your Laundry Name" is printed 54 108 162 343 574 825

FUNNY STUFF (Also see Captain Marvel & Flash Comics)
National Periodical Publications (Wheaties Giveaway): 1946 (6-1/2x8-1/4")

nn-(Scarce)-Dodo & the Frog, Three Mouseketeers, etc.; came taped to Wheaties box; never found in better than fine 45 90 315 450 – –

FUTURE COP: L.A.P.D. (Electronic Arts video game)
DC Comics (WildStorm): 1998

nn-Ron Lim-a/Dave Johnson-c 4.00

GABBY HAYES WESTERN (Movie star)
Fawcett Publications

Quaker Oats Giveaway nn's(#1-5, 1951, 2-1/2x7") (Kagran Corp.)-...In Tracks of Guilt, ...In the Fence Post Mystery, ...In the Accidental Sherlock, ...In the Frame-Up, ...In the Double Cross Brand known 10 20 30 54 72 90
Mailing Envelope (has illo of Gabby on front) 10 20 30 54 72 90

GARY GIBSON COMICS (Donut club membership)
National Dunking Association: 1950 (Included in donut box with pin and card)

1-Western soft-c, 16 pgs.; folded into the box 5 10 15 24 30 35

GENE AUTRY COMICS
Dell Publishing Co.

...Adventure Comics And Play-Fun Book ('47)-32 pgs., 8x6-1/2"; games, comics, magic (Pillsbury premium) 20 40 60 120 196 270
Quaker Oats Giveaway(1950)-2-1/2x6-3/4"; 5 different versions; "Death Card Gang", "Phantoms of the Cave", "Riddle of Laughing Mtn.", "Secret of Lost Valley", "Bond of the Broken Arrow" (came in wrapper) each... 10 20 30 58 79 100
Mailing Envelope (has illo. of Gene on front) 10 20 30 58 79 100
3-D Giveaway(1953)-Pocket-size; 5 different 10 20 30 58 79 100
Mailing Envelope (no art on front) 8 16 24 44 57 70

GENE AUTRY TIM (Formerly Tim) (Becomes Tim in Space)
Tim Stores: 1950 (Half-size) (B&W Giveaway)

nn-Several issues (All Scarce) 19 38 57 109 172 235

GENERAL FOODS SUPER-HEROES
DC Comics: 1979, 1980

1-4 (1979), 1-4 (1980) each... 12.00

G. I. COMICS (Also see Jeep & Overseas Comics)
Giveaways: 1945 - No. 73?, 1946 (Distributed to U. S. Armed Forces)

1-73-Contains Prince Valiant by Foster, Blondie, Smilin' Jack, Mickey Finn, Terry & the Pirates, Donald Duck, Alley Oop, Moon Mullins & Capt. Easy strip reprints (at least 73 issues known to exist) 8 16 24 44 57 70

GODZILLA VS. MEGALON
Cinema Shares Int.: 1976 (4 pgs. on newsprint) (Movie theater giveaway)

Grenada © CCC

History of Gas © AGA

Hoppy the Marvel Bunny (Well Known Comics) © FAW

	GD 2.0	VG 4.0	FN 6.0	VF 8.0	VF/NM 9.0	NM- 9.2
nn-1st. comic app. Godzilla in U.S.	5	10	15	31	53	75
GOLDEN ARROW						
Fawcett Publications						
...Well Known Comics (1944; 12 pgs.; 8-1/2x10-1/2"; paper-c; glued binding)- Bestmaid/ Samuel Lowe giveaway; printed in green	10	20	30	58	79	100
GOLDILOCKS & THE THREE BEARS						
K. K. Publications: 1943 (Giveaway)						
nn	13	26	39	74	105	135
GREAT PEOPLE OF GENESIS, THE						
David C. Cook Publ. Co.: No date (Religious giveaway, 64 pgs.)						
nn-Reprint/Sunday Pix Weekly	5	10	15	23	28	32
GREAT SACRAMENT, THE						
Catechetical Guild: 1953 (Giveaway, 36 pgs.)						
nn	5	10	15	22	26	30
GREEN JET COMICS, THE (See Comic Books, Series 1)						
GRENADA						
Commercial Comics Co.: 1983 (Giveaway produced by the CIA)						
1-Air dropped over Grenada during 1983 invasion	4	8	12	25	40	55
GRIT (YOU'VE GOT TO HAVE...)						
GRIT Publishing Co.: 1959						
nn-GRIT newspaper sales recruitment comic; Schaffenberger-a. Later version has altered artwork	5	10	15	22	26	30
GROWING UP WITH JUDY						
1952						
nn-General Electric giveaway	4	8	12	18	22	25
GULF FUNNY WEEKLY (Gulf Comic Weekly No. 1-4)(See Standard Oil Comics)						
Gulf Oil Company (Giveaway): 1933 - No. 422, 5/23/41 (in full color; 4 pgs.; tabloid size to 2/3/39; 2/10/39 on, regular comic book size)(early issues undated)						
1	77	154	231	493	847	1200
2-5	37	74	111	222	361	500
6-30	21	42	63	124	202	280
31-100	15	30	45	86	133	180
101-196	12	24	36	67	94	120
197-Wings Winfair begins(1/29/37); by Fred Meagher beginning in 1938	26	52	78	154	252	350
198-300 (Last tabloid size)	15	30	45	86	133	180
301-350 (Regular size)	10	20	30	54	72	90
351-422	8	16	24	42	54	65
GULLIVER'S TRAVELS						
Macy's Department Store: 1939, small size						
nn-Christmas giveaway	15	30	45	84	127	170
GUN THAT WON THE WEST, THE						
Winchester-Western Division & Olin Mathieson Chemical Corp.: 1956 (Giveaway, 24 pgs.)						
nn-Painted-c	6	12	18	28	34	40
HAPPINESS AND HEALING FOR YOU (Also see Oral Roberts'...)						
Commercial Comics: 1955 (36 pgs., slick cover) (Oral Roberts Giveaway)						
nn	10	20	30	58	79	100
NOTE: *The success of this book prompted Oral Roberts to go into the publishing business himself to produce his own material.*						
HAPPI TIME FUN BOOK						
Sears, Roebuck & Co.: 1940s - 1950s (32 pgs., soft-c)						
nn-Comics, games, puzzles, & magic tricks cut -outs	4	9	13	18	22	26
HAPPY CHAMP, THE (The Story of Joker Osborn)						
Western Publ.: 1965						
nn-About water-skiing	3	6	9	19	30	40
HAPPY TOOTH						
DC Comics: 1996						
1						3.00
HARLEM YOUTH REPORT (Also see All-Negro Comics and Negro Romances)						
Custom Comics, Inc.: 1964 (Giveaway)(No issues #1-4)						
5-"Youth in the Ghetto" and "The Blueprint For Change"; distr. in Harlem only; has map of central Harlem on back-c; hypo-c (scarce)	59	118	177	472	1061	1650
HAVE MORE FUN BY PLAYING SAFE						
Commercial Comics: 1965 (Sheriff's Youth Foundation, 16 pages, paper-c)						
nn	3	6	9	19	30	40

	GD 2.0	VG 4.0	FN 6.0	VF 8.0	VF/NM 9.0	NM- 9.2
HAWKMAN - THE SKY'S THE LIMIT						
DC Comics: 1981 (General Foods giveaway, 8 pages, 3-1/2 x 6-3/4", oblong)						
nn	2	4	6	10	14	18
HAWTHORN-MELODY FARMS DAIRY COMICS						
Everybody's Publishing Co.: No date (1950's) (Giveaway)						
nn-Cheerie Chick, Tuffy Turtle, Robin Koo Koo, Donald & Longhorn Legends	2	4	6	9	13	16
H-BOMB AND YOU						
Commercial Comics: (? date) (small size, slick-c)						
nn - H–Bomb explosion-c	39	78	117	240	395	550
HENRY ALDRICH COMICS (TV)						
Dell Publishing Co.: 1951 (16 pgs., soft-c)						
Giveaway - Capehart radio	4	8	12	23	37	50
HERE IS SANTA CLAUS						
Goldsmith Publ. Co. (Kann's in Washington, D.C.): 1930s (16 pgs., 8 in color) (stiff paper covers)						
nn	14	28	42	82	121	160
HERE'S HOW AMERICA'S CARTOONISTS HELP TO SELL U.S. SAVINGS BONDS						
Harvey Comics: 1950? (16 pgs., giveaway, paper cover)						
Contains: Joe Palooka, Donald Duck, Archie, Kerry Drake, Red Ryder, Blondie & Steve Canyon	20	40	60	120	195	270
HISTORY OF GAS						
American Gas Assoc.: Mar, 1947 (Giveaway, 16 pgs., soft-c)						
nn-Miss Flame narrates	10	20	30	54	72	90
HOME DEPOT, SAFETY HEROES						
Marvel Comics.: Oct, 2005 (Giveaway)						
nn-Spider-Man and the Fantastic Four on the cover; Olliffe-a/c; Roseman-s						3.00
HONEYBEE BIRDWHISTLE AND HER PET PEPI (Introducing...)						
Newspaper Enterprise Assoc.: 1969 (Giveaway, 24 pgs., B&W, slick cover)						
nn-Contains Freckles newspaper strips with a short biography of Henry Fornhals (artist) & Fred Fox (writer) of the strip	4	8	12	28	47	65
HOODS UP						
Fram Corp.: 1953 (15¢, distributed to service station owners, 16 pgs.)						
1-(Very Rare; only 2 known); Eisner-c/a in all (a CGC 9.0 copy sold for $1840 in 2006)						
2-6-(Very Rare; only 1 known of #3, 2 known of #2,4) (a CGC 8.0 copy of #4 sold for $500 in 2012)	53	106	159	334	567	800
NOTE: *Convertible Connie gives tips for service stations, selling Fram oil filters.*						
HOOKED (Anti-drug comic distributed at NYC methadone clinics)						
U.S. Dept. of Health: 1966 (giveaway, oblong)						
nn-Distributed between May and July, 1966	5	10	15	35	63	90
HOPALONG CASSIDY						
Fawcett Publications						
Grape Nuts Flakes giveaway (1950,9x6")	14	28	42	80	115	150
...& the Mad Barber (1951 Bond Bread giveaway)-7x5"; used in **SOTI**, pgs. 308,309	19	38	57	111	176	240
...Meets the Brend Brothers Bandits (1951 Bond Bread giveaway, color, paper-c, 16 pgs., 3-1/2x7")- Fawcett Publ.	9	18	27	50	65	80
...Strange Legacy (1951 Bond Bread giveaway)	9	18	27	50	65	80
White Tower Giveaway (1946, 16pgs., paper-c)	10	20	30	54	72	90
HOPPY THE MARVEL BUNNY (WELL KNOWN COMICS)						
Fawcett Publications: 1944 (8-1/2x10-1/2", paper-c)						
Bestmaid/Samuel Lowe (printed in red or blue)	11	22	33	64	90	115
HOT STUFF, THE LITTLE DEVIL						
Harvey Publications (Illustrated Humor):1963						
Shoestore Giveaway	3	6	9	21	33	45
HOW KIDS ENJOY NEW YORK						
American Airlines: 1966 (Giveaway, 40 pgs., 4x9")						
nn-Includes 8 color pages by Bob Kane featuring a tour of New York and his studio (a FN+ copy sold for $250 in 2004, and a VF copy sold for $800 in 2018)						
HOW STALIN HOPES WE WILL DESTROY AMERICA						
Joe Lowe Co. (Pictorial Media): 1951 (Giveaway, 16 pgs.)						
nn	40	80	120	214	402	560
HURRICANE KIDS, THE (Also See Magic Morro, The Owl, Popular Comics #45)						
R.S. Callender: 1941 (Giveaway, 7-1/2x5-1/4", soft-c)						
nn-Will Ely-a.	9	18	27	50	65	80

The Iron Giant #1 © WB

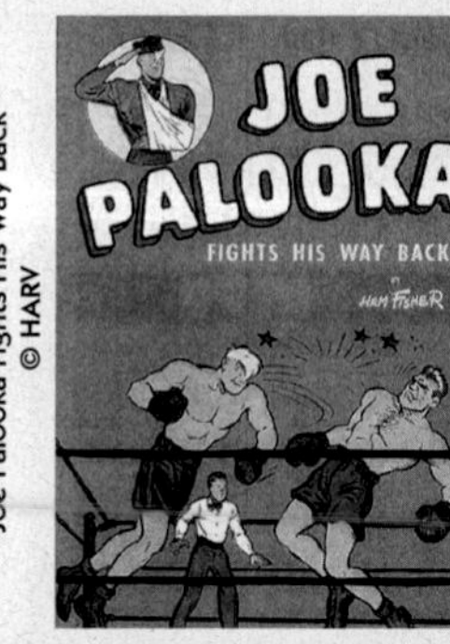

Joe Palooka Fights His Way Back © HARV

Joe the Genie 1950 © USSC

GD 2.0 | VG 4.0 | FN 6.0 | VF 8.0 | VF/NM 9.0 | NM- 9.2

IF THE DEVIL WOULD TALK
Roman Catholic Catechetical Guild/Impact Publ.: 1950; 1958 (32 pgs.; paper cover; in full color)
nn-(Scarce)-About secularism (20-30 copies known to exist); very low distribution 121 242 363 768 1322 1875
1958 Edition-(Impact Publ.); art & script changed to meet church criticism of earlier edition; 80 plus copies known to exist 34 68 102 199 325 450
Black & White version of nn edition; small size; only 4 known copies exist 36 72 108 216 351 485
NOTE: *The original edition of this book was printed and killed by the Guild's board of directors. It is believed that a very limited number of copies were distributed. The 1958 version was a complete bomb with very limited, if any, circulation. In 1979, 11 original, 4 1958 reprints, and 4 B&W's surfaced from the Guild's old files in St. Paul, Minnesota.*

IKE'S STORY
Sponsored Comics, Inc.: 1952 (soft-c)
nn-Dwight D. Eisenhower campaign (A 9.6 sold for $288 in 2018)

IN LOVE WITH JESUS
Catechetical Educational Society: 1952 (Giveaway, 36 pgs.)
nn 7 14 21 37 46 55

INTERSTATE THEATRES' FUN CLUB COMICS
Interstate Theatres: Mid 1940's (10¢ on cover) (B&W cover) (Premium)
Cover features MLJ characters looking at a copy of Top-Notch Comics, but contains an early Detective Comic on inside; many combinations 37 74 111 222 361 500

IN THE GOOD HANDS OF THE ROCKEFELLER TEAM
Country Art Studios: No date (paper cover, 8 pgs.)
nn-Joe Simon-a 9 18 27 47 61 75

IRON GIANT
DC Comics: 1999 (4 pages, theater giveaway)
1-Previews movie 5.00

IRON HORSE GOES TO WAR, THE
Association of American Railroads: 1960 (Giveaway, 16 pgs.)
nn-Civil War & railroads 3 6 9 17 26 35

IS THIS TOMORROW?
Catechetical Guild: 1947 (One Shot) (3 editions) (52 pgs.)
1-Theme of communists taking over the USA; (no price on cover) Used in **POP**, pg. 102 39 78 117 240 395 550
1-(10¢ on cover)(Red price on yellow circle) 39 78 117 240 395 550
1-(10¢ on cover)(Yellow price on red circle) 39 78 117 240 395 550
1-(10¢ on cover)(Yellow price on black circle) 39 78 117 240 395 550
1-Has blank circle with no price on cover 39 78 117 240 395 550
Black & White advance copy titled "Confidential" (52 pgs.)-Contains script and art edited out of the color edition, including one page of extreme violence showing mob nailing a Cardinal to a door; (only two known copies). A VF+ sold in 2/08 for $3346. A NM 9.2 sold in 11/16 for $2629.
NOTE: *The original color version first sold for 10 cents. Since sales were good, it was later printed as a giveaway. Approximately four million in total were printed. The two black and white copies listed plus two other versions as well as a full color untrimmed version surfaced in 1979 from the Guild's old files in St. Paul, Minnesota.*

IT'S FUN TO STAY ALIVE
National Automobile Dealers Association: 1948 (Giveaway, 16 pgs., heavy stock paper)
Featuring: Bugs Bunny, The Berrys, Dixie Dugan, Elmer, Henry, Tim Tyler, Bruce Gentry, Abbie & Slats, Joe Jinks, The Toodles, & Cokey; all art copyright 1946-48 drawn especially for this book 15 30 45 88 137 185

IT'S TIME FOR REASON - NOT TREASON
Liberty Lobby: 1967 (Reg. size, soft-c) (Anti-communist)
nn 6 12 18 41 76 110

JACK AND CHUCK LEARN THE HARD WAY
Commercia Comics/Wagner Electric Co.: 1950s (Reg. size, soft-c)
nn-Automotive giveaway 9 18 27 47 61 75

JACK & JILL VISIT TOYTOWN WITH ELMER THE ELF
Butler Brothers (Toytown Stores): 1949 (Giveaway, 16 pgs., paper cover)
nn 5 10 15 23 28 32

JACK ARMSTRONG (Radio)(See True Comics)
Parents' Institute: 1949
12-Premium version (distr. in Chicago only); Free printed on upper right-c; no price (Rare) 18 36 54 107 169 230

JACKIE JOYNER KERSEE IN HIGH HURDLES (Kellogg's Tony's Sports Comics)
DC Comics: 1992 (Sports Illustrated)
nn 5.00

JACKPOT OF FUN COMIC BOOK
DCA Food Ind.: 1957, giveaway (paper cover, regular size)
nn-Features Howdy Doody 12 24 36 67 94 120

JEDLICKA SHOES
DC Comics: 1961 (Funny animal-c)
nn-Contains Superman #142 9 18 27 58 114 170

JEEP COMICS
R. B. Leffingwell & Co.: 1945 - 1946 (16 pgs.)(King Features Syndicate)
1-(Giveaways)-Strip reprints in all issues; Tarzan, Flash Gordon, Blondie, The Nebbs, Little Iodine, Red Ryder, Don Winslow, The Phantom, Johnny Hazard, Katzenjammer Kids; distr. to U.S. Armed Forces from 1945-1946 19 38 57 111 176 240
2-5 15 30 45 85 130 175
6-46 6 12 18 31 38 45

JINGLE BELLS CHRISTMAS BOOK
Montgomery Ward (Giveaway): 1971 (20 pgs., B&W inside, slick-c)
nn 1 2 3 5 6 8

JOAN OF ARC
Catechetical Guild (Topix) (Giveaway): No date (28 pgs., blank back-c)
nn-Ingrid Bergman photo-c; Addison Burbank-a 14 28 42 76 108 140
NOTE: *Unpublished version exists which came from the Guild's files.*

JOE PALOOKA (2nd Series)
Harvey Publications
...Body Building Instruction Book (1958 B&M Sports Toy giveaway, 16 pgs., 5-1/4x7")-Origin 8 16 24 42 54 65
...Fights His Way Back (1945 Giveaway, 24 pgs.) Family Comics 11 22 33 62 86 110
...in Hi There! (1949 Red Cross giveaway, 12 pgs., 4-3/4x6") 7 14 21 37 46 55
...in It's All in the Family (1945 Red Cross giveaway, 16 pgs., regular size) 8 16 24 40 50 60

JOE THE GENIE OF STEEL (Also see "Return of...")
U.S. Steel Corp., Pittsburgh, PA: 1950 (16 pgs, reg size)
nn-Joe Magarac, the Paul Bunyan of steel 9 18 27 50 65 80

JOHNNY GETS THE WORD
Dept. of Health of New York City: 1963 (small size)
nn - Prevention of venereal diseases 5 10 15 33 57 80
NOTE: *A CGC 9.6 copy sold in 2016 for $263.*

JOHNNY JINGLE'S LUCKY DAY
American Dairy Assoc.: 1956 (16 pgs.; 7-1/4x5-1/8") (Giveaway) (Disney)
nn 5 10 15 24 30 35

JOHNSON MAKES THE TEAM
B.F. Goodrich: 1950 (Reg. size) (Football giveaway)
nn 6 12 18 31 38 45

JO-JOY (The Adventures of...)
W. T. Grant Dept. Stores: 1945 - 1953 (Christmas gift comic, 16 pgs., 7-1/16x10-1/4")
1945-53 issues 8 16 24 40 50 60

JOLLY CHRISTMAS BOOK (See Christmas Journey Through Space)
Promotional Publ. Co.: 1951; 1954; 1955 (36 pgs.; 24 pgs.)
1951-(Woolworth giveaway)-slightly oversized; no slick cover; Marv Levy-c/a 8 16 24 40 50 60
1954-(Hot Shoppes giveaway)-regular size-reprints 1951 issue; slick cover added; 24 pgs.; no ads 7 14 21 35 43 50
1955-(J. M. McDonald Co. giveaway)-reg. size 6 12 18 31 38 45

JOURNEY OF DISCOVERY WITH MARK STEEL (See Mark Steel)

JUMPING JACKS PRESENTS THE WHIZ KIDS
Jumping Jacks Stores giveaway: 1978 (In 3-D) with glasses (4 pgs.)
nn 1 2 3 5 6 8

JUNGLE BOOK FUN BOOK, THE (Disney)
Baskin Robbins: 1978
nn-Ice Cream giveaway 2 4 6 9 12 15

JUSTICE LEAGUE OF AMERICA
DC Comics: 1999 (included in Justice League of America Monopoly game)
nn - Reprints 1st app. in Brave and the Bold #28 3.00

KASCO KOMICS
Kasko Grainfeed (Giveaway): 1945; No. 2, 1949 (Regular size, paper-c)
1(1945)-Similar to Katy Keene; Bill Woggon-a; 28 pgs.; 6-7/8x9-7/8"

Kite Book 1953 - Pinocchio © DIS

Kolynos Presents the White Guard © Whitehall Pharmacal

The Little Fir Tree © W.T. Grant

	GD 2.0	VG 4.0	FN 6.0	VF 8.0	VF/NM 9.0	NM- 9.2
	22	44	66	128	209	290
2(1949)-Woggon-c/a	15	30	45	88	137	185

KATY AND KEN VISIT SANTA WITH MISTER WISH
S. S. Kresge Co. : 1948 (Giveaway, 16 pgs., paper-c)

nn	6	12	18	31	38	45

KELLOGG'S CINNAMON MINI-BUNS SUPER-HEROES
DC Comics: 1993 (4 1/4" x 2 3/4")

4 editions: Flash, Justice League America, Superman, Wonder Woman and the Star Riders each..... 4.00

KERRY DRAKE DETECTIVE CASES
Publisher's Syndicate

...in the Case of the Sleeping City-(1951)-16 pg. giveaway for armed forces; paper cover 7 14 21 37 46 55

KEY COMICS
Key Clothing Co./Peterson Clothing: 1951 - 1956 (32 pgs.) (Giveaway)
Contains a comic from different publishers bound with new cover. Cover changed each year. Many combinations possible. Distributed in Nebraska, Iowa, & Kansas. Contents would determine price, 40-60 percent of original.

KING JAMES "THE KING OF BASKETBALL"
DC Comics: 2004 (Promo comic for LeBron James and Powerade Flava23 sports drink)

nn - Ten different covers by various artists; 4 covers for retail, 4 for mail-in, 1 for military commissaries, and 1 general market; Damion Scott-a/Gary Phillips-s 3.00

KIRBY'S SHOES COMICS
Kirby's Shoes: 1959 - 1961 (8 pgs., soft-c, several different editions)

nn-Features Kirby the Golden Bear	4	7	10	14	17	20

KITE FUN BOOK
Pacific, Gas & Electric/Sou. California Edison/Florida Power & Light/ Missouri Public Service Co.: 1952 - 1998 (16 pgs, 5x7-1/4", soft-c)

	GD	VG	FN	VF	VF/NM	NM-
1952-Having Fun With Kites (P.G.&E.)	10	20	30	58	79	100
1953-Pinocchio Learns About Kites (Disney)	41	82	123	250	418	585
1954-Donald Duck Tells About Kites-Fla. Power, S.C.E. & version with label issues -Barks pencils-8 pgs.; inks-7 pgs. (Rare)	206	412	618	1318	2259	3200
1954-Donald Duck Tells About Kites-P.G.&E. issue -7th page redrawn changing middle 3 panels to show P.G.&E. in story line; (All Barks-a) Scarce	187	374	561	1197	2049	2900
1955-Brer Rabbit in "A Kite Tail" (Disney)	24	48	72	144	237	330
1956-Woody Woodpecker (Lantz)	12	24	36	67	94	120
1957-Ruff and Reddy (exist?)						
1958-Tom And Jerry (M.G.M.)	9	18	27	52	69	85
1959-Bugs Bunny (Warner Bros.)	4	8	12	27	44	60
1960-Porky Pig (Warner Bros.)	4	8	12	28	47	65
1960-Bugs Bunny (Warner Bros.)	4	8	12	28	47	65
1961-Huckleberry Hound (Hanna-Barbera)	5	10	15	31	53	75
1962-Yogi Bear (Hanna-Barbera)	4	8	12	25	40	55
1963-Rocky and Bullwinkle (TV)(Jay Ward)	5	10	15	35	63	90
1963-Top Cat (TV)(Hanna-Barbera)	3	6	9	19	30	40
1964-Magilla Gorilla (TV)(Hanna-Barbera)	3	6	9	17	26	35
1965-Jinks, Pixie and Dixie (TV)(Hanna-Barbera)	3	6	9	15	22	28
1965-Tweety and Sylvester (Warner); S.C.E. version with Reddy Kilowatt app.	2	4	6	9	13	16
1966-Secret Squirrel (Hanna-Barbera); S.C.E. version with Reddy Kilowatt app.	5	10	15	30	50	70
1967-Beep! Beep! The Road Runner (TV)(Warner)	2	4	6	11	16	20
1968-Bugs Bunny (Warner Bros.)	2	4	6	13	18	22
1969-Dastardly and Muttley (TV)(Hanna-Barbera)	3	6	9	19	30	40
1970-Rocky and Bullwinkle (TV)(Jay Ward)	4	8	12	27	44	60
1971-Beep! Beep! The Road Runner (TV)(Warner)	2	4	6	11	16	20
1972-The Pink Panther (TV)	2	4	6	10	14	18
1973-Lassie (TV)	3	6	9	15	22	28
1974-Underdog (TV)	2	4	6	11	16	20
1975-Ben Franklin	2	4	6	8	10	12
1976-The Brady Bunch (TV)	3	6	9	16	23	30
1977-Ben Franklin (exist?)	2	4	6	8	10	12
1977-Popeye	2	4	6	9	13	16
1978-Happy Days (TV)	2	4	6	11	16	20
1979-Eight is Enough (TV)	2	4	6	9	13	16
1980-The Waltons (TV, released in 1981)	2	4	6	9	13	16
1982-Tweety and Sylvester	2	4	6	8	11	14
1984-Smokey Bear	1	3	4	6	8	10
1986-Road Runner	1	2	3	5	6	8
1997-Thomas Edison						4.00
1998-Edison Field (Anaheim Stadium)						3.00

KNOWING'S NOT ENOUGH
Commercial Comics: 1956 (Reg. size, paper-c) (United States Steel safety giveaway)

nn	7	14	21	35	43	50

KNOW YOUR MASS
Catechetical Guild: No. 303, 1958 (35¢, 100 Pg. Giant) (Square binding)

303-In color	7	14	21	35	43	50

KOLYNOS PRESENTS THE WHITE GUARD
Whitehall Pharmacal Co.: 1949 (paper cover, 8 pgs.)

nn	6	12	18	31	38	45

KOLYNOS PRESENTS THE WICKED WITCH
Whitehall Pharmacal Co.: 1951 (paper cover, 8 pgs.)

nn-Anti-tooth decay	4	7	10	14	17	20

K. O. PUNCH, THE (Also see Lucky Fights It Through & Sidewalk Romance)
E. C. Comics: 1948 (VD Educational giveaway)

nn-Feldstein-splash; Kamen-a	123	246	369	787	1344	1900

KOREA MY HOME (Also see Yalta to Korea)
Johnstone and Cushing: nd (1950s, slick-c, regular size)

nn-Anti-communist; Korean War	26	52	78	152	249	345

KRIM-KO KOMICS
Krim-ko Chocolate Drink: 5/18/35 - No. 6, 6/22/35; 1936 - 1939 (weekly)

1-(16 pgs., soft-c, Dairy giveaways)-Tom, Mary & Sparky Advs. by Russell Keaton, Jim Hawkins by Dick Moores, Mystery Island! by Rick Yager begin	14	28	42	81	118	155
2-6 (6/22/35)	11	22	33	60	83	105
Lola, Secret Agent; 184 issues, 4 pg. giveaways - all original stories each....	8	16	24	42	54	65

LABOR IS A PARTNER
Catechetical Guild Educational Society: 1949 (32 pgs., paper-c)

nn-Anti-communism	45	90	135	284	480	675

Confidential Preview-(8-1/2x11", B&W, saddle stitched)-only one known copy; text varies from color version, advertises next book on secularism (If the Devil Would Talk)
(A VF- copy sold for $2629 in 11/2016 and a VG/FN copy sold for $454 in 1/2017)

LADIES - WOULDN'T IT BE BETTER TO KNOW
American Cancer Society: 1969 (Reg. size)

nn	4	8	12	22	35	48

LADY AND THE TRAMP IN "BUTTER LATE THAN NEVER"
American Dairy Assoc. (Premium): 1955 (16 pgs., 5x7-1/4", soft-c) (Disney)

nn	9	18	27	47	61	75

LASSIE (TV)
Dell Publ. Co

The Adventures of... nn-(Red Heart Dog Food giveaway, 1949)-16 pgs, soft-c; 1st app. Lassie in comics	39	78	117	231	378	525

LIFE OF THE BLESSED VIRGIN
Catechetical Guild (Giveaway): 1950 (68pgs.) (square binding)

nn-Contains "The Woman of the Promise" & "Mother of Us All" rebound	10	20	30	56	76	95

LIGHTNING RACERS
DC Comics: 1989

1 4.50

LI'L ABNER (Al Capp's) (Also see Natural Disasters!)
Harvey Publ./Toby Press

...& the Creatures from Drop-Outer Space-nn (Job Corps giveaway; 36 pgs., in color) (entire book by Frank Frazetta)	21	42	63	124	202	280
...Joins the Navy (1950) (Toby Press Premium)	11	22	33	62	86	110
Al Capp by Li'l Abner (Circa 1946, nd, giveaway) Al Capp bio and his life as an amputee	11	22	33	62	86	110

LITTLE ALONZO
Macy's Dept. Store: 1938 (B&W, 5-1/2x8-1/2")(Christmas giveaway)

nn-By Ferdinand the Bull's Munro Leaf	10	20	30	54	72	90

LITTLE ARCHIE (See Archie Comics)

LITTLE DOT
Harvey Publications

Shoe store giveaway 2	4	8	12	28	47	65

LITTLE FIR TREE, THE
W. T. Grant Co. : nd (1942) (8-1/2x11") (12 pgs. with cover, color & B&W, heavy paper)

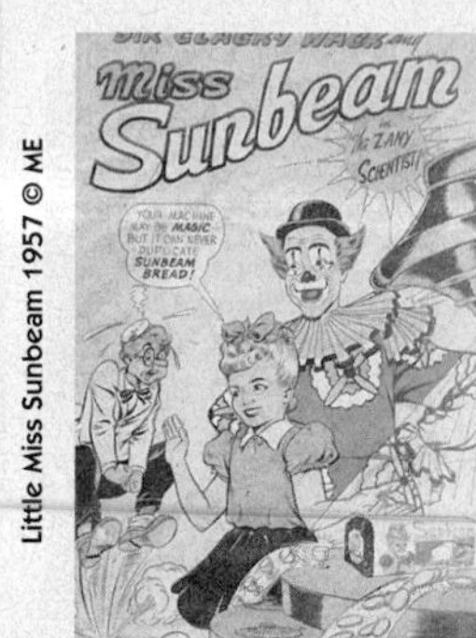

Little Miss Sunbeam 1957 © ME

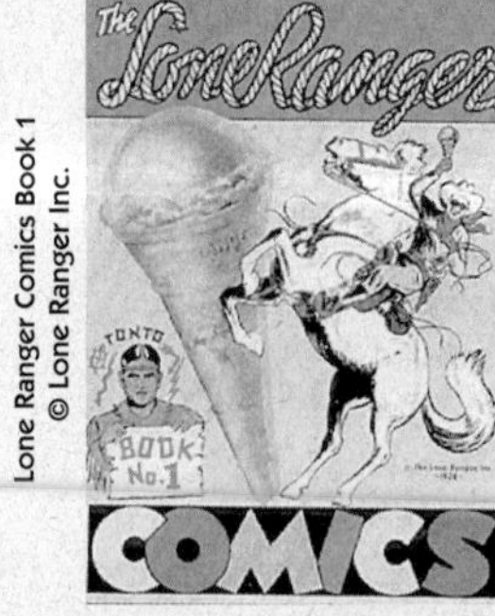

Lone Ranger Comics Book 1 © Lone Ranger Inc.

March of Comics #20 © DIS

	GD 2.0	VG 4.0	FN 6.0	VF 8.0	VF/NM 9.0	NM- 9.2

(Christmas giveaway)
nn-Story by Hans Christian Anderson; 8 pg. Kelly-r/Santa Claus Funnies (not signed); X-Mas-c 95 190 285 603 1039 1475

LITTLE KLINKER
Little Klinker Ventures: Nov, 1960 (20 pgs.) (slick cover) (Montgomery Ward Giveaway)
nn - Christmas; Santa-c 3 6 9 14 20 25

LITTLE MISS SUNBEAM COMICS
Magazine Enterprises/Quality Bakers of America
Bread Giveaway 1-4(Quality Bakers, 1949-50)-14 pgs. each 7 14 21 37 46 55
Bread Giveaway (1957,61; 16pgs, reg. size) 6 12 18 31 38 45

LITTLE ORPHAN ANNIE
David McKay Publ./Dell Publishing Co.
Junior Commandos Giveaway (same-c as 4-Color #18, K.K. Publ.)(Big Shoe Store); same back cover as '47 Popped Wheat giveaway; 16 pgs; flag-c; r/strips 9/7/42-10/10/42 26 52 78 154 252 350
Popped Wheat Giveaway ('47)-16 pgs. full color; reprints strips from 5/3/40 to 6/20/40 5 10 15 22 26 30
Quaker Sparkies Giveaway (1940) 18 36 54 103 162 220
Quaker Sparkies Giveaway (1941, full color, 20 pgs.); "LOA and the Rescue"; r/strips 4/13/39-6/21/39 & 7/6/39-7/17/39. "LOA and the Kidnappers"; r/strips 11/28/38-1/28/39 15 30 45 94 147 200
Quaker Sparkies Giveaway (1942, full color, 20 pgs.); "LOA and Mr. Gudge"; r/strips 2/13/38-3/21/38 & 4/18/37-5/30/37. "LOA and the Great Am" 15 30 45 88 137 185

LITTLE TREE THAT WASN'T WANTED, THE
W. T. Grant Co. (Giveaway): 1960, (Color, 28 pgs.)
nn-Christmas story, puzzles and games 3 6 9 21 33 45

LONE RANGER, THE
Dell Publishing Co.
Cheerios Giveaways (1954, 16 pgs., 2-1/2x7", soft-c) #1- "The Lone Ranger, His Mask & How He Met Tonto". #2- "The Lone Ranger & the Story of Silver" each.... 12 24 36 69 97 125
Doll Giveaways (Gabriel Ind.)(1973, 3-1/4x5")- "The Story of The Lone Ranger," "The Carson City Bank Robbery" & "The Apache Buffalo Hunt" 2 4 6 12 16 20
How the Lone Ranger Captured Silver Book(1936)-Silvercup Bread giveaway 55 110 165 352 601 850
...In Milk for Big Mike (1955, Dairy Association giveaway), soft-c; 5x7-1/4", 16 pgs. 10 20 30 58 79 100
Legend of The Lone Ranger (1969, 16 pgs., giveaway)-Origin The Lone Ranger 4 8 12 21 33 45
Merita Bread giveaway (1954, 16 pgs., 5x7-1/4")- "How to Be a Lone Ranger Health & Safety Scout" 14 28 42 80 115 150
Merita Bread giveaway (1955, 16 pgs., 5x7-1/4")- "Official Lone Ranger and Tonto Coloring Book" 12 24 36 69 97 125
Merita Bread giveaway (1956, 16 pgs., 5x7-1/4")- "Tells the Story of Branding" 12 24 36 69 97 125

LONE RANGER COMICS, THE
Lone Ranger, Inc. : Book 1, 1939(inside) (shows 1938 on-c) (52 pgs. in color; regular size) (Ice cream mail order)
Book 1-(Scarce)-The first western comic devoted to a single character; not by Vallely 571 1142 1713 4000 - -
2nd version w/large full color promo poster pasted over centerfold & a smaller poster pasted over back cover; includes new additional premiums not originally offered (Rare) (A CGC 6.5 copy sold in 2020 for $2,160) 643 1286 1929 4500 - -

LOONEY TUNES
DC Comics: 1991, 1998
Claritin promotional issue (1998); Colgate mini-comic (1998) 3.00
Tyson's 1-10 (1991) 4.00

LUCKY FIGHTS IT THROUGH (Also see The K. O. Punch & Sidewalk Romance)
Educational Comics: 1949 (Giveaway, 16 pgs. in color, paper-c)
nn-(Very Rare)-1st Kurtzman work for E.C.; V.D. prevention 181 362 543 1158 1979 2800
nn-Reprint in color (1977) 7.00
NOTE: *Subtitled "The Story of That Ignorant, Ignorant Cowboy". Prepared for Communications Materials Center, Columbia University.*

LUDWIG VON DRAKE (See Frito-Lay Giveaway)

MACO TOYS COMIC
Maco Toys/Charlton Comics: 1959 (Giveaway, 36 pgs.)
1-All military stories featuring Maco Toys 4 9 13 18 22 26

MAD MAGAZINE
DC Comics: 1997, 1999, 2008
Special Edition (1997, Tang giveaway) 3.00
Stocking Stuffer (1999) 3.00
San Diego Comic-Con Edition (2008) Watchmen parody with Fabry-a; Aragonés cartoons 3.00

MAGAZINELAND USA
DC Comics: 1977
nn-Kubert-c/a 3 6 9 16 24 32

MAGIC MORRO (Also see Super Comics #21, The Owl, & The Hurricane Kids)
K. K. Publications: 1941 (7-1/2 x 5-1/4", giveaway, soft-c)
nn-Ken Ernst-a. 10 20 30 56 76 95

MAGIC OF CHRISTMAS AT NEWBERRYS, THE
E. S. London: 1967 (Giveaway) (B&W, slick-c, 20 pgs.)
nn 1 3 4 6 8 10

MAGIC SHOE ADVENTURE BOOK
Western Publications: 1962 - No. 3, 1963 (Shoe store giveaway, Reg. size)
nn-(1962) 5 10 15 34 60 85
1 (1963)-And the Flaming Threat 4 8 12 28 47 65
2 (1963)-And the Winning Run 4 8 12 28 47 65
3 (1963)-And the Missing Masterpiece Mystery 4 8 12 28 47 65

MAJOR INAPAK THE SPACE ACE
Magazine Enterprises (Inapac Foods): 1951 (20 pgs.) (Giveaway)
1-Bob Powell-c/a 2 4 6 8 10 12
NOTE: *Many warehouse copies surfaced in 1973.*

MAMMY YOKUM & THE GREAT DOGPATCH MYSTERY
Toby Press: 1951 (Giveaway)
nn-Li'l Abner 16 32 48 92 144 195
nn-Reprint (1956) 5 10 15 24 30 35

MAN NAMED STEVENSON, A
Democratic National Committee: 1952 (20 pgs., 5 1/4 x 7")
nn 9 18 27 47 61 75

MAN OF PEACE, POPE PIUS XII
Catechetical Guild: 1950 (See Pope Pius XII... & To V2#8)
nn-All Powell-a 7 14 21 35 43 50

MAN OF STEEL BEST WESTERN
DC Comics: 1997 (Best Western hotels promo)
3-Reprints Superman's first post-Crisis meeting with Batman 4.00

MAN WHO RUNS INTERFERENCE
General Comics, Inc./Institute of Life Insurance: 1946 (Paper-c)
nn-Football premium 6 12 18 28 34 40

MAN WHO WOULDN'T QUIT, THE
Harvey Publications Inc.: 1952 (16 pgs., paper cover)
nn-The value of voting 4 8 12 18 22 25

MARCH OF COMICS (Boys' and Girls'...#3-353)
K. K. Publications/Western Publishing Co.: 1946 - No. 488, April, 1982 (#1-4 are not numbered) (K.K. Giveaway) (Founded by Sig Feuchtwanger)
Early issues were full size, 32 pages, and were printed with and without an extra cover of slick stock, just for the advertiser. The binding was stapled if the slick cover was added; otherwise, the pages were glued together at the spine. Most 1948 - 1951 issues were full size,24 pages, pulp covers. Starting in 1952 they were half-size (with a few exceptions) and 32 pages with slick covers.1959 and later issues had only 16 pages plus covers. 1952 -1959 issues read oblong; 1960 and later issues read upright. All have new stories except where noted.
nn (#1, 1946)-Goldilocks; Kelly back-c (16 pgs., stapled) 52 104 156 328 552 775
nn (#2, 1946)-How Santa Got His Red Suit; Kelly-a (11 pgs., r/4-Color #61 from 1944) (16pgs., stapled) 32 64 96 188 307 425
nn (#3, 1947)-Our Gang (Walt Kelly) 36 72 108 216 351 485
nn (#4)-Donald Duck by Carl Barks, "Maharajah Donald", 28 pgs.; Kelly-c? (Disney) 784 1568 2352 5723 10,112 14,500
5-Andy Panda (Walter Lantz) 18 36 54 103 162 220
6-Popular Fairy Tales; Kelly-c; Noonan-a(2) 18 36 54 105 165 225
7-Oswald the Rabbit 20 40 60 117 189 260
8-Mickey Mouse, 32 pgs. (Disney) 42 84 126 265 445 625
9(nn)-The Story of the Gloomy Bunny 12 24 36 69 97 125
10-Out of Santa's Bag 11 22 33 64 90 115
11-Fun With Santa Claus 10 20 30 58 79 100

March of Comics #47 © Roy Rogers

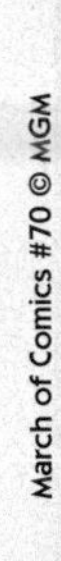

March of Comics #70 © MGM

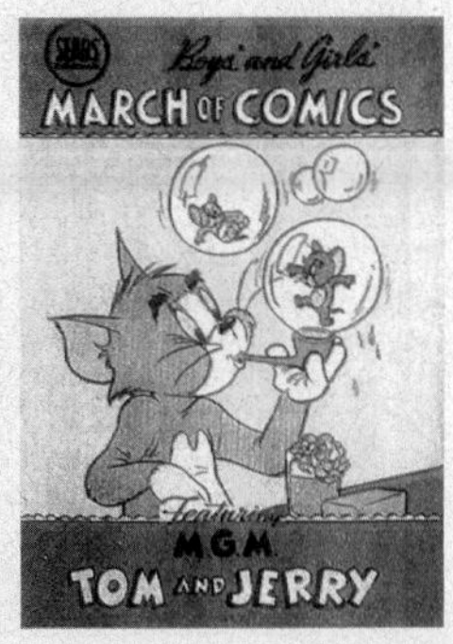

March of Comics #141 © DIS

	GD 2.0	VG 4.0	FN 6.0	VF 8.0	VF/NM 9.0	NM- 9.2
12-Santa's Toys	10	20	30	58	79	100
13-Santa's Surprise	10	20	30	58	79	100
14-Santa's Candy Kitchen	10	20	30	58	79	100
15-Hip-It-Ty Hop & the Big Bass Viol	10	20	30	56	76	95
16-Woody Woodpecker (1947)(Walter Lantz)	14	28	42	78	112	145
17-Roy Rogers (1948)	20	40	60	120	195	270
18-Popular Fairy Tales	12	24	36	67	94	120
19-Uncle Wiggily	10	20	30	58	79	100
20-Donald Duck by Carl Barks, "Darkest Africa", 22 pgs.; Kelly-c (Disney)	271	542	813	1734	2967	4200
21-Tom and Jerry	11	22	33	62	86	110
22-Andy Panda (Lantz)	11	22	33	62	86	110
23-Raggedy Ann & Andy; Kerr-a	13	26	39	72	101	130
24-Felix the Cat, 1932 daily strip reprints by Otto Messmer	16	32	48	94	147	200
25-Gene Autry	17	34	51	100	158	215
26-Our Gang; Walt Kelly	16	32	48	96	151	205
27-Mickey Mouse; r/in M. M. #240 (Disney)	29	58	87	172	281	390
28-Gene Autry	17	34	51	98	154	210
29-Easter Bonnet Shop	9	18	27	47	61	75
30-Here Comes Santa	8	16	24	44	57	70
31-Santa's Busy Corner	8	16	24	44	57	70
32-No book produced						
33-A Christmas Carol (12/48)	9	18	27	47	61	75
34-Woody Woodpecker	11	22	33	62	86	110
35-Roy Rogers (1948)	19	38	57	112	179	245
36-Felix the Cat(1949); by Messmer; '34 strip-r	14	28	42	82	121	160
37-Popeye	14	28	42	78	112	145
38-Oswald the Rabbit	8	16	24	44	57	70
39-Gene Autry	16	32	48	94	147	200
40-Andy and Woody	8	16	24	44	57	70
41-Donald Duck by Carl Barks, "Race to the South Seas", 22 pgs.; Kelly-c	245	490	735	1568	2684	3800
42-Porky Pig	9	18	27	47	61	75
43-Henry	8	16	24	42	54	65
44-Bugs Bunny	9	18	27	52	69	85
45-Mickey Mouse (Disney)	20	40	60	120	195	270
46-Tom and Jerry	9	18	27	52	69	85
47-Roy Rogers	15	30	45	90	140	190
48-Greetings from Santa	6	12	18	31	38	45
49-Santa Is Here	6	12	18	31	38	45
50-Santa Claus' Workshop (1949)	6	12	18	31	38	45
51-Felix the Cat (1950) by Messmer	14	28	42	80	115	150
52-Popeye	11	22	33	62	86	110
53-Oswald the Rabbit	8	16	24	40	50	60
54-Gene Autry	15	30	45	84	127	170
55-Andy and Woody	8	16	24	40	50	60
56-Donald Duck; not by Barks; Barks art on back-c (Disney)	20	40	60	114	182	260
57-Porky Pig	8	16	24	40	50	60
58-Henry	7	14	21	35	43	50
59-Bugs Bunny	9	18	27	47	61	75
60-Mickey Mouse (Disney)	20	40	60	120	195	270
61-Tom and Jerry	8	16	24	40	50	60
62-Roy Rogers	15	30	45	90	140	190
63-Welcome Santa (1/2-size, oblong)	6	12	18	31	38	45
64(nn)-Santa's Helpers (1/2-size, oblong)	6	12	18	31	38	45
65(nn)-Jingle Bells (1950) (1/2-size, oblong)	6	12	18	31	38	45
66-Popeye (1951)	12	24	36	67	94	120
67-Oswald the Rabbit	7	14	21	35	43	50
68-Roy Rogers	14	28	42	80	115	150
69-Donald Duck; Barks-a on back-c (Disney)	20	40	60	117	189	260
70-Tom and Jerry	8	16	24	40	50	60
71-Porky Pig	8	16	24	42	54	65
72-Krazy Kat	9	18	27	47	61	75
73-Roy Rogers	14	28	42	82	121	160
74-Mickey Mouse (1951)(Disney)	20	40	60	114	182	250
75-Bugs Bunny	9	18	27	47	61	75
76-Andy and Woody	8	16	24	40	50	60
77-Roy Rogers	14	28	42	82	121	160
78-Gene Autry (1951); last regular size issue	14	28	42	80	115	150

Note: All pre #79 issues came with or without a slick protective wrap-around cover over the regular cover which advertised Poll Parrot Shoes, Sears, etc. This outer cover protects the inside pages making them in nicer condition.
Issues with the outer cover are worth 15-25% more

	GD 2.0	VG 4.0	FN 6.0	VF 8.0	VF/NM 9.0	NM- 9.2
79-Andy Panda (1952, 5x7" size)	7	14	21	35	43	50
80-Popeye	8	16	24	40	50	60
81-Oswald the Rabbit	6	12	18	29	36	42
82-Tarzan; Lex Barker photo-c	15	30	45	84	127	170
83-Bugs Bunny	7	14	21	37	46	55
84-Henry	6	12	18	29	36	42
85-Woody Woodpecker	6	12	18	29	36	42
86-Roy Rogers	11	22	33	62	86	110
87-Krazy Kat	8	16	24	44	57	70
88-Tom and Jerry	6	12	18	31	38	45
89-Porky Pig	6	12	18	29	36	42
90-Gene Autry	11	22	33	62	86	110
91-Roy Rogers & Santa	11	22	33	62	86	110
92-Christmas with Santa	5	10	15	24	30	35
93-Woody Woodpecker (1953)	5	10	15	23	28	32
94-Indian Chief	10	20	30	54	72	90
95-Oswald the Rabbit	5	10	15	23	28	32
96-Popeye	10	20	30	54	72	90
97-Bugs Bunny	7	14	21	35	43	50
98-Tarzan; Lex Barker photo-c	14	28	42	82	121	160
99-Porky Pig	5	10	15	23	28	32
100-Roy Rogers	10	20	30	58	79	100
101-Henry	5	10	15	22	26	30
102-Tom Corbett (TV)('53, early app).; painted-c	12	24	36	67	94	120
103-Tom and Jerry	5	10	15	23	28	32
104-Gene Autry	10	20	30	56	76	95
105-Roy Rogers	10	20	30	56	76	95
106-Santa's Helpers	5	10	15	24	30	35
107-Santa's Christmas Book - not published						
108-Fun with Santa (1953)	5	10	15	24	30	35
109-Woody Woodpecker (1954)	5	10	15	24	30	35
110-Indian Chief	6	12	18	31	38	45
111-Oswald the Rabbit	5	10	15	22	26	30
112-Henry	4	9	13	18	22	26
113-Porky Pig	5	10	15	22	26	30
114-Tarzan; Russ Manning-a	14	28	42	82	121	160
115-Bugs Bunny	6	12	18	27	33	38
116-Roy Rogers	10	20	30	56	76	95
117-Popeye	10	20	30	54	72	90
118-Flash Gordon; painted-c	11	22	33	64	90	115
119-Tom and Jerry	5	10	15	22	26	30
120-Gene Autry	10	20	30	58	76	95
121-Roy Rogers	10	20	30	58	76	95
122-Santa's Surprise (1954)	5	10	15	22	26	30
123-Santa's Christmas Book	5	10	15	22	26	30
124-Woody Woodpecker (1955)	4	9	13	18	22	26
125-Tarzan; Lex Barker photo-c	14	28	42	78	112	145
126-Oswald the Rabbit	4	9	13	18	22	26
127-Indian Chief	7	14	21	35	43	50
128-Tom and Jerry	4	9	13	18	22	26
129-Henry	4	8	12	17	21	24
130-Porky Pig	4	9	13	18	22	26
131-Roy Rogers	10	20	30	56	76	95
132-Bugs Bunny	5	10	15	23	28	32
133-Flash Gordon; painted-c	11	22	33	62	86	110
134-Popeye	8	16	24	42	54	65
135-Gene Autry	10	20	30	56	76	95
136-Roy Rogers	10	20	30	56	76	95
137-Gifts from Santa	4	7	10	14	17	20
138-Fun at Christmas (1955)	4	7	10	14	17	20
139-Woody Woodpecker (1956)	4	9	13	18	22	26
140-Indian Chief	7	14	21	35	43	50
141-Oswald the Rabbit	4	9	13	18	22	26
142-Flash Gordon	12	24	36	69	97	125
143-Porky Pig	4	9	13	18	22	26
144-Tarzan; Russ Manning-a; painted-c	13	26	39	72	101	130
145-Tom and Jerry	4	9	13	18	22	26
146-Roy Rogers; photo-c	10	20	30	56	76	95
147-Henry	4	8	11	16	19	22
148-Popeye	8	16	24	42	54	65
149-Bugs Bunny	5	10	15	22	26	30
150-Gene Autry	10	20	30	56	76	95
151-Roy Rogers	10	20	30	56	76	95
152-The Night Before Christmas	4	8	11	16	19	22
153-Merry Christmas (1956)	4	9	13	18	22	26
154-Tom and Jerry (1957)	4	9	13	18	22	26
155-Tarzan; photo-c	12	24	36	69	97	125

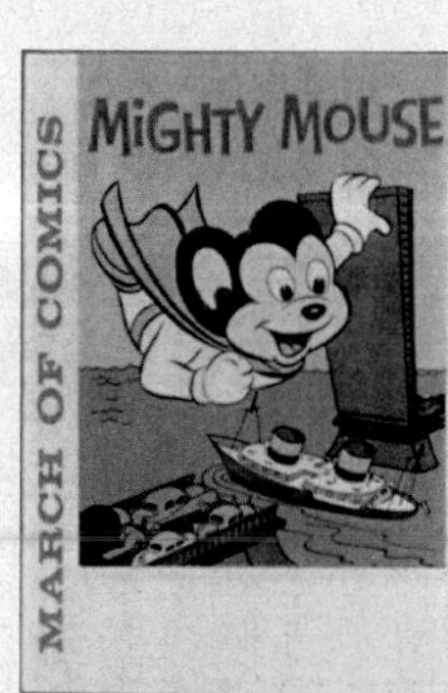

March of Comics #205 © Terry Toons

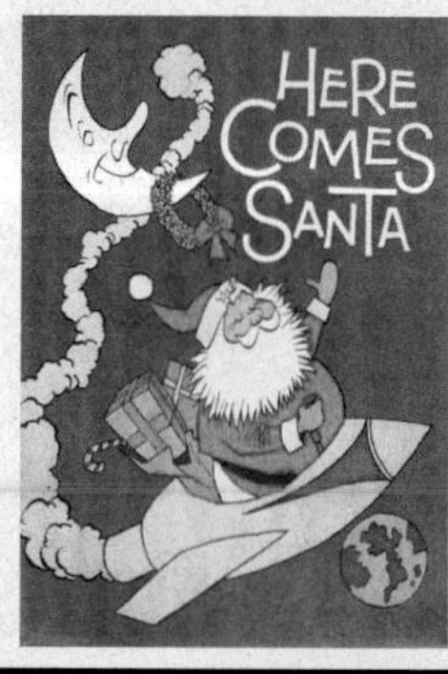

March of Comics #213 © WEST

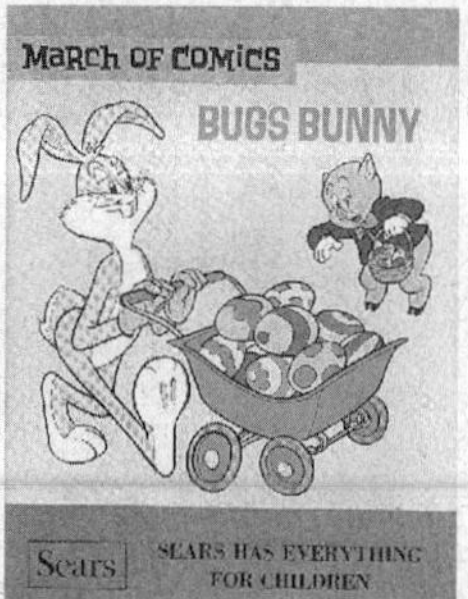

March of Comics #301 © WB

	GD 2.0	VG 4.0	FN 6.0	VF 8.0	VF/NM 9.0	NM- 9.2
156-Oswald the Rabbit	4	9	13	18	22	26
157-Popeye	7	14	21	35	43	50
158-Woody Woodpecker	4	9	13	18	22	26
159-Indian Chief	7	14	21	35	43	50
160-Bugs Bunny	5	10	15	22	26	30
161-Roy Rogers	9	18	27	52	69	85
162-Henry	4	8	11	16	19	22
163-Rin Tin Tin (TV)	8	16	24	42	54	65
164-Porky Pig	4	9	13	18	22	26
165-The Lone Ranger	9	18	27	50	65	80
166-Santa and His Reindeer	4	7	10	14	17	20
167-Roy Rogers and Santa	9	18	27	52	69	85
168-Santa Claus' Workshop (1957, full size)	4	8	11	16	19	22
169-Popeye (1958)	7	14	21	35	43	50
170-Indian Chief	7	14	21	35	43	50
171-Oswald the Rabbit	4	8	12	17	21	24
172-Tarzan	11	22	33	60	83	105
173-Tom and Jerry	4	8	12	17	21	24
174-The Lone Ranger	9	18	27	50	65	80
175-Porky Pig	4	8	12	17	21	24
176-Roy Rogers	9	18	27	47	61	75
177-Woody Woodpecker	4	8	12	17	21	24
178-Henry	4	8	11	16	19	22
179-Bugs Bunny	4	8	12	17	21	24
180-Rin Tin Tin (TV)	7	14	21	37	46	55
181-Happy Holiday	4	7	9	14	16	18
182-Happi Tim	4	8	11	16	19	22
183-Welcome Santa (1958, full size)	4	7	9	14	16	18
184-Woody Woodpecker (1959)	4	8	11	16	19	22
185-Tarzan; photo-c	10	20	30	58	79	100
186-Oswald the Rabbit	4	8	11	16	19	22
187-Indian Chief	6	12	18	28	34	40
188-Bugs Bunny	4	8	11	16	19	22
189-Henry	4	7	10	14	17	20
190-Tom and Jerry	4	8	11	16	19	22
191-Roy Rogers	8	16	24	44	57	70
192-Porky Pig	4	8	11	16	19	22
193-The Lone Ranger	9	18	27	47	61	75
194-Popeye	6	12	18	31	38	45
195-Rin Tin Tin (TV)	7	14	21	35	43	50
196-Sears Special - not published						
197-Santa Is Coming	4	7	10	14	17	20
198-Santa's Helpers (1959)	4	7	10	14	17	20
199-Huckleberry Hound (TV)(1960, early app.)	8	16	24	42	54	65
200-Fury (TV)	6	12	18	28	34	40
201-Bugs Bunny	4	8	11	16	19	22
202-Space Explorer	8	16	24	42	54	65
203-Woody Woodpecker	4	7	10	14	17	20
204-Tarzan	9	18	27	52	69	85
205-Mighty Mouse	6	12	18	33	41	48
206-Roy Rogers; photo-c	8	16	24	42	54	65
207-Tom and Jerry	4	7	10	14	17	20
208-The Lone Ranger; Clayton Moore photo-c	10	20	30	54	72	90
209-Porky Pig	4	7	10	14	17	20
210-Lassie (TV)	6	12	18	33	41	48
211-Sears Special - not published						
212-Christmas Eve	4	7	10	14	17	20
213-Here Comes Santa (1960)	4	7	10	14	17	20
214-Huckleberry Hound (TV)(1961)	7	14	21	35	43	50
215-Hi Yo Silver	8	16	24	40	50	60
216-Rocky & His Friends (TV)(1961); predates Rocky and His Fiendish Friends #1 (see Four Color #1128)	9	18	27	52	69	85
217-Lassie (TV)	6	12	18	31	38	45
218-Porky Pig	4	7	10	14	17	20
219-Journey to the Sun	5	10	15	24	30	35
220-Bugs Bunny	4	8	11	16	19	22
221-Roy and Dale; photo-c	8	16	24	42	54	65
222-Woody Woodpecker	4	7	10	14	17	20
223-Tarzan	9	18	27	50	65	80
224-Tom and Jerry	4	7	10	14	17	20
225-The Lone Ranger	8	16	24	40	50	60
226-Christmas Treasury (1961)	4	7	10	14	17	20
227-Letters to Santa (1961)	4	7	10	14	17	20
228-Sears Special - not published?						
229-The Flintstones (TV)(1962); early app.; predates 1st Flintstones Gold Key issue (#7)	10	20	30	54	72	90
230-Lassie (TV)	6	12	18	27	33	38
231-Bugs Bunny	4	8	11	16	19	22
232-The Three Stooges	9	18	27	52	69	85
233-Bullwinkle (TV) (1962, very early app.)	9	18	27	52	69	85
234-Smokey the Bear	5	10	15	23	28	32
235-Huckleberry Hound (TV)	7	14	21	35	43	50
236-Roy and Dale	7	14	21	35	43	50
237-Mighty Mouse	6	12	18	27	33	38
238-The Lone Ranger	8	16	24	40	50	60
239-Woody Woodpecker	4	7	10	14	17	20
240-Tarzan	8	16	24	44	57	70
241-Santa Claus Around the World	4	7	9	14	16	18
242-Santa's Toyland (1962)	4	7	9	14	16	18
243-The Flintstones (TV)(1963)	8	16	24	44	57	70
244-Mister Ed (TV); early app.; photo-c	7	14	21	35	43	50
245-Bugs Bunny	4	8	11	16	19	22
246-Popeye	6	12	18	27	33	38
247-Mighty Mouse	6	12	18	27	33	38
248-The Three Stooges	10	20	30	54	72	90
249-Woody Woodpecker	4	7	10	14	17	20
250-Roy and Dale	7	14	21	35	43	50
251-Little Lulu & Witch Hazel	11	22	33	60	83	105
252-Tarzan; painted-c	8	16	24	42	54	65
253-Yogi Bear (TV)	8	16	24	40	50	60
254-Lassie (TV)	6	12	18	27	33	38
255-Santa's Christmas List	4	7	10	14	17	20
256-Christmas Party (1963)	4	7	10	14	17	20
257-Mighty Mouse	6	12	18	27	33	38
258-The Sword in the Stone (Disney)	8	16	24	42	54	65
259-Bugs Bunny	4	8	11	16	19	22
260-Mister Ed (TV)	6	12	18	31	38	45
261-Woody Woodpecker	4	7	10	14	17	20
262-Tarzan	8	16	24	40	50	60
263-Donald Duck; not by Barks (Disney)	9	18	27	52	69	85
264-Popeye	6	12	18	27	33	38
265-Yogi Bear (TV)	6	12	18	31	38	45
266-Lassie (TV)	5	10	15	23	28	32
267-Little Lulu; Irving Tripp-a	10	20	30	56	76	95
268-The Three Stooges	9	18	27	47	61	75
269-A Jolly Christmas	3	6	8	12	14	16
270-Santa's Little Helpers	3	6	8	12	14	16
271-The Flintstones (TV)(1965)	8	16	24	44	57	70
272-Tarzan	8	16	24	40	50	60
273-Bugs Bunny	4	8	11	16	19	22
274-Popeye	6	12	18	27	33	38
275-Little Lulu; Irving Tripp-a	9	18	27	50	65	80
276-The Jetsons (TV)	12	24	36	67	94	120
277-Daffy Duck	4	8	11	16	19	22
278-Lassie (TV)	5	10	15	23	28	32
279-Yogi Bear (TV)	6	12	18	31	38	45
280-The Three Stooges; photo-c	9	18	27	47	61	75
281-Tom and Jerry	4	7	9	14	16	18
282-Mister Ed (TV)	6	12	18	31	38	45
283-Santa's Visit	4	7	9	14	16	18
284-Christmas Parade (1965)	4	7	9	14	16	18
285-Astro Boy (TV); 2nd app. Astro Boy	32	64	96	192	314	435
286-Tarzan	7	14	21	37	46	55
287-Bugs Bunny	4	8	11	16	19	22
288-Daffy Duck	4	7	10	14	17	20
289-The Flintstones (TV)	8	16	24	44	57	70
290-Mister Ed (TV); photo-c	5	10	15	24	30	35
291-Yogi Bear (TV)	6	12	18	27	33	38
292-The Three Stooges; photo-c	9	18	27	47	61	75
293-Little Lulu; Irving Tripp-a	8	16	24	42	54	65
294-Popeye	5	10	15	24	30	35
295-Tom and Jerry	4	7	9	14	16	18
296-Lassie (TV); photo-c	5	10	15	22	26	30
297-Christmas Bells	3	6	8	12	14	16
298-Santa's Sleigh (1966)	3	6	8	12	14	16
299-The Flintstones (TV)(1967)	8	16	24	44	57	70
300-Tarzan	7	14	21	37	46	55
301-Bugs Bunny	4	7	10	14	17	20
302-Laurel and Hardy (TV); photo-c	6	12	18	28	34	40
303-Daffy Duck	3	6	8	12	14	16
304-The Three Stooges; photo-c	7	14	21	35	43	50
305-Tom and Jerry	3	6	8	12	14	16

March of Comics #337 © H-B

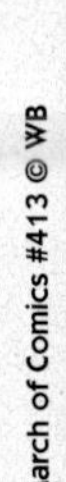
March of Comics #413 © WB

March of Comics #441 © Pink Panther Inc.

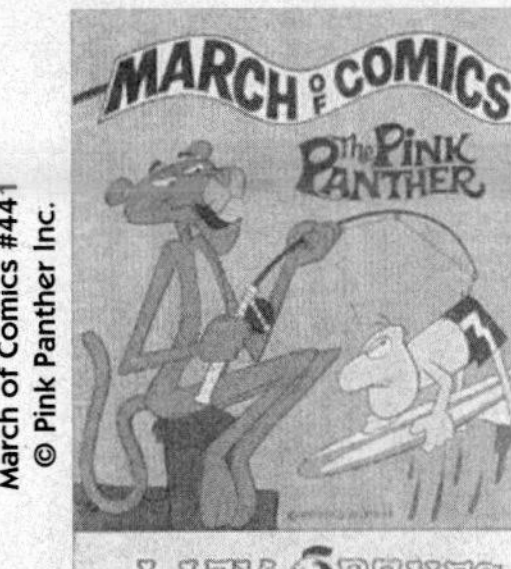

	GD 2.0	VG 4.0	FN 6.0	VF 8.0	VF/NM 9.0	NM- 9.2
306-Daniel Boone (TV); Fess Parker photo-c	7	14	21	35	43	50
307-Little Lulu; Irving Tripp-a	7	14	21	37	46	55
308-Lassie (TV); photo-c	5	10	15	22	26	30
309-Yogi Bear (TV)	5	10	15	24	30	35
310-The Lone Ranger; Clayton Moore photo-c	10	20	30	54	72	90
311-Santa's Show	4	7	9	14	16	18
312-Christmas Album (1967)	4	7	9	14	16	18
313-Daffy Duck (1968)	3	6	8	12	14	16
314-Laurel and Hardy (TV)	6	12	18	27	33	38
315-Bugs Bunny	4	7	10	14	17	20
316-The Three Stooges	8	16	24	40	50	60
317-The Flintstones (TV)	8	16	24	42	54	65
318-Tarzan	7	14	21	35	43	50
319-Yogi Bear (TV)	5	10	15	24	30	35
320-Space Family Robinson (TV); Spiegle-a	11	22	33	62	86	110
321-Tom and Jerry	3	6	8	12	14	16
322-The Lone Ranger	7	14	21	37	46	55
323-Little Lulu; not by Stanley	5	10	15	24	30	35
324-Lassie (TV); photo-c	5	10	15	22	26	30
325-Fun with Santa	4	7	9	14	16	18
326-Christmas Story (1968)	4	7	9	14	16	18
327-The Flintstones (TV)(1969)	8	16	24	42	54	65
328-Space Family Robinson (TV); Spiegle-a	11	22	33	62	86	110
329-Bugs Bunny	4	7	10	14	17	20
330-The Jetsons (TV)	10	20	30	56	76	95
331-Daffy Duck	3	6	8	12	14	16
332-Tarzan	6	12	18	28	34	40
333-Tom and Jerry	3	6	8	12	14	16
334-Lassie (TV)	4	9	13	18	22	26
335-Little Lulu	5	10	15	24	30	35
336-The Three Stooges	8	16	24	40	50	60
337-Yogi Bear (TV)	5	10	15	24	30	35
338-The Lone Ranger	7	14	21	37	46	55
339-(Was not published)						
340-Here Comes Santa (1969)	3	6	8	12	14	16
341-The Flintstones (TV)	8	16	24	42	54	65
342-Tarzan	3	6	9	19	30	40
343-Bugs Bunny	2	4	6	10	14	18
344-Yogi Bear (TV)	3	6	9	16	23	30
345-Tom and Jerry	2	4	6	9	13	16
346-Lassie (TV)	3	6	9	15	21	26
347-Daffy Duck	2	4	6	9	13	16
348-The Jetsons (TV)	5	10	15	34	60	85
349-Little Lulu; not by Stanley	3	6	9	16	23	30
350-The Lone Ranger	3	6	9	17	26	35
351-Beep-Beep, the Road Runner (TV)	2	4	6	11	16	20
352-Space Family Robinson (TV); Spiegle-a	6	12	18	41	76	110
353-Beep-Beep, the Road Runner (1971) (TV)	2	4	6	11	16	20
354-Tarzan (1971)	3	6	9	17	26	35
355-Little Lulu; not by Stanley	3	6	9	16	23	30
356-Scooby Doo, Where Are You? (TV)	6	12	18	40	73	105
357-Daffy Duck & Porky Pig	2	4	6	8	11	14
358-Lassie (TV)	3	6	9	14	19	24
359-Baby Snoots	2	4	6	10	14	18
360-H. R. Pufnstuf (TV); photo-c	6	12	18	37	66	95
361-Tom and Jerry	2	4	6	8	11	14
362-Smokey Bear (TV)	2	4	6	8	11	14
363-Bugs Bunny & Yosemite Sam	2	4	6	9	13	16
364-The Banana Splits (TV); photo-c	5	10	15	33	57	80
365-Tom and Jerry (1972)	2	4	6	8	11	14
366-Tarzan	3	6	9	17	26	35
367-Bugs Bunny & Porky Pig	2	4	6	9	13	16
368-Scooby Doo (TV)(4/72)	5	10	15	34	60	85
369-Little Lulu; not by Stanley	3	6	9	14	19	24
370-Lassie (TV); photo-c	3	6	9	14	19	24
371-Baby Snoots	2	4	6	9	13	16
372-Smokey the Bear (TV)	2	4	6	8	11	14
373-The Three Stooges	4	8	12	23	37	50
374-Wacky Witch	2	4	6	8	11	14
375-Beep-Beep & Daffy Duck (TV)	2	4	6	8	11	14
376-The Pink Panther (1972) (TV)	2	4	6	10	14	18
377-Baby Snoots (1973)	2	4	6	9	13	16
378-Turok, Son of Stone; new-a	6	12	18	42	79	115
379-Heckle & Jeckle New Terrytoons (TV)	2	4	6	8	11	14
380-Bugs Bunny & Yosemite Sam	2	4	6	8	11	14
381-Lassie (TV)	2	4	6	11	16	20

	GD 2.0	VG 4.0	FN 6.0	VF 8.0	VF/NM 9.0	NM- 9.2
382-Scooby Doo, Where Are You? (TV)	5	10	15	31	53	75
383-Smokey the Bear (TV)	2	4	6	8	11	14
384-Pink Panther (TV)	2	4	6	8	11	14
385-Little Lulu	2	4	6	13	18	22
386-Wacky Witch	2	4	6	8	11	14
387-Beep-Beep & Daffy Duck (TV)	2	4	6	8	11	14
388-Tom and Jerry (1973)	2	4	6	8	11	14
389-Little Lulu; not by Stanley	2	4	6	13	18	22
390-Pink Panther (TV)	2	4	6	8	11	14
391-Scooby Doo (TV)	4	8	12	27	44	60
392-Bugs Bunny & Yosemite Sam	2	4	6	8	10	12
393-New Terrytoons (Heckle & Jeckle) (TV)	2	4	6	8	10	12
394-Lassie (TV)	2	4	6	9	13	16
395-Woodsy Owl	2	4	6	8	10	12
396-Baby Snoots	2	4	6	8	11	14
397-Beep-Beep & Daffy Duck (TV)	2	4	6	8	10	12
398-Wacky Witch	2	4	6	8	10	12
399-Turok, Son of Stone; new-a	6	12	18	40	73	105
400-Tom and Jerry	2	4	6	8	10	12
401-Baby Snoots (1975) (r/#371)	2	4	6	8	11	14
402-Daffy Duck (r/#313)	1	3	4	6	8	10
403-Bugs Bunny (r/#343)	2	4	6	8	10	12
404-Space Family Robinson (TV)(r/#328)	5	10	15	35	63	90
405-Cracky	1	3	4	6	8	10
406-Little Lulu (r/#355)	2	4	6	10	14	18
407-Smokey the Bear (TV)(r/#362)	2	4	6	8	10	12
408-Turok, Son of Stone; c-r/Turok #20 w/changes; new-a	5	10	15	35	63	90
409-Pink Panther (TV)	1	3	4	6	8	10
410-Wacky Witch	1	2	3	5	6	8
411-Lassie (TV)(r/#324)	2	4	6	9	13	16
412-New Terrytoons (1975) (TV)	1	2	3	5	6	8
413-Daffy Duck (1976)(r/#331)	1	2	3	5	6	8
414-Space Family Robinson (r/#328)	5	10	15	34	60	85
415-Bugs Bunny (r/#329)	1	2	3	5	6	8
416-Beep-Beep, the Road Runner (r/#353)(TV)	1	2	3	5	6	8
417-Little Lulu (r/#323)	2	4	6	10	14	18
418-Pink Panther (r/#384) (TV)	1	2	3	5	6	8
419-Baby Snoots (r/#377)	1	3	4	6	8	10
420-Woody Woodpecker	1	2	3	5	6	8
421-Tweety & Sylvester	1	2	3	5	6	8
422-Wacky Witch (r/#386)	1	2	3	5	6	8
423-Little Monsters	1	3	4	6	8	10
424-Cracky (12/76)	1	2	3	5	6	8
425-Daffy Duck	1	2	3	5	6	8
426-Underdog (TV)	3	6	9	21	33	45
427-Little Lulu (r/#335)	2	4	6	8	11	14
428-Bugs Bunny	1	2	3	4	5	7
429-The Pink Panther (TV)	1	2	3	4	5	7
430-Beep-Beep, the Road Runner (TV)	1	2	3	4	5	7
431-Baby Snoots	1	2	3	5	6	8
432-Lassie (TV)	2	4	6	8	10	12
433-437: 433-Tweety & Sylvester. 434-Wacky Witch. 435-New Terrytoons (TV). 436-Wacky Advs. of Cracky. 437-Daffy Duck	1	2	3	4	5	7
438-Underdog (TV)	3	6	9	19	30	40
439-Little Lulu (r/#349)	2	4	6	8	11	14
440-442,444-446: 440-Bugs Bunny. 441-The Pink Panther (TV). 442-Beep-Beep, the Road Runner (TV). 444-Tom and Jerry. 445-Tweety and Sylvester. 446-Wacky Witch	1	2	3	5	6	8
443-Baby Snoots	1	2	3	5	6	8
447-Mighty Mouse	2	4	6	8	10	12
448-455,457,458: 448-Cracky. 449-Pink Panther (TV). 450-Baby Snoots. 451-Tom and Jerry. 452-Bugs Bunny. 453-Popeye. 454-Woody Woodpecker. 455-Beep-Beep, the Road Runner (TV). 457-Tweety & Sylvester. 458-Wacky Witch	1	2	3	5	6	8
456-Little Lulu (r/#369)	2	4	6	8	10	12
459-Mighty Mouse	2	4	6	8	10	12
460-466: 460-Daffy Duck. 461-The Pink Panther (TV). 462-Baby Snoots. 463-Tom and Jerry. 464-Bugs Bunny. 465-Popeye. 466-Woody Woodpecker	1	2	3	5	6	8
467-Underdog (TV)	3	6	9	17	26	35
468-Little Lulu (r/#385)	1	2	3	5	6	8
469-Tweety & Sylvester	1	2	3	5	6	8
470-Wacky Witch	1	2	3	5	6	8
471-Mighty Mouse	1	3	4	6	8	10
472-474,476-478: 472-Heckle & Jeckle(12/80). 473-Pink Panther(1/81)(TV). 474-Baby Snoots. 476-Bugs Bunny. 477-Popeye. 478-Woody Woodpecker						

Martin Luther King and The Montgomery Story
© Fellowship Reconciliation

Marvel Comics Presents Care Bears
© MAR

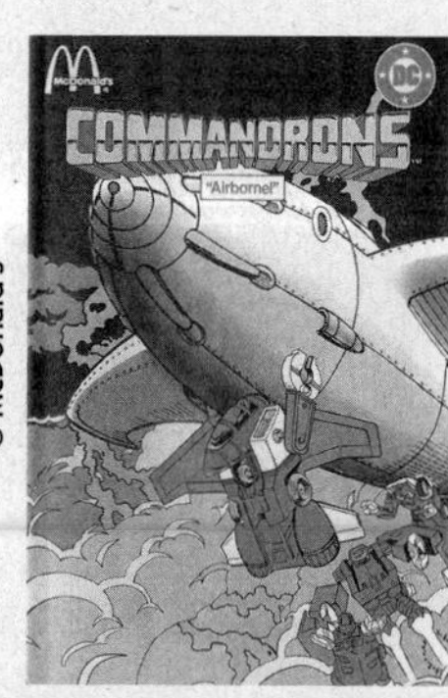

McDonald's Commandrons nn
© McDonald's

	GD	VG	FN	VF	VF/NM	NM-
	2.0	4.0	6.0	8.0	9.0	9.2
	1	2	3	5	6	8
475-Little Lulu (r/#323)	1	3	4	6	8	10
479-Underdog (TV)	3	6	9	16	23	30
480-482: 480-Tom and Jerry. 481-Tweety and Sylvester. 482-Wacky Witch	1	2	3	4	5	8
483-Mighty Mouse	1	3	4	6	8	10
484-487: 484-Heckle & Jeckle. 485-Baby Snoots. 486-The Pink Panther (TV). 487-Bugs Bunny	1	2	3	4	5	8
488-Little Lulu (4/82) (r/#335) (Last issue)	2	4	6	10	14	18

MARCH TO MARKET, THE
Pictorial Media/Swift & Co.: 1948, 1950 (Giveaway)
nn-The story of meat 4 7 10 14 17 20

MARGARET O'BRIEN (See The Adventures of...)

MARK STEEL
American Iron & Steel Institute: 1967, 1968, 1972 (Giveaway) (24 pgs.)
1967,1968- "Journey of Discovery with..."; Neal Adams art
4 8 12 23 37 50
1972- "...Fights Pollution"; N. Adams-a 2 4 6 9 13 15

MARTIN LUTHER KING AND THE MONTGOMERY STORY
Fellowship Reconciliation: 1957 (Giveaway, 16 pgs.) (A Spanish edition also exists)
nn-In color with paper-c (a VF copy sold for $261 in 2013, a FN/VF copy sold for $76 in 2015, a CGC 8.0 copy sold for $185 in 2017, and a VF+ copy sold for $675 in 2019)

MARTIN LUTHER KING AND THE MONTGOMERY STORY
Top Shelf/Fellowship Reconciliation: 2011, 2013 ($5.00, newsprint-c, 16 pgs.)
nn-(2011) Reprint of the 1957 giveaway published by Fellowship Reconciliation; stapled 10.00
nn-(2013) Reprint has glued binding unlike the stapled 2011 version 10.00

MARVEL COLLECTOR'S EDITION: X-MEN
Marvel Comics: 1993 (3-3/4x6-1/2")
1-4-Pizza Hut giveaways 6.00

MARVEL COMICS PRESENTS
Marvel Comics: 1987, 1988 (4 1/4 x 6 1/4, 20 pgs.)
...Mini Comic Giveaway
nn-(1988) Alf 1 3 4 6 8 10
nn-(1987) Captain America r/ #250 1 3 4 6 8 10
nn-(1987) Care Bears (Star Comics...) 1 3 4 6 8 10
nn-(1988) Flintstone Kids 1 3 4 6 8 10
nn-(1987) Heathcliffe (Star Comics...) 1 3 4 6 8 10
nn-(1987) Spider-Man-r/Spect. Spider-Man #21 1 3 4 6 8 10
nn-(1988) Spider-Man-r/Amazing Spider-Man #1 1 3 4 6 8 10
nn-(1988) X-Men-reprints X-Men #53; B. Smith-a 1 3 4 6 8 10

MARVEL GUIDE TO COLLECTING COMICS, THE
Marvel Comics: 1982 (16 pgs., newsprint pages and cover)
1-Simonson-c 1 3 4 6 8 10

MARVEL MINI-BOOKS
Marvel Comics Group: 1966 (50 pgs., B&W; 5/8x7/8") (6 different issues) (Smallest comics ever published) (Marvel Mania Giveaways)
Captain America, Millie the Model, Sgt. Fury, Hulk, Thor
each... 3 6 9 19 30 40
Spider-Man 3 6 9 19 30 40
NOTE: *Each came from gum machines in six different color covers, usually one color: Pink, yellow, green, etc.*

MARVEL SUPER-HERO ISLAND ADVENTURES
Marvel Comics: 1999 (Sold at the park polybagged with Captain America V3 #19, one other comic, 5 trading cards and a cloisonn´e pin)
1-Promotes Universal Studios Islands of Adventures theme park 5.00

MARY'S GREATEST APOSTLE (St. Louis Grignion de Montfort)
Catechetical Guild (Topix) (Giveaway): No date (16 pgs.; paper cover)
nn 5 10 15 23 28 32

MASK (Made for Kenner Toys)
DC Comics: 1985
1-3 1 2 3 5 6 8

MASKED PILOT, THE (See Popular Comics #43)
R.S. Callender: 1939 (7-1/2x5-1/4", 16 pgs., premium, non-slick-c)
nn-Bob Jenney-a 9 18 27 50 65 80

MASTERS OF THE UNIVERSE (He-Man)
DC Comics: 1982 (giveaways with action figures, at least 35 different issues, unnumbered)
nn 2 4 6 9 13 16

MATRIX, THE (1999 movie)
Warner Brothers: 1999 (Recalled by Warner Bros. over questionable content)
nn-Paul Chadwick-s/a (16 pgs.); Geof Darrow-c 4 8 12 23 37 50

McCRORY'S CHRISTMAS BOOK
Western Printing Co: 1955 (36 pgs., slick-c) (McCrory Stores Corp. giveaway)
nn-Painted-c 6 12 18 28 34 40

McCRORY'S TOYLAND BRINGS YOU SANTA'S PRIVATE EYES
Promotional Publ. Co.: 1956 (16 pgs.) (Giveaway)
nn-Has 9 pg. story plus 7 pgs. toy ads 4 8 12 18 22 25

McCRORY'S WONDERFUL CHRISTMAS
Promotional Publ. Co.: 1954 (20 pgs., slick-c) (Giveaway)
nn 6 12 18 28 34 40

McDONALDS COMMANDRONS
DC Comics: 1985
nn-Four editions 5.00

MEDAL FOR BOWZER, A (Giveaway)
American Visuals Corp.: 1966 (8 pgs.)
nn-Eisner-c/script; Bowzer (a dog) survives untried pneumonia cure and earns his medal; (medical experimentation on animals) 19 38 57 129 287 445

MEET HIYA A FRIEND OF SANTA CLAUS
Julian J. Proskauer/Sundial Shoe Stores, etc.: 1949 (18 pgs.?, paper-c)(Giveaway)
nn 7 14 21 37 46 55

MEET THE NEW POST-GAZETTE SUNDAY FUNNIES
Pittsburgh Post Gazette: 3/12/49 (7-1/4x10-1/4", 16 pgs., paper-c)
Commercial Comics (insert in newspaper) (Rare)
Dick Tracy by Gould, Gasoline Alley, Terry & the Pirates, Brenda Starr, Buck Rogers by Yager, The Gumps, Peter Rabbit by Fago, Superman, Funnyman by Siegel & Shuster, The Saint, Archie, & others done especially for this book. A fine copy sold at auction in 1985 for $276.00.
260 520 780 1700 - -

MEN OF COURAGE
Catechetical Guild: 1949
Bound Topix comics-V7#2,4,6,8,10,16,18,20 7 14 21 35 43 50

MEN WHO MOVE THE NATION
Publisher unknown: (Giveaway) (B&W)
nn-Neal Adams-a 7 14 21 35 43 50

MERRY CHRISTMAS, A
K. K. Publications (Child Life Shoes): 1948 (Giveaway)
nn-Santa cover 8 16 24 44 57 70

MERRY CHRISTMAS
K. K. Publications (Blue Bird Shoes Giveaway): 1956 (7-1/4x5-1/4")
nn-Santa cover 4 8 12 18 22 25

MERRY CHRISTMAS FROM MICKEY MOUSE
K. K. Publications: 1939 (16 pgs.) (Color & B&W) (Shoe store giveaway)
nn-Donald Duck & Pluto app.; text with art (Rare); c-reprint/Mickey Mouse Mag. V3#3 (12/37)(Rare) 252 504 756 1613 2757 3900

MERRY CHRISTMAS FROM SEARS TOYLAND (See Santa's Christmas Comic, Bob & Betty & Santa's Wishing Whistle, and A Christmas Carol)
Sears Roebuck Giveaway: 1939 (16 pgs.) (Color)(Die-cut)
nn-Dick Tracy, Little Orphan Annie, The Gumps, Terry & the Pirates
105 210 315 667 1146 1625

MICKEY MOUSE (Also see Frito-Lay Giveaway)
Dell Publ. Co
...& Goofy Explore Business(1978) 2 4 6 8 10 12
...& Goofy Explore Energy(1976-1978, 36 pgs.); Exxon giveaway in color; regular size 2 4 6 8 10 12
...& Goofy Explore Energy Conservation(1976-1978)-Exxon
2 4 6 8 10 12
...& Goofy Explore The Universe of Energy(1985, 20 pgs.); Exxon giveaway in color; regular size 1 2 3 5 7 9
The Perils of Mickey nn (1993, 5-1/4x7-1/4", 16 pgs.)-Nabisco giveaway w/ games, Nabisco coupons & 6 pgs. of stories; Phantom Blot app. 6.00

MICKEY MOUSE MAGAZINE
Walt Disney Productions: V1#1, Jan, 1933 - V1#9, Sept, 1933 (5-1/4x7-1/4")
No. 1-3 published by Kamen-Blair (Kay Kamen, Inc.)
(Scarce)-Distributed by dairies and leading stores through their local theatres. First few issues had 5¢ listed on cover, later ones had no price.
V1#1 425 850 1700 5100 - -

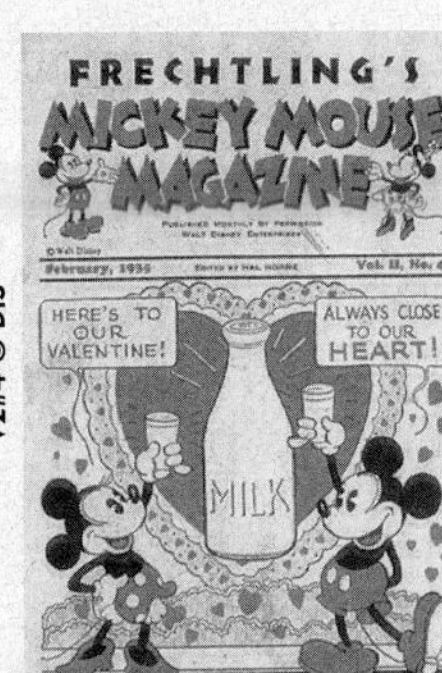
Mickey Mouse Magazine V2#4 © DIS

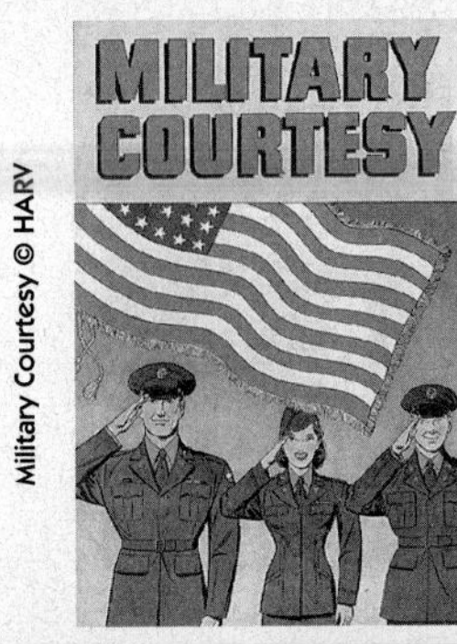

Military Courtesy © HARV

Nolan Ryan in The Winning Pitch © DC

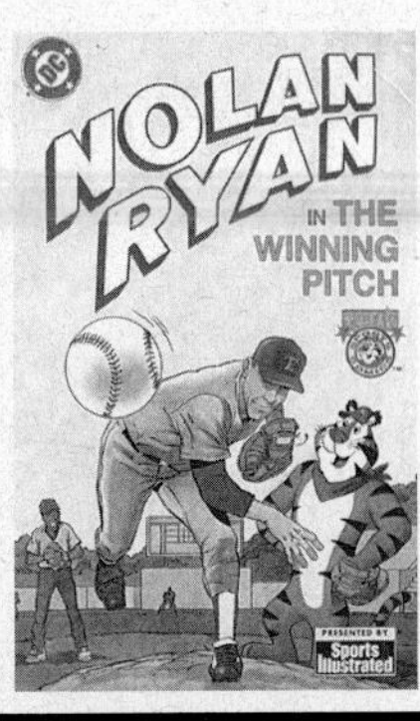

GD 2.0 VG 4.0 FN 6.0 VF 8.0 VF/NM 9.0 NM- 9.2

2 200 400 800 1600 - -
3,4 155 310 620 1250 - -
5-9 100 200 400 825 - -

NOTE: *A rare V1#1 Hardbound copy with a glassine dust jacket sold in July 2017 for $13,145.*

MICKEY MOUSE MAGAZINE (Digest size)
Walt Disney Productions: V1#1, 11/33 - V2#12, 10/35 (Mills giveaways issued by different dairies)

V1#1 160 320 480 1040 1750 -
2-12: 2-X-Mas issue 54 108 162 343 574 825
V2#1 (11/34) Donald Duck in sailor suit pg. 6 (cameo) 41 82 123 256 428 600
V2#2-4,6-12: 2-X-Mas issue. 4-St. Valentine-c 39 78 117 240 395 550
V2#5 (3/35) 1st app. Donald Duck in sailor outfit on-c 106 212 318 673 1162 1650

MICKEY MOUSE MAGAZINE
K.K. Publications: V4#1, Oct, 1938 (Giveaway)

V4#1 42 84 126 265 445 625

MIGHTY ATOM, THE
Whitman

Giveaway (1959, '63, Whitman)-Evans-a 3 6 9 16 23 30
Giveaway ('64r, '65r, '66r, '67r, '68r)-Evans-r? 2 4 6 10 14 18
Giveaway ('73r, '76r) 2 4 6 8 11 14

MILES THE MONSTER (Initially sold only at the Dover Speedway track)
Dover International Speedway, Inc.: 2006 ($3.00)

1,2-Allan Gross & Mark Wheatley-s/Wheatley-a 3.00

MILITARY COURTESY
Harvey Publications: (16 pgs.)

nn-Regulations and saluting instructions 5 10 14 20 24 28

MINUTE MAN
Sovereign Service Station giveaway: No date (16 pgs., B&W, paper-c blue & red)

nn-American history 4 7 10 14 17 20

MINUTE MAN ANSWERS THE CALL, THE
By M. C. Gaines: 1942,1943,1944,1945 (4 pgs.) (Giveaway inserted in Jr. JSA Membership Kit)

nn-Sheldon Moldoff-a 22 44 66 132 216 300

MIRACLE ON BROADWAY
Broadway Comics: Dec, 1995 (Giveaway)

1-Ernie Colon-c/a; Jim Shooter & Co. story; 1st known digitally printed comic book; 1st app. Spire & Knights on Broadway (1150 print run) 20.00

NOTE: *Miracle on Broadway was a limited edition comic given to 1100 VIPs in the entertainment industry for the 1995 Holiday Season.*

MISS SUNBEAM (See Little Miss Sunbeam Comics)

MR. BUG GOES TO TOWN (See Cinema Comics Herald)
K.K. Publications: 1941 (Giveaway, 52 pgs.)

nn-Cartoon movie (scarce) 69 138 207 442 759 1075

MR. PEANUT, THE PERSONAL STORY OF
Planters Nut & Chocolate Co.: 1956

nn 4 8 12 23 37 50

MOTHER OF US ALL
Catechetical Guild Giveaway: 1950? (32 pgs.)

nn 5 10 15 23 28 32

MOTION PICTURE FUNNIES WEEKLY (Amazing Man #5 on?)
First Funnies, Inc.: 1939 (Giveaway)(B&W, 36 pgs.) No month given; last panel in Sub-Mariner story dated 4/39 (Also see Colossus, Green Giant & Invaders No. 20)

1-Origin & 1st printed app. Sub-Mariner by Bill Everett (8 pgs.); Fred Schwab-c; reprinted in Marvel Mystery #1 with color added over the craft tint which was used to shade the black & white version; Spy Ring, American Ace (reprinted in Marvel Mystery #3) app. (Rare)-only eight known copies, one near mint with white pages, the rest with brown pages. 8700 17,400 26,100 43,500 61,000 -
Covers only to #2-4 (set) 900

NOTE: Eight copies (plus one coverless) were discovered in 1974 in the estate of the deceased publisher. Covers only to issues No. 2-4 were also found which evidently were printed in advance along with #1. #1 was to be distributed only through motion picture movie houses. However, it is believed that only advanced copies were sent out and the motion picture houses not going for the idea. Possible distribution at local theaters in Boston suspected. The "pay" copy (graded at 9.0) was discovered after 1974, bringing the total known to nine. The last panel of Sub-Mariner contains a rectangular box with "Continued Next Week" printed in it. When reprinted in Marvel Mystery, the box was left in with lettering omitted.

MY DOG TIGE (Buster Brown's Dog)
Buster Brown Shoes: 1957 (Giveaway)

nn 5 10 15 24 30 35

MY GREATEST THRILLS IN BASEBALL
Mission of California: 1957 (16 pg. Giveaway)

nn-By Mickey Mantle 53 106 159 334 567 800

MYSTERIOUS ADVENTURES WITH SANTA CLAUS
Lansburgh's: 1948 (paper cover)

nn 14 28 42 80 115 150

NAKED FORCE!
Commercial Comics: 1958 (Small size)

nn 3 6 8 11 13 15

NATURAL DISASTERS!
Graphic Information Service/ Civil Defense: 1956 (16 pgs., soft-c)

nn-Al Capp Li'l Abner-c; Li'l Abner cameo (1 panel); narrated by Mr. Civil Defense 10 20 30 56 76 95

NAVY: HISTORY & TRADITION
Stokes Walesby Co./Dept. of Navy: 1958 - 1961 (nn) (Giveaway)

1772-1778, 1778-1782, 1782-1817, 1817-1865, 1865-1936, 1940-1945:
1772-1778-16 pg. in color 5 10 15 22 26 30
1861: Naval Actions of the Civil War: 1865-36 pg. in color; flag-c 5 10 15 22 26 30

NEW ADVENTURE OF WALT DISNEY'S SNOW WHITE AND THE SEVEN DWARFS, A
(See Snow White Bendix Giveaway)

NEW ADVENTURES OF PETER PAN (Disney)
Western Publishing Co.: 1953 (5x7-1/4", 36 pgs.) (Admiral giveaway)

nn 13 26 39 72 101 130

NEW AVENGERS... (Giveaway for U.S Military personnel)
Marvel Comics: 2005 - Present (Distributed by Army & Air Force Exchange Service)

... Guest Starring the Fantastic Four (4/05) Bendis-s/Jurgens-a/c 5.00
...: Pot of Gold (AAFES 110th Anniversary Issue) (10/05) Jenkins-s/Nolan-a/c 5.00
(#3) ...: Avengers & X-Men Time Trouble (4/06) Kirkman-s 5.00
(#4) ...: Letters Home (12/06) Capt. America, Punisher, Silver Surfer, Ghost Rider on-c 5.00
5-The Spirit of America (10/05) Captain America app. 5.00
6-Fireline (8/08) Spider-Man, Iron Man & Hulk app. Richards-a/Dave Ross-c 5.00
7-An Army of One (2009) Frank Cho pin-up on back-c 5.00
8-The Promise (12/09) Captain America (Bucky) app. 5.00

NEW FRONTIERS
Harvey Information Press (United States Steel Corp.) : 1958 (16 pgs., paper-c)

nn-History of barbed wire 4 8 12 18 22 25

NEW TEEN TITANS, THE
DC Comics: Nov. 1983

nn(11/83-Keebler Co. Giveaway)-In cooperation with "The President's Drug Awareness Campaign"; came in Presidential envelope w/letter from White House (Nancy Reagan) 1 2 3 5 6 8
nn-(re-issue of above on Mando paper for direct sales market); American Soft Drink Industry version; I.B.M. Corp. version 5.00

NEW USES FOR GOOD EARTH
Mined Land Conservation: 1960 (paper-c)

nn 3 6 9 19 30 40

NOLAN RYAN IN THE WINNING PITCH (Kellogg's Tony's Sports Comics)
DC Comics: 1992 (Sports Illustrated)

nn 5.00

OLD GLORY COMICS
Chesapeake & Ohio Railway: 1944 (Giveaway)

nn-Capt. Fearless reprint 8 16 24 42 54 65

ON THE AIR
NBC Network Comic: 1947 (Giveaway, paper-c, regular size)

nn-(Rare) 20 40 60 114 182 250

OPERATION SURVIVAL!
Graphic Information Service/ Civil Defense: 1957 (16 pgs., soft-c)

nn-Al Capp Li'l Abner-c; Li'l Abner cameo (1 panel); narrated by Mr. Civil Defense 10 20 30 56 76 95

OUT OF THE PAST A CLUE TO THE FUTURE
E. C. Comics (Public Affairs Comm.): 1946? (16 pgs.) (paper cover)

nn-Based on public affairs pamphlet "What Foreign Trade Means to You" 21 42 63 124 202 280

OUTSTANDING AMERICAN WAR HEROES
The Parents' Institute: 1944 (16 pgs., paper-c)

Overseas Comics

The Plot to Steal the World © Work & Unity Group

Poll Parrot #2 © K.K. Pub

	GD 2.0	VG 4.0	FN 6.0	VF 8.0	VF/NM 9.0	NM- 9.2
nn-Reprints from True Comics	5	10	15	24	30	35

OVERSEAS COMICS (Also see G.I. Comics & Jeep Comics)
Giveaway (Distributed to U.S. Armed Forces): 1944 - No. 105?, 1946 (7-1/4x10-1/4"; 16 pgs. in color)

	GD	VG	FN	VF	VF/NM	NM-
23-105-Bringing Up Father (by McManus), Popeye, Joe Palooka, Dick Tracy, Superman, Gasoline Alley, Buz Sawyer, Li'l Abner, Blondie, Terry & the Pirates, Out Our Way	7	14	21	37	46	55

OWL, THE (See Crackajack Funnies #25 & Popular Comics #72)(Also see The Hurricane Kids & Magic Morro
Western Pub. Co./R.S. Callender: 1940 (Giveaway)(7-1/2x5-1/4")(Soft-c, color)

	GD	VG	FN	VF	VF/NM	NM-
nn-Frank Thomas-a	15	30	45	90	140	190

OXYDOL-DREFT
Toby Press:1950 (Set of 6 pocket-size giveaways; distributed through the mail as a set) (Scarce)

	GD	VG	FN	VF	VF/NM	NM-
1-3: 1-Li'l Abner. 2-Daisy Mae. 3-Shmoo	9	18	27	50	65	80
4-John Wayne; Williamson/Frazetta-c from John Wayne #3	13	26	39	72	101	130
5-Archie	12	24	36	67	94	120
6-Terrytoons Mighty Mouse	9	18	27	52	69	85
Mailing Envelope (has All Capp's Shmoo on front)	9	18	27	52	69	85

OZZIE SMITH IN THE KID WHO COULD (Kellogg's Tony's Sports Comics)
DC Comics: 1992 (Sports Illustrated)

nn-Ozzie Smith app. 5.00

PADRE OF THE POOR
Catechetical Guild: nd (Giveaway) (16 pgs., paper-c)

	GD	VG	FN	VF	VF/NM	NM-
nn	6	12	18	27	33	38

PAUL TERRY'S HOW TO DRAW FUNNY CARTOONS
Terrytoons, Inc. (Giveaway): 1940's (14 pgs.) (Black & White)

	GD	VG	FN	VF	VF/NM	NM-
nn-Heckle & Jeckle, Mighty Mouse, etc.	13	26	39	72	101	130

PERKY AND PAM
Kay Kamen: Late 1940's (soft-c)

nn-Christmas themes (a VF copy sold for $320 in 2019)

PETER PAN (See New Adventures of Peter Pan)

PETER PENNY AND HIS MAGIC DOLLAR
American Bankers Association, N. Y. (Giveaway): 1947 (16 pgs.; paper-c; regular size)

	GD	VG	FN	VF	VF/NM	NM-
nn-(Scarce)-Used in **SOTI**, pg. 310, 311	21	42	63	124	202	280
Diff. version (7-1/4x11")-redrawn, 16 pgs., paper-c	10	20	30	58	79	100

PETER WHEAT (The Adventures of...)
Bakers Associates Giveaway: 1948 - 1957? (16 pgs. in color) (paper covers)

	GD	VG	FN	VF	VF/NM	NM-
nn(No.1)-States on last page, end of 1st Adventure of...; Kelly-a	27	54	81	158	259	360
nn(4 issues)-Kelly-a	15	30	45	84	127	170
6-10-All Kelly-a	10	20	30	54	72	90
11-20-All Kelly-a	9	18	27	50	65	80
21-35-All Kelly-a	8	16	24	40	50	60
36-66	6	12	18	28	34	40
...Artist's Workbook ('54, digest size)	6	12	18	28	34	40
...Four-In-One Fun Pack (Vol. 2, '54), oblong, comics w/puzzles	7	14	21	35	43	50
...Fun Book ('52, 32 pgs., paper-c, B&W & color, 8-1/2x10-3/4")-Contains cut-outs, puzzles, games, magic & pages to color	8	16	24	44	57	70

NOTE: *Al Hubbard art #36 on; written by Del Connell.*

PETER WHEAT NEWS
Bakers Associates: 1948 - No. 63, 1953 (4 pgs. in color)

	GD	VG	FN	VF	VF/NM	NM-
Vol. 1-All have 2 pgs. Peter Wheat by Kelly	22	44	66	130	213	295
2-10	13	26	39	72	101	130
11-20	8	16	24	40	50	60
21-30	6	12	18	28	34	40
31-63	4	7	10	14	17	20

NOTE: *Early issues have no date & **Kelly** art.*

PINOCCHIO
Cocomalt/Montgomery Ward Co.: 1940 (10 pgs.; giveaway, linen-like paper)

	GD	VG	FN	VF	VF/NM	NM-
nn-Cocomalt edition	43	86	129	271	461	650
nn-store edition	37	74	111	222	361	500

PIUS XII MAN OF PEACE
Catechetical Guild: No date (12 pgs.; 5-1/2x8-1/2") (B&W)

	GD	VG	FN	VF	VF/NM	NM-
nn-Catechetical Guild Giveaway	6	12	18	33	41	48

PLOT TO STEAL THE WORLD, THE
Work & Unity Group: 1948, 16pgs., paper-c

	GD	VG	FN	VF	VF/NM	NM-
nn-Anti commumism	19	38	57	112	179	245

POCAHONTAS
Pocahontas Fuel Company (Coal): 1941 - No. 2, 1942

	GD	VG	FN	VF	VF/NM	NM-
nn(#1), 2-Feat. life story of Indian princess Pocahontas & facts about Pocahontas coal, Pocahontas, VA.	18	36	54	103	162	220

POLL PARROT
Poll Parrot Shoe Store/International Shoe
K. K. Publications (Giveaway): 1950 - No. 4, 1951; No. 2, 1959 - No. 16, 1962

	GD	VG	FN	VF	VF/NM	NM-
1 ('50)-Howdy Doody; small size	18	36	54	107	169	230
2-4('51)-Howdy Doody	15	30	45	88	137	185
2('59)-16('62): 2-The Secret of Crumbley Castle. 5-Bandit Busters. 6-Fortune Finders. 7-The Make-Believe Mummy. 8-Mixed Up Mission('60). 10-The Frightful Flight. 11-Showdown at Sunup. 12-Maniac at Mubu Island. 13-...and the Runaway Genie. 14-Bully for You. 15-Trapped In Tall Timber. 16-...& the Rajah's Ruby('62)	2	4	6	11	16	20

POPEYE
Whitman

	GD	VG	FN	VF	VF/NM	NM-
Bold Detergent giveaway (Same as regular issue #94)	2	4	6	9	13	16
Quaker Cereal premium (1989, 16pp, small size,4 diff.)(Popeye & the Time Machine, --On Safari, --& Big Foot, --vs. Bluto)	2	4	6	8	10	12

POPEYE
Charlton (King Features) (Giveaway): 1972 - 1974 (36 pgs. in color)

	GD	VG	FN	VF	VF/NM	NM-
E-1 to E-15 (Educational comics)	2	4	6	9	13	16
nn-Popeye Gettin' Better Grades-4 pgs. used as intro. to above giveaways (in color)	2	4	6	9	13	16

POPSICLE PETE FUN BOOK (See All-American Comics #6)
Joe Lowe Corp.: 1947, 1948

	GD	VG	FN	VF	VF/NM	NM-
nn-36 pgs. in color; Sammy 'n' Claras, The King Who Couldn't Sleep & Popsicle Pete stories, games, cut-outs	11	22	33	62	86	110
Adventure Book ('48)-Has Classics ad with checklist to HRN #343 (Great Expectations #43)	10	20	30	54	72	90

PORKY'S BOOK OF TRICKS
K. K. Publications (Giveaway): 1942 (8-1/2x5-1/2", 48 pgs.)

	GD	VG	FN	VF	VF/NM	NM-
nn-7 pg. comic story, text stories, plus games & puzzles	55	110	165	352	601	850

POST GAZETTE (See Meet the New...)

PUNISHER: COUNTDOWN (Movie)
Marvel Comics: 2004 (7 1/4" X 4 3/4" mini-comic packaged with Punisher DVD)

nn-Prequel to 2004 movie; Ennis-s/Dillon-a/Bradstreet-c 3.00

PURE OIL COMICS (Also see Salerno Carnival of Comics, 24 Pages of Comics, & Vicks Comics)
Pure Oil Giveaway: Late 1930's (24 pgs., regular size, paper-c)

	GD	VG	FN	VF	VF/NM	NM-
nn-Contains 1-2 pg. strips; i.e., Hairbreadth Harry, Skyroads, Buck Rogers by Calkins & Yager, Olly of the Movies, Napoleon, S'Matter Pop, etc. Also a 16 pg. 1938 giveaway with Buck Rogers	36	72	108	214	347	480

QUAKER OATS (Also see Cap'n Crunch)
Quaker Oats Co.: 1965 (Giveaway) (2-1/2x5-1/2") (16 pgs.)

	GD	VG	FN	VF	VF/NM	NM-
"Plenty of Glutton", starring Quake & Quisp;	3	6	9	14	19	24
"Lava Come-Back", "Kite Tale"	1	3	4	6	8	10

RAILROADS DELIVER THE GOODS!
Assoc. of American Railroads: Dec, 1954; Sept, 1957 (16 pgs., paper-c)

	GD	VG	FN	VF	VF/NM	NM-
nn-The story of railway freight	6	12	18	28	34	40

RAILS ACROSS AMERICA!
Assoc. of American Railroads: nd (16 pgs.)

	GD	VG	FN	VF	VF/NM	NM-
nn	6	12	18	28	34	40

READY THEN, READY NOW
Western Publications: 1966 (National Guard military giveaway, regular size)

	GD	VG	FN	VF	VF/NM	NM-
nn	5	10	15	33	57	80

REAL FUN OF DRIVING!!, THE
Chrysler Corp.: 1965, 1966, 1967 (Regular size, 16 pgs.)

	GD	VG	FN	VF	VF/NM	NM-
nn-Schaffenberger-a (12 pgs.)	1	2	3	5	6	8

REAL HIT
Fox Feature Publications: 1944 (Savings Bond premium)

	GD	VG	FN	VF	VF/NM	NM-
1-Blue Beetle-r; Blue Beetle on-c	18	36	54	107	169	230

NOTE: *Two versions exist, with and without covers. The coverless version has the title, No. 1 and price printed at top of splash page.*

RED BALL COMIC BOOK

Reddy Goose #3 © WEST

Richie Rich, Casper and Wendy National League © HARV

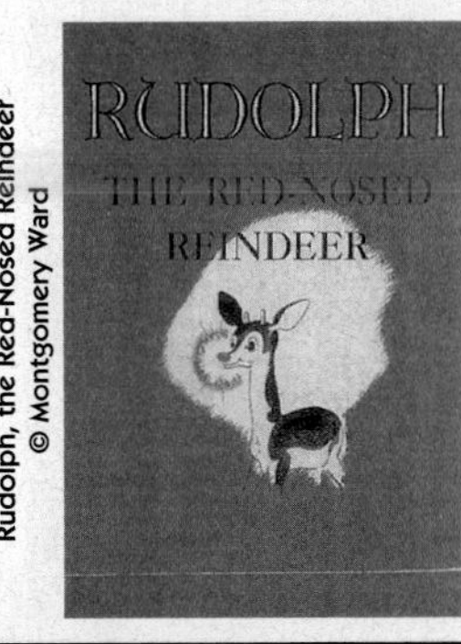

Rudolph, the Red-Nosed Reindeer © Montgomery Ward

	GD 2.0	VG 4.0	FN 6.0	VF 8.0	VF/NM 9.0	NM- 9.2

Parents' Magazine Institute: 1947 (Red Ball Shoes giveaway)
nn-Reprints from True Comics 4 8 12 17 21 24

REDDY GOOSE
International Shoe Co. (Western Printing): No number, 1958?; No. 2, Jan, 1959 - No. 16, July, 1962 (Giveaway)
nn (#1) 4 8 12 23 37 50
2-16 3 6 9 14 20 25

REDDY KILOWATT (5¢) (Also see Story of Edison)
Educational Comics (E. C.): 1946 - No. 2, 1947; 1956 - 1965 (no month) (16 pgs., paper-c)
nn-A Visit With Reddy (1948-1954?) 9 18 27 52 69 85
nn-Reddy Made Magic (1946, 5¢) 13 26 39 74 105 135
nn-Reddy Made Magic (1958) 9 18 27 52 69 85
2-Edison, the Man Who Changed the World (3/4" smaller than #1) (1947, 5¢) 13 26 39 74 105 135
...Comic Book 2 (1954)- "Light's Diamond Jubilee" 10 20 30 56 76 95
...Comic Book 2 (1956, 16 pgs.)- "Wizard of Light" 9 18 27 52 69 85
...Comic Book 2 (1958, 16 pgs.)- "Wizard of Light" 9 18 27 50 65 78
...Comic Book 2 (1965, 16 pgs.)- "Wizard of Light" 4 8 12 28 44 60
...Comic Book 3 (1956, 8 pgs.)- "The Space Kite"; Orlando story; regular size 9 18 27 52 69 85
...Comic Book 3 (1960, 8 pgs.)- "The Space Kite"; Orlando story; regular size 5 10 15 30 50 70

NOTE: *Several copies surfaced in 1979.*

REDDY MADE MAGIC
Educational Comics (E. C.): 1956, 1958 (16 pgs., paper-c)
1-Reddy Kilowatt-r (splash panel changed) 11 22 33 60 83 105
1 (1958 edition) 6 12 18 31 38 45

RED ICEBERG, THE
Impact Publ. (Catechetical Guild): 1960 (10¢, 16 pgs., Communist propaganda)
nn-(Rare)- "We The People" back-c 35 70 105 252 564 875
2nd version- "Impact Press" back-c 27 54 81 194 435 675
3rd version- "Explains comic" back-c 27 54 81 194 435 675
4th version- "Impact Press w/World Wide Secret Heart Program ad" 27 54 81 194 435 675
5th version- "Chicago Inter-Student Catholic Action" back-c 27 54 81 194 435 675

NOTE: *This book was the Guild's last anti-communist propaganda book and had very limited circulation. 3 - 4 copies surfaced in 1979 from the defunct publisher's files. Other copies do turn up.*

RED RYDER COMICS
Dell Publ. Co.
Buster Brown Shoes Giveaway (1941, color, soft-c, 32 pgs.) 20 40 60 117 189 260
Red Ryder Super Book of Comics (1944, paper-c, 32 pgs.; blank back-c) Magic Morro app. 20 40 60 117 189 260
Red Ryder Victory Patrol-nn(1942, 32 pgs.)(Langendorf bread; includes cut-out membership card and certificate, order blank and "Slide-Up" decoder, and a Super Book of Comics in color (same content as Super Book #4 w/diff. cover (Pan-Am)) (Rare) 87 174 261 553 952 1350
Red Ryder Victory Patrol-nn(1943, 32 pgs.)(Langendorf bread; includes cut-out "Rodeomatic" radio decoder, order coupon for "Magic V-Badge", cut-out membership card and certificate and a full color Super Book of comics comic book) (Rare) 61 122 183 390 670 950
Red Ryder Victory Patrol-nn(1944, 32 pgs.)-r-/#43,44; comic has a paper-c & is stapled inside a triple cardboard fold-out-c; contains membership card, decoder, map of R.R. home range, etc. Herky app. (Langendorf Bread giveaway; sub-titled 'Super Book of Comics') (Rare) 61 122 183 390 670 950
Wells Lamont Corp. giveaway (1950)-16 pgs. in color; regular size; paper-c; 1941-r 14 28 42 76 108 140

RETURN OF JOE THE GENIE OF STEEL (Also see Joe The Genie of Steel)
U. S. Steel Corp., Pittsburgh, PA/Commercial Comics: 1951 (U. S. Steel Corp. giveaway)
nn-Joe Magarac, the Paul Bunyan of steel 5 10 15 31 53 75

REX MORGAN M.D. TALKS ABOUT YOUR UNBORN CHILD
(No publisher) Fetal Alcohol, Tobacco & Firearms giveaway, 1980 (Reg. size, paper-c)
nn 3 6 9 19 30 40

RICHIE RICH, CASPER & WENDY NATIONAL LEAGUE
Harvey Publications: June, 1976 (52 pgs.) (newsstand edition also exists)
1 (Released-3/76 with 6/76 date) 3 6 9 16 23 30
1 (6/76)-2nd version w/San Francisco Giants & KTVU 2 logos; has "Compliments of Giants and Straw Hat Pizza" on-c 3 6 9 16 23 30
1-Variants for other 11 NL teams, similar to Giants version but with different ad on inside front-c 3 6 9 16 23 30

RIDE THE HIGH IRON!
Assoc. of American Railroads: Jan, 1957 (16 pgs.)
nn-The Story of modern passenger trains 5 10 15 24 30 35

RIPLEY'S BELIEVE IT OR NOT!
Harvey Publications
J. C. Penney giveaway (1948) 10 20 30 54 72 90

ROBIN HOOD (New Adventures of...)
Walt Disney Productions: 1952 (Flour giveaways, 5x7-1/4", 36 pgs.)
"New Adventures of Robin Hood", "Ghosts of Waylea Castle", & "The Miller's Ransom" each.... 4 7 10 14 17 20

ROBIN HOOD'S FRONTIER DAYS (...Western Tales, Adventures of... #1)
Shoe Store Giveaway (Robin Hood Stores): 1956 (20 pgs., slick-c)(7 issues?)
nn 6 12 18 31 38 45
nn-Issues with Crandall-a 8 16 24 42 54 65

ROCKETS AND RANGE RIDERS
Richfield Oil Corp.: May, 1957 (Giveaway, 16 pgs., soft-c)
nn-Toth-a 20 40 60 117 189 260

ROMANCE OF MONEY, THE
Natamsa Publishing Co.: 1937,1947 (4-7/8" x 6-1/4")
1937 ed. -(Scarce) 24 pgs with blue logo and artwork; distributed by the National Savings Bank, Albany, NY. Art by H.T. Elmo, a pseudonym for Jacob Kurtzberg (Jack Kirby). Believed to be Kirby's first published comic book work 250 375 800 - - -
1947 ed. -(Scarce) 16 pgs with red logo and artwork 125 250 425 - - -

ROUND THE WORLD GIFT
National War Fund (Giveaway): No date (mid 1940's) (4 pgs.)
nn 13 26 39 72 101 130

ROY ROGERS COMICS
Dell Publishing Co.
...& the Man From Dodge City (Dodge giveaway, 16 pgs., 1954)-Frontier, Inc. (5x7-1/4") 12 24 36 69 97 125
Official Roy Rogers Riders Club Comics (1952; 16 pgs., reg. size, paper-c) 15 30 45 86 133 180

RUDOLPH, THE RED-NOSED REINDEER
Montgomery Ward: 1939 (2,400,000 copies printed); Dec, 1951 (Giveaway)
Paper cover-1st app. in print; written by Robert May; ill. by Denver Gillen 19 38 57 112 179 245
Hardcover version 20 40 60 120 195 270
1951 Edition (Has 1939 date)-36 pgs., slick-c printed in red & brown; pulp interior printed in four mixed-ink colors: red, green, blue & brown 12 24 36 67 94 120
1951 Edition with red-spiral promotional booklet printed on high quality stock, 8-1/2"x11", in red & brown, 25 pages composed of 4 fold outs, single sheets and the Rudolph comic book inserted (rare) 48 96 144 302 514 725

SABRINA THE TEENAGE WITCH AND HER BOOK OF MAGIC
Archie Comic Publications: 1970 (small size giveaway)
2 (A graded 9.4 copy sold for $121 in 2014 and a graded 7.5 copy sold for $31 in 2018)

SAD CASE OF WAITING ROOM WILLIE, THE
American Visuals Corp. (For Baltimore Medical Society): (nd, 1950?) (14 pgs. in color; paper covers; regular size)
nn-By Will Eisner (Rare) 50 100 150 315 533 750

SAD SACK COMICS
Harvey Publications: 1957-1962
Armed Forces Complimentary copies, HD #1 (1957) 5 10 15 33 57 80
2-40 (1957-1962) 3 6 9 16 23 30

SALERNO CARNIVAL OF COMICS (Also see Pure Oil Comics, 24 Pages of Comics, & Vicks Comics)
Salerno Cookie Co.: Late 1930s (Giveaway, 16 pgs, paper-c)
nn-Color reprints of Calkins' Buck Rogers & Skyroads, plus other strips from Famous Funnies 45 90 135 284 480 675

SALUTE TO THE BOY SCOUTS
Association of American Railroads: 1960 (16 pgs., paper-c, regular size)
nn-History of scouting and the railroad 3 6 9 16 23 30

SANTA AND POLLYANNA PLAY THE GLAD GAME
Western Publ.: Aug, 1960 (16 pgs.) (Disney giveaway)
nn 3 6 9 14 20 25

SANTA & THE BUCCANEERS
Promotional Publ. Co.: 1959 (Giveaway, paper-c)

Santa's Fun Book © Promo. Pub. Co.

Sidewalk Romance © Health Publ.

Skippy's Own Book of Comics © Percy Crosby

	GD 2.0	VG 4.0	FN 6.0	VF 8.0	VF/NM 9.0	NM- 9.2
nn-Reprints 1952 Santa & the Pirates	2	4	6	13	18	22
SANTA & THE CHRISTMAS CHICKADEE						
Murphy's: 1974 (Giveaway, 20 pgs.)						
nn	2	4	6	8	10	12
SANTA & THE PIRATES						
Promotional Publ. Co.: 1952 (Giveaway)						
nn-Marv Levy-c/a	5	10	14	20	24	28
SANTA CLAUS FUNNIES (Also see The Little Fir Tree)						
W. T. Grant Co./Whitman Publishing: nd; 1940 (Giveaway, 8x10"; 12 pgs., color & B&W, heavy paper)						
nn-(2 versions- no date and 1940)	43	86	129	271	461	650
SANTA IS HERE!						
Western Publ. (Giveaway): 1949 (oblong, slick-c)						
nn	6	12	18	33	41	48
SANTA ON THE JOLLY ROGER						
Promotional Publ. Co. (Giveaway): 1965						
nn-Marv Levy-c/a	2	4	6	8	10	12
SANTA! SANTA!						
R. Jackson: 1974 (20 pgs.) (Montgomery Ward giveaway)						
nn	1	3	4	6	8	10
SANTA'S BUNDLE OF FUN						
Gimbels: 1969 (Giveaway, B&W, 20 pgs.)						
nn-Coloring book & games	2	4	6	8	10	12
SANTA'S CHRISTMAS COMIC VARIETY SHOW (See Merry Christmas From Sears Toyland, Bob & Betty & Santa's Wishing Whistle, and A Christmas Carol)						
Sears Roebuck & Co.: 1943 (24 pgs.)						
Contains puzzles & new comics of Dick Tracy, Little Orphan Annie, Moon Mullins, Terry & the Pirates, etc.	54	108	162	343	574	825
SANTA'S CHRISTMAS TIME STORIES						
Premium Sales, Inc.: nd (Late 1940s) (16 pgs., paper-c) (Giveaway)						
nn	7	14	21	35	43	50
SANTA'S CIRCUS						
Promotional Publ. Co.: 1964 (Giveaway, half-size)						
nn-Marv Levy-c/a	2	4	6	9	12	15
SANTA'S FUN BOOK						
Promotional Publ. Co.: 1951, 1952 (Regular size, 16 pgs., paper-c) (Murphy's giveaway)						
nn	6	12	18	28	34	40
SANTA'S GIFT BOOK						
No Publisher: No date (16 pgs.)						
nn-Puzzles, games only	4	9	13	18	22	26
SANTA'S NEW STORY BOOK						
Wallace Hamilton Campbell: 1949 (16 pgs., paper-c) (Giveaway)						
nn	7	14	21	35	43	50
SANTA'S REAL STORY BOOK						
Wallace Hamilton Campbell/W. W. Orris: 1948, 1952 (Giveaway, 16 pgs.)						
nn	7	14	21	35	43	50
SANTA'S RIDE						
W. T. Grant Co.: 1959 (Giveaway)						
nn	4	9	13	18	22	26
SANTA'S RODEO						
Promotional Publ. Co.: 1964 (Giveaway, half-size)						
nn-Marv Levy-a	2	4	6	9	12	15
SANTA'S SECRET CAVE						
W.T. Grant Co.: 1960 (Giveaway, half-size)						
nn	2	4	6	11	16	20
SANTA'S SECRETS						
Sam B. Anson Christmas giveaway: 1951, 1952? (16 pgs., paper-c)						
nn-Has games, stories & pictures to color	5	10	14	20	24	28
SANTA'S STORIES						
K. K. Publications (Klines Dept. Store): 1953 (Regular size, paper-c)						
nn-Kelly-a	16	32	48	94	147	200
nn-Another version (1953, glossy-c, half-size, 7-1/4x5-1/4")-Kelly-a	15	30	45	88	137	185
SANTA'S SURPRISE						
K. K. Publications: 1947 (Giveaway, 36 pgs., slick-c)						
nn	8	16	24	44	57	70
SANTA'S TOYTOWN FUN BOOK						
Promotional Publ. Co.: 1953 (Giveaway)						
nn-Marv Levy-c	4	8	12	17	21	24
SANTA TAKES A TRIP TO MARS						
Bradshaw-Diehl Co., Huntington, W.VA.: 1950s (nd) (Giveaway, 16 pgs.)						
nn	4	8	12	23	37	50
SCHWINN BIKE THRILLS						
Schwinn Bicycle Co.: 1959 (Reg. size)						
nn	8	16	24	44	57	70
SCIENCE FAIR STORY OF ELECTRONICS						
Radio Shack/Tandy Corp.: 1975 - 1987 (Giveaway)						
11 different issues (approx. 1 per year) each....						4.00
SECRETS BEHIND THE COMICS						
Famous Enterprises, Inc.: 1947 (Small size; advertised in Timely comics)						
nn - By Stan Lee; profile of Syd Shores (w/4 pgs. of his Blonde Phantom), Mike Sekowsky, Basil Wolverton, Al Jaffee & Martin Goodman; description of Captain America's creation with images	145	290	435	921	1586	2250
SEEING WASHINGTON						
Commercial Comics: 1957 (also sold at 25¢)(Slick-c, reg. size)						
nn	6	12	18	28	34	40
SERGEANT PRESTON OF THE YUKON						
Quaker Cereals: 1956 (4 comic booklets) (Soft-c, 16 pgs., 7x2-1/2" & 5x2-1/2") Giveaways						
"How He Found Yukon King", "The Case That Made Him A Sergeant", "How Yukon King Saved Him From The Wolves", "How He Became A Mountie" each...	9	18	27	47	61	75
SHAZAM! (Visits Portland Oregon in 1943)						
DC Comics: 1989 (69¢ cover)						
nn-Promotes Super-Heroes exhibit at Oregon Museum of Science and Industry; reprints Golden Age Captain Marvel story	2	4	6	11	16	20
SHERIFF OF COCHISE, THE (TV)						
Mobil: 1957 (16 pgs.) Giveaway						
nn-Schaffenberger-a	4	9	13	18	22	26
SIDEWALK ROMANCE (Also see The K. O. Punch & Lucky Fights It Through)						
Health Publications: 1950						
nn-VD educational giveaway	48	96	144	302	514	725
SILLY PUTTY MAN						
DC Comics: 1978						
1	2	4	6	11	16	20
SKATING SKILLS						
Custom Comics, Inc./Chicago Roller Skates: 1957 (36 & 12 pgs.; 5x7", two versions) (10¢)						
nn-Resembles old ACG cover plus interior art	4	7	10	14	17	20
SKIPPY'S OWN BOOK OF COMICS (See Popular Comics)						
No publisher listed: 1934 (Giveaway, 52 pgs., strip reprints)						
nn-(Scarce)-By Percy Crosby	330	650	1000	2200	4100	5800
Published by Max C. Gaines for Phillip's Dental Magnesia to be advertised on the Skippy Radio Show and given away with the purchase of a tube of Phillip's Tooth Paste. This is the first four-color comic book of reprints about one character.						
SKY KING "RUNAWAY TRAIN" (TV)						
National Biscuit Co.: 1964 (Regular size, 16 pgs.)						
nn	5	10	15	35	63	90
SLAM BANG COMICS						
Post Cereal Giveaway: No. 9, No date						
9-Dynamic Man, Echo, Mr. E, Yankee Boy app.	10	20	30	54	72	90
SMILIN' JACK						
Dell Publishing Co.						
Popped Wheat Giveaway (1947)-1938 strip reprints; 16 pgs. in full color	2	4	6	9	13	16
Shoe Store Giveaway-1938 strip reprints; 16 pgs.	5	10	15	24	30	35
Sparked Wheat Giveaway (1942)-16 pgs. in full color	5	10	15	24	30	35
SMOKEY BEAR (See Forest Fire for 1st app.)						
Dell Publ. Co.: 1959,1960						

Sparky © NFPA

The Spirit 6/02/40 © Will Eisner

The Spirit 1/09/44 © Will Eisner

	GD 2.0	VG 4.0	FN 6.0	VF 8.0	VF/NM 9.0	NM- 9.2
True Story of..., The -U.S. Forest Service giveaway-Publ. by Western Printing Co.; reprints 1st 16 pgs. of Four Color #932. Inside front-c differs slightly in 1959 & 1960 editions	6	12	18	28	34	40
1964,1969 reprints	2	4	6	11	16	20

SMOKEY STOVER
Dell Publishing Co.

	GD 2.0	VG 4.0	FN 6.0	VF 8.0	VF/NM 9.0	NM- 9.2
General Motors giveaway (1953)	8	16	24	42	54	65
National Fire Protection giveaway(1953 & 1954)-16 pgs., paper-c	8	16	24	42	54	65

SNOW FOR CHRISTMAS
W. T. Grant Co.: 1957 (16 pgs.) (Giveaway)

	GD 2.0	VG 4.0	FN 6.0	VF 8.0	VF/NM 9.0	NM- 9.2
nn	4	8	12	18	22	25

SNOW WHITE AND THE SEVEN DWARFS
Bendix Washing Machines: 1952 (32 pgs., 5x7-1/4", soft-c) (Disney)

	GD 2.0	VG 4.0	FN 6.0	VF 8.0	VF/NM 9.0	NM- 9.2
nn	13	26	39	72	101	130

SNOW WHITE AND THE SEVEN DWARFS
Promotional Publ. Co.: 1957 (Small size)

	GD 2.0	VG 4.0	FN 6.0	VF 8.0	VF/NM 9.0	NM- 9.2
nn	7	14	21	35	43	50

SNOW WHITE AND THE SEVEN DWARFS
Western Printing Co.: 1958 (16 pgs, 5x7-1/4", soft-c) (Disney premium)

	GD 2.0	VG 4.0	FN 6.0	VF 8.0	VF/NM 9.0	NM- 9.2
nn- "Mystery of the Missing Magic"	6	12	18	31	38	45

SNOW WHITE AND THE 7 DWARFS IN "MILKY WAY"
American Dairy Assoc.: 1955 (16 pgs., soft-c, 5x7-1/4") (Disney premium)

	GD 2.0	VG 4.0	FN 6.0	VF 8.0	VF/NM 9.0	NM- 9.2
nn	7	14	21	37	46	55

SOLDIER OF GOD
Conventual Franciscans of Marytown: 1982 ($1.00)

	GD 2.0	VG 4.0	FN 6.0	VF 8.0	VF/NM 9.0	NM- 9.2
nn-Story of Father Maximilian Kobe, priest in WWII Poland; Ray Chatton-a						5.00

SPACE GHOST COAST TO COAST
Cartoon Network: Apr, 1994 (giveaway to Turner Broadcasting employees)

	GD 2.0	VG 4.0	FN 6.0	VF 8.0	VF/NM 9.0	NM- 9.2
1-(8 pgs.); origin of Space Ghost	1	2	3	5	6	8

SPACE PATROL (TV)
Ziff-Davis Publishing Co. (Approved Comics)

	GD 2.0	VG 4.0	FN 6.0	VF 8.0	VF/NM 9.0	NM- 9.2
...'s Special Mission (8 pgs., B&W, Giveaway)	47	94	141	296	498	700

SPARKY
Fire Protection Association: 1961 (Reg. size, paper-c)

	GD 2.0	VG 4.0	FN 6.0	VF 8.0	VF/NM 9.0	NM- 9.2
nn	3	6	9	16	24	32

SPECIAL AGENT
Assoc. of American Railroads: Oct, 1959 (16 pgs.)

	GD 2.0	VG 4.0	FN 6.0	VF 8.0	VF/NM 9.0	NM- 9.2
nn-The Story of the railroad police	6	12	18	29	36	42

SPECIAL DELIVERY
Post Hall Synd.: 1951 (32 pgs.; B&W) (Giveaway)

nn-Origin of Pogo, Swamp, etc.; 2 pg. biog. on Walt Kelly (One copy sold in 1980 for $150.00)

SPECIAL EDITION (U. S. Navy Giveaways)
National Periodical Publs.: 1944 - 1945 (Reg. comic format with wording simplified, 52 pgs.)

	GD 2.0	VG 4.0	FN 6.0	VF 8.0	VF/NM 9.0	NM- 9.2
1-Action (1944)-Reprints Action #80	84	168	252	538	919	1300
2-Action (1944)-Reprints Action #81	84	168	252	538	919	1300
3-Superman (1944)-Reprints Superman #33	84	168	252	538	919	1300
4-Detective (1944)-Reprints Detective #97	84	168	252	538	919	1300
5-Superman (1945)-Reprints Superman #34	84	168	252	538	919	1300
6-Action (1945)-Reprints Action #84	84	168	252	538	919	1300

NOTE: ***Wayne Boring** c-1, 2, 6. **Dick Sprang** c-4.*

SPIDER-MAN (See Amazing Spider-Man, The)

SPIRIT, THE (Weekly Comic Book)(Distributed through various newspapers & other sources)
Will Eisner: 6/2/40 - 10/5/52 (16 pgs.; 8 pgs.) (no cover) (in color)

NOTE: **Eisner** script, pencils/inks for the most part from 6/2/40-4/26/42; a few stories assisted by Jack Cole, Fine, Powell and Kotsky.

	GD 2.0	VG 4.0	FN 6.0	VF 8.0	VF/NM 9.0	NM- 9.2
6/2/40(#1)-Origin/1st app. The Spirit; reprinted in Police #11; Lady Luck (Brenda Banks) (1st app.) by Chuck Mazoujian & Mr. Mystic (1st. app.) by S. R. (Bob) Powell begin (rare)	486	972	1458	3550	6275	9000
6/9/40(#2)	94	188	282	597	1024	1450
6/16/40(#3)-Black Queen app. in Spirit	43	86	129	271	461	650
6/23/40(#4)-Mr. Mystic receives magical necklace	33	66	99	194	320	445
6/30/40(#5)	33	66	99	194	320	445
7/7/40(#6)-1st app. Spirit carplane; Black Queen app. in Spirit	35	70	105	208	339	470
7/14/40(#7)-8/4/40(#10): 7/21/40-Spirit becomes fugitive wanted for murder	29	58	87	172	281	390
8/11/40-9/22/40: 9/15/40-Racist-c	27	54	81	160	263	365
9/29/40-Ellen drops engagement with Homer Creep	23	46	69	134	220	305
10/6/40-11/3/40	23	46	69	134	220	305
11/10/40-The Black Queen app.	23	46	69	134	220	305
11/17/40, 11/24/40	23	46	69	134	220	305
12/1/40-Ellen spanking by Spirit on cover & inside; Eisner-1st 3 pgs., J. Cole rest	32	64	96	192	314	435
12/8/40-3/9/41	16	32	48	96	151	205
3/16/41-Intro. & 1st app. Silk Satin	22	44	66	128	209	290
3/23/41-6/1/41: 5/11/41-Last Lady Luck by Mazoujian. 5/18/41-Lady Luck by Nick Viscardi begins, ends 2/22/42	16	32	48	94	147	200
6/8/41-2nd app. Satin; Spirit learns Satin is also a British agent	18	36	54	107	169	230
6/15/41-1st app. Twilight	18	36	54	105	165	225
6/22/41-Hitler app. in Spirit	17	34	51	98	154	210
6/29/41-1/25/42,2/8/42	14	28	42	82	121	160
2/1/42-1st app. Duchess	16	32	48	96	151	205
2/15/42-4/26/42-Lady Luck by Klaus Nordling begins 3/1/42	15	30	45	90	140	190
5/3/42-8/16/42-Eisner/Fine/Quality staff assists on Spirit	12	24	36	69	97	125
8/23/42-Satin cover splash; Spirit by Eisner/Fine although signed by Fine	18	36	54	107	169	230
8/30/42,9/27/42-10/11/42,10/25/42-11/8/42-Eisner/Fine/Quality staff assists on Spirit	12	24	36	67	94	120
9/6/42-9/20/42,10/18/42-Fine/Belfi art on Spirit; scripts by Manly Wade Wellman	9	18	27	50	65	80
11/15/42-12/6/42,12/20/42,12/27/42,1/17/43-4/18/43,5/9/43-8/8/43-Wellman/ Woolfolk scripts, Fine pencils, Quality staff inks	9	18	27	50	65	80
12/13/42,1/3/43,1/10/43,4/25/43,5/2/43-Eisner scripts/layouts; Fine pencils, Quality staff inks	10	20	30	54	72	90
8/15/43-Eisner script/layout; pencils/inks by Quality staff; Jack Cole-a	8	16	24	44	57	70
8/22/43-12/12/43-Wellman/Woolfolk scripts, Fine pencils, Quality staff inks; Mr. Mystic by Guardineer-10/10/43-10/24/43	8	16	24	44	57	70
12/19/43-8/13/44-Wellman/Woolfolk/Jack Cole scripts; Cole, Fine & Robin King-a; Last Mr. Mystic-5/14/44	8	16	24	42	54	65
8/20/44-12/16/45-Wellman/Woolfolk scripts; Fine art with unknown staff assists	8	16	24	42	54	65

NOTE: *Scripts/layouts by Eisner, or Eisner/Nordling, Eisner/Mercer or Spranger/Eisner; inks by Eisner or Eisner/Spranger in issues 12/23/45-2/2/47.*

	GD 2.0	VG 4.0	FN 6.0	VF 8.0	VF/NM 9.0	NM- 9.2
12/23/45-1/6/46: 12/23/45-Christmas-c	9	18	27	52	69	85
1/13/46-Origin Spirit retold	13	26	39	72	101	130
1/20/46-1st postwar Satin app.	11	22	33	64	90	115
1/27/46-3/10/46: 3/3/46-Last Lady Luck by Nordling	10	20	30	54	72	90
3/17/46-Intro. & 1st app. Nylon	11	22	33	64	90	115
3/24/46,3/31/46,4/14/46	9	18	27	52	69	85
4/7/46-2nd app. Nylon	10	20	30	56	76	95
4/21/46-Intro. & 1st app. Mr. Carrion & His Pet Buzzard Julia	13	26	39	72	101	130
4/28/46-5/12/46,5/26/46-6/30/46: Lady Luck by Fred Schwab in issues 5/5/46-11/3/46	9	18	27	52	69	85
5/19/46-2nd app. Mr. Carrion	10	20	30	56	76	95
7/7/46-Intro. & 1st app. Dulcet Tone & Skinny	11	22	33	64	90	115
7/14/46-9/29/46	9	18	27	52	69	85
10/6/46-Intro. & 1st app. P'Gell	13	26	39	74	105	135
10/13/46-11/3/46,11/16/46-11/24/46	9	18	27	52	69	85
11/10/46-2nd app. P'Gell	11	22	33	62	86	110
12/1/46-3rd app. P'Gell	10	20	30	54	72	90
12/8/46-2/2/47	9	18	27	50	65	80

NOTE: *Scripts, pencils/inks by Eisner except where noted in issues 2/9/47-12/19/48.*

	GD 2.0	VG 4.0	FN 6.0	VF 8.0	VF/NM 9.0	NM- 9.2
2/9/47-7/6/47: 6/8/47-Eisner self satire	9	18	27	50	65	80
7/13/47- "Hansel & Gretel" fairy tales	11	22	33	64	90	115
7/20/47-Li'L Abner, Daddy Warbucks, Dick Tracy, Fearless Fosdick parody; A-Bomb blast-c	13	26	39	72	101	130
7/27/47-9/14/47	9	18	27	50	65	80
9/21/47-Pearl Harbor flashback	11	22	33	60	83	105
9/28/47-1st mention of Flying Saucers in comics - three months after 1st sighting in Idaho on 6/25/47	19	38	57	111	176	240
10/5/47- "Cinderella" fairy tales	11	22	33	64	90	115
10/12/47-11/30/47	9	18	27	50	65	80
12/7/47-Intro. & 1st app. Powder Pouf	13	26	39	72	101	130
12/14/47-12/28/47	9	18	27	50	65	80
1/4/48-2nd app. Powder Pouf	10	20	30	54	72	90
1/11/48-1st app. Sparrow Fallon; Powder Pouf app.	10	20	30	54	72	90

The Spirit 4/03/49 © Will Eisner

The Spirit 5/07/50 © Will Eisner

Standard Oil Comics #5B © Standard Oil

	GD 2.0	VG 4.0	FN 6.0	VF 8.0	VF/NM 9.0	NM- 9.2
1/18/48-He-Man ad cover; satire issue	10	20	30	54	72	90
1/25/48-Intro. & 1st app. Castanet	13	26	39	72	101	130
2/1/48-2nd app. Castanet	9	18	27	52	69	85
2/8/48-3/7/48	9	18	27	50	65	80
3/14/48-Only app. Kretchma	9	18	27	52	69	85
3/21/48,3/28/48,4/11/48-4/25/48	9	18	27	50	65	80
4/4/48-Only app. Wild Rice	9	18	27	52	69	85
5/2/48-2nd app. Sparrow	9	18	27	50	65	80
5/9/48-6/27/48,7/11/48,7/18/48: 6/13/48-TV issue	9	18	27	50	65	80
7/4/48-Spirit by Andre Le Blanc	8	16	24	42	54	65
7/25/48-Ambrose Bierce's "The Thing" adaptation classic by Eisner/Grandenetti	15	30	45	90	140	190
8/1/48-8/15/48,8/29/48-9/12/48	9	18	27	50	65	80
8/22/48-Poe's "Fall of the House of Usher" classic by Eisner/Grandenetti	16	32	48	94	147	200
9/19/48-Only app. Lorelei	10	20	30	54	72	90
9/26/48-10/31/48	9	18	27	50	65	80
11/7/48-Only app. Plaster of Paris	11	22	33	64	90	115
11/14/48-12/19/48	9	18	27	50	65	80

NOTE: *Scripts by Eisner or Feiffer or Eisner/Feiffer or Nordling. Art by Eisner with backgrounds by Eisner, Grandenetti, Le Blanc, Stallman, Nordling, Dixon and/or others in issues 12/26/48-4/1/51 except where noted.*

	GD 2.0	VG 4.0	FN 6.0	VF 8.0	VF/NM 9.0	NM- 9.2
12/26/48-Reprints some covers of 1948 with flashbacks	9	18	27	50	65	80
1/2/49-1/16/49	9	18	27	50	65	80
1/23/49,1/30/49-1st & 2nd app. Thorne	10	20	30	54	72	90
2/6/49-8/14/49	9	18	27	50	65	80
8/21/49,8/28/49-1st & 2nd app. Monica Veto	10	20	30	54	72	90
9/4/49,9/11/49	9	18	27	50	65	80
9/18/49-Love comic cover; has gag love comic ads on inside	10	20	30	54	72	90
9/25/49-Only app. Ice	9	18	27	52	69	85
10/2/49,10/9/49-Autumn News appears & dies in 10/9 issue	9	18	27	52	69	85
10/16/49-11/27/49,12/18/49,12/25/49	9	18	27	50	65	80
12/4/49,12/11/49-1st & 2nd app. Flaxen	9	18	27	52	69	85
1/1/50-Flashbacks to all of the Spirit girls-Thorne, Ellen, Satin, & Monica	14	28	42	78	112	145
1/8/50-Intro. & 1st app. Sand Saref	15	30	45	88	137	185
1/15/50-2nd app. Saref	13	26	39	72	101	130
1/22/50-2/5/50	9	18	27	50	65	80
2/12/50-Roller Derby issue	10	20	30	54	72	90
2/19/50-Half Dead Mr. Lox - Classic horror	12	24	36	67	94	120
2/26/50-4/23/50,5/14/50,5/28/50,7/23/50-9/3/50	9	18	27	50	65	80
4/30/50-Script/art by Le Blanc with Eisner framing	8	16	24	40	50	60
5/7/50,6/4/50-7/16/50-Abe Kanegson-a	8	16	24	40	50	60
5/21/50-Script by Feiffer/Eisner, art by Blaisdell, Eisner framing	8	16	24	40	50	60
9/10/50-P'Gell returns	10	20	30	54	72	90
9/17/50-1/7/51	9	18	27	50	65	80
1/14/51-Life Magazine cover; brief biography of Comm. Dolan, Sand Saref, Silk Satin, P'Gell, Sammy & Willum, Darling O'Shea, & Mr. Carrion & His Pet Buzzard Julia, with pin-ups by Eisner	11	22	33	64	90	115
1/21/51,2/4/51-4/1/51	9	18	27	50	65	80
1/28/51- "The Meanest Man in the World" by Eisner	11	22	33	64	90	115
4/8/51-7/29/51,8/12/51-Last Eisner issue	9	18	27	50	65	80
8/5/51,8/19/51-7/20/52-Not Eisner	8	16	24	40	50	60
7/27/52-(Rare)-Denny Colt in Outer Space by Wally Wood; 7 pg. S/F story of E.C. vintage	55	110	165	352	601	850
8/3/52-(Rare)- "Mission...The Moon" by Wood	55	110	165	352	601	850
8/10/52-(Rare)- "A DP On The Moon" by Wood	55	110	165	352	601	850
8/17/52-(Rare)- "Heart" by Wood/Eisner	55	110	165	352	601	850
8/24/52-(Rare)- "Rescue" by Wood	55	110	165	352	601	850
8/31/52-(Rare)- "The Last Man" by Wood	55	110	165	352	601	850
9/7/52-(Rare)- "The Man in The Moon" by Wood	55	110	165	352	601	850
9/14/52-(Rare)-Eisner/Wenzel-a	37	74	111	222	361	500
9/21/52-(Rare)- "Denny Colt, Alias The Spirit/Space Report" by Eisner/Wenzel	37	74	111	222	361	500
9/28/52-(Rare)- "Return From The Moon" by Wood	50	100	150	315	533	750
10/5/52-(Rare)- "The Last Story" by Eisner	34	68	102	199	325	450

Large Tabloid pages from 1946 on (Eisner) - Price 200 percent over listed prices.

NOTE: *Spirit sections came out in both large and small format. Some newspapers went to the 8-pg. format months before others. Some printed the pages so they cannot be folded into a small comic book section; these are worth less. (Also see Three Comics & Spiritman).*

SPY SMASHER
Fawcett Publications

	GD 2.0	VG 4.0	FN 6.0	VF 8.0	VF/NM 9.0	NM- 9.2
Well Known Comics (1944, 12 pgs., 8-1/2x10-1/2"), paper-c, glued binding, printed in green; Bestmaid/Samuel Lowe giveaway	15	30	45	88	137	185

STANDARD OIL COMICS (Also see Gulf Funny Weekly)
Standard Oil Co.: 1932-1934 (Giveaway, tabloid size, 4 pgs. in color)

	GD 2.0	VG 4.0	FN 6.0	VF 8.0	VF/NM 9.0	NM- 9.2
nn (Dec. 1932)	65	130	195	416	708	1000
1-Series has original art	53	106	159	334	567	800
2-5	22	44	66	132	216	300
6-14: 14-Fred Opper strip, 1 pg.	15	30	45	85	130	175
1A (Jan 1933)	53	106	159	334	567	800
2A-14A (1933)	37	74	111	222	361	500
1B (1934)	41	82	123	256	428	600
2B-7B (1934)	37	74	111	222	361	500

NOTE: *Series A contains Frederick Opper's Si & Mirandi; Series B contains Goofus: He's From The Big City; McVittie by Walter O'Ehrle; interior strips include Pesty And His Pop & Smiling Slim by Sid Hicks.*

STARS AND STRIPES
Centaur Publications: Oct. 1942 (regular size)

5 - World's Greatest Parade of Comics and Fun Promotional Cover Edition (Atlas Theater)
(A certified CGC 2.5 copy sold for $460 in 2019)

STAR TEAM
Marvel Comics Group: 1977 (6-1/2x5", 20 pgs.) (Ideal Toy Giveaway)

	GD 2.0	VG 4.0	FN 6.0	VF 8.0	VF/NM 9.0	NM- 9.2
nn	3	6	9	14	19	24

STEVE CANYON COMICS
Harvey Publications

	GD 2.0	VG 4.0	FN 6.0	VF 8.0	VF/NM 9.0	NM- 9.2
Dept. Store giveaway #3(6/48, 36pp)	10	20	30	54	72	90
...'s Secret Mission (1951, 16 pgs., Armed Forces giveaway); Caniff-a	9	18	27	47	61	75
Strictly for the Smart Birds (1951, 16 pgs.)-Information Comics Div. (Harvey) Premium	8	16	24	40	50	60

STORIES OF CHRISTMAS
K. K. Publications: 1942 (Giveaway, 32 pgs., paper cover)

	GD 2.0	VG 4.0	FN 6.0	VF 8.0	VF/NM 9.0	NM- 9.2
nn-Adaptation of "A Christmas Carol"; Kelly story "The Fir Tree"; Infinity-c	52	104	156	328	552	775

STORY HOUR SERIES (Disney)
Whitman Publ. Co.: 1948, 1949; 1951-1953 (36 pgs., paper-c) (4-3/4x6-1/2")
Given away with subscription to Walt Disney's Comics & Stories

	GD 2.0	VG 4.0	FN 6.0	VF 8.0	VF/NM 9.0	NM- 9.2
nn(1948)-Mickey Mouse and the Boy Thursday	12	24	36	67	94	120
nn(1948)-Mickey Mouse the Miracle Master	12	24	36	67	94	120
nn(1948)-Minnie Mouse and Antique Chair	12	24	36	67	94	120
nn(1949)-The Three Orphan Kittens(B&W & color)	9	18	27	47	61	75
nn(1949)-Danny-The Little Black Lamb	9	18	27	47	61	75
800(1948)-Donald Duck in "Bringing Up the Boys"	15	30	45	88	137	185
1953 edition	11	22	33	64	90	115
801(1948)-Mickey Mouse's Summer Vacation	10	20	30	56	76	95
1951, 1952 editions	7	14	21	35	43	50
802(1948)-Bugs Bunny's Adventures	9	18	27	50	65	80
803(1948)-Bongo	8	16	24	40	50	60
804(1948)-Mickey and the Beanstalk	9	18	27	47	61	75
805-15(1949)-Andy Panda and His Friends	8	16	24	40	50	60
806-15(1949)-Tom and Jerry	8	16	24	44	57	70
808-15(1949)-Johnny Appleseed	8	16	24	40	50	60

1948, 1949 Hard Cover Edition of each....30% - 40% more.

STOP AND GO, THE SAFETY TWINS
J.C. Penney: no date (giveaway)

	GD 2.0	VG 4.0	FN 6.0	VF 8.0	VF/NM 9.0	NM- 9.2
nn	5	10	15	24	30	35

STORY OF CHECKS THE
Federal Reserve Bank: 1979 (Reg. size)

	GD 2.0	VG 4.0	FN 6.0	VF 8.0	VF/NM 9.0	NM- 9.2
nn	1	3	4	6	8	10

STORY OF CHECKS AND ELECTRONIC PAYMENTS
Federal Reserve Bank: 1983 (Reg size)

	GD 2.0	VG 4.0	FN 6.0	VF 8.0	VF/NM 9.0	NM- 9.2
nn	1	2	3	5	6	8

STORY OF CONSUMER CREDIT
Federal Reserve Bank: 1980 (Reg. size)

	GD 2.0	VG 4.0	FN 6.0	VF 8.0	VF/NM 9.0	NM- 9.2
nn	1	2	3	5	6	8

STORY OF EDISON, THE
Educational Comics: 1956 (16 pgs.) (Reddy Killowatt)

	GD 2.0	VG 4.0	FN 6.0	VF 8.0	VF/NM 9.0	NM- 9.2
nn-Reprint of Reddy Kilowatt #2(1947)	7	14	21	37	46	55

STORY OF FOREIGN TRADE AND EXCHANGE
Federal Reserve Bank: 1985 (Reg. size)

	GD 2.0	VG 4.0	FN 6.0	VF 8.0	VF/NM 9.0	NM- 9.2
nn	1	2	3	5	6	8

The Story of Harry S. Truman © DNC

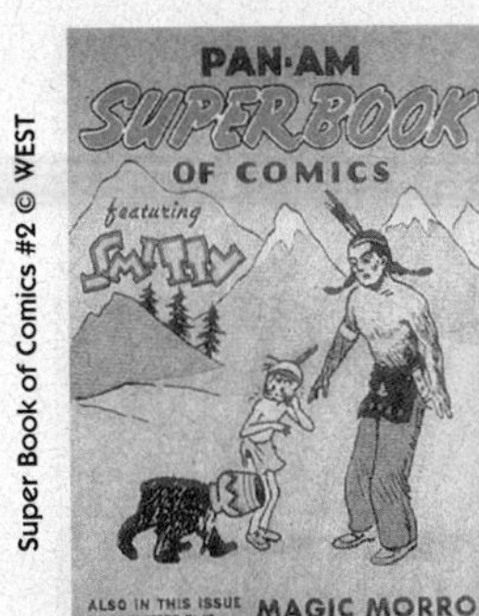

Super Book of Comics #2 © WEST

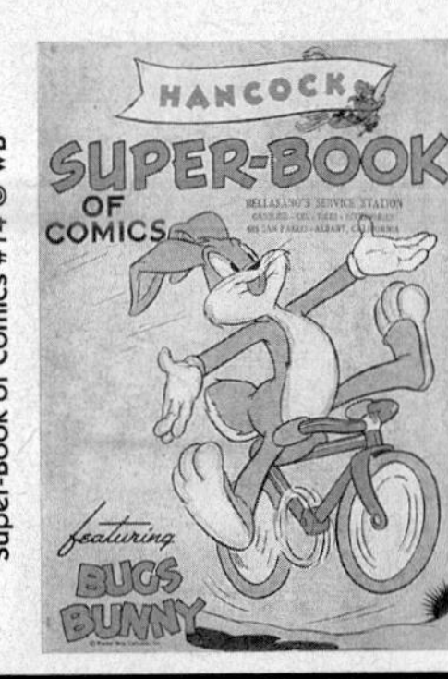

Super-Book of Comics #14 © WB

	GD 2.0	VG 4.0	FN 6.0	VF 8.0	VF/NM 9.0	NM- 9.2
STORY OF HARRY S. TRUMAN, THE						
Democratic National Committee: 1948 (Giveaway, regular size, soft-c, 16 pg.)						
nn-Gives biography on career of Truman; used in **SOTI**, pg. 311	14	28	42	80	115	150
STORY OF INFLATION, THE						
Federal Reserve Bank: 1980s (Reg size)						
nn	1	3	4	6	8	10
STORY OF MONEY						
William C. Popper: 1962, 1965						
nn-Soft-c	3	6	9	16	23	30
STORY OF MONEY						
Federal Reserve Bank: 1984 (Reg. size)						
nn	1	3	4	6	8	10
STORY OF THE BALLET, THE						
Selva and Sons, Inc.: 1954 (16 pgs., paper cover)						
nn	4	8	12	18	22	25
STRANGE AS IT SEEMS						
McNaught Syndicate: 1936 (B&W, 5" x 7", 24 pgs.)						
nn-Ex-Lax giveaway	9	18	27	52	69	85
STRIKES AND THE PUBLIC						
Socialist Labor Party: no date						
nn-Calling worker class to organize against capitalist class (a FN/VF copy sold for $216 in 2018)						
SUGAR BEAR						
Post Cereal Giveaway: No date, circa 1975? (2 1/2" x 4 1/2", 16 pgs.)						
"The Almost Take Over of the Post Office", "The Race Across the Atlantic", "The Zoo Goes Wild" each...	1	2	3	5	6	8
SUNDAY WORLD'S EASTER EGG FULL OF EASTER MEAT FOR LITTLE PEOPLE						
Supplement to the New York World: 3/27/1898 (soft-c, 16pg, 4"x8" approx., opens at top, color & B&W)(Giveaway)(shaped like an Easter egg)						
nn-By R.F. Outcault	20	40	60	114	182	250
SUPER BOOK OF COMICS						
Western Publ. Co.: nd (1942-1943?) (Soft-c, 32 pgs.) (Pan-Am/Gilmore Oil/Kelloggs premiums)						
nn-Dick Tracy (Gilmore)-Magic Morro app. (2 versions: Dick Tracy Jr. on cover and a filing cabinet cover)	39	78	117	240	395	550
1-Dick Tracy & The Smuggling Ring; Stratosphere Jim app. (Rare) (Pan-Am)	31	62	93	182	296	410
1-Smilin' Jack, Magic Morro (Pan-Am)	14	28	42	76	108	140
2-Smilin' Jack, Stratosphere Jim (Pan-Am)	14	28	42	76	108	140
2-Smitty, Magic Morro (Pan-Am)	14	28	42	76	108	140
3-Captain Midnight, Magic Morro (Pan-Am)	22	44	66	131	216	300
3-Moon Mullins?	13	26	39	74	105	135
4-Red Ryder, Magic Morro (Pan-Am). Same content as Red Ryder Victory Patrol comic w/diff. cover	15	30	45	85	130	175
4-Smitty, Stratosphere Jim (Pan-Am)	13	26	39	74	105	135
5-Don Winslow, Magic Morro (Gilmore)	15	30	45	85	130	175
5-Don Winslow, Stratosphere Jim (Pan-Am)	15	30	45	85	130	175
5-Terry & the Pirates	17	34	51	98	154	210
6-Don Winslow, Stratosphere Jim (Pan-Am)-McWilliams-a	15	30	45	85	130	175
6-King of the Royal Mounted, Magic Morro (Pan-Am)	15	30	45	85	130	175
7-Dick Tracy, Magic Morro (Pan-Am)	19	38	57	112	179	245
7-Little Orphan Annie	11	22	33	64	90	115
8-Dick Tracy, Stratosphere Jim (Pan-Am)	17	34	51	98	154	210
8-Dan Dunn, Magic Morro (Pan-Am)	11	22	33	64	90	115
9-Terry & the Pirates, Magic Morro (Pan-Am)	17	34	51	98	154	210
10-Red Ryder, Magic Morro (Pan-Am)	15	30	45	85	130	175
SUPER-BOOK OF COMICS						
Western Publishing Co.: (Omar Bread & Hancock Oil Co. giveaways) 1944 - No. 30, 1947 (Omar); 1947 - 1948 (Hancock) (16 pgs.)						
NOTE: The Hancock issues are all exact reprints of the earlier Omar issues. The issue numbers were removed in some of the reprints.						
1-Dick Tracy (Omar, 1944)	17	34	51	98	154	210
1-Dick Tracy (Hancock, 1947)	14	28	42	78	112	145
2-Bugs Bunny (Omar, 1944)	8	16	24	40	50	60
2-Bugs Bunny (Hancock, 1947)	6	12	18	32	39	46
3-Terry & the Pirates (Omar, 1944)	11	22	33	60	83	105
3-Terry & the Pirates (Hancock, 1947)	10	20	30	54	72	90
4-Andy Panda (Omar, 1944)	8	16	24	40	50	60
4-Andy Panda (Hancock, 1947)	6	12	18	32	39	46
5-Smokey Stover (Omar, 1945)	6	12	18	32	39	46
5-Smokey Stover (Hancock, 1947)	5	10	15	24	30	35
6-Porky Pig (Omar, 1945)	8	16	24	40	50	60
6-Porky Pig (Hancock, 1947)	6	12	18	32	39	46
7-Smilin' Jack (Omar, 1945)	8	16	24	40	50	60
7-Smilin' Jack (Hancock, 1947)	6	12	18	32	39	46
8-Oswald the Rabbit (Omar, 1945)	6	12	18	32	39	46
8-Oswald the Rabbit (Hancock, 1947)	5	10	15	24	30	35
9-Alley Oop (Omar, 1945)	11	22	33	64	90	115
9-Alley Oop (Hancock, 1947)	11	22	33	60	83	105
10-Elmer Fudd (Omar, 1945)	6	12	18	32	39	46
10-Elmer Fudd (Hancock, 1947)	5	10	15	24	30	35
11-Little Orphan Annie (Omar, 1945)	8	16	24	42	53	64
11-Little Orphan Annie (Hancock, 1947)	7	14	21	36	45	54
12-Woody Woodpecker (Omar, 1945)	6	12	18	32	39	46
12-Woody Woodpecker (Hancock, 1947)	5	10	15	24	30	35
13-Dick Tracy (Omar, 1945)	11	22	33	64	90	115
13-Dick Tracy (Hancock, 1947)	11	22	33	60	83	105
14-Bugs Bunny (Omar, 1945)	6	12	18	32	39	46
14-Bugs Bunny (Hancock, 1947)	5	10	15	24	30	35
15-Andy Panda (Omar, 1945)	6	12	18	28	34	40
15-Andy Panda (Hancock, 1947)	5	10	15	24	30	35
16-Terry & the Pirates (Omar, 1945)	11	22	33	60	83	105
16-Terry & the Pirates (Hancock, 1947)	9	18	27	47	61	75
17-Smokey Stover (Omar, 1946)	6	12	18	32	39	46
17-Smokey Stover (Hancock, 1948?)	5	10	15	24	30	35
18-Porky Pig (Omar, 1946)	6	12	18	28	34	40
18-Porky Pig (Hancock, 1948?)	5	10	15	24	30	35
19-Smilin' Jack (Omar, 1946)	6	12	18	32	39	46
nn-Smilin' Jack (Hancock, 1948)	5	10	15	24	30	35
20-Oswald the Rabbit (Omar, 1946)	6	12	18	28	34	40
nn-Oswald the Rabbit (Hancock, 1948)	5	10	15	24	30	35
21-Gasoline Alley (Omar, 1946)	8	16	24	42	53	64
nn-Gasoline Alley (Hancock, 1948)	7	14	21	36	45	54
22-Elmer Fudd (Omar, 1946)	6	12	18	28	34	40
nn-Elmer Fudd (Hancock, 1948)	5	10	15	24	30	35
23-Little Orphan Annie (Omar, 1946)	8	16	24	40	50	60
nn-Little Orphan Annie (Hancock, 1948)	6	12	18	32	39	46
24-Woody Woodpecker (Omar, 1946)	6	12	18	28	34	40
nn-Woody Woodpecker (Hancock, 1948)	5	10	15	24	30	35
25-Dick Tracy (Omar, 1946)	11	22	33	60	83	105
nn-Dick Tracy (Hancock, 1948)	9	18	27	50	65	80
26-Bugs Bunny (Omar, 1946))	6	12	18	28	34	40
nn-Bugs Bunny (Hancock, 1948)	5	10	15	24	30	35
27-Andy Panda (Omar, 1946)	6	12	18	28	34	40
27-Andy Panda (Hancock, 1948)	5	10	15	24	30	35
28-Terry & the Pirates (Omar, 1946)	11	22	33	60	83	105
28-Terry & the Pirates (Hancock, 1948)	9	18	27	47	61	75
29-Smokey Stover (Omar, 1947)	6	12	18	28	34	40
29-Smokey Stover (Hancock, 1948)	5	10	15	24	30	35
30-Porky Pig (Omar, 1947)	6	12	18	28	34	40
30-Porky Pig (Hancock, 1948)	5	10	15	24	30	35
nn-Bugs Bunny (Hancock, 1948)-Does not match any Omar book	6	12	18	28	34	40
SUPER CIRCUS (TV)						
Cross Publishing Co.						
1-(1951, Weather Bird Shoes giveaway)	8	16	24	44	57	70
SUPER FRIENDS						
DC Comics: 1981 (Giveaway, no ads, no code or price)						
...Special 1 -r/Super Friends #19 & 36	2	4	6	10	14	18
SUPERGEAR COMICS						
Jacobs Corp.: 1976 (Giveaway, 4 pgs. in color, slick paper)						
nn-(Rare)-Superman, Lois Lane; Steve Lombard app. (500 copies printed, over half destroyed?)	19	38	57	132	294	455
SUPERGIRL						
DC Comics: 1984, 1986 (Giveaway, Baxter paper)						
nn-(American Honda/U.S. Dept. Transportation) Torres-c/a	2	4	6	9	13	16
SUPER HEROES PUZZLES AND GAMES						
General Mills Giveaway (Marvel Comics Group): 1979 (32 pgs., regular size)						
nn-Four 2-pg. origin stories of Spider-Man, Captain America, The Hulk, & Spider-Woman	3	6	9	15	22	28

Superman Adventures #1 (WBSS) © DC

Superman-Tim 1/48 © DC

Tastee-Freez Comics nn © HARV

SUPERMAN
National Periodical Publ./DC Comics

	GD 2.0	VG 4.0	FN 6.0	VF 8.0	VF/NM 9.0	NM- 9.2
72-Giveaway(9-10/51)-(Rare)-Price blackened out; came with banner wrapped around book; without banner	77	154	231	493	847	1200
72-Giveaway with banner	124	248	372	787	1356	1925

Bradman birthday custom (1988)(extremely limited distribution) - a CGC 9.6 copy sold for $2600, a NM copy sold for $1125, and a FN/VF copy sold for $800 in 2011-2012, plus a CGC 9.0 sold for $421 in 12/12 and a CGC 9.6 copy sold for $1314 in 8/15

	GD 2.0	VG 4.0	FN 6.0	VF 8.0	VF/NM 9.0	NM- 9.2
... For the Animals (2000, Doris Day Animal Foundation, 30 pgs.) polybagged with Gotham Adventures #22, Hourman #12, Impulse #58, Looney Tunes #62, Stars and S.T.R.I.P.E. #8 and Superman Adventures #41						4.00
Kelloggs Giveaway-(2/3 normal size, 1954)-r-two stories/Superman #55	31	62	93	186	303	420
Kenner: Man of Steel (Doomsday is Coming) (1995, 16 pgs.) packaged with set of Superman and Doomsday action figures						5.00
...Meets the Quik Bunny (1987, Nestles Quik premium, 36 pgs.)	1	2	3	5	7	9
Pizza Hut Premiums (12/77)-Exact reprints of 1950s comics except for paid ads (set of 6 exist?); Vol. 1-r#97 (#113-r also known)	2	4	6	9	12	15
Radio Shack Giveaway-36 pgs. (7/80) "The Computers That Saved Metropolis", Starlin/ Giordano-a; advertising insert in Action #509, New Advs. of Superboy #7, Legion of Super-Heroes #265, & House of Mystery #282. (All comics were 68 pgs.) Cover of inserts printed on newsprint. Giveaway contains 4 extra pgs. of Radio Shack advertising that inserts do not have	1	2	3	5	7	9
Radio Shack Giveaway-(7/81) "Victory by Computer"	1	2	3	5	7	9
Radio Shack Giveaway-(7/82) "Computer Masters of Metropolis"	1	2	3	5	7	9

SUPERMAN ADVENTURES, THE (TV)
DC Comics: 1996 (Based on animated series)

	GD 2.0	VG 4.0	FN 6.0	VF 8.0	VF/NM 9.0	NM- 9.2
1-(1996) Preview issue distributed at Warner Bros. stores						5.00
Titus Game Edition (1998)						4.00

SUPERMAN AND THE GREAT CLEVELAND FIRE
National Periodical Publ.: 1948 (Giveaway, 4 pgs., no cover) (Hospital Fund)

	GD 2.0	VG 4.0	FN 6.0	VF 8.0	VF/NM 9.0	NM- 9.2
nn-In full color	81	162	243	518	884	1250

SUPERMAN AT THE GILBERT HALL OF SCIENCE
National Periodical Publ.: 1948 (Giveaway) (Gilbert Chemistry Sets / A.C. Gilbert Co.)

	GD 2.0	VG 4.0	FN 6.0	VF 8.0	VF/NM 9.0	NM- 9.2
nn-(8 1/2" x 5 1/2")	39	78	117	240	395	560

SUPERMAN (Miniature)
National Periodical Publ.: 1942; 1955 - 1956 (3 issues, no #'s, 32 pgs.)
The pages are numbered in the 1st issue: 1-32; 2nd: 1A-32A, and 3rd: 1B-32B

	GD 2.0	VG 4.0	FN 6.0	VF 8.0	VF/NM 9.0	NM- 9.2
No date-Py-Co-Pay Tooth Powder giveaway (8 pgs.; circa 1942)(The Adventures of...) Japanese air battle	39	78	117	240	395	560
1-The Superman Time Capsule (Kellogg's Sugar Smacks)(1955)	22	44	66	128	209	290
1A-Duel in Space (1955)	20	40	60	120	195	270
1B-The Super Show of Metropolis (also #1-32, no B)(1955)	20	40	60	120	195	270

NOTE: *Numbering variations exist. Each title could have any combination-#1, 1A, or 1B.*

SUPERMAN RECORD COMIC
National Periodical Publications: 1966 (Golden Records)

	GD 2.0	VG 4.0	FN 6.0	VF 8.0	VF/NM 9.0	NM- 9.2
(With record)-Record reads origin of Superman from comic; came with iron-on patch, decoder, membership card & button; comic-r/Superman #125,146	11	22	33	75	160	245
Comic only	6	12	18	37	66	95

SUPERMAN'S BUDDY (Costume Comic)
National Periodical Publs.: 1954 (4 pgs., slick paper-c; one-shot) (Came in box w/costume)

	GD 2.0	VG 4.0	FN 6.0	VF 8.0	VF/NM 9.0	NM- 9.2
1-With box & costume	132	264	396	838	1444	2050
Comic only	58	116	174	371	636	900
1-(1958 edition)-Printed in 2 colors	18	36	54	105	165	225

SUPERMAN'S CHRISTMAS ADVENTURE
National Periodical Publications: 1940, 1944 (Giveaway, 16 pgs.)
Distributed by Nehi drinks, Bailey Store, Ivey-Keith Co., Kennedy's Boys Shop, Macy's Store, Boston Store

	GD 2.0	VG 4.0	FN 6.0	VF 8.0	VF/NM 9.0	NM- 9.2
1(1940)-Burnley-a; F. Ray-c/r from Superman #6 (Scarce)-Superman saves Santa Claus. Santa makes real Superman Toys offered in 1940. 1st merchandising story; versions with Royal Crown Cola ad on front-c & Boston Store ad on front-c; cover art on each has the same layout but different art	530	1060	1590	3869	6835	9800
nn(1944) w/Santa Claus & X-mas tree-c	116	232	348	742	1271	1800
nn(1944) w/Candy cane & Superman-c	116	232	348	742	1271	1800
nn(1944) w/1940-c (Santa over chimney); Superman image (from Superman #6) on back-c	116	232	348	742	1271	1800

SUPERMAN-TIM (Becomes Tim)
Superman-Tim Stores/National Periodical Publ.: Aug, 1942 - May, 1950 (Half size) (B&W Giveaway w/2 color covers) (Publ. monthly 2/43 on)(All have Superman illos)

	GD 2.0	VG 4.0	FN 6.0	VF 8.0	VF/NM 9.0	NM- 9.2
8/42 (#1)- 2 pg. Superman story	152	304	456	965	1658	2350
9/42 (#2) Superman/Uncle Sam flag-c	58	116	174	371	636	900
12/42-Christmas-c	47	94	141	296	498	700
1/43	45	90	135	284	480	675
2/43, 3/43-Classic flag-c	42	84	126	265	445	625
4/43, 5/43, 6/43, 8/43	39	78	117	231	378	525
7/43-Classic Superman bomb-c	42	84	126	265	445	625
9/43, 10/43, 11/43, 12/43	31	62	93	182	296	410
1/44-12/44	24	48	72	144	237	330
1/45-5/45, 8/45, 10-12/45 (X-mas-c), 1/46-8/46	22	44	66	132	216	300
6/45-Classic Superman-c	24	48	72	142	234	325
7/45-Classic Superman flag-c	24	48	72	142	234	325
9/45-1st stamp album issue	48	96	114	302	514	725
9/46-2nd stamp album issue	42	84	126	265	445	625
10/46-1st Superman story	29	58	87	174	285	395
11/46, 12/46, 1/47-8/47 issues-Superman story in each; 2/47-Infinity-c. All 36 pgs.	29	58	87	174	285	395
9/47-Stamp album issue & Superman story	41	82	123	256	428	600
10/47, 11/47, 12/47-Superman stories (24 pgs.)	29	58	87	174	285	395
1/48-7/48,10/48, 11/48, 12/48, 2/49, 4/49-11/49	24	48	72	142	234	325
8/48-Contains full page ad for Superman-Tim watch giveaway	24	48	72	142	234	325
9/48-Stamp album issue	32	64	96	192	314	435
1/49-Full page Superman bank cut-out	24	48	72	142	234	325
3/49-Full page Superman boxing game cut-out	24	48	72	142	234	325
12/49-3/50, 5/50-Superman stories	26	52	78	154	252	350
4/50-Superman story, baseball stories; photo-c without Superman	31	62	93	182	296	410

NOTE: *All issues have Superman illustrations throughout. The page count varies depending on whether a Superman-Tim comic story is inserted. If it is, the page count is either 36 or 24 pages. Otherwise all issues are 16 pages. Each issue has a special place for inserting a full color Superman stamp. The stamp album issues had spaces for the stamps given away the past year. The books were mailed as a subscription premium. The stamps were given away free (or when you made a purchase) only when you physically came into the store.*

SUPER SEAMAN SLOPPY
Allied Pristine Union Council, Buffalo, NY: 1940s, 8pg., reg. size (Soft-c)

	GD 2.0	VG 4.0	FN 6.0	VF 8.0	VF/NM 9.0	NM- 9.2
nn	12	24	36	67	94	120

SURVEY
Marvel Comics Group: 1948 (Readership survey for advertisers, reg. size)

	GD 2.0	VG 4.0	FN 6.0	VF 8.0	VF/NM 9.0	NM- 9.2
nn-Harvey Kurtzman-c/a	100	200	300	635	1093	1550

SWAMP FOX, THE
Walt Disney Productions: 1960 (14 pgs, small size) (Canada Dry Premiums)

	GD 2.0	VG 4.0	FN 6.0	VF 8.0	VF/NM 9.0	NM- 9.2
Titles: (A)-Tory Masquerade, (B)-Turnabout Tactics, (C)-Rindau Rampage; each came in paper sleeve, books 1,2 & 3; Set with sleeves	5	10	15	31	53	75
Comic only	2	4	6	13	18	22

SWORDQUEST
DC Comics/Atari Pub.: 1982, 52pg., 5"x7" (Giveaway with video games)

	GD 2.0	VG 4.0	FN 6.0	VF 8.0	VF/NM 9.0	NM- 9.2
1,2-Roy Thomas & Gerry Conway-s; George Pérez & Dick Giordano-c/a in all	2	4	6	10	14	18
3-Low print	3	6	9	15	22	28

SYNDICATE FEATURES (Sci/fi)
Harry A. Chesler Syndicate: V1#3, 11/15/37; V1#5, 12/15/37 (Tabloid size, 3 colors, 4 pgs.) (Editors premium) (Came folded)

	GD 2.0	VG 4.0	FN 6.0	VF 8.0	VF/NM 9.0	NM- 9.2
V1#3,5-Dan Hastings daily strips-Guardineer-a	158	316	474	1003	1727	2450

TAKING A CHANCE
American Cancer Society: no date (giveaway)

	GD 2.0	VG 4.0	FN 6.0	VF 8.0	VF/NM 9.0	NM- 9.2
nn-Anti-smoking	2	4	6	11	16	20

TASTEE-FREEZ COMICS (Also see Harvey Hits and Richie Rich)
Harvey Comics: 1957 (10¢, 36 pgs.)(6 different issues given away)

	GD 2.0	VG 4.0	FN 6.0	VF 8.0	VF/NM 9.0	NM- 9.2
1-Little Dot on cover; Richie Rich "Ride 'Em Cowboy" story published one year prior to being printed in Harvey Hits #9.	8	16	24	54	102	150
2,4,5: 2-Rags Rabbit. 4-Sad Sack. 5-Mazie	2	4	6	8	10	12
3-Casper	2	4	6	11	16	20
6-Dick Tracy	2	4	6	11	16	20
nn-Brings You Space Facts and Fun Book	1	2	3	5	6	8

TAYLOR'S CHRISTMAS TABLOID
Dept. Store Giveaway: Mid 1930s, Cleveland, Ohio (Tabloid size; in color)
nn-(Very Rare)-Among the earliest pro work of Siegel & Shuster; one full color page called

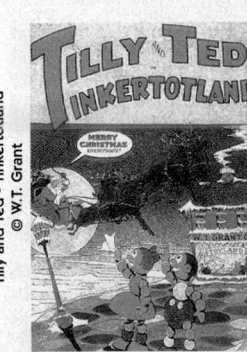

Tilly and Ted - Tinkertotland © W.T. Grant

Tom Mix Comics #5 © FAW

Trapped © HARV

GD 2.0 | VG 4.0 | FN 6.0 | VF 8.0 | VF/NM 9.0 | NM- 9.2

"The Battle in the Stratosphere", with a pre-Superman look; Shuster art thoughout. (Only 1 known copy) Estimated value... 5000.00

TAZ'S 40TH BIRTHDAY BLOWOUT
DC Comics: 1994 (K-Mart giveaway, 16 pgs.)
nn-Six pg. story, games and puzzles 4.00

TEE AND VEE CROSLEY IN TELEVISION LAND COMICS (Also see Crosley's House of Fun)
Crosley Division, Avco Mfg. Corp. : 1951 (52 pgs.; 8x11"; paper cover; in color) (Giveaway)
Many stories, puzzles, cut-outs, games, etc. 8 16 24 42 54 65

TEEN-AGE BOOBY TRAP
Commercial Comics: 1970 (Small size)
nn 3 6 9 16 23 30

TENNESSEE JED (Radio)
Fox Syndicate? (Wm. C. Popper & Co.): nd (1945) (16 pgs.; paper-c; reg. size; giveaway)
nn 20 40 60 120 195 270

TENNIS (...For Speed, Stamina, Strength, Skill)
Tennis Educational Foundation: 1956 (16 pgs.; soft cover; 10¢)
Book 1-Endorsed by Gene Tunney, Ralph Kiner, etc. showing how tennis has helped them 6 12 18 28 34 40

TERRY AND THE PIRATES
Dell Publishing Co.: 1939 - 1953 (By Milton Caniff)
Buster Brown Shoes giveaway(1938)-32 pgs.; in color 20 40 60 120 195 270
Canada Dry Premiums-Books #1-3(1953, 36 pgs.; 2x5")-Harvey; #1-Hot Shot Charlie Flies Again; 2-In Forced Landing; 3-Dragon Lady in Distress) 14 28 42 80 115 150
Gambles Giveaway (1938, 16 pgs.) 10 20 30 54 72 90
Gillmore Giveaway (1938, 24 pgs.) 10 20 30 56 76 95
Popped Wheat Giveaway(1938)-Strip reprints in full color; Caniff-a 3 6 8 12 14 16
Shoe Store giveaway (Weatherbird & Poll-Parrot)(1938, 16 pgs., soft-c)(2-diff.) 10 20 30 56 76 95
Sparked Wheat Giveaway(1942, 16 pgs.)-In color 10 20 30 56 76 95

TERRY AND THE PIRATES
Libby's Radio Premium: 1941 (16 pgs.; reg. size)(shipped folded in the mail)
"Adventure of the Ruby of Genghis Khan" - Each pg. is a puzzle that must be completed to read the story 410 820 1230 2650 - -

THAT THE WORLD MAY BELIEVE
Catechetical Guild Giveaway: No date (16 pgs.) (Graymoor Friars distr.)
nn 5 10 14 20 24 28

THREAT TO FREEDOM
1965 (Small size)
nn - Anti-communism pamphlet; hammer & sickle-c 9 18 27 58 114 170

3-D COLOR CLASSICS (Wendy's Kid's Club)
Wendy's Int'l Inc.: 1995 (5 1/2" x 8", comes with 3-D glasses)
The Elephant's Child, Gulliver's Travels, Peter Pan, The Time Machine, 20,000 Leagues Under the Sea: Neal Adams-a in all each.... 3.50

350 YEARS OF AMERICAN DAIRY FOODS
American Dairy Assoc.: 1957 (5x7", 16 pgs.)
nn-History of milk 4 7 9 14 16 18

THUMPER (Disney)
Grosset & Dunlap: 1942 (50¢, 32pgs., hardcover book, 7"x8-1/2" w/dust jacket)
nn-Given away (along with a copy of Bambi) for a $2.00, 2-year subscription to WDC&S in 1942. (Xmas offer). Book only 17 34 51 100 158 215
Dust jacket only 10 20 30 58 79 100

TILLY AND TED-TINKERTOTLAND
W. T. Grant Co.: 1945 (Giveaway, 20 pgs.)
nn-Christmas comic 9 18 27 52 69 85

TIM (Formerly Superman-Tim; becomes Gene Autry-Tim)
Tim Stores: June, 1950 - Oct, 1950 (B&W, half-size)
4 issues; 6/50, 9/50, 10/50 known 17 34 51 100 158 215

TIM AND SALLY'S ADVENTURES AT MARINELAND
Marineland Restaurant & Bar, Marineland, CA: 1957 (5x7", 16 pgs., soft-c)
nn-copyright Oceanarium, Inc. 2 4 6 9 13 16

TIME OF DECISION
Harvey Publications Inc.: (16 pgs., paper cover)
nn-ROTC recruitment 5 10 15 22 26 30

TIM IN SPACE (Formerly Gene Autry Tim; becomes Tim Tomorrow)
Tim Stores: 1950 (1/2 size giveaway) (B&W)
nn 14 28 42 88 121 160

TIM TOMORROW (Formerly Tim In Space)
Tim Stores: 8/51, 9/51, 10/51, Christmas, 1951 (5x7-3/4")
nn-Prof. Fumble & Captain Kit Comet in all 14 28 42 88 121 160

TIM TYLER'S LUCK
Standard Comics (King Feat. Syndicate): 1950s (Reg. size, slick-c)
nn-Felix the Cat app. 4 8 12 17 21 24

TOM MIX (...Commandos Comics #10-12)
Ralston-Purina Co.: Sept, 1940 - No. 12, Nov, 1942 (36 pgs.); 1983 (one-shot)
Given away for two Ralston box-tops; 1983 came in cereal box
1-Origin (life) Tom Mix; Fred Meagher-a 216 432 648 1372 2361 3350
2 47 94 141 296 498 700
3-9 39 78 117 231 378 525
10-12: 10-Origin Tom Mix Commando Unit; Speed O'Dare begins; Japanese sub-c. 12-Sci/fi-c 31 62 93 182 296 410
1983- "Taking of Grizzly Grebb", Toth-a; 16 pg. miniature 2 4 6 9 12 15

TOM SAWYER COMICS
Giveaway: 1951? (Paper cover)
nn-Contains a coverless Hopalong Cassidy from 1951; other combinations known 3 6 9 15 22 28

TOO MUCH, TOO LITTLE
Federal Reserve Bank: 1989 (Reg. size)
9-13 1 3 4 6 8 10

TOP-NOTCH COMICS
MLJ Magazines/Rex Theater: 1940s (theater giveaway, sepia-c)
1-Black Hood-c; content & covers can vary 61 122 183 390 670 950

TOWN THAT FORGOT SANTA, THE
W. T. Grant Co.: 1961 (Giveaway, 24 pgs.)
nn 3 6 9 16 23 30

TOY LAND FUNNIES (See Funnies On Parade)
Eastern Color Printing Co.: 1934 (32 pgs., Hecht Co. store giveaway)
nn-Reprints Buck Rogers Sunday pages #199-201 from Famous Funnies #5. A rare variation of Funnies On Parade; same format, similar contents, same cover except for large Santa placed in center (value will be based on sale)

TOY WORLD FUNNIES (See Funnies On Parade)
Eastern Color Printing Co.: 1933 (36 pgs., slick cover, Golden Eagle and Wanamaker giveaway)
nn-Contains contents from Funnies On Parade/Century Of Comics. A rare variation of Funnies On Parade; same format, similar contents, same cover except for large Santa placed in center. A GD/VG 3.0 copy sold for $5258 in May 2016.

TRAPPED
Harvey Publications (Columbia Univ. Press): 1951 (Giveaway, soft-c, 16 pgs)
nn-Drug education comic (30,000 printed?) distributed to schools.; mentioned in **SOTI**, pgs. 256,350 5 10 14 20 24 28
NOTE: *Many copies surfaced in 1979 causing a setback in price; beware of trimmed edges, because many copies have a brittle edge.*

TRIPLE-A BASEBALL HEROES
Marvel Comics: 2007 (Minor league baseball stadium giveaway)
1-Special John Watson painted-c for Memphis, Durham and Buffalo; generic cover with team logos for each of the other 27 teams; Spider-Man, Iron Man, FF app. 4.00

TRIP TO OUTER SPACE WITH SANTA
Sales Promotions, Inc/Peoria Dry Goods: 1950s (paper-c)
nn-Comics, games & puzzles 5 10 15 24 29 34

TRIP WITH SANTA ON CHRISTMAS EVE, A
Rockford Dry Goods Co.: No date (Early 1950s) (Giveaway, 16 pgs., paper-c)
nn 5 10 15 24 29 34

TRUTH BEHIND THE TRIAL OF CARDINAL MINDSZENTY, THE (See Cardinal Mindszenty)

TURNING WHEELS
Studebaker: 1954 (paper-c)
nn-The Studebaker story (A CGC 9.6 sold in 2018 for $1016 & a CGC 9.6 sold in 2019 for $156)

24 PAGES OF COMICS (No title) (Also see Pure Oil Comics, Salerno Carnival of Comics, & Vicks Comics)

Unkept Promise © Legion of Truth

Wheaties B-1 © DIS

Whiz Comics Wheaties Giveaway © FAW

GD 2.0 | VG 4.0 | FN 6.0 | VF 8.0 | VF/NM 9.0 | NM- 9.2

Giveaway by various outlets including Sears: Late 1930s
nn-Contains strip reprints-Buck Rogers, Napoleon, Sky Roads, War on Crime 34 68 102 204 332 460

TWO FACES OF COMMUNISM (Also see Double Talk)
Christian Anti-Communism Crusade, Houston, Texas: 1961 (Giveaway, paper-c, 36 pgs.)
nn 28 56 84 165 270 375

2001, A SPACE ODYSSEY (Movie)
Marvel Comics Group
Howard Johnson giveaway (1968, 8pp); 6 pg. movie adaptation, 2 pg. games, puzzles; McWilliams-a 2 4 6 10 14 18

UNCLE SAM'S CHRISTMAS STORY
Promotional Publ. Co.: 1958 (Giveaway)
nn-Reprints 1956 Christmas USA 2 4 6 11 16 20

UNCLE WIGGILY COMICS
Herberger's Clothing Store: 1942 (32 pgs., paper cover)
nn-Comic panels with 6 pages of puzzles 14 28 42 82 121 160

UNKEPT PROMISE
Legion of Truth: 1949 (Giveaway, 24 pgs.)
nn-Anti-alcohol 11 22 33 60 83 105

UNTOLD LEGEND OF THE BATMAN, THE
DC Comics: 1989 (28 pgs., 6X9", limited series of cereal premiums)
1-1st & 2nd printings known; Byrne-a 2 4 6 8 10 12
2,3: 1st & 2nd printings known 1 2 3 5 7 9

UNTOUCHABLES, THE (TV)
Leaf Brands, Inc.
Topps Bubblegum premiums produced by Leaf Brands, Inc.-2-1/2x4-1/2", 8 pgs. (3 diff. issues) "The Organization, Jamaica Ginger, The Otto Frick Story (drug), 3000 Suspects, The Antidote, Mexican Stakeout, Little Egypt, Purple Gang, Bugs Moran Story, & Lily Dallas Story" 3 6 9 17 25 34

VICKS COMICS (See Pure Oil Comics, Salerno Carnival of Comics & 24 Pages of Comics)
Eastern Color Printing Co. (Vicks Chemical Co.): nd (circa 1938) (Giveaway, 68 pgs. in color)
nn-Famous Funnies-r (before #40); contains 5 pgs. Buck Rogers (4 pgs. from F.F. #15, & 1 pg. from #16) Joe Palooka, Napoleon, etc. app. 63 126 189 403 689 975
nn-16 loose, untrimmed page giveaway; paper-c; r/Famous Funnies #14; Buck Rogers, Joe Palooka app. Has either "Vicks Comics" printed on cover or only a local store name as the logo. 26 52 78 152 249 345

WALT DISNEY'S COMICS & STORIES
K.K. Publications: 1942-1963 known (7-1/3"x10-1/4", 4 pgs. in color, slick paper) (folded horizontally once or twice as mailers) (Xmas subscription offer)
1942 mailer-r/Kelly cover to WDC&S 25; 2-year subscription + two Grosset & Dunlap hardcover books (32-pages each), of Bambi and of Thumper, offered for $2.00; came in an illustrated C&S envelope with an enclosed postage paid envelope
(Rare) Mailer only 25 50 75 150 245 340
with envelopes 30 60 90 177 289 400
1947,1948 mailer 19 38 57 111 176 240
1949 mailer-A rare Barks item: Same WDC&S cover as 1942 mailer, but with art changed so that nephew is handing teacher Donald a comic book rather than an apple, as originally drawn by Kelly. The tiny, 7/8"x1-1/4" cover shown was a rejected cover by Barks that was intended for C&S 110, but was redrawn by Kelly for C&S 111. The original art has been lost and this is its only app. (Rare) 40 80 120 246 411 575
1950 mailer-P.1 r/Kelly cover to Dell Xmas Parade 1 (without title); p.2 r/Kelly cover to C&S 101 (w/o title), but with the art altered to show Donald reading C&S 122 (by Kelly); hardcover book, "Donald Duck in Bringing Up the Boys" given with a $1.00 one-year subscription; P.4 r/full Kelly Xmas cover to C&S 99 (Rare) 18 36 54 107 167 230
1952 mailer-P1 r/cover WDC&S #88 15 30 45 86 133 180
1953 mailer-P.1 r/cover Dell Xmas Parade 4 (w/o title); insides offer "Donald Duck Full Speed Ahead," a 28-page, color, 5-5/8"x6-5/8" book, not of the Story Hour series; P.4 r/full Barks C&S 148 cover (Rare) 15 30 45 86 133 180
1963 mailer-Pgs. 1,2 & 4 r/GK Xmas art; P.3 r/a 1963 C&S cover (Scarce) 7 14 21 44 82 120
NOTE: *It is assumed a different mailer was printed each Xmas for at least twenty years.*

WALT DISNEY'S COMICS & STORIES
Walt Disney Productions: 1943 (36 pgs.) (Dept. store Xmas giveaway)
nn-X-Mas-c with Donald & the Boys; Donald Duck by Jack Hannah; Thumper by Ken Hultgren 77 154 231 493 847 1200

WARLORD
DC Comics: (Remco Toy giveaway, 2-3/4x4")
nn 5.00

WATCH OUT FOR BIG TALK
General Comics: 1950
nn-Dan Barry-a; about crooked politicians 8 16 24 40 50 60

WEATHER-BIRD (See Comics From..., Dick Tracy, Free Comics to You..., Super Circus & Terry and the Pirates)
International Shoe Co./Western Printing Co.: 1958 - No. 16, July, 1962 (Shoe store giveaway)
1 4 8 12 24 38 52
2-16 3 6 9 14 19 24
NOTE: *The numbers are located in the lower bottom panel, pg. 1. All feature a character called Weather-Bird.*

WEATHER BIRD COMICS (See Comics From Weather Bird)
Weather Bird Shoes: 1955 - 1958 (Giveaway)
nn-Contains a comic bound with new cover. Several combinations possible; contents determine price (40 - 60 percent of contents).

WEEKLY COMIC MAGAZINE
Fox Publications: May 12, 1940 (16 pgs.) (Others exist w/o super-heroes)
(1st Version)-8 pg. Blue Beetle story, 7 pg. Patty O'Day story; two copies known to exist. (a VF copy sold in 5/07 for $1553)
(2nd Version)-7 two-pg. adventures of Blue Beetle, Patty O'Day, Yarko, Dr. Fung, Green Mask, Spark Stevens, & Rex Dexter (two known copies, a FN sold in 2007 for $1912, other is GD)
(3rd version)-Captain Valor (only one known copy, in VG+; it sold in 2005 for $480)
Discovered with business papers, letters and exploitation material promoting **Weekly Comic Magazine** for use by newspapers in the same manner of **The Spirit** weeklies. Interesting note: these are dated three weeks before the first Spirit comic. Letters indicate that samples may have been sent to a few newspapers. These sections were actually 15-1/2x22" pages which will fold down to an approximate 8x10" comic booklet. Other various comic sections were found with the above, but were more like the Sunday comic sections in format.

WE HIT THE JACKPOT
General Comics, Inc./American Affairs: 1947 (Promotional comic)(Paper-c)
nn 7 14 21 35 43 50

WHAT DO YOU KNOW ABOUT THIS COMICS SEAL OF APPROVAL?
No publisher listed (DC Comics giveaway): nd (1955) (4 pgs., slick paper-c)
nn-(Rare) 129 287 387 826 1413 2000

WHAT IF THEY CALL ME "CHICKEN"?
Kiwanis International: 1970 (giveaway)
nn-Educational anti-marijuana comic 4 8 12 25 40 55

WHAT'S BEHIND THESE HEADLINES
William C. Popper Co.: 1948 (16 pgs.)
nn-Comic insert "The Plot to Steal the World" 7 14 21 35 43 50

WHAT'S IN IT FOR YOU?
Harvey Publications Inc.: (16 pgs., paper cover)
nn-National Guard recruitment 4 7 10 14 17 20

WHEATIES (Premiums)
Walt Disney Productions: 1950 & 1951 (32 titles, pocket-size, 32 pgs.)
Mailing Envelope (no art on front)(Designates sets A,B,C or D on front) 7 14 21 37 46 55

(Set A-1 to A-8, 1950)
A-1-Mickey Mouse & the Disappearing Island, A-5-Mickey Mouse, Roving Reporter each... 6 12 18 31 38 45
A-2-Grandma Duck, Homespun Detective, A-6-Li'l Bad Wolf, Forest Ranger, A-7-Goofy, Tightrope Acrobat, A-8-Pluto & the Bogus Money each... 6 12 18 28 34 40
A-3-Donald Duck & the Haunted Jewels, A-4-Donald Duck & the Giant Ape each... 8 16 24 44 57 70

(Set B-1 to B-8, 1950)
B-1-Mickey Mouse & the Pharoah's Curse, B-4-Mickey Mouse & the Mystery Sea Monster each... 7 14 21 35 43 50
B-2-Pluto, Canine Cowpoke, B-5-Li'l Bad Wolf in the Hollow Tree Hideout, B-7-Goofy & the Gangsters each... 6 12 18 28 34 40
B-3-Donald Duck & the Buccaneers, B-6-Donald Duck,Trail Blazer, B-8 Donald Duck, Klondike Kid each... 8 16 24 44 57 70

(Set C-1 to C-8, 1951)
C-1-Donald Duck & the Inca Idol, C-5-Donald Duck in the Lost Lakes, C-8-Donald Duck Deep-Sea Diver each... 8 16 24 44 57 70
C-2-Mickey Mouse & the Magic Mountain, C-6-Mickey Mouse & the Stagecoach Bandits each... 7 14 21 35 45 50
C-3-Li'l Bad Wolf, Fire Fighter, C-4-Gus & Jaq Save the Ship, C-7-Goofy, Big Game Hunter each... 6 12 18 28 34 40

(Set D-1 to D-8, 1951)
D-1-Donald Duck in Indian Country, D-5-Donald Duck, Mighty Mystic each... 8 16 24 44 57 70

Wisco - Tex Farnum, Frontiersman © Vital

World's Finest Comics #176 (Best Western) © DC

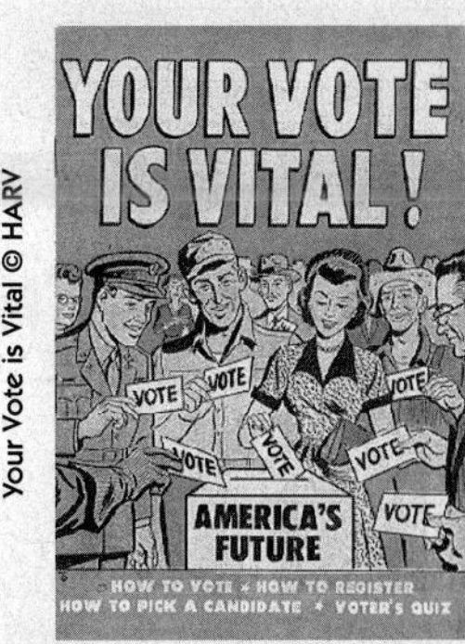

Your Vote is Vital © HARV

	GD 2.0	VG 4.0	FN 6.0	VF 8.0	VF/NM 9.0	NM- 9.2

D-2-Mickey Mouse and the Abandoned Mine, D-6-Mickey Mouse & the Medicine Man each... 7 14 21 35 43 50
D-3-Pluto & the Mysterious Package, D-4-Bre'r Rabbit's Sunken Treasure, D-7-Li'l Bad Wolf and the Secret of the Woods, D-8-Minnie Mouse, Girl Explorer each... 6 12 18 28 34 40
NOTE: *Some copies lack the Wheaties ad.*

WHEEL OF PROGRESS, THE
Assoc. of American Railroads: Oct, 1957 (16 pgs.)
nn-Bill Bunce 6 12 18 28 34 40

WHIZ COMICS (Formerly Flash Comics & Thrill Comics #1)
Fawcett Publications
Wheaties Giveaway(1946, Miniature, 6-1/2x8-1/4", 32 pgs.); all copies were taped at each corner to a box of Wheaties and are never found in very fine or mint condition; "Capt. Marvel & the Water Thieves", plus Golden Arrow, Ibis, Crime Smasher stories 83 166 415 – – –

WILD KINGDOM (TV) (Mutual of Omaha's...)
Western Printing Co.: 1965, 1966 (Giveaway, regular size, slick-c, 16 pgs.)
nn-Front & back-c are different on 1966 edition 2 4 6 9 12 15

WISCO/KLARER COMIC BOOK (Miniature)
Marvel Comics/Vital Publ./Fawcett Publ.: 1948 - 1964 (3-1/2x6-3/4", 24 pgs.)
Given away by Wisco "99" Service Stations, Carnation Malted Milk, Klarer Health Wieners, Fleers Dubble Bubble Gum, Rodeo All-Meat Wieners, Perfect Potato Chips, & others; see ad in Tom Mix #21
Blackstone & the Gold Medal Mystery (1948) 8 16 24 40 50 60
Blackstone "Solves the Sealed Vault Mystery" (1950) 8 16 24 40 50 60
Blaze Carson in "The Sheriff Shoots It Out" (1950) 8 16 24 40 50 60
Captain Marvel & Billy's Big Game (r/Capt. Marvel Adv. #76) (Prices vary widely on this book) 26 52 78 154 252 350
China Boy in "A Trip to the Zoo" #10 (1948) 4 8 12 18 22 25
Indoors-Outdoors Game Book 3 6 9 11 13 15
Jim Solar Space Sheriff in "Battle for Mars", "Between Two Worlds", "Conquers Outer Space", "The Creatures on the Comet", "Defeats the Moon Missile Men", "Encounter Creatures on Comet", "Meet the Jupiter Jumpers", "Meets the Man From Mars", "On Traffic Duty", "Outlaws of the Spaceways", "Pirates of the Planet X", "Protects Space Lanes", "Raiders From the Sun", "Ring Around Saturn", "Robots of Rhea", "The Sky Ruby", "Spacetts of the Sky", "Spidermen of Venus", "Trouble on Mercury" 6 12 18 29 36 42
Johnny Starboard & the Underseas Pirates (1948) 4 8 12 18 22 25
Kid Colt in "He Lived by His Guns" (1950) 8 16 24 40 50 60
Little Aspirin as the "Crook Catcher" #2 (1950) 3 6 9 11 13 15
Little Aspirin in "Naughty But Nice" #6 (1950) 3 6 9 11 13 15
Return of the Black Phantom (not M.E. character)(Roy Dare)(1948) 6 12 18 27 33 38
Secrets of Magic 4 7 9 14 16 18
Slim Morgan "Brings Justice to Mesa City" #3 4 7 9 14 16 18
Super Rabbit(1950)-Cuts Red Tape, Stops Crime Wave! 8 16 24 44 57 70
Tex Farnum, Frontiersman (1948) 4 8 12 18 22 25
Tex Taylor in "Draw or Die, Cowpoke!" (1950) 6 12 18 28 34 40
Tex Taylor in "An Exciting Adventure at the Gold Mine" (1950) 6 12 18 27 33 38
Wacky Quacky in "All-Aboard" 3 5 7 10 12 14
When School Is Out 3 5 7 10 12 14
Willie in a "Comic-Comic Book Fall" #1 4 7 9 14 16 18
Wonder Duck "An Adventure at the Rodeo of the Fearless Quacker!" (1950) 8 16 24 44 57 70
Rare uncut version of three; includes Capt. Marvel, Tex Farnum, Black Phantom (A VG copy sold in Sept. 2015 for $147)
Rare uncut version of three; includes China Boy, Blackstone, Johnny Starboard & the Underseas Pirates (A FN/VF copy sold in Sept. 2015 for $137)
Rare uncut version of three; all Jim Solar (A VG copy sold in Sept. 2015 for $79)
Rare uncut version of three; includes Willie in a "Comic-Comic Book Fall", Little Aspirin #2, Slim Morgan Brings Justice to Mesa City (a VF/FN copy sold for $54 in Nov. 2007)

WIZARD OF OZ
MGM: 1967 (small size)
"Dorothy and Friends Visit Oz", "Dorothy Meets the Wizard", "The Tin Woodsman Saves Dorothy" each... 2 4 6 10 14 18

WOLVERINE
Marvel Comics
145-(1999 Nabisco mail-in offer) Sienkiewicz-c 10 20 30 64 132 200
...Son of Canada (4/01, ed. of 65,000) Spider-Man & The Hulk app.; Lim-a 5.00

WOMAN OF THE PROMISE, THE
Catechetical Guild: 1950 (General Distr.) (Paper cover, 32 pgs.)
nn 6 12 18 28 34 40

WONDER BOOK OF RUBBER
B.F. Goodrich: 1947 (Promo giveaway
nn 5 10 15 22 26 30

WONDERFUL WORLD OF DUCKS (See Golden Picture Story Book)
Colgate Palmolive Co.: 1975
1-Mostly-r 1 3 4 6 8 10

WONDER WOMAN
DC Comics: 1977
Pizza Hut Giveaways (12/77)-Reprints #60,62 2 4 6 10 14 18
... - The Minotaur (1981, General Foods giveaway, 8 pages, 3-1/2 x 6-3/4", oblong) 3 6 9 14 19 24

WONDER WORKER OF PERU
Catechetical Guild: No date (5x7", 16 pgs., B&W, giveaway)
nn 6 12 18 28 34 40

WOODY WOODPECKER
Dell Publishing Co.
Clover Stamp-Newspaper Boy Contest('56)-9 pg. story-(Giveaway) 8 16 24 40 50 60
In Chevrolet Wonderland(1954-Giveaway)(Western Publ.)-20 pgs., full story line; Chilly Willy app. 18 36 54 105 165 225
...Meets Scotty MacTape(1953-Scotch Tape giveaway)-16 pgs., full size 18 36 54 105 165 225

WOOLWORTH'S CHRISTMAS STORY BOOK (See Jolly Christmas Book)
Promotional Publ. Co.(Western Printing Co.): 1952 - 1954 (16 pgs., paper-c)
nn: 1952 issue-Marv Levy c/a 8 16 24 40 50 60

WOOLWORTH'S HAPPY TIME CHRISTMAS BOOK
F. W. Woolworth Co. (Western Printing Co.): 1952 (Christmas giveaway)
nn-36 pgs. 7 14 21 37 46 55

WORLD'S FINEST COMICS
National Periodical Publ./DC Comics
Giveaway (c. 1944-45, 8 pgs., in color, paper-c)-Johnny Everyman-r/World's Finest 22 44 66 128 209 290
Giveaway (c. 1949, 8 pgs., in color, paper-c)- "Make Way For Youth" r/World's Finest; based on film of same name 20 40 60 114 182 250
#176, #179- Best Western reprint edition (1997) 3.00

WORLD'S GREATEST SUPER HEROES
DC Comics (Nutra Comics) (Child Vitamins, Inc.): 1977 (Giveaway, 3-3/4x3-3/4", 24 pgs.)
nn-Batman & Robin app.; health tips 2 4 6 11 16 20

WYOMING THE COWBOY STATE
1954 (Giveaway, slick-c)
nn 5 10 15 22 26 30

XMAS FUNNIES
Kinney Shoes: No date (Giveaway, paper cover, 36 pgs.?)
Contains 1933 color strip-r; Mutt & Jeff, etc. 32 64 96 188 307 425

X-MEN THE MOVIE
Marvel Comics/Toys R' Us: 2000
Special Movie Prequel Edition 1 2 3 5 6 8

X2 PRESENTS THE ULTIMATE X-MEN #2
Marvel Comics/New York Post: July, 2003
Reprint distributed inside issue of the New York Post 3.00

YALTA TO KOREA (Also see Korea My Home)
M. Phillip Corp. (Republican National Committee): 1952 (Giveaway, paper-c)
nn-(8 pgs.)-Anti-communist propaganda book 19 38 57 112 179 245

YOGI BEAR (TV)
Dell Publishing Co.
Giveaway ('84, '86)-City of Los Angeles, "Creative First Aid" & "Earthquake Preparedness for Children" 1 2 3 4 5 7

YOUR TRIP TO NEWSPAPERLAND
Philadelphia Evening Bulletin (Printed by Harvey Press): June, 1955 (14x11-1/2", 12 pgs.)
nn-Joe Palooka takes kids on newspaper tour 6 12 18 27 33 38

YOUR VOTE IS VITAL!
Harvey Publications Inc.: 1952 (5" x 7", 16 pgs., paper cover)
nn-The importance of voting 5 10 14 20 24 28

THE PIONEER AGE

The American Comic Book: 1500s-1828

For the last few years, we have featured a tremendous article by noted historian and collector Eric C. Caren on the foundations of what we now call "The Pioneer Age" of comics. We look forward to a new article on this significant topic in a future edition of *The Overstreet Comic Book Price Guide*. In the meantime, should you need it, Caren's article may be found in the 35th through 39th editions.

That said, even with the space constraints in this edition of the *Guide*, we could not possibly exclude reference to these incredible, formative works.

Why are these illustrations and sequences of illustrations important to the comic books of today?

German broadsheet, dated 1569.

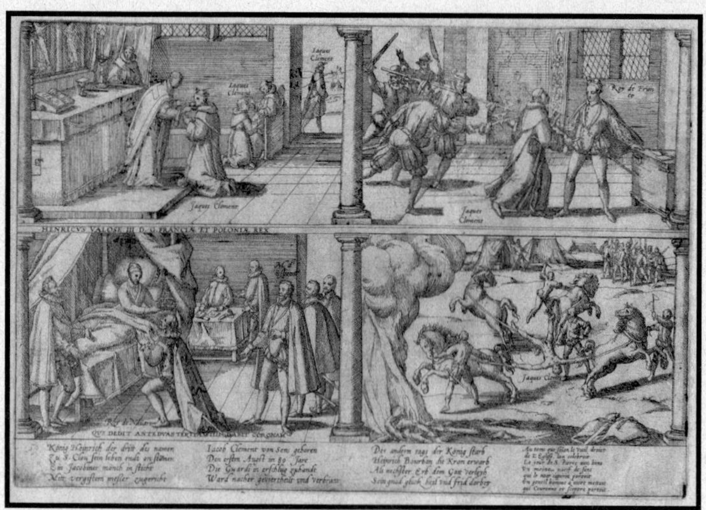

The Murder of King Henry III (1589).

Quite frankly, because we can see in them the very building blocks of the comic art form.

The shooting of the Italian Concini (1617).

Over the course of just a few hundred years, we the evolution of narration, word balloons, panel-to-panel progression of story, and so much more. If these stories aren't developed first, how would be every have reached the point that that *The Adventures of Mr. Obadiah Oldbuck* could have come along in 1842?

As the investigation of comic book history has blown away the notion that comic books were a 20 century invention, it hasn't been easy to convince some, even with the clear, linear progression of the artful melding of illustration and words.

"Want to avoid an argument in social discourse? Steer clear of politics and religion. In the latter category, the most controversial subject is human evolution. Collectors can become just as squeamish when you start messing with the evolution of a particular collectible," Eric Caren wrote in his article. "In most cases, the origin of a particular comic character will be universally agreed upon, but try tackling the origin of printed comics and you are asking for trouble."

"The Bubblers Medley" (1720).

"Join, or Die" from the **Pennsylvania Gazette**, *May 9, 1754.*

"Amusement for John Bull..." from **The European Magazine** *(1783).*

But the evidence is there for any who choose to look. Before the original comics of the Golden Age, there were comic strip reprints collected in comic book form. The practice dated back decades earlier, of course, but coalesced into the current form when the realities of the Great Depression spawned the modern incarnation of the comic book and its immediate cousin, the Big Little Book.

Everything that came later, though, did so because the acceptance of the visual language had already been worked out. Before Spider-Man and the Hulk, before Superman and Batman, before the Yellow Kid, Little Nemo, and the Brownies, cartoonists and editorial illustrators were working out how to tell a story or simply convey their ideas in this new artform.

Without this sort of work, without these pioneers, we simply wouldn't be where we are today.

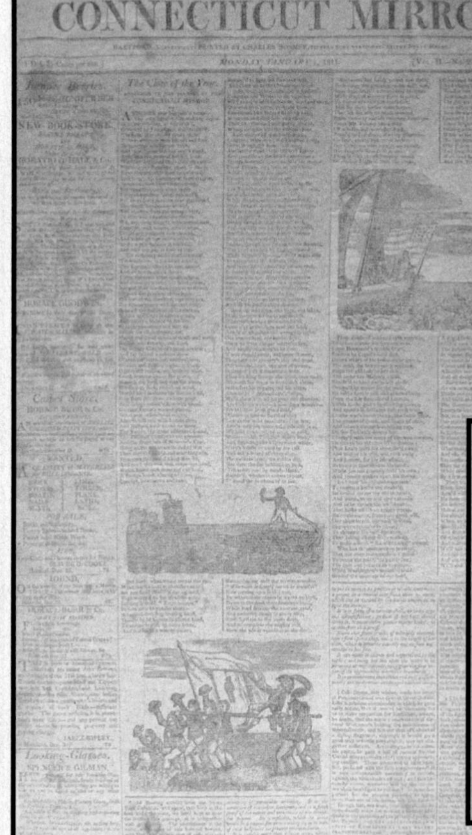
CONNECTICUT MIRROR.

Cartoons satirizing Napoleon on the front page of the **Connecticut Mirror**, *dated January 7, 1811.*

Another Napoleon cartoon, this time dubbing him "The Corsican Munchausen," from the **London Strand**, *December 4, 1813.*

"A Consultation at the Medical Board" from **The Pasquin or General Satirist** *(1821).*

THE NEW-HAMPSHIRE JOURNAL.

CONCORD, MONDAY, OCTOBER 20, 1828.

☞ *Monumental Inscriptions.*

... ILLEGALLY AND WANTONLY SHED THE BLOOD OF HIS COUNTRYMEN AND FELLOW SOLDIERS, ENTRUST NOT THE LIBERTY AND HAPPINESS OF THIS MOST FREE AND MOST HAPPY COUNTRY TO HIS KEEPING.

JACOB WEBB,

EDWARD LINDSEY,

HENRY LEWIS,

JOHN HARRIS,

David Morrow,

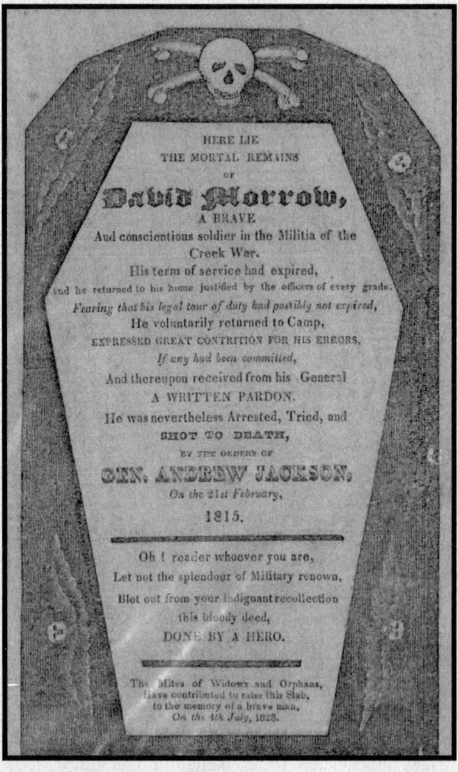

HERE LIE
THE MORTAL REMAINS
OF
David Morrow,
A BRAVE
And conscientious soldier in the Militia of the
Creek War.
His term of service had expired,
and he returned to his home justified by the officers of every grade.
Fearing that his legal tour of duty had possibly not expired,
He voluntarily returned to Camp,
EXPRESSED GREAT CONTRITION FOR HIS ERRORS,
If any had been committed,
And thereupon received from his General
A WRITTEN PARDON.
He was nevertheless Arrested, Tried, and
SHOT TO DEATH,
BY THE ORDERS OF
GEN. ANDREW JACKSON,
On the 21st February,
1815.

Oh! reader whoever you are,
Let not the splendour of Military renown,
Blot out from your indignant recollection
this bloody deed,
DONE BY A HERO.

The Mites of Widows and Orphans,
Have contributed to raise this Slab,
to the memory of a brave man,
On the 4th July, 1828.

Above left, the front page of **The New Hampshire Journal**, *dated October 20, 1828, with multiple tombstone "panels." To the right is a detail of the bottom right tombstone.*

THE VICTORIAN AGE

Comic Strips and Books: 1646-1900

By Carrie Wood

Comics were appearing in publications long before caped heroes graced the newsstands around the country. The Victorian and Platinum Ages of comics pre-date the Golden Age arrival of superheroes by decades, though these eras are notable for far more than just the publication dates. We'll delve into the Platinum Age in the following section, and here we'll be focusing on Victorian comics, which began in the 1840s and ran through the end of the century, overlapping with the Platinum Age for a few years.

In terms of subject matter, the commonly-held attitudes and beliefs of 19th century America can be found throughout these cartoons – for better or for worse, by today's standards. And when it comes to the layout of the comics themselves, there's several things worth noting. For instance, word balloons in the Victorian Age were almost never used, and on the rare occasions they were found they were almost completely inconsequential. Typical comics of this time were single-panel illustrations, with narration or dialogue found beneath the panels rather than within the art itself.

There's a wealth of information to discuss about the Victorian Age, and especially with regards to pricing these historical comics, but we found it prudent to hit some of the most important events here before moving into this year's pricing section:

- The Victorian Age began in different countries at different times, depending entirely on when the first sequential comic art was published. Many European countries had a significant head start on the U.S. in this regard.
- America had non-sequential comic art in the years before the Victorian Age began, with woodcut prints occurring as early as the mid-1600s. The 1800s also introduced the States to memorable cartoon artwork, with one of the best-remembered being Benjamin Franklin's "Join or Die" piece, published in 1754; it represented the American Colonies at the time as severed snake parts. These early political cartoons helped introduce an initial baseline for comic art in publications around the country.
- In America, the Victorian Age began proper with the publication of *The Adventures of Mr. Obadiah Oldbuck* in 1842. This story was an unlicensed copy of the original work, *Histoire de M. Vieux Bois*, by Rodolphe Topffer, who had not granted permission of any sort to the periodical that published it (*Brother Jonathan Extra*).
- Topffer was a novelist, artist and teacher from Switzerland who began working on what he referred to

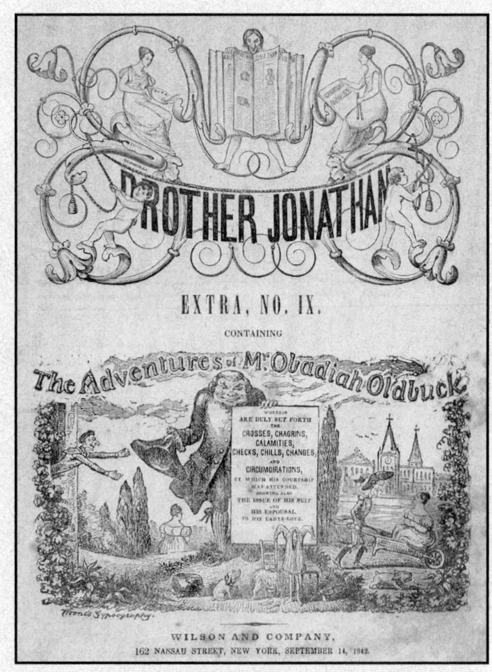
BROTHER JONATHAN

EXTRA, NO. IX.

CONTAINING

The Adventures of Mr. Obadiah Oldbuck

WHEREIN ARE DULY SET FORTH THE CROSSES, CHAGRINS, CALAMITIES, CHECKS, CHILLS, CHANGES, AND CIRCUMGYRATIONS,

WILSON AND COMPANY,
162 NASSAU STREET, NEW YORK, SEPTEMBER 14, 1842.

The earliest-known sequential comic book published in America, ***The Adventures of Mr. Obadiah Oldbuck****, from September 1842.*

The Strange and Wonderful Adventures of Bachelor Butterfly
by Rodolphe Töpffer (New York, 1846), America's 3rd comic book.

as "picture novels" or "graphic literature" by the late 1820s. By the time his work found its way to Paris, they were a significant success. The demand for his work quickly outmatched the supply available, leading to the widespread piracy of his comics; in a world that didn't yet have any sort of international copyright law, this was perfectly legal at the time.

- *Brother Jonathan* began in 1839, with the newspaper being created to exploit a loophole in the postage rates, as magazines were held to a higher postage rate than newspapers. Despite being printed in newspaper format, it didn't contain any news, and instead focused on fictional stories, most of which were pirated from European works. Later that year, the publisher introduced *Brother Jonathan Extra*, a book-sized publication that reprinted novels. The publication of *Obadiah Oldbuck* in this format, which was reformatted from the European original, closely resembled a modern American comic book.
- George Cruikshank was another British cartoonist popular during this era. He was known for his caricature work during his early working years, and he later moved into providing illustrations for books such as *Grimms' Fairy Tales* and for his friend, novelist Charles Dickens. Cruikshank produced numerous cartoons over the course of his career, many of which saw international success.
- Thanks to the success of *Obadiah Oldbuck* in the U.S., it was followed up with printings of Cruikshank's *The Bachelor's Own Book*, which became the second known sequential comic book in the U.S.
- Cruikshank's *The Bottle* debuted in London in 1847 and told the story of a man with alcoholism and how it ruined his family and his life. It was reprinted in a British-American co-publication later that year. Both printings were in a large folio format. This was followed up with a smaller printing the following year, included in the volume *Temperance Tales; Or, Six Nights with the Washing-tonians*. *The Bottle* would see reprintings again and again by numerous publishers well into the 20th century.
- It was during this era that the humor magazine first made its debut, largely in part to the success of published comics in other periodicals. These included *Punch*, a British comic weekly which debuted in 1841. It was a huge success in both England and in the U.S., with thousands of copies being exported to the States with every issue.
- With the success of *Punch*, American businessmen quickly tried to seize upon the market for humorous content, founding the various short-lived publications of *Yankee Doodle*, *Judy*, *The John-Donkey* and *The Elephant* – none of which lasted more than a year, though all of which helped the comics market grow.

George Cruikshank's ***The Bottle*** *from 1847, popular enough to be reprinted numerous times into the 20th century.*

***Journey to the Gold Diggins By Jeremiah Saddlebags**, June 1849, so far the earliest known sequential comic book by American creators, J.A. and D.F. Read, shown with a pair of sample pages.*

- The earliest-known American-created comic book appeared in 1849: *Journey to the Gold Diggins by Jeremiah Saddlebags*, created by cartoonists James and Donald Read. The brothers had worked for *Yankee Doodle* before creating this work, which told of the California gold rush (a wildly popular subject matter for cartoonists of the era).
- Following the international success of *Punch* were collections that reprinted cartoons from the popular magazine, including *Merry Pictures by the Comic Hands* (1859) and others for decades to come. Newspapers would also reprint cartoons from *Punch*, which later would often be replaced by new original American cartoon work.
- *Harper's Monthly* began publishing comics shortly after it began publication in late 1850. The periodical began by reprinting *Punch* cartoons at the end of every issue, later moving into reprints from the British publication *Town Talk* before hiring Frank Bellew to create original comics.
- Bellew provided a huge number of sequential cartoon work during this era, and his work could be found in nearly every American comic or humor publication for decades. His work included contributions to *The Lantern, New York Picayune, The Comic Monthly, Wild Oats, Punchinello, Momus,* and plenty more. His work would go on to influence further generations of comic creators.
- Thomas Nast is another artist of note from this era, known more for his political cartoons than for his sequential comic artwork. Nast's work could be found in *Harper's Weekly*, where he worked from 1862-1886. His work helped to popularize the double-page folio-sized cartoon, a size which he practically invented on his own.
- The German humor magazine *Puck* launched first in 1871, founded by Joseph Keppler. An English-language version of the magazine launched the following year, though both were shut down by the end of 1872. Keppler relaunched *Puck* in 1876, this time to much greater success; it featured lithographed cartoons, and in color, and on top of that was being published on an ambitious weekly schedule. By 1880, *Puck* was a massive success, becoming the benchmark by which all other humor magazines were measured against.
- In 1881, *Judge* debuted, seeking to be the rival to *Puck*. This periodical was founded by former *Puck* artist James A. Wales, and it struggled financially for several years up until the point where politicians realized the power of these cartoons to influence the public. This led the Republican party at the time to help finance W.J. Arkell's purchase of the publication in 1886.
- *Life* arrived in 1883, becoming the third pillar of the comic scene during this era. Though it was priced the same as *Puck* and *Judge*, it was smaller in size and printed in black and white – though that didn't stop it from gaining a significant audience. Its earliest artists included Palmer Cox and Charles Dana Gibson. While *Puck* and *Judge* both altered their content as the world entered the 20th century, *Life* stayed almost exactly the same and maintained its audience better for it.
- On top of magazines, numerous almanacs and other publications rose around this time to start publishing comic art. We also started seeing promotional comics enter the scene during this era – you can learn more about those in our Promotional Comics section of this book.

***Puck** (January 27, 1885 shown) and **Judge** (June 7, 1890 shown) were the top two humor magazine titles of the late 19th century.*

The American Comic Almanac #11
1835 © Charles Ellms, NYC

The Strange and Wonderful Adventures
of Bachelor Butterfly by Rodolphe Töpffer
1870s © Dick & Fitzgerald, NYC

Barker's "Komic" Picture Souvenir, 3rd Edition
1894 © Barker, Moore & Klein Medicine Co.

COLLECTOR'S NOTE: Most of the books listed in this section were published well over a century before organized comics fandom began archiving and helping to preserve these fragile popular culture artifacts. With some of these comics now over 160 years old, they almost never surface in Fine+ or better shape. Be happy when you simply find a copy.

This year has seen price growth in quite a few comic books in this era. Since this section began growing almost a decade now, comic books from Wilson, Brother Jonathan, Huestis & Cozans, Garrett, Dick & Fitzgerald, Frank Leslie, Street & Smith and others continue to be recognized by the more savvy in this fine hobby as legitimate comic book collectors' items. We had been more concerned with simply establishing what is known to exist. For the most part, that work is now a *fait accompli* in this section compiled, revised, and expanded by Robert Beerbohm with special thanks this year to Terrance Keegan plus acknowledgment to Bill Blackbeard, Chris Brown, Alfredo Castelli, Darrell Coons, Leonardo De Sá, Scott Deschaine, Joe Evans, Ron Friggle, Tom Gordon III, Michel Kempeneers, Andy Konkykru, Don Kurtz, Richard Olson, Robert Quesinberry, Joseph Rainone, Steve Rowe, Randy Scott, John Snyder, Art Spiegelman, Steve Thompson, Richard Samuel West, Doug Wheeler and Richard Wright. Special kudos to long-time collector and scholar Gabriel Laderman.

The prices given for Fair, Good and Fine categories are for strictly graded editions. If you need help grading your item, we refer you to the grading section in this book or contact the authors of this essay. Items marked Scarce, Rare or Very Rare we are still trying to figure out how many copies might still be in existence. We welcome additions and corrections from any interested collectors and scholars at feedback@gemstonepub.com.

For ease ascertaining the contents of each item of this listing and the Platinum index list, we offer the following list of categories found immediately following most of the titles:

E - EUROPEAN ORIGINAL COMICS MATERIAL; Printed in Europe or reprinted in USA
G - GRAPHIC NOVEL (LONGER FORMAT COMIC TELLING A SINGLE STORY)
H - "HOW TO DRAW CARTOONS" BOOKS
I - ILLUSTRATED BOOKS NOTABLE FOR THE ARTIST, BUT NOT A COMIC.
M - MAGAZINE / PERIODICAL COMICS MATERIAL REPRINTS
N - NEWSPAPER COMICS MATERIAL REPRINTS
O - ORIGINAL COMIC MATERIAL NOT REPRINTED FROM ANOTHER SOURCE
P - PROMOTIONAL COMIC, EITHER GIVEN AWAY FOR FREE, OR A PREMIUM GIVEN IN CONJUNCTION WITH THE PURCHASE OF A PRODUCT.
S - SINGLE PANEL / NON-SEQUENTIAL CARTOONS

Measurements are in inches. The first dimension given is Height and the second is Width. Some original British editions are included in the section, so as to better explain and differentiate their American counterparts.

ACROBATIC ANIMALS
R.H. Russell: 1899 (9x11-7/8", 72 pgs, B&W, hard-c)

nn (Scarce) 175.00 360.00 725.00
NOTE: *Animal strips by Gustave Verbeck, presented 1 panel per page.*

ALMY'S SANTA CLAUS (P,E)
Edward C. Almy & Co., Providence, R.I.: nd (1880's) (5-3/4x4-5/8", 20 pgs, B&W, paper-c

nn - (Rare) 12.50 40.00 125.00
NOTE: *Department store Christmas giveaway containing an abbreviated 28-panel reprinting of George Cruikshank's* ***The Tooth-ache****. Santa Claus cover.*

AMERICAN COMIC ALMANAC, THE (OLD AMERICAN COMIC ALMANAC 1839-1846)
Charles Ellms: 1831-1846 (5x8, 52 pgs, B&W)

1-First American comic almanac ever prrinted 650.00 1300.00 2700.00
2-16 125.00 210.00 475.00
NOTE:#1 from 1831 is the First American Comic Almanac

AMERICAN PUNCH
American Punch Publishing Co: Jan 1879-March 1881, J.A. Cummings Engraving Co (last 3 issues) (Quarto Monthly)

Most issues 25.00 50.00 175.00

THE AMERICAN WIT
Richardson & Collins, NY: 1867-68 (18-1/2x13. 8 pgs, B&W)

2/3 Frank Bellew single panels 50.00 100.00 250.00

AMERICAN WIT AND HUMOR
Harper & Bros, NY: 1859 (

nn - numerous McLenan sequential comic strips 130.00 260.00 550.00

ATTWOOD'S PICTURES - AN ARTIST'S HISTORY OF THE LAST TEN YEARS OF THE NINETEENTH CENTURY (M,S)
Life Publishing Company, New York: 1900 (11-1/4x9-1/8", 156 pgs, B&W, gilted blue hard-c)

nn - By Attwood 50.00 100.00 200.00
NOTE: *Reprints monthly calendar cartoons which appeared in* ***LIFE****, for 1887 through 1899.*

BACHELOR BUTTERFLY, THE VERITABLE HISTORY OF MR. (E,G)
D. Bogue, London: 1845 (5-1/2x10-1/4", 74 pgs, B&W, gilted hardcover)

nn - By Rodolphe Töpffer (Scarce) 500.00 1250.00 3200.00
nn - Hand colored edition (Very Rare) (no known sales)
NOTE: *This is the British Edition, translated from the re-engraved by Cham serialization found in* ***L'Illustration*** *- a periodical from Paris publisher Dubochet. Predates the first French collected edition. Third Töpffer comic book published in English. The first story page is numbered Page 3. Page 17 shows Bachelor Butterfly being swallowed by a whale.*

BACHELOR BUTTERFLY, THE STRANGE ADVENTURES OF (E,G)
Wilson & Co., New York: 1846 (5-3/8x10-1/8", 68 pgs, B&W, soft-c)

nn - By Rodolphe Töpffer (Very Rare) 600.00 1500.00 3400.00
nn - At least one hand colored copy exists (Very Rare) (no known sales)
NOTE: *2nd Töpffer comic book printed in the U.S., 3rd earliest known sequential comic book in the USA. Reprinted from the British D. Bogue 1845 edition, itself from the earlier French language* ***Histoire de Mr. Cryptogame****. Released the same year as the French Dubochet edition. Two variations known, the earlier printing with Page number 17 placed on the inside (left) bottom corner in error, with slightly later printings corrected to place page number 17 on the outside (right) bottom corner of that page. Another first printing indicator is pages 17 and 20 are printed on the wrong side of the page. For both printings: the first story page is numbered 2. Page 17 shows Bachelor Butterfly already in the whale. In most panels with 3 lines of text, the third line is indented further than the second, which is in turn indented further than the first.*

BACHELOR BUTTERFLY, THE STRANGE ADVENTURES
Brother Jonathan Press, NY: 1854 (5-1/2x10-5/8", 68 pgs, paper-c, B&W) (Very Rare)

nn - By Rodolphe Töpffer 250.00 500.00 1400.00

BACHELOR BUTTERFLY,THE STRANGE & WONDERFUL ADVENTURES OF
Dick & Fitzgerald, New York: 1870s-1888 (various printings 30 Cent cover price, 68 pgs, B&W, paper cover) (all versions Rare) (E,G)

nn - Black print on blue cover (5-1/2x10-1/2"); string bound 150.00 300.00 600.00
nn - Black print on green cover (5-1/2x10-1/2"); string bound 100.00 200.00 475.00
NOTE: *Reprints the earlier Wilson & Co. edition. Page 2 is the first story page. Page 17 shows Bachelor Butterfly already in the whale. In most panels with 3 lines of text, the second and third lines are equally indented in from the first. Unknown which cover (blue or green) is earlier.*

BACHELOR'S OWN BOOK. BEING THE PROGRESS OF MR. LAMBKIN, (GENT.) IN THE PURSUIT OF PLEASURE AND AMUSEMENT (E,O,G)
(See also PROGRESS OF MR. LAMBKIN)
D. Bogue, London: August 1, 1844 (5x8-1/4", 28 pgs printed one side only, cardboard cover & interior) (all versions Rare)

nn - First printing hand colored 225.00 450.00 1000.00
nn - First printing black & white 225.00 450.00 1000.00
NOTE: *First printing has misspellings in the title. "PURSUIT" is spelled "PERSUIT", and "AMUSEMENT" is spelled "AMUSEMEMT".*
nn - Second printing hand colored 225.00 450.00 1000.00
nn - Second printing black & white 225.00 450.00 1000.00
NOTE: Second printing. The misspelling of "PURSUIT" has been corrected, but "AMUSEMEMT" error is still present.
nn - Third printing hand colored No misspellings 225.00 450.00 1000.00
nn - Third printing black & white 225.00 450.00 1000.00
NOTE: *By George Cruikshank. This is the British Edition. Issued both in black & white, and professionally hand-colored editions. Hand-colored editions have survived in higher quantities than uncolored. Originally made with thin paper sheets covering the plates.*

BACHELOR'S OWN BOOK; OR, THE PROGRESS OF MR. LAMBKIN, (GENT.), IN THE PURSUIT OF PLEASURE AND AMUSEMENT, AND ALSO IN SEARCH OF HEALTH AND HAPPINESS, THE (E,O,G)
David Bryce & Son: Glasgow: 1884 (one shilling; 7-5/8 x5-7/8", 62 pgs printed one side only, illustrated hardcover, page edges guilt

nn - Reprints the 1844 edition with altered title 25.00 50.00 150.00
nn - soft cover edition exists 20.00 35.00 70.00

BACHELOR'S OWN BOOK. BEIN-G TWENTY-FOUR PASSAGES IN THE LIFE OF MR. LAMBKIN, GENT. (E,G)
Burgess, Stringer & Co., New York on cover; Carey & Hart, Philadelphia on title page: 1845 (31-1/4 cents, 7-1/2x4-5/8", 52 pgs, B&W, paper cover)

nn - By George Cruikshank (Very Rare) (no known sales)
NOTE: *This is the second known sequential comic book story published in America. Reprints the earlier British edition. Pages printed on one side only. New cover art by an unknown artist.*

BAD BOY'S FIRST READER (O,S)
G.W. Carleton & Co.: 1881 (5-3/4 x 4-1/8", 44 pgs, B&W, paper cover)

nn - By Frank Bellew (Senior) 60.00 125.00 285.00
NOTE: *Parody of a children's ABC primer, one cartoon illustration plus text per page. Includes one panel of Boss Tweed. Frank Bellew is considered the "Father of the American Sequential Comics."*

BALL OF YARN OR, QUEER, QUIANT & QUIZZICAL STORIES, UNRAVELED WITH NEARLY 200 COMIC ENGRAVINGS OF FREAKS, FOLLIES & FOIBLES OF QUEER FOLKS BY THAT PRINCE OF COMICS, ELTON, THE (M)
Philip. J. Cozans, 116 Nassau St, NY: early 1850s (7-1/4x3-1/2", 76 pgs, yellow-wraps)

nn - sequential comic strips plus singles (no known sales)
NOTE: Mose Keyser-r, Jones, Smith & Robinson Goes To A Ball-r; The Adventures of Mr Goliah Starvemouse-r are all sequential comic strips printed in a number of sources

BARKER'S ILLUSTRATED ALMANAC (O,P,S)
Barker, Moore & Mein Medicine Co: 1878-1932+ (36 pgs, B&W, color paper-cr)

1878-1879 (Rare) 60.00 125.00 335.00
NOTE: *Not known yet what the cover art is.*
1880 Farmer Plowing Field-c 50.00 100.00 295.00
1881-1883 (Scarce,7-3/4x6-1/8") *4-mast ships & lighthouse-c* 50.00 100.00 295.00
1884-1889 (8x6-1/4") *Horse & Rider jumping picket fence-c* 50.00 100.00 295.00
1890-1897 (8-1/8x6-1/4") 50.00 100.00 295.00
1898-1899 (7-3/8x5-7/8") 50.00 100.00 295.00
1900+: see the Platinum Age Comics section (7x5-7/8")
NOTE: *Barker's Almanacs were actually issued in November of the year preceding the year which appears on the almanac. For example, the 1878 dated almanac was issued November 1877. They were given away to retailers of Barker's farm animal medicinal products, to in turn be given away to customers. Each Barker's Almanac contains 10 full page cartoons. These frequently included racist stereotypes of blacks. Each cartoon contained advertisements for Barker's products. It is unknown whether the cartoons appeared only in the*

The Comical Adventures of Beau Ogleby
1843 © Tlit & Bogue, London

The Bottle by George Cruikshank
1871 © Geo. Gebbie

Buzz A Buzz Or The Bees By Wilhelm Busch
1873 © Henry Holt And Company, New York

almanacs, or if they also ran as newspaper ads or flyers. Originally issued with a metal hook attached in the upper left hand corner, which could be used to hang the almanac.

BARKER'S "KOMIC" PICTURE SOUVENIR (P,S)
Barker, Moore & Mein Medicine Co: nd (1892-94) (color cardboard cover, B&W interior) (all unnumbered editions Very Rare)

nn - (1892) (1st edition, 6-7/8x10-1/2, 150 pgs) wraparound cover showing people headed towards Chicago for the 1893 World's Fair 285.00 655.00 1450.00
nn - (1893) (2nd edition, ??? pgs) same cover as 1st edition 285.00 655.00 1450.00
nn - (1894) (3rd edition, 180 pgs, 6-3/4x10-3/8") 285.00 655.00 1450.00
NOTE: *New cover art showing crowd of people laughing with a copy of Barker's Almanac.The crowd picture is flanked on both sides by picture of a tall thin person.*
nn - (1894) (4th edition, 124 pgs, 6-3/8x9-3/8") same-c as 3rd edition 260.00 415.00 1150.00
NOTE: *Essentially same-c as 3rd edition, except flanking picture on left edge is now gone. The 2nd through 4th editions state their printing on the first interior page, in the paragraph beneath the picture of the Barker's Building. These have been confirmed as premium comic books, predating the Buster Brown premiums. They reprint advertising cartoons from Barker's Illustrated Almanac. For the 50 page booklets by this same name, numbered as "Part"s, see the PLATINUM AGE SECTION. All "Editions in Parts", without exception, were published after 1900.*

BEAU OGLEBY, THE COMICAL ADVENTURES OF (E,G)
Tilt & Bogue: nd (c1843) (5-7/8x9-1/8", 72 pgs, printed one side only, green gilted hard-c, B&W)

nn - By Rodolphe Töpffer (Rare) 500.00 1000.00 2400.00
nn - Hand coloured edition (Very Rare) (no known sales)
NOTE: *British Edition; no known American Edition. 2nd Töpffer comic book published in English. Translated from Paris publisher Aubert's unauthorized redrawn 1839 bootleg edition of Töpffer's* ***Histoire de Mr. Jabot***. *The back most interior page is an advertisement for* ***Obadiah Oldbuck***, *showing its comic book cover*

BEE, THE
Bee Publishing Co: May 16 1898-Aug 2 1898 (Chromolithographic Weekly)

most issues 50.00 100.00 200.00
8 June Yellow Kid Hearst cover issue 185.00 380.00 775.00

BEFORE AND AFTER. A LOCOFOCO CHRISTMAS PRESENT. (O, C)
D.C. Johnston, Boston: 1837 (4-3/4x3", 1 page, hand colored cardboard)

nn - (Very Rare) by David Claypoole Johnston (sold at auction for $400 in GD)
NOTE: *Pull-tab cartoon envelope, parodying the 1836 New York City mayoral election, picturing the candidate of the Locofoco Party smiling "Before the N.York election", then, when the tab is pulled, picturing him with an angry sneer "After the N.York election".*

BILLY GOAT AND OTHER COMICALITIES, THE (M)
Charles Scribner's Sons: 1898 (6-3/4x8-1/2", 116 pgs., B&W, Hardcover)

nn - By E. W. Kemble 125.00 250.00 660.00

BLACKBERRIES, THE (N.S) (see Coontown's 400)
R. H. Russell: 1897 (9"x12", 76 pgs, hard-c, every other page in color, every other page in one color sepia tone)

nn - By E. W. Kemble 340.00 680.00 2050.00
NOTE: *Tastefully done comics about Black Americana during the USA's Jim Crow days.*

BOOK OF BUBBLES, YE (S)
Endicott & Co., New York: March 1864 (6-1/4 x 9-7/8",160 pgs, guilt-illus. hard-c, B&W

nn - By unknown 150.00 300.00 600.00
NOTE: *Subtitle: A contribution to the New York Fair in aid of the Sanitary Commission; 68 single-sided pages of B&W cartoons, each with an accompanying limerick. A few are sequential.*

BOOK OF DRAWINGS BY FRED RICHARDSON (N,S)
Lakeside Press, Chicago: 1899 (13-5/8x10-1/2", 116 pgs, B&W, hard-c)

nn - 80.00 160.00 360.00
NOTE: *Reprinted from the* ***Chicago Daily News***. *Mostly single panel. Includes one* ***Yellow Kid*** *parody, some Spanish-American War cartoons.*

BOTTLE, THE (E,O) (see also THE DRUNKARD'S CHILDREN, and TEA GARDEN TO TEA POT, and TEMPERANCE TALES; OR, SIX NIGHTS WITH THE WASHINGTONIANS)
D. Bogue, London, with others in later editions: nd (1846) (16-1/2x11-1/2", 16 pgs, printed one side only, paper cover)

D. Bogue, London (nd; 1846): first edition:
nn - Black & white (Scarce) 250.00 450.00 1250.00
nn - Hand colored (Rare) (no known sales)
D. Bogue, London, and Wiley and Putnam, New York (nd; 1847) : second edition, misspells American publisher "Putnam" as "Putman":
nn - Black & white (Scarce) 150.00 300.00 750.00
nn - Hand colored (Rare) (no known sales)
D. Bogue, London, and Wiley and Putnam, New York (nd; 1847) : third edition has "Putnam" spelled correctly.
nn - Black & white (Scarce) 150.00 300.00 750.00
nn - Hand colored (Rare) (no known sales)
D. Bogue, London, Wiley and Putnam, New York, and J. Sands, Sydney, New South Wales: (nd; 1847) : fourth edition with no misspellings
nn - Black & white (Scarce) 150.00 300.00 750.00
nn - Hand colored (Rare) (no known sales)
NOTE: *By George Cruikshank. Temperance/anti-alcohol story. All editions are in precisely identical format. The only difference is to be found on the cover, where it lists who published it. Cover is text only - no cover art.*

BOTTLE, THE HISTORY OF THE
J.C. Becket, 22 Grea St James St, Montreal, Canada: 1851 (9-1/8x6", B&W)

nn - From Engravings by Cruikshank 175.00 325.00 735.00
NOTE: *As published in The Canada Temperance Advocate.*

BOTTLE, THE (E)
W. Tweedie, London: nd (1862) (11-1/2x17-1/3", 16 pgs, printed one side only, paper cover)

nn - Black & white; By George Cruikshank (Scarce) 100.00 200.00 420.00
nn - Hand colored (Scarce) (no known sales)

BOTTLE, THE (E)
Geo. Gebbie, Philadelphia: nd (c.1871) (11-3/8x17-1/8", 42 pgs, tinted interior, hard-c)

nn - By George Cruikshank 100.00 200.00 425.00
NOTE: *New cover art (cover not by Cruikshank).*

BOTTLE, THE (E)
National Temperance, London: nd (1881) (11-1/2x16-1/2", 16 pgs, printed one side only, paper-c, color)

nn - By George Cruikshank 100.00 200.00 425.00
NOTE: *See Platinum Age section for 1900s printings.*

BOTTLE, THE (E)
Marques, Pittsburgh, PA: 1884/85 (6x8", 8 plates, full color, illustrated envelope)

nn - art not by Cruickshank; New Art 75.00 125.00 260.00
NOTE: Says Presented by J.M. Gusky, Dealer in Boots and Shoes

BROAD GRINS OF THE LAUGHING PHILOSOPHER
Dick & Fitzgerald,NY: 1870s

nn - (4) panel sequential strip 25.00 50.00 150.00

BROTHER JONATHAN
Wilson & Co/Benj H Day, 48 Beekman, NYC: 1839-???

July 4 1846 - ads for Obadiah & Butterfly 75.00 125.00 250.00
July 4 1856 catalog list - front cover comic strip 100.00 200.00 400.00
Xmas/New Years 1856 75.00 150.00 300.00
average large size issues 25.00 50.00 100.00
NOTE: has full page advert for Fredinand Flipper comic book116

BULL CALF, THE (P,M)
Various: nd (c1890's) (3-7/8x4-1/8", 16 pgs, B&W, paper-c)

nn - By A.B. Frost Creme Oatmeal Toilet Soap 50.00 75.00 220.00
nn - By A.B. Frost Thompson & Taylor Spice Co, Chicago 50.00 75.00 220.00
NOTE: *Reprints the popular strip story by Frost, with the art modified to place a sign for Creme Oatmeal Soap within each panel. The back cover advertises the specific merchant who gave this booklet away - multiple variations exist.*

BULL CALF AND OTHER TALES, THE (M)
Charles Scribner's Sons: 1892 (120 pgs., 6-3/4x8-7/8", B&W, illus. hard cover)

nn - By Arthur Burdett Frost 50.00 150.00 500.00
NOTE: *Blue, grey, tan hard covers known to exist.*

BULL CALF, THE STORY OF THE MAN OF HUMANITY AND THE (P,M)
C.H. Fargo & Co.: 1890 (5-1/4x6-1/4", 24 pgs, B&W, color paper-c)

nn - By A.B. Frost 50.00 100.00 200.00
NOTE: *Fargo shoe company giveaway; pages alternate between shoe advertisements and the strip story.*

BUSHEL OF MERRY THOUGHTS, A (see Mischief Book, The) (E)
Sampson Low Son & Marsten: 1868 (68 pgs, handcolored hardcover, B&W)

nn - (6-1/4 x 9-7/8", 138 pgs) red binding, publisher's name on title page only; has hand colored interior by publisher 250.00 500.00 1100.00
nn - (6-1/2 x 10", 134 pgs) green binding, publisher's name on cover & title page; has hand colored interior by publisher 250.00 500.00 1100.00
NOTE: *Cover plus story title pages designed by Leighton Brothers, based on Busch art. Translated by Harry Rogers (who is credited instead of Busch). This is a British publication, notable as the earliest known English language anthology collection of Wilhelm Busch comic strips. Page 13 of second story missing from all editions (panel dropped). Unknown which of the two editions was published first. A modern reprint, by Dover in 1971.*

BUTTON BURSTER, THE (M) (says on cover "ten cents hard cash")
M.J. Ivers & Co., 86 Nassau St., New York: 1873 (11x8-1/8", soft paper, B&W)

By various cartoonists (Very Rare) 150.00 300.00 625.00
NOTE: *Reprints from various 1873 issues of Wild Oats; has (5) different sequential comic strips: (3) by Livingston Hopkins, (1) by Thomas Worth, other one creator presently unknown; Bellew, Sr. single panel cartoons.*

BUZZ A BUZZ OR THE BEES (E)
Griffith & Farran, London: September 1872 (8-1/2x5-1/2", 168 pgs, printed one side only, orange, black & white hardcover, B&W interior)

nn - By Wilhelm Busch (Scarce) 112.00 225.00 550.00
NOTE: *Reprint published by Phillipson & Golder, Chester; text written by English to accompany Busch art.*

BUZZ A BUZZ OR THE BEES (E)
Henry Holt & Company, New York: 1873 (9x6", 96 pgs, gilted hardcover, hand colored)

nn - By Wilhelm Busch (Scarce) 125.00 250.00 550.00
NOTE: *Completely different translation than the Griffith & Farran version. Also, contains 28 additional illustrations by Park Benjamin. The lower page count is because the Henry Holt edition prints on both sides of each page, and the Griffith & Farran edition is printed one side only.*

CALENDAR FOR THE MONTH; YE PICTORIAL LYSTE OF YE MATTERS OF INTEREST FOR SUMMER READING (P,M)
S.E. Bridgman & Company, Northampton, Mass: nd (c. late 1880's-1890's)

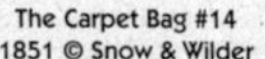

The Carpet Bag #14
1851 © Snow & Wilder

Centennial Fun (Keppler cover)
July 1876 © Frank Leslie

Comic Monthly v6 #8
March 1865 © J.C.Haney, NY

FR1.0 GD2.0 FN6.0

(5-5/8x7-1/4", 64 pgs, paper-c, B&W)
nn - (Very Rare) T.S. Sullivant-c/a 125.00 250.00 500.00
NOTE: *Book seller's catalog, with every other page reprinting cartoons and strips (from Life??). Art by: Chips Bellew, Gibson, Howarth, Kemble, Sullivant, Townsend, Woolf.*

CARICATURE AND OTHER COMIC ART
Harper & Brothers, NY: 1877 (9-5/16x7-1/8", 360 pgs, B&W, green hard-c)
nn - By James Parton (over 200 illustrations) 30.00 60.00 275.00
NOTE: *This is the earliest known serious history of comics & related genre from around the world produced by an American. Parton was a cousin of Thomas Nast's wife Sarah. A large portion of this book was first serialized in* ***Harper's Monthly*** *in 1875.*

CARPET BAG, THE
Snow & Wilder, later Wilder & Pickard, Boston: March 21 1851-March 26 1853
Each average issue 25.00 50.00 100.00
Samuel "Mark Twain" Clemmons issues (first app in print) 800.00 1500.00 3500.00
NOTE: *Many issues contain cartoons by DC Johnston, Frank Bellew, others; literature includes Artemus Ward's Miss Partington who had a mischevious little Katzenjammer Kids-like brat. Carpet Bag was not considered derogatory pre-Civil War.*

CARROT-POMADE (O.G)
James G. Gregory, Publisher, New York: 1864 (9x6-7/8", 36 pgs, B&W)
nn - By Augustus Hoppin 75.00 150.00 300.00
NOTE: *The story of a quack remedy for baldness, sequentially told in the format parodying ABC primers. Has protective tissue pages (not part of page count).*

CARTOONS BY HOMER C. DAVENPORT (M,N,S)
De Witt Publishing House: 1898 (16-1/8x12", 102 pgs, hard-c, B&W)
nn 100.00 200.00 425.00
NOTE: *Reprinted from Harper's Weekly and the New York Journal. Includes cartoons about the Spanish-American War. Title page reads "Davenport's Cartoons".*

CARTOONS BY WILL E. CHAPIN (P,N,S)
The Times-Mirror Printing and Binding House, Los Angeles: 1899 (15-1/4x12", 98 pgs, hard-c, B&W)
nn - scarce 100.00 200.00 425.00
NOTE: *Premium item for subscribing to the Los-Angeles Times-Mirror newspaper, from which these cartoons were reprinted. Includes cartoons about the Spanish-American War.*

CARTOONS OF OUR WAR WITH SPAIN (N,S)
Frederick A. Stokes Company: 1898 (11-1/2x10", 72 pgs, hardcover, B&W)
nn - By Charles Nelan (r-New York Herald) 40.00 100.00 200.00
nn - 2nd printing noted on copy right page 30.00 60.00 120.00

CARTOONS OF THE WAR OF 1898 (E,M,N,S)
Belford, Middlebrook & Co., Chicago: 1898 (7x10-3/8",190 pgs, B&W, hard-c)
nn 50.00 100.00 210.00
NOTE: *Reprints single panel editorial cartoons on the Spanish-American War, from American, Spanish, Latino, and European newspapers and magazines, at rate of 2 to 6 cartoons per page. Art by Bart, Berryman, Bowman, Bradley, Chapin, Gillam, Nelan, Tenniel, others.*

CENTENNIAL FUN (O,S) (Rare)
Frank Leslie, Philadelphia: (July) 1876 (25¢, 11x8", 32 pgs, paper cover, B&W)
nn - By Joseph Keppler-c/a;Thomas Worth-a 175.00 350.00 725.00
NOTE: *Issued for the 1876 Centennial Exposition in Philadelphia. Exists with both black & white, and orange, black & white covers. One copy of the latter had an embossed newstand label from Partland, Maine, implying that the orange cover version, at least, was distributed and sold outside of Philadelphia.*

CHAMPAIGNE
Frank Leslie: June-Dec 1871
1-7 scarce 150.00 225.00 400.00

CHIC
Chic Publishing Co: 1880-81 (Chromolithographic Weekly)
1-38 Livingston Hopkins, Charles Kendrick, CW Weldon 75.00 150.00 325.00

CHILDREN'S CHRISTMAS BOOK, THE
The New York Sunday World: 1897 (10-1/4x8-3/4", 16 pgs, full color)
Dec 12, 1897 - By George Luks, G.H. Grant, Will Crawford, others) (Rare)
75.00 125.00 325.00

CHIP'S DOGS (M)
R.H. Russell and Son Publishers: 1895 hardcover, B&W)
nn - By Frank P. W. "Chip" Bellew 25.00 50.00 100.00
Early printing 80 pgs, 8-7/8x11-7/8"; dark green border of hardcover surrounds all four sides of pasted on cover image; pages arranged in error -- see NOTE below. (more scarce)
nn - By Frank P. W. "Chip" Bellew 12.50 25.00 50.00
Later printing 72 pgs, 8-7/8x11-3/4";green border only on the binding side (one side) of the cover image.
NOTE: *Both are strip reprints from* ***LIFE***. *The difference in page count is due to more blank pages in the first printing -- all printings have the same comics contents, but with the pages in the first printing arranged differently. This is noticeable particularly in the 2-page strip "Getting a Pointer", which appears on the 2nd & 3rd to last pages of the later printings, but in the early printing the first half of this strip is near the middle of the book, while the last half appears on the 2nd to last story page.*

CHIP'S OLD WOOD CUTS (M,S)
R.H. Russell & Son: 1895 (8-7/8x11-3/4", 72 pgs, hardcover, B&W)
nn - By Frank P. W. ("Chip") Bellew 30.00 60.00 120.00
nn - 1897 reprint 15.00 30.00 60.00

CHIP'S UN-NATURAL HISTORY (O,S)

FR1.0 GD2.0 FN6.0

Frederick A. Stokes & Brother: 1888 (7x5-1/4", 64 pgs, hardcover, B&W)
nn - By Frank P. W. ("Chip") Bellew 12.50 25.00 50.00
NOTE: *Title page lists publisher as "Successors to White, Stokes & Allen."*

CLOWN, OR THE BANQUET OF WIT, THE (E,M,O)
Fisher & Brother, Philadelphia, Baltimore, New York, Boston: nd (c.1851) (7-3/8x4-1/2", 88 pgs, paper cover, B&W)
nn - (Very Rare; 3 known copies) 675.00 1300.00 2800.00
NOTE: *Earliest known multi-artist anthology of sequential comics; contains multiple sequential comics, plus numerous single panel cartoons. A mixture of reprinted and original material, involving both European and American artists. "Jones, Smith, and Robinson Goes to a Ball" by Richard Doyle (1st app. of Doyle's "Foreign Tour" in America, reprinted from PUNCH, August 24, 1850); "Moses Keyser The Bowery Bully's Trip to the Californian Gold Mines", by John H. Manning; "The Adventures of Mr. Gulp" (by the Read brothers?); more comics by artists unknown; cartoons by George Cruikshank, Grandville, Elton.*

COLD CUTS AND PICKLED EELS' FEET; DONE BROWN BY JOHN BROWN
P.J. Cozans, New York: nd (c1855-60) (B&W)
nn - (Very Rare) 100.00 200.00 300.00
NOTE: *Mostly a children's book. But, pages 87 to 110, and 111 to 122, contain narrative sequential stories.*

COLLEGE SCENES (O,G)
N. Hayward, Boston: 1850 (5x6-3/4", 72 pgs, printed one side only, B&W lithography)
nn - (Rare) by Nathan Hayward 200.00 400.00 750.00
NOTE: *This is the 2nd such production for an American University; the first issued at Yale circa 1845, decent funny art of story about life of a Harvard student from his entrance thru graduation entirely in caricature. Has art on back cover as well.*

COLLEGE CUTS Chosen From The Columbia Spectator 1880-81-82 (S)
White & Stokes, NY: 1882 (8x9-5/8", 92 pgs, B&W)
By F. Benedict Herzog, H. McVickar, W. Bard McVickar, others 25.00 55.00 125.00
nn - 2nd edition reprint (1888) (8-1/4x10-3/8) 10.00 20.00 50.00

COMICAL COONS (M)
R.H. Russell: 1898 (8-7/8 x 11-7/8", 68 pgs, hardcover, B&W)
nn - By E. W. Kemble 400.00 800.00 1600.00
NOTE: *Black Americana collection of 2-panel stories.*

COMICAL ALMANAC
Anton Bicker, Cinncinati, OH: 1885 (9x6, 260 pgs, B&W, illustrated-c)
nn - two (12) page sequential Busch comic strips 50.00 100.00 275.00

COMIC ALMANAC, THE
John Berger. Baltimore: 1854-? (7-1/2x6-1/4, 36 pgs, B&W)
nn - 65.00 125.00 275.00

COMIC ANNUAL, AMERICAN (O,I)
Richardson, Lord, & Holbrook, Boston: 1831 (6-7/8x4-3/8", 268 pgs, B&W, hard-c)
nn - (Scarce) 160.00 320.00 675.00
NOTE: *Mostly text; front & back cover illustrations, 13 full page, and scattered smaller illustrations by David Claypoole Johnston; edited by Henry J. Finn.*

COMIC HISTORY OF THE UNITED STATES, (I)
Carleton & Co., NY: 1876 (6-7/8x5-1/8", 336 pgs, hardcover, B&W)
nn - By Livingston Hopkins. 25.00 50.00 100.00
2nd printing: Cassell, Petter, Galpin & Co.: 1880 (6-7/8x5-1/8", 336 pgs, hardcover, B&W)
nn - By Livingston Hopkins. 25.00 50.00 100.00
NOTE: *Text with many B&W illustrations; some are multi-panel comics. Not to beconfused with* ***Bill Nye's Comic History Of The U.S.*** *which contains Frederick Opper illustrations.*

COMIC MONTHLY, THE
J.C. Haney, N.Y.: March 1859-1880 (16 x 11-1/2", 30 pgs average, B&W)
Certain average issues with sequential comics 50.00 100.00 225.00
11 (Jan 1860) Bellew-c 25.00 50.00 110.00
v2#2 (Apr 1860) Bellew-c 25.00 50.00 110.00
v2#3 (May 1860) Bellew-c 25.00 50.00 110.00
v2#4 (June 1860) Comic Strip Cover 50.00 100.00 225.00
v2#5 (July 1860) Bellew-c; (12) panel Explaining American Politics To An Intelligent Foreigner; (10) panel The Art of Stump Speaking; (15) panel Mr. Dibbs Goes to Pike's Peak and Comes Back Again 125.00 250.00 525.00
v2#7 (Sept 1860) Comic Strip Cover; (24) panel double page spread The Prince of Wales In America 50.00 100.00 225.00
v2#8 (18) panel The Three Young Friends Sillouette Strip 25.00 50.00 110.00
v2#9 (Nov 1860) (9) panel sequential 25.00 50.00 110.00
v2#10 11 not indexed 25.00 50.00 110.00
v2#12 (Jan 1861) (12) panel double page spread 25.00 50.00 110.00

COMIC TOKEN FOR 1836, A COMPANION TO THE COMIC ALMANAC, THE
Charles Ellms, Boston: 1836 (8x5', 48 pgs, B&W)
nn - 50.00 100.00 225.00

COMIC WEEKLY, THE
???, NYC: 1881-???
issues with comic strips (Chips, etc) 60.00 125.00 250.00

COMIC WORLD
???: 1876-1879 (Quarto Monthly)
issues with comic strips 37.50 75.00 150.00

Comics From Scribner's Magazine
1891 © Scribner's

The Daily Graphic #158
Sept. 4, 1873 © The Graphic Company, NY

Elton's Californian Comic All-My-Nack #17
1850 © Elton's, NY

FR1.0 GD2.0 FN6.0

FR1.0 GD2.0 FN6.0

COMICS FROM SCRIBNER'S MAGAZINE (M)
Scribner's: nd (1891) (10 cents, 9-1/2x6-5/8", 24 pgs, paper cover, side stapled, B&W)

nn - (Rare) F.M.Howarth C&A 175.00 350.00 725.00

NOTE: *Advertised in SCRIBNER'S MAGAZINE in the June 1891 issue, page 793, as available by mail order for 10 cents. Collects together comics material which ran in the back pages of Scribner's Magazine. Art by Attwood, "Chip" Bellew, Dōes, Frost, Gibson, Zim.*

COMUS OFFERING CONTAINING HUMOROUS SCRAPS OF DIVERTING COMICALITIES, THE (O, S)
B. Franklin Edmands, 25 Court St, Boston: c1830-31 (8-7/8x10-3/4", 16 pgs, thin brown paper-c, blank on backs,

nn - (William F Straton, Engraver, 15 Water St, Boston) (no known sales)

NOTE: All hand-colored single panel cartoons format definitely inspired by D.C. Johnston's Scraps with every panel character using well-defined word balloons. Might become a seminal step in the evolution of the American comic book. More research is needed.

CONTRASTS AND CONCEITS FOR CONTEMPLATION BY LUKE LIMNER (O)
Ackerman & Co, 96 Strand, London: c1848 (9-3/4x6-1/4, 48 pgs, B&W)
nn - By John Leighton 60.00 110.00 210.00

COONTOWN'S 400 (M) (see **Blackberries**) (M)
The Life (Magazine) Co.: 1899 (10-15/16x8-7/8, 68 pgs, cloth light-brown hard-c, B&W

nn - By E.W. Kemble (scarce) 400.00 650.00 2000.00

NOTE: *Tastefully drawn depictions of Black Americana over one hundred years ago during Jim Crow days.*

CROSSING THE ATLANTIC (O,G)
James R. Osgood & Co., Boston: 1872 (10-7/8x16", 68 pgs, hardcover, B&W);
Houghton, Osgood & Co., Boston: 1880

1st printing - by Augustus Hoppin 50.00 100.00 200.00
2nd printing (1880; 66 pgs; 8-1/8x11-1/8") 32.50 65.00 150.00

C.R. PITT'S COMIC ALMANAC
C.R. Pitt: 1880 (7-1/2x4-5/8", 28 pgs)

nn - contains (8) panel sequential 50.00 100.00 200.00

CRUIKSHANK'S OMNIBUS: A VEHICLE FOR FUN AND FROLIC (E,S)
E. Ferrett & Co., Philadelphia: 1845 (25 cents, 7-1/2" x 4-5/8", 96 pgs, B&W, paper-c)

nn - By George Cruikshank c/a (Very Rare) 160.00 320.00 825.00

NOTE: *Mostly prose, with 10 plates of cartoons printed on one-side (about half the plates with multiple cartoons), plus illustrated cover, all by George Cruikshank. First (perhaps only) American printing of Cruikshank's Omnibus, which was published first in Britain. It is only a partial reprinting.*

CYCLISTS' DICTIONARY (S)
Morgan & Wright, Chicago: 1894 (5 x3-3/4, 80 pgs, soft-c, B&W

nn - By Unknown 37.50 75.00 150.00

THE DAILY GRAPHIC
The Graphic Company, 39 Park Place, NY: 1873-Sept 23, 1889 (14x20-1/2, 8 pgs, B&W)

Average issues with comic strips 15.00 20.00 40.00
Average issues without comic strips 10.00 15.00 30.00

DAVY CROCKETT'S COMIC ALMANACK
???, Nashville, TN, then elsewhere: 1835-end (32 pages plus wraps)

1 600.00 1150.00 2400.00
2-13 15 end 275.00 550.00 1200.00
14 contains (17) panel Crocket comic strip bio 1848 1050.00 1600.00 3300.00

DAY'S DOINGS (was The Last Sensation) (Becomes New York Illustrated Times)
James Watts, NYC: #1 June 6 1868-early 1876 (11x16, 16 pgs, B&W)

average issue with comic strips 10.00 15.00 25.00
Paul Pry & Alley Sloper character issues 25.00 50.00 100.00
Aug 19 1871 - First Alley Sloper in America?? 50.00 100.00 200.00

NOTE: *James Watts was a shadow company for Frank Leslie; outright sold to Frank Leslie in 1873. There are a lot of issues with comic strips from 1868 up.*

DAY'S SPORT - OR, HUNTING ADVENTURES OF S. WINKS WATTLES, A SHOPKEEPER, THOMAS TITT, A "LEGAL GENT," AND MAJOR NICHOLAS NOGGIN, A JOLLY GOOD FELLOW GENERALLY, A (O)
Brother Jonathan, NY: c1850s (5-7/8x8-1/4, 44 pgs)

nn - By Henry L. Stephens, Philadelphia (Very Rare) (no known sales)

DEVIL'S COMICAL OLDMANICK WITH COMIC ENGRAVINGS OF THE PRINCIPAL EVENTS OF TEXAS, THE
Turner & Fisher, NY & Philadelphia: 1837 (7-7/8x5", 24 pgs)

nn - many single panel cartoons 125.00 250.00 550.00

DIE VEHME, ILLUSTRIRTES WOCHENBLATT FUR SCHERZ UND ERNEST (M,O)
Heinrich Binder, St. Louis: No.1 Aug 28, 1869 - No.?? Aug 20, 1870 (10 cents, 8 pgs, B&W, paper-c) (see also PUCK)

1-?? (Very Rare) by Joseph Keppler 100.00 210.00 425.00

NOTE: *Joseph Keppler's first attempt at a weekly American humor periodical. Entirely in German. The title translates into: "The Star Chamber: An Illustrated Weekly Paper in Fun and Ernest".*

DOMESTIC MANNERS OF THE AMERICANS
The Imprint Society, Barre, Mass: 1969 (9-3/4 x 7-1/4", 390 pgs, hard-c in slipcase, B&W)

nn - 15.00 25.00 60.00

NOTE: *Reprints the 1832 edition of this book by Mrs. Trollope with an added insert. The 28-page insert is what is of primary interest to us -- it reproduces SCRAPS No. 4 (1833) by D.C. Johnston.*

DRUNKARD'S CHILDREN, THE (see also THE BOTTLE) (E,O)
David Bogue, London; John Wiley and G.P. Putnam, New York; J. Sands, Sydney, New South Wales: July 1, 1848 (16x11", 16 pgs, printed on one side only, paper-c)

nn - Black & white edition (Scarce) 400.00 850.00 1250.00
nn - Hand colored edition (Rare) (no known sales)

NOTE: *Sequel story to THE BOTTLE, by George Cruikshank. Temperance/anti-alcohol story. British-American-Australian co-publication. Cover is text only - no cover art.*

DRUNKARD'S PROGRESS, OR THE DIRECT ROAD TO POVERTY, WRETCHEDNESS & RUIN, THE
J. W. Barber, New Haven, Conn.: Sept 1826 (single sheet)

nn - By John Warner Barber (Very Rare) (no known sales)

NOTE: *Broadside designed and printed by barber contains four large wood engravings showing "The Morning Dram" which is "The Beginning of Sorrow"; "The Grog Shop" with its "Bad Company"; "The Confirmed Drunkard" in a state of "Beastly Intoxication"; and the "Concluding Scene" with the family being drive off to the alms house. It is an interesting set of cuts, faintly reminiscent of Hogarth. Many modern reprints exist.*

DUEL FOR LOVE, A (O,P)
E.C. DeWitt & Co., Chicago: nd (c1880's) (3-3/8" x 2-5/8", 12 pgs, B&W, paper-c)

nn - Art by F.M. Howarth (Rare) 25.00 50.00 125.00

NOTE: *Advertising giveaway for DeWitt's Little Early Risers, featuring an 8-panel strip story, spread out 1 panel per page.*

DURHAM WHIFFS (O, P)
Blackwells Durham Tobacco Co: Jan 8 1878 (9x6.5", 8 pgs, color-c, B&W)

v1 #1 w/Trade Card Insert 150.00 250.00 600.00

NOTE: Sold in 2008 CGC 9.4 $1250

DYNALENE LAFLETS (P)
The Dynalene Company: nd (3 x 3-1/2", 16 pgs, B&W, paper cover)

nn - Dynalene Dyes promo (9) panel comic strip 25.00 50.00 75.00

ELEPHANT, THE
William H Graham, Tribune Building, NYC: Jan 22 1848-Feb 19 1848 (11x8.5", B&W)

1-5 Rare - single panel cartoons 175.00 325.00 675.00

ELTON'S COMIC ALL-MY-NACK (E,O.S)
Elton, Publisher, 18 Division & 98 Nassau St, NY: 1833-1852 (7-1/2x4-1/2", 36pgs, B&W

1-5 99% single panel cartoons 100.00 200.00 425.00
6 (1839) 100.00 200.00 425.00

NOTE: Two different covers & different interiors exist for this title and number

7-15 - 99% single panel cartoons 100.00 200.00 400.00
16 - contains 6 panel "A Tales of A Tayl-or" 1848-49 200.00 400.00 675.00
17 - contains "Moses Keyser, The Bowery Bully's Trip To the California Gold Mines" 1850
By John H. Manning, early comics creator, told in 15 panels 200.00 400.00 675.00
18-19 presently unknown contents 100.00 200.00 425.00

NOTE: *Contains both original American, and pirated European, cartoons. All single panel material, except where noted. Almanacs are published near the end of the year prior to that for which they are printed -- like calendars today. Thus, the 1833 No. 1 issue was really published in the last months of 1832. #17 has Elton's Californian Comic-All-My-Nack on the cover.*

ELTON'S COMIC ALMANAC (Publsiher change)
GW Cottrell & Co, Publishers & C Cornhill, Boston, Mass: 1853 (7-7/8x4-5/8,36pgs,B&W

20 - (2) sequential comic strips (9) panel "Jones, Smith and Robinson Goes To A Ball;
(21) panel "The Adventures of Mr. Gulp" Rare 400.00 800.00 1600.00

NOTE: *Both strips appear in* The Clown, Or The Banquet of Wit

ELTON'S FUNNY ALMANACK (title change to Almanac)
Elton Publisher and Engraver, New York: 1846 (8x6-1/2", 36 pgs)

1 50.00 100.00 225.00

ELTON'S FUNNY ALMANAC (#1 titled Almanack)
Elton & Co, New York: 1847-1853 (8x6-1/4, 36 pgs, B&W)

2 (1847) #3 (1848) 50.00 100.00 225.00
nn 1853 (8-1/8x4-7/8"; (5) panel comic strip "The Adventures of Mr. Goliah Starvemouse"

ELTON'S RIPSNORTER COMIC ALMANAC
Elton, 90 Nassau St, NY: 1850 (8x5, 24 pgs, B&W, paper-c)

nn - scarce 50.00 100.00 250.00

ENGLISH SOCIETY (S)
Harper & Brothers, Publishers, New York: 1897 (9-5/8x12-1/4", 206 pgs, B&W)

nn - by George Du Maurier 50.00 75.00 110.00

ENGLISH SOCIETY AT HOME (S)
James R. Osgood and Company: 1881 (10-7/8x8-5/8, 182 pgss, protective sheets on some pages - not included in pages count, hard-c, B&W 50.00 75.00 110.00

nn - by George Du Maurier

ENTER: THE COMICS (E,G)
University of Nebraska Press: 1965 (6-7/8x9-1/4", 120 pgs, hard-c)

nn - By Ellen Weisse 25.00 50.00 100.00

NOTE: *Contains overview of Töpffer's life and career plus only published English translation of Töpffer's Monsieur Crepin (1837); appears to have been re-drawn by Weisse in the days before xerox machines.*

ESQUIRE BROWN AND HIS MULE, STORY OF
A.C. Meyer, Baltimore, Maryland: 1880s (5x3/7/8", 28 pgs, B&W)

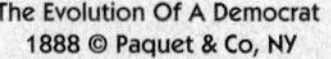

The Evolution Of A Democrat
1888 © Paquet & Co, NY

Flying Leaves
1880s © E.R. Herrick & Company, New York

The Fools Paradise Mirth and Fun
For Old and Young
1883 © E.P. Dutton & Co, NYC

FR1.0 GD2.0 FN6.0

Booklet (9 panel story plus cough remedies catalog) 40.00 80.00 160.00
Fold-Out of Booklet (9 panel version) 40.00 80.00 160.00

"EVENTS OF THE WEEK" REPRINTED FROM THE CHICAGO TRIBUNE
Henry O. Shepard Co, Chicago: 1894 (5-3/8x15-7/8", 110 pg, B&W, hard-c)
First Series, Second Series - By HR Heaton 37.50 75.00 150.00

EVERYBODY'S COMICK ALMANACK
Turner & Fisher, NY & Philadelphia: 1837 (7-7/8x5", 36 pgs, B&W)
nn 50.00 100.00 220.00

EVOLUTION OF A DEMOCRAT - A DARWINIAN TALE, THE (O,G)
Paquet & Co., New York: 1888 (25 cents, 7-7/8x5-1/2", 100 pgs, printed one side only, orange paper cover, B&W) (Very Rare)
nn - Written by Henry Liddell, art by G. Roberty 400.00 800.00 1600.00
NOTE: *Political parody about the rise of an Irishman through Tammany Hall. Grover Cleveland appears as linked with Tammany. Ireland becomes the next state in the USA.*

FABLES FOR THE TIMES (S, I)
R.H. Russell & Son, New York: 1896 (9-1/8x12-1/8", 52 pgs, yellow hard-c)
nn - By H.W. Phillips and T.S. Sullivant Scarce 75.00 150.00 300.00

FERDINAND FLIPPER, ESQ., THE FORTUNES OF (O,G)
Brother Jonathan, Publisher, NY: nd (1851) (5-3/4 x 9-3/8", 84 pgs, B&W, printed both sides)
nn - By Various (Very Rare) 700.00 1200.00 3450.00
NOTE: *Extended title: "...Commencing With A Period of Four Months And Anterior To His Birth Going Thru The Various Stages of His Infancy, Childhood, Verdant Years, Manhood, Middle Life, and Green and Ripe Old Age, And Ending A Short Time Subsequent to His Sudden Decease With His Final Exit, Funeral And Burial." Extremely unique comic book, put together by gathering 145 independent single illustrations and cartoons, by various artists, and stringing them together into a sequential story. The majority of panels are by Grandville. Also included are at least 19 signed Charles Martin, reprinted from 1847 issues of Yankee Doodle, 5 panels from D.C. Johnston, plus other panels by F.O.C. Darley, T.H. Matheson, and others. The story also contains several panels of Gold Rush content . Printed by E.A. Alverds. The 1851 date is derived from an advertisement found in the Oct-Dec 1851 issue of the Brother Jonathan newspaper. It ispossible, however, that it actually came out even earlier.*

FERDINAND FLIPPER, ESQ., THE FORTUNES OF (G)
Dick & Fitzgerald, New York: nd (1870's to 1888) (30 Cents, 84 pgs, B&W, paper cover)
nn - (Very Rare reprint - several editions possible) 375.00 750.00 1800.00

FINN'S COMIC ALMANAC
Marsh, Capen, & Lyon; Boston: 1835-??? (4.5x7.5, 36 pgs, B&W)
nn 90.00 175.00 350.00

FINN'S COMIC SKETCHBOOK (S)
Peabody & Co., 223 Broadway, NY: 1831 (10-1/2x16", 12 pgs, B&W)
nn - By Henry J. Finn (Very Rare) (no known sales)
NOTE: *Designs on copper plates; etched by J. Harris, NY; should have tissue paper in front of each plate.*

50 GREAT CARTOONS (M,P,S)
Ram's Horn Press: 1899 (14x10-3/4, 112 pgs, hard-c)
nn - By Frank Beard 30.00 60.00 125.00
NOTE: *Premium in return for a subscription to **The Ram's Horn** magazine.*

FISHER'S COMIC ALMANAC
Ames Fisher and Brother, No 12 North Sixth St, Philadelphia , Charles Small in NYC, Also in Boston: 1841-1868 (4-1/2 x 7-1/4, 36 pgs, B&W)
1-7 (1841-1847) 125.00 250.00 450.00
12 reprints mermaid-c with word balloon (1868) 125.00 250.00 450.00

F**** A*** K*****, OUTLINES ILLUSTRATIVE OF THE JOURNAL OF** (O,S)
D.C. Johnston, Boston: 1835 (9-5/16 x 6", 12 pgs, printed one side only, blue paper cover, B&W interior) (see also **SCRAPS**)
nn - by David Claypoole Johnston (Scarce) 650.00 1100.00 1800.00
NOTE: *This is a series of 8 plates parodying passages from the Journal of Fanny (Frances) A. Kemble, a British woman who wrote a highly negative book about American Culture after returning from the U.S. Though remembered now for her campaign against slavery, she was prejudiced against most everything American culture, thus inspiring Johnston's satire. Contains 4 protective sheets (not part of page count.)*

FLYING DUTCHMAN; OR, THE WRATH OF HERR VONSTOPPELNOZE, THE (E)
Carleton Publishing, New York: 1862 (7-5/8x5-1/4", 84 pgs, printed on one side only, gilted hardcover, B&W)
nn - By Wilhelm Busch (Scarce) 35.00 70.00 160.00
nn - 1975 Scarce 100 copy-r 74 pgs Visual Studies Workshop 5.00 10.00 20.00
NOTE: *This is the earliest known English language book publication of a Wilhelm Busch work. The story is plagiarized by American poet John G. Saxe, who is credited with the text, while the uncredited Busch cartoons are described merely as accompanying illustrations.*

FLYING LEAVES (E)
E.R. Herrick & Company, New York: nd (c1889/1890's) (8-1/4" x 11-1/2", 76 pgs, B&W interior, orange, b&w hard-c)
nn- (Scarce) 85.00 175.00 260.00
NOTE: *Reprints strips and single panel cartoons from 1888 Fliegende Blatter issues, translated into English. Various artists, including Bechstein, Adolf Hengeler, Lothar Meggendorfer, Emil Reinicke.*

FOOLS PARADISE WITH THE MANY ADVENTURES THERE AS SEEN IN THE STRANGE SURPRISING PEEP SHOW OF PROFESSOR WOLLEY COBBLE, THE (E) (see also THE COMICAL PEEP SHOW)
John Camden Hotten, London: Nov 1871 (1 crown, 9-7/8x7-3/8", 172 pgs, printed one side only, gilted green hardcover, hand colored interior)
nn - By Wilhelm Busch (Rare) 500.00 1000.00 2100.00
NOTE: *Title on cover is: **WALK IN! WALK IN!! JUST ABOUT TO BEGIN!!! the FOOLS PARADISE**; below the above title page. Anthology of Wilhelm Busch comics, translated into English.*

FOOLS PARADISE WITH THE MANY WONDERFUL SIGHTS AS SEEN IN THE STRANGE SURPRISING PEEP SHOW OF PROFESSOR WOLLEY COBBLE, FURTHER ADVENTURES IN (E)
Chatto & Windus, London: 1873 (10x7-3/8", 128 pgs, printed one side only, brown hardcover, hand colored interior)
nn - By Wilhelm Busch (Rare) 400.00 800.00 1700.00
NOTE: *Sequel to the 1871 **FOOLS PARADISE**, containing a completely different set of Busch stories, translated into English.*

FOOLS PARADISE MIRTH AND FUN FOR THE OLD & YOUNG (E)
Griffith & Farran, London: May 1883 (9-3/4x7-5/8", 78 pgs, color cover, color interior)
nn - By Wilhelm Busch (Rare) 110.00 225.00 525.00
NOTE: *Collection of selected stories reprinted from both the 1871 & 1873 **FOOLS PARADISE**.*

FOOLS PARADISE - MIRTH AND FUN FOR THE OLD & YOUNG (E)
E.P. Dutton and Co., NY: May 1883 (9-3/4x7-5/8", 78 pgs, color cover, color interior)
nn - By Wilhelm Busch (Rare) 100.00 200.00 470.00
NOTE: *Collection of selected stories reprinted from both the 1871 & 1873 **FOOLS PARADISE**.*

FOREIGN TOUR OF MESSRS. BROWN, JONES, AND ROBINSON, THE (see Messrs....)

FRANK LESLIE'S BOYS AND GIRLS
Frank Leslie, NYC: Oct 13 1866-#905 Feb 9 1884
average issue with comic strip 20.00 30.00 50.00

FRANK LESLIE'S BUDGET OF FUN
Frank Leslie, Ross & Tousey, 121 Nassau St, NYC: Jan 1859-1878 (newspaper size)
1-5 no comic strips 50.00 100.00 275.00
6 June 1859 (9) panel "The Wonderful Hunting Tour of Mr Borridge After the Deer" 75.00 150.00 450.00
7-9 no comic strips 25.00 50.00 130.00
10 Sept 1859 sequential comic strip 50.00 100.00 260.00
11 (8) panel sequential "Apropos of the Great Eastern" 50.00 100.00 260.00
12-14 25.00 50.00 130.00
15 Feb 1860 (12) panel "The Ballet Girl" strip 50.00 100.00 250.00
16-18 25.00 50.00 130.00
19 June 1860 comic strip front cover 100.00 200.00 420.00
NOTE: Cover is (11) panel "The Very Latest Fashionable Amusement..."; Back cover comic strip "Mr Jogg's Reasons For Preferring to Board to Keeping House" (7) panels using word balloons. Plus centerfold double page (18) panel spread "The New York May, Moving in General, and Mrs. Grundy's In Particular."
20 24 25 no comic strips 25.00 50.00 130.00
21 (7/15/60) (8) panel Mr Septimus Verdilater Visits the Baltimore Convention" 50.00 100.00 275.00
22 (8/1/60) (3) panel 25.00 50.00 130.00
23 (8/15/60) (12) panel "Superb Scheme For Perfecting of Dramatic Entertainment" 50.00 100.00 275.00
25 (9/15/60 (9) panel sequential 25.00 50.00 130.00
27 AbrahamLincoln Word Balloon cover 50.00 100.00 275.00
28 Wilhelm Busch sequential strip-r begin 50.00 100.00 275.00
29, 31-51 25.00 50.00 130.00
30 (12/15/60) (3) panel sequential strip 25.00 50.00 130.00
31 (Jan 1861) (12) panel The Boarding School Miss 25.00 50.00 130.00
32 (Feb 1861) (10) panel Telegraphic Horrors; Or, Mr Buchanan Undergoing A Series of Electric Shocks 50.00 100.00 275.00
35 (4/1/61) Abraham Lincoln Word Balloon cover 50.00 100.00 275.00
43 44 no sequential comic strips 25.00 50.00 130.00
45 (Nov 1861) (6) panel sequential; (11) panel The Budget Army and Infantry Tactics; First Bellew here? - Many Bellew full pagers begin 50.00 100.00 275.00
48 (Feb 1862) Bellew-c; (2) panel Bellew strip plus singles 50.00 100.00 275.00
49 (Mar 1862) Bellew-c; (16) panel Wilhelm Busch "The Fly Or The Disturbed Dutchman A Story without Words" 50.00 100.00 260.00
50 (April 1862) Bellew-c "Succession Bath" plus singles 25.00 50.00 130.00
51 (May 1862) Bellew-c; (25) panel Busch The Toothache (6) panel Definitions of the Day 50.00 100.00 275.00
52 (June 1862) Bellew-c; (9) panel A Cock & A Bull Expedition; (6) panel Bellew The First Campaign of the Home Guard 50.00 100.00 275.00
NOTE: Johnny Bull & Louis Napolean with Brother Jonathan
53-67 To Be Indexed in the Future 25.00 50.00 150.00
68 (11/18///63) (6) panel Bellew strip "Cuts On Cowards" 25.00 50.00 150.00
NOTE: contains (1) panel William Newman 1817-1870, mentor to Thomas Nast
71 (Feb 1864) Word Balloon Jefferson Davis-c 25.00 50.00 150.00
72 (Mar 1864) Word Balloon-c 25.00 50.00 150.00
73 (April 1864) Word Balloon-c in (6) panels 25.00 50.00 150.00
74 (May 1864) Newman Word Balloon-c 25.00 50.00 150.00
75 77 78 no sequentials 25.00 50.00 150.00
76 (July 1864) Newman Word Balloon-c 25.00 50.00 150.00
79 (Oct 1864) Word Balloon-c 25.00 50.00 150.00
80 (Nov 1864) Robt E Lee & Jeff Davis-c; no sequentials 25.00 50.00 150.00
81 (Dec 1864) Word Balloon "Abyss of War"-c 25.00 50.00 150.00

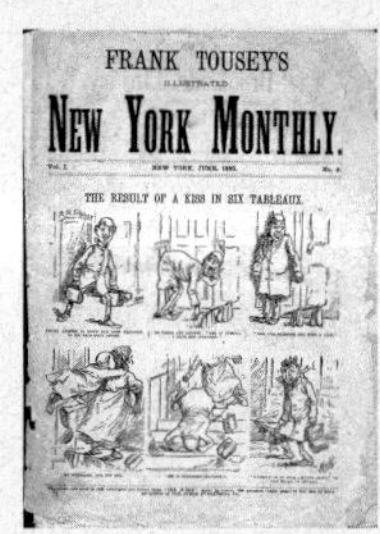

Frank Tousey's Illustrated New York Monthly #9
June 1882 © Frank Tousey

The Funnyest Of Awl And The Funniest Sort Of Phun v4#4
1865 © A.T. Bellew Word Balloon Cover

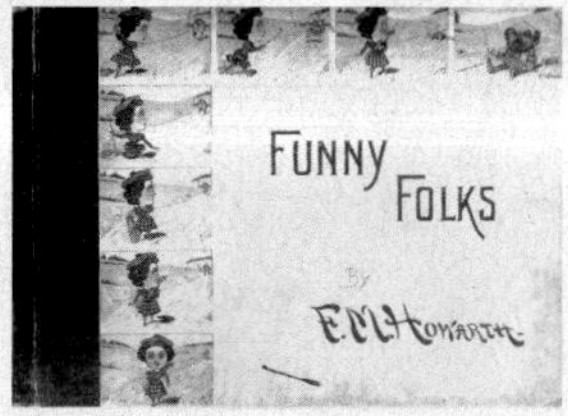

Funny Folk by F.M. Howarth
1899© E.P. Dutton

FR1.0 GD2.0 FN6.0

83 (2/18/65) Back-c (6) panel "Petroleum" 25.00 50.00 150.00
84 (Mar 1865) (6) panel sequential 25.00 50.00 150.00
85 (Apr 1865) Word Balloon-c 25.00 50.00 150.00
86 89 90 92 no sequentials 25.00 50.00 150.00
88 (7/6/65) (6) panel "Marriage" 25.00 50.00 150.00
91 (Oct 1865) (6) panel "Brief Confab At The Corner 25.00 50.00 150.00
93-98 yet to be indexed 25.00 50.00 150.00
99 (June 1866) (18) panel Mr Paul Peters Adventures While Trout-Fishing In The Adirondacks 50.00 100.00 275.00
100 (July 1866) (4) panel sequential comic strip 25.00 50.00 130.00
102 (Sept 1866) (6) panel sequential comic strip 25.00 50.00 130.00
103 (Oct 1866) (9) panel strip; (12) pane;l back cover Adventures of McTiffin At Long Branch 50.00 100.00 275.00
104 (Nov 1866) (4) panel; (23) panel "The Budget Rebuses; (2) panel Glut On Treason Market;back-c; (6) sequential strip 25.00 50.00 130.00
105 (12/18/66) Word Balloon-c; (20) panel sequential back-c 37.50 65.00 156.00
NOTE: Artists include William Newman (1863-1868), William Henry Shelton, Joseph Keppler (1873-1876), James A. Wales (1876-1878), Frederick Burr Opper (1878)

FRANK LESLIE'S LADY'S MAGAZINE
Frank Leslie, NYC: Feb 1863-Dec 1882 (8.5x12", typically 152 pgs)
issues with comic strips 20.00 40.00 60.00

FRANK LESLIE'S PICTORIAL WEEKLY
Frank Leslie, Ross & Tousey, 121 Nassau St, NYC:
average issue (Very Rare) 55.00 110.00 220.00

FRANK TOUSEY'S NEW YORK COMIC MONTHLY
Frank Tousey, NYC: (no known sales)

FREAKS
???, Philadelphia: Jan 8, 1881-April? 1881 (Chromolithographic Weekly)
(Very Rare) 125.00 250.00 550.00

FREELANCE, THE
A.M. Soteldo Jr, Edito, 292 Broadway, NYC: 1874-75 (Folio Weekly)
(Rare) 25.00 50.00 100.00

FREE MASONRY EXPOSED
Winchell & Small, 113 Fulton, NY: 1871 (7-5/8x10-1/2", 36pgs, blue paper-c, B&W)
nn- Thomas Worth Scarce 110.00 225.00 525.00
NOTE: Scathing satircal look at Free Masons thru many cartoons, their power waning by the 1870s

FREETHINKERS' PICTORIAL TEXT-BOOK, THE (S,O)
The Truth Seeker Company, New York: 1890, 1896, 1898 (9x12, hard-c, B&W)
1 (1890 edition) - Scarce 382 pgs By Watson Heston 225.00 450.00 1150.00
1 (1896 edition) - Scarce 378 pgs By Watson Heston (1890-r)130.00 260.00 625.00
2 (1898 edition) - Scarce 408 pgs By Watson Heston 130.00 260.00 625.00
NOTE: *Sought after by collectors of Freethought/Atheism material. There is also 200 copy Modern Reprint.*

FRITZ SPINDLE-SHANKS, THE RAVEN BLACK
Cosack & C o, Buffalo, NY: 1870/80s (4-3/8x2-3/4", color)
(10) card comic strip set by Wilhelm Busch 25.00 50.00 100.00

FUN BY RALL
Unknown: circa 1865 (11x7-7/8", 68 pgs, soft-c, B&W)
nn - By presently unknown (Very Rare) 125.00 250.00 500.00
NOTE: *Wraparound soft cover like modern comic book; yellow paper cover with red & black ink.*

FUN FOR THE FAMILY IN PICTURES
D. Lothrop and Company: 1886 (4 x 7", 48 pgs, Silver & Red stiff-c; interior pages have various single color inks)
nn - By unknown hand 75.00 125.00 250.00
NOTE: *Single panel cartoons and sequential stories.*

FUN FROM LIFE
Frederick A Stokes & Brother, New York: 1889 (9 1/8 by 7 1/8, 72 pages, hard-c)
nn - Mostly by Frank "Chips" Bellew Jr 62.50 125.00 250.00
NOTE: *Contains both single panel and many sequential comics reprints from Life.*

FUNNYEST OF AWL AND THE FUNNIEST SORT OF PHUN, THE
AT Bellew Or W. Jennings Demorest, 121 Nassau St, NY : 1865-67 (30 issues, 16x11 tabloid 16 pgs B&W Monthly, 1-8 © American News; 9-on © A.T. Bellews)
1 (April 1864) Bellew-c 50.00 100.00 225.00
4 (1865) Bellew-c 50.00 100.00 225.00
5 (1865) Busch (20) panel comic srtip The Toothache 75.00 150.00 400.00
7 (1865) Bellew-c 50.00 100.00 225.00
8 (1865) Special Petroleum oil issue - much cartoon art 100.00 200.00 500.00
9 (July 1865) Bellew Bullfrog-c; centerfold double page spread hanging many Confederates; (6) panel strip hanging Jeff Davis 100.00 200.00 500.00
10 (Aug 1865) Bellew-c (13) panel Busch strip with two ducks, a frog and a butcher who gets the ducks in the end 100.00 200.00 500.00
11 (Sept 1865) Bellew Bull Frog Anti-French-c 50.00 100.00 225.00
13 14 15 (12/65-1/66) Bellew-c no sequential comic strips 50.00 100.00 225.00
16 (March 1866) address change to 39 Park Ave 50.00 100.00 225.00
22 (Sept 1866) 133 Nassau St 50.00 100.00 225.00

FR1.0 GD2.0 FN6.0

34 (Oct 1867) 133 Nassau St (7) panel Baseball comic strip; Last Known Issue - were there more? 100.00 200.00 500.00
NOTE: *Radical Republican politics distributed by Great American News Company; owned by Frank Bellew's wife as a front for her husband. When the Civil War ended, the brutal anti-Confederate comic strips and jokes switched to frogs and began attacking France. Funny thing, history says without France's help in the 1700s, there just might not have been a United States.*

FUNNY ALMANAC
Elton & Co., NY: 1853 (8-1/8x4-7/8, 36 pgs)
nn - sequential comic strip 50.00 100.00 200.00
NOTE: (5) panel strip "The Adventures of Mr. Goliah Starvemouse"

FUNNY FELLOWS OWN BOOK, A COMPANION FOR THE LOVERS OF FROLIC AND GLEE, THE (M,N)
Philip. J. Cozans, 116 Nassau ST, NY: 1852 (4-1/2x7-1/2", 196 pgs, burnt orange paper-c)
nn - contains many sequential comic strips (Very Rare) (no known sales)
NOTE: Collected from many different Comic Alamac(k)s including Mose Keyser (Calif Gold Rush); Jones, Smith and Robinson Goes To A Ball; Adventures of Mr. Gulp, Or the Effects of A Dinner Party; The Bowery Bully's Trip To The California Gold Mines plus lots more. This one is a sleeper so far.

FUNNY FOLK (M)
E. P. Dutton: 1899 (12x16-1/2", 90 pgs,14 strips in color-rest in b&w, hard-c)
nn - By Franklin Morris Howarth 250.00 500.00 1900.00
nn - London: J.M. Dent, 1899 embossed-c; same interior 250.00 500.00 1200.00
NOTE: *Reprints many sequential strips & single panel cartoons from* ***Puck.*** *This is considered by many to be yet another "missing link" between Victorian & Platinum Age comic books. Most comic books 1900-1917 reprinting Sunday newspaper comic strips follow this size format, except using cardboard-c rather than hard-c.*

FUNNY SKETCHES...Also Embracing Comic Illustrations
Frank Harrison, New York: 1881 (6-5/8x5", 68 pgs, B&W, Color-c)
nn - contains (3) sequential comic strips; one strip is (6) pages long; plus one (3) pages; one more (2) pager 75.00 150.00 330.00

GIBSON BOOK, THE (M,S)
Charles Scribner's Sons & R.H. Russell, New York: 1906 (11-3/8x17-5/8", gilted red hard-c, B&W)
Book I 50.00 100.00 225.00
NOTE: *Reprints in whole the books: Drawings, Pictures of People, London,Sketches and Cartoons, Education of Mr. Pipp, Americans. 414 pgs. 1907 2nd editions exist same value.*
Book II 50.00 100.00 225.00
NOTE: *Reprints in whole the books: A Widow and Her Friends, The Weaker Sex, Everyday People, Our Neighbors. 314 pgs 1907 second edition for both also exists. Same value.*

GIBSON'S PUBLISHED DRAWINGS, MR. (M,S) (see Plat index for later issues post 1900)
R.H. Russell, New York: No.1 1894 - No. 9 1904 (11x17-3/4", hard-c, B&W)
nn (No.1; 1894) Drawings 96 pgs 30.00 60.00 125.00
nn (No.2; 1896) Pictures of People 92 pgs 30.00 60.00 125.00
nn (No.3; 1898) Sketches and Cartoons 94 pgs 30.00 60.00 125.00
nn (No.4; 1899) The Education of Mr. Pipp 88 pgs 30.00 60.00 125.00
nn (No.5; 1900) Americans 30.00 60.00 125.00
NOTE: *By Charles Dana Gibson cartoons, reprinted from magazines, primarily* ***LIFE.*** *The Education of Mr. Pipp tells a story. Series continues how long after 1904? Each of these books originally came in a boxx and are worth more with the box.*

GIRL WHO WOULDN'T MIND GETTING MARRIED, THE (O)
Frederick Warne & Co., London & New York: nd (c1870's) (9-1/2x11-1/2", 28 pgs, printed 1 side, paper-c, B&W)
nn - By Harry Parkes 75.00 150.00 300.00
NOTE: *Published simultaneously with its companion volume,* ***The Man Who Would Like to Marry.***

GOBLIN SNOB, THE (O)
DeWitt & Davenport, New York: nd (c1853-56) (24 x 17 cm, 96 pgs, B&W, color hard-c)
nn - (Rare) by H.L. Stephens 375.00 600.00 1200.00

GOLDEN ARGOSY
Frank A. Munsey, 81 Warren St, NYC: 1880s (10-1/2x12, 16 pgs, B&W)
issues with full page comic strips by Chips and Bisbee 20.00 40.00 60.00

GOLDEN DAYS, THE
James Elverson, Publisher, NYC: March 6 1880-May 11 1907 weekly, 16 pgs
issues with comic strips 4.00 7.50 15.00
Horatio Alger issues 10.00 20.00 40.00
v10 #49-v11#1 1889 first Stratemeyer story 25.00 50.00 100.00

GOLDEN WEEKLY, THE
Frank Tousey, NYC: #1 Sept 25 1889-#145 Aug 18 1892 (10-3/4x14-1/2, 16 pgs, B&W)
average issue with comic striips 15.00 25.00 50.00

GREAT LOCOFOCO JUGGERNAUT, THE (S)
publisher unknown: Fall/Winter 1837 (7-5/8x3-1/4, handbill single page)
nn - By David Claypoole Johnston (a VG copy sold for $2000 in 2005)
nn - **Imprint Society:** 1971 (reprint) 6.00 12.00 25.00

HALF A CENTURY OF ENGLISH HISTORY (S. M)
G.P. Putnam's Sons - The Knickerbocker Press, New York and London: 1884 (7-3/4 x 5-3/4", 316 pgs., illustrated hard-c)
nn - By Various 50.00 75.00 225.00
NOTE: *Subtitle: Pictorially Presented in a Series of Cartoons from the Collection of Mr. Punch. Comprising 150*

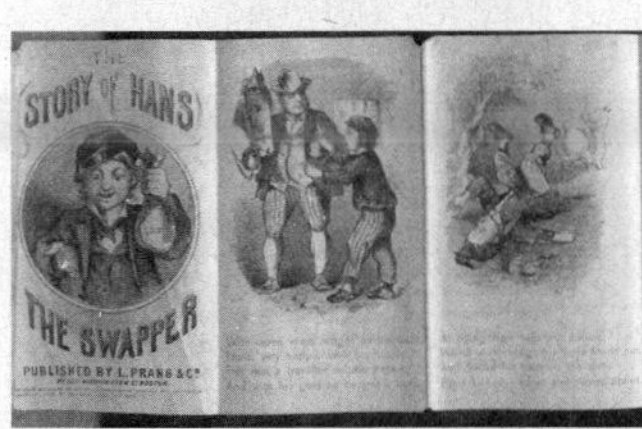

The Story of Han's The Swapper Cover & First Two Panels
1865 © L. Pranc & Co, Boston

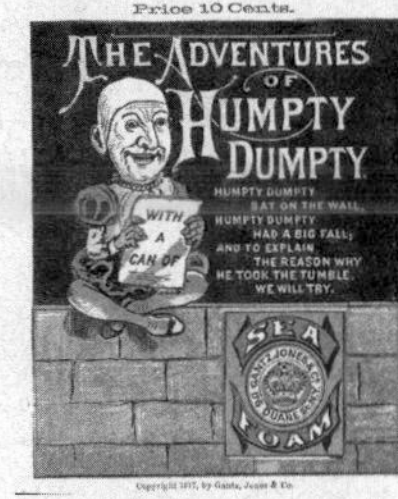

Humpty Dumpty, The Adventures of...
© Gantz, Jones and Co.

Imagerie d'Epinal
1888 © Mumoristic Publishing Co.

FR1.0 GD2.0 FN6.0

plates by Doyle, Leech, Tenniel, and others, in which are portrayed the political careers of Peel, Palmerston, Russell, Cobden, Bright, Beaconsfield, Derby, Salisbury, Gladstone and other English statesmen.

HAIL COLUMBIA! HISTORICAL, COMICAL, AND CENTENNIAL (O,S)
The Graphic Co., New York & Walter F. Brown, Providence, RI: 1876 (10x11-3/8", 60 pgs, red gilted hard-c, B&W)

nn - by Walter F. Brown (Scarce) 125.00 250.00 550.00

HANS HUCKEBEIN'S BATCH OF ODD STORIES ODDLY ILLUSTRATEDED
McLoughlin Bros., New York: 1880s (9-3/4x7-3/8, 36?? pg?

nn - By Wilhelm Busch (Rare) 75.00 150.00 310.00

HANS THE SWAPPER, THE STORY OF (O)
L. Pranc & Co., 159 Washington St, Boston: 1865 (33 inch long fold out in colors)

nn - Unique fold out comic book on one long piece of paper 75.00 150.00 310.00

HARPER'S NEW MONTHLY MAGAZINE
Harper & Brothers, Franklin Square, NY: 1850-1870s (6-3/4x10, 140 pgs, paper-c, B&W)
1850s issues with comic strips in back advert section 20.00 35.00 90.00

HEALTH GUYED (I)
Frederick A. Stokes Company: 1890 (5-3/8 x 8-3/8, 56 pgs, hardcover, B&W)

nn - By Frank P.W. ("Chip") Bellew (Junior) 50.00 75.00 210.00
NOTE: *Text & cartoon illustration parody of a health guide.*

HEATHEN CHINEE, THE (O)
Western News Co.: 1870 (5-1/32x7-1/4, B&W, paper)
nn - 10 sheets printed on one side came in envelope 75.00 150.00 325.00

HITS AT POLITICS (M,S)
R.H. Russell, New York: 1899 (15" x 12", 156 pgs, B&W, hard-c)

nn - W.A. Rogers c/a 100.00 200.00 335.00
NOTE: *Collection of W.A. Rogers cartoons, all reprinted from Harper's Weekly. Includes Spanish-American War cartoons.*

THE HOME CIRCLE
Garrett & Co, NY: 1854-56 (26x19", 4 pgs, B&W)

1 (1/54) beautiful ad of Garrett Building 100.00 200.00 430.00
2/4 (4/66) Cover ad for Yale College Scraps 100.00 200.00 430.00
2/5 (5/55) First ad for Oscas Shanghai 75.00 150.00 300.00
2/6 (6/55) another ad forOscas Snanghai 75.00 150.00 300.00
2/8 (#20) (8/55) Oscar Shanghai comic book cover repro 200.00 400.00 1100.00
3/1 (#25) (1/56) 200.00 400.00 1100.00
NOTE: Garrett's 2nd comic book Courtship of Chavalier Slyfox-Wikoff
3/8 (#32) (8/56) 50.00 100.00 200.00
NOTE: First print ad for Foreign Tour of Messrs. Brown, Jones, and Robinson
35 (11/56) first official Garrett, Dick & Fitzgerald issue 50.00 100.00 200.00
37 (1/57) 100.00 200.00 450.00
NOTE: Front page comic strip repro ad for Messrs. Brown, Jones, and Robinson's Foreign Tour; Back cover full of short sequentials, singles panel

HOME MADE HAPPY. A ROMANCE FOR MARRIED MEN IN SEVEN CHAPTERS (O,P)
Genuine Durham Smoking Tobacco & The Graphic Co.: nd (c1870's) (5-1/4 tall x 3-3/8" wide folded, 27" wide unfolded, color cardboard)

nn - With all 8 panels attached (Scarce) 30.00 60.00 200.00
nn - Individual panels/cards 5.00 10.00 25.00
NOTE: *Consists of 8 attached cards, printed on one side, which unfold into a strip story of title card & 7 panels. Scrapbook hobbyists in the 19th Century tended to pull the panels apart to paste into their scrapbooks, making copies with all panels still attached scarce.*

HOME PICTURE BOOK FOR LITTLE CHILDREN (E,P)
Home Insurance Company, New York: July 1887 (8 x 6-1/8", 36 pgs, b&w, color paper-c)

nn (Scarce) 55.00 110.00 200.00
NOTE: *Contains an abbreviated 32-panel reprinting of "The Toothache" by George Cruikshank. Remainder of booklet does not contain comics. Some copies known to exist do not contain The Toothache - buyer beware!*

HOOD'S COMICALITIES. COMICAL PICTURES FROM HIS WORKS (E,S)
Porter & Coates: 1880 (8-1/2x10-3/8", 104 pgs, printed one side, hard-c, B&W)

nn 30.00 50.00 100.00
NOTE: *Reprints 4 cartoon illustrations per page from the British Hood's Comic Annuals, which were poetry books by Thomas Hood.*

HOOKEYBEAK THE RAVEN, AND OTHER TALES (see also JACK HUCKABACK, THE SCAPEGRACE RAVEN) (E)
George Routledge and Sons, London & New York: nd (1878) (7-1/4x5-5/8", 104 pgs, hardcover, B&W)

nn - By Wilhelm Busch (Rare) 100.00 200.00 475.00

HOW ADOLPHUS SLIM-JIM USED JACKSON'S BEST, AND WAS HAPPY. A LENGTHY TALE IN 7 ACTS. (O,P)
Jackson's Best Chewing Tobacco & Donaldson Brothers: nd(c1870's) (5-1/8 tall x 3-3/8" wide folded, 27" wide unfolded, color cardboard)

nn - With all 8 panels attached (Scarce) 25.00 50.00 200.00
nn - Individual panels/cards 10.00 15.00 30.00
NOTE: *Consists of 8 attached cards, printed on one side, which unfold into a strip story of title card & 7 panels. Scrapbook hobbyists in the 19th Century tended to pull the panels apart topaste into their scrapbooks, making copies with all panels still attached scarce.*

HOW DAYS' DURHAM STANDARD OF THE WORLD SMOKING TOBACCO MADE

TWO PAIRS OF TWINS HAPPY (O,P)
J.R. Day & Bro. Standard Durham Smoking Tobacco, Durham, NC: nd (c late 1870's/ early 1880's) (3-5/8" x 5-1/2", folded, 21-3/4" tall unfolded, color cardboard)

nn- With all 6 panels attached (Scarce) 160.00 320.00 650.00
nn- Individual panels/cards 20.00 40.00 60.00
NOTE: *Highly sought by both Black Americana and Tobacciana collectors. Recurring mid-19th Century story about two African-American twin brothers who romance and marry a pair of African-American twin sisters. Although the text is racist at points, the art is not. Consists of 6 attached cards, printed on one side, which unfold downwards into a strip story of title card & 5 panels. Scrapbook hobbyists in the 19th Century tended to pull the panels apart and paste into their scrapbooks, making copies with all panels attached scarce. Note, there are numerous cartoon tellings of this same story, including several card series versions (with different art, and story variations, each time). But, the above is the only version which unfolds as a strip of attached cards. The cards from all the unattached versions are smaller sized, and thus distinguishable.*

HUGGINIANA; OR, HUGGINS' FANTASY, BEING A COLLECTION OF THE MOST ESTEEMED MODERN LITERARY PRODUCTIONS (I,S,P)
H.C. Southwick, New York: 1808 (296 pgs, printed one side, B&W, hard-c)

nn - (Very Rare)) (no known sales)
NOTE: *The earliest known surviving collected promotional cartoons in America. This is a booklet collecting 7 folded plus 1 full page flyer advertisements for barber John Richard Desborus Huggins, who hired American artists Elkanah Tisdale and William S. Leney to modify previously published illustrations into cartoons referring to his barber shop.*

HUMOROUS MASTERPIECES - PICTURES BY JOHN LEECH (E,M)
Frederick A. Stokes: nd (late 1900's - early 1910's) No.1-2 (5-5/8x3-7/8", 68 pgs, cardboard covers, B&W)

1- John Leech (single panel cartoon-r from **Punch**) 25.00 50.00 110.00
2- John Leech (single panel cartoon-r from **Punch**) 25.00 50.00 110.00

HUMOURIST, THE (E,I,S)
C.V. Nickerson and Lucas and Deaver, Baltimore: No.1 Jan 1829 - No.12 Dec 1829 (5-3/4x3-1/2", B&W text w/hand colored cartoon pg.)

Bound volume No.1-12 (Very Rare; copies in libraries 270 pgs) (no known sales)
NOTE: *Earliest known American published periodical to contain a cartoon every issue. Surviving individual issues currently unknown -- all information comes from 1 surviving bound volume. Each issue is mostly text, with one full page hand-colored cartoon. Bound volume contains an additional hand-colored cartoons at front of each six month set (total of 14 cartoons in volume). Cartoons appear to be of British origin, possibly by George Cruikshank.*

HUMPTY DUMPTY, ADVENTURES OF...(I,P)
1877 (Promotional 4x3-1/2", 12 page chapbook from Gantz, Jones & Co, 10¢-c.)

nn-Promotes Gantz Sea Foam Baking Powder; early app. of a costumed character, dressed as Humpty Dumpty 250.00 400.00 1050.00

HUSBAND AND WIFE, OR THE STORY OF A HAIR. (O,P)
Garland Stoves and Ranges, Michigan Stove Co.: 1883 (4-3/16 tall x 2-11/16" wide folded, 16" wide unfolded, color cardboard)

nn - With all 6 panels attached (Scarce) 50.00 75.00 150.00
nn - Individual panels/cards 5.00 10.00 25.00
NOTE: *Consists of 6 attached cards, printed on one side, which unfold into a strip story of title card & 5 panels. Scrapbook hobbyists in the 19th Century tended to pull the panels apart topaste into their scrapbooks, making copies with all panels still attached scarce.*

ICHABOD ACADEMICUS, THE COLLEGE EXPERIENCES OF (O,G)
William T. Peters, New Haven, CT: 1850 (5-1/2x9-3/4",108 pgs, B&W)

nn - By William T. Peters (Rare) 1000.00 2000.00 4300.00
NOTE: *Pages are not uniform in size. Also, a copy showed up on eBay with misspelled Academicus. Has "n" instead of "m" - not known yet which printing is earliest version.*

ICHABOD ACADEMICUS, THE COLLEGE EXPERIENCES OF (O,G)
Dick & Fitzgerald, New York: nd (1870s-1888) (paper-c, B&W)

nn - By William T. Peters (Very Rare) 300.00 575.00 1150.00
NOTE: *Pages are uniform in size.*

ILLUSTRATED SCRAP-BOOK OF HUMOR AND INTELLIGENCE (M)
John J. Dyer & Co.: nd (c1859-1860)

nn - Very Rare 250.00 550.00 1000.00
NOTE: *A "printed scrapbook" of images culled from some unidentified periodical. About half of it is illustrations that would have accompanied prose pieces. There are pages of single panel cartoons (multiple per page). And there are roughly 8 to 12 pages of sequential comics (all different stories, but appears to all be by the same presently unidentified artist).*

ILLUSTRATED WEEKLY, THE
Chars C Lucas & Co, 11 Dey St, NY: 1876 (15x18", 8pgs, 8¢ per issue)

2/8 (2/19/76) back-c all sequential comic strips 100.00 200.00 425.00
2/12 (3/18/76) full page of British-r sequentials 100.00 200.00 425.00
2/14 (4/1/76) April Fool Issue - (6) panel center; plus more 100.00 200.00 425.00
2/15 (4/8/76) (6) panel sequential 100.00 200.00 425.00
issues without comic strips 12.50 25.00 50.00

ILLUSTRATIONS OF THE POETS: FROM PASSAGES IN THE LIFE OF LITTLE BILLY VIDKINS (See A Day's Sport...)
S. Robinson, Philadelphia: May 1849 (14.7 cm x 11.3 cm, 32 pgs, B&W)

nn - by Henry Stephens (very rare) (no known sales)
NOTE: *Predates Journey to the Gold Diggins By Jeremiah Saddlebags by a few months and is an original American proto-comic strip book. More research needs to be done. A later edition brought $800 in G/VG 2007*

IMAGERIE d'EPINAL (untrimmed individual sheets) (E)

Jingo No. 3, Sept 24
1884 © Art Newspaper Co, Boston & NYC

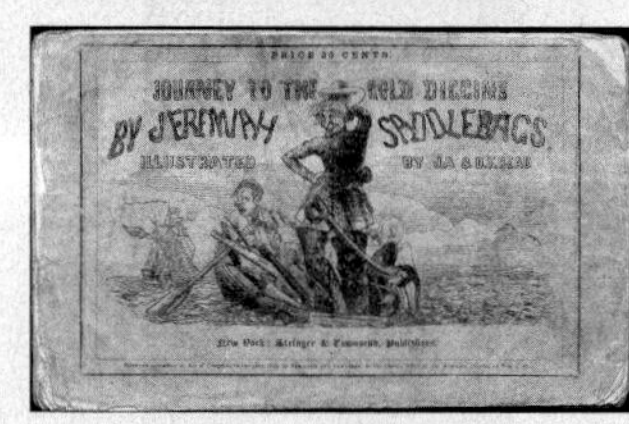

Journey To The Gold Diggings By Jeremiah Saddlebags
1849 © Various - First Original USA Comic Book

The Lantern Dec 18
1852 © Stringer & Townsend

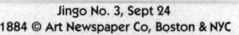

Pellerin for Humoristic Publishing Co, Kansas City, Mo.: nd (1888) No.1-60 (15-7/8x11-3/4",single sheets, hand colored) (All are Rare)

1-14, 21, 22, 25-46, 49-60 - in the Album d'Images 20.00 45.00 75.00
15-20, 23,24, 47, 48 - not in the Album d'Images 30.00 60.00 125.00
NOTE: *Printed and hand colored in France expressly for the Humoristic Publishing Company. Printed on one side only. These are single sheets, sold separately. Reprints and translates the sheets from their original French.*

IMAGERIE d'EPINAL ALBUM d'IMAGES (E)
Pellerin for Humoristic Publishing Co., Kansas City. Mo: nd (1888) (15-1/2x11-1/2",108 pgs plus full color hard-c, hand colored interior)

nn - Various French artists (Rare) 500.00 1000.00 2000.00
NOTE: *Printed and hand colored in France expressly for the Humoristic Publishing Company. Printed on one side only. This is supposedly a collection of sixty broadsheets, originally sold separately. All copies known only have fifty of the sixty known of these broadsheets (slightly bigger, before binding, trimming the margins in the process, down to 15-1/4x11-3/8".). Three slightly different covers known to exist, with or without the indication in French "Textes en Anglais" ("Texts in English), with or without the general title "Contes de FÉes" ("Fairy Tales"). All known copies were collected with sheets 15-20, 23,24, 47, and 48 missing.*

IN LAUGHLAND (M)
R.H. Russell, New York: 1899 (14-9/16x12", 72 pgs, hard-c)

nn - By Henry "Hy" Mayer (scarce) 150.00 300.00 650.00
NOTE: *Mostly strips plus single panel cartoon-r from various magazines. The majority are reprinted from Life, with the rest from: Truth, Dramatic Mirror, Black and White, Figaro Illustre, Le Rire, and Fliegende Blatter.*

IN THE "400" AND OUT (M,S) (see also **THE TAILOR-MADE GIRL**)
Keppler & Schwarzmann, New York: 1888 (8-1/4x12", 64 pgs, hardc, B&W)

nn - By C.J. Taylor 42.50 85.00 210.00
NOTE: *Cartoons reprinted from **Puck**. The "400" is a reference to New York City's aristocratic elite.*

IN VANITY FAIR (M,S)
R.H.Russell & Son, New York: 1896 (11-7/8x17-7/8", 80 pgs, hard-c, B&W)

nn - By A.B.Wenzell, r-LIFE and HARPER'S 50.00 100.00 210.00

JACK HUCKABACK, THE SCAPEGRACE RAVEN (see also HOOKEYBEAK THE RAVEN) (E)
Stroefer & Kirchner, New York: nd (c1877) (9-3/8x6-3/8", 56 pgs, printed one side only, hand colored hardcover, B&W interior)

nn - By Wilhelm Busch (Rare) 100.00 200.00 425.00
NOTE: *The 1877 date is derived from a gift signature on one known copy. The publication date might in truth be earlier. There are also professionally hand colored copies known to exist which would be worth more.*

JEFF PETTICOATS
American News Company, NY: July 1865 (23 inches folded out; 6-1/4x8 folded,, B&W)
nn - Very Rare Frank Bellew (6) panel sequential foldout (10¢) (no known sales)
NOTE: printed also in **FUNNYEST OF AWL AND THE FUNNIEST SORT OF PHUN #**9 (July 1865) (6) panel strip hanging Jeff Davis; This sold hundreds of thousand of copies in its day

JINGO (M,O)
Art Newspaper Co., Boston & New York: No.1 Sept 10, 1884 - No.11 Nov 19, 1884 (10 cents, 13-7/8" x 10-1/4",16 pgs, color front/back-c and center, remainder B&W, paper-c)

1-11(Rare) 55.00 125.00 250.00
NOTE: *Satirical Republican propaganda magazine, modeled after **Puck** and **Judge**, which was published during the last couple months of the 1884 Presidential Election campaign. The Republicans lost, **Jingo** ceased publication, and Republican backers soon after purchased **Judge** magazine.*

JOHN-DONKEY, THE (O, S)
George Dexter, Burgess, Stringer & Co., NYC: 1848 (10x7.5",16 pgs,B&W, 6¢

1 Jan 1 1848 75.00 150.00 325.00
2-end (last issue Aug 12 1848) 50.00 100.00 200.00

JOLLY JOKER
Frank Leslie, NY: 1862-1878 (B&W, 10¢)

20/6 (July 1877) (Bellew Opper cover & single panels 150.00 300.00 650.00

JOLLY JOKER, OR LAUGH ALL-ROUND
Dick & Fitzgerald, NY: 1870s? (8-1/4x4-7/8", 148, B&W, illustrated green cover)

nn - cartoons on every page 100.00 200.00 420.00

JONATHAN'S WHITTLINGS OF THE WAR (O, S)
T.W. Strong, 98 Nassau St, NYC: April 1854-July 8 1854 (11.5x8.5", 16 pgs, B&W)

1 April 1854 100.00 200.00 410.00
NOTE: *Begins Frank Bellew's sequential comic strip* "Mr. Hookemcumsnivey, A Russian Gentleman, Hears That His Country Is In A State of War"
2-12 (July 8 1854) Many Bellew & Hopkins 100.00 200.00 410.00

JOURNAL CARRIER'S GREETING
???, Minn, Minn: 1897-98? (giveaway promo, 10-1/8x8-1/4, 36, B&W, paper-c)
nn - rare 50.00 100.00 190.00

JOURNEY TO THE GOLD DIGGINS BY JEREMIAH SADDLEBAGS (O,G)
Various publishers: 1849 (25 cents, 5-5/8 x 8-3/4", 68 pgs, green & black paper cover, B&W interior)

nn -- New York edition, Stringer & Townsend, Publishers (Very Rare) By J.A. and D.F. Read. 5500.00 8800.00 13,500.00
nn -- Cincinnati, Ohio edition, published by U.P. James (Very Rare) By J.A. and D.F. Read. 5500.00 8800.00 13,500.00
nn -- 1950 reprint, with introduction, published by William P. Wreden, Burlingame, California: 1950 (5-7/8 x 9", 92 pgs, hardcover, color interior) (390 copies printed) By J.A. and D.F. Read. 75.00 150.00 300.00
NOTE: *Earliest known original sequential comic book by an American creator; directly inspired by Töpffer's **Obadiah Oldbuck** and **Bachelor Butterfly** The New York and Cincinnati editions were both published in 1849, one soon after the other. Antiquarian Book sources have traditionally cited that the Cincinnati edition preceded the New York, but without referencing their evidence. Conflicting with this, the Cincinnati edition lists the New York publishers' 1849 copyright, while the New York edition makes no reference to the Cincinnati publishers. Such would indicate that the New York edition was first. Both are very rare, and until resolved both will be regarded as published simultaneously. A New York copy with missing back cover, detached front cover, and G/VG interior sold for $2000 in 2000. Two copies sold at auction in 2006 for $11,500 and 12,000. (Prices vary widely.)*

JUDGE (M,O)
Judge Publishing, New York: No.1 Oct 29, 1881 - No. 950, Dec ??, 1899 (10 cents, color front/back c and centerspread, remainder B&W, paper-c)

1 (Scarce) (no known sales)
2-26 (Volume 1; Scarce) 30.00 55.00 125.00
27-790,792-950 12.50 25.00 50.00
791 (12/12/1896; Vol.31) - classic satirical-c depicting Tammany Hall politicians as the Yellow Kid & Cox's Brownies 100.00 250.00 550.00
Bound Volumes (six month, 26 issue run each):
Vol. 1 (Scarce) (no known sales)
Vol. 2-30,32-37 140.00 280.00 600.00
Vol. 31 - includes issue 791 **YK/Brownies** parody 200.00 300.00 900.00
NOTE: *Rival publication to Puck. Purchased by Republican Party backers, following their loss in the 1884 Presidential Election, to become a Republican propaganda satire magazine.*

JUDGE, GOOD THINGS FROM
Judge Publishing Co., NY: 1887 (13-3/4x10.5", 68 pgs, color paper-c)

1 first printing 50.00 100.00 200.00
NOTE: Zimmerman, Hamilton, Victor, Woolf, Beard, Ehrhart, De Meza, Howarth, Smith, Alfred Mitchell

JUDGE'S LIBRARY (M)
Judge Publishing, New York: No.1, April 1890 - No. 141, Dec 1899 (10 cents, 11x8-1/8", 36 pgs, color paper-c, B&W)

1 15.00 30.00 65.00
2-141 15.00 30.00 65.00
151-??? (post-1900 issues; see Platinum Age section)
NOTE: ***Judge's Library** was a monthly magazine reprinting cartoons & prose from **Judge**, with each issue's material organized around the same subject. The cover art was often original. All issues were kept in print for the duration of the series, so later issues are more scarce than earlier ones.*

JUDGE'S QUARTERLY (M)
Judge Publishing Company/Arkell Publishing Company, New York: No.1 April 1892 - 31 Oct 1899 (25¢, 13-3/4x10-1/4", 64 pgs, color paper-c, B&W)

1-11 13-31 contents presently unknown to us 15.00 30.00 65.00
12 ZIM Sketches From Judge Jan 1895 100.00 225.00 450.00
NOTE: *Similar to **Judge's Library**, except larger in size, and issued quarterly. All reprint material, except for the cover art.*

JUDGE'S SERIALS (M,S)
Judge Publishing, New York: March 1888 (10x7.5", 36 pgs)

#3 - Eugene Zimmerman 100.00 200.00 400.00
NOTE: *A bit of sequential comic strips; mostly single panel cartoons. This series runs to at least #8.*

JUDY
Burgess, Stringer & Co., 17 Ann St, NYC: Nov 28 1846-Feb 20 47 (11x8.5",12 pgs,B&W)

1 Nov 28 1846 67.50 125.00 250.00
2-13 50.00 100.00 200.00

JUVENILE GEM, THE (see also THE ADVENTURES OF MR. TOM PLUMP, and OLD MOTHER MITTEN) (O,I)
Huestis & Cozans: nd (1850-1852) (6x3-7/8", 64 pgs, hand colored paper-c, B&W) (all versions Very Rare)

nn - First printing(s) publisher's address is 104 Nassau Street (1850-1851) (1 copy sold for $800.00 in Fair)
nn - 2nd printing(s) publisher's address is 116 Nassau Street (1851-1852) (no known sales)
nn - 3rd printing(s) publisher's address is 107 Nassau Street (1852+) (no known sales)
NOTE: *The JUVENILE GEM is a gathering of multiple booklets under a single, hand colored cover (none of the interior booklets have the covers which they were given when sold separately). The publisher appears to have gathered whichever printings of each booklet were available when copies of THE JUVENILE GEM was assembled, so that the booklets within, and the conglomerate cover, may be from a mixture of printings. Contains two sequential comic booklets: THE ADVENTURES OF MR. TOM PLUMP, and OLD MOTHER MITTEN AND HER FUNNY KITTEN, plus five heavily illustrated children's booklets - **The Pretty Primer**, **The Funny Book**, **The Picture Book**, **The Two Sisters**, and **Story Of The Little Drummer**. Six of these -- including the two comic books -- were reprinted in the 1960's by Americana Review as a set of individual booklets, and included in a folder collectively titled "Six Children's Books of the 1850's".*

LANTERN, THE
Stringer & Townsend:1852-1853 (11x8-3/8", 12 pgs, soft paper, 6 ¢)

1 Jan 10, 1852 37.50 75.00 175.00
2 25.00 50.00 120.00
3-First Frank Bellew cartoons onwards each issue 37.50 75.00 175.00
4-Bellew 's Mr Blobb begins 1/31/52 50.00 100.00 250.00
NOTE: *Bellew serial sequential comic strip "Mr Blobb In Search Of A Physician" becomes 2nd earliest known recurring character in American comic strips plus full page single panel Bellew cartoon "The Modern Frankenstein" take-off on Shelly's story.*
5-Hunsdale 2-panel "The Horrors of Slavery"; Mr Blobb 50.00 100.00 230.00
6-DF Read 15 panel "A Volley of Valentines"; Mr Blobb 50.00 100.00 230.00

Leslie's Young America #1
1881 © Leslie & Company, NYC

Life Jan 3
1884 © J.A. Mitchell

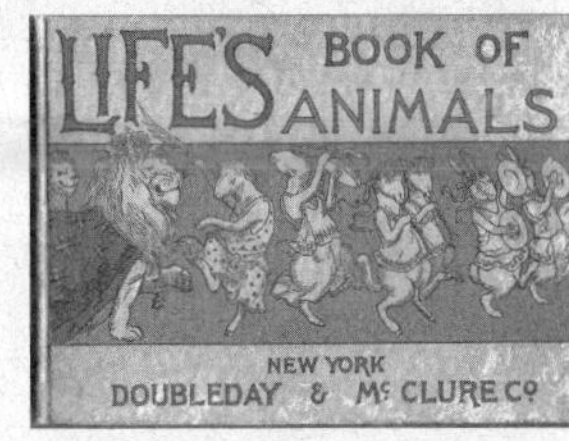

Life's Book of Animals
1888 © Doubleday & McClure Co.

	FR1.0	GD2.0	FN6.0
7-8,10-Bellew's Mr Blobb continues	25.00	50.00	125.00
9-Four panel "The Perils of Leap Year" MrBlobb	50.00	100.00	230.00
11-no Mr Blobb	20.00	40.00	115.00
12-Bellew's Mr Blobb continues 3/27/52	50.00	100.00	230.00
13-Bellew (10) panel sequential "Stump Speaking Studied"	50.00	100.00	230.00
14-no comic strips	20.00	40.00	110.00
15-Bellew's Mr Blobb ends (5) panel 4/17/52	50.00	100.00	230.00
16-Bellew begins new comic strip serial, "Mr. Bulbear, A Stockbroker, After having Supped at Delmonicos, Has A Dream", Part One, (6) panels	50.00	100.00	230.00
17-Bellew's Mr Bulbear continues	25.00	50.00	125.00
18-Bellew (8) panel "Trials of a Witness"	50.00	100.00	230.00
19-Bellew's Mr Bulbear's Dream continues	25.00	50.00	125.00
20-23-No comic strips	20.00	40.00	115.00
24 Bellew "Trials of a Publisher" (6) panel	50.00	100.00	230.00
25 comic strip "Travels of Jonathan Verdant"recurring character	25.00	50.00	125.00
26-49 contents still to be indexed			
50 (12/18/52) (2) panel Impertinent Smile	25.00	50.00	125.00
58 (2/12/53) (6) panel Trip to California	25.00	50.00	125.00
66 (4/9/53) (3) panel sequential strip	25.00	50.00	125.00

LAST SENSATION, THE (Becomes Day's Doings)
James Watts, NYC: Dec 27 1867-May 30 1868 (11x16 folio-size, 16 pgs, B&W)

Issues with comic strips	50.00	100.00	215.00

LAUGH AND GROW FAT COMIC ALMANAC
Fisher & Brother, Philadelphia, New York & Boston: 1860-? (36 pgs)

nn	60.00	120.00	275.00

LEGEND OF SAM'L OF POSEN (O)
M.B. Curtis Company: 1884-85 (8x3-3/8", 44 pgs, Color-c, B&W interior)

nn - By M.B. Curtis	50.00	100.00	215.00

NOTE: Cover blurb says: From Early Days in Fatherland to affluence And Success in the Land of His Adoption, America

LESLIE'S YOUNG AMERICA (O. S)
Leslie & Co, 98 Chamber St, NY: 1881-82 (11-1/2x8", 5¢, B&W)

1 (7/9/81) back cover (6) panel strip	150.00	300.00	650.00
2 (7/16/81) back cover (9) panel strip	50.00	100.00	260.00
3 (7/23/81) back cover (16) panel Busch strip	67.50	125.00	300.00
9 (9/3/81) sequentials; Hopkins singles	50.00	100.00	260.00
15 (10/15/81) Zim or Frost? (6) panel strip	50.00	100.00	260.00
19 (11/12/81) (9) panel back-c strip	50.00	100.00	260.00
24 (4) panel strip 25 (2) panel back-c strip	50.00	100.00	260.00
26 27 (6) panel back-c strip	50.00	100.00	260.00
29 31 (12) panel strip	50.00	100.00	260.00
32 (2/11/82) (8) panel strip	50.00	100.00	260.00
issues without comic strips or Jules Verne	25.00	50.00	125.00

NOTE: Jules Verne stories begin with #1 and run thru at least #42

LIFE (M,O) (continues with Vol.35 No. 894+ in the Platinum Age section)
J.A.Mitchell: Vol.1 No.1 Jan. 4, 1883 - Vol.1 No.26 June 29, 1883 (10-1/4x8", 16 pgs, B&W, paper cover); J.A. Mitchell: Vol. 2 No. 27, July 5, 1883 - Vol. 6 No.148, Oct 29, 1885 (10-1/4x8-1/4", 16 pgs., B&W, paper cover); Mitchell & Miller: Vol.6 No.149, Nov. 5, 1885 - Vol. 31, No. 796, March 17, 1898 (10-3/8x8-3/8", 16 pgs., B&W, paper cover); Life Publishing Company: Vol. 31 No. 797, March 24, 1898 - Vol. 34 No. 893, Dec 28, 1899 (10-3/8 x 8-1/2", 20 pgs., B&W, paper cover)

1-26 (Scarce)	(no known sales)		
27-799	5.00	10.00	20.00
800 (4/7/1898) parody Yellow Kid / Spanish-American War cover (not by Outcault)	75.00	150.00	300.00
801-893	5.00	10.00	20.00

NOTE: *All covers for issues 1 - 26 are identical, apart from issue number & date.*

Hard bound collected volumes:

V. 1 (No.1-26) (Scarce)	67.50	125.00	275.00
V. 2-34	45.00	90.00	180.00
V. 31 YK #800 parody-c not by RFO	70.00	140.00	325.00

NOTE: *Because the covers of all issues in Volume 1 are identical, it was common practice to remove the covers before binding the issues together. This is not true of later volumes, though, in all volumes it was common to drop the advertising pages which appeared at the rear of each issue. Information on many more individual issues will expand next Guide.*

LIFE AND ADVENTURES OF JEFF DAVIS (I)
J.C. Haney & Co., NY: 1865 (10 cents, 7-1/2" x 4", 36 pgs, B&W, paper-c)

nn - By McArone (Scarce)	200.00	400.00	800.00
nn - 1974 Reprint (350) copies 6-3/4x4-3/8	50.00	10.00	20.00
nn - 1997 Reprint (7th Fla. Sutler, Clearwater, 6-3/4x4-1/4")	–	–	2.00

NOTE: *Humorous telling of the capture of Confederate President Jeff Davis in women's clothing, from the publisher of Merryman's Monthly. It contains an ad page for that publication; the material is perhaps reprinted from it. J.C. Haney licensed it to local printers, and so various publishers are found -- all printings currently regarded as simultaneous. (The Geo. H. Hees printing, Oswego, NY, contains an ad for the upcoming October 1865 issue of Merryman's Monthly, thus placing that printing in September 1865). Modern facsimile editions have been produced.*

LIFE IN PHILADELPHIA
W. Simpson, 66 Chestnut, Philadelphia; Siltart, No. 65 South Third St, Philadelphia: 1830 (7-3/4x6-7/8", 15 loose plates, hand colored copies exist, maybe B&W also)

nn - By Edward Williams Clay (1799-1857) (Very Rare)	(no known sales)		

NOTE: *First 13 plates etched, with many word balloons; scenes of exaggerated Black Americana in Philadelphia viewed one by one as broadsides. Had several publishers over the years. Was also eventually collected into a book of same name but only with the first 13 plates used; the last two not used in book. Collected book not yet viewed to share info.*

LIFE'S BOOK OF ANIMALS (M,S)
Doubleday & McClure Co.: 1898 (7-1/4x10-1/8", 88 pgs, color hardcover, B&W)

nn	30.00	55.00	110.00

NOTE: *Reprints funny animal single panel and strip cartoons reprinted from LIFE. Art by Blaisdell, Chip Bellew, Kemble, Hy Mayer, Sullivant, Woolf.*

LIFE'S COMEDY (M,S)
Charles Scribner's Sons: Series 1 1897 - Series 3 1898 (12x9-3/8", hardcover, B&W)

1 (142 pgs). 2, 3 (138 pgs)	60.00	120.00	250.00

NOTE: *Gibson a-1-3; c-3. Hy Mayer a-1-3. Rose O'Neill a-2-3. Stanlaws a-2-3. Sullivant a-1-2. Verbeek a-2. Wenzell a-1-3; c(painted)-2.*

LIFE, THE GOOD THINGS OF (M,S)
White, Stokes, & Allen, NY: 1884 - No.3 1886 ; Frederick A. Stokes, NY: No.4 1887; Frederick Stokes & Brother, NY: No.5 1888 - No.6 1889; Frederick A. Stokes Company, NY: No. 7 1890 - No.10 1893 (8-3/8x10-1/2", 74 pgs, gilted hardcover, B&W)

nn - 1884 (most common issue)	35.00	75.00	160.00
2 - 1885	35.00	75.00	160.00
3 - 1886 (76 pgs)	35.00	75.00	160.00
4 - 1887 (76 pgs)	35.00	75.00	160.00
5 - 1888	35.00	75.00	160.00
6 - 1889	35.00	75.00	160.00
7 - 1890	35.00	75.00	160.00
8 - 1891 (scarce)	75.00	150.00	320.00
9 - 1892	35.00	75.00	160.00
10 - 1893	35.00	75.00	160.00

NOTE: *Contains mostly single panel, and some sequential, comics reprinted from LIFE. Attwood a-1-4,10. Roswell Bacon a-5. Chip Bellew a-4-6. Frank Bellew a-4,6. Palmer Cox a-1. H. E. Dey a-5. C. D. Gibson a-4-10. F.M. Howarth a-5-6. Kemble a-1-3. Klapp a-5. Walt McDougall a-1-2. H. McVickar a-5; J. A. Mitchell a-5. Peter Newell a-2-3. Gray Parker a-4-5,7. J. Smith a-5. Albert E. Steiner a-5; T. S. Sullivant a-7-9. Wenzell a-8-10. Wilder a-3. Woolf a-3-6.*)

LIFE, THE SPICE OF (E,M,)
White and Allen: NY & London: 1888 (8-3/8x10-1/2",76 pgs, hard-c, B&W)

nn	50.00	100.00	230.00

NOTE: *Resembles **THE GOOD THINGS OF LIFE** in layout and format, and appears to be an attempt to compete with their former partner Frederick A. Stokes. However, the material is not from **LIFE**, but rather is reprinted and translated German sequential and single panel comics.*

LIFE'S PICTURE GALLERY (becomes LIFE'S PRINTS) (M,S,P)
Life Publishing Company, New York: nd (1898-1899) (paper cover, B&W) (all are scarce)

nn - (nd; 1898, 100 pgs, 5-1/4x8-1/2") Gibson-c of a woman with closed umbrella; 1st interior page announcing that after January 1, 1899 Gibson will draw exclusively for LIFE; the word "SPECIMEN" is printed in red, diagonally, across every print; a-Gibson, Rose O'Neill, Sullivant	37.50	75.00	150.00
nn - (nd; 1899, 128 pgs, 4-7/8x7-3/8") Gibson-c of a woman golfer; 1st interior page announcing that Gibson & Hanna, Jr. draw exclusively for LIFE; the word "SPECIMEN" is printed in red, horizontally, across every print. Includes prints from Gibson's **THE EDUCATION OF MR. PIPP**; a-Gibson, Sullivant	37.50	75.00	150.00

NOTE: *Catalog of prints reprinted from **LIFE** covers & centerspreads. The first catalog was given away free to anyone requesting it, but after many people got the catalog without ordering anything, subsequent catalogs were sold at 10 cents.*

LIGHT AND SHADE
William Drey Doppel Soap: 1892 (3-3/4x5-3/8", 20 pgs, B&W, color cover)

nn - By J.C.	50.00	100.00	220.00

NOTE: Contains (8) panel comic strip of black boy whose skin turns white using this soap.

LITTLE SICK BEAR, THE
Edwin W. Joy Co, San Francisco, CA: 1897 (6-1/4x5", 20 pgs, B&W, Scarce)

nn - By James Swinnerton one long sequential comic strip	225.00	450.00	900.00

LONDON OUT OF TOWN, OR THE ADVENTURES OF THE BROWNS AT THE SEA SIDE BY LUKE LIMNER, ESQ. (O)
David Bogue, 86 Fleet St, London: c1847 (5-1/2x4-1/4, 32 pgs, yellow paper hard-c, B&W)

nn - By John Leighton	150.00	350.00	725.00

NOTE: one long sequential comic strip multiple-panel per page story; each page crammed with panels inspired by the Töpffer comic books Bogue began several years earlier.

LORGNETTE, THE (S)
George J Coombes, New York: 1886 (6-1/2x8-3/4, 38 pgs, hard-c, B&W

nn - By J.K. Bangs	50.00	100.00	200.00

LOVING BALLAD OF LORD BATEMAN, THE (E,I)
G.W. Carleton & Co., Publishers, Madison Square, NY: 1871 (9x5-7/8",16 pgs, soft-c, 6¢)

nn - By George Cruikshank	50.00	100.00	200.00

MADISON'S EXPOSITION OF THE AWFUL & TERRIFYING CEREMONIES

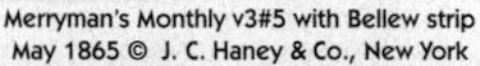

Merryman's Monthly v3#5 with Bellew strip
May 1865 © J. C. Haney & Co., New York

Minneapolis Journal Cartoons Second Series
1895 © Minneapolis Journal

The Mischief Book by Wilhelm Busch
color cover art variation
1880 © R. Worthington, New York

FR1.0 GD2.0 FN6.0

OF THE ODD FELLOWS
T.E. Peterson & Brothers, 306 Chestnut St, Phila: 1870s? (5-3/4x9-1/4, 68 pgs, B&W)
nn - single panel cartoons 50.00 100.00 200.00

MANNERS AND CUSTOMS OF YE HARVARD STUDENTE (M,S)
Houghton Mifflin & Co., Boston & Moses King, Cambridge: 1877 (7-7/8x11", 72 pgs, printed one side, hardc, B&W)
nn - by F.G. Attwood 125.00 250.00 500.00
NOTE: *Collection of cartoons originally serialized in the* ***Harvard Lampoon****. Attwood later became a major cartoonist for* ***Life****.*

MAN WHO WOULD LIKE TO MARRY, THE (O)
Frederick Warne & Co., London & New York: nd (c 1880's) (9-1/2x11-1/2", 28 pgs, printed 1 side, paper-c, B&W)
nn - By Harry Parkes 75.00 150.00 300.00
NOTE: *Published simultaneously with its companion volume,* ***The Girl Who Wouldn't Mind Getting Married****.*

MAX AND MAURICE: A JUVENILE HISTORY IN SEVEN TRICKS (E)
(see also Teasing Tom and Naughty Ned)
Roberts Brothers, Boston: 1871 first edition (8-1/8 x 5-1/2", 76 pgs, hard & soft-c B&W)
nn - By Wilhelm Busch (green or brown cloth hardbound) 300.00 600.00 1300.00
nn - exactly the same, but soft paper cover 175.00 350.00 700.00
NOTE: *Page count includes 56 pgs of art, two blank endpapers at the front (one colored), 8 pgs of ads at the back, two blank endpapers at the end (one colored), and the covers. Green or brown illustrated hardcover. The name of the author is given on the title page as "William Busch." We assume this to be the 1st edition. Back side of title page states: Entered according to Act of Congress, in the year 1870, by Roberts Brothers, In the office of the Librarian of Congress at Washington.*
nn - By Wilhelm Busch (1872 edition) 250.00 500.00 1300.00
nn - 1875 reprint 100.00 200.00 450.00
nn - 1882 reprint (76 pgs, hand colored- c/a, 75¢) 100.00 200.00 400.00
nn- 1889 reprint with new art on cover printed in full color 100.00 200.00 400.00
NOTE: *Each of the above contains 56 pages of art and text in a transitional format between a regular children's book and a comic book (the page count difference is ad pages in back). Seminal inspiration for William Randolph Hearst to acquire as a "new comic" (following the wild success of Outcault's Yellow Kid) to license M&M from Busch and hire Rudolph Dirks in late 1897 to create a New York American newspaper incarnation. In Hearst's English language newspapers it was called The Katzenjammer Kids and in his German language NYC newspaper it was titled Max & Moritz, Busch's original title. At least 50 other reprints versions are reputed to exist printed thru 1900. Translated from the 1865 German original. We are still sorting out the edition confusion.*

MAX AND MAURICE: A JUVENILE HISTORY IN SEVEN TRICKS (E)
(see also Teasing Tom and Naughty Ned)
Little, Brown, and Company, Boston: 1898-1902 (8-1/8 x 5-3/4", 72 pgs, hardcover, black ink on orange paper) (various early reprints)
nn - 1898 , 1899 By Wilhelm Busch 75.00 150.00 330.00
nn - 1902 (64 pages, B&W) 20.00 35.00 100.00

MERRY MAPLE LEAVES Or A Summer In The Country (S)
E.P. Dutton And Company, New York: 1872 (9-3/8x7-3/8", 90 and 86 pgs pgs, hard-c)
nn - By Abner Perk 25.00 50.00 150.00
NOTE: *Each drawing contained in a maple leaf motif by Livingston Hopkins and others.*

MERRYMAN'S MONTHLY A COMIC MAGAZINE FOR THE FAMILY (M,O,E)
J.C. Haney & Co, NY: 1863-1875 (10-7/8x7-13/16", 30 pgs average, B&W)
Certain issues with sequential comics 100.00 200.00 450.00
NOTE: *Sequential strips by Frank Bellew Sr, Wilhelm Busch found so far; others?*

MERRYTHOUGHT, OR LAUGHTER FROM YEAR TO YEAR, THE
Fisher & Brother, Phila, Baltimore: early 1850s (4-1/2x7", B&W)
nn - many singles, some sequential (Very Rare) (no known sales)
NOTE: See Vict article for back cover pic which is earliest known use of the term Comic Book

MESSRS. BROWN, JONES, AND ROBINSON, THE FOREIGN TOUR OF
(see also **THE CLOWN, OR THE BANQUET OF WIT**) (E,M,O,G)
Bradbury & Evans, London: 1854 (11-5/8x9-1/2", 196 pgs, gilted hard-c, B&W)
nn - By Richard Doyle 35.00 70.00 250.00
nn - Bradbury & Evans 1900 reprint 25.00 50.00 100.00
NOTE: *Protective sheets between each page (not part of page count). Expanded and redrawn sequential comics story from the serialized episodes originally published in PUNCH. Also comes in a 174 pg 8-3/4x11" version.*

MESSRS. BROWN, JONES, AND ROBINSON, THE LAUGHABLE ADVENTURES OF (E,M,G)
Garrett, Dick & Fitzgerald, NY: nd (1856 or 1857) (5-3/4x9-1/4", 100 pgs, printed one side only, paper-c, B&W)
nn - (Very Rare) by Richard Doyle c/a 350.00 600.00 1425.00
NOTE: *1st American reprinting of the "Foreign Tour"; reformatted into a small oblong format. Links the earlier Garrett & Co. to the later Dick & Fitzgerald. Back cover reprints full size the Garrett & Co. version cover for Oscar Shanghai. Interior front cover reprints full size the Garrett & Co. version cover for Slyfox-Wikof. Issued without a title page.*

MESSRS. BROWN, JONES, AND ROBINSON, THE FOREIGN TOUR OF (E,M,G)
D. Appleton & Co., New York: 1860 & 1877 (11-5/8x9-1/2", 196 pgs, gilted hard-c, B&W)
nn - (1860 printing) by Richard Doyle 30.00 60.00 220.00
nn - (1871 printing) by Richard Doyle 30.00 60.00 150.00
nn - (1877 printing) by Richard Doyle 30.00 60.00 150.00
NOTE: *Protective sheets between each page (not part of page count). Reprints the Bradbury & Evans edition.*

MESSRS BROWN JONES AND ROBINSON, THE AMERICAN TOUR OF (O,G)
D. Appleton & Co., New York: 1872 (11-5/8x9-1/2", 158 pgs, printed one side only, B&W, green gilted hard-c)
nn - By Toby 100.00 200.00 600.00
NOTE: *Original American graphic novel sequel to Richard Doyle's Foreign Tour of Brown, Jones, and Robinson, with the same characters visiting New York, Canada, and Cuba. Protective sheets between each page (not part of page count).*

MESSRS. BROWN, JONES, AND ROBINSON, THE LAUGHABLE ADVEN. OF (E,M,G)
Dick & Fitzgerald, NY: nd (late 1870's - 1888) (5-3/4x9-1/4", 100 pgs, printed one side only, green paper-c, B&W)
nn - (Scarce) by Richard Doyle 110.00 210.00 500.00
NOTE: *Reprints the Garrett, Dick & Fitzgerald printing, with the following changes: Takes what had been page 12 in the Garrett, D&F printing (art by M.H. Henry), and makes it a title page, which is numbered page 1. The first story page, "Go to the Races", is numbered 2 (whereas it is numbered 1 in the Garrett, Dick & Fitzgerald version). Numbering stays ahead of the G,D&F edition by 1 page up through page 12, after which the page numbering becomes identical.*

MINNEAPOLIS JOURNAL CARTOONS (N,S)
Minneapolis Journal: nn 1894 - No.2 1895 (7-3/4" x 10-7/8", 76 pgs, B&W, paper-c)
nn (1894) (Rare) 50.00 100.00 210.00
Second Series (1895) (Rare) 50.00 100.00 210.00
nn- "War Cartoons" Jan 1899 (9x8", 160 pgs, paperback, punched & string bound) (Scarce) 25.00 100.00 180.00
NOTE: *Reprints single panel cartoons from the prior year, by Charles "Bart" L. Bartholomew.*

MINNEAPOLIS TRIBUNE CARTOON BOOK FOR 1901
Roland C. Bowman: 1901
nn (a FR/GD copy sold in 2010 for $134)

MISCHIEF BOOK, THE (E)
R. Worthington, New York: 1880 (7-1/8 x 10-3/4", 176 pgs, hard-c, B&W)
nn - Green cloth binding; green on brown cover; cover art by R. Lewis based on Busch art by Wilhelm Busch 200.00 400.00 850.00
nn - Blue cloth binding; hand colored cover; completely different cover art based on Busch by Wilhelm Busch 200.00 400.00 850.00
NOTE: *Translated by Abby Langdon Alger. American published anthology collection of Wilhelm Busch comic strips. Includes two of the strips found in the British "Bushel of Merry-Thoughts" collection, translated better, and with the dropped panel restored. Unknown which cover version was first.*

MISSES BROWN, JONES AND ROBINSON, THE FOREIGN TOUR OF THE (E,O,G)
Bickers & Sons, London: nd (c1850's) (12-1/4" x 9-7/8", 108 pgs, printed on one side, B&W, hard-c)
nn- "by Miss Brown" (Rare) 100.00 200.00 410.00
NOTE: *A female take on Doyle's Foreign Tour, by an unknown woman artist, using the pseudonym "Miss Brown."*

MISS MILLY MILLEFLEUR'S CAREER (S)
Sheldon & Co., NY: 1869 (10-3/4x9-7/8", 74 pgs, purple hard-c)
nn - Artist unknown (Rare) 75.00 150.00 300.00

MR PODGER AT COUP'S GREATEST SHOW ON EARTH HIS HAPS AND MISHAPS, THE ADVENTURES OF (O,S)
W.C. Coup, New York: 1884 (5-5/8x4-1/4", 20 pgs, color-c, B&W)
nn - Circus Themes; Similar to Barker's Comic Almanacs 30.00 60.00 115.00

MR. TOODLES' GREAT ELEPHANT HUNT (See Peter Piper in Bengal)
Brother Jonathan, NYC: 1850s (4-1/4x7-7/8", page count presently unknown)
nn - catalog contains comic strip (Very Rare) (no known sales)

MR. TOODLES' TERRIFIC ELEPHANT HUNT
Dick & Fitzgerald, NYC: 1860s (5-3/4x9-1/4", 32 pgs, paper-c, B&W) (Very Rare)
nn - catalog reprint contains 28 panel comic strip 175.00 350.00 700.00

MRS GRUNDY
Mrs Grundy Publishing Co, NYC: July 8 1865-Sept 30 1865 (weekly)
1-13 Thomas Nast, Hoppin, Stephens, 50.00 100.00 200.00

MUSEUM OF WONDERS, A (O,I)
Routledge & Sons: 1894 (13x10", 64 pgs, color-c, color thru out)
nn - By Frederick Opper 125.00 250.00 525.00

MY FRIEND WRIGGLES, A (Laughter) Moving Panorama, of His Fortunes And Misfortunes, Illustrated With Over 200 Engravings, of Most Comic Catastrophes And Side-Splitting Merriment) (O,G)
Stearn & Co, 202 Williams St, NY: 1850s (5-7/8x9-3/4", 100 pgs, B&W)
nn - By S. P. Avery (also the engraver) (Very Rare) 250.00 500.00 1100.00

MY SKETCHBOOK (E,S)
Dana Estes & Charles E. Lauriat, Boston; J. Sabins & Sons, New York: circa 1880s (9-3/8x12", brown hard-c)
nn - By George Cruikshank 25.00 50.00 150.00
NOTE: *Reprints British editions 1834-36; extensive usage of word balloons.*

NASBY'S LIFE OF ANDY JONSON (O, M)
Jesse Haney Co., Publishers No. 119 Nassau St, NY: 1866 (4-1/2x7-1/2, 48 pgs, B&W)
nn - President Andrew Johnson satire 150.00 300.00 600.00
NOTE: Blurb further reads: With a True Pictorial History of His STumping Tour Out West By Petroleum V. Nasby,

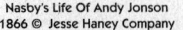

Nasby's Life Of Andy Jonson
1866 © Jesse Haney Company

99 "Woolf's" from Truth
1896 © Truth Company

The Adventures of Obadiah Oldbuck 4th printing
mid-1850s © Brother Jonathan Offices, NY

FR1.0 GD2.0 FN6.0

A Dimmicrat of Thirty Years Standing, And Who Allus Tuk His Licker Straight. Front of book has long sequential comic strip satire on President Andrew Johnson, misspelling his name on the cover on purpose.

NAST'S ILLUSTRATED ALMANAC
Harper & Brothers, Franklin Square, NYC: 1872-1874 (8x5.5", 80 pgs, B&W, 35¢)

nn 65.00 125.00 275.00

NAST'S WEEKLY (O,S)
???: 1892-93 (Quarto Weekly)

all issues scarce 50.00 100.00 200.00

NATIONAL COMIC ALMANAC
An Association of Gentlemen, Boston: 1838-?? (8.25x4.75", 34 pgs, B&W)

nn 60.00 120.00 250.00

NEW AMERICAN COMIC ALL-IMAKE (ELTON'S BASKET OF COMICAL SCRAPS), THE
Elton, Publisher, New York: 1839 (7-1/2x4-5/8, 24 pgs)

1 100.00 200.00 400.00

NEW BOOK OF NONSENSE, THE: A Contribution To The Great Central Fair In Aid of the Sanitary Commission (O,S)
Ashmead & Evans, No. 724 Chestnut St, Philadelphia: June 1864 (red hard-c)

nn - Artists unknown (Scarce) 50.00 150.00 320.00

NEW YORK ILLUSTRATED NEWS
Frank Leslie, NYC: 10/14/76-June 1884

average issues with comic strips 25.00 50.00 100.00

NEW YORK PICAYUNE (see PHUN FOTOCRAFT)
Woodward & Hutchings: 1850-1855 newspaper-size weekly; 1856-1857 Folio Monthly 16x10.5; 1857-1858 Quarto Weekly; 1858-1860 Quarto Weekly

Average Issue With Comic Strips 50.00 100.00 225.00
Issues with Full Front Page Comic Strip 100.00 200.00 400.00

NOTE: *Many issues contain Frank Bellew sequential comic strips & single panel cartoons. Later issues published by Woodward, Levison & Robert Gun (1853-1857) ; Levison & Thompson (1857-1860)*

NICK-NAX
Levison & Haney, NY: 1857-1858? (11x7-3/4", 32 pgs, B&W, paper-c)
v2 #10 Feb 1858 has many single panel cartoons 50.00 100.00 200.00

99 "WOOLFS" FROM TRUTH (see Sketches of Lowly Life in a Great City, Truth)
Truth Company, NY: 1896 (9x5-1/2", 72 pgs, varnished paper-like cloth hard-c, 25 cents)

nn - By Michael Angelo Woolf (Rare) 150.00 310.00 675.00

NOTE: *Woolf's cartoons are regarded as a primary influence on R.F. Outcault in the later development of The Yellow Kid newspaper strip. Copy sold in 2002 on eBay for $800.00.*

NONSENSE OR, THE TREASURE BOX OF UNCONSIDERED TRIFLES
Fisher & Brother, 12 North Sixth St, Phila, PA, 64 Baltimore St, Baltimore, MD: early 1850s (4-1/2x7", 128 pgs, B&W)
nn - much Davy Crocket sequential story-telling comic strips 310.00 640.00 1325.00

OBADIAH OLDBUCK, THE ADVENTURES OF MR. (E,G)
Tilt & Bogue, London: nd (1840-41) (5-15/16x9-3/16", 176 pgs,B&W, gilted hard-c)

nn - By Rodolphe Töpffer 825.00 1325.00 3300.00
nn - Hand coloured edition (Very Rare) (no known sales)

NOTE: *This is the British edition, translating the unauthorized redrawn 1839 edition from Parisian publisher Aubert, adapted from Töpffer's "Les Amours de Mr. Vieux Bois" (aka "Histoire de Mr. Vieux Bois"), originally published in French in Switzerland, in 1837 (2nd ed. 1839). Early 19th century books are often found rebound, with original cover and/or title page gone. To distinguish editions having no cover or title page: the British oblong editions (published by Tilt & Bogue) use Roman Numerals to number pages. American oblong shaped editions use Arabic Numerals. British are printed on one side only. This is the earliest known English language sequential comic book. Has a new title page with art by Robert Cruikshank.*

OBADIAH OLDBUCK, THE ADVENTURES OF MR. (E,G)
Wilson and Company, New York: September 14, 1842 (11-3/4x9", 44 pgs, B&W, yellow paper-c on bookstand editions, hemp paper interior)

Brother Jonathan Extra No. IX - Rare bookstand edition 2800.00 6000.00 12,000.00
Brother Jonathan Extra No. IX Very Rare subscriber/mailorder
2800.00 6000.00 12,000.00

NOTE: *By Rodolphe Töpffer. Earliest known sequential American comic book, reprinting the 1841 British edition. Pages are numbered via Roman numerals. States "BROTHER JONATHAN EXTRA - ADVENTURES OF MR. OBADIAH OLDBUCK." at the top of each page. Prints 2 to 3 tiers of panels on both sides of each page. Copies could be had for ten cents according to adverts in* **Brother Jonathan**. *By Rodolphe Töpffer with cover masthead design by David Claypool Johnston, and cover art beneath the masthead reprinting Robert Cruik-shank's title page art from the Tilt & Bogue edition. A special, additional cover was added for copies sold on stands (it was not issued with mail order or subscriber copies). Only 1 known copy possesses (partially) this very thin outer yellow cover. A decent (subscriber) copy sold on eBay in later October 2002 for over $3500.00.*
In 2005, a GD/VG for $20,000; and a VG for $20,000. An apparent GD copy sold in auction in 2007 for $9560. A FR/GD copy sold in 2008 for $4182.50. A bound edition sold in 2010 for $2270.50. A copy in GD (restored) sold in 2012 for $5377. A Poor condition copy sold in 2014 for $4780. A Fair condition copy sold for $3107 in 2018. (Prices vary widely.)

OBADIAH OLDBUCK, THE ADVENTURES OF MR. (E,G)
Wilson & Co, New York: nd (1849) (5-11/16x8-3/8", 84 pgs, B&W,paper-c)

nn - by Rodolphe Töpffer; title page by Robert Cruikshank (Very Rare)
600.00 1400.00 4300.00

NOTE: *2nd Wilson & Co printing, reformatted into a small oblong format, with nine panels edited out, and text modified to smooth out this removal. Results in four less printed tiers/strips. Pages are numbered via Arabic numerals. Every panel on Pages 11, 14, 19, 21, 24, 34, 35 has one line of text. Reformatted to conform with British first edition.*

FR1.0 GD2.0 FN6.0

OBADIAH OLDBUCK, THE ADVENTURES OF MR. (E,G)
Wilson & Co, 162 Nassau, NY: nd (early-1850s) (5-11/16x8-3/8", 84 pgs, B&W, yellow-c

nn - 3rd USA Printing by Rodolphe Töpffer; title page by Robert Cruikshank (Very Rare)
Says By Timothy Crayon, an obvious pseudonym 800.00 1600.00 4300.00

NOTE: Front cover banner the giant is holding says "Done With Drawings By Timothy Crayon, Gypsographer, 188 Comic Etchings On Antimony" Title page changes address to No. 15 Spruce-Street. (Late 162 Nassau Street.)

OBADIAH OLDBUCK, THE ADVENTURES OF MR..
Brother Jonathan Offices: ND (mid-1850s) (5-11/16x8-3/8", 84 pages, B&W, oblong)

nn - 4th printing; Originally by Rodolphe Töpffer (Very Rare) 600.00 1400.00 4300.00

NOTE: *Cover States: "New York: Published at the Brother Jonathan Office". Front cover banner the giant is holding says "Done With Drawings By Timothy Crayon, Gypsographer, 188 Comic Designs On Antimony."*

OBADIAH OLDBUCK, THE ADVENTURES OF MR. (E,G)
Dick & Fitzgerald, New York: nd (various printings; est. 1870s to 1888)
(Thirty Cents, 84 pgs, B&W, paper-c) (all versions scarce)

nn - Black print on green cover(5-11/16x8-15/16"); string bound 250.00 500.00 1100.00
nn - Black print on blue cover; same format as green-c 250.00 500.00 1100.00
nn - Black print on white cover(5-13/16x9-3/16"); staple bound beneath cover);
this is a later printing than the blue or green-c 250.00 500.00 1100.00

NOTE: *Reprints the abbreviated 1849 Wilson & Co. 2nd printing. Pages are numbered via Arabic numerals. Many of the panels on Pages 11, 14, 19, 21, 24, 34, 35 take two lines to print the same words found in the Wilson & Co version, which used only one text line for the same panels. Unknown whether the blue or green cover is earlier. White cover version has "thirty cents" line blackened out on the two copies known to exist. Robert Cruikshank's title page has been made the cover in the D&F editions.*

OLD FOGY'S COMIC ALMANAC
Philip J. Cozans, NY: 1858 (4-7/8x7-1/4, 48 pgs)

nn - sequential comic strip told one panel per page 50.00 100.00 220.00

NOTE: Contains (12) panel "Fourth of July in New York" sequential

OLD MOTHER MITTEN AND HER FUNNY KITTEN (see also **The Juvenile Gem**) (O)
Huestis & Cozans: nd(1850-1852) (6x3-7/8"12pgs, hand colored paper-c, B&W)

nn - first printing(s) publisher's address is 104 Nassau Street (1850-1851)
(Very Rare) (no known sales)

NOTE: *A hand colored outer cover is highly rare, with only 1 recorded copy possessing it. Front cover image and text is repeated precisely on page 3 (albeit b&w), and only interior pages are numbered, together leading owners of coverless copies to believe they have the cover. The true back cover has ads for the publisher. Cover was issued only with copies which were sold separately - books which were bound together as part of THE JUVENILE GEM never had such covers.*

OLD MOTHER MITTEN AND HER FUNNY KITTEN (see JUVENILE GEM) (O)
Philip J. Cozans: nd (1850-1852) (6x3-7/8",12 pgs, hand colored paper-c, B&W)

nn - Second printing(s) publisher's address is 116 Nassau Street (1851-1852)
(Very Rare) (no known sales)
nn - Third printing(s) publisher's address is 107 Nassau Street (1852+)
(Very Rare) (no known sales)

OLD MOTHER MITTEN AND HER FUNNY KITTEN
Americana Review, Scotia, NY: nd (1960's) (6-1/4x4-1/8", 8 pgs, side-stapled, cardboard, B&W)

nn - Modern reprint 6.00 12.00 20.00

NOTE: *Issued within a folder titled SIX CHILDREN'S BOOKS OF THE 1850'S. States "Reprinted by American Review" at bottom of front cover. Reprints the 104 Nassau Street address.*

ON THE NILE (O,G)
James R. Osgood & Co., Boston: 1874 ; **Houghton, Osgood & Co., Boston:** 1880 (112 pgs, gilted green hardcover, B&W)

1st printing (1874; 10-3/4x16") - by Augustus Hoppin 50.00 100.00 200.00
2nd printing (1880; smaller sized) 32.50 65.00 130.00

OSCAR SHANGHAI, THE EXTRAORDINARY AND MIRTH-PROVKING ADVENTURES BY SEA & LAND OF (O, G)
Garrett & Co., Publishers, No. 18 Ann Street, New York: May 1855 (5-3/4x9-1/4", 100 pgs, printed one side only, paper-c, 25¢, B&W)

nn - Samuel Avery-c; interior by ALC Very Rare) 1100.00 2200.00 4200.00

NOTE: *Not much is known of this first edition as the data comes from a recently rediscovered* **Brother Jonathan** *catalog issued circa 1853-55. No original known yet to exist.*

OSCAR SHANGHAI, THE WONDERFUL AND AMUSING DOINGS BY SEA AND LAND OF (G)
Dick & Fitzgerald, 10 Ann St, NY: nd (1870s-1888) (25 ¢, 5-3/4x9-1/4", 100 pgs, printed one side only, green paper c, B&W)

nn - Cover by Samuel Avery; interior by ALC (Rare) 310.00 550.00 1200.00

NOTE: *Exact reprint of Garrett & Co original.*

OUR ARTIST IN CUBA (O)
Carleton, New York: 1865 (6-5/8x4-3/8", 120 pgs, printed one side only, gilted hard-c, B&W)

nn - By Geo. W. Carleton 50.00 100.00 200.00

OUR ARTIST IN CUBA, PERU, SPAIN, AND ALGIERS (O)
Carleton: 1877 (6-1/2x5-1/8", 156 pgs, hard-c, B&W)

nn - By Geo. W. Carleton 50.00 100.00 200.00
nn - By Geo. W. Carleton (wraps paper cover) (Rare) 50.00 100.00 200.00

NOTE: *Reprints OUR ARTIST IN CUBA and OUR ARTIST IN PERU, then adds new section on Spain and Algiers.*

OUR ARTIST IN PERU (O)

The Wonderful and Amusing Doings by Sea & Land of Oscar Shanghai
1870s © Dick & Fitzgerald, New York

Pictorial History of Senator Slim's Voyage To Europe
1860 © Dr. Herrick & Brother, Albany, NY

Puck #1
1877 © Keppler & Schwarzman, NY

FR1.0 GD2.0 FN6.0

Carleton, New York: 1866 (7-3/4x5-7/8", 68 pgs, gilted hardcover, B&W)
nn- By Geo. W. Carleton 37.50 75.00 150.00
NOTE: *Contains advertisement for the upcoming books **OUR ARTIST IN ITALY** and **OUR ARTIST IN FRANCE**, but no such publications have been found to date.*

PARSON SOURBALL'S EUROPEAN TOUR (O)
Duff and Ashmead: 1867 (6x7-1/2", 76 pgs, blue embossed title hard-c)
nn - By Horace Cope 100.00 200.00 425.00
NOTE: see **REV. MR. SOURBALL'S EUROPEAN TOUR, THE** for the soft paper cover version

PEN AND INK SKETCHES OF YALE NOTABLES (O,S)
Soule, Thomas and Winsor, St. Louis: 1872 (12-1/4x9-3/4", B&W)
By Squills 30.00 60.00 120.00
NOTE: *Printed by Steamlith Press, The R.P. Studley Company, St Louis.*

PETER PIPER IN BENGAL
Bengamin H Day.Publisher, Brother Jonathan Cheap Book Establishment, 48 Beekman, NY: 1953-55 (6-5/8x4-1/4, 36 pgs, yellow paper-c, B&W, 3 cents - two dollars per hundred) (Very Rare)
nn - By John Tenniel - 32 panel comic strip Punch-r 550.00 1100.00 2400.00
NOTE: *Actually also a catalog of inexpensive books, prints, maps and half a dozen comic books for sale on separate pages from publishers Day and Garrett - see full story of this brand new find in the Victorian Era essay. A complete copy with split spine sold in November 2002 for $750.00. Published date most likely 1855.*

THE PHILADELPHIA COMIC ALMANAC (S)
G. Strong, 44 Strawberry St, NYC: 1835 (8-1/2x5", 36 pgs)
nn - 100.00 200.00 625.00
NOTE: 77 engravings full of recurring cartoon characters but not sequential; early use of recurring characters.

PHIL MAY'S SKETCH BOOK (E,S,M)
R.H. Russell, New York: 1899 (14-5/8x10", 64 pgs, brown hard-c, B&W)
nn - By Phil May 40.00 75.00 150.00
NOTE: *American reprint of the British edition.*

PHUNNY PHELLOW, THE
Oakie, Dayton & Jones: Oct 1859-1876; **Street & Smith** 1876: (Folio Monthly)
average issue with Thomas Nast 50.00 100.00 220.00

PHUN FOTOCRAFT, KEWREUS KONSEETS KOMICALLY ILLUSTRATED BY A KWEER FELLER (N) (see **NEW YORK PICAYUNE)**
The New York Picayune, NY: 1850s (104 pgs)
nn - Mostly Frank Bellew, some John Leach 300.00 600.00 1200.00
NOTE: *Many sequential comic strips as well as single cartoons all collected from The New York Picayune. Ross & Tousey, Agents, 121 Nassau St, NY. The Picayune ran many sequential comic strips in its decade.*

PICTORIAL HISTORY OF SENATOR SLIM'S VOYAGE TO EUROPE
Dr. Herrick & Brother, Chemists, Albany, NY: 1860 (3-1/4x4-3/4", 32 pgs, B&W)
nn - By John McLenan Very Rare 150.00 300.00 600.00

PICTURES OF ENGLISH SOCIETY (Parchment-Paper Series, No.4) (M,S,E)
D. Appleton & Co., New York: 1884 (5-5/8x4-3/8", 108 pgs, paper-c, B&W)
4 - By George du Maurier; Punch-r 30.00 60.00 125.00
NOTE: *Every other page is a full page cartoon, with the opposite page containing the cartoon's caption.*

PICTURES OF LIFE AND CHARACTER (M,S,E)
Bradbury and Evans, London: No.1 1855 - No.5 c1864 (12-1/2x18", 100 pgs, illustrated hard-c, B&W)
nn (No.1) (1855) 40.00 80.00 180.00
2 (1858), 3 (1860) 40.00 80.00 180.00
4 (nd; c1862) 5 (nd; c1864) 40.00 80.00 180.00
nn (nd (late 1860's) 35.00 70.00 160.00
NOTE: 2-1/2x18-1/4", 494 pgs, green gilted-c) reprints 1-5 in one book
1-3 John Leech's... (nd; 12-3/8x10", ? pgs, red gilted-c). 30.00 60.00 110.00
NOTE: *Reprints John Leech cartoons from **Punch**. note that the Volume Number is mentioned only on the last page of these versions.*

PICTURES OF LIFE AND CHARACTER (E,M,S)
G.P. Putnam's Sons: 1880's (8-5/8x6-1/4", 218 pgs, hardcover, color-cr, B&W)
nn - John Leech (single panel **Punch** cartoon-r) 25.00 50.00 180.00
NOTE: *Leech reprints which extend back to the 1850s.*

PICTURES OF LIFE AND CHARACTER (Parchment-Paper Series) (E,M,S)
(see also Humerous Masterpieces)
D. Appleton & Co., NY: 1884 (30¢, 5-3/4 x 4-1/2", 104 pgs, paper-c, B&W)
nn - John Leech (single panel **Punch** cartoon-r) 20.00 40.00 160.00
NOTE: *An advertisment in the back refers to a cloth-bound edition for 50 cents.*

PIPPIN AMONG THE WIDE-AWAKES (O,S)
Werill & Chapin, 113 Nassau St, NYC, NY): 1860 (6x4-1/2", 36 pgs, 6 cents)
nn - Artist unknown (Very Rare) 100.00 200.00 410.00

PLISH AND PLUM (E.G)
Roberts Brothers, Boston: 1883 (8-1/8x5-3/4", 80 pgs, hardcover, B&W)
nn - By Wilhelm Busch 50.00 100.00 230.00
nn - Reprint (Roberts Brothers, 1895) 40.00 80.00 200.00
nn - Reprint (Little, Brown & Co., 1899) 40.00 80.00 200.00
NOTE: *The adventures of two dogs.*

POUNDS OF FUN
Frank Tousey, 34 North Moore St, NY: 1881 (6-1/2x9-1/2", 68pgs, B&W)
nn - Bellew, Worth, Woolf, Chips 40.00 80.00 200.00

PRESIDENTS MESSAGE, THE
G.P. Putnam's Sons, NY: 1887 (5-3/4x7-5/8, 44 pgs)
nn - (19) Thomas Nast single panel full page cartoons 50.00 100.00 220.00

PROTECT THE U.S. FROM JOHN BULL - PROTECTION PICTURES FROM JUDGE
Judge Publishing, New York: 1888 ((10 cents, 6-7/8x10-3/8", 36 pgs, paper-c, B&W)
nn - (Scarce) 30.00 60.00 140.00
NOTE: *Reprints both cartoons and commentary from **Puck**, concerning the issue of tariffs which were then being debated in Congress. Art by Gillam, Hamilton, Victor.*

PUCK (German language edition, St. Louis) (M,O) (see also Die Vehme)
Publisher unknown, St. Louis: No.1, March 18, 1871 - No. ??, Aug. 24, 1872 (B&W, paper-c)
1-?? (Very Rare) by Joseph Keppler (no known sales)
NOTE: *Joseph Keppler's second attempt at a weekly humor periodical, following **Die Vehme** one year earlier. This was his first attempt to launch using the title **Puck**. This German language version ran for a full year before being joined by an English language version.*

PUCK (English language edition, St. Louis) (M,O)
Publisher unknown, St. Louis: No.1, March ?? 1872 - No. ??, Aug. 24, 1872 (B&W, paper c)
1-?? (Very Rare) by Joseph Keppler (no known sales)
NOTE: *Same material as in the German language edition, but in English.*

PUCK, ILLUSTRIRTES HUMORISTISCHES WOCHENBLATT (German language edition, NYC) (M,O)
Keppler & Schwarzmann, New York: No.1 Sept (27) 1876 - 1164 Dec ?? 1899 (10 cents, color front/back-c and centerspread, remainder B&W, paper-c)
1-26 (Volume 1; Rare) by Joseph Keppler - these issues precede the English language version, and contain cartoons not found in them. Includes cartoons on the controversial Tilden-Hayes 1876 Presidential Election debacle. (no known sales)
27-52 (Volume 2; Rare) by Joseph Keppler - contains some cartoon material not found in the English language editions. Particularly in the earlier issues. (no known sales)
53-1164 15.00 30.00 60.00
Bound Volumes (six month, 26 issue run each):
Vol. 1 (Rare) (no known sales)
Vol. 2-4 (Rare) (no known sales)
Vol. 5-47 75.00 150.00 310.00
NOTE: *Joseph Keppler's second, and successful, attempt to launch **Puck**. In German. The first six months precede the launch of the English language edition. Soon after (but not immediately after) the launch of the English edition, both editions began sharing the same cartoons, but, their prose material always remained different. The German language edition ceased publication at the end of 1899, while the English language edition continued into the early 20th Century. First American periodical to feature printed color every issue.*

PUCK (English language edition, NYC) (M,O)
Keppler & Schwarzmann, New York: No.1 March (14) 1877 - 1190 Dec ?? 1899 (10 cents, color front/back-c and centerspread, remainder B&W, paper-c)
1 (Rare) by Joseph Keppler (no known sales)
2-26 (Rare) by Joseph Keppler (no known sales)
27-1190 12.50 25.00 50.00
(see Platinum Age section for year 1900+ issues)
Bound volumes (six month, 26 issue run each):
Vol. 1 (Rare) (one set sold on eBay for $2300.00)
Vol. 2 (Scarce) (one set sold on eBay for $1500.00)
Vol. 3-6 (pre-1880 issues) 200.00 400.00 800.00
Vol. 7-46 140.00 300.00 600.00
NOTE: *The English language editions began six months after the German editions, and so the English edition numbering is always one volume number, and 26 issue numbers, behind its parallel German language edition. Pre-1880 & post-1900 issues are more scarce than 1880's & 1890's.*

PUCK (miniature) (M,P,I)
Keppler & Schwarzmann, New York: nd (c1895) (7x5-1/8", 12 pgs, color front & back paper-c, B&W interior)
nn - Scarce 25.00 50.00 110.00
NOTE: *C.J. Taylor-c; F.M. Howarth-a; F. Opper-a; giveaway item promoting **Puck's** various publications. Mostly text, with art reprinted from **Puck**.*

PUCK, CARTOONS FROM (M,S)
Keppler & Schwarzmann, New York: 1893 (14-1/4x11-1/2", 244 pgs, hard-c, mostly B&W)
nn - by Joseph Keppler (Signed and Numbered) 105.00 225.00 475.00
NOTE: *Reprints Keppler cartoons from 1877 to 1893, mostly in B&W, though a few in color, with a text opposite each cartoon explaining the situation then being satirized. Issued only in an edition of 300 numbered issues, signed by Keppler. Only 1/4 of the pages are cartoons.*

PUCK'S LIBRARY (M)
Keppler & Schwarzmann, New York: No.1, July, 1887 - No. 174, Dec, 1899 (10 cents, 11-1/2x8-1/4", 36 pgs, color paper-c, B&W)
1- "The National Game" (Baseball) 70.00 130.00 285.00
2-149 10.00 20.00 50.00
NOTE: ***Puck's Library** was a monthly magazine reprinting cartoons & prose from **Puck**, with each issue's material organized around the same subject. The cover art was often original. All issues were kept in print for the duration of the series, so later issues are more scarce than earlier ones.*

PUCK, PICKINGS FROM (M)
Keppler & Schwarzmann, New York: No.1, Sept, 1891 - No. 34, Dec, 1899

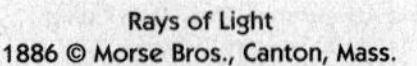
Rays of Light
1886 © Morse Bros., Canton, Mass.

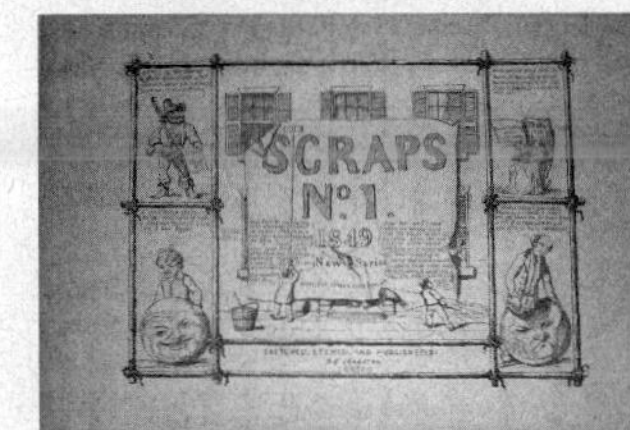
Scraps, New Series #1 by D.C. Johnston
1849 © D.C. Johnston, Boston

Shakespeare Would Ride The Bicycle If Alive Today
1896 © Cleveland Bicycles, Toledo, OH.

(25 cents, 13-1/4x10-1/4", 68 pgs, color paper-c, B&W)

1-34 Scarce 25.00 50.00 110.00

NOTE: *Similar to **Puck's Library**, except larger in size, and issued quarterly. All reprint material, except for the cover art. There also exist variations with "RAILROAD EDITION 30 CENTS" printed on the cover in place of the standard 25 cent price.*

PUCK'S OPPER BOOK (M)
Keppler & Schwarzmann, New York: 1888 (11-3/4x13-7/8", color paper-c, 68 pgs,interior B&W, 30¢)

nn - (Very Rare) by F. Opper 225.00 450.00 810.00

NOTE: *Puck's first book collecting work by a single artist.; mostly sequential comic strips.*

PUCK'S PRINTING BOOK FOR CHILDREN (S,O.I)
Keppler & Schwarzman, Pubs, NY: 1891 (10-3/8x7-7/8", 52 pgs, color-c, B&W and color)

nn - Frederick B Opper (Very Rare) (no known sales)

NOTE: *Left side printed in color; Right side B&W to be colored in.*

PUCK PROOFS (M,P,S)
Keppler & Schwarzmann, New York: nd (1906-1909) (74 pgs, paper cover; B&W) (all are Scarce)

nn - (c.1906, no price, 4-1/8x5-1/4") B&W painted -c of couple kissing over a chess board; 1905 & 1906-r 25.00 50.00 100.00

nn- (c.1909, 10 cents, 4-3/8x5-3/8") plain green paper-c; 76 pgs 1905-1909-r 25.00 50.00 100.00

NOTE: *Catalog of prints available from **Puck**, reprinting mostly cover & centerspread art from **Puck**. There likely exist more as yet unreported **Puck Proofs** catalogs. Art by Rose O'Neill.*

PUCK, THE TARIFF ?, CARTOONS AND COMMENTS FROM (M,S)
Keppler & Schwarzmann, New York: 1888 (10 cents, 6-7/8x10-3/8", 36 pgs, paper-c, B&W)

nn - (Scarce) 37.50 75.00 200.00

NOTE: *Reprints both cartoons and commentary from **Puck**, concerning the issue of tariffs which were then being debated in Congress. Art by Gillam, Keppler, Opper, Taylor.*

PUCK, WORLD'S FAIR
Keppler & Schwarzmann, PUCK BUILDING, World's Fair Grounds, Chicago: No.1 May 1, 1893 - No.26 Oct 30, 1893 (10 cents, 11-1/4x8-3/4, 14 pgs, paper-c, color front/back/center pages, rest B&W)(All issues Scarce to Rare)

1-26 35.00 70.00 140.00
1-26 bound volume: 600.00 1200.00 2400.00

NOTE: *Art by Joseph Keppler, F. Opper, F.M. Howarth, C.J. Taylor, W.A. Rogers. This was a separate, parallel run of **Puck**, published during the 1893 Chicago World's Fair from within the fairgrounds, and containing all new and different material than the regular weekly **Puck**. Smaller sized and priced the same, this originally sold poorly, and had not as wide distribution as **Puck**, and so consequently issues are much more rare than regular **Puck** issues from the same period. Not to be confused with the larger sized regular **Puck** issues from 1893 which sometimes also contained World's Fair related material, and sometimes had the words "World's Fair" appear on the cover. Can also be distinguished by the fact that **Puck's** issue numbering was in the 800's in 1893, while these issue number 1 through 26.*

PUNCHINELLO
Punchinello Publishing Co, NYC: April 2-Dec 24 1870 (weekly)

1-39 Henry L. Stephens, Frank Bellew, Bowlend 25.00 50.00 100.00

NOTE: *Funded by the Tweed Ring, mild politics attacking Grant Admin & other NYC newspapers. Bound copies exist.*

QUIDDITIES OF AN ALASKAN TRIP (O,G)
G.A. Steel & Co., Portland, OR: 1873 (6-3/4x10-1/2", 80 pgs, gilted hard-c, Red-c and Blue-c exist, B&W)

nn - By William H. Bell (Scarce) 350.00 750.00 1800.00

NOTE: *Highly sought Western Americana collectors. Parody of a trip from Washington DC to Alaska, by a member of the team which went to survey Alaska, purchase commonly known then as "Seward's Folly".*

"RAG TAGS" AND THEIR ADVENTURES, THE (N,S)
A. M. Robertson, San Francisco: 1899 (10-1/4x13-7/8, 84 pgs, color hard-c, B&W inside)

nn - By Arthur M. Lewis (SF Chronicle newspaper-r) (Scarce) 65.00 125.00 310.00

RAYS OF LIGHT (O,P)
Morse Bros., Canton, Mass.: No.1 1886 (7-1/8x5-1/8", 8 pgs, color paper-c, B&W)

1- (Rare) 50.00 100.00 200.00

NOTE: *Giveaway pamphlet in guise of an educational publication, consisting entirely of a sequential story in which a teacher instructs her classroom of young girls in the use of Rising Sun Stove Polish. Color front & back covers.*

RELIC OF THE ITALIAN REVOLUTION OF 1849, A
Gabici's Music Stores, New Orleans: 1849 (10-1/8x12-3/4", 144 pgs, hardcover)

nn - By G. Daelli (Scarce) 100.00 210.00 425.00

NOTE: *From the title page: "Album of fifty line engravings, executed on copper, by the most eminent artists at Rome in 1849; secreted from the papal police after the 'Restoration of Order,' And just imported into America."*

REMARKS ON THE JACOBINIAD (I,S)
E.W. Weld & W. Greenough, Boston: 1795-98 (8-1/4x5-1/8", 72 pgs, a number of B&W plates with text)

nn - Written by Rev. James Sylvester Gardner,artist unknown (Rare) (no known sales)

NOTE: *Early comics-type characters. Not sequential comics, but uses word balloons. Satire directed against "The Jacobin Club," supporters of the French Revolution and Radical Republicans. Gardner came to America from England in 1783, was minister of Trinity Church, Boston. There appears to be some reprints of this done as late as 1798.*

REV. MR. SOURBALL'S EUROPEAN TOUR, THE RECREATION OF A CITY, THE
Duffield Ashmead, Philadelphia: 1867 (7-5/8x6-1/4", 72 pgs, turquoise blue soft wrappers)

By Horace Cope (Rare) 50.00 100.00 225.00

NOTE: *see* **PARSON SOURBALL'S EUROPEAN TOUR** *for the hard cover version.*

RHYMES OF NONSENSE TRUTH & FICTION (S)
G.W. Carleton & Co, Publishers, NY: 1874 (10x7-3/4", 44 pgs, hard-c, B&W) (Very Rare)

nn - By Chaucer Jones and Michael Angelo Raphael Smith 100.00 200.00 475.00

NOTE: *Creator names obviously pseudonyms; looks like weak A.B. Frost.*

ROMANCE OF A HAMMOCK, THE - AS RECITED BY MR. GUS WILLIAMS IN "ONE OF THE FINEST" (O,P)
Unknown: 1880s (5-1/2x3-5/8" folded, 7 attached cardboard cards which fold out into a strip, color)

nn - By presently unknown Scarce 100.00 200.00 400.00

NOTE: *12-panel story, which one begins reading on one side of the folded-out strip, then flip to the other side to continue -- unlike the vast majority of folded strips, which are printed on only one side. This was a promotional handout, for a play titled "One of the Finest". The story pictured comes from a poem read in the play by then famous New York stage actor Gus Williams, who is pictured on the "cover"/title card."*

SAD TALE OF THE COURTSHIP OF CHEVALIER SLYFOX-WIKOF, SHOWING HIS HEART-RENDING ASTOUNDING & MOST WONDERFUL LOVE ADVENTURES WITH FANNY ELSSLER AND MISS GAMBOL, THE (O,G)
Garrett & Co., NY: Jan 1856 (25 ¢, 5-3/4x9-1/4", 100 pages, paper-c, B&W)

nn - By T.C. Bond ?? (Very Rare) 550.00 1100.00 2325.00

NOTE: *No surviving copies yet reported -- known via ads in Home Circle published by Garrett. Cover art by John McLenan and Samuel Avery. Graphic novel parodying the real-life romance between European actress/dancer Fanny Elssler and American aristocrat Henry Wikoff. The entire graphic novel is reprinted in the 1976 book "Fanny Elssler in America."*

SAD TALE OF THE COURTSHIP OF CHEVALIER SLYFOX-WIKOF, SHOWING HIS HEART-RENDING ASTOUNDING & MOST WONDERFUL LOVE ADVENTURES WITH FANNY ELSSLER AND MISS GUMBEL, THE (G) (25 cents printed on cover)
Dick And Fitzgerald, NY: 1870s-1888 (5-3/4x9-1/4", ??? pages, soft paper-c, B&W)

nn - By T.C. Bond ?? (Very Rare) 250.00 500.00 1225.00

NOTE: *Reprint of Garrett original printing before G,D&F partnership begins.*

SALT RIVER GUIDE FOR DISAPPOINTED POLITICIANS
Winchell, Small & Co., 113 Fulton St, NY: 1870s (16 pgs, 10¢)

nn - single panel cartoons from Wlld Oats (Rare) 75.00 150.00 300.00

SAM SLICK'S COMIC ALMANAC
Philip J. Cozans, NYC: 1857 (7.5x4.5, 48 pgs, B&W) 100.00 200.00 400.00

NOTE: *Contains reprint of* "Moses Keyser the Bowery Bully's Trip to the California Gold Mines" *from* Elton's Comic Almanac *#17 1850.*

SCRAPS (O,S) (see also **F****** A*** K*******)
D.C. Johnston, Boston: 1828 - No.8 1840; New Series No.1 1849 (12 pgs, printed one side only, paper-c, B&W)

1 - 1828 (9-1/4 x 11-3/4") (Very Rare) (no known sales)
2 - 1830 (9-3/4 x 12-3/4") (Very Rare) (no known sales)
3 - 1832 (10-7/8 x 13-1/8") (Very Rare) (no known sales)
4 - 1833 (11 x 13-5/8") (Very Rare) (no known sales)
5- 1834 (10-3/8 x 13-3/8") (Very Rare) (no known sales)
6 - 1835 (10-3/8 x 13-1/4") red lettering in title SCRAPS (Very Rare) 300.00 600.00 1300.00
6 - 1835 (10-3/8 x 13-1/4") no red lettering in title (Rare) 225.00 500.00 1100.00
7 - 1837 (10-3/4 x 13-7/8") 1st Edition (Very Rare) 200.00 400.00 900.00
7 - 1837 (10-3/4 x 13-3/4") 2nd Edition (so stated) 100.00 175.00 375.00

NOTE: *20 pgs. of text (double-sided), 4 pgs. of art (single-sided), plus the covers. There are no protective sheets between the art pages.*

8 - 1840 (10-1/2 x 13-7/8") (Rare) 200.00 400.00 900.00
New Series 1- 1849 (10-7/8 x 13-3/4") 125.00 250.00 500.00

NOTE: *By David Claypoole Johnston. All issues consist of four one-sided sheets with 9 to 12 single panel cartoons per sheet. The other pages are blank or text. With #1-5 the size of the pages can vary up to an inch. Contains 4 protective sheets (not part of page count) Only 1 3 4 and the 1849 New Series Number 1 has cover art along with 4 art pgs. (single sided) with 4 protective sheets and no text pages.New Series Number 1, as well as #6 with bo red lettering and the second printing of issue 7, have survived in higher numbers due to a 1940s warehouse discovery.*

THE SETTLEMENT OF RHODE ISLAND (O)
The Graphic Co. Photo-Lith 39 & 41, Park Place, New York: 1874 (11-3/8x10, 40 pgs, gilted blue hard-c

nn - Charles T. Miller & Walter F. Brown 75.00 150.00 300.00

NOTE: *This is also the Same Walter F. Brown that did "Hail Columbia".*

SHAKESPEARE WOULD RIDE THE BICYCLE IF ALIVE TODAY. "THE REASON WHY" (O,P,S)
Cleveland Bicycles H.A. Lozier & Co., Toledo, OH: 1896 (5-1/2x4",16 pgs, paper-c, color)

nn - By F. Opper (Rare) 75.00 150.00 360.00

NOTE: *Original cartoons of Shakespearian characters riding bicycles; also popular amongst collectors of bicycle ephemera.*

SHAKINGS - ETCHINGS FROM THE NAVAL ACADEMY BY A MEMBER OF THE CLASS OF '67 (O,S)
Lee & Shepard, Boston: 1867 (7-7/8x10", 132 pages, blue hard-c)

By: Park Benjamin 38.00 75.00 150.00

Stumping It
1876 © Collin & Lee, NY

Texas Siftings v6 #2 May 15
1886 ©Texas Siftings Publishing Co.

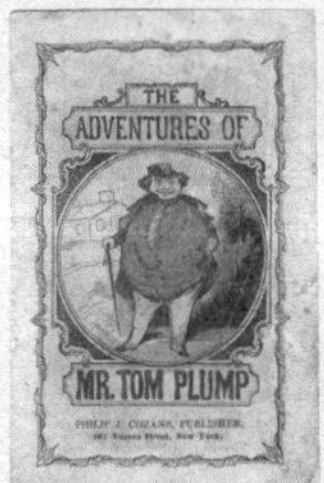

The Adventures Of Mr. Tom Plump
1851 © Huestis & Cozans, NY

NOTE: *Park Benjamin later became editor of Harper's Bazaar magazine.*

SHOO FLY PICTORIAL (S)
John Stetson, Chestnut sT Theatre, Phila, PA: June 1870 (15-1/2x11-1/2", 8 pgs, B&W)
1 75.00 150.00 275.00

SHYS AT SHAKSPEARE
J.P. and T.C.P., Philadelphia: 1869 (9-1/4x6", 52 pgs)
nn - Artist unknown 75.00 150.00 310.00

SKETCHES OF LOWLY LIFE IN A GREAT CITY (M,S) (See 99 "Woolfs" From Truth)
G. P. Puntam's Sons: 1899 (8-5/8x11-1/4", 200 pgs, hard-c, B&W)
(reprints from Life and Judge of Woolf's cartoons of NYC slum children)
nn - By Michael Angelo Woolf 105.00 190.00 425.00
NOTE: *Woolf's cartoons are regarded as a primary influence on R.F. Outcault in the later development of The Yellow Kid newspaper strip.*

SNAP (O,S)
Valentine & Townsend, Tribune Bldg, NYC: March 13,1885 (17x11, 8 pgs, B&W)
1-Contains a sequential comic strip 50.00 100.00 200.00

SOCIETY PICTURES (M,S,E)
Charles H. Sergel Company, Chicago: 1895 (5-1/4x7-3/4", 168 pgs, printed 1 side, paper-c, B&W)
nn - By George du Maurier; reprints from **Punch**. 25.00 50.00 125.00

SOLDIERS AND SAILORS HALF DIME TALES OF THE LATE REBELLION
Soldiers & Sailors Publishing Co: 1868 (5-1/4x7-7/8", 32 pgs)
v1#1-#16 v2#1-#10 15.00 30.00 60.00
v2 #11 contains (5) page comic strip 25.00 50.00 100.00
NOTE: *Changes to Soldiers & Sailors Half Dime Magazine with v2 #1.*

SOUVENIR CONTAINING CARTOONS ISSUED BY THE PRESS BUREAU OF THE OHIO STATE REPUBLICAN EXECUTIVE COMMITTEE, A (S)
Ohio State Republican Executive Committee, Columbus, OH: 1899 (10-3/8x13-1/2, 248 pgs, Hard-c, B&W
nn - By William L. Bloomer (Scarce) 105.00 225.00 450.00

SOUVENIR OF SOHMER CARTOONS FROM PUCK, JUDGE, AND FRANK LESLIE'S (M,S,P)
Sohmer Piano Co.: nd(c.1893) (6x4-3/4", 16 pgs, paper-c, B&W)
nn 25.00 50.00 100.00
NOTE: *Reprints painted "cartoon" Sohmer Piano advertisements which appeared in the above publications. Artists include Keppler, Gillam, others.*

SPORTING NEW YORKER, THE
Ornum & Co, Beekman ST, NYC: 1870s
issues with sequential comic strips (Rare) 50.00 100.00 200.00

STORY OF THE MAN OF HUMANITY AND THE BULL CALF, THE
(see Bull Calf, The Story of The Man Of Humanity And The)
NOTE: *Reprints of two of A. B. Frost's mostfamous sequential comic strips.*

STREET & SMITH'S LITERARY ALBUM
Street & Smith, NY: #1 Dec 23 1865-#225 Apr 9 1870 (11-3/4x16-3/4", 16 pgs, B&W)
1 (23 Dec 1865) 15.00 50.00 100.00
2-129 131-225 (issues with short sequential strips) 15.00 50.00 100.00
130 (Steam Man satire parody) 105.00 210.00 350.00

STUFF AND NONSENSE (Harper's Monthly strip-r) (M)
Charles Scribner's Sons: 1884 (10-1/4x7-3/4", 100 pgs, hardcover, B&W)
nn - By Arthur Burdett Frost 125.00 200.00 400.00
nn - By A.B. Frost (1888 reprint, 104 pgs) 50.00 100.00 200.00
NOTE: *Earliest known anthology devoted to collecting the comic strips of a single American artist. 1888 2nd printing has a different cover and is layed out somewhat differently inside with a new title page, 3 added pages of cartoons, and a couple more illustrations. For more Frost, the 2nd is worth checki ng out also.*

STUMPING IT (LAUGHING SERIES BRICKTOP STORIES #8) (O,S)
Collin & Small, NY: 1876 (6-5/8x9-1/4, 68 pgs, perfect bound, B&W)
nn - Thomas Worth art abounds (some sequentials) 110.00 200.00 400.00
NOTE: Mainly single panel cartoons w/text; however, some sequential comic strips inside worth picking up

SUMMER SCHOOL OF PHILOSOPHY AT MT. DESERT, THE
Henry Holt & Co.: 1881 (10-3/8x8-5/8", 60 pgs, illus. gilt hard-c, B&W)
nn - By J. A. Mitchell 60.00 120.00 250.00
NOTE: *J.A.Mitchell went on to found **LIFE** two years later in 1883. Also, the long-running mascot for **LIFE** was Cupid - which you see multitudes of Cupids flying around in this story.*

SURE WATER CURE, THE
Carey Grey & Hart, Phila, PA: c1841-43 (8-/2x5, 32 pgs, B&W
nn - proto-comic-strip Very Rare 175.00 350.00 725.00

TAILOR-MADE GIRL, HER FRIENDS, HER FASHIONS, AND HER FOLLIES, THE
(see also IN THE "400" AND OUT) (M)
Charles Scribner's Sons, New York: 1888 (8-3/8x10-1/2", 68 pgs, hard-c, B&W)
nn - Art by C.J. Taylor 25.00 50.00 110.00
NOTE: *Format is a full page cartoon on every other page, with a script style vignette, written by Philip H. Welch, on every page opposite the art.*

FR1.0 GD2.0 FN6.0

TALL STUDENT, THE
Roberts Brothers, Boston: 1873 (7x5", 48 pgs, printed one side only, gilted hard-c, B&W)
nn - By Wilhelm Busch (Scarce) 37.50 75.00 150.00

TARIFF ?, CARTOONS AND COMMENTS FROM PUCK, THE (see Puck, The Tariff...)

TEASING TOM AND NAUGHTY NED WITH A SPOOL OF CLARK'S COTTON, THE ADVENTURES OF (O,P)
Clark's O.N.T. Spool Cotton: 1879 (4-1/4x3", 12 pgs, B&W, paper-c)
nn 17.50 35.00 80.00
NOTE: *Knock-off of the "First Trick" in Wilhelm Busch's **Max and Maurice**, modified to involve Clark's Spool Cotton in the story, with similar but new art by an artist identified as "HB". The back cover advertises the specific merchant who gave this booklet away -- multiple variations of back cover suspected.*

TEMPERANCE TALES; OR, SIX NIGHTS WITH THE WASHINGTONIANS, VOL I & II
W.A. Leary & Co., Philadelphia: 1848 (50¢, 6-1/8x4", 328 pgs, B&W, hard-c)
nn 160.00 320.00 625.00
NOTE: *Mostly text. This edition gathers Volume I & II together. The first 8 pages reprints George Cruikshank's **THE BOTTLE**, re-drawn & re-engraved by Phil A. Pilliner. Later editions of this book do not include **THE BOTTLE** reprint and are therefore of little interest to comics collectors.*

TEXAS SIFTINGS
Texas Siftings Publishing Co, Austin, Texas (1881-1887), **NYC** (1887-1897): 1881-1885 newspaper-size weekly; 1886-1897 folio weekly (15x10-3/4", 16 pgs, B&W 10¢
1881-1885 issues 25.00 50.00 120.00
v6#1 (5/8/86) (8) panel strip Afterwhich He Emigrated;
(16) panel The Tenor's Triumph Veni Vidi Vici 12.50 25.00 100.00
v6#2 (5/16/86 (5) panel sewuential 12.50 25.00 100.00
v6#3 no sequentials 12.50 25.00 100.00
v6#4 (5/29/86) Worth-c (4) panel Worth strip; (2) panel 12.50 25.00 100.00
v6#5 no sequentials 12.50 25.00 100.00
v6#6 (6/12/86) Comic Strip Cover (11) panels The Rise of a Great Artist
(5) panel sequential 50.00 100.00 205.00
v6#7 (6/19/86) Worth-c (2) panel Wiorth;
(10) panel Ha! Ha! The Honest Youth & the Lordly Villain 25.00 50.00 110.00
v6#8 (6/26/86) Worth-c; (15) panel The Kangaroo Hunter 25.00 50.00 110.00
v6#9 (7/3/86) Worth-c; Bellew (2) panel How Wives Get What They Want
12.50 25.00 100.00
v6#10 ((7/10/86) Baseball-c; (3) panel;
(5) panel A Story Without Words from Fliegende Blätter 12.50 25.00 100.00
v6 #11 12 13 Worth-c no sequentials 12.50 25.00 100.00
v6#14 (8/7/86) Wiorth-c; (7) panel Mrs Cleveland Presents
The President With A New Rocking Chair 12.50 25.00 100.00
v6#15 (8/14/86) Worth-c; (6) panel Worth strip 12.50 25.00 100.00
v6#16 (8/21/86) Worth-c Asleep At Post USA/Mexico Border
(6) panel sequential 12.50 25.00 100.00
v6#17 no sequrntials 12.50 25.00 100.00
v6#18 (9/4/86) Worth-c; (3) panel from Fliegende 12.50 25.00 100.00
v6#19 (9/11/86) Worth Anarchist & Uncle Sam-c;
(5) panel Duel of the Dudes 12.50 25.00 100.00
v6#20 (9/18/86) Worth-c (6) panel sequential 12.50 25.00 100.00
v6#21 (9/25/86) Worth-c; Verbeck single panel; (9) panel 12.50 25.00 100.00
v6#22 (10/2/86) Verbeck-c plus interiors 12.50 25.00 100.00
v6#23 (10/9/86) Worth-c Geronimo & Devil cover;
Verbeck and Chips singles 25.00 50.00 110.00
v6#24 (10/16/86) Worth-c Verbeck strip "Evolution" 12.50 25.00 100.00
v6#25 no sequential strips 12.50 25.00 100.00
v6#26 (10/30/86) Worth-c; (6) panel Verbeck "A Warning To Smokers"
12.50 25.00 100.00
NOTE: *Many Thomas Worth sequential comic strips. Frank Bellew and Dan McCarthy appear. Wilhelm Busch-r from German Fligende Blaetter. Later issues in 1890s comics become sporadic*

THAT COMIC PRIMER (S)
G.W. Carleton & Co., Publishers: 1877 (6-5/8x5", 52 pgs, paper soft-c, B&W)
nn - By Frank Bellew 75.00 150.00 300.00
NOTE: *Premium for the United States Life Insurance Company, New York.*

TIGER, THE LEFTENANT AND THE BOSUN, THE
Prudential Insurance Home Office, 878 & 880 Broad St, Newark, NJ: 1889 (4.5x3.25", 12 pgs) (Scarce)
nn - 8 panel sequential story in color 50.00 100.00 225.00

TOM PLUMP, THE ADVENTURES OF MR. (see also The Juvenile Gem) (O)
Huestis & Cozans, New York: nd (c1850-1851) (6x3-7/8", 12 pgs, hand colored paper-c, B&W)
nn- First printing(s) publisher's address is 104 Nassau Street (1850-1851)
(Very Rare) 800.00 1600.00 3350.00
NOTE: *California Gold Rush story. The hand colored outer cover is highly rare, with only 1 recorded copy possessing it. The front cover image and text is repeated precisely on page 3 (albeit b&w), and only interior pages are numbered, together leading owners of coverless copies to believe they have the cover. The true back cover contains ads for the publisher. The cover was issued only with copies which were sold separately - booklets which were bound together as part of **THE JUVENILE GEM** never had such covers.*

TOM PLUMP, THE ADVENTURES OF MR. (see also The Juvenile Gem) (O)
Philip J. Cozans: nd (1851-1852) (6x3-7/8", 12 pgs,hand colored paper-c, B&W)
nn- Second printing(s) publisher's address is 116 Nassau Street (1851-1852)

Truth #372 (first app. The Yellow Kid)
June 2 1894 © Truth Company, NY

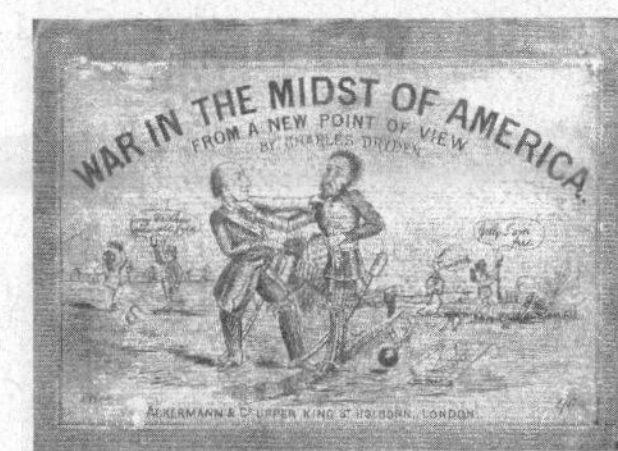

War in the Midst of America
1864 © Ackermann & Co.

Wild Oats #115 March 10
1875 © Winchell & Small, NYC

FR1.0 GD2.0 FN6.0

(Very Rare) 450.00 900.00 1800.00
nn- Third printing(s) publisher's address is 107 Nassau Street (1852+)
(Very Rare) 450.00 900.00 1800.00

TOM PLUMP, THE ADVENTURES OF MR.
Americana Review, Scotia, NY: nd(1960's) (6-1/4x4-1/8", 8 pgs, side-stapled, cardboard-c, B&W)
nn - Modern reprint - 25.00 50.00
NOTE: *Issued within a folder titled SIX CHILDREN'S BOOKS OF THE 1850'S. States "Reprinted by American Review" at bottom of front cover. Reprints the 104 Nassau Street address.)*
nn - Modern rep. (Scarce 1980s) (5-1/2x4-1/4", 8 pgs,side-stapled) - 10.00 20.00
NOTE: *Photocopy reprint by a comix zine publisher, from an Americana Review cop; vailable by mail order*

TOOTH-ACHE, THE (E,O)
D. Bogue, London: 1849 (5-1/4x3-3/4)
nn - By Cruikshank, B&W (Very Rare) 330.00 660.00 1425.00
nn - By Cruikshank, hand colored (Rare) (no known sales)
NOTE: *Scripted by Horace Mayhew, art by George Cruikshank. This is the British edition. Price 1/6 b&w, 3 hand colored. In British editions, the panels are not numbered. Publisher's name appears on cover. Booklet's "pages" unfold into a single, long, strip.*
J.L. Smith, Philadelphia, PA: nd (1849) (5-1/8"x 3-3/4" folded, 86-7/8" wide unfolded, 26 pgs, cardboard-c, color, 15¢)
nn - By Cruikshank, hand colored (Very Rare) 400.00 800.00 1700.00
NOTE: *Reprints the D. Bogue edition. In American editions, the panels are numbered (43 panels, not counting front & back cover). Publisher's name stamped on inside front cover, plus printed along left-hand side of first interior page. Page 1 is pasted to inside back cover, and unfolds from there. Front cover not attached to back cover by design. Booklet's "pages" unfold into a single, long, strip (made from four individual strips pasted together on the blank back side). There is a fairly common1974 British Arts Council reprint.*

TRAMP, THE: His Tricks, Tallies, and Tell-Tales, with His Signs, Countersigns, Grips, Passwords and Villainies Exposed (O,S)
Dick & Fitzgerald, New York: 1878 (11-3/8x8, 36 pgs, paper-c, B&W, 25¢) (Rare)
1 Frank Bellew 160.00 350.00 700.00
NOTE: *Edited by Frank Bellew, A Bee And A Chip (Bellew's daughter and son Frank).*

TRUTH (See Platinum Age section for 1900-1906 issues)
Truth Company, NY: 1886-1906? (13-11/16x10-5/16", 16 pgs, process color-c & centerfolds, rest B&W)
1886-1887 issues 20.00 40.00 100.00
1888-1895 issues non Outcault issues 15.00 30.00 80.00
Mar 10 1894 - precursor Yellow Kid RFO 60.00 180.00 450.00
#372 June 2 1894 - first app Yellow Kid RFO 200.00 600.00 1200.00
June 23 1894 - precursor Yellow Kid R. F. Outcault 60.00 180.00 425.00
July 14 1894 -2nd app Yellow Kid RFO 110.00 330.00 700.00
Sept 15 1894 - (2) 3rd app YK RFO plus YK precursor 110.00 330.00 700.00
Feb 9 1895 - 4th app Yellow Kid RFO 110.00 330.00 700.00
1896-1899 issues 10.00 20.00 55.00
NOTE: *This magazine contains the earliest known appearances of* ***The Yellow Kid*** *by Richard Felton Outcault. Feb 9 1895 issue's YK cartoon was reprinted one week later in the* ***New York World*** *Feb 17 1895 edition. We are still sorting out further Outcault appearances. Truth also contained full color sequential strips by Hy Mayer on the back plus Woolf, Verbeek, etc.*

TRUTH, SELECTIONS FROM
Truth Company, NY: 1894-Spr 1897 (13-11/16x10-1/4, color-c, quarterly)
1-4 25.00 50.00 100.00
5-Outcault's early Yellow Kid 125.00 250.00 500.00
6-13 20.00 40.00 80.00
NOTE: *#5 reprints all early Outcault Yellow Kid appearances*

TURNER'S COMIC ALMANAC
Charles Strong, 298 Pearl St, NYC: ???-1843 (7.25x4.5", 36 pgs, B&W)
nn 65.00 125.00 250.00

TURNER'S COMICK ALMA-NACK
Turner & Fisher, NYC: 1844-?? (7.25x4.5", 36 pgs, B&W)
nn 65.00 125.00 250.00

TWO HUNDRED SKETCHES, HUMOROUS AND GROTESQUE, BY GUSTAVE DORE (E)
Frederick Warne & Co, London: 1867 (13-3/4x11-3/8, 94 pgs, hard-c, B&W)
nn - (1867) by Gustave Dore 100.00 200.00 525.00
nn - (Second Edition; 1871)- by Gustave Dore 60.00 125.00 260.00
nn - (Third Edition; 1870's)- by Gustave Dore 60.00 125.00 260.00
nn - (Fourth Edition; 1870's- by Gustave Dore 60.00 125.00 260.00
NOTE: *Contains sequential comics stories, single panel cartoons, and sketches. Reprints and translates material which originally appeared in the French publications "Le Journal pour Rire", circa 1848-49. Although dated 1867, it was likely published & available for the 1866 Christmas Season, as has been confirmed for the American edition. Printed by Dalziel. The American & first British editions were printed simultaneously, the American edition is not a reprint of the British.*

TWO HUNDRED SKETCHES, HUMOROUS AND GROTESQUE, BY GUSTAVE DORE (E)
Roberts Brothers, Boston: 1867 (13-3/4x11-3/8", 96 pgs, hard-c, B&W)
nn - By Gustave Dore 110.00 225.00 620.00
NOTE: *Although dated 1867, it was published & available for the 1866 Christmas Season. Printed by Dalziel, in England, and imported to the USA expressly for a USA publisher.*

UNCLE JOSH'S TRUNK-FUL OF FUN
Dick & Fitzgerald, 18 Ann St, NY: 1870s (5-3/4x9", 68 pgs, B&W & Red-c, B&W inside)
nn - Rare 75.00 125.00 200.00
NOTE: *Many single panel cartoons; (2) pages of early boxing sequential strip*

UNCLE SAM'S COMIC ALMANAC
M.J. Meyers, NY: 1879 (11x8", 32 pgs)
nn - 50.00 100.00 200.00

UNDER THE GASLIGHT
Gaslight Publishing Co (Frank Tousey): Oct 13 1878-Apr 12 1879 (Folio, 16pgs)
1-27 75.00 125.00 200.00

UNITED STATES COMIC ALMANAC
King & Baird, Philadelphia: 1851-?? (7.5x4.5", 36 pgs, B&W)
nn 60.00 120.00 260.00

UPS AND DOWNS ON LAND AND WATER (O.G)
James R. Osgood & Co., Boston: 1871 ; **Houghton, Osgood & Co., Boston:** 1880 (108 pgs, gilted hard-c, B&W)
1st printing (1871; 10-3/4x16") - By Augustus Hoppin 50.00 100.00 200.00
2nd printing (1880; smaller sized) 32.50 65.00 130.00
NOTE: *Exists as blue or orange hard covers.*

VANITY FAIR
William A. Stephens (for Thompson & Camac): Dec 29 1859-July 4 1863 Quarto Weekly
Average issues with comic strips 20.00 30.00 100.00

VERDICT, THE
Verdict Publishing Co: Dec 19 1898-Nov 12 1900 (Chromolithographic Weekly)
Average Issues 60.00 125.00 250.00
NOTE: *Artists included George B. Luks, Horace Taylor, MIRS. Striking anti-Republican weekly full o fsome of the most savage political cartoons of the era. The last brilliant burst of energy for the political cartoon weekly*

VERY VERY FUNNY (M,S)
Dick & Fitzgerald, New York: nd(c1880's) (10¢, 7-1/2x5", 68 pgs, paper-c, B&W)
nn - (Rare) 75.00 150.00 350.00
NOTE: *Unauthorized reprints of prose and cartoons extracted from Puck, Texas Siftings, and other publications. Includes art by Chips Bellew, Bisbee, Graetz, Opper, Wales, Zim.*

VIM
H. Wimmel, NYC: June 22-Aug 24 1898 (Chromolithographic Weekly)
average issue 50.00 100.00 200.00
Yellow Kid by Leon Barritt issues 75.00 150.00 380.00

WAR IN THE MIDST OF AMERICA. FROM A NEW POINT OF VIEW. (E,O,G)
Ackermann & Co., London: 1864 (4-3/8" x 5-7/8", folded, 36 feet wide unfolded, 80 pgs, hard-c, B&W)
nn- by Charles Dryden (rare) 500.00 1000.00 2100.00
NOTE: *British graphic novel about the American Civil War, with a pro-Confederate bent. Adventures of a British artist who decides to visually summarize the American Civil War for his countrymen, from newspaper accounts. Reaching current events, he finds he can not finish the story until the War ends, and so he travels to America, to end it. Book unfolds into a single long strip (binding was issued split, to enable the unfolding).*

WASP, THE ILLUSTRATED SAN FRANCISCO
F. Korbel & Bros and Numerous Others: August 5 1876-April 25 1941 (Chromolithographic Weekly)
average 1800s issues with comic strips 50.00 100.00 200.00

WHAT I KNOW OF FARMING: Founded On The Experience of Horace Greeley (S)
The American News Company, New York: 1871 (7-1/4x4-1/2", paper-c, B&W)
nn - By Joseph Hull (Scarce) 35.00 70.00 175.00
NOTE: *Pay & Cox, Printers & Engravers, NY; political tract regarding Presidential elections.*

WILD FIRE
Wild Fire Co, NYC: Nov 30 1877-at least#16 Mar 1878 (Folio, 16 pgs)
1-16 30.00 60.00 125.00

WILD OATS, An Illustrated Weekly Journal of Fun, Satire, Burlesque, and Nits at Persons and Events of the Day (O)
Winchell & Small, 113 Fulton St /48 Ann St, NYC: Feb 1870-1881 (16-1/4x11", generally 16 pages, B&W, began as monthly, then bi-weekly, then weekly) All loose issues Very Rare (See *The Overstreet Price Guide #35* 2005 for a detailed index of single issue contents)
1-25 Very Rare - contents to be indexed in a future edition 50.00 100.00 275.00
26-28 30 32 35 36 39 40 41 43-46 1872 (sequential strips) 50.00 100.00 250.00
29 33 37 42 no sequential strips 40.00 80.00 180.00
31 34 38 47 Hopkins sequential comic strips 50.00 100.00 250.00
48 (1/16/73) Worth 13 panel sequential; first Woolf-c 50.00 100.00 250.00
49 51 53 54 60 62 61 64 65 66 67 69 1873 sequential strips 50.00 100.00 250.00
50 52 56 59 63 71 no sequential strips 40.00 80.00 180.00
51 (Worth 18 panel double page spread, Woolf 9 panel 50.00 100.00 250.00
55 Hopkins 22 panel double page spread; Bellew-c 50.00 150.00 325.00
57 Intense unknown 6 panel "Two Relics of Barbarism, or A Few Contrasted Pictures, Showing the origin of the North American Indian 50.00 100.00 250.00
58 (6/5/73) unknown 19 panel double pager "The Terrible Adventures of Messrs Buster & Stumps, About Exterminating the Indians" reads across both pages like Popeye #2095 (1933); Woolf-c 100.00 200.00 460.00
68 (10/16/73) unknown 9 panel "Adv of New jersey Mosquito" looks like Winsor McCay

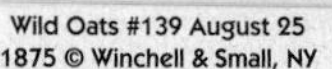

Wild Oats #139 August 25
1875 © Winchell & Small, NY

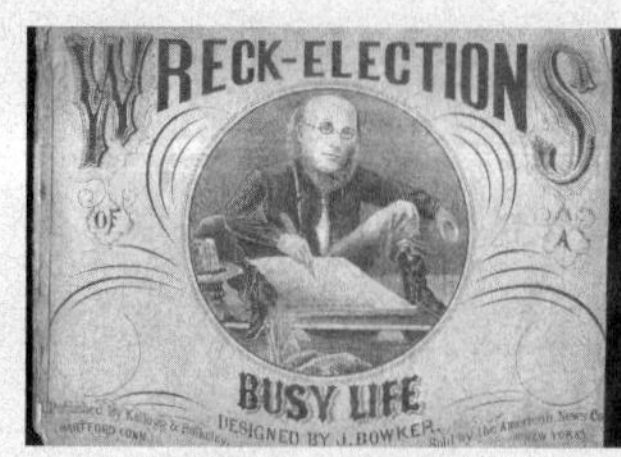

Wreck-Elections Of Busy Life
Kellogg & Buckeley © 1864?

Yankee Notions #7 (v2#1)
July 1852 © T.W. Strong, NY

type style: early inspiration for McCay's animated cartoon? 50.00 100.00 250.00
70 unknown 6 panel; Hopkins 6 panel "Hopkins novel: A Tale of True Love, with all the variations"; Bellew-c 50.00 100.00 230.00
72 (12/11/73) Worth 11 panel; Wales President Grant war-c 50.00 100.00 230.00
73 74 75 Hopkins sequential comic strip 75.00 150.00 310.00
76 77 sequential strips 50.00 100.00 230.00
78 Bellew 5 panel double pager 50.00 100.00 230.00
79-105 (March 1874-Dec 1874) contents presently unknown 50.00 100.00 230.00
106 107 111 no sequentials;Bellew-c #106 110;Wales-c #107 50.00 100.00 230.00
108 (1/20/75) Wales 12 panel double pg spread; Bellew-c 50.00 100.00 230.00
109 (1/27/75) unknown 6 panel; Wales-c 50.00 100.00 230.00
111 Busch 13 panel "The Conundrum of the Day - Is Lager Beer Intoxicating?"; Bellew-c 50.00 100.00 230.00
112 116 sequential comic strips 50.00 100.00 230.00
113 114 115 no sequentials Worth-c #114 40.00 80.00 180.00
117 intense Wales 6 panel "One of the Oppresions of the Civil Rights Laws"' Bellew-c 75.00 150.00 330.00
118-137 (3/31/75-8/4/75) no sequential comic strips 40.00 80.00 180.00
138 (8/18/75) Bellew Sr & Bellew "Chips" Jr singles appear 50.00 100.00 225.00
139-143 145-147 154-157 159 no sequentials 40.00 80.00 180.00
144 (9/29/75) Hopkins 8 panel sequential; Wales-c 50.00 100.00 230.00
148 (10/27/75) Opper's first cover; many Opper singles 75.00 150.00 320.00
149 150 151 152 153 all Opper-c and much interior work 50.00 100.00 230.00
158 (1/5/76) Palmer Cox 1rst comic strip 24 panel double page spread "The Adv of Mr & Mrs Sprowl And Their Christmas Turkey - A Crashing Chasing Tearful Tragedy But Happily Ending Well"; Opper-c 100.00 200.00 450.00
159 160 162 165 167 169-173 no sequentials 40.00 80.00 180.00
161 163 164 166 168 179 182 Palmer Cox sequential strips 100.00 200.00 450.00
174 (4/26/76) Cox 24 panel double pager "The Tramp's Progress; A Story of the West And the Union Pacific Railroad" 100.00 200.00 450.00
175-178 183-189 no sequentials 40.00 80.00 180.00
180 (6/7/76) Beard & Opper jam; Woolf, Bellew singles 50.00 100.00 230.00
181 more Mann two panel jobs; Opper-c 50.00 100.00 230.00
190 Bellew 9 panel "Rodger's Patent Mosquito Armour" 75.00 150.00 320.00
191-end contents to be indexed in the near future 40.00 80.00 180.00

NOTE: *There are very few lknown oose issues. All loose issues are Very Rare. Prices vary widely on this magazine. Issues with sequential comic strips would be in higher demand than issues with no comic strips. We present this index from the Library of Congress and New York Historical Society bound sets. We would love to hear from any one who turns up loose copies. This scarce humor bi-weekly contains easily a couple hundred original first-time published sequential comic strips found in most issues plus innumerable single panel cartoons in every issue*

WOMAN IN SEARCH OF HER RIGHTS, THE ADVENTURES OF (G)
Lee & Shepard, Boston And New York: early 1870s (8-3/8x13", 40 pgs, hard-c)

By Florence Claxton (Very Rare) 560.00 1120.00 2200.00

NOTE: *Earliest known original comic book sequential story by a woman; contains "nearly 100 original drawings by the author, which have been reproduced in fac-simile by the graphotype process of engraving." Tinted two color lithography; orange tint printed first, then printed 2nd time with black ink; early women's sufferage.*

WORLD OVER, THE (I)
G. W. Dillingham Company, New York: 1897 (192 pgs, hard-c)

nn - By Joe Kerr; 80 illustrations by R.F. Outcault (Rare) 330.00 660.00 1300.00

NOTE: soft cover editions also exist

WRECK-ELECTIONS OF BUSY LIFE (S)
Kellogg & Bulkeley: 1867 (9-1/4x11-3/4", ??? pages, soft-c)

nn - By J. Bowker (Rare) 110.00 225.00 450.00

NOTE: *Says "Sold by American News Company, New York" on cover.*

WYMAN'S COMIC ALMANAC FOR THE TIMES
T.W. Strong, NY: 1854 (8x5", 24 pgs)

nn - 50.00 100.00 200.00

YANKEE DOODLE
W.H. Graham, Tribune Building, NYC: Oct 10 1846-Oct 2 1847 (Quarto weekly)

average issue 110.00 125.00 250.00

YANKEE NOTIONS, OR WHITTLINGS OF JONATHAN'S JACK-KNIFE
T.W. Strong, 98 Nassau St, NYC: Jan. 1852-1875 (11x8, 32 pgs, paper-c, 12.5¢, monthly)

1 Brother Jonathan character single panel cartoons 60.00 125.00 250.00

NOTE: *Begins continuing character sequential comic strip, "The Adventures of Jeremiah Oldpot" in "A Bird in the Hand Is Worth Two in The Bush"*

2-4 25.00 50.00 130.00
5 British X-Over 25.00 50.00 130.00

NOTE: *Single panel of John Bull & Brother Jonathan exchanging civilities (issues of* Punch & Yankee Notions*)*

6 end of Jeremiah Oldpot continued strip 25.00 50.00 130.00
v2#1 begin "Hoosier Bragg" sequential strip - six issue serial 25.00 50.00 130.00
v2#2 Feb 1853 two pg 12 panel sequential "Mr Vanity's Exploits, Arising Out Of A Valentine" 37.50 75.00 200.00
v2#3-v2#5 continues Hoosier Bragg 25.00 50.00 130.00
v2#6 June 1853 Lion Eats Hoosier Bragg, end of story 25.00 50.00 130.00
v3#1 begins referring to its cartoons as "Comic Art" 37.50 75.00 200.00
v4#1-V4#6 v5#1-v5#2 no sequential comic strips 20.00 40.00 100.00
v5#3 two sequential comic strips 37.50 75.00 210.00

NOTE: *Mr Take-A-Drop And The Maine Law (5) panels and The First Segar (7) panels (about smoking tobacco)*

v5#4 April 1856 begin Billy Vidkins 37.50 75.00 210.00

NOTE: *Begins reprinting "From Passages in the Life of Little Billy Vidkins, first issued as a stand alone proto-comic book in 1849 Illustrations of the Poets*

v5#5 The McBargem Guards (9) panel sequential; Vidkins 25.00 50.00 130.00
v5#6 v5 #9 no comics 20.00 40.00 105.00
v5#7 Billy Vidkins continues 25.00 50.00 130.00
v5#8 end of Vidkins By HL Stephens, Esq. 25.00 50.00 130.00
v5#10 (6) panel "How We Learn To Ride"; Timber is hero 25.00 50.00 130.00
v5#11 (7) panel "How Mr. Green Sparrowgrass Voted-A Warning For the Benefit of Quiet Citizens About To Excercize the Elective Franchise" plus Pt Two "How We Learn to Ride" 37.50 75.00 200.00
v5#12 (6) panel "How Mr Pipp Got Struck"; "The Eclipse" featuring Mr Phips; Pt 3 "How We Learn to Ride" 25.00 50.00 130.00
v6#1 (Jan 1857) (12) panel "A Tale of An Umbrella; (4) panel begins a serial "The Man Who Bought The Elephant; (8) panel How Our Young New Yorkers Celebrate New Years Day 25.00 50.00 130.00
v6#2 (Feb 1857) Pt 2 (4) panels The Man Who Bought the Elephant; (7) panel A Game of All Fours 25.00 50.00 130.00
v6#3 (Mar 1857) Pt 3 (4) panels The Man Who Bought the Elephant ending; (4) panel Ye Great Crinoline Monopoly 25.00 50.00 130.00
v6#4 no comic strips 25.00 50.00 130.00
v6#5 (May 1850) (3) panel A Short Trip to Mr Bumps, And How It Ended; (2) panel How mr Trembles Was Garrotted 25.00 50.00 130.00
v6#6 no comic strips 25.00 50.00 130.00
v6#7 (July 1857) (5) panel Alma Mater; (3) panel Three Tableaux In the Life of A Broadway Swell 25.00 50.00 130.00
v6 #8 9 no comic strips 25.00 50.00 130.00
v6#10 (Oct 1857) (3) panel Adv of Mr Near-Sight 25.00 50.00 130.00
v6#11 (Nov 1857) (11) panel Mrs Champignon's Dinner Party And the Way She Arranged Her Guests; (4) panel A Stroll in August 25.00 50.00 130.00
v6#12 (Dec 1857) (8) panel strip; (12) panel Young Fitz At A Blow Out in the Fifth Ave 25.00 50.00 130.00
v10#1 (Jan 1860) comic strip Bibbs at Central Park Skating Pond using word balloons 25.00 50.00 130.00

YE TRUE ACCOUNTE OF YE VISIT TO SPRINGFIELDE BY YE CONSTABEL HIS SPECIAL REPORTER
Frank Leslie: 1861 (5-1/8 x 5-1/4 or 93 inches when folded out, paper-c, B&W)

nn - Very Rare fold-out of 18 comic strip panels plus covers (a FN copy sold in 2010 for $101.85)

NOTE: *8 panels contain word balloons (Very Rare - only one copy known to exist.) First printed in Frank Leslie's Budget of Fun Jan 1 1861 issue. Abraham Lincoln Biography.*

YE VERACIOUS CHRONICLE OF GRUFF & POMPEY IN 7 TABLEAUX. (O,P)
Jackson's Best Chewing Tobacco & Donaldson Brothers: nd (c1870's) (5-1/8 tall x 3-3/8" wide folded, 27" wide unfolded, color cardboard)

nn - With all 8 panels attached (Scarce) 45.00 90.00 200.00
nn - Individual panels/cards 6.00 12.00 24.00

NOTE: *Black Americana interest. Consists of 8 attached cards, printed on one side, which unfold into a strip story of title card & 7 panels. Scrapbook hobbyists in the 19th Century tended to pull the panels apart and paste into their scrapbooks, making copies with all panels attached scarce.*

YOUNG AMERICA (continues as Yankee Doodle)
T.W. Strong, NYC: 1856

1-30 John McLennon 60.00 110.00 250.00

YOUNG AMERICA'S COMIC ALMANAC
T.W. Strong, NY: 1857 (7-1/2x5", 24 pgs)

nn 60.00 110.00 250.00

THE YOUNG MEN OF AMERICA (becomes Golden Weekly) (S)
Frank Tousey, NYC: 1887-88 (14x10-1/4", 16 pgs, B&W)

527 (10/13/87) Bellew strip "Story of A Black Eye" 25.00 50.00 115.00
530 (11/3/87) Thomas Worth (6) panel strip 32.00 64.00 125.00
531 (11/10/87) Thomas Worth(3) panel strip
537 (12/22/87) H.E. Patterson (3) panel strip
544 (2/9/88) Caran s'Ache (6) panel strip-r 37.50 75.00 115.00
555 (4/26/88) Thomas Worth (3) panel strip
556 (5/3/88) Thomas Worth (6) panel strip; Kit Carson-c 75.00 150.00 360.00
569 (8/21/88) Frank Bellew (2) panel strip
570 (8/9/88) Kemble (2) panel strip
571 (8/16/88) Kemble (2) panel strip; first Davy Crockett 75.00 150.00 360.00
Issues with just single panel cartoons 10.00 20.00 50.00

ZIM'S QUARTERLY (M)
(13-13/16x10-1/4", 60 pgs, color-c; mostly B&W, some interior color)

1 - Eugene Zimmerman 112.50 225.00 500.00

NOTE: *Approx. half sequential comic strips, other half single panel cartoons.*

Any addititions or corrections to this section are always welcome, very much encouraged and can be sent to **feedback@gemstonepub.com** to be processed for next year's Guide.

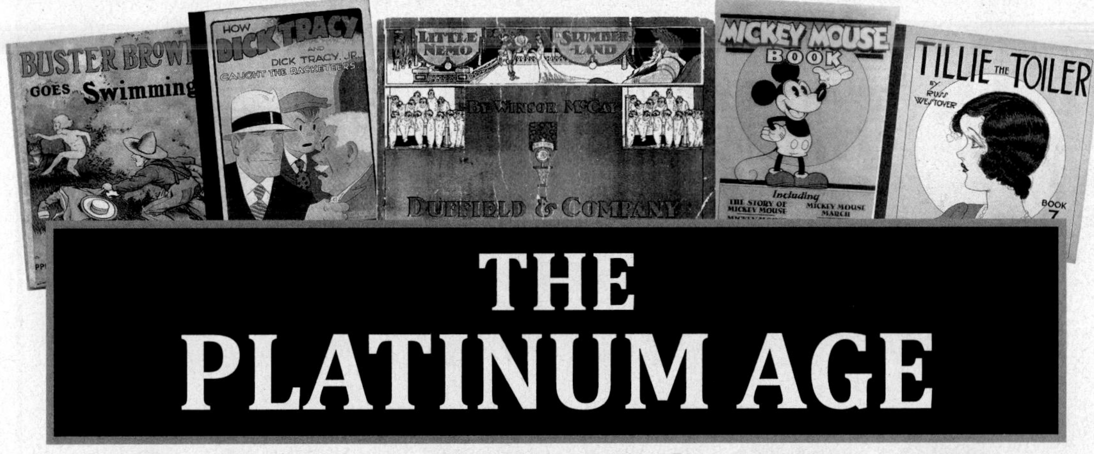

THE PLATINUM AGE

The American Comic Book: 1883-1938

The comic book ages tend to overlap a bit with one another – DC's Silver Age started with *Showcase* #4, but Marvel's didn't begin until *Fantastic Four* #1, for instance – so it's not surprising that the Platinum Age and Victorian Age tend to overlap a bit, with the Victorian Age in some ways running through the end of the 19th century. The Platinum Age of comics is marked by the introduction of several important elements, including three distinct and important features: the rise of licensed character merchandise, panel formats, and the evolution of the speech balloon.

The Platinum Age of Comics began with Palmer Cox's creation of *The Brownies* in 1883. Cox introduced a significant change to the medium with his work, and all at once rather than slowly and incrementally – he produced his art specifically with children in mind, and then merchandised his characters extensively. *The Brownies* became the first North American comic characters to be internationally merchandised. Their first standalone book, *The Brownies: Their Book*, debuted in 1887.

By the mid-1890s, newspaper publishers had caught on to the idea that comic characters could help sell more papers, having seen what they did to boost circulation of various magazines. The idea of a Sunday "comic supplement" was born at this time.

Throughout the Platinum Age, there are numerous important landmarks: James Swinnerton's *The Little Bears* (later *Little Bears & Tykes*), debuted in 1892, Richard F. Outcault's *Hogan's Alley* first appeared in 1894 in the *New York World* and The Yellow Kid first appeared in 1895 and had his first word balloon on October 25, 1896.

By the early 1900s, many other characters and strips were enjoying successful collections in volume format. Strips like *The Blackberries*, *Opper's Folks in Funnyville*, *Vaudevilles and Other Things*, *Mutt & Jeff*, *Bringing Up Father*, *The Katzenjammer Kids* and many others had circulations significantly higher than the early superheroes.

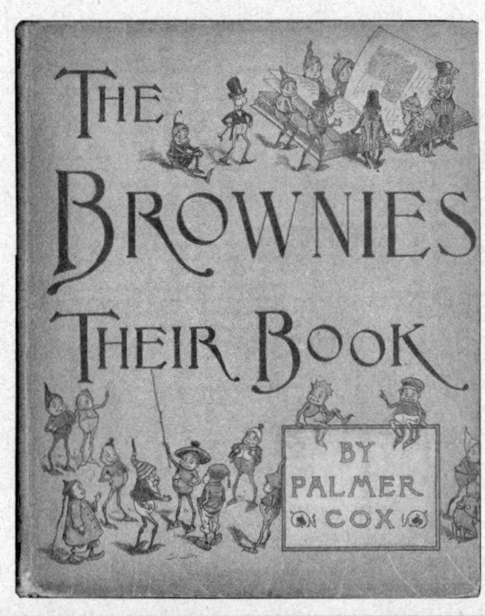

The Brownies' first book in 1887 set a precedent for the Platinum Age, collecting and reprinting previously published material.

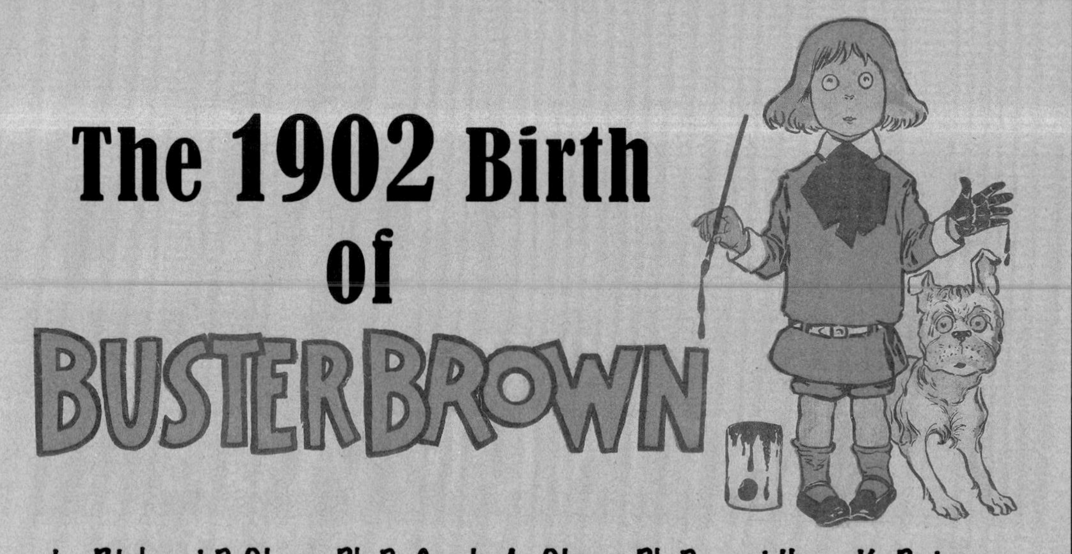

The 1902 Birth of Buster Brown

by Richard D. Olson, Ph.D., Gayle A. Olson, Ph.D., and Hans K. Pedersen

The economic success of a newspaper has always been based on its circulation figures, because they determined the price for ad space in the paper. Thus, owners were always looking for ways to increase circulation. One prime example was the circulation battle between Joseph Pulitzer's *The New York World* and William Randolph Hearst's *The New York Journal*. These two owners hated each other and never missed an opportunity to help their respective papers dominate the New York City market, beginning in the 1890s.

Accordingly, when *The San Francisco Examiner* added a color section and James Swinnerton drew iconic cartoon, *Little Bears* beginning on October 14, 1893, its success with the public was immediate. New components in a paper like a colored section and a cartoon helped sell papers. Pulitzer had already started publishing cartoons, often borrowed from humor magazines, in 1889. He added a color press to make a colored humor section in 1894, and in 1895 he hit the jackpot with Richard F. Outcault's *Yellow Kid* cartoons. The Yellow Kid took New York by storm, increased circulation numbers, and was also used to merchandise a wide variety of products. He was not the first cartoon character, but he was the first cartoon superstar.

Hearst quickly followed suit, hired Outcault and let the Yellow Kid sell his papers. Readers loved to follow the exploits of the Yellow Kid as he and friends from the Irish tenements caused trouble, ridiculed Society's 400, and later took a trip around the world.

Following the success of the *Yellow Kid*, Hearst added another strip with children causing trouble. He hired Rudolph Dirks to create a comic probably based on Wilhelm Busch's famous German troublemakers, *Max and Moritz*. On December 12, 1897 the *Katzenjammer Kids* made their debut, and Hearst had another winner for his *New York Journal*. The timing was perfect, leave it to the zeitgeist to ensure that, because the popularity of the Yellow Kid was waning.

Outcault tried a couple of group comics, *Casey's Corner* in 1898 followed by *Kelley's Kids* in 1898-1899 but neither seemed to resonate with the public. Apparently, the readers wanted a focal character to follow rather than a group. This led Outcault to try something different and he created *Pore Li'l Mose*, the first strip starring a black character, which ran in 1900-1902. Mose was a young boy living in Cottonville until he moved to New York City. The strip proved to be very popular and set the stage for the creation and development of Outcault's most popular character, Buster Brown.

On May 4, 1902, *Buster Brown* made his debut in many of the *Herald* papers from coast to coast, and ushered in a new era in Sunday comics. While the Yellow Kid just appeared in New York City papers and focused on events and places in that general area, Buster Brown appeared nationally. For nearly 20 years his story focused on a wealthy boy who found a multitude of ways to get into trouble that could have occurred in any city. What probably endeared the strip to adults was that Buster was nearly always caught, spanked, and in the last panel of the comic, resolved to be better in the future. Buster was not based on his son as some early readers thought, but rather probably modelled after another boy in the area, Granville Fisher. His name was likely due to the popularity of child star, Buster Keaton. His sister in the comic, Mary Jane, however, was Outcault's daughter.

Buster's best friend was Tige, his pet dog, an American Pit Bull Terrier. Tige may have been the first talking animal in the comics and was nearly always Buster's partner in mischief even when he tried to talk him out of doing something bad. He might even be viewed as a precursor to Jiminy Cricket, who tried to serve as Pinocchio's conscience.

In the first several comics, Buster often had a wild look as he got into trouble, with crazed eyes and wild hair sticking straight out like straw from under his cap. He wore a red or purple suit, with the purple suit ultimately being discarded later in the year as the red suit became a permanent fixture. As the year progressed, his wild look was toned down and he looked like a regular boy with a twinkle in his eyes.

As was often the case with new strips, he did not appear every week in 1902 and he was sometimes presented in black and white rather than color when he was published on an interior page in the comic section. As the popularity of the strip grew, however, he became a fixture on page one and was always in color. By the end of 1902, he was so popular that games and toys were starting to appear in the marketplace. Merchandise from 1902 is fairly rare, and any material carrying Outcault's signature is very collectible.

Buster's popularity continued to grow, and the merchandise followed. After he became associated with the Brown Shoe Company in 1904, shoes and clothing followed, and he became one of the most widely recognized comic characters in the country.

Acknowledgements: The authors would like to thank Jenny E. Robb, Susan Liberator, and the rest of the staff at The Billy Ireland Cartoon Library and Museum at The Ohio State University. We would also like to thank the research staff at the New York Public Library.

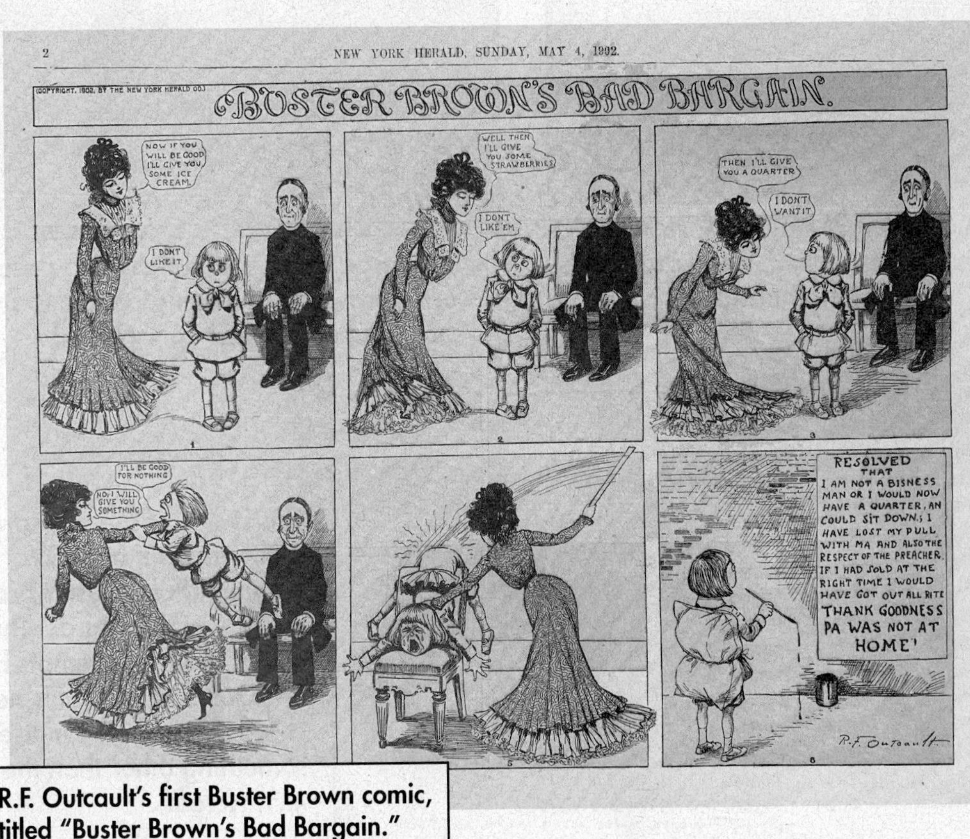

R.F. Outcault's first Buster Brown comic, titled "Buster Brown's Bad Bargain." It was published May 4, 1902.

The front of a 1902 *New York Herald* advertising card drawn by a staff artist showing Buster Brown being punished as Tige watches.

The reverse of that card saying that Buster Brown wants every boy and girl to see him in next Sunday's *N.Y. Herald*.

Another early *New York Herald* advertising card, this one drawn by R.F. Outcault.

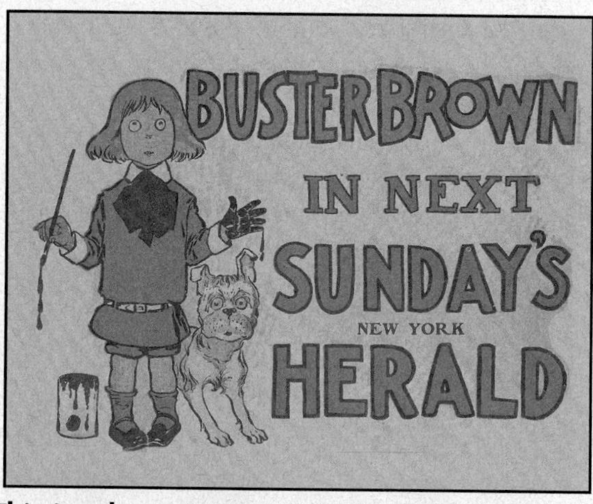

This is a large 11″ x 14″ advertising poster for Buster Brown encouraging people to buy next Sunday's *New York Herald*.

This is one of the postcards in the rare set of 1902 Bloomingdales Buster Brown private mailing cards. This is one of the first attempts by R.F. Outcault to use his new character to merchandise something other than the *N.Y. Herald*.

This is the front of the Christmas advertising card for Buster Brown's first Christmas special.

The Christmas Number of the

NEW YORK HERALD

WILL BE ISSUED

SUNDAY, DEC. 14TH.

DON'T MISS IT.

"I will be in it."—BUSTER BROWN.

The reverse of that card saying Buster Brown will be in the Sunday, December 14, 1902 issue of the *New York Herald*.

THE NEW YORK HERALD.

PRICE FIVE CENTS.

A Buster Brown Sunday comic dated November 2, 1902 showing him in his purple suit but much less crazed and disheveled.

A cell from the June 1, 1902 Buster Brown Sunday comic showing how crazed and disheveled he looked in the first few months of the strip.

A cell showing Buster and Tige meeting Pore Li'l Mose and his animals. Buster was also visited several times by the Yellow Kid.

Date	Title
5/04/1902	Buster Brown's Bad Bargain
5/11/1902	Everything is Runnning Smoothly in the Brown Family Now
5/18/1902	Buster Brown's Bath
5/25/1902	Buster Brown Earns a Five Dollar Bill
6/01/1902	Buster Brown Visits the Zoo
6/08/1902	
6/15/1902	
6/22/1902	
6/29/1902	Buster Brown in More Trouble
7/06/1902	Buster Brown's Experience at the Dentists
7/13/1902	Buster Brown Makes Another Resolution
7/20/1902	Buster Brown and Pore Li'l Mose
7/27/1902	Buster Brown Learns Another Sad Lesson
8/03/1902	Buster Brown in More Trouble
8/10/1902	Buster Brown Kisses Venus Green and Gets into Trouble
8/17/1902	Buster Brown Receives His Mother's Callers and a Licking--Poor Buster Brown
8/24/1902	
8/31/1902	Buster Brown has His Sunday School Lesson, a Side-Ache and a Licking
9/07/1902	
9/14/1902	Buster Brown Starts to School
9/21/1902	Buster Brown Gets Everything All Smeared up to Beat the Band
9/28/1902	Buster Brown Has His Fortune Told
10/05/1902	Buster Brown Transacts a Little Business with the Old Clothes Man
10/12/1902	Buster Brown Suffers, but Doesn't Get a Beating
10/19/1902	Buster Brown Has a Birthday Party
10/26/1902	Buster Brown Takes Some Medicine
11/02/1902	This Time Buster Brown Wins
11/09/1902	Buster Brown is Prevailed upon to Sing a Song
11/16/1902	Buster Brown Gets Every Body into Trouble Again
11/23/1902	Buster Brown Frightens His Parents
11/30/1902	Buster Brown Paints His Face and Frightens His Mama
12/07/1902	Buster Brown Puts Tacks on Every Old Chair in the House
12/14/1902	What Buster Brown Got for Christmas
12/21/1902	Buster Brown's Dog Meets His Old Side Partner and they do their Old Stunt
12/28/1902	Buster Brown's Happy New Year

The Adventures of Willie Green
© Frank M. Acton

Alphonse and Gaston by Opper
1902 © Hearst's NY American & Journal

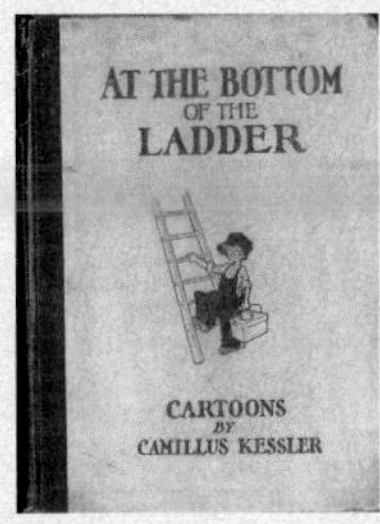

At The Bottom Of The Ladder
1926 © J.P. Lippincott Company

GD2.0 FN6.0 VF8.0

COLLECTOR'S NOTE: The books listed in this section were published many decades before organized comics fandom began archiving and helping to preserve these fragile popular culture artifacts. Consequently, copies of most all of these comics do not often surface in Fine+ or better shape. eBay has proven after more than a decade that many items once considered rare actually are not, though they almost always are in higher grades. For items marked scarce, we are trying to ascertain how many copies might still be in existence. Your input is always welcome.

Most Platinum Age comic books are in the Fair to VG range. If you want to collect these only in high grade, your collection will be extremely small. The prices given for Good, Fine and Very Fine categories are for strictly graded editions. If you need help grading your item, we refer you to the grading section in the front of this price guide or contact the authors of the Platinum essay. Most measurements are in inches. A few measurements are in centimeters. The first dimension given is Height and the second is Width.

For ease of ascertaining the contents of each item of this listing, there is a code letter or two following most titles we have been adding in over the years to aid you. A helpful list of categories pertaining to these codes can be found at the beginning of the Victorian Age pricing sections. This section created, revised, and expanded by Robert Beerbohm and Richard Olson with able assistance from Ray Agricola, Jon Berk, Bill Blackbeard, Roy Bonario, Ray Bottorff Jr., Chris Brown, Alfredo Castelli, Darrell Coons, Sol Davidson, Leonardo De Sá, Scott Deschaine, Mitchell Duval, Joe Evans, Tom Gordon III, Bruce Hamilton, Andy Konkykru, Don Kurtz, Gabriel Laderman, Bruce Mason, Donald Puff, Robert Quesinberry, Steve Rowe, Randy Scott, John Snyder, Art Spiegelman, Steve Thompson, Joan Crosby Tibbets, Richard Samuel West, Doug Wheeler, Richard Wright and Craig Yoe.

ADVENTURES OF EVA, PORA AND TED (M)
Evaporated Milk Association: 1932 (5x15", 16 pgs, B&W)
nn - By Steve 20.00 40.00 105.00
NOTE: *Appears to have had green, blue or white paper cover versions.*

ADVENTURES OF HAWKSHAW (N) (See Hawkshaw The Detective)
The Saalfield Publishing Co.: 1917 (9-3/4x13-1/2", 48 pgs., color & two-tone)
nn - By Gus Mager (only 24 pgs. of strips, reverse of each pg. is blank)
50.00 175.00 400.00
nn - 1927 Reprints 1917 issue 30.00 150.00 260.00
NOTE: *Started Feb 23, 1913-Sept 4, 1922, then begins again Dec 13, 1931-Feb 11, 1952.*

ADVENTURES OF SLIM AND SPUD, THE (M)
Prairie Farmer Publ. Co.: 1924 (3-3/4x 9-3/4", 104 pgs., B&W strip reprints)
nn 25.00 90.00 180.00
NOTE: *Illustrated mailing envelope exists postmarked out of Chicago, add 50%.*

ADVENTURES OF WILLIE WINTERS, THE (O,P)
Kelloggs Toasted Corn Flake Co.: 1912 (6-7/8x9-1/2", 20 pgs, full color)
nn - By Byron Williams & Dearborn Melvill 54.00 189.00 360.00

ADVENTURES OF WILLIE GREEN, THE (N) (see The Willie Green Comics)
Frank M. Acton Co.: 1915 (50¢, 52 pgs, 8-1/2X16", B&W, soft-c)
Book 1 - By Harris Brown; strip-r 54.00 189.00 360.00

A. E. F. IN CARTOONS BY WALLY, THE (N)
Don Sowers & Co.: 1933 (12x10-1/8", 88 pgs, hardcover B&W)
nn - By Wally Wallgren (WW One Stars & Stripes-r) 60.00 125.00 250.00

AFTER THE TOWN GOES DRY (I)
The Howell Publishing Co, Chicago: 1919 (48 pgs, 6-1/2x4", hardbound two color-c)
nn - By Henry C. Taylor; illus by Frank King 25.00 75.00 160.00

AIN'T IT A GRAND & GLORIOUS FEELING? (N) (Also see Mr. & Mrs.)
Whitman Publishing Co.: 1922 (9x9-3/4", 52 pgs., stiff cardboard-c)
nn - 1921 daily strip-r; B&W, color-c; Briggs-a 36.00 143.00 250.00
nn -(9x9-1/2", 28pgs., stiff cardboard-c)-Sunday strip-r in color (inside front-c says "More of the Married Life of Mr. & Mrs".) 36.00 143.00 250.00
NOTE: *Strip started in 1917; This is the 2nd Whitman comic book, after Brigg's MR. & MRS.*

ALL THE FUNNY FOLKS (I)
World Press Today, Inc.: 1926 (11-1/2x8-1/2", 112 pgs., color, hard-c)
nn-Barney Google, Spark Plug, Jiggs & Maggie, Tillie The Toiler, Happy Hooligan, Hans & Fritz, Toots & Casper, etc. 100.00 400.00 725.00
With Dust Jacket By Louis Biedermann 225.00 850.00 1600.00
NOTE: *Booklength race horse story masterfully enveloping all major King Features characters.*

ALPHONSE AND GASTON AND THEIR FRIEND LEON (N)
Hearst's New York American & Journal: 1902,1903 (10x15-1/4", Sunday strip reprints in color)
nn - (1902) - By Frederick Opper (scarce) 600.00 2200.00 –
nn - (1903) - By Frederick Opper (scarce) (72 pages) 600.00 2200.00 –
NOTE: *Strip ran Sept 22, 1901 to at least July 17, 1904.*

ALWAYS BELITTLIN' (see Skippy; That Rookie From the 13th Squad; Between Shots)
Henry Holt & Co.: 1927 (6x8", hard-c with DJ,
nn -By Percy Crosby (text with cartoons) 43.00 172.00 325.00

ALWAYS BELITTLIN' (I) (see Skippy; That Rookie From the 13th Squad, Between Shots)
Percy Crosby, Publisher: 1933 (14 1/4 x 11", 72 pgs, hard-c, B&W)
nn - By Percy Crosby 43.00 172.00 320.00
NOTE: *Self-published; primarily political cartoons with text pages denouncing prohibition's gang warfare effects and cuts in the national defense budget as Crosby saw war looming in Europe and with Japan.*

AMERICAN-JOURNAL-EXAMINER JOKE BOOK SPECIAL SUPPLEMENT (O)
New York American: 1911-12 (12 x 9 3/4", 16 pgs) (known issues) (Very Rare)
1 Tom Powers Joke Book(12/10/11) 80.00 320.00 –
2 Mutt & Jeff Joke Book (Bud Fisher 12/17/11) 100.00 375.00 –
3 TAD's Joke Book (Thomas Dorgan 12/24/11) 80.00 320.00 –
4 F. Opper's Joke Book (Frederick Burr Opper 12/31/11) (contains Happy Hooligan) 100.00 365.00 –
5 not known to exist
6 Swinnerton's Joke Book (Jimmy Swinnerton 01/14/12) (contains Mr. Jack) 100.00 420.00 –
7 The Monkey's Joke Book (Gus Mager 01/21/12) (contains Sherlocko the Monk) 100.00 370.00 –
8 Joys And Glooms Joke Book (T. E. Powers 01/28/12) 80.00 320.00 –
9 The Dingbat Family's Joke Book (George Herriman 02/04/12) (contains early Krazy Kat & Ignatz) 200.00 820.00 –
10 Valentine Joke Book, A (Opper, Howarth, Mager, T. E. Powers 02/11/12) 80.00 325.00 –
11 Little Hatchet Joke Book (T. E. Powers 02/18/12) 80.00 325.00 –
12 Jungle Joke Book (Dirks, McCay 02/25/12) 100.00 420.00 –
13 The Hayseeds Joke Book (03/03/12) 80.00 320.00 –
14 Married Life Joke Book (T.E. Powers 03/10/12) 80.00 320.00 –
NOTE: *These were insert newspaper supplements similar to Eisner's later Spirit sections. A Valentine Joke Book recently surfaced from Hearst's Boston Sunday American proving that other cities besides New York City had these special supplements. Each issue also contains work by other cartoonists besides the cover featured creator and those already listed above such as Sidney Smith, Winsor McCay, Hy Mayer, Grace Weiderseim (later Drayton), others.*

AMERICA'S BLACK & WHITE BOOK 100 Pictured Reasons Why We Are At War (N,S)
Cupples & Leon: 1917 (10 3/4 x 8", 216 pgs)
nn - W. A. Rogers (New York Herald-r) 35.00 118.00 220.00

AMONG THE FOLKS IN HISTORY
Rand McNally Print Guild: 1935 (192 pgs, 8-1/2x9-1/2", hard-c, B&W)
nn - By Gaar Williams 21.00 84.00 160.00

AMONG THE FOLKS IN HISTORY
The Book and Print Guild: 1935 (200 pgs, 8-1/2x9-1/2:,
nn - By Gaar Williams 21.00 84.00 160.00
NOTE: *Both the above are evidently different editions and contain largely full-page, single panel cartoons similar to Briggs' work of that sort. 8 or 10 pages are broken into panels, usually with a "this is how it was in the old days, this is how it is today theme."*

ANGELIC ANGELINA (N)
Cupples & Leon Company: 1909 (11-1/2x17", 56 pgs., 2 colors)
nn - By Munson Paddock 67.00 233.00 425.00
NOTE: *Strip ran March 22, 1908-Feb 7, 1909.*

ANDY GUMP, HIS LIFE STORY (I)
The Reilly & Lee Co, Chicago: 1924 (192 pgs, hardbound)
nn - By Sidney Smith (over 100 illustrations) 30.00 100.00 250.00

ANIMAL CIRCUS, THE (from Puggery Wee)
Rand McNally + Company: 1908 (48 pgs, 11x8-1/2", color-c, 3-color insides)
nn - By unknown 25.00 80.00 160.00
NOTE: *Illustrated verse, many pages with multiple illustrations.*

ANIMAL SERIALS
T. Y. Crowell: 1906 (9x6-7/8", 214 pgs, hard-c, B&W)
nn - By E Warde Blaisdell 20.00 80.00 160.00
NOTE: *Multi-page comic strip stories. Reprints of Sunday strip "Bunny Bright He's All-Right".*

A NOBODY'S SCRAP BOOK
Frederik A. Stokes Co., New York: 1900 (11" x 8-5/8", hard-c, color)
nn- (Scarce) 67.00 233.00 450.00
NOTE: *Designed in England, printed in Holland, on English paper -- which likely explains the mispelling of Frederick Stokes' name. Highly fragile paper. Strips and cartoons, all by the same unidentified artist, "A Nobody", almost certainly reprinted from somewhere, as they are very professional.*

AT THE BOTTOM OF THE LADDER (M)
J.P. Lippincott Company: 1926 (11x8-1/4", 296 pgs, hardcover, B&W)
nn - By Camillus Kessler 45.00 157.50 300.00
NOTE: *Hilarious single panel cartoons showing first jobs of then important "captains of industry."*

AUTO FUN, PICTURES AND COMMENTS FROM "LIFE"
Thomas Y. Crowell & Co.: 1905 (152 pgs, 9x7", hard-c, B&W)
nn -By various 55.00 170.00 435.00
NOTE: *The cover just has "Auto Fun" but the title page also has the subheading listed here. This is similar to other reprint books of Life cartoons printed in the guide. Largely single panel cartoons but also several sequential. One or more cartoons by Kemble, Levering, Dirks, Flagg, Sullivant. Sequential cartoons by Kemble, Levering, Sullivant, and the highpoint, a 2 pg 6 panel piece by Winsor McCay.*

BANANA OIL (N) (see also HE DONE HER WRONG)
MS Publ. Co.: 1924 (9-7/8x10", 52 pgs., B&W)

Barney Google and Spark Plug #1
© C&L

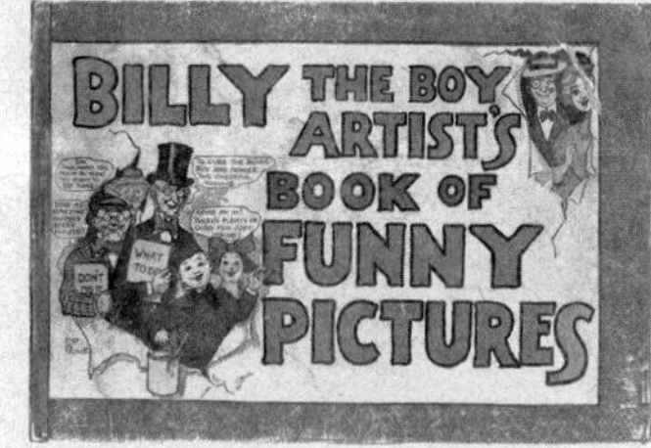

Bill the Boy Artist's Book by Ed Payne
1910 © C.M. Clark Publishing Co

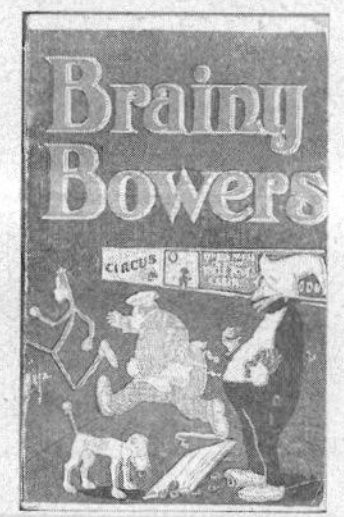

Brainy Bowers and Drowsy Duggan by R.W. Taylor
1905 © Star Publishing Co. - the first daily reprints

	GD2.0	FN6.0	VF8.0
nn - Milt Gross comic strips; not reprints	200.00	500.00	1000.00

BARKER'S ILLUSTRATED ALMANAC (O,P,S) (See Barkers in Victorian Era section)
Barker, Moore & Mein Medicine Co: 1900-1932+ (36 pgs, B&W, color paper-c)

1900-1932+ (7x5-7/8")	50.00	100.00	225.00

BARKER'S "KOMIC" PICTURE SOUVENIR (P,S) (see Barker's in Victorian)
Barker, Moore & Mein Medicine Co: nd (Parts 1-3, 1901-1903; Parts 1-4, 1906+) (color cardboard-c, B&W interior, 50 pages)

Parts 1-3 (Rare, earliest printing, nd (1901)) 225.00 450.00 900.00
NOTE: *Same cover as 4th edition in Victorian Age Section, except has "Part 1", "Part 2", or "Part 3" printed in the blank space beneath the crate on which central figure is sitting. States "Edition in 3 Parts" on the first interior page, beneath the picture of the Barker's Building.*
Parts 1-3 (nd, c1901-1903) 125.00 280.00 700.00
NOTE: *New cover art on all Parts. States "Edition in 3 Parts" on the first interior page.*
Parts 1-4 (nd, c1906+) 125.00 240.00 500.00
NOTE: *States "Edition in 4 Parts" on the first interior page. Various printings known.These have been confirmed as premium comic books, predating the Buster Brown premiums. They reprint advertising cartoons from Barker's Illustrated Almanac. For the 50 page booklets by this same name, numbered as "Part"s, without exception, were published after 1900. Some editions are found to have 54 pages.*

BARNEY GOOGLE AND SPARK PLUG (N) (See **Comic Monthly**)
Cupples & Leon Co.: 1923 - No.6, 1928 (9-7/8x9-3/4"; 52 pgs., B&W, daily-r)

1 (nn)-By Billy DeBeck 65.00 250.00 675.00
2-4 (#5 & #6 do not exist) 46.00 186.00 350.00
NOTE: *Started June 17, 1919 as newspaper strip; Spark Plug introduced July 17, 1922; strip still running making it one of the oldest still in existence.*

BART'S CARTOONS FOR 1902 FROM THE MINNEAPOLIS JOURNAL (N,S)
Minneapolis Journal: 1903 (11x9", 102 pgs, paperback, B&W)

nn - By Charles L. Bartholomew 30.00 100.00 180.00

BELIEVE IT OR NOT! by Ripley (N,S)
Simon & Schuster: 1929 (8x 5-1/4", 68 pgs, red, B&W cover, B&W interior)

nn - By Robert Ripley (strip-r text & art) 60.00 125.00 275.00
NOTE: *1929 was the first printing of many reprintings . Strip began Dec 19, 1918 and is still running.*

BEN WEBSTER (N)
Standard Printing Company: 1928-1931 (13-3/4x4-7/16", 768 pgs, soft-c)

1 - "Bound to Win" 58.00 160.00 315.00
2 - "...in old Mexico 58.00 160.00 315.00
3 - "...At Wilderness Lake 58.00 160.00 315.00
4 - "...in the Oil Fields 58.00 160.00 315.00
NOTE: *Self Published by Edwin Alger, also contains fan's letter pages.*

BIG SMOKER
W.T. Blackwell & Co.: 1908 (16 pgs, 5-1/2x3-1/2", color-c & interior)

nn - By unknown 20.00 55.00 100.00
NOTE: *Stated reprint of 1878 version. no known copies yet of original printing.*

BILLY BOUNCE (I)
Donohue & Co.: 1906 (288 pgs, hardbound)

nn - By W.W. Denslow & Dudley Bragdon 210.00 630.00 1250.00
NOTE: *Billy Bounce was created in 1901 as a comic strip by W. W. Denslow (strip ran from 1901 NOV 11 to 1905 DEC 3), but the series is best remembered in the C. W. Kahles version (from 1902 SEP 28). Denslow resumed his character in the above illustrated book.*

BILLY HON'S FAMOUS CARTOON BOOK (H)
Wasley Publishing Co.: 1927 (7-1/2x10", 68 pgs, softbound wraparound)

nn - By Billy Hon 15.00 50.00 100.00

BILLY THE BOY ARTIST'S BOOK OF FUNNY PICTURES (N)
C.M.Clark Publishing Co.: 1910 (9x12", hardcover-c, Boston Globe strip-r)

nn - By Ed Payne 125.00 400.00 775.00
NOTE: *This long lived strip ran in **The Boston Globe** from Nov 5 1899-Jan 7 1955; one of the longer run strips.*

BILLY THE BOY ARTIST'S PAINTING BOOK OF FUNNY PICTURES
(known to exist; more data required) – – –

BIRD CENTER CARTOONS: A Chronicle of Social Happenings (N,S)
A. C. McClurg & Co.: 1904 (12-3/8x9-1/2", 216 pgs, hardcover, B&W, single panels)

nn - By John McCutcheon 40.00 140.00 260.00
NOTE: *Strip began in **The Chicago Tribune** in 1903. Satirical cartoons and text concerning a mythical town.*

BLASTS FROM THE RAM'S HORN
The Rams Horn Company: 1902 (330 pgs, 7x9", B&W)

nn - By various 40.00 100.00 150.00
NOTE: *Cartoons reprinted from what was, apparently, a religious newspaper. Many cartoons by Frank Beard. Mostly single panel but occasionally sequential. Allegorical cartoons similar to the Christian Cartoons book. This book mixes cartoons and text sort of like the Caricature books. One or more cartoons on every page.*

BOBBY THATCHER & TREASURE CAVE (N)
Altemus Co.: 1932 (9x7", 86 pgs., B&W, hard-c)

nn - Reprints; Storm-a 65.00 200.00 410.00

BOBBY THATCHER'S ROMANCE (N)
The Bell Syndicate/Henry Altemus Co.: 1931 (8-3/4x7", color cover, B&W)

nn - By Storm 65.00 200.00 410.00

GD2.0 FN6.0 VF8.0

BOOK OF CARTOONS, A (M,S)
Edward T. Miller: 1903 (12-1/4x9-1/4", 120 pgs, hardcover, B&W)

nn - By Harry J. Westerman (Ohio State Journal-r) 20.00 70.00 125.00

BOOK OF DRAWINGS BY A.B. FROST, A (M,S)
P.F. Collier & Son: 1904 (15-3/8 x 11", 96 pgs, B&W)

nn - A.B. Frost 55.00 105.00 300.00
NOTE: *Pages alternate verses by Wallace Irwin and full-page plated by A.B.Frost. 39 plates.*

BOTTLE, THE (E) (see Victorian Age section for earlier printings)
Gowans & Gray, London & Glasgow: June 1905 (3-3/4x6", 72 pgs, printed one side only, paper cover, B&W)

nn - 1st printing (June 1905) 20.00 50.00 145.00
nn - 2nd printing (March 1906) 20.00 50.00 115.00
nn - 3rd printing (January 1911) 20.00 50.00 115.00
NOTE: *By George Cruikshank. Reprints both THE BOTTLE and THE DRUNKARD'S CHILDREN. Cover is text only - no cover art.*

BOTTLE, THE (E)
Frederick A. Stokes: nd (c1906) (3-3/4x6", 72 pgs, printed one side only, paper-c, B&W)

nn- by George Cruikshank 30.00 55.00 115.00
NOTE: *Reprint of the Gowans & Gray edition. Reprints both THE BOTTLE and THE DRUNKARD'S CHILDREN. Cover is text only - no cover art.*

BOYS AND FOLKS (N).
George H. Dornan Company: 1917 (10-1/4 x 8-1/4", 232 pgs. (single-sided), B&W strip-r.

nn - By Webster 21.00 64.00 150.00
NOTE: *Four sections: Life's Darkest Moments, Mostly About Folks, The Thrill That Comes Once in a Lifetime, and Our Boyhood Ambitions. Most are single-panel cartoons, but there are some sequential comic strips.*

BOY'S & GIRLS' BIG PAINTING BOOK OF INTERESTING COMIC PICTURES (N)
M. A. Donohue & Co.: 1914-16 (9x15, 70 pgs)

nn - By Carl "Bunny" Schultze (Foxy Grandpa-r) 105.00 310.00 –
#2 (1914) 105.00 310.00 –
#337 (1914) (sez "Big Painting & Drawing Book") 105.00 310.00 –
nn - (1916) (sez "Big Painting Book")(9-1/4x15") 105.00 310.00 –
NOTE: *These are all **Foxy Grandpa** items.*

BRAIN LEAKS: Dialogues of Mutt & Flea (N)
O. K. Printing Co. (Rochester Evening Times): 1911 (76 pgs, 6-5/8x4-5/8, hard-c, B&W)

nn - By Leo Edward O'Melia; newspaper strip-r 29.00 100.00 200.00

BRAINY BOWERS AND DROWSY DUGGAN (N)
Star Publishing: 1905 (7-1/4 x 4-9/16", 98 pgs., blue, brown & white color cover, B&W interior, 25¢) (daily strip-r 1902-04 Chicago Daily News)

#74 - By R. W. Taylor (Scarce) 600.00 1950.00 –
NOTE: *Part of a series of Atlantic Library Heart Series. Strip begins in 1901 and runs thru 1915. Taylor also created Yen the Janitor for the **New York World.***

BRAIN BOWERS AND DROWSY DUGAN (N)
Max Stein Pub. House, Chicago: 1905 (6-3/16x4-3/8", 64 pgs, B&W)

nn - By R.W. Taylor (Scarce) 600.00 2000.00 –
NOTE: *A coverless copy of this surfaced on eBay in 2002 selling for $700.00.;*

BRAINY BOWERS AND DROWSY DUGGAN GETTING ON IN THE WORLD WITH NO VISIBLE MEANS OF SUPPORT (STORIES TOLD IN PICTURES TO MAKE THEIR TELLING SHORT) (N)
Max Stein/Star Publishing: 1905 (7-3/8x5 1/8", 164 pgs, slick black, red & tan color cover, interior newsprint) (daily strip-r 1902-04 Chicago Daily News)

nn - By R. W. Taylor (Scarce) 500.00 1900.00 –
nn - Possible hard cover edition also? – – –
NOTE: *These Brainy Bowers editions are the earliest known daily newspaper strip reprint books.*

BRINGING UP FATHER (N)
Star Co. (King Features): 1917 (5-1/2x16-1/2", 100 pgs., B&W, cardboard-c)

nn - (Scarcer)-Daily strip- by George McManus 160.00 560.00 1150.00

BRINGING UP FATHER (N)
Cupples & Leon Co.: 1919 - No. 26, 1934 (10x10", 52 pgs., B&W, stiff cardboard-c) (No. 22 is 9-1/4x9-1/2")

1-Daily strip-r by George McManus in all 30.00 110.00 400.00
2-10 28.00 105.00 300.00
11-20 40.00 200.00 400.00
21-26 (Scarcer) 65.00 310.00 600.00
The Big Book 1 (1926)-Thick book (hardcover, 142 pgs.) 127.00 508.00 1000.00
w/dust jacket (rare) 183.00 732.00 1500.00
The Big Book 2 (1929) 96.00 384.00 800.00
w/dust jacket (rare) 183.00 732.00 1400.00
NOTE: *The Big Books contain 3 regular issues rebound. Strip began Jan 2 1913-May 28 2000.*

BRINGING UP FATHER, THE TROUBLE OF (N)
Embee Publ. Co.: 1921 (9-3/4x15-3/4", 46 pgs, Sunday-r in color)

nn - (Rare) 100.00 350.00 725.00
NOTE: *Ties with Mutt & Jeff (EmBee) and Jimmie Dugan And The Reg'lar Fellers (C&L) as the last of the oblong size era. This was self published by George McManus.*

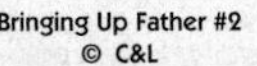
Bringing Up Father #2
© C&L

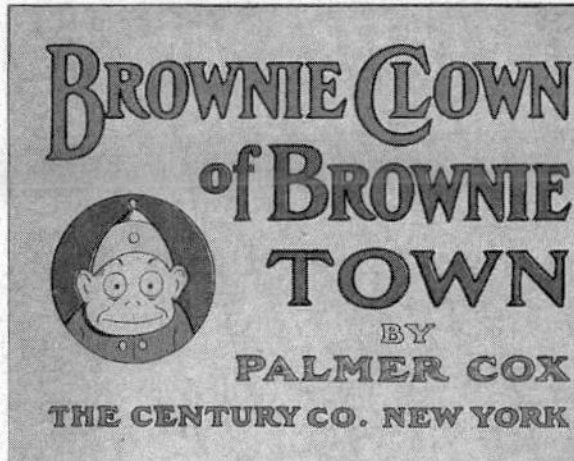

Brownie Clown of Brownie Town
© The Century Co.

Buster Brown Nuggets - Goes Swimming
1907 © Cupples & Leon

GD2.0 FN6.0 VF8.0

BRINGING UP FATHER (N) (see SAGARA'S ENGLISH CARTOONS
Publisher unknown (actually, unreadable), Tokyo: October 1924 (9-7/8" x 7-1/2", 90 pgs, color hard-c, B&W)

nn- (Scarce) by George McManus C&A (no known sales)
NOTE: *Published in Tokyo, Japan, with all strips in both English and Japanese, to facilitate learning English. Introduction by George McManus. Scarce in USA.*

BRONX BALLADS (I)
Simon & Schuster, NY: 1927 (9-1/2x7-1/4", hard-c, B&W)

nn - By Robert Simon and Harry Hershfield 75.00 150.00 300.00

BROWNIES, THE (not sequential comic strips)
The Century Co.: 1887 - 1914 (all came with dust jackets; add $100-150 to value if original dust jacket is included and intact)

Book 1 - The Brownies: Their Book (1887) 200.00 800.00 1200.00
Book 2 - Another Brownies Book (1890) 150.00 635.00 1000.00
Book 3 - The Brownies at Home (1893) 125.00 530.00 825.00
Book 4 - The Brownies Around the World (1894) 100.00 425.00 675.00
Book 5 - The Brownies Through the Union (1895) 100.00 425.00 675.00
Book 6 - The Brownies Abroad (1899) 100.00 425.00 675.00
Book 7 - The Brownies in the Philippines (1904) 100.00 425.00 675.00
Book 8 - The Brownies' Latest Adventures (1910) 100.00 425.00 675.00
Book 9 - The Brownies Many More Nights (1914) 100.00 425.00 675.00
...Raid on Kleinmaier Bros. (c. 1910, 16 pages) Kleinmaier Bros. Clothing, Marion, Ohio (no known sales)

BROWNIE CLOWN OF BROWNIE TOWN (N)
The Century Co.: 1908 (6-7/8 x 9-3/8", 112 pgs, color hardcover & interior)

nn - By Palmer Cox (rare; 1907 newspaper comic strip-r) 250.00 800.00 1100.00
NOTE: *The Brownies created 1883 in **St Nicholas Magazine.***

BUDDY TUCKER & HIS FRIENDS (N) (Also see **Buster Brown Nuggets**)
Cupples & Leon Co.: 1906 (11-5/8 x17", 58 pgs, color) (Scarce)

nn - 1905 Sunday strip-r by R. F. Outcault 525.00 1550.00 2900.00
NOTE: *Strip began Apr 30, 1905 thru at least Oct 1905.*

BUFFALO BILL'S PICTURE STORIES
Street & Smith Publications: 1909 (Soft cardboard cover)

nn - Very rare 100.00 275.00 460.00

BUGHOUSE FABLES (N) (see also **Comic Monthly**)
Embee Distributing Co. (King Features): 1921 (10¢, 4x4-1/2", 48 pgs.)

1-By Barney Google (Billy DeBeck) 50.00 200.00 400.00

BUG MOVIES (O) (Also see Clancy The Cop & Deadwood Gulch)
Dell Publishing Co.: 1931 (9-13/16x9-7/8", 52 pgs., B&W)

nn - Original material; Stookie Allen-a 150.00 300.00 600.00

BULL
Bull Publishing Company, New York: No.1, March, 1916 - No.12, Feb, 1917 (10 cents, 10-3/4x8-3/4", 24 pgs, color paper-c, B&W)

1-12 (Very Rare) – – –
NOTE: *Pro-German, Anti-British cartoon/humor monthly, whose goal was to keep the U.S. neutral and out of World War I. We know of no copies which have sold in the past few years.*

BUNNY'S BLUE BOOK (see also Foxy Grandpa) (N)
Frederick A. Stokes Co.: 1911 (10x15, 60¢)

nn - By Carl "Bunny" Schultze strip-r 125.00 375.00 –

BUNNY'S RED BOOK (see also Foxy Grandpa) (N)
Frederick A. Stokes Co.: 1912 (10-1/4x15-3/4", 64 pgs.)

nn - By Carl "Bunny" Schultze strip-r 125.00 375.00 –

BUNNY'S GREEN BOOK (see also Foxy Grandpa) (N)
Frederick A. Stokes Co.: 1913 (10x15")

nn - By Carl "Bunny" Schultze 125.00 375.00 –

BUSTER BROWN (C) (Also see Brown's Blue Ribbon Book of Jokes and Jingles & Buddy Tucker & His Friends)
Frederick A. Stokes Co.: 1903 - 1916 (Daily strip-r in color)

1903...& His Resolutions (11-1/4x16", 66 pgs.) by R. F. Outcault (Rare)-1st nationally distributed comic. Distr. through Sears & Roebuck 1650.00 3400.00 –
1904...His Dog Tige & Their Troubles (11-1/4x16-1/4", 66 pgs.)(Rare) 600.00 1800.00 –
1905...Pranks (11-1/4x16-3/8", 66 pgs.) 400.00 1550.00 –
1906...Antics (11x16-3/8", 66 pgs.) 400.00 1550.00 –
1906...And Company (11x16-1/2", 66 pgs.) 300.00 1100.00 –
1906...Mary Jane & Tige (11-1/4x16, 66 pgs.) 300.00 1100.00 –
NOTE: ***Yellow Kid** pictured on two pages.*
1908 Collection of Buster Brown Comics 250.00 835.00 –
1909 Outcault's Real Buster and The Only Mary Jane (11x16, 66 pgs, Stokes) 250.00 835.00 –
1910...Up to Date (10-1/8x15-3/4", 66 pgs.) 208.00 729.00 1100.00
1911...Fun And Nonsense (10-1/8x15-3/4", 66 pgs.) 183.00 642.00 1200.00
1912...The Fun Maker (10-1/8x15-3/4", 66 pgs.) -Yellow Kid (4 pgs.) 183.00 642.00 1200.00
1913...At Home (10-1/8x15-3/4", 56 pgs.) 167.00 583.00 1100.00
1914...And Tige Here Again (10x16, 62 pgs, Stokes) 153.00 535.00 900.00
1915...And His Chum Tige (10x16, Stokes) 153.00 535.00 900.00
1916...The Little Rogue (10-1/8x15-3/4", 62 pgs.) 162.00 567.00 1100.00
1917...And the Cat (5-1/2x 6-1/2, 26 pgs, Stokes) 115.00 402.00 700.00
1917...Disturbs the Family (5-1/2x 6 1/2, 26 pgs, Stokes
NOTE: *Story featuring statue of "the Chinese Yellow Kid"* 115.00 402.00 700.00
1917...The Real Buster Brown (5-1/2x 6 -/2, 26 pgs, Stokes 115.00 402.00 700.00

Frederick A. Stokes Co. Hard Cover Series (I)

...Abroad (1904, 10-1/4x8", 86 pgs., B&W, hard-c)-R. F. Outcault-a (Rare) 180.00 600.00 900.00
...Abroad (1904, B&W, 67 pgs.)-R. F. Outcault-a 180.00 600.00 900.00
NOTE: *Buster Brown Abroad is not an actual comic book, but prose with illustrations.*
..."Tige" His Story 1905 (10x8", 63 pgs., B&W) (63 illos.)
nn-By RF Outcault 143.00 500.00 –
...My Resolutions 1906 (10x8", B&W, 68 pgs.)-R.F. Outcault-a (Rare) 233.00 817.00 1400.00
...Autobiography 1907 (10x8", B&W, 71 pgs.) (16 color plates & 36 B&W illos) 65.00 230.00 420.00
...And Mary Jane's Painting Book 1907 (10x13-1/4", 60 pgs, both card & hardcover versions exist
nn-RFO (first printing blank on top of cover) 67.00 233.00 440.00
First Series- this is a reprint if it says First Series 67.00 233.00 440.00
Volume Two - By RFO 67.00 233.00 440.00
... My Resolutions by Buster Brown (1907, 68 pgs, small size, cardboard covers) scarce 43.00 150.00 285.00
NOTE: *Not actual comic book per se, but a compilation of the Resolutions panels found at the end of Outcault's Buster Brown newspaper strips.*

BUSTER BROWN (N)
Cupples & Leon Co./N. Y. Herald Co.: 1906 - 1917 (11x17", color, strip-r)
NOTE: *Early issues by R. F. Outcault; most C&L editions are not by Outcault.*

1906...His Dog Tige And Their Jolly Times (11-3/8x16-5/8", 68 pgs.) 300.00 1100.00 1900.00
1906...His Dog Tige & Their Jolly Times (11x16, 46 pgs.) 163.00 600.00 1100.00
1907...Latest Frolics (11-3/8x16-5/8", 66 pgs., r/'05-06 strips)163.00 600.00 1000.00
1908...Amusing Capers (58 pgs.) 129.00 475.00 775.00
1909...The Busy Body (11-3/8x16-5/8", 62 pgs.) 129.00 475.00 775.00
1910...On His Travels (11x16", 58 pgs.) 115.00 402.00 775.00
1911...Happy Days (11-3/8x16-5/8", 58 pgs.) 115.00 402.00 775.00
1912...In Foreign Lands (10x16", 58 pgs) 115.00 402.00 775.00
1913...And His Pets (11x16", 58 pgs.) STOKES???? 115.00 402.00 775.00
1913...And His Pets (26 pg partial reprint) – – –
1914...Funny Tricks (11-3/8x16-5/8", 58 pgs.) 115.00 402.00 775.00
1916...At Play (10x16, 58 pgs) 115.00 402.00 775.00

BUSTER BROWN NUGGETS (N)
Cupples & Leon Co./N.Y.Herald Co.: 1907 (1905, 7-1/2x6-1/2", 36 pgs., color, strip-r, hard-c)(By R. F. Outcault) (NOTE: books are all unnumbered)

Buster Brown Goes Fishing, Goes Swimming, Plays Indian, Goes Shooting, Plays Cowboy, On Uncle Jack's Farm, Tige And the Bull, And Uncle Buster 40.00 150.00 360.00
Buddy Tucker Meets Alice in Wonderland 56.00 200.00 425.00
Buddy Tucker Visits The House That Jack Built 40.00 150.00 360.00

BUSTER BROWN MUSLIN SERIES (N)
Saalfield: 1907 (also contain copyright Cupples & Leon)

...Goes Fishing, Plays Indian, And the Donkey (1907, 6-7/8x6-1/8", 24 pgs., color)-r/1905 Sunday comics page by Outcault (Rare) 50.00 175.00 330.00
...Plays Cowboy (1907, 6-3/4x6", 10 pgs., color)-r/1905 Sunday comics page by Outcault (Rare) 50.00 175.00 325.00
NOTE: *These are muslin versions of the C&L BB Nugget series. Muslin books are all cloth books, made to be washable so as not easily stained/destroyed by very young children. The Muslin books contain one strip each (the title strip), to the more common NUGGET's three strips.*

BUSTER BROWN PREMIUMS (Advertising premium booklets)
Various Publishers: 1904 - 1912 (3x5" to 5x7"; sizes vary)

American Fruit Product Company, Rochester, NY

Buster Brown Duffy's 1842 Cider (1904, 7x5". 12 pgs, C.E. Sherin Co, NYC)
nn - By R. F. Outcault (scarce) 100.00 350.00 600.00

The Brown Shoe Company, St. Louis, USA
Set of five books (5x7", 16 pgs., color)

Brown's Blue Ribbon Book of Jokes and Jingles Book 1 (nn, 1904)-By R. F. Outcault; Buster Brown & Tige, Little Tommy Tucker, Jack & Jill, Little Boy Blue, Dainty Jane; The Yellow Kid app. on back-c (1st BB comic book premium) 350.00 1100.00 2200.00
Buster Brown's Blue Ribbon Book of Jokes and Jingles Book 2 (1905)-
Original color art by Outcault 200.00 600.00 1200.00

Buster Brown Nuggets -Buster Brown Plays Cowboy
© C&L

Captain Easy and Wash Tubbs by Roy Crane
1934 © Whitman Famous Comics Cartoon Book

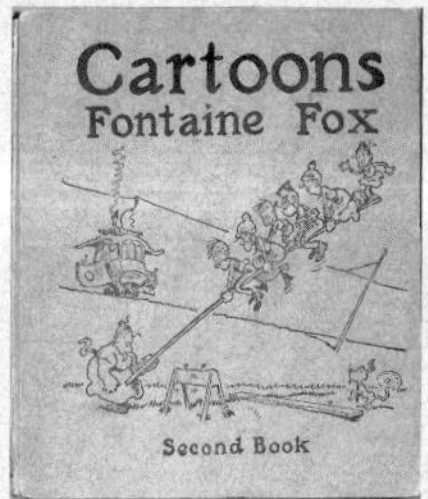

Cartoons Fontaine Fox Second Book
early 1920s © Harper & Bros, NY

GD2.0 FN6.0 VF8.0

Buster's Book of Jokes & Jingles Book 3 (1909)
not by R.F. Outcault 200.00 450.00 900.00
NOTE: *Reprinted from the Blue Ribbon post cards with advert jingles added.*
Buster's Book of Instructive Jokes and Jingles Book 4 (1910)-Original color art
not by R.F. Outcault 150.00 585.00 1100.00
...Book of Travels nn (1912, 3x5")-Original color art not signed by Outcault
117.00 408.00 725.00
NOTE: *Estimated 5 or 6 known copies exist of books #1-4.*

The Buster Brown Bread Company
"Buster Brown" Bread Book of Rhymes, The (1904, 4x6", 12 pgs., half color, half B&W)- Original color art not signed by RFO 158.00 553.00 1100.00

Buster Brown's Hosiery Mills
"Buster Brown's Latest" nn (1909, 7x5-1/4". 20 pgs, color paper cover and color interior By R.F. Outcault (a GD+ copy sold for $150)
"How Buster Brown Got The Pie" nn (nd, 7x5-1/4". 16 pgs, color paper cover and color interior By R.F. Outcault 85.00 300.00 600.00
"The Autobiography of Buster Brown" nn (nd,9x6-1/8", 36 pgs, text story & art by R.F. Outcault 85.00 300.00 600.00
NOTE: *Similar to, but a distinctly different item than "Buster Brown's Autobiography."*

The Buster Brown Stocking Company
Buster Brown Drawing Book, The nn (nd, 5x6", 20 pgs.)-B&W reproductions of 1903 R.F. Outcault art to trace 65.00 165.00 400.00
NOTE: *Reprints a comic strip from Burr McIntosh Magazine, which includes Buster, Yellow Kid, and Pore Li'l Mose (only known story involving all three.)*
Buster Brown Stocking Magazine nn (Jan. 1906, 7-3/4x5-3/8", 36 pgs.) R.F. Outcault
50.00 100.00 275.00
NOTE: *This was actually a store bought item selling for 5 cents per copy.*

Collins Baking Company
Buster Brown Drawing Book nn (1904, 5x3", 12 pgs.)-Original B&W art to trace, not signed by R.F. Outcault 50.00 200.00 400.00

C. H. Morton, St. Albans, VT
Merry Antics of Buster Brown, Buddy Tucker & Tige nn (nd, 3-1/2x5-1/2", 16 pgs.) -Original B&W art by R.F. Outcault 83.00 292.00 500.00

Ivan Frank & Company
Buster Brown nn (1904, 3x5", 12 pgs.)-B&W repros of R. F. Outcault Sunday pages (First premium to actually reproduce Sunday comic pages – may be first premium comic strip-r book?) 125.00 438.00 900.00
Buster Brown's Pranks (1904, 3-1/2x5-1/8", 12 pgs.)-reprints intro of Buddy Tucker into the BB newspaper strip before he was spun off into his own short lived newspaper strip
125.00 438.00 800.00

Kaufmann & Strauss
Buster Brown Drawing Book (1906, 28 pages, 5x3-1/2") Color Cover, B+W original story signed by Outcault, tracing paper inserted as alternate pages. Back cover imprinted for Nox' Em All Shoes 50.00 150.00 330.00

Pond's Extract
Buster Brown's Experiences With Pond's Extract nn (1904, 6-3/4x4-1/2", 28 pgs.) Original color art by R.F. Outcault (may be the first BB premium comic book with original art) 130.00 320.00 700.00

C. A. Cross & Co.
Red Cross Drawing Book nn (1906, 4-7/8x3-1/2", color paper -c, B&W interior, 12 pgs.)
75.00 175.00 325.00
NOTE: *This is for Red Cross coffee; not the health organization.*

Ringen Stove Company
Quick Meal Steel Ranges nn (nd, 5x3", 16 pgs.)-Original B&W art not signed by R.F. Outcault 80.00 205.00 410.00

Steinwender Stoffregen Coffee Co.
"Buster Brown Coffee" (1905, 4-7/8x3", color paper cover, B&W interior, 12 printed pages, plus 1 tracing paper page above each interior image (total of 8 sheets) (Very Rare)
105.00 310.00 625.00
NOTE: *Part of a BB drawing contest. If instructions had been followed, most copies would have ended up destroyed.*

U. S. Playing Card Company
Buster Brown - My Own Playing Cards (1906, 2-1/2x1-3/4", full color)
nn - By R. F. Outcault 42.00 147.00 250.00
NOTE: *Series of full color panels tell stories, average about 5 cards per story.*

Publisher Unknown
The Drawing Book nn (1906, 3-9/16x5", 8 pgs.)-Original B&W art to trace not by R.F. Outcault 50.00 150.00 325.00

BUTLER BOOK A Series of Clever Cartoons of Yale Undergraduate Life
Yale Record: June 16, 1913 (10-3/4 x 17", 34 pgs, paper cover B&W)
nn - By Alban Bernard Butler 25.00 75.00 150.00
NOTE: *Cartoons and strips reprinted from The Yale Record student newspaper.*

BUTTONS & FATTY IN THE FUNNIES
Whitman Publishing Co.: nd 1927 (10-1/4x15-1/2", 28pg., color)
W936 - Signed "M.E.B.", probably M.E. Brady; strips in color copyright The Brooklyn Daily Eagle; (very rare) 61.00 244.00 450.00

BY BRIGGS (M,N,P) (see also OLD GOLD THE SMOOTHER AND BETTER CIGARETTE)
Old Gold Cigarettes: nd (c1920's) (11" x 9-11/16", 44 pgs, cardboard-c, B&W)
nn- (Scarce) 45.00 90.00 185.00
NOTE: *Collection reprinting strip cartoons by Clare Briggs, advertising Old Gold Cigarettes. These strips originally appeared in various magazines, play program booklets, newspapers, etc. Some of the strips involve regular Briggs strip series. Contains all of the strips in the smaller, color "OLD GOLD" giveaways, plus more.*

CAMION CARTOONS
Marshall Jones Company: 1919 (7-1/2x5", 136 pgs, B&W)
nn - By Kirkland H. Day (W.W.One occupation) 20.00 70.00 125.00

CANYON COUNTRY KIDDIES (M)
Doubleday, Page & Co: 1923 (8x10-1/4", 88 pgs, hard-c, B&W)
nn - By James Swinnerton 39.00 137.00 260.00

CARLO (H)
Doubleday, Page & Co.: 1913 (8 x 9-5/8, 120 pgs, hardcover, B&W)
nn - By A.B. Frost 40.00 140.00 300.00
NOTE: *Original sequential strips about a dog. Became short lived newspaper comic strip in 1914. Originally published with a dust jacket which increases value 50%.*

CARTOON BOOK, THE
Bureau of Publicity, War Loan Organization, Treasury Department, Washington, D.C.: 1918 (6-1/2x4-7/8", 48 pgs, paper cover, B&W)
nn - By various artists 38.00 115.00 225.00
NOTE: *U.S. government issued booklet of WW I propaganda cartoons by 46 artists promoting the third sale of Liberty Loan bonds. The artists include: Berryman, Clare Briggs, Cesare, J. N. "Ding" Darling, Rube Goldberg, Kemble, McCutcheon, George McManus, F. Opper, T. E. Powers, Ripley, Satterfield, H. T. Webster, Gaar Williams.*

CARTOON CATALOGUE (S)
The Lockwood Art School, Kalamazoo, Mich.: 1919 (11-5/8x9, 52 pgs, B&W)
nn - Edited by Mr. Lockwood 20.00 60.00 150.00
NOTE: *Jammed with 100s of single panel cartoons and some sequential comics; Mr Lockwood began the very first cartoonist school back in 1892. Clare Briggs was one of his students.*

CARTOON COMICS
Lasco Publications, Detroit, Mich: #1, April 1930 - #2, May 1930 (8-3/6x5-1/5")
1, 2 - By Lu Harris 25.00 65.00 125.00
NOTE: *Contains recurring characters Hollywood Horace, Campus Charlie, Pair-A-Dice Alley and Jocko Monkey. Not much is presently known about the creator(s) or publisher.*

CARTOON HISTORY OF ROOSEVELT'S CAREER, A
The Review of Reviews Company: 1910 (276 pgs, 8-1/4x11",
nn - By various 105.00 210.00 425.00
NOTE: *Reprints editorial cartoons about Teddy Roosevelt from U.S. and international newspapers and cartoons from the humor magaines (Puck, Judge, etc.). A few cartoonists whose work is included are Dalrymple, Opper, McDougall, McCutcheon, Remington, Rogers, Kemble. Mostly single panel but 10 or so are sequential strips.*

CARTOON HUMOR
Collegian Press: 1938 (102 pgs, squarebound, B&W)
nn 20.00 70.00 125.00
NOTE: *Contains cartoons & strips by Otto Soglow, Syd Hoff, Peter Arno, Abner Dean, others.*

CARTOONIST'S PHILOSOPHY, A
Percy Crosby: 1931, HC, 252 pgs, 5-1/2x7-1/2", hard-c, celluloid dust wrapper
nn - By Percy Crosby (10 plates, 6 are of Skippy) 30.00 70.00 140.00
NOTE: *Crosby's partial autobiography regarding his return to France in 1929, and portrayals of Normandy, the "cliff dwellers" on Normandy cliffs (destroyed in WWII), his visit to London, comments on art, philosophy, several poems, and political dialogue. His description of his Cockney driver, "Harold" is amusing. Also describes his experience visiting Chicago to speak out against Capone, his concerns over the evils of Prohibition, and the economy prior to the 1929 crash. This book reveals he was aware of the dangers of his outspoken views, and is prophetic, re: his later years as political prisoner. Also reveals his religious beliefs.*

CARTOONS BY BRADLEY: CARTOONIST OF THE CHICAGO DAILY NEWS
Rand McNally & Company: 1917 (11-1/4x8-3/4", 112 pgs, hardcover, B&W)
nn - By Luther D. Bradley (editorial) 20.00 70.00 120.00

CARTOONS BY FONTAINE FOX (Toonerville Trolley) (S)
Harper & Brothers Publishers: nd early '20s (9x7-7/8",102 pgs., hard-c, B&W)
Second Book- By Fontaine Fox (Toonerville-r) 150.00 300.00 575.00

CARTOONS BY HALLADAY (N,S)
Providence Journal Co., Rhode Island: Dec 1914 (116 pgs, 10-1/2x 7-3/4", hard-c, B&W)
nn- (Scarce) 50.00 125.00 250.00
NOTE: *Cartoons on Rhode Island politics, plus some Teddy Roosevelt & WW I cartoons.*

CARTOONS BY McCUTCHEON (S)
A. C. McClurg & Co.: 1903 (12-3/8x9-3/4", 212 pgs., hardcover, B&W)
nn - By John McCutcheon 20.00 70.00 125.00

CARTOONS BY W. A. IRELAND (S)
The Columbus-Evening Dispatch: 1907 (13-3/4 x 10-1/2", 66 pgs, hardcover)
nn - By W. A. Ireland (strip-r) 20.00 70.00 125.00

CARTOONS MAGAZINE (I,N,S)
H. H. Windsor, Publisher: Jan 1912-June 1921; July 1921-1923; 1923-1924; 1924-1927 (1912-July 1913 issues 12x9-1/4", 68-76 pgs; 1913-1921 issues 10x7", average 112 to 188 pgs, color covers)
1912-Jan-Dec 30.00 75.00 160.00

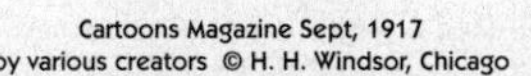
Cartoons Magazine Sept, 1917
by various creators © H. H. Windsor, Chicago

Charlie Chaplin in the Army by Segar
1917 © Essaney

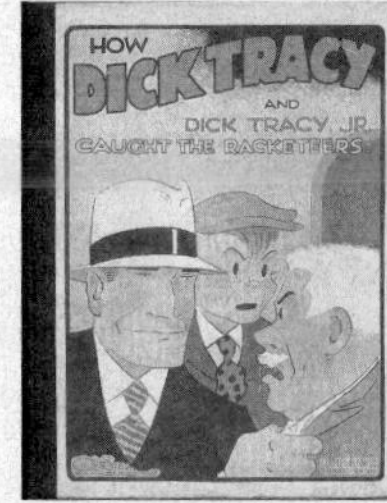

How Dick Tracy and Dick Tracy, Jr.
Caught the Racketeers by Chester Gould
1933 © Cupples & Leon

GD2.0 FN6.0 VF8.0

1913-1917 30.00 75.00 160.00
1917-(Apr) "How Comickers Regard Their Characters" 30.00 105.00 170.00
1917-(June) "A Genius of the Comic Page" - long article on George Herriman, Krazy Kat, etc with lots of Herriman art; "Cartoonists and Their Cars" 150.00 300.00 760.00
1918-1919 30.00 75.00 155.00
1920-June 1921 30.00 75.00 155.00
July 1921-1923 titled Wayside Tales & Cartoons Magazine 30.00 75.00 155.00
1923-1924 becomes Cartoons Magazine again 30.00 75.00 155.00
1924-1927 becomes Cartoons & Movie Magazine 30.00 75.00 155.00
NOTE: *Many issues contain a wealth of historical background on then current cartoonists of the day with an international slant; each issue profusely illustrated with many cartoons. We are unsure if this magazine continued after 1927.*

CARTOONS BY J. N. DARLING (S,N - some sequential strips)
The Register & Tribune Co., Des Moines, Iowa: 1909?-1920 (12x8-7/8",B&W)

Book 1 20.00 55.00 150.00
Book 2 Education of Alonzo Applegate (1910) 18.00 52.00 120.00
2nd printing 18.00 52.00 120.00
Book 3 Cartoons From The Files (1911) 18.00 52.00 120.00
Book 4 18.00 52.00 120.00
Book 5 In Peace And War (1916) 18.00 52.00 120.00
Book 6 Aces & Kings War Cartoons (Dec 1, 1918) 18.00 52.00 120.00
Book 7 The Jazz Era (Dec 1920) 18.00 52.00 120.00
Book 8 Our Own Outlines of History (1922) 18.00 52.00 120.00
NOTE: *Some of the most inspired hard hitting cartoons ever printed. Are there more?*

CARTOONS THAT MADE PRINCE HENRY FAMOUS, THE (N,S)
The Chicago Record-Herald: Feb/March 1902 (12-1/8" x 9", 32 pgs, paper-c, B&W)

nn- (Scarce) by McCutcheon 15.00 51.00 100.00
NOTE: *Cartoons about the visit of the British Prince Henry to the U.S.*

CAVALRY CARTOONS (O)
R. Montalboddi: nd (c1918) (14-1/4" x 11", 30 pgs, printed on one side, olive & black construction paper-c, B&W interior)

nn - By R.Montalboddi 20.00 55.00 100.00
NOTE: *Comics about life in the U.S.Cavalry during World War I, by a soldier who was in the 1st Cavalry.*

CAWS AND EFFECT
L.D. Gallison Pub., NY: nd (7 two-sided panels, 4-5/8 x 3", B&W)

nn - By Edgar Ape O. (a GVG copy sold for $111.55 in 2010)

CHARLIE CHAPLIN (N)
Essanay/M. A. Donohue & Co.: 1917 (9x16", B&W, large size soft-c)

Series 1, #315-Comic Capers (9-3/4x15-3/4")-20 pgs. by Segar;
Series 1, #316-In the Movies 165.00 525.00 1200.00
#317-Up in the Air (20 pgs), #318-In the Army 165.00 525.00 1400.00
Funny Stunts-(12-1/2x16-3/8",16 color pgs) 165.00 525.00 1400.00
NOTE: *All contain pre-Thimble Theatre Segar art. The thin paper used makes high grade copies very scarce.*

CHASING THE BLUES
Doubleday Page: 1912 (7-1/2x10", 108 pgs., B&W, hard-c)

nn - By Rube Goldberg 150.00 525.00 1100.00
NOTE: *Contains a dozen Foolish Questions, baseball, a few Goldberg poems and lots of sequential strips.*

CHRISTIAN CARTOONS (N,S)
The Sunday School Times Company: 1922 (7-1/4 x 6-1/8,104 pgs, brown hard-c, B&W)

nn - E.J. Pace 15.00 51.00 100.00
NOTE: *Religious cartoons reprinted from The Sunday School Times.*

CLANCY THE COP (O)
Dell Publishing Co.: 1930 - No. 2, 1931 (10x10", 52 pgs., B&W, cardboard-c)
(Also see Bug Movies & Deadwood Gulch)

1, 2-By VEP Victor Pazimino (original material; not reprints) 110.00 275.00 550.00

CLIFFORD MCBRIDE'S IMMORTAL NAPOLEON & UNCLE ELBY (N)
The Castle Press: 1932 (12x17"; soft-c cartoon book)

nn - Intro. by Don Herod 36.00 144.00 250.00

COLLECTED DRAWINGS OF BRUCE BAIRNSFATHER, THE
W. Colston Leigh: 1931 (11-1/4x8-1/4 ", 168 pages, hardcover, B&W)

nn - By Bruce Bairnsfather 25.00 100.00 200.00

COMICAL PEEP SHOW
McLoughlin Bros: 1902 (36 pgs, B&W)

nn 24.00 96.00 165.00
NOTE: *Comic stories of Wilhelm Busch redrawn; two versions with green or gold front cover logos; back covers different.*

COMIC ANIMALS (I)
Charles E. Graham & Co.: 1903 (9-3/4x7-1/4", 90 pgs, color cover)

nn - By Walt McDougall (not comic strips) 80.00 160.00 275.00

COMIC CUTS (O)
H. L. Baker Co., Inc.: 5/19/34-7/28/34 (Tabloid size 10-1/2x15-1/2", 24 pgs., 5¢)
(full color, not reprints; published weekly; created for news stand sales)

GD2.0 FN6.0 VF8.0

V1#1 - V1#7(6/30/34), V1#8(7/14/34), V1#9(7/28/34)-Idle Jack strips 250.00 500.00 1000.00
NOTE: *According to a 1958 Lloyd Jacquet interview, this short-lived comics mag was the direct inspiration for Major Malcolm Wheeler-Nicholson's **New Fun Comics**, not **Famous Funnies**.*

COMIC MONTHLY (N)
Embee Dist. Co.: Jan, 1922 - No. 12, Dec, 1922 (10¢, 8-1/2"x9", 28 pgs., 2-color covers) (1st monthly newsstand comic publication) (Reprints 1921 B&W dailies)

1-Polly & Her Pals by Cliff Sterrett 400.00 1200.00 2500.00
2-Mike & Ike by Rube Goldberg 150.00 500.00 1000.00
3-S'Matter, Pop? 150.00 500.00 1000.00
4-Barney Google by Billy DeBeck 150.00 500.00 1000.00
5-Tillie the Toiler by Russ Westover 150.00 500.00 1000.00
6-Indoor Sports by Tad Dorgan 150.00 500.00 1000.00
NOTE: *#6 contains more Judge Rummy than Indoor Sports.*
7-Little Jimmy by James Swinnerton 150.00 500.00 1000.00
8-Toots and Casper b y Jimmy Murphy 150.00 500.00 1000.00
9-New Bughouse Fables by Barney Google 150.00 500.00 1000.00
10-Foolish Questions by Rube Goldberg 150.00 500.00 1000.00
11-Barney Google & Spark Plug by Billy DeBeck 150.00 500.00 1000.00
12-Polly & Her Pals by Cliff Sterrett 150.00 500.00 1000.00
NOTE: *This series was published by George McManus (Bringing Up Father) as Em & Rudolph Block, Jr., son of Hearst's cartoon editor for many years, as "Bee." One would have thought this series would have done very well considering the tremendous amount of talent assembled. All issues are extremely hard to find these days and rarely show up in any type of higher grade.*

COMIC PAINTING AND CRAYONING BOOK (H)
Saalfield Publ. Co.: 1917 (13-1/2x10", 32 pgs.) (No price on-c)

nn - Tidy Teddy by F. M. Follett, Clarence the Cop, Mr. & Mrs. Butt-In; regular comic stories to read or color 50.00 175.00 330.00

COMPLETE TRIBUNE PRIMER, THE (I)
Mutual Book Company: 1901 (7 1/4 x 5", 152 pgs, red hard-c)

nn - By Frederick Opper; has 75 Opper cartoons 25.00 75.00 150.00

COURTSHIP OF TAGS, THE (N)
McCormick Press: pre-1910 (9x4", 88 pgs, red & B&W-c, B&W interior)

nn - By O. E. Wertz (strip-r Wichita Daily Beacon) 25.00 75.00 150.00

DAFFYDILS (N)
Cupples & Leon Co.: 1911 (5-3/4x7-7/8", 52 pgs., B&W, hard-c)

nn - By "Tad" Dorgan 58.00 204.00 350.00
NOTE: *Also exists in self-published TAD edition: The T.A. Dorgan Company; unknown which is first printing.*

DAN DUNN SECRET OPERATIVE 48 (Also See Detective Dan) (N)
Whitman Publishing: 1937 ((5 1/2 x 7 1/4", 68pgs., color cardboard-c, B&W)

1010 And The Gangsters' Frame-Up 50.00 150.00 350.00
NOTE: *There are two versions of the book the later printing has a 5 cent cover price. Dick Tracy look-alike character by Norman Marsh.*

DANGERS OF DOLLY DIMPLE, THE (N)
Penn Tobacco Co.: nd (1930's) (9-3/8x7-7/8", 28 pgs, red cardboard-c, B&W)

nn - (Rare) by Walter Enright 25.00 88.00 150.00
NOTE: *Reprints newspaper comic strip advertisements, in which in every episode, Dolly Dimple's life is saved by Penn's Smoking Tobacco. - how very un-P.C. by today's standards.*

DEADWOOD GULCH (O) (See The Funnies 1929)(also see Bug Movies & Clancy The Cop)
Dell Publishing Co.: 1931 (10x10", 52 pgs., B&W, color covers, B&W interior)

nn - By Charles "Boody" Rogers (original material) 150.00 300.00 600.00

DESTINY A Novel In Pictures (O)
Farrar & Rinehart: 1930 (8x7", 424 pgs, B&W, hard-c, dust jacket?)

nn - By Otto Nuckel (original graphic novel) 25.00 100.00 200.00

DICK TRACY & DICK TRACY JR. CAUGHT THE RACKETEERS, HOW
Cupples & Leon Co.: 1933 (8-1/2x7", 88 pgs., hard-c) (See Treasure Box of Famous Comics) (N)

2-(Numbered on pg. 84)-Continuation of Stooge Viller book (daily strip reprints from 8/3/33 thru 11/8/33)(Rarer than #1) 100.00 400.00 800.00
With dust jacket... 175.00 500.00 1200.00

DICK TRACY & DICK TRACY JR. AND HOW THEY CAPTURED "STOOGE" VILLER (N)
Cupples & Leon Co.: 1933 (8-1/2x7", 100 pgs., hard-c, one-shot)
Reprints 1932 & 1933 Dick Tracy daily strips

nn(No.1)-1st app. of "Stooge" Viller 100.00 400.00 800.00
With dust jacket... 175.00 500.00 1100.00

DIMPLES By Grace Drayton (N) (See Dolly Dimples)
Hearst's International Library Co.: 1915 (6 1/4 x 5 1/4, 12 pgs) (5 known)

nn-Puppy and Pussy; nn-She Goes For a Walk; nn-She Had A Sneeze; nn-She Has a Naughty Play Husband; nn-Wait Till Fido Comes Home 21.00 74.00 175.00

DOINGS OF THE DOO DADS, THE (N)
Detroit News (Universal Feat. & Specialty Co.): 1922 (50¢, 7-3/4x7-3/4", 34 pgs, B&W, red & white-c, square binding)

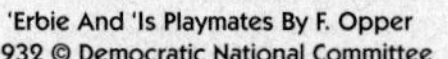
'Erbie And 'Is Playmates By F. Opper
1932 © Democratic National Committee

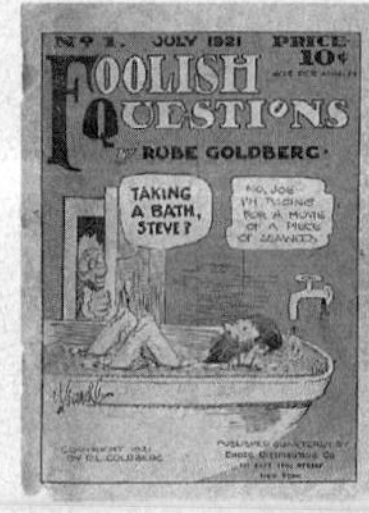

Foolish Questions by Rube Goldberg
1921 © EmBee Distributing Co., NY.

The Latest Adventures of Foxy Grandpa 1905
© Bunny Publ.

nn-Reprints 1921 newspaper strip "Text & Pictures" given away as prize in the Detroit News Doo Dads contest; by Arch Dale 43.00 173.00 360.00

DOING THE GRAND CANYON
Fred Harvey: 1922 (7 x 4-3/4", 24 pgs, B&W, paper cover)

nn - John McCutcheon 30.00 60.00 125.00
NOTE: *Text & 8 cartoons about visiting the Grand Canyon.*

DOINGS OF THE VAN-LOONS (N) (from same company as Mutt & Jeff #1-#5)
Ball Publications: 1912 (5-3/4X15-1/2", 68pg., B&W, hard-c)

nn - By Fred I. Leipziger (scarce) 72.00 252.00 600.00

DOLLY DIMPLES & BOBBY BOUNCE (See Dimples)
Cupples & Leon Co.: 1933 (8-3/4x7", color hardcover, B&W)

nn - Grace Drayton-a 24.00 96.00 165.00

DOO DADS, THE (Sleepy Sam and Tiny the Elephant)
Universal Feature * Specialty Co: 1922 (5-1/4x14", 36 pgs.,B&W, R&W-c,square binding)

nn - By Arch Dale 35.00 125.00 250.00

DRAWINGS BY HOWARD CHANDLER CHRISTIE (S, M)
Moffat, Yard & Company, NY: 1905 (11-7/8x16-1/2", 68 pgs, hard-c, B&W)

nn - Howard C. Christie 30.00 60.00 125.00
NOTE: *Reprints1898-1905 from Haprer & Bros, Ch. Scribners Sons, Leslie's, MacMillians, McLurg, Russell.*

DREAMS OF THE RAREBIT FIEND (N)
Frederick A. Stokes Co.:1905 (10-1/4x7-1/2", 68 pgs, thin paper cover all B&W) newspaper reprints from the New York Evening Telegram printed on yellow paper

nn-By Winsor "Silas" McCay (Very Rare) (Five copies known to exist)
Estimated value.... 1100.00 2800.00 –
NOTE: *A G/VG copy sold for $2,045 in May 2004. This item usually turns up with fragile paper.*

DRISCOLL'S BOOK OF PIRATES (O)
David McKay Publ.: 1934 (9x7", 124 pgs, B&W, hardcover)

nn - By Montford Amory ("Pieces of Eight strip-r) 21.00 64.00 150.00

DUCKY DADDLES
Frederick A. Stokes Co: July 1911 (15x10")

nn - By Grace Weiderseim (later Drayton) strip-r 50.00 175.00 310.00

DUMBUNNIES AND THEIR FRIENDS IN RABBITBORO, THE (O)
Albertine Randall Wheelan: 1931 (8-3/4x7-1/8", 82 pgs, color hardcover, B&W)

nn - By Albertine Randall Wheelan (self-pub) 65.00 110.00 220.00

EDISON - INSPIRATION TO YOUTH (N)(Also see Life of Thomas---)
Thomas A. Edison, Incorporated: 1939 (9-1/2 x 6-1/2, paper cover, B&W)

nn - Photo-c 50.00 150.00 300.00
NOTE: *Reprints strip material found in the 1928 Life of Thomas A. Edison in Word and Picture.*

'ERBIE AND 'IS PLAYMATES
Democratic National Committee: 1932 (8x9-1/2, 16 pgs, B&W)

nn - By Frederick Opper (Rare) 100.00 200.00 425.00
NOTE: *Anti-Hoover/Pro-Roosevelt political comics.*

EXPANSION BEING BART'S BEST CARTOONS FOR 1899
Minneapolis Journal: 1900 (10-1/4x8-1/4", 124 pgs, paperback, B&W)

v2#1 - By Charles L. Bartholomew 24.00 84.00 150.00

FAMOUS COMICS (N)
King Features Synd. (Whitman Pub. Co.): 1934 (100 pgs., daily newspaper-r) (3-1/2x8-1/2"; paper cover)(came in an illustrated box)

684 (#1) - Little Jimmy, Katz Kids & Barney Google 40.00 100.00 260.00
684 (#2) - Polly, Little Jimmy, Katzenjammer Kids 40.00 100.00 260.00
684 (#3) - Little Annie Rooney, Polly and Her Pals, Katzenjammer Kids 40.00 100.00 260.00
Box price... 75.00 150.00 450.00

FAMOUS COMICS CARTOON BOOKS (N)
Whitman Publishing Co.: 1934 (8x7-1/4", 72 pgs, B&W hard-c, daily strip-r)

1200-The Captain & the Kids; Dirks reprints credited to Bernard Dibble 29.00 86.00 215.00
1202-Captain Easy & Wash Tubbs by Roy Crane; 2 slightly different versions of cover exist 34.00 103.00 250.00
1203-Ella Cinders By Conselman & Plumb 28.00 84.00 215.00
1204-Freckles & His Friends 25.00 75.00 205.00
NOTE: *Called Famous Funnies Cartoon Books inside back area sales advertisement.*

FANTASIES IN HA-HA (M)
Meyer Bros & Co.: 1900 (14 x 11-7/8", 64 pgs, color cover hardcover, B&W)

nn - By Hy Mayer 50.00 150.00 300.00

FELIX (N)
Henry Altemus Company: 1931 (6-1/2"x8-1/4", 52 pgs., color, hard-c w/dust jacket)

1-3-Sunday strip reprints of Felix the Cat by Otto Messmer. Book No. 2 r/1931 Sunday panels mostly two to a page in a continuity format oddly arranged so each tier of panels reads across two pages, then drops to the next tier. (Books 1 & 3 have not been documented.)(Rare)
Each 250.00 500.00 1000.00
With dust jacket 250.00 750.00 1500.00

FELIX THE CAT BOOK (N)
McLoughlin Bros.: 1927 (8"x15-3/4", 52 pgs, half in color-half in B&W)

nn - Reprints 23 Sunday strips by Otto Messmer from 1926 & 1927, every other one in color, two pages per strip. (Rare) 200.00 900.00 1850.00
260-Reissued (1931), reformatted to 9-1/2"x10-1/4" (same color plates, but one strip per every three pages), retitled ("Book" dropped from title) and abridged (only eight strips repeated from first issue, 28 pgs.).(Rare) 90.00 350.00 660.00

F. FOX'S FUNNY FOLK (see Toonerville Trolley; Cartoons by Fontaine Fox) (C)
George H. Doran Company: 1917 (10-1/4x8-1/4", 228 pgs, red, B&W cover, B&W interior, hardcover; dust jacket?)

nn - By Fontaine Fox (Toonerville Trolley strip-r) 150.00 450.00 800.00

52 CAREY CARTOONS (O,S)
Carey Cartoon Service, NY: 1915 (25 cents, 6-3/4" x 10-1/2", 118 pgs, printed on one side, color cardboard-c, B&W)

nn - (1915) War – – –
NOTE: *The Carey Cartoon Service supplied a weekly, hand-colored single panel cartoon broadsheet, on current news events, starting in 1906 or 1907, for window display in Carey Fountain Pen chain stores. These broadsheets were 22-1/2" x 33" in size. Starting circa 1915, Carey Fountain Pens began offering subscriptions for the broadsheets to other merchants, for window display in their stores as well. This collects, in B&W, the cartoons for 1915. An "Edition Deluxe" was also advertised, with all cartoons hand colored. It is currently unknown whether a reprint collection was only issued in 1915, or if other editions exist.*

52 LETTERS TO SALESMEN
Steven-Davis Company: 1927 (???)

nn - (Rare) 25.00 100.00 150.00
NOTE: *52 motivational letters to salesmen, with page of comics for each week, bound into embossed leather binder.*

FOLKS IN FUNNYVILLE (S)
R.H. Russell: 1900 (12"x9-1/4", 48 pgs.)(cardboard-c)

nn - By Frederick Opper 300.00 1000.00 –
NOTE: *Reprinted from Hearst's NY Journal American Humorist supplements.*

FOOLISH QUESTIONS (S)
Small, Maynard & Co.: 1909 (6-7/8 x 5-1/2", 174 pgs, hardcover, B&W)

nn - By Rube Goldberg (first Goldberg item) 100.00 300.00 500.00
NOTE: *Comic strip began Oct 23, 1908 running thru 1941. Also drawn by George Frink in 1909.*

FOOLISH QUESTIONS THAT ARE ASKED BY ALL
Levi Strauss & Co./Small, Maynard & Co.: 1909 (5-1/2x5-3/4", 24 pgs, paper-c, B&W)

nn- (Rare) by Rube Goldberg 65.00 175.00 350.00

FOOLISH QUESTIONS (Boxed card set) (S)
Wallie Dorr Co., N.Y.: 1919 (5-1/4x3-3/4")(box & card backs are red)

nn - Boxed set w/52 B&W comics on cards; each a single panel gag complete set w/box 75.00 263.00 500.00
NOTE: *There are two diff sets put out simultaneously with the first set, by the same company. One set continues/picks up the numbering of the cards from the other set.*

FOOLISH QUESTIONS (S)
EmBee Distributing Co.: 1921 (10¢, 4x5 1/2; 52 pgs, 3 color covers; B&W)

1-By Rube Goldberg 46.00 160.00 300.00

FOXY GRANDPA
Foxy Grandpa Company, 33 Wall St, NY : 1900 (9x15", 84 pgs, full color, cardboard-c)

nn - By Carl Schultze (By Permission of New York Herald) 271.00 1200.00 –
NOTE: *This seminal comic strip began Jan 7, 1900 and was collected later that same year.*

FOXY GRANDPA (Also see The Funnies, 1st series) (N)
N. Y. Herald/Frederick A. Stokes Co./M. A. Donahue & Co./Bunny Publ. (L. R. Hammersly Co.): 1901 - 1916 (Strip-r in color, hard-c)

1901- 9x15" in color-N. Y. Herald 313.00 1000.00 –
1902- "Latest Larks of...", 32 pgs., 9-1/2x15-1/2" 164.00 575.00 –
1902- "The Many Advs. of...", 9x12", 148 pgs., Hammersly Co. 179.00 625.00 –
1903- "Latest Advs.", 9x15", 24 pgs., Hammersly Co. 164.00 575.00 –
1903- "...'s New Advs.", 11x15", 66 pgs., Stokes 164.00 575.00 –
1904- "Up to Date", 10x15", 66 pgs., Stokes 146.00 510.00 920.00
1904- "The Many Adventures of...", 9x15, 144pgs, Donohue 146.00 510.00 920.00
1905- "& Flip-Flaps", 9-1/2x15-1/2", 52 pgs. 146.00 510.00 920.00
1905- "The Latest Advs. of...", 9x15", 28, 52, & 68 pgs, M.A. Donohue Co.; re-issue of 1902 issue 104.00 365.00 710.00
1905- "Latest Larks of...", 9-1/2x15-1/2", 52 pgs., Donahue; re-issue of 1902 issue with more pages added 104.00 365.00 710.00
1905- "Latest Larks of...", 9-1/2x15-1/2", 24 pgs. edition, Donahue; re-issue of 1902 issue 104.00 365.00 710.00
1905- "Merry Pranks of...", 9-1/2x15-1/2", 28, 52 & 62 pgs., Donahue 104.00 365.00 710.00

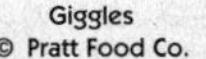
Giggles
© Pratt Food Co.

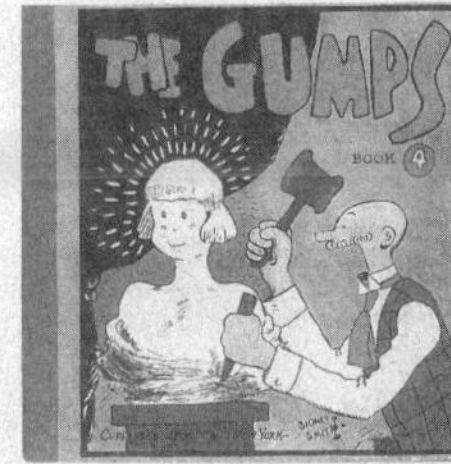

The Gumps by Sidney Smith
1927? © Cupples & Leon

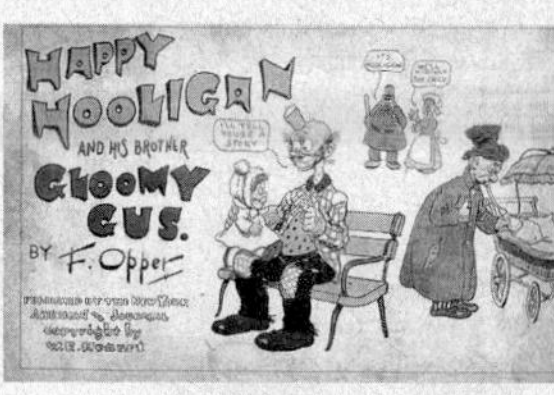

Happy Hooligan Book 1 1902
© Frederick A. Stokes

GD2.0 FN6.0 VF8.0

1905-"...Surprises",10x15", color, 64 pg,Stokes, 60¢ 104.00 365.00 710.00
1906- "Frolics", 10x15", 30 pgs., Stokes 104.00 365.00 710.00
1907?-"...& His Boys",10x15", 64 color pgs, Stokes 104.00 365.00 710.00
1907- "Triumphs", 10x15", 62 pgs, Stokes 104.00 365.00 710.00
1908-"...Mother Goose", Stokes 104.00 365.00 710.00
1909- "...& Little Brother", 10x15, 58 pgs, Stokes 104.00 365.00 710.00
1911- "Latest Tricks", r-1910,1911 Sundays-Stokes Co. 104.00 365.00 710.00
1914-(9-1/2x15-1/2", 24 pgs.)-6 color cartoons/page, Bunny Publ. Co. 88.00 306.00 615.00
1915 - ...Always Jolly (10x16, Stokes) 88.00 306.00 615.00
1916- "Merry Book", (10x15", 64 pgs, Stokes) 88.00 306.00 615.00
1917-"...Adventures (5 1/2 x 6 1/2, 26 pgs, Stokes) 57.00 200.00 460.00
1917-"...Frolics (5 1/2 x 6 1/2, 26 pgs, Stokes) 57.00 200.00 460.00
1917-"...Triumphs (5 1/2 x 6 1/2, 26 pgs, Stokes) 57.00 200.00 460.00

FOXY GRANDPA, FUNNY TRICKS OF (The Stump Books)
M.A. Donahue Co, Chicago: approx 1903 (1-7/8x6-3/8", 44 pgs, blue hardcover)
nn - By Carl Schultze 54.00 189.00 330.00
NOTE: *One of a series of ten "stump" books; the only comics one.*

FOXY GRANDPA'S MOTHER GOOSE (I)
Stokes: October 1903 (10-11/16x8-1/2", 86 pgs, hard-c)
nn - By Carl Schultze (not comics - illustrated book) 54.00 189.00 330.00

FOXY GRANDPA SPARKLETS SERIES (N)
M. A. Donahue & Co.: 1908 (7-3/4x6-1/2"; 24 pgs., color)
"... Rides the Goat", "...& His Boys", "...Playing Ball", "...Fun on the Farm", "...Fancy Shooting", "...Show His Boys Up-To-Date Sports", "...Plays Santa Claus"
each.... 88.00 306.00 575.00
900- "Playing Ball"; Bunny illos; 8 pgs., linen like pgs., no date 73.00 254.00 440.00

FOXY GRANDPA VISITS RICHMOND (O,P)
Dietz Printing Co., Richmond, VA / Hotel Rueger: nd (c1920's) (5-7/8" x 4-1/2", 16 pgs, paper-c, B&W)
nn - (Scarce) By Bunny 50.00 100.00 275.00
NOTE: *Promotional comic given away to its guests by the Hotel Rueger, about Foxy Grandpa visiting and enjoying the Hotel. Originally came in an envelope, with the words "Foxy Grandpa Visits Richmond -- and Rueger's" printed on it.*

FOXY GRANDPA VISITS WASHINGTON, D.C. (P)
Dietz Printing Co., Richmond, VA / Hamilton Hotel: nd (c1920's) (5-7/8" x 4-1/2", 16 pgs, paper-c, B&W)
nn - (Scarce) By Bunny 55.00 105.00 200.00
NOTE: *Mostly reprints "... Visits Richmond", changing all references to Hotel Rueger, to Hamilton Hotel instead. Also, changes depictions of a waiter and a cook from black to white, plus incompletely erases the cover art on a book Foxy Grandpa falls asleep with (the latter is how we know that the Richmond version was first).*

FRAGMENTS FROM FRANCE (S)
G. P. Putnam & Sons: 1917 (9x6-1/4", 168 pgs, hardcover, $1.75)
nn - By Bruce Bairnsfather 25.00 88.00 150.00
NOTE: *WW1 trench warfare cartoons; color dust jacket.*

FUNNIES, THE (H) (See Clancy the Cop, Deadwood Gulch, Bug Movies)
Dell Publishing Co.: 1929 - No. 36, 10/18/30 (10¢; 5¢ No. 22 on) (16 pgs.)
Full tabloid size in color; not reprints; published every Saturday
1-My Big Brudder, Jonathan, Jazzbo & Jim, Foxy Grandpa, Sniffy, Jimmy Jams & other strips begin; first four-color comic newsstand publication; also contains magic, puzzles & stories 300.00 800.00 1600.00
2-21 (1930, 10¢) 155.00 310.00 620.00
22(nn-7/12/30-5¢) 155.00 310.00 620.00
23(nn-7/19/30-5¢), 24(nn-7/26/30-5¢), 25(nn-8/2/30), 26(nn-8/9/30), 27(nn-8/16/30), 28(nn-8/23/30), 29(nn-8/30/30), 30(nn-9/6/30), 31(nn-9/13/30), 32(nn-9/20/30), 33(nn-9/27/30), 34(nn-10/4/30), 35(nn-10/11/30), 36(nn, no date-10/18/30)
each.... 150.00 300.00 580.00

GASOLINE ALLEY (Also see Popular Comics & Super Comics) (N)
Reilly & Lee Publishers: 1929 (8-3/4x7", B&W daily strip-r, hard-c)
nn - By King (96 pgs.) 125.00 300.00 600.00
with scarce Dust Wrapper 250.00 500.00 1000.00
NOTE: *Of all the Frank King reprint books, this is the only one to reprint actual complete newspaper strips - all others are illustrated prose text stories.*

GIBSON'S PUBLISHED DRAWINGS, MR. (M,S) (see Victorian index for earlier issues)
R.H. Russell, New York: No.1 1894 - No. 9 1904 (11x17-3/4", hard-c, B&W)
nn (No.6; 1901) A Widow and her Friends (90 pgs.) 30.00 60.00 115.00
nn (No.7; 1902) The Social Ladder (88 pgs.) 30.00 60.00 115.00
8 - 1903 The Weaker Sex (88 pgs.) 30.00 60.00 115.00
9 - 1904 Everyday People (88 pgs.) 30.00 60.00 115.00
NOTE: *By Charles Dana Gibson cartoons, reprinted from magazines, primarily LIFE. The Education of Mr. Pipp tells a story. Series continues how long after 1904?*

GIGGLES
Pratt Food Co., Philadelphia, PA: 1908-09? (12x9", 8 pgs, color, 5 cents-c)
1-8: By Walt McDougall (#8 dated March 1909) 40.00 175.00 -

GD2.0 FN6.0 VF8.0

NOTE: *Appears to be monthly; almost tabloid size; yearly subscriptions was 25 cents.*

GOD'S MAN (H)
Jonathan Cape and Harrison Smith Inc.: 1929 (8-1/4x6", 298 pgs, B&W hardcover w/dust jacket) (original graphic novel in wood cuts)
nn - By Lynd Ward 43.00 171.00 300.00

GOLD DUST TWINS
N. K. Fairbank Co.: 1904 (4-5/8x6-3/4", 18 pgs, color and B&W)
nn - By E. W. Kemble (Rare) 50.00 100.00 225.00
NOTE: *Promo comic for Gold DustWashing Powder; includes page of watercolor paints.*

GOLF
Volland Co.: 1916 (9x12-3/4", 132 pgs, hard-c, B&W)
nn - By Clair Briggs 100.00 200.00 400.00

GUMPS, THE (N)
Landfield-Kupfer: No. 1, 1918 - No. 6, 1921; (B&W Daily strip-r)
Book No. 1(1918)(scarce)-cardboard-c, 5-1/4x13-1/3", 64 pgs., daily strip-r by Sidney Smith 75.00 250.00 500.00
Book No.2(1918)-(scarce); 5-1/4x13-1/3"; paper cover; 36 pgs. daily strip reprints by Sidney Smith 75.00 250.00 500.00
Book No. 3 100.00 350.00 700.00
Book No. 4 (1918) 5-3/8x13-7/8", 20 pgs. Color card-c 100.00 350.00 700.00
Book No. 5 10-1/4x13-1/2", 20 pgs. Color paper-c 100.00 350.00 700.00
Book No. 6 (Rare, 20 pgs, 8x13-3/8, strip-r 1920-21) 121.00 423.00 750.00

GUMPS, ANDY AND MIN, THE (N)
Landfield-Kupfer Printing Co., Chicago/Morrison Hotel: nd (1920s) (Giveaway, 5-1/2"x14", 20 pgs., B&W, soft-c)
nn - Strip-r by Sidney Smith; art & logo embossed on cover w/hotel restaurant menu on back-c or a hotel promo ad; 4 different contents of issues known 50.00 175.00 300.00

GUMPS, THE (N)
Cupples & Leon: 1924-1930 (10x10, 52 pgs, B&W)
1 - By Sidney Smith 75.00 250.00 400.00
2-7 39.00 154.00 265.00

THE GUMPS (P)
Cupples & Leon Company: 1924 (9 x 7-1/2", 28 pgs, paper cover)
nn (1924) 50.00 175.00 275.00
NOTE: *Promotional comic for Sunshine Andy Gump Biscuits. Daily strip-r from 1922-24.*

GUMP'S CARTOON BOOK, THE (N)
The National Arts Company: 1931 (13-7/8x10", 36 pgs, color covers, B&W)
nn - By Sidney Smith 57.00 228.00 400.00

GUMPS PAINTING BOOK, THE (N)
The National Arts Company: 1931 (11 x 15 1/4", 20 pgs, half in full color)
nn - By Sidney Smith 57.00 228.00 400.00

HALT FRIENDS! (see also **HELLO BUDDY**)
???: 1918? (4-3/8x5-3/4", 36 pgs, color-c, B&W, no cover price listed)
nn - Unknown 20.00 40.00 100.00
NOTE: *Says on front cover: "Comics of War Facts of Service Sold on its merits by Unemployed or Disabled Ex-Service Men. Credentials Shown On Request. Price - Pay What You Please." These are very common; contents vary widely.*

HAMBONE'S MEDITATIONS
Jahl & Co.: 1917, no date (1920) (6-1/8 x 7-1/2, 108 pgs, paper cover, B&W)
nn - (1917, 68 pgs.) By J. P. Alley (a copy in GD sold in 2010 for $278)
nn - (nd, 108 pgs.) By J. P. Alley 50.00 150.00 325.00
NOTE: *Reprint of racist single panel newspaper series, 2 cartoons per page.*

HAN OLA OG PER (N)
Anundsen Publishing Co, Decorah, Iowa: 1927 (10-3/8 x 15-3/4", 54 pgs, paper-c, B&W)
nn - American origin Norwegian language strips-r 33.00 131.00 230.00
NOTE: *1940s and modern reprints exist.*

HANS UND FRITZ (N)
The Saalfield Publishing Co.: 1917, 1927-29 (10x13-1/2", 28 pgs., B&W)
nn - By R. Dirks (1917, r-1916 strips) 96.00 335.00 575.00
nn - By R. Dirks (1923 edition- reprint of 1917 edition) 58.00 204.00 300.00
nn - By R. Dirks (1926 edition- reprint of 1917 edition) 58.00 204.00 300.00
The Funny Larks Of... By R. Dirks (©1917 outside cover; ©1916 inside indicia) 96.00 335.00 575.00
The Funny Larks Of... (1927) reprints 1917 edition of 1916 strips Halloween-c 58.00 204.00 300.00
The Funny Larks Of... 2 (1929) 58.00 204.00 300.00
193 - By R. Dirks; contains 1916 Sunday strip reprints of Katzenjammer Kids & Hawkshaw the Detective - reprint of 1917 nn edition (1929) this edition is not rare 58.00 204.00 300.00

HAPPY DAYS (S)
Coward-McCann Inc.: 1929 (12-1/2x9-5/8", 110 pgs, hardcover B&W)

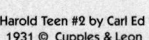

Harold Teen #2 by Carl Ed
1931 © Cupples & Leon

Jimmy and His Scrapes
© Frederick A. Stokes

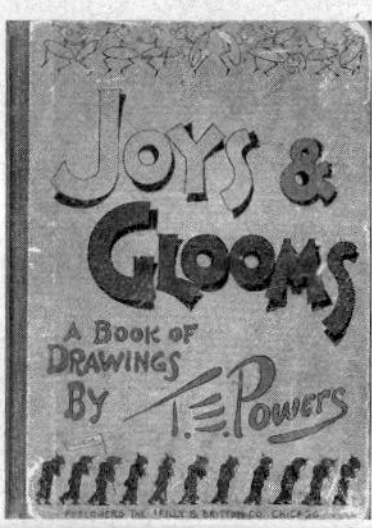

Joys & Glooms By T.E. Powers
1912 © Reilly & Britton Co.

GD2.0 FN6.0 VF8.0

nn - By Alban Butler (WW 1 cartoons) 20.00 60.00 125.00

HAPPY HOOLIGAN (See Alphonse...) (N)
Hearst's New York American & Journal: 1902,1903

Book 1-(1902)-"And His Brother Gloomy Gus", By Fred Opper; has 1901-02-r; (yellow & black)(86 pgs.)(10x15-1/4") 600.00 1800.00 3400.00
New Edition, 1903 -10x15" 82 pgs. in color 350.00 1400.00 –
NOTE: *Strip ran March 26, 1900-Aug 14, 1932 and is widely recognized as setting the format standard for all newspaper comic strips which came after it. Opper (1857-1937) was going blind towards the end.*

HAPPY HOOLIGAN (N) (By Fredrick Opper)
Frederick A. Stokes Co.: 1906-08 (10-1/4x15-3/4", cardboard color-c)

1906 - :Travels of...), 68 pgs,10-1/4x15-3/4", 1905-r 350.00 900.00 –
1907 - "--Home Again", 68 pgs., 10x15-3/4", 60¢; full color-c 350.00 900.00 –
1908 - "Handy--", 68 pgs, color 350.00 900.00 –

HAPPY HOOLIGAN, THE STORY OF (G)
McLoughlin Bros.: No. 281, 1932 (12x9-1/2", 20 pgs., soft-c)

281-Three-color text, pictures on heavy paper 57.00 228.00 400.00
NOTE: *An homage to Opper's creation on its 30th Anniversary in 1932.*

HAROLD HARDHIKE'S REJUVENATION
O'Sullivan Rubber: 1917 (6-1/4x3-1/2, 16 pgs, B&W)

nn 25.00 100.00 200.00
NOTE: *Comic book to promote rubber shoe heels.*

HAROLD TEEN (N)
Cupples & Leon Co.: 1929 (9-7/8x9-7/8", 52 pgs, cardboard covers)

1 - By Carl Ed 50.00 200.00 525.00
nn - (1931, 8-11/16x6-7/8", 96 pgs, hardcover w/dj) 41.00 164.00 280.00
NOTE: *Title 2nd book:* ***HAROLD TEEN AND HIS OLD SIDE-KICK– POP JENKINS,*** *(Adv. of...). Precursor for Archie Andrews & crew; strip began May 4, 1919 running into 1959.*

HAROLD TEEN PAINT AND COLOR BOOK (N)
McLoughlin Bros Inc.: 1932 (13x9-3/4, 28 pgs, B&W and color)

#2054 25.00 100.00 200.00

HAWKSHAW THE DETECTIVE (See Advs. of..., Hans Und Fritz & Okay) (N)
The Saalfield Publishing Co.: 1917 (10-1/2x13-1/2", 24 pgs., B&W)

nn - By Gus Mager (Sunday strip-r) 54.00 190.00 350.00
nn - By Gus Mayer (1923 reprint of 1917 edition) 25.00 100.00 160.00
nn - By Gus Mager (1926 reprint of 1917 edition) 25.00 100.00 160.00
NOTE: *Runs Feb 23, 1913-Sept 4, 1922, starts again from Dec 13, 1931-Feb 11, 1952; Sherlock Holmes spoof.*

HEALTH IN PICTURES
American Public Health Association, NYC: 1930 (6-1/2" x 5-3/16", 76 pgs, green & black paper-c, B&W interior)

nn - By various 20.00 55.00 125.00
NOTE: *Collection of strips and cartoons put out by the Public Health Association, on topics ranging from boating and food safety, to small pox and typhoid prevention.*

HE DONE HER WRONG (O) (see also BANANA OIL)
Doubleday, Doran & Company: 1930 (8-1/4x 7-1/4", 276pgs, hard-c with dust jacket, B&W interiors)

nn - By Milt Gross 75.00 225.00 400.00
NOTE: *A seminal original-material wordless graphic novel, not reprints. Several modern reprints.*

HELLO BUDDY (see also **HALT FRIENDS**)
???: 1919? (4-3/8x5-3/4", 36 pgs, color-c, B&W, 15¢)

nn - Unknown 10.00 30.00 100.00
NOTE: *Says on front cover: "Comics of War Facts of Service Sold on its merits by Unemployed or Disabled Ex-Service Men." These are very common; contents vary widely.*

HENRY (N)
David McKay Co.: 1935 (25¢, soft-c)

Book 1 - By Carl Anderson 57.00 200.00 425.00
NOTE: *Strip began March 19 1932; this book ties with Popeye (David McKay) and Little Annie Rooney (David McKay) as the last of the 10x10" Platinum Age comic books.*

HENRY (M)
Greenberg Publishers Inc.: 1935 (11-1/4x 8-5/8", 72 pgs, red & blue color hard-c, dust jacket, B&W interiors) (strip-r from Saturday Evening Post)

nn - By Carl Anderson 57.00 200.00 400.00

HIGH KICKING KELLYS, THE (M)
Vaudeville News Corporation, NY: 1926 (5x11", B&W, two color soft-c)

nn - By Jack A. Ward (scarce) 40.00 160.00 300.00

HIGHLIGHTS OF HISTORY (N)
World Syndicate Publishing Co.: 1933-34 (4-1/2x4", 288 pgs)

nn - 5 different unnumbered issues; daily strip-r 25.00 50.00 100.00
NOTE: *Titles include Buffalo Bill, Daniel Boone, Kit Carson, Pioneers of the Old West, Winning of the Old Northwest. There are line drawing color covers and embossed hardcover versions. It is unknown which came out first.*

HOMER HOLCOMB AND MAY (N)
no publisher listed: 1920s (4 x 9-1/2", 40 pgs, paper cover, B&W)

nn - By Doc Bird Finch (strip-r) 10.00 40.00 70.00

HOME, SWEET HOME (N)
M.S. Publishing Co.: 1925 (10-1/4x10")

nn - By Tuthill 33.00 134.00 235.00

HOW THEY DRAW PROHIBITION (S)
Association Against Prohibition: 1930 (10x9", 100 pgs.)

nn - Single panel and multi-panel comics (rare) 100.00 300.00 600.00
NOTE: *Contains art by J.N. "Ding" Darling, James Flagg, Rollin Kirby, Winsor McCay, T.E. Powers, H.T. Webster, others. Also comes with a loose sheet listing all the newspapers where the cartoons originally appeared.*

HOW TO BE A CARTOONIST (H)
Saalfield Pub. Co: 1936 (10-3/8x12-1/2", 16 pgs, color-c, B&W)

nn - By Chas. H. Kuhn 15.00 50.00 100.00

HOW TO DRAW: A PRACTICAL BOOK OF INSTRUCTION (H)
Harper & Brothers: 1904 (9-1/4x12-3/8", 128 pgs, hardcover, B&W)

nn - Edited By Leon Barritt 57.00 228.00 400.00
NOTE: *Strips reprinted include: "Buster Brown" by Outcault, "Foxy Grandpa" by Bunny, "Happy Hooligan" by Opper, "Katzenjammer Kids" by Dirks, "Lady Bountiful" by Gene Carr, "Mr. Jack" by Swinnerton, "Panhandle Pete" by George McManus, "Mr E.Z. Mark" by F.M. Howarth others; non-character strips by Hy Mayer, Winsor McCay, T.E. Powers, others; single panel cartoons by Davenport, Frost, McDougall, Nast, W.A. Rogers, Sullivant, others.*

HOW TO DRAW CARTOONS (H)
Garden City Publishing Co.: 1926, 1937 (10 1/4 x 7 1/2, 150 pgs)

1926 first edition By Clare Briggs 25.00 75.00 160.00
1937 2nd edition By Clare Briggs 20.00 60.00 110.00
NOTE: *Seminal "how to" break into the comics syndicates with art by Briggs, Fisher, Goldberg, King, Webster, Opper, Tad, Hershfield, McCay, Ding, others. Came with Dust Jacket -add 50%.*

HOW TO DRAW FUNNY PICTURES: A Complete Course in Cartooning (H)
Frederick J. Drake & Co., Chicago: 1936 (10-3/8x6-7/8", 168 pgs, hardcover, B&W)

nn - By E.C. Matthews (200 illus by Eugene Zimmerman) 20.00 60.00 120.00

HY MAYER (M)
Puck Publishing: 1915 (13-1/2 x 20-3/4", 52 pgs, hardcover cover, color & B&W interiors)

nn - By Hy Mayer(strip reprints from Puck) 40.00 140.00 300.00

HYSTERICAL HISTORY OF THE CIVILIAN CONSERVATION CORPS
Peerless Engraving: 1934 (10-3/4x7-1/2", 104 pgs, soft-c, B&W)

nn - By various 35.00 70.00 140.00
NOTE: *Comics about CCC life, includes two color insert postcards in back.*

INDOOR SPORTS (N,S)
National Specials Co., New York: nd circa 1912 (25 cents, 6 x 9", 68 pgs, B&W)

nn - Tad 35.00 125.00 250.00
NOTE: *Cartoons reprinted from Hearst papers.*

IT HAPPENS IN THE BEST FAMILIES (N)
Powers Photo Engraving Co.: 1920 (52 pgs.)(9-1/2x10-3/4")

nn - By Briggs; B&W Sunday strips-r 29.00 114.00 220.00
Special Railroad Edition (30¢)-r/strips from 1914-1920 26.00 103.00 200.00

JIMMIE DUGAN AND THE REG'LAR FELLERS (N)
Cupples & Leon: 1921, 46 pgs. (11"x16")

nn - By Gene Byrne 71.00 284.00 500.00
NOTE: *Ties with EmBee's Mutt & Jeff and Trouble of Bringing Up Father as the last of this size.*

JIMMY (N) (see Little Jimmy Picture & Story Book)
N. Y. American & Journal: 1905 (10x15", 84 pgs., color)

nn - By Jimmy Swinnerton (scarce) 335.00 875.00 2100.00
NOTE: *James Swinnerton was one of the original first pioneers of the American newspaper comic strip.*

JIMMY AND HIS SCRAPES (N)
Frederick A. Stokes: 1906, (10-1/4x15-1/4", 66 pgs, cardboard-c, color)

nn - By Jimmy Swinnerton (scarce) 300.00 800.00 1800.00

JOE PALOOKA (N)
Cupples & Leon Co.: 1933 (9-13/16x10", 52 pgs., B&W daily strip-r)

nn - By Ham Fisher (scarce) 150.00 500.00 1100.00

JOHN, JONATHAN AND MR. OPPER BY F. OPPER (S,I,N)
Grant, Richards, 48 Leicester Square, W.C.: 1903 (9-5/8x8-3/8", 108 pgs, hard-c B&W)

nn - Opper (Scarce) 50.00 200.00 400.00
NOTE: *British precursor-type companion to* Willie And His Poppa *reprints from Hearst's NY American & Journal Opper cartoons interfacing* Uncle Sam *precursor* Brother Jonathan, John Bull. *Uses name* Happy Hooligan *in one cartoon, has John Bull smoking opium in another.*

JOLLY POLLY'S BOOK OF ENGLISH AND ETIQUETTE (S)
Jos. J. Frisch: 1931 (60 cents, 8 x 5-1/8, 88 pgs, paper-c, B&W)

nn - By Jos. J. Frisch 20.00 60.00 125.00
NOTE: *Reprint of single panel newspaper series, 4 per page, of English and etiquette lessons taught by a flapper.*

JOYS AND GLOOMS (N)

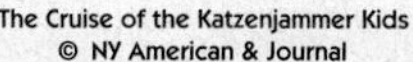
The Cruise of the Katzenjammer Kids
© NY American & Journal

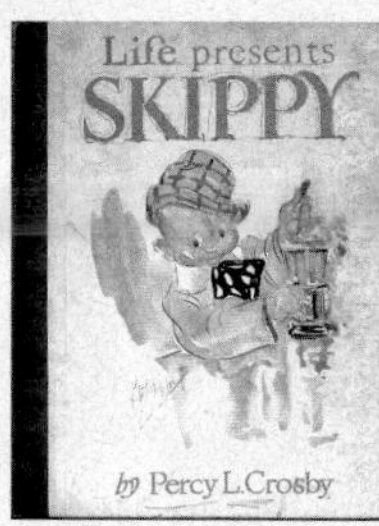

Life Presents Skippy by Percy L. Crosby
1924 © Life Publishing Company

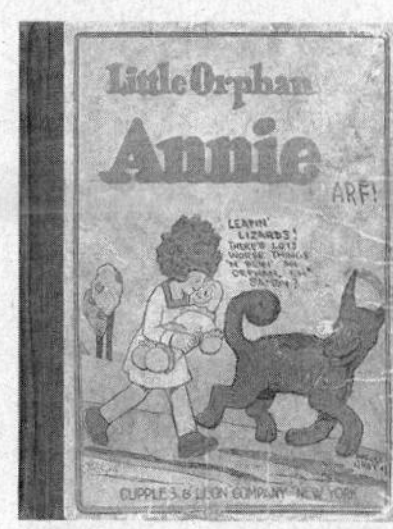

Little Orphan Annie 1926
© C&L

GD2.0 FN6.0 VF8.0

Reilly & Britton Co.: 1912 (11x8", 72 pgs, hard-c, B&W interior)
nn - By T. E. Powers (newspaper strip-r) 39.00 156.00 325.00

JUDGE - yet to be indexed

JUDGE'S LIBRARY - yet to be indexed

JUST KIDS COMICS FOR CRAYON COLORING
King Features. NYC: 1928 (11x8-1/2, 16 pgs, soft-c)
nn - By Ad Carter 33.00 100.00 200.00
NOTE: *Porous better grade paper; top pics printed in color; lower in b&w to color.*

JUST KIDS, THE STORY OF (I)
McLoughlin Bros.: 1932 (12x9-1/2", 20 pgs., paper-c)
283-Three-color text, pictures on heavy paper 30.00 125.00 275.00

KAPTIN KIDDO AND PUPPO (N)
Frederick A. Stokes Co.: 1910-1913 (11x16-1/2", 62 pgs)
1910-By Grace Wiederseim (later Drayton) 50.00 150.00 275.00
1910-Turr-ble Tales of... By Grace Wiederseim (Edward Stern & Co., 11x16-1/2", 64 pgs.) 50.00 150.00 260.00
1913- ...'Speriences By Grace Drayton 50.00 150.00 260.00
NOTE: *Strip ran approx. 1909-1912.*

KATZENJAMMER KIDS, THE (Also see Hans Und Fritz) (N)
New York American & Journal: 1902,1903 (10x15-1/4", 86 pgs., color)
(By Rudolph Dirks; strip first appeared in 1897) © W.R. Hearst
NOTE: *All KK books 1902-1905 all have the same exact title page with a 1902 copyright by W.R. Hearst; almost always look instead on the front cover.*
1902 (Rare) (red & black); has 1901-02 strips 1000.00 2800.00 -
1903- **A New Edition** (Rare), 86 pgs 800.00 2200.00 -
1904- 10x15", 84 pgs 250.00 950.00 -
1905?-The Cruise of the, 10x15", 60¢, in color 250.00 950.00 -
1905-A Series of Comic Pictures, 10x15", 84 pgs. in color, possible reprint of 1904 edition 250.00 810.00 -
1905-Tricks of... (10x15", 66 pgs, Stokes) 250.00 810.00 -
1906-Stokes (10x16", 32 pgs. in color) 186.00 810.00 -
1907- The Cruise of the, 10x15", 62 pgs 1905-r? 186.00 810.00 -
1910-The Komical...(10x15) 150.00 450.00 810.00
1921-Embee Dist. Co., 10x16", 20 pgs. in color 150.00 450.00 810.00

KATZENJAMMER KIDS MAGIC DRAWING AND COLORING BOOK (N)
Sam L Gabriel Sons And Company: 1931 (8 1/2 x 12", 36 pages, stiff-c
838-By Knerr 50.00 200.00 375.00

KEEPING UP WITH THE JONESES (N)
Cupples & Leon Co.: 1920 - No. 2, 1921 (9-1/4x9-1/4",52 pgs.,B&W daily strip-r)
1,2-By Pop Momand 39.00 154.00 300.00

KID KARTOONS (N,S)
The Century Co.: 1922 (232 pgs, printed 1 side, 9-3/4 x 7-3/4", hard-c, B&W)
nn - By Gene Carr (Metropolitan Movies strip-r) 60.00 245.00 -

KING OF THE ROYAL MOUNTED (Also See Dan Dunn) (N)
Whitman Publishing: 1937 (5 1/2 x 7 1/4", 68 pgs., color cardboard-c, B&W)
1010 35.00 135.00 240.00

LADY BOUNTIFUL (N)
Saalfield Publ. Co./Press Publ. Co.: 1917 (13-3/8x10", 36 pgs, color cardboard-c, B&W interiors)
nn - By Gene Carr; 2 panels per page 50.00 150.00 300.00
1935 - 2nd printing (13-1/8x10",28 pgs color-c, B&W) 33.00 117.00 200.00

LAUGHS YOU MIGHT HAVE HAD From The Comic Pages of Six Week Day Issues of the Post-Dispatch (N)
St. Louis Post-Dispatch: 1921 (9 x 10 1/2", 28 pgs, B&W, red ink cover)
nn - Various comic strips 39.00 154.00 270.00

LIFE, DOGS FROM (M)
Doubleday, Page & Company: nn 1920 - No.2 1926 (130 pgs, 11-1/4 x 9", color painted-c, hard-c, B&W)
nn (No.1) 120.00 360.00 -
Second Litter 80.00 320.00 -
NOTE: *Reprints strips & cartoons featuring dogs, from Life Magazine. Editted by Thomas L. Masson. Highly sought by collectors of dog ephemera. Art in both books is mostly by Robert L. Dickey. Other art: Carl Anderson-1,2; Barbes-1; Chip Bellew-1; Lang Campbell-1,2; Percy Crosby-1,2; Edwina-2; Frueh-2; R.B. Fuller-1; Gibson-1,2; Don Herold-2; Gus Mager-2; Orr-1; J.R. Shaver-1,2; T.S. Sullivant-2; Russ Westover-1,2; Crawford Young-1.*

LIFE OF DAVY CROCKETT IN PICTURE AND STORY, THE
Cupples & Leon: 1935 (8-3/4x7", 64 pgs, B&W hard-c, dust jacket)
nn - By C. Richard Schaare 29.00 116.00 230.00

LIFE OF THOMAS A. EDISON IN WORD AND PICTURE, THE (N)(Also see Edison...)
Thomas A. Edison Industries: 1928 (10x8", 56 pgs, paper cover, B&W)
nn - Photo-c 100.00 250.00 410.00

GD2.0 FN6.0 VF8.0

NOTE: *Reprints newspaper strip which ran August to November 1927.*

LIFE'S LITTLE JOKES (S)
M.S. Publ. Co.: No date (1924)(10-1/16x10", 52 pgs., B&W)
nn - By Rube Goldberg 64.00 257.00 550.00

LIFE, MINIATURE (see also LIFE (miniature reprint of of issue No. 1)) (M,P,S)
Life Publishing Co.: No. 1 - No. 4 1913, 1916, 1919 (5-3/4x4-5/8", 20 pgs, color paper-c
1- 3 (1913) 4 (1916) 5 (1919) 35.00 10.00 210.00
NOTE: *Giveaway item from Life, to promote subscriptions. All reprint material. No.2: James Montgomery Flagg-c; a-Chip Bellew, Gus Dirks, Gibson, F.M.Howarth, Art Young.*

LIFE'S PRINTS (was **LIFE'S PICTURE GALLERY** - See Victorian Age section) (M,S,P)
Life Publishing Company, New York: nd (c1907) (7x4-1/2", 132 pgs, paper cover, B&W)
nn - (nd; c1907) unillustrated black construction paper cover; reprints art from 1895-1907; art by J.M.Flagg, A.B.Frost, Gibson (Scarce) - - -
nn - (nd; c1908) b&w cardboard painted cover by Gibson, showing angel raising a champagne glass; reprints art from 1901-1908; art by J.M.Flagg, A.B.Frost, Gibson, Walt Kuhn, Art Young (Scarce) - - -
NOTE: *Catalog of prints reprinted from LIFE covers & centerspreads. There are likely more as yet unreported catalogs.*

LIFE, THE COMEDY OF LIFE
Life Publishing Company: 1907 (130 pgs, 11-3/4x9-1/4",embossed printed cloth covered board-c, B+W
nn - By various 30.00 100.00 150.00
NOTE: *Single cartoons and some sequential cartoons). Artists include Charles Dana Gibson, Harrison Cady, E.W. Kemble, James Montgomery Flagg.*

LILY OF THE ALLEY IN THE FUNNIES
Whitman Publishing Co.: No date (1927) (10-1/4x15-1/2"; 28 pgs., color)
W936 - By T. Burke (Rare) 57.00 228.00 400.00

LITTLE ANNIE ROONEY (N)
David McKay Co.: 1935 (25¢, soft-c)
Book 1 43.00 172.00 350.00
NOTE: *Ties with Henry & Popeye (David McKay) as the last of the 10x10" size Plat comic books.*

LITTLE ANNIE ROONEY WISHING BOOK (G) (See Happy Hooligan, Story of #281)
McLoughlin Bros.: 1932 (12x9-1/2", 16 pgs., soft-c, 3-color text, heavier paper)
282 - By Darrell McClure 41.00 144.00 285.00

LITTLE BIRD TOLD ME, A (E)
Life Publishing Co.: 1905? (96 pgs, hardbound)
nn - By Walt Kuhn (Life-r) 41.00 144.00 285.00

LITTLE FOLKS PAINTING BOOK (N)
The National Arts Company: 1931 (10-7/8 x 15-1/4", 20 pgs, half in full color)
nn - By "Tack" Knight (strip-r) 41.00 144.00 285.00

LITTLE JIMMY PICTURE AND STORY BOOK (I) (see Jimmy)
McLaughlin Bros., Inc.: 1932 (13-1/4 x 9-3/4", 20 pgs, cardstock color cover)
284 Text by Marion Kincaird; illus by Swinnerton 57.00 228.00 425.00

LITTLE JOHNNY & THE TEDDY BEARS (Judge-r) (M) (see Teddy Bear Books)
Reilly & Britton Co.: 1907 (10x14".; 68 pgs, green, red, black interior color)
nn - By J. R. Bray-a/Robert D. Towne-s 67.00 233.00 425.00

LITTLE JOURNEY TO THE HOME OF BRIGGS THE SKY-ROCKET, THE
Lockhart Art School: 1917 (10-3/4x7-7/8", 20 pgs, B&W) (I)
nn - About Clare Briggs (bio & lots of early art) 41.00 144.00 280.00

LITTLE KING, THE (see New Yorker Cartoon Albums for 1st appearance) (M)
Farrar & Reinhart, Inc: 1933 (10-1/4 x 8-3/4, 80 pgs, hardcover w/dust jacket
nn - By Otto Soglow (strip-r The New Yorker) 125.00 250.00 550.00
NOTE: *Copies with dust jacket are worth 50% more. Also exists in a 12x8-3/4 edition.*

LITTLE LULU BY MARGE (M)
Rand McNally & Company, Chicago: 1936 (6-9/16x6", 68 pgs, yellow hard-c, B&W)
nn - By Marjorie Henderson Buell 50.00 130.00 305.00
NOTE: *Begins reprinting single panel Little Lulu cartoons which began with Saturday Evening Post Feb. 23, 1935. This book was reprinted several times as late as 1940.*

LITTLE NAPOLEON
No publisher listed: 1924 , 50 pages, 10" by 10"; Color cardstock-c, B&W
nn - By Bud Counihan (Cupples &Leon format) 25.00 100.00 250.00

LITTLE NEMO (...in Slumberland) (N) (see also Little Sammy Sneeze, Dreams...Rarebit F)
Doffield & Co.(1906)/Cupples & Leon Co.(1909): 1906, 1909 (Sunday strip-r in color, cardboard covers)
1906-11x16-1/2" by Winsor McCay; 30 pgs. (scarce) 1500.00 5200.00 -
1909-10x14" by Winsor McCay (scarce) 1300.00 4000.00 -

LITTLE ORPHAN ANNIE (See Treasure Box of Famous Comics) (N)
Cupples & Leon Co.: 1926 - 1934 (8-3/4x7", 100 pgs., B&W daily strip-r, hard-c)
1 (1926)-Little Orphan Annie (softback see Treasure Box) 50.00 200.00 400.00

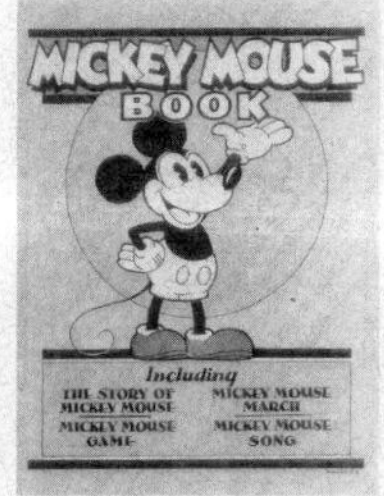

The Trials of Lulu and Leander by Howarth
1906 © NY American & Journal

Maud the Mirthful Mule by Opper
1908 © Frederick A. Stokes

Mickey Mouse Book
1930 © Bibo & Lang

	GD2.0	FN6.0	VF8.0
2 (1927)-In the Circus (softback see Wonder Box...)	36.00	144.00	260.00
3 (1928)-The Haunted House (softback see Wonder Box...)	36.00	144.00	260.00
4 (1929)-Bucking the World	36.00	144.00	260.00
5 (1930)-Never Say Die	30.00	120.00	225.00
6 (1931)-Shipwrecked	30.00	120.00	225.00
7 (1932)-A Willing Helper	25.00	100.00	180.00
8 (1933)-In Cosmic City	25.00	100.00	180.00
9 (1934)-Uncle Dan (not rare)	25.00	100.00	180.00

NOTE: *Each book reprints dailies from the previous year. Each hardcover came with a dust jacket. Books with out dust jackets are worth 50% less. Many of copies of #9 Uncle Dan have been turning up on eBay recently.*

LITTLE ORPHAN ANNIE RUMMY CARDS (N)
Whitman Publishing Co., Racine: 1935 (box: 5 x 6 1/2" Cards: 3 1/2 x 2 1/4")

nn-Harold Gray 20.00 60.00 125.00
NOTE: *36 cards, including 1 instruction card, 5 character cards and 30 cards forming 5 sequential stories (6 cards each).*

LITTLE SAMMY SNEEZE (N) (see also Little Nemo, Dreams of A Rarebit Fiend)
New York Herald Co.: Dec 1905 (11x16-1/2", 72 pgs., color)

nn - By Winsor McCay (Very Rare) 3500.00 8500.00 –
NOTE: *Rarely found in fine to mint condition.*

LIVE AND LET LIVE
Travelers Insurance Co.: 1936 (5-3/4x7/3/4", 16 pgs. color and B&W)

nn - Bill Holman, Carl Anderson, etc 20.00 60.00 115.00

LULU AND LEANDER (N) (see also Funny Folk, 1899, in Victorian section)
New York American & Journal: 1904 (76 pgs); **William A Stokes & Co:** 1906

nn - By F.M. Howarth 400.00 800.00 1600.00
nn - The Trials of...(1906, 10x16", 68 pgs. in color) 400.00 800.00 1600.00
NOTE: *F. M. Howarth helped pioneer the American comic strip in the pages of PUCK magazine in the early 1890s before the Yellow Kid.*

MADMAN'S DRUM (O)
Jonathan Cape and Harrison Smith Inc.: 1930 (8-1/4x6", 274 pgs, B&W hardcover w/dust jacket) (original graphic novel in wood cuts)

nn - By Lynd Ward 50.00 175.00 305.00

MAMA'S ANGEL CHILD IN TOYLAND (I)
Rand McNally, Chicago: 1915 (128 pgs, hardbound)

nn - By M.T. "Penny" Ross & Marie C, Sadler 40.00 140.00 240.00
NOTE: *Mamma's Angel Child published as a comic strip by the "Chicago Tribune" 1908 Mar 1 to 1920 Oct 17.This novel dedicated to Esther Starring Richartz, "the original Mamma's Angel Kid."*

MAUD (N) (see also **Happy Hooligan**)
Frederick A. Stokes Co.: 1906 - 1908? (10x15-1/2", cardboard-c)

1906-By Fred Opper (Scarce), 66 pgs. color 400.00 1300.00 –
1907-The Matchless, 10x15" 70 pgs in color 300.00 1000.00 –
1908-The Mirthful Mule, 10x15", 64 pgs in color 300.00 1000.00 –
NOTE: *First run of strip began July 24, 1904 to at least Oct 6, 1907, spun out of* ***Happy Hooligan.***

MEMORIAL EDITION The Drawings of Clare Briggs (S)
Wm H. Wise & Company: 1930 (7-1/2x8-3/4", 284 pgs, pebbled false black leather, B&W) (posthumous boxed set of 7 books by Clare Briggs)

nn - The Days of Real Sport; nn-Golf; nn-Real Folks at Home; nn-Ain't it a Grand and Glorious Feeling?; nn-That Guiltiest Feeling; nn-Somebody's Always Taking the Joy Out of Life; nn-When a Feller Needs a Friend
Each book... 25.00 75.00 125.00
NOTE: *Also exists in a whitish cream colored paper back edition; first edition unknown presently.*

MENACE CARTOONS (M, S)
Menace Publishing Company, Aurora, Missouri: 1914 (10-3/8x8", 80 pgs, cardboard-c, B&W)

nn - (Rare) 50.00 150.00 675.00
NOTE: *Reprints anti-Catholic cartoons from K.K.K. related publication* ***The Menace.***

MEN OF DARING (N)
Cupples & Leon Co.: 1933 (8-3/4x7", 100 pgs)

nn - By Stookie Allen, intro by Lowell Thomas 30.00 90.00 200.00

MICKEY MOUSE BOOK
Bibo & Lang: 1930-1931 (12x9", stapled-c, 20 pgs., 4 printings)

nn - First Disney licensed publication (a magazine, not a book–see first book, Adventures of Mickey Mouse). Contains story of how Mickey met Walt and got his name; games, cartoons & song "Mickey Mouse (You Cute Little Feller)," written by Irving Bibo; Minnie, Clarabelle Cow, Horace Horsecollar & caricature of Walt shaking hands with Mickey. The changes made with the 2nd printing have been verified by billing affidavits in the Walt Disney Archives and include:Two Win Smith Mickey strips from 4/15/30 and 4/17/30 added to page 8 & back-c; "Printed in U.S.A." added to front cover; Bobette Bibo's age of 11 years added to title page; faulty type on the word "tail" corrected top of page 3; the word "start" added to bottom of page 7, removing the words "start 1 2 3 4" from the top of page 7; music and lyrics were rewritten on pages 12-14. A green ink border was added beginning with 2nd printing and some covers have inking variations. Art by Albert Barbelle, drawn in an Ub Iwerks style. Total circulation : 97,938 copies varying from 21,000 to 26,000 per printing.

1st printing. Contains the song lyrics **censored** in later printings, "When little Minnie's pursued by a big bad villain we feel so bad then we're glad when you up and kill him." Attached to the Nov. 15, 1930 issue of the Official Bulletin of the Mickey Mouse Club notes: "Attached to this Bulletin is a new Mickey Mouse Book that has just been published." This is thought to be the reason why a slightly disproportionate larger number of copies of the first printing still exist 600.00 1200.00 5100.00
1st printing (variant) All white-c and has advertising on inside front & back-cvrs. All other examples have blank inside cvrs. Has word "kill" in the song. One of the ads is for a Mickey Mouse Club. A Fine copy sold on 12/24/17 for $2375.
2nd printing with a theater/advertising. Christmas greeting added to inside front cover (1 copy known with Dec. 27, 1930 date) – 8000.00 –
2nd-4th printings 500.00 1100.00 3400.00
NOTE: *Theater/advertising copies do not qualify as separate printings. Most copies are missing pages 9 & 10 which had a puzzle to be cut out. Puzzle (pages 9 and 10) cut out or missing, subtract 60% to 75%.*

MICKEY MOUSE COLORING BOOK (S)
Saalfield Publishing Company:1931 (15-1/4x10-3/4", 32 pgs, color soft cover, half printed in full color interior, rest B&W

871 - By Ub Iwerks & Floyd Gottfredson (rare) 450.00 1300.00 2600.00
NOTE: *Contains reprints of first MM daily strip ever, including the "missing" speck the chicken is after found only on the original daily strip art by Iwerks plus other very early MM art. There were several other Saalfield Mickey Mouse coloring books manufactured around the same time.*

MICKEY MOUSE, THE ADVENTURES OF (I)
David McKay Co., Inc.: Book I, 1931 - Book II, 1932 (5-1/2"x8-1/2", 32 pgs.)

Book I-First Disney book, by strict definition (1st printing-50,000 copies)(see Mickey Mouse Book by Bibo & Lang). Illustrated text refers to Clarabelle Cow as "Carolyn" and Horace Horsecollar as "Henry". The name "Donald Duck" appears with a non-costumed generic duck on back cover & inside, not in the context of the character that later debuted in the Wise Little Hen.
Hardback w/characters on back-c 150.00 450.00 1000.00
Softcover w/characters on back-c 40.00 165.00 420.00
Version without characters on back-c 50.00 200.00 460.00
Book II-Less common than Book I. Character development brought into conformity with the Mickey Mouse cartoon shorts and syndicated strips. Captain Church Mouse, Tanglefoot, Peg-Leg Pete and Pluto appear with Mickey & Minnie 125.00 300.00 750.00

MICKEY MOUSE COMIC (N)
David McKay Co.: 1931 - No. 4, 1934 (10"x9-3/4", 52 pgs., card board-c)
(Later reprints exist)

1 (1931)-Reprints Floyd Gottfredson daily strips in black & white from 1930 & 1931, including the famous two week sequence in which Mickey tries to commit suicide 300.00 1200.00 2400.00
2 (1932)-1st app. of Pluto reprinted from 7/8/31 daily. All pgs. from 1931 164.00 656.00 1250.00
3 (1933)-Reprints 1932 & 1933 Sunday pages in color, one strip per page, including the "Lair of Wolf Barker" continuity pencilled by Gottfredson and inked by Al Taliaferro & Ted Thwaites. First app. Mickey's nephews, Morty & Ferdie, one identified by name of Mortimer Fieldmouse, not to be confused with Uncle Mortimer Mouse who is introduced in the Wolf Barker story 214.00 856.00 1800.00
4 (1934)-1931 dailies, include the only known reprint of the infamous strip of 2/4/31 where the villainous Kat Nipp snips off the end of Mickey's tail with a pair of scissors 140.00 560.00 1100.00

MICKEY MOUSE (N)
Whitman Publishing Co.: 1933-34 (10x8-3/4", 34 pgs, cardboard-c)

948-1932 & 1933 Sunday strips in color, printed from the same plates as Mickey Mouse Book #3 by David McKay, but only pages 5-17 & 32-48 (including all of the "Wolf Barker" continuity) 157.00 629.00 1300.00
NOTE: *Some copies bound with back cover upside down. Variance doesn't affect value. Same art appears on front and back covers of all copies. Height of Whitman reissue trimmed 1/2 inch.*

MILITARY WILLIE
J. I. Austen Co.: 1907 (7x9-1/2", 12 pgs., every other page in color, stapled)

nn - By F. R. Morgan 70.00 245.00 375.00

MINNEAPOLIS TRIBUNE CARTOON BOOK (S)
Minneapolis Tribune: 1899-1903 (11-3/8x9-3/8", B&W, paper cover)

	GD2.0	FN6.0	VF8.0
nn (#1) (1899)	45.00	100.00	200.00
nn (#2) (1900)	45.00	100.00	200.00
nn (#3) (1901) (published Jan 01, 1901)	45.00	100.00	200.00
nn (#4) (1902) (114 pgs)	45.00	100.00	200.00
nn (#5) (1903) (9x10-3/4",110 pgs, B&W; color-c)	45.00	100.00	200.00

NOTE: *All by Roland C. Bowman (editorial-r).*

MINUTE BIOGRAPHIES: INTIMATE GLIMPSES INTO THE LIVES OF 150 FAMOUS MEN AND WOMEN
Grossett & Dunlap: 1931, 1933 (10-1/4x7-3/4", 168 pgs, hardcover, B&W)

nn - By Nisenson (art) & Parker(text) 25.00 75.00 165.00
More.... (1933) 25.00 75.00 165.00

MISCHIEVOUS MONKS OF CROCODILE ISLE, THE (N)
J. I. Austen Co., Chicago: 1908 (8-1/2x11-1/2", 12 pgs., 4 pgs. in color)

nn - By F. R. Morgan; reads longwise 125.00 375.00 600.00

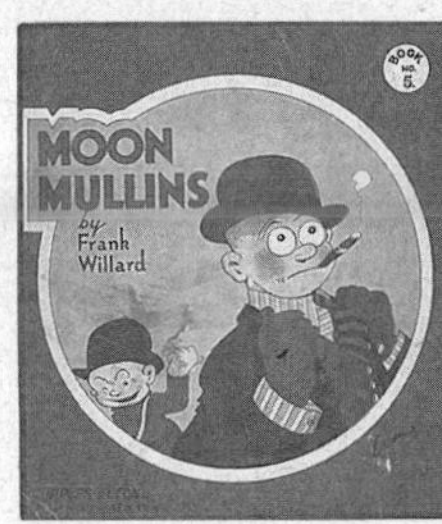

Moon Mullins #5 by Frank Willard
1931 @ Cupples & Leon

The Nebbs
© C&L

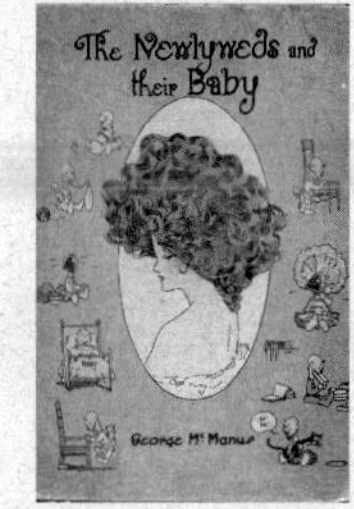

The Newlyweds by George McManus
1907 © Saalfield Publishing Co.

GD2.0 FN6.0 VF8.0 **GD2.0 FN6.0 VF8.0**

MR. & MRS. (Also see Ain't It A Grand and Glorious Feeling?) (N)
Whitman Publishing Co.: 1922 (9x9-1/2", 52 & 28 pgs., cardboard-c)
nn - By Briggs (B&W, 52 pgs.) 37.00 149.00 260.00
nn - 28 pgs.-(9x9-1/2")-Sunday strips-r in color 41.00 163.00 285.00
NOTE: *The earliest presently-known Whitman comic books*

MR. BLOCK (N)
Industrial Workers of the World (IWW): 1913, 1919
nn - By Ernest Riebe (C) 55.00 160.00 –
...And The Profiteers (original material) (H) 55.00 160.00 –
NOTE: *Mr Block was a daily strip published from 1912 NOV 7 to 1913 SEP ? by the socialist newspaper "Industrial Worker"; Mr Block was a "square" guy (his head was in fact a block) who enthusiastically supported the same system that exploited him. The noted Joe Hill wrote a song about him (Mr Block,1913, on the air of "It loooks me like a big time tonight") for the "Industrial Worker Songbook".*

MR. TWEE-DEEDLE (N)
Cupples & Leon: 1913, 1917 (11-3/8 x 16-3/4" color strips-r from NY Herald)
nn - By John B. Gruelle (later of Raggedy Ann fame) 350.00 900.00 2100.00
nn - "Further Adventures of..." By Gruelle 350.00 900.00 2100.00
NOTE: *Strip ran Feb 5, 1911-March 10, 1918.*

MONKEY SHINES OF MARSELEEN AND SOME OF HIS ADVENTURES (C)
McLaughlin Bros. New York: 1906 (10 x 12-3/8", 36 pgs, full color hardcover)
nn - By Norman E. Jennett strip-r NY Evening Telegram 100.00 250.00 500.00
NOTE: *Strip began in 1906 until at least March 13, 1910.*

MONKEY SHINES OF MARSELEEN (N)
Cupples & Leon Co.: 1909 (11-1/2 x 17", 58 pgs. in two colors)
nn - By Norman E. Jennett (strip-r New York Herald) 100.00 250.00 465.00

MOON MULLINS (N)
Cupples & Leon Co.: 1927 - 1933 (52 pgs., B&W daily strip-r)
Series 1 ('27)-By Willard 63.00 250.00 560.00
Series 2 ('28), Series 3 ('29), Series 4 ('30) 39.00 156.00 310.00
Series 5 ('31), 6 ('32), 7 ('33) 39.00 156.00 310.00
Big Book 1 ('30)-B&W (scarce) 100.00 400.00 750.00
w/dust jacket (rare) 183.00 732.00 1150.00

MOVING PICTURE FUNNIES
Saml Gabriel Sons & Company: 1918 (5-1/4 x 10-1/4", 52 pgs, B&W, illustrated hard-c)
nn 25.00 50.00 100.00
NOTE: *823 Comical illustrations that show a different scene when folded.*

MUTT & JEFF (...Cartoon, The) (N)
Ball Publications: 1911 - No. 5, 1916 (5-3/4 x 15-1/2", 72 pgs, B&W, hard-c)
1 (1910)(50¢) very common 75.00 290.00 565.00
2,3: 2 (1911)-Opium den panels; Jeff smokes opium (pipe dreams).
3 (1912) both very common 71.00 286.00 500.00
2-(1913) Reprint of 1911 edition with black ink cover 50.00 175.00 300.00
4 (1915) (50¢) (Scarce) 150.00 350.00 650.00
5 (1916) (Rare) -Photos of Fisher, 1st pg. (68 pages) 200.00 480.00 1000.00
5-Scarce 84 page reprint edition 150.00 450.00 850.00
NOTE: *Mutt & Jeff first appeared in newspapers in 1907. Cover variations exist showing Mutt & Jeff reading various newspapers; i.e., The Oregon Journal, The American, and The Detroit News. Reprinting of each issue began soon after publication. No. 4 and 5 may not have been reprinted. Values listed include the reprints. Mutt & Jeff was the first successful American daily newspaper comic strip and as such remains one of the seminal strips of all time.*

MUTT & JEFF (N)
Cupples & Leon Co.: No. 6, 1919 - No. 22, 1934? (9-1/2x9-1/2", 52 pgs., B&W dailies, stiff-c)
6, 7 - By Bud Fisher (very common) 32.00 128.00 215.00
8-10 46.00 186.00 325.00
11-18 (Somewhat Scarcer) (#19-#22 do not exist) 60.00 240.00 420.00
nn (1920) (Advs. of...) 11x16"; 44 pgs.; full color reprints of 1919 Sunday strips 93.00 372.00 675.00
Big Book nn (1926, 144 pgs., hardcovers) 114.00 456.00 800.00
w/dust jacket 193.00 772.00 1400.00
Big Book 1 (1928) - Thick book (hardcovers) 114.00 456.00 800.00
w/dust jacket (rare) 182.00 729.00 1300.00
Big Book 2 (1929) - Thick book (hardcovers) 114.00 456.00 800.00
w/dust jacket (rare) 182.00 729.00 1300.00
NOTE: *The Big Books contain three previous issues rebound.*

MUTT & JEFF (N)
Embee Publ. Co.: 1921 (9x15", color cardboard-c & interior)
nn - Sunday strips in color (Rare)- BY Bud Fisher 150.00 600.00 1200.00
NOTE: *Ties with The Trouble of Bringing Up Father (EmBee) and Jimmie Dugan & The Reg'lar Fellers (C&L) as the last of this size.*

MYSTERIOUS STRANGER AND OTHER CARTOONS, THE
McClure, Phillips & Co.: 1905 (12-3/8x9-3/4", 338 pgs, hardcover, B&W)
nn - By John McCutcheon 32.00 128.00 250.00

MY WAR - Szeged (Szuts)
Wm. Morrow Co.: 1932 (7x10-1/2", 210 pgs, hard-c, B&W)
nn - (All story panels, no words - powerful) 32.00 128.00 250.00

NAUGHTY ADVENTURES OF VIVACIOUS MR. JACK, THE
New York American & Journal: 1904 (15x10", color strips)
nn - By James Swinnerton; (Very Rare - 3 known copies) 1100.00 1800.00 2600.00

NEBBS, THE (N)
Cupples & Leon Co.: 1928 (52 pgs., B&W daily strip-r)
nn - By Sol Hess; Carlson-a 40.00 160.00 285.00

NERVY NAT'S ADVENTURES (E)
Leslie-Judge Co.: 1911 (90 pgs, 85¢, 1903 strip reprints from **Judge**)
nn - By James Montgomery Flagg 75.00 263.00 450.00

THE NEWLYWEDS AND THEIR BABY (N)
Saalfield Publ. Co.: 1907 (13x10", 52 pgs., hardcover)
...& Their Baby' by McManus; daily strips 50% color 350.00 1100.00 –
NOTE: *Strip ran Apr 10, 1904 thru Jan 14, 1906 and then May 19, 1907-Dec 5, 1916; was a huge success with Baby Snookums long before McManus invented Bringing Up Father; Snookums brought back as a topper strip over BUF Nov 19, 1944-Dec 30, 1956.*

THE NEWLYWEDS AND THEIR BABY'S COMIC PICTURES FOR PAINTING AND CRAYONING (N)
Saalfield Publishign Company: 1916 (10-1/4x14-3/4", 52 pgs. Cardboard-c)
nn - 44 B&W pages, covers, and one color wrap glued to B&W title page.
Color wrap: color title pg. & 3 pgs of color strips 83.00 290.00 575.00
nn - (1917, 10x14", 20 pgs, oblong, cardboard-c) partial reprint of 1916 edition 31.00 124.00 300.00

THE NEWLYWEDS AND THEIR BABY (N)
Saalfield Publishing Company: 1917 (10-1/8x13-9/16 ", 52 pgs, full color cardstock-c, some pages full color, others two color (orange, blue))
nn 83.00 290.00 465.00

NEW YORKER CARTOON ALBUM, THE (M)
Doubleday, Doran & Company Inc.: (1928-1931); **Harper & Brothers.:** (1931-1933); **Random House** (1935-1937), 12x9", various pg counts, hardcovers w/dust jackets)
1928: nn-114 pgs Arno, Held, Soglow, Williams, etc 20.00 60.00 140.00
1928: SECOND-114 pgs Arno, Bairnsfather, Gross, Held, Soglow, Williams 10.00 30.00 85.00
1930: THIRD-172 pgs Arno, Bairnsfather, Held, Soglow, Art Young 10.00 30.00 85.00
1931: FOURTH-154 pgs Arno, Held, Soglow, Steig, Thurber, Williams, Art Young, "Little King" by Soglow begins 10.00 30.00 85.00
1932: FIFTH-156 pgs Arno, Bairnsfather, Held, Hoff, Soglow, Steig, Thurber, Williams 10.00 30.00 85.00
1933: SIXTH-156 pgs same as above 10.00 30.00 85.00
1935: SEVENTH-164 pgs 10.00 30.00 85.00
1937: 168 pgs; Charles Addams plus same as above but no Little King, two page "Gone With The Wind" parody strip 10.00 30.00 85.00
NOTE: *Some sequential strips but mostly single panel cartoons.*

NIPPY'S POP (N)
The Saalfield Publishing Co.: 1917 (10-1/2x13-1/2", 36 pgs., B&W, Sunday strip-r)
nn - Charles M Payne (better known as S'Matter Pop) 50.00 160.00 270.00

OH, MAN (A Bully Collection of Those Inimitable Humor Cartoons) (S)
P.F. Volland & Co.: 1919 (8-1/2x13"; 136 pgs.)
nn - By Briggs 50.00 160.00 270.00
NOTE: *Originally came in illustrated box with Briggs art (box is Rare - worth 50% more with box).*

OH SKIN-NAY! (S)
P.F. Volland & Co.: 1913 (8-1/2x13", 136 pgs.)
nn - The Days Of Real Sport by Briggs 43.00 152.00 250.00
NOTE: *Originally came in illustrated box with Briggs art (box is Rare - worth 50% more with box).*

OLD GOLD THE SMOOTHER AND BETTER CIGARETTE...NOT A COUGH IN A CARLOAD (M,N,P) (see also BY BRIGGS)
Old Gold Cigarettes: nd (c1920's) (16 pgs, paper-c, color) (both Scarce)
nn- (4-1/4" x 3-7/8") cover strip is "Oh, Man!"; also contains: "Real Folks at Home", "Ain't It a Grand and Glorious Feelin?", "It Happens in the Best Regulated Families", and "Mr. and Mrs." (no known sales)
1440- (5-9/16" x 5-1/4") cover strip is "Frank and Ernest"; also contains: "That Guiltiest Feeling", "Real Folks at Home", "Oh, Man!", "When a Feller Needs a Friend". (no known sales)
NOTE: *Collection reprinting strip cartoons by Clare Briggs, advertising Old Gold Cigarettes. These strips originally appeared in various magazines, play program booklets, newspapers, etc. Some of the strips involve regular Briggs strip series. The two booklets contain a completely different set of comics.*

ON AND OFF MOUNT ARARAT (also see **Tigers**) (N)
Hearst's New York American & Journal: 1902, 86pgs. 10x15-1/4"
nn - Rare Noah's Ark satire by Jimmy Swinnerton (rare) 450.00 1600.00 –

ON THE LINKS (N)
Associated Feature Service: Dec, 1926 (9x10", 48 pgs.)
nn - Daily strip-r 50.00 125.00 210.00

The Adventures of Peck's Bad Boy With the Teddy Bear Show by McDougall
1907 © Charles C. Thompson, Co.

Popeye Cartoon Book
1934 © The Saalfield Co.

Roger Bean, R.G. #4
1917 © Indiana News Co., Distributors

GD2.0 FN6.0 VF8.0

ONE HUNDRED WAR CARTOONS (S)
Idaho Daily Statesman: 1918 (7-3/4x10", 102 pgs, paperback, B&W)
nn - By Villeneuve (WW I cartoons) 20.00 60.00 130.00

OUR ANTEDILUVIAN ANCESTORS (N,S)
New York Evening Journal, NY: 1903 (11-3/8x8-7/8", hardcover)
nn - By F Opper 75.00 200.00 450.00
NOTE: *There is a simultaneously published British edition, identical size and contents, from C. Arthur Pearson Ltd, London. A collection of single panel cartoons about cavemen. Similar to an earlier British cartoon book "Prehistoric Peeps from Punch", by E.T. Reed.*

OUTBURSTS OF EVERETT TRUE, THE (N)
Saalfield Publ. Co.(Werner Co.): 1907 (92 pgs, 9-7/16x5-1/4")
1907 (2-4 panel strips-r)-By Condo & Raper 125.00 350.00 700.00
1921-Full color-c; reprints 56 of 88 cartoons from 1907 ed. (10x10", 32 pgs B&W) 125.00 225.00 350.00

OVER THERE COMEDY FROM FRANCE
Observer House Printing: nd (WW 1 era) (6x14", 60 pgs, paper cover)
nn - Artist(s) unknown 15.00 53.00 110.00

OWN YOUR OWN HOME (I)
Bobbs-Merrill Company, Indianapolis: 1919 (7-7/16x5-1/4")
nn - By Fontaine Fox – – –

PECKS BAD BOY (N)
Charles C. Thompson Co, Chicago (by Walt McDougal): 1906-1908 (strip-r)
The Adventures of... (1906) 11-1/2x16-1/4", 68 pgs 100.00 400.00 830.00
...& His Country Cousin Cynthia (1907) 12x16-1/2," 34 pgs In color 100.00 400.00 830.00
Advs. of...And His Country Cousins (1907) 5-1/2x10 1/2", 18 pgs In color 50.00 175.00 390.00
Advs. of...And His Country Cousins (1907) 11-1/2x16-1/4", 36 pgs 50.00 175.00 390.00
...& Their Advs With The Teddy Bear (1907) 5-1/2x10-1/2", 18 pgs in color 50.00 175.00 390.00
...& Their Balloon Trip To the Country (1907) 5-1/2x 10-1/2, 18 pgs in color 50.00 175.00 390.00
...With the Teddy Bear Show (1907) 5-1/2x 10-1/2 50.00 175.00 390.00
...With The Billy Whiskers Goats (1907) 5-1/2 x 10-1/2, 18 pgs in color 50.00 175.00 390.00
...& His Chums (1908) - 11x16-3/8", 36 pgs. Stanton & Van Vliet Co 100.00 400.00 830.00
...& His Chums (1908)-Hardcover; full color;16 pgs. 100.00 350.00 675.00
Advs. of...in Pictures (1908) (11x17, 36 pgs)-In color; Stanton & Van V. Liet Co. 100.00 400.00 830.00

PERCY & FERDIE (N)
Cupples & Leon Co.: 1921 (10x10", 52 pgs., B&W dailies, cardboard-c)
nn - By H. A. MacGill (Rare) 61.00 244.00 500.00

PETER RABBIT (N)
John H. Eggers Co. The House of Little Books Publishers: 1922 - 1923
B1-B4-(Rare)-(Set of 4 books which came in a cardboard box)-Each book reprints half of a Sunday page per page and contains 8 B&W and 2 color pages; by Harrison Cady (9-1/4x6-1/4", paper-c) each.... 43.00 172.00 335.00
Box only 57.00 228.00 425.00

PHILATELIC CARTOONS (M)
Essex Publishing Company, Lynn, Mass.: 1916 (8-11/16" x 5-7/8", 40 pgs, light blue construction paper-c, B&W interior)
nn - By Leroy S. Bartlett 50.00 100.00 200.00
NOTE: *Comics reprinted from The New England Philatelist.*

PICTORIAL HISTORY OF THE DEPARTMENT OF COMMERCE UNDER HERBERT HOOVER (see Picture Life of a Great American) (O)
Hoover-Curtis Campaign Committee of New York State: no date, 1928 (3-1/4 x 5-1/4, 32 pgs, paper cover, B&W)
nn - By Satterfield (scarce) 50.00 150.00 300.00
NOTE: *1928 Presidential Campaign giveaway. Original material, contents completely different from Picture Life of a Great American.*

PICTURE LIFE OF A GREAT AMERICAN (see Pictorial History of the Department of Commerce under Herbert Hoover) (O)
Hoover-Curtis Campaign Committee of New York State: no date, 1928 (paper cover, B&W)
nn - (8-3/4 x 7, 20 pgs) Text cover, 2 page text introduction, 18 pgs of comics (scarcer first print) 43.00 129.00 275.00
nn - (9 x 6-3/4,24 pgs) Illustrated cover,5 page text introduction, 18 pgs of comics (scarce) 43.00 129.00 275.00
NOTE: *1928 Presidential Campaign giveaway. Unknown which above version was published first. Both contain the same original comics material by Satterfield.*

PINK LAFFIN (I)
Whitman Publishing Co.: 1922 (9x12")(Strip-r; some of these actually text joke books)

GD2.0 FN6.0 VF8.0

...the Lighter Side of Life, ...He Tells 'Em, ...and His Family, ...Knockouts; Ray Gleason-a (All rare) each... 26.00 104.00 200.00

POLLY (AND HER PALS) - (N)
Newspaper Feature Service: 1916 (3x2-1/2", color)
Altogether: Three Rahs and a Tiger! by Cliff Sterrett 40.00 80.00 160.00
There Is A Limit To Pa's Patience by Cliff Sterrett 40.00 80.00 160.00
Pa's Lil Book Has Some Uncut Pages by Sterrett 40.00 80.00 160.00
NOTE: *Single newsprint sheet printed in full color on both sides, unfolds to show 12 panel story.*

POPEYE PAINT BOOK (N)
McLaughlin Bros, Inc., Springfield, Mass.: 1932 (9-7/8x13", 28 pgs, color-c)
2052 - By E. C. Segar 90.00 300.00 675.00
NOTE: *Contains a full color panel above and the exact same art in below panel n B&W which one was to color in; strip-r panels.*

POPEYE CARTOON BOOK (N)
The Saalfield Co.: 1934 (8-1/2x13", 40 pgs, cardboard-c)
2095-(scarce)-1933 strip reprints in color by Segar. Each page contains a vertical half of a Sunday strip, so the continuity reads row by row completely across each double page spread. If each page is read by itself, the continuity makes no sense. Each double page spread reprints one complete Sunday page from 1933 300.00 700.00 2400.00
12 Page Version 125.00 350.00 1000.00

POPEYE (See **Thimble Theatre** for earlier Popeye-r from Sonnett) (N)
David McKay Publications: 1935 (25¢; 52 pgs, B&W) (By Segar)
1-Daily strip reprints- "The Gold Mine Thieves" 200.00 400.00 950.00
2-Daily strip-r (scarce) 200.00 400.00 1000.00
NOTE: *Ties with Henry & Little Annie Rooney (David McKay) as the last of the 10x10" size books.*

PORE LI'L MOSE (N)
New York Herald Publ. by Grand Union Tea
Cupples & Leon Co.: 1902 (10-1/2x15", 78 pgs., color)
nn - By R. F. Outcault; Earliest known C&L comic book (scarce in high grade - very high demand) 1200.00 4100.00 –
NOTE: *Black Americana one page newspaper strips; falls in between Yellow Kid & Buster Brown. Complete copies have become scarce. Some have cut this book apart thinking that reselling individual pages will bring them more money.*

PRETTY PICTURES (M)
Farrar & Rinehart: 1931 (12 x 8-7/8", 104 pgs, color hardcover w/dust jacket, B&W; reprints from New Yorker, Judge, Life, Collier's Weekly)
nn - By Otto Soglow (contains "The Little King") 33.00 134.00 250.00

QUAINT OLD NEW ENGLAND (S)
Triton Syndicate: 1936 (5-1/4x6-1/4", 100 pgs, soft-c squarebound, B&W)
nn - By Jack Withycomb 36.00 144.00 250.00
NOTE: *Comics about weird doings in Old New England.*

RED CARTOONS (S)
Daily Worker Publishing Company: 1926 (12 x 9", 68 pgs,cardboard cover, B&W)
nn - By Various (scarce) 40.00 160.00 280.00
NOTE: *Reprint of American Communist Party editorial cartoons, from The Daily Worker, The Workers Monthly, and the Liberator. Art by Fred Ellis, William Gropper, Clive Weed, Art Young.*

REG'LAR FELLERS (See All-American Comics, Jimmie Dugan & The..., Popular Comics & Treasure Box of Famous Comics) (N)
Cupples & Leon Co./MS Publishing Co.: 1921-1929
1 (1921)-52 pgs. B&W dailies (Cupples & Leon, 10x10") 43.00 171.00 325.00
1925, 48 pgs. B&W dailies (MS Publ.) 39.00 157.00 300.00
Hardcover (1929, 8-3/4x7-1/2"; 96 pgs.)-B&W-r 54.00 214.00 400.00

REG'LAR FELLERS STORY PAINT BOOK
Whitman, Racine, Wisc.: 1932 (8-3/4x12-1/8", 132 pgs, red soft-c)
By Gene Byrnes 25.00 75.00 150.00

ROGER BEAN, R. G. (Regular Guy) (N)
The Indiana News Co, Distributers.: 1915 - No. 2, 1915 (5-3/8x17", 68 pgs., B&W, hardcovers); #3-#5 published by **Chas. B. Jackson:** 1916-1919
(No. 1 2 4 & 5 bound on side, No. 3 bound at top)
1-By Chas B. Jackson (68pgs.)(Scarce) 55.00 200.00 380.00
2- 5-5/8x17-1/8", 66 pgs (says 1913 inside - an obvious printing error) (red or green binding) 55.00 200.00 380.00
3-Along the Firing Line... (1916; 68 pgs, 6x17") 55.00 200.00 380.00
3-Along the Firing Line side-bound version 55.00 200.00 380.00
4-Into the Trenches and Out Again with... (1917, 68 pgs) 55.00 200.00 380.00
5 ...And The Reconstruction Period (1919, 5-3/8x15-1/2", 84 pgs) (Scarce) (has $1 printed on cover) 55.00 200.00 380.00
Baby Grand Editions 1-5 (10x10", cardboard-c) 55.00 200.00 380.00
NOTE: *No. 1 & 2 of the Twin Baby Grands (nd) 8-1/4x10-7/8", 52 pgs. #3 & #4 9x10-7/8" Cardboard cover. B&W strip reprints. Cover also says "Politics Pickles People Police."*
nn - 9x11, 68 pgs 55.00 200.00 380.00
NOTE: Has picture of Chic Jackson and a posthumous dedication from his three children. strip-r 1931-32

ROGER BEAN PHILOSOPHER
Schnull & Co: 1917 (5-1/2x17", 36 pgs., B&W, brown & black paper-c, square binding)

Seaman Si
© Pierce Publ. Co.

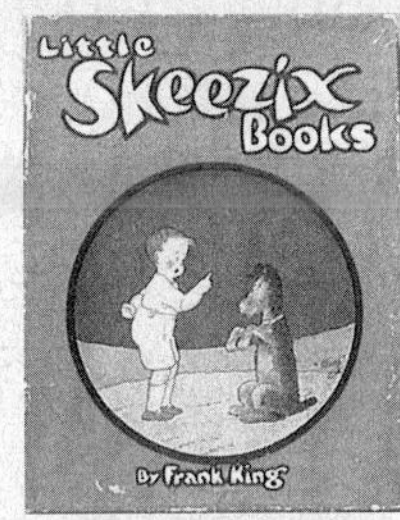

Little Skeezix Books by Frank King
1929 © Reilly & Lee

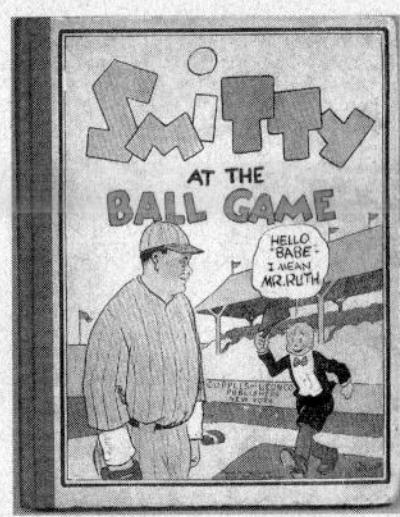

Smitty #2 By Walter Berndt
1929 © Cupples & Leon

GD2.0 FN6.0 VF8.0

nn - By Chic Jackson (no known sales)

ROOKIE FROM THE 13TH SQUAD, THAT (N) (also Between Shots; Always Belittlin';Skippy)
Harper & Brothers Publishers: Feb. 1918 (8x9-1/4", 72 pgs, hardcover, B&W)

nn - By Lieut. P(ercy) L. Crosby 75.00 225.00 400.00
NOTE: *Strip began in 1917 at an Army base during basic training.*

ROUND THE WORLD WITH THE DOO-DADS (see Doings of the Doo-Dads, Doo Dads)
Universal Feature And Specialty Co, Chicago: 1922 (12x10-1/2", 52 pgs, B&W, red & light blue-c, square binding)

nn - By Arch Dale newspaper strip-r 43.00 173.00 300.00
NOTE: *Intermixed single panel and sequential comic strips with scenes from Scotland, Ireland, England, Holland, Italy, Spain, Egypt, Africa, and Lions & Elephants along the Nile River, China, Australia & back home.*

RUBAIYKT OF THE EGG
The John C Winston Co, Philadelphia: 1905 (7x5/12", 64 pgs, purple-c, B&W)

nn - By Clare Victor Dwiggins 40.00 80.00 180.00
NOTE: *Book is printed & cut into the shape of an egg.*

RULING CLAWSS, THE (N,S)
The Daily Worker: 1935 (192 pgs, 10-1/4 x 7-3/8", hard-c, B&W)

nn - By Redfield 75.00 250.00 –
NOTE: *Reprints cartoons from the American Communist Party newspaper The Daily Worker.*

SAGARA'S ENGLISH CARTOONS AND CARTOON STORIES (N)
Bunkosha, Tokyo: nd (c1925) (6-5/8" x 4-1/4", 272 pgs, hard-c, B&W)

nn- (Scarce) – – –
NOTE: *Published in Tokyo, Japan, with all strips in both English and Japanese, to facilitate learning English. Majority of book is Bringing Up Father by George McManus. Also contains Japanese strip Father Takes it Easy, by T. Sagara, reprinted from the Kokusai News Agency.*

SAM AND HIS LAUGH (N)
Frederick A. Stokes: 1906 (10x15", cardboard-c, Sunday strip-r in color)

nn - By Jimmy Swinnerton (Extremely Rare) 800.00 1400.00 3100.00
NOTE: *Strip ran July 24, 1904-Dec 26 1906; its ethnic humor might be considered racist by today's standards.*

SCHOOL DAYS (N)
Harper & Bros.: 1919 (9x8", 104 pgs.)

nn - By Clare Victor Dwiggins 75.00 150.00 305.00

SEAMAN SI - A Book of Cartoons About the Funniest "Gob" in the Navy (N)
Pierce Publishing Co.: 1916 (4x8-1/2, 200 pgs, hardcover, B&W); 1918 (4-1/8x8-1/4, 104 pgs, hardcover, B&W)

nn - By Perce Pearce (1916) 50.00 150.00 300.00
nn - 1918 - (Reilly & Britton Co.) 30.00 125.00 200.00
NOTE: *There exists two different covers for the 1918 reprints. The earlier edition was self published by the artist. The newspaper strip is sometimes also known as "The American Sailor."*

SECRET AGENT X-9 (N)
David McKay Pbll.: 1934 (Book 1: 84 pgs; Book 2: 124 pgs.) (8x7-1/2")

Book 1-Contains reprints of the first 13 weeks of the strip by Dashiell Hammett & Alex Raymond, complete except for 2 dailies 100.00 300.00 630.00
Book 2-Contains reprints immediately following contents of Book 1, for 20 weeks by Dashiell Hammett & Alex Raymond; complete except for two dailies. Last 5 strips misdated from 6/34, continuity correct 100.00 300.00 630.00

SILK HAT HARRY'S DIVORCE SUIT (N)
M. A. Donoghue & Co.: 1912 (5-3/4x15-1/2", oblong, B&W)

nn - Newspaper-r by Tad (Thomas A. Dorgan) 33.00 117.00 425.00

SINBAD A DOG'S LIFE (M)
Coward - McCann, Inc.: 1930 (11x 8-3/4", 104 pgs., single-sided, illustrated hard-c, B&W

nn - By Edwina 11.00 33.00 110.00
Sinbad...Again (1932, 10-15/16x 8-9/16", 104 pgs.) 11.00 33.00 110.00
NOTE: *Wordless comic strips from LIFE.*

SIS HOPKINS OWN BOOK AND MAGAZINE OF FUN
Leslie-Judge Co.: 1899-July 1911 (36 pgs, color-c, B&W) (merged into Judge's Library, later titled Film Fun)

Any issue - By various 11.00 33.00 100.00
NOTE: *Zim, Flagg, Young, Newell, Adams, etc.*

SKEEZIX (Also see Gasoline Alley & Little Skeezix Books listed below) (I)
Reilly & Lee Co.: 1925 - 1928 (Strip-r, soft covers) (pictures & text)

...and Uncle Walt (1924)-Origin 26.00 104.00 225.00
...and Pal (1925), ...at the Circus (1926) 21.00 84.00 175.00
...& Uncle Walt (1927) (does this actually exist? reprint? never seen one yet)
...Out West (1928) 30.00 100.00 225.00
Hardback Editions... 34.00 136.00 245.00

SKEEZIX BOOKS, LITTLE (Also see Skeezix, Gasoline Alley) (G)
Reilly & Lee Co.: No date (1928, 1929) (Boxed set of three Skeezix books)

nn - Box with 3 issues of Skeezix. Skeezix & Pal, Skeezix at the Circus, Skeezix & Uncle Walt known. 1928 Set... 60.00 180.00 360.00
nn - Box with 4 issues of (3) above Skeezix plus "Out West" 80.00 330.00 550.00

SKEEZIX COLOR BOOK (N)
McLaughlin Bros. Inc, Springfield, Mass: 1929 (9-1/2x10-1/4", 28 pgs, one third in full color, rest in B&W)

2023 - By Frank King; strip-r to color 20.00 75.00 150.00

SKIPPY (see also Life Presents Skippy, Always Belittlin', That Rookie From 13th Squad)
No publisher listed: Circa 1920s (10x8", 16 pgs., color/B&W cartoons)

nn - By Percy Crosby 20.00 84.00 160.00

SKIPPY, LIFE PRESENTS (M)
Life Publishing Company & Henry Holt, NY: nd 1924 (134 pgs, 10-13/16x8-3/4", color hard-c, B&W

nn - By Percy L Crosby 100.00 300.00 550.00
NOTE: *Many sequential & single panel reprints from Skippy's earliest appearances in Life Magazine.*

SKIPPY
Greenberg, Publisher, Inc, NY: 1925. (11-14x8-5/8, 72 pgs, hard-c, B&W and color

nn - By Percy L. Crosby 50.00 150.00 275.00

NOTE: *Some but not all of these comics were also in Life Presents Skippy; issued with dust wrapper.*

SKIPPY AND OTHER HUMOR
Greenberg: Publisher, NY: 1929 (11-1/4x8-1/2",72 pgs,tan hard-c, B&W and color)

nn - By Percy L. Crosby 25.00 75.00 160.00
NOTE: *Came with a dust jacket.*

SKIPPY (I)
Grossett & Dunlap: 1929 (7-3/8x6, 370 pgs, hardcover text with some art)

nn - By Percy Crosby (issued with a dust jacket) 23.00 92.00 200.00
NOTE: *This is worth very little without the dust wrapper; very common without the dust jacket.*

SKIPPY
Greenberg Press: 1930 (soft cover, ca. 16 pp.,

nn - By Percy Crosby (scarce) 50.00 175.00 300.00
NOTE: *Reprints from LIFE cartoons, color, b/w. Crosby told Greenberg to withdraw from the market as it cheapened the hard cover prior editions. Greenberg then stopped publishing per agreement, and sent Crosby all the copper & zinc bookplates, which were in Crosby estate until 1996.*

SKIPPY CRAYON AND COLORING BOOK (N)
McLoughlin Bros, Inc., Springfield, MA: 1931 (13x9-3/4", 28 pgs, color-c, color & B&W)

2050 - By Percy Crosby 30.00 90.00 200.00
NOTE: *This item says on the front cover: "Licensed by Percy Crosby" because he owned his creation. About half the pages have one panel pre-printed in full color with same one b&w below for person to copy the colors.*

SKIPPY RAMBLES (I)
G.P. Putnam's Sons: 1932 (7 1/8 x 5 1/8, 202 pgs)

nn - By Percy Crosby 30.00 90.00 180.00
NOTE: *Issued with a dustjacket. Has Skippy plates by Crosby every 4 or 5 pages.*

SKUDDABUD STARRY STORY SERIES - FOLK FROM THE FUTURE (O,G)
no publisher listed: 1936 (9" x 11-7/8", 48 pgs, cardboard-c, B&W)

Book One (Rare) "Parachuting" (a VG/FN copy sold for $268 in 2010) 21.00 84.00 165.00
NOTE: *By Columba Krebs. Top half of each page is a continuing strip story, while bottom half are different stories, in prose, about the same characters -- a race of aliens who have migrated to Earth, from their dying world.*

S'MATTER POP? (N)
Saalfield Publ. Co.: 1917 (10x14", 44 pgs., B&W, cardboard-c,)

nn - By Charlie Payne; in full color; pages printed on one side 48.00 169.00 280.00

S'MATTER POP? (N) (25 ¢ cover price)
E.I. Company, New York: 1927 (8-15/16x7-1/8", 52 pgs, yellow soft-c perfect bound

nn - By C.M. Payne (scarce) 24.00 84.00 150.00
NOTE: *First comic book published by Hugo Gernsback, noted for inventing Amazing Stories among other memorable science fiction pulps. The World Science Fiction Convention Award, The Hugo, is named for him.*

SMITTY (See Treasure Box of Famous Comics) (N)
Cupples & Leon Co.: 1928 - 1933 (9x7", 96 pgs., B&W strip-r, hardcover)

1928-(96 pgs. 7x8-3/4") By Walter Berndt 50.00 185.00 350.00
1929-At the Ball Game (Babe Ruth on cover) 60.00 235.00 500.00
1930-The Flying Office Boy, 1931-The Jockey, 1932-In the North Woods each... 45.00 150.00 300.00
1933-At Military School 45.00 150.00 300.00
NOTE: *Each hardbound was published with a dust jacket; worth 50% more with dust jacket. The 1929 edition is very popular with baseball collectors. Strip debuted Nov 27, 1922.*

SMOKEY STOVER (See Dan Dunn & King of the Royal Mounted) (N)
Whitman Publishing: 1937 (5 1/2 x 7 1/4", 68pgs., color cardboard-c, B&W)

1010 36.00 150.00 300.00

SOCIAL COMEDY (M)
Life Publishing Company: 1902 (11-3/4 x 9-1/2", 128 pgs, B&W, illustrated hardcover)

nn - Artists include C.D. Gibson & Kemble. 25.00 75.00 150.00
NOTE: *Reprints cartoons and a few sequential comics from LIFE. Came in unmarked slipcase.*

SOCIAL HELL, THE (O)
Rich Hill: 1902

nn - By Ryan Walker 25.00 75.00 150.00
NOTE: *"The conditions of workers and the corruption of a political system beholden to corporate interests have*

Thimble Theater #1 by E.C. Segar
1931 © Sonnet Publishing Co.

Tillie the Toiler #7 by Russ Westover
1932 © Cupples & Leon

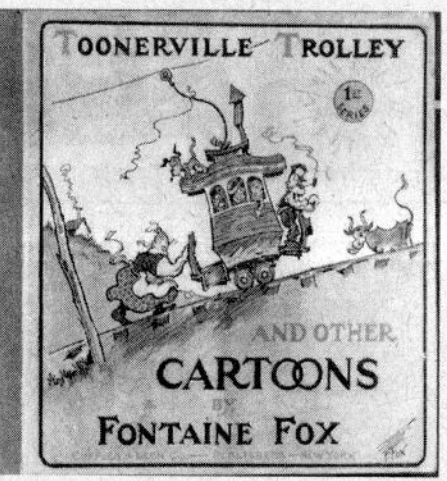

Toonerville Trolley And Other Cartoons
1921 © Cupples & Leon

GD2.0 FN6.0 VF8.0

been a major focus of human rights concerns since the 19th century. This early graphic novel depicts the social evils of unreformed capitalism. Ryan Walker was a syndicate cartoonist for many mainstream newspapers as well as for the communist Daily Worker." This description comes from http://www.lib.uconn.edu/DoddCenter/ascexh3.html, where you can find also a reproduction of the cover. I add that Ryan Walker was the editor of "The Saint Louis Republic" comic section since its inception in 1897; the supplement published "Alma and Oliver", George McManus's first series.

SPORT AND THE KID (see The Umbrella Man) (N)
Lowman & Hanford Co.: 1913 (6-1/4x6-5/8",114 pgs, hardcover, B&W&orange)
nn - By J.R. "Dok" Hager 20.00 70.00 150.00

STORY OF CONNECTICUT (N)
The Hartford Times: Vol.1 1935 - Vol.3 1936 (10-1/2" x 7-3/8",304 pgs,color hard-c, B&W)
Vol.1 - 3 20.00 70.00 150.00
NOTE: *Collects a newspaper strip on Connecticut State history, which ran in the Hartford Times. Strip is in a similar format to "Texas History Movies". Also published in a plain, blue hardcover.*

STORY OF JAPAN IN CHINA, THE (N,S)
Trans-Pacific News Service, NYC: Vol. 3, No.1 March 10, 1938 (9" x 6", 36 pgs, construction paper-c, B&W)
Vol.3 No.1 21.00 64.00 150.00
NOTE: *Part of the "China Reference Series" of booklets, detailing the Japanese occupation and brutalization of China. Consists entirely of cartoons. The other booklets in the series have no cartoons. Art by: Ding, Fitzpatrick, Herblock, Herman, Rollin Kirby, Knox, Low, Manning, Orr, Shoemaker, Talburt.*

STRANGE AS IT SEEMS (S)
Blue-Star Publishing Co.: 1932 (64 pgs., B&W, square binding)
1-Newspaper-r (*Published with & without No. 1 and price on cover.*) 32.00 128.00 200.00
Ex-Lax giveaway (1936, B&W, 24 pgs., 5x7") - McNaught Synd.
20.00 55.00 100.00

SULLIVANT'S ABC ZOO (I)
The Old Wine Press: 1946 (11-3/4x9-3/8", hardcover)
nn - By T.S. Sullivant (Rare) – – –
NOTE: *Reprints Mitchell & Miller material 1895-1898 and Life Publishing 1898-1926.*

TAILSPIN TOMMY STORY & PICTURE BOOK (N)
McLoughlin Bros.: No. 266, 1931? (nd) (10x10-1/2", color strip-r)
266 - By Forrest 43.00 172.00 300.00

TAILSPIN TOMMY (Also see Famous Feature Stories & The Funnies)(N)
Cupples & Leon Co.: 1932 (100 pgs., hard-c) (B&W 1930 strip reprints)
nn - (Scarce)- by Hal Forrest & Glenn Chaffin 50.00 150.00 400.00

TALES OF DEMON DICK AND BUNKER BILL (O)
Whitman Publishing Co.: 1934 (5-1/4x10-1/2", 80 pgs, color hardcover, B&W)
793 - By Spencer 33.00 100.00 300.00

TARZAN BOOK (The Illustrated...) (N)
Grosset & Dunlap: 1929 (9x7", 80 pgs.)
1(Rare)-Contains 1st B&W Tarzan newspaper comics from 1929. By Hal Foster Cloth reinforced spine & dust jacket (50¢); Foster-c
With dust jacket... 100.00 350.00 630.00
Without dust jacket... 55.00 200.00 310.00
2nd Printing(1934, 25¢, 76 pgs.)-4 Foster pgs. dropped; paper spine, circle in lower right cover with 25¢ price. The 25¢ is barely visible on some copies
40.00 145.00 250.00
1967-House of Greystoke reprint-7x10", using the complete 300 illustrations/text from the 1929 edition minus the original indicia, foreword, etc. Initial version bound in gold paper & sold for $5.00. Officially titled **Burroughs Bibliophile #2**. A very few additional copies were bound in heavier blue paper. Gold binding... 2.25 6.75 20.00
Blue binding... 2.50 7.50 27.00

TARZAN OF THE APES TO COLOR (N)
Saalfield Publishing Co.: No. 988, 1933 (15-1/4x10-3/4", 24 pgs) (Coloring book)
988-(Very Rare)-Contains 1929 daily reprints with some new art by Hal Foster. Two panels blown up large on each page with one at the top of opposing pages on every other double-page spread. Believed to be the only time these panels appeared in color. Most color panels are reproduced a second time in B&W to be colored
275.00 1100.00 2300.00

TARZAN OF THE APES The Big Little Cartoon Book (N)
Whitman Publishing Company: 1933 (4-1/2x3 5/8", 320 pgs, color-c, B&W)
744 - By Hal Foster (comic strips on every page) 60.00 175.00 350.00

TECK HASKINS AT OHIO STATE (S)
Lea-Mar Press: 1908 (7-1/4x5-3/8", 84 pgs, B&W hardcover)
nn - By W.A. Ireland; football cartoons-r from Columbus Ohio Evening Dispatch
30.00 100.00 180.00
NOTE: *Small blue & white patch of cover art pasted atop a color cloth quilt patter; pasted patch can easily peel off some copies.*

TECK 1909 (S)
Lea-Mar Press: 1909 (8-5/8 x 8-1/8", 124 pgs., B&W hardcover, 25¢)
nn - By W.A. Ireland; Ohio State University baseball cartoons-r from Columbus Evening Dispatch 30.00 100.00 180.00

TEDDY BEAR BOOKS, THE (M) (see also LITTLE JOHNNY AND THE TEDDY BEARS)
Reilly & Britton Co., Chicago: 1907 (7-1/16" x 5-3/8", 24 pgs, hard-c, color
The Teddy Bears Come to Life, The Teddy Bears at the Circus, The Teddy Bears in a Smashup, The Teddy Bears on a Lark, The Teddy Bears on a Toboggan, The Teddy Bears at School, The Teddy Bears Go Fishing, The Teddy Bears in Hot Water
25.00 75.00 160.00
NOTE: *Books are all unnumbered. C & A by J.R. Bray; s-Robert D. Towne. Reprints "Little Johnny & the Teddy Bears" strips, from Judge Magazine. Similar in format to the Buster Brown Nuggets series. All eight books debuted simultaneously.*

TEDDY BEARS IN FUN AND FROLIC (M) (see LITTLE JOHNNY & THE TEDDY BEARS)
Reilly & Britton Co., Chicago: 1908 (8-3/4" x 8-3/4", 50 pgs, cardboard-c, color)
nn - (Rare) by J.R. Bray-a; Robert D. Towne-s 100.00 400.00 750.00
NOTE: *Reprints "Little Johnny & the Teddy Bears" strips, from Judge Magazine. Unknown if there were any other "Teddy Bear" titles published in this format.*

TEENIE WEENIES, THE
Reilly & Britton, Chicago: 1916 (16-3/8x10-1/2", 52 pgs, cardboard-c, full color)
nn - By Wm. Donahey (Chicago Tribune-r) 175.00 450.00 950.00

TERROR OF THE TINY TADS (see also UPSIDE DOWNS OF LITTLE LADY LOVEKINS AND OLD MAN MUFFAROO)
Cupples & Leon: 1909 (11x17, 26 Sunday strips in Black & Red, Stiff cardboard-c)
nn - By Gustave Verbeek (Very Rare) (no known sales)

TEXAS HISTORY MOVIES (N)
Various editions, 1928 to 1986 (B&W)
Book I -1928 Southwest Press (7-1/4 x 5-3/8, 56 pgs, cardboard cover) for the Magnolia Petroleum Company 50.00 125.00 300.00
nn - 1928 Southwest Press (12-3/8 x 9-1/4, 232 pgs, HC) 75.00 200.00 410.00
nn - 1935 Magnolia Petroleum Company (6 x 9, 132 pgs, paper cover)
21.00 63.00 145.00
NOTE: *Exists with either Wagon Train or Texas Flag & Lafitte/pirate covers.*
nn - 1943 Magnolia Petroleum Company (132 pgs, paper-c) 25.00 55.00 125.00
nn - 1963 Graphic Ideas Inc (11 x 8-1/2, softcover) 12.00 37.00 75.00
NOTE: *Reprints daily newspaper strips from the Dallas News, on Texas history. 1935 editions onward distributed within the Texas Public School System. Prior to that they appear to be giveaway comic books for the Magnolia Petroleum Company. There are many more editions than the ones pointed out above.*

THAT ROOKIE FROM THE 13TH SQUAD
Harper & Brothers Publ.: 1918 (B&W)
1-By Lieut. Percy Crosby 25.00 75.00 150.00

THAT SON-IN-LAW OF PA'S! (N)
Newspaper Feature Service: 1914 (2-1/2 by 3", color)
nn - *Imprinted on back for THE LESTER SHOE STORE.* 15.00 30.00 65.00
NOTE: *Single sheet printed in full color on both sides, unfolds to show 12 panel story.*

THIMBLE THEATRE STARRING POPEYE (See also Popeye) (N)
Sonnet Publishing Co.: 1931 - No. 2, 1932 (25¢, B&W, 52 pgs.)(Rare)
1-Daily strip serial-r in both by Segar 165.00 700.00 1500.00
2 140.00 600.00 1200.00
NOTE: *The very first Popeye reprint book. The first Thimble Theatre Sunday page appeared Dec 19, 1919. Popeye first entered Thimble Theatre on Jan 17, 1929.*

THREE FUN MAKERS, THE (N)
Stokes and Company: 1908 (10x15", 64 pgs., color) (1904-06 Sunday strip-r)
nn - Maud, Katzenjammer Kids, Happy Hooligan 800.00 2100.00 –
NOTE: *This is the first comic book to compile more than one newspaper strip together.*

TIGERS (Also see On and Off Mount Ararat) (N)
Hearst's New York American & Journal: 1902, 86 pgs. 10x15-1/4"
nn - Funny animal strip-r by Jimmy Swinnerton 600.00 1600.00 –
NOTE: *The strip began as The Journal Tigers in The New York Journal Dec 12, 1897-Sept 28 1903*

TILLIE THE TOILER (N)
Cupples & Leon Co.: 1925 - No. 8, 1933 (52 pgs., B&W, daily strip-r)
nn (#1) By Russ Westover 54.00 216.00 425.00
2-8 50.00 175.00 350.00
NOTE: *First newspaper strip appearance was in January, 1921.*

TILLIE THE TOILER MAGIC DRAWING AND COLORING BOOK
Sam L Gabriel Sons And Company: 1931 (8-1/2 x 12", 36 pages, stiff-c)
838-By Russ Westover 39.00 156.00 270.00

TIMID SOUL, THE (N)
Simon & Schuster: 1931 (12-1/4x9", 136 pgs, B&W hardcover, dust jacket?)
nn - By H. T. Webster (newspaper strip-r) 40.00 120.00 260.00

TIM McCOY, POLICE CAR 17 (O)
Whitman Publishing Co.: 1934 (14-3/4x11", 32 pgs, stiff color covers)
674-1933 original material 75.00 300.00 460.00
NOTE: *Historically important as first movie adaptation in comic books.*

TOAST BOOK
John C. Winston Co: 1905 (7-1/4 x 6,104 pgs, skull-shaped book, feltcover, B&W)
nn - By Clare Dwiggins 50.00 175.00 300.00
NOTE: *Cartoon illustrations accompanying toasts/poems, most involving alcohol.*

TOM SAWYER & HUCK FINN (N)

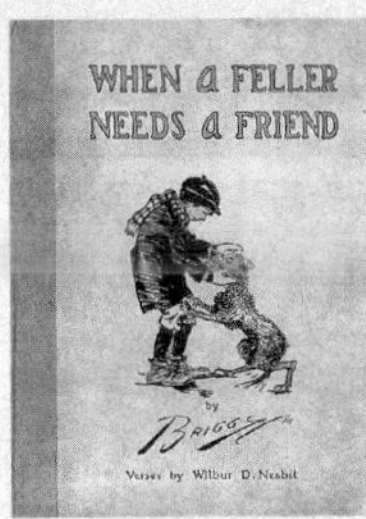

When a Feller Needs a Friend
© P.F. Volland & Co.

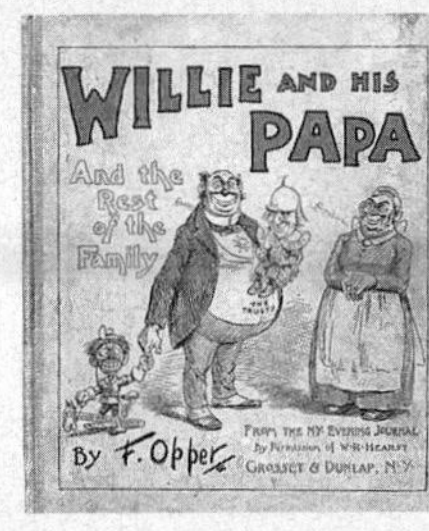

Willie and His Papa & the Rest of the Family by Opper
1901 © Grossett & Dunlap

The Yellow Kid #4 cover by Outcault
1897 © Howard, Ainslee & Co.

	GD2.0	FN6.0	VF8.0

Stoll & Edwards Co.:1925 (10x10-3/4", 52 pgs, stiff covers)

nn - By "Dwig" Dwiggins; 1923, 1924-r color Sunday strips	50.00	200.00	350.00

NOTE: *By Permission of the Estate of Samuel L. Clemons and the Mark Twain Company.*

TOONERVILLE TROLLEY AND OTHER CARTOONS (N) (See Cartoons by Fontaine Fox)
Cupples & Leon Co.: 1921 (10 x10", 52 pgs., B&W, daily strip-r)

1 - By Fontaine Fox	75.00	300.00	600.00

TRAINING FOR THE TRENCHES (M)
Palmer Publishing Company: 1917 (5-3/8 x 7", 20 pgs., paper-c, 10¢)

nn - By Lieut. Alban B. Butler, Jr.	21.00	84.00	150.00

NOTE: *Subtitle: "A book of humorous cartoons on a serious subject." Single-panels about military training.*

TREASURE BOX OF FAMOUS COMICS (N) (see Wonder Chest of Famous Comics)
Cupples & Leon Co.: 1934 (8-1/2 x 6-7/8", 36 pgs, soft covers) (Boxed set of 5 books)

Little Orphan Annie (1926)	45.00	90.00	180.00
Reg'lar Fellers (1928)	19.00	76.00	160.00
Smitty (1928)	19.00	76.00	160.00
Harold Teen (1931)	19.00	76.00	160.00
How Dick Tracy & Dick Tracy Jr. Caught The Racketeers (1933)	26.00	104.00	210.00
Softcover set of five books in box	160.00	640.00	1500.00
Box only	57.00	228.00	475.00

NOTE: *Dates shown are copyright dates; all books actually came out in 1934 or later. The softcovers are abbreviated versions of the hardcover editions listed under each character.*

T.R. IN CARTOONS (N)
A.C. McClurg & Co., Chicago: June 13, 1910 (10-5/8" x 8", 104? pgs, paper-c, B&W)

nn - By McCutcheon about Teddy Roosevelt	-	-	-

TRUTH (See Victorian section for earlier issues including the first Yellow Kid appearances)
Truth Company, NY: 1886-1906? (13-11/16x10-5/16", 16 pgs, process color-c & centerfolds, rest B&W)

1900-1906 issues	25.00	50.00	110.00

TRUTH SAVE IT FROM ABUSE & OVERWORK BEING THE EPISODE OF THE HIRED HAND & MRS. STIX PLASTER, CONCERTIST (N)
Radio Truth Society of WBAP: no date, 1924 (6-3/8 x 4-7/8, 40 pgs, paper cover, B&W)

nn - By V.T. Hamlin (Very Rare)	100.00	400.00	725.00

NOTE: *Radio station WBAP giveaway reprints strips from the Ft. Worth Texas Star-Telegram set at local radio station. 1st collected work by V.T. Hamlin, pre-Alley Oop.*

TWENTY FIVE YEARS AGO (see At The Bottom Of The Ladder) (M,S)
Coward-McCann: 1931 (5-3/4x8-1/4, 328 pgs, hardcover, B&W)

nn - By Camillus Kessler	32.00	128.00	250.00

NOTE: *Multi-image panel cartoons showing historical events for dates during the year.*

UMBRELLA MAN, THE (N) (See Sport And The Kid)
Lowman & Hanford Co.: 1911 (8-7/8x5-7/8",112 pgs, hard-c, B&W & orange)

nn - By J.R. "Dok" Hager (Seattle Times-r)	20.00	70.00	125.00

UNCLE REMUS AND BRER RABBIT (N)
Frederick A. Stokes Co.: 1907 (64 pgs, hardbound, color)

nn - By Joel C Harris & J.M. Conde	75.00	200.00	325.00

UPSIDE DOWNS OF LITTLE LADY LOVEKINS AND OLD MAN MUFFAROO
(see also TERROR OF THE TINY TADS)
New York Herald: 1905 (?) (N)

nn - By Gustav Verbeck	150.00	450.00	850.00

VAUDEVILLES AND OTHER THINGS (N)
Isaac H. Blandiard Co.: 1900 (13x10-1/2", 22 pgs., color) plus two reprints

nn - By Bunny (Scarce)	400.00	1000.00	-
nn - 2nd print "By the Creator of Foxy Grandpa" on-c but only has copyright info of 1900 (10-1/2x15 1/2, 28 pgs, color)	450.00	850.00	-
nn - 3rd print. "By the creator of Foxy Grandpa" on-c; has both 1900 and 1901 copyright info (11x13")	350.00	650.00	-

WALLY - HIS CARTOONS OF THE A.E.F. (N)
Stars & Stripes: 1917 (96 and 108 pgs, B&W)

nn - By Abian A "Wally" Wallgren (7x18; 96 pgs)	25.00	75.00	150.00
nn - another edition (108 pgs, 7x17-1/2)	25.00	75.00	150.00

NOTE: *World War One cartoons reprints from Stars & Stripes; sold to U.S. servicemen with profits to go to French War Orphans Fund. various editions from 1917-1920; there might be more than what we list here.*

WAR CARTOONS (S)
Dallas News: 1918 (11x9", 112 pgs, hardcover, B&W)

nn - By John Knott (WWOne cartoons)	20.00	70.00	130.00

WAR CARTOONS FROM THE CHICAGO DAILY NEWS (N,S)
Chicago Daily News: 1914 (10 cents, 7-3/4x10-3/4", 68 pgs, paper-c, B&W)

nn - By L.D. Bradley	20.00	70.00	130.00

WEBER & FIELD'S FUNNYISMS (S,M,O)
Arkell Comoany, NY: 1904 (10-7/8x8", 112 pgs, color-c, B&W)

1 - By various (only issue?)	20.00	70.00	150.00

NOTE: *Contains some sequential & many single panel strips by Outcault, George Luks, CA David, Houston, L Smith, Hy Mayer, Verbeck, Woolf, Sydney Adams, Frank "Chip" Bellew, Eugene "ZIM" Zimmerman, Phil May, FT Richards, Billy Marriner, Grosvenor and many others.*

WE'RE NOT HEROES (O,S)
E.C. Wells and J.W. Moss: 1933 (8-11/16" x 5-7/8", 52 pgs, B&W interior)

nn - By Eddie Wells; red & black paper-c	20.00	40.00	80.00

NOTE: *Amateurish cartoons about World War I vets in the Walter Reed Veteran's Hospital.*

WHEN A FELLER NEEDS A FRIEND (S)
P. F. Volland & Co.: 1914 (11-11/16x8-7/8)

nn - By Clare Briggs	37.00	131.00	220.00

NOTE: *Originally came in box with Briggs art (box is Rare); also numerous more modern reprints)*

WILD PILGRIMAGE (O)
Harrison Smith & Robert Haas: 1932 (9-7/8x7", 210 pgs, B&W hardcover w/dust jacket) (original wordless graphic novel in woodcuts)

nn - By Lynd Ward	50.00	175.00	300.00

WILLIE AND HIS PAPA AND THE REST OF THE FAMILY (I)
Grossett & Dunlap: 1901 (9-1/2x8", 200 pgs, hardcover from N.Y. Evening Journal by Permission of W. R. Hearst) (pictures & text)

nn - By Frederick Opper	100.00	260.00	425.00

NOTE: *Political satire series of single panel cartoons, involving whiny child Willie (President William McKinley), his rambunctious and uncontrollable cousin Teddy (Vice President Roosevelt), and Willie's Papa (trusts/ monopolies) and their Maid (Senator) Hanna.*

WILLIE GREEN COMICS, THE (N) (see Adventures of Willie Green)
Frank M. Acton Co./Harris Brown: 1915 (8x15, 36 pgs); 1921 (6x10-1/8", 52 pgs, color paper cover, B&W interior, 25¢)

Book No. 1 By Harris Brown	45.00	158.00	300.00
Book 2 (#2 sold via mail order directly from the artist)(very rare)	45.00	172.00	325.00

NOTE: *Book No. 1 possible reprint of Adv. of Willie Green; definitely two different editions.*

WILLIE WESTINGHOUSE EDISON SMITH THE BOY INVENTOR (N)
William A. Stokes Co.: 1906 (10x16", 36 pgs. in color)

nn - By Frank Crane (Scarce)	400.00	1000.00	1500.00

NOTE: *Comic strip began May 27, 1900 and ran thru 1914. Parody of inventors Westinghouse and Edison.*

WINNIE WINKLE (N)*Strip began as a daily Sept 20, 1920.*
Cupples & Leon Co.: 1930 - No. 4, 1933 (52 pgs., B&W daily strip-r)

1	40.00	160.00	360.00
2-4	25.00	110.00	300.00

WISDOM OF CHING CHOW, THE (see also The Gumps)
R. J. Jefferson Printing Co.: 1928 (4x3", 100 pgs, red & B&W cardboard cover) (newspaper strip-r The Chicago Tribune)

nn - By Sidney Smith (scarce)	30.00	90.00	150.00

WONDER CHEST OF FAMOUS COMICS (N) see Treasure Chest of Famous Comics)
Cupples & Leon Co.: 1935? 8-1/2x(6-7/8", 36 pgs, soft covers) (Boxed set of 5 books)

Little Orphan Annie #2 (1927) (Haunted House)	21.00	84.00	150.00
Little Orphan Annie #3 (1928) (in the Circus)	19.00	76.00	150.00
Smitty #2 (1929) (Babe Ruth app.)	19.00	76.00	150.00
Dolly Dimples and Bobby Bounce (1933) by Grace Drayton	19.00	76.00	150.00
How Dick Tracy & Dick Tracy Jr. Caught The Racketeers (1933)	26.00	104.00	220.00
Softcover set of five books in box	160.00	640.00	1300.00
Box only	57.00	228.00	430.00

NOTE: *Dates shown are original copyright dates of the first printings; all actually came out in 1934 or later. Extremely abbreviated versions of the hardcover editions listed under each character. It is suspected this came out the Christmas season following Treasure Chest of Famous Comics. which contains earlier editions.*

WORLD OF TROUBLE, A (S)
Minneapolis Journal: 1901 (10x8-3/4", 100 pgs, 40 pgs full color)

v3#1 - By Charles L. Bartholomew (editorial-r)	28.00	99.00	170.00

WRIGLEY'S "MOTHER GOOSE"
Wm. Wrigley Jr. Company, Chicago: 1915 (6" x 4", 28 pgs, full color)

nn - *Promotional comics for Wrigley's gum. Intro Wrigley's "Spearmen*	20.00	70.00	150.00
Book No. 2	20.00	70.00	150.00

YELLOW KID, THE (Magazine)(I) (becomes **The Yellow Book** #10 on)
Howard, Ainslee & Co., N.Y.: Mar. 20, 1897 - #9, July 17, 1897
(5¢, B&W w/color covers, 52p., stapled) (not a comic book)

1-R.F. Outcault Yellow kid on-c only #1-6. The same Yellow Kid color ad app. on back-c #1-6 (advertising the New York Sunday Journal)	1000.00	4000.00	-
2-6 (#2 4/3/97, #5 5/22/97, #6, 6/5/97)	775.00	3000.00	-
7-9 (Yellow Kid not on-c)	300.00	800.00	-

NOTE: *Richard Outcault's Yellow Kid from the Hearst New York American represents the very first successful newspaper comic strip in America. Listed here due to historical importance. A set of #1-9 sold in 2015 for $20,315.*

YELLOW KID IN MCFADDEN'S FLATS, THE (N)
G. W. Dillingham Co., New York: 1897 (50¢, 7-1/2x5-1/2", 196 pgs., B&W, squarebound)

nn - The first "comic" book featuring The Yellow Kid; E. W. Townsend narrative w/R. F. Outcault Sunday comic page art-r & some original drawings (Prices vary widely. Rare.)	7000.00	15,000.00	-

NOTE: *A Fair condition copy sold for $2,901 in August 2004.; restored app VF sold for $10,500 in 2005. A copy in Fine+ (spine intact) and loose back cover sold for $17,000 in 2006. An apparent FN+ copy sold for $6,572.50 in 2011. An apparent FN/VF copy sold for $4,182 in 2012.*

YESTERDAYS (S)
The Reilly & Lee Co.: 1930 (8-3/4 x 7-1/2", 128 pgs, illustrated hard-c with dust jacket

nn - Text and cartoons about Victorian times by Frank Wing	25.00	50.00	100.00

DICK TRACY AT 90

By Ed Catto

There's a theory that you must be a little mad to be a successful entrepreneur with a groundbreaking idea. You need a clear vision and unbridled passion to make it come alive and a clarity to your vision, even if no one else can understand it.

Chester Gould had that when he created Dick Tracy. He was like a slightly deranged railroad engineer, piloting his train at breakneck speed along a twisty track – with navigation that made sense only to him. His vision for Dick Tracy was unlike anything the public had ever seen before in the newspaper funnies. And it worked!

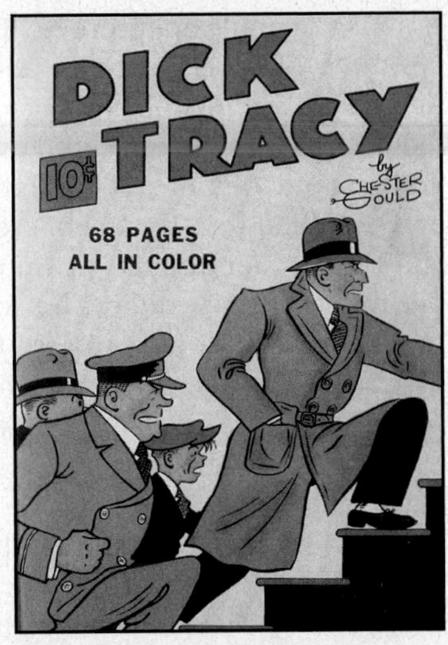

"The Dick Tracy strip was inspired by Melvin Purvis and Al Capone. It debuted the same year that Capone was convicted of tax evasion," John Siuntres, creator and host of *The Word Balloon Podcast*, said.

"When it comes to iconic heroes firmly entrenched in the pulp mythos, Dick Tracy should be up there alongside names like the Shadow, Batman, and more," said Alex Segura, writer and Co-President of Archie Comic Publications. "The yellow-coated detective's rogues gallery is on par with those of the Dark Knight, Spider-Man, and beyond. It's the rare strip that continues to evolve and change over time, whether it's Gould's original, gritty crime tales, Max Allan Collins' sharp reinvention of the strip, or Kyle Baker's cinematic and stylistic masterpiece, Dick Tracy is a hidden gem of the sequential medium."

Dick Tracy is a sort of hidden gem, but that's hard to reconcile with his 90 years of success.

"Dick Tracy, as befits a plainclothes detective, exists in a pretty tight spot for fans of comic books," author Laurence Maslon said. An arts professor at New York University's Tisch School of the Arts, as well as associate chair of the Graduate Acting Program, Maslon is also a writer and coproducer of several books and documentaries including *Superheroes! Capes, Cowls and the Creation of Comic Book Culture.* Maslon observed:

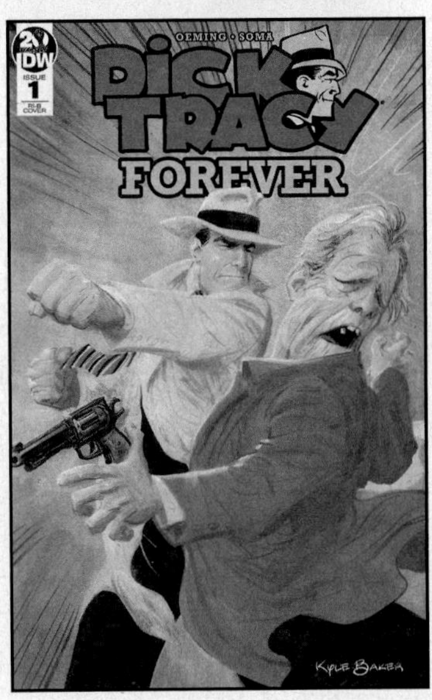

> "He [Dick Tracy] is, without a doubt, one of the three most famous action heroes created for the comic strips, along with Flash Gordon and the Phantom. He's a combination of Sherlock Holmes, Philip Marlowe, and Officer Joe Bolton. But he is probably also the action hero with the least amount of personality ever – no wonder Warren Beatty was better at playing one of the most infamous criminals of the Great Depression than he was at playing one of its most famous lawmen."

"Like many superheroes, Tracy had a costume, of sorts, to help make him distinctive – an inexplicably canary yellow fedora and trench coat (kinda would make Tracy stand out in a gun fight, wouldn't it?). Combined with a razor's edge profile and the frequent gimcrack (most famously the two-way wrist radio), he was certainly recognizable as a pop culture figure, even if he was impossible to imitate or impersonate because of his one-dimensional determined personality.

"One of most appealing things about the *Dick Tracy* comic strip itself was how unappealing it was. Readers and/or consumers who only know Tracy from Gould's irrelevant science fiction "Moon" narratives from the 1950s and 1960s or from the variety of cheap (and in some cases politically incorrect) Saturday morning cartoon versions of Tracy from a slightly later time would be shocked to read the daily and Sunday strips from the 1930s to the mid-1940s (which again dovetail perfectly with the Roosevelt Administration). It's not just the criminals who are loathsome and pernicious – it's their deeds, graphically depicted by Gould day after day, week after week: asphyxiation, mutilation, amputation, burning, scalding, poisoning, suffocation, death by axe, death by hatchet, and, of course, barrages of bullets from machine guns, hand guns, rifles, you name it, all punctuated by buckets of blood, slathered on the page, out of Gould's copious inkwell. Some of the strips even hint at sexual abuse, transvestism, and pedophilia."

A CAST OF CHARACTERS, AND WE DO MEAN "CHARACTERS"

Dick Tracy started with a few narrative standards for a supporting cast – a villain, a true love, a boss and an impressionable young protégé.

Tracy's sweetheart, Tess Trueheart would prove to be his anchor, but also integral to establishing Tracy's true calling. It was her father's murder that started Tracy's lifelong quest to crush crime.

Junior, an orphan later adopted by Tracy, would fulfill the sidekick role similar to Jimmy Olsen or Robin. Junior was a pivotal figure in the *Dick Tracy* radio show. He served as a surrogate for the young listeners – just as excited about the secret code and the Dick Tracy clubs in each episode as he was at solving the mystery or capturing the storyline's villain.

It is staggeringly impressive to see the cast grown from that initial line-up. Tracy enjoys a large family and the respect and partnership of his many colleagues.

But the bad apples, in this case, may be the most appealing.

In popular fiction, so often the heroes are defined by their villains. Evildoers are the ones looking to shake things up, while the heroes fight for stability and the status quo. The *Dick Tracy* strip is all this and more: his villains are so creepy and grotesque that they have become unforgettable.

In the mob era, it was common to assign nicknames, either as the natural course of things or via the media. Ben Siegel, for example, was assigned the name "Bugsy"

Newspaper strip from 1945.

(meaning "crazy"), which he revealed he loathed. Al Capone was the original "Scarface."

Gould took this tradition to the extreme. Dick Tracy and his police cohorts found themselves locked in combat with the likes of Big Boy, Flattop Jones, the Brow, Measles, Itchy Oliver, Shoulders, Pruneface, Wormy, B.B. Eyes, Rughead and the Blank.

Some villains even had their own spin-offs – often as the original was unavailable (due to a grisly demise). So Pruneface begat Mrs. Pruneface. Big Boy begat Little Boy. Years after the death of Breathless Mahoney, Restless Mahoney was introduced. And Breathless' sister, Heartless Mahoney, would later take center stage to seek revenge against Dick Tracy.

"I think Dick Tracy's legacy is more than introducing forensic science and grotesque villains to the masses," said Christopher Irving, Associate Professor, Narrative Media at VCU Communication Arts. "His influence on Batman alone, as Bob Kane was aping Chester Gould's stiff figures and heavy shadows (while also unapologetically swiping Alex Raymond) and Bill Finger and company were creating Batman's own similar Rogue's Gallery, still resonates in everyone from Joker to Two-Face to Harley Quinn."

Flattop spawned an entire larcenous lineage. This twisted family tree includes Flattop Jr., Mrs. Flattop, Sharptop, Blowtop and Angela "Angeltop" Jones, Flattop's daughter. Current Tracy strip writer Mike Curtis revealed that Hi-Top, Angeltop's son and thus Flattop's grandson, won't be seen again – as he just makes Grandpa Tracy seem too old!

Gould villains were especially nasty. For example, when Influence uses his strangely charismatic influence on Tracy's longtime pal, Vitamin Smith, the businessman is forced to eat only dried peas – and like it – and smilingly accept cigarette burns on his skin (reminiscent of a cult branding).

The villains mostly took it out on Tracy himself. "He was (almost) starved to death; terrible things happen to Tracy," current Tracy strip artist Joe Staton said.

While Gould's convoluted plots might reveal the circumstances to how things got so out of control for any of these vile characters, there wasn't room for a lot of sympathy. Likewise, Tracy never came across as vengeful or righteous – he was a just a man with a clear job to do and a society to protect.

Their grisly ends would punctuate their bizarre lives. While gunshot wounds would often prove fatal, Lips Manlis was encased in cement and dumped in the river. Ugly Christine fell to her doom from a flying Police Magnetic Air Car. Spud Spaldoni died in a car bombing. The Governor would fall from atop a Ferris Wheel in freezing weather.

BURSTING BEYOND THE NEWSPAPERS

Dick Tracy, the comic strip character, jumped to movies and radio with the speed and urgency of a rooftop chase scene. By 1937 he starred in a long line of movies, debuting with *Dick Tracy*. His cinematic endeavors were more substantial than his four-color compatriots. Unlike Captain America or Superman, Dick Tracy was awarded more movies.

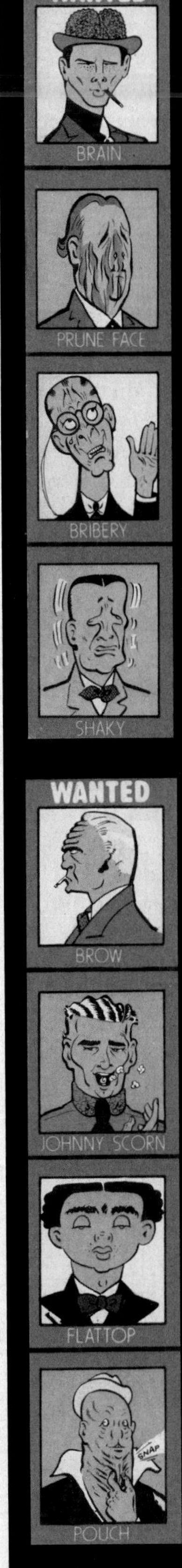

The *Dick Tracy* radio serial was clearly aimed at kids. Serialized episodes plodded along the adventures ever so slowly, making sure there was plenty of time for the sponsor's message and the obligatory secret message. Kids would have to nag mom to purchase the sponsors' products and send in package box tops in return for a secret decoder. The whole notion was reinforced further as kids were urged to join The Dick Tracy Club and even ascend the ranks.

"He was even featured in one of pop culture's more eccentric amalgamations, an original radio musical entitled *Dick Tracy in B-Flat*, made expressly for the U.S. Armed Forces in February of 1945," Maslon said. "The cast included Bing Crosby as Tracy (mocked for his relentless squareness), Bob Hope as Flattop, and, in a moment of incomparable perfection, Frank 'Wizard of Oz' Morgan as the chemically dependent thespian Vitamin Flintheart. Dinah Shore, Judy Garland, and Jimmy Durante (as the Mole) also participated; rumor has it that Larry Gelbart (of *M*A*S*H* fame) wrote some of the jokes for one of his first jobs."

TEAM TRACY – OVER THE YEARS

Unlike so many other pop culture heroes, Tracy's destiny has been shaped by just a handful of creators.

Much has been written about series creator, Chester Gould. He was an illustrator focusing on advertising. He didn't believe in suffering for one's art and would dress like a banker in all his professional interactions. After ten years of trying to break into comics, and extensive networking with Captain Joseph Patterson of the *Chicago Tribune*, Gould finally hit paydirt.

Patterson liked Gould's basic idea behind the detective strip *Plainclothes Tracy.* Of note: the surname "Tracy" was a play on "tracing," meaning to track down criminals. There was a request, however, to change the title to Dick Tracy – as "dick" was slang for detective. At age 31 Gould had found the endeavor that he would focus on for the rest of his career.

Gould took chances but would always maintain his vision for the strip. "What makes this fascinating is that, at the time, Gould was going rogue himself – at least as far as censorship in popular culture was concerned," Maslon said. "There was no Comics Code Authority back then, but there sure was a Production Code in Hollywood and a strong series of Standards and Practices for radio broadcast. If Gould had to submit any of his actual strips to either of those regulation bureaus, they would have tossed out (and tossed back) one strip out of every five. Quite simply, there was nothing as graphic when it came to crime and violence in American culture as the daily *Dick Tracy* strip – which of course was read avidly by every kid who could get his dad to bring home a Chicago Tribune Syndicate newspaper."

"Chet lived, slept and dreamt Tracy," remembered his friend and one-time assistant, Rick Fletcher.

He ended up working on the strip for almost 50 years – 46 years, 2 months and 21 days, to be precise.

"We always think of old comics as being vanilla and boring, but Gould's Tracy was dark and violent, yet oddly considered wholesome for his being a religious character," Irving said.

In 1977, Gould passed the torch to Chicago enthusiast and mystery writer Max Allan Collins. A gifted writer, Collins was more than comfortable with crime stories and comics, as he was writing both, most notably with his Nate Heller true crime novels and his groundbreaking *Ms. Tree* comic series, with artist Terry Beatty. Collins had a respect and passion for the *Dick Tracy* strip, having been first exposed to his adventures in the Harvey comics series reprinting and reformatting the stories from the newspaper strips.

Collins would be joined by "Chet's assistant, Rick Fletcher, then later by another assistant, Dick Locher," Collins said. Both of these artists' contributions to the mythology were significant.

Collins' tenure was followed by Mike Kilian, who wrote the strip from 1993 until his death in 2005. Currently, the Dick Tracy strip is helmed by writer Curtis and beloved comics artist Staton. But there are changes and improvements to tradition. "One thing we do now – we credit entire staff," said Curtis. "We have a team – just like Tracy has."

CONSTANT INNOVATION

"Calling Dick Tracy!" was a call to arms for Dick Tracy fans of all ages. Like the popular "Calling All Cars," used as a war cry to mobilize a police fleet, this phrase worked within the narrative but also made fans sit up straight in anticipation of the adventures ahead.

With all that in mind, it makes sense that Dick Tracy would be on the forefront of personal communication with his two-way-wrist radio. Over the years, his wonderful gadget would metamorphize into a two-way wrist TV and even a two-way wrist computer.

"The whole look of Tracy speaking into his wrist radio has become iconic. It's very important, like Superman standing with his hands on his hips," Curtis, the current series writer, said. In fact, he would soon work with Staton to redesign the watch.

The prescience of the device for all of us who now live in the Apple Watch era is uncanny. Today we take for granted concepts like instantaneous messaging and the ability to carry a worldwide communication device in our pockets. But when Dick Tracy debuted these incredible devices, it was the stuff of dreams.

The Space Coupe, introduced in 1964, was invented by a Diet Smith Industries employee, Dyne O' Matick. This vehicle harnessed magnetic energy, although it also needed "16 atomic energizers to ramp up the magnetic attraction." Despite a two-year atomic power supply, the bizarre contraption wore thin quickly. Toy company Aurora, and later it's fan-focused descendant, Polar Lights, would immortalize this strange craft with a plastic model kit.

Likewise, the magnetic Air Cars, resembling oversized flying garbage cans to many readers, would be introduced in 1964. The first one was a gift to Earth from the Moon Governor, who ruled Moon Valley. These peculiar vehicles were like mini-helicopters, but quieter as they relied on magnetism to power their flight. Improvements would be made and by 1973, the Air Cars could fit two policemen and were enclosed with a windshield.

The Space Coupe and the Air Cars may have foretold Japan's high speed bullet trains. These Maglev trains have successfully harnessed the power of magnetic repulsion to actually levitate the passenger cars above the tracks.

Sometimes *Dick Tracy* would instead showcase what was just around the corner. For example, during the Collins-Fletcher era and Tracy's conflict with the art thief Art Dekko, the star detective employed the Nite-Site. This device, attached to his .357 Magnum, allowed Tracy to see in the dark. In fact, the co-inventor of this device, Deputy Sheriff Julio Santiago, had presented artist Fletcher, a gun enthusiast himself, with his own Nite-Site.

And shortly thereafter, the comic strip narrative shifted focus to entrepreneur

Vitamin Flint contemplating a "Fusion Now" marketing campaign for nuclear energy.

OFF TRACK: A MOON MAID, A MUSTACHE AND MATRIMONIAL DISCORD

Dick Tracy didn't need a mission statement. His sense of purpose was as chiseled into fan's hearts as his profile was into each Sunday page. And yet, in his lengthy run, there are many instances where Dick Tracy strayed far from his film noir roots.

For example, in the '60s, the tales became untethered from traditional film noir or police procedurals as Gould introduced adventures focusing on the Moon People, the Moon Governor and the pursuit of magnetism as an alternative fuel source. Tracy's granddaughter, Honey Moon, was born from the union of Junior and a Moon Maid.

These tales featured outlandish stories focusing on strange aliens. It is interesting to note that when Collins took over the strip from Gould, one of the very first things he did was to summarily excise the Moon focused elements.

For a brief period, Dick Tracy even sported a mustache. Thankfully, his mustache did not significantly impact his signature profile. Nonetheless, it was soon shaved off in a comic strip sequence with that deadly seriousness usually reserved for a firing squad.

In 1994, both Dick Tracy and legions of newspaper readers were shocked and surprised when Tess Trueheart, his wife of 44 years, presented him with divorce papers. Maybe no one should have been surprised. Locher and Kilian had researched and found the sad fact that in New York City, the divorce rate among policemen was 85% at the time.

The story quickly grew beyond the funny pages. *USAToday* ran it on the front page. *Newsweek* and the *Today Show* both featured the story. Dan Rather even reached out to Locher.

"I want to be the first to know *when* the reconciliation happens," Rather told Locher. And that was the thing – calmer heads knew that true love, or at least Trueheart, would prevail.

The detective and wife reconciled and promptly went on a second honeymoon to get away from it all. Of course, even in the sunshine and on a beach, Tracy stumbled across another case to solve. Some guys never learn.

FOUR COLORS AND TWO STAPLES

Dick Tracy first leapt from the Sunday funny pages to Dell's *Feature Comics*, and then to *Dick Tracy Feature Comics*, which was published by David McKay Publications. During the initial heyday *Dick Tracy* Big Little Books and other collectible publications were published and sold. Dell soon started publishing *Dick Tracy Monthly* and enjoyed a healthy run from 1939 to 1949.

Harvey Publications picked up right where Dell had left off and published Dick Tracy until 1961. It is notable that this Harvey series inspired Tracy writers Collins and Curtis.

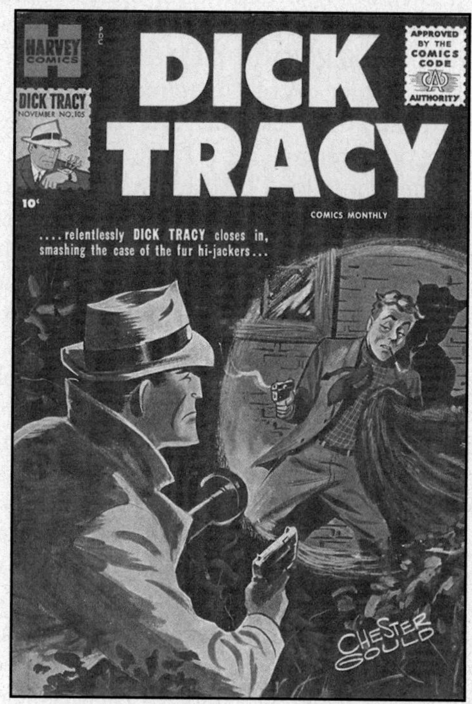

Dick Tracy Comics Monthly #105, 1956, from Harvey Publications.

Kyle Baker's three-part *Dick Tracy: Big City Blues* comic series from Walt Disney Comics, ostensibly tied to the 1990 movie, was fresh, innovative and generally well-regarded by fans.

Other comics publishers would include Gladstone and Blackthorne.

LOOKING FORWARD WHILE LOOKING BACK

In recent years, IDW, through the Library of American Comics, provided a comprehensive Dick Tracy library, with high quality reprints of *Dick Tracy* daily and Sunday strips through the years. Each volume is lovingly designed celebrating the strips with an austere reverence.

When a minor reprint slip-up occurs, it's treated with the seriousness of a heart attack. Like a political figure owning up to a misdeed, the Tracy volumes waste no time with excuses, but boldly, confidently and quickly work to correct it,

Each volume is stuffed with text pieces. Collins grabs readers and guides them through the fascinating ins and outs of the Tracy stories. Collins routinely provides a clear-eyed period analysis of the state of the country, the strip, and the creator. Fascinating additional essays, presented at the end of the books offer deep dives into various aspect of the Tracy mythology, like the serials or the licensed merchandise.

Recently IDW cleared the stage for current creatives to take a crack at the iconic detective. *Dick Tracy Dead or Alive* by Michael Allred, Lee Allred, Rich Tommaso, and Laura Allred. This 2018 four-issue series added a pop sheen to the usual pulpy noir of Tracy. The covers especially, by Mike and Laura Allred, showcase Tracy's lemon hued coat and hat with an eye towards strong design. Of note, there's a clever bit included as an homage to Tracy's ill-fated mustache.

Michael Avon Oeming's uses his thick expressive lines that would make Gould proud in the four-issue series, *Dick Tracy Forever*. Oeming explores the concepts of the characters as part of specific time periods to show how Tracy shines during the corrupt prohibition days or a time of the police embracing technology.

THE STRIP TODAY

Being the writer of the current Dick Tracy newspaper strip brings it all full circle for Curtis. He's always loved Dick Tracy. He explained how as a child in the 1950s, childcare was difficult since his parents were both working, and his brother was in school. The solution was for him to go to work with his dad, who was a manager at the Wonder Bread plant in Memphis, Tennessee. They started giving him issues of the old Harvey reprints. When he'd get an oversized 25¢ Harvey *Dick Tracy* issue, that would keep him busy for the entire day.

Artist Staton has a similar story. He recalls a favorite family story when they found him on the kitchen floor reading Dick Tracy in the Sunday Funnies – before he could even read. Staton proudly teases he's had long stints on pop culture's two most beloved detectives – Dick Tracy and Scooby Doo. He's drawn Batman stories too.

Curtis may have misunderstood the strip at first. He explained how one of the first newspaper stories he read, when fighting Measles, Dick Tracy got his coat stuck in a car and was brutally dragged. And in the Harvey comic that young Curtis bought, Tracy was again dragged by a car. Curtis thought, at that point, every story included a part where Dick Tracy would be dragged by a car.

Years later, when Staton and Curtis accepted the Harvey award, they made a promise they would include a car-dragging sequence and they eventually did.

Curtis has read the entire library of Dick Tracy adventures, so he can better present the new adventures with fresh eyes – and avoid any duplication of past efforts.

DICK TRACY – THE FATHER FIGURE

Under the management of Staton and Curtis – Dick Tracy has a taken a leadership role in the world of comics – devoting adventures to team-up with comics characters of days gone like Little Orphan Annie, The Spirit, Steve Roper, and Mike Nomad. "It all started with Hank O'Hare from *Brenda Starr*," recalled Curtis. "But for just one panel."

Next up was Hot Shot Charlie from *Terry and the Pirates* – for just three days. It all went so well they decided to make in an ongoing tradition.

The team also wanted to resolve the dangling *Little Orphan Annie* storyline. When that long-running strip ended, Annie had been kidnapped and held prisoner on a villain's yacht. It all came to a close with a message to the reader explaining "this is where we will leave Annie for now."

Leave it to Dick Tracy, and Curtis and Staton, to see that justice was done. "We did a five-month story resolving the Little Orphan Annie storyline," said Curtis.

In fact, one crossover with Little Orphan Annie has teamed her up with Honey Moon, Tracy's granddaughter.

Curtis is planning for the future, "2024 is *Little Orphan Annie's* anniversary we'll have a big crossover adventure with her that year."

These clever crossovers have historical precedent: Gould occasionally would have celebrities like Spike Jones and his City Slicker's, pop up in the *Dick Tracy* comic strip.

WINDY CITY WIND-UP

Why has Dick Tracy persevered? "Superman was the first superhero, but Dick Tracy was the first strip with gunfights. It was as action strip with violence. The first and the best. And it had never been done before," Curtis said.

"Tracy was the hero in the ultimate Manichean battles of his time," Maslon said. "He was most at home, not on the magazine rack or on the radio console, but in the back of the newspapers in black and white – Dick Tracy was himself the black and white crusader of a desperate black and white age in American history."

Could Gould ever have envisioned that his policeman strip would last 90 years? If he shared the same square-jawed confidence of Dick Tracy himself, I believe he might have.

Ed Catto is a marketing and start-up strategist, with a specialty in pop culture. As founder of Agendae, Ed is dedicated to helping brands and companies innovate and grow. As part of the faculty at Ithaca College's School of Business, Ed teaches entrepreneurial courses and one unique class focusing on comic conventions and geek culture. Ed's also an illustrator, having won the 2019 Pulp Factory Award and a retropreneur, rejuvenating brands like Captain Action.

Abbott and Costello #4 © STJ

Abbott: 1973 #1 © Saladin Ahmed

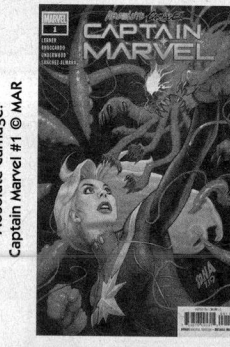

Absolute Carnage: Captain Marvel #1 © MAR

	GD 2.0	VG 4.0	FN 6.0	VF 8.0	VF/NM 9.0	NM- 9.2

The correct title listing for each comic book can be determined by consulting the indicia (publication data) on the beginning interior pages of the comic. The official title is determined by those words of the title in capital letters only, and not by what is on the cover. Titles are listed in this book as if they were one word, ignoring spaces, hyphens, and apostrophes, to make finding titles easier. Exceptions are made in rare cases. Comic books listed should be assumed to be in color unless noted "B&W".

PRICING IN THIS GUIDE: Prices for **GD 2.0** (Good), **VG 4.0** (Very Good), **FN 6.0** (Fine), **VF 8.0** (Very Fine), **VF/NM 9.0** (Very Fine/Near Mint),and **NM– 9.2** (Near Mint–) are listed in whole U.S. dollars except for prices below $7 which show dollars and cents. **The minimum price listed is $3.00**, the cover price for current new comics. Many books listed at this price can be found in $1.00 boxes at conventions and dealers stores.

A-1 (See A-One)

A&A: THE ADVENTURES OF ARCHER & ARMSTRONG
Valiant Entertainment: Mar, 2016 - No. 12, Feb, 2017 ($3.99)

1-12: 1-Rafer Roberts-s/David Lafuente-a. 5-Faith app. 5-12-Norton-a 4.00
10-Cat cosplay photo variant-c 4.00

AARDVARK COMICS (Reprints from Cerebus in Hell)(Also see Batvark)
Aardvark-Vanaheim: Sept, 2017 ($4.00, B&W)

1-Cerebus figures placed over original Gustave Doré artwork of Hell; Action #1-c swipe 4.00

ABADAZAD
CrossGen (Code 6): Mar, 2004 - No. 3, May, 2004 ($2.95)

1-3-Ploog-a/c; DeMatteis-s 3.00
1-2nd printing with new cover 3.00

ABATTOIR
Radical Comics: Oct, 2010 - No. 6, Aug, 2011 ($3.99/$3.50, limited series)

1-($3.99) Cansino-a/Levin & Peteri-s 4.00
2-6-($3.50) 3.50

ABBIE AN' SLATS (...With Becky No. 1-4) (See Comics On Parade, Fight for Love, Giant Comics Edition 2, Giant Comics Editions #1, Sparkler Comics, Tip Topper, Treasury of Comics, & United Comics)
United Features Syndicate: 1940; March, 1948 - No. 4, Aug, 1948 (Reprints)

	GD	VG	FN	VF	VF/NM	NM-
Single Series 25 ('40)	42	84	126	265	445	625
Single Series 28	37	74	111	218	354	490
1 (1948)	17	34	51	98	154	210
2-4: 3-r/Sparkler #68-72	10	20	30	58	79	100

ABBOTT
BOOM! Studios: Jan, 2018 - No. 5, May, 2018 ($3.99, limited series)

1-5-Saladin Ahmed-s/Sami Kivelä 4.00

ABBOTT AND COSTELLO (...Comics)(See Giant Comics Editions #1 & Treasury of Comics)
St. John Publishing Co.: Feb, 1948 - No. 40, Sept, 1956 (Mort Drucker-a in most issues)

	GD	VG	FN	VF	VF/NM	NM-
1	92	184	276	584	1005	1425
2	54	108	162	343	574	825
3-9 (#8, 8/49; #9, 2/50)	35	70	105	208	339	470
10-Son of Sinbad story by Kubert (new)	39	78	117	240	395	550
11,13-20 (#11, 10/50; #13, 8/51; #15, 12/52)	22	44	66	132	216	300
12-Movie issue	24	48	72	144	237	330
21-30: 28-r/#8. 29,30-Painted-c	17	34	51	98	154	210
31-40: 33,36,38-Reprints	14	28	42	82	121	160
3-D #1 (11/53, 25¢)-Infinity-c	33	66	99	194	317	440

ABBOTT AND COSTELLO (TV)
Charlton Comics: Feb, 1968 - No. 22, Aug, 1971 (Hanna-Barbera)

	GD	VG	FN	VF	VF/NM	NM-
1	7	14	21	49	92	135
2	4	8	12	27	44	60
3-10	3	6	9	21	33	45
11-22	3	6	9	17	26	35

ABBOTT: 1973
BOOM! Studios: Jan, 2021 - No. 5 ($3.99, limited series)

1,2-Saladin Ahmed-s/Sami Kivelä 4.00

ABC (See America's Best TV Comics)

ABC: A-Z (one-shots)
America's Best Comics: Nov, 2005 - July, 2006 ($3.99, one-shots)

... Greyshirt and Cobweb (1/06) character bios; Veitch-s/a; Gebbie-a; Dodson-c 4.00
... Terra Obscura and Splash Brannigan (3/06) character bios; Barta-a; Dodson-c 4.00
... Tom Strong and Jack B. Quick (11/05) character bios; Sprouse-a; Nowlan-a; Dodson-c 4.00
... Top Ten and Teams (7/06) character bios; Ha & Cannon-a; Veitch-a; Dodson-c 4.00

ABE SAPIEN... (Hellboy character)
Dark Horse Comics: Apr, 2013 - No. 36, Aug, 2016 ($3.50/$3.99)

1-33: 1,2-Subtitled "Dark and Terrible"; Mignola & Allie-s/Fiumara-a/c. 8-Oeming-a. 23-Hellboy app.; Nowlan-a 3.50
34-36-($3.99) 4.00
...: Drums of the Dead (3/98, $2.95) 1-Thompson-a. Hellboy back-up; Mignola-s/a/c 4.00
...: The Abyssal Plain (6/10 - No. 2, 7/10, $3.50) 1,2-Mignola & Arcudi-s/Snejbjerg-a 3.50
...: The Devil Does Not Jest (9/11 - No. 2, 10/11, $3.50) Mignola & Arcudi-s. 1-Two covers by Johnson & Francavilla 3.50
...: The Drowning (2/08 - No. 5, 6/08, $2.99) 1-5-Mignola-s/c; Alexander-a 3.50
...: The Haunted Boy (10/09, $3.50) 1-Mignola & Arcudi-s/Reynolds-a/Johnson-c 3.50

ABIGAIL AND THE SNOWMAN
Boom Entertainment (KaBOOM!): Dec, 2014 - No. 4, Mar, 2015 ($3.99, limited series)

1-4-Roger Langridge-s/a. 1-Covers by Langridge & Liew 4.00

A. BIZARRO
DC Comics: Jul, 1999 - No. 4, Oct, 1999 ($2.50, limited series)

1-4-Gerber-s/Bright-a 4.00

ABOMINATIONS (See Hulk)
Marvel Comics: Dec, 1996 - No. 3, Feb, 1997 ($1.50, limited series)

1-3-Future Hulk storyline 4.00

ABRAHAM LINCOLN LIFE STORY (See Dell Giants)

ABRAHAM STONE
Marvel Comics (Epic): July, 1995 - No. 2, Aug, 1995 ($6.95, limited series)

1,2-Joe Kubert-s/a 7.00

ABSENT-MINDED PROFESSOR, THE (see Shaggy Dog & The... under Movie Comics)

ABSOLUTE CARNAGE
Marvel Comics: Oct, 2019 - No. 5, Jan, 2020 ($7.99/$4.99, limited series)

1-($7.99) Donny Cates-s/Ryan Stegman-a; Venom, Carnage Spider-Man app. 8.00
2-5-($4.99) 2-Miles Morales & The Grendel Symbiote app. 3-Hulk app. 5-Knull freed 5.00
...: Avengers 1 (12/19, $4.99) Captain America, Hawkeye, The Thing, Wolverine app. 5.00
...: Captain Marvel 1 (1/20, $4.99) Carnage possesses the Flerkin Chewie 5.00
...: Immortal Hulk 1 (12/19, $4.99) Ewing-s/Andrade-a; Betty Ross & Venom app. 5.00
...: Separation Anxiety 1 (10/19, $4.99) The Life Foundation symbiotes app. 5.00
...: Symbiote of Vengeance 1 (11/19, $4.99) Ghost Rider vs. Carnage 5.00
...: Symbiote Spider-Man 1 (11/19, $4.99) Peter David-s; White Rabbit app. 5.00
...: Weapon Plus 1 (1/20, $4.99) Raffaele-a; Weapon Plus vs. Carnage 5.00

ABSOLUTE CARNAGE: LETHAL PROTECTORS
Marvel Comics: Oct, 2019 - No. 3, Dec, 2019 ($3.99, limited series)

1-3-Iron Fist, Misty Knight, Cloak & Dagger, Firestar & Morbius 4.00

ABSOLUTE CARNAGE: MILES MORALES
Marvel Comics: Oct, 2019 - No. 3, Dec, 2019 ($3.99, limited series)

1-3-Scorpion & Silver Sable app.; Ahmed-s/Vicentini-a 4.00

ABSOLUTE CARNAGE: SCREAM
Marvel Comics: Oct, 2019 - No. 3, Dec, 2019 ($3.99, limited series)

1-3-Bunn-s/Sandoval-a; Andi Benton app. 4.00

ABSOLUTE CARNAGE VS. DEADPOOL
Marvel Comics: Oct, 2019 - No. 3, Dec, 2019 ($3.99, limited series)

1-3-Tieri-s/Ferreira-a; Spider-Man app. 4.00

ABSOLUTE VERTIGO
DC Comics (Vertigo): Winter, 1995 (99¢, mature)

	GD	VG	FN	VF	VF/NM	NM-
nn-1st app. Preacher. Previews upcoming titles including Jonah Hex: Riders of the Worm, The Invisibles (King Mob), The Eaters, Ghostdancing & Preacher	3	6	9	14	20	25

ABYSS, THE (Movie)
Dark Horse Comics: June, 1989 - No. 2, July, 1989 ($2.25, limited series)

1,2-Adaptation of film; Kaluta & Moebius-a 3.00

ACCELERATE
DC Comics (Vertigo): Aug, 2000 - No. 4, Nov, 2000 ($2.95, limited series)

1-4-Pander Bros.-a/Kadrey-s 3.00

ACCLAIM ADVENTURE ZONE
Acclaim Books: 1997 ($4.50, digest size)

1-Short stories of Turok, Troublemakers, Ninjak and others 4.50

ACCUSED, THE (Civil War II tie-in)
Marvel Comics: Oct, 2016 ($4.99, one-shot)

1-The trial of Hawkeye; Matt Murdock app.; Guggenheim-s/Bachs & Brown-a/Mack-c 5.00

Ace Comics #30 © DMP

Action Comics #7 © DC

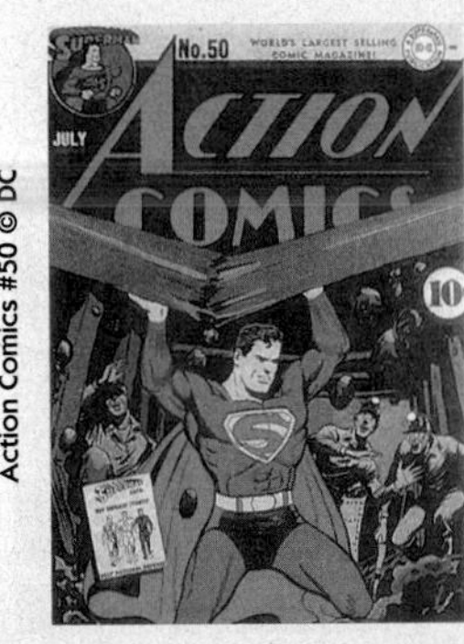

Action Comics #50 © DC

GD VG FN VF VF/NM NM-
2.0 4.0 6.0 8.0 9.0 9.2

ACE COMICS
David McKay Publications: Apr, 1937 - No. 151, Oct-Nov, 1949 (All contain some newspaper strip reprints)

1-Jungle Jim by Alex Raymond, Blondie, Ripley's Believe It Or Not, Krazy Kat begin (1st app. of each) 360 720 1080 2520 4410 6300
2 106 212 318 673 1162 1650
3-5 71 142 213 454 777 1100
6-10 54 108 162 343 574 825
11-The Phantom begins (1st app., 2/38) (in brown costume) 423 846 1269 3000 5250 7500
12-20 42 84 126 265 445 625
21-25,27-30 39 78 117 231 378 525
26-Origin & 1st app. Prince Valiant (5/39); begins series? 155 310 465 992 1696 2400
31-40: 37-Krazy Kat ends 22 44 66 132 216 300
41-60 15 30 45 88 137 185
61-64,66-76-(7/43; last 68 pgs.) 14 28 42 80 115 150
65-(8/42)-Flag-c 18 36 54 105 165 225
77-84 (3/44; all 60 pgs.) 12 24 36 67 94 120
85-99 (52 pgs.) 11 22 33 60 83 105
100 (7/45; last 52 pgs.) 12 24 36 67 94 120
101-134: 128-(11/47)-Brick Bradford begins. 134-Last Prince Valiant (all 36 pgs.) 10 20 30 56 76 95
135-151: 135-(6/48)-Lone Ranger begins 9 18 27 52 69 85

ACE KELLY (See Tops Comics & Tops In Humor)

ACE KING (See Adventures of Detective...)

ACES
Acme Press (Eclipse): Apr, 1988 - No. 5, Dec, 1988 ($2.95, B&W, magazine)

1-5 3.00

ACES HIGH
E.C. Comics: Mar-Apr, 1955 - No. 5, Nov-Dec, 1955

1-Not approved by code 30 60 90 240 383 525
2 16 32 48 128 207 285
3-5 15 30 45 120 190 260

NOTE: *All have stories by* **Davis, Evans, Krigstein,** *and* **Wood. Evans** *c-1-5.*

ACES HIGH
Gemstone Publishing: Apr, 1999 - No. 5, Aug, 1999 ($2.50)

1-5-Reprints E.C. issues 4.00
Annual 1 ($13.50) r/#1-5 14.00

ACME NOVELTY LIBRARY, THE
Fantagraphics Books: Winter 1993-94 - Present (quarterly, various sizes)

1-Introduces Jimmy Corrigan; Chris Ware-s/a in all 3 6 9 17 26 35
1-2nd and later printings 1 3 4 6 8 10
2,3: 2-Quimby 2 4 6 10 14 18
4-Sparky's Best Comics & Stories 3 6 9 14 20 25
5-12: Jimmy Corrigan in all 2 4 6 9 12 15
13,15-($10.95-c) 2 4 6 11 16 20
14-($12.95-c) Concludes Jimmy Corrigan saga 22.00
16,19-($15.95, hardcover) Rusty Brown 22.00
17-($16.95, hardcover) Rusty Brown 22.00
18-($17.95, hardcover) 22.00
Jimmy Corrigan, The Smartest Kid on Earth (2000, Pantheon Books, Hardcover, $27.50, 380 pgs.) Collects Jimmy Corrigan stories; folded dust jacket 35.00
Jimmy Corrigan, The Smartest Kid on Earth (2003, Softcover, $17.95) 20.00

NOTE: *Multiple printings exist for most issues.*

ACROSS THE UNIVERSE: THE DC UNIVERSE STORIES OF ALAN MOORE (Also see DC Universe: The Stories of Alan Moore)
DC Comics: 2003 ($19.95, TPB)

nn-Reprints selected Moore stories from '85-'87; Superman, Batman, Swamp Thing app. 20.00

ACTION ADVENTURE (War) (Formerly Real Adventure)
Gillmor Magazines: V1#2, June, 1955 - No. 4, Oct, 1955

V1#2-4 8 16 24 40 50 60

ACTION COMICS (...Weekly #601-642) (Also see The Comics Magazine #1, More Fun #14-17 & Special Edition) (Also see Promotional Comics section)
National Periodical Publ./Detective Comics/DC Comics: 6/38 - No. 583, 9/86; No. 584, 1/87 - No. 904, Oct, 2011

1-Origin & 1st app. Superman by Siegel & Shuster, Marco Polo, Tex Thomson, Pep Morgan, Chuck Dawson & Scoop Scanlon; 1st app. Zatara & Lois Lane; Superman story missing 4 pgs. which were included when reprinted in Superman #1; Clark Kent works for Daily Star; story continued in #2 263,000 526,000 920,500 1,840,000 3,420,000 5,000,000

1-Reprint, Oversize 13-1/2x10". **WARNING:** for its size. DC published it in 1974 with a second cover titling it as a Famous First Edition. There have been many reported cases of the outer cover being removed and the interior sold as the original edition. The reprint with the new outer cover removed is practically worthless. See Famous First Edition for value.

2-O'Mealia non-Superman covers thru #6 13,000 26,000 39,000 97,500 168,750 240,000
3 (Scarce)-Superman apps. in costume in only one panel 8600 17,200 25,800 64,500 112,250 160,000
4,5 3800 7600 11,400 28,500 49,250 70,000
6-1st Jimmy Olsen (called office boy) 3900 7800 11,700 29,250 50,625 72,000
7-1st time the name Superman is printed on a comic cover; 2nd Superman cover 40,000 92,000 138,000 276,000 425,500 575,000
8,9 3000 6000 9000 22,500 39,250 56,000
10-3rd Superman cover by Shuster; splash panel used as cover art for Superman #1 31,000 62,000 93,000 186,000 285,500 385,000
11,14: 1st X-Ray Vision? 14-Clip Carson begins, ends #41; Zatara-c 1400 2800 4200 10,500 18,250 26,000
12-Has 1 panel Batman ad for Det. #27 (5/39); Zatara sci-fi cover 3100 6200 9300 23,200 40,600 58,000
13-Shuster Superman-c; last Scoop Scanlon; centerspread has a 2-page ad for Superman #1 16,700 33,400 50,100 100,000 150,000 200,000
15-Guardineer Superman-c; has ad mentioning Detective Comics and Batman; full page ad for New York World's Fair 1939 with 25¢-c 3080 6160 9240 23,000 40,000 57,000
16-Has full page ad and 1 panel ad for New York World's Fair 1939 25¢ cover edition 780 1560 2340 5850 10,175 14,500
17-Superman cover; last Marco Polo; full page ad for New York World's Fair 1939 with 15¢-c 1840 3680 5520 13,800 23,900 34,000
18-Origin 3 Aces; has a 1 panel ad for New York World's Fair 1939 at the end of the Superman story (ad also in #16,17,19) 780 1560 2340 5850 10,175 14,500
19-Superman covers begin 1730 3460 5190 13,000 22,500 32,000
20-The 'S' left off Superman's chest; Clark Kent works at 'Daily Star' 1675 3350 5025 12,550 21,775 31,000
21-Has 2 ads for More Fun #52 (1st Spectre) 865 1730 2595 6315 11,158 16,000
22 703 1406 2109 5132 9066 13,000
23-1st app. Luthor (w/red hair) & Black Pirate; Black Pirate by Moldoff; 1st mention of The Daily Planet (4/40)-Has 1 panel ad for Spectre in More Fun 5000 10,000 15,000 35,000 57,500 80,000
24,25: 24-Kent at Daily Planet. 25-Last app. Gargantua T. Potts, Tex Thomson's sidekick 524 1048 1572 3825 6763 9700
26,28,30 465 930 1395 3395 5998 8600
27-(8/40) 1st Lois Lane-c 524 1048 1572 3825 6763 9700
29-2nd Lois Lane-c 508 1016 1524 3708 6554 9400
31,32: 32-Intro/1st app. Krypto Ray Gun in Superman story by Burnley 326 652 978 2282 3991 5700
33-Origin Mr. America; Superman by Burnley; has half page ad for All Star Comics #3 349 698 1047 2443 4272 6100
34,35,38,39 314 628 942 2198 3849 5500
36,40: 36-Classic robot-c. 40-(9/41)-Intro/1st app. Star Spangled Kid & Stripesy; Jerry Siegel photo 366 732 1098 2562 4481 6400
37-Origin Congo Bill 314 628 942 2198 3849 5500
41,43-46,48-50: 44-Fat Man's i.d. revealed to Mr. America. 45-1st app. Stuff (Vigilante's Asian sidekick) 300 600 900 1950 3375 4800
42-1st app./origin Vigilante; Bob Daley becomes Fat Man; origin Mr. America's magic flying carpet; The Queen Bee & Luthor app; Black Pirate ends; not in #41 303 606 909 2121 3711 5300
47-1st Luthor cover in comics (4/42) 423 846 1269 3088 5444 7800
51-1st app. The Prankster 300 600 900 1920 3310 4700
52-Fat Man & Mr. America become the Ameri-commandos; origin Vigilante retold; classic Superman and back-ups-c 366 732 1098 2562 4481 6400
53-56,59: 56-Last Fat Man 258 516 774 1651 2826 4000
57-3rd Lois Lane-c in Action (2/43) 265 530 795 1694 2897 4100
58-"Slap a Jap"-c 476 952 1428 3475 6138 8800
60-First app. Lois Lane as Super-woman 290 580 870 1856 3178 4500
61-Historic Atomic Radiation-c (6/43) 300 600 900 2010 3505 5000
62-Japan war-c 252 504 756 1613 2757 3900
63-Japan war-c; last 3 Aces 300 600 900 1950 3375 4800
64-Intro Toyman 216 432 648 1372 3086 3350
65-70: 66-69-Kubert-i on Vigilante 177 354 531 1124 1937 2750
71-79: 74-Last Mr. America 139 278 417 883 1517 2150
80-2nd app. & 1st Mr. Mxyztplk-c (1/45) 166 332 498 1054 1815 2575
81-88,90: 83-Intro Hocus & Pocus 126 252 378 806 1378 1950
89-Classic rainbow cover 158 316 474 1003 1727 2450
91-99: 93-X-Mas-c. 99-1st small logo (8/46) 106 212 318 673 1162 1650
100 145 290 435 921 1586 2250
101-Nuclear explosion-c (10/46) 258 516 774 1651 2826 4000
102-Mxyztplk-c 106 212 318 673 1162 1650

Action Comics #130 © DC

Action Comics #376 © DC

Action Comics #489 © DC

	GD 2.0	VG 4.0	FN 6.0	VF 8.0	VF/NM 9.0	NM- 9.2
103,104,106,107,109-116,118-120:	100	200	300	635	1093	1550
105,117-Christmas covers	103	206	309	659	1130	1600
108-Classic molten metal-c	126	252	378	806	1378	1950
121,122,124-126,128-140: 135,136,138-Zatara by Kubert	95	190	285	603	1039	1475
123-(8/48) Superman flies (See Superman #30 for 1st time he flies, not leaps)	126	252	378	806	1378	1950
127-Vigilante by Kubert; Tommy Tomorrow begins (12/48, see Real Fact #6)	97	194	291	621	1061	1500
141-150,152-155,157,159-161: 161- Last 52 pgs.	97	194	291	621	1061	1400
151-Luthor/Mr. Mxyztplk/Prankster team-up	132	264	396	838	1444	2050
156-Lois as Super Woman	103	206	309	659	1130	1600
158-Origin Superman retold	145	290	435	921	1586	2250
162-180: 168,176-Used in **POP**, pg. 90. 173-Robot-c	86	172	248	546	936	1325
181-201: 191-Intro. Janu in Congo Bill. 198-Last Vigilante. 201-Last pre-code issue	81	162	243	518	884	1250
202-220,232: 212-(1/56)-Includes 1956 Superman calendar that is part of story. 232-1st Curt Swan-c in Action	63	126	189	403	689	975
221-231,233-240: 221-1st S.A. issue. 224-1st Golden Gorilla story. 228-(5/57)-Kongorilla in Congo Bill story (Congorilla try-out)	53	106	159	334	567	800
241,243-251: 241-Batman x-over. 248-Origin/1st app. Congorilla; Congo Bill renamed Congorilla. 251-Last Tommy Tomorrow	45	90	135	284	480	675
242-Origin & 1st app. Brainiac (7/58); 1st mention of Shrunken City of Kandor	825	1650	3300	9900	21,450	33,000
252-Origin & 1st app. Supergirl (5/59); 1st app. Metallo	750	1500	3000	9000	19,500	30,000
253-2nd app. Supergirl	89	178	267	565	970	1375
254-1st meeting of Bizarro & Superman-c/story; 3rd app. Supergirl	65	130	195	416	708	1000
255-1st Bizarro Lois Lane-c/story & both Bizarros leave Earth to make Bizarro World; 4th app. Supergirl	54	108	162	343	574	825
256-260: 259-Red Kryptonite used	36	72	108	216	351	485
261-1st X-Kryptonite which gave Streaky his powers; last Congorilla in Action; origin & 1st app. Streaky The Super Cat	41	82	123	256	428	600
262,264-266,268-270	32	64	96	188	307	425
263-Origin Bizarro World (continues in #264)	40	80	120	246	411	575
267(8/60)-3rd Legion app; 1st app. Chameleon Boy, Colossal Boy, & Invisible Kid, 1st app. of Supergirl as Superwoman.	73	146	219	467	796	1125
271-275,277-282: 274-Lois Lane as Superwoman. 280-Brief origin of Superman & Supergirl retold; Brainiac-c. 282-Last 10¢ issue	26	52	78	152	249	345
276(5/61)-6th Legion app; 1st app. Brainiac 5, Phantom Girl, Triplicate Girl, Bouncing Boy, Sun Boy, & Shrinking Violet; Supergirl joins Legion	69	138	207	442	759	1075
283(12/61)-Legion of Super-Villains app. 1st 12¢	14	28	42	96	211	325
284(1/62)-Mon-El app.	14	28	42	96	211	325
285(2/62)-12th Legion app; Brainiac 5 cameo; Supergirl's existence revealed to world; JFK & Jackie, LBJ & Khrushchev cameos	29	58	87	209	467	725
286-287,289-292,294-299: 286(3/62)-Legion of Super Villains app. 287(4/62)-15th Legion app. (cameo). 289(6/62)-16th Legion app. (Adult); Lightning Man & Saturn Woman's marriage 1st revealed. 290(7/62)-Legion app. (cameo); Phantom Girl app. 1st Supergirl emergency squad. 291-1st meeting Supergirl & Mr. Mxyzptlk. 292-2nd app. Superhorse (see Adv.#293). 297-General Zod, Phantom Zone villains & Mon-El app. 298-General Zod app.; Legion cameo	11	22	33	76	163	250
288-Mon-El app.; r-origin Supergirl	12	24	36	79	170	260
293-Origin Comet (Superhorse)	14	28	42	96	211	325
300-(5/63)	14	28	42	94	207	320
301-303,305,307,308,310-312,315-320: 307-Saturn Girl app. 317-Death of Nor-Kan of Kandor. 319-Shrinking Violet app.	9	18	27	58	114	170
304,306,313: 304-Origin/1st app. Black Flame (9/63). 306-Brainiac 5, Mon-El app. 313-Batman app.	9	18	27	60	120	180
309-(2/64)-Legion app.; Batman & Robin-c & cameo; JFK app. (he died 11/22/63; on stands last week of Dec, 1963)	12	24	36	82	179	275
314-Retells origin Supergirl; J.L.A. x-over	9	18	27	61	123	185
321-333,335-339: 336-Origin Akvar (Flamebird)	7	14	21	48	89	130
334-Giant G-20; origin Supergirl, Streaky, Superhorse & Legion (all-r)	10	20	30	66	138	210
340-Origin, 1st app. of the Parasite; 2 pg. pin-up	16	32	48	111	246	380
341,344,350,358: 341-Batman app. in Supergirl back-up story. 344-Batman x-over. 350-Batman, Green Arrow & Green Lantern app. in Supergirl back-up story. 358-Superboy meets Supergirl	6	12	18	41	76	110
342,343,345,346,348,349,351-357,359: 342-UFO story. 345-Allen Funt/Candid Camera story.	6	12	18	40	73	105
347,360-Giant Supergirl G-33,G-45; 347-Origin Comet-r plus Bizarro story. 360-Legion app.-r; r/origin Supergirl	8	16	24	55	105	155
361-2nd app. Parasite	7	14	21	46	86	125
362-364,367-372,374-378: 362-366-Leper/Death story. 370-New facts about Superman's origin. 376-Last Supergirl in Action; last 12¢-c. 377-Legion begins (thru #392)	5	10	15	33	57	80
365,366: 365-JLA & Legion app. 366-JLA app.	5	10	15	35	63	90
373-Giant Supergirl G-57; Legion-r	8	16	24	52	99	145
379-399,401: 388-Sgt. Rock app. 392-Batman-c/app.; last Legion in Action; Saturn Girl gets new costume. 393-401-All Superman issues. 395-Bonus "Secrets of Superman's Fortress" 2-page spread	3	6	9	19	30	40
400	4	8	12	28	47	65
402-Last 15¢ issue; Superman vs. Supergirl duel	3	6	9	20	31	42
403-413: All 52 pg. issues. 411-Origin Eclipso-(r). 413-Metamorpho begins, ends #418	3	6	9	19	30	40
414-424: 419-Intro. Human Target. 421-Intro Capt. Strong; Green Arrow begins. 422,423-Origin Human Target	2	4	6	9	13	16
425-Neal Adams-a(p); The Atom begins	3	6	9	16	23	30
426-431,433-436,438,439	2	4	6	8	10	12
432-1st Bronze Age Toyman app. (2/74)	3	6	9	14	19	24
437,443-(100 pg. Giants)	4	8	12	28	47	65
440-1st Grell-a on Green Arrow	2	4	6	13	18	22
441,442,444-448: 441-Grell-a on Green Arrow continues	2	4	6	8	10	12
449-(68 pgs.)	2	4	6	10	14	18
450-465,467-470,474-483,486,489-499: 454-Last Atom. 456-Grell Jaws-c. 458-Last Green Arrow	1	2	3	4	5	7
466,487,488: 466-Batman, Flash app. 487,488-(44 pgs.). 487-Origin & 1st app. Microwave Man; origin Atom retold	1	2	3	5	7	9
471-(5/77) 1st app. Faora Hu-Ul	2	4	6	12	16	20
472,473-Faora app. 473-Faora, General Zod app.	2	4	6	10	14	18
481-483,486-492,495-499,501-505,507,508-Whitman variants (low print run; none show issue # on cover)	2	4	6	8	10	12
484-Earth II Superman & Lois Lane wed; 40th anniversary issue(6/78)	2	4	6	10	14	18
484-Variant includes 3-D Superman punchout doll in cello. pack; 4 different inserts; (Canadian promo?)	6	12	18	42	79	115
485-Classic Neal Adams Superman-c	2	4	6	11	16	20
485-Whitman variant	3	6	9	14	20	26
500-($1.00, 68 pgs.)-Infinity-c; Superman life story retold; shows Legion statues in museum	2	4	6	13	18	22
501-520,522-543,545,547-551: 511-514-Airwave II solo stories. 513-The Atom begins. 517-Aquaman begins; ends #541. 528-530-Three-part Brainiac storyline. 532,536-New Teen Titans cameo. 535,536-Omega Men app. 551-Starfire becomes Red-Star						6.00
521-1st app. The Vixen	5	10	15	31	53	75
544-(6/83, Mando paper, 68 pgs.)-45th Anniversary issue; origins new Luthor & Brainiac; Omega Men cameo; Shuster-a (pin-up); article by Siegel	2	4	6	10	14	18
546-J.L.A., New Teen Titans app.	2	4	6	8	10	12
552,553-Animal Man, Cave Carson, Congorilla, Sea Devils-c/app.; Dolphin, Immortal Man, Rip Hunter, Suicide Squad app (2/84 & 3/84)	1	2	3	5	6	7
554-582: 577-Intro. Caitiff, the First Vampire						5.00
583-(9/86) Alan Moore scripts; last Earth 1 Superman story (cont'd from Superman #423)	3	6	9	14	20	26
584-(1/87) Byrne-a begins; New Teen Titans app.						6.00
585-599: 586-Legends x-over. 595-1st app. Silver Banshee. 596-Millennium x-over; Spectre app. 598-1st Checkmate						4.00
600-($2.50, 84 pgs., 5/88)	1	3	4	6	8	10
601-642: (#601-642 are weekly issues) ($1.50, 52 pgs.) 601-Re-intro The Secret Six; death of Katma Tui. 611-614-Catwoman stories (new costume in #611). 613-618-Nightwing stories						5.00
643-Superman & monthly issues begin again; Perez-c/a/scripts begin; swipes cover to Superman #1						6.00
644-649,651-661,663-666,668-673,675-682: 645-1st app. Maxima. 654-Part 3 of Batman storyline. 655-Free extra 8 pgs. 660-Death of Lex Luthor. 661-Begin $1.00-c. 675-Deathstroke cameo. 679-Last $1.00 issue						4.00
650,667: 650-($1.50, 52 pgs.)-Lobo cameo (last panel). 667-($1.75, 52 pgs.)						5.00
662-Clark Kent reveals i.d. to Lois Lane; story cont'd in Superman #53						5.00
674-Supergirl logo & c/story (reintro)	1	2	3	5	6	8
683-1st Jackal; Doomsday cameo	3	6	9	15	22	28
683-685-2nd & 3rd printings						3.00
684,685: 684-Doomsday battle issue. 685-Funeral for a Friend issue; Supergirl app.	2	4	6	10	14	18
686-Funeral for a Friend issue; Supergirl app.						5.00
687-($1.95)-Collector's Ed.w/die-cut-c						5.00
687-($1.50)-Newsstand Edition with mini-poster						4.00
688-699,701-703-($1.50): 688-Guy Gardner-c/story. 697-Bizarro-c/story. 703-(9/94)-Zero Hour						4.00

Action Comics #745 © DC

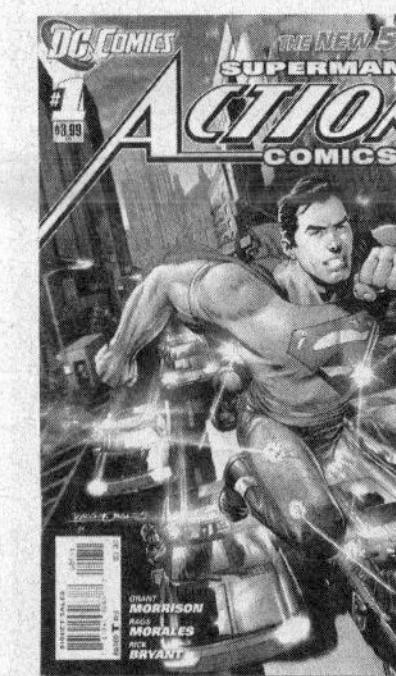

Action Comics (2011 series) #1 © DC

Action Comics #1018 © DC

	GD	VG	FN	VF	VF/NM	NM-
	2.0	4.0	6.0	8.0	9.0	9.2

695-($2.50)-Collector's Edition w/embossed foil-c 500

700-($2.95, 68 pgs.)-Fall of Metropolis Pt 1, Guice-a; Pete Ross marries Lana Lang and Smallville flashbacks with Curt Swan art & Murphy Anderson inks 5.00

700-Platinum 18.00

700-Gold 20.00

0(10/94), 704(11/94)-719,721-731: 710-Begin $1.95-c. 714-Joker app. 719-Batman-c/app. 721-Mr. Mxyzptlk app. 723-Dave Johnson-c. 727-Final Night x-over. 4.00

720-Lois breaks off engagement w/Clark 5.00

720-2nd print. 4.00

732-749,751-764,767,767: 732-New powers. 733-New costume, Ray app. 738-Immonen-s/a(p) begins. 741-Legion app. 744-Millennium Giants x-over. 745-747-70's-style Superman vs. Prankster. 753-JLA-c/app. 757-Hawkman-c. 760-1st Encantadora. 761-Wonder Woman app. 766-Batman-c/app. 4.00

750-($2.95) 5.00

765-Joker & Harley-c/app. 2 4 6 8 11 14

768,769,771-774: 768-Begin $2.25-c; Marvel Family-c/app. 771-Nightwing-c/app. 772,773-Ra's al Ghul app. 774-Martian Manhunter-c/app. 4.00

770-($3.50) Conclusion of Emperor Joker x-over 6.00

775-($3.75) Bradstreet-c; intro. The Elite 3 6 9 14 19 24

775-(2nd printing) 1 3 4 6 8 10

776-799: 776-Farewell to Krypton; Rivoche-c. 780-782-Our Worlds at War x-over. 781-Hippolyta and Major Lane killed. 782-War ends. 784-Joker: Last Laugh; Batman & Green Lantern app. 793-Return to Krypton. 795-The Elite app. 798-Van Fleet-c 3.00

800-(4/03, $3.95) Struzan painted-c; guest artists include Ross, Jim Lee, Jurgens, Sale 1 3 4 6 8 10

801-811: 801-Raney-a. 809-The Creeper app. 811-Mr. Majestic app. 3.00

812-Godfall part 1; Turner-c; Caldwell-a(p) 4.00

812-2nd printing; B&W sketch-c by Turner 3.00

813-Godfall pt. 4; Turner-c; Caldwell-a(p) 4.00

814-824,826-828,830-834,836: 814-Reis-a/Art Adams-c; Darkseid app.; begin $2.50-c. 815,816-Teen Titans-c/app. 820-Doomsday app. 826-Capt. Marvel app. 827-Byrne-c/a begin. 831-Villains United tie-in. 836-Infinite Crisis; revised origin 3.00

825-($2.99, 40 pgs.) Doomsday app. 4.00

829-Omac Project x-over Sacrifice pt. 2 5.00

829-(2nd printing) red tone cover 4.00

835-1st Livewire app. in regular DCU 2 4 6 11 16 20

837-843-One Year Later; powers return after Infinite Crisis; Johns & Busiek-s 3.00

844-Donner & Johns-s/Adam Kubert-a/c begin; brown-toned cover 4.00

844-Andy Kubert variant-c 6.00

844-2nd printing with red-toned Adam Kubert cover 3.00

845-849,851-857: 845-Bizarro-c/app.; re-intro. General Zod, Ursa & Non. 846-Jax-Ur app. 847-849-No Kubert-a. 851-Kubert-a/c. 855-857-Bizarro app.; Powell-a/c 3.00

850-($3.99) Supergirl and LSH app., origin re-told; Guedes-a/c 4.00

858-($3.50) Legion of Super-Heroes app.; 1st meeting re-told; Johns-s/Frank-a/c 4.00

858-Variant-c (Superman & giant Brainiac robot) by Frank 5.00

858-Second printing with regular cover with red background instead of yellow 3.00

858-Special Edition (7/10, $1.00) r/#858 with "What's Next?" cover logo 3.00

859-878: 859-863-Legion of Super-Heroes app.; var-c on each (859-Andy Kubert. 860-Lightle. 861-Grell. 862-Giffen. 863-Frank) 864-Batman and Lightning Lad app. 866-Brainiac returns 869-"Soda Pop" cover edition, 870-Pa Kent dies. 871-New Krypton; Ross-c 3.00

869-Initial printing recalled because of beer bottles on cover 6 12 18 38 69 100

879-896: 879-($3.99) Back-up Capt. Atom feature begins. 890-Luthor stories begin. 893-Comics debut of Chloe Sullivan (Smallville TV show) in regular DCU. 894-Death (Sandman) app. 896-Secret Six app. 4.00

897-899, 901-903-($2.99) 897-Joker app. 898-Larfleeze app. 899-Brainiac app. 3.00

900 (6/11, $5.99, 96 pgs.) Conclusion of Luthor Black Ring saga; Doomsday app.; bonus short stories by various; Superman renounces U.S. citizenship 6.00

904-(10/11) Last issue of first volume; Doomsday app.; Rocafort-c 3.00

904-Variant-c by Ordway 5.00

#1,000,000 (11/98) Gene Ha-c; 853rd Century x-over 3.00

Annual 1 ('87, $2.95) Art Adams-c/a(p); Batman app. 1 2 3 5 6 8

Annual 2-6 ('89-'94, $2.95)-2-Pérez-c/a(i). 3-Armageddon 2001. 4-Eclipso vs. Shazam. 5-Bloodlines; 1st app. Loose Cannon. 6-Elseworlds story 4.00

Annual 7,9 ('95, '97, $3.95) 7-Year One story. 9-Pulp Heroes story 4.00

Annual 8 (1996, $2.95) Legends of the Dead Earth story 4.00

Annual 10 ('07, $3.99) Short stories by Johns & Donner and various incl. A. Adams, J. Kubert, Wight, Morales; origin of Phantom Zone, Mon-El; Metallo app.; Adam & Joe Kubert-c 6.00

Annual 11 (7/08, $4.99) Conclusion to General Zod story continued from #851; Kubert-a 5.00

Annual 12 (8/09, $4.99) Origin of Nightwing and Flamebird 5.00

Annual 13 (2/11, $4.99) 1st meeting of Luthor and Darkseid; Ra's al Ghul app. 5.00

NOTE:***Supergirl's*** *origin in 262, 280, 285, 291, 305, 309.* **N. Adams** *c-356, 358, 359, 361-364, 366, 367, 370-374, 377-379i, 398-400, 402, 404,405, 419p, 466, 468, 469, 473i, 485.* **Aparo** *a-642.* **Austin** *c/a-682i.* **Baily** *a-24, 25.* **Boring** *a-164, 194, 211, 223, 233, 241, 250, 261, 266-268, 346, 348, 352, 356, 357.* **Burnley** *a-28-33; c-48?, 53-55, 58, 59?, 60-63, 65, 66p, 67p, 70p, 71p, 79p, 82p, 84-86p, 90-92p, 93p?, 94p, 107p, 108p.* **Byrne** *a-584-598p, 599i, 600p; c-584-591, 596-600.* **Ditko** *a-642.* **Giffen** *a-560, 563, 565, 577, 579; c-539, 560, 563, 565, 577, 579.* **Grell** *a-440-442, 444-446, 450-452, 456-458; c-456.* **Guardineer** *a-24, 25; c-8, 11, 12, 14-16, 18. 25.* **Guice** *a(p)-676-681, 683-698, 700; c-683, 685, 686, 687(direct), 688-693i, 694-696, 697i, 698-700.* **Infantino** *a-642.* **Kaluta** *c-613.* **Bob Kane's** *Clip Carson-14-41.* **Gil Kane** *a-443r, 493r, 539-541, 544-546, 551-554, 601-605, 642; c-535p, 540, 541, 544p, 545-549, 551-554, 580, 627.* **Kirby** *c-638.* **Meskin** *a-42-121(most).* **Mignola** *a-600, Annual 2; c-c-614.* **Moldoff** *a-23-25, 443r.* **Mooney** *a-667p.* **Mortimer** *c-153, 154, 159-172, 174, 178-181, 184, 186-189, 191-193, 196, 200, 206.* **Orlando** *a-617p; c-621.* **Perez** *a-600i, 643-652p, Annual 2p; c-529p, 602, 643-651, Annual 2p.* **Quesada** *c-Annual 4p.* **Fred Ray** *c-34, 36-46, 50-52.* **Siegel & Shuster** *a-1-27.* **Paul Smith** *c-608.* **Starlin** *a-509; c-631.* **Leonard Starr** *a-597i(part),* **Staton** *a-525p, 526p, 531p, 535p, 536p.* **Swan/Moldoff** *c-281, 286, 287, 293, 298, 334.* **Thibert** *c-676, 677p, 678-681, 684.* **Toth** *a-406, 407, 413, 431; c-616.* **Tuska** *a-486p, 550.* **Williamson** *a-568i.* **Zeck** *c-Annual 5*

ACTION COMICS (2nd series)(DC New 52)(Numbering reverts to original V1 #957 after #52)
DC Comics: Nov, 2011 - No. 52, Jul, 2016 ($3.99)

1-Grant Morrison-s/Rags Morales-a/c; re-introduces Superman 2 4 6 8 11 14

1-Variant-c by Jim Lee of Superman in new armor costume 2 4 6 10 14 18

1-(2nd - 5th printings) 4.00

2-12: 2-Morales & Brent Anderson-a; behind the scenes sketch art and commentary. 3-Gene Ha & Morales-a. 4-Re-intro. Steel. 5-Flashback to Krypton; Andy Kubert-a. 6-Legion of Super-Heroes app.; Andy Kubert-a. 7-Gets the new costume; intro. Steel 4.00

2-12-Variant covers. 2-Van Sciver. 3-Ha. 4-Choi. 5,6-Morales. 8-Frank 5.00

13-17,19-23: 13-Re-intro of Krypto. 14-Neil deGrasse Tyson app. 15-Legion app. 4.00

18-($4.99) Last Morrison-s; Mxyzptlk, The Legion and the Wanderers app. 5.00

23.1, 23.2, 23.3, 23.4 (11/13, $2.99, regular covers) 3.00

23.1 (11/13, $3.99, 3-D cover) "Cyborg Superman #1" on cover; Zor-El & Brainiac app. 5.00

23.2 (11/13, $3.99, 3-D cover) "Zod #1" on cover; origin of Zod on Krypton; Faora app. 5.00

23.3 (11/13, $3.99, 3-D cover) "Lex Luthor #1" on cover; Kuder-c 5.00

23.4 (11/13, $3.99, 3-D cover) "Metallo #1" on cover; Fisch-s/Pugh-a 5.00

24-49,51,52: 25-Zero Year. 30-Doomsday app. 31-35-Doomed x-over. 40-Bizarro app. 51-Supergirl app. 52-Wonder Woman, Batman and pre-Flashpoint Superman app. 4.00

50-($4.99) Vandal Savage and the Justice League app. 5.00

#0 (11/12, $3.99) Flashback to Lois' 1st Superman sighting; Oliver-a; 4.00

Annual 1 (12/12, $4.99) Superman vs. K-Man; Fisch-s/Hamner-a; Atomic Skull app. 5.00

Annual 2 (12/13, $4.99) Rocafort & Jurgens-a; H'El & Faora app.; back-up Mad sampler 5.00

Annual 3 (9/14, $4.99) Superman Doomed x-over; Brainiac app. 5.00

...: Futures End 1 (11/14, $2.99, regular-c) Five years later; Alixe-a 3.00

...: Futures End 1 (11/14, $3.99, 3-D cover) 4.00

ACTION COMICS (Numbering reverts to original V1 #957 after #52 from 2011-2016 series)
DC Comics: No. 957, Aug, 2016 - Present ($2.99/$3.99)

957-974: 957-Jurgens-s/Zircher-a; the pre-52 Superman vs. Lex Luthor & Doomsday. 960-962-Wonder Woman app. 973-Superwoman & Steel app. 3.00

975-($3.99) Superman Reborn pt. 2; back-up with Mxyzptlk; Dini-s/Churchill-a 4.00

976-986,992-999: 976-Superman Reborn pt. 4. 977,978-Origin revised. 979-Cyborg Superman returns. 984-Intro Ursa and Lor-Zod. 992-998-Booster Gold app. 3.00

987-991-($2.99) The Oz Effect regular covers; Jor-El returns 3.00

987-991-($3.99) The Oz Effect lenticular covers 4.00

1000-(6/18, $7.99) Short stories and pin-ups by various incl. Jurgens, Swan, Coipel, Ordway, Gleason, García-López; intro. Rogol Zaar; Bendis-s/Jim Lee-a; 9 covers 8.00

1001-1028: 1001-Intro. Red Cloud; Gleason-a. 1004-1006-Sook-a. 1007-1011-Leviathan Rising; Epting-a. 1012-1016-Kudranski-a; Red Cloud and Thorn app. 1015-1016-Batman & Naomi app. 1017-1027-Romita, Jr.-a. 1017-1021-Legion of Doom app. 1020-1022-Young Justice app. 4.00

... Special 1 (7/18, $4.99) Jurgens-s/Conrad-a; Russell-s/Thompson-a; Landis-s/Manapul-a 5.00

ACTION COMICS
DC Comics: (no date)

1-Ashcan comic, not distributed to newsstands, only for in-house use. Cover art is the rejected art to Detective Comics #2 and interior from Detective Comics #1. A CGC certified 9.0 copy sold for $17,825 in 2002, $29,000 in 2008, and $50,000 in 2010.

ACTION FORCE (Also see G.I. Joe European Missions)
Marvel Comics Ltd. (British): Mar, 1987 - No. 50, 1988 ($1.00, weekly, magazine)

1,3: British G.I. Joe series. 3-w/poster insert 2 4 6 9 13 16

2,4 1 2 3 5 6 8

5-10 5.00

11-50 3.00

...Special 1 (7/87) Summer holiday special; Snake Eyes-c/app. 2 4 6 8 10 12

...Special 2 (10/87) Winter special 5.00

ACTION FUNNIES
DC Comics: 1937/1938

nn - Ashcan comic, not distributed to newsstands, only for in house use. Cover art is Action Comics #3 and interior from Detective Comics #10. The Mallette/Brown copy in VG+ condition sold for $15,000 in 2005. A VF+ copy sold for $10,157.50 in 2012.

ACTION GIRL
Slave Labor Graphics: Oct, 1994 - No. 19 ($2.50/$2.75/$2.95, B&W)

Adam Strange (2004 series) #1 © DC

Addams Family: The Bodies Issue © MGM

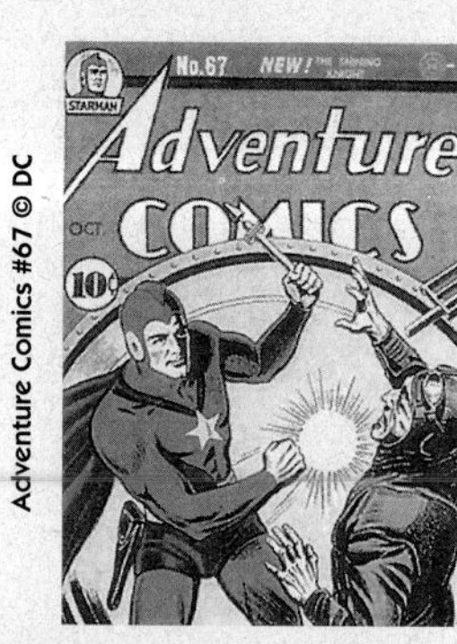

Adventure Comics #67 © DC

	GD	VG	FN	VF	VF/NM	NM-
	2.0	4.0	6.0	8.0	9.0	9.2

1-19: 4-Begin $2.75-c. 19-Begin $2.95-c 4.00
1-6 ($2.75, 2nd printings): All read 2nd Print in indicia. 1-(2/96). 2-(10/95). 3-(2/96). 4-(7/96). 5-(2/97). 6-(9/97) 3.00
1-4 ($2.75, 3rd printings): All read 3rd Print in indicia. 3.00

ACTION MAN (Based on the Hasbro G.I. Joe-type action figure)
IDW Publishing: Jun, 2016 - No. 4, Sept, 2016 ($3.99, limited series)
1-4-John Barber-s/Paolo Villanelli-a 4.00
...: Revolution (10/16, $3.99) Tie-in to Hasbro toy titles x-over; Barber-s/Villanelli-a 4.00

ACTION PHILOSOPHERS!
Dark Horse Comics: Oct, 2014 ($1.00, one-shot)
1-Van Lente-s/Dunlavey-a 3.00

ACTION PLANET COMICS
Action Planet: 1996 - No. 3, Sept, 1997 ($3.95, B&W, 44 pgs.)
1-3: 1-Intro Monster Man by Mike Manley & other stories 4.00
Giant Size Action Planet Halloween Special (1998, $5.95, oversized) 6.00

ACTUAL CONFESSIONS (Formerly Love Adventures)
Atlas Comics (MPI): No. 13, Oct, 1952 - No. 14, Dec, 1952
13,14 14 28 42 76 108 140

ACTUAL ROMANCES (Becomes True Secrets #3 on?)
Marvel Comics (IPS): Oct, 1949 - No. 2, Jan, 1950 (52 pgs.)
1-Photo-c 20 40 60 115 185 255
2-Photo-c 14 28 42 80 115 150

A.D.: AFTER DEATH
Image Comics: Book 1, Nov, 2016 - Book 3, May, 2017 ($5.99, limited series, square-bound 8"x11")
1-3-Scott Snyder-s/Jeff Lemire-a 6.00

ADAM AND EVE
Spire Christian Comics (Fleming H. Revell Co.): 1975,1978 (35¢/39¢/49¢)
nn-By Al Hartley (1975 edition) 3 6 9 14 20 25
nn (1978 edition) 2 4 6 10 14 18

ADAM: LEGEND OF THE BLUE MARVEL
Marvel Comics: Jan, 2009 - No. 5, May, 2009 ($3.99, limited series)
1-First app. Blue Marvel (Adam Brashear); Grevioux-s/Broome-a; Avengers app.
17 34 51 117 259 400
2 6 12 18 41 76 110
3-5: 4-Namor app. 4 8 12 23 37 50

ADAM STRANGE (Also see Green Lantern #132, Mystery In Space #53 & Showcase #17)
DC Comics: 1990 - No. 3, 1990 ($3.95, 52 pgs, limited series, squarebound)
Book One - Three: Andy & Adam Kubert-c/a 4.00
...: The Man of Two Worlds (2003, $19.95, TPB) r/#1-3; sketch pages by Andy Kubert 20.00

ADAM STRANGE (Leads into the Rann/Thanagar War mini-series)
DC Comics: Nov, 2004 - No. 8, June, 2005 ($2.95, limited series)
1-8-Andy Diggle-s/Pascal Ferry-a/c. 1-Superman app. 3.00
...: Planet Heist TPB (2005, $19.99) r/series; sketch pages 20.00
... Special (11/08, $3.50) Takes place during Rann/Thanagar Holy War series; Starlin-s 4.00

ADAM STRANGE / FUTURE QUEST SPECIAL
DC Comics: May, 2017 ($4.99, one-shot)
1-Adam Strange meets Jonny Quest and team; back-up Top Cat story; Batman app. 5.00

ADAM-12 (TV)
Gold Key: Dec, 1973 - No. 10, Feb, 1976 (Photo-c)
1 6 12 18 38 69 100
2-10 4 8 12 23 37 50

ADDAMS FAMILY (TV cartoon)
Gold Key: Oct, 1974 - No. 3, Apr, 1975 (Hanna-Barbera)
1 8 16 24 51 96 140
2,3 5 10 15 34 60 85

ADDAMS FAMILY
IDW Publishing: Oct, 2019 ($4.99, one-shot)
...: The Bodies Issue - Zöe Quinn-s/Philip Murphy-a 5.00

ADLAI STEVENSON
Dell Publishing Co.: Dec, 1966
12-007-612-Life story; photo-c 3 6 9 21 33 45

ADOLESCENT RADIOACTIVE BLACK BELT HAMSTERS (See Clint)
Comic Castle/Eclipse Comics: 1986 - No. 9, Jan, 1988 ($1.50, B&W)
1-9: 1st & 2nd printings exist 4.00
1-Limited Edition 7.00
1-In 3-D (7/86), 2-4 ($2.50) 4.00
Massacre The Japanese Invasion #1 (8/89, $2.00) 4.00

ADOLESCENT RADIOACTIVE BLACK BELT HAMSTERS
Dynamite Entertainment: 2008 - No. 4, 2008 ($3.50, limited series)
1-4-Tom Nguyen-a/Keith Champagne-s; 2 covers by Nguyen and Oeming 3.50

ADRENALYNN (See The Tenth)
Image Comics: Aug, 1999 - No. 4, Feb, 2000 ($2.50)
1-4-Tony Daniel-s/Marty Egeland-a; origin of Adrenalynn 3.00

ADULT TALES OF TERROR ILLUSTRATED (See Terror Illustrated)

ADVANCED DUNGEONS & DRAGONS (Also see TSR Worlds)
DC Comics: Dec, 1988 - No. 36, Dec, 1991 (Newsstand #1 is Holiday, 1988-89) ($1.25-$1.75)
1-Based on TSR role playing game 1 3 4 6 8 10
2-36: 25-$1.75-c begins 4.00
Annual 1 (1990, $3.95, 68 pgs.) 5.00

ADVENTURE BOUND
Dell Publishing Co.: Aug, 1949
Four Color 239 6 12 18 38 69 100

ADVENTURE COMICS (Formerly New Adventure)(...Presents Dial H For Hero #479-490)
National Periodical Publications/DC Comics: No. 32, 11/38 - No. 490, 2/82; No. 491, 9/82 - No. 503, 9/83
32-Anchors Aweigh (ends #52), Barry O'Neil (ends #60, not in #33), Captain Desmo (ends #47), Dale Daring (ends #47), Federal Men (ends #70), The Golden Dragon (ends #36), Rusty & His Pals (ends #52) by Bob Kane, Todd Hunter (ends #38) and Tom Brent (ends #39) begin 550 1100 1650 2970 4485 6000
33-35,38 370 740 1110 1998 2999 4000
36 (scarce) 650 1300 1950 3510 5255 7000
37-Cover used on Double Action #2 460 920 1380 2484 3742 5000
39(6/39)- Jack Wood begins, ends #42; early mention of Marijuana in comics
390 780 1170 2106 3153 4200
40-(Rare, 7/39, on stands 6/10/39)-The Sandman begins by Bert Christman (who died in WWII); believed to be 1st conceived story (see N.Y. World's Fair for 1st published app.); Socko Strong begins, ends #54 7400 14,800 22,200 54,800 119,900 185,000
41-O'Mealia shark-c 660 1320 1980 4818 8509 12,200
42,44-Sandman-c by Flessel. 44-Opium story 919 1838 2757 6709 11,855 17,000
43,45: 45-Full page ad for Flash Comics #1 470 940 1410 3431 6066 8700
46,47-Sandman covers by Flessel. 47-Steve Conrad Adventurer begins, ends #76
692 1384 2076 5052 8926 12,800
48-1st app. The Hourman by Bernard Baily; Baily-c (Hourman c-48,50,52-59)
2800 5600 8400 20,900 43,450 66,000
49 300 600 900 2010 3505 5000
50-2nd Hourman-c; Cotton Carver by Jack Lehti begins, ends #64
320 640 960 2240 3920 5600
51,60-Sandman-c: 51-Sandman-c by Flessel. 400 800 1200 2800 4900 7000
52-59: 53-1st app. Jimmy "Minuteman" Martin & the Minutemen of America in Hourman; ends #78. 58-Paul Kirk Manhunter begins (1st app.), ends #72
271 542 813 1734 2967 4200
61-1st app. Starman by Jack Burnley (4/41); Starman c-61-72; Starman by Burnley in #61-80
1340 2680 4020 10,000 19,500 29,000
62-65,67,68,70: 67-Origin & 1st app. The Mist; classic Burnley-c. 70-Last Federal Men
258 516 774 1651 2826 4000
66-Origin/1st app. Shining Knight (9/41) 300 600 900 1950 3375 4800
69-1st app. Sandy the Golden Boy (Sandman's sidekick) by Paul Norris (in a Bob Kane style); Sandman dons new costume 298 596 894 1907 3279 4650
71-Jimmy Martin becomes costumed aide to the Hourman; 1st app. Hourman's Miracle Ray machine 258 516 774 1651 2826 4000
72-1st Simon & Kirby Sandman (3/42, 1st DC work)
975 1950 2919 7100 13,050 19,000
73-Origin Manhunter by Simon & Kirby; begin new series; Manhunter-c (scarce)
1275 2550 3825 9550 18,275 27,000
74-78,80: 74-Thorndyke replaces Jimmy, Hourman's assistant; new Sandman-c begin by S&K. 75-Thor app. by Kirby; 1st Kirby Thor (see Tales of the Unexpected #16). 77-Origin Genius Jones; Mist story. 80-Last S&K Manhunter & Burnley Starman
194 388 582 1242 2121 3000
79-Classic Manhunter-c 303 606 909 2121 3711 5300
81-90: 83-Last Hourman. 84-Mike Gibbs begins, ends #102
123 246 369 787 1344 1900
91-Last Simon & Kirby Sandman 126 252 378 808 1378 1950
92-99,101,102: 92-Last Manhunter. 101-Shining Knight origin retold. 102-Last Starman, Sandman, & Genius Jones; most-S&K-c (Genius Jones cont'd in More Fun #108)
97 194 291 621 1061 1500
100-S&K-c 135 270 405 864 1482 2100

Adventure Comics #143 © DC

Adventure Comics #297 © DC

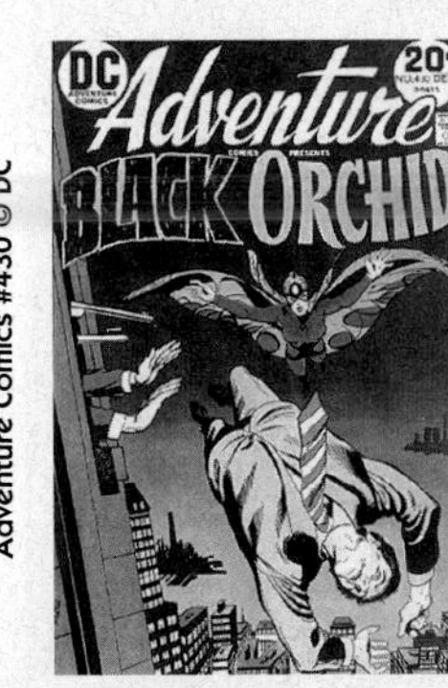

Adventure Comics #430 © DC

	GD 2.0	VG 4.0	FN 6.0	VF 8.0	VF/NM 9.0	NM- 9.2
103-Aquaman, Green Arrow, Johnny Quick & Superboy all move over from More Fun Comics #107; 8th app. Superboy; Superboy-c begin; 1st small logo (4/46)	309	618	927	2163	3782	5400
104	123	246	369	787	1344	1900
105-110	84	168	252	538	919	1300
111-120: 113-X-Mas-c	74	148	222	470	810	1150
121,122-126,128-130: 128-1st meeting Superboy & Lois Lane	69	138	207	442	759	1075
127-Brief origin Shining Knight retold	71	142	213	454	777	1100
131-141,143-149: 132-Shining Knight 1st return to King Arthur time; origin aide Sir Butch	61	122	183	390	670	950
142-Origin Shining Knight & Johnny Quick retold	77	154	231	493	847	1200
150,151,153,155,157,159,161,163-All have 6 pg. Shining Knight stories by Frank Frazetta. 159-Origin Johnny Quick. 161-1st Lana Lang app. in this title	74	148	222	470	810	1150
152,154,156,158,160,162,164-169: 166-Last Shining Knight. 168-Last 52 pg. issue	54	108	162	343	574	825
170-180	52	104	156	328	552	775
181-199: 189-B&W and color illo in **POP**	50	100	150	315	533	750
200 (5/54)	60	120	180	381	653	925
201-208: 207-Last Johnny Quick (not in 205)	47	94	141	296	498	700
209-Last pre-code issue; origin Speedy	50	100	150	315	535	750
210-1st app. Krypto (Superdog)-c/story (3/55)	700	1400	2800	6300	11,150	16,000
211-213,215-219	45	90	135	284	480	675
214-2nd app. Krypto	103	206	309	659	1130	1600
220-Krypto-c/sty	54	108	162	343	574	825
221-228,230-246: 237-1st Intergalactic Vigilante Squadron (6/57). 239-Krypto-c	37	74	111	222	361	500
229-1st S.A. issue; Green Arrow & Aquaman app.	30	60	90	216	483	750
247(4/58)-1st Legion of Super Heroes app.; 1st app. Cosmic Boy, Saturn Girl & Lightning Boy (later Lightning Lad in #267) (origin)	975	1950	3900	9750	20,375	31,000
248-252,254,255-Green Arrow in all: 255-Intro. Red Kryptonite in Superboy (used in #252 but with no effect)	34	68	102	199	325	450
253-1st meeting of Superboy & Robin; Green Arrow by Kirby in #250-255 (also see World's Finest #96-99)	41	82	123	256	428	600
256-Origin Green Arrow by Kirby	75	150	225	488	1069	1650
257-259: 258-Green Arrow x-over in Superboy	27	54	81	162	266	370
260-1st Silver Age origin Aquaman (5/59)	106	212	318	848	1699	2550
261-265,268,270: 262-Origin Speedy in Green Arrow. 270-Congorilla begins, ends #281,283	22	44	66	128	209	290
266-(11/59)-Origin & 1st app. Aquagirl (tryout, not same as later character)	34	68	102	199	325	450
267(12/59)-2nd Legion of Super Heroes; Lightning Boy now called Lightning Lad; new costumes for Legion	98	196	294	617	1784	2950
269-Intro. Aqualad (2/60); last Green Arrow (not in #206)	61	122	183	390	670	950
271-Origin Luthor retold	52	104	156	328	552	775
272-274,277-280: 279-Intro White Kryptonite in Superboy. 280-1st meeting Superboy & Lori Lemaris	20	40	60	118	192	265
275-Origin Superman-Batman team retold (see World's Finest #94)	34	68	102	204	332	460
276-(9/60) Robinson Crusoe-like story	21	42	63	122	199	275
281,284,287-289: 281-Last Congorilla. 284-Last Aquaman in Adv.; Mooney-a. 287,288-Intro Dev-Em, the Knave from Krypton. 287-1st Bizarro Perry White & Jimmy Olsen. 288-Bizarro-c. 289-Legion cameo (statues)	19	38	57	111	176	240
282(3/61)-5th Legion app; intro/origin Star Boy	42	84	126	265	445	625
283-Intro. The Phantom Zone; 1st app. of General Zod (cameo in 2 panels)	90	180	270	576	988	1400
285-1st Tales of the Bizarro World-c/story (ends #299) in Adv. (see Action #255)	25	50	75	150	245	340
286-1st Bizarro Mxyzptlk; Bizarro-c	23	46	69	136	223	310
290(11/61)-9th Legion app; origin Sunboy in Legion (last 10¢ issue)	37	74	111	222	361	500
291,292,295-298: 291-1st 12¢ ish, (12/61). 292-1st Bizarro Lana Lang & Lucy Lane. 295-Bizarro-c; 1st Bizarro Titano	10	20	30	64	132	200
293(2/62)-13th Legion app; Mon-El app.; Legion of Super Pets 1st app./origin; 1st Superhorse; 2nd app. General Zod; 1st Bizarro Luthor & Kandor	39	78	117	231	378	525
294-1st Bizarro Marilyn Monroe, Pres. Kennedy.	13	26	39	86	188	290
299-1st Gold Kryptonite (8/62)	10	20	30	69	147	225
300-Tales of the Legion of Super-Heroes series begins (9/62); Mon-El leaves Phantom Zone (temporarily), joins Legion	55	110	165	440	1120	1800
301-Origin Bouncing Boy	16	32	48	108	239	370
302-305: 303-1st app. Matter-Eater Lad. 304-Death of Lightning Lad in Legion	13	26	39	86	188	290
306-310: 306-Intro. Legion of Substitute Heroes. 307-1st app. Element Lad in Legion. 308-1st app. Lightning Lass in Legion. 309-1st app. Legion of Super-Monsters	12	24	36	79	170	260
311-320: 312-Lightning Lad back in Legion. 315-Last new Superboy story; Colossal Boy app. 316-Origins & powers of Legion given. 317-Intro. Dream Girl in Legion; Lightning Lass becomes Light Lass; Hall of Fame series begins. 320-Dev-Em 2nd app.	10	20	30	64	132	200
321-Intro. Time Trapper	9	18	27	60	120	180
322-330: 327-Intro/1st app. Lone Wolf in Legion. 329-Intro The Bizarro Legionnaires; intro. Legion flight rings	8	16	24	55	105	155
331-340: 337-Chlorophyll Kid & Night Girl app. 340-Intro Computo in Legion	8	16	24	51	96	140
341-Triplicate Girl becomes Duo Damsel	7	14	21	48	89	130
342-345,347-351: 345-Last Hall of Fame; returns in 356,371. 348-Origin Sunboy; intro Dr. Regulus in Legion. 349-Intro Universo & Rond Vidar. 351-1st app. White Witch	6	12	18	42	79	115
346-1st app. Karate Kid, Princess Projectra, Ferro Lad, & Nemesis Kid.	22	44	66	154	340	525
352,354-360: 354,355-Superman meets the Adult Legion. 355-Insect Queen joins Legion (4/67)	6	12	18	38	69	100
353-Death of Ferro Lad in Legion	10	20	30	68	144	220
361-364,366,368-370: 369-Intro Mordru in Legion	5	10	15	35	63	90
365,367: 365-Intro Shadow Lass (memorial to Shadow Woman app. in #354's Adult Legion-s); lists origins & powers of L.S.H. 367-New Legion headquarters	7	14	21	48	89	130
371,372: 371-Intro. Chemical King (mentioned in #354's Adult Legion-s). 372-Timber Wolf & Chemical King join	6	12	18	42	79	115
373,374,376-380: 373-Intro. Tornado Twins (Barry Allen Flash descendants). 374-Article on comics fandom. 380-Last Legion in Adventure; last 12¢-c	5	10	15	34	60	85
375-Intro Quantum Queen & The Wanderers	6	12	18	37	66	95
381-Supergirl begins; 1st full length Supergirl story & her 1st solo book (6/69)	14	28	42	98	217	335
382-389	5	10	15	31	53	75
390-Giant Supergirl G-69	6	12	18	41	76	110
391-396,398	4	8	12	23	37	50
397-1st app. new Supergirl	5	10	15	33	57	80
399-Unpubbed G.A. Black Canary story	4	8	12	27	44	60
400-New costume for Supergirl (12/70)	5	10	15	35	63	90
401,402,404-408-(15¢-c)	3	6	9	17	26	35
403-68 pg. Giant G-81; Legion-r/#304,305,308,312	6	12	18	38	69	100
409-411,413-415,417-420-(52 pgs.): 413-Hawkman by Kubert r/B&B #44; G.A. Robotman-r/Det. #178; Zatanna by Morrow. 414-r-2nd Animal Man/Str. Advs. #184. 415-Animal Man-r/Str. Adv.#190 (origin recap). 417-Morrow Vigilante; Frazetta Shining Knight-r/Adv. #161; origin The Enchantress; no Zatanna. 418-Prev. unpub. Dr. Mid-Nite story from 1948; no Zatanna. 420-Animal Man-r/Str. Adv. #195	3	6	9	18	28	38
412-(52 pgs.) Reprints origin & 1st app. of Animal Man from Strange Adventures #180	3	6	9	19	30	40
416-Also listed as DC 100 Pg. Super Spectacular #10; Golden Age-r; r/1st app. Black Canary from Flash #86; no Zatanna	10	20	30	68	144	220
421-424: 424-Last Supergirl in Adventure	3	6	9	14	20	25
425-New look, content change to adventure; Kaluta-c; Toth-a, origin Capt. Fear	3	6	9	16	23	30
426,427: 426-1st Adventurers Club. 427-Last Vigilante	2	4	6	9	12	15
428-Origin/1st app. Black Orchid (c/story, 6-7/73)	7	14	21	49	92	135
429,430-Black Orchid-c/stories	3	6	9	20	31	42
431-Spectre by Aparo begins, ends #440.	5	10	15	35	63	90
432-439-Spectre app. 433-437-Cover title is Weird Adventure Comics. 436-Last 20¢ issue	3	6	9	21	33	45
440-New Spectre origin	4	8	12	25	40	55
441-458: 441-452-Aquaman app. 443-Fisherman app. 445-447-The Creeper app. 446-Flag-c. 449-451-Martian Manhunter app. 450-Weather Wizard app. in Aquaman story. 453-458-Superboy app. 453-Intro. Mighty Girl. 457,458-Eclipso app.	1	3	4	6	8	10
459,460 (68 pgs.): 459-New Gods/Darkseid storyline concludes from New Gods #19 (#459 is dated 9-10/78) without missing a month. 459-Flash (ends #466), Deadman (ends #466), Wonder Woman (ends #464), Green Lantern (ends #460). 460-Aquaman (ends #478)	3	6	9	15	22	28
461-($1.00, 68 pgs.) Justice Society begins; ends 466	4	8	12	25	40	55
462-($1.00, 68 pgs.) Death Earth II Batman	5	10	15	34	60	85
463-466 ($1.00 size, 68 pgs.)	2	4	6	10	14	18
467-Starman by Ditko & Plastic Man begins; 1st app. Prince Gavyn (Starman).	2	4	6	10	14	18
468-490: 470-Origin Starman. 479-Dial 'H' For Hero begins, ends #490. 478-Last Starman & Plastic Man. 480-490: Dial 'H' For Hero						5.00

Adventureman #1 © Milkfed & Dodson

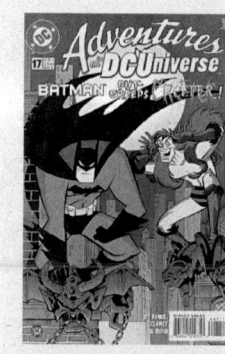

Adventures in the DC Universe #17 © DC

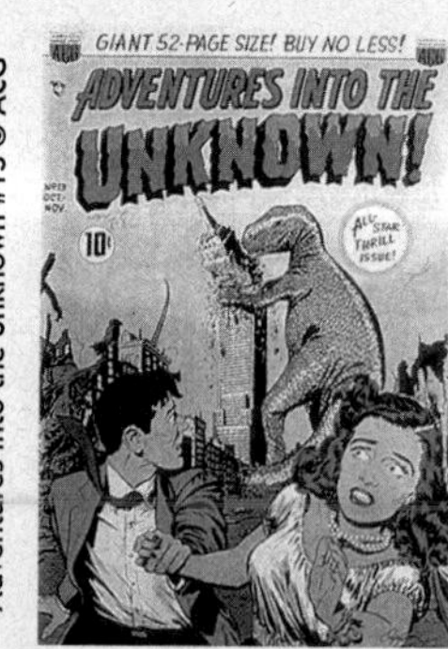

Adventures Into the Unknown #13 © ACG

GD	VG	FN	VF	VF/NM	NM-
2.0	4.0	6.0	8.0	9.0	9.2

491-503: 491-100pg. Digest size begins; r/Legion of Super Heroes/Adv. #247, 267; Spectre, Aquaman, Superboy, S&K Sandman, Black Canary-r & new Shazam by Newton begin. 492,495,496,499-S&K Sandman-r/Adventure in all. 493-Challengers of the Unknown begins by Tuska w/brief origin. 493-495,497-499-G.A. Captain Marvel-r. 494-499-Spectre-r/Spectre 1-3, 5-7. 496-Capt. Marvel Jr. new-s, Cockrum-a. 498-Mary Marvel new-s; Plastic Man-r begin; origin Bouncing Boy-r/ #301. 500-Legion-r (Digest size, 148 pgs.).

501-503: G.A.-r 2 4 6 9 13 16

... 80 Page Giant (10/98, $4.95) Wonder Woman, Shazam, Superboy, Supergirl, Green Arrow, Legion, Bizarro World stories 5.00

NOTE: *Bizarro covers-285, 286, 288, 294, 295, 329. Vigilante app.-420, 426, 427.* ***N. Adams*** *a(r)-495i-498i; c-365-369, 371-373, 375-379, 381-383.* ***Aparo*** *a-431-433, 434i, 435, 436, 437i, 438i, 439-452, 503r; c-431-452.* ***Austin*** *a-449i 451i.* ***Bernard Baily*** *c-48, 50, 52-59.* ***Bolland*** *c-475.* ***Burnley*** *c-61-72, 116-120p.* ***Chaykin*** *a-438.* ***Ditko*** *a-467-478p; c-467p.* ***Creig Flessel*** *c-32, 33, 40, 42, 44, 46, 47, 51, 60.* ***Giffen*** *c-491p-494p, 500p.* ***Grell*** *a-435-437, 440.* ***Guardineer*** *c-34, 35, 45.* ***Infantino*** *a-416r.* ***Kaluta*** *c-425.* ***Bob Kane*** *a-38.* ***G. Kane*** *a-414r, 425; c-496-499, 537.* ***Kirby*** *a-250-256.* ***Kubert*** *a-413.* ***Meskin*** *a-81,125,127.* ***Moldoff*** *a-494i; c-49.* ***Morrow*** *a-413-415, 417, 422, 502r, 503r.* ***Netzer/Nasser*** *a-449-451.* ***Newton*** *a-459-461, 464-466, 491p, 492p.* ***Paul Norris*** *a-69.* ***Orlando*** *a-457p, 458p.* ***Perez*** *c-484-486, 490p.* ***Simon/Kirby*** *a-503r; c-73-97, 100-102.* ***Starlin*** *c-471.* ***Staton*** *a-445-447i, 456-458p, 459, 460, 461p-465p, 466,467p-478p, 502p(r); c-458, 461(back).* ***Toth*** *a-418, 419, 425, 431, 495p-497p.* ***Tuska*** *a-494p.*

ADVENTURE COMICS (Also see All Star Comics 1999 crossover titles)
DC Comics: May, 1999 ($1.99, one-shot)

1-Golden Age Starman and the Atom; Snejbjerg-a 4.00

ADVENTURE COMICS (See Final Crisis: Legion of Three Worlds)
DC Comics: No. 0, Apr, 2009 - No. 12, Aug, 2010; No. 516, Sept, 2010 - No. 529, Oct, 2011 ($1.00/$3.99)

0-($1.00) R/Adventure Comics #247; new Luthor & Brainiac back-up-s; Lopresti-c 3.00
1-7-($3.99) Superboy stories; Johns-s/Manapul-a; Legion back-up-s. 5-7-Blackest Night 4.00
1-12-Variant 7-panel covers by various numbered with original #504-#515 5.00
8-12: 8-11-New Krypton x-over. 11-Mon-El leaves 21st century. 12-Legion; Levitz-s 4.00
516-521: 516-(9/10, resumes original numbering) flashback to Legion formation; Atom back-ups. 521-Adult Legion resumes; Mon-El joins Green Lanterns 4.00
522-529-($2.99) Legion Academy. 523-527-Jimenez-a/c 3.00

ADVENTURE COMICS SPECIAL (See New Krypton issues in 2009 Superman titles)
DC Comics: Jan, 2009 ($2.99, one-shot)

... Featuring the Guardian - James Robinson-s/Pere Pérez-a; origin re-told; intro. Gwen 3.00

ADVENTURE INTO MYSTERY
Atlas Comics (BFP No. 1/OPI No. 2-8): May, 1956 - No. 8, July, 1957

1-Powell s/f-a; Forte-a; Everett-c 77 154 231 493 847 1200
2-Flying Saucer story 37 74 111 222 361 500
3,6-Everett-c 34 68 102 199 325 450
4,5,7: 4-Williamson-a, 4 pgs; Powell-a. 5-Everett-c/a, Orlando-a. 7-Torres-a; Everett-c 36 72 108 211 343 475
8-Moreira, Sale, Torres, Woodbridge-a, Severin-c 34 68 102 199 325 450

ADVENTURE IS MY CAREER
U.S. Coast Guard Academy/Street & Smith: 1945 (44 pgs.)

nn-Simon, Milt Gross-a 23 46 69 136 223 310

ADVENTUREMAN
Image Comics: Jun, 2020 - No. 4, Oct, 2020 ($3.99, limited series)

1-4-Matt Fraction-s/Terry Dodson-a 4.00

ADVENTURERS, THE
Aircel Comics/Adventure Publ.: Aug, 1986 - No. 10, 1987? ($1.50, B&W)
V2#1, 1987 - V2#9, 1988; V3#1, Oct, 1989 - V3#6, 1990

1-Peter Hsu-a 1 2 3 5 6 8
1-Cover variant, limited ed. 2 4 6 9 12 15
1-2nd print (1986); 1st app. Elf Warrior 3.00
2,3, 0 (#4, 12/86)-Origin, 5-10, Book II, reg. & Limited Ed. #1 3.50
Book II, #2,3,0,4-9 3.00
Book III, #1 (10/89, $2.25)-Reg. & limited-c, Book III, #2-6 3.00

ADVENTURES (No. 2 Spectacular... on cover)
St. John Publishing Co.: Nov, 1949 - No. 2, Feb, 1950 (No. 1 ...in Romance on cover) (Slightly larger size)

1(Scarce); Bolle, Starr-a(2) 40 80 120 246 411 575
2(Scarce)-Slave Girl; China Bombshell app.; Bolle, L. Starr-a 52 104 156 328 552 775

ADVENTURES FOR BOYS
Bailey Enterprises: Dec, 1954

nn-Comics, text, & photos 8 16 24 40 50 60

ADVENTURES IN PARADISE (TV)
Dell Publishing Co.: Feb-Apr, 1962

Four Color 1301 6 12 18 37 66 95

ADVENTURES IN ROMANCE (See Adventures)

ADVENTURES IN SCIENCE (See Classics Illustrated Special Issue)

ADVENTURES IN THE DC UNIVERSE
DC Comics: Apr, 1997 - No. 19, Oct, 1998 ($1.75/$1.95/$1.99)

1-Animated style in all: JLA-c/app 5.00
2-11,13-17,19: 2-Flash app. 3-Wonder Woman. 4-Green Lantern. 6-Aquaman. 7-Shazam Family. 8-Blue Beetle & Booster Gold. 9-Flash. 10-Legion. 11-Green Lantern & Wonder Woman. 13-Impulse & Martian Manhunter. 14-Superboy/Flash race 3.50
12,18-JLA-c/app 3.50
Annual 1(1997, $3.95)-Dr. Fate, Impulse, Rose & Thorn, Superboy, Mister Miracle app. 4.50

ADVENTURES IN THE RIFLE BRIGADE
DC Comics (Vertigo): Oct, 2000 - No. 3, Dec, 2000 ($2.50, limited series)

1-3-Ennis-s/Ezquerra-a/Bolland-c 3.00
TPB (2004, $14.95) r/series and Operation Bollock series 15.00

ADVENTURES IN THE RIFLE BRIGADE: OPERATION BOLLOCK
DC Comics (Vertigo): Oct, 2001 - No. 3, Jan, 2002 ($2.50, limited series)

1-3-Ennis-s/Ezquerra-a/Fabry-c 3.00

ADVENTURES IN 3-D (With glasses)
Harvey Publications: Nov, 1953 - No. 2, Jan, 1954 (25¢)

1-Nostrand, Powell-a, 2-Powell-a 14 28 42 80 115 150

ADVENTURES INTO DARKNESS (See Seduction of the Innocent 3-D)
Better-Standard Publications/Visual Editions: No. 5, Aug, 1952- No. 14, 1954

5-Katz-c/a; Toth-a(p) 77 154 231 493 847 1200
6-Tuska, Katz-a 55 110 165 352 601 850
7-Classic horror-c; Katz-c/a 161 322 483 1030 1765 2500
8,9-Toth-a(p) 54 108 162 343 574 825
10-Jack Katz-a 50 100 150 315 533 750
11,12-Classic horror-c: 11-Jack Katz-a. 12-Toth-a; lingerie panel 65 130 195 416 708 1000
13-Toth-a(p); Cannibalism story cited by T. E. Murphy articles 71 142 213 454 777 1100
14 65 130 195 416 708 1000

NOTE: ***Fawcette*** *a-13.* ***Moreira*** *a-5.* ***Sekowsky*** *a-10, 11, 13(2).*

ADVENTURES INTO TERROR (Formerly Joker Comics)
Marvel/Atlas Comics (CDS): No. 43, Nov, 1950 - No. 31, May, 1954

43(#1) 103 206 309 659 1130 1600
44(#2, 2/51)-Sol Brodsky-c 54 108 162 343 574 825
3(4/51), 4 43 86 129 271 461 650
5-Wolverton-c panel/Mystic #6; Rico-c panel also; Atom Bomb story 47 94 141 296 498 700
6,8: 8-Wolverton text illo r-/Marvel Tales #104; prototype of Spider-Man villain The Lizard 43 86 129 271 461 650
7-Wolverton-a "Where Monsters Dwell", 6 pgs.; Tuska-c; Maneely-c panels 73 146 219 467 796 1125
9,10,12-Krigstein-a. 9-Decapitation panels 41 82 123 256 428 600
11,13-20 39 78 117 236 388 540
21-24,26-31 39 78 117 231 378 525
25-Matt Fox-a 41 82 123 256 428 600

NOTE: ***Ayers*** *a-21.* ***Colan*** *a-3, 5, 14, 21, 24, 25, 28, 29; c-27.* ***Colletta*** *a-30.* ***Everett*** *c-13, 21, 25.* ***Fass*** *a-28, 29.* ***Forte*** *a-28.* ***Heath*** *a-43, 44, 4-6, 22, 24, 26; c-43, 9, 11.* ***Lazarus*** *a-7.* ***Maneely*** *a-7(3 pg.), 10, 11, 21., 22 c-15, 29.* ***Don Rico*** *a-4, 5(3 pg.).* ***Sekowsky*** *a-43, 3, 4.* ***Sinnott*** *a-8, 9, 11, 24, 28.* ***Tuska*** *a-14; c-7.*

ADVENTURES INTO THE UNKNOWN
American Comics Group: Fall, 1948 - No. 174, Aug, 1967 (No. 1-33: 52 pgs.)
(1st continuous series Supernatural comic; see Eerie #1)

1-Guardineer-a; adapt. of 'Castle of Otranto' by Horace Walpole 277 554 831 1759 3030 4300
2,3: 3-Feldstein-a (9 pgs) 97 194 291 621 1061 1500
4,5: 5- 'Spirit Of Frankenstein' series begins, ends #12 (except #11) 50 100 150 315 533 750
6-10 39 78 117 231 378 525
11-16,18-20: 13-Starr-a. 15-Hitler app. 32 64 96 192 314 435
17-Story similar to movie 'The Thing' 36 72 108 211 343 475
21-26,28-30 27 54 81 158 259 360
27-Williamson/Krenkel-a (8 pgs.) 41 82 123 256 428 600
31-37,39-50 21 42 63 122 199 275
38-Atom bomb panels; Devil-c 15 30 45 103 227 350
51-(1/54)-(3-D effect-c/story)-Only white cover 55 110 165 352 601 850
52-58: (3-D effect-c/stories with black covers). 52-E.C. swipe/Haunt Of Fear #14 52 104 156 328 552 775
59-3-D effect story only; new logo 36 72 108 211 343 475
60-Wood*esque*-a by Landau 16 32 48 94 147 200

Adventures of Alan Ladd #8 © DC

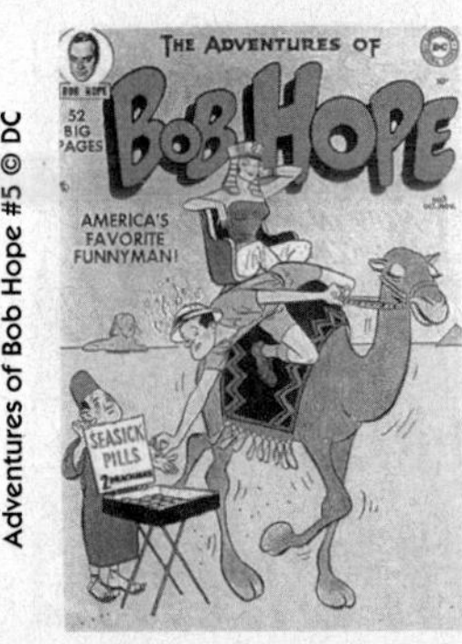

Adventures of Bob Hope #5 © DC

Adventures of Jerry Lewis #60 © DC

GD 2.0 | VG 4.0 | FN 6.0 | VF 8.0 | VF/NM 9.0 | NM- 9.2

61-Last pre-code issue (1-2/55) 16 32 48 94 147 200
62-70 7 14 21 49 92 135
71-90: 80-Hydrogen bomb panel 6 12 18 38 69 100
91,96(#95 on inside),107,116-All have Williamson-a 6 12 18 41 76 110
92-95,97-99,101-106,108-115,117-128: 109-113,118-Whitney painted-c. 128-Williamson/Krenkel/Torres-a(r)/Forbidden Worlds #63; last 10¢ issue
5 10 15 33 57 80
100 5 10 15 35 63 90
129-153,157: 153,157-Magic Agent app. 4 8 12 25 40 55
154-Nemesis series begins (origin), ends #170 5 10 15 30 50 70
155,156,158-167,170-174: 174-Flying saucer-c 4 8 12 23 37 50
168-Ditko-a(p) 4 8 12 28 47 65
169-Nemesis battles Hitler 4 8 12 28 47 65
Nemesis Archives: Vol. One (Dark Horse Books, 9/08, $59.95) r/#154-170; creator bios 60.00
NOTE: *"Spirit of Frankenstein" series in 5, 6, 8-10, 12, 16.* ***Buscema*** *a-100, 106, 108-110, 158r, 165r.* ***Cameron*** *a-34.* ***Craig*** *a-152, 160.* ***Goode*** *a-45, 47, 60.* ***Landau*** *a-51, 59-63.* ***Lazarus*** *a-34, 48, 51, 52, 56, 58, 79, 87; c-31-56, 58.* ***Reinman*** *a-102, 111, 112, 115-118, 124, 130, 137, 141, 145, 164.* ***Whitney*** *c-12-30, 57, 59-on (most.)* ***Torres/Williamson*** *a-116.*

ADVENTURES INTO WEIRD WORLDS
Marvel/Atlas Comics (ACI): Jan, 1952 - No. 30, June, 1954

1-Atom bomb panels 142 284 426 909 1555 2200
2-Sci/fic stories (2); one by Maneely 54 108 162 343 574 825
3-10: 7-Tongue ripped out. 10-Krigstein, Everett-a 47 94 141 296 498 700
11-20 41 82 123 256 428 600
21-Hitler in Hell story 48 96 144 302 514 725
22-26: 24-Man holds hypo & splits in two-c 40 80 120 246 411 575
27-Matt Fox end of world story-a; severed head-c 61 122 183 390 670 950
28-Atom bomb story; decapitation panels 43 86 129 271 461 650
29,30 37 74 111 218 354 490
NOTE: ***Ayers*** *a-8, 26.* ***Everett*** *a-4, 5; c-6, 8, 10-13, 18, 19, 22, 24, 25; a-4, 25.* ***Fass*** *a-7.* ***Forte*** *a-21, 24.* ***Al Hartley*** *a-2.* ***Heath*** *a-1, 4, 17, 22; c-7, 9, 20.* ***Maneely*** *a-2, 3, 11, 20, 22, 23, 25; c-1, 3, 22, 25-27, 29.* ***Reinman*** *a-24, 28.* ***Rico*** *a-13.* ***Robinson*** *a-13.* ***Sinnott*** *a-25, 30.* ***Tuska*** *a-1, 2, 12, 15.* ***Whitney*** *a-7.* ***Wildey*** *a-28. Bondage c-22.*

ADVENTURES IN WONDERLAND (Also see Uncle Charlies Fables)
Lev Gleason Publications: April, 1955 - No. 5, Feb, 1956 (Jr. Readers Guild)

1-Maurer-a 13 26 39 74 105 135
2-4 8 16 24 42 54 65
5-Christmas issue 8 16 24 44 57 70

ADVENTURES OF ALAN LADD, THE
National Periodical Publ.: Oct-Nov, 1949 - No. 9, Feb-Mar, 1951 (All 52 pgs.)

1-Photo-c 84 168 252 538 919 1300
2-Photo-c 41 82 123 256 428 600
3-6: Last photo-c 36 72 108 211 343 475
7-9 30 60 90 177 289 400
NOTE: ***Dan Barry*** *a-1.* ***Moreira*** *a-3-7.*

ADVENTURES OF ALICE (Also see Alice in Wonderland) (Becomes Alice at Monkey Island #3)
Civil Service Publ./Pentagon Publishing Co.: 1945

1 16 32 48 94 147 200
2-Through the Magic Looking Glass 13 26 39 74 105 135

ADVENTURES OF BARON MUNCHAUSEN, THE
Now Comics: July, 1989 - No. 4, Oct, 1989 ($1.75, limited series)

1-4: Movie adaptation 3.00

ADVENTURES OF BARRY WEEN, BOY GENIUS, THE
Image Comics: Mar, 1999 - No. 3, May, 1999 ($2.95, B&W, limited series)

1-3-Judd Winick-s/a 3.00
...: Secret Crisis Origin Files (Oni, 7/04, Free Comic Book Day giveaway) - Winick-s/a 3.00
TPB (Oni Press, 11/99, $8.95) r/#1-3 9.00

ADVENTURES OF BARRY WEEN, BOY GENIUS 2.0, THE
Oni Press: Feb, 2000 - No. 3, Apr, 2000 ($2.95, B&W, limited series)

1-3-Judd Winick-s/a 3.00
TPB (2000, $8.95) 9.00

ADVENTURES OF BARRY WEEN, BOY GENIUS 3, THE : MONKEY TALES
Oni Press: Feb, 2001 - No. 6, Feb, 2002 ($2.95, B&W, limited series)

1-6-Judd Winick-s/a 3.00
TPB (2001, $8.95) r/#1-3; intro. by Peter David 9.00
...4 TPB (5/02, $8.95) r/#4-6 9.00

ADVENTURES OF BAYOU BILLY, THE (Based on video game)
Archie Comics: Sept, 1989 - No. 5, June, 1990 ($1.00)

1-5: Esposito-c/a(i). 5-Kelley Jones-c 3.00

ADVENTURES OF BOB HOPE, THE (Also see True Comics #59)
National Per. Publ.: Feb-Mar, 1950 - No. 109, Feb-Mar, 1968 (#1-10: 52pgs.)

GD 2.0 | VG 4.0 | FN 6.0 | VF 8.0 | VF/NM 9.0 | NM- 9.2

1-Photo-c 258 516 774 1651 2826 4000
2-Photo-c 92 184 276 584 1005 1425
3,4-Photo-c 57 114 171 362 619 875
5-10: 9-Horror-c 41 82 123 256 428 600
11-20 29 58 87 170 278 385
21-31 (2-3/55; last precode) 20 40 60 117 189 260
32-40 9 18 27 61 123 185
41-50 8 16 24 54 102 150
51-70 7 14 21 46 86 125
71-93 5 10 15 35 63 90
94-Aquaman cameo 6 12 18 42 79 115
95-1st app. Super-Hip & 1st monster issue (11/65) 9 18 27 58 114 170
96-105: Super-Hip and monster stories in all. 103-Batman, Robin, Ringo Starr cameos
6 12 18 38 69 100
106-109-All monster-c/stories by N. Adams-c/a 8 16 24 55 105 155
NOTE: *Buzzy in #34. Kitty Karr of Hollywood in #15, 17-20, 23, 28. Liz in #26, 109. Miss Beverly Hills of Hollywood in #7, 8, 10, 13, 14. Miss Melody Lane of Broadway in #15. Rusty in #23, 25. Tommy in #24. No 2nd feature in #2-4, 6, 8, 11, 12, 28-108.*

ADVENTURES OF CAPTAIN AMERICA
Marvel Comics: Sept, 1991 - No. 4, Jan, 1992 ($4.95, 52 pgs., squarebound, limited series)

1-4: 1-Origin in WW2; embossed-c; Nicieza scripts; Maguire-c/a(p) begins, ends #3. 2-4-Austin-c/a(i). 3,4-Red Skull app. 5.00

ADVENTURES OF CYCLOPS AND PHOENIX (Also See Askani'son & The Further Adventures of Cyclops And Phoenix)
Marvel Comics: May, 1994 - No. 4, Aug, 1994 ($2.95, limited series)

1-4-Characters from X-Men; origin of Cable 4.00
Trade paperback ($14.95)-reprints #1-4 15.00

ADVENTURES OF DEAN MARTIN AND JERRY LEWIS, THE
(The Adventures of Jerry Lewis #41 on) (See Movie Love #12)
National Periodical Publications: July-Aug, 1952 - No. 40, Oct, 1957

1 194 388 582 1242 2121 3000
2-Three pg. origin on how they became a team 60 120 180 381 653 925
3-10: 3- I Love Lucy text featurette 36 72 108 211 343 475
11-19: Last precode (2/55) 22 44 66 132 216 300
20-30 17 34 51 98 154 210
31-40 15 30 45 83 124 165

ADVENTURES OF DETECTIVE ACE KING, THE (Also see Bob Scully-- & Detective Dan)
Humor Publ. Corp.: No date (1933) (36 pgs., 9-1/2x12") (10¢, B&W, one-shot) (paper-c)

Book 1-Along with Bob Scully & Detective Dan, the first comic w/original art & the first of a single theme.; Not reprints; Ace King by Martin Nadle (The American Sherlock Holmes). A Dick Tracy look-alike 775 1550 2325 6200 - -

ADVENTURES OF EVIL AND MALICE, THE
Image Comics: June, 1999 - No. 3, Nov, 1999 ($3.50/$3.95, limited series)

1-3-Jimmie Robinson-s/a. 3-($3.95-c) 4.00

ADVENTURES OF FELIX THE CAT, THE
Harvey Comics: May, 1992 ($1.25)

1-Messmer-r 5.00

ADVENTURES OF FORD FAIRLANE, THE
DC Comics: May, 1990 - No. 4, Aug, 1990 ($1.50, limited series, mature)

1-4: Andrew Dice Clay movie tie-in; Don Heck inks 4.00

ADVENTURES OF HOMER COBB, THE
Say/Bart Prod. : Sept, 1947 (Oversized) (Published in the U.S., but printed in Canada)

1-(Scarce)-Feldstein-c/a 50 100 150 315 533 750

ADVENTURES OF HOMER GHOST (See Homer The Happy Ghost)
Atlas Comics: June, 1957 - No. 2, Aug, 1957

V1#1,2: 2-Robot-c 18 36 54 107 169 230

ADVENTURES OF JERRY LEWIS, THE (Adventures of Dean Martin & Jerry Lewis No. 1-40) (See Super DC Giant)
National Periodical Publ.: No. 41, Nov, 1957 - No. 124, May-June, 1971

41 9 18 27 62 126 190
42-60 7 14 21 49 92 135
61-67,69-73,75-80 6 12 18 41 76 110
68,74-Photo-c (movie) 9 18 27 60 120 180
81,82,85-87,90,91,94,96,98,99 5 10 15 34 60 85
83,84,88: 83-1st Monsters-c/s. 84-Jerry as a Super-hero-c/s. 88-1st Witch, Miss Kraft
6 12 18 38 69 100
89-Bob Hope app.; Wizard of Oz & Alfred E. Neuman in MAD parody
7 14 21 44 82 120
92-Superman cameo 7 14 21 44 82 120

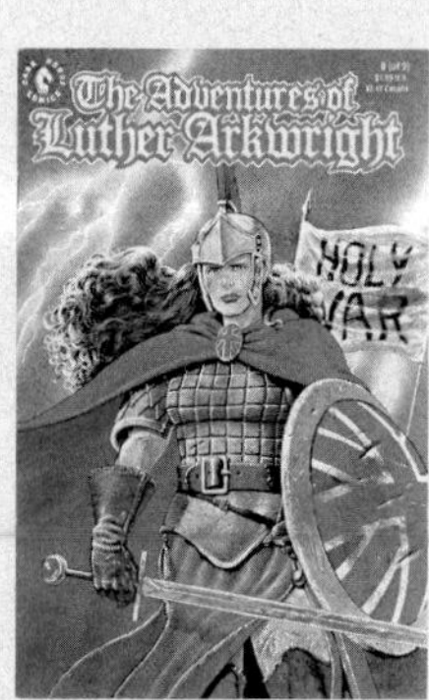

Adventures of Luther Arkwright #8 © DH

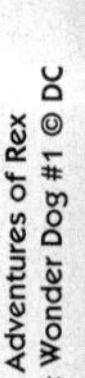
Adventures of Rex the Wonder Dog #1 © DC

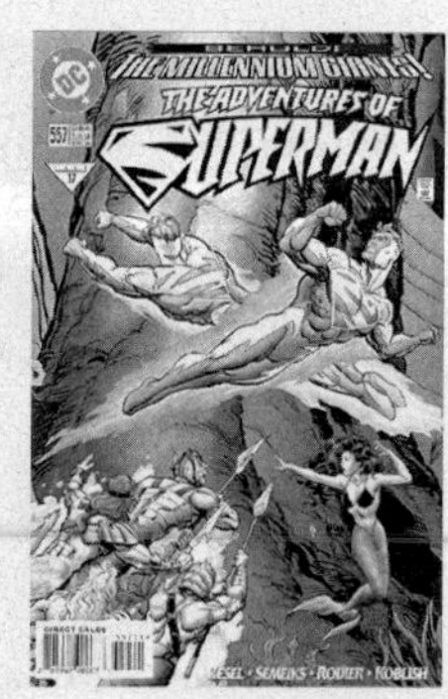

Adventures of Superman #557 © DC

	GD 2.0	VG 4.0	FN 6.0	VF 8.0	VF/NM 9.0	NM- 9.2
93-Beatles parody as babies	6	12	18	38	69	100
95-1st Uncle Hal Wack-A-Boy Camp-c/s	6	12	18	38	69	100
97-Batman/Robin/Joker-c/story; Riddler & Penguin app; Dick Sprang-c.	9	18	27	59	117	175
100	6	12	18	40	73	105
101,103,104-Neal Adams-c/a	7	14	21	46	86	125
102-Beatles app.; Neal Adams c/a	9	18	27	57	111	165
105-Superman x-over	6	12	18	41	76	110
106-111,113-116	4	8	12	28	47	65
112,117: 112-Flash x-over. 117-W. Woman x-over	6	12	18	40	73	105
118-124	4	8	12	27	44	60

NOTE: *Monster-c/s-90,93,96,98,101. Wack-A-Buy Camp-c/s-96,99,102,107,108.*

ADVENTURES OF JO-JOY, THE (See Jo-Joy)

ADVENTURES OF LASSIE, THE (See Lassie)

ADVENTURES OF LUTHER ARKWRIGHT, THE
Valkyrie Press/Dark Horse Comics: Oct, 1987 - No. 9, Jan, 1989 ($2.00, B&W) V2, #1, Mar, 1990 - V2#9, 1990 ($1.95, B&W)

	GD 2.0	VG 4.0	FN 6.0	VF 8.0	VF/NM 9.0	NM- 9.2
1-9: 1-Alan Moore intro., V2#1-9 (Dark Horse): r-1st series; new-c						4.00
TPB (1997, $14.95) r/#1-9 w/Michael Moorcock intro.						15.00

ADVENTURES OF MIGHTY MOUSE (Mighty Mouse Adventures No. 1)
St. John Publishing Co.: No. 2, Jan, 1952 - No. 18, May, 1955

	GD 2.0	VG 4.0	FN 6.0	VF 8.0	VF/NM 9.0	NM- 9.2
2	29	58	87	172	281	390
3-5	15	30	45	90	140	190
6-18	13	26	39	72	101	130

ADVENTURES OF MIGHTY MOUSE (2nd Series) (Becomes Mighty Mouse #161 on)
(Two No. 144's; formerly Paul Terry's Comics; No. 129-137 have nn's)
St. John/Pines/Dell/Gold Key: No. 126, Aug, 1955 - No. 160, Oct, 1963

	GD 2.0	VG 4.0	FN 6.0	VF 8.0	VF/NM 9.0	NM- 9.2
126(8/55), 127(10/55), 128(11/55)-St. John	10	20	30	56	76	95
nn(129, 4/56)-144(8/59)-Pines	5	10	15	30	50	70
144(10-12/59)-155(7-9/62) Dell	4	8	12	27	44	60
156(10/62)-160(10/63) Gold Key	4	8	12	27	44	60

NOTE: *Early issues titled "Paul Terry's Adventures of ...."*

ADVENTURES OF MIGHTY MOUSE (Formerly Mighty Mouse)
Gold Key: No. 166, Mar, 1979 - No. 172, Jan, 1980

	GD 2.0	VG 4.0	FN 6.0	VF 8.0	VF/NM 9.0	NM- 9.2
166-172	1	2	3	5	6	8

ADVS. OF MR. FROG & MISS MOUSE (See Dell Junior Treasury No. 4)

ADVENTURES OF OZZIE & HARRIET, THE (See Ozzie & Harriet)

ADVENTURES OF PATORUZU
Green Publishing Co.: Aug, 1946 - Winter, 1946

	GD 2.0	VG 4.0	FN 6.0	VF 8.0	VF/NM 9.0	NM- 9.2
nn's-Contains Animal Crackers reprints	6	12	18	31	38	45

ADVENTURES OF PINKY LEE, THE (TV)
Atlas Comics: July, 1955 - No. 5, Dec, 1955

	GD 2.0	VG 4.0	FN 6.0	VF 8.0	VF/NM 9.0	NM- 9.2
1	28	56	84	165	270	375
2-5	17	34	51	98	154	210

ADVENTURES OF PIPSQUEAK, THE (Formerly Pat the Brat)
Archie Publications (Radio Comics): No. 34, Sept, 1959 - No. 39, July, 1960

	GD 2.0	VG 4.0	FN 6.0	VF 8.0	VF/NM 9.0	NM- 9.2
34	3	6	9	21	33	45
35-39	3	6	9	17	26	35

ADVENTURES OF QUAKE & QUISP, THE (See Quaker Oats "Plenty of Glutton")

ADVENTURES OF REX THE WONDER DOG, THE (Rex...No. 1)
National Periodical Publ.: Jan-Feb, 1952 - No. 45, May-June, 1959; No. 46, Nov-Dec, 1959

	GD 2.0	VG 4.0	FN 6.0	VF 8.0	VF/NM 9.0	NM- 9.2
1-(Scarce)-Toth-c/a	232	464	696	1485	2543	3600
2-(Scarce)-Toth-c/a	89	178	267	565	970	1375
3-(Scarce)-Toth-a	63	126	189	403	689	975
4,5	50	100	150	315	533	750
6-10	41	82	123	256	428	600
11-Atom bomb-c/story; dinosaur-c/sty	48	96	144	302	514	725
12-19: 19-Last precode (1-2/55)	32	64	96	188	307	425
20-46	22	44	66	132	216	300

NOTE: ***Infantino, Gil Kane** art in 5-19 (most)*

ADVENTURES OF ROBIN HOOD, THE (Formerly Robin Hood)
Magazine Enterprises (Sussex Publ. Co.): No. 6, Jun, 1957 - No. 8, Nov, 1957
(Based on Richard Greene TV Show)

	GD 2.0	VG 4.0	FN 6.0	VF 8.0	VF/NM 9.0	NM- 9.2
6-8-Richard Greene photo-c. 6,7-Powell-a	15	30	45	83	124	165

ADVENTURES OF ROBIN HOOD, THE
Gold Key: Mar, 1974 - No. 7, Jan, 1975 (Disney cartoon) (36 pgs.)

	GD 2.0	VG 4.0	FN 6.0	VF 8.0	VF/NM 9.0	NM- 9.2
1(90291-403)-Part-r of $1.50 editions	2	4	6	13	18	22
2-7: 1-7 are part-r	2	4	6	8	11	14

ADVENTURES OF SNAKE PLISSKEN
Marvel Comics: Jan, 1997 ($2.50, one-shot)

	GD 2.0	VG 4.0	FN 6.0	VF 8.0	VF/NM 9.0	NM- 9.2
1-Based on Escape From L.A. movie; Brereton-c						4.00

ADVENTURES OF SPAWN, THE
Image Comics (Todd McFarlane Prods.): Jan, 2007; Nov, 2008 ($5.99)

	GD 2.0	VG 4.0	FN 6.0	VF 8.0	VF/NM 9.0	NM- 9.2
1,2-Printed adaptation of the Spawn.com web comic; Khary Randolph-a	2	4	6	9	12	15

ADVENTURES OF SPIDER-MAN, THE (Based on animated TV series)
Marvel Comics: Apr, 1996 - No. 12, Mar, 1997 (99¢)

	GD 2.0	VG 4.0	FN 6.0	VF 8.0	VF/NM 9.0	NM- 9.2
1-12: 1-Punisher app. 2-Venom cameo. 3-X-Men. 6-Fantastic Four						4.00

ADVENTURES OF SUPERBOY, THE (See Superboy, 2nd Series)

ADVENTURES OF SUPERGIRL (Based on the TV series)
DC Comics: Early Jul, 2016 - No. 6, Sept, 2016 ($2.99)(Printing of stories first appearing online)

	GD 2.0	VG 4.0	FN 6.0	VF 8.0	VF/NM 9.0	NM- 9.2
1-6: 1-Rampage app.; Bengal-a/Staggs-c						3.00

ADVENTURES OF SUPERMAN (Formerly Superman)
DC Comics: No. 424, Jan, 1987 - No. 499, Feb, 1993; No. 500, Early June, 1993 - No. 649, Apr, 2006 (This title's numbering continues with Superman #650, May, 2006)

	GD 2.0	VG 4.0	FN 6.0	VF 8.0	VF/NM 9.0	NM- 9.2
424-Ordway-c/a; Wolfman-s begin following Byrne's Superman revamp; 1st Cat Grant	1	3	4	6	8	10
425-435,437-462: 426-Legends x-over. 432-1st app. Jose Delgado who becomes Gangbuster in #434. 437-Millennium x-over. 438-New Brainiac app. 440-Batman app. 449-Invasion						4.00
436-Byrne scripts begin; Millennium x-over						5.00
463-Superman/Flash race; cover swipe/Superman #199						7.00
464-Lobo-c & app. (pre-dates Lobo #1)	1	2	3	5	6	8
465-1st app. Hank Henshaw (later becomes Cyborg Superman)	2	4	6	8	11	14
466-479,481-495: 467-Part 2 of Batman story. 473-Hal Jordan, Guy Gardner x-over. 477-Legion app. 491-Last $1.00-c. 495-Forever People-c/story; Darkseid app.						4.00
480,496,497: 480-($1.75, 52 pgs.). 496-Doomsday cameo. 497-Doomsday battle issue						4.00
496,497-2nd printings						4.00
498,499-Funeral for a Friend; Supergirl app.						5.00
498-2nd & 3rd printings						3.00
500-($2.95, 68 pgs.)-Collector's edition w/card	1	2	3	5	6	8
500-($2.50, 68 pgs.)-Regular edition w/different-c						4.00
500-Platinum edition						60.00
501-($1.95)-Collector's edition with die-cut-c						5.00
501-($1.50)-Regular edition w/mini-poster & diff.-c						4.00
502-516: 502-Supergirl-c/story. 508-Challengers of the Unknown app. 510-Bizarro-c/story. 516-(9/94)-Zero Hour						3.00
505-($2.50)-Holo-grafx foil-c edition						5.00
0,517-523: 0-(10/94). 517-(11/94)						3.00
524-549,551-580: 524-Begin $1.95-c. 527-Return of Alpha Centurion (Zero Hour). 533-Impulse-c/app. 535-Luthor-c/app. 536-Brainiac app. 537-Parasite app. 540-Final Night x-over. 541-Superboy-c/app.; Lois & Clark honeymoon. 545-New powers. 546-New costume. 555-Red & Blue Supermen battle. 557-Millennium Giants x-over. 558-560: Superman Silver Age-style story; Krypto app. 561-Begin $1.99-c. 565-JLA app.						3.00
550-($3.50)-Double sized						4.00
581-588: 581-Begin $2.25-c. 583-Emperor Joker. 588-Casey-s						3.00
589-595: 589-Return to Krypton; Rivoche-c. 591-Wolfman-s. 593-595-Our Worlds at War x-over. 593-New Suicide Squad formed. 594-Doomsday-c/app.						3.00
596-Aftermath of "War" x-over has panel showing damaged World Trade Center buildings; issue went on sale the day after the Sept. 11 attack						6.00
597-599,601-624: 597-Joker: Last Laugh. 604,605-Ultraman, Owlman, Superwoman app. 606-Return to Krypton. 612-616,619-623-Nowlan-c. 624-Mr. Majestic app.						3.00
600-($3.95) Wieringo-a; painted-c by Adel; pin-ups by various						4.00
625,626-Godfall parts 2,5; Turner-c; Caldwell-a(p)						4.00
627-641,643-648: 627-Begin $2.50-c, Rucka-s/Clark-a/Ha-c begin. 628-Wagner-c. 631-Bagged with Sky Captain CD; Lois shot. 634-Mxyzptlk visits DC offices. 639-Capt. Marvel & Eclipso app. 641-OMAC app. 643-Sacrifice aftermath; Batman & Wonder Woman app.						3.00
642-OMAC Project x-over Sacrifice pt. 3; JLA app.						5.00
642-(2nd printing) red tone cover						3.00
649-Last issue; Infinite Crisis x-over, Superman vs. Earth-2 Superman						4.00
#1,000,000 (11/98) Gene Ha-c; 853rd Century x-over						3.00
Annual 1 (1987, $1.25, 52 pgs.)-Starlin-c & scripts						4.00
Annual 2,3 (1990, 1991, $2.00, 68 pgs.): 2-Byrne-c/a(i); Legion '90 (Lobo) app. 3-Armageddon 2001 x-over						4.00
Annual 4-6 ('92-'94, $2.50, 68 pgs.): 4-Guy Gardner/Lobo-c/story; Eclipso storyline; Quesada-c(p). 5-Bloodlines storyline. 6-Elseworlds sty.						4.00
Annual 7,9('95, '97, $3.95)-7-Year One story. 9-Pulp Heroes sty						4.00

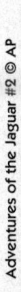

Adventures of the Jaguar #2 © AP

Adventures of the Outsiders #36 © DC

Adventure Time #57 © CN

	GD 2.0	VG 4.0	FN 6.0	VF 8.0	VF/NM 9.0	NM- 9.2
Annual 8 (1996, $2.95)-Legends of the Dead Earth story						4.00

NOTE: *Erik Larsen a-431.*

ADVENTURES OF SUPERMAN
DC Comics: Jul, 2013 - No. 17, Nov, 2014 ($3.99)

	GD	VG	FN	VF	VF/NM	NM-
1-17-Short story anthology by various. 1-Lemire-s/a. 4-Timm-c. 6-Mongul app. 14-Joker app.; Sugar & Spike app.; Hester-a						4.00

ADVENTURES OF THE DOVER BOYS
Archie Comics (Close-up): September, 1950 - No. 2, 1950 (No month given)

	GD	VG	FN	VF	VF/NM	NM-
1,2	11	22	33	60	83	105

ADVENTURES OF THE FLY (The Fly #1-6; Fly Man No. 32-39; See The Double Life of Private Strong, The Fly, Laugh Comics & Mighty Crusaders)
Archie Publications/Radio Comics: Aug, 1959 - No. 30, Oct, 1964; No. 31, May, 1965

	GD	VG	FN	VF	VF/NM	NM-
1-Shield app.; origin The Fly; S&K-c/a	52	104	156	411	931	1450
2-Williamson, S&K-a	29	58	87	209	467	725
3-Origin retold; Davis, Powell-a	25	50	75	175	388	600
4-Neal Adams-a(p)(1 panel); S&K-c; Powell-a; 2 pg. Shield story	32	64	96	230	515	800
5,6,9,10: 9-Shield app. 9-1st app. Cat Girl. 10-Black Hood app.	11	22	33	76	163	250
7,8: 7-1st S.A. app. Black Hood (7/60). 8-1st S.A. app. Shield (9/60)	15	30	45	103	227	350
11-13,15-20: 13-1st app. Fly Girl w/o costume. 16-Last 10¢ issue. 20-Origin Fly Girl retold	7	14	21	49	92	135
14-Origin & 1st app. Fly Girl in costume	8	16	24	55	105	155
21-30: 23-Jaguar cameo. 27-29-Black Hood 1 pg. strips. 30-Comet x-over (1st S.A. app.) in Fly Girl	6	12	18	38	69	100
31-Black Hood, Shield, Comet app.	6	12	18	40	73	105
Vol. 1 TPB ('04, $12.95) r/#1-4 & Double Life of Private Strong #1,2; foreward by Joe Simon						13.00

NOTE: *Simon c-2-4. Tuska a-1. Cover title to #31 is Flyman; Advs. of the Fly inside.*

ADVENTURES OF THE JAGUAR, THE (See Blue Ribbon Comics, Laugh Comics & Mighty Crusaders)
Archie Publications (Radio Comics): Sept, 1961 - No. 15, Nov, 1963

	GD	VG	FN	VF	VF/NM	NM-
1-Origin Jaguar (1st app?) by J. Rosenberger	23	46	69	156	348	540
2,3: 3-Last 10¢ issue	10	20	30	70	150	230
4-6-Catgirl app. (#4's-c is same as splash pg.)	8	16	24	56	108	160
7-10: 10-Dinosaur-c	7	14	21	46	86	125
11-15: 13,14-Catgirl, Black Hood app. in both	6	12	18	40	73	105

ADVENTURES OF THE MASK (TV cartoon)
Dark Horse Comics: Jan, 1996 - No. 12, Dec, 1996 ($2.50)

	GD	VG	FN	VF	VF/NM	NM-
1-12: Based on animated series						3.00

ADVENTURES OF THE NEW MEN (Formerly Newmen #1-21)
Maximum Press: No. 22, Nov, 1996; No. 23, March, 1997 ($2.50)

	GD	VG	FN	VF	VF/NM	NM-
22,23-Sprouse-c/a						3.00

ADVENTURES OF THE OUTSIDERS, THE (Formerly Batman & The Outsiders; also see The Outsiders)
DC Comics: No. 33, May, 1986 - No. 46, June, 1987

	GD	VG	FN	VF	VF/NM	NM-
33-46: 39-45-r/Outsiders #1-7 by Aparo						4.00

ADVENTURES OF THE SUPER MARIO BROTHERS (See Super Mario Bros.)
Valiant: 1990 - No. 9, Oct, 1991 ($1.50)

	GD	VG	FN	VF	VF/NM	NM-
V2#1	3	6	9	16	23	30
2-9	2	4	6	8	11	14

ADVENTURES OF THE SUPER SONS (Jon Kent and Damian Wayne)
DC Comics: Oct, 2018 - No. 12, Sept, 2019 ($3.99)

	GD	VG	FN	VF	VF/NM	NM-
1-12: 1-Intro Rex Luthor and Joker Jr.; Tomasi-s/Barberi-a. 6-Tommy Tomorrow app.						4.00

ADVENTURES OF THE THING, THE (Also see The Thing)
Marvel Comics: Apr, 1992 - No. 4, July, 1992, ($1.25, limited series)

	GD	VG	FN	VF	VF/NM	NM-
1-4: 1-r/Marvel Two-In-One #50 by Byrne; Kieth-c. 2-4-r/Marvel Two-In-One #80,51 & 77; 2-Ghost Rider-c/story; Quesada-c. 3-Miller-r/Quesada-c; new Perez-a (4 pgs.)						4.00

ADVENTURES OF THE X-MEN, THE (Based on animated TV series)
Marvel Comics: Apr, 1996 - No. 12, Mar, 1997 (99¢)

	GD	VG	FN	VF	VF/NM	NM-
1-12: 1-Wolverine/Hulk battle. 3-Spider-Man-c. 5,6-Magneto-c/app.						4.00

ADVENTURES OF TINKER BELL (See Tinker Bell, 4-Color No. 896 & 982)

ADVENTURES OF TOM SAWYER (See Dell Junior Treasury No. 10)

ADVENTURES OF YOUNG DR. MASTERS, THE
Archie Comics (Radio Comics): Aug, 1964 - No. 2, Nov, 1964

	GD	VG	FN	VF	VF/NM	NM-
1	4	8	12	23	37	50
2	3	6	9	16	23	30

ADVENTURES ON OTHER WORLDS (See Showcase #17 & 18)

ADVENTURES ON THE PLANET OF THE APES (Also see Planet of the Apes)
Marvel Comics Group: Oct, 1975 - No. 11, Dec, 1976

	GD	VG	FN	VF	VF/NM	NM-
1-Planet of the Apes magazine-r in color; Starlin-c; adapts movie thru #6	5	10	15	30	50	70
2-5: 5-(25¢-c edition)	3	6	9	16	23	30
5-7-(30¢-c variants, limited distribution)	5	10	15	34	60	85
6-10: 6,7-(25¢-c edition). 7-Adapts 2nd movie (thru #11)	3	6	9	14	20	25
11-Last issue; concludes 2nd movie adaptation	3	6	9	17	26	35

NOTE: *Alcala a-6-11r. Buckler c-2p. Nasser c-7. Ploog a-1-9. Starlin c-6. Tuska a-1-5r.*

ADVENTURES WITH THE DC SUPER HEROES (Interior also inserted into some DC issues)
DC Comics/Geppi's Entertainment Museum: 2007 Free Comic Book Day giveaway

	GD	VG	FN	VF	VF/NM	NM-
"The Batman and Cal Ripken, Jr. Hall of Fame Edition "A Rare Catch" " in indicia						4.00

ADVENTURE TIME (With Finn & Jake) (Based on the Cartoon Network animated series)
Boom Entertainment (KaBOOM!): Feb, 2012 - No. 75, Apr, 2018 ($3.99)

	GD	VG	FN	VF	VF/NM	NM-
1-Cover A						25.00
1-Covers B & C; interlocking image						25.00
1-Cover D variant by Jeffrey Brown						30.00
1-Cover E wraparound						40.00
1-Second & third printings						5.00
2-Four covers						10.00
3-24,26-49,51-74-Multiple covers on all						4.00
25-($4.99) Art by Dustin Nguyen, Jess Fink, Jeffrey Brown & others; multiple covers						5.00
50-($4.99) Hastings-s/McGinty-a; multiple covers						5.00
75-($4.99) Last issue; multiple covers						5.00
2013 Annual #1 (5/13, $4.99) Three covers; s/a by Langridge, Nguyen & others						5.00
2013 Spoooktacular (10/13, $4.99) Halloween-themed; s/a by Fraser Irving & others						5.00
2013 Summer Special (7/13, $4.99) Multiple covers						5.00
2014 Annual #1 (4/14, $4.99) Three covers; stories printed sideways						5.00
2014 Winter Special (1/14, $4.99) Multiple covers						5.00
2015 Spoooktacular (10/15, $4.99) a Marceline story; s/a by Hanna K						5.00
2016 Spoooktacular (9/16, $4.99) Short stories by various; 2 covers by Bartel & McClaren						5.00
2017 Spoooktacular (10/17, $4.99) Short stories by various; 2 covers						5.00
... BMO Bonanza 1 (3/18, $7.99) Short stories by various						8.00
... Cover Showcase (12/12, $3.99) Gallery of variant covers for #1-9; Paul Pope-c						4.00
... Free Comic Book Day Edition (5/12) Giveaway flip book with Peanuts						3.00
... with Fionna and Cake 2018 Free Comic Book Day Special (5/18) Giveaway						3.00

ADVENTURE TIME: BANANA GUARD ACADEMY (Cartoon Network)
Boom Entertainment (KaBOOM!): Jul, 2014 - No. 6, Dec, 2014 ($3.99, limited series)

	GD	VG	FN	VF	VF/NM	NM-
1-6-Multiple covers on all; Mad Rupert-a						4.00

ADVENTURE TIME: BEGINNING OF THE END (Cartoon Network)
Boom Entertainment (KaBOOM!): May, 2018 - No. 3, Jul, 2018 ($3.99, limited series)

	GD	VG	FN	VF	VF/NM	NM-
1-3-Multiple covers on all; Ted Anderson-s/Marina Julia-a						4.00

ADVENTURE TIME: CANDY CAPERS (Cartoon Network)
Boom Entertainment (KaBOOM!): Jul, 2013 - No. 6, Dec, 2013 ($3.99, limited series)

	GD	VG	FN	VF	VF/NM	NM-
1-6-Multiple covers on all; McGinty-a						4.00

ADVENTURE TIME COMICS (Cartoon Network)
Boom Entertainment (KaBOOM!): Jul, 2016 - No. 25, Jul, 2018 ($3.99)

	GD	VG	FN	VF	VF/NM	NM-
1-24-Short stories by various. 1-Baltazar, Cook, Millionaire, Leyh-s/a						4.00
25-($4.99) Sonny Liew-s/a; Morgan Beem-s/a						5.00

ADVENTURE TIME: ICE KING (Cartoon Network)
Boom Entertainment (KaBOOM!): Jan, 2016 - No. 6, Jun, 2016 ($3.99, limited series)

	GD	VG	FN	VF	VF/NM	NM-
1-6-Multiple covers on all; Naujokaitis-s/Andrewson-a						4.00

ADVENTURE TIME: MARCELINE AND THE SCREAM QUEENS (Cartoon Network)
Boom Entertainment (KaBOOM!): Jul, 2012 - No. 6, Dec, 2012 ($3.99, limited series)

	GD	VG	FN	VF	VF/NM	NM-
1-6-Multiple covers on all						4.00

ADVENTURE TIME: MARCELINE GONE ADRIFT (Cartoon Network)
Boom Entertainment (KaBOOM!): Jan, 2015 - No. 6, Jun, 2015 ($3.99, limited series)

	GD	VG	FN	VF	VF/NM	NM-
1-6-Multiple covers on all; Meredith Gran-s/Carey Pietsch-a						4.00

ADVENTURE TIME: MARCY & SIMON (Cartoon Network)
Boom Entertainment (KaBOOM!): Jan, 2019 - No. 6, Jun, 2019 ($3.99, limited series)

	GD	VG	FN	VF	VF/NM	NM-
1-6-Multiple covers on all; Olivia Olson-s/Slimm Fabert; former Ice King apology tour						4.00

ADVENTURE TIME/ REGULAR SHOW (Cartoon Network)
Boom Entertainment (KaBOOM!): Aug, 2017 - No. 6, Jan, 2018 ($3.99, limited series)

	GD	VG	FN	VF	VF/NM	NM-
1-6-McCreery-s/Di Meo-a; multiple covers on each						4.00

Aero #8 © MAR

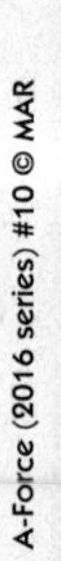

A-Force (2016 series) #10 © MAR

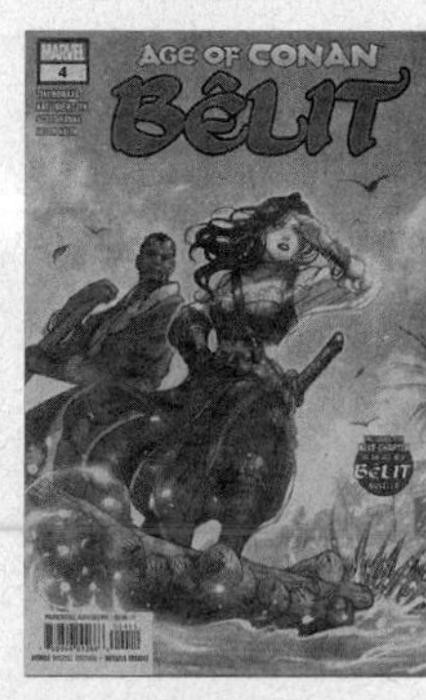

Age of Conan: Belit #4 © CPI

GD	VG	FN	VF	VF/NM	NM-
2.0	4.0	6.0	8.0	9.0	9.2

GD VG FN VF VF/NM NM-
2.0 4.0 6.0 8.0 9.0 9.2

ADVENTURE TIME: SEASON 11 (Cartoon Network)
Boom Entertainment (KaBOOM!): Oct, 2018 - No. 6, Mar, 2019 ($3.99)

1-6-Follows the television finale; Ted Anderson-s/Marina Julia-a 4.00

ADVENTURE TIME: THE FLIP SIDE (Cartoon Network)
Boom Entertainment (KaBOOM!): Jan, 2014 - No. 6, Jun, 2014 ($3.99, limited series)

1-6-Multiple covers on all; Tobin & Coover-s; Wook Jin Clark-a 4.00

ADVENTURE TIME WITH FIONNA & CAKE (Cartoon Network)
Boom Entertainment (KaBOOM!): Jan, 2013 - No. 6, Jun, 2013 ($3.99, limited series)

1-6-Multiple covers on all 4.00

ADVENTURE TIME WITH FIONNA & CAKE CARD WARS (Cartoon Network)
Boom Entertainment (KaBOOM!): Jul, 2015 - No. 6, Dec, 2015 ($3.99, limited series)

1-6-Multiple covers on all; Jen Wang-s/Britt Wilson-a. 1-Polybagged with a game card 4.00

AEON FLUX (Based on the 2005 movie which was based on the MTV animated series)
Dark Horse Comics: Oct, 2005 - No. 4, Jan, 2006 ($2.99, limited series)

1-4-Timothy Green II-a/Mike Kennedy-s 3.00
TPB (5/06, $12.95) r/series; cover gallery 13.00

AERO (See War of the Realms: New Agents of Atlas #4)
Marvel Comics: Sept, 2019 - No. 12, Dec, 2020 ($3.99)

1-10: 1-Liefen-s/Kang-a; Shanghai-based heroine; origin back-up by Pak-s/Mhan-a 4.00

A-FORCE (Secret Wars tie-in)
Marvel Comics: Jul, 2015 - No. 5, Dec, 2015 ($3.99, limited series)

1-5-All-Female Avengers team; Bennett & Willow Wilson-s/Molina-a. 1-Intro. Singularity 4.00

A-FORCE (Follows Secret Wars)
Marvel Comics: Mar, 2016 - No. 10, Dec, 2016 ($3.99)

1-10: 1-Medusa, She-Hulk, Dazzler, Nico, Capt. Marvel, Singularity team; Wilson-s/Molina-a. 5-7-Thompson-s/Caldwell-a. 8-10-Civil War II tie-in 4.00

AFRICA
Magazine Enterprises: 1955

1(A-1 #137)-Cave Girl, Thun'da; Powell-c/a(4) 37 74 111 222 361 500

AFRICAN LION (Disney movie)
Dell Publishing Co.: Nov, 1955

Four Color 665 5 10 15 34 60 85

AFTER DARK
Sterling Comics: No. 6, May, 1955 - No. 8, Sept, 1955

6-8-Sekowsky-a in all 10 20 30 54 72 90

AFTER DARK (Co-created by Wesley Snipes)
Radical Comics: No. 0, Jun, 2010 - No. 3 ($1.00/$4.99, limited series)

0-($1.00) Milligan-s/Nentrup & Mattina-a 3.00
1-3-($4.99) Milligan-s/Manco-a 5.00

AFTERLIFE WITH ARCHIE
Archie Comic Publications: Sept, 2013 - Present ($2.99/$3.99)

1-Aguirre-Sacasa-s/Francavilla-a; zombies in Riverdale; Sabrina app.; 4 covers 24.00
1-Second printing; new cover by Francavilla 6.00
2-Covers by Francavilla & Seeley; back-up short story r/Chilling Advs. in Sorcery 12.00
3-6: 3,4-Covers by Francavilla & Seeley on each; back-up r/Chilling Advs. in Sorcery. 5,6-Pepoy variant-c. 6-Back-up preview of Chilling Advs. of Sabrina #1 6.00
7-10-($3.99) 7-Covers by Francavilla & Pepoy; back-up r/Chilling Advs. in Sorcery 5.00
... Halloween ComicFest Edition 1 (2014, giveaway) Grey-toned reprint of #1 3.00
... Halloween ComicFest Edition 1 (2016, giveaway) Grey-toned reprint of #7 3.00

AFTER REALM QUARTERLY, THE
Image Comics: Feb, 2020 - Present ($5.99, quarterly)

1-3-Michael Avon Oeming-s/a; intro/origin of Oona Lightfoot 6.00

AFTERSHOCK GENESIS
AfterShock Comics: May, 2016 ($1.00, one-shot)

1-Short stories by various and previews of upcoming AfterShock titles 3.00

AFTER THE CAPE
Image Comics (Shadowline): Mar, 2007 - No. 3, May, 2007 ($2.99, B&W, limited series)

1-3-Jim Valentino-s/Marco Rudy-a 3.00
... Volume One TPB (9/07, $12.99) r/series; scripts, sketch pages, character profiles 13.00
...II (11/07 - No. 3, 1/08, $2.99) 1-3-Jim Valentino-s/Sergio Carrera-a 3.00

AGENCY, THE
Image Comics (Top Cow): August, 2001 - No. 6, Mar, 2002 ($2.50/$2.95/$4.95)

1-5: 1-Jenkins-s/Hotz-a; three covers by Hotz, Turner, Silvestri. 3-5-($2.95) 3.00
6-($4.95) Flip-c preview of Jeremiah TV series 5.00
Preview (2001, 16 pgs.) B&W pages, cover previews, sketch pages 3.00

AGENT CARTER: S.H.I.E.L.D. 50TH ANNIVERSARY
Marvel Comics: Nov, 2015 ($3.99, one-shot)

1-Kathryn Immonen-s/Rich Ellis-a; set in 1966; Sif, Dum Dum and Nick Fury app. 4.00

AGENT 47: BIRTH OF THE HITMAN (Based on the Io-Anteractive video game)
Dynamite Entertainment: 2017 - No. 6, 2018 ($3.99)

1-6: 1-Sebela-s/Lau-a; multiple covers on each 4.00

AGENT LIBERTY SPECIAL (See Superman, 2nd Series)
DC Comics: 1992 ($2.00, 52 pgs, one-shot)

1-1st solo adventure; Guice-c/a(i) 4.00

AGENTS, THE
Image Comics: Apr, 2003 - No. 6, Sept, 2003 ($2.95, B&W)

1-5-Ben Dunn-c/a in all 3.00
6-Five pg. preview of The Walking Dead #1 3 6 9 17 26 35

AGENTS OF ATLAS
Marvel Comics: Oct, 2006 - No. 6, Mar, 2007 ($2.99, limited series)

1-6: 1-Golden Age heroes Marvel Boy & Venus app.; Kirk-a 3.00
... MGC 1 (7/10, $1.00) r/#1 with "Marvel's Greatest Comics" logo on cover 3.00
HC (2007, $24.99, dustjacket) r/#1-6, What If? #9, agents' debuts in '40s-'50s Atlas comics, creator interviews, character design art 25.00

AGENTS OF ATLAS (Dark Reign)
Marvel Comics: Apr, 2009 - No. 11, Nov, 2009 ($3.99)

1-11: 1-Pagulayan-a; 2 covers by Art Adams and McGuinness; back-up with Wolverine app. 5-New Avengers app. 8-Hulk app. 4.00

AGENTS OF ATLAS (Continues in Atlantis Attacks #1)(Also see Future Fight Firsts)
Marvel Comics: Oct, 2019 - No. 5, Feb, 2020 ($4.99/$3.99)

1-($4.99) Team of Shang-Chi, Brawn, Silk, Jimmy Woo, Luna Snow, Aero & others 5.00
2-5-($3.99) Greg Pak-s/Nico Leon-a. 5-Namor app. 4.00

AGENTS OF LAW (Also see Comic's Greatest World)
Dark Horse Comics: Mar, 1995 - No. 6, Sept, 1995 ($2.50)

1-6: 5-Predator app. 6-Predator app.; death of Law 3.00

AGENTS OF S.H.I.E.L.D. (Characters from the TV series)
Marvel Comics: Mar, 2016 - No. 10, Dec, 2016 ($3.99)

1-10: 1-Guggenheim-s/Peralta-a; Tony Stark app. 3,4-Standoff tie-in. 5-Spider-Man app. 7-10-Civil War II tie-in. 9,10-Elektra app. 4.00

AGENT X (Continued from Deadpool)
Marvel Comics: Sept. 2002 - No. 15, Dec, 2003 ($2.99/$2.25)

1-($2.99) Simone-s/Udon Studios-a; Taskmaster app. 4.00
2-9-($2.25) 2-Punisher app. 3.00
10-15-($2.99) 10,11-Evan Dorkin-s. 12-Hotz-a 3.00

AGE OF APOCALYPSE (See Uncanny X-Force)
Marvel Comics: May, 2012 - No. 14, Jun, 2013 ($2.99)

1-14: 1-Lapham-s/De La Torre-a/Ramos-c. 13-Leads into X-Termination x-over 3.00

AGE OF APOCALYPSE (Secret Wars tie-in)
Marvel Comics: Sept, 2015 - No. 5, Dec, 2015 ($4.99/$3.99, limited series)

1-($4.99) Nicieza-s/Sandoval-a; alternate X-Men vs. Apocalypse 5.00
2-5-($3.99) Covers #1-5 form one image; Blink, Sabretooth & Magneto app. 4.00

AGE OF APOCALYPSE: THE CHOSEN
Marvel Comics: Apr, 1995 ($2.50, one-shot)

1-Wraparound-c 5.00

AGE OF BRONZE
Image Comics: Nov, 1998 - Present ($2.95/$3.50, B&W)

1-6-Eric Shanower-c/s/a 3.50
7-33-($3.50) 3.50
...Behind the Scenes (5/02, $3.50) background info and creative process 3.50
Image Firsts: Age of Bronze #1 (4/10, $1.00) r/#1 with "Image Firsts" cover logo 3.00
...Special (6/99, $2.95) Story of Agamemnon and Menelaus 3.50
A Thousand Ships (7/01, $19.95, TPB) r/#1-9 20.00
Sacrifice (9/04, $19.95, TPB) r/#10-19 20.00

AGE OF CONAN: BELIT
Marvel Comics: May, 2019 - No. 5, Sept, 2019 ($3.99, limited series)

1-5-Tini Howard-s/Kate Niemczyk-a/Sana Takeda-c; back-up serialized text story 4.00

AGE OF CONAN: VALERIA
Marvel Comics: Oct, 2019 - No. 5, Feb, 2020 ($3.99, limited series)

Age of Heroes #4 © MAR

Aggie Mack #8 © SUPR

Airboy Comics V3 #1 © HILL

	GD	VG	FN	VF	VF/NM	NM-
	2.0	4.0	6.0	8.0	9.0	9.2

1-5-Meredith Finch-s/Aneke-a; origin from childhood; back-up serialized text story 4.00

AGE OF HEROES, THE
Halloween Comics/Image Comics #3 on: 1996 - No. 5, 1999 ($2.95, B&W)

1-5: James Hudnall scripts; John Ridgway-c/a 3.00
...Special ($4.95) r/#1,2 5.00
...Special 2 ($6.95) r/#3,4 7.00
...Wex 1 ('98, $2.95) Hudnall-s/Angel Fernandez-a 3.00

AGE OF HEROES (The Heroic Age)
Marvel Comics: Jul, 2010 - No. 4, Oct, 2010 ($3.99, limited series)

1-4-Short stories of Avengers members by various. 4-Jae Lee-c 4.00

AGE OF INNOCENCE: THE REBIRTH OF IRON MAN
Marvel Comics: Feb, 1996 ($2.50, one-shot)

1-New origin of Tony Stark 3.00

AGE OF REPTILES
Dark Horse Comics: Nov, 1993 - No. 4, Feb, 1994 ($2.50, limited series)

1-4: Delgado-c/a/scripts in all 4.00
... Ancient Egyptians 1-4 (6/15 - No. 4, 9/15, $3.99) Delgado-c/a/scripts; wraparound-c 4.00
... The Hunt 1-5 (5/96 - No. 5, 9/96, $2.95) Delgado-c/a/scripts in all; wraparound-c 4.00
... The Journey 1-4 (11/09 - No. 4, 7/10, $3.50) Delgado-c/a/scripts in all; wraparound-c 3.50

AGE OF THE SENTRY, THE
Marvel Comics: Nov, 2008 - No. 6, Mar, 2010 ($2.99, limited series)

1-6-Silver Age style stories. 1-Origin retold; Bullock-c. 3-Coover-a 3.00

AGE OF ULTRON
Marvel Comics: May, 2013 - No. 10, Aug, 2013 ($3.99, limited series)

1-Wraparound cardstock foil-c; Hitch-a/c 6.00
2-9: 2-5-Hitch-a/c. 6-Peterson & Pacheco-a, Hank Pym killed 4.00
10-Polybagged; Angela joins the Marvel Universe 6.00
10AU (8/13, $3.99) Waid-s/Aralijo-a/Pichelli-c; Hank Pym's origin re-told
1 3 4 6 8 10

AGE OF ULTRON VS. MARVEL ZOMBIES (Secret Wars tie-in)
Marvel Comics: Aug, 2015 - No. 4, Nov, 2015 ($3.99, limited series)

1-4-James Robinson-s/Steve Pugh-a; Vision, Wonder Man & Jim Hammond app. 4.00

AGE OF X (X-Men titles crossover)
Marvel Comics: ($3.99, limited series)

... Alpha 1 (3/11, $3.99) Short stories by various; covers by Bachalo & Coipel 6.00
...: Universe 1,2 (5/11 - No. 2, 6/11, $3.99) Pham-a; Bianchi-c; Avengers & Spider-Man app. 6.00

AGE OF X-MAN
Marvel Comics: Mar, 2019 - Sept, 2019 ($4.99/$3.99, limited series)

... Alpha 1 (3/19, $4.99) Rosanas-a; world where everyone is a mutant 5.00
...: Apocalypse and the X-Tracts 1-5 (5/19 - No. 5, 9/19 $3.99) Seeley-s/Espin-a 4.00
...: Nextgen 1-5 (4/19 - No. 5, 8/19, $3.99) 1-4-To-a; Bachalo-c. 5-Werneck-a 4.00
...: Omega 1 (9/19, $4.99) Conclusion; leads into House of X #1; Buonfantino-a 5.00
...: Prisoner X 1-5 (5/19 - No. 5, 9/19, $3.99) Peralta-a; Bishop, Polaris, Beast, Gabby app. 4.00
...: The Amazing Nightcrawler 1-5 (4/19 - No. 5, 8/19, $3.99) Frigeri-a 4.00
...: The Marvelous X-Men 1-5 (4/19 - No. 5, 8/19, $3.99) Failla-a/Noto-c; X-Man app. 4.00
...: X-Tremists 1-5 (4/19 - No. 5, 8/19, $3.99) Jeanty-a/Rahzzah-c 4.00

AGGIE MACK
Four Star Comics Corp./Superior Comics Ltd.: Jan, 1948 - No. 8, Aug, 1949

1-Feldstein-a, "Johnny Prep" 48 96 144 302 514 725
2,3-Kamen-c 29 58 87 170 278 385
4-Feldstein "Johnny Prep"; Kamen-c 36 72 108 215 350 485
5-8-Kamen-c/a. 7-Burt Lancaster app. on-c 31 62 93 182 296 410

AGGIE MACK
Dell Publishing Co.: Apr - Jun, 1962

Four Color 1335 5 10 15 33 57 80

AIR
DC Comics (Vertigo): Oct, 2008 - No. 24, Oct, 2010 ($2.99)

1-6,8-24-G. Willow Wilson-s/M.K. Perker-a 3.00
7-($1.00) Includes story re-cap 3.00
... A History of the Future TPB (2011, $14.99) r/#18-24 15.00
... Flying Machine TPB (2009, $12.99) r/#6-10; Wilson intro. 13.00
... Letters From Lost Countries TPB (2009, $9.99) r/#1-5; character sketch pages 10.00
... Pure Land TPB (2010, $14.99) r/#11-17 15.00

AIR ACE (Formerly Bill Barnes No. 1-12)
Street & Smith Publications: V2#1, Jan, 1944 - V3#8(No. 20), Feb-Mar, 1947

V2#1-Nazi concentration camp-c 65 130 195 416 708 1000
V2#2-Classic Japanese WWII-c 277 554 831 1759 3030 4300
V2#3-12: 3-WWII-c. 7-Powell-a 18 36 54 107 169 230
V3#1-6: 2-Atomic explosion on-c 15 30 45 84 127 170
V3#7-Powell bondage-c/a; all atomic issue 47 94 141 296 498 700
V3#8 (V5#8 on-c)-Powell-c/a 16 32 48 94 147 200

AIRBOY (Also see Airmaidens, Skywolf, Target: Airboy & Valkyrie)
Eclipse Comics: July, 1986 - No. 50, Oct, 1989 (#1-8, 50¢, 20 pgs., bi-weekly; #9-on, 36 pgs.; #34-on monthly)

1-4: 2-1st Marisa; Skywolf gets new costume. 3-The Heap begins 5.00
5-Valkyrie returns; Dave Stevens-c 2 4 6 9 13 16
6-49: 9-Begin $1.25-c; Skywolf begins. 11-Origin of G.A. Airboy & his plane Birdie. 28-Mr. Monster vs. The Heap. 33-Begin $1.75-c. 38-40-The Heap by Infantino. 41-r/1st app. Valkyrie from Air Fighters. 42-Begin $1.95-c. 46,47-part-r/Air Fighters. 48-Black Angel-r/A.F 4.00
50 ($4.95, 52 pgs.)-Kubert-c 5.00
51-(It's Alive Press, Oct, 2019, $9.99) Chuck Dixon-s/Brent McKee-a; The Heap back-up 10.00

NOTE: ***Evans*** *c-21.* ***Gulacy*** *c-7, 20.* ***Spiegle*** *a-34, 35, 37.* ***Ken Steacy*** *painted c-17, 33.*

AIRBOY
Image Comics: Jun, 2015 - No. 4, Nov, 2015 ($2.99, limited series, mature)

1-4: 1-Airboy meets writer James Robinson and artist Greg Hinkle. 3,4-Valkyrie app. 3.00

AIRBOY COMICS (Air Fighters Comics No. 1-22)
Hillman Periodicals: V2#11, Dec, 1945 - V10#4, May, 1953 (No V3#3)

V2#11 61 122 183 390 670 950
12-Valkyrie-c/app. 60 120 180 381 653 925
V3#1,2(no #3) 40 80 120 246 411 575
4-The Heap app. in Skywolf 39 78 117 236 388 540
5,7,8,10,11 33 66 99 194 317 440
6-Valkyrie-c/app. 39 78 117 231 378 525
9-Origin The Heap 39 78 117 231 378 525
12-Skywolf & Airboy x-over; Valkyrie-c/app. 40 80 120 246 411 575
V4#1-Iron Lady app. 33 66 99 194 317 440
2,3,12: 2-Rackman begins 26 52 78 154 252 350
4-Simon & Kirby-c 31 62 93 186 303 420
5-7,9,11-All S&K-a 30 60 90 177 289 400
8-Classic bondage/torture-c; S&K-a 226 452 678 1446 2473 3500
10-Valkyrie-c/app. 36 72 108 211 343 475
V5#1-4,6-11: 4-Infantino Heap. 10-Origin The Heap 20 40 60 120 195 270
5-Skull-c. 24 48 72 144 237 330
12-Krigstein-a(p) 21 42 63 124 202 280
V6#1-3,5-12: 6,8-Origin The Heap 20 40 60 114 182 250
4-Origin retold 22 44 66 132 216 300
V7#1-12: 7,8,10-Origin The Heap. 12-(1/51) 19 38 57 112 179 245
V8#1-3,5-12: 5-UFO-c (6/51) 18 36 54 105 165 225
4-Krigstein-a 19 38 57 109 172 235
V9#1,3,4,6-12: 7-One pg. Frazetta ad 15 30 45 90 140 190
2-Valkyrie app. 16 32 48 94 147 200
5(#100) 16 32 48 94 147 200
V10#1-4 15 30 45 85 130 175

NOTE: ***Barry*** *a-V2#3, 7.* ***Bolle*** *a-V4#12.* ***McWilliams*** *a-V3#7, 9.* ***Powell*** *a-V7#2, 3, V8#1, 6.* ***Starr*** *a-V5#1, 12.* ***Dick Wood*** *a-V4#12. Bondage-c V5#8.*

AIRBOY MEETS THE PROWLER
Eclipse Comics: Aug, 1987 ($1.95, one-shot)

1-John Snyder, III-c/a 4.00

AIRBOY-MR. MONSTER SPECIAL
Eclipse Comics: Aug, 1987 ($1.75, one-shot)

1 4.00

AIRBOY VERSUS THE AIR MAIDENS
Eclipse Comics: July, 1988 ($1.95)

1 4.00

AIR FIGHTERS CLASSICS
Eclipse Comics: Nov, 1987 - No. 6, May, 1989 ($3.95, 68 pgs., B&W)

1-6: Reprints G.A. Air Fighters #2-7. 1-Origin Airboy 4.00

AIR FIGHTERS COMICS (Airboy Comics #23 (V2#11) on)
Hillman Periodicals: Nov, 1941; No. 2, Nov, 1942 - V2#10, Fall, 1945

V1#1-(Produced by Funnies, Inc.); No Airboy; Black Commander only app.
226 452 678 1446 2473 3500
2(11/42)-(Produced by Quality artists & Biro for Hillman); Origin & 1st app. Airboy & Iron Ace; Black Angel (1st app.), Flying Dutchman & Skywolf (1st app.) begin; Fuje-a; Biro-c/a 508 1016 1524 3701 6551 9400
3-Origin/1st app. The Heap; origin Skywolf; 2nd Airboy app./c

Air Fighters Comics #7 © HILL

Akiko #16 © Mark Crilley

Albedo Anthropomorphics #2 © AP

	GD 2.0	VG 4.0	FN 6.0	VF 8.0	VF/NM 9.0	NM- 9.2
	206	412	618	1318	2259	3200
4-Japan war-c	181	362	543	1158	1979	2800
5-Japanese octopus War-c	194	388	582	1242	2121	3000
6-Japanese soldiers as rats-c	226	452	678	1446	2473	3500
7-Classic Nazi swastika-c	206	412	618	1318	2259	3200
8-12: 8,10,11-War covers	90	180	270	576	988	1400
V2#1-Classic Nazi War-c	100	200	300	635	1093	1550
2-Skywolf by Giunta; Flying Dutchman by Fuje; 1st meeting Valkyrie & Airboy (she worked for the Nazis in beginning); 1st app. Valkyrie (11/43); Valkyrie-c	219	438	657	1402	2401	3400
3,4,6,8,9	61	122	183	390	670	950
5-Flag-c; Fuje-a	68	136	204	435	743	1050
7-Valkyrie app.	90	180	270	576	988	1400
10-Origin The Heap & Skywolf	70	140	210	445	765	1085

NOTE: *Fuje a-V1#2, 5, 7, V2#2, 3, 5, 7-9.* ***Giunta*** *a-V2#2, 3, 7, 9.*

AIRFIGHTERS MEET SGT. STRIKE SPECIAL, THE
Eclipse Comics: Jan, 1988 ($1.95, one-shot, stiff-c)

1-Airboy, Valkyrie, Skywolf app.						4.00

AIR FORCES (See American Air Forces)

AIRMAIDENS SPECIAL
Eclipse Comics: August, 1987 ($1.75, one-shot, Baxter paper)

1-Marisa becomes La Lupina (origin)						3.00

AIR RAIDERS
Marvel Comics (Star Comics)/Marvel #3 on: Nov, 1987- No. 5, Mar, 1988 ($1.00)

1,5: Kelley Jones-a in all						4.00
2-4: 2-Thunderhammer app.						3.00

AIRTIGHT GARAGE, THE (Also see Elsewhere Prince)
Marvel Comics (Epic Comics): July, 1993 - No. 4, Oct, 1993 ($2.50, lim. series, Baxter paper)

1-4: Moebius-c/a/scripts	1	3	4	6	8	10

AIR WAR STORIES
Dell Publishing Co.: Sept-Nov, 1964 - No. 8, Aug, 1966

1-Painted-c; Glanzman-c/a begins	4	8	12	27	44	60
2-8: 2,3-Painted-c	3	6	9	17	26	35

A.K.A. GOLDFISH
Caliber Comics: 1994 - 1995 (B&W, $3.50/$3.95)

...:Ace; ...:Jack; ...:Queen; ...:Joker; ...:King -Brian Michael Bendis-s/a						4.00
TPB (1996, $17.95)						20.00
Goldfish: The Definitive Collection (Image, 2001, $19.95) r/series plus promo art and new prose story; intro. by Matt Wagner						20.00
10th Anniversary HC (Image, 2002, $49.95)						50.00

AKIKO
Sirius: Mar, 1996 - No. 52, Feb, 2004 ($2.50/$2.95, B&W)

1-Crilley-c/a/scripts in all						5.00
2						4.00
3-49,51,52: 25-($2.95, 32 pgs.)-w/Asala back-up pages. 40-Begin $2.95-c						3.00
50-($3.50)						3.50
Flights of Fancy TPB (5/02, $12.95) r/various features, pin-ups and gags						13.00
TPB Volume 1,4 ('97, 2/00, $14.95) 1-r/#1-7. 4-r/#19-25						15.00
TPB Volume 2,3 ('98, '99, $11.95) 2-r/#8-13. 3- r/#14-18						12.00
TPB Volume 5 (12/01, $12.95) r/#26-31						13.00
TPB Volume 6,7 (6/03, 4/04, $14.95) 6-r/#32-38. 7-r/#40-47						15.00

AKIKO ON THE PLANET SMOO
Sirius: Dec, 1995 ($3.95, B&W)

V1#1-($3.95)-Crilley-c/a/scripts; gatefold-c						5.00
Ashcan ('95, mail offer)						3.00
Hardcover V1#1 (12/95, $19.95, B&W, 40 pgs.)						20.00
The Color Edition(2/00,$4.95)						5.00

AKIRA
Marvel Comics (Epic): Sept, 1988 - No. 38, Dec, 1995 ($3.50/$3.95/$6.95, deluxe, 68 pgs.)

1-1st English translation of Katsuhiro Otomo's manga	3	6	9	20	31	42
1,2-2nd printings (1989, $3.95)						5.00
2	2	4	6	9	12	15
3-5	2	4	6	8	10	12
6-16	1	2	3	5	7	9
17-33: 17-$3.95-c begins						6.00
34,35: 34-(1994)-$6.95-c begins. 35-(1995)	2	4	6	10	14	18
36-MIyako's Last Stand	4	8	12	23	37	50
37-Texeira back-up, Gibbons, Williams pin-ups	5	10	15	30	50	70
38-Moebius, Allred, Pratt, Toth, Romita, Van Fleet, O'Neill, Madureira pin-ups; last Otomo issue	8	16	24	54	102	150

ALABASTER: THE GOOD, THE BAD AND THE BIRD
Dark Horse Comics: Dec, 2015 - No. 5, Apr, 2016 ($3.99, limited series)

1-5-Caitlin Kiernan-s/Daniel Johnson-a						4.00

ALADDIN & HIS WONDERFUL LAMP (See Dell Jr Treasury #2)

ALAN LADD (See The Adventures of...)

ALAN MOORE'S AWESOME UNIVERSE HANDBOOK (Also see Across the Universe:...)
Awesome Entertainment: Apr, 1999 ($2.95, B&W)

1-Alan Moore-text/ Alex Ross-sketch pages and 2 covers						5.00

ALAN MOORE...
DC Comics (WildStorm): TPB

...'s Complete WildC.A.T.S. (2007, $29.99) r/#21-34,50; ...Homecoming & ...Gang War						30.00
...: Wild Worlds (2007, $24.99) r/various WildStorm one-shots and limited series						25.00

ALARMING ADVENTURES
Harvey Publications: Oct, 1962 - No. 3, Feb, 1963

1-Crandall/Williamson-a	8	16	24	52	99	145
2-Williamson/Crandall-a	5	10	15	33	57	80
3-Torres-a	5	10	15	30	50	70

NOTE: ***Bailey*** *a-1, 3.* ***Crandall*** *a-1p, 2i.* ***Powell*** *a-2(2).* ***Severin*** *c-1-3.* ***Torres*** *a-2?* ***Tuska*** *a-1.* ***Williamson*** *a-1i, 2p.*

ALARMING TALES
Harvey Publications (Western Tales): Sept, 1957 - No. 6, Nov, 1958

1-Kirby-c/a(4); Kamandi prototype story by Kirby	34	68	102	204	332	460
2-Kirby-a(4)	22	44	66	132	216	300
3,4-Kirby-a. 4-Powell, Wildey-a	17	34	51	98	154	210
5-Kirby/Williamson-a; Wildey-a; Severin-c	18	36	54	105	165	225
6-Williamson-a?; Severin-c	14	28	42	82	121	160

ALBEDO
Thoughts And Images: Summer, 1983 - No. 14, Spring, 1989 (B&W)
Antarctic Press: (Vol. 2) Jun, 1991 - No. 10 ($2.50)

0-Yellow cover; 50 copies	16	32	48	110	243	375
0-White cover, 450 copies	9	18	27	59	117	175
0-Blue, 1st printing, 500 copies	8	16	24	54	102	150
0-Blue, 2nd printing, 1000 copies	4	8	12	27	44	60
0-3rd & 4th printing	3	6	9	14	19	24
1-Dark red, 1st printing - low print run	12	24	36	79	170	260
1-Bright red, later printings - low print run	6	12	18	41	76	110
2-(11/84) 1st app. Usagi Yojimbo by Stan Sakai; 2000 copies - no 2nd printing	400	800	1200	2800	4400	6000
3	4	8	12	23	37	50
4-Usagi Yojimbo-c	5	10	15	34	60	85
5-14						6.00
(Vol. 2) 1	1	3	4	6	8	10
2-10, Color Special	1	2	3	4	5	7

ALBEDO ANTHROPOMORPHICS
Antarctic Press: (Vol. 3) Spring, 1994 - No. 4, Jan, 1996 ($2.95, color);
(Vol. 4) Dec, 1999 - No. 2, Jan, 1999 ($2.95/$2.99, B&W)

V3#1-Steve Gallacci-c/a	2	4	6	8	10	12
V3#2-4-Steve Gallacci-c/a. V4#1,2	1	2	3	5	6	8

ALBERTO (See The Crusaders)

ALBERT THE ALLIGATOR & POGO POSSUM (See Pogo Possum)

ALBION (Inspired by 1960s IPC British comics characters)
DC Comics (WildStorm): Aug, 2005 - No. 6, Nov, 2006 ($2.99, limited series)

1-6-Alan Moore, Leah Moore & John Reppion-s/Shane Oakley-a; Dave Gibbons-c						3.00
TPB (2007, $19.99) r/series; intro by Neil Gaiman; reprints from 1960s British comics						20.00

ALBUM OF CRIME (See Fox Giants)

ALBUM OF LOVE (See Fox Giants)

AL CAPP'S DOGPATCH (Also see Mammy Yokum)
Toby Press: No. 71, June, 1949 - No. 4, Dec, 1949

71(#1)-Reprints from Tip Top #112-114	16	32	48	92	144	195
2-4: 4-Reprints from Li'l Abner #73	13	26	39	72	101	130

AL CAPP'S SHMOO (Also see Oxydol-Dreft & Washable Jones & Shmoo)
Toby Press: July, 1949 - No. 5, Apr, 1950 (None by Al Capp)

1-1st app. Super-Shmoo	31	62	93	182	296	410
2-5: 3-Sci-fi trip to moon. 4-X-Mas-c	20	40	60	120	195	270

AL CAPP'S WOLF GAL
Toby Press: 1951 - No. 2, 1952

Alex + Ada #1 © Luna & Vaughn

Alias #25 © MAR

Alien Encounters #10 © ECL

	GD 2.0	VG 4.0	FN 6.0	VF 8.0	VF/NM 9.0	NM- 9.2
1-Edited-r from Li'l Abner #63	34	68	102	199	325	475
2-Edited-r from Li'l Abner #64	19	38	57	111	176	250
ALEISTER ARCANE						
IDW Publishing: Apr, 2004 - No. 3, June, 2004 ($3.99, limited series)						
1-3-Steve Niles-s/Breehn Burns-a						4.00
TPB (10/04, $17.99) r/series; sketch pages						18.00
ALEXANDER THE GREAT (Movie)						
Dell Publishing Co.: No. 688, May, 1956						
Four Color 688-Buscema-a; photo-c	6	12	18	42	79	115
ALEX + ADA						
Image Comics: Nov, 2013 - No. 15, Jun, 2015 ($2.99/$3.99)						
1-14-Jonathan Luna-a/c; Sarah Vaughn & Luna-s						3.00
15-($3.99) Conclusion						4.00
ALF (TV) (See Star Comics Digest)						
Marvel Comics: Mar, 1988 - No. 50, Feb, 1992 ($1.00)						
1-Photo-c	2	4	6	9	12	15
1-2nd printing						3.00
2-19: 6-Photo-c						4.00
20-22: 20-Conan parody. 21-Marx Brothers. 22-X-Men parody						5.00
23-30: 24-Rhonda-c/app. 29-3-D cover						4.00
31-43,46,47,49						4.00
44,45: 44-X-Men parody. 45-Wolverine, Punisher, Capt. America-c						5.00
48-(12/91) Risqué Alf with seal cover	5	10	15	34	60	85
50-($1.75, 52 pgs.)-Final issue; photo-c						5.00
Annual 1-3: 1-Rocky & Bullwinkle app. 2-Sienkiewicz-c. 3-TMNT parody						5.00
...Comics Digest 1,2: 1-(1988)-Reprints Alf #1,2	2	4	6	8	10	12
Holiday Special 1,2 ('88, Wint. '89, 68 pgs.): 2-X-Men parody-c						5.00
Spring Special 1 (Spr/89, $1.75, 68 pgs.) Invisible Man parody						5.00
TPB (68 pgs.) r/#1-3; photo-c						5.00
ALFRED HARVEY'S BLACK CAT						
Lorne-Harvey Productions: 1995 ($3.50, B&W/color)						
1-Origin by Mark Evanier & Murphy Anderson; contains history of Alfred Harvey & Harvey Publications; 5 pg. B&W Sad Sack story; Hildebrandts-c						6.00
ALGIE (LITTLE...)						
Timor Publ. Co.: Dec, 1953 - No. 3, 1954						
1-Teenage	9	18	27	52	69	85
1-Algie #1 cover w/Secret Mysteries #19 inside	11	22	33	62	86	110
2,3	6	12	18	29	36	42
Accepted Reprint #2(nd)	3	6	8	12	14	16
Super Reprint #15	2	4	6	8	11	14
ALIAS:						
Now Comics: July, 1990 - No. 5, Nov, 1990 ($1.75)						
1-5: 1-Sienkiewicz-c						3.00
ALIAS (Also see Jessica Jones apps. in New Avengers and The Pulse)						
Marvel Comics (MAX Comics): Nov, 2001 - No. 28, Jan, 2004 ($2.99)						
1-Bendis-s/Gaydos-a/Mack-c; intro Jessica Jones; Luke Cage app.	4	8	12	28	47	65
2-4	1	2	3	4	5	7
5-23: 7,8-Sienkiewicz-a (2 pgs.) 16-21-Spider-Woman app. 22,23-Jessica's origin						3.00
24-28-Purple Man app.; Avengers app.; flashback-a by Bagley						5.00
... MGC 1 (6/10, $1.00) r/#1 with "Marvel's Greatest Comics" logo on cover						3.00
HC (2002, $29.99) r/#1-9; intro. by Jeph Loeb						30.00
Omnibus (2006, $69.99, hardcover with dustjacket) r/#1-28 and What If Jessica Jones Had Joined the Avengers?; original pitch, script and sketch pages						70.00
Vol. 1: TPB (2003, $19.99) r/#1-9						20.00
Vol. 2: Come Home TPB (2003, $13.99) r/#11-15						14.00
Vol. 3: The Underneath TPB (2003, $16.99) r/#10,16-21						17.00
ALICE (New Adventures in Wonderland)						
Ziff-Davis Publ. Co.: No. 10, 7-8/51 - No. 11(#2), 11-12/51						
10-Painted-c; Berg-a	31	62	93	184	300	415
11-(#2 on inside) Dave Berg-a	20	40	60	115	185	255
ALICE AT MONKEY ISLAND (Formerly The Adventures of Alice)						
Pentagon Publ. Co. (Civil Service): No. 3, 1946						
3	11	22	33	62	86	110
ALICE COOPER (Also see Last Temptation)						
Dynamite Entertainment: 2014 - No. 6, 2015 ($3.99)						
1-6: 1-5-Joe Harris-s/Eman Casallos-a/David Mack-c. 6-Jerwa-s/Tenorio-a						4.00
ALICE COOPER VS. CHAOS!						
Dynamite Entertainment: 2015 - No. 6, 2016 ($3.99, limited series)						
1-6-Chastity, Purgatori, Evil Ernie, Lady Demon & The Queen of Sorrows app.						4.00
ALICE IN WONDERLAND (Disney; see Advs. of Alice, Dell Jr. Treasury #1, The Dreamery, Movie Comics, Walt Disney Showcase #22, and World's Greatest Stories)						
Dell Publishing Co.: No. 24, 1940; No. 331, 1951; No. 341, July, 1951						
Single Series 24 (#1)(1940)	61	122	183	390	670	950
Four Color 331, 341-"Unbirthday Party w/..."	16	32	48	112	249	385
1-(Whitman, 3/84, pre-pack only)-r/4-Color #331	3	6	9	21	33	45
ALIENATED						
BOOM! Studios: Feb, 2020 - No. 6, Sept, 2020 ($3.99, limited series)						
1-6-Spurrier-s/Wildgoose-a						4.00
ALIEN ENCOUNTERS (Replaces Alien Worlds)						
Eclipse Comics: June, 1985 - No. 14, Aug, 1987 ($1.75, Baxter paper, mature)						
1-10: Nudity, strong language in all. 9-Snyder-a						4.00
11-14-Low print run						5.00
ALIEN LEGION (See Epic & Marvel Graphic Novel #25)						
Marvel Comics (Epic Comics): Apr, 1984 - No. 20, Sept, 1987						
nn-With bound-in trading card; Austin-i						5.00
2-20: 2-$1.50-c. 7,8-Portacio-i						3.00
ALIEN LEGION (2nd Series)						
Marvel Comics (Epic): Aug, 1987(indicia)(10/87 on-c) - No. 18, Aug, 1990						
V2#1-18-Stroman-a in all. 7-18-Farmer-i						4.00
....: Force Nomad TPB (Checker Book Pub. Group, 2001, $24.95) r/#1-11						25.00
....: Piecemaker TPB (Checker Book Pub. Group, 2002, $19.95) r/#12-18						20.00
ALIEN LEGION: (Series of titles; all Marvel/Epic Comics)						
--BINARY DEEP, 1993 ($3.50, one-shot, 52 pgs.), nn-With bound-in trading card						4.00
--JUGGER GRIMROD, 8/92 ($5.95, one-shot, 52 pgs.) Book 1						6.00
--ONE PLANET AT A TIME, 5/93 - Book 3, 7/93 ($4.95, squarebound, 52 pgs.) Book 1-3: Hoang Nguyen-a						5.00
--ON THE EDGE (The... #2 & 3), 11/90 - No. 3, 1/91 ($4.50, 52 pgs.) 1-3-Stroman & Farmer-a						4.50
--TENANTS OF HELL, '91 - No. 2, '91 ($4.50, squarebound, 52 pgs.) Book 1,2-Stroman-c/a(p)						4.50
ALIEN LEGION: UNCIVIL WAR						
Titan Comics: Jul, 2014 - No. 4, Oct, 2014 ($3.99)						
1-4-Dixon-s/Stroman-a						4.00
ALIEN NATION (Movie)						
DC Comics: Dec, 1988 ($2.50; 68 pgs.)						
1-Adaptation of film; painted-c						4.00
ALIEN PIG FARM 3000						
Image Comics (RAW Studios): Apr, 2007 - No. 4, July, 2007 ($2.99, limited series)						
1-4-Steve Niles, Thomas Jane & Todd Farmer-s/Don Marquez-a						3.00
ALIEN RESURRECTION (Movie)						
Dark Horse Comics: Oct, 1997 - No. 2, Nov, 1997 ($2.50; limited series)						
1,2-Adaptation of film; Dave McKean-c						4.00
ALIENS, THE (Captain Johner and...)(Also see Magnus Robot Fighter...)						
Gold Key: Sept-Dec, 1967; No. 2, May, 1982						
1-Reprints from Magnus #1,3,4,6-10; Russ Manning-a in all	3	6	9	19	30	40
2-(Whitman) Same contents as #1	1	2	3	5	6	8
ALIENS (Movie) (See Alien: The Illustrated..., Dark Horse Comics & Dark Horse Presents #24)						
Dark Horse Comics: May, 1988 - No. 6, July, 1989 ($1.95, B&W, limited series)						
1-Based on movie sequel; 1st app. Aliens in comics	10	20	30	58	79	100
1-2nd - 6th printings; 4th w/new inside front-c						4.00
2	4	7	10	14	17	20
2-2nd & 3rd printing, 3-6-2nd printings						3.00
3	2	4	5	7	8	10
4-6						5.00
Mini Comic #1 (2/89, 4x6")-Was included with Aliens Portfolio						4.00
Collection 1 ($10.95,)-r/#1-6 plus Dark Horse Presents #24 plus new-a						12.00
Collection 1-2nd printing (1991, $11.95)-On higher quality paper than 1st print; Dorman painted-c						12.00
Hardcover ('90, $24.95, B&W)-r/1-6, DHP #24						30.00
... Omnibus Vol. 1 (7/07, $24.95, 9x6") r/1st & 2nd series and Aliens: Earth War						25.00
... Omnibus Vol. 2 (12/07, $24.95, 9x6") r/Genocide, Harvest and Colonial Marines series						25.00

Aliens: Defiance #3 © 20FOX

Aliens vs. Parker #4 © BOOM

Alien: The Original Screenplay #1 © 20FOX

	GD	VG	FN	VF	VF/NM	NM-
	2.0	4.0	6.0	8.0	9.0	9.2

... Omnibus Vol. 3 (3/08, $24.95, 9x6") r/Rogue, Salvation and Sacrifice, Labyrinth series 25.00
... Omnibus Vol. 4 (8/08, $24.95, 9x6") r/Music of the Spears, Stronghold, Berserker, Mondo Pest and Mondo Heat series and one-shots 25.00
... Omnibus Vol. 5 (11/08, $24.95, 9x6") r/Alchemy, Survival, Havoc series and various 25.00
... Omnibus Vol. 6 (2/09, $24.95, 9x6") r/Apocalypse GN, Xenogenesis & one-shots 25.00
... Outbreak (3rd printing, 8/96, $17.95)-Bolton-c 18.00
Platinum Edition - (See Dark Horse Presents: Aliens Platinum Edition) -

ALIENS
Dark Horse Comics: V2#1, Aug, 1989 - No. 4, 1990 ($2.25, limited series)

	GD	VG	FN	VF	VF/NM	NM-
V2#1-Painted art by Denis Beauvais	2	4	5	7	8	10
1-2nd printing (1990), 2-4						3.00
...: Nightmare Asylum TPB (12/96, $16.95) r/series; Bolton-c						17.00

ALIENS
Dark Horse Comics: May, 2009 - No. 4, Nov, 2009 ($3.50, limited series)

1-Howard-c 6.00
2-4-John Arcudi-s/Zach Howard-a. 2-Howard-c. 3,4-Swanland-c 4.00

ALIENS: (Series of titles, all Dark Horse)
--ALCHEMY, 10/97 - No. 3, 11/97 ($2.95),1-3-Corben-c/a, Arcudi-s 4.00
--APOCALYPSE - THE DESTROYING ANGELS, 1/99 - No. 4, 4/99 ($2.95)
1-4-Doug Wheatly-a/Schultz-s 4.00
--BERSERKERS, 1/95 - No. 4, 4/95 ($2.50) 1-4 4.00
--COLONIAL MARINES, 1/93 - No. 10, 7/94 ($2.50) 1-10 4.00
--DEAD ORBIT, 4/17 - No. 4, 12/17 ($3.99) 1-4-James Stokoe-s/a 4.00
--DEFIANCE, 4/16 - No. 12, 6/17 ($3.99) 1-12: 1,2-Brian Wood-s/Tristan Jones-a 4.00
--DUST TO DUST, 4/18 - No. 4, 1/19 ($3.99) 1-4-Gabriel Hardman-s/a 4.00
--EARTH ANGEL, 8/94 ($2.95) 1-Byrne-a/story; wraparound-c 4.00
--EARTH WAR, 6/90 - No. 4, 10/90 ($2.50) 1-All have Sam Kieth-a & Bolton painted-c 5.00
1-2nd printing, 3,4 4.00
2 4.00
--GENOCIDE, 11/91 - No. 4, 2/92 ($2.50) 1-4-Suydam painted-c. 4-Wraparound-c, poster 4.00
--GLASS CORRIDOR, 6/98 ($2.95) 1-David Lloyd-s/a 4.00
--HARVEST (See Aliens: Hive)
--HAVOC, 6/97 - No. 2, 7/97 ($2.95) 1,2: Schultz-s, Kent Williams-c, 40 artists including Art Adams, Kelley Jones, Duncan Fegredo, Kevin Nowlan 4.00
--HIVE, 2/92 - No. 4,5/92 ($2.50) 1-4: Kelley Jones-c/a in all 4.00
...Harvest TPB ('98, $16.95) r/series; Bolton-c 17.00
--KIDNAPPED, 12/97 - No. 3, 2/98 ($2.50) 1-3 4.00
--LABYRINTH, 9/93 - No. 4, 1/94 ($2.50) 1-4: 1-Painted-c 4.00
--LIFE AND DEATH, 9/16 - No. 4, 12/16 ($3.99) 1-4-Abnett-s/Moritat-a 4.00
--LOVESICK, 12/96 ($2.95) 1 4.00
--MONDO HEAT, 2/96 ($2.50) nn-Sequel to Mondo Pest 4.00
--MONDO PEST, 4/95 ($2.95, 44 pgs.) nn-r/Dark Horse Comics #22-24 5.00
--MUSIC OF THE SPEARS, 1/94 - No. 4, 4/94 ($2.50) 1-4 4.00
--NEWT'S TALE, 6/92 - No. 2, 7/92 ($4.95) 1,2-Bolton-c 5.00
--PIG, 3/97 ($2.95)1 4.00
--PREDATOR: THE DEADLIEST OF THE SPECIES, 7/93 - No. 12,8/95 ($2.50)
1-Bolton painted-c; Guice-a(p) 6.00
1-Embossed foil platinum edition 10.00
2-12: Bolton painted-c. 2,3-Guice-a(p) 4.00
--PURGE, 8/97 ($2.95) nn-Hester-a 4.00
--RESCUE, 7/19 - No. 4, 10/19 ($3.99) 1-4-Brian Wood-s/Kieran McKeown-a 4.00
--RESISTANCE, 1/19 - No. 4, 4/19 ($3.99) 1-4-Brian Wood-s/Robert Carey-a 4.00
--ROGUE, 4/93 - No. 4, 7/93 ($2.50) 1-4: Painted-c 4.00
--SACRIFICE, 5/93 ($4.95, 52 pgs.) nn-P. Milligan scripts; painted-c/a 5.00
--SALVATION, 11/93 ($4.95, 52 pgs.) nn-Mignola-c/a(p); Gibbons script 5.00
--SPECIAL, 6/97 ($2.50) 1 4.00
--STALKER, 6/98 ($2.50)1-David Wenzel-s/a 4.00
--STRONGHOLD, 5/94 - No. 4, 9/94 ($2.50) 1-4 4.00
--SURVIVAL, 2/98 - No. 3, 4/98 ($2.95) 1-3-Tony Harris-c 4.00
--TRIBES, 1992 ($24.95, hardcover graphic novel) Bissette text-s with Dorman painted-a 25.00
...softcover ($9.95) 10.00

ALIENS: FIRE AND STONE (Crossover with AvP, Predator, and Prometheus)
Dark Horse Comics: Sept, 2014 - No. 4, Dec, 2014 ($3.50, limited series)
1-4-Roberson-s/Reynolds-a 4.00

ALIENS/ VAMPIRELLA (See Vampirella/Aliens)

ALIENS VS. PARKER (Not based on the Alien movie series)
BOOM! Studios: Mar, 2013 - No. 4, May, 2013 ($3.99, limited series)
1-4: 1-Paul Scheer & Nick Giovannetti-s; Bracchi-a/Noto-c 4.00

ALIENS VS. PREDATOR (See Dark Horse Presents #36)
Dark Horse Comics: June, 1990 - No. 4, Dec, 1990 ($2.50, limited series)

	GD	VG	FN	VF	VF/NM	NM-
1-Painted-c	3	6	8	11	13	15
1-2nd printing						3.00
0-(7/90, $1.95, B&W)-r/Dark Horse Pres. #34-36	3	6	8	11	13	15
2,3						6.00
4-Dave Dorman painted-c						5.00
Annual (7/99, $4.95) Jae Lee-c						5.00
... : Booty (1/96, $2.50) painted-c						4.00
... Omnibus Vol. 1 (5/07, $24.95, 9x6") r/#1-4 & Annual; ...: War; ...: Eternal						25.00
... Omnibus Vol. 2 (10/07, $24.95, 9x6") r/...: Xenogenesis #1-4; ...: Deadliest of the Species; ...: Booty and stories from ... Annual						25.00
...: One For One (8/10, $1.00) r/#1 with red cover frame						4.00
... : Thrill of the Hunt (9/04, $6.95, digest-size TPB) Based on 2004 movie						7.00
... Wraith 1 (7/98, $2.95) Jay Stephens-s						4.00

--VS. PREDATOR: DUEL, 3/95 - No. 2, 4/95 ($2.50) 1,2 4.00
--VS. PREDATOR: ETERNAL, 6/98 - No. 4, 9/98 ($2.50)1-4: Edginton-s/Maleev-a; Fabry-c 4.00
--VS. PREDATOR: THREE WORLD WAR, 1/10 - No. 6, 9/10 ($3.50) 1-6-Leonardi-a 4.00
--VS. PREDATOR VS. THE TERMINATOR, 4/00 - No. 4, 7/00 ($2.95) 1-4: Ripley app. 4.00
--VS. PREDATOR: WAR, No. 0, 5/95 - No. 4, 8/95 ($2.50) 0-4: Corben painted-c 4.00
--VS. PREDATOR: XENOGENESIS, 12/99 - No. 4, 3/00 ($2.95) 1-4: Watson-s/Mel Rubi-a 4.00
--XENOGENESIS, 8/99 - No. 4, 11/99 ($2.95) 1-4: T&M Bierbaum-s 4.00

ALIENS VS. ZOMBIES (Not based on the Alien movie series)
Zenescope Entertainment: Jul, 2015 - No. 5, Dec, 2015 ($3.99, limited series)
1-5: 1-Brusha-s/Riccardi-a; multiple covers on each 4.00

ALIEN TERROR (See 3-D Alien Terror)

ALIEN: THE ILLUSTRATED STORY (Also see Aliens)
Heavy Metal Books: 1980 ($3.95, soft-c, 8x11")

	GD	VG	FN	VF	VF/NM	NM-
nn-Movie adaptation; Simonson-a	3	6	9	19	30	40

ALIEN: THE ORIGINAL SCREENPLAY
Dark Horse Comics: Aug, 2020 - Present ($3.99, limited series)
1-5-Adaptation of Dan O'Bannon's original 1976 screenplay; Seixas-s/Balbi-a 4.00

ALIEN 3 (Movie)
Dark Horse Comics: June, 1992 - No. 3, July, 1992 ($2.50, limited series)
1-3: Adapts 3rd movie; Suydam painted-c 4.00

ALIEN 3 (WILLIAM GIBSON'S...) (Movie)
Dark Horse Comics: Nov, 2018 - No. 5, Mar, 2019 ($3.99, limited series)
1-5-Adapts William Gibson's unproduced screenplay for Alien 3; Johnnie Christmas-s/a 4.00

ALIEN VS. PREDATOR: FIRE AND STONE (Crossover with Aliens, Predator, and Prometheus)
Dark Horse Comics: Oct, 2014 - No. 4, Jan, 2015 ($3.50, limited series)
1-4-Sebela-s/Olivetti-a 3.50

ALIEN VS. PREDATOR: LIFE AND DEATH (Crossover with Aliens, Predator, and Prometheus)
Dark Horse Comics: Dec, 2016 - No. 4, Mar, 2017 ($3.99, limited series)
1-4-Abnett-s/Theis-a 4.00

ALIEN VS. PREDATOR: THICKER THAN BLOOD
Dark Horse Comics: Dec, 2019 - No. 4 ($3.99, limited series)
1,2-Jeremy Barlow-s/Doug Wheatey-a 4.00

ALIEN WORLDS (Also see Eclipse Graphic Album #22)
Pacific Comics/Eclipse: Dec, 1982 - No. 9, Jan, 1985

	GD	VG	FN	VF	VF/NM	NM-
1,2,4: 2,4-Dave Stevens-c/a						6.00
3,5-7						4.00
8,9	1	2	3	4	5	7
3-D No. 1-Art Adams 1st published art	1	2	3	4	5	7

ALISON DARE, LITTLE MISS ADVENTURES (Also see Return of ...)
Oni Press: Sept, 2000 ($4.50, B&W, one-shot)
1-J. Torres-s/J.Bone-c/a 4.50

ALISON DARE & THE HEART OF THE MAIDEN

All-American Comics #18 © DC

All-American Men of War #7 © DC

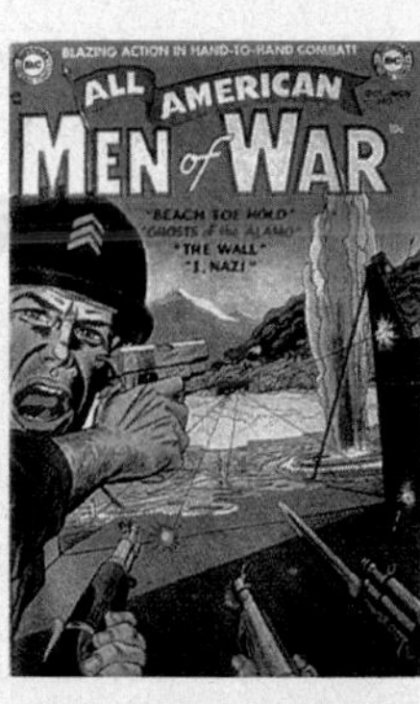

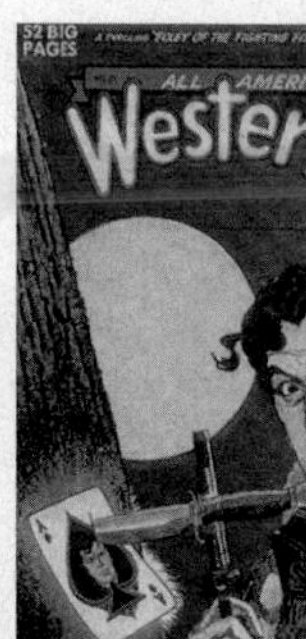

All-American Western #112 © DC

Oni Press: Jan, 2002 - No. 2, Feb, 2002 ($2.95, B&W, limited series)

1,2-J. Torres-s/J.Bone-c/a 3.00

ALISTER THE SLAYER

Midnight Press: Oct, 1995 ($2.50)

1-Boris-c 3.00

ALL-AMERICAN COMICS (...Western #103-126, ...Men of War #127 on; also see The Big All-American Comic Book)

All-American/National Periodical Publ.: April, 1939 - No. 102, Oct, 1948

	GD 2.0	VG 4.0	FN 6.0	VF 8.0	VF/NM 9.0	NM- 9.2
1-Hop Harrigan (1st app.), Scribbly by Mayer (1st DC app.), Toonerville Folks, Ben Webster, Spot Savage, Mutt & Jeff, Red White & Blue (1st app.), Adventures in the Unknown, Tippie, Reg'lar Fellers, Skippy, Bobby Thatcher, Mystery Men of Mars, Daiseybelle, Wiley of West Point begin	715	1430	2145	5000	8750	12,500
2-Ripley's Believe It or Not begins, ends #24	239	478	717	1530	2615	3700
3-5: 5-The American Way begins, ends #10	203	406	609	1289	2220	3150
6,7: 6-Last Spot Savage; Popsicle Pete begins, ends #26, 28. 7-Last Bobby Thatcher	148	296	444	947	1624	2300
8-The Ultra Man begins & 1st-c app.	454	908	1362	3314	5857	8400
9,10: 10-X-Mas-c	135	270	405	864	1482	2100
11,15: 11-Ultra Man-c. 15-Last Tippie & Reg'lar Fellars; Ultra Man-c	200	400	600	1280	2190	3100
12-14: 12-Last Toonerville Folks	132	264	396	838	1444	2050
16-(Rare)-Origin/1st app. Green Lantern by Sheldon Moldoff (c/a)(7/40) & begin series; appears in costume on-c & only one panel inside; created by Martin Nodell. Inspired in 1940 by a switchman's green lantern that would give trains the go ahead to proceed. G.L. cover pose swiped from last panel of a Jan, 1939 Flash Gordon Sunday page.	28,000	56,000	84,000	207,000	566,000	925,000
17-2nd Green Lantern	1375	2750	4125	10,300	21,650	33,000
18-N.Y. World's Fair-c/story (scarce); The Atom app. in one panel announcing debut in next issue	1300	2600	3900	9750	20,375	31,000
19-Origin/1st app. The Atom (10/40); last Ultra Man	2875	5750	8625	21,500	44,250	67,000
20-Atom dons costume; Ma Hunkle becomes Red Tornado (1st app.)(1st DC costumed heroine, before Wonder Woman, 11/40); Rescue on Mars begins, ends #25; 1 pg. origin Green Lantern	703	1406	2109	5132	9066	13,000
21-Last Wiley of West Point & Skippy; classic Moldoff-c	541	1082	1623	3950	6975	10,000
22,23: 23-Last Daiseybelle; 3 Idiots begin, end #82	366	732	1098	2562	4481	6400
24-Sisty & Dinky become the Cyclone Kids; Ben Webster ends; origin Dr. Mid-Nite & Sargon, The Sorcerer in text with app.	383	766	1149	2681	4691	6700
25-Origin & 1st story app. Dr. Mid-Nite by Stan Asch; Hop Harrigan becomes Guardian Angel; last Adventure in the Unknown (scarce)	1230	2460	3690	9220	19,360	29,500
26-Origin/1st story app. Sargon, the Sorcerer	394	788	1182	2758	4829	6900
27: #27-32 are misnumbered in indicia with correct No. appearing on-c. Intro. Doiby Dickles, Green Lantern's sidekick	400	800	1200	2800	4900	7000
28-Hop Harrigan gives up costumed i.d.	213	426	639	1363	2332	3300
29,30	213	426	639	1363	2332	3300
31-40: 35-Doiby learns Green Lantern's i.d.	177	354	531	1124	1937	2750
41-50: 50-Sargon ends	142	284	426	909	1555	2200
51-60: 59-Scribbly & the Red Tornado ends	119	238	357	762	1306	1850
61-Origin/1st app. Solomon Grundy (11/44)	2050	4100	6150	15,400	29,700	44,000
62-70: 70-Kubert Sargon; intro Sargon's helper, Maximillian O'Leary	105	210	315	667	1146	1625
71-88: 71-Last Red White & Blue. 72-Black Pirate begins (not in #74-82); last Atom. 73-Winky, Blinky & Noddy begins, ends #82. 79,83-Mutt & Jeff-c. 85-1st Crusher Crock (becomes Sportsmaster); Hasen "Derby" cover	82	164	246	528	902	1275
89-Origin & 1st app. Harlequin	276	552	828	1753	3027	4300
90,92,96-99: 90-Origin/1st app. Icicle. 98-Sportsmaster-c. 99-Last Hop Harrigan	158	316	474	1003	1727	2450
91,93,94,95-Harlequin-c	200	400	600	1280	2190	3100
100-1st app. Johnny Thunder by Alex Toth (8/48); western theme begins (Scarce)	206	412	618	1318	2259	3200
101-Last Mutt & Jeff (Scarce)	142	284	426	909	1555	2200
102-Last Green Lantern, Black Pirate & Dr. Mid-Nite (Scarce)	271	542	813	1734	2967	4200

NOTE: *No Atom in 47, 62-69.* ***Kinstler*** *Black Pirate-89.* ***Stan Aschmeier*** *a (Dr. Mid-Nite) 25-84; c-7.* ***Mayer*** *c-1, 2(part), 6, 10.* ***Moldoff*** *c-16-23.* ***Nodell*** *c-31.* ***Paul Reinman*** *a (Green Lantern)-53-55p, 56-84, 87; (Black Pirate)-83-88, 90; c-52, 55-76, 78, 80, 81, 87.* ***Toth*** *a-88, 92, 96, 98-102; c(p)-92, 96-102. Scribbly by* ***Mayer*** *in #1-59. Ultra Man by* ***Mayer*** *in #8-19.*

ALL AMERICAN COMICS

DC Comics: April 1939

nn - Ashcan comic, not distributed to newsstands, only for in house use. Cover art is Adventure Comics #33 and interior from Detective Comics #23. A CGC 7.5 copy sold for $7466 in December 2014 and for $15,000 in July 2017.

ALL-AMERICAN COMICS (Also see All Star Comics 1999 crossover titles)

DC Comics: May, 1999 ($1.99, one-shot)

1-Golden Age Green Lantern and Johnny Thunder; Barreto-a 4.00

ALL-AMERICAN MEN OF WAR (Previously All-American Western)

National Periodical Publ.: No. 127, Aug-Sept, 1952 - No. 117, Sept-Oct, 1966

	GD 2.0	VG 4.0	FN 6.0	VF 8.0	VF/NM 9.0	NM- 9.2
127 (#1, 1952)	139	278	417	1112	2506	3900
128 (1952)	57	114	171	456	1016	1575
2(12-1/'52-53)-5	53	106	159	424	950	1475
6-Devil Dog story; Ghost Squadron story	38	76	114	285	641	1000
7-10: 8-Sgt. Storm Cloud-s	38	76	114	285	641	1000
11-16,18: 18-Last precode; 1st Kubert-c (2/55)	35	70	105	252	564	875
17-1st Frogman-s in this title	36	72	108	259	580	900
19,20,22-27	27	54	81	194	435	675
21-Easy Co. prototype	34	68	102	245	548	850
28 (12/55)-1st Sgt. Rock prototype; Kubert-a	61	122	183	488	1094	1700
29,30,32-Wood-a	27	54	81	194	435	675
31,33,34,36-38,40: 34-Gunner prototype-s. 36-Little Sure Shot prototype-s. 38-1st S.A. issue	25	50	75	175	388	600
35-Greytone-c	31	62	93	223	499	775
39 (11/56)-2nd Sgt. Rock prototype; 1st Easy Co.?	41	82	123	303	689	1075
41,43-47,49,50: 46-Tankbusters-c/s	21	42	63	150	330	510
42-Pre-Sgt. Rock Easy Co.-c/s	27	54	81	189	420	650
48-Easy Co.-c/s; Nick app.; Kubert-a	27	54	81	189	420	650
51-56,58-62,65,66: 61-Gunner-c/s	17	34	51	117	259	400
57(5/58),63,64-Pre-Sgt. Rock Easy Co.-c/s	23	46	69	161	356	550
67-1st Gunner & Sarge by Andru & Esposito	54	108	162	432	966	1500
68,69: 68-2nd app. Gunner & Sarge. 69-1st Tank Killer-c/s	22	42	63	147	324	500
70	14	28	42	96	211	325
71-80: 71,72,76-Tank Killer-c/s. 74-Minute Commandos-c/s	12	24	36	82	179	275
81-Greytone-c	12	24	36	81	176	270
82-Johnny Cloud begins(1st app.), ends #117	31	62	93	222	496	770
83-2nd Johnny Cloud	15	30	45	100	220	340
84-88: 88-Last 10¢ issue	10	20	30	69	147	225
89-100: 89-Battle Aces of 3 Wars begins, ends #98. 89,90-Panels from these issues used by artist Roy Lichtenstein for famous paintings	8	16	24	56	108	160
101-111,113-116: 110,11-Greytone-c. 111,114,115-Johnny Cloud	6	12	18	40	73	105
112-Balloon Buster series begins, ends #114,116	6	12	18	41	76	110
117-Johnny Cloud-c & 3-part story	6	12	18	41	76	110

NOTE: *Frogman stories in 17, 38, 44, 45, 50, 51, 53, 55-58, 63, 65, 66, 72, 76, 77.* ***Colan*** *a-112.* ***Drucker*** *a-47, 58, 61, 63, 65, 69, 71, 74, 77.* ***Grandenetti*** *c(p)-127, 128, 2-17(most).* ***Heath*** *a-14, 27, 32, 38, 41, 45, 47, 50, 51, 55-58, 62, 64, 71, 75, 76, 78, 95, 111-117; c-85, 91, 94-96, 100, 101, 110-112, others?* ***Infantino*** *a-8.* ***Kirby*** *a-29.* ***Krigstein*** *a-128('52), 2, 3, 5.* ***Kubert*** *a-22, 24, 28, 29, 33, 34, 36, 38, 39, 41-43, 47-50, 52, 53, 55, 56, 59, 60, 63-65, 69, 71-73, 76, 102, 103, 105, 106, 108, 114; c-41, 44, 52, 54, 55, 58, 64, 69, 76, 77, 79, 102-106, 108, 113-117, others? Tank Killer in 69, 71, 76 by* ***Kubert. P. Reinman*** *c-55, 57, 61, 62, 71, 72, 74-76, 80.* ***J. Severin*** *a-58.*

ALL AMERICAN MEN OF WAR

DC Comics: Aug/Sept. 1952

nn - Ashcan comic, not distributed to newsstands, only for in-house use. Cover art is All Star Western #58 and interior from Mr. District Attorney #21. A GD+ copy sold for $1195 in 2012.

ALL-AMERICAN SPORTS

Charlton Comics: Oct, 1967

	GD 2.0	VG 4.0	FN 6.0	VF 8.0	VF/NM 9.0	NM- 9.2
1	3	6	9	19	30	45

ALL-AMERICAN WESTERN (Formerly All-American Comics; Becomes All-American Men of War)

National Periodical Publ.: No. 103, Nov, 1948 - No. 126, June-July, 1952 (103-121: 52 pgs.)

	GD 2.0	VG 4.0	FN 6.0	VF 8.0	VF/NM 9.0	NM- 9.2
103-Johnny Thunder & his horse Black Lightning continues by Toth, ends #126; Foley of The Fighting 5th, Minstrel Maverick, & Overland Coach begin; Captain Tootsie by Beck; mentioned in Love and Death	54	108	162	343	574	825
104-Kubert-a	39	78	117	234	385	535
105,107-Kubert-a	34	68	102	199	325	450
106,108-110,112: 112-Kurtzman's "Pot-Shot Pete" (1 pg.)	28	56	84	165	270	375
111,114-116-Kubert-a	29	58	87	172	281	390
113-Intro. Swift Deer, J. Thunder's new sidekick (4-5/50); classic Toth-c; Kubert-a	32	64	96	188	307	425
117-126: 121-Kubert-a; bondage-c	21	42	63	122	199	275

NOTE: ***G. Kane*** *c(p)-112, 119, 120, 123.* ***Kubert*** *a-103-105, 107, 111, 112(1 pg.), 113-116, 121.* ***Toth*** *a-103-125; c(p)-103-111,113-116, 121, 122, 124-126. Some copies of #125 have #12 on-c.*

ALL COMICS

Chicago Nite Life News: 1945

Alley Cat #2 © Alley Baggett

All-Flash #18 © DC

All Great Comics #1 © FOX

	GD 2.0	VG 4.0	FN 6.0	VF 8.0	VF/NM 9.0	NM- 9.2
1	16	32	48	94	147	200

ALLEGRA
Image Comics (WildStorm): Aug, 1996 - No. 4, Dec, 1996 ($2.50)

	GD	VG	FN	VF	VF/NM	NM-
1-4						3.00

ALLEY CAT (Alley Baggett)
Image Comics: July, 1999 - No. 6, Mar, 2000 ($2.50/$2.95)

	GD	VG	FN	VF	VF/NM	NM-
Preview Edition						6.00
Prelude						5.00
Prelude w/variant-c						6.00
1-Photo-c						3.00
1-Painted-c by Dorian						4.00
1-Another Universe Edition, 1-Wizard World Edition						7.00
2-4: 4-Twin towers on-c						3.00
5,6-($2.95)						3.00
Lingerie Edition (10/99, $4.95) Photos, pin-ups, cover gallery						5.00
...Vs. Lady Pendragon ('99, $3.00) Stinsman-c						3.00

ALLEY OOP (See The Comics, The Funnies, Red Ryder and Super Book #9)
Dell Publishing Co.: No. 3, 1942

	GD	VG	FN	VF	VF/NM	NM-
Four Color 3 (#1)	49	98	147	382	866	1350

ALLEY OOP
Argo Publ.: Nov, 1955 - No. 3, Mar, 1956 (Newspaper reprints)

	GD	VG	FN	VF	VF/NM	NM-
1	18	36	54	107	169	230
2,3	13	26	39	72	101	130

ALLEY OOP
Dell Publishing Co.: 12-2/62-63 - No. 2, 9-11/63

	GD	VG	FN	VF	VF/NM	NM-
1	5	10	15	35	63	90
2	5	10	15	31	53	75

ALLEY OOP
Standard Comics: No. 10, Sept, 1947 - No. 18, Oct, 1949

	GD	VG	FN	VF	VF/NM	NM-
10	32	64	96	188	307	425
11-16	24	48	72	142	234	325
17,18-Schomburg-c	39	78	117	231	378	525

ALLEY OOP ADVENTURES
Antarctic Press: Aug, 1998 - No. 3, Dec, 1998 ($2.95)

	GD	VG	FN	VF	VF/NM	NM-
1-3-Jack Bender-s/a						3.00

ALLEY OOP ADVENTURES (Alley Oop Quarterly in indicia)
Antarctic Press: Sept, 1999 - No. 3, Mar, 2000 ($2.50/$2.99, B&W)

	GD	VG	FN	VF	VF/NM	NM-
1-3-Jack Bender-s/a						3.00

ALL-FAMOUS CRIME (2nd series - Formerly Law Against Crime #1-3; becomes All-Famous Police Cases #6 on)
Star Publications: No. 8, 5/51 - No. 10, 11/51; No. 4, 2/52 - No. 5, 5/52;

	GD	VG	FN	VF	VF/NM	NM-
8 (#1-1st series)	32	64	96	188	307	425
9 (#2)-Used in **SOTI**, illo- "The wish to hurt or kill couples in lovers' lanes is a not uncommon perversion;" L.B. Cole-c/a(r)/Law-Crime #3	43	86	129	271	461	650
10 (#3)	25	50	75	147	241	335
4 (#4-2nd series)-Formerly Law-Crime	25	50	75	147	241	335
5 (#5) Becomes All-Famous Police Cases #6	24	48	72	140	230	320

NOTE: *All have **L.B. Cole** covers.*

ALL FAMOUS CRIME STORIES (See Fox Giants)

ALL-FAMOUS POLICE CASES (Formerly All Famous Crime #5)
Star Publications: No. 6, Feb, 1952 - No. 16, Sept, 1954

	GD	VG	FN	VF	VF/NM	NM-
6	34	68	102	199	325	450
7-Matt Baker story	58	116	174	396	636	900
8-Marijuana story	26	52	78	154	252	350
9-16	22	44	66	132	216	300

NOTE: ***L. B. Cole** c-all; a-15, 1pg. **Hollingsworth** a-15.*

ALL-FLASH (...Quarterly No. 1-5)
National Per. Publ./All-American: Summer, 1941 - No. 32, Dec-Jan, 1947-48

	GD	VG	FN	VF	VF/NM	NM-
1-Origin The Flash retold by E. E. Hibbard; Hibbard c-1-10,12-14,16,31p.	1250	2500	3750	8750	14,875	21,000
2-Origin recap	271	542	813	1734	2967	4200
3,4	161	322	483	1030	1765	2500
5-Winky, Blinky & Noddy begins (1st app.), ends #32	116	232	348	742	1271	1800
6-Has full page ad for Wonder Woman #1	111	222	333	705	1215	1725
7-10	106	212	318	673	1162	165
11,13: 13-The King app.	94	188	282	597	1024	1450
12-Origin/1st The Thinker	106	212	318	673	1162	1650
14-Green Lantern cameo	110	220	330	704	1202	1700
15-20: 18-Mutt & Jeff begins, ends #22	86	172	258	546	936	1325
21-31	71	142	213	454	777	1100
32-Origin/1st app. The Fiddler; 1st Star Sapphire	258	516	774	1651	2826	4000
All-Flash Quarterly ashcan	(a CGC 7.0 copy sold for $8150 in 2012)					

NOTE: *Book length stories in 2-13, 16. Bondage c-31, 32. **Martin Nodell** c-15, 17-28.*

ALL FLASH (Leads into Flash [2nd series] #231)
DC Comics: Sept, 2007 ($2.99, one-shot)

	GD	VG	FN	VF	VF/NM	NM-
1-Wally West hunts down Bart's killers; Waid-s; two covers by Middleton & Sienkiewicz						3.00

ALL FOR LOVE (Young Love V3#5-on)
Prize Publications: Apr-May, 1957 - V3#4, Dec-Jan, 1959-60

	GD	VG	FN	VF	VF/NM	NM-
V1#1	10	20	30	65	135	205
2-6: 5-Orlando-c	6	12	18	37	66	95
V2#1-5(1/59), 5(3/59)	5	10	15	34	60	85
V3#1(5/59), 1(7/59)-4: 2-Powell-a	5	10	15	31	53	75

ALL FUNNY COMICS
Tilsam Publ./National Periodical Publications (Detective): Winter, 1943-44 - No. 23, May-June, 1948

	GD	VG	FN	VF	VF/NM	NM-
1-Genius Jones (see Adventure #77 for debut), Buzzy (1st app., ends #4), Dover & Clover (see More Fun #93) begin; Bailey-a	54	108	162	343	574	825
2	23	46	69	136	223	310
3-10	15	30	45	85	130	175
11-13,15,18,19-Genius Jones app.	14	28	42	80	115	150
14,17,20-23	10	20	30	56	76	95
16-DC Super Heroes app.	32	64	96	192	314	435

ALL GOOD
St. John Publishing Co.: Oct, 1949 (50¢, 260 pgs.)

	GD	VG	FN	VF	VF/NM	NM-
nn-(8 St. John comics bound together)	113	226	339	718	1234	1750

NOTE: *Also see Li'l Audrey Yearbook & Treasury of Comics.*

ALL GOOD COMICS (See Fox Giants)
Fox Feature Syndicate: No.1, Spring, 1946 (36 pgs.)

	GD	VG	FN	VF	VF/NM	NM-
1-Joy Family, Dick Transom, Rick Evans, One Round Hogan	29	58	87	170	278	385

ALL GREAT
William H. Wise & Co.: nd (1945?) (132 pgs.)

	GD	VG	FN	VF	VF/NM	NM-
nn-Capt. Jack Terry, Joan Mason, Girl Reporter, Baron Doomsday; Torture scenes	48	96	144	302	514	725

ALL GREAT COMICS (See Fox Giants)
Fox Feature Syndicate: 1946 (36 pgs.)

	GD	VG	FN	VF	VF/NM	NM-
1-Crazy House, Bertie Benson Boy Detective, Gussie the Gob	27	54	81	158	259	360

ALL GREAT COMICS (Formerly Phantom Lady #13? Dagar, Desert Hawk No. 14 on)
Fox Feature Syndicate: No. 14, Oct, 1947 - No. 13, Dec, 1947 (Newspaper strip reprints)

	GD	VG	FN	VF	VF/NM	NM-
14(#12)-Brenda Starr & Texas Slim-r (Scarce)	60	120	180	381	653	925
13-Origin Dagar, Desert Hawk; Brenda Starr (all-r); Kamen-c; Dagar covers begin	68	136	204	435	743	1050

ALL-GREAT CONFESSION MAGAZINE (See Fox Giants)

ALL-GREAT CONFESSIONS (See Fox Giants)

ALL GREAT CRIME STORIES (See Fox Giants)

ALL GREAT JUNGLE ADVENTURES (See Fox Giants)

ALL HALLOW'S EVE
Innovation Publishing: 1991 ($4.95, 52 pgs.)

	GD	VG	FN	VF	VF/NM	NM-
1-Painted-c/a	1	3	4	6	8	10

ALL HERO COMICS
Fawcett Publications: Mar, 1943 (100 pgs., cardboard-c)

	GD	VG	FN	VF	VF/NM	NM-
1-Capt. Marvel Jr., Capt. Midnight, Golden Arrow, Ibis the Invincible, Spy Smasher, Lance O'Casey; 1st Banshee O'Brien; Raboy-c	198	396	594	1257	2166	3075

ALL HUMOR COMICS
Quality Comics Group: Spring, 1946 - No. 17, December, 1949

	GD	VG	FN	VF	VF/NM	NM-
1	24	48	72	140	230	320
2-Atomic Tot story; Gustavson-a	14	28	42	76	108	140
3-9: 3-Intro Kelly Poole who is cover feature #3 on. 5-1st app. Hickory? 8-Gustavson-a	9	18	27	52	69	85
10-17	9	18	27	47	61	75

ALL LOVE (...Romances No. 26)(Formerly Ernie Comics)
Ace Periodicals (Current Books): No. 26, May, 1949 - No. 32, May, 1950

	GD	VG	FN	VF	VF/NM	NM-
26 (No. 1)-Ernie, Lily Belle app.	15	30	45	84	127	170

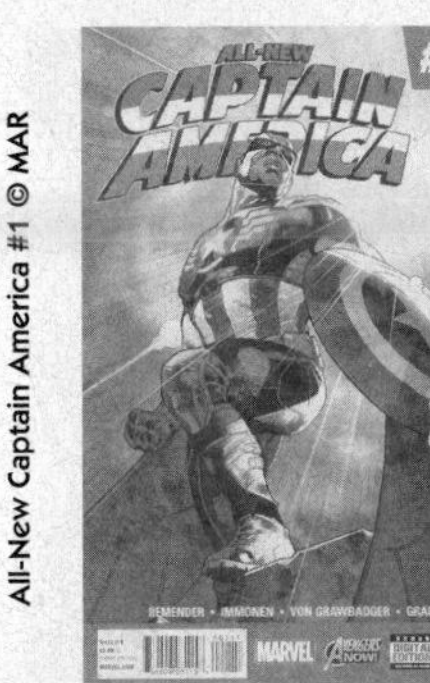

All-New Captain America #1 © MAR

All-New Comics #9 © HARV

All-New Hawkeye (2016 series) #6 © MAR

	GD 2.0	VG 4.0	FN 6.0	VF 8.0	VF/NM 9.0	NM- 9.2
27-L. B. Cole-a	16	32	48	94	147	200
28-32	11	22	33	64	90	115

ALL-NEGRO COMICS
All-Negro Comics: June, 1947 (15¢)

	GD	VG	FN	VF	VF/NM	NM-
1 (Rare)	2400	4800	7200	13,000	18,500	24,000

NOTE: *Seldom found in fine or mint condition; many copies have brown pages.*

ALL-NEW ALL-DIFFERENT AVENGERS (Follows Secret Wars event)
Marvel Comics: Jan, 2016 - No. 15, Dec, 2015 ($4.99/$3.99)

1-($4.99) Spider-Man (Miles), Ms. Marvel, Nova join; Waid-s/Adam Kubert & Asrar-a 5.00
2-15-($3.99) Main cover by Alex Ross. 2,3-Warbringer app.; Kubert-a. 4-6,9,10-Asrar-a. 7,8-Standoff tie-ins; Adam Kubert-a. 9-Intro. new Wasp (Nadia). 13-15-Civil War II tie-in 4.00
Annual 1(10/16, $4.99) Fan-fic short stories by various incl. Waid/Zdarsky & Allegri 5.00

ALL-NEW ALL-DIFFERENT MARVEL UNIVERSE
Marvel Comics: May, 2016 ($4.99, one-shot)

1-Handbook-style entries; profiles of major characters; Marquez-c 5.00

ALL-NEW ALL-DIFFERENT POINT ONE (Follows Secret Wars event)
Marvel Comics: Dec, 2015 ($5.99, one-shot)

1-Preludes to new titles: Carnage, Daredevil, All-New Inhumans, Agents of S.H.I.E.L.D., Rocket Raccoon & Groot, and Contest of Champions; Del Mundo-c 6.00

ALL-NEW ATOM, THE (See The Atom and DCU Brave New World)
DC Comics: Sept, 2006 - No. 25, Sept, 2008 ($2.99)

1-25: 1-18-Simone-s. 1-Intro Ryan Choi; Byrne-a thru #3. 4-11-Barrows-a. 12,13-Chronos app. 14,15-Countdown x-over. 17,18-Wonder Woman app. 3.00
...: Future/Past TPB (2007, $14.99) r/#7-11 15.00
...: My Life in Miniature TPB (2007, $14.99) r/#1-6 and app. in DCU Brave New World #1 15.00
...: Small Wonder TPB (2008, $17.99) r/#17,18,21-25 18.00
...: The Hunt For Ray Palmer TPB (2008, $14.99) r/#12-16 15.00

ALL-NEW BATMAN: BRAVE & THE BOLD (See Batman: The Brave and the Bold)

ALL-NEW CAPTAIN AMERICA (See Captain America #25 - 2014 series)
Marvel Comics: Jan, 2015 - No. 6, Jun, 2015 ($3.99)

1-6: 1-Sam Wilson as Captain America, Ian as Nomad; Immonen-a 4.00
... Special 1 (7/15, $4.99) Loveness-s/Morgan-a; Inhumans & Spider-Man app. 5.00

ALL-NEW CAPTAIN AMERICA: FEAR HIM (Sam Wilson as Cap)
Marvel Comics: Jan, 2015 - No. 4, Apr, 2015 ($3.99, limited series)

1-4-Hopeless & Remender-s/Kudranski-a/Bianchi-c; The Scarecrow app. 4.00

ALL-NEW CLASSIC CAPTAIN CANUCK
Chapterhouse Comics: No. 0, Feb, 2016 - No. 4, Apr, 2017 ($4.99/$3.99)

0-($4.99) Short stories; Ed Brisson-s; art by various 5.00
1-4-($3.99) Brisson-s/Freeman-a; 2 covers on each 4.00

ALL-NEW COLLECTORS' EDITION (Formerly Limited Collectors' Edition: see for C-57, C-59)
DC Comics, Inc.: Jan, 1978 - Vol. 8, No. C-62, 1979 (No. 54-58: 76 pgs.)

	GD	VG	FN	VF	VF/NM	NM-
C-53-Rudolph the Red-Nosed Reindeer	5	10	15	31	53	75
C-54-Superman Vs. Wonder Woman	5	10	15	33	57	80
C-55-Superboy & the Legion of Super-Heroes; Wedding of Lightning Lad & Saturn Girl; Grell-c/a	4	8	12	27	44	60
C-56-Superman Vs. Muhammad Ali: Wraparound Neal Adams-c/a; Adams & O'Neil-s (see "Superman Vs. Muhammad Ali" for reprint)	11	22	33	73	157	240
C-56-Superman Vs. Muhammad Ali (Whitman variant)-low print	13	26	39	86	188	290
C-57,C-59-(See Limited Collectors' Edition)						
C-58-Superman Vs. Shazam; Buckler-c/a; Black Adam's 2nd Bronze Age app.	5	10	15	31	53	75
C-60-Rudolph's Summer Fun(8/78)	4	8	12	28	47	65
C-61-(See Famous First Edition-Superman #1)						
C-62-Superman the Movie (68 pgs.; 1979)-Photo-c from movie plus photos inside (also see DC Special Series #25 for Superman II)	3	6	9	17	26	35

ALL-NEW COMICS (...Short Story Comics No. 1-3)
Family Comics (Harvey Publications): Jan, 1943 - No. 14, Nov, 1946; No. 15, Mar-Apr, 1947 (10 x 13-1/2")

	GD	VG	FN	VF	VF/NM	NM-
1-Steve Case, Crime Rover, Johnny Rebel, Kayo Kane, The Echo, Night Hawk, Ray O'Light, Detective Shane begin (all 1st app.?); Red Blazer on cover only; Sultan-a; Nazi WWII-c	300	600	900	2010	3505	5000
2-Origin Scarlet Phantom by Kubert; Nazi WWII-c	142	284	426	909	1555	2200
3-Nazi WWII-c	121	242	363	768	1322	1875
4-Sci-fi Nazi monsters bondage-c	219	438	657	1402	2401	3400
5-Classic Schomburg Japanese WWII-c showing Japanese using Human Suicide bombs falling on the Capitol building	219	438	657	1402	2401	3400
6-11: Schomburg-c on all. 9-11-Japanese WWII-c. 6-8 Nazi WWII-c. 6-The Boy Heroes & Red Blazer (text story) begin, end #12; Black Cat app.; intro. Sparky in Red Blazer. 7-Kubert, Powell-a; Black Cat & Zebra app. 8,9: 8-Shock Gibson app.; Kubert, Powell-a; Schomburg-c. 9-Black Cat app.; Kubert-a. 10-The Zebra app. (from Green Hornet Comics); Kubert-a(3). 11-Girl Commandos, Man In Black app.	168	336	504	1075	1838	2600
12-Kubert-a; Japanese WWII-c	71	142	213	454	777	1100
13-Stuntman by Simon & Kirby; Green Hornet, Joe Palooka, Flying Fool app.; Green Hornet-c	52	104	156	328	552	775
14-The Green Hornet & The Man in Black Called Fate by Powell, Joe Flying Fool app.; Flying Fool app.; J. Palooka-c by Ham Fisher	42	84	126	265	445	625
15-(Rare)-Small size (5-1/2x8-1/2"; B&W; 32 pgs.). Distributed to mail subscribers only. Black Cat and Joe Palooka app.	181	362	543	1158	1979	2800

NOTE: *Also see Boy Explorers No. 2, Flash Gordon No. 5, and Stuntman No. 3.* **Powell** *a-11.* **Schomburg** *c-5-11. Captain Red Blazer & Spark on c-5-11 (w/Boy Heroes #12).*

ALL-NEW DOOP (X-Men)
Marvel Comics: Jun, 2014 - No. 5, Nov, 2014 ($3.99, limited series)

1-5-Milligan-s/Lafuente-a; Kitty Pryde and X-Men app. 3-5-The Anarchist app. 4.00

ALL-NEW EXECUTIVE ASSISTANT: IRIS (Volume 4) (Also see Executive Assistant: Iris)
Aspen MLT: Sept, 2013 - No. 5, Jun, 2014 ($1.00/$3.99)

1-($1.00) Buccellato-s/Qualano-a; multiple covers 3.00
2-5-($3.99) Multiple covers 4.00
...: Enemies Among Us 1 (12/16, $4.99) Wohl-s/Cafaro-a; Hernandez-s/Green-a; multiple-c 5.00

ALL NEW FATHOM (See Fathom)

ALL-NEW GHOST RIDER (Also see the 2017 Ghost Rider series)
Marvel Comics: May, 2014 - No. 12, May, 2015 ($3.99)

1-12: 1-Felipe Smith-s/Tradd Moore-a; origin of Robbie Reyes. 6-10-Damion Scott-a 4.00

ALL-NEW GUARDIANS OF THE GALAXY (Continues in Guardians of the Galaxy #146)
Marvel Comics: Jul, 2017 - No. 12, Dec, 2017 ($3.99)

1-12: 1-Grandmaster app.; Duggan-s/Kuder-a. 2,4-The Collector app. 3-Irving-a 4.00
Annual 1 (8/17, $4.99) Tie-in to Secret Empire; Beyruth-a; Yondu & Mantis app. 5.00

ALL-NEW HAWKEYE
Marvel Comics: May, 2015 - No. 5, Nov, 2015 ($3.99)

1-5-Jeff Lemire-s/Ramón Pérez-a/c; Kate Bishop app.; flashback to circus childhood 4.00

ALL-NEW HAWKEYE
Marvel Comics: Jan, 2016 - No. 6, Jun, 2016 ($3.99)

1-6-Lemire-s/Pérez-a/c; Kate Bishop app. 1-3-Flashforward 30 years; Mandarin app. 4.00

ALL-NEW INHUMANS
Marvel Comics: Feb, 2016 - No. 11, Nov, 2016 ($3.99)

1-($4.99)-Asmus & Soule-s/Caselli-a; Crystal & Gorgon app. 5.00
2-11-($3.99) 2-4-The Commissar app. 5,6-Spider-Man app. 4.00

ALL-NEW INVADERS
Marvel Comics: Mar, 2014 - No. 15, Apr, 2015 ($3.99)

1-15: 1-Capt. America, Bucky, Namor & Jim Hammond team; Robinson-s/Pugh-a. 6,7-Original Sin tie-in 4.00

ALL-NEW MARVEL NOW! POINT ONE
Marvel Comics: Mar, 2014 ($5.99, one-shot preview of upcoming series)

1-Previews of Loki, Silver Surfer, Black Widow, Ms. Marvel, Avengers, All-New Invaders 6.00

ALL NEW MICHAEL TURNER'S FATHOM (See Fathom)

ALL NEW MICHAEL TURNER'S SOULFIRE (See Soulfire)

ALL-NEW OFFICIAL HANDBOOK OF THE MARVEL UNIVERSE A TO Z
Marvel Comics: 2006 - No. 12, 2006 ($3.99, limited series)

1-12-Profile pages of Marvel characters not covered in 2004-2005 Official Handbooks 4.00
...: Update 1-4 (2007, $3.99) Profile pages 4.00

ALL-NEW ULTIMATES
Marvel Comics: Jun, 2014 - No. 12, Mar, 2015 ($3.99)

1-12: 1-Miles Morales Spider-Man, Spider-Woman, Cloak and Dagger, Kitty Pryde and Bombshell team. 5,6-Crossbones app. 4.00

ALL-NEW WOLVERINE (Laura Kinney X-23 as Wolverine)
Marvel Comics: Jan, 2016 - No. 35, Jul, 2018 ($4.99/$3.99)

	GD	VG	FN	VF	VF/NM	NM-
1-($4.99) Tom Taylor-s/David Lopez-a; Angel app.	1	2	3	5	6	8

2-35-($3.99) 2-Intro. Gabby. 2,3-Taskmaster app. 4-Doctor Strange app. 5-Janet Van Dyne app. 7-Squirrel Girl app. 8,9-Fin Fang Foom app. 10-12-Civil War II tie-in. 16-18-Gambit app.19-21-Ironheart app. 22-24-Guardians of the Galaxy app.; Yu-c. 25-30-Daken app. 31-Deadpool app. 33-"Old Woman Laura"; future against Doom 4.00
Annual 1 (10/16, $4.99) Gwen Stacy app.; Tom Taylor-s/Marcio Takara-a 5.00

ALL-NEW X-FACTOR

All-New X-Men #1 © MAR

All Star Batman & Robin, the Boy Wonder #4 © DC

All Star Comics #4 © DC

	GD	VG	FN	VF	VF/NM	NM-
	2.0	4.0	6.0	8.0	9.0	9.2

Marvel Comics: Mar, 2014 - No. 20, Mar, 2015 ($3.99)

1-20: 1-12-David-s/DiGiandomenico-a; Gambit, Polaris, Quicksilver, Danger app. 13,14-Mhan-a. 14-Scarlet Witch app. 15-17-Axis tie-in 4.00

ALL-NEW X-MEN
Marvel Comics: Jan, 2013 - No. 41, Aug, 2015 ($3.99)

1-Bendis-s; Immonen-a and wraparound-c; original X-Men time travel to present 4.00
2-24: 6-8-Marquez-a; Mystique app. 8-Avengers app. 16,17-Battle of the Atom tie-ins. 18-New uniforms. 22-24-Trial of Jean Grey; Guardians of the Galaxy app. 4.00
25-($4.99) Art by Marquez with pages by Timm, Mack, Young, Campbell & many others 5.00
26-41: 30-Pichelli-a. 31-36-X-Men in Ultimate universe; Miles Morales app. 38,39-Black Vortex x-over; Ronan & Guardians of the Galaxy app.; Sorrentino-a. 40-Iceman revealed as gay 4.00
Annual 1 (2/15, $4.99) Sorrentino-a; Eva Bell and Morgana Le Fey in the past 5.00
Special #1 (12/13, $4.99) Superior Spider-Man and the Hulk app. 5.00

ALL-NEW X-MEN
Marvel Comics: Feb, 2016 - No. 19, May, 2017 ($3.99)

1-8-Hopeless-s/Bagley-a; original X-Men, Wolverine (X-23), Kid Apocalypse app. 4.00
9-($4.99) Apocalypse Wars x-over; Beast & Kid Apocalypse in ancient Egypt 5.00
10-19: 10,11-Apocalypse Wars; young Apocalypse app. 17,18-Inhumans app. 4.00
Annual 1 (1/17, $4.99) Spotlight on Idie; Sina Grace-s/Cory Smith-a 5.00
#1.MU (4/17, $4.99) Monsters Unleashed tie-in; Barberi & Lim-a; Gambit app. 5.00

ALL NIGHTER
Image Comics: Jun, 2011 - No. 5, Oct, 2011 ($2.99, B&W, limited series)

1-5-David Haun-s/a/c 3.00

ALL-OUT WAR
DC Comics: Sept-Oct, 1979 - No. 6, Aug, 1980 ($1.00, 68 pgs.)

1-The Viking Commando (origin), Force Three(origin), & Black Eagle Squadron begin
2 4 6 13 18 22
2-6 2 4 6 8 10 12

NOTE: *Ayers a(p)-1-6. Elias r-2. Evans a-1-6. Kubert c-16.*

ALL PICTURE ADVENTURE MAGAZINE
St. John Publishing Co.: Oct, 1952 - No. 2, Nov, 1952 (100 pg. Giants, 25¢, squarebound)

1-War comics 54 108 162 343 574 825
2-Horror-crime comics 68 136 204 435 743 1050

NOTE: *Above books contain three St. John comics rebound; variations possible. **Baker** art known in both.*

ALL PICTURE ALL TRUE LOVE STORY
St. John Publishing Co.: Oct., 1952 - No. 2, Nov., 1952 (100 pgs., 25¢)

1-Canteen Kate by Matt Baker 84 168 252 538 919 1300
2-Baker-c/a 74 148 222 470 810 1150

ALL-PICTURE COMEDY CARNIVAL
St. John Publishing Co.: October, 1952 (100 pgs., 25¢)(Contains 4 rebound comics)

1-Contents can vary; Baker-a 52 104 156 328 552 775

ALL REAL CONFESSION MAGAZINE (See Fox Giants)

ALL ROMANCES (Mr. Risk No. 7 on)
A. A. Wyn (Ace Periodicals): Aug, 1949 - No. 6, June, 1950

1 20 40 60 114 182 250
2 12 24 36 69 97 125
3-6 11 22 33 62 86 110

ALL-SELECT COMICS (Blonde Phantom No. 12 on)
Timely Comics (Daring Comics): Fall, 1943 - No. 11, Fall, 1946

1-Capt. America (by Rico #1), Human Torch, Sub-Mariner begin; Black Widow story (4 pgs.); Classic Schomburg-c 2100 4200 6000 13,900 28,950 44,000
2-Red Skull app. 811 1622 2433 5920 10,460 15,000
3-The Whizzer begins 459 918 1377 3350 5925 8500
4,5-Last Sub-Mariner 383 766 1149 2681 4691 6700
6-9: 6-The Destroyer app. 8-No Whizzer 300 600 900 1965 3433 4900
10-The Destroyer & Sub-Mariner app.; last Capt. America & Human Torch issue
300 600 900 2010 3505 5000
11-1st app. Blonde Phantom; Miss America app.; all Blonde Phantom-c by Shores
300 600 900 2070 3635 5200

NOTE: *Schomburg c-1-10. Sekowsky a-7. #7 & 8 show 1944 in indicia, but should be 1945.*

ALL SELECT COMICS 70th ANNIVERARY SPECIAL
Marvel Comics: Sept, 2009 ($3.99, one-shot)

1-New stories of Blonde Phantom and Marvex the Super Robot; r/Marvex G.A. app. 5.00

ALL SPORTS COMICS (Formerly Real Sports Comics; becomes All Time Sports Comics No. 4 on)
Hillman Periodicals: No. 2, Dec-Jan, 1948-49; No. 3, Feb-Mar, 1949

2-Krigstein-a(p), Powell, Starr-a 37 74 111 222 361 500

	GD	VG	FN	VF	VF/NM	NM-
	2.0	4.0	6.0	8.0	9.0	9.2

3-Mort Lawrence-a 24 48 72 142 234 325

ALL STAR BATMAN
DC Comics: Oct, 2016 - No. 14, Dec, 2017 ($4.99)

1-5-Snyder-s/Romita Jr.-a; Two-Face app.; back-up with Shalvey-a 5.00
1-Director's Cut ($5.99) r/#1 with B&W art and original script; variant cover gallery 6.00
6-9-Back-up w/Francavilla-a. 6-Jock-a; Mr. Freeze app. 7-Lotay-a; Poison Ivy app 5.00
10-14-Albuquerque-a; back-up with Fiumara-a 5.00

ALL STAR BATMAN & ROBIN, THE BOY WONDER
DC Comics: Sept, 2005 - No. 10, Aug, 2008 ($2.99)

1-Two covers; retelling of Robin's origin; Frank Miller-s/Jim Lee-a/c 5.00
1-Diamond Retailer Summit Edition (9/05) sketch-c 60.00
2-10: 2-7-Two covers by Lee and Miller. 3-Black Canary app. 4-Six pg. Batcave gatefold. 10-Edition without profanity 3.00
8-10: 8,9-Variant cover by Neal Adams. 10-Variant-c by Quitely 5.00
10-Recalled edition with insufficiently covered profanity inside; Jim Lee-c 20.00
10-Recalled edition with variant Quitely-c 40.00
... Special Edition (2/06, $3.99) r/#1 with Lee pencil pages and Miller script; new Miller-c 4.00
Vol. 1 HC (2008, $24.99, dustjacket) r/#1-9; cover gallery, sketch pages; Schreck intro. 25.00
Vol. 1 SC (2009, $19.99) r/#1-9; cover gallery, sketch pages; Schreck intro. 20.00

ALL STAR COMICS
DC Comics: Spring 1940

1-Ashcan comic, not distributed to newsstands, only for in-house use. Cover art is Flash Comics #1 and interior from Detective Comics #37. A CGC certified 7.0 copy sold for $15,600 in 2002 and for $21,000 in May 2014.

ALL STAR COMICS (All Star Western No. 58 on)
National Periodical Publ./All-American/DC Comics: Sum, 1940 - No. 57, Feb-Mar, 1951; No. 58, Jan-Feb, 1976 - No. 74, Sept-Oct, 1978

1-The Flash (#1 by E.E. Hibbard), Hawkman (by Shelly), Hourman (by Bernard Baily), The Sandman (by Creig Flessel), The Spectre (by Baily), Biff Bronson, Red White & Blue (ends #2) begin; Ultra Man's only app. (#1-3 are quarterly; #4 begins bi-monthly issues)
1250 2500 3750 9375 17,688 26,000
2-Green Lantern (by Martin Nodell), Johnny Thunder begin; Green Lantern figure swipe from the cover of All-American Comics #16; Flash figure swipe from cover of Flash Comics #8; Moldoff/Bailey-c (cut & paste-c.) 541 1082 1623 3950 6975 10,000
3-Origin & 1st app. The Justice Society of America (Win/40); Dr. Fate & The Atom begin, Red Tornado cameo 6200 12,400 18,600 49,600 96,300 143,000
3-Reprint, Oversize 13-1/2x10". **WARNING:** This comic is an exact reprint of the original except for its size. DC published it in 1974 with a second cover titling it as a Famous First Edition. There have been many reported cases of the outer cover being removed and the interior sold as the original edition. The reprint with the new outer cover removed is practically worthless. See Famous First Edition for value.
4-1st adventure for J.S.A. 622 1244 1866 4541 8021 11,500
5-1st app. Shiera Sanders as Hawkgirl (1st costumed super-heroine, 6-7/41)
514 1028 1542 3750 6625 9500
6-Johnny Thunder joins JSA 300 600 900 1980 3440 4900
7-First time ever Superman and Batman appear in a story together; Superman, Batman and Flash become honorary members; last Hourman; Doiby Dickles app.
423 846 1269 3067 5384 7700
8-Origin & 1st app. Wonder Woman (12-1/41-42)(added as 9 pgs. book is 76 pgs.; origin cont'd in Sensation #1; see W.W. #1 for more detailed origin); Dr. Fate dons new helmet; Hop Harrigan text stories & Starman begin; Shiera app.; Hop Harrigan JSA guest; Starman & Dr. Mid-Nite become members
21,625 43,250 64,875 173,000 274,000 375,000
9-11: 9-JSA's girlfriends cameo; Shiera app.; J. Edgar Hoover of FBI made associate member of JSA. 10-Flash, Green Lantern cameo; Sandman new costume. 11-Wonder Woman begins; Spectre cameo; Shiera app.; Moldoff Hawkman-c
300 600 900 2070 3635 5200
12-Wonder Woman becomes JSA Secretary 300 600 900 2010 3505 5000
13,15: Sandman w/Sandy in #14 & 15. 13-Hitler app. in book-length sci-fi story. 15-Origin & 1st app. Brain Wave; Shiera app. 252 504 756 1613 2757 3900
14-(12/42) Junior JSA Club begins; w/membership offer & premiums
258 516 774 1651 2826 4000
16-20: 19-Sandman w/Sandy. 20-Dr. Fate & Sandman cameo
239 478 717 1530 2615 3700
21-23: 21-Spectre & Atom cameo; Dr. Fate by Kubert; Dr. Fate, Sandman end. 22-Last Hop Harrigan; Flag-c. 23-Origin/1st app. Psycho Pirate; last Spectre & Starman 181 362 543 1158 1979 2800
24-Flash & Green Lantern cameo; Mr. Terrific only app.; Wildcat, JSA guest; Kubert Hawkman begins; Hitler-c 187 374 561 1197 2049 2900
25-27: 25-Flash & Green Lantern start again. 26-Robot-c. 27-Wildcat, JSA guest (#24-26: only All-American imprint) 161 322 483 1030 1765 2500
28-32 148 296 444 947 1624 2300
33-Solomon Grundy & Doiby Dickles app; classic Solomon Grundy cover
420 840 1260 2940 5170 7400

All Star Comics #58 © DC

All-Star Squadron #1 © DC

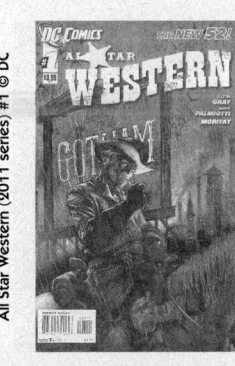

All Star Western (2011 series) #1 © DC

	GD 2.0	VG 4.0	FN 6.0	VF 8.0	VF/NM 9.0	NM- 9.2
34,35-Johnny Thunder cameo in both	135	270	405	864	1482	2100
36-Batman & Superman JSA guests	300	600	900	2010	3505	5000
37-Johnny Thunder cameo; origin & 1st app. Injustice Society; last Kubert Hawkman	194	388	582	1242	2121	3000
38-Black Canary begins; JSA Death issue	252	504	756	1613	2757	3900
39,40: 39-Last Johnny Thunder	129	258	387	826	1413	2000
41-Black Canary joins JSA; Injustice Society app. (2nd app.?)	155	310	465	992	1696	2400
42-Atom & the Hawkman don new costumes	148	296	444	947	1624	2300
43-49,51-56: 43-New logo; Robot-c. 55-Sci/Fi story. 56-Robot-c	129	258	387	826	1413	2000
50-Frazetta art, 3 pgs.	139	278	417	883	1517	2150
57-Kubert-a, 6 pgs. (Scarce); last app. G.A. Green Lantern, Flash & Dr. Mid-Nite	203	406	609	1289	2220	3150
V12 #58-(1976) JSA (Flash, Hawkman, Dr. Mid-Nite, Wildcat, Dr. Fate, Green Lantern, Robin & Star Spangled Kid) app.; intro. Power Girl	10	20	30	67	141	215
V12 #59,60: 59-Estrada & Wood-a	3	6	9	20	31	42
V12 #61-68: 62-65-Superman app. 64,65-Wood-c/a; Vandal Savage app. 66-Injustice Society app. 68-Psycho Pirate app.	3	6	9	20	31	42
V12 #69-1st Earth-2 Huntress (Helena Wayne)	6	12	18	41	76	110
V12 #70-73: 70-Full intro. of Huntress. 72-Thorn on-c	3	6	9	20	31	42
V12 #74-(44 pgs.) Last issue, story continues in Adventure Comics #461 & 462 (death of Earth-2 Batman; Staton-c/a	4	8	12	28	47	65

(See Justice Society Vol. 1 TPB for reprints of V12 revival)

NOTE: *No Atom-27, 36; no Dr. Fate-13; no Flash-8, 9, 11-23; no Green Lantern-8, 9,11-23; Hawkman in 1-57 (only one to app. in all 57 issues); no Johnny Thunder-5, 36; no Wonder Woman-9, 10, 23. Book length stories in 4-9, 11-14, 18-22, 25, 26, 29, 30, 32-36, 40, 42, 43. Johnny Peril in #42-46, 48, 49, 51, 52,54-57.* ***Baily*** *a-1-10, 12, 13, 14i, 15-20.* ***Burnley*** *Starman-8-13; c-12, 13.* ***Grell*** *c-58.* ***E.E. Hibbard*** *c-3, 4, 6-10.* ***Infantino*** *c-40.* ***Kubert*** *Hawkman-24-30, 33-37.* ***Lampert/Baily/Flessel*** *c-1, 2.* ***Moldoff*** *Hawkman-3-23; c-11.* ***Mart Nodell*** *c-25i, 26i, 27-32.* ***Purcell*** *c-5.* ***Simon & Kirby*** *Sandman 14-17, 19.* ***Staton*** *a-66-74p. c-74p.* ***Toth*** *a-37(2), 38(2), 40, 41; c-38, 41.* ***Wood*** *a-58i-63i, 64, 65; c-63i, 64, 65. Issues 1-7, 9-16 are 68 pgs.; #8 is 76 pgs.; #17-19 are 60 pgs.; #20-57 are 52 pgs.*

ALL STAR COMICS (Also see crossover 1999 editions of Adventure, All-American, National, Sensation, Smash, Star Spangled and Thrilling Comics)
DC Comics: May, 1999 - No. 2, May, 1999 ($2.95, bookends for JSA x-over)

1,2-Justice Society in World War 2; Robinson-s/Johnson-c	4.00
1-RRP Edition	45.00
...80-Page Giant (9/99, $4.95) Phantom Lady app.	5.00

ALL STAR INDEX, THE
Independent Comics Group (Eclipse): Feb, 1987 ($2.00, Baxter paper)

	GD	VG	FN	VF	VF/NM	NM-
1	1	2	3	5	6	8

ALL-STAR SECTION EIGHT (Also see Sixpack and Dogwelder: Hard Travelin' Heroz)
DC Comics: Aug, 2015 - No. 6, Feb, 2016 ($2.99, limited series)

1-6-Ennis-s/McCrea-a/Conner-c. 1-Batman app. 4-Wonder Woman app. 6-Superman 4.00

ALL-STAR SQUADRON (See Justice League of America #193)
DC Comics: Sept, 1981 - No. 67, Mar, 1987

	GD	VG	FN	VF	VF/NM	NM-
1-Original Atom, Hawkman, Dr. Mid-Nite, Robotman (origin), Plastic Man, Johnny Quick, Liberty Belle, Shining Knight begin	2	4	6	9	12	15
2-10: 3-Solomon Grundy app. 4,7-Spectre app. 8-Re-intro Steel, the Indestructable Man						6.00
11-24,26-46,48,49: 12-Origin G.A. Hawkman retold. 15-JLA, JSA & Crime Syndicate app. 23-Origin/1st app. The Amazing Man. 24-Batman app. 26-Origin Infinity, Inc.(2nd app.); Robin app. 27-Dr. Fate vs. The Spectre. 30-35-Spectre app. 33-Origin Freedom Fighters of Earth-X. 36,37-Superman vs. Capt. Marvel; Ordway-c. 41-Origin Starman						5.00
25-1st app. Nuklon (Atom Smasher) & Infinity, Inc. (9/83)	2	4	6	10	14	18
47-Origin Dr. Fate; McFarlane-a (1st full story)/part-c (7/85)	3	6	9	14	19	24
50-Double size; Crisis x-over	1	3	4	6	8	10
51-66: 51-56-Crisis x-over. 61-Origin Liberty Belle. 62-Origin The Shining Knight. 63-Origin Robotman. 65-Origin Johnny Quick. 66-Origin Tarantula						6.00
67-Last issue; retells first case of the Justice Society	1	2	3	5	7	9
Annual 1-3: 1(11/82)-Retells origin of G.A. Atom, Guardian & Wildcat; Jerry Ordway's 1st pencils for DC. (1st work was inking Carmine Infantino in Mystery in Space #117). 2(11/83)-Infinity, Inc. app. 3(9/84)						6.00

NOTE: ***Buckler*** *a-1-5; c-1, 3-5, 51.* ***Kubert*** *c-2, 7-18. JLA app. in 14, 15. JSA app. in 4, 14, 15, 19, 27, 28.*

ALL-STAR STORY OF THE DODGERS, THE
Stadium Communications: Apr, 1979 ($1.00)

	GD	VG	FN	VF	VF/NM	NM-
1	2	4	6	10	14	18

ALL-STAR SUPERMAN (Also see FCBD edition in the Promotional Comics section)
DC Comics: Jan, 2006 - No. 12, Oct, 2008 ($2.99)

1-Grant Morrison-s/Frank Quitely-a/c	5.00
1-Variant-c by Neal Adams	20.00
1-Special Edition (2009, $1.00) r/#1 with "After Watchmen" cover logo frame	3.00
2-12: 3-Lois gets super powers. 7,8-Bizarro app.	3.00
Free Comic Book Day giveaway (6/08) reprints #1	3.00
Vol. 1 HC (2007, $19.99, dustjacket) r/#1-6; Bob Schreck intro.	20.00
Vol. 1 SC (2008, $12.99) r/#1-6; Schreck intro.	13.00
Vol. 2 HC (2009, $19.99, dustjacket) r/#7-12; Mark Waid intro.	20.00
Vol. 2 SC (2009, $12.99) r/#7-12; Mark Waid intro.	13.00

ALL STAR WESTERN (Formerly All Star Comics No. 1-57)
National Periodical Publ.: No. 58, Apr-May, 1951 - No. 119, June-July, 1961

	GD	VG	FN	VF	VF/NM	NM-
58-Trigger Twins (ends #116), Strong Bow, The Roving Ranger & Don Caballero begin	52	104	156	328	552	775
59,60: Last 52 pgs.	31	62	93	186	303	420
61-66: 61-64-Toth-a	25	50	75	150	245	340
67-Johnny Thunder begins; Gil Kane-a	36	72	108	211	343	475
68-81: Last precode (2-3/55)	17	34	51	98	154	210
82-98: 97-1st S.A. issue	15	30	45	84	127	170
99-Frazetta-r/Jimmy Wakely #4	15	30	45	85	130	175
100	15	30	45	85	130	175
101-107,109-116,118,119: 103-Grey tone-c	14	28	42	80	115	150
108-Origin J. Thunder; J. Thunder logo begins	26	52	78	154	252	350
117-Origin Super Chief	19	38	57	111	176	240

NOTE: ***Gil Kane*** *c(p)-58, 59, 61, 63, 64, 68, 69, 70-95(most), 97-199(most).* ***Infantino*** *art in most issues. Madame .44 app.- #117-119.*

ALL-STAR WESTERN (Weird Western Tales No. 12 on)
National Periodical Publications: Aug-Sept, 1970 - No. 11, Apr-May, 1972

	GD	VG	FN	VF	VF/NM	NM-
1-Pow-Wow Smith-r; Infantino-a	6	12	18	38	69	100
2-Outlaw begins; El Diablo by Morrow begins; has cameos by Williamson, Torres, Kane, Giordano & Phil Seuling	5	10	15	35	63	90
3-Origin El Diablo	5	10	15	31	53	75
4-6: 5-Last Outlaw issue. 6-Billy the Kid begins, ends #8	4	8	12	23	37	50
7-9-(52 pgs.) 9-Frazetta-a, 3pgs.(r)	4	8	12	25	40	55
10-(52 pgs.) Jonah Hex begins (1st app., 2-3/72)	36	72	108	259	580	900
11-(52 pgs.) 2nd app. Jonah Hex; 1st cover	13	26	39	89	195	300

NOTE: ***Neal Adams*** *c-2-5;* ***Aparo*** *a-5.* ***G. Kane*** *a-3, 4, 6, 8.* ***Kubert*** *a-4r, 7-9r.* ***Morrow*** *a-2-4, 10, 11. No. 7-11 have 52 pgs.*

ALL STAR WESTERN (DC New 52)
DC Comics: Nov, 2011 - No. 34, Oct, 2014 ($3.99)

1-34: 1-Jonah Hex in 1880s Gotham City; Gray & Palmiotti-s/Moritat-a. 2,3-El Diablo back-up. 9-11-Court of Owls. 10-Bat Lash back-up; Garcia-López-a. 13-16-Tomahawk back-up. 19-21-Booster Gold app. 21-28-Hex in present day. 22-Batman app. 27-Superman app. 30,31-Madame .44 back-up; Garcia-López-a. 34-Darwyn Cooke-c/a	4.00
#0 (11/12, $3.99) Jonah Hex's full origin; Gray & Palmiotti-s/Moritat-a	4.00

ALL SURPRISE (Becomes Jeanie #13 on) (Funny animal)
Timely/Marvel (CPC): Fall, 1943 - No. 12, Winter, 1946-47

	GD	VG	FN	VF	VF/NM	NM-
1-Super Rabbit, Gandy & Sourpuss begin	63	126	189	403	689	975
2	27	54	81	158	259	360
3-10,12	20	40	60	120	195	270
11-Kurtzman "Pigtales" art	21	42	63	126	206	285

ALL TEEN (Formerly All Winners; All Winners & Teen Comics No. 21 on)
Marvel Comics (WFP): No. 20, January, 1947

	GD	VG	FN	VF	VF/NM	NM-
20-Georgie, Mitzi, Patsy Walker, Willie app.; Syd Shores-c	40	80	120	246	411	575

ALL-TIME SPORTS COMICS (Formerly All Sports Comics)
Hillman Per.: V2, No. 4, Apr-May, 1949 - V2, No. 7, Oct-Nov, 1949 (All 52 pgs.)

	GD	VG	FN	VF	VF/NM	NM-
V2#4	26	52	78	154	252	350
5-7: 5-(V1#5 inside)-Powell-a; Ty Cobb sty. 7-Krigstein-p; Walter Johnson & Knute Rockne sty	19	38	57	112	179	245

ALL TOP
William H. Wise Co.: 1944 (132 pgs.)

	GD	VG	FN	VF	VF/NM	NM-
nn-Capt. V, Merciless the Sorceress, Red Robbins, One Round Hogan, Mike the M.P., Snooky, Pussy Katnip app.	53	106	159	334	567	800

ALL TOP COMICS (My Experience No. 19 on)
Fox Feature Synd./Green Publ./Norlen Mag.: 1945; No. 2, Sum, 1946 - No. 18, Jul, 1949; 1957 - 1959

	GD	VG	FN	VF	VF/NM	NM-
1-Cosmo Cat & Flash Rabbit begin (1st app.)	36	72	108	211	343	475
2 (#1-7 are funny animal)	17	34	51	98	154	210
3-7: 7-Two diff. issues (7/47 & 9/47)	14	28	42	82	121	160
8-Blue Beetle, Phantom Lady, & Rulah, Jungle Goddess begin (11/47); Kamen-c	300	600	900	2040	3570	5100
9-Kamen-c	161	322	483	1030	1765	2500

All True Romance #1 © Artful

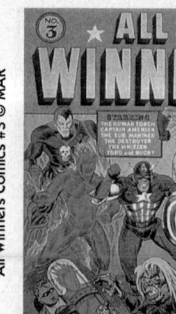

All Winners Comics #3 © MAR

Alpha Flight #95 © MAR

GD VG FN VF VF/NM NM-
2.0 4.0 6.0 8.0 9.0 9.2

10-Classic Kamen bondage/torture/dwarf-c 203 406 609 1289 2220 3150
11-13,15,17: 11,12-Rulah-c. 15-No Blue Beetle 132 264 396 838 1444 2050
14-No Blue Beetle; used in **SOTI**, illo- "Corpses of colored people strung up by their wrists" 203 406 609 1289 2220 3150
16-Classic Good Girl octopus-c 300 600 900 2010 3505 5000
18-Dagar, Jo-Jo app; no Phantom Lady or Blue Beetle 103 206 309 659 1130 1600
6(1957-Green Publ.)-Patoruzu the Indian; Cosmo Cat on cover only. 6(1958-Literary Ent.)-Muggy Doo; Cosmo Cat on cover only. 6(1959-Norlen)-Atomic Mouse; Cosmo Cat on-c only. 6(1959)-Little Eva. 6(Cornell)-Supermouse on-c 5 10 15 24 30 35
NOTE: *Jo-Jo by* ***Kamen****-12,18.*

ALL TRUE ALL PICTURE POLICE CASES
St. John Publishing Co.: Oct, 1952 - No. 2, Nov, 1952 (100 pgs.)

1-Three rebound St. John crime comics 58 116 174 371 636 900
2-Three comics rebound 43 86 129 271 461 650
NOTE: *Contents may vary.*

ALL-TRUE CRIME (...Cases No. 26-35; formerly Official True Crime Cases)
Marvel/Atlas Comics: No. 26, Feb, 1948 - No. 52, Sept, 1952
(OFI #26,27/CFI #28,29/LCC #30-46/LMC #47-52)

26(#1)-Syd Shores-c 43 86 129 271 461 650
27(4/48)-Electric chair-c 37 74 111 222 361 500
28-41,43-48,50-52: 35-37-Photo-c 17 34 51 98 154 210
42,49-Krigstein-a. 49-Used in **POP**, Pg 79 18 36 54 103 162 220
NOTE: ***Colan*** *a-46.* ***Keller*** *a-46.* ***Robinson*** *a-47, 50.* ***Sale*** *a-46.* ***Shores*** *c-26.* ***Tuska*** *a-48(3).*

ALL-TRUE DETECTIVE CASES (Kit Carson No. 5 on)
Avon Periodicals: #2, Apr-May, 1954 - No. 4, Aug-Sept, 1954

2(#1)-Wood-a 32 64 96 188 307 425
3-Kinstler-c 18 36 54 103 162 220
4-r/Gangsters And Gun Molls #2; Kamen-a 23 46 69 136 223 310
nn(100 pgs.)-7 pg. Kubert-a, Kinstler back-c 54 108 162 343 574 825

ALL TRUE ROMANCE (...Illustrated No. 3)
Artful Publ. #1-3/Harwell(Comic Media) #4-20?/Ajax-Farrell(Excellent Publ.) No. 22 on/Four Star Comic Corp.: 3/51 - No. 20, 12/54; No. 22, 3/55 - No. 30?, 7/57; No. 3(#31), 9/57;No. 4(#32), 11/57; No. 33, 2/58 - No. 34, 6/58

1 (3/51) 28 56 84 165 270 375
2 (10/51; 11/51 on-c) 15 30 45 90 140 190
3(12/51) - #5(5/52) 14 28 42 82 121 160
6-Wood-a, 9 pgs. (exceptional) 24 48 72 142 234 325
7-10 [two #7s: #7(11/52, 9/52 inside), #7(11/52, 11/52 inside)]. 10-Hollingsworth-c 14 28 42 80 115 150
11-13,16-19(9/54),20(12/54) (no #21): 11,13-Heck-a 13 26 39 72 101 130
14-Marijuana story 13 26 39 74 105 135
22: Last precode issue (1st Ajax, 3/55) 13 26 39 72 101 130
23-27,29,30(7/57): 29-Disbrow-a 11 22 33 62 86 110
28 (9/56)-L. B. Cole, Disbrow-a 15 30 45 83 124 165
3(#31, 9/57),4(#32, 11/57),33,34 (Farrell, '57- '58) 10 20 30 56 76 95

ALL WESTERN WINNERS (Formerly All Winners; becomes Western Winners with No. 5; see Two-Gun Kid No. 5)
Marvel Comics(CDS): No. 2, Winter, 1948-49 - No. 4, April, 1949

2-Black Rider (origin/1st app.) & his horse Satan, Kid Colt & his horse Steel, & Two-Gun Kid & his horse Cyclone begin; Shores c-2-4 84 168 252 538 919 1300
3-Anti-Wertham editorial 40 80 120 246 411 575
4-Black Rider i.d. revealed; Heath, Shores-a 40 80 120 246 411 575

ALL WINNERS COMICS (All Teen #20) (Also see Timely Presents: ...)
USA No. 1-7/WFP No. 10-19/YAI No. 21: Summer, 1941 - No. 19, Fall, 1946; No. 21, Winter, 1946-47; (No #20) (No. 21 continued from Young Allies No. 20)

1-The Angel & Black Marvel only app.; Capt. America by Simon & Kirby, Human Torch & Sub-Mariner begin (#1 was advertised as All Aces); 1st app. All-Winners Squad in text story by Stan Lee 1900 3800 5700 13,500 25,750 38,000
2-The Destroyer & The Whizzer begin; Simon & Kirby Captain America 676 1352 2028 4935 8718 12,500
3 481 962 1443 3511 6206 8900
4-Classic War-c by Al Avison 541 1082 1623 3950 6975 10,000
5 400 800 1200 2800 4900 7000
6-The Black Avenger only app.; no Whizzer story; Hitler, Hirohito & Mussolini-c 703 1406 2109 5132 9066 13,000
7-10 394 788 1182 2758 4829 6900
11,13-15: 11-1st Atlas globe on-c (Winter, 1943-44; also see Human Torch #14). 14,15-No Human Torch 300 600 900 2010 3455 4900
12-Red Skull story; last Destroyer; no Whizzer story 389 778 1167 2723 4762 6800
16-18: 16-No Human Torch 252 504 756 1613 2757 3900

GD VG FN VF VF/NM NM-
2.0 4.0 6.0 8.0 9.0 9.2

19-(Scarce)-1st story app. & origin All Winners Squad (Capt. America & Bucky, Human Torch & Toro, Sub-Mariner, Whizzer, & Miss America; r-in Fantasy Masterpieces #10 965 1930 2895 7050 14,775 22,500
21-(Scarce)-All Winners Squad; bondage-c 690 1380 2070 5030 10,765 16,500
NOTE: ***Everett*** *Sub-Mariner-1, 3, 4;* ***Burgos*** *Torch-1, 3, 4.* ***Schomburg*** *c-1, 7-18.* ***Shores*** *c-19p, 21.*
(2nd Series - August, 1948, Marvel Comics (CDS))
(Becomes All Western Winners with No. 2)
1-The Blonde Phantom, Capt. America, Human Torch, & Sub-Mariner app. 320 640 960 2240 3920 5600

ALL WINNERS COMICS 70th ANNIVERARY SPECIAL
Marvel Comics: Oct, 2009 ($3.99, one-shot)

1-New story of All Winners Squad; r/G.A. Capt America app. from All Winners #12 5.00

ALL-WINNERS SQUAD: BAND OF HEROES
Marvel Comics: Aug, 2011 - No. 5, Dec, 2011 ($2.99, unfinished limited series of 8 issues)

1-5-WWII story of the Young Avenger and Captain Flame; Jenkins-s/DiGiandomenico-a 3.00

ALL YOUR COMICS (See Fox Giants)
Fox Feature Syndicate (R. W. Voight): Spring, 1946 (36 pgs.)

1-Red Robbins, Merciless the Sorceress app. 32 64 96 188 307 425

ALMANAC OF CRIME (See Fox Giants)

AL OF FBI (See Little Al of the FBI)

ALOHA, HAWAIIAN DICK (Also see Hawaiian Dick)
Image Comics: Apr, 2016 - No. 5, Aug, 2016 ($3.99, limited series)

1-5-B. Clay Moore-s. 1-4-Jacob Wyatt-a. 5-Paul Reinwand-a 4.00

ALONE IN THE DARK (Based on video game)
Image Comics: Feb, 2003 ($4.95)

1-Matt Haley-c/a; Jean-Marc & Randy Lofficier-s 5.00

ALPHA AND OMEGA
Spire Christian Comics (Fleming H. Revell): 1978 (49¢)

nn 2 4 6 9 13 16

ALPHA: BIG TIME (See Amazing Spider-Man #692-694)
Marvel Comics: Apr, 2013 - No. 5, Aug, 2015 ($2.99)

1-5-Fialkov-s/Plati-a/Ramos-c. 1,3,5-Superior Peter Parker app. 4-Thor app. 3.00

ALPHA CENTURION (See Superman, 2nd Series & Zero Hour)
DC Comics: 1996 ($2.95, one-shot)

1 3.00

ALPHA FLIGHT (See X-Men #120,121 & X-Men/Alpha Flight)
Marvel Comics: Aug, 1983 - No. 130, Mar, 1994 (#52-on are direct sales only)

1-(52 pgs.) Byrne-a begins (thru #28) -Wolverine & Nightcrawler cameo 2 4 6 10 14 18
2-11,13-28: 2-Vindicator becomes Guardian; origin Marrina & Alpha Flight. 3-Concludes origin Alpha Flight. 6-Origin Shaman. 7-Origin Snowbird. 10,11-Origin Sasquatch. 13-Wolverine app. 16,17-Wolverine cameo. 17-X-Men x-over (mostly r-/X-Men #109). 19-Origin/1st app. Talisman. 20-New headquarters. 25-Return of Guardian. 28-Last Byrne issue 4.00
12-(52 pgs.)-Death of Guardian 5.00
29-32,35-49: 39-47,49-Portacio-a(i) 3.00
33-1st app. Lady Deathstrike; Wolverine app. 2 4 6 11 16 20
34-2nd app. Lady Deathstrike; origin Wolverine 6.00
50-Double size; Portacio-a(i) 4.00
51-Jim Lee's 1st work at Marvel (10/87); Wolverine cameo; 1st Lee Wolverine; Portacio-a(i) 2 4 6 8 10 12
52,53-Wolverine app.; Lee-a on Wolverine; Portacio-a(i); 53-Lee/Portacio-a 4.00
54-73,76-86,91-99,101-105: 54,63,64-No Jim Lee-a. 54-Portacio-a(i). 55-62-Jim Lee-a(p). 71-Intro The Sorcerer (villain). 91-Dr. Doom app. 94-F.F. x-over. 99-Galactus, Avengers app. 102-Intro Weapon Omega 3.00
74,75,87-90,100: 74-Wolverine, Spider-Man & The Avengers app. 75-Double size ($1.95, 52 pgs.). 87-90-Wolverine. 4 part story w/Jim Lee-c. 89-Original Guardian returns. 100-($2.00, 52 pgs.)-Avengers & Galactus app. 4.00
106-Northstar revealed to be gay 1 3 4 6 8 10
106-2nd printing (direct sale only) 3.00
107-109,112-119,121-129: 107-X-Factor x-over. 112-Infinity War x-overs. 115-1st Wyre 3.00
110,111: Infinity War x-overs, Wolverine app. (brief). 111-Thanos cameo 3.00
120-($2.25)-Polybagged w/Paranormal Registration Act poster 4.00
130-($2.25, 52 pgs.) 4.00
Annual 1,2 (9/86, 12/87) 4.00
...Classics Vol. 1 TPB (2007, $24.99) r/#1-8; character profile pages; Byrne interview 25.00
... No. 1 Facsimile Edition (7/19, $4.99) r/#1 with original 1983 ads and letter column 5.00
Special V2#1(6/92, $2.50, 52 pgs.)-Wolverine-c/story 4.00
NOTE: ***Austin*** *c-1i, 2i, 53i.* ***Byrne*** *c-81, 82.* ***Guice*** *c-85, 91-99.* ***Jim Lee*** *a(p)-51, 53, 55-62, 64; c-53, 87-90.* ***Mignola***

Alpha Flight: True North #1 © MAR

Amazing Adult Fantasy #9 © MAR

Amazing Adventures #1 © Z-D

	GD 2.0	VG 4.0	FN 6.0	VF 8.0	VF/NM 9.0	NM- 9.2

*a-29-31p. **Whilce Portacio** a(i)-39-47, 49-54.*

ALPHA FLIGHT (2nd Series)
Marvel Comics: Aug, 1997 - No. 20, Mar, 1999 ($2.99/$1.99)

	GD	VG	FN	VF	VF/NM	NM-
1-($2.99)-Wraparound cover						6.00
2,3: 2-Variant-c						4.00
4-11: 8,9-Wolverine-c/app.						3.00
12-($2.99) Death of Sasquatch; wraparound-c						4.00
13-15,18-20						3.00
16-1st app. cameo Honey Lemon (Big Hero 6)	1	2	3	5	6	8
17-1st app. Big Hero 6	2	4	6	10	14	18
.../Inhumans '98 Annual ($3.50) Raney-a						4.00

ALPHA FLIGHT (3rd Series)
Marvel Comics: May, 2004 - No. 12, April, 2005 ($2.99)

	GD	VG	FN	VF	VF/NM	NM-
1-12: 1-6-Lobdell-s/Henry-c/a						3.00
... Vol. 1: You Gotta Be Kiddin' Me (2004, $14.99) r/#1-6						15.00

ALPHA FLIGHT (4th Series)
Marvel Comics: No. 0.1, Jul, 2011 - No. 8, Mar, 2012 ($2.99)

	GD	VG	FN	VF	VF/NM	NM-
0.1-Pak & Van Lente-s/Oliver & Green-a; Kara Killgrave app.						3.00
1-(8/11, $3.99) Fear Itself tie-in; Eaglesham-a/Jimenez-c; bonus design sketch pages						4.00
2-8-($2.99) Fear Itself tie-ins. 2-Puck returns. 5-Taskmaster app. 7,8-Wolverine app.						3.00

ALPHA FLIGHT: IN THE BEGINNING
Marvel Comics: July, 1997 ($1.95, one-shot)

	GD	VG	FN	VF	VF/NM	NM-
(-1)-Flashback w/Wolverine						3.00

ALPHA FLIGHT SPECIAL
Marvel Comics: July, 1991 - No. 4, Oct, 1991 ($1.50, limited series)

	GD	VG	FN	VF	VF/NM	NM-
1-4: 1-3-r-A. Flight #97-99 w/covers. 4-r-A.Flight #100						3.00

ALPHA FLIGHT: TRUE NORTH
Marvel Comics: Nov, 2019 ($4.99, one-shot)

	GD	VG	FN	VF	VF/NM	NM-
1-Short stories by Canadian creators incl. Jim Zub, Dunbar, Brisson, MacKay, Hepburn						5.00

ALPHA KING (3 FLOYDS:...)
Image Comics: May, 2016 - No. 5, Nov, 2017 ($3.99)

	GD	VG	FN	VF	VF/NM	NM-
1-5-Azzarello & Floyd-s/Bisley-a/c						4.00

ALTERED IMAGE
Image Comics: Apr, 1998 - No. 3, Sept, 1998 ($2.50, limited series)

	GD	VG	FN	VF	VF/NM	NM-
1-3-Spawn, Witchblade, Savage Dragon; Valentino-s/a						3.00

ALTERED STATES
Dynamite Entertainment: 2015 ($3.99, series of one-shots)

	GD	VG	FN	VF	VF/NM	NM-
...: Doc Savage - Alternate reality Doc Savage in caveman past; Philip Tan-c						4.00
...: Red Sonja - Alternate reality Sonja in modern day New York City; Philip Tan-c						4.00
...: The Shadow - Alternate reality Shadow in sci-fi future; Philip Tan-c						4.00
...: Vampirella - Alternate reality Vampirella as a mortal on Drakulon; Collins-s						4.00

ALTER EGO
First Comics: May, 1986 - No. 4, Nov, 1986 (Mini-series)

	GD	VG	FN	VF	VF/NM	NM-
1-4						3.00

ALTER NATION
Image Comics: Feb, 2004 - No. 4, Jun, 2004 ($2.95, limited series)

	GD	VG	FN	VF	VF/NM	NM-
1-4: 1-Two covers by Art Adams and Barberi; Barberi-a						3.00

ALTERS
AfterShock Comics: Sept, 2016 - No. 10, Feb, 2018 ($3.99)

	GD	VG	FN	VF	VF/NM	NM-
1-10: 1-Paul Jenkins-s/Leila Leiz-a						4.00

ALVIN (TV) (See Four Color Comics No. 1042 or Three Chipmunks #1)
Dell Publishing Co.: Oct-Dec, 1962 - No. 28, Oct, 1973

	GD	VG	FN	VF	VF/NM	NM-
12-021-212 (#1)	8	16	24	56	108	160
2	5	10	15	33	57	80
3-10	4	8	12	28	47	65
11-"Chipmunks sing the Beatles' Hits"	5	10	15	31	53	75
12-28	4	8	12	23	37	50
Alvin For President (10/64)	4	8	12	28	47	65
...& His Pals in Merry Christmas with Clyde Crashcup & Leonardo 1 (25¢ Giant) (02-120-402)-(12-2/64)	6	12	18	42	79	115
Reprinted in 1966 (12-023-604)	4	8	12	23	37	50

ALVIN & THE CHIPMUNKS
Harvey Comics: July, 1992 - No. 5, May, 1994

	GD	VG	FN	VF	VF/NM	NM-
1-5: 1-Richie Rich app.						5.00

AMALGAM AGE OF COMICS, THE: THE DC COMICS COLLECTION
DC Comics: 1996 ($12.95, trade paperback)

	GD	VG	FN	VF	VF/NM	NM-
nn-r/Amazon, Assassins, Doctor Strangefate, JLX, Legends of the Dark Claw, & Super Soldier						13.00

AMANDA AND GUNN
Image Comics: Apr, 1997 - No. 4, Oct, 1997 ($2.95, B&W, limited series)

	GD	VG	FN	VF	VF/NM	NM-
1-4						3.00

AMAZING ADULT FANTASY (Formerly Amazing Adventures #1-6; becomes Amazing Fantasy #15) (See Amazing Fantasy for Omnibus HC reprint of #1-15)
Marvel Comics Group (AMI): No. 7, Dec, 1961 - No. 14, July, 1962

	GD	VG	FN	VF	VF/NM	NM-
7-Ditko-c/a begins, ends #14	56	112	168	448	999	1550
8-Last 10¢ issue	46	92	138	368	834	1300
9-13: 12-1st app. Mailbag. 13-Anti-communist story	47	94	141	364	820	1275
13-2nd printing (1994)	2	4	6	9	12	15
14-Prototype issue (Professor X)	57	114	171	456	1028	1600

AMAZING ADVENTURE FUNNIES (Fantoman No. 2 on)
Centaur Publications: June, 1940 - No. 2, Sept. 1940

	GD	VG	FN	VF	VF/NM	NM-
1-The Fantom of the Fair by Gustavson (r/Amaz. Mystery Funnies V2#7,V2#8), The Arrow, Skyrocket Steele From the Year X by Everett (r/AMF #2); Burgos-a	219	438	657	1402	2401	3400
2-Reprints; Published after Fantoman #2	145	290	435	921	1586	2250

NOTE: ***Burgos** a-1(2). **Everett** a-1(3). **Gustavson** a-1(5), 2(3). **Pinajian** a-2.*

AMAZING ADVENTURES (Also see Boy Cowboy & Science Comics)
Ziff-Davis Publ. Co.: 1950; No. 1, Nov, 1950 - No. 6, Fall, 1952 (Painted covers)

	GD	VG	FN	VF	VF/NM	NM-
1950 (no month given) (8-1/2x11) (8 pgs.) Has the front & back cover plus Schomburg story used in Amazing Advs. #1 (Sent to subscribers of Z-D s/f magazines & ordered through mail for 10¢. Used to test market)	90	180	270	576	988	1400
1-Wood, Schomburg, Anderson, Whitney-a	106	212	318	673	1162	1650
2,3,5: 2-Schomburg-a. 2,5-Anderson-a. 3,5-Starr-a	53	106	159	334	567	800
4-Classic-c; Anderson-a	142	284	426	909	1555	2200
6-Krigstein-a	50	100	150	315	533	750

AMAZING ADVENTURES (Becomes Amazing Adult Fantasy #7 on) (See Amazing Fantasy for Omnibus HC reprint of #1-15)
Atlas Comics (AMI)/Marvel Comics No. 3 on: June, 1961 - No. 6, Nov, 1961

	GD	VG	FN	VF	VF/NM	NM-
1-Origin Dr. Droom (1st Marvel-Age Superhero who later becomes Doctor Druid) by Kirby; Kirby/Ditko-a (5 pgs.) Ditko & Kirby-a in all; Kirby monster c-1-6	141	282	423	1142	2571	4000
2	53	106	159	424	950	1475
3-6: 6-Last Dr. Droom	49	98	147	382	866	1350

AMAZING ADVENTURES
Marvel Comics Group: Aug, 1970 - No. 39, Nov, 1976

	GD	VG	FN	VF	VF/NM	NM-
1-Inhumans by Kirby(p) & Black Widow (1st app. in Tales of Suspense #52) double feature begins	8	16	24	52	99	145
2-4: 2-F.F. brief app. 4-Last Inhumans by Kirby	3	6	9	21	33	45
5-8: Adams-a(p); 8-Last Black Widow; last 15¢-c	5	10	15	30	50	70
9,10: Magneto app. 10-Last Inhumans (origin-r by Kirby)	5	10	15	30	50	70
11-New Beast begins(1st app. in mutated form; origin in flashback); X-Men cameo in flashback (#11-17 are X-Men tie-ins)	19	38	57	131	291	450
12-17: 12-Beast battles Iron Man. 13-Brotherhood of Evil Mutants x-over from X-Men. 15-X-Men app. 16-Rutland Vermont - Bald Mountain Halloween x-over; Juggernaut app. 17-Last Beast (origin); X-Men app.	7	14	21	48	89	130
18-War of the Worlds begins (5/73); 1st app. Killraven; Neal Adams-a(p)	5	10	15	30	50	70
19-35,38,39: 19-Chaykin-a. 25-Buckler-a. 35-Giffen's first published story (art), along with Deadly Hands of Kung-Fu #22 (3/76)	1	3	4	6	8	10
36,37-(Regular 25¢ edition)(7-8/76)	1	3	4	6	8	10
36,37-(30¢-c variants, limited distribution)	5	10	15	30	50	70

NOTE: ***N. Adams** c-6-8. **Buscema** a-1p, 2p. **Colan** a-3-5p, 26p. **Ditko** a-24r. **Everett** a(i)3-5, 7-9. **Giffen** a-35i, 38p. **G. Kane** c-11, 25p, 29p. **Ploog** a-12i. **Russell** a-27-32, 34-37, 39; c-28, 30-32, 33i, 34, 35, 37, 39i. **Starliing** a-17. **Starlin** c-15p, 16, 17, 27. **Sutton** a-11-15p.*

AMAZING ADVENTURES
Marvel Comics Group: Dec, 1979 - No. 14, Jan, 1981

	GD	VG	FN	VF	VF/NM	NM-
V2#1-Reprints story/X-Men #1 & 38 (origins)	3	6	9	16	24	32
2-14: 2-6-Early X-Men-r. 7,8-Origin Iceman	2	4	6	8	10	12

NOTE: ***Byrne** c-6p, 9p. **Kirby** a-1-14r; c-7, 9. **Steranko** a-12r. **Tuska** a-7-9.*

AMAZING ADVENTURES
Marvel Comics: July, 1988 ($4.95, squarebound, one-shot, 80 pgs.)

	GD	VG	FN	VF	VF/NM	NM-
1-Anthology; Austin, Golden-a						5.00

AMAZING ADVENTURES OF CAPTAIN CARVEL AND HIS CARVEL CRUSADERS, THE
(See Carvel Comics in the Promotional Comics section)

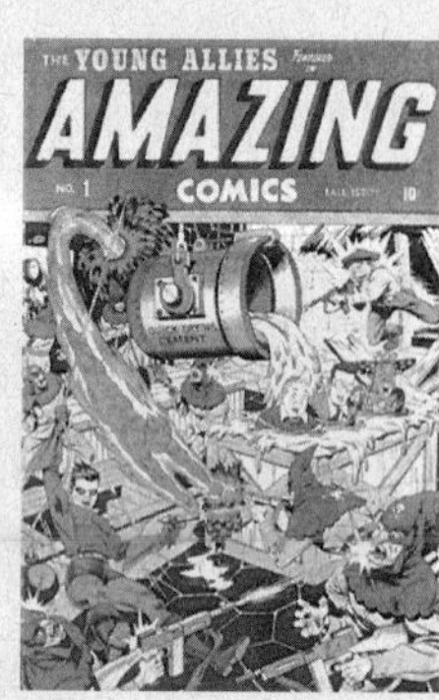

Amazing Comics #1 © MAR

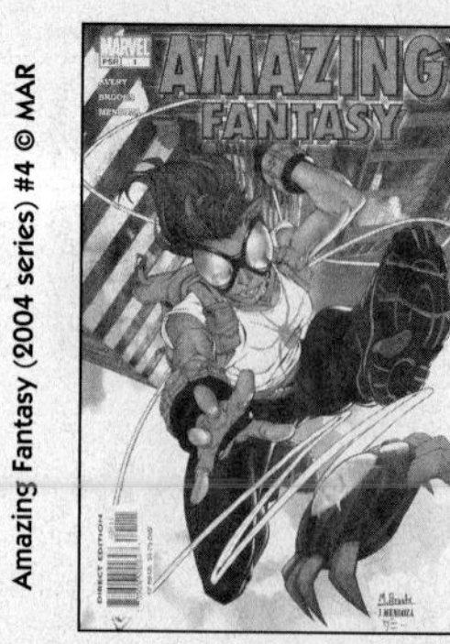

Amazing Fantasy (2004 series) #4 © MAR

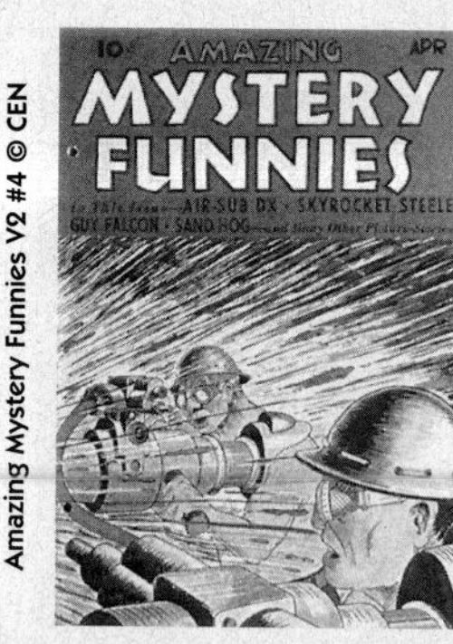

Amazing Mystery Funnies V2 #4 © CEN

	GD	VG	FN	VF	VF/NM	NM-
	2.0	4.0	6.0	8.0	9.0	9.2

AMAZING BATVARK (Cerebus in Hell)
Aardvark-Vanaheim: Feb, 2021 ($4.00, B&W)

1-Cerebus figures placed over Doré artwork of Hell; Amazing Spider-Man #50-c swipe 4.00

AMAZING CEREBUS (Reprints from Cerebus in Hell)(Also see Aardvark Comics)
Aardvark-Vanaheim: Feb, 2018 ($4.00, B&W)

1-Cerebus figures placed over original Doré artwork; Amazing Spider-Man #300-c swipe 4.00

AMAZING CHAN & THE CHAN CLAN, THE (TV)
Gold Key: May, 1973 - No. 4, Feb, 1974 (Hanna-Barbera)

1-Warren Tufts-a in all 4 8 12 25 40 55
2-4 3 6 9 16 24 32

AMAZING COMICS (Complete Comics No. 2)
Timely Comics (EPC): Fall, 1944

1-The Destroyer, The Whizzer, The Young Allies (by Sekowsky), Sergeant Dix; Schomburg-c 297 594 891 1901 3251 4600

AMAZING DETECTIVE CASES (Formerly Suspense No. 2?)
Marvel/Atlas Comics (CCC): No. 3, Nov, 1950 - No. 14, Sept, 1952

3 34 68 102 204 332 460
4-6: 6-Jerry Robinson-a 20 40 60 117 189 260
7-10 19 38 57 109 172 235
11,12: 11-(3/52)-Horror format begins. 12-Krigstein-a 57 114 171 362 619 875
13-(Scarce)-Everett-a; electrocution-c/story 61 122 183 390 670 950
14 53 106 159 334 567 800

NOTE: *Colan a-9. Maneely c-13. Sekowsky a-12. Sinnott a-13. Tuska a-10.*

AMAZING FANTASY (Formerly Amazing Adult Fantasy #7-14)
Atlas Magazines/Marvel: #15, Aug, 1962 (Sept, 1962 shown in indicia); #16, Dec, 1995 - #18, Feb, 1996

15-Origin/1st app. of Spider-Man by Steve Ditko (11 pgs.); 1st app. Aunt May & Uncle Ben; Kirby/Ditko-c 9600 19,200 38,400 110,400 280,000 450,000
16-18 ('95-'96, $3.95): Kurt Busiek scripts; painted-c/a by Paul Lee 4.00
Amazing Fantasy #15 Facsimile Edition (12/19, $3.99) r/#15 with original 1962 ads 4.00
Amazing Fantasy #15: Spider-Man! (8/12, $3.99) recolored rep. of #15 and ASM #1 4.00
Amazing Fantasy Omnibus HC ("Amazing Adult Fantasy" on-c) (2007, $75.00, dustjacket) r/Amazing Adventures #1-6, Amazing Adult Fantasy #7-14 and Amazing Fantasy #15 with letter pages; foreword by Bissette; cover gallery from '70s reprint titles 75.00

AMAZING FANTASY (Continues from #6 in Araña: The Heart of the Spider)
Marvel Comics: Aug, 2004 - No. 20, June, 2006 ($2.99)

1-Intro. Anya Corazon; Avery-s/Brooks-c/a 3 6 9 16 23 30
2-14,16-20: 3,4-Roger Cruz-a. 7-Intro. new Scorpion; Kirk-a. 10-Intro. Vampire By Night 13,14-Back-up Captain Universe stories. 16-20-Death's Head 3.00
15-($3.99, 1/06) Spider-Man app.; intro 6 new characters incl. Amadeus Cho/Mastermind Excello seen in World War Hulk series; s/a by various 8 16 24 54 102 150
Death's Head 3.0: Unnatural Selection TPB (2006, $13.99) r/#16-20 14.00
Scorpion: Poison Tomorrow (2005, $7.99, digest) r/#7-13 8.00

AMAZING GHOST STORIES (Formerly Nightmare)
St. John Publishing Co.: No. 14, Oct, 1954 - No. 16, Feb, 1955

14-Pit & the Pendulum story by Kinstler; Baker-c 194 388 582 1242 2121 3000
15-r/Weird Thrillers #5; Baker-c, Powell-a 53 106 159 334 567 800
16-Kubert reprints of Weird Thrillers #4; Baker-c; Roussos, Tuska-a; Kinstler-a (1 pg.) 48 96 144 302 514 725

AMAZING HIGH ADVENTURE
Marvel Comics: 8/84; No. 2, 10/85; No. 3, 10/86 - No. 5, 1986 ($2.00)

1-5: Painted-c on all. 3,4-Baxter paper. 4-Bolton-c/a. 5-Bolton-a 4.00

NOTE: *Bissette a-4. Severin a-1, 3. Sienkiewicz a-1,2. Paul Smith a-2. Williamson a-2i.*

AMAZING JOY BUZZARDS
Image Comics: 2005 - No. 4, 2005 ($2.95, B&W with pink spot color in #1)

1-4-Mark Andrew Smith-s/Dan Hipp-a. 1-Mahfood back-c. 2-Morse back-c 3.00
Vol. 1 TPB (2005, $11.95) r/#1-4; bonus art and character design sketches 12.00
TPB (2008, $19.99) r/#1-4 and Vol. 2 #1-5 20.00

AMAZING JOY BUZZARDS (Volume 2)
Image Comics: Oct, 2005 - No. 5, Aug, 2006 ($2.99, B&W)

1-5: 1-Mark Andrew Smith-s/Dan Hipp-a. 4-Mahfood-a; Crosland-a. 5-Holgate-a 3.00
Vol. 2 TPB (2006, $12.99) r/#1-4; bonus art, pin-ups and character sketches 13.00

AMAZING-MAN COMICS (Formerly Motion Picture Funnies Weekly?)
(Also see Stars And Stripes Comics, and Amazing Mystery Funnies nn)
Centaur Publications: No. 5, Sept, 1939 - No. 26, Jan, 1942

5(#1)(Rare)-Origin/1st app. A-Man the Amazing Man by Bill Everett; The Cat-Man by Tarpe Mills (also #8), Mighty Man by Filchock, Minimidget & sidekick Ritty, & The Iron Skull by Burgos begins 2150 4300 6450 17,200 30,600 44,000
6-Origin The Amazing Man retold; The Shark begins; Ivy Menace by Tarpe Mills app. 470 940 1410 3431 6066 8700
7-Magician From Mars begins; ends #11 320 640 960 2240 3920 5600
8-Cat-Man dresses as woman 277 554 831 1759 3030 4300
9-Magician From Mars battles the 'Elemental Monster,' swiped into The Spectre in More Fun #54 & 55. Ties w/Marvel Mystery #4 for 1st Nazi War-c on a comic (2/40) 290 580 870 1856 3178 4500
10,11: 11-Zardi, the Eternal Man begins; ends #16; Amazing Man dons costume; last Everett issue 213 426 639 1363 2332 3300
12,13 200 400 600 1280 2190 3100
14-Reef Kinkaid, Rocke Wayburn (ends #20), & Dr. Hypno (ends #21) begin; no Zardi or Chuck Hardy 174 348 522 1114 1907 2700
15,17-20: 15-Zardi returns; no Rocke Wayburn. 17-Dr. Hypno returns; no Zardi 142 284 426 909 1555 2200
16-Mighty Man's powers of super strength & ability to shrink & grow explained; Rocke Wayburn returns; no Dr. Hypno; Al Avison (a character) begins, ends #18 (a tribute to the famed artist) 155 310 465 992 1696 2400
21-Origin Dash Dartwell (drug-use story); origin & only app. T.N.T. 168 336 504 1075 1838 2600
22-Dash Dartwell, the Human Meteor & The Voice app; last Iron Skull & The Shark; Silver Streak app. (classic Nazi monster-c) 2000 4000 6000 15,200 27,600 40,000
23-Two Amazing Man stories; intro/origin Tommy the Amazing Kid; The Marksman only app. 148 296 444 947 1624 2300
24-King of Darkness, Nightshade, & Blue Lady begin; end #26; 1st app. Super-Ann 148 296 444 947 1624 2300
25 (Scarce) Meteor Martin by Wolverton 541 1082 1623 3950 6975 10,000
26 (Scarce) Meteor Martin by Wolverton; Electric Ray app. 1000 2000 3000 7600 13,800 20,000

NOTE: *Everett a-5-11; c-5-11. Gilman a-14-20. Giunta/Mirando a-7-10. Sam Glanzman a-14-16, 18-21, 23. Louis Glanzman a-6, 9-11, 14-21; c-13-19, 21. Robert Golden a-9. Gustavson a-6; c-22, 23. Lubbers a-14-21. Simon a-10. Frank Thomas a-6, 9-11, 14, 15, 17-21.*

AMAZING MARY JANE (Mary Jane Watson)
Marvel Comics: Dec, 2019 - No. 6, May 2020 ($3.99)

1-6-Mary Jane & Mysterio filming a super-hero movie; Savage Six app.;Leah Williams-s 4.00

AMAZING MYSTERIES (Formerly Sub-Mariner Comics No. 31)
Marvel Comics (CCC): No. 32, May, 1949 - No. 35, Jan, 1950 (1st Marvel Horror Comic)

32-The Witness app. 139 278 417 883 1517 2150
33-Horror format 68 136 204 435 743 1050
34,35: Changes to Crime. 34,35-Photo-c 28 56 84 165 270 375

AMAZING MYSTERY FUNNIES
Centaur Publications: Aug, 1938 - No. 24, Sept, 1940 (All 52 pgs.)

V1#1-Everett-c(1st); Dick Kent Adv. story; Skyrocket Steele in the Year X on cover only 649 1298 1947 4738 8369 12,000
2-Everett 1st-a (Skyrocket Steele) 389 778 1167 2723 4762 6800
3 252 504 756 1613 2757 3900
3(#4, 12/38)-nn on cover, #3 on inside; bondage-c 284 568 852 1818 3109 4400
V2#1,3,4,6: 3-Air-Sub DX begins by Burgos. 4-Dan Hastings, Sand Hog begins (ends #5). 6-Last Skyrocket Steele 219 438 657 1402 2401 3400
2-Classic-c; drug use story 432 864 1296 3154 5577 8000
5-Classic Everett-c 703 1406 2109 5132 9066 13,000
7 (Scarce)-Intro. The Fantom of the Fair & begins; Everett, Gustavson, Burgos-a 470 940 1410 3431 6066 8700
8-Origin & 1st app. Speed Centaur 219 438 657 1402 2401 3400
9-11: 11-Self portrait and biog. of Everett; Jon Linton begins; early Robot cover (11/39) 168 336 504 1075 1838 2600
12 (Scarce)-1st Space Patrol; Wolverton-a (12/39); new costume Phantom of the Fair 277 554 831 1759 3030 4300
V3#1(#17, 1/40)-Intro. Bullet; Tippy Taylor serial begins, ends #24 (continued in The Arrow #2) 142 284 426 909 1555 2200
18,20: 18-Fantom of the Fair by Gustavson 135 270 405 864 1482 2100
19,21-24: Space Patrol by Wolverton in all 161 322 483 1030 1765 2500

NOTE: *Burgos a-V2#3-9. Eisner a-V1#2, 3(2). Everett a-V1#2-4, V2#1, 3-6; c-V1#1-4,V2#3, 5, 18. Filchock a-V2#9. Flessel a-V2#6. Guardineer a-V1#4, V2#4-6; Gustavson a-V2#4, 5, 9-12, V3#1, 18, 19; c-V2#7, 9, 12, V3#1, 21, 22; McWilliams a-V2#9, 10. TarpeMills a-V2#2, 4-6, 9-12, V3#1. Leo Morey(Pulp artist) c-V2#10; text illo-V2#11. FrankThomas a-6-V2#11. Webster a-V2#4.*

AMAZING MYSTERY FUNNIES
Centaur Publications: 1942

nn (#23)-Cover from Amazing Man Comics #23 w/interior from Amazing Man Comics #25. (2 known copies). A CGC 2.0 copy sold in 2020 for $4,400.

AMAZING SAINTS
Logos International: 1974 (39¢)

Amazing Spider-Girl #4 © MAR

Amazing Spider-Man #33 © MAR

Amazing Spider-Man #121 © MAR

GD VG FN VF VF/NM NM-
2.0 4.0 6.0 8.0 9.0 9.2

nn-True story of Phil Saint 2 4 6 9 13 16

AMAZING SCARLET SPIDER
Marvel Comics: Nov, 1995 - No. 2, Dec, 1995 ($1.95, limited series)

1,2: Replaces "Amazing Spider-Man" for two issues. 1-Venom/Carnage cameos. 2-Green Goblin & Joystick-c/app. 3.00

AMAZING SCREW-ON HEAD, THE
Dark Horse Comics (Maverick): May, 2002 ($2.99, one-shot)

1-Mike Mignola-s/a/c 3.00

AMAZING SPIDER-GIRL (Also see Spider-Girl and What If...? (2nd series) #105)
Marvel Comics: No. 0, 2006; No. 1, Dec, 2006 - No. 30, May, 2009 ($2.99)

0-($1.99) Recap of the Spider-Girl series and character profiles; A.F. #15 cover swipe 1 2 3 5 6 8
1-14,16-24,26-($2.99) Frenz & Buscema-a. 9-Carnage returns. 19-Has #17 on cover 3.00
15,25,30-($3.99) 15-10th Anniversary issue. 25-Three covers 4.00
... Vol. 1: What Ever Happened to the Daughter of Spider-Man? TPB (2007, $14.99) r/#0-6 15.00
... Vol. 2: Comes the Carnage! TPB (2007, $13.99) r/#7-12 14.00
... Vol. 3: Mind Games TPB (2008, $13.99) r/#13-18 14.00

AMAZING SPIDER-MAN, THE (See All Detergent Comics, Amazing Fantasy, America's Best TV Comics, Aurora, Deadly Foes of..., Fireside Book Series, Friendly Neighborhood..., Giant-Size..., Giant Size Super-Heroes Featuring..., Marvel Age..., Marvel Collectors Item Classics, Marvel Fanfare, Marvel Graphic Novel, Marvel Knights..., Marvel Spec. Ed., Marvel Tales, Marvel Team-Up, Marvel Treasury Ed., New Avengers, Nothing Can Stop the Juggernaut, Official Marvel Index To..., Peter Parker..., Power Record Comics, Spectacular..., Spider-Man, Spider-Man Digest, Spider-Man Saga, Spider-Man 2099, Spider-Man Vs. Wolverine, Spidey Super Stories, Strange Tales Annual #2, Superior Spider-Man, Superman Vs. ..., Try-Out Winner Book, Ultimate Marvel Team-Up, Ultimate Spider-Man, Web of Spider- Man & Within Our Reach)

AMAZING SPIDER-MAN, THE
Marvel Comics Group: March, 1963 - No. 441, Nov, 1998

1-Retells origin by Steve Ditko; 1st Fantastic Four x-over (ties with F.F. #12 as first Marvel x-over); intro. John Jameson & The Chameleon; Spider-Man's 2nd app.; Kirby/Ditko-c; Ditko-c/a #1-38 2900 5800 8700 21,800 54,900 88,000
1-Reprint from the Golden Record Comic set 36 72 108 259 580 900
With record (1966) 44 88 132 326 738 1200
2-1st app. the Vulture & the Terrible Tinkerer 570 1140 1710 4300 10,150 16,000
3-1st app. Doc Octopus; 1st full-length story; Human Torch cameo; Spider-Man pin-up by Ditko 410 820 1230 3500 8000 12,500
4-Origin & 1st app. The Sandman (see Strange Tales #115 for 2nd app.); 1st monthly issue; intro. Betty Brant & Liz Allen 333 666 1000 2831 6416 10,000
5-Dr. Doom app. 241 482 723 1988 4494 7000
6-1st app. Lizard 207 414 621 1708 3854 6000
7-Vs. The Vulture 141 282 423 1163 2632 4100
8-Fantastic Four app. in back-up story by Kirby & Ditko 107 214 321 856 1928 3000
9-Origin & 1st app. Electro (2/64) 145 290 435 1196 2698 4200
10-1st app. Big Man & The Enforcers 100 200 300 800 1800 2800
11-1st app. Bennett Brant 129 258 387 1032 2316 3600
12-Doc Octopus unmasks Spider-Man-c/story 91 182 273 728 1639 2550
13-1st app. Mysterio 241 482 723 1988 4494 7000
14-(7/64)-1st app. The Green Goblin (c/story)(Norman Osborn); Hulk x-over 300 600 900 2550 5775 9000
15-1st app. Kraven the Hunter; 1st mention of Mary Jane Watson (not shown) 172 344 516 1419 3210 5000
16-Spider-Man battles Daredevil (1st x-over 9/64); still in old yellow costume 79 158 237 632 1416 2200
17-2nd app. Green Goblin (c/story); Human Torch x-over (also in #18 & #21) 82 164 246 656 1478 2300
18-1st app. Ned Leeds who later becomes Hobgoblin; Fantastic Four cameo; 3rd app. Sandman 50 100 150 400 900 1400
19-Sandman app. 40 80 120 296 673 1050
20-Origin & 1st app. The Scorpion 79 158 237 632 1416 2200
21-2nd app. The Beetle (see Strange Tales #123) 42 84 126 311 706 1100
22-1st app. Princess Python 39 78 117 289 657 1025
23-3rd app. The Green Goblin-c/story; Norman Osborn app.; Marvel Masterwork pin-up by Ditko; fan letter by Jim Shooter 49 98 147 382 866 1350
24 37 74 111 274 612 950
25-(6/65)-1st brief app. Mary Jane Watson (face not shown); 1st app. Spencer Smythe; Norman Osborn app. 44 88 132 326 738 1150
26-4th app. The Green Goblin-c/story; 1st app. Crime Master; dies in #27; Norman Osborn app. 42 84 126 311 706 1100
27-5th app. The Green Goblin-c/story; Norman Osborn app. 40 80 120 296 673 1050
28-Origin & 1st app. Molten Man (9/65, scarcer in high grade) 121 242 363 968 2184 3400
29,30 30 60 90 216 483 750
31-(12/65)-1st app. Gwen Stacy, Prof. Warren, and Harry Osborn who later becomes 2nd Green Goblin 79 158 237 632 1416 2200
32-38: 34-4th app. Kraven the Hunter. 36-1st app. Looter. 37-Intro. Norman Osborn. 38-(7/66)-2nd brief app. Mary Jane Watson (face not shown); last Ditko issue 23 46 69 164 362 560
39-The Green Goblin-c/story; Green Goblin's identity revealed as Norman Osborn; Osborn learns Spider-Man's secret identity; Romita-a begins (8/66; see Daredevil #16 for 1st Romita-a on Spider-Man) 54 108 162 432 966 1500
40-1st told origin The Green Goblin-c/story 42 84 126 311 706 1100
41-1st app. Rhino 61 122 183 488 1094 1700
42-(11/66)-3rd app. Mary Jane Watson (cameo in last 2 panels); 1st time face is shown 27 54 81 189 420 650
43-45,47-49: 43-Origin of the Rhino. 44,45-2nd & 3rd app. The Lizard. 47-M.J. Watson & Peter Parker 1st date. 47-Green Goblin cameo; Harry & Norman Osborn app. 47,49-5th & 6th app. Kraven the Hunter. 48-1st new Vulture (Blackie Drago) 18 36 54 126 281 435
46-Intro/origin The Shocker 36 72 108 259 580 900
50-1st app. Kingpin (7/67) 141 282 423 1142 2571 4000
51-2nd app. Kingpin; Joe Robertson 1-panel cameo 27 54 81 189 420 650
52-58,60: 52-1st app. Joe Robertson & 3rd app. Kingpin. 56-1st app. Capt. George Stacy. 57,58-Ka-Zar app. 13 26 39 87 191 295
59-1st app. Brainwasher (alias Kingpin); 1st-c app. M. J. Watson 14 28 42 93 204 315
61-74: 61-1st Gwen Stacy cover app. 67-1st app. Randy Robertson. 69-Kingpin-c. 69,70-Kingpin app. 70-1st app. Vanessa Fisk (Kingpin's wife)(only seen in shadow). 73-1st app. Silvermane. 74-Last 12¢ issue 10 20 30 68 144 220
75-77,79-83,87-89,91,92,95,99: 79-The Prowler app. 83-1st app. Schemer; Vanessa Fisk app. (only previously seen in shadow in #70) 9 18 27 60 120 180
78-1st app. The Prowler 15 30 45 103 227 350
84,85,93: 84,85-Kingpin-c/story. 93-1st app. Arthur Stacy 9 18 27 61 123 185
86-Re-intro & origin Black Widow in new costume 13 26 39 89 195 300
90-Death of Capt. Stacy 12 24 36 79 170 260
94-Origin retold 10 20 30 64 132 200
96-98-Green Goblin app. (97,98-Green Goblin-c); drug books not approved by CCA 10 20 30 69 147 225
100-Anniversary issue (9/71); Green Goblin cameo (2 pgs.) 15 30 45 103 227 350
101-1st app. Morbius the Living Vampire; Lizard cameo; Stan Lee co-plots with Roy Thomas; last 15¢ issue (10/71) 50 100 150 400 900 1400
101-Silver ink 2nd printing (9/92, $1.75) 3 6 9 19 30 40
101 Facsimile Edition 1 (4/21, $3.99) r/#101 with original 1971 ads and letter column 5.00
102-Origin & 2nd app. Morbius (25¢, 52 pgs.) 12 24 36 81 176 270
103-118: 103,104-Roy Thomas-s. 104,111-Kraven the Hunter-c/stories. 105-109-Stan Lee-s. 108-1st app. Sha-Shan. 109-Dr. Strange-c/story. 110-1st app. Gibbon; Conway-s begin. 113-1st app. Hammerhead. 116-118-Reprints story from Spectacular Spider-Man Mag. in color with some changes 6 12 18 41 76 110
119,120-Spider-Man vs. Hulk (4 & 5/73) 9 18 27 61 123 185
121-Death of Gwen Stacy (6/73) (killed by Green Goblin)(reprinted in Marvel Tales #98 & 192); Harry Osborn LSD overdose 32 64 96 230 515 800
122-Death of The Green Goblin-c/story (7/73) (reprinted in Marvel Tales #99 & 192) 24 48 72 168 372 575
123-Cage app. 7 14 21 48 89 130
124-1st app. Man-Wolf (9/73) 10 20 30 69 149 225
125-Man-Wolf origin 6 12 18 41 76 110
126-128: 126-1st mention of Harry Osborn becoming Green Goblin 6 12 18 38 69 100
129-1st app. The Punisher (2/74); 1st app. Jackal 250 500 750 1250 1875 2500
130-133: 131-Last 20¢ issue 5 10 15 34 60 85
134-(7/74); 1st app. Tarantula; Harry Osborn discovers Spider-Man's ID; Punisher cameo 7 14 21 48 89 130
135-2nd full Punisher app. (8/74) 11 22 33 76 163 250
136-1st app. Harry Osborn in Green Goblin costume 8 16 24 54 102 150
137-Green Goblin-c/story (2nd Harry Osborn Goblin) 6 12 18 38 69 100
138-141: 139-1st Grizzly. 140-1st app. Glory Grant 4 8 12 25 40 55
142,143-Gwen Stacy clone cameos: 143-1st app. Cyclone 5 10 15 31 53 75
144-147: 144-Full app. of Gwen Stacy clone. 145,146-Gwen Stacy clone storyline continues. 147-Spider-Man learns Gwen Stacy is clone 4 8 12 25 40 55
148-Jackal revealed 5 10 15 35 63 90
149-Spider-Man clone story begins, clone dies (?); origin of Jackal 10 20 30 69 147 225
150-Spider-Man decides he is not the clone 5 10 15 31 53 75
151-Spider-Man disposes of clone body; Len Wein-s begins; thru #180 6 12 18 41 76 110

Amazing Spider-Man #186 © MAR

Amazing Spider-Man #246 © MAR

Amazing Spider-Man #330 © MAR

	GD 2.0	VG 4.0	FN 6.0	VF 8.0	VF/NM 9.0	NM- 9.2
152-160-(Regular 25¢ editions). 152-vs. the Shocker. 154-vs. Sandman. 156-1st Mirage. 157-159-Doc Octopus & Hammerhead app. 159-Last 25¢ issue(8/76). 160-Spider-Mobile destroyed	3	6	9	21	33	45
155-159-(30¢-c variants, limited distribution)	9	18	27	57	111	165
161-Nightcrawler app. from X-Men; Punisher cameo; Wolverine & Colossus app.	4	8	12	28	47	65
162-Punisher, Nightcrawler app.; 1st Jigsaw	5	10	15	30	53	75
163-168: 163-164-vs. the Kingpin. 165-vs. Stegron. 166-Stegron & the Lizard app. 167-1st app. Will O' The Wisp. 168-Will O' The Wisp app.	3	6	9	16	23	30
169-170,172-173: 169-Clone story recapped; Stan Lee Cameo. 170-Dr. Faustus app. 172-1st Rocket Racer. 173-vs Molten Man	3	6	9	16	23	30
171-Nova app. x-over w/Nova #12	3	6	9	19	30	40
169-173-(35¢-c variants, limited dist.)(6-10/77)	20	40	60	138	307	475
174,175-Punisher app.	3	6	9	19	30	40
176-180-Green Goblin (Barton Hamilton) app.; Harry Osborn Green Goblin in #180 only. 177-180-Silvermane app.	3	6	9	18	28	38
181-186: 181-Origin retold; gives life history of Spidey; Punisher cameo in flashback (1 panel). 182-(7/78)-Peter's first proposal to Mary Jane, but she declines (in #183). 183-Rocket Racer & the Big Wheel app. 184-vs. the second White Dragon. 185-Peter graduates college	3	6	9	14	20	25
187,188: 187-Captain America app. 188-vs. Jigsaw	3	6	9	19	30	40
189,190-Byrne-a; Man-Wolf app.	3	6	9	19	30	40
191-193,196-199: 191-vs. the Spider-Slayer. 192-Death of Spencer Smythe. 193-Peter & Mary Jane break up; the Fly app. 196-Faked death of Aunt May. 197-vs. the Kingpin. 198,199-Mysterio app.	2	4	6	11	16	20
NOTE: *Whitman 3-packs containing #192-194,196 exist.*						
194-1st app. Black Cat	11	22	33	76	163	250
195-2nd app. Black Cat & origin Black Cat	3	6	9	20	31	42
200-Giant origin issue (1/80); death of the burglar (from Amazing Fantasy #15)	3	6	9	21	33	45
201,202-Punisher app. 201-Classic bullseye-c	3	6	9	17	25	34
203-208,210,211,213-219: 203-3rd Dazzler (4/80). 204,205-Black Cat app. 204-Last Wolfman-s. 206-Byrne-a. 207-vs Mesmero. 210-1st app. Madame Web. 211-Sub-Mariner app. 214,215-New Frightful Four app: Wizard, Trapster, Sandman & Llyra (Namor foe). 216-Madame Web app. 217-Sandman vs Hydro-Man. 219-Grey Gargoyle app.; Frank Miller-c	2	4	6	9	12	15
209-Kraven the Hunter app; 1st app. origin Calypso	3	6	9	14	19	24
212-1st app. & origin Hydro-Man	4	8	12	25	40	55
220-225,228: 220-Moon Knight app. 222-1st app. of the Whizzer as Speed Demon. 223-vs. The Red Ghost & the Super-Apes; Roger Stern-s begins. 224-Vulture app. 225-Foolkiller II-c/story.	1	3	4	6	8	10
226,227-Black Cat returns	3	6	9	14	19	24
229,230: Classic 'Nothing can stop the Juggernaut' story	3	6	9	14	20	26
231-237: 231,232-Cobra & Mr Hyde app. 233-Tarantula app. 234-Free 16 pg. insert "Marvel Guide to Collecting Comics", Tarantula & Will O' The Wisp app. 235-Origin Will 'O The Wisp. 236-Tarantula dies. 237-Stilt-Man app.	1	3	4	6	8	10
238-(3/83)-1st app. Hobgoblin (Ned Leeds); came with skin "Tattooz" decal.						
NOTE: The same decal appears in the more common Fantastic Four #252 which is being removed & placed in this issue as incentive to increase value. (No "Tattooz" were included in the Canadian edition)						
(Value with tattooz)	10	20	30	69	147	225
(Value without tattooz)	5	10	15	35	63	90
239-2nd app. Hobgoblin & 1st battle w/Spidey	4	8	12	23	37	50
240-243,246-248: 240,241-Vulture app. (origin in #241). 242-Mary Jane Watson cameo (last panel). 243-Reintro Mary Jane after 4 year absence. 248-Classic 'The Kid Who Collects Spider-Man' story; Spider-Man tells origin & reveals identity to young boy with leukemia	1	3	4	6	8	10
244-3rd app. Hobgoblin (cameo)	2	4	6	13	18	22
245-(10/83)-4th app. Hobgoblin (cameo); Lefty Donovan gains powers of Hobgoblin & battles Spider-Man	3	6	9	14	20	25
249-251: 3 part Hobgoblin/Spider-Man battle. 249-Retells origin & death of 1st Green Goblin. 251-Last old costume	2	4	6	9	13	16
252-Spider-Man dons new black costume (5/84); ties with Marvel Team-Up #141 & Spectacular Spider-Man #90 for 1st new costume in regular title (See Marvel Super-Heroes Secret Wars #8 (12/84) for acquisition of costume); last Roger Stern-s	6	12	18	42	79	115
252 Facsimile Edition 1 (6/19, $4.99) r/#252 with original 1984 ads and letter column						5.00
253-1st app. The Rose; Tom DeFalco-s begin	2	4	6	11	16	20
254,255,257,258: 254-Jack O' Lantern app. 255-1st app Black Fox. 257-Hobgoblin cameo; 2nd app. Puma; M.J. Watson reveals she knows Spidey's i.d. 258-Spider-Man discovers black costume is an alien symbiote; Mister Fantastic, Human Torch, Hobgoblin app.	1	3	4	6	8	10
256-1st app. Puma	3	6	9	16	23	30
259-Full Hobgoblin app.; Spidey back to old costume; origin Mary Jane Watson	2	4	6	13	18	22

	GD 2.0	VG 4.0	FN 6.0	VF 8.0	VF/NM 9.0	NM- 9.2
260-Hobgoblin app.	2	4	6	13	18	22
261-Hobgoblin-c/story; painted-c by Vess	3	6	9	14	19	24
262-Spider-Man unmasked; photo-c	2	4	6	9	12	15
263,264,266-268: 266-Toad & Frogman app.; Peter David-s. 268-Secret Wars II x-over	1	2	3	5	6	8
265-1st app. Silver Sable (6/85)	4	8	12	23	37	50
265-Silver ink 2nd printing ($1.25)	2	4	6	9	13	16
269-270: 269-Spider-Man vs Firelord. 270 Avengers app.	1	3	4	6	8	10
271-274,277-280,282-283: 272-1st app. Slyde. 273-Secret Wars II x-over; Beyonder app. 274-Secret Wars II x-over; Zarathos app. (The Spirit of Vengeance). 277-Vess-c & back-up art. 278-Scourge app; death of the Wraith. 279-Jack O' Lantern-c/s. 280-1st Sinister Syndicate: Beetle, Boomerang, Hydro-Man, Rhino, Speed Demon. 282-X-Factor app.	1	2	3	5	6	8
275-($1.25, 52 pgs.)-Hobgoblin-c/story; origin-r by Ditko	3	6	9	16	23	30
276-Hobgoblin app.	2	4	6	9	13	16
281-Hobgoblin battles Jack O'Lantern	2	4	6	10	14	18
284,285: 284-Punisher cameo; Gang War Pt. 1; Hobgoblin-c/story. 285-Punisher app.; minor Hobgoblin app.; last Tom DeFalco-s; Gang War Pt. 2	2	4	6	8	10	12
286-288: Gang War Parts 3-5. 286-Hobgoblin-c & app. (minor). 287-Hobgoblin app. (minor). 288-Full Hobgoblin app.; Gang War ends	1	3	4	6	8	10
289-(6/87, $1.25, 52 pgs.)-Hobgoblin's i.d. revealed as Ned Leeds; death of Ned Leeds; Macendale (Jack O'Lantern) becomes new Hobgoblin (1st app.)	3	6	9	15	22	28
290-292,295-297: 290-Peter proposes to Mary Jane; 1st David Michelinie-s. 291,292-Spider-Slayer app. 292-She accepts; leads into wedding in Amazing Spider-Man Annual #21. 295-'Mad Dog Ward' Pt. 2; x-over w/Web of Spider-Man #33 & Spectacular Spider-Man #133. 296-297-Doc Octopus app.	1	2	3	5	6	8
293,294-Part 2 & 5 of Kraven story from Web of Spider-Man. 293-Continued from Web of Spider-Man #31; continues into Spectacular Spider-Man #131. 294-Death of Kraven; continued from Web of Spider-Man #32; continues in Spectacular Spider-Man #132	2	4	6	13	18	22
298-Todd McFarlane-c/a begins (3/88); 1st brief app. Eddie Brock who becomes Venom; (last pg.)	5	10	15	34	60	85
299-1st brief app. Venom with costume	6	12	18	37	66	95
300 ($1.50, 52 pgs.; 25th Anniversary)-1st full Venom app.; last black costume (5/88)	60	120	180	300	400	500
301-$1.00 issues begin. Classic McFarlane-c	4	8	12	27	44	60
302-305: 302-303-Silver Sable app. 304,305-Black Fox app. 304-1st bi-weekly issue	2	4	6	10	14	18
306-311,313,314: 306-Swipes-c from Action #1. 307-Chameleon app. 308-Taskmaster app. 309-1st app. Styx & Stone. 310-Killer Shrike app. 311-Inferno x-over; Mysterio app. 313-Lizard app.; origin retold. 314-Christmas-c	2	4	6	9	13	16
312-Hobgoblin battles Green Goblin; Inferno x-over	3	6	9	15	22	28
315,317-Venom app.	3	6	9	17	26	35
316-Classic Venom-c	6	12	18	38	69	100
318-323,325: 318-Scorpion app. 319-Bi-weekly begins again; Scorpion, Rhino, Backlash app. 320-'Assassination Nation Plot' Pt.1 (ends in issue #325); Paladin & Silver Sable app. 321-Paladin & Silver Sable app. 322-Silver Sable app.; fan letters from Stan Lee and Charlie Novinskie. 323-Captain America app. 325-Captain America & Red Skull app.	1	3	4	6	8	10
324-Sabretooth app.; McFarlane cover only	2	4	6	10	14	18
326,327,329: 326-Acts of Vengeance x-over; vs Graviton. 327-Acts of Vengeance x-over; vs. Magneto; Cosmic storyline continues from Spectacular Spider-Man; Erik Larsen-a. 329-Acts of Vengeance x-over; vs. the Tri-Sentinel; Sebastian Shaw app.; Erik Larsen-a (continuous through issue #344)						6.00
328-Acts of Vengeance x-over; vs. the Hulk; last McFarlane issue	3	6	9	14	20	25
330,331-Punisher app. 331-Minor Venom app.	1	2	3	5	6	8
332,333-Venom-c/story	2	4	6	10	14	18
334-343: 334-339-Return of the Sinister Six. 337-Hobgoblin app. 341-Tarantula app; Spider-Man loses his cosmic powers. 342,343-Black Cat app.						6.00
344-(2/91) 1st app. Cletus Kasady (Carnage)	4	8	12	22	35	48
345-1st full app. Cletus Kasady; Venom cameo on last pg.; 1st Mark Bagley-a on Spider-Man	3	6	9	14	19	24
346,347-Venom app.	2	4	6	13	18	22
347 Facsimile Edition (3/20, $3.99) r/#347 with original 1991 ads and letter column						4.00
348,349,351-359: 348-Avengers x-over. 351-Bagley-a begins. 351,352-Nova of New Warriors app. 353-Darkhawk app.; brief Punisher app. 354-Punisher cameo & Nova, Night Thrasher (New Warriors), Darkhawk & Moon Knight app. 357,358-Punisher, Darkhawk, Moon Knight, Night Thrasher, Nova x-over. 358-3 part gatefold-c; last $1.00-c						4.00
350-($1.50, 52pgs.)-Origin retold; Spidey vs. Dr. Doom; last Erik Larsen-a pin-ups; Uncle Ben app.						5.00

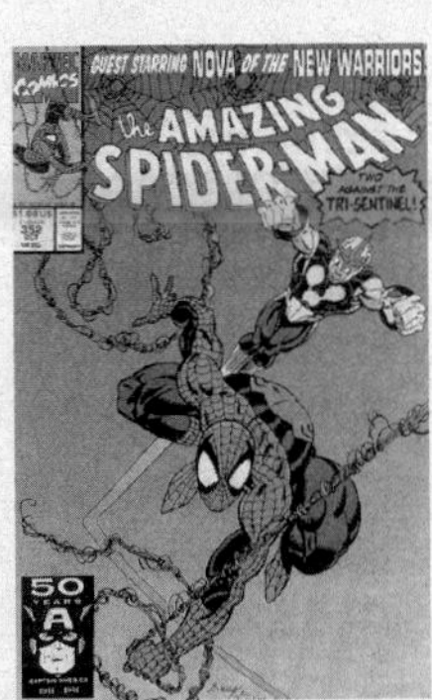

Amazing Spider-Man #352 © MAR

Amazing Spider-Man #400 © MAR

Amazing Spider-Man Special #5 © MAR

	GD 2.0	VG 4.0	FN 6.0	VF 8.0	VF/NM 9.0	NM- 9.2

360-Carnage cameo 3 6 9 14 20 25
361-(4/92) Intro. Carnage (the Spawn of Venom); begin 3 part story; recap of how Spidey's alien costume became Venom 7 14 21 44 82 120
361-($1.25)-2nd printing; silver-c 4 8 12 27 44 60
362,363-Carnage & Venom-c/story 2 4 6 13 18 22
362-2nd printing 2 4 6 9 12 15
364,366-373,376,377,381-387: 364-The Shocker app. (old villain). 366-Peter's parents-c/story; Red Skull, Viper & Taskmaster app. 367-Red Skull, Viper & Taskmaster app. 368-Invasion of the Spider-Slayers Pt.1 (through Pt.6 in #373). 369-Harry Osborn back-up (Gr. Goblin II). Electro app. 370-Black Cat & Scorpion app. 373-Venom back-up. 376,377-Cardiac app. 381,382-Hulk app. 383-The Jury app. 383-385-vs The Jury. 384-Venom/Carnage app. 386-Vulture app. 387-Vulture is de-aged & gets new costume 3.00
365-($3.95, 84 pgs.)-30th anniversary issue w/silver hologram on-c; Spidey/Venom/Carnage pull-out poster; contains 5 pg. preview of Spider-Man 2099 (1st app.); Spidey's origin retold; Lizard app.; reintro Peter's parents in Stan Lee 3 pg. text w/illo (story continues thru #370) 3 6 9 15 22 28
374-Venom-c/story 6.00
375-(3/93, $3.95, 68 pgs.)-Holo-grafx foil-c; vs. Venom; ties into Venom: Lethal Protector #1; intro. Ann Weying; Pat Olliffe-a. 3 6 9 14 19 24
378-380: Parts 3,7 and 11 of Maximum Carnage. 378-Continued from Web of Spider-Man #101; Venom vs Carnage; continues in Spider-Man #35. 379-Continued from Web of Spider-Man #102; Deathlok, Firestar, Black Cat & Morbius app.; continued in Spider-Man #36. 380-Continued from Web of Spider-Man #103; Captain America & Cloak and Dagger app.; continued in Spider-Man #37 5.00
388-($2.25, 68 pgs.)-Newsstand edition; Venom back-up & Cardiac & chance back-up; last David Michelinie-s (6-year run) 4.00
388-($2.95, 68 pgs.)-Collector's edition w/foil-c 5.00
389-1st JM DeMatteis-s; Trading Card insert (3 cards) attached to the staples; harder to find in true high grade due to indents caused by the cards; Green Goblin app. 4.00
390-393,395,396: 390-393-vs. Shriek. 395-Puma app. 396-Daredevil & the Owl app. 3.00
390-($2.95)-Collector's edition polybagged w/16 pg. insert of new animated Spidey TV show plus animation cel 5.00
394-($2.95, 48 pgs.)-Deluxe edition; flip book w/Birth of a Spider-Man Pt. 2; silver foil both-c; Power & Responsibility Pt. 2; Judas Traveller, the Jackal and the Gwen Stacy Clone app. 1st app. Scrier 5.00
394-Newstand edition ($1.50-c) 7.00
397-($2.25)-Flip book w/Ultimate Spider-Man 4.00
398,399: 398-Web of Death Pt.3; continued from Spectacular Spider-Man #220; Doc Octopus & Kaine app.; continued in Spectacular Spider-Man #221. 399-Smoke and Mirrors Pt.2; continued from Web of Spider-Man #122; Jackal, Scarlet Spider, Gwen Stacy Clone app; continued in Spider-Man #56 5.00
400-($2.95)-Death of Aunt May; newsstand edition 3 6 9 18 28 38
400-($3.95)-Death of Aunt May; embossed grey overlay cover 3 6 9 14 19 24
400-Collector's Edition; white embossed-c; (10,000 print run) 5 10 15 30 50 70
401,402,405,406-409: 401-The Mark of Kaine Pt.2; continued from Web of Spider-Man #124; Scarlet Spider app; continues in Spider-Man #58. 402-Judas Traveller & Scrier app. 405-Exiled Pt.2; continued from Web of Spider-Man #128; Scarlet Spider app.; continues in Spider-Man #62. 406-1st full app. of the female Doc Octopus (Carolyn Trainer); continues in Spider-Man #63; Marvel Overpower card insert; harder to find in higher grades due to card indenting; last JM DeMatteis-s. 407-Human Torch, Sandman & Silver Sable app. Tom DeFalco-s (returns to Spider-Man; last-s in 1987). 408-Regular ed; Media Blizzard pt.2; Mysterio app; continued from Sensational Spider-Man #1; continues in Spider-Man #65. 409-The Return of Kaine Pt.3; continued from Spectacular Spider-Man #231; Kaine & Rhino app.; continues in Spider-Man #66 5.00
403-The Trial of Peter Parker Pt. 2; continued from Web of Spider-Man #126; Carnage app; continues in Spider-Man #60. 1 2 3 5 6 8
404-Maximum Clonage Pt.3; continued from Web of Spider-Man #127; Scarlet Spider, Jackal, Scrier & Kaine app; continued in Spider-Man #61 5.00
408-($2.95)-Polybagged version with TV theme song cassette; scarce in high grade due to damage caused by the cassette indenting the actual comic 9 18 27 60 120 180
408-Direct edition (without cassette & out of polybag) 4 8 12 23 37 50
408-Newstand edition; variant cover 5 10 15 31 53 75
410-Web of Carnage Pt.2; continued from Sensational Spider-Man #3; Carnage app; continues in Spider-Man #67 3 6 9 16 23 30
411,412,414,417-419,421-424: 411-Blood Brothers Pt.2; continued from Sensational Spider-Man #4; Gaunt app; continued in Spider-Man #68. 412-Blood Brothers Pt.6; continued from Sensational Spider-Man #5; vs Gaunt. 414-The Rose app. 417-Death of Scrier. 418-Revelations Pt.3; continued from Spectacular Spider-Man #240; Norman Osborn returns; 'death' of Peter and Mary Jane's baby (May Parker); continued in Spider-Man #75. 419-1st minor app. of The Black Tarantula. 422,423-Electro app. 424-Elektra app. 5.00
413-Contains a free packet of Island Twists Kool-Aid and Spider-Man For Kids magazine subscriber card; harder to find in true high grade 7.00
415-Onslaught Impact 2; Green Goblin (Phil Urich) app. vs. Mark IV Sentinels; last Mark Bagley-a (5 year run) 6.00
416-Epilogue to Onslaught; harder to find in high grade due to Marvel Overpower card insert 1 3 4 6 8 10
420-X-Man app. 1 2 3 4 5 7
425-($2.99)-48 pgs., wraparound-c; X-Man app 1 2 3 4 5 7
426,428,429,432,435-437,440: 426-Female Dr. Octopus app. 428-Dr. Octopus app. 429-Absorbing Man app. 432-Spider-Hunt Pt.2; continued from Sensational Spider-Man #25; Black Tarantula & Norman Osborn app. 433-Mr. Hyde app. 435-Identity Crisis; Black Tarantula & Kaine app. 436-Black Tarantula app. 437-Plantman app. 440-Gathering of Five Pt.2; continued from Sensational Spider-Man #32; John Byrne-s; Molten Man & Norman Osborn app; continued in Spider-Man #96 6.00
427-Return of Dr. Octopus; double-gatefold-c. 1 2 3 4 5 7
430-Carnage & Silver Surfer app. 3 6 9 19 30 40
431-Cosmic-Carnage vs Silver Surfer; Galactus cameo 4 8 12 25 40 55
432-Variant yellow-c 'Wanted Dead or Alive' 2 4 6 10 14 18
434-Identity Crisis; Black Tarantula app. 2 4 6 9 12 15
434-Variant 'Amazing Ricochet #1'-c 2 4 6 9 12 15
438-Daredevil app. 7.00
439-Alternate future story; Avengers app; last Tom DeFalco-s 2 4 6 8 10 12
441-The Final Chapter Pt.1; John Byrne-s; Norman Osborn app; last issue (Dec. 1998); story continues in Spider-Man #97 1 3 4 6 8 10
#500-up (See Amazing Spider-Man Vol. 2; series resumed original numbering after Vol. 2 #58)
#(-1) Flashback issue (7/97, $1.95-c) 4.00
Annual 1 (1964, 72 pgs.) Origin Spider-Man; 1st app. Sinister Six (Dr. Octopus, Electro, Kraven the Hunter, Mysterio, Sandman, Vulture) (new 41 pg. story); plus gallery of Spidey foes; early X-Men app. 207 414 621 1708 3854 6000
Annual 2 (1965, 25¢, 72 pgs.) Reprints from #1,2,5 plus new Doctor Strange story 36 72 108 266 596 925
Special 3 (11/66, 25¢, 72 pgs.) New Avengers story & Hulk x-over; Doctor Octopus-r from #11,12; Romita-a 19 38 57 131 291 450
Special 4 (11/67, 25¢, 68 pgs.) Spidey battles Human Torch (new 41 pg. story) 13 26 39 89 195 300
Special 5 (11/68, 25¢, 68 pgs.) New 40 pg. Red Skull story; 1st app. Peter Parker's parents; last annual with new-a 11 22 33 76 163 250
Special 5-2nd printing (1994) 2 4 6 8 10 12
Special 6 (11/69, 25¢, 68 pgs.) Reprints 41 pg. Sinister Six story from annual #1 plus 2 Kirby/Ditko stories (r) 8 16 24 51 96 140
Special 7 (12/70, 25¢, 68 pgs.) All-r(#1,2) new Vulture-c 5 10 15 35 63 90
Special 8 (12/71) All-r 5 10 15 35 63 90
King Size 9 ('73) Reprints Spectacular Spider-Man (mag.) #2; 40 pg. Green Goblin-c/story (re-edited from 58 pgs.) 5 10 15 35 63 90
Annual 10 (1976) Origin Human Fly (vs. Spidey); new-a begins 3 6 9 16 24 32
Annual 11-13 ('77-'79): 12-Spidey vs. Hulk-r/#119,120. 13-New Byrne/Austin-a; Dr. Octopus x-over w/Spectacular S-M Ann. #1 2 4 6 11 16 20
Annual 14 (1980) Miller-c/a(p); Doctor Strange and Doctor Doom app. 3 6 9 14 20 25
Annual 15 (1981) Miller-c/a(p); Punisher and Doctor Octopus app.; 4 bonus pin-ups (Man-Wolf, The Jackal, Punisher and Tarantula) 3 6 9 17 26 35
Annual 16 (1982)-Origin/1st app. new Captain Marvel (female heroine Monica Rambeau) 8 16 24 51 96 140
Annual 17-20: 17 ('83)-Kingpin app. 18 ('84)-Scorpion app.; JJJ weds. 19 ('85). 20 ('86)-Origin Iron Man of 2020 2 4 6 8 10 12
Annual 21 (1987) Special wedding issue; newsstand & direct sale versions exist & are worth same 3 6 9 19 30 40
Annual 22 (1988, $1.75, 68 pgs.) 1st app. Speedball; Evolutionary War x-over; Daredevil app. 2 4 6 13 18 22
Annual 23 (1989, $2.00, 68 pgs.) Atlantis Attacks; origin Spider-Man retold; She-Hulk app.; Byrne-c; Liefeld-a(p), 23 pgs. 1 3 4 5 6 8
Annual 24 (1990, $2.00, 68 pgs.) -Ant-Man app. 5.00
Annual 25 (1991, $2.00, 68 pgs.) 3 pg. origin recap; Iron Man app.; 1st Venom solo story; Ditko-a (6 pgs.) 1 3 4 5 6 8
Annual 26 (1992, $2.25, 68 pgs.) New Warriors-c/story; Venom solo story cont'd in Spectacular Spider-Man Annual #12 2 4 6 8 10 12
Annual 27 ('93, $2.95, 68 pgs.) Bagged w/card; 1st app. Annex 5.00
Annual 28 ('94, $2.95, 68 pgs.) Carnage-c/story 2 4 6 8 10 12
'96 Special-($2.95, 64 pgs.)-"Blast From The Past" 5.00
'97 Special-($2.99)-Wraparound-c,Sundown app. 5.00
... : Carnage (6/93, $6.95)-r/ASM #344,345,359-363 2 4 6 8 10 12
Marvel Graphic Novel - Parallel Lives (3/89, $8.95) 2 4 6 8 10 12

Amazing Spider-Man V2 #5 © MAR

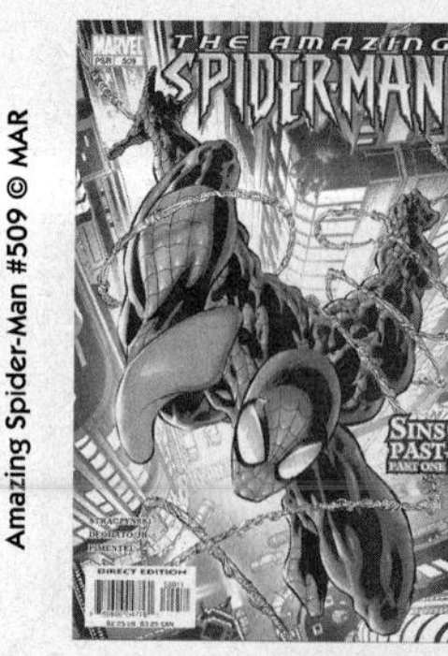

Amazing Spider-Man #509 © MAR

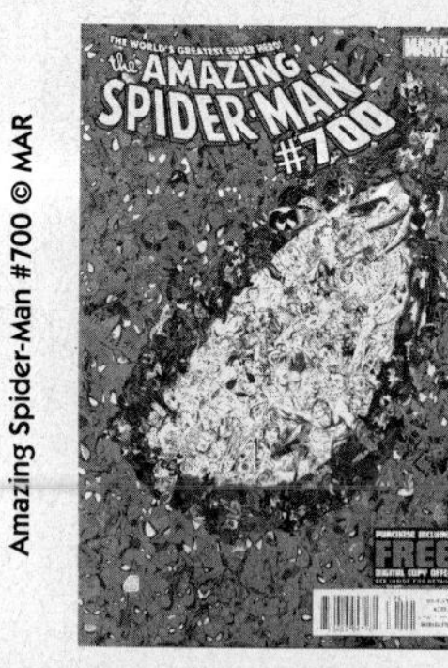

Amazing Spider-Man #700 © MAR

GD VG FN VF VF/NM NM-
2.0 4.0 6.0 8.0 9.0 9.2

...: Parallel Lives 1 (2012, $4.99) r/1989 GN 5.00
Marvel Graphic Novel - Spirits of the Earth (1990, $18.95, HC)
2 4 6 10 15 19
Super Special 1 (4/95, $3.95)-Flip Book 2 4 6 11 16 20
...: Skating on Thin Ice 1(1990, $1.25, Canadian)-McFarlane-c; anti-drug issue; Electro app.
1 2 3 5 7 9
...: Skating on Thin Ice 1 (2/93, $1.50, American) 4.00
...: Double Trouble 2 (1990, $1.25, Canadian) 6.00
...: Double Trouble 2 (2/93, $1.50, American) 3.00
...: Hit and Run 3 (1990, $1.25, Canadian)-Ghost Rider-c/story
1 2 3 5 7 9
...: Hit and Run 3 (2/93. $1.50, American) 3.00
...: Chaos in Calgary 4 (Canadian; part of 5 part series)-Turbine,Night Rider, Frightful app. 2 4 6 8 11 14
...: Chaos in Calgary 4 (2/93, $1.50, American) 3.00
...: Deadball 5 (1993, $1.60, Canadian)-Green Goblin-c/story; features Montreal Expos 2 4 6 10 14 18
Note: Prices listed above are for English Canadian editions. French editions are worth double.
...: Soul of the Hunter nn (8/92, $5.95, 52 pgs.)-Zeck-c/a(p) 6.00
...: Venom 3D No. 1 (10/19, $7.99) Reprints ASM #300 in 3D; bagged with glasses 8.00
Wizard #1 Ace Edition ($13.99) r/#1 w/ new Ramos acetate-c 14.00
Wizard #129 Ace Edition ($13.99) r/#129 w/ new Ramos acetate-c 14.00
NOTE: ***Austin*** *a(i)-248, 335, 337, Annual 13; c(i)-188, 241, 242, 248, 331, 334, 343, Annual 25.* ***J. Buscema*** *a(p)-72, 73, 76-81, 84, 85.* ***Byrne*** *a-189p, 190p, 206p, Annual 3r, 6r, 7r, 13p; c-189p, 268, 296, Annual 12.* ***Ditko*** *a-1-38, Annual 1, Special 3(r), 2, 24(2); c-1i, 2-38, Annual 1.* ***Guice*** *c/a-Annual 18i.* ***Gil Kane*** *a(p)-89-105, 120-124, 150, Annual 10, 12i, 24p; c-90p, 96, 98, 99, 101-105p, 129p, 131p, 132p, 137-140p, 143p, 148p, 149p, 151p, 153p, 160p, 161p, Annual 10p, 24.* ***Kirby*** *a-8.* ***Erik Larsen*** *a-324, 327, 329-350; c-327, 329-350, 354i, Annual 25.* ***McFarlane*** *a-298p, 299p, 300-303, 304-323p, 325p, 328; c-298-325, 328.* ***Miller*** *c-218, 219.* ***Mooney*** *a-65i, 67-82i, 84-88i, 173i, 178i, 189i, 190i, 192i, 193i, 196-202i, 207i, 211-219i, 221i, 222i, 226i, 227i, 229-233i, Annual 11i, 17i.* ***Nasser*** *c-228p.* ***Nebres*** *a-Annual 24i.* ***Russell*** *c-357i.* ***Simonson*** *c-222, 337i.* ***Starlin*** *a-113i, 114i, 187p.* ***Williamson*** *a-365i.*

AMAZING SPIDER-MAN (Volume 2) (Some issues reprinted in "Spider-Man, Best Of" hardcovers)
Marvel Comics: Jan, 1999 - No. 700, Feb, 2013 ($2.99/$1.99/$2.25)

1-($2.99)-Byrne-a; Avengers, Fantastic Four & Green Goblin app.
1 3 4 6 8 10
1-Sunburst variant-c 2 4 6 9 12 15
1-($6.95) Dynamic Forces variant-c by the Romitas 2 4 6 10 14 18
1-Marvel Matrix sketch variant-c 1 3 4 6 8 10
2-($1.99) Two covers -by John Byrne and Andy Kubert 5.00
3-11: 4-Fantastic Four app. 5-Spider-Woman-c 3.00
12-($2.99) Sinister Six return (cont. in Peter Parker #12) 4.00
13-17: 13-Mary Jane's plane explodes 3.00
18,19,21-24,26-28: 18-Begin $2.25-c. 19-Venom-c. 24-Maximum Security 3.00
20-($2.99, 100 pgs.) Spider-Slayer issue; new story and reprints 4.00
25-($2.99) Regular cover; Peter Parker becomes the Green Goblin 4.00
25-($3.99) Holo-foil enhanced cover 5.00
29-Peter is reunited with Mary Jane 4.00
30-Straczynski-s/Campbell-c begin; intro. Ezekiel 6.00
31-35: Battles Morlun 4.00
36-Black cover; aftermath of the Sept. 11 tragedy in New York
4 8 12 23 37 50
37-49: 39-'Nuff Said issue 42-Dr. Strange app. 43-45-Doctor Octopus app. 46-48-Cho-c 3.00
50-Peter and MJ reunite; Captain America & Dr. Doom app.; Campbell-c 4.00
51-58: 51,52-Campbell-c. 55,56-Avery scripts. 57,58-Avengers, FF, Cyclops app. 3.00
(After #58 [Nov, 2003] numbering reverts back to original Vol. 1 with #500, Dec, 2003)
500-($3.50) J. Scott Campbell-c; Romita Jr. & Sr.-a; Uncle Ben app.
2 4 6 9 12 15
501-524: 501-Harris-c. 503-504-Loki app. 506-508-Ezekiel app. 509-514-Sins Past; intro. Gabriel and Sarah Osborn; Deodato-a. 519-Moves into Avengers HQ. 521-Begin $2.50-c 524-Harris-c 3.00
525,526-Evolve or Die x-over. 525-David-s. 526-Hudlin-s; Spider-Man loses eye 4.00
525-528-2nd printings with variant-c. 525-Ben Reilly costume. 526-Six-Armed Spidey. 527-Spider-Man 2099. 528-Spider-Ham 5.00
527,528: Evolve or Die pt. 9,12 3.00
529-Debut of red and gold costume (Iron Spider); Garney-a 24.00
529-2nd printing 5.00
529-3rd printing with Wieringo-c 3.00
530,531-Titanium Man app.; Kirkham-a. 531-Begin $2.99-c 8.00
532-538-Civil War tie-in. 538-Aunt May shot 5.00
539-543-Back in Black. 539-Peter wears the black costume 3.00
544-($3.99) "One More Day" pt. 1; Quesada-a/Straczynski-s 4.00
545-(12/08, $3.99) "One More Day" pt. 4; Quesada-a/Straczynski-s, Peter & MJ's marriage un-done; r/wedding from ASM Annual #21; 2 covers by Quesada and Djurdjevic 4.00
546-($3.99) Brand New Day begins; McNiven-a; Deodato, Winslade, Land, Romita Jr.-a; 1st app. Mr. Negative 6.00
546-Variant-c by Bryan Hitch 12.00
546-Second printing with new McNiven-c of Peter Parker 4.00
546-MGC (7/10, $1.00) r/#546 with "Marvel's Greatest Comics" logo on cover 3.00
547-567: 547,548-McNiven-a. 549-551-Larroca-a. 550-Intro. Menace. 555-557-Bachalo-a. 559-Intro. Screwball. 560,561-MJ app. 565-New Kraven intro. 566,567-Spidey in Daredevil costume 3.00
568-($3.99) Romita Jr.-a begins; two covers by Romita Jr. and Alex Ross 10.00
568-Variant-c by John Romita Sr. 25.00
568-2nd printing with Romita Jr. Anti-Venom costume cover 4.00
569-Debut of Anti-Venom; Norman Osborn and Thunderbolts app.; Romita Jr.-c 45.00
569-Variant Venom-c by Granov 50.00
569-2nd printing with Romita Jr.-c 100.00
570-572-Two covers on each 8.00
573-($3.99) New Ways to Die conclusion; Spidey meets Stephen Colbert back-up; Ollife-a; two covers by Romita Jr. and Maguire 6.00
573-Variant cover with Stephen Colbert; cover swipe of AF #15 by Quesada 25.00
574-582: 577-Punisher app. 3.00
583-($3.99) Spidey meets Obama back-up story; regular Romita Sr. "Cougars" cover 10.00
583-($3.99) Obama variant-c with Spidey on left; Spidey meets Obama back-up story 60.00
583-($3.99) Second printing Obama variant-c with Spidey on right and yellow bkgrd 8.00
583-($3.99) 3rd-5th printings Obama variant-c: 3rd-Blue bkgrd w/flag. 4th-White bkgrd w/flag. 5th-Lincoln Memorial bkgrd 5.00
584-587, 589-599: 585-Menace ID revealed. 590,591-Fantastic Four app. 594-Aunt May engaged. 595-599-American Son; Osborn Avengers app. app. 3.00
588-($3.99) Conclusion to "Character Assassination"; Romita Jr.-a 4.00
600-(9/09, $4.99) Aunt May's wedding; Romita Jr.-a; Doc Octopus, FF app.; Mary Jane cameo; back-up story by Stan Lee; back-up with Doran-a; 2 covers by Romita Jr. & Ross 12.00
600-Variant covers by Romita Sr. and Quesada 18.00
601-Mary Jane cover by Campbell; back-up w/Quesada-a 50.00
602-1st new Slyde 10.00
603,604,608-610,613-616,618-621,623-627: 612-The Gauntlet begins; Waid-s. 615,616-Sandman app. 621-Black Cat app. 624-Peter Parker fired. 626-Gaydos-a 3.00
605,612,617,622,628-($3.99): 605-Mayhew-c. 613-Rhino back-up story. 617-New Rhino. 622-Bianchi-c; Morbius app. 628-Captain Universe app. 4.00
606,607-Black Cat app.; Campbell-c 50.00
611-Deadpool-c/app. 20.00
629-633-($2.99)-Bachalo-a; Lizard app. 3.00
634-636,638-641-($3.99) 634-637-Grim Hunt; Kaine app. 635-Kraven returns. 638-641-"One Moment in Time" wedding flashback/retcon; Quesada-s 4.00
637-1st Araña(Anya Corazon) as Spider-Girl 30.00
638-641-Variant covers by Quesada 15.00
642-646-($2.99) Waid-s/Azaceta-a; interlocking covers by Djurdjevic 3.00
647-($4.99) Short stories by various; Djurdjevic-c; cover gallery of Brand New Day issues 5.00
648-691-($3.99) 648-Big Time begins; Ramos-a; Hobgoblin app. 654-Flash Thompson becomes Venom; Marla Jameson killed. 655-Martin-a. 657-660-Fantastic Four app. 666-673-Spider Island. 667-672-Ramos-a; Avengers app. 677-X-over w/Daredevil #8. 682-687-Avengers app. 4.00
654.1-(4/11, $2.99) Flash Thompson as Venom; Ramos-a 3.00
679.1-(4/12, $2.99) Morbius the Living Vampire app. 3.00
692-($5.99) Debut of Alpha; Ramos-a; back-up short stories 6.00
693-697: 694-Cover swipe of Superman vs. Spider-Man 4.00
698, 699, 699.1: 698-Doctor Octopus brain switch revealed. 699.1-Morbius origin 4.00
700-($7.99) Collage cover; Leads into Superior Spider-Man #1; back-up short stories 28.00
700-Variant skyline-c by Marcos 45.00
700-Second printing cover with Doctor Octopus on an ASM #300 swipe 8.00
700.1 - 700.5 (2/14, weekly limited series, $3.99) 700.1-Janson-a/Ferry-c 4.00
1999, 2000 Annual (6/99, '00, $3.50) 1999-Buscema-a 4.00
2001 Annual ($2.99) Follows Peter Parker: S-M #29; last Mackie-s 4.00
Annual 1 (2008, $3.99) McKone-a; secret of Jackpot revealed; death of Jackpot 4.00
Annual 36 (9/09, $3.99) Debut of Raptor; Olliffe-a 4.00
Annual 37 (7/10, $3.99) Untold 1st meeting with Captain America; back-up w/Olliffe-a 4.00
Annual 38 (6/11, $3.99) Deadpool & Hulk app.; Garbett-a/McNiven-c 4.00
Annual 39 (7/12, $3.99) Avengers app.; Garbett-a/c 4.00
...: Big Time 1 (8/11, $5.99) r/#648-650 6.00
Collected Edition #30-32 ($3.95) reprints #30-32 w/cover #30 4.00
... 500 Covers HC (2004, $49.99) reprints covers for #1-500 & Annuals; yearly re-caps 50.00
...: Ends of the Earth (7/12, $3.99) Silas-a/Fiumara-c; Big Hero Six app. 4.00
...: Family Business HC (2014, $24.99) Kingpin app.; Waid & Robinson-s/Dell'Otto-a 25.00
Free Comic Book Day 2011 (Spider-Man) 1-Ramos-c/a; Spider-Woman & Shang-Chi app. 3.00
.../Ghost Rider: Motorstorm 1 ('11, $2.99) r/#558-560 3.00
...: Hooky 1 (2012, $4.99) r/Marvel Graphic Novel #22 (1986) with Wrightson-a 5.00
...: Infested 1 (11/11, $3.99) Spider Island tie-in; short stories by various; Ramos-c 4.00
... Omnibus HC (2007, $99.99, dustjacket) r/Amazing Fantasy #15, Amazing Spider-Man #1-38, Annual #1,2, Strange Tales Annual #2 & Fantastic Four Annual #1; letter pages, bonus art, intro. by Stan Lee; bios, essays, Marvel Tales cover gallery 100.00
Spider-Man: Brand New Day - Extra!! #1 (9/08, $3.99) short stories; Bachalo,Olliffe-a 4.00
Spider-Man: Brand New Day Yearbook #1 (2008, $4.99) plot synopses; profile pages 5.00

Amazing Spider-Man (2014 series) #4 © MAR

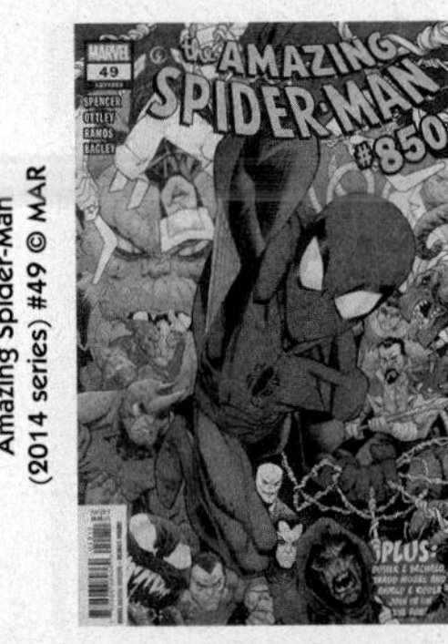

Amazing Spider-Man (2014 series) #49 © MAR

Amazing World of DC Comics #9 © DC

	GD	VG	FN	VF	VF/NM	NM-
	2.0	4.0	6.0	8.0	9.0	9.2

... Spidey Sunday Spectacuar (7/11, $3.99) collects back-ups from ASM #634-645 4.00
...: Swing Shift (2007 FCBD Edition) Jimenez-c/a; Slott-s 4.00
...: Swing Shift Director's Cut (2008, $3.99) story from 2007 FCBD; Brand New Day info 4.00
The Many Loves of the Amazing Spider-Man (7/10, $3.99) short stories of Black Cat, Gwen & Carlie, and Mary Jane; s/a by various 4.00
...: The Short Halloween (7/09, $3.99) Bill Hader & Seth Meyers-s/Maguire-a 4.00
...: You're Hired 1 (5/11, $3.99) r/story from New York Daily News insert 4.00
...Vol. 1: Coming Home (2001, $15.95) r/#30-35; J. Scott Campbell-c 16.00
...Vol. 2: Revelations (2002, $8.99) r/#36-39; Kaare Andrews-c 9.00
...Vol. 3: Until the Stars Turn Cold (2002, $12.99) r/#40-45; Romita Jr.-c 13.00
...Vol. 4: The Life and Death of Spiders (2003, $11.99) r/#46-50; Campbell-c 12.00
...Vol. 5: Unintended Consequences (2003, $12.99) r/#51-56; Dodson-c 13.00
...Vol. 6: Happy Birthday (2003, $12.99) r/#57,58,500-502 13.00
...Vol. 7: The Book of Ezekiel (2004, $12.99) r/#503-508; Romita Jr.-c 13.00
...Vol. 8: Sins Past (2005, $12.99) r/#509-514; cover sketch gallery 13.00
...Vol. 9: Skin Deep (2005, $9.99) r/#515-518 10.00
...Vol. 10: New Avengers (2005, $14.99) r/#519-524 15.00
Brand New Day #1-3 (11/08-1/09, $3.99) reprints #546-551 4.00
Civil War: Amazing Spider-Man TPB (2007, $17.99) r/#532-538; variant covers 18.00

AMAZING SPIDER-MAN (Follows Superior Spider-Man)(Also see Spider-Verse Team-Up)
Marvel Comics: Jun, 2014 - No. 20.1 , Oct, 2015 ($3.99)(there was no #19 or 20)

1-($5.99) 1st app. Cindy Moon (cameo, becomes Silk in #3); Slott-s/Ramos-a; bonus shorts with Electro, Black Cat, Spider-Man 2099, Kaine; bonus r/Inhuman #1; Ramos-c 6.00
1-Variant-c by J. Scott Campbell 8.00
2,3-Cindy Moon app.; Electro app. 2-Avengers app. 3-Black Cat app. 4.00
4-1st app. Silk (Cindy Moon); Original Sin tie-in 75.00
5-8: 5,6-Silk, Black Cat app. 7,8-Ms. Marvel app.; back-up Spider-Verse; Morlun app. 4.00
9-($4.99) Spider-Verse part 1; Variant Spider-Men & Spider-Gwen app.; Coipel-a 6.00
10-15-Spider-Verse; Superior Spider-Man returns. 13,14-Uncle Ben app.; Camuncoli-a 4.00
16-18-Ghost app.; Ramos-a; back-up with Black Cat 4.00
16.1, 17.1, 18.1, 19.1, 20.1-($3.99) Spiral parts 1-5; Conway-s/Barberi-a 4.00
Annual 1 (2/15, $4.99) Sean Ryan-s/Peterson-a/c; Nitz-s/Salas-a 5.00
Special 1(5/15, $4.99) Crossover with Inhumans and All-New Captain America specials 5.00
#1.1-1.5 (Learning to Crawl) (7/14-11/14, $3.99) Re-tells early career; Alex Ross-c 4.00

AMAZING SPIDER-MAN (Follows Secret Wars)
Marvel Comics: Dec, 2015 - No. 32, Nov, 2017; No. 789, Dec, 2017 - No. 801, Aug, 2018 ($5.99/$3.99)

1-($5.99) Slott-s/Camuncoli-a; main-c by Alex Ross; back-up previews of Spider-titles 6.00
2-18-($3.99) 3,5-Human Torch app. 6-8-Cloak & Dagger app. 13-15-Iron Man app. 15-Mary Jane in the Iron Spider suit. 17-New female Electro 4.00
19-($4.99) Clone Conspiracy tie-in; Kingpin & Rhino app. 5.00
20-24: Clone Conspiracy tie-ins. 20-Doctor Octopus gets his body back. 21-Kaine returns 4.00
25-($9.99) Osborn Identity begins; Silver Sable returns; debut of The Superior Octopus 10.00
26-32: 26-28,32-Norman Osborn app.; Immonen-a. 29-31-Secret Empire tie-ins 4.00

[Title switches to legacy numbering after #32 (11/17)]

789-799,801: 789-791-"Fall of Parker"; Immonen-a. 792,793-Venom Inc. x-over. 795-Osborn merges with Carnage; Loki app. 4.00
800-(7/18, $9.99, 80 pages) Spider-Man vs. Red Goblin; death of Flash Thompson; art by Immonen, Ramos, Bradshaw, Camuncoli, Martin 10.00
#1.1-1.6 (Amazing Grace) (2/16-9/16, $3.99) The Santerians app.; Bianchi-a 4.00
Annual 1 (1/17, $4.99) Short stories by various incl. Wayne Brady, Ramos, Gage, Asmus 5.00
Annual 42 (4/18, $4.99) Dan Slott-s/Cory Smith-a 5.00

AMAZING SPIDER-MAN
Marvel Comics: Sept, 2018 - Present ($5.99/$3.99)

1-($5.99) Spencer-s/Ottley-a; Mysterio app. 6.00
2-15-($3.99) 2-Taskmaster app. 6-10-Ramos-a. 8-10-Black Cat app. 14,15-Bachalo-a 4.00
16,17-($4.99) Kraven & Arcade app. 5.00
18-24: 18-23-Hunted. 18,20,22-Ramos-a. 22-Kraven dies. 23-Ottley-a. 24-Mysterio app. 4.00
16HU-($3.99) Hunted story arc; Coello-a; Black Cat, Taskmaster, Black Ant app. 4.00
18HU,19HU,20HU-($3.99) Hunted; 18-The Gibbon. 19-The Lizard; Bachalo-a. 20-Vulture 4.00
25-($7.99) Mysterio and Electro app.; art by Ottley, Ramos, Gleason, Walker 8.00
26-44,46-48: 30,31-Absolute Carnage tie-ins. 32-36-Spider-Man 2099. 41-Lethal Legion returns. 46-48-Sins Rising. 47,48-Norman Osborn app. 4.00
45-($4.99) Sins Rising begins; Spencer-s/Bagley-a; The Sin-Eater app. 5.00
49-($9.99) 850th issue celebration; Spidey vs. Green Goblin; back-up stories by various 10.00
50-($5.99) Last Remains; Dr. Strange app.; Kindred revealed as Harry Osborn 6.00
51-54,57-59: 51-54-Last Remains. 58,59-Mr. Negative app. 4.00
53.LR,54.LR-($3.99) Last Remains; Order of the Web vs. Kindred 4.00
55-Last Remains ends 20.00
56-($4.99) Last Remains Post Mortem; Norman Osborn, Kingpin app.; Bagley-a 5.00
Annual 1 (11/18, $4.99) Flashback to early days with the black costume (Venom) 5.00
...: Full Circle 1 (12/19, $9.99) Seven creative teams with successive chapters of 1 story; Hickman, Duggan, Zdarsky & others-s/Bachalo, Allred, Bagley & others-a 10.00
...: Going Big 1 (11/19, $4.99) Conway-s/Bagley-a; Macchio-s/Nauck-a; Larsen-s/a 5.00
...: Sins Rising Prelude 1 (9/20, $4.99) Spencer-s/Sanna-a; story of the Sin-Eater 5.00
...: The Sins of Norman Osborn 1 (11/20, $4.99) Spencer-s/Vicentini-a; leads into #49 5.00

AMAZING SPIDER-MAN & SILK: THE SPIDER(FLY) EFFECT
Marvel Comics: May, 2016 - No. 4, Aug, 2016 ($4.99, limited series)

1-4: 1-Robbie Thompson-s/Todd Nauck-a; time-travelling Peter & Silk meet Ben Parker 5.00

AMAZING SPIDER-MAN EXTRA! (Continued from Spider-Man: Brand New Day - Extra!! #1)
Marvel Comics: No. 2, Mar, 2009 - No. 3, May, 2009 ($3.99)

2,3: 2-Anti-Venom app.; Bachalo-a. 3-Ana Kraven app.; Jimenez-a 4.00

AMAZING SPIDER-MAN FAMILY (Also see Spider-Man Family)
Marvel Comics: Oct, 2008 - No. 8, Sept, 2009 ($4.99, anthology)

1-8-New tales and reprints. 1-Includes r/ASM #300; Granov-c. 2-Deodato-c. 5-Spider-Girl new story. 6-Origin of Jackpot 5.00

AMAZING SPIDER-MAN PRESENTS: AMERICAN SON
Marvel Comics: Jul, 2010 - No. 4, Oct, 2010 ($3.99, limited series)

1-4-Reed-s/Briones-a/Djurdjevic-c; Gabriel Stacy app. 4.00

AMAZING SPIDER-MAN PRESENTS: ANTI-VENOM - NEW WAYS TO LIVE
Marvel Comics: Nov, 2009 - No. 3, Feb, 2010 ($3.99, limited series)

1-3-Wells-s/Siqueira-a; Punisher app. 4.00

AMAZING SPIDER-MAN PRESENTS: JACKPOT
Marvel Comics: Mar, 2010 - No. 3, Jun, 2010 ($3.99, limited series)

1-3-Guggenheim-s/Melo-a; Boomerang and White Rabbit app. 4.00

AMAZING SPIDER-MAN: RENEW YOUR VOWS (Secret Wars tie-in)
Marvel Comics: Aug, 2015 - No. 5, Nov, 2015 ($3.99, limited series)

1-5-Adam Kubert-a; wife Mary Jane and daughter Annie app. 1-Venom app. 4.00

AMAZING SPIDER-MAN: RENEW YOUR VOWS (Series) (Leads into Spider-Girls #1)
Marvel Comics: Jan, 2017 - No. 23, Nov, 2018 ($4.99/$3.99)

1-($4.99) Conway-s/Stegman-a; Mole Man app.; back-up Holden-s/a; Leth-s/Sauvage-a 5.00
2-23-($3.99) 6,7-X-Men & Magneto app. 8,9-Venom app. 13-Jumps to 8 years later 4.00

AMAZING SPIDER-MAN: THE DAILY BUGLE
Marvel Comics: Mar, 2020 - No. 5 ($3.99, limited series)

1,2-Mat Johnson-s/Mack Chater-a 4.00

AMAZING SPIDER-MAN: THE MOVIE
Marvel Comics: Aug, 2012 - No. 2, Aug, 2012 ($3.99, limited series)

1,2-Partial adaptation of the 2012 movie; Neil Edwards-a; photo covers 4.00

AMAZING SPIDER-MAN: THE MOVIE ADAPTATION
Marvel Comics: Mar, 2014 - No. 2, Apr, 2014 ($2.99, limited series)

1,2-Adaptation of the 2012 movie; Wellington Alves-a; photo covers 3.00

AMAZING SPIDER-MAN: VENOM INC. (Crossover with ASM #792,793 & Venom #159,160)
Marvel Comics: 2018 ($4.99, bookends of crossover series)

... Alpha 1 (2/18, $4.99) Part 1 of x-over; Stegman-a; Eddie Brock & Anti-Venom app. 5.00
... Omega 1 (3/18, $4.99) Concluding Part 6 of x-over; Stegman-a 5.00

AMAZING SPIDER-MAN: WAKANDA FOREVER (Crossover with Wakanda Forever title)
Marvel Comics: Aug, 2018 ($4.99, one-shot)

1-Spider-Man teams with Dora Milaje; Nnedi Okorafor-s/Rafael Albuquerque-a 5.00

AMAZING WILLIE MAYS, THE
Famous Funnies Publ.: No date (Sept, 1954)

	GD	VG	FN	VF	VF/NM	NM-
nn	87	174	261	553	952	1350

AMAZING WORLD OF DC COMICS
DC Comics: Jul, 1974 - No. 17, 1978 ($1.50, B&W, mail-order DC Pro-zine)

	GD	VG	FN	VF	VF/NM	NM-
1-Kubert interview; unpublished Kirby-a; Infantino-c	6	12	18	42	79	115
2-4: 3-Julie Schwartz profile. 4-Batman; Robinson-c	5	10	15	31	53	75
5-Sheldon Mayer	4	8	12	28	47	65
6,8,13: 6-Joe Orlando; EC-r; Wrightson pin-up. 8-Infantino; Batman-r from Pop Tart giveaway. 13-Humor; Aragonés-c; Wood/Ditko-a; photos from serials of Superman, Batman, Captain Marvel	4	8	12	22	35	48
7,10-12: 7-Superman; r/1955 Pep comic giveaway. 10-Behind the scenes at DC; Showcase article. 11-Super-Villains; unpubl. Secret Society of S.V. story. 12-Legion; Grell-c/interview;	4	8	12	23	37	50
9-Legion of Super-Heroes; lengthy bios and history; Cockrum-c	6	12	18	42	79	115
14-Justice League	4	8	12	25	40	55
15-Wonder Woman; Nasser-c	5	10	15	30	50	70
16-Golden Age heroes	4	8	12	28	47	65
17-Shazam; G.A., '70s, TV and Fawcett heroes	4	8	12	25	40	55

Amazing X-Men (2014 series) #1 © MAR

Ame-Comi Girls #1 © DC

American Carnage #4 © Hill & Fernandez

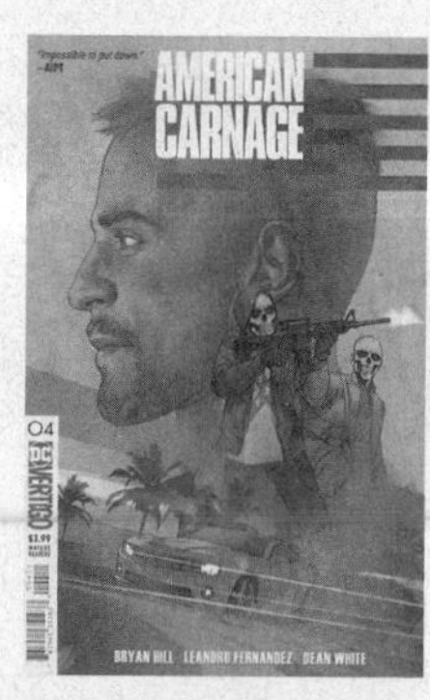

	GD 2.0	VG 4.0	FN 6.0	VF 8.0	VF/NM 9.0	NM- 9.2

Special 1 (Digest size) 3 6 9 20 31 42

AMAZING WORLD OF GUMBALL, THE (Based on the Cartoon Network series)
Boom Entertainment (kaBOOM!): Jun, 2014 - No. 8, Mar, 2015 ($3.99)

1-8-Multiple covers on each 4.00
... 2015 Grab Bag Special (9/15, $4.99) Short stories and pin-ups by various; 3 covers 5.00
... 2015 Special (1/15, $4.99) Short stories by various; 3 covers 5.00
... 2016 Grab Bag Special (8/16, $4.99) Short stories and pin-ups by various 5.00
... 2017 Grab Bag Special (8/17, $7.99) Short stories and pin-ups by various 8.00
... 2018 Grab Bag Special (8/18, $7.99) Short stories by various; Aguirre-c 8.00
... Spring Break Smash 1 (2/19, $7.99) Short stories by various 8.00

AMAZING WORLD OF SUPERMAN (See Superman)

AMAZING X-MEN
Marvel Comics: Mar, 1995 - No. 4, July, 1995 ($1.95, limited series)

1-Age of Apocalypse; Andy Kubert-c/a 5.00
2-4 3.00

AMAZING X-MEN
Marvel Comics: Jan, 2014 - No. 19, Jun, 2015 ($3.99)

1-19: 1-Nightcrawler returns; Aaron-s/McGuinness-a; wraparound-c. 7-Firestar, Iceman and Spider-Man app. 8-12-World War Wendigo. 19-Colossus vs. The Juggernaut 4.00
Annual 1 (8/14, $4.99) Larroca-a/c; back-up w/Juan Doe-a 5.00

AMAZON
Comico: Mar, 1989 - No. 3, May, 1989 ($1.95, limited series)

1-3: Ecological theme; Steven Seagle-s/Tim Sale-a 5.00
1-3-(Dark Horse, 3/09 - No. 3, 5/09, $3.50) recolored reprint with creator interviews 3.50

AMAZON (Also see Marvel Versus DC #3 & DC Versus Marvel #4)
DC Comics (Amalgam): Apr, 1996 ($1.95, one-shot)

1-John Byrne-c/a/scripts 6.00

AMAZON ATTACK 3-D
The 3-D Zone: Sept, 1990 ($3.95, 28 pgs.)

1-Chaykin-a 6.00

AMAZONS ATTACK (See Wonder Woman #8 - 2006 series)
DC Comics: Jun, 2007 - No. 6, Late Oct, 2007 ($2.99, limited series)

1-6-Queen Hippolyta and Amazons attacks Wash., DC; Pfeifer-s/Woods-a 3.00

AMAZON WOMAN (1st Series)
FantaCo: Summer, 1994 - No. 2, Fall, 1994 ($2.95, B&W, limited series, mature)

1,2: Tom Simonton-c/a/scripts 3 6 9 14 19 24

AMAZON WOMAN (2nd Series)
FantaCo: Feb, 1996 - No. 4, May, 1996 ($2.95, B&W, limited series, mature)

1-4: Tom Simonton-a/scripts 2 4 6 11 16 20
...: Invaders of Terror ('96, $5.95) Simonton-a/s 1 3 4 6 8 10

AMBER BLAKE
IDW Publishing: Feb, 2019 - No. 4, May, 2019 ($3.99, oversized 8-3/8" x 11", limited series)

1-4:-Jade Lagardére-s/Butch Guice-a; 2 covers on each 3.00

AMBUSH BUG (Also see Son of...)
DC Comics: June, 1985 - No. 4, Sept, 1985 (75¢, limited series)

1-4: Giffen-c/a in all 4.00
Nothing Special 1 (9/92, $2.50, 68 pg.)-Giffen-c/a 4.00
Stocking Stuffer (2/86, $1.25)-Giffen-c/a 4.00

AMBUSH BUG: YEAR NONE
DC Comics: Sept, 2008 - No. 5, Jan, 2009; No. 7, Dec, 2009 ($2.99, limited series, no #6)

1-5,7-Giffen-s/a; Jonni DC app. 4-Conner-c. 7-Baltazar & Franco-a; Giffen-a 3.00

AME-COMI GIRLS (Based on the Anime-styled statue series)
DC Comics: Dec, 2012 - No. 5, Apr, 2013 ($3.99, printed version of digital-first series)

1-5: 1-Wonder Woman; Conner-c/a. 2-Batgirl. 3-Duela Dent; Naifeh-a 4.00

AME-COMI GIRLS (Based on the Anime-styled statue series)
DC Comics: May, 2013 - No. 8, Dec, 2013 ($3.99)

1-8: 1-Palmiotti & Gray-s/Francisco-a; story continues from earlier series 4.00

AMERICA (From Young Avengers and The Ultimates)
Marvel Comics: May, 2017 - No. 12, Apr, 2018 ($3.99)

1-12: 1-Gabby Rivera-s/Joe Quinones-a; Captain Marvel & Spectrum app. 2-Moon Girl app. 3-Storm & the X-Men app. 4.00

AMERICA AT WAR - THE BEST OF DC WAR COMICS (See Fireside Book Series)

AMERICA IN ACTION
Dell (Imp. Publ. Co.)/ Mayflower House Publ.: 1942; Winter, 1945 (36 pgs.)

	GD 2.0	VG 4.0	FN 6.0	VF 8.0	VF/NM 9.0	NM- 9.2

1942-Dell-(68 pgs.) 20 40 60 114 182 250
1-(1945)-Has 3 adaptations from American history; Kiefer, Schrotter & Webb-a 15 30 45 83 124 165

AMERICAN, THE
Dark Horse Comics: July, 1987 - No. 8, 1989 ($1.50/$1.75, B&W)

1-8: ($1.50) 3.00
Collection ($5.95, B&W)-Reprints 6.00
Special 1 (1990, $2.25, B&W) 3.00

AMERICAN AIR FORCES, THE (See A-1 Comics)
William H. Wise(Flying Cadet Publ. Co./Hasan(No.1)/Life's Romances/ Magazine Ent. No. 5 on): Sept-Oct, 1944-No. 4, 1945; No. 5, 1951-No. 12, 1954

1-Article by Zack Mosley, creator of Smilin' Jack; German war-c 50 100 150 315 533 750
2-Classic-Japan war-c 116 232 348 742 1271 1800
3,4-Japan war-c 20 40 60 118 192 265
NOTE: *All part comic, part magazine. Art by* **Whitney, Chas. Quinlan, H. C. Kiefer,** *and* **Tony Dipreta.**
5(A-1 45)(Formerly Jet Powers), 6(A-1 54), 7(A-1 58), 8(A-1 65), 9(A-1 67), 10(A-1 74), 11(A-1 79), 12(A-1 91) 10 20 30 56 76 95
NOTE: ***Powell** c/a-5-12.*

AMERICAN CARNAGE
DC Comics (Vertigo): Jan, 2019 - No. 9, Sept, 2019 ($3.99)

1-9: 1-Bryan Hill-s/Leandro Fernandez-a 4.00

AMERICAN CENTURY
DC Comics (Vertigo): May, 2001 - No. 27, Oct, 2003 ($2.50/$2.75)

1-Chaykin-s/painted-c; Tischman-s; Laming-a 4.00
2-27: 5-New story arc begins. 10-16,22-27-Orbik-c. 17-21-Silke-c. 18-$2.75-c begins 3.00
Hollywood Babylon (2002, $12.95, TPB) r/#5-9; w/sketch-to-art pages 13.00
Scars & Stripes (2001, $8.95, TPB) r/#1-4; Tischman intro. 9.00

AMERICAN DREAM (From the M2 Avengers)
Marvel Comics: Jul, 2008 - No. 5, Sept, 2008 ($2.99, limited series)

1-5-DeFalco-s/Nauck-a 3.00

AMERICAN FLAGG! (See First Comics Graphic Novel 3,9,12,21 & Howard Chaykin's..)
First Comics: Oct, 1983 - No. 50, Mar, 1988

1,21-27: 1-Chaykin-c/a begins. 21-27-Alan Moore scripts 4.00
2-20,28-49: 31-Origin Bob Violence 3.00
50-Last issue 4.00
Special 1 (11/86)-Introduces Chaykin's Time2 4.00
...: Hard Times TPB (6/85, $11.95) r/#1-7; intro. by Michael Moorcock; bonus materials 12.00
...: Definitive Collection Volume 1 HC (2008, $49.99) r/#1-14 and material from the...: Hard Times TPB; intro by Michael Chabon; afterword by Jim Lee 50.00

AMERICAN FREAK: A TALE OF THE UN-MEN
DC Comics (Vertigo): Feb, 1994 - No. 5, Jun, 1994 ($1.95, mini-series, mature)

1-5 3.00

AMERICAN GODS (Based on the Neil Gaiman novel)
Dark Horse Comics: Mar, 2017 - No. 9, Nov, 2017 ($3.99)

1-9: 1-Gaiman & Russell-s/Scott Hampton-a. 3-Simonson-a (4 pgs). 4-Doran-a (9 pgs.) 4.00

AMERICAN GODS: MY AINSEL (Based on the Neil Gaiman novel)
Dark Horse Comics: Mar, 2018 - No. 9, Dec, 2018 ($3.99)

1-9: 1-Gaiman & Russell-s/Scott Hampton-a. 5-Buckingham-a 4.00

AMERICAN GODS: THE MOMENT OF THE STORM (Based on the Neil Gaiman novel)
Dark Horse Comics: Apr, 2019 - No. 9, Jan, 2020 ($3.99)

1-9-Gaiman & Russell-s/Scott Hampton-a 4.00

AMERICAN GRAPHICS
Henry Stewart: No. 1, 1954; No. 2, 1957 (25¢)

1-The Maid of the Mist, The Last of the Eries (Indian Legends of Niagara) (sold at Niagara Falls) 14 28 42 82 121 160
2-Victory at Niagara & Laura Secord (Heroine of the War of 1812) 9 18 27 47 61 75

AMERICAN INDIAN, THE (See Picture Progress)

AMERICAN JESUS: THE NEW MESSIAH (Also see Chosen)
Image Comics: Dec, 2019 - No. 3, Feb, 2020 ($3.99, limited series)

1-3-Mark Millar-s/Peter Gross-a 4.00

AMERICAN LIBRARY
David McKay Publ.: 1943 - No. 6, 1944 (15¢, 68 pgs., B&W, text & pictures)

nn (#1)-Thirty Seconds Over Tokyo (movie) 48 96 144 302 514 725
nn (#2)-Guadalcanal Diary; painted-c (only 10¢) 36 72 108 211 343 475

American Ronin #1 © AWA Inc.

American Vampire #30 © Snyder & DC

America's Best Comics #9 © STD

	GD 2.0	VG 4.0	FN 6.0	VF 8.0	VF/NM 9.0	NM- 9.2

3-6: 3-Look to the Mountain. 4-Case of the Crooked Candle (Perry Mason). 5-Duel in the Sun. 6-Wingate's Raiders 18 36 54 105 165 225

AMERICAN: LOST IN AMERICA, THE
Dark Horse Comics: July, 1992 - No. 4, Oct, 1992 ($2.50, limited series)
1-4: 1-Dorman painted-c. 2-Phillips painted-c. 3-Mignola-c. 4-Jim Lee-c 3.00

AMERICAN MONSTER
AfterShock Comics: Jan, 2016 - No. 6, May, 2017 ($3.99)
1-6-Brian Azzarello-s/Juan Doe-a 4.00

AMERICAN MYTHOLOGY ARCHIVES: LAUREL AND HARDY
American Mythology Prods.: 2020 ($3.99)
1-Reprints Laurel and Hardy #1 (1972) 4.00

AMERICAN MYTHOLOGY ARCHIVES PRESENTS ZORRO
American Mythology Prods.: 2019 ($3.99)
1-Reprints Four Color #882; art by Alex Toth 4.00

AMERICAN MYTHOLOGY DARK: WEREWOLVES VS DINOSAURS
American Mythology Prods.: 2016 - No. 2, 2017 ($3.99)
1,2-Chris Scalf & Eric Dobson-s/a; 3 covers 4.00

AMERICAN RONIN
AWA Inc.: Oct, 2020 - No. 5 ($3.99, limited series)
1-4-Peter Milligan-s/Aco-a 4.00

AMERICAN SPLENDOR: (Series of titles)
Dark Horse Comics: Aug, 1996 - Apr, 2001 (B&W, all one-shots)
--**COMIC-CON COMICS** (8/96) 1-H. Pekar script. --**MUSIC COMICS** (11/97) nn-H. Pekar-s/ Sacco-a; r/Village Voice jazz strips. --**ODDS AND ENDS** (12/97) 1-Pekar-s. --**ON THE JOB** (5/97) 1-Pekar-s. --**A STEP OUT OF THE NEST** (8/94) 1-Pekar-s. --**TERMINAL** (9/99) 1-Pekar-s. --**TRANSATLANTIC** (7/98) 1-"American Splendour" on cover; Pekar-s 3.00
--**A PORTRAIT OF THE AUTHOR IN HIS DECLINING YEARS** (4/01, $3.99) 1-Photo-c. --**BEDTIME STORIES** (6/00, $3.95) 4.00

AMERICAN SPLENDOR
DC Comics: Nov, 2006 - No. 4, Feb, 2007 ($2.99, B&W)
1-4-Pekar-s/art by Haspiel and various. 1-Fabry-c 3.00
...: Another Day TPB (2007, $14.99) r/#1-4 15.00

AMERICAN SPLENDOR (Volume 2)
DC Comics (Vertigo): Jun, 2008 - No. 4, Sept, 2008 ($2.99, B&W)
1-4-Pekar-s/art by Haspiel and various. 1-Bond-c. 3-Cooke-c 3.00
...: Another Dollar TPB (2009, $14.99) r/#1-4 15.00

AMERICAN SPLENDOR: UNSUNG HERO
Dark Horse Comics: Aug, 2002 - No. 3, Oct, 2002 ($3.99, B&W, limited series)
1-3-Pekar script/Collier-a; biography of Robert McNeill 4.00
TPB (8/03, $11.95) r/#1-3 12.00

AMERICAN SPLENDOR: WINDFALL
Dark Horse Comics: Sept, 1995 - No. 2, Oct,1995 ($3.95, B&W, limited series)
1,2-Pekar script 4.00

AMERICAN TAIL: FIEVEL GOES WEST, AN
Marvel Comics: Early Jan, 1992 - No. 3, Early Feb, 1992 ($1.00, limited series)
1-3-Adapts Universal animated movie; Wildman-a 4.00
1-($2.95-c, 69 pgs.) Deluxe squarebound edition 5.00

AMERICAN VAMPIRE
DC Comics (Vertigo): May, 2010 - No. 34, Feb, 2013 ($3.99/$2.99)
1-Snyder-s/Albuquerque-a; back-up story by Stephen King 1 2 3 5 6 8
1-5-Variant-c: 1-Jim Lee. 2-Berni Wrightson. 3-Andy Kubert. 5-Paul Pope 1 2 4 6 8 10
2-10: 2-9-Snyder-s/Albuquerque-a. 2-5-Back-up story by Stephen King continues 4.00
11-34-($2.99) 11-Santolouco-a. 12-Zezelj-a. 19-21-Bernet-a 3.00
... Anthology 1 (10/13, $7.99) Short stories by various; Albuquerque-c 8.00
...: The Long Road to Hell 1 (8/13, $6.99) Snyder-s/Albuquerque-a 7.00
HC (2010, $24.99, d.j.) r/#1-5; intro. by Stephen King; script pages and sketch art 25.00
...Volume Two HC (2011, $24.99, d.j.) r/#6-11; cover design art 25.00

AMERICAN VAMPIRE: LORD OF NIGHTMARES
DC Comics (Vertigo): Aug, 2012 - No. 5, Dec, 2012 ($2.99, limited series)
1-5-Set in 1954 England; Snyder-s/Nguyen-a/c. 2-Origin of Dracula 3.00

AMERICAN VAMPIRE: 1976
DC Comics (Vertigo): Dec, 2020 - No. 9 ($3.99, limited series)
1-5-Snyder-s/Albuquerque-a/c 4.00

AMERICAN VAMPIRE: SECOND CYCLE
DC Comics (Vertigo): May, 2014 - No. 11, Jan, 2016 ($3.99/$2.99, limited series)
1,8-10-($3.99) Snyder-s/Albuquerque-a/c 4.00
2-7-($2.99) 5-Bergara-a 3.00
11-($4.99) Snyder-s/Albuquerque-a/c 5.00

AMERICAN VAMPIRE: SURVIVAL OF THE FITTEST
DC Comics (Vertigo): Aug, 2011 - No. 5, Dec, 2011 ($2.99, limited series)
1-5-Set during WWII; Snyder-s/Murphy-a/c 3.00

AMERICAN VIRGIN
DC Comics (Vertigo): May, 2006 - No. 23, Mar, 2008 ($2.99)
1-23-Steven Seagle-s/Becky Cloonan-a in most. 1-3-Quitely-c. 4-14-Middleton-c 3.00
...: Head (2006, $9.99, TPB) r/#1-4; interviews with the creators and page development 10.00
...: Going Down (2007, $14.99, TPB) r/#5-9 15.00
...: Wet (2007, $12.99, TPB) r/#10-14 13.00
...: Around the World (Vol. 4) (2008, $17.99, TPB) r/#15-23 18.00

AMERICAN WAY, THE
DC Comics (WildStorm): Apr, 2006 - No. 8, Nov, 2006 ($2.99, limited series)
1-8-John Ridley-s/Georges Jeanty-a/c 3.00

AMERICAN WAY, THE: THOSE ABOVE AND THOSE BELOW
DC Comics (Vertigo): Sept, 2017 - No. 6, Apr, 2018 ($3.99, limited series)
1-6-John Ridley-s/Georges Jeanty-a/c; sequel set in 1972 4.00

AMERICA'S BEST COMICS
Nedor/Better/Standard Publications: Feb, 1942; No. 2, Sept, 1942 - No. 31, July, 1949 (New logo with #9)

	GD 2.0	VG 4.0	FN 6.0	VF 8.0	VF/NM 9.0	NM- 9.2
1-The Woman in Red, Black Terror, Captain Future, Doc Strange, The Liberator, & Don Davis, Secret Ace begin	383	766	1149	2681	4691	6700
2-Origin The American Eagle; The Woman in Red ends	171	342	513	1086	1868	2650
3-Pyroman begins (11/42, 1st app.; also see Startling Comics #18, 12/42)	165	330	495	1048	1799	2550
4-6: 5-Last Capt. Future (not in #4); Lone Eagle app. 6-American Crusader app.	126	252	378	806	1378	1950
7-Hitler, Mussolini & Hirohito-c	337	674	1011	2359	4130	5900
8-Last Liberator	126	252	378	806	1378	1950
9-The Fighting Yank begins; The Ghost app.	126	252	378	806	1378	1950
10-Flag-c	119	238	357	762	1306	1850
11-Hirohito & Tojo-c. (10/44)	145	290	435	921	1586	2250
12	95	190	285	603	1039	1475
13-Japanese WWII-c	110	220	330	704	1202	1700
14-17: 14-American Eagle ends; Doc Strange vs. Hitler story	76	152	228	486	831	1175
18-Classic-c	116	232	348	742	1271	1800
19-21: 21-Infinity-c	66	132	198	419	722	1025
22-Capt. Future app.	58	116	174	371	636	900
23-Miss Masque begins; last Doc Strange	90	180	270	576	988	1400
24-Miss Masque bondage-c	87	174	261	553	952	1350
25-Last Fighting Yank; Sea Eagle app.	65	130	195	416	708	1000
26-Miss Masque motorcycle-c; The Phantom Detective & The Silver Knight app.; Frazetta text illo & some panels in Miss Masque	71	142	213	454	777	1100
27-31: 27,28-Commando Cubs. 27-Doc Strange. 28-Tuska Black Terror. 29-Last Pyroman	58	116	174	371	636	900

NOTE: *American Eagle not in 3, 8, 9, 13. Fighting Yank not in 10, 12. Liberator not in 2, 6, 7. Pyroman not in 9, 11, 14-16, 23, 25-27.* ***Schomburg (Xela)*** *c-5, 7-31. Bondage c-18, 24.*

AMERICA'S BEST COMICS
America's Best Comics: 1999 - 2008
... Preview (1999, Wizard magazine supplement) - Previews Tom Strong, Top Ten, Promethea, Tomorrow Stories 3.00
... Primer (2008, $4.99, TPB) r/Tom Strong #1, Tom Strong's Terrific Tales, Top Ten #1, Promethea #1, Tomorrow Stories #1,6 5.00
... Sketchbook (2002, $5.95, square-bound)-Design sketches by Sprouse, Ross, Adams, Nowlan, Ha and others 6.00
Special 1 (2/01, $6.95)-Short stories of Alan Moore's characters; art by various; Ross-c 7.00
TPB (2004, $17.95) Reprints short stories and sketch pages from ABC titles 18.00

AMERICA'S BEST TV COMICS (TV)
American Broadcasting Co. (Prod. by Marvel Comics): 1967 (25¢, 68 pgs.)
1-Spider-Man, Fantastic Four (by Kirby/Ayers), Casper, King Kong, George of the Jungle, Journey to the Center of the Earth stories (promotes new TV cartoon show) 10 20 30 69 147 225

AMERICA'S BIGGEST COMICS BOOK
William H. Wise: 1944 (196 pgs., one-shot)

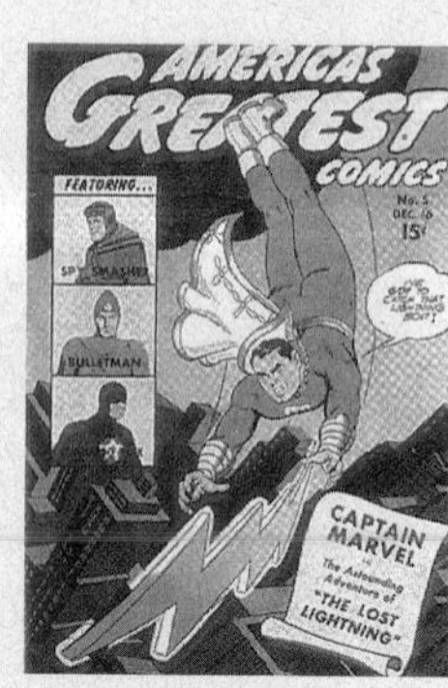

America's Greatest Comics #5 © FAW

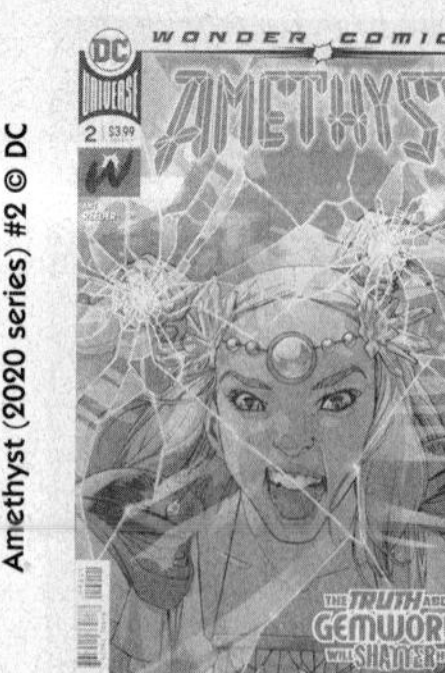

Amethyst (2020 series) #2 © DC

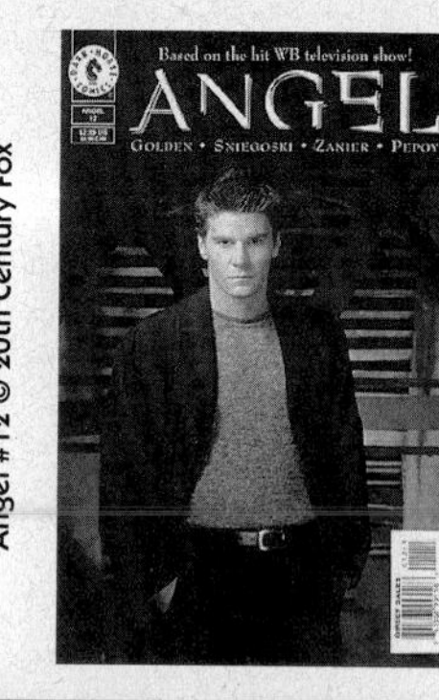

Angel #12 © 20th Century Fox

	GD 2.0	VG 4.0	FN 6.0	VF 8.0	VF/NM 9.0	NM- 9.2
1-The Grim Reaper, The Silver Knight, Zudo, the Jungle Boy, Commando Cubs, Thunderhoof app.	53	106	159	334	567	800

AMERICA'S FUNNIEST COMICS
William H. Wise: 1944 - No. 2, 1944 (15¢, 80 pgs.)

	GD 2.0	VG 4.0	FN 6.0	VF 8.0	VF/NM 9.0	NM- 9.2
nn(#1), 2-Funny Animal	24	48	72	142	234	325

AMERICA'S GOT POWERS
Image Comics: Apr, 2012 - No. 7, Oct, 2013 ($2.99, limited series)

	GD 2.0	VG 4.0	FN 6.0	VF 8.0	VF/NM 9.0	NM- 9.2
1-7-Jonathan Ross-s/Bryan Hitch-a/c. 1-Wraparound-c						3.00

AMERICA'S GREATEST COMICS
Fawcett Publications: May?, 1941 - No. 8, Summer, 1943 (15¢, 100 pgs., soft cardboard-c)

	GD 2.0	VG 4.0	FN 6.0	VF 8.0	VF/NM 9.0	NM- 9.2
1-Bulletman, Spy Smasher, Capt. Marvel, Minute Man & Mr. Scarlet begin; Classic Mac Raboy-c. 1st time that Fawcett's major super-heroes appear together as a group on a cover. Fawcett's 1st squarebound comic	349	698	1047	2443	4272	6100
2	145	290	435	921	1586	2250
3	113	226	339	718	1234	1750
4,5: 4-Commando Yank begins; Golden Arrow, Ibis the Invincible & Spy Smasher cameo in Captain Marvel	77	154	231	489	837	1185
6,7: 7-Balbo the Boy Magician app.; Captain Marvel, Bulletman cameo in Mr. Scarlet	68	136	204	435	743	1050
8-Capt. Marvel Jr. & Golden Arrow app.; Spy Smasher x-over in Capt. Midnight; no Minute Man or Commando Yank	68	136	204	435	743	1050

AMERICA'S SWEETHEART SUNNY (See Sunny, ...)

AMERICA VS. THE JUSTICE SOCIETY
DC Comics: Jan, 1985 - No. 4, Apr, 1985 ($1.00, limited series)

	GD 2.0	VG 4.0	FN 6.0	VF 8.0	VF/NM 9.0	NM- 9.2
1-Double size; Alcala-a(i) in all	2	4	6	8	10	12
2-4: 3,4-Spectre cameo	1	2	3	5	7	9

AMERICOMICS
Americomics: April, 1983 - No. 6, Mar, 1984 ($2.00, Baxter paper/slick paper)

	GD 2.0	VG 4.0	FN 6.0	VF 8.0	VF/NM 9.0	NM- 9.2
1-Intro/origin The Shade; Intro. The Slayer, Captain Freedom and The Liberty Corps; Perez-c						5.00
1,2-2nd printings ($2.00)						3.00
2-6: 2-Messenger app. & 1st app. Tara on Jungle Island. 3-New & old Blue Beetle battle. 4-Origin Dragonfly & Shade. 5-Origin Commando D. 6-Origin the Scarlet Scorpion						3.00
Special 1 (8/83, $2.00)-Sentinels of Justice (Blue Beetle, Captain Atom, Nightshade & The Question)						5.00

AMETHYST
DC Comics: Jan, 1985 - No. 16, Aug, 1986 (75¢)

	GD 2.0	VG 4.0	FN 6.0	VF 8.0	VF/NM 9.0	NM- 9.2
1-16: 8-Fire Jade's i.d. revealed						3.00
Special 1 (10/86, $1.25)						4.00
1-4 (11/87 - 2/88)(Limited series)						3.00

AMETHYST (Princess of Gemworld)(Also see Young Justice)
DC Comics (Wonder Comics): Apr, 2020 - No. 6, Feb, 2021 ($3.99)

	GD 2.0	VG 4.0	FN 6.0	VF 8.0	VF/NM 9.0	NM- 9.2
1-6: 1-Amy Reeder-s/a; origin re-told in flashback						4.00

AMETHYST, PRINCESS OF GEMWORLD (See Legion of Super-Heroes #298)
DC Comics: May, 1983 - No. 12, Apr, 1984 (Maxi-series)

	GD 2.0	VG 4.0	FN 6.0	VF 8.0	VF/NM 9.0	NM- 9.2
1-(60¢)						5.00
1,2-(35¢): tested in Austin & Kansas City	5	10	15	34	60	85
2-12, Annual 1(9/84): 5-11-Pérez-c(p)						4.00

NOTE: *Issues #1 & 2 also have Canadian variants with a 75¢ cover price.*

AMORY WARS (Based on the Coheed and Cambria album The Second Stage Turbine Blade)
Image Comics: Jun, 2007 - No. 5, Jan, 2008 ($2.99, limited series)

	GD 2.0	VG 4.0	FN 6.0	VF 8.0	VF/NM 9.0	NM- 9.2
1-5: 1-Claudio Sanchez-s/Gus Vasquez-a						3.00

AMORY WARS II
Image Comics: Jun, 2008 - No. 5, Oct, 2008 ($2.99, limited series)

	GD 2.0	VG 4.0	FN 6.0	VF 8.0	VF/NM 9.0	NM- 9.2
1-5-Claudio Sanchez-s/Gabriel Guzman-a						3.00

AMORY WARS: GOOD APOLLO, I'M BURNING STAR IV
BOOM! Studios: Apr, 2017 - No. 12, Oct, 2018 ($3.99)

	GD 2.0	VG 4.0	FN 6.0	VF 8.0	VF/NM 9.0	NM- 9.2
1-12: 1-Claudio Sanchez & Chondra Echert-s/Rags Morales-a. 1-Four covers						4.00

AMORY WARS IN KEEPING SECRETS OF SILENT EARTH: 3
BOOM! Studios: May, 2010 - No. 12, Jun, 2011 ($3.99)

	GD 2.0	VG 4.0	FN 6.0	VF 8.0	VF/NM 9.0	NM- 9.2
1-12: 1-Claudio Sanchez & Peter David-s/Chris Burnham-a. 1-Four covers						4.00

AMY RACECAR COLOR SPECIAL (See Stray Bullets)
El Capitán Books: July, 1997; Oct, 1999 ($2.95/$3.50)

	GD 2.0	VG 4.0	FN 6.0	VF 8.0	VF/NM 9.0	NM- 9.2
1,2-David Lapham-a/scripts. 2-($3.50)						3.50

ANALOG
Image Comics: Apr, 2018 - No. 10, Mar, 2020 ($3.99)

	GD 2.0	VG 4.0	FN 6.0	VF 8.0	VF/NM 9.0	NM- 9.2
1-10-Gerry Duggan-s/David O'Sullivan-a						4.00

ANARCHO DICTATOR OF DEATH (See Comics Novel)

ANARKY (See Batman titles)
DC Comics: May, 1997 - No. 4, Aug, 1997 ($2.50, limited series)

	GD 2.0	VG 4.0	FN 6.0	VF 8.0	VF/NM 9.0	NM- 9.2
1						3.50
2-4						3.00

ANARKY (See Batman titles)
DC Comics: May, 1999 - No. 8, Dec, 1999 ($2.50)

	GD 2.0	VG 4.0	FN 6.0	VF 8.0	VF/NM 9.0	NM- 9.2
1-8: 1-JLA app.; Grant-s/Breyfogle-a. 3-Green Lantern app. 7-Day of Judgment; Haunted Tank app. 8-Joker-c/app.						3.00

ANCHORS ANDREWS (The Saltwater Daffy)
St. John Publishing Co.: Jan, 1953 - No. 4, July, 1953 (Anchors the Saltwater... No. 4)

	GD 2.0	VG 4.0	FN 6.0	VF 8.0	VF/NM 9.0	NM- 9.2
1-Canteen Kate by Matt Baker (9 pgs.)	28	56	84	165	270	375
2-4	11	22	33	62	86	110

ANDY & WOODY (See March of Comics No. 40, 55, 76)

ANDY BURNETT (TV, Disney)
Dell Publishing Co.: Dec, 1957

	GD 2.0	VG 4.0	FN 6.0	VF 8.0	VF/NM 9.0	NM- 9.2
Four Color 865-Photo-c	8	16	24	54	102	150

ANDY COMICS (Formerly Scream Comics; becomes Ernie Comics)
Current Publications (Ace Magazines): No. 20, June, 1948-No. 21, Aug, 1948

	GD 2.0	VG 4.0	FN 6.0	VF 8.0	VF/NM 9.0	NM- 9.2
20,21: Archie-type comic	14	28	42	80	115	150

ANDY DEVINE WESTERN
Fawcett Publications: Dec, 1950 - No. 2, 1951

	GD 2.0	VG 4.0	FN 6.0	VF 8.0	VF/NM 9.0	NM- 9.2
1-Photo-c	47	94	141	296	498	700
2-Photo-c	32	64	96	192	314	435

ANDY GRIFFITH SHOW, THE (TV)(1st show aired 10/3/60)
Dell Publishing Co.: #1252, Jan-Mar, 1962; #1341, Apr-Jun, 1962

	GD 2.0	VG 4.0	FN 6.0	VF 8.0	VF/NM 9.0	NM- 9.2
Four Color 1252(#1)	38	76	114	285	641	1000
Four Color 1341-Photo-c	35	70	105	252	564	875

ANDY HARDY COMICS (See Movie Comics #3 by Fiction House)
Dell Publishing Co.: April, 1952 - No. 6, Sept-Nov, 1954

	GD 2.0	VG 4.0	FN 6.0	VF 8.0	VF/NM 9.0	NM- 9.2
Four Color 389(#1)	6	12	18	40	73	105
Four Color 447,480,515, #5,#6	4	8	12	27	44	60

ANDY PANDA (Also see Crackajack Funnies #39, The Funnies, New Funnies & Walter Lantz...)
Dell Publishing Co.: 1943 - No. 56, Nov-Jan, 1961-62 (Walter Lantz)

	GD 2.0	VG 4.0	FN 6.0	VF 8.0	VF/NM 9.0	NM- 9.2
Four Color 25(#1, 1943)	50	100	150	390	870	1350
Four Color 54(1944)	25	50	75	175	388	600
Four Color 85(1945)	15	30	45	103	227	350
Four Color 130(1946),154,198	10	20	30	70	150	230
Four Color 216,240,258,280,297	8	16	24	55	105	155
Four Color 326,345,358	6	12	18	41	76	110
Four Color 383,409	5	10	15	35	63	90
16(11-1/52-53) - 30	4	8	12	28	47	65
31-56	4	8	12	23	37	50

(See March of Comics #5, 22, 79, & Super Book #4, 15, 27.)

A-NEXT (See Avengers)
Marvel Comics: Oct, 1998 - No. 12, Sept, 1999 ($1.99)

	GD 2.0	VG 4.0	FN 6.0	VF 8.0	VF/NM 9.0	NM- 9.2
1-6,8-11: 1-Next generation of Avengers; Frenz-a. 2-Two covers. 3-Defenders app.						3.00
7-1st app. of Hope Pym	2	4	6	11	16	20
12-1st full app. of Hope Pym	1	3	4	6	8	10
Spider-Girl Presents Avengers Next Vol. 1: Second Coming (2006, $7.99, digest) r/#1-6						8.00

ANGEL
Dell Publishing Co.: Aug, 1954 - No. 16, Nov-Jan, 1958-59

	GD 2.0	VG 4.0	FN 6.0	VF 8.0	VF/NM 9.0	NM- 9.2
Four Color 576(#1, 8/54)	5	10	15	31	53	75
2(5-7/55) - 16	3	6	9	17	26	35

ANGEL (TV) (Also see Buffy the Vampire Slayer)
Dark Horse Comics: Nov, 1999 - No. 17, Apr, 2001 ($2.95/$2.99)

	GD 2.0	VG 4.0	FN 6.0	VF 8.0	VF/NM 9.0	NM- 9.2
1-17: 1-3,5-7;10-14-Zanier-a. 1-4,7,10-Matsuda & photo-c. 16-Buffy-c/app.						3.00
...: Earthly Possessions TPB (4/01, $9.95) r/#5-7, photo-c						10.00
...: Surrogates TPB (12/00, $9.95) r/#1-3; photo-c						10.00

ANGEL (Buffy the Vampire Slayer)
Dark Horse Comics: Sept, 2001 - No. 4, May, 2002 ($2.99, limited series)

	GD 2.0	VG 4.0	FN 6.0	VF 8.0	VF/NM 9.0	NM- 9.2
1-4-Joss Whedon & Matthews-s/Rubi-a; photo-c and Rubi-c on each						3.00

ANGEL (Buffy the Vampire Slayer) (Previously titled Angel: After the Fall)
IDW Publishing: No. 18, Feb, 2009 - No. 44, Apr, 2011 ($3.99)

Angela: Asgard's Assassin #6 © MAR

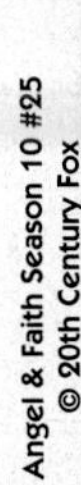
Angel & Faith Season 10 #25 © 20th Century Fox

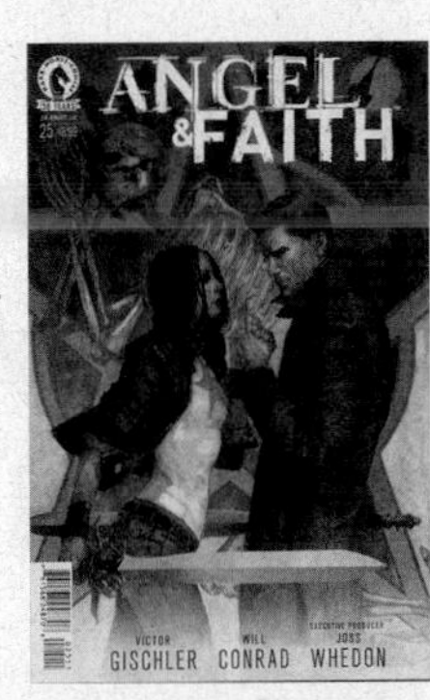

Angry Birds Comics #6 © Rovio

	GD 2.0	VG 4.0	FN 6.0	VF 8.0	VF/NM 9.0	NM- 9.2

18-44: Multiple covers on all. 25-Juliet Landau-s 4.00

ANGEL (one-shots) (Buffy the Vampire Slayer)
IDW Publishing: ($3.99/$7.49)

...: Connor (8/06, $3.99) Jay Faerber-s/Bob Gill-a; 4 covers + 1 retailer cover 4.00
...: Doyle (7/06, $3.99) Jeff Mariotte-s/David Messina-a; 4 covers + 1 retailer cover 4.00
...: Gunn (5/06, $3.99) Dan Jolley-s/Mark Pennington-a; 4 covers + 2 retailer covers 4.00
...: Illyria (4/06, $3.99) Peter David-s/Nicola Scott-a; 4 covers + 2 retailer covers 4.00
...: Masks (10/06, $7.49) short stories of Angel, Illyria, Cordilia & Lindsay; puppet Angel app. 8.00
... 100-Page Spectacular (4/11, $7.99) reprints of 4 issues; Runge-c 8.00
... Special • Lorne (3/10, $7.99) John Byrne-s/a; The Groosalugg app. 8.00
Team Angel 100-Page Spectacular (4/11, $7.99) reprints; Runge-c 8.00
...: Vs. Frankenstein (10/09, $3.99) John Byrne-s/a/c 4.00
...: Vs. Frankenstein II (10/10, $3.99) John Byrne-s/a/c 4.00
...: Wesley (6/06, $3.99) Scott Tipton-s/Mike Norton-a; 4 covers + 1 retailer cover 4.00
Spotlight TPB (12/06, $19.99) r/Connor, Doyle, Gunn, Illyria & Wesley one-shots 20.00
... Yearbook (5/11, $7.99) short stories by various; 3 covers 8.00

ANGEL (Buffy the Vampire Slayer)(Title changes to Angel + Spike with #9)
BOOM! Studios: No. 0, Apr, 2019 - No. 8, Jan, 2020 ($3.99)

0-Bryan Edward Hill-s/Gleb Melnikov-a; Angel in Los Angeles; origin re-told 4.00
1-8: 1-(5/19). 3-Intro. Fred. 4-Intro. Gunn. 5-8-Hellmouth tie-ins with Buffy 4.00

ANGELA
Image Comics (Todd McFarlane Prod.): Dec, 1994 - No. 3, Feb, 1995 ($2.95, lim. series)

	GD	VG	FN	VF	VF/NM	NM-
1-Gaiman scripts & Capullo-c/a in all; Spawn app.	1	2	3	5	6	8
2						6.00
3						5.00
Special Edition (1995)-Pirate Spawn-c	3	6	9	14	20	25
Special Edition (1995)-Angela-c	3	6	9	14	20	25
TPB ($9.95, 1995) reprints #1-3 & Special Ed. w/additional pin-ups						10.00

ANGELA: ASGARD'S ASSASSIN (The Image Comics character in the Marvel Universe)
Marvel Comics: Feb, 2015 - No. 6, Jul, 2015 ($3.99)

1-6: 1-Gillen-s/Jimenez-a; multiple covers. 4-6-Guardians of the Galaxy app. 4.00

ANGEL: AFTER THE FALL (Buffy the Vampire Slayer) (Follows the last TV episode)
IDW Publishing: Nov, 2007 - No. 17, Feb, 2009 ($3.99)(Continues as Angel with #18)

1-Whedon & Lynch-s; multiple covers 5.00
2-17: Multiple covers on all 4.00

ANGELA/GLORY: RAGE OF ANGELS (See Glory/Angela: Rage of Angels)
Image Comics (Todd McFarlane Productions): Mar, 1996 ($2.50, one-shot)

1-Liefeld-c/Cruz-a(p); Darkchylde preview flip book 4.00
1-Variant-c 4.00

ANGEL: A HOLE IN THE WORLD (Adaptation of the 2-part TV episode)
IDW Publishing: Dec, 2009 - No. 5, Apr, 2010 ($3.99, limited series)

1-5-Fred becomes Illyria; Casagrande-a/c 4.00

ANGEL & FAITH (Follows Buffy the Vampire Slayer Season Eight)
Dark Horse Comics: Aug, 2011 - No. 25, Aug, 2013 ($2.99)

1-Gage-s/Isaacs-a; two covers by Morris & Chen 3.00
2-25-Two covers by Morris & Isaacs. 5-Harmony & Clem app.; Noto-a. 7-Drusilla app. 11-14-Willow & Connor app. 20-Spike app.; Archie style-c 3.00

ANGEL & FAITH SEASON 10 (Buffy the Vampire Slayer)
Dark Horse Comics: Apr, 2014 - No. 25, Apr, 2016 ($3.50/$3.99)

1-15-Two covers on each. 1-Gischler-s/Conrad-a. 5-Santacruz-a. 6-10-Amy app. 10-Fred returns 3.50
16-25-($3.99) 17-Drusilla returns 4.00

ANGEL AND THE APE (Meet Angel No. 7) (See Limited Collector's Edition C-34 & Showcase #77)
National Periodical Publications: Nov-Dec, 1968 - No. 6, Sept-Oct, 1969

	GD	VG	FN	VF	VF/NM	NM-
1-(11-12/68)-Not Wood-a	5	10	15	34	60	85
2-5-Wood inks in all. 4-Last 12¢ issue	3	6	9	21	33	46
6-Wood inks	4	8	12	25	40	55

ANGEL AND THE APE (2nd Series)
DC Comics: Mar, 1991 - No. 4, June, 1991 ($1.00, limited series)

1-4 4.00

ANGEL AND THE APE (3rd Series)
DC Comics (Vertigo): Oct, 2001 - No. 4, Jan 2002 ($2.95, limited series)

1-4-Chaykin & Tischman-s/Bond-a/Art Adams-c 3.00

ANGELA: QUEEN OF HEL (The Image Comics character in the Marvel Universe)
Marvel Comics: Dec, 2015 - No. 7, Jun, 2016 ($3.99)

1-5: 1-Bennett-s/Jacinto & Hans-a. 4,5-Hela app. 6,7-Thor (Jane) app. 4.00

	GD 2.0	VG 4.0	FN 6.0	VF 8.0	VF/NM 9.0	NM- 9.2

ANGEL: AULD LANG SYNE (Buffy the Vampire Slayer)
IDW Publishing: Nov, 2006 - No. 5, Mar, 2007 ($3.99, limited series)

1-5: 1-Three covers plus photo-c; Tipton-s/Messina-a 4.00

ANGEL: BARBARY COAST (Buffy the Vampire Slayer)
IDW Publishing: Apr, 2010 - No. 3, Jun, 2010 ($3.99, limited series)

1-3-Angel in 1906 San Francisco; Tischman-s/Urru-a; 2 covers on each 4.00

ANGEL: BLOOD & TRENCHES (Buffy the Vampire Slayer)
IDW Publishing: Mar, 2009 - No. 4, June, 2009 ($3.99, B&W&Red, limited series)

1-4-Angel in World War II Europe; John Byrne-s/a/c 4.00

ANGEL: ILLYRIA: HAUNTED (Buffy the Vampire Slayer)
IDW Publishing: Nov, 2010 - No. 4, Feb, 2011 ($3.99, limited series)

1-4-Tipton & Huehner-s/Casagrande-a; 2 covers 4.00

ANGEL LOVE
DC Comics: Aug, 1986 - No. 8, Mar, 1987 (75¢, limited series)

1-8, Special 1 (1987, $1.25, 52 pgs.) 4.00

ANGEL: NOT FADE AWAY (Buffy the Vampire Slayer)
IDW Publishing: May, 2009 - No. 3, July, 2009 ($3.99, limited series)

1-3-Adaptation of TV show's final episodes; Mooney-a 4.00

ANGEL OF LIGHT, THE (See The Crusaders)

ANGEL: OLD FRIENDS (Buffy the Vampire Slayer)
IDW Publishing: Nov, 2005 - No. 5, Mar, 2006 ($3.99, limited series)

1-5: Four covers plus photo-c on each; Mariotte-s/Messina-a; Gunn, Spike and Illyria app. 4.00
... Cover Gallery (6/06, $3.99) gallery of variant covers for the series 4.00
... Cover Gallery (12/06, $3.99) gallery of variant covers; preview of Angel: Auld Lang Syne 4.00
TPB (2006, $19.99) r/series; gallery of Messina covers 20.00

ANGEL: ONLY HUMAN (Buffy the Vampire Slayer)
IDW Publishing: Aug, 2009 - No. 5, Dec, 2009 ($3.99, limited series)

1-5-Lobdell-s/Messina-a; covers by Messina and Dave Dorman 4.00

ANGEL + SPIKE (Buffy the Vampire Slayer)(Title changed from Angel after #8)
BOOM! Studios: No. 9, Feb, 2020 - No. 16, Nov, 2020 ($3.99)

9-16: 9-12-Hill-s/Melnikov-a. 13-Kowalski-a. 14-16-Sherman-a 4.00

ANGEL: REVELATIONS (X-Men character)
Marvel Comics: July, 2008 - No. 5, Nov, 2008 ($3.99, limited series)

1-5-Origin from childhood re-told; Adam Pollina-a/Aguirre-Sacasa-s 4.00

ANGEL SEASON 11 (Buffy the Vampire Slayer)
Dark Horse Comics: Jan, 2017 - No. 12, Dec, 2017 ($3.99)

1-12: 1-4-Bechko-s/Borges-a; Fred & Illyria app. 4.00

ANGEL: SMILE TIME (Buffy the Vampire Slayer)
IDW Publishing: Dec, 2008 - No. 3, Apr, 2009 ($3.99, limited series)

1-3-Adaptation of TV episode; Messina-a; Messina and photo covers for each 4.00

ANGEL: THE CURSE (Buffy the Vampire Slayer)
IDW Publishing: June, 2005 - No. 5, Oct, 2005 ($3.99, limited series)

1-5-Four covers on each; Mariotte-s/Messina-a 4.00
TPB (1/06, $19.99) r/#1-5; cover gallery of Messina covers 20.00

ANGELTOWN
DC Comics (Vertigo): Jan, 2005 - No. 5, May, 2005 ($2.95, limited series)

1-5-Gary Phillips-s/Shawn Martinbrough-a 3.00

ANGELUS
Image Comics (Top Cow): Dec, 2007; Dec, 2009 - Nov, 2010 ($2.99)

... Pilot Season 1-(12/07) Sejic-a/c; Edington-s; origin re-told 3.00
1-6-Marz-s/Sejic-a; multiple covers on each 3.00

ANGRY BIRDS COMICS (Based on the Rovio videogame)(Also see Super Angry Birds)
IDW Publishing: Jun, 2014 - No. 12, Jun, 2015 ($3.99)

1-12-Short stories by Jeff Parker, Paul Tobin and various; wraparound-c on most 4.00
Volume 2 (1/16 - 12/16, $3.99) 1-12-Wraparound-c on all 4.00
...: Holiday Special (12/14, $5.99) Terence in charge of the North Pole 6.00
... Quarterly: Furious Fowl (8/17, $5.99) Short stories by various 6.00
... Quarterly: Monsters and Mistletoe (12/17, $5.99) Short stories by various 6.00

ANGRY BIRDS: FLIGHT SCHOOL (Based on the Rovio videogame)
IDW Publishing: Feb, 2017 - No. 3, Jun, 2017 ($3.99)

1-3-Short stories by various 4.00

ANGRY BIRDS GAME PLAY (Based on the Rovio videogame)
IDW Publishing: Jan, 2017 - No. 3, May, 2017 ($3.99)

Animal Comics #17 © Bobbs-Merrill

Animal Man #13 © DC

Animosity #24 © Bennett & AfterShock

	GD	VG	FN	VF	VF/NM	NM-
	2.0	4.0	6.0	8.0	9.0	9.2

GD VG FN VF VF/NM NM- 2.0 4.0 6.0 8.0 9.0 9.2

1-3-Short stories by various; wraparound-c 4.00

ANGRY BIRDS TRANSFORMERS (Based on the Rovio videogame)
IDW Publishing: Nov, 2014 - No. 4, Feb, 2015 ($3.99, limited series)

1-4-Barber-s; the Eggspark lands on Piggy Island 4.00

ANGRY CHRIST COMIX (See Cry For Dawn)

ANIMA
DC Comics: Mar, 1994 - No. 15, July, 1995 ($1.75/$1.95/$2.25)

1-7,0,8-15: 7-(9/94)-Begin $1.95-c; Zero Hour x-over 3.00

ANIMAL ADVENTURES
Timor Publications/Accepted Publ. (reprints): Dec, 1953 - No. 3, May?, 1954

1-Funny animal 9 18 27 47 61 75
2,3: 2-Featuring Soopermutt (2/54) 7 14 21 35 43 50
1-3 (reprints, nd) 3 6 8 11 13 15

ANIMAL ANTICS
DC Comics: Feb, 1946

nn - Ashcan comic, not distributed to newsstands, only for in-house use. Cover art is Star Spangled Comics #49 and interior is Boy Commandos #12; a NM cover sold for $1000 in 2012, and FN/VF copy sold for $1553.50 in 2012.

ANIMAL ANTICS (Movietown... No. 24 on)
National Periodical Publ: Mar-Apr, 1946 - No. 23, Nov-Dec, 1949 (All 52 pgs.?)

1-Raccoon Kids begins by Otto Feuer; many-c by Grossman; Seaman Sy Wheeler by Kelly in some issues; Grossman-a in most issues 48 96 114 302 514 725
2 25 50 75 147 241 335
3-10: 10-Post-c/a 16 32 48 94 147 200
11-23: 14,15,18,19-Post-a 12 24 36 69 97 125

ANIMAL COMICS
Dell Publishing Co.: Dec-Jan, 1941-42 - No. 30, Dec-Jan, 1947-48

1-1st Pogo app. by Walt Kelly (Dan Noonan art in most issues) 135 270 405 864 1482 2100
2-Uncle Wiggily begins 58 116 174 371 636 900
3,5 27 54 81 189 420 650
4,6,7-No Pogo 16 32 48 110 243 375
8-10 19 38 57 131 291 450
11-15 12 24 36 79 170 260
16-20 9 18 27 58 114 170
21-30: 24-30- "Jigger" by John Stanley 8 16 24 51 96 140

NOTE: ***Dan Noonan** a-18-30. **Gollub** art in most later issues; c-29, 30. **Kelly** c-7-26, part #27-30.*

ANIMAL CRACKERS (Also see Adventures of Patoruzu)
Green Publ. Co./Norlen/Fox Feat.(Hero Books): 1946; No. 31, July, 1950; No. 9, 1959

1-Super Cat begins (1st app.) 21 42 63 124 202 280
2 11 22 33 64 90 115
31(Fox)-Formerly My Love Secret 9 18 27 50 65 80
9(1959-Norlen)-Infinity-c 5 10 15 22 26 30
nn, nd ('50s), no publ.; infinity-c 5 10 15 22 26 30

ANIMAL FABLES
E. C. Comics (Fables Publ. Co.): July-Aug, 1946 - No. 7, Nov-Dec, 1947

1-Freddy Firefly (clone of Human Torch), Korky Kangaroo, Petey Pig, Danny Demon begin 69 138 207 442 759 1075
2-Aesop Fables begin 40 80 120 246 411 575
3-6 36 72 108 215 350 485
7-Origin Moon Girl 90 180 270 576 988 1400

ANIMAL FAIR (Fawcett's...)
Fawcett Publications: Mar, 1946 - No. 11, Feb, 1947

1-Hoppy the Marvel Bunny-c 31 62 93 182 296 410
2 15 30 45 84 127 170
3-6 12 24 36 67 94 120
7-11 10 20 30 54 72 90

ANIMAL FUN
Premier Magazines: 1953 (25¢, came w/glasses)

1-(3-D)-Ziggy Pig, Silly Seal, Billy & Buggy Bear 40 80 120 246 411 575

ANIMAL MAN (See Action Comics #552, 553, DC Comics Presents #77, 78, Last Days of Animal Man, Secret Origins #39, Strange Adventures #180 & Wonder Woman #267, 268)
DC Comics (Vertigo imprint #57 on): Sept, 1988 - No. 89, Nov, 1995 ($1.25/$1.50/$1.75/$1.95/$2.25, mature)

1-Grant Morrison scripts begin, ends #26 2 4 6 8 11 14
2-10: 2-Superman cameo. 6-Invasion tie-in. 9-Manhunter-c/story. 10-Psycho Pirate app. 1 2 3 4 5 7
11-49,51-55,57-89: 23,24-Psycho Pirate app. 24-Arkham Asylum story; Bizarro Superman app. 25-Inferior Five app. 26-Morrison apps. in story; part photo-c (of Morrison?) 4.00
50-($2.95, 52 pgs.)-Last issue w/Veitch scripts 5.00
56-($3.50, 68 pgs.) 5.00
Annual 1 (1993, $3.95, 68 pgs.)-Bolland-c; Children's Crusade Pt. 3 6.00
...: Deus Ex Machina TPB (2003, $19.95) r/#18-26; Morrison-s; new Bolland-c 20.00
...: Origin of the Species TPB (2002, $19.95) r/#10-17 & Secret Origins #39 20.00

NOTE: ***Bolland** c-1-63. 71-**Sutton**-a(i)*

ANIMAL MAN (DC New 52)
DC Comics: Nov, 2011 - No. 29, May, 2014 ($2.99)

1-Jeff Lemire-s/Travel Foreman-a/c; 1st printing with yellow cover background 8.00
1-Second printing (red cover background), Third printing (grey cover background) 3.00
2-29: 2-4 Foreman-a. 5-Huat-a. 10 Justice League Dark app. 13-17-Rotworld 3.00
#0 (11/12, $2.99) Lemire-s/Pugh-a/c; Buddy Baker's origin re-told 3.00
Annual 1 (7/12, $4.99) Swamp Thing app.; Lemire-s/Green-a 5.00
Annual 2 (9/13, $4.99) Lemire-s/Foreman-a 5.00

ANIMAL MYSTIC (See Dark One...)
Cry For Dawn/Sirius: 1993 - No. 4, 1995 ($2.95?/$3.50, B&W)

1 6.00
1-Alternate 2 4 6 9 12 15
1-2nd printing 4.00
2 4.00
2,3-2nd prints (Sirius) 3.50
3,4: 4-Color poster insert, Linsner-s 4.00
TPB ($14.95) r/series 15.00

ANIMAL MYSTIC WATER WARS
Sirius: 1996 - No. 6, Oct, 1998 ($2.95, limited series)

1-6-Dark One-c/a/scripts 4.00

ANIMAL WORLD, THE (Movie)
Dell Publishing Co.: No. 713, Aug, 1956

Four Color 713 5 10 15 33 57 80

ANIMANIACS (TV)
DC Comics: May, 1995 - No. 59, Apr, 2000 ($1.50/$1.75/$1.95/$1.99)

1 1 2 3 5 6 8
2-20: 13-Manga issue. 19-X-Files parody; Miran Kim-c; Adlard-a (4 pgs.) 5.00
21-59: 26-E.C. parody-c. 34-Xena parody. 43-Pinky & the Brain take over 3.00
A Christmas Special (12/94, $1.50, "1" on-c) 2 4 6 9 12 15

ANIMATED COMICS
E. C. Comics: No date given (Summer, 1947?)

1 (Rare) Funny Animal 106 212 318 673 1162 1650

ANIMATED FUNNY COMIC TUNES (See Funny Tunes)

ANIMATED MOVIE-TUNES (Movie Tunes No. 3)
Margood Publishing Corp. (Timely): Fall, 1945 - No. 2, Sum, 1946

1,2-Super Rabbit, Ziggy Pig & Silly Seal 41 82 123 256 428 600

ANIMAX
Marvel Comics (Star Comics): Dec, 1986 - No. 4, June, 1987

1-4: Based on toys; Simonson-a 3.00

ANIMOSITY (Also see World of Animosity one-shot)
AfterShock Comics: Aug, 2016 - Present ($3.99)

1-Marguerite Bennett-s/Rafael de Latorre-a; 2 covers 15.00
2 8.00
3-28: 17-Savarese-a. 19-28-Thomasi-a 4.00
... Tales 1 (5/19, Free Comic Book Day giveaway) Bennett-s/Thomasi-a 3.00

ANIMOSITY: EVOLUTION
AfterShock Comics: Oct, 2017 - No. 10, Jan, 2019 ($3.99, limited series)

1-10-Bennett-s/Gapstur-a; San Francisco one month after the awakening 4.00

ANIMOSITY: THE RISE
AfterShock Comics: Jan, 2017 - No. 3, Sept, 2017 ($3.99, limited series)

1-3-Bennett-s/Juan Doe-a; the early days after the animals awoke 4.00

ANITA BLAKE (Circus of the Damned - The Charmer on cover)
Marvel Comics: July, 2010 - No. 5, Dec, 2010 ($3.99, limited series)

1-5-Laurell K. Hamilton & Jess Ruffner-s/Ron Lim-a/ Brett Booth-c 4.00
... - The Ingenue 1-5 (3/11 - No. 5, 10/11, $3.99) Hamilton & Ruffner-s/Lim-a/Booth-c 4.00
... - The Scoundrel 1-4 (11/11 - No. 5, 5/12, $3.99) Hamilton & Ruffner-s/Lim-a/Booth-c 4.00

ANITA BLAKE: VAMPIRE HUNTER GUILTY PLEASURES
Marvel Comics (Dabel Brothers): Dec, 2006 - No. 12, Aug, 2008 ($2.99)

Anita Blake: Vampire Hunter Guilty Pleasures #9 © L.K. Hamilton

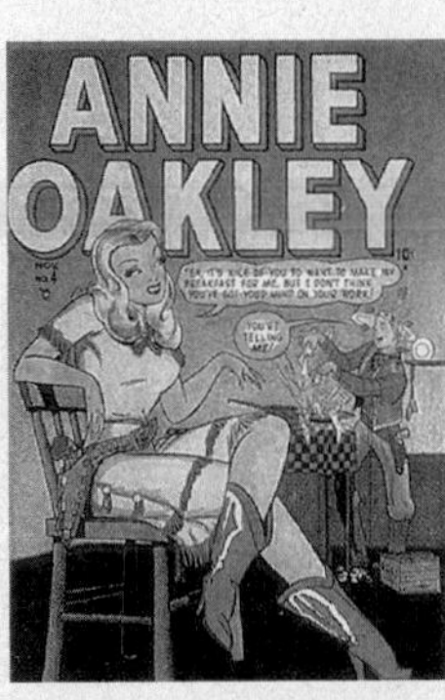

Annie Oakley #4 © MAR

Annihilation: Conquest #1 © MAR

	GD 2.0	VG 4.0	FN 6.0	VF 8.0	VF/NM 9.0	NM- 9.2

1-Laurell K. Hamilton-s/Brett Booth-a; blue cover 6.00
1-Variant-c by Greg Horn 20.00
1-Sketch cover 25.00
1-2nd printing with red cover 3.00
2-Two covers 5.00
3-12 3.00
...: Handbook (2007, $3.99) profile pages of characters; glossary 4.00
... Volume One HC (6/07, $19.99, dust jacket) r/#1-6; cover gallery 20.00

ANITA BLAKE: VAMPIRE HUNTER THE FIRST DEATH, (LAURELL K. HAMILTON'S...)
Marvel Comics (Dabel Brothers): July, 2007 - No. 2, Dec, 2007 ($3.99)

1,2-Laurell K. Hamilton & Jonathon Green-s/Wellington Alves-a. 2-Marvel Zombie var-c 4.00
... HC (2008, $19.99, dust jacket) r/#1,2 & Guilty Pleasures Handbook 20.00

ANITA BLAKE, VAMPIRE HUNTER: THE LAUGHING CORPSE
Marvel Comics: Dec, 2008 - No. 5, Apr, 2009 ($3.99)

... - Book One (12/08 - No. 5, 4/09) 1-5-Laurell K. Hamilton-s/Ron Lim-a/c 4.00
... - Necromancer 1-5 (6/09 - No. 5, 11/09, $3.99) Lim-a/c 4.00
Anita Blake (Executioner on-c) #11-15 (12/09 - No. 15, 5/10) numbering continued; Lim-a 4.00

ANNE RICE'S INTERVIEW WITH THE VAMPIRE
Innovation Books: 1991 - No. 12, Jan, 1994 ($2.50, limited series)

1-Adapts novel; Moeller-a 1 3 4 6 8 10
2-12-Continues adaptation 4.00

ANNE RICE'S THE MASTER OF RAMPLING GATE
Innovation Books: 1991 ($6.95, one-shot)

1-Bolton painted-c; Colleen Doran painted-a 7.00

ANNE RICE'S THE MUMMY OR RAMSES THE DAMNED
Millennium Publications: Oct, 1990 - No. 12, Feb, 1992 ($2.50, limited series)

1-Adapts novel; Mooney-p in all 1 3 4 6 8 10
2-12-Continues adaptation 4.00

ANNE RICE'S THE WITCHING HOUR
Millennium Publ./Comico: 1992 - No. 13, Jan, 1993 ($2.50, limited series)

1-13 3.00

ANNETTE (Disney, TV)
Dell Publishing Co.: No. 905, May, 1958; No. 1100, May, 1960
(Mickey Mouse Club)

Four Color 905-Annette Funicello photo-c 23 46 69 156 348 540
Four Color 1100-...'s Life Story (Movie); A. Funicello photo-c
18 36 54 122 271 420

ANNEX (See Amazing Spider-Man Annual #27 for 1st app.)
Marvel Comics: Aug, 1994 - No. 4, Nov, 1994 ($1.75)

1-4: 1,4-Spider-Man app. 3.00

ANNIE
Marvel Comics Group: Oct, 1982 - No. 2, Nov, 1982 (60¢)

1,2-Movie adaptation 4.00
Treasury Edition ($2.50, tabloid size) 3 6 9 17 26 35

ANNIE OAKLEY (See Tessie The Typist #19, Two-Gun Kid & Wild Western)
Marvel/Atlas Comics(MPI No. 1-4/CDS No. 5 on): Spring, 1948 - No. 4, 11/48; No. 5, 6/55 - No. 11, 6/56

1 (1st Series, 1948)-Hedy Devine app. 74 148 222 470 810 1150
2 (7/48, 52 pgs.)-Kurtzman-a, "Hey Look", 1 pg; Intro. Lana; Hedy Devine
app; Captain Tootsie by Beck 39 78 117 240 395 550
3,4 32 64 96 192 314 435
5 (2nd Series, 1955)-Reinman-a; Maneely-c 22 44 66 132 216 300
6-9: 6,8-Woodbridge-a. 9-Williamson-a (4 pgs.) 16 32 48 94 147 200
10,11: 11-Severin-c 16 32 48 94 147 200

ANNIE OAKLEY AND TAGG (TV)
Dell Publishing Co./Gold Key: 1953 - No. 18, Jan-Mar, 1959; July, 1965 (Gail Davis photo-c #3 on)

Four Color 438 (#1) 13 26 39 89 195 300
Four Color 481,575 (#2,3) 9 18 27 59 117 175
4(7-9/55)-10 7 14 21 46 86 125
11-18(1-3/59) 6 12 18 38 69 100
1(7/65-Gold Key)-Photo-c (c-r/#6) 4 8 12 27 44 60
NOTE: *Manning a-13. Photo back c-4, 9, 11.*

ANNIHILATION
Marvel Comics: May, 2006 - No. 6, Mar, 2007 ($3.99/$2.99, limited x-over series)

Prologue (5/06, $3.99, one-shot) Nova, Thanos and Silver Surfer app. 4.00
1-6: 1-(10/06) Giffen-s/DiVito-a; Annihilus app. 3.00
...: Heralds of Galactus 1,2 (4/07-5/07, $3.99) 2-Silver Surfer app. 4.00
...: Nova 1-4 (6/06-9/06, $2.99) Abnett & Lanning-s/Walker-a/Dell'Otto-c. 2,3-Quasar app. 3.00
...: Ronan 1-4 (6/06-9/06, $2.99) Furman-s/Lucas-a/Dell'Otto-c 3.00
... Saga (2007, $1.99) re-cap of the series; DiVito-c 3.00
...: Silver Surfer 1-4 (6/06-9/06, $2.99) Giffen-s/Arlem-a/Dell'Otto-c 3.00
...: Super-Skrull 1-4 (6/06-9/06, $2.99) Grillo-Marxuach-s/Titus-a/Dell'Otto-c 3.00
...: The Nova Corps Files (2006, $3.99) profile pages of characters and alien races 4.00
Annihilation Book 1 HC (2007, $29.99, dustjacket) r/Drax the Destroyer #1-4, Annihilation Prologue and Annihilation: Nova #1-4; sketch and layout pages 30.00
Annihilation Book 1 SC (2007, $24.99) same content as HC 25.00
Annihilation Book 2 HC (2007, $29.99, dustjacket) r/Annihilation: Silver Surfer #1-4, ...: Super Skrull #1-4 and ...: Ronan #1-4; sketch and layout pages 30.00
Annihilation Book 2 SC (2007, $24.99) same content as HC 25.00
Annihilation Book 3 HC (2007, $29.99, dustjacket) r/Annihilation #1-6, Annihilation: Heralds of Galactus #1,2 and Annihilation: Nova Corps Files; sketch pages 30.00
Annihilation Book 3 SC (2007, $24.99) same content as HC 25.00

ANNIHILATION: CONQUEST (Also see Nova 2007 series)
Marvel Comics: Jan, 2008 - No. 6, Jun, 2008 ($3.99/$2.99, limited x-over series)

Prologue (8/07, $3.99, one-shot) the new Quasar, Moondragon app.; Perkins-a 5.00
1-5-Raney-a; Ultron app. 3-Moondragon dies 5.00
6-($3.99) Guardians of the Galaxy team forms 3 6 9 17 26 35
... - Quasar 1-4 (9/07-No. 4, 12/07, $2.99) Gage-s/Lilly-a. 1-Super-Adaptoid app. 3.00
... - Starlord 1-4 (9/07-No. 4, 12/07, $2.99) Giffen-s/Green-a 6.00
... - Wraith 1-4 (9/07-No. 4, 12/07, $2.99) Hotz-a/Grillo-Marxuach-s 3.00
Annihilation: Conquest Book 1 HC (2008, $29.99, dustjacket) r/Prologue; ...Quasar #1-4, ...Star-Lord #1-4; Annihilation Saga; design pages 30.00

ANNIHILATION – SCOURGE
Marvel Comics: Jan, 2020 - Feb, 2020 ($4.99, limited series)

Alpha (1/20, $4.99) Annihilus, Blastaar, Nova, and The Sentry app. 5.00
Omega 1 (2/20, $4.99) Conclusion of series; Lockjaw, Beta Ray Bill, Fantastic Four app. 5.00
...: Beta Ray Bill 1 (2/20, $4.99) Lockjaw and The Sentry app. 5.00
...: Fantastic Four 1 (2/20, $4.99) Gage-s/Olortegui-a 5.00
...: Nova 1 (2/20, $4.99) Rosenberg-s/Roberson-a; Richard Rider app. 5.00
...: Silver Surfer 1 (2/20, $4.99) Abnett-s/Davidson-a; Surfer merges with Bob Reynolds 5.00

ANNIHILATOR
Legendary Comics: Sept, 2014 - No. 6, Jun, 2015 ($3.99)

1-6-Grant Morrison-s/Frazer Irving-a/c 4.00

ANNIHILATORS
Marvel Comics: May, 2011 - No. 4, Aug, 2011 ($4.99, limited series)

1-4: Quasar, Silver Surfer, Beta-Ray Bill, Ronan, Gladiator app.; Huat-a 5.00

ANNIHILATORS: EARTHFALL
Marvel Comics: Nov, 2011 - No. 4, Feb, 2012 ($3.99, limited series)

1-4-Avengers app.; Abnett & Lanning-s/Huat-a/Christopher-c 4.00

ANNO DRACULA: 1895 SEVEN DAYS IN MAYHEM (Based on the Kim Newman novels)
Titan Comics: Apr, 2017 - No. 5, Sept, 2017 ($3.99, limited series)

1-5-Kim Newman-s/Paul McCaffrey-a; multiple covers on each 4.00

ANOTHER WORLD (See Strange Stories From...)

ANSWER!, THE
Dark Horse Comics: Jan, 2013 - No. 4 ($3.99, limited series)

1-3-Dennis Hopeless-s/Mike Norton-a 4.00

ANT
Image Comics: Aug, 2005 - No. 11 ($2.99)

1-11: 1-Mario Gulley-s/a. 2-Savage Dragon & Spawn app. 3-Spawn-c/app. 3.00
Vol. 1: Reality Bites TPB (2006, $12.99) r/#1-4; sketch and concept art 13.00

ANTHEM (Based on the Electronic Arts videogame)
Dark Horse Comics: Feb, 2019 - No. 3, May, 2019 ($3.99, limited series)

1-3-Freed-s/Francisco-a 4.00

ANTHRO (See Showcase #74)
National Periodical Publications: July-Aug, 1968 - No. 6, July-Aug, 1969

1-(7-8/68)-Howie Post-a in all 5 10 15 33 57 80
2-5: 5-Last 12¢ issue 3 6 9 21 33 45
6-Wood-c/a (inks) 4 8 12 25 40 55

ANTI-HITLER COMICS
New England Comics Press: Summer, 1992 ($2.75, B&W, one-shot)

1-Reprints Hitler as Devil stories from wartime comics 1 2 3 5 6 8

ANT-MAN (See Irredeemable Ant-Man, The)

ANT-MAN (Also see Astonishing Ant-Man)

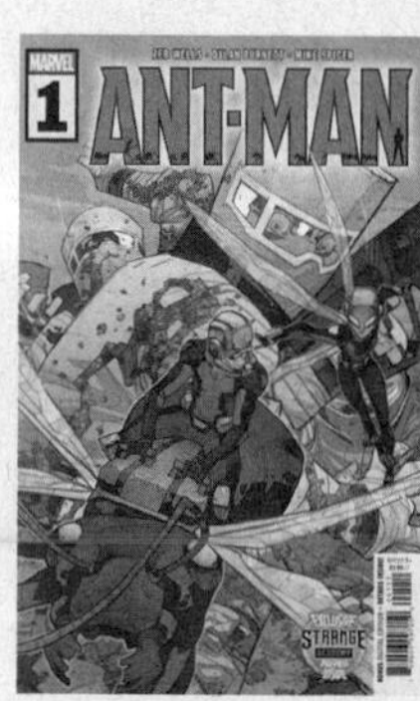

Ant-Man (2020 series) #1 © MAR

A-1 Comics #49 © ME

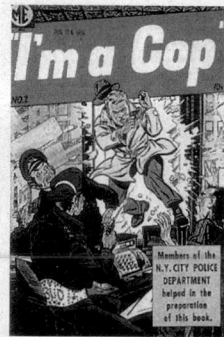

A-1 Comics #126 © ME

	GD 2.0	VG 4.0	FN 6.0	VF 8.0	VF/NM 9.0	NM- 9.2

Marvel Comics: Mar, 2015 - No. 5, Jul, 2015 ($3.99)

1-($4.99) Scott Lang as Ant-Man; Spencer-s/Rosanas-a; main-c by Brooks 5.00
2-5-($3.99) 2,3-Taskmaster app. 4-Darren Cross returns 4.00
Annual 1 (9/15, $4.99) Giant-Man & Egghead app.; intro. Raz Malhotra 5.00
...: Larger Than Life 1 (8/15, $3.99) movie Hank Pym story; r/Tales to Astonish #27 & #35 4.00
...: Last Days 1 (10/15, $3.99) Secret Wars tie-in; Spencer-s; Miss Patriot app. 4.00

ANT-MAN
Marvel Comics: Apr, 2020 - No. 5, Oct, 2020 ($3.99)

1-5-Wells-s/Burnett-a; Scott Lang & Stinger (Cassie). 3-Spider-Man & Black Cat app. 4.00

ANT-MAN & THE WASP
Marvel Comics: Aug, 2018 - No. 5, Nov, 2018 ($3.99, limited series)

1-5-Waid-s/Garrón-a; Scott Lang & Nadia Van Dyne 4.00
...: Living Legends 1 (8/18, $3.99) Macchio-s/Di Vito-a; Scott Lang & Janet Van Dyne 4.00

ANT-MAN & WASP
Marvel Comics: Jan, 2011 - No. 3, Mar, 2011 ($3.99, limited series)

1-3-Tim Seeley-s/a; Espin-c; Tigra app. 5.00

ANT-MAN'S BIG CHRISTMAS
Marvel Comics: Feb, 2000 ($5.95, square-bound, one-shot)

1-Bob Gale-s/Phil Winslade-a; Avengers app. 6.00

ANT-MAN: SEASON ONE
Marvel Comics: 2012 ($24.99, hardcover graphic novel)

HC - Origin story; DeFalco-s/Domingues-a/Tedesco painted-c 25.00

ANTONY AND CLEOPATRA (See Ideal, a Classical Comic)

ANYTHING GOES
Fantagraphics Books: Oct, 1986 - No. 6, 1987 ($2.00, #1-5 color & B&W/#6 B&W, lim. series)

1-6: 1-Flaming Carrot app. (1st in color?); G. Kane-c. 2-6: 2-Miller-c(p); Alan Moore scripts; Kirby-a; early Sam Kieth-a (2 pgs.). 3-Capt. Jack, Cerebus app.; Cerebus-c by N. Adams. 4-Perez-c. 5-3rd color Teenage Mutant Ninja Turtles app. 4.00

A-1
Marvel Comics (Epic Comics): 1992 - No. 4, 1993 ($5.95, limited series, mature)

1-4: 1-Fabry-c/a, Russell-a, S. Hampton-a. 3-Bisley-c; Kent Williams-a. 4-McKean-a; Dorman-s/a 1 2 3 4 5 7

A-1 COMICS (A-1 appears on covers No. 1-17 only)(See individual title listings for #11-139) (1st two issues not numbered.)
Life's Romances Publ.-No. 1/Compix/Magazine Ent.: 1944 - No. 139, Sept-Oct, 1955 (No #2)

nn-(1944) (See Kerry Drake Detective Cases)

	GD 2.0	VG 4.0	FN 6.0	VF 8.0	VF/NM 9.0	NM- 9.2
1-Dotty Dripple (1 pg.), Mr. Ex, Bush Berry, Rocky, Lew Loyal (20 pgs.)	21	42	63	126	206	285
3-8,10: Texas Slim & Dirty Dalton, The Corsair, Teddy Rich, Dotty Dripple, Inca Dinca, Tommy Tinker, Little Mexico & Tugboat Tim, The Masquerader & others. 7-Corsair-c/s. 8-Intro Rodeo Ryan	13	26	39	72	101	130
9-All Texas Slim	13	26	39	74	105	135

(See Individual Alphabetical listings for prices)

11-Teena; Ogden Whitney-c
12,15-Teena
13-Guns of Fact & Fiction (1948). Used in **SOTI**, pg. 19; Ingels & Johnny Craig-a
14-Tim Holt Western Adventures #1
16-Vacation Comics; The Pixies, Tom Tom, Flying Fredd, & Koko & Kola
17-Tim Holt #2; photo-c; last issue to carry A-1 on cover (9-10/48)
18,20-Jimmy Durante; photo covers on both
19-Tim Holt #3; photo-c
21-Joan of Arc (1949)-Movie adaptation; Ingrid Bergman photo-covers & interior photos; Whitney-a
22-Dick Powell (1949)-Photo-c
23-Cowboys and Indians #6; Doc Holiday-c/story
24-Trail Colt #1-Frazetta-r in-Manhunt #13; Ingels-c; L. B. Cole-a
25-Fibber McGee & Molly (1949) (Radio)
26-Trail Colt #2-Ingels-c
27-Ghost Rider #1(1950)-Origin
28-Christmas-(Koko & Kola #6) ("50)
29-Ghost Rider #2-Frazetta-c (1950)
30-Jet Powers #1-Powell-a
31-Ghost Rider #3-Frazetta-c & origin ('51)
32-Jet Powers #2
33-Muggsy Mouse #1('51)
34-Ghost Rider #4-Frazetta-c (1951)
35-Jet Powers #3-Williamson/Evans-a
36-Muggsy Mouse #2; Racist-c
37-Ghost Rider #5-Frazetta-c (1951)
38-Jet Powers #4-Williamson/Wood-a
39-Muggsy Mouse #3
40-Dogface Dooley #1('51)
41-Cowboys 'N' Indians #7 (1951)
42-Best of the West #1-Powell-a
43-Dogface Dooley #2
44-Ghost Rider #6
45-American Air Forces #5-Powell-c/a
46-Best of the West #2
47-Thun'da, King of the Congo #1-Frazetta-c/a('52)
48-Cowboys 'N' Indians #8
49-Dogface Dooley #3
50-Danger Is Their Business #11 ('52)-Powell-a
51-Ghost Rider #7 ('52)
52-Best of the West #3
53-Dogface Dooley #4
54-American Air Forces #6(8/52)-Powell-a
55-U.S. Marines #5-Powell-a
56-Thun'da #2-Powell-c/a
57-Ghost Rider #8
58-American Air Forces #7-Powell-a
59-Best of the West #4
60-The U.S. Marines #6-Powell-a
61-Space Ace #5('53)-Guardineer-a
62-Starr Flagg, Undercover Girl #5 (#1) reprinted from A-1 #24
63-Manhunt #13-Frazetta
64-Dogface Dooley #5
65-American Air Forces #8-Powell-a
66-Best of the West #5
67-American Air Forces #9-Powell-a
68-U.S. Marines #7-Powell-a
69-Ghost Rider #9(10/52)
70-Best of the West #6
71-Ghost Rider #10(12/52)-Vs. Frankenstein
72-U.S. Marines #8-Powell-a(3)
73-Thun'da #3-Powell-c/a
74-American Air Forces #10-Powell-a
75-Ghost Rider #11(3/52)
76-Best of the West #7
77-Manhunt #14
78-Thun'da #4-Powell-c/a
79-American Air Forces #11-Powell-a
80-Ghost Rider #12(6/52)-One-eyed Devil-c
81-Best of the West #8
82-Cave Girl #11(1953)-Powell-c/a; origin (#1)
83-Thun'da #5-Powell-c/a
84-Ghost Rider #13(7-8/53)
85-Best of the West #9
86-Thun'da #6-Powell-c/a
87-Best of the West #10(9-10/53)
88-Bobby Benson's B-Bar-B Riders #20
89-Home Run #3-Powell-a; Stan Musial photo-c
90-Red Hawk #11(1953)-Powell-c/a
91-American Air Forces #12-Powell-a
92-Dream Book of Romance #5-Photo-c; Guardineer-a
93-Great Western #8('54)-Origin The Ghost Rider; Powell-a
94-White Indian #11-Frazetta-a(r); Powell-c
95-Muggsy Mouse #4
96-Cave Girl #12, with Thun'da; Powell-c/a
97-Best of the West #11
98-Undercover Girl #6-Powell-c
99-Muggsy Mouse #5
100-Badmen of the West #1-Meskin-a(?)
101-White Indian #12-Frazetta-a(r)
101-Dream Book of Romance #6 (4-6/54); Marlon Brando photo-c; Powell, Bolle, Guardineer-a
103-Best of the West #12-Powell-a
104-White Indian #13-Frazetta-a(r) ('54)
105-Great Western #9-Ghost Rider app.; Powell-a, 6 pgs.; Bolle-c
106-Dream Book of Love #1 (6-7/54) -Powell, Bolle-a; Montgomery Clift, Donna Reed photo-c
107-Hot Dog #1
108-Red Fox #15 (1954)-L.B. Cole-c/a; Powell-a
109-Dream Book of Romance #7 (7-8/54). Powell-a; movie photo-c
110-Dream Book of Romance #8 (10/54)-Movie photo-c
111-I'm a Cop #1 ('54); drug mention story; Powell-a
112-Ghost Rider #14 ('54)
113-Great Western #10; Powell-a
114-Dream Book of Love #2- Guardineer, Bolle-a; Piper Laurie, Victor Mature photo-c
115-Hot Dog #3
116-Cave Girl #13-Powell-c/a
117-White Indian #14
118-Undercover Girl #7-Powell-c
119-Straight Arrow's Fury #1 (origin); Fred Meagher-c/a
120-Badmen of the West #2
121-Mysteries of Scotland Yard #1; reprinted from Manhunt (5 stories)
122-Black Phantom #1 (11/54)
123-Dream Book of Love #3 (10-11/54)-Movie photo-c
124-Dream Book of Romance #8 (10-11/54)
125-Cave Girl #14-Powell-c/a
126-I'm a Cop #2-Powell-a
127-Great Western #11('54)-Powell-a
128-I'm a Cop #3-Powell-a
129-The Avenger #1('55)-Powell-c
130-Strongman #1-Powell-a (2-3/55)
131-The Avenger #2('55)-Powell-c/a
132-Strongman #2
133-The Avenger #3-Powell-c/a
134-Strongman #3
135-White Indian #15
136-Hot Dog #4
137-Africa #1-Powell-c/a(4)
138-The Avenger #4-Powell-c/a
139-Strongman #4-Powell-a

NOTE: ***Bolle** a-110. Photo-c-17-22, 89, 92, 101, 106, 109, 110, 114, 123, 124.*

APACHE
Fiction House Magazines: 1951

	GD 2.0	VG 4.0	FN 6.0	VF 8.0	VF/NM 9.0	NM- 9.2
1	23	46	69	138	227	315
I.W. Reprint No. 1-r/#1 above	3	6	9	17	26	35

APACHE KID (Formerly Reno Browne; Western Gunfighters #20 on) (Also see Two-Gun Western & Wild Western)
Marvel/Atlas Comics(MPC No. 53-10/CPS No. 11 on): No. 53, 12/50 - No. 10, 1/52; No. 11, 12/54 - No. 19, 4/56

	GD 2.0	VG 4.0	FN 6.0	VF 8.0	VF/NM 9.0	NM- 9.2
53(#1)-Apache Kid & his horse Nightwind (origin), Red Hawkins by Syd Shores begins	41	82	123	256	428	600
2(2/51)	19	38	57	111	176	240
3-5	14	28	42	82	121	160
6-10 (1951-52): 7-Russ Heath-a	13	26	39	72	101	130
11-19 (1954-56)	11	22	33	60	83	105

NOTE: ***Heath** a-7. c-11, 13. **Maneely** a-53; c-53(#1), 12, 14-16. **Powell** a-14. **Severin** c-17.*

APACHE MASSACRE (See Chief Victorio's...)

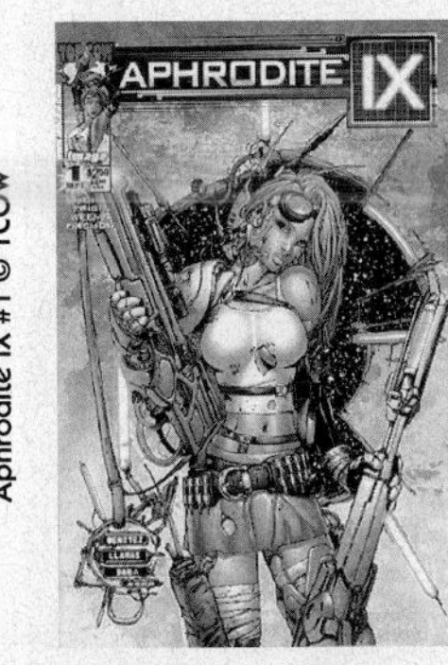

Aphrodite IX #1 © TCOW

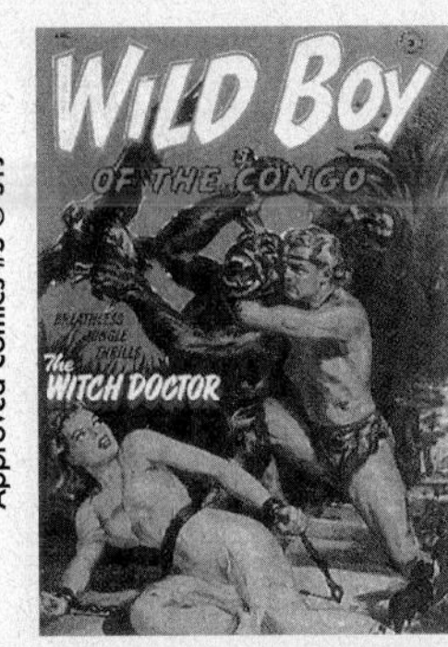

Approved Comics #3 © STJ

Aquaman #3 © DC

APACHE SKIES
Marvel Comics: Sept, 2002 - No. 4, Dec, 2002 ($2.99, limited series)

	GD 2.0	VG 4.0	FN 6.0	VF 8.0	VF/NM 9.0	NM- 9.2
1-4-Apache Kid app.; Ostrander-s/Manco-c/a						3.00
TPB (2003, $12.99) r/#1-4						13.00

APACHE TRAIL
Steinway/America's Best: Sept, 1957 - No. 4, June, 1958

	GD 2.0	VG 4.0	FN 6.0	VF 8.0	VF/NM 9.0	NM- 9.2
1	13	26	39	72	101	130
2-4: 2-Tuska-a	8	16	24	42	54	65

APE (Magazine)
Dell Publishing Co.: 1961 (52 pgs., B&W)

	GD 2.0	VG 4.0	FN 6.0	VF 8.0	VF/NM 9.0	NM- 9.2
1-Comics and humor	5	10	15	30	50	70

APHRODITE IX
Image Comics (Top Cow): Sept, 2000 - No. 4, Mar, 2002 ($2.50)

	GD 2.0	VG 4.0	FN 6.0	VF 8.0	VF/NM 9.0	NM- 9.2
1-3: 1-Four covers by Finch, Turner, Silvestri, Benitez						4.00
1-Tower Record Ed.; Finch-c						3.00
1-DF Chrome ($14.99)						15.00
4-($4.95) Double-sized issue; Finch-c						5.00
Convention Preview						10.00
...: Time Out of Mind TPB (6/04, $14.99) r/#1-4, & #0; cover gallery						15.00
Wizard #0 (4/00, bagged w/Tomb Raider magazine) Preview & sketchbook						5.00
#0-(6/01, $2.95) r/Wizard #0 with cover gallery						3.00

APHRODITE IX (Volume 2)
Image Comics (Top Cow): May, 2013 - No. 11, Jun, 2014 ($2.99/$3.99)

	GD 2.0	VG 4.0	FN 6.0	VF 8.0	VF/NM 9.0	NM- 9.2
1-Free Comic Book Day giveaway; Hawkins-s/Sejic-a						3.00
2-10-($2.99) Hawkins-s/Sejic-a						3.00
11-($3.99) Leads into Aphrodite IX Cyber Force #1						4.00
...: Ares #1 (9/18, $3.99) Glaser-s/Knaepen-a; Marsh-s/Renna-a						4.00
... Cyber Force #1 (7/14, $5.99) Hawkins-s/Sejic-a; leads into IXth Generation #1						6.00
... Hidden Files 1 (1/14, $2.99) Character profiles; Sejic-a						3.00

APHRODITE V
Image Comics (Top Cow): Jul, 2018 - No. 4, Oct, 2018 ($3.99)

	GD 2.0	VG 4.0	FN 6.0	VF 8.0	VF/NM 9.0	NM- 9.2
1-4-Bryan Hill-s/Jeff Spokes-a. 1-Origin re-told						4.00

A+X (Avengers Plus X-Men)
Marvel Comics: Dec, 2012 - No. 18, May, 2014 ($3.99)

	GD 2.0	VG 4.0	FN 6.0	VF 8.0	VF/NM 9.0	NM- 9.2
1-18: 1-Hulk & Wolverine team-up; Keown-c. 2-Black Widow/Rogue; Bachalo-c/a. 14-Superior Spider-Man app.						4.00
1-Variant baby-c by Skottie Young						5.00

APOCALYPSE NERD
Dark Horse Comics: January, 2005 - No. 6, Oct, 2007 ($2.99, B&W)

	GD 2.0	VG 4.0	FN 6.0	VF 8.0	VF/NM 9.0	NM- 9.2
1-6-Peter Bagge-s/a						3.00

APOLLO IX (See Aphrodite IX)
Image Comics (Top Cow): Aug, 2015 ($3.99, one-shot)

	GD 2.0	VG 4.0	FN 6.0	VF 8.0	VF/NM 9.0	NM- 9.2
1-Ashley Robinson-s/Fernando Argosino-a; 2 covers						4.00

APPARITION
Caliber Comics: 1995 ($3.95, 52 pgs., B&W)

	GD 2.0	VG 4.0	FN 6.0	VF 8.0	VF/NM 9.0	NM- 9.2
1 ($3.95)						4.00
V2#1-6 ($2.95)						3.00
Visitations						4.00

APPLESEED
Eclipse Comics: Sept, 1988 - Book 4, Vol. 4, Aug, 1991 ($2.50/$2.75/$3.50, 52/68 pgs, B&W)

	GD 2.0	VG 4.0	FN 6.0	VF 8.0	VF/NM 9.0	NM- 9.2
Book One, Vol. 1-5: 5-(1/89), Book Two, Vol. 1(2/89) -5(7/89): Art Adams-c, Book Three, Vol. 1(8/89) -4 ($2.75), Book Three, Vol. 5 ($3.50), Book Four, Vol. 1 (1/91) - 4 (8/91) ($3.50, 68 pgs.)	1	2	3	5	6	8

APPLESEED DATABOOK
Dark Horse Comics: Apr, 1994 - No. 2, May, 1994 ($3.50, B&W, limited series)

	GD 2.0	VG 4.0	FN 6.0	VF 8.0	VF/NM 9.0	NM- 9.2
1,2: 1-Flip book format						4.00

APPROVED COMICS (Also see Blue Ribbon Comics)
St. John Publishing Co. (Most have no c-price): March, 1954 - No. 12, Aug, 1954 (Painted-c on #1-5,7,8,10)

	GD 2.0	VG 4.0	FN 6.0	VF 8.0	VF/NM 9.0	NM- 9.2
1-The Hawk #5-r	11	22	33	62	86	110
2-Invisible Boy (3/54)-Origin; Saunders-c	17	34	51	98	154	210
3-Wild Boy of the Congo #11-r (4/54)	11	22	33	62	86	110
4,5: 4-Kid Cowboy-r. 5-Fly Boy-r	11	22	33	62	86	110
6-Daring Adv.-r (5/54); Krigstein-a(2); Baker-c	47	94	141	296	498	700
7-The Hawk #6-r	11	22	33	62	86	110
8-Crime on the Run (6/54); Powell-a; Saunders-c	11	22	33	62	86	110
9-Western Bandit Trails #3-r, with new-c; Baker-c/a	30	60	90	177	289	400
10-Dinky Duck (Terrytoons)	8	16	24	40	50	60
11-Fightin' Marines #3-r (8/54); Canteen Kate app; Baker-c/a	37	74	111	222	361	500
12-Northwest Mounties #4-r(8/54); new Baker-c	34	68	102	199	325	450

AQUAMAN (See Adventure Comics #260, Brave & the Bold, DC Comics Presents #5, DC Special #28, DC Special Series #1, DC Super Stars #7, Detective Comics, JLA, Justice League of America, More Fun #73, Showcase #30-33, Super DC Giant, Super Friends, and World's Finest Comics)

AQUAMAN (1st Series)
National Periodical Publications/DC Comics: Jan-Feb, 1962 - No. 56, Mar-Apr, 1971; No. 57, Aug-Sept, 1977 - No. 63, Aug-Sept, 1978

	GD 2.0	VG 4.0	FN 6.0	VF 8.0	VF/NM 9.0	NM- 9.2
1-(1-2/62)-Intro. Quisp	207	414	621	1708	3854	6000
2	36	72	108	259	580	900
3-5	21	42	63	147	324	500
6-10	14	28	42	96	211	325
11-1st app. Mera	93	186	279	744	1672	2600
12-17,19,20	11	22	33	76	163	250
18-Aquaman weds Mera; JLA cameo	16	32	48	112	249	385
21-28,30-32: 23-Birth of Aquababy. 26-Huntress app.(3-4/66). 30-Batman & Superman-c & cameo	8	16	24	52	99	145
29-1st app. Ocean Master, Aquaman's step-brother	40	80	120	296	673	1050
33-1st app. Aqua-Girl (see Adventure #266)	15	30	45	103	227	350
34,36-40: 40-Jim Aparo's 1st DC work (8/68)	6	12	18	42	79	115
35-1st app. Black Manta	63	126	189	504	1127	1750
41,43-46,47,49: 45-Last 12¢-c	6	12	18	37	66	95
42-Black Manta-c	12	24	36	83	182	280
48-Origin reprinted	6	12	18	41	76	110
50-52-Deadman by Neal Adams	8	16	24	51	96	140
53-56('71): 56-1st app. Crusader; last 15¢-c	3	6	9	21	33	45
57-('77) Black Manta-c	3	6	9	16	23	30
58-63: 58-Origin retold	2	4	6	9	12	15
...: Death of a Prince TPB (2011, $29.99) r/#58-63 and Adventure #435-437,441-455						30.00

NOTE: ***Aparo** a-40-45, 46p, 47-59; c-58-63. **Nick Cardy** c-1-40. **Newton** a-60-63.*

AQUAMAN (1st limited series)
DC Comics: Feb, 1986 - No. 4, May, 1986 (75¢, limited series)

	GD 2.0	VG 4.0	FN 6.0	VF 8.0	VF/NM 9.0	NM- 9.2
1-New costume; 1st app. Nuada of Thierna Na Oge	2	4	6	8	10	12
2-4: 3-Retelling of Aquaman & Ocean Master's origins.						5.00
Special 1 (1988, $1.50, 52 pgs.)						4.00

NOTE: ***Craig Hamilton** c/a-1-4p. **Russell** c-2-4i.*

AQUAMAN (2nd limited series)
DC Comics: June, 1989 - No. 5, Oct, 1989 ($1.00, limited series)

	GD 2.0	VG 4.0	FN 6.0	VF 8.0	VF/NM 9.0	NM- 9.2
1-Giffen plots/breakdowns; Swan-a(p) in all						6.00
2-5						4.00
Special 1 (Legend of..., $2.00, 1989, 52 pgs.)-Giffen plots/breakdowns; Swan-a(p)						4.00

AQUAMAN (2nd Series)
DC Comics: Dec, 1991 - No. 13, Dec, 1992 ($1.00/$1.25)

	GD 2.0	VG 4.0	FN 6.0	VF 8.0	VF/NM 9.0	NM- 9.2
1-5						3.00
6-13: 6-Begin $1.25-c. 9-Sea Devils app.						3.00

AQUAMAN (3rd Series)(Also see Atlantis Chronicles)
DC Comics: Aug, 1994 - No. 75, Jan, 2001 ($1.50/$1.75/$1.95/$1.99/$2.50)

	GD 2.0	VG 4.0	FN 6.0	VF 8.0	VF/NM 9.0	NM- 9.2
1-(8/94)-Peter David scripts begin; reintro Dolphin						6.00
2-(9/94)-Aquaman loses hand						6.50
0-(10/94)-Aquaman replaces lost hand with hook.						6.50
3-8: 3-(11/94)-Superboy-c/app. 4-Lobo app. 6-Deep Six app.						3.50
9-69: 9-Begin $1.75-c. 10-Green Lantern app. 11-Reintro Mera. 15-Re-intro Kordax. 16-vs. JLA. 18-Reintro Ocean Master & Atlan (Aquaman's father). 19-Reintro Garth (Aqualad). 23-1st app. Deep Blue (Neptune Perkins & Tsunami's daughter). 23,24-Neptune Perkins, Nuada, Tsunami, Arion, Power Girl, & The Sea Devils app. 26-Final Night. 28-Martian Manhunter-c/app. 29-Black Manta-c/app. 32-Swamp Thing-c/app. 37-Genesis x-over. 41-Maxima-c/app. 43-Millennium Giants x-over; Superman-c/app. 44-G.A. Flash & Sentinel app. 50-Larsen-s begins. 53-Superman app. 60-Tempest marries Dolphin; Teen Titans app. 63-Kaluta covers begin. 66-JLA app.						3.00
70-75: 70-Begin $2.50-c. 71-73-Warlord-c/app. 75-Final issue						3.00
#1,000,000 (11/98) 853rd Century x-over						3.00
Annual 1 (1995, $3.50)-Year One story						4.00
Annual 2 (1996, $2.95)-Legends of the Dead Earth story						4.00
Annual 3 (1997, $3.95)-Pulp Heroes story						4.00
Annual 4,5 ('98, '99, $2.95)-4-Ghosts; Wrightson-c. 5-JLApe						4.00
...Secret Files 1 (12/98, $4.95) Origin-s and pin-ups						5.00

NOTE: ***Art Adams**-c, Annual 5. **Mignola** c-6. **Simonson** c-15.*

AQUAMAN (4th Series)(Titled Aquaman: Sword of Atlantis #40-on) (Also see JLA #69-75)
DC Comics: Feb, 2003 - No. 57, Dec, 2007 ($2.50/$2.99)

Aquaman (2016 series) #6 © DC

Araña The Heart of the Spider #12 © MAR

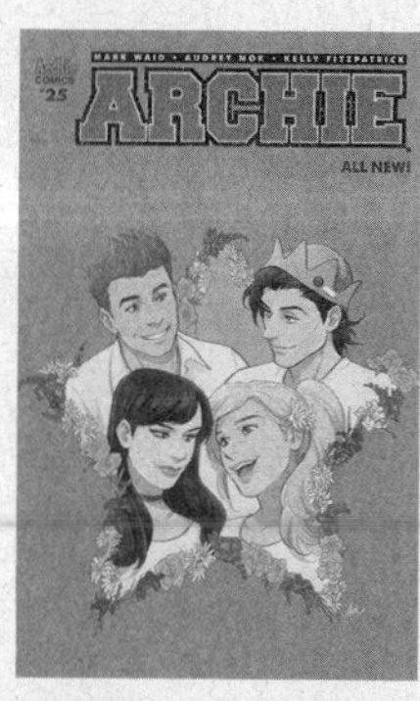
Archie #25 © ACP

	GD	VG	FN	VF	VF/NM	NM-
	2.0	4.0	6.0	8.0	9.0	9.2

1-Veitch-s/Guichet-a/Maleev-c 4.00
2-14: 2-Martian Manhunter app. 8-11-Black Manta app. 3.00
15-39: 15-San Diego flooded; Pfeifer-s/Davis-c begin. 23,24-Sea Devils app. 33-Mera returns. 39-Black Manta app. 3.00
40-Sword of Atlantis; One Year Later begins ($2.99-c) Guice-a ; two covers 4.00
41-49,51-57: 41-Two covers. 42-Sea Devils app. 44-Ocean Master app. 3.00
50-($3.99) Tempest app.; McManus-a 4.00
...Secret Files 2003 (5/03, $4.95) background on Aquaman's new powers; pin-ups 5.00
...: Once and Future TPB (2006, $12.99) r/#40-45 13.00
...: The Waterbearer TPB (2003, $12.95) r/#1-4, stories from Aquaman Secret Files and JLA/JSA Secret Files #1; JG Jones-c 13.00

AQUAMAN (DC New 52)
DC Comics: Nov, 2011 - No. 52, Jul, 2016 ($2.99/$3.99)

1-Geoff Johns-s/Ivan Reis-a/c 1 2 3 5 6 8
2-23,24,26-40: 7-13-Black Manta app. 14-17-Throne of Atlantis. 15,16-Justice League app. 24-Story of Atlan. 26-Pelletier-a. 31-Swamp Thing app. 37-Grodd app. 3.00
23.1, 23.2 (11/13, $2.99, regular covers) 3.00
23.1 (11/13, $3.99, 3-D cover) "Black Manta #1" on cover; Crime Syndicate app. 5.00
23.2 (11/13, $3.99, 3-D cover) "Ocean Master #1" on cover; Crime Syndicate app. 5.00
25-($3.99) "Death of a King" finale; last Johns-s 4.00
41-49,51,52: 41-($3.99-c begin) 4.00
50-($4.99) Booth-a 5.00
#0 (11/12, $2.99) Aquaman & Vulko's return to Atlantis; Johns-s/Reis-a/c 3.00
Annual 1 (12/13, $4.99) The Others app.; Pelletier-c/Ostrander-s 5.00
Annual 2 (9/14, $4.99) Wonder Woman app.; Parker-s/Guichet-a 5.00
...: Futures End 1 (11/14, $2.99, regular-c) Five years later; Jurgens-s 3.00
...: Futures End 1 (11/14, $3.99, 3-D cover) 4.00

AQUAMAN (DC Rebirth) (Also see Mera: Queen of Atlantis)
DC Comics: Aug, 2016 - No. 66, Feb, 2021 ($2.99/$3.99)

1-24: 1-Abnett-s/Walker-a; Black Manta app. 5,6-Superman app. 14,15-Black Manta app. 3.00
25-49-($3.99) 25-Sejic-a; leads into Justice League #24. 34-Kelley Jones-a. 39-X-over with Suicide Squad #45,46. 41,42-Drowned Earth. 43-DeConnick-s begin 4.00
50-($4.99) Black Manta returns; Wonder Woman app. 5.00
51-66: 51-54-Year of The Villain tie-ins; Black Manta app. 54-Acetate-c. 57-Princess Andy born. 57-61-Ocean Master app. 62,63-Black Manta app. 66-Endless Winter pt. 4 4.00
Annual 1 (1/18, $4.99) Fiumara-a; future Aquaman & Mera with son Tom 5.00
Annual 2 (12/19, $4.99) Year of the Villain tie-in; Aqualad app.; Ibáñez-a 5.00
.../ Jabberjaw Special 1 (7/18, $4.99) Abnett-s/Pelletier-a; back-up Capt. Caveman story 5.00
.../ Justice League: Drowned Earth Special 1 (1/19, $4.99) Leads into #43; Manapul-a 5.00
...: Rebirth (8/16, $2.99) Abnett-s/Eaton & Jiménez-a; Black Manta app. 3.00

AQUAMAN AND THE OTHERS (DC New 52)
DC Comics: Jun, 2014 - No. 11, May, 2015 ($2.99)

1-11: 1-Jurgens-s/Medina-a 3.00
...: Futures End 1 (11/14, $2.99, regular-c) Five years later; Cont'd from Aquaman: FE #1 3.00
...: Futures End 1 (11/14, $3.99, 3-D cover) 4.00

AQUAMAN GIANT
DC Comics: 2019 - No. 4, 2020 ($4.99, 100 pgs., squarebound, Mass Market & Direct Market editions exist for each issue, with different covers)

1-4-Two new stories and reprints in each. 1-Black Manta app. 2-Sea Devils app. 5.00

AQUAMAN: TIME & TIDE (3rd limited series) (Also see Atlantis Chronicles)
DC Comics: Dec, 1993 - No. 4, Mar, 1994 ($1.50, limited series)

1-4: Peter David scripts; origin retold. 3.00
Trade paperback ($9.95) 10.00

AQUANAUTS (TV)
Dell Publishing Co.: May - July, 1961

Four Color 1197-Photo-c 6 12 18 41 76 110

ARABIAN NIGHTS (See Cinema Comics Herald)

ARACHNOPHOBIA (Movie)
Hollywood Comics (Disney Comics): 1990 ($5.95, 68 pg. graphic novel)

nn-Adaptation of film; Spiegle-a 6.00
Comic edition ($2.95, 68 pgs.) 4.00

ARAK/SON OF THUNDER (See Warlord #48)
DC Comics: Sept, 1981 - No. 50, Nov, 1985

1,24,50: 1-1st app. Angelica, Princess of White Cathay. 24,50-(52 pgs.) 4.00
2-23,25-49: 3-Intro Valda. 12-Origin Valda. 20-Origin Angelica 3.00
Annual 1(10/84) 4.00

ARAÑA THE HEART OF THE SPIDER (See Amazing Fantasy (2004) #1-6)
Marvel Comics: March, 2005 - No. 12, Feb, 2006 ($2.99)

1-12: 1-Avery-s/Cruz-a. 4-Spider-Man-c/app. 3.00
Vol. 1: Heart of the Spider (2005, $7.99, digest) r/Amazing Fantasy (2004) #1-6 8.00
Vol. 2: In the Beginning (2005, $7.99, digest) r/#1-6 8.00
Vol. 3: Night of the Hunter (2006, $7.99, digest) r/#7-12 8.00

ARCADIA
BOOM! Studios: May, 2015 - No. 8, Feb, 2016 ($3.99)

1-8-Paknadel-s/Pfeiffer-a 4.00

ARCANA (Also see Books of Magic limited & ongoing series and Mister E)
DC Comics (Vertigo): 1994 ($3.95, 68 pgs., annual)

1-Bolton painted-c; Children's Crusade/Tim Hunter story 4.00

ARCANUM
Image Comics (Top Cow Productions): Apr, 1997 - No. 8, Feb, 1998 ($2.50)

1/2 Gold Edition 12.00
1-Brandon Peterson-s/a(p), 1-Variant-c, 4-American Ent. Ed. 3.50
2-8 3.00
3-Variant-c 4.00
...: Millennium's End TPB (2005, $16.99) r/#1-8 & #1/2; cover gallery and sketch pages 17.00

ARCHANGEL (See Uncanny X-Men, X-Factor & X-Men)
Marvel Comics: Feb, 1996 ($2.50, B&W, one-shot)

1-Milligan story 3.00

ARCHANGEL 8
AWA Studios: Mar, 2020 - No. 5, Sept, 2020 ($3.99, limited series)

1-5-Michael Moreci-s/C.P. Smith-a 4.00

ARCHARD'S AGENTS (See Ruse)
CrossGeneration Comics: Jan, 2003; Nov, 2003; Apr, 2004 ($2.95)

1-Dixon-s/Perkins-a 3.00
...: The Case of the Puzzled Pugilist (11/03) Dixon-s/Perkins-a 3.00
Vol. 3 - Deadly Dare (4/04) Dixon-s/McNiven-a; preview of Lady Death: The Wild Hunt 3.00

ARCHENEMIES
Dark Horse Comics: Apr, 2006 - No. 4, July, 2006 ($2.99, limited series)

1-4-Melbourne-s/Guichet-a 3.00

ARCHER & ARMSTRONG
Valiant: July (June inside), 1992 - No. 26, Oct, 1994 ($2.50)

0-(7/92)-B. Smith-c/a; Reese-i assists 1 2 3 5 6 8
0-(with Gold Valiant Logo) 6 12 18 37 66 95
1,2: 1-(8/92)-Origin & 1st app. Archer; Miller-c; B. Smith/Layton-a. 2-2nd app. Turok (c/story); Smith/Layton-a; Simonson-c 5.00
3-7: 3,4-Smith-c&a(p) & scripts 4.00
8-($4.50, 52 pgs.)-Combined with Eternal Warrior #8; B. Smith-c/a & scripts; 1st app. Ivar the Time Walker 5.00
9-26: 10-2nd app. Ivar. 10,11-B. Smith-c. 21,22-Shadowman app. 22-w/bound-in trading card. 25-Eternal Warrior app. 26-Flip book w/Eternal Warrior #26 3.00
...: First Impressions HC (2008, $24.95) recolored reprints #0-6; new "Formation of the Sect" story by Jim Shooter and Sal Velutto; Shooter commentary; new cover by Golden 25.00

ARCHER & ARMSTRONG
Valiant Entertainment: Aug, 2012 - No. 25, Oct, 2014 ($3.99)

1-24: 1-Van Lente-s/Henry-a; two covers; origin. 5-8-Eternal Warrior app. 4.00
1,4-8-Pullbox variants: 1-Clayton Henry. 4-Juan Doe. 7,8-Emanuela Lupacchino 4.00
1-Variant-c by David Aja 10.00
1-Variant-c by Neal Adams 28.00
25-($4.99) Van Lente-s/Henry-a; back-up short stories by various; cover gallery 5.00
#0-(5/13, $3.99) Van Lente-s/Henry-a 4.00
...Archer #0-(2/14, $3.99) Van Lente-s/Pere Pérez-a; childhood origin 4.00
...: The One Percent #1 (11/14, $3.99) Fawkes-s/Eisma-a/Juan Doe-c 4.00

ARCHIE (See Archie Comics) (Also see Afterlife With..., Christmas & Archie, Everything's..., Explorers of the Unknown, Jackpot, Life With..., Little..., Oxydol-Dreft, Pep, Riverdale High, Teenage Mutant Ninja Turtles Adventures & To Riverdale and Back Again)

ARCHIE
Archie Comic Publs.: Sept, 2015 - No. 32, Sept, 2018; No. 699, Nov, 2018 - Present ($3.99)

1-32-Mark Waid-s; multiple covers on all; back-up classic reprints. 1-3-Fiona Staples-a. 4-Annie Wu-a. 5-10-Veronica Fish-a. 13-Re-intro. Cheryl Blossom; back-up r/1st app. from B&V #320. 13-17-Eisma-a. 18-22-Pete Woods-a. 23-32-Audrey Mok-a 4.00
699-(11/18, $1.00) Recaps of events from #1-32; preview of #700; Sauvage-c 3.00
700-713: 700-704-($3.99) Spencer-s/Sauvage-a; Sabrina app. 705-709-"Archie and Sabrina" on cover. 710-713-"Archie and Katy Keene" on cover 4.00
... Collector's Edition (2/16, $9.99) r/#1-3 with creator intros and variant cover gallery 10.00
FCBD Edition (2016, giveaway) r/#1; Staples-c; back-up Jughead story 3.00

ARCHIE ALL CANADIAN DIGEST
Archie Publications: Aug, 1996 ($1.75, 96 pgs.)

Archie & Friends #99 © ACP

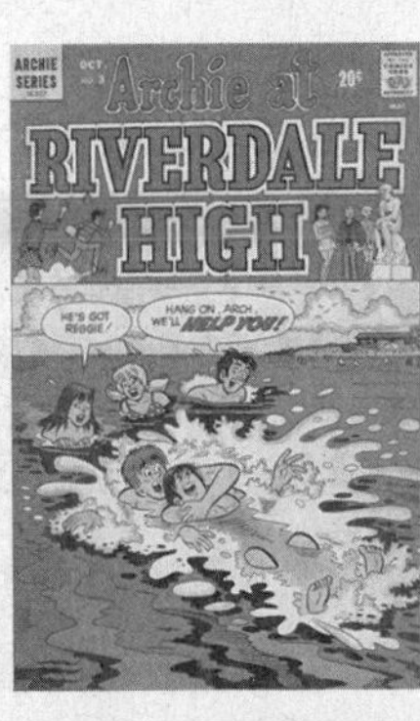

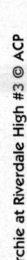

Archie at Riverdale High #3 © ACP

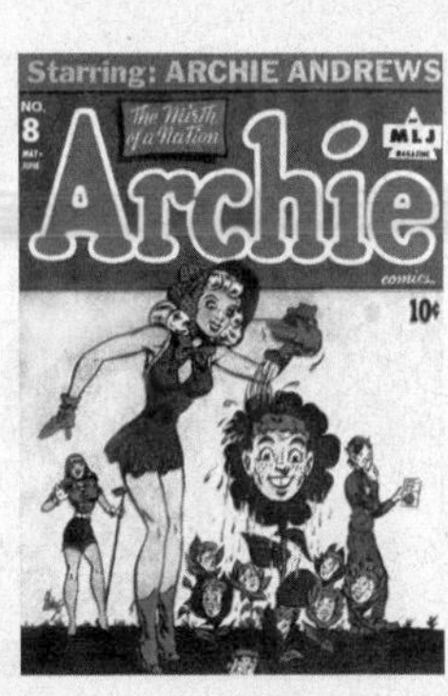

Archie Comics #8 © ACP

	GD 2.0	VG 4.0	FN 6.0	VF 8.0	VF/NM 9.0	NM- 9.2
1	1	2	3	5	6	8

ARCHIE AMERICANA SERIES, BEST OF THE FORTIES
Archie Publications: 1991, 2002 ($10.95, trade paperback)

	GD 2.0	VG 4.0	FN 6.0	VF 8.0	VF/NM 9.0	NM- 9.2
Vol. 1,2-r/early strips from 1940s 1-Intro. by Steven King. 2-Intro. by Paul Castiglia						12.00

ARCHIE AMERICANA SERIES, BEST OF THE FIFTIES
Archie Publications: 1991 ($8.95, trade paperback)

	GD 2.0	VG 4.0	FN 6.0	VF 8.0	VF/NM 9.0	NM- 9.2
Vol. 2-r/strips from 1950's						12.00
2nd printing (1998, $9.95)						12.00
Book 2 (2003, $10.95)						12.00

ARCHIE AMERICANA SERIES, BEST OF THE SIXTIES
Archie Publications: 1995 ($9.95, trade paperback)

	GD 2.0	VG 4.0	FN 6.0	VF 8.0	VF/NM 9.0	NM- 9.2
Vol. 3-r/strips from 1960s; intro. by Frankie Avalon						12.00

ARCHIE AMERICANA SERIES, BEST OF THE SEVENTIES
Archie Publications: 1997, 2008 ($9.95/$10.95, trade paperback)

	GD 2.0	VG 4.0	FN 6.0	VF 8.0	VF/NM 9.0	NM- 9.2
Vol. 4 (1997, $9.95)-r/strips from 1970s						12.00
Vol. 8 Book 2 (2008, $10.95)-r/other strips from 1970s						12.00

ARCHIE AMERICANA SERIES, BEST OF THE EIGHTIES
Archie Publications: 2001 ($10.95, trade paperback)

	GD 2.0	VG 4.0	FN 6.0	VF 8.0	VF/NM 9.0	NM- 9.2
Vol. 5-r/strips from 1980s; foreward by Steve Geppi						12.00

ARCHIE AMERICANA SERIES, BEST OF THE '90S
Archie Publications: 2008 ($11.95, trade paperback)

	GD 2.0	VG 4.0	FN 6.0	VF 8.0	VF/NM 9.0	NM- 9.2
Vol. 9-r/strips from 1990s; new Lindsey cover						12.00

ARCHIE AND BIG ETHEL
Spire Christian Comics (Fleming H. Revell Co.): 1982 (69¢)

	GD 2.0	VG 4.0	FN 6.0	VF 8.0	VF/NM 9.0	NM- 9.2
nn-(Low print run)	2	4	6	13	18	22

ARCHIE & FRIENDS
Archie Comics: Dec, 1992 - No. 159, Feb, 2012 ($1.25-$2.99)

	GD 2.0	VG 4.0	FN 6.0	VF 8.0	VF/NM 9.0	NM- 9.2
1						5.00
2,4,10-14,17,18,20-Sabrina app. 20-Archie's Band-c						4.00
3,5-9,16						3.00
15-Babewatch-s with Sabrina app.						6.00
19-Josie and the Pussycats app.; E.T. parody-c/s						5.00
21-46						3.00
47-All Josie and the Pussycats issue; movie and actress profiles/photos						4.00
48-142: 48-56,58,60,96-Josie and the Pussycats-c/s. 79-Cheryl Blossom returns. 100-The Veronicas-c/app. 101-Katy Keene begins. 129-Begin $2.50. 130,131-Josie and the Pussycats. 137-Cosmo, Super Duck, Pat the Brat and other old characters app.						3.00
143-159: 143-Begin $2.99-c. 145-Jersey Shore spoof. 146,147-Twilite. 154-Little Archie						3.00

ARCHIE & FRIENDS (Classic-style reprints)
Archie Publications: Apr, 2019 - Present ($2.99, quarterly)

	GD 2.0	VG 4.0	FN 6.0	VF 8.0	VF/NM 9.0	NM- 9.2
...: Music #1; ...: Beach Party #1 (#2), ...: Back to School #1 (#3), ...: Travel #1 (#4), ...: Winter Wonderland #1 (#5), ...: Geeks and Games #1 (#6), ...: Endless Summer #1 (#7), ...: Fall Festival #1 (#8), ...: Guide to Dating #1 (#9)						3.00

ARCHIE & FRIENDS DOUBLE DIGEST MAGAZINE
Archie Comics: Feb, 2011 - No. 33, Jan, 2014 ($3.99, digest-size)

	GD 2.0	VG 4.0	FN 6.0	VF 8.0	VF/NM 9.0	NM- 9.2
1-32: 1-Staton-a. 7-13-SuperTeens app.						4.00
33-($5.99, 320 pages) Double Double Digest						6.00

ARCHIE AND ME (See Archie Giant Series Mag. #578, 591, 603, 616, 626)
Archie Publications: Oct, 1964; No. 2, Aug, 1965 - No. 161, Feb, 1987

	GD 2.0	VG 4.0	FN 6.0	VF 8.0	VF/NM 9.0	NM- 9.2
1	19	38	57	133	297	460
2-(8/65)	10	20	30	64	132	200
3-5: 3-(12/65)	6	12	18	40	73	105
6-10: 6-(8/66)	5	10	15	30	50	70
11-20: 11-(4/68)	3	6	9	21	33	45
21(6/68)-26,28-30: 21-UFO story. 26-X-Mas-c	3	6	9	16	24	32
27-Groovyman & Knowman superhero-s; UFO-sty	3	6	9	19	30	40
31-42: 37-Japan Expo '70-c/s	3	6	9	14	19	24
43-48,50-63-(All Giants): 43-(8/71) Mummy-s. 44-Mermaid-s. 62-Elvis cameo-c. 63-(2/74)	3	6	9	15	22	28
49-(Giant) Josie & the Pussycats-c/app.	3	6	9	20	31	42
64-66,68-99-(Regular size): 85-Bicentennial-s. 98-Collectors Comics	2	4	6	8	10	12
67-Sabrina app.(8/74)	2	4	6	10	14	18
100-(4/78)	2	4	6	8	11	14
101-120: 107-UFO-s	1	2	3	5	6	8
121(8/80)-159: 134-Riverdale 2001						6.00
160,161: 160-Origin Mr. Weatherbee; Caveman Archie gang story. 161-Last issue	1	2	3	5	6	8

ARCHIE & ME COMICS DIGEST
Archie Comics: Dec, 2017 - Present ($6.99/$7.99, digest-size)

	GD 2.0	VG 4.0	FN 6.0	VF 8.0	VF/NM 9.0	NM- 9.2
1-20-Reprints include Archie Babies in early issues						7.00
21-23-($7.99)						8.00

ARCHIE AND MR. WEATHERBEE
Spire Christian Comics (Fleming H. Revell Co.): 1980 (59¢)

	GD 2.0	VG 4.0	FN 6.0	VF 8.0	VF/NM 9.0	NM- 9.2
nn - (Low print run)	3	6	9	14	19	24

ARCHIE...ARCHIE ANDREWS, WHERE ARE YOU? (...Comics Digest #9, 10; ...Comics Digest Mag. No. 11 on)
Archie Publications: Feb, 1977 - No. 114, May, 1998 (Digest size, 160-128 pgs., quarterly)

	GD 2.0	VG 4.0	FN 6.0	VF 8.0	VF/NM 9.0	NM- 9.2
1	3	6	9	17	26	35
2,3,5,7-9-N. Adams-a; 8-r-/origin The Fly by S&K. 9-Steel Sterling-r	2	4	6	10	14	18
4,6,10 ($1.00/$1.50)	2	4	6	8	11	14
11-20: 17-Katy Keene story	2	3	4	6	8	10
21-50,100	1	2	3	5	6	8
51-70						4.00
71-99,101-114: 113-Begin $1.95-c						3.00

ARCHIE AS PUREHEART THE POWERFUL (Also see Archie Giant Series #142, Jughead as Captain Hero, Life With Archie & Little Archie)
Archie Publications (Radio Comics): Sept, 1966 - No. 6, Nov, 1967

	GD 2.0	VG 4.0	FN 6.0	VF 8.0	VF/NM 9.0	NM- 9.2
1-Super hero parody	12	24	36	79	170	260
2	6	12	18	42	79	115
3-6	6	12	18	37	66	95

NOTE: *Evilheart cameos in all. Title: Archie As Pureheart the Powerful #1-3; ...As Capt. Pureheart-#4-6.*

ARCHIE AT RIVERDALE HIGH (See Archie Giant Series Magazine #573, 586, 604 & Riverdale High)
Archie Publications: Aug, 1972 - No. 113, Feb, 1987

	GD 2.0	VG 4.0	FN 6.0	VF 8.0	VF/NM 9.0	NM- 9.2
1	8	16	24	52	99	145
2	4	8	12	27	44	60
3-5	3	6	9	16	23	30
6-10	2	4	6	11	16	20
11-30	2	4	6	8	10	12
31(12/75)-46,48-50(12/77)	1	3	4	6	8	10
47-Archie in drag-s; Betty mud wrestling-s	2	4	6	10	14	18
51-80,100 (12/84)	1	2	3	5	6	8
81(8/81)-88, 91,93-95,98						6.00
89,90-Early Cheryl Blossom app. 90-Archies Band app.	3	6	9	14	20	26
92,96,97,99-Cheryl Blossom app. 96-Anti-smoking issue	2	4	6	11	16	20
101,102,104-109,111,112: 102-Ghost-c						6.00
103-Archie dates Cheryl Blossom-s	2	4	6	11	16	20
110,113: 110-Godzilla-s. 113-Last issue	1	2	3	5	6	8

ARCHIE CHRISTMAS SPECTACULAR
Archie Comics: Feb, 2018; Feb, 2019; Feb, 2020; Feb, 2021 ($2.99)

	GD 2.0	VG 4.0	FN 6.0	VF 8.0	VF/NM 9.0	NM- 9.2
1, nn (2019), nn (2020), nn (2021)-Christmas-themed reprints						3.00

ARCHIE COMICS (See Pep Comics #22 [12/41] for Archie's debut) (1st Teen-age comic; Radio show first aired 6/2/45 by NBC)
MLJ Magazines No. 1-19/Archie Publ. No. 20 on: Winter, 1942-43 - No. 19, 3-4/46; No. 20, 5-6/46 - No. 666, Jul, 2015

	GD 2.0	VG 4.0	FN 6.0	VF 8.0	VF/NM 9.0	NM- 9.2
1 (Scarce)-Jughead, Veronica app.; 1st app. Mrs. Andrews	13,200	26,400	46,200	92,400	148,700	205,000
2 (Scarce)	1880	3760	5640	14,100	23,550	33,000
3 (60 pgs.)(scarce)	946	1892	2838	6906	12,203	17,500
4-Article about Archie radio series	535	1070	1605	3906	6903	9900
5-Halloween-c	481	962	1443	3511	6206	8900
6-Christmas-c	343	686	1029	2400	4200	6000
7-1st definitive love triangle story	389	778	1167	2723	4762	6800
8-10: 9-1st Miss Grundy cover	309	618	927	2163	3782	5400
11-15: 15-Dotty & Ditto by Woggon	171	342	513	1086	1868	2650
16-20: 15,17,18-Dotty & Ditto by Woggon. 16,19-Woggon-a. 18-Halloween pumpkin-c.	148	296	444	947	1624	2300
21-30: 23-Betty & Veronica by Woggon. 25-Woggon-a. 30-Coach Piffle app., a Coach Kleats prototype. 34-Pre-Dilton try-out (named Dilbert)	90	180	270	576	988	1400
31-40	55	110	165	352	601	850
41-49	43	86	129	271	461	650
50-Classic Montana Betty headlight-c (5-6/51)	432	864	1296	3154	5577	8000
51-60	18	36	54	124	275	425
61-70 (1954): 65-70, Katy Keene app.	15	30	45	103	227	350
71-80: 72-74-Katy Keene app.	12	24	36	82	179	275

Archie Comics #88 © ACP

Archie Comics #606 © ACP

Archie Giant Series Magazine #9 © ACP

	GD 2.0	VG 4.0	FN 6.0	VF 8.0	VF/NM 9.0	NM- 9.2
81-93,95-99	9	18	27	60	120	180
94-1st Coach Kleats in this title (see Pep #24)	11	22	33	76	163	250
100	14	28	42	96	211	325
101-122,126,128-130 (1962): 101-Headlight-c	6	12	18	40	73	105
123-125,127-Horror/SF covers. 123-UFO-c/s	10	20	30	69	147	225
131,132,134-157,159,160: 137-1st Caveman Archie gang story. 159-James Bond on cover	4	8	12	28	47	65
133 (12/62)-1st app. Cricket O'Dell	5	10	15	33	57	80
158-Archie in drag story	5	10	15	34	60	85
161(2/66)-184,186-188,190-195,197-199: 168-Superhero gag-c. 176,178-Twiggy-c 183-Caveman Archie gang story	3	6	9	17	26	35
185-1st "The Archies" Band story	4	8	12	25	40	55
189 (3/69)-Archie's band meets Don Kirshner who developed the Monkees	3	6	9	19	30	40
196 (12/69)-Early Cricket O'Dell app.	3	6	9	19	30	40
200 (6/70)	3	6	9	18	28	38
201-230(11/73): 213-Sabrina/Josie-c cameos. 229-Lost Child issue	2	4	6	11	16	20
231-260(3/77): 253-Tarzan parody	2	4	6	8	11	14
261-282, 284-299	1	3	4	6	8	10
283(8/79)-Cover/story plugs "International Children's Appeal" which was a fraudulent charity, according to TV's 20/20 news program broadcast July 20, 1979	2	4	6	8	10	12
300(1/81)-Anniversary issue	2	4	6	8	11	14
301-321,323-325,327-335,337-350: 323-Cheryl Blossom pin-up. 325-Cheryl Blossom app.						6.00
322-E.T. story	1	2	3	5	6	8
326-Early Cheryl Blossom story	2	4	6	11	16	20
336-Michael Jackson/Boy George parody	2	4	6	8	10	12
351-399: 356-Calgary Olympics Special. 393-Infinity-c; 1st comic book printed on recycled paper						5.00
400 (6/92)-Shows 1st meeting of Little Archie and Veronica						6.00
401-428						4.00
429-Love Showdown part 1						5.00
430-599: 467- "A Storm Over Uniforms" x-over parts 3,4. 538-Comic-Con issue						3.00
600-602: 600-(10/09) Archie proposes to Veronica. 601-Marries Veronica. 602-Twins born						4.00
603-605: 603-(1/10) Archie proposes to Betty. 604-Marries Betty. 605-Twins born						4.00
606-615,618-626: 609-Begin $2.99-c. 610-613-Man From RIVERDALE. 625-70th Anniversary. 626-Michael Strahan app.						3.00
616,617-Obama & Palin app.; two covers on each						4.00
627-630-Archie Meets KISS; 2 covers on each by Parent & Francavilla						4.00
631-658: 632-634-Archie marries Valerie from the Pussycats. 635-Jill Thompson var-c. 636-Gender swap. 641-644-Crossover with Glee; 2 covers. 648-Simonson var-c. 655-Cosmo the Merry Martian app. 656-Intro. Harper Lodge						3.00
650-Variant "Battle of the Bands" cover by Fiona Staples						5.00
659-665-($3.99) Two covers on each. 664-Game of Thrones parody. 665-Harper app.						4.00
666-Last issue; 6 interlocking covers with vintage title logos (Archie Comics, Blue Ribbon Comics, Top-Notch Comics, Pep Comics, Zip Comics, and Jackpot Comics)						4.00
Annual 1 ('50)-116 pgs. (Scarce)	310	620	930	2015	4208	6400
Annual 2 ('51)	116	232	348	742	1496	2250
Annual 3 ('52)	66	132	198	419	810	1200
Annual 4,5 (1953-54)	51	102	153	321	586	850
Annual 6-10 (1955-59): 8,9-(100 pgs.). 10-(84 pgs.) Elvis record on-c	17	34	51	117	259	400
Annual 11-15 (1960-65): 12,13-(84 pgs.) 14,15-(68 pgs.)	9	18	27	63	129	195
Annual 16-20 (1966-70)(all 68 pgs.): 20-Archie's band-c	6	12	18	40	73	105
Annual 21,22,24-26 (1971-75): 21,22-(68 pgs.). 22-Archie's band-s. 24-26-(52 pgs.). 25-Cavemen-s	4	8	12	23	37	50
Annual 23-Archie's band-c/s; Josie/Sabrina-c	5	10	15	30	50	70
Annual Digest 27 ('75)	4	8	12	23	37	50
...28-30	3	6	9	14	20	25
...31-34	2	4	6	9	13	16
...35-40 (...Magazine #35 on)	1	3	4	6	8	10
...41-65 ('94)						5.00
...66-69						3.00
...All-Star Specials (Winter '75, $1.25)-6 remaindered Archie comics rebound in each; titles: "The World of Giant Comics", "Giant Grab Bag of Comics", "Triple Giant Comics" & "Giant Spec. Comics	6	12	18	37	66	95

NOTE: *Archies Band-s-185, 188-192, 197, 198, 201, 204, 205, 208, 209, 215, 329, 330; Band-c-191, 330. Cavemen Archie Gang-s-183, 192, 197, 208, 210, 220, 223, 282, 333, 335, 338, 340.* ***Al Fagly*** *c-17-35.* ***Bob Montana*** *c-38, 41-50, 58, Annual 1-4.* ***Bill Woggon*** *c-53, 54.*

ARCHIE COMICS DIGEST (...Magazine No. 37-95)
Archie Publications: Aug, 1973 - No. 267, Nov, 2010 (Digest-size, 160-128 pgs.)

	GD 2.0	VG 4.0	FN 6.0	VF 8.0	VF/NM 9.0	NM- 9.2
1-1st Archie digest	10	20	30	67	141	215
2	5	10	15	33	57	80
3-5	4	8	12	23	37	50
6-10	3	6	9	16	23	30
11-33: 32,33-The Fly-r by S&K	2	4	6	10	14	18
34-60	1	3	4	6	8	10
61-80,100	1	2	3	5	6	8
81-99						5.00
101-140: 36-Katy Keene story						4.00
141-165						3.00
166-235,237-267: 194-Begin $2.39-c. 225-Begin $2.49-c						3.00
236-65th Anniversary issue, r/1st app. in Pep #22 and entire Archie Comics #1 (1942)						5.00

NOTE: ***Neal Adams*** *a-1, 2, 4, 5, 19-21, 24, 25, 27, 29, 31, 33. X-mas c-88, 94, 100, 106.*

ARCHIE COMICS DIGEST (Continues from Archie's Double Digest #252)
Archie Publications: No. 253, Sept, 2014 - Present ($4.99-$7.99, digest-size)

	NM- 9.2
253,254,257-259,261,262,264,267,269,270,272,273,275,277,279,281-($4.99)	5.00
255,260,266,274,276,282,283,285-301-($6.99) Titled Archie Jumbo Comics Digest	7.00
256,263,265,268,271,278,280,284-($5.99): 256,263,268,278-Titled Archie Comics Annual	6.00
301-317-($7.99)	8.00

ARCHIE COMICS (Free Comic Book Day editions) (Also see Pep Comics)
Archie Publications: 2003 - Present

	NM- 9.2
... Free Comic Book Day Edition 1,2: 1-(7/03). 2-(9/04)	3.00
Little Archie "The Legend of the Lost Lagoon" FCBD Edition (5/07) Bolling-s/a	3.00
... Presents the Mighty Archie Art Players ('09) Free Comic Book Day giveaway	3.00
...'s 65th Anniversary Bash ('06) Free Comic Book Day giveaway	3.00
...'s Summer Splash FCBD Edition (5/10) Parent-a; Cheryl Blossom app.	3.00

ARCHIE COMICS PRESENTS: THE LOVE SHOWDOWN COLLECTION
Archie Publications: 1994 ($4.95, squarebound)

	GD 2.0	VG 4.0	FN 6.0	VF 8.0	VF/NM 9.0	NM- 9.2
nn-r/Archie #429, Betty #19, Betty & Veronica #82, & Veronica #39	1	3	4	6	8	10

ARCHIE COMICS SUPER SPECIAL
Archie Publications: Dec, 2012 - No. 7, Jan, 2017 ($9.99, squarebound magazine-sized, quarterly)

	NM- 9.2
1-7: 1-Christmas themed. 2-Valentine's themed	10.00

ARCHIE DIGEST (Free Comic Book Day edition)
Archie Comic Publications: June/July 2014 (digest-size giveaway)

	NM- 9.2
1-Reprints; Parent-c	3.00

ARCHIE DOUBLE DIGEST (See Archie's Double Digest Quarterly Magazine)

ARCHIE 80TH ANNIVERSARY JUMBO COMICS DIGEST
Archie Comic Publications: Mar, 2021 - Present ($7.99, digest-size)

	NM- 9.2
1-Reprints from all eras including Archie's debut in Pep Comics #22	8.00

ARCHIE GETS A JOB
Spire Christian Comics (Fleming H. Revell Co.): 1977

	GD 2.0	VG 4.0	FN 6.0	VF 8.0	VF/NM 9.0	NM- 9.2
nn	2	4	6	13	18	22

ARCHIE GIANT SERIES MAGAZINE
Archie Publications: 1954 - No. 632, July, 1992 (No #36-135, no #252-451)
(#1 not code approved) (#1-233 are Giants; #12-184 are 68 pgs.,#185-194,197-233 are 52 pgs.; #195,196 are 84 pgs.; #234-up are 36 pgs.)

	GD 2.0	VG 4.0	FN 6.0	VF 8.0	VF/NM 9.0	NM- 9.2
1-Archie's Christmas Stocking	181	362	543	1158	1979	2800
2-Archie's Christmas Stocking('55)	87	174	261	553	952	1350
3-6-Archie's Christmas Stocking('56- '59)	55	110	165	352	601	850
7-10: 7-Katy Keene Holiday Fun(9/60); Bill Woggon-c. 8-Betty & Veronica Summer Fun (10/60); baseball story w/Babe Ruth & Lou Gehrig. 9-The World of Jughead (12/60); Neal Adams-a. 10-Archie's Christmas Stocking(1/61)	39	78	117	240	395	550
11,13,16,18: 11-Betty & Veronica Spectacular (6/61). 13-Betty & Veronica Summer Fun (10/61). 16-Betty & Veronica Spectacular (6/62). 18-Betty & Veronica Summer Fun (10/62)	26	52	78	154	252	350
12,14,15,17,19,20: 12-Katy Keene Holiday Fun (9/61). 14-The World of Jughead (12/61); Vampire-s. 15-Archie's Christmas Stocking (1/62). 17-Archie's Jokes (9/62); Katy Keene app. 19-The World of Jughead (12/62). 20-Archie's Christmas Stocking (1/63)	19	38	57	112	179	245
21,23,28: 21-Betty & Veronica Spectacular (6/63). 23-Betty & Veronica Summer Fun (10/63). 28-Betty & Veronica Summer Fun (9/64)	9	18	27	59	117	175
22,24,25,27,29,30: 22-Archie's Jokes (9/63). 24-The World of Jughead (12/63). 25-Archie's Christmas Stocking (1/64). 27-Archie's Jokes (8/64). 29-Around the World with Archie (10/64); Doris Day-s. 30-The World of Jughead (12/64)	8	16	24	54	102	150
26-Betty & Veronica Spectacular (6/64); all pin-ups; DeCarlo-c/a	10	20	30	64	132	200
31,33-35: 31-Archie's Christmas Stocking (1/65). 33-Archie's Jokes (8/65). 34-Betty & Veronica Summer Fun (9/65). 35-Around the World with Archie (10/65).	6	12	18	38	69	100

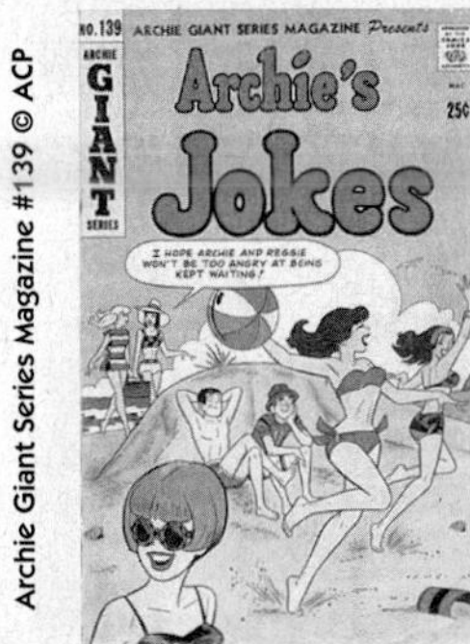

Archie Giant Series Magazine #139 © ACP

Archie Giant Series Magazine #250 © ACP

Archie Giant Series Magazine #617 © ACP

GD VG FN VF VF/NM NM-
2.0 4.0 6.0 8.0 9.0 9.2

32-Betty & Veronica Spectacular (6/65); all pin-ups; DeCarlo-c/a
8 16 24 54 102 150

36-135-**Do not exist**

136-141: 136-The World of Jughead (12/65). 137-Archie's Christmas Stocking (1/66). 138-Betty & Veronica Spect. (6/66). 139-Archie's Jokes (6/66). 140-Betty & Veronica Summer Fun (8/66). 141-Around the World with Archie (9/66) 6 12 18 38 69 100

142-Archie's Super-Hero Special (10/66)-Origin Capt. Pureheart, Capt. Hero, and Evilheart
8 16 24 55 105 155

143-The World of Jughead (12/66); Capt. Hero-c/s; Man From R.I.V.E.R.D.A.L.E., Pureheart, Superteen app. 6 12 18 38 69 100

144-160: 144-Archie's Christmas Stocking (1/67). 145-Betty & Veronica Spectacular (6/67). 146-Archie's Jokes (6/67). 147-Betty & Veronica Summer Fun (8/67) 148-World of Archie (9/67). 149-World of Jughead (10/67). 150-Archie's Christmas Stocking (1/68). 151-World of Archie (2/68). 152-World of Jughead (2/68). 153-Betty & Veronica Spectacular (6/68). 154-Archie Jokes (6/68). 155-Betty & Veronica Summer Fun (8/68). 156-World of Archie (10/68). 157-World of Jughead (12/68). 158-Archie's Christmas Stocking (1/69). 159-Betty & Veronica Christmas Spectacular (1/69). 160-World of Archie (2/69); Frankenstein-s each... 4 8 12 23 37 50

161-World of Jughead (2/69); Super-Jughead-s; 11 pg. early Cricket O'Dell-s
4 8 12 25 40 55

162-183: 162-Betty & Veronica Spectacular (6/69). 163-Archie's Jokes(8/69). 164-Betty & Veronica Summer Fun (9/69). 165-World of Archie (9/69). 166-World of Jughead (9/69). 167-Archie's Christmas Stocking (1/70). 168-Betty & Veronica Christmas Spect. (1/70). 169-Archie's Christmas Love-In (1/70). 170-Jughead's Eat-Out Comic Book Mag. (12/69). 171-World of Archie (2/70). 172-World of Jughead (2/70). 173-Betty & Veronica Spectacular (6/70). 174-Archie's Jokes (8/70). 175-Betty & Veronica Summer Fun (9/70). 176-Li'l Jinx Giant Laugh-Out (8/70). 177-World of Archie (9/70). 178-World of Jughead (9/70). 179-Archie's Christmas Stocking(1/71). 180-Betty & Veronica Christmas Spect. (1/71). 181-Archie's Christmas Love-In (1/71). 182-World of Archie (2/71). 183-World of Jughead (2/71)-Last squarebound each... 3 6 9 17 26 35

184-189,193,194,197-199 (52 pgs.): 184-Betty & Veronica Spectacular (6/71). 185-Li'l Jinx Giant Laugh-Out (6/71). 186-Archie's Jokes (8/71). 187-Betty & Veronica Summer Fun (9/71). 188-World of Archie (9/71). 189-World of Jughead (9/71). 193-World of Archie (3/72).194-World of Jughead (4/72). 197-Betty & Veronica Spectacular (6/72). 198-Archie's Jokes (8/72). 199-Betty & Veronica Summer Fun (9/72)
each... 3 6 9 15 22 28

190-Archie's Christmas Stocking (12/71); Sabrina-c 4 8 12 28 47 65

191-Betty & Veronica Christmas Spect.(2/72); Sabrina app.
4 8 12 28 47 65

192-Archie's Christmas Love-In (1/72); Archie Band-c/s
3 6 9 20 31 42

195-(84 pgs.)-Li'l Jinx Christmas Bag (1/72). 3 6 9 21 33 45

196-(84 pgs.)-Sabrina's Christmas Magic (1/72) 6 12 18 38 69 100

200-(52 pgs.)-World of Archie (10/72) 3 6 9 20 31 42

201-206,208-219,221-230,232,233 (All 52 pgs.): 201-Betty & Veronica Spectacular (10/72). 202-World of Jughead (11/72). 203-Archie's Christmas Stocking (12/72). 204-Betty & Veronica Christmas Spectacular (2/73). 205-Archie's Christmas Love-In (1/73). 206-Li'l Jinx Christmas Bag (12/72). 208-World of Archie (3/73). 209-World of Jughead (4/73). 210-Betty & Veronica Spectacular (6/73). 211-Archie's Jokes (8/73). 212-Betty & Veronica Summer Fun (9/73). 213-World of Archie (10/73). 214-Betty & Veronica Spectacular (10/73). 215-World of Jughead (11/73). 216-Archie's Christmas Stocking (12/73). 217-Betty & Veronica Christmas Spectacular (2/74). 218-Archie's Christmas Love-In (1/74). 219-Li'l Jinx Christmas Bag (12/73). 221-Betty & Veronica Spectacular (Advertised as World of Archie) (6/74). 222-Archie's Jokes (advertised as World of Jughead) (8/74). 223-Li'l Jinx (8/74). 224-Betty & Veronica Summer Fun (9/74). 225-World of Archie (9/74). 226-Betty & Veronica Spectacular (10/74). 227-World of Jughead (10/74). 228-Archie's Christmas Stocking (12/74). 229-Betty & Veronica Christmas Spectacular (12/74). 230-Archie's Christmas Love-In (1/75). 232-World of Archie (3/75). 233-World of Jughead (4/75)
each... 2 4 6 11 16 20

207,220,231,243: Sabrina's Christmas Magic. 207-(12/72). 220-(12/73). 231-(1/75). 243-(1/76)
each... 3 6 9 17 25 34

234-242,244-251 (36 pgs.): 234-Betty & Veronica Spectacular (6/75). 235-Archie's Jokes (8/75). 236-Betty & Veronica Summer Fun (9/75). 237-World of Archie (9/75) 238-Betty & Veronica Spectacular (10/75). 239-World of Jughead (10/75). 240-Archie's Christmas Stocking (12/75). 241-Betty & Veronica Christmas Spectacular (12/75). 242-Archie's Christmas Love-In (1/76). 244-World of Archie (3/76). 245-World of Jughead (4/76). 246-Betty & Veronica Spectacular (6/76). 247-Archie's Jokes (8/76). 248-Betty & Veronica Summer Fun (9/76). 249-World of Archie (9/76). 250-Betty & Veronica Spectacular (10/76). 251-World of Jughead each.... 2 4 6 9 12 15

252-451-**Do not exist**

452-454,456-466,468-478, 480-490,492-499: 452-Archie's Christmas Stocking (12/76). 453-Betty & Veronica Christmas Spectacular (12/76). 454-Archie's Christmas Love-In (1/77). 456-World of Archie (3/77). 457-World of Jughead (4/77). 458-Betty & Veronica Spectacular (6/77). 459-Archie's Jokes (8/77)-Shows 8/76 in error. 460-Betty & Veronica Summer Fun (9/77). 461-World of Archie (9/77). 462-Betty & Veronica Spectacular (10/77). 463-World of Jughead (10/77). 464-Archie's Christmas Stocking (12/77). 465-Betty & Veronica Christmas Spectacular (12/77). 466-Archie's Christmas Love-In (1/78). 468-World of Archie (2/78). 469-World of Jughead (2/78). 470-Betty & Veronica Spectacular(6/78). 471-Archie's Jokes (8/78). 472-Betty & Veronica Summer Fun (9/78). 473-World of Archie (9/78). 474-Betty & Veronica Spectacular (10/78). 475-World of Jughead (10/78). 476-Archie's Christmas Stocking (12/78). 477-Betty & Veronica Christmas Spectacular (12/78). 478-Archie's Christmas Love-In (1/79). 480-The World of Archie (3/79). 481-World of Jughead (4/79). 482-Betty & Veronica Spectacular (6/79). 483-Archie's Jokes (8/79). 484-Betty & Veronica Summer Fun(9/79). 485-The World of Archie (9/79). 486-Betty & Veronica Spectacular (10/79). 487-The World of Jughead (10/79). 488-Archie's Christmas Stocking (12/79). 489-Betty & Veronica Christmas Spectacular (1/80). 490-Archie's Christmas Love-in (1/80). 492-The World of Archie (2/80). 493-The World of Jughead (4/80). 494-Betty & Veronica Spectacular (6/80). 495-Archie's Jokes (8/80). 496-Betty & Veronica Summer Fun (9/80). 497-The World of Archie (9/80). 498-Betty & Veronica Spectacular (10/80). 499-The World of Jughead (10/80) each... 2 4 6 8 10 12

455,467,479,491,503-Sabrina's Christmas Magic: 455-(1/77). 467-(1/78). 479-(1/79) Dracula/Werewolf-s. 491-(1/80), 503(1/81) 2 4 6 13 18 22

500-Archie's Christmas Stocking (12/80) 2 4 6 8 11 14

501-514,516-527,529-532,534-539,541-543,545-550: 501-Betty & Veronica Christmas Spectacular (12/80). 502-Archie's Christmas Love-in (1/81). 504-The World of Archie (3/81). 505-The World of Jughead (4/81). 506-Betty & Veronica Spectacular (6/81). 507-Archie's Jokes (8/81). 508-Betty & Veronica Summer Fun (9/81). 509-The World of Archie (9/81). 510-Betty & Vernonica Spectacular (9/81). 511-The World of Jughead (10/81). 512-Archie's Christmas Stocking (12/81). 513-Betty & Veronica Christmas Spectacular (12/81). 514-Archie's Christmas Love-in (1/82). 516-The World of Archie(3/82). 517-The World of Jughead (4/82). 518-Betty & Veronica Spectacular (6/82). 519-Archie's Jokes (8/82). 520-Betty & Veronica Summer Fun (9/82). 521-The World of Archie (9/82). 522-Betty & Veronica Spectacular (10/82). 523-The World of Jughead (10/82).524-Archie's Christmas Stocking (1/83). 525-Betty and Veronica Christmas Spectacular (1/83). 526-Betty and Veronica Spectacular (5/83). 527-Little Archie (8/83). 529-Betty and Veronica Summer Fun (8/83). 530-Betty and Veronica Spectacular (9/83). 531-The World of Jughead (9/83). 532-The World of Archie (10/83). 534-Little Archie (1/84). 535-Archie's Christmas Stocking (1/84). 536-Betty and Veronica Christmas Spectacular (1/84). 537-Betty and Veronica Spectacular (6/84). 538-Little Archie (8/84). 539-Betty and Veronica Summer Fun (8/84). 541-Betty and Veronica Spectacular (9/84). 542-The World of Jughead (9/84). 543-The World of Archie (10/84). 545-Little Archie (12/84). 546-Archie's Christmas Stocking (12/84). 547-Betty and Veronica Christmas Spectacular (12/84). 548-Betty and Veronica Spectacular (6/85). 549-Little Archie. 550-Betty and Veronica Summer Fun
each... 1 2 3 5 7 9

515,528,533,540,544: 515-Sabrina's Christmas Magic (1/82). 528-Josie and the Pussycats (8/83). 533-Sabrina; Space Pirates by Frank Bolling (10/83). 540-Josie and the Pussycats (8/84). 544-Sabrina the Teen-Age Witch (10/84).
each... 2 4 6 11 16 20

551,562,571,584,597-Josie and the Pussycats 2 4 6 9 12 15

552-561,563-570,572-583,585-596,598-600: 552-Betty & Veronica Spectacular. 553-The World of Jughead. 554-The World of Archie. 555-Betty's Diary. 556-Little Archie (1/86). 557-Archie's Christmas Stocking (1/86). 558-Betty & Veronica Christmas Spectacular (1/86). 559-Betty & Veronica Spectacular. 560-Little Archie. 561-Betty & Veronica Summer Fun. 563-Betty & Veronica Spectacular. 564-World of Jughead. 565-World of Archie. 566-Little Archie. 567-Archie's Christmas Stocking. 568-Betty & Veronica Christmas Spectacular. 569-Betty & Veronica Spring Spectacular. 570-Little Archie. 571-Dracula-c/s. 572-Betty & Veronica Summer Fun. 573-Archie At Riverdale High. 574-World of Archie. 575-Betty & Veronica Spectacular. 576-Pep. 577-World of Jughead. 578-Archie And Me. 579-Archie's Christmas Stocking. 580-Betty and Veronica Christmas Spectacular. 581-Little Archie Christmas Special. 582-Betty & Veronica Spring Spectacular. 583-Little Archie. 585-Betty & Veronica Summer Fun. 586-Archie At Riverdale High. 587-The World of Archie (10/88); 1st app. Explorers of the Unknown. 588-Betty & Veronica Spectacular. 589-Pep (10/88). 590-The World of Jughead. 591-Archie & Me. 592-Archie's Christmas Stocking. 593-Betty & Veronica Christmas Spectacular. 594-Little Archie. 595-Betty & Veronica Spring Spectacular. 596-Little Archie. 598-Betty & Veronica Summer Fun. 599-The World of Archie (10/89); 2nd app. Explorers of the Unknown. 600-Betty and Veronica Spectacular
each.... 6.00

601,602,604-609,611-629: 601-Pep. 602-The World of Jughead. 604-Archie at Riverdale High. 605-Archie's Christmas Stocking. 606-Betty and Veronica Christmas Spectacular. 607-Little Archie. 608-Betty and Veronica Spectacular. 609-Little Archie. 611-Betty and Veronica Summer Fun. 612-The World of Archie. 613-Betty and Veronica Spectacular. 614-Pep (10/90). 615-Veronica's Summer Special. 616-Archie and Me. 617-Archie's Christmas Stocking. 618-Betty & Veronica Christmas Spectacular. 619-Little Archie. 620-Betty and Veronica Spectacular. 621-Betty and Veronica Summer Fun. 622-Josie & the Pussycats; not published. 623-Betty and Veronica Spectacular. 624-Pep Comics. 625-Veronica's Summer Special. 626-Archie and Me. 627-World of Archie. 628-Archie's Pals 'n' Gals Holiday Special. 629-Betty & Veronica Christmas Spectacular.
each.... 4.00

603-Archie and Me; Titanic app. 5.00

610-Josie and the Pussycats 1 2 3 4 5 7

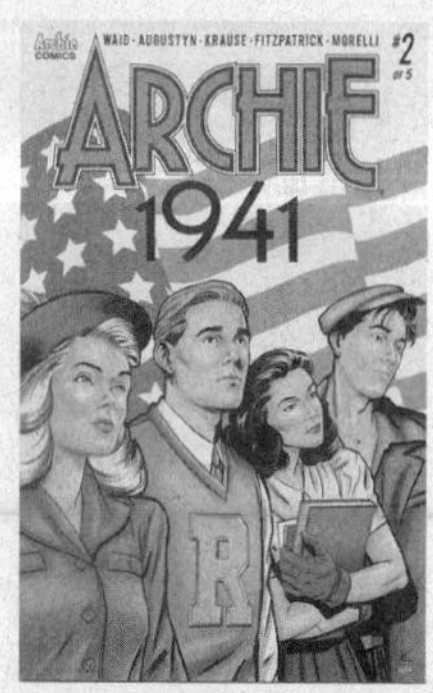

Archie 1941 #2 © ACP

Archie's Christmas Stocking #5 © ACP

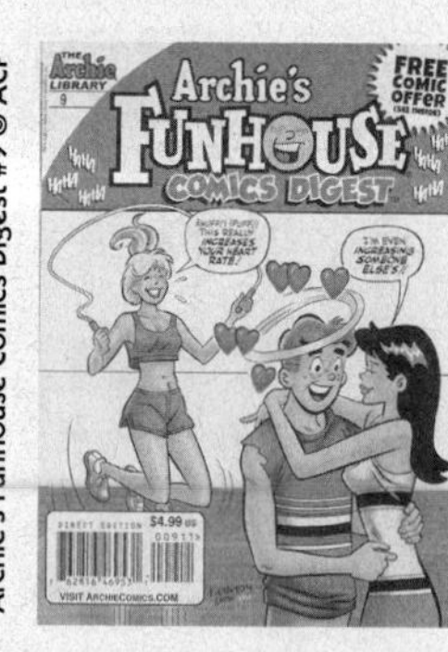

Archie's Funhouse Comics Digest #9 © ACP

	GD 2.0	VG 4.0	FN 6.0	VF 8.0	VF/NM 9.0	NM- 9.2
630-631: 630-Archie's Christmas Stocking. 631-Archie's Pals 'n' Gals						4.00
632-Last issue; Betty & Veronica Spectacular	1	2	3	4	5	7

NOTE: *Archies Band-c-173,180,192; s-189,192. Archie Cavemen-165,225,232,244,249. Little Sabrina-527,534, 538,545,556,566. UFO-s-178,487,594.*

ARCHIE HALLOWEEN SPECTACULAR
Archie Comic Publications: Dec, 2017; Dec, 2018; Dec, 2019; Dec, 2020 ($2.99)

	GD 2.0	VG 4.0	FN 6.0	VF 8.0	VF/NM 9.0	NM- 9.2
1-Halloween-themed reprints; Shultz-c						3.00
nn (12/18) Parent-c; nn (12/19) Parent-c; Sabrina app.; nn (12/20)						3.00

ARCHIE JUMBO COMICS DIGEST (See Archie Comic Digest)

ARCHIE MEETS BATMAN '66
Archie Comic Publications: Sept, 2018 - No. 6, Mar, 2019 ($3.99, limited series)

	GD 2.0	VG 4.0	FN 6.0	VF 8.0	VF/NM 9.0	NM- 9.2
1-6-Parker & Moreci-s/Parent-a; multiple covers; Poison Ivy, Bookworm, Siren app. 2-6-Joker, Riddler, Penguin & Catwoman app. 6-Super Teens app.						5.00

ARCHIE MEETS RAMONES
Archie Comic Publications: 2016 ($4.99, one-shot)

	GD 2.0	VG 4.0	FN 6.0	VF 8.0	VF/NM 9.0	NM- 9.2
1-Segura & Rosenberg-s/Lagacé-a; multiple covers; The Archies go to 1976; Sabrina app.	1	2	3	5	6	8

ARCHIE MEETS THE B-52s
Archie Comic Publications: Apr, 2020 ($3.99, one-shot)

	GD 2.0	VG 4.0	FN 6.0	VF 8.0	VF/NM 9.0	NM- 9.2
1-Set in the '80s with the original line-up; Segura & Rosenberg-s/Parent-a; multiple covers						4.00

ARCHIE MEETS THE PUNISHER (Same contents as The Punisher Meets Archie)
Marvel Comics & Archie Comics Publ.: Aug, 1994 ($2.95, 52 pgs., one-shot)

	GD 2.0	VG 4.0	FN 6.0	VF 8.0	VF/NM 9.0	NM- 9.2
1-Batton Lash story, John Buscema-a on Punisher, Stan Goldberg-a on Archie	2	4	6	8	10	12

ARCHIE MILESTONES JUMBO COMICS DIGEST
Archie Comics: Apr, 2019 - No. 12, Feb, 2021 ($6.99/$7.99, digest-size)

	GD 2.0	VG 4.0	FN 6.0	VF 8.0	VF/NM 9.0	NM- 9.2
1-5-($6.99)						7.00
6-12-($7.99)						8.00

ARCHIE 1941
Archie Comic Publications: Nov, 2018 - No. 5, Mar, 2019 ($3.99, limited series)

	GD 2.0	VG 4.0	FN 6.0	VF 8.0	VF/NM 9.0	NM- 9.2
1-5-Set in 1941 during WWII; Augustyn & Waid-s/Krause-a						4.00

ARCHIE 1955
Archie Comic Publications: Nov, 2019 - No. 5, Apr, 2020 ($3.99, limited series)

	GD 2.0	VG 4.0	FN 6.0	VF 8.0	VF/NM 9.0	NM- 9.2
1-5-Set in 1955 at the dawn of Rock 'n' Roll; Augustyn & Waid-s/Grummett-a						4.00

ARCHIES, THE
Archie Comic Publications: Jul, 2017; Nov, 2017 - No. 7, Jul, 2018 ($4.99/$3.99)

	GD 2.0	VG 4.0	FN 6.0	VF 8.0	VF/NM 9.0	NM- 9.2
1-7-($3.99) Segura & Rosenberg-s/Eisma-a. 3-Chvrches app. 4-The Monkees app. 6-Blondie app. 7-Josie and the Pussycats app.						4.00
..., One-Shot (7/17, $4.99) Segura & Rosenberg-s/Eisma-a; Archie forms the band						5.00

ARCHIE'S ACTIVITY COMICS DIGEST MAGAZINE
Archie Enterprises: 1985 - No. 4 (Annual, 128 pgs., digest size)

	GD 2.0	VG 4.0	FN 6.0	VF 8.0	VF/NM 9.0	NM- 9.2
1 (Most copies are marked)	2	4	6	9	13	16
2-4	1	2	3	5	7	9

ARCHIE'S CAR
Spire Christian Comics (Fleming H. Revell co.): 1979 (49¢)

	GD 2.0	VG 4.0	FN 6.0	VF 8.0	VF/NM 9.0	NM- 9.2
nn	3	6	9	14	19	24

ARCHIE'S CHRISTMAS LOVE-IN (See Archie Giant Series Mag. No. 169, 181,192, 205, 218, 230, 242, 454, 466, 478, 490, 502, 514)

ARCHIE'S CHRISTMAS STOCKING (See Archie Giant Series Mag. No. 1-6,10, 15, 20, 25, 31, 137, 144, 150, 158, 167, 179, 190, 203, 216, 228, 240, 452, 464, 476, 488, 500, 512, 524, 535, 546, 557, 567, 579, 592, 605, 617, 630)

ARCHIE'S CHRISTMAS STOCKING
Archie Comics: 1993 - No. 7, 1999 ($2.00-$2.29, 52 pgs.)(Bound-in calendar poster in all)

	GD 2.0	VG 4.0	FN 6.0	VF 8.0	VF/NM 9.0	NM- 9.2
1-Dan DeCarlo-c/a						5.00
2-5						4.00
6,7: 6-(1998, $2.25). 7-(1999, $2.29)						4.00

ARCHIE'S CIRCUS
Barbour Christian Comics: 1990 (69¢)

	GD 2.0	VG 4.0	FN 6.0	VF 8.0	VF/NM 9.0	NM- 9.2
nn	2	4	6	10	14	18

ARCHIE'S CLASSIC CHRISTMAS STORIES
Archie Comics: 2002 ($10.95, TPB)

	GD 2.0	VG 4.0	FN 6.0	VF 8.0	VF/NM 9.0	NM- 9.2
Volume 1 - Reprints stories from 1955-1964 Archie's Christmas Stocking issues						12.00

ARCHIE'S CLEAN SLATE
Spire Christian Comics (Fleming H. Revell Co.): 1973 (35/49¢)

	GD 2.0	VG 4.0	FN 6.0	VF 8.0	VF/NM 9.0	NM- 9.2
1-(35¢-c edition)(Some issues have nn)	3	6	9	14	19	24
1-(49¢-c edition)	2	4	6	10	14	18

ARCHIE'S DATE BOOK
Spire Christian comics (Fleming H. Revell Co.): 1981

	GD 2.0	VG 4.0	FN 6.0	VF 8.0	VF/NM 9.0	NM- 9.2
nn-(Low print)	2	4	6	13	18	22

ARCHIE'S DOUBLE DIGEST QUARTERLY MAGAZINE
Archie Comics: 1981 - No. 252, Aug, 2014 ($1.95-$3.99, 256 pgs.) (Archie's Double Digest Magazine No. 10 on)(Title becomes Archie's Comics Digest #253 on)

	GD 2.0	VG 4.0	FN 6.0	VF 8.0	VF/NM 9.0	NM- 9.2
1	3	6	9	16	23	30
2-10; 6-Katy Keene story.	2	4	6	10	14	18
11-30: 29-Pureheart story	2	4	6	8	10	12
31-50	1	2	3	4	5	7
51-70,100						5.00
71-99,101-237,239-251: 123-Begin $3.29-c. 170-Begin $3.69. 197-Begin $3.99-c						4.00
238-Titled Archie Double Double Digest (4/13, $5.99, 320 pages)						6.00
252-($4.99) Title changes to Archie's Comics Digest with #253						5.00

ARCHIE'S FAMILY ALBUM
Spire Christian Comics (Fleming H. Revell Co.): 1978 (39¢/49¢, 36 pgs.)

	GD 2.0	VG 4.0	FN 6.0	VF 8.0	VF/NM 9.0	NM- 9.2
nn	2	4	6	13	18	22
nn (49¢-c edition)	2	4	6	9	13	16

ARCHIE'S FESTIVAL
Spire Christian Comics (Fleming H. Revell Co.): 1980 (49¢)

	GD 2.0	VG 4.0	FN 6.0	VF 8.0	VF/NM 9.0	NM- 9.2
nn	2	4	6	13	18	22

ARCHIE'S FUNHOUSE DOUBLE DIGEST
Archie Comics: Feb, 2014 - No. 28, Nov, 2017 ($3.99-$7.99, digest-size)

	GD 2.0	VG 4.0	FN 6.0	VF 8.0	VF/NM 9.0	NM- 9.2
1-5						4.00
6,19,21: 6,19-Titled Archie's Funhouse Double Double Digest ($5.99, 320 pgs.)						6.00
7-10,12-14,16,18,25,28-($4.99) Title becomes Archie's Funhouse Comics Digest						5.00
11-($7.99) Titled Archie's Funhouse Jumbo Comics Digest						8.00
15,17,20,22-($6.99) Archie's Funhouse Jumbo Comics Digest						7.00
23,24,26,27-($5.99) 23-Titled Archie's Funhouse Christmas Annual Double Digest						6.00

ARCHIE'S GIRLS, BETTY AND VERONICA (Becomes Betty & Veronica)(Also see Veronica)
Archie Publications (Close-Up): 1950 - No. 347, Apr, 1987

	GD 2.0	VG 4.0	FN 6.0	VF 8.0	VF/NM 9.0	NM- 9.2
1	349	698	1047	2443	4272	6100
2	148	296	444	947	1624	2300
3-5: 3-Betty's 1st ponytail. 4-Dan DeCarlo's 1st Archie work	90	180	270	576	988	1400
6-10: 10-Katy Keene app. (2 pgs.)	61	122	183	390	670	950
11-20: 11,13,14,17-19-Katy Keene app. 17-Last pre-code issue (3/55). 20-Debbie's Diary (2 pgs.)	43	86	129	271	461	650
21-30: 27,30-Katy Keene app. 29-Tarzan	36	72	108	211	343	475
31-43,45-50: 41-Marilyn Monroe and Brigitte Bardot mentioned. 45-Fabian 1 pg. photo & bio. 46-Bobby Darin 1 pg. photo & bio	21	42	63	126	206	285
44-Elvis Presley 1 pg. photo & bio	24	48	72	144	237	330
51-55,57-74: 67-Jackie Kennedy homage. 73-Sci-fi-c	9	18	27	57	111	165
56-Elvis and Bobby Darin records parody	10	20	30	66	138	210
75-Betty & Veronica sell souls to Devil	25	50	75	175	388	600
76-99: 82-Bobby Rydell 1 pg. illustrated bio; Elvis mentioned on-c. 83-Rick Nelson illo/text page. 84-Connie Francis 1 pg. illustrated bio	6	12	18	38	69	100
100	6	12	18	42	79	115
101-104, 106-117,120 (12/65): 113-Monsters-s	4	8	12	28	47	65
105-Beatles wig parody (5 pg. story)(9/64)	5	10	15	31	53	75
118-(10/65) 1st app./origin Superteen (also see Betty & Me #3)	6	12	18	41	76	110
119-2nd app./last Superteen story	5	10	15	31	53	75
121,122,124-126,128-140 (8/67): 135,140-Mod-c. 136-Slave Girl-s	3	6	9	19	30	40
123-"Jingo"-Ringo parody-c	4	8	12	23	37	50
127-Beatles Fan Club-s	5	10	15	31	53	75
141-156,158-163,165-180 (12/70)	3	6	9	15	22	28
157,164-Archies Band	3	6	9	18	28	38
181-193,195-199	2	4	6	11	16	20
194-Sabrina-c/s	4	8	12	23	37	50
200-(8/72)	3	6	9	14	19	24
201-205,207,209,211-215,217-240	2	4	6	8	10	12
206,208,210, 216: 206,208,216-Sabrina c/app. 206-Josie-c. 210-Sabrina app.	3	6	9	15	22	28
241 (1/76)-270 (6/78)	1	3	4	6	8	10
271-299: 281-UFO-s	1	2	3	5	7	9
300 (12/80)-Anniversary issue	2	4	6	8	10	12
301-309	1	2	3	4	5	7
310-John Travolta parody story	1	3	4	6	8	10
311-319						6.00

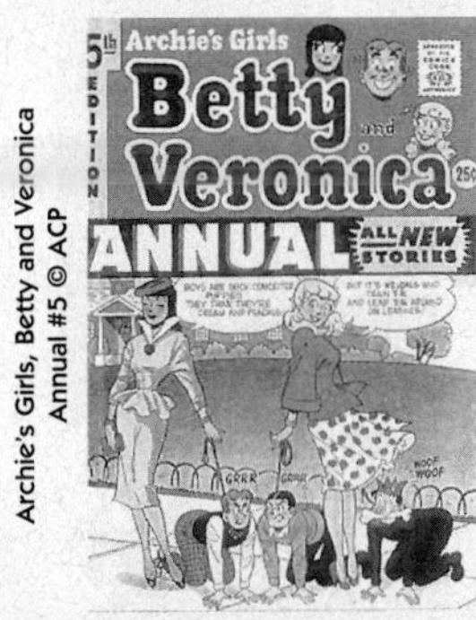

Archie's Girls, Betty and Veronica Annual #5 © ACP

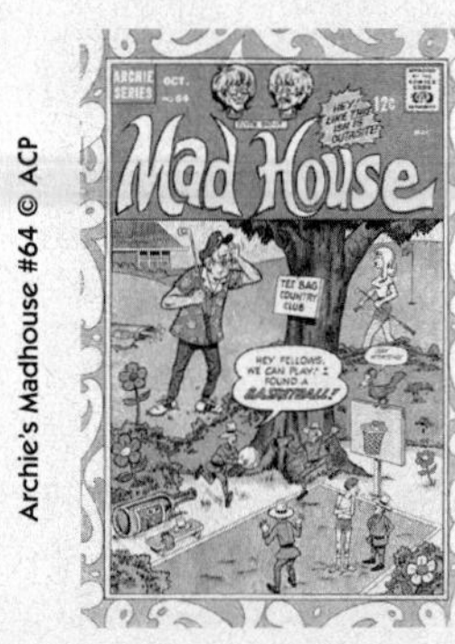

Archie's Madhouse #64 © ACP

Archie's Pal, Jughead #2 © ACP

GD VG FN VF VF/NM NM-
2.0 4.0 6.0 8.0 9.0 9.2

320 (10/82)-Intro. of Cheryl Blossom on cover and inside story (she also appears, but not on the cover, in Jughead #325 with same 10/82 publication date) 20 40 60 138 307 475
321-Cheryl Blossom app. 7 14 21 44 82 120
322-Cheryl Blossom app.; Cheryl meets Archie for the 1st time 7 14 21 49 92 135
323,326,329,330,331,333-338: 333-Monsters-s 6.00
324,325-Crickett O'Dell app. 2 4 6 9 12 15
327,328-Cheryl Blossom app. 3 6 9 20 31 42
332,339: 332-Superhero costume party. 339-(12/85) Betty dressed as Madonna. 2 4 6 10 14 18
340-346 Low print 1 3 4 6 8 10
347 (4/87) Last issue; low print 2 4 6 8 10 12
Annual 1 (1953) 142 284 426 909 1555 2200
Annual 2 (1954) 55 110 165 352 601 850
Annual 3-5 (1955-1957) 42 84 126 265 445 625
Annual 6-8 (1958-1960) 30 60 90 177 289 400

ARCHIE'S HOLIDAY FUN DIGEST
Archie Comics: Feb, 1997 - No. 12, Dec, 2007 ($1.75/$1.95/$1.99/$2.19/$2.39/$2.49, annual)
1-12-Christmas stories 4.00

ARCHIE SHOWCASE DIGEST
Archie Comics: Sept, 2020 - Present ($7.99, digest)
1,2-Reprints from all eras. 2-Jughead spotlight 8.00

ARCHIE'S JOKEBOOK COMICS DIGEST ANNUAL (See Jokebook...)

ARCHIE'S JOKE BOOK MAGAZINE (See Joke Book ...)
Archie Publ: 1953 - No. 3, Sum, 1954; No. 15, Fall, 1954 - No. 288, 11/82 (subtitled...Laugh-In #127-140; ...Laugh-Out #141-194)
1953-One Shot (#1) 155 310 465 992 1696 2400
2 55 110 165 352 601 850
3 (no #4-14) 41 82 123 256 428 600
15-20: 15-Formerly Archie's Rival Reggie #14; last pre-code issue (Fall/54). 15-17-Katy Keene app. 27 54 81 158 259 360
21-30 16 32 48 94 147 200
31-43: 42-Bio of Ed "Kookie" Byrnes. 43-story about guitarist Duane Eddy 14 28 42 76 108 140
44-1st professional comic work by Neal Adams, 4 pgs. 34 68 102 199 325 450
45-47-N. Adams-a in all, 2-6 pgs. 20 40 60 114 182 250
48-Four pgs. N. Adams-a 20 40 60 114 182 250
49,50 6 12 18 41 66 90
51-56,60 (1962) 4 8 12 27 44 60
57-Elvis mentioned; Marilyn Monroe cameo 6 12 18 37 66 95
58,59-Horror/Sci-Fi-c 8 16 24 51 96 140
61-80 (8/64): 66-(12¢ cover). 76-Robot-c 3 6 9 17 26 35
66-(15¢ cover variant) 4 8 12 27 44 60
81-89,91,92,94-99 3 6 9 14 20 25
90,93: 90-Beatles gag. 93-Beatles cameo 3 6 9 16 24 32
100 (5/66) 3 6 9 16 23 30
101,103-117,119-123,127,129,131-140 (9/69): 105-Superhero gag-c. 108-110-Archies Archers Band-s. 116-Beatles/Monkees/Bob Dylan cameos (posters) 2 4 6 11 16 20
102 (7/66) Archie Band prototype-c; Elvis parody panel, Rolling Stones mention 3 6 9 17 26 35
118,124,125,126,128,130: 118-Archie Band-c; Veronica & Groovers band-s. 124-Archies Band-c/app. 125-Beatles cameo (poster). 126,130-Monkees cameo. 128-Veronica/Archies Band app. 3 6 9 16 23 30
141-173,175-181,183-199 2 4 6 8 11 14
174-Sabrina-c. 182-Sabrina cameo 2 4 6 9 13 16
200 (9/74) 2 4 6 9 13 16
201-230 (3/77) 1 2 3 5 6 8
231-239,241-287 6.00
240-Elvis record-c 2 3 4 6 8 10
288-Last issue 1 2 3 4 5 7

NOTE: *Archies Band-c-118,124,147,172; 1 pg.-s-127,128,138,140,143,147,167; 2 pg.-s-124,131, 155. Sabrina app.-247,248,252-259,261,262,264,266-270,274,277,284-286.*

ARCHIE'S JOKES (See Archie Giant Series Mag. No. 17, 22, 27, 33, 139, 146, 154, 163, 174, 186, 198, 211, 222, 235, 247, 459, 471, 483, 495, 519)

ARCHIE'S LOVE SCENE
Spire Christian Comics (Fleming H. Revell Co.): 1973 (35¢/39¢/49¢/no price)
1-(35¢ Edition) 3 6 9 14 20 26
1-(39¢/49¢ Edition/no price) (Some copies have nn) 2 4 6 10 14 18

ARCHIE'S LOVE SHOWDOWN SPECIAL
Archie Publications: 1994 ($2.00, one-shot)
1-Concludes x-over from Archie #429, Betty #19, B&V #82, Veronica #39 1 3 4 6 8 10

ARCHIE'S MADHOUSE (Madhouse Ma-ad No. 67 on)
Archie Publications: Sept, 1959 - No. 66, Feb, 1969
1-Archie begins 38 76 114 285 641 1000
2 13 26 39 89 195 300
3-5 9 18 27 60 120 180
6-10 6 12 18 41 76 110
11-17 (Last w/regular characters) 5 10 15 35 63 90
18-21,23,29: 18-New format begins. 19-1st app. Witch Hilda. 23-No Sabrina. 29-Flying saucer-c 5 10 15 31 53 75
22-1st app. Sabrina, the Teen-age Witch and Salem the cat (10/62) 152 304 456 1254 2827 4400
24-2nd app. Sabrina and Salem; 1st app. Witch Hazel in a Sabrina story 20 40 60 138 307 475
25,26,28-Sabrina app. 25-1st app. Captain Sprocket (4/63); 3rd app. Sabrina; sci-fi/horror-c 12 24 36 83 182 280
27-Sabrina-c; no story 9 18 27 61 123 185
30-33,36,37-Sabrina app. 37-Witch Hilda now called Aunt Hilda 8 16 24 51 96 140
34,38-40: No Sabrina. 34-Bordered-c begin. 4 8 12 25 40 55
35-Beatles cameo. No Sabrina 4 8 12 28 47 65
41-44,46,47,51,54,56,57,60-62,64,66: No Sabrina. 43-Mighty Crusaders cameo. 44-Swipes Mad #4 (Super-Duperman) in "Bird Monsters From Outer Space". 3 6 9 20 31 42
45,48-50,52,53,55,58,59,63,65-Sabrina stories. 45-1st app. Rosalind. 65-1st app. Aunt Zelda 6 12 18 37 66 95
Annual 1 (1962-63) no Sabrina 11 22 33 72 154 235
Annual 2 (1964) no Sabrina 5 10 15 35 63 90
Annual 3 (1965)-r/1st app. Sabrina from #22 12 24 36 82 179 275
Annual 4,5('66-68)(Becomes Madhouse Ma-ad Annual #7 on); no Sabrina 4 8 12 28 47 65
Annual 6 (1969)-Sabrina the Teen-Age Witch-sty 7 14 21 44 82 120

NOTE: *Cover title to #61-65 is "Madhouse" and to #66 is "Madhouse Ma-ad Jokes". Sci-Fi/Horror covers 6, 8, 11, 13, 15-26, 29, 35, 36, 38, 42, 43, 48, 51, 58, 60.*

ARCHIE'S MECHANICS
Archie Publications: Sept, 1954 - No. 3, 1955
1-(15¢; 52 pgs.) 111 222 333 705 1215 1725
2-(10¢)-Last pre-code issue 61 122 183 390 670 950
3-(10¢) 53 106 159 334 567 800

ARCHIE'S MYSTERIES (Continued from Archie's Weird Mysteries)
Archie Comics: No. 25, Feb, 2003 - No. 34, June, 2004 ($2.19)
25-34- Archie and gang as "Teen Scene Investigators" 4.00

ARCHIE'S ONE WAY
Spire Christian Comics (Fleming H. Revell Co.): 1972 (35¢/39¢/49¢, 36 pgs.)
nn-(35¢ Edition) 3 6 9 14 20 26
nn-(39¢, 49¢, no price editions) 2 4 6 11 16 20

ARCHIE'S PAL, JUGHEAD (Jughead No. 127 on)
Archie Publications: 1949 - No. 126, Nov, 1965
1 (1949)-1st app. Moose (see Pep #33) 300 600 900 2040 3495 4950
2 (1950) 106 212 318 673 1162 1650
3-5 58 116 174 371 636 900
6-10: 7-Suzie app. 39 78 117 240 395 550
11-20: 20-Jughead as Sherlock Holmes parody 26 52 78 154 252 350
21-30: 23-25,28-30-Katy Keene app. 23-Early Dilton-s. 28-Debbie's Diary app. 18 36 54 103 162 220
31-50: 49-Archies Rock 'N' Rollers band-c 7 14 21 48 89 130
51-57,59-70: 59- Bio of Will Hutchins of TV's Sugarfoot. 68-Early Archie Gang Cavemen-s 5 10 15 34 60 85
58-Neal Adams-a 6 12 18 40 73 105
71-76,83,89-99: 72-Jughead dates Betty & Veronica. 83 (4/62) 1st mention of Secret Society of Jughead Hating Girls. 95-2nd app. Cricket O'Dell 4 8 12 27 44 60
77,78,80-82,85,86,88-Horror/Sci-Fi-c. 86(7/62) 1st app. The Brain 8 16 24 51 96 140
79-Creature From the Black Lagoon-c 38 76 114 285 641 1000
84-1st app. Big Ethyl (5/62) 10 20 30 64 132 200
87-2nd app. of Big Ethyl; UGAJ (United Girls Against Jughead)-s 5 10 15 33 57 80
100 6 12 18 38 69 100
101-Return of Big Ethyl 4 8 12 27 44 60

Archie's Pals 'n' Gals #2 © ACP

Archie's Rival Reggie #9 © ACP

Archie's TV Laugh-Out #11 © ACP

	GD 2.0	VG 4.0	FN 6.0	VF 8.0	VF/NM 9.0	NM- 9.2
102-126	3	6	9	19	30	40
Annual 1 (1953, 25¢)	103	206	309	659	1130	1600
Annual 2 (1954, 25¢)-Last pre-code issue	53	106	159	334	567	800
Annual 3-5 (1955-57, 25¢)	36	72	108	211	343	475
Annual 6-8 (1958-60, 25¢)	22	44	66	132	216	300

ARCHIE'S PAL JUGHEAD COMICS (Formerly Jughead #1-45)
Archie Comic Publ.: No. 46, June, 1993 - No. 214, Sept, 2012 ($1.25-$2.99)

	GD 2.0	VG 4.0	FN 6.0	VF 8.0	VF/NM 9.0	NM- 9.2
46-214: 100-"A Storm Over Uniforms" x-over part 1,2. 166-Three Geeks cameo. 200-Tom Root-s; Sabrina cameo. 201-Begin $2.99-c						4.00

ARCHIE'S PALS 'N' GALS (Also see Archie Giant Series Magazine #628)
Archie Publ: 1952-53 - No. 6, 1957-58; No. 7, 1958 - No. 224, Sept, 1991
(...All News Stories on-c #49-59)

	GD 2.0	VG 4.0	FN 6.0	VF 8.0	VF/NM 9.0	NM- 9.2
1-(116 pgs., 25¢)	126	252	378	806	1378	1950
2(Annual)('54, 25¢)	53	106	159	334	567	800
3-5(Annual, '55-57, 25¢): 3-Last pre-code issue	39	78	117	231	378	525
6-10('58-'60)	24	48	72	142	234	325
11,13,14,16,17,20-(84 pgs.): 17-B&V paper dolls	14	28	42	80	115	150
12,15-(84 pgs.) Neal Adams-a. 12-Harry Belafonte 2 pg. photos & bio.	15	30	45	90	140	190
18-(84 pgs.) Horror/Sci-Fi-c	18	36	54	105	165	225
19-Marilyn Monroe app.	20	40	60	114	182	250
21,22,24-28,30 (68 pgs.)	6	12	18	41	76	110
23-(Wint./62) 6 pg. Josie-s with Pepper and Melody (1st app.) by DeCarlo; Betty in towel pin-up	68	136	204	544	1222	1900
29-Beatles satire (68 pgs.)	9	18	27	60	120	180
31(Wint. 64/65)-39 -(68 pgs.)	5	10	15	33	57	80
40-Early Superteen-s; with Pureheart	6	12	18	41	76	110
41(8/67)-43,45-50(2/69) (68 pgs.)	4	8	12	25	40	55
44-Archies Band-s; WEB cameo	4	8	12	28	47	65
51(4/69),52,55-64(6/71): 62-Last squarebound	3	6	9	18	28	38
53-Archies Band-c/s	3	6	9	21	33	45
54-Satan meets Veronica-s	5	10	15	34	60	85
65(8/70),67-70,73,74,76-81,83(6/74) (52 pgs.)	3	6	9	21	33	45
66,82-Sabrina-c	4	8	12	22	34	45
71,72-Two part drug story (8/72,9/72)	3	6	9	21	33	45
75-Archies Band-s	3	6	9	16	24	32
84-99	2	4	6	8	10	12
100 (12/75)	2	4	6	9	13	16
101-130(3/79): 125,126-Riverdale 2001-s	1	2	3	5	6	8
131-160,162-170 (7/84)						6.00
161 (11/82) 3rd app./1st solo Cheryl Blossom-s and pin-up; 2nd Jason Blossom	6	12	18	40	73	105
171-173,175,177-197,199: 197-G. Colan-a						5.00
174,176,198: 174-New Archies Band-s. 176-Cyndi Lauper-c. 198-Archie gang on strike at Archie Ent. offices						6.00
200(9/88)-Illiteracy-s						6.00
201,203-223: Later issues $1.00 cover						4.00
202-Explains end of Archie's jalopy; Dezerland-c/s; James Dean cameo						6.00
224-Last issue						6.00

NOTE: *Archies Band-c-45,47,49,53,56; s-44,53,75,174. UFO-s-50,63,209,220.*

ARCHIE'S PALS 'N' GALS DOUBLE DIGEST MAGAZINE
Archie Comic Publications: Nov, 1992 - No. 146, Dec, 2010 ($2.50-$3.99)

	GD 2.0	VG 4.0	FN 6.0	VF 8.0	VF/NM 9.0	NM- 9.2
1-Capt. Hero story; Pureheart app.	2	4	6	8	10	12
2-10: 2-Superduck story; Little Jinx in all. 4-Begin $2.75-c	1	2	3	4	5	7
11-29						4.00
30-146: 40-Begin $2.99-c. 48-Begin $3.19-c. 56-Begin $3.29-c. 72-Begin $3.59-c. 100-Story uses screen captures from classic animated series. 102-Begin $3.69-c. 125-128-"New Look" art; Moose and Midge break up. 130-Begin $3.99-c. 133-Reggie spotlight, also reprints early apps.						4.00

ARCHIE'S PARABLES
Spire Christian Comics (Fleming H. Revell Co.): 1973,1975 (39/49¢, 36 pgs.)

	GD 2.0	VG 4.0	FN 6.0	VF 8.0	VF/NM 9.0	NM- 9.2
nn-By Al Hartley; 39¢ Edition	3	6	9	14	20	25
49¢, no price editions	2	4	6	10	14	18

ARCHIE'S R/C RACERS (Radio controlled cars)
Archie Comics: Sept, 1989 - No. 10, Mar, 1991 (95¢/$1)

	GD 2.0	VG 4.0	FN 6.0	VF 8.0	VF/NM 9.0	NM- 9.2
1						6.00
2,5-7,10: 5-Elvis parody. 7-Supervillain-c/s. 10-UFO-c/s						4.00
3,4,8,9						3.00

ARCHIE'S RIVAL REGGIE (Reggie & Archie's Joke Book #15 on)
Archie Publications: 1949 - No. 14, Aug, 1954

	GD 2.0	VG 4.0	FN 6.0	VF 8.0	VF/NM 9.0	NM- 9.2
1-Reggie 1st app. in Jackpot Comics #5	116	232	348	742	1271	1800
2	53	106	159	334	567	800
3-5	37	74	111	222	361	500
6-10	25	50	75	150	245	340
11-14: Katy Keene in No. 10-14, 1-2 pgs.	20	40	60	117	189	260

ARCHIE'S RIVERDALE HIGH (See Riverdale High)

ARCHIE'S ROLLER COASTER
Spire Christian Comics (Fleming H. Revell Co.): 1981 (69¢)

	GD 2.0	VG 4.0	FN 6.0	VF 8.0	VF/NM 9.0	NM- 9.2
nn-(Low print)	2	4	6	13	18	22

ARCHIE'S SOMETHING ELSE
Spire Christian Comics (Fleming H. Revell Co.): 1975 (39/49¢, 36 pgs.)

	GD 2.0	VG 4.0	FN 6.0	VF 8.0	VF/NM 9.0	NM- 9.2
nn-(39¢-c) Hell's Angels Biker on motorcycle-c	3	6	9	14	19	24
nn-(49¢-c)	2	4	6	10	14	18
Barbour Christian Comics Edition ('86, no price listed)	2	3	4	6	8	10

ARCHIE'S SONSHINE
Spire Christian Comics (Fleming H. Revell Co.): 1973, 1974 (39/49¢, 36 pgs.)

	GD 2.0	VG 4.0	FN 6.0	VF 8.0	VF/NM 9.0	NM- 9.2
39¢ Edition	3	6	9	14	19	24
49¢, no price editions	2	4	6	9	13	16

ARCHIE'S SPORTS SCENE
Spire Christian Comics (Fleming H. Revell Co.): 1983 (no cover price)

	GD 2.0	VG 4.0	FN 6.0	VF 8.0	VF/NM 9.0	NM- 9.2
nn-(Low print)	2	4	6	13	18	22

ARCHIE'S SPRING BREAK
Archie Comics: 1996 - No. 5, 2000 ($2.00/$2.49, 48 pgs., annual)

	GD 2.0	VG 4.0	FN 6.0	VF 8.0	VF/NM 9.0	NM- 9.2
1-5: 1,2-Dan DeCarlo-c						4.00

ARCHIE'S STORY & GAME COMICS DIGEST MAGAZINE
Archie Enterprises: Nov, 1986 - No. 39, Jan, 1998 ($1.25-$1.95, 128 pgs., digest-size)

	GD 2.0	VG 4.0	FN 6.0	VF 8.0	VF/NM 9.0	NM- 9.2
1: Marked-up copies are common	2	4	6	11	16	20
2-10	2	4	6	8	10	12
11-20	1	2	3	4	5	7
21-39: 39-($1.95)						4.00

ARCHIE'S SUPER HERO SPECIAL (See Archie Giant Series Mag. No. 142)

ARCHIE'S SUPER HERO SPECIAL (...Comics Digest Mag. 2)
Archie Publications (Red Circle): Jan, 1979 - No. 2, Aug, 1979 (95¢, 148 pgs.)

	GD 2.0	VG 4.0	FN 6.0	VF 8.0	VF/NM 9.0	NM- 9.2
1-Simon & Kirby r-/Double Life of Pvt. Strong #1,2; Black Hood, The Fly, Jaguar, The Web app.	3	6	9	15	22	28
2-Contains contents to the never published Black Hood #1; origin Black Hood; N. Adams, Wood, Channing, McWilliams, Morrow, S&K-a(r); N. Adams-c. The Shield, The Fly, Jaguar, Hangman, Steel Sterling, The Web, The Fox-r	3	6	9	14	20	25

ARCHIE'S SUPER TEENS
Archie Comic Publications, Inc.: 1994 - No. 4, 1996 ($2.00, 52 pgs.)

	GD 2.0	VG 4.0	FN 6.0	VF 8.0	VF/NM 9.0	NM- 9.2
1-Staton/Esposito-c/a; pull-out poster						5.00
2-4: 2-Fred Hembeck script; Bret Blevins/Terry Austin-a						4.00

ARCHIE'S SUPER TEENS VERSUS CRUSADERS
Archie Comic Publications: Aug, 2018 - No. 2, Sept, 2018 ($3.99, limited series)

	GD 2.0	VG 4.0	FN 6.0	VF 8.0	VF/NM 9.0	NM- 9.2
1,2-Black Hood, Steel Sterling, The Fox, The Web, The Comet, and The Shield app.						4.00

ARCHIE'S TV LAUGH-OUT ("...Starring Sabrina" on-c #1-50)
Archie Publications: Dec, 1969 - No. 105, Feb, 1986 (#1-7: 68 pgs.)

	GD 2.0	VG 4.0	FN 6.0	VF 8.0	VF/NM 9.0	NM- 9.2
1-Sabrina begins, thru #105. 1st app. Ambrose Spellman (Sabrina's cousin) and Harvey Kinkle (Sabrina's boyfriend). 1st app. of the Archie gang (Archie, Jughead, Reggie, Betty and Veronica) in a Sabrina story as Sabrina now attends Riverdale High	11	22	33	77	166	255
2 (68 pgs.)	6	12	18	37	66	95
3-6 (68 pgs.)	5	10	15	30	50	70
7-Josie begins, thru #105; Archie's & Josie's Bands cover logos begin	7	14	21	49	92	135
8-23 (52 pgs.): 10-1st Josie on-c. 12-1st Josie and Pussycats on-c. 14-Beatles cameo on poster	4	8	12	25	40	55
24-40: 37,39,40-Bicenntennial-c	3	6	9	14	20	25
41,47,56: 41-Alexandra rejoins J&P band. 47-Fonz cameo; voodoo-s. 56-Fonz parody; B&V with Farrah hair-c	3	6	9	15	22	28
42-46,48-55,57-60	2	4	6	9	12	15
61-68,70-80: 63-UFO-s. 79-Mummy-s	1	3	4	6	8	10
69-Sherlock Holmes parody	1	3	4	6	8	10
81-90,94,95,97-99: 84 Voodoo-s	1	2	3	5	6	8
91-Early Cheryl Blossom-s; Sabrina/Archies Band-c	3	6	9	19	30	40
92-A-Team parody	1	3	4	6	8	10
93-(2/84) Archie in drag-s; Hill Street Blues-s; Groucho Marx parody; cameo parody app. of Batman, Spider-Man, Wonder Woman and others	2	4	6	9	12	15

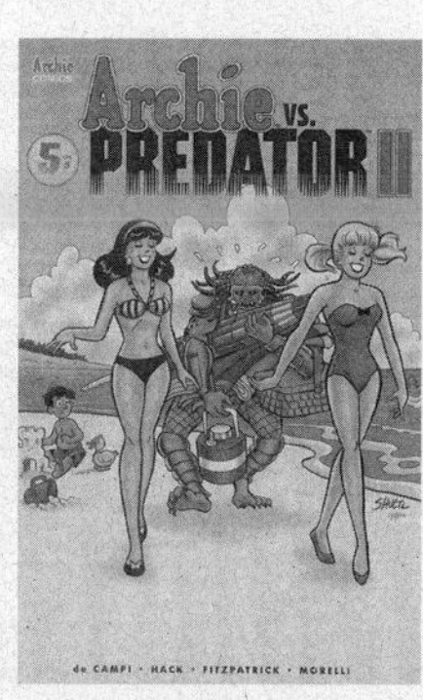

Archie vs. Predator II #5 © ACP & DH

Aria #2 © Haberlin & Holguin

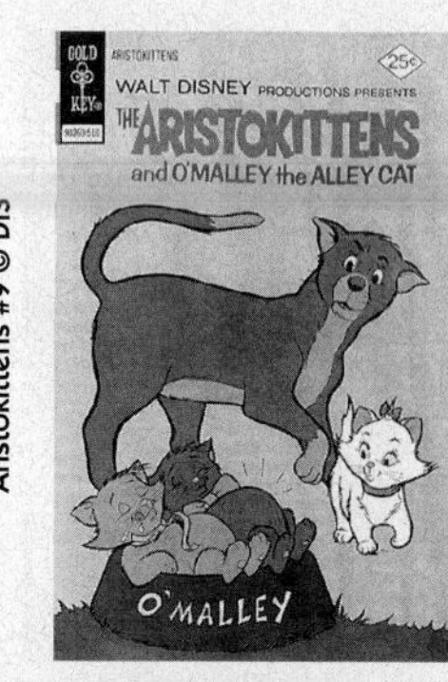

Aristokittens #9 © DIS

	GD 2.0	VG 4.0	FN 6.0	VF 8.0	VF/NM 9.0	NM- 9.2

96-MASH parody-s; Jughead in drag; Archies Band-c 1 3 4 6 8 10
100-(4/85) Michael Jackson parody-c/s; J&P band and Archie band on-c 2 4 6 10 14 18
101-104-Lower print run. 104-Miami Vice parody-c 1 2 3 5 7 9
105-Wrestling/Hulk Hogan parody-c; J&P band-s 2 4 6 9 12 15
NOTE: ***Dan DeCarlo-a** 78-up(most), **c**-89-up(most). **Archies Band-s** 2,7,9-11,15,20,25,37,64,65,67,68,70,73, 76,78,79,83,84,86,90,96,100,101; **Archies Band-c** 2,17,20,91,94,96,99-103. **Josie-s** 12,21,26,35,52,78,80,90. **Josie-c** 10,91,94. **Josie and the Pussycats (as a band in costume)-s** 7,9,10,37,38,41,42,66,84,99-101,105. **Josie w/Pussycats member Valerie &/or Melody-s** 17,20,22,25,27-29,31,33,36,39,40,43-51,53-65,67-77,79,81-83,85-89,92-94,102-104. **Josie w/Pussycats band-c** 12,14,17,18,22,24. **Sabrina-s** 1-9,11-86,88-106. **Sabrina-c** 1-18,21,23,27,49,91,94.*

ARCHIE'S VACATION SPECIAL
Archie Publications: Winter, 1994 - No. 8, 2000 ($2.00/$2.25/$2.29/$2.49, annual)
1 5.00
2-8: 8-(2000, $2.49) 4.00

ARCHIE'S WEIRD MYSTERIES (Continues as Archie's Mysteries)
Archie Comics: Feb, 2000 - No. 24, Dec, 2002 ($1.79/$1.99)
1 6.00
2-24: 3-Mighty Crusaders app. 14-Super Teens-c/app.; Mighty Crusaders app. 4.00

ARCHIE'S WORLD
Spire Christian Comics (Fleming H. Revell Co.): 1973, 1976 (39/49¢)
39¢ Edition 3 6 9 14 19 24
49¢ Edition, no price editions 2 4 6 9 13 16

ARCHIE: THE MARRIED LIFE – 10TH ANNIVERSARY
Archie Comics: Sept, 2019 - No. 6, Mar, 2020 ($3.99, limited series)
1-6-Sequel to future stories in Archie #600-605; Uslan-s/Parent-a; multiple covers 4.00

ARCHIE 3000
Archie Comics: May, 1989 - No. 16, July, 1991 (75¢/95¢/$1.00)
1,16: 16-Aliens-c/s 5.00
2-15: 6-Begin $1.00-c; X-Mas-c 4.00

ARCHIE VS. PREDATOR
Dark Horse Comics: Apr, 2015 - No. 4, Jul, 2015 ($3.99, limited series)
1-4-The Archie gang hunted by the Predator; de Campi-s/Ruiz-a; 3 covers on each 4.00

ARCHIE VS. PREDATOR II
Archie Comics: Sept, 2019 - No. 5, Mar, 2020 ($3.99, limited series)
1-5-Multiverse Archie gangs; de Campi-s/Hack-a; 3 covers on each 4.00

ARCHIE VS. SHARKNADO
Archie Comics: 2015 ($4.99, one-shot)
1-Based on the Sharknado movie series; Ferrante-s/Parent-a; 3 covers 5.00

ARCOMICS PREMIERE
Arcomics: July, 1993 ($2.95)
1-1st lenticular-c on a comic (flicker-c) 4.00

AREA 52
Image Comics: Jan, 2001 - No. 4, June, 2001 ($2.95)
1-4-Haberlin-s/Henry-a 3.00

ARES
Marvel Comics: Mar, 2006 - No. 5, July, 2006 ($2.99, limited series)
1-5-Oeming-s/Foreman-a 3.00
...: God of War TPB (2006, $13.99) r/series 14.00

ARES IX: THE DARKNESS
Image Comics (Top Cow): Dec, 2018 ($3.99, one-shot)
1-Hodgdon-s/Valyogos-a; Crapo-s/Whitaker-a; The Darkness app. 4.00

ARGUS (See Flash, 2nd Series) (Also see Showcase '95 #1,2)
DC Comics: Apr, 1995 - No. 6, Oct, 1995 ($1.50, limited series)
1-6: 4-Begin $1.75-c 3.00

ARIA
Image Comics (Avalon Studios): Jan, 1999 - No. 4, Nov, 1999 ($2.50)
Preview (11/98, $2.95) 5.00
1-Anacleto-c/a 1 2 3 5 6 8
1-Variant-c by Michael Turner 1 2 3 5 6 8
1-($10.00) Alternate-c by Turner 1 3 4 6 8 10
1,2-(Blanc & Noir) Black and white printing of pencil art 3.00
1-(Blanc & Noir) DF Edition 5.00
2-4: 2,4-Anacleto-c/a. 3-Martinez-a 3.00
4-($6.95) Glow in the Dark-c 1 3 4 6 8 10
Aria Angela 1 (2/00, $2.95) Anacleto-a; 4 covers by Anacleto, JG Jones, Portacio and Quesada 3.00
Aria Angela Blanc & Noir 1 (4/00, $2.95) Anacleto-c 3.00
Aria Angela European Ashcan 10.00
Aria Angela 2 (10/00, $2.95) Anacleto-a/c 3.00
...: A Midwinter's Dream 1 (1/02, $4.95, 7"x7") text-s w/Anacleto panels 5.00
...: Heavenly Creatures (2/21, $6.99) Reprints Aria Angela issues with Angela replaced 7.00
...: The Enchanted Collection (5/04, $16.95) r/Summer's Spell & The Uses of Enchantment 17.00

ARIA: SUMMER'S SPELL
Image Comics (Avalon Studios): Mar, 2002 - No. 2, Jun, 2002 ($2.95)
1,2-Anacleto-c/Holguin-s/Pajarillo & Medina-a 3.00

ARIA: THE SOUL MARKET
Image Comics (Avalon Studios): Mar, 2001 - No. 6, Dec, 2001 ($2.95)
1-6-Anacleto-c/Holguin-s 3.00
HC (2002, $26.95, 8.25" x 12.25") oversized r/#1-6 27.00
SC (2004, $16.95, 8.25" x 12.25") oversized r/#1-6 17.00

ARIA: THE USES OF ENCHANTMENT
Image Comics (Avalon Studios): Feb, 2003 - No. 4, Sept, 2003 ($2.95)
1-4-Anacleto-c/Holguin-s/Medina-a 3.00

ARIANE AND BLUEBEARD (See Night Music #8)

ARIEL & SEBASTIAN (See Cartoon Tales & The Little Mermaid)

ARION, LORD OF ATLANTIS (Also see Crisis on Infinite Earths & Warlord #55)
DC Comics: Nov, 1982 - No. 35, Sept, 1985
1-Story cont'd from Warlord #62 4.00
2-35 3.00
... Special #1 (11/85) 4.00

ARION THE IMMORTAL (Also see Arion, Lord of Atlantis & Showcase '95 #7)
DC Comics: July, 1992 - No. 6, Dec, 1992 ($1.50, limited series)
1-6: 4-Gustovich-a(i) 3.00

ARISTOCATS (See Movie Comics & Walt Disney Showcase No. 16)

ARISTOKITTENS, THE (...Meet Jiminy Cricket No. 1)(Disney)
Gold Key: Oct, 1971 - No. 9, Oct, 1975
1 3 6 9 19 30 40
2-5,7-9 3 6 9 14 19 24
6-(52 pgs.) 3 6 9 15 22 28

ARIZONA KID, THE (Also see The Comics & Wild Western)
Marvel/Atlas Comics(CSI): Mar, 1951 - No. 6, Jan, 1952
1 27 54 81 158 259 360
2-4: 2-Heath-a(3) 14 28 42 80 115 150
5,6 12 24 36 67 94 120
NOTE: ***Heath** a-1-3; c-1-3. **Maneely** c-4-6. **Morisi** a-4-6. **Sinnott** a-6.*

ARK, THE (See The Crusaders)

ARKAGA
Image Comics: Sept, 1997 ($2.95, one-shot)
1-Jorgensen-s/a 3.00

ARKANIUM
Dreamwave Productions: Sept, 2002 - No. 5 ($2.95)
1-5: 1-Gatefold wraparound-c 3.00

ARKHAM ASYLUM: LIVING HELL
DC Comics: July, 2003 - No. 6, Dec, 2003 ($2.50, limited series)
1-6-Ryan Sook-a; Batman app. 3-Batgirl-c/app. 3.00

ARKHAM ASYLUM: MADNESS
DC Comics: 2010 ($19.99, HC graphic novel, dustjacket)
HC-Sam Kieth-s/a/c; Joker, Two-Face, Harley and Ivy app. 20.00
SC-(2011, $14.99) Sam Kieth-s/a/c; Joker, Two-Face, Harley and Ivy app. 15.00

ARKHAM MANOR (Follows events in Batman Eternal #30)
DC Comics: Dec, 2014 - No. 6, May, 2015 ($2.99)
1-6-Arkham Asylum re-opens in Wayne Manor; Duggan-s/Crystal-a 3.00
...: Endgame 1 (6/15, $2.99) Tieri-s/Albuquerque-c; tie-in with other Batman titles 3.00

ARKHAM REBORN
DC Comics: Dec, 2009 - No. 3, Feb, 2010 ($2.99, limited series)
1-3-David Hine-s/Jeremy Haun-a 3.00
Batman: Arkham Reborn TPB (2010, $12.99) r/#1-3, Detective Comics #864,865 and Batman: Battle For the Cowl: Arkham Asylum #1 13.00

ARMAGEDDON
Chaos! Comics: Oct, 1999 - No. 4, Jan, 2000 ($2.95, limited series)
Preview 5.00

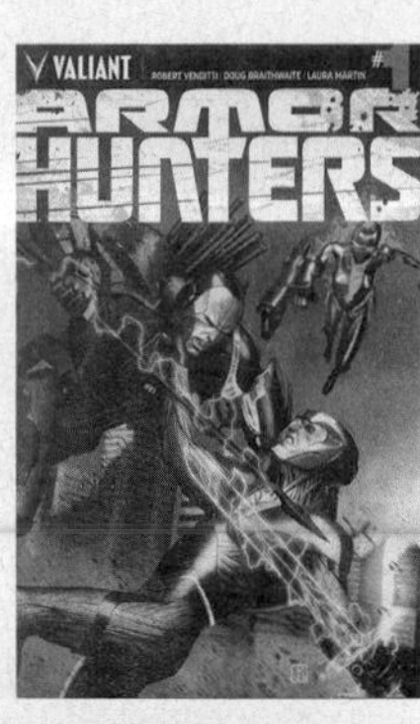

Armor Hunters #1 © VAL

Army @ Love #12 © Rick Veitch

Army of Darkness V4 #1 © Orion

	GD	VG	FN	VF	VF/NM	NM-
	2.0	4.0	6.0	8.0	9.0	9.2

1-4-Lady Death, Evil Ernie, Purgatori app. 3.00

ARMAGEDDON: ALIEN AGENDA
DC Comics: Nov, 1991 - No. 4, Feb, 1992 ($1.00, limited series)
1-4 3.00

ARMAGEDDON FACTOR, THE
AC Comics: 1987 - No. 2, 1987; No. 3, 1990 ($1.95)
1,2: Sentinels of Justice, Dragonfly, Femforce 3.00
3-($3.95, color)-Almost all AC characters app. 4.00

ARMAGEDDON: INFERNO
DC Comics: Apr, 1992 - No. 4, July, 1992 ($1.00, limited series)
1-4: Many DC heroes app. 3-A. Adams/Austin-a 3.00

ARMAGEDDON 2001
DC Comics: May, 1991 - No. 2, Oct, 1991 ($2.00, squarebound, 68 pgs.)
1-Features many DC heroes; intro Waverider 5.00
1-2nd & 3rd printings; 3rd has silver ink-c 4.00
2 4.00

ARMED & DANGEROUS
Acclaim Comics (Armada): Apr, 1996 - No.4, July, 1996 ($2.95, B&W)
1-4-Bob Hall-c/a & scripts 3.00
Special 1 (8/96, $2.95, B&W)-Hall-c/a & scripts. 3.00

ARMED & DANGEROUS HELL'S SLAUGHTERHOUSE
Acclaim Comics (Armada): Oct, 1996 - No. 4, Jan, 1997 ($2.95, B&W)
1-4: Hall-c/a/scripts. 3.00

ARMOR (AND THE SILVER STREAK) (Revengers Featuring... in indicia for #1-3)
Continuity Comics: Sept, 1985 - No.13, Apr, 1992 ($2.00)
1-13: 1-Intro/origin Armor & the Silver Streak; Neal Adams-c/a. 7-Origin Armor; Nebres-i 4.00

ARMOR (DEATHWATCH 2000)
Continuity Comics: Apr, 1993 - No. 6, Nov, 1993 ($2.50)
1-6: 1-3-Deathwatch 2000 x-over 3.00

ARMOR HUNTERS
Valiant Entertainment: Jun, 2014 - No. 4, Sept, 2014 ($3.99)
1-4-Venditti-s/Braithwaite-a; X-O vs. the Hunters. 2-4-Bloodshot app. 4-Ninjak app. 4.00
...: Aftermath 1 (10/14, $3.99) Venditti-s/Cafu-a; leads into Unity #0 4.00

ARMOR HUNTERS: BLOODSHOT
Valiant Entertainment: Jul, 2014 - No. 3, Sept, 2014 ($3.99, limited series)
1-3-Joe Harris-s/Hairsine-a; Malgam app. 4.00

ARMOR HUNTERS: HARBINGER
Valiant Entertainment: Jul, 2014 - No. 3, Sept, 2014 ($3.99, limited series)
1-3-Dysart-s/Gill-a 4.00

ARMORINES (See X-O Manowar #25 for 16 pg. bound-in Armorines #0)
Valiant: June, 1994 - No. 12, June, 1995 ($2.25)
0-Stand-alone edition with cardstock-c 30.00
0-Gold 25.00
1 4.00
2-12: 7-Wraparound-c. 12-Byrne-c/swipe (X-Men, 1st Series #138) 3.00

ARMORINES (Volume 2)
Acclaim Comics: Oct, 1999 - No. 4 ($3.95/$2.50, limited series)
1-($3.95) Calafiore & P. Palmiotti-a 4.00
2,3-($2.50) 3.00

ARMOR WARS (Secret Wars tie-in)
Marvel Comics: Aug, 2015 - No. 5, Nov, 2015 ($3.99, limited series)
1-5-Tony Stark and other armor-clad citizens of Technopolis; Robinson-s/Takara-a 4.00

ARMOR X
Image Comics: March, 2005 - No. 4, June, 2005 ($2.95, limited series)
1-Keith Champagne-s/Andy Smith-a; flip covers on #2-4 3.00

ARMSTRONG AND THE VAULT OF SPIRITS (Archer and Armstrong)
Valiant Entertainment: Feb, 2018 ($3.99, one-shot)
1-Van Lente-s/Cafu & Robertson-a; Archer, Faith, Quantum & Woody, Ivar app. 4.00

ARMY AND NAVY COMICS (Supersnipe No. 6 on)
Street & Smith Publications: May, 1941 - No. 5, July, 1942

	GD 2.0	VG 4.0	FN 6.0	VF 8.0	VF/NM 9.0	NM- 9.2
1-Cap Fury & Nick Carter	61	122	183	390	670	950
2-Cap Fury & Nick Carter	37	74	111	222	361	500
3,4: 4-Jack Farr-c/a	29	58	87	170	278	385
5-Supersnipe app.; see Shadow V2#3 for 1st app.; Story of Douglas MacArthur; George Marcoux-c/a	58	116	174	371	636	900

ARMY @ LOVE
DC Comics (Vertigo): May, 2007 - No. 12, Apr, 2008; V2 #1, Oct, 2008 - No. 6, Mar, 2009 ($2.99)
1-12-Rick Veitch-s/a(p); Gary Erskine-a(i) 3.00
(Vol. 2) 1-6-Veitch-s/a(p); Erskine-a(i) 3.00
...: Generation Pwned TPB (2008, $12.99) r/#6-12 13.00
...: The Hot Zone Club TPB (2007, $9.99) r/#1-5; intro. by Peter Kuper 10.00

ARMY ATTACK
Charlton Comics: July, 1964 - No. 4, Feb, 1965; V2#38, July, 1965 - No. 47, Feb, 1967

	GD 2.0	VG 4.0	FN 6.0	VF 8.0	VF/NM 9.0	NM- 9.2
V1#1	5	10	15	30	50	70
2-4(2/65)	3	6	9	19	30	40
V2#38(7/65)-47 (formerly U.S. Air Force #1-37)	3	6	9	16	23	30

NOTE: *Glanzman a-1-3. Montes/Bache a-44.*

ARMY AT WAR (Also see Our Army at War & Cancelled Comic Cavalcade)
DC Comics: Oct-Nov, 1978

	GD 2.0	VG 4.0	FN 6.0	VF 8.0	VF/NM 9.0	NM- 9.2
1-Kubert-c; all new story and art	3	6	9	14	20	25

ARMY OF DARKNESS (Movie)
Dark Horse Comics: Nov, 1992 - No. 2, Dec, 1992; No. 3, Oct, 1993 ($2.50, limited series)

	GD 2.0	VG 4.0	FN 6.0	VF 8.0	VF/NM 9.0	NM- 9.2
1-Bolton painted-c/a in all	3	6	9	17	26	35
2,3	2	4	6	11	16	20

... Movie Adaptation TPB (2006, $14.99) r/#1-3; intro. by Busiek; Bruce Campbell interview 15.00

ARMY OF DARKNESS (Also see Marvel Zombies vs. Army of Darkness)
Dynamite Entertainment: 2005 - No. 13, 2007 ($2.99)
1-4 (Vs. Re-Animator):1,2-Four covers; Greene-a/Kuhoric-s. 3,4-Three covers 4.00
5-13: 5-7-Kuhoric-s/Sharpe-a; four covers. 8-11-Ash Vs. Dracula. 12,13-Death of Ash 4.00

ARMY OF DARKNESS: ... (Also see Death to the Army of Darkness)
Dynamite Entertainment: 2007 - No. 27, 2010 ($3.50/$3.99)
... From the Ashes 1-4-Kuhoric-s/Blanco-a; covers by Blanco & Suydam 4.00
5-8-(The Long Road Home); two covers on each 4.00
9-25: 9-12-(Home Sweet Hell), 13-King For a Day. 14-17-Hellbillies and Deadnecks 4.00
26,27-($3.99) Raicht-s/Cohn-a/c 4.00
#1992.1 (2014, $7.99, squarebound) Short stories by Kuhoric, Niles and others 8.00
...: Ash's Christmas Horror Special (2008, $4.99) Kuhoric-s/Simons-a; 2 covers 5.00
...: Convention Invasion (2014, $7.99, squarebound) Moreci-s/Peeples-a 8.00
... Election Special 1 (2016, $5.99) Serrano-s/Galindo-a 6.00
... Halloween Special One-Shot (2018, $4.99) art by Marron & Lofti; Blackbeard app. 5.00
.../ Reanimator One Shot (2013, $4.99) Rahner-s/Valiente-a 5.00

ARMY OF DARKNESS VOLUME 3
Dynamite Entertainment: 2012 - No. 13, 2013 ($3.99)
1-13: 1-Female Ash; Michaels-a 4.00

ARMY OF DARKNESS VOLUME 4
Dynamite Entertainment: 2014 - No. 5, 2015 ($3.99)
1-5-Ash in space; Bunn-s/Watts-a; multiple covers 4.00

ARMY OF DARKNESS: ASHES 2 ASHES (Movie)
Devil's Due Publ.: July, 2004 - No. 4, 2004 ($2.99, limited series)
1-4-Four covers for each; Nick Bradshaw-a 4.00
1-Director's Cut (12/04, $4.99) r/#1, cover gallery, script and sketch pages 5.00
TPB (2005, $14.99) r/series; cover gallery; Bradshaw interview and sketch pages 15.00

ARMY OF DARKNESS: ASH GETS HITCHED
Dynamite Entertainment: 2014 - No. 4, 2014 ($3.99, limited series)
1-4-Ash in medieval times; Niles-s/Tenorio-a; multiple covers 4.00

ARMY OF DARKNESS: ASH SAVES OBAMA
Dynamite Entertainment: 2009 - No. 4, 2009 ($3.50, limited series)
1-4-Serrano-s/Padilla-a; covers by Parrillo and Nauck. 4-Obama app. 4.00

ARMY OF DARKNESS/BUBBA HO-TEP
Dynamite Entertainment/IDW: 2019 - No. 4, 2019 ($3.99, limited series)
1-4-Ash meets Elvis; Duvall-s/Federici-a; multiple covers 4.00

ARMY OF DARKNESS FURIOUS ROAD
Dynamite Entertainment: 2016 - No. 6, 2016 ($3.99, limited series)
1-6-Nancy Collins-s/Kewber Baal-a. 1-Multiple covers 4.00

ARMY OF DARKNESS: SHOP TILL YOU DROP DEAD (Movie)
Devil's Due Publ.: Jan, 2005 - No. 4, July, 2005 ($2.99, limited series)
1-4:1-Five covers; Bradshaw-a/Kuhoric-s. 2-4: Two covers. 3-Greene-a 4.00

ARMY OF DARKNESS VS. HACK/SLASH
Dynamite Entertainment: 2013 - No. 6, 2014 ($3.99, limited series)

Arrow #1 © DC

Artifact One #2 © AspenMLT

Ascencia #1 © John Dolmayan

	GD	VG	FN	VF	VF/NM	NM-
	2.0	4.0	6.0	8.0	9.0	9.2

1-6-Tim Seeley-s/Daniel Leister-a; multiple covers on each 4.00

ARMY OF DARKNESS / XENA
Dynamite Entertainment: 2008 - No. 4, 2008 ($3.50, limited series)
1-4-Layman-s/Montenegro-a; two covers on each 4.00

ARMY OF DARKNESS XENA: WARRIOR PRINCESS FOREVER... AND A DAY
Dynamite Entertainment: 2016 - No. 6, 2017 ($3.99, limited series)
1-6-Lobdell-s. 1-Multiple covers. 1,2-Fernandez-a. 3-6-Galindo-a 4.00

ARMY SURPLUS KOMIKZ FEATURING CUTEY BUNNY
Army Surplus Komikz/Eclipse Comics: 1982 - No. 5, 1985 ($1.50, B&W)
1-Cutey Bunny begins 2 4 6 8 10 12
2-5: 5-(Eclipse)-JLA/X-Men/Batman parody 4.50

ARMY WAR HEROES (Also see Iron Corporal)
Charlton Comics: Dec, 1963 - No. 38, June, 1970
1 6 12 18 41 76 110
2-10 3 6 9 21 33 45
11-21,23-30: 24-Intro. Archer & Corp. Jack series 3 6 9 16 23 30
22-Origin/1st app. Iron Corporal series by Glanzman 5 10 15 30 50 70
31-38 2 4 6 10 14 18
Modern Comics Reprint 36 ('78) 5.00
NOTE: *Montes/Bache a-1, 16, 17, 21, 23-25, 27-30.*

AROUND THE BLOCK WITH DUNC & LOO (See Dunc and Loo)

AROUND THE WORLD IN 80 DAYS (Movie) (See A Golden Picture Classic)
Dell Publishing Co.: Feb, 1957
Four Color 784-Photo-c 7 14 21 46 86 125

AROUND THE WORLD UNDER THE SEA (See Movie Classics)

AROUND THE WORLD WITH ARCHIE (See Archie Giant Series Mag. #29, 35, 141)

AROUND THE WORLD WITH HUCKLEBERRY & HIS FRIENDS (See Dell Giant No. 44)

ARRGH! (Satire)
Marvel Comics Group: Dec, 1974 - No. 5, Sept, 1975 (25¢)
1-Dracula story; Sekowsky-a(p) 3 6 9 20 31 42
2-5: 2-Frankenstein. 3-Mummy. 4-Nightstalker(TV); Dracula-c/app., Hunchback. 5-Invisible Man, Dracula 3 6 9 14 20 25
NOTE *Alcala a-2; c-3. Everett a-1r, 2r. Grandenetti a-4. Maneely a-4r. Sutton a-1-3.*

ARROW (See Protectors)
Malibu Comics: Oct, 1992 ($1.95, one-shot)
1-Moder-a(p) 4.00

ARROW (Based on the 2012 television series)
DC Comics: Jan, 2013 - No. 12, Dec, 2013 ($3.99, printings of digital-first stories)
1-Photo-c; origin retold; Grell-a 1 2 3 5 6 8
1-Special Edition (2012, giveaway) Grell-c; back-up preview of Green Arrow #0 3.00
2-12: 8-12-Photo-c 4.00

ARROW SEASON 2.5 (Follows the second season of the 2012 television series)
DC Comics: Dec, 2014 - No. 12, Nov, 2015 ($2.99, printings of digital-first stories)
1-12-Photo-c on most. 1-5-Brother Blood app. 5,6-Suicide Squad app. 3.00

ARROW, THE (See Funny Pages)
Centaur Publications: Oct, 1940 - No. 2, Nov, 1940; No. 3, Oct, 1941
1-The Arrow begins(r/Funny Pages) 415 830 1245 2905 5103 7300
2,3: 2-Tippy Taylor serial continues from Amazing Mystery Funnies #24. 3-Origin Dash Dartwell, the Human Meteor; origin The Rainbow-r; bondage-c 271 542 813 1734 2967 4200
NOTE: *Gustavson a-1, 2; c-3.*

ARROWHEAD (See Black Rider and Wild Western)
Atlas Comics (CPS): April, 1954 - No. 4, Nov, 1954
1-Arrowhead & his horse Eagle begin 23 46 69 136 223 310
2-4: 4-Forte-a 15 30 45 83 124 165
NOTE: *Heath c-3. Jack Katz a-3. Maneely c-2. Pakula a-2. Sinnott a-1-4; c-1.*

ARROWSMITH (Also see Astro City/Arrowsmith flip book)
DC Comics (Cliffhanger): Sept, 2003 - No. 6, May, 2004 ($2.95)
1-6-Pacheco-a/Busiek-s 3.00
...: So Smart in Their Fine Uniforms TPB (2004, $14.95) r/#1-6 15.00

ARSENAL (Teen Titans' Speedy)
DC Comics: Oct, 1998 - No. 4, Jan, 1999 ($2.50, limited series)
1-4: Grayson-s. 1-Black Canary app. 2-Green Arrow app. 4.00

ARSENAL SPECIAL (See New Titans, Showcase '94 #7 & Showcase '95 #8)
DC Comics: 1996 ($2.95, one-shot)
1 4.00

ARTBABE
Fantagraphics Books: May, 1996 - Apr, 1999 ($2.50/$2.95/$3.50, B&W)
V1 #5, V2 #1-3 3.00
#4-($3.50) 3.50

ARTEMIS & THE ASSASSIN
AfterShock Comics: Mar, 2020 - No. 5, Sept, 2020 ($4.99/$3.99)
1-($4.99) Stephanie Phillips-s/Meghan Hetrick & Francesca Fantini-a 5.00
2-5-($3.99) 3-5-Fantini-a 4.00

ARTEMIS IX (See Aphrodite IX)
Image Comics (Top Cow): Aug, 2015 ($3.99, one-shot)
1-Dan Wickline-s/Johnny Desjardins-a; 2 covers 4.00

ARTEMIS: REQUIEM (Also see Wonder Woman, 2nd Series #90)
DC Comics: June, 1996 - No. 6, Nov, 1996 ($1.75, limited series)
1-6: Messner-Loebs scripts & Benes-c/a in all. 1,2-Wonder Woman app. 3.00

ARTIFACT ONE
Aspen MLT: No. 0, Aug, 2018 - No. 4, Mar, 2019 ($3.99)
0-($1.50) Krul & Hernandez-s/Moranelli-a 3.00
1-4: 1-(10/18, $3.99) Krul & Hernandez-s/Moranelli-a; bonus Aspen Mascots story 4.00

ARTIFACTS
Image Comics (Top Cow): Jul, 2010 - No. 40, Nov, 2014 ($3.99, intended as a limited series)
0-(5/10, free) Free Comic Book Day edition; Sejic-a 3.00
1-39: 1-6-Marz-s/Broussard-a. 1-Multiple covers; back-up origin of Witchblade. 7,8-Portacio-a. 9-12-Haun-a. 10-Wraparound-c by Sejic. 13-Keown-a. 14-25-Sejic-a 4.00
40-($5.99) Steve Foxe-s/Adalor Alvarez-a/Sejic-c; back-up stories 6.00
... Lost Tales 1 (5/15, $3.99) Short stories by Talent Hunt runners-up 4.00
...Origins (1/12, $3.99) Two-page spread origins of the 13 artifacts; wraparound-c 4.00

ART OF HOMAGE STUDIOS, THE
Image Comics: Dec, 1993 ($4.95, one-shot)
1-Short stories and pin-ups by Jim Lee, Silvestri, Williams, Portacio & Chiodo 5.00

ART OF ZEN INTERGALACTIC NINJA, THE
Entity Comics: 1994 - No. 2, 1994 ($2.95)
1,2 3.00

ART OPS
DC Comics (Vertigo): Dec, 2015 - No. 12, Dec, 2016 ($3.99)
1-12: Shaun Simon-s/Mike Allred-c. 1-5,8,9,12-Mike Allred-a. 6,7-Eduardo Risso-a 4.00

ARZACH (See Moebius...)
Dark Horse Comics: 1996 ($6.95, one-shot)
nn-Moebius-c/a/scripts 4 8 12 27 44 60

ASCENCIA
Wake Entertainment: Jan, 2021 - Present ($3.99)
1-John Dolmayan-s/Tony Parker-a 4.00

ASCENDER (Also see Descender)
Image Comics: Apr, 2019 - Present ($3.99)
1-14-Lemire-s/Nguyen-a/c in all. 4-Telsa app. 4.00

ASCENSION
Image Comics (Top Cow Productions): Oct, 1997 - No. 22, Mar, 2000 ($2.50)
Preview 5.00
Preview Gold Edition 8.00
Preview San Diego Edition 2 4 6 8 10 12
0 4.00
1/2 6.00
1-David Finch-s/a(p)/Batt-s/a(i) 4.00
1-Variant-c w/Image logo at lower right 6.00
2-22 3.00
... Collected Edition 1,2 (1998 - No. 2, $4.95, squarebound) 1-r/#1,2. 2-r/#3,4 5.00
Fan Club Edition 5.00

ASGARDIANS OF THE GALAXY
Marvel Comics: Nov, 2018 - No. 10, Aug, 2019 ($3.99)
1-10-Angela, Valkyrie, Skurge, Thunderstrike, Throg (Thor Frog), The Destroyer team 4.00

ASH
Event Comics: Nov, 1994 - No. 6, Dec, 1995; No. 0, May, 1996 ($2.50/$3.00)
0-Present & Future (Both 5/96, $3.00, foil logo-c)-w/pin-ups 3.00
0-Blue Foil logo-c (Present and Future) (1000 each) 4.00
0-Silver Prism logo-c (Present and Future) (500 each) 10.00

Ash: Cinder & Smoke #2 © Q&P

Aspen Universe: Decimation #1 © AspenMLT

Assassin's Creed #9 © Ubisoft

	GD 2.0	VG 4.0	FN 6.0	VF 8.0	VF/NM 9.0	NM- 9.2
0-Red Prism logo-c (Present and Future) (250 each)						20.00
0-Gold Hologram logo-c (Present and Future) (1000 each)						8.00
1-Quesada-p/story; Palmiotti-i/story: Barry Windsor-Smith pin-up	2	4	6	8	10	12
2-Mignola Hellboy pin-up	1	2	3	4	5	7
3,4: 3-Big Guy pin-up by Geoff Darrow. 4-Jim Lee pin-up						4.00
4-Fahrenheit Gold						7.00
4-6-Fahrenheit Red (5,6-1000)						8.00
4-6-Fahrenheit White						12.00
5, 6-Double-c w/Hildebrandt Bros.-a, Quesada & Palmiotti. 6-Texeira-c						3.00
5,6-Fahrenheit Gold (2000)						4.00
6-Fahrenheit White (500)-Texeira-c						12.00
Volume 1 (1996, $14.95, TPB)-r/#1-5, intro by James Robinson						15.00
Wizard Mini-Comic (1996, magazine supplement)						3.00
Wizard #1/2 (1997, mail order)						4.00

ASH AND THE ARMY OF DARKNESS (Leads into Army of Darkness: Ash Gets Hitched)
Dynamite Entertainment: 2013 - No. 8, 2014 ($3.99)

1-8: 1-5-Niles-s/Calero-a. 1-Three covers. 2-8-Two covers. 6-8-Tenorio-a 4.00

ASH & THORN
AHOY Comics: 2020 - No. 5, 2020 ($3.99)

1-5-Mariah McCourt-s/Soo Lee-a/ Jill Thompson-c 4.00

ASH: CINDER & SMOKE
Event Comics: May, 1997 - No. 6, Oct, 1997 ($2.95, limited series)

1-6: Ramos-a/Waid, Augustyn-s in all. 2-6-variant covers by Ramos and Quesada 3.00

ASH: FILES
Event Comics: Mar, 1997 ($2.95, one-shot)

1-Comics w/text 3.00

ASH: FIRE AND CROSSFIRE
Event Comics: Jan, 1999 - No. 5 ($2.95, limited series)

1,2-Robinson-s/Quesada & Palmiotti-c/a 3.00

ASH: FIRE WITHIN, THE
Event Comics: Sept, 1996 - No. 2, Jan, 1997 ($2.95, unfinished limited series)

1,2: Quesada & Palmiotti-c/s/a 3.00

ASH/ 22 BRIDES
Event Comics: Dec, 1996 - No. 2, Apr, 1997 ($2.95, limited series)

1,2: Nicieza-s/Ramos-c/a 3.00

ASH VS. THE ARMY OF DARKNESS
Dynamite Entertainment: No. 0, 2017 - No. 5, 2017 ($3.99)

0-5: 0-Sims & Bowers-s/Vargas-a; multiple covers on each 4.00

ASKANI'SON (See Adventures of Cyclops & Phoenix limited series)
Marvel Comics: Jan, 1996 - No. 4, May, 1996 ($2.95, limited series)

1-4: Story cont'd from Advs. of Cyclops & Phoenix; Lobdell/Loeb story; Gene Ha-c/a(p) 3.00
TPB (1997, $12.99) r/#1-4; Gene Ha painted-c 13.00

ASPEN (MICHAEL TURNER PRESENTS:...) (Also see Fathom)
Aspen MLT, Inc.: July, 2003 - No. 3, Aug, 2003 ($2.99)

1-Fathom story; Turner-a/Johns-s; interviews w/Turner & Johns; two covers by Turner 3.00
2,3:2-Fathom story; Turner-a/Johns-s; two covers by Turner; pin-ups and interviews 3.00
... Presents: The Adventures of the Aspen Universe (10/16, free) coloring book; Oum-a3.00
... Seasons: Fall 2005 (12/05, $2.99) short stories by various; Turner-c 3.00
... Seasons: Spring 2005 (4/05, $2.99) short stories by various; Turner-c 3.00
... Seasons: Summer 2006 (10/06, $2.99) short stories by various; Turner-c 3.00
... Seasons: Winter 2009 (3/09, $2.99) short stories by various; Benitez-c 3.00
... Showcase: Aspen Matthews 1 (7/08, $2.99) Caldwell-a 3.00
... Showcase: Kiani 1 (10/09, $2.99) Scott Clark-a; covers by Clark and Caldwell 3.00
... Sketchbook 1 (2003, $2.99) sketch pages by Michael Turner and Talent Caldwell 3.00
... Splash: 2006 Swimsuit Spectacular 1 (3/06, $2.99) pin-up pages by various; Turner-c 3.00
... Splash: 2007 Swimsuit Spectacular 1 (8/07, $2.99) pin-up pages by various; Turner-c 3.00
... Splash: 2008 Swimsuit Spectacular 1 (7/08, $2.99) pin-up pages by various; Turner-c 3.00
... Splash: 2010 Swimsuit Spectacular 1 (8/10, $2.99) pin-up pages by various; 2 covers 3.00
... Splash: 2018 Swimsuit Spectacular 1 (7/18, $3.99) pin-up pages by various; 2 covers 4.00
...: The Year Ahead 2019 1 (2/19, 25¢) Previews, summaries of TPBs, creator profiles 3.00
... Universe Sourcebook 1 (7/16, $5.99) Character profiles for Fathom, Soulfire, Iris 6.00

ASPEN SHOWCASE
Aspen MLT: Oct, 2008 ($2.99)

...: Benoist 1 (10/08) - Krul-s/Gunnell-a; two covers by Gunnell & Manapul 3.00
...: Ember 1 (2/09) - Randy Green-a; two covers by Gunnell & Green 3.00

ASPEN UNIVERSE: DECIMATION
Aspen MLT: No. 0, May, 2017; No. 1, Oct, 2017 - No. 4, Jan, 2018 (free/$3.99)

0-(5/17, free) Prelude to Aspen crossover series; Hernandez-s/Renna & Bazaldua-a 3.00
1-4-($3.99) Hernandez-s/Renna-a 4.00

ASPEN UNIVERSE: REVELATIONS
Aspen MLT: Jul, 2016 - No. 5, Dec, 2016 ($3.99)

1-5-Fathom & Soulfire crossover; Fialkov & Krul-s/Gunderson-a; multiple covers 4.00

ASPEN VISIONS
Aspen MLT: Jan, 2019 - Mar, 2019 ($3.99)

...: Executive Assistant: Iris: The Midst of Chaos 1 (1/19) - Northcott-s/Tran-a; 4 covers 4.00
...: Fathom: Spinning Our Fate 1 (2/19) - Northcott-s/Sta Maria-a; 4 covers 4.00
...: Soulfire: The Heart of Eternity 1 (3/19) - Northcott-s/Cafaro-a; 4 covers 4.00

ASSASSINISTAS
IDW Publishing (Black Crown): Dec, 2017 - No. 6, May, 2018 ($3.99)

1-6-Tini Howard-s/Gilbert Hernandez-a 4.00

ASSASSIN NATION
Image Comics (Skybound): Mar, 2019 - No. 5, Jul, 2019 ($3.99, limited series)

1-5-Kyle Starks-s/Erica Henderson-a/c 4.00

ASSASSINS
DC Comics (Amalgam): Apr, 1996 ($1.95)

1 3.00

ASSASSIN'S CREED (Based on the Ubisoft Entertainment videogame)
Titan Comics: Nov, 2015 - No. 14, Feb, 2017 ($3.99/$4.99)

1-Trial By Fire; Del Col & McCreery-s/Edwards-a; multiple-c 6.00
2-12: 2-5-Trial By Fire. 6-11-Setting Sun 4.00
13,14-($4.99) Homecoming 5.00
... Free Comic Book Day (5/16, giveaway) Alves-a; Great Wall back-up w/Calero-a 3.00

ASSASSIN'S CREED: AWAKENING (Based on the Ubisoft Entertainment videogame)
Titan Comics: Dec, 2016 - No. 6, May, 2017 ($4.99, B&W manga style, reads right to left)

1-6-Takashi Yano-s/Kenji Oiwa-a 5.00

ASSASSIN'S CREED: CONSPIRACIES (Based on the Ubisoft Entertainment videogame)
Titan Comics: Sept, 2018 - No. 2, Oct, 2018 ($5.99, limited series)

1,2: 1-Dorison-s/Hostache-a. 2-Pion-a 6.00

ASSASSIN'S CREED: LOCUS (Based on the Ubisoft Entertainment videogame)
Titan Comics: Oct, 2016 - No. 4, Jan, 2017 ($3.99, limited series)

1-4-Edginton-s/Wijngaard-a 4.00

ASSASSIN'S CREED: ORIGINS (Based on the Ubisoft Entertainment videogame)
Titan Comics: Mar, 2018 - No. 4, Jul, 2018 ($3.99, limited series)

1-4-Del Col-s/Kaiowa-a. 1-Four covers. 2-4-Two covers 4.00

ASSASSIN'S CREED: REFLECTIONS (Based on the Ubisoft Entertainment videogame)
Titan Comics: Apr, 2017 - No. 4, Aug, 2017 ($3.99, limited series)

1-4-Edginton-s/Favoccia-a 4.00

ASSASSIN'S CREED: THE FALL (Based on the Ubisoft Entertainment videogame)
DC Comics: Jan, 2011 - No. 3, Mar, 2011 ($3.99, limited series)

1-3-Cam Stewart & Karl Kerschl-s/a 4.00

ASSASSIN'S CREED: UPRISING (Based on the Ubisoft Entertainment videogame)
Titan Comics: Feb, 2017 - No. 8, Nov, 2017 ($3.99)

	GD	VG	FN	VF	VF/NM	NM-
1-Paknadel & Watters-s/Holder-a; multiple covers	1	2	3	5	6	8
2-8-Paknadel & Watters-s/Holder-a; multiple covers						5.00

ASSASSIN'S CREED VALHALLA: SONG OF GLORY (Ubisoft Entertainment videogame)
Dark Horse Comics: Oct, 2020 - No. 3, Dec, 2020 ($3.99)

1-3-Cavan Scott-s/Martín Túnica-a 4.00

ASSIGNMENT, THE (Adapts screenplay of 2017 movie The Assignment)
Titan Comics (Hard Case Crime): Feb, 2017 - No. 3, Apr, 2017 ($5.99)

1-3-Walter Hill & Denis Hamill-s/Jef-a; English version of French comic 6.00

ASSAULT ON NEW OLYMPUS PROLOGUE
Marvel Comics: Jan, 2010 ($3.99, one-shot)

1-Spider-Man, Hercules, Amadeus Cho app.; Granov-c; leads into Inc. Hercules #138 4.00

ASTONISHING (Formerly Marvel Boy No. 1, 2)
Marvel/Atlas Comics(20CC): No. 3, Apr, 1951 - No. 63, Aug, 1957

	GD	VG	FN	VF	VF/NM	NM-
3-Marvel Boy continues; 3-5-Marvel Boy-c	187	374	561	1197	2049	2900
4-Classic skeletons-c; 4-Stan Lee app.	174	348	522	1114	1907	2700
5,6-Last Marvel Boy	126	252	378	806	1378	1950
7-10: 7-Maneely s/f story. 10-Sinnott s/f story	58	116	174	371	636	900

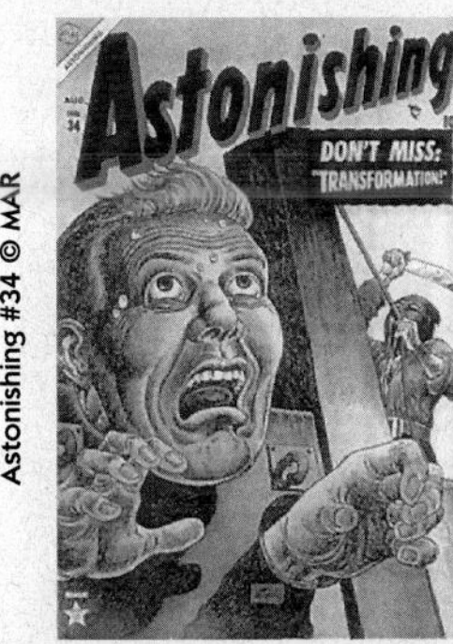

Astonishing #34 © MAR

Astonishing X-Men (2004 series) #5 © MAR

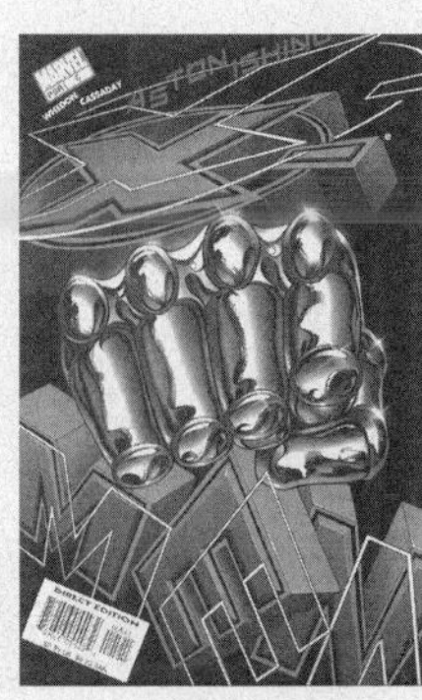

Astounding Wolf-Man #5 © Kirkman & Howard

	GD 2.0	VG 4.0	FN 6.0	VF 8.0	VF/NM 9.0	NM- 9.2
11,12,15,17,20	52	104	156	328	552	775
13,14,16,18,19-Krigstein-a. 18-Jack The Ripper sty	53	106	159	334	567	800
21,22,24	41	82	123	256	428	600
23-E.C. swipe "The Hole In The Wall" from Vault Of Horror #16	43	86	129	271	461	650
25,29: 25-Crandall-a. 29-Decapitation-c	40	80	120	246	411	575
26-28	39	78	117	240	395	550
30-Tentacled eyeball-c/story; classic-c	194	388	582	1242	2121	3000
31-Classic story: man develops atomic powers after exposure to A-bomb; four A-bomb panels	68	136	204	435	743	1050
32-37-Last pre-code issues	34	68	102	204	332	460
38-43,46,48-52,56,58,59,61	26	52	78	156	256	355
44,45,47,53-55,57,60: 44-Crandall swipe/Weird Fantasy #22. 45,47-Krigstein-a. 53-Ditko-a. 54-Torres-a, 55-Crandall, Torres-a. 57-Williamson/Krenkel-a (4 pgs.). 60-Williamson/Mayo-a (4 pgs.)	29	58	87	172	281	390
62,63: 62-Torres, Powell-a. 63-Woodbridge-a	29	58	87	172	281	390

NOTE: ***Ayers*** *a-16, 49.* ***Berg*** *a-36, 53, 56.* ***Cameron*** *a-50.* ***Gene Colan*** *a-12, 20, 29, 56.* ***Ditko*** *a-53.* ***Drucker*** *a-41, 62.* ***Everett*** *a-3-6(3), 6, 10, 12, 37, 47, 48, 58; c-3-5, 13,15, 16, 18, 29, 47, 49, 51, 53-55, 57, 59-63.* ***Fass*** *a-11, 34.* ***Forte*** *a-26, 48, 53, 58, 60.* ***Fuje*** *a-11.* ***Heath*** *a-8, 29; c-8, 9, 19, 22, 25, 26.* ***Kirby*** *a-56.* ***Lawrence*** *a-28, 37, 38, 42.* ***Maneely*** *a-7(2), 19; c-7, 31, 33, 34, 56.* ***Moldoff*** *a-33.* ***Morisi*** *a-10, 60.* ***Morrow*** *a-52, 61.* ***Orlando*** *a-47, 58, 61.* ***Pakula*** *a-10.* ***Powell*** *a-43, 44, 48.* ***Ravielli*** *a-26, 28.* ***Reinman*** *a-32, 34, 38.* ***Robinson*** *a-20.* ***J. Romita*** *a-7, 18, 24, 43, 57,61.* ***Roussos*** *a-55.* ***Sale*** *a-28, 38, 59; c-32.* ***Sekowsky*** *a-13.* ***Severin*** *c-46.* ***Shores*** *a-16, 60.* ***Sinnott*** *a-11, 30, 31.* ***Whitney*** *a-13.* ***Ed Win*** *a-20. Canadian reprints exist.*

ASTONISHING ANT-MAN (Scott Lang)
Marvel Comics: Dec, 2015 - No. 13, Dec, 2016 ($3.99)

1-12: 1-Spencer-s/Rosanas-a; Cassie Lang app. 2,3-Capt. America (Sam Wilson) app. 4.00
13-($4.99) Spencer-s/Schoonover & Rosanas-a; Yellowjacket app. 5.00

ASTONISHING SPIDER-MAN AND WOLVERINE
Marvel Comics: Jul, 2010 - No. 6, Jul. 2011 ($3.99, limited series)

1-6-Adam Kubert-a/Jason Aaron-s. 1-Bonus pin-up gallery; wraparound-c 4.00
1-Director's Cut (10/10, $4.99) r/#1 with full script & B&W art 5.00
...: Another Fine Mess (6/11, $4.99) r/#1-3; wraparound-c 5.00

ASTONISHING TALES (See Ka-Zar)
Marvel Comics Group: Aug, 1970 - No. 36, July, 1976 (#1-7: 15¢; #8: 25¢)

	GD	VG	FN	VF	VF/NM	NM-
1-Ka-Zar (by Kirby(p) #1,2; by B. Smith #3-6) & Dr. Doom (by Wood #1-4; by Tuska #5,6; by Colan #7,8; 1st Marvel villain solo series) double feature begins; Kraven the Hunter-c/story; Nixon cameo	6	12	18	41	76	110
2-Kraven the Hunter-c/story; Kirby, Wood-a	4	8	12	23	37	50
3-5: B. Smith-p; Wood-a-#3,4. 5-Red Skull app.	4	8	12	25	40	55
6-1st app. Bobbi Morse (later becomes Mockingbird); Doctor Doom vs. Black Panther-c/sty;	6	12	18	41	76	110
7-Last 15¢ issue; Black Panther app.	3	6	9	17	26	35
8-(25¢, 52 pgs.)-Last Dr. Doom of series	4	8	12	25	40	55
9-All Ka-Zar issues begin; Lorna-r/Lorna #14	2	4	6	11	16	20
10-B. Smith/Sal Buscema-a.	3	6	9	14	20	25
11-Origin Ka-Zar & Zabu; death of Ka-Zar's father	3	6	9	14	20	25
12-2nd app.Man-Thing; by Neal Adams (see Savage Tales #1 for 1st app.)	6	12	18	38	69	100
13-3rd app.Man-Thing	4	8	12	27	44	60
14-20: 14-Jann of the Jungle-r (1950s); reprints censored Ka-Zar-s from Savage Tales #1. 17-S.H.I.E.L.D. begins. 19-Starlin-a(p). 20-Last Ka-Zar (continues into 1974 Ka-Zar series); Nick Fury & S.H.I.E.L.D. app.	1	3	4	6	8	10
21-(12/73)-It! the Living Colossus begins, ends #24 (see Supernatural Thrillers #1)	4	8	12	23	37	50
22	3	6	9	17	26	35
23,24-It! the Living Colossus vs. Fin Fang Foom	4	8	12	27	44	60
25-1st app. Deathlok the Demolisher; full length stories begin, end #36; Perez's 1st work, 2 pgs. (8/74)	9	18	27	60	120	180
26-28,30	3	6	9	14	20	25
29-Reprints origin/1st app. Guardians of the Galaxy from Marvel Super-Heroes #18 plus-c w/4 pgs. omitted; no Deathlok story	4	8	12	25	40	55
31-34: 31-Watcher-r/Silver Surfer #3	2	4	6	10	14	18
35,36-(Regular 25¢ edition)(5,7/76)	2	4	6	10	14	18
35,36-(30¢-c, low distribution)	7	14	21	44	82	120

NOTE: ***Buckler*** *a-13i, 16p, 25, 26p, 27p, 28, 29p-36p; c-13, 25p, 26-30, 32-35p, 36.* ***John Buscema*** *a-9, 12p-14p, 16p; c-4-6p, 12p.* ***Colan*** *a-7p, 8p.* ***Ditko*** *a-21r.* ***Everett*** *a-6i.* ***G. Kane*** *a-11p, 15p; c-9, 10p, 11p, 14, 15p, 21p.* ***McWilliams*** *a-30i.* ***Starlin*** *a-19p; c-16p.* ***Sutton & Trimpe*** *a-8.* ***Tuska*** *a-5p, 6p, 8p.* ***Wood*** *a-1-4.* ***Wrightson*** *c-31i.*

ASTONISHING TALES (Anthology)
Marvel Comics: Apr, 2009 - No. 6, Sept, 2009 ($3.99, limited series)

1-6-Wolverine, Punisher, Iron Man and Iron Man 2020 app. 1-Wraparound-c 4.00

ASTONISHING THOR
Marvel Comics: Jan, 2011 - No. 5, Sept, 2011 ($3.99, limited series)

1-5: 1-Robert Rodi-s/Mike Choi-a/Esad Ribic-c 4.00

ASTONISHING X-MEN
Marvel Comics: Mar, 1995 - No. 4, July, 1995 ($1.95, limited series)

1-Age of Apocalypse; Magneto-c 5.00
2-4 3.00

ASTONISHING X-MEN
Marvel Comics: Sept, 1999 - No. 3, Nov, 1999 ($2.50, limited series)

1-3-New team, Cable & X-Man app.; Peterson-a 3.00
TPB (11/00, $15.95) r/#1-3, X-Men #92 & #95, Uncanny X-Men #375 16.00

ASTONISHING X-MEN (See Giant-Size Astonishing X-Men for story folllowing #24)
Marvel Comics: July, 2004 - No. 68, Dec, 2013 ($2.99/$3.99)

1-Whedon-s/Cassaday-c/a; team of Cyclops, Beast, Wolverine, Emma Frost & Kitty Pryde 4.00
1-Director's Cut (2004, $3.99) different Cassaday partial sketch-c; cover gallery, sketch pages and script excerpt 5.00
1-Variant-c by Cassaday 10.00
1-Variant-c by Dell'Otto 5.00
2,3,5,6-X-Men battle Ord 3.00
4-Colossus returns 4.00
4-Variant Colossus cover by Cassaday 5.00
7-24: 7-Fantastic Four app. 9,10-X-Men vs. the Danger Room 3.00
7,9,10-12,19-24-Second printing variant covers 3.00
25-35: 25-Ellis-s/Bianchi-a begins; Bianchi wraparound-c. 31-Jimenez-a begins 3.00
36-68-($3.99): 36-Pearson wraparound-c; Way-s/Pearson-a. 44-47-McKone-a. 51-Northstar wedding; wraparound-c. 60-X-Termination tie-in 4.00
Annual 1 (1/13, $4.99) Gage-s/Baldeon-a; bonus r/Alpha Flight #106 5.00
.../Amazing Spider-Man: The Gauntlet Sketchbook ('09, giveaway) flip book preview 3.00
...: Ghost Boxes 1,2 (12/08-1/09, $3.99) Ellis-s/Davis & Granov-a; full Ellis script 4.00
... Saga (2006, $3.99) reprints highlights from #1-12; sketch pages and cover gallery 4.00
... Sketchbook Special ('08, $2.99) Costume sketches & blueprints by Bianchi & Larroca 3.00
...Vol. 1 HC (2006, $29.99, dust jacket) r/#1-12; interviews, sketch pages and covers 30.00
...Vol. 1: Gifted (2004, $14.99) r/#1-6; variant cover gallery 15.00
...Vol. 2: Dangerous (2005, $14.99) r/#7-12; variant cover gallery 15.00
...Vol. 3: Torn (2007, $14.99) r/#13-18; variant & sketch cover gallery 15.00

ASTONISHING X-MEN
Marvel Comics: Sept, 2017 - No. 17, Jan, 2019 ($4.99/$3.99)

1-($4.99) Soule-s/Cheung-a; Old Man Logan, Rogue, Bishop, Gambit, Psylocke app. 5.00
2-17-($3.99) 2-Deodato-a; Mystique app. 3-McGuinness-a. 4-Pacheco-a. 7-Xavier returns; Noto-a. 13,14-Havok & Banshee return; Land-a 4.00
Annual 1 (10/18, $4.99) Rosenberg-s/Foreman-a; Xavier & Lucifer app. 5.00

ASTONISHING X-MEN: XENOGENESIS
Marvel Comics: July, 2010 - No. 5, Apr, 2011 ($3.99, limited series)

1-5-Warren Ellis-s/Kaare Andrews-a/c. 1-Wraparound-c; script 4.00
1-Director's Cut (10/10, $4.99) r/#1 with full script & B&W art; cover sketches 5.00

ASTOUNDING SPACE THRILLS: THE COMIC BOOK
Image Comics: Apr, 2000 - No. 4, Dec, 2000 ($2.95, limited series)

1-4-Steve Conley-s/a. 2,3-Flip book w/Crater Kid 3.00
Galaxy-Sized Astounding Space Thrills 1 (10/01, $4.95) 5.00

ASTOUNDING WOLF-MAN
Image Comics: Jun, 2007 - No. 25, Nov, 2010 ($2.99)

1-Free Comic Boy Day issue; Kirkman-s/Howard-a; origin story 3.00
2-24: 11-Invincible x-over from Invincble #57 3.00
25-($4.99) Wraparound-c; Wolfcorps app. 5.00
Vol. 1 TPB (2008, $14.99) r/#1-7; sketch pages; Kirkman intro. 15.00

ASTRA
CPM Manga: 2001 - No. 8 ($2.95, B&W, limited series)

1-8: Created by Jerry Robinson; Tanaka-a. 1-Balent variant-c 3.00
TPB (2002, $15.95) r/#1-8; JH Williams III-c from #3 16.00

ASTRO BOY (TV) (See March of Comics #285 & The Original...)
Gold Key: August, 1965 (12¢)

	GD	VG	FN	VF	VF/NM	NM-
1(10151-508) 1st app. Astro Boy in comics	29	58	87	209	467	725

ASTRO BOY THE MOVIE (Based on the 2009 CGI movie)
IDW Publishing: 2009 ($3.99, limited series)

...Official Movie Adaptation 1-4 (8/09 - No. 4, 9/09, $3.99) EJ Su-a 4.00
...Official Movie Prequel 1-4 (5/09 - No. 4, 8/09) Jourdan-a/c; Ashley Wood var-c on each 4.00

ASTRO CITY (Also see Kurt Busiek's Astro City)
DC Comics (WildStorm Productions): Dec, 2004 - Dec, 2009 (one-shots)

...#1 Special Edition (8/10, $1.00) reprints first issue with "What's Next? cover logo 3.00
...: Astra Special 1,2 (11/09, 12/09, $3.99) Busiek-s/Anderson-a/Ross-c 4.00
... A Visitor's Guide (12/04, $5.95) short story, city guide and pin-ups by various; Ross-c 6.00

Astro City (2013 series) #14 © Juke Box

Atlantis Attacks #4 © MAR

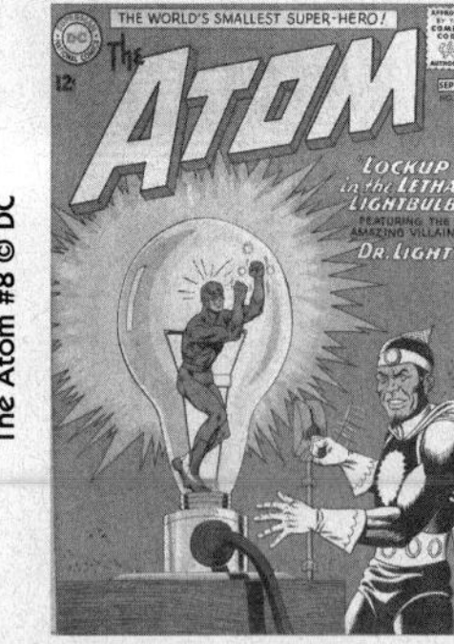

The Atom #8 © DC

	GD 2.0	VG 4.0	FN 6.0	VF 8.0	VF/NM 9.0	NM- 9.2

...: Beautie (4/08, $3.99) Busiek-s/Anderson-a/Ross-c; origin 4.00
...: Samaritan (9/06, $3.99) Busiek-s/Anderson-a/Ross-c; origin of Infidel 4.00
...: Shining Stars HC (2011, $24.99, d.j) r/...: Astra Special 1,2, ...: Beautie, ...: Samaritan, and ...: Silver Agent 1,2; bonus design art and Ross cover sketch art 25.00
...: Silver Agent 1,2 (8,9/10, $3.99) Busiek-s/Anderson-a/Ross-c 4.00

ASTRO CITY (Also see Kurt Busiek's Astro City)
DC Comics (Vertigo): Aug, 2013 - No. 52, Aug, 2018 ($3.99)

1-52-Busiek-s/Ross-c; Anderson-a in most. 12-Nolan-a. 17-Grummett-a. 22,25-Merino-a. 35,36-Ron Randall-a; Jack-In-The Box app. 39,40-Carnero-a. 47-Origin G-Dog 4.00

ASTRO CITY / ARROWSMITH (Flip book)
DC Comics (WildStorm Productions): Jun, 2004 ($2.95, one-shot flip book)

1-Intro. Black Badge; Ross-c; Arrowsmith a/c by Pacheco 3.00

ASTRO CITY: DARK AGE
DC Comics (WildStorm Productions): Aug, 2005 - No. 4, Dec, 2005 ($2.95, limited series)

Book One 1-4-Busiek-s/Anderson-a/Ross-c; Silver Agent and The Blue Knight app. 3.00
Book Two #1-4 (1/07-11/07, $2.99) Busiek-s/Anderson-a/Ross-c 3.00
Book Three #1-4 (7/09-10/09, $3.99) Busiek-s/Anderson-a/Ross-c 4.00
Book Four #1-4 (3/10-6/10, $3.99) Busiek-s/Anderson-a/Ross-c 4.00
... 1: Brothers and Other Strangers HC (2008, $29.99, d.j.) r/Book One #1-4, Book Two #1-4, and story from Astro City/Arrowsmith #1; Marc Guggenheim intro.; new Ross-c 30.00
... 1: Brothers and Other Strangers SC (2009, $19.99) same contents as HC 20.00
... 2: Brothers in Arms HC ('10, $29.99, d.j.) r/Book Three #1-4, Book Four #1-4, Ross-c 30.00

ASTRO CITY: LOCAL HEROES
DC Comics (WildStorm Productions): Apr, 2003 - No. 5, Feb, 2004 ($2.95, limited series)

1-5-Busiek-s/Anderson-a/Ross-c 3.00
HC (2005, $24.95) r/series; Kurt Busiek's Astro City V2 #21,22; stories from Astro City/Arrowsmith #1; and 9-11, The World's Finest... Vol. 2; Alex Ross sketch pages 25.00
SC (2005, $17.99) same contents as HC 18.00

ASTRO HUSTLE
Dark Horse Comics: Mar, 2019 - No. 2, Apr, 2019 ($3.99, unfinished limited series of 4 issues)

1,2-Jai Nitz-s/Tom Reilly-a 4.00

ASTRONAUTS IN TROUBLE
Image Comics: Jun, 2015 - No. 11 ($2.99, B&W, reprints of earlier Astronauts in Trouble)

1-11-Larry Young-s. 1-3-Reprints the Space: 1959 series; Charlie Adlard-a. 4-9-Reprints the Live From the Moon series. 4-6-Matt Smith-a. 7-11-Adlard-a 3.00

ASYLUM
Millennium Publications: 1993 ($2.50)

1-3: 1-Bolton-c/a; Russell 2-pg. illos 3.00

ASYLUM
Maximum Press: Dec, 1995 - No. 11, Jan, 1997 ($2.95/$2.99, anthology)
(#1-6 are flip books)

1-11: 1-Warchild by Art Adams, Beanworld, Avengelyne, Battlestar Galactica. 2-Intro Mike Deodato's Deathkiss. 4-1st app.Christian; painted Battlestar Galactica story begins. 6-Intro Bionix (Six Million Dollar Man & the Bionic Woman). 7-Begin $2.99-c. 8-B&W-a. 9- Foot Soldiers & Kid Supreme. 10-Lady Supreme by Terry Moore-c/app. 4.00

ATARI FORCE (Also see Promotional comics section)
DC Comics: Jan, 1984 - No. 20, Aug, 1985 (Mando paper)

1-(1/84)-Intro Tempest, Packrat, Babe, Morphea, & Dart; García-López-a 4.00
2-20 3.00
Special 1 (4/86) 4.00
NOTE: ***Byrne*** *c-Special 1i.* ***Giffen*** *a-12p, 13i.* ***Rogers*** *a-18p, Special 1p.*

A-TEAM, THE (TV) (Also see Marvel Graphic Novel)
Marvel Comics Group: Mar, 1984 - No. 3, May, 1984 (limited series)

	GD	VG	FN	VF	VF/NM	NM-
1-Marie Severin-a/John Romita-c	2	4	6	9	12	15
2,3: 2-Mooney-a. 3-Kupperberg-s/a	1	2	3	5	6	8
1,2-(Whitman bagged set) w/75¢-c	2	4	6	10	14	18
3-(Whitman, no bag) w/75¢-c	1	3	4	6	8	10

A-TEAM: SHOTGUN WEDDING (Based on the 2010 movie)
IDW Publishing: Mar, 2010 - No. 4, Apr, 2010 ($3.99, limited series)

1-4-Co-plotted by Joe Carnahan; Stephen Mooney-a; Snyder III-c 4.00

A-TEAM: WAR STORIES (Based on the 2010 movie)
IDW Publishing: Mar, 2010 - Apr, 2010 ($3.99, series of one-shots)

...: B.A. (3/10) Dixon & Burnham-s/Maloney-a/Gaydos & photo-c 4.00
...: Face (4/10) Dixon & Burnham-s/Muriel-a/Gaydos & photo-c 4.00
...: Hannibal (3/10) Dixon & Burnham-s/Petrus-a/Gaydos & photo-c 4.00
...: Murdock (4/10) Dixon & Burnham-s/Vilanova-a/Gaydos & photo-c 4.00

ATHENA INC. THE MANHUNTER PROJECT
Image Comics: Dec, 2001; Apr, 2002 - No. 6 ($2.95/$4.95/$5.95)

...The Beginning (12/01, $5.95) Anacleto-c/a; Haberlin-s 6.00
1-5: 1-(4/02, $2.95) two covers by Anacleto 3.00
6-($4.95) 5.00
...: Agents Roster #1 (11/02, $5.95, 8 1/2 x 11") bios and sketch pages by Anacleto 6.00
Vol. 1 TPB (4/03, $19.95) r/#1-6 & Agents Roster; cover gallery 20.00

ATHENA
Dynamite Entertainment: 2009 - No. 4, 2010 ($3.50)

1-4-Murray-s/Neves-a; multiple covers on each. 1-Obama flip cover 3.50

ATHENA IX (See Aphrodite IX)
Image Comics (Top Cow): Jul, 2015 ($3.99, one-shot)

1-Ryan Cady-s/Phillip Sevy; 3 covers 4.00

ATLANTIS ATTACKS (Continued from Agents of Atlas 2019-2020 series)
Marvel Comics: Mar, 2020 - No. 5, Feb, 2021 ($3.99, limited series)

1-5-Greg Pak-s/Ario Anindito-a; the current and the original Agents of Atlas app. 4.00

ATLANTIS CHRONICLES, THE (Also see Aquaman, 3rd Series & Aquaman: Time & Tide)
DC Comics: Mar, 1990 - No. 7, Sept, 1990 ($2.95, limited series, 52 pgs.)

1-7: 1-Peter David scripts. 7-True origin of Aquaman; nudity panels 4.00

ATLANTIS, THE LOST CONTINENT
Dell Publishing Co.: May, 1961

	GD	VG	FN	VF	VF/NM	NM-
Four Color 1188-Movie, photo-c	9	18	27	60	120	180

ATLAS (See 1st Issue Special)

ATLAS
Dark Horse Comics: Feb, 1994 - No. 4, 1994 ($2.50, limited series)

1-4 3.00

ATLAS (Agents of Atlas)(The Heroic Age)
Marvel Comics: Jul, 2010 - No. 5, Nov, 2010 ($3.99/$2.99)

1-($3.99) Parker-s/Hardman-a/Dodson-c; 3-D Man app.; profile page 4.00
2-5-($2.99) 2,3,5-Pagulayan-c. 4-Jae Lee-c 3.00

ATLAS UNIFIED
Atlas Comics: No. 0, Oct, 2011 - No. 2, Feb, 2012 ($2.99, unfinished limited series)

0 Prelude: Midnight (10/11) Phoenix, Kromag, Sgt. Hawk app.; bonus sketch pages 3.00
1,2: 1-Three covers; Peyer-s/Salgado-a; x-over of Grim Ghost, Wulf, Phoenix & others 3.00

ATMOSPHERICS
Avatar Press: June, 2002 ($5.95, B&W, one-shot graphic novel)

1-Warren Ellis-s/Ken Meyer Jr.-painted-a/c 6.00

ATOM, THE (See Action #425, All-American #19, Brave & the Bold, D.C. Special Series #1, Detective Comics, Flash Comics #80, Hawkman, Identity Crisis, JLA, Power Of The Atom, Showcase #34 -36, Super Friends, Sword of The Atom, Teen Titans & World's Finest)

ATOM, THE (...& the Hawkman No. 39 on)
National Periodical Publ.: June-July, 1962 - No. 38, Aug-Sept, 1968

	GD	VG	FN	VF	VF/NM	NM-
1-(6-7/62)-Intro Plant-Master; 1st app. Maya	111	222	333	888	1994	3100
2	31	62	93	223	499	775
3-1st Time Pool story; 1st app. Chronos (origin)	24	48	72	168	372	575
4,5: 4-Snapper Carr x-over	15	30	45	103	227	350
6,9,10	11	22	33	76	163	250
7-Hawkman x-over (6-7/63; 1st Atom & Hawkman team-up); 1st app. Hawkman since Brave & the Bold tryouts	23	46	69	161	356	550
8-Justice League, Dr. Light app.	13	26	39	87	191	295
11-15: 13-Chronos-c/story	9	18	27	60	120	180
16-18,20	7	14	21	46	86	125
19-Zatanna x-over; 2nd app.	15	30	45	103	227	350
21-28,30: 26-Two-page pin-up. 28-Chronos-c/story	6	12	18	41	76	110
29-1st solo Golden Age Atom x-over in S.A.	12	24	36	79	170	260
31-35,37,38: 31-Hawkman x-over. 37-Intro. Major Mynah; Hawkman cameo	5	10	15	35	63	90
36-G.A. Atom x-over	7	14	21	44	82	120

NOTE: ***Anderson*** *a-1-11i, 13i; c-inks-1-25, 31-35, 37.* ***Sid Greene*** *a-8i-37i.* ***Gil Kane*** *a-1p-37p; c-1p-28p, 29, 33p, 34; c-26i.* ***George Roussos*** *a-38i.* ***Mike Sekowsky*** *a-38p. Time Pool stories also in 6, 9,12, 17, 21, 27, 35.*

ATOM, THE (See All New Atom and Tangent Comics/ The Atom)

ATOM AGE (See Classics Illustrated Special Issue)

ATOM-AGE COMBAT
St. John Publishing Co.: June, 1952 - No. 5, Apr, 1953; Feb, 1958

	GD	VG	FN	VF	VF/NM	NM-
1-Buck Vinson in all	58	116	174	371	636	900
2-Flying saucer story	37	74	111	222	361	500
3,5: 3-Mayo-a (6 pgs.). 5-Flying saucer-c/story	32	64	96	188	307	425
4 (Scarce)	37	74	111	222	361	500

Atomic Comics #2 © Green Pub. Co.

The Atomics #3 © Mike Allred

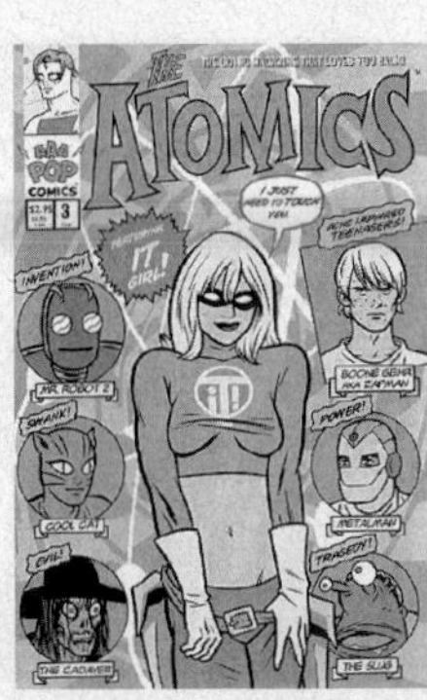

Attack #4 © YM

	GD 2.0	VG 4.0	FN 6.0	VF 8.0	VF/NM 9.0	NM- 9.2
1(2/58-St. John)	27	54	81	162	266	370
ATOM-AGE COMBAT						
Fago Magazines: No. 2, Jan, 1959 - No. 3, Mar, 1959						
2-A-Bomb explosion-c;	33	66	99	194	320	445
3	24	48	72	144	237	330
ATOMAN						
Spark Publications: Feb, 1946 - No. 2, April, 1946						
1-Origin & 1st app. Atoman; Robinson/Meskin-a; Kidcrusaders, Wild Bill Hickok, Marvin the Great app.	82	164	246	528	902	1275
2-Robinson/Meskin-a; Robinson c-1,2	47	94	141	296	498	700
ATOM & HAWKMAN, THE (Formerly The Atom)						
National Periodical Publ: No. 39, Oct-Nov, 1968 - No. 45, Oct-Nov, 1969; No. 46, Mar, 2010						
39-43: 40-41-Kubert/Anderson-a. 43-(7/69)-Last 12¢ issue; 1st S.A. app. Gentleman Ghost	5	10	15	34	60	85
44,45: 44-(9/69)-1st 15¢-c; origin Gentleman Ghost	5	10	15	34	60	85
46-(3/10, $2.99) Blackest Night crossover one-shot; Geoff Johns-s/Ryan Sook-a/c						3.00
NOTE: *M. Anderson a-39, 40i, 41i, 43, 44. Sid Greene a-40i-45i. Kubert a-40p, 41p; c-39-45.*						
ATOM ANT (TV) (See Golden Comics Digest #2) (Hanna-Barbera)						
Gold Key: January, 1966 (12¢)						
1(10170-601)-1st app. Atom Ant, Precious Pup, and Hillbilly Bears	15	30	45	103	227	350
ATOM ANT & SECRET SQUIRREL (See Hanna-Barbera Presents)						
ATOMIC AGE						
Marvel Comics (Epic Comics): Nov, 1990 - No. 4, Feb, 1991 ($4.50, limited series, squarebound, 52 pgs.)						
1-4: Williamson-a(i); sci-fi story set in 1957						4.50
ATOMIC ATTACK (True War Stories; formerly Attack, first series)						
Youthful Magazines: No. 5, Jan, 1953 - No. 8, Oct, 1953 (1st story is sci/fi in all issues)						
5-Atomic bomb-c; science fiction stories in all	52	104	156	328	552	775
6-8	34	68	102	204	332	460
ATOMIC BOMB						
Jay Burtis Publications: 1945 (36 pgs.)						
1-Superheroes Airmale & Stampy (scarce)	74	148	222	470	810	1150
ATOMIC BUNNY (Formerly Atomic Rabbit)						
Charlton Comics: No. 12, Aug, 1958 - No. 19, Dec, 1959						
12	12	24	36	69	97	125
13-19	8	16	24	42	54	65
ATOMIC COMICS						
Daniels Publications (Canadian): Jan, 1946 (Reprints, one-shot)						
1-Rocketman, Yankee Boy, Master Key app.	47	94	141	296	498	700
ATOMIC COMICS						
Green Publishing Co.: Jan, 1946 - No. 4, July-Aug, 1946 (#1-4 were printed w/o cover gloss)						
1-Radio Squad by Siegel & Shuster; Barry O'Neal app.; Fang Gow cover-r/ Detective Comics (Classic-c)	89	178	267	565	970	1375
2-Inspector Dayton; Kid Kane by Matt Baker; Lucky Wings, Congo King, Prop Powers (only app.) begin; atomic monster-c	61	122	183	390	670	950
3,4: 3-Zero Ghost Detective app.; Baker-a(2) each; 4-Baker-c	43	86	129	271	461	650
ATOMIC KNIGHTS (See Strange Adventures #117)						
DC Comics: 2010 ($39.99, HC with dustjacket)						
HC-Reprints the original 1960-64 run from debut in Strange Adventures #117 to S.A. #160; new intro. by Murphy Anderson						40.00
ATOMIC MOUSE (TV, Movies) (See Blue Bird, Funny Animals, Giant Comics Edition & Wotalife Comics)						
Capitol Stories/Charlton Comics: 3/53 - No. 52, 2/63; No. 1, 12/84; V2#10, 9/85 - No. 12, 1/86						
1-Origin & 1st app.; Al Fago-c/a in most	40	80	120	244	402	560
2	15	30	45	86	133	180
3-10: 5-Timmy The Timid Ghost app.; see Zoo Funnies	10	20	30	58	79	100
11-13,16-25	8	16	24	40	50	60
14,15-Hoppy The Marvel Bunny app.	9	18	27	50	65	80
26-(68 pgs.)	12	24	36	67	94	120
27-40: 36,37-Atom The Cat app.	6	12	18	29	36	42
41-52	5	10	15	22	26	30
1 (1984)-Low print run; rep/#7-c w/diff. stories	2	4	6	8	10	12
V2#10 (9/85) -12(1/86)-Low print run	1	3	4	6	8	10
ATOMIC RABBIT (Atomic Bunny #12 on; see Giant Comics #3 & Wotalife)						

	GD 2.0	VG 4.0	FN 6.0	VF 8.0	VF/NM 9.0	NM- 9.2
Charlton Comics: Aug, 1955 - No. 11, Mar, 1958						
1-Origin & 1st app.; Al Fago-c/a in all?	36	72	108	214	347	480
2	14	28	42	82	121	160
3-10	10	20	30	58	79	100
11-(68 pgs.)	14	28	42	82	121	160
ATOMICS, THE						
AAA Pop Comics: Jan, 2000 - No. 15, Nov, 2001 ($2.95)						
1-11-Mike Allred-s/a; 1-Madman-c/app.						3.00
12-15-($3.50): 13-15-Savage Dragon-c/app. 15-Afterword by Alex Ross; colored reprint of 1st Frank Einstein story						3.50
...King-Size Giant Spectacular: Jigsaw (2000, $10.00) r/#1-4						10.00
...King-Size Giant Spectacular: Lessons in Light, Lava, & Lasers (2000, $8.95) r/#5-8						9.00
...King-Size Giant Spectacular: Running With the Dragon ('02, $8.95) r/#13-15 and r/1st Frank Einstein app. in color						9.00
...King-Size Giant Spectacular: Worlds Within Worlds ('01, $8.95) r/#9-12						9.00
Madman and the Atomics, Vol. 1 TPB (2007, $24.99) r/#1-15, cover gallery, pin-ups, afterword by Alex Ross						25.00
...: Spaced Out & Grounded in Snap City TPB (10/03, $12.95) r/one-shots - It Girl, Mr. Gum, Spaceman and Crash Metro & the Star Squad; sketch pages						13.00
ATOMIC SPY CASES						
Avon Periodicals: Mar-Apr, 1950 (Painted-c)						
1-No Wood-a; A-bomb blast panels; Fass-a	47	94	141	296	498	700
ATOMIC THUNDERBOLT, THE						
Regor Company: Feb, 1946 (one-shot) (scarce)						
1-Intro. Atomic Thunderbolt & Mr. Murdo	84	168	252	538	919	1300
ATOMIC TOYBOX						
Image Comics: Dec, 1999 ($2.95)						
1- Aaron Lopresti-c/s/a						3.00
ATOMIC WAR!						
Ace Periodicals (Junior Books): Nov, 1952 - No. 4, Apr, 1953						
1-Atomic bomb-c	187	374	561	1197	2049	2900
2,3: 3-Atomic bomb-c	73	146	219	467	796	1125
4-Used in **POP**, pg. 96 & illo.	74	148	222	470	810	1150
ATOMIKA						
Speakeasy Comics/Mercury Comics: Mar, 2005 - No. 12, Jun, 2011 ($2.99)						
1-12: 1-Alex Ross-c/Sal Abbinanti-a/Dabb-s. 3-Fabry-c. 4-Four covers; Romita back-c						3.00
... God is Red TPB (5/06, $19.99) r/#1-6; cover gallery; Dabb foreword						20.00
ATOMIK ANGELS						
Crusade Comics: May, 1996 - No. 4, Nov. 1996 ($2.50)						
1-4: 1-Freefall from Gen 13 app.						3.00
1-Variant-c						4.00
Intrep-Edition (2/96, B&W, giveaway at launch party)-Previews Atomik Angels #1; includes Billy Tucci interview.						4.00
ATOM SPECIAL (See Atom & Justice League of America)						
DC Comics: 1993/1995 ($2.50/$2.95)(68pgs.)						
1,2: 1-Dillon-c/a. 2-McDonnell-a/Bolland-c/Peyer-s						4.00
ATOM THE CAT (Formerly Tom Cat; see Giant Comics #3)						
Charlton Comics: No. 9, Oct, 1957 - No. 17, Aug, 1959						
9	10	20	30	54	72	90
10,13-17	7	14	21	35	43	50
11,12: 11(64 pgs)-Atomic Mouse app. 12(100 pgs.)	11	22	33	62	86	110
ATTACK						
Youthful Mag./Trojan No. 5 on: May, 1952 - No. 4, Nov, 1952; No. 5, Jan, 1953 - No. 5, Sept, 1953						
1-(1st series)-Extreme violence	53	106	159	334	567	800
2,3-Both Harrison-c/a; bondage, whipping	29	58	87	170	278	385
4-Krenkel-a (7 pgs.); Harrison-a (becomes Atomic Attack #5 on)	29	58	87	170	278	385
5-(#1, Trojan, 2nd series)	19	38	57	109	172	235
6-8 (#2-4), 5	14	28	42	82	121	160
ATTACK						
Charlton Comics: No. 54, 1958 - No. 60, Nov, 1959						
54 (25¢, 100 pgs.)	13	26	39	74	105	135
55-60	8	16	24	40	50	60
ATTACK!						
Charlton Comics: 1962 - No. 15, 3/75; No. 16, 8/79 - No. 48, 10/84						
nn(#1)-('62) Special Edition	7	14	21	44	82	120

Authentic Police Cases #6 © STJ

The Authority V2 #1 © WSP

Autumn Adventures #1 © DIS

GD VG FN VF VF/NM NM-
2.0 4.0 6.0 8.0 9.0 9.2

2('63), 3(Fall, '64) 4 8 12 23 37 50
V4#3(10/66), 4(10/67)-(Formerly Special War Series #2; becomes Attack At Sea V4#5):
3-Tokyo Rose story 3 6 9 19 30 40
1(9/71)-D-Day story 3 6 9 16 23 30
2-5: 2-Hitler app. 4-American Eagle app. 2 4 6 9 12 15
6-15(3/75): 8-Nixon app. 1 3 4 6 8 10
16(8/79) - 40 5.00
41-47 Low print run 7.00
48(10/84)-Wood-r; S&K-c (low print) 1 3 4 6 8 10
Modern Comics 13('78)-r 5.00
NOTE: *Sutton a-9,10,13.*

ATTACK!
Spire Christian Comics (Fleming H. Revell Co.): 1975 (39¢/49¢, 36 pgs.)
nn 2 4 6 10 14 18

ATTACK AT SEA (Formerly Attack!, 1967)
Charlton Comics: V4#5, Oct, 1968 (one-shot)
V4#5 3 6 9 19 30 40

ATTACK ON PLANET MARS (See Strange Worlds #18)
Avon Periodicals: 1951
nn-Infantino, Fawcette, Kubert & Wood-a; adaptation of Tarrano the Conqueror by Ray Cummings 106 212 318 673 1162 1650

ATTRACTIVE COUSINS (Cerebus)
Aardvark-Vanaheim: Aug, 2020 ($4.00, B&W)
1-Cerebus figures with original Gustave Doré artwork; Supergirl Action #252-c swipe 4.00

AUDREY & MELVIN (Formerly Little...)(See Little Audrey & Melvin)
Harvey Publications: No. 62, Sept, 1974
62 2 4 6 9 13 16

AUGIE DOGGIE (TV) (See Hanna-Barbera Band Wagon, Quick-Draw McGraw, Spotlight #2, Top Cat & Whitman Comic Books)
Gold Key: October, 1963 (12¢)
1-Hanna-Barbera character 15 30 45 100 220 340

AUNTIE AGATHA'S HOME FOR WAYWARD RABBITS
Image Comics: Nov, 2018 - No. 6, Apr, 2019 ($3.99, limited series)
1-6-Keith Giffen-s/Benjamin Roman-a 4.00

AUTHENTIC POLICE CASES
St. John Publishing Co.: 2/48 - No. 6, 11/48; No. 7, 5/50 - No. 38, 3/55
1-Hale the Magician by Tuska begins 65 130 195 416 708 1000
2-Lady Satan, Johnny Rebel app. 43 86 129 271 461 650
3-Veiled Avenger app.; blood drainage story plus 2 Lucky Coyne stories; used in **SOTI**, illo. from Red Seal #16 69 138 207 442 759 1075
4,5: 4-Masked Black Jack app. 5-Late 1930s Jack Cole-a(r); transvestism story 43 86 129 271 461 650
6-Matt Baker-c; used in **SOTI**, illo- "An invitation to learning", r-in Fugitives From Justice #3; Jack Cole-a; also used by the N.Y. Legis. Comm. 168 336 504 1075 1838 2600
7,8,10-14: 7-Jack Cole-a; Matt Baker-a begins #8, ends #?; Vic Flint in #10-14. 10-12-Baker-a(2 each) 55 110 165 352 601 850
9-No Vic Flint 53 106 159 334 567 800
15-Drug-c/story; Vic Flint app.; Baker-c 103 206 309 659 1130 1600
16,17,19,22-Baker-c 52 104 156 328 552 775
18,20,21,23: Baker-a(i) 40 80 120 244 402 560
24-28 (All 100 pgs.): 26-Transvestism 58 116 174 371 636 900
29,31,32-Baker-c 45 90 135 284 480 675
30 31 62 93 182 296 410
33-38: 33-Baker-c. 34-Baker-c; drug story; r/#9. 35-Baker-c/a(2); r/#10. 36-r/#11; Vic Flint strip-r; Baker-c/a(2) unsigned. 37-Baker-c; r/#17. 38- Baker-c/a; r/#18 45 90 135 284 480 675
NOTE: *Matt Baker c-6-16, 17, 19, 22, 27, 29, 31-38; a-13, 16. Bondage c-1, 3.*

AUTHORITY, THE (See Stormwatch and Jenny Sparks: The Secret History of...)
DC Comics (WildStorm): May, 1999 - No. 29, Jul, 2002 ($2.50)
1-Wraparound-c; Warren Ellis-s/Bryan Hitch and Paul Neary-a 1 3 4 6 8 10
1-Special Edition (7/10, $1.00) r/#1 with "What's Next?" logo on cover 3.00
2-4 5.00
5-12: 12-Death of Jenny Sparks; last Ellis-s 4.00
13-Mark Millar-s/Frank Quitely-c/a begins 6.00
14-16-Authority vs. Marvel-esque villains 4.00
17-29: 17,18-Weston-a. 19,20,22-Quitely-a. 21-McCrea-a. 23-26-Peyer-s/Nguyen-a; new Authority. 25,26-Jenny Sparks app. 27,28-Millar-s/Art Adams-a/c 3.00
Annual 2000 ($3.50) Devil's Night x-over; Hamner-a/Bermejo-c 4.00

GD VG FN VF VF/NM NM-
2.0 4.0 6.0 8.0 9.0 9.2

Absolute Authority Slipcased Hardcover (2002, $49.95) oversized r/#1-12 plus script pages by Ellis and sketch pages by Hitch 50.00
...: Earth Inferno and Other Stories TPB (2002, $14.95) r/#17-20, Annual 2000, and Wildstorm Summer Special; new Quitely-c 15.00
...: Human on the Inside HC (2004, $24.95, dust jacket) Ridley-s/Oliver-a/c 25.00
...: Human on the Inside SC (2004, $17.99) Ridley-s/Oliver-a/c 18.00
...: Kev (10/02, $4.95) Ennis-s/Fabry-c/a 5.00
...: Relentless TPB (2000, $17.95) r/#1-8 18.00
...: Scorched Earth (2/03, $4.95) Robbie Morrison-s/Frazer Irving-a/Ashley Wood-c 5.00
...: Transfer of Power TPB (2002, $17.95) r/#22-29 18.00
...: Under New Management TPB (2000, $17.95) r/#9-16; new Quitely-c 18.00

AUTHORITY, THE (See previews in Sleeper, Stormwatch: Team Achilles and Wildcats Version 3.0)
DC Comics (WildStorm): Jul, 2003 - No. 14, Oct, 2004 ($2.95)
1-14: 1-Robbie Morrison-s/Dwayne Turner-a. 5-Huat-a. 14-Portacio-a 3.00
#0 (10/03, $2.95) r/preview back-up-s listed above; Turner sketch pages 3.00
...: Fractured Worlds TPB (2005, $17.95) r/#6-14; cover gallery 18.00
...: Harsh Realities TPB (2004, $14.95) r/#0-5; cover gallery 15.00
.../Lobo: Jingle Hell (2/04, $4.95) Bisley-c/a; Giffen & Grant-s 5.00
.../Lobo: Spring Break Massacre (8/05, $4.99) Bisley-c/a; Giffen & Grant-s 5.00

AUTHORITY, THE (Volume 4) (The Lost Year)
DC Comics (WildStorm): Dec, 2006 - No. 2, May 2007; No. 3, Jan, 2010 - No. 12, Oct, 2010 ($2.99)
1,2-Grant Morrison-s/Gene Ha-a/c 3.00
1-Variant cover by Art Adams 5.00
3-12: 3-(1/10) Morrison & Giffen-s/Robertson-a. 3-12-Ha-c. 12-Ordway-a 3.00
...Reader: The Lost Year (1/10, $2.99) r/#1,2 3.00
... Book One (2010, $17.99) r/#1-7; cover sketch art 18.00

AUTHORITY, THE (Volume 5) (World's End)
DC Comics (WildStorm): Oct, 2008 - No. 29, Jan, 2011 ($2.99)
1-29: 1-5-Simon Coleby-a/c; Lynch back-up story w/Hairsine-a/Gage-s. 21-Simonson-c 3.00
...: Rule Britannia TPB (2010, $19.99) r/#8-17 20.00
...: World's End TPB (2009, $17.99) r/#1-7 18.00

AUTHORITY, THE: MORE KEV
DC Comics (WildStorm): Jul, 2004 - No. 4, Dec, 2004 ($2.95, limited series)
1-4-Garth Ennis-s/Glenn Fabry-c/a 3.00
...: Kev TPB (2005, $14.99) r/Authority: Kev one-shot and Authority: More Kev series 15.00

AUTHORITY, THE: PRIME
DC Comics (WildStorm): Dec, 2007 - No. 6, May, 2008 ($2.99, limited series)
1-6-Gage-s/Robertson-c/a; Bendix app. 3.00
TPB (2008, $17.99) r/#1-6 18.00

AUTHORITY, THE: REVOLUTION
DC Comics (WildStorm): Dec, 2004 - No. 12, Dec, 2005 ($2.95/$2.99)
1-12-Brubaker-s/Nguyen-a. 5-Henry Bendix returns. 7-Jenny Sparks app. 3.00
...: Book One TPB (2005, $14.99) r/#1-6; cover gallery and Nguyen sketch pages 15.00
...: Book Two TPB (2006, $14.99) r/#7-12; cover gallery and Nguyen sketch pages 15.00

AUTHORITY, THE: THE MAGNIFICENT KEV
DC Comics (WildStorm): Nov, 2005 - No. 5, Feb, 2006 ($2.99, limited series)
1-5-Garth Ennis-s/Carlos Ezquerra-a/Glenn Fabry-c 3.00
TPB (2006, $14.99) r/#1-5 15.00

AUTOMATIC KAFKA
DC Comics (WildStorm): Sept, 2002 - No. 9, Jul, 2003 ($2.95)
1-9-Ashley Wood-c/a; Joe Casey-s 3.00

AUTUMN ADVENTURES (Walt Disney's...)
Disney Comics: Autumn, 1990; No. 2, Autumn, 1991 ($2.95, 68 pgs.)
1-Donald Duck-r(2) by Barks, Pluto-r, & new-a 4.00
2-D. Duck-r by Barks; new Super Goof story 4.00

AUTUMNLANDS: TOOTH & CLAW (Titled Tooth & Claw for issue #1, Autumnlands for #7-14)
Image Comics: Nov, 2014 - No. 14, Jan, 2017 ($2.99)
1-14: 1-Busiek-s/Dewey-a. 2-Variant-c by Alex Ross 3.00

AVANT-GUARDS, THE
BOOM! Studios (Boom! Box): Jan, 2019 - No. 8, Sept, 2019 ($3.99)
1-8-Carly Usdin-s/Noah Hayes-a 4.00

AVATAARS: COVENANT OF THE SHIELD
Marvel Comics: Sept, 2000 - No. 3, Nov, 2000 ($2.99, limited series)
1-3-Kaminski-s/Oscar Jimenez-a 3.00

AVATAR
DC Comics: Feb, 1991 - No. 3, Apr, 1991 ($5.95, limited series, 100 pgs.)

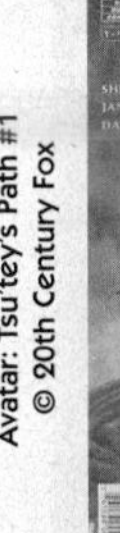
Avatar: Tsu'tey's Path #1 © 20th Century Fox

Avengers #4 © MAR

Avengers #67 © MAR

GD VG FN VF VF/NM NM-
2.0 4.0 6.0 8.0 9.0 9.2

1-3: Based on TSR's Forgotten Realms 6.00

AVATAR: THE NEXT SHADOW (Based on the James Cameron movie)
Dark Horse Comics: Jan, 2021 - No. 4 ($3.99, limited series)

1,2-Takes place 2 weeks after the movie; Jeremy Barlow-s/Josh Hood-a 4.00

AVATAR: TSU'TEY'S PATH (Based on the James Cameron movie)
Dark Horse Comics: Jan, 2019 - No. 6, Aug, 2019 ($3.99, limited series)

1-6-Sherri L. Smith-s/Jan Duursema-a 4.00

AVENGELYNE
Maximum Press: May, 1995 - No. 3, July, 1995 ($2.50/$3.50, limited series)

1/2 2 4 6 8 10 12
1/2 Platinum 15.00
1-Newstand ($2.50)-Photo-c; poster insert 6.00
1-Direct Market ($3.50)-Chromium-c; poster 1 2 3 4 5 7
1-Glossy edition 2 4 6 12 16 20
1-Gold 12.00
2-3: 2-Polybagged w/card 3.00
3-Variant-c; Deodato pin-up 5.00
...Bible (10/96, $3.50) 4.00
.../Glory (9/95, $3.95) 2 covers 4.00
.../Glory Swimsuit Special (6/96, $2.95) photo and illos. covers 3.00
.../Glory: The Godyssey (9/96, $2.99) 2 covers (1 photo) 3.00
...Revelation One (Avatar, 1/01, $3.50) 3 covers by Haley, Rio, Shaw; Shaw-a 3.50
.../Shi (Avatar, 11/01, $3.50) Eight covers; Waller-a 3.50
...Swimsuit (8/95, $2.95)-Pin-ups/photos. 3-Variant-c exist (2 photo, 1 Liefeld-a) 4.00
...Swimsuit (1/96, $3.50, 2nd printing)-photo-c 4.00
Trade paperback (12/95, $9.95) 10.00
.../Warrior Nun Areala 1 (11/96, $2.99) also see Warrior Nun/Avengelyne 3.00

AVENGELYNE
Maximum Press: V2#1, Apr, 1996 - No. 14, Apr, 1997 ($2.95/$2.50)

V2#1-Four covers exist (2 photo-c). 4.00
V2#2-Three covers exist (1 photo-c); flip book w/Darkchylde 5.00
V2#0, 3-14: 0-(10/96).3-Flip book w/Priest preview. 5-Flip book w/Blindside 3.00

AVENGELYNE (Volume 3)
Awesome Comics: Mar, 1999 ($2.50)

1-Fraga & Liefeld-a 3.00

AVENGELYNE (4th series)
Image Comics: Jul, 2011 - No. 8, May, 2012 ($2.99)

1-8-Liefeld & Poulson-s/Gieni-a. 1-Three covers by Liefeld, Gieni, and Benitez 3.00

AVENGELYNE: ARMAGEDDON
Maximum Press: Dec, 1996 - No. 3, Feb, 1997 ($2.99, limited series)

1-3-Scott Clark-a(p) 3.00

AVENGELYNE: DEADLY SINS
Maximum Press: Feb, 1996 - No. 2, Mar, 1996 ($2.95, limited series)

1,2: 1-Two-c exist (1 photo, 1 Liefeld-a). 2-Liefeld-c; Pop Mhan-a(p) 3.00

AVENGELYNE/POWER
Maximum Press: Nov, 1995 - No.3, Jan, 1996 ($2.95, limited series)

1-3: 1,2-Liefeld-c. 3-Three variant-c. exist (1 photo-c) 3.00

AVENGELYNE · PROPHET
Maximum Press: May, 1996; No. 2, Feb. 1997 ($2.95, unfinished lim. series)

1,2-Liefeld-c/a(p) 3.00

AVENGER, THE (See A-1 Comics)
Magazine Enterprises: Feb-Mar, 1955 - No. 4, Aug-Sept, 1955

1(A-1 #129)-Origin 54 108 162 343 574 825
2(A-1 #131), 3(A-1 #133) Robot-c, 4(A-1 #138) 54 108 162 343 574 825
IW Reprint #9('64)-Reprints #1 (new cover) 3 6 9 19 30 40
NOTE: *Powell a-2-4; c-1-4.*

AVENGER, THE (Pulp Hero from Justice Inc.)
Dynamite Entertainment: 2014 ($7.99)

... Special 2014: The Television Killers - Rahner-s/Menna-a/Hack-c 8.00

AVENGERS, THE (TV)(Also see Steed and Mrs. Peel)
Gold Key: Nov, 1968 ("John Steed & Emma Peel" cover title) (15¢)

1-Photo-c 10 20 30 84 132 200
1-(Variant with photo back-c) 17 34 51 117 259 400

AVENGERS, THE (See Essential..., Giant-Size..., JLA/..., Kree/Skrull War Starring..., Marvel Graphic Novel #27, Marvel Super Action, Marvel Super Heroes('66), Marvel Treasury Ed., Marvel Triple Action, New Avengers, Solo Avengers, Tales Of Suspense #49, West Coast Avengers & X-Men Vs....)

AVENGERS, THE (The Mighty Avengers on cover only #63-69)
Marvel Comics Group: Sept, 1963 - No. 402, Sept, 1996

1-Origin & 1st app. The Avengers (Thor, Iron Man, Hulk, Ant-Man, Wasp); Loki app. 920 1840 3680 10,200 28,100 46,000
2-Hulk leaves Avengers 121 242 363 968 2184 3400
3-2nd Sub-Mariner x-over outside the F.F. (see Strange Tales #107 for 1st); Sub-Mariner & Hulk team-up & battle Avengers; Spider-Man cameo (1/64) 93 186 279 744 1672 2600
4-Revival of Captain America who joins the Avengers; 1st Silver Age app. of Captain America & Bucky (3/64) 287 574 861 2440 5520 8600
4-Reprint from the Golden Record Comic set 19 38 57 131 291 450
With Record (1966) 25 50 75 175 388 600
5-Hulk app. 54 108 162 432 966 1500
6-1st app. original Zemo & his Masters of Evil 46 92 138 340 770 1200
7-Rick Jones app. in Bucky costume 42 84 126 311 706 1100
8-Intro Kang 89 178 267 712 1606 2500
9-Intro Wonder Man who dies in same story 57 114 171 456 1028 1600
10-Intro/1st app. Immortus; early Hercules app. (11/64) 32 64 96 230 515 800
11-Spider-Man-c & x-over (12/64) 37 74 111 274 612 950
12-15: 15-Death of original Zemo 19 38 57 133 297 460
16-New Avengers line-up (Hawkeye, Quicksilver, Scarlet Witch join; Thor, Iron Man, Giant-Man, Wasp leave) 38 76 114 285 641 1000
17,18: 17-Minor Hulk app. 14 28 42 96 211 325
19-1st app. Swordsman; origin Hawkeye (8/65) 17 34 51 117 259 400
20-22: Wood inks. 20-Intro. Power Man (Erik Josten) 11 22 33 72 154 235
23,24,26,27,29,30: 23-Romita Sr. inks (1st Silver Age Marvel work). 23,24-Avengers vs. Kang. 9 18 27 63 129 195
25-Dr. Doom-c/story 19 38 57 133 297 460
28-(5/66) First app. of The Collector; Giant-Man becomes Goliath 27 54 81 194 435 675
31-40: 32-1st Sons of the Serpent. 34-Last full Stan Lee plot/script. 35-1st Roy Thomas script w/Stan Lee plot. 38-40-Hercules app. 40-Sub-Mariner app. 8 16 24 54 102 150
41-46,50: 43-1st app. Red Guardian (dies in #44). 45-Hercules joins. 46-Ant-Man returns (re-intro, 11/67) 7 14 21 49 92 135
47-Magneto-c/story 18 36 54 124 275 425
48-Origin/1st app. new Black Knight (1/68) 36 72 108 259 580 900
49-Magneto-c/story 8 16 24 52 99 145
51-The Collector app. 8 16 24 54 102 150
52-Black Panther joins; 1st app. The Grim Reaper 10 20 30 66 138 210
53-X-Men app. 10 20 30 64 132 200
54-1st Ultron app. (1 panel); new Masters of Evil 11 22 33 76 163 250
55-1st full app. Ultron (8/68) (1 panel reveal in #54) 19 38 57 131 291 450
56-Zemo app; story explains how Capt. America became imprisoned in ice during WWII, only to be rescued in Avengers #4 9 18 27 58 114 170
57-1st app. S.A. Vision (10/68); death of Ultron-5 49 98 147 382 866 1350
57 Facsimile Edition (1/21, $3.99) Reprints #57 with original ads and letter column 4.00
58-Origin The Vision 11 22 33 72 154 235
59-Intro. Yellowjacket 12 24 36 82 179 275
60-65: 60-Wasp & Yellowjacket wed. 61-Dr. Strange app. 62-1st Man-Ape. 63-Goliath becomes Yellowjacket; Hawkeye becomes the new Goliath. 65-Last 12¢ issue 7 14 21 44 82 120
66-B. Smith-a; vs. Ultron-6; 1st mention of adamantium metal 8 16 24 54 102 150
67-Ultron-6 cvr/sty; B. Smith-a 9 18 27 61 123 185
68-Buscema-a 6 12 18 40 73 105
69-1st brief app. Squadron Sinister (Dr. Spectrum, Hyperion, Nighthawk) 10 20 30 70 150 230
70-1st full app. Nighthawk 10 20 30 64 132 200
71-1st app. The Invaders (12/69); Black Knight joins 11 22 33 72 154 235
72-79,81,82,84,86,90-91: 72-1st Zodiak; Captain Marvel & Nick Fury app. 73,74-Sons of the Serpent. 75-1st app. Arkon. 78-1st app. Lethal Legion (Man-Ape, Living Laser, Power Man, Grimm Reaper, Swordsman). 82-Daredevil app. 86-2nd Squadron Supreme app. 6 12 18 38 69 100
80-1st app. Red Wolf 8 16 24 55 105 155
83-Intro. The Liberators (Wasp, Valkyrie, Scarlet Witch, Medusa & the Black Widow) 14 28 42 96 211 325
85-1st app. Squadron Supreme (American Eagle, Dr. Spectrum, Hawkeye (Wyatt McDonald), Hyperion, Lady Lark, Nighthawk (Kyle Richmond), Tom Thumb, Whizzer) 8 16 24 56 108 160
87-Origin The Black Panther 11 22 33 73 157 240
88-Written by Harlan Ellison; Hulk app. 6 12 18 37 66 95
88-2nd printing (1994) 2 4 6 8 10 12
89-Classic Captain Marvel execution-c; beginning of Kree/Skrull War (runs through issue #97)

Avengers #141 © MAR

Avengers #189 © MAR

Avengers #254 © MAR

	GD 2.0	VG 4.0	FN 6.0	VF 8.0	VF/NM 9.0	NM- 9.2
	7	14	21	48	89	130
92-Last 15¢ issue; Neal Adams-c	8	16	24	54	102	150
93-(52 pgs.)-Neal Adams-c/a	15	30	45	100	220	340
94-96-Neal Adams-c/a	8	16	24	54	102	150
97-G.A. Capt. America, Sub-Mariner, Human Torch, Patriot, Vision, Blazing Skull, Fin, Angel, & new Capt. Marvel x-over	8	16	24	51	96	140
98,99: 98-Goliath becomes Hawkeye; Smith c/a(i). 99-Smith-c, Smith/Sutton-a	5	10	15	31	53	75
100-(6/72)-Smith-c/a; featuring everyone who was an Avenger	10	20	30	64	132	200
101-Harlan Ellison scripts	4	8	12	28	47	65
102-106,108,109	4	8	12	23	37	50
107-Starlin-a(p)	4	8	12	27	44	60
110,111-X-Men and Magneto app.	6	12	18	40	73	105
112-1st app. Mantis	10	20	30	64	132	200
113-115,119-124,126,128-130: 114-Swordsman returns; joins Avengers, first Mantis-c. 115-Prologue to Avengers/Defenders War. 119-Rutland, Vermont Halloween issue. 120-123-vs. Zodiac. 123,124-Mantis origin. 124-1st Star-Stalker. 126-Klaw & Solarr app. 129-Kang app; story continues in Giant-Size Avengers #2	3	6	9	19	30	40
116-118-Avengers/Defenders War; x-over w/Defenders #8-11. 116-Silver Surfer vs Vision. 117-Captain America vs. Sub-Mariner. 118-Avengers & Defenders vs. Loki & Dormammu	5	10	15	35	63	90
125-Thanos-c & brief app.; story continues in Captain Marvel #33	7	14	21	46	86	125
127-Ultron-7 app; story continues in Fantastic Four #150	4	8	12	23	37	50
131-133,136-140: 131,132-Vs. Kang. 131-1st Legion of the Unliving. 132-Continues in Giant-Size Avengers #3. 133-Origin of the Kree. 136-Ploog-r/Amazing Advs. #12. 137-Moondragon joins; Beast app; becomes provisional member; officially joins in #151; Wasp & Yellowjacket return	3	6	9	16	23	30
134,135-Origin of the Vision revised (also see Avengers Forever mini-series). 135-Continues in Giant-Size Avengers #4	4	8	12	23	37	50
141-143: 141-Squadron Supreme app; Pérez-a(p) begins. 142,143-Marvel Western heroes app. (Kid Colt, Rawhide Kid, Two-Gun Kid, Ringo Kid, Night Rider). 143-Vs. Kang (last 1970s app.)	2	4	6	12	15	20
144-Origin & 1st app. Hellcat (Patsy Walker)	7	14	21	49	92	135
145,146: Published out of sequence; Tony Isabella-s; originally intended to be in Giant-Size Avengers #5	2	4	6	9	12	15
146-149-(30¢-c variants, limited distribution)	6	12	18	40	73	105
147-149-(Reg. 25¢ editions)(5-7/76) Squadron Supreme app.	2	4	6	11	16	20
150-Kirby-a(r) pgs. 7-18 (from issue #16); pgs. 1-6 feature new-a by Pérez; new line-up: Capt. America, Iron Man, Scarlet Witch, Wasp, Yellowjacket, Vision & The Beast	3	6	9	14	20	25
150-(30¢-c variant, limited distribution)	6	12	18	40	73	105
151-Wonder Man returns w/new costume; Champions app.; The Collector app.	3	6	9	15	22	28
152-154,157,159,160,163: 152-1st app Black Talon. 154-vs. Attuma; continues in Super-Villain Team-up #9. 160-Grimm Reaper app. 163-Vs. The Champions	2	4	6	9	12	15
155,156-Dr. Doom app.	2	4	6	10	14	18
158-1st app. Graviton; Wonder Man vs. Vision; Jim Shooter plots begin	2	4	6	11	16	20
160-164-(35¢-c variants, limited dist.)(6-10/77)	9	18	27	61	123	185
161,162-Ultron-8 app; Henry Pym appears as Ant-Man. 162-1st app. Jocasta	3	6	9	15	22	28
164,165-Byrne-a; vs. Lethal Legion	2	4	6	10	14	18
166-Byrne-a; vs. Count Nefaria	2	4	6	13	18	22
167,168-Guardians of the Galaxy app.	2	4	6	11	16	20
169,172,178-180: 172-Hawkeye rejoins	1	3	4	6	8	10
170,171-Ultron & Jocasta app. 170-Minor Guardians of the Galaxy app.	2	4	6	11	16	20
173-177-Korvac Saga issues; 173-175-The Collector app. 173,177-Guardians of the Galaxy app. 174-Thanos cameo. 176-Starhawk app.	2	4	6	8	10	12
181-(3/79) Byrne-a/Pérez-c; new line-up: Capt. America, Scarlet Witch, Iron Man, Wasp, Vision, Beast & The Falcon; debut of Scott Lang who becomes Ant-Man in Marvel Premiere #47 (4/79)	6	12	18	40	73	105
182-191-Byrne-a: 183-Ms. Marvel joins. 184-vs. Absorbing Man. 185-Origin Quicksilver & Scarlet Witch. 186-187-vs. Morded the Mystic. 188-Intro. The Elements of Doom. 189-Deathbird app. 190,191-vs. Grey Gargoyle	2	4	6	8	10	12
192-194,197-199: 197-199-vs Red Ronin	1	2	3	5	6	8
195-1st Taskmaster cameo	3	6	9	19	30	40
196-1st full Taskmaster app.	8	16	24	51	96	140
200-(10/80, 52 pgs.)-Ms. Marvel leaves; 1st actual app. of Marcus Immortus	2	4	6	13	18	22
201,203-210,212: 204,205-vs. Yellow Claw						6.00
202-Ultron app.	2	4	6	11	16	20
211-New line-up: Capt. America, Iron Man, Tigra, Thor, Wasp & Yellowjacket; Angel, Beast, Dazzler app.	1	3	4	6	8	10
213,215,216,239,240,250: 213-Controversial Yellowjacket slapping Wasp issue; Yellowjacket leaves. 215,216-Silver Surfer app. 216-Tigra leaves. 239-(1/84) Avengers app. on David Letterman show. 240-Spider-Woman revived. 250-($1.00, 52 pgs; West Coast Avengers app. vs. Maelstrom	1	2	3	5	6	8
214-Ghost Rider app.	1	3	4	6	8	10
217-218,222,224-226,228-235,238: 217-Yellowjacket & Wasp return. 222-1st app. Egghead's Masters of Evil. 225,226-Black Knight app. 229-Death of Egghead. 230-Yellowjacket quits. 231-Iron Man leaves. 232-Starfox (Eros) joins. 233-Byrne-a. 234-Origin Quicksilver & Scarlet Witch. 238-Origin Blackout						6.00
219,220-Drax the Destroyer app. 220-Moondragon vs. Drax	1	3	4	6	8	10
221-Hawkeye & She-Hulk join; Spider-Man, Spider-Woman, Dazzler app.	1	2	3	5	6	8
223-Taskmaster app.	3	6	9	14	19	24
227-Captain Marvel (Monica Rambeau) joins; Roger Stern plots begin	2	4	6	8	11	14
236,237-Spider-Man tries to join the Avengers	1	2	3	5	6	8
241-249,251-256,258-262: 242-Dr. Strange app. 243-Vision becomes chairman. 244,245-vs. Dire Wraiths. 246-248-Eternals app. 249-x-over with Thor #350. 252-vs. the Blood Brothers. 253-Vision vs. Quasimodo. 254-West Coast Avengers app. 255-John Buscema & Tom Palmer return as artists; 1st app Nebula's pirate crew. 256-Terminus app. 258-x-over with Amazing Spider-Man #269-270; Spider-Man & Firelord app. 258-260-Nebula app. 260-261-Secret Wars II X-over; Beyonder app. 262-Hercules vs. Sub-Mariner						5.00
257-1st app. Nebula (from the Guardians of the Galaxy movie)	4	8	12	22	35	48
263-(1/86) Return of Jean Grey, leading into X-Factor #1(story continues in FF #286)	1	2	3	5	6	8
264-265,267-269: 264-1st new Yellowjacket (Rita Demara) 266-Secret Wars II x-over; vs. The Beyonder. 267-269-Kang app.						4.00
266-Secret Wars II epilogue; Silver Surfer & Molecule Man app.						5.00
270-273-Baron Zemo and the new Masters of Evil app. 272-Alpha Flight app.						5.00
274-277-Baron Zemo and the new Masters of Evil app. in 'Siege of Avengers mansion'. 274-Hercules injured. 275-Jarvis severely beaten. 276-Thor returns. 277-Capt. America vs. Baron Zemo						6.00
278-283: 279-Capt. Marvel (Monica Rambeau) becomes Avengers leader; Dr. Druid joins. 280-Jarvis flashback issue. 281-283-Olympian Gods app. 282-Sub-Mariner rejoins						4.00
284,285-vs. the Olympian Gods. 285 Avengers vs. Zeus; Hercules recovers						5.00
286-299: 286-Fixer app. Awesome Android & Super Adaptoid app. 287-Mentallo app. 288-1st app. 'Heavy Metal' (TESS-One, Intergalactic Sentry #459, Machine Man, Super-Adaptoid). 290-West Coast Avengers app. 291-$1.00 issues begin. 292-1st app. the Leviathan (Marrina). 293-Death of Marrina. 294-Capt. Marvel (Monica Rambeau) leaves. 295-vs. the Cross-Time Kangs. 297-Dr. Druid leaves; Thor, Black Knight & She-Hulk resign. 298-Inferno x-over. 299-Inferno x-over; New Mutants app.						4.00
300-(2/89, $1.75, 68 pgs., squarebound) New line-up; the Captain (Steve Rogers), Thor, Invisible Woman, Mr. Fantastic & Gilgamesh (formerly the Forgotten one) Inferno x-over; Simonson-a						6.00
301-304,306-313,319-325,327,330-343: 301-Firelord app; 1st app. Super-Nova. 302-Re-intro Quasar; Firelord app. 303-vs. Super-Nova. Quasar, Firelord & West Coast Avengers app.; Mr. Fantastic & Invisible Woman leave. 308-310-Eternals app. 311-313-Acts of Vengeance x-over. 312-Freedom Force app. 320-324-Alpha Flight app. 327-2nd app. Rage. 332,333-Dr. Doom app. 334-Intro. Thane Ector & the Brethren; Inhumans & Quicksilver app. 335-339-vs. the Brethren. 335-1st Steve Epting art. 341,342-New Warriors & Sons of the Serpent app. 343-Intro. the Gatherers; Bob Harras scripts begin (end #395); last $1.00-c						4.00
305,314-318: 305-Byrne scripts begin; most current & non-active Avengers app. 314-318-Spider-Man x-over.						5.00
326-1st app. Rage (11/90)	1	2	3	5	6	8
328,329: 328-Origin Rage. 329-New line-up (Capt. America, Quasar, Sersi, She-Hulk, Thor, Vision, Black Widow) Spider-Man becomes a reserve member; Rage & Sandman become probationary members						5.00
344-346, 348-349,351-359: 344-1st app. Proctor, leader of the Gatherers. 345,346-Operation Galactic Storm x-overs. 345-Pt.5-Deathbird app. 346-Pt.12-Intro. Starforce (super-powered Kree warriors) 349-Thor vs. Hercules. 351-Starjammers app. 352-354-Grimm Reaper app.						4.00
347-Double-sized issue ($1.75, 39, pgs.) Operation Galactic Storm conclusion (Pt.19) end of the Kree/Shi'ar War; 'death' of the Supreme Intelligence						5.00
350-($2.50, 68 pgs.) Double gatefold-c showing-c to #1; r/#53 w/cover in flip book format; vs. The Starjammers						6.00
360-($2.95, 52 pgs.) Embossed all-foil-c; 30th ann.						6.00

Avengers #396 © MAR

Avengers V2 #11 © MAR

Avengers V3 #25 © MAR

	GD	VG	FN	VF	VF/NM	NM-
	2.0	4.0	6.0	8.0	9.0	9.2

361,362,364,365,367: 361-362-vs. the Gatherers. 364-365-vs. Galen-Kor of the Kree 4.00
363-($2.95, 52 pgs.)-All silver foil-c; vs. Proctor & the Gatherers; 1st cameo app. Deathcry (unnamed) 5.00
366-($3.95, 68 pgs.)-Embossed all gold foil-c; Deadpool app. in back-up story 5.00
368,376-378: 368-Bloodties pt.1; Avengers/X-Men x-over 4.00
369-($2.95)-Foil embossed-c; Bloodties pt.5; X-Men/Avengers vs. Exodus 5.00
370-373: 370-371-Ghaur the Deviant app. 372-373-vs. Proctor & the Gatherers 4.00
374-Bound-in trading card sheet; origin of Proctor as an alternate-Earth Black Knight revealed (scarcer in NM due to the card insert) 5.00
375-($2.00, 52 pgs.)-Regular ed.; Thunderstrike returns; leads into Malibu Comic's Black September; end of the Gatherers saga (since #343); death of Proctor; Black Knight & Sersi leave; last Epting-a 5.00
375-($2.50, 52 pgs.)-Collectors ed. 6.00
379-382-Regular editions: 379-Galen Kor & Kree Lunatic Legion app. 380-382-High Evolutionary app. 380-1st Mike Deodato-a. 381-Exodus app. 4.00
379-382-Marvel Double Feature editions ($2.50, 45 pgs.)-All have Giant-Man stories in a flip-book format 5.00
383-385: 383-Fantastic Force app. 384-Hercules stripped of immortality & banished from Olympus. 385-Red Skull app. 5.00
386-389, 398-399: 386-Red Skull app.; 'Taking of AIM' prelude; continues in Capt. America #440. 387-Taking of AIM Pt.2; Red Skull app.; re-intro Modok; continues in Capt. America #441. 388-Taking of AIM Pt.4; Red Skull & Modok app. 1 2 3 5 6 8
390-393: 390-'The Crossing' prelude; leads into Avengers: the Crossing #1. 391,392-The Crossing. 391-Overpower game card insert; scarcer in NM. 392-393-The Crossing 6.00
394,397: 394-The Crossing; 1st new Wasp; story cont. in Avengers Timeslide #1; 397-x-over w/Hulk #440-441 1 2 3 4 5 7
395-The Crossing/Timeslide; 'death' of Tony Stark; Bob Harras co-plot only, last work on Avengers 1 2 3 5 6 8
396-First Sign Pt.4; vs. the Zodiac 8.00
400-(Double-size, 32 pgs.)-Mark Waid scripts; Loki app. 7.00
401,402: 401-Onslaught Impact #1; Magneto app. 402-Onslaught Impact #2; vs. Onslaught & Holocaust; last issue; continues in X-Men #56 6.00
#500-503 (See Avengers Vol. 3; series resumed original numbering after Vol. 3 #84)
Special 1 (9/67, 25¢, 68 pgs.)-New-a; original & new Avengers team-up 13 26 39 87 191 295
Special 2 (9/68, 25¢, 68 pgs.)-New-a; original vs. new Avengers 9 18 27 63 129 195
Special 3 (9/69, 25¢, 68 pgs.)-r/Avengers #4 plus 3 Capt. America stories by Kirby (art); origin Red Skull 6 12 18 37 66 95
Special 4 (1/71, 25¢, 68 pgs.)-Kirby-r/Avengers #5,6 4 8 12 25 40 55
Special 5 (1/72, 52 pgs.)-All-reprint issue; Kirby-r Avengers #8/Heck-r w/Spider-Man from issue #11 4 8 12 23 37 50
Annual 6 (11/76) Pérez-a; Kirby-c; vs. Nuklo 3 6 9 14 19 24
Annual 7 (11/77)-Starlin-c/a; Warlock dies; Thanos app.; x-over w/Marvel Two-in-one Ann #2 6 12 18 38 69 100
Annual 8 (1978)-Dr. Strange, Ms. Marvel app. vs. Hyperion, Dr. Spectrum & Whizzer 2 4 6 9 13 16
Annual 9 (1979)-Newton-a(p); Intro. Arsenal 2 4 6 9 12 15
Annual 10 (1981)-Golden-a; X-Men cameo; 1st app. Rogue & Madelyne Pryor 6 12 18 38 69 100
Annual 11-13: 11 (1982)-Vs. The Defenders. 12 ('83)-Inhumans app. 13 ('84)-Ditko/Byrne-a 6.00
Annual 14-15,17-18: 14 ('85)-x-over w/Fantastic Four Ann. #19; vs. the Skrulls. 15 ('86)-vs. Freedom Force; x-over w/Avengers West Coast Ann. #1. 17('88)-Evolutionary War x-over. 18('89)-Atlantis Attacks 5.00
Annual 16 (1987)-x-over w/Avengers West Coast Ann. #2; Silver Surfer app. vs. the Grandmaster and Legion of the Unliving (including Drax, Captain Marvel & Green Goblin) 6.00
Annual 19-22: 19 ('90)-Terminus Factor Pt.5 (conclusion) continued from Avengers West Coast Ann. #5. 20 ('91)-Subterranean Saga Pt.1; cont. in Hulk Ann. #17. 21 ('92)-Citizen Kang pt.4; vs. Terminatrix. 22 ('93)-Bagged w/card; 1st app. Bloodwraith 4.00
Annual 23 (1994)-Buscema-a; Roy Thomas-s; vs. Loki & Pluto; x-over w/Thor Ann. #195.00
Avengers 1: The Coming of the Avengers! (2012, $3.99) recolored reprint/#1 5.00
...: Galactic Storm Vol. 1 ('06, $29.99, TPB) r/Kree-Shi'ar war from Avengers #345-346, Capt. America #398-399, Avengers West Coast #80-81, Quasar #32-33, Wonder Man #7-8, Iron Man #278 and Thor #445; new Epting-c 30.00
...: Galactic Storm Vol. 2 ('06, $29.99, TPB) r/Kree-Shi'ar war from Avengers #347, Capt. America #400-401, Avengers West Coast #82, Quasar #34-36, Wonder Man #9, Iron Man #279, Thor #446 and What If #55-56 30.00
...: Kang - Time and Time Again ('05, $19.99, TPB) r/Avengers #69-71 & 267-269, Thor #140 and Incredible Hulk #135 20.00
...Kree-Skrull War ('00, $24.95, TPB) new Neal Adams-c 25.00
...: Legends Vol. 3: George Perez ('03, $16.99)-r/#161,162,194-196,201, Ann. #6 & 8 17.00
Marvel Double Feature...Avengers/Giant-Man #379 ($2.50, 52 pgs.)-Same as Avengers #379 w/Giant-Man flip book 4.00

Marvel Graphic Novel - Deathtrap: The Vault (1991, $9.95) Venom-c/app. 2 4 6 11 16 20
The Korvac Saga TPB (2003, $19.95)-r/#167,168,170-177; Perez-c 20.00
The Serpent Crown TPB (2005, $15.99)-r/#141-144,147-149; Hellcat app. 16.00
The Yesterday Quest ($6.95)-r/#181,182,185-187 1 2 3 4 5 7
Under Siege ('98, $16.95, TPB) r/#270,271,273-277 17.00
...: Vision and the Scarlet Witch TPB (2005, $15.99) r/wedding from Giant-Size Avengers #4 and "Vision and the Scarlet Witch" mini-series #1-4 16.00
...: Visionaries ('99, $16.95)-r/early George Perez art 17.00
NOTE: ***Austin*** *c(i)-157, 167, 168, 170-177, 181, 183-188, 198-201, Annual 8.* ***John Buscema*** *a-41-44p, 46p, 47p, 49, 50, 51-62p, 74-77, 79-85, 87-91, 97, 105p, 121p, 124p,125p, 152, 153p, 255-279p, 281-302p; c-41-66, 68-71, 73-91, 97-99, 178, 256-259p, 261-279p, 281-302p.* ***Byrne*** *a-164-166p, 181-191p, 233p, Annual 13i, 14p; c-186-190p, 233p, 260, 305p; scripts-305-312.* ***Colan*** *a(p)-63-65, 111, 206-208, 210, 211; c(p)-65, 206-208, 210, 211.* ***Ditko*** *a-Annual 13.* ***Guice*** *a-Annual 12p.* ***Don Heck*** *a-9-15, 17-40, 157.* ***Kane*** *c-37p, 159p.* ***Kane/Everett*** *c-97.* ***Kirby*** *a-1-8p, Special 3r, 4r(p); c-1-30, 148, 151-158; layouts-14-16.* ***Ron Lim*** *c(p)-335-341.* ***Miller*** *c-193p.* ***Mooney*** *a-86i, 179p, 180p.* ***Nebres*** *a-178i; c-179i.* ***Newton*** *a-204p, Annual 9p.* ***Perez*** *a(p)-141, 143, 144, 148, 150, 154, 155, 160, 161, 162, 167,168, 170, 171, 194-196, 198-202, Annual 6, 8; c(p)-160-162, 164-166, 170-174, 181,183-185, 191, 192, 194-201, 379-382, Annual 8.* ***Starlin*** *c-121, 135.* ***Staton*** *a-127-134i.* ***Tuska*** *a-47i,48i, 51i, 53i, 54i, 106p, 107p, 135p, 137-140p, 163p. Guardians of the Galaxy app. in #167, 168, 170, 173, 175, 181.*

AVENGERS, THE (Volume Two)
Marvel Comics: V2#1, Nov, 1996 - No. 13, Nov, 1997 ($2.95/$1.95/$1.99) (Produced by Extreme Studios)

1-($2.95)-Heroes Reborn begins; intro new team (Captain America, Swordsman, Scarlet Witch, Vision, Thor, Hellcat & Hawkeye); 1st app. Avengers Island; Loki & Enchantress app.; Rob Liefeld-p & plot; Chap Yaep-p; Jim Valentino scripts; variant-c exists 5.00
1-($1.95)-Variant-c 6.00
2-13: 2,3-Jeph Loeb scripts begin, Kang app. 4-Hulk-c/app. 5-Thor/Hulk battle; 2 covers. 10,11,13-"World War 3"-pt. 2, x-over w/Image characters. 12-($2.99) "Heroes Reunited"-pt. 2 4.00
Heroes Reborn: Avengers (2006, $29.99, TPB) r/#1-12; pin-up and cover gallery 30.00

AVENGERS, THE (Volume Three)(See New Avengers for next series)
Marvel Comics: Feb, 1998 - No. 84, Aug, 2004; No. 500, Sept, 2004 - No. 503, Dec, 2004 ($2.99/$1.99/$2.25)

1-($2.99, 48 pgs.) Busiek-s/Pérez-a/wraparound-c; Avengers reassemble after Heroes Return; many Avengers app. vs. Morgan Le Fey 5.00
1-Variant Heroes Return sunburst cover 1 2 3 4 5 7
1-Dynamic Forces Ltd Edition (1500 copies); sunburst-c signed by Perez 4 8 12 23 37 50
1-Rough Cut-Features original script and pencil pages 4.00
2-($1.99) Pérez-c; vs. Morgan Le Fey, alternate painted-c by Lago 4.00
3,4: 3-Wonder Man-c/app. & "dies". 4-Final roster chosen; Captain America, Thor, Hawkeye, Iron Man, Scarlet Witch, Vision, Warbird (formally Ms. Marvel: Carol Danvers) 3.00
5-6,8-11; 5-6: Squadron Supreme-c/app.: Hyperion, Dr. Spectrum, Power Princess, Whizzer, Haywire, Lady Lark, Shape & Moonglow. 8-1st app; Triathlon & Silverclaw; vs. Moses Magnum. 9-1st mention of the Triune Understanding. 10-Grimm Reaper & Ultron app; return of the Legion of the Unliving: Captain Mar-Vell, Dr. Druid, Mockingbird, Swordsman, Wonder Man & Thunderstrike. 11-Legion of the Unliving app; Hellcat, Spider-Man, Daredevil & Fantastic Four guest app; Wonder Man returns to life 3.00
7-Live Kree or Die pt. 4; continued from Quicksilver #10; Warbird leaves; vs. Kree Lunatic Legion 4.00
12-($2.99, 38 pgs.) Thunderbolts app; Firebird and Justice (of the New Warriors) join the Avengers. 4.00
12-Alternate-c of Avengers w/white background; no logo 3 6 9 16 23 30
12-Dynamic Forces alternate-c; ltd. to 5000 copies 2 4 6 8 10 12
12-Dynamic Forces alternate-c; ltd. to 1500 copies; signed by Pérez, Vey and Smith 3 6 9 15 22 28
13-18,23,26: 13-New Warriors app.; 1st app. Lord Templar; 1st (shadowed) app. Jonathan Tremont – leader of the Triune Understanding. 14-Beast app. vs. Lord Templar; 1st app. Pagan. 15-1st full app. of Jonathan Tremont; Pagan and Lord Templar, the Wrecking Crew and Ultron app. 16-18-Ordway-s/a; vs. the Doomsday Man in #17; vs. the Wrecking Crew in #18. 23-Vision & Scarlet Witch history retold. 26-Immonen-a; Lord Templar & Taskmaster app. 3.00
16-Variant-c w/purple background 5.00
19,20: Ultron Unlimited pt. 1-2; Black Panther app.; Giant-Man (Henry Pym app. in #20-22) 1 2 3 5 6 8
21,22-Ultron Unlimited pt. 3-4; vs. Ultron; Black Panther app. 6.00
24-Continued from Juggernaut: the Eighth Day #1; vs. the Exemplars 4.00
25-Vs. the Exemplars; Spider-Man, New Warriors, Juggernaut and Quicksilver app. 5.00
27-($2.99, 100 pgs. 'Monster') New line up - Justice, Firestar & Thor leave, Triathlon & She-Hulk join, Wonder Man becomes a reserve member; Ant-Man app.; reprints issues (all Vol.1) #101,150,151, Annual #19; Note: Due to the 100 pages, this issue often suffers from tears around the staples. 6.00
28-32: 28-30-vs. Kulan Gath. 31-Vision rejoins; vs. Grimm Reaper. 32-Life story & secret origin of Madame Masque revealed 3.00

Avengers V3 #65 © MAR

Avengers (2013 series) #1 © MAR

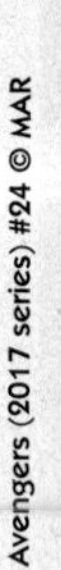

Avengers (2017 series) #24 © MAR

GD VG FN VF VF/NM NM-
2.0 4.0 6.0 8.0 9.0 9.2

33-Thunderbolts x-over w/Thunderbolts #44; Madame Masque & Count Nefaria app.
1 3 4 6 9 12
34-($2.99, 38 pgs.) Last Perez-a; continued from Thunderbolts #44; vs. Count Nefaria; Black Widow app 6.00
35-37: 35-Maximum Security x-over; Romita Jr.-a; 36-37; vs. Bloodwraith; Epting-a 4.00
38-Davis-a begins ($1.99-c); new line-up: Captain America, Goliath (Henry Pym), Thor, Quicksilver, Wasp, Iron Man, Vision, Scarlet Witch, Triathlon, Wonder Man & Warbird (Carol Danvers) 4.00
39,40: Hulk app. 5.00
41-47,49: 41-Vs. Scarlet Centurion; Kang app. 42-44-Kang, Scarlet Centurion & the Presence app. 43-Jack of Hearts joins; last Davis-a. 45-Origin of the Scarlet Centurion; Kang & the Master of the World (from Alpha Flight issues) app. 46-Vs. Kang and his army; Scarlet Centurion & the Master of the World app. 47-Origin of Scarlet Centurion continued with flashback to issue #200 w/Ms. Marvel (Carol Danvers); 1st full app of the Triple Evil (ancient cosmic menace). 49-'Nuff Said story; Kang attacks Washington DC 3.00
48-($3.50, 100 pgs); vs. Kang and his legions; Scarlet Centurion app; death of Master of the World; Triple Evil app.; r/#98-100 4.00
50-($3.50); vs. the Triple Evil (destroyed); Lord Pagan & Templar app. (both die); Jonathan Tremont & the Triune Understanding revealed as villains; 3-D Man app. 5.00
51,52: 51-Kang app. as ruler of the Earth; Wonder Man and Scarlet Witch app.; features 2 pg. tribute to the late John Buscema who passed away on January 10th 2002. 52-Avengers vs. Kang; Scarlet Centurion & the Presence app. 4.00
53-Avengers vs. Kang; death of Jonathan Tremont. 6.00
54-56: 54-Conclusion of the Kang war w/Kang defeated; death of Scarlet Centurion. 55-Kang war aftermath; Thor leaves. 56-Beast app; last Busiek issue 4.00
57-62,65-84: 57-Geoff Johns-s begins; 'World Trust' pt. 1; ends with pt. 4 in issue #60. 64-Solo Falcon story; vs Scarecrow. 65-70-Red Zone pt. 1-6; vs. the Red Skull. Wasp and Yellowjacket (Henry Pym) story; vs. Plantman and Whirlwind. 71-74; Search for She-Hulk pt. 1-4; Hulk app. in #73-74. 77-Last Johns issue. 78-81; Chuck Austen-s begin; Lionheart of Avalon pt. 1-5; special 50-¢t issue. 79-81; Captain Britain (Brian Braddock) app. 82-84-Once an Invader pt. 1-4; intro. New invaders team: Blazing Skull, Spitfire, US Agent & Union Jack; Namor app. in #83-84 4.00
63-Standoff pt. 3; continued from Thor (Vol. 2) #58; Thor vs. Iron Man; Dr. Doom app.
2 4 6 9 12 15

(After #84 [Aug, 2004], numbering reverted back to original Vol. 1 with #500, Sept, 2004)

500-($3.50) "Avengers Disassembled" begins; Bendis-s/Finch-a; Ant-Man (Scott Lang) and Jack of Hearts killed, Vision destroyed by the Scarlet Witch 5.00
500-Director's Cut ($4.99) Cassaday foil variant-c plus interviews and galleries
1 3 4 6 8 10
501, 502-($2.25): 501-Numerous Avengers and ex-team members app. 502-Hawkeye killed 5.00
503-($3.50) "Avengers Disassembled" ends; reprint pages from Avengers V1#16; Dr. Strange and Magneto app; story continues in Avengers Finale #1 4.00
#11/2 (12/99, $2.50) Timm-c/a; Stern-s; 1963-style issue 3.00
.../ Squadron Supreme '98 Annual ($2.99) 4.00
1999, 2000 Annual (7/99, '00, $3.50) 1999-Manco-a. 2000-Breyfogle-a 4.00
2001 Annual ($2.99) Reis-a; back-up-s art by Churchill 4.00
...: Above and Beyond TPB ('05, $24.99) r/#36-40,56, Annual 2001, & Avengers: The Ultron Imperative; Alan Davis-c 25.00
... Assemble HC ('04, $29.95, oversized) r/#1-11 & '98 Annual; Busiek intro.; Pérez pencil art and Busiek script from Avengers #1 30.00
... Assemble Vol. 2 HC ('05, $29.95, oversized) r/#12-22, #0 & Ann. 1999; Ordway intro. 30.00
... Assemble Vol. 3 HC ('06, $34.99, oversized) r/#23-34, #1 1/2 & Thunderbolts #42-44 35.00
... Assemble Vol. 4 HC ('07, $34.99, oversized) r/#35-40, Avengers 2000, Avengers 2001, Avengers: The Ultron Imperative, Maximum Security #1-3 & ...Dangerous Planet 35.00
... Assemble Vol. 5 HC ('07, $39.99, oversized) r/#41-56 and Avengers 2001 40.00
...: Clear and Present Dangers TPB ('01, $19.95) r/#8-15 20.00
...: Defenders War HC ('07, $19.99) r/#115-118 & Defenders #8-11; Englehart intro. 20.00
...: Disassembled HC ('06, $24.99) r/#500-503 & Avengers Finale; Director's Cut extras 25.00
...: Disassembled TPB ('05, $15.99) r/#500-503 & Avengers Finale; Director's Cut extras 16.00
...Finale 1 (1/05, $3.50) Epilogue to Avengers Disassembled; Neal Adams-c; art by various incl. Peréz, Maleev, Oeming, Powell, Mayhew, Mack, McNiven, Cheung, Frank 4.00
Free Comic Book Day (5/09, giveaway) New Avengers 1st battle vs. Dark Avengers 4.00
...: Living Legends TPB ('04, $19.99) r/#23-30; last Busiek/Pérez arc 20.00
...Supreme Justice TPB (4/01, $17.95) r/Squadron Supreme appearances in Avengers #5-7, '98 Annual, Iron Man #7, Capt. America #8, Quicksilver #10; Pérez-c 18.00
The Kang Dynasty TPB ('02, $29.99) r/#41-55 & 2001 Annual 30.00
The Morgan Conquest TPB ('00, $14.95) r/#1-4 15.00
.../Thunderbolts Vol. 1: The Nefaria Protocols (2004, $19.99) r/#31-34, 42-44 20.00
Ultron Unleashed TPB (8/99, $3.50) reprints early app. 4.00
Ultron Unlimited TPB (4/01, $14.95) r/#19-22 & #0 prelude 15.00
Wizard #0-Ultron Unlimited prelude 4.00
Vol. 1: World Trust TPB ('03, $14.99) r/#57-62 & Marvel Double-Shot #2 15.00
Vol. 2: Red Zone TPB ('04, $14.99) r/#64-70 15.00
Vol. 3: The Search For She-Hulk TPB ('04, $12.99) r/#71-76 13.00
Vol. 4: The Lionheart of Avalon TPB ('04, $11.99) r/#77-81 12.00
Vol. 5: Once an Invader TPB ('04, $14.99) r/#82-84, V1 #71; Invaders #0 & Ann #1 ('77) 15.00

AVENGERS (The Heroic Age)
Marvel Comics: July, 2010 - No. 34, Jan, 2013 ($3.99)

1-New team assembled; Bendis-s/Romita Jr.-a; Kang app.; back-up text Avengers history 6.00
1-Variant-c by Land 8.00
1-Variant covers by Djurdjevic and John Romita Sr. 12.00
1-3-Second printings 4.00
2,3: 2-Wonder Man app. 5.00
4-12: 4-6-Ultron app. 7-Red Hulk app. 12-Red Hulk joins 4.00
12.1 -(6/11, $2.99) Hitch & Neary-c/a; The Wizard & The Intelligencia app.; Ultron returns 3.00
13-24: 13-17-Fear Itself tie-ins. 13,15-Bachalo-a. 17-New Avengers app. 18-20-Acuña-a. 19-Vision returns, Storm joins 4.00
24.1 -(5/12, $2.99) Peterson-a; Magneto, She-Hulk app. 3.00
25-33: 25-30-Avengers vs. X-Men tie-in; Simonson-a. 31-34-Janet Van Dyne app. 4.00
34-($4.99) Art by Peterson, Mayhew & Dodson; Deodato, Simonson, Yu, Cheung, Coipel art pages; Bendis afterword 5.00
... Annual 1 (3/12, $4.99) Bendis-s/Dell'Otto-c/a; Wonder Man app. 5.00
... Assemble 1 (7/10, $3.99) Handbook-style profiles of Avengers, enemies, allies 4.00
...: Infinity Quest 1 (8/11, $4.99) r/#7-9 with variant covers 5.00
... Roll Call 1 (2012, $4.99) Updated handbook-style profiles of Avengers & enemies 5.00
... Spotlight (7/10, $3.99) Creator interviews, previews, history of the team; trivia 4.00

AVENGERS (Marvel NOW!)
Marvel Comics: Feb, 2013 - No. 44, Jun, 2015 ($3.99)

1-13: 1-Hickman-s/Opeña-a/Weaver-c. 4-6-Adam Kubert-a 4.00
14-23: 14-17-Prelude to Infinity. 18-23-Infinity tie-ins 4.00
24-($4.99) Rogue Planet; Ribic-a; Iron Man 3030 app. 5.00
25-28-Hickman-s/Larroca-a. 27-Includes reprint of All-New Invaders #1 4.00
29-($4.99) Original Sin tie-in; Yu-a/Cho-c 5.00
30-34-Original Sin tie-in; Hickman-s/Yu-a 4.00
34.1 (11/14), 34.2 (3/15), 35-($4.99) 34.1-Spotlight on Hyperion; Keown-a. 34.2-Spotlight on Starbrand; Bengal-a. 35-Cheung, Medina-a 5.00
36-39,41-43: 37,39,41-Deodato-a. 39-Leads into New Avengers #28 4.00
40-($4.99) Thanos-c/app.; Caselli-a 5.00
44-($4.99) Follows New Avengers #33; Thanos app.; leads into Secret Wars #1 5.00
Annual (2/14, $4.99) Christmas-themed; Lafuente-a 5.00
...: Endless Wartime HC (2013, $24.99, OGN) Ellis-s/McKone-a; intro by Clark Gregg 25.00
...: No More Bullying (3/15, $1.99) Short stories; Avengers, Spider-Man, GOTG app. 3.00
... Now! Handbook 1 (2/15, $4.99) Updated version with new characters from 2014 5.00
...: The Enemy Within (7/13, $2.99) DeConnick-s/Hepburn-a; Captain Marvel tie-in 3.00
...: Vs 1 (7/15, $5.99) Printing of 4 digital-first stories; Raney-c 6.00
100th Anniversary Special: Avengers 1 (9/14, $3.99) James Stokoe-s/a 4.00

AVENGERS (After Secret Wars)
Marvel Comics: No. 0, Dec, 2015 ($5.99)

0-Short story preludes for the various Avengers 2016 titles; Deadpool app. 6.00

AVENGERS (Follows events of Civil War II)
Marvel Comics: Jan, 2017 - No. 11, Nov, 2017; No. 672, Dec, 2017 - No. 690, Jun, 2018 ($4.99/$3.99)

1-($4.99) Spider-Man, Capt. America (Sam), Thor (Jane), Wasp, Vision, Hercules team 5.00
2-11-($3.99) 2-6-Kang app.; Waid-s/del Mundo-a. 7,8-Infamous Iron Man app.; Noto-a. 9,10-Secret Empire tie-ins 4.00

[Title switches to legacy numbering after #11 (11/17)]

672-674,676-683,685-688,690: 672-674-The Champions app. 676-690-No Surrender. 681-Origin of Voyager. 682-Hulk returns 4.00
675-($4.99) No Surrender Part 1; "return" of Voyager; lenticular wraparound-c by Brooks 5.00
684-($4.99) No Surrender Part 10; re-cap of Hulk origin and many deaths 5.00
689-($4.99) No Surrender Part 15; Larraz-a 5.00
#1.MU (3/17, $4.99) Monsters Unleashed tie-in; Zub-s/Izaakse-a 5.00
...: Shards of Infinity 1 (6/18, $3.99) Macchio-s/Di Vito-a; Black Panther app. 4.00

AVENGERS
Marvel Comics: Jul, 2018 - Present ($4.99/$3.99)

1-($4.99) Aaron-s/McGuinness-a; Avengers re-form vs. the Celestials 5.00
2-9-($3.99) Loki app. 7-Origin of prehistoric Ghost Rider; Pichelli-a. 9-Namor app. 4.00
10-($5.99) 700th issue; Namor and The Winter Guard app.; McGuinness-a 6.00
11-30,32-41: 11-Phil Coulson app. 12-Blade joins. 15-17-Marquez-a. 16-Johnny Blaze app. 18-20-War of the Realms tie-ins; McGuinness-a. 18,21-Squadron Supreme app. 22,23-Hellstrom app. 23-25-Cosmic Ghost Rider app. 32-Mephisto & Dracula app. 39,41-Enter The Phoenix. 39-Keown-a. 40-Doom app. 4.00
31-($4.99) "The Temptation of Anthony Stark"; Aaron-s; art by various 5.00
...: Edge of Infinity 1 (6/19, $3.99) Macchio-s/Di Vito-a; M.O.D.O.K. app. 4.00
... Halloween Special 1 (12/18, $4.99) Short stories by various; Geoff Shaw-c 5.00
...: Loki Unleashed 1 (11/19, $4.99) Takes place after Avengers #277; Stern-s/Lim-a 5.00

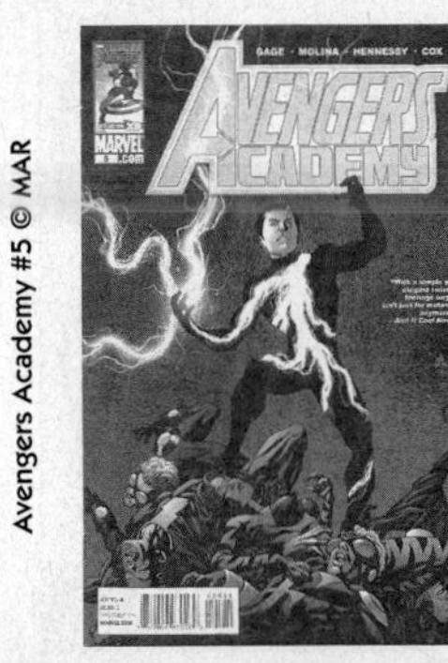

Avengers Academy #5 © MAR

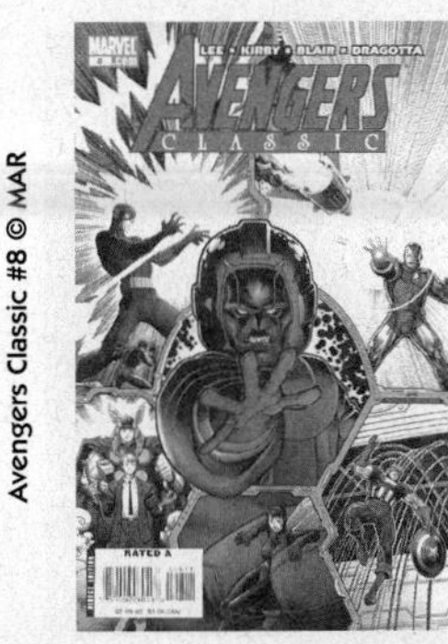

Avengers Classic #8 © MAR

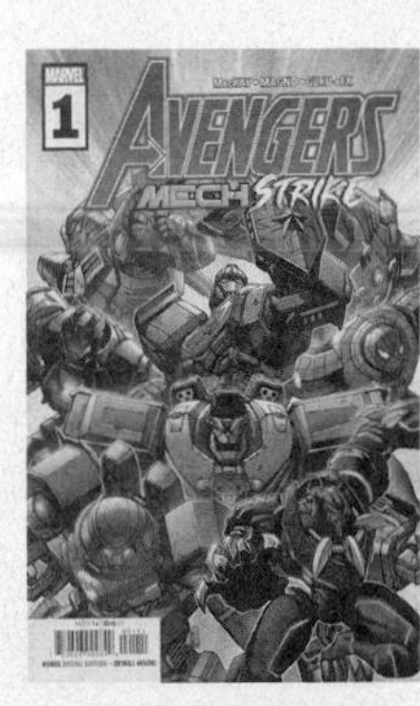

Avengers Mech Strike #1 © MAR

...: Marvels Snapshots 1 (1/21, $4.99) Barbara Kesel-s/Staz Johnson-a 5.00

AVENGERS (Flashback to new team roster from Avengers #16 [1965])
Marvel Comics: No. 1.1, Jan, 2017 - No. 5.1, May, 2017 ($3.99)

1.1, 2.1, 3.1, 4.1, 5.1- Hawkeye, Quicksilver and Scarlet Witch join team; Waid-s/Kitson-a 4.00

AVENGERS (Marvel Action all ages)(Title changes to Marvel Action: Avengers with #6)
IDW Publishing: Dec, 2018 - No. 5, Apr, 2019 ($3.99)

1-5-Iron Man, Captain America, Thor, Hawkeye, Black Widow, Black Panther & Hulk app. 4.00

AVENGERS ACADEMY (The Heroic Age)(Also see Avengers Arena)
Marvel Comics: Aug, 2010 - No. 39, Jan, 2013 ($3.99/$2.99)

1-($3.99) Gage-s/McKone-a/c; Intro. team of Veil, Hazmat, Striker, Mettle, Finesse, Reptil 4.00
1-Variant-c by Djurdjevic 8.00
2-14,14.1 -($2.99) 3,4-Juggernaut app. 5-Molina-a. 7-Absorbing Man app.; Raney-a. 3.00
15-39: 15-20-Fear Itself tie-in. 22-Magneto app. 27,28-Runaways app. 29-33-Tie in to Avengers vs. X-Men event 3.00
... Giant Size 1 (7/11, $7.99) Young Allies and Arcade app.; Tobin-s/Baldeon-a 8.00

AVENGERS: AGE OF ULTRON POINT ONE (Free Comic Book Day)
Marvel Comics: 2012 (Free giveaway)

#0.1 - Reprints Avengers 12.1 (6/11); Bendis-s/Hitch & Neary-c/a 4.00

AVENGERS: A.I. (Follows Age of Ultron series)
Marvel Comics: Sept, 2013 - No. 12, Jun, 2014 ($2.99)

1-12: 1-Humphries-s/Araújo-a; Hank Pym, Vision app. 7-Daredevil app. 3.00

AVENGERS AND POWER PACK ASSEMBLE!
Marvel Comics: June, 2006 - No. 4, Sept, 2006 ($2.99, limited series)

1-4-GuriHiru-a/Sumerak-s. 1-Capt. America app. 2-Iron Man. 3-Spider-Man, Kang app. 3.00
TPB (2006, $6.99, digest-size) r/#1-4 7.00

AVENGERS AND THE INFINITY GAUNTLET
Marvel Comics: Oct, 2010 - No. 4, Jan, 2011 ($2.99, limited series)

1-4: 1-Clevinger-s/Churilla-a; Dr. Doom and Thanos app. 1-Ramos-c. 2-Lim-c 3.00

AVENGERS & X-MEN: AXIS
Marvel Comics: Dec, 2014 - No. 9, Feb, 2015 ($4.99/$3.99, limited series)

1-($4.99) Remender-s/Adam Kubert-a; Red Skull as Red Onslaught 5.00
2-8-($3.99): 2,7-Kubert-a. 3,4,8-Yu-a. 3-Adult Apocalypse app. 5,6-Dodson-a 4.00
9-($4.99) Cheung, Dodson, Yu & Kubert-a 5.00

AVENGERS ARENA
Marvel Comics: Feb, 2013 - No. 18, Jan, 2014 ($2.99)

1-18: 1-Avengers Academy members & Runaways in Arcade's Murder World; Walker-a 3.00

AVENGERS ASSEMBLE (Also see Marvel Universe Avengers Assemble)
Marvel Comics: May, 2012 - No. 25, May, 2014 ($3.99)

1-25: 1-Bendis-s/Bagley-a/c; movie roster in regular Marvel universe. 3-Thanos returns. 4-8-Guardians of the Galaxy app. 9-DeConnick-s begin. 13,14-Age of Ultron tie-in. 18-20-Infinity tie-in. 21-23-Inhumanity 4.00
Annual 1 (3/13, $4.99) Gage-s/Coker-a; spotlight on The Vision 5.00

AVENGERS: BACK TO BASICS
Marvel Comics: 2018 ($14.99, squarebound, printing of original digital comics)

nn-Peter David-s/Brian Level & Juanan Ramírez-a; Ms. Marvel & Kang app. 15.00

AVENGERS: CELESTIAL QUEST
Marvel Comics: Nov, 2001 - No. 8, June, 2002 ($2.50/$3.50, limited series)

1-7-Englehart-s/Santamaría-a; Thanos app. 3.00
8-($3.50) 4.00

AVENGERS: CLASSIC
Marvel Comics: Aug, 2007 - No. 12, Juy, 2008 ($3.99/$2.99)

1,12-($3.99) 1-Reprints Avengers #1 ('63) with new stories about that era; Art Adams-c 4.00
2-11-($2.99) R/#2-11 with back-up w/art by Oeming and others 3.00

AVENGERS COLLECTOR'S EDITION, THE
Marvel Comics: 1993 (Ordered through mail w/candy wrapper, 20 pgs.)

1-Contains 4 bound-in trading cards 5.00

AVENGERS: EARTH'S MIGHTIEST HEROES
Marvel Comics: Jan, 2005 - No. 8, Apr, 2005 ($3.50, limited series)

1-8-Retells origin; Casey-s/Kolins-a 4.00
HC (2005, $24.99, 7 1/2" x 11" with dustjacket) r/#1-8 25.00

AVENGERS: EARTH'S MIGHTIEST HEROES (Based on the Disney animated series)
Marvel Comics: Jan, 2011 - No. 4, Apr, 2011 ($3.99)

1-4-Yost-s/Wegener-a. 1-Hero profile pages. 2-Villain profile pages 4.00

AVENGERS EARTH'S MIGHTIEST HEROES (Titled Marvel Universe... for #1)
Marvel Comics: Jun, 2012 - No. 17, Oct, 2013 ($2.99)

1-17-All ages title. 13-FF & Dr. Doom app. 17-Ant-Man, Luke Cage & Iron Fist app. 4.00

AVENGERS: EARTH'S MIGHTIEST HEROES II
Marvel Comics: Jan, 2007 - No. 8, May, 2007 ($3.99, limited series)

1-8-Retells time when the Vision joined; Casey-s/Rosado-a. 6-Hank & Janet's wedding 4.00
HC (2007, $24.99, 7 1/2" x 11" with dustjacket) r/#1-8; cover sketches 25.00

AVENGERS FAIRY TALES
Marvel Comics: May, 2008 - No. 4, Dec, 2008 ($2.99, limited series)

1-4: 1-Peter Pan-style tale; Cebulski-a/Lemos-a. 2-The Vision. 3-Miyazawa-a 3.00

AVENGERS FOREVER
Marvel Comics: Dec, 1998 - No. 12, Feb, 2000 ($2.99)

1-Busiek-s/Pacheco-a in all 5.00
2-12: 4-Four covers. 6-Two covers. 8-Vision origin revised. 12-Rick Jones becomes Capt. Marvel 4.00
TPB (1/01, $24.95) r/#1-12; Busiek intro.; new Pacheco-c 25.00

AVENGERS INFINITY
Marvel Comics: Sept, 2000 - No. 4, Dec, 2000 ($2.99, limited series)

1-4-Stern-s/Chen-a 4.00

AVENGERS/ INVADERS
Marvel Comics: Jul, 2008 - No. 12, Aug, 2009 ($2.99, limited series)

1-Invaders journey to the present; Alex Ross-c/Sadowski-a; Thunderbolts app. 3.00
2-12: 2-New Avengers app.; Perkins variant-c. 3-12-Variant-c on each 3.00
... Sketchbook (2008, giveaway) Ross and Sadowski sketch art; Krueger commentary 3.00

AVENGERS/ JLA (See JLA/Avengers for #1 & #3)
DC Comics: No, 2, 2003; No. 4, 2003 ($5.95, limited series)

2-Busiek-s/Pérez-a; wraparound-c; Krona, Galactus app. 6.00
4-Busiek-s/Pérez-a; wraparound-c 6.00

AVENGERS LOG, THE
Marvel Comics: Feb, 1994 ($1.95)

1-Gives history of all members; Pérez-c 4.00

AVENGERS MECH STRIKE
Marvel Comics: Apr, 2021 - No. 5 ($3.99, limited series)

1-Avengers with new giant robots vs. giant monsters; Jed MacKay-s/Carlos Magno-a 4.00

AVENGERS: MILLENNIUM
Marvel Comics: Jun, 2015 - No. 4, Jun, 2015 ($3.99, weekly limited series)

1-4-Di Giandomenico-a; Scarlet Witch & Quicksilver app. 1-Yu-c. 2-4-Deodato-c. 4.00

AVENGERS NEXT (See A-Next and Spider-Girl)
Marvel Comics: Jan, 2007 - No. 5, Mar, 2007 ($2.99, limited series)

1-5-Lim-a/Wieringo-c; Spider-Girl app. 1-Avengers vs. zombies. 2-Thena app. 3.00
...: Rebirth TPB (2007, $13.99) r/#1-5 14.00

AVENGERS 1959
Marvel Comics: Dec, 2011 - No. 5, Mar, 2012 ($2.99, limited series)

1-5-Chaykin-s/a/c; Nick Fury, Kraven, Namora, Sabretooth, Dominic Fortune app. 3.00

AVENGERS NO ROAD HOME
Marvel Comics: Apr, 2019 - No. 10, Jun, 2019 ($4.99/$3.99, weekly limited series)

1-($4.99) Waid, Ewing & Zub-s/Medina-a; intro Nyx; Rocket Raccoon & Hercules app. 5.00
2-5,7-9-($3.99) 2-Nightmare app. 4-Izaakse-a. 5-Conan cameo on last page. 7-9-Conan app. 7,9-Medina-a. 8-Barberi-a 4.00
6-($4.99) Conan the Barbarian and Scarlet Witch team-up; Izaakse-a 5.00
10-($4.99) Izaakse-a; Conan goes to the Savage Land 5.00

AVENGERS OF THE WASTELANDS
Marvel Comics: Mar, 2020 - No. 5, Nov, 2020 ($3.99, limited series)

1-5-Brisson-s/Scharf-a; set in the future during Old Man Logan & Dead Man Logan series 4.00

AVENGERS: OPERATION HYDRA
Marvel Comics: Jun, 2015 ($3.99, one-shot)

1-Movie team; Pilgrim-s/Di Vito-a; bonus reprint of Avengers #16 (1965) 4.00

AVENGERS ORIGINS (Series of one-shots)
Marvel Comics: Jan, 2012 ($3.99)

...: Ant-Man & The Wasp 1 (1/12) Aguirre-Sacasa-s/Hans-a/Djurdjevic-c; origin of both 4.00
...: Luke Cage 1 (1/12) Glass & Benson-s/Talajic-a/Djurdjevic-c; 4.00
...: Scarlet Witch & Quicksilver 1 (1/12) McKeever-s/Pierfederici-a/Djurdjevic-c 4.00
...: Thor 1 (1/12) K. Immonen-s/Barrionuevo-a/Djurdjevic-c 4.00
...: Vision 1 (1/12) Higgins & Siegel-s/Perger-a/Djurdjevic-c; Ultron-5 app. 4.00

AVENGERS PRIME (The Heroic Age)

Avengers: The Children's Crusade #1 © MAR

Avengers: The Origin #5 © MAR

Avengers vs. X-Men #6 © MAR

	GD	VG	FN	VF	VF/NM	NM-
	2.0	4.0	6.0	8.0	9.0	9.2

Marvel Comics: Aug, 2010 - No. 5, Mar, 2011 ($3.99, limited series)

1-5-Thor, Iron Man & Steve Rogers; Bendis-s/Davis-a; Enchantress app. 4.00
1-Variant-c by Djurdjevic 8.00

AVENGERS: RAGE OF ULTRON
Marvel Comics: 2015 ($24.99, hardcover graphic novel)

HC - Remender-s/Opeña-a; intro by Busiek 25.00

AVENGERS: SEASON ONE
Marvel Comics: 2013 ($24.99, hardcover graphic novel)

HC - Origin story; Peter David-a/Tedesco painted-c; bonus script outline 25.00

AVENGERS: SOLO
Marvel Comics: Dec, 2011 - No. 5, Apr, 2012 ($3.99, limited series)

1-5-Hawkeye; back-up Avengers Academy 4.00

AVENGERS SPOTLIGHT (Formerly Solo Avengers #1-20)
Marvel Comics: No. 21, Aug, 1989 - No. 40, Jan, 1991 (75¢/$1.00)

21-Byrne-c/a 5.00
22-40: 26-Acts of Vengeance story. 31-34-U.S. Agent series. 36-Heck-i. 37-Mortimer-i. 40-The Black Knight app. 4.00

AVENGERS STANDOFF (Crossover with Avengers titles and other Marvel titles)
Marvel Comics: Apr, 2016 - Jun, 2016 ($4.99)

...: Assault on Pleasant Hill Alpha 1 (5/16) Part 2 of crossover; Spencer-s/Saiz-a 5.00
...: Assault on Pleasant Hill Omega 1 (6/16) Part 3 of crossover; Spencer-s/Acuña-a; new Quasar debut; Red Skull app. 5.00
...: Welcome to Pleasant Hill 1 (4/16) Part 1 of crossover; Spencer-s/Bagley-a/Acuña-c 5.00

AVENGERS STRIKEFILE
Marvel Comics: Jan, 1994 ($1.75, one-shot)

1 4.00

AVENGERS: THE CHILDREN'S CRUSADE
Marvel Comics: Sept, 2010 - No. 9, May, 2012 ($3.99, limited series)

1-9-Young Avengers search for Scarlet Witch; Heinberg-s/Cheung-a. 6-9-X-Men app. 4.00
1-4-Variant-c. 1-Jelena Djurdjevic. 2-Travis Charest. 3,4-Art Adams 6.00
... - Young Avengers (5/11, $3.99) Takes place between #4&5; Alan Davis-a/c 4.00

AVENGERS: THE CROSSING
Marvel Comics: July, 1995 ($4.95, one-shot)

1-Deodato-c/a; 1st app. Thor's new costume 5.00

AVENGERS: THE INITIATIVE (See Civil War and related titles)
Marvel Comics: Jun, 2007 - No. 35, Jun, 2010 ($2.99)

1-Caselli-a/Slott-s/Cheung-c; War Machine app. 4.00
2-35: 4,5-World War Hulk. 6-Uy-a. 14-19-Secret Invasion; 3-D Man app. 16-Skrull Kill Krew returns. 20-Tigra pregnancy revealed, 21-25-Ramos-a. 32-35-Siege 3.00
Annual 1 (1/08, $3.99) Secret Invasion tie-in; Cheung-c 4.00
... Featuring Reptil (5/09, $3.99) Gage-s/Uy-a 4.00
... Special 1 (1/09, $3.99) Slott & Gage-s/Uy-a 4.00
...: Vol. 1 - Basic Training HC (2007, $19.99, d.j.) r/#1-6 20.00
...: Vol. 1 - Basic Training SC (2008, $14.99) r/#1-6 15.00

AVENGERS: THE ORIGIN
Marvel Comics: Jun, 2010 - No. 5, Oct, 2010 ($3.99, limited series)

1-5-Casey-s/Noto-a/c; team origin (pre-Capt. America) re-told; Loki app. 4.00

AVENGERS: THE TERMINATRIX OBJECTIVE
Marvel Comics: Sept, 1993 - No. 4, Dec, 1993 ($1.25, limited series)

1 ($2.50)-Holo-grafx foil-c 5.00
2-4-Old vs. current Avengers 4.00

AVENGERS: THE ULTRON IMPERATIVE
Marvel Comics: Nov, 2001 ($5.99, one-shot)

1-Follow-up to the Ultron Unlimited ending in Avengers #42; BWS-c 6.00

AVENGERS, THOR & CAPTAIN AMERICA: OFFICIAL INDEX TO THE MARVEL UNIVERSE
Marvel Comics: Jun, 2010 - No. 15, 2001 ($3.99)

1-15-Each issue has chronological synopsies, creator credits, character lists for 30-40 issues of Avengers, Captain America and Journey Into Mystery starting with debuts 4.00

AVENGERS/THUNDERBOLTS
Marvel Comics: May, 2004 - No. 6, Sept, 2004 ($2.99, limited series)

1-6: Busiek & Nicieza-s/Kitson-c. 1,2-Kitson-a. 3-6-Grummett-a 3.00
Vol. 2: Best Intentions (2004, $14.99) r/#1-6 15.00

AVENGERS: TIMESLIDE
Marvel Comics: Feb, 1996 ($4.95, one-shot)

1-Foil-c 5.00

AVENGERS TWO: WONDER MAN & BEAST
Marvel Comics: May, 2000 - No. 3, July, 2000 ($2.99, limited series)

1-3: Stern-s/Bagley-c/a 3.00

AVENGERS/ULTRAFORCE (See Ultraforce/Avengers)
Marvel Comics: Oct, 1995 ($3.95, one-shot)

1-Wraparound foil-c by Pérez 4.00

AVENGERS: ULTRON FOREVER
Marvel Comics: Jun, 2015 ($4.99)(Continues in New Avengers: Ultron Forever)

1-Part 1 of 3-part crossover with New Avengers and Uncanny Avengers; Ewing-s/Alan Davis-a; team-up of past, present and future Avengers vs. Ultron 5.00

AVENGERS UNDERCOVER (Follows Avengers Arena series)
Marvel Comics: May, 2014 - No. 10, Nov, 2014 ($2.99)

1-10: Hopeless-s in all; Masters of Evil app. 1,2,4,5,7,Kev Walker-a. 3,6,9-Green-a 3.00

AVENGERS UNITED THEY STAND
Marvel Comics: Nov, 1999 - No. 7, June, 2000 ($2.99/$1.99)

1-Based on the animated series 5.00
2-6-($1.99) 2-Avengers battle Hydra. 6-The Collector app. 4.00
7-($2.99) Devil Dinosaur-c/app.; The Collector app.; r/Avengers Action Figure Comic 5.00

AVENGERS UNIVERSE
Marvel Comics: Jun, 2000 - No. 3, Oct, 2000 ($3.99)

1-3-Reprints recent stories 4.00

AVENGERS UNPLUGGED
Marvel Comics: Oct, 1995 - No. 6, Aug, 1996 (99¢, bi-monthly)

1-6 4.00

AVENGERS VS. ATLAS (Leads into Atlas #1)
Marvel Comics: Mar, 2010 - No. 4, Jun, 2010 ($3.99, limited series)

1-4-Hardman-a; Ramos-c. 1-Back-up w/Miyazawa-a. 2-4-Original Avengers app. 4.00

AVENGERS VS INFINITY
Marvel Comics: Jan, 2016 ($5.99, one-shot)

1-Short stories with The Wrecker, Doctor Doom, Bossman & Dracula; Alves & Lim-a 6.00

AVENGERS VS. PET AVENGERS
Marvel Comics: Dec, 2010 - No. 4, Mar, 2011 ($2.99, limited series)

1-4-Eliopoulos-s/Guara-a; Fin Fang Foom app. 3.00

AVENGERS VS. X-MEN (Also see AVX: VS and AVX: Consequences)
Marvel Comics: No. 0, May, 2012 - No. 12, Dec, 2012 ($3.99/$4.99, bi-weekly limited series)

0-Bendis & Aaron-s; Frank Cho-a/c; Scarlet Witch and Hope featured 4.00
1-11: 1-5-Romita Jr. -a. 6,7,11-Coipel-a. 8-10-Adam Kubert-a. 11-Hulk app. 4.00
12-($4.99) Adam Kubert-a; Cyclops as Dark Phoenix 5.00

AVENGERS WEST COAST (Formerly West Coast Avengers)
Marvel Comics: No. 48, Sept, 1989 - No. 102, Jan, 1994 ($1.00/$1.25)

48,49: 48-Byrne-c/a & scripts continue thru #57 4.00
50-Re-intro original Human Torch 5.00
51-69,71-74,76-83,85,86,89-99: 54-Cover swipe/F.F. #1. 78-Last $1.00-c. 79-Dr. Strange x-over. 93-95-Darkhawk app. 4.00
70,75,84,87,88: 70-Spider-Woman app. 75 (52 pgs.)-Fantastic Four x-over. 84-Origin Spider-Woman retold; Spider-Man app. (also in #85,86). 87,88-Wolverine-c/story 5.00
100-($3.95, 68 pgs.)-Embossed all red foil-c 5.00
101,102: 101-X-Men x-over 5.00
Annual 5-8 ('90- '93, 68 pgs.)-5,6-West Coast Avengers in indicia. 7-Darkhawk app. 8-Polybagged w/card 4.00
...: Darker Than Scarlet TPB (2008, $24.99) r/#51-57,60-62; Byrne-s/a 25.00
...: Vision Quest TPB (2005, $24.99) r/#42-50; Byrne-s/a 25.00

AVENGERS WORLD
Marvel Comics: Mar, 2014 - No. 21, Jul, 2015 ($3.99)

1-21: 1-Hickman & Spencer-s/Caselli-a. 6-Neal Adams-c. 15,16-Doctor Doom app. 16-Cassie Lang brought back to life. 21-Leads into Secret Wars #1 4.00

AVENGERS: X-SANCTION
Marvel Comics: Feb, 2012 - No. 4, May, 2012 ($3.99, limited series)

1-4-Loeb-s/McGuinness-a/c; Cable battles the Avengers. 3,4-Wolverine & Spidey app. 4.00

AVENGING SPIDER-MAN (Spider-Man and Avengers member team-ups)
Marvel Comics: Jan, 2012 - No. 22, Aug, 2013 ($3.99)

	GD	VG	FN	VF	VF/NM	NM-
1-Madureira-a/Wells-s; Madureira-c; Red Hulk & Avengers app.	1	2	3	5	6	8
1-Variant-c by Ramos	1	3	4	6	8	10
1-Variant-c by J. Scott Campbell	1	3	4	6	8	10

Axis: Revolutions #1 © MAR

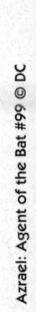

Azrael: Agent of the Bat #99 © DC

Babe #6 © Prize

	GD	VG	FN	VF	VF/NM	NM-
	2.0	4.0	6.0	8.0	9.0	9.2

GD VG FN VF VF/NM NM-
2.0 4.0 6.0 8.0 9.0 9.2

2-8,10-15: 2,3-Madureira-a/Wells-s; Madureira-c. 2,3-Red Hulk & Avengers app. 4-Hawkeye. 5-Captain America app.; Yu-a. 11-Dillon-a. 12,13-Deadpool app. 14,15-Devil Dinosaur 4.00
9-(9/12) Carol Danvers (Ms. Marvel) takes the name Captain Marvel 5 10 15 35 63 90
15.1 (2/13, $2.99) Follows Amazing Spider-Man #700; 1st Superior Spider-Man 5.00
16-22-Superior Spider-Man. 16-Wolverine & X-Men app. 18-Thor app. 22-Punisher app. 4.00
Annual 1 (12/12, $4.99) Spider-Man (Peter Parker) and The Thing; Zircher-c 5.00

AVIATION ADVENTURES AND MODEL BUILDING (True Aviation Advs. ...No. 15)
Parents' Magazine Institute: No. 16, Dec, 1946 - No. 17, Feb, 1947
16,17-Half comics and half pictures 8 16 24 44 57 70

AVIATION CADETS
Street & Smith Publications: 1943
nn 19 37 57 111 176 240

A-V IN 3-D
Aardvark-Vanaheim: Dec, 1984 ($2.00, 28 pgs. w/glasses)
1-Cerebus, Flaming Carrot, Normalman & Ms. Tree 4.00

AVX: CONSEQUENCES (Aftermath of Avengers Vs. X-Men series)
Marvel Comics: Dec, 2012 - No. 5, Jan, 2013 ($3.99, weekly limited series)
1-5-Cyclops in prison; Gillen-s/art by various 4.00

AVX: VS (Tie-in to Avengers Vs. X-Men series)
Marvel Comics: Jun, 2012 - No. 6, Nov, 2012 ($3.99, limited series)
1-6-Spotlight on the individual fights from Avengers Vs. X-Men #2; art by various 4.00

AWAKEN SKIES
Aspen MLT: No. 0, Jun, 2018 ($1.50, one-shot)
0-($1.50) Mastromauro-s/Lorenzana-a; two covers 3.00

AWESOME ADVENTURES
Awesome Entertainment: Aug, 1999 ($2.50)
1-Alan Moore-s/ Steve Skroce-a; Youngblood story 3.00

AWESOME HOLIDAY SPECIAL
Awesome Entertainment: Dec, 1997 ($2.50, one-shot)
1-Flip book w/covers of Fighting American & Coven. Holiday stories also featuring Kaboom and Shaft by regular creators. 3.00
1-Gold Edition 5.00

AWFUL OSCAR (Formerly & becomes Oscar Comics with No. 13)
Marvel Comics: No. 11, June, 1949 - No. 12, Aug, 1949
11,12 17 34 51 98 154 210

AW YEAH COMICS: ACTION CAT & ADVENTURE BUG
Dark Horse Graphics: Mar, 2016 - No. 4, Jun, 2016 ($2.99, limited series)
1-4-Art Baltazar & Franco-s/a 3.00

AXA
Eclipse Comics: Apr, 1987 - No. 2, Aug, 1987 ($1.75)
1,2 6.00

AXCEND
Image Comics: Oct, 2015 - No. 5, Jul, 2016 ($3.50/$3.99)
1-3-Shane Davis-s/a 3.50
4,5-($3.99) 4.00

AXE COP: BAD GUY EARTH
Dark Horse Comics: Mar, 2011 - No. 3, May, 2011 ($3.50, limited series)
1-3-Malachai Nicolle-s/Ethan Nicolle-a 3.50

AXE COP: PRESIDENT OF THE WORLD
Dark Horse Comics: Jul, 2012 - No. 3, Sept, 2012 ($3.50, limited series)
1-3-Malachai Nicolle-s/Ethan Nicolle-a 3.50

AXE COP: THE AMERICAN CHOPPERS
Dark Horse Comics: May, 2014 - No. 3, Jul, 2014 ($3.99, limited series)
1-3-Malachai Nicolle-s/Ethan Nicolle-a. 3-Origin of Axe Cop 4.00

AXEL PRESSBUTTON (Pressbutton No. 5; see Laser Eraser &...)
Eclipse Comics: Nov, 1984 - No. 6, July, 1985 ($1.50/$1.75, Baxter paper)
1-6: Reprints Warrior (British mag.). 1-Bolland-c; origin Laser Eraser & Pressbutton 4.00

AXIS ALPHA
Axis Comics: Feb, 1994 ($2.50, one-shot)
V1-Previews Axis titles including, Tribe, Dethgrip, B.E.A.S.T.I.E.S. & more; Pitt app. in Tribe story. 4.00

AXIS: CARNAGE (Tie-in to Avengers & X-Men Axis series)
Marvel Comics: Dec, 2014 - No. 3, Feb, 2015 ($3.99, limited series)
1-3-Spears-s/Peralta-a; Carnage as a hero; Sin-Eater app. 4.00

AXIS: HOBGOBLIN (Tie-in to Avengers & X-Men Axis series)
Marvel Comics: Dec, 2014 - No. 3, Feb, 2015 ($3.99, limited series)
1-3-Shinick-s/Rodriguez-a; Hobgoblin as a hero; Goblin King app. 4.00

AXIS: RESOLUTIONS (Tie-in to Avengers & X-Men Axis series)
Marvel Comics: Dec, 2014 - No. 4, Feb, 2015 ($3.99, limited series)
1-4-Two stories per issue; s/a by various. 1-Lashley-a. 4-Chaykin-s/a 4.00

AZRAEL (...Agent of the Bat #47 on)(Also see Batman: Sword of Azrael)
DC Comics: Feb, 1995 - No. 100, May, 2003 ($1.95/$2.25/$2.50/$2.95)
1-Dennis O'Neil scripts begin 1 2 3 5 6 8
2,3 4.00
4-46,48-62: 5,6-Ras Al Ghul app. 13-Nightwing-c/app. 15-Contagion Pt. 5 (Pt. 4 on-c). 16-Contagion Pt. 10. 22-Batman-c/app. 23,27-Batman app. 27,28-Joker app. 35-Hitman app. 36-39-Batman, Bane app. 50-New costume. 53-Joker-c/app. 56,57,60-New Batgirl app. 3.00
47-($3.95) Flip book with Batman: Shadow of the Bat #80 4.00
63-74,76-92: 63-Huntress-c/app.; Azrael returns to old costume. 67-Begin $2.50-c. 70-79-Harris-c. 83-Joker x-over. 91-Bruce Wayne: Fugitive pt. 15 3.00
75-($3.95) New costume; Harris-c 4.00
93-100: 93-Begin $2.95-c. 95,96-Two-Face app. 100-Last issue; Zeck-c 3.00
#1,000,000 (11/98) Giarrano-a 3.00
Annual 1 (1995, $3.95)-Year One story 4.00
Annual 2 (1996, $2.95)-Legends of the Dead Earth story 4.00
Annual 3 (1997, $3.95)-Pulp Heroes story; Orbik-c 4.00
.../Ash (1997, $4.95) O'Neil-s/Quesada, Palmiotti-a 5.00
Plus (12/96, $2.95)-Question-c/app. 4.00

AZRAEL
DC Comics: Dec, 2009 - No. 18, May, 2011 ($2.99)
1-18: 1-9-Nicieza-s/Bachs-a. 1-Covers by Jock & Irving. 2,3-Jock-c. 5-Ragman app. 3.00
...: Angel in the Dark TPB (2010, $17.99) r/#1-6; cover gallery 18.00

AZRAEL: DEATH'S DARK KNIGHT
DC Comics: May, 2009 - No. 3, Jul, 2009 ($2.99, limited series)
1-Battle For the Cowl tie-in; Nicieza-s/Irving-a/March-c 3.00
TPB (2010, $14.99) r/#1-3, Batman Annual #27 and Detective Annual #11 15.00

AZTEC ACE
Eclipse Comics: Mar, 1984 - No. 15, Sept, 1985 ($2.25/$1.50/$1.75, Baxter paper)
1-$2.25-c (52 pgs.) 4.00
2-15: 2-Begin 36 pgs. 3.00
NOTE: *N. Redondo a-1i-8i, 10i. c-6-8i.*

AZTEK: THE ULTIMATE MAN
DC Comics: Aug, 1996 - No. 10, May 1997 ($1.75)
1-1st app. Aztek & Synth; Grant Morrison & Mark Millar scripts in all 6.00
2-9: 2-Green Lantern app. 3-1st app. Death-Doll. 4-Intro The Lizard King. 5-Origin. 6-Joker app.; Batman cameo. 7-Batman app. 8-Luthor app. 9-vs. Parasite-c/app. 4.00
10-Joins the JLA; JLA-c/app. 1 2 4 6 8 10
JLA Presents: Aztek the Ultimate Man TPB (2008, $19.99) r/#1-10 20.00
NOTE: *Breyfogle c-5p. N. Steven Harris a-1-5p. Porter c-1p. Wieringo c-2p.*

BABE (...Darling of the Hills, later issues)(See Big Shot and Sparky Watts)
Prize/Headline/Feature: June-July, 1948 - No. 11, Apr-May, 1950
1-Boody Rogers-a 55 110 165 352 601 850
2-Boody Rogers-a 36 72 108 211 343 475
3-11-All by Boody Rogers 28 56 84 165 270 375

BABE
Dark Horse Comics (Legend): July, 1994 - No. 4, Jan, 1994 ($2.50, lim. series)
1-4: John Byrne-c/a/scripts; ProtoTykes back-up story 4.00

BABE RUTH SPORTS COMICS (Becomes Rags Rabbit #11 on?)
Harvey Publications: April, 1949 - No. 11, Feb, 1951
1-Powell-a 41 82 123 256 428 600
2-Powell-a 27 54 81 158 259 360
3-11: Powell-a in most 22 44 66 130 213 295
NOTE: *Baseball c-2-4, 9. Basketball c-1, 6. Football c-5. Yogi Berra c/story-8. Joe DiMaggio c/story-3. Bob Feller c/story-4. Stan Musial c-9.*

BABES IN TOYLAND (Disney, Movie) (See Golden Pix Story Book ST-3)
Dell Publishing Co.: No. 1282, Feb-Apr, 1962
Four Color 1282-Annette Funicello photo-c 13 26 39 86 188 290

BABES OF BROADWAY
Broadway Comics: May, 1996 ($2.95, one-shot)

Baby Huey Duckland #12 © HARV

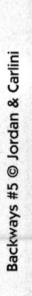

Babyteeth #13 © Cates & Brown

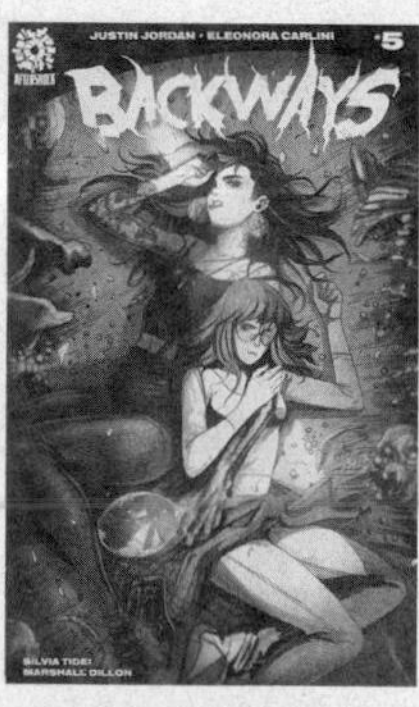

Backways #5 © Jordan & Carlini

	GD 2.0	VG 4.0	FN 6.0	VF 8.0	VF/NM 9.0	NM- 9.2
1-Pin-ups of Broadway Comics' female characters; Alan Davis, Michael Kaluta, J.G. Jones, Alan Weiss, Guy Davis & others-a; Giordano-c.						5.00

BABE 2
Dark Horse Comics (Legend): Mar, 1995 - No. 2, May, 1995 ($2.50, lim. series)

	GD	VG	FN	VF	VF/NM	NM-
1,2: John Byrne-c/a/scripts						3.00

BABY HUEY
Harvey Comics: No. 1, Oct, 1991 - No. 9, June, 1994 ($1.00/$1.25/$1.50, quarterly)

	GD	VG	FN	VF	VF/NM	NM-
1 ($1.00): 1-Cover says "Big Baby Huey"						5.00
2-9 ($1.25-$1.50)						3.00

BABY HUEY AND PAPA (See Paramount Animated...)
Harvey Publications: May, 1962 - No. 33, Jan, 1968 (Also see Casper The Friendly Ghost)

	GD	VG	FN	VF	VF/NM	NM-
1	13	26	39	86	188	290
2	7	14	21	49	92	135
3-5	5	10	15	33	57	80
6-10	3	6	9	20	31	42
11-20	3	6	9	15	22	28
21-33	2	4	6	13	18	22

BABY HUEY DIGEST
Harvey Publications: June, 1992 (Digest-size, one-shot)

	GD	VG	FN	VF	VF/NM	NM-
1-Reprints	1	3	4	6	8	10

BABY HUEY DUCKLAND
Harvey Publications: Nov, 1962 - No. 15, Nov, 1966 (25¢ Giants, 68 pgs.)

	GD	VG	FN	VF	VF/NM	NM-
1	10	20	30	66	138	210
2-5	5	10	15	34	60	85
6-15	3	6	9	21	33	45

BABY HUEY, THE BABY GIANT (Also see Big Baby Huey, Casper, Harvey Hits #22, Harvey Comics Hits #60, & Paramount Animated Comics)
Harvey Publ: 9/56 - #97, 10/71; #98, 10/72; #99, 10/80; #100, 10/90; #101, 11/90

	GD	VG	FN	VF	VF/NM	NM-
1-Infinity-c	53	106	159	419	947	1475
2	21	42	63	147	324	500
3-Baby Huey takes anti-pep pills	13	26	39	89	195	300
4,5	9	18	27	61	123	185
6-10	6	12	18	40	73	105
11-20	5	10	15	31	53	75
21-40	4	8	12	23	37	50
41-60	3	6	9	16	23	30
61-79 (12/67)	2	4	6	13	18	22
80(12/68) - 95-All 68 pg. Giants	3	6	9	16	24	32
96,97-Both 52 pg. Giants	3	6	9	14	19	24
98-Regular size	2	4	6	9	12	15
99-Regular size	1	2	3	5	6	8
100,101 ($1.00)						4.00

BABYLON 5 (TV)
DC Comics: Jan, 1995 - No. 11, Dec, 1995 ($1.95/$2.50)

	GD	VG	FN	VF	VF/NM	NM-
1	2	4	6	8	11	14
2-5	1	2	3	5	7	9
6-11: 7-Begin $2.50-c	1	2	3	4	5	7
... The Price of Peace (1998, $9.95, TPB) r/#1-4,11						10.00

BABYLON 5: IN VALEN'S NAME
DC Comics: Mar, 1998 - No. 3, May, 1998 ($2.50, limited series)

	GD	VG	FN	VF	VF/NM	NM-
1-3						4.00

BABY SNOOTS (Also see March of Comics #359,371,396,401,419,431,443,450,462,474,485)
Gold Key: Aug, 1970 - No. 22, Nov, 1975

	GD	VG	FN	VF	VF/NM	NM-
1	3	6	9	19	30	50
2-11	2	4	6	11	16	20
12-22: 22-Titled Snoots, the Forgetful Elefink	2	4	6	8	10	12

BABYTEETH
AfterShock Comics: Jun, 2017 - No. 16, Sept, 2019 ($3.99)

	GD	VG	FN	VF	VF/NM	NM-
1-16-Donny Cates-s/Garry Brown-a						4.00
... #1: Halloween Edition (10/17, giveaway) r/#1 in B&W; Elizabeth Torque-c						3.00

BACCHUS (Also see Eddie Campbell's ...)
Harrier Comics (New Wave): 1988 - No. 2, Aug, 1988 ($1.95, B&W)

	GD	VG	FN	VF	VF/NM	NM-
1,2: Eddie Campbell-c/a/scripts.						3.00

BACHELOR FATHER (TV)
Dell Publishing Co.: No. 1332, 4-6/62 - No. 2, Sept.-Nov., 1962

	GD	VG	FN	VF	VF/NM	NM-
Four Color 1332 (#1), 2-Written by Stanley	7	14	21	46	86	125

BACHELOR'S DIARY
Avon Periodicals: 1949 (15¢)

	GD	VG	FN	VF	VF/NM	NM-
1(Scarce)-King Features panel cartoons & text-r; pin-up, girl wrestling photos; similar to Sideshow	148	296	444	947	1624	2300

BACKLASH (Also see The Kindred)
Image Comics (WildStorm Prod.): Nov,1994 - No. 32, May, 1997 ($1.95/$2.50)

	GD	VG	FN	VF	VF/NM	NM-
1-Double-c; variant-double-c						4.00
2-24,26-32: 5-Intro Mindscape; 2 pinups. 8-Wildstorm Rising Pt 8 (newsstand & Direct Market versions. 19-Fire From Heaven Pt 2. 20-Fire From Heaven Pt 10. 31-WildC.A.T.S app.						3.00
25-($3.95)-Double-size						4.00
...& Taboo's African Holiday (9/99, $5.95) Booth-s/a(p)						6.00

BACKLASH/SPIDER-MAN
Image Comics (WildStorm Productions): Aug, 1996 - No. 2, Sept, 1996 ($2.50, lim. series)

	GD	VG	FN	VF	VF/NM	NM-
1,2: Pike (villain from WildC.A.T.S) & Venom app.						3.00

BACKPACK MARVELS (B&W backpack-sized reprint collections)
Marvel Comics: Nov, 2000 ($6.95, B&W, digest-size)

	GD	VG	FN	VF	VF/NM	NM-
Avengers 1 -r/Avengers #181-189; profile pages						7.00
Spider-Man 1-r/ASM #234-240						7.00
X-Men 1-r/Uncanny X-Men #167-173						7.00
X-Men 2-r/Uncanny X-Men #174-179; new painted-c by Greg Horn						7.00

BACKSTAGERS, THE
Boom Entertainment (BOOM! Box): Aug, 2016 - No. 8, Mar, 2017 ($3.99)

	GD	VG	FN	VF	VF/NM	NM-
1-8: 1-James Tynion IV-s/Rian Sygh-a/Veronica Fish-c						4.00
...: Halloween Intermission 1 (10/18, $7.99) Short stories by Tynion, Sygh and others						8.00
...: Valentine's Intermission 1 (2/18, $7.99) Short stories by Tynion, Sygh and others						8.00

BACK TO THE FUTURE (Movie, TV cartoon)
Harvey Comics: Nov, 1991 - No. 4, June, 1992 ($1.25)

	GD	VG	FN	VF	VF/NM	NM-
1-4: 1,2-Gil Kane-c; based on animated cartoon						4.00

BACK TO THE FUTURE (Movie, TV cartoon)
IDW Publishing: Oct, 2015 - No. 25, Oct, 2017 ($3.99)

	GD	VG	FN	VF	VF/NM	NM-
1-Story by Bob Gale; multiple covers; Doc & Marty's first meeting						6.00
2-24-Multiple covers. 3-Archie variant-c						4.00
25-($4.99)						

BACK TO THE FUTURE: BIFF TO THE FUTURE
IDW Publishing: Jan, 2017 - No. 6, Jun, 2017 ($3.99, limited series)

	GD	VG	FN	VF	VF/NM	NM-
1-5-Biff's rise to power with the sports almanac; Gale & Fridolfs-s/Alan Robinson-a						4.00

BACK TO THE FUTURE: CITIZEN BROWN (Based on the Telltale Games video game)
IDW Publishing: May, 2016 - No. 5, Sept, 2016 ($4.99, limited series)

	GD	VG	FN	VF	VF/NM	NM-
1-5-Erik Burnham-s/Alan Robinson-a; multiple covers on all						5.00

BACK TO THE FUTURE: FORWARD TO THE FUTURE
Harvey Comics: Oct, 1992 - No. 3, Feb, 1993 ($1.50, limited series)

	GD	VG	FN	VF	VF/NM	NM-
1-3						4.00

BACK TO THE FUTURE: TALES FROM THE TIME TRAIN
IDW Publishing: Dec, 2017 - No. 6, May, 2018 ($3.99, limited series)

	GD	VG	FN	VF	VF/NM	NM-
1-6-Doc Brown, Clara and their kids; Gale & Barber-s/Levens-a. 2-6-1939 World's Fair						4.00

BACKWAYS
AfterShock Comics: Dec, 2107 - No. 5, May, 2018 ($3.99)

	GD	VG	FN	VF	VF/NM	NM-
1-5-Justin Jordan-s/Eleonora Carlini-a						4.00

BAD ASS
Dynamite Entertainment: 2014 - No. 4. 2014 ($3.99)

	GD	VG	FN	VF	VF/NM	NM-
1-4-Hanna-s/Bessadi-a						4.00

BAD BLOOD
Dark Horse Comics: Jan, 2014 - No. 5, May, 2014 ($3.99, limited series)

	GD	VG	FN	VF	VF/NM	NM-
1-5-Vampire story; Jonathan Maberry-s/Tyler Crook-a						4.00

BAD BOY
Oni Press: Dec, 1997 ($4.95, one-shot)

	GD	VG	FN	VF	VF/NM	NM-
1-Frank Miller-s/Simon Bisley-a/painted-c						5.00

BAD COMPANY
Quality Comics/Fleetway Quality #15 on: Aug, 1988 - No. 19?, 1990 ($1.50/$1.75, high quality paper)

	GD	VG	FN	VF	VF/NM	NM-
1-19: 5,6-Guice-c						3.00

BADGE OF JUSTICE (Formerly Crime And Justice #21)
Charlton Comics: No. 22, Jan, 1955; No. 2, Apr, 1955 - No. 4, Oct, 1955

	GD	VG	FN	VF	VF/NM	NM-
22(#1)-Giordano-c	13	26	39	72	101	130
2-4	9	18	27	47	61	75

Badger #20 © First Pub.

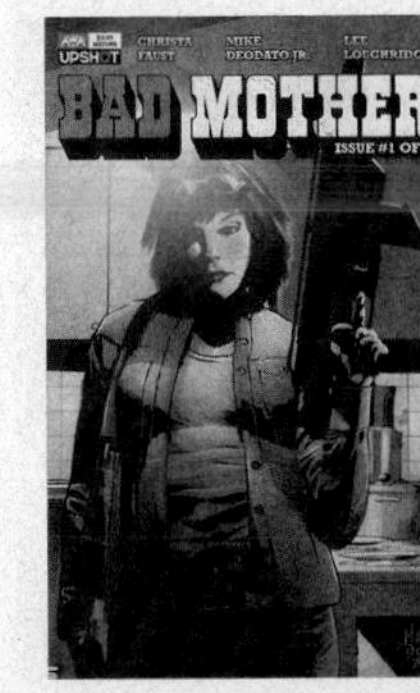

Bad Mother #1 © AWA Inc.

Ballistic Imagery #1 © TCOW

	GD	VG	FN	VF	VF/NM	NM-
	2.0	4.0	6.0	8.0	9.0	9.2

BADGER, THE
Capital Comics(#1-4)/First Comics: Dec, 1983 - No. 70, Apr, 1991; V2#1, Spring, 1991

1	1	3	4	6	8	10
2-49,51-70: 52-54-Tim Vigil-c/a						3.00
50-($3.95, 52 pgs.)						4.00
V2#1 (Spring, 1991, $4.95)						5.00

BADGER, THE
Image Comics: V3#78, May, 1997 - V3#88 ($2.95, B&W)

78-Cover lists #1, Baron-s 3.00
79/#2, 80/#3, 81(indicia lists #80)/#4,82-88/#5-11 3.00

BADGER, THE
Devil's Due/1First Comics: 2016 - No. 5, 2016 ($3.99)

1-5: 1-Mike Baron-s/Jim Fern-a/Val Mayerik-c; origin story. 2-5-Putin app. 4.00

BADGER GOES BERSERK
First Comics: Sept, 1989 - No. 4, Dec, 1989 ($1.95, lim. series, Baxter paper)

1-4: 2-Paul Chadwick-c/a(2pgs.) 3.00

BADGER: SHATTERED MIRROR
Dark Horse Comics: July, 1994 - No. Oct, 1994 ($2.50, limited series)

1-4 3.00

BADGER: ZEN POP FUNNY-ANIMAL VERSION
Dark Horse Comics: July, 1994 - No. 2, Aug, 1994 ($2.50, limited series)

1,2 3.00

BAD GIRLS
DC Comics: Oct, 2003 - No. 5, Feb, 2004 ($2.50, limited series)

1-5-Steve Vance-s/Jennifer Graves-a/Darwyn Cooke-c 3.00
TPB (2009, $14.99) r/#1-5; Graves sketch pages 15.00

BAD IDEAS
Image Comics: Apr, 2004 - No. 2, July, 2004 ($5.95, B&W, limited series)

1,2-Chinsang-s/Mahfood & Crosland-a 6.00
..., Vol. 1: Collected! (2005, $12.99) r/#1,2 13.00

BAD KITTY ONE SHOT (CHAOS!...)
Dynamite Entertainment: 2014 ($5.99)

1-Spence-s/Rafael-a/c; origin 6.00

BADLANDS
Vortex Comics: May, 1990 ($3.00, glossy stock, mature)

1-Chaykin-c 3.00

BADLANDS
Dark Horse Comics: July, 1991 - No. 6, Dec, 1991 ($2.25, B&W, limited series)

1-6: 1-John F. Kennedy-c; reprints Vortex Comics issue 3.00

BAD LUCK CHUCK
Dark Horse Comics: Mar, 2019 - No. 4, Jun, 2019 ($3.99, limited series)

1-4-Lela Gwenn-s/Matthew Dow Smith-a 4.00

BADMEN OF THE WEST
Avon Periodicals: 1951 (Giant) (132 pgs., painted-c)

1-Contains rebound copies of Jesse James, King of the Bad Men of Deadwood, Badmen of Tombstone; other combinations possible. Issues with Kubert-a...	53	106	159	334	567	800

BADMEN OF THE WEST! (See A-1 Comics)
Magazine Enterprises: 1953 - No. 3, 1954

1 (A-1 100)-Meskin-a?	24	48	72	144	237	330
2 (A-1 120), 3: 2-Larsen-a	16	32	48	92	144	195

BADMEN OF TOMBSTONE
Avon Periodicals: 1950

nn	20	40	60	114	182	250

BAD MOTHER
AWA Studios: Aug, 2020 - No. 5, Dec, 2020 ($3.99, limited series)

1-5-Christa Faust-s/Mike Deodato Jr.-a 4.00

BAD PLANET
Image Comics (Raw Studios): Dec, 2005 - No. 6, Nov, 2008 ($2.99)

1-6: 1-Thomas Jane & Steve Niles-s/Larosa & Bradstreet-a/c. 2-Wrightson-c. 3-3-D pages3.00

BAD RECEPTION
AfterShock Comics: Aug, 2019 - No. 5, Jul, 2020 ($3.99, limited series)

1-5-Juan Doe-s/a 4.00

BADROCK (Also see Youngblood)
Image Comics (Extreme Studios): Mar, 1995 - No. 2, Jan, 1996 ($1.75/$2.50)

1-Variant-c (3) 4.00
2-Liefeld-c/a & story; Savage Dragon app, flipbook w/Grifter/Badrock #2; variant-c exist 3.00
Annual 1(1995,$2.95)-Arthur Adams-c 4.00
Annual 1 Commemorative ($9.95)-3,000 printed 10.00
.../Wolverine (6/96, $4.95, squarebound)-Sauron app; pin-ups; variant-c exists 5.00
.../Wolverine (6/96)-Special Comicon Edition 5.00

BADROCK AND COMPANY (Also see Youngblood)
Image Comics (Extreme Studios): Sept, 1994 - No.6, Feb, 1995 ($2.50)

1-6 : 6-Indicia reads "October 1994"; story cont'd in Shadowhawk #17 3.00

BAFFLING MYSTERIES (Formerly Indian Braves No. 1-4; Heroes of the Wild Frontier No. 26-on)
Periodical House (Ace Magazines): No. 5, Nov, 1951 - No. 26, Oct, 1955

5	53	106	159	334	567	800
6-19,21-24: 8-Woodish-a by Cameron. 10-E.C. Crypt Keeper swipe on-c. 24-Last pre-code issue	39	78	117	240	395	550
20-Classic bondage-c	47	94	141	296	498	700
25-Reprints; surrealistic-c	32	64	96	188	307	425
26-Reprints	26	52	78	152	249	345

NOTE: ***Cameron*** *a-8, 10, 16-18, 20-22.* ***Colan*** *a-5, 11, 25r/5.* ***Sekowsky*** *a-5, 6, 22. Bondage c-20, 23. Reprints in 18(1), 19(1), 24(3).*

BAKER STREET PECULIARS, THE
Boom Entertainment (kaboom!): Mar, 2016 - No. 4, Jun, 2016 ($3.99, limited series)

1-4-Roger Langridge-s/Andy Hirsch-a 4.00

BALBO (See Master Comics #33 & Mighty Midget Comics)

BALDER THE BRAVE (Character from Thor)
Marvel Comics Group: Nov, 1985 - No. 4, 1986 (Limited series)

1-4: Walt Simonson-c/s; Sal Buscema-a 4.00

BALLAD OF HALO JONES, THE
Quality Comics: Sept, 1987 - No. 12, Aug, 1988 ($1.25/$1.50)

1-12: Alan Moore scripts in all 3.00

BALL AND CHAIN
DC Comics (Homage): Nov, 1999 - No. 4, Feb, 2000 ($2.50, limited series)

1-4-Lobdell-s/Garza-a 5.00

BALLISTIC (Also See Cyberforce)
Image Comics (Top Cow Productions): Sept, 1995 - No. 3, Dec, 1995 ($2.50, limited series)

1-3: Wetworks app, Turner-c/a 3.00
... Action (5/96, $2.95) Pin-ups of Top Cow characters participating in outdoor sports 3.00
... Imagery (1/96, $2.50, anthology) Cyberforce app. 3.00
.../ Wolverine (2/97, $2.95) Devil's Reign pt. 4; Witchblade cameo (1 page) 4.00

BALOO & LITTLE BRITCHES (Disney)
Gold Key: Apr, 1968

1-From the Jungle Book	4	8	12	23	37	50

BALTIMORE: ... (One-shots)
Dark Horse Comics: ($3.50)

... The Inquisitor (6/13) Mignola & Golden-s; Stenbeck-a/c 3.50
... The Play (11/12) Mignola & Golden-s; Stenbeck-a/c 3.50
... The Widow and the Tank (2/13) Mignola & Golden-s; Stenbeck-a/c 3.50

BALTIMORE: CHAPEL OF BONES
Dark Horse Comics: Jan, 2014 - No. 2, Feb, 2014 ($3.50, limited series)

1,2-Mignola & Golden-s; Stenbeck-a/c 3.50

BALTIMORE: EMPTY GRAVES
Dark Horse Comics: Apr, 2016 - No. 5, Aug, 2016 ($3.99, limited series)

1-5-Mignola & Golden-s; Bergting-a; Stenbeck-c 4.00

BALTIMORE: DR. LESKOVAR'S REMEDY
Dark Horse Comics: Jun, 2012 - No. 2, Jul, 2012 ($3.50, limited series)

1,2-Mignola & Golden-s; Stenbeck-a/c 3.50

BALTIMORE: THE CULT OF THE RED KING
Dark Horse Comics: May, 2015 - No. 5, Sept, 2015 ($3.99, limited series)

1-5-Mignola & Golden-s; Bergting-a; Stenbeck-c 4.00

BALTIMORE: THE CURSE BELLS
Dark Horse Comics: Aug, 2011 - No. 5, Dec, 2011 ($3.50, limited series)

1-5-Mignola-s/c; Stenbeck-a. 1-Variant-c by Francavilla 3.50

BALTIMORE: THE INFERNAL TRAIN
Dark Horse Comics: Sept, 2013 - No. 3, Nov, 2013 ($3.50, limited series)

Baltimore: The Red Kingdom #4 © Mignola & Golden

Barbalien: Red Planet #3 © 171 Studios & Ormston

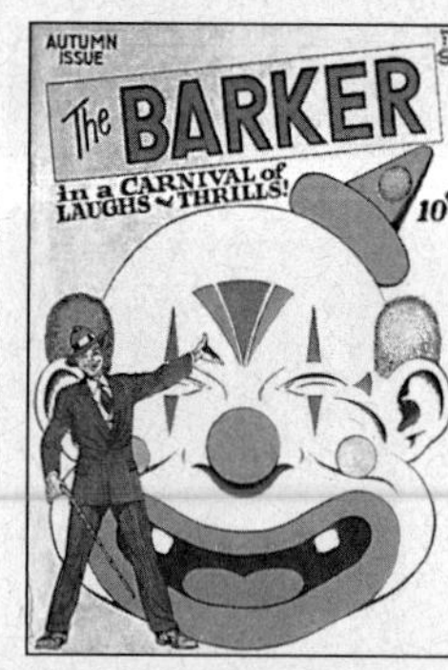

The Barker #1 © QUA

	GD	VG	FN	VF	VF/NM	NM-
	2.0	4.0	6.0	8.0	9.0	9.2

1-3-Mignola & Golden-s; Stenbeck-a/c 3.50

BALTIMORE: THE PLAGUE SHIPS
Dark Horse Comics: Aug, 2010 - No. 5, Dec, 2010 ($3.50, limited series)
1-5-Mignola-s/c; Stenbeck-a; Lord Baltimore hunting vampires in 1916 Europe 3.50

BALTIMORE: THE RED KINGDOM
Dark Horse Comics: Feb, 2017 - No. 5, Jun, 2017 ($3.99, limited series)
1-5-Mignola & Golden-s; Bergting-a; Stenbeck-c 4.00

BALTIMORE: THE WITCH OF HARJU
Dark Horse Comics: Jul, 2014 - No. 3, Sept, 2014 ($3.50, limited series)
1-3-Mignola & Golden-s; Bergting-a; Stenbeck-c 3.50

BALTIMORE: THE WOLF AND THE APOSTLE
Dark Horse Comics: Oct, 2014 - No. 2, Nov, 2014 ($3.50, limited series)
1,2-Mignola & Golden-s; Stenbeck-a/c 3.50

BAMBI (Disney) (See Movie Classics, Movie Comics, and Walt Disney Showcase No. 31)
Dell Publishing Co.: No. 12, 1942; No. 30, 1943; No. 186, Apr, 1948; 1984
Four Color 12-Walt Disney's... 46 92 138 359 805 1250
Four Color 30-Bambi's Children (1943) 41 82 123 303 689 1075
Four Color 186-Walt Disney's...; reprinted as Movie Classic Bambi #3 (1956)
14 28 42 98 217 335
1-(Whitman, 1984; 60¢)-r/Four Color #186 (3-pack) 2 4 6 10 14 18

BAMBI (Disney)
Grosset & Dunlap: 1942 (50¢, 7"x8-1/2", 32 pg, hard-c w/dust jacket)
nn-Given away w/a copy of Thumper for a $2.00, 2-yr. subscription to WDC&S
in 1942 (Xmas offer). Book only 24 48 72 140 230 320
w/dust jacket 40 80 120 244 402 560

BAMM BAMM & PEBBLES FLINTSTONE (TV)
Gold Key: Oct, 1964 (Hanna-Barbera)
1 8 16 24 55 105 155

BANANA SPLITS, THE (TV) (See Golden Comics Digest & March of Comics No. 364)
Gold Key: June, 1969 - No. 8, Oct, 1971 (Hanna-Barbera)
1-Photo-c on all 9 18 27 61 123 185
2-8 5 10 15 34 60 85

BAND WAGON (See Hanna-Barbera Band Wagon)

BANE: CONQUEST
DC Comics: Jul, 2017 - No. 12, Aug, 2018 ($3.99, limited series)
1-12: 1-Chuck Dixon-s/Graham Nolan-a; covers by Nolan and Kelley Jones. 4,5-Catwoman app. 6-12-Kobra app. 4.00

BANG!
Dark Horse Comics: Feb, 2020 - No. 5, Nov, 2020 ($3.99, limited series)
1-5-Matt Kindt-s/Wilfredo Torres-a 4.00

BANG! TANGO
DC Comics (Vertigo): Apr, 2009 - No. 6, Sept, 2009 ($2.99, limited series)
1-6-Kelly-s/Sibar-a/Chaykin-c 3.00

BANG-UP COMICS
Progressive Publishers: Dec, 1941 - No. 3, June, 1942
1-Nazi WWII-c; Cosmo Mann & Lady Fairplay begin; Buzz Balmer by Rick Yager in all
(origin #1) 126 252 378 806 1378 1950
2-Nazi zeppelin WWII-c 81 162 243 518 884 1250
3-Japanese WWII-c 68 136 204 435 743 1050

BANISHED KNIGHTS (See Warlands)
Image Comics: Dec, 2001 - No. 4, June, 2002 ($2.95)
1-4-Two covers (Alvin Lee, Pat Lee) 3.00

BANNER COMICS (Becomes Captain Courageous No. 6)
Ace Magazines: No. 3, Sept, 1941 - No. 5, Jan, 1942
3-Captain Courageous (1st app.) & Lone Warrior & Sidekick Dicky begin;
Nazi WWII-c by Jim Mooney 271 542 813 1734 2967 4200
4,5: 4-Flag-c 181 362 543 1158 1979 2800

BARACK OBAMA (See Presidential Material: Barack Obama, Amazing Spider-Man #583, Savage Dragon #137)

BARACK THE BARBARIAN
Devil's Due Publishing: Jun, 2009 - No. 4, Oct, 2009 ($3.50/$3.99, limited series)
...Quest For The Treasure of Stimuli 1-3-($3.50) Conan spoof with Barack Obama; Hama-s 3.50
...Quest For The Treasure of Stimuli 4-($3.99) 4.00
...: The Red of Red Sarah 1 ($5.99, B&W) Sarah Palin satire; Hama-s 6.00

BARBALIEN: RED PLANET (From Black Hammer)

	GD	VG	FN	VF	VF/NM	NM-
	2.0	4.0	6.0	8.0	9.0	9.2

Dark Horse Comics: Nov, 2020 - No. 5 ($3.99, limited series)
1-4-Lemire & Brombal-s/Walta-a 4.00

BARBARELLA (Volume 1)
Dynamite Entertainment: 2017 - No. 12, 2018 ($3.99)
1-12-Mike Carey-s/Kenan Yarar-a in most; multiple covers on each. 4-Fornés-a 4.00
... Holiday Special One Shot (2018, $5.99) Niklaus von Claus app.; J-M Lofficier-s 6.00

BARBARELLA / DEJAH THORIS
Dynamite Entertainment: 2019 - No. 4, 2019 ($3.99, limited series)
1-4-Leah Williams-s/Germán García-a; multiple covers on each 4.00

BARBARIANS, THE
Atlas Comics/Seaboard Periodicals: June, 1975
1-Origin, only app. Andrax; Iron Jaw app.; Marcos-a 3 6 9 15 22 28

BARBIE
Marvel Comics: Jan, 1991 - No. 63, Mar, 1996 ($1.00/$1.25/$1.50)
1-Polybagged w/doorknob hanger; Romita-c 2 4 6 11 16 20
2-49,51-62 1 2 3 5 7 9
50,63: 50-(Giant). 63-Last issue 2 4 6 8 10 12
... And Baby Sister Kelly (1995, 99¢-c, part of a Marvel 4-pack) scarce
3 6 9 14 20 25

BARBIE & KEN
Dell Publishing Co.: May-July, 1962 - No. 5, Nov-Jan, 1963-64
01-053-207(#1)-Based on Mattel toy dolls 37 74 111 274 612 950
2-4 26 52 78 182 404 625
5 (Last issue) 27 54 81 189 420 650

BARBIE FASHION
Marvel Comics: Jan, 1991 - No. 53, May, 1995 ($1.00/$1.25/$1.50)
1-Polybagged w/Barbie Pink Card 2 4 6 11 16 20
2-49,51,52: 4-Contains preview to Sweet XVI 1 2 3 5 7 9
50,53: 50-(Giant). 53-Last issue 2 4 6 8 10 12

BARB WIRE (See Comics' Greatest World)
Dark Horse Comics: Apr, 1994 - No. 9, Feb, 1995 ($2.00/$2.50)
1-9: 1-Foil logo 4.00
Trade paperback (1996, $8.95)-r/#2,3,5,6 w/Pamela Anderson bio 9.00

BARB WIRE (Volume 2)
Dark Horse Comics: Jul, 2015 - No. 8, Feb, 2016 ($3.99)
1-8-Adam Hughes-c on all. 1-Warner-s/Olliffe-a; two covers by Hughes 4.00

BARB WIRE: ACE OF SPADES
Dark Horse Comics: May, 1996 - No. 4, Sept, 1996 ($2.95, limited series)
1-4: Chris Warner-c/a(p)/scripts; Tim Bradstreet-c/a(i) in all 4.00

BARB WIRE COMICS MAGAZINE SPECIAL
Dark Horse Comics: May, 1996 ($3.50, B&W, magazine, one-shot)
nn-Adaptation of film; photo-c; poster insert. 5.00

BARB WIRE MOVIE SPECIAL
Dark Horse Comics: May, 1996 ($3.95, one-shot)
nn-Adaptation of film; photo-c; 1st app. new look 4.00

BARKER, THE (Also see National Comics #42)
Quality Comics Group/Comic Magazine: Autumn, 1946 - No. 15, Dec, 1949
1 29 58 87 170 278 385
2 15 30 45 90 140 190
3-10 13 26 39 72 101 130
11-14 10 20 30 54 72 90
15-Jack Cole-a(p) 10 20 30 56 76 95
NOTE: *Jack Cole art in some issues.*

BARNABY
Civil Service Publications Inc.: 1945 (25¢,102 pgs., digest size)
V1#1-r/Crocket Johnson strips from 1942 6 12 18 28 34 40

BARNEY AND BETTY RUBBLE (TV) (Flintstones' Neighbors)
Charlton Comics: Jan, 1973 - No. 23, Dec, 1976 (Hanna-Barbera)
1 4 8 12 27 44 60
2-11: 11(2/75)-1st Mike Zeck-a (illos) 3 6 9 14 20 25
12-23: 17-Columbo parody 2 4 6 10 14 18
Digest Annual (1972, B&W, 100 pgs.) (scarce) 4 8 12 27 44 60

BARNEY BAXTER (Also see Magic Comics)
David McKay/Dell Publishing Co./Argo: 1938 - No. 2, 1956
Feature Books 15(McKay-1938) 45 90 135 284 480 675

Barney Google & Snuffy Smith #4 © TOBY

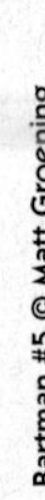
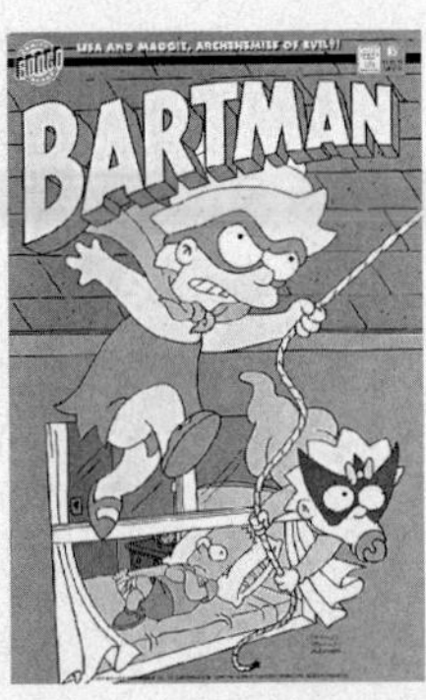

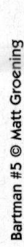

Bartman #5 © Matt Groening

Basketful of Heads #4 © Joe Hill

GD VG FN VF VF/NM NM-
2.0 4.0 6.0 8.0 9.0 9.2

Four Color 20(1942) 25 50 75 175 388 600
1,2 (1956-Argo) 9 18 27 50 65 80

BARNEY BEAR ...
Spire Christian Comics (Fleming H. Revell Co.): 1977-1982
...Home Plate nn-(1979, 49¢), ...In Toyland nn-(1982, 49¢),...Lost and Found nn-(1979, 49¢), Out of The Woods nn-(1980, 49¢), Sunday School Picnic nn-(1981, 69¢), The Swamp Gang!-(1977, 39¢) 2 4 6 9 13 16

BARNEY GOOGLE & SNUFFY SMITH
Dell Publishing Co./Gold Key: 1942 - 1943; April, 1964
Four Color 19(1942) 52 104 156 323 549 775
Four Color 40(1944) 20 40 60 135 300 465
Large Feature Comic 11(1943) 39 78 117 240 395 550
1(10113-404)-Gold Key (4/64) 4 8 12 25 40 55

BARNEY GOOGLE & SNUFFY SMITH
Toby Press: June, 1951 - No. 4, Feb, 1952 (Reprints)
1 14 28 42 80 115 150
2,3 9 18 27 47 61 75
4-Kurtzman-a "Pot Shot Pete", 5 pgs.; reprints John Wayne #5
12 24 36 69 97 125

BARNEY GOOGLE AND SNUFFY SMITH
Charlton Comics: Mar, 1970 - No. 6, Jan, 1971
1 3 6 9 16 24 32
2-6 2 4 6 11 16 20

BARNUM!
DC Comics (Vertigo): 2003; 2005 ($29.95, $19.95)
Hardcover (2003, $29.95, with dust jacket)-Chaykin & Tischman-s/Henrichon-a 30.00
Softcover (2005, $19.95)-Chaykin & Tischman-s/Henrichon-a 20.00

BARNYARD COMICS (Dizzy Duck No. 32 on)
Nedor/Polo Mag./Standard(Animated Cartoons): Jun, 1944 - No. 31, Sept, 1950; No. 10, 1957
1 (nn, 52 pgs.)-Funny animal 26 52 78 154 252 350
2 (52 pgs.) 15 30 45 84 127 170
3-5 11 22 33 64 90 115
6-12,16 10 20 30 58 79 100
13-15,17,21,23,26,27,29-All contain Frazetta text illos
11 22 33 64 90 115
18-20,22,24,25-All contain Frazetta-a & text illos 14 28 42 80 115 150
28,30,31 9 18 27 52 69 85
10 (1957)(Exist?) 4 7 10 14 17 20

BARRIER
Image Comics: May, 2018 - No. 5, May, 2018 ($4.99/$3.99, limited series, printed sideways)
1,5-($4.99) Brian K. Vaughan-s/Marcos Martin-a 5.00
2-4-($3.99) 4.00

BARRY M. GOLDWATER
Dell Publishing Co.: Mar, 1965 (Complete life story)
12-055-503-Photo-c 4 8 12 25 40 55

BARRY WINDSOR-SMITH: STORYTELLER
Dark Horse Comics: Oct, 1996 - No. 9, July, 1997 ($4.95, oversize)
1-9: 1-Intro Young Gods, Paradox Man & the Freebooters; Barry Smith-c/a/scripts 5.00
Preview 4.00

BAR SINISTER (Also see Shaman's Tears)
Acclaim Comics (Windjammer): Jun, 1995 - No. 4, Sept, 1995 ($2.50, lim. series)
1-4: Mike Grell-c/a/scripts 3.00

BARTMAN (Also see Simpsons Comics & Radioactive Man)
Bongo Comics: 1993 - No. 6, 1994 ($1.95/$2.25)
1-($2.95)-Foil-c; bound-in jumbo Bartman poster 1 3 4 6 8 10
2-6: 3-w/trading card 5.00
...: Spectacularly Super Secret Saga (2018, $7.99) Adult Bartman 20 years in the future 8.00

BART SIMPSON (See Simpsons Comics Presents Bart Simpson)

BASEBALL COMICS
Will Eisner Productions: Spring, 1949 (Reprinted later as a Spirit section)
1-Will Eisner-c/a 71 142 213 454 777 1100

BASEBALL COMICS
Kitchen Sink Press: 1991 ($3.95, coated stock)
1-r/1949 ish. by Eisner; contains trading cards 6.00

BASEBALL HEROES
Fawcett Publications: 1952 (one-shot)
nn (Scarce)-Babe Ruth photo-c; baseball's Hall of Fame biographies
87 174 261 553 952 1350

BASEBALL'S GREATEST HEROES
Magnum Comics: Dec, 1991 - No. 2, May, 1992 ($1.75)
1-Mickey Mantle #1; photo-c; Sinnott-a(p) 5.00
2-Brooks Robinson #1; photo-c; Sinnott-a(i) 4.00

BASEBALL THRILLS
Ziff-Davis Publ. Co.: No. 10, Sum, 1951 - No. 3, Sum, 1952 (Saunders painted-c No.1,2)
10(#1)-Bob Feller, Musial, Newcombe & Boudreau stories
44 88 132 277 469 660
2-Powell-a(2)(Late Sum, '51); Feller, Berra & Mathewson stories
32 64 96 188 307 425
3-Kinstler-c/a; Joe DiMaggio story 32 64 96 188 307 425

BASEBALL THRILLS 3-D
The 3-D Zone: May, 1990 ($2.95, w/glasses)
1-New L.B. Cole-c; life stories of Ty Cobb & Ted Williams 6.00

BASICALLY STRANGE (Magazine)
John C. Comics (Archie Comics Group): Dec, 1982 ($1.95, B&W)
1-(21,000 printed; all but 1,000 destroyed; pgs. out of sequence)
3 6 9 16 24 32
1-Wood, Toth-a; Corben-c; reprints & new art 2 4 6 13 18 22

BASIC HISTORY OF AMERICA ILLUSTRATED
Pendulum Press: 1976 (B&W) (Soft-c $1.50; Hard-c $4.50)
07-1999-America Becomes a World Power 1890-1920. 07-2251-The Industrial Era 1865-1915. 07-226x-Before the Civil War 1830-1860. 07-2278-Americans Move Westward 1800-1850. 07-2286-The Civil War 1850-1876; Redondo-a. 07-2294-The Fight for Freedom 1750-1783. 07-2308-The New World 1500-1750. 07-2316-Problems of the New Nation 1800-1830. 07-2324-Roaring Twenties and the Great Depression 1920-1940. 07-2332-The United States Emerges 1783-1800. 07-2340-America Today 1945-1976. 07-2359-World War II 1940-1945
Softcover editions each 1 2 3 4 5 7
Hardcover editions each 14.00

BASIL (...the Royal Cat)
St. John Publishing Co.: Jan, 1953 - No. 4, Sept, 1953
1-Funny animal 9 18 27 47 61 75
2-4 6 12 18 28 34 40

BASIL WOLVERTON'S FANTASTIC FABLES
Dark Horse Comics: Oct, 1993 - No. 2, Dec, 1993 ($2.50, B&W, limited series)
1,2-Wolverton-c/a(r) 1 2 3 5 6 8

BASIL WOLVERTON'S GATEWAY TO HORROR
Dark Horse Comics: June, 1988 ($1.75, B&W, one-shot)
1-Wolverton-r 1 2 3 5 6 8

BASIL WOLVERTON'S PLANET OF TERROR
Dark Horse Comics: Oct, 1987 ($1.75, B&W, one-shot)
1-Wolverton-r; Alan Moore-c 1 2 3 5 6 8

BASKETFUL OF HEADS
DC Comics (Hill House Comics): Dec, 2019 - No. 7, Jun, 2020 ($3.99, limited series)
1-7-Joe Hill-s/Leomacs-a; back-up serial Sea Dogs in each; Murakami-c 4.00
1-($4.99) Variant cardstock-c by Josh Middleton 5.00

BASTARD SAMURAI
Image Comics: Apr, 2002 - No. 3, Aug, 2002 ($2.95)
1-3-Oeming & Gunter-s; Shannon-a/Oeming-i 3.00
TPB (2003, $12.95) r/#1-3; plus sketch pages and pin-ups 13.00

BATGIRL (See Batman: No Man's Land stories)
DC Comics: Apr, 2000 - No. 73, Apr, 2006 ($2.50)
1-Scott & Campanella-a 2 4 6 8 10 12
1-(2nd printing) 3.00
2-10: 8-Lady Shiva app. 5.00
11-24: 12-"Officer Down" x-over. 15-Joker-c/app. 24-Bruce Wayne: Murderer pt. 2. 4.00
25-($3.25) Batgirl vs Lady Shiva 4.50
26-29: 27- Bruce Wayne: Fugitive pt. 5; Noto-a. 29-B.W.:F. pt. 13 4.00
30-49,51-73: 30-32-Connor Hawke app. 39-Intro. Black Wind. 41-Superboy-c/app. 53-Robin (Spoiler) app. 54-Bagged with Sky Captain CD. 55-57-War Games. 63,64-Deathstroke app. 67-Birds of Prey app. 70-1st app. Lazara (Nora Fries). 73-Lady Shiva origin; Sale-c 4.00
50-($3.25) Batgirl vs Batman 5.00
Annual 1 ('00, $3.50) Planet DC; intro. Aruna 5.00
...: A Knight Alone (2001, $12.95, TPB) r/#7-11,13,14 13.00
...: Death Wish (2003, $14.95, TPB) r/#17-20,22,23,25 & Secret Files and Origins #1 15.00
...: Destruction's Daughter (2006, $19.99, TPB) r/#65-73 20.00

Batgirl (2011 series) #27 © DC

Batgirl (2016 series) #50 © DC

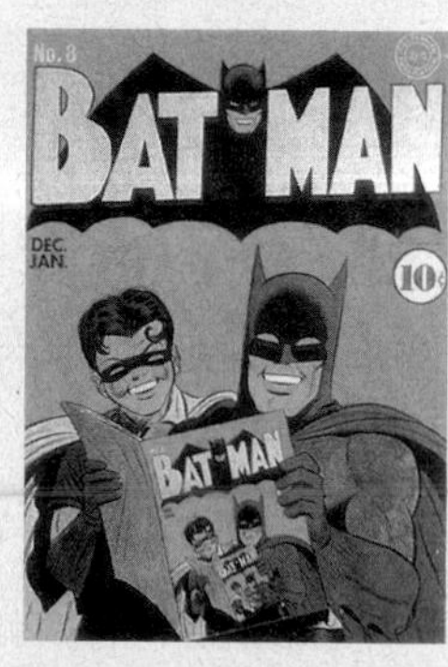

Batman #8 © DC

	GD	VG	FN	VF	VF/NM	NM-
	2.0	4.0	6.0	8.0	9.0	9.2

...: Fists of Fury (2004, $14.95, TPB) r/#15,16,21,26-28 15.00
...: Kicking Assassins (2005, $14.99, TPB) r/#60-64 15.00
... Secret Files and Origins (8/02, $4.95) origin-s Noto-a; profile pages and pin-ups 5.00
...: Silent Running (2001, $12.95, TPB) r/#1-6 13.00

BATGIRL (Cassandra Cain)
DC Comics: Sept, 2008 - No. 6, Feb, 2009 ($2.99)

1-6-Beechen-s/Calafiore-a 4.00

BATGIRL (Spoiler/Stephanie Brown)(Batman: Reborn)
DC Comics: Oct, 2009 - No. 24, Oct, 2011 ($2.99)

1-Garbett-a/Noto-c 1 3 4 6 8 10
1-Variant-c by Hamner 2 4 6 9 12 15
2-24: 2-7-Garbett-a/Noto-c. 3-New costume. 8-Caldwell-a. 9-14-Lau-c. 14-Supergirl app. 4.00
...: Batgirl Rising TPB (2010, $17.99) r/#1-7 20.00
...: The Flood TPB (2011, $14.99) r/#9-14 15.00

BATGIRL (Barbara Gordon)(DC New 52)(See Secret Origins #10)
DC Comics: Nov, 2011 - No. 52, Jul, 2016 ($2.99)

1-Barbara Gordon back in costume; Simone-s/Syaf-a/Hughes-c 18.00
1-Second & Third printings 5.00
2-12: 2-6-Hughes-c. 3-Nightwing app. 7-12-Syaf-c. 9-Night of the Owls. 12-Batwoman app. 3.00
13-Die-cut cover; Death of the Family tie-in; Batwoman app. 10.00
13-24: 14-16-Death of the Family tie-in; Joker app. 20,21-Intro. The Ventriloquist 3.00
25-($3.99) Zero Year tie-in; Bennett-s/Pasarin-a 4.00
26-34: 27-Gothtopia tie-in. 28,29-Strix app. 31-34-Simone-s. 31-Ragdoll app. 3.00
35-49,51,52: 35-New costume; Tarr-a/Stewart-c. 37-Dagger Type app. 41,42-Batman (Gordon) & Livewire app. 45-Dick Grayson app. 48,49-Black Canary app. 3.00
50-($4.99) Black Canary, Spoiler & Bluebird app.; Tarr-a 5.00
#0 (11/12, $2.99) Batgirl origin updated; Simone-s/Benes-a 3.00
Annual 1 (12/12, $4.99) Catwoman and the Talons app.; Simone-s/Wijaya-a/Benes-c 5.00
Annual 2 (6/14, $4.99) Poison Ivy app.; Simone-s/Gill-a/Benes-c 5.00
Annual 3 (9/15, $4.99) Dick Grayson, Spoiler & Batwoman app. 5.00
...: Endgame 1 (5/15, $2.99) Tie-in with other Endgame stories in Batman titles 3.00
...: Futures End 1 (11/14, $2.99, regular-c) Five years later; Bane app.; Simone-s 3.00
...: Futures End 1 (11/14, $3.99, 3-D cover) 4.00

BATGIRL (DC Rebirth)
DC Comics: Sept, 2016 - No. 50, Dec, 2020 ($2.99/$3.99)

1-9: 1-Hope Larson-s/Rafael Albuquerque-a. 6-Poison Ivy app. 9-Penguin app. 3.00
10-24-($3.99): 10,11-Penguin app. 13-Catwoman app. 18-Harley Quinn app. 4.00
25-($4.99) Short stories by various; art by Derenick, Panosian, Pelletier, Lupacchino 5.00
26-49: 26-New costume. 30-34-Jason Bard app. 34-36-Terrible Trio app. 37-41-Year of the Villain tie-ins; new Oracle app. 41-Acetate-c. 47,48-Joker War tie-ins 4.00
50-($5.99) Intro. Ryan Wilder (1 pg.); Lupacchino-a; back-up w/Sauvage-a 6.00
Annual 1 (5/17, $4.99) Supergirl app. (story cont'd in Supergirl #9); Larson-s; Bengal-c 5.00
Annual 2 (10/18, $4.99) Casagrande-a; brother James Gordon app. 5.00

BATGIRL ADVENTURES (See Batman Adventures, The)
DC Comics: Feb, 1998 ($2.95, one-shot) (Based on animated series)

1-Harley Quinn and Poison Ivy app.; Timm-c 4 8 12 27 44 60

BATGIRL AND THE BIRDS OF PREY (DC Rebirth)
DC Comics: Aug, 2016 - No. 22, Jul, 2018 ($2.99/$3.99)

1-8: 1-Julie & Shawna Benson-s/Claire Roe-a. 3-6,8-Antonio-a. 8-Nightwing app. 3.00
9-22-($3.99) 10-Nightwing & Green Arrow app. 12-17-Catwoman & Poison Ivy app. 4.00
...: Rebirth 1 (9/16, $2.99) Batgirl, Black Canary & Huntress team up; Claire Roe-a 3.00

BATGIRL SPECIAL
DC Comics: 1988 ($1.50, one-shot, 52 pgs)

1-Kitson-a/Mignola-c 2 4 6 9 13 16

BATGIRL: YEAR ONE
DC Comics: Feb, 2003 - No. 9, Oct, 2003 ($2.95, limited series)

1-Barbara Gordon becomes Batgirl; Killer Moth app.; Beatty & Dixon-s
2 4 6 8 10 12
2-9 4.00
TPB (2003, $17.95) r/#1-9 25.00

BAT LASH (See DC Special Series #16, Showcase #76, Weird Western Tales)
National Periodical Publications: Oct-Nov, 1968 - No. 7, Oct-Nov, 1969 (12¢/15¢)

1-(10-11/68, 12¢-c)-2nd app. Bat Lash; classic Nick Cardy-c/a in all
7 14 21 46 86 125
2-7: 6,7-(15¢-c) 4 8 12 27 44 60

BAT LASH
DC Comics: Feb, 2008 - No. 6, Jul, 2008 ($2.99, limited series)

1-6-Aragonés & Brandvold-s/John Severin-a. 1-Two covers by Severin and Simonson 3.00

BATMAN (See All Star Batman & Robin, Anarky, Aurora [in Promo. Comics section], Azrael, The Best of DC #2, Blind Justice, The Brave & the Bold, Cosmic Odyssey, DC 100-Page Super Spec. #14,20, DC Special, DC Special Series, Detective Comics, Dynamic Classics, 80-Page Giants, Gotham By Gaslight, Gotham Nights, Greatest Batman Stories Ever Told, Greatest Joker Stories Ever Told, Heroes Against Hunger, JLA, The Joker, Justice League of America, Justice League Int., Legends of the Dark Knight, Limited Coll. Ed., Man-Bat, Nightwing, Power Record Comics, Real Fact #5, Robin, Saga of Ra's al Ghul, Shadow of the..., Star Spangled, Super Friends, 3-D Batman, Untold Legend of..., Wanted... & World's Finest Comics)

BATMAN
National Per. Publ./Detective Comics/DC Comics: Spring, 1940 - No. 713, Oct, 2011 (#1-5 were quarterly)

1-Origin The Batman reprinted (2 pgs.) from Detective Comics #33 w/splash from #34 by Bob Kane; 1st app. Joker (2 stories intended for 2 separate issues of Detective which would have been 1st & 2nd app.); splash pg. to 2nd Joker story is similar to cover of Detective #40 (story intended for #40); 1st app. The Cat (Catwoman)(1st villainess in comics); has Batman story (w/Hugo Strange) without Robin originally planned for Detective #38; mentions location (Manhattan) where Batman lives (see Detective #31). This book was created entirely from the inventory of Detective Comics; 1st Batman/Robin pin-up on back-c; has text piece & photo of Bob Kane
61,500 123,000 184,500 418,000 671,500 925,000

1-Reprint, oversize 13-1/2x10". **WARNING**: This comic is an exact duplicate reprint of the original except for its size. DC published it in 1974 with a second cover titling it as a Famous First Edition. There have been many reported cases of the outer cover being removed and the interior sold as the original edition. The reprint with the new outer cover removed is practically worthless. See Famous First Edition for value.

2-2nd app. The Joker; 2nd app. Catwoman (out of costume) in Joker story; 1st time called Catwoman (NOTE: A 15¢-c for Canadian distr. exists.)
3150 6300 9450 22,400 42,200 62,000
3-3rd app Catwoman (1st in costume & 1st costumed villainess); 1st Puppet Master app.; classic Kane & Robinson-c 1380 2760 4140 10,300 20,150 30,000
4-4th app. The Joker (see Det. #45 for 3rd); 1st mention of Gotham City in a Batman comic (on newspaper)(Win/40) 1100 2200 3300 8400 15,200 22,000
5-1st app. the Batmobile with its bat-head front 892 1784 2676 6512 11,506 16,500
6,7: 7-Bullseye-c; Joker app. 730 1460 2190 5329 9415 13,500
8-Infinity-c by Fred Ray; Joker app. 649 1298 1947 4738 8369 12,000
9,10: 9-1st Batman Christmas story; Burnley-c. 10-Catwoman story (gets new costume)
541 1082 1623 3950 6975 10,000
11-Classic Joker-c by Ray/Robinson (3rd Joker-c, 6-7/42); Joker & Penguin app.
1600 3200 4800 12,200 22,100 32,000
12,15: 12-Joker app. 15-New costume Catwoman 400 800 1200 2800 4900 7000
13-Jerry Siegel (Superman's co-creator) appears in a Batman story; Batman parachuting on black-c 423 846 1269 3067 5384 7700
14-2nd Penguin-c; Penguin app. (12-1/42-43) 411 822 1233 2877 5039 7200
16-Intro/origin Alfred (4-5/43); cover is a reverse of #9 cover by Burnley; 1st small logo
865 1730 2595 6315 11,158 16,000
17,20: 17-Classic war-c; Penguin app. 20-1st Batmobile-c (12-1/43-44); Joker app.
354 708 1062 2478 4339 6200
18-Hitler, Hirohito, Mussolini-c. 530 1060 1590 3869 6835 9800
19-Joker app. 265 530 795 1694 2897 4100
21,22,24,26,28-30: 21-1st skinny Alfred in Batman (2-3/44). 21,30-Penguin app. 22-1st Alfred solo-c/story (Alfred solo stories in 22-32,36); Catwoman & The Cavalier app. 28-Joker story
210 420 630 1334 2292 3250
23-Joker-c/story; classic black-c 649 1298 1947 4738 8369 12,000
25-Only Joker/Penguin team-up; 1st team-up between two major villains
309 618 927 2163 3782 5400
27-Classic Burnley Christmas-c; Penguin app. 258 516 774 1651 2826 4000
31,32,34-36,39: 32-Origin Robin retold; Joker app. 35-Catwoman story (in new costume w/o cat head mask). 36-Penguin app. 155 310 465 992 1696 2400
33-Christmas-c 181 362 543 1158 1979 2800
37-Joker spotlight on black-c 400 800 1200 2800 4900 7000
38-Penguin-c/story 226 452 678 1446 2473 3500
40-Joker-c/story 271 542 813 1734 2967 4200
41-1st Sci-fi cover/story in Batman; Penguin app.(6-7/47)
145 290 435 921 1586 2250
42-2nd Catwoman-c (1st in Batman)(8-9/47); Catwoman story also.
300 600 900 1950 3375 4800
43-Penguin-c/story 161 322 483 1030 1765 2500
44-Classic Joker-c 400 800 1200 2800 4900 7000
45,46: 45-Christmas-c/story; Catwoman story. 46-Joker app.
129 258 387 826 1413 2000
47-1st detailed origin The Batman (6-7/48); 1st Bat-signal-c this title (see Detective #108); Batman tracks down his parent's killer and reveals i.d. to him
703 1406 2109 5132 9066 13,000
48-1000 Secrets of the Batcave; r-in #203; Penguin story
300 600 900 2010 3505 5000
49-Joker-c/story; 1st app. Mad Hatter; 1st app. Vicki Vale

Batman #52 © DC

Batman #182 © DC

Batman #227 © DC

	GD 2.0	VG 4.0	FN 6.0	VF 8.0	VF/NM 9.0	NM- 9.2
	400	800	1200	2800	4900	7000
50-Two-Face impostor app.	200	400	600	1280	2190	3100
51,54,56,57,60: 57-Centerfold is a 1950 calendar; Joker app.	123	246	369	787	1344	1900
52-Joker-c/story	343	686	1029	2400	4200	6000
53-Joker story	174	348	522	1114	1907	2700
55-Joker-c/stories	300	600	900	2010	3505	5000
58,61: 58-Penguin-c. 61-Origin Batplane II	194	388	582	1242	2121	3000
59-1st app. Deadshot; Batman in the future-c/sty	432	864	1296	3154	5577	8000
62-Origin Catwoman; Catwoman-c	343	686	1029	2400	4200	6000
63-1st app. Killer Moth; Joker story; flying saucer story(2-3/51)	194	388	582	1242	2121	3000
64,70-72,74-77,79: 70-Robot-c. 72-Last 52 pg. issue. 74-Used in **POP**, Pg. 90. 75-Gorilla-c. 76-Penguin story. 79-Vicki Vale in "The Bride of Batman"	103	206	309	659	1130	1600
65,69-Catwoman-c/stories	258	516	774	1651	2826	4000
66,73-Joker-c/stories. 66-Pre-2nd Batman & Robin team try-out. 73-Vicki Vale story	271	542	813	1734	2967	4200
67-Joker story	129	258	387	826	1413	2000
68,81-Two-Face-c/stories	258	516	774	1651	2826	4000
78-(8-9/53)-Roh Kar, The Man Hunter from Mars story-the 1st lawman of Mars to come to Earth (green skinned)	258	516	774	1651	2826	4000
80-Joker stories	129	258	387	826	1413	2000
82,83,87-89: 89-Last pre-code issue	97	194	291	621	1061	1500
84-Catwoman-c/story; Two-Face app.	194	388	582	1242	2121	3000
85,86-Joker story. 86-Intro Batmarine (Batman's submarine)	103	206	309	659	1130	1600
90,91,93-96,98,99: 99-(4/56)-Last G.A. Penguin app.	84	168	252	538	919	1300
92-1st app. Bat-Hound-c/story	258	516	774	1651	2826	4000
97-2nd app. Bat-Hound-c/story; Joker story	129	258	387	826	1413	2000
100-(6/56)	326	652	978	2282	3991	5700
101-(8/56)-Clark Kent x-over who protects Batman's i.d. (3rd story)	84	168	252	538	919	1300
102-104,106-109: 103-1st S.A. issue; 3rd Bat-Hound-c/story	77	154	231	493	847	1200
105-1st Batwoman in Batman (2nd anywhere)	161	322	483	1030	1765	2500
110-Joker story	81	162	243	518	884	1250
111-120: 112-1st app. Signalman (super villain). 113-1st app. Fatman; Batman meets his counterpart on Planet X w/a chest plate similar to S.A. Batman's design (yellow oval w/black design inside).	65	130	195	416	708	1000
121-Origin/1st app. of Mr. Zero (Mr. Freeze)	784	1568	2352	5723	10,112	14,500
122,124-126,128,130: 122,126-Batwoman-c/story. 124-2nd app. Signal Man. 128-Batwoman cameo. 130-Lex Luthor app.	57	114	171	362	619	875
123,127: 123-Joker story; Bat-Hound-c/app. 127-(10/59)-Batman vs. Thor the Thunder God c/story; Joker story; Superman cameo	57	114	171	362	619	875
129-Origin Robin retold; bondage-c; Batwoman-c/story (reprinted in Batman Family #8)	69	138	207	442	759	1075
131-135,137,138,141-143: 131-Intro 2nd Batman & Robin series (see #66; also in #135,145, 154,159,163). 133-1st Bat-Mite in Batman (3rd app. anywhere). 134-Origin The Dummy (not Vigilante's villain). 141-2nd app. original Bat-Girl. 143-(10/61)-Last 10¢ issue	47	94	141	296	498	700
136-Joker-c/story	55	110	165	352	601	850
139-Intro 1st original Bat-Girl; only app. Signalman as the Blue Bowman	135	270	405	864	1482	2100
140-Joker story, Batwoman-c/s; Superman cameo	47	94	141	296	498	700
144-(12/61)-1st 12¢ issue; Joker story	28	56	84	202	451	700
145,148-Joker-c/stories	38	76	114	285	641	1000
146,147,149,150	24	48	72	168	372	575
151-154,156-158,160-162,164-168,170: 152-Joker story. 156-Ant-Man/Robin team-up(6/63). 164-New Batmobile(6/64) new look & Mystery Analysts series begins	18	36	54	126	281	435
155-1st S.A. app. The Penguin (5/63)	71	142	213	568	1284	2000
159,163-Joker-c/stories. 159-Bat-Girl app. 163-Last Bat-Girl app. until Teen Titans #50	27	54	81	189	420	650
169-2nd SA Penguin app.	24	48	72	168	372	575
171-1st Riddler app.(5/65) since Dec. 1948	86	172	258	688	1544	2400
172-175,177,178,180,184	11	22	33	76	163	250
176-(80-Pg. Giant G-17); Joker-c/story; Penguin app. in strip-r; Catwoman reprint	14	28	42	98	217	335
179-2nd app. Silver Age Riddler	24	48	72	168	372	575
181-Intro. Poison Ivy; Batman & Robin poster insert	136	272	408	1088	2444	3800
181-(Facsimile Edition)(2019, $3.99) reprints issue with original ads and letter column						4.00
182,187-(80 Pg. Giants G-24, G-30); Joker-c/stories	12	24	36	82	179	275
183-2nd app. Poison Ivy	15	30	45	105	233	360

	GD 2.0	VG 4.0	FN 6.0	VF 8.0	VF/NM 9.0	NM- 9.2
185-(80 Pg. Giant G-27)	12	24	36	79	170	260
186-Joker-c/story	12	24	36	82	179	275
188,191,192,194-196,199	9	18	27	61	123	185
189-1st S.A. app. Scarecrow; retells origin of G.A. Scarecrow from World's Finest #3 (1st app.)	38	76	114	281	628	975
190-Penguin-c/app.	13	26	39	91	201	310
193-(80-Pg. Giant G-37)	10	20	30	68	144	220
197-4th S.A. Catwoman app. cont'd from Det. #369; 1st new Batgirl app. in Batman (5th anywhere)	16	32	48	112	249	385
198-(80-Pg. Giant G-43); Joker-c/story-r/World's Finest #61; Catwoman-r/Det. #211; Penguin-r; origin-r/#47	11	22	33	75	160	245
200-(3/68)-Scarecrow app.; Joker, Penguin, Killer Moth cameos; retells origin of Batman & Robin; 1st Neal Adams work this title (cover only)	13	26	39	86	188	290
201-Joker story	8	16	24	51	96	140
202,204-207,209-212: 210-Catwoman-c/app. 212-Last 12¢ issue	7	14	21	46	86	125
203-(80 Pg. Giant G-49); r/#48, 61, & Det. 185; Batcave Blueprints	9	18	27	60	120	180
208-(80 Pg. Giant G-55); New origin Batman by Gil Kane plus 3 G.A. Batman reprints w/Catwoman, Vicki Vale & Batwoman	9	18	27	58	114	170
213-(80-Pg. Giant G-61); 30th anniversary issue (7-8/69); origin Alfred (r/Batman #16), Joker(r/Det. #168), Clayface; new origin Robin with new facts	9	18	27	61	123	185
214-217: 216-Alfred given a new last name- "Pennyworth" (see Detective #96)	6	12	18	38	69	100
218-(68 pg. Giant G-67)	9	18	27	63	129	195
219-Neal Adams-a	9	18	27	63	129	195
220,221,224-226,229-231	5	10	15	35	63	90
222-Beatles take-off; art lesson by Joe Kubert	19	38	57	129	287	445
223,228,233: 223,228-(68 pg. Giants G-73,G-79). 233-G-85-(68 pgs., "64 pgs." on-c)	7	14	21	48	89	130
227-Neal Adams cover swipe of Detective #31	46	92	138	368	834	1300
232-(6/71) Adams-a. Intro/1st app. Ra's al Ghul; origin Batman & Robin retold; last 15¢ issue (see Detective #411 (5/71) for Talia's debut)	38	76	114	285	641	1000
232-(Facsimile Edition)(2019, $3.99) reprints issue with original ads and letter column						4.00
234-(9/71)-1st modern app. of Harvey Dent/Two-Face with origin re-told in brief; (see World's Finest #173 for Batman as Two-Face; only S.A. mention of character); N. Adams-a; 52 pg. issues begin, end #242	23	46	69	161	356	550
235,236,239-242: 239-XMas-c. 241-Reprint/#5	6	12	18	41	76	110
237-N. Adams-c/a. 1st Rutland Vermont - Bald Mountain Halloween x-over. 1st app. The Reaper; Holocaust reference; Wrightson/Ellison plots; G.A. Batman-r/Detective #37	15	30	45	100	220	340
238-Also listed as DC 100 Page Super Spectacular #8; Batman, Legion, Aquaman-r; G.A. Atom, Sargon (r/Sensation #57), Plastic Man (r/Police #14) stories; Doom Patrol origin-r; N. Adams wraparound-c	15	30	45	103	227	350
243-245-Neal Adams-a	10	20	30	66	138	210
246-250,252,253: 246-Scarecrow app. 253-Shadow-c & app.	6	12	18	37	66	95
251-(9/73)-N. Adams-c/a; Joker-c/story	42	84	126	311	706	1100
251-(Facsimile Edition)(2019, $3.99) reprints issue with original ads and letter column						4.00
254,256,257,259,261-All 100 pg. editions; part-r: 254-(2/74)-Man-Bat-c/app. 256-Catwoman app. 257-Joker & Penguin app. 259-Shadow-c/app.	7	14	21	49	92	135
255-(100 pgs.)-N. Adams-c/a; tells of Bruce Wayne's father who wore bat costume & fought crime (r/Det. #235); r/story Batman #22	8	16	24	54	102	150
258-First mention of Arkham (Hospital, renamed Arkham Asylum in #260)	8	16	24	54	102	150
260-(100 pgs.) Joker-c/story; 2nd Arkham Asylum (see #258 for 1st mention)	8	16	24	54	102	150
262 (68 pgs.)	5	10	15	33	57	80
263,264,266-285,287-290,292,293,295-299: 266-Catwoman back to old costume	3	6	9	14	20	25
265-Wrightson-a(i)	3	6	9	15	22	28
286,291,294: 294-Joker-c/stories	3	6	9	17	26	35
300-Double-size	4	8	12	27	44	60
301-(7/78)-306,308-310,312,314,315,317-320,325-331,333-352: 304-(44 pgs.). 306-3rd app. Black Spider. 308-Mr. Freeze app. 310-1st modern app. The Gentleman Ghost in Batman; Kubert-c. 312,314-Two-Face-c/stories. 318-Intro Firebug. 319-2nd modern age app. of The Gentleman Ghost; Kubert-c. 331-1st app./death original Electrocutioner. 344-Poison Ivy app. 345-1st app. new Dr. Death. 345,346,351-Catwoman back-ups. 346-Two-Face-c/app.	2	4	6	9	12	15
306-308,311-320,323,324,326-(Whitman variants; low print run; none show issue # on cover)	3	6	9	15	22	28
307-1st app. Lucius Fox (1/79)	3	6	9	17	26	35
311,316,322-324: 311-Batgirl-c/story; Batgirl reteams w/Batman. 316-Robin returns. 322-324-Catwoman (Selina Kyle) app. 322,323-Cat-Man cameos (1st in Batman, 1 panel						

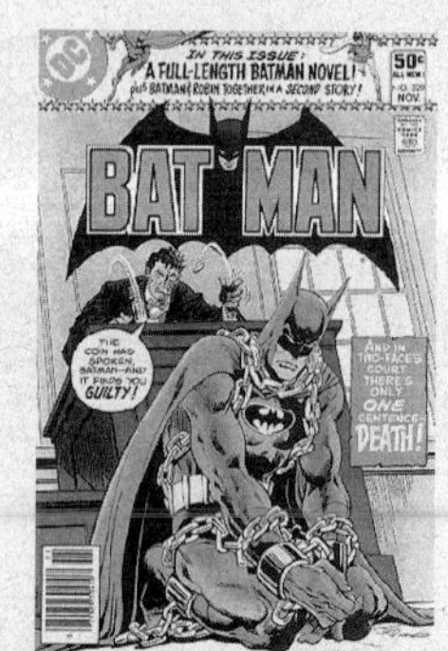

Batman #329 © DC

Batman #463 © DC

Batman #628 © DC

GD VG FN VF VF/NM NM-
2.0 4.0 6.0 8.0 9.0 9.2

each). 323-1st meeting Catwoman & Cat-Man. 324-1st full app. Cat-Man this title 2 4 6 10 14 18
313-1st app. Timothy Fox (7/79)(see Future State: The Next Batman); Two-Face app.; 2nd app. Calendar Man 3 6 9 14 19 24
321,359-Joker-c/stories 3 6 9 16 24 32
332-Catwoman's 1st solo 3 6 9 14 20 25
353-Joker-c/story; preview of Masters of the Universe 3 6 9 19 30 40
354-356,358,360,362-365,369,370: 362-Riddler-c/story with origin retold in brief 1 3 4 6 8 10
357-1st app. Jason Todd (3/83); see Det. #524; brief app. Croc (see Detective #523 (2/83) for earlier cameo 8 16 24 56 108 160
361-Debut of Harvey Bullock (7/83)(see Detective #441,('74) for a similar Lt. Bullock, no first name given, appeared in 3 panels) 3 6 9 16 24 32
366-Jason Todd 1st in Robin costume; Joker-c/story 4 8 12 23 37 50
367-Jason in red & green costume (not as Robin) 2 4 6 10 14 18
368-1st new Robin in costume (Jason Todd) 3 6 9 21 33 45
371-385,388-399,401-403: 371-Cat-Man-c/story; brief origin Cat-Man (cont'd in Det. #538). 390-391-Catwoman app. 398-Catwoman & Two-Face app. 401-2nd app. Magpie (see Man of Steel #3 for 1st). 403-Joker cameo 1 3 4 6 8 10

NOTE: *Issues 397-399, 401-403, 408-416, 421-425, 430-432 all have 2nd printings in 1989; some with up to 8 printings. Some are not identified as reprints but have newer ads copyrighted after cover dates. All reprints have different back-c ads. All reprints are scarcer than 1st prints and have same value to variant collectors.*

386-Intro Black Mask (villain) 6 12 18 37 66 95
387-Intro Black Mask continues 2 4 6 11 16 20
400 ($1.50, 68pgs.)-Dark Knight special; intro by Stephen King; Art Adams/Austin-a 3 6 9 21 33 45
404-Miller scripts begin (end 407); Year 1; 1st modern app. Catwoman (2/87) 3 6 9 21 33 45
405-407: 407-Year 1 ends (See Detective Comics #575-578 for Year 2) 3 6 9 14 20 25
408-410: New Origin Jason Todd (Robin) 2 4 6 13 18 22
411-416,421,422,424,425: 411-Two-face app. 412-Origin/1st app. Mime. 414-Starlin scripts begin, end #429. 416-Nightwing-c/story 1 2 3 5 6 8
417-420: "Ten Nights of the Beast" storyline 2 4 6 8 10 12
423-McFarlane-c 7 14 21 46 86 125
426-($1.50, 52 pgs.)- "A Death In The Family" storyline begins, ends #429 3 6 9 20 31 42
427- "A Death In The Family" part 2. (Direct Sales version has inside back-c page for phone poll; newsstand version has an ad on inside back-c and UPC code on front-c) 3 6 9 16 23 30
428-Death of Robin (Jason Todd) 4 8 12 23 37 50
429-Joker-c/story; Superman app. 3 6 9 14 20 25
430-435: 433-435-Many Deaths of the Batman story by John Byrne-c/scripts 6.00
436-Year 3 begins (ends #439); origin original Robin retold by Nightwing (Dick Grayson); 1st app. Timothy Drake (8/89) 2 4 6 11 16 20
436-441: 436-2nd printing. 437-Origin Robin cont. 440,441: "A Lonely Place of Dying" Parts 1 & 3 6.00
442-1st app. Timothy Drake in Robin costume 2 4 6 8 10 12
443-456,458,459,462-464: 445-447-Batman goes to Russia. 448,449-The Penguin Affair Pts 1 & 3. 450-Origin Joker. 450,451-Joker-c/stories. 452-454-Dark Knight Dark City storyline; Riddler app. 455-Alan Grant scripts begin, ends #466, 470. 464-Last solo Batman story; free 16 pg. preview of Impact Comics line 5.00
457-Timothy Drake officially becomes Robin & dons new costume 2 4 6 9 12 15
457-Direct sale edition (has #000 in indicia) 2 4 6 10 14 18
460,461,465-487: 460,461-Two part Catwoman story. 465-Robin returns to action with Batman. 470-War of the Gods x-over. 475-1st app. Renee Montoya. 475,476-Return of Scarface. 476-Last $1.00-c. 477,478-Photo-c 5.00
488-Cont'd from Batman: Sword of Azrael #4; Azrael-c & app. 1 2 3 5 6 8
489-Bane-c/story; 1st app. Azrael in Bat-costume 2 4 6 9 12 15
490-Riddler-c/story; Azrael & Bane app. 1 3 4 6 8 10
491,492: 491-Knightfall lead-in; Joker-c/story; Azrael & Bane app.; Kelley Jones-c begin. 492-Knightfall part 1; Bane app. 1 2 3 5 6 8
492-Platinum edition (promo copy) 2 4 6 11 16 20
493-496: 493-Knightfall Pt. 3. 494-Knightfall Pt. 5; Joker-c & app. 495-Knightfall Pt. 7; brief Bane & Joker apps. 496-Knightfall Pt. 9, Joker-c/story; Bane cameo 6.00
497-(Late 7/93)-Knightfall Pt. 11; Bane breaks Batman's back; B&W outer-c; Aparo-a(p); Giordano-a(i) 2 4 6 10 14 18
497-499: 497-2nd printing. 497-Newsstand edition w/o outer cover. 498-Knightfall part 15; Bane & Catwoman-c & app. (see Showcase 93 #7 & 8) 499-Knightfall Pt. 17; Bane app. 5.00
500-($2.50, 68 pgs.)-Knightfall Pt. 19; Azrael in new Bat-costume; Bane-c/story 1 3 4 6 8 10
500-($3.95, 68 pgs.)-Collector's Edition w/die-cut double-c w/foil by Joe Quesada & 2 bound-in post cards 1 3 4 6 8 10

GD VG FN VF VF/NM NM-
2.0 4.0 6.0 8.0 9.0 9.2

501-508,510,511: 501-Begin $1.50-c. 501-508-Knightquest. 503,504-Catwoman app. 507-Ballistic app.; Jim Balent-a(p). 510-KnightsEnd Pt. 7. 511-(9/94)-Zero Hour; Batgirl-c/story 4.00
509-($2.50, 52 pgs.)-KnightsEnd Pt. 1 6.00
512-514,516-518: 512-(11/94)-Dick Grayson assumes Batman role 4.00
515-Special Ed.($2.50)-Kelley Jones-a begins; all black embossed-c; Troika Pt. 1 1 2 3 5 6 8
515-Regular Edition 4.00
519-534,536-549: 519-Begin $1.95-c. 521-Return of Alfred, 522-Swamp Thing app. 525-Mr. Freeze app. 527,528-Two Face app. 529-Contagion Pt. 6. 530-532-Deadman app. 533-Legacy prelude. 534-Legacy Pt. 5. 536-Final Night x-over; Man-Bat-c/app. 540,541-Spectre-c-app. 544-546-Joker & The Demon. 548,549-Penguin-c/app. 4.00
530-532 ($2.50)-Enhanced edition; glow-in-the-dark-c. 5.00
535-(10/96, $2.95)-1st app. The Ogre 5.00
535-(10/96, $3.95)-1st app. The Ogre; variant, cardboard, foldout-c 6.00
550-($3.50)-Collector's Ed., includes 4 collector cards; intro. Chase, return of Clayface; Kelley Jones-c 6.00
550-($2.95)-Standard Ed.; Williams & Gray-c 5.00
551-562: 551,552-Ragman c/app. 553-Cataclysm pt.3. 554-Cataclysm pt. 12. 4.00
563-No Man's Land; Joker-c by Campbell; Gale-s 2 4 6 8 10 12
564-566,568,569,571-574: 569-New Batgirl-c/app. 4.00
567-1st Cassandra Cain 4 8 12 22 35 48
570-Joker and Harley Quinn story 3 6 9 16 23 30
575-579: 575-New look Batman begins; McDaniel-a 4.00
580-599: 580-Begin $2.25-c. 587-Gordon shot. 591,592-Deadshot-c/app. 599-Bruce Wayne: Murderer pt. 7 4.00
600-($3.95) Bruce Wayne: Fugitive pt. 1; back-up homage stories in '50s, 60's, & 70s styles; by Aragonés, Gaudiano, Shanower and others 5.00
600-(2nd printing) 4.00
601-604, 606,607: 601,603-Bruce Wayne: Fugitive pt.3,13. 606,607-Deadshot-c/app. 4.00
605-($2.95) Conclusion to Bruce Wayne: Fugitive x-over; Noto-c 4.00
608-(12/02) Hush begins; Jim Lee-a/c & Jeph Loeb-s begin; Poison Ivy & Catwoman app. 2 4 6 11 16 20
608-2nd printing; has different cover with Batman standing on gargoyle 150.00
608-Special Edition; has different cover; 200 printed; used for promotional purposes (a CGC certified 9.2 copy sold for $700, and a CGC certified 9.8 copy sold for $2,100)
608-Special Edition (9/09, $1.00) printing has new "After Watchmen" logo cover frame 6.00
609-Huntress app. 2 4 6 11 16 20
610,611: 610-Killer Croc-c/app.; Batman & Catwoman kiss 1 3 4 6 8 10
612-Batman vs. Superman; 1st printing with full color cover 24.00
612-2nd printing with B&W sketch cover 34.00
613-Harley Quinn & Joker-c/app. 2 4 6 9 13 16
614-Joker-c/app. 1 3 4 6 8 10
615-617: 615-Reveals ID to Catwoman. 616-Ra's al Ghul app. 617-Scarecrow app. 6.00
618-Batman vs. "Jason Todd" 5.00
619-Newsstand cover; Hush story concludes; Riddler app. 5.00
619-Two variant tri-fold covers; one Heroes group, one Villains group 5.00
619-2nd printing with Riddler chess cover 5.00
620-Broken City pt. 1; Azzarello-s/Risso-a/c begin; Killer Croc app. 5.00
621-633: 621-625-Azzarello-s/Risso-a/c. 626-630-Winick-s/Nguyen-a/Wagner-c; Penguin & Scarecrow app. 631-633-War Games. 633-Conclusion to War Games x-over 4.00
634,636,637-Winick-s/Nguyen-a/Wagner-c; Red Hood app. 637-Amazo app. 5.00
635-1st app. Red Hood (later revealed as Jason Todd in #638) 150.00
638-Red Hood unmasked as Jason Todd; Nguyen-a 2 4 6 9 13 16
639-650: 640-Superman app. 641-Begin $2.50-c. 643,644-War Crimes; Joker app. 650-Infinite Crisis; Joker and Jason Todd app. 4.00
651-654-One Year Later; Bianchi-c 5.00
655-Begin Grant Morrison-s/Andy Kubert-a; Kubert-c w/red background 34.00
655-Variant cover by Adam Kubert, brown-toned image 110.00
656-Intro. Damian, son of Talia and Batman (see Batman: Son of the Demon) 3 6 9 14 20 25
657-Damian in Robin costume 2 4 6 8 10 12
658-665: 659-662-Mandrake-a. 663-Van Fleet-a. 664-Bane app. 4.00
666-Future story of adult Damian; Andy Kubert-a 3 6 9 16 24 32
667-675: 667-669-Williams III-a. 670,671-Resurrection of Ra's al Ghul; Daniel-a. 671-2nd printing 4.00
676-Batman R.I.P. begins; Morrison-s/Daniel-a/Alex Ross-c 8.00
676-Variant-c by Tony Daniel 14.00
676-Second (red-tinted Daniel-c) & third (B&W Daniel-c) printings 4.00
677-685: Batman R.I.P.; Alex Ross-c. 678-Bat-Mite app. 681-($3.99) Batman R.I.P. conclusion. 682-685-Last Rites 4.00
677-Variant-c with Red Hood by Tony Daniel 12.00
677-Second printing with B&W&red-tinted Daniel-c 4.00
686-($3.99) Gaiman-s/Andy Kubert-a; continues in Detective #853; Kubert sketch pgs.;

Batman #713 © DC

Batman (2011 series) #38 © DC

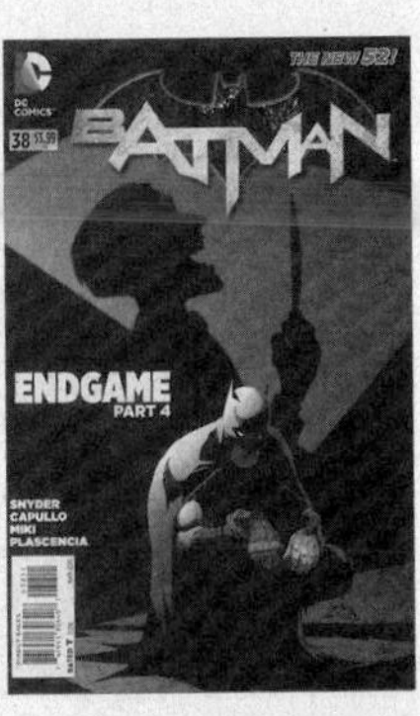

Batman (2016 series) #98 © DC

GD VG FN VF VF/NM NM-
2.0 4.0 6.0 8.0 9.0 9.2

covers by Kubert and Ross; 2nd & 3rd printings exist 4.00
687-($3.99) Batman: Reborn begins; Dick Grayson becomes Batman; Winick-s/Benes-a 4.00
688-699: 688-691-Bagley-a. 692-697,699-Tony Daniel-s/a. 692-Catwoman app. 5.00
700-(8/10, $4.99) Morrison-s; art by Daniel, Quitely, Finch & Andy Kubert; Finch-c 14.00
700-Variant-c by Mignola 50.00
701-712: 701,702-Morrison-s; R.I.P story. 704-Batman Inc. begins; Daniel-s/a 4.00
713-(10/11) Last issue of first volume; Nicieza-s; Robin flashbacks 10.00
#0 (10/94)-Zero Hour issue released between #511 & #512; Origin retold 4.00
#1,000,000 (11/98) 853rd Century x-over 4.00
Annual 1 (8-10/61)-Swan-c 59 118 177 472 1061 1650
Annual 2 26 52 78 182 404 625
Annual 3 (Summer, '62)-Joker-c/story 25 50 75 175 388 600
Annual 4,5 14 28 42 93 204 315
Annual 6 (80 pgs., 25¢) 12 24 36 82 179 275
Annual 7 (7/64, 25¢, 80 pgs.) 12 24 36 79 170 260
Annual V5#8 (1982)-Painted-c 2 4 6 8 10 12
Annual 9,10,12: 9(7/85). 10(1986). 12(1988, $1.50) 1 2 3 5 7 9
Annual 11 (1987, $1.25)-Penguin-c/story; Moore-s 2 4 6 8 10 12
Annual 13 (1989, $1.75, 68 pgs.)-Gives history of Bruce Wayne, Dick Grayson, Jason Todd, Alfred, Comm. Gordon, Barbara Gordon (Batgirl) & Vicki Vale; Morrow-i 6.00
Annual 14-17 ('90-'93, 68 pgs.)-14-Origin Two-Face. 15-Armageddon 2001 x-over; Joker app. 5.00
15 (2nd printing). 16-Joker-c/s; Kieth-c. 17 (1993, $2.50, 68 pgs.)-Azrael in Bat-costume; intro Ballistic 5.00
Annual 18 (1994, $2.95) 5.00
Annual 19 (1995, $3.95)-Year One story; retells Scarecrow's origin 5.00
Annual 20 (1996, $2.95)-Legends of the Dead Earth story; Giarrano-a 5.00
Annual 21 (1997, $3.95)-Pulp Heroes story 5.00
Annual 22,23 ('98, '99, $2.95)-22-Ghosts; Wrightson-c. 23-JLApe; Art Adams-c 5.00
Annual 24 ('00, $3.50) Planet DC; intro. The Boggart; Aparo-a 5.00
Annual 25 ('06, $4.99) Infinite Crisis-revised story of Jason Todd; unused Aparo page 12.00
Annual 26 ('07, $3.99) Origin of Ra's al Ghul; Damian app. 5.00
Annual 27 ('09, $4.99) Azrael app.; Calafiore-a; back-up story w/Kelley Jones-a 5.00
Annual 28 (2/11, $4.99) The Question, Nightrunner and Veil app.; Lau-c 5.00

NOTE: **Art Adams** *a-400p.* **Neal Adams** *c-200, 203, 210, 217, 219-222, 224-227, 229, 230, 232, 234, 236-241, 243-246, 251, 255, Annual 14.* **Aparo** *a-414-420, 426-435, 440-448, 450, 451, 480-483, 486-491, 494-500; c-414-416, 481, 482, 463i, 486, 487i.* **Bolland** *a-400; c-445-447.* **Burnley** *a-10, 12-18, 20, 22, 25, 27; c-9, 15, 16, 27, 28p, 40p, 42p.* **Byrne** *c-401, 433-435, 533-535, Annual 11.* **Travis Charest** *c-488-490p.* **Colan** *a-340p, 343-345p, 348-351p, 373p, 383p; c-343p, 345p, 350p.* **J. Cole** *a-238r.* **Cowan** *a-Annual 10p.* **Golden** *a-295p, 303p, 484, 485.* **Alan Grant** *scripts-455-466, 470, 474-476, 479, 480, Annual 16(part).* **Grell** *a-287, 288p, 289p, 290; c-287-290.* **Infantino/Anderson** *c-167, 173, 175, 181, 186, 191, 192, 194, 195, 198, 199.* **Infantino/Giella** *c-190.* **Kelley Jones** *a-513-519, 521-525, 527; c-491-499, 500(newsstand), 501-510, 513.* **Kaluta** *c-242, 248, 253, Annual 12.* **G. Kane/Anderson** *c-178-180.* **Bob Kane** *a-1, 2, 5; c-1-5, 7, 17.* **G. Kane** *a-(r)-254, 255, 259, 261, 353i.* **Kubert** *a-238r, 400; c-310, 319p, 327, 328, 344.* **McFarlane** *c-423.* **Mignola** *c-426-429, 452-454, Annual 18.* **Moldoff** *c-101-140.* **Moldoff/Giella** *a-164-175, 177-181, 183, 184, 186.* **Moldoff/Greene** *a-169, 172-174, 177-179, 181, 184.* **Mooney** *a-255r.* **Morrow** *a-Annual 13i.* **Newton** *a-305, 306, 328p, 331p, 332p, 337p, 338p, 346p, 352-357p, 360-372p, 374-378p; c-374p, 378p.* **Nino** *a-Annual 9.* **Irv Novick** *c-201, 202.* **Perez** *a-400; c-436-442.* **Fred Ray** *c-8, 10; w/* **Robinson**-*11.* **Robinson/Roussos** *a-12-17, 20, 22, 24, 25, 27, 28, 31, 33, 37.* **Robinson** *a-12, 14, 18, 22-32,34, 36, 37, 255r, 260r, 261r; c-6, 10, 12-14, 18, 21, 24, 26, 30, 37, 39.* **Simonson** *a-300p, 312p, 321p; c-300p, 312p, 366, 413i.* **P. Smith** *a-Annual 9.* **Dick Sprang** *c-19, 20, 22, 23, 25, 29, 31-36, 38, 51, 55, 66, 73, 76.* **Starlin** *c/a-402.* **Staton** *a-334.* **Sutton** *a-400.* **Wrightson** *a-265i, 400; c-320r. Bat-Hound app. in 92, 97, 103, 123, 125, 133, 156, 158. Bat-Mite app. in 133, 136, 144, 146, 158, 161. Batwoman app. in 105, 116, 122, 125, 128, 129, 131, 133, 139, 140, 141, 144, 145, 150, 151, 153, 154, 157, 159, 162, 163.* **Zeck** *c-417-420. Catwoman back-ups in 332, 345, 346, 348-351. Joker app. in 1, 2, 4, 5, 7-9, 11-13, 19, 20, 23, 25, 28, 32 & many more. Robin solo back-up stories in 337-339, 341-343.*

BATMAN (DC New 52)
DC Comics: Nov, 2011 - No. 52, Jul, 2016 ($2.99/$3.99)

1-Snyder-s/Capullo-a/c 5 10 15 33 57 80
1-Variant-c by Van Sciver 5 10 15 30 50 70
1-2nd-5th printings 3 6 9 17 26 35
2-4 2 4 6 9 13 16
2-5-Variant covers. 2-Jim Lee. 3-Ivan Reis. 4-Mike Choi, 5-Burnham. 6-Gary Frank 2 4 6 10 14 18
5-7-Court of Owls. 7-Debut Harper Row 1 3 4 6 8 10
5-7 Combo Pack ($3.99) polybagged with digital download code 2 4 6 8 10 12
8-11: 8-Begin $3.99-c. 8,9-Night of the Owls. 11-Court of the Owls finale 6.00
12-Story of Harper Row; Cloonan-a 5.00
13-Death of the Family; Joker and Harley Quinn app.; die-cut-c 2 4 6 8 11 14
14-20: 14-17-Death of the Family. 17-Death of the Family conclusion. 18-Andy Kubert-a 5.00
21-23: 21-Zero Year begins; 1st app. Duke Thomas (unnamed) 5.00
23.1, 23.2, 23.3, 23.4 (11/13, $2.99, regular covers) 4.00
23.1 (11/13, $3.99, 3-D cover) "Joker #1" on cover; Andy Kubert-s/Andy Clarke-a 12.00
23.2 (11/13, $3.99, 3-D cover) "Riddler #1" on cover; Jeremy Haun-a 8.00
23.3 (11/13, $3.99, 3-D cover) "Penguin #1" on cover; Tieri-s/Duce-a/Fabok-c 8.00
23.4 (11/13, $3.99, 3-D cover) "Bane #1" on cover; Nolan-a/March-c 8.00
24-(12/13, $6.99) Batman vs. Red Hood at Ace Chemicals re-told; Dark City begins 10.00
24-New York Comic Con variant with Detective #27 cover swipe

GD VG FN VF VF/NM NM-
2.0 4.0 6.0 8.0 9.0 9.2

3 6 9 15 22 28
25,29,33-($4.99) 25-All black cover; Doctor Death app. 33-Zero Year finale 6.00
26-28,30-32,34: 28-Nguyen-a; Harper Row as Bluebird; Stephanie Brown returns 4.00
35-($4.99) Endgame pt. 1; Justice League app.; back-up with Kelley Jones-a 5.00
36-39-Endgame; Joker app.; (back-up stories in each; 37-McCrea-a, 38-Kieth-a, 39-Nguyen) 39-Alfred attacked 4.00
40-($4.99) Endgame conclusion 5.00
41-43,45-49,51,52: 41-Gordon dons the robot suit. 49-Paquette-a. 52-Tynion-s 4.00
44-($4.99) Snyder & Azzarello-s/Jock-a 5.00
50-($5.99) Bruce Wayne back as Batman; new costume 6.00
#0 (11/12, $3.99) Flashbacks; Red Hood gang app. 5.00
Annual 1 (7/12, $4.99) Origin of Mr. Freeze; Snyder-s/Fabok-a 2 4 6 11 16 20
Annual 2 (9/13, $4.99) Origin of the Anchoress; Jock-c 6.00
Annual 3 (2/15, $4.99) Joker app.; Tynion-s/Antonio-a/Albuquerque-c 5.00
Annual 4 (11/15, $4.99) Joker app.; Tynion-s/Antonio-a/Murphy-c 5.00
... Endgame 40 Director's Cut 1 (1/16, $5.99) Pencil art and original script for #40 6.00
...: Futures End 1 (11/14, $2.99, regular-c) Five years later; Fawkes-s; Bizarro app. 3.00
...: Futures End 1 (11/14, $3.99, 3-D cover) 4.00
... Zero Year Director's Cut (9/13, $5.99) Reprints Batman #21 original pencil art pages with word balloons; Scott Snyder's script 6.00

BATMAN (DC Rebirth)
DC Comics: Aug, 2016 - Present ($2.99/$3.99)

1-King-s/Finch-a/c; intro. Gotham and Gotham Girl 5.00
1-Director's Cut (1/17, $5.99) r/#1 in pencil-a; original script; variant cover gallery 6.00
2-20: 2-Hugo Strange app. 3-Psycho Pirate returns. 5-Justice League app. 7,8-Night of the Monster Men x-overs; Batwoman & Nightwing app. 9-13-I Am Suicide; Bane app. 3.00
21,22-The Button x-over with Flash #21,22; Eobard Thawne & Flashpoint Batman app. 3.00
23,24: 23-Swamp Thing app. 24-Batman proposes to Catwoman 3.00
25-($3.99) War of Jokes and Riddles part 1; Joker & Riddler app. 4.00
26-35,38-49: 26-32-War of Jokes and Riddles. 27-Kite Man app. 33-35,39,40,44-Joëlle Jones-a. 42-Justice League app. 45-47-Booster Gold app. 3.00
36,37-Superman & Lois app.; Clay Mann-a 3.00
50-(9/18, $4.99) The Wedding; art by Janin with pages by Adams, Miller, Kubert, Sale, Conner, Garcia-Lopez, Finch, Jim Lee, Capullo, Cloonan, Fabok and others 5.00
51-74: 51-53-Weeks-a; trial of Mr. Freeze. 54-Wagner-a. 55-Nightwing shot. 64,65-X-over with Flash #64,65; tie-in to Heroes in Crisis. 67-Weeks-a. 68-Conner-a 4.00
75-($4.99) City of Bane part 1; Gotham Girl app.; Daniel-a 5.00
76-84-City of Bane. 77-Alfred killed by Bane. 80,81-Romita Jr.-a. 82-Acetate-c 4.00
85-($4.99) City of Bane conclusion 5.00
86-88,90,91,93,94: 86-Tynion IV-s begin; Deathstroke & Cheshire app.; 1st app. the Nightclimber. 91,93-Harley Quinn app. 93,94-Joker and Punchline app. 4.00
89-1st app. Punchline in cameo; intro. The Designer 50.00
92-1st full app. Punchline in title; Joker & Harley app. 1 3 4 6 8 10
95-99-Joker War: 96-1st app. Clownhunter 4.00
100-(Early 12/20, $6.99) Conclusion to Joker War; intro. The Ghost-Maker 7.00
101-105: 101-Grifter app. 102-105-The Ghost-Maker & Clownhunter app. 4.00
Annual 1 (1/17, $4.99) Short stories by various incl. Adams, Dini, Snyder, Finch; Finch-c 5.00
Annual 2 (1/18, $4.99) King-s/Weeks & Lark-a; Batman & Catwoman's early encounters 5.00
Annual 3 (2/19, $4.99) Taylor-s/Schmidt-a; spotlight on Alfred 5.00
Annual 4 (2/20, $4.99) King-s/Fornes & Norton-a; Alfred's diary of Batman's exploits 5.00
Annual 5 (2/21, $4.99) Origin of Clownhunter; Tynion IV-s/Stokoe-a 5.00
...: Rebirth 1 (8/16, $2.99) King & Snyder-s/Janín-a; Duke Thomas & Calendar Man app. 3.00

BATMAN (Hardcover books and trade paperbacks)
...: ABSOLUTION (2002, $24.95)-Hard-c.; DeMatteis-s/Ashmore painted-a 25.00
...: ABSOLUTION (2003, $17.95)-Soft-c.; DeMatteis-s/Ashmore painted-a 18.00
...: A LONELY PLACE OF DYING (1990, $3.95, 132 pgs.)-r/Batman #440-442 & New Titans #60,61; Perez-c 18.00
...: ANARKY TPB (1999, $12.95) r/early appearances 18.00
...AND DRACULA: RED RAIN nn (1991, $24.95)-Hard-c; Elseworlds storyline 35.00
...AND DRACULA: RED RAIN nn (1992, $9.95)-SC 16.00
...AND SON HC (2007, $24.99, dustjacket) r/Batman #655-658,663-666 25.00
...AND SON SC (2008, $14.99) r/Batman #655-658,663-666 15.00
...ANNUALS (See DC Comics Classics Library for reprints of early Annuals)
ARKHAM ASYLUM Hard-c; Morrison-s/McKean-a (1989, $24.95) 30.00
ARKHAM ASYLUM Soft-c ($14.95) 20.00
ARKHAM ASYLUM 15TH ANNIVERSARY EDITION Hard-c (2004, $29.95) reprint with Morrison's script and annotations, original page layouts; Karen Berger afterword 30.00
ARKHAM ASYLUM 15TH ANNIVERSARY EDITION Soft-c (2005, $17.99) 18.00
...: AS THE CROW FLIES-(2004, $12.95) r/#626-630; Nguyen sketch pages 13.00
BIRTH OF THE DEMON Hard-c (1992, $24.95)-Origin of Ra's al Ghul 40.00
BIRTH OF THE DEMON Soft-c (1993, $12.95) 20.00
BLIND JUSTICE nn (1992, $7.50)-r/Det. #598-600 12.00
BLOODSTORM (1994, $24.95,HC) Kelley Jones-c/a 28.00

Batman: Bruce Wayne - The Road Home HC © DC

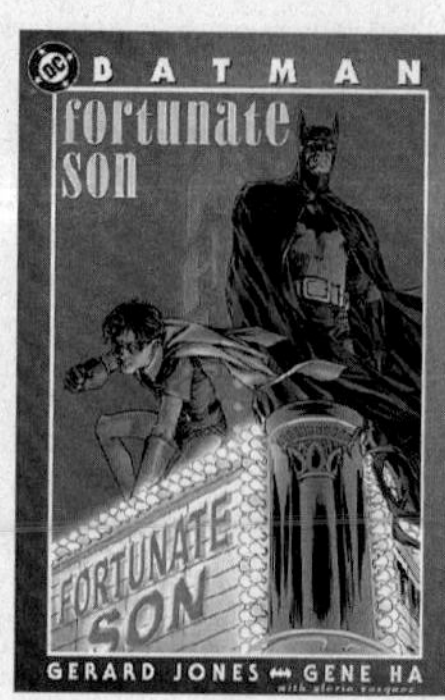

Batman: Fortunate Son HC © DC

Batman: Prey TPB © DC

GD VG FN VF VF/NM NM-
2.0 4.0 6.0 8.0 9.0 9.2

BRIDE OF THE DEMON Hard-c (1990, $19.95) 25.00
BRIDE OF THE DEMON Soft-c ($12.95) 15.00
...: BROKEN CITY HC-(2004, $24.95) r/#620-625; new Johnson-c; intro by Schreck 25.00
...: BROKEN CITY SC-(2004, $14.99) r/#620-625; new Johnson-c; intro by Schreck 15.00
...: BRUCE WAYNE: FUGITIVE Vol. 1 ('02, $12.95)-r/ story arc 15.00
...: BRUCE WAYNE: FUGITIVE Vol. 2 ('03, $12.95)-r/ story arc 15.00
...: BRUCE WAYNE: FUGITIVE Vol. 3 ('03, $12.95)-r/ story arc 15.00
...: BRUCE WAYNE-MURDERER? ('02, $19.95)-r/ story arc 25.00
...: BRUCE WAYNE - THE ROAD HOME HC ('11, $24.99) r/Bruce Wayne: The Road Home one-shots 25.00
...: CATACLYSM ('99, $17.95)-r/ story arc 35.00
...: CHILD OF DREAMS (2003, $24.95, B&W, HC) Reprint of Japanese manga with Kia Asamiya-s/a/c; English adaptation by Max Allan Collins; Asamiya interview 25.00
...: CHILD OF DREAMS (2003, $19.95, B&W, SC) 20.00
...CHRONICLES VOL. 1 (2005, $14.99)-r/apps. in Detective Comics #27-38; Batman #1 15.00
...CHRONICLES VOL. 2 (2006, $14.99)-r/apps. in Detective Comics #39-45 and NY World's Fair 1940; Batman #2,3 15.00
...CHRONICLES VOL. 3 (2007, $14.99)-r/apps. in Detective Comics #46-50 and World's Best Comics #1; Batman #4,5 15.00
...CHRONICLES VOL. 4 (2007, $14.99)-r/apps. in Detective Comics #51-56 and World's Finest Comics #2,3; Batman #6,7 15.00
...CHRONICLES VOL. 5 (2008, $14.99)-r/apps. in Detective Comics #57-61 and World's Finest Comics #4; Batman #8,9 15.00
...CHRONICLES VOL. 6 (2008, $14.99)-r/apps. in Detective Comics #62-65 and World's Finest Comics #5,6; Batman #10,11 15.00
...CHRONICLES VOL. 7 (2009, $14.99)-r/apps. in Detective Comics #66-70 and World's Finest Comics #7; Batman #12,13 15.00
...CHRONICLES VOL. 8 (2009, $14.99)-r/apps. in Detective Comics #71-74 and World's Finest Comics #8,9; Batman #14,15 15.00
...CHRONICLES VOL. 9 (2010, $14.99)-r/apps. in Detective Comics #75-77 and World's Finest Comics #10; Batman #16,17 15.00
...CHRONICLES VOL. 10 (2010, $14.99)-r/apps. in Detective Comics #78-81 and World's Finest Comics #11; Batman #18,19 15.00
...: CITY OF CRIME (2006, $19.99) r/Detective Comics #800-808,811-814; Lapham-s 20.00
...: COLLECTED LEGENDS OF THE DARK KNIGHT nn (1994, $12.95)-r/Legends of the Dark Knight #32-34,38,42,43 18.00
...: CRIMSON MIST (1999, $24.95,HC)-Vampire Batman Elseworlds story Doug Moench-s/Kelley Jones-c/a 45.00
...: CRIMSON MIST (2001, $14.95,SC) 20.00
...: DARK JOKER-THE WILD (1993, $24.95,HC)-Elseworlds story; Moench-s/Jones-c/a 30.00
...: DARK JOKER-THE WILD (1993, $9.95,SC) 12.00
...DARK KNIGHT DYNASTY nn (1997, $24.95)-Hard-c.; 3 Elseworlds stories; Barr-s/ S. Hampton painted-a, Gary Frank, McDaniel-a(p) 28.00
...DARK KNIGHT DYNASTY Softcover (2000, $14.95) Hampton-c 15.00
...DEADMAN: DEATH AND GLORY nn (1996, $24.95)-Hard-c.; Robinson-s/ Estes-c/a 32.00
...DEADMAN: DEATH AND GLORY ($12.95)-SC 18.00
DEATH AND THE CITY (2007, $14.99, TPB)-r/Detective #827-834 15.00
DEATH BY DESIGN (2012, $24.99, HC)-Chip Kidd-s/Dave Taylor-s 25.00
DEATH IN THE FAMILY (1988, $3.95, trade paperback)-r/Batman #426-429 by Aparo 20.00
DEATH IN THE FAMILY: (2nd - 5th printings) 9.00
...: DETECTIVE (2007, $14.99, SC)-r/Detective Comics #821-826 15.00
...: DETECTIVE #27 HC (2003, $19.95)-Elseworlds; Uslan-s/Snejbjerg-a 20.00
...: DETECTIVE #27 SC (2004, $12.95)-Elseworlds; Uslan-s/Snejbjerg-a 13.00
DIGITAL JUSTICE nn (1990, $24.95, Hard-c.)-Computer generated art 25.00
... EARTH ONE HC (2012, $22.99)-Updated re-imagining of Batman's origin & debut; Geoff Johns-s/Gary Frank-a 23.00
... : EGO AND OTHER TALES HC (2007, $24.99)-r/Batman: Ego, Catwoman: Selina's Big Score, and stories from Batman Black and White and Solo; Darwyn Cooke-s/a 25.00
... : EGO AND OTHER TALES SC (2008, $17.99) same contents as HC 18.00
... :EVOLUTION (2001, $12.95, SC)-r/Detective Comics #743-750 13.00
... FACES (1995, $9.95, TPB) r/Legends of the Dark Knight #28-30 15.00
... FACES (2008, $12.99, TPB) Second printing 13.00
...: FACE THE FACE (2006, $14.99, TPB)-r/Batman #651-654, Detective #817-820 15.00
...: FALSE FACES HC (2008, $19.99)-r/Batman #588-590, Wonder Woman #160,161; Batman: Gotham City Secret Files #1 and Detective #787; Brian K. Vaughn intro. 20.00
...: FALSE FACES SC (2008, $14.99)-r/Batman #588-590, Wonder Woman #160,161; Batman: Gotham City Secret Files #1 and Detective #787; Brian K. Vaughn intro. 15.00
...: FORTUNATE SON HC (1999, $24.95) Gene Ha-a 25.00
...: FORTUNATE SON SC (2000, $14.95) Gene Ha-a 15.00
FOUR OF A KIND TPB (1998, $14.95)-r/1995 Year One Annuals featuring Poison Ivy, Riddler, Scarecrow, & Man-Bat 30.00
... GOING SANE (2008, $14.95, TPB) r/Legends of the Dark Knight #65-68,200 15.00
...: GOTHAM BY GASLIGHT (2006, $12.99, TPB) r/Gotham By Gaslight & Master of the Future one-shots; Elseworlds Batman vs. Jack the Ripper 13.00
...GOTHIC (1992, $12.95, TPB)-r/Legends of the Dark Knight #6-10 20.00

GD VG FN VF VF/NM NM-
2.0 4.0 6.0 8.0 9.0 9.2

...GOTHIC (2007, $14.99, TPB)-r/Legends of the Dark Knight #6-10 15.00
...: HARVEST BREED-(2000, $24.95) George Pratt-s/painted-a 25.00
...: HARVEST BREED-(2003, $17.95) George Pratt-s/painted-a 18.00
...: HAUNTED KNIGHT-(1997, $12.95) r/ Halloween specials 18.00
...: HEART OF HUSH HC-(2009, $19.99) r/#Detective #846-850; pin-ups 20.00
...: HEART OF HUSH SC-(2010, $14.99) r/#Detective #846-850; pin-ups 15.00
...: HONG KONG HC (2003, $24.95, with dustjacket) Doug Moench-s/Tony Wong-a 25.00
...: HONG KONG SC (2004, $17.95) Doug Moench-s/Tony Wong-a 18.00
...: HUSH DOUBLE FEATURE-(2003, $3.95) r/#608,609(1st 2 Jim Lee-a issues) 6.00
...: HUSH SC-(2009, $24.99) r/#608-619; Wizard 0; variant cover gallery; Loeb intro 25.00
...: HUSH UNWRAPPED-(2011, $39.99, HC) r/#608-619's original Jim Lee pencil art 40.00
...: HUSH VOLUME 1 HC-(2003, $19.95) r/#608-612; & new 2 pg. origin w/Lee-a 20.00
...: HUSH VOLUME 1 SC-(2004, $12.95) r/#608-612; includes CD of DC GN art 13.00
...: HUSH VOLUME 2 HC-(2003, $19.95) r/#613-619; Lee intro & sketchpages 20.00
...: HUSH VOLUME 2 SC-(2004, $12.95) r/#613-619; Lee intro & sketchpages 13.00
...: ILLUSTRATED BY NEAL ADAMS VOLUME 1 HC-(2003, $49.95) r/Batman, Brave and the Bold, and Detective Comics stories and covers 50.00
...: ILLUSTRATED BY NEAL ADAMS VOLUME 2 HC-(2004, $49.95) r/Adams' Batman art from 1969-71; intro. by Dick Giordano 50.00
...: ILLUSTRATED BY NEAL ADAMS VOLUME 3 HC-(2006, $49.99) r/Adams' Batman art from 1971-74; covers, pin-ups and design art; intro. by Denny O'Neil 50.00
... IMPOSTERS TPB (2011, $14.99) r/Detective Comics #867-870 15.00
... INTERNATIONAL TPB (2010, $17.99) R/Batman: Scottish Connection, Batman in Barcelona: Dragon's Knight and Batman: Legends of the DK #52,53; Jim Lee-c 18.00
... IN THE FORTIES TPB ($19.95) Intro. by Bill Schelly 20.00
... IN THE FIFTIES TPB ($19.95) Intro. by Michael Uslan 20.00
... IN THE SIXTIES TPB ($19.95) Intro. by Adam West 20.00
... IN THE SEVENTIES TPB ($19.95) Intro. by Dennis O'Neil 20.00
... IN THE EIGHTIES TPB ($19.95) Intro. by John Wells 20.00
.../ JUDGE DREDD FILES (2004, $14.95) reprints cross-overs 15.00
... :KING TUT'S TOMB TPB (2010, $14.99) r/Batman Confidential #26-28, Batman #353 and Brave and the Bold #164,171 15.00
... LEGACY-(1996, $17.95) reprints Legacy 30.00
...: LIFE AFTER DEATH HC-(2010, $19.99, dustjacket) r/#Batman #692-699 20.00
...: LONG SHADOWS HC-(2010, $19.99, dustjacket) r/#Batman #687-691 20.00
...: LONG SHADOWS SC-(2011, $14.99) r/#Batman #687-691 15.00
...: LOVERS & MADMEN-(See Batman Confidential)
...: MAD LOVE AND OTHER STORIES HC (2009, $19.99) r/Batman Adventures: Mad Love, Batman Advs. Holiday Special and other Dini/Timm collaborations; commentary 20.00
...: THE MANY DEATHS OF THE BATMAN (1992, $3.95, 84 pgs.)-r/Batman #433-435 w/new Byrne-c 12.00
...: MONSTERS (2009, $19.99, TPB)-r/Legends of the Dark Knight #71-73,83,84,89,90 20.00
...: THE MOVIES (1997, $19.95)-r/movie adaptations of Batman, Batman Returns, Batman Forever, Batman and Robin 30.00
...: NINE LIVES HC (2002, $24.95, sideways format) Motter-s/Lark-a 25.00
...: NINE LIVES SC (2003, $17.95, sideways format) Motter-s/Lark-a 18.00
...: OFFICER DOWN (2001, $12.95)-r/Commissioner shot x-over; Talon-c 13.00
.../ PLANETARY DELUXE HC (2011, $22.99)-r/Planetary/Batman: Night on Earth; script 23.00
...: PREY (1992, $12.95)-Gulacy/Austin-a 24.00
...: PRIVATE CASEBOOK HC (2008, $19.99)-r/Detective Comics #840-845 and story from DC Infinite Halloween Special #1 20.00
...: PRODIGAL (1997, $14.95)-Gulacy/Austin-a 45.00
...: R.I.P.: THE DELUXE EDITION HC (2009, $24.99)-r/Batman #676-683 and story from DC Universe #0 25.00
...: R.I.P.: SC (2010, $14.99)-r/Batman #676-683 and story from DC Universe #0 15.00
... SCARECROW TALES (2005, $19.99, TPB) r/Scarecrow stories & pin-ups from World's Finest #3 to present 20.00
...: SECRETS OF THE BATCAVE (2007, $17.99, TPB) r/Batcave stories 18.00
SHAMAN (1993, $12.95)-r/Legends/D.K. #1-5 45.00
...: SNOW (2007, $14.99, TPB)-r/Legends of the Dark Knight #192-196; Fisher-a 15.00
...: SON OF THE DEMON Hard-c (9/87, $14.95) (see Batman #655-658) 35.00
...: SON OF THE DEMON limited signed & numbered Hard-c (1,700) 60.00
...: SON OF THE DEMON Soft-c w/new-c ($8.95) 20.00
...: SON OF THE DEMON Soft-c (1989, $9.95, 2nd printing - 5th printing) 10.00
... : STRANGE APPARITIONS ($12.95) r/'77-'78 Englehart/Rogers stories from Detective #469-479; also Simonson-a 25.00
...: TALES OF THE DEMON (1991, $17.95, 212 pgs.)-Intro by Sam Hamm; reprints by Neal Adams(3) & Golden; contains Saga of Ra's al Ghul #1 20.00
TALES OF THE MULTIVERSE: BATMAN - VAMPIRE (2007, $19.99) r/Batman & Dracula: Red Rain, Batman: Bloodstorm and Batman: Crimson Mist; Van Lustbader foreword 20.00
...: TEN NIGHTS OF THE BEAST (1994, $5.95)-r/Batman #417-420 18.00
...: TERROR (2003, $12.95, TPB)-r/Legends of the Dark Knight #137-141; Gulacy-c 13.00
...: THE BLACK GLOVE (2009, $17.99, TPB) r/Batman #667-669,672-675 18.00
...: THE CHALICE (HC, '99, $24.95) Van Fleet painted-a 25.00
...: THE CHALICE (SC, '00, $14.95) Van Fleet painted-a 15.00

Batman: The Last Angel TPB © DC

Batman: Full Circle © DC

Batman: Poison Ivy © DC

	GD	VG	FN	VF	VF/NM	NM-
	2.0	4.0	6.0	8.0	9.0	9.2

...: THE GREATEST STORIES EVER TOLD (2005, $19.99, TPB) Les Daniels intro. 20.00
...: THE GREATEST STORIES EVER TOLD VOLUME TWO (2007, $19.99, TPB) 20.00
...: THE JOKER'S LAST LAUGH ('08, $17.99) r/Joker's Last Laugh series #1-6 18.00
...: THE LAST ANGEL (1994, $12.95, TPB) Lustbader-s 15.00
...: THE RESURRECTION OF RA'S AL GHUL (2008, $29.99, HC w/DJ) r/x-over 30.00
...: THE RESURRECTION OF RA'S AL GHUL (2009, $19.99, SC) r/x-over 20.00
...: THE RING, THE ARROW AND THE BAT (2003, $19.95, TPB) r/Legends of the DCU #7-9 & Batman: Legends of the Dark Knight #127-131; Green Lantern & Green Arrow app. 20.00
...: THE STRANGE DEATHS OF BATMAN ('09, $19.99) r/Batman #291-294, Det. #347, World's Finest #184,269, Brave & the Bold #115, Nightwing #52; Aparo-c 20.00
...: THE WRATH ('09, $17.99) r/Batman Special #1 and Batman Confidential #13-16 18.00
...: THRILLKILLER (1998, $12.95, TPB)-r/series & Thrillkiller '62 20.00
...: TIME AND THE BATMAN HC ('11, $19.99) r/Batman #700-703; cover gallery 20.00
...: TWO-FACE AND SCARECROW YEAR ONE (2009, $19.99, TPB)-r/Year One: Batman Scarecrow #1,2 and Two Face: Year One #1,2 20.00
...: UNDER THE COWL (2010, $17.99, TPB)-r/app. Dick Grayson, Tim Drake, Damian Wayne, Jean Paul Valley and Terry McGinnis as Batman 18.00
...: UNDER THE HOOD (2005, $9.99, TPB)-r/Batman #635-641 10.00
...: UNDER THE HOOD Vol. 2 (2006, $9.99, TPB)-r/Batman #645-650 & Annual #25 10.00
...: UNDER THE RED HOOD (2011, $29.99, TPB)-r/Batman #635-641,645-650, Ann. #25 30.00
...: VENOM (1993, $9.95, TPB)-r/Legends of the Dark Knight #16-20; embossed-c 25.00
... VS. TWO-FACE (2008, $19.99, TPB) r/initial (Det. #80) & classic battles; Bianchi-c 20.00
...: WAR CRIMES (2006, $12.99, TPB) r/x-over; James Jean-c 13.00
... WAR DRUMS (2004, $17.95) r/Detective #790-796 & Robin #126-128 18.00
...: WAR GAMES ACT 1,2,3 (2005, $14.95/$14.99, TPB) r/x-over; James Jean-c; each.. 15.00
...: WHATEVER HAPPENED TO THE CAPED CRUSADER? HC-(2009, $24.99, d.j.) r/Batman #686, Detective #853 and other Gaiman Batman stories; Gaiman intro.; Andy Kubert sketch pages; new Kubert cover 25.00
...: WHATEVER HAPPENED TO THE CAPED CRUSADER? SC-(2010, $14.99) 15.00
YEAR ONE Hard-c (1988, $12.95) r/Batman #404-407 25.00
YEAR ONE (1988, $9.95, TPB)-r/Batman #404-407 by Miller; intro by Miller 15.00
YEAR ONE (TPB, 2nd & 3rd printings) 10.00
YEAR ONE Deluxe HC (2005, $19.99, die-cut d.j.) new intro. by Miller and developmental material from Mazzucchelli; script pages and sketches 20.00
YEAR ONE (Deluxe) SC (2007, $14.99) r/story plus bonus material from 2005 HC 15.00
YEAR TWO (1990, $9.95, TPB)-r/Det. 575-578 by McFarlane; wraparound-c 15.00

BATMAN (one-shots)
... ABDUCTION, THE (1998, $5.95) 6.00
... ALLIES SECRET FILES AND ORIGINS 2005 (8/05, $4.99) stories/pin-ups by various 5.00
... & ROBIN (1997, $5.95)-Movie adaptation 8.00
...: ARKHAM ASYLUM - TALES OF MADNESS (5/98, $2.95) Cataclysm x-over pt. 16 8.00
... : BANE (1997, $4.95)-Dixon-s/Burchett-a; Stelfreeze-c; cover art interlocks w/Batman:(Batgirl, Mr. Freeze, Poison Ivy) 10.00
... : BATGIRL (1997, $4.95)-Puckett-s/Haley,Kesel-a; Stelfreeze-c; cover art interlocks w/Batman:(Bane, Mr. Freeze, Poison Ivy) 6.00
... : BATGIRL (6/98, $1.95)-Girlfrenzy; Balent-a 4.00
... : BLACKGATE (1/97, $3.95) Dixon-s 5.00
... : BLACKGATE - ISLE OF MEN (4/98, $2.95) Cataclysm x-over pt. 8; Moench-s/Aparo-a 4.00
... BOOK OF SHADOWS, THE (1999, $5.95) 6.00
BROTHERHOOD OF THE BAT (1995, $5.95)-Elseworlds-s 8.00
... BULLOCK'S LAW (8/99, $4.95) Dixon-s 5.00
.../CAPTAIN AMERICA (1996, $5.95, DC/Marvel) Elseworlds story; Byrne-c/s/a 10.00
...: CASTLE OF THE BAT ($5.95)-Elseworlds story 6.00
... : CATWOMAN DEFIANT nn (1992, $4.95, prestige format)-Milligan scripts; cover art interlocks w/Batman: Penguin Triumphant; special foil logo 8.00
.../CATWOMAN: FOLLOW THE MONEY (1/11, $4.99) Chaykin-c/s/a 8.00
... /DANGER GIRL (2/05, $4.95)-Leinil Yu-a/c; Joker, Harley Quinn & Catwoman app. 8.00
... /DAREDEVIL (2000, $5.95)-Barreto-a 12.00
...: DARK ALLEGIANCES (1996, $5.95)-Elseworlds story, Chaykin-c/a 7.00
...: DARK KNIGHT GALLERY (1/96, $3.50)-Pin-ups by Pratt, Balent, & others 4.00
...:DAY OF JUDGMENT (11/99, $3.95) 5.00
... DAY SPECIAL EDITION 1 (10/17, giveaway) r/Batman #16 (2017) with Harley Quinn framing pages by Palmiotti & Conner-s/Blevins-a 3.00
...:DEATH OF INNOCENTS (12/96, $3.95)-O'Neil-s/ Staton-a(p) 8.00
.../DEMON (1996, $4.95)-Alan Grant scripts 8.00
.../DEMON: A TRAGEDY (2000, $5.95)-Grant-s/Murray painted-a 12.00
...:D.O.A. (1999, $6.95)-Bob Hall-s/a 7.00
...:/DOC SAVAGE SPECIAL (2010, $4.99)-Azzarello-s/Noto-a/covers by JG Jones & Morales; preview of First Wave line (Batman, Doc Savage, The Spirit, Blackhawks) 5.00
...:DREAMLAND (2000, $5.95)-Grant-s/Breyfogle-a 6.00
... : EGO (2000, $6.95)-Darwyn Cooke-s/a 7.00
... 80-PAGE GIANT (8/98, $4.95) Stelfreeze-c 6.00
... 80-PAGE GIANT 1 (2/10, $5.99) Andy Kubert-c; Catwoman, Poison Ivy app. 6.00
... 80-PAGE GIANT 2 (10/99, $4.95) Luck of the Draw 6.00
... 80-PAGE GIANT 3 (7/00, $5.95) Calendar Man 6.00
... 80-PAGE GIANT 2011 (2/11, $5.95) Nguyen-c; short stories of villains by various 6.00
... 80-PAGE GIANT 2011 (10/11, $5.99) Nguyen-c; art by Naifeh & others 6.00
... /ELMER FUDD SPECIAL 1 (8/17, $4.99) Tom King-s/Lee Weeks-a; cartoony back-up with Bugs Bunny; King-s/Vaughns-a 12.00
... /ELMER FUDD SPECIAL 1 (10/17, $4.99) 2nd printing; brighter red bkgd on cover 8.00
... FOREVER (1995, $5.95, direct market) 8.00
... FOREVER (1995, $3.95, newsstand) 6.00
FULL CIRCLE nn (1991, $5.95, 68 pgs.)-Sequel to Batman: Year Two 8.00
...GALLERY, The 1 (1992, $2.95)-Pin-ups by Miller, N. Adams & others 4.00
...GOLDEN STREETS OF GOTHAM (2003, $6.95) Elseworlds in early 1900s 14.00
...GOTHAM BY GASLIGHT (1989, $3.95) Elseworlds; Mignola-a/Augustyn-s 10.00
...GOTHAM CITY SECRET FILES 1 (4/00, $4.95) Batgirl app. 6.00
...: GOTHAM NOIR (2001, $6.95)-Elseworlds; Brubaker-s/Phillips-c/a 20.00
.../GREEN ARROW: THE POISON TOMORROW nn (1992, $5.95, square-bound, 68 pgs.) Netzer-c/a 8.00
... HALLOWEEN COMIC FEST SPECIAL EDITION 1 (11/17, giveaway) r/Batman #7 ('16) 3.00
...: HIDDEN TREASURES 1 (12/10, $4.99) unpubl. story Wrightson-a; r/Swamp Thing #7 5.00
HOLY TERROR nn (1991, $4.95, 52 pgs.)-Elseworlds story 6.00
.../HOUDINI: THE DEVIL'S WORKSHOP (1993, $5.95) 7.00
... :HUNTRESS/SPOILER - BLUNT TRAUMA (5/98, $2.95) Cataclysm pt. 13; Dixon-s/Barreto & Sienkiewicz-a 4.00
...: I, JOKER nn (1998, $4.95)-Elseworlds story; Bob Hall-s/a 8.00
...: IN BARCELONA: DRAGON'S KNIGHT 1 (7/09, $3.99) Waid-s/Olmos-a/Jim Lee-c 4.00
...: IN DARKEST KNIGHT nn (1994, $4.95, 52 pgs.)-Elseworlds story; Batman w/Green Lantern's ring. 8.00
...:JOKER'S APPRENTICE (5/99, $3.95) Von Eeden-a 5.00
...:JOKER'S DAUGHTER (4/14, $4.99) Bennett-s/Hetrick-a/Jeanty-c 5.00
.../ JOKER: SWITCH (2003, $6.95)-Bolton-a/Grayson-s 7.00
...:JUDGE DREDD: JUDGEMENT ON GOTHAM nn (1991, $5.95, 68 pgs.) Simon Bisley-c/a; Grant/Wagner scripts 8.00
...:JUDGE DREDD: JUDGEMENT ON GOTHAM nn (2nd printing) 6.00
...:JUDGE DREDD: THE ULTIMATE RIDDLE (1995, $4.95) 6.00
...:JUDGE DREDD: VENDETTA IN GOTHAM (1993, $5.95) 7.00
...: KNIGHTGALLERY (1995, $3.50)-Elseworlds sketchbook. 4.00
.../ LOBO (2000, $5.95)-Elseworlds; Joker app.; Bisley-a 6.00
...: MASK OF THE PHANTASM (1994, $2.95)-Movie adapt. 4.00
...: MASK OF THE PHANTASM (1994, $4.95)-Movie adapt. 6.00
...: MASQUE (1997, $6.95)-Elseworlds; Grell-c/s/a 7.00
...: MASTER OF THE FUTURE nn (1991, $5.95, 68 pgs.)-Elseworlds; sequel to Gotham By Gaslight; Barreto-a; embossed-c 6.00
...: MITEFALL (1995, $4.95)-Alan Grant script, Kevin O'Neill-a 6.00
... : MR. FREEZE (1997, $4.95)-Dini-s/Buckingham-a; Stelfreeze-c; cover art interlocks w/Batman:(Bane, Batgirl, Poison Ivy) 8.00
... /NIGHTWING: BLOODBORNE (2002, $5.95) Cypress-a; McKeever-c 6.00
...: NOEL (2011, $22.99, HC graphic novel with dustjacket) Lee Bermejo-s/a; Jim Lee intro.; Catwoman, Superman & The Joker app.; bonus sketch & layout art pages 23.00
...: NOSFERATU (1999, $5.95) McKeever-a 6.00
...: OF ARKHAM (2000, $5.95)-Elseworlds; Grant-s/Alcatena-a 6.00
...: OUR WORLDS AT WAR (8/01, $2.95)-Jae Lee-c 3.00
...: PENGUIN TRIUMPHANT nn (1992, $4.95)-Staton-a(p); foil logo 6.00
...: PENNYWORTH R.I.P. 1 (4/20, $4.99) Short story reminisces after Alfred's death 5.00
...•PHANTOM STRANGER nn (1997, $4.95) nn-Grant-s/Ransom-a 6.00
... : PLUS (2/97, $2.95) Arsenal-c/app. 4.00
... : POISON IVY (1997, $4.95)-J.F. Moore-s/Apthorp-a; Stelfreeze-c; cover art interlocks w/Batman:(Bane, Batgirl, Mr. Freeze) 6.00
.../POISON IVY: CAST SHADOWS (2004, $6.95) Van Fleet-c/a; Nocenti-s 7.00
.../PUNISHER: LAKE OF FIRE (1994, $4.95, DC/Marvel) 6.00
... :REIGN OF TERROR ('99, $4.95) Elseworlds 6.00
...RETURNS MOVIE SPECIAL (1992, $3.95) 4.00
...RETURNS MOVIE PRESTIGE (1992, $5.95, squarebound)-Dorman painted-c 6.00
...:RIDDLER-THE RIDDLE FACTORY (1995, $4.95)-Wagner script 6.00
...: ROOM FULL OF STRANGERS (2004, $5.95) Scott Morse-s/c/a 6.00
...: SCARECROW 3-D (12/98, $3.95) w/glasses 6.00
.../ SCARFACE: A PSYCHODRAMA (2001, $5.95)-Adlard-a/Sienkiewicz-c 6.00
...: SCAR OF THE BAT nn (1996, $4.95)-Elseworlds; Max Allan Collins script; Barreto-a 6.00
... :SCOTTISH CONNECTION (1998, $5.95) Quitely-a 6.00
... :SEDUCTION OF THE GUN nn (1992, $2.50, 68 pgs.) 5.00
.../SPAWN: WAR DEVIL nn (1994, $4.95, 52 pgs.) 6.00
... SPECIAL 1 (4/84)-Mike W. Barr story; Golden-c/a 1 2 3 5 6 8
.../SPIDER-MAN (1997, $4.95) Dematteis-s/Nolan & Kesel-a 6.00
... : THE ABDUCTION ('98, $5.95) 6.00
...: THE BLUE, THE GREY, & THE BAT (1992, $5.95)-Weiss/Lopez-a 7.00
... :THE HILL (5/00, $2.95)-Priest-s/Martinbrough-a 3.00
...: THE JOKER WAR ZONE (11/20, $5.99)-Short stories by various incl. Coipel, Stokoe 6.00
... :THE KILLING JOKE (1988, deluxe 52 pgs., mature readers)-Bolland-c/a; Alan Moore

Batman Adventures #14 © DC

Batman and Robin #22 © DC

Batman and Robin Adventures #16 © DC

GD 2.0 | VG 4.0 | FN 6.0 | VF 8.0 | VF/NM 9.0 | NM- 9.2

scripts; Joker cripples Barbara Gordon 5 10 15 31 53 75
...: THE KILLING JOKE (2nd thru 14th printings) 3 6 9 14 20 25
...: THE KILLING JOKE : THE DELUXE EDITION (2008, $17.99, HC) re-colored version along with Bolland-s/a from Batman Black and White #4; sketch pages; Tim Sale intro. 18.00
...: THE MAN WHO LAUGHS (2005, $6.95)-Retells 1st meeting with the Joker; Mahnke-a 7.00
...: THE OFFICIAL COMIC ADAPTATION OF THE WARNER BROS. MOTION PICTURE (1989, $2.50, regular format, 68 pgs.)-Ordway-c 6.00
...: THE OFFICIAL COMIC ADAPTATION OF THE WARNER BROS. MOTION PICTURE (1989, $4.95, prestige format, 68 pgs.)-same interiors but different-c 1 2 3 5 6 8
...: THE ORDER OF BEASTS (2004, $5.95)-Elseworlds; Eddie Campbell-a 6.00
...: THE SMILE KILLER (8/20, $5.99)-Epilogue to Joker: Killer Smile series; Sorrentino-a 6.00
...: THE SPIRIT (1/07, $4.99)-Loeb-s/Cooke-a; P'Gell & Commissioner Dolan app. 5.00
...: THE 10-CENT ADVENTURE (3/02, 10¢) intro. to the "Bruce Wayne: Murderer" x-over; Rucka-s/Burchett & Janson-a/Dave Johnson-c 3.00

NOTE: (Also see Promotional Comics section for alternate copies with special outer half-covers promoting local comic shops)

...: THE 12-CENT ADVENTURE (10/04, 12¢) intro. to the "War Games" x-over; Grayson-s/Bachs-a; Catwoman & Spoiler app. 3.00
...: TWO-FACE-CRIME AND PUNISHMENT-(1995, $4.95)-McDaniel-a 6.00
... : TWO FACES (11/98, $4.95) Elseworlds 6.00
...Vs. THE INCREDIBLE HULK (1995, $3.95)-r/DC Special Series #27 15.00
...: VILLAINS SECRET FILES (10/98, $4.95) Origin-s 6.00
... VILLAINS SECRET FILES AND ORIGINS 2005 (7/05, $4.99) Clayface origin w/ Mignola-a; Black Mask story, pin-up of villains by various; Barrionuevo-c 6.00

BATMAN ADVENTURES, THE (Based on animated series)(See DC Classics for reprints)
DC Comics: Oct, 1992 - No. 36, Oct, 1995 ($1.25/$1.50)

1-Penguin-c/story 2 4 6 10 14 18
1 ($1.95, Silver Edition)-2nd printing 3.00
2,4-6,8-11,13-15,17-19: 2-Catwoman-c/story. 5-Scarecrow-c/story. 10-Riddler-c/story. 11-Man-Bat-c/story. 18-Batgirl-c/story. 19-Scarecrow-c/story 5.00
3-Joker-c/story 2 4 6 10 14 18
7-Special edition polybagged with Man-Bat trading card 1 2 3 5 6 8
12-(9/93) 1st Harley Quinn app. in comics; 1st animated-version Batgirl app. in title 50 100 150 240 370 500
16-Joker-c/story; begin $1.50-c 3 6 9 16 23. 30
20-24,26,27,29-32: 26-Batgirl app. 4.00
25-($2.50, 52 pgs.)-Superman app. 2 4 6 8 10 12
28-Joker & Harley Quinn-c; 2nd app. Harley Quinn 3 6 9 19 30 40
33-36: 33-Begin $1.75-c 4.00
Annual 1 ('94) 3rd app. Harley Quinn 3 6 9 19 30 40
Annual 2 ('95) Demon-c/story; Ra's al Ghul app. 5.00
...: Dangerous Dames & Demons (2003, $14.95, TPB) r/Annual 1,2, Mad Love & Adventures in the DC Universe #3; Bruce Timm painted-c 30.00
Holiday Special 1 (1995, $2.95) Harley Quinn app. 3 6 9 15 22 28
The Collected Adventures Vol. 1,2 ('93, '95, $5.95) 15.00
TPB ('98, $7.95) r/#1-6; painted wraparound-c 10.00

BATMAN ADVENTURES (Based on animated series)
DC Comics: Jun, 2003 - No. 17, Oct, 2004 ($2.25)

1-Timm-c 2 4 6 8 10 12
1-Free Comic Book Day edition (6/03) Timm-c 4.00
1-Halloween Fest Special Edition (12/15) Timm-c 4.00
2,4-9,11-15,17: 4-Ra's al Ghul app. 6-8-Phantasm app. 14-Grey Ghost app. 4.00
3-Joker & Harley Quinn-c/app. 3 6 9 18 28 38
10-Catwoman-c/app. 3 6 9 14 20 26
16-Joker & Harley Quinn-c/app. 5 10 15 31 53 75
Batman/Scooby-Doo Halloween Fest 1 (12/12, giveaway flipbook with Scooby-Doo) r/#1 1 2 3 5 6 8
Vol. 1: Rogues Gallery (2004, $6.95, digest size) r/#1-4 & Batman: Gotham Advs. #50 7.00
Vol. 2: Shadows & Masks (2004, $6.95, digest size) r/#5-9 7.00

BATMAN ADVENTURES, THE: MAD LOVE
DC Comics: Feb, 1994 ($3.95/$4.95)

1-Origin of Harley Quinn; Dini-s/Timm-c/a 7 14 21 48 89 130
1-($4.95, Prestige format) new Timm painted-c 5 10 15 35 63 90

BATMAN ADVENTURES, THE: THE LOST YEARS (TV)
DC Comics: Jan, 1998 - No. 5, May, 1998 ($1.95) (Based on animated series)

1-5-Leads into Fall '97's new animated episodes. 4-Tim Drake becomes Robin. 5-Dick becomes Nightwing 5.00
TPB-(1999, $9.95) r/series 35.00

BATMAN/ALIENS
DC Comics/Dark Horse: Mar, 1997 - No. 2, Apr, 1997 ($4.95, limited series)

GD 2.0 | VG 4.0 | FN 6.0 | VF 8.0 | VF/NM 9.0 | NM- 9.2

1,2: Wrightson-c/a. 1 3 4 6 8 10
TPB-(1997, $14.95) w/prequel from DHP #101,102 30.00

BATMAN/ALIENS II
DC Comics/Dark Horse: 2003 - No. 3, 2003 ($5.95, limited series)

1-3-Edginton-s/Staz Johnson-a 1 3 4 6 8 10
TPB-(2003, $14.95) r/#1-3 20.00

BATMAN AND... (See Batman and Robin [2011 series] #19-on)

BATMAN AND ROBIN (See Batman R.I.P. and Batman: Battle For The Cowl series)
DC Comics: Aug, 2009 - No. 26, Oct, 2011 ($2.99)

1-Grant Morrison-s/Frank Quitely-a/c; Dick Grayson & Damian Wayne team 8.00
1-Variant cover by J.G. Jones 20.00
1-Second thru Fourth printings - recolored Quitely covers 3.00
2-16-Quitely-c. 2-Three printings. 4-6-Tan-a. 7-9-Stewart-a; Batwoman & Squire app. 13-15-Joker app.; Irving-a. 16-Bruce Wayne returns; Batman Inc. announced 3.00
2-Variant-c by Adam Kubert 10.00
17-26: 17-McDaniel-a/March-c. 21,22-Gleason-a. 23-25-Red Hood app. 3.00
... #1 Special Edition (6/10, $1.00) r/#1 with "What's Next?" cover logo 3.00
...: Batman and Robin Must Die - The Deluxe Edition HC (2011, $24.99) r/#13-16; cover and costume design sketch art 25.00
...: Batman Reborn - The Deluxe Edition HC (2010, $24.99) r/#1-6; design sketch art 25.00
...: Batman Reborn SC (2011, $14.99) r/#1-6; cover and character design sketch art 15.00
...: Batman vs. Robin - The Deluxe Edition HC (2010, $24.99) r/#7-12; cover sketch art 25.00

BATMAN AND ROBIN (DC New 52)(Cover title changes each issue from #19-32)
DC Comics: Nov, 2011 - No. 40, May, 2015 ($2.99)

1-Bruce and Damian Wayne in costume; Tomasi-s/Gleason-a 4.00
2-14: 5,6-Ducard flashback. 9-Night of the Owls 3.00
15-Death of the Family tie-in; die-cut Joker cover 5.00
16-18: 16-Death of the Family tie-in. 18-Requiem 3.00
19-23: 19-Red Robin. 20-Red Hood. 21-Batgirl. 22-Catwoman. 23-Nightwing 3.00
23.1, 23.2, 23.3, 23.4 (11/13, $2.99, regular covers) 3.00
23.1 (11/13, $3.99, 3-D cover) "Two Face #1" on cover; March-a; Scarecrow app. 6.00
23.2 (11/13, $3.99, 3-D cover) "Court of Owls #1" on cover; history of the Owls 5.00
23.3 (11/13, $3.99, 3-D cover) "Ra's al Ghul #1" on cover; history of Ra's retold 5.00
23.4 (11/13, $3.99, 3-D cover) "Killer Croc #1" on cover; Croc's origin 5.00
24-40: 24-28-Two-Face. 25-Matches Malone app. 29-Aquaman. 30-Wonder Woman. 31-Frankenstein. 32-Ra's al Ghul. 33-38-Title back to Batman and Robin. 37-Darkseid app.; Damian returns; cont'd in Robin Rises: Alpha. 39,40-Justice League app. 3.00
#0 (11/12, $2.99) Damian's childhood training with Talia; Tomasi-s/Gleason-a 3.00
Annual 1 (3/13, $4.99) Damian in the Batman #666 costume; Andy Kubert-c 5.00
Annual 2 (3/14, $4.99) Mahnke-a; flashback to Dick Grayson's first week as Robin 5.00
Annual 3 (6/15, $4.99) Ryp-a/Syaf-c 5.00
...: Futures End 1 (11/14, $2.99, regular-c) Five years later; Nguyen-a; 1st app. Duke Thomas as future Robin 3.00
...: Futures End 1 (11/14, $3.99, 3-D cover) 4.00

BATMAN AND ROBIN ADVENTURES (TV)
DC Comics: Nov, 1995 - No. 25, Dec, 1997 ($1.75) (Based on animated series)

1-Dini-s 2 4 6 8 11 14
2-4,6,7,9-15,17,19,20,22,23: 2-4-Dini script. 4-Penguin-c/app. 9-Batgirl & Talia-c/app. 10-Ra's al Ghul-c/app. 11-Man-Bat app. 12-Bane-c/app. 13-Scarecrow-c/app. 15 Deadman-c/app. 4.00
5-Joker-c/story 1 2 3 5 6 8
8-Poison Ivy & Harley Quinn-c/app. 3 6 9 14 20 25
16,18,24: 16-Catwoman-c/app. 18-Joker-c/app. 24-Poison Ivy app. 2 4 6 8 10 12
21-Batgirl-c 3 6 9 19 30 40
25-($2.95, 48 pgs.) 6.00
Annual 1 (11/96) Phantasm-c/app. 3 6 9 19 30 40
Annual 2 (11/97) Zatara & Zatanna-c/app. 1 2 3 5 6 8
...: Sub-Zero(1998, $3.95) Adaptation of animated video 6.00

BATMAN & ROBIN ETERNAL (Sequel to Batman Eternal)
DC Comics: Dec, 2015 - No. 26, May, 2016 ($3.99/$2.99, weekly series)

1-($3.99) Tynion IV & Snyder-s/Daniel-a; Cassandra Cain app. 4.00
2-25-($2.99) Dick Grayson, Red Hood, Red Robin, Bluebird, Spoiler app. 6-1st app. Mother. 9,10,15,16,24,25-Azrael app. 23-25-Midnighter app. 3.00
26-($3.99) Conclusion; Tony Daniel-c 4.00

BATMAN AND SUPERMAN ADVENTURES: WORLD'S FINEST
DC Comics: 1997 ($6.95, square-bound, one-shot) (Based on animated series)

1-Adaptation of animated crossover episode; Dini-s/Timm-c; Harley Quinn on cover 2 4 6 11 16 20

BATMAN AND SUPERMAN: WORLD'S FINEST

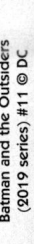

Batman and the Outsiders (2019 series) #11 © DC

Batman Beyond (2016 series) #38 © DC

Batman: Black & White (2021 series) #1 © DC

	GD	VG	FN	VF	VF/NM	NM-
	2.0	4.0	6.0	8.0	9.0	9.2

DC Comics: Apr, 1999 - No. 10, Jan, 2000 ($4.95/$1.99, limited series)

1,10-($4.95, squarebound) Taylor-a 5.00
2-9-($1.99) 5-Batgirl app. 8-Catwoman-c/app. 3.00
TPB (2003, $19.95) r/#1-10 20.00

BATMAN AND THE OUTSIDERS (The Adventures of the Outsiders #33 on)
(Also see Brave & The Bold #200 & The Outsiders) (Replaces The Brave and the Bold)
DC Comics: Aug, 1983 - No. 32, Apr, 1986 (Mando paper #5 on)

1-Batman, Halo, Geo-Force, Katana, Metamorpho & Black Lightning begin
2 4 6 8 11 14
2-32: 5-New Teen Titans x-over. 9-Halo begins. 11,12-Origin Katana. 18-More info on Metamorpho's origin. 28-31-Lookers origin. 32-Team disbands 4.00
Annual 1,2 (9/84, 9/85): 2-Metamorpho & Sapphire Stagg wed 5.00
NOTE: ***Aparo** a-1-9, 11-13p, 16-20; c-1-4, 5i, 6-21, Annual 1, 2. **B. Kane** a-3r. **Layton** a-19i, 20i. **Lopez** a-3p. **Miller** c-Annual 1. **Perez** c-5p. **B. Willingham** a-14p.*

BATMAN AND THE OUTSIDERS (Continues as The Outsiders for #15-39)
DC Comics: Dec, 2007 - No. 14, Feb, 2009; No. 40, Jul, 2011 ($2.99)

1-14: 1-Batman, Catwoman, Martian Manhunter, Katana, Metamorpho, Thunder & Grace begin. 4-Batgirl joins. 11-13-Batman R.I.P. 3.00
40 (7/11) Final issue; Didio-s/Tan-a; history of the team 3.00
... Special (3/09, $3.99) Alfred assembles a new team; Andy Kubert-a; two covers 4.00
...: The Chrysalis TPB (2008, $14.99) r/#1-5 15.00
...: The Snare TPB (2008, $14.99) r/#6-10 15.00

BATMAN & THE OUTSIDERS
DC Comics: Jul, 2019 - No. 17, Dec, 2020 ($3.99)

1-17: 1-Batman, Black Lightning, Katana, The Signal and Orphan team; Hill-s/Soy-a 4.00
Annual 1 (12/19, $4.99) Max Raynor-a; spotlight on Katana 5.00

BATMAN & THE SIGNAL
DC Comics: Mar, 2018 - No. 3, Jun, 2018 ($3.99)

1-3-Batman and Duke Thomas; Hamner-a 4.00

BATMAN: ARKHAM CITY (Prequel to the video game)
DC Comics: Early Jul, 2011 - No. 5, Oct, 2011 ($2.99, limited series)

1-5-Dini-s/D'Anda-a; Joker app. 3.00
...: End Game (1/13, $6.99) Story bridges Arkham City and Arkham Unhinged series 7.00

BATMAN: ARKHAM KNIGHT (Prequel to the Arkham video game trilogy finale)
DC Comics: May, 2015 - No. 12, Feb, 2016 ($3.99)

1-Tomasi-s/Bogdanovic-a/Panosian-c; 1st comic app. of Arkham Knight 6.00
2-12: 2-Harley Quinn cover 4.00
Annual 1 (11/15, $4.99) Tomasi-s/Segovia-a; Firefly app. 5.00
...: Robin 1 (1/16, $2.99) Tomasi-s/Rocha-a 3.00

BATMAN: ARKHAM KNIGHT: GENESIS
DC Comics: Oct, 2015 - No. 6 ($2.99, limited series)

1-4: 1-Tomasi-s/Borges-a/Sejic-c; Jason Todd's origin. 4-Harley Quinn cover 3.00

BATMAN: ARKHAM UNHINGED (Based on the Batman: Arkham City video game)
DC Comics: Jun, 2012 - No. 20, Jan, 2014 ($2.99)

1-20: 1-Wilkins-c; Catwoman, Two-Face & Hugo Strange app. 3.00

BATMAN: BANE OF THE DEMON
DC Comics: Mar, 1998 - No. 4, June, 1998 ($1.95, limited series)

1-4-Dixon-s/Nolan-a; prelude to Legacy x-over 4.00

BATMAN: BATTLE FOR THE COWL (Follows Batman R.I.P. storyline)
DC Comics: May, 2009 - No. 3, Jul, 2009 ($3.99, limited series)

1-3-Tony Daniel-s/a/c; 2 covers on each 4.00
...: Arkham Asylum (6/09, $2.99) Hine-s/Haun-a/Ladronn-c 3.00
...: Commissioner Gordon (5/09, $2.99) Mandrake-a/Ladronn-c; Mr. Freeze app. 3.00
...: Man-Bat (6/09, $2.99) Harris-s/Calafiore-a/Ladronn-c; Dr. Phosphorus app. 3.00
...: The Network (7/09, $2.99) Nicieza-s/Calafiore & Kramer-a/Ladronn-c 3.00
...: The Underground (6/09, $2.99) Yost-s/Raimondi-a/Ladronn-c; Harley Quinn app. 3.00
Companion SC (2009, $14.99) r/ five one-shots 15.00
HC (2009, $19.99) r/#1-3 & Gotham Gazette: Batman Dead & Gotham Gazette: Batman Alive; gallery of variant covers and sketch art 20.00
SC (2010, $14.99) same contents as HC 15.00

BATMAN BEYOND (Based on animated series)
DC Comics: Mar, 1999 - No. 6, Aug, 1999 ($1.99, limited series)

	GD	VG	FN	VF	VF/NM	NM-
1-Adaptation of pilot episode, Timm-c	12	24	36	82	179	275
2-Adaptation of pilot episode cont., Timm-c	4	8	12	23	37	50
3	3	6	9	19	30	40
4-6: 4-Darwyn Cooke-c; The Demon app.	2	4	6	8	11	14
TPB (1999, $9.95) r/#1-6						15.00

BATMAN BEYOND (Based on animated series)(Continuing series)
DC Comics: Nov, 1999 - No. 24, Oct, 2001 ($1.99)

	GD	VG	FN	VF	VF/NM	NM-
1-Rousseau-a; Batman vs. Batman	2	4	6	8	11	14
2,3,5-24: 14-Demon-c/app. 21,22-Justice League Unlimited-c/app.						6.00
4-1st app. Melanie Walker/Ten (Royal Flush Gang)	4	8	12	23	37	50
...: Return of the Joker (2/01, $2.95) adaptation of video release	4	8	12	23	37	50

BATMAN BEYOND (Animated series)(See Superman/Batman Annual #4)
DC Comics: Aug, 2010 - No. 6, Jan, 2011 ($2.99, limited series)

	GD	VG	FN	VF	VF/NM	NM-
1-Benjamin-a; Nguyen-c; return of Hush	1	3	4	6	8	10
1-Variant-c by J.H. Williams III	2	4	6	8	10	12
2-6						4.00
...: Hush Beyond TPB (2011, $14.99) r/#1-6						15.00

BATMAN BEYOND
DC Comics: Mar, 2011 - No. 8, Oct, 2011 ($2.99)

1-8: 1-3-Justice League app.; Beechen-s/Benjamin-a/Nguyen-c. 8-Inque app. 4.00
1-Variant-c by Darwyn Cooke 5.00

BATMAN BEYOND (Tim Drake as Batman)
DC Comics: Aug, 2015 - No. 16, Nov. 2016 ($2.99)

1-16: 1-Jurgens-s/Chang-a. 2-Inque app. 5-New suit. 7,16-Stephen Thompson-a. 10-Tuftan app. 11-Superman's son app. 12-Tan-a. 16-Terry McGinnis back as Batman 3.00

BATMAN BEYOND (DC Rebirth)
DC Comics: Dec, 2016 - No. 50, Feb, 2021 ($2.99/$3.99)

1-6: 1-3,6-Dan Jurgens-s/Bernard Chang-a. 4,5-Pete Woods-a 3.00
7-24,26-50-($3.99) 8-11,44-47-Damian app. 22-24-New Scarecrow. 26-30-Joker app. 36-Flash app. 37-Intro. new Batwoman. 40-Batwoman ID revealed; Dick Grayson app. 48,49-Booster Gold app. 50-Wonder Woman & Inque app. 4.00
25-($4.99) Jurgens-s/Hamner-a; Joker app. 5.00
...: Rebirth 1 (11/16, $2.99) Terry McGinnis in the suit; Jurgens-s/Sook-a 3.00

BATMAN BEYOND UNIVERSE
DC Comics: Oct, 2013 - No. 16, Jan, 2015 ($3.99)

1-12: 1-Superman & the JLB app.; Sean Murphy-c. 8-12-Wonder Woman app. 9-12-Justice Lords app. 13,14-Phantasm returns. 15-Royal Flush Gang app. 4.00

BATMAN BEYOND UNLIMITED
DC Comics: Apr, 2012 - No. 18, Sept, 2013 ($3.99)

1-18: 1-Beechen-s/Breyfogle-a; Superman & Justice League back-ups; Nguyen-c. 17-Metal Men return; Marvel Family app. 18-New Batgirl 4.00

BATMAN: BLACK & WHITE
DC Comics: June, 1996 - No. 4, Sept, 1996 ($2.95, B&W, limited series)

1-Stories by McKeever, Timm, Kubert, Chaykin, Goodwin; Jim Lee-c; Allred inside front-c; Mœbius inside back-c 4.00
2-4: 2-Stories by Simonson, Corben, Bisley & Gaiman; Miller-c. 3-Stories by M. Wagner, Janson, Sienkiewicz, O'Neil & Kristiansen; B. Smith-c; Russell inside front-c; Silvestri inside back-c. 4-Stories by Bolland, Goodwin & Gianni, Strnad & Nowlan, O'Neil & Stelfreeze; Toth-c; pin-ups by Neal Adams & Alex Ross 3.00
Hardcover ('97, $39.95) r/series w/new art & cover plate 40.00
Softcover ('00, $19.95) r/series 20.00
Volume 2 HC ('02, $39.95, 7 3/4"x12") r/B&W back-up-s from Batman: Gotham Knights #1-16; stories and art by various incl. Ross, Buscema, Byrne, Ellison, Sale; Mignola-c 40.00
Volume 2 SC ('03, $19.95, 7 3/4"x12") same contents as HC 20.00
Volume 2 SC ('08, $19.99, reg. size) same contents as HC 20.00
Volume 3 HC ('07, $24.99, reg. size) r/B&W back-up-s from Batman: Gotham Knights #17-49; stories and art by various incl. Davis, DeCarlo, Morse, Schwartz, Thompson; Miller-c 25.00

BATMAN: BLACK & WHITE
DC Comics: Nov, 2013 - No. 6, Apr, 2014 ($4.99, B&W, limited series)

1-6-Short story anthology by various. 1-Silvestri-c; Neal Adams-a. 2-Steranko-c; Nino-a. 3-Bermejo-s/a. 4-Conner-c; Allred-s/a. 6-Mahnke-c; Hughes, Cloonan, Chiang-a 5.00

BATMAN: BLACK & WHITE
DC Comics: Jan, 2021 - No. 6 ($5.99, B&W, limited series)

1-3-Short story anthology by various. 1-Dini-s/Kubert-a; JH Williams III-s/a. 2-King-s/Gerads-a. 3-Future State Batman by Ridley-s/Coipel-a; Bengal-s/a; Kelley Jones-a 6.00

BATMAN: BOOK OF THE DEAD
DC Comics: Jun, 1999 - No. 2, July, 1999 ($4.95, limited series, prestige format)

1,2-Elseworlds; Kitson-a 8.00

BATMAN CACOPHONY
DC Comics: Jan, 2009 - No. 3, Mar, 2009 ($3.99, limited series)

1-3-Kevin Smith-s/Walt Flanagan-a; Joker and Onomatoapoeia app.; Adam Kubert-c 4.00

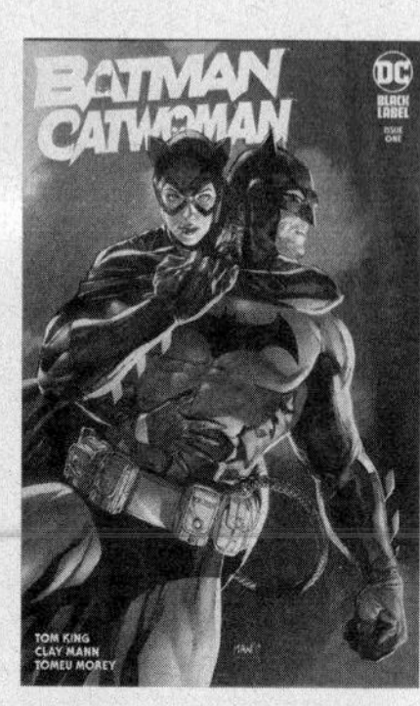

Batman / Catwoman #1 © DC

Batman Eternal #27 © DC

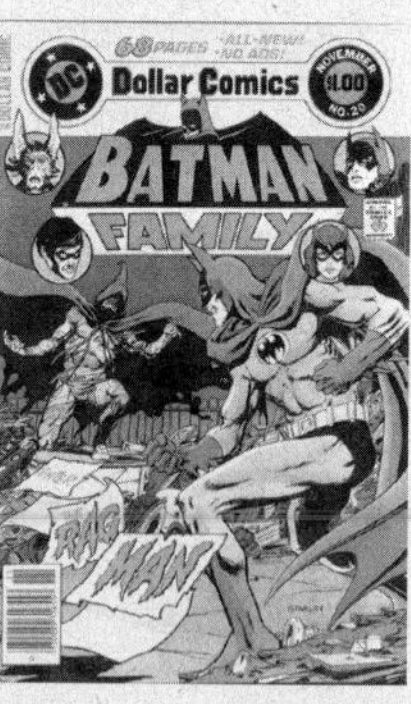

Batman Family #20 © DC

	GD 2.0	VG 4.0	FN 6.0	VF 8.0	VF/NM 9.0	NM- 9.2
1-3-Variant-c by Sienkiewicz						15.00
HC (2009, $19.99, d.j.) r/#1-3; Kevin Smith intro.; script for #3, cover gallery						20.00
SC (2010, $14.99) r/#1-3; Kevin Smith intro.; script for #3, cover gallery						15.00

BATMAN / CATWOMAN
DC Comics (Black Label): Feb, 2021 - Present ($4.99)

1-3-King-s/Mann-a; Andrea Beaumont and The Joker app. 3-Intro. Helena Wayne — 5.00

BATMAN: CATWOMAN DEFIANT (See Batman one-shots)

BATMAN/ CATWOMAN: TRAIL OF THE GUN
DC Comics: 2004 - No. 2, 2004 ($5.95, limited series, prestige format)

1,2-Elseworlds; Van Sciver-a/Nocenti-s — 8.00

BATMAN CHRONICLES, THE (See the Batman TPB listings for the Golden Age reprint series that shares this title)
DC Comics: Summer, 1995 - No. 23, Winter, 2001 ($2.95, quarterly)

	GD 2.0	VG 4.0	FN 6.0	VF 8.0	VF/NM 9.0	NM- 9.2
1-3,5-19: 1-Dixon/Grant/Moench script. 3-Bolland-c. 5-Oracle Year One story, Richard Dragon app., Chaykin-c. 6-Kaluta-c; Ra's al Ghul story. 7-Superman-c/app.11-Paul Pope-s/a. 12-Cataclysm pt. 10. 18-No Man's Land						5.00
4-Hitman story by Ennis, Contagion tie-in; Balent-c	2	4	6	9	12	15
20,22,23: 20-Catwoman and Relative Heroes-c/app.						4.00
21-Brian Michael Bendis-s (1st for DC)/Gaydos-a; Giordano-a; Pander Bros.-a/c						6.00
...Gallery (3/97, $3.50) Pin-ups						4.00
...Gauntlet, The (1997, $4.95, one-shot)						6.00

BATMAN: CITY OF LIGHT
DC Comics: Dec, 2003 - No. 8, July, 2004 ($2.95, limited series)

1-8-Pander Brothers-a/s; Paniccia-s — 3.00

BATMAN CONFIDENTIAL
DC Comics: Feb, 2007 - No. 54, May, 2011 ($2.99)

	NM- 9.2
1-49,51-54: 1-6-Diggle-s/Portacio-a/c. 7-12-Cowan-a; Joker's origin. 13-16-Morales-a. 17-21-Batgirl vs. Catwoman; Maguire-a. 22-25-McDaniel-a; Joker app. 26-28-King Tut app.; Garcia-Lopez-a. 40-43-Kieth-s/a. 44-48-Mandrake-a/c	3.00
50-($4.99) Bingham-a; back-up Silver Age-style JLA story	5.00
...: Dead to Rights SC (2010, $14.99) r/#22-25,29,30	15.00
...: Lovers and Madmen HC (2008, $24.99, dustjacket) r/#7-12; Brad Meltzer intro.	25.00
...: Lovers and Madmen SC (2009, $14.99) r/#7-12; Brad Meltzer intro.	15.00
...: Rules of Engagement HC (2007, $24.99, dustjacket) r/#1-6	25.00
...: The Bat and the Beast SC (2010, $12.99) r/#31-35	13.00
...: The Cat and the Bat SC (2009, $12.99) r/#17-21	13.00
...: Vs. The Undead SC (2010, $14.99) r/#44-48	15.00

BATMAN: CREATURE OF THE NIGHT
DC Comics: Jan, 2018 - No. 4, Jan, 2020 ($5.99, squarebound, limited series)

1-4-Kurt Busiek-s/John Paul Leon-a; story of Bruce Wainwright — 6.00

BATMAN: CURSE OF THE WHITE KNIGHT (Sequel to Batman: White Knight series)
DC Comics (Black Label): Sept, 2019 - No. 8, May, 2020 ($4.99, limited series)

1-8-Sean Murphy-s/a; flashbacks to 1685 Edmond Wayne in Gotham; Azrael returns — 6.00

BATMAN: DAMNED
DC Comics (Black Label): Nov, 2018 - No. 3, Aug, 2019 ($6.99, squarebound, oversized, limited series)

	NM- 9.2
1-Azzarello-s/Bermejo-a/c; Constantine & Deadman app.; nudity	35.00
1-Variant cover by Jim Lee	40.00
2,3-Harley Quinn, Constantine & Deadman app.; covers by Bermejo & Lee	10.00

BATMAN: DARK DETECTIVE
DC Comics: Early July, 2005 - No. 6, Late September, 2005 ($2.99, limited series)

	GD 2.0	VG 4.0	FN 6.0	VF 8.0	VF/NM 9.0	NM- 9.2
1-Englehart-s/Rogers & Austin-a; Silver St. Cloud and The Joker app.; Joker-c	1	3	4	6	8	10
2-6						4.00

BATMAN: DARK KNIGHT OF THE ROUND TABLE
DC Comics: 1999 - No. 2, 1999 ($4.95, limited series, prestige format)

1,2-Elseworlds; Giordano-a — 7.00

BATMAN: DARK VICTORY
DC Comics: 1999 - No. 13, 2000 ($4.95/$2.95, limited series)

	NM- 9.2
Wizard #0 Preview	3.00
1-($4.95) Loeb-s/Sale-c/a	5.00
2-12-($2.95)	3.00
13-($4.95)	5.00
Hardcover (2001, $29.95) with dust jacket; r/#0,1-13	30.00
Softcover (2002, $19.95) r/#0,1-13	20.00

BATMAN: DEATH AND THE MAIDENS
DC Comics: Oct, 2003 - No. 9, Aug, 2004 ($2.95, limited series)

	NM- 9.2
1-Ra's al Ghul app.; Rucka-s/Janson-a	4.00
2-9: 9-Ra's al Ghul dies	3.00
TPB (2004, $19.95) r/#1-9 & Detective #783	20.00

BATMAN/ DEATHBLOW: AFTER THE FIRE
DC Comics/WildStorm: 2002 - No. 3, 2002 ($5.95, limited series)

	NM- 9.2
1-3-Azzarello-s/Bermejo & Bradstreet-a	6.00
TPB (2003, $12.95) r/#1-3; plus concept art	13.00

BATMAN: DEATH MASK
DC Comics/CMX: Jun, 2008 - No. 4, Sept, 2008 ($2.99, B&W, lim. series, right-to-left manga style)

	NM- 9.2
1-4-Yoshinori Natsume-s/a	3.00
TPB (2008, $9.99, digest size) r/#1-4; interview with Yoshinori Natsume	10.00

BATMAN ETERNAL (Also see Arkham Manor series)
DC Comics: Jun, 2014 - No. 52, Jun, 2015 ($2.99, weekly series)

	NM- 9.2
1-Snyder-s/Fabok-a; Professor Pyg & Jason Bard app.	5.00
2-51: 2-Carmine Falcone returns. 3-Stephanie Brown app. 6,14-17,26,29,30,37-Joker's Daughter app. 20-Spoiler dons costume. 30-Arkham Asylum destroyed. 41-Bluebird in costume	3.00
52-($3.99) Jae Lee-c; art by various	4.00

BATMAN: EUROPA
DC Comics: Jan, 2016 - No. 4, Apr, 2016 ($4.99, limited series)

	NM- 9.2
1-4: 1-Joker app.; Casali & Azzarello-a/Camuncoli & Jim Lee-a. 2-Camuncoli-a	5.00
... Director's Cut 1 (8/16, $5.99) r/#1 with Jim Lee's pencil art; bonus original script	6.00

BATMAN FAMILY, THE
National Periodical Pub./DC Comics: Sept-Oct, 1975 - No. 20, Oct-Nov, 1978
(#1-4, 17-on: 68 pgs.) (Combined with Detective Comics with No. 481)

	GD 2.0	VG 4.0	FN 6.0	VF 8.0	VF/NM 9.0	NM- 9.2
1-Origin/2nd app. Batgirl-Robin team-up (The Dynamite Duo); reprints plus one new story begins; N. Adams-a(r); r/1st app. Man-Bat from Det. #400	5	10	15	30	50	70
2-5: 2-r/Det. #369. 3-Batgirl & Robin learn each's i.d.; r/Batwoman app. from Batman #105. 4-r/1st Fatman app. from Batman #113. 5-r/1st Bat-Hound app. from Batman #92	3	6	9	16	23	30
6-(7-8/76) Joker's daughter on cover (1st app.)	7	14	21	49	92	135
7,8,14-16: 8-r/Batwoman app.14-Batwoman app. 15-3rd app. Killer Moth. 16-Bat-Girl cameo (last app. in costume until New Teen Titans #47)	2	4	6	13	18	22
9-Joker's daughter-c/app.	5	10	15	33	57	80
10-1st revival Batwoman; Cavalier app.; Killer Moth app.	3	6	9	18	28	38
11-13,17-20: 11-13-Rogers-a(p): 11-New stories begin; Man-Bat begins. 13-Batwoman cameo. 17-($1.00 size)-Batman, Huntress begin; Batwoman & Catwoman 1st meet. 18-20: Huntress by Staton in all. 20-Origin Ragman retold	3	6	9	17	26	35

NOTE: ***Aparo*** *a-17; c-11-16.* ***Austin*** *a-12i.* ***Chaykin*** *a-14p.* ***Michael Golden*** *a-15-17,18-20p.* ***Grell*** *a-1; c-1.* ***Gil Kane*** *a-2r.* ***Kaluta*** *c-17, 19.* ***Newton*** *a-13.* ***Robinson*** *a-1r, 3i(r), 9r.* ***Russell*** *a-18i, 19i.* ***Starlin*** *a-17; c-18, 20.*

BATMAN: FAMILY
DC Comics: Dec, 2002 - No. 8, Feb, 2003 ($2.95/$2.25, weekly limited series)

	NM- 9.2
1,8-($2.95): 1-John Francis Moore-s/Hoberg & Gaudiano-a	5.00
2-7-($2.25): 3-Orpheus & Black Canary app.	3.00

BATMAN: GATES OF GOTHAM
DC Comics: Jul, 2011 - No. 5, Late Oct, 2011 ($2.99, limited series)

1-5-Flashbacks to 1880s Gotham City; Snyder-s/Higgins-a — 4.00

BATMAN: GCPD
DC Comics: Aug, 1996 - No. 4, Nov, 1996 ($2.25, limited series)

1-4: Features Jim Gordon; Aparo/Sienkiewicz-a — 4.00

BATMAN GIANT (See reprint of new stories in Batman Universe)
DC Comics: 2018 - No. 14, 2019 ($4.99, 100 pgs., squarebound, Walmart exclusive)

	NM- 9.2
1-New story Palmiotti-s/Zircher-a; reprints from Batman #608 (Hush), Nightwing ('11), and Harley Quinn ('14) in all	10.00
2,3,5-14: 2-Palmiotti-s/Zircher-a plus reprints. 3-Bendis-s/Derrington-a begins plus reprints. 8-Green Lantern & Jonah Hex app. in new story; Batgirl reprints replace Harley Quinn	5.00
4-Debut of Ginny Hex (Young Justice) in new story; Bendis-s/Derrington-a	8.00

BATMAN GIANT
DC Comics: 2019 - Present ($4.99, 100 pgs., squarebound, Mass Market & Direct Market editions exist for each issue, with different covers)

1-3-Two new stories and reprints in each. 1-Batwoman vs. Lord Death Man — 5.00

BATMAN: GORDON OF GOTHAM
DC Comics: June, 1998 - No. 4, Sept, 1998 ($1.95, limited series)

1-4: Gordon's early days in Chicago — 4.00

BATMAN: GORDON'S LAW

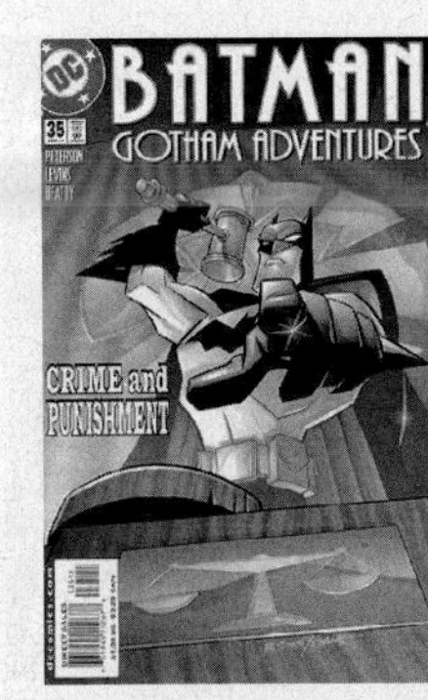

Batman: Gotham Adventures #35 © DC

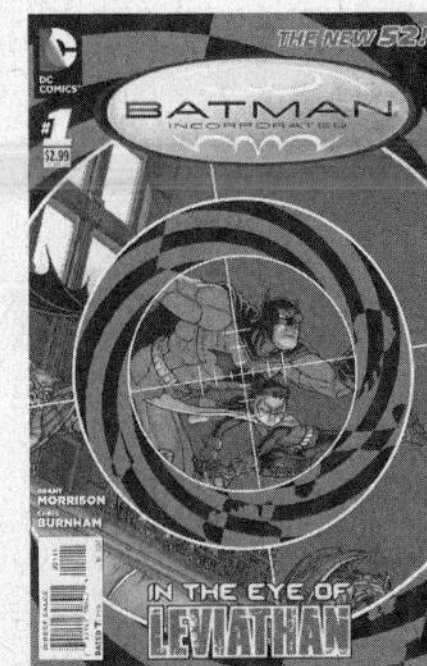

Batman Incorporated #1 © DC

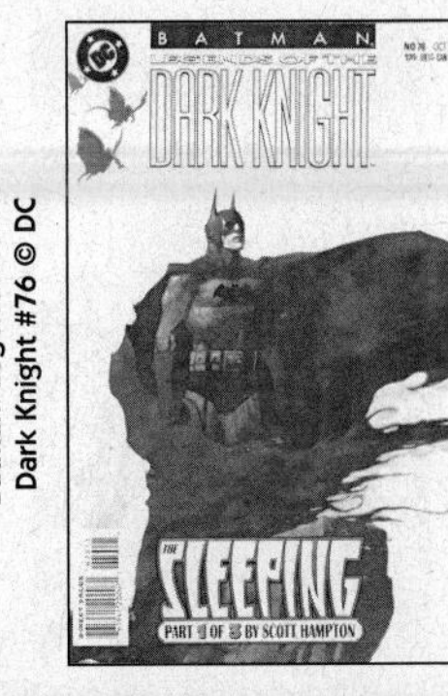

Batman: Legends of the Dark Knight #76 © DC

	GD 2.0	VG 4.0	FN 6.0	VF 8.0	VF/NM 9.0	NM- 9.2

DC Comics: Dec, 1996 - No. 4, Mar, 1997 ($1.95, limited series)

1-4: Dixon-s/Janson-c/a 4.00

BATMAN: GOTHAM ADVENTURES (Based on Kids WB Batman animated series)
DC Comics: June, 1998 - No. 60, May, 2003 ($2.95/$1.95/$1.99/$2.25)

1-($2.95) 2 4 6 11 16 20
2-3-($1.95): 2-Two-Face-c/app. 5.00
4-9,11-13,15-28: 4-Begin $1.99-c. 5-Deadman-c. 13-MAD #1 cover swipe 4.00
10,14-Harley Quinn c/app. 2 4 6 11 16 20
29,43-Harley Quinn c/app. 2 4 6 11 16 20
30,32-42,44,46-52,54-59: 50-Catwoman-c/app. 58-Creeper-c/app. 4.00
31-Joker-c/app. 6.00
45-Harley Quinn c/app. 3 6 9 16 24 35
53-Poison Ivy-c/app.; Harley Quinn cameo 2 4 6 9 12 15
60-Joker-c/app. 2 4 6 11 16 20
TPB (2000, $9.95) r/#1-6 24.00

BATMAN: GOTHAM AFTER MIDNIGHT
DC Comics: July, 2008 - No. 12, Jun, 2009 ($2.99, limited series)

1-12-Steve Niles-s/Kelley Jones-a/c. 1-Scarecrow app. 2-Man-Bat app. 5,6-Joker app. 4.00
TPB (2009, $19.99) r/#1-12; John Carpenter intro.; Jones sketch pages 20.00

BATMAN: GOTHAM COUNTY LINE
DC Comics: 2005 - No. 3, 2005 ($5.99, square-bound, limited series)

1-3-Steve Niles-s/Scott Hampton-a. 2,3-Deadman app. 6.00
TPB (2006, $17.99) r/#1-3 18.00

BATMAN: GOTHAM KNIGHTS
DC Comics: Mar, 2000 - No. 74, Apr, 2006 ($2.50/$2.75)

1-Grayson-s; B&W back-up by Warren Ellis & Jim Lee 6.00
2-10-Grayson-s; B&W back-ups by various. 6-Killing Joke flashback 3.00
11-($3.25) Bolland-c; Kyle Baker back-up story 4.00
12-24: 13-Officer Down x-over; Ellison back-up-s. 15-Colan back-up. 20-Superman-c/app. 3.00
25,26-Bruce Wayne: Murderer pt. 4,10 3.50
27-31: 28,30,31-Bruce Wayne: Fugitive pt. 7,14,17 3.00
32-49: 32-Begin $2.75-c; Kaluta-a back-up. 33,34-Bane-c/app. 35-Mahfood-a back-up. 38-Bolton-a back-up. 43-Jason Todd & Batgirl app. 44-Jason Todd flashback 3.00
50-54-Hush returns-Barrionuevo-a/Bermejo-c. 53,54-Green Arrow app. 4.00
55-($3.75) Batman vs. Hush; Joker & Riddler app. 5.00
56-74: 56-58-War Games; Jae Lee-c. 60-65-Hush app. 66-Villains United tie-in; Talia app. 3.00
Batman: Hush Returns TPB (2006, $12.99) r/#50-55,66; cover gallery 13.00

BATMAN: GOTHAM NIGHTS II (First series listed under Gotham Nights)
DC Comics: Mar, 1995 - No. 4, June, 1995 ($1.95, limited series)

1-4 4.00

BATMAN/GRENDEL (1st limited series)
DC Comics: 1993 - No. 2, 1993 ($4.95, limited series, squarebound; 52 pgs.)

1,2: Batman vs. Hunter Rose. 1-Devil's Riddle; Matt Wagner-c/a/scripts. 2-Devil's Masque; Matt Wagner-c/a/scripts 7.00

BATMAN/GRENDEL (2nd limited series)
DC Comics: June, 1996 - No. 2, July, 1996 ($4.95, limited series, squarebound)

1,2: Batman vs. Grendel Prime. 1-Devil's Bones. 2-Devil's Dance; Wagner-c/a/s 6.00

BATMAN: HARLEY & IVY
DC Comics: Jun, 2004 - No. 3, Aug, 2004 ($2.50, limited series)

1-Paul Dini-s/Bruce Timm-c/a in all 3 6 9 20 31 42
2,3 3 6 9 14 20 26
TPB (2007, $14.99) r/series; newly colored story from Batman: Gotham Knights #14 and Harley and Ivy: Love on the Lam series 20.00

BATMAN: HARLEY QUINN
DC Comics: 1999 ($5.95, prestige format)

1-Intro. of Harley Quinn into regular DC continuity; Dini-s/Alex Ross-c 8 16 24 51 96 140
1-(2nd printing) 4 8 12 27 44 60

BATMAN: HAUNTED GOTHAM
DC Comics: 2000 - No. 4, 2000 ($4.95, limited series, squarebound)

1-4-Doug Moench-s/Kelley Jones-c/a 6.00
TPB (2009, $19.99) r/#1-4 20.00

BATMAN/ HELLBOY/STARMAN
DC Comics/Dark Horse: Jan, 1999 - No. 2, Feb, 1999 ($2.50, limited series)

1,2: Robinson-s/Mignola-a. 2-Harris-c 6.00

BATMAN: HOLLYWOOD KNIGHT
DC Comics: Apr, 2001 - No. 3, Jun, 2001 ($2.50, limited series)

1-3-Elseworlds Batman as a 1940's movie star; Giordano-a/Layton-s 3.00

BATMAN/ HUNTRESS: CRY FOR BLOOD
DC Comics: Jun, 2000 - No. 6, Nov, 2000 ($2.50, limited series)

1-6: Rucka-s/Burchett-a; The Question app. 3.00
TPB (2002, $12.95) r/#1-6 13.00

BATMAN, INC.
DC Comics: Jan, 2011 - No. 8, Aug, 2011 ($3.99/$2.99)

1-3-Morrison-s/Paquette-a; covers by Paquette & Williams 4.00
4-8-($2.99) 4-Burnham-a, original Batwoman (Kathy Kane) app. 3.00
...: Leviathan Strikes (2/12, $6.99) Morrison-s/Burnham & Stewart-a; cover gallery 7.00

BATMAN INCORPORATED
DC Comics: Jul, 2012 - No. 13, Sept, 2013 ($2.99)

1-7-Morrison-s/Burnham-a/c. 2-Origin of Talia. 3-Matches Malone returns 3.00
1-Variant-c by Quitely 5.00
8-Death of Damian 5.00
9-13: 9,10,12,13-Morrison-s/Burnham-a/c 3.00
#0 (11/12, $2.99) Frazer Irving-a; the start of Batman Incorporated 3.00
... Special 1 (10/13, $4.99) Short stories about international Batmen; s/a by various 5.00

BATMAN: JEKYLL & HYDE
DC Comics: June, 2005 - No. 6, Nov, 2005 ($2.99, limited series)

1-6-Paul Jenkins-s; Two-Face app. 1-3-Jae Lee-a. 4-6-Sean Phillips-a 3.00
TPB (2008, $14.99) r/#1-6 15.00

BATMAN: JOKER TIME (...: It's Joker Time! on cover)
DC Comics: 2000 - No. 3 ($4.95, limited series, squarebound)

1-3-Bob Hall-s/a 6.00

BATMAN: JOURNEY INTO KNGHT
DC Comics: Oct, 2005 - No. 12, Nov, 2006 ($2.50/$2.99, limited series)

1-9-Andrew Helfer-s/Tan Eng Huat-a/Pat Lee-c 3.00
10-12-($2.99) Joker app. 3.00

BATMAN/ JUDGE DREDD "DIE LAUGHING"
DC Comics: 1998 - No. 2, 1999 ($4.95, limited series, squarebound)

1,2: 1-Fabry-c/a. 2-Jim Murray-c/a 1 2 3 5 6 8

BATMAN: KINGS OF FEAR
DC Comics: Oct, 2018 - No. 6, Mar, 2019 ($3.99, limited series)

1-6-Scott Peterson-s/Kelley Jones-a; Scarecrow app. 4.00

BATMAN: KNIGHTGALLERY (See Batman one-shots)

BATMAN: LAST KNIGHT ON EARTH
DC Comics: Jul, 2019 - No. 3, Feb, 2020 ($5.99, limited series, squarebound)

1-3-Snyder-s/Capullo-a 6.00

BATMAN: LEAGUE OF BATMEN
DC Comics: 2001 - No. 2, 2001 ($5.95, limited series, squarebound)

1,2-Elseworlds; Moench-s/Bright & Tanghal-a/Van Fleet-c 6.00

BATMAN: LEGENDS OF THE DARK KNIGHT (Legends of the Dark...#1-36)
DC Comics: Nov, 1989 - No. 214, Mar, 2007 ($1.50/$1.75/$1.95/$1.99/$2.25/$2.50/$2.99)

1- "Shaman" begins, ends #5; outer cover has four different color variations, all worth same 6.00
2-10: 6-10- "Gothic" by Grant Morrison (scripts) 4.00
11-15: 11-15-Gulacy/Austin-a. 13-Catwoman app. 4.00
16-Intro drug Bane uses; begin Venom story 6.00
17-20 5.00
21-49,51-63: 38-Bat-Mite-c/story. 46-49-Catwoman app. w/Heath-c/a. 51-Ragman app.; Joe Kubert-c. 59,60,61-Knightquest x-over. 62,63-KnightsEnd Pt. 4 & 10 3.00
50-($3.95, 68 pgs.)-Bolland embossed gold foil-c; Joker-c/story; pin-ups by Chaykin, Simonson, Williamson, Kaluta, Russell, others 2 4 6 9 12 15
64-99: 64-(9/94)-Begin $1.95-c. 71-73-James Robinson-s,Watkiss-c/a. 74,75-McKeever-c/a/s. 76-78-Scott Hampton-c/a/s. 81-Card insert. 83,84-Ellis-s. 85-Robinson-s. 91-93-Ennis-s. 94-Michael T. Gilbert-s/a. 3.00
100-($3.95) Alex Ross painted-c; gallery by various 5.00
101-115: 101-Ezquerra-a. 102-104-Robinson-s 3.00
116-No Man's Land stories begin; Huntress-c 4.00
117-119,121-126: 122-Harris-c 3.00
120-ID of new Batgirl revealed 2 4 6 8 10 12
127-131: Return to Legends stories; Green Arrow app. 3.00
132-199, 201-204: 132-136 ($2.25-c) Archie Goodwin-s/Rogers-a. 137-141-Gulacy-a. 142-145-Joker and Ra's al Ghul app. 146-148-Kitson-a. 158-Begin $2.50-c 169-171-Tony Harris-c/a. 182-184-War Games. 182-Bagged with Sky Captain CD 3.00
200-($4.99) Joker-c/app. 1 2 3 5 6 8

Batman: Li'l Gotham #2 © DC

The Batman's Grave #4 © DC

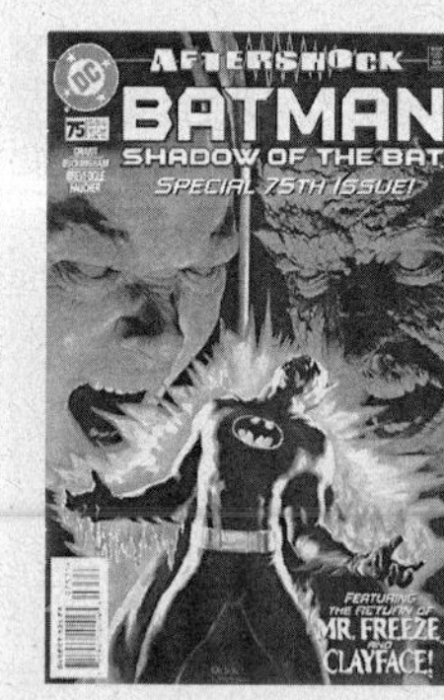

Batman: Shadow of the Bat #75 © DC

GD	VG	FN	VF	VF/NM	NM-
2.0	4.0	6.0	8.0	9.0	9.2

205-214: 205-Begin $2.99-c. 207,208-Olivetti-a. 214-Deadshot app. 3.00
#0-(10/94)-Zero Hour; Quesada/Palmiotti-c; released between #64&65 3.00
Annual 1-7 ('91-'97, $3.50-$3.95, 68 pgs.): 1-Joker app. 2-Netzer-c/a. 3-New Batman (Azrael) app. 4-Elseworlds story. 5-Year One; Man-Bat app. 6-Legend of the Dead Earth story. 7-Pulp Heroes story 4.00
... Halloween Special 1 (12/93, $6.95, 84 pgs.)-Embossed & foil stamped-c 1 2 3 5 6 8
... Halloween Special Edition 1 (12/14, giveaway) Sale-a/c 3.00
Batman Madness-...Halloween Special (1994, $4.95) 6.00
Batman Ghosts-...Halloween Special (1995, $4.95) 6.00
NOTE: ***Aparo*** *a-Annual 1.* ***Chaykin*** *scripts-24-26.* ***Giffen*** *a-Annual 1.* ***Golden*** *a-Annual 1.* ***Alan Grant*** *scripts-38, 52, 53.* ***Gil Kane*** *c/a-24-26.* ***Mignola*** *a-54; c-54, 62.* ***Morrow*** *a-Annual 3i.* ***Quesada*** *a-Annual 1.* ***James Robinson*** *scripts- 71-73.* ***Russell*** *c/a-42, 43.* ***Sears*** *a-21, 23; c-21, 23.* ***Zeck*** *a-69, 70; c-69, 70.*

BATMAN-LEGENDS OF THE DARK KNIGHT: JAZZ
DC Comics: Apr, 1995 - No. 3, June, 1995 ($2.50, limited series)
1-3 3.00

BATMAN: LI'L GOTHAM
DC Comics: Jun, 2013 - No. 12, May, 2014 ($2.99, printings of stories that 1st appeared online)
1-12-Dustin Nguyen-a/c; Nguyen & Fridolfs-s; holiday themed short stories 3.00
Halloween Comic Fest 2013 (12/13, no cover price) Halloween giveaway; r/#1 3.00

BATMAN/LOBO
DC Comics: Oct, 2007 - No. 2, Nov, 2007 ($5.99, squarebound, limited series)
1,2-Sam Kieth-s/a 1 2 3 5 6 8

BATMAN: LOST (Tie-in to Dark Nights: Metal series)
DC Comics: Jan, 2018 ($4.99, one-shot)
1-Snyder, Tynion IV & Williamson-s/Mahnke, Paquette & Jimenez-a; Coipel foil-c 5.00

BATMAN: MANBAT
DC Comics: Oct, 1995 - No. 3, Dec, 1995 ($4.95, limited series)
1-3-Elseworlds-Delano-script; Bolton-a 6.00
TPB-(1997, $14.95) r/#1-3 15.00

BATMAN: MITEFALL (See Batman one-shots)

BATMAN MINIATURE (See Batman Kellogg's)

BATMAN: NEVERMORE
DC Comics: June, 2003 - No. 5, Oct, 2003 ($2.50, limited series)
1-5-Elseworlds Batman & Edgar Allan Poe; Wrightson-c/Guy Davis-a/Len Wein-s 4.00

BATMAN: NO MAN'S LAND (Also see 1999 Batman titles)
DC Comics: (one shots)
nn (3/99, $2.95) Alex Ross-c; Bob Gale-s; begins year-long story arc 4.00
Collector's Ed. (3/99, $3.95) Ross lenticular-c 6.00
#0 (: Ground Zero on cover) (12/99, $4.95) Orbik-c 6.00
...: Gallery (7/99, $3.95) Jim Lee-c 4.00
...: Secret Files (12/99, $4.95) Maleev-c 6.00
TPB ('99, $12.95) r/early No Man's Land stories; new Batgirl early app. 13.00
No Law and a New Order TPB(1999, $5.95) Ross-c 8.00
Volume 2 ('00, $12.95) r/later No Man's Land stories; Batgirl(Huntress) app.; Deodato-c 13.00
Volume 3-5 ('00,'01 $12.95) 3-Intro. new Batgirl. 4-('00). 5-('01) Land-c 13.00

BATMAN: ODYSSEY
DC Comics: Sept, 2010 - No. 6, Feb, 2011 ($3.99, limited series)
1-6-Neal Adams-s/a/c. 1-Man-Bat app.; bonus sketch pages. 5,6-Joker app. 4.00
1-6-Variant B&W-version cover 5.00
Vol. 2 (12/11 - No. 7, 6/12) 1-7-Neal Adams-s/a/c 4.00

BATMAN: ORPHANS
DC Comics: Early Feb, 2011 - No. 2, Late Feb, 2011 ($3.99, limited series)
1,2-Berganza-s/Barberi-a/c 4.00

BATMAN: ORPHEUS RISING
DC Comics: Oct, 2001 - No. 5, Feb, 2002 ($2.50, limited series)
1-5-Intro. Orpheus; Simmons-s/Turner & Miki-a 3.00

BATMAN: OUTLAWS
DC Comics: 2000 - No. 3, 2000 ($4.95, limited series)
1-3-Moench-s/Gulacy-a 5.00

BATMAN: PENGUIN TRIUMPHANT (See Batman one-shots)

BATMAN/PREDATOR III: BLOOD TIES
DC Comics/Dark Horse Comics: Nov, 1997 - No. 4, Feb, 1998 ($1.95, lim. series)
1-4: Dixon-s/Damaggio-c/a 1 2 3 5 6 8
TPB-(1998, $7.95) r/#1-4 15.00

BATMAN: PRELUDE TO THE WEDDING
DC Comics: Jul, 2018 - Aug, 2018 ($3.99, series of one-shots)
...: Batgirl vs. Riddler 1 (8/18) Tim Seeley-s/Minkyu Jung-a 4.00
...: Harley Quinn vs. Joker 1 (8/18) Tim Seeley-s/Sami Basri-a; leads into Batman #48 4.00
...: Nightwing vs. Hush 1 (8/18) Tim Seeley-s/Travis Moore-a; Superman app. 4.00
...: Red Hood vs. Anarky 1 (8/18) Tim Seeley-s/Javier Fernandez-a; Joker app. 4.00
...: Robin vs. Ra's al Ghul 1 (7/18) Tim Seeley-s/Brad Walker-a; Selina Kyle app. 4.00

BATMAN/RA'S AL GHUL (See Year One:...)

BATMAN RETURNS MOVIE SPECIAL (See Batman one-shots)

BATMAN: RIDDLER-THE RIDDLE FACTORY (See Batman one-shots)

BATMAN: RUN, RIDDLER, RUN
DC Comics: 1992 - Book 3, 1992 ($4.95, limited series)
Book 1-3: Mark Badger-a & plot 6.00

BATMAN SCARECROW (See Year One:...)

BATMAN: SECRET FILES
DC Comics: Oct, 1997; Dec, 2018; Sept, 2019; Jun, 2020 ($4.95/$4.99)
1-New origin-s and profiles 6.00
1-(12/18, $4.99) Short stories by various; Detective Chimp app. 5.00
2-(9/19, $4.99) Short stories by various; Joker, Riddler, Bane, Hugo Strange app. 5.00
3-(6/20, $4.99) Short stories; Deathstroke, Cheshire, Merlyn, Mr. Teeth & Gunsmith 5.00

BATMAN: SECRETS
DC Comics: May, 2006 - No. 5, Sept, 2006 ($2.99, limited series)
1-5-Sam Kieth-s/a/c; Joker app. 3.00
TPB (2007, $12.99) r/series 13.00

BATMAN'S GRAVE, THE
DC Comics: Dec, 2019 - No. 12, Feb, 2021 ($3.99, limited series)
1-12-Warren Ellis-s/Bryan Hitch-a 4.00

BATMAN / SHADOW (Pulp hero)
DC Comics: June, 2017 - No. 6, Nov, 2017 ($3.99, limited series)
1-6: Snyder & Orlando-s/Rossmo-a; Lamont Cranston in current Gotham City 4.00

BATMAN: SHADOW OF THE BAT
DC Comics: June, 1992 - No. 94, Feb, 2000 ($1.50/$1.75/$1.95/$1.99)
1-The Last Arkham-c/story begins; 1st app. Victor Zsasz; Alan Grant scripts in all 2 4 6 9 12 15
1-($2.50)-Deluxe edition polybagged w/poster, pop-up & book mark 1 3 4 6 8 10
2-7: 4-The Last Arkham ends. 7-Last $1.50-c 4.00
8-28: 14,15-Staton-a(p). 16-18-Knightfall tie-ins. 19-28-Knightquest tie-ins w/Azrael as Batman. 25-Silver ink-c; anniversary issue 4.00
29-($2.95, 52 pgs.)-KnightsEnd Pt. 2 5.00
30-72: 30-KnightsEnd Pt. 8. 31-(9/94)-Begin $1.95-c; Zero Hour. 32-(11/94). 33-Robin-c. 35-Troika-Pt.2. 43,44-Cat-Man & Catwoman-c. 48-Contagion Pt. 1; card insert. 49-Contagion Pt.7. 56,57,58-Poison Ivy-c/app. 62-Two-Face app. 69,70-Fate app. 4.00
35-($2.95)-Variant embossed-c 5.00
73,74,76-78: Cataclysm x-over pts. 1,9. 76-78-Orbik-c 4.00
75-($2.95) Mr. Freeze & Clayface app.; Orbik-c 5.00
79,81,82: 79-Begin $1.99-c; Orbik-c 4.00
80-($3.95) Flip book with Azrael #47 5.00
83-No Man's Land; intro. new Batgirl (Huntress) 2 4 6 9 12 15
84,85-No Man's Land 5.00
86-92,94: 87-Deodato-a. 90-Harris-c. 92-Superman app. 94-No Man's Land ends 4.00
93-Joker and Harley app. 5.00
#0 (10/94) Zero Hour; released between #31&32 4.00
#1,000,000 (11/98) 853rd Century x-over; Orbik-c 4.00
Annual 1-5 ('93-'97 $2.95-$3.95, 68 pgs.): 3-Year One story; Poison Ivy app. 4-Legends of the Dead Earth story; Starman cameo. 5-Pulp Heroes story; Poison Ivy app. 5.00

BATMAN: SINS OF THE FATHER (Based on the Batman: The Telltale Series video game)
DC Comics: Apr, 2018 - No. 6, Sept, 2018 ($2.99, printing of digital first stories)
1-6-Gage-s/Ienco-a; Deadshot app. 3.00

BATMAN '66 (Characters and likenesses based on the 1966 television series)
DC Comics: Sept, 2013 - No. 30, Feb, 2016 ($3.99/$2.99, printings of stories that first appeared online)
1-Jeff Parker-s/Jonathan Case-a/Mike Allred-c; Riddler & Catwoman app. 1 3 4 6 8 10
1-Variant-c by Jonathan Case 2 4 6 8 10 12
1-San Diego Comic-Con variant action figure photo-c3 6 9 17 26 35
2-12: 2-Penguin & Mr. Freeze app.; Templeton-a. 3,11,20-Joker app. 5,10,11-Batgirl app. 8-King Tut app. 4.00
13-24,26-30: 14-Selfie variant-c. 16,20-Egghead app. 18,21,27,29-Batgirl app.

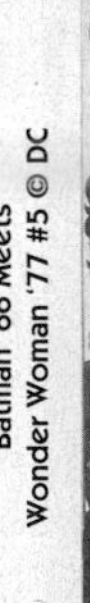

Batman '66 Meets Wonder Woman '77 #5 © DC

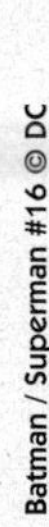

Batman / Superman #16 © DC

Batman: The Adventures Continue #5 © DC

GD 2.0 VG 4.0 FN 6.0 VF 8.0 VF/NM 9.0 NM- 9.2

21-Lord Death Man app. 22-Oeming-a. 26-Poison Ivy app. 27-Bane app. 30-Allred-a 3.00
25-1st app. The Harlequin; back-up Mad Men spoof with Batgirl 1 3 4 6 8 10
... Meets the Legion of Super-Heroes 1 (9/17, $3.99) Lee Allred-s/Mike Allred-a/c 4.00
... The Lost Episode 1 (1/15, $9.99) Harlan Ellison 1960s script adapted by Len Wein; García-López-a; Two-Face app.; covers by García-López & Ross; original pencil art 10.00

BATMAN '66 MEETS STEED AND MRS. PEEL (TV's The Avengers)
DC Comics: Sept, 2016 - No. 6, Feb, 2017 ($2.99, printings of stories that first appeared online)
1-6-Edginton-s/Dow Smith-a/Allred-c. 1,2-Catwoman app. 3-6-Mr. Freeze app. 3.00

BATMAN '66 MEETS THE GREEN HORNET
DC Comics: Aug, 2014 - No. 6, Jan, 2015 ($2.99, printings of stories that first appeared online)
1-6-Kevin Smith & Ralph Garman-s/Ty Templeton-a/Alex Ross-c 3.00

BATMAN '66 MEETS THE MAN FROM U.N.C.L.E.
DC Comics: Feb, 2016 - No. 6, Jul, 2016 ($2.99, limited series)
1-6-Jeff Parker-s/David Haun-a/Allred-c. 1-Olga and Penguin app. 3.00

BATMAN '66 MEETS WONDER WOMAN '77
DC Comics: Mar, 2017 - No. 6, Aug, 2017 ($3.99, limited series)
1-6-Parker & Andreyko-s/Haun-a; Ra's al Ghul & Talia app. 5,6-Robin as Nightwing 6.00

BATMAN: SON OF THE DEMON (Also see Batman #655-658 and Batman Hardcovers)
DC Comics: 2006 ($5.99, reprints the 1987 HC in comic book format)
nn-Talia has Batman's son; Mike W. Barr-s/Jerry Bingham-a; new Andy Kubert-c 6.00

BATMAN-SPAWN: WAR DEVIL (See Batman one-shots)

BATMAN SPECTACULAR (See DC Special Series No. 15)

BATMAN: STREETS OF GOTHAM (Follows Batman: Battle For The Cowl series)
DC Comics: Aug, 2009 - No. 21, May, 2011 ($3.99$2.99)
1-18: 1-Dini-s/Nguyen-a; back-up Manhunter feature; Jeanty-a. 10,11-Zsasz app. 4.00
19-21-($2.99) 19-Joker app. 3.00
...- Hush Money HC (2010, $19.99) r/#1-4, Detective #852 and Batman #685 20.00
...- Hush Money SC (2011, $14.99) r/#1-4, Detective #852 and Batman #685 15.00
...- Leviathan HC (2010, $19.99) r/#5-11 20.00
...- The House of Hush HC (2011, $22.99) r/#12-14,16-21 23.00

BATMAN STRIKES!, THE (Based on the 2004 animated series)
DC Comics: Nov, 2004 - No. 50, Dec, 2008 ($2.25)
1,2,4-27,29-31,33,34,36-38,40,42,44,46,48-50: 1,11-Penguin app. 2-Man-Bat app. 4-Bane app. 9-Joker app. 18-Batgirl debut. 29-Robin debuts. 33-Cal Ripken 8-pg. insert. 44-Superman app. 3.00
1-Free Comic Book Day edition (6/05) Penguin app. 3.00
3-($2.95) Joker-c/app.; Catwoman & Wonder Woman-r from Advs. in the DCU 4.00
28,32-Joker-c/app. 32-Cal Ripken 8-pg. insert. 5.00
35-Joker & Harley Quinn-c/app. 2 4 6 9 12 15
39,47-Black Mask-c/app. 6.00
41-Harley Quinn & Poison Ivy-c/app. 2 4 6 10 14 18
43-Harley Quinn-c/app. 2 4 6 9 12 15
45-Harley Quinn, Poison Ivy, Catwoman-c/app. 2 4 6 11 16 20
Jam Packed Action (2005, $7.99, digest) adaptations of two TV episodes 8.00
... Vol. 1: Crime Time (2005, $6.99, digest) r/#1-5 7.00
... Vol. 2: In Darkest Knight (2005, $6.99, digest) r/#6-10 7.00

BATMAN/ SUPERMAN
DC Comics: Aug, 2013 - No. 32, Jul, 2016 ($3.99)
1-4-Greg Pak-s/Jae Lee-a/c; Catwoman & Wonder Woman app. 4.00
3.1 (11/13, $2.99, regular cover) 3.00
3.1 (11/13, $3.99, 3-D cover) "Doomsday #1" on cover; Booth-a; Zod app. 6.00
5-7-Booth-a; reads sideways; Mongul app. 4.00
8,9-First Contact x-over with Worlds' Finest #20,21; Power Girl & Huntress app.; Lee-a 4.00
10-31: 11-Doomed tie-in. 13-Jae Lee-a. 13-15-Catwoman app. 17-Lobo app. 21-Batman (Gordon in robot suit). 23,24-Aquaman app. 25-27-Vandal Savage app. 4.00
32-The Great Ten app.; 1st app. Chinese Super-Man (Kong Kenan) 5.00
Annual 1 (5/14, $5.99) Supergirl, Krypto, Cyborg, Batgirl, Red Hood app.; Jae Lee-c 6.00
Annual 2 (5/15, $4.99) Killer Croc, Cheshire & Bane app.; Syaf-c 5.00
...: Futures End 1 (11/14, $2.99, regular-c) Five years later; Pak-s 3.00
...: Futures End 1 (11/14, $3.99, 3-D cover) 4.00

BATMAN/ SUPERMAN
DC Comics: Oct, 2019 - Present ($3.99)
1-15: 1-5-The Batman Who Laughs app.; Williamson-s/Marquez-a. 4-Acetate-c. 7,8-General Zod & Ra's al Ghul app. 9-11-Ultra-Humanite app. 15-Solomon Grundy app. 4.00
Annual 1 (11/20, $4.99) Bat-Mite and Mr. Mxyzptlk app.; Eaglesham & Melnikov-a 5.00

BATMAN/ SUPERMAN/WONDER WOMAN: TRINITY
DC Comics: 2003 - No. 3, 2003 ($6.95, limited series, squarebound)
1-3-Matt Wagner-s/a/c. 1-Ra's al Ghul & Bizarro app. 7.00
HC (2004, $24.95, with dust-jacket) r/series; intro. by Brad Meltzer 30.00
SC (2004, $17.99) r/series; intro. by Brad Meltzer 18.00

BATMAN: SWORD OF AZRAEL (Also see Azrael & Batman #488,489)
DC Comics: Oct, 1992 - No. 4, Jan, 1993 ($1.75, limited series)
1-Wraparound gatefold-c; Quesada-c/a(p) in all; 1st app. Azrael 2 4 6 11 16 20
2-4: 4-Cont'd in Batman #488 1 2 3 5 6 8
Silver Edition 1-4 (1993, $1.95)-Reprints #1-4 3.00
Trade Paperback (1993, $9.95)-Reprints #1-4 12.00
Trade Paperback Gold Edition 18.00

BATMAN/ TARZAN: CLAWS OF THE CAT-WOMAN
Dark Horse Comics/DC Comics: Sept, 1999 - No. 4, Dec, 1999 ($2.95, limited series)
1-4: Marz-s/Kordey-a 3.00

BATMAN/ TEENAGE MUTANT NINJA TURTLES
DC Comics: Feb, 2016 - No. 6, Jul, 2016 ($3.99, limited series)
1-6-Tynion IV-s/Williams II-a; Penguin, Croc & Shredder app. 5.00
... Director's Cut 1 (11/16, $5.99) r/#1 in B&W and pencil-a; original script 6.00

BATMAN/ TEENAGE MUTANT NINJA TURTLES II
DC Comics: Feb, 2018 - No. 6, Jun, 2018 ($3.99, limited series)
1-6-Tynion IV-s/Williams II-a; Bane app. 4.00

BATMAN/ TEENAGE MUTANT NINJA TURTLES III
DC Comics: Jul, 2019 - No. 6, Dec, 2019 ($3.99, limited series)
1-6-Tynion IV-s/Williams II-a; Crisis in a Half Shell; Anti-Monitor and Krang app. 4.00

BATMAN/ TEENAGE MUTANT NINJA TURTLES ADVENTURES
IDW Publishing: Nov, 2016 - No. 6, Apr, 2017 ($3.99, limited series)
1-6-Manning-s/Sommariva-a; Clayface, Joker and Harley Quinn app.; multiple covers 4.00
... Director's Cut 1 (2/17, $4.99) r/#1 in B&W and pencil-a; original script 5.00

BATMAN: TENSES
DC Comics: 2003 - No. 2, 2003 ($6.95, limited series)
1,2-Joe Casey-s/Cully Hamner-a; Bruce Wayne's first year back in Gotham 7.00

BATMAN: THE ADVENTURES CONTINUE (Set in Batman: The Animated Series continuity)
DC Comics: Jun, 2020 - No. 8, Mar, 2021 ($3.99, printing of digital first stories)
1-7-Dini & Burnett-s/Templeton-a. 2,3-Deathstroke app. 4-Azrael app. 5,6-Red Hood app.; Jason Todd origin as Robin. 6-Joker & Harley Quinn app. 4.00
8-($4.99) Harley Quinn, Poison Ivy, Scarface and Joker app. 5.00

BATMAN: THE ANKH
DC Comics: 2002 - No. 2, 2002 ($5.95, limited series)
1,2-Dixon-s/Van Fleet-a 6.00

BATMAN: THE BRAVE AND THE BOLD (Based on the 2008 animated series)
DC Comics: Mar, 2009 - No. 22, Dec, 2010 ($2.50/$2.99)
1-18: 1-Power Girl app. 4-Sugar & Spike cameo. 7-Doom Patrol app. 9-Catman app. 3.00
19-22-($2.99) Cyborg Superman and the Green Lantern Corps app. 22-Aquaman app. 3.00
TPB (2009, $12.99) r/#1-6 13.00
...: Emerald Knight TPB (2011, $12.99) r/#13,14,16,18,19,21 13.00
...: The Fearsome Fangs Strike Again TPB (2010, $12.99) r/#7-12 13.00

BATMAN: THE BRAVE AND THE BOLD (Titled "All New Batman: Brave & the Bold" for #1-13)
DC Comics: Jan, 2011 - No. 16, Apr, 2012 ($2.99)
1-16: 1-Superman. 4-Wonder Woman app. 8-Aquaman app. 9-Hawkman app. 3.00

BATMAN: THE CULT
DC Comics: 1988 - No. 4, Nov, 1988 ($3.50, deluxe limited series)
1-Wrightson-a/painted-c in all 1 2 3 5 6 8
2-4 6.00
Trade Paperback (1991, $14.95)-New Wrightson-c; Starlin intro. 25.00
Trade Paperback (2009, $19.99) 20.00

BATMAN: THE DARK KNIGHT
DC Comics: Jan, 2011 - No. 5, Oct, 2011 ($3.99/$2.99)
1-David Finch-s/a; Penguin & Killer Croc app.; covers by Finch and Clarke 4.00
2-5-($2.99) Demon app. 3.00

BATMAN: THE DARK KNIGHT (DC New 52)
DC Comics: Nov, 2011 - No. 29, May, 2014 ($2.99)
1-29: 1-Jenkins & Finch-s/Finch-a/c; White Rabbit debut. 3-Flash app. 5,6-Superman app. 6,7-Bane app. 9-Night of the Owls. 22-25-Maleev-a. 28-Van Sciver-a/c 3.00
23.1, 23.2, 23.3, 23.4 (11/13, $2.99, regular covers) 3.00
23.1 (11/13, $3.99, 3-D cover) "Ventriloquist #1" on cover; Simone-s/Santacruz-a 6.00
23.2 (11/13, $3.99, 3-D cover) "Mr. Freeze #1" on cover; Gray & Palmiotti-s 5.00

Batman: The Return of Bruce Wayne #4 © DC

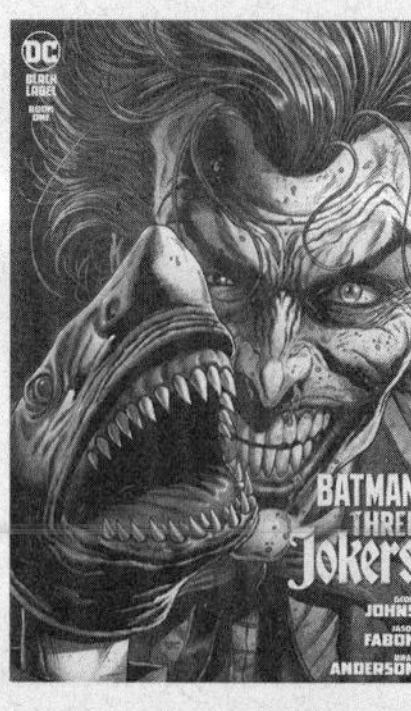

Batman: Three Jokers #1 © DC

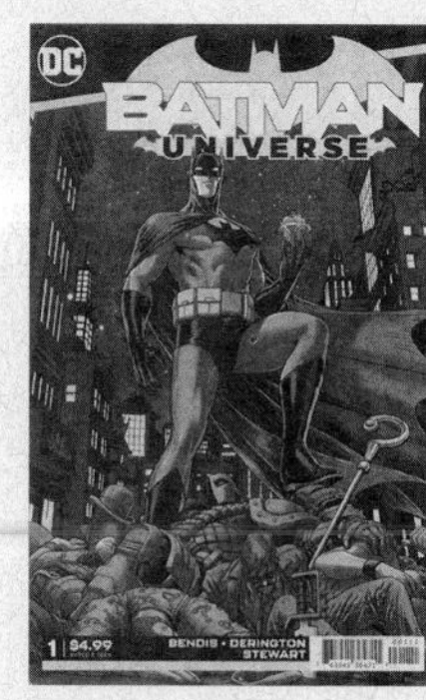

Batman Universe #1 © DC

	GD	VG	FN	VF	VF/NM	NM-
	2.0	4.0	6.0	8.0	9.0	9.2

23.3 (11/13, $3.99, 3-D cover) "Clayface#1" on cover; Richards-a 5.00
23.4 (11/13, $3.99, 3-D cover) "Joker's Daughter #1" on cover; origin story; Jeanty-a 12.00
#0 (11/12, $2.99) Hurwitz-s/Suayan & Ryp-a; flashback to aftermath of parents' murder3.00
Annual 1 (7/13, $4.99) Hurwitz-s/Kudranski-a/Maleev-c; Scarecrow, Penguin Mad Hatter 5.00

BATMAN: THE DARK KNIGHT RETURNS (Also see Dark Knight Strikes Again)
DC Comics: Mar, 1986 - No. 4, 1986 ($2.95, squarebound, limited series)

1-Miller story & c/a(p); set in the future 7 14 21 48 89 130
1,2-2nd & 3rd printings, 3-2nd printing 3 6 9 16 23 30
2-Carrie Kelley becomes 1st female Robin 4 8 12 25 40 55
3-Death of Joker; Superman app. 3 6 9 19 30 40
4-Death of Alfred; Superman app. 3 6 9 19 30 40
Hardcover, signed & numbered edition ($40.00)(4000 copies) 285.00
Hardcover, trade edition 65.00
Softcover, trade edition (1st printing only) 2 4 6 11 16 20
Softcover, trade edition (2nd thru 8th printings) 2 4 6 8 10 12
10th Anniv. Slipcase set ('96, $100.00): Signed & numbered hard-c edition (10,000 copies), sketchbook, copy of script for #1, 2 color prints 135.00
10th Anniv. Hardcover ('96, $45.00) 50.00
10th Anniv. Softcover ('97, $14.95) 18.00
Hardcover 2nd printing ('02, $24.95) with 3 1/4" tall partial dustjacket 25.00
NOTE: *The #2 second printings can be identified by matching the grey background colors on the inside front cover and facing page. The inside front cover of the second printing has a dark grey background which does not match the lighter grey of the facing page. On the true 1st printings, the backgrounds are both light grey. All other issues are clearly marked.*

BATMAN: THE DARK PRINCE CHARMING
DC Comics: Jan, 2018 - No. 2, Jun, 2018 ($12.99, HC, limited series)

1,2-Enrico Marini-s/a; Joker & Harley Quinn app. 13.00

BATMAN: THE DAWNBREAKER (Tie-in to Dark Nights: Metal series)
DC Comics: Dec, 2017 ($3.99, one-shot)

1-Humphries-s/Van Sciver-a; Fabok foil-c; Wayne as Dark Multiverse Green Lantern 4.00

BATMAN: THE DOOM THAT CAME TO GOTHAM
DC Comics: 2000 - No. 3, 2001 ($4.95, limited series)

1-3-Elseworlds; Mignola-c/s; Nixey-a; Etrigan app. 6.00

BATMAN: THE DEVASTATOR (Tie-in to Dark Nights: Metal series)
DC Comics: Jan, 2018 ($3.99, one-shot)

1-Tieri-s/Daniel-a; Fabok foil-c; Bruce Wayne as Dark Multiverse Doomsday 4.00

BATMAN: THE DROWNED (Tie-in to Dark Nights: Metal series)
DC Comics: Dec, 2017 ($3.99, one-shot)

1-Abnett-s/Tan-a; Fabok foil-c; female Bryce Wayne as Dark Multiverse Aquawoman 4.00

BATMAN: THE KILLING JOKE (See Batman one-shots)

BATMAN: THE LONG HALLOWEEN
DC Comics: Oct, 1996 - No. 13, Oct, 1997 ($2.95/$4.95, limited series)

1-($4.95)-Loeb-s/Sale-c/a in all 4 8 12 23 37 50
2,4,5 ($2.95): 2-Solomon Grundy-c/app. 1 3 4 6 8 10
3-Joker-c/app., Catwoman, Poison Ivy app. 2 4 6 9 12 15
6,8-10: 6-Poison Ivy-c 6.00
7-Riddler-c/app. 2 4 6 8 11 14
11,12 6.00
13-($4.95, 48 pgs.)-Killer revelations 2 4 6 8 10 12
Special Edition (Halloween Comic Fest 2013) (12/13, free giveaway) r/#1 3.00
Absolute Batman: The Long Halloween (2007, $75.00, oversized HC) r/series; interviews with the creators; Sale sketch pages; action figure line; unpubbed 4-page sequence 100.00
HC-($29.95) r/series 50.00
SC-($19.95) 20.00

BATMAN: THE MAD MONK ("Batman & the Mad Monk" on cover)
DC Comics: Oct, 2006 - No. 6, Mar, 2007 ($3.50, limited series)

1-6-Matt Wagner-s/a/c. 1-Catwoman app. 3.50
TPB (2007, $14.99) r/#1-6 15.00

BATMAN / THE MAXX: ARKHAM DREAMS
IDW Publishing/DC Comics: Sept, 2018 - No. 5 ($4.99, limited series)

1-3-Sam Kieth-s/a; 3 covers on each. 2-Joker app. 5.00
... The Lost Year Compendium (9/20, $7.99) Reprints #1-3; thumbnail previews of #4 8.00

BATMAN: THE MERCILESS (Tie-in to Dark Nights: Metal series)
DC Comics: Dec, 2017 ($3.99, one-shot)

1-Tomasi-s/Manapul-a; Fabok foil-c; Bruce Wayne as Dark Multiverse God of War 4.00

BATMAN: THE MONSTER MEN ("Batman & the Monster Men" on cover)
DC Comics: Jan, 2006 - No. 6, June, 2006 ($2.99, limited series)

1-6-Matt Wagner-s/a/c 3.00
TPB (2006, $14.99) r/#1-6 15.00

BATMAN: THE MURDER MACHINE (Tie-in to Dark Nights: Metal series)
DC Comics: Nov, 2017 ($3.99, one-shot)

1-Tieri-s/Federici-a; Fabok foil-c; Bruce Wayne as Dark Multiverse Cyborg 4.00

BATMAN: THE OFFICIAL COMIC ADAPTATION OF THE WARNER BROS. MOTION PICTURE
(See Batman one-shots)

BATMAN: THE RED DEATH (Tie-in to Dark Nights: Metal series)
DC Comics: Nov, 2017 ($3.99, one-shot)

1-Williamson-s/Di Giandomenico-a; Fabok foil-c; Bruce Wayne as Dark Multiverse Flash 4.00

BATMAN: THE RETURN
DC Comics: Jan, 2011 ($4.99, one-shot)

1-Morrison-s/Finch-a; covers by Finch & Ha; costume design sketch art; script pages 5.00

BATMAN: THE RETURN OF BRUCE WAYNE (Follows Batman's "death" in Final Crisis #6)
DC Comics: Early Jul, 2010 - No. 6, Dec, 2010 ($3.99, limited series)

1-6-Bruce Wayne's time travels; Morrison-s/Andy Kubert-c. 1-Sprouse-a. 4-Jeanty-a 4.00
1-Second & third printings; 4.00
1-6-Variant covers: 1-Sprouse. 2-Irving. 3-Paquette. 4-Jeanty. 5-Sook. 6-Garbett 8.00
... - The Deluxe Edition HC (2011, $29.99) r/#1-6; sketch pages 30.00

BATMAN: THE ULTIMATE EVIL
DC Comics: 1995 ($5.95, limited series, prestige format)

1,2-Barrett, Jr. adaptation of Vachss novel. 6.00

BATMAN: THE WIDENING GYRE
DC Comics: Oct, 2009 - No. 6, Sept, 2010 ($3.99/$2.99/$4.99, limited series)

1-($3.99) Kevin Smith-s/Walt Flanagan-a; debut Baphomet; Demon app.; Sienkiewicz-c 4.00
1-5-Variant covers by Gene Ha 8.00
2-5-($2.99) 2-Silver St. Cloud returns. 5-Catwoman app. 3.00
6-($4.99) Joker, Deadshot & Catwoman app. 5.00
6-Variant cover by Gene Ha 10.00
HC (2010, $19.99, dj) r/#1-6; variant covers; afterword by Kevin Smith 20.00

BATMAN 3-D (Also see 3-D Batman)
DC Comics: 1990 ($9.95, w/glasses, 8-1/8x10-3/4")

nn-Byrne-a/scripts; Riddler, Joker, Penguin & Two-Face app. plus r/1953 3-D Batman; pin-ups by many artists 2 4 6 9 13 16

BATMAN: THREE JOKERS
DC Comics (Black Label): Oct, 2020 - No. 3, Dec, 2020 ($6.99, limited series)

1-3-Johns-s/Fabok-a. 1-Red Hood & Batgirl app. 2,3-Joe Chill app. 7.00

BATMAN: TOYMAN
DC Comics: Nov, 1998 - No. 4, Feb, 1999 ($2.25, limited series)

1-4-Hama-s 3.00

BATMAN: TURNING POINTS
DC Comics: Jan, 2001 - No. 5, Jan, 2001 ($2.50, weekly limited series)

1-5: 2-Giella-a. 3-Kubert-c/Giordano-a. 4-Chaykin-c/Brent Anderson-a. 5-Pope-c/a 3.00
TPB (2007, $14.99) r/#1-5 15.00

BATMAN: TWO-FACE-CRIME AND PUNISHMENT (See Batman one-shots)

BATMAN: TWO-FACE STRIKES TWICE
DC Comics: 1993 - No. 2, 1993 ($4.95, 52 pgs.)

1,2-Flip book format w/Staton-a (G.A. side) 6.00

BATMAN UNIVERSE (Reprints serialized story from Walmart exclusive Batman Giant)
DC Comics: Sept, 2019 - No. 6, Feb, 2020 ($4.99, limited series)

1-6: 1-Ginny Hex debut. 2-Green Arrow & Vandal Savage app. 3,4,6-Jonah Hex app. 5.00

BATMAN UNSEEN
DC Comics: Early Dec, 2009 - No. 5, Feb, 2010 ($2.99, limited series)

1-5-Doug Moench-s/Kelley Jones-a/c. Black Mask app. 3.00
SC (2010, $14.99) r/#1-5 15.00

BATMAN: VENGEANCE OF BANE (Also see Batman #491)
DC Comics: Jan, 1993; 1995 ($2.50, 68 pgs.)

... Special 1 - Origin & 1st app. Bane; Dixon-s/Nolan & Barreto-a/Fabry-c 5 10 15 31 53 75
... Special 1 (2nd printing) 2 4 6 10 14 18
.... II nn (1995, $3.95)-sequel; Dixon-s/Nolan & Barreto-a/Fabry-c 2 4 6 9 12 15

BATMAN VERSUS PREDATOR
DC Comics/Dark Horse Comics: 1991 - No. 3, 1992 ($4.95/$1.95, limited series)
(1st DC/Dark Horse x-over)

The Batman Who Laughs #7 © DC

Battle #3 © MAR

Battle Chasers #1 © Joe Madureira

	GD 2.0	VG 4.0	FN 6.0	VF 8.0	VF/NM 9.0	NM- 9.2

1 (Prestige format, $4.95)-1 & 3 contain 8 Batman/Predator trading cards;
Andy & Adam Kubert-a; Suydam painted-c 1 2 3 5 6 8
1-3 (Regular format, $1.95)-No trading cards 4.00
2,3-(Prestige)-2-Extra pin-ups inside; Suydam-c 6.00
TPB (1993, $5.95, 132 pgs.)-r/#1-3 w/new introductions & forward plus new wraparound-c
by Dave Gibbons 2 4 6 8 10 12

BATMAN VERSUS PREDATOR II: BLOODMATCH
DC Comics: Late 1994 - No. 4, 1995 ($2.50, limited series)
1-4-Huntress app.; Moench scripts; Gulacy-a 4.00
TPB (1995, $6.95)-r/#1-4 1 3 4 6 8 10

BATMAN VS. RA'S AL GHUL
DC Comics: Nov, 2019 - No. 6 ($3.99, limited series)
1-4-Neal Adams-s/a; Deadman app. 4.00

BATMAN VS. THE INCREDIBLE HULK (See DC Special Series No. 27)

BATMAN: WAR ON CRIME
DC Comics: Nov, 1999 ($9.95, treasury size, one-shot)
nn-Painted art by Alex Ross; story by Alex Ross and Paul Dini 20.00

BATMAN: WHITE KNIGHT
DC Comics: Dec, 2017 - No. 8, Jul, 2018 ($3.99, limited series)
1-7-Sean Murphy-s/a; Joker is cured. 2-7-Harley Quinn app. 4.00
8-($4.99) Murphy-s/a 5.00
... Presents Von Freeze (Black Label, 1/20, $5.99) Murphy-s/Janson-a; Fries flashback 6.00

BATMAN: WHITE KNIGHT PRESENTS HARLEY QUINN
DC Comics (Black Label): Dec, 2020 - No. 6 ($4.99, limited series)
1-5-Katana Collins & Sean Murphy-s/Matteo Scalera-a 5.00

BATMAN WHO LAUGHS, THE (See Dark Nights: Metal)
DC Comics: Feb, 2019 - No. 7, Sept, 2019 ($4.99, limited series)
1-7-Snyder-s/Jock-a; Joker and The Grim Knight app. 5.00
...: The Grim Knight 1 (5/19, $4.99) origin of the Grim Knight; Risso-a 5.00

BATMAN/ WILDCAT
DC Comics: Apr, 1997 - No. 3, June, 1997 ($2.25, mini-series)
1-3: Dixon/Smith-s: 1-Killer Croc app. 3.00

BATMAN: YEAR 100
DC Comics: 2006 - No. 4, 2006 ($5.99, squarebound, limited series)
1-4-Paul Pope-s/a/c 6.00
TPB (2007, $19.99) r/series 20.00

BAT MASTERSON (TV) (Also see Tim Holt #28)
Dell Publishing Co.: Aug-Oct, 1959; Feb-Apr, 1960 - No. 9, Nov-Jan, 1961-62
Four Color 1013 (#1) (8-10/59) 10 20 30 69 147 225
2-9: Gene Barry photo-c on all. 2,3,6-Two different back-c exist; variants have a comic strip
on the back-c 6 12 18 40 73 105

BAT-MITE
DC Comics: Aug, 2015 - No. 6, Jan, 2016 ($2.99, limited series)
1-6: 1-Jurgens-s/Howell-a; Batman app. 4-Booster Gold app. 5-Inferior Five app. 3.00

BATS (See Tales Calculated to Drive You Bats)

BATS, CATS & CADILLACS
Now Comics: Oct, 1990 - No. 2, Nov, 1990 ($1.75)
1,2: 1-Gustovich-a(i); Snyder-c 3.00

BAT-THING
DC Comics (Amalgam): June, 1997 ($1.95, one-shot)
1-Hama-s/Damaggio & Sienkiewicz-a 3.00

BATTLE
Marvel/Atlas Comics(FPI #1-62/ Male #63 on): Mar, 1951 - No. 70, Jun, 1960
1 68 136 204 435 743 1050
2 36 72 108 214 347 480
3-10: 4-1st Buck Pvt. O'Toole. 10-Pakula-a 29 58 87 174 285 395
11-20: 11-Check-a. 17-Classic Hitler story 24 48 72 140 230 320
21,23-Krigstein-a 24 48 72 140 230 320
22,24-36: 32-Tuska-a. 36-Everett-a 21 42 63 122 199 275
37-Kubert-a (Last precode, 2/55) 22 44 66 132 216 300
38-40,42-48 20 40 60 115 185 255
41,49: 41-Kubert/Moskowitz-a. 49-Davis-a 21 42 63 122 199 275
50-54,56-58: 56-Colan-a; Ayers-a 19 38 57 111 176 240
55-Williamson-a (5 pgs.) 20 40 60 118 192 265
59-Torres-a 19 38 57 112 174 245
60-62: 60,62-Combat Kelly app. 61-Combat Casey app.
19 38 57 111 176 240
63-Ditko-a 27 54 81 160 263 365
64-66-Kirby-a. 66-Davis-a; has story of Fidel Castro in pre-Communism days
(an admiring profile) 30 60 90 177 289 400
67,68: 67-Williamson/Crandall-a (4 pgs.); Kirby, Davis-a. 68-Kirby/Williamson-a (4 pgs.);
Kirby/Ditko-a 32 64 96 190 310 430
69,70: 69-Kirby-a. 70-Kirby/Ditko-a 30 60 90 177 289 400
NOTE: ***Andru** a-37. **Berg** a-8, 38, 14, 60-62. **Colan** a-19, 33, 43, 55. **Everett** a-36, 50, 70; c-56, 57. **Heath** a-6, 9, 13, 31, 69; c-6, 9, 12, 26, 35, 37. **Kirby** c-64-69. **Maneely** a-4-7, 31, 61; c-4, 22, 27, 33, 43, 48, 59, 61. **Orlando** a-47. **Powell** a-53, 55. **Reinman** a-4, 8-10, 14, 26, 32, 48. **Robinson** a-9, 39. **Romita** a-14, 26. **Severin** a-28, 32-34, 66-69; c-36, 50, 55. **Sinnott** a-33, 37, 63, 66. **Whitney** s-10.**Woodbridge** a-52, 55.*

BATTLE ACTION
Atlas Comics (NPI): Feb, 1952 - No. 12, 5/53; No. 13, 10/54 - No. 30, 8/57
1-Pakula-a 48 96 144 302 514 725
2 26 52 78 154 252 350
3,4,6,7,9,10: 6-Robinson-c/a. 7-Partial nudity 19 38 57 109 172 235
5-Used in **POP**, pg. 93,94 19 38 57 111 176 240
8-Krigstein-a 19 38 57 112 179 245
11-15 (Last precode, 2/55) 18 36 54 105 165 225
16-30: 20-Romita-a. 22-Pakula-a. 27,30-Torres-a 16 32 48 94 147 200
NOTE: *Battle Brady app. 5-7, 10-12. **Berg** a-3. **Check** a-11. **Everett** a-7; c-13, 25. **Heath** a-3, 8, 18; c-3,15, 18, 21. **Maneely** a-1; c-5. **Reinman** a-1, 2, 20. **Robinson** a-6, 7; c-6. **Shores** a-7(2), 12, 20; c-11. **Sinnott** a-3, 27. **Woodbridge** a-28, 30.*

BATTLE ATTACK
Stanmor Publications: Oct, 1952 - No. 8, Dec, 1955
1 17 34 51 98 154 210
2 10 20 30 58 79 100
3-8: 3-Hollingsworth-a 9 18 27 52 69 85

BATTLEAXES
DC Comics (Vertigo): May, 2000 - No. 4, Aug, 2000 ($2.50, limited series)
1-4: Terry LaBan-s/Alex Horley-a 3.00

BATTLE BEASTS
Blackthorne Publishing: Feb, 1988 - No. 4, 1988 ($1.50/$1.75, B&W/color)
1-4: 1-3- (B&W)-Based on Hasbro toys. 4-Color 3.00

BATTLE BEASTS
IDW Publishing: Jul, 2012 - No. 4, Oct, 2012 ($3.99, limited series)
1-4-Curnow-s/Schiti-a; 2 covers on each 4.00

BATTLE BRADY (Formerly Men in Action No. 1-9; see 3-D Action)
Atlas Comics (IPC): No. 10, Jan, 1953 - No. 14, June, 1953
10: 10-12-Syd Shores-c 29 58 87 170 278 385
11-Used in **POP**, pg. 95 plus B&W & color illos 19 38 57 112 179 245
12-14 17 34 51 100 158 215

BATTLE CHASERS
Image Comics (Cliffhanger): Apr, 1998 - No. 4, Dec, 1998;
DC Comics (Cliffhanger): No. 5, May, 1999 - No. 8, May, 2001 ($2.50)
Image Comics: No. 9, Sept, 2001 ($3.50)
Prelude (2/98) 1 3 4 6 8 10
Prelude Gold Ed. 1 3 4 6 8 10
1-Madureira & Sharrieff-s/Madureira-a(p)/Charest-c 1 2 3 5 7 9
1-American Ent. Ed. w/"racy" cover 1 3 4 6 8 10
1-Gold Edition 12.00
1-Chromium cover 24.00
1-2nd printing 3.00
2 5.00
2-Dynamic Forces BattleChrome cover 2 4 6 8 10 12
3-Red Monika cover by Madureira 4.00
4-8: 4-Four covers. 6-Back-up by Adam Warren-s/a. 7-Three covers (Madureira, Ramos, Campbell) 3.00
9-($3.50, Image) Flip cover/story by Adam Warren 4.00
...: A Gathering of Heroes HC ('99, $24.95) r/#1-5, Prelude, Frank Frazetta Fantasy Ill.;
cover gallery 25.00
...: A Gathering of Heroes SC ('99, $14.95) 15.00
...Collected Edition 1,2 (11/98, 5/99, $5.95) 1-r/#1,2. 2-r/#3,4 6.00

BATTLE CLASSICS (See Cancelled Comic Cavalcade)
DC Comics: Sept-Oct, 1978 (44 pgs.)
1-Kubert-r; new Kubert-c 2 4 6 8 10 12

BATTLE CRY
Stanmor Publications: 1952 (May) - No. 20, Sept, 1955
1 37 74 111 222 361 500
2-(7/52) 14 28 42 82 121 160

Battlefront #4 © MAR

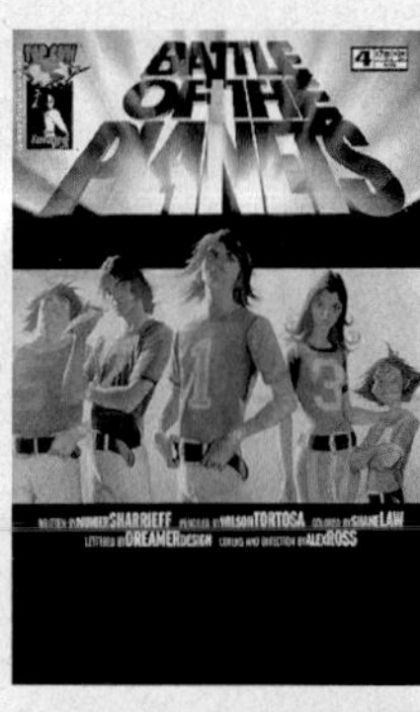
Battle of the Planets (2002 series) #4 © Sandy Frank

Battler Britton #1 © DC & IPC Media

GD VG FN VF VF/NM NM-
2.0 4.0 6.0 8.0 9.0 9.2

3,5-10: 8-Pvt. Ike begins, ends #13,17 12 24 36 69 97 125
4-Classic E.C. swipe 22 44 66 132 216 300
11-20 11 22 33 62 86 110
NOTE: ***Hollingsworth** a-9; c-20.*

BATTLEFIELD (War Adventures on the...)
Atlas Comics (ACI): April, 1952 - No. 11, May, 1953

1-Pakula, Reinman-a 42 84 126 265 445 625
2-5: 2-Heath, Maneely, Pakula, Reinman-a 21 42 63 126 206 285
6-11 19 38 57 111 176 240
NOTE: ***Colan** a-11. **Everett** a-8. **Heath** a-1, 2, 5p,7; c-2, 8, 9, 11. **Ravielli** a-11.*

BATTLEFIELD ACTION (Formerly Foreign Intrigues)
Charlton Comics: No. 16, Nov, 1957 - No. 62, 2-3/66; No. 63, 7/80 - No. 89, 11/84

V2#16 9 18 27 52 69 85
17,20-30: 29-D-Day story 6 12 18 28 34 40
18,19-Check-a (2 stories in #18) 3 6 9 21 33 45
31-34,36-62(1966): 40-Panel from this issue used by artist Roy Lichtenstein for famous painting. 55,61-Hitler app. 3 6 9 16 23 30
35-Hitler-c 4 8 12 28 47 65
63-80(1983-84) 5.00
81-83,85-89 (Low print run) 1 2 3 4 5 7
84-Kirby reprints; 3 stories 1 3 4 6 8 10
NOTE: ***Montes/Bache** a-43, 55, 62. **Glanzman** a-87r.*

BATTLEFIELDS
Dynamite Entertainment: 2008 - No. 9, 2010 ($3.50, limited series then numbered issues)

...: Dear Billy 1-3 ('09 - No. 3, '09, $3.50) Ennis-s/Snejbjerg-a/Cassaday-c.1-Leach var-c 3.50
...: Happy Valley 1-3 ('09 - No. 3, '09, $3.50) Ennis-s/Holden-a/Leach-c 3.50
...: The Night Witches 1-3 ('08 - No. 3, '09, $3.50) Ennis-s/Braun-a/Cassaday-c; Russian female pilots in WW2. 1-Leach var-c 3.50
...: The Tankies 1-3 ('09 - No. 3, '09, $3.50) Ennis-s/Ezquerra-a/Cassaday-c.1-Leach var-c 3.50
4-9: 4-6-Ezquerra-a/Leach-c. 7-9-Sequel to "The Night Witches"; Braun-a 3.50

BATTLEFIELDS (Volume 2)
Dynamite Entertainment: 2012 - No. 6, 2013 ($3.99, limited series)

1-6: 1-3-Ennis-s/Ezquerra-a/Leach-c. 4-6-Braun-a 4.00

BATTLE FIRE
Aragon Magazine/Stanmor Publications: Apr, 1955 - No. 7, 1955

1 17 34 51 98 154 210
2-(6/55) 11 22 33 62 86 110
3-7 10 20 30 56 76 95

BATTLE FOR A THREE DIMENSIONAL WORLD
3D Cosmic Publications: May, 1983 (20 pgs., slick paper w/stiff-c, $3.00)

nn-Kirby c/a in 3-D; shows history of 3-D 2 4 6 8 11 14

BATTLEFORCE
Blackthorne Publishing: Nov, 1987 - No. 2, 1988 ($1.75, color/B&W)

1,2: Based on game. 1-In color. 2-B&W 3.00

BATTLE FOR INDEPENDENTS, THE (Also See Cyblade/Shi & Shi/Cyblade: The Battle For Independents)
Image Comics (Top Cow Productions)/Crusade Comics: 1995 ($29.95)

nn-Boxed set of all editions of Shi/Cyblade & Cyblade/Shi plus new variant 3 6 9 19 30 40

BATTLE FOR THE PLANET OF THE APES (See Power Record Comics)

BATTLEFRONT
Atlas Comics (PPI): June, 1952 - No. 48, Aug, 1957

1-Heath-c 54 108 162 343 574 825
2-Robinson-a(4) 29 58 87 170 278 385
3-5-Robinson-a 23 46 69 136 223 310
6-10: Combat Kelly in No. 6-10. 6-Romita-a 20 40 60 118 192 265
11-22,24-28: 14,16-Battle Brady app. 22-Teddy Roosevelt & His Rough Riders story. 28-Last pre-code (2/55) 19 38 57 111 176 240
23,43-Check-a 19 38 57 112 179 245
29-39,41,44-47 18 36 54 103 162 220
40,42-Williamson-a 19 38 57 111 176 240
48-Crandall-a 18 36 54 107 169 230
NOTE: ***Ayers** a-18, 19, 25, 32, 35. **Berg** a-44. **Colan** a-21, 22, 24, 25, 32, 33-35, 38, 40, 42, 43, 45. **Drucker** a-28, 29. **Everett** a-44. **Heath** c-23, 26, 27, 29, 32. **Maneely** a-21-23, 26; c-2, 7, 13, 22, 24, 25, 34, 35, 41. **Morisi** a-42. **Morrow** a-41.**Orlando** a-47. **Powell** a-19, 21, 25, 29, 32, 40, 47. **Robinson** a-1-3, 4&5(4); c-4, 5. **Robert Sale** a-19, 24. **Severin** a-32; c-40, 42, 45. **Sinnott** a-26, 45, 48. **Woodbridge** a-45, 46.*

BATTLEFRONT
Standard Comics: No. 5, June, 1952

5-Toth-a 18 36 54 103 162 220

GD VG FN VF VF/NM NM-
2.0 4.0 6.0 8.0 9.0 9.2

BATTLE GODS: WARRIORS OF THE CHAAK
Dark Horse Comics: Apr, 2000 - No. 4, July, 2000 ($2.95)

1-4-Francisco Ruiz Velasco-s/a 3.00

BATTLE GROUND
Atlas Comics (OMC): Sept, 1954 - No. 20, Sept, 1957

1 41 82 123 256 428 600
2-Jack Katz-a (11/54) 21 42 63 126 206 285
3,4: 3-Jack Katz-a. 4-Last precode (3/55) 19 38 57 112 179 245
5-8,10 (3/56) 18 36 54 103 162 220
9,11,13,18: 9-Krigstein-a. 11,13,18-Williamson-a in each 19 38 57 112 179 245
12,15-17,19,20 17 34 51 98 154 210
14-Kirby-a 21 42 63 124 202 280
NOTE: ***Ayers** a-4, 6, 13, 16. **Colan** a-3, 11, 13. **Drucker** a-7, 12, 13, 20. **Heath** c-2, 3, 5, 7, 13. **Maneely** a-3, 14, 19; c-1, 6, 18, 19. **Orlando** a-17. **Pakula** a-6, 11. **Reinman** a-2. **Severin** a-4, 5, 12, 19. c-20. **Sinnott** a-7, 16. **Tuska** a-11.*

BATTLE HEROES
Stanley Publications: Sept, 1966 - No. 2, Nov, 1966 (25¢, squarebound giants)

1 4 8 12 23 37 50
2 3 6 9 17 26 35

BATTLE HYMN
Image Comics: Jan, 2005 - No. 5, Oct, 2005 ($2.95/$2.99, limited series)

1-5-WW2 super team; B. Clay Moore-s/Jeremy Haun-a; flip cover on #1-4 3.00

BATTLE OF THE BULGE (See Movie Classics)

BATTLE OF THE PLANETS (Based on syndicated cartoon by Sandy Frank)
Gold Key/Whitman No. 6 on: 6/79 - No. 10, 12/80

1: Mortimer a-1-4,7-10 8 16 24 54 102 150
2-6,10 3 6 9 21 33 45
7-Low print run 7 14 21 44 82 120
8,9-Low print run: 8(11/80). 9-(3-pack only?) 5 10 15 35 63 90

BATTLE OF THE PLANETS (Also see Thundercats/...)
Image Comics (Top Cow): Aug, 2002 - No. 12, Sept, 2003 ($2.95/$2.99)

1-($2.95) Alex Ross-c & art director; Tortosa-a(p); re-intro. G-Force 3.00
1-($5.95) Holofoil-c by Ross 6.00
2-11-($2.99) Ross-c on all 3.00
12-($4.99) 5.00
#1/2 (7/03, $2.99) Benitez-c; Alex Ross sketch pages 3.00
... Battle Book 1 (5/03, $4.99) background info on characters, equipment, stories 5.00
... : Jason 1 (7/03, $4.99) Ross-c; Erwin David-a; preview of Tomb Raider: Epiphany 5.00
... : Mark 1 (5/03, $4.99) Ross-c; Erwin David-a; preview of BotP: Jason 5.00
.../Thundercats 1 (Image/WildStorm, 5/03, $4.99) 2 covers by Ross & Campbell 5.00
.../Witchblade 1 (2/03, $5.95) Ross-c; Christina and Jo Chen-a 6.00
Vol. 1: Trial By Fire (2003, $7.99) r/#1-3 8.00
Vol. 2: Blood Red Sky (9/03, $16.95) r/#4-9 17.00
Vol. 3: Destroy All Monsters (11/03, $19.95) r/#10-12, ...: Jason, ...: Mark, .../Witchblade 20.00
Vol. 1: Digest (1/04, $9.99, 7-3/8x5", B&W) r/#1-9 & ...: Mark 10.00
Vol. 2: Digest (8/04, $9.99, B&W) r/#10-12, ...: Jason, ...: Manga #1-3, .../Witchblade 10.00

BATTLE OF THE PLANETS: MANGA
Image Comics (Top Cow): Nov, 2003 - No. 3, Jan, 2004 ($2.99, B&W)

1-3-Edwin David-a/David Wohl-s; previews for Wanted & Tomb Raider #35 3.00

BATTLE OF THE PLANETS: PRINCESS
Image Comics (Top Cow): Nov, 2004 - No. 6, May, 2005 ($2.99, B&W, limited series)

1-6-Tortosa-a/Wohl-s. 1-Ross-c. 2-Tortosa-c 3.00

BATTLE POPE
Image Comics: June, 2005 - No. 14, Apr, 2007 ($2.99/$3.50, reprints 2000 B&W series in color)

1-5-Kirkman-s/Moore-a 3.50
6-10,12-14-($3.50) 14-Wedding 3.50
11-($4.99) Christmas issue 5.00
... Vol. 1: Genesis TPB (2006, $12.95) r/#1-4; sketch pages 13.00
... Vol. 2: Mayhem TPB (2006, $12.99) r/#5-8; sketch pages 13.00
... Vol. 3: Pillow Talk TPB (2007, $12.99) r/#9-11; sketch pages 13.00

BATTLEPUG
Image Comics: Sept, 2019 - No. 5, Jan, 2020 ($3.99)

1-5-Mike Norton-s/a 4.00

BATTLER BRITTON (British comics character who debuted in 1956)
DC Comics (WildStorm): Sept, 2006 - No. 5, Jan, 2007 ($2.99, limited series)

1-5-WWII fighter pilots; Garth Ennis-s/Colin Wilson-a 3.00
TPB (2007, $19.99) r/#1-5; background of the character's British origins in the 1950s 20.00

BATTLE REPORT

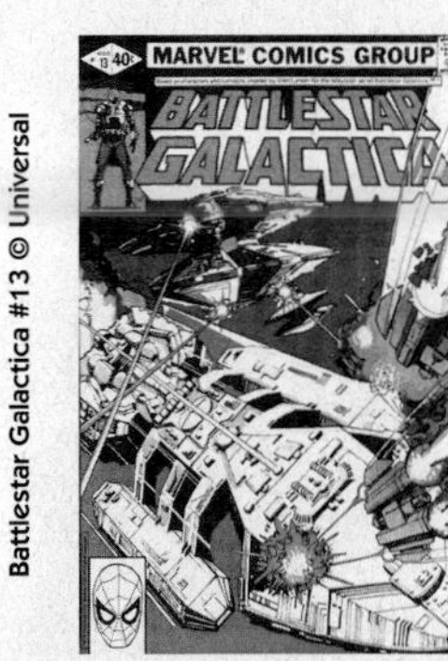

Battlestar Galactica #13 © Universal

Battlestar Galactica: Origins #1 © Universal

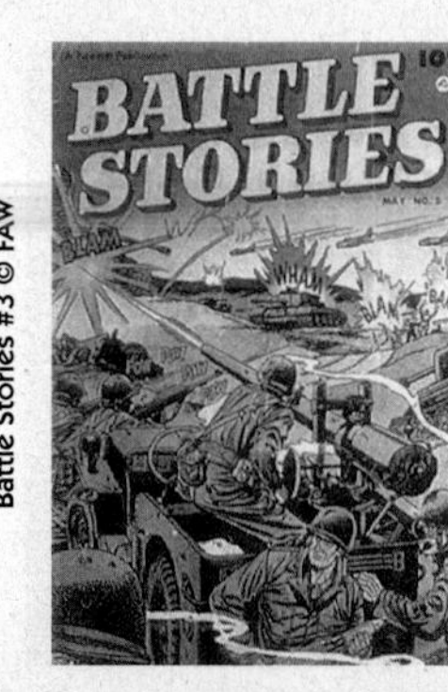

Battle Stories #3 © FAW

	GD 2.0	VG 4.0	FN 6.0	VF 8.0	VF/NM 9.0	NM- 9.2

Ajax/Farrell Publications: Aug, 1952 - No. 6, June, 1953

1	16	32	48	92	144	195
2-6	11	22	33	60	83	105

BATTLE SCARS
Marvel Comics: Jan, 2012 - No. 6, Jun, 2012 ($2.99, limited series)

1-Intro. Marcus Johnson and Cheese (later ID'd as Phil Coulson in #6); Eaton-a/Pagulayan-c	2	4	6	8	10	12
2-5: 4-Deadpool app. 5-Nick Fury app.						4.00
6-Marcus Johnson becomes Nick Fury Jr.; resembles movie version; Cheese joins SHIELD and is ID'd as Agent Coulson	2	4	6	8	10	12

BATTLE SQUADRON
Stanmor Publications: April, 1955 - No. 5, Dec, 1955

1	15	30	45	85	130	175
2-5: 3-Iwo Jima & flag-c	10	20	30	56	76	95

BATTLESTAR GALACTICA (TV) (Also see Marvel Comics Super Special #8)
Marvel Comics Group: Mar, 1979 - No. 23, Jan, 1981

1: 1-5 adapt TV episodes	4	9	13	18	22	26
2-23: 1-3-Partial-r	2	4	6	8	10	12

NOTE: ***Austin** c-9i, 10i. **Golden** c-18. **Simonson** a(p)-4, 5, 11-13, 15-20, 22, 23; c(p)-4, 5,11-17, 19, 20, 22, 23.*

BATTLESTAR GALACTICA (TV) (Also see Asylum)
Maximum Press: July, 1995 - No. 4, Nov, 1995 ($2.50, limited series)

1-4: Continuation of 1978 TV series 4.00
Trade paperback (12/95, $12.95)-reprints series 13.00

BATTLESTAR GALACTICA (1978 TV series)
Realm Press: Dec, 1997 - No. 5, July, 1998 ($2.99)

1-5-Chris Scalf-s/painted-a/c 3.00
...Search For Sanctuary (9/98, $2.99) Scalf & Kuhoric-s 3.00
...Search For Sanctuary Special (4/00, $3.99) Kuhoric-s/Scalf & Scott-a 4.00

BATTLESTAR GALACTICA (2003-2009 TV series)
Dynamite Entertainment: No. 0, 2006 - No. 12, 2007 (25¢/$2.99)

0-(25¢-c) Two covers; Pak-s/Raynor-a 3.00
1-($2.99) Covers by Turner, Tan, Raynor & photo-c; Pak-s/Raynor-a 3.00
2-12-Four covers on each 3.00
... Pegasus (2007, $4.99) story of Battlestar Pegasus & Admiral Cain; 2 covers 5.00
... Volume 1 HC (2007, $19.99) r/#0-4; cover gallery; Raynor sketch pages; commentary 20.00
... Volume 1 TPB (2007, $14.99) r/#0-4; cover gallery; Raynor sketch pages; commentary 15.00
... Volume 2 HC (2007, $19.99) r/#5-8; cover gallery; Raynor sketch pages 20.00
... Volume 2 TPB (2007, $14.99) r/#5-8; cover gallery; Raynor sketch pages 15.00

BATTLESTAR GALACTICA, (Classic...) (1978 TV series characters)
Dynamite Entertainment: 2006 - No. 5,2006 ($2.99)

1-5: 1-Two covers by Dorman & Caldwell; Rafael-a. 2-Two covers 3.00

BATTLESTAR GALACTICA, (Classic...) (Volume 2) (1978 TV series characters)
Dynamite Entertainment: 2013 - No. 12, 2014 ($3.99)

1-12: 1-5-Two covers by Alex Ross & Chris Eliopoulos on each; Abnett & Lanning-s 4.00

BATTLESTAR GALACTICA, (Classic...) (Volume 3) (1978 TV series characters)
Dynamite Entertainment: 2016 - No. 5, 2016 ($3.99)

1-5: 1-Cullen Bunn-s/Alex Sanchez-a; multiple covers 4.00

BATTLESTAR GALACTICA, (Classic...) (Volume 4) (1978 TV series characters)
Dynamite Entertainment: No. 0, 2018 - No. 5, 2019 ($3.99)

0-(35¢, listed as #1 in indicia) John Jackson Miller-s/Daniel HDR-a; multiple covers 3.00
1-5-Multiple covers on each 4.00

BATTLESTAR GALACTICA: APOLLO'S JOURNEY (1978 TV series)
Maximum Press: Apr, 1996 - No. 3, June, 1996 ($2.95, limited series)

1-3: Richard Hatch scripts 4.00

BATTLESTAR GALACTICA: BSG VS. BSG (1978 characters meet 2003 characters)
Dynamite Entertainment: 2018 - No. 6, 2018 ($3.99, limited series)

1-6-Peter David-s; multiple covers. 1-3-Johnny DesJardins-a. 4-6-Edu Menna-a 3.00

BATTLESTAR GALACTICA: CYLON APOCALYPSE (1978 TV series characters)
Dynamite Entertainment: 2007 - No. 4, 2007 ($2.99, limited series)

1-4-Carlos Rafael-a; 4 covers on each 3.00
TPB (2007, $14.99) r/series with cover gallery 15.00

BATTLESTAR GALACTICA: CYLON WAR (2003-2009 TV series)
Dynamite Entertainment: 2009 - No. 4, 2010 ($3.99, limited series)

1-3-First cylon war 40 years before the Caprica attack; Raynor-a; 2 covers 4.00

BATTLESTAR GALACTICA 1880, STEAMPUNK... (1978 TV series characters)
(Title changes from "(Classic) Battlestar Galactica Vol. 2" after #1)
Dynamite Entertainment: 2014 - No. 4, 2014 ($3.99, limited series)

1-4-Tony Lee-s/Aneke-a; multiple covers 4.00

BATTLESTAR GALACTICA: GHOSTS (2003-2009 TV series)
Dynamite Entertainment: 2008 - No. 4, 2009 ($4.99, 40 pgs., limited series)

1-4-Intro. of the Ghost Squadron; Jerwa-s/Lau-a/Calero-c 5.00

BATTLESTAR GALACTICA: GODS AND MONSTERS (2003-2009 TV series)
Dynamite Entertainment: 2016 - No. 5, 2017 ($3.99, limited series)

1-5-Karl Kesel-s/Alec Morgan & Dan Schkade-a 4.00

BATTLESTAR GALACTICA: JOURNEY'S END (1978 TV series)
Maximum Press: Aug, 1996 - No. 4, Nov, 1996 ($2.99, limited series)

1-4-Continuation of the T.V. series 4.00

BATTLESTAR GALACTICA: ORIGINS (2003-2009 TV series)
Dynamite Entertainment: 2007 - No. 11, 2008 ($3.50)

1-11: 1-4-Baltar's origin; multiple covers. 5-8-Adama's origin. 9-11-Starbuck & Helo 3.50

BATTLESTAR GALACTICA: SEASON III
Realm Press: June/July, 1999 - No. 3, Sept, 1999 ($2.99)

1-3: 1-Kuhoric-s/Scalf & Scott-a; two covers by Scalf & Jae Lee. 2,3-Two covers 3.00
Gallery (4/00, $3.99) short story and pin-ups 4.00
1999 Tour Book (5/99, $2.99) 3.00
1999 Tour Book Convention Edition (6.99) 7.00
...Special: Centurion Prime (12/99, $3.99) Kuhoric-s 4.00

BATTLESTAR GALACTICA: SEASON ZERO (2003-2009 TV series)
Dynamite Entertainment: 2007 - No. 12, 2008 ($2.99)

1-12-Set 2 years before the Cylon attack; multiple covers 3.00
.../The Lone Ranger 2007 Free Comic Book Day Edition; flip book with Cassaday Lone Ranger-c 3.00

BATTLESTAR GALACTICA: SIX (2003-2009 TV series)
Dynamite Entertainment: No. 1, 2014 - No. 5, 2015 ($3.99, limited series)

1-5: 1-J.T. Krul-s/Igor Lima-a; multiple covers. 3-5-Rodolfo-a. 5-Baltar app. 4.00

BATTLESTAR GALACTICA: SPECIAL EDITION (TV)
Maximum Press: Jan, 1997 ($2.99, one-shot)

1-Fully painted; Scalf-c/s/a; r/Asylum 3.00

BATTLESTAR GALACTICA: STARBUCK (TV)
Maximum Press: Dec, 1995 - No. 3, Mar, 1996 ($2.50, limited series)

1-3 4.00

BATTLESTAR GALACTICA: STARBUCK, (Classic...) (1978 TV series characters)
Dynamite Entertainment: 2013 - No. 4, 2014 ($3.99, limited series)

1-4-Tony Lee-s/Eman Casallos-a. 1-Childhood flashback 4.00

BATTLESTAR GALACTICA: THE COMPENDIUM (TV)
Maximum Press: Feb, 1997 ($2.99, one-shot)

1 3.00

BATTLESTAR GALACTICA: THE DEATH OF APOLLO, (Classic...) (1978 TV series)
Dynamite Entertainment: 2014 - No. 6, 2015 ($3.99, limited series)

1-6-Dan Abnett-s/Dietrich Smith-a; multiple covers on each 4.00

BATTLESTAR GALACTICA: THE ENEMY WITHIN (TV)
Maximum Press: Nov, 1995 - No. 3, Feb, 1996 ($2.50, limited series)

1-3: 3-Indicia reads Feb, 1995 in error. 4.00

BATTLESTAR GALACTICA: THE FINAL FIVE (2003 series)
Dynamite Entertainment: 2009 - No. 4, 2009 ($3.99, limited series)

1-4-Raynor-a; 2 covers on each 4.00

BATTLESTAR GALACTICA: TWILIGHT COMMAND (2003 series)
Dynamite Entertainment: 2019 - No. 5, 2019 ($3.99, limited series)

1-5-Moreci-s/Tamura-a; 2 covers; takes place during season 3 of the 2003 series 4.00

BATTLESTAR GALACTICA ZAREK (2003 series)
Dynamite Entertainment: 2007 - No. 4, 2007 ($3.50, limited series)

1-4-Origin story of political activist Tom Zarek; 2 covers on each 3.50

BATTLE STORIES (See XMas Comics)
Fawcett Publications: Jan, 1952 - No. 11, Sept, 1953

1-Evans-a (Korean War)	19	38	57	112	179	245
2	12	24	36	69	97	125
3-11	10	20	30	58	79	100

BATTLE STORIES

Batwoman #10 © DC

The Beagle Boys #9 © DIS

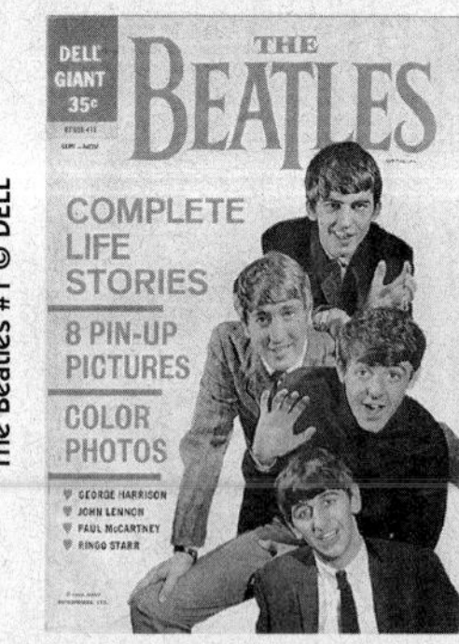

The Beatles #1 © DELL

	GD	VG	FN	VF	VF/NM	NM-
	2.0	4.0	6.0	8.0	9.0	9.2

GD VG FN VF VF/NM NM- 2.0 4.0 6.0 8.0 9.0 9.2

Super Comics: 1963 - 1964

Reprints #10-13,15-18: 10-r/U.S Tank Commandos #? 11-r/? 11, 12,17-r/Monty Hall #?; 13-Kintsler-a (1pg).15-r/American Air Forces #7 by Powell; Bolle-r. 18-U.S. Fighting Air Force #? 2 4 6 10 14 18

BATTLETECH (See Blackthorne 3-D Series #41 for 3-D issue)
Blackthorne Publishing: Oct, 1987 - No. 6, 1988 ($1.75/$2.00)

1-6: Based on game. 1-Color. 2-Begin B&W 3.00
Annual 1 ($4.50, B&W) 5.00

BATTLETECH
Malibu Comics: Feb, 1995 ($2.95)

0 3.00

BATTLETECH FALLOUT
Malibu Comics: Dec, 1994 - No. 4, Mar, 1995 ($2.95)

1-4-Two edi. exist #1; normal logo 3.00
1-Gold version w/foil logo stamped "Gold Limited Edition 8.00
1-Full-c holographic limited edition 6.00

BATTLETIDE (Death's Head II & Killpower...)
Marvel Comics UK, Ltd.: Dec, 1992 - No. 4, Mar, 1993 ($1.75, mini-series)

1-4: Wolverine, Psylocke, Dark Angel app. 3.00

BATTLETIDE II (Death's Head II & Killpower...)
Marvel Comics UK, Ltd.: Aug, 1993 - No. 4, Nov, 1993 ($1.75, mini-series)

1-($2.95)-Foil embossed logo 4.00
2-4: 2-Hulk-c/story 3.00

BATVARK (Reprints from Cerebus in Hell)
Aardvark-Vanaheim: Aug, 2017 ($4.00, B&W)

1-Cerebus figures placed over original Gustave Doré artwork of Hell; Batman #1-c swipe 4.00
... Penis (9/20, $4.00) Homage to Batman: Damned; Michelangelo's David app. 4.00
... XXXXX (1/21, $4.00) 2nd printing 4.00

BATWING (DC New 52)
DC Comics: Nov, 2011 - No. 34, Oct, 2014 ($2.99)

1-24: 1-3,5-Judd Winick-s/Ben Oliver-a. 4-Origin; Chriscross-a. 9-Night of the Owls 3.00
25-($3.99) Zero Year tie-in; Luke Fox's first meeting with Batman; Conner-c 4.00
26-34: 26,27-Darwyn Cooke-c 3.00
#0 (11/12, $2.99) origin of David Zavimbe; Winick-s/To-a 3.00
...: Futures End 1 (11/14, $2.99, regular-c) Five years later; Panosian-c 3.00
...: Futures End 1 (11/14, $3.99, 3-D cover) 4.00

BATWOMAN (See 52 #9 & 11 for debut and Detective Comics #854-860)
DC Comics: No. 0, Jan, 2011; No. 1, Nov, 2011 - No. 40, May, 2015 ($2.99)

0-(1/11) Williams III-s; art by Williams III and Reeder; Williams III-c 3.00
0-(1/11)-Variant-c by Reeder 5.00
1-New DC 52; Williams III-a; Williams III & Blackman-s; Bette Kane app. 5.00
2-24: 2-Cameron Chase returns. 6-8-Reeder-a/c. 9-11,15,18-20,22,23-McCarthy-a. 12-17-Wonder Woman app. 21-Francavilla-a; Killer Croc app. 3.00
25-($3.99) Zero Year tie-in; Maggie Sawyer & Bruce Wayne app. 4.00
26-40: 26-31-Wolf Spider. 35-Etrigan, Clayface, Ragman & Alice app. 3.00
#0 (11/12, $2.99) Flashback to Kate's training; Williams III-a 3.00
Annual 1 (6/14, $4.99) Continued from #24; Batman app.; McCarthy & Moritat-a 5.00
Annual 2 (6/15, $4.99) Continued from #40; Jeanty-c/a 5.00
... Elegy The Deluxe Edition HC (2010, $24.99, d.j.) r/Detective #854-860; gallery of variant covers, sketch art and script pages; intro. by Rachel Maddow 25.00
... Elegy SC (2011, $17.99) same contents as Deluxe HC 18.00
...: Futures End 1 (11/14, $2.99, regular-c) Five years later; Red Alice app. 3.00
...: Futures End 1 (11/14, $3.99, 3-D cover) 4.00

BATWOMAN (DC Rebirth)
DC Comics: May, 2017 - No. 18, Oct, 2018 ($2.99/$3.99)

1-18: 1-($3.99) M. Bennett & Tynion IV-s/Epting-a; covers by Epting & JG Jones. 6-Arlem-a 8-10-Scarecrow app. 13-Alice returns 4.00
...: Rebirth 1 (4/17, $2.99) Bennett & Tynion-s/Epting-a; origin re-capped 3.00

BATWOMAN/SUPERGIRL: WORLD'S FINEST GIANT
DC Comics: 2019 - Present ($4.99, 100 pgs., squarebound, Mass Market & Direct Market editions exist for each issue, with different covers)

1-Three new stories plus reprints; Alice app.; Joëlle Jones-c 5.00

BAY CITY JIVE
DC Comics (WildStorm): Jul, 2001 - No. 3, Sept, 2001 ($2.95, limited series)

1-3: Intro Sugah Rollins in 1970s San Francisco; Layman-s/Johnson-a 3.00

BAYWATCH COMIC STORIES (TV) (Magazine)
Acclaim Comics (Armada): May, 1996 - No. 4, 1997 ($4.95) (Photo-c on all)

1-4: Photo comics based on TV show 1 3 4 6 8 10

BEACH BLANKET BINGO (See Movie Classics)

BEAGLE BOYS, THE (Walt Disney)(See The Phantom Blot)
Gold Key: 11/64; No. 2, 11/65; No. 3, 8/66 - No. 47, 2/79 (See WDC&S #134)

	GD	VG	FN	VF	VF/NM	NM-
1	5	10	15	33	57	80
2-5	3	6	9	17	26	35
6-10	3	6	9	15	22	28
11-20: 11,14,19-r	2	4	6	11	16	20
21-30: 27-r	2	4	6	8	11	14
31-47	1	3	4	6	8	10

BEAGLE BOYS VERSUS UNCLE SCROOGE
Gold Key: Mar, 1979 - No. 12, Feb, 1980

	GD	VG	FN	VF	VF/NM	NM-
1	2	4	6	9	13	16
2-12: 9-r	1	2	3	5	6	8

BEANBAGS
Ziff-Davis Publ. Co. (Approved Comics): Winter, 1951 - No. 2, Spring, 1952

1,2 15 30 45 86 133 180

BEANIE THE MEANIE
Fago Publications: No. 3, May, 1959

3 6 12 18 31 38 45

BEANY AND CECIL (TV) (Bob Clampett's...)
Dell Publishing Co.: Jan, 1952 - 1955; July-Sept, 1962 - No. 5, July-Sept, 1963

	GD	VG	FN	VF	VF/NM	NM-
Four Color 368	24	48	72	168	372	575
Four Color 414,448,477,530,570,635(1/55)	13	26	39	87	191	295
01-057-209 (#1)	12	24	36	79	170	260
2-5	9	18	27	59	117	175

BEAR COUNTRY (Disney)
Dell Publishing Co.: No. 758, Dec, 1956

Four Color 758-Movie 5 10 15 34 60 85

BEAST (See X-Men)
Marvel Comics: May, 1997 - No. 3, 1997 ($2.50, mini-series)

1-3-Giffen-s/Nocon-a 4.00

BEAST BOY (See Titans)
DC Comics: Jan, 2000 - No. 4, Apr, 2000 ($2.95, mini-series)

1-4-Justiano-c/a; Raab & Johns-s 4.00

BEASTS OF BURDEN (See Dark Horse Book of Hauntings, ...Monsters, ...The Dead, ...Witchcraft)
Dark Horse Comics: Sept, 2009 - No. 4, Dec, 2009 ($2.99, limited series)

1-4-Evan Dorkin-s/Jill Thompson-a/c 3.00
...: Hunters & Gatherers (3/14, $3.50) Evan Dorkin-s/Jill Thompson-a/c 3.50
...: Neighborhood Watch (8/12, $3.50) Evan Dorkin-s/Jill Thompson-a/c 3.50
...: What the Cat Dragged In (5/16, $3.99) Evan Dorkin & Sarah Dyer-s/Jill Thompson-a/c 4.00
Volume 1: Animal Rites HC (6/10, $19.99) r/#1-4 & short stories from Dark Horse Books 20.00

BEASTS OF BURDEN: THE PRESENCE OF OTHERS
Dark Horse Comics: May, 2019 - No. 2, Jun, 2019 ($3.99, limited series)

1,2-Evan Dorkin-s/Jill Thompson-a/c 4.00

BEASTS OF BURDEN: WISE DOGS AND ELDRITCH MEN
Dark Horse Comics: Aug, 2018 - No. 4, Dec, 2018 ($3.99, limited series)

1-4-Evan Dorkin-s/Benjamin Dewey-a/c 4.00

BEATLES, THE (See Girls' Romances #109, Go-Go, Heart Throbs #101, Herbie #5, Howard the Duck Mag. #4, Laugh #166, Marvel Comics Super Special #4, My Little Margie #54, Not Brand Echh, Strange Tales #130, Summer Love, Superman's Pal Jimmy Olsen #79, Teen Confessions #37, Tippy's Friends & Tippy Teen)

BEATLES, THE (Life Story)
Dell Publishing Co.: Sept-Nov, 1964 (35¢)

1-(Scarce)-Stories with color photo pin-ups; Paul S. Newman-s/Joe Sinnott-a; photo-c 49 98 147 382 854 1325

BEATLES EXPERIENCE, THE
Revolutionary Comics: Mar, 1991 - No. 8, 1991 ($2.50, B&W, limited series)

1-8: 1-Gold logo 5.00

BEATLES YELLOW SUBMARINE (See Movie Comics under Yellow...)

BEAUTIFUL KILLER
Black Bull Comics: Sept., 2002 - No. 3, Jan, 2003 ($2.99, limited series)

...Limited Preview Edition (5/02, $5.00) preview pgs. & creator interviews 5.00
1-Noto-a/Palmiotti-s; Hughes-c; intro Brigit Cole 3.00
2,3: 2-Jusko-c. 3-Noto-c 3.00
TPB (5/03, $9.99) r/#1-3; cover gallery and Adam Hughes sketch pages 10.00

The Beauty #29 © Haun & Hurley

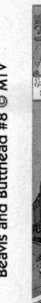

Beavis and Butthead #8 © MTV

Beetlejuice #1 © Geffen Film Co.

GD VG FN VF VF/NM NM-
2.0 4.0 6.0 8.0 9.0 9.2

BEAUTIFUL PEOPLE
Slave Labor Graphics: Apr, 1994 ($4.95, 8-1/2x11", one-shot)
nn 5.00

BEAUTIFUL STORIES FOR UGLY CHILDREN
DC Comics (Piranha Press): 1989 - No. 30, 1991 ($2.00/$2.50, B&W, mature)
Vol. 1-20: 12-$2.50-c begins 5.00
21-25 5.00
26-29-(Lower print run) 1 2 3 5 6 8
30-(Lower print run) 2 4 6 9 12 15
A Cotton Candy Autopsy ($12.95, B&W)-Reprints 1st two volumes 20.00

BEAUTY, THE (Also see Pilot Season: The Beauty)
Image Comics: Aug, 2015 - Present ($3.50/$3.99)
1-6-Jeremy Haun & Jason Hurley-s/Haun-a. 1-Three covers; reprints Pilot Season issue 4.00
7-29-($3.99) 7-Huddleston-a. 8-10-Weldele-a. 12-Haun-a. 13-29-Nachlik-a 4.00

BEAUTY AND THE BEAST, THE
Marvel Comics Group: Jan, 1985 - No. 4, Apr, 1985 (limited series)
1-4: Dazzler & the Beast from X-Men; Sienkiewicz-c on all 5.00

BEAUTY AND THE BEAST (Graphic novel)(Also see Cartoon Tales & Disney's New Adventures of...)
Disney Comics: 1992
nn-($4.95, prestige edition)-Adapts animated film 7.00
nn-($2.50, newsstand edition) 4.00

BEAUTY AND THE BEAST
Disney Comics: Sept., 1992 - No. 2, 1992 ($1.50, limited series)
1,2 4.00

BEAUTY AND THE BEAST: PORTRAIT OF LOVE (TV)
First Comics: May, 1989 - No. 2, Mar, 1990 ($5.95, 60 pgs., squarebound)
1,2: 1-Based on TV show, Wendy Pini-a/scripts. 2-...: Night of Beauty; by Wendy Pini 6.00

BEAVER VALLEY (Movie)(Disney)
Dell Publishing Co.: No. 625, Apr, 1955
Four Color 625 6 12 18 37 66 95

BEAVIS AND BUTTHEAD (MTV's...)(TV cartoon)
Marvel Comics: Mar, 1994 - No. 28, June, 1996 ($1.95)
1-Silver ink-c. 1, 2-Punisher & Devil Dinosaur app. 2 4 6 8 10 12
1-2nd printing 4.00
2,3: 2-Wolverine app. 3-Man-Thing, Spider-Man, Venom, Carnage, Mary Jane & Stan Lee cameos; John Romita, Sr. art (2 pgs.) 6.00
4-28: 5-War Machine, Thor, Loki, Hulk, Captain America & Rhino cameos. 6-Psylocke, Polaris, Daredevil & Bullseye app. 7-Ghost Rider & Sub-Mariner app. 8-Quasar & Eon app. 9-Prowler & Nightwatch app. 11-Black Widow app. 12-Thunderstrike & Bloodaxe app. 13-Night Thrasher app. 14-Spider-Man 2099 app. 15-Warlock app. 16-X-Factor app. 25-Juggernaut app. 5.00

BECK & CAUL INVESTIGATIONS
Gauntlet Comics (Caliber): Jan, 1994 - No. 5, 1995? ($2.95, B&W)
1-5 3.00
Special 1 ($4.95) 5.00

BEDKNOBS AND BROOMSTICKS (See Walt Disney Showcase No. 6 & 50)

BEDLAM!
Eclipse Comics: Sept, 1985 - No. 2, Sept, 1985 (B&W-r in color)
1,2: Bissette-a 4.00

BEDTIME STORIES FOR IMPRESSIONABLE CHILDREN
Moonstone Books/American Mythology: Nov, 2010; Feb, 2017 ($3.99, B&W)
1-(11/10) Short story anthology; Vaughn, Kuhoric & Tinnell-s; 3 covers 4.00
1-(2/17) Short story anthology; Vaughn, Shooter & Nelms-s; 4 covers 4.00

BEDTIME STORY (See Cinema Comics Herald)

BEE AND PUPPYCAT
Boom Entertainment (KaBOOM!): May, 2014 - No. 11, Apr, 2016 ($3.99)
1-11: Multiple covers on each. 1,2-Natasha Allegri-s/a 4.00

BEELZELVIS
Slave Labor Graphics: Feb, 1994 ($2.95, B&W, one-shot)
1 3.00

BEEP BEEP, THE ROAD RUNNER (TV) (See Dell Giant Comics Bugs Bunny Vacation Funnies #8 for 1st app.) (Also see Daffy & Kite Fun Book)
Dell Publishing Co./Gold Key No. 1-88/Whitman No. 89 on: July, 1958 - No. 14, Aug-Oct, 1962; Oct, 1966 - No. 105, 1984
Four Color 918 (#1, 7/58) 12 24 36 84 185 285
Four Color 1008,1046 (11-1/59-60) 8 16 24 51 96 140
4(2-4/60)-14(Dell) 6 12 18 37 66 95
1(10/66, Gold Key) 6 12 18 42 79 115
2-5 4 8 12 27 44 60
6-14 3 6 9 19 30 40
15-18,20-40 3 6 9 16 23 30
19-With pull-out poster 4 8 12 25 40 55
41-50 3 6 9 14 19 24
51-70 2 4 6 9 13 16
71-88 2 3 4 6 8 10
89,90,94-101: 100(3/82), 101(4/82) 2 4 6 8 10 12
91(8/80), 92(9/80), 93 (3-pack?) (low printing) 8 16 24 51 96 140
102-105 (All #90189 on-c; nd or date code; pre-pack) 102(6/83), 103(7/83), 104(5/84), 105(6/84) 3 6 9 19 30 40
#63-2970 (Now Age Books/Pendulum Pub. Comic Digest, 1971, 75¢, 100 pages, B&W) collection of one-page gags 4 8 12 27 44 60
NOTE: *See March of Comics #351, 353, 375, 387, 397, 416, 430, 442, 455. #5, 8-10, 35, 53, 59-62, 68-r; 96-102, 104 are 1/3-r.*

BEETLE BAILEY (See Giant Comic Album, Sarge Snorkel; also Comics Reading Libraries in the Promotional Comics section)
Dell Publishing Co./Gold Key #39-53/King #54-66/Charlton #67-119/Gold Key #120-131/ Whitman #132: #459, 5/53 - #38, 5-7/62; #39, 11/62 - #53, 5/66; #54, 8/66 - #65, 12/67;#67, 2/69 - #119, 11/76; #120, 4/78 - #132, 4/80
Four Color 469 (#1)-By Mort Walker 13 26 39 86 188 290
Four Color 521,552,622 7 14 21 49 92 135
5(2-4/56)-10(5-7/57) 5 10 15 35 63 90
11-20(4-5/59) 4 8 12 28 47 65
21-38(5-7/62) 3 6 9 20 31 42
39-53(5/66) 3 6 9 17 26 35
54-65 3 6 9 16 23 30
66 (only exists as U.S. published complimentary copies given away overseas) 3 6 9 16 23 30
67-69: 69-Last 12¢ issue 3 6 9 14 20 25
70-99 2 4 6 9 13 16
100 2 4 6 11 16 20
101-111,114-119 1 3 4 6 8 10
112,113-Byrne illos. (4 each) 2 4 6 9 12 18
120-132 1 2 3 4 5 7

BEETLE BAILEY
Harvey Comics: V2#1, Sept, 1992 - V2#9, Aug, 1994 ($1.25/$1.50)
V2#1 5.00
2-9-($1.50) 3.50
Big Book 1(11/92),2(5/93)(Both $1.95, 52 pgs.) 4.00
Giant Size V2#1(10/92),2(3/93)(Both $2.25,68 pgs.) 4.00

BEETLEJUICE (TV)
Harvey Comics: Oct, 1991 ($1.25)
1 2 4 6 11 16 20

BEETLEJUICE CRIMEBUSTERS ON THE HAUNT
Harvey Comics: Sept, 1992 - No. 3, Jan, 1993 ($1.50, limited series)
1-3 2 4 6 11 16 20

BEE 29, THE BOMBARDIER
Neal Publications: Feb, 1945
1-(Funny animal) 39 78 117 231 378 525

BEFORE THE FANTASTIC FOUR: BEN GRIMM AND LOGAN
Marvel Comics: July, 2000 - No. 3, Sept, 2000 ($2.99, limited series)
1-3-The Thing and Wolverine app.; Hama-s 3.00

BEFORE THE FANTASTIC FOUR: REED RICHARDS
Marvel Comics: Sept, 2000 - No. 3, Dec, 2000 ($2.99, limited series)
1-3-Peter David-s/Duncan Fegredo-c/a 3.00

BEFORE THE FANTASTIC FOUR: THE STORMS
Marvel Comics: Dec, 2000 - No. 3, Feb, 2001 ($2.99, limited series)
1-3-Adlard-a 3.00

BEFORE WATCHMEN: COMEDIAN (Prequel to 1986 Watchmen series)
DC Comics: Aug, 2012 - No. 6, Jun, 2013 ($3.99, limited series)
1-6-Brian Azzarello-s/J.G. Jones-a/c; The Comedian during the Vietnam War; back-up Crimson Corsair serial in #1-4; Higgins-a 4.00
1-Variant-c by Jim Lee 60.00
1-6-Variant covers. 1-Risso. 2-Bradstreet. 3-Leon. 4-Stelfreeze. 5-Frank. 6-Albuquerque 8.00

BEFORE WATCHMEN: DOLLAR BILL (Prequel to 1986 Watchmen series)

Before Watchmen: Dr. Manhattan #1 © DC

Ben Reilly: Scarlet Spider #18 © MAR

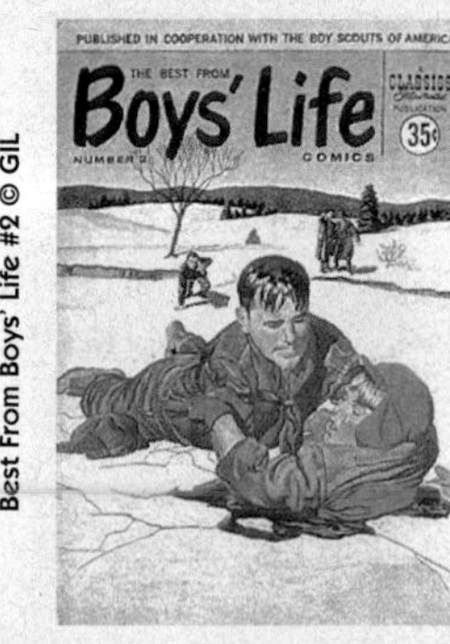

Best From Boys' Life #2 © GIL

	GD 2.0	VG 4.0	FN 6.0	VF 8.0	VF/NM 9.0	NM- 9.2
DC Comics: Mar, 2013 ($3.99, one-shot)						
1-Len Wein-s/Steve Rude-a/c; origin and demise of Dollar Bill						4.00
1-Variant-c by Jim Lee						60.00
1-Variant-c by Darwyn Cooke						8.00
BEFORE WATCHMEN: DR. MANHATTAN (Prequel to 1986 Watchmen series)						
DC Comics: Oct, 2012 - No. 4, Apr, 2013 ($3.99, limited series)						
1-4-Straczynski-s/Hughes-a/c; back-up Crimson Corsair serial in #1-3; Higgins-a						4.00
1-Variant-c by Jim Lee						60.00
1-4-Variant covers. 1-Pope. 2-Russell. 3-Neal Adams. 4-Sienkiewicz						8.00
BEFORE WATCHMEN: MINUTEMEN (Prequel to 1986 Watchmen series)						
DC Comics: Aug, 2012 - No. 6, Mar, 2013 ($3.99, limited series)						
1-6-Darwyn Cooke-a/c; The team flashback to 1939; back-up Crimson Corsair serial in #1-5; Higgins-a						4.00
1-Variant-c by Jim Lee						40.00
1-6-Variant covers. 1-Golden. 2-Garcia-Lopez-c. 3-Chiang. 4-Rude. 6-Cloonan						8.00
BEFORE WATCHMEN: MOLOCH (Prequel to 1986 Watchmen series)						
DC Comics: Jan, 2013 - No. 2, Feb, 2013 ($3.99, limited series)						
1,2-Straczynski-s/Risso-a/c; origin; back-up Crimson Corsair serial in both; Higgins-a						4.00
1-Variant-c by Jim Lee						40.00
1,2-Variant covers. 1-Matt Wagner. 2-Olly Moss						8.00
BEFORE WATCHMEN: NITE OWL (Prequel to 1986 Watchmen series)						
DC Comics: Aug, 2012 - No. 4, Feb, 2013 ($3.99, limited series)						
1-4-Straczynski-s/Andy Kubert-a/c; Joe Kubert-a(i) in #1-3; back-up Crimson Corsair serial in #1-3; Higgins-a						4.00
1-Variant-c by Jim Lee						50.00
1-4-Variant covers. 1-Nowlan. 2-Finch. 3-Samnee. 4-Van Sciver						8.00
BEFORE WATCHMEN: OZYMANDIAS (Prequel to 1986 Watchmen series)						
DC Comics: Sept, 2012 - No. 6, Apr, 2013 ($3.99, limited series)						
1-6-Len Wein-s/Jae Lee-a/c; origin of master plan; back-up Crimson Corsair serial in #1-4; Higgins-a						4.00
1-Variant-c by Jim Lee						50.00
1-6-Variant covers. 1-Jimenez. 2-Noto. 3-Carnevale. 4-Kaluta. 5-Thompson. 6-Sook						8.00
BEFORE WATCHMEN: RORSCHACH (Prequel to 1986 Watchmen series)						
DC Comics: Oct, 2012 - No. 4, Apr, 2013 ($3.99, limited series)						
1-4-Azzarello-s/Bermejo-a/c; back-up Crimson Corsair serial in #1-3; Higgins-a						5.00
1-Variant-c by Jim Lee						75.00
1-4-Variant covers. 1-Steranko. 2-Jock. 3-Kidd. 4-Reis						10.00
BEFORE WATCHMEN: SILK SPECTRE (Prequel to 1986 Watchmen series)						
DC Comics: Aug, 2012 - No. 4, Dec, 2013 ($3.99, limited series)						
1-4-Cooke & Conner-s/Conner-a/c; back-up Crimson Corsair serial in all; Higgins-a						4.00
1-Variant-c by Jim Lee						60.00
1-4-Variant covers. 1-Dave Johnson. 2-Middleton. 3-Allred. 4-Timm						8.00
BEHIND PRISON BARS						
Realistic Comics (Avon): 1952						
1-Kinstler-c	42	84	126	265	445	625
BEHOLD THE HANDMAID						
George Pflaum: 1954 (Religious) (25¢ with a 20¢ sticker price)						
nn	7	14	21	35	43	50
BELIEVE IT OR NOT (See Ripley's...)						
BEN AND ME (Disney)						
Dell Publishing Co.: No. 539, Mar, 1954						
Four Color 539	5	10	15	30	50	70
BEN BOWIE AND HIS MOUNTAIN MEN						
Dell Publishing Co.: 1952 - No. 17, Nov-Jan, 1958-59						
Four Color 443 (#1)	9	18	27	63	129	195
Four Color 513,557,599,626,657	5	10	15	34	60	85
7(5-7/56)-11: 11-Intro/origin Yellow Hair	4	8	12	25	40	55
12-17	4	8	12	23	37	50
BEN CASEY (TV)						
Dell Publishing Co.: June-July, 1962 - No. 10, June-Aug, 1965 (Photo-c)						
12-063-207 (#1)	5	10	15	35	63	90
2(10/62),3,5-10	4	8	12	23	37	50
4-Marijuana & heroin use story	4	8	12	27	44	60
BEN CASEY FILM STORIES (TV)						
Gold Key: Nov, 1962 (25¢) (Photo-c)						
30009-211-All photos	6	12	18	38	69	100

	GD 2.0	VG 4.0	FN 6.0	VF 8.0	VF/NM 9.0	NM- 9.2
BENEATH THE PLANET OF THE APES (See Movie Comics & Power Record Comics)						
BEN FRANKLIN (See Kite Fun Book)						
BEN HUR						
Dell Publishing Co.: No. 1052, Nov, 1959						
Four Color 1052-Movie, Manning-a	9	18	27	61	123	185
BEN ISRAEL						
Logos International: 1974 (39¢)						
nn-Christian religious	2	4	6	10	14	18
BEN REILLY: SCARLET SPIDER						
Marvel Comics: Jun, 2017 - No. 25, Dec, 2018 ($3.99)						
1-25: 1-Peter David-s/Mark Bagley-a. 6,7-Sliney-a. 7-Death app. 8-10-The Hornet app. 15-17-Damnation tie-in; Mephisto app. 23,25-Mephisto app.						4.00
BEN 10 (Cartoon Network)						
IDW Publishing: Nov, 2013 - No. 4, Feb, 2014 ($3.99, limited series)						
1-4: Henderson-s/Purcell-a; multiple covers on each						4.00
BEOWULF (Also see First Comics Graphic Novel #1)						
National Periodical Publications: Apr-May, 1975 - No. 6, Feb-Mar, 1976						
1	2	4	6	10	14	18
2,3,5,6: 5-Flying saucer-c/story	1	2	3	5	6	8
4-Dracula-c/s	1	3	4	6	8	10
BERNI WRIGHTSON, MASTER OF THE MACABRE						
Pacific Comics/Eclipse Comics No. 5: July, 1983 - No. 5, Nov, 1984 ($1.50, Baxter paper)						
1-5: Wrightson-c/a(r). 4-Jeff Jones-r (11 pgs.)						6.00
BERRYS, THE (Also see Funny World)						
Argo Publ.: May, 1956						
1-Reprints daily & Sunday strips & daily Animal Antics by Ed Nofziger	6	12	18	29	36	42
BERZERKER (Milo Ventimiglia Presents...)						
Image Comics (Top Cow): No. 0, Feb, 2009 - No. 6, Jun, 2010 ($2.99/$3.99)						
0-3-Jeremy Haun-a/Rick Loverd-s/Dale Keown-c. 0-Creator interviews						3.00
4-6-($3.99) Covers by Haun & Keown						4.00
BERZERKERS (See Youngblood V1#2)						
Image Comics (Extreme Studios): Aug, 1995 - No. 3, Oct, 1995 ($2.50, limited series)						
1-3: Beau Smith scripts, Fraga-a						3.00
BERZERKER UNBOUND						
Dark Horse Comics: Aug, 2019 - No. 4, Nov, 2019 ($3.99, limited series)						
1-4-Jeff Lemire-s/Mike Deodato-a/c. 1-Mignola var-c. 2-Sorrentino var-c. 3-Nguyen var-c						4.00
BEST COMICS						
Better Publications: Nov, 1939 - No. 4, Feb, 1940(10-11/16" wide x 8" tall, reads sideways)						
1-(Scarce)-Red Mask begins (1st app., 1st African American superhero in comics) & c/s-all	423	846	1269	3000	5250	7500
2-4: 3-Racist-c. 4-Cannibalism story	226	452	678	1446	2473	3500
BEST FROM BOY'S LIFE, THE						
Gilberton Company: Oct, 1957 - No. 5, Oct, 1958 (35¢)						
1-Space Conquerors & Kam of the Ancient Ones begin, end #5; Bob Cousy photo/story	14	28	42	76	108	140
2,3,5	8	16	24	42	54	65
4-L.B. Cole-a	8	16	24	44	57	70
BEST LOVE (Formerly Sub-Mariner Comics No. 32)						
Marvel Comics (MPI): No. 33, Aug, 1949 - No. 36, April, 1950 (Photo-c 33-36)						
33-Kubert-a	18	36	54	105	165	225
34 (10/49)	13	26	39	72	101	130
35,36-Everett-a	14	28	42	78	112	145
BEST OF ARCHIE, THE						
Perigee Books: 1980 ($7.95, softcover TPB)						
nn-Intro by Michael Uslan & Jeffrey Mendel	5	10	15	34	60	85
BEST OF BUGS BUNNY, THE						
Gold Key: Oct, 1966 - No. 2, Oct, 1968						
1,2-Giants	4	8	12	27	44	60
BEST OF DC, THE (Blue Ribbon Digest) (See Limited Coll. Ed. C-52)						
DC Comics: Sept-Oct, 1979 - No. 71, Apr, 1986 (100-148 pgs; mostly reprints)						
1-Superman, w/"Death of Superman"-r	3	6	9	14	20	25
2,5-9: 2-Batman 40th Ann. Special. 5-Best of 1979. 6,8-Superman. 7-Superboy. 9-Batman, Creeper app.	2	4	6	8	10	12

The Best of DC #45 © DC

The Best of the Brave and the Bold #6 © DC

Bettie Page Unbound #5 © Bettie Page LLC

	GD 2.0	VG 4.0	FN 6.0	VF 8.0	VF/NM 9.0	NM- 9.2

3-Superfriends 2 4 6 9 12 15
4-Rudolph the Red Nosed Reindeer 2 4 6 9 13 16
10-Secret Origins of Super Villains; 1st ever Penguin origin-s
3 6 9 16 23 30
11-16,18-20: 11-The Year's Best Stories. 12-Superman Time and Space Stories.13-Best of DC Comics Presents. 14-New origin stories of Batman villains. 15-Superboy. 16-Superman Anniv. 18-Teen Titans new-s., Adams, Kane-a; Perez-c. 19-Superman. 20-World's Finest
1 2 3 5 7 9
17-Supergirl 2 4 6 8 10 12
21,22: 21-Justice Society. 22-Christmas; unpublished Sandman story w/Kirby-a
2 4 6 10 14 18
23-27: 23-(148 pgs.)-Best of 1981. 24 Legion, new story and 16 pgs. new costumes. 25-Superman. 26-Brave & Bold. 27-Superman vs. Luthor
2 4 6 9 12 15
28,29: 28-Binky, Sugar & Spike app. 29-Sugar & Spike, 3 new stories; new Stanley & his Monster story 2 4 6 9 13 16
30,32-36,38,40: 30-Detective Comics. 32-Superman. 33-Secret origins of Legion Heroes and Villains. 34-Metal Men; has #497 on-c from Adv. Comics. 35-The Year's Best Comics Stories (148 pgs.). 36-Superman vs. Kryptonite. 38-Superman. 40-World of Krypton
2 4 6 9 12 15
31-JLA 2 4 6 10 14 18
34-Corrected version with "#34" on cover 2 4 6 10 14 18
37,39: 37-"Funny Stuff", Mayer-a. 39-Binky 2 4 6 10 14 18
41,43,45,47,49,53,55,58,60,63,65,68,70: 41-Sugar & Spike new stories with Mayer-a. 43,49,55-Funny Stuff. 45,53,70-Binky. 47,65,68-Sugar & Spike. 58-Super Jrs. Holiday Special; Sugar & Spike. 60-Plop!; Wood-c(r) & Aragonés-r (5/85). 63-Plop!; Wrightson-a(r)
3 6 9 14 19 24
42,44,46,48,50-52,54,56,57,59,61,62,64,66,67,69,71: 42,56-Superman vs. Aliens. 44,57,67-Superboy & LSH. 46-Jimmy Olsen. 48-Superman Team-ups. 50-Year's best Superman. 51-Batman Family. 52 Best of 1984. 54,56,59-Superman. 61-(148 pgs.)Year's best. 62-Best of Batman 1985. 69-Year's best Team stories. 71-Year's best
2 4 6 10 14 18

NOTE: ***N. Adams** a-2r, 14r, 18r, 26, 51. **Aparo** a-9, 14, 26, 30; c-9, 14, 26. **Austin** a-51i. **Buckler** a-40p; c-16, 22. **Giffen** a-50, 52; c-33p. **Grell** a-33p. **Grossman** a-37. **Heath** a-26. **Infantino** a-10r, 18. **Kaluta** a-40. **G. Kane** a-10r, 18r; c-40, 44. **Kubert** a-10r, 21, 26. **Layton** a-21. **S. Mayer** c-29, 37, 41, 43, 47; a-28, 29, 37, 41, 43, 47, 58, 65, 68. **Moldoff** c-64p. **Morrow** a-40; c-40. **W. Mortimer** a-39p. **Newton** a-5, 51. **Perez** a-24, 50p; c-18, 21, 23. **Rogers** a-14, 51p. **Simonson** a-11r. **Spiegle** a-52. **Starlin** a-51. **Staton** a-5, 21. **Tuska** a-24. **Wolverton** a-60. **Wood** a-60, 63; c-60, 63. **Wrightson** a-60. New art in #14, 18, 24.*

BEST OF DENNIS THE MENACE, THE
Hallden/Fawcett Publications: Summer, 1959 - No. 5, Spring, 1961 (100 pgs.)
1-All reprints; Wiseman-a 6 12 18 41 76 110
2-5: 2-Christmas-c 5 10 15 34 50 65

BEST OF DONALD DUCK, THE
Gold Key: Nov, 1965 (12¢, 36 pgs.)(Lists 2nd printing in indicia)
1-Reprints Four Color #223 by Barks 7 14 21 49 92 135

BEST OF DONALD DUCK & UNCLE SCROOGE, THE
Gold Key: Nov, 1964 - No. 2, Sept, 1967 (25¢ Giants)
1(30022-411)('64)-Reprints 4-Color #189 & 408 by Carl Barks; cover of F.C. #189 redrawn by Barks 8 16 24 54 102 150
2(30022-709)('67)-Reprints 4-Color #256 & "Seven Cities of Cibola" & U.S. #8 by Barks
7 14 21 44 82 120

BEST OF HORROR AND SCIENCE FICTION COMICS
Bruce Webster: 1987 ($2.00)
1-Wolverton, Frazetta, Powell, Ditko-r 2 4 6 8 10 12

BEST OF JOSIE AND THE PUSSYCATS
Archie Comics: 2001 ($10.95, TPB)
1-Reprints 1st app. and noteworthy stories 12.00

BEST OF MARMADUKE, THE
Charlton Comics: 1960
1-Brad Anderson's strip reprints 3 6 9 21 33 45

BEST OF MS. TREE, THE
Pyramid Comics: 1987 - No. 4, 1988 ($2.00, B&W, limited series)
1-4 3.00

BEST OF THE BRAVE AND THE BOLD, THE (See Super DC Giant)
DC Comics: Oct, 1988 - No. 6, Jan, 1989 ($2.50, limited series)
1-6: Neal Adams-r, Kubert-r & Heath-r in all 4.00

BEST OF THE SPIRIT, THE
DC Comics: 2005 ($14.99, TPB)
nn-Reprints 1st app. and noteworthy stories; intro by Neil Gaiman; Eisner bio. 15.00

BEST OF THE WEST (See A-1 Comics)

Magazine Enterprises: 1951 - No. 12, April-June, 1954
1(A-1 42)-Ghost Rider, Durango Kid, Straight Arrow, Bobby Benson begin
41 82 123 256 428 600
2(A-1 46) 22 44 66 128 209 290
3(A-1 52), 4(A-1 59), 5(A-1 66) 18 36 54 105 165 225
6(A-1 70), 7(A-1 76), 8(A-1 81), 9(A-1 85), 10(A-1 87), 11(A-1 97), 12(A-1 103) 15 30 45 84 127 170
NOTE: ***Bolle** a-9. **Borth** a-12. **Guardineer** a-5, 12. **Powell** a-1, 12.*

BEST OF UNCLE SCROOGE & DONALD DUCK, THE
Gold Key: Nov, 1966 (25¢)
1(30030-611)-Reprints part 4-Color #159 & 456 & Uncle Scrooge #6,7 by Carl Barks
7 14 21 44 82 120

BEST OF WALT DISNEY COMICS, THE
Western Publishing Co.: 1974 ($1.50, 52 pgs.) (Walt Disney)
(8-1/2x11" cardboard covers; 32,000 printed of each)
96170-Reprints 1st two stories less 1 pg. each from 4-Color #62
6 12 18 37 66 95
96171-Reprints Mickey Mouse and the Bat Bandit of Inferno Gulch from 1934 (strips) by Gottfredson 6 12 18 37 66 95
96172-r/Uncle Scrooge #386 & two other stories 6 12 18 37 66 95
96173-Reprints "Ghost of the Grotto" (from 4-Color #159) & "Christmas on Bear Mountain" (from 4-Color #178) 6 12 18 37 66 95

BEST ROMANCE
Standard Comics (Visual Editions): No. 5, Feb-Mar, 1952 - No. 7, Aug, 1952
5-Toth-a; photo-c 18 36 54 105 165 225
6,7-Photo-c 12 24 36 69 97 125

BEST SELLER COMICS (See Tailspin Tommy)

BEST WESTERN (Formerly Terry Toons? or Miss America Magazine
Marvel Comics (IPC): V7#24(#57)?; Western Outlaws & Sheriffs No. 60 on)
No. 58, June, 1949 - No. 59, Aug, 1949
58,59-Black Rider, Kid Colt, Two-Gun Kid app.; both have Syd Shores-c
22 44 66 130 213 295

BETA RAY BILL: GODHUNTER
Marvel Comics: Aug, 2009 - No. 3, Oct, 2009 ($3.99, limited series)
1-3-Kano-a; Thor and Galactus app.; reprints form Thor #337-339. 2,3-Silver Surfer app. 4.00

BETRAYAL OF THE PLANET OF THE APES (Set 20 years before the first movie)
BOOM! Studios: Nov, 2011 - No. 4, Feb, 2012 ($3.99, limited series)
1-4-Dr. Zaius app.; Bechko-s/Hardman-a. 1-Three covers. 2-Two covers 4.00

BETROTHED
AfterShock Comics: Mar, 2018 - No. 5, Jul, 2018 ($3.99, limited series)
1-5-Sean Lewis-s/Steve Uy-a 4.00

BETTIE PAGE
Dynamite Entertainment: 2017 - No. 8, 2018 ($3.99)
1-8: 1-Bettie Page in 1951 Hollywood; Avallone-s/Worley-a; multiple covers on each 4.00
... Halloween Special One-Shot (2018, $4.99) Avallone-s; art by Ohta & Ruiz 5.00
... Halloween Special One-Shot (2019, $4.99) Avallone-s; art by Martinez & Ruiz 5.00

BETTIE PAGE COMICS
Dark Horse Comics: Mar, 1996 ($3.95)
1-Dave Stevens-c; Blevins & Heath-a; Jaime Hernandez pin-up
2 4 6 13 18 22

BETTIE PAGE COMICS: QUEEN OF THE NILE
Dark Horse Comics: Dec, 1999 - No. 3, Apr, 2000 ($2.95, limited series)
1-3-Silke-s/a; Stevens-c 2 4 6 8 10 12

BETTIE PAGE COMICS: SPICY ADVENTURE
Dark Horse Comics: Jan, 1997 ($2.95, one-shot, mature)
nn-Silke-c/s/a 2 4 6 8 10 12

BETTIE PAGE UNBOUND (Volume 3)
Dynamite Entertainment: 2019 - No. 10, 2020 ($3.99)
1-10-Multiple covers on each: 1-Bettie as Red Sonja. 2-Bettie as Vampirella 4.00

BETTIE PAGE: VOLUME 2
Dynamite Entertainment: 2018 - No. 5, 2019 ($3.99)
1-5-Bettie Page in 1952 England. 1-4-Avallone-s/Ohta-a; multiple covers on each 4.00

BETTIE PAGE: VOLUME 3
Dynamite Entertainment: 2020 - No. 5, 2020 ($3.99)
1-5-Bettie Page shooting a movie in the Caribbean; multiple covers on each 4.00

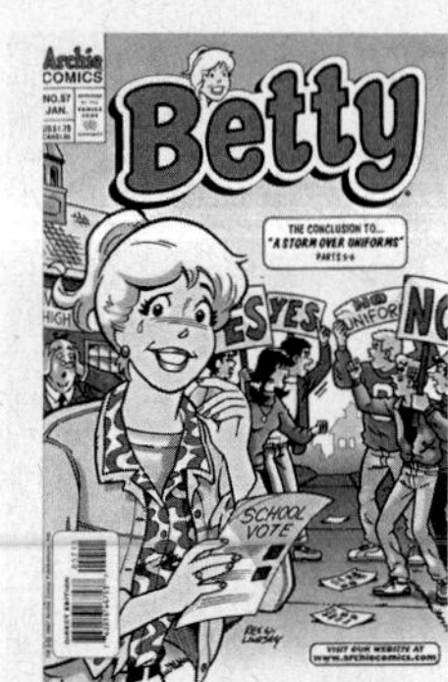

Betty #57 © ACP

Betty and Veronica #175 © ACP

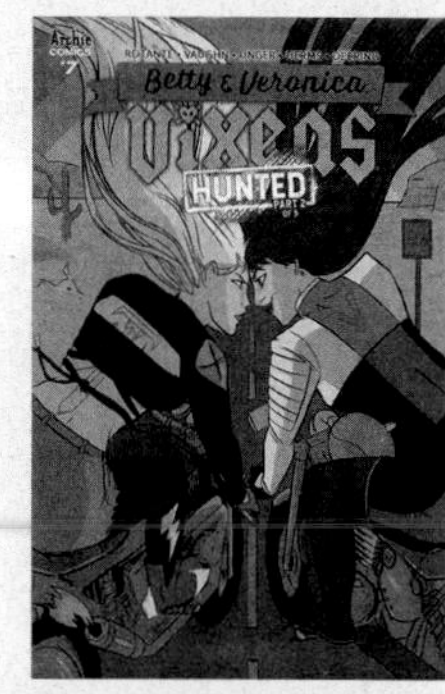

Betty & Veronica: Vixens #7 © ACP

	GD	VG	FN	VF	VF/NM	NM-
	2.0	4.0	6.0	8.0	9.0	9.2

BETTY (See Pep Comics #22 for 1st app.)
Archie Comics: Sept, 1992 - No. 195, Jan, 2012 ($1.25-$2.99)

1 6.00
2-18,20-24: 20-1st Super Sleuther-s 4.00
19-Love Showdown part 2 5.00
25-Pin-up page of Betty as Marilyn Monroe, Madonna, Lady Di 5.00
26-50 3.00
51-195: 57- "A Storm Over Uniforms" x-over part 5,6. 186-Begin $2.99-c 3.00

BETTY AND HER STEADY (Going Steady with Betty No. 1)
Avon Periodicals: No. 2, Mar-Apr, 1950

2 14 28 42 81 118 155

BETTY AND ME
Archie Publications: Aug, 1965 - No. 200, Aug, 1992

1 18 36 54 124 275 425
2,3: 3-Origin Superteen 7 14 21 46 86 125
4-8: Superteen in new costume #4-7; dons new helmet in #5, ends #8. 5 10 15 34 60 85
9,10: Girl from R.I.V.E.R.D.A.L.E. 9-UFO-s 4 8 12 27 44 60
11-15,17-20(4/69) 3 6 9 21 33 45
16-Classic cover; w/risqué cover dialogue 30 60 90 216 483 750
21,24-35: 33-Paper doll page 3 6 9 16 23 30
22-Archies Band-s 3 6 9 16 24 32
23-I Dream of Jeannie parody 3 6 9 19 30 40
36(8/71),37,41-55 (52 pgs.): 42-Betty as vamp-s 3 6 9 16 23 30
38-Sabrina app. 4 8 12 23 37 50
39-Josie and Sabrina cover cameos 3 6 9 19 30 40
40-Archie & Betty share a cabin 3 6 9 17 26 35
56(4/71)-80(12/76): 79 Betty Cooper mysteries thru #86. 79-81-Drago the Vampire-s 2 4 6 9 13 16
81-99: 83-Harem-c. 84-Jekyll & Hyde-c/s 2 4 6 8 10 12
100(3/79) 2 4 6 9 12 15
101,118: 101-Elvis mentioned. 118-Tarzan mentioned 1 2 3 5 7 9
102-117,119-130(9/82): 103,104-Space-s. 124-DeCarlo-c begins 7.00
131-138,140,142-147,149-154,156-158: 135,136-Jason Blossom app. 136-Cheryl Blossom cameo. 137-Space-s. 138-Tarzan parody 5.00
139,141,148: 139-Katy Keene collecting-s; Archie in drag-s. 141-Tarzan parody-s. 148-Cyndi Lauper parody-s 6.00
155,159,160(8/87): 155-Archie in drag-s. 159-Superhero gag-c. 160-Wheel of Fortune parody 6.00
161-169,171-199 4.00
170,200: 170-New Archie Superhero-s 6.00

BETTY AND VERONICA (Also see Archie's Girls...)
Archie Enterprises: June, 1987 - No. 278, Dec, 2015 (75¢-$3.99)

1 2 3 4 6 8 10
2-10 6.00
11-30 4.00
31-81 3.00
82-Love Showdown part 3 5.00
83-271: 242-Begin $2.50-c. 247-Begin $2.99-c. 264-271-Two covers 3.00
267-Mermaid variant-c by Fiona Staples 10.00
272-274,276-278-($3.99): 272-274,276,277-Two covers. 278-Last issue; 6 covers 4.00
275-($4.99) Five covers by Adam Hughes, Ramona Fradon & others 5.00
... Free Comic Book Day Edition #1 (6/05) Katy Keene-c/app.; Cheryl Blossom app. 3.00

BETTY AND VERONICA (Volume 3)
Archie Comic Publications: Sept, 2016 - No. 3, Aug, 2017 ($3.99, limited series)

1-3-Adam Hughes-s/a; multiple covers on each; back-up classic pin-ups 4.00
... No. 1: FCBD Edition (5/17, giveaway) r/#1; bonus Riverdale TV show character guide 3.00

BETTY AND VERONICA (Volume 4)
Archie Comic Publications: Feb, 2019 - No. 5, Jul, 2019 ($3.99, limited series)

1-5-Rotante-s/Lanz-a; Senior year in high school 4.00

BETTY & VERONICA ANNUAL DIGEST (...Digest Magazine #1-4, 44 on; ...Comics Digest Mag. #5-43)(Continues as Betty & Veronica Friends Double Digest #209-on)
Archie Publications: Nov, 1980 - No. 208, Nov, 2010 ($1.00/-$2.69, digest size)

1 3 6 9 16 23 30
2-10: 2(11/81-Katy Keene story), 3(8/82) 2 4 6 9 13 16
11-30 1 3 4 6 8 10
31-50 1 2 3 4 5 7
51-70 4.00
71-191: 110-Begin $2.19-c. 135-Begin $2.39-c. 165-Begin $2.49. 185-Includes reprint of Archie's Girls B&V #1 (1950) and new story where 1950 & 2008 B&V meet 3.00
192-208: 192-Begin $2.69-c 3.00

BETTY & VERONICA ANNUAL DIGEST MAGAZINE
Archie Comics: Sept, 1989 - No. 16, Aug, 1997 ($1.50/$1.75/$1.79, 128 pgs.)

1 1 2 3 5 7 9
2-10: 9-Neon ink logo 5.00
11-16: 16-Begin $1.79-c 3.00

BETTY & VERONICA CHRISTMAS SPECTACULAR (See Archie Giant Series Magazine #159, 168, 180, 191, 204, 217, 229, 241, 453, 465, 477, 489, 501, 513, 525, 536, 547, 558, 568, 580, 593, 606, 618)

BETTY & VERONICA DOUBLE DIGEST MAGAZINE
Archie Enterprises: 1987 - Present ($2.25-$7.99, digest size, 256 pgs.)(...Digest #12 on)

1 2 4 6 8 10 12
2-10 1 2 3 4 5 7
11-25: 5,17-Xmas-c. 16-Capt. Hero story 5.00
26-50 4.00
51-150: 87-Begin $3.19-c. 95-Begin $3.29-c. 114-Begin $3.59-c. 142-Begin $3.69-c 4.00
151-211,213-222: 151-(7/07)-Realistic style Betty & Veronica debuts (thru #154). 160-Cheryl Blossom spotlight. 170-173-Realistic style 4.00
212,223,237,240-($5.99) Titled Betty & Veronica Double Double Digest (320 pages) 6.00
224-($5.99) Titled Betty & Veronica Comics Annual (192 pgs.) 6.00
225,228,238,242,247,250,255,257,260-275-($6.99) Titled Betty & Veronica Jumbo Comics Digest (320 pgs.) 7.00
226,227,229-232,234-236,239,241,243,245,246,249,251,254,256-($4.99) Titled Betty & Veronica Comics Digest or Comics Double Digest 5.00
244,248,252,253,258-($5.99) 244,253-Titled Betty & Veronica Summer Ann. 6.00
276-291-($7.99): 287-Halloween-c 8.00
Betty & Veronica: in Bad Boy Trouble Vol.1 TPB (2007, $7.49) r/new style from #151-154 8.00

BETTY & VERONICA FRIENDS DOUBLE DIGEST (Continues from B&V Digest Mag. #208)
Archie Publications: No. 209, Jan, 2011 - Present ($3.99-$7.99, digest size)

209-236,238: 209-Cheryl Blossom app. 4.00
237,246-Titled Betty & Veronica Friends Double Double Digest ($5.99, 320 pages) 6.00
239-($4.99) Double Digest 5.00
240,245,250,252,254,256,257-273-($6.99) 257-Winter Annual 7.00
241-244,248-($4.99) Titled Betty & Veronica Friends Comics Digest. 244-Pussycats app. 5.00
247,249,251,253,255-($5.99) 247-Easter Annual. 251-Halloween Annual 6.00
274-286-($7.99) 8.00

BETTY & VERONICA FRIENDS FOREVER
Archie Publications: Jun, 2018 - Present ($2.99, quarterly)

1-Classic-style stories; Parent-a 3.00
1-(#2) Travel Tales on cover, 1-(#3) Storybook Tales, 1-(#4) Go To Work, 1-(#5) Pets, 1-(#6) Return to Storybook Land, 1-(#7) Supernatural Stories, 1-(#8) What If...?, 1(#9) It's All Relative. 1-(#10) Danger Zone. 1-(#11) Good Citizens. 1-(#12) Winterfest 3.00

BETTY & VERONICA SPECTACULAR (See Archie Giant Series Mag. #11, 16, 21, 26, 32, 138, 145, 153, 162, 173, 184, 197, 201, 210, 214, 221, 226, 234, 238, 246, 250, 458, 462, 470, 482, 486, 494, 498, 506, 510, 518, 522, 526, 530, 537, 552, 559, 563, 569, 575, 582, 588, 600, 608, 613, 620, 623, and Betty & Veronica)

BETTY AND VERONICA SPECTACULAR
Archie Comics: Oct, 1992 - No. 90, Sept, 2009 ($1.25/$1.50/$1.75/$1.99/$2.19/$2.25/$2.50)

1-Dan DeCarlo-c/a 5.00
2-90: 48-Cheryl Blossom leaves Riverdale. 64-Cheryl Blossom returns 3.00

BETTY & VERONICA SPRING SPECTACULAR (See Archie Giant Series Magazine #569, 582, 595)

BETTY & VERONICA SUMMER FUN (See Archie Giant Series Mag. #8, 13, 18, 23, 28, 34, 140, 147, 155, 164, 175, 187, 199, 212, 224, 236, 248, 460, 484, 496, 508, 520, 529, 539, 550, 561, 572, 585, 598, 611, 621)
Archie Comics: 1994 - No. 6, 1999 ($2.00/$2.25/$2.29, annual)

1-($2.00, 52 pgs. plus poster) 4.00
2-6: 5-($2.25-c). 6-($2.29-c) 3.00
Vol. 1 (2003, $10.95) reprints stories from Archie Giant Series editions 12.00

BETTY & VERONICA: VIXENS
Archie Comics Publications: Jan, 2018 - No. 10, Nov, 2018 ($3.99)

1-10: 1-Betty & Veronica form a biker gang; Cabrera-a; South Side Serpents app. 4.00

BETTY BOOP (Volume 1)
Dynamite Entertainment: 2016 - No. 4, 2017 ($3.99)

1-4-Langridge-s/Lagacé-a; Koko app.; multiple covers on each 4.00

BETTY BOOP'S BIG BREAK
First Publishing: 1990 ($5.95, 52 pgs.)

nn-By Joshua Quagmire; 60th anniversary ish. 6.00

BETTY PAGE 3-D COMICS
The 3-D Zone: 1991 ($3.95, "7-1/2x10-1/4," 28 pgs., no glasses)

1-Photo inside covers; back-c nudity 2 4 6 9 13 16

BETTY'S DIARY (See Archie Giant Series Magazine No. 555)
Archie Enterprises: April, 1986 - No. 40, Apr, 1991 (#1:65¢; 75¢/95¢)

Beverly Hillbillies #5 © DELL

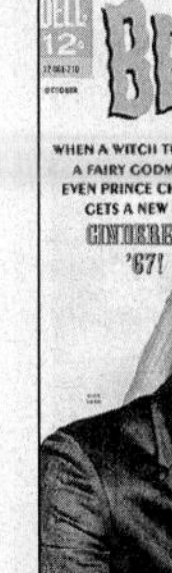
Bewitched #11 © Screen Gems

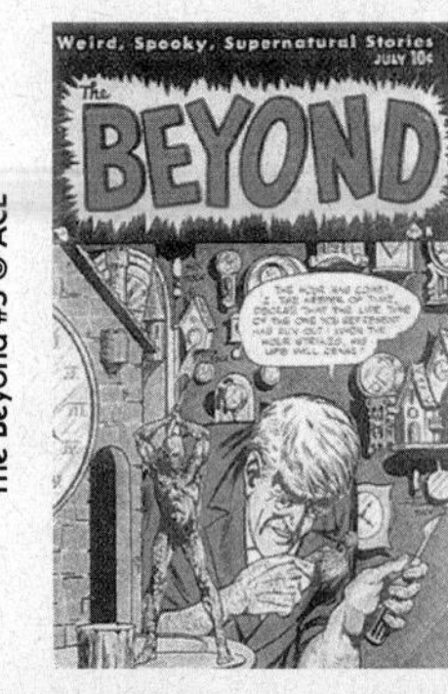

The Beyond #5 © ACE

	GD 2.0	VG 4.0	FN 6.0	VF 8.0	VF/NM 9.0	NM- 9.2
1	1	2	3	4	5	7
2-10						4.00
11-40						3.00

BETTY'S DIGEST
Archie Enterprises: Nov, 1996 - No. 2 ($1.75/$1.79)

	GD	VG	FN	VF	VF/NM	NM-
1,2						3.00

BEVERLY HILLBILLIES (TV)
Dell Publishing Co.: 4-6/63 - No. 18, 8/67; No. 19, 10/69; No. 20, 10/70; No. 21, Oct, 1971

	GD	VG	FN	VF	VF/NM	NM-
1-Photo-c	15	30	45	101	223	345
2-Photo-c	8	16	24	55	105	155
3-9: All have photo covers	6	12	18	40	73	105
10: No photo cover	5	10	15	30	50	70
11-21: All have photo covers. 18-Last 12¢ issue. 19-21-Reprint #1-3 (covers and insides)	5	10	15	33	57	80

NOTE: *#1-9, 11-21 are photo covers.*

BEWARE (Formerly Fantastic; Chilling Tales No. 13 on)
Youthful Magazines: No. 10, June, 1952 - No. 12, Oct, 1952

	GD	VG	FN	VF	VF/NM	NM-
10-E.A. Poe's Pit & the Pendulum adaptation by Wildey; Harrison/Bache-a; atom bomb and shrunken head-c	84	168	252	538	919	1300
11-Harrison-a; Ambrose Bierce adapt.	58	116	174	371	636	900
12-Used in **SOTI**, pg. 388; Harrison-a	58	116	174	371	636	900

BEWARE
Trojan Magazines/Merit Publ. No. ?: No. 13, 1/53 - No. 16, 7/53; No. 5, 9/53 - No. 15, 5/55

	GD	VG	FN	VF	VF/NM	NM-
13(#1)-Harrison-a	87	174	261	553	952	1350
14(#2, 3/53)-Krenkel/Harrison-c; dismemberment, severed head panels; Good Girl-c	135	270	405	864	1482	2100
15,16(#3, 5/53; #4, 7/53)-Harrison-a	50	100	150	315	533	750
5,9,12,13(1/55)	48	96	144	302	514	725
6-Ill. in **SOTI**- "Children are first shocked and then desensitized by all this brutality." Corpse on cover swipe/V.O.H. #26; girl on cover swipe/Advs. Into Darkness #10	206	412	618	1318	2259	3200
7,8-Check-a	54	108	162	343	574	825
10-Frazetta/Check-c; Disbrow, Check-a	290	580	870	1856	3178	4500
11-Disbrow-a; heart torn out, blood drainage story	58	116	174	371	636	900
14,15: 14-Myron Fass-c. 15-Harrison-a	45	90	135	284	480	675

NOTE: ***Fass** a-5, 6, 8; c-6, 11, 14. **Forte** a-8. **Hollingsworth** a-15(#3), 16(#4), 9; c-16(#4), 8, 9. **Kiefer** a-16(#4), 5, 6, 10.*

BEWARE (Becomes Tomb of Darkness No. 9 on)
Marvel Comics Group: Mar, 1973 - No. 8, May, 1974 (All reprints)

	GD	VG	FN	VF	VF/NM	NM-
1-Everett-c; Kirby & Sinnott-r ('54)	5	10	15	31	53	75
2-8: 2-Forte, Colan-r. 6-Tuska-a. 7-Torres-r/Mystical Tales #7	3	6	9	21	33	45

NOTE: ***Infantino** a-4r. **Gil Kane** c-4. **Wildey** a-7r.*

BEWARE TERROR TALES
Fawcett Publications: May, 1952 - No. 8, July, 1953

	GD	VG	FN	VF	VF/NM	NM-
1-E.C. art swipe/Haunt of Fear #5 & Vault of Horror #26	71	142	213	454	777	1100
2	47	94	141	296	498	700
3-5,7	41	82	123	256	428	600
6-Classic skeleton-c	65	130	195	416	708	1000
8-Tothish-a; people being cooked-c	71	142	213	454	777	1100

NOTE: ***Andru** a-2. **Bernard Bailey** a-1; c-1-5. **Powell** a-1, 2, 8. **Sekowsky** a-2.*

BEWARE THE BATMAN (Based on the Cartoon Network series)
DC Comics: Dec, 2013 - No. 6, May, 2014 ($2.99)

	GD	VG	FN	VF	VF/NM	NM-
1-6: 1-Anarky app. 4-Man-Bat app. 6-Killer Croc app.						3.00

BEWARE THE CREEPER (See Adventure, Best of the Brave & the Bold, Brave & the Bold, 1st Issue Special, Flash #318-323, Showcase #73, World's Finest Comics #249)
National Periodical Publications: May-June, 1968 - No. 6, Mar-Apr, 1969 (All 12¢ issues)

	GD	VG	FN	VF	VF/NM	NM-
1-(5-6/68)-Classic Ditko-c; Ditko-a in all	8	16	24	54	102	150
2-6: 2-5-Ditko-c. 2-Intro. Proteus. 6-Gil Kane-c	5	10	15	31	53	75

BEWARE THE CREEPER
DC Comics (Vertigo): June, 2003 - No. 5, Oct, 2003 ($2.95, limited series)

	GD	VG	FN	VF	VF/NM	NM-
1-5-Female vigilante in 1920s Paris; Jason Hall-s/Cliff Chiang-a						3.00

BEWITCHED (TV)
Dell Publishing Co.: 4-6/65 - No. 11, 10/67; No. 12, 10/68 - No. 13, 1/69; No. 14, 10/69

	GD	VG	FN	VF	VF/NM	NM-
1-Photo-c	14	28	42	96	211	325
2-No photo-c	8	16	24	51	96	140
3-13-All have photo-c. 12-Rep. #1. 13-Last 12¢-c	6	12	18	41	76	110
14-No photo-c; reprints #2	5	10	15	33	57	80

BEYOND!
Marvel Comics: Sept, 2006 - No. 6, Feb, 2007 ($2.99, limited series)

	GD	VG	FN	VF	VF/NM	NM-
1-6-McDuffie-s/Kolins-a; Spider-Man, Venom, Gravity, Wasp app. 6-Gravity dies						3.00

BEYOND, THE
Ace Magazines: Nov, 1950 - No. 30, Jan, 1955

	GD	VG	FN	VF	VF/NM	NM-
1-Bakerish-a(p)	71	142	213	454	777	1100
2-Bakerish-a(p)	42	84	126	265	445	625
3-10: 10-Woodish-a by Cameron	36	72	108	214	347	480
11-20: 18-Used in **POP**, pgs. 81,82	30	60	90	177	289	400
21-26,28-30	27	54	81	162	266	370
27-Used in **SOTI**, pg. 111	53	106	159	334	567	800

NOTE: ***Cameron** a-10, 11p, 12p, 15, 16, 21-27, 30; c-20. **Colan** a-6, 13, 17. **Sekowsky** a-2, 3, 5, 7, 11, 14, 27r. No. 1 was to appear as Challenge of the Unknown No. 7.*

BEYONDERS
AfterShock Comics: Aug, 2018 - No. 5, Mar, 2019 ($3.99, limited series)

	GD	VG	FN	VF	VF/NM	NM-
1-5-Paul Jenkins-s/Wesley St. Claire-a						4.00

BEYOND THE FRINGE (Based on the TV series Fringe)
DC Comics: May, 2012 ($3.99, one-shot)

	GD	VG	FN	VF	VF/NM	NM-
1-Joshua Jackson-s/Jorge Jimenez-a/Drew Johnson-c						4.00

BEYOND THE GRAVE
Charlton Comics: July, 1975 - No. 6, June, 1976; No. 7, Jan, 1983 - No. 17, Oct, 1984

	GD	VG	FN	VF	VF/NM	NM-
1-Ditko-a (6 pgs.); Sutton painted-c	4	8	12	28	47	65
2-6: 2-5-Ditko-a; Ditko c-2,3,6	3	6	9	16	24	32
7-17: ('83-'84) Reprints. 8,11,16-Ditko-a. 11-Staton-a. 13-Aparo-c(r). 15-Sutton-c (low print run). 16-Palais-a	1	2	3	5	6	8
Modern Comics Reprint 2('78)						6.00

NOTE: ***Howard** a-4. **Kim** a-1. **Larson** a-4, 6.*

BIBLE, THE: EDEN
IDW Publishing: 2003 ($21.99, hardcover graphic novel)

	GD	VG	FN	VF	VF/NM	NM-
HC-Scott Hampton painted-a; adaptation of Genesis by Dave Elliot and Keith Giffen						22.00

BIBLE TALES FOR YOUNG FOLK (...Young People No. 3-5)
Atlas Comics (OMC): Aug, 1953 - No. 5, Mar, 1954

	GD	VG	FN	VF	VF/NM	NM-
1	30	60	90	177	289	400
2-Everett, Krigstein, Maneely-a; Robinson-c	19	38	57	109	172	235
3-5: 4,5-Robinson-c	16	32	48	92	144	195

BIG (Movie)
Hit Comics (Dark Horse Comics): Mar, 1989 ($2.00)

	GD	VG	FN	VF	VF/NM	NM-
1-Adaptation of film; Paul Chadwick-c						3.00

BIG ALL-AMERICAN COMIC BOOK, THE (See All-American Comics)
All-American/National Per. Publ.: 1944 (132 pgs., one-shot) (Early DC Annual)

	GD	VG	FN	VF	VF/NM	NM-
1-Wonder Woman, Green Lantern, Flash, The Atom, Wildcat, Scribbly, The Whip, Ghost Patrol, Hawkman by Kubert (1st on Hawkman), Hop Harrigan, Johnny Thunder, Little Boy Blue, Mr. Terrific, Mutt & Jeff app.; Sargon on cover only; cover by Kubert/Hibbard/Mayer and others	650	1300	1950	4750	8875	13,000

BIG BABY HUEY (See Baby Huey)

BIG BANG COMICS (Becomes Big Bang #4)
Caliber Press: Spring, 1994 - No. 4, Feb, 1995; No. 0, May, 1995 ($1.95, lim. series)

	GD	VG	FN	VF	VF/NM	NM-
1-4-($1.95-c)						4.00
0-(5/95, $2.95) Alex Ross-c; color and B&W pages						3.00
Your Big Book of Big Bang Comics TPB ('98, $11.00) r/#0-2						11.00

BIG BANG COMICS (Volume 2)
Image Comics (Highbrow Ent.): V2#1, May, 1996 - No. 35, Jan, 2001 ($1.95-$3.95)

	GD	VG	FN	VF	VF/NM	NM-
1-23,26: 1-Mighty Man app. 2-4-S.A. Shadowhawk app. 5-Begin $2.95-c. 6-Curt Swan/Murphy Anderson-c. 7-Begin B&W. 12-Savage Dragon-c/app. 16,17,21-Shadow Lady						3.00
24,25,27-35-($3.95): 35-Big Bang vs. Alan Moore's "1963" characters						4.00
...Presents the Ultiman Family (2/05, $3.50)						3.50
...Round Table of America (2/04, $3.95) Don Thomas-a						4.00
...Summer Special (8/03, $4.95) World's Nastiest Nazis app.						5.00

BIG BANG PRESENTS (Volume 3)
Big Bang Comics: July, 2006 - No. 5 ($2.95/$3.95, B&W)

	GD	VG	FN	VF	VF/NM	NM-
1,2: 1-Protoplasman (Plastic Man homage)						3.00
3-5-($3.95) 3-Origin of Protoplasman. 4-Flip book						4.00

BIG BANG UNIVERSE
AC Comics: 2015 ($9.95, B&W)

	GD	VG	FN	VF	VF/NM	NM-
1-Four new stories; Ultiman, Knight Watchman, Galahad & Whiz Kids app.						10.00

BIG BLACK KISS

Big Chief Wahoo #5 © EAS

Big Girls #1 © Jason Howard

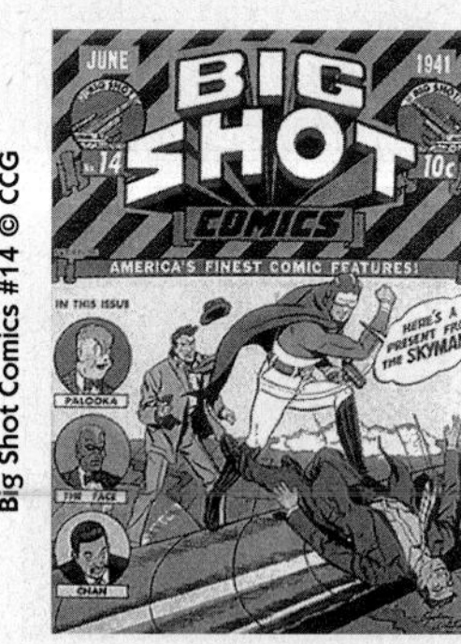

Big Shot Comics #14 © CCG

GD 2.0 | VG 4.0 | FN 6.0 | VF 8.0 | VF/NM 9.0 | NM- 9.2

Vortex Comics: Sep, 1989 - No, 3, Nov, 1989 ($3.75, B&W, lim. series, mature)
1-3-Chaykin-s/a 5.00

BIG BLOWN BABY (Also see Dark Horse Presents)
Dark Horse Comics: Aug, 1996 - No. 4, Nov, 1996 ($2.95, lim. series, mature)
1-4: Bill Wray-c/a/scripts 3.00

BIG BOOK OF ..., THE
DC Comics (Paradox Press): 1994 - 1999 (B&W)($12.95 - $14.95)
nn-...**BAD**,1998 ($14.95),...**CONSPIRACIES**, 1995 ($12.95), ...**DEATH**,1994 ($12.95), ...**FREAKS**, 1996 ($14.95), ...**GRIMM**, 1999 ($14.95), ...**HOAXES**, 1996 ($14.95), ...**LITTLE CRIMINALS**, 1996 ($14.95), ...**LOSERS**,1997 ($14.95), **MARTYRS**, 1997 ($14.95), ...**SCANDAL**,1997 ($14.95), ...**THE WEIRD WILD WEST**,1998 ($14.95), ...**THUGS**, 1997 ($14.95), ...**UNEXPLAINED**, 1997 ($14.95), ...**URBAN LEGENDS**, 1994 ($12.95), ...**VICE**, 1999 ($14.95), ...**WEIRDOS**, 1995 ($12.95) cover price

BIG BOOK OF FUN COMICS (See New Book of Comics)
National Periodical Publications: Spring, 1936 (Large size, 52 pgs.)
(1st comic book annual & DC annual)
1 (Very rare)-r/New Fun #1-5 2400 4800 7200 15,500 - -

BIG BOOK ROMANCES
Fawcett Publications: Feb, 1950 (no date given) (148 pgs.)
1-Contains remaindered Fawcett romance comics - several combinations possible 87 174 261 553 952 1350

BIG CHIEF WAHOO
Eastern Color Printing/George Dougherty (distr. by Fawcett): July, 1942 - No. 7, Wint., 1943/44?(no year given)(Quarterly)
1-Newspaper-r (on sale 6/15/42) 47 94 141 296 498 700
2-Steve Roper app. 24 48 72 140 230 320
3-5: 4-Chief is holding a Katy Keene comic in one panel 19 38 57 109 172 235
6-7 14 28 42 82 121 160
NOTE: *Kerry Drake in some issues.*

BIG CIRCUS, THE (Movie)
Dell Publishing Co.: No. 1036, Sept-Nov, 1959
Four Color 1036-Photo-c 6 12 18 40 73 105

BIG CON JOB, THE (PALMIOTTI & BRADY'S...)
BOOM! Studios: Mar, 2015 - No. 4, Jun, 2015 ($3.99, limited series)
1-4-Palmiotti & Brady-s/Stanton-a/Conner-c 4.00

BIG COUNTRY, THE (Movie)
Dell Publishing Co.: No. 946, Oct, 1958
Four Color 946-Photo-c 6 12 18 42 79 115

BIG DADDY DANGER
DC Comics: Oct, 2002 - No. 9, June, 2003 ($2.95, limited series)
1-9-Adam Pollina-s/a/c 3.00

BIG DADDY ROTH (Magazine)
Millar Publications: Oct-Nov, 1964 - No. 4, Apr-May, 1965 (35¢)
1-Toth-a; Batman & Robin parody 20 40 60 136 303 470
2-4-Toth-a 12 24 36 84 185 285

BIGFOOT
IDW Publishing: Feb, 2005 - No. 4, May, 2005 ($3.99, limited series)
1-4-Steve Niles & Rob Zombie-s/Richard Corben-a/c 4.00

BIG GIRLS
Image Comics: Aug, 2020 - No. 6, Jan, 2021 ($3.99)
1-6-Jason Howard-s/a 4.00

BIGG TIME
DC Comics (Vertigo): 2002 ($14.95, B&W, graphic novel)
nn-Ty Templeton-s/c/a 15.00

BIG GUY AND RUSTY THE BOY ROBOT, THE (Also See Madman Comics #6,7 & Martha Washington Stranded In Space)
Dark Horse (Legend): July, 1995 - No. 2, Aug, 1995 ($4.95, oversize, limited series)
1,2-Frank Miller scripts & Geoff Darrow-c/a 1 2 3 4 5 8

BIG HERO ADVENTURES (See Jigsaw)

BIG HERO 6 (Also see Sunfire & Big Hero Six)
Marvel Comics: Nov, 2008 - No. 5, Mar, 2009 ($3.99, limited series)
1-Claremont-s/Nakayama-a; 1-Character design pages & Handbook entries 3 6 9 17 26 35
2-5 1 2 3 5 6 8

...: Brave New Heroes 1 (11/12, $8.99) r/#1-5 9.00

BIG HERO 6: THE SERIES (Based on the Disney Channel animated series)
IDW Publishing: Nov, 2019 - Present ($3.99)
1-Blumenreich & Caramagna-s/Baldari-a; two covers 4.00

BIG JON & SPARKIE (Radio)(Formerly Sparkie, Radio Pixie)
Ziff-Davis Publ. Co.: No. 4, Sept-Oct, 1952 (Painted-c)
4-Based on children's radio program 20 40 60 114 182 250

BIG LAND, THE (Movie)
Dell Publishing Co.: No. 812, July, 1957
Four Color 812-Alan Ladd photo-c 8 16 24 52 99 145

BIG LIE, THE
Image Comics: Sept, 2011 ($3.99, one-shot)
1-Revisits the 9-11 attacks; Rick Veitch-s/a(p); Thomas Yeates-c 4.00

BIG MAN PLANS
Image Comics: Mar, 2015 - No. 4 ($3.50, limited series)
1-4-Eric Powell & Tim Wiesch-s/Powell-a/c 3.50

BIG MOOSE (Character from Archie Comics)
Archie Comics Publications: Jun, 2017 ($4.99, limited series)
..., One Shot - short stories by various; art by Cory Smith, Pitilli & Jampole 4.00

BIG RED (See Movie Comics)

BIG SHOT COMICS
Columbia Comics Group: May, 1940 - No. 104, Aug, 1949
1-Intro. Skyman; The Face (1st app.; Tony Trent), The Cloak (Spy Master), Marvelo, Monarch of Magicians, Joe Palooka, Charlie Chan, Tom Kerry, Dixie Dugan, Rocky Ryan begin; Charlie Chan moves over from Feature Comics #31 (4/40) 300 600 900 1920 3310 4700
2 100 200 300 635 1093 1550
3-The Cloak called Spy Chief; Skyman-c 94 188 282 597 1024 1450
4,5 61 122 183 390 670 950
6-10: 8-Christmas-c 50 100 150 315 533 750
11-13 47 94 141 296 498 700
14-Origin & 1st app. Sparky Watts (6/41) 50 100 150 315 533 750
15-Origin The Cloak 60 120 180 381 653 925
16-20 39 78 117 240 395 550
21-23,27,30: 30-X-Mas-c, WWII-c 34 68 102 204 332 460
24-Classic Tojo-c. 129 258 387 826 1413 2000
25-Hitler-c 94 188 282 597 1024 1450
26,29-Japanese WWII-c. 29-Intro. Capt. Yank; Bo (a dog) newspaper strip-r by Frank Beck begin, ends #104. 41 82 123 256 428 600
28-Hitler, Tojo & Mussolini-c 135 270 405 864 1482 2100
31,33-40 24 48 72 142 234 325
32-Vic Jordan newspaper strip reprints begin, ends #52; Hitler, Tojo & Mussolini-c 116 232 348 742 1271 1800
41,42,44,45,47-50: 42-No Skyman. 50-Origin The Face retold 21 42 63 122 199 275
43-Hitler-c 110 220 330 704 1202 1700
46-Hitler, Tojo-c (6/44) 103 206 309 659 1130 1600
51-Tojo Japanese war-c 42 84 126 265 445 625
52-56,58-60: 18 36 54 105 165 225
57-Hitler, Tojo Halloween mask-c 43 86 129 271 461 650
61-70: 63 on-Tony Trent, the Face 14 28 42 82 121 160
71-80: 73-The Face cameo. 74-(2/47)-Mickey Finn begins. 74,80-The Face app. in Tony Trent. 78-Last Charlie Chan strip-r 14 28 42 76 108 140
81-90: 85-Tony Trent marries Babs Walsh. 86-Valentines-c 11 22 33 62 86 110
91-99,101-104: 69-94-Skyman in Outer Space. 96-Christmas-c 10 20 30 56 76 95
100 11 22 33 64 90 115
NOTE: ***Mart Bailey** art on "The Face" No. 1-104. **Guardineer** a-5. Sparky Watts by **Boody Rogers**-No. 14-42, 77-104, (by others No. 43-76). Others than Tony Trent wear "The Face" mask in No. 46-63, 93. Skyman by **Ogden Whitney**-No. 1, 2, 4, 12-37, 49, 70-101. Skyman covers-No. 1, 3, 7-12, 14, 16, 20, 27, 89, 95, 100.*

BIG SMASH BARGAIN COMICS
No publisher listed: 1950 - No. 6, 1951 (25¢, 160pgs., Canadian reprints)
1-6: Contains 4 comics from various companies bundled with new cover (scarce) 45 90 135 284 480 675

BIG TEX
Toby Press: June, 1953
1-Contains (3) John Wayne stories-r with name changed to Big Tex 14 28 42 78 112 145

Big-3 #6 © FOX

Bill & Ted Are Doomed #1 © B&T FTM

Billionaire Island #2 © Mark Russell

	GD	VG	FN	VF	VF/NM	NM-
	2.0	4.0	6.0	8.0	9.0	9.2

BIG-3
Fox Feature Syndicate: Fall, 1940 - No. 7, Jan, 1942

1-Blue Beetle, The Flame, & Samson begin	258	516	774	1651	2826	4000
2	116	232	348	742	1271	1800
3-5	87	174	261	553	952	1350
6-Last Samson	65	130	195	416	708	1000
7-WWII Nazi-c; V-Man app.	81	162	243	518	884	1250

BIG THUNDER MOUNTAIN RAILROAD (Disney Kingdoms)
Marvel Comics: May, 2015 - No. 5, Oct, 2015 ($3.99, limited series)

1-5: 1-Dennis Hopeless-s/Tigh Walker-a/Pasqual Ferry-c. 3-Ruiz-a 4.00

BIG TOP COMICS, THE (TV's Great Circus Show)
Toby Press: 1951 - No. 2, 1951 (No month)

1	14	28	42	78	112	145
2	10	20	30	58	79	100

BIG TOWN (Radio/TV) (Also see Movie Comics, 1946)
National Periodical Publ: Jan, 1951 - No. 50, Mar-Apr, 1958 (No. 1-9: 52pgs.)

1-Dan Barry-a begins	69	138	207	442	759	1075
2	37	74	111	222	361	500
3-10	22	44	66	132	216	300
11-20	18	36	54	105	165	225
21-31: Last pre-code (1-2/55)	14	28	42	76	108	140
32-50: 46-Grey tone cover	10	20	30	56	76	95

BIG TROUBLE IN LITTLE CHINA (Based on the 1986 Kurt Russell movie)
BOOM! Studios: Jun, 2014 - No. 25, Jun, 2016 ($3.99)

1-12-Continuing advs. of Jack Burton; John Carpenter & Eric Powell-s; Brian Churilla-a; multiple covers by Powell and others on each 4.00
13-24: 13-16-Van Lente-s/Eisma-a. 17-20-McDaid-a. 21-24-Santos-a 4.00
25-($4.99) Van Lente-s/Santos-a 5.00

BIG TROUBLE IN LITTLE CHINA / ESCAPE FROM NEW YORK (Based on the movies)
BOOM! Studios: Oct, 2016 - No. 6, Mar, 2017 ($3.99)

1-6-Jack Burton meets Snake Plisskin; Greg Pak-s/Daniel Bayliss-a 4.00

BIG TROUBLE IN LITTLE CHINA: OLD MAN JACK (Based on the movie)
BOOM! Studios: Sept, 2017 - No. 12, Aug, 2018 ($3.99)

1-12-Old Jack Burton battles Lo Pan; Carpenter & Burch-s/Corona-a; multiple covers 4.00

BIG VALLEY, THE (TV)
Dell Publishing Co.: June, 1966 - No. 5, Oct, 1967; No. 6, Oct, 1969

1: Photo-c #1-5	5	10	15	31	53	75
2-6: 6-Reprints #1	3	6	9	21	33	45

BIKER MICE FROM MARS (TV)
Marvel Comics: Nov, 1993 - No. 3, Jan, 1994 ($1.50, limited series)

1-3: 1-Intro Vinnie, Modo & Throttle. 2-Origin 5.00

BILL & TED ARE DOOMED (Movie)
Dark Horse Comics: Sept, 2020 - No. 4, Dec, 2020 ($3.99, limited series)

1-4-Evan Dorkin-s/Roger Langridge-a; set in the year 2000 after the 2nd movie 4.00

BILL & TED GO TO HELL (Movie)
BOOM! Studios: Feb, 2016 - No. 4, May, 2016 ($3.99, limited series)

1-4-Joines-s/Bachan-a 4.00

BILL & TED SAVE THE UNIVERSE (Movie)
BOOM! Studios: Jun, 2017 - No. 5, Oct, 2017 ($3.99, limited series)

1-5-Joines-s/Bachan-a 4.00

BILL & TED'S BOGUS JOURNEY
Marvel Comics: Sept, 1991 ($2.95, squarebound, 84 pgs.)

1-Adapts movie sequel 6.00

BILL & TED'S EXCELLENT COMIC BOOK (Movie)
Marvel Comics: Dec, 1991 - No. 12, 1992 ($1.00/$1.25)

1-12: 3-Begin $1.25-c 4.00

BILL & TED'S MOST TRIUMPHANT RETURN (Movie)
BOOM! Studios: Mar, 2015 - No. 6, Aug, 2015 ($3.99, limited series)

1-6: 1-Follows the end of the second movie; Lynch-s/Gaylord-a/Guillory-c 4.00

BILL BARNES COMICS (...America's Air Ace Comics No. 2 on) (Becomes Air Ace V2#1 on; also see Shadow Comics)
Street & Smith Publications: Oct, 1940(No. month given) - No. 12, Oct, 1943

1-23 pgs.-comics; Rocket Rooney begins	113	226	339	718	1234	1750
2-Barnes as The Phantom Flyer app.; Tuska-a	58	116	174	371	636	900
3-5-War covers	47	94	141	296	498	700
6,8,10,12-War covers	41	82	123	256	428	600
7-(1942) Story about dropping atomic bomb on Japan	219	438	657	1402	2401	3400
9-Classic WWII cover	65	130	195	416	708	1000
11-Japanese WWII Gremlin cover	47	94	141	296	498	700

BILL BATTLE, THE ONE MAN ARMY (Also see Master Comics No. 133)
Fawcett Publications: Oct, 1952 - No. 4, Apr, 1953 (All photo-c)

1	15	30	45	88	137	185
2	10	20	30	54	72	90
3,4	9	18	27	50	65	80

BILL BLACK'S FUN COMICS
Paragon #1-3/Americomics #4: Dec, 1982 - No. 4, Mar, 1983 ($1.75/$2.00, Baxter paper) (1st AC comic)

1-(B&W fanzine; 7x8-1/2"; low print) Intro. Capt. Paragon, Phantom Lady & Commando D	3	6	9	15	22	28
2-4: 2,3-(B&W fanzines; 8-1/2x11"). 3-Kirby-c. 4-($2.00, color)-Origin Nightfall (formerly Phantom Lady); Nightveil app.; Kirby-a	2	4	6	8	10	12

BILL BOYD WESTERN (Movie star; see Hopalong Cassidy & Western Hero)
Fawcett Publ: Feb, 1950 - No. 23, June, 1952 (1-3,7,11,14-on: 36 pgs.)

1-Bill Boyd & his horse Midnite begin; photo front/back-c	32	64	96	188	307	425
2-Painted-c	16	32	48	94	147	200
3-Photo-c begin, end #23; last photo back-c	14	28	42	80	115	150
4-6(52 pgs.)	12	24	36	69	97	125
7,11(36 pgs.)	10	20	30	56	76	95
8-10,12,13(52 pgs.)	10	20	30	58	79	100
14-22	9	18	27	52	69	85
23-Last issue	10	20	30	56	76	95

BILL BUMLIN (See Treasury of Comics No. 3)

BILL ELLIOTT (See Wild Bill Elliott)

BILLI 99
Dark Horse Comics: Sept, 1991 - No. 4, 1991 ($3.50, B&W, lim. series, 52 pgs.)

1-4: Tim Sale-c/a 4.00

BILLIONAIRE ISLAND
AHOY Comics: 2020 - No. 6, 2020 ($3.99, limited series)

1-6-Mark Russell-s/Steve Pugh-a 4.00

BILL STERN'S SPORTS BOOK
Ziff-Davis Publ. Co.(Approved Comics): Spring-Sum, 1951 - V2#2, Win, 1952

V1#10-(1951) Whitney painted-c	21	42	63	122	199	275
2-(Sum/52; reg. size)	16	32	48	94	147	200
V2#2-(1952, 96 pgs.)-Krigstein, Kinstler-a	21	42	63	126	206	285

BILL THE BULL: ONE SHOT, ONE BOURBON, ONE BEER
Boneyard Press: Dec, 1994 ($2.95, B&W, mature)

1 3.00

BILLY AND BUGGY BEAR (See Animal Fun)
I.W. Enterprises/Super: 1958; 1964

I.W. Reprint #1, #7('58)-All Surprise Comics #?(Same issue-r for both)	2	4	6	10	14	18
Super Reprint #10(1964)	2	4	6	8	11	14

BILLY BATSON AND THE MAGIC OF SHAZAM! (Follows Shazam: The Monster Society of Evil mini-series)
DC Comics: Sept, 2008 - No. 21, Dec, 2010 ($2.25/$2.50, all ages title)

1-17: 1-4-Mike Kunkel-s/a/c; Theo (Black) Adam app. 5-DeStefano-a. 13-16-Black Adam 4.00
1-Variant B&W sketch cover 4.00
18-21 ($2.99) 21-Justice League cameo 4.00
TPB (2010, $12.99) r/#1-6; cover and haracter sketches 13.00
...: Mr. Mind Over Matter TPB (2011, $12.99) r/#7-12 13.00

BILLY BUCKSKIN WESTERN (2-Gun Western No. 4)
Atlas Comics (IMC No. 1/MgPC No. 2,3): Nov, 1955 - No. 3, Mar, 1956

1-Mort Drucker-a; Maneely-c/a	18	36	54	107	169	230
2-Mort Drucker-a	11	22	33	64	90	115
3-Williamson, Drucker-a	14	28	42	76	108	140

BILLY BUNNY (Black Cobra No. 6 on)
Excellent Publications: Feb-Mar, 1954 - No. 5, Oct-Nov, 1954

1	10	20	30	56	76	95
2	7	14	21	35	43	50
3-5	6	12	18	28	34	40

Billy the Kid #5 © TOBY

Bionic Man #1 © Universal

Birds of Prey #1 © DC

BILLY BUNNY'S CHRISTMAS FROLICS
Farrell Publications: 1952 (25¢ Giant, 100 pgs.)

	GD 2.0	VG 4.0	FN 6.0	VF 8.0	VF/NM 9.0	NM- 9.2
1	22	44	66	132	216	300

BILLY MAKE BELIEVE
United Features Syndicate: No. 14, 1939

	GD 2.0	VG 4.0	FN 6.0	VF 8.0	VF/NM 9.0	NM- 9.2
Single Series 14	32	64	96	192	314	435

BILLY NGUYEN, PRIVATE EYE
Caliber Press: V2#1, 1990 ($2.50)

	GD 2.0	VG 4.0	FN 6.0	VF 8.0	VF/NM 9.0	NM- 9.2
V2#1						3.00

BILLY THE KID (Formerly The Masked Raider; also see Doc Savage Comics & Return of the Outlaw)
Charlton Publ. Co.: No. 9, Nov, 1957 - No. 121, Dec, 1976; No. 122, Sept, 1977 - No. 123, Oct, 1977; No. 124, Feb, 1978 - No. 153, Mar, 1983

	GD 2.0	VG 4.0	FN 6.0	VF 8.0	VF/NM 9.0	NM- 9.2
9	10	20	30	58	79	100
10,12,14,17-19: 12-2 pg Check-sty	8	16	24	40	50	60
11-(68 pgs.)-Origin & 1st app. The Ghost Train	9	18	27	50	65	80
13-Williamson/Torres-a	8	16	24	44	57	70
15-Origin; 2 pgs. Williamson-a	8	16	24	44	57	70
16-Williamson-a, 2 pgs.	8	16	24	42	54	65
20-26-Severin-a(3-4 each)	8	16	24	44	57	70
27-30: 30-Masked Rider app.	3	6	9	18	28	38
31-40	3	6	9	15	22	28
41-60	2	4	6	13	18	22
61-65	2	4	6	10	14	18
66-Bounty Hunter series begins.	3	6	9	14	20	25
67-80: Bounty Hunter series; not in #79,82,84-86	2	4	6	10	14	18
81-84,86-90: 87-Last Bounty Hunter. 88-1st app. Mr. Young of the Boothill Gazette	2	4	6	8	10	12
85-Early Kaluta-a (4 pgs.)	2	4	6	9	13	16
91-123: 110-Mr. Young of Boothill app. 111-Origin The Ghost Train. 117-Gunsmith & Co., The Cheyenne Kid app.	1	2	3	5	6	8
124(2/78)-153						6.00
Modern Comics 109 (1977 reprint)						5.00

NOTE: ***Boyette** a-88-110. **Kim** a-73. **Morsi** a-12,14. **Sattler** a-118-123. **Severin** a(r)-121-129, 134; c-23, 25. **Sutton** a-111.*

BILLY THE KID ADVENTURE MAGAZINE
Toby Press: Oct, 1950 - No. 29, 1955

	GD 2.0	VG 4.0	FN 6.0	VF 8.0	VF/NM 9.0	NM- 9.2
1-Williamson/Frazetta-a (2 pgs) r/from John Wayne Adventure Comics #2; photo-c	32	64	96	188	307	425
2-Photo-c	13	26	39	74	105	135
3-Williamson/Frazetta "The Claws of Death", 4 pgs. plus Williamson art	34	68	102	204	332	460
4,5,7,8,10: 4,7-Photo-c	9	18	27	52	69	85
6-Frazetta assist on "Nightmare"; photo-c	15	30	45	83	124	165
9-Kurtzman Pot-Shot Pete; photo-c	11	22	33	64	90	115
11,12,15-20: 11-Photo-c	8	16	24	42	54	65
13-Kurtzman-r/John Wayne #12 (Genius)	9	18	27	47	61	75
14-Williamson/Frazetta; r-of #1 (2 pgs.)	10	20	30	56	76	95
21,23-29	7	14	21	37	46	55
22-Williamson/Frazetta-r(1pg.)/#1; photo-c	8	16	24	42	54	65

BILLY THE KID AND OSCAR (Also see Fawcett's Funny Animals)
Fawcett Publications: Winter, 1945 - No. 3, Fall, 1946 (Funny animal)

	GD 2.0	VG 4.0	FN 6.0	VF 8.0	VF/NM 9.0	NM- 9.2
1	15	30	45	90	140	190
2,3	11	22	33	62	86	110

BILLY THE KID'S OLD TIMEY ODDITIES
Dark Horse Comics: Apr, 2005 - No. 4, July, 2005 ($2.99, limited series)

	GD 2.0	VG 4.0	FN 6.0	VF 8.0	VF/NM 9.0	NM- 9.2
1-4-Eric Powell-s/c; Kyle Hotz-a						4.00
TPB (2005, $13.95) r/series						14.00
... and the Ghostly Fiend of London (9/10 - No. 4, 12/10, $3.99) 1-4-Powell-s/c; Kyle Hotz-a; Goon back-up; Powell-s/a						4.00
... and the Orm of Loch Ness (10/12 - No. 4, 1/13, $3.50) 1-4-Powell-s/Hotz-a/c						4.00

BILLY WEST (Bill West No. 9,10)
Standard Comics (Visual Editions): 1949-No. 9, Feb, 1951; No. 10, Feb, 1952

	GD 2.0	VG 4.0	FN 6.0	VF 8.0	VF/NM 9.0	NM- 9.2
1	20	40	60	114	182	250
2	13	26	39	72	101	130
3-6,9,10	10	20	30	56	76	95
7,8-Schomburg-c	12	24	36	69	97	125

NOTE: ***Celardo** a-1-6, 9; c-1-3. **Moreira** a-3. **Roussos** a-2.*

BING CROSBY (See Feature Films)

BINGO (...Comics) (H. C. Blackerby)
Howard Publ.: 1945 (Reprints National material)

	GD 2.0	VG 4.0	FN 6.0	VF 8.0	VF/NM 9.0	NM- 9.2
1-L. B. Cole opium-c; blank back-c	41	82	123	256	428	600

BINGO, THE MONKEY DOODLE BOY
St. John Publishing Co.: Aug, 1951; Oct, 1953

	GD 2.0	VG 4.0	FN 6.0	VF 8.0	VF/NM 9.0	NM- 9.2
1(8/51)-By Eric Peters	11	22	33	62	86	110
1(10/53)	9	18	27	47	61	75

BINKY (Formerly Leave It to...)
National Periodical Publ./DC Comics: No. 72, 4-5/70 - No. 81, 10-11/71; No. 82, Summer/77

	GD 2.0	VG 4.0	FN 6.0	VF 8.0	VF/NM 9.0	NM- 9.2
72-76	4	8	12	27	44	60
77-79: (68 pgs.). 77-Bobby Sherman 1pg. story w/photo. 78-1 pg. sty on Barry Williams of Brady Bunch. 79-Osmonds 1pg. story	5	10	15	35	63	90
80,81 (52 pgs.)-Sweat Pain story	5	10	15	31	53	75
82 (1977, one-shot)	4	8	12	27	44	60

BINKY'S BUDDIES
National Periodical Publications: Jan-Feb, 1969 - No. 12, Nov-Dec, 1970

	GD 2.0	VG 4.0	FN 6.0	VF 8.0	VF/NM 9.0	NM- 9.2
1	8	16	24	52	99	145
2-12: 3-Last 12¢ issue	4	8	12	27	47	65

BIONIC MAN (TV)
Dynamite Entertainment: 2011 - No. 26, 2013 ($3.99)

	GD 2.0	VG 4.0	FN 6.0	VF 8.0	VF/NM 9.0	NM- 9.2
1-26: 1-Kevin Smith & Phil Hester-s; Lau-a; multiple covers. 12-15-Bigfoot app.						4.00
Annual 1 (2013, $4.99) The Venus Probe; Beatty-s/Mayhew-c						5.00

BIONIC MAN VS. THE BIONIC WOMAN (TV)
Dynamite Entertainment: 2013 - No. 5, 2013 ($3.99, limited series)

	GD 2.0	VG 4.0	FN 6.0	VF 8.0	VF/NM 9.0	NM- 9.2
1-5-Champagne-s/Luis-a; 3 covers on each						4.00

BIONIC WOMAN, THE (TV)
Charlton Publications: Oct, 1977 - No. 5, June, 1978

	GD 2.0	VG 4.0	FN 6.0	VF 8.0	VF/NM 9.0	NM- 9.2
1	5	10	15	33	57	80
2-5	3	6	9	21	33	45

BIONIC WOMAN, THE (TV)
Dynamite Entertainment: 2013 - No. 10, 2013 ($3.99)

	GD 2.0	VG 4.0	FN 6.0	VF 8.0	VF/NM 9.0	NM- 9.2
1-10: 1-Tobin-s/Renaud-c/Carvalho-a; origin re-told						4.00

BIONIC WOMAN, THE: SEASON FOUR (TV)
Dynamite Entertainment: 2014 - No. 4, 2014 ($3.99, limited series)

	GD 2.0	VG 4.0	FN 6.0	VF 8.0	VF/NM 9.0	NM- 9.2
1-4-Jerwa-s/Cabrera-a. 1-Reg & photo-c						4.00

BIRDS OF PREY (Also see Black Canary/Oracle: Birds of Prey)
DC Comics: Jan, 1999 - No. 127, Apr, 2009 ($1.99/$2.50/$2.99)

	GD 2.0	VG 4.0	FN 6.0	VF 8.0	VF/NM 9.0	NM- 9.2
1-Dixon-s/Land-c/a	2	4	6	10	14	18
2-4						6.00
5-7,9-15: 15-Guice-a begins.						4.00
8-Nightwing-c/app.; Barbara & Dick's circus date	4	8	12	27	44	60
16-38: 23-Grodd-c/app. 26-Bane app. 32-Noto-c begin						3.00
39,40-Bruce Wayne: Murderer pt. 5,12						3.50
41-Bruce Wayne: Fugitive pt. 2						4.00
42-46: 42-Fabry-a. 45-Deathstroke-c/app.						3.00
47-74,77-91: 47-49-Terry Moore-s/Conner & Palmiotti-a; Noto-c. 50-Gilbert Hernandez-s begin. 52,54-Metamorpho app. 56-Simone-s/Benes-a begin. 65,67,68,70-Land-c. 86-Timm-a (7 pgs.)						3.00
75-($2.95) Pearson-c; back-up story of Lady Blackhawk						4.00
76-Debut of Black Alice (from Day of Vengeance)	2	4	6	8	10	12
92-99,101-127: 92-One Year Later. 94-Begin $2.99-c; Prometheus app. 96,97-Black Alice app. 98,99-New Batgirl app. 99-Black Canary leaves the team. 104-107-Secret Six app.						3.00
100-($3.99) new team recruited; Black Canary origin re-told						4.00
TPB (1999, $17.95) r/ previous series and one-shots						18.00
...: Batgirl 1 (2/98, $2.95) Dixon-s/Frank-c						5.00
...: Batgirl/Catwoman 1 ('03, $5.95) Robertson-a; cont'd in BOP: Catwoman/Oracle 1						6.00
...: Between Dark & Dawn TPB (2006, $14.99) r/#69-75						15.00
...: Blood and Circuits TPB (2007, $17.99) r/#96-103						18.00
...: Catwoman/Oracle 1 ('03, $5.95) Cont'd from BOP: Batgirl/Catwoman 1; David Ross-a						6.00
...: Club Kids TPB (2008, $17.99) r/#109-112,118						18.00
...: Dead of Winter TPB (2008, $17.99) r/#104-108						18.00
...: Metropolis or Dust TPB (2008, $17.99) r/#113-117						18.00
...: Of Like Minds TPB (2004, $14.95) r/#55-61						15.00
...: Old Friends, New Enemies TPB (2003, $17.95) r/#1-6, ...: Batgirl, ...: Wolves						18.00
...: Perfect Pitch TPB (2007, $17.99) r/#86-90,92-95						18.00
...: Platinum Flats TPB (2009, $17.99) r/#119-124						18.00
...: Revolution 1 (1997, $2.95) Frank-c/Dixon-s						5.00
... Secret Files 2003 (8/03, $4.95) Short stories, pin-ups and profile pages; Noto-c						5.00
...: Sensei and Student TPB (2005, $17.95) r/#62-68						18.00
...: The Battle Within TPB (2006, $17.99) r/#76-85						18.00
...: The Ravens 1 (6/98, $1.95)-Dixon-s; Girlfrenzy issue						4.00

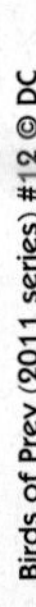
Birds of Prey (2011 series) #12 © DC

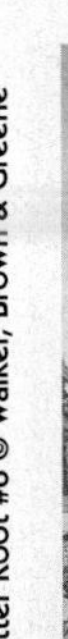
Bitter Root #6 © Walker, Brown & Greene

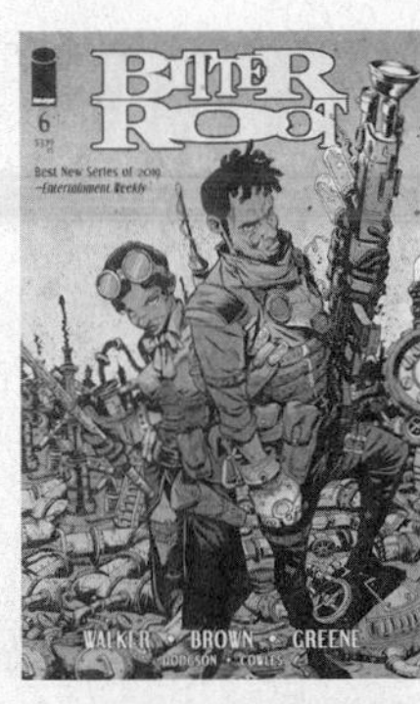

Black Adam #4 © DC

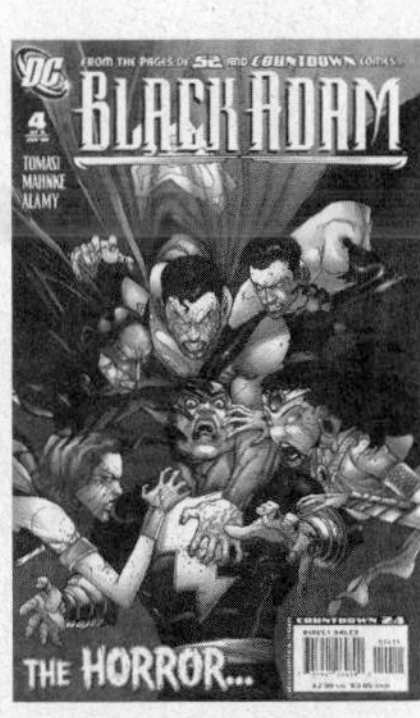

	GD 2.0	VG 4.0	FN 6.0	VF 8.0	VF/NM 9.0	NM- 9.2

...: Wolves 1 (10/97, $2.95) Dixon-s/Giordano & Faucher-a 5.00

BIRDS OF PREY (Brightest Day)
DC Comics: Jul, 2010 - No. 15, Oct, 2011 ($2.99)

1-Simone-s/Benes-a/c; Hawk and Dove join team, Penguin app. 4.00
1-Variant cover by Chiang 6.00
2-15: 2-4-Penguin app. 7-10-"Death of Oracle". 11-Catman app. 14,15-Tucci-a 3.00
... End Run HC (2011, $22.99, d.j.) r/#1-6 23.00

BIRDS OF PREY (DC New 52)
DC Comics: Nov, 2011 - No. 34, Oct, 2014 ($2.99)

1-24: 1-Swierczynski-s/Saiz-a; intro. Starling. 2-Katana & Poison Ivy join. 4-Batgirl joins. 9-Night of the Owls. 16-Strix joins. 18-20-Mr. Freeze app. 3.00
25-($3.99) Zero Year tie-in; flashback to Dinah's childhood; John Lynch app. 4.00
26-34: 26-Birds vs. Basilisk. 28-Gothtopia tie-in; Ra's al Ghul app. 32-34-Suicide Squad 3.00
#0 (11/12, $2.99) Black Canary and Batgirl first meeting; Molenaar-a/Lau-c 3.00
...: Futures End 1 (11/14, $2.99, regular-c) Five years later; The Red League 3.00
...: Futures End 1 (11/14, $3.99, 3-D cover) 4.00

BIRDS OF PREY GIANT
DC Comics: 2019 - Present ($4.99, 100 pgs., squarebound, Mass Market & Direct Market editions exist for each issue, with different covers)

1-Three new stories plus reprints; Harley Quinn app.; Lupacchino-c 5.00

BIRDS OF PREY: MANHUNT
DC Comics: Sept, 1996 - No. 4, Dec, 1996 ($1.95, limited series)

1-Features Black Canary, Oracle, Huntress, & Catwoman; Chuck Dixon scripts; Gary Frank-c on all. 1-Catwoman cameo only 1 2 3 5 6 8
2-4 6.00
NOTE: *Gary Frank c-1-4. Matt Haley a-1-4p. Wade Von Grawbadger a-1i.*

BIRTH CAUL, THE
Eddie Campbell Comics: 1999 ($5.95, B&W, one-shot)

1-Alan Moore-s/Eddie Campbell-a 6.00

BIRTH OF THE DEFIANT UNIVERSE, THE
Defiant: May, 1993

nn-Contains promotional artwork & text; limited print run of 1000 copies. 3 6 9 21 33 45

BIRTHRIGHT
Image Comics (Skybound): Oct, 2014 - Present ($2.99/$3.99)

1-25-Joshua Williamson-s/Andrei Bressan-a 3.00
26-46-($3.99) 27-Regular & Walking Dead tribute covers. 45-Bonus preview of Stillwater 4.00

BISHOP (See Uncanny X-Men & X-Men)
Marvel Comics: Dec, 1994 - No.4, Mar, 1995 ($2.95, limited series)

1-4: Foil-c; Shard & Mountjoy in all. 1-Storm app. 4.00

BISHOP THE LAST X-MAN
Marvel Comics: Oct, 1999 - No. 16, Jan, 2001 ($2.99/$1.99/$2.25)

1-($2.99)-Jeanty-a 4.00
2-8-($1.99): 2-Two covers 3.00
9-11,13-16: 9-Begin $2.25-c. 15-Maximum Security x-over; Xavier app. 3.00
12-($2.99) 4.00

BISHOP: XAVIER SECURITY ENFORCER
Marvel Comics: Jan, 1998 - No.3, Mar, 1998 ($2.50, limited series)

1-3: Ostrander-s 3.00

BITCH PLANET
Image Comics: Dec, 2014 - No. 9, Apr, 2017 ($3.50/$3.99)

1-DeConnick-s/De Landro-a/c 5.00
2-9: 3-Origin of Penny Rolle. 5-Begin $3.99-c. 6-Meiko flashback 4.00

BITCH PLANET: TRIPLE FEATURE
Image Comics: Jun, 2017 - No. 5, Oct, 2017 ($3.99)

1-5-Short story anthology by various; De Landro-c. 5-Charretier-a 4.00

BITE CLUB
DC Comics (Vertigo): Jun, 2004 - No. 6, Nov, 2004 ($2.95, limited series)

1-6-Chaykin-s/Tischman-a/Quitely-c 3.00
TPB Digest (2005, $9.99) r/#1-6; cover gallery 10.00
The Complete Bite Club TPB (2007, $19.99) r/#1-6 and ...: Vampire Crime Unit #1-5 20.00

BITE CLUB: VAMPIRE CRIME UNIT
DC Comics (Vertigo): Jun, 2006 - No. 5, Oct, 2006 ($2.99, limited series)

1-5: 1-Chaykin & Tischman-s/Hahn-a/Quitely-c. 4-Chaykin-c 3.00

BITTER ROOT
Image Comics: Nov, 2018 - No. 10, Sept, 2020 ($3.99)

1-10-David F. Walker & Chuck Brown-s/Sanford Greene-a 4.00
... Red Summer Special 1 (7/19, $5.99) Short stories by various; Greene-c 6.00

BIZARRE ADVENTURES (Formerly Marvel Preview)
Marvel Comics Group: No. 25, 3/81 - No. 34, 2/83 (#25-33: Magazine-$1.50)

25-Lethal Ladies 3 6 9 16 23 30
26-King Kull; Bolton-c/a 2 4 6 10 14 18
27,28: 27-Phoenix, Iceman & Nightcrawler app. 28-The Unlikely Heroes; Elektra by Miller; Neal Adams-a 2 4 6 13 18 22
29,30,32,33: 29-Stephen King's Lawnmower Man. 30-Tomorrow; 1st app. Silhouette. 32-Gods; Thor-c/s. 33-Horror; Dracula app.; photo-c 2 3 4 6 8 10
31-After The Violence Stops; new Hangman story; Miller-a 2 4 6 8 12 15
34 ($2.00, Baxter paper, comic size)-Son of Santa; Christmas special; Howard the Duck by Paul Smith 1 3 4 6 8 10
No. 1 (12/19, $4.99) Short stories; Bloodstone, Shang-Chi, Dracula; Black Goliath app. 5.00
NOTE: ***Alcala** a-27i. **Austin** a-25i, 28i. **Bolton** a-26, 32. **J. Buscema** a-27p, 29, 30p; c-26. **Byrne** a-31 (2 pg.). **Golden** a-25p, 28p. **Perez** a-27p. **Rogers** a-25p. **Simonson** a-29; c-29. **Paul Smith** a-34.*

BIZARRO
DC Comics: Aug, 2015 - No. 6, Jan, 2016 ($2.99, limited series)

1-6-Corson-s/Duarte-a; Jimmy Olsen app. 4-Zatanna app. 6-Superman app. 3.00

BIZARRO COMICS!
DC Comics: 2001 ($29.95, hardcover, one-shot)

HC-Short stories of DC heroes by various alternative cartoonists including Dorkin, Pope, Haspiel, Kidd, Kochalka, Millionaire, Stephens, Wray; includes "Superman's Babysitter" by Kyle Baker from Elseworlds 80-Page Giant recalled by DC; Groening-c 30.00
Softcover (2003, $19.95) 20.00

BIZARRO WORLD
DC Comics: 2005 ($29.95, hardcover, one-shot)

HC-Short stories by various alternative cartoonists including Bagge, Baker, Dorkin, Dunn, Kupperman, Morse, Oswalt, Pekar, Simpson, Stewart; Jaime Hernandez-c 30.00
Softcover (2006, $19.99) 20.00

BLACK ADAM (See 52 and Countdown)
DC Comics: Oct, 2007 - No. 6, Mar, 2008 ($2.99, limited series)

1-Mahnke-a/c; Isis returns; Felix Faust app. 1 2 3 5 6 8
1-Variant-c by Alex Ross 5 10 15 34 60 85
2-6 5.00
....: Endless Winter Special (2/21, $3.99) Part 8 of crossover event; Frost King app. 4.00
...: The Dark Age TPB (2008, $17.99) r/#1-6; Alex Ross-c 18.00
...: Year of the Villain 1 (12/19, $4.99) Jenkins-s/Miranda-a; battles King Shazam 5.00

BLACK AND WHITE (See Large Feature Comic, Series I)

BLACK & WHITE (Also see Codename: Black & White)
Image Comics (Extreme): Oct, 1994 - No. 3, Jan, 1995 ($1.95, limited series)

1-3: Thibert-c/story 3.00

BLACK & WHITE MAGIC
Innovation Publishing: 1991 ($2.95, 98 pgs., B&W w/30 pgs. color, squarebound)

1-Contains rebound comics w/covers removed; contents may vary 4.00

BLACK AXE
Marvel Comics (UK): Apr, 1993 - No. 7, Oct, 1993 ($1.75)

1-4: 1-Romita Jr.-c. 2-Sunfire-c/s 3.00
5-7: 5-Janson-c; Black Panther app. 6,7-Black Panther-c/s 3.00

BLACK BADGE
BOOM! Studios: Aug, 2018 - No. 12, Jul, 2019 ($3.99)

1-12-Matt Kindt-s/Tyler Jenkins-a 4.00

BLACKBALL COMICS
Blackball Comics: Mar, 1994 ($3.00)

1-Trencher-c/story by Giffen; John Pain by O'Neill 3.00

BLACK BAT, THE
Dynamite Entertainment: 2013 - No. 12, 2014 ($3.99)

1-12-Buccellato-s/Cliquet-a; multiple covers on each 4.00

BLACKBEARD'S GHOST (See Movie Comics)

BLACK BEAUTY (See Son of Black Beauty)
Dell Publishing Co.: No. 440, Dec, 1952

Four Color 440 5 10 15 35 63 90

BLACK BEETLE, THE
Dark Horse Comics: Jan, 2013 - No. 4, Jun, 2013 ($3.99, limited series)

1-4-Francavilla-s/a/c 4.00

Black Bolt #9 © MAR

Black Cat (2019 series) #12 © MAR

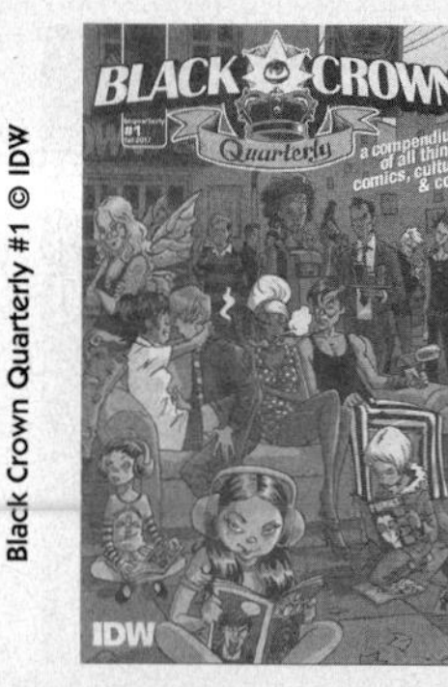

Black Crown Quarterly #1 © IDW

	GD 2.0	VG 4.0	FN 6.0	VF 8.0	VF/NM 9.0	NM- 9.2

BLACKBIRD
Image Comics: Oct, 2018 - No. 6, Mar, 2019 ($3.99)

1-6-Sam Humphries-s/Jen Bartel-a 4.00

BLACK BOLT (The Inhumans)
Marvel Comics: Jul, 2017 - No. 12, Jun, 2018 ($3.99)

1-12: 1-6-Saladin Ahmed-s/Christian Ward-a; Absorbing Man app. 7-Irving-a 4.00

BLACK BOLT: SOMETHING INHUMAN THIS WAY COMES
Marvel Comics: Sept, 2013 ($7.99, one-shot)

1-Reprints Black Bolt app. in Amazing Adventures #5-10 & Avengers #95 8.00

BLACKBURNE COVENANT, THE
Dark Horse Comics: Apr, 2003 - No. 4, July, 2003 ($2.99, limited series)

1-4-Nicieza-s/Raffaele-a 3.00
TPB (2003, $12.95) r/#1-4 13.00

BLACK CANARY (See All Star Comics #38, Flash Comics #86, Justice League of America #75 & World's Finest #244)
DC Comics: Nov, 1991 - No. 4, Feb, 1992 ($1.75, limited series)

1-4 3.00

BLACK CANARY
DC Comics: Jan, 1993 - No. 12, Dec, 1993 ($1.75)

1-Sarah Byam-s/Trevor Von Eeden-a/c 6.00
2-7 3.00
8-12: 8-The Ray-c/story. 9,10-Huntress-c/story 3.00

BLACK CANARY (Follows Oliver Queen's marriage proposal in Green Arrow #75)
DC Comics: Early Sept, 2007 - No. 4, Late Oct, 2007 ($2.99, bi-weekly limited series)

1-4-Bedard-s/Siqueira-a 3.00
... Wedding Planner 1 (11/07, $2.99) Roux-c/Ferguson & Norrie-a 3.00

BLACK CANARY
DC Comics: Aug, 2015 - No. 12, Aug, 2016 ($2.99)

1-12: 1-Fletcher-s/Annie Wu-a/c. 4,5-Guerra-a. 8-Vixen app. 9-Moritat-a. 10-Batgirl app. 3.00

BLACK CANARY AND ZATANNA; BLOODSPELL
DC Comics: 2014 ($22.99, hardcover graphic novel, dustjacket)

HC-Paul Dini-s/Joe Quinones-a; includes script and sketch art 23.00

BLACK CANARY/ORACLE: BIRDS OF PREY (Also see Showcase '96 #3)
DC Comics: 1996 ($3.95, one-shot)

1-Chuck Dixon scripts & Gary Frank-c/a.	3	6	9	17	25	34

BLACK CAT (From Spider-Man)
Marvel Comics: Aug, 2019 - No. 12, Oct, 2020 ($4.99/$3.99)

1-($4.99) MacKay-s/Foreman-a; back-up story with The Black Fox & Dracula 5.00
2-12-($3.99) 4,5-Johnny Storm app. 9,10-Wolverine app. 11,12-Iron Man app. 4.00
Annual 1 (1/20, $4.99) MacKay-s; "Wedding" of Spider-Man & Black Cat 5.00

BLACK CAT (From Spider-Man)
Marvel Comics: Feb, 2021 - Present ($3.99)

1-3-"King In Black" tie-ins; MacKay-s/Villa-a 4.00

BLACK CAT (AMAZING SPIDER-MAN PRESENTS...)
Marvel Comics: Aug, 2010 - No. 4, Dec, 2010 ($3.99, limited series)

1-4-Van Meter-s/Pulido-a/Conner-c; Spider-Man & Ana Kraven app. 5.00

BLACK CAT COMICS (...Western #16-19; ...Mystery #30 on)
(See All-New #7,9, The Original Black Cat, Pocket & Speed Comics)
Harvey Publications (Home Comics): June-July, 1946 - No. 29, June, 1951

	GD	VG	FN	VF	VF/NM	NM-
1-Kubert-a; Joe Simon c-1,2	90	180	270	576	988	1400
2-Kubert-a	45	90	135	284	480	675
3,4: 4-The Red Demons begin (The Demon #4 & 5)	37	74	111	222	361	500
5,6,7: 5,6-The Scarlet Arrow app. in ea. by Powell; S&K-a in both. 6-Origin Red Demon. 7-Vagabond Prince by S&K plus 1 more story	41	82	123	256	428	600
8-S&K-a; Kerry Drake begins, ends #13	39	78	117	240	395	550
9-Origin Stuntman (r/Stuntman #1)	40	80	120	246	411	575
10-20: 14,15,17-Mary Worth app. plus Invisible Scarlet O'Neil-#15,20,24	28	56	84	168	274	380
21-26	22	44	66	132	216	300
27,28: 27-Used in **SOTI**, pg. 193; X-Mas-c; 2 pg. John Wayne story. 28-Intro. Kit, Black Cat's new sidekick	26	52	78	152	249	345
29-Black Cat bondage-c; Black Cat stories	28	56	84	165	270	375

BLACK CAT MYSTERY (Formerly Black Cat; ...Western Mystery #54; ...Western #55,56; ...Mystery #57; ...Mystic #58-62; Black Cat #63-65)
Harvey Publications: No. 30, Aug, 1951 - No. 65, Apr, 1963

	GD	VG	FN	VF	VF/NM	NM-
30-Black Cat on cover and first page only	40	80	120	246	411	575
31,32,34,37,38,40	32	64	96	192	314	435
33-Used in **POP**, pg. 89; electrocution-c	55	110	165	352	601	850
35-Atomic disaster cover/story	43	86	129	271	461	650
36,39-Used in **SOTI**: #36-Pgs. 270,271; #39-Pgs. 386-388	41	82	123	256	428	600
41-43	31	62	93	186	303	420
44-Eyes, ears, tongue cut out; Nostrand-a	39	78	117	240	395	550
45-Classic "Colorama" by Powell; Nostrand-a	94	188	282	597	1024	1450
46-49,51-Nostrand-a in all. 51-Story has blank panel covering censored art (post-Code)	36	72	108	211	343	475
50-Check-a; classic Warren Kremer-c showing a man's face & hands burning away	865	1730	2595	6315	11,158	16,000
52,53 (r/#34 & 35)	20	40	60	120	195	270
54-Two Black Cat stories (2/55, last pre-code)	23	46	69	136	223	310
55,56-Black Cat app.	20	40	60	120	195	270
57(7/56)-Kirby-c	22	44	66	132	216	300
58-60-Kirby-a(4). 58,59-Kirby-c. 60,61-Simon-c	26	52	78	154	252	350
61-Nostrand-a; "Colorama" r/#45	24	48	72	140	230	320
62 (3/58)-E.C. story swipe	20	40	60	120	195	270
63-65: Giants(10/62,1/63, 4/63); Reprints; Black Cat app. 63-origin Black Kitten. 65-1 pg. Powell-a	23	46	69	136	223	310

NOTE: ***Kremer** a-37, 39, 43; c-36, 37, 47. **Meskin** a-51. **Palais** a-30, 31(2), 32(2), 33-35, 37-40. **Powell** a-32-35, 36(2), 40, 41, 43-53, 57. **Simon** c-63-65. **Sparling** a-44. Bondage c-32, 34, 43.*

BLACK CLOUD
Image Comics: Apr, 2017 - No. 10, Jun, 2018 ($3.99)

1-10: 1-Latour & Brandon-s/Hinkle-a 4.00

BLACK COBRA (Bride's Diary No. 4 on) (See Captain Flight #8)
Ajax/Farrell Publications(Excellent Publ.): No. 1, 10-11/54; No. 6(No. 2), 12-1/54-55; No. 3, 2-3/55

	GD	VG	FN	VF	VF/NM	NM-
1-Re-intro Black Cobra & The Cobra Kid (costumed heroes)	41	82	123	256	428	600
6(#2)-Formerly Billy Bunny	23	46	69	136	223	310
3-(Pre-code)-Torpedoman app.	22	44	66	132	216	300

BLACK CONDOR (Also see Crack Comics, Freedom Fighters & Showcase '94 #10,11)
DC Comics: June, 1992 - No. 12, May, 1993 ($1.25)

1-8-Heath-c 3.00
9-12: 9,10,12-Heath-c. 9,10-The Ray app. 12-Batman-c/app. 3.00

BLACK CROSS SPECIAL (See Dark Horse Presents)
Dark Horse Comics: Jan, 1988 ($1.75, B&W, one-shot)(Reprints & new-a)

1-1st printing 4.00
1-(2nd printing) has 2 pgs. new-a 3.00
...: Dirty Work 1 (4/97, $2.95) Chris Warner-c/s/a 3.00

BLACK CROWN QUARTERLY
IDW Publishing: Oct, 2017 - No. 3, Apr, 2018 ($6.99, quarterly)

1-3-Short story anthology with creator interviews and series previews 7.00

BLACK DIAMOND
Americomics: May, 1983 - No. 5, 1984 (no month)($2.00-$1.75, Baxter paper)

1-3-Movie adapt.; 1-Colt back-up begins 4.00
4,5 3.00

NOTE: ***Bill Black** a-1i; c-1. **Gulacy** c-2-5. Sybil Danning photo back-c-1.*

BLACK DIAMOND WESTERN (Formerly Desperado No. 1-8)
Lev Gleason Publ: No. 9, Mar, 1949 - No. 60, Feb, 1956 (No. 9-28: 52 pgs.)

	GD	VG	FN	VF	VF/NM	NM-
9-Black Diamond & his horse Reliapon begin; origin & 1st app. Black Diamond	21	42	63	126	206	285
10	12	24	36	69	97	125
11-15	10	20	30	54	72	90
16-28(11/49-11/51)-Wolverton's Bingbang Buster	14	28	42	76	108	140
29-40: 31-One pg. Frazetta anti-drug ad	9	18	27	47	61	75
41-50,53-59	8	16	24	40	50	60
51-3-D effect-c/story	15	30	45	85	130	175
52-3-D effect story	14	28	42	81	118	155
60-Last issue	8	16	24	44	57	70

NOTE: ***Biro** c-9-35?. **Cooper** a-12. **Myron Foss** a-54-58, c-54-56, 58. **Guardineer** a-9, 12, 15, 18. **Jack Keller** a-12. **Kida** a-9. **Maurer** a-10. **Ed Moore** a-16. **Morisi** a-55. **William Overgard** a-9-23. **Tuska** a-10, 48. **Bill Walton** a-57.*

BLACK DRAGON, THE
Marvel Comics (Epic Comics): May, 1985 - No. 6, Oct, 1985 (Baxter paper, mature)

1-6: 1-Chris Claremont story & John Bolton painted-c/a in all 4.00
TPB (Dark Horse, 4/96, $17.95, B&W, trade paperback) r/#1-6; intro by Anne McCaffrey 18.00

BLACK DYNAMITE (Based on the Michael Jai White film)

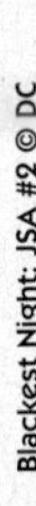
Blackest Night: JSA #2 © DC

Black Goliath #1 © MAR

Black Hammer: Visions #1 © 171 Studios & Ormston

GD VG FN VF VF/NM NM-
2.0 4.0 6.0 8.0 9.0 9.2

GD VG FN VF VF/NM NM-
2.0 4.0 6.0 8.0 9.0 9.2

IDW Publishing: Dec, 2013 - No. 4, Aug, 2014 ($3.99)

1-4: 1-Ash-s/Wimberly-a; multiple covers. 2,3-Ferreira-a 4.00

BLACKEST NIGHT (2009 Green Lantern & DC crossover) (Leads into Brightest Day series)
DC Comics: No. 0, Jun, 2009 - No. 8, May, 2010 ($3.99, limited series)

0-Free Comic Book Day edition; Johns-s/Reis-a; profile pages of different corps 3.00
1-8: 1-($3.99) Black Lantern Corps arises; Johns-s/Reis-c/a; Hawkman & Hawkgirl killed. 4-Nekron rises. 8-Dead heroes return 5.00
1-Variant cover by Van Sciver 10.00
1-3,5: 2nd-4th printings 4.00
2-8: 2-Cascioli variant-c. 3-Van Sciver variant-c. 4-7-Migliari variant-c. 8-Mahnke var-c 8.00
... Director's Cut (6/10, $5.99) Commentary with story panels; cover gallery, script pgs. 6.00
HC (2010, $29.99, d.j.) r/#0-8 & Blackest Night Director's Cut; variant cover gallery 30.00
SC (2011, $19.99) r/#0-8 & Blackest Night Director's Cut; variant cover gallery 20.00
...: Black Lantern Corps Vol. 1 HC (2010, $24.99, d.j.) r/BN: Batman, BN: Superman, and BN: Titans series; cover gallery and character sketch designs 25.00
...: Black Lantern Corps Vol. 1 SC (2011, $19.99) same contents as HC edition 20.00
...: Black Lantern Corps Vol. 2 HC (2010, $24.99, d.j.) r/BN: The Flash, BN: JSA, and BN: Wonder Woman series; cover gallery and character sketch designs 25.00
...: Rise of the Black Lanterns HC (2010, $24.99) r/one-shots Atom and Hawkman #46, Catwoman #83, Phantom Stranger #42, Power of Shazam #48, The Question #37, Starman #81, Weird Western Tales #71, Green Arrow #30 & Adventure Comics #7; sketch art 25.00
...: Rise of the Black Lanterns SC (2011, $19.99) same contents as HC edition 20.00

BLACKEST NIGHT: BATMAN (2009 Green Lantern & DC crossover)
DC Comics: Oct, 2009 - No. 3, Dec, 2009 ($2.99, limited series)

1-3: 1-Bat-parents rise as Black Lanterns; Deadman app.; Syaf-a/Andy Kubert-c; 2 printings. 3-Flying Graysons return 3.00
1-3-Variant-c by Sienkiewicz 5.00

BLACKEST NIGHT: JSA (2009 Green Lantern & DC crossover)
DC Comics: Feb, 2010 - No. 3, Apr, 2010 ($2.99, limited series)

1-3-Original Sandman, Dr. Midnite and Mr. Terrific rise; Barrows-a/c 3.00
1-3-Variant-c by Gene Ha 5.00

BLACKEST NIGHT: SUPERMAN (2009 Green Lantern & DC crossover)
DC Comics: Oct, 2009 - No. 3, Dec, 2009 ($2.99, limited series)

1-3-Earth-2 Superman and Lois become Black Lanterns; Barrows-a/c; 2 printings 3.00
1-3-Variant-c by Shane Davis 5.00

BLACKEST NIGHT: TALES OF THE CORPS (2009 Green Lantern & DC crossover)
DC Comics: Sept, 2009 - No. 3, Sept, 2009 ($3.99, weekly limited series)

1-3-Short stories by various; interlocking cover images. 3-Commentary on B.N. #0 4.00
HC (2010, $24.99) r/#1-3 & Adventure Comics #4,5 & Green Lantern #49; sketch art 25.00
SC (2011, $19.99) r/#1-3 & Adventure Comics #4,5 & Green Lantern #49; sketch art 20.00

BLACKEST NIGHT: THE FLASH (2009 Green Lantern & DC crossover)
DC Comics: Feb, 2010 - No. 3, Apr, 2010 ($2.99, limited series)

1-3-Rogues vs. Dead Rogues; Johns-s/Kolins-a 3.00
1-3-Variant-c by Manapul 5.00

BLACKEST NIGHT: TITANS (2009 Green Lantern & DC crossover)
DC Comics: Oct, 2009 - No. 3, Dec, 2009 ($2.99, limited series)

1-3-Terra and the original Hawk return; Benes-a/c 3.00
1-3-Variant-c by Brian Haberlin 5.00

BLACKEST NIGHT: WONDER WOMAN (2009 Green Lantern & DC crossover)
DC Comics: Feb, 2010 - No. 3, Apr, 2010 ($2.99, limited series)

1-3-Maxwell Lord returns; Rucka-s/Scott-a/Horn-c. 2,3-Mera app.; Star Sapphire 3.00
1-3-Variant-c by Ryan Sook 5.00

BLACK-EYED KIDS
AfterShock Comics: Apr, 2016 - No. 15, Dec, 2017 ($3.99)

1-15: 1-($1.99) Joe Pruett-s/Szymon Kudranski-a/Francesco Francavilla-c. 2-15-($3.99) 4.00

BLACK FLAG (See Asylum #5)
Maximum Press: Jan, 1995 - No.4, 1995; No. 0, July, 1995 ($2.50, B&W) (No. 0 in color)

Preview Edition (6/94, $1.95, B&W)-Fraga/McFarlane-c. 3.00
0-4: 0-(7/95)-Liefeld/Fraga-c. 1-(1/95). 3.00
1-Variant cover 5.00
2,4-Variant covers 3.00
NOTE: *Fraga a-0-4, Preview Edition; c-1-4.* ***Liefeld/Fraga*** *c-0.* ***McFarlane/Fraga*** *c-Preview Edition.*

BLACK FURY (Becomes Wild West No. 58) (See Blue Bird)
Charlton Comics Group: May, 1955 - No. 57, Mar-Apr, 1966 (Horse stories)

1 12 24 36 67 94 120
2 7 14 21 37 46 55
3-10 6 12 18 28 34 40
11-15,19,20 4 8 10 18 22 25
16-18-Ditko-a 12 24 36 67 94 120
21-30 4 7 10 14 17 20
31-57 3 6 8 12 14 16

BLACK GOLIATH (See Avengers #32-35,41,54 and Civil War #4)
Marvel Comics Group: Feb, 1976 - No. 5, Nov, 1976

1-Tuska-a(p) thru #3 4 8 12 23 37 50
2-5: 2-4-(Regular 25¢ editions). 4-Kirby-c/Buckler-a 2 4 6 10 14 18
2-4-(30¢-c variants, limited distribution)(4,6,8/76) 5 10 15 31 53 75

BLACK HAMMER
Dark Horse Comics: Jul, 2016 - No. 13, Sept, 2017 ($3.99)

1-13: 1-8,10,11,13-Lemire-s/Ormston-a; covers by Ormston & Lemire. 9,12-Rubín-a 4.00
...: Cthu-Louise (12/18, $3.99) Lemire-s/Lenox-a; two covers by Lenox & Jill Thompson 4.00
... Director's Cut (1/19, $4.99) r/#1 in original B&W ink with original script 6.00
... Giant-Sized Annual (1/17, $5.99) Short stories by various incl. Nguyen, Allred, Kindt 6.00

BLACK HAMMER: AGE OF DOOM
Dark Horse Comics: Apr, 2018 - No. 12, Sept, 2019 ($3.99)

1-12: 1-5,8-12-Lemire-s/Ormston-a. 6,7-Tammaso-a 4.00

BLACK HAMMER '45
Dark Horse Comics: Mar, 2019 - No. 4, Jun, 2019 ($3.99, limited series)

1-4-Fawkes-s/Kindt-a; flashbacks to the Black Hammer Squadron in WWII 4.00

BLACK HAMMER / JUSTICE LEAGUE: HAMMER OF JUSTICE!
Dark Horse Comics: Jul, 2019 - No. 5, Nov, 2019 ($3.99, limited series)

1-5-Lemire-s/Walsh-a; Justice League switches places with the Black Hammer crew 4.00

BLACK HAMMER: VISIONS
Dark Horse Comics: Feb, 2021 - No. 8 ($3.99, limited series)

1-Spotlight on Golden Gail; Patton Oswalt-s/Dean Kotz-a 4.00

BLACKHAWK (Formerly Uncle Sam #1-8; see Military Comics & Modern Comics)
Comic Magazines(Quality)No. 9-107(12/56); National Periodical Publications No. 108 (1/57) -250; DC Comics No. 251 on: No. 9, Winter, 1944 - No. 243, 10-11/68; No. 244, 1-2/76 - No. 250, 1-2/77; No. 251, 10/82 - No. 273, 11/84

9 (1944) 284 568 852 1818 3109 4400
10 (1946) 116 232 348 742 1271 1800
11-15: 14-Ward-a; 13,14-Fear app. 84 168 252 538 919 1300
16-19 68 136 204 435 743 1050
20-Classic Crandall bondage-c; Ward Blackhawk 119 238 357 762 1306 1850
21-30 (1950) 52 104 156 328 552 775
31-40: 31-Chop Chop by Jack Cole 41 82 123 250 418 585
41-49,51-60: 42-Robot-c 36 72 108 216 351 485
50-1st Killer Shark; origin in text 39 78 117 240 395 550
61,62: 61-Used in **POP**, pg. 91. 62-Used in **POP**, pg. 92 & color illo 33 66 99 195 320 445
63-70,72-80: 65-H-Bomb explosion panel. 66-B&W & color illos **POP**. 67-Hitler-s. 70-Return of Killer Shark; atomic explosion panel. 75-Intro. Blackie the Hawk 31 62 93 182 296 410
71-Origin retold; flying saucer-c; A-Bomb panels 35 70 105 208 339 470
81-86: Last precode (3/55) 27 54 81 162 266 370
87-92,94-99,101-107: 91-Robot-c. 105-1st S.A. 22 44 66 132 216 300
93-Origin in text 23 46 69 136 223 310
100 30 60 90 177 289 400
108-1st DC issue (1/57); re-intro. Blackie, the Hawk, their mascot; not in #115 41 82 123 303 689 1075
109-117: 117-(10/57)-Mr. Freeze app. 15 30 45 100 220 340
118-(11/57)-Frazetta-r/Jimmy Wakely #4 (3 pgs.) 15 30 45 103 227 350
119-130 (11/58): 120-Robot-c 12 24 36 79 170 260
131,132,134-140 (9/59) 10 20 30 66 138 210
133-Intro. Lady Blackhawk 135 270 405 864 1482 2100
141-150,152-163,165,166: 141-Cat-Man returns-c/s. 143-Kurtzman-r/Jimmy Wakely #4. 150-(7/60)-King Condor returns. 166-Last 10¢ issue 8 16 24 54 102 150
151-Lady Blackhawk receives & loses super powers 9 18 27 59 117 175
164-Origin retold 9 18 27 58 114 170
167-180 6 12 18 37 66 95
181-190 5 10 15 31 53 75
191-196,199: 196-Combat Diary series begins 4 8 12 27 44 60
197,198,200: 197-New look for Blackhawks. 198-Origin retold 4 8 12 28 47 65
201,202,204-210 3 6 9 21 33 45
203-Origin Chop Chop (12/64) 4 8 12 25 40 55
211-227,229-243(1968): 230-Blackhawks become superheroes; JLA cameo 242-Return to old costumes 3 6 9 17 26 35

Blackhawk #261 © DC

Black Knight (1955 series) #4 © MAR

Black Lightning #1 © DC

GD VG FN VF VF/NM NM-
2.0 4.0 6.0 8.0 9.0 9.2

228-Batman, Green Lantern, Superman, The Flash cameos. 4 8 12 28 47 65
244 ('76) -250: 250-Chuck dies 1 2 3 5 6 8
251-273: 251-Origin retold; Black Knights return. 252-Intro Domino. 253-Part origin Hendrickson. 258-Blackhawk's Island destroyed. 259-Part origin Chop-Chop. 265-273 (75¢ cover price) 5.00
NOTE: ***Chaykin** a-260; c-257-260, 262. **Crandall** a-10, 11, 13, 16?, 18-20, 22-26, 30-33, 35p, 36(2), 37, 38?, 39-44, 46-50, 52-58, 60, 63, 64, 66, 67; c-14-20, 22-63(most except #28-33, 36, 37, 39). **Evans** a-244, 245,246i, 248-250i. **G. Kane** c-263, 264. **Kubert c**-244, 245. **Newton** a-266p. **Severin** a-257.**Spiegle** a-261-267, 269-273; c-265-272. **Toth** a-260p. **Ward** a-16-27(Chop Chop, 8pgs. ea.); pencilled stories-No. 17-63(approx.). **Wildey** a-268. Chop Chop solo stories in #10-95?*

BLACKHAWK
DC Comics: Mar, 1988 - No. 3, May, 1988 ($2.95, limited series, mature)
1-3: Chaykin painted-c/a/scripts 4.00

BLACKHAWK (Also see Action Comics #601)
DC Comics: Mar, 1989 - No. 16, Aug, 1990 ($1.50, mature)
1 4.00
2-6,8-16: 16-Crandall-c swipe 3.00
7-($2.50, 52 pgs.)-Story-r/Military #1 4.00
Annual 1 (1989, $2.95, 68 pgs.)-Recaps origin of Blackhawk, Lady Blackhawk, and others 4.00
Special 1 (1992, $3.50, 68 pgs.)-Mature readers 4.00

BLACKHAWK INDIAN TOMAHAWK WAR, THE
Avon Periodicals: 1951 (Also see Fighting Indians of the Wild West)
nn-Kinstler-c; Kit West story 22 44 66 132 216 300

BLACKHAWKS (DC New 52)
DC Comics: Nov, 2011 - No. 8, Jun, 2012 ($2.99)
1-8: 1-Costa-s/Nolan & Lashley-a 3.00

BLACK HOLE (See Walt Disney Showcase #54) (Disney, movie)
Whitman Publishing Co.: Mar, 1980 - No. 4, Sept, 1980
11295(#1) (1979, Golden, $1.50-c, 52 pgs., graphic novel; 8 1/2x11") Photo-c; Spiegle-a. 3 6 9 15 22 28
1-3: 1,2-Movie adaptation. 2,3-Spiegle-a. 3-McWilliams-a; photo-c.
3-New stories 2 4 6 10 14 18
4-Sold only in pre-packs; new story; Spiegle-a 25 50 75 175 388 600

BLACK HOOD, THE (See Blue Ribbon, Flyman & Mighty Comics)
Red Circle Comics (Archie): June, 1983 - No. 3, Oct, 1983 (Mandell paper)
1-Morrow, McWilliams, Wildey-a; Toth-c 6.00
2,3: The Fox by Toth-c/a; Boyette-a. 3-Morrow-a; Toth wraparound-c 4.00
NOTE: *Also see Archie's Super-Hero Special Digest #2*

BLACK HOOD
DC Comics (Impact Comics): Dec, 1991 - No. 12, Dec, 1992 ($1.00)
1 4.00
2-12: 11-Intro The Fox. 12-Origin Black Hood 3.00
Annual 1 (1992, $2.50, 68 pgs.)-w/Trading card 4.00

BLACK HOOD, THE
Archie Comic Publications (Dark Circle Comics): Apr, 2015 - No. 11, Aug, 2016 ($3.99)
1-11: 1-Origin retold; Swierczynski-s/Gaydos-a; five covers. 6-Chaykin-a. 8-Hack-a 4.00

BLACK HOOD, THE (Volume 2)
Archie Comic Publications (Dark Circle Comics): Dec, 2016 - No. 5, Aug, 2017 ($3.99)
1-5-Swierczynski-s/Greg Scott-a 4.00

BLACK HOOD COMICS (Formerly Hangman #2-8; Laugh Comics #20 on; also see Black Swan, Jackpot, Roly Poly & Top-Notch #9)
MLJ Magazines: No. 9, Wint., 1943-44 - No. 19, Sum., 1946 (on radio in 1943)
9-The Hangman & The Boy Buddies cont'd 148 296 444 947 1624 2300
10-Hangman & Dusty, the Boy Detective app. 90 180 270 376 988 1400
11-Dusty app.; no Hangman 74 148 222 470 810 1150
12,13,15-18: 17-Hal Foster swipe from Prince Valiant; 1st issue with "An Archie Magazine" on-c 68 136 204 435 743 1050
14-Kinstler blood-c 119 238 357 762 1306 1850
19-I.D. exposed; last issue 84 168 252 538 919 1300
NOTE: *Hangman by **Fuje** in 9, 10. **Kinstler** a-15, c-14-16.*

BLACK JACK (Rocky Lane's...; formerly Jim Bowie)
Charlton Comics: No. 20, Nov, 1957 - No. 30, Nov, 1959
20 9 18 27 52 69 85
21,27,29,30 6 12 18 31 38 45
22,23: 22-(68 pgs.). 23-Williamson/Torres-a 8 16 24 42 54 65
24-26,28-Ditko-a 10 20 30 56 76 95

BLACK KNIGHT, THE
Toby Press: May, 1953; 1963
1-Bondage-c 161 322 483 1030 1765 2500
Super Reprint No. 11 (1963)-Reprints 1953 issue 3 6 9 19 25 32

BLACK KNIGHT, THE
Atlas Comics (MgPC): May, 1955 - No. 5, April, 1956
1-Origin Crusader; Maneely-c/a 300 600 900 2010 3505 5000
2-Maneely-c/a(4) 161 322 483 1030 1765 2500
3-5: 4-Maneely-c/a. 5-Maneely-c, Shores-a 148 296 444 947 1624 2300
...No. 1 Facsimile Edition (4/21, $3.99) Reprints #1 with original ads 4.00

BLACK KNIGHT (See The Avengers #48, Marvel Super Heroes & Tales To Astonish #52)
Marvel Comics: June, 1990 - No. 4, Sept, 1990 ($1.50, limited series)
1-Original Black Knight returns 2 4 6 9 12 15
2-4: 3,4-Dr. Strange app. 3.00
... (MDCU) 1 (01/10, $3.99) Origin re-told; Frenz-a; originally from Marvel Digital Comics 4.00
NOTE: ***Buckler** c-1-4p*

BLACK KNIGHT (See Weirdworld and Secret Wars 2015 series)
Marvel Comics: Jan, 2016 - No. 5, May, 2016 ($3.99)
1-5: 1-Tieri-s/Pizzari-a. 2-5-Uncanny Avengers app. 4.00

BLACK KNIGHT: EXODUS
Marvel Comics: Dec, 1996 ($2.50, one-shot)
1-Raab-s; Apocalypse-c/app. 3.00

BLACK LAMB, THE
DC Comics (Helix): Nov, 1996 - No, 6, Apr, 1997 ($2.50, limited series)
1-6: Tim Truman-c/a/scripts 3.00

BLACK LAUGHTER
Black Laughter Publ.: Nov, 1972 (35¢)
V1#1-African American humor; James Dixon-s/a; 1st app. of Mr. Habeus Corpus (a 9.2 copy sold for $2629 and a 7.0 copy sold for $335 in 2018, and a CGC 7.5 sold for $617 in 2020)

BLACKLIGHT (From ShadowHawk)
Image Comics: June, 2005 - No. 2, Jul, 2005 ($2.99)
1,2-Toledo & Deering-a/Wherle-s 3.00

BLACK LIGHTNING (See The Brave & The Bold, Cancelled Comic Cavalcade, DC Comics Presents #16, Detective Comics #490 and World's Finest #257)
National Periodical Publ./DC Comics: Apr, 1977 - No. 11, Sept-Oct, 1978
1-Origin Black Lightning; 1st app. Tobias Whale 5 10 15 34 60 85
2,3,6-10: 2-Talia and Merlyn app. 2 4 6 8 11 14
4,5-Superman-c/s. 4-Intro Cyclotronic Man 2 4 6 11 16 20
11-The Ray new solo story 2 4 6 10 14 18
NOTE: ***Buckler** c-1-3p, 6-11p. #11 is 44 pgs.*

BLACK LIGHTNING (2nd Series)
DC Comics: Feb, 1995 - No. 13, Feb, 1996 ($1.95/$2.25)
1-Tony Isabella scripts begin, ends #8 1 3 4 6 8 10
2-1st app. Painkiller 1 3 4 6 8 10
3-13: 6-Begin $2.25-c. 13-Batman-c/app. 3.00

BLACK LIGHTNING: COLD DEAD HANDS
DC Comics: Jan, 2018 - No. 6, Jun, 2018 ($3.99, limited series)
1-6-Tony Isabella-s/Clayton Henry-a; Tobias Whale app. 4.00

BLACK LIGHTNING / HONG KONG PHOOEY SPECIAL
DC Comics: Jul, 2018 ($3.99, one-shot)
1-Cowan & Sienkiewicz-a/Hill-s; takes place in 1976; Funky Phantom back-up story 4.00

BLACK LIGHTNING: YEAR ONE
DC Comics: Mar, 2009 - No. 6, May, 2009 ($2.99, bi-weekly limited series)
1-6-Van Meter-s/Hamner-a. 1-Two printings (white and yellow cover title logos) 3.00
TPB (2009, $17.99) r/#1-6 18.00

BLACK LIST, THE (Based on the TV show)
Titan Comics: Aug, 2015 - No. 10, Jul, 2016 ($3.99)
1-10-Art & photo-c for each: 1-Nicole Phillips-s/Beni Lobel-a. 4.00

BLACK MAGIC (...Magazine) (Becomes Cool Cat V8#6 on)
Crestwood Publ. V1#1-4,V6#1-V7#5/Headline V1#5-V5#3,V7#6-V8#5: 10-11/50 - V4#1, 6-7/53: V4#2, 9-10/53 - V5#3, 11-12/54; V6#1, 9-10/57 - V7#2, 11-12/58: V7#3, 7-8/60 - V8#5, 11-12/61 (V1#1-5, 52pgs.; V1#6-V3#3, 44pgs.)
V1#1-S&K-a, 10 pgs.; Meskin-a(2) 177 354 531 1124 1937 2750
2-S&K-a, 17 pgs.; Meskin-a 76 152 228 486 831 1175
3-6(8-9/51)-S&K, Roussos, Meskin-a 63 126 189 403 689 975
V2#1(10-11/51),4,5,7(#13),9(#15),12(#18)-S&K-a 41 82 123 256 428 600
2,3,6,8,10,11(#17) 36 72 108 211 343 475
V3#1(#19, 12/52) - 6(#24, 5/53)-S&K-a 36 72 108 216 348 485

Black Magick #8 © Rucka & Scott

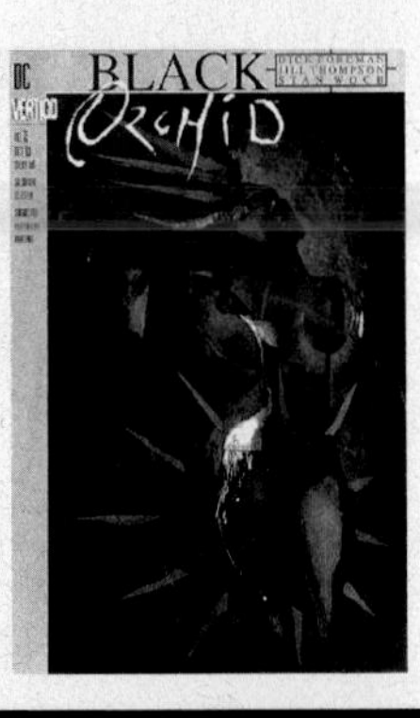
Black Orchid #2 © DC

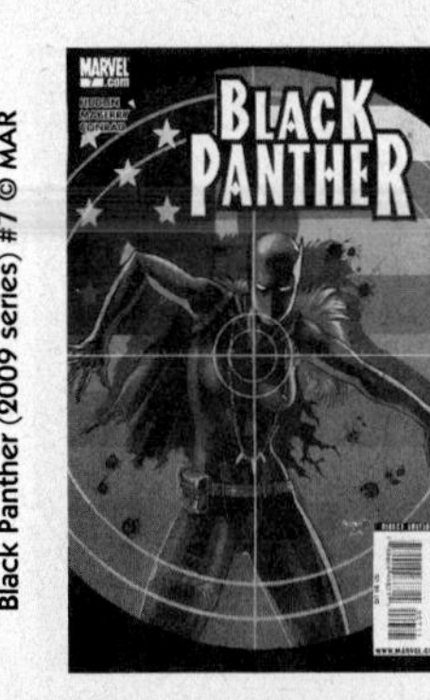
Black Panther (2009 series) #7 © MAR

GD VG FN VF VF/NM NM-
2.0 4.0 6.0 8.0 9.0 9.2

V4#1(#25, 6-7/53), 2(#26, 9-10/53)-S&K-a(3-4) 37 74 111 222 361 500
3(#27, 11-12/53)-S&K-a; Ditko-a (2nd published-a); also see Captain 3-D, Daring Love #1, Strange Fantasy #9, & Fantastic Fears #5 (Fant. Fears was 1st drawn, but not 1st publ.)
68 136 204 435 743 1050
4(#28)-Eyes ripped out/story-S&K, Ditko-a 50 100 150 315 533 750
5(#29, 3-4/54)-S&K, Ditko-a 39 78 117 229 375 520
6(#30, 5-6/54)-S&K, Powell?-a 31 62 93 186 303 420
V5#1(#31, 7-8/54 - 3(#33, 11-12/54)-S&K-a 21 42 63 122 199 275
V6#1(#34, 9-10/57), 2(#35, 11-12/57) 12 24 36 69 97 125
3(1-2/58) - 6(7-8/58) 12 24 36 69 97 125
V7#1(9-10/58) - 3(7-8/60), 4(9-10/60) 10 20 30 56 76 95
5(11-12/60)-Hitler-c; Torres-a 21 42 63 122 199 275
6(1-2/61)-Powell-a(2) 10 20 30 56 76 95
V8#1(3-4/61)-Powell-c/a 10 20 30 56 76 95
2(5-6/61)-E.C. story swipe/W.F. #22; Ditko, Powell-a
11 22 33 62 86 110
3(7-8/61)-E.C. story swipe/W.F. #22; Powell-a(2) 11 22 33 62 86 110
4(9-10/61)-Powell-a(5) 10 20 30 56 76 95
5-E.C. story swipe/W.S.F. #28; Powell-a(3) 11 22 33 60 83 105

NOTE: ***Bernard Baily*** *a-V4#6?, V5#3(2).* ***Grandenetti*** *a-V2#3, 11.* ***Kirby*** *c-V1#1-6, V2#1-12, V3#1-6, V4#1, 2, 4-6, V5#1-3.* ***McWilliams*** *a-V3#2i.* ***Meskin*** *a-V1#1(2), 2, 3, 4(2), 5(2), 6, V2/1, 2, 3(2), 4(3), 5, 6(2), 7-9, 11, 12i, V3#1(2), 5, 6, V5#1(2), 2.* ***Orlando*** *a-V6#1, 4, V7#2; c-V6/1-6.* ***Powell*** *a-V5#1?.* ***Roussos*** *a-V1#3-5, 6(2), V2#3(2), 4, 5(2), 6, 8, 9, 10(2), 11, 12p, V3#1(2), 2i, 5, V5#2.* ***Simon*** *a-V2#12, V3#2, V7#5? c-V4#3?, V7#3?, 4, 5?, 6?, V8#1-5.* ***Simon & Kirby*** *a-V1#1, 2(2), 3-6, V2#1, 4, 5, 7, 9, 12, V3#1-6, V4#1(3), 2(4), 3(2), 4(2), 5, 6, V5#1-3; c-V2#1.* ***Leonard Starr*** *a-V1#1.* ***Tuska*** *a-V6#3, 4.* ***Woodbridge*** *a-V7#4.*

BLACK MAGIC
National Periodical Publications: Oct-Nov, 1973 - No. 9, Apr-May, 1975
1-S&K reprints 3 6 9 17 25 34
2-8-S&K reprints 2 4 6 10 14 18
9-S&K reprints 2 4 6 11 16 20

BLACK MAGICK
Image Comics: Oct, 2015 - Present ($3.99)
1-16-Greg Rucka-s/Nicola Scott-a 4.00

BLACKMAIL TERROR (See Harvey Comics Library)

BLACK MARKET
BOOM! Studios: Jul, 2014 - No. 4, Oct, 2014 ($3.99, limited series)
1-4-Barbiere-s/Santos-a 4.00

BLACK MASK
DC Comics: 1993 - No. 3, 1994 ($4.95, limited series, 52 pgs.)
1-3 5.00

BLACK MASK: YEAR OF THE VILLAIN
DC Comics: Oct, 2019 ($4.99, one-shot)
1-Tom Taylor-s/Cully Hamner-a; Apex Lex Luthor & Batwoman app. 5.00

BLACK MONDAY MURDERS, THE
Image Comics: Aug, 2016 - No. 8, Feb, 2018 ($4.99/$3.99, limited series)
1-4-Jonathan Hickman-s/Tomm Coker-a 5.00
5-8-($3.99) 4.00

BLACK OPS
Image Comics (WildStorm): Jan, 1996 - No. 5, May, 1996 ($2.50, lim. series)
1-5 3.00

BLACK ORCHID (See Adventure Comics #428 & Phantom Stranger)
DC Comics: Holiday, 1988-89 - No. 3, 1989 ($3.50, lim. series, prestige format)
Book 1,3: Gaiman scripts & McKean painted-a in all 6.00
Book 2-Arkham Asylum story; Batman app. 1 2 3 5 6 8
TPB (1991, $19.95) r/#1-3; new McKean-c 20.00

BLACK ORCHID
DC Comics: Sept, 1993 - No. 22, June, 1995 ($1.95/$2.25)
1-22: Dave McKean-c all issues 3.00
1-Platinum Edition 12.00
Annual 1 (1993, $3.95, 68 pgs.)-Children's Crusade 4.00

BLACK ORDER (The Warmasters of Thanos)
Marvel Comics: Jan, 2019 - No. 5, May, 2019 ($3.99, limited series)
1-5: 1-Landy-s/Tan-a. 3-5-Nova app. 5-Magno-a 4.00

BLACKOUT
Dark Horse Comics: Mar, 2014 - No. 4, Jul, 2014 ($2.99, limited series)
1-4-Barbiere-s/Lorimer-a; King Tiger back-up by Stradley-s/Doug Wheatley-a 3.00

BLACKOUTS (See Broadway Hollywood...)

BLACK PANTHER, THE (Also see Avengers #52, Fantastic Four #52, Jungle Action, Marvel Premiere #51-53 and Rise of the Black Panther)
Marvel Comics Group: Jan, 1977 - No. 15, May, 1979

GD VG FN VF VF/NM NM-
2.0 4.0 6.0 8.0 9.0 9.2

1-Jack Kirby-s/a thru #12 9 18 27 58 114 170
2 3 6 9 21 33 45
3-5: 4,5-(Regular 30¢ editions). 3 6 9 19 30 40
4,5-(35¢-c variants, limited dist.)(7,9/77) 9 18 27 59 117 175
6-13: 8-Origin 3 6 9 17 26 35
14,15-Avengers x-over. 14-Origin 3 6 9 18 28 38
...By Jack Kirby Vol. 1 TPB (2005, $19.99) r/#1-7; unused covers and sketch pages 20.00
...By Jack Kirby Vol. 2 TPB (2006, $19.99) r/#8-12 by Kirby and #13 non-Kirby 20.00
NOTE: ***J. Buscema*** *c-15p.* ***Layton*** *c-13i.*

BLACK PANTHER
Marvel Comics Group: July, 1988 - No. 4, Oct, 1988 ($1.25)
1-4-Gillis-s/Cowan & Delarosa-a 1 2 3 5 6 8

BLACK PANTHER (Marvel Knights)
Marvel Comics: Nov, 1998 - No. 62, Sept, 2003 ($2.50)
1-Texeira-a/c; Priest-s 2 4 6 11 16 20
1-($6.95) DF edition w/Quesada & Palmiotti-c 2 4 6 13 18 22
2,3: 2-Two covers by Texeira and Timm. 3-Fantastic Four app. 5.00
4-1st White Wolf 2 4 6 11 16 20
5-22,24-35,37-40: 5-Evans-a. 6-8-Jusko-a. 8-Avengers-c/app. 15-Hulk app. 22-Moon Knight app. 25-Maximum Security x-over. 26-Storm-c/app. 28-Magneto & Sub-Mariner-c/app. 29-WWII flashback meeting w/Captain America. 35-Defenders-c/app. 37-Luke Cage and Falcon-c/app. 3.00
23-Deadpool & the Avengers app. 3 6 9 14 20 25
36-($3.50, 100 pgs.) 35th Anniversary issue incl. r/1st app. in FF #52 4.00
41-56: 41-44-Wolverine app. 47-Thor app. 48,49-Magneto app. 3.00
57-62: 57-Begin $2.99-c. 59-Falcon app. 3.00
...: The Client (6/01, $14.95, TPB) r/#1-5 15.00
... 2099 #1 (11/04, $2.99) Kirkman-s/Hotz-a/Pat Lee-c 3.00

BLACK PANTHER (Marvel Knights)
Marvel Comics: Apr, 2005 - No. 41, Nov, 2008 ($2.99)
1-Reginald Hudlin-s/John Romita Jr. & Klaus Janson-a; covers by Romita & Ribic
2 4 6 9 12 15
2-1st app. Shuri 8 16 24 54 102 150
3-7,9-15,17-20: 7-House of M; Hairsine-a. 10-14-Luke Cage app. 12,13-Blade app. 17-Linsner-c. 19-Doctor Doom app. 3.00
8-Cho-c; X-Men app. 5.00
8-2nd printing variant-c 3.00
16-($3.99) Wedding of T'Challa and Storm; wraparound Cho-c; Hudlin-s/Eaton-a 4.00
21-Civil War x-over; Namor app. 8.00
21-2nd printing with new cover and Civil War logo 3.00
22-25-Civil War: 23-25-Turner-c 4.00
26-41: 26-30-T'Challa and Storm join the Fantastic Four. 27-30-Marvel Zombies app. 28-30-Suydam-c. 39-41-Secret Invasion 3.00
Annual 1 (4/08, $3.99) Hudlin-s/Stroman & Lashley-a; alternate future; Uatu app. 4.00
...: Bad Mutha TPB (2006, $10.99) r/#10-13 11.00
...: Civil War TPB (2007, $17.99) r/#19-25 18.00
...: Four the Hard Way TPB (2007, $13.99) r/#26-30; page layouts and character designs 14.00
...: Little Green Men TPB (2008, $10.99) r/#31-34 11.00
...: The Bride TPB (2006, $14.99) r/#14-18; interview with the dress designer 15.00
...: Who Is The Black Panther HC (2005, $21.99) r/#1-6; Hudlin afterword; cover gallery 22.00
...: Who Is The Black Panther SC (2006, $14.99) r/#1-6; Hudlin afterword; cover gallery 15.00

BLACK PANTHER
Marvel Comics: Apr, 2009 - No. 12, Mar, 2010 ($3.99/$2.99)
1-($3.99) Hudlin-s/Lashley-a; covers by Campbell & Lashley; Dr. Doom & Shuri app.
7 14 21 46 86 125
2-12-($2.99) 2-6-Campbell-c. 6-Shuri becomes female Black Panther 4.00

BLACK PANTHER
Marvel Comics: Jun, 2016 - No. 18, Nov, 2017; No. 166, Dec, 2017 - No. 172, Jun, 2018 ($4.99/$3.99)
1-($4.99) Ta-Nehisi Coates-s/Brian Stelfreeze-a; bonus Stelfreeze interview & art
1 3 4 6 8 10
2-18-($3.99) 2-4,9,12-Stelfreeze-a. 5-8,10-12,16-18-Sprouse-a. 13-17-Ororo app. 4.00
[Title switches to legacy numbering after #18 (11/17)]
166-172: 166-Klaw app.; Coates-s/Kirk-a 4.00
Annual 1 (4/18, $4.99) Stories by Priest, Perkins, McGregor, Acuña, Hudlin & Lashley 5.00

BLACK PANTHER
Marvel Comics: Jul, 2018 - Present ($4.99/$3.99)
1-($4.99) Ta-Nehisi Coates-s/Daniel Acuña-a; Intergalactic Empire of Wakanda 5.00
2-23-($3.99) 2-Intro Emperor N'Jadaka. 6,12-Jen Bartel-a. 7-11-Walker-a. 14-17-Acuña-a 4.00

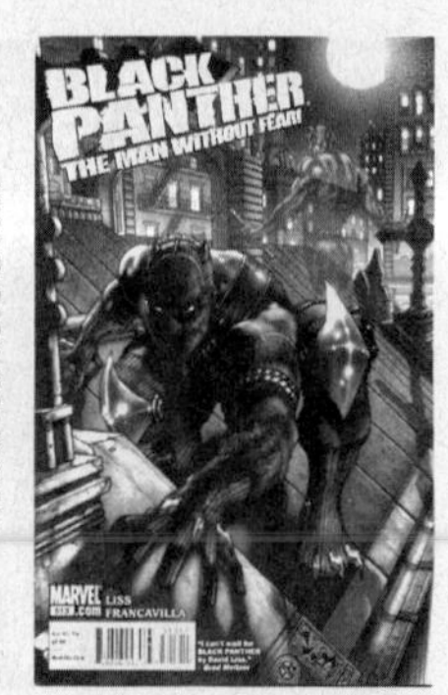

Black Panther: The Man Without Fear #513 © MAR

Black Science #2 © Rick Remender

Black Terror #14 © BP

GD VG FN VF VF/NM NM-
2.0 4.0 6.0 8.0 9.0 9.2

BLACK PANTHER (All ages title)
IDW Publishing (Marvel): Jan, 2019 - No. 6, Jun, 2019 ($3.99, limited series)
1-6: 1-3-Kyle Baker-s; Shuri app. 4-6-Vita Ayala-s 4.00

BLACK PANTHER AND THE AGENTS OF WAKANDA
Marvel Comics: Nov, 2019 - Present ($3.99)
1-8: 1-Team with Janet Van Dyne, Okoye, Gorilla-Man, and Broo. 5,6-Deadpool app. 4.00

BLACK PANTHER AND THE CREW
Marvel Comics: Jun, 2017 - No. 6, Oct, 2017 ($3.99)
1-6-Storm, Luke Cage, Misty Knight & Manifold app.; Ta-Nehisi Coates-s/Butch Guice-a 4.00

BLACK PANTHER/CAPTAIN AMERICA: FLAGS OF OUR FATHERS
Marvel Comics: Jun, 2010 - No. 4, Sept, 2010 ($3.99, limited series)
1-4-Hudlin-s/Cowan-a; WW2 story; Howling Commandos & Red Skull app. 4.00

BLACK PANTHER: PANTHER'S PREY
Marvel Comics: May, 1991 - No. 4, Oct, 1991 ($4.95, squarebound, lim. series, 52 pgs.)
1-4: McGregor-s/Turner-a 6.00

BLACK PANTHER: THE MAN WITHOUT FEAR (Continues from Daredevil #512)
Marvel Comics: No. 513, Feb, 2011 - No. 523, Nov, 2011 ($2.99)
513-523: 513-Shadowland aftermath; Liss-s/Francavilla-a/Bianchi-c. 521-523-Fear Itself 3.00
513-Variant-c by Francavilla 5.00

BLACK PANTHER: THE MOST DANGEROUS MAN ALIVE
Marvel Comics: No. 523.1, Nov, 2011 - No. 529, Apr, 2012 ($2.99)
523.1, 524-529: 523.1-Palo-a/Zircher-c. 524-Spider Island tie-in; Lady Bullseye app. 3.00

BLACK PANTHER: THE SOUND AND THE FURY
Marvel Comics: Apr, 2018 ($3.99, one-shot)
1-Klaw app.; Macchio-s/Di Vito-a; reprint of Fantastic Four #53 (origin/1st app. Klaw) 4.00

BLACK PANTHER VS. DEADPOOL
Marvel Comics: Dec, 2018 - No. 5, Apr, 2019 ($3.99, limited series)
1-5: 1-Kibblesmith-s/Ortiz-a; Willie Lumpkin app. 4.00

BLACK PANTHER: WORLD OF WAKANDA
Marvel Comics: Jan, 2017 - No. 6, Jun, 2017 ($4.99/$3.99, limited series)
1-($4.99) Roxanne Gay-s/Alitha E. Martinez-a; spotlight on The Dora Milaje 5.00
2-6-($3.99) 6-Rembert Browne-s/Joe Bennett-a; White Tiger app. 4.00

BLACK PEARL, THE
Dark Horse Comics: Sept, 1996 - No. 5, Jan, 1997 ($2.95, limited series)
1-5: Mark Hamill scripts 3.00

BLACK PHANTOM (See Tim Holt #25, 38)
Magazine Enterprises: Nov, 1954 (one-shot) (Female outlaw)
1 (A-1 #122)-The Ghost Rider story plus 3 Black Phantom stories; Headlight-c/a
65 130 195 416 708 1000

BLACK PHANTOM
AC Comics: 1989 - No. 3, 1990 ($2.50, B&W; #2 color)(Reprints & new-a)
1-3: 1-Ayers-r, Bolle-r/B.P. #1-3-Redmask-r 4.00

BLACK PHANTOM, RETURN OF THE (See Wisco)

BLACK RACER AND SHILO NORMAN SPECIAL, THE (Jack Kirby 100th Birthday tribute)
DC Comics: Oct, 2017 ($4.99, one-shot)
1-Black Racer origin; Hudlin-s/Cowan-a; reprint pages from New Gods #5,7,8 5.00

BLACK RIDER (Western Winners #1-7; Western Tales of Black Rider #28-31; Gunsmoke Western #32 on)(See All Western Winners, Best Western, Kid Colt, Outlaw Kid, Rex Hart, Two-Gun Kid, Two-Gun Western, Western Gunfighters, Western Winners, & Wild Western)
Marvel/Atlas Comics(CDS No. 8-17/CPS No. 19 on): No. 8, 3/50 - No. 18, 1/52; No. 19, 11/53 - No. 27, 3/55
8 (#1)-Black Rider & his horse Satan begin; 36 pgs; Stan Lee photo-c as Black Rider) 61 122 183 390 670 950
9-52 pgs. begin, end #14 30 60 90 177 289 400
10-Origin Black Rider 34 68 102 204 332 460
11-14: 14-Last 52pgs. 20 40 60 118 192 265
15-19: 19-Two-Gun Kid app. 18 36 54 105 165 225
20-Classic-c; Two-Gun Kid app. 20 40 60 120 195 270
21-27: 21-23-Two-Gun Kid app. 24,25-Arrowhead app. 26-Kid Colt app. 27-Last issue; last precode. Kid Colt app. The Spider (a villain) burns to death
16 32 48 92 144 195

NOTE: ***Ayers** c-22. **Jack Keller** a-15, 26, 27. **Maneely** a-14; c-9, 16, 17, 24, 25, 27. **Syd Shores** a-19, 21, 22, 23(3), 24(3), 25-27; c-19, 21, 23. **Sinnott** a-24, 25. **Tuska** a-12, 19-21.*

BLACK RIDER RIDES AGAIN!, THE
Atlas Comics (CPS): Sept, 1957
1-Kirby-a(3); Powell-a; Severin-c 40 80 120 246 411 575

GD VG FN VF VF/NM NM-
2.0 4.0 6.0 8.0 9.0 9.2

BLACK ROAD
Image Comics: Apr, 2016 - No. 10, May, 2017 ($3.99)
1-10-Brian Wood-s/Garry Brown-a 4.00

BLACK SCIENCE
Image Comics: Nov, 2013 - No. 43, Sept, 2019 ($3.50/$3.99)
1-Remender-s/Scalera-a; multiple covers 2 4 6 8 10 12
2 6.00
3-33: 11,16,21-33,35-43-$3.99-c 4.00
34-($4.99) 5.00

BLACK SEPTEMBER (Also see Avengers/Ultraforce, Ultraforce (1st series) #10 & Ultraforce/Avengers)
Malibu Comics (Ultraverse): 1995 ($1.50, one-shot)
Infinity-Intro to the new Ultraverse; variant-c exists. 3.00

BLACKSTONE (See Super Magician Comics & Wisco Giveaways)

BLACKSTONE, MASTER MAGICIAN COMICS
Vital Publ./Street & Smith Publ.: Mar-Apr, 1946 - No. 3, July-Aug, 1946
1 40 80 120 246 411 575
2,3 24 48 72 142 234 325

BLACKSTONE, THE MAGICIAN (...Detective on cover only #3 & 4)
Marvel Comics (CnPC): No. 2, May, 1948 - No. 4, Sept, 1948 (No #1) (Cont'd from E.C. #1?)
2-The Blonde Phantom begins, ends #4 100 200 300 635 1093 1550
3,4: 3-Blonde Phantom by Sekowsky 57 114 171 362 619 875

BLACKSTONE, THE MAGICIAN DETECTIVE FIGHTS CRIME
E. C. Comics: Fall, 1947
1-1st app. Happy Houlihans 65 130 195 416 708 1000

BLACK SUN (X-Men Black Sun on cover)
Marvel Comics: Nov, 2000 - No. 5, Nov, 2000 ($2.99, weekly limited series)
1-(...: X-Men), 2-(...: Storm), 3-(...: Banshee and Sunfire), 4-(...: Colossus and Nightcrawler), 5-(...: Wolverine and Thunderbird); Claremont-s in all; Evans interlocking painted covers; Magik returns 4.00

BLACK SUN
DC Comics (WildStorm): Nov, 2002 - No. 6, Jun, 2003 ($2.95, limited series)
1-6-Andreyko-s/Scott-a 3.00

BLACK SWAN COMICS
MLJ Magazines (Pershing Square Publ. Co.): 1945
1-The Black Hood reprints from Black Hood No. 14; Bill Woggon-a; Suzie app. Caribbean Pirates-c 26 52 78 154 252 350

BLACK TARANTULA (See Feature Presentations No. 5)

BLACK TERROR (See America's Best Comics & Exciting Comics)
Better Publications/Standard: Winter, 1942-43 - No. 27, June, 1949
1-Black Terror, Crime Crusader begin; Japanese WWII-c
423 864 1269 3000 5250 7500
2 206 412 618 1318 2259 3200
3-Nazi WWII-c 194 388 582 1242 2121 3000
4,5-Nazi & Japanese WWII-c 155 310 465 992 1696 2400
6-8: 6,8-Classic Nazi WWII-c. 7-Classic Japanese WWII-c; The Ghost app.
187 374 561 1197 2049 2900
9,10-Nazi & Japanese WWII-c 139 278 417 883 1517 2150
11,13-19 68 136 204 435 743 1050
12-Japanese WWII-c 87 174 261 553 952 1350
20-Classic-c; The Scarab app. 110 220 330 704 1202 1700
21-Miss Masque app. 84 168 252 538 919 1300
22-Part Frazetta-a on one Black Terror story 71 142 213 454 777 1100
23,25-27 58 116 174 371 636 900
24-Frazetta-a (1/4 pg.) 90 180 270 576 988 1400

NOTE: ***Schomburg (Xela)** c-2-27; bondage c-2, 17, 24. **Meskin** a-27. **Moreira** a-27. **Robinson/Meskin** a-23, 24(3), 25, 26. **Roussos/Mayo** a-24. **Tuska** a-26, 27.*

BLACK TERROR, THE (Also see Total Eclipse)
Eclipse Comics: Oct, 1989 - No. 3, June, 1990 ($4.95, 52 pgs., squarebound, limited series)
1-3: Beau Smith & Chuck Dixon scripts; Dan Brereton painted-c/a 5.00

BLACK TERROR (Also see Project Superpowers)
Dynamite Entertainment: 2008 - No. 14, 2011 ($3.50/$3.99)
1-14-Golden Age hero. 1-Alex Ross-c/Mike Lilly-a; various variant-c exist 4.00

BLACK TERROR VOLUME 2
Dynamite Entertainment: 2019 - No. 5, 2020 ($3.99, limited series)

Black Widow (2020 series) #1 © MAR

Blackwood: The Mourning After #1 © Dorkin & Fish

Blade Runner 2019 #6 © Alcon Pub.

GD 2.0 | VG 4.0 | FN 6.0 | VF 8.0 | VF/NM 9.0 | NM- 9.2

1-5: 1-Set in 1974; Bemis-s/Gaudio-a. 2-5-Coleman-a; multiple covers for each 4.00

BLACKTHORNE 3-D SERIES
Blackthorne Publishing Co.: May, 1985 - No. 80, 1989 ($2.25/$2.50)

1-Sheena in 3-D #1. D. Stevens-c/retouched-a 1 3 4 6 8 10
2-10: 2-MerlinRealm in 3-D #1. 3-3-D Heroes #1. Goldyn in 3-D #1. 5-Bizarre 3-D Zone #1. 6-Salimba in 3-D #1. 7-Twisted Tales in 3-D #1. 8-Dick Tracy in 3-D #1. 9-Salimba in 3-D #2. 10-Gumby in 3-D #1 6.00
11-19: 11-Betty Boop in 3-D #1. 12-Hamster Vice in 3-D #1. 13-Little Nemo in 3-D #1. 14-Gumby in 3-D #2. 15-Hamster Vice #6 in 3-D. 16-Laffin' Gas #6 in 3-D. 17-Gumby in 3-D #3. 18-Bullwinkle and Rocky in 3-D #1. 19-The Flintstones in 3-D #1 6.00
20(#1),26(#2),35(#3),39(#4),52(#5),62,71(#6)-G.I. Joe in 3-D. 62-G.I. Joe Annual 2 4 6 8 11 14
21-24,27-28: 21-Gumby in 3-D #4. 22-The Flintstones in 3-D #2. 23-Laurel & Hardy in 3-D #1. 24-Bozo the Clown in 3-D #1. 27-Bravestarr in 3-D #1. 28- Gumby in 3-D #5 6.00
25,29,37-The Transformers in 3-D 2 4 6 11 16 20
30-Star Wars in 3-D #1 3 6 9 17 26 35
31-34,36,38,40: 31-The California Raisins in 3-D #1. 32-Richie Rich & Casper in 3-D #1. 33-Gumby in 3-D #6. 34-Laurel & Hardy in 3-D #2. 36-The Flintstones in 3-D #3. 38-Gumby in 3-D #7. 40-Bravestarr in 3-D #2 6.00
41-46,49,50: 41-Battletech in 3-D #1. 42-The Flintstones in 3-D #4. 43-Underdog in 3-D #1 44-The California Raisins in 3-D #2. 45-Red Heat in 3-D #1 (movie adapt.). 46-The California Raisins in 3-D #3. 49-Rambo in 3-D #1. 49-Sad Sack in 3-D #1. 50-Bullwinkle For President in 3-D #1 6.00
47,48-Star Wars in 3-D #2,3 3 6 9 14 19 24
51,53-60: 51-Kull in 3-D #1. 53-Red Sonja in 3-D #1. 54-Bozo in 3-D #2. 55-Waxwork in 3-D #1 (movie adapt.). 57-Casper in 3-D #1. 58-Baby Huey in 3-D #1. 59-Little Dot in 3-D #1. 60-Solomon Kane in 3-D #1 6.00
61,63-70,72-74,76-80: 61-Werewolf in 3-D #1. 63-The California Raisins in 3-D #4. 64-To Die For in 3-D #1. 65-Capt. Holo in 3-D #1. 66-Playful Little Audrey in 3-D #1. 67-Kull in 3-D #2. 69-The California Raisins in 3-D #5. 70-Wendy in 3-D #1. 72-Sports Hall of Shame #1. 74-The Noid in 3-D #1. 80-The Noid in 3-D #2 1 2 3 4 5 7
75-Moonwalker in 3-D #1 (Michael Jackson movie adapt.) 4 8 12 28 47 65

BLACK VORTEX (See Guardians of the Galaxy & X-Men: The Black Vortex)

BLACK WIDOW (Marvel Knights) (Also see Marvel Graphic Novel)
Marvel Comics: May, 1999 - No. 3, Aug, 1999 ($2.99, limited series)

1-(June on-c) Devin Grayson-s/J.G. Jones-c/a; intro. Yelena Belova; Daredevil app. 3 6 9 15 22 28
1-Variant-c by J.G. Jones 4 8 12 23 37 50
2,3 5.00
...Web of Intrigue (6/99, $3.50) r/origin & early appearances 4.00
TPB (7/01, $15.95) r/Vol. 1 & 2; Jones-c 16.00

BLACK WIDOW (Marvel Knights) (Volume 2)
Marvel Comics: Jan, 2001 - No. 3, May, 2001 ($2.99, limited series)

1-3-Grayson & Rucka-s/Scott Hampton-c/a; Daredevil app. 4.00

BLACK WIDOW (Marvel Knights)
Marvel Comics: Nov, 2004 - No. 6, Apr, 2005 ($2.99, limited series)

1-6-Sienkiewicz-a/Land-c 4.00

BLACK WIDOW (Continues in Widowmaker #1)
Marvel Comics: Jun, 2010 - No. 8, Jan, 2011 ($3.99/$2.99)

1-($3.99) Liu-s/Acuña-a; Wolverine app.; back-up history text 5.00
1-Variant photo-c of Scarlett Johansson from Iron Man 2 movie 7 14 21 44 82 120
2-8-($2.99) 2-5-Acuña-a. 2,3-Elektra app. 3.00

BLACK WIDOW (All-New Marvel Now!)
Marvel Comics: Mar, 2014 - No. 20, Sept, 2015 ($3.99)

1-20: 1-Edmonson-s/Noto-a/c. 7-Daredevil app. 8-Winter Soldier app. 11-X-23 app. 4.00

BLACK WIDOW
Marvel Comics: May, 2016 - No. 12, May, 2017 ($3.99)

1-12: 1-Waid-s/Samnee-s&a. 6-Iron Man app. 9,10-Winter Soldier app. 4.00

BLACK WIDOW
Marvel Comics: Mar, 2019 - No. 5, Jul, 2019 ($3.99, limited series)

1-5: 1-Jen & Sylvia Soska-s/Flaviano-a; Captain America app. 2,3-Madame Masque app. 4.00

BLACK WIDOW
Marvel Comics: Jun, 2020 - Present ($3.99)

1-5: 1-Kelly Thompson-s/Elena Casagrande; Yelena Belova & Arcade app. 4.00
...: Widow's Sting 1 (12/20, $3.99) Macchio-s/Buonfantino-a 4.00

BLACK WIDOW & THE MARVEL GIRLS
Marvel Comics: Feb, 2010 - No. 4, Apr, 2010 ($2.99, limited series)

1-4-Tobin-s. 1-Enchantress app. 2-Avengers app. 4-Storm app.; Miyazawa-a 4.00

BLACK WIDOW: DEADLY ORIGIN
Marvel Comics: Jan, 2010 - No. 4, Apr, 2010 ($3.99, limited series)

1-4-Granov-c; origin retold. 1-Wolverine and Bucky app. 3-Daredevil app. 4.00

BLACK WIDOW: PALE LITTLE SPIDER (Marvel Knights) (Volume 3)
Marvel Comics: Jun, 2002 - No. 3, Aug, 2002 ($2.99, limited series)

1-3-Rucka-s/Kordey-a/Horn-c 4.00

BLACK WIDOW 2 (THE THINGS THEY SAY ABOUT HER) (Marvel Knights)
Marvel Comics: Nov, 2005 - No. 6, Apr, 2006 ($2.99, limited series)

1-6-Phillips & Sienkiewicz-a/Morgan-s; Daredevil app. 4.00
TPB (2006, $15.99) r/#1-6 16.00

BLACKWOOD
Dark Horse Comics: May, 2018 - No. 4, Aug, 2018 ($3.99, limited series)

1-4-Evan Dorkin-s/Veronica Fish-a 4.00

BLACKWOOD: THE MOURNING AFTER
Dark Horse Comics: Feb, 2020 - No. 4, Sept, 2020 ($3.99, limited series)

1-4-Evan Dorkin-s/Veronica Fish-a 4.00

BLACKWULF
Marvel Comics: June, 1994 - No. 10, Mar, 1995 ($1.50)

1-($2.50)-Embossed-c; Angel Medina-a 4.00
2-10 3.00

BLADE (The Vampire Hunter)
Marvel Comics

1-(3/98, $3.50) Colan-a(p)/Christopher Golden-s 6.00
... Black & White TPB (2004, $15.99, B&W) reprints from magazines Vampire Tales #8,9; Marvel Preview #3,6; Crescent City Blues #1 and Marvel Shadow and Light #1 16.00
San Diego Con Promo (6/97) Wesley Snipes photo-c 3.00
...Sins of the Father (10/98, $5.99) Sears-a; movie adaption 6.00
Blade 2: Movie Adaptation (5/02, $5.95) Ponticelli-a/Bradstreet-c 6.00

BLADE (The Vampire Hunter)
Marvel Comics: Nov, 1998 - No. 3, Jan, 1999 ($3.50/$2.99)

1-($3.50) Contains Movie insider pages; McKean-a 6.00
2,3-($2.99): 2-Two covers 3.00

BLADE (Volume 2)
Marvel Comics (MAX): May, 2002 -No. 6, Oct, 2002 ($2.99)

1-6-Bradstreet-c/Hinz-s. 1-5-Pugh-a. 6-Homs-a 3.00

BLADE
Marvel Comics: Nov, 2006 - No. 12, Oct, 2007 ($2.99)

1-12: 1-Chaykin-a/Guggenheim-s; origin retold; Spider-Man app. 2-Dr. Doom-c/app. 5-Civil War tie-in; Wolverine app. 6-Blade loses a hand. 10-Spider-Man app. 3.00
...: Sins of the Father TPB (2007, $14.99) r/#7-12; afterword by Guggenheim 15.00
...: Undead Again TPB (2007, $14.99) r/#1-6; letters pages from #1&2 15.00

BLADE OF THE IMMORTAL (Manga)
Dark Horse Comics: June, 1996 - No. 131, Nov, 2007 ($2.95/$2.99/$3.95, B&W)

1-Hiroaki Samura-s/a in all 2 4 6 8 10 12
2-5: 2-#1 on cover in error 6.00
6-10 5.00
11,19,20,34-($3.95, 48 pgs.): 34-Food one-shot 4.00
12-18,21-33,35-41,43-105,107-131: 12-20-Dreamsong. 21-28-On Silent Wings. 29-33-Dark Shadow. 35-42-Heart of Darkness. 43-57-The Gathering 3.00
42-($3.50) Ends Heart of Darkness 3.50
106-($3.99) 4.00

BLADE RUNNER (Movie)
Marvel Comics Group: Oct, 1982 - No. 2, Nov, 1982

1,2-r/Marvel Super Special #22; 1-Williamson-c/a. 2-Williamson-a 2 4 6 9 13 16

BLADE RUNNER 2019
Titan Comics: Aug, 2019 - No. 12, Dec, 2020 ($3.99)

1-12: 1-Green & Johnson-s/Guinaldo-a; multiple covers on each. 5-Jumps to 2026 4.00

BLADE RUNNER 2029
Titan Comics: Jan, 2021 - Present ($3.99)

1,2: 1-Mike Johnson-s/Andres Guinaldo-a; multiple covers on each 4.00

BLADE: THE VAMPIRE-HUNTER
Marvel Comics: July, 1994 - No. 10, Apr, 1995 ($1.95)

Blair Witch: Dark Testaments #1 © Haxan Films

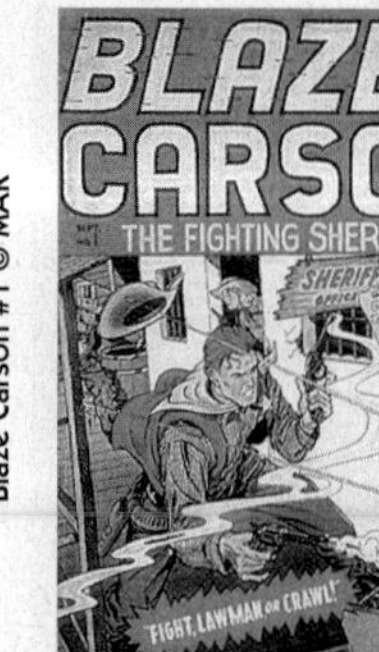
Blaze Carson #1 © MAR

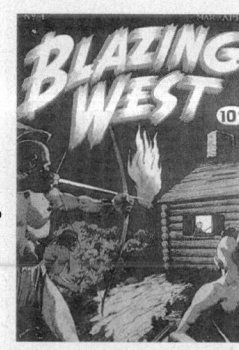

Blazing West #4 © ACG

GD 2.0 | VG 4.0 | FN 6.0 | VF 8.0 | VF/NM 9.0 | NM- 9.2

1-($2.95)-Foil-c; Dracula returns; Wheatley-c/a 2 4 6 11 16 20
2-10: 2,3,10-Dracula-c/app. 8-Morbius app. 4.00

BLADE: VAMPIRE-HUNTER
Marvel Comics: Dec, 1999 - No. 6, May, 2000 ($3.50/$2.50)
1-($3.50)-Bart Sears-s; Sears and Smith-a 1 2 3 5 6 8
2-6-($2.50): 2-Regular & Wesley Snipes photo-c 4.00

BLAIR WITCH CHRONICLES, THE
Oni Press: Mar, 2000 - No. 4, July, 2000 ($2.95, B&W, limited series)
1-4-Van Meter-s.1-Guy Davis-a. 2-Mireault-a 4.00
1-DF Alternate-c by John Estes 5.00
TPB (9/00, $15.95) r/#1-4 & Blair Witch Project one-shot 16.00

BLAIR WITCH: DARK TESTAMENTS
Image Comics: Oct, 2000 ($2.95, one-shot)
1-Edington-s/Adlard-a; story of murderer Rustin Parr 3.00

BLAIR WITCH PROJECT, THE (Movie companion, not adaptation)
Oni Press: July, 1999 ($2.95, B&W, one-shot)
1-(1st printing) History of the Blair Witch, art by Edwards, Mireault, and Davis; Van Meter-s; only the stick figure is red on the cover 1 2 3 5 6 8
1-(2nd printing) Stick figure and title lettering are red on cover 4.00
1-(3rd printing) Stick figure, title, and creator credits are red on cover 3.00
DF Glow in the Dark variant-c ($10.00) 10.00

BLAST (Satire Magazine)
G & D Publications: Feb, 1971 - No. 2, May, 1971
1-Wrightson & Kaluta-a/Everette-c 7 14 21 48 89 130
2-Kaluta-c/a 5 10 15 35 63 90

BLAST CORPS
Dark Horse Comics: Oct, 1998 ($2.50, one-shot, based on Nintendo game)
1-Reprints from Nintendo Power magazine; Mahn-a 4.00

BLASTERS SPECIAL
DC Comics: 1989 ($2.00, one-shot)
1-Peter David scripts; Invasion spin-off 4.00

BLAST-OFF (Three Rocketeers)
Harvey Publications (Fun Day Funnies): Oct, 1965 (12¢)
1-Kirby/Williamson-a(2); Williamson/Crandall-a; Williamson/Torres/Krenkel-a; Kirby/Simon-c 6 12 18 41 76 110

BLAZE
Marvel Comics: Aug, 1994 - No. 12, July, 1995 ($1.95)
1-($2.95)-Foil embossed-c 4.00
2-12: 2-Man-Thing-c/story. 11,12-Punisher app. 3.00

BLAZE CARSON (Rex Hart #6 on)(See Kid Colt, Tex Taylor, Wild Western, Wisco)
Marvel Comics (USA): Sept, 1948 - No. 5, June, 1949
1-Tex Taylor app.; Shores-c 34 68 102 202 329 455
2,4,5: 2-Tex Morgan app.; Shores-c. 4-Two-Gun Kid app. 5-Tex Taylor app. 21 42 63 126 206 285
3-Used by N.Y. State Legis. Comm. (injury to eye splash); Tex Morgan app. 22 44 66 132 216 300

BLAZE: LEGACY OF BLOOD (See Ghost Rider & Ghost Rider/Blaze)
Marvel Comics (Midnight Sons imprint): Dec, 1993 - No. 4, Mar, 1994 ($1.75, limited series)
1-4 3.00

BLAZE OF GLORY
Marvel Comics: Feb, 2000 - No. 4, Mar, 2000 ($2.99, limited series)
1-4-Ostrander-s/Manco-a; Two-Gun Kid, Rawhide Kid, Red Wolf and Ghost Rider app. 3.00
TPB (7/02, $9.99) r/#1-4 10.00

BLAZE THE WONDER COLLIE (Formerly Molly Manton's Romances #1?)
Marvel Comics(SePI): No. 2, Oct, 1949 - No. 3, Feb, 1950 (Both have photo-c)
2(#1), 3-(Scarce) 30 60 90 177 289 400

BLAZING BATTLE TALES
Seaboard Periodicals (Atlas): July, 1975
1-Intro. Sgt. Hawk & the Sky Demon; Severin, McWilliams, Sparling-a; Nazi-c by Thorne 3 6 9 16 23 30

BLAZING COMBAT (Magazine)
Warren Publishing Co.: Oct, 1965 - No. 4, July, 1966 (35¢, B&W)
1-Frazetta painted-c on all 38 76 114 285 641 1000
2 9 18 27 60 120 180
3,4: 4-Frazetta half pg. ad 8 16 24 56 108 160

GD 2.0 | VG 4.0 | FN 6.0 | VF 8.0 | VF/NM 9.0 | NM- 9.2

nn-Anthology (reprints from No. 1-4) (low print) 8 16 24 56 108 160
NOTE: *Adkins a-4. Colan a-3,4,nn. Crandall a-all. Evans a-1,4. Heath a-4,nn. Morrow a-1-3,nn. Orlando a-1-3,nn. J. Severin a-all. Torres a-1-4. Toth a-all. Williamson a-2. and Wood a-3,4,nn.*

BLAZING COMBAT: WORLD WAR I AND WORLD WAR II
Apple Press: Mar, 1994 ($3.75, B&W)
1,2: 1-r/Colan, Toth, Goodwin, Severin, Wood-a. 2-r/Crandall, Evans, Severin, Torres, Williamson-a 6.00

BLAZING COMICS (Also see Blue Circle Comics and Red Circle Comics)
Enwil Associates/Rural Home: 6/44 - #3, 9/44; #4, 2/45; #5, 3/45; #5(V2#2), 3/55 - #6(V2#3), 1955?
1-The Green Turtle, Red Hawk, Black Buccaneer begin; origin Jun-Gal; classic Japanese WWII splash 71 142 213 454 777 1100
2-5: 2-Japanese WWII-c. 3-Briefer-a. 5-(V2#2 inside) 42 84 126 265 445 625
5(3/55, V2#2-inside)-Black Buccaneer-c, 6(V2#3-inside, 1955)-Indian/Japanese-c; cover is from Apr. 1945 26 52 78 152 249 345
NOTE: *No. 5 & 6 contain remaindered comics rebound and the contents can vary. Cloak & Dagger, Will Rogers, Superman 64, Star Spangled 130, Kaanga known. Value would be half of contents.*

BLAZING SIXGUNS
Avon Periodicals: Dec, 1952
1-Kinstler-c/a; Larsen/Alascia-a(2), Tuska?-a; Jesse James, Kit Carson, Wild Bill Hickok app. 39 78 117 240 395 550

BLAZING SIXGUNS
I.W./Super Comics: 1964
I.W. Reprint #1,8,9: 1-r/Wild Bill Hickok #26, Western True Crime #? & Blazing Sixguns #1 by Avon; Kinstler-c. 8-r/Blazing Western #?; Kinstler-c. 9-r/Blazing Western #1; Ditko-r; Kintsler-c reprinted from Dalton Boys #1 2 4 6 10 14 18
Super Reprint #10,11,15-17: 10,11-r/The Rider #2,1. 15-r/Silver Kid Western #?. 16-r/Buffalo Bill #?; Wildey-r; Severin-c. 17(1964)-r/Western True Crime #? 2 4 6 10 14 18
12-Reprints Bullseye #3; S&K-a 3 6 9 18 28 38
18-r/Straight Arrow #? by Powell; Severin-c 2 4 6 10 14 18

BLAZING SIX-GUNS (Also see Sundance Kid)
Skywald Comics: Feb, 1971 - No. 2, Apr, 1971 (52 pgs.)
1-The Red Mask (3-D effect, not true 3-D), Sundance Kid begin (new-s), Avon's Geronimo reprint by Kinstler; Wyatt Earp app. 3 6 9 14 20 25
2-Wild Bill Hickok, Jesse James, Kit Carson-r plus M.E. Red Mask-r (3-D effect) 2 4 6 10 14 18

BLAZING WEST (The Hooded Horseman #21 on)(52 pgs.)
American Comics Group (B&I Publ./Michel Publ.): Fall, 1948 - No. 20, Nov-Dec, 1951
1-Origin & 1st app. Injun Jones, Tenderfoot & Buffalo Belle; Texas Tim & Ranger begins, ends #13 24 48 72 142 234 325
2,3 (1-2/49) 14 28 42 78 112 145
4-Origin & 1st app. Little Lobo; Starr-a (3-4/49) 13 26 39 74 105 135
5-10: 5-Starr-a 10 20 30 56 76 95
11-13 9 18 27 50 65 80
14(11-12/50)-Origin/1st app. The Hooded Horseman 15 30 45 86 133 180
15-20: 15,16,18,19-Starr-a 10 20 30 56 76 95

BLAZING WESTERN
Timor Publications: Jan, 1954 - No. 5, Sept, 1954
1-Ditko-a (1st Western-a?); text story by Bruce Hamilton 20 40 60 120 195 270
2-4 10 20 30 54 72 90
5-Disbrow-a; L.B. Cole-c 10 20 30 56 76 95

BLINDSIDE
Image Comics (Extreme Studios): Aug, 1996 ($2.50)
1-Variant-c exists 3.00

BLINK (See X-Men Age of Apocalypse storyline)
Marvel Comics: March, 2001 - No. 4, June, 2001 ($2.99, limited series)
1-4-Adam Kubert-c/Lobdell-s/Winick-script; leads into Exiles #1 3.00

BLIP
Marvel Comics Group: 2/1983 - 1983 (Video game mag. in comic format)
1-1st app. Donkey Kong & Mario Bros. in comics, 6pgs. comics; photo-c 4 8 12 25 40 55
2-Spider-Man photo-c; 6pgs. Spider-Man comics w/Green Goblin 2 4 6 11 16 20
3,4,6 1 2 3 5 6 8
5-E.T., Indiana Jones; Rocky-c 1 2 3 5 7 9
7-6pgs. Hulk comics; Pac-Man & Donkey Kong Jr. Hints

Blitzkrieg #3 © DC

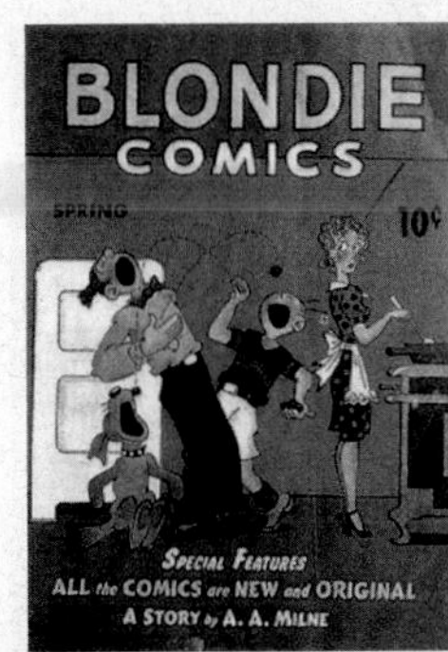

Blondie Comics #1 © HARV

Blood of the Demon #16 © DC

GD	VG	FN	VF	VF/NM	NM-
2.0	4.0	6.0	8.0	9.0	9.2
1	3	4	6	8	10

BLISS
Image Comics: Jul, 2020 - Present ($3.99)
1-5-Sean Lewis-s/Caitlin Yarsky-a 4.00

BLISS ALLEY
Image Comics: July, 1997 - No. 2, Sept, 1997 ($2.95, B&W)
1,2-Messner-Loebs-s/a 3.00

BLITZKRIEG
National Periodical Publications: Jan-Feb, 1976 - No. 5, Sept-Oct, 1976
1-Kubert-c on all 4 8 12 28 47 65
2-5 3 6 9 16 24 32

BLOCKBUSTERS OF THE MARVEL UNIVERSE
Marvel Comics: March, 2011 ($4.99, one-shot)
1-Handbook-style summaries of Marvel crossover events like Civil War & Heroes Reborn 5.00

BLONDE PHANTOM (Formerly All-Select #1-11; Lovers #23 on)(Also see Blackstone, Marvel Mystery, Millie The Model #2, Sub-Mariner Comics #25 & Sun Girl)
Marvel Comics (MPC): No. 12, Winter, 1946-47 - No. 22, Mar, 1949
12-Miss America begins, ends #14 232 464 696 1485 2543 3600
13-Sub-Mariner begins (not in #16) 142 284 426 909 1555 2200
14,15: 15-Kurtzman's "Hey Look" 135 270 405 864 1482 2100
16-Captain America with Bucky story by Rico(p), 6 pgs.; Kurtzman's "Hey Look" (1 pg.) 165 330 495 1048 1799 2550
17-22: 22-Anti Wertham editorial 119 238 357 762 1306 1850
NOTE: *Shores c-12-18.*

BLONDIE (See Ace Comics, Comics Reading Libraries (Promotional Comics section), Dagwood, Daisy & Her Pups, Eat Right to Work..., King & Magic Comics)
David McKay Publications: 1942 - 1946
Feature Books 12 (Rare) 100 200 300 635 1093 1550
Feature Books 27-29,31,34(1940) 23 46 69 136 223 310
Feature Books 36,38,40,42,43,45,47 20 40 60 120 195 270
...1944 (Hard-c, 1938, B&W, 128 pgs.)-1944 daily strip-r 18 36 54 103 162 220

BLONDIE & DAGWOOD FAMILY
Harvey Publ. (King Features Synd.): Oct, 1963 - No. 4, Dec, 1965 (68 pgs.)
1 5 10 15 30 50 70
2-4 3 6 9 19 30 40

BLONDIE COMICS (...Monthly No. 16-141)
David McKay #1-15/Harvey #16-163/King #164-175/Charlton #177 on: Spring, 1947 - No. 163, Nov, 1965; No. 164, Aug, 1966 - No. 175, Dec, 1967; No. 177, Feb, 1969 - No. 222, Nov, 1976
1 50 100 150 315 533 750
2 21 42 63 126 206 285
3-5 16 32 48 94 147 200
6-10 14 28 42 80 115 150
11-15 10 20 30 56 76 95
16-(3/50; 1st Harvey issue) 11 22 33 62 86 110
17-20: 20-(3/51)-Becomes Daisy & Her Pups #21 & Chamber of Chills #21 5 10 15 34 60 85
21-30 5 10 15 31 53 75
31-50 4 8 12 27 44 60
51-80 4 8 12 23 37 50
81-99 3 6 9 21 33 45
100 4 8 12 25 40 55
101-124,126-130 3 6 9 17 26 35
125 (80 pgs.) 4 8 12 27 44 60
131-136,138,139 3 6 9 16 24 32
137,140-(80 pgs.) 4 8 12 25 40 55
141-147,149-154,156,160,164-167 3 6 9 16 23 30
148,155,157-159,161-163 are 68 pgs. 3 6 9 21 33 45
168-175 2 4 6 11 16 20
177-199 (no #176)-Moon landing-c/s 2 4 6 9 13 16
200-Anniversary issue; highlights of the Bumsteads 2 4 6 10 14 18
201-210,213-222 2 4 6 8 10 12
211,212-1st & 2nd app. Super Dagwood 2 4 6 9 13 16
Blondie, Dagwood & Daisy by Chic Young #1(Harvey, 1953, 100 pg. squarebound giant) new stories; Popeye (1 pg.) and Felix (1pg.) app. 10 20 30 58 79 100

BLOOD
Marvel Comics (Epic Comics): Feb, 1988 - No. 4, Apr, 1988 ($3.25, mature)
1-4: DeMatteis scripts & Kent Williams-c/a 5.00

BLOOD AND GLORY (Punisher & Captain America)
Marvel Comics: Oct, 1992 - No. 3, Dec, 1992 ($5.95, limited series)
1-3: 1-Embossed wraparound-c by Janson; Chichester & Clarke-s 6.00

BLOOD & ROSES: FUTURE PAST TENSE (Bob Hickey's...)
Sky Comics: Dec, 1993 ($2.25)
1-Silver ink logo 3.00

BLOOD & ROSES: SEARCH FOR THE TIME-STONE (Bob Hickey's...)
Sky Comics: Apr, 1994 ($2.50)
1 3.00

BLOOD AND SHADOWS
DC Comics (Vertigo): 1996 - Book 4, 1996 ($5.95, squarebound, mature)
Books 1-4: Joe R. Lansdale scripts; Mark A. Nelson-c/a. 6.00

BLOOD AND WATER
DC Comics (Vertigo): May, 2003 - No. 5, Sept, 2003 ($2.95, limited series)
1-5-Judd Winick-s/Tomm Coker-a/Brian Bolland-c 3.00
TPB (2009, $14.99) r/#1-5 15.00

BLOOD: A TALE
DC Comics (Vertigo): Nov, 1996 - No. 4, Feb, 1997 ($2.95, limited series)
1-4: Reprints Epic series w/new-c; DeMatteis scripts; Kent Williams-c/a 3.00
TPB (2004, $19.95) r/#1-4 20.00

BLOODBATH
DC Comics: Early Dec, 1993 - No. 2, Late Dec, 1993 ($3.50, 68 pgs.)
1-Neon ink-c; Superman app.; new Batman-c /app. 4.00
2-Hitman 2nd app. 1 2 3 4 5 7

BLOOD BLISTER
AfterShock Comics: Jan, 2017 - No. 2, Apr, 2017 ($3.99)
1,2-Phil Hester-s/Tony Harris-a 4.00

BLOODBORNE (Based on the Sony computer game)
Titan Comics: Mar, 2018 - No. 16, Nov, 2019 ($3.99)
1-16-Ales Kot-s/Piotr Kowalski-a 4.00

BLOODHOUND
DC Comics: Sept, 2004 - No. 10, June, 2005 ($2.95)
1-10: 1-Jolley-s/Kirk-a/Johnson-c. 5-Firestorm app. (cont. from Firestorm #7) 3.00

BLOODHOUND: CROWBAR MEDICINE
Dark Horse Comics: Oct, 2013 - No. 5, Mar, 2014 ($3.99)
1-5-Jolley-s/Kirk-a/c 4.00

BLOOD LEGACY
Image Comics (Top Cow): May, 2000 - No. 4, Nov, 2000; Apr, 2003 ($2.50/$4.99)
...: The Story of Ryan 1-4-Kerri Hawkins-s. 1-Andy Park-a(p); 3 covers 3.00
...: The Young Ones 1 (4/03, $4.99, one-shot) Basaldua-c/a 5.00
Preview Special ('00, $4.95) B&W flip-book w/The Magdalena Preview 5.00

BLOODLINES
DC Comics: Jun, 2016 - No. 6, Nov, 2016 ($2.99, limited series)
1-6: 1-Krul-s/Marion-a 3.00

BLOODLINES: A TALE FROM THE HEART OF AFRICA (See Tales From the Heart of Africa)
Marvel Comics (Epic Comics): 1992 ($5.95, 52 pgs.)
1-Story cont'd from Tales From... 6.00

BLOOD OF DRACULA
Apple Comics: Nov, 1987 - No. 20?, 1990 ($1.75/$1.95, B&W)($2.25 #14,16 on)
1-3,5-14,20: 1-10-Chadwick-c 4.00
4,16-19-Lost Frankenstein pgs. by Wrightson 1 2 3 4 5 7
15-Contains stereo flexidisc ($3.75) 5.00

BLOOD OF THE DEMON (Etrigan the Demon)
DC Comics: May, 2005 - No. 17, Sept, 2006 ($2.50/$2.99)
1-14-Byrne-a(p) & plot/Pfeifer-script. 3,4-Batman app. 13-One Year Later 3.00
15-17-($2.99) 3.00

BLOOD OF THE INNOCENT (See Warp Graphics Annual)
WaRP Graphics: 1/7/86 - No. 4, 1/28/86 (Weekly mini-series, mature)
1-4 3.00

BLOODPACK
DC Comics: Mar, 1995 - No. 4, June,1995 ($1.50, limited series)
1-4 3.00

BLOODPOOL

Blood Red Dragon #0 © POW

Bloodshot Salvation #6 © VAL

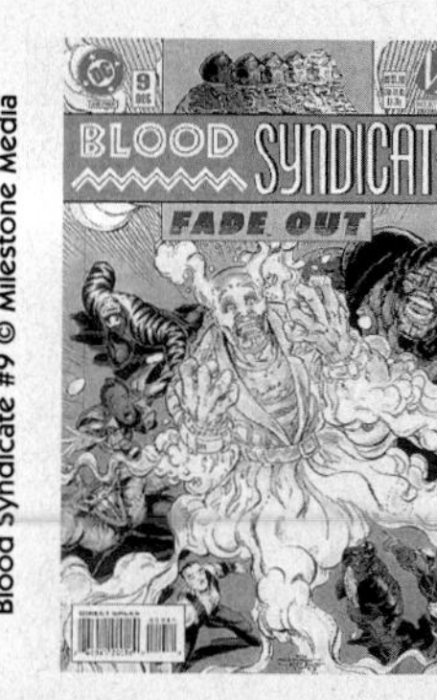

Blood Syndicate #9 © Milestone Media

GD VG FN VF VF/NM NM-
2.0 4.0 6.0 8.0 9.0 9.2

Image Comics (Extreme): Aug, 1995 - No. 4, Nov, 1995 ($2.50, limited series)

1-4: Jo Duffy scripts in all 3.00
Special (3/96, $2.50)-Jo Duffy scripts 3.00
Trade Paperback (1996, $12.95)-r/#1-4 13.00

BLOOD QUEEN, THE
Dynamite Entertainment: 2014 - No. 6, 2014 ($3.99, limited series)

1-6-Brownfield-s/Casas-a/Anacleto-c; variant covers on each 4.00
Annual 2014 ($7.99) Prequel stories to the series 8.00

BLOOD QUEEN VS. DRACULA
Dynamite Entertainment: 2015 - No. 4, 2015 ($3.99, limited series)

1-4-Brownfield-s/Baal-a/Anacleto-c; variant covers on each 4.00

BLOOD RED DRAGON (Stan Lee and Yoshiki's...)
Image Comics: No. 0, Aug, 2011 - No. 3, Nov, 2011 ($3.99)

0-3-Goff-s/Soriano-a 4.00

BLOODSCENT
Comico: Oct, 1988 ($2.00, one-shot, Baxter paper)

1-Colan-p 3.00

BLOODSEED
Marvel Comics (Frontier Comics): Oct, 1993 - No. 2, Nov, 1993 ($1.95)

1,2: Sharp/Cam Smith-a 3.00

BLOODSHOT (See Eternal Warrior #4 & Rai #0)
Valiant/Acclaim Comics (Valiant): Feb, 1993 - No. 51, Aug, 1996 ($2.25/$2.50)

0-(3/94, $3.50)-Wraparound chromium-c by Quesada(p); origin 5.00
0-Gold variant; no cover price 30.00
Note: There is a "Platinum variant" ; press run error of Gold ed. (25 copies exist)
(A CGC certified 9.8 copy sold for $2,067 in 2004)
1-($3.50)-Chromium embossed-c by B. Smith w/poster
2 4 6 8 10 12
2-5,8-14: 3-$2.25-c begins; cont'd in Hard Corps #5. 4-Eternal Warrior-c/story. 5-Rai & Eternal Warrior app. 14-(3/94)-Reese-c(i) 4.00
6,7: 6-1st app. Ninjak (out of costume). 7-Ninjak in costume
2 4 6 8 10 12
15(4/94)-50: 16-w/bound-in trading card 3.00
51-Bloodshot dies? 4 8 12 23 37 50
Yearbook 1 (1994, $3.95) 4.00
Special 1 (3/94, $5.95)-Zeck-c/a(p); Last Stand 6.00
...: Blood of the Machine HC (2012, $24.99) r/#1-8; new 8 pg. story; intro. by VanHook 25.00

BLOODSHOT (Volume Two)
Acclaim Comics (Valiant): July, 1997 - No. 16, Oct, 1998 ($2.50)

1-16: 1-Two covers. 5-Copycat-c. X-O Manowar-c/app 3.00

BLOODSHOT (Re-titled Bloodshot and H.A.R.D.Corps for #14-23)
Valiant Entertainment: July, 2012 - No. 25, Nov, 2014 ($3.99)

1-13: 1-Sweirczynski-s/Garcia & Lozzi-a. 10-13-Harbinger Wars tie-ins 4.00
1-9-Pullbox variants 4.00
1-Variant-c by David Aja 15.00
1-Variant-c by Esad Ribic 20.00
14-24: 14-23-Bloodshot and H.A.R.D.Corps 4.00
25-($4.99) Milligan-s/Larosa-a; back-up Chaykin-s/a; short features by various 5.00
#0 (8/13) Kindt-s/ChrisCross-a; covers by Lupacchino & Bullock 4.00
Bloodshot and H.A.R.D.Corps #0 (2/14, $3.99) History of Project Rising Spirit 4.00
Bloodshot's Day Off 1 (7/17, $3.99) Rahal-s/Evans-a; Viet Man app. 4.00

BLOODSHOT
Valiant Entertainment: Sept, 2019 - Present ($3.99)

1-11: 1-Tim Seeley-s/Brett Booth-a; multiple covers on each 4.00
#0 (2/20, $3.99) Tim Seeley-s/Marc Laming-a; Bloodshot in Siberia; leads into issue #7 4.00

BLOODSHOT REBORN
Valiant Entertainment: Apr, 2015 - No. 18, Oct, 2016 ($3.99)

1-18: 1-4-Lemire-s/Suayan-a. 1-1st app. Bloodsquirt. 6-9-Guice-a. 10-13-Set 30 years later. 14-1st app. Deathmate 4.00
#0 (3/17, $3.99) Lemire-s/Guedes-a 4.00
Annual 2016 #1 (3/16, $5.99) Short stories by various incl. Kano, Lemire, Bennett 6.00
...: Bloodshot Island - Director's Cut 1 (6/16, $4.99) r/#1 in B&W; original script 5.00

BLOODSHOT RISING SPIRIT
Valiant Entertainment: Nov, 2018 - No. 8, Jun, 2019 ($3.99)

1-8: 1-Grevioux-s/Lashley-a; Bloodshot prototype; bonus Livewire #12 preview 4.00

BLOODSHOT SALVATION
Valiant Entertainment: Sept, 2017 - No. 12, Aug, 2018 ($3.99)

GD VG FN VF VF/NM NM-
2.0 4.0 6.0 8.0 9.0 9.2

1-12: 1-Lemire-s/LaRosa-a; bonus Ninjak #1 preview 4.00

BLOODSHOT U.S.A.
Valiant Entertainment: Oct, 2016 - No. 4, Jan, 2017 ($3.99, limited series)

1-4-Lemire-s/Braithwaite-a; Ninjak and Deathmate app. 4.00

BLOODSTONE
Marvel Comics: Dec, 2001 - No. 4, Mar, 2002 ($2.99)

1-4-Intro. Elsa Bloodstone; Abnett & Lanning-s/Lopez-a
1 3 4 6 8 10

BLOODSTRIKE (See Supreme V2#3) (Issue #25 published between #10 & #11)
Image Comics (Extreme Studios): 1993 - No. 22, May, 1995; No. 25, May, 1994 ($1.95/$2.50)

1-22, 25: Liefeld layouts in early issues. 1-Blood Brothers prelude. 2-1st app. Lethal. 5-1st app. Noble. 9-Black and White part 6 by Art Thibert; Liefeld pin-up. 9,10-Have coupon #3 & 7 for Extreme Prejudice #0. 10-(4/94). 11-(7/94). 16:Platt-c; Prophet app. 17-19-polybagged w/card . 25-(5/94)-Liefeld/Fraga-c 3.00
#0-(6/18, $3.99) Brutalists part 1; origin of the team; Michel Fiffe-s/a 4.00
#23,24-(6/18, $3.99) Brutalists parts 2&3; retroactively fills story gap between #22&25 4.00
... #1 Remastered Edition (7/17, $3.99) Two covers by Fraga & Liefeld 4.00
NOTE: ***Giffen** story/layouts-4-6. **Jae Lee** c-7, 8. **Rob Liefeld** layouts-1-3. **Art Thibert** c-6i.*

BLOODSTRIKE
Image Comics: No. 26, Mar, 2012 - No. 33, Dec, 2012 ($2.99/$3.99)

26-29: 26-Two covers by Seeley & Liefeld; Seeley-s/Gaston-a 3.00
30-33-($3.99) 32,33-Suprema app. 4.00

BLOODSTRIKE (Volume 2)
Image Comics: Jul, 2015 - No. 2, Sept, 2015 ($2.99/$3.99)

1-($3.99) Liefeld-s/a 4.00
2-(9/15, $2.99) Liefeld-s/a 3.00

BLOODSTRIKE ASSASSIN
Image Comics (Extreme Studios): June, 1995 - No. 3, Aug, 1995; No. 0, Oct, 1995 ($2.50, limited series)

0-3: 3-(8/95)-Quesada-c. 0-(10/95)-Battlestone app. 3.00

BLOOD SWORD, THE
Jademan Comics: Aug, 1988 - No. 53, Dec, 1992 ($1.50/$1.95, 68 pgs.)

1-53-Kung Fu stories in all 4.00

BLOOD SWORD DYNASTY
Jademan Comics: 1989 - No. 41, Jan, 1993 ($1.25, 36 pgs.)

1-Ties into Blood Sword 4.00
2-41: Ties into Blood Sword 3.00

BLOOD SYNDICATE
DC Comics (Milestone): Apr, 1993 - No. 35, Feb, 1996 ($1.50/-$3.50)

1-($2.95)-Collector's Edition; polybagged with poster, trading card, & acid-free backing board (direct sale only) 4.00
1-9,11-24,26,27,29,33-34: 8-Intro Kwai. 15-Byrne-c. 16-Worlds Collide Pt. 6; Superman-c/app. 17-Worlds Collide Pt. 13. 29-(99¢); Long Hot Summer x-over 3.00
10,28,30-32: 10-Simonson-c. 30-Long Hot Summer x-over 3.00
25-($2.95, 52 pgs.) 4.00
35-Kwai disappears; last issue 4.00

BLOODWULF
Image Comics (Extreme): Feb, 1995 - No. 4, May, 1995 ($2.50, limited series)

1-4: 1-Liefeld-c w/4 diferent captions & alternate-c. 3.00
Summer Special (8/95, $2.50)-Jeff Johnson-c/a; Supreme app; story takes place between Legend of Supreme #3 & Supreme #23. 3.00

BLOODY MARY
DC Comics (Helix): Oct, 1996 - No. 4, Jan, 1997 ($2.25, limited series)

1-4: Garth Ennis scripts; Ezquerra-c/a in all 3.50
TPB (2005, $19.99) r/#1-4 and Bloody Mary: Lady Liberty #1-4 20.00

BLOODY MARY: LADY LIBERTY
DC Comics (Helix): Sept, 1997 - No. 4, Dec, 1997 ($2.50, limited series)

1-4: Garth Ennis scripts; Ezquerra-c/a in all 3.00

BLOSSOMS: 666 (Archie Comics' Cheryl & Jason Blossom Satanic Horror)
Archie Comic Publications: Mar, 2019 - No. 5, Sept, 2019 ($3.99, limited series)

1-5-Cullen Bunn-s/Laura Braga-a; multiple covers. 2-Intro. Julian Blossom 4.00

BLUE
Image Comics (Action Toys): Aug, 1999 - No. 2, Apr, 2000 ($2.50)

1,2-Aronowitz-s/Struzan-c 3.00

BLUEBEARD
Slave Labor Graphics: Nov, 1993 - No. 3, Mar, 1994 ($2.95, B&W, lim. series)

Blue Beetle #51 © FOX

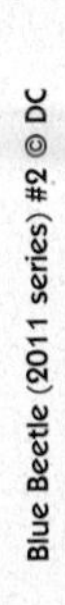
Blue Beetle (2011 series) #2 © DC

Blue Bolt V6 #2 © NOVP

GD 2.0 | VG 4.0 | FN 6.0 | VF 8.0 | VF/NM 9.0 | NM- 9.2

1-3: James Robinson scripts. 2-(12/93) 3.00
Trade paperback (6/94, $9.95) 13.00
Trade paperback (2nd printing, 7/96, $12.95)-New-c 13.00

BLUE BEETLE, THE (Also see All Top, Big-3, Mystery Men & Weekly Comic Magazine)
Fox Publ. No. 1-11, 31-60; Holyoke No. 12-30: Winter, 1939-40 - No. 57, 7/48; No. 58, 4/50 - No. 60, 8/50

1-Reprints from Mystery Men #1-5; Blue Beetle origin; Yarko the Great-r/from Wonder Comics /Wonderworld #2-5 all by Eisner; Master Magician app.; (Blue Beetle in 4 different costumes) 730 1460 2190 5329 9415 13,500
2-K-51-r by Powell/Wonderworld #8,9 265 530 795 1694 2897 4100
3-Simon-c 187 374 561 1197 2049 2900
4-Marijuana drug mention story 135 270 405 864 1482 2100
5-Zanzibar The Magician by Tuska 110 220 330 704 1202 1700
6-Dynamite Thor begins (1st); origin Blue Beetle 106 212 318 673 1162 1650
7,8-Dynamo app. in both. 8-Last Thor 103 206 309 659 1130 1600
9-12: 9,10-The Blackbird & The Gorilla app. 10-Bondage/hypo-c. 11(2/42)-Bondage-c; The Gladiator app. 12(6/42)-The Black Fury app. 94 188 282 597 1024 1450
13-V-Man begins (1st app.), ends #19; Kubert-a; centerfold spread 97 194 291 621 1061 1500
14,15-Kubert-a in both. 14-Intro. side-kick (c/text only), Sparky (called Spunky #17-19); BB vs. The Red Robe (Red Skull swipe) 87 174 261 553 952 1350
16-18: 17-Brodsky-c 65 130 195 416 708 1000
19-Kubert-a 68 136 204 435 743 1050
20-Origin/1st app. Tiger Squadron; Arabian Nights begin 71 142 213 454 777 1100
21-26: 24-Intro. & only app. The Halo. 26-General Patton story & photo 55 110 165 352 601 850
27-Tamaa, Jungle Prince app. 50 100 150 315 533 750
28-30(2/44): 29-WWII Nazi bondage-c(1/44) 47 94 141 296 498 700
31(6/44), 33,34,36-40: 34-38-"The Threat from Saturn" serial. 40-Shows #20 in indicia 40 80 120 244 402 560
32-Hitler-c 132 264 396 838 1444 2050
35-Extreme violence 45 90 135 284 480 675
41-45 (#43 exist?) 39 78 117 231 378 525
46-The Puppeteer app. 42 84 126 265 445 625
47-Kamen & Baker-a begin 200 400 600 1280 2190 3100
48-50 135 270 405 864 1482 2100
51,53 119 238 357 762 1306 1850
52-Kamen bondage-c; true crime stories begin 203 406 609 1289 2220 3150
54-Used in **SOTI**. Illo, "Children call these 'headlights' comics"; classic-c 703 1406 2109 5132 9066 13,000
55-57: 56-Used in **SOTI**, pg. 145. 57(7/48)-Last Kamen issue; becomes Western Killers? 116 232 348 742 1271 1800
58(4/50)-60-No Kamen-a 28 56 84 165 270 375
NOTE: ***Kamen** a-47-51, 53, 55-57; c-47, 49-52. **Powell** a-4(2). Bondage-c 9-12, 46, 52. Headlight-c 46, 48, 57.*

BLUE BEETLE (Formerly The Thing; becomes Mr. Muscles No. 22 on) (See Charlton Bullseye & Space Adventures)
Charlton Comics: No. 18, Feb, 1955 - No. 21, Aug, 1955

18,19-(Pre-1944-r). 18-Last pre-code issue. 19-Bouncer, Rocket Kelly-r 41 82 123 256 428 600
20-Joan Mason by Kamen 43 86 129 271 461 650
21-New material 36 72 108 211 343 475

BLUE BEETLE (Unusual Tales #1-49; Ghostly Tales #55 on)(See Captain Atom #83 & Charlton Bullseye)
Charlton Comics: V2#1, June, 1964 - V2#5, Mar-Apr, 1965; V3#50, July, 1965 - V3#54, Feb-Mar, 1966; #1, June, 1967 - #5, Nov, 1968

V2#1-Origin/1st S.A. app. Dan Garrett-Blue Beetle 27 54 81 189 420 650
2-5: 5-Weiss illo; 1st published-a? 7 14 21 44 82 120
V3#50-54-Formerly Unusual Tales 6 12 18 41 76 110
1(1967)-Question series begins by Ditko 26 52 78 182 404 625
2-Origin Ted Kord-Blue Beetle (see Capt. Atom #83 for 1st Ted Kord Blue Beetle); Dan Garrett x-over 8 16 24 56 108 160
3-5 (All Ditko-c/a in #1-5) 6 12 18 41 76 110
1,3(Modern Comics-1977)-Reprints 2 4 6 9 12 15
NOTE: *#6 only appeared in the fanzine 'The Charlton Portfolio.'*

BLUE BEETLE (Also see Americomics, Crisis On Infinite Earths, Justice League & Showcase '94 #2-4)
DC Comics: June, 1986 - No. 24, May, 1988

1-Origin retold; intro. Firefist 2 4 6 8 10 12
2-10,15-19,21-24: 2-Origin Firefist. 5-7-The Question app. 21-Millennium tie-in 4.00
11-14,20: 11-14-New Teen Titans x-over. 20-Justice League app.; Millennium tie-in 4.00

BLUE BEETLE (See Infinite Crisis, Teen Titans, and Booster Gold #21)
DC Comics: May, 2006 - No. 36, Apr, 2009 ($2.99)

1-Hamner-a/Giffen & Rogers-s; Guy Gardner app. 4.00
1-2nd & 3rd printings 3.00
2-36: 2-2nd printing exists. 2-4-Oracle app. 5-Phantom Stranger app. 16-Eclipso app. 18,33-Teen Titans app. 20-Sinestro Corps. 21-Spectre app. 26-Spanish issue 3.00
...: Black and Blue TPB (2010, $17.99) r/#27,28,35,36 & Booster Gold #21-25,28,29 18.00
...: Boundaries TPB (2009, $14.99) r/#29-34 15.00
...: End Game TPB (2008, $14.99) r/#20-26; English script for #26 15.00
...: Reach For the Stars TPB (2008, $14.99) r/#13-19 15.00
...: Road Trip TPB (2007, $12.99) r/#7-12 13.00
...: Shellshocked TPB (2006, $12.99) r/#1-6 13.00

BLUE BEETLE (DC New 52) (Also see Threshold)
DC Comics: Nov, 2011 - No. 16, Mar, 2013 ($2.99)

1-16: 1-Bedard-s/Ig Guara-a; new origin. 9-Green Lantern (Kyle) app. 11-Booster Gold 3.00
#0 (11/12, $2.99) Origin of the scarab 3.00

BLUE BEETLE (DC Rebirth)
DC Comics: Nov, 2016 - No. 18, Apr, 2018 ($2.99/$3.99)

1-7-Giffen-s/Kolins-a. 4-7-Doctor Fate app. 3.00
8-18-($3.99) 8-11-Doctor Fate, Arion and OMAC app. 12-Batman app. 4.00
...: Rebirth 1 (10/16, $2.99) Giffen-s/Kolins-a; Ted Kord & Doctor Fate app. 3.00

BLUEBERRY (See Lt. Blueberry & Marshal Blueberry)
Marvel Comics (Epic Comics): 1989 - No. 5, 1990 ($12.95/$14.95, graphic novel)

1-($12.95) Moebius-a 4 8 12 28 47 65
2-5: 2-($14.95). 3,4,5-($12.95)-Moebius-a in all 3 6 9 17 26 35

BLUE BOLT
Funnies, Inc. No. 1/Novelty Press/Premium Group of Comics: June, 1940 - No. 101 (V10#2), Sept-Oct, 1949

V1#1-Origin Blue Bolt by Joe Simon, Sub-Zero Man, White Rider & Super Horse, Dick Cole, Wonder Boy & Sgt. Spook (1st app. of each) 411 822 1233 2817 5039 7200
2-Simon & Kirby's 1st art & 1st super-hero (Blue Bolt) 290 580 870 1856 3178 4500
3-1 pg. Space Hawk by Wolverton; 2nd S&K-a on Blue Bolt (same cover date as Red Raven #1); Simon-c 265 530 795 1694 2897 4100
4-S&K-a; classic Everett shark-c 239 478 717 1530 2615 3700
5-S&K-a; Everett-a begins on Sub-Zero; 1st time S&K names app. in a comic 200 400 600 1280 2190 3100
6,8-10-S&K-a 174 348 522 1114 1907 2700
7-Classic S&K-c/a (scarce) 245 490 735 1568 2684 3800
11-Classic Everett Giant Robot-c (scarce) 219 438 657 1402 2401 3400
12-Nazi submarine-c 174 348 522 1114 1907 2700
V2#1-Origin Dick Cole & The Twister; Twister x-over in Dick Cole, Sub-Zero, & Blue Bolt; origin Simba Karno who battles Dick Cole thru V2#5 & becomes main supporting character V2#6 on; battle-c 54 108 162 343 574 825
2-Origin The Twister retold in text 42 84 126 265 445 625
3-5: 5-Intro. Freezum 37 74 111 218 354 490
6-Origin Sgt. Spook retold 33 66 99 194 317 440
7-12: 7-Lois Blake becomes Blue Bolt's costume aide; last Twister. 12-Text-sty by Mickey Spillaine 27 54 81 162 266 370
V3#1-3 22 44 66 132 216 300
4-12: 4-Blue Bolt abandons costume 20 40 60 114 182 250
V4#1-Hitler, Tojo, Mussolini-c 123 246 369 787 1344 1900
V4#2-Liberty Bell-c 19 38 57 111 176 240
V4#3-12: 3-Shows V4#3 on-c, V4#4 inside (9-10/43). 5-Infinity-c. 8-Last Sub-Zero 16 32 48 92 144 195
V5#1-8, V6#1-3,5-7,9,10, V7#1-12 15 30 45 83 124 165
V6#4-Racist cover 40 80 120 244 402 560
V6#8-Girl fight-c 18 36 54 105 165 225
V8#1-6,8-12, V9#1-4,7,8, V10#1(#100),V10#2(#101)-Last Dick Cole, Blue Bolt 12 24 36 69 97 125
V8#7,V9#6,9-L. B. Cole-c 24 48 72 142 234 325
V9#5-Classic fish in the face-c 34 68 102 199 325 450
NOTE: ***Everett** c-V1#4, 11, V2#1, 2. **Gustavson** a-V1#1-12, V2#1-7. **Kiefer** c-V3#1. **Rico** a-V6#10, V7#4. Blue Bolt not in V9#8.*

BLUE BOLT (Becomes Ghostly Weird Stories #120 on; continuation of Novelty Blue Bolt) (...Weird Tales of Terror #111,112,...Weird Tales #113-119)
Star Publications: No. 102, Nov-Dec, 1949 - No. 119, May-June, 1953

102-The Chameleon, & Target app. 47 94 141 296 498 700
103,104-The Chameleon app. 104-Last Target 42 84 126 265 445 625
105-Origin Blue Bolt (from #1) retold by Simon; Chameleon & Target app.; opium den story 226 452 678 1446 2473 3500
106-Blue Bolt by S&K begins; Spacehawk reprints from Target by Wolverton begin, ends #110; Sub-Zero begins; ends #109 110 220 330 704 1202 1700
107-110: 108-Last S&K Blue Bolt reprint. 109-Wolverton-c(r)/inside Spacehawk splash.

Blue Circle Comics #6 © Enwil

Blue Ribbon Comics (1983 series) #7 © ACP

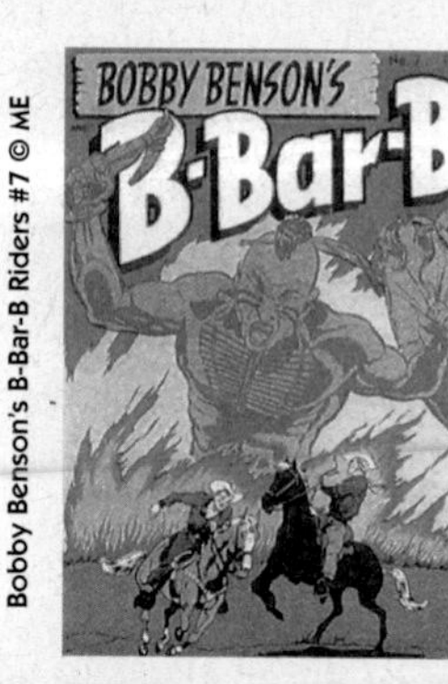

Bobby Benson's B-Bar-B Riders #7 © ME

	GD 2.0	VG 4.0	FN 6.0	VF 8.0	VF/NM 9.0	NM- 9.2
110-Target app.	84	168	252	538	919	1300
111,112: 111-Red Rocket & The Mask-r; last Blue Bolt; 1pg. L. B. Cole-a; classic-c 112-Last Torpedo Man app.	110	220	330	704	1202	1700
113-Wolverton's Spacehawk-r/Target V3#7	94	188	282	597	1024	1450
114,116: 116-Jungle Jo-r	90	180	270	576	988	1400
115-Classic-c; Sgt. Spook app.	194	388	582	1242	2121	3000
117-Jo-Jo & Blue Bolt-r; Hollingsworth-a	97	194	291	621	1061	1500
118-"White Spirit" by Wood	94	188	282	597	1024	1450
119-Disbrow/Cole-c; Jungle Jo-r	90	180	270	576	988	1400
Accepted Reprint #103(1957?, nd)	15	30	45	86	133	180

NOTE: ***L. B. Cole*** *c-102-108, 110 on.* ***Disbrow*** *a-112(2), 113(3), 114(2), 115(2), 116-118.* ***Hollingsworth*** *a-117.* ***Palais*** *a-112r. Sci/Fi c-105-110. Horror c-111.*

BLUE BULLETEER, THE (Also see Femforce Special)
AC Comics: 1989 ($2.25, B&W, one-shot)

	GD 2.0	VG 4.0	FN 6.0	VF 8.0	VF/NM 9.0	NM- 9.2
1-Origin by Bill Black; Bill Ward-a						4.00

BLUE BULLETEER (Also see Femforce Special)
AC Comics: 1996 ($5.95, B&W, one-shot)

	GD 2.0	VG 4.0	FN 6.0	VF 8.0	VF/NM 9.0	NM- 9.2
1-Photo-c						6.00

BLUE CIRCLE COMICS (Also see Red Circle Comics, Blazing Comics & Roly Poly Comic Book)
Enwil Associates/Rural Home: June, 1944 - No. 6, Apr, 1945

	GD 2.0	VG 4.0	FN 6.0	VF 8.0	VF/NM 9.0	NM- 9.2
1-The Blue Circle begins (1st app.); origin & 1st app. Steel Fist	43	86	129	271	461	650
2	25	50	75	150	245	340
3-Hitler parody-c	58	116	174	371	636	900
4-6: 5-Last Steel Fist.	22	44	66	128	209	290
6-(Dated 4/45, Vol. 2#3 inside)-Leftover covers to #6 were later restapled over early 1950's coverless comics; variations of the coverless comics exist. Colossal Features known.	22	44	66	128	209	290

BLUE DEVIL (See Fury of Firestorm #24, Underworld Unleashed, Starman (2nd) #38, Infinite Crisis and Shadowpact)
DC Comics: June, 1984 - No. 31, Dec, 1986 (75¢/$1.25)

	GD 2.0	VG 4.0	FN 6.0	VF 8.0	VF/NM 9.0	NM- 9.2
1						4.00
2-16,19-31: 4-Origin Nebiros. 7-Gil Kane-a. 8-Giffen-a						3.00
17,18-Crisis x-over						3.50
Annual 1 (11/85)-Team-ups w/Black Orchid, Creeper, Demon, Madame Xanadu, Man-Bat & Phantom Stranger						4.00

BLUE MONDAY: ... (one-shots)
Oni Press: Feb, 2002 - Dec, 2008 (B&W, Chynna Clugston-Major-s/a/c in all)

	GD 2.0	VG 4.0	FN 6.0	VF 8.0	VF/NM 9.0	NM- 9.2
Dead Man's Party (10/02, $2.95) Dan Brereton painted back-c						3.00
Inbetween Days (9/03, $9.95, 8" x 5-1/2") r/Dead Man's Party, Lovecats, & Nobody's Fool						10.00
Lovecats (2/02, $2.95) Valentine's Day themed						3.00
Nobody's Fool (2/03, $2.95) April Fool's Day themed						3.00
Thieves Like Us (12/08, $3.50) Part 1 of an unfinished 5-part series						3.50

BLUE MONDAY: ABSOLUTE BEGINNERS
Oni Press: Feb, 2001 - No. 4, Sept, 2001 ($2.95, B&W, limited series)

	GD 2.0	VG 4.0	FN 6.0	VF 8.0	VF/NM 9.0	NM- 9.2
1-4-Chynna Clugston-Major-s/a/c						3.00
TPB (12/01, $11.95, 8" x 6") r/series						12.00

BLUE MONDAY: PAINTED MOON
Oni Press: Feb, 2004 - No. 4, Mar, 2005 ($2.99, B&W, limited series)

	GD 2.0	VG 4.0	FN 6.0	VF 8.0	VF/NM 9.0	NM- 9.2
1-4-Chynna Clugston-Major-s/a/c						3.00
TPB (4/05, $11.95, digest-sized) r/series; sketch pages						12.00

BLUE MONDAY: THE KIDS ARE ALRIGHT
Oni Press: Feb, 2000 - No. 3, May, 2000 ($2.95, B&W, limited series)

	GD 2.0	VG 4.0	FN 6.0	VF 8.0	VF/NM 9.0	NM- 9.2
1-3-Chynna Clugston-Major-s/a/c. 1-Variant-c by Warren. 2-Dorkin-c						3.00
3-Variant cover by J. Scott Campbell						4.00
TPB (12/00, $10.95, digest-sized) r/#1-3 & earlier short stories						11.00

BLUE PHANTOM, THE
Dell Publishing Co.: June-Aug, 1962

	GD 2.0	VG 4.0	FN 6.0	VF 8.0	VF/NM 9.0	NM- 9.2
1(01-066-208)-by Fred Fredericks	3	6	9	20	31	42

BLUE RIBBON COMICS (...Mystery Comics No. 9-18)
MLJ Magazines: Nov, 1939 - No. 22, Mar, 1942 (1st MLJ series)

	GD 2.0	VG 4.0	FN 6.0	VF 8.0	VF/NM 9.0	NM- 9.2
1-Dan Hastings, Richy the Amazing Boy, Rang-A-Tang the Wonder Dog begin (1st app. of each); Little Nemo app. (not by W. McCay); Jack Cole-a(3) (1st MLJ comic)	271	542	813	1734	2967	4200
2-Bob Phantom, Silver Fox (both in #3), Rang-A-Tang Club & Cpl. Collins begin (1st app. of each); Jack Cole-a	142	284	426	909	1555	2200
3-J. Cole-a	97	194	291	621	1061	1500
4-Doc Strong, The Green Falcon, & Hercules begin (1st app. each); origin & 1st app. The Fox & Ty-Gor, Son of the Tiger	106	212	318	673	1162	1650
5-8: 8-Last Hercules; 6,7-Biro, Meskin-a. 7-Fox app. on-c	84	168	252	538	919	1300
9-(Scarce)-Origin & 1st app. Mr. Justice (2/41)	354	708	1062	2478	4339	6200
10-13: 12-Last Doc Strong. 13-Inferno, the Flame Breather begins, ends #19; Devil-c	155	310	465	992	1696	2400
14,15,17,18: 15-Last Green Falcon	129	258	387	826	1413	2000
16-Origin & 1st app. Captain Flag (9/41)	187	374	561	1197	2049	2900
19,20,22: 20-Last Ty-Gor. 22-Origin Mr. Justice retold	113	226	339	718	1234	1750
21-Classic Black Hood-c	206	412	618	1318	2259	3200

NOTE: ***Biro*** *c-3-5; a-2 (Cpl. Collins & Scoop Cody).* ***S. Cooper*** *c-9-17. 20-22 contain "Tales From the Witch's Cauldron" (same strip as "Stories of the Black Witch" in Zip Comics). Mr. Justice c-9-18. Captain Flag c-16-18 (w/ Mr. Justice), 19-22.*

BLUE RIBBON COMICS (Becomes Teen-Age Diary Secrets #4)
(Also see Approved Comics, Blue Ribbon Comics and Heckle & Jeckle)
Blue Ribbon (St. John): Feb, 1949 - No. 6, Aug, 1949

	GD 2.0	VG 4.0	FN 6.0	VF 8.0	VF/NM 9.0	NM- 9.2
1-Heckle & Jeckle (Terrytoons)	17	34	51	98	154	210
2(4/49)-Diary Secrets; Baker-c	63	126	189	403	689	975
3-Heckle & Jeckle (Terrytoons)	12	24	36	69	97	125
4(6/49)-Diary Secrets; Baker c/a(2)	71	142	213	454	777	1100
5(8/49)-Teen-Age Diary Secrets; Oversize; photo-c; Baker-a(2)- Continues as Teen-Age Diary Secrets	81	162	243	518	884	1250
6-Dinky Duck(8/49)(Terrytoons)	8	16	24	44	57	70

BLUE RIBBON COMICS
Red Circle Prod./Archie Ent. No. 5 on: Nov, 1983 - No. 14, Dec, 1984

	GD 2.0	VG 4.0	FN 6.0	VF 8.0	VF/NM 9.0	NM- 9.2
1-S&K-r/Advs. of the Fly #1,2; Williamson/Torres-r/Fly #2; Ditko-c	1	2	3	5	6	8
2-7,9,10: 3-Origin Steel Sterling. 5-S&K Shield-r; new Kirby-c. 6,7-The Fox app.						6.00
8-Toth centerspread; Black Hood app.; Neal Adams-a(r)	1	2	3	4	5	7
11,13,14: 11-Black Hood. 13-Thunder Bunny. 14-Web & Jaguar						6.00
12-Thunder Agents; Noman new Ditko-a	1	2	3	5	6	8

NOTE: ***N. Adams*** *a(r)-8.* ***Buckler*** *a-4i.* ***Nino*** *a-2i.* ***McWilliams*** *a-8.* ***Morrow*** *a-8.*

BLUE STREAK (See Holyoke One-Shot No. 8)

BLUNTMAN AND CHRONIC TPB(Also see Jay and Silent Bob, Clerks, and Oni Double Feature)
Image Comics: Dec, 2001 ($14.95, TPB)

	GD 2.0	VG 4.0	FN 6.0	VF 8.0	VF/NM 9.0	NM- 9.2
nn-Tie-in for "Jay & Silent Bob Strike Back" movie; new Kevin Smith-s/Michael Oeming-a; r/app. from Oni Double Feature #12 in color; Ben Affleck & Jason Lee afterwords						15.00

BLYTHE (Marge's)
Dell Publishing Co.: No. 1072, Jan-Mar, 1960

	GD 2.0	VG 4.0	FN 6.0	VF 8.0	VF/NM 9.0	NM- 9.2
Four Color 1072	5	10	15	34	60	85

B-MAN (See Double-Dare Adventures)

BO (Tom Cat #4 on) (Also see Big Shot #29 & Dixie Dugan)
Charlton Comics Group: June, 1955 - No. 3, Oct, 1955 (A dog)

	GD 2.0	VG 4.0	FN 6.0	VF 8.0	VF/NM 9.0	NM- 9.2
1-3: Newspaper reprints by Frank Beck; Noodnik the Eskimo app.	8	16	24	40	50	60

BOATNIKS, THE (See Walt Disney Showcase No. 1)

BOB BURDEN'S ORIGINAL MYSTERYMEN PRESENTS
Dark Horse Comics: 1999 - No. 4 ($2.95/$3.50)

	GD 2.0	VG 4.0	FN 6.0	VF 8.0	VF/NM 9.0	NM- 9.2
1-3-Bob Burden-s/Sadowski-a(p)						3.50
4-($3.50) All Villain issue						3.50

BOBBY BENSON'S B-BAR-B RIDERS (Radio) (See Best of The West, The Lemonade Kid & Model Fun)
Magazine Enterprises/AC Comics: May-June, 1950 - No. 20, May-June, 1953

	GD 2.0	VG 4.0	FN 6.0	VF 8.0	VF/NM 9.0	NM- 9.2
1-The Lemonade Kid begins; Powell-a (Scarce)	45	90	135	284	480	675
2	18	36	54	103	162	220
3-5: 4,5-Lemonade Kid-c (#4-Spider-c)	14	28	42	78	112	145
6-8,10	13	26	39	74	105	135
9,11,13-Frazetta-c; Ghost Rider in #13-15 by Ayers-a. 13-Ghost Rider-c	40	80	120	246	411	575
12,17-20: 20-(A-1 #88)	12	24	36	67	94	120
14-Decapitation/Bondage-c & story; classic horror-c	43	86	129	271	461	650
15-Ghost Rider-c	23	46	69	136	223	310
16-Photo-c	14	28	42	81	118	155
1 (1990, $2.75, B&W)-Reprints; photo-c & inside covers						3.00

NOTE: ***Ayers*** *a-13-15, 20.* ***Powell*** *a-1-12(4 ea.), 13(3), 14-16(Red Hawk only); c-1-8,1 0, 12. Lemonade Kid in most 1-13.*

BOBBY COMICS
Universal Phoenix Features: May, 1946

	GD 2.0	VG 4.0	FN 6.0	VF 8.0	VF/NM 9.0	NM- 9.2
1-By S. M. Iger	15	30	45	84	127	170

Bob Colt #4 © FAW

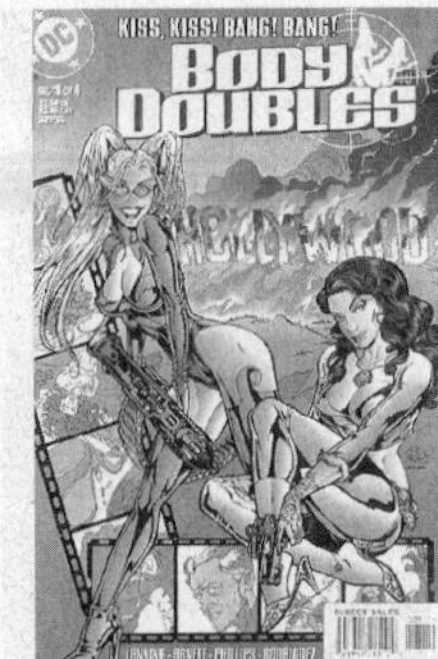

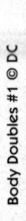

Body Doubles #1 © DC

Bomber Comics #2 © EP

GD VG FN VF VF/NM NM-
2.0 4.0 6.0 8.0 9.0 9.2

BOBBY SHERMAN (TV)
Charlton Comics: Feb, 1972 - No. 7, Oct, 1972
1-Based on TV show "Getting Together" 5 10 15 33 57 80
2-7: Photo-c on all. 7-Bobby Sherman for President 4 8 12 23 37 50

BOB COLT (See XMas Comics)
Fawcett Publications: Nov, 1950 - No. 10, May, 1952
1-Bob Colt, his horse Buckskin & sidekick Pablo begin; photo front/back-c begin 26 52 78 154 252 350
2 14 28 42 80 115 150
3-5 12 24 36 67 94 120
6-Flying Saucer story 10 20 30 58 79 100
7-10: 9-Last photo back-c 9 18 27 52 69 85

BOB HOPE (See Adventures of... & Calling All Boys #12)

BOB MARLEY, TALE OF THE TUFF GONG (Music star)
Marvel Comics: Aug, 1994 - No, 3, Nov, 1994 ($5.95, limited series)
1-3 6.00

BOB POWELL'S TIMELESS TALES
Eclipse Comics: March, 1989 ($2.00, B&W)
1-Powell-r/Black Cat #5 (Scarlet Arrow), 9 & Race for the Moon #1 3.00

BOB'S BURGERS (TV)
Dynamite Entertainment: 2014 - No. 5, 2014 ($3.99)
1-Short stories by various; multiple covers 3 6 9 14 20 25
2-5-Short stories by various 4.00

BOB'S BURGERS (Volume 2)(TV)
Dynamite Entertainment: 2015 - No. 16, 2016 ($3.99)
1-Short stories by various; multiple covers 1 3 4 6 8 10
2-16-Short stories by various; multiple covers on all 4.00
... Free Comic Book Day 2015 (giveaway) Reprints various short stories from Vol. 1 3.00
... Free Comic Book Day 2016 (giveaway) Reprints various short stories 3.00
... Free Comic Book Day 2018 (giveaway) Reprints various short stories 3.00
... Free Comic Book Day 2019 (giveaway) Reprints various short stories 3.00

BOB SCULLY, THE TWO-FISTED HICK DETECTIVE (Also see Advs. of Detective Ace King and Detective Dan)
Humor Publ. Co.: No date (1933) (36 pgs., 9-1/2x11", B&W, paper-c; 10¢-c)
nn-By Howard Dell; not reprints; along with Advs. of Detective Ace King and Detective Dan, the first comic w/original art & the first of a single theme; has a blue 2-tone cover 675 1350 2025 5400 -- --

BOB SON OF BATTLE
Dell Publishing Co.: No. 729, Nov, 1956
Four Color 729 4 8 12 28 47 65

BOB STEELE WESTERN (Movie star)
Fawcett Publications/AC Comics: Dec, 1950 - No. 10, June, 1952; 1990
1-Bob Steele & his horse Bullet begin; photo front/back-c begin 37 74 111 222 361 500
2 19 38 57 109 172 235
3-5: 4-Last photo back-c 14 28 42 82 121 160
6-10: 10-Last photo-c 13 26 39 72 101 130
1 (1990, $2.75, B&W)-Bob Steele & Rocky Lane reprints; photo-c & inside covers 3.00

BOB SWIFT (Boy Sportsman)
Fawcett Publications: May, 1951 - No. 5, Jan, 1952
1 10 20 30 58 79 100
2-5: Saunders painted-c #1-5 7 14 21 35 43 50

BOB, THE GALACTIC BUM
DC Comics: Feb, 1995 - No. 4, June, 1995 ($1.95, limited series)
1-4: 1-Lobo app. 3.00

BODIES
DC Comics (Vertigo): Sept, 2014 - No. 8, Apr, 2015 ($3.99, limited series)
1-8-Spencer-s; art by Hetrick, Ormston, Lotay & Winslade 4.00

BODY BAGS
Dark Horse Comics (Blanc Noir): Sept, 1996 - No. 4, Jan, 1997 ($2.95, mini-series, mature) (1st Blanc Noir series)
1,2-Jason Pearson-c/a/scripts in all. 1-Intro Clownface & Panda 5.00
3,4 4.00
Body Bags 1 (Image Comics, 7/05, $5.99) r/#1&2 6.00
Body Bags 2 (Image Comics, 8/05, $5.99) r/#3&4 6.00
...: 3 The Hard Way (Image, 2/06, $5.99) new story & r/Dark Horse Presents Annual 1997 and Dark Horse Maverick 2000; Pearson-c 6.00
...: One Shot (Image, 11/08, $5.99) wraparound-c; Pearson-c/a/s 6.00

BODYCOUNT (Also see Casey Jones & Raphael)
Image Comics (Highbrow Entertainment): Mar, 1996 - No. 4, July, 1996 ($2.50, lim. series)
1-4: Kevin Eastman-a(p)/scripts; Simon Bisley-c/a(i); Turtles app. 1 3 4 6 8 10
2-4 5.00

BODY DOUBLES (See Resurrection Man)
DC Comics: Oct, 1999 - No. 4, Jan, 2000 ($2.50, limited series)
1-4-Lanning & Abnett-s. 2-Black Canary app. 4-Wonder Woman app. 3.00
... (Villains) (2/98, $1.95, one-shot) 1-Pearson-c; Deadshot app. 3.00

BOFFO LAFFS
Paragraphics: 1986 - No. 5 ($2.50/$1.95)
1-($2.50) First comic cover with hologram 4.00
2-5 3.00

BOLD ADVENTURE
Pacific Comics: Nov, 1983 - No. 3, June, 1984 ($1.50)
1-Time Force, Anaconda, & The Weirdling begin 3.00
2,3: 2-Soldiers of Fortune begins. 3-Spitfire 3.00
NOTE: *Kaluta c-3. Nebres a-1-3. Nino a-2, 3. Severin a-3.*

BOLD STORIES (Also see Candid Tales & It Rhymes With Lust)
Kirby Publishing Co.: Mar, 1950 - July, 1950 (Digest size, 144 pgs.)
March issue (Very Rare) - Contains "The Ogre of Paris" by Wood 277 554 831 1759 3030 4300
May issue (Very Rare) - Contains "The Cobra's Kiss" by Graham Ingels (21 pgs.) 229 458 687 1454 2502 3550
July issue (Very Rare) - Contains "The Ogre of Paris" by Wood 229 458 687 1454 2502 3550

BOLT AND STAR FORCE SIX
Americomics: 1984 ($1.75)
1-Origin Bolt & Star Force Six 3.00
Special 1 (1984, $2.00, 52pgs., B&W) 4.00

BOMBARDIER (See Bee 29, the Bombardier & Cinema Comics Herald)

BOMBAST
Topps Comics: 1993 ($2.95, one-shot) (Created by Jack Kirby)
1-Polybagged w/Kirbychrome trading card; Savage Dragon app.; Kirby-c; has coupon for Amberchrome Secret City Saga #0 4.00

BOMBA THE JUNGLE BOY (TV)
National Periodical Publ.: Sept-Oct, 1967 - No. 7, Sept-Oct, 1968 (12¢)
1-Intro. Bomba; Infantino/Anderson-c 5 10 15 34 60 85
2-7 3 6 9 19 30 40

BOMBER COMICS
Elliot Publ. Co./Melverne Herald/Farrell/Sunrise Times: Mar, 1944 - No. 4, Winter, 1944-45
1-Wonder Boy, & Kismet, Man of Fate begin 103 206 309 659 1130 1600
2-Hitler-c and 8 pg. story 148 296 444 947 1624 2300
3: 2-4-Have Classics Comics ad to HRN 20 55 110 165 352 601 850
4-Hitler, Tojo & Mussolini-c; Sensation Comics #13-c/swipe; has Classics Comics ad to HRN 20. 148 296 444 947 1624 2300

BOMB QUEEN
Image Comics (Shadowline): Feb, 2006 - No. 4, May, 2006 ($3.50, mature)
1-Jimmie Robinson-s/a in all 3 6 9 16 23 30
2-4 1 2 3 5 6 8
... Vs. Blacklight One Shot #1 (8/06, $3.50) Robinson-a; Shadowhawk app. 5.00
..., Vol. 1: WMD: Woman of Mass Destruction TPB (7/06, $12.99) r/#1-4; bonus art 13.00

BOMB QUEEN II
Image Comics (Shadowline): Oct, 2006 - No. 3, Dec, 2006 ($3.50, mature)
1-Jimmie Robinson-s/a; intro. The Four Queens 1 3 4 6 8 10
2,3 6.00
..., Vol. 2: Dirty Bomb - Queen of Hearts TPB (7/07, $14.99) r/#1-3 & Blacklight One Shot; bonus art; Robinson interview 15.00

BOMB QUEEN III THE GOOD, THE BAD & THE LOVELY
Image Comics (Shadowline): Mar, 2007 - No. 4, Jun, 2007 ($3.50, mature)
1-4-Jimmie Robinson-a/Jim Valentino-s; Blacklight & Rebound app. 1-Linsner-c 4.00

BOMB QUEEN IV SUICIDE BOMBER
Image Comics (Shadowline): Aug, 2007 - No. 4, Dec, 2007 ($3.50, mature)
1-4-Jim Robinson-s/a. 3-She-Spawn app. 4.00

BOMB QUEEN (Volumes 5-8)

Bombshells: United #4 © DC

Bone #3 © Jeff Smith

Book of the Dead #2 © MAR

GD 2.0 | VG 4.0 | FN 6.0 | VF 8.0 | VF/NM 9.0 | NM- 9.2

Image Comics (Shadowline): May, 2008 - Present ($3.50/$3.99, mature)

Vol. 5 #1-6 (5/08 - No. 6, 3/09) Jimmie Robinson-s/a 4.00
Vol. 6 #1-4 (9/09 - No. 4, 1/11, $3.50) Obama satire 3.50
Vol. 7 #1-4 (12/11 - No. 4, 5/12, $3.50) Bomb Queen returns in 2112 3.50
Vol. 8 #1-4 (8/20 - No. 4, 12/20, $3.99) Donald Trump satire 4.00
... Presents: All Girl Comics (5/09, $3.50) Dee Rail, Blacklight, Rebound, Tempest app. 3.50
... Presents: All Girl Special (7/11, $3.50) President Palin app. 3.50
... vs. Hack/Slash (2/11, $3.50) Cassie and Vlad app.; Robinson-s/a 3.50

BOMBSHELLS: UNITED (Continued from DC Comics: Bombshell series)
DC Comics: Nov, 2017 - No. 19, Early Aug, 2018 ($2.99)

1-19: 1-Bennett-s/Sauvage-a/Dodson-c; intro. Dawnstar & Clayface. 9,17-Siya Oum-a3.00

BONANZA (TV)
Dell/Gold Key: June-Aug, 1960 - No. 37, Aug, 1970 (All Photo-c)

	GD	VG	FN	VF	VF/NM	NM-
Four Color 1110 (6-8/60)	30	60	90	216	483	750
Four Color 1221,1283, & #01070-207, 01070-210	15	30	45	100	220	340
1(12/62-Gold Key)	16	32	48	110	243	375
2 9	18	27	58	114	170	
3-10	7	14	21	44	82	120
11-20	5	10	15	34	60	85
21-37: 29-Reprints	5	10	15	30	50	70

BONE
Cartoon Books #1-20, 28 on/Image Comics #21-27: Jul, 1991 - No. 55, Jun, 2004 ($2.95, B&W)

	GD	VG	FN	VF	VF/NM	NM-
1-Jeff Smith-c/a in all	54	108	162	432	966	1500
1-2nd printing	3	6	9	14	20	25
1-3rd thru 5th printings						5.00
2-1st printing	10	20	30	69	147	225
2-2nd & 3rd printings						5.00
3-1st printing	6	12	18	42	79	115
3-2nd thru 4th printings						4.00
4,5	5	10	15	33	57	80
6-10	2	4	6	13	18	22
11-20						6.00
13 1/2 (1/95, Wizard)	2	4	6	8	10	12
13 1/2 (Gold)	2	4	6	9	12	15
21-37: 21-1st Image issue						5.00
38-($4.95) Three covers by Miller, Ross, Smith	1	2	3	4	5	7
39-55-($2.95)						4.00
1-27-($2.95): 1-Image reprints begin w/new-c. 2-Allred pin-up.						3.00
nn (2008, 8-1/2" x 5-3/8" Halloween mini-comic giveaway)						3.00
... Holiday Special (1993, giveaway)	2	3	4	6	8	10
... Reader -($9.95) Behind the scenes info						10.00
... Sourcebook-San Diego Edition						4.00
...10th Anniversary Edition (8/01, $5.95) r/#1 in color; came with figure						6.00
Complete Bone Adventures Vol 1,2 ('93, '94, $12.95, r/#1-6 & #7-12)						15.00
...: One Volume Edition (2004, $39.95, 1300 pgs.) r/#1-54; extra material						40.00
...: One Volume Limited Edition HC (2004, signed by Jeff Smith, numbered edition of 2000)	21	42	63	147	324	500
Volume 1-($19.95, hard-c)-"Out From Boneville"						20.00
Volume 1-($12.95, soft-c)						13.00
Volume 2,5-($22.95, hard-c)-"The Great Cow Race" & "Rock Jaw"						23.00
Volume 2,5-($14.95, soft-c)						15.00
Volume 3,4-($24.95, hard-c)-"Eyes of the Storm" & "The Dragonslayer"						25.00
Volume 3,4,7-($16.95, soft-c)						17.00
Volume 6-($15.95, soft-c)-"Old Man's Cave"						16.00
Volume 7-($24.95, hard-c)-"Ghost Circles"						25.00
Volume 8-($23.95, hard-c)-"Treasure Hunters"						24.00

NOTE: *Printings not listed sell for cover price.*

BONE PARISH
BOOM! Studios: Jul, 2018 - No. 12, Aug, 2019 ($3.99)

1-12-Cullen Bunn-s/Jonas Scharf-a 4.00

BONGO (See Story Hour Series)

BONGO & LUMPJAW (Disney, see Walt Disney Showcase #3)
Dell Publishing Co.: No. 706, June, 1956; No. 886, Mar, 1958

	GD	VG	FN	VF	VF/NM	NM-
Four Color 706 (#1)	6	12	18	41	76	110
Four Color 886	5	10	15	31	53	75

BONGO COMICS ...
Bongo Comics: 2005 - Present (Free Comic Book Day giveaways)

Gimme Gimme Giveaway! (2005) - Short stories from Simpsons Comics, Futurama Comics and Radioactive Man 3.00
Free-For-All! (2006, 2007, 2008, 2009, 2010, 2011, 2013-2018) - Short stories 3.00
Free-For-All! 2012 - Flip book with SpongeBob Comics 3.00

BONGO COMICS PRESENTS RADIOACTIVE MAN (See Radioactive Man)

BON VOYAGE (See Movie Classics)

BOOF
Image Comics (Todd McFarlane Prod.): July, 1994 - No. 6, Dec, 1994 ($1.95)

1-6 3.00

BOOF AND THE BRUISE CREW
Image Comics (Todd McFarlane Prod.): July, 1994 - No. 6, Dec, 1994 ($1.95)

1-6 3.00

BOOK AND RECORD SET (See Power Record Comics)

BOOK OF ALL COMICS
William H. Wise: 1945 (196 pgs.)(Inside f/c has Green Publ. blacked out)

	GD	VG	FN	VF	VF/NM	NM-
nn-Green Mask, Puppeteer & The Bouncer	69	138	207	442	759	1075

BOOK OF ANTS, THE
Artisan Entertainment: 1998 ($2.95, B&W)

1-Based on the movie Pi; Aronofsky-s 4.00

BOOK OF BALLADS AND SAGAS, THE
Green Man Press: Oct, 1995 - No. 4 ($2.95/$3.50/$3.25, B&W)

1-4: 1-Vess-c/a; Gaiman story. 3.50

BOOK OF COMICS, THE
William H. Wise: No date (1944) (25¢, 132 pgs.)

	GD	VG	FN	VF	VF/NM	NM-
nn-Captain V app.; WWII-c	54	108	162	343	574	825

BOOK OF DEATH
Valiant Entertainment: Jul, 2015 - No. 4, Oct, 2015 ($3.99, limited series)

1-4-Venditti-s/Gill & Braithwaite-a; multiple covers on each. 4-Flip book with preview for Wrath of the Eternal Warrior series 4.00
...: Fall of Bloodshot (7/15, $3.99) Lemire-s/Braithwaite-a; Armstrong app. 4.00
...: Fall of Harbinger (9/15, $3.99) Dysart-s/Kano-a; future deaths of the team 4.00
...: Fall of Ninjak (8/15, $3.99) Kindt-s/Hairsine-a 4.00
...: Fall of X-O Manowar (10/15, $3.99) Venditti-s/Henry-a; future death of Aric 4.00

BOOK OF FATE, THE (See Fate)
DC Comics: Feb, 1997 - No. 12, Jan, 1998 ($2.25/$2.50)

1-12: 4-Two-Face-c/app. 6-Convergence. 11-Sentinel app. 3.00

BOOK OF LOST SOULS, THE
Marvel Comics (Icon): Dec, 2005 - No. 6, June, 2006 ($2.99)

1-6-Colleen Doran-a/c; J. Michael Straczynski-s 3.00
... Vol. 1: Introductions All Around (2006, $16.99, TPB) r/series 17.00

BOOK OF LOVE (See Fox Giants)

BOOK OF NIGHT, THE
Dark Horse Comics: July, 1987 - No. 3, 1987 ($1.75, B&W)

1-3: Reprints from Epic Illustrated; Vess-a 3.00
TPB-r/#1-3 15.00
Hardcover-Black-c with red crest 100.00
Hardcover w/slipcase (1991) signed and numbered 50.00

BOOK OF THE DEAD
Marvel Comics: Dec, 1993 - No. 4, Mar, 1994 ($1.75, limited series, 52 pgs.)

	GD	VG	FN	VF	VF/NM	NM-
1-4: 1-Ploog Frankenstein & Morrow Man-Thing-r begin; Wrightson-r/Chamber of Darkness #7. 2-Morrow new painted-c; Chaykin/Morrow Man-Thing; Krigstein-r/Uncanny Tales #54; r/Fear #10. 3-r/Astonishing Tales #10 & Starlin Man-Thing. 3,4-Painted-c	1	2	3	5	6	8

BOOKS OF DOOM (Dr. Doom from Fantastic Four)
Marvel Comics: Jan, 2006 - No. 6, June, 2006 ($2.99, limited series)

1-6-Life story/origin of Dr. Doom; Brubaker-s/Raimondi-a/Rivera-c 3.00
Fantastic Four: Books of Doom HC (2006, $19.99) r/#1-6 20.00
Fantastic Four: Books of Doom SC (2007, $14.99) r/#1-6 15.00

BOOKS OF FAERIE, THE
DC Comics (Vertigo): Mar, 1997 - No. 3, May, 1997 ($2.50, limited series)

1-3-Gross-a 4.00
TPB (1998, $14.95) r/#1-3 & Arcana Annual #1 15.00

BOOKS OF FAERIE, THE : AUBERON'S TALE
DC Comics (Vertigo): Aug, 1998 - No. 3, Oct, 1998 ($2.50, limited series)

1-3-Gross-a 4.00

BOOKS OF FAERIE, THE : MOLLY'S STORY
DC Comics (Vertigo): Sept, 1999 - No. 4, Dec, 1999 ($2.50, limited series)

1-4-Ney Rieber-s/Mejia-a 4.00

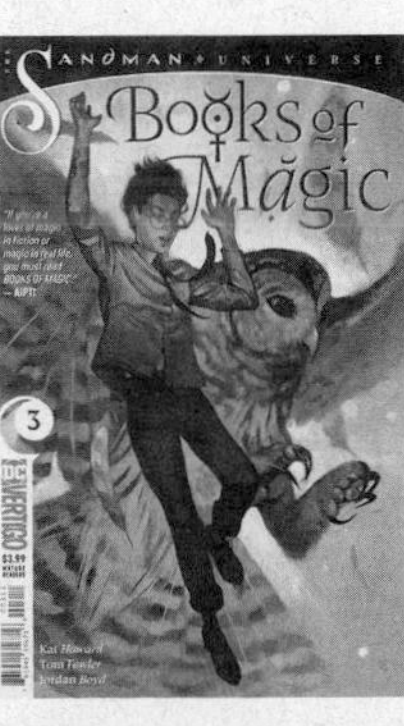

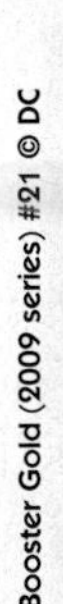
Books of Magic (2018 series) #3 © DC

Booster Gold (2009 series) #21 © DC

Borderlands: Origins #2 © Gearbox

	GD 2.0	VG 4.0	FN 6.0	VF 8.0	VF/NM 9.0	NM- 9.2

BOOKS OF MAGIC
DC Comics: 1990 - No. 4, 1991 ($3.95, 52 pgs., limited series, mature)
1-Bolton painted-c/a; Phantom Stranger app.; Gaiman scripts in all — 1 3 4 6 8 10
2,3: 2-John Constantine, Dr. Fate, Spectre, Deadman app. 3-Dr. Occult app.; minor Sandman app. — 1 2 3 4 5 7
4-Early Death-c/app. (early 1991) — 1 2 3 5 6 8
Trade paperback-($19.95)-Reprints limited series — 20.00

BOOKS OF MAGIC (Also see Hunter: The Age of Magic and Names of Magic)
DC Comics (Vertigo): May, 1994 - No. 75, Aug, 2000 ($1.95/$2.50, mature)
1-Charles Vess-c — 2 4 6 8 10 12
1-Platinum — 2 4 6 13 18 22
2-4: 4-Death app. — 1 2 3 4 5 7
5-14; Charles Vess-c — 4.00
15-75: 15-$2.50-c begins. 22-Kaluta-c. 25-Death-c/app; Bachalo-c. 51-Peter Gross-s/a begins. 55-Medley-a — 3.00
Annual 1-3 (2/97, 2/98, '99, $3.95) — 4.00
Bindings (1995, $12.95, TPB)-r/#1-4 — 13.00
Death After Death (2001, $19.95, TPB)-r/#42-50 — 20.00
Girl in the Box (1999, $14.95, TPB)-r/#26-32 — 15.00
Reckonings (1997, $12.95, TPB)-r/#14-20 — 13.00
Summonings (1996, $17.50, TPB)-r/#5-13, Vertigo Rave #1 — 17.50
The Burning Girl (2000, $17.95, TPB)-r/#33-41 — 18.00
Transformations (1998, $12.95, TPB)-r/#21-25 — 13.00

BOOKS OF MAGIC (The Sandman Universe)
DC Comics (Vertigo for #1-13, Black Label #14-on): Dec, 2018 - No. 23, Nov, 2020 ($3.99)
1-23: 1-Howard-s/Fowler-a; Tim Hunter's story continues from 1990 series; Dr. Rose app. 19-Barnett-s begins — 4.00

BOOKS OF MAGICK, THE : LIFE DURING WARTIME (See Books of Magic)
DC Comics (Vertigo): Sept, 2004 - No. 15, Dec, 2005 ($2.50/$2.75)
1-15: 1-Spencer-s/Ormston-a/Quitely-c; Constantine app. 2-Bagged with Sky Captain CD 6-Fegredo-a. 7-Constantine & Zatanna-c — 3.00
... Book One TPB (2005, $9.95) r/#1-5 — 10.00

BOOM! STUDIOS...
BOOM! Studios
... Free Comic Book Day 2019 No. 1 (5/19) Short stories of Buffy, Angel, Firefly — 3.00
... Ten Year Celebration 2015 Free Comic Book Day Special (5/15, giveaway) short stories of Adventure Time, Peanuts, Garfield, Lumberjanes, Regular Show & others — 3.00
... Summer Blast (5/16, FCBD giveaway) Mouse Guard, Labyrinth, Adventure Time — 3.00
... 2017 Summer Blast (5/17) FCBD giveaway; Mouse Guard, Brave Chef Brianna — 3.00

BOONDOCK SAINTS (Based on the movie)
12-Gauge Comics: May, 2010 - No. 2, Jun, 2010 ($3.99, limited series)
...: In Nomine Patris 1,2-Troy Duffy-s/Guus Floor-a — 4.00
...: In Nomine Patris Vol. 2 (10/10 - No. 2, 11/10): 1,2-Duffy-s/Floor-a — 4.00
...: In Nomine Patris Vol. 3 (3/11 - No. 2, 4/11): 1,2-Duffy-s/Floor-a — 4.00

BOOSTER GOLD (See Justice League #4)
DC Comics: Feb, 1986 - No. 25, Feb, 1988 (75¢)
1-Dan Jurgens-s/a(p); 1st app. of Booster Gold — 4 8 12 23 37 50
2-25: 4-Rose & Thorn app. 6-Origin. 6,7,23-Superman app. 8,9-LSH app. 22-JLI app. 24,25-Millennium tie-ins — 5.00
NOTE: *Austin c-22i. Byrne c-23i.*

BOOSTER GOLD (See DC's weekly series 52)
DC Comics: Oct, 2007 - No. 47, Oct, 2011 ($3.50/$2.99/$3.99)
1-Geoff Johns-s/Dan Jurgens-a(p); covers by Jurgens and Art Adams; Rip Hunter app. — 5.00
2-4,6-20: 3-Jonah Hex app. 4-Barry Allen app. 8-Superman app. — 3.00
5-Joker and Batgirl app.; Killing Joke-style-c — 6.00
21-29-($3.99) 21-Blue Beetle back-ups begin. 22-New Teen Titans app. 23-Photo-c. 26,27-Blackest Night; Ted Kord rises. 29-Cyborg Superman app. — 4.00
30-47-($2.99): 32-34-Giffen & DeMatteis-s. 32-Emerald Empress app. 40-Origin retold. 43-Legion of S.H. app. 44-47-Flashpoint tie-in; Doomsday app. — 3.00
#0-(4/08) Blue Beetle (Ted Cord) returns; takes place between #6&7 — 3.00
#1,000,000-(9/08) Michelle Carter returns; takes place between #10&11 — 3.00
...: Futures End 1 (11/14, $2.99, regular-c) Jurgens-s; Kamandi, LSH, Captain Atom app. — 3.00
...: Futures End 1 (11/14, $3.99, 3-D cover) — 4.00
.../ The Flintstones Special 1 (5/17, $4.99) Russell-s/Leonardi-a; Jetsons back-up — 5.00

BOOTS AND HER BUDDIES
Standard Comics/Visual Editions/Argo (NEA Service):
No. 5, 9/48 - No. 9, 9/49; 12/55 - No. 3, 1956
5-Strip-r — 22 44 66 132 216 300
6,8 — 15 30 45 83 124 165
7-(Scarce) — 17 34 51 98 154 210
9-(Scarce)-Frazetta-a (2 pgs.) — 34 68 102 199 325 450
1-3(Argo-1955-56)-Reprints — 6 12 18 31 38 45

BOOTS & SADDLES (TV)
Dell Publ. Co.: No. 919, July, 1958; No. 1029, Sept, 1959; No. 1116, Aug, 1960
Four Color 919 (#1)-Photo-c — 7 14 21 48 89 130
Four Color 1029, 1116-Photo-c — 5 10 15 34 60 85

BORDERLANDS: ... (Based on the video game)
IDW Publishing: Jul, 2014 - No. 8, Feb, 2015 ($3.99)
1-8: 1-4-The Fall of Fyerstone. 5-8-Tannis and the Vault — 4.00

BORDERLANDS: ORIGINS (Based on the video game)
IDW Publishing: Nov, 2012 - No. 4, Feb, 2013 ($3.99, limited series)
1-4: 1-Spotlight on Roland. 2-Lilith. 3-Mordecai. 4-Brick — 4.00

BORDER PATROL
P. L. Publishing Co.: May-June, 1951 - No. 3, Sept-Oct, 1951
1 — 17 34 51 96 154 210
2,3 — 11 22 33 62 86 110

BORDER TOWN
DC Comics (Vertigo): Dec, 2018 - No. 4, Feb, 2019 ($3.99, unfinished series)
1-4-Esquivel-s/Villalobos-a — 4.00

BORDER WORLDS (Also see Megaton Man)
Kitchen Sink Press: 7/86 - No. 7, 1987; V2#1, 1990 - No. 4, 1990 ($1.95-$2.00, B&W, mature)
1-7, V2#1-4: Donald Simpson-c/a/scripts — 3.00

BORIS KARLOFF TALES OF MYSTERY (TV) (...Thriller No. 1,2)
Gold Key: No. 3, April, 1963 - No. 97, Feb, 1980
3-5-(Two #5's, 10/63,11/63): 5-(10/63)-11 pgs. Toth-a. — 5 10 15 35 63 90
6-8,10: 10-Orlando-a — 4 8 12 27 44 60
9-Wood-a — 4 8 12 28 47 65
11-Williamson-a, 8 pgs.; Orlando-a, 5 pgs. — 4 8 12 28 47 65
12-Torres, McWilliams-a; Orlando-a(2) — 4 8 12 21 33 45
13,14,16-20 — 3 6 9 18 28 38
15-Crandall — 3 6 9 19 30 40
21-Jeff Jones-a(3 pgs.) "The Screaming Skull" — 3 6 9 19 30 40
22-Last 12¢ issue — 3 6 9 16 23 30
23-30: 23-Reprint; photo-c — 3 6 9 15 22 28
31-50: 36-Weiss-a — 3 6 9 14 19 24
51-74: 74-Origin & 1st app. Taurus — 2 4 6 10 14 18
75-79,87-97: 90-r/Torres, McWilliams-a/#12; Morrow-c2 — 4 6 9 12 15
80-86-(52 pgs.) — 2 4 6 10 14 18
Story Digest 1(7/70-Gold Key)-All text/illos.; 148 pp. — 5 10 15 31 53 75
(See Mystery Comics Digest No. 2, 5, 8, 11, 14, 17, 20, 23, 26)
NOTE: *Bolle a-51-54, 56, 58, 59. McWilliams a-12, 14, 18, 19, 72, 80, 81, 93. Orlando a-11-15, 21. Reprints: 78, 81-86, 88, 90, 92, 95, 97.*

BORIS KARLOFF THRILLER (TV) (Becomes Boris Karloff Tales...)
Gold Key: Oct, 1962 - No. 2, Jan, 1963 (84 pgs.)
1-Photo-c — 10 20 30 70 150 230
2 — 6 12 18 41 76 110

BORIS THE BEAR
Dark Horse Comics/Nicotat Comics #13 on: Aug, 1986 - No. 34, 1990 ($1.50/$1.75/$1.95, B&W)
1, 8, Annual 1 (1988, $2.50): 8-(44 pgs.) — 4.00
1 (2nd printing),2,3,4A,4B,5-12, 14-34 — 3.00
13-1st Nicotat Comics issue — 3.00

BORIS THE BEAR INSTANT COLOR CLASSICS
Dark Horse Comics: July, 1987 - No. 3, 1987 ($1.75/$1.95)
1-3 — 3.00

BORN
Marvel Comics: 2003 - No. 4, 2003 ($3.50, limited series)
1-4-Frank Castle (the Punisher) in 1971 Vietnam; Ennis-s/Robertson-a — 4.00
HC (2004, $17.99) oversized reprint of series; proposal, layout pages — 18.00
Punisher: Born SC (2004, $13.99) r/series; proposal, layout pages — 14.00

BORN AGAIN
Spire Christian Comics (Fleming H. Revell Co.): 1978 (39¢)
nn-Watergate, Nixon, etc. — 3 6 9 19 30 40

BOUNCE, THE
Image Comics: May, 2013 - No. 12, May, 2014 ($2.99)
1-12-Casey-s/Messina-a — 3.00

Box Office Poison #21 © Alex Robinson

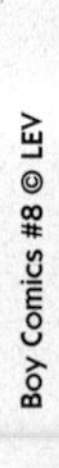
Boy Comics #8 © LEV

Boy Commandos #8 © DC

	GD 2.0	VG 4.0	FN 6.0	VF 8.0	VF/NM 9.0	NM- 9.2

BOUNCER, THE (Formerly Green Mask #9)
Fox Feature Syndicate: 1944 - No. 14, Jan, 1945

nn(1944, #10?) 36 72 108 211 343 475
11 (9/44)-Origin; Rocket Kelly, One Round Hogan app.
25 50 75 150 245 340
12-14: 14-Reprints no # issue 20 40 60 117 189 260

BOUNTY
Dark Horse Comics: Jul, 2016 - No. 5, Dec, 2016 ($3.99, limited series)

1-5-Kurtis Wiebe-s/Mindy Lee-a 4.00

BOUNTY GUNS (See Luke Short's..., Four Color 739)

BOX OFFICE POISON
Antarctic Press: 1996 - No. 21, Sept, 2000 ($2.95, B&W)

1-Alex Robinson-s/a in all 1 2 3 4 5 7
2-5 4.00
6-21, ...Kolor Karnival 1 (5/99, $2.99) 3.00
...Super Special 0 (5/97, $4.95) 5.00
Sherman's March: Collected BOP Vol. 1 (9/98, $14.95) r/#0-4 15.00
TPB (2002, $29.95, 608 pgs.) r/entire series 30.00

BOX OFFICE POISON COLOR COMICS
IDW Publishing: Jan, 2017 - No. 5, May, 2017 ($3.99)

1-5-Colored reprints of 1996 series; Alex Robinson-s/a in all; bonus commentary 4.00

BOY AND THE PIRATES, THE (Movie)
Dell Publishing Co.: No. 1117, Aug, 1960

Four Color 1117-Photo-c 6 12 18 37 66 95

BOY COMICS (Captain Battle No. 1 & 2; Boy Illustories No. 43-108) (Stories by Charles Biro) (Also see Squeeks)
Lev Gleason Publ. (Comic House): No. 3, Apr, 1942 - No. 119, Mar, 1956

3 (No.1)-1st app. & origin Crimebuster (ends #110), Bombshell (ends #8) Young Robin Hood (ends # 32), Yankee Longago (ends #28), Hero of the Month (ends #31), Case 1001-1005, 1006-1009 (ends #10); Swoop Storm begins (ends #32); Pepper Casey only app.; 1st app. Iron Jaw; Crimebuster's pet monkey Squeeks begins
331 662 993 2317 4059 5800
4-Hitler, Tojo Mussolini-c; Iron Jaw app. Little Wise Guys (prototype of later version) begins, ends #5 219 438 657 1402 2401 3400
5-Japanese war-c 142 284 426 909 1555 2200
6-Origin Iron Jaw; origin & death of Iron Jaw's son killed by his father; Hitler app.; Little Dynamite begins, ends #39; 1st Iron Jaw-c 331 662 993 2317 4059 5800
7-Flag & Hitler, Tojo, Mussolini-c; Dickey Dean app. 226 452 678 1446 2473 3500
8-Death of Iron Jaw; Iron Jaw-c & spash pg. 106 212 318 673 1162 1650
9-Iron Jaw classic-c (does not appear in story) 258 516 774 1651 2826 4000
10-Return of Iron Jaw; classic Biro Iron Jaw/Nazi-c 213 426 639 1363 2332 3300
11-Iron Jaw sty/classic-c 148 296 444 947 1624 2300
12-Classic Japanese WWII bondage torture interrogation-c
126 252 378 806 1378 1950
13-Nazi firing squad-c 94 188 282 597 1024 1450
14-Iron Jaw-c 86 172 258 546 936 1325
15-Death of Iron Jaw, killed by The Rodent 100 200 300 635 1093 1550
16,18,20 (2/45) 48 96 144 302 514 725
17-(8/44)-Flag-c; The Moth app. 53 106 159 334 567 800
19-One of the greatest all-time stories 57 114 171 362 619 875
21-24: 24-Concentration camp story 36 72 108 211 343 475
25-Devil-c; hanging story (52 pgs.) 41 82 123 256 428 600
26-Bondage, torture-c/story (68 pgs.) 48 96 144 302 514 725
27-29,31,32-(All 68 pgs.). 28-Yankee Longago ends. 32-Swoop Storm & Young Robin Hood end 36 72 108 211 343 475
30-(10/46, 68 pgs.)-Origin Crimebuster retold from #3 w/Iron Jaw; Nazi work camp story
41 82 123 256 428 600
33-40: 34-Crimebuster story (2); suicide-c/story 23 46 69 136 223 310
41-50-41-Daredevil illus. text story 19 38 57 111 176 240
51-59: 57(9/50)-Dilly Duncan begins, ends #71 16 32 48 94 147 200
60-(12/50)-Iron Jaw returns c/sty 18 36 54 105 165 225
61-Origin Crimebuster & Iron Jaw retold c/sty 20 40 60 114 182 250
62-(2/51)-Death of Iron Jaw explained w/Iron Jaw-c 19 38 57 111 176 240
63-67,69-72: 63-McWilliams-a 14 28 42 76 108 140
68,73-Iron Jaw c/sty; 73-Frazetta 1 pg. ad 14 28 42 80 115 150
74,78,81-Iron Jaw c/sty (2-3) 12 24 36 67 94 120
75-77,84 11 22 33 62 86 110
79,80-Iron Jaw sty: 80(8/52)-1st app. Rocky X of the Rocketeers; becomes "Rocky X" #101; Iron Jaw, Sniffer & the Deadly Dozen in #80-118 11 22 33 64 90 115
82-Iron Jaw-c (apps. in one panel) 11 22 33 62 86 110
83,85-88-Iron Jaw c/sty. 87-The Deadly Dozen begins; becomes Iron Jaw #88 (4/53)
11 22 33 64 90 115
89(5/53)-92-The Claw serial app. in Rocky X (also see Silver Streak & Daredevil); on-c. 89-"Iron Jaw" becomes "Sniffrer & Iron Jaw" (ends #118); Iron Jaw c/story in all
12 24 36 67 94 120
93-Claw cameo & last app.; Woodesque-a on Rocky X by Sid Check; Iron Jaw-c/sty
11 22 33 64 90 115
94-97-Iron Jaw-c/sty in all 11 22 33 60 83 105
98,100:(4/54): 98-Rocky X by Sid Check 11 22 33 62 86 110
99,101-107,109,111,119: 101-Rocky X becomes spy strip. 106-Robin Hood app. 111-Crimebuster becomes Chuck Chandler, ends #119
10 20 30 54 72 90
108-(2/55)-Kubert & Ditko-a (Crimebuster, 8 pgs.) 11 22 33 62 86 110
110,112-118-Kubert-a 10 20 30 58 79 100
(See Giant Boy Book of Comics)
NOTE: *Boy Movies in 3-5,40,41. Iron Jaw app. 3,4,6,8,10,11,13-15; returns-60,62, 68, 69, 72-79, 81-118; c-60-62, 73, 74, 78, 81-83, 85-97.* ***Biro*** *c-all.* ***Jack Alderman*** *a-26.* ***Dan Barry*** *a-31,32, 35-38.* ***Al Borth*** *a- 51.* ***Dick Briefer*** *a-3-28, 124.* ***Sid Check*** *a-93, 98.* ***Ditko*** *a-108.* ***Bob Fujitani (Fuje)*** *a-55, 18pgs.* ***Jerry Gandenetti*** *a-52.* ***R. W. Hall*** *a-19-22.* ***Hubbell*** *a-30, 106, 108, 110, 111.* ***Joe Kubert*** *a-108, 110, 112-118.* ***Kenneth Landau*** *a-92.* ***George Mandel*** *a-3-30.* ***Norman Maurer*** *a-4-9, 11-13, 31, 32, 35, 41, 43, 46, 51, 57, 61, 73, 74, 78-83.* ***Bob Montana*** *a-4, 16, 19.* ***Pete Morisi*** *a-111.* ***William Overgard*** *a-68, 71, 74, 86, 88.* ***Palais*** *a-14, 16, 17, 19, 20, 25, 26. among others.* ***Tuska*** *a-30.* ***Bob Wood*** *a-8-13.*

BOY COMMANDOS (See Detective #64 & World's Finest Comics #8)
National Periodical Publications: Winter, 1942-43 - No. 36, Nov-Dec, 1949

1-Origin Liberty Belle; The Sandman & The Newsboy Legion x-over in Boy Commandos; S&K-a, 48 pgs.; S&K cameo? (classic WWII-c) 400 800 1200 2800 4900 7000
2-Last Liberty Belle; Hitler-c; S&K-a, 46 pgs.; WWII-c
252 504 756 1613 2757 3900
3-S&K-a, 45 pgs.; WWII-c 135 270 405 864 1482 2100
4-6: All WWII-c. 6-S&K-a 86 172 258 546 936 1325
7-10: All WWII-c 54 108 162 343 574 825
11-13: All WWII-c. 11-Infinity-c 40 80 120 244 402 560
14,16,18-19-All have S&K-a. 18-2nd Crazy Quilt-c 34 68 102 199 325 450
15-1st app. Crazy Quilt, their arch nemesis 42 84 126 265 445 625
17,20-Sci/fi-c/stories 40 80 120 246 411 575
21,22,25: 22-3rd Crazy Quilt-c; Judy Canova x-over 27 54 81 158 259 360
23-S&K-c/a(all) 36 72 108 214 347 480
24-1st costumed superhero satire-c (11-12/47) 39 78 117 231 378 525
26-Flying Saucer story (3-4/48)-4th of this theme; see The Spirit 9/28/47(1st), Shadow Comics V7#10 (2nd, 1/48) & Captain Midnight #60 (3rd, 2/48)
34 68 102 199 325 450
27,28,30: 30-Cleveland Indians story 26 52 78 154 252 350
29-S&K story (1) 27 54 81 162 266 370
31-35: 32-Dale Evans app. on-c & in story. 33-Last Crazy Quilt-c. 34-Intro. Wolf, their mascot 23 46 69 136 223 310
36-Intro The Atomobile c/sci-fi story (Scarce) 42 84 126 265 445 625
The Boy Commandos by Joe Simon & Jack Kirby Volume One HC (2010, $49.99) reprints apps. in Detective #64-72, World's Finest #8,9 & Boy Commandos #1,2; Buhle intro. 50.00
NOTE: *Most issues signed by* ***Simon & Kirby*** *are not by them.* ***S&K*** *c-1-9, 13, 14, 17, 21, 23, 24, 30-32.* ***Feller*** *c-30.*

BOY COMMANDOS
National Per. Publ.: Sept-Oct, 1973 - No. 2, Nov-Dec, 1973 (G.A. S&K reprints)

1,2: 1-Reprints story from Boy Commandos #1 plus-c & Detective #66 by S&K. 2-Infantino/Orlando-c 2 4 6 10 14 18

BOY COMMANDOS COMICS
DC Comics: Sept/Oct. 1942

1-Ashcan comic, not distributed to newsstands, only for in-house use. Cover art is the splash page from the Boy Commandos story in Detective Comics #68 interior is from an unidentified issue of Detective Comics (A FN- copy sold for $1912 in 2012)
nn - (9-10/42) Ashcan comic, not distributed to newsstands, only for in-house use. Cover art is the splash page from the Boy Commandos story in Detective Comics #68 interior is from Detective Comics #68 (no known sales)

BOY COWBOY (Also see Amazing Adventures & Science Comics)
Ziff-Davis Publ. Co.: 1950 (8 pgs. in color)

nn-Sent to subscribers of Ziff-Davis mags. & ordered through mail for 10¢; used to test market for Kid Cowboy 36 72 108 216 351 485

BOY DETECTIVE
Avon Periodicals: May-June, 1951 - No. 4, May, 1952

1 26 52 78 152 249 345
2-4: 3,4-Kinstler-c 15 30 45 90 140 190

BOY EXPLORERS COMICS (Terry and The Pirates No. 3 on)
Family Comics (Harvey Publ.): May-June, 1946 - No. 2, Sept-Oct, 1946

1-Intro The Explorers, Duke of Broadway, Calamity Jane & Danny Dixon...Cadet; S&K-c/a, 24 pgs. 84 168 252 538 919 1300
2-(Rare)-Small size (5-1/2x8-1/2"; B&W; 32 pgs.) Distributed to mail subscribers only;

Boy Meets Girl #4 © LEV

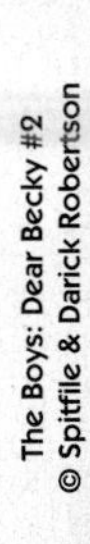
The Boys: Dear Becky #2 © Spitfile & Darick Robertson

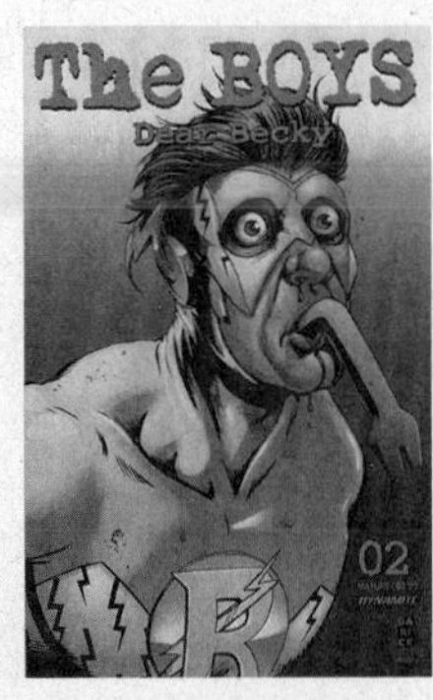

B.P.R.D.: Hell on Earth #120 © Mignola

GD VG FN VF VF/NM NM-
2.0 4.0 6.0 8.0 9.0 9.2

S&K-a 158 316 474 1003 1727 2450
(Also see All New No. 15, Flash Gordon No. 5, and Stuntman No. 3)

BOY ILLUSTORIES (See Boy Comics)

BOY LOVES GIRL (Boy Meets Girl No. 1-24)
Lev Gleason Publications: No. 25, July, 1952 - No. 57, June, 1956
25(#1) 15 30 45 90 140 190
26,27,29-33: 30-33-Serial, 'Loves of My Life 11 22 33 62 86 110
34-42: 39-Lingerie panels 11 22 33 60 83 105
28-Drug propaganda story 11 22 33 62 86 110
43-Toth-a 11 22 33 64 90 115
44-50: 47-Toth-a? 49-Roller Derby-c. 50-Last pre-code (2/55)
10 20 30 56 76 95
51-57: 57-Ann Brewster-a 9 18 27 52 69 85

BOY MEETS GIRL (Boy Loves Girl No. 25 on)
Lev Gleason Publications: Feb, 1950 - No. 24, June, 1952 (No. 1-17: 52 pgs.)
1-Guardineer-a 23 46 69 136 223 310
2 14 28 42 81 118 155
3-10 14 28 42 76 108 140
11-24 12 24 36 67 94 120
NOTE: *Briefer a-24. Fuje c-3,7. Painted-c 1-17. Photo-c 19-21, 23.*

BOYS, THE (Inspired the 2019 Amazon Prime TV series)
DC Comics (WildStorm)/Dynamite Ent. #7 on: Oct, 2006 - No. 72, 2012 ($2.99/$3.99)
1-Garth Ennis-s/Darick Robertson-a 6 12 18 38 69 100
2,3 3 6 9 21 33 45
4,5 3 6 9 14 20 25
6-20 1 3 4 6 8 10
21-50: 19-Origin of the Homelander. 23-Variant-c by Cassaday
1 2 3 5 6 8
50-64,66-71-($3.99) Russ Braun-a in most. 54,55-McCrea-a 5.00
65,72-($4.99): 65-End of the Homelander. 72-Last issue; bonus pin-ups; cover gallery
1 2 3 5 6 8
#1: Dynamite Edition (2009, $1.00) r/#1; flip book with Battlefields Night Witches 5.00
...: Herogasm 1-6 (2009 - No. 6, 2009, $2.99) Ennis-s/McCrea-a 3.00
... Volume 1: The Name of the Game TPB (2007, $14.99) r/#1-6; intro. by Simon Pegg 15.00
... Volume 2: Get Some TPB (2008, $19.99) r/#7-14 20.00
... Volume 3: Good For The Soul TPB (2008, $19.99) r/#15-22 20.00
... Volume 4: We Gotta Go Now TPB (2009, $19.99) r/#23-30; cover gallery 20.00
... Volume 5: Herogasm TPB (2009, $19.99) r/#Herogasm #1-6 20.00

BOYS, THE: BUTCHER, BAKER, CANDLESTICKMAKER
Dynamite Entertainment: 2011 - No. 6, 2011 ($3.99, mature)
1-6-Garth Ennis-s/Darick Robertson-a; Billy Butcher's early years 4.00

BOYS, THE: DEAR BECKY
Dynamite Entertainment: 2020 - No. 8, 2020 ($3.99, mature)
1-8-Garth Ennis-s/Russ Braun-a/Darick Robertson-c; set 12 years later, plus flashbacks 4.00

BOYS, THE: HIGHLAND LADDIE
Dynamite Entertainment: 2010 - No. 6, 2011 ($3.99, mature)
1-6-Garth Ennis-s/John McCrea-a 4.00

BOYS' AND GIRLS' MARCH OF COMICS (See March of Comics)

BOYS' RANCH (Also see Western Tales & Witches' Western Tales)
Harvey Publ.: Oct, 1950 - No. 6, Aug, 1951 (No.1-3, 52 pgs.; No. 4-6, 36 pgs.)
1-S&K-c/a(3) 61 122 183 390 670 950
2-S&K-c/a(3) 41 82 123 250 418 585
3-S&K-c/a(2); Meskin-a 39 78 117 236 388 540
4-S&K-c/a, 5 pgs. 34 68 102 204 332 460
5,6-S&K-c, splashes & centerspread only; Meskin-a
20 40 60 117 189 260

BOZO (Larry Harmon's Bozo, the World's Most Famous Clown)
Innovation Publishing: 1992 ($6.95, 68 pgs.)
1-Reprints Four Color #285(#1) 1 2 3 4 5 7

BOZO THE CLOWN (TV) (Bozo No. 7 on)
Dell Publishing Co.: July, 1950 - No. 4, Oct-Dec, 1963
Four Color 285(#1) 18 36 54 122 271 420
2(7-9/51)-7(10-12/52) 9 18 27 63 129 195
Four Color 464,508,551,594(10/54) 9 18 27 58 114 170
1(nn, 5-7/62) 7 14 21 44 82 120
2 - 4(1963) 5 10 15 35 63 90

BOZZ CHRONICLES, THE
Marvel Comics (Epic Comics): Dec, 1985 - No. 6, 1986 (Lim. series, mature)

GD VG FN VF VF/NM NM-
2.0 4.0 6.0 8.0 9.0 9.2

1-6-Logan/Wolverine look alike in 19th century. 1,3,5-Blevins-a 3.00

B.P.R.D. (Bureau of Paranormal Research and Defense) (Also see Hellboy titles)
Dark Horse Comics: (one-shots)
... Dark Waters (7/03, $2.99) Guy Davis-c/a; Augustyn-s 3.00
... Night Train (9/03, $2.99) Johns & Kolins-s; Kolins & Stewart-a 3.00
... The Ectoplasmic Man (6/08, $2.99) Stenbeck-a/Mignola-c; origin of Johann Kraus 3.00
... There's Something Under My Bed (11/03, $2.99) Pollina-a/c 3.00
... The Soul of Venice (5/03, $2.99) Oeming-a/c; Gunter & Oeming-s 3.00
... The Soul of Venice and Other Stories TPB (8/04, $17.95) r/one-shots & new story by Mignola and Cam Stewart; sketch pages by various 18.00
... War on Frogs (6/08,12/08, 6/09, 12/09, $2.99) 1-Trimpe-a/Mignola-c; Abe Sapien app. 2-Severin-a. 3-Moline-a. 4-Snejbjerg 3.00

B.P.R.D.: GARDEN OF SOULS
Dark Horse Comics: Mar, 2007 - No. 5, July, 2007 ($2.99, limited series)
1-5-Mignola & Arcudi-s/Guy Davis-a/Mignola-c 3.00

B.P.R.D.: HELL ON EARTH
Dark Horse Comics: ($3.50, limited series)
... Exorcism (6/12 - No. 2, 7/12) 1,2-Mignola-s/Stewart-a/Kalvachev -c 3.50
... Gods (1/11 - No. 3, 3/11) 1-Mignola & Arcudi-s/Guy Davis-a; Ryan Sook-c 3.50
... Monsters (7/11 - No. 2, 8/11) 1,2-Mignola & Arcudi-s. 1-Sook & Francavilla covers 3.50
... New World (8/10 - No. 5, 12/10) 1-5-Mignola & Arcudi-s/Guy Davis-a/c 3.50
... Russia (9/11 - No. 5, 1/12) 1-5-Mignola & Arcudi-s/Crook-a 3.50
... The Devil's Engine (5/12 - No. 3, 7/12) 1-3-Mignola & Arcudi-s/Crook-a/Fegredo-c 3.50
... The Long Death (2/12 - No. 3, 4/12) 1-3-Mignola & Arcudi-s/Harren-a/Fegredo-c 3.50
... The Pickens County Horror (3/12 - No. 2, 4/12) 1,2-Mignola & Allie-s/Latour-a 3.50
... The Transformation of J.H. O'Donnell (5/12) 1-Mignola & Allie-s/Fiumara-a 3.50
... The Return of the Master (8/12 - No. 5, 12/12) 1-5-Mignola & Arcudi-s/Crook-a; 3-5-Also numbered as #100-102 on cover and indicia 3.50
103-141: 103-(1/13). 103,104-The Abyss of Time. 105,106-A Cold Day in Hell 3.50
142-147-($3.99) 4.00

B.P.R.D.: HOLLOW EARTH (Mike Mignola's...)
Dark Horse Comics: Jan, 2002 - No. 3, June, 2002 ($2.99, limited series)
1-3-Mignola, Golden & Sniegoski-s/Sook-a/Mignola-c; Hellboy and Abe Sapien app. 5.00
... and Other Stories TPB (1/03; 7/04, $17.95) r/#1-3, Hellboy: Box Full of Evil, Abe Sapien: Drums of the Dead, and Dark Horse Extra; plus sketch pages 18.00

B.P.R.D.: KILLING GROUND
Dark Horse Comics: Aug, 2007 - No. 5, Dec, 2007 ($2.99, limited series)
1-5-Mignola & Arcudi-s/Guy Davis-a/c 3.00

B.P.R.D.: KING OF FEAR
Dark Horse Comics: Jan, 2010 - No. 5, May, 2010 ($2.99, limited series)
1,2-Mignola & Arcudi-s/Guy Davis-a; Mignola-c 3.00

B.P.R.D.: 1946
Dark Horse Comics: Jan, 2008 - No. 5, May, 2008 ($2.99, limited series)
1-5-Mignola & Dysart-s/Azaceta-a; Mignola-c 3.00

B.P.R.D.: 1947
Dark Horse Comics: Jul, 2009 - No. 5, Nov, 2009 ($2.99, limited series)
1-5-Mignola & Dysart-s/Bá & Moon-a; Mignola-c 3.00

B.P.R.D.: 1948
Dark Horse Comics: Oct, 2012 - No. 5, Feb, 2013 ($3.50, limited series)
1-5-Mignola & Arcudi-s/Fiumara-a; Johnson-c 3.50

B.P.R.D.: PLAGUE OF FROGS
Dark Horse Comics: Mar, 2004 - No. 5, July, 2004 ($2.99, limited series)
1-5-Mignola-s/Guy Davis-c/a 3.00
TPB (1/05, $17.95) r/series; sketchbook pages & afterword by Davis & Mignola 18.00

B.P.R.D.: THE BLACK FLAME
Dark Horse Comics: Sept, 2005 - No. 6, Jan, 2006 ($2.99, limited series)
1-6-Mignola & Arcudi-s/Guy Davis-a/ Mignola-c 3.00
TPB (7/06, $17.95) r/series; sketchbook pages & afterword by Davis & Mignola 18.00

B.P.R.D.: THE BLACK GODDESS
Dark Horse Comics: Jan, 2009 - No. 5, May, 2009 ($2.99, limited series)
1-5-Mignola & Arcudi-s/Guy Davis-a/Nowlan-c 3.00

B.P.R.D.: THE DEAD
Dark Horse Comics: Nov, 2004 - No. 5, Mar, 2005 ($2.99, limited series)
1-5-Mignola-s/Guy Davis-c/a 3.00

B.P.R.D.: THE DEAD REMEMBERED
Dark Horse Comics: Apr, 2011 - No. 3, Jun, 2011 ($3.50, limited series)

Brain Boy (2013 series) #3 © DH

The Brave and the Bold #2 © DC

The Brave and the Bold #55 © DC

	GD 2.0	VG 4.0	FN 6.0	VF 8.0	VF/NM 9.0	NM- 9.2

1-3-Mignola-s; Moline-a; Jo Chen-c. 1-Variant-c by Moline 3.50

B.P.R.D.: THE DEVIL YOU KNOW
Dark Horse Comics: Jul, 2017 - No. 15, Apr, 2019 ($3.99, limited series)
1-15: 1-Mignola & Allie-s/Laurence Campbell-a/Fegredo-c. 6-8-Fiumara-a 4.00

B.P.R.D.: THE UNIVERSAL MACHINE
Dark Horse Comics: Apr, 2006 - No. 5, Aug, 2006 ($2.99, limited series)
1-5-Mignola & Arcudi-s/Guy Davis-a/Mignola-c. 5-Mignola-a (5 pgs.) 3.00
TPB (1/07, $17.95) r/series; sketchbook pages by Davis; Mignola afterword 18.00

B.P.R.D.: THE WARNING
Dark Horse Comics: July, 2008 - No. 5, Nov, 2008 ($2.99, limited series)
1-5-Mignola & Arcudi-s/Guy Davis-c/a 3.00

B.P.R.D.: VAMPIRE
Dark Horse Comics: Mar, 2013 - No. 5, Jul, 2013 ($3.50, limited series)
1-5-Mignola-s/Bá & Moon-a; Moon-c 3.50

BRADLEYS, THE (Also see Hate)
Fantagraphics Books: Apr, 1999 - No. 6, Jan, 2000 ($2.95, B&W, limited series)
1-6-Reprints Peter Bagge's-s/a 3.00

BRADY BUNCH, THE (TV)(See Kite Fun Book and Binky #78)
Dell Publishing Co.: Feb, 1970 - No. 2, May, 1970 (photo-c)

	GD	VG	FN	VF	VF/NM	NM-
1	12	24	36	79	170	260
2	9	18	27	60	120	180

BRAIN, THE
Sussex Publ. Co./Magazine Enterprises: Sept, 1956 - No. 7, 1958

	GD	VG	FN	VF	VF/NM	NM-
1-Dan DeCarlo-a in all including reprints	13	26	39	74	105	135
2,3	9	18	27	47	61	75
4-7	4	8	12	27	44	60
I.W. Reprints #1-4,8-10('63),14: 2-Reprints Sussex #2 with new cover added	2	4	6	9	13	16
Super Reprint #17,18(nd)	2	4	6	9	13	16

BRAINBANX
DC Comics (Helix): Mar, 1997 - No. 6, Aug, 1997 ($2.50, limited series)
1-6: Elaine Lee-s/Temujin-a 3.00

BRAIN BOY
Dell Publishing Co.: Apr-June, 1962 - No. 6, Sept-Nov, 1963 (Painted c-#1-6)

	GD	VG	FN	VF	VF/NM	NM-
Four Color 1330(#1)-Gil Kane-a; origin	10	20	30	66	138	210
2(7-9/62),3-6: 4-Origin retold	6	12	18	41	76	110

BRAIN BOY
Dark Horse Comics: Sept, 2013 - No. 3, Nov, 2013 ($2.99, limited series)
1-3-Van Lente-s/Silva-a/Olivetti-c 3.00
#0-(12/13, $2.99) Reprints stories from Dark Horse Presents #23-25; Olivetti-c 3.00

BRAIN BOY: THE MEN FROM G.E.S.T.A.L.T.
Dark Horse Comics: May, 2014 - No. 4, Aug, 2014 ($2.99, limited series)
1-4-Van Lente-s/Freddie Williams II-a/c 3.00

BRAM STOKER'S DRACULA (Movie)(Also see Dracula: Vlad the Impaler)
Topps Comics: Oct, 1992 - No. 4, Jan, 1993 ($2.95, limited series, polybagged)
1-(1st & 2nd printing)-Adaptation of film begins; Mignola-c/a in all; 4 trading cards & poster; photo scenes of movie 5.00
1-Crimson foil edition (limited to 500) 20.00
2-4: 2-Bound-in poster & cards. 4 trading cards in both. 3-Contains coupon to win 1 of 500 crimson foil-c edition of #1. 4-Contains coupon to win 1 of 500 uncut sheets of all 16 trading cards 4.00

BRAND ECHH (See Not Brand Echh)

BRAND OF EMPIRE (See Luke Short's...Four Color 771)

BRASS
Image Comics (WildStorm Productions): Aug, 1996 - No. 3, May, 1997 ($2.50, lim. series)
1-($4.50) Folio Ed.; oversized 4.50
1-3: Wiesenfeld-s/Bennett-a. 3-Grunge & Roxy(Gen 13) cameo 3.00

BRASS
DC Comics (WildStorm): Aug, 2000 - No. 6, Jan, 2001 ($2.50, limited series)
1-6-Arcudi-s 3.00

BRATH
CrossGeneration Comics: Feb, 2003 - No. 14, June, 2004 ($2.95)
Prequel-Dixon-s/Di Vito-a 3.00
1-14: 1-(3/03)-Dixon-s/Di Vito-a 3.00
Vol. 1: Hammer of Vengeance (2003, $9.95) Digest-sized reprint of Prequel & #1-6 10.00

BRATS BIZARRE
Marvel Comics (Epic/Heavy Hitters): 1994 - No. 4, 1994 ($2.50, limited series)
1-4: All w/bound-in trading cards 3.00

BRAVADOS, THE (See Wild Western Action)
Skywald Publ. Corp.: Aug, 1971 (52 pgs., one-shot)

	GD	VG	FN	VF	VF/NM	NM-
1-Red Mask, The Durango Kid, Billy Nevada-r; Bolle-a; 3-D effect story	3	6	9	15	22	28

BRAVE AND THE BOLD, THE (See Best Of... & Super DC Giant) (Replaced by Batman & The Outsiders)
National Periodical Publ./DC Comics: Aug-Sept, 1955 - No. 200, July, 1983

	GD	VG	FN	VF	VF/NM	NM-
1-Viking Prince by Kubert, Silent Knight, Golden Gladiator begin; part Kubert-c	350	700	1050	3000	6750	10,500
2	139	278	417	1112	2506	3900
3,4	75	150	225	600	1350	2100
5-Robin Hood begins (4-5/56, 1st DC app.), ends #15; see Robin Hood Tales #7	79	158	237	632	1416	2200
6-10: 6-Robin Hood by Kubert; last Golden Gladiator app.; Silent Knight; no Viking Prince. 8-1st S.A. issue	50	100	150	400	900	1400
11-22,24: 12,14-Robin Hood-c. 18,21-23-Grey tone-c. 22-Last Silent Knight. 24-Last Viking Prince by Kubert (2nd solo book)	40	80	120	296	673	1050
23-Viking Prince origin by Kubert; 1st B&B single theme issue & 1st Viking Prince solo book	50	100	150	400	900	1400
25-1st app. Suicide Squad (8-9/59)	307	614	921	2533	5717	8900
26,27-Suicide Squad	42	84	126	311	706	1100
28-(2-3/60)-Justice League 1st app.; battle Starro; origin/1st app. Snapper Carr	1400	2800	5600	18,000	55,000	92,000
28 (Facsimile Edition)(2020, $3.99) Reprints #28 with original ads and letter column						4.00
29-Justice League (4-5/60)-2nd app. battle the Weapons Master; robot-c	238	416	714	1964	4432	6900
30-Justice League (6-7/60)-3rd app.; vs. Amazo	197	394	591	1625	3663	5700
31-1st app. Cave Carson (8-9/60); scarce in high grade; 1st try-out series	49	98	147	382	866	1350
32,33-Cave Carson	26	52	78	182	404	625
34-Origin/1st app. Silver-Age Hawkman, Hawkgirl & Byth (2-3/61); Gardner Fox story, Kubert-c/a ; 1st S.A. Hawkman tryout series; 2nd in #42-44; both series predate Hawkman #1 (4-5/64)	169	338	507	1394	3147	4900
35-Hawkman by Kubert (4-5/61)-2nd app.	38	76	114	285	641	1000
36-Hawkman by Kubert; origin & 1st app. Shadow Thief (6-7/61)-3rd app.	35	70	105	252	564	875
37-Suicide Squad (2nd tryout series)	27	54	81	194	435	675
38,39-Suicide Squad. 38-Last 10¢ issue	20	40	60	141	313	485
40,41-Cave Carson Inside Earth (2nd try-out series). 40-Kubert-a. 41-Meskin-a	13	26	39	90	198	305
42-Hawkman by Kubert (2nd tryout series); Hawkman earns helmet wings; Byth app.	20	40	60	141	313	485
43-Hawkman by Kubert; more detailed origin	23	46	69	161	356	550
44-Hawkman by Kubert; grey-tone-c	20	40	60	141	313	485
45-49-Strange Sports Stories by Infantino	8	16	24	56	108	160
50-The Green Arrow & Manhunter From Mars (10-11/63); 1st Manhunter x-over outside of Detective Comics (pre-dates House of Mystery #143); team-ups begin	19	38	57	131	291	450
51-Aquaman & Hawkman (12-1/63-64); pre-dates Hawkman #1	19	38	57	129	287	445
52-(2-3/64)-3 Battle Stars; Sgt. Rock, Haunted Tank, Johnny Cloud, & Mlle. Marie team-up for 1st time by Kubert (c/a)	24	48	72	168	372	575
53-Atom & The Flash by Toth	9	18	27	63	129	195
54-Kid Flash, Robin & Aqualad; 1st app./origin Teen Titans (6-7/64)	82	164	246	656	1478	2300
55-Metal Men & The Atom	9	18	27	57	111	165
56-The Flash & Manhunter From Mars	9	18	27	57	111	165
57-Origin & 1st app. Metamorpho (12-1/64-65)	24	48	72	168	372	575
58-2nd app. Metamorpho by Fradon	9	18	27	61	123	185
59-Batman & Green Lantern; 1st Batman team-up in Brave and the Bold	12	24	36	80	173	265
60-Teen Titans (2nd app.)-1st app. new Wonder Girl (Donna Troy), who joins Titans (6-7/65)	50	100	150	400	900	1400
61-Origin Starman & Black Canary by Anderson	12	24	36	82	179	275
62-Origin Starman & Black Canary cont'd. 62-1st S.A. app. Wildcat (10-11/65); 1st S.A. app. of G.A. Huntress (W.W. villain)	10	20	30	69	147	225
63-Supergirl & Wonder Woman	9	18	27	62	126	190
64-Batman Versus Eclipso (see H.O.S. #61)	8	16	24	51	96	140
65-Flash & Doom Patrol (4-5/66)	6	12	18	38	69	100

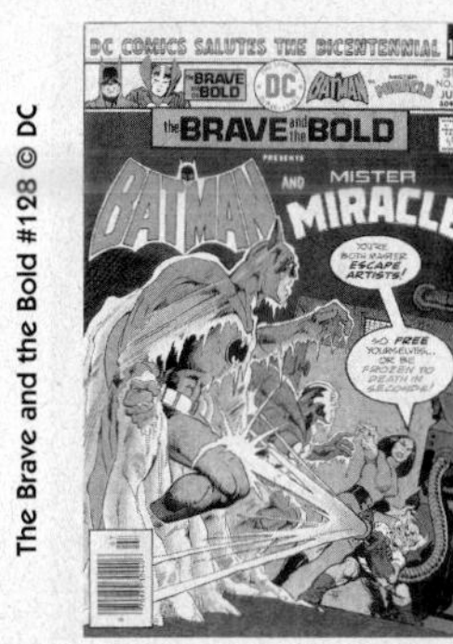

The Brave and the Bold #128 © DC

The Brave and the Bold #197 © DC

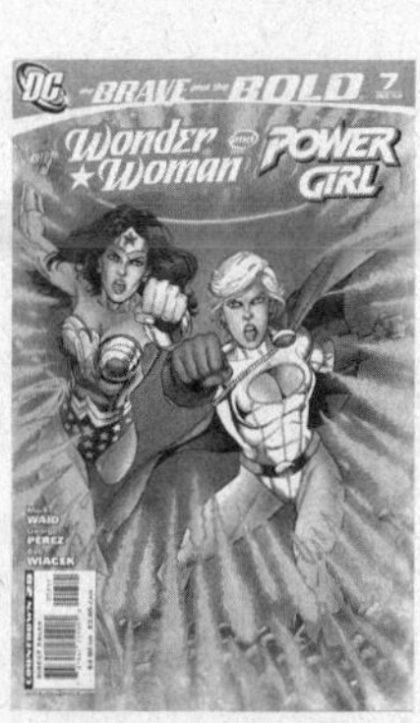

The Brave and the Bold (2007 series) #7 © DC

GD VG FN VF VF/NM NM-
2.0 4.0 6.0 8.0 9.0 9.2

66-Metamorpho & Metal Men (6-7/66) 6 12 18 38 69 100
67-Batman & The Flash by Infantino; Batman team-ups begin, end #200 (8-9/66) 7 14 21 49 92 135
68-Batman/Metamorpho/Joker/Riddler/Penguin-c/story; Batman as Bat-Hulk (Hulk parody) 8 16 24 51 96 140
69-Batman & Green Lantern 6 12 18 38 69 100
70-Batman & Hawkman; Craig-a(p) 6 12 18 38 69 100
71-Batman & Green Arrow 6 12 18 38 69 100
72-Spectre & Flash (6-7/67); 4th app. The Spectre; predates Spectre #1 6 12 18 40 73 105
73-Aquaman & The Atom 6 12 18 37 66 95
74-Batman & Metal Men 6 12 18 37 66 95
75-Batman & The Spectre (12-1/67-68); 6th app. Spectre; came out between Spectre #1 & #2 6 12 18 41 76 110
76-Batman & Plastic Man (2-3/68); came out between Plastic Man #8 & #9 6 12 18 37 66 95
77-Batman & The Atom 6 12 18 37 66 95
78-Batman, Wonder Woman & Batgirl 7 14 21 44 82 120
79-Batman & Deadman by Neal Adams (8-9/68); early Deadman app. 10 20 30 65 135 205
80-Batman & Creeper (10-11/68); N. Adams-a; early app. The Creeper; came out between Creeper #3 & #4 8 16 24 52 99 145
81-Batman & Flash; N. Adams-a 8 16 24 52 99 145
82-Batman & Aquaman; N. Adams-a; origin Ocean Master retold (2-3/69) 9 18 27 57 111 165
83-Batman & Teen Titans; N. Adams-a (4-5/69) 8 16 24 52 99 145
84-Batman (G.A., 1st S.A. app.) & Sgt. Rock; N. Adams-a; last 12¢ issue (6-7/69) 8 16 24 52 99 145
85-Batman & Green Arrow; 1st new costume for Green Arrow by Neal Adams (8-9/69) 14 28 42 94 207 320
86-Batman & Deadman (10-11/69); N. Adams-a; story concludes from Strange Adventures #216 (1-2/69) 8 16 24 55 105 155
87-Batman & Wonder Woman 4 8 12 27 44 60
88-Batman & Wildcat 4 8 12 27 44 60
89-Batman & Phantom Stranger (4-5/70); early Phantom Stranger app. (came out between Phantom Stranger #6 & 7 4 8 12 27 44 60
90-Batman & Adam Strange 4 8 12 27 44 60
91-Batman & Black Canary (8-9/70) 4 8 12 27 44 60
92-Batman; intro the Bat Squad 4 8 12 27 44 60
93-Batman-House of Mystery; N. Adams-a 9 18 27 59 117 175
94-Batman-Teen Titans 4 8 12 28 47 65
95-Batman & Plastic Man 3 6 9 21 33 45
96-Batman & Sgt. Rock; last 15¢ issue 3 6 9 21 33 45
97-Batman & Wildcat; 52 pg. issues begin, end #102; reprints origin & 1st app. Deadman from Strange Advs. #205 3 6 9 21 33 45
98-Batman & Phantom Stranger; 1st Jim Aparo Batman-a? 3 6 9 21 33 45
99-Batman & Flash 3 6 9 21 33 45
100-(2-3/72, 25¢, 52 pgs.)-Batman-Green Lantern-Green Arrow-Black Canary-Robin; Deadman-r by Adams/Str. Advs. #210 5 10 15 35 63 90
101-Batman & Metamorpho; Kubert Viking Prince 3 6 9 20 31 42
102-Batman-Teen Titans; N. Adams-a(p) 5 10 15 31 53 75
103-107,109,110: Batman team-ups: 103-Metal Men. 104-Deadman. 105-Wonder Woman. 106-Green Arrow. 107-Black Canary. 109-Demon. 110-Wildcat 3 6 9 15 22 28
108-Sgt. Rock 3 6 9 16 23 30
111-Batman/Joker-c/story 4 8 12 25 40 55
112-117: All 100 pgs.; Batman team-ups: 112-Mr. Miracle. 113-Metal Men; reprints origin/1st Hawkman from Brave and the Bold #34; r/origin Multi-Man/Challengers #14. 114-Aquaman. 115-Atom; r/origin Viking Prince from #23; r/Dr. Fate/Hourman/Solomon Grundy/Green Lantern from Showcase #55. 116-Spectre. 117-Sgt. Rock; last 100 pg. issue 5 10 15 30 50 70
118-Batman/Wildcat/Joker-c/story 3 6 9 19 30 40
119,121-123,125-128,132-140: Batman team-ups: 119-Man-Bat. 121-Metal Men. 122-Swamp Thing. 123-Plastic Man/Metamorpho. 125-Flash. 126-Aquaman. 127-Wildcat. 128-Mr. Miracle. 132-Kung-Fu Fighter. 133-Deadman. 134-Green Lantern. 135-Metal Men. 136-Metal Men/Green Arrow. 137-Demon. 138-Mr. Miracle. 139-Hawkman. 140-Wonder Woman 2 4 6 8 10 12
120-Kamandi (68 pgs.) 3 6 9 14 19 24
124-Sgt. Rock; Jim Aparo app. on cover & in story 2 4 6 10 14 18
129,130-Batman/Green Arrow/Atom parts 1 & 2; Joker & Two Face-c/stories 3 6 9 15 22 28
131-Batman & Wonder Woman vs. Catwoman-c/sty 2 4 6 11 16 20
141-Batman/Black Canary vs. Joker-c/story 3 6 9 14 19 24
142-160: Batman team-ups: 142-Aquaman. 143-Creeper; origin Human Target (44 pgs.). 144-Green Arrow; origin Human Target part 2 (44 pgs.). 145-Phantom Stranger. 146-G.A. Batman/Unknown Soldier. 147-Supergirl. 148-Plastic Man; X-Mas-c. 149-Teen Titans. 150-Anniversary issue; Superman. 151-Flash. 152-Atom. 153-Red Tornado. 154-Metamorpho. 155-Green Lantern. 156-Dr. Fate. 157-Batman vs. Kamandi (ties into Kamandi #59). 158-Wonder Woman. 159-Ra's Al Ghul. 160-Supergirl. 1 3 4 6 8 10
145(11/79)-147,150-159,165(8/80)-(Whitman variants; low print run; none show issue # on cover) 2 4 6 10 14 18
161-181,183-190,192-195,198,199: Batman team-ups: 161-Adam Strange. 162-G.A. Batman/Sgt. Rock. 163-Black Lightning. 164-Hawkman. 165-Man-Bat. 166-Black Canary; Nemesis (intro) back-up story begins, ends #192; Penguin-c/story. 167-G.A. Batman/Blackhawk; origin Nemesis. 168-Green Arrow. 169-Zatanna. 170-Nemesis. 171-Scalphunter. 172-Firestorm. 173-Guardians of the Universe. 174-Green Lantern. 175-Lois Lane. 176-Swamp Thing. 177-Elongated Man. 178-Creeper. 179-Legion. 180-Spectre. 181-Hawk & Dove. 183-Riddler. 184-Huntress & Earth II Batman. 185-Green Arrow. 186-Hawkman. 187-Metal Men. 188,189-Rose & the Thorn. 190-Adam Strange. 192-Superboy vs. Mr. I.Q. 194-Flash. 195-I...Vampire. 198-Karate Kid. 199-Batman vs. The Spectre 6.00
182-G.A. Robin; G.A. Starman app.; 1st modern app. G.A. Batwoman 2 4 6 8 11 14
191-Batman/Joker-c/story; Nemesis app. 3 6 9 14 20 25
196-Ragman; origin Ragman retold. 1 2 3 5 6 8
197-Catwoman; Earth II Batman & Catwoman marry; 2nd modern app. of G.A. Batwoman; Scarecrow story in Golden Age style 3 6 9 14 20 26
200-Double-sized (64 pgs.); printed on Mando paper; Earth One & Earth Two Batman app. in separate stories; intro/1st app. Batman & The Outsiders; 1st app. Katana 3 6 9 18 28 38

NOTE: ***Neal Adams*** *a-79-86, 93, 100r, 102; c-75, 76, 79-86, 88-90, 93, 95, 99, 100r.* ***M. Anderson*** *a-115r; c-72i, 96i.* ***Andru/Esposito*** *c-25-27.* ***Aparo*** *a-98, 100-102, 104-125, 126i, 127-136, 138-145, 147, 148i, 149-152, 154, 155, 157-162, 168-170, 173-178, 180-182, 184, 186i-189i, 191i-193i, 195, 196, 200; c-105-109, 111-136, 137i, 138-175, 177, 180-184, 186-200.* ***Austin*** *a-166i.* ***Bernard Baily*** *c-32, 33, 58.* ***Buckler*** *a-185, 186p; c-137, 178p, 185p, 186p.* ***Giordano*** *a-143, 144.* ***Infantino*** *a-67p, 72p, 97r, 98r, 115r, 172p, 183p, 190p, 194p; c-45-49, 67p, 69p, 70p, 72p, 96p, 98r.* ***Kaluta*** *c-176.* ***Kane*** *a-115r; c-59, 64.* ***Kubert*** *&/or* ***Heath*** *a-1-24; reprints-101, 113, 115, 117.* ***Kubert*** *a-99r; c-22-24, 34-36, 40, 42-44, 52.* ***Mooney*** *a-114r.* ***Mortimer*** *a-64, 69.* ***Newton*** *a-153p, 156p, 165p.* ***Irv Novick*** *c-1(part), 2-21.* ***Fred Ray*** *a-78r.* ***Roussos*** *a-50, 76i, 114r.* ***Staton*** *148p. 52 pgs.-97, 100; 68 pgs.-120; 100 pgs.-112-117.*

BRAVE AND THE BOLD, THE
DC Comics: Dec, 1991 - No. 6, June, 1992 ($1.75, limited series)

1-6: Green Arrow, The Butcher, The Question in all; Grell scripts in all 4.00
NOTE: ***Grell*** *c-3, 4-6.*

BRAVE AND THE BOLD, THE
DC Comics: Apr, 2007 - No. 35, Aug, 2010 ($2.99)

1-Batman & Green Lantern team-up; Roulette app.; Waid-s/Peréz-c/a; 2 covers 5.00
2-32,34,35: 2-GL & Supergirl. 3-Batman & Blue Beetle vs. Fatal Five; Lobo app. 4-6-LSH app. 12-Megistus conclusion; Ordway-a. 14-Kolins-a. 16-Superman & Catwoman. 28-Blackhawks app. 29-Batman/Brother Power the Geek. 31-Atom/Joker 3.00
33-Batgirl, Zatanna & W.W.; prelude to Killing Joke 3 6 9 16 23 30
...: Demons and Dragons HC (2009, $24.99, dustjacket) r/#13-16; Brave & the Bold V1 #181, Flash V3 #107 and Impulse #17; Mark Waid commentary 25.00
...: Demons and Dragons SC (2010, $17.99) same contents as HC 18.00
...: Milestone SC (2010, $17.99) r/#24-26 and Static #12, Hardware #16, Xombi #6 18.00
Team-ups of the Brave and the Bold HC (2010, $24.99) r/#27-33 25.00
...: The Book of Destiny HC (2008, $24.99, dustjacket) r/#7-12; Ordway sketch pages 25.00
...: The Book of Destiny SC (2009, $17.99) r/#7-12; Ordway sketch pages 18.00
...: The Lords of Luck HC (2007, $24.99, dustjacket) r/#1-6 with Waid intro & annotations 25.00
...: The Lords of Luck SC (2008, $17.99) r/#1-6 with Waid intro & annotations 18.00
...: Without Sin SC (2009, $17.99) r/#17-22 18.00

BRAVE AND THE BOLD ANNUAL NO. 1 1969 ISSUE, THE
DC Comics: 2001 ($5.95, one-shot)

1-Reprints Silver Age team-ups in 1960s-style 80 pg. Giant format 6.00

BRAVE AND THE BOLD: BATMAN AND WONDER WOMAN, THE
DC Comics: Apr, 2018 - No. 6, Sept, 2018 ($3.99, limited series)

1-6-Liam Sharp-s/a 4.00

BRAVE AND THE BOLD SPECIAL, THE (See DC Special Series No. 8)

BRAVE EAGLE (TV)
Dell Publishing Co.: No. 705, June, 1956 - No. 929, July, 1958

Four Color 705 (#1)-Photo-c 6 12 18 42 79 115
Four Color 770, 816, 879 (2/58), 929-All photo-c 5 10 15 31 53 75

BRAVE NEW WORLD (See DCU Brave New World)

BRAVE OLD WORLD (V2K)
DC Comics (Vertigo): Feb, 2000 - No. 4, May, 2000 ($2.50, mini-series)

1-4-Messner-Loeb-s/Guy Davis & Phil Hester-a 3.00

BRAVE ONE, THE (Movie)

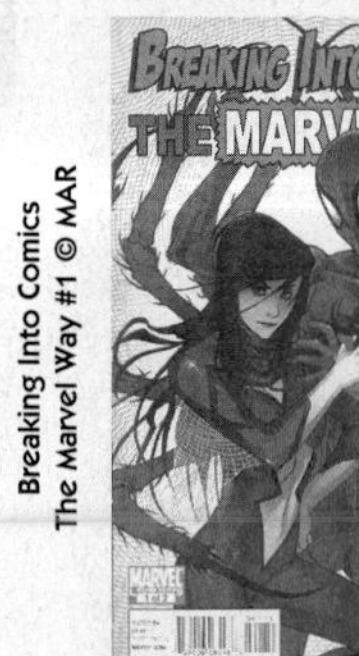

Breaking Into Comics The Marvel Way #1 © MAR

Brenda Starr #13 (#1) © SUPR

Brigade #3 © Image

	GD 2.0	VG 4.0	FN 6.0	VF 8.0	VF/NM 9.0	NM- 9.2

Dell Publishing Co.: No. 773, Mar, 1957

Four Color 773-Photo-c	5	10	15	34	60	85

BRAVEST WARRIORS (Based on the animated web series)
BOOM! Entertainment (KaBOOM): Oct, 2012 - No. 36, Sept, 2015 ($3.99)

1-36-Multiple covers on each						4.00
2014 Annual (1/14, $4.99) Short stories featuring Catbug; multiple covers						5.00
2014 Impossibear Special 1 (6/14, $4.99) Short stories; multiple covers						5.00
... Paralyzed Horse Giant 1 (11/14, $4.99) Short stories; multiple covers						5.00
...: Tales From the Holo John 1 (5/15, $4.99) Short stories; multiple covers						5.00

BRAVURA
Malibu Comics (Bravura): 1995 (mail-in offer)

0-wraparound holographic-c; short stories and promo pin-ups of Chaykin's Power & Glory, Gil Kane's & Steven Grant's Edge, Starlin's Breed, & Simonson's Star Slammers						5.00
1 1/2						7.00

BREACH
DC Comics: Mar, 2005 - No. 11, Jan, 2006 ($2.95/$2.50)

1-11: 1-Marcos Martin-a/Bob Harras-s; origin. 4-JLA-c/app.						3.00

BREAKDOWN
Devil's Due Publ.: Oct, 2004 - No. 6, Apr, 2005 ($2.95)

1-6: 1-Two covers by Dave Ross and Leinil Yu; Dixon-s/Ross-a						3.00

BREAKFAST AFTER NOON
Oni Press: May, 2000 - No. 6, Jan, 2001 ($2.95, B&W, limited series)

1-6-Andi Watson-s/a						3.00
TPB (2001, $19.95) r/series						20.00

BREAKING INTO COMICS THE MARVEL WAY
Marvel Comics: May, 2010 - No. 2, May, 2010 ($3.99, limited series)

1,2-Short stories by various newcomer artists; artist profiles						4.00

BREAKNECK BLVD.
MotioN Comics/Slave Labor Graphics Vol. 2: No. 0, Feb, 1994 - No. 2, Nov, 1994; Vol. 2#1, Jul, 1995 - #6, Dec., 1996 ($2.50/$2.95, B&W)

0-2, V2#1-6: 0-Pérez/Giordano-c						3.00

BREAK-THRU (Also see Exiles V1#4)
Malibu Comics (Ultraverse): Dec, 1993 - No. 2, Jan, 1994 ($2.50, 44 pgs.)

1,2-Pérez-c/a(p); has x-overs in Ultraverse titles						4.00

BREATH OF BONES: A TALE OF THE GOLEM
Dark Horse Comics: Jun, 2013 - No. 3, Aug, 2013 ($3.99, B&W, limited series)

1-3-Niles-s/Wachter-a						4.00

BREATHTAKER
DC Comics: 1990 - No. 4, 1990 ($4.95, 52 pgs., prestige format, mature)

Book 1-4: Mark Wheatley-painted-c/a & scripts; Marc Hempel-a						5.00
TPB (1994, $14.95) r/#1-4; intro by Neil Gaiman						15.00

'BREED
Malibu Comics (Bravura): Jan, 1994 - No. 6, 1994 ($2.50, limited series)

1-(48 pgs.)-Origin/1st app. of 'Breed by Starlin; contains Bravura stamps; spot varnish-c						4.00
2-6: 2-5-contains Bravura stamps. 6-Death of Rachel						3.00
...:Book of Genesis (1994, $12.95)-reprints #1-6						13.00

'BREED II
Malibu Comics (Bravura): Nov, 1994 - No. 6, Apr, 1995 ($2.95, limited series)

1-6: Starlin-c/a/scripts in all. 1-Gold edition						3.00

'BREED III
Image Comics: May, 2011 - No. 7, Dec, 2011 ($2.99)

1-7: Starlin-c/a/scripts in all						3.00

BREEZE LAWSON, SKY SHERIFF (See Sky Sheriff)

BRENDA LEE'S LIFE STORY
Dell Publishing Co.: July-Sept., 1962

01-078-209	8	16	24	51	86	120

BRENDA STARR (Also see All Great)
Four Star Comics Corp./Superior Comics Ltd.: No. 13, 9/47; No. 14, 3/48; V2#3, 6/48 - V2#12, 12/49

V1#13-By Dale Messick	113	226	339	718	1234	1750
14-Classic Kamen bondage-c	541	1082	1623	3950	6975	10,000
V2#3-Baker-a?	84	168	252	538	919	1300
4-Used in **SOTI**, pg. 21; Kamen-c	110	220	330	704	1202	1700
5-10	74	148	222	470	810	1150
11,12 (Scarce)	77	154	231	493	847	1200

NOTE: *Newspaper reprints plus original material through #6. All original #7 on.*

BRENDA STARR (...Reporter)(Young Lovers No. 16 on?)
Charlton Comics: No. 13, June, 1955 - No. 15, Oct, 1955

13-15-Newspaper-r	33	66	99	197	321	445

BRENDA STARR REPORTER
Dell Publishing Co.: Oct, 1963

1	10	20	30	68	144	220

BRER RABBIT (See Kite Fun Book, Walt Disney Showcase #28 and Wheaties)
Dell Publishing Co.: No. 129, 1946; No. 208, Jan, 1949; No. 693, 1956 (Disney)

Four Color 129 (#1)-Adapted from Disney movie "Song of the South"	25	50	75	175	388	600
Four Color 208 (1/49)	10	20	30	70	150	230
Four Color 693-Part-r #129	8	16	24	51	96	140

BRIAN PULIDO'S LADY DEATH... (See Lady Death)

BRICK BRADFORD (Also see Ace Comics & King Comics)
King Features Syndicate/Standard: No. 5, July, 1948 - No. 8, July, 1949 (Ritt & Grey reprints)

5	21	42	63	124	202	280
6-Robot-c (by Schomburg?).	226	452	678	1446	2473	3500
7-Schomburg-c. 8-Says #7 inside, #8 on-c	18	36	54	103	162	220

BRICKLEBERRY (Based on the animated series)
Dynamite Entertainment: 2016 - No. 4, 2016 ($3.99, limited series)

1-4-Waco O'Guin & Roger Black-s						4.00

BRIDE'S DIARY (Formerly Black Cobra No. 3)
Ajax/Farrell Publ.: No. 4, May, 1955 - No. 10, Aug, 1956

4 (#1)	13	26	39	74	105	135
5-8	10	20	30	54	72	90
9,10-Disbrow-a	11	22	33	62	86	110

BRIDES IN LOVE (Hollywood Romances & Summer Love No. 46 on)
Charlton Comics: Aug, 1956 - No. 45, Feb, 1965

1	15	30	45	84	127	170
2	9	18	27	47	61	75
3-6,8-10	4	8	12	25	40	55
7-(68 pgs.)	5	10	15	30	50	70
11-20	3	6	9	17	26	35
21-45	3	6	9	14	20	25

BRIDES OF HELHEIM
Oni Press: Oct, 2014 - No. 6, May, 2015 ($3.99)

1-6-Cullen Bunn-s/Joëlle Jones-a						4.00

BRIDES ROMANCES
Quality Comics Group: Nov, 1953 - No. 23, Dec, 1956

1	22	44	66	130	213	295
2	14	28	42	76	108	140
3-10: Last precode (3/55)	13	26	39	74	105	135
11-17,19-22: 15-Baker-a(p)?; Colan-a	12	24	36	67	94	120
18-Baker-a	14	28	42	82	121	160
23-Baker-c/a	22	44	66	132	216	300

BRIDE'S SECRETS
Ajax/Farrell(Excellent Publ.)/Four-Star: Apr-May, 1954 - No. 19, May, 1958

1	19	38	57	109	172	235
2	13	26	39	72	101	130
3-6: Last precode (3/55)	11	22	33	60	83	105
7-11,13-19: 18-Hollingsworth-a	10	20	30	56	76	95
12-Disbrow-a	11	22	33	62	86	110

BRIDE-TO-BE ROMANCES (See True...)

BRIGADE
Image Comics (Extreme Studios): Aug, 1992 - No. 4, 1993 ($1.95, lim. series)

1-Liefeld part plots/scripts in all, Liefeld-c(p); contains 2 Brigade trading cards						4.00
1-Gold foil stamped logo edition						8.00
2-Contains coupon for Image Comics #0 & 2 trading cards						3.00
2-With coupon missing						2.00
3,4: 3-Contains 2 trading cards; 1st Birds of Prey. 4-Flip book featuring Youngblood #5						3.00

BRIGADE
Image Comics (Extreme): V2#1, May, 1993 - V2#22, July, 1995, V2#25, May, 1996 ($1.95/$2.50)

V2#1-22,25: 1-Gatefold-c; Liefeld co-plots; Blood Brothers part 1; Bloodstrike app. 2-(6/93, V2#1 on inside)-Foil merricote-c (newsstand ed. w/out foil-c exists). 3-Perez-c(i); Liefeld scripts.

Briggs Land: Lone Wolves #3 © Brian Wood

Broadway Romances #2 © QUA

The Brotherhood #4 © MAR

	GD 2.0	VG 4.0	FN 6.0	VF 8.0	VF/NM 9.0	NM- 9.2

8,9-Coupons #2 & 6 for Extreme Prejudice #0 bound-in. 11-(8/94, $2.50) WildC.A.T.S app.
16-Polybagged w/ trading card. 22-"Supreme Apocalypse" Pt. 4; w/ trading card 3.00
0-(9/93)-Liefeld scripts; 1st app. Warcry; Youngblood & Wildcats app.; 3.00
20-Variant-c. by Quesada & Palmiotti 3.00
Sourcebook 1 (8/94, $2.95) 3.00
1-(Awesome Ent., 7/00, $2.99) Flip book w/Century preview 4.00
1-(6/10, $3.99) Liefeld-s/Mychaels-a; covers by Liefeld & Mychaels 4.00

BRIGAND, THE (See Fawcett Movie Comics No. 18)

BRIGGS LAND
Dark Horse Comics: Aug, 2016 - No. 6, Jan, 2017 ($3.99)
1-6-Brian Wood-s/Mack Chater-a/Tula Lotay-c 4.00

BRIGGS LAND: LONE WOLVES
Dark Horse Comics: Jun, 2017 - No. 6, Nov, 2017 ($3.99)
1-6: 1-Brian Wood-s/Mack Chater-a/Matthew Woodson-c. 4-Del Ray-a 4.00

BRIGHTEST DAY (Also see Blackest Night and Green Lantern)
DC Comics: No. 0, Jun, 2010 - No. 24, Late Jun, 2011 ($3.99/$2.99)
0-($3.99) Johns & Tomasi-s/Pasarin-a/Finch-c 4.00
0-Variant-c by Reis 8.00
1-23-($2.99) 1-Black Manta returns. 4-Intro. Jackson (new Aqualad) 16-Aqualad origin.
18-Hawkman & Hawkgirl killed. 20-Aquaman killed 3.00
1-23: Variant covers. 1-6,9-18,20-23-by Reis, 7,8 White Lantern by Sook. 19-by Frank 6.00
24-($4.99) Swamp Thing and John Constantine return to DC universe 5.00
24-($4.99) Variant cover by Reis 8.00
...: The Atom Special (9/10, $2.99) Lemire-s/Asrar-a/Frank-c 3.00
... Volume 1 HC (2010, $29.99) r/#0-7; cover gallery 30.00
... Volume 2 HC (2011, $29.99) r/#8-16; cover gallery 30.00

BRIGHTEST DAY AFTERMATH: THE SEARCH FOR SWAMP THING
DC Comics: Aug, 2011 - No. 3, Oct, 2011 ($2.99, limited series)
1-3-Vankin-s/Castiello-a; covers by Syaf & Jones; John Constantine & Zatanna app. 3.00

BRILLIANT
Marvel Comics (Icon): Jul, 2011 - No. 5, Mar, 2014 ($3.95, limited series)
1-5-Bendis-s/Bagley-a/c 4.00

BRILLIANT TRASH
AfterShock Comics: Nov, 2017 - No. 6, May, 2018 ($3.99)
1-6: 1-Tim Seeley-s/Priscilla Petraites-a. 6-Steve Kurth-a 4.00

BRING BACK THE BAD GUYS (Also see Fireside Book Series)
Marvel Comics: 1998 ($24.95, TPB)
1-Reprints stories of Marvel villains' secrets 25.00

BRINGING UP FATHER
Dell Publishing Co.: No. 9, 1942 - No. 37, 1944

	GD	VG	FN	VF	VF/NM	NM-
Large Feature Comic 9	37	74	111	222	361	500
Four Color 37	19	38	57	129	287	445

BRING ON THE BAD GUYS (See Fireside Book Series)

BRING THE THUNDER
Dynamite Entertainment: 2010 - No. 4, 2011 ($3.99)
1-4-Alex Ross-c/Ross & Nitz-s/Tortosa-a 4.00

BRITANNIA
Valiant Entertainment: Sept, 2016 - No. 4, Dec, 2016 ($3.99, limited series)
1-4-Milligan-a/Ryp-a; set in 60-66 A.D.; Emperor Nero app. 4.00
... One Dollar Debut #1 (5/19, $1.00) r/#1 3.00

BRITANNIA: LOST EAGLES OF ROME
Valiant Entertainment: Jul, 2018 - No. 4, Oct, 2018 ($3.99, limited series)
1-4-Milligan-a/Gill-a; Antonius Axia and Achillia in Egypt; multiple covers on each 4.00

BRITANNIA: WE WHO ARE ABOUT TO DIE
Valiant Entertainment: Apr, 2017 - No. 4, Jul, 2017 ($3.99, limited series)
1-4-Milligan-a/Ryp-a; further story of Antonius Axia; multiple covers on each 4.00

BROADWAY HOLLYWOOD BLACKOUTS
Stanhall: Mar-Apr, 1954 - No. 3, July-Aug, 1954

	GD	VG	FN	VF	VF/NM	NM-
1	31	62	93	182	296	410
2,3	20	40	60	117	189	260

BROADWAY ROMANCES
Quality Comics Group: January, 1950 - No. 5, Sept, 1950

	GD	VG	FN	VF	VF/NM	NM-
1-Ward-c/a (9 pgs.); Gustavson-a	47	94	141	296	498	700
2-Ward-a (9 pgs.); photo-c	31	62	93	182	296	410
3-5: All-Photo-c	18	36	54	103	162	220

BROKEN ARROW (TV)
Dell Publishing Co.: No. 855, Oct, 1957 - No. 947, Nov, 1958

	GD	VG	FN	VF	VF/NM	NM-
Four Color 855 (#1)-Photo-c	6	12	18	38	69	100
Four Color 947-Photo-c	5	10	15	31	53	75

BROKEN CROSS, THE (See The Crusaders)

BROKEN MOON
American Gothic Press: Sept, 2015 - No. 4, Jan, 2016 ($3.99, limited series)
1-4-Steve Niles-s/Nat Jones-a; covers by Jones & Sanjulian 4.00

BROKEN PIECES
Aspen MLT: No. 0, Sept, 2011; Oct, 2011 - No. 5, Dec, 2012 ($2.50/$3.50, limited series)
0-($2.50)-Roslan-s/Kaneshiro-a; three covers 3.00
1-5: 1-($3.50)-Roslan-s/Kaneshiro-a; three covers 3.50

BROKEN TRINITY
Image Comics (Top Cow): July, 2008 - No. 3, Nov, 2008 ($2.99, limited series)
1-3-Witchblade, Darkness & Angelus app.; Marz-s/Sejic & Hester-a; two covers 3.00
...: Aftermath 1 (4/09, $2.99) Marz & Hill-s/Lucas & Kirkham-a 3.00
...: Angelus 1 (12/08, $2.99) Marz-s/Stelfreeze-a; two covers 3.00
...: Pandora's Box 1-6 (2/10 - No. 6, 4/11 $3.99) Tommy Lee Edwards-c 4.00
...: The Darkness 1 (8/08, $2.99) Hester-s/Lucas-a; two covers 3.00
...: Witchblade 1 (12/08, $2.99) Marz-s/Blake-a; two covers 3.00

BRONCHO BILL (See Comics On Parade, Sparkler & Tip Top Comics)
United Features Syndicate/Standard(Visual Editions) No. 5-on: 1939 - 1940; No. 5, 1?/48 - No. 16, 8?/50

	GD	VG	FN	VF	VF/NM	NM-
Single Series 2 ('39)	57	114	171	362	619	875
Single Series 19 ('40)(#2 on cvr)	43	86	129	271	461	650
5	15	30	45	88	137	185
6(4/48)-10(4/49)	10	20	30	58	79	100
11(6/49)-16	9	18	27	52	69	85

NOTE: ***Schomburg** c-6, 7, 9-13, 15, 16.*

BRONZE AGE BOOGIE
AHOY Comics: 2019 - No. 6, 2019 ($3.99, limited series)
1-6-Stuart Moore-s/Alberto Ponticelli-a 4.00

BROOKLYN ANIMAL CONTROL
IDW Publishing: Dec, 2015 ($7.99, square-bound, one-shot)
1-J.T. Petty-s/Stephen Thompson-a; werewolves in Brooklyn 8.00

BROOKS ROBINSON (See Baseball's Greatest Heroes #2)

BROTHER BILLY THE PAIN FROM PLAINS
Marvel Comics Group: 1979 (68pgs.)

	GD	VG	FN	VF	VF/NM	NM-
1-B&W comics, satire, Jimmy Carter-c & x-over w/Brother Billy peanut jokes. Joey Adams-a (scarce)	5	10	15	31	53	75

BROTHERHOOD, THE (Also see X-Men titles)
Marvel Comics: July, 2001 - No. 9, Mar, 2002 ($2.25)
1-Intro. Orwell & the Brotherhood; Ribic-a/X-s/Sienkiewicz-c 3.00
2-9: 2-Two covers (JG Jones & Sienkiewicz). 4-6-Fabry-c. 7-9-Phillips-c/a 3.00

BROTHER POWER, THE GEEK (See Saga of Swamp Thing Annual & Vertigo Visions)
National Periodical Publications: Sept-Oct, 1968 - No. 2, Nov-Dec, 1968

	GD	VG	FN	VF	VF/NM	NM-
1-Origin; Simon-c(i?)	5	10	15	31	53	75
2	3	6	9	19	30	40

BROTHERS DRACUL
AfterShock Comics: Apr, 2018 - No. 5, Aug, 2018 ($3.99, limited series)
1-5-Cullen Bunn-s/Mirko Colak-a 4.00

BROTHERS, HANG IN THERE, THE
Spire Christian Comics (Fleming H. Revell Co.): 1979 (49¢)

	GD	VG	FN	VF	VF/NM	NM-
nn	2	4	6	13	18	22

BROTHERS IN ARMS (Based on the World War II military video game)
Dynamite Entertainment: 2008 - No. 4, 2008 ($3.99/$3.50)
1-($3.99) Fabbri-a; two covers by Fabbri & Sejic 4.00
2-4-($3.50) Two covers by Fabbri & Sejic on each 3.50

BROTHERS OF THE SPEAR (Also see Tarzan)
Gold Key/Whitman No. 18: June, 1972 - No. 17, Feb, 1976; No. 18, May, 1982

	GD	VG	FN	VF	VF/NM	NM-
1	5	10	15	31	53	75
2-Painted-c begin, end #17	3	6	9	18	28	38
3-10	3	6	9	15	22	28
11-18: 12-Line drawn-c. 13-17-Spiegle-a. 18(5/82)-r/#2; Leopard Girl-r	2	4	6	11	16	20

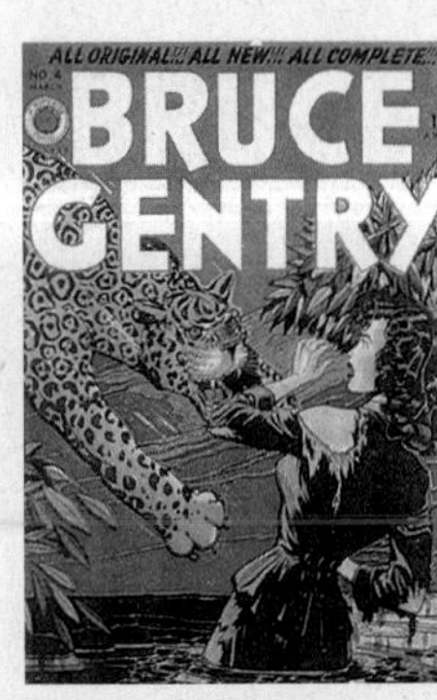
Bruce Gentry #4 © SUPR

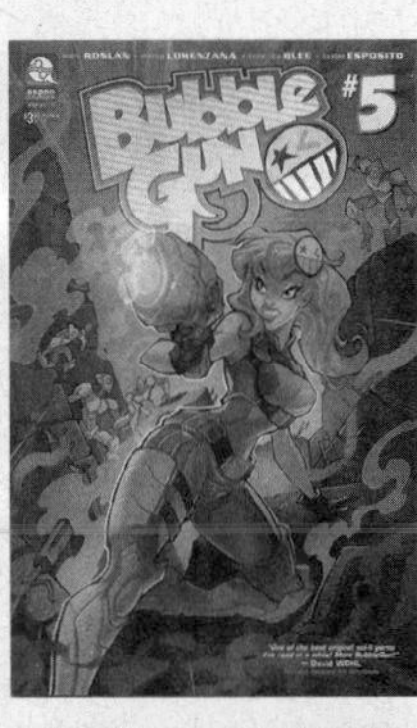
BubbleGun V2 #5 © AspenMLT

Buck Jones #2 © DELL

	GD 2.0	VG 4.0	FN 6.0	VF 8.0	VF/NM 9.0	NM- 9.2

BROTHERS, THE CULT ESCAPE, THE
Spire Christian Comics (Fleming H. Revell Co.): 1980 (49¢)

nn	3	6	9	14	19	24

BROWNIES (See New Funnies)
Dell Publishing Co.: No. 192, July, 1948 - No. 605, Dec, 1954

Four Color 192(#1)-Kelly-a	13	26	39	91	201	310
Four Color 244(9/49), 293 (9/50)-Last Kelly c/a	10	20	30	64	132	200
Four Color 337(7-8/51), 365(12-1/51-52), 398(5/52)	6	12	18	38	69	100
Four Color 436(11/52), 482(7/53), 522(12/53), 605	5	10	15	35	63	90

BRUCE GENTRY
Better/Standard/Four Star Publ./Superior No. 3: Jan, 1948 - No. 8, Jul, 1949

1-Ray Bailey strip reprints begin, end #3; E.C. emblem appears as a monogram on stationery in story; negligee panels	77	154	231	493	847	1200
2,3: 2-Negligee panels	41	82	123	256	428	600
4-8	30	60	90	177	289	400

NOTE: *Kamenish a-2-7; c-1-8.*

BRUCE JONES' OUTER EDGE
Innovation: 1993 ($2.50, B&W, one-shot)

1-Bruce Jones-c/a/script 3.00

BRUCE LEE (Also see Deadly Hands of Kung Fu)
Malibu Comics: July, 1994 - No. 6, Dec, 1994 ($2.95, 36 pgs.)

1-6: 1-(44 pgs.)-Mortal Kombat prev., 1st app. in comics. 2,6-(36 pgs.) 6.00

BRUCE WAYNE: AGENT OF S.H.I.E.L.D. (Also see Marvel Vs. DC #3 & DC Vs. Marvel #4)
Marvel Comics (Amalgam): Apr, 1996 ($1.95, one-shot)

1-Chuck Dixon scripts & Cary Nord-c/a. 3.00

BRUCE WAYNE: THE ROAD HOME (See Batman: The Return of Bruce Wayne)
(See Batman: Bruce Wayne - The Road Home HC for reprints)
DC Comics: Dec, 2010 ($2.99, series of one-shots with interlocking covers)

...: Batgirl 1 - Bryan Miller-s/Pere Pérez-a 5.00
...: Batman and Robin 1 - Nicieza-s/Richards-a; Vicki Vale app. 5.00
...: Catwoman 1 - Fridolfs-s/Nguyen-a; Harley & Ivy app. 5.00
...: Commissioner Gordon 1 - Beechen-s/Kudranski-a; Penguin app. 5.00
...: Oracle 1 - Andreyko-s/Padilla-a; Man-Bat & Manhunter app. 5.00
...: Outsiders 1 - Barr-s/Saltares-a 5.00
...: Ra's al Ghul 1 - Nicieza-s/McDaniel-a 5.00
...: Red Robin 1 - Nicieza-s/Bachs-a; Ra's al Ghul app. 5.00

BRUTAL NATURE
IDW Publishing: May, 2016 - No. 4, Aug, 2016 ($3.99, limited series)

1-4-Ariel Olivetti-a/Luciano Saracino-s 4.00

BRUTAL NATURE: CONCRETE FURY
IDW Publishing: Mar, 2017 - No. 5, Jul, 2017 ($3.99, limited series)

1-5-Ariel Olivetti-a/Luciano Saracino-s 4.00

BRUTE, THE
Seaboard Publ. (Atlas): Feb, 1975 - No. 3, July, 1975

1-Origin & 1st app; Sekowsky-a(p)	3	6	9	17	26	35
2-Sekowsky-a(p); Fleisher-s	2	4	6	10	14	18
3-Brunner/Starlin/Weiss-a(p)	2	4	6	13	18	22

BRUTE & BABE
Ominous Press: July, 1994 - No. 2, Aug, 1994

1-($3.95, 8 tablets plus-c)-"...It Begins..."; tablet format 4.00
2-($2.50, 36 pgs.)-"Mael's Rage", 2-(40 pgs.)-Stiff additional variant-c 3.00

BRUTE FORCE
Marvel Comics: Aug, 1990 - No. 4, Nov, 1990 ($1.00, limited series)

1-4: Animal super-heroes; Delbo & DeCarlo-a 3.00

B-SIDES (The Craptacular...)
Marvel Comics: Nov, 2002 - No. 3, Jan, 2003 ($2.99, limited series)

1-3-Kieth-c/Weldele-a. 2-Dorkin-a (1 pg.) 2-FF cameo. 3-FF app. 3.00

BUBBA HO-TEP AND THE COSMIC BLOODSUCKERS
IDW Publications: Mar, 2018 - No. 5, Jul, 2018 ($3.99, limited series)

1-5-Jabcuga-s/Galusha-a; Elvis Presley vs. vampires and voodoo; Nixon app. 4.00

BUBBLEGUM CRISIS: GRAND MAL
Dark Horse Comics: Mar, 1994 - No. 4, June, 1994 ($2.50, limited series)

1-4-Japanese manga 4.00

BUBBLEGUN
Aspen MLT: Jun, 2013 - No. 5, Mar, 2014 ($1.00/$3.99)

1-($1.00) Roslan-s/Bowden-a; multiple covers 3.00
2-5-($3.99) Multiple covers on each 4.00

BUBBLEGUN (Volume 2)
Aspen MLT: May, 2017 - No. 5, Sept, 2017 ($3.99)

1-5-Roslan-s/Tovar-a; multiple covers 4.00

BUCCANEER
I. W. Enterprises: No date (1963)

I.W. Reprint #1(r-/Quality #20), #8(r-/#23): Crandall-a in each	3	6	9	16	23	30

BUCCANEERS (Formerly Kid Eternity)
Quality Comics: No. 19, Jan, 1950 - No. 27, May, 1951 (No. 24-27: 52 pgs.)

19-Captain Daring, Black Roger, Eric Falcon & Spanish Main begin; Crandall-a	50	100	150	315	533	750
20,23-Crandall-a	37	74	111	222	361	500
21-Crandall-c/a	39	78	117	240	395	550
22-Bondage-c	29	58	87	170	278	385
24-26: 24-Adam Peril, U.S.N. begins. 25-Origin & 1st app. Corsair Queen. 26-Last Spanish Main	24	48	72	142	234	325
27-Crandall-c/a	34	68	102	205	335	465
Super Reprint #12 (1964)-Crandall-r/#21	3	6	9	16	23	30

BUCCANEERS, THE (TV)
Dell Publishing Co.: No. 800, 1957

Four Color 800-Photo-c	6	12	18	42	79	115

BUCKAROO BANZAI (Movie)
Marvel Comics Group: Dec, 1984 - No. 2, Feb, 1985

1-Movie adaptation; r/Marvel Super Special #33; Texiera-c/a	1	2	3	5	6	8
2-Adaptation continues						5.00

BUCKAROO BANZAI: RETURN OF THE SCREW
Moonstone: 2006 - No. 3, 2006 ($3.50, limited series)

1-3: 1-Three covers by Haley, Stribling, Beck; Thompson-a 3.50
Preview (2006, 50¢) B&W preview; history of movie and spin-off projects 3.00

BUCK DUCK
Atlas Comics (ANC): June, 1953 - No. 4, Dec, 1953

1-Funny animal stories in all	20	40	60	117	189	260
2-4: 2-Ed Win-a(5)	13	26	39	72	101	130

BUCK JONES (Also see Crackajack Funnies, Famous Feature Stories, Master Comics #7 & Wow Comics #1, 1936)
Dell Publishing Co.: No. 299, Oct, 1950 - No. 850, Oct, 1957 (All Painted-c)

Four Color 299(#1)-Buck Jones & his horse Silver-B begin; painted back-c begins, ends #5	13	26	39	86	188	290
2(4-6/51)	7	14	21	46	86	125
3-8(10-12/52)	6	12	18	38	69	100
Four Color 460,500,546,589	6	12	18	42	79	115
Four Color 652,733,850	5	10	15	35	63	90

BUCK ROGERS (Also see Famous Funnies, Pure Oil Comics, Salerno Carnival of Comics, 24 Pages of Comics, & Vicks Comics)
Famous Funnies: Winter, 1940-41 - No. 6, Sept, 1943
NOTE: Buck Rogers first appeared in the pulp magazine Amazing Stories Vol. 3 #5 in Aug, 1928.

1-Sunday strip reprints by Rick Yager; begins with strip #190; Calkins-c	360	720	1080	2520	4410	6300
2 (7/41)-Calkins-c	142	284	426	909	1555	2200
3 (12/41), 4 (7/42)	119	238	357	762	1306	1850
5,6: 5-Story continues with Famous Funnies No. 80; Buck Rogers, Sky Roads. 6-Reprints of 1939 dailies; contains B.R. story "Crater of Doom" (2 pgs.) by Calkins not-r from Famous Funnies	100	200	300	635	1093	1550

BUCK ROGERS
Toby Press: No. 100, Jan, 1951 - No. 9, May-June, 1951

100(#7)-All strip-r begin; Anderson, Chatton-a	34	68	102	199	325	450
101(#8), 9-All Anderson-a(1947-49-r/dailies)	26	52	78	154	252	350

BUCK ROGERS (...in the 25th Century No. 5 on) (TV)
Gold Key/Whitman No. 7 on: Oct, 1964; No. 2, July, 1979 - No. 16, May, 1982 (No #10; story was written but never released. #17 exists only as a press proof without covers and was never published)

1(10128-410, 12¢)-1st S.A. app. Buck Rogers & 1st new B. R. in comics since 1933 giveaway; painted-c; back-c pin-up	12	24	36	79	170	260
2(7/79)-6: 3,4,6-Movie adaptation; painted-c	2	4	6	9	12	15

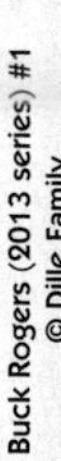
Buck Rogers (2013 series) #1 © Dille Family

Buffalo Bill #2 © YM

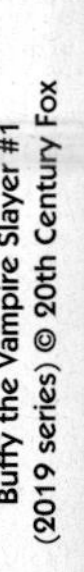
Buffy the Vampire Slayer #1 (2019 series) © 20th Century Fox

GD 2.0 | VG 4.0 | FN 6.0 | VF 8.0 | VF/NM 9.0 | NM- 9.2

7,11 (Whitman) 2 4 6 11 16 20
8,9 (prepack)(scarce) 5 10 15 30 50 70
12-16: 14(2/82), 15(3/82), 16(5/82) 2 4 6 8 10 12
Giant Movie Edition 11296(64pp, Whitman, $1.50), reprints GK #2-4 minus cover; tabloid size; photo-c (See Marvel Treasury) 3 6 9 17 26 35
Giant Movie Edition 02489(Western/Marvel, $1.50), reprints GK #2-4 minus cover 3 6 9 16 24 32
NOTE: *Bolle a-2p,3p, Movie Ed.(p).* **McWilliams** *a-2i,3i, 5-11, Movie Ed.(i). Painted c-1-9,11-13.*

BUCK ROGERS (Comics Module)
TSR, Inc.: 1990 - No. 10, 1991 ($2.95, 44 pgs.)
1-10 (1990): 1-Begin origin in 3 parts. 2-Indicia says #1. 2,3-Black Barney back-up story. 4-All Black Barney issue; B. B.-c. 5-Indicia says #6; Black Barney-c & lead story; Buck Rogers back-up story. 10-Flip book (72pgs.) 4.00

BUCK ROGERS
Dynamite Entertainment: No. 0, 2009 - No. 12, 2010 (25¢/$3.50)
0-(25¢) Beatty-s/Rafael-a/Cassaday-c 3.00
1-12: 1-($3.50) Three covers by Cassaday, Ross and Wagner; origin re-told 3.50
Annual 1 (2011, $4.99) Rafael-a; covers by Rafael & Sadowski 5.00

BUCK ROGERS
Hermes Press: 2013 - No. 4, 2013 ($3.99)
1-4-Howard Chaykin-s/a/c 4.00

BUCKSKIN (TV)
Dell Publishing Co.: No. 1011, July, 1959 - No. 1107, June-Aug, 1960
Four Color 1011 (#1)-Photo-c 7 14 21 44 82 120
Four Color 1107-Photo-c 6 12 18 40 73 105

BUCKY BARNES: THE WINTER SOLDIER (See Captain America titles)
Marvel Comics: Dec, 2014 - No. 11, Nov, 2015 ($3.99)
1-11: 1-Ales Kot-s/Marco Rudy-a; Daisy Johnson app. 2,8,9,10-Loki app. 4-7,9-Crossbones app. 7-Foss-a 4.00

BUCKY O'HARE (Funny Animal)
Continuity Comics: 1986 ($5.95, graphic novel)
1-Golden-c/a(r); r/serial-Echo of Futurepast #1-6 2 4 6 9 12 15
Deluxe Hardcover ($40.00, 52 pg., 8 x 11") 40.00

BUCKY O'HARE
Continuity Comics: Jan, 1991 - No. 5, 1991 ($2.00)
1-Michael Golden-c/a 2 4 6 9 12 15
2 6.00
3-6 4.00

BUDDIES IN THE U.S. ARMY
Avon Periodicals: Nov, 1952 - No. 2, 1953
1-Lawrence-c 23 46 69 138 227 315
2-Mort Lawrence-c/a 13 26 39 74 105 135

BUFFALO BEE (TV)
Dell Publishing Co.: No. 957, Nov, 1958 - No. 1061, Dec-Feb, 1959-60
Four Color 957 (#1) 8 16 24 54 102 150
Four Color 1002 (8-10/59), 1061 6 12 18 41 76 110

BUFFALO BILL (See Frontier Fighters, Super Western Comics & Western Action Thrillers)
Youthful Magazines: No. 2, Oct, 1950 - No. 9, Dec, 1951
2-Annie Oakley story 15 30 45 84 127 170
3-9: 2-4-Walter Johnson-c/a. 9-Wildey-a 11 22 33 60 83 105

BUFFALO BILL CODY (See Cody of the Pony Express)

BUFFALO BILL, JR. (TV) (See Western Roundup)
Dell/Gold Key: Jan, 1956 - No. 13, Aug-Oct, 1959; 1965 (All photo-c)
Four Color 673 (#1) 9 18 27 57 111 165
Four Color 742,766,798,828,856(11/57) 6 12 18 37 66 95
7(2-4/58)-13 5 10 15 31 53 75
1(6/65, Gold Key)-Photo-c(r/F.C. #798); photo-b/c 4 8 12 23 37 50

BUFFALO BILL PICTURE STORIES
Street & Smith Publications: June-July, 1949 - No. 2, Aug-Sept, 1949
1,2-Wildey, Powell-a in each 14 28 42 82 121 160

BUFFY: THE HIGH SCHOOL YEARS (Based on the TV series)
Dark Horse Comics
... – Glutton For Punishment (10/16, $10.99, 6" x 9") McDonald-s/Li-a 11.00
... – Parental Parasite (6/17, $10.99, 6" x 9") McDonald-s/Li-a 11.00

BUFFY THE VAMPIRE SLAYER (Based on the TV series)(Also see Angel and Faith, Spike, Tales of the Vampires and Willow)
Dark Horse Comics: 1998 - No. 63, Nov, 2003 ($2.95/$2.99)
1-Bennett-a/Watson-s; Art Adams-c 2 4 6 8 10 12
1-Variant photo-c 2 4 6 9 12 15
1-Gold foil logo Art Adams-c 15.00
1-Gold foil logo photo-c 20.00
2-4-Photo-c 1 3 4 6 8 10
5-15-Regular and photo-c. 4-7-Gomez-a. 5,8-Green-c 5.00
16-49: 29,30-Angel x-over. 43-45-Death of Buffy. 47-Lobdell-s begin. 48-Pike returns 3.00
50-($3.50) Scooby gang battles Adam; back-up story by Watson 4.00
51-63: 51-54-Viva Las Buffy; pre-Sunnydale Buffy & Pike in Vegas 3.00
Annual '99 ($4.95)-Two stories and pin-ups 1 2 3 4 5 7
...: A Stake to the Heart TPB (3/04, $12.95) r/#60-63 13.00
...: Chaos Bleeds (6/03, $2.99) Based on the video game; photo & Campbell-c 3.00
...: Creatures of Habit (3/02, $17.95) text with Horton & Paul Lee-a 18.00
...: Jonathan 1 (1/01, $2.99) two covers; Richards-a 3.00
...: Lost and Found 1 (3/02, $2.99) aftermath of Buffy's death; Richards-a 3.00
... Lovers Walk (2/01, $2.99) short stories by various; Richards & photo-c 3.00
...: Note From the Underground (3/03, $12.95) r/#47-50 13.00
...: Omnibus Vol. 1 (7/07, $24.95, 9x6") r/Spike & Dru #3, Origin #1-3 and Buffy #51-59 25.00
...: Omnibus Vol. 2 (9/07, $24.95, 9x6") r/Buffy #60-63 and various one-shots & specials 25.00
...: Omnibus Vol. 3 (1/08, $24.95, 9x6") r/Buffy #1-8,12,16, Annual '99 25.00
...: Omnibus Vol. 4 (5/08, $24.95, 9x6") r/Buffy #9-11,13-15,17-20,50 and various 25.00
...: Omnibus Vol. 5 (9/08, $24.95, 9x6") r/Buffy #21-28 and various one-shots & specials 25.00
...: Omnibus Vol. 6 (2/09, $24.95, 9x6") r/Buffy #29-38 and various one-shots & specials 25.00
...: One For One (9/10, $1.00) r/#1 with red cover frame 3.00
...: Reunion (6/02, $3.50) Buffy & Angel's; Espenson-s; art by various 3.50
...: Slayer Interrupted TPB (2003, $14.95) r/#56-59 15.00
...: Tales of the Slayers (10/02, $3.50) art by Matsuda and Colan; art & photo-c 3.50
...: The Death of Buffy TPB (8/02, $15.95) r/#43-46 16.00
...: Viva Las Buffy TPB (7/03, $12.95) r/#51-54 13.00
Wizard #1/2 1 2 3 6 8 9

BUFFY THE VAMPIRE SLAYER ("Season Eight" of the TV series)
Dark Horse Comics: Mar, 2007 - No. 40, Jan, 2011 ($2.99)
1-Joss Whedon-s/Georges Jeanty-a/Jo Chen-c 6.00
1-Variant cover by Jeanty 6.00
1-RRP with B&W Jeanty cover (edition of 1000) 85.00
1-4: 1-2nd thru 5th printings. 2-2nd-4th printings. 3,4-2nd & 3rd printings 3.00
2-5-Jeanty-a; covers by Chen & Jeanty 4.00
6-13,16-19-Two covers by Chen & Jeanty. 6-9-Faith app.; Vaughan-s. 10,11-Whedon-s. 12-15-Goddard-s; Dracula app. 16-19-Fray app.; Whedon-s/Moline-a 3.00
20-40: 20-28,31-40-Two covers by Chen and Jeanty. 20-Animation style flashback. 21,26-30-Espenson-s. 30-Hughes-c. 31-Whedon-s. 32-35-Meltzer-s. 36-40-Whedon-s 3.00
...: Riley (8/10, $3.50) Espensen-s/Moline-a; Riley Finn and Sam; Angel app. 3.50
... Tales of the Vampires (6/09, $2.99) Cloonan-s/Lolos-a; covers by Chen & Bá/Moon 3.00
...: Willow (12/09, $3.50) Whedon-s/Moline-a; Willow meets the Snake Guide 3.50

BUFFY THE VAMPIRE SLAYER ("Season Nine" of the TV series)
Dark Horse Comics: Sept, 2011 - No. 25, Sept, 2013 ($2.99)
1-25: 1-Whedon-s/Jeanty-a; covers by Morris & Chen. 2-5-Chambliss-s; two covers by Morris & Jeanty. 5-Moline-a; Nikki flashback. 6,7-Two covers by Jeanty & Noto. 8-10-Richards-a. 14-Espenson-s; intro. Billy. 16-19-Illyria app. 3.00
....: Buffyverse Sampler (1/13, $4.99) r/#1, Angel & Faith #1, Spike #1, Willow #1 5.00
FCBD (5/12, giveaway) Buffy vs. Alien; Jeanty-a; flip book with The Guild 3.00

BUFFY THE VAMPIRE SLAYER (SEASON TEN)
Dark Horse Comics: Mar, 2014 - No. 30, Aug, 2016 ($3.50/$3.99)
1-16: 1-Gage-s/Isaacs-a; covers by Morris & Isaacs. 2-5-Dracula app. 3-5,7,12,13-Nicholas Brendon & Gage-s. 8-Corben-a (3 pgs) 3.50
17-30-($3.99) 19-Nicholas Brendon & Gage-s. 25-Levens-a 4.00

BUFFY THE VAMPIRE SLAYER SEASON ELEVEN
Dark Horse Comics: Nov, 2016 - No. 12, Oct, 2017 ($3.99)
1-12: 1-Gage-s/Isaacs-a; covers by Morris & Isaacs. 5,9-Jeanty-a 4.00

BUFFY THE VAMPIRE SLAYER SEASON 12
Dark Horse Comics: Jun, 2018 - No. 4, Sept, 2018 ($3.99)
1-4-Gage & Whedon-s/Jeanty-a; Melaka Fray, Angel, Illyria app. 4.00

BUFFY THE VAMPIRE SLAYER
Dark Horse Comics: Jan, 2019 - Present ($3.99)
1-22: 1-Rebooted Buffy first meets the Scooby gang in high school; Bellaire-s/Mora-a. 4-Xander attacked. 5-12-David López-a. 8-12-Hellmouth x-over with Angel #5-8. 10-Intro. Kendra. 11-Intro. Anya. 13-Valero-O'Connell-a. 19-Faith arrives 4.00
...: Chosen Ones 1 (8/19, $7.99) Short stories of previous slayers 8.00
...: Every Generation 1 (4/20, $7.99) Short stories of previous slayers; Andolfo-c 8.00
...: Faith 1 (2/21, $7.99) Lambert-s/Carlini-a; flashbacks to childhood and recruitment 8.00

Buffy the Vampire Slayer: Willow #1 © 20th Century Fox

Bugs Bunny #100 © WB

Bulletman #11 © FAW

	GD 2.0	VG 4.0	FN 6.0	VF 8.0	VF/NM 9.0	NM- 9.2

BUFFY THE VAMPIRE SLAYER: ANGEL
Dark Horse Comics: May, 1999 - No. 3, July, 1999 ($2.95, limited series)

1-3-Gomez-a; Matsuda-c & photo-c for each						4.00

BUFFY THE VAMPIRE SLAYER: GILES
Dark Horse Comics: Oct, 2000 ($2.95, one-shot)

1-Eric Powell-a; Powell & photo-c						4.00

BUFFY THE VAMPIRE SLAYER: HAUNTED
Dark Horse Comics: Dec, 2001 - No. 4, Mar, 2002 ($2.99, limited series)

1-4-Faith and the Mayor app.; Espenson-s/Richards-a						4.00
TPB (9/02, $12.95) r/series; photo-c						13.00

BUFFY THE VAMPIRE SLAYER: OZ
Dark Horse Comics: July, 2001 - No. 3, Sept, 2001 ($2.99, limited series)

1-3-Totleben & photo-c; Golden-s						4.00

BUFFY THE VAMPIRE SLAYER: SPIKE AND DRU
Dark Horse Comics: Apr, 1999; No. 2, Oct, 1999; No. 3, Dec, 2000 ($2.95)

1-3: 1,2-Photo-c. 3-Two covers (photo & Sook)						4.00

BUFFY THE VAMPIRE SLAYER: THE ORIGIN (Adapts movie screenplay)
Dark Horse Comics: Jan, 1999 - No. 3, Mar, 1999 ($2.95, limited series)

1-3-Brereton-s/Bennett-a; reg & photo-c for each						4.00

BUFFY THE VAMPIRE SLAYER: WILLOW
BOOM! Studios: Jul, 2020 - No. 5, Nov, 2020 ($3.99, limited series)

1-5-Mariko Tamaki-s/Natacha Bustos-a						4.00

BUFFY THE VAMPIRE SLAYER: WILLOW & TARA
Dark Horse Comics: Apr, 2001 ($2.99, one-shot)

1-Terry Moore-a/Chris Golden & Amber Benson-s; Moore-c & photo-c						4.00
TPB (4/03, $9.95) r/#1 & W&T - Wilderness; photo-c						10.00

BUFFY THE VAMPIRE SLAYER: WILLOW & TARA - WILDERNESS
Dark Horse Comics: Jul, 2002 - No. 2, Sept, 2002 ($2.99, limited series)

1,2-Chris Golden & Amber Benson-s; Jothikaumar-c & photo-c						4.00

BUG
Marvel Comics: Mar, 1997 ($2.99, one-shot)

1-Micronauts character						3.00

BUGALOOS (Sid & Marty Kroft TV show)
Charlton Comics: Sept, 1971 - No. 4, Feb, 1972

1	5	10	15	31	53	75
2-4	3	6	9	20	31	42

NOTE: *No. 3(1/72) went on sale late in 1972 (after No. 4) with the 1/73 issues.*

BUGHOUSE (Satire)
Ajax/Farrell (Excellent Publ.): Mar-Apr, 1954 - No. 4, Sept-Oct, 1954

V1#1	28	56	84	165	270	375
2-4	15	30	45	90	140	190

BUGS BUNNY (See The Best of..., Camp Comics, Comic Album #2, 6, 10, 14, Dell Giant #28, 32, 46, Dynabrite, Golden Comics Digest #1, 3, 5, 6, 8, 10, 14, 15, 17, 21, 26, 30, 34, 39, 42, 47, Kite Fun Book, Large Feature Comic #8, Looney Tunes and Merry Melodies, March of Comics #44, 59, 75, 83, 97, 115, 132, 149, 160, 179, 188, 201, 220, 231, 245, 259, 273, 287, 301, 315, 329, 343, 363, 367, 380, 392, 403, 415, 428, 440, 452, 464, 476, 487, Porky Pig, Puffed Wheat, Story Hour Series #802, Super Book #14, 26 and Whitman Comic Books)

BUGS BUNNY (See Dell Giants for annuals)
Dell Publishing Co./Gold Key No. 86-218/Whitman No. 219 on: 1942 - No. 245, April, 1984

Large Feature Comic 8(1942)-(Rarely found in fine-mint condition)	300	600	900	1888	3319	4750
Four Color 33 ('43) Bondage/torture-c	118	236	354	944	2122	3300
Four Color 51	37	74	111	274	612	950
Four Color 88-Sci-fi-c	23	46	69	164	362	560
Four Color 123('46),142,164	16	32	48	110	243	375
Four Color 187,200,217,233	12	24	36	79	170	260
Four Color 250-Used in **SOTI**, pg. 309	12	24	36	81	176	270
Four Color 266,274,281,289,298('50)	9	18	27	62	126	190
Four Color 307,317(#1),327(#2),338,347,355,366,376,393	8	16	24	55	105	155
Four Color 407,420,432(10/52)	7	14	21	48	89	130
Four Color 498(9/53),585(9/54),647(9/55)	6	12	18	38	69	100
Four Color 724(9/56),838(9/57),1064(12/59)	5	10	15	34	60	85
28(12-1/52-53)-30	5	10	15	34	60	85
31-50	4	8	12	28	47	65
51-85(7-9/62)	4	8	12	23	37	50
86(10/62)-88-Bugs Bunny's Showtime-(25¢, 80pgs.)	5	10	15	35	63	90
89-99	3	6	9	16	24	32
100	3	6	9	17	26	35
101-118: 108-1st Honey Bunny. 118-Last 12¢ issue	3	6	9	14	19	24
119-140	2	4	6	11	16	20
141-170	2	4	6	9	12	15
171-218: 218-Publ. by Whitman only?	2	4	6	8	10	12
219,220,225-237(5/82): 229-Swipe of Barks story/WDC&S #223. 233(2/82)	2	4	6	8	10	12
221(9/80),222(11/80)-Pre-pack? (Scarce)	4	8	12	28	47	65
223 (1/81, 50¢-c), 224 (3/81)-Low distr.	3	6	9	14	20	25
223 (1/81, 40¢-c) Cover price error variant	3	6	9	17	26	35
238-245 (#90070 on-c, nd, nd code; pre-pack): 238(5/83), 239(6/83), 240(7/83), 241(7/83), 242(8/83), 243(8/83), 244(3/84), 245(4/84)	3	6	9	15	22	28

NOTE: *Reprints-100,102-104,110,115,123,143,144,147,167,173,175-177,179-185,187,190.*

nn (Xerox Pub. Comic Digest, 1971, 100 pages, B&W) collection of one-page gags	4	8	12	23	37	50
...Comic-Go-Round 11196-(224 pgs.)($1.95)(Golden Press, 1979)	4	8	12	25	40	55
...Winter Fun 1(12/67-Gold Key)-Giant	5	10	15	30	50	70

BUGS BUNNY
DC Comics: June, 1990 - No. 3, Aug, 1990 ($1.00, limited series)

1-3: Daffy Duck, Elmer Fudd, others app.						4.00

BUGS BUNNY (...Monthly on-c)
DC Comics: 1993 - No. 3, 1994? ($1.95)

1-3-Bugs, Porky Pig, Daffy, Road Runner						3.50

BUGS BUNNY (Digest-size reprint from Looney Tunes)
DC Comics: 2005 ($6.99, digest)

Vol. 1: What's Up Doc? - Reprints from Looney Tunes #37,41,43-45,48,52,55,57-59,63						7.00

BUGS BUNNY & PORKY PIG
Gold Key: Sept, 1965 (Paper-c, giant, 100 pgs.)

1(30025-509)	6	12	18	38	69	100

BUGS BUNNY'S ALBUM (See Bugs Bunny, Four Color No. 498,585,647,724)

BUGS BUNNY LIFE STORY ALBUM (See Bugs Bunny, Four Color No. 838)

BUGS BUNNY MERRY CHRISTMAS (See Bugs Bunny, Four Color No. 1064)

BUG! THE ADVENTURES OF FORAGER (From New Gods)
DC Comics (Young Animal): Jul, 2017 - No. 6, Feb, 2018 ($3.99)

1-6-Lee Allred-s/Mike Allred-a/c. 1-Sandman, Brute & Glob app. 2-G.A. Sandman, Sandy, Blue Beetle and The Losers app. 3-Atlas app. 5-Omac app.						4.00

BUILDING, THE
Kitchen Sink Press: 1987; 2000 (8 1/2" x 11" sepia toned graphic novel)

nn-Will Eisner-s/c/a						15.00
nn-(DC Comics, 9/00, $9.95) reprints 1987 edition						10.00

BULLET CROW, FOWL OF FORTUNE
Eclipse Comics: Mar, 1987 - No. 2, Apr, 1987 ($2.00, B&W, limited series)

1,2-The Comic Reader-r & new-a						3.00

BULLETMAN (See Fawcett Miniatures, Master Comics, Mighty Midget Comics, Nickel Comics & XMas Comics)
Fawcett Publications: Sum, 1941 - #12, 2/12/43; #14, Spr, 1946 - #16, Fall, 1946 (No #13)

1-Silver metallic-c	406	812	1218	2842	4971	7100
2-Raboy-c	177	354	531	1124	1937	2750
3,5-Raboy-c each	142	284	426	909	1555	2200
4	98	196	294	622	1074	1525
6,8,9	84	168	252	538	919	1300
7-Ghost Stories told by night watchman of cemetery begins; Eisnerish-a; hidden message "Chic Stone is a jerk".	94	188	282	597	1024	1450
10-Intro. Bulletdog	92	184	276	584	1005	1425
11,12,14-16 (nn 13): 12-Robot-c	61	122	183	390	670	950

NOTE: ***Mac Raboy** c-1-3, 5, 6, 10. "Bulletman the Flying Detective" on cover #8 on.*

BULLET POINTS
Marvel Comics: Jan, 2007 - No. 5, May, 2007 ($2.99, limited series)

1-5: 1-Steve Rogers becomes Iron Man; Straczynski-s/Edwards-a. 4,5-Galactus app.						3.00
TPB (2007, $13.99) r/#1-5; layout pages by Edwards						14.00

BULLETPROOF MONK (Inspired the 2003 film)
Image Comics (Flypaper Press): 1998 - No. 3, 1999 ($2.95, limited series)

1-3-Oeming-a						3.00
...: Tales of the BPM (3/03, $2.95) Flip book; 2 covers by Sale; art by Sale, Oeming, Dave Johnson; Seann William Scott afterword						3.00
TPB (2002, $9.95) r/#1-3; foreword by John Woo						10.00

Bullwinkle #8 © Jay Ward

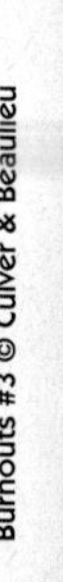
Burnouts #3 © Culver & Beaulieu

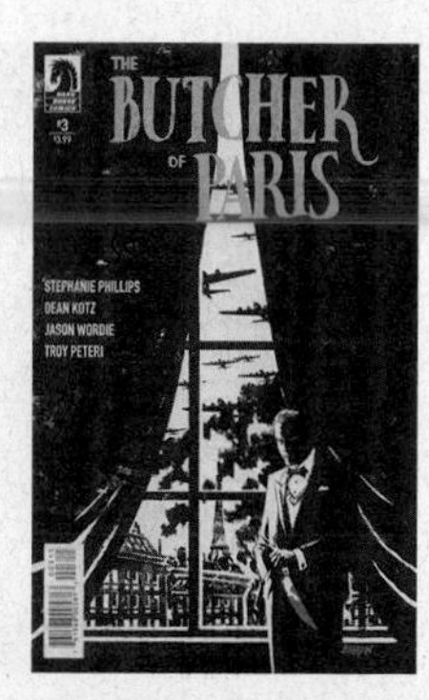

The Butcher of Paris #3 © Phillips & Kotz

	GD 2.0	VG 4.0	FN 6.0	VF 8.0	VF/NM 9.0	NM- 9.2

BULLETS AND BRACELETS (Also see Marvel Versus DC #3 & DC Versus Marvel #4)
Marvel Comics (Amalgam): Apr, 1996 ($1.95)

1-John Ostrander script & Gary Frank-c/a 4.00

BULLSEYE (Daredevil villain)
Marvel Comics: Apr, 2017 - No. 5, Aug, 2017 ($4.99/$3.99, limited series)

1-($4.99) Brisson-s/Sanna-a; back-up with Wolfman-s/Morgan-a 5.00
2-5-($3.99) Brisson-s/Sanna-a 4.00

BULLS-EYE (Cody of The Pony Express No. 8 on)
Mainline No. 1-5/Charlton No. 6,7: 7-8/54-No. 5, 3-4/55; No. 6, 6/55; No. 7, 8/55

	GD	VG	FN	VF	VF/NM	NM-
1-S&K-c, 2 pgs.-a	81	162	243	518	884	1250
2-S&K-c/a	60	120	180	381	653	925
3-5-S&K-c/a(2 each). 4-Last pre-code issue (1-2/55). 5-Censored issue with tomahawks removed in battle scene	50	100	150	315	533	750
6-S&K-c/a	42	84	126	265	445	625
7-S&K-c/a(3)	48	96	144	302	514	725

BULLS-EYE COMICS (Formerly Komik Pages #10; becomes Kayo #12)
Harry 'A' Chesler: No. 11, 1944

	GD	VG	FN	VF	VF/NM	NM-
11-Origin K-9, Green Knight's sidekick, Lance; The Green Knight, Lady Satan, Yankee Doodle Jones app.	161	322	483	1030	1765	2500

BULLSEYE: GREATEST HITS (Daredevil villain)
Marvel Comics: Nov, 2004 - No. 5, Mar, 2005 ($2.99, limted series)

1-5-Origin of Bullseye; Steve Dillon-a/Deodato-c. 3-Punisher app. 3.00
TPB (2005, $13.99) r/#1-5 14.00

BULLSEYE: PERFECT GAME (Daredevil villain)
Marvel Comics: Jan, 2011 - No. 2, Feb, 2011 ($3.99, limited series)

1,2-Huston-s/Martinbrough-a; Bullseye as baseball pitcher 4.00

BULLWHIP GRIFFIN (See Movie Comics)

BULLWINKLE (...and Rocky No. 22 on; See March of Comics #233 and Rocky & Bullwinkle) (TV) (Jay Ward)
Dell/Gold Key: 3-5/62 - #11, 4/74; #12, 6/76 - #19, 3/78; #20, 4/79 - #25, 2/80

	GD	VG	FN	VF	VF/NM	NM-
Four Color 1270 (3-5/62)	16	32	48	112	249	385
01-090-209 (Dell, 7-9/62)	13	26	39	89	195	300
1(11/62, Gold Key)	12	24	36	82	179	275
2(2/63)	8	16	24	54	102	150
3(4/72)-11(4/74-Gold Key)	5	10	15	31	53	75
12-14: 12(6/76)-Reprints. 13(9/76), 14-New stories	3	6	9	17	26	35
15-25	2	4	6	11	16	20
Mother Moose Nursery Pomes 01-530-207 (5-7/62, Dell)	15	30	45	103	227	350

NOTE: *Reprints: 6, 7, 20-24.*

BULLWINKLE AND ROCKY (TV)
Charlton Comics: July, 1970 - No. 7, July, 1971

	GD	VG	FN	VF	VF/NM	NM-
1-Has 1 pg. pin-up	6	12	18	40	73	105
2-7: 3-Snidely Whiplash app.	5	10	15	30	50	70

BULLWINKLE AND ROCKY
Star Comics/Marvel Comics No. 3 on: Nov, 1987 - No. 9, Mar, 1989

	GD	VG	FN	VF	VF/NM	NM-
1-9: Boris & Natasha in all. 3,5,8-Dudley Do-Right app. 4-Reagan-c						5.00
Marvel Moosterworks (1/92, $4.95)	2	4	6	8	10	12

BULLY WARS
Image Comics: Sept, 2018 - No. 5, Jan, 2019 ($3.99, limited series)

1-5-Skottie Young-s/Aaron Conley-a 4.00

BUMMER
Fantagraphics Books: June, 1995 ($3.50, B&W, mature)

1 3.50

BUNNY (Also see Harvey Pop Comics and Fruitman Special)
Harvey Publications: Dec, 1966 - No. 20, Dec, 1971; No. 21, Nov, 1976

	GD	VG	FN	VF	VF/NM	NM-
1-68 pg. Giants begin	7	14	21	49	92	135
2-10: 3-1st app. Fruitman. 6,8-10-Fruitman	4	8	12	28	47	65
11-18: 18-Last 68 pg. Giant	4	8	12	27	44	60
19-21-52 pg. Giants: 21-Fruitman app.	4	8	12	25	40	55

BURKE'S LAW (TV)
Dell Publ.: 1-3/64; No. 2, 5-7/64; No. 3, 3-5/65 (All have Gene Barry photo-c)

	GD	VG	FN	VF	VF/NM	NM-
1-Photo-c	5	10	15	31	53	75
2,3-Photo-c	4	8	12	23	37	50

BURNING FIELDS
BOOM! Studios: Jan, 2015 - No. 8, Sept, 2015 ($3.99, limited series)

1-6-Moreci & Daniel-s/Lorimer-a 4.00

BURNING ROMANCES (See Fox Giants)

BURNOUTS
Image Comics: Sept, 2018 - No. 5, Jan, 2019 ($3.99)

1-5-Dennis Culver-s/Geoffo-a 4.00

BUSTER BEAR
Quality Comics Group (Arnold Publ.): Dec, 1953 - No. 10, June, 1955

	GD	VG	FN	VF	VF/NM	NM-
1-Funny animal	13	26	39	74	105	135
2	7	14	21	37	46	55
3-10	6	12	18	31	38	45
I.W. Reprint #9,10 (Super on inside)	2	4	6	9	13	16

BUSTER BROWN COMICS (See Promotional Comics section)

BUSTER BUNNY
Standard Comics(Animated Cartoons)/Pines: Nov, 1949 - No. 16, Oct, 1953

	GD	VG	FN	VF	VF/NM	NM-
1-Frazetta 1 pg. text illo.	14	28	42	82	121	160
2	8	16	24	42	54	65
3-14,16	7	14	21	37	46	55
15-Racist-c	14	28	42	76	108	140

BUSTER CRABBE (TV)
Famous Funnies Publ.: Nov, 1951 - No. 12, 1953

	GD	VG	FN	VF	VF/NM	NM-
1-1st app.(?) Frazetta anti-drug ad; text story about Buster Crabbe & Billy the Kid	41	82	123	256	428	600
2-Williamson/Evans-c; text story about Wild Bill Hickok & Pecos Bill	39	78	117	231	378	525
3-Williamson/Evans-c/a	40	80	120	246	411	575
4-Frazetta-c/a, 1pg.; bondage-c	65	130	195	416	708	1000
5-Classic Frazetta sci-fi cover; Williamson/Krenkel/Orlando-a, 11pgs. (per Mr. Williamson)	174	348	522	1114	1907	2700
6,8	23	46	69	136	223	310
7-Frazetta one pg. ad	21	42	63	126	206	285
9-One pg. Frazetta Boy Scouts ad (1st?)	18	36	54	103	162	220
10-12	14	28	42	76	108	140

NOTE: Eastern Color sold 3 dozen each NM file copies of #s 9-12 a few years ago.

BUSTER CRABBE (The Amazing Adventures of...)(Movie star)
Lev Gleason Publications: Dec, 1953 - No. 4, June, 1954

	GD	VG	FN	VF	VF/NM	NM-
1,4: 1-Photo-c. 4-Flash Gordon-c	23	46	69	136	223	310
2,3-Toth-a	20	40	60	117	189	260

BUTCH CASSIDY
Skywald Comics: June, 1971 - No. 3, Oct, 1971 (52 pgs.)

	GD	VG	FN	VF	VF/NM	NM-
1-Pre-code reprints and new material; Red Mask reprint, retitled Maverick; Bolle-a; Sutton-a	3	6	9	15	22	28
2,3: 2-Whip Wilson-r. 3-Dead Canyon Days reprint/Crack Western No. 63; Sundance Kid app.; Crandall-a	2	4	6	10	14	18

BUTCH CASSIDY (...& the Wild Bunch)
Avon Periodicals: 1951

	GD	VG	FN	VF	VF/NM	NM-
1-Kinstler-c/a	25	50	75	150	245	340

NOTE: ***Reinman** story; Issue number on inside spine.*

BUTCH CASSIDY (See Fun-In No. 11 & Western Adventure Comics)

BUTCHER, THE (Also see Brave and the Bold, 2nd Series)
DC Comics: May, 1990 - No. 5, Sept, 1990 ($1.50, mature)

1-5: 1-No indicia inside 3.00

BUTCHER KNIGHT
Image Comics (Top Cow): Jan, 2001 - No. 4, June, 2001 ($2.95, limited series)

Preview (B&W, 16 pgs.) Dwayne Turner-c/a 3.00
1-4-Dwayne Turner-c/a 3.00

BUTCHER OF PARIS, THE
Dark Horse Comics: Dec, 2019 - No. 5, Apr, 2020 ($3.99, limited series)

1-5-Serial killer in 1944 Paris; Stephanie Phillips-s/Dean Kotz-a 4.00

BUTTERFLY
Archaia: Sept, 2014 - No. 4, Dec, 2014 ($3.99, limited series)

1-4: Phil Noto-c on all. 1-Marguerite Bennett-s/Antonio Fuso-a. 3,4-Simeone-a 4.00

BUZ SAWYER (Sweeney No. 4 on)
Standard Comics: June, 1948 - No. 3, 1949

	GD	VG	FN	VF	VF/NM	NM-
1-Roy Crane-a	30	60	90	177	289	400
2-Intro his pal Sweeney	17	34	51	98	154	210
3	13	26	39	72	101	130

By Night #9 © Allison & Larsen

Cable (2020 series) #1 © MAR

Cadillacs and Dinosaurs #1 © Topps

GD 2.0 | VG 4.0 | FN 6.0 | VF 8.0 | VF/NM 9.0 | NM- 9.2

BUZ SAWYER'S PAL, ROSCOE SWEENEY (See Sweeney)

BUZZ, THE (Also see Spider-Girl)
Marvel Comics: July, 2000 - No. 3, Sept, 2000 ($2.99, limited series)

1-3-Buscema-a/DeFalco & Frenz-s 3.00

BUZZARD (See The Goon)
Dark Horse Comics: Jun, 2010 - No. 3, Aug, 2010 ($3.50, limited series)

1-3-Eric Powell-c; Buzzard story w/Powell-s/a; Billy The Kid back-up; Powell-s/Hotz-a 3.50

BUZZ BUZZ COMICS MAGAZINE
Horse Press: May, 1996 ($4.95, B&W, over-sized magazine)

1-Paul Pope-c/a/scripts; Moebius-a 5.00

BUZZY (See All Funny Comics)
National Periodical Publications/Detective Comics: Winter, 1944-45 - No. 75, 1-2/57; No. 76, 10/57; No. 77, 10/58

1 (52 pgs. begin); "America's favorite teenster" 41 82 123 256 428 600
2 (Spr, 1945) 21 42 63 126 206 285
3-5 17 34 51 98 154 210
6-10 15 30 45 84 127 170
11-20 14 28 42 78 112 145
21-30 13 26 39 72 101 130
31,35-38 11 22 33 64 90 115
32-34,39-Last 52 pgs. Scribbly story by Mayer in each (these four stories were done for Scribbly #14 which was delayed for a year) 12 24 36 69 97 125
40-77: 62-Last precode (2/55) 11 22 33 62 86 110

BUZZY THE CROW (See Harvey Comics Hits #60 & 62, Harvey Hits #18 & Paramount Animated Comics #1)

BY BIZARRE HANDS
Dark Horse Comics: Apr, 1994 - No. 3, June, 1994 ($2.50, B&W, mature)

1-3: Lansdale stories 3.00

BY NIGHT
Boom Entertainment (BOOM! Box): Jun, 2018 - No. 12, Jun, 2019 ($3.99)

1-12-John Allison-s/Christine Larsen-a 4.00

BYTE-SIZED
AWA , Inc.: Dec, 2020 - No. 4 ($3.99, limited series)

1-3-Cullen Bunn-s/Nelson Blake II-a 4.00

CABBOT: BLOODHUNTER (Also see Bloodstrike & Bloodstrike: Assassin)
Maximum Press: Jan, 1997 ($2.50, one-shot)

1-Rick Veitch-a/script; Platt-c; Thor, Chapel & Prophet cameos 3.00

CABLE (See Ghost Rider &..., & New Mutants #87) (Title becomes Soldier X)
Marvel Comics: May, 1993 - No. 107, Sept, 2002 ($3.50/$1.95/$1.50-$2.25)

1-($3.50, 52 pgs.)-Gold foil & embossed-c; Thibert a-1-4p; c-1-3 2 4 6 8 10 12
2,4-15: 4-Liefeld-a assist; last Thibert-a(p). 6-8-Reveals that Baby Nathan is Cable; gives background on Stryfe. 9-Omega Red-c/story. 11-Bound-in trading card sheet 4.00
3-1st Weasel; extra 16 pg. X-Men/Avengers ann. preview 1 2 3 5 6 8
16-Newsstand edition 3.00
16-Enhanced edition 5.00
17-20-($1.95)-Deluxe edition, 20-w/bound in '95 Fleer Ultra cards 4.00
17-20-($1.50)-Standard edition 3.00
21-24, 26-44, -1(7/97): 21-Begin $1.95-c; return from Age of Apocalyse. 24-Grizzly dies. 28-vs. Sugarman; Mr. Sinister app. 30-X-Man-c/app.; Exodus app. 31-vs. X-Man. 32-Post app. 33-Post-c/app; Mandarin app (flashback); includes "Onslaught Update". 34-Onslaught x-over; Hulk-c/app; Apocalypse app. (cont'd in Hulk #444). 35-Onslaught x-over; Apocalypse vs. Cable. 36-w/card insert. 38-Weapon X-c/app; Psycho Man & Micronauts app. 40-Scott Clark-a(p). 41-Bishop-c/app. 3.00
25 ($3.95)-Foil gatefold-c 5.00
45-49,51-74: 45-Operation Zero Tolerance. 51-1st Casey-s. 54-Black Panther. 55-Domino-c/app. 62-Nick Fury-c/app.63-Stryfe-c/app. 67,68-Avengers-c/app. 71,73-Liefeld-a 3.00
50-($2.99) Double sized w/wraparound-c 4.00
75 -($2.99) Liefeld-c/a; Apocalypse: The Twelve x-over 4.00
76-79: 76-Apocalypse: The Twelve x-over 3.00
80-96: 80-Begin $2.25-c. 87-Mystique-c/app. 3.00
97-99,101-107: 97-Tischman-s/Kordey-a/c begin 3.00
100-($3.99) Dialogue-free 'Nuff Said back-up story 4.00
... Classic Vol. 1 TPB (2008, $29.99) r/#1-4, New Mutants #87, Cable: Blood & Metal #1,2 30.00
.../Machine Man '98 Annual ($2.99) Wraparound-c 4.00
.../X-Force '96 Annual ($2.95) Wraparound-c 4.00
...'99 Annual ($3.50) vs. Sinister; computer photo-c 4.00
...Second Genesis 1 (9/99, $3.99) r/New Mutants #99, 100 and X-Force #1; Liefeld-c 4.00
...: The End (2002, $14.99, TPB) r/#101-107 15.00

CABLE
Marvel Comics: May, 2008 - No. 25, Jun, 2010 ($2.99/$3.99)

1-23: 1-10-Olivetti-c/a. 1-Liefeld var-c. 2-Finch var-c. 3-Romita Jr. var-c. 4-Bishop app.; Djurdjevic var-c. 5-Silvestri var-c. 6-Liefeld var-c. 13-15-Messiah War x-over; Deadpool app. 16,17-Gulacy-a 3.00
24-($3.99) Bishop app. 4.00
25-($3.99) Deadpool app.; Medina-a 1 2 3 5 6 8

CABLE
Marvel Comics: Jul, 2017 - No. 5, Nov, 2017; No. 150, Dec, 2017 - No. 159, Sept, 2018 ($3.99)

1-5: 1-Robinson-s/Pacheco-a. 4,5-Cinar-a. 4-Rasputin app. 4.00
[Title switches to legacy numbering after #5 (11/17)]
150-159: 150-154-The Externals app. 4.00
... Deadpool Annual 1 (10/18, $4.99) David F. Walker-s; art by various 5.00

CABLE
Marvel Comics: May, 2020 - Present ($4.99/$3.99)

1-($4.99) Duggan-s/Noto-a; young Cable on Krakoa; Wolverine app. 5.00
2-8-($3.99) 3-Space Knights and Deadpool app. 4-6-"X of Swords" tie-ins 4.00

CABLE AND X-FORCE (Marvel NOW!)
Marvel Comics: Feb, 2013 - No. 19, Mar, 2014 ($3.99)

1-19: 1-Hopeless-s/Larroca-a; Cable, Colossus, Domino, Forge & Dr. Nemesis team 4.00

CABLE - BLOOD AND METAL (Also see New Mutants #87 & X-Force #8)
Marvel Comics: Oct, 1992 - No. 2, Nov, 1992 ($2.50, limited series, 52 pgs.)

1-Fabian Nicieza scripts; John Romita, Jr.-c/a in both; Cable vs. Stryfe; 2nd app. of The Wild Pack (becomes The Six Pack); wraparound-c 5.00
2-Prelude to X-Cutioner's Song 5.00

CABLE/DEADPOOL ("Cable & Deadpool" on cover)
Marvel Comics: May, 2004 - No. 50, Apr, 2008 ($2.99)

1-Nicieza-s/Liefeld-c 4 8 12 27 44 60
2,3 2 4 6 8 10 12
4-23,25-37: 7-9-X-Men app. 17-House of M. 21-Heroes For Hire app. 30,31-Civil War. 30-Great Lakes Avengers app. 33-Liefeld-c 5.00
24-Spider-Man app. 1 3 4 6 8 10
38-1st Bob, Agent of HYDRA 2 4 6 13 18 22
39-49: 43,44-Wolverine app. 4.00
50-($3.99) Final issue; Spider-Man and the Avengers app.; 1st Venompool 3 6 9 21 33 45
Cable & Deadpool MCG 1 (7/11, $1.00) r/#1 with "Marvel's Greatest Comics" cover logo 3.00
... Vol. 1: If Looks Could Kill TPB (2004, $14.99) r/#1-6 15.00
... Vol. 2: The Burnt Offering TPB (2005, $14.99) r/#7-12 15.00
... Vol. 3: The Human Race TPB (2005, $14.99) r/#13-18 15.00
... Vol. 4: Bosom Buddies TPB (2006, $14.99) r/#19-24 15.00
... Vol. 5: Living Legends TPB (2006, $13.99) r/#25-29 14.00
... Vol. 6: Paved With Good Intentions TPB (2007, $14.99) r/#30-35 15.00
... Vol. 7: Separation Anxiety TPB (2007, $17.99) r/#36-42; sketch pages 18.00
Deadpool Vs. The Marvel Universe TPB (2008, $24.99) r/#43-50 25.00

CADET GRAY OF WEST POINT (See Dell Giants)

CADILLACS & DINOSAURS (TV)
Marvel Comics (Epic Comics): Nov, 1990 - No. 6, Apr, 1991 ($2.50, limited series)

1-6: r/Xenozoic Tales in color w/new-c 3.00
...In 3-D #1 (7/92, $3.95, Kitchen Sink)-With glasses 6.00

CADILLACS AND DINOSAURS (TV)
Topps Comics: V2#1, Feb, 1994 - V2#9, 1995 ($2.50, limited series)

V2#1-($2.95)-Collector's edition w/Stout-c & bound-in poster; Buckler-a; foil stamped logo; Giordano-a in all 6.00
V2#1-9: 1-Newsstand edition w/Giordano-c. 2,3-Collector's editions w/Stout-c & posters. 2,3-Newsstand ed. w/Giordano-c; w/o posters. 4-6-Collectors & Newsstand editions; Kieth-c. 7-9-Linsner-c 3.00

CAGE (Also see Hero for Hire, Power Man & Punisher)
Marvel Comics: Apr, 1992 - No. 20, Nov, 1993 ($1.25)

1,3,10,12: 3-Punisher-c & minor app. 10-Rhino & Hulk-c/app. 12-(52 pgs.)-Iron Fist app. 4.00
2,4-9,11,13-20: 9-Rhino-c/story; Hulk cameo 3.00

CAGE (Volume 3)
Marvel Comics (MAX): Mar, 2002 - No. 5, Sept, 2002 ($2.99, mature)

1-5-Corben-c/a; Azzarello-s 3.00
HC (2002, $19.99, with dustjacket) r/#1-5; intro. by Darius James; sketch pages 20.00
SC (2003, $13.99) r/#1-5; intro. by Darius James 14.00

CAGE! (Luke Cage)
Marvel Comics: Dec, 2016 - No. 4, Mar, 2017 ($3.99, limited series)

The Call #1 © MAR

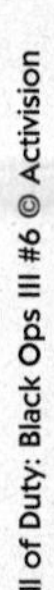
Call of Duty: Black Ops III #6 © Activision

Camp Comics #2 © WHIT

GD VG FN VF VF/NM NM-
2.0 4.0 6.0 8.0 9.0 9.2

1-4-Genndy Tartakovsky-s/a; set in 1977 4.00

CAGED HEAT 3000 (Movie)
Roger Corman's Cosmic Comics: Nov, 1995 - No. 3, Jan, 1996 ($2.50)
1-3: Adaptation of film 3.00

CAGE HERO
Dynamite Entertainment: 2015 - No. 4, 2016 ($3.99, limited series)
1-4-Kevin Eastman & Ian Parker-s/Renalto Rei-a 4.00

CAGES
Tundra Publ.: 1991 - No. 10, May, 1996 ($3.50/$3.95/$4.95, limited series)
1-Dave McKean-c/a in all 2 4 6 8 10 12
2-Misprint exists 1 2 3 5 6 8
3-9: 5-$3.95-c begins 4.00
10-($4.95) 5.00

CAIN'S HUNDRED (TV)
Dell Publishing Co.: May-July, 1962 - No. 2, Sept-Nov, 1962
nn (01-094-207) 3 6 9 19 30 40
2 3 6 9 15 22 28

CAIN/VAMPIRELLA FLIP BOOK
Harris Comics: Oct, 1994 ($6.95, one-shot, squarebound)
nn-contains Cain #3 & #4; flip book is r/Vampirella story from 1993 Creepy Fearbook 1 2 3 5 7 9

CALAMITY KATE
Dark Horse Comics: Mar, 2019 - No. 4, Jun, 2019 ($3.99, limited series)
1-4-Magdalene Visaggio-s/Corin Howell-a 4.00

CALIBER PRESENTS
Caliber Press: Jan, 1989 - No. 24, 1991 ($1.95/$2.50, B&W, 52 pgs.)
1-Anthology; 1st app. The Crow; Tim Vigil-c/a 12 24 36 82 179 275
2-Deadworld story; Tim Vigil-a 2 4 6 11 16 20
3-24: 15-24 ($3.50, 68 pgs.) 4.00
...: Cinderella on Fire 1 (1994, $2.95, B&W, mature) 3.00

CALIBER SPOTLIGHT
Caliber Press: May, 1995 ($2.95, B&W)
1-Kabuki app. 3.50

CALIFORNIA GIRLS
Eclipse Comics: June, 1987 - No. 8, May, 1988 ($2.00, 40 pgs, B&W)
1-8: All contain color paper dolls 4.00

CALL, THE
Marvel Comics: June, 2003 - No. 4, Sept, 2003 ($2.25)
1-4-Austen-s/Olliffe-a 3.00

CALLING ALL BOYS (Tex Granger No. 18 on)
Parents' Magazine Institute: Jan, 1946 - No. 17, May, 1948 (Photo c-1-5,7,8)
1 21 42 63 122 199 275
2-Contains Roy Rogers article 11 22 33 64 90 115
3-7,9,11,14-17: 6-Painted-c. 11-Rin Tin Tin photo on-c; Tex Granger begins. 14-J. Edgar Hoover photo on-c. 15-Tex Granger-c begin 10 20 30 54 72 90
8-Milton Caniff story 11 22 33 64 90 115
10-Gary Cooper photo on-c 11 22 33 64 90 115
12-Bob Hope photo on-c 15 30 45 88 137 185
13-Bing Crosby photo on-c 14 28 42 82 121 160

CALLING ALL GIRLS
Parents' Magazine Institute: Sept, 1941 - No. 89, Sept, 1949 (Part magazine, part comic)
1-Photo-c 29 58 87 170 278 385
2-Photo-c 15 30 45 85 130 175
3-Shirley Temple photo-c 20 40 60 117 189 260
4-10: 4,5,7,9-Photo-c. 9-Flag-c 13 26 39 74 105 135
11-Tina Thayer photo-c; Mickey Rooney photo-b/c; B&W photo inside of Gary Cooper as Lou Gehrig in "Pride of Yankees" 14 28 42 82 121 160
12-20 11 22 33 60 83 105
21-39,41-43(10-11/45)-Last issue with comics 10 20 30 56 76 95
40-Liz Taylor photo-c 29 58 87 170 278 385
44-51(7/46)-Last comic book size issue 9 18 27 50 65 80
52-89 8 16 24 44 57 70
NOTE: ***Jack Sparling*** *art in many issues; becomes a girls' magazine "Senior Prom" with #90.*

CALLING ALL KIDS (Also see True Comics)
Parents' Magazine Institute: Dec-Jan, 1945-46 - No. 26, Aug, 1949
1-Funny animal 19 38 57 112 179 245
2 11 22 33 64 90 115
3-10 9 18 27 52 69 85
11-26 9 18 27 47 61 75

CALL OF DUTY: BLACK OPS III (Based on the Activision video game)
Dark Horse Comics: Nov, 2015 - No. 6, Oct, 2016 ($3.99, limited series)
1-6-Prequel to the game; Hama-s/Ferreira-a 4.00

CALL OF DUTY: ZOMBIES (Based on the Activision video game)
Dark Horse Comics: Oct, 2016 - No. 6, Aug, 2017 ($3.99, limited series)
1-6-Justin Jordan-s/Jonathan Wayshak-a/Simon Bisley-c 4.00

CALL OF DUTY: ZOMBIES 2 (Based on the Activision video game)
Dark Horse Comics: Sept, 2018 - No. 3, Dec, 2018 ($3.99, limited series)
1-3-Justin Jordan-s/Andres Ponce-a/E.M. Gist-c 4.00

CALL OF DUTY, THE : THE BROTHERHOOD
Marvel Comics: Aug, 2002 - No. 6, Jan, 2003 ($2.25)
1-Exploits of NYC Fire Dept.; Finch-c/a; Austen & Bruce Jones-s 4.00
2-6-Austen-s 3.00
...Vol 1: The Brotherhood & The Wagon TPB (2002, $14.99) r/#1-6 & ...The Wagon #1-4 15.00

CALL OF DUTY, THE : THE PRECINCT
Marvel Comics: Sept, 2002 - No. 5, Jan, 2003 ($2.25, limited series)
1-Exploits of NYC Police Dept.; Finch-c; Bruce Jones-s/Mandrake-a 3.00
2-4 3.00
...Vol 2: The Precinct TPB (2003, $9.99) r/#1-4 10.00

CALL OF DUTY, THE : THE WAGON
Marvel Comics: Oct, 2002 - No. 4, Jan, 2003 ($2.25, limited series)
1-4-Exploits of NYC EMS Dept.; Finch-c; Austen-s/Zelzej-a 3.00

CALVIN (See Li'l Kids)

CALVIN & THE COLONEL (TV)
Dell Publishing Co.: No. 1354, Apr-June, 1962 - No. 2, July-Sept, 1962
Four Color 1354(#1) (The last Four Color issue) 9 18 27 58 114 170
2 5 10 15 35 63 90

CAMELOT 3000
DC Comics: Dec, 1982 - No. 11, July, 1984; No. 12, Apr, 1985 (Direct sales, maxi series, Mando paper)
1-12: 1-Mike Barr scripts & Brian Bolland-c/a in all. 5-Intro Knights of New Camelot 5.00
TPB (1988, $12.95) r/#1-12 15.00
...: The Deluxe Edition (2008, $34.99, HC) r/#1-12; oversized & recolored; Barr intro.; design and promotional art; original proposal page 40.00
NOTE: ***Austin*** *a-7i-12i.* ***Bolland*** *a-1-12p; c-1-12.*

CAMERA COMICS
U.S. Camera Publishing Corp./ME: July, 1944 - No. 9, Summer, 1946
nn (7/44) 41 82 123 256 428 600
nn (9/44) 30 60 90 177 289 400
1(10/44)-The Grey Comet (slightly smaller page size than subsequent issues); WWII-c 34 68 102 204 332 460
2-16 pgs. of photos with 32 pgs. of comics 22 44 66 128 209 290
3-Nazi WW II-c; photos 39 78 117 240 395 550
4-9: All 1/3 photos 19 38 57 111 176 240

CAMP CANDY (TV)
Marvel Comics: May, 1990 - No. 6, Oct, 1990 ($1.00, limited series)
1-6: Post-c/a(p); featuring John Candy 5.00

CAMP COMICS
Dell Publishing Co.: Feb, 1942 - No. 3, April, 1942 (All have photo-c)(All issues are scarce)
1- "Seaman Sy Wheeler" by Kelly, 7 pgs.; Bugs Bunny app.; Mark Twain adaptation 95 190 285 603 1039 1475
2-Kelly-a, 12 pgs.; Bugs Bunny app.; classic-c 94 188 282 597 1024 1450
3-(Scarce)-Dave Berg & Walt Kelly-a 65 130 195 416 708 1000

CAMP RUNAMUCK (TV)
Dell Publishing Co.: Apr, 1966
1-Photo-c 3 6 9 21 33 45

CAMPUS LOVES
Quality Comics Group (Comic Magazines): Dec, 1949 - No. 5, Aug, 1950
1-Ward-c/a (9 pgs.) 43 86 129 271 461 650
2-Ward-c/a 34 68 102 204 332 460
3-5 19 38 57 109 172 235
NOTE: ***Gustavson*** *a-1-5. Photo c-3-5.*

CAMPUS ROMANCE (...Romances on cover)
Avon Periodicals/Realistic: Sept-Oct, 1949 - No. 3, Feb-Mar, 1950

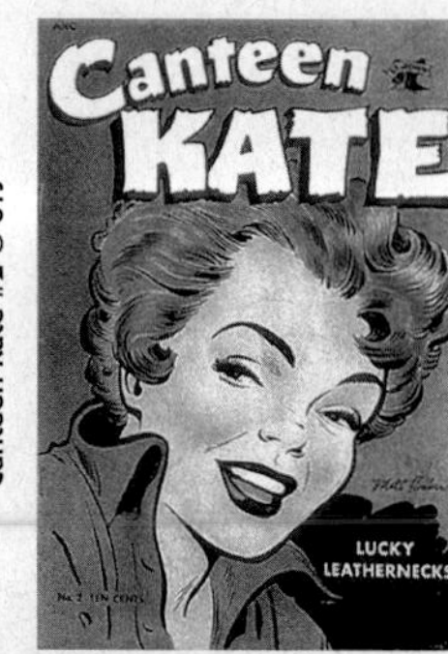

Canteen Kate #2 © STJ

The Cape: Fallen #2 © Joe Hill

Captain Aero Comics #1 © HOKE

	GD 2.0	VG 4.0	FN 6.0	VF 8.0	VF/NM 9.0	NM- 9.2

1-Walter Johnson-a; c-/Avon paperback #348 48 96 144 302 514 725
2-Grandenetti-a; c-/Avon paperback #151 34 68 102 204 332 460
3-c-/Avon paperback #201 34 68 102 204 332 460
Realistic reprint 19 38 57 111 176 240

CANADA DRY PREMIUMS (See Swamp Fox, The & Terry & The Pirates in the Promotional Comics section)

CANADIAN VARK! (Reprints from Cerebus in Hell)
Aardvark-Vanaheim: Dec, 2018 ($4.00, B&W)
1-Cerebus figures placed over original Doré artwork of Hell; American Flagg #1-c swipe 4.00

CANCELLED COMIC CAVALCADE (See the Promotional Comics section)

CANDID TALES (Also see Bold Stories & It Rhymes With Lust)
Kirby Publ. Co.: April, 1950; June, 1950 (Digest size) (144 pgs.) (Full color)
nn-(Scarce) Contains Wood female pirate story, 15 pgs., and 14 pgs. in June issue; Powell-a
200 400 600 1280 2190 3100
NOTE: *Another version exists with Dr. Kilmore by Wood; no female pirate story.*

CANDY (Teen-age)(Also see Police Comics #37)
Quality Comics Group (Comic Magazines): Autumn, 1947 - No. 64, Jul, 1956
1-Gustavson-a 34 68 102 202 329 455
2-Gustavson-a 17 34 51 98 154 210
3-10 13 26 39 74 105 135
11-30 10 20 30 58 79 100
31-64: 64-Ward-c(p)? 9 18 27 50 65 80
Super Reprint No. 2,10,12,16,17,18('63- '64):17-Candy #12
2 4 6 10 14 18
NOTE: ***Jack Cole** 1-2 pg. art in many issues.*

CANDY COMICS
William H. Wise & Co.: Fall, 1944 - No. 3, Spring, 1945
1-Two Scoop Scuttle stories by Wolverton 43 86 124 271 461 650
2,3-Scoop Scuttle by Wolverton, 2-4 pgs. 30 60 90 177 289 400

CANNON (See Heroes, Inc. Presents Cannon)

CANNIBAL
Image Comics: Oct, 2016 - No. 8, Oct, 2017 ($3.99)
1-8-Young & Buccellato-s/Bergara-a 4.00

CANNON: DAWN OF WAR (Michael Turner's...)
Aspen MLT, Inc.: Nov, 2004 ($2.99)
1-Turnbull-a; two covers by Turnbull and Turner 3.00

CANNONBALL COMICS
Rural Home Publishing Co.: Feb, 1945 - No. 2, Mar, 1945
1-The Crash Kid, Thunderbrand, The Captive Prince & Crime Crusader begin; skull-c
168 336 504 1075 1838 2600
2-Devil-c 129 258 387 826 1413 2000

CANTEEN KATE (See All Picture All True Love Story & Fightin' Marines)
St. John Publishing Co.: June, 1952 - No. 3, Nov, 1952
1-Matt Baker-c/a 110 220 330 704 1202 1700
2-Matt Baker-c/a 60 120 180 381 653 925
3-(Rare)-Used in **POP**, pg. 75; Baker-c/a 71 142 213 454 777 1100

CAPE, THE
IDW Publishing: Dec, 2010; Jul, 2011 - No. 4, Jan, 2012 ($3.99)
1-(12/10) Zach Howard-c/a; Jason Ciaramella-s 4.00
1-4: 1-(7/11) Story continues from 12/10 issue 4.00
...: Fallen (6/18 - No. 4, 12/18, $3.99) 1-4-Ciaramella-s; Zach Howard-a 4.00
...: Greatest Hits (6/18, $1.00) reprints #1 (12/10) and previews The Cape: Fallen series 3.00
...: Legacy Edition (6/11, $5.99) r/#1 (12/10) with Joe Hill's original short story 6.00
...: 1969 (7/12 - No. 4, 10/12, $3.99) 1-4-Ciaramella-s; origin in Vietnam 4.00

CAPER
DC Comics: Dec, 2003 - No. 12, Nov, 2004 ($2.95, limited series)
1-12: 1-4-Judd Winick-s/Farel Dalrymple-a. 5-8-John Severin-a. 9-12-Fowler-a 3.00

CAPES
Image Comics: Sept, 2003 - No. 3, Nov, 2003 ($3.50)
1-Robert Kirkman-s; 5 pg. preview of The Walking Dead #1
4 8 12 22 35 48
2,3-Robert Kirkman-s/Mark Englert-a/c 3.50

CAP'N QUICK & A FOOZLE (Also see Eclipse Mag. & Monthly)
Eclipse Comics: July, 1984 - No. 3, Nov, 1985 ($1.50, color, Baxter paper)
1-3-Rogers-c/a 3.00

CAPTAIN ACTION (Toy)
National Periodical Publications: Oct-Nov, 1968 - No. 5, June-July, 1969 (Based on Ideal toy)
1-Origin; Wally Wood-a; Superman-c app. 7 14 21 46 86 125
2,3,5-Gil Kane/Wally Wood-a 5 10 15 31 53 75
4- Gil Kane-c 4 8 12 27 44 60

CAPTAIN ACTION CAT: THE TIMESTREAM CATASTROPHE
Dynamite Entertainment: 2014 - No. 4, 2014 ($3.99, limited series)
1-4-Art Baltazar-s/a; Franco & Smits-s; all ages cat version of Capt. Action characters; Ghost, X, Captain Midnight, Skyman & The Occultist app. 4.00

CAPTAIN ACTION COMICS (Toy)
Moonstone: No. 0, 2008 - No. 5 (Based on the Ideal toy)
0-($1.99) Origin re-told; Sparacio-a; three covers; character history by Michael Eury 3.00
1-5: 1-($3.99) Sparacio-a; intro. by Jim Shooter 4.00
... Comics Special 1 (2010, $5.99) 3 covers by Barreto, Ordway & Spiegle 6.00
... Exclusive Special 1 (2011, no price) Gulacy-c; Barreto-a 4.00
...: First Mission, Last Day (2008, $3.99) origin story re-told; Nicieza-s/Procopio-a 4.00
... King Size Special 1 (2011, $6.99) 1-Covers by Byrne, Wheatley & M. Benes 7.00
... Season 2 (2010, $3.99) 1-3: 1-Covers by Allred & Texiera; Obama app. 4.00
... Winter Special (2011, $4.99) Green Hornet & Kato on-c & text story 5.00

CAPTAIN AERO COMICS (Samson No. 1-6; also see Veri Best Sure Fire & Veri Best Sure Shot Comics)
Holyoke Publishing Co.: V1#7(#1), Dec, 1941 - V2#4(#10), Jan, 1943; V3#9(#11), Sept, 1943 -V4#3(#17), Oct, 1944; #21, Dec, 1944 - #26, Aug, 1946 (No #18-20)
V1#7(#1)-Flag-Man & Solar, Master of Magic, Captain Aero, Cap Stone, Adventurer begin; Nazi WWII-c 219 438 657 1402 2401 3400
8,10: 8(#2)-Pals of Freedom app. 10(#4)-Origin The Gargoyle; Kubert-a
106 212 318 673 1162 1650
9(#3)-Hitler-sty; Catman back-c; Alias X begins; Pals of Freedom app.; Nazi WWII-c
119 238 357 762 1306 1850
11,12(#5,6)-Kubert-a; Miss Victory in #6 86 172 258 546 936 1325
V2#1,2(#7,8): 8-Origin The Red Cross; Miss Victory app.; Brodsky-c(i)
68 136 204 435 743 1050
3(#9)-Miss Victory app. 116 232 348 742 1271 1800
4(#10)-Miss Victory app.; Japanese WWII-c 102 204 306 648 1112 1575
V3#9 - V3#12(#11-14): All Quinlan Japanese WWII-c. 9-Miss Victory app.
86 172 258 546 936 1325
V3#13(#15),V4#2(#16): Schomburg Japanese WWII-c. 13-Miss Victory app.
102 204 306 648 1112 1575
V4#3(#17)-Miss Victory app.; L.B. Cole Japanese WWII-c
76 152 228 486 831 1175
21-24-L.B. Cole Japanese WWII covers. 22-Intro/origin Mighty Mite
65 130 195 416 708 1000
25-L.B. Cole Sci-fi-c 82 164 246 528 902 1275
26-L.B. Cole Sci-fi-c; Palais-a(2) (scarce) 300 600 900 1980 3440 4900
NOTE: ***L.B. Cole** c-17, 21-26. **Hollingsworth** a-23. **Infantino** a-23, 26. **Schomburg** c-15, 16.*

CAPTAIN AMERICA (See Adventures of..., All-Select, All Winners, Aurora, Avengers #4, Blood and Glory, Captain Britain 16-20, Giant-Size..., The Invaders, Marvel Double Feature, Marvel Fanfare, Marvel Mystery, Marvel Super-Action, Marvel Super Heroes V2#3, Marvel Team-Up, Marvel Treasury Special, Power Record Comics, Ultimates, USA Comics, Young Allies & Young Men)

CAPTAIN AMERICA (Formerly Tales of Suspense #1-99) (Captain America and the Falcon #134-223 & Steve Rogers: Captain America #444-454 appears on cover only)
Marvel Comics Group: No. 100, Apr, 1968 - No. 454, Aug, 1996
100-Flashback on Cap's revival with Avengers & Sub-Mariner; story continued from Tales of Suspense #99; Kirby-c/a begins 55 110 165 380 715 1050
101-The Sleeper-c/story; Red Skull app. 9 18 27 62 126 190
102-104: 102-Sleeper-c/s. 103,104-Red Skull-c/sty 7 14 21 48 89 130
105,106,108 6 12 18 38 69 100
107-Red Skull & Hitler-c 8 16 24 51 96 140
109-Origin Capt. America retold in detail 10 20 30 69 147 225
109-2nd printing (1994) 2 4 6 8 10 12
110-Rick Jones dons Bucky's costume & becomes Cap's partner; Hulk x-over; Steranko-a Classic Steranko-c 12 24 36 79 170 260
111-Classic Steranko-c/a; Death of Steve Rogers 10 20 30 68 144 220
112-S.A. recovery retold; last Kirby-c/a 6 12 18 42 79 115
113-Cap's funeral; Avengers app.; classic Steranko-c/a
9 18 27 62 126 190
114-116,119,120: 114-Red Skull Cosmic Cube story. 115,116-Red Skull app; last 12c issue. 119-Cap vs. Red Skull; Cosmic Cube "destroyed"; Falcon app.
5 10 15 30 50 70
117-1st app. The Falcon (9/69) 37 74 111 274 612 950
117 Facsimile Edition (3/21, $3.99) Reprints #117 with original ads and letter column 4.00
118-2nd app. The Falcon 9 18 27 57 111 165
121-136,139,140: 121-Retells origin; Avengers app. 122-Cap vs. Scorpion. 124-Modok app. 125-Mandarin app. 129-Red Skull app. 133-The Falcon becomes Cap's partner; origin Modok. 139,140-Grey Gargoyle app; origin in #140

Captain America #179 © MAR

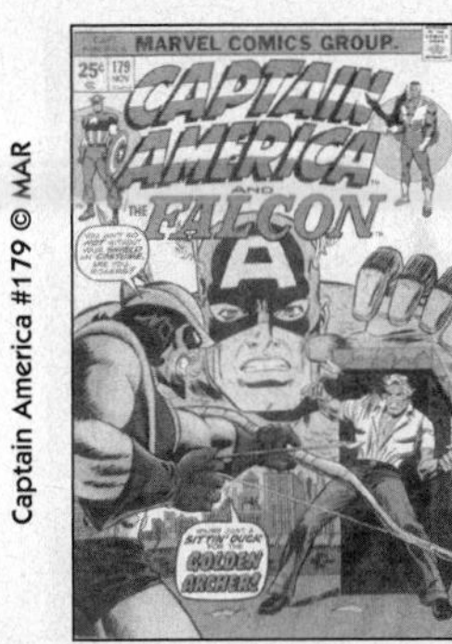

Captain America #357 © MAR

Captain America #431 © MAR

	GD 2.0	VG 4.0	FN 6.0	VF 8.0	VF/NM 9.0	NM- 9.2
	4	8	12	23	37	50
137,138-Spider-Man x-over	5	10	15	30	50	70
141,142-Grey Gargoyle app. 141-Last Stan Lee issue. 142-Last 15¢ issue	3	6	9	21	33	45
143-(52 pgs) Cap vs. Red Skull	4	8	12	25	40	55
144-New costume Falcon	3	6	9	21	33	45
145-152: 145-147-Cap vs. the Supreme Hydra. 146-1st Sal Buscema-a on title. 147-Supreme Hydra revealed to be Kingpin's son. 148-Red Skull app. 150-The Stranger app. 151,152- Cap vs. Mr. Hyde & The Scorpion. 152-1st app. Boss Morgan	3	6	9	14	20	25
153-155: 153-1st brief app. Jack Monroe; return of 1950s Captain America. 154-1st full app. Jack Monroe (Nomad); 1950s Captain America and Avengers app. 155-Origin retold; origin Jack Monroe and the 1950s Captain America	3	6	9	21	33	45
156-Cap vs. the 1950s Captain America; Jack Monroe app; classic Cap vs Cap cover	3	6	9	19	30	40
157-162,165-167,177-179: 157-1st app. Viper. 159-Cap vs. Eel, Porcupine & Scarecrow. 160-1st app. Solarr. 161,162-Peggy Carter app. 164-1st Nightshade. 165-167-Cap vs. Yellow Claw. 177-Lucifer app. 178-1st time Peggy Carter meets Steve Rogers. 179-Hawkeye app. as the Golden Archer	2	4	6	10	14	18
163-1st Serpent Squad: Viper, Eel and Cobra	2	4	6	10	14	18
164-1st app. Nightshade, Queen of Werewolves	2	4	6	10	14	18
168-1st Helmut Zemo (as the Phoenix)	3	6	9	19	30	40
169-1st app. Quentin Harderman; Moonstone 1st app. (cameo)	2	4	6	10	14	18
170-New Falcon costume with wings for flying; Moonstone 1st full app. & origin	2	4	6	10	14	18
171-Black Panther & Iron Man app.	4	8	12	22	35	48
172-175: X-Men x-over. 174-1st app. Number 1	3	6	9	16	23	30
176-Steve Rogers quits being Cap.; Avengers app.	2	4	6	13	18	22
180-Intro/origin of Nomad (Steve Rogers)	8	16	24	54	102	150
181-Intro/origin new Cap.	3	6	9	17	26	35
182,184,185,187-192: 182,184,185-Red Skull app. 182-Frank Robbins-a. 189,190-Cap vs. Nightshade. 191-Iron Man app. 192-Intro Dr. Karla Sofen (later becomes Moonstone)	2	4	6	8	10	12
183-Death of new Cap; Steve Rogers drops Nomad I.D; returns to being Capt. America	2	4	6	9	12	15
186-True origin The Falcon; Red Skull app.	3	6	9	14	19	24
193-Kirby-c/a begins	4	8	12	25	40	55
194-199-(Regular 25¢ edition)(4-7/76)	2	4	6	10	14	18
196-199-(30¢-c variants, limited distribution)	6	12	18	37	66	95
200-(Regular 25¢ edition)(8/76)	2	4	6	11	16	20
200-(30¢-c variant, limited distribution)	7	14	21	44	82	120
201-214-Kirby-c/a. 208-1st Arnim Zola. 209,210- Arnim Zola app. 210-212 –vs Red Skull	2	4	6	8	11	14
210-214-(35¢-c variants, limited dist.)(6-10/77)	10	20	30	66	138	210
215,216,218-229: 215-Origin retold. 216-r/Strange Tales #114. 218-Sal Buscema-a resumes. 226,227-Red Skull app. 228-Cap vs. Constrictor. 229-Marvel Man app.	1	3	4	6	8	10
217-Intro. Marvel Boy (Wendell Vaughan); becomes Marvel Man in #218; later becomes Quasar (2/78)	6	12	18	38	69	100
230,235: 230-Battles Hulk-c/story cont'd in Inc. Hulk #232. 235-(7/79) Daredevil x-over; Miller-a(p)	2	4	6	8	10	12
231-234,236-240,242-246: 233-"Death" of Sharon Carter. 234-Daredevil app. 244,245-Miller-c	1	2	3	5	6	8
241-Punisher app.; Miller-c	5	10	15	31	53	75
241-2nd print	1	2	3	5	6	8
247-252-Byrne-a	1	3	4	6	8	10
253,255: 253-Byrne-a; Baron Blood app. 255-Origin retold; Miller-c	2	4	6	9	12	15
254-Byrne-a; death of Baron Blood; intro new Union Jack	2	4	6	13	18	22
256-262: 257-Hulk app. 258-Zeck-a begins. 259-Cap vs. Dr. Octopus. 261,262-Red Skull app.						6.00
263-266: 263-Red Skull-c/story. 264-Original X-Men app. 265,266-Spider-Man app.	1	2	3	5	6	8
267-280: 267-1st app. & origin Everyman. 268-Defenders app. 269-1st Team America. 272-1st Vermin. 273,274-Baron Strucker. 275-1st Baron Zemo (formally the Phoenix). 276-278-Cap vs. Baron Zemo. 279-(3/83)-Contains Tattooz skin decals. 280-Scarecrow app.						5.00
281-1950's Bucky returns. Spider-Woman and Viper app.	1	2	3	4	6	8
282-Bucky becomes new Nomad (Jack Monroe)	2	4	6	8	10	12
282-Silver ink 2nd print ($1.75) w/original date (6/83)						4.00
283-289,291-300: 283-Cap vs. Viper. 284-Patriot (Jack Mace) app. 285-Death of Patriot. 286-288-Deathlok app. 293,294-Nomad app. 293-299-Red Skull and Baron Zemo app. 298-Origin Red Skull. 300- "Death" of Red Skull						6.00
290-1st Mother Superior (Red Skull's daughter, later becomes Sin)	2	4	6	8	10	12
301-304,307-322,324-331: 301-Avengers app. 307-1st Madcap; 1st Mark Gruenwald-s (begins 8-year run). 308-Secret Wars II x-over. 310-1st Serpent Society. 312-1st Flag Smasher. 313-Death of Modok. 314-Squadron Supreme x-over. 317-Hawkeye & Mockingbird app. 318-Scourge app; death of Blue Streak and Adder. 319-Scourge kills numerous villians. 320-"Death"of Scourge. 321-Cap vs. Flag Smasher; classic Zeck cover Cap with machine gun. 322-Cap vs. Flag Smasher. 325-Nomad app. 327-Cap vs Super-Patriot. 328,330-Demolition Man (D-Man) app.						5.00
305,306-Captain Britain app.						6.00
323-1st app. new Super-Patriot (see Nick Fury)	5	10	15	31	53	75
332-Old Captain America resigns	2	4	6	9	13	16
333-Super Patriot becomes new Captain America	3	6	9	14	20	25
334-340: 334-Intro new Bucky; Freedom Force app. 337-Serpent Society app; Avengers #4 homage-c; Steve Rogers becomes 'the Captain'; becomes Captain America again in issue #350. 339-Fall of the Mutants tie-in						5.00
341-343,345-349: 341-Cap vs Iron Man; x-over with Iron Man #228. 342-Cap vs. Viper and the Serpent Squad						5.00
344-($1.50, 52 pgs.)-Ronald Reagan cameo as a snake man						6.00
350-($1.75, 68 pgs.)-Return of Steve Rogers (original Cap) to original costume	1	3	4	6	8	10
351-353-355-358,361-382,384-396: 351-Nick Fury app. 357-Bloodstone hunt Pt. 1 (of 6). 358-Baron Zemo app. 365,366-Acts of Vengeance x-overs. 367-Magneto vs Red Skull. 372-378-Streets of Poison. 374-Bullseye app. 375-Daredevil app. 376-Black Widow app. 377-Bullseye vs. Crossbones; Red Skull app. 379-Quasar app. 380-382-Serpent Society app. 386-U.S. Agent app. 387-392-Superia Stratagem. 387-389-Red Skull back-up stories. 394-Red Skull app. 395-Thor app. (Eric Masterson; also in #396-397); Red Skull app. 396-Red Skull and new (1st) Jack O Lantern app.						5.00
354-John Walker's 1st app. as U.S.Agent	5	10	15	33	57	80
354 Facsimile Edition (3/21, $3.99) Reprints #354 with original ads and letter column						4.00
359-Crossbones debut (cameo); Baron Zemo app.	2	4	6	8	10	12
360-1st app. Crossbones; Baron Zemo app.	3	6	9	16	24	32
383-($2.00, 68 pgs., squarebound)-50th anniversary issue; Red Skull story; Jim Lee-c(i)						6.00
397-399,401-424: 397-New Jack O Lantern app. 398,399-Operation Galactic Storm x-overs. 401-Operation Galactic storm epilogue. 402-Begin 6 part Man-Wolf story w/Wolverine in #403-407. 405-410-New Jack O Lantern app. in back-up story. 406-Cable & Shatterstar cameo. 407-Capwolf vs. Cable-c/story. 408-Infinity War x-over; Falcon back-up story. 409-Red Skull & Crossbones app. 410-Crossbones app. 414-Black Panther app. 419-Red Skull app; x-over with Silver Sable #15. 423- Cap vs. Namor-c/story						4.00
400-($2.25, 84 pgs.) Flip book format w/double gatefold-c; Operation Galactic Storm x-over; r/Avengers #4 plus-c contains cover pin-ups	1	2	3	5	6	8
425-($2.95, 52 pgs.)-Embossed Foil-c edition; Fighting Chance Pt. 1						5.00
425-($1.75, 52 pgs.)-non-embossed-c edition; Fighting Chance Pt. 1						5.00
426-439,442,443: 426-437-Fighting Chance Pt. 2-12. 427-Begins $1.50-c; bound-in trading card sheet. 428-1st Americop. 431-1st Free Spirit. 434-1st Jack Flag. 438-Fighting Chance epilogue. 443-Last Gruenwald issue						4.00
440,441,444,445: 440,441-Avengers x-overs; 'Taking A.I.M" story. 444-Mark Waid-s (1st on Cap) & Ron Garney-c/a(p) begins, ends #454; Avengers app. 445-Operation rebirth Pt.1; vs. Red Skull; Sharon Carter returns						5.00
446,447 – Operation Rebirth; Red Skull app. 446-Hitler app.						6.00
448-($2.95, double-sized issue) Waid script & Garney-c/a; Red Skull "dies"						5.00
449-Thor app; story x-overs with Thor, Iron Man and Avengers titles						5.00
450- "Man Without a Country" begins; Steve Rogers-c						6.00
450-Captain America-c with white background	1	2	3	5	6	8
451-453: 451-1st app. Cap's new costume. 453-Cap gets old costume back; Bill Clinton app.						4.00
454-Last issue of the regular series (8/96)						5.00
#600-up (See Captain America 2005 series, resumed original numbering after #50)						
Special 1(1/71)-All reprint issue from Tales Of Suspense #63,69,70,71,75	6	12	18	40	73	105
Special 2(1/72, 52 pgs.)-All reprint issue from Tales Of Suspense #72-74 and Not Brand Echh #5	4	8	12	27	44	60
Annual 3('76, 52 pgs.)-Kirby-c/a(new)	3	6	9	16	23	30
Annual 4('77, 34 pgs.)-Magneto-c/story	3	6	9	16	23	30
Annual 5-7: (52 pgs.)('81-'83)						5.00
Annual 8(9/86)-Wolverine-c/story;Zeck-c	4	8	12	23	37	50
Annual 9-13('90-'94, 68 pgs.)-9-Nomad back-up. 10-Origin retold (2 pgs.). 11-Falcon solo story. 12-Bagged w/card. 13-Red Skull-c/story						6.00
...Ashcan Edition ('95, 75¢)						4.00
... and the Falcon: Madbomb TPB (2004, $16.99) r/#193-200; Kirby-s/a						17.00
... and the Falcon: Nomad TPB (2006, $24.99) r/#177-186; Cap becomes Nomad						25.00
... and the Falcon: Secret Empire TPB (2005, $19.99) r/#169-176						20.00
... and the Falcon: The Swine TPB (2006, $29.99) r/#206-214 & Annual #3,4						30.00

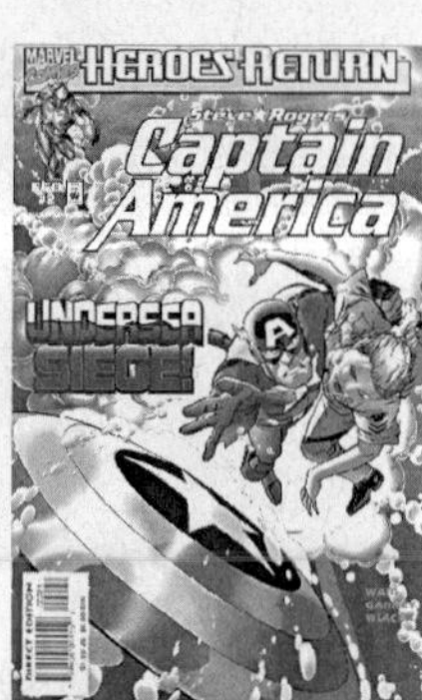
Captain America V3 #2 © MAR

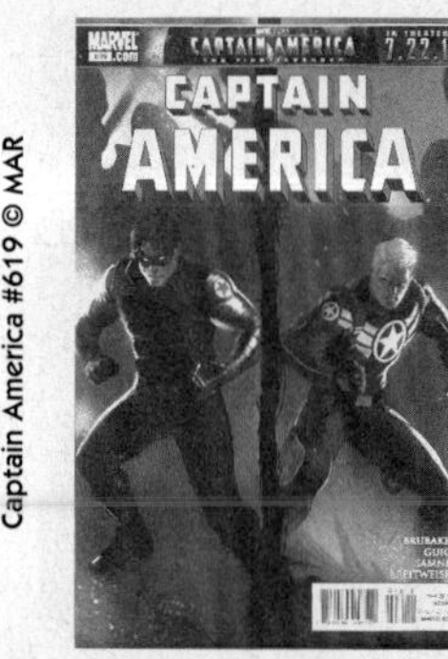
Captain America #619 © MAR

Captain America (2013 series) #1 © MAR

GD VG FN VF VF/NM NM-
2.0 4.0 6.0 8.0 9.0 9.2

... By Jack Kirby: Bicentennial Battles TPB (2005, $19.99) r/#201-205 & Marvel Treasury Special Featuring Captain America's Bicentennial Battles; Kirby-s/a 20.00
...: Deathlok Lives! nn(10/93, $4.95)-r/#286-288 6.00
...Drug War 1-(1994, $2.00, 52 pgs.)-New Warriors app. 4.00
...Man Without a Country(1998, $12.99, TPB)-r/#450-453 13.00
...Medusa Effect 1 (1994, $2.95, 68 pgs.)-Origin Baron Zemo 4.00
...Operation Rebirth (1996, $9.95)-r/#445-448 10.00
... 65th Anniversary Special (5/06, $3.99) WWII flashback with Bucky; Brubaker-s 5.00
...Streets of Poison ($15.95)-r/#372-378 16.00
...: The Movie Special nn (5/92, $3.50, 52 pgs.)-Adapts movie; printed on coated stock; The Red Skull app. 4.00

NOTE: **Austin** *c-225i, 239i, 246i.* **Buscema** *a-115p, 217p; c-136p, 217, 297.* **Byrne** *c-223(part), 238, 239, 247p-254p, 290, 291, 313p; a-247-254p, 255, 313p, 350.* **Colan** *a(p)-116-137, 256, Annual 5; c(p)-116-123, 126, 129.* **Everett** *a-136i, 137i; c-126i.* **Garney** *a(p)-444-454.* **Gil Kane** *a-145p; c-147p, 149p, 150p, 170p, 172-174, 180, 181p, 183-190p, 215, 216, 220, 221.* **Kirby** *a(p)-100-109, 112, 193-214, 216, Special 1, 2(layouts), Annual 3, 4; c-100-109, 112, 126p, 193-214.* **Ron Lim** *a(p)-366, 368-378, 380-386; c-366p, 368-378p, 379, 380-393p.* **Miller** *c-241p, 244p, 245p, 255p, Annual 5.* **Mooney** *a-149i.* **Morrow** *a-144.* **Perez** *c-243p, 246p.* **Robbins** *c(p)-183-187, 189-192, 225.* **Roussos** *a-140i, 168i.* **Shores** *a-102i, 107i, 109i.* **Starlin/Sinnott** *c-162.* **Sutton** *a-244i.* **Tuska** *a-112i, 215p, Special 2.* **Waid** *scripts-444-454.* **Williamson** *a-313i.* **Wood** *a-127i.* **Zeck** *a-263-289; c-300.*

CAPTAIN AMERICA (Volume Two)
Marvel Comics: V2#1, Nov, 1996 - No. 13, Nov, 1997($2.95/$1.95/$1.99)
(Produced by Extreme Studios)

1-($2.95)-Heroes Reborn begins; Liefeld-c/a; Loeb scripts; reintro Nick Fury 1 3 4 6 8 10
1-($2.95)-(Variant-c)-Liefeld-c/a 1 2 3 5 6 8
1-(7/96, $2.95)-(Exclusive Comicon Ed.)-Liefeld-c/a 2 4 6 8 10 12
2-4,6-11,13: 6-Cable-c/app. 13-"World War 3"-pt. 4, x-over w/Image 3.00
5-1st cover app. of Rikki Barnes; two covers 1 3 4 6 8 10
12-($2.99) "Heroes Reunited"-pt. 4 4.00
Heroes Reborn: Captain America (2006, $29.99, TPB) r/#1-12 & Heroes Reborn #1/2 30.00

CAPTAIN AMERICA (Vol. Three) (Also see Capt. America: Sentinel of Liberty)
Marvel Comics: Jan, 1998 - No. 50, Feb, 2002 ($2.99/$1.99/$2.25)

1-($2.99) Mark Waid-s/Ron Garney-a 4.00
1-Variant cover 6.00
2-($1.99): 2-Two covers 3.00
3-11: 3-Returns to old shield. 4-Hawkeye app. 5-Thor-c/app. 7-Andy Kubert-c/a begin. 9-New shield 3.00
12-($2.99) Battles Nightmare; Red Skull back-up story 4.00
13-17,19-Red Skull returns 3.00
18-($2.99) Cap vs. Korvac in the Future 4.00
20-24,26-29: 20,21-Sgt. Fury back-up story painted by Evans 3.00
25-($2.99) Cap & Falcon vs. Hatemonger 4.00
30-49: 30-Begin $2.25-c. 32-Ordway-a. 33-Jurgens-s/a begins; U.S. Agent app. 36-Maximum Security x-over. 41,46-Red Skull app. 3.00
50-($5.95) Stories by various incl. Jurgens, Quitely, Immonen; Ha-c 6.00
.../Citizen V '98 Annual ($3.50) Busiek & Kesel-s 4.00
1999 Annual ($3.50) Flag Smasher app. 4.00
2000 Annual ($3.50) Continued from #35 vs. Protocide; Jurgens-s 4.00
2001 Annual ($2.99) Golden Age flashback; Invaders app. 4.00
...: To Serve and Protect TPB (2/02, $17.95) r/Vol. 3 #1-7 18.00

CAPTAIN AMERICA (Volume 4)
Marvel Comics: Jun, 2002 - No. 32, Dec, 2004 ($3.99/$2.99)

1-Ney Rieber-s/Cassaday-c/a 4.00
2-9-($2.99) 3-Cap reveals Steve Rogers ID. 7-9-Hairsine-a 3.00
10-32: 10-16-Jae Lee-a. 17-20-Gibbons-s/Weeks-a. 21-26-Bachalo-a. 26-Bucky flashback. 27,28-Eddie Campbell-a. 29-32-Red Skull app. 3.00
...Vol. 1: The New Deal HC (2003, $22.99) r/#1-6; foreword by Max Allan Collins 23.00
...Vol. 2: The Extremists TPB (2003, $13.99) r/#7-11; Cassaday-c 14.00
...Vol. 3: Ice TPB (2003, $12.99) r/#12-16; Jae Lee-a; Cassaday-c 13.00
...Vol. 4: Cap Lives TPB (2004, $12.99) r/#17-22 & Tales of Suspense #66 13.00
Avengers Disassembled: Captain America TPB (2004, $17.99) r/#29-32 and Captain America and the Falcon #5-7 18.00

CAPTAIN AMERICA
Marvel Comics: Jan, 2005 - No. 50, Jul, 2009; No. 600, Aug, 2009 - No. 619, Aug, 2011 ($2.99/$3.99)

1-Brubaker-s/Epting-c/a; Red Skull app. 2 4 6 11 16 20
2-5 6.00
6-1st full app. of the Winter Soldier; swastika-c 3 6 9 21 33 45
6-Retailer variant cover 4 8 12 27 44 60
7-24: 10-House of M. 11-Origin of the Winter Soldier. 13-Iron Man app. 24-Civil War 4.00
8-Variant Red Skull cover 2 4 6 8 10 12
25-($3.99) Captain America shot dead; handcuffed red glove cover by Epting 12.00
25-($3.99) Variant edition with running Cap cover by McGuinness 8.00
25-($3.99) 2nd printing with "The Death of The Dream" cover by Epting 5.00
25-Director's Cut-($4.99) w/script with Brubaker commentary; pencil pages, variant and un-used covers gallery; article on media hype 6.00
26-33-Falcon & Winter Soldier app. 3.00
34-(3/08) Bucky becomes the new Captain America; Alex Ross-c 10.00
34-Variant-c by Steve Epting 8.00
34-($3.99) Director's Cut; includes script; pencil art, costume designs, cover gallery 5.00
34-DF Edition with Alex Ross portrait cover; signed by Ross 40.00
35-49-Bucky as Captain America. 43-45-Batroc app. 46,47-Sub-Mariner app. 3.00
50-(7/09, $3.99) Bucky's birthday flashbacks; Captain America's life synopsis; Martin-a 4.00
(After #50, numbering reverts to original with #600, Aug, 2009)
600-(8/09, $4.99) Covers by Ross and Epting; leads into Captain America: Reborn series; art by Guice, Chaykin, Ross, Eaglesham; commentary by Joe Simon; cover gallery 5.00
601-615,617-619-($3.99) 601-Gene Colan-a; 3 covers. 602-Nomad back-up feature begins. 606-Baron Zemo returns. 611-615-Trial of Captain America 4.00
615.1 (5/11, $2.99) Brubaker-s/Breitweiser-a/Acuña-c 3.00
616-(5/11, $4.99) 70th Anniversary Issue; short stories by Brubaker, Chaykin, Deodato, McGuinness, Grist and others, Charest-c 5.00
616-Variant-c by Epting 8.00
...: America's Avenger (8/11, $4.99) Handbook format profiles of friends and foes 5.00
... and Batroc (5/11, $3.99) Gillen-s/Arlem-a; Bucky vs. Batroc in Paris 4.00
... and Crossbones (5/11, $3.99) Harms-s/Shalvey-a/Tocchini-c 4.00
... and Falcon (5/11, $3.99) Williams-s/Isaacs-a/Tocchini-c 4.00
... and the First Thirteen (5/11, $3.99) Peggy Carter in WWII France 1943 4.00
... and the Secret Avengers (5/11, $3.99) DeConnick-s/Tocchini-a/c; Black Widow app. 4.00
... and Thor: Avengers 1 (9/11, $4.99) Movie version Cap; prequel to Thor movie; Lim-c 5.00
... By Ed Brubaker Omnibus Vol. 1 HC (2007, $74.99, dustjacket) r/#1-25; Capt. America 65th Anniv. Spec. and Winter Soldier: Winter Kills; Brubaker intro.; bonus material 75.00
Civil War: Captain America TPB (2007, $11.99) r/#22-24 & Winter Soldier: Winter Kills 12.00
...: Fighting Avenger (6/11, $4.99) 1st WWII mission; Gurihiru-a/c; Kitson var-c 5.00
...MGC #1 (5/10, $1.00) r/#1 with "Marvel's Greatest Comics" cover logo 3.00
...: Rebirth 1 (8/11, $4.99) r/origin & Red Skull apps. from Tales of Suspense #63,65-68 5.00
...: Red Menace Vol. 1 SC (2006, $11.99) r/#15-17 and 65th Anniversary Special 12.00
...: Red Menace Vol. 2 SC (2006, $10.99) r/#18-21; Brubaker interview 11.00
... Spotlight (7/11, $3.99) creator interviews; features on the movie and The Invaders 4.00
... Theater of War: America First! (2/09, $4.99) 1950s era tale; Chaykin-s/a; reprints 5.00
... Theater of War: America the Beautiful (3/09, $4.99) WW2 tale; Jenkins-s/Erskine-a 5.00
... Theater of War: Operation Zero-Point (12/08, $3.99) WW2 tale; Breitweiser-a 4.00
...: The Death of Captan America Vol. 1 HC (2007, $19.99) r/#25-30; variant covers 20.00
...: The Death of Captan America Vol. 2 HC (2008, $19.99) r/#31-36; variant covers 20.00
...Vol. 1: Winter Soldier HC (2005, $21.99) r/#1-7; concept sketches 22.00
...Vol. 1: Winter Soldier SC (2006, $16.99) r/#1-7; concept sketches 17.00
...: Who Won't Wield the Shield (6/10, $3.99) Deadpool & Forbush Man app. 4.00
...: Winter Soldier Vol. 2 HC (2006, $19.99) r/#8,9,11-14 20.00
...: Winter Soldier Vol. 2 SC (2006, $14.99) r/#8,9,11-14 15.00

CAPTAIN AMERICA
Marvel Comics: Sept, 2011 - No. 19, Dec, 2012 ($3.99)

1-19: 1-5-Brubaker-s/McNiven-c/a. 1-Nick Fury & Baron Zemo app. 6-10-Davis-a/c 4.00
1-Variant-c by John Romita Sr. 1 3 4 6 8 10
1-Movie photo variant-c of Chris Evans in costume 4 8 12 23 37 50

CAPTAIN AMERICA (Marvel NOW!)
Marvel Comics: Jan, 2013 - No. 25, Dec, 2014 ($3.99)

1-10-Remender-s/Romita Jr.-a/c; Cap in Dimension Z; Arnim Zola app.; 1st app. Jet Black. 10-Sharon Carter supposedly killed 4.00
11-24: 11,12,14,15-Pacheco-a; Nuke returns. 16-Red Skull app.; Alixe-a. 21-Steve Rogers rapidly aged. 22-24-Pacheco-a; Avengers app. 23-Sharon Carter returns 4.00
25-($4.99) Sam Wilson becomes the new Captain America; Pacheco-a 5.00
...: Homecoming 1 (5/14, $3.99) Van Lente-s/Grummett-a; bonus rep of Capt. Am. #117 4.00
...: Peggy Carter, Agent of S.H.I.E.L.D. (2014, $7.99) r/notable appearances 8.00

CAPTAIN AMERICA (Secret Empire tie-in)(Follows Captain America: Sam Wilson #24)
Marvel Comics: No. 25, Oct, 2017 ($4.99)

25-Leads into Secret Empire #8; Black Panther, Namor app.; Spencer-s/Saiz-a 5.00

CAPTAIN AMERICA (Marvel Legacy)
Marvel Comics: No. 695, Jan, 2018 - No. 704, Aug, 2018 ($3.99)

695-699: 695-Follows Secret Empire; Waid-s/Samnee-a. 697-Kraven app. 4.00
700-(6/18, $5.99) Waid-s/Samnee-a; back-up story by Waid using unpublished Kirby art 6.00
701-704-Romero-a. 701-Hughes-a (4 pgs). 702-Chaykin-a (5 pgs). 703-Davis-a (5 pgs) 4.00

CAPTAIN AMERICA
Marvel Comics: Sept, 2018 - Present ($4.99/$3.99)

1-($4.99) Ta-Nehisi Coates-s/Leinil Francis Yu-a; wraparound-c by Alex Ross 5.00
2-24,26-($3.99) 3-Black Panther app. 4,5-Taskmaster app. 7-12-Adam Kubert-a. 12-Daughters of Liberty regroup; back in Steve Rogers uniform. 14-Sin app. 16-John Walker app. 22,23-Shuri app. 23-Sharon Carter de-aged. 24-Red Skull app. 26-Red Hulk app. 4.00

Captain America and the Mighty Avengers #1 © MAR

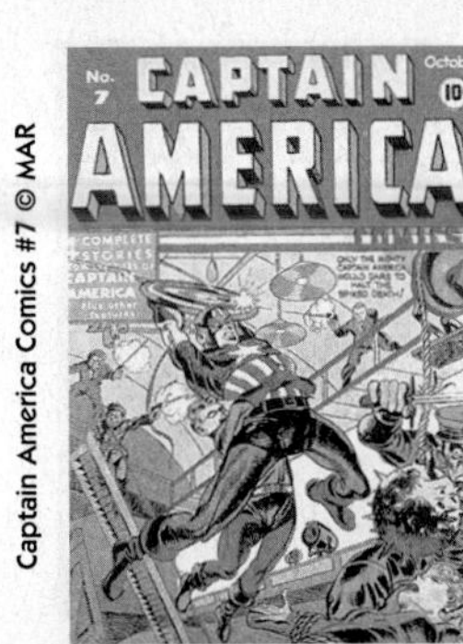

Captain America Comics #7 © MAR

Captain America: Man Out of Time #1 © MAR

	GD 2.0	VG 4.0	FN 6.0	VF 8.0	VF/NM 9.0	NM- 9.2

25-($4.99) Red Skull, Falcon, Winter Soldier app.; back-up with Michael Cho-a 5.00
Annual 1 (11/18, $4.99) Howard-s/Sprouse & Lim-a; takes place in 1940; Bucky app. 5.00
... & The Invaders: Bahamas Triangle 1 (9/19, $4.99) Roy Thomas-s/Jerry Ordway-a 5.00
... The End 1 (4/20, $4.99) Erik Larsen-s/a; M.O.D.O.K. app. 5.00

CAPTAIN AMERICA AND ... (Numbering continues from Captain America #619)
Marvel Comics: No. 620, Sept, 2011 - No. 640, Feb, 2013 ($2.99)

... Bucky 620-628: 620-624-Brubaker & Andreyko-s/Samnee-a/McGuinness-c. 620-Bucky's early WWII days. 625-628-Francavilla-c/a 3.00
... Hawkeye 629-632: 629-(6/12) Bunn-s/Vitti-a/Dell'Otto-c 3.00
... Iron Man 633-635: 635-(8/12) Bunn-s/Kitson-a/Andrasofszky-c; Batroc app. 3.00
... Namor 635.1 (10/12) World War II flashback; Will Conrad-a/Immonen-c 3.00
... Black Widow 636-640: 636-(11/12) Bunn-s/Francavilla-a/c 3.00

CAPTAIN AMERICA AND THE FALCON
Marvel Comics: May, 2004 - No. 14, June, 2005 ($2.99, limited series)

1-4-Priest-s/Sears-a 3.00
5-14: 5-8-Avengers Disassembled x-over. 6,7-Scarlet Witch app. 8-12-Modok app. 3.00
... Vol. 1: Two Americas (2005, $9.99) r/#1-4 10.00
... Vol. 2: Brothers and Keepers (2005, $17.99) r/#8-14 18.00

CAPTAIN AMERICA & THE KORVAC SAGA
Marvel Comics: Feb, 2011 - No. 4, May, 2011 ($2.99, limited series)

1-4-McCool-s/Rousseau-a/c. 4-Galactus app. 3.00

CAPTAIN AMERICA & THE MIGHTY AVENGERS (Sam Wilson as Captain America)
Marvel Comics: Jan, 2015 - No. 9, Aug, 2015 ($3.99)

1-9: 1-3-AXIS tie-ins; Luke Ross-a. 8,9-Secret Wars tie-in 4.00

CAPTAIN AMERICA/BLACK PANTHER (See Black Panther/Captain America: Flags of Our Fathers)

CAPTAIN AMERICA COMICS
Timely/Marvel Comics (TCI 1-20/CmPS 21-68/MjMC 69-75/Atlas Comics (PrPI 76-78):
Mar, 1941 - No. 75, Feb, 1950; No. 76, 5/54 - No. 78, 9/54
(No. 74 & 75 titled Capt. America's Weird Tales)

	GD 2.0	VG 4.0	FN 6.0	VF 8.0	VF/NM 9.0	NM- 9.2
1-Origin & 1st app. Captain America & Bucky by Simon & Kirby; Hurricane, Tuk the Caveboy begin by S&K; 1st app. Red Skull; Hitler-c (by Simon?); intro of the "Capt. America Sentinels of Liberty Club" (advertised on inside front-c.); indicia reads Vol. 2, Number 1	31,000	62,000	93,000	207,000	341,000	600,000
2-S&K Hurricane; Tuk by Avison (Kirby splash); classic Hitler-c; 1st app. Cap's round shield	2900	5800	8700	21,800	45,900	70,000
3-Classic Red Skull-c & app; Stan Lee's 1st text (1st work for Marvel)	2800	5600	8400	21,000	43,100	65,000
4-Early use of full pg. panel in comic; back-c pin-up of Captain America and Bucky	1300	2600	3900	9700	18,350	27,000
5-Classic Kirby Nazi/torture Wheel of Death/Red Skull-c	1175	2350	3525	8930	16,215	23,500
6-Origin Father Time; Tuk the Caveboy ends	1025	2050	3075	7790	14,145	20,500
7-Red Skull app.; classic-c	1150	2300	3450	8700	15,850	23,000
8-10-Last S&K issue, (S&K centerfold #6-10)	919	1838	2757	6709	11,855	17,000
11-Last Hurricane, Headline Hunter; Al Avison Captain America begins, ends #20; Avison-c(p)	676	1352	2028	4935	8718	12,500
12-The Imp begins, ends #16; last Father Time	676	1352	2028	4935	8718	12,500
13-Origin The Secret Stamp; classic "Remember Pearl Harbor"-c	1100	2200	3300	8360	15,180	22,000
14-"Remember Pearl Harbor" Japanese bondage/torture-c	757	1514	2271	5526	9763	14,000
15	676	1352	2028	4935	8718	12,500
16-Red Skull unmasks Cap; Red Skull-c	975	1950	2919	7100	12,550	18,000
17-The Fighting Fool only app.	508	1016	1526	3708	6554	9400
18-Classic-c	508	1082	1623	3950	6975	10,000
19-Human Torch begins #19	481	962	1443	3511	6206	8900
20-Sub-Mariner app.; no Human Torch	476	952	1428	3475	6138	8800
21-23,25: 25-Cap drinks liquid opium	470	940	1410	3431	6066	8700
24-Classic Japanese torture-c with boiling tar and fingernail removal	595	1190	1785	4350	7675	11,000
26-30: 27-Last Secret Stamp; Nazi WWII-c; last 68 pg. issue. 28-60 pg. issues begin.	465	930	1395	3395	5998	8600
31-35,38-40: 34-Centerfold poster of Cap. 38-Japanese bondage-c	423	846	1269	3067	5384	7700
36-Classic Hitler-c	1000	2000	3000	7400	13,200	19,000
37-Red Skull app.	919	1338	2757	6709	11,855	17,000
41-Last Japan War-c	377	754	1131	2639	4620	6600
42-45	300	600	900	1980	3440	4900
46-German Holocaust-c; classic	2700	5400	8100	18,000	31,500	45,000
47-Last German War-c	337	674	1011	2359	4130	5900
48-58,60	245	490	735	1568	2684	3800
59-Origin retold	383	766	1149	2681	4690	6700
61-Red Skull-c/story	423	846	1269	3046	5323	7600
62,64,65: 65-Kurtzman's "Hey Look"	284	568	852	1818	3109	4400
63-Intro/origin Asbestos Lady	297	594	891	1888	3244	4600
66-Bucky is shot; Golden Girl teams up with Captain America & learns his i.d; origin Golden Girl	383	766	1149	2681	4690	6700
67-69: 67-Captain America/Golden Girl team-up; Mxyztplk swipe; last Toro in Human Torch. 68-Sub-Mariner/Namora, and Captain America/Golden Girl team-up. 69-Human Torch/Sun Girl team-up.	349	698	1047	2443	4272	6100
70-73: 70-Sub-Mariner/Namora, and Captain America/Golden Girl team-up. 70-SciFi-c/story. 71-Anti Wertham editorial; The Witness, Bucky app.	400	800	1200	2800	4900	7000
74-(Scarce)(10/49)-Titled "Captain America's Weird Tales"; Red Skull-c & app.; classic-c	2350	4700	7050	17,860	32,430	47,000
75(2/50)-Titled "C.A.'s Weird Tales"; no C.A. app.; horror cover/stories	383	766	1149	2681	4690	6700
76-78(1954): Human Torch/Toro stories; all have communist-c/stories	277	554	831	1759	3030	4300
132-Pg. Issue (B&W-1942)(Canadian)-Very rare. Has blank inside-c and back-c; contains Marvel Mystery #33 & Captain America #18 w/cover from Captain America #22; same contents as one version of the Marvel Mystery annuals	5450	10,900	16,350	41,000	--	--

NOTE: ***Crandall*** *a-2i, 3i, 9i, 10i.* ***Kirby*** *c-1, 2, 5-8p.* ***Rico*** *c-69-71.* ***Romita*** *c-77, 78.* ***Schomburg*** *c-3, 4, 26-29, 31, 33, 37-39, 41, 42, 45-54, 58.* ***Sekowsky*** *c-55, 56.* ***Shores*** *c-1i, 2i, 5-7i, 11i, 20-25, 30, 32, 34, 35, 40, 57, 59-67.* ***S&K*** *c-9, 10. Bondage c-3, 7, 15, 16, 34, 38.*

CAPTAIN AMERICA COMICS #1 70TH ANNIVERSARY EDITION
Marvel Comics: May, 2011 ($4.99, one-shot)

	GD 2.0	VG 4.0	FN 6.0	VF 8.0	VF/NM 9.0	NM- 9.2
1-Recolored reprint of entire 1941 issue including Hurricane & Tuk stories; Ching-c	1	3	4	6	8	10

CAPTAIN AMERICA COMICS 70TH ANNIVERSARY SPECIAL
Marvel Comics: June, 2009 ($3.99, one-shot)

	GD 2.0	VG 4.0	FN 6.0	VF 8.0	VF/NM 9.0	NM- 9.2
1-WWII flashback; Marcos Martin-a; Marcos-2 covers; r/Capt. America Comics #7	1	3	4	6	8	10

CAPTAIN AMERICA CORPS
Marvel Comics: Aug, 2011 - No. 5, Dec, 2011 ($2.99, limited series)

1-5-Stern-s/Briones-a/Jimenez-a; various versions of Captain America team-up 3.00

CAPTAIN AMERICA: DEAD MEN RUNNING
Marvel Comics: Mar, 2002 - No. 3, May, 2002 ($2.99, limited series)

1-3-Macan-s/Zezelj-a 3.00

CAPTAIN AMERICA: FIRST VENGEANCE (Based on the 2011 movie version)
Marvel Comics: Jul, 2011 - No. 4, Aug, 2011 ($2.99, limited series)

1-4-Van Lente-s; art by Luke Ross & others. 2-Movie photo-c 3.00

CAPTAIN AMERICA: FOREVER ALLIES
Marvel Comics: Oct, 2010 - No. 4, Jan, 2011 ($3.99, limited series)

1-4-Stern-s/Dragotta-a; Bucky in present & WW2 flashbacks; Young Allies app. 4.00

CAPTAIN AMERICA: HAIL HYDRA
Marvel Comics: Mar, 2011 - No. 5, Jul, 2011 ($2.99, limited series)

1-5-Cap vs. Hydra; Granov-c. 1-WWII flashback. 2-Kirby-style art by Scioli. 4-Hotz-a 3.00

CAPTAIN AMERICA: LIVING LEGEND
Marvel Comics: Dec, 2013 - No. 4, Feb, 2014 ($3.99, limited series)

1-4: 1-Diggle-s/Granov-a/c. 2-4-Alessio-a 4.00

CAPTAIN AMERICA: MAN OUT OF TIME
Marvel Comics: Jan, 2011 - No. 5, May, 2011 ($3.99, limited series)

1-5-Waid-s/Molina-a/Hitch-c; Cap's unfreezing in modern times re-told 4.00

CAPTAIN AMERICA/NICK FURY: BLOOD TRUCE
Marvel Comics: Feb, 1995 ($5.95, one-shot, squarebound)

nn-Chaykin story 6.00

CAPTAIN AMERICA/NICK FURY: THE OTHERWORLD WAR
Marvel Comics: Oct, 2001 ($6.95, one-shot, squarebound)

nn-Manco-a; Bucky and Red Skull app. 7.00

CAPTAIN AMERICA: PATRIOT
Marvel Comics: Nov, 2010 - No. 4, Feb, 2011 ($3.99, limited series)

1-4-Kesel-s/Breitweiser-a; 1-WW2 story; Patriot & the Liberty Legion app. 4.00

CAPTAIN AMERICA: REBORN (Titled Reborn in #1-3)
Marvel Comics: Sept, 2009 - No. 6, Mar, 2010 ($3.99, limited series)

1-6-Steve Rogers returns from the dead; Brubaker-s/Hitch & Guice-a. 1-Covers by Hitch, Ross & Quesada. 2-Origin re-told. 4-Joe Kubert var-c. 5-Cassaday var-c 4.00

Captain America: Steve Rogers #6 © MAR

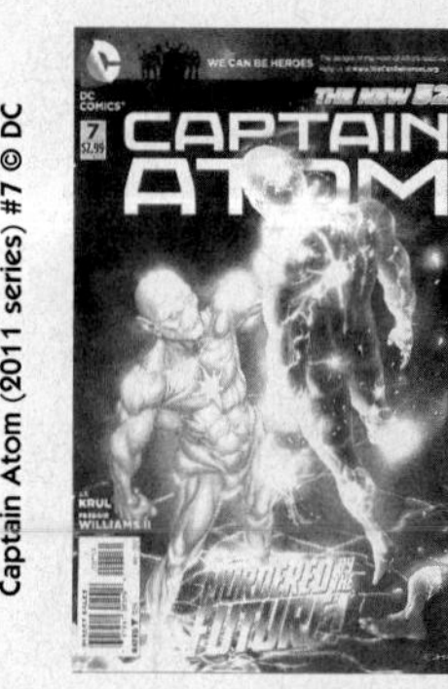

Captain Atom (2011 series) #7 © DC

Captain Battle #1 © LEV

	GD 2.0	VG 4.0	FN 6.0	VF 8.0	VF/NM 9.0	NM- 9.2

1-4-Variant-c by Cassaday. 2-Variant-c by Sale. 5-Finch var-c 10.00
... MGC #1 (5/11, $1.00) r/#1 with "Marvel's Greatest Comics" logo on cover 3.00
...: Who Will Wield the Shield? (2/10, $3.99) Aftermath of series; Guice & Luke Ross-a 4.00

CAPTAIN AMERICA: RED, WHITE & BLUE
Marvel Comics: Sept, 2002 ($29.99, one-shot, hardcover with dustjacket)

nn-Reprints from Lee & Kirby, Steranko, Miller and others; and new short stories and pin-ups by various incl. Ross, Dini, Timm, Waid, Dorkin, Sienkiewicz, Miller, Bruce Jones, Collins, Piers-Rayner, Pope, Deodato, Quitely, Nino; Stelfreeze-c 30.00
TPB (2007, $19.99) 20.00

CAPTAIN AMERICA: ROAD TO WAR
Marvel Comics: Jun, 2016 ($4.99, one-shot)

1-Prelude to Captain America: Civil War movie; bonus r/Tales of Suspense #58 5.00

CAPTAIN AMERICA: SAM WILSON (Leads into Captain America #25 (Oct. 2017))
Marvel Comics: Dec, 2015 - No. 24, Sept, 2017 ($3.99)

1-6: 1-Spencer-s/Acuña-a; Misty Knight & D-Man app. 3-6-Sam as CapWolf 4.00
7-($5.99) 75th Anniversary issue; Steve Rogers regains his youth; Standoff tie-in; bonus short stories by Whedon & Cassaday, Tim Sale, and Rucka & Perkins 6.00
8-24: 8-Standoff tie-in; Baron Zemo app. 10-13-Civil War II tie-in. 11-13-U.S. Agent app. 22-24-Secret Empire tie-ins 4.00

CAPTAIN AMERICA, SENTINEL OF LIBERTY (See Fireside Book Series)

CAPTAIN AMERICA: SENTINEL OF LIBERTY
Marvel Comics: Sept, 1998 - No. 12, Aug, 1999 ($1.99)

1-Waid-s/Garney-a 5.00
1-Rough Cut ($2.99) Features original script and pencil pages 4.00
2-5: 2-Two-c; Invaders WW2 story 3.00
6-($2.99) Iron Man-c/app. 4.00
7-11: 8-Falcon-c/app. 9-Falcon poses as Cap 3.00
12-($2.99) Final issue; Bucky-c/app. 4.00

CAPTAIN AMERICA SPECIAL EDITION
Marvel Comics Group: Feb, 1984 - No. 2, Mar, 1984 ($2.00, Baxter paper)

1-Steranko-c/a(r) in both; r/Capt. America #110,111 1 2 3 5 6 8
2-Reprints the scarce Our Love Story #5, and C.A. #113 1 2 3 5 6 8

CAPTAIN AMERICA: STEVE ROGERS (Also see Captain America: Sam Wilson)
Marvel Comics: Jul, 2016 - No. 19, Sept, 2017 ($4.99/$3.99)

1-Spencer-s/Saiz-a; childhood flashbacks to Hydra recruitment; Red Skull app. 5.00
2-19-($3.99) 2-Kobik app. 4-6-Civil War II tie-in. 14,15-Red Skull app. 16-19-Secret Empire tie-ins. 18-Namor app. 19-Leads into Captain America #25 (10/17) 4.00

CAPTAIN AMERICA THEATER OF WAR
Marvel Comics: 2009 - 2010 ($3.99, series of one-shots)

...: A Brother in Arms (6/09) Jenkins-s/McCrea-a; WWII story 4.00
...: Ghosts of My Country (12/09) Jenkins-s/Bonetti-a/Guice-c 4.00
...: Prisoners of Duty (2/10) Higgins & Siegel-s/Padilla-a; WWII story 4.00
...: To Soldier On (10/09) Jenkins-s/Blanco-a/Noto-c; Captain America in Iraq 4.00

CAPTAIN AMERICA: THE CHOSEN
Marvel Comics: Nov, 2007 - No. 6, Mar, 2008 ($3.99, limited series)

1-6-Breitweiser-a/Morrell-s 4.00

CAPTAIN AMERICA: THE CLASSIC YEARS
Marvel Comics: Jun, 1998 - No. 2 (trade paperbacks)

1-($19.95) Reprints Captain America Comics #1-5 25.00
2-($24.95) Reprints Captain America Comics #6-10 25.00

CAPTAIN AMERICA: THE FIRST AVENGER ADAPTATION (MARVEL'S...)
Marvel Comics: Jan, 2014 - No. 2, Feb, 2014 ($2.99, limited series)

1,2-Adaptation of the 2011 movie; Peter David-s/Wellinton Alves-a/photo-c 3.00

CAPTAIN AMERICA: THE LEGEND
Marvel Comics: Sept, 1996 ($3.95, one-shot)

1-Tribute issue; wraparound-c 5.00

CAPTAIN AMERICA: THE 1940S NEWSPAPER STRIP
Marvel Comics: Aug, 2010 - No. 3, Oct, 2010 ($3.99, limited series)

1-3-Karl Kesel-s/a; new stories set in WW2, formatted like 1940s newspaper comics 4.00

CAPTAIN AMERICA: WHAT PRICE GLORY
Marvel Comics: May, 2003 - No. 4, May, 2003 ($2.99, weekly limited series)

1-4-Bruce Jones-s/Steve Rude & Mike Royer-a 3.00

CAPTAIN AMERICA: WHITE
Marvel Comics: No. 0, Sept, 2008; No. 1, Nov, 2015 - No. 5, Feb, 2016 (limited series)

0-Bucky's origin retold; Loeb-s/Sale-a in all; interviews with creators; Sale sketch art 3.00
1-($4.99) Flashback to 1941; Sgt. Fury and the Howling Commandos app. 5.00
2-5-($3.99) 3-5-Red Skull app. 4.00

CAPTAIN AMERICA: WINTER SOLDIER DIRECTOR'S CUT
Marvel Comics: Jun, 2014 ($4.99, one-shot)

1-Reprints Captain America (2005) #1; bonus Brubaker script & series proposal 5.00

CAPTAIN AND THE KIDS, THE (See Famous Comics Cartoon Books)

CAPTAIN AND THE KIDS, THE (See Comics on Parade, Katzenjammer Kids, Okay Comics & Sparkler Comics)
United Features Syndicate/Dell Publ. Co.: 1938 -12/39; Sum, 1947 - No. 32, 1955; Four Color No. 881, Feb, 1958

Single Series 1(1938) 119 238 357 762 1306 1850
Single Series 1(Reprint)(12/39- "Reprint" on-c) 48 96 144 302 514 725
1(Summer, 1947-UFS)-Katzenjammer Kids 19 38 57 111 176 240
2 11 22 33 62 86 110
3-10 10 20 30 54 72 90
11-20 8 16 24 44 57 70
21-32 (1955) 8 16 24 40 50 60
50th Anniversary issue-(1948)-Contains a 2 pg. history of the strip, including an account of the famous Supreme Court decision allowing both Pulitzer & Hearst to run the same strip under different names 19 38 57 111 176 240
Special Summer issue, Fall issue (1948) 12 24 36 69 97 125
Four Color 881 (Dell) 5 10 15 30 50 70

CAPTAIN ATOM
Nationwide Publishers: 1950 - No. 7, 1951 (5¢, 5x7-1/4", 52 pgs.)

1-Science fiction 42 84 126 265 445 625
2-7 26 52 78 154 252 350

CAPTAIN ATOM (Formerly Strange Suspense Stories #77)(Also see Space Adventures and Thunderbolt)
Charlton Comics: V2#78, Dec, 1965 - V2#89, Dec, 1967

V2#78-Origin retold; Bache-a (3 pgs.) 8 16 24 51 96 145
79-81: 79-1st app. Dr. Spectro; 3 pg. Ditko cut & paste /Space Adventures #24. 6 12 18 37 66 95
82-Intro. Nightshade (9/66) 11 22 33 75 160 245
83-(11/66)-1st app. Ted Kord/Blue Beetle 44 88 132 326 738 1150
84-86: Ted Kord Blue Beetle in all. 84-1st app. new Captain Atom. 85-1st app. Punch and Jewelee 5 10 15 34 60 85
87-89: Nightshade by Aparo in all 5 10 15 33 57 80
83-(Modern Comics-1977)-reprints 3 6 9 19 30 40
84,85-(Modern Comics-1977)-reprints 1 2 3 5 6 8
NOTE: ***Aparo** a-87-89. **Ditko** c/a(p) 78-89. #90 only published in fanzine 'The Charlton Bullseye' #1, 2.*

CAPTAIN ATOM (Also see Americomics & Crisis On Infinite Earths)
DC Comics: Mar, 1987 - No. 57, Sept, 1991 (Direct sales only #35 on)

1-(44 pgs.)-Origin/1st app. with new costume 6.00
2-49: 5-Firestorm x-over. 6-Intro. new Dr. Spectro. 11-Millennium tie-in. 14-Nightshade app. 16-Justice League app. 17-$1.00-c begins; Swamp Thing app. 20-Blue Beetle x-over. 24,25-Invasion tie-in 4.00
50-($2.00, 52 pgs.) 5.00
51-57: 57-War of the Gods x-over 4.00
Annual 1,2 ('88, '89)-1-Intro Major Force 5.00

CAPTAIN ATOM (DC New 52)
DC Comics: Nov, 2011 - No. 12, Oct, 2012; No. 0, Nov, 2012 ($2.99)

1-12-J.T. Krul-s/Freddie Williams II-a. 3-Flash app. 3.00
#0 (11/12, $2.99) origin of Captain Atom re-told 3.00

CAPTAIN ATOM: ARMAGEDDON (Restarts the WildStorm Universe)
DC Comics (WildStorm): Dec, 2005 - No. 9, Aug, 2006 ($2.99, limited series)

1-9-Captain Atom appears in WildStorm Universe; Pfeifer-s/Camuncoli-a. 1-Lee-c 3.00
TPB (2007, $19.99) r/series 20.00

CAPTAIN BATTLE (Boy Comics #3 on) (See Silver Streak Comics)
New Friday Publ./Comic House: Summer, 1941 - No. 2, Fall, 1941

1-Origin Blackout by Rico; Captain Battle begins (1st appeared in Silver Streak #10, 5/41) classic hooded villain bondage/torture-c 206 412 618 1318 2259 3200
2-Origin Doctor Horror & only app.; classic story "House of Giants" 97 194 291 621 1061 1500

CAPTAIN BATTLE (2nd Series)
Magazine Press/Picture Scoop No. 5: No. 3, Wint, 1942-43; No. 5, Sum, 1943 (No #4)

3-Origin Silver Streak-r/SS#3; origin Lance Hale-r/SS #2; Cloud Curtis, Presto Martin 1st app.-r/SS #7; Simon-a(r) (52 pgs., nd) 97 194 291 621 1061 1500
5-Origin Blackout-r/#1 (68 pgs.); Japanese WWII-c 97 194 291 621 1061 1500

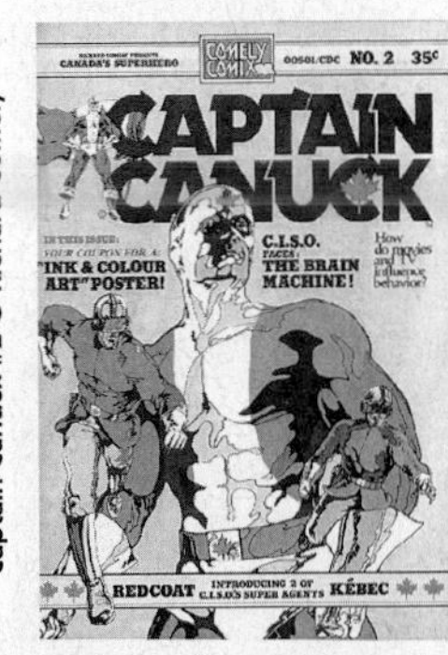

Captain Canuck #2 © Richard Comely

Captain Easy #14 © NEA

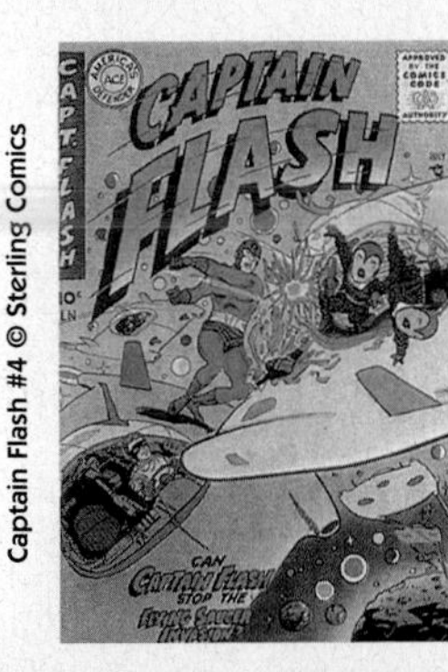

Captain Flash #4 © Sterling Comics

	GD	VG	FN	VF	VF/NM	NM-
	2.0	4.0	6.0	8.0	9.0	9.2

CAPTAIN BATTLE, JR.
Comic House (Lev Gleason): Fall, 1943 - No. 2, Winter, 1943-44

1-Nazi WWII-c by Rico. Hitler/Claw sty; The Claw vs. The Ghost 158 316 474 1003 1721 2450
2-Wolverton's Scoop Scuttle; Don Rico-c/a; The Green Claw story is reprinted from Silver Streak #6; Japanese WWII bondage/torture-c by Rico 97 194 291 621 1061 1500

CAPTAIN BEN DIX (See Promotional Comics section)

CAPTAIN BRITAIN (Also see Marvel Team-Up No. 65, 66)
Marvel Comics International: Oct. 13, 1976 - No. 39, July 6, 1977 (Weekly)

1-1st app & origin of Captain Britain (Brian Broddock); with Capt. Britain's face mask inside Claremont-s/Trimpe-a 16 32 48 112 249 385
2-Origin, part II; Capt. Britain's Boomerang inside 4 8 12 27 44 60
3-7: 3-Vs. Bank Robbers. 4-7-Vs. Hurricane 2 4 6 10 14 18
8-(12/76) 1st app. Betsy Braddock, the sister of Capt. Britain (Brian Braddock) who later becomes Psylocke (X-Men); 1st app. Dr. Synne 23 46 69 161 356 550
9-11-Battles Dr. Synne. 9,10-Betsy Braddock app. 2 4 6 8 11 14
12-23,25-27: (low print run)-12,13-Vs. Dr. Synne. 14,15-Vs. Mastermind. 16-23,25,26-With Captain America. 17-Misprinted & color section reprinted in #18. 27-Origin retold 3 6 9 15 22 28
24-With Capt. Britain's Jet Plane inside 4 8 12 23 37 50
28-32,36-39: 28-32-Vs. Lord Hawk. 30-32-Inhumans app. 35-Dr. Doom app. 37-39-Vs. Highwayman & Munipulator 1 3 4 6 8 10
33-35-More on origin 2 4 6 8 10 12
Annual (1978, Hardback, 64 pgs.)-Reprints #1-7 with pin-ups of Marvel characters 3 6 9 16 23 30
Summer Special (1980, 52 pgs.)-Reprints 1 3 4 6 8 10

NOTE: *No. 1, 2, & 24 are rarer in mint due to inserts. Distributed in Great Britain only. Nick Fury-r by* ***Steranko*** *in 1-20, 24-31, 35-37. Fantastic Four-r by* ***J. Buscema*** *in all. New* ***Buscema****-a in 24-30. Story from No. 39 continues in Super Spider-Man (British weekly) No. 231-247. Following cancellation of his series, new Captain Britain stories appeared in "Super Spider-Man" (British weekly) No. 231-247. Captain Britain stories which appear in Super-Spider-Man No 248-253 are reprints of Marvel Team-Up No. 65&66. Capt. Britain strips also appeared in Hulk Comic (weekly) 1, 3-30, 42-55, 57-60, in Marvel Superheroes (monthly) 377-388, in Daredevils (monthly) 1-11, Mighty World of Marvel (monthly) 7-16 & Captain Britain (monthly) 1-14. Issues 1-23 have B&W & color, paper-c, & are 32 pgs. Issues 24 on are all B&W w/glossy-c & are 36 pgs.*

CAPTAIN BRITAIN AND MI: 13 (Also see Secret Invasion x-over titles)
Marvel Comics: Jul, 2008 - No. 15, Sept, 2009 ($2.99)

1-Skrull invasion; Black Knight app.; Kirk-a 1 2 3 5 6 8
1-2nd printing with Kirk variant-c; 3rd printing with B&W cover 3.00
2-15: 5-Blade app. 9,10-Dracula app. 3.00
... Annual 1 (8/09, $3.99) Land-c; Meggan in Hell; Dr. Doom cameo; Collins-a 4.00

CAPTAIN BRITAIN AND THE MIGHTY DEFENDERS (Secret Wars tie-in)
Marvel Comics: Sept, 2015 - No. 2, Oct, 2015 ($3.99, limited series)

1,2-Ho Yinsen, Faiza Hussain, White Tiger, She-Hulk app.; Al Ewing-s/Alan Davis-a 4.00

CAPTAIN CANUCK
Comely Comix (Canada)(All distr. in U. S.): Jul,1975 - No. 4, Jul, 1977; No. 4, Jul-Aug, 1979 - No. 14, Mar-Apr, 1981

1-1st app. Captain Canuck, C.I.S.O. & Bluefox; Richard Comely-c/a 3 6 9 14 19 24
2,3(5-7/76): 2-1st app. Dr. Walker, Redcoat & Kebec. 3-1st app. Heather 1 2 3 5 6 8
4 (1st printing-2/77)-10x14-1/2"; (5.00); B&W; 300 copies serially numbered and signed with one certificate of authenticity 9 18 27 63 129 195
4 (2nd printing-7/77)-11x17", B&W; only 15 copies printed; signed by creator Richard Comely, serially #'d and two certificates of authenticity inserted; orange cardboard covers (Very Rare) 13 26 39 89 195 300
4-14: 4(7-8/79)-1st app. Tom Evans & Mr. Gold; origin The Catman. 5-Origin Capt. Canuck's powers; 1st app. Earth Patrol & Chaos Corps. 5-7-Three-part neo-Nazi story set in 1994. 8-Jonn 'The Final Chapter'; 1st app. Mike & Saskia. 9-1st World Beyond. 11-1st 'Chariots of Fire' story. 12-A-bomb explosion panel 6.00
15-(8/04, $15.00) Limited edition of unpublished issue from 1981; serially #'d edition of 150; signed by creator Richard Comely 7 14 21 48 89 130
... Legacy 1 (9-10/06) Comely-s/a 4.00
... Legacy Special Edition ($7.95, 52 pgs., limited ed. of 1000) Comely-s/a 1 3 4 6 8 10
Special Collectors Pack (#1 & #2 polybagged) 2 4 6 8 11 14
Summer Special 1(7-9/80, 95¢, 64 pgs.) George Freeman-c/a; pin-ups by Gene Day, Tom Grummett, Dave Sim and others 6.00
Summer Special / Canada Day Edition #1 (2014, no cover price) 2 new stories, background on animated web series; regular-c shows a parade; variants exist 5.00

NOTE: *30,000 copies of No. 2 were destroyed in Winnipeg.*

CAPTAIN CANUCK
Chapterhouse Comics: May, 2015 - No. 12, May, 2017 ($3.99)

1-Kalman Andrasofszky-s/a; 3 covers 1 3 4 6 8 10
2-12: 2-Andrasofszky-s/a. 3-12-Leonard Kirk-a 4.00
#0/FCBD Edition (5/15, giveaway) previews #1; origin re-told; character profiles 3.00
... Free Comic Book Day Issue 2019 (5/19) Intro. of a new Captain Canuck 3.00

CAPTAIN CANUCK (Season 5)
Chapterhouse Comics: Nov, 2020 - Present ($4.99)

1-Ho Che Anderson-s/Felipe Cunha-a 5.00

CAPTAIN CANUCK: UNHOLY WAR
Comely Comix: Oct, 2004 - No. 3, Jan, 2005; No. 4, Sept, 2007 ($2.50, limited series)

1-3-Riel Langlois-s/Drue Langlois-a: 1-1st app. David Semple (West Coast Capt. Canuck); Clair Sinclair as Bluefox 3.00
4-(Low print run) Black Mack the Lumberjack, Torchie, Splatter app. 6.00

CAPTAIN CANUCK YEAR ONE
Chapterhouse Comics: May, 2017; Nov, 2017 ($1.99)

1-($1.99) Baruchel & Andrasofszky-s; Marcus To-a; back-up Die Kitty Die story 3.00
#1/FCBD Edition (5/17, giveaway) back-up Die Kitty Die story 3.00

CAPTAIN CARROT AND HIS AMAZING ZOO CREW (Also see New Teen Titans & Oz-Wonderland War)
DC Comics: Mar, 1982 - No. 20, Nov, 1983

1-Superman app. 1 3 4 6 8 10
2-20: 3-Re-intro Dodo & The Frog. 9-Re-intro Three Mouseketeers, the Terrific Whatzit. 10,11-Pig Iron reverts back to Peter Porkchops. 20-Changeling app. 4.00

CAPTAIN CARROT AND THE FINAL ARK (DC Countdown tie-in)
DC Comics: Dec, 2007 - No. 3, Feb, 2008 ($2.99, limited series)

1-3-Bill Morrison-s/Scott Shaw!-a. 3-Batman, Red Arrow, Hawkgirl & Zatanna app. 3.00
TPB (2008, $19.99) r/#1-3; Captain Carrot and His Amazing Zoo Crew #1,14,15; New Teen Titans #16 and stories from Teen Titans (2003 series) #30,31; cover gallery 20.00

CAPTAIN CARVEL AND HIS CARVEL CRUSADERS (See Carvel Comics)

CAPTAIN CONFEDERACY
Marvel Comics (Epic Comics): Nov, 1991 - No. 4, Feb, 1992 ($1.95)

1-All new stories 1 2 3 5 6 8
2-4-All new stories 4.00

CAPTAIN COURAGEOUS COMICS (Banner #3-5; see Four Favorites #5)
Periodical House (Ace Magazines): No. 6, March, 1942

6-Origin & 1st app. The Sword; Lone Warrior, Capt. Courageous app.; Capt. moves to Four Favorites #5 in May 126 252 378 806 1378 1950

CAPT'N CRUNCH COMICS (See Cap'n...)

CAPTAIN DAVY JONES
Dell Publishing Co.: No. 598, Nov, 1954

Four Color 598 6 12 18 37 66 95

CAPTAIN EASY (See The Funnies & Red Ryder #3-32)
Hawley/Dell Publ./Standard(Visual Editions)/Argo: 1939 - No. 17, Sept, 1949; April, 1956

nn-Hawley(1939)-Contains reprints from The Funnies & 1938 Sunday strips by Roy Crane 103 206 309 659 1130 1600
Four Color 24 (1943) 57 114 171 362 619 875
Four Color 111(6/46) 13 26 39 86 188 290
10(Standard-10/47) 15 30 45 84 127 170
11,12,14,15,17: 11-17 all contain 1930s & '40s strip-r 10 20 30 58 79 100
13,16: Schomburg-c 16 32 48 94 147 200
Argo 1(4/56)-Reprints 7 14 21 37 46 55

CAPTAIN EASY & WASH TUBBS (See Famous Comics Cartoon Books)

CAPTAIN ELECTRON
Brick Computer Science Institute: Aug, 1986 ($2.25)

1-Disbrow-a 3.00

CAPTAIN EO 3-D (Michael Jackson Disney theme parks movie)
Eclipse Comics: July, 1987 (Eclipse 3-D Special #18, $3.50, Baxter)

1-Adapts 3-D movie; Michael Jackson-c/app. 3 6 9 17 26 35
1-2-D limited edition 5 10 15 33 57 80
1-Large size (11x17", 8/87)-Sold only at Disney Theme parks ($6.95) 4 8 12 27 44 60

CAPTAIN FEARLESS COMICS (Also see Holyoke One-Shot #6, Old Glory Comics & Silver Streak #1)
Helnit Publishing Co. (Holyoke Publ. Co.): Aug, 1941 - No. 2, Sept, 1941

1-Origin Mr. Miracle, Alias X, Captain Fearless, Citizen Smith Son of the Unknown Soldier; Miss Victory (1st app.) begins (1st patriotic heroine? before Wonder Woman) 119 238 357 762 1306 1850

Captain Flight Comics #10 © Four Star

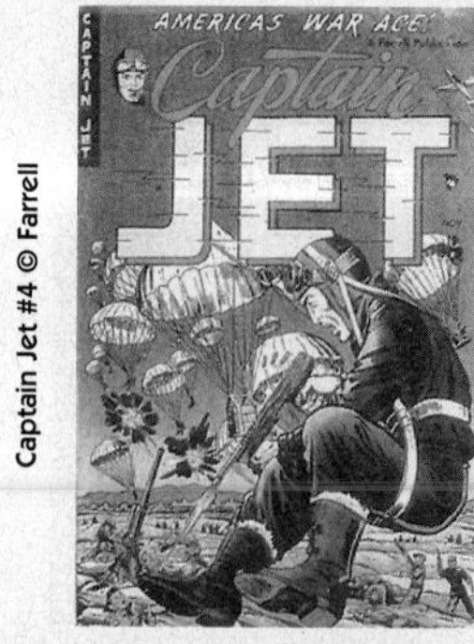

Captain Jet #4 © Farrell

Captain Marvel (1989 series) #1 © MAR

	GD 2.0	VG 4.0	FN 6.0	VF 8.0	VF/NM 9.0	NM- 9.2
2-Grit Grady, Captain Stone app.	60	120	180	381	653	925

CAPTAIN FLAG (See Blue Ribbon Comics #16)

CAPTAIN FLASH
Sterling Comics: Nov, 1954 - No. 4, July, 1955

	GD 2.0	VG 4.0	FN 6.0	VF 8.0	VF/NM 9.0	NM- 9.2
1-Origin; Sekowsky-a; Tomboy (female super hero) begins; only pre-code issue; atomic rocket-c	52	104	156	328	552	775
2-4: 4-Flying saucer invasion-c	32	64	96	192	314	435

CAPTAIN FLEET (Action Packed Tales of the Sea)
Ziff-Davis Publishing Co.: Fall, 1952

	GD 2.0	VG 4.0	FN 6.0	VF 8.0	VF/NM 9.0	NM- 9.2
1-Painted-c	21	42	63	126	206	285

CAPTAIN FLIGHT COMICS
Four Star Publications: May, 1944 - No. 10, Dec, 1945; No. 11, Feb-Mar, 1947

	GD 2.0	VG 4.0	FN 6.0	VF 8.0	VF/NM 9.0	NM- 9.2
nn-Captain Flight begins	82	164	246	528	902	1275
2-4: 4-Rock Raymond begins, ends #7	52	104	156	328	552	775
5-Bondage, classic torture-c; Red Rocket begins; the Grenade app. (scarce)	239	478	717	1530	2615	3700
6-L. B. Cole-a, 8 pgs.	52	104	156	328	552	775
7-10: 7-L. B. Cole covers begin, end #11. 7-9-Japanese WWII-c. 8-Yankee Girl begins; intro. Black Cobra & Cobra Kid & begins. 9-Torpedoman app.; last Yankee Girl; Kinstler-a. 10-Deep Sea Dawson, Zoom of the Jungle, Rock Raymond, Red Rocket, & Black Cobra app; bondage-c	68	136	204	435	743	1050
11-Torpedoman, Blue Flame (Human Torch clone) app.; last Black Cobra, Red Rocket; classic L. B. Cole sci-fi robot-c (scarce)	354	708	1062	2478	4339	6200

CAPTAIN GALLANT (...of the Foreign Legion) (TV) (Texas Rangers in Action No. 5 on?)
Charlton Comics: 1955; No. 2, Jan, 1956 - No. 4, Sept, 1956

	GD 2.0	VG 4.0	FN 6.0	VF 8.0	VF/NM 9.0	NM- 9.2
Non-Heinz version (#1)-Buster Crabbe photo on-c; full page Buster Crabbe photo inside front-c	8	16	24	44	57	70
(Heinz version is listed in the Promotional Comics section)						
2-4: Buster Crabbe in all. 2-Crabbe photo back-c	6	12	18	31	38	45

CAPTAIN GINGER
AHOY Comics: 2018 - Present ($3.99)

1-4: Space-faring cats; Stuart Moore-s/June Brigman-a; back-up text stories by various						4.00
... Season Two (2020 - Present) 1,2-Moore-s/Brigman-a						4.00

CAPTAIN GLORY
Topps Comics: Apr, 1993 ($2.95) (Created by Jack Kirby)

1-Polybagged w/Kirbychrome trading card; Ditko-a & Kirby-c; has coupon for Amberchrome Secret City Saga #0 — 4.00

CAPTAIN HERO (See Jughead as...)

CAPTAIN HERO COMICS DIGEST MAGAZINE
Archie Publications: Sept, 1981

	GD 2.0	VG 4.0	FN 6.0	VF 8.0	VF/NM 9.0	NM- 9.2
1-Reprints of Jughead as Super-Guy	2	4	6	10	14	18

CAPTAIN HOBBY COMICS
Export Publication Ent. Ltd. (Dist. in U.S. by Kable News Co.): Feb, 1948 (Canadian)

	GD 2.0	VG 4.0	FN 6.0	VF 8.0	VF/NM 9.0	NM- 9.2
1	15	30	45	83	124	165

CAPT. HOLO IN 3-D (See Blackthorne 3-D Series #65)

CAPTAIN HOOK & PETER PAN (Movie)(Disney)
Dell Publishing Co.: No. 446, Jan, 1953

	GD 2.0	VG 4.0	FN 6.0	VF 8.0	VF/NM 9.0	NM- 9.2
Four Color 446	9	18	27	61	123	185

CAPTAIN JET (Fantastic Fears No. 7 on)
Four Star Publ./Farrell/Comic Media: May, 1952 - No. 5, Jan, 1953

	GD 2.0	VG 4.0	FN 6.0	VF 8.0	VF/NM 9.0	NM- 9.2
1-Bakerish-a	27	54	81	158	259	360
2	15	30	45	90	140	190
3-5,6(?)	13	26	39	74	105	135

CAPTAIN JOHNER & THE ALIENS
Valiant: May, 1995 - No. 2, May, 1995 ($2.95, shipped in same month)

1,2: Reprints Magnus Robot Fighter 4000 A.D. back-up stories; new Paul Smith-c — 3.00

CAPTAIN JUSTICE (TV)
Marvel Comics: Mar, 1988 - No. 2, Apr, 1988 (limited series)

1,2-Based on the 1987 "Once a Hero" television series — 3.00

CAPTAIN KANGAROO (TV)
Dell Publishing Co.: No. 721, Aug, 1956 - No. 872, Jan, 1958

	GD 2.0	VG 4.0	FN 6.0	VF 8.0	VF/NM 9.0	NM- 9.2
Four Color 721 (#1)-Photo-c	13	26	39	91	201	310
Four Color 780, 872-Photo-c	12	24	36	79	170	260

CAPTAIN KID
AfterShock Comics: Jul, 2016 - No. 5, Mar, 2017 ($3.99)

1-5-Mark Waid & Tom Peyer-s/Wilfredo Torres-a — 4.00

CAPTAIN KIDD (Formerly Dagar; My Secret Story #26 on)(Also see Comic Comics & Fantastic Comics)
Fox Feature Syndicate: No. 24, June, 1949 - No. 25, Aug, 1949

	GD 2.0	VG 4.0	FN 6.0	VF 8.0	VF/NM 9.0	NM- 9.2
24,25: 24-Features Blackbeard the Pirate	15	30	45	88	137	185

CAPTAIN KRONOS - VAMPIRE HUNTER (Based on the 1974 Hammer film)
Titan Comics (Hammer Comics): Oct, 2017 - No. 4, Jan, 2018 ($3.99)

1-4-Abnett-s/Mandrake-a; multiple covers on each (art & photo) — 4.00

CAPTAIN MARVEL (See All Hero, All-New Collectors' Ed., America's Greatest, Fawcett Miniature, Gift, JSA, Kingdom Come, Legends, Limited Collectors' Ed., Marvel Family, Master No. 21, Mighty Midget Comics, Power of Shazam!, Shazam, Special Edition Comics, Whiz, Wisco (in Promotional Comics section), World's Finest #253 and XMas Comics)

CAPTAIN MARVEL (Becomes ...Presents the Terrible 5 No. 5)
M. F. Enterprises: April, 1966 - No. 4, Nov, 1966 (25¢ Giants)

	GD 2.0	VG 4.0	FN 6.0	VF 8.0	VF/NM 9.0	NM- 9.2
nn-(#1 on pg. 5)-Origin; created by Carl Burgos	6	12	18	40	73	105
2-4: 3-(#3 on pg. 4)-Fights the Bat	5	10	15	31	53	75

CAPTAIN MARVEL (Marvel's Space-Born Super-Hero! Captain Marvel #1-6; see Giant-Size..., Life Of..., Marvel Graphic Novel #1, Marvel Spotlight V2#1 & Marvel Super-Heroes #12)
Marvel Comics Group: May, 1968 - No. 19, Dec, 1969; No. 20, June, 1970 - No. 21, Aug, 1970; No. 22, Sept, 1972 - No. 62, May, 1979

	GD 2.0	VG 4.0	FN 6.0	VF 8.0	VF/NM 9.0	NM- 9.2
1	18	36	54	126	281	435
2-Super Skrull-c/story	8	16	24	51	96	140
3-5: 4-Captain Marvel battles Sub-Mariner	6	12	18	38	69	100
6-11: 11-Capt. Marvel given great power by Zo the Ruler; Smith/Trimpe-c; Death of Una	4	8	12	25	40	55
12,13,15,19,20	3	6	9	17	26	35
14-Capt. Marvel vs. Iron Man; last 12¢ issue.	4	8	12	28	47	65
16-1st new Captain Marvel (cameo)	4	8	12	28	47	65
17-1st new Captain Marvel app.	9	18	27	61	123	185
18-Carol Danvers gets powers	10	20	30	69	147	225
21-Capt. Marvel battles Hulk; last 15¢ issue	5	10	15	31	53	75
22-24	3	6	9	17	26	35
25-Starlin-c/a begins; Starlin's 1st Thanos saga begins (3/73), ends #34; Thanos cameo (5 panels)	7	14	21	49	92	135
26-2nd app. Thanos (see Iron Man #55); 1st Thanos-c	9	18	27	59	117	175
27-3rd app. Thanos	7	14	21	46	86	125
28-Thanos-c/s (4th app.); Avengers app.	9	18	27	59	117	175
29,30-Thanos cameos. 29-C.M. gains more powers	5	10	15	31	53	75
31-Thanos app.; last 20¢ issue; Avengers app.	5	10	15	30	50	70
32-Thanos-c & app.; Avengers app.	5	10	15	33	57	80
33-Thanos-c & app.; Capt. Marvel battles Thanos; Thanos origin re-told	8	16	24	55	105	155
34-1st app. Nitro; C.M. contracts cancer which eventually kills him; last Starlin-c/a	4	8	12	27	44	60
35,37-40,42,46-48,50,53-56,59-62: 39-Origin Watcher. 42,59-62-Drax app.	2	4	6	8	10	12
36,41,43,49: 36-R-origin/1st app. Capt. Marvel from Marvel Super-Heroes #12. 41,43-Drax app.; Wrightson part inks; #43-c(i). 49-Starlin & Weiss-p assists	2	4	6	8	11	14
44,45-(Regular 25¢ editions)(5,7/76)	2	4	6	8	10	12
44,45-(30¢-c variants, limited distribution)	4	8	12	27	44	60
51,52-(Regular 30¢ editions)(7,9/77)	2	4	6	8	10	12
51,52-(35¢-c variants, limited distribution)	7	14	21	48	89	130
57-Thanos appears in flashback	2	4	6	13	18	22
58-Thanos cameo; Drax app.	2	4	6	10	14	18

NOTE: ***Alcala** a-35. **Austin** a-46i, 49-53i; c-52i. **Buscema** a-18p-21p. **Colan** a(p)-1-4; c(p)-1-4, 8, 9. **Heck** a-5-10p, 16p. **Gil Kane** a-17-21p; c-17-24p, 37p, 53. **Starlin** a-36. **McWilliams** a-40i. #25-34 were reprinted in The Life of Captain Marvel.*

CAPTAIN MARVEL
Marvel Comics: Nov, 1989 ($1.50, one-shot, 52 pgs.)

	GD 2.0	VG 4.0	FN 6.0	VF 8.0	VF/NM 9.0	NM- 9.2
1-Monica Rambeau gains new powers; McDuffie-s	4	8	12	23	37	50

CAPTAIN MARVEL
Marvel Comics: Feb, 1994 ($1.75, 52 pgs.)

1-(Indicia reads Vol 2 #2)-Minor Captain America app. — 6.00

CAPTAIN MARVEL
Marvel Comics: Dec, 1995 - No. 6, May, 1996 ($2.95/$1.95)

1 ($2.95)-Advs. of Mar-Vell's son begins; Fabian Nicieza scripts; foil-c						4.00
2-6: 2-Begin $1.95-c						3.00

CAPTAIN MARVEL (Vol. 3) (See Avengers Forever)
Marvel Comics: Jan, 2000 - No. 35, Oct, 2002 ($2.50)

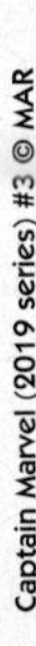
Captain Marvel (2019 series) #3 © MAR

Captain Marvel Adventures #21 © FAW

Captain Marvel, Jr. #33 © FAW

	GD 2.0	VG 4.0	FN 6.0	VF 8.0	VF/NM 9.0	NM- 9.2

1-Peter David-s in all; two covers 4.00
2-10: 2-Two covers; Hulk app. 9-Silver Surfer app. 3.00
11-35: 12-Maximum Security x-over. 17,18-Starlin-a. 27-30-Spider-Man 2099 app. 3.00
Wizard #0-Preview and history of Rick Jones 4.00
...: First Contact (8/01, $16.95, TPB) r/#0,1-6 17.00

CAPTAIN MARVEL (Vol. 4) (See Avengers Forever)
Marvel Comics: Nov, 2002 - No. 25, Sept, 2004 ($2.25/$2.99)

1-Peter David-s/Chriscross-a ; 3 covers by Ross, Jusko & Chriscross 5.00
2-7: 2,3-Punisher app. 3-Alex Ross-c; new costume debuts. 4-Noto-c. 7-Thor app. 3.00
3-Sketchbook Edition-($3.50) includes Ross' concept design pages for new costume 4.00
8-25: 8-Begin $2.99-c; Thor app.; Manco-c. 10-Spider-Man-c/app. 15-Neal Adams-c 3.00
Vol. 1: Nothing To Lose (2003, $14.99, TPB) r/#1-6 15.00
Vol. 2: Coven (2003, $14.99, TPB) r/#7-12 15.00
Vol. 3: Crazy Like a Fox (2004, $14.99, TPB) r/#13-18 15.00
Vol. 4: Odyssey (2004, $16.99, TPB) r/#19-25 17.00

CAPTAIN MARVEL (Vol. 5) (See Secret Invasion x-over titles)
Marvel Comics: Jan, 2008 - No. 5, Jun, 2008 ($2.99)

1-5-Mar-Vell "from the past in the present"; McGuinness-c/Weeks-a 3.00
3,4-Skrull variant-c 4.00

CAPTAIN MARVEL
Marvel Comics: Sept, 2012 - No. 17, Jan, 2014 ($2.99)

1-Carol Danvers as Captain Marvel; DeConnick-s/Soy-a
3 6 9 16 24 32
2-5 6.00
6-13,15,16: 13-The Enemy Within. 15,16-Infinity tie-in 5.00
14-1st cameo of Kamala Khan (new Ms. Marvel); Andrade-a; The Enemy Within cont'd
10 20 30 69 147 225
17-($3.99) Cameo of Kamala Khan (new Ms. Marvel); Andrade-a
3 6 9 19 30 40
17-($3.99, 2nd printing) Kamala Khan (new Ms. Marvel) in costume on cover
21 42 63 147 324 500

CAPTAIN MARVEL
Marvel Comics: May, 2014 - No. 15, Jul, 2015 ($3.99)

1-Carol Danvers; DeConnick-s/Lopez-a 3 6 9 14 20 25
2,3-Guardians of the Galaxy app. 6.00
4-9,11-15: 7,8-Rocket Raccoon app. 14-Black Vortex x-over 4.00
10-($4.99) 100th issue; War Machine & Spider-Woman app.; Lopez & Takara-a 5.00

CAPTAIN MARVEL (Follows Secret Wars event)(Also see Mighty Captain Marvel)
Marvel Comics: Mar, 2016 - No. 10, Jan, 2017 ($3.99)

1-5-Carol Danvers; Fazekas & Butters-s/Anka-a; Aurora, Sasquatch & Puck app. 4.00
6-9-Civil War II tie-ins 4.00
10-($4.99) Civil War II tie-in; Gage & Gage-s/Silas-a; Alpha Flight app. 5.00

CAPTAIN MARVEL (Follows Mighty Captain Marvel)
Marvel Comics: No. 125, Dec, 2017 - No. 129, Apr, 2018 ($3.99)

125-129-Carol Danvers; Stohl-s/Bandini-a; Alpha Flight app. 4.00

CAPTAIN MARVEL (Carol Danvers)(Also see Star series)
Marvel Comics: Mar, 2019 - Present ($4.99/$3.99)

1-($4.99) Thompson-s/Carnero-a; Spider-Woman, Hazmat, Nuclear Man app. 5.00
2-25-($3.99) 2,3-Echo & She-Hulk app. 3-5-Rogue app. 6,7-War of The Realms tie-in.
8-Debut of Star. 11-Star gets the Reality Stone. 12-16-The Last Avenger. 17-Wolverine app.
18-21-Empyre tie-in; Carol as The Accuser; intro. Lauri-ell 4.00
...: Braver & Mightier 1 (4/19, $3.99) Houser-s/Buonfantino-a 4.00
...: Marvels Snapshots 1 (4/21, $4.99) Mark Waid-s/Claire Roe-a; Kamala app. 5.00
...: The End 1 (3/20, $4.99) Carol's last adventure, set in 2051; Thompson-s/Carnero-a 5.00

CAPTAIN MARVEL ADVENTURES (See Special Edition Comics for pre #1)
Fawcett Publications: 1941 (March) - No. 150, Nov, 1953 (#1 on stands 1/16/41)

nn(#1)-Captain Marvel & Sivana by Jack Kirby. The cover was printed on unstable paper stock and is rarely found in Fine or Mint condition; blank back inside-c
6000 12,000 24,000 48,000 79,000 110,000
2-(Advertised as #3, which was counting Special Edition Comics as the real #1); Tuska-a 470 940 1410 3431 6066 8700
3-Metallic silver-c 337 574 1011 2359 4130 5900
4-Three Lt. Marvels app. 235 470 705 1492 2571 3650
5 181 362 543 1158 1979 2800
6-10: 9-1st Otto Binder scripts on Capt. Marvel 135 270 405 864 1482 2100
11-15: 12-Capt. Marvel joins the Army. 13-Two pg. Capt. Marvel pin-up.
15-Comix Cards on back-c begin, end #26 106 212 318 673 1162 1650
16,17: 17-Painted-c 97 194 291 621 1061 1500
18-Origin & 1st app. Mary Marvel & Marvel Family (12/11/42); classic painted-c;
Mary Marvel by Marcus Swayze 838 1676 2514 6117 10,809 15,500
19-Mary Marvel x-over; classic Christmas-c 95 190 285 603 1039 1475
20,21,23-Attached to the cover, each has a miniature comic just like the Mighty Midget Comics #11, except that each has a full color promo ad on the back cover. Most copies were circulated without the miniature comic. These issues with miniatures attached are very rare, and should not be mistaken for copies with the similar Mighty Midget glued in its place. The Mighty Midgets had blank back covers except for a small victory stamp seal. Only the Capt. Marvel, Captain Marvel Jr. and Golden Arrow No. 11 miniatures have been positively documented as having been affixed to these covers. Each miniature was only partially glued by its back cover to the Captain Marvel comic making it easy to see if it's the genuine miniature rather than a Mighty Midget.
with comic attached.... 470 940 1410 3431 6066 8700
20,23-Without miniature 76 152 228 486 831 1175
21-Without miniature; Hitler-c 148 296 444 947 1624 2300
22-Mr. Mind serial begins; Mr. Mind first heard 103 206 309 659 1130 1600
24,25 69 138 207 442 759 1075
26-28,30: 26-Flag-c; subtle Mr. Mind 2-panel cameo. 27-1st full Mr. Mind app. (his voice was only heard over the radio before now) (9/43) 57 114 171 362 619 875
29-1st Mr. Mind-c (11/43) 68 136 204 435 743 1050
31-35: 35-Origin Radar (5/44, see Master #50) 51 102 153 318 539 760
36-40: 37-Mary Marvel x-over 47 94 141 296 498 700
41-46: 42-Christmas-c. 43-Capt. Marvel 1st meets Uncle Marvel; Mary Batson cameo.
46-Mr. Mind serial ends 39 78 117 240 395 550
47-50 37 74 111 222 361 500
51-53,55-60: 51-63-Bi-weekly issues. 52-Origin & 1st app. Sivana Jr.; Capt. Marvel Jr. x-over
34 68 102 199 325 450
54-Special oversize 68 pg. issue 36 72 108 211 343 475
61-The Cult of the Curse serial begins 36 72 108 216 351 485
62-65-Serial cont.; Mary Marvel x-over in #65 34 68 102 199 325 450
66-Serial ends; Atomic War-c 40 80 120 246 411 575
67-77,79: 69-Billy Batson's Christmas; Uncle Marvel, Mary Marvel, Capt. Marvel Jr. x-over.
71-Three Lt. Marvels app. 72-Empire State Building photo-c. 79-Origin Mr. Tawny
31 62 93 182 296 410
78-Origin Mr. Atom 34 68 102 204 322 460
80-Origin Capt. Marvel retold; origin scene-c 97 194 291 621 1061 1500
81-84,86-90: 81,90-Mr. Atom app. 82-Infinity-c. 82,86,88,90-Mr. Tawny app.
31 62 93 182 296 410
85-Freedom Train issue 34 68 102 204 332 460
91-99: 92-Mr. Tawny app. 96-Gets 1st name "Tawky" 30 60 90 177 289 400
100-Origin retold; silver metallic-c 54 108 162 343 574 825
101-115,117-120 30 60 90 177 289 400
116-Flying Saucer issue (1/51) 34 68 102 199 325 450
121-Origin retold 37 74 111 222 361 500
122-137,139,140 30 60 90 177 289 400
138-Flying Saucer issue (11/52) 34 68 102 204 332 460
141-Pre-code horror story "The Hideous Head-Hunter"
36 72 108 211 343 475
142-149: 142-used in **POP**, pgs. 92,96 33 66 99 194 317 440
150-(Low distribution) 61 122 183 390 670 950
NOTE: ***Swayze** a-12, 14, 15, 18, 19, 40; c-12, 15, 19.*

CAPTAIN MARVEL AND THE CAROL CORPS (Secret Wars tie-in)
Marvel Comics: Aug, 2015 - No. 4, Nov, 2015 ($3.99, limited series)

1-4: 1-Carol Danvers' squad; DeConnick & Thompson-s/Lopez-a. 4-Braga-a 4.00

CAPTAIN MARVEL AND THE GOOD HUMOR MAN (Movie)
Fawcett Publications: 1950

nn-Partial photo-c w/Jack Carson & the Captain Marvel Club Boys
54 108 162 343 574 825

CAPTAIN MARVEL COMIC STORY PAINT BOOK (See Comic Story...)

CAPTAIN MARVEL, JR. (See Fawcett Miniatures, Marvel Family, Master Comics, Mighty Midget Comics, Shazam & Whiz Comics)

CAPTAIN MARVEL, JR.
Fawcett Publications: Nov, 1942 - No. 119, June, 1953 (No #34)

1-Origin Capt. Marvel Jr. retold (Whiz #25); Capt. Nazi app. Classic Raboy-c
622 1244 1866 4541 8021 11,500
2-Vs. Capt. Nazi; origin Capt. Nippon 223 446 669 1416 2433 3450
3 123 246 369 787 1344 1900
4-Classic Raboy-c 135 270 405 864 1482 2100
5-Vs. Capt. Nazi 103 206 309 659 1130 1600
6-8: 8-Vs. Capt. Nazi 81 162 243 518 884 1250
9-Classic flag-c 100 200 300 635 1093 1550
10-Hitler-c 200 400 600 1280 2190 3100
11,12,15-Capt. Nazi app. 74 148 222 470 810 1150
13-Classic Hitler, Tojo and Mussolini football-c 200 400 600 1280 2190 3100
14,16-20: 14-Christmas-c. 16-Capt. Marvel & Sivana x-over. 17-Futuristic city-c; Raboy-c/a(3).
19-Capt. Nazi & Capt. Nippon app. 57 114 171 362 619 875
21-30: 25-Flag-c 45 90 135 284 480 675
31-33,36-40: 37-Infinity-c 33 66 99 194 317 440

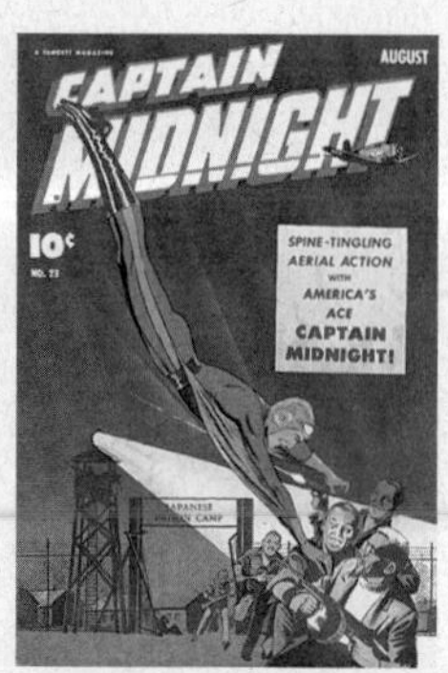

Captain Midnight #23 © FAW

Capt. Savage and His Leatherneck Raiders #4 © MAR

Captain Thunder and Blue Bolt #1 © Hero

	GD 2.0	VG 4.0	FN 6.0	VF 8.0	VF/NM 9.0	NM- 9.2
35-#34 on inside; cover shows origin of Sivana Jr. which is not on inside. Evidently the cover to #35 was printed out of sequence and bound with contents to #34	34	68	102	199	325	450
41-70: 42-Robot-c. 53-Atomic Bomb-c/story	27	54	81	160	263	365
71-99,101-104: 87,93-Robot-c. 104-Used in **POP**, pg. 89	24	48	72	142	234	325
100	29	58	87	170	278	385
105-114,116-118: 116-Vampira, Queen of Terror app.	28	56	84	165	270	375
115-Classic injury to eye-c; Eyeball story w/injury-to-eye panels	168	336	504	1075	1838	2600
119-Electric chair-c (scarce)	84	168	252	538	919	1300

NOTE: *Mac Raboy c-1-28, 30-32, 57, 59 among others.*

CAPTAIN MARVEL PRESENTS THE TERRIBLE FIVE
M. F. Enterprises: Aug, 1966; V2#5, Sept, 1967 (No #2-4) (25¢)

	GD	VG	FN	VF	VF/NM	NM-
1	5	10	15	35	63	90
V2#5-(Formerly Captain Marvel)	4	8	12	27	44	60

CAPTAIN MARVEL'S FUN BOOK
Samuel Lowe Co.: 1944 (1/2" thick) (cardboard covers)(25¢)

	GD	VG	FN	VF	VF/NM	NM-
nn-Puzzles, games, magic, etc.; infinity-c	47	94	141	296	498	700

CAPTAIN MARVEL SPECIAL EDITION (See Special Edition)

CAPTAIN MARVEL STORY BOOK
Fawcett Publications: Summer, 1946 - No. 4, Summer?, 1948

	GD	VG	FN	VF	VF/NM	NM-
1-Half text	64	128	183	390	670	950
2-4	43	86	129	271	461	650

CAPTAIN MARVEL THRILL BOOK (Large-Size)
Fawcett Publications: 1941 (B&W w/color-c)

	GD	VG	FN	VF	VF/NM	NM-
1-Reprints from Whiz #8,10, & Special Edition #1 (Rare)	460	920	1380	4600	--	--

NOTE: *Rarely found in Fine or Mint condition.*

CAPTAIN MIDNIGHT (TV, radio, films) (See The Funnies, Popular Comics & Super Book of Comics)(Becomes Sweethearts No. 68 on)
Fawcett Publications: Sept, 1942 - No. 67, Fall, 1948 (#1-14: 68 pgs.)

	GD	VG	FN	VF	VF/NM	NM-
1-Origin Captain Midnight, star of radio and movies; Captain Marvel cameo on cover	331	662	993	2317	4059	5800
2-Smashes the Jap Juggernaut	158	316	474	1003	1727	2450
3-Classic Nazi war-c	155	310	465	992	1696	2400
4,5: 4-Grapples the Gremlins	116	232	348	742	1271	1800
6-8: 7-WWII-c	69	138	207	442	759	1075
9-Raboy-c	81	162	243	518	884	1250
10-Raboy Flag-c/WWII-c	77	154	231	493	847	1200
11-20: 11,17,18-Raboy-c. 16 (1/44)	50	100	150	315	533	750
21-Classic WWII-c	61	122	183	390	670	950
22,25-30: 22-War savings stamp-c	40	80	120	246	411	575
23-WWII Concentration Camp-c	57	114	171	362	619	875
24-Japan flag sunburst-c	63	126	189	403	689	975
31-40	32	64	96	188	307	425
41-59,61-67: 50-Sci/fi theme begins?	25	50	75	150	245	340
60-Flying Saucer issue (2/48)-3rd of this theme; see The Spirit 9/28/47 (1st), Shadow Comics V7#10 (2nd, 1/48) & Boy Commandos #26 (4th, 3-4/48)	40	80	120	244	402	560

CAPTAIN MIDNIGHT
Dark Horse Comics: No. 0, Jun, 2013 - No. 24, Jun, 2015 ($2.99)

	GD	VG	FN	VF	VF/NM	NM-
0-24: 0-Williamson-s/Ibáñez-a; WWII hero appears in modern times. 4,5-Skyman app.						3.00
One For One: Captain Midnight #1 (1/14, $1.00) r/#1						3.00

CAPTAIN NICE (TV)
Gold Key: Nov, 1967 (one-shot)

	GD	VG	FN	VF	VF/NM	NM-
1(10211-711)-Photo-c	6	12	18	37	66	95

CAPTAIN N: THE GAME MASTER (TV)
Valiant Comics: 1990 - No. 5, 1990 ($1.95, thick stock, coated-c)

	GD	VG	FN	VF	VF/NM	NM-
1-5: 3-Quesada-a (1st pro work). 4,5-Layton-c						5.00

CAPTAIN PARAGON (See Bill Black's Fun Comics)
Americomics: Dec, 1983 - No. 4, 1985

	GD	VG	FN	VF	VF/NM	NM-
1-Intro/1st app. Ms. Victory						4.00
2-4						3.00

CAPTAIN PARAGON AND THE SENTINELS OF JUSTICE
AC Comics: April, 1985 - No. 6, 1986 ($1.75)

	GD	VG	FN	VF	VF/NM	NM-
1-6: 1-Capt. Paragon, Commando D., Nightveil, Scarlet Scorpion, Stardust & Atoman						3.00

CAPTAIN PLANET AND THE PLANETEERS (TV cartoon)
Marvel Comics: Oct, 1991 - No. 12, Oct, 1992 ($1.00/$1.25)

	GD	VG	FN	VF	VF/NM	NM-
1-N. Adams painted-c	1	2	3	5	6	8
2-12: 3-Romita-c						3.00

CAPTAIN POWER AND THE SOLDIERS OF THE FUTURE (TV)
Continuity Comics: Aug, 1988 - No. 2, 1988 ($2.00)

	GD	VG	FN	VF	VF/NM	NM-
1,2: 1-Neal Adams-c/layouts/inks; variant-c exists.						4.00

CAPTAIN PUREHEART (See Archie as...)

CAPTAIN ROCKET
P. L. Publ. (Canada): Nov, 1951

	GD	VG	FN	VF	VF/NM	NM-
1-Harry Harrison-a	60	120	180	381	653	925

CAPT. SAVAGE AND HIS LEATHERNECK RAIDERS (...And His Battlefield Raiders #9 on)
Marvel Comics Group (Animated Timely Features): Jan, 1968 - No. 19, Mar, 1970
(See Sgt. Fury No. 10)

	GD	VG	FN	VF	VF/NM	NM-
1-Sgt. Fury & Howlers cameo	6	12	18	41	76	110
2,7,11: 2-Origin Hydra. 7-Pre-"Thing" Ben Grimm story. 11-Sgt. Fury app.	3	6	9	17	26	35
3-6,8-10,12-14: 4-Origin Hydra. 14-Last 12¢ issue	3	6	9	16	23	30
15-19	3	6	9	14	19	24

NOTE: *Ayres/Shores a-1-8,11. Ayres/Severin a-9,10,17-19. Heck/Shores a-12-15.*

CAPTAIN SCIENCE (Fantastic No. 8 on)
Youthful Magazines: Nov, 1950; No. 2, Feb, 1951 - No. 7, Dec, 1951

	GD	VG	FN	VF	VF/NM	NM-
1-Wood-a; origin; 2 pg. text w/ photos of George Pal's "Destination Moon."	110	220	330	704	1202	1700
2-Flying saucer-c swipes Weird Science #13(#2)-c	60	120	180	381	653	925
3,7; 3-Bondage c-swipes/Wings #94	55	110	165	352	601	850
4,5-Wood/Orlando-c/a(2) each	97	194	291	621	1061	1500
6-Bondage c-swipes/Wings #91	129	258	387	826	1413	2000

NOTE: *Fass a-4. Bondage c-3, 6, 7.*

CAPTAIN SILVER'S LOG OF SEA HOUND (See Sea Hound)

CAPTAIN SINBAD (Movie Adaptation) (See Fantastic Voyages of... & Movie Comics)

CAPTAIN STERNN: RUNNING OUT OF TIME
Kitchen Sink Press: Sept, 1993 - No. 5, 1994 ($4.95, limited series, coated stock, 52 pgs.)

	GD	VG	FN	VF	VF/NM	NM-
1-5: Berni Wrightson-c/a/scripts						6.00
1-Gold ink variant						10.00

CAPTAIN STEVE SAVAGE (...& His Jet Fighters, No. 2-13)
Avon Periodicals: 1950 - No. 8, 1/53; No. 5, 9-10/54 - No. 13, 5-6/56

	GD	VG	FN	VF	VF/NM	NM-
nn(1st series)-Harrison/Wood art, 22 pgs. (titled "...Over Korea")	48	96	144	302	514	725
1(4/51)-Reprints nn issue (Canadian)	22	44	66	132	216	300
2-Kamen-a	19	38	57	109	172	235
3-11 (#6, 11-12/54, last precode)	15	30	45	85	130	175
12-Wood-a (6 pgs.)	18	36	54	107	169	230
13-Check, Lawrence-a	15	30	45	86	133	180

NOTE: *Kinstler c-2-5, 7-9, 11. Lawrence a-8. Ravielli a-5, 9.*

	GD	VG	FN	VF	VF/NM	NM-
5(9-10/54-2nd series)(Formerly Sensational Police Cases)	12	24	36	69	97	125
6-Reprints nn issue; Harrison/Wood-a	13	26	39	72	101	130
7-13: 9,10-Kinstler-c. 10-r/cover #2 (1st series). 13-r/cover #8 (1st series)	10	20	30	58	79	100

CAPTAIN STONE (See Holyoke One-Shot No. 10)

CAPT. STORM (Also see G. I. Combat #138)
National Periodical Publications: May-June, 1964 - No. 18, Mar-Apr, 1967

	GD	VG	FN	VF	VF/NM	NM-
1-Origin	10	20	30	69	147	225
2-7,9-18: 3,6,13-Kubert-a. 4-Colan-a. 12-Kubert-c	7	14	21	44	82	120
8-Grey-tone-c	8	16	24	54	102	150

CAPTAIN 3-D (Super hero)
Harvey Publications: December, 1953 (25¢, came with 2 pairs of glasses)

	GD	VG	FN	VF	VF/NM	NM-
1-Kirby/Ditko-a (Ditko's 3rd published work tied with Strange Fantasy #9, see also Daring Love #1 & Black Magic V4 #3); shows cover in 3-D on inside; Kirby/Meskin-c	14	28	42	78	112	145

NOTE: *Half price without glasses*

CAPTAIN THUNDER AND BLUE BOLT
Hero Comics: Sept, 1987 - No. 10, 1988 ($1.95)

	GD	VG	FN	VF	VF/NM	NM-
1-10: 1-Origin Blue Bolt. 3-Origin Capt. Thunder. 6-1st app. Wicket. 8-Champions x-over						3.00

CAPTAIN TOOTSIE & THE SECRET LEGION (Advs. of...)(Also see Monte Hale #30,39 & Real Western Hero)
Toby Press: Oct, 1950 - No. 2, Dec, 1950

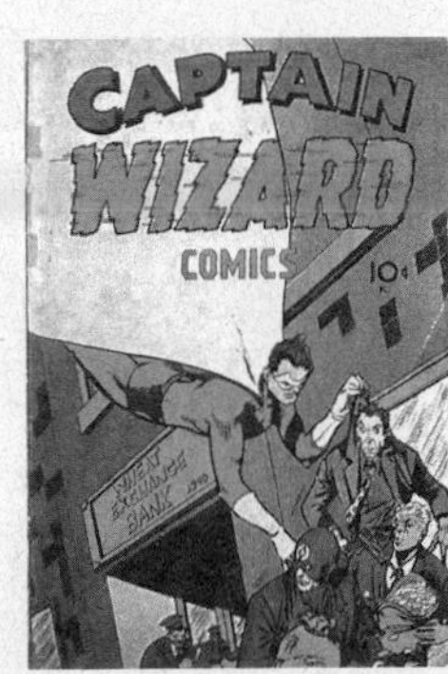
Captain Wizard Comics #1 © Rural Home

Career Girl Romances #46 © CC

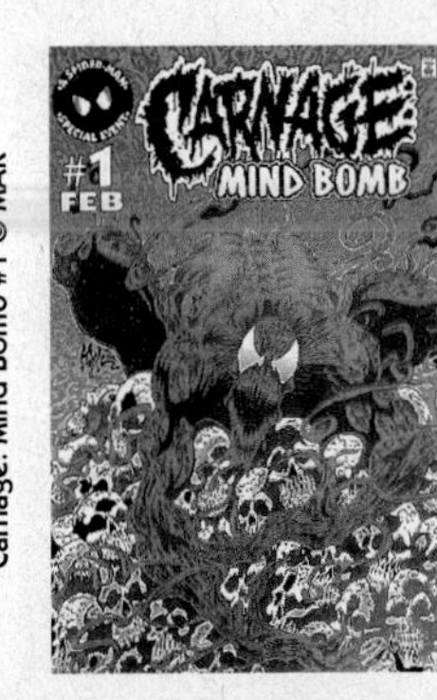

Carnage: Mind Bomb #1 © MAR

	GD 2.0	VG 4.0	FN 6.0	VF 8.0	VF/NM 9.0	NM- 9.2
1-Not Beck-a; both have sci/fi covers	37	74	111	222	361	500
2-The Rocketeer Patrol app.; not Beck-a	22	44	66	128	209	290

CAPTAIN TRIUMPH (See Crack Comics #27)

CAPTAIN UNIVERSE... (5-part x-over)
Marvel Comics: 2005; Jan, 2006

.../ Daredevil 1 (1/06, $2.99) Part 2; Faerber-s/Santacruz-a 3.00
.../ Hulk 1 (1/06, $2.99) Part 1; Faerber-s/Magno-a 3.00
.../ Invisible Woman 1 (1/06, $2.99) Part 4; Faerber-s/Raiz-a; Gladiator app. 3.00
.../ Silver Surfer 1 (1/06, $2.99) Part 5; Faerber-s/Magno-a 3.00
.../ X-23 1 (1/06, $2.99) Part 3; Faerber-s/Portella-a; Scorpion app. 3.00
....: Power Unimaginable TPB (2005, $19.99)-Reprints from Marvel Spotlight #9-11, Incredible Hulk Ann. #10, Marvel Fanfare #25, Web of Spider-Man Ann. #5&6, Marvel Comics Presents #148, Cosmic Power Unlimited #5 20.00
....: The Hero Who Could Be You 1 (7/13, $7.99) r/Marvel Spotlight #9-11 & early apps. 8.00
....: Universal Heroes TPB (2005, $13.99) reprints .../Hulk, .../Daredevil, ...X-23 and back-up stories from Amazing Fantasy (2005) #13,14 14.00

CAPTAIN VENTURE & THE LAND BENEATH THE SEA (See Space Family Robinson)
Gold Key: Oct, 1968 - No. 2, Oct, 1969

1-r/Space Family Robinson serial; Spiegle-a 4 8 12 28 47 65
2-Spiegle-a 4 8 12 23 37 50

CAPTAIN VICTORY AND THE GALACTIC RANGERS (Also see Kirby: Genesis)
Pacific Comics: Nov, 1981 - No. 13, Jan, 1984 ($1.00, direct sales, 36-48 pgs.)
(Created by Jack Kirby)

1-1st app. Mr. Mind 6.00
2-13: 3-N. Adams-a 3.00
Special 1-(10/83)-Kirby c/a(p) 4.00
*NOTE: **Conrad** a-10, 11. **Ditko** a-6. **Kirby** a-1-3p; c-1-13.*

CAPTAIN VICTORY AND THE GALACTIC RANGERS
Jack Kirby Comics: July, 2000 - No. 2, Sept, 2000 ($2.95, B&W)

1,2-New Jeremy Kirby-s with reprinted Jack Kirby-a; Liefeld pin-up art 3.00

CAPTAIN VICTORY AND THE GALACTIC RANGERS
Dynamite Entertainment: 2014 - No. 6, 2015 ($3.99)

1-6-Joe Casey-s; art by various. 3-Dalrymple & Mahfood-a 4.00

CAPTAIN VIDEO (TV) (See XMas Comics)
Fawcett Publications: Feb, 1951 - No. 6, Dec, 1951 (No. 1,5,6-36 pgs.; 2-4, 52 pgs.)

1-George Evans-a(2); 1st TV hero comic 103 206 309 659 1130 1600
2-Used in **SOTI**, pg. 382 68 136 204 435 743 1050
3-6-All Evans-a except #5 mostly Evans 55 110 165 352 601 850
NOTE: *Minor **Williamson** assists on most issues. Photo c-1, 5, 6; painted c-2-4.*

CAPTAIN WILLIE SCHULTZ (Also see Fightin' Army)
Charlton Comics: No. 76, Oct, 1985 - No. 77, Jan, 1986

76,77-Low print run 1 2 3 5 6 8

CAPTAIN WIZARD COMICS (See Meteor, Red Band & Three Ring Comics)
Rural Home: 1946

1-Capt. Wizard dons new costume; Impossible Man, Race Wilkins app.
43 86 129 271 461 650

CAPTAIN WONDER
Image Comics: Feb, 2011 ($4.99, 3-D comic with glasses)

1-Haberlin-s/Tan-a; sketch pages, crossword puzzle, paper dolls 5.00

CAPTURE CREATURES
BOOM! Entertainment (kaboom!): Nov, 2014 - No. 4, May, 2015 ($3.99)

1-4-Frank Gibson-s/Becky Dreistadt-a; multiple covers on each 4.00

CARBON GREY
Image Comics: Mar, 2011 - No. 3, May, 2011 ($2.99, limited series)

1-3-Khari Evans, Kinsun Loh & Hoang Nguyen-a; Nguyen-c 3.00
... Origins 1,2 (11/11 - No. 2, 3/12, $3.99) 1-Pop Mhan-a 4.00
Vol. 2 (7/12 - No. 3, 2/13, $3.99) 1-3-Gardner-s/Evans & Nguyen-a 4.00
Vol. 3 (12/13 - No. 2, 1/14) 1,2-Gardner-s/Evans & Nguyen-a 4.00

CARE BEARS (TV, Movie)(See Star Comics Magazine)
Star Comics/Marvel Comics No. 15 on: Nov, 1985 - No. 20, Jan, 1989

1-Post-a begins 3 6 9 15 22 28
2-20: 11-$1.00-c begins. 13-Madballs app. 1 3 4 6 8 10

CARE BEARS (TV, Movie)(Subtitled "Unlock the Magic" on cover)
IDW Publishing: Jul, 2019 - No. 3, Sept, 2019 ($3.99, limited series)

1-3-Garbowska-a 4.00

CAREER GIRL ROMANCES (Formerly Three Nurses)
Charlton Comics: June, 1964 - No. 78, Dec, 1973

V4#24-31 3 6 9 17 25 34
32-Elvis Presley, Herman's Hermits, Johnny Rivers line drawn-c
10 20 30 69 147 225
33-37,39-50: 39-Tiffany Sinn app. 3 6 9 15 22 28
38-(2/67) 1st app. Tiffany Sinn, C.I.A. Sweetheart, Undercover Agent (also see Secret Agent #10; Dominguel-a 3 6 9 18 28 38
51-78: 54-Jonnie Love anti-drup PSA. 67-Susan Dey pin-up. 70-David Cassidy pin-up
2 4 6 13 18 22

CAR 54, WHERE ARE YOU? (TV)
Dell Publishing Co.: Mar-May, 1962 - No. 7, Sept-Nov, 1963; 1964 - 1965 (All photo-c)

Four Color 1257(#1, 3-5/62) 8 16 24 56 108 160
2(6-8/62)-7 5 10 15 30 50 70
2,3(10-12/64), 4(1-3/65)-Reprints #2,3,&4 of 1st series
3 6 9 19 30 40

CARL BARKS LIBRARY OF WALT DISNEY'S GYRO GEARLOOSE COMICS AND FILLERS IN COLOR, THE
Gladstone: 1993 ($7.95, 8-1/2x11", limited series, 52 pgs.)

1-6: Carl Barks reprints 1 3 4 6 8 10

CARL BARKS LIBRARY OF WALT DISNEY'S COMICS AND STORIES IN COLOR, THE
Gladstone: Jan, 1992 - No. 51, Mar, 1996 ($8.95, 8-1/2x11", 60 pgs.)

1,2,6,8-51: 1-Barks Donald Duck-r/WDC&S #31-35; 2-r/#36,38-41; 6-r/#57-61; 8-r/#67-71; 9-r/#72-76; 10-r/#77-81; 11-r/#82-86; 12-r/#87-91; 13-r/#92-96; 14-r/#97-101; 15-r/#102-106; 16-r/#107-111; 17-r/#112,114,117,124,125; 18-r/#126-130; 19-r/#131,132(2),133,134; 20-r/#135-139; 21-r/#140-144; 22-r/#145-149; 23-r/#150-154; 24-r/#155-159; 25-r/#160-164; 26-r/#165-169; 27-r/#170-174;28-r/#175-179; 29-r/#180-184; 30-r/#185-189; 31-r/#190-194; 32-r/#195-199;33-r/#200-204; 34-r/#205-209; 35-r/#210-214; 36-r/#215-219; 37-r/#220-224; 38-r/#225-229; 39-r/#230-234; 40-r/#235-239; 41-r/#240-244; 42r/#245-249; 43-r/#250-254; 44-50; All contain one Heroes & Villains trading card each
2 4 6 9 12 15
3,4,7: 3-r/#42-46. 4-r/#47-51. 7-r/#62-66. 2 4 6 11 16 20
5-r/#52-56 3 6 9 16 23 30

CARL BARKS LIBRARY OF WALT DISNEY'S DONALD DUCK ADVENTURES IN COLOR, THE
Gladstone: Jan, 1994 - No. 25, Jan, 1996 ($7.95-$9.95, 44-68 pgs., 8-1/2"x11")
(all contain one Donald Duck trading card each)

1-5,7-25-Carl Barks-r: 1-r/FC #9; 2-r/FC #29; 3-r/FC #62; 4-r/FC #108; 5-r/FC #147 & #79(Mickey Mouse); 7-r/FC #159. 8-r/FC #178 & 189. 9-r/FC #199 & 203; 10-r/FC 223 & 238; 11-r/Christmas Parade #1 & 2; 12-r/FC #296; 13-r/FC #263; 14-r/MOC #20 & 41; 15-r/FC 275 & 282; 16-r/FC #291&300; 17-r/FC #308 & 318; 18-r/Vac. Parade #1 & Summer Fun #2; 19-r/FC #328 & 367 2 4 6 9 12 15
6-r/MOC #4, Cheerios "Atom Bomb," D.D. Tells About Kites
3 6 9 14 20 25

CARL BARKS LIBRARY OF WALT DISNEY'S DONALD DUCK CHRISTMAS STORIES IN COLOR, THE
Gladstone: 1992 ($7.95, 44pgs., one-shot)

nn-Reprints Firestone giveaways 1945-1949 2 4 6 10 14 18

CARL BARKS LIBRARY OF WALT DISNEY'S UNCLE SCROOGE COMICS ONE PAGERS IN COLOR, THE
Gladstone: 1992 - No. 2, 1993 ($8.95, limited series, 60 pgs., 8-1/2x11")

1-Carl Barks one pg. reprints 3 6 9 16 23 30
2-Carl Barks one pg. reprints 2 4 6 10 14 18

CARNAGE
Marvel Comics: Dec, 2010 - No. 5, Aug, 2011 ($3.99, limited series)

1-5-Spider-Man & Iron Man app.; Clayton Crain-a/c; Wells-s 4.00
...: It's a Wonderful Life (10/96, $1.95) David Quinn scripts 3.00
...: Mind Bomb (2/96, $2.95) Warren Ellis script; Kyle Hotz-a 4.00

CARNAGE
Marvel Comics: Jan, 2016 - No. 16, Mar, 2017 ($3.99)

1-16: 1-Conway-s/Perkins-a; Eddie Brock app. 3-Man-Wolf app. 4,5-Toxin app. 4.00

CARNAGE, U.S.A.
Marvel Comics: Feb, 2012 - No. 5, Jun, 2012 ($3.99, limited series)

1-4-Clayton Crain-a/c; Wells-s; Spider-Man & Avengers app. 3,4-Venom app. 4.00

CARNATION MALTED MILK GIVEAWAYS (See Wisco/Klarer in the Promotional Comics section)

CARNEYS, THE
Archie Comics: Summer, 1994 ($2.00, 52 pgs)

1-Bound-in pull-out poster 4.00

CARNIVAL COMICS (Formerly Kayo #12; becomes Red Seal Comics #14)

Cars 2 #1 © DIS & Pixar

Casanova #10 © Fraction & Bá

Casper and Friends #1 © HARV

	GD	VG	FN	VF	VF/NM	NM-
	2.0	4.0	6.0	8.0	9.0	9.2

Harry 'A' Chesler/Pershing Square Publ. Co.: 1945
nn (#13)-Guardineer-a 21 42 63 122 199 275

CAROLINE KENNEDY
Charlton Comics: 1961 (one-shot)
nn-Interior photo covers of Kennedy family 10 20 30 69 147 225

CAROUSEL COMICS
F. E. Howard, Toronto: V1#8, April, 1948
V1#8 14 28 42 80 115 150

CARS (Based on the 2006 Pixar movie)
Boom Entertainment: No. 0, Nov, 2009 - No. 7, Jun, 2010 ($2.99)
0-7: 0,1-Three covers on each. 2-7-Two covers on each 3.00
...: Adventures of Tow Mater 1-4 (7/10 - No. 4, 10/10, $2.99) 1-Two covers 3.00
...: Radiator Springs 1-4 (7/09 - No. 4, 10/09, $2.99) Two covers on each 3.00
...: The Rookie 1-4 (3/09 - No. 4, 6/09, $2.99) Origin of Lightning McQueen 3.00

CARS 2 (Based on the 2011 Pixar movie)
Marvel Worldwide (Disney Comics): Aug, 2011 - No. 2, Aug, 2011 ($3.99)
1,2-Movie adaptation; car profile pages 4.00

CARS, WORLD OF (Free Comic Book Day giveaway)
BOOM Kids!: May, 2009
1-Based on the Disney/Pixar movie 3.00

CARSON OF VENUS (Also see Edgar Rice Burroughs'...)
American Mythology Prods.: 2020 - 2020 ($3.99, limited series)
...: Realm of the Dead 1-3 - Wolfer-s/Mesarcia-a 4.00
...: The Eye of Amtor 1-3 - Wolfer-s/Carratu-a 4.00

CARTOON CARTOONS (Anthology)
DC Comics: Mar, 2001 - No. 33, Oct, 2004 ($1.99/$2.25)
1-33-Short stories of Cartoon Network characters. 3,6,10,13,15-Space Ghost. 13-Begin $2.25-c. 17-Dexter's Laboratory begins 3.00

CARTOON KIDS
Atlas Comics (CPS): 1957 (no month)
1-Maneely-c/a; Dexter The Demon, Willie The Wise-Guy, Little Zelda app. 17 34 51 100 158 215

CARTOON NETWORK ACTION PACK (Anthology)
DC Comics: July, 2006 - No. 67, May, 2012 ($2.25/$2.50/$2.99)
1-31-Short stories of Cartoon Network characters. 1,4,6-Rowdyruff Boys app. 3.00
32-67: 32-Begin $2.50-c. 50-Ben 10/Generator Rex team-up 3.00

CARTOON NETWORK BLOCK PARTY (Anthology)
DC Comics: Nov, 2004 - No. 59, Sept, 2009 ($2.25/$2.50)
1,2,4-51-Short stories of Cartoon Network characters 3.00
3-($2.95) Bonus pages 4.00
52-59: 52-Begin $2.50-c. 59-Last issue; Powerpuff Girls app. 3.00
Cartoon Network 2-in-1: Ben 10 Alien Force/The Secret Saturdays TPB (2010, $12.99) reprints stories from #26-42 13.00
Cartoon Network 2-in-1: Foster's Home For Imaginary Friends/Powerpuff Girls TPB (2010, $12.99) reprints stories from #19-21,23,25,26,28,30-32,34-38,41 13.00
... Vol. 1: Get Down! (2005, $6.99, digest) reprints from Dexter's Lab and Cartoon Cartoons 7.00
... Vol. 2: Read All About It! (2005, $6.99, digest) reprints 7.00
... Vol. 3: Can You Dig It?; ... Vol. 4: Blast Off! (2006, $6.99, digest) reprints 7.00

CARTOON NETWORK PRESENTS
DC Comics: Aug, 1997 - No. 24, Aug, 1999 ($1.75-$1.99, anthology)
1-Dexter's Lab 2 4 6 9 12 15
1-Platinum Edition 2 4 6 8 10 12
2-10: 2-Space Ghost 4.00
11-24: 12-Bizarro World 3.00

CARTOON NETWORK PRESENTS SPACE GHOST
Archie Comics: Mar, 1997 ($1.50)
1-Scott Rosema-p 2 4 6 10 14 18

CARTOON NETWORK STARRING... (Anthology)
DC Comics: Sept, 1999 - No. 18, Feb, 2001 ($1.99)
1-Powerpuff Girls 4 8 12 27 44 60
2-18: 2,8,11,14,17-Johnny Bravo. 12,15,18-Space Ghost 4.00

CARTOON TALES (Disney's...)
W.D. Publications (Disney): nd, nn (1992) ($2.95, 6-5/8x9-1/2", 52 pgs.)
nn-Ariel & Sebastian-Serpent Teen; Beauty and the Beast; A Tale of Enchantment; Darkwing Duck - Just Us Justice Ducks; 101 Dalmatians - Canine Classics; Tale Spin - Surprise in the Skies; Uncle Scrooge - Blast to the Past 4.00

CARVERS
Image Comics (Flypaper Press): 1998 - No. 3, 1999 ($2.95)
1-3-Pander Bros.-a/Fleming-s 3.00

CAR WARRIORS
Marvel Comics (Epic): June, 1991 - No. 4, Sept, 1991 ($2.25, lim. series)
1-4: 1-Says April in indicia 3.00

CASANOVA
Image Comics: June, 2006 - No. 14, May, 2008 ($1.99, B&W & olive green or blue)
1-14: 1-7-Matt Fraction-s/Gabriel Bá-a/c. 8-14-Fabio Moon-a 3.00
...: Luxuria TPB (2008, $12.99) r/#1-7; sketch pages and cover gallery 13.00
1-4 (Marvel Comics, 10/10 - No. 4, 12/10, $3.99) Recolored reprints Image series #1-7 4.00
...: Acedia 1-8 (Image, 1/15 - No. 8, 3/17) Fraction-s/Moon-a; back-up by Chabon-s/Bá-a 4.00
...: Avaritia (III) 1-4 (Marvel, 11/11 - No. 4, 8/12, $4.99) new story; Fraction-s/Bá-a 5.00
...: Gula (Marvel, 1/11 - No. 4, 4/11) r/Image series #8-14. 4-New story pages 4.00

CASE FILES: SAM & TWITCH (Also see the Spawn titles)
Image Comics: May, 2003 - No. 25, July, 2006 ($2.50/$2.95, color #1-6/B&W #7-on)
1-25: 1-5-Scott Morse-a/Marc Andreyko-s. 7-13-Paul Lee-a. 13-Niles-s 3.00

CASE OF THE SHOPLIFTER'S SHOE (See Perry Mason, Feature Book No.50)

CASE OF THE WINKING BUDDHA, THE
St. John Publ. Co.: 1950 (132 pgs.; 25¢; B&W; 5-1/2x7-5-1/2x8")
nn-Charles Raab-a; reprinted in Authentic Police Cases No. 25 53 106 159 334 567 800

CASEY BLUE
DC Comics (WildStorm): Jul, 2008 - No. 6, Dec, 2008 ($2.99, limited series)
1-6-B. Clay Moore-s/Carlos Barberi-a 3.00
...: Beyond Tomorrow TPB (2009, $19.99) r/#1-6; Barberi sketch pages 20.00

CASEY-CRIME PHOTOGRAPHER (Two-Gun Western No. 5 on)(Radio)
Marvel Comics (BFP): Aug, 1949 - No. 4, Feb, 1950
1-Photo-c; 52 pgs. 37 74 111 222 361 500
2-4: Photo-c 22 44 66 132 216 300

CASEY JONES (TV)
Dell Publishing Co.: No. 915, July, 1958
Four Color 915-Alan Hale photo-c 6 12 18 37 66 95

CASEY JONES & RAPHAEL (See Bodycount)
Mirage Studios: Oct, 1994 ($2.75, unfinished limited series)
1-Bisley-c; Eastman story & pencils 3.00

CASEY JONES: NORTH BY DOWNEAST
Mirage Studios: May, 1994 - No. 2, July, 1994 ($2.75, limited series)
1,2-Rick Veitch script & pencils; Kevin Eastman story & inks 3.00

CASPER... (One-shots)
American Mythology Prods.: 2018 - 2019 ($3.99)
.. & Hot Stuff #1 (2018) Wolfer-s/Shanower-a and Shand-s/Scherer-a; r/Devil Kids #87 4.00
.. & Wendy #1 (2018) Check-s/Scherer-a and Shand-s/Sosa-a; r/Casper and Wendy #1 4.00
Casper's Classic Christmas #1 (2019, $3.99) Christmas-themed reprints; Hot Stuff app. 4.00
Casper's Haunted Halloween #1 (2019) Spooky, Nightmare and the Ghostly Trio reprints 4.00
... Spotlight: The Ghostly Trio #1 (2020) Reprints from 1971-1990 4.00
Casper's Spooksville #1 (2019) New stories by various 4.00

CASPER ADVENTURE DIGEST
Harvey Comics: V2#1, Oct, 1992 - V2#8, Apr, 1994 ($1.75/$1.95, digest-size)
V2#1: Casper, Richie Rich, Spooky, Wendy 5.00
2-8 3.50

CASPER AND...
Harvey Comics: Nov, 1987 - No. 12, June, 1990 (75¢/$1.00, all reprints)
1-Ghostly Trio 5.00
2-12: 2-Spooky; begin $1.00-c. 3-Wendy. 4-Nightmare. 5-Ghostly Trio. 6-Spooky. 7-Wendy. 8-Hot Stuff. 9-Baby Huey. 10-Wendy.11-Ghostly Trio. 12-Spooky 3.00

CASPER AND FRIENDS
Harvey Comics: Oct, 1991 - No. 5, July, 1992 ($1.00/$1.25)
1-Nightmare, Ghostly Trio, Wendy, Spooky 4.00
2-5 3.00

CASPER AND FRIENDS MAGAZINE: Mar, 1997 - No. 3, July, 1997 ($3.99)
1-3 4.00

CASPER AND NIGHTMARE (See Harvey Hits# 37, 45, 52, 56, 59, 62, 65, 68,71, 75)

Casper and the Ghostly Trio #6 © HARV

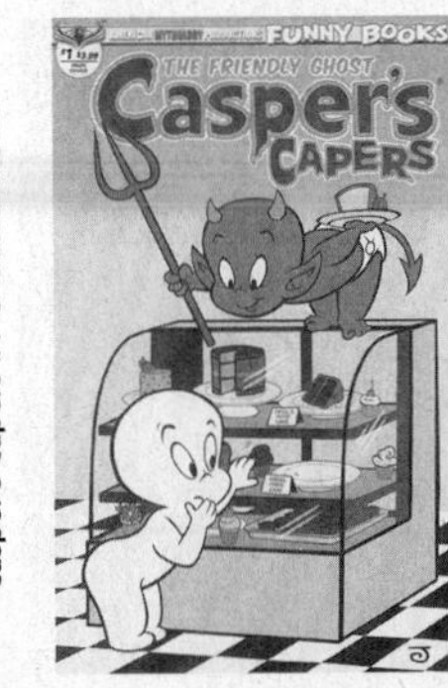

Casper's Capers #1 © Classic Media

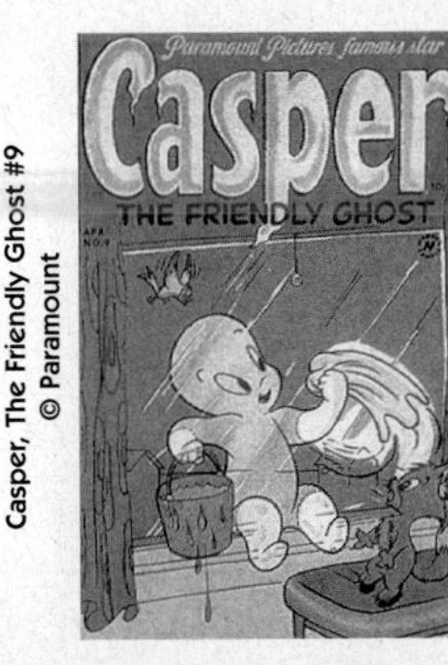

Casper, The Friendly Ghost #9 © Paramount

	GD 2.0	VG 4.0	FN 6.0	VF 8.0	VF/NM 9.0	NM- 9.2

GD VG FN VF VF/NM NM- 2.0 4.0 6.0 8.0 9.0 9.2

CASPER AND NIGHTMARE (Nightmare & Casper No. 1-5)
Harvey Publications: No. 6, 11/64 - No. 44, 10/73; No. 45, 6/74 - No. 46, 8/74 (25¢)

	GD	VG	FN	VF	VF/NM	NM-
6: 68 pg. Giants begin, ends #32	5	10	15	33	57	80
7-10	3	6	9	21	33	45
11-20	3	6	9	17	26	35
21-37: 33-37-(52 pg. Giants)	3	6	9	14	20	26
38-46	2	4	6	10	14	18

NOTE: *Many issues contain reprints.*

CASPER AND SPOOKY (See Harvey Hits No. 20)
Harvey Publications: Oct, 1972 - No. 7, Oct, 1973

	GD	VG	FN	VF	VF/NM	NM-
1	3	6	9	19	30	40
2-7	2	4	6	10	14	18

CASPER AND THE GHOSTLY TRIO
Harvey Pub.: Nov, 1972 - No. 7, Nov, 1973; No. 8, Aug, 1990 - No. 10, Dec, 1990

	GD	VG	FN	VF	VF/NM	NM-
1	3	6	9	19	30	40
2-7	2	4	6	10	14	18
8-10						6.00

CASPER AND WENDY
Harvey Publications: Sept, 1972 - No. 8, Nov, 1973

	GD	VG	FN	VF	VF/NM	NM-
1: 52 pg. Giant	3	6	9	19	30	40
2-8	2	4	6	10	14	18

CASPER BIG BOOK
Harvey Comics: V2#1, Aug, 1992 - No. 3, May, 1993 ($1.95, 52 pgs.)

	GD	VG	FN	VF	VF/NM	NM-
V2#1-Spooky app.						4.00
2,3						4.00

CASPER CAT (See Dopey Duck)
I. W. Enterprises/Super: 1958; 1963

	GD	VG	FN	VF	VF/NM	NM-
1,7: 1-Wacky Duck #?.7-Reprint, Super No. 14('63)	2	4	6	9	13	16

CASPER DIGEST (...Magazine #?; ...Halloween Digest #8, 10)
Harvey Publications: Oct, 1986 - No. 18, Jan, 1991 ($1.25/$1.75, digest-size)

	GD	VG	FN	VF	VF/NM	NM-
1	1	3	4	6	8	10
2-18: 11-Valentine-c. 18-Halloween-c						6.00

CASPER DIGEST (...Magazine #? on)
Harvey Comics: V2#1, Sept, 1991 - V2#14, Nov, 1994 ($1.75/$1.95, digest-size)

	GD	VG	FN	VF	VF/NM	NM-
V2#1						5.00
2-14						3.50

CASPER DIGEST STORIES
Harvey Publications: Feb, 1980 - No. 4, Nov, 1980 (95¢, 132 pgs., digest size)

	GD	VG	FN	VF	VF/NM	NM-
1	2	4	6	9	13	16
2-4	1	2	3	5	7	9

CASPER DIGEST WINNERS
Harvey Publications: Apr, 1980 - No. 3, Sept, 1980 (95¢, 132 pgs., digest size)

	GD	VG	FN	VF	VF/NM	NM-
1	2	4	6	9	13	16
2,3	1	2	3	5	7	9

CASPER ENCHANTED TALES DIGEST
Harvey Comics: May, 1992 - No. 10, Oct, 1994 ($1.75, digest-size, 98 pgs.)

	GD	VG	FN	VF	VF/NM	NM-
1-Casper, Spooky, Wendy stories						5.00
2-10						4.00

CASPER GHOSTLAND
Harvey Comics: May, 1992 ($1.25)

	GD	VG	FN	VF	VF/NM	NM-
1						3.00

CASPER GIANT SIZE
Harvey Comics: Oct, 1992 - No. 4, Nov, 1993 ($2.25, 68 pgs.)

	GD	VG	FN	VF	VF/NM	NM-
V2#1-Casper, Wendy, Spooky stories						5.00
2-4						4.00

CASPER HALLOWEEN TRICK OR TREAT
Harvey Publications: Jan, 1976 (52 pgs.)

	GD	VG	FN	VF	VF/NM	NM-
1	3	6	9	17	26	35

CASPER IN SPACE (Formerly Casper Spaceship)
Harvey Publications: No. 6, June, 1973 - No. 8, Oct, 1973

	GD	VG	FN	VF	VF/NM	NM-
6-8	2	4	6	10	14	18

CASPER'S CAPERS
American Mythology Prods.: 2018 - No. 6, 2019 ($3.99)

	GD	VG	FN	VF	VF/NM	NM-
1-6-Classic reprints with digital recoloring. 1-Includes 1st apps. of Casper and Wendy						4.00

CASPER'S GHOSTLAND
Harvey Publications: Winter, 1958-59 - No. 97, 12/77; No. 98, 12/79 (25¢)

	GD	VG	FN	VF	VF/NM	NM-
1-84 pgs. begin, ends #10	18	36	54	126	281	435
2	9	18	27	59	117	175
3-10	7	14	21	44	82	120
11-20: 11-68 pgs. begin, ends #61. 13-X-Mas-c	5	10	15	35	63	90
21-40	4	8	12	28	47	65
41-61	3	6	9	16	24	32
62-77: 62-52 pgs. begin	2	4	6	9	13	16
78-98: 94-X-Mas-c	2	4	6	8	10	12

NOTE: *Most issues contain reprints w/new stories.*

CASPER'S GHOSTLAND
American Mythology Prods.: 2018 - No. 2, 2018 ($3.99)

	GD	VG	FN	VF	VF/NM	NM-
1,2-New stories; art by Shanower & others; Wendy, Hot Stuff, Ghostly Trio app.						4.00

CASPER SPACESHIP (Casper in Space No. 6 on)
Harvey Publications: Aug, 1972 - No. 5, April, 1973

	GD	VG	FN	VF	VF/NM	NM-
1: 52 pg. Giant	3	6	9	18	28	38
2-5	2	4	6	11	16	20

CASPER'S SCARE SCHOOL
Ape Entertainment: 2011 - No. 2 ($3.99, limited series)

	GD	VG	FN	VF	VF/NM	NM-
1,2-New short stories and classic reprints						4.00

CASPER'S SPOOKSVILLE
American Mythology Prods.: 2020 - No. 4, 2020 ($3.99)

	GD	VG	FN	VF	VF/NM	NM-
1-4-New stories & reprints; art by Shanower & others; Wendy, Hot Stuff, Spooky app.						4.00
... FCBD Edition 1 (2019, giveaway) New stories & reprints; art by Shanower						3.00

CASPER STRANGE GHOST STORIES
Harvey Publications: October, 1974 - No. 14, Jan, 1977 (All 52 pgs.)

	GD	VG	FN	VF	VF/NM	NM-
1	3	6	9	18	28	38
2-14	2	4	6	11	16	20

CASPER, THE FRIENDLY GHOST (See America's Best TV Comics, Famous TV Funday Funnies, The Friendly Ghost..., Nightmare &..., Richie Rich and..., Tastee-Freez, Treasury of Comics, Wendy the Good Little Witch & Wendy Witch World)

CASPER, THE FRIENDLY GHOST (Becomes Harvey Comics Hits No. 61 (No. 6), and then continued with Harvey issue No. 7)(1st Series)
St. John Publishing Co.: Sept, 1949 - No. 5, Aug, 1951

	GD	VG	FN	VF	VF/NM	NM-
1(1949)-Origin & 1st app. Baby Huey & Herman the Mouse (1st comic app. of Casper and the 1st time the name Casper app. in any media, even films)	649	1298	1947	4738	8369	12,000
2,3 (2/50 & 8/50)	152	304	456	965	1658	2350
4,5 (3/51 & 8/51)	100	200	300	635	1093	1550

CASPER, THE FRIENDLY GHOST (Paramount Picture Star...)(2nd Series)
Harvey Publications (Family Comics): No. 7, Dec, 1952 - No. 70, July, 1958
Note: No. 6 is Harvey Comics Hits No. 61 (10/52)

	GD	VG	FN	VF	VF/NM	NM-
7-Baby Huey begins, ends #9	44	88	132	326	738	1150
8,9	23	46	69	161	356	550
10-Spooky begins (1st app., 6/53), ends #70?	40	80	120	296	673	1050
11,12: 2nd & 3rd app. Spooky	15	30	45	103	227	350
13-18: Alfred Harvey app. in story	12	24	36	81	176	270
19-1st app. Nightmare (4/54)	27	54	81	194	435	675
20-Wendy the Witch begins (1st app., 5/54)	49	98	147	382	866	1350
21-30: 24-Infinity-c	9	18	27	61	123	185
31-40: 38-Early Wendy app. 39-1st app. Samson Honeybun. 40-1st app. Dr. Brainstorm	7	14	21	49	92	135
41-1st Wendy app. on-c	15	30	45	101	223	345
42-50: 43-2nd Wendy-c. 46-1st app. Spooky's girl Pearl.	6	12	18	38	69	100
51-70 (Continues as Friendly Ghost... 8/58) 58-Early app. Bat Balfrey. 63-2nd app. Something the Baby Ghost. 66-1st app. Wildcat Witch	5	10	15	33	57	80
Harvey Comics Classics Vol. 1 TPB (Dark Horse Books, 6/07, $19.95) Reprints Casper's earliest appearances in this title, Little Audrey, and The Friendly Ghost Casper, mostly B&W with some color stories; history, early concept drawings and animation art						20.00

NOTE: *Baby Huey app. 7-9, 11, 121, 14, 16, 20. Buzzy app. 14, 16, 20. Nightmare app. 19, 27, 36, 37, 42, 46, 51, 53, 56, 70. Spooky app. 10-70. Wendy app. 20, 29-31, 35, 37, 38, 41-49, 51, 52, 54-58, 61, 64, 68.*

CASPER THE FRIENDLY GHOST (Formerly The Friendly Ghost...)(3rd Series)
Harvey Comics: No. 254, July, 1990 - No. 260, Jan, 1991 ($1.00)

	GD	VG	FN	VF	VF/NM	NM-
254-260						3.00

CASPER THE FRIENDLY GHOST (4th Series)
Harvey Comics: Mar, 1991 - No. 28, Nov, 1994 ($1.00/$1.25/$1.50)

	GD	VG	FN	VF	VF/NM	NM-
1-Casper becomes Mighty Ghost; Spooky & Wendy app.						5.00
2-28: 7,8-Post-a. 11-28-($1.50)						3.00

The Cat #1 © MAR

Cataclysm: Ultimate Spider-Man #1 © MAR

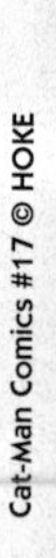
Cat-Man Comics #17 © HOKE

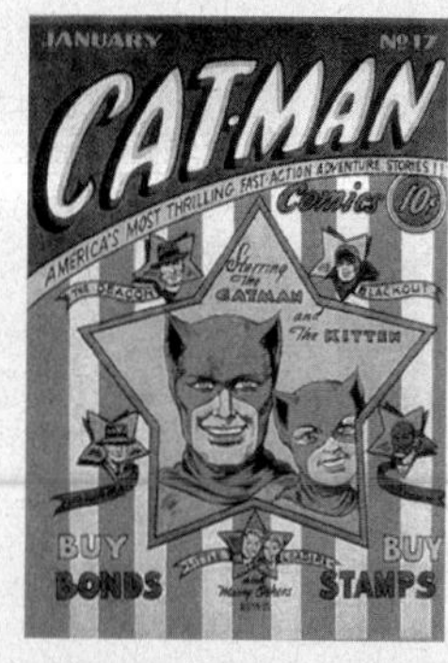

	GD 2.0	VG 4.0	FN 6.0	VF 8.0	VF/NM 9.0	NM- 9.2

CASPER THE FRIENDLY GHOST (5th Series)
American Mythology Prods.: 2017 - Present ($3.99)

1,2-New stories and reprints; Hot Stuff, Spooky & Wendy app. 4.00
... Presents Hot Stuff Sizzlers 1 (2020) Reprints Hot Stuff from 1958-62 4.00
... Presents Wendy & the Witch Widow 1 (2020) Reprints Casper from 1955-56 4.00

CASPER T.V. SHOWTIME
Harvey Comics: Jan, 1980 - No. 5, Oct, 1980

1 2 4 6 9 13 16
2-5 1 2 3 5 7 9

CASSETTE BOOKS (Classics Illustrated)
Cassette Book Co./I.P.S. Publ.: 1984 (48 pgs, b&w comic with cassette tape)
NOTE: *This series was illegal. The artwork was illegally obtained, and the Classics Illustrated copyright owner, Twin Circle Publ. sued to get an injunction to prevent the continued sale of this series. Many C.I. collectors obtained copies before the 1987 injunction, but now they are already scarce. Here again the market is just developing, but sealed mint copies of com ic and tape should be worth at least $25.*
1001 (CI#1-A2)New-PC 1002(CI#3-A2)CI-PC 1003(CI#13-A2)CI-PC
1004(CI#25)CI-LDC 1005(CI#10-A2)New-PC 1006(CI#64)CI-LDC

CASTILIAN (See Movie Classics)

CASTLE: A CALM BEFORE STORM (Based on the ABC TV series Castle)
Marvel Comics: Feb, 2013 - No. 5, Jul, 2013 ($3.99, limited series)

1-5-Peter David-s/Robert Atkins-a/Mico Suayan-c 4.00

CASTLE: RICHARD CASTLE'S ... (Based on the ABC TV series Castle)
Marvel Comics: 2011, 2012 ($19.99, hardcover graphic novels with dustjacket)

Deadly Storm HC (2011) - An "adaptation" of the show's fictional Derrick Storm novel; Bendis & DeConnick-s 20.00
Storm Season HC (2012) - Bendis & DeConnick-s/Lupacchino-a 20.00

CASTLEVANIA: THE BELMONT LEGACY
IDW Publishing: March 2005 - No. 5, July, 2005 ($3.99, limited series)

1-5-Marc Andreyko-s/E.J. Su-a 4.00

CASTLE WAITING
Olio: 1997 - No. 7, 1999 ($2.95, B&W)
Cartoon Books: Vol. 2, Aug, 2000 - No. 16 ($2.95/$3.95, B&W)
Fantagraphics Books: Vol. 3, 2006 - No. 18, 2012 ($5.95/$3.95, B&W)

1-Linda Medley-s/a in all 1 2 3 5 6 8
2 4.00
3-7 3.00
The Lucky Road TPB r/#1-7 17.00
Hiatus Issue (1999) Crilley-c; short stories and previews 3.00
Vol. 2 #1-6,14-16 (#5&6 also have #12&13 on cover, for series numbering) 3.00
Vol. 3 #1 ($5.95) r/#15,16 and new story 6.00
Vol. 3 #2-18 ($3.95) 4.00

CASUAL FLING
AWA Studios: Feb, 2021 - No. 4 ($3.99, limited series)

1-Jason Starr-s/Dalibor Talajic-a 4.00

CASUAL HEROES
Image Comics (Motown Machineworks): Apr, 1996 ($2.25, unfinished lim. series)

1-Steve Rude-c 3.00

CAT, T.H.E. (TV) (See T.H.E. Cat)

CAT, THE (See Movie Classics)

CAT, THE (Female hero)
Marvel Comics Group: Nov, 1972 - No. 4, June, 1973

1-Origin & 1st app. The Cat (who later becomes Tigra); Mooney-a(i); Wood-c(i)/a(i)
9 18 27 63 129 195
2,3: 2-Marie Severin/Mooney-a. 3-Everett inks 3 6 9 19 30 40
4-Starlin/Weiss-a(p) 3 6 9 21 33 45

CATACLYSM
Marvel Comics: No. 0.1, Dec, 2013 ($3.99)

0.1-Fialkov-s; Galactus threatens the Ultimate Universe 4.00

CATACLYSM: THE ULTIMATES LAST STAND (Leads into Survive #1)
Marvel Comics: Jan, 2014 - No. 5, Apr, 2014 ($3.99, limited series)

1-5-Galactus in the Ultimate Universe; Ultimates & Spider-Man app.; Bendis-s/Bagley-a 4.00

CATACLYSM: ULTIMATES
Marvel Comics: Jan, 2014 - No. 3, Mar, 2014 ($3.99, limited series)

1-3-Ultimates vs. Galactus; Fialkov-s/Giandomenico-a 4.00

CATACLYSM: ULTIMATE SPIDER-MAN
Marvel Comics: Jan, 2014 - No. 3, Mar, 2014 ($3.99, limited series)

1-3-Spider-Man vs. Galactus; Bendis-s/Marquez-a 4.00

CATACLYSM: ULTIMATE X-MEN
Marvel Comics: Jan, 2014 - No. 3, Mar, 2014 ($3.99, limited series)

1-3-Fialkov-s/Martinez-a; Captain Marvel app. 4.00

CATALYST: AGENTS OF CHANGE (Also see Comics' Greatest World)
Dark Horse Comics: Feb, 1994 - No. 7, Nov, 1994 ($2.00, limited series)

1-7: 1-Foil stamped logo 3.00

CATALYST COMIX (From Comics' Greatest World)
Dark Horse Comics: Jul, 2013 - No. 9, Mar, 2014 ($2.99)

1-9: Amazing Grace, Frank Wells, and Agents of Change app.; Casey-s/Grampá-c 3.00

CATECHISM IN PICTURES
Catechetical Guild: Jan, 1958

311-Addison Burbank-a 8 16 24 42 54 65

CAT FROM OUTER SPACE (See Walt Disney Showcase #46)

CATHOLIC COMICS (See Heroes All Catholic...)
Catholic Publications: June, 1946 - V3#10, July, 1949

1 31 62 93 186 303 420
2 17 34 51 98 154 210
3-13(7/47): 11-Hollingsworth-a 15 30 45 84 127 170
V2#1-10 11 22 33 62 86 110
V3#1-10: Reprints 10-part Treasure Island serial from Target V2#2-11 (see Key Comics #5)
11 22 33 64 90 115
NOTE: ***Orlando** c-V2#10, V3#5, 6, 8.*

CATHOLIC PICTORIAL
Catholic Guild: 1947

1-Toth-a(2) (Rare) 40 80 120 246 411 575

CAT-MAN COMICS (Formerly Crash Comics No. 1-5)
Holyoke Publishing Co./Continental Magazines V2#12, 7/44 on:
5/41 - No. 17, 1/43; No. 18, 7/43 - No. 22, 12/43; No. 23, 3/44 - No. 26, 11/44; No. 27, 4/45 - No. 30, 12/45; No. 31, 6/46 - No. 32, 8/46

1(V1#6)-The Cat-Man new costume (see Crash Comics for 1st app.) by Charles Quinlan; Origin The Deacon & Sidekick Mickey, Dr. Diamond & Rag-Man; The Black Widow app. Blaze Baylor begins 703 1406 2109 5132 9066 13,000
2(V1#7) 271 542 813 1734 2967 4200
3(V1#8)-The Pied Piper begins; classic Hitler, Stalin & Mussolini-c
480 960 1458 3550 6275 9000
4(V1#9) 252 504 756 1613 2757 3900
5(V2#10, 12/41)-Origin/1st app. The Kitten, Cat-Man's sidekick; The Hood begins. (cover re-dated w/cat image printed over Nov. date). Most of The Kitten's cover image blocked with sidebar 297 594 891 1901 3251 4600
6(V2#11) Mad scientist-c 300 600 900 1920 3310 4700
7(V2#12) 252 504 756 1613 2757 3900
8(V2#13,3/42)-Origin Little Leaders; Volton by Kubert begins (his 1st comic book work)
300 600 900 2070 3635 5200
9 (V2#14, 4/42)-Classic-c showing a laughing Kitten slaughtering Japanese soldiers with a machine gun 377 754 1131 2639 4620 6600
10 (V2#15, 5/42)-Origin Blackout; Phantom Falcon begins
232 464 696 1485 2543 3600
11 (V3#1, 6/42)-Kubert-a 232 464 696 1485 2543 3600
12 (V3#2),15,17(1/43): 12-Volton by Brodsky, not Kubert
219 438 657 1402 2401 3400
13-(9/42)(scarce) Weed of Doom (marijuana) 811 1622 2433 5920 10,460 15,000
14-(10/42) World War II-c; Brodsky-a 252 504 756 1613 2757 3900
16 (V3#5, 12/42)-Hitler, Tojo, Mussolini, Goehring-c
738 1476 2214 3875 6738 9600
18 (V3#8, 7/43)-(scarce) 323 646 969 1696 2948 4200
19 (V2#6, 9/43)-Hitler, Tojo, Mussolini-c 723 1446 2169 3796 6598 9400
20 (V2#7, 10/43)-Classic Hitler-c 1423 2846 4269 7471 12,986 18,500
21,22 (V2#8, V2#9) 187 374 561 1197 2049 2900
23 (V2#10, 3/44) World War II-c 219 438 657 1402 2401 3400
nn(V3#13, 5/44) Rico-a; Schomburg Japanese WWII bondage-c (Rare)
371 742 1113 2600 4550 6500
nn(V2#12, 7/44) L.B. Cole-a (4 pgs) 155 310 465 992 1696 2400
nn(V3#1, 9/44)-Origin The Golden Archer; Leatherface app.
155 310 465 992 1696 2400
nn(V3#2, 11/44)-L. B. Cole-c 181 362 543 1158 1979 2800
27-Origins Catman & Kitten retold; L. B. Cole Flag-c; Infantino-a
232 464 696 1485 2543 3600
28-Dr. Macabre app.; L. B. Cole-c/a 354 708 1062 2478 4339 6200
29-32-L. B. Cole-c; bondage-#30 232 464 696 1485 2543 3600

Catwoman #19 © DC

Catwoman (2018 series) #13 © DC

Catwoman / Wildcat #1 © DC

	GD 2.0	VG 4.0	FN 6.0	VF 8.0	VF/NM 9.0	NM- 9.2

NOTE: *Fuje a-11, 27, 28(2), 29(3), 30.* ***Palais*** *a-11, 16, 27, 28, 29(2), 30(2), 32; c-25(7/44).* ***Rico*** *a-11(2), 23, 27, 28.*

CAT TALES (3-D)
Eternity Comics: Apr, 1989 ($2.95)

1-Felix the Cat-r in 3-D 5.00

CATWOMAN (Also see Action Comics Weekly #611, Batman #404-407, Detective Comics, & Superman's Girlfriend Lois Lane #70, 71)
DC Comics: Feb, 1989 - No. 4, May, 1989 ($1.50, limited series, mature)

1 2 4 6 8 11 14
2-4: 3-Batman cameo. 4-Batman app. 1 2 3 5 7 9
Her Sister's Keeper (1991, $9.95, trade paperback)-r/#1-4 12.00

CATWOMAN (Also see Showcase '93, Showcase '95 #4, & Batman #404-407)
DC Comics: Aug, 1993 - No. 94, Jul, 2001 ($1.50-$2.25)

0-(10/94)-Zero Hour; origin retold. Released between #14&15 4.00
1-($1.95)-Embossed-c; Bane app.; Balent c-1-10; a-1-10p 1 2 3 5 6 8
2-20: 3-Bane flashback cameo. 4-Brief Bane app. 6,7-Knightquest tie-ins; Batman (Azrael) app. 8-1st app. Zephyr. 12-KnightsEnd pt. 6. 13-new Knights End Aftermath. 14-(9/94)-Zero Hour 4.00
21-24, 26-30, 33-49: 21-$1.95-c begins. 28,29-Penguin cameo app. 36-Legacy pt. 2. 38-40-Year Two; Batman, Joker, Penguin & Two-Face app. 46-Two-Face app. 3.00
25,31,32: 25-($2.95)-Robin app. 31,32-Contagion pt. 4 (Reads pt. 5 on-c) & pt. 9. 4.00
50-($2.95, 48 pgs.)-New armored costume 4.00
50-($2.95, 48 pgs.)-Collector's Ed. w/metallic ink-c 5.00
51-77: 51-Huntress-c/app. 54-Grayson-s begins. 56-Cataclysm pt.6. 57-Poison Ivy-c/app. 63-65-Joker-c/app. 72-No Man's Land; Ostrander-s begins 3.00
78-82: 80-Catwoman goes to jail 3.00
83,84,89-Harley Quinn-c/app. 83-Begin $2.25-c 2 4 6 8 10 12
85-88,90-94 3.00
#1,000,000 (11/98) 853rd Century x-over 3.00
Annual 1 (1994, $2.95, 68 pgs.)-Elseworlds story; Batman app.; no Balent-a 4.00
Annual 2,4 ('95, '97, $3.95) 2-Year One story. 4-Pulp Heroes 4.00
Annual 3 (1996, $2.95)-Legends of the Dead Earth story 4.00
...Plus 1 (11/97, $2.95) Screamqueen (Scare Tactics) app. 4.00
TPB ($9.95) r/#15-19, Balent-c 12.00

CATWOMAN (Also see Detective Comics #759-762)
DC Comics: Jan, 2002 - No. 82, Oct, 2008; No. 83, Mar, 2010 ($2.50/$2.99)

1-Darwyn Cooke & Mike Allred-a; Ed Brubaker-s 2 4 6 8 11 14
2-4 1 2 3 5 6 8
5-43: 5-9-Rader-a/Paul Pope-c. 10-Morse-c. 16-JG Jones-c. 22-Batman-c/app. 34-36-War Games. 43-Killer Croc app. 4.00
44-Adam Hughes-c begin 1 3 4 6 8 10
45-Headlights-c; Hush & Clayface app. 4 8 12 23 37 50
46-Captain Cold app. 3 6 9 15 22 28
47,49,52-57,59-68,71,73,75-79: 52-Catwoman kills Black Mask. 53-One Year Later; Helena born. 55-Begin $2.99-c. 56-58-Wildcat app. 75-78-Salvation Run 5.00
48,69 1 2 3 5 6 8
50,58,72-Zatanna-c/app. 1 3 4 6 8 10
51-Classic Selina Kyle mugshot-c 6 12 18 38 69 100
70-Classic-c; "Amazons Attack" tie-in 3 6 9 21 33 45
74-Zatanna app. 4 8 12 27 44 60
80-82 1 3 4 6 8 10
83-(3/10, $2.99) Blackest Night one-shot; Harley Quinn & Black Mask app.; Adam Hughes-c 1 3 4 6 8 10
...: Catwoman Dies TPB (2008, $14.99) r/#66-72; Hughes cover gallery 15.00
...: Crime Pays TPB (2008, $14.99) r/#73-77 15.00
...: Crooked Little Town TPB (2003, $14.95) r/#5-10 & Secret Files; Oeming-c 15.00
...: It's Only a Movie TPB (2007, $19.99) r/#59-65 20.00
...: Relentless TPB (2005, $19.95) r/#12-19 & Secret Files 20.00
... Secret Files and Origins (10/02, $4.95) origin-s Oeming-a; profiles and pin-ups 5.00
...Selina's Big Score HC (2002, $24.95) Cooke-s/a; pin-ups by various 25.00
...Selina's Big Score SC (2003, $17.95) Cooke-s/a; pin-ups by various 18.00
...: The Dark End of the Street TPB (2002, $12.95) r/#1-4 & Slam Bradley back-up stories from Detective Comics #759-762 13.00
...: The Long Road Home TPB (2009, $17.99) r/#78-82 18.00
...: The Replacements TPB (2007, $14.99) r/#53-58 15.00
...: Wild Ride TPB (2005, $14.99) r/#20-24 & Secret Files #1 15.00

CATWOMAN (DC New 52)
DC Comics: Nov, 2011 - No. 52, Jul, 2016 ($2.99)

1-Winick-s/March-a; Batman app. 5.00
2-12: 2-6-March-a. 7,8-Melo-a. 9-Night of the Owls 3.00
13-(12/12) Death of the Family tie-in; die-cut Joker mask-c 12.00
13-Second printing with chessboard-c 5.00
14-22: 14-Death of the Family tie-in; Joker app 3.00
23,24: 23-(10/13) Debut of Joker's Daughter in final panel. 24-Joker's Daughter app. 5.00
25,26,28-49: 25-Zero Year. 26-Joker's Daughter app. 28-Gothtopia. 35-40-Jae Lee-c 3.00
27-($3.99) Gothtopia x-over with Detective Comics #27; Olliffe & Richards-a 4.00
50-($4.99) Harley Quinn, Poison Ivy app.; back-up origin of Black Mask's mask 5.00
51,52: Black Mask & the False Face Society app.; Middleton-c 3.00
#0 (11/12, $2.99) Origin re-told; Nocenti-s/Melo-a/March-c 3.00
Annual 1 (7/13, $4.99) Nocenti-s/Duce-a; Penguin app. 5.00
Annual 2 (2/15, $4.99) Olliffe & McCrea-a 5.00
...: Election Night 1 (1/17, $4.99) Meredith Finch-s/Shane Davis-a; Prez app. 5.00
...: Futures End 1 (11/14, $2.99, regular-c) Five years later; Olliffe-a/Dodson-c 3.00
...: Futures End 1 (11/14, $3.99, 3-D cover) 4.00

CATWOMAN (Follows Batman #50 [2018])
DC Comics: Sept, 2018 - Present ($3.99)

1-12: 1-Joëlle Jones-s/a; new costume. 7,8-Casagrande-a; Penguin app. 9-Timms-a 4.00
13-24,26-28: 13-17-Year of the Villain tie-ins. 15-Andolfo-a. 17-Acetate-c. 18-Zatanna app. 23-24-Sean Murphy-c 4.00
13-($4.99) Year of the Villain cardstock-c by Artgerm 5.00
25-($5.99) Joker War tie-in; Riddler and Penguin app.; 2 back-up stories; J.P. Leon-a 6.00
Annual 1 (7/19, $4.99) Casagrande & Petrus-a 5.00
.../Tweety & Sylvester 1 (10/18, $4.99) Simone-s/Miranda-a; Black Canary app. 5.00

CATWOMAN 80TH ANNIVERSARY 100-PAGE SUPER SPECTACULAR
DC Comics: Jun, 2020 ($9.99, squarebound, one-shot)

1-Short stories & pin-ups by various; birth of Helena by King-s/Janin-a; multiple covers 10.00

CATWOMAN/ GUARDIAN OF GOTHAM
DC Comics: 1999 - No. 2, 1999 ($5.95, limited series)

1,2-Elseworlds; Moench-s/Balent-a 1 3 4 6 8 10

CATWOMAN: NINE LIVES OF A FELINE FATALE
DC Comics: 2004 ($14.95, TPB)

nn-Reprints notable stories from Batman #1 to the present; pin-ups by various; Bolland-c 15.00

CATWOMAN: THE MOVIE (2004 Halle Berry movie)
DC Comics: 2004 ($4.95/$9.95)

1-($4.95) Movie adaptation; Jim Lee-c and sketch pages; Derenick-a 5.00
... & Other Cat Tales TPB (2004, $9.95)-r/Movie adaptation; Jim Lee sketch pages, r/Catwoman #0, Catwoman (2nd series) #11 & 25; photo-c 10.00

CATWOMAN/VAMPIRELLA: THE FURIES
DC Comics/Harris Publ.: Feb, 1997 ($4.95, squarebound, 46 pgs.) (1st DC/Harris x-over)

nn-Reintro Pantha; Chuck Dixon scripts; Jim Balent-c/a 1 2 3 5 6 8

CATWOMAN: WHEN IN ROME
DC Comics: Nov, 2004 - No. 6, Aug, 2005 ($3.50, limited series)

1-6-Jeph Loeb-s/Tim Sale-a/c; Riddler app. 3.50
HC (2005, $19.99, dustjacket) r/series; intro by Mark Chiarello; sketch pages 20.00
SC (2007, $12.99) r/series; intro by Mark Chiarello; sketch pages 13.00

CATWOMAN/WILDCAT
DC Comics: Aug, 1998 - No. 4, Nov, 1998 ($2.50, limited series)

1-4-Chuck Dixon & Beau Smith-s; Stelfreeze-c 4.00

CAUGHT
Atlas Comics (VPI): Aug, 1956 - No. 5, Apr, 1957

1 29 58 87 170 278 385
2-4: 3-Maneely, Pakula, Torres-a. 4-Maneely-a 16 32 48 94 147 200
5-Crandall, Krigstein-a 17 34 51 98 154 210
NOTE: ***Drucker*** *a-2.* ***Heck*** *a-4.* ***Severin*** *c-1, 2, 4, 5.* ***Shores*** *a-4.*

CAVALIER COMICS
A. W. Nugent Publ. Co.: 1945; 1952 (Early DC reprints)

2(1945)-Speed Saunders, Fang Gow 22 44 66 128 209 290
2(1952) 14 28 42 76 108 140

CAVALRY, THE : S.H.I.E.L.D. 50TH ANNIVERSARY
Marvel Comics: Nov, 2015 ($3.99, one-shot)

1-Agent Melinda May on a training mission; Luke Ross-a; Keown-c 4.00

CAVE CARSON HAS A CYBERNETIC EYE
DC Comics (Young Animal): Dec, 2016 - No. 12, Nov, 2017 ($3.99)

1-12-Jonathan Rivera & Gerald Way-s/Michael Avon Oeming-a; back-up Tom Scioli-s/a in #1-6. 7-Superman-c/app. 4.00
.../ Swamp Thing Special 1 (4/18, $4.99) Part 4 of Milk Wars crossover; Rivera-a/Foss-a 5.00

CAVE CARSON HAS AN INTERSTELLAR EYE
DC Comics (Young Animal): May, 2018 - No. 6, Oct, 2018 ($3.99)

1-6-Jonathan Rivera-s/Michael Avon Oeming-a; back-up with Maybury-a in #1-5 4.00

Centipede #5 © Atari

Cerebus #272 © Dave Sim & Gerhard

The Challenger #4 © Interfaith

	GD 2.0	VG 4.0	FN 6.0	VF 8.0	VF/NM 9.0	NM- 9.2

CAVE GIRL (Also see Africa)
Magazine Enterprises: No. 11, 1953 - No. 14, 1954

11(A-1 82)-Origin; all Cave Girl stories 60 120 180 381 653 925
12(A-1 96), 13(A-1 116), 14(A-1 125)-Thunda by Powell in each
41 82 123 256 428 600

NOTE: ***Powell*** *c/a in all.*

CAVE GIRL
AC Comics: 1988 ($2.95, 44 pgs.) (16 pgs. of color, rest B&W)

1-Powell-r/Cave Girl #11; Nyoka photo back-c from movie; Powell/Bill Black-c; Special Limited Edition on-c 4.00

CAVE KIDS (TV) (See Comic Album #16)
Gold Key: Feb, 1963 - No. 16, Mar, 1967 (Hanna-Barbera)

1 6 12 18 38 69 100
2-5 4 8 12 23 37 50
6-16: 7,12-Pebbles & Bamm Bamm app. 16-1st Space Kidettes
3 6 9 19 30 40

CAVEWOMAN
Basement Comics: Jan, 1994 - No. 6, 1995 ($2.95)

1 6 12 18 41 76 110
2 3 6 9 21 33 45
3-6 2 4 6 10 14 18
...: Meets Explorers ('97, $2.95) 5.00
...: One-Shot Special (7/00, $2.95) Massey-s/a 5.00

CBLDF (Comic Book Legal Defense Fund) (See Liberty Comics)

CELESTINE (See Violator Vs. Badrock #1)
Image Comics (Extreme): May, 1996 - No. 2, June, 1996 ($2.50, limited series)

1,2: Warren Ellis scripts 3.00

CEMETERY BEACH
Image Comics: Sept, 2018 - No. 7, Mar, 2019 ($3.99)

1-7-Warren Ellis-s/Jason Howard-a 4.00

CENTIPEDE (Based on Atari videogame)
Dynamite Entertainment: 2017 - No. 5, 2017 ($3.99)

1-5: 1-Bemis-s/Marron-a; covers by Marron, Francavilla & Schkade 4.00

CENTURION OF ANCIENT ROME, THE
Zondervan Publishing House: 1958 (no month listed) (B&W, 36 pgs.)

(Rare) All by Jay Disbrow 113 226 339 718 1234 1750

CENTURIONS (TV)
DC Comics: June, 1987 - No. 4, Sept, 1987 (75¢, limited series)

1-4 4.00

CENTURY: DISTANT SONS
Marvel Comics: Feb, 1996 ($2.95, one-shot)

1-Wraparound-c 4.00

CENTURY OF COMICS (See Promotional Comics section)

CENTURY WEST
Image Comics: Sept, 2013 ($7.99, squarebound, graphic novel)

nn-Howard Chaykin-s/a/c 8.00

CEREBUS BI-WEEKLY
Aardvark-Vanaheim: Dec. 2, 1988 - No. 27, Nov. 24, 1989 ($1.25, B&W)

Reprints Cerebus The Aardvark #1-27
1-16, 18, 19, 21-27: 3.00
17-Hepcats app. 2 4 6 8 10 12
20-Milk & Cheese app. 2 4 6 10 12 15

CEREBUS: CHURCH & STATE
Aardvark-Vanaheim: Feb, 1991 - No. 30, Apr, 1992 ($2.00, B&W, bi-weekly)

1-30: r/Cerebus #51-80 3.00

CEREBUS: HIGH SOCIETY
Aardvark-Vanaheim: Feb, 1990 - No. 25, 1991 ($1.70, B&W)

1-25: r/Cerebus #26-50 3.00

CEREBUS IN HELL?
Aardvark-Vanaheim: No. 0, 2016; No. 1, Jan, 2017 - No. 4, Apr, 2017 ($4.00, B&W)

0-4-Sim & Atwal-s; Cerebus figures placed over original Gustave Doré artwork of Hell 4.00
Cerberus In Hell 1 (12/18, $4.00) new pages and reprints; cover swipe of Cerebus #1 4.00
Cerebus The Vark Knight Returns 1 (12/17, $4.00) new pages and reprints 4.00
The Death of Cerebus in Hell 1 (11/17, $4.00) new pages and reprints 4.00
... 2021 1 (1/21, $4.00) Cerebus figures with Doré art; calendar pages with parody covers 4.00

CEREBUS JAM
Aardvark-Vanaheim: Apr, 1985

1-Eisner, Austin, Dave Sim-a (Cerebus vs. Spirit) 6.00

CEREBUS THE AARDVARK (See A-V in 3-D, Nucleus, Power Comics)
Aardvark-Vanaheim: Dec, 1977 - No. 300, March, 2004 ($1.70/$2.00/$2.25, B&W)

0 3.00
0-Gold 20.00
1-1st app. Cerebus; 2000 print run; most copies poorly printed
141 282 423 1142 2571 4000

Note: *There is a counterfeit version known to exist. It can be distinguished from the original in the following ways: inside cover is glossy instead of flat, black background on the front cover is blotted or spotty. Reports show that a counterfeit #2 also exists.*

2-Dave Sim art in all 15 30 45 103 227 350
3-Origin Red Sophia 11 22 33 76 163 250
4-Origin Elrod the Albino 9 18 27 62 126 190
5,6 7 14 21 49 92 135
7-10 6 12 18 37 66 95
11,12: 11-Origin The Cockroach 5 10 15 31 53 75
13-15: 14-Origin Lord Julius 4 8 12 28 47 65
16-20 3 6 9 21 33 45
21-B. Smith letter in letter column 5 10 15 35 63 90
22-Low distribution; no cover price 4 8 12 25 40 55
23-30: 23-Preview of Wandering Star by Teri S. Wood. 26-High Society begins, ends #50
3 6 9 16 23 30
31-Origin Moonroach 3 6 9 16 24 32
32-40, 53-Intro. Wolveroach (brief app.) 2 4 6 8 10 12
41-50,52: 48-1st app. Joshua "Wolverine" MacAlistaire in back-up. 52-Church & State begins, ends #111; Cutey Bunny app. 1 2 3 5 7 9
51,54: 51-Cutey Bunny app. 54-1st full Wolveroach story
2 4 6 8 11 14
55,56-Wolveroach app.; Normalman back-ups by Valentino
1 3 4 6 8 10
57-100: 61,62: Flaming Carrot app. 65-Gerhard begins 4.00
101-160: 104-Flaming Carrot app. 112/113-Double issue. 114-Jaka's Story begins, ends #136. 139-Melmoth begins, ends #150. 151-Mothers & Daughters begins, ends #200 3.00
161-Bone app. 1 3 4 6 8 10
162-231: 175-($2.25, 44 pgs). 186-Strangers in Paradise cameo. 201-Guys storyline begins; Eddie Campbell's Bacchus app. 220-231-Rick's Story 3.00
232-265-Going Home 3.00
266-288,291-299-Latter Days: 267-Five-Bar Gate. 276-Spore (Spawn spoof) 3.00
289&290 ($4.50) Two issues combined 5.00
300-Final issue 3.00
Free Cerebus (Giveaway, 1991-92?, 36 pgs.)-All-r 4.00

CEREBUS WOMAN
Aardvark-Vanaheim: May, 2019 ($4.00, B&W, one-shot)

1-Cerebus figures placed over original Gustave Doré artwork; Wonder Woman #1 c-swipe 4.00

CHAIN GANG WAR
DC Comics: July, 1993 - No. 12, June, 1994 ($1.75)

1-($2.50)-Embossed silver foil-c, Dave Johnson-c/a 4.00
2-4,6-12: 3-Deathstroke app. 4-Brief Deathstroke app. 6-New Batman (Azrael) cameo. 11-New Batman-c/story. 12-New Batman app. 3.00
5-($2.50)-Foil-c; Deathstroke app; new Batman cameo (1 panel) 4.00

CHAINS OF CHAOS
Harris Comics: Nov, 1994 - No. 3, Jan, 1995 ($2.95, limited series)

1-3-Re-Intro of The Rook w/ Vampirella 5.00

CHALLENGE OF THE UNKNOWN (Formerly Love Experiences)
Ace Magazines: No. 6, Sept, 1950 (See Web Of Mystery No. 19)

6- "Villa of the Vampire" used in N.Y. Joint Legislative Comm. Publ; Sekowsky-a
53 106 159 334 567 800

CHALLENGER, THE
Interfaith Publications/T.C. Comics: 1945 - No. 4, Oct-Dec, 1946

nn; nd; 32 pgs.; Origin the Challenger Club; Anti-Fascist with funny animal filler
106 212 318 673 1162 1650
2-Classic Pandora's Box demons-c; Kubert-a 89 178 267 565 970 1375
3,4: Kubert-a; 4-Fuje-a 54 108 162 343 574 825

CHALLENGERS OF THE FANTASTIC
Marvel Comics (Amalgam): June 1997 ($1.95, one-shot)

1-Karl Kesel-s/Tom Grummett-a 4.00

CHALLENGERS OF THE UNKNOWN (See Showcase #6, 7, 11, 12, Super DC Giant, and Super Team Family) (See Showcase Presents for B&W reprints)

Challengers of the Unknown #63 © DC

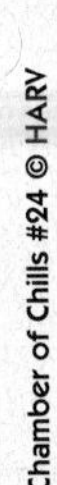
Chamber of Chills #24 © HARV

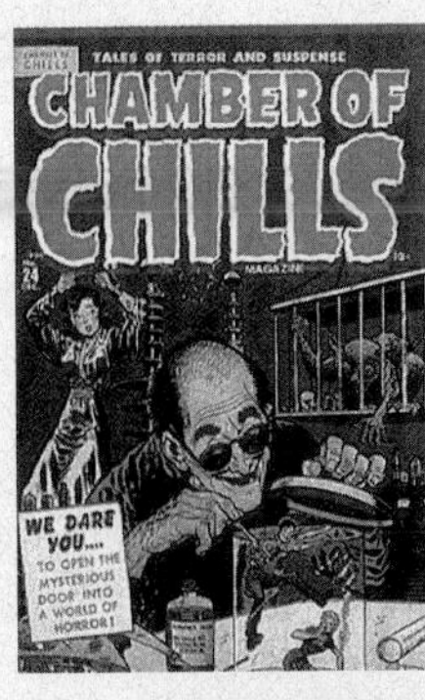

The Champions #13 © MAR

	GD	VG	FN	VF	VF/NM	NM-
	2.0	4.0	6.0	8.0	9.0	9.2

National Per. Publ./DC Comics: 4-5/58 - No. 77, 12-1/70-71; No. 78, 2/73 - No. 80, 6-7/73; No. 81, 6-7/77 - No. 87, 6-7/78

1-(4-5/58)-Kirby/Stein-a(2); Kirby-c 236 472 708 1947 4399 6850
2-Kirby/Stein-a(2) 68 136 204 544 1222 1900
3-Kirby/Stein-a(2); Rocky returns from space with powers similar to the Fantastic Four (9/58)
61 122 183 488 1094 1700
4-8-Kirby/Wood-a plus cover to #8 43 86 129 318 722 1125
9,10 25 50 75 175 388 600
11-Grey tone-c 32 64 96 230 515 800
12-15: 14-Origin/1st app. Multi-Man (villain) 17 34 51 119 265 410
16-22: 18-Intro. Cosmo, the Challengers Spacepet. 22-Last 10¢ issue
12 24 36 81 176 270
23-30 8 16 24 56 108 160
31-Retells origin of the Challengers 9 18 27 57 111 165
32-40 6 12 18 41 76 110
41-47,49,50,52-60: 43-New look begins. 47-1st Sponge-Man. 49-Intro. Challenger Corps.
55-Death of Red Ryan. 60-Red Ryan returns 5 10 15 31 53 75
48,51: 48-Doom Patrol app. 51-Sea Devils app. 5 10 15 33 57 80
61-68: 64,65-Kirby origin-r, parts 1 & 2. 66-New logo. 68-Last 12¢ issue.
4 8 12 23 37 50
69-73,75-80: 69-1st app. Corinna. 77-Last 15¢ issue 3 6 9 16 23 30
74-Deadman by Tuska/Adams; 1 pg. Wrightson-a 6 12 18 41 76 110
81,83-87: 81-(6-7/77). 83-87-Swamp Thing app. 84-87-Deadman app.
2 4 6 8 10 12
82-Swamp Thing begins (thru #87, c/s 2 4 6 9 12 15

NOTE: ***N. Adams** c-67, 68, 70, 72, 74i, 81i. **Buckler** c-83-86p. **Giffen** a-83-87p. **Kirby** a-75-80r; c-75, 77, 78. **Kubert** c-64, 66, 69, 76, 79. **Nasser** c/a-81p, 82p. **Tuska** a-73. **Wood** r-76.*

CHALLENGERS OF THE UNKNOWN
DC Comics: Mar, 1991 - No. 8, Oct, 1991 ($1.75, limited series)

1-Jeph Loeb scripts & Tim Sale-a in all (1st work together); Bolland-c 5.00
2-8: 2-Superman app. 3-Dr. Fate app. 6-G. Kane-c(p). 7-Steranko-c/swipe by Art Adams 4.00
... Must Die! (2004, $19.95, TPB) r/series; intro by Bendis; Sale sketch pages 20.00

NOTE: ***Art Adams** c-7. **Hempel** c-5. **Gil Kane** c-6p. **Sale** a-1-8; c-3, 8. **Wagner** c-4.*

CHALLENGERS OF THE UNKNOWN
DC Comics: Feb, 1997 - No. 18, July, 1998 ($2.25)

1-18: 1-Intro new team; Leon-c/a(p) begins. 4-Origin of new team. 11,12-Batman app.
15-Millennium Giants x-over; Superman-c/app. 4.00

CHALLENGERS OF THE UNKNOWN
DC Comics: Aug, 2004 - No. 6, Jan, 2005 ($2.95, limited series)

1-6-Intro. new team; Howard Chaykin-s/a 3.00

CHALLENGE TO THE WORLD
Catechetical Guild: 1951 (10¢, 36 pgs.)

nn 7 14 21 35 43 50

CHAMBER (See Generation X and Uncanny X-Men)
Marvel Comics: Oct, 2002 - No. 4, Jan, 2003 ($2.99, limited series)

1-4-Bachalo-c/Vaughan-s/Ferguson-a. 1-Cyclops app. 3.00

CHAMBER OF CHILLS (Formerly Blondie Comics #20; ...of Clues No. 27 on)
Harvey Publications/Witches Tales: No. 21, June, 1951 - No. 26, Dec, 1954

21 (#1) 90 180 270 576 988 1400
22,24 (#2,4) 50 100 150 315 533 750
23 (#3)-Excessive violence; eyes torn out 53 106 159 334 567 800
5(2/52)-Decapitation, acid in face scene 45 90 135 284 480 675
6-Woman melted alive 43 86 129 271 461 650
7-Used in **SOTI**, pg. 389; decapitation/severed head panels
45 90 135 284 480 675
8-10: 8-Decapitation panels 41 82 123 256 428 600
11,12 36 72 108 216 350 485
13,15-18,20-22,24-Nostrand-a in all. 13,21-Decapitation panels. 18-Atom bomb panels.
20-Nostrand-c 40 80 120 246 411 575
14-Spider-Man precursor (11/52) 43 86 129 271 461 650
19-Classic-c; Nostrand-a 400 800 1200 2800 4900 7000
23-Classic-c of corpse kissing woman; Nostrand-a 343 686 1029 2400 4200 6000
25,26 29 58 87 170 278 385

NOTE: *About half the issues contain bondage, torture, sadism, perversion, gore, cannabalism, eyes ripped out, acid in face, etc. **Elias** c-4-11, 14-19, 21-26. **Kremer** a-12, 17. **Palais** a-21(1), 23. **Nostrand/Powell** a-13, 15, 16. **Powell** a-21, 23, 24('51), 5-8, 11, 13, 18-21, 23-25. Bondage-c-21, 24('51), 7. 25-r/#5; 26-r/#9.*

CHAMBER OF CHILLS
Marvel Comics Group: Nov, 1972 - No. 25, Nov, 1976

1-Harlan Ellison adaptation 5 10 15 33 57 80
2-5: 2-1st app. John Jakes' Brak the Barbarian 3 6 9 17 26 35
6-25: 22,23-(Regular 25¢ editions) 3 6 9 16 23 30
22,23-(30¢-c variants, limited distribution)(5,7/76) 6 12 18 41 76 110

NOTE: ***Adkins** a-1i, 2i. **Brunner** a-2-4; c-4. **Chaykin** a-4. **Ditko** r-14, 16, 19, 23, 24. **Everett** a-3i, 11r,21r. **Heath** a-1r. **Gil Kane** c-2p. **Kirby** r-11, 18, 19, 22. **Powell** a-13r. **Russell** a-1p, 2p. **Shores** a-5 . **Williamson/Mayo** a-13r. **Robert E. Howard** horror story adaptation-2, 3.*

CHAMBER OF CLUES (Formerly Chamber of Chills)
Harvey Publications: No. 27, Feb, 1955 - No. 28, April, 1955

27-Kerry Drake-r/#19; Powell-a; last pre-code 8 16 24 40 50 60
28-Kerry Drake 6 12 18 31 38 45

CHAMBER OF DARKNESS (Monsters on the Prowl #9 on)
Marvel Comics Group: Oct, 1969 - No. 8, Dec, 1970

1-Buscema-a(p) 7 14 21 48 89 130
2,3: 2-Neal Adams scripts. 3-Smith, Buscema-a 4 8 12 28 47 65
4-A Conan-esque tryout by Smith (4/70); reprinted in Conan #16; Marie
Severin/Everett-c 9 18 27 58 114 170
5,8: 5-H.P. Lovecraft adaptation. 8-Wrightson-c 4 8 12 25 40 55
6 3 6 9 21 33 45
7-Wrightson-c/a, 7pgs. (his 1st work at Marvel); Wrightson draws himself in
1st & last panels; Kirby/Ditko-r; last 15¢-c 6 12 18 38 69 100
1-(1/72; 25¢ Special, 52 pgs.) 4 8 12 25 40 55

NOTE: ***Adkins/Everett** a-8. **Buscema** a-Special 1r. **Craig** a-5. **Ditko** a-6-8r. **Heck** a-1, 2, 8, Special 1r. **Kirby** a(p)-4, 5, 7r. **Kirby/Everett** c-5. **Severin/Everett** c-6. **Shores** a-2, 3i, Special 1r. **Sutton** a-1, 2i, 4, 7, Special 1r. **Wrightson** c-7, 8.*

CHAMP COMICS (Formerly Champion No. 1-10)
Worth Publ. Co./Champ Publ./Family Comics(Harvey Publ.): No. 11, Oct, 1940 - No. 24, Dec, 1942; No. 25, April, 1943

11-Human Meteor cont'd. from Champion 152 304 456 965 1658 2350
12-17,20: 14,15-Crandall-c. 20-The Green Ghost app.; Japanese WWII-c
126 252 378 806 1378 1950
18,19-Simon-c. 19-The Wasp app. 152 304 456 965 1658 2350
21-23,25: 22-The White Mask app. 23-Flag-c 97 194 291 621 1061 1500
24-Hitler, Tojo & Mussolini-c 271 542 813 1734 2967 4200

CHAMPION (See Gene Autry's...)

CHAMPION COMICS
Worth Publ. Co.: Oct, 1939 (ashcan)

nn-Ashcan comic, not distributed to newsstands, only for in house use. A FN/VF copy sold for $2,261.76 in 2010.

CHAMPION COMICS (Formerly Speed Comics #1?; Champ Comics No. 11 on)
Worth Publ. Co.(Harvey Publications): No. 2, Dec, 1939 - No. 10, Aug, 1940 (no No.1)

2-The Champ, The Blazing Scarab, Neptina, Liberty Lads, Jungleman, Bill
Handy, Swingtime Sweetie begin 142 284 426 909 1555 2200
3-7: 7-The Human Meteor begins? 95 190 285 603 1039 1475
8,10: 8-Simon-c. 10-Bondage-c by Kirby 300 600 900 2010 3505 5000
9-1st S&K-c (1st collaboration together) 354 708 1062 2478 4339 6200

CHAMPIONS, THE
Marvel Comics Group: Oct, 1975 - No. 17, Jan, 1978

1-Origin & 1st app. The Champions (The Angel. Black Widow, Ghost Rider, Hercules, Iceman) Venus x-over 5 10 15 31 53 75
2-10: 2-3 vs. Pluto, Venus x-over. 5-7-(Regular 25¢ edition)(4-8/76). 5-1st Rampage. 6-Kirby-c. 7-1st Darkstar, Griffin & Titanium Man app. 8-Champions vs. Darkstar, Griffin & Titanium Man; 1st Yuri Petrovitch as new Crimson Dynamo. 10-Champions vs. Crimson Dynamo & Titanium Man 2 4 6 11 16 20
5-7-(30¢-c variants, limited distribution) 5 10 15 31 53 75
11-15: 11-Byrne-a begins; Black Goliath app; Darkstar joins. 12-Stilt-Man, Black Goliath & The Stranger app. 13-Black Goliath & The Stranger app. 14,15-(Regular 30¢ edition). 14-1st Swarm; Iceman dons new costume. 15-Origin Swarm
2 4 6 13 18 22
14,15-(35¢-c variant, limited distribution) 6 12 18 42 79 115
16-Continued from Super-Villain Team-Up #14; Magneto & Dr. Doom app; Hulk & Beast guest app. 2 4 6 13 18 25
17-Last issue; vs. The Brotherhood of Evil Mutants; Sentinels app.; Champions app. next in Spectacular Spider-Man #17 2 4 6 13 18 22
... Classic Vol. 1 TPB (2006, $19.99) r/#1-11; unused cover to #7 20.00
... Classic Vol. 2 TPB (2007, $19.99) r/#12-17, Iron Man Ann. #4, Avengers #163, Super-Villain Team-Up #14 and Peter Parker, The Spectacular Spider-Man #17-18 20.00
...: No Time For Losers (2016, $7.99) r/#1-3,14,15; art by Heck, Tuska & Byrne 8.00

NOTE: ***Buckler/Adkins** c-3. **Byrne** a-11-15, 17. **Kane/Adkins** c-1. **Kane/Layton** c-11. **Tuska** a-3p, 4p, 6p, 7p. Ghost Rider c-1-4, 7, 8, 10, 14, 16, 17 (4, 10, 14 are more prominent).*

CHAMPIONS (Game)
Eclipse Comics: June, 1986 - No. 6, Feb, 1987 (limited series)

1-6: 1-Intro Flare; based on game. 5-Origin Flare 4.00

CHAMPIONS (Also see The League of Champions)

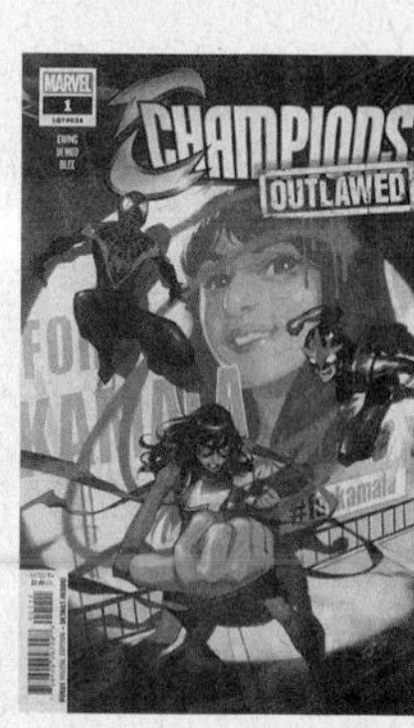

Champions (2020 series) #1 © MAR

Chapel #2 © Rob Liefeld

Charlton Arrow V2 #1 © Staton & 1First

	GD	VG	FN	VF	VF/NM	NM-
	2.0	4.0	6.0	8.0	9.0	9.2

Hero Comics: Sept, 1987 - No. 12, 1989 ($1.95)

1-12: 1-Intro The Marksman & The Rose. 4-Origin Malice — 4.00
Annual 1(1988, $2.75, 52 pgs.)-Origin of Giant — 5.00

CHAMPIONS
Marvel Comics: Dec, 2016 - No. 27, Feb, 2019 ($4.99/$3.99)

1-($4.99) Ms. Marvel, Spider-Man (Miles), Hulk (Amadeus), Nova, Viv Vision team — 5.00
2-24,26,27-($3.99) 3-Young Cyclops joins. 5-Gwenpool app. 9-Intro. Red Locust. 10,11-Secret Empire tie-ins. 13-15-Avengers app. 21-Zub-s/Izaakse-a begins. 22-New Ironheart armor. 23-Man-Thing app. 27-Champions in Weirdworld — 4.00
25-($4.99) Champions go to Weirdworld; Man-Thing app. — 5.00
#1.MU (4/17, $4.99) Monsters Unleashed tie-in; Whitely-s/Stein & Brandt-a — 5.00
Annual 1 (2/19, $4.99) Spotlight on Snowguard; Marcus To-a — 5.00

CHAMPIONS
Marvel Comics: Mar, 2019 - No. 10, Dec, 2019 ($3.99)

1-10: 1-Zub-s/Cummings-a; Mephisto app. 5,6-War of The Realms tie-in — 4.00

CHAMPIONS (Takes place after Outlawed #1)
Marvel Comics: Dec, 2020 - Present ($3.99)

1-4: 1-Eve L. Ewing-s/Simone Di Meo-a; Ms. Marvel, Nova, Spider-Man (Miles) app. — 4.00

CHAMPION SPORTS
National Periodical Publications: Oct-Nov, 1973 - No. 3, Feb-Mar, 1974

	GD	VG	FN	VF	VF/NM	NM-
1	3	6	9	16	23	30
2,3	2	4	6	9	12	15

CHANNEL ZERO
Image Comics: Feb, 1998 - No. 5 ($2.95, B&W, limited series)

1-5, ...Dupe (1/99) -Brian Wood-s/a — 3.00

CHAOS (See The Crusaders)

CHAOS!
Dynamite Entertainment: 2014 - No. 6, 2014 ($3.99, limited series)

1-6-Seeley-s/Andolfo-a; multiple covers on each. Purgatori, Evil Ernie, Chastity app. — 4.00
... Holiday Special 2014 ($5.99) Short stories by various; Lupacchino-c — 6.00
...: Smiley The Psychotic Button 1 (2015, $4.99) origin re-told; Andolfo-c — 5.00

CHAOS! BIBLE
Chaos! Comics: Nov, 1995 ($3.30, one-shot)

1-Profiles of characters & creators — 3.50

CHAOS! CHRONICLES
Chaos! Comics: Feb, 2000 ($3.50, one-shot)

1-Profiles of characters, checklist of Chaos! comics and products — 3.50

CHAOS EFFECT, THE
Valiant: 1994

Alpha (Giveaway w/trading card checklist) — 3.00
Alpha-Gold variant, Alpha-Red variant, Omega-Gold variant — 5.00
Omega (11/94, $2.25); Epilogue Pt. 1, 2 (12/94, 1/95; $2.95) — 3.00

CHAOS! GALLERY
Chaos! Comics: Aug, 1997 ($2.95, one-shot)

1-Pin-ups of characters — 3.00

CHAOS! QUARTERLY
Chaos! Comics: Oct, 1995 -No. 3, May, 1996 ($4.95, quarterly)

1-3: 1-Anthology; Lady Death-c by Julie Bell. 2-Boris "Lady Demon"-c — 5.00
1-Premium Edition (7,500) — 25.00

CHAOS WAR
Marvel Comics: Dec, 2010 - No. 4, Mr, 2011 ($3.99, limited series)

1-5-Hercules, Thor and others vs. Chaos King; Pham-a. 3-5-Galactus app. — 4.00
...: Alpha Flight 1 (1/11, $3.99) McCann-s/Brown-a — 4.00
...: Ares 1 (2/11, $3.99) Oeming-s/Segovia-a — 4.00
...: Chaos King 1 (1/11, $3.99) Kaluta-a/c; Monclair-s — 4.00
...: Dead Avengers 1-3 (1/11 - No. 3, 3/11, $3.99) Grummett-a; Capt. Marvel app. — 4.00
...: God Squad 1 (2/11, $3.99) Sumerak-s/Panosian-a — 4.00
...: Thor 1,2 (1/11 - No. 2, 2/11, $3.99) DeMatteis-s/Ching-a — 4.00
...: X-Men 1,2 (2/11 - No. 2, 3/11, $3.99) Braithwaite-a; Thunderbird, Banshee app. — 4.00

CHAPEL (Also see Youngblood & Youngblood Strikefile #1-3)
Image Comics (Extreme Studios): No. 1 Feb, 1995 - No. 2, Mar, 1995 ($2.50, limited series)

1,2 — 4.00

CHAPEL (Also see Youngblood & Youngblood Strikefile #1-3)
Image Comics (Extreme Studios): V2 #1, Aug, 1995 - No. 7, Apr, 1996 ($2.50)

V2#1-7: 4-Babewatch x-over. 5-vs. Spawn. 7-Shadowhawk-c/app; Shadowhunt x-over — 4.00
#1-Quesada & Palmiotti variant-c — 4.00

CHAPEL (Also see Youngblood & Youngblood Strikefile #1-3)
Awesome Entertainment: Sept, 1997 ($2.99, one-shot)

1 (Reg. & alternate covers) — 4.00

CHARISMAGIC
Aspen MLT: No. 0, Mar, 2011 - No. 6, Jul, 2012 ($1.99/$2.99/$3.50)

0-($1.99) Khary Randolph-a/ Vince Hernandez-s; 3 covers — 3.00
1-4-($2.99) 1-4-Four covers on each — 3.00
5,6-($3.50) Multiple covers on each — 3.50
... Primer 1 (2/18, 25¢) Character profiles and story histories — 3.00
...: The Death Princess 1-3 (11/12 - No. 3, 7/13, $3.99) Hernandez-s/Emilio Lopez-a — 4.00

CHARISMAGIC (Volume 2)
Aspen MLT: May, 2013 - No. 6, Nov, 2013 ($1.00/$3.99)

1-($1.00) Vincenzo Cucca-a/ Vince Hernandez-s; multiple covers — 3.00
2-6-($3.99) Multiple covers on each — 4.00

CHARISMAGIC (Volume 3)
Aspen MLT: Feb, 2018 - No. 5, Jun, 2018 ($3.99)

1-5-Joey Vazquez-a/ Vince Hernandez-s; multiple covers — 4.00

CHARLEMAGNE (Also see War Dancer)
Defiant: Mar, 1994 - No. 5, July, 1994 ($2.50)

1-(3/94, $3.50, 52 pgs.)-Adam Pollina-c/a. — 4.00
2,3,5: Adam Pollina-c/a. 2-War Dancer app. 5-Pre-Schism issue. — 3.00
4-($3.25, 52 pgs.) — 4.00
#0 (Hero Illustrated giveaway)-Adam Pollina-c/a; 1st app. of Ngu — 3.00

CHARLIE CHAN (See Big Shot Comics, Columbia Comics, Feature Comics & The New Advs. of...)

CHARLIE CHAN (The Adventures of...) (Zaza The Mystic No. 10 on) (TV)
Crestwood(Prize) No. 1-5; Charlton No. 6(6/55) on: 6-7/48 - No. 5, 2-3/49; No. 6, 6/55 - No. 9, 3/56

	GD	VG	FN	VF	VF/NM	NM-
1-S&K-c, 2 pgs.; Infantino-a	94	188	282	597	1024	1450
2-5-S&K-c: 3-S&K-c/a	52	104	156	328	552	775
6 (6/55-Charlton)-S&K-c	39	78	117	231	378	525
7-9	21	42	63	122	199	275

CHARLIE CHAN
Dell Publishing Co.: Oct-Dec, 1965 - No. 2, Mar, 1966

	GD	VG	FN	VF	VF/NM	NM-
1-Springer-a/c	5	10	15	31	53	75
2-Springer-a/c	3	6	9	21	33	45

CHARLIE McCARTHY (See Edgar Bergen Presents...)
Dell Publishing Co.: No. 171, Nov, 1947 - No. 571, July, 1954 (See True Comics #14)

	GD	VG	FN	VF	VF/NM	NM-
Four Color 171	26	52	78	182	404	625
Four Color 196-Part photo-c; photo back-c	16	32	48	111	246	380
1(3-5/49)-Part photo-c; photo back-c	12	24	36	84	185	285
2-9(7/52; #5,6-52 pgs.)	7	14	21	48	89	130
Four Color 445,478,527,571	6	12	18	41	76	110

CHARLIE'S ANGELS (Based on the 1970s TV series)
Dynamite Entertainment: 2018 - No. 5, 2018 ($3.99)

1-5-John Layman-s/Joe Eisma-a; multiple covers on each; Jimmy Carter app. — 4.00

CHARLIE'S ANGELS VS. THE BIONIC WOMAN (Based on the 1970s TV series)
Dynamite Entertainment: 2019 - No. 4, 2019 ($3.99)

1-4-Cameron DeOrdio-s/Soo Lee-a; multiple covers on each — 4.00

CHARLTON ACTION: FEATURING "STATIC" (Also see Eclipse Monthly)
Charlton Comics: No, 11, Oct, 1985 - No. 12, Dec, 1985

	GD	VG	FN	VF	VF/NM	NM-
11,12-Ditko-c/a; low print run	1	2	3	5	6	8

CHARLTON ARROW
Charlton Neo: 2017 ($7.99)

1-New E-Man and Nova by Cuti & Staton; Monster Hunter, Mr. Mixit — 8.00

CHARLTON BULLSEYE
CPL/Gang Publications: 1975 - No. 5, 1976 ($1.50, B&W, bi-monthly, magazine format)

	GD	VG	FN	VF	VF/NM	NM-
1: 1 & 2 are last Capt. Atom by Ditko/Byrne intended for the never published Capt. Atom #90; Nightshade app.; Jeff Jones-a	5	10	15	30	50	70
2-Part 2 Capt. Atom story by Ditko/Byrne	3	6	9	21	33	45
3-Wrong Country by Sanho Kim	2	4	6	13	18	22
4-Doomsday + 1 by John Byrne	3	6	9	16	24	32
5-Doomsday + 1 by Byrne, The Question by Toth; Neal Adams back-c; Toth-c	5	10	15	31	53	75

CHARLTON BULLSEYE
Charlton Publications: June, 1981 - No. 10, Dec, 1982; Nov, 1986

Charmed Season 10 #1 © Spelling

Chastity: Crazytown #2 © Chaos!

Cheryl Blossom #25 © ACP

GD VG FN VF VF/NM NM-
2.0 4.0 6.0 8.0 9.0 9.2

GD VG FN VF VF/NM NM-
2.0 4.0 6.0 8.0 9.0 9.2

1-1st Blue Beetle app. since '74, 1st app. The Question since '75; 1st app. Rocket Rabbit; Neil The Horse shown on preview page 3 6 9 18 28 38
2-5: 2-Charlton debut of Neil The Horse; Rocket Rabbit app. 4-Vanguards 6.00
6-10: Low print run. 6-Origin & 1st app. Thunderbunny. 7-1st apps. of Captain Atom & Nightshade since '75. 9-1st app. Bludd. 2 4 6 8 10 12
NOTE: *Material intended for issue #11-up was published in **Scary Tales** #37-up.*

CHARLTON CLASSICS
Charlton Comics: Apr, 1980 - No. 9, Aug, 1981
1-Hercules-r by Glanzman in all 6.00
2-9 5.00

CHARLTON CLASSICS LIBRARY (1776)
Charlton Comics: V10 No.1, Mar, 1973 (one-shot)
1776 (title) - Adaptation of the film musical "1776"; given away at movie theatres; also a newsstand version 3 6 9 14 19 24

CHARLTON PREMIERE (Formerly Marine War Heroes)
Charlton Comics: V1#19, July, 1967; V2#1, Sept, 1967 - No. 4, May, 1968
V1#19, V2#1,2,4: V1#19-Marine War Heroes. V2#1-Trio; intro. Shape, Tyro Team & Spookman. 2-Children of Doom; Boyette classic-a. 4-Unlikely Tales; Aparo, Ditko-a 3 6 9 15 22 28
V2#3-Sinistro Boy Fiend; Blue Beetle & Peacemaker x-over 3 6 9 17 26 35

CHARLTON SPORT LIBRARY - PROFESSIONAL FOOTBALL
Charlton Comics: Winter, 1969-70 (Jan. on cover) (68 pgs.)
1 3 6 9 19 30 40

CHARMED (TV)
Zenescope Entertainment: No. 0, Jun, 2010 - No. 24, Oct, 2012 ($3.50)
0-24-Multiple covers on most 3.50

CHARMED SEASON 10 (TV)
Zenescope Entertainment: Oct, 2014 - No. 17, Mar, 2016 ($3.99)
1-17: 1-Shand-s/Feliz-a/Seidman-c 4.00

CHARMED (Volume 1) (TV)
Dynamite Entertainment: 2017 - No. 5, 2017 ($3.99)
1-5-Schultz-s/Sanapo-a; multiple covers on all 4.00

CHASE (See Batman #550 for 1st app.)(Also see Batwoman)
DC Comics: Feb, 1998 - No. 9, Oct, 1998; #1,000,000 Nov, 1998 ($2.50)
1-9: Williams III & Gray-a. 1-Includes 4 Chase cards. 4-Teen Titans app. 7,8-Batman app. 9-GL Hal Jordan-c/app. 3.00
#1,000,000 (11/98) Final issue; 853rd Century x-over 3.00

CHASING DOGMA (See Jay and Silent Bob)

CHASSIS
Millenium Publications: 1996 - No. 3 ($2.95)
1-3: 1-Adam Hughes-c. 2-Conner var-c. 3.00

CHASSIS
Hurricane Entertainment: 1998 - No. 3 ($2.95)
0,1-3: 1-Adam Hughes-c. 0-Green var-c. 3.00

CHASSIS (Vol. 3)
Image Comics: Nov, 1999 - No. 4 ($2.95, limited series)
1-4: 1-Two covers by O'Neil and Green. 2-Busch var-c. 3.00
1-($6.95) DF Edition alternate-c by Wieringo 7.00

CHASTITY
Chaos! Comics: (one-shots)
#1/2 (1/01, $2.95) Batista-a 3.00
Heartbreaker (3/02, $2.99) Adrian-a/Molenaar-c 3.00
Love Bites (3/01, $2.99) Vale-a/Romano-c 3.00
Reign of Terror 1 (10/00, $2.95) Grant-s/Ross-a/Rio-c 3.00
Re-Imagined 1 (7/02, $2.99) Conner-c; Toledo-a 3.00

CHASTITY
Dynamite Entertainment: 2014 - No. 6, 2014 ($3.99, limited series)
1-6: 1-Andreyko-s/Acosta-a; origin retold. Multiple covers on each 4.00

CHASTITY (VOLUME 2)
Dynamite Entertainment: 2019 - No. 5, 2020 ($3.99, limited series)
1-5: 1-Leah Williams-s/Daniel Maine-a; multiple covers on each 4.00

CHASTITY: CRAZYTOWN
Chaos! Comics: Apr, 2002 - No. 3, June, 2002 ($2.99, limited series)
1-3-Nicieza-s/Batista-c/a 3.00

CHASTITY: LUST FOR LIFE
Chaos! Comics: May, 1999 - No. 3, July, 1999 ($2.95, limited series)
1-3-Nutman-s/Benes-c/a 3.00

CHASTITY: ROCKED
Chaos! Comics: Nov, 1998 - No. 4, Feb, 1999 ($2.95, limited series)
1-4-Nutman-s/Justiniano-c/a 3.00

CHASTITY: SHATTERED
Chaos! Comics: Jun, 2001 - No. 3, Sept, 2001 ($2.99, limited series)
1-3-Kaminski & Pulido-s/Batista-c/a 3.00

CHASTITY: THEATER OF PAIN
Chaos! Comics: Feb, 1997 - No. 3, June, 1997 ($2.95, limited series)
1-3-Pulido-s/Justiniano-c/a 3.00
TPB (1997, $9.95) r/#1-3 10.00

CHECKMATE (TV)
Gold Key: Oct, 1962 - No. 2, Dec, 1962
1-Photo-c on both 5 10 15 33 57 80
2 5 10 15 30 50 70

CHECKMATE! (See Action Comics #598 and The OMAC Project)
DC Comics: Apr, 1988 - No. 33, Jan, 1991 ($1.25)
1-33: 13: New format begins 3.00
NOTE: ***Gil Kane** c-2, 4, 7, 8, 10, 11, 15-19.*

CHECKMATE (See Infinite Crisis and The OMAC Project)
DC Comics: Jun, 2006 - No. 31, Dec, 2008 ($2.99)
1-Rucka-s/Saiz-a/Bermejo-c; Alan Scott, Mr. Terrific, Sasha Bordeaux app. 4.00
1-2nd printing with B&W cover 3.00
2-31: 2,3-Kobra, King Faraday, Amanda Waller, Fire app. 4-The Great Ten app. 13-15-Outsiders app. 26-Chimera origin 3.00
...: A King's GameTPB (2007, $14.99) r/#1-7 15.00
...: Chimera TPB (2009, $17.99) r/#26-31 18.00
...: Fall of the Wall TPB (2008, $14.99) r/#16-22 15.00
...: Pawn Breaks TPB (2007, $14.99) r/#8-12 15.00

CHERYL BLOSSOM (See Archie's Girls, Betty and Veronica #320 for 1st app.)
Archie Publications: Sept, 1995 - No. 3, Nov, 1995 ($1.50, limited series)
1 2 4 6 13 18 22
2,3 1 2 3 5 7 9
Special 1-4 ('95, '96, $2.00) 1 2 3 5 7 9

CHERYL BLOSSOM (Cheryl's Summer Job)
Archie Publications: July, 1996 - No. 3, Sept, 1996 ($1.50, limited series)
1-3 1 2 3 4 5 7

CHERYL BLOSSOM (...Goes Hollywood)
Archie Publications: Dec, 1996 - No. 3, Feb, 1997 ($1.50, limited series)
1-3 1 2 3 4 5 7

CHERYL BLOSSOM
Archie Publications: Apr, 1997 - No. 37, Mar, 2001 ($1.50/$1.75/$1.79/$1.99)
1-Dan DeCarlo-c/a 2 4 6 8 10 12
2-10: 2-7-Dan DeCarlo-c/a 6.00
11-37: 32-Begin $1.99-c. 34-Sabrina app. 4.00

CHESTY SANCHEZ
Antarctic Press: Nov, 1995 - No. 2, Mar, 1996 ($2.95, B&W)
1,2 1 2 3 5 6 8
...Super Special (2/99, $5.99) 1 2 3 5 6 8

CHEVAL NOIR
Dark Horse Comics: 1989 - No. 48, Nov, 1993 ($3.50, B&W, 68 pgs.)
1 ($3.50) Dave Stevens-c 2 4 6 13 18 24
2-6,8,10 ($3.50): 6-Moebius poster insert 1 2 3 5 6 8
7-Dave Stevens-c 3 6 9 16 23 30
9,11,13,15,17,20,22 ($4.50, 84 pgs.) 1 2 3 5 6 8
12,18,19,21,23 ($3.95): 12-Geary-a; Mignola-c 6.00
14 ($4.95, 76 pgs.)(7 pgs. color) 1 2 3 5 6 8
16,24 ($3.75): 16-19-Contain trading cards 6.00
25,26 ($3.95): 26-Moebius-a begins 6.00
27-48 ($2.95): 33-Snyder III-c 5.00
NOTE: ***Bolland** a-2, 6, 7, 13, 14. **Bolton** a-2, 4, 45; c-4, 20. **Chadwick** c-13. **Dorman** painted c-16. **Geary** a-13, 14. **Kelley Jones** c-27. **Kaluta** a-6; c-6, 18. **Moebius** c-5, 9, 26. **Dave Stevens** c-1, 7. **Sutton** painted c-36.*

CHEW (See Walking Dead #61 for preview)(Also see Chu)
Image Comics: Jun, 2009 - No. 60, Nov, 2016 ($2.99/$3.50/$3.99)
1-Layman-s/Guillory-a 11 22 33 72 154 235

Cheyenne #17 © DELL

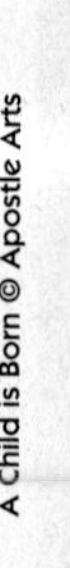
A Child is Born © Apostle Arts

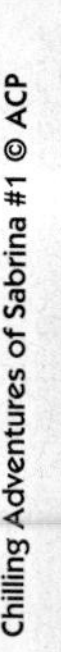
Chilling Adventures of Sabrina #1 © ACP

	GD 2.0	VG 4.0	FN 6.0	VF 8.0	VF/NM 9.0	NM- 9.2
1-(2nd-4th printings)	2	4	6	9	12	15
2-1st printing	3	6	9	21	33	45
2-5-(2nd & 3rd printings)						6.00
3-1st printing	2	4	6	13	18	22
4,5-1st printings	2	4	6	9	12	15
6-10	1	3	4	6	8	10
11-15: 15-Gatefold wraparound-c	1	2	3	5	6	8
16-24: 19-Neon green cover ink						5.00
25-44,46-49: 27-(6/12) Second Helping Edition						3.00
27-(5/11) Future issue released between #18 & #19						5.00
45,50-55-($3.50) 49-Poyo cover. 53-Flintstones cover						3.50
56-59-($3.99)						4.00
60-($5.99) Final issue; double cover with gatefold; set in the future						6.00
...: Demon Chicken Poyo One-Shot (4/16, $3.99) Layman-s/Guillory-a; pin-up gallery						4.00
.../ Revival One Shot (5/14, $4.99) Flip book: Layman-s/Guillory-a & Selley-s/Norton-a						5.00
...: Warrior Chicken Poyo (7/14, $3.50) Layman-s/Guillory-a; bonus pin-up gallery						3.50
Image Firsts: Chew #1 (4/10, $1.00) r/#1 with "Image Firsts" cover logo						5.00

CHEWBACCA (Star Wars)
Marvel Comics: Dec, 2015 - No. 5, Feb, 2016 ($3.99, limited series)

	GD	VG	FN	VF	VF/NM	NM-
1-5-Duggan-s/Noto-a; takes place after Episode 4 Battle of Yavin						4.00

CHEYENNE (TV)
Dell Publishing Co.: No. 734, Oct, 1956 - No. 25, Dec-Jan, 1961-62

	GD	VG	FN	VF	VF/NM	NM-
Four Color 734(#1)-Clint Walker photo-c	13	26	39	86	188	290
Four Color 772,803: Clint Walker photo-c	8	16	24	51	96	140
4(8-10/57) - 20: 4-9,13-20-Clint Walker photo-c. 10-12-Ty Hardin photo-c	6	12	18	37	66	95
21-25-Clint Walker photo-c on all	6	12	18	38	69	100

CHEYENNE AUTUMN (See Movie Classics)

CHEYENNE KID (Formerly Wild Frontier No. 1-7)
Charlton Comics: No. 8, July, 1957 - No. 99, Nov, 1973

	GD	VG	FN	VF	VF/NM	NM-
8 (#1)	8	16	24	42	54	65
9,15-19	6	12	18	29	36	42
10-Williamson/Torres-a(3); Ditko-c	11	22	33	60	83	105
11-(68 pgs.)-Cheyenne Kid meets Geronimo	10	20	30	58	79	100
12-Williamson/Torres-a(2)	10	20	30	58	79	100
13-Williamson/Torres-a (5 pgs.)	8	16	24	44	57	70
14-Williamson-a (5 pgs.?)	8	16	24	42	54	65
20-22,24,25-Severin c/a(3) each	4	8	12	21	33	45
23,27-29	3	6	9	15	22	28
26,30-Severin-a	3	6	9	17	26	35
31-59	2	4	6	10	14	18
60-65	2	4	6	8	11	14
66-Wander by Aparo begins, ends #87	2	4	6	10	14	18
67-80	2	4	6	8	11	14
81-99: Apache Red begins #88, origin in #89	2	4	6	8	11	14
Modern Comics Reprint 87,89(1978)						5.00

CHIAROSCURO (THE PRIVATE LIVES OF LEONARDO DA VINCI)
DC Comics (Vertigo): July, 1995 - No. 10, Apr, 1996 ($2.50/$2.95, limited series, mature)

	GD	VG	FN	VF	VF/NM	NM-
1-9: McGreal and Rawson-s/Truog & Kayanan-a						3.00
10-($2.95)						3.00
TPB (2005, $24.99) r/series; intro. by Alisa Kwitney, afterword by Pat McGreal						25.00

CHICAGO MAIL ORDER (See C-M-O Comics in the Promotional Comics section)

CHIEF, THE (Indian Chief No. 3 on)
Dell Publishing Co.: No. 290, Aug, 1950 - No. 2, Apr-June, 1951

	GD	VG	FN	VF	VF/NM	NM-
Four Color 290(#1)	8	16	24	54	102	150
2	5	10	15	35	63	90

CHIEF CRAZY HORSE (See Wild Bill Hickok #21)
Avon Periodicals: 1950 (Also see Fighting Indians of the Wild West!)

	GD	VG	FN	VF	VF/NM	NM-
nn-Fawcette-c	25	50	75	150	245	340

CHIEF VICTORIO'S APACHE MASSACRE (See Fight Indians of/Wild West!)
Avon Periodicals: 1951

	GD	VG	FN	VF	VF/NM	NM-
nn-Williamson/Frazetta-a (7 pgs.); Larsen-a; Kinstler-c	63	126	189	403	689	975

CHILD IS BORN, A
Apostle Arts: Nov, 2011 ($5.99, one-shot)

	GD	VG	FN	VF	VF/NM	NM-
nn-Story of the birth of Jesus; Billy Tucci-s/a; cover by Tucci & Sparacio						6.00
HC (7/12, $15.99) Includes bonus interview with Billy Tucci and sketch art						16.00

CHILDREN OF FIRE
Fantagor Press: Nov, 1987 - No. 3, 1988 ($2.00, limited series)

	GD 2.0	VG 4.0	FN 6.0	VF 8.0	VF/NM 9.0	NM- 9.2
1-3: by Richard Corben						4.00

CHILDREN OF THE VOYAGER (See Marvel Frontier Comics Unlimited)
Marvel Frontier Comics: Sept, 1993 - No. 4, Dec, 1993 ($1.95, limited series)

	GD	VG	FN	VF	VF/NM	NM-
1-($2.95)-Embossed glow-in-the-dark-c; Paul Johnson-c/a						4.00
2-4						3.00

CHILDREN'S BIG BOOK
Dorene Publ. Co.: 1945 (25¢, stiff-c, 68 pgs.)

	GD	VG	FN	VF	VF/NM	NM-
nn-Comics & fairy tales; David Icove-a	16	32	48	94	147	200

CHILDREN'S CRUSADE, THE
DC Comics (Vertigo): Dec, 1993 - No. 2, Jan, 1994 ($3.95, limited series)

	GD	VG	FN	VF	VF/NM	NM-
1,2-Gaiman scripts & Bachalo-a; framing issues for Children's Crusade x-over						4.00

CHILD'S PLAY: THE SERIES (Movie)
Innovation Publishing: May, 1991 - #3, 1991 ($2.50, 28pgs.)

	GD	VG	FN	VF	VF/NM	NM-
1-3						5.00

CHILD'S PLAY 2 THE OFFICIAL MOVIE ADAPTATION (Movie)
Innovation Publishing: 1990 - No. 3, 1990 ($2.50, bi-weekly limited series)

	GD	VG	FN	VF	VF/NM	NM-
1-3: Adapts movie sequel						5.00

CHILI (Millie's Rival)
Marvel Comics Group: 5/69 - No. 17, 9/70; No. 18, 8/72 - No. 26, 12/73

	GD	VG	FN	VF	VF/NM	NM-
1	9	18	27	62	126	190
2,4,5	5	10	15	34	60	85
3-Millie & Chili visit Marvel and meet Stan Lee & Stan Goldberg (6 pgs.)	6	12	18	38	69	100
6-17	5	10	15	30	50	70
18-26	4	8	12	27	44	60
Special 1(12/71, 52 pgs.)	5	10	15	35	63	90

CHILLER
Marvel Comics (Epic): Nov, 1993 - No. 2, Dec, 1993 ($7.95, lim. series)

	GD	VG	FN	VF	VF/NM	NM-
1,2-(68 pgs.)	1	2	3	5	6	8

CHILLING ADVENTURES IN SORCERY (...as Told by Sabrina #1, 2)
(Red Circle Sorcery No. 6 on)
Archie Publications (Red Circle Prods.): 9/72 - No. 2, 10/72; No. 3, 10/73 - No. 5, 2/74

	GD	VG	FN	VF	VF/NM	NM-
1-Sabrina cameo as narrator	5	10	15	35	63	90
2-Sabrina cameo as narrator	3	6	9	20	31	42
3-5: Morrow-c/a, all. 4,5-Alcazar-a	2	4	6	11	16	20

CHILLING ADVENTURES OF SABRINA (Inspired the 2018 Netflix series)(See Madam Satan)
Archie Comic Publications: Dec, 2014 - No. 8, Aug, 2017 ($3.99, mature content)

	GD	VG	FN	VF	VF/NM	NM-
1-8: 1-Aguirre-Sacasa-s/Hack-a; two covers; origin re-told, set in the 1960s						4.00
1-(12/18, $1.00) r/#1 with Netflix art cover						3.00
... - Halloween ComicFest Edition 1 (2015, free) r/#1 in B&W						3.00
... - Halloween ComicFest Edition #1 2017 (free) r/#7 in B&W						3.00
... Monster-Sized One-Shot 1 (5/19, $7.99) r/#6-8; Hack-c						8.00

CHILLING TALES (Formerly Beware)
Youthful Magazines: No. 13, Dec, 1952 - No. 17, Oct, 1953

	GD	VG	FN	VF	VF/NM	NM-
13(No.1)-Harrison-a; Matt Fox-c/a	258	516	774	1651	2826	4000
14-Harrison-a	97	194	291	621	1061	1500
15-Matt Fox-c; Harrison-a	110	220	330	704	1202	1700
16-Poe adapt.-'Metzengerstein'; Rudyard Kipling adapt.- 'Mark of the Beast,' by Kiefer; bondage-c	129	258	387	826	1413	2000
17-Matt Fox-c; Sir Walter Scott & Poe adapt.	103	206	309	659	1130	1600

CHILLING TALES OF HORROR (Magazine)
Stanley Publications: V1#1, 6/69 - V1#7, 12/70; V2#2, 2/71 - V2#6, 10/71(50¢, B&W, 52 pgs.)

	GD	VG	FN	VF	VF/NM	NM-
V1#1	9	18	27	61	123	185
2-4,(no #5),6,7: 7-Cameron-a	6	12	18	41	76	110
V2#2-6: 2-Two different #2 issues exist (2/71 & 4/71). 2-(2/71) Spirit of Frankenstein -r/Adventures into the Unknown #16. 4-(8/71) different from other V2#4(6/71)	6	12	18	37	66	95
V2#4-(6/71) r/9 pg. Feldstein-a from Adventures into the Unknown #3	6	12	18	38	69	100

NOTE: *Two issues of V2#2 exist, Feb, 1971 and April, 1971. Two issues of V2#4 exist, Jun, 1971 and Aug, 1971.*

CHILLY WILLY (Also see New Funnies #211)
Dell Publ. Co.: No. 740, Oct, 1956 - No. 1281, Apr-June, 1962 (Walter Lantz)

	GD	VG	FN	VF	VF/NM	NM-
Four Color 740 (#1)	8	16	24	54	102	150
Four Color 852 (2/58),967 (2/59),1017 (9/59),1074 (2-4/60),1122 (8/60), 1177 (4-6/61),1212 (7-9/61),1281	5	10	15	34	60	85

CHIMERA
CrossGeneration Comics: Mar, 2003 - No. 4, July, 2003 ($2.95, limited series)

Chip 'n' Dale #71 © DIS

Christmas Carnival © Z-D

Christmas with the Super-Heroes #1 © DC

	GD 2.0	VG 4.0	FN 6.0	VF 8.0	VF/NM 9.0	NM- 9.2
1-4-Marz-s/Peterson-c/a						3.00
Vol. 1 TPB (2003, $15.95) r/#1-4 plus sketch pages, 3-D models, how-to guides						16.00

CHIMICHANGA
Albatross Exploding Funny Books: 2010 ($3.00, B&W)

	GD	VG	FN	VF	VF/NM	NM-
1-3-Eric Powell-s/a/c						3.00

CHIMICHANGA: THE SORROW OF THE WORLD'S WORST FACE
Dark Horse Comics: Oct, 2016 - No. 4, Dec, 2017 ($3.99, limited series)

	GD	VG	FN	VF	VF/NM	NM-
1-4-Eric Powell-s/Stephanie Buscema-a						4.00

CHINA BOY (See Wisco in the Promotional Comics section)

CHIN MUSIC
Image Comics: May, 2013 - No. 2, Aug, 2013 ($2.99)

	GD	VG	FN	VF	VF/NM	NM-
1,2-Steve Niles-s/Tony Harris-a/c						3.00

CHIP 'N' DALE (Walt Disney)(See Walt Disney's C&S #204)
Dell Publishing Co./Gold Key/Whitman No. 65 on: Nov, 1953 - No. 30, June-Aug, 1962; Sept, 1967 - No. 83, July, 1984

	GD	VG	FN	VF	VF/NM	NM-
Four Color 517(#1)	11	22	33	76	163	250
Four Color 581,636	6	12	18	42	79	115
4(12/55-2/56)-10	5	10	15	33	57	80
11-30	4	8	12	28	47	65
1(Gold Key, 1967)-Reprints	3	6	9	19	30	40
2-10	2	4	6	13	18	22
11-20	2	4	6	9	12	15
21-40	2	4	6	8	10	12
41-64,70-77: 75(2/82), 76(2-3/82), 77(3/82)	1	2	3	5	7	9
65,66 (Whitman)	2	4	6	8	11	14
67-69 (3-pack? 1980): 67(8/80), 68(10/80) (scarce)	4	8	12	28	47	65
78-83 (All #90214; 3-pack, nd, nd code): 78(4/83), 79(5/83), 80(7/83), 81(8/83), 82(5/84), 83(7/84)	3	6	9	15	22	28

NOTE: *All Gold Key/Whitman issues have reprints except No. 32-35, 38-41, 45-47. No. 23-28, 30-42, 45-47, 49 have new covers.*

CHIP 'N DALE RESCUE RANGERS
Disney Comics: June, 1990 - No. 19, Dec, 1991 ($1.50)

	GD	VG	FN	VF	VF/NM	NM-
1-New stories; origin begins						4.00
2-19: 2-Origin continued						3.00

CHIP 'N' DALE RESCUE RANGERS
BOOM! Studios: Dec, 2010 - No. 8, Jul, 2011 ($3.99)

	GD	VG	FN	VF	VF/NM	NM-
1-8: 1-Brill-s/Castellani-a; 3 covers						4.00
... Free Comic Book Day Edition (5/11) Flip book with Darkwing Duck						3.00

CHITTY CHITTY BANG BANG (See Movie Comics)

C.H.I.X.
Image Comics (Studiosaurus): Jan, 1998 ($2.50)

	GD	VG	FN	VF	VF/NM	NM-
1-Dodson, Haley, Lopresti, Randall, and Warren-s/c/a						3.00
1-($5.00) "X-Ray Variant" cover						5.00
C.H.I.X. That Time Forgot 1 (8/98, $2.95)						3.00

CHOICE COMICS
Great Publications: Dec, 1941 - No. 3, Feb, 1942

	GD	VG	FN	VF	VF/NM	NM-
1-Origin Secret Circle; Atlas the Mighty app.; Zomba, Jungle Fight, Kangaroo Man, & Fire Eater begin	155	310	465	992	1696	2400
2	77	154	231	493	847	1200
3-Double feature; Features movie "The Lost City" (classic cover); continued from Great Comics #3	213	426	639	1363	2332	3300

CHOLLY AND FLYTRAP (Arthur Suydam's...)(Also see New Adventures of...)
Image Comics: Nov, 2004 - No. 4, June, 2005 ($4.95/$5.95, limited series)

	GD	VG	FN	VF	VF/NM	NM-
1-($4.95) Arthur Suydam-s/a/c						6.00
2-4-($5.95)						6.00

CHOO CHOO CHARLIE
Gold Key: Dec, 1969

	GD	VG	FN	VF	VF/NM	NM-
1-John Stanley-a	5	10	15	35	63	90

CHOSEN
Dark Horse Comics: Jan, 2004 - No. 3, Aug, 2004 ($2.99, limited series)

	GD	VG	FN	VF	VF/NM	NM-
1-Story of the second coming; Mark Millar-s/Peter Gross-a						4.00
2,3						3.00

CHRIS CLAREMONT ANNIVERSARY SPECIAL
Marvel Comics: Mar, 2021 ($4.99, one-shot)

	GD	VG	FN	VF	VF/NM	NM-
1-Claremont-s; art by Sienkiewicz, Chen, Olortegui, and Booth; Dani Moonstar app.						5.00

CHRISTIAN (See Asylum)
Maximum Press: Jan, 1996 ($2.99, one-shot)

	GD	VG	FN	VF	VF/NM	NM-
1-Pop Mhan-a						3.00

CHRISTIAN HEROES OF TODAY
David C. Cook: 1964 (36 pgs.)

	GD	VG	FN	VF	VF/NM	NM-
nn	3	6	9	17	26	35

CHRISTMAS (Also see A-1 Comics)
Magazine Enterprises: No. 28, 1950

	GD	VG	FN	VF	VF/NM	NM-
A-1 28	11	22	33	62	86	110

CHRISTMAS ADVENTURE, A (See Classics Comics Giveaways, 12/69)

CHRISTMAS ALBUM (See March of Comics No. 312)

CHRISTMAS ANNUAL
Golden Special: 1975 ($1.95, 100 pgs., stiff-c)

	GD	VG	FN	VF	VF/NM	NM-
nn-Reprints Mother Goose stories with Walt Kelly-a	3	6	9	21	33	45

CHRISTMAS & ARCHIE
Archie Comics: Jan, 1975 ($1.00, 68 pgs., 10-1/4x13-1/4" treasury-sized)

	GD	VG	FN	VF	VF/NM	NM-
1-(scarce)	5	10	15	34	60	85

CHRISTMAS BELLS (See March of Comics No. 297)

CHRISTMAS CARNIVAL
Ziff-Davis Publ. Co./St. John Publ. Co. No. 2: 1952 (25¢, one-shot, 100 pgs.)

	GD	VG	FN	VF	VF/NM	NM-
nn	39	78	117	235	385	535
2-Reprints Ziff-Davis issue plus-c	18	36	54	105	165	225

CHRISTMAS CAROL, A (See March of Comics No. 33)

CHRISTMAS EVE, A (See March of Comics No. 212)

CHRISTMAS IN DISNEYLAND (See Dell Giants)

CHRISTMAS PARADE (See Dell Giant No. 26, Dell Giants, March of Comics No. 284, Walt Disney Christmas Parade & Walt Disney's...)

CHRISTMAS PARADE (Walt Disney's)
Gold Key: 1962 (no month listed) - No. 9, Jan, 1972 (#1,5: 80 pgs.; #2-4,7-9: 36 pgs.)

	GD	VG	FN	VF	VF/NM	NM-
1 (30018-301)-Giant	8	16	24	52	99	145
2-6: 2-r/F.C. #367 by Barks. 3-r/F.C. #178 by Barks. 4-r/F.C. #203 by Barks. 5-r/Christmas Parade #1 (Dell) by Barks; giant. 6-r/Christmas Parade #2 (Dell) by Barks (64 pgs.); giant	5	10	15	35	63	90
7-Pull-out poster (half price w/o poster)	5	10	15	30	50	70
8-r/F.C. #367 by Barks; pull-out poster	5	10	15	35	63	90
9	4	8	12	25	40	55

CHRISTMAS PARTY (See March of Comics No. 256)

CHRISTMAS STORIES (See Little People No. 959, 1062)

CHRISTMAS STORY (See March of Comics No. 326 in the Promotional Comics section)

CHRISTMAS STORY, THE
Catechetical Guild: 1955 (15¢)

	GD	VG	FN	VF	VF/NM	NM-
393-Addison Burbank-a	8	16	24	42	54	65

CHRISTMAS STORY BOOK (See Woolworth's Christmas Story Book)

CHRISTMAS TREASURY, A (See Dell Giants & March of Comics No. 227)

CHRISTMAS WITH ARCHIE
Spire Christian Comics (Fleming H. Revell Co.): 1973, 1974 (49¢, 52 pgs.)

	GD	VG	FN	VF	VF/NM	NM-
nn-Low print run	3	6	9	15	22	28

CHRISTMAS WITH MOTHER GOOSE
Dell Publishing Co.: No. 90, Nov, 1945 - No. 253, Nov, 1949

	GD	VG	FN	VF	VF/NM	NM-
Four Color 90 (#1)-Kelly-a	15	30	45	103	227	350
Four Color 126 ('46), 172 (11/47)-By Walt Kelly	11	22	33	76	163	250
Four Color 201 (10/48), 253-By Walt Kelly	10	20	30	64	132	200

CHRISTMAS WITH SANTA (See March of Comics No. 92)

CHRISTMAS WITH THE SUPER-HEROES (See Limited Collectors' Edition)
DC Comics: 1988; No. 2, 1989 ($2.95)

	GD	VG	FN	VF	VF/NM	NM-
1,2: 1-(100 pgs.)-All reprints; N. Adams-r, Byrne-c; Batman, Superman, JLA, LSH Christmas stories; r-Miller's 1st Batman/DC Special Series #21. 2-(68 pgs.)-Superman by Chadwick; Batman, Wonder Woman, Deadman, Green Lantern, Flash app.; Morrow-a; Enemy Ace by Byrne; all new-a	1	2	3	5	6	8

CHROMA-TICK, THE (...Special Edition, #1,2) (Also see The Tick)
New England Comics Press: Feb, 1992 - No. 8, Nov, 1993 ($3.95/$3.50, 44 pgs.)

	GD	VG	FN	VF	VF/NM	NM-
1,2-Includes serially numbered trading card set						6.00
3-8 ($3.50, 36 pgs.): 6-Bound-in card						4.00

CHROME

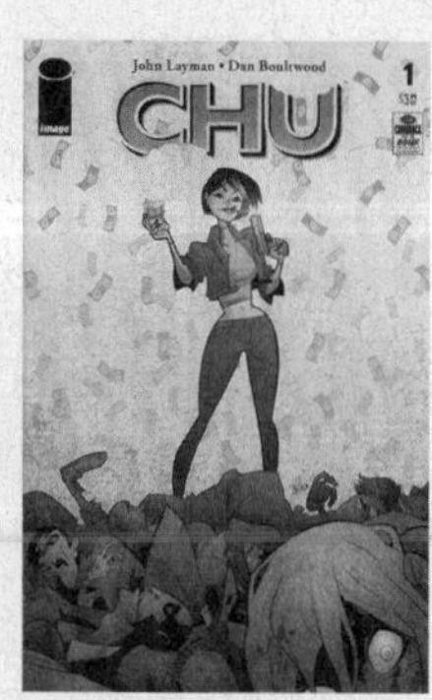

Chu #1 © Mighty Layman Prods.

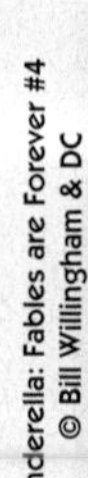
Cinderella: Fables are Forever #4 © Bill Willingham & DC

Cinderella Love #11 © Z-D

	GD 2.0	VG 4.0	FN 6.0	VF 8.0	VF/NM 9.0	NM- 9.2

Hot Comics: 1986 - No. 3, 1986 ($1.50, limited series)
1-3 3.00

CHROMIUM MAN, THE
Triumphant Comics: Aug, 1993 - No.10, May, 1994 ($2.50)
1-1st app. Mr. Death; all serially numbered 3.00
2-10: 2-1st app. Prince Vandal. 3-1st app. Candi, Breaker & Coil. 4,5-Triumphant Unleashed x-over. 8,9-(3/94). 10-(5/94) 3.00
0-(4/94)-Four color-c, 0-All pink-c & all blue-c; no cover price 3.00

CHROMIUM MAN: VIOLENT PAST, THE
Triumphant Comics: Jan, 1994 - No. 2, Jan, 1994 ($2.50, limited series)
1,2-Serially numbered to 22,000 each 3.00

CHRONICLES OF CONAN, THE (See Conan the Barbarian)

CHRONICLES OF CORUM, THE (Also see Corum...)
First Comics: Jan, 1987 - No. 12, Nov, 1988 ($1.75/$1.95, deluxe series)
1-12: Adapts Michael Moorcock's novel; Thomas-s; Mignola-a/c 3.00

CHRONONAUTS
Image Comics: Mar, 2015 - No. 4, Jun, 2015 ($3.50/$5.99)
1-3-Mark Millar-s/Sean Murphy-a 3.50
4-($5.99) 6.00

CHRONONAUTS: FUTURE SHOCK
Image Comics: Oct, 2019 - No. 4, Oct, 2019 ($3.99/$5.99, all 4 issues released the same day)
1-3-Mark Millar-s/Eric Canete-a/Pasqual Ferry-c 3.50
4-($5.99) 6.00

CHRONOS
DC Comics: Mar, 1998 - No. 11, Feb. 1999 ($2.50)
1-11-J.F. Moore-s/Guinan-a 3.00
#1,000,000 (11/98) 853rd Century x-over 3.00

CHU (Characters from Chew)
Image Comics: Jul, 2020 - No. 5, Nov, 2020 ($3.99)
1-5-Layman-s/Boultwood-a; Tony Chu and Saffron Chu app. 4.00

CHUCK (Based on the NBC TV series)
DC Comics (WildStorm): Aug, 2008 - No. 6, Jan, 2009 ($2.99, limited series)
1-6-Jeremy Haun-a/Kristian Donaldson-c; Noto back-up-a 3.00
TPB (2009, $19.99) r/#1-6; photo-c 20.00

CHUCKLE, THE GIGGLY BOOK OF COMIC ANIMALS
R. B. Leffingwell Co.: 1945 (132 pgs., one-shot)

	GD	VG	FN	VF	VF/NM	NM-
1-Funny animal	28	56	84	165	270	375

CHUCK NORRIS (TV)
Marvel Comics (Star Comics): Jan, 1987 - No. 4, July, 1987

	GD	VG	FN	VF	VF/NM	NM-
1-Ditko-a	3	6	9	14	19	24
2,3: Ditko-a	1	2	3	5	6	8
4-No Ditko-a (low print run)	1	3	4	6	8	10

CHUCK WAGON (See Sheriff Bob Dixon's...)

CHUCKY (Based on the 1988 killer doll movie Child's Play)
Devil's Due Publishing: Apr, 2007 - No. 4, Nov, 2007 ($3.50/$5.50)

	GD	VG	FN	VF	VF/NM	NM-
1-3-Pulido-s/Medors-a; art & photo covers						5.00
4-($5.50)	1	2	3	4	5	7
TPB (2007, $18.99) r/series; gallery of variant covers; 4 pages of script and sketch art						19.00

CHYNA (WWF Wrestling)
Chaos! Comics: Sept, 2000; July, 2001 ($2.95/$2.99, one-shots)
1-Grant-s/Barrows-a; photo-c 3.00
1-($9.95) Premium Edition; Cleavenger-c 10.00
II -(7/01, $2.99) Deodato-a; photo-c 3.00

CICERO'S CAT
Dell Publishing Co.: July-Aug, 1959 - No. 2, Sept-Oct, 1959

	GD	VG	FN	VF	VF/NM	NM-
1-Cat from Mutt & Jeff	4	8	12	28	47	65
2	4	8	12	25	40	55

CIMARRON STRIP (TV)
Dell Publishing Co.: Jan, 1968

	GD	VG	FN	VF	VF/NM	NM-
1-Stuart Whitman photo-c	4	8	12	23	37	50

CIMMERIAN: QUEEN OF THE BLACK COAST
Ablaze Publishing: 2020 - No. 2, 2020 ($3.99)
1,2-Conan adaptation from Queen of the Black Coast; Morvan-s/Alary-a; text back-up 4.00

CIMMERIAN, THE: PEOPLE OF THE BLACK CIRCLE
Ablaze Publishing: 2020 - No. 3, 2020 ($3.99, limited series)
1-3-Conan adaptation; Yasmina app.; Runberg-s/Jae Kwang Park-a; text back-up 4.00

CIMMERIAN, THE: FROST-GIANT'S DAUGHTER
Ablaze Publishing: 2020 - No. 3, 2020 ($3.99, limited series)
1-3-Conan adaptation; Atali app.; Robin Recht-a; text back-up 4.00

CIMMERIAN, THE: RED NAILS
Ablaze Publishing: 2020 - No. 2, 2020 ($3.99)
1,2-Conan adaptation; Valeria app.; Hautiere-s/Vatine & Cassegrain-a; text back-up 4.00

CINDER AND ASHE
DC Comics: May, 1988 - No. 4, Aug, 1988 ($1.75, limited series)
1-4: Mature readers 3.00

CINDERELLA (Disney) (See Movie Comics)
Dell Publishing Co.: No. 272, Apr, 1950 - No. 786, Apr, 1957

	GD	VG	FN	VF	VF/NM	NM-
Four Color 272	12	24	36	84	185	285
Four Color 786-Partial-r #272	6	12	18	42	79	115

CINDERELLA
Whitman Publishing Co.: Apr, 1982

	GD	VG	FN	VF	VF/NM	NM-
nn-Reprints 4-Color #272	1	2	3	4	5	7

CINDERELLA: FABLES ARE FOREVER (See Fables)
DC Comics (Vertigo): Apr, 2011 - No. 6, Sept, 2011 ($2.99, limited series)
1-6-Roberson-s/McManus-a/Zullo-c; Dorothy Gale app. 3.00

CINDERELLA: FROM FABLETOWN WITH LOVE (See Fables)
DC Comics (Vertigo): Jan, 2010 - No. 6, Jun, 2010 ($2.99, limited series)
1-6: Roberson-s/McManus-a/Zullo-c 3.00
TPB (2010, $14.99) r/#1-6 15.00

CINDERELLA LOVE
Ziff-Davis/St. John Publ. Co. No. 12 on: No. 10, 1950; No. 11, 4-5/51; No. 12, 9/51; No. 4, 10-11/51 - No. 11, Fall, 1952; No. 12, 10/53 - No. 15, 8/54; No. 25, 12/54 - No. 29, 10/55 (No #16-24)

	GD	VG	FN	VF	VF/NM	NM-
10(#1)(1st Series, 1950)-Painted-c	28	56	84	168	274	380
11(#2, 4-5/51)-Crandall-a; Saunders painted-c	20	40	60	115	185	255
12(#3, 9/51)-Photo-c	16	32	48	94	147	200
4-8: 4,6,7-Photo-c	15	30	45	86	133	180
9-Kinstler-a; photo-c	16	32	48	92	144	195
10,11(Fall/'52): 10,11-Photo-c	15	30	45	86	133	180
12(St. John-10/53)-#13: 13-Painted-c.	15	30	45	85	130	175
14-Matt Baker-a	33	66	99	194	317	440
15(8/54)-Matt Baker-c	94	188	282	597	1024	1450
25(2nd Series)(Formerly Romantic Marriage) Classic Matt Baker-c	148	296	444	947	1624	2300
26-Matt Baker-c; last precode (2/55)	113	226	339	718	1234	1750
27-29: Matt Baker-c	94	188	282	597	1024	1450

CINDY COMICS (...Smith No. 39, 40; Crime Can't Win No. 41 on)(Formerly Krazy Komics) (See Junior Miss & Teen Comics)
Timely Comics: No. 27, Fall, 1947 - No. 40, July, 1950

	GD	VG	FN	VF	VF/NM	NM-
27-Kurtzman-a, 3 pgs: Margie, Oscar begin	47	94	141	296	498	700
28-31-Kurtzman-a	30	60	90	177	289	400
32-36,38-40: 33-Georgie story; anti-Wertham editorial. 39-Louise Altson painted-c	26	52	78	152	249	345
37-Classic greytone-c	350	700	1050	1750	2625	3500

NOTE: *Kurtzman's "Hey Look"-#27(3), 29(2), 30(2), 31; "Giggles 'n' Grins"-28.*

CINNAMON: EL CICLO
DC Comics: Oct, 2003 - No. 5, Feb, 2004 ($2.50, limited series)
1-5-Van Meter-s/Chaykin-c/Paronzini-a 3.00

CIRCUS (...the Comic Riot)
Globe Syndicate: June, 1938 - No. 3, Aug, 1938

	GD	VG	FN	VF	VF/NM	NM-
1-(Scarce)-Spacehawks (2 pgs.), & Disk Eyes by Wolverton (2 pgs.), Pewee Throttle by Cole (2nd comic book work; see Star Comics V1#11), Beau Gus, Ken Craig & The Lords of Crillon, Jack Hinton by Eisner, Van Bragger by Kane	508	1016	1524	3708	6554	9400
2,3-(Scarce)-Eisner, Cole, Wolverton, Bob Kane-a in each	297	594	891	1901	3251	4600

CIRCUS BOY (TV) (See Movie Classics)
Dell Publishing Co.: No. 759, Dec, 1956 - No. 813, July, 1957

	GD	VG	FN	VF	VF/NM	NM-
Four Color 759 (#1)-The Monkees' Mickey Dolenz photo-c	12	24	36	81	176	270
Four Color 785 (4/57), 813-Mickey Dolenz photo-c	9	18	27	62	126	190

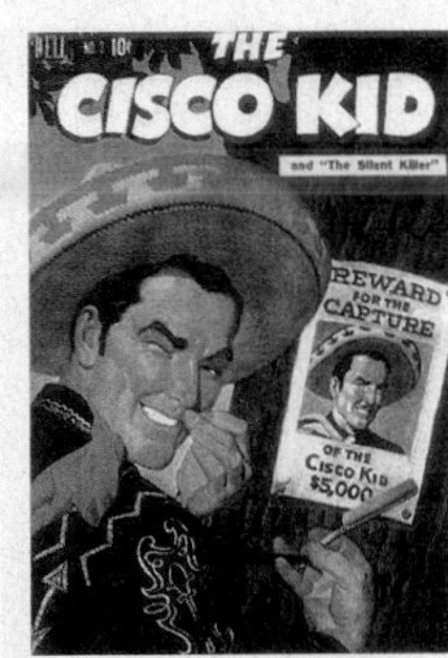

The Cisco Kid #3 © DELL

Civil War #6 © MAR

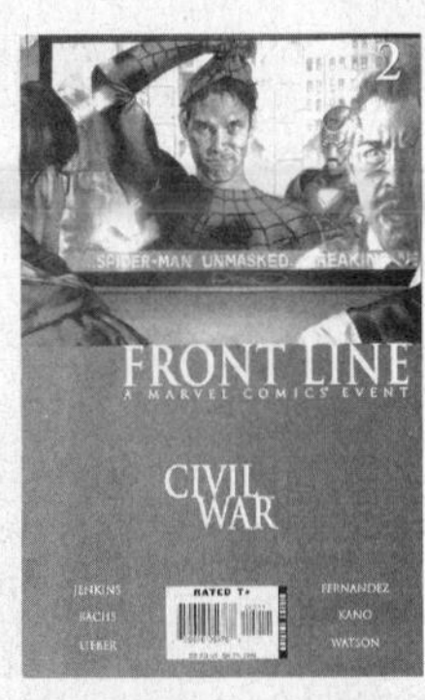

Civil War: Frontline #2 © MAR

CIRCUS COMICS
Farm Women's Pub. Co./D. S. Publ.: Apr, 1945 - No. 2, Jun, 1945; Wint., 1948-49

	GD 2.0	VG 4.0	FN 6.0	VF 8.0	VF/NM 9.0	NM- 9.2
1-Funny animal	16	32	48	92	144	195
2	11	22	33	62	86	110
1(1948)-D.S. Publ.; 2 pgs. Frazetta	27	54	81	158	259	360

CIRCUS OF FUN COMICS
A. W. Nugent Publ. Co.: 1945 - No. 3, Dec, 1947 (A book of games & puzzles)

	GD 2.0	VG 4.0	FN 6.0	VF 8.0	VF/NM 9.0	NM- 9.2
1	15	30	45	90	140	190
2,3	10	20	30	54	72	90

CISCO KID, THE (TV)
Dell Publishing Co.: July, 1950 - No. 41, Oct-Dec, 1958

	GD 2.0	VG 4.0	FN 6.0	VF 8.0	VF/NM 9.0	NM- 9.2
Four Color 292(#1)-Cisco Kid, his horse Diablo, & sidekick Pancho & his horse Loco begin; line drawn cover	21	42	63	147	324	500
2(1/51) Painted-c begin	10	20	30	64	132	200
3-5	9	18	27	59	117	175
6-10	8	16	24	51	96	140
11-20	7	14	21	44	82	120
21-36-Last painted-c	6	12	18	37	66	95
37-41: All photo-c	7	14	21	46	86	125

NOTE: ***Buscema** a-40. **Ernest Nordli** painted c-5-16, 20, 35.*

CISCO KID COMICS
Bernard Bailey/Swappers Quarterly: Winter, 1944 (one-shot)

	GD 2.0	VG 4.0	FN 6.0	VF 8.0	VF/NM 9.0	NM- 9.2
1-Illustrated Stories of the Operas: Faust; Funnyman by Giunta; Cisco Kid (1st app.) & Superbaby begin; Giunta-c	47	94	141	296	498	700

CITIZEN JACK
Image Comics: Nov, 2015 - No. 6, May, 2016 ($3.99, limited series)

	GD 2.0	VG 4.0	FN 6.0	VF 8.0	VF/NM 9.0	NM- 9.2
1-6-Sam Humphries-s/Tommy Patterson-a						4.00

CITIZEN SMITH (See Holyoke One-Shot No. 9)

CITIZEN V AND THE V-BATTALION (See Thunderbolts)
Marvel Comics: June, 2001 - No. 3, Aug, 2001 ($2.99, limited series)

	GD 2.0	VG 4.0	FN 6.0	VF 8.0	VF/NM 9.0	NM- 9.2
1-3-Nicieza-a; Michael Ryan-c/a						3.00
...: The Everlasting 1-4 (3/02 - No. 4, 7/02) Nicieza-s/LaRosa-a(p)						3.00

CITY OF HEROES (Online game)
Dark Horse Comics/Blue King Studios: Sept, 2002; May, 2004 - No. 7 ($2.95)

	GD 2.0	VG 4.0	FN 6.0	VF 8.0	VF/NM 9.0	NM- 9.2
1-(no cover price) Dakan-s/Zombo-a						3.00
1-7-($2.95)						3.00

CITY OF HEROES (Online game)
Image Comics: June, 2005 - No. 20, Aug, 2007 ($2.99)

	GD 2.0	VG 4.0	FN 6.0	VF 8.0	VF/NM 9.0	NM- 9.2
1-20: 1-Waid-s; Pérez-c. 6-Flip-c with City of Villains. 7-9-Jurgens-s						3.00

CITY OF OTHERS
Dark Horse Comics: Apr, 2007 - No. 4, Aug, 2007 ($2.99, limited series)

	GD 2.0	VG 4.0	FN 6.0	VF 8.0	VF/NM 9.0	NM- 9.2
1-4-Bernie Wrightson-a/c; Steve Niles & Wrightson-s						3.00
TPB (2/08, $14.95) r/#1-4; Wrightson sketch pages						15.00

CITY OF SILENCE
Image Comics: May, 2000 - No. 3, July, 2000 ($2.50)

	GD 2.0	VG 4.0	FN 6.0	VF 8.0	VF/NM 9.0	NM- 9.2
1-3-Ellis-s/Erskine-a						3.00
TPB (6/04, $9.95) r/#1-3; pin-up gallery						10.00

CITY OF THE LIVING DEAD (See Fantastic Tales No. 1)
Avon Periodicals: 1952

	GD 2.0	VG 4.0	FN 6.0	VF 8.0	VF/NM 9.0	NM- 9.2
nn-Hollingsworth-c/a	103	206	309	659	1130	1600

CITY OF TOMORROW
DC Comics (WildStorm): June, 2005 - No. 6, Nov, 2005 ($2.99, limited series)

	GD 2.0	VG 4.0	FN 6.0	VF 8.0	VF/NM 9.0	NM- 9.2
1-6-Howard Chaykin-s/a						3.00
TPB (2006, $19.99) r/#1-6						20.00

CITY PEOPLE NOTEBOOK
Kitchen Sink Press: 1989 ($9.95, B&W, magazine sized)

	GD 2.0	VG 4.0	FN 6.0	VF 8.0	VF/NM 9.0	NM- 9.2
nn-Will Eisner-s/a						15.00
nn-(DC Comics, 2000) Reprint						10.00

CITY SURGEON (Blake Harper...)
Gold Key: August, 1963

	GD 2.0	VG 4.0	FN 6.0	VF 8.0	VF/NM 9.0	NM- 9.2
1(10075-308)-Painted-c	4	8	12	23	37	50

CIVIL WAR (Also see Amazing Spider-Man for TPB)
Marvel Comics: July, 2006 - No. 7, Jan, 2007 ($3.99/$2.99, limited series)

	GD 2.0	VG 4.0	FN 6.0	VF 8.0	VF/NM 9.0	NM- 9.2
1-($3.99) Millar-s/McNiven-a & wraparound-c	2	4	6	11	16	20
1-Variant cover by Michael Turner	3	6	9	19	30	40
1-Aspen Comics Variant cover by Turner	3	6	9	19	30	40
1-Sketch Variant cover	4	8	12	23	37	50
1-Director's Cut (2006, $4.99) r/#1 plus promo art, variant covers, sketches and script	1	2	3	5	6	8
2-($2.99) Spider-Man unmasks	2	4	6	8	10	12
2-Turner variant cover	2	4	6	11	16	20
2-B&W sketch variant cover	3	6	9	17	26	35
2-2nd printing						5.00
3-7: 3-Thor returns. 4-Goliath killed	1	2	3	5	6	8
3-7-Turner variant covers	1	2	3	6	8	10
3-7-B&W sketch variant covers	3	6	9	14	20	25
TPB (2007, $24.99) r/#1-7; gallery of variant covers						25.00
...: Battle Damage Report (2007, $3.99) Post-Civil War character profiles; McGuinness-c						4.00
...: Choosing Sides (2/07, $3.99) Colan-c; Howard the Duck app.; 2 covers by Yu & Colan						5.00
... Companion TPB (2007, $13.99) r/Civil War Files, ...:Battle Damage Report, Marvel Spotlight: Millar/McNiven, Marvel Spotlight: Civil War Aftermath and Daily Bugle CW						14.00
Daily Bugle Civil War Newspaper Special #1 (9/06, 50¢, newsprint) Daily Bugle "newspaper" overview of the crossover; Mayhew-a						3.00
...Files (2006, $3.99) profile pages of major Civil War characters; McNiven-c						4.00
...: Marvels Snapshots 1 (2/21, $4.99) Ahmed-s/Kelly-a; Alex Ross-c; Captain America app.						5.00
...: Marvel Universe TPB (2007, $11.99) r/Civil War: Choosing Sides, CW: The Return, She-Hulk #8, CW: The Initiative; She-Hulk sketch page; variant cover gallery						12.00
...: MGC #1 (6/10, $1.00) r/#1 with "Marvel's Greatest Comics" cover logo						3.00
...: The Confession (5/07, $2.99) Maleev-c/a; Bendis-s						3.00
...: The Initiative (4/07, $4.99) Silvestri-c/a; previews of post-Civil War series						5.00
...: The Return (3/07, $2.99) Captain Marvel returns; The Sentry app.; Raney-a						3.00
...: The Road to Civil War TPB (2007, $14.99) r/New Avengers: Illuminati, Fantastic Four #536 & 537, Amazing Spider-Man #529-531; Spider-Man costume sketches by Bachalo						15.00
... War Crimes (2/07, $3.99) Kingpin in prison; Tieri-s/Staz Johnson-a						4.00
... War Crimes TPB (2007, $17.99) r/Civil War: War Crimes one-shot and Underworld #1-5						18.00
... X-Men Universe TPB (2007, $13.99) r/Cable & Deadpool #30-32; X-Factor #8,9						14.00

CIVIL WAR (Secret Wars tie-in)
Marvel Comics: Sept, 2015 - No. 5, Dec, 2015 ($4.99/$3.99, limited series)

	GD 2.0	VG 4.0	FN 6.0	VF 8.0	VF/NM 9.0	NM- 9.2
1-($4.99) Soule-s/Yu-a; Stark vs. Rogers on Battleworld						5.00
2-5-($3.99)						4.00

CIVIL WAR CHRONICLES (Reprints of Civil War and related Marvel issues)
Marvel Comics: Oct, 2007 - No. 12, Sept, 2008 ($4.99, limited series)

	GD 2.0	VG 4.0	FN 6.0	VF 8.0	VF/NM 9.0	NM- 9.2
1-12: Reprints Civil War, Civil War: Frontline and x-over issues						5.00

CIVIL WAR: FRONTLINE (Tie-in to Civil War and related Marvel issues)
Marvel Comics: Aug, 2006 - No. 11, Apr, 2007 ($2.99, limited series)

	GD 2.0	VG 4.0	FN 6.0	VF 8.0	VF/NM 9.0	NM- 9.2
1-Jenkins-s/Bachs-a/Watson-c; back-up stories by various						4.00
2-11: 3-Green Goblin app. 11-Aftermath of Civil War #7						3.00
... Book 1 TPB (2007, $14.99) r/#1-6						15.00
... Book 2 TPB (2007, $14.99) r/#7-11						15.00

CIVIL WAR: HOUSE OF M
Marvel Comics: Nov, 2008 - No. 5, Mar, 2009 ($2.99, limited series)

	GD 2.0	VG 4.0	FN 6.0	VF 8.0	VF/NM 9.0	NM- 9.2
1-5-Gage-s/DiVito-a						3.00

CIVIL WAR MUSKET, THE (Kadets of America Handbook)
Custom Comics, Inc.: 1960 (25¢, half-size, 36 pgs.)

	GD 2.0	VG 4.0	FN 6.0	VF 8.0	VF/NM 9.0	NM- 9.2
nn	3	6	9	15	22	28

CIVIL WAR II
Marvel Comics: No. 0, Jul, 2016 - No. 8, Feb, 2017 ($4.99/$5.99, limited series)

	GD 2.0	VG 4.0	FN 6.0	VF 8.0	VF/NM 9.0	NM- 9.2
0-($4.99) Bendis-s/Coipel-a; intro. Ulysses						5.00
1-($5.99) Bendis-s/Marquez-a; Thanos kills War Machine						6.00
2-8-($4.99) 3-Banner killed. 4,5-Guardians of the Galaxy app. 7-Sorrentino-a (2 pgs.)						5.00
...: The Oath 1 (3/17, $4.99) Spencer-s; Capt. America named Director of SHIELD						5.00

CIVIL WAR II: AMAZING SPIDER-MAN
Marvel Comics: Aug, 2016 - No. 4, Nov, 2016 ($3.99, limited series)

	GD 2.0	VG 4.0	FN 6.0	VF 8.0	VF/NM 9.0	NM- 9.2
1-4-Gage-s/Foreman-a; Ulysses app.; Clash returns						4.00

CIVIL WAR II: CHOOSING SIDES
Marvel Comics: Aug, 2016 - No. 6, Nov, 2016 ($4.99/$3.99, limited series)

	GD 2.0	VG 4.0	FN 6.0	VF 8.0	VF/NM 9.0	NM- 9.2
1-($4.99) Short stories; Nick Fury, Night Thrasher & Damage Control app.						5.00
2-6-($3.99) Nick Fury story in all. 2-War Machine. 4-Punisher. 6-Jessica Jones						4.00

CIVIL WAR II: GODS OF WAR
Marvel Comics: Aug, 2016 - No. 4, Nov, 2016 ($3.99, limited series)

	GD 2.0	VG 4.0	FN 6.0	VF 8.0	VF/NM 9.0	NM- 9.2
1-4-Abnett-s/Laiso-a/Anacleto-c. 1-Amadeus Cho app. 3-Avengers app.						4.00

CIVIL WAR II: KINGPIN
Marvel Comics: Sept, 2016 - No. 4, Dec, 2016 ($4.99/$3.99, limited series)

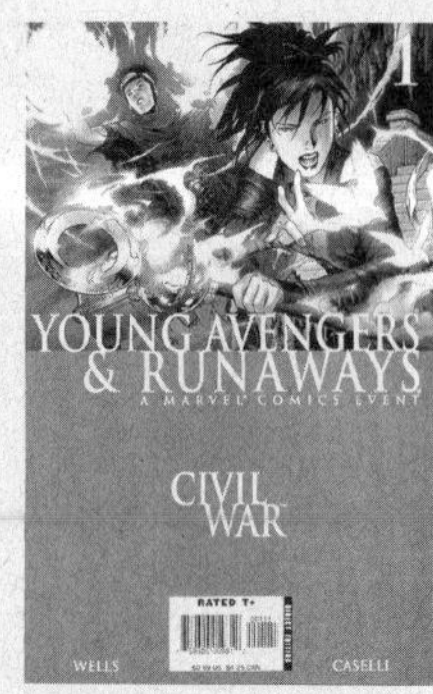

Civil War: Young Avengers & Runaways #1 © MAR

Clandestine #4 © MAR

Clash #1 © Tom Veitch & Adam Kubert

	GD 2.0	VG 4.0	FN 6.0	VF 8.0	VF/NM 9.0	NM- 9.2
1-($4.99) Two stories; Rosenberg-s/Ortiz-a; Talajic-a; intro./origin Janus Jardeesh						5.00
2-4-($3.99) Rosenberg-s/Ortiz-a. 3-Punisher app.						4.00

CIVIL WAR II: ULYSSES
Marvel Comics: Oct, 2016 - No. 3, Dec, 2016 ($4.99, limited series)

1-3-Ewing-s/Kesel & Palo-a/Francavilla-c; Karnak and the Inhumans app. 4.00

CIVIL WAR II: X-MEN
Marvel Comics: Aug, 2016 - No. 4, Nov, 2016 ($3.99, limited series)

1-4-Bunn-s/Broccardo-a; Magneto app. 2-The Brood & Fantomex app. 4-Ulysses app. 4.00

CIVIL WAR: X-MEN (Tie-in to Civil War)
Marvel Comics: Sept, 2006 - No. 4, Dec, 2006 ($2.99, limited series)

1-4-Paquette-a/Hine-s; Bishop app. 3.00
1-Variant cover by Michael Turner 10.00
TPB (2007, $11.99) r/#1-4, profile pages of minor characters 12.00

CIVIL WAR: YOUNG AVENGERS & RUNAWAYS (Tie-in to Civil War)
Marvel Comics: Sept, 2006 - No. 4, Dec, 2006 ($2.99, limited series)

1-4-Caselli-a/Wells-s/Cheung-c 3.00
TPB (2007, $11.99) r/#1-4, profile pages of characters 12.00

CLAIRE VOYANT (Also see Keen Teens)
Leader Publ./Standard/Pentagon Publ.: 1946 - No. 4, 1947 (Sparling strip reprints)

	GD	VG	FN	VF	VF/NM	NM-
nn	94	188	282	597	1024	1450
2-Kamen-c	71	142	213	454	777	1100
3-Kamen bridal-c; contents mentioned in Love and Death, a book by Gershom Legman(1949) referenced by Dr. Wertham in **SOTI**	103	206	309	659	1130	1600
4-Kamen bondage-c	90	180	270	576	988	1400

CLANDESTINE (Also see Marvel Comics Presents & X-Men: ClanDestine)
Marvel Comics: Oct, 1994 - No.12, Sept, 1995 ($2.95/$2.50)

1-($2.95)-Alan Davis-c/a(p)/scripts & Mark Farmer-c/a(i) begin, ends #8; Modok app.; Silver Surfer cameo; gold foil-c 4.00
2-12: 2-Wraparound-c. 2,3-Silver Surfer app. 5-Origin of ClanDestine. 6-Capt. America, Hulk, Spider-Man, Thing & Thor-c; Spider-Man cameo. 7-Spider-Man-c/app; Punisher cameo. 8-Invaders & Dr. Strange app. 10-Captain Britain-c/app. 11-Sub-Mariner app. 3.00
Preview (10/94, $1.50) 3.00
... Classic HC (2008, $29.99, DJ) r/#1-8, Marvel Comics Presents #158, X-Men and Clandestine #1&2, sketch pages and cover gallery; Alan Davis afterword 30.00

CLANDESTINE
Marvel Comics: Apr, 2008 - No. 5, Aug, 2008 ($2.99, limited series)

1-5: 1-Alan Davis-c/a(p)/scripts & Mark Farmer-c/a(i). 2-5-Excalibur app. 3.00

CLARENCE (Based on the Cartoon Network series)
BOOM! Studios (kaboom): Jun, 2015 - No. 4, Sept, 2015 ($3.99)

1-4-Short stories by various; multiple covers on each 4.00
...: Quest 1 (6/16, $4.99) Cron-DeVico-s; art by Smigiel & Omac 5.00
...: Rest Stops 1 (12/15, $4.99) Short stories by various; two covers 5.00

CLANKILLERS
AfterShock Comics: Jul, 2018 - No. 5, Dec, 2018 ($3.99, limited series)

1-5-Sean Lewis-s/Antonio Fuso-a 4.00

CLASH
DC Comics: 1991 - No. 3, 1991 ($4.95, limited series, 52 pgs.)

Book One - Three: Adam Kubert-c/a 5.00

CLASSIC BATTLESTAR GALACTICA (See Battlestar Galactica, Classic...)

CLASSIC COMICS/ILLUSTRATED - INTRODUCTION
by Dan Malan

Since the first publication of this special introduction to the **Classics** section, a number of revisions have been made to further clarify the listings. **Classics** reprint editions prior to 1963 had either incorrect dates or no dates listed. Those reprint editions should be identified only by the highest number on the reorder list (HRN). Past *Guides* listed what were calculated to be approximately correct dates, but many people found it confusing for the *Guide* to list a date not listed in the comic itself.

We have also attempted to clear up confusion about edition variations, such as color, printer, etc. Such variations are identified by letters. Editions are determined by three categories. Original edition variations are designated as Edition 1A, 1B, etc. All reprint editions prior to 1963 are identified by HRN only. All reprint editions from 9/63 on are identified by the correct date listed in the comic.

Information is also included on four reprintings of **Classics**. From 1968-1976, Twin Circle, the Catholic newspaper, serialized over 100 **Classics** titles. That list can be found under non-series items at the end of this section. In 1972, twelve **Classics** were reissued as **Now Age Books Illustrated**. They are listed under **Pendulum Illustrated Classics**. In 1982, 20 **Classics** were reissued, adapted for teaching English as a second language. They are listed under **Regents Illustrated Classics**. Then in 1984, six **Classics** were reissued with cassette tapes. See the listing under **Cassette Books**.

UNDERSTANDING CLASSICS ILLUSTRATED
by Dan Malan

Since **Classics Illustrated** is the most complicated comic book series, with all its reprint editions and variations, changes in covers and artwork, a variety of means of identifying editions, and the most extensive worldwide distribution of any comic-book series, this introductory section is provided to assist you in gaining expertise about this series.

THE HISTORY OF CLASSICS

The **Classics** series was the brain child of Albert L. Kanter, who saw in the new comic-book medium a means of introducing children to the great classics of literature. In October of 1941 his Gilberton Co. began the **Classic Comics** series with **The Three Musketeers**, with 64 pages of storyline. In those early years, the struggling series saw irregular schedules and numerous printers, not to mention variable art quality and liberal story adaptations. With No.13 the page total was reduced to 56 (except for No. 33, originally scheduled to be No. 9), and with No. 15 the coming-next ad on the outside back cover moved inside. In 1945 the Jerry Iger Shop began producing all new CC titles, beginning with No. 23. In 1947 the search for a classier logo resulted in **Classics Illustrated**, beginning with No. 35, **Last Days of Pompeii**. With No. 45 the page total dropped again to 48, which was to become the standard.

Two new developments in 1951 had a profound effect upon the success of the series. One was the introduction of painted covers, instead of the old line drawn covers, beginning with No. 81, **The Odyssey**. The second was the switch to the major national distributor Curtis. They raised the cover price from 10 to 15 cents, making it the highest priced comic-book, but it did not slow the growth of the series, because they were marketed as books, not comics. Because of this higher quality image, **Classics** flourished during the fifties while other comic series were reeling from outside attacks. They diversified with their new **Juniors**, **Specials**, and **World Around Us** series.

Classics artwork can be divided into three distinct periods. The pre-Iger era (1941-44) was mentioned above for its variable art quality. The Iger era (1945-53) was a major improvement in art quality and adaptations. It came to be dominated by artists Henry Kiefer and Alex Blum, together accounting for some 50 titles. Their styles gave the first real personality to the series. The EC era (1954-62) resulted from the demise of the EC horror series, when many of their artists made the major switch to classical art.

But several factors brought the production of new CI titles to a complete halt in 1962. Gilberton lost its 2nd class mailing permit. External factors like television, cheap paperback books, and Cliff Notes were all eating away at their market. Production halted with No.167, **Faust**, even though many more titles were already in the works. Many of those found their way into foreign series, and are very desirable to collectors. In 1967, **Classics Illustrated** was sold to Patrick Frawley and his Catholic publication, Twin Circle. They issued two new titles in 1969 as part of an attempted revival, but succumbed to major distribution problems in 1971. In 1988, First Publishing acquired the rights to use the old CI series art, logo, and name from the Frawley Group, and released a short-lived series featuring contributions of modern creators. Acclaim Books and Twin Circles issued a series of **Classics** reprints from 1997-1998.

One of the unique aspects of the **Classics Illustrated** (CI) series was the proliferation of reprint variations. Some titles had as many as 25 editions. Reprinting began in 1943. Some **Classic Comics** (CC) reprints (r) had the logo format revised to a banner logo, and added a motto under the banner. In 1947 CC titles changed to the CI logo, but kept their line drawn covers (LDC). In 1948, Nos. 13, 18, 29 and 41 received second covers (LDC2), replacing covers considered too violent, and reprints of Nos. 13-44 had pages reduced to 48, except for No. 26, which had 48 pages to begin with.

Starting in the mid-1950s, 70 of the 80 LDC titles were reissued with new painted covers (PC). Thirty of them also received new interior artwork (A2). The new artwork was generally higher quality with larger art panels and more faithful but abbreviated storylines. Later on, there were 29 second painted covers (PC2), mostly by Twin Circle. Altogether there were 199 interior art variations (169 (O)s and 30 A2 editions) and 272 different covers (169 (O)s, four LDC2s, 70 new PCs of LDC (O)s, and 29 PC2s). It is mildly astounding to realize that there are nearly 1400 different editions in the U.S. CI series.

FOREIGN CLASSICS ILLUSTRATED

If U.S. Classics variations are mildly astounding, the veritable plethora of foreign CI variations will boggle your imagination. While we still anticipate additional discoveries, we presently know about series in 25 languages and 27 countries. There were 250 new CI titles in foreign series, and nearly 400 new foreign covers of U.S. titles. The 1400 U.S. CI editions pale in comparison to the 4000 plus foreign editions. The very nature of CI lent itself to flourishing as an international series. Worldwide, they published over one billion copies! The first foreign CI series consisted of six Canadian Classic Comic reprints in 1946.

The following chart shows when CI series first began in each country:
1946: Canada. 1947: Australia. 1948: Brazil/The Netherlands. 1950: Italy. 1951: Greece/Japan/ Hong Kong(?)/England/Argentina/Mexico. 1952: West Germany. 1954: Norway. 1955: New Zealand/South Africa. 1956: Denmark/Sweden/Iceland. 1957: Finland/France. 1962: Singapore(?). 1964: India (8 languages). 1971: Ireland (Gaelic). 1973: Belgium(?) / Philippines(?) & Malaysia(?).

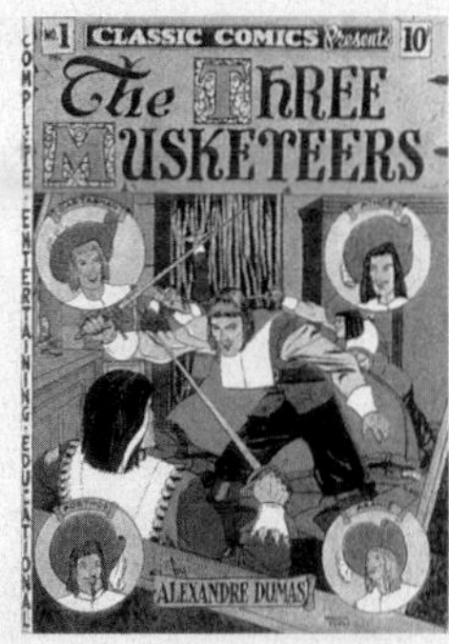

Classic Comics #1 © GIL

Classic Comics #2 © GIL

Classic Comics #3 © GIL

	GD	VG	FN	VF	VF/NM	NM-
	2.0	4.0	6.0	8.0	9.0	9.2

Significant among the early series were Brazil and Greece. In 1950, Brazil was the first country to begin doing its own new titles. They issued nearly 80 new CI titles by Brazilian authors. In Greece in 1951 they actually had debates in parliament about the effects of Classics Illustrated on Greek culture, leading to the inclusion of 88 new Greek History & Mythology titles in the CI series.

But by far the most important foreign CI development was the joint European series which began in 1956 in 10 countries simultaneously. By 1960, CI had the largest European distribution of any American publication, not just comics! So when all the problems came up with U.S. distribution, they literally moved the CI operation to Europe in 1962, and continued producing new titles in all four CI series. Many of them were adapted and drawn in the U.S., the most famous of which was the British CI #158A. Dr. No, drawn by Norman Nodel. Unfortunately, the British CI series ended in late 1963, which limited the European CI titles available in English to 15. Altogether there were 82 new CI art titles in the joint European series, which ran until 1976.

IDENTIFYING CLASSICS EDITIONS

HRN: This is the highest number on the reorder list. It should be listed in ( ) after the title number. It is crucial to understanding various CI editions.

ORIGINALS (O): This is the all-important First Edition. To determine (O)s,there is one primary rule and two secondary rules (with exceptions):

Rule No. 1: All (O)s and only (O)s have coming-next ads for the next number. **Exceptions**: No. 14(15) (reprint) has an ad on the last inside text page only. No. 14(0) also has a full-page outside back cover ad (also rule 2). Nos.55(75) and 57(75) have coming-next ads. (Rules 2 and 3 apply here). Nos. 168(0) and 169(0) do not have coming-next ads. No.168 was never reprinted; No. 169(0) has HRN (166). No. 169(169) is the only reprint.

Rule No. 2: On nos.1-80, all (O)s and only (O)s list 10c on the front cover. **Exceptions**: Reprint variations of Nos. 37(62), 39(71), and 46(62) list 10c on the front cover. (Rules 1 and 3 apply here.)

Rule No. 3: All (O)s have HRN close to that title No. **Exceptions**: Some reprints also have HRNs close to that title number: a few CC(r)s, 58(62), 60(62), 149(149), 152(149) 153(149), and title nos. in the 160's. (Rules 1 and 2 apply here.)

DATES: Many reprint editions list either an incorrect date or no date. Since Gilberton apparently kept track of CI editions by HRN, they often left the (O) date on reprints. Often, someone with a CI collection for sale will swear that all their copies are originals. That is why we are so detailed in pointing out how to identify original editions. Except for original editions, which should have a coming-next ad, etc., all CI dates prior to 1963 are incorrect! So you want to go by HRN only if it is (165) or below, and go by listed date if it is 1963 or later. There are a few (167) editions with incorrect dates. They could be listed either as (167) or (62/3), which is meant to indicate that they were issued sometime between late 1962 and early 1963.

COVERS: A change from CC to LDC indicates a logo change, not a cover change; while a change from LDC to LDC2, LDC to PC, or from PC to PC2 does indicate a new cover. New PCs can be identified by HRN, and PC2s can be identified by HRN and date. Several covers had color changes, particularly from purple to blue.

Notes: If you see 15 cents in Canada on a front cover, it does not necessarily indicate a Canadian edition. Editions with an HRN between 44 and 75, with 15 cents on the cover are Canadian. Check the publisher's address. An HRN listing two numbers with a / between them indicates that there are two different reorder lists in the front and back covers. Official Twin Circle editions have a full-page back cover ad for their TC magazine, with no CI reorder list. Any CI with just a Twin Circle sticker on the front is not an official TC edition.

TIPS ON LISTING CLASSICS FOR SALE

It may be easy to just list Edition 17, but Classics collectors keep track of CI editions in terms of HRN and/or date, (O) or (r), CC or LDC, PC or PC2, A1 or A2, soft or stiff cover, etc. Try to help them out. For originals, just list (0), unless there are variations such as color (Nos. 10 and 61), printer (Nos. 18-22), HRN (Nos. 95, 108, 160), etc. For reprints, just list HRN if it's (165) or below. Above that, list HRN and date. Also, please list type of logo/cover/art for the convenience of buyers. They will appreciate it.

CLASSIC COMICS (Also see Best from Boys Life, Cassette Books, Famous Stories, Fast Fiction, Golden Picture Classics, King Classics, Marvel Classics Comics, Pendulum Illustrated Classics, Picture Parade, Picture Progress, Regents Ill. Classics, Spitfire, Stories by Famous Authors, Superior Stories, and World Around Us.)

CLASSIC COMICS (Classics Illustrated No. 35 on)
Elliot Publishing #1-3 (1941-1942)/Gilberton Publications #4-167 (1942-1967) /Twin Circle Pub. (Frawley) #168-169 (1968-1971):
10/41 - No. 34, 2/47; No. 35, 3/47 - No. 169, Spring 1969
(Reprint Editions of almost all titles 5/43 - Spring 1971)
(Painted Covers (0)s No. 81 on, and (r)s of most Nos. 1-80)

Abbreviations:
A–Art; C or c–Cover; CC–Classic Comics; CI–Classics Ill.; Ed–Edition; LDC–Line Drawn Cover; PC–Painted Cover; r–Reprint

1. The Three Musketeers

Ed	HRN	Date	Details	A	C	GD 2.0	VG 4.0	FN 6.0	VF 8.0	VF/NM 9.0	NM- 9.2
1	–	10/41	Date listed-1941; Elliot Pub; 68 pgs.	1	1	516	1032	1548	3767	6659	9550
2	10	–	10¢ price removed on all (r)s; Elliot Pub; CC-r	1	1	37	74	111	222	361	500
3	15	–	Long Isl. Ind. Ed.; CC-r	1	1	26	52	78	154	252	350
4	18/20	–	Sunrise Times Ed.; CC-r	1	1	19	38	57	109	172	235
5	21	–	Richmond Courier Ed.; CC-r	1	1	17	34	51	98	154	210
6	28	1946	CC-r	1	1	14	28	42	80	115	150
7	36	–	LDC-r	1	1	8	16	24	42	54	65
8	60	–	LDC-r	1	1	6	12	18	27	33	38
9	64	–	LDC-r	1	1	5	10	15	22	26	30
10	78	–	C-price 15¢;LDC-r	1	1	4	9	13	18	22	26
11	93	–	LDC-r	1	1	4	9	13	18	22	26
12	114	–	Last LDC-r	1	1	4	8	11	16	19	22
13	134	–	New-c; old-a; 64 pg. PC-r	1	2	3	6	9	18	28	38
14	143	–	Old-a; PC-r; 64 pg.	1	2	2	4	6	11	16	20
15	150	–	New-a; PC-r; Evans/Crandall-a	2	2	3	6	9	16	24	32
16	149	–	PC-r	2	2	2	4	6	8	11	14
17	167	–	PC-r	2	2	2	4	6	8	11	14
18	167	4/64	PC-r	2	2	2	4	6	8	11	14
19	167	1/65	PC-r	2	2	2	4	6	8	11	14
20	167	3/66	PC-r	2	2	2	4	6	8	11	14
21	166	11/67	PC-r	2	2	2	4	6	8	11	14
22	166	Spr/69	C-price 25¢ ; stiff-c; PC-r	2	2	2	4	6	8	11	14
23	169	Spr/71	PC-r; stiff-c	2	2	2	4	6	8	11	14

2. Ivanhoe

Ed	HRN	Date	Details	A	C	GD 2.0	VG 4.0	FN 6.0	VF 8.0	VF/NM 9.0	NM- 9.2
1	(O)	12/41?	Date listed-1941; Elliot Pub; 68 pgs.	1	1	245	490	735	1568	2684	3800
2	10	–	Price & 'Presents' removed; Elliot Pub; CC-r	1	1	32	64	96	188	307	425
3	15	–	Long Isl. Ind. ed.; CC-r	1	1	21	42	63	124	202	280
4	18/20	–	Sunrise Times ed.; CC-r	1	1	18	36	54	103	162	225
5	21	–	Richmond Courier ed.; CC-r	1	1	16	32	48	94	147	200
6	28	1946	Last 'Comics'-r	1	1	14	28	42	80	115	150
7	36	–	1st LDC-r	1	1	9	18	27	47	61	75
8	60	–	LDC-r	1	1	6	12	18	27	33	38
9	64	–	LDC-r	1	1	5	10	15	22	26	30
10	78	–	C-price 15¢; LDC-r	1	1	4	9	13	18	22	26
11	89	–	LDC-r	1	1	4	8	12	17	21	24
12	106	–	LDC-r	1	1	4	7	10	14	17	20
13	121	–	Last LDC-r	1	1	4	7	10	14	17	20
14	136	–	New-c&a; PC-r	2	2	5	10	15	25	31	36
15	142	–	PC-r	2	2	2	4	6	9	13	16
16	153	–	PC-r	2	2	2	4	6	9	13	16
17	149	–	PC-r	2	2	2	4	6	9	13	16
18	167	–	PC-r	2	2	2	4	6	8	11	14
19	167	5/64	PC-r	2	2	2	4	6	8	11	14
20	167	1/65	PC-r	2	2	2	4	6	8	11	14
21	167	3/66	PC-r	2	2	2	4	6	8	11	14
22A	166	9/67	PC-r	2	2	2	4	6	8	11	14
22B	166	–	Center ad for Children's Digest & Young Miss; rare; PC-r	2	2	6	12	18	40	73	105
23	166	R/68	C-Price 25¢; PC-r	2	2	2	4	6	8	11	14
24	169	Win/69	Stiff-c	2	2	2	4	6	8	11	14
25	169	Win/71	PC-r; stiff-c	2	2	2	4	6	8	11	14

3. The Count of Monte Cristo

Ed	HRN	Date	Details	A	C	GD 2.0	VG 4.0	FN 6.0	VF 8.0	VF/NM 9.0	NM- 9.2
1	(O)	3/42	Elliot Pub; 68 pgs.	1	1	161	322	483	1030	1765	2500
2	10	–	Conray Prods; CC-r1		1	29	58	87	170	278	385
3	15	–	Long Isl. Ind. ed.; CC-r	1	1	22	44	66	128	209	290
4	18/20	–	Sunrise Times ed.; CC-r	1	1	19	38	57	111	176	240

Classic Comics #4 © GIL

Classic Comics #5 © GIL

Classic Comics #7 © GIL

Ed	HRN	Date	Details	A	C	GD 2.0	VG 4.0	FN 6.0	VF 8.0	VF/NM 9.0	NM- 9.2
5	20	–	Sunrise Times ed.; CC-r	1	1	17	34	51	98	154	210
6	21	–	Richmond Courier ed.; CC-r	1	1	16	32	48	94	147	200
7	28	1946	CC-r; new Banner logo	1	1	14	28	42	80	115	150
8	36	–	1st LDC-r	1	1	9	18	27	47	61	75
9	60	–	LDC-r	1	1	6	12	18	27	33	38
10	62	–	LDC-r	1	1	6	12	18	29	36	42
11	71	–	LDC-r	1	1	5	10	14	20	24	28
12	87	–	C-price 15¢; LDC-r	1	1	4	9	13	18	22	26
13	113	–	LDC-r	1	1	4	7	10	14	17	20
14	135	–	New-c&a; PC-r; Cameron-a	2	2	3	6	9	17	26	35
15	143	–	PC-r	2	2	2	4	6	8	13	16
16	153	–	PC-r	2	2	2	4	6	8	13	
16											
17	161	–	PC-r	2	2	2	4	6	8	13	16
18	167	–	PC-r	2	2	2	4	6	8	11	14
19	167	7/64	PC-r	2	2	2	4	6	8	11	14
20	167	7/65	PC-r	2	2	2	4	6	8	11	14
21	167	7/66	PC-r	2	2	2	4	6	8	11	14
22	166	R/68	C-price 25¢; PC-r	2	2	2	4	6	8	11	14
23	169	–	Win/69 Stiff-c; PC-r	2	2	2	4	6	8	11	14

4. The Last of the Mohicans

Ed	HRN	Date	Details	A	C	GD 2.0	VG 4.0	FN 6.0	VF 8.0	VF/NM 9.0	NM- 9.2
1	(O)	8/42	Date listed-1942; Gilberton #4(0) on; 68 pgs.	1	1	139	278	417	883	1517	2150
2	12	–	Elliot Pub; CC-r	1	1	27	54	81	158	259	360
3	15	–	Long Isl. Ind. ed.; CC-r	1	1	20	40	60	120	195	270
4	20	–	Long Isl. Ind. ed.; CC-r; banner logo	1	1	18	36	54	105	165	225
5	21	–	Queens Home News ed.; CC-r	1	1	16	32	48	94	147	200
6	28	1946	Last CC-r; new	1	1	14	28	42	80	115	150
7	36	–	1st LDC-r	1	1	9	18	27	47	61	75
8	60	–	LDC-r	1	1	6	12	18	27	33	38
9	64	–	LDC-r	1	1	5	10	14	20	24	28
10	78	–	C-price 15¢; LDC-r	1	1	4	9	13	18	22	26
11	89	–	LDC-r	1	1	4	8	12	17	21	24
12	117	–	Last LDC-r	1	1	4	7	10	14	17	20
13	135	–	New-c; PC-r	1	2	5	10	15	24	30	35
14	141	–	PC-r	1	2	4	7	9	14	16	18
15	150	–	New-a; PC-r; Severin, L.B. Cole-a	2	2	6	12	18	27	33	38
16	161	–	PC-r	2	2	2	4	6	8	11	14
17	167	–	PC-r	2	2	2	4	6	8	11	14
18	167	6/64	PC-r	2	2	2	4	6	8	11	14
19	167	8/65	PC-r	2	2	2	4	6	8	11	14
20	167	8/66	PC-r	2	2	2	4	6	8	11	14
21	166	R/67	C-price 25¢; PC-r	2	2	2	4	6	8	11	14
22	169	Spr/69	Stiff-c; PC-r	2	2	2	4	6	8	11	14

5. Moby Dick

Ed	HRN	Date	Details	A	C	GD 2.0	VG 4.0	FN 6.0	VF 8.0	VF/NM 9.0	NM- 9.2
1A	(O)	9/42	Date listed-1942; Gilberton; 68 pgs.	1	1	171	342	513	1086	1868	2650
1B			inside-c, rare free promo			258	516	774	1651	2826	4000
2	10	–	Conray Prods; Pg. 64 changed from 105 title list to letter from Editor; CC-r	1	1	28	56	84	165	270	375
3	15	–	Long Isl. Ind. ed.; Pg. 64 changed from Letter to the Editor to Ill. poem-Concord Hymn; CC-r	1	1	23	46	69	136	223	310
4	18/20	–	Sunrise Times ed.; CC-r	1	1	19	38	57	109	172	235
5	20	–	Sunrise Times ed.; CC-r	1	1	18	36	54	105	165	225
6	21	–	Sunrise Times ed.; CC-r	1	1	16	32	48	94	147	200
7	28	1946	CC-r; new banner logo	1	1	14	28	42	81	118	155
8	36	–	1st LDC-r	1	1	9	18	27	47	61	75
9	60	–	LDC-r	1	1	6	12	18	27	33	38
10	62	–	LDC-r	1	1	6	12	18	29	36	42
11	71	–	LDC-r	1	1	5	10	15	22	26	30
12	87	–	C-price 15¢; LDC-r	1	1	5	10	14	20	24	28
13	118	–	LDC-r	1	1	4	8	12	17	21	24
14	131	–	New c&a; PC-r	2	2	5	10	15	25	31	36
15	138	–	PC-r	2	2	2	4	6	9	12	16
16	148	–	PC-r	2	2	2	4	6	9	12	16
17	158	–	PC-r	2	2	2	4	6	9	12	16
18	167	–	PC-r	2	2	2	4	6	8	11	14
19	167	6/64	PC-r	2	2	2	4	6	8	11	14
20	167	7/65	PC-r	2	2	2	4	6	8	11	14
21	167	3/66	PC-r	2	2	2	4	6	8	11	14
22	166	9/67	PC-r	2	2	2	4	6	8	11	14
23	166	Win/69	New-c & c-price 25¢; Stiff-c; PC-r	2	3	3	6	9	16	23	30
24	169	Win/71	PC-r	2	3	3	6	9	14	19	24

6. A Tale of Two Cities

Ed	HRN	Date	Details	A	C	GD 2.0	VG 4.0	FN 6.0	VF 8.0	VF/NM 9.0	NM- 9.2
1	(O)	10/42	Date listed-1942; 68 pgs. Zeckerberg c/a	1	1	132	264	396	838	1444	2050
2	14	–	Elliot Pub; CC-r	1	1	24	48	72	142	234	325
3	18	–	Long Isl. Ind. ed.; CC-r	1	1	20	40	60	114	182	250
4	20	–	Sunrise Times ed.; CC-r	1	1	18	36	54	105	165	225
5	28	1946	Last CC-r; new banner logo	1	1	14	28	42	80	115	150
6	51	–	1st LDC-r	1	1	8	16	24	42	54	65
7	64	–	LDC-r	1	1	5	10	15	23	28	32
8	78	–	C-price 15¢; LDC-r	1	1	5	10	14	20	24	28
9	89	–	LDC-r	1	1	4	7	10	14	17	20
10	117	–	LDC-r	1	1	4	7	10	14	17	20
11	132	–	New-c&a; PC-r; Joe Orlando-a	2	2	5	10	15	25	31	36
12	140	–	PC-r	2	2	2	4	6	8	11	14
13	147	–	PC-r	2	2	2	4	6	8	11	14
14	152	–	PC-r; very rare	2	2	17	34	51	98	154	210
15	153	–	PC-r	2	2	2	4	6	9	13	16
16	149	–	PC-r	2	2	2	4	6	9	13	16
17	167	–	PC-r	2	2	2	4	6	8	11	14
18	167	6/64	PC-r	2	2	2	4	6	8	11	14
19	167	8/65	PC-r	2	2	2	4	6	8	11	14
20	166	5/67	PC-r	2	2	2	4	6	8	11	14
21	166	Fall/68	New-c & 25¢; PC-r	2	3	3	6	9	16	24	32
22	169	Sum/70	Stiff-c; PC-r	2	3	2	4	6	13	18	22

7. Robin Hood

Ed	HRN	Date	Details	A	C	GD 2.0	VG 4.0	FN 6.0	VF 8.0	VF/NM 9.0	NM- 9.2
1	(O)	12/42	Date listed-1942; first Gift Box ad-bc; 68 pgs.	1	1	102	204	306	648	1112	1575
2	12	–	Elliot Pub; CC-r	1	1	24	48	72	140	230	320
3	18	–	Long Isl. Ind. ed.; CC-r	1	1	19	38	57	111	176	240
4	20	–	Nassau Bulletin ed.; CC-r	1	1	18	36	54	103	162	220
5	22	–	Queens Cty. Times ed.; CC-r	1	1	16	32	48	94	147	200
6	28	–	CC-r	1	1	14	28	42	81	118	155
7	51	–	LDC-r	1	1	8	16	24	42	54	65
8	64	–	LDC-r	1	1	5	10	15	24	30	35
9	78	–	LDC-r	1	1	4	9	13	18	22	26
10	97	–	LDC-r	1	1	4	8	12	17	21	24
11	106	–	LDC-r	1	1	4	7	10	14	17	20
12	121	–	LDC-r	1	1	4	7	10	14	17	20
13	129	–	New-c; PC-r	1	2	5	10	15	25	31	36
14	136	–	New-a; PC-r	2	2	5	10	15	24	29	34
15	143	–	PC-r	2	2	2	4	6	9	13	16

Classic Comics #10 © GIL

Classic Comics #12 © GIL

Classic Comics #13 © GIL

Ed	HRN	Date	Details	A	C	GD 2.0	VG 4.0	FN 6.0	VF 8.0	VF/NM 9.0	NM- 9.2
16	153	–	PC-r	2	2	2	4	6	9	13	16
17	164	–	PC-r	2	2	2	4	6	8	11	14
18	167	–	PC-r	2	2	2	4	6	8	11	14
19	167	6/64	PC-r	2	2	2	4	6	8	11	14
20	167	5/65	PC-r	2	2	2	4	6	8	11	14
21	167	7/66	PC-r	2	2	2	4	6	8	11	14
22	166	12/67	PC-r	2	2	2	4	6	8	11	14
23	169	Sum/69	Stiff-c; c-price 25¢; PC-r	2	2	2	4	6	8	11	14

8. Arabian Nights

Ed	HRN	Date	Details	A	C	GD 2.0	VG 4.0	FN 6.0	VF 8.0	VF/NM 9.0	NM- 9.2
1	(O)	2/43	Original; 68 pgs. Lilian Chestney-c/a	1	1	152	304	456	965	1658	2350
2	17	–	Long Isl. ed.; pg. 64 changed from Gift Box ad to Letter from British Medical Worker; CC-r	1	1	52	104	156	323	549	775
3	20	–	Nassau Bulletin; Pg. 64 changed from letter to article-Three Men Named Smith; CC-r	1	1	42	84	126	265	445	625
4A	28	1946	CC-r; new banner logo, slick-c	1	1	31	62	93	182	296	410
4B	28	1946	Same, but w/stiff-c	1	1	31	62	93	182	296	410
5	51	–	LDC-r	1	1	22	44	66	128	209	290
6	64	–	LDC-r	1	1	19	38	57	111	176	240
7	78	–	LDC-r	1	1	18	36	54	105	165	225
8	164	–	New-c&a; PC-r	2	2	15	30	45	90	140	190

9. Les Miserables

Ed	HRN	Date	Details	A	C	GD 2.0	VG 4.0	FN 6.0	VF 8.0	VF/NM 9.0	NM- 9.2
1A	(O)	3/43	Original; slick paper cover; 68 pgs.	1	1	103	206	309	659	1130	1600
1B	(O)	3/43	Original; rough, pulp type-c; 68 pgs.	1	1	123	246	369	787	1344	1900
2	14	–	Elliot Pub; CC-r	1	1	26	52	78	154	252	350
3	18	3/44	Nassau Bul. Pg. 64 changed from Gift Box ad to Bill of Rights article; CC-r	1	1	22	44	66	128	209	290
4	20	–	Richmond Courier ed.; CC-r	1	1	19	38	57	111	176	240
5	28	1946	Gilberton; pgs. 60-64 rearranged/ illos added; CC-r	1	1	14	28	42	81	118	155
6	51	–	LDC-r	1	1	9	18	27	47	61	75
7	71	–	LDC-r	1	1	6	12	18	29	36	42
8	87	–	C-price 15¢; LDC-r	1	1	6	12	18	27	33	38
9	161	–	New-c&a; PC-r	2	2	7	14	21	37	46	55
10	167	9/63	PC-r	2	2	2	4	6	11	16	20
11	167	12/65	PC-r	2	2	2	4	6	11	16	20
12	166	R/1968	New-c & price 25¢; PC-r	2	3	3	6	9	17	26	35

10. Robinson Crusoe (Used in **SOTI**, pg. 142)

Ed	HRN	Date	Details	A	C	GD 2.0	VG 4.0	FN 6.0	VF 8.0	VF/NM 9.0	NM- 9.2
1A	(O)	4/43	Original; Violet-c; 68 pgs; Zuckerberg c/a	1	1	86	172	258	546	936	1325
1B	(O)	4/43	Original; blue-grey-c, 68 pgs.	1	1	94	188	282	597	1024	1450
2A	14	–	Elliot Pub; violet-c; 68 pgs; CC-r	1	1	29	58	87	170	278	385
2B	14	–	Elliot Pub; blue-grey-c; CC-r	1	1	25	50	75	147	241	335
3	18	–	Nassau Bul. Pg. 64 changed from Gift Box ad to Bill of Rights article; CC-r	1	1	19	38	57	111	176	240
4	20	–	Queens Home News ed.; CC-r	1	1	16	32	48	94	147	200
5	28	1946	Gilberton; pg. 64 changes from Bill of Rights to WWII article-One Leg Shot Away; last CC-r	1	1	14	28	42	80	115	150
6	51	–	LDC-r	1	1	8	16	24	42	54	65
7	64	–	LDC-r	1	1	6	12	18	27	33	38
8	78	–	C-price 15¢; LDC-r	1	1	5	10	14	20	24	28
9	97	–	LDC-r	1	1	4	9	13	18	22	26
10	114	–	LDC-r	1	1	4	7	10	14	17	20
11	130	–	New-c; PC-r	1	2	5	10	15	25	31	36
12	140	–	New-a; PC-r	2	2	5	10	15	24	29	34
13	153	–	PC-r	2	2	2	4	6	8	11	14
14	164	–	PC-r	2	2	2	4	6	8	11	14
15	167	–	PC-r	2	2	2	4	6	8	11	14
16	167	7/64	PC-r	2	2	2	4	6	10	14	18
17	167	5/65	PC-r	2	2	2	4	6	10	14	18
18	167	6/66	PC-r	2	2	2	4	6	8	11	14
19	166	Fall/68	C-price 25¢; PC-r	2	2	2	4	6	8	11	14
20	166	R/68	(No Twin Circle ad)	2	2	2	4	6	9	13	16
21	169	Sm/70	Stiff-c; PC-r	2	2	2	4	6	9	13	16

11. Don Quixote

Ed	HRN	Date	Details	A	C	GD 2.0	VG 4.0	FN 6.0	VF 8.0	VF/NM 9.0	NM- 9.2
1	10	5/43	First (O) with HRN list; 68 pgs.	1	1	89	178	267	565	970	1375
2	18	–	Nassau Bulletin ed.; CC-r	1	1	23	46	69	136	223	310
3	21	–	Queens Home News ed.; CC-r	1	1	19	38	57	111	176	240
4	28	–	CC-r	1	1	14	28	42	81	118	155
5	110	–	New-PC; PC-r	1	2	7	14	21	35	43	50
6	156	–	Pgs. reduced 68 to 52; PC-r	1	2	4	7	10	14	17	20
7	165	–	PC-r	1	2	2	4	6	9	13	16
8	167	1/64	PC-r	1	2	2	4	6	9	13	16
9	167	11/65	PC-r	1	2	2	4	6	9	13	16
10	166	R/1968	New-c & price 25¢; PC-r	1	3	3	6	9	18	27	36

12. Rip Van Winkle and the Headless Horseman

Ed	HRN	Date	Details	A	C	GD 2.0	VG 4.0	FN 6.0	VF 8.0	VF/NM 9.0	NM- 9.2
1	11	6/43	Original; 68 pgs.	1	1	92	184	276	584	1005	1425
2	15	–	Long Isl. Ind. ed.; CC-r	1	1	24	48	72	142	234	325
3	20	–	Long Isl. Ind. ed.;	1	1	20	40	60	114	182	250
4	22	–	Queens Cty. Times ed.; CC-r	1	1	16	32	48	94	147	200
5	28	–	CC-r	1	1	14	28	42	80	115	150
6	60	–	1st LDC-r	1	1	8	16	24	40	50	60
7	62	–	LDC-r	1	1	5	10	15	23	28	32
8	71	–	LDC-r	1	1	4	9	13	18	22	26
9	89	–	C-price 15¢; LDC-r	1	1	4	8	12	17	21	24
10	118	–	LDC-r	1	1	4	7	10	14	17	20
11	132	–	New-c; PC-r	1	2	5	10	15	25	31	36
12	150	–	New-a; PC-r	2	2	5	10	15	24	29	34
13	158	–	PC-r	2	2	2	4	6	9	13	16
14	167	–	PC-r	2	2	2	4	6	9	13	16
15	167	12/63	PC-r	2	2	2	4	6	8	11	14
16	167	4/65	PC-r	2	2	2	4	6	8	11	14
17	167	4/66	PC-r	2	2	2	4	6	8	11	14
18	166	R/1968	New-c&price 25¢; PC-r; stiff-c	2	3	3	6	9	14	20	26
19	169	Sm/70	PC-r; stiff-c	2	3	2	4	6	10	14	18

13. Dr. Jekyll and Mr. Hyde (Used in **SOTI**, pg. 143)(1st horror comic?)

Ed	HRN	Date	Details	A	C	GD 2.0	VG 4.0	FN 6.0	VF 8.0	VF/NM 9.0	NM- 9.2
1	12	8/43	Original 60 pgs.	1	1	145	290	435	921	1586	2250
2	15	–	Long Isl. Ind. ed.; CC-r	1	1	36	72	108	211	343	475
3	20	–	Long Isl. Ind. ed.; CC-r	1	1	24	48	72	142	234	325
4	28	–	No c-price; CC-r	1	1	19	38	57	109	172	235
5	60	–	New-c; Pgs. reduced from 60 to 52; H.C. Kiefer-c; LDC-r	1	2	9	18	27	47	61	75
6	62	–	LDC-r	1	2	6	12	18	28	34	40
7	71	–	LDC-r	1	2	5	10	15	23	28	32

Classic Comics #14 © GIL

Classic Comics #16 © GIL

Classic Comics #19 © GIL

Ed	HRN	Date	Details	A	C	GD 2.0	VG 4.0	FN 6.0	VF 8.0	VF/NM 9.0	NM- 9.2
8	87	–	Date returns (erroneous); LDC-r	1	2	5	10	15	22	26	30
9	112	–	New-c&a; PC-r; Cameron-a	2	3	7	14	21	35	43	50
10	153	–	PC-r	2	3	2	4	6	9	13	16
11	161	–	PC-r	2	3	2	4	6	9	13	16
12	167	–	PC-r	2	3	2	4	6	8	11	14
13	167	8/64	PC-r	2	3	2	4	6	8	11	14
14	167	11/65	PC-r	2	3	2	4	6	8	11	14
15	166	R/68	C-price 25¢; PC-r	2	3	2	4	6	8	11	14
16	169	Wn/69	PC-r; stiff-c	2	3	2	4	6	8	11	14

14. Westward Ho!

Ed	HRN	Date	Details	A	C	GD 2.0	VG 4.0	FN 6.0	VF 8.0	VF/NM 9.0	NM- 9.2
1	13	9/43	Original; last outside bc coming-next ad; 60 pgs.	1	1	194	388	582	1242	2121	3000
2	15	–	Long Isl. Ind. ed.; CC-r	1	1	58	116	174	371	636	900
3	21	–	Queens Home News; Pg. 56 changed from coming-next ad to Three Men Named Smith; CC-r	1	1	46	92	138	290	488	685
4	28	1946	Gilberton; Pg. 56 changed again to WWII article-Speaking for America; last CC-r	1	1	39	78	117	242	401	560
5	53	–	Pgs. reduced from 60 to 52; LDC-r	1	1	36	72	108	216	351	485

15. Uncle Tom's Cabin (Used in **SOTI**, pgs. 102, 103)

Ed	HRN	Date	Details	A	C	GD 2.0	VG 4.0	FN 6.0	VF 8.0	VF/NM 9.0	NM- 9.2
1	14	11/43	Original; Outside-bc ad: 2 Gift Boxes; 60 pgs.; color var. on-c; green trunk,root on left & brown trunk, root on left	1	1	84	168	252	538	919	1300
2	15	–	Long Isl. Ind. listed- bottom inside-fc; also Gilberton listed bottom-pg. 1; CC-r; portion of root to the left of the price circle can be green or brown	1	1	26	52	78	154	252	350
3	21	–	Nassau Bulletin ed.; CC-r	1	1	20	40	60	117	189	260
4	28	–	No c-price; CC-r	1	1	14	28	42	82	121	160
5	53	–	Pgs. reduced 60 to 52; LDC-r	1	1	8	16	24	42	54	65
6	71	–	LDC-r	1	1	6	12	18	27	33	38
7	89	–	C-price 15¢; LDC-r	1	1	5	10	15	24	30	35
8	117	–	New-c/lettering changes; PC-r	1	2	5	10	15	25	31	36
9	128	–	'Picture Progress' promo; PC-r	1	2	2	4	6	10	14	18
10	137	–	PC-r	1	2	2	4	6	9	13	16
11	146	–	PC-r	1	2	2	4	6	9	13	16
12	154	–	PC-r	1	2	2	4	6	9	13	16
13	161	–	PC-r	1	2	2	4	6	8	11	14
14	167	–	PC-r	1	2	2	4	6	8	11	14
15	167	6/64	PC-r	1	2	2	4	6	8	11	14
16	167	5/65	PC-r	1	2	2	4	6	8	11	14
17	166	5/67	PC-r	1	2	2	4	6	8	11	14
18	166	Wn/69	New-stiff-c; PC-r	1	3	3	6	9	15	22	28
19	169	Sm/70	PC-r; stiff-c	1	3	2	4	6	10	14	18

16. Gulliver's Travels

Ed	HRN	Date	Details	A	C	GD 2.0	VG 4.0	FN 6.0	VF 8.0	VF/NM 9.0	NM- 9.2
1	15	12/43	Original-Lilian Chestney c/a; 60 pgs.	1	1	81	162	243	518	884	1250
2	18/20	–	Price deleted; Queens Home News ed; CC-r	1	1	22	44	66	128	209	290
3	22	–	Queens Cty. Times ed.; CC-r	1	1	18	36	54	105	165	225
4	28	–	CC-r	1	1	14	28	42	80	115	150
5	60	–	Pgs. reduced to 48; LDC-r	1	1	6	12	18	31	38	45
6	62	–	LDC-r	1	1	5	10	15	23	28	32
7	78	–	C-price 15¢; LDC-r	1	1	5	10	14	20	24	28
8	89	–	LDC-r	1	1	4	8	12	17	21	24
9	155	–	New-c; PC-r	1	2	5	10	15	25	31	36
10	165	–	PC-r	1	2	2	4	6	8	11	14
11	167	5/64	PC-r	1	2	2	4	6	8	11	14
12	167	11/65	PC-r	1	2	2	4	6	8	11	14
13	166	R/1968	C-price 25¢; PC-r	1	2	2	4	6	8	11	14
14	169	Wn/69	PC-r; stiff-c	1	2	2	4	6	8	11	14

17. The Deerslayer

Ed	HRN	Date	Details	A	C	GD 2.0	VG 4.0	FN 6.0	VF 8.0	VF/NM 9.0	NM- 9.2
1	16	1/44	Original; Outside-bc ad: 3 Gift Boxes; 60 pgs.	1	1	66	132	198	419	872	1025
2A	18	–	Queens Cty Times (inside-fc); CC-r	1	1	23	46	69	136	223	310
2B	18	–	Gilberton (bottom-pg. 1); CC-r; Scarce	1	1	33	66	99	194	317	440
3	22	–	Queens Cty. Times ed.; CC-r	1	1	19	38	57	109	172	235
4	28	–	CC-r	1	1	14	28	42	81	118	155
5	60	–	Pgs.reduced to 52; LDC-r	1	1	7	14	21	37	46	55
6	64	–	LDC-r	1	1	5	10	15	22	26	30
7	85	–	C-price 15¢; LDC-r	1	1	4	8	12	17	21	24
8	118	–	LDC-r	1	1	4	7	10	14	17	20
9	132	–	LDC-r	1	1	4	7	10	14	17	20
10	167	11/66	Last LDC-r	1	1	2	4	6	11	16	20
11	166	R/1968	New-c & price 25¢; PC-r	1	2	3	6	9	17	26	35
12	169	Spr/71	Stiff-c; letters from parents & educators; PC-r	1	2	2	4	6	10	14	18

18. The Hunchback of Notre Dame

Ed	HRN	Date	Details	A	C	GD 2.0	VG 4.0	FN 6.0	VF 8.0	VF/NM 9.0	NM- 9.2
1A	17	3/44	Orig.; Gilberton ed; 60 pgs.	1	1	103	206	309	659	1130	1600
1B	17	3/44	Orig.; Island Pub. Ed.; 60 pgs.	1	1	87	174	261	553	952	1350
2	18/20	–	Queens Home News ed.; CC-r	1	1	28	56	84	165	270	375
3	22	–	Queens Cty. Times ed.; CC-r	1	1	22	44	66	132	216	300
4	28	–	CC-r	1	1	21	42	63	122	199	275
5	60	–	New-c; 8pgs. deleted; Kiefer-c; LDC-r	1	2	9	18	27	50	65	80
6	62	–	LDC-r	1	2	5	10	15	22	26	30
7	78	–	C-price 15¢; LDC-r	1	2	5	10	14	20	24	28
8A	89	–	H.C.Kiefer on bottom right-fc; LDC-r	1	2	4	9	13	18	22	26
8B	89	–	Name omitted; LDC-r	1	2	5	10	15	24	30	35
9	118	–	LDC-r	1	2	4	8	12	17	21	24
10	140	–	New-c; PC-r	1	3	7	14	21	35	43	50
11	146	–	PC-r	1	3	4	9	13	18	22	26
12	158	–	New-c&a; PC-r; Evans/Crandall-a	2	4	5	10	15	25	31	36
13	165	–	PC-r	2	4	2	4	6	9	13	16
14	167	9/63	PC-r	2	4	2	4	6	9	13	16
15	167	10/64	PC-r	2	4	2	4	6	9	13	16
16	167	4/66	PC-r	2	4	2	4	6	8	11	14
17	166	R/1968	New price 25¢; PC-r	2	4	2	4	6	8	11	14
18	169	Sp/70	Stiff-c; PC-r	2	4	2	4	6	8	11	14

19. Huckleberry Finn

Ed	HRN	Date	Details	A	C	GD 2.0	VG 4.0	FN 6.0	VF 8.0	VF/NM 9.0	NM- 9.2
1A	18	4/44	Orig.; Gilberton ed.; 60 pgs.	1	1	55	110	165	352	601	850
1B	18	4/44	Orig.; Island Pub.; 60 pgs.	1	1	58	116	174	371	636	900
2	18	–	Nassau Bulletin	1	1	23	46	69	136	223	310

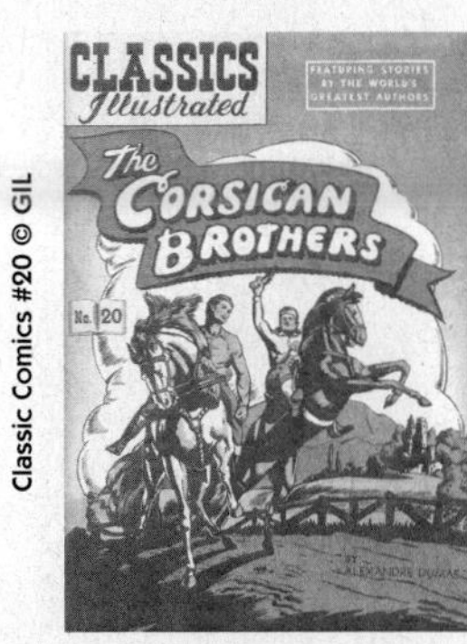

Classic Comics #20 © GIL

Classic Comics #22 © GIL

Classic Comics #25 © GIL

Ed	HRN	Date	Details	A	C	GD 2.0	VG 4.0	FN 6.0	VF 8.0	VF/NM 9.0	NM- 9.2
			ed.; fc-price 15¢-Canada; no coming-next ad; CC-r								
3	22	–	Queens City Times ed.; CC-r	1	1	19	38	57	111	176	240
4	28	–	CC-r	1	1	14	28	42	80	115	150
5	60	–	Pgs. reduced to 48; LDC-r	1	1	6	12	18	31	38	45
6	62	–	LDC-r	1	1	5	10	15	23	28	32
7	78	–	LDC-r	1	1	4	9	13	18	22	26
8	89	–	LDC-r	1	1	4	8	12	17	21	24
9	117	–	LDC-r	1	1	4	7	10	14	17	20
10	131	–	New-c&a; PC-r	2	2	5	10	15	24	30	35
11	140	–	PC-r	2	2	2	4	6	9	13	16
12	150	–	PC-r	2	2	2	4	6	9	13	16
13	158	–	PC-r	2	2	2	4	6	9	13	16
14	165	–	PC-r (scarce)	2	2	3	6	9	14	19	24
15	167	–	PC-r	2	2	2	4	6	8	11	14
16	167	6/64	PC-r	2	2	2	4	6	8	11	14
17	167	6/65	PC-r	2	2	2	4	6	8	11	14
18	167	10/65	PC-r	2	2	2	4	6	8	11	14
19	166	9/67	PC-r	2	2	2	4	6	8	11	14
20	166	Win/69	C-price 25¢; PC-r; stiff-c	2	2	2	4	6	8	11	14
21	169	Sm/70	PC-r; stiff-c	2	2	2	4	6	8	11	14

20. The Corsican Brothers

Ed	HRN	Date	Details	A	C	GD 2.0	VG 4.0	FN 6.0	VF 8.0	VF/NM 9.0	NM- 9.2
1A	20	6/44	Orig.; Gilberton ed.; bc-ad: 4 Gift Boxes; 60 pgs.	1	1	50	100	150	315	533	750
1B	20	6/44	Orig.; Courier ed.; 60 pgs.	1	1	42	84	126	265	445	625
1C	20	6/44	Orig.; Long Island Ind. ed.; 60 pgs.	1	1	42	84	126	265	445	625
2	22	–	Queens Cty. Times ed.; white logo banner; CC-r	1	1	20	40	60	114	182	250
3	28	–	CC-r	1	1	19	38	57	109	172	235
4	60	–	CI logo; no price; 48 pgs.; LDC-r	1	1	15	30	45	90	140	190
5A	62	–	LDC-r; Classics Ill. logo at top of pgs.	1	1	15	30	45	83	124	165
5B	62	–	w/o logo at top of pg. (scarcer)	1	1	15	30	45	86	133	180
6	78	–	C-price 15¢; LDC-r	1	1	14	28	42	81	118	155
7	97	–	LDC-r	1	1	14	28	42	78	112	145

21. 3 Famous Mysteries ("The Sign of the 4", "The Murders in the Rue Morgue", "The Flayed Hand")

Ed	HRN	Date	Details	A	C	GD 2.0	VG 4.0	FN 6.0	VF 8.0	VF/NM 9.0	NM- 9.2
1A	21	7/44	Orig.; Gilberton ed.; 60 pgs.	1	1	100	200	300	635	1093	1550
1B	21	7/44	Orig. Island Pub. Co.; 60 pgs.	1	1	103	206	309	659	1130	1600
1C	21	7/44	Original; Courier Ed.; 60 pgs.	1	1	90	180	270	576	988	1400
2	22	–	Nassau Bulletin ed.; CC-r	1	1	40	80	120	244	402	560
3	30	–	CC-r	1	1	28	56	84	165	270	375
4	62	–	LDC-r; 8 pgs. deleted; LDC-r	1	1	22	44	66	128	209	290
5	70	–	LDC-r	1	1	20	40	60	117	189	260
6	85	–	C-price 15¢; LDC-r	1	1	18	36	54	107	169	230
7	114	–	New-c; PC-r	1	2	18	36	54	107	169	230

22. The Pathfinder

Ed	HRN	Date	Details	A	C	GD 2.0	VG 4.0	FN 6.0	VF 8.0	VF/NM 9.0	NM- 9.2
1A	22	10/44	Orig.; No printer listed; ownership statement inside fc lists Gilberton & date; 60 pgs.	1	1	47	94	141	296	498	725
1B	22	10/44	Orig.; Island Pub. ed.; 60 pgs.	1	1	48	96	144	302	514	625
1C	22	10/44	Orig.; Queens Cty Times ed. 60 pgs.	1	1	48	96	144	302	514	625
2	30	–	C-price removed; CC-r	1	1	15	30	45	85	130	175
3	60	–	Pgs. reduced to 52; LDC-r	1	1	6	12	18	27	33	38
4	70	–	LDC-r	1	1	5	10	15	22	26	30
5	85	–	C-price 15¢; LDC-r	1	1	4	9	13	18	22	26
6	118	–	LDC-r	1	1	4	8	12	17	21	24
7	132	–	LDC-r	1	1	4	7	10	14	17	20
8	146	–	LDC-r	1	1	4	7	10	14	17	20
9	167	11/63	New-c; PC-r	1	2	4	8	12	23	37	50
10	167	12/65	PC-r	1	2	2	4	6	11	16	20
11	166	8/67	PC-r	1	2	2	4	6	11	16	20

23. Oliver Twist (1st Classic produced by the Iger Shop)

Ed	HRN	Date	Details	A	C	GD 2.0	VG 4.0	FN 6.0	VF 8.0	VF/NM 9.0	NM- 9.2
1	23	7/45	Original; 60 pgs.	1	1	48	96	144	302	514	725
2A	30	–	Printers Union logo on bottom left-fc same as 23(Orig.) (very rare); CC-r	1	1	30	60	90	177	289	400
2B	30	–	Union logo omitted; CC-r	1	1	15	30	45	84	127	170
3	60	–	Pgs. reduced to 48; LDC-r	1	1	6	12	18	29	36	42
4	62	–	LDC-r	1	1	5	10	15	23	28	32
5	71	–	LDC-r	1	1	5	10	14	20	24	28
6	85	–	C-price 15¢; LDC-r	1	1	4	9	13	18	22	26
7	94	–	LDC-r	1	1	4	7	10	14	17	20
8	118	–	LDC-r	1	1	4	7	10	14	17	20
9	136	–	New-PC, old-a; PC-r	1	2	5	10	15	24	30	35
10	150	–	Old-a; PC-r	1	2	4	7	10	14	17	20
11	164	–	Old-a; PC-r	1	2	4	8	11	16	19	22
12	164	–	New-a; PC-r; Evans/Crandall-a	2	2	4	8	12	23	37	50
13	167	–	PC-r	2	2	2	4	6	11	16	20
14	167	8/64	PC-r	2	2	2	4	6	8	11	14
15	167	12/65	PC-r	2	2	2	4	6	8	11	14
16	166	R/1968	New 25¢; PC-r	2	2	2	4	6	8	11	14
17	169	Win/69	Stiff-c; PC-r	2	2	2	4	6	8	11	14

24. A Connecticut Yankee in King Arthur's Court

Ed	HRN	Date	Details	A	C	GD 2.0	VG 4.0	FN 6.0	VF 8.0	VF/NM 9.0	NM- 9.2
1	–	9/45	Original	1	1	43	86	129	271	461	650
2	30	–	No price circle; CC-r	1	1	15	30	45	84	127	170
3	60	–	8 pgs. deleted; LDC-r	1	1	6	12	18	27	33	38
4	62	–	LDC-r	1	1	5	10	15	23	28	32
5	71	–	LDC-r	1	1	5	10	15	22	26	30
6	87	–	C-price 15¢; LDC-r	1	1	4	9	13	18	22	26
7	121	–	LDC-r	1	1	4	8	12	17	21	24
8	140	–	New-c&a; PC-r	2	2	5	10	15	25	31	36
9	153	–	PC-r	2	2	2	4	6	9	13	16
10	164	–	PC-r	2	2	2	4	6	8	11	14
11	167	–	PC-r	2	2	2	4	6	8	11	14
12	167	7/64	PC-r	2	2	2	4	6	8	11	14
13	167	6/66	PC-r	2	2	2	4	6	8	11	14
14	166	R/1968	C-price 25¢; PC-r	2	2	2	4	6	8	11	14
15	169	Spr/71	PC-r; stiff-c	2	2	2	4	6	8	11	14

25. Two Years Before the Mast

Ed	HRN	Date	Details	A	C	GD 2.0	VG 4.0	FN 6.0	VF 8.0	VF/NM 9.0	NM- 9.2
1	–	10/45	Original; Webb/Heames-a&c	1	1	42	84	126	265	445	625
2	30	–	Price circle blank; CC-r	1	1	15	30	45	84	127	170
3	60	–	8 pgs. deleted; LDC-r	1	1	6	12	18	27	33	38
4	62	–	LDC-r	1	1	5	10	15	23	28	32
5	71	–	LDC-r	1	1	4	9	13	18	22	26
6	85	–	C-price 15¢; LDC-r	1	1	4	8	12	17	21	24
7	114	–	LDC-r	1	1	4	7	10	14	17	20
8	156	–	3 pgs. replaced by fillers; new-c; PC-r	1	2	5	10	15	25	31	36
9	167	12/63	PC-r	1	2	2	4	6	8	11	14
10	167	12/65	PC-r	1	2	2	4	6	8	11	14

Classic Comics #27 © GIL

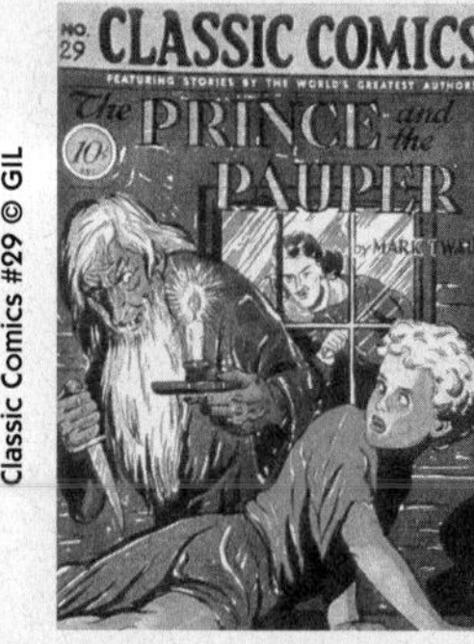

Classic Comics #29 © GIL

Classic Comics #31 © GIL

Ed	HRN	Date	Details	A	C	GD 2.0	VG 4.0	FN 6.0	VF 8.0	VF/NM 9.0	NM- 9.2
11	166	9/67	PC-r	1	2	2	4	6	8	11	14
12	169	Win/69	C-price 25¢; stiff-c PC-r	1	2	2	4	6	8	11	14

26. Frankenstein (2nd horror comic?)

Ed	HRN	Date	Details	A	C	GD 2.0	VG 4.0	FN 6.0	VF 8.0	VF/NM 9.0	NM- 9.2
1	26	12/45	Orig.; Webb/Brewster a&c; 52 pgs.	1	1	123	246	369	787	1344	1900
2A	30	–	Price circle blank; no indicia; CC-r	1	1	34	68	102	199	325	450
2B	30	–	With indicia; scarce; CC-r	1	1	39	78	117	231	378	525
3	60	–	LDC-r	1	1	17	34	51	98	154	210
4	62	–	LDC-r	1	1	15	30	45	88	137	185
5	71	–	LDC-r	1	1	8	16	24	42	54	65
6A	82	–	C-price 15¢; soft-c LDC-r	1	1	7	14	21	37	46	55
6B	82	–	Stiff-c; LDC-r	1	1	8	16	24	42	54	65
7	117	–	LDC-r	1	1	5	10	15	22	26	30
8	146	–	New Saunders-c; PC-r	1	2	6	12	18	31	38	45
9	152	–	Scarce; PC-r	1	2	8	16	24	42	54	65
10	153	–	PC-r	1	2	2	4	6	10	14	18
11	160	–	PC-r	1	2	2	4	6	10	14	18
12	165	–	PC-r	1	2	2	4	6	9	13	16
13	167	–	PC-r	1	2	2	4	6	9	13	16
14	167	6/64	PC-r	1	2	2	4	6	9	13	16
15	167	6/65	PC-r	1	2	2	4	6	9	13	16
16	167	10/65	PC-r	1	2	2	4	6	9	13	16
17	166	9/67	PC-r	1	2	2	4	6	9	13	16
18	169	Fall/69	C-price 25¢; stiff-c PC-r	1	2	2	4	6	9	13	16
19	169	Spr/71	PC-r; stiff-c	1	2	2	4	6	9	13	16

27. The Adventures of Marco Polo

Ed	HRN	Date	Details	A	C	GD 2.0	VG 4.0	FN 6.0	VF 8.0	VF/NM 9.0	NM- 9.2
1	–	4/46	Original	1	1	42	84	126	265	445	625
2	30	–	Last 'Comics' reprint; CC-r	1	1	15	30	45	86	133	180
3	70	–	8 pgs. deleted; no c-price; LDC-r	1	1	5	10	15	24	30	35
4	87	–	C-price 15¢; LDC-r	1	1	4	9	13	18	22	26
5	117	–	LDC-r	1	1	4	7	10	14	17	20
6	154	–	New-c; PC-r	1	2	5	10	15	24	30	35
7	165	–	PC-r	1	2	2	4	6	8	11	14
8	167	4/64	PC-r	1	2	2	4	6	8	11	14
9	167	6/66	PC-r	1	2	2	4	6	8	11	14
10	169	Spr/69	New price 25¢; stiff-c; PC-r	1	2	2	4	6	8	11	14

28. Michael Strogoff

Ed	HRN	Date	Details	A	C	GD 2.0	VG 4.0	FN 6.0	VF 8.0	VF/NM 9.0	NM- 9.2
1	–	6/46	Original	1	1	41	82	123	256	428	600
2	51	–	8 pgs. cut; LDC-r	1	1	15	30	45	84	127	170
3	115	–	New-c; PC-r	1	2	6	12	18	31	38	45
4	155	–	PC-r	1	2	4	7	10	14	17	20
5	167	11/63	PC-r	1	2	2	4	6	9	13	16
6	167	7/66	PC-r	1	2	2	4	6	9	13	16
7	169	Sm/69	C-price 25¢; stiff-c PC-r	1	3	3	6	9	15	21	26

29. The Prince and the Pauper

Ed	HRN	Date	Details	A	C	GD 2.0	VG 4.0	FN 6.0	VF 8.0	VF/NM 9.0	NM- 9.2
1	–	7/46	Orig.; "Horror"-c	1	1	60	120	180	381	653	925
2	60	–	8 pgs. cut; new-c by Kiefer; LDC-r	1	2	9	18	27	52	69	85
3	62	–	LDC-r	1	2	5	10	15	24	30	35
4	71	–	LDC-r	1	2	4	9	13	18	22	26
5	93	–	LDC-r	1	2	4	8	12	17	21	24
6	114	–	LDC-r	1	2	4	7	10	14	17	20
7	128	–	New-c; PC-r	1	3	5	10	15	24	30	35
8	138	–	PC-r	1	3	2	4	6	9	13	16
9	150	–	PC-r	1	3	2	4	6	9	13	16
10	164	–	PC-r	1	3	2	4	6	8	11	14
11	167	–	PC-r	1	3	2	4	6	8	11	14
12	167	7/64	PC-r	1	3	2	4	6	8	11	14
13	167	11/65	PC-r	1	3	2	4	6	8	11	14
14	166	R/68	C-price 25¢; PC-r	1	3	2	4	6	8	11	14
15	169	Sm/70	PC-r; stiff-c	1	3	2	4	6	8	11	14

30. The Moonstone

Ed	HRN	Date	Details	A	C	GD 2.0	VG 4.0	FN 6.0	VF 8.0	VF/NM 9.0	NM- 9.2
1	–	9/46	Original; Rico-c/a	1	1	41	82	123	256	428	600
2	60	–	LDC-r; 8pgs. cut	1	1	9	18	27	50	65	80
3	70	–	LDC-r	1	1	8	16	24	42	54	65
4	155	–	New L.B. Cole-c; PC-r	1	2	4	8	12	28	44	60
5	165	–	PC-r; L.B. Cole-c	1	2	3	6	9	16	23	30
6	167	1/64	PC-r; L.B. Cole-c	1	2	2	4	6	11	16	20
7	167	9/65	PC-r; L.B. Cole-c	1	2	2	4	6	10	14	18
8	166	R/1968	C-price 25¢; PC-r	1	2	2	4	6	9	13	16

31. The Black Arrow

Ed	HRN	Date	Details	A	C	GD 2.0	VG 4.0	FN 6.0	VF 8.0	VF/NM 9.0	NM- 9.2
1	30	10/46	Original	1	1	39	78	117	235	385	535
2	51	–	CI logo; LDC-r 8pgs. deleted	1	1	6	12	18	33	41	48
3	64	–	LDC-r	1	1	4	9	13	18	22	26
4	87	–	C-price 15¢; LDC-r	1	1	4	8	12	17	21	24
5	108	–	LDC-r	1	1	4	7	10	14	17	20
6	125	–	LDC-r	1	1	4	7	10	14	17	20
7	131	–	New-c; PC-r	1	2	5	10	15	24	30	35
8	140	–	PC-r	1	2	2	4	6	9	13	16
9	148	–	PC-r	1	2	2	4	6	9	13	16
10	161	–	PC-r	1	2	2	4	6	8	11	14
11	167	–	PC-r	1	2	2	4	6	8	11	14
12	167	7/64	PC-r	1	2	2	4	6	8	11	14
13	167	11/65	PC-r	1	2	2	4	6	8	11	14
14	166	R/1968	C-price 25¢; PC-r	1	2	2	4	6	8	11	14

32. Lorna Doone

Ed	HRN	Date	Details	A	C	GD 2.0	VG 4.0	FN 6.0	VF 8.0	VF/NM 9.0	NM- 9.2
1	–	12/46	Original; Matt Baker c&a	1	1	47	94	141	296	498	700
2	53/64	–	8 pgs. deleted; LDC-r	1	1	9	18	27	52	69	85
3	85	1951	C-price 15¢; LDC-r; Baker c&a	1	1	7	14	21	37	46	55
4	118	–	LDC-r	1	1	4	9	13	18	22	26
5	138	–	New-c; old-c becomes new title pg.; PC-r	1	2	6	12	18	28	34	40
6	150	–	PC-r	1	2	2	4	6	8	11	14
7	165	–	PC-r	1	2	2	4	6	8	11	14
8	167	1/64	PC-r	1	2	2	4	6	9	13	16
9	167	11/65	PC-r	1	2	2	4	6	9	13	16
10	166	R/1968	New-c; PC-r	1	3	3	6	9	16	24	32

33. The Adventures of Sherlock Holmes

Ed	HRN	Date	Details	A	C	GD 2.0	VG 4.0	FN 6.0	VF 8.0	VF/NM 9.0	NM- 9.2
1	33	1/47	Original; Kiefer-c; contains Study in Scarlet & Hound of the Baskervilles; 68 pgs.	1	1	139	278	417	883	1517	2150
2	53	–	"A Study in Scarlet" (17 pgs.) deleted; LDC-r	1	1	50	100	150	315	533	750
3	71	–	LDC-r	1	1	39	78	117	231	378	525
4A	89	–	C-price 15¢; LDC-r	1	1	30	60	90	117	289	400
4B	89	–	Kiefer's name omitted from-c	1	1	31	62	93	186	303	420

34. Mysterious Island (Last "Classic Comics" issue)

Ed	HRN	Date	Details	A	C	GD 2.0	VG 4.0	FN 6.0	VF 8.0	VF/NM 9.0	NM- 9.2
1	35	2/47	Original; Webb/Heames-c/a	1	1	41	82	123	256	428	600
2	60	–	8 pgs. deleted; LDC-r	1	1	7	14	21	37	46	55
3	62	–	LDC-r	1	1	5	10	15	23	28	32
4	71	–	LDC-r	1	1	6	12	18	31	38	45
5	78	–	C-price 15¢ in circle; LDC-r	1	1	5	10	14	20	24	28
6	92	–	LDC-r	1	1	4	9	13	18	22	26
7	117	–	LDC-r	1	1	4	7	10	14	17	20
8	140	–	New-c; PC-r	1	2	5	10	15	24	30	35

Classics Illustrated #36 © GIL

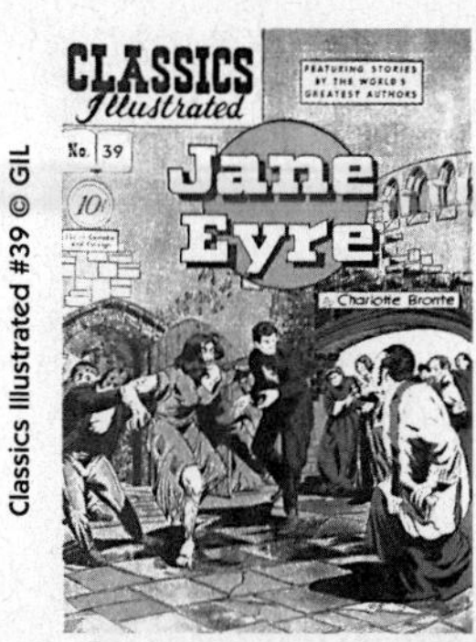

Classics Illustrated #39 © GIL

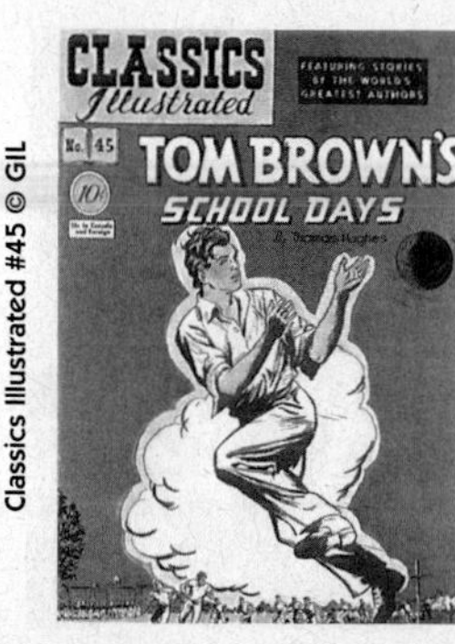

Classics Illustrated #45 © GIL

Ed	HRN	Date	Details	A	C	GD 2.0	VG 4.0	FN 6.0	VF 8.0	VF/NM 9.0	NM- 9.2
9	156	–	PC-r	1	2	2	4	6	9	13	16
10	167	10/63	PC-r	1	2	2	4	6	8	11	14
11	167	5/64	PC-r	1	2	2	4	6	8	11	14
12	167	6/66	PC-r	1	2	2	4	6	8	11	14
13	166	R/1968	C-price 25¢; PC-r	1	2	2	4	6	8	11	14

35. Last Days of Pompeii (First "Classics Illustrated")

Ed	HRN	Date	Details	A	C	GD 2.0	VG 4.0	FN 6.0	VF 8.0	VF/NM 9.0	NM- 9.2
1	35	3/47	Original; LDC; Kiefer-c/a	1	1	41	82	123	256	428	600
2	161	–	New c&a; 15¢; PC-r; Kirby/Ayers-a	2	2	5	10	15	31	53	75
3	167	1/64	PC-r	2	2	3	6	9	16	22	28
4	167	7/66	PC-r	2	2	3	6	9	16	22	28
5	169	Spr/70	New price 25¢; stiff-c; PC-r	2	2	3	6	9	16	22	28

36. Typee

Ed	HRN	Date	Details	A	C	GD 2.0	VG 4.0	FN 6.0	VF 8.0	VF/NM 9.0	NM- 9.2
1	36	4/47	Original	1	1	30	60	90	177	289	400
2	64	–	No c-price; 8 pg. ed.; LDC-r	1	1	8	16	24	40	50	60
3	155	–	New-c; PC-r	1	2	5	10	15	24	30	35
4	167	9/63	PC-r	1	2	2	4	6	9	13	16
5	167	7/65	PC-r	1	2	2	4	6	9	13	16
6	169	Sm/69	C-price 25¢; stiff-c PC-r	1	2	2	4	6	9	13	16

37. The Pioneers

Ed	HRN	Date	Details	A	C	GD 2.0	VG 4.0	FN 6.0	VF 8.0	VF/NM 9.0	NM- 9.2
1	37	5/47	Original; Palais-c/a	1	1	27	54	81	162	266	370
2A	62	–	8 pgs. cut; LDC-r; price circle blank	1	1	6	12	18	28	34	40
2B	62	–	10¢; LDC-r;	1	1	29	58	87	170	278	385
3	70	–	LDC-r	1	1	4	8	12	17	21	24
4	92	–	15¢; LDC-r	1	1	4	8	11	16	19	22
5	118	–	LDC-r	1	1	4	7	10	14	17	20
6	131	–	LDC-r	1	1	4	7	10	14	17	20
7	132	–	LDC-r	1	1	4	7	10	14	17	20
8	153	–	LDC-r	1	1	4	7	10	14	17	20
9	167	5/64	LDC-r	1	1	2	4	6	9	13	16
10	167	6/66	LDC-r	1	1	2	4	6	9	13	16
11	166	R/1968	New-c; 25¢; PC-r	1	2	3	6	9	18	27	36

38. Adventures of Cellini

Ed	HRN	Date	Details	A	C	GD 2.0	VG 4.0	FN 6.0	VF 8.0	VF/NM 9.0	NM- 9.2
1	–	6/47	Original; Froehlich c/a	1	1	32	64	96	192	314	435
2	164	–	New-c&a; PC-r	2	2	3	6	9	18	27	36
3	167	12/63	PC-r	2	2	2	4	6	10	14	18
4	167	7/66	PC-r	2	2	2	4	6	10	14	18
5	169	Spr/70	Stiff-c; new price 25¢; PC-r	2	2	2	4	6	11	16	20

39. Jane Eyre

Ed	HRN	Date	Details	A	C	GD 2.0	VG 4.0	FN 6.0	VF 8.0	VF/NM 9.0	NM- 9.2
1	–	7/47	Original	1	1	31	62	93	186	303	420
2	60	–	No c-price; 8 pgs. cut; LDC-r	1	1	6	12	18	31	38	45
3	62	–	LDC-r	1	1	5	10	15	24	30	35
4	71	–	LDC-r; c-price 10¢	1	1	5	10	15	22	26	30
5	92	–	C-price 15¢; LDC-r	1	1	4	9	13	18	22	26
6	118	–	LDC-r	1	1	4	8	12	17	21	24
7	142	–	New-c; old-a; PC-r	1	2	6	12	18	28	34	40
8	154	–	Old-a; PC-r	1	2	4	8	12	17	21	24
9	165	–	New-a; PC-r	2	2	3	6	9	17	26	35
10	167	12/63	PC-r	2	2	3	6	9	14	19	24
11	167	4/65	PC-r	2	2	2	4	6	13	18	22
12	167	8/66	PC-r	2	2	2	4	6	13	18	22
13	166	R/1968	New-c; PC-r	2	3	5	10	15	31	53	75

40. Mysteries ("The Pit and the Pendulum", "The Advs. of Hans Pfall" & "The Fall of the House of Usher")

Ed	HRN	Date	Details	A	C	GD 2.0	VG 4.0	FN 6.0	VF 8.0	VF/NM 9.0	NM- 9.2
1	40	8/47	Original; Kiefer-c/a, Froehlich, Griffiths-a	1	1	61	122	183	390	670	950
2	62	–	LDC-r; 8pgs. cut	1	1	25	50	75	147	241	335
3	75	–	LDC-r	1	1	19	38	57	111	176	240
4	92	–	C-price 15¢; LDC-r	1	1	15	30	45	94	147	200

41. Twenty Years After

Ed	HRN	Date	Details	A	C	GD 2.0	VG 4.0	FN 6.0	VF 8.0	VF/NM 9.0	NM- 9.2
1	–	9/47	Original; 'horror'-c	1	1	39	78	117	235	385	535
2	62	–	New-c; no c-price 8 pgs. cut; LDC-r; Kiefer-c	1	2	7	14	21	37	46	55
3	78	–	C-price 15¢; LDC-r	1	2	5	10	15	23	28	32
4	156	–	New-c; PC-r	1	3	5	10	15	24	30	35
5	167	12/63	PC-r	1	3	2	4	6	8	11	14
6	167	11/66	PC-r	1	3	2	4	6	8	11	14
7	169	Spr/70	New price 25¢; stiff-c; PC-r	1	3	2	4	6	8	11	14

42. Swiss Family Robinson

Ed	HRN	Date	Details	A	C	GD 2.0	VG 4.0	FN 6.0	VF 8.0	VF/NM 9.0	NM- 9.2
1	42	10/47	Orig.; Kiefer-c&a;	1	1	25	50	75	150	245	340
2A	62	–	8 pgs. cut; outside bc: Gift Box ad; LDC-r	1	1	6	12	18	31	38	45
2B	62	–	8 pgs. cut; outside-bc: Reorder list; scarce; LDC-r	1	1	13	26	39	74	105	135
3	75	–	LDC-r	1	1	5	10	14	20	24	28
4	93	–	LDC-r	1	1	5	10	14	20	24	28
5	117	–	LDC-r	1	1	3	6	9	14	19	24
6	131	–	New-c; old-a; PC-r	1	2	3	6	9	15	21	26
7	137	–	Old-a; PC-r	1	2	2	4	6	10	14	18
8	141	–	Old-a; PC-r	1	2	2	4	6	10	14	18
9	152	–	New-a; PC-r	2	2	3	6	9	16	23	30
10	158	–	PC-r	2	2	2	4	6	8	11	14
11	165	–	PC-r	2	2	3	6	9	16	24	32
12	167	12/63	PC-r	2	2	2	4	6	8	11	14
13	167	4/65	PC-r	2	2	2	4	6	8	11	14
14	167	5/66	PC-r	2	2	2	4	6	8	11	14
15	166	11/67	PC-r	2	2	2	4	6	8	11	14
16	169	Spr/69	PC-r; stiff-c	2	2	2	4	6	8	11	14

43. Great Expectations (Used in **SOTI**, pg. 311)

Ed	HRN	Date	Details	A	C	GD 2.0	VG 4.0	FN 6.0	VF 8.0	VF/NM 9.0	NM- 9.2
1	43	11/47	Original; Kiefer-a/c	1	1	90	180	270	576	988	1400
2	62	–	No c-price; 8 pgs. cut; LDC-r	1	1	57	114	171	362	624	885

44. Mysteries of Paris (Used in **SOTI**, pg. 323)

Ed	HRN	Date	Details	A	C	GD 2.0	VG 4.0	FN 6.0	VF 8.0	VF/NM 9.0	NM- 9.2
1A	44	12/47	Original; 56 pgs.; Kiefer-c/a	1	1	65	130	195	416	708	1000
1B	44	12/47	Orig.; printed on white/heavier paper; (rare)	1	1	76	152	228	486	831	1175
2A	62	–	8 pgs. cut; outside-bc: Gift Box ad; LDC-r	1	1	30	60	90	177	289	400
2B	62	–	8 pgs. cut; outside-bc: reorder list; LDC-r	1	1	30	60	90	177	289	400
3	78	–	C-price 15¢; LDC-r	1	1	25	50	75	147	241	335

45. Tom Brown's School Days

Ed	HRN	Date	Details	A	C	GD 2.0	VG 4.0	FN 6.0	VF 8.0	VF/NM 9.0	NM- 9.2
1	44	1/48	Original; 1st 48pg. issue	1	1	20	40	60	114	182	250
2	64	–	No c-price; LDC-r	1	1	7	14	21	35	43	50
3	161	–	New-c&a; PC-r	2	2	3	6	9	16	24	32
4	167	2/64	PC-r	2	2	2	4	6	9	13	16
5	167	8/66	PC-r	2	2	2	4	6	9	13	16
6	166	R/1968	C-price 25¢; PC-r	2	2	2	4	6	9	13	16

46. Kidnapped

Ed	HRN	Date	Details	A	C	GD 2.0	VG 4.0	FN 6.0	VF 8.0	VF/NM 9.0	NM- 9.2
1	47	4/48	Original; Webb-c/a	1	1	21	42	63	122	199	275
2A	62	–	Price circle blank; LDC-r	1	1	7	14	21	35	43	50
2B	62	–	C-price 10¢; rare; LDC-r	1	1	31	62	93	182	296	410
3	78	–	C-price 15¢; LDC-r	1	1	5	10	14	20	24	28
4	87	–	LDC-r	1	1	4	9	13	18	22	26

Classics Illustrated #48 © GIL

Classics Illustrated #51 © GIL

Classics Illustrated #53 © GIL

Ed	HRN	Date	Details	A	C	GD 2.0	VG 4.0	FN 6.0	VF 8.0	VF/NM 9.0	NM- 9.2
5	118	–	LDC-r	1	1	4	7	10	14	17	20
6	131	–	New-c; PC-r	1	2	5	10	15	23	28	32
7	140	–	PC-r	1	2	2	4	6	9	13	
16											
8	150	–	PC-r	1	2	2	4	6	9	13	16
9	164	–	Reduced pg.width; PC-r	1	2	2	4	6	8	11	14
10	167	–	PC-r	1	2	2	4	6	8	11	14
11	167	3/64	PC-r	1	2	2	4	6	8	11	14
12	167	6/65	PC-r	1	2	2	4	6	8	11	14
13	167	12/65	PC-r	1	2	2	4	6	8	11	14
14	166	9/67	PC-r	1	2	2	4	6	8	11	14
15	166	Win/69	New price 25¢; PC-r; stiff-c	1	2	2	4	6	8	11	14
16	169	Sm/70	PC-r; stiff-c	1	2	2	4	6	8	11	14

47. Twenty Thousand Leagues Under the Sea

Ed	HRN	Date	Details	A	C	GD	VG	FN	VF	VF/NM	NM-
1	47	5/48	Orig.; Kiefer-a&c;	1	1	21	42	63	126	206	285
2	64	–	No c-price; LDC-r	1	1	6	12	18	28	34	40
3	78	–	C-price 15¢; LDC-r	1	1	4	9	13	18	22	26
4	94	–	LDC-r	1	1	4	8	12	17	21	24
5	118	–	LDC-r	1	1	4	7	10	14	17	20
6	128	–	New-c; PC-r	1	2	5	10	15	24	30	35
7	133	–	PC-r	1	2	2	4	6	10	14	18
8	140	–	PC-r	1	2	2	4	6	9	13	16
9	148	–	PC-r	1	2	2	4	6	9	13	16
10	156	–	PC-r	1	2	2	4	6	9	13	16
11	165	–	PC-r	1	2	2	4	6	9	13	16
12	167	–	PC-r	1	2	2	4	6	9	13	16
13	167	3/64	PC-r	1	2	2	4	6	9	13	16
14	167	8/65	PC-r	1	2	2	4	6	9	13	16
15	167	10/66	PC-r	1	2	2	4	6	9	13	16
16	166	R/1968	C-price 25¢; new-c PC-r	1	3	3	6	9	15	22	28
17	169	Spr/70	Stiff-c; PC-r	1	3	2	4	6	13	18	22

48. David Copperfield

Ed	HRN	Date	Details	A	C	GD	VG	FN	VF	VF/NM	NM-
1	47	6/48	Original; Kiefer-c/a	1	1	20	40	60	117	189	260
2	64	–	Price circle replaced by motif of boy reading; LDC-r	1	1	6	12	18	28	34	40
3	87	–	C-price 15¢; LDC-r	1	1	4	8	12	17	21	24
4	121	–	New-c; PC-r	1	2	5	10	15	22	26	30
5	130	–	PC-r	1	2	2	4	6	9	13	16
6	140	–	PC-r	1	2	2	4	6	9	13	16
7	148	–	PC-r	1	2	2	4	6	9	13	16
8	156	–	PC-r	1	2	2	4	6	9	13	16
9	167	–	PC-r	1	2	2	4	6	8	11	14
10	167	4/64	PC-r	1	2	2	4	6	8	11	14
11	167	6/65	PC-r	1	2	2	4	6	8	11	14
12	166	5/67	PC-r	1	2	2	4	6	8	11	14
13	166	R/67	PC-r; C-price 25¢	1	2	2	4	6	10	14	18
14	166	Spr/69	C-price 25¢; stiff-c PC-r	1	2	2	4	6	8	11	14
15	169	Win/69	Stiff-c; PC-r	1	2	2	4	6	8	11	14

49. Alice in Wonderland

Ed	HRN	Date	Details	A	C	GD	VG	FN	VF	VF/NM	NM-
1	47	7/48	Original; 1st Blum a & c	1	1	34	68	102	204	332	460
2	64	–	No c-price; LDC-r	1	1	9	18	27	47	61	75
3A	85	–	C-price 15¢; soft-c LDC-r	1	1	8	16	24	40	50	60
3B	85	–	Stiff-c; LDC-r	1	1	8	16	24	42	54	65
4	155	–	New PC, similar to orig.; PC-r	1	2	4	8	12	27	44	60
5	165	–	PC-r	1	2	3	6	9	18	28	38
6	167	3/64	PC-r	1	2	3	6	9	16	24	32
7	167	6/66	PC-r	1	2	4	8	12	28	47	65
8A	166	Fall/68	New-c; soft-c; 25¢ c-price; PC-r	1	3	4	8	12	27	44	60
8B	166	Fall/68	New-c; stiff-c; 25¢ c-price; PC-r	1	3	6	12	18	41	76	110

50. Adventures of Tom Sawyer (Used in **SOTI**, pg. 37)

Ed	HRN	Date	Details	A	C	GD	VG	FN	VF	VF/NM	NM-
1A	51	8/48	Orig.; Aldo Rubano a&c	1	1	20	40	60	114	182	250
1B	51	9/48	Orig.; Rubano c&a	1	1	20	40	60	114	182	250
1C	51	9/48	Orig.; outside-bc: blue & yellow only; rare	1	1	25	50	75	147	241	335
2	64	–	No c-price; LDC-r	1	1	5	10	15	23	28	32
3	78	–	C-price 15¢; LDC-r	1	1	4	8	12	17	21	24
4	94	–	LDC-r	1	1	4	7	10	14	17	20
5	117	–	LDC-r	1	1	2	4	6	10	14	18
6	132	–	LDC-r	1	1	2	4	6	10	14	18
7	140	–	New-c; PC-r	1	2	3	6	9	17	26	35
8	150	–	PC-r	1	2	2	4	6	9	13	16
9	164	–	New-a; PC-r	2	2	3	6	9	17	26	35
10	167	–	PC-r	2	2	2	4	6	9	13	16
11	167	1/65	PC-r	2	2	2	4	6	8	11	14
12	167	5/66	PC-r	2	2	2	4	6	8	11	14
13	166	12/67	PC-r	2	2	2	4	6	8	11	14
14	169	Fall/69	C-price 25¢; stiff-c; PC-r	2	2	2	4	6	8	11	14
15	169	Win/71	PC-r	2	2	2	4	6	8	11	14

51. The Spy

Ed	HRN	Date	Details	A	C	GD	VG	FN	VF	VF/NM	NM-
1A	51	9/48	Original; inside-bc illo: Christmas Carol	1	1	19	38	57	112	179	245
1B	51	9/48	Original; inside-bc illo: Man in Iron Mask	1	1	19	38	57	112	179	245
1C	51	8/48	Original; outside-bc: full color	1	1	19	38	57	112	179	245
1D	51	8/48	Original; outside-bc: blue & yellow only; scarce	1	1	20	40	60	118	192	265
2	89	–	C-price 15¢; LDC-r	1	1	5	10	14	20	24	28
3	121	–	LDC-r	1	1	4	8	12	17	21	24
4	139	–	New-c; PC-r	1	2	3	6	9	18	27	35
5	156	–	PC-r	1	2	2	4	6	9	13	16
6	167	11/63	PC-r	1	2	2	4	6	8	11	14
7	167	7/66	PC-r	1	2	2	4	6	8	11	14
8A	166	Win/69	C-price 25¢; soft-c; scarce; PC-r	1	2	3	6	9	15	21	26
8B	166	Win/69	C-price 25¢; stiff-c; PC-r	1	2	2	4	6	8	11	14

52. The House of the Seven Gables

Ed	HRN	Date	Details	A	C	GD	VG	FN	VF	VF/NM	NM-
1	53	10/48	Orig.; Griffiths a&c	1	1	19	38	57	112	179	245
2	89	–	C-price 15¢; LDC-r	1	1	5	10	15	22	26	30
3	121	–	LDC-r	1	1	4	8	12	17	21	24
4	142	–	New-c&a; PC-r; Woodbridge-a	2	2	5	10	15	25	31	36
5	156	–	PC-r	2	2	2	4	6	9	13	16
6	165	–	PC-r	2	2	2	4	6	8	11	14
7	167	5/64	PC-r	2	2	2	4	6	9	13	16
8	167	3/66	PC-r	2	2	2	4	6	8	11	14
9	166	R/1968	C-price 25¢; PC-r	2	2	2	4	6	8	11	14
10	169	Spr/70	Stiff-c; PC-r	2	2	2	4	6	8	11	14

53. A Christmas Carol

Ed	HRN	Date	Details	A	C	GD	VG	FN	VF	VF/NM	NM-
1	53	11/48	Original & only ed; Kiefer-c/a	1	1	29	58	87	170	278	385

54. Man in the Iron Mask

Ed	HRN	Date	Details	A	C	GD	VG	FN	VF	VF/NM	NM-
1	55	12/48	Original; Froehlich-a, Kiefer-c	1	1	19	38	57	112	179	245
2	93	–	C-price 15¢; LDC-r	1	1	5	10	15	23	28	32
3A	111	–	(O) logo lettering; scarce; LDC-r	1	1	6	12	18	31	38	45
3B	111	–	New logo as PC; LDC-r	1	1	5	10	15	23	28	32
4	142	–	New-c&a; PC-r	2	2	5	10	15	24	30	35
5	154	–	PC-r	2	2	2	4	6	9	13	16
6	165	–	PC-r	2	2	2	4	6	8	11	14
7	167	5/64	PC-r	2	2	2	4	6	8	11	14
8	167	4/66	PC-r	2	2	2	4	6	8	11	14

Classics Illustrated #56 © GIL

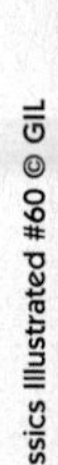
Classics Illustrated #60 © GIL

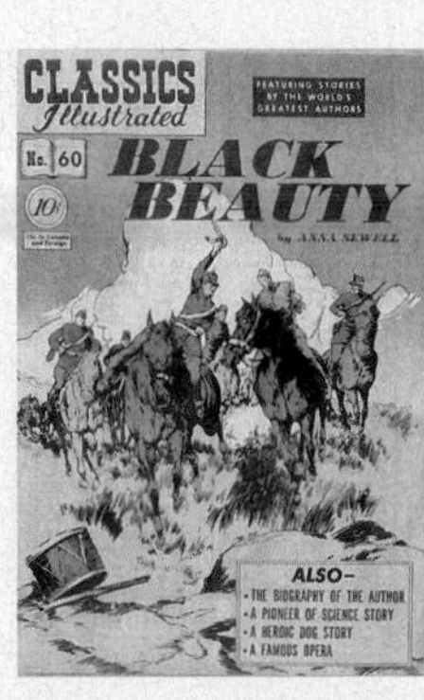

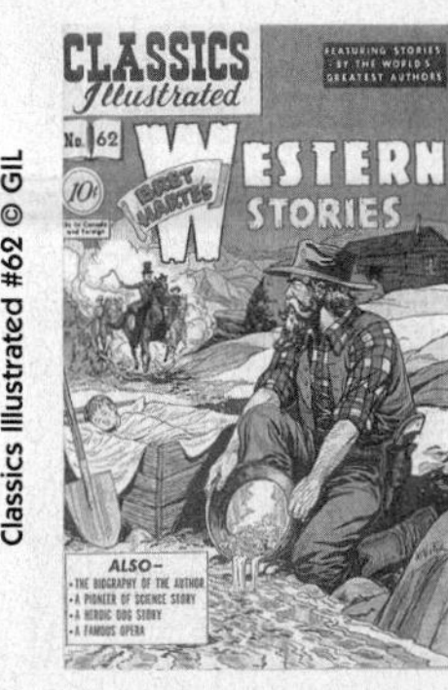

Classics Illustrated #62 © GIL

Ed	HRN	Date	Details	A	C	GD 2.0	VG 4.0	FN 6.0	VF 8.0	VF/NM 9.0	NM- 9.2
9A	166	Win/69	C-price 25¢; soft-c PC-r	2	2	3	6	9	15	21	26
9B	166	Win/69	Stiff-c	2	2	2	4	6	8	11	14

55. Silas Marner (Used in **SOTI**, pgs. 311, 312)

Ed	HRN	Date	Details	A	C	GD	VG	FN	VF	VF/NM	NM-
1	55	1/49	Original-Kiefer-c	1	1	19	38	57	109	172	235
2	75	–	Price circle blank; 'Coming Next' ad; LDC-r	1	1	5	10	15	24	30	35
3	97	–	LDC-r	1	1	3	6	9	14	19	24
4	121	–	New-c; PC-r	1	2	3	6	9	18	27	35
5	130	–	PC-r	1	2	2	4	6	9	13	16
6	140	–	PC-r	1	2	2	4	6	9	13	16
7	154	–	PC-r	1	2	2	4	6	9	13	16
8	165	–	PC-r	1	2	2	4	6	8	11	14
9	167	2/64	PC-r	1	2	2	4	6	8	11	14
10	167	6/65	PC-r	1	2	2	4	6	8	11	14
11	166	5/67	PC-r	1	2	2	4	6	8	11	14
12A	166	Win/69	C-price 25¢; soft-c PC-r	1	2	3	6	9	15	21	26
12B	166	Win/69	C-price 25¢; stiff-c PC-r	1	2	2	4	6	8	11	14

56. The Toilers of the Sea

Ed	HRN	Date	Details	A	C	GD	VG	FN	VF	VF/NM	NM-
1	55	2/49	Original; A.M. Froehlich-c/a	1	1	25	50	75	147	241	335
2	165	–	New-c&a; PC-r; Angelo Torres-a	2	2	8	16	24	40	50	60
3	167	3/64	PC-r	2	2	3	6	9	16	23	30
4	167	10/66	PC-r	2	2	3	6	9	16	23	30

57. The Song of Hiawatha

Ed	HRN	Date	Details	A	C	GD	VG	FN	VF	VF/NM	NM-
1	55	3/49	Original; Alex Blum-c/a	1	1	18	36	54	107	169	230
2	75	–	No c-price w/15¢ sticker; 'Coming Next' ad; LDC-r	1	1	5	10	15	24	30	35
3	94	–	C-price 15¢; LDC-r	1	1	5	10	14	20	24	28
4	118	–	LDC-r	1	1	3	6	9	14	19	24
5	134	–	New-c; PC-r	1	2	3	6	9	17	26	35
6	139	–	PC-r	1	2	2	4	6	9	13	16
7	154	–	PC-r	1	2	2	4	6	9	13	16
8	167	–	Has orig.date; PC-r	1	2	2	4	6	8	11	14
9	167	9/64	PC-r	1	2	2	4	6	8	11	14
10	167	10/65	PC-r	1	2	2	4	6	8	11	14
11	166	F/1968	C-price 25¢; PC-r	1	2	2	4	6	8	11	14

58. The Prairie

Ed	HRN	Date	Details	A	C	GD	VG	FN	VF	VF/NM	NM-
1	60	4/49	Original; Palais c/a	1	1	18	36	54	107	169	230
2A	62	–	No c-price; no coming-next ad; LDC-r	1	1	9	18	27	47	61	75
2B	62		10¢ (rare)	1	1	20	40	60	115	185	255
3	78	–	C-price 15¢ in dbl. circle; LDC-r	1	1	5	10	15	22	26	30
4	114	–	LDC-r	1	1	4	8	12	17	21	24
5	131	–	LDC-r	1	1	4	7	10	14	17	20
6	132	–	LDC-r	1	1	4	7	10	14	17	20
7	146	–	New-c; PC-r	1	2	5	10	15	23	28	32
8	155	–	PC-r	1	2	2	4	6	9	13	16
9	167	5/64	PC-r	1	2	2	4	6	8	11	14
10	167	4/66	PC-r	1	2	2	4	6	8	11	14
11	169	Sm/69	New price 25¢; stiff-c; PC-r	1	2	2	4	6	8	11	14

59. Wuthering Heights

Ed	HRN	Date	Details	A	C	GD	VG	FN	VF	VF/NM	NM-
1	60	5/49	Original; Kiefer-c/a	1	1	19	38	57	111	176	240
2	85	–	C-price 15¢; LDC-r	1	1	6	12	18	31	38	45
3	156	–	New-c; PC-r	1	2	5	10	15	25	31	36
4	167	1/64	PC-r	1	2	2	4	6	9	13	16
5	167	10/66	PC-r	1	2	2	4	6	9	13	16
6	169	Sm/69	C-price 25¢; stiff-c; PC-r	1	2	2	4	6	9	13	16

60. Black Beauty

Ed	HRN	Date	Details	A	C	GD	VG	FN	VF	VF/NM	NM-
1	62	6/49	Original; Froehlich-c/a	1	1	18	36	54	103	162	220
2	62	–	No c-price; no coming-next ad; LDC-r (rare)	1	1	20	40	60	114	182	250
3	85	–	C-price 15¢; LDC-r	1	1	5	10	15	23	28	32
4	158	–	New L.B. Cole-c/a; PC-r	2	2	7	14	21	35	43	50
5	167	2/64	PC-r	2	2	2	4	6	11	16	20
6	167	3/66	PC-r	2	2	2	4	6	11	16	20
7	166	R/1968	New-c&price, 25¢; PC-r	2	3	5	10	15	30	50	70

61. The Woman in White

Ed	HRN	Date	Details	A	C	GD	VG	FN	VF	VF/NM	NM-
1A	62	7/49	Original; Blum-c/a fc-purple; bc: top illos light blue	1	1	20	40	60	120	195	270
1B	62	7/49	Original; Blum-c/a fc-pink; bc: top illos light violet	1	1	20	40	60	120	195	270
2	156	–	New-c; PC-r	1	2	6	12	18	28	34	40
3	167	1/64	PC-r	1	2	2	4	6	11	16	20
4	166	R/1968	C-price 25¢; PC-r	1	2	2	4	6	11	16	20

62. Western Stories ("The Luck of Roaring Camp" and "The Outcasts of Poker Flat")

Ed	HRN	Date	Details	A	C	GD	VG	FN	VF	VF/NM	NM-
1	62	8/49	Original; Kiefer-c/a	1	1	18	36	54	103	162	220
2	89	–	C-price 15¢; LDC-r	1	1	5	10	15	23	28	32
3	121	–	LDC-r	1	1	3	6	9	15	21	26
4	137	–	New-c; PC-r	1	2	3	6	9	17	26	35
5	152	–	PC-r	1	2	2	4	6	8	11	14
6	167	10/63	PC-r	1	2	2	4	6	8	11	14
7	167	6/64	PC-r	1	2	2	4	6	8	11	14
8	167	11/66	PC-r	1	2	2	4	6	8	11	14
9	166	R/1968	New-c&price 25¢; PC-r	1	3	3	6	9	16	24	32

63. The Man Without a Country

Ed	HRN	Date	Details	A	C	GD	VG	FN	VF	VF/NM	NM-
1	62	9/49	Original; Kiefer-c/a	1	1	20	40	60	117	189	260
2	78	–	C-price 15¢ in double circle; LDC-r	1	1	5	10	15	23	28	32
3	156	–	New-c, old-a; PC-r	1	2	6	12	18	28	34	40
4	165	–	New-a & text pgs.; PC-r; A. Torres-a	2	2	5	10	15	23	28	32
5	167	3/64	PC-r	2	2	2	4	6	8	11	14
6	167	8/66	PC-r	2	2	2	4	6	8	11	14
7	169	Sm/69	New price 25¢; stiff-c; PC-r	2	2	2	4	6	8	11	14

64. Treasure Island

Ed	HRN	Date	Details	A	C	GD	VG	FN	VF	VF/NM	NM-
1	62	10/49	Original; Blum-c/a	1	1	19	38	57	109	172	235
2A	82	–	C-price 15¢; soft-c LDC-r	1	1	5	10	15	22	26	30
2B	82	–	Stiff-c; LDC-r	1	1	5	10	15	23	28	32
3	117	–	LDC-r	1	1	3	6	9	15	21	26
4	131	–	New-c; PC-r	1	2	3	6	9	17	26	35
5	138	–	PC-r	1	2	2	4	6	9	13	16
6	146	–	PC-r	1	2	2	4	6	9	13	16
7	158	–	PC-r	1	2	2	4	6	9	13	16
8	165	–	PC-r	1	2	2	4	6	8	11	14
9	167	–	PC-r	1	2	2	4	6	8	11	14
10	167	6/64	PC-r	1	2	2	4	6	8	11	14
11	167	12/65	PC-r	1	2	2	4	6	8	11	14
12A	166	10/67	PC-r	1	2	2	4	6	8	11	14
12B	166	10/67	w/Grit ad stapled in book	1	2	10	20	30	66	138	210
13	169	Spr/69	New price 25¢; stiff-c; PC-r	1	2	2	4	6	9	13	16
14	–	1989	Long John Silver's Seafood Shoppes;	1	2						5.00

Classics Illustrated #65 © GIL

Classics Illustrated #73 © GIL

Classics Illustrated #78 © GIL

						GD 2.0	VG 4.0	FN 6.0	VF 8.0	VF/NM 9.0	NM- 9.2
			$1.95, First/Berkley Publ.; Blum-r								

65. Benjamin Franklin

Ed	HRN	Date	Details	A	C	GD 2.0	VG 4.0	FN 6.0	VF 8.0	VF/NM 9.0	NM- 9.2
1	64	11/49	Original; Kiefer-c; Iger Shop-a	1	1	10	20	30	70	150	230
2	131	–	New-c; PC-r	1	2	6	12	18	28	34	40
3	154	–	PC-r	1	2	2	4	6	9	13	16
4	167	2/64	PC-r	1	2	2	4	6	9	13	16
5	167	4/66	PC-r	1	2	2	4	6	9	13	16
6	169	Fall/69	New price 25¢; stiff-c; PC-r	1	2	2	4	6	9	13	16

66. The Cloister and the Hearth

Ed	HRN	Date	Details	A	C	GD 2.0	VG 4.0	FN 6.0	VF 8.0	VF/NM 9.0	NM- 9.2
1	67	12/49	Original & only ed; Kiefer-a & c	1	1	36	72	108	211	343	475

67. The Scottish Chiefs

Ed	HRN	Date	Details	A	C	GD 2.0	VG 4.0	FN 6.0	VF 8.0	VF/NM 9.0	NM- 9.2
1	67	1/50	Original; Blum-a&c	1	1	15	30	45	90	140	190
2	85	–	C-price 15¢; LDC-r	1	1	5	10	15	23	28	32
3	118	–	LDC-r	1	1	3	6	9	15	21	26
4	136	–	New-c; PC-r	1	2	3	6	9	18	27	36
5	154	–	PC-r	1	2	2	4	6	9	13	16
6	167	11/63	PC-r	1	2	2	4	6	10	14	18
7	167	8/65	PC-r	1	2	2	4	6	9	13	16

68. Julius Caesar (Used in **SOTI**, pgs. 36, 37)

Ed	HRN	Date	Details	A	C	GD 2.0	VG 4.0	FN 6.0	VF 8.0	VF/NM 9.0	NM- 9.2
1	70	2/50	Original; Kiefer-c/a	1	1	16	32	48	94	147	200
2	85	–	C-price 15¢; LDC-r	1	1	5	10	15	22	26	30
3	108	–	LDC-r	1	1	4	9	13	18	22	26
4	156	–	New L.B. Cole-c; PC-r	1	2	6	12	18	28	34	40
5	165	–	New-a by Evans, Crandall; PC-r	2	2	5	10	15	24	30	35
6	167	2/64	PC-r	2	2	2	4	6	8	11	14
7	167	10/65	Tarzan books inside cover; PC-r	2	2	2	4	6	8	11	14
8	166	R/1967	PC-r	2	2	2	4	6	8	11	14
9	169	Win/69	PC-r; stiff-c	2	2	2	4	6	8	11	14

69. Around the World in 80 Days

Ed	HRN	Date	Details	A	C	GD 2.0	VG 4.0	FN 6.0	VF 8.0	VF/NM 9.0	NM- 9.2
1	70	3/50	Original; Kiefer-c/a	1	1	16	32	48	94	147	200
2	87	–	C-price 15¢; LDC-r	1	1	5	10	15	22	26	30
3	125	–	LDC-r	1	1	4	9	13	18	22	26
4	136	–	New-c; PC-r	1	2	5	10	15	25	31	36
5	146	–	PC-r	1	2	2	4	6	9	13	16
6	152	–	PC-r	1	2	2	4	6	9	13	16
7	164	–	PC-r	1	2	2	4	6	8	11	14
8	167	–	PC-r	1	2	2	4	6	8	11	14
9	167	7/64	PC-r	1	2	2	4	6	8	11	14
10	167	11/65	PC-r	1	2	2	4	6	8	11	14
11	166	7/67	PC-r	1	2	2	4	6	8	11	14
12	169	Spr/69	C-price 25¢; stiff-c; PC-r	1	2	2	4	6	8	11	14

70. The Pilot

Ed	HRN	Date	Details	A	C	GD 2.0	VG 4.0	FN 6.0	VF 8.0	VF/NM 9.0	NM- 9.2
1	71	4/50	Original; Blum-c/a	1	1	15	30	45	83	124	165
2	92	–	C-price 15¢; LDC-r	1	1	5	10	15	23	28	32
3	125	–	LDC-r	1	1	4	9	13	18	22	26
4	156	–	New-c; PC-r	1	2	6	12	18	28	34	40
5	167	2/64	PC-r	1	2	2	4	6	11	16	20
6	167	5/66	PC-r	1	2	2	4	6	9	13	16

71. The Man Who Laughs

Ed	HRN	Date	Details	A	C	GD 2.0	VG 4.0	FN 6.0	VF 8.0	VF/NM 9.0	NM- 9.2
1	71	5/50	Original; Blum-c/a	1	1	21	42	63	122	199	275
2	165	–	New-c&a; PC-r	2	2	15	30	45	83	124	165
3	167	4/64	PC-r	2	2	11	22	33	62	86	115

72. The Oregon Trail

Ed	HRN	Date	Details	A	C	GD 2.0	VG 4.0	FN 6.0	VF 8.0	VF/NM 9.0	NM- 9.2
1	73	6/50	Original; Kiefer-c/a	1	1	14	28	42	81	118	155
2	89	–	C-price 15¢; LDC-r	1	1	5	10	15	23	28	32
3	121	–	LDC-r	1	1	4	9	13	18	22	26
4	131	–	New-c; PC-r	1	2	5	10	15	25	31	36
5	140	–	PC-r	1	2	2	4	6	9	13	16
6	150	–	PC-r	1	2	2	4	6	9	13	16
7	164	–	PC-r	1	2	2	4	6	8	11	14
8	167	–	PC-r	1	2	2	4	6	8	11	14
9	167	8/64	PC-r	1	2	2	4	6	8	11	14
10	167	10/65	PC-r	1	2	2	4	6	8	11	14
11	166	R/1968	C-price 25¢; PC-r	1	2	2	4	6	8	11	14

73. The Black Tulip

Ed	HRN	Date	Details	A	C	GD 2.0	VG 4.0	FN 6.0	VF 8.0	VF/NM 9.0	NM- 9.2
1	75	7/50	1st & only ed.; Alex Blum-c/a	1	1	39	78	117	231	378	525

74. Mr. Midshipman Easy

Ed	HRN	Date	Details	A	C	GD 2.0	VG 4.0	FN 6.0	VF 8.0	VF/NM 9.0	NM- 9.2
1	75	8/50	1st & only edition	1	1	38	76	114	228	369	510

75. The Lady of the Lake

Ed	HRN	Date	Details	A	C	GD 2.0	VG 4.0	FN 6.0	VF 8.0	VF/NM 9.0	NM- 9.2
1	75	9/50	Original; Kiefer-c/a	1	1	15	30	45	83	124	165
2	85	–	C-price 15¢; LDC-r	1	1	5	10	15	24	30	35
3	118	–	LDC-r	1	1	5	10	14	20	24	28
4	139	–	New-c; PC-r	1	2	5	10	15	25	31	36
5	154	–	PC-r	1	2	2	4	6	9	13	16
6	165	–	PC-r	1	2	2	4	6	8	11	14
7	167	4/64	PC-r	1	2	2	4	6	8	11	14
8	167	5/66	PC-r	1	2	2	4	6	8	11	14
9	169	Spr/69	New price 25¢; stiff-c; PC-r	1	2	2	4	6	8	11	14

76. The Prisoner of Zenda

Ed	HRN	Date	Details	A	C	GD 2.0	VG 4.0	FN 6.0	VF 8.0	VF/NM 9.0	NM- 9.2
1	75	10/50	Original; Kiefer-c/a	1	1	15	30	45	83	124	165
2	85	–	C-price 15¢; LDC-r	1	1	5	10	15	23	28	32
3	111	–	LDC-r	1	1	3	6	9	16	21	26
4	128	–	New-c; PC-r	1	2	3	6	9	17	26	35
5	152	–	PC-r	1	2	2	4	6	9	13	16
6	165	–	PC-r	1	2	2	4	6	8	11	14
7	167	4/64	PC-r	1	2	2	4	6	8	11	14
8	167	9/66	PC-r	1	2	2	4	6	8	11	14
9	169	Fall/69	New price 25¢; stiff-c; PC-r	1	2	2	4	6	8	11	14

77. The Iliad

Ed	HRN	Date	Details	A	C	GD 2.0	VG 4.0	FN 6.0	VF 8.0	VF/NM 9.0	NM- 9.2
1	78	11/50	Original; Blum-c/a	1	1	14	28	42	81	118	155
2	87	–	C-price 15¢; LDC-r	1	1	5	10	15	24	30	35
3	121	–	LDC-r	1	1	3	6	9	15	21	26
4	139	–	New-c; PC-r	1	2	3	6	9	16	24	32
5	150	–	PC-r	1	2	2	4	6	9	13	16
6	165	–	PC-r	1	2	2	4	6	8	11	14
7	167	10/63	PC-r	1	2	2	4	6	8	11	14
8	167	7/64	PC-r	1	2	2	4	6	8	11	14
9	167	5/66	PC-r	1	2	2	4	6	8	11	14
10	166	R/1968	C-price 25¢; PC-r	1	2	2	4	6	8	11	14

78. Joan of Arc

Ed	HRN	Date	Details	A	C	GD 2.0	VG 4.0	FN 6.0	VF 8.0	VF/NM 9.0	NM- 9.2
1	78	12/50	Original; Kiefer-c/a	1	1	14	28	42	81	118	155
2	87	–	C-price 15¢; LDC-r	1	1	5	10	15	23	28	32
3	113	–	LDC-r	1	1	3	6	9	15	21	26
4	128	–	New-c; PC-r	1	2	3	6	9	17	26	35
5	140	–	PC-r	1	2	2	4	6	9	13	16
6	150	–	PC-r	1	2	2	4	6	9	13	16
7	159	–	PC-r	1	2	2	4	6	9	13	16
8	167	–	PC-r	1	2	2	4	6	8	11	14
9	167	12/63	PC-r	1	2	2	4	6	8	11	14
10	167	6/65	PC-r	1	2	2	4	6	8	11	14
11	166	6/67	PC-r	1	2	2	4	6	8	11	14
12	166	Win/69	New-c&price, 25¢; PC-r; stiff-c	1	3	3	6	9	16	24	32

79. Cyrano de Bergerac

Ed	HRN	Date	Details	A	C	GD 2.0	VG 4.0	FN 6.0	VF 8.0	VF/NM 9.0	NM- 9.2
1	78	1/51	Orig.; movie promo inside front-c; Blum-c/a	1	1	14	28	42	81	118	155
2	85	–	C-price 15¢; LDC-r	1	1	5	10	15	23	28	32
3	118	–	LDC-r	1	1	3	6	9	17	23	28

Classics Illustrated #81 © GIL

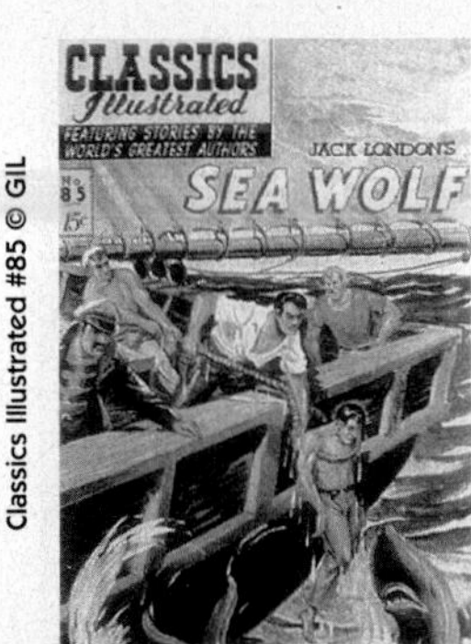

Classics Illustrated #85 © GIL

Classics Illustrated #94 © GIL

Ed	HRN	Date	Details	A	C	GD 2.0	VG 4.0	FN 6.0	VF 8.0	VF/NM 9.0	NM- 9.2
4	133	–	New-c; PC-r	1	2	3	6	9	16	24	32
5	156	–	PC-r	1	2	2	4	6	11	16	20
6	167	8/64	PC-r	1	2	2	4	6	11	16	20

80. White Fang (Last line drawn cover)

Ed	HRN	Date	Details	A	C	GD 2.0	VG 4.0	FN 6.0	VF 8.0	VF/NM 9.0	NM- 9.2
1	79	2/51	Orig.; Blum-c/a	1	1	14	28	42	81	118	155
2	87	–	C-price 15¢; LDC-r	1	1	5	10	15	24	30	35
3	125	–	LDC-r	1	1	3	6	9	15	21	26
4	132	–	New-c; PC-r	1	2	3	6	9	16	24	32
5	140	–	PC-r	1	2	2	4	6	9	13	16
6	153	–	PC-r	1	2	2	4	6	9	13	16
7	167	–	PC-r	1	2	2	4	6	8	11	14
8	167	9/64	PC-r	1	2	2	4	6	8	11	14
9	167	7/65	PC-r	1	2	2	4	6	8	11	14
10	166	6/67	PC-r	1	2	2	4	6	8	11	14
11	169	Fall/69	New price 25¢; PC-r; stiff-c	1	2	2	4	6	8	11	14

81. The Odyssey (1st painted cover)

Ed	HRN	Date	Details	A	C	GD 2.0	VG 4.0	FN 6.0	VF 8.0	VF/NM 9.0	NM- 9.2
1	82	3/51	First 15¢ Original; Blum-c	1	1	14	28	42	81	118	155
2	167	8/64	PC-r	1	1	2	4	6	11	16	20
3	167	10/66	PC-r	1	1	2	4	6	11	16	20
4	169	Spr/69	New, stiff-c; PC-r	1	2	3	6	9	18	27	36

82. The Master of Ballantrae

Ed	HRN	Date	Details	A	C	GD 2.0	VG 4.0	FN 6.0	VF 8.0	VF/NM 9.0	NM- 9.2
1	82	4/51	Original; Blum-c	1	1	14	28	42	76	108	140
2	167	8/64	PC-r	1	1	3	6	9	14	19	24
3	166	Fall/68	New, stiff-c; PC-r	1	2	3	6	9	18	27	36

83. The Jungle Book

Ed	HRN	Date	Details	A	C	GD 2.0	VG 4.0	FN 6.0	VF 8.0	VF/NM 9.0	NM- 9.2
1	85	5/51	Original; Blum-c Bossert/Blum-a	1	1	14	28	42	80	115	150
2	110	–	PC-r	1	1	2	4	6	10	14	18
3	125	–	PC-r	1	1	2	4	6	9	13	16
4	134	–	PC-r	1	1	2	4	6	9	13	16
5	142	–	PC-r	1	1	2	4	6	9	13	16
6	150	–	PC-r	1	1	2	4	6	9	13	16
7	159	–	PC-r	1	1	2	4	6	9	13	16
8	167	–	PC-r	1	1	2	4	6	8	11	14
9	167	3/65	PC-r	1	1	2	4	6	8	11	14
10	167	11/65	PC-r	1	1	2	4	6	8	11	14
11	167	5/66	PC-r	1	1	2	4	6	8	11	14
12	166	R/1968	New c&a; stiff-c; PC-r	2	2	3	6	9	18	28	38

84. The Gold Bug and Other Stories ("The Gold Bug", "The Tell-Tale Heart", "The Cask of Amontillado")

Ed	HRN	Date	Details	A	C	GD 2.0	VG 4.0	FN 6.0	VF 8.0	VF/NM 9.0	NM- 9.2
1	85	6/51	Original; Blum-c/a; Palais, Laverly-a	1	1	15	30	45	88	137	185
2	167	7/64	PC-r	1	1	11	22	33	64	90	115

85. The Sea Wolf

Ed	HRN	Date	Details	A	C	GD 2.0	VG 4.0	FN 6.0	VF 8.0	VF/NM 9.0	NM- 9.2
1	85	7/51	Original; Blum-c/a	1	1	11	22	33	64	90	115
2	121	–	PC-r	1	1	2	4	6	9	13	16
3	132	–	PC-r	1	1	2	4	6	9	13	16
4	141	–	PC-r	1	1	2	4	6	9	13	16
5	161	–	PC-r	1	1	2	4	6	8	11	14
6	167	2/64	PC-r	1	1	2	4	6	8	11	14
7	167	11/65	PC-r	1	1	2	4	6	8	11	14
8	169	Fall/69	New price 25¢; stiff-c; PC-r	1	1	2	4	6	8	11	14

86. Under Two Flags

Ed	HRN	Date	Details	A	C	GD 2.0	VG 4.0	FN 6.0	VF 8.0	VF/NM 9.0	NM- 9.2
1	87	8/51	Original; first delBourgo-a	1	1	11	22	33	64	90	115
2	117	–	PC-r	1	1	2	4	6	10	14	18
3	139	–	PC-r	1	1	2	4	6	9	13	16
4	158	–	PC-r	1	1	2	4	6	9	13	16
5	167	2/64	PC-r	1	1	2	4	6	8	11	14
6	167	8/66	PC-r	1	1	2	4	6	8	11	14
7	169	Sm/69	New price 25¢; stiff-c; PC-r	1	1	2	4	6	8	11	14

87. A Midsummer Nights Dream

Ed	HRN	Date	Details	A	C	GD 2.0	VG 4.0	FN 6.0	VF 8.0	VF/NM 9.0	NM- 9.2
1	87	9/51	Original; Blum c/a	1	1	11	22	33	64	90	115
2	161	–	PC-r	1	1	2	4	6	9	13	16
3	167	4/64	PC-r	1	1	2	4	6	8	11	14
4	167	5/66	PC-r	1	1	2	4	6	8	11	14
5	169	Sm/69	New price 25¢; stiff-c; PC-r	1	1	2	4	6	8	11	14

88. Men of Iron

Ed	HRN	Date	Details	A	C	GD 2.0	VG 4.0	FN 6.0	VF 8.0	VF/NM 9.0	NM- 9.2
1	89	10/51	Original	1	1	12	24	36	67	94	120
2	154	–	PC-r	1	1	2	4	6	9	13	16
3	167	1/64	PC-r	1	1	2	4	6	8	11	14
4	166	R/1968	C-price 25¢; PC-r	1	1	2	4	6	8	11	14

89. Crime and Punishment (Cover illo. in **POP**)

Ed	HRN	Date	Details	A	C	GD 2.0	VG 4.0	FN 6.0	VF 8.0	VF/NM 9.0	NM- 9.2
1	89	11/51	Original; Palais-a	1	1	14	28	42	76	108	140
2	152	–	PC-r	1	1	2	4	6	9	13	16
3	167	4/64	PC-r	1	1	2	4	6	8	11	14
4	167	5/66	PC-r	1	1	2	4	6	8	11	14
5	169	Fall/69	New price 25¢ stiff-c; PC-r	1	1	2	4	6	8	11	14

90. Green Mansions

Ed	HRN	Date	Details	A	C	GD 2.0	VG 4.0	FN 6.0	VF 8.0	VF/NM 9.0	NM- 9.2
1	89	12/51	Original; Blum-c/a	1	1	12	24	36	67	94	120
2	148	–	New L.B. Cole-c; PC-r	1	2	5	10	15	24	29	34
3	165	–	PC-r	1	2	2	4	6	8	11	14
4	167	4/64	PC-r	1	2	2	4	6	8	11	14
5	167	9/66	PC-r	1	2	2	4	6	8	11	14
6	169	Sm/69	New price 25¢; stiff-c; PC-r	1	2	2	4	6	8	11	14

91. The Call of the Wild

Ed	HRN	Date	Details	A	C	GD 2.0	VG 4.0	FN 6.0	VF 8.0	VF/NM 9.0	NM- 9.2
1	92	1/52	Orig.; delBourgo-a	1	1	12	24	36	69	97	125
2	112	–	PC-r	1	1	2	4	6	9	13	16
3	125	–	'Picture Progress' on back-c; PC-r	1	1	2	4	6	9	13	16
4	134	–	PC-r	1	1	2	4	6	9	13	16
5	143	–	PC-r	1	1	2	4	6	9	13	16
6	165	–	PC-r	1	1	2	4	6	9	13	16
7	167	–	PC-r	1	1	2	4	6	8	11	14
8	167	4/65	PC-r	1	1	2	4	6	8	11	14
9	167	3/66	PC-r	1	1	2	4	6	8	11	14
10	166	11/67	PC-r	1	1	2	4	6	8	11	14
11	169	Spr/70	New price 25¢; stiff-c; PC-r	1	1	2	4	6	8	11	14

92. The Courtship of Miles Standish

Ed	HRN	Date	Details	A	C	GD 2.0	VG 4.0	FN 6.0	VF 8.0	VF/NM 9.0	NM- 9.2
1	92	2/52	Original; Blum-c/a	1	1	12	24	36	69	97	125
2	165	–	PC-r	1	1	2	4	6	9	13	16
3	167	3/64	PC-r	1	1	2	4	6	9	13	16
4	166	5/67	PC-r	1	1	2	4	6	9	13	16
5	169	Win/69	New price 25¢ stiff-c; PC-r	1	1	2	4	6	9	13	16

93. Pudd'nhead Wilson

Ed	HRN	Date	Details	A	C	GD 2.0	VG 4.0	FN 6.0	VF 8.0	VF/NM 9.0	NM- 9.2
1	94	3/52	Orig.; Kiefer-c/a;	1	1	12	24	36	69	97	125
2	165	–	New-c; PC-r	1	2	2	4	6	11	16	25
3	167	3/64	PC-r	1	2	2	4	6	9	13	16
4	166	R/1968	New price 25¢; soft-c; PC-r	1	2	2	4	6	9	13	16

94. David Balfour

Ed	HRN	Date	Details	A	C	GD 2.0	VG 4.0	FN 6.0	VF 8.0	VF/NM 9.0	NM- 9.2
1	94	4/52	Original; Palais-a	1	1	11	22	33	64	90	115
2	167	5/64	PC-r	1	1	2	4	6	11	16	20
3	166	R/1968	C-price 25¢; PC-r	1	1	2	4	6	13	18	22

95. All Quiet on the Western Front

Ed	HRN	Date	Details	A	C	GD 2.0	VG 4.0	FN 6.0	VF 8.0	VF/NM 9.0	NM- 9.2
1A	96	5/52	Orig.; del Bourgo-a	1	1	15	30	45	83	124	165
1B	99	5/52	Orig.; del Bourgo-a	1	1	14	28	42	76	108	140
2	167	10/64	PC-r	1	1	3	6	9	15	22	28

Classics Illustrated #98 © GIL

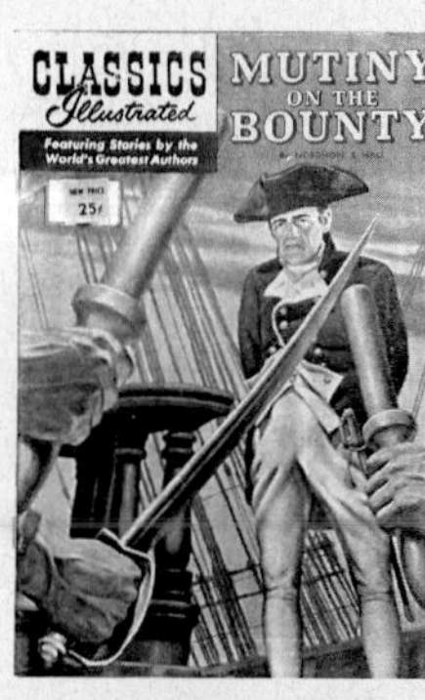

Classics Illustrated #100 © GIL

Classics Illustrated #106 © GIL

Ed	HRN	Date	Details	A	C	GD 2.0	VG 4.0	FN 6.0	VF 8.0	VF/NM 9.0	NM- 9.2
3	167	11/66	PC-r	1	1	3	6	9	15	22	28

96. Daniel Boone

Ed	HRN	Date	Details	A	C	GD 2.0	VG 4.0	FN 6.0	VF 8.0	VF/NM 9.0	NM- 9.2
1	97	6/52	Original; Blum-a	1	1	11	22	33	62	86	110
2	117	–	PC-r	1	1	2	4	6	9	13	16
3	128	–	PC-r	1	1	2	4	6	9	13	16
4	132	–	PC-r	1	1	2	4	6	9	13	16
5	134	–	"Story of Jesus" on back-c; PC-r	1	1	2	4	6	9	13	16
6	158	–	PC-r	1	1	2	4	6	9	13	16
7	167	1/64	PC-r	1	1	2	4	6	8	11	14
8	167	5/65	PC-r	1	1	2	4	6	8	11	14
9	167	11/66	PC-r	1	1	2	4	6	8	11	14
10	166	Win/69	New-c; price 25¢; PC-r; stiff-c	1	2	3	6	9	15	22	28

97. King Solomon's Mines

Ed	HRN	Date	Details	A	C	GD 2.0	VG 4.0	FN 6.0	VF 8.0	VF/NM 9.0	NM- 9.2
1	96	7/52	Orig.; Kiefer-a	1	1	12	24	36	67	94	120
2	118	–	PC-r	1	1	2	4	6	9	13	16
3	131	–	PC-r	1	1	2	4	6	9	13	16
4	141	–	PC-r	1	1	2	4	6	9	13	16
5	158	–	PC-r	1	1	2	4	6	9	13	16
6	167	2/64	PC-r	1	1	2	4	6	8	11	14
7	167	9/65	PC-r	1	1	2	4	6	8	11	14
8	169	Sm/69	New price 25¢; stiff-c; PC-r	1	1	2	4	6	8	11	14

98. The Red Badge of Courage

Ed	HRN	Date	Details	A	C	GD 2.0	VG 4.0	FN 6.0	VF 8.0	VF/NM 9.0	NM- 9.2
1	98	8/52	Original	1	1	12	24	36	67	94	120
2	118	–	PC-r	1	1	2	4	6	9	13	16
3	132	–	PC-r	1	1	2	4	6	9	13	16
4	142	–	PC-r	1	1	2	4	6	9	13	16
5	152	–	PC-r	1	1	2	4	6	9	13	16
6	161	–	PC-r	1	1	2	4	6	9	13	16
7	167	–	Has orig.date; PC-r	1	1	2	4	6	9	13	16
8	167	9/64	PC-r	1	1	2	4	6	9	13	16
9	167	10/65	PC-r	1	1	2	4	6	9	13	16
10	166	R/1968	New-c&price 25¢; PC-r; stiff-c	1	2	3	6	9	16	23	30

99. Hamlet (Used in **POP**, pg. 102)

Ed	HRN	Date	Details	A	C	GD 2.0	VG 4.0	FN 6.0	VF 8.0	VF/NM 9.0	NM- 9.2
1	98	9/52	Original; Blum-a	1	1	11	22	33	64	90	115
2	121	–	PC-r	1	1	2	4	6	9	13	16
3	141	–	PC-r	1	1	2	4	6	9	13	16
4	158	–	PC-r	1	1	2	4	6	9	13	16
5	167	–	Has orig.date; PC-r	1	1	2	4	6	8	11	14
6	167	7/65	PC-r	1	1	2	4	6	8	11	14
7	166	4/67	PC-r	1	1	2	4	6	8	11	14
8	169	Spr/69	New-c&price 25¢; PC-r; stiff-c	1	2	3	6	9	16	23	30

100. Mutiny on the Bounty

Ed	HRN	Date	Details	A	C	GD 2.0	VG 4.0	FN 6.0	VF 8.0	VF/NM 9.0	NM- 9.2
1	100	10/52	Original	1	1	11	22	33	62	86	110
2	117	–	PC-r	1	1	2	4	6	9	13	16
3	132	–	PC-r	1	1	2	4	6	9	13	16
4	142	–	PC-r	1	1	2	4	6	9	13	16
5	155	–	PC-r	1	1	2	4	6	9	13	16
6	167	–	Has orig. date;PC-r	1	1	2	4	6	8	11	14
7	167	5/64	PC-r	1	1	2	4	6	8	11	14
8	167	3/66	PC-r	1	1	2	4	6	8	11	14
9	169	Spr/70	PC-r; stiff-c	1	1	2	4	6	8	11	14

101. William Tell

Ed	HRN	Date	Details	A	C	GD 2.0	VG 4.0	FN 6.0	VF 8.0	VF/NM 9.0	NM- 9.2
1	101	11/52	Original; Kiefer-c delBourgo-a	1	1	12	24	36	67	94	120
2	118	–	PC-r	1	1	2	4	6	9	13	16
3	141	–	PC-r	1	1	2	4	6	9	13	16
4	158	–	PC-r	1	1	2	4	6	9	13	16
5	167	–	Has orig.date; PC-r	1	1	2	4	6	8	11	14
6	167	11/64	PC-r	1	1	2	4	6	8	11	14
7	166	4/67	PC-r	1	1	2	4	6	8	11	14
8	169	Win/69	New price 25¢; stiff-c; PC-r	1	1	2	4	6	8	11	14

102. The White Company

Ed	HRN	Date	Details	A	C	GD 2.0	VG 4.0	FN 6.0	VF 8.0	VF/NM 9.0	NM- 9.2
1	101	12/52	Original; Blum-a	1	1	14	28	42	80	115	150
2	165	–	PC-r	1	1	3	6	9	16	23	30
3	167	4/64	PC-r	1	1	3	6	9	16	23	30

103. Men Against the Sea

Ed	HRN	Date	Details	A	C	GD 2.0	VG 4.0	FN 6.0	VF 8.0	VF/NM 9.0	NM- 9.2
1	104	1/53	Original; Kiefer-c; Palais-a	1	1	12	24	36	67	94	120
2	114	–	PC-r	1	1	4	8	11	16	19	22
3	131	–	New-c; PC-r	1	2	5	10	15	24	30	35
4	158	–	PC-r	1	2	4	7	10	14	17	20
5	149	–	White reorder list; came after HRN-158; PC-r	1	2	5	10	15	22	26	30
6	167	3/64	PC-r	1	2	2	4	6	9	13	16

104. Bring 'Em Back Alive

Ed	HRN	Date	Details	A	C	GD 2.0	VG 4.0	FN 6.0	VF 8.0	VF/NM 9.0	NM- 9.2
1	105	2/53	Original; Kiefer-c/a	1	1	11	22	33	62	86	110
2	118	–	PC-r	1	1	2	4	6	9	13	16
3	133	–	PC-r	1	1	2	4	6	9	13	16
4	150	–	PC-r	1	1	2	4	6	9	13	16
5	158	–	PC-r	1	1	2	4	6	9	13	16
6	167	10/63	PC-r	1	1	2	4	6	8	11	14
7	167	9/65	PC-r	1	1	2	4	6	8	11	14
8	169	Win/69	New price 25¢; stiff-c; PC-r	1	1	2	4	6	8	11	14

105. From the Earth to the Moon

Ed	HRN	Date	Details	A	C	GD 2.0	VG 4.0	FN 6.0	VF 8.0	VF/NM 9.0	NM- 9.2
1	106	3/53	Original; Blum-a	1	1	11	22	33	62	86	110
2	118	–	PC-r	1	1	2	4	6	9	13	16
3	132	–	PC-r	1	1	2	4	6	9	13	16
4	141	–	PC-r	1	1	2	4	6	9	13	16
5	146	–	PC-r	1	1	2	4	6	9	13	16
6	156	–	PC-r	1	1	2	4	6	9	13	16
7	167	–	Has orig. date; PC-r	1	1	2	4	6	8	11	14
8	167	5/64	PC-r	1	1	2	4	6	8	11	14
9	167	5/65	PC-r	1	1	2	4	6	8	11	14
10A	166	10/67	PC-r	1	1	2	4	6	8	11	14
10B	166	10/67	w/Grit ad stapled in book	1	1	9	18	27	59	117	175
11	169	Sm/69	New price 25¢; stiff-c; PC-r	1	1	2	4	6	8	11	14
12	169	Spr/71	PC-r	1	1	2	4	6	8	11	14

106. Buffalo Bill

Ed	HRN	Date	Details	A	C	GD 2.0	VG 4.0	FN 6.0	VF 8.0	VF/NM 9.0	NM- 9.2
1	107	4/53	Orig.; delBourgo-a	1	1	11	22	33	60	83	105
2	118	–	PC-r	1	1	2	4	6	9	13	16
3	132	–	PC-r	1	1	2	4	6	9	13	16
4	142	–	PC-r	1	1	2	4	6	9	13	16
5	161	–	PC-r	1	1	2	4	6	8	11	14
6	167	3/64	PC-r	1	1	2	4	6	8	11	14
7	166	7/67	PC-r	1	1	2	4	6	8	11	14
8	169	Fall/69	PC-r; stiff-c	1	1	2	4	6	8	11	14

107. King of the Khyber Rifles

Ed	HRN	Date	Details	A	C	GD 2.0	VG 4.0	FN 6.0	VF 8.0	VF/NM 9.0	NM- 9.2
1	108	5/53	Original; Ditko-a (earliest published; about 1/3 of book)	1	1	11	22	33	64	90	115
2	118	–	PC-r	1	1	2	4	6	9	13	16
3	146	–	PC-r	1	1	2	4	6	9	13	16
4	158	–	PC-r	1	1	2	4	6	9	13	16
5	167	–	Has orig.date; PC-r	1	1	2	4	6	8	11	14
6	167	10/66	PC-r	1	1	2	4	6	8	11	14

108. Knights of the Round Table

Ed	HRN	Date	Details	A	C	GD 2.0	VG 4.0	FN 6.0	VF 8.0	VF/NM 9.0	NM- 9.2
1A	108	6/53	Original; Blum-a	1	1	12	24	36	69	97	125
1B	109	6/53	Original; scarce	1	1	13	26	39	72	101	130
2	117	–	PC-r	1	1	2	4	6	9	13	16
3	165	–	PC-r	1	1	2	4	6	8	11	14
4	167	4/64	PC-r	1	1	2	4	6	8	11	14

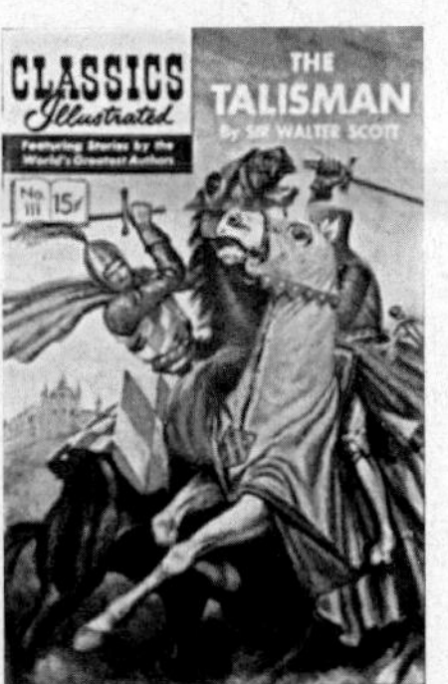

Classics Illustrated #111 © GIL

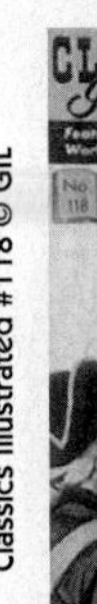

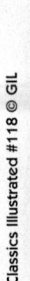

Classics Illustrated #118 © GIL

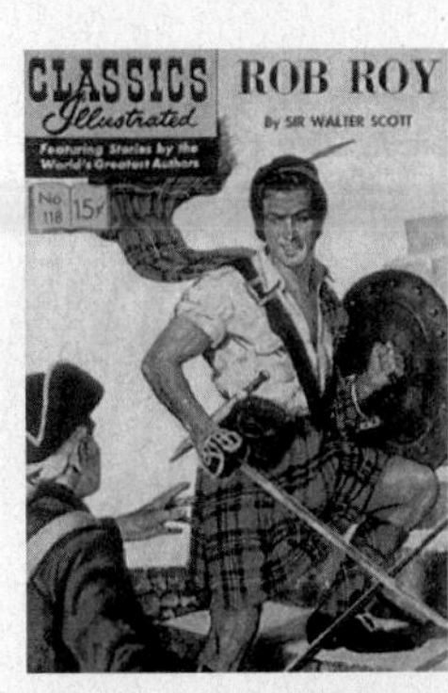

Classics Illustrated #125 © GIL

Ed	HRN	Date	Details	A	C	GD 2.0	VG 4.0	FN 6.0	VF 8.0	VF/NM 9.0	NM- 9.2
5	166	4/67	PC-r	1	1	2	4	6	8	11	14
6	169	Sm/69	New price 25¢; stiff-c; PC-r	1	1	2	4	6	8	11	14

109. Pitcairn's Island

Ed	HRN	Date	Details	A	C	GD 2.0	VG 4.0	FN 6.0	VF 8.0	VF/NM 9.0	NM- 9.2
1	110	7/53	Original; Palais-a	1	1	11	22	33	64	90	115
2	165	–	PC-r	1	1	2	4	6	9	13	16
3	167	3/64	PC-r	1	1	2	4	6	9	13	16
4	166	6/67	PC-r	1	1	2	4	6	9	13	16

110. A Study in Scarlet

Ed	HRN	Date	Details	A	C	GD 2.0	VG 4.0	FN 6.0	VF 8.0	VF/NM 9.0	NM- 9.2
1	111	8/53	Original	1	1	15	30	45	84	127	170
2	165	–	PC-r	1	1	11	22	33	62	86	110

111. The Talisman

Ed	HRN	Date	Details	A	C	GD 2.0	VG 4.0	FN 6.0	VF 8.0	VF/NM 9.0	NM- 9.2
1	112	9/53	Original; last H.C. Kiefer-a	1	1	11	22	33	64	90	115
2	165	–	PC-r	1	1	2	4	6	9	13	16
3	167	5/64	PC-r	1	1	2	4	6	9	13	16
4	166	Fall/68	C-price 25¢; PC-r	1	1	2	4	6	9	13	16

112. Adventures of Kit Carson

Ed	HRN	Date	Details	A	C	GD 2.0	VG 4.0	FN 6.0	VF 8.0	VF/NM 9.0	NM- 9.2
1	113	10/53	Original; Palais-a	1	1	11	22	33	62	86	110
2	129	–	PC-r	1	1	2	4	6	9	13	16
3	141	–	PC-r	1	1	2	4	6	9	13	16
4	152	–	PC-r	1	1	2	4	6	9	13	16
5	161	–	PC-r	1	1	2	4	6	8	11	14
6	167	–	PC-r	1	1	2	4	6	8	11	14
7	167	2/65	PC-r	1	1	2	4	6	8	11	14
8	167	5/66	PC-r	1	1	2	4	6	8	11	14
9	166	Win/69	New-c&price 25¢; PC-r; stiff-c	1	2	3	6	9	14	20	25

113. The Forty-Five Guardsmen

Ed	HRN	Date	Details	A	C	GD 2.0	VG 4.0	FN 6.0	VF 8.0	VF/NM 9.0	NM- 9.2
1	114	11/53	Orig.; delBourgo-a	1	1	14	28	42	76	108	140
2	166	7/67	PC-r	1	1	4	8	12	23	37	50

114. The Red Rover

Ed	HRN	Date	Details	A	C	GD 2.0	VG 4.0	FN 6.0	VF 8.0	VF/NM 9.0	NM- 9.2
1	115	12/53	Original	1	1	14	28	42	76	108	140
2	166	7/67	PC-r	1	1	4	8	12	23	37	50

115. How I Found Livingstone

Ed	HRN	Date	Details	A	C	GD 2.0	VG 4.0	FN 6.0	VF 8.0	VF/NM 9.0	NM- 9.2
1	116	1/54	Original	1	1	14	28	42	80	115	150
2	167	1/67	PC-r	1	1	4	8	12	27	44	60

116. The Bottle Imp

Ed	HRN	Date	Details	A	C	GD 2.0	VG 4.0	FN 6.0	VF 8.0	VF/NM 9.0	NM- 9.2
1	117	2/54	Orig.; Cameron-a	1	1	14	28	42	80	115	150
2	167	1/67	PC-r	1	1	4	8	12	27	44	60

117. Captains Courageous

Ed	HRN	Date	Details	A	C	GD 2.0	VG 4.0	FN 6.0	VF 8.0	VF/NM 9.0	NM- 9.2
1	118	3/54	Orig.; Costanza-a	1	1	13	26	39	74	105	135
2	167	2/67	PC-r	1	1	3	6	9	14	20	26
3	169	Fall/69	New price 25¢; stiff-c; PC-r	1	1	3	6	9	14	20	26

118. Rob Roy

Ed	HRN	Date	Details	A	C	GD 2.0	VG 4.0	FN 6.0	VF 8.0	VF/NM 9.0	NM- 9.2
1	119	4/54	Original; Rudy & Walter Palais-a	1	1	14	28	42	80	115	150
2	167	2/67	PC-r	1	1	4	8	12	27	44	60

119. Soldiers of Fortune

Ed	HRN	Date	Details	A	C	GD 2.0	VG 4.0	FN 6.0	VF 8.0	VF/NM 9.0	NM- 9.2
1	120	5/54	Schaffenberger-a	1	1	13	26	39	72	101	130
2	166	3/67	PC-r	1	1	3	6	9	14	20	26
3	169	Spr/70	New price 25¢; stiff-c; PC-r	1	1	3	6	9	14	20	26

120. The Hurricane

Ed	HRN	Date	Details	A	C	GD 2.0	VG 4.0	FN 6.0	VF 8.0	VF/NM 9.0	NM- 9.2
1	121	6/54	Orig.; Cameron-a	1	1	14	28	42	76	108	140
2	166	3/67	PC-r	1	1	4	8	12	22	34	50

121. Wild Bill Hickok

Ed	HRN	Date	Details	A	C	GD 2.0	VG 4.0	FN 6.0	VF 8.0	VF/NM 9.0	NM- 9.2
1	122	7/54	Original	1	1	11	22	33	60	83	105
2	132	–	PC-r	1	1	2	4	6	9	13	16
3	141	–	PC-r	1	1	2	4	6	9	13	16
4	154	–	PC-r	1	1	2	4	6	9	13	16
5	167	–	PC-r	1	1	2	4	6	8	11	14
6	167	8/64	PC-r	1	1	2	4	6	8	11	14
7	166	4/67	PC-r	1	1	2	4	6	8	11	14
8	169	Win/69	PC-r; stiff-c	1	1	2	4	6	8	11	14

122. The Mutineers

Ed	HRN	Date	Details	A	C	GD 2.0	VG 4.0	FN 6.0	VF 8.0	VF/NM 9.0	NM- 9.2
1	123	9/54	Original	1	1	11	22	33	64	90	115
2	136	–	PC-r	1	1	2	4	6	9	13	16
3	146	–	PC-r	1	1	2	4	6	9	13	16
4	158	–	PC-r	1	1	2	4	6	9	13	16
5	167	11/63	PC-r	1	1	2	4	6	8	11	14
6	167	3/65	PC-r	1	1	2	4	6	8	11	14
7	166	8/67	PC-r	1	1	2	4	6	8	11	14

123. Fang and Claw

Ed	HRN	Date	Details	A	C	GD 2.0	VG 4.0	FN 6.0	VF 8.0	VF/NM 9.0	NM- 9.2
1	124	11/54	Original	1	1	11	22	33	64	90	115
2	133	–	PC-r	1	1	2	4	6	9	13	16
3	143	–	PC-r	1	1	2	4	6	9	13	16
4	154	–	PC-r	1	1	2	4	6	9	13	16
5	167	–	Has orig.date; PC-r	1	1	2	4	6	8	11	14
6	167	9/65	PC-r	1	1	2	4	6	8	11	14

124. The War of the Worlds

Ed	HRN	Date	Details	A	C	GD 2.0	VG 4.0	FN 6.0	VF 8.0	VF/NM 9.0	NM- 9.2
1	125	1/55	Original; Cameron-c/a	1	1	14	28	42	82	121	160
2	131	–	PC-r	1	1	2	4	6	10	14	18
3	141	–	PC-r	1	1	2	4	6	10	14	18
4	148	–	PC-r	1	1	2	4	6	10	14	18
5	156	–	PC-r	1	1	2	4	6	10	14	18
6	165	–	PC-r	1	1	2	4	6	13	18	22
7	167	–	PC-r	1	1	2	4	6	9	13	16
8	167	11/64	PC-r	1	1	2	4	6	10	14	18
9	167	11/65	PC-r	1	1	2	4	6	9	13	16
10	166	R/1968	C-price 25¢; PC-r	1	1	2	4	6	9	13	16
11	169	Sm/70	PC-r; stiff-c	1	1	2	4	6	9	13	16

125. The Ox Bow Incident

Ed	HRN	Date	Details	A	C	GD 2.0	VG 4.0	FN 6.0	VF 8.0	VF/NM 9.0	NM- 9.2
1	–	3/55	Original; Picture Progress replaces reorder list	1	1	11	22	33	60	83	105
2	143	–	PC-r	1	1	2	4	6	9	13	16
3	152	–	PC-r	1	1	2	4	6	9	13	16
4	149	–	PC-r	1	1	2	4	6	9	13	16
5	167	–	PC-r	1	1	2	4	6	8	11	14
6	167	11/64	PC-r	1	1	2	4	6	8	11	14
7	166	4/67	PC-r	1	1	2	4	6	8	11	14
8	169	Win/69	New price 25¢; stiff-c; PC-r	1	1	2	4	6	8	11	14

126. The Downfall

Ed	HRN	Date	Details	A	C	GD 2.0	VG 4.0	FN 6.0	VF 8.0	VF/NM 9.0	NM- 9.2
1	–	5/55	Orig.; 'Picture Progress' replaces reorder list; Cameron-c/a	1	1	11	22	33	64	90	115
2	167	8/64	PC-r	1	1	2	4	6	13	18	22
3	166	R/1968	C-price 25¢; PC-r	1	1	2	4	6	13	18	22

127. The King of the Mountains

Ed	HRN	Date	Details	A	C	GD 2.0	VG 4.0	FN 6.0	VF 8.0	VF/NM 9.0	NM- 9.2
1	128	7/55	Original	1	1	11	22	33	64	90	115
2	167	6/64	PC-r	1	1	2	4	6	11	16	20
3	166	F/1968	C-price 25¢; PC-r	1	1	2	4	6	11	16	20

128. Macbeth (Used in **POP**, pg. 102)

Ed	HRN	Date	Details	A	C	GD 2.0	VG 4.0	FN 6.0	VF 8.0	VF/NM 9.0	NM- 9.2
1	128	9/55	Orig.; last Blum-a	1	1	11	22	33	64	90	115
2	143	–	PC-r	1	1	2	4	6	9	13	16
3	158	–	PC-r	1	1	2	4	6	9	13	16
4	167	–	PC-r	1	1	2	4	6	8	11	14
5	167	6/64	PC-r	1	1	2	4	6	8	11	14
6	166	4/67	PC-r	1	1	2	4	6	8	11	14

Classics Illustrated #131 © GIL

Classics Illustrated #138 © GIL

Classics Illustrated #140 © GIL

Ed	HRN	Date	Details	A	C	GD 2.0	VG 4.0	FN 6.0	VF 8.0	VF/NM 9.0	NM- 9.2
7	166	R/1968	C-Price 25¢; PC-r	1	1	2	4	6	8	11	14
8	169	Spr/70	Stiff-c; PC-r	1	1	2	4	6	8	11	14

129. Davy Crockett

Ed	HRN	Date	Details	A	C	GD 2.0	VG 4.0	FN 6.0	VF 8.0	VF/NM 9.0	NM- 9.2
1	129	11/55	Orig.; Cameron-a	1	1	14	28	42	82	121	160
2	167	9/66	PC-r	1	1	11	22	33	62	86	110

130. Caesar's Conquests

Ed	HRN	Date	Details	A	C	GD 2.0	VG 4.0	FN 6.0	VF 8.0	VF/NM 9.0	NM- 9.2
1	130	1/56	Original; Orlando-a	1	1	11	22	33	64	90	115
2	142	–	PC-r	1	1	2	4	6	9	13	16
3	152	–	PC-r	1	1	2	4	6	9	13	16
4	149	–	PC-r	1	1	2	4	6	9	13	16
5	167	–	PC-r	1	1	2	4	6	8	11	14
6	167	10/64	PC-r	1	1	2	4	6	8	11	14
7	167	4/66	PC-r	1	1	2	4	6	8	11	14

131. The Covered Wagon

Ed	HRN	Date	Details	A	C	GD 2.0	VG 4.0	FN 6.0	VF 8.0	VF/NM 9.0	NM- 9.2
1	131	3/56	Original	1	1	6	12	18	40	73	105
2	143	–	PC-r	1	1	2	4	6	9	13	16
3	152	–	PC-r	1	1	2	4	6	9	13	16
4	158	–	PC-r	1	1	2	4	6	9	13	16
5	167	–	PC-r	1	1	2	4	6	8	11	14
6	167	11/64	PC-r	1	1	2	4	6	8	11	14
7	167	4/66	PC-r	1	1	2	4	6	8	11	14
8	169	Win/69	New price 25¢; stiff-c; PC-r	1	1	2	4	6	8	11	14

132. The Dark Frigate

Ed	HRN	Date	Details	A	C	GD 2.0	VG 4.0	FN 6.0	VF 8.0	VF/NM 9.0	NM- 9.2
1	132	5/56	Original	1	1	11	22	33	64	90	115
2	150	–	PC-r	1	1	2	4	6	9	13	16
3	167	1/64	PC-r	1	1	2	4	6	9	13	16
4	166	5/67	PC-r	1	1	2	4	6	9	13	16

133. The Time Machine

Ed	HRN	Date	Details	A	C	GD 2.0	VG 4.0	FN 6.0	VF 8.0	VF/NM 9.0	NM- 9.2
1	132	7/56	Orig.; Cameron-a	1	1	7	14	21	46	86	125
2	142	–	PC-r	1	1	2	4	6	10	14	18
3	152	–	PC-r	1	1	2	4	6	10	14	18
4	158	–	PC-r	1	1	2	4	6	9	13	16
5	167	–	PC-r	1	1	2	4	6	9	13	16
6	167	6/64	PC-r	1	1	2	4	6	10	14	18
7	167	3/66	PC-r	1	1	2	4	6	9	13	16
8	166	12/67	PC-r	1	1	2	4	6	9	13	16
9	169	Win/71	New price 25¢; stiff-c; PC-r	1	1	2	4	6	9	13	16

134. Romeo and Juliet

Ed	HRN	Date	Details	A	C	GD 2.0	VG 4.0	FN 6.0	VF 8.0	VF/NM 9.0	NM- 9.2
1	134	9/56	Original; Evans-a	1	1	6	12	18	42	79	115
2	161	–	PC-r	1	1	2	4	6	9	13	16
3	167	9/63	PC-r	1	1	2	4	6	8	11	14
4	167	5/65	PC-r	1	1	2	4	6	8	11	14
5	166	6/67	PC-r	1	1	2	4	6	8	11	14
6	166	Win/69	New c&price 25¢; stiff-c; PC-r	1	2	3	6	9	17	25	32

135. Waterloo

Ed	HRN	Date	Details	A	C	GD 2.0	VG 4.0	FN 6.0	VF 8.0	VF/NM 9.0	NM- 9.2
1	135	11/56	Orig.; G. Ingels-a	1	1	6	12	18	42	79	115
2	153	–	PC-r	1	1	2	4	6	9	13	16
3	167	–	PC-r	1	1	2	4	6	8	11	14
4	167	9/64	PC-r	1	1	2	4	6	8	11	14
5	166	R/1968	C-price 25¢; PC-r	1	1	2	4	6	8	11	14

136. Lord Jim

Ed	HRN	Date	Details	A	C	GD 2.0	VG 4.0	FN 6.0	VF 8.0	VF/NM 9.0	NM- 9.2
1	136	1/57	Original; Evans-a	1	1	6	12	18	42	79	115
2	165	–	PC-r	1	1	2	4	6	8	11	14
3	167	3/64	PC-r	1	1	2	4	6	8	11	14
4	167	9/66	PC-r	1	1	2	4	6	8	11	14
5	169	Sm/69	New price 25 ¢; stiff-c; PC-r	1	1	2	4	6	8	11	14

137. The Little Savage

Ed	HRN	Date	Details	A	C	GD 2.0	VG 4.0	FN 6.0	VF 8.0	VF/NM 9.0	NM- 9.2
1	136	3/57	Original; Evans-a	1	1	6	12	18	42	79	115
2	148	–	PC-r	1	1	2	4	6	9	13	16
3	156	–	PC-r	1	1	2	4	6	9	13	16
4	167	–	PC-r	1	1	2	4	6	8	11	14
5	167	10/64	PC-r	1	1	2	4	6	8	11	14
6	166	8/67	PC-r	1	1	2	4	6	8	11	14
7	169	Spr/70	New price 25¢; stiff-c; PC-r	1	1	2	4	6	8	11	14

138. A Journey to the Center of the Earth

Ed	HRN	Date	Details	A	C	GD 2.0	VG 4.0	FN 6.0	VF 8.0	VF/NM 9.0	NM- 9.2
1	136	5/57	Original	1	1	8	16	24	51	96	140
2	146	–	PC-r	1	1	2	4	6	11	16	20
3	156	–	PC-r	1	1	2	4	6	11	16	20
4	158	–	PC-r	1	1	2	4	6	9	13	16
5	167	–	PC-r	1	1	2	4	6	8	11	14
6	167	6/64	PC-r	1	1	2	4	6	13	18	22
7	167	4/66	PC-r	1	1	2	4	6	13	18	22
8	166	R/68	C-price 25¢; PC-r	1	1	2	4	6	10	14	18

139. In the Reign of Terror

Ed	HRN	Date	Details	A	C	GD 2.0	VG 4.0	FN 6.0	VF 8.0	VF/NM 9.0	NM- 9.2
1	139	7/57	Original; Evans-a	1	1	6	12	18	40	73	105
2	154	–	PC-r	1	1	2	4	6	9	13	16
3	167	–	Has orig.date; PC-r	1	1	2	4	6	8	11	14
4	167	7/64	PC-r	1	1	2	4	6	8	11	14
5	166	R/1968	C-price 25¢; PC-r	1	1	2	4	6	8	11	14

140. On Jungle Trails

Ed	HRN	Date	Details	A	C	GD 2.0	VG 4.0	FN 6.0	VF 8.0	VF/NM 9.0	NM- 9.2
1	140	9/57	Original	1	1	6	12	18	40	73	105
2	150	–	PC-r	1	1	2	4	6	9	13	16
3	160	–	PC-r	1	1	2	4	6	9	13	16
4	167	9/63	PC-r	1	1	2	4	6	8	11	14
5	167	9/65	PC-r	1	1	2	4	6	8	11	14

141. Castle Dangerous

Ed	HRN	Date	Details	A	C	GD 2.0	VG 4.0	FN 6.0	VF 8.0	VF/NM 9.0	NM- 9.2
1	141	11/57	Original	1	1	7	14	21	44	82	120
2	152	–	PC-r	1	1	2	4	6	9	13	16
3	167	–	PC-r	1	1	2	4	6	9	13	16
4	166	7/67	PC-r	1	1	2	4	6	9	13	16

142. Abraham Lincoln

Ed	HRN	Date	Details	A	C	GD 2.0	VG 4.0	FN 6.0	VF 8.0	VF/NM 9.0	NM- 9.2
1	142	1/58	Original	1	1	6	12	18	42	79	115
2	154	–	PC-r	1	1	2	4	6	9	13	16
3	158	–	PC-r	1	1	2	4	6	9	13	16
4	167	10/63	PC-r	1	1	2	4	6	8	11	14
5	167	7/65	PC-r	1	1	2	4	6	8	11	14
6	166	11/67	PC-r	1	1	2	4	6	8	11	14
7	169	Fall/69	New price 25¢; stiff-c; PC-r	1	1	2	4	6	8	11	14

143. Kim

Ed	HRN	Date	Details	A	C	GD 2.0	VG 4.0	FN 6.0	VF 8.0	VF/NM 9.0	NM- 9.2
1	143	3/58	Original; Orlando-a	1	1	6	12	18	40	73	105
2	165	–	PC-r	1	1	2	4	6	8	11	14
3	167	11/63	PC-r	1	1	2	4	6	8	11	14
4	167	8/65	PC-r	1	1	2	4	6	8	11	14
5	169	Win/69	New price 25¢; stiff-c; PC-r	1	1	2	4	6	8	11	14

144. The First Men in the Moon

Ed	HRN	Date	Details	A	C	GD 2.0	VG 4.0	FN 6.0	VF 8.0	VF/NM 9.0	NM- 9.2
1	143	5/58	Original; Woodbridge/Williamson/Torres-a	1	1	7	14	21	49	92	135
2	152	–	(Rare)-PC-r	1	1	8	16	24	54	102	150
3	153	–	PC-r	1	1	2	4	6	9	13	16
4	161	–	PC-r	1	1	2	4	6	8	11	14
5	167	–	PC-r	1	1	2	4	6	8	11	14
6	167	12/65	PC-r	1	1	2	4	6	8	11	14
7	166	Fall/68	New-c&price 25¢; PC-r; stiff-c	1	2	3	6	9	16	23	30
8	169	Win/69	Stiff-c; PC-r	1	2	2	4	6	10	16	20

145. The Crisis

Ed	HRN	Date	Details	A	C	GD 2.0	VG 4.0	FN 6.0	VF 8.0	VF/NM 9.0	NM- 9.2
1	143	7/58	Original; Evans-a	1	1	6	12	18	42	79	115
2	156	–	PC-r	1	1	2	4	6	9	13	16
3	167	10/63	PC-r	1	1	2	4	6	8	11	14

Classics Illustrated #148 © GIL

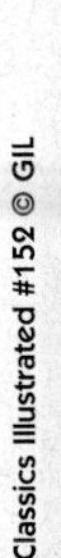
Classics Illustrated #152 © GIL

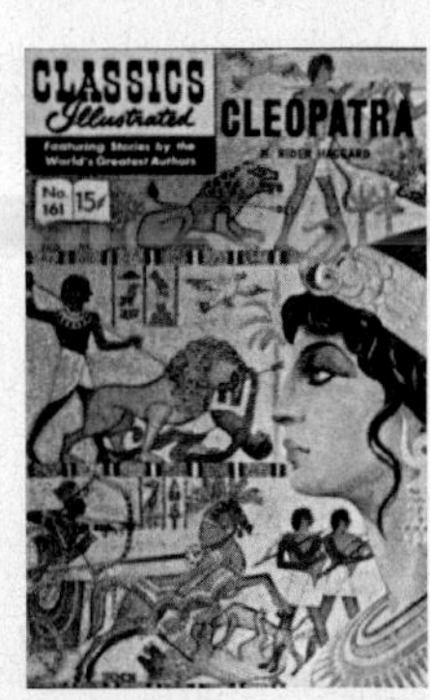

Classics Illustrated #161 © GIL

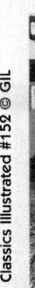

Ed	HRN	Date	Details	A	C	GD 2.0	VG 4.0	FN 6.0	VF 8.0	VF/NM 9.0	NM- 9.2
4	167	3/65	PC-r	1	1	2	4	6	8	11	14
5	166	R/68	C-price 25¢; PC-r	1	1	2	4	6	8	11	14

146. With Fire and Sword

Ed	HRN	Date	Details	A	C	GD 2.0	VG 4.0	FN 6.0	VF 8.0	VF/NM 9.0	NM- 9.2
1	143	9/58	Original; Woodbridge-a	1	1	6	12	18	42	79	115
2	156	–	PC-r	1	1	2	4	6	10	14	18
3	167	11/63	PC-r	1	1	2	4	6	9	13	16
4	167	3/65	PC-r	1	1	2	4	6	9	13	16

147. Ben-Hur

Ed	HRN	Date	Details	A	C	GD 2.0	VG 4.0	FN 6.0	VF 8.0	VF/NM 9.0	NM- 9.2
1	147	11/58	Original; Orlando-a	1	1	7	14	21	44	82	120
2	152	–	Scarce; PC-r	1	1	7	14	21	46	86	125
3	153	–	PC-r	1	1	2	4	6	9	13	16
4	158	–	PC-r	1	1	2	4	6	9	13	16
5	167	–	Orig.date; but PC-r	1	1	2	4	6	8	11	14
6	167	2/65	PC-r	1	1	2	4	6	8	11	14
7	167	9/66	PC-r	1	1	2	4	6	8	11	14
8A	166	Fall/68	New-c&price 25¢; PC-r; soft-c	1	2	3	6	9	16	24	32
8B	166	Fall/68	New-c&price 25¢; PC-r; stiff-c; scarce	1	2	3	6	9	21	33	45

148. The Buccaneer

Ed	HRN	Date	Details	A	C	GD 2.0	VG 4.0	FN 6.0	VF 8.0	VF/NM 9.0	NM- 9.2
1	148	1/59	Orig.; Evans/Jenny-a; Saunders-c	1	1	6	12	18	40	73	105
2	568	–	Juniors list only PC-r	1	1	2	4	6	9	13	16
3	167	–	PC-r	1	1	2	4	6	8	11	14
4	167	9/65	PC-r	1	1	2	4	6	8	11	14
5	169	Sm/69	New price 25¢; PC-r; stiff-c	1	1	2	4	6	8	11	14

149. Off on a Comet

Ed	HRN	Date	Details	A	C	GD 2.0	VG 4.0	FN 6.0	VF 8.0	VF/NM 9.0	NM- 9.2
1	149	3/59	Orig.;G.McCann-a; blue reorder list	1	1	6	12	18	42	79	115
2	155	–	PC-r	1	1	2	4	6	9	13	16
3	149	–	PC-r; white reorder list; no coming-next ad	1	1	2	4	6	9	13	16
4	167	12/63	PC-r	1	1	2	4	6	8	11	14
5	167	2/65	PC-r	1	1	2	4	6	8	11	14
6	167	10/66	PC-r	1	1	2	4	6	8	11	14
7	166	Fall/68	New-c & price 25¢; PC-r	1	2	3	6	9	16	23	30

150. The Virginian

Ed	HRN	Date	Details	A	C	GD 2.0	VG 4.0	FN 6.0	VF 8.0	VF/NM 9.0	NM- 9.2
1	150	5/59	Original	1	1	7	14	21	44	82	120
2	164	–	PC-r	1	1	2	4	6	11	16	20
3	167	10/63	PC-r	1	1	3	6	9	15	21	26
4	167	12/65	PC-r	1	1	2	4	6	11	16	20

151. Won By the Sword

Ed	HRN	Date	Details	A	C	GD 2.0	VG 4.0	FN 6.0	VF 8.0	VF/NM 9.0	NM- 9.2
1	150	7/59	Original	1	1	6	12	18	42	79	115
2	164	–	PC-r	1	1	2	4	6	10	14	18
3	167	10/63	PC-r	1	1	2	4	6	10	14	18
4	166	7/67	PC-r	1	1	2	4	6	10	14	18

152. Wild Animals I Have Known

Ed	HRN	Date	Details	A	C	GD 2.0	VG 4.0	FN 6.0	VF 8.0	VF/NM 9.0	NM- 9.2
1	152	9/59	Orig.; L.B. Cole c/a	1	1	7	14	21	46	86	125
2A	149	–	PC-r; white reorder list; no coming-next ad; IBC: Jr. list #572	1	1	2	4	6	9	13	16
2B	149	–	PC-r; inside-bc: Jr. list to #555	1	1	2	4	6	9	13	16
2C	149	–	PC-r; inside-bc: has World Around Us ad; scarce	1	1	3	6	9	15	21	26
3	167	9/63	PC-r	1	1	2	4	6	8	11	14
4	167	8/65	PC-r	1	1	2	4	6	8	11	14
5	169	Fall/69	New price 25¢; stiff-c; PC-r	1	1	2	4	6	8	11	14

153. The Invisible Man

Ed	HRN	Date	Details	A	C	GD 2.0	VG 4.0	FN 6.0	VF 8.0	VF/NM 9.0	NM- 9.2
1	153	11/59	Original	1	1	8	16	24	52	99	145
2A	149	–	PC-r; white reorder list; no coming-next ad; inside-bc: Jr. list to #572	1	1	3	6	9	14	19	24
2B	149	–	PC-r; inside-bc: Jr. list to #555	1	1	3	6	9	14	20	26
3	167	–	PC-r	1	1	2	4	6	9	13	16
4	167	2/65	PC-r	1	1	2	4	6	9	13	16
5	167	9/66	PC-r	1	1	2	4	6	9	13	16
6	166	Win/69	New price 25¢; PC-r; stiff-c	1	1	2	4	6	9	13	16
7	169	Spr/71	Stiff-c; letters spelling 'Invisible Man' are 'solid' not 'invisible;' PC-r	1	1	2	4	6	9	13	16

154. The Conspiracy of Pontiac

Ed	HRN	Date	Details	A	C	GD 2.0	VG 4.0	FN 6.0	VF 8.0	VF/NM 9.0	NM- 9.2
1	154	1/60	Original	1	1	7	14	21	41	82	120
2	167	11/63	PC-r	1	1	2	4	6	13	18	22
3	167	7/64	PC-r	1	1	2	4	6	13	18	22
4	166	12/67	PC-r	1	1	2	4	6	13	18	22

155. The Lion of the North

Ed	HRN	Date	Details	A	C	GD 2.0	VG 4.0	FN 6.0	VF 8.0	VF/NM 9.0	NM- 9.2
1	154	3/60	Original	1	1	6	12	18	42	79	115
2	167	1/64	PC-r	1	1	2	4	6	11	16	20
3	166	R/1967	C-price 25¢; PC-r	1	1	2	4	6	10	14	18

156. The Conquest of Mexico

Ed	HRN	Date	Details	A	C	GD 2.0	VG 4.0	FN 6.0	VF 8.0	VF/NM 9.0	NM- 9.2
1	156	5/60	Orig.; Bruno Premiani-c/a	1	1	6	12	18	42	79	115
2	167	1/64	PC-r	1	1	2	4	6	10	14	18
3	166	8/67	PC-r	1	1	2	4	6	10	14	18
4	169	Spr/70	New price 25¢; stiff-c; PC-r	1	1	2	4	6	9	13	16

157. Lives of the Hunted

Ed	HRN	Date	Details	A	C	GD 2.0	VG 4.0	FN 6.0	VF 8.0	VF/NM 9.0	NM- 9.2
1	156	7/60	Orig.; L.B. Cole-c	1	1	7	14	21	44	82	120
2	167	2/64	PC-r	1	1	2	4	6	13	18	22
3	166	10/67	PC-r	1	1	2	4	6	13	18	22

158. The Conspirators

Ed	HRN	Date	Details	A	C	GD 2.0	VG 4.0	FN 6.0	VF 8.0	VF/NM 9.0	NM- 9.2
1	156	9/60	Original	1	1	7	14	21	44	82	120
2	167	7/64	PC-r	1	1	2	4	6	13	18	22
3	166	10/67	PC-r	1	1	2	4	6	13	18	22

159. The Octopus

Ed	HRN	Date	Details	A	C	GD 2.0	VG 4.0	FN 6.0	VF 8.0	VF/NM 9.0	NM- 9.2
1	159	11/60	Orig.; Gray Morrow-a; L.B. Cole-c	1	1	7	14	21	48	89	130
2	167	2/64	PC-r	1	1	2	4	6	13	18	22
3	166	R/1967	C-price 25¢; PC-r	1	1	2	4	6	13	18	22

160. The Food of the Gods

Ed	HRN	Date	Details	A	C	GD 2.0	VG 4.0	FN 6.0	VF 8.0	VF/NM 9.0	NM- 9.2
1A	159	1/61	Original	1	1	7	14	21	49	92	135
1B	160	1/61	Original; same, except for HRN	1	1	7	14	21	46	86	125
2	167	1/64	PC-r	1	1	2	4	6	13	18	22
3	166	6/67	PC-r	1	1	2	4	6	13	18	22

161. Cleopatra

Ed	HRN	Date	Details	A	C	GD 2.0	VG 4.0	FN 6.0	VF 8.0	VF/NM 9.0	NM- 9.2
1	161	3/61	Original	1	1	7	14	21	48	89	130
2	167	1/64	PC-r	1	1	3	6	9	14	19	24
3	166	8/67	PC-r	1	1	3	6	9	14	19	24

162. Robur the Conqueror

Ed	HRN	Date	Details	A	C	GD 2.0	VG 4.0	FN 6.0	VF 8.0	VF/NM 9.0	NM- 9.2
1	162	5/61	Original	1	1	7	14	21	44	82	120
2	167	7/64	PC-r	1	1	3	6	9	14	19	24
3	166	8/67	PC-r	1	1	3	6	9	14	19	24

163. Master of the World

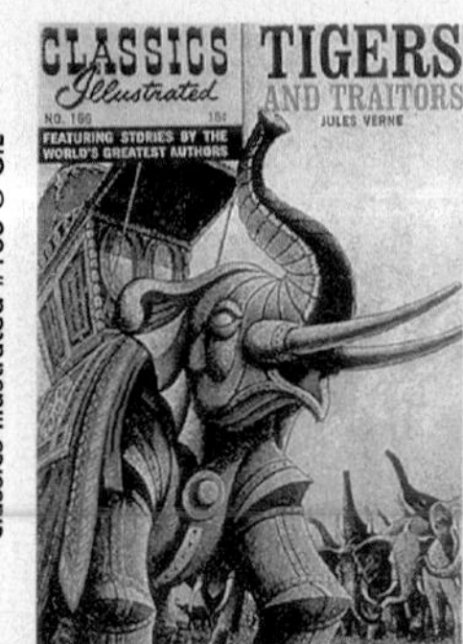

Classics Illustrated #166 © GIL

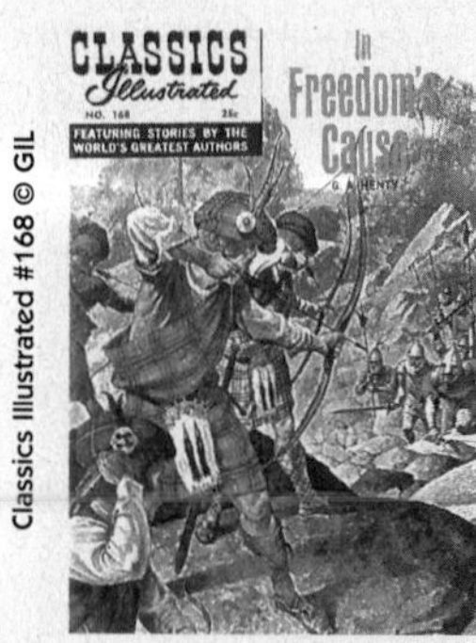

Classics Illustrated #168 © GIL

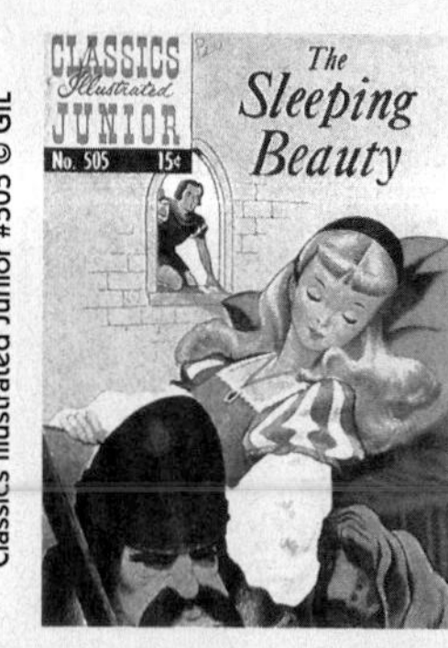

Classics Illustrated Junior #505 © GIL

Ed	HRN	Date	Details	A	C	GD 2.0	VG 4.0	FN 6.0	VF 8.0	VF/NM 9.0	NM- 9.2
1	163	7/61	Original; Gray Morrow-a	1	1	7	14	21	44	82	120
2	167	1/65	PC-r	1	1	2	4	6	13	18	22
3	166	R/1968	C-price 25¢; PC-r	1	1	2	4	6	13	18	22

164. The Cossack Chief

Ed	HRN	Date	Details	A	C	GD	VG	FN	VF	VF/NM	NM-
1	164	(1961)	Orig.; nd(10/61?)	1	1	6	12	18	41	76	110
2	167	4/65	PC-r	1	1	2	4	6	13	18	22
3	166	Fall/68	C-price 25¢; PC-r	1	1	2	4	6	13	18	22

165. The Queen's Necklace

Ed	HRN	Date	Details	A	C	GD	VG	FN	VF	VF/NM	NM-
1	164	1/62	Original; Morrow-a	1	1	7	14	21	44	82	120
2	167	4/65	PC-r	1	1	2	4	6	13	18	22
3	166	Fall/68	C-price 25¢; PC-r	1	1	2	4	6	13	18	22

166. Tigers and Traitors

Ed	HRN	Date	Details	A	C	GD	VG	FN	VF	VF/NM	NM-
1	165	5/62	Original	1	1	8	16	24	55	105	155
2	167	2/64	PC-r	1	1	3	6	9	21	33	45
3	167	11/66	PC-r	1	1	3	6	9	21	33	45

167. Faust

Ed	HRN	Date	Details	A	C	GD	VG	FN	VF	VF/NM	NM-
1	165	8/62	Original	1	1	11	22	33	77	166	255
2	167	2/64	PC-r	1	1	5	10	15	34	60	85
3	166	6/67	PC-r	1	1	5	10	15	34	60	85

168. In Freedom's Cause

Ed	HRN	Date	Details	A	C	GD	VG	FN	VF	VF/NM	NM-
1	169	Win/69	Original; Evans/ Crandall-a; stiff-c; 25¢; no coming-next ad;	1	1	13	26	39	86	188	290

169. Negro Americans The Early Years

Ed	HRN	Date	Details	A	C	GD	VG	FN	VF	VF/NM	NM-
1	166	Spr/69	Orig. & last issue; 25¢; Stiff-c; no coming-next ad; other sources indicate publication date of 5/69	1	1	12	24	36	82	179	275
2	169	Spr/69	Stiff-c	1	1	7	14	21	48	89	130

NOTE: *Many other titles were prepared or planned but were only issued in British/European series.*

CLASSIC POPEYE (See Popeye, Classic)

CLASSIC PUNISHER (Also see Punisher)
Marvel Comics: Dec, 1989 ($4.95, B&W, deluxe format, 68 pgs.)

1-Reprints Marvel Super Action #1 & Marvel Preview #2 plus new story — 6.00

CLASSIC RED SONJA
Dynamite Entertainment: 2010 - No. 4, 2010 ($3.99)

1-4-Newly colored reprints of stories from Savage Sword of Conan magazine — 4.00

CLASSICS ILLUSTRATED
First Publishing/Berkley Publishing: Feb, 1990 - No. 27, July, 1991 ($3.75/$3.95, 52 pgs.)

1-27: 1-Gahan Wilson-c/a. 4-Sienkiewicz painted-c/a. 6-Russell scripts/layouts. 7-Spiegle-a. 9-Ploog-c/a. 16-Staton-a. 18-Gahan Wilson-c/a; 20-Geary-a. 26-Aesop's Fables (6/91). 26,27-Direct sale only — 5.00

CLASSICS ILLUSTRATED
Acclaim Books/Twin Circle PublishingCo.: Feb, 1997 - Jan, 1998 ($4.99, digest-size) (Each book contains study notes)

A Christmas Carol-(12/97), A Connecticut Yankee in King Arthur's Court-(5/97), All Quiet on the Western Front-(1/98), A Midsummer's Night Dream-(4/97) Around the World in 80 Days-(1/98), A Tale of Two Cities-(2/97)Joe Orlando-r, Captains Courageous-(11/97), Crime and Punishment-(3/97), Dr. Jekyll and Mr. Hyde-(10/97), Don Quixote-(12/97), Frankenstein-(10/97), Great Expectations-(4/97), Hamlet-(3/97), Huckleberry Finn-(3/97), Jane Eyre-(2/97), Kidnapped-(1/98), Les Miserables-(5/97), Lord Jim-(9/97), Macbeth-(5/97), Moby Dick-(4/97), Oliver Twist-(5/97), Robinson Crusoe-(9/97), Romeo & Juliet-(2/97), Silas Marner-(11/97), The Call of the Wild-(9/97), The Count of Monte Cristo-(1/98), The House of the Seven Gables-(9/97), The Iliad-(12/97), The Invisible Man-(10/97), The Last of the Mohicans-(12/97), The Master of Ballantrae-(11/97), The Odyssey-(3/97), The Prince and the Pauper-(4/97), The Red Badge Of Courage-(9/97), Tom Sawyer-(2/97) Wuthering Heights-(11/97) — 5.00

NOTE: *Stories reprinted from the original Gilberton Classic Comics and Classics Illustrated.*

CLASSICS ILLUSTRATED GIANTS
Gilberton Publications: Oct, 1949 (One-Shots - "OS")

These Giant Editions, all with new front and back covers, were advertised from 10/49 to 2/52. They were 50¢ on the newsstand and 60¢ by mail. They are actually four Classics in one volume. All the stories are reprints of the Classics Illustrated Series.
NOTE: There were also British hardback Adventure & Indian Giants in 1952, with the same covers but different contents: Adventure - 2, 7, 10; Indian - 17, 22, 37, 58. They are also rare.

	GD 2.0	VG 4.0	FN 6.0	VF 8.0	VF/NM 9.0	NM- 9.2
"An Illustrated Library of Great Adventure Stories" - reprints of No. 6,7,8,10 (Rare); Kiefer-c	161	322	483	1030	1765	2500
"An Illustrated Library of Exciting Mystery Stories" - reprints of No. 30,21,40, 13 (Rare); Blum-c	173	346	519	1099	1887	2675
"An Illustrated Library of Great Indian Stories" - reprints of No. 4,17,22,37 (Rare); Blum-c	165	330	495	1048	1799	2550

INTRODUCTION TO CLASSICS ILLUSTRATED JUNIOR

Collectors of Juniors can be put into one of two categories: those who want any copy of each title, and those who want all the originals. Those seeking every original and reprint edition are a limited group, primarily because Juniors have no changes in art or covers to spark interest, and because reprints are so low in value it is difficult to get dealers to look for specific reprint editions.

In recent years it has become apparent that most serious Classics collectors seek Junior originals. Those seeking reprints seek them for low cost. This has made the previous note about the comparative market value of reprints inadequate. Three particular reprint editions are worth even more. For the 535-Twin Circle edition, see Giveaways. There are also reprint editions of 501 and 503 which have a full-page bc ad for the very rare Junior record. Those may sell as high as $10-$15 in mint. Original editions of 557 and 558 also have that ad.

There are no reprint editions of 577. The only edition, from 1969, is a 25 cent stiff-cover edition with no ad for the next issue. All other original editions have coming-next ad. But 577, like C.I. #168, was prepared in 1962 but not issued. Copies of 577 can be found in 1963 British/European series, which then continued with dozens of additional new Junior titles.

PRICES LISTED BELOW ARE FOR ORIGINAL EDITIONS, WHICH HAVE AN AD FOR THE NEXT ISSUE.

NOTE: *Non HRN 576 copies- many are written on or colored . Reprints with 576 HRN are worth about 1/3 original prices. All other HRN #'s are 1/2 original price*

CLASSICS ILLUSTRATED JUNIOR
Famous Authors Ltd. (Gilberton Publications): Oct, 1953 - Spring, 1971

	GD	VG	FN	VF	VF/NM	NM-
501-Snow White & the Seven Dwarfs; Alex Blum-a	12	24	36	69	97	125
502-The Ugly Duckling	9	18	27	47	61	75
503-Cinderella	8	16	24	40	50	60
504-512: 504-The Pied Piper. 505-The Sleeping Beauty. 506-The Three Little Pigs. 507-Jack & the Beanstalk. 508-Goldilocks & the Three Bears. 509-Beauty and the Beast. 510-Little Red Riding Hood. 511-Puss-N Boots. 512-Rumpelstiltskin	6	12	18	27	33	38
513-Pinocchio	7	14	21	37	46	55
514-The Steadfast Tin Soldier	8	16	24	44	57	70
515-Johnny Appleseed	6	12	18	27	33	38
516-Aladdin and His Lamp	6	12	18	29	36	42
517-519: 517-The Emperor's New Clothes. 518-The Golden Goose. 519-Paul Bunyan	6	12	18	27	33	38
520-Thumbelina	6	12	18	29	36	42
521-King of the Golden River	6	12	18	27	33	38
522,523,530: 522-The Nightingale. 523-The Gallant Tailor. 530-The Golden Bird	5	10	15	24	30	35
524-The Wild Swans	6	12	18	29	36	42
525,526: 525-The Little Mermaid. 526-The Frog Prince	6	12	18	29	36	42
527-The Golden-Haired Giant	6	12	18	27	33	38
528-The Penny Prince	6	12	18	27	33	38
529-The Magic Servants	6	12	18	27	33	38
531-Rapunzel	6	12	18	27	33	38
532-534: 532-The Dancing Princesses. 533-The Magic Fountain. 534-The Golden Touch	5	10	15	23	28	32
535-The Wizard of Oz	8	16	24	44	57	70
536-The Chimney Sweep	6	12	18	27	33	38
537-The Three Fairies	6	12	18	28	34	40
538-Silly Hans	5	10	15	23	28	32
539-The Enchanted Fish	6	12	18	31	38	45
540-The Tinder-Box	6	12	18	31	38	45
541-Snow White & Rose Red	5	10	15	24	30	35
542-The Donkey's Tale	5	10	15	24	30	35
543-The House in the Woods	6	12	18	27	33	38
544-The Golden Fleece	6	12	18	31	38	45
545-The Glass Mountain	5	10	15	24	30	35
546-The Elves & the Shoemaker	5	10	15	24	30	35
547-The Wishing Table	6	12	18	27	33	38
548-551: 548-The Magic Pitcher. 549-Simple Kate. 550-The Singing Donkey. 551-The Queen Bee	5	10	15	23	28	32
552-The Three Little Dwarfs	6	12	18	27	33	38

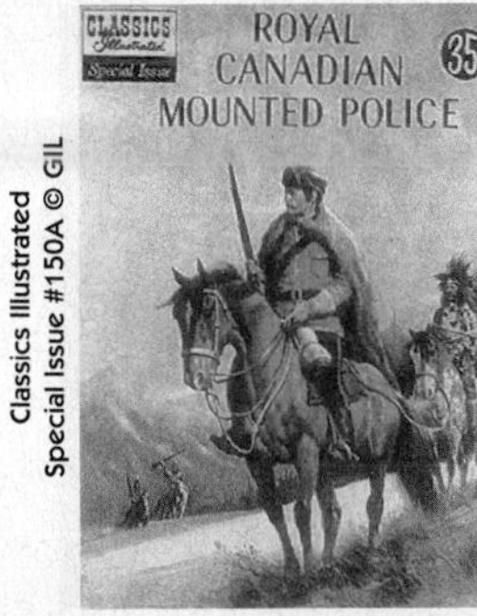

Classics Illustrated Special Issue #150A © GIL

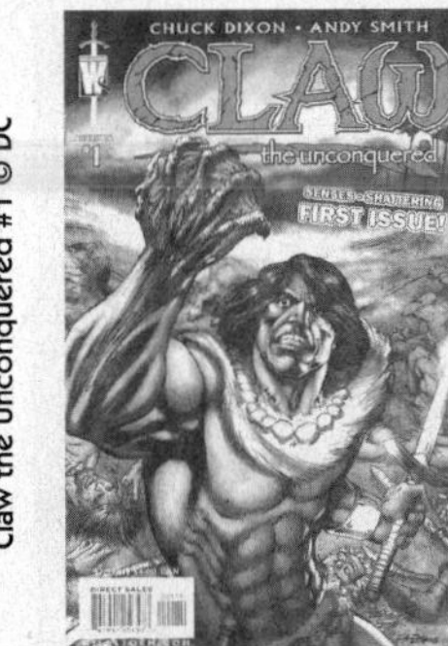

Claw the Unconquered #1 © DC

Clerks: The Lost Scene #1 © View Askew

	GD 2.0	VG 4.0	FN 6.0	VF 8.0	VF/NM 9.0	NM- 9.2
553,556: 553-King Thrushbeard. 556-The Elf Mound	5	10	15	23	28	32
554-The Enchanted Deer	6	12	18	29	36	42
555-The Three Golden Apples	5	10	15	24	30	35
557-Silly Willy	6	12	18	28	34	40
558-The Magic Dish; L.B. Cole-c; soft and stiff-c exist on original	7	14	21	35	43	50
559-The Japanese Lantern; 1 pg. Ingels-a; L.B. Cole-c	7	14	21	35	43	50
560-The Doll Princess; L.B. Cole-c	7	14	21	35	43	50
561-Hans Humdrum; L.B. Cole-c	6	12	18	29	36	42
562-The Enchanted Pony; L.B. Cole-c	7	14	21	35	43	50
563,565-568,570: 563-The Wishing Well; L.B. Cole-c. 565-The Silly Princess; L.B. Cole-c. 566-Clumsy Hans; L.B. Cole-c. 567-The Bearskin Soldier; L.B. Cole-c. 570-The Pearl Princess	6	12	18	27	33	38
564-The Salt Mountain; L.B.Cole-c. 568-The Happy Hedgehog; L.B. Cole-c.	6	12	18	28	34	40
569,573: 569-The Three Giants.573-The Crystal Ball	5	10	15	23	28	32
571,572: 571-How Fire Came to the Indians. 572-The Drummer Boy	6	12	18	29	36	42
574-Brightboots	5	10	15	24	30	35
575-The Fearless Prince	6	12	18	28	34	40
576-The Princess Who Saw Everything	7	14	21	35	43	50
577-The Runaway Dumpling	8	16	24	44	57	70

NOTE: *Prices are for original editions. Last reprint - Spring, 1971.* ***Costanza*** *&* ***Schaffenberger*** *art in many issues.*

CLASSICS ILLUSTRATED SPECIAL ISSUE
Gilberton Co.: (Came out semi-annually) Dec, 1955 - Jul, 1962 (35¢, 100 pgs.)

	GD 2.0	VG 4.0	FN 6.0	VF 8.0	VF/NM 9.0	NM- 9.2
129-The Story of Jesus (titled ...Special Edition) "Jesus on Mountain" cover	18	36	54	105	165	225
"Three Camels" cover (12/58)	19	38	57	109	172	235
"Mountain" cover (no date)-Has checklist on inside b/c to HRN #161 & different testimonial on back-c	14	28	42	76	108	140
"Mountain" cover (1968 re-issue; has white 50¢ circle)	10	20	30	56	76	95
132A-The Story of America (6/56); Cameron-a	12	24	36	67	94	120
135A-The Ten Commandments(12/56)	11	22	33	64	90	115
138A-Adventures in Science(6/57); HRN to 137	11	22	33	60	83	105
138A-(6/57)-2nd version w/HRN to 149	7	14	21	35	43	50
138A-(12/61)-3rd version w/HRN to 149	7	14	21	35	43	50
141A-The Rough Rider (Teddy Roosevelt)(12/57); Evans-a	11	22	33	62	86	110
144A-Blazing the Trails West(6/58)- 73 pgs. of Crandall/Evans plus Severin-a	11	22	33	64	90	115
147A-Crossing the Rockies(12/58)-Crandall/Evans-a	11	22	33	62	86	110
150A-Royal Canadian Police(6/59)-Ingels, Sid Check-a	11	22	33	62	86	110
153A-Men, Guns & Cattle(12/59)-Evans-a (26 pgs.); Kinstler-a	11	22	33	62	86	110
156A-The Atomic Age(6/60)-Crandall/Evans, Torres-a	11	22	33	62	86	110
159A-Rockets, Jets and Missiles(12/60)-Evans, Morrow-a	11	22	33	62	86	110
162A-War Between the States(6/61)-Kirby & Crandall/Evans-a; Ingels-a	17	34	51	100	158	215
165A-To the Stars(12/61)-Torres, Crandall/Evans, Kirby-a	14	28	42	76	108	140
166A-World War II('62)-Torres, Crandall/Evans, Kirby-a	15	30	45	83	124	165
167A-Prehistoric World(7/62)-Torres & Crandall/Evans-a; two versions exist (HRN to 165 & HRN to 167)	14	28	42	81	118	155
nn Special Issue-The United Nations (1964; 50¢; scarce); this is actually part of the European Special Series, which cont'd on after the U.S. series stopped issuing new titles in 1962. This English edition was prepared specifically for sale at the U.N. It was printed in Norway	50	100	150	315	533	750

NOTE: *There was another U.S. Special Issue prepared in 1962 with artwork by* ***Torres*** *entitled World War I. Unfortunately, it was never issued in any English-language edition. It was issued in 1964 in West Germany, The Netherlands, and some Scandanavian countries, with another edition in 1974 with a new cover.*

CLASSICS LIBRARY (See King Classics)

CLASSIC STAR WARS (Also see Star Wars)
Dark Horse Comics: Aug, 1992 - No. 20, June, 1994 ($2.50)

	GD 2.0	VG 4.0	FN 6.0	VF 8.0	VF/NM 9.0	NM- 9.2
1-Begin Star Wars strip-r by Williamson; Williamson redrew portions of the panels to fit comic book format						6.00
2-10: 8-Polybagged w/Star Wars Galaxy trading card. 8-M. Schultz-c						4.00
11-19: 13-Yeates-c. 17-M. Schultz-c. 19-Evans-c						3.00
20-($3.50, 52 pgs.)-Polybagged w/trading card						4.00
Escape To Hoth TPB ($16.95) r/#15-20						17.00
The Rebel Storm TPB - r/#8-14						17.00
Trade paperback ($29.95, slip-cased)-Reprints all movie adaptations						30.00

NOTE: *Williamson c-1-5,7,9,10,14,15,20.*

CLASSIC STAR WARS: (Title series). **Dark Horse Comics**

	GD 2.0	VG 4.0	FN 6.0	VF 8.0	VF/NM 9.0	NM- 9.2
--A NEW HOPE, 6/94 - No. 2, 7/94 ($3.95) 1,2: 1-r/Star Wars #1-3, 7-9 publ; 2-r/Star Wars #4-6, 10-12 publ. by Marvel Comics						6.00
--DEVILWORLDS, 8/96 - No.2, 9/96 ($2.50s)1,2: r/Alan Moore-s						4.00
--HAN SOLO AT STARS' END, 3/97 - No. 3, 5/97 ($2.95) 1-3: r/strips by Alfredo Alcala						4.00
--RETURN OF THE JEDI, 10/94 - No.2, 11/94 ($3.50) 1,2: 1-r/1983-84 Marvel series; polybagged with w/trading card						5.00
--THE EARLY ADVENTURES, 8/94 - No. 9, 4/95 ($2.50)1-9						4.00
--THE EMPIRE STRIKES BACK, 8/94 - No. 2, 9/94 ($3.95) 1-r/Star Wars #39-44 published by Marvel Comics						4.00

CLASSIC X-MEN (Becomes X-Men Classic #46 on)
Marvel Comics Group: Sept, 1986 - No. 45, Mar, 1990

	GD 2.0	VG 4.0	FN 6.0	VF 8.0	VF/NM 9.0	NM- 9.2
1-Begins-r of New X-Men	2	4	6	9	12	15
2-10: 10-Sabretooth app.						5.00
11-42,44,45: 11-1st origin of Magneto in back-up story. 17-Wolverine-c. 27-r/X-Men #121. 26-r/X-Men #120; Wolverine-c/app. 35-r/X-Men #129. 39-New Jim Lee back-up story (2nd-a on X-Men)						3.00
43-Byrne-c/a(r); ($1.75, double-size)						4.00

NOTE: ***Art Adams*** *c(p)-1-10, 12-16, 18-23.* ***Austin*** *c-10,15-21,24-28i.* ***Bolton*** *back up stories in 1-28,30-35.* ***Williamson*** *c-12-14i.*

CLAW (See Capt. Battle, Jr., Daredevil Comics & Silver Streak Comics)

CLAWS (See Wolverine & Black Cat: Claws 2 for sequel)
Marvel Comics: Oct, 2006 - No. 3, Dec, 2006 ($3.99, limited series)

	GD 2.0	VG 4.0	FN 6.0	VF 8.0	VF/NM 9.0	NM- 9.2
1-3-Wolverine and Black Cat team-up; Linsner-a/c						4.00
Wolverine & Black Cat: Claws HC (2007, $17.99, dustjacket) r/#1-3 & bonus Linsner art						18.00

CLAW THE UNCONQUERED (See Cancelled Comic Cavalcade)
National Periodical Publications/DC Comics: 5-6/75 - No. 9, 9-10/76; No. 10, 4-5/78 - No. 12, 8-9/78

	GD 2.0	VG 4.0	FN 6.0	VF 8.0	VF/NM 9.0	NM- 9.2
1-1st app. Claw	2	4	6	8	11	14
2-12: 3-Nudity panel. 9-Origin	1	2	3	4	5	7

NOTE: ***Giffen*** *a-8-12p.* ***Kubert*** *c-10-12.* ***Layton*** *a-9i, 12i.*

CLAW THE UNCONQUERED (See Red Sonja/Claw: The Devil's Hands)
DC Comics: Aug, 2006 - No. 6, Jan, 2007 ($2.99)

	GD 2.0	VG 4.0	FN 6.0	VF 8.0	VF/NM 9.0	NM- 9.2
1-6: 1,2-Chuck Dixon-s/Andy Smith; two covers by Smith & Van Sciver						3.00
TPB (2007, $17.99) r/#1-6; cover gallery						18.00

CLAY CODY, GUNSLINGER
Pines Comics: Fall, 1957

	GD 2.0	VG 4.0	FN 6.0	VF 8.0	VF/NM 9.0	NM- 9.2
1-Painted-c	6	12	18	31	38	45

CLEAN FUN, STARRING "SHOOGAFOOTS JONES"
Specialty Book Co.: 1944 (10¢, B&W, oversized covers, 24 pgs.)

	GD 2.0	VG 4.0	FN 6.0	VF 8.0	VF/NM 9.0	NM- 9.2
nn-Humorous situations involving Negroes in the Deep South						
White cover issue...	29	58	87	172	281	390
Dark grey cover issue...	29	58	87	170	278	385

CLEAN ROOM
DC Comics (Vertigo): Dec, 2015 - No. 18, Jun, 2017 ($3.99)

	GD 2.0	VG 4.0	FN 6.0	VF 8.0	VF/NM 9.0	NM- 9.2
1-18: 1-Gail Simone-s/Jon Davis-Hunt-a/Jenny Frison-c						4.00

CLEMENTINA THE FLYING PIG (See Dell Jr. Treasury)

CLEOPATRA (See Ideal, a Classical Comic No. 1)

CLERKS: THE COMIC BOOK (Also see Tales From the Clerks and Oni Double Feature #1)
Oni Press: Feb, 1998 ($2.95, B&W, one-shot)

	GD 2.0	VG 4.0	FN 6.0	VF 8.0	VF/NM 9.0	NM- 9.2
1-Kevin Smith-s	2	4	6	11	16	20
1-Second printing						4.00
...Holiday Special (12/98, $2.95) Smith-s						6.00
...The Lost Scene (12/99, $2.95) Smith-s/Hester-a	1	2	3	5	6	8

CLIFFHANGER (See Battle Chasers, Crimson, and Danger Girl)
WildStorm Prod./Wizard Press: 1997 (Wizard supplement)

	GD 2.0	VG 4.0	FN 6.0	VF 8.0	VF/NM 9.0	NM- 9.2
0-Sketchbook preview of Cliffhanger titles						6.00

CLIMAX! (Mystery)
Gillmor Magazines: July, 1955 - No. 2, Sept, 1955

	GD 2.0	VG 4.0	FN 6.0	VF 8.0	VF/NM 9.0	NM- 9.2
1	19	38	57	109	172	235
2	14	28	42	81	118	155

Clive Barker's Nightbreed #12 © Barker & BOOM

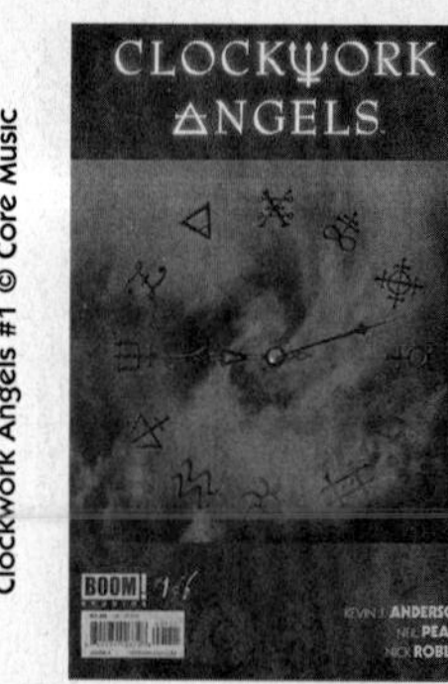

Clockwork Angels #1 © Core Music

Clue #4 © Hasbro

GD VG FN VF VF/NM NM-
2.0 4.0 6.0 8.0 9.0 9.2

CLINT (Also see Adolescent Radioactive Black Belt Hamsters)
Eclipse Comics: Sept, 1986 - No. 2, Jan, 1987 ($1.50, B&W)
1,2 4.00

CLINT & MAC (TV, Disney)
Dell Publishing Co.: No. 889, Mar, 1958
Four Color 889-Alex Toth-a, photo-c 10 20 30 64 132 200

CLIVE BARKER'S BOOK OF THE DAMNED: A HELLRAISER COMPANION
Marvel Comics (Epic): Oct, 1991 - No. 3, Nov, 1992 ($4.95, semi-annual, 52 pgs.)
1-Simon Bisley-c 1 3 4 6 8 10
2,3: 2-(4/92). 3-(11/92)-McKean-a (1 pg.) 5.00

CLIVE BARKER'S HELLRAISER (Also see Epic, Hellraiser Nightbreed –Jihad, Revelations, Son of Celluloid, Tapping the Vein & Weaveworld)
Marvel Comics (Epic Comics): 1989 - No. 20, 1993 ($4.50-6.95, mature, quarterly, 68 pgs.)
Book 1-4,10-16,18,19: Based on Hellraiser & Hellbound movies; Bolton-c/a; Spiegle & Wrightson-a (graphic album). 10-Foil-c. 12-Sam Kieth-a 1 2 3 5 6 8
Book 5-9 ($5.95): 7-Bolton-a. 8-Morrow-a 1 2 3 5 6 8
Book 17-Alex Ross-a, 34 pgs. 2 4 6 8 10 12
Book 20-By Gaiman/McKean 1 2 3 5 6 8
...Collected Best (Checker Books, '02, $21.95)-r/by various incl. Ross, Gaiman, Mignola 22.00
...Collected Best II ('03, $19.95)-r/by various incl. Bolton, L. Wachowski, Dorman 20.00
...Collected Best III ('04, $26.95)-r/by various incl. Bolton, L. Wachowski, Wrightson 27.00
...Dark Holiday Special ('92, $4.95)-Conrad-a 6.00
...Spring Slaughter 1 ('94, $6.95, 52 pgs.)-Painted-c 7.00
...Summer Special 1 ('92, $5.95, 68 pgs.) 6.00

CLIVE BARKER'S HELLRAISER
BOOM! Studios: Mar, 2011 - No. 20, Nov, 2012 ($3.99)
1-20: 1-Barker & Monfette-s/Manco-a; preview of Hellraiser Masterpieces; 3 covers 4.00
Annual 1 (3/12, $4.99) Hervás-a; three covers 5.00
2013 Annual (10/13, $4.99) Seifert-s/Hervás-a; Barker & Meares-s/Ordon-a 5.00
...: Bestiary 1-6 (8/14 - No. 6, 1/15, $3.99) short stories by various; multiple covers 4.00
... Masterpieces 1-12 (11/11 - No. 12, 4/12, $3.99) reps from Marvel series. 1-Wrightson-a 4.00
...: The Dark Watch 1-12 (2/13 - No. 12, 1/14, $3.99) Tom Garcia-a; multiple covers 4.00
...: The Road Below 1-4 (10/12 - No. 4, 1/13, $3.99) Haemi Jang-a; multiple covers 4.00

CLIVE BARKER'S NEXT TESTAMENT
BOOM! Studios: May, 2013 - No. 12, Aug, 2014 ($3.99)
1-12: 1-Clive Barker & Mark Miller-s/Haemi Jang-a. 1-Four covers 4.00

CLIVE BARKER'S NIGHTBREED (Also see Epic)
Marvel Comics (Epic Comics): Apr, 1990 - No. 25, Mar, 1993 ($1.95/$2.25/$2.50, mature)
1-25: 1-4-Adapt horror movie. 5-New stories; Guice-a(p) 3.00

CLIVE BARKER'S NIGHTBREED
BOOM! Studios: May, 2014 - No. 12, Apr, 2015 ($3.99)
1-12: 1-8-Andreyko-s/Kowalski-a. 9-11-Javier & Pramanik-a 4.00

CLIVE BARKER'S THE HARROWERS
Marvel Comics (Epic Comics): Dec, 1993 - No. 6, May, 1994 ($2.50)
1-($2.95)-Glow-in-the-dark-c; Colan-c/a in all 4.00
2-6 3.00
NOTE: ***Colan** a(p)-1-6; c-1-3, 4p, 5p. **Williamson** a(i)-2, 4, 5(part).*

CLOAK AND DAGGER
Ziff-Davis Publishing Co.: Fall, 1952
1-Saunders painted-c 40 80 120 246 411 575

CLOAK AND DAGGER (Also see Marvel Fanfare and Spectacular Spider-Man #64)
Marvel Comics Group: Oct, 1983 - No. 4, Jan, 1984 (Mini-series)
1-Mantlo-s/Leonardi-a/Austin-a(i) in all 1 2 3 5 6 8
2-4: 4-Origin 5.00

CLOAK AND DAGGER (2nd Series)(Also see Marvel Graphic Novel #34 & Strange Tales)
Marvel Comics Group: July, 1985 - No. 11, Jan, 1987
1-Mantlo-s/Leonardi-a/Austin-a(i) 1 2 3 5 6 8
2-11: 7,8-Mignola-c. 9-Art Adams-p 4.00
...And Power Pack (1990, $7.95, 68 pgs.) 8.00

CLOAK AND DAGGER (3rd Series listed as Mutant Misadventures Of...)

CLOAK AND DAGGER
Marvel Comics: May, 2010 ($3.99, one-shot)
1-Stuart Moore-s/Mark Brooks-a; X-Men app. 6.00

CLOAK AND DAGGER: NEGATIVE EXPOSURE
Marvel Comics: 2019 ($19.99, squarebound TPB, printing of digital-first story)
nn-Hopeless-s/Manna & Coleman-a; Mister Negative app.; bonus inked art pages 20.00

GD VG FN VF VF/NM NM-
2.0 4.0 6.0 8.0 9.0 9.2

CLOAK AND DAGGER: SHADES OF GREY
Marvel Comics: 2018 ($19.99, squarebound TPB, printing of digital-first story)
nn-Hopeless-s/Messina-a; bonus inked art pages 20.00

CLOAKS
BOOM! Studios: Sept, 2014 - No. 4, Dec, 2014 ($3.99, limited series)
1-4-Monroe-s/Navarro-a 4.00

CLOBBERIN' TIME
Marvel Comics: Sept, 1995 ($1.95) (Based on card game)
nn-Overpower game guide; Ben Grimm story 3.00

CLOCK, THE
Image Comics: Jan, 2020 - Present ($3.99)
1,2-Matt Hawkins-s/Colleen Doran-a 4.00

CLOCK MAKER, THE
Image Comics: Jan, 2003 - No. 4, May, 2003 ($2.50, comic unfolds to 10"x13" pages)
1-4-Krueger-s 3.00
... Act Two (4/04, $4.95, standard format) Krueger-s/Matt Smith-c 5.00

CLOCKWORK ANGELS (Based on Neil Peart's story and lyrics from Rush's album)
BOOM! Studios: Mar, 2014 - No. 6, Nov, 2014 ($3.99, limited series)
1-6-Kevin J. Anderson-s/Nick Robles-a; two covers on each 4.00

CLONE CONSPIRACY, THE (Also see Amazing Spider-Man [2017] #18)
Marvel Comics: Dec, 2016 - No. 5, Apr, 2017 ($4.99/$3.99)
1-($4.99) Slott-s/Cheung-a; Miles Warren, Gwen Stacy, Doc Ock & Rhino app. 5.00
2-5-($3.99) Kaine app. 3-Ben Reilly returns 4.00
...: Omega 1 (5/17, $4.99) Three short stories by various; aftermath of series 5.00

CLONEZONE SPECIAL
Dark Horse Comics/First Comics: 1989 ($2.00, B&W)
1-Back-up series from Badger & Nexus 3.00

CLOSE ENCOUNTERS (See Marvel Comics Super Special & Marvel Special Edition)

CLOSE SHAVES OF PAULINE PERIL, THE (TV cartoon)
Gold Key: June, 1970 - No. 4, March, 1971
1 4 8 12 23 37 50
2-4 3 6 9 16 23 30

CLOUDBURST
Image Comics: June, 2004 ($7.95, squarebound)
1-Gray & Palmiotti-s/Shy & Gouveia-a 8.00

CLOUDFALL
Image Comics: Nov, 2003 ($4.95, B&W, squarebound)
1-Kirkman-s/Su-a/c 5.00

CLOWN COMICS (No. 1 titled Clown Comic Book)
Clown Comics/Home Comics/Harvey Publ.: 1945 - No. 3, Win, 1946
nn (#1) 15 30 45 86 133 180
2,3 10 20 30 56 76 95

CLOWNS, THE (I Pagliacci)
Dark Horse Comics: 1998 ($2.95, B&W, one-shot)
1-Adaption of the opera; P. Craig Russell-script 3.00

CLUBHOUSE RASCALS (#1 titled ...Presents?) (Also see Three Rascals)
Sussex Publ. Co. (Magazine Enterprises): June, 1956 - No. 2, Oct, 1956
1-The Brain app. in both; DeCarlo-a 9 18 27 50 65 80
2 7 14 21 37 46 55

CLUB "16"
Famous Funnies: June, 1948 - No. 4, Dec, 1948
1-Teen-age humor 24 48 72 140 230 320
2-4 15 30 45 84 127 170

CLUE (Based on the boardgame)
IDW Publishing: Jun, 2017 - No. 6, Nov, 2017 ($3.99)
1-6-Paul Allor-s/Nelson Daniel-a; multiple covers on each 4.00

CLUE: CANDLESTICK (Based on the boardgame)
IDW Publishing: May, 2019 - No. 3, Jul, 2019 ($4.99, limited series)
1-3-Dash Shaw-s/a; multiple covers on each 5.00

CLUE COMICS (Real Clue Crime V2#4 on)
Hillman Periodicals: Jan, 1943 - No. 15(V2#3), May, 1947
1-Origin The Boy King, Nightmare, Micro-Face, Twilight, & Zippo
184 368 552 1168 2009 2850

Cluster #1 © Brisson & Couceiro

Codename: Stryke Force #8 © TCOW

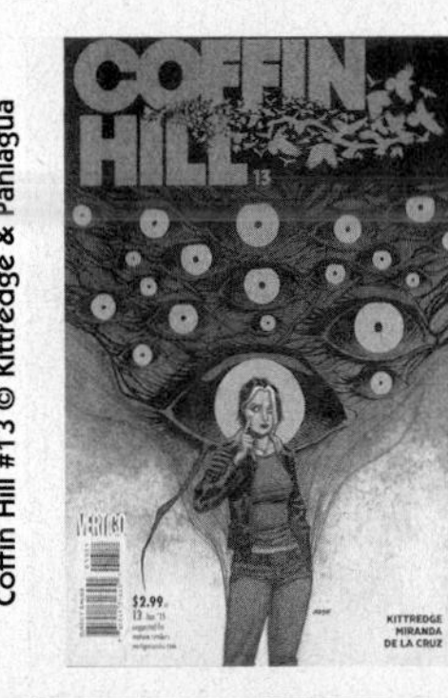

Coffin Hill #13 © Kittredge & Paniagua

	GD 2.0	VG 4.0	FN 6.0	VF 8.0	VF/NM 9.0	NM- 9.2
2 (scarce)	90	180	270	576	988	1400
3-5 (9/43)	47	94	141	296	498	700
6,8,9: 8-Palais-c/a(2)	36	72	108	211	343	475
7-Classic concentration camp torture-c (3/44)	94	188	282	597	1024	1450
10-Origin/1st app. The Gun Master & begin series; content changes to crime (10/46)	39	78	117	231	378	525
11 (12/46)	27	54	81	160	263	365
12-Origin Rackman; McWilliams-a, Guardineer-a(2)	37	74	111	218	354	490
V2#1-Nightmare new origin; Iron Lady app.; Simon & Kirby-a (3/47)	58	116	174	371	636	900
V2#2-S&K-a(2)-Bondage/torture-c; man attacks & kills people with electric iron. Infantino-a	87	174	261	553	952	1350
V2#3-S&K-a(3)	60	120	180	381	653	925

CLUELESS: SENIOR YEAR (Movie)
Boom Entertainment (BOOM Box): Aug, 2017 ($14.99, SC, graphic novel)

nn-Sarah Kuhn & Amber Benson-s/Siobhan Keenan-a; sequel to the movie; bonus art 15.00

CLUELESS SPRING SPECIAL (TV)
Marvel Comics: May, 1997 ($3.99, magazine sized, one-shot)

1-Photo-c from TV show 4.00

CLUSTER
BOOM! Studios: Feb, 2015 - No. 8, Oct, 2015 ($3.99, limited series)

1-8-Ed Brisson-s/Damian Couceiro-a 4.00

CLUTCHING HAND, THE
American Comics Group: July-Aug, 1954

	GD	VG	FN	VF	VF/NM	NM-
1-Gustavson, Moldoff-a	58	116	174	371	636	900

CLYDE BEATTY COMICS (Also see Crackajack Funnies)
Commodore Productions & Artists, Inc.: October, 1953 (84 pgs.)

	GD	VG	FN	VF	VF/NM	NM-
1-Photo front/back-c; movie scenes and comics	22	44	66	132	216	300

CLYDE CRASHCUP (TV)
Dell Publishing Co.: Aug-Oct, 1963 - No. 5, Sept-Nov, 1964

	GD	VG	FN	VF	VF/NM	NM-
1-All written by John Stanley	6	12	18	41	76	110
2-5	4	8	12	27	44	60

COBB
IDW Publishing: May, 2006 - No. 3, July, 2007 ($3.99, B&W)

1-3-Beau Smith-s/Eduardo Barreto-a/c; regular and retailer incentive covers 4.00

COBRA (G.I. Joe)
IDW Publishing: No. 10, Feb, 2012 - No. 21, Jan, 2013 ($3.99)

10-21 4.00
... Annual 2012: The Origin of Cobra Commander (1/12, $7.99) Dixon-s 8.00

COBRA KAI: THE KARATE KID SAGA CONTINUES (Based on the Karate Kid movie)
IDW Publishing: Oct, 2019 - Present ($3.99)

1-3-Johnny Lawrence's story before & during the movie; Kagan McLeod-a 4.00

CODENAME: ACTION
Dynamite Entertainment: 2013 - No. 5, 2014 ($3.99, limited series)

1-5-Captain Action; Chris Roberson-s/Jonathan Lau-a; multiple covers on each 4.00

CODE NAME: ASSASSIN (See 1st Issue Special)

CODENAME: BABOUSHKA
Image Comics: Oct, 2015 - No. 5, Mar, 2016 ($3.99, limited series)

1-5: 1-Antony Johnston-s/Shari Chankhamma-a 4.00

CODENAME: DANGER
Lodestone Publishing: Aug, 1985 - No. 4, May, 1986 ($1.50)

1-4 3.00

CODENAME: FIREARM (Also see Firearm)
Malibu Comics (Ultraverse): June, 1995 - No. 5, Sept, 1995 ($2.95, bimonthly limited series)

0-5: 0-2-Alec Swan back-up story by James Robinson. 0-Pérez-c 3.00

CODENAME: GENETIX
Marvel Comics UK: Jan, 1993 - No. 4, May, 1993 ($1.75, limited series)

1-4: Wolverine in all 3.00

CODENAME: KNOCKOUT
DC Comics (Vertigo): No. 0, Jun, 2001 - No. 23, June, 2003 ($2.50/$2.75)

0-15: Rodi-s in all. 0-5-Small Jr. -a. 1-Two covers by Chiodo & Cho. 7,8,10,11,12-Paquette-a. 6,9,13,14-Conner-a 3.00
16-23: 16-Begin $2.75-c. 23-Last issue; JG Jones-c 3.00

CODENAME SPITFIRE (Formerly Spitfire And The Troubleshooters)
Marvel Comics Group: No. 10, July, 1987 - No. 13, Oct, 1987

10-13: 10-Rogers-c/a (low printing) 3.50

CODENAME: STRYKE FORCE (Also See Cyberforce V1#4 & Cyberforce/Stryke Force: Opposing Forces
Image Comics (Top Cow Productions): Jan, 1994 - No. 14, Sept, 1995 ($1.95-$2.25)

0,1-14: 1-12-Silvestri stories, Peterson-a. 4-Stormwatch app. 14-Story continues in Cyberforce/Stryke Force: Opposing Forces; Turner-a 3.00
1-Gold, 1-Blue 4.00

CODE OF HONOR
Marvel Comics: Feb, 1997 - No. 4, May, 1997 ($5.95, limited series)

1-4-Fully painted by various; Dixon-s 6.00

CODY OF THE PONY EXPRESS (See Colossal Features Magazine)
Fox Feature Syndicate: Sept, 1950 (See Women Outlaws)(One shot)

	GD	VG	FN	VF	VF/NM	NM-
1-Painted-c	15	30	45	86	133	180

CODY OF THE PONY EXPRESS (Buffalo Bill...) (Outlaws of the West #11 on; Formerly Bullseye)
Charlton Comics: No. 8, Oct, 1955; No. 9, Jan, 1956; No. 10, June, 1956

	GD	VG	FN	VF	VF/NM	NM-
8-Bullseye on splash pg; not S&K-a	8	16	24	44	57	70
9,10: Buffalo Bill app. in all	6	12	18	29	36	42

CODY STARBUCK (1st app. in Star Reach #1)
Star Reach Productions: July, 1978

	GD	VG	FN	VF	VF/NM	NM-
nn-Howard Chaykin-c/a	3	6	9	14	20	25
2nd printing	2	4	6	8	10	12

NOTE: Both printings say First Printing. True first printing is on lower-grade paper, somewhat off-register, and snow in snow sequence has green tint.

CO-ED ROMANCES
P. L. Publishing Co.: November, 1951

	GD	VG	FN	VF	VF/NM	NM-
1	14	28	42	80	115	150

COFFEE WORLD
World Comics: Oct, 1995 ($1.50, B&W, anthology)

1-Shannon Wheeler's Too Much Coffee Man story 4.00

COFFIN, THE
Oni Press: Sept, 2000 - No. 4, May, 2001 ($2.95, B&W, limited series)

1-4-Hester-s/Huddleston-a 3.00

COFFIN BOUND
Image Comics: Aug, 2019 - No. 8, Nov, 2020 ($3.99/$4.99, limited series)

1-3,5,6,8-($3.99) Dan Watters-s/Dani-a 4.00
4,7-($4.99) 4-Bonus preview of Protector #1 5.00

COFFIN HILL
DC Comics (Vertigo): Dec, 2013 - No. 20, Sept, 2015 ($2.99/$3.99)

1-18: 1-Caitlin Kittredge-s/Inaki Miranda-a; covers by Dave Johnson & Gene Ha 3.00
19,20-($3.99) Johnson-c 4.00

COLDER
Dark Horse Comics: Nov, 2012 - No. 5, Mar, 2013 ($3.99, limited series)

1-5-Tobin-s/Ferreyra-a/c 4.00

COLDER: THE BAD SEED
Dark Horse Comics: Oct, 2014 - No. 5, Feb, 2015 ($3.99, limited series)

1-5-Tobin-s/Ferreyra-a/c 4.00

COLDER: TOSS THE BONES
Dark Horse Comics: Sept, 2015 - No. 5, Jan, 2016 ($3.99, limited series)

1-5-Tobin-s/Ferreyra-a/c 4.00

COLD WAR
IDW Publishing: Oct, 2011 - No. 4, Jan, 2012 ($3.99, limited series)

1-4-John Byrne-s/a/c; two covers on each 4.00

COLD WAR
AfterShock Comics: Feb, 2018 - No. 5, Jun, 2018 ($3.99, limited series)

1-5-Sebela-a/Sherman-a 4.00

COLLAPSER
DC Comics (Young Animal): Sept, 2019 - No. 6, Feb, 2020 ($3.99, limited series)

1-6-Mikey Way & Shaun Simon-s/Ilias Kyriazis-a. 5-Superman #1 cover swipe 4.00

COLLECTORS DRACULA, THE
Millennium Publications: 1994 - No. 2, 1994 ($3.95, color/B&W, 52 pgs., limited series)

1,2-Bolton-a (7 pgs.) 4.00

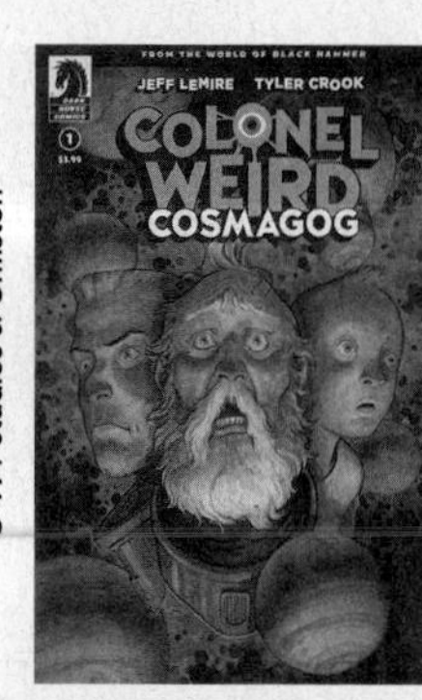

Colonel Weird: Cosmagog #1 © 171 Studios & Ormston

Combat Kelly #8 © MAR

Comedy Comics #14 © MAR

	GD	VG	FN	VF	VF/NM	NM-
	2.0	4.0	6.0	8.0	9.0	9.2

COLLECTORS ITEM CLASSICS (See Marvel Collectors Item Classics)

COLLIDER (See FBP: Federal Bureau Of Physics; title changed after issue #1)

COLONEL WEIRD: COSMAGOG (From Black Hammer)
Dark Horse Comics: Oct, 2020 - No. 4, Jan, 2021 ($3.99, limited series)
1-4-Jeff Lemire-s/Tyler Crook-a 3.00

COLONIZED, THE
IDW Publishing: Apr, 2013 - No. 4, Jul, 2013 ($3.99, limited series)
1-4-Aliens vs. Zombies; Dave Sim-c/Chris Ryall-s/Drew Moss-a 4.00

COLORS IN BLACK
Dark Horse Comics: Mar, 1995 - No. 4, June, 1995 ($2.95, limited series)
1-4 3.00

COLOSSAL FEATURES MAGAZINE (Formerly I Loved) (See Cody of the Pony Express)
Fox Feature Syndicate: No. 33, 5/50 - No. 34, 7/50; No. 3, 9/50 (Based on Columbia serial)
33,34: Cody of the Pony Express begins. 33-Painted-c. 34-Photo-c
17 34 51 98 154 210
3-Authentic criminal cases 41 82 123 256 428 600

COLOSSAL SHOW, THE (TV cartoon)
Gold Key: Oct, 1969
1 5 10 15 30 50 70

COLOSSUS (See X-Men)
Marvel Comics: Oct, 1997 ($2.99, 48 pgs., one-shot)
1-Raab-s/Hitch & Neary-a, wraparound-c 4.00

COLOSSUS COMICS (See Green Giant & Motion Picture Funnies Weekly)
Sun Publications (Funnies, Inc.?): March, 1940
1-(Scarce)-Tulpa of Tsang(hero); Colossus app. 1000 2000 3000 7600 13,800 20,000
NOTE: *Cover by artist that drew Colossus in Green Giant Comics.*

COLOUR OF MAGIC, THE (Terry Pratchett's...)
Innovation Publishing: 1991 - No. 4, 1991 ($2.50, limited series)
1-4: Adapts 1st novel of the Discworld series 3.00

COLOUR YOUR OWN CEREBUS IN HELL?
Aardvark-Vanaheim: Oct, 2019 ($4.00, B&W)
1-Cerebus figures placed over original Gustave Doré artwork of Hell 4.00

COLT .45 (TV)
Dell Publishing Co.: No. 924, 8/58 - No. 1058, 11-1/59-60; No. 4, 2-4/60 - No. 9, 5-7/61
Four Color 924(#1)-Wayde Preston photo-c on all 9 18 27 62 126 190
Four Color 1004,1058: 1004-Photo-b/c 7 14 21 48 89 130
4,5,7-9 7 14 21 48 89 130
6-Toth-a 8 16 24 51 96 140

COLUMBIA COMICS
William H. Wise Co.: 1943
1-Joe Palooka, Charlie Chan, Capt. Yank, Sparky Watts, Dixie Dugan app.
34 68 102 204 332 460

COMANCHE
Dell Publishing Co.: No. 1350, Apr-Jun, 1962
Four Color 1350-Disney movie; reprints FC #966 with title change from "Tonka" to "Comanche"; Sal Mineo photo-c 5 10 15 33 57 80

COMANCHEROS, THE
Dell Publishing Co.: No. 1300, Mar-May, 1962
Four Color 1300-Movie, John Wayne photo-c 14 28 42 94 207 320

COMBAT
Atlas Comics (ANC): June, 1952 - No. 11, April, 1953
1 48 96 144 302 514 725
2-Heath-c/a 27 54 81 158 259 360
3,5-9,11: 3-Romita-a. 6-Robinson-c; Romita-a 20 40 60 115 185 255
4-Krigstein-a 20 40 60 114 182 250
10-B&W and color illos. in **POP**; Sale-a, Forte-a 22 44 66 132 216 300
NOTE: *Combat Casey in 7-11.* ***Heath*** *a-2, 3; c-1, 2, 5, 9.* ***Maneely*** *a-1; c-3, 10.* ***Pakula*** *a-1.* ***Reinman*** *a-1.*

COMBAT
Dell Publishing Co.: Oct-Nov, 1961 - No. 40, Oct, 1973 (No #9)
1-Painted-c (thru #17) 8 16 24 51 96 140
2,3,5 5 10 15 31 53 75
4-John F. Kennedy c/story (P.T. 109) 6 12 18 38 69 100
6,7,8(4-6/63), 8(7-9/63) 4 8 12 27 44 60
10-26: 26-Last 12¢ issue 3 6 9 21 33 45
27-40(reprints #1-14). 30-r/#4 3 6 9 14 19 24

	GD	VG	FN	VF	VF/NM	NM-
	2.0	4.0	6.0	8.0	9.0	9.2

COMBAT CASEY (Formerly War Combat)
Atlas Comics (SAI): No. 6, Jan, 1953 - No. 34, July, 1957
6 (Indicia shows 1/52 in error) 34 68 102 204 332 460
7-R.Q. Sale-a 20 40 60 115 185 255
8-Used in **POP**, pg. 94 19 38 57 109 172 235
9,10,13-19-Violent art by R.Q. Sale; Battle Brady x-over #10
21 42 63 126 206 285
11,12,20-Last Precode (2/55) 16 32 48 94 147 200
21-34: 22,25-R.Q. Sale-a 15 30 45 88 137 185
NOTE: ***Everett*** *a-6.* ***Heath*** *c-10, 17, 19, 23, 30.* ***Maneely*** *c-6, 8, 15.* ***Powell*** *a-29(5), 30(5), 34.* ***Severin*** *c-26, 33, 34.*

COMBAT KELLY
Atlas Comics (SPI): Nov, 1951 - No. 44, Aug, 1957
1-1st app. Combat Kelly; Heath-a 50 100 150 315 533 750
2 26 52 78 154 252 350
3-10 20 40 60 115 185 255
11-Used in **POP**, pgs. 94,95 plus color illo. 20 40 60 117 189 260
12-Color illo. in **POP** 19 38 57 109 172 235
13-16 17 34 51 98 154 210
17-Violent art by R. Q. Sale; Combat Casey app. 21 42 63 124 202 280
18-20,22-28: 18-Battle Brady app. 28-Last precode (1/55)
16 32 48 94 147 200
21-Transvestism-c 19 38 57 111 176 240
29-44: 38-Green Berets story (8/56) 15 30 45 88 137 185
NOTE: ***Berg*** *a-8, 12-14, 15-17, 19-23, 25, 26, 28, 31-37, 39, 41-44; c-2.* ***Colan*** *a-42.* ***Heath*** *a-4, 18; c-31.* ***Lawrence*** *a-23.* ***Maneely*** *a-3-5(2), 6, 7(3), 8, 9(2), 11; c-4, 5, 7, 8, 10, 11, 25, 29, 39.* ***R.Q. Sale*** *a-17, 25.* ***Severin*** *c-41, 42.* ***Whitney*** *a-5.*

COMBAT KELLY (...and the Deadly Dozen)
Marvel Comics Group: June, 1972 - No. 9, Oct, 1973
1-Intro & origin new Combat Kelly; Ayers/Mooney-a; Severin-c (20¢)
4 8 12 27 44 60
2,5-8 2 4 6 13 18 22
3,4: 3-Origin. 4-Sgt. Fury-c/s 3 6 9 15 22 28
9-Death of the Deadly Dozen 3 6 9 19 30 40

COMBAT ZONE: TRUE TALES OF GIS IN IRAQ
Marvel Comics: 2005 ($19.99, squarebound)
Vol. 1-Karl Zinsmeister scripts adapted from his non-fiction books; Dan Jurgens-a 20.00

COMBINED OPERATIONS (See The Story of the Commandos)

COMEBACK (See Zane Grey 4-Color 357)

COMEDY CARNIVAL
St. John Publishing Co.: no date (1950's) (100 pgs.)
nn-Contains rebound St. John comics 39 78 117 240 395 550

COMEDY COMICS (1st Series) (Daring Mystery #1-8) (Becomes Margie Comics #35 on)
Timely Comics (TCI 9,10): No. 9, April, 1942 - No. 34, Fall, 1946
9-(Scarce)-The Fin by Everett, Capt. Dash, Citizen V, & The Silver Scorpion app.; Wolverton-a; 1st app. Comedy Kid; satire on Hitler & Stalin; The Fin, Citizen V & Silver Scorpion cont. from Daring Mystery 303 606 909 2121 3711 5300
10-(Scarce)-Origin The Fourth Musketeer, Victory Boys; Monstro, the Mighty app.
235 470 705 1492 2571 3650
11-Vagabond, Stuporman app. 68 136 204 435 743 1050
12,13 32 64 96 188 307 425
14-Origin/1st app. Super Rabbit (3/43) plus-c 94 188 282 597 1024 1450
15-19 28 56 84 165 270 375
20-Hitler parody-c 74 148 222 470 810 1150
21-Tojo-c 57 114 171 362 619 875
22-Hitler parody-c 100 200 300 635 1093 1550
23-32 20 40 60 120 195 270
33-Kurtzman-a (5 pgs.) 21 42 63 126 206 285
34-Intro Margie; Wolverton-a (5 pgs.) 40 80 120 246 411 575

COMEDY COMICS (2nd Series)
Marvel Comics (ACI): May, 1948 - No. 10, Jan, 1950
1-Hedy, Tessie, Millie begin; Kurtzman's "Hey Look" (he draws himself)
84 168 252 538 919 1300
2 53 106 159 334 567 800
3,4-Kurtzman's "Hey Look": 3-(1 pg). 4-(3 pgs) 68 136 204 435 743 1050
5-10 30 60 90 177 289 400

COMET, THE (See The Mighty Crusaders & Pep Comics #1)
Red Circle Comics (Archie): Oct, 1983 - No. 2, Dec, 1983
1-Re-intro & origin The Comet; The American Shield begins. Nino & Infantino art in both. Hangman in both 6.00
2-Origin continues. 5.00

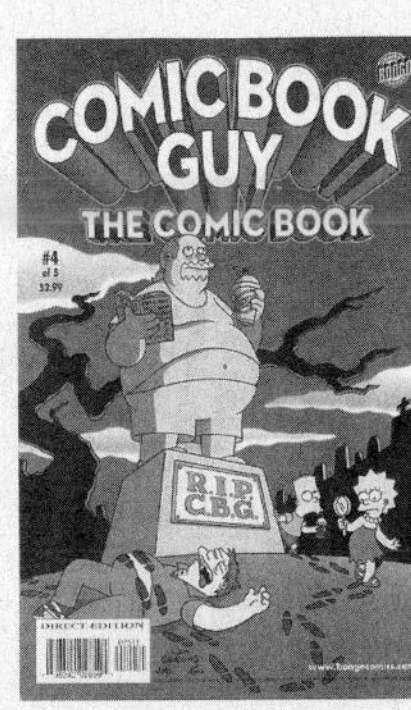

Comic Book Guy: The Comic Book #4 © Bongo

Comic Cavalcade #5 © DC

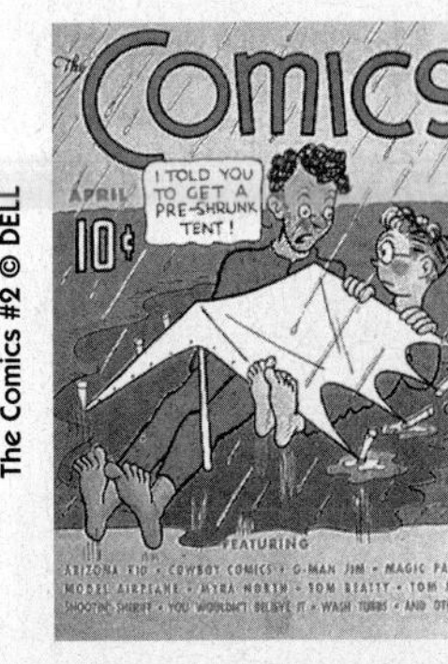

The Comics #2 © DELL

GD VG FN VF VF/NM NM-
2.0 4.0 6.0 8.0 9.0 9.2

COMET, THE
DC Comics (Impact Comics): July, 1991 - No. 18, Dec, 1992 ($1.00/$1.25)
1 4.00
2-18: 4-Black Hood app. 6-Re-intro Hangman. 8-Web x-over. 10-Contains Crusaders trading card. 4-Origin. Netzer (Nasser) c(p)-11,14-17 3.00
Annual 1 (1992, $2.50, 68 pgs.)-Contains Impact trading card; Shield back-up story 4.00

COMET MAN, THE (Movie)
Marvel Comics Group: Feb, 1987 - No. 6, July, 1987 (limited series)
1-6: 3-Hulk app. 4-She-Hulk shower scene-c/s. Fantastic 4 app. 5-Fantastic 4 app. 3.00
NOTE: *Kelley Jones a-1-6p.*

COMIC ALBUM (Also see Disney Comic Album)
Dell Publishing Co.: Mar-May, 1958 - No. 18, June-Aug, 1962
1-Donald Duck 9 18 27 59 117 175
2-Bugs Bunny 5 10 15 31 53 75
3-Donald Duck 6 12 18 41 76 110
4-6,8-10: 4-Tom & Jerry. 5-Woody Woodpecker. 6,10-Bugs Bunny. 8-Tom & Jerry. 9-Woody Woodpecker 4 8 12 27 44 60
7,11,15: Popeye. 11-(9-11/60) 4 8 12 28 47 65
12-14: 12-Tom & Jerry. 13-Woody Woodpecker. 14-Bugs Bunny 4 8 12 27 44 60
16-Flintstones (12-2/61-62)-3rd app. Early Cave Kids app. 7 14 21 46 86 125
17-Space Mouse (3rd app.) 5 10 15 30 50 70
18-Three Stooges; photo-c 7 14 21 46 86 125

COMIC BOOK
Marvel Comics-#1/Dark Horse Comics-#2: 1995 ($5.95, oversize)
1-Spumco characters by John K. 1 2 3 4 5 7
2-(Dark Horse) 6.00

COMIC BOOK GUY: THE COMIC BOOK (BONGO COMICS PRESENTS...) (Simpsons)
Bongo Comics: 2010 - No. 5, 2010 ($3.99/$2.99, limited series)
1-($3.99) Four-layer cover w/classic swipes incl. FF#1; intro Graphic Novel Kid 3 6 9 14 20 25
2-5-($2.99) 2-Stan Lee cameo. 3-Includes Little Lulu spoof. 4-Comic Book Guy origin 6.00

COMIC CAPERS
Red Circle Mag./Marvel Comics: Fall, 1944 - No. 6, Fall, 1946
1-Super Rabbit, The Creeper, Silly Seal, Ziggy Pig, Sharpy Fox begin 45 90 135 284 480 675
2 24 48 72 140 230 320
3-6: 4-(Summer 1945) 22 44 66 130 213 295

COMIC CAVALCADE
All-American/National Periodical Publications: Winter, 1942-43 - No. 63, June-July, 1954 (Contents change with No. 30, Dec-Jan, 1948-49 on)
1-The Flash, Green Lantern, Wonder Woman, Wildcat, The Black Pirate by Moldoff (also #2), Ghost Patrol, and Red White & Blue begin; Scribbly app.; Minute Movie 1000 2000 3000 7500 13,500 19,500
2-Mutt & Jeff begin; last Ghost Patrol & Black Pirate; Minute Movies 284 568 852 1818 3109 4400
3-Hop Harrigan & Sargon, the Sorcerer begin; The King app. 181 362 543 1158 1979 2800
4,5: 4-The Gay Ghost, The King, Scribbly, & Red Tornado app. 5-Christmas-c. 5-Prints ad for Jr. JSA membership kit that includes "The Minute Man Answers The Call" 174 348 522 1114 1907 2700
6-10: 7-Red Tornado & Black Pirate app.; last Scribbly. 9-Fat & Slat app.; X-Mas-c 148 296 444 947 1624 2300
11-Wonder Woman vs. The Cheetah 126 252 378 806 1378 1950
12,14: 12-Last Red White & Blue 113 226 339 718 1234 1750
13-Solomon Grundy app.; X-Mas-c 216 432 648 1372 2361 3350
15-Just a Story begins 111 222 333 705 1215 1725
16-20: 19-Christmas-c 103 206 309 659 1130 1600
21-23: 22-Johnny Peril begins. 23-Harry Lampert-c (Toth swipes) 94 188 282 597 1024 1450
24-Solomon Grundy x-over in Green Lantern 126 252 378 806 1378 1950
25-28: 25-Black Canary app.; X-Mas-c. 26-28-Johnny Peril app. 28-Last Mutt & Jeff 87 174 261 553 952 1350
29-(10-11/48)-Last Flash, Wonder Woman, Green Lantern & Johnny Peril; Wonder Woman invents "Thinking Machine"; 2nd computer in comics (after Flash Comics #52); Leave It to Binky story (early app.) 123 246 369 787 1344 1900
30-(12-1/48-49)-The Fox & the Crow, Dodo & the Frog & Nutsy Squirrel begin 45 90 135 284 480 675
31-35 23 46 69 136 223 310
36-49: 41-Last squarebound issue 17 34 51 100 158 215
50-62(Scarce) 21 42 63 122 199 275
63(Rare) 37 74 111 222 361 500
NOTE: ***Grossman** a-30-63. **E.E. Hibbard** c-(Flash only)-1-4, 7-14, 16-19, 21. **Sheldon Mayer** a(2-3)-40-63. **Moulson** c(G.L.)-7, 15. **Nodell** c(G.L.)-9. **H.G. Peter** c(W. Woman only)-1, 3-21, 24. **Post** a-31, 36. **Purcell** c(G.L.)-2-5, 10. **Reinman** a(Green Lantern)-4-6, 8, 9, 13, 15-21; c(Gr. Lantern)-6, 8, 19. **Toth** a(Green Lantern)-26-28; c-27. Atom app.-22, 23.*

COMIC COMICS
Fawcett Publications: Apr, 1946 - No. 10, Feb, 1947
1-Captain Kid; Nutty Comics #1 in indicia 18 36 54 103 162 220
2-10-Wolverton-a, 4 pgs. each. 5-Captain Kidd app. Mystic Moot by Wolverton in #2-10? 16 32 48 96 151 205

COMIC LAND
Fact and Fiction Publ.: March, 1946
1-Sandusky & the Senator, Sam Stupor, Sleuth, Marvin the Great, Sir Passer, Phineas Gruff app.; Irv Tirman & Perry Williams art 16 32 48 96 151 205

COMICO CHRISTMAS SPECIAL
Comico: Dec, 1988 ($2.50, 44 pgs.)
1-Rude/Williamson-a; Dave Stevens-c 5.00

COMICO COLLECTION (Also see Grendel)
Comico: 1987 ($9.95, slipcased collection)
nn-Contains exclusive Grendel: Devil's Vagary, 9 random Comico comics, a poster and newsletter in black slipcase w/silver ink 25.00

COMICO PRIMER (See Primer)

COMIC PAGES (Formerly Funny Picture Stories)
Centaur Publications: V3#4, July, 1939 - V3#6, Dec, 1939
V3#4-Bob Wood-a 123 246 369 787 1344 1900
5,6: 6-Schwab-c 110 220 330 704 1202 1700

COMICS (See All Good)

COMICS, THE
Dell Publ. Co.: Mar, 1937 - No. 11, Nov, 1938 (Newspaper strip-r; bi-monthly)
1-1st app. Tom Mix in comics; Wash Tubbs, Tom Beatty, Myra North, Arizona Kid, Erik Noble & International Spy w/Doctor Doom begin 187 374 561 1197 2049 2900
2 87 174 261 553 952 1350
3-11: 3-Alley Oop begins 71 142 213 454 777 1100

COMICS AND STORIES (See Walt Disney's Comics and Stories)

COMICS & STORIES (Also see Wolf & Red)
Dark Horse Comics: Apr, 1996 - No. 4, July, 1996 ($2.95, lim. series) (Created by Tex Avery)
1-4: Wolf & Red app; reads Comics and Stories on-c. 1-Terry Moore-a. 2-Reed Waller-a 3.00

COMICS CALENDAR, THE (The 1946...)
True Comics Press (ordered through the mail): 1946 (25¢, 116 pgs.) (Stapled at top)
nn-(Rare) Has a "strip" story for every day of the year in color 43 86 129 271 461 650

COMICS DIGEST (Pocket size)
Parents' Magazine Institute: Winter, 1942-43 (B&W, 100 pgs)
1-Reprints from True Comics (non-fiction World War II stories) 12 24 36 67 94 120

COMICS EXPRESS
Eclipse Comics: Nov, 1989 - No. 2, Jan, 1990 ($2.95, B&W, 68pgs.)
1,2: Collection of strip-r; 2(12/89-c, 1/90 inside) 4.00

COMICS FOR KIDS
London Publ. Co./Timely: 1945 (no month); No. 2, Sum, 1945 (Funny animal)
1-Puffy Pig, Sharpy Fox 36 72 108 216 350 485
2-Puffy Pig, Sharpy Fox 24 48 72 142 234 325

COMICS' GREATEST WORLD
Dark Horse Comics: Jun, 1993 - V4#4, Sept, 1993 ($1.00, weekly, lim. series)
Arcadia (Wk 1): V1#1,2,4: 1-X: Frank Miller-c. 2-Pit Bulls. 4-Monster. 3.00
1-B&W Press Proof Edition (1500 copies) 1 3 4 6 8 10
1-Silver-c; distr. retailer bonus w/print & cards 1 2 3 5 6 8
3-Ghost, Dorman-c; Hughes-a 4.00
Retailer's Prem. Emb. Silver Foil Logo-r/V1#1-4 1 3 4 6 8 10
Golden City (Wk 2: V2#1-4: 1-Rebel; Ordway-c. 2-Mecha; Dave Johnson-c.
3-Titan; Walt Simonson-c. 4-Catalyst; Perez-c. 3.00
1-Gold-c; distr. retailer bonus w/print & cards. 6.00
Retailer's Prem. Embos. Gold Foil Logo-r/V2#1-4 1 2 3 5 6 8
Steel Harbor (Week 3): V3#1-Barb Wire; Dorman-c; Gulacy-a(p) 4.00
2-4: 2-The Machine. 3-Wolfgang. 4-Motorhead 3.00

Comics on Parade #12 © UFS

Commanders in Crisis #1 © Steve Orlando

Commando Adventures #1 © MAR

	GD 2.0	VG 4.0	FN 6.0	VF 8.0	VF/NM 9.0	NM- 9.2
1-Silver-c; distr. retailer bonus w/print & cards	1	2	3	5	6	8
Retailer's Prem. Emb. Red Foil Logo-r/V3#1-4.	1	3	4	6	8	10

Vortex (Week 4): V4#1-4: 1-Division 13; Dorman-c. 2-Hero Zero; Art Adams-c. 3-King Tiger; Chadwick-a(p); Darrow-c. 4-Vortex; Miller-c. 3.00
1-Gold-c; distr. retailer bonus w/print & cards. 6.00

	GD	VG	FN	VF	VF/NM	NM-
Retailer's Prem. Emb. Blue Foil Logo-r/V4#1-4.	1	2	3	5	6	8

COMICS' GREATEST WORLD: OUT OF THE VORTEX (See Out of The Vortex)

COMICS HITS (See Harvey Comics Hits)

COMICS MAGAZINE, THE (...Funny Pages #3)(Funny Pages #6 on)
Comics Magazine Co. (1st Comics Mag./Centaur Publ.): May, 1936 - No. 5, Sept, 1936 (Paper covers)

	GD	VG	FN	VF	VF/NM	NM-
1-1st app. Dr. Mystic (a.k.a. Dr. Occult) by Siegel & Shuster (the 1st app. of a Superman prototype in comics). Dr. Mystic is not in costume but later appears in costume as a more pronounced prototype in More Fun #14-17. (1st episode of "The Koth and the Seven"; continues in More Fun #14; originally scheduled for publication at DC). 1 pg. Kelly-a; Sheldon Mayer-a	4100	8200	12,300	24,500	--	--
2-Federal Agent (a.k.a. Federal Men) by Siegel & Shuster; 1 pg. Kelly-a	440	880	1320	2650	3525	4400
3-5	380	760	1140	2280	3040	3800

COMICS NOVEL (Anarcho, Dictator of Death)
Fawcett Publications: 1947

	GD	VG	FN	VF	VF/NM	NM-
1-All Radar; 51 pg anti-fascism story	43	86	129	271	461	650

COMICS ON PARADE (No. 30 on are a continuation of Single Series)
United Features Syndicate: Apr, 1938 - No. 104, Feb, 1955

	GD	VG	FN	VF	VF/NM	NM-
1-Tarzan by Foster; Captain & the Kids, Little Mary Mixup, Abbie & Slats, Ella Cinders, Broncho Bill, Li'l Abner begin	400	800	1200	2800	4900	7000
2 (Tarzan & others app. on-c of #1-3,17)	145	290	435	921	1586	2250
3	115	230	345	730	1253	1775
4,5	82	164	246	528	902	1275
6-10	55	110	165	352	601	850
11-16,18-20	42	84	126	267	451	635
17-Tarzan-c	55	110	165	352	601	850
21-29: 22-Son of Tarzan begins. 22,24,28-Tailspin Tommy-c. 29-Last Tarzan issue	36	72	108	216	351	485
30-Li'l Abner	20	40	60	114	182	250
31-The Captain & the Kids	15	30	45	85	130	175
32-Nancy & Fritzi Ritz	14	28	42	78	112	145
33,36,39,42-Li'l Abner	16	32	48	94	147	200
34,37,40-The Captain & the Kids (10/41,6/42,3/43)	15	30	45	83	124	165
35,38-Nancy & Fritzi Ritz. 38-Infinity-c	14	28	42	76	108	140
41-Nancy & Fritzi Ritz	12	24	36	67	94	120
43-The Captain & the Kids	15	30	45	83	124	165
44 (3/44),47,50: Nancy & Fritzi Ritz	12	24	36	67	94	120
45-Li'l Abner	15	30	45	84	127	170
46,49-The Captain & the Kids	13	26	39	74	105	135
48-Li'l Abner (3/45)	15	30	45	84	127	170
51,54-Li'l Abner	14	28	42	76	108	140
52-The Captain & the Kids (3/46)	12	24	36	69	97	125
53,55,57-Nancy & Fritzi Ritz	11	22	33	62	86	110
56-The Captain & the Kids (r/Sparkler)	11	22	33	62	86	110
58-Li'l Abner; continues as Li'l Abner #61?	14	28	42	76	108	140
59-The Captain & the Kids	10	20	30	54	72	90
60-70-Nancy & Fritzi Ritz	9	18	27	47	61	75
71-99,101-104-Nancy & Sluggo: 71-76-Nancy only	8	16	24	42	54	65
100-Nancy & Sluggo	14	28	42	76	108	140
Special Issue, 7/46; Summer, 1948 - The Captain & the Kids app.	14	28	42	76	108	140
NOTE: Bound Volume (Very Rare) includes No. 1-12; bound by publisher in pictorial comic boards & distributed at the 1939 World's Fair and through mail order from ads in comic books (also see Tip Top)	300	600	900	2010	3505	5000

NOTE: *Li'l Abner reprinted from Tip Top.*

COMICS READING LIBRARIES (See the Promotional Comics section)

COMICS REVUE
St. John Publ. Co. (United Features Synd.): June, 1947 - No. 5, Jan, 1948

	GD	VG	FN	VF	VF/NM	NM-
1-Ella Cinders & Blackie	15	30	45	85	130	175
2,4: 2-Hap Hopper (7/47). 4-Ella Cinders (9/47)	10	20	30	54	72	90
3,5: 3-Iron Vic (8/47). 5-Gordo No. 1 (1/48)	9	18	27	52	69	85

COMIC STORY PAINT BOOK
Samuel Lowe Co.: 1943 (Large size, 68 pgs.)

	GD	VG	FN	VF	VF/NM	NM-
1055-Captain Marvel & a Captain Marvel Jr. story to read & color; 3 panels in color per pg. (reprints)	87	174	261	553	952	1350

COMING OF RAGE
Liquid Comics: 2015 - No. 5, 2016 ($3.99, limited series)

1-5-Wes Craven & Steve Niles-s/Francesco Biagini-a. 1-Afterword by Wes Craven 4.00

COMIX BOOK
Marvel Comics Group/Krupp Comics Works No. 4,5: 1974 - No. 5, 1976 ($1.00, B&W, magazine) (#1-3 newsstand; #4,5 were direct distribution only)

	GD	VG	FN	VF	VF/NM	NM-
1-Underground comic artists; 2 pgs. Wolverton-a	3	6	9	15	22	28
2,3: 2-Wolverton-a (1 pg.)	3	6	9	14	19	24
4(2/76), 4(5/76), 5 (Low distribution)	3	6	9	16	23	30

NOTE: *Print run No. 1-3: 200,000-250,000; No. 4&5: 10,000 each.*

COMIX INTERNATIONAL
Warren Magazines: Jul, 1974 - No. 5, Spring, 1977 (Full color, stiff-c, mail only)

	GD	VG	FN	VF	VF/NM	NM-
1-Low distribution; all Corben story remainders from Warren; Corben-c on all	9	18	27	62	126	190
2,4: 2-Two Dracula stories; Wood, Wrightson-r; Crandall-a; Maroto-a. 4-Printing w/ 3 Corben sty	6	12	18	37	66	95
3-5: 3-Dax story. 4-(printing without Corben story). 4-Crandall-a. 4,5-Vampirella stories. 5-Spirit story; Eisner-a	5	10	15	33	57	80

NOTE: *No. 4 had two printings with extra **Corben** story in one. No. 3 may also have a variation. No. 3 has two Jeff Jones reprints from Vampirella.*

COMMANDER BATTLE AND THE ATOMIC SUB
Amer. Comics Group (Titan Publ. Co.): Jul-Aug, 1954 - No. 7, Aug-Sep, 1955

	GD	VG	FN	VF	VF/NM	NM-
1 (3-D effect)-Moldoff flying saucer-c	68	136	204	435	743	1050
2,4-7: 2-Moldoff-c. 4-(1-2/55)-Last pre-code; Landau-a. 5-3-D effect story (2 pgs.). 6,7-Landau-a. 7-Flying saucer-c	40	80	120	246	411	575
3-H-Bomb-c; Atomic Sub becomes Atomic Spaceship	47	94	141	296	498	700

COMMANDERS IN CRISIS
Image Comics: Oct, 2020 - Present ($3.99)

1-5-Steve Orlando-s/Davide Tinto-a 4.00

COMMANDO ADVENTURES
Atlas Comics (MMC): June, 1957 - No. 2, Aug, 1957

	GD	VG	FN	VF	VF/NM	NM-
1-Severin-c	19	38	57	109	172	235
2-Severin-c; Reinman & Romita-a; Drucker-a?	14	28	42	76	108	140

COMMANDOS
DC Comics: Oct. 1942

1-Ashcan comic, not distributed to newsstands, only for in-house use. Cover art is Boy Commandos #1 with interior being a Boy Commandos story from an unidentified issue of Detective Comics (a VF copy sold for $2629 in 2018)

COMMANDO YANK (See The Mighty Midget Comics & Wow Comics)

COMMON GROUNDS
Image Comics (Top Cow): Feb, 2004 - No. 6, July, 2004 ($2.99)

1-6: 1-Two covers; art by Jurgens and Oeming. 3-Bachalo, Jurgens-a. 4-Peréz-a 3.00
...: Baker's Dozen TPB (12/04, $14.99) r/#1-6; cover gallery; Holey Crullers pages 15.00

COMPLETE ALICE IN WONDERLAND (Adaptation of Carroll's original story)
Dynamite Entertainment: 2009 - No. 4 ($4.99, limited series)

1-4-Leah Moore & John Reppion-s/Erica Awano-a/John Cassaday-c 5.00

COMPLETE BOOK OF COMICS AND FUNNIES
William H. Wise & Co.: 1944 (25¢, one-shot, 196 pgs.)

	GD	VG	FN	VF	VF/NM	NM-
1-Origin Brad Spencer, Wonderman; The Magnet, The Silver Knight by Kinstler, & Zudo the Jungle Boy app.	69	138	207	442	759	1075

COMPLETE BOOK OF TRUE CRIME COMICS
William H. Wise & Co.: No date (Mid 1940's) (25¢, 132 pgs.)

	GD	VG	FN	VF	VF/NM	NM-
nn-Contains Crime Does Not Pay rebound (includes #22)	174	348	522	1114	1907	2700

COMPLETE COMICS (Formerly Amazing Comics No. 1)
Timely Comics (EPC): No. 2, Winter, 1944-45

	GD	VG	FN	VF	VF/NM	NM-
2-The Destroyer, The Whizzer, The Young Allies & Sergeant Dix; Schomburg-c	187	374	561	1197	2049	2900

COMPLETE DRACULA (Adaptation of Stoker's original story)
Dynamite Entertainment: 2009 - No. 5, 2009 ($4.99, limited series)

1-5-Leah Moore & John Reppion-s/Colton Worley-a/John Cassaday-c 5.00

COMPLETE FRANK MILLER BATMAN, THE
Longmeadow Press: 1989 ($29.95, hardcover, silver gilded pages)

HC-Reprints Batman: Year One, Wanted: Santa Claus--Dead or Alive, and The Dark Knight Returns 45.00

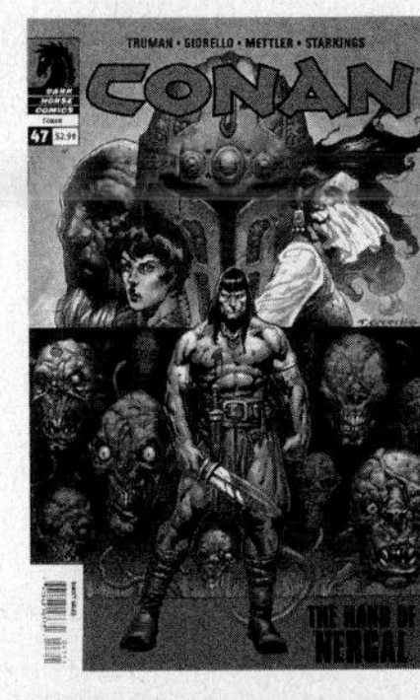

Conan #47 © CPI

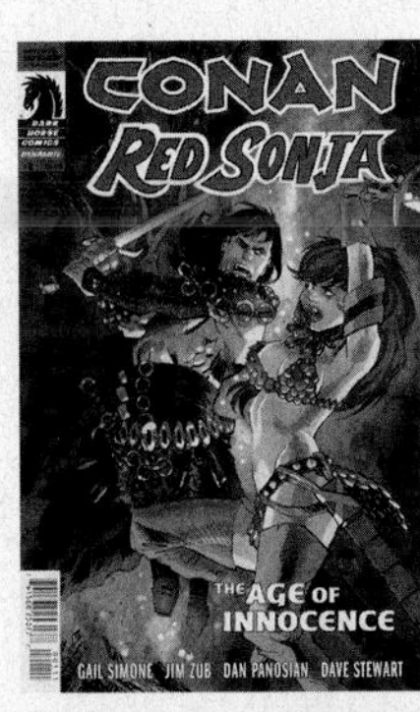

Conan Red Sonja #1 © CPI & RSLLC

Conan the Barbarian #11 © CPI

	GD	VG	FN	VF	VF/NM	NM-
	2.0	4.0	6.0	8.0	9.0	9.2

COMPLETE GUIDE TO THE DEADLY ARTS OF KUNG FU AND KARATE
Marvel Comics: 1974 (68 pgs., B&W magazine)

V1#1-Bruce Lee-c and 5 pg. story (scarce) 7 14 21 46 86 125

COMPLETE LOVE MAGAZINE (Formerly a pulp with same title)
Ace Periodicals (Periodical House): V26#2, May-June, 1951 - V32#4(#191), Sept, 1956

V26#2-Painted-c (52 pgs.) 16 32 48 96 151 205
V26#3-6(2/52), V27#1(4/52)-6(1/53) 13 26 39 74 105 135
V28#1(3/53), V28#2(5/53), V29#3(7/53)-6(12/53) 12 24 36 67 94 120
V30#1(2/54), V30#1(#176, 4/54),2,4-6(#181, 1/55) 12 24 36 67 94 120
V30#3(#178)-Rock Hudson photo-c 13 26 39 72 101 130
V31#1(#182, 3/55)-Last precode 11 22 33 64 90 115
V31#2(5/55)-6(#187, 1/56) 11 22 33 62 86 110
V32#1(#188, 3/56)-4(#191, 9/56) 11 22 33 62 86 110
NOTE: *(34 total issues). Photo-c V27#5-on. Painted-c V26#3.*

COMPLETE MYSTERY (True Complete Mystery No. 5 on)
Marvel Comics (PrPl): Aug, 1948 - No. 4, Feb, 1949 (Full length stories)

1-Seven Dead Men 60 120 180 381 653 925
2-4: 2-Jigsaw of Doom!; Shores-a. 3-Fear in the Night; Burgos-c/a (28 pgs.).
4-A Squealer Dies Fast 47 94 141 296 498 700

COMPLETE ROMANCE
Avon Periodicals: 1949

1-(Scarce)-Reprinted as Women to Love 61 122 183 390 670 950

CONAN (See Chamber of Darkness #4, Giant-Size..., Handbook of..., King Conan, Marvel Graphic Novel #19, 28, Marvel Treasury Ed., Power Record Comics, Robert E. Howard's.., Savage Sword of Conan, and Savage Tales)

CONAN
Dark Horse Comics: Feb, 2004 - No. 50, May, 2008 ($2.99)

0-(11/03, 25¢-c) Busiek-s/Nord-a 3.00
1-($2.99) Linsner-c/Busiek-s/Nord-a 5.00
1-(2nd printing) J. Scott Campell-c 3.00
1-(3rd printing) Nord-c 3.00
2-49: 18-Severin & Timm-a. 22-Kaluta-a (6 pgs.) 24-Harris-c. 29-31-Mignola-s 3.00
24-Variant-c with nude woman (also see Conan and the Demons of Khitai #3 for ad) 90.00
50-($4.99) Harris-c; new story and reprint from Conan the Barbarian #30 5.00
... and the Daughters of Midora (10/04, $4.99) Texiera-a/c 5.00
...: Born on the Battlefield TPB (6/08, $17.95) r/#0,8,15,23,32,45,46; Ruth sketch pages 18.00
...: FCBD 2006 Special (5/06) Paul Lee-a; flip book with Star Wars FCBD 2006 Special 3.00
...: One For One (8/10, $1.00) r/#1 with red cover frame 3.00
...: The Blood-Stained Crown and Other Stories TPB (1/08, $14.95) r/#18,26-28,39 15.00
....: The Weight of the Crown (1/10, $3.50) Darick Robertson-s/a; 2 covers by Robertson 3.50
HC Vol. 1: The Frost Giant's Daughter and Other Stories (2005, $24.95) r/#1-6, partial #7; signed by Busiek; Nord sketch pages 25.00
Vol. 1: The Frost Giant's Daughter and Other Stories (2005, $15.95) r/#1-6, partial #7 16.00
Vol. 2: The God in the Bowl and Other Stories HC (2005, $24.95) r/#9-14 25.00
Vol. 2: The God in the Bowl and Other Stories SC (2006, $15.95) r/#9-14 16.00
Vol. 3: The Tower of the Elephant and Other Stories HC (5/06, $24.95) r/#0,16,17,19-22 25.00
Vol. 3: The Tower of the Elephant and Other Stories SC (6/06, $15.95) r/#0,16,17,19-22 16.00
Vol. 4: The Hall of the Dead and Other Stories HC (5/07, $24.95) r/#0,24,25,29-31,33,34 25.00
Vol. 4: The Hall of the Dead and Other Stories SC (6/07, $17.95) r/#0,24,25,29-31,33,34 18.00
Vol. 5: Rogues in the House and Other Stories SC (3/08, $17.95) r/#0,37,38,41-44 18.00
Vol. 6: The Hand of Nergal HC (10/08, $24.95) r/#0,47-50; sketch pages 25.00

CONAN AND THE DEMONS OF KHITAI
Dark Horse Comics: Oct, 2005 - No. 4, Jan, 2006 ($2.99, limited series)

1,2,4-Paul Lee-a/Akira Yoshida-s/Pat Lee-c 3.00
3-1st printing with red cover logo; letters page has image of Conan #24 nude variant-c 5.00
3-2nd printing with black cover logo; letters page has image of Conan #24 regular-c 3.00
TPB (7/06, $12.95) r/series 13.00

CONAN AND THE JEWELS OF GWAHLUR
Dark Horse Comics: Apr, 2005 - No. 3, June, 2005 ($2.99, limited series)

1-3-P. Craig Russell-s/a/c 3.00
HC (12/05, $13.95) r/series; P. Craig Russell interview and sketch pages 14.00

CONAN AND THE MIDNIGHT GOD
Dark Horse Comics: Dec, 2006 - No. 5, May, 2007 ($2.99, limited series)

1-5-Dysart-s/Conrad-a/Alexander-c 3.00
TPB (10/07, $14.95) r/#1-5 and Age of Conan: Hyborian Adventures one-shot 15.00

CONAN AND THE PEOPLE OF THE BLACK CIRCLE
Dark Horse Comics: Oct, 2013 - No. 4, Jan, 2014 ($3.50, limited series)

1-4-Van Lente-s/Olivetti-a/c 3.50

CONAN AND THE SONGS OF THE DEAD
Dark Horse Comics: July, 2006 - No. 5, Nov, 2006 ($2.99, limited series)

	GD	VG	FN	VF	VF/NM	NM-
	2.0	4.0	6.0	8.0	9.0	9.2

1-5-Timothy Truman-a/c; Joe Lansdale-s 3.00
TPB (4/07, $14.95) r/series; Truman sketch pages 15.00

CONAN: (Title Series): Marvel Comics

CONAN, 8/95 - No. 11, 6/96 ($2.95), 1-11: 4-Malibu Comic's Rune app. 3.00

...CLASSIC, 6/94 - No. 11, 4/95 ($1.50), 1-11: 1-r/Conan #1 by B. Smith, r/covers w/changes. 2-11-r/Conan #2-11 by Smith. 2-Bound w/cover to Conan The Adventurer #2 by mistake 3.00

...DEATH COVERED IN GOLD, 9/99 - No. 3, 11/99 ($2.99), 1-3-Roy Thomas-s/ John Buscema-a 3.00

...FLAME AND THE FIEND, 8/00 - No. 3, 10/00 ($2.99), 1-3-Thomas-s 3.00

...RETURN OF STYRM, 9/98 - No. 3, 11/98 ($2.99), 1-3-Parente & Soresina-a; painted-c 3.00

...RIVER OF BLOOD, 6/98 - No. 3, 8/98 ($2.50), 1-3 3.00

...SCARLET SWORD, 12/98 - No. 3, 2/99 ($2.99), 1-3-Thomas-s/Raffaele-a 3.00

CONAN: BATTLE FOR THE SERPENT CROWN
Marvel Comics: Apr, 2020 - No. 5, Nov, 2020 ($3.99, limited series)

1-5-Saladin Ahmed-s/Luke Ross-a; set in the present; Black Cat & Mephisto app. 3-Black Panther app. 4-Namor app. 4.00

CONAN: ISLAND OF NO RETURN
Dark Horse Comics: Jun, 2011 - No. 2, Jul, 2011 ($3.50, limited series)

1,2-Marz-s/Sears-a 3.50

CONAN RED SONJA
Dark Horse Comics: Jan, 2015 - No. 4, Apr, 2015 ($3.99, limited series)

1-4-Gail Simone & Jim Zub-s/Dan Panosian-a/c 4.00

CONAN: ROAD OF KINGS
Dark Horse Comics: Dec, 2010 - No. 12, Jan, 2012 ($3.50)

1-12: 1-Roy Thomas-s/Mike Hawthorne-a; covers by Wheatley & Keown 3.50

CONAN SAGA, THE
Marvel Comics: June, 1987 - No. 97, Apr, 1995 ($2.00/$2.25, B&W, magazine)

1-Barry Smith-r; new Smith-c 2 4 6 9 13 16
2-27: 2-9,11-new Barry Smith-c. 13,15-Boris-c. 17-Adams-r.18,25-Chaykin-r. 22-r/Giant-Size Conan 1,2 4.00
28-90: 28-Begin $2.25-c. 31-Red Sonja-r by N. Adams/SSOC #1; 1 pg. Jeff Jones-r. 32-Newspaper strip-r begin by Buscema. 33-Smith/Conrad-a. 39-r/Kull #1('71) by Andru & Wood. 44-Swipes-c/Savage Tales #1. 57-Brunner-r/SSOC #30. 66-r/Conan Annual #2 by Buscema. 79-r/Conan #43-45 w/Red Sonja. 85-Based on Conan #57-63 3.00
91-96 5.00
97-Last issue 1 2 3 5 6 8
NOTE: ***J. Buscema** r-32-on; c-86. **Chaykin** r-34. **Chiodo** painted c-63, 65, 66, 82. **G. Colan** a-47p. **Jusko** painted c-64, 83. **Kaluta** c-84. **Nino** a-37. **Ploog** a-50. **N. Redondo** painted c-48, 50, 51, 53, 57, 62. **Simonson** r-50-54, 56. **B. Smith** r-51. **Starlin** c-34. **Williamson** r-50i.*

CONAN: SERPENT WAR
Marvel Comics: Feb, 2020 - No. 4, Mar, 2020 ($4.99/$3.99, limited series)

1-($4.99) Jim Zub-s/Scot Eaton-a; Moon Knight, Solomon Kane and Dark Agnes app.; back-up Solomon Kane text serial 5.00
2-4-($3.99) Solomon Kane text serial in each. 2-Segovia-a. 3-Pizzari-a. 4-Guara-a 4.00

CONAN THE ADVENTURER
Marvel Comics: June, 1994 - No. 14, July, 1995 ($1.50)

1-($2.50)-Embossed foil-c; Kayaran-a 4.00
2-14 3.00
2-Contents are Conan Classics #2 by mistake 3.00

CONAN THE AVENGER
Dark Horse Comics: Apr, 2014 - No. 25, Apr, 2016 ($3.99/$3.50)

1-25: 1-Van Lente-s/Ching-a. 4-Staples-c. 13-15-Powell-c. 25-Bisley-c 4.00

CONAN THE BARBARIAN
Marvel Comics: Oct, 1970 - No. 275, Dec, 1993

1-Origin/1st app. Conan (in comics) by Barry Smith; 1st brief app. Kull; #1-9 are 15¢ issues 28 56 84 202 431 700
2 9 18 27 63 129 195
3-(Low distribution in some areas) 12 24 36 84 185 285
4,5 7 14 21 49 92 135
6-9: 8-Hidden panel message, pg. 14. 9-Last 15¢-c 6 12 18 37 66 95
10,11 (25¢ 52 pg. giants): 10-Black Knight-r; Kull story by Severin 7 14 21 44 82 120
12,13: 12-Wrightson-c(i) 5 10 15 34 60 85
14,15-Elric app. 6 12 18 40 73 105
16,19,20: 16-Conan-r/Savage Tales #1 5 10 15 33 57 80
17,18-No Barry Smith-a 4 8 12 27 44 60

Conan the Barbarian #144 © CPI

Conan the Barbarian (2019 series) #17 © CPI

Conan the Cimmerian #0 © CPI

	GD 2.0	VG 4.0	FN 6.0	VF 8.0	VF/NM 9.0	NM- 9.2
21,22: 22-Has reprint from #1	4	8	12	28	47	65
23-1st app. Red Sonja (2/73)	10	20	30	64	132	200
24-1st full Red Sonja story; last Smith-a	10	20	30	64	132	200
25-John Buscema-c/a begins	3	6	9	16	24	32
26-30: 28-Centerfold ad by Mark Jewelers	2	4	6	13	18	22
31-36,38-40	2	4	6	9	12	15
37-Neal Adams-c/a; last 20¢ issue; contains pull-out subscription form	3	6	9	18	27	36
41-43,46-50: 48-Origin retold	2	4	6	8	10	12
44,45-N. Adams-i(Crusty Bunkers). 45-Adams-c	2	4	6	9	12	15
51-57,59,60: 59-Origin Belit	1	2	3	5	6	8
58-2nd Belit app. (see Giant-Size Conan #1)	2	4	6	8	11	14
61-65-(Regular 25¢ editions)(4-8/76)	1	2	3	4	5	7
61-65-(30¢-c variants, limited distribution)	5	10	15	35	63	90
66-99: 68-Red Sonja story cont'd from Marvel Feature #7. 75-79-(Reg. 30¢-c). 84-Intro. Zula. 85-Origin Zula. 87-r/Savage Sword of Conan #3 in color						6.00
75-79-(35¢-c variants, limited distribution)	8	16	24	51	96	140
100-(52 pg. Giant)-Death of Belit	2	4	6	8	11	14
101-114						5.00
115-Double size						6.00
116-199,201-231,233-249: 116-r/Power Record Comic PR31. 244-Zula returns						5.00
200,232: 200-(52 pgs.). 232-Young Conan storyline begins; Conan is born						5.00
250-(60 pgs.)						6.00
251-270: 262-Adapted from R.E. Howard story						5.00
271-274	1	2	3	5	6	8
275-($2.50, 68 pgs.)-Final issue; painted-c (low print)	4	8	12	25	40	55
King Size 1(1973, 35¢)-Smith-r/#2,4; Smith-c	4	8	12	27	44	60
Annual 2(1976, 50¢)-New full length story	2	4	6	11	16	20
Annual 3,4: 3('78)-Chaykin/N. Adams-r/SSOC #2. 4('78)-New full length story	2	4	6	8	10	12
Annual 5,6: 5(1979)-New full length Buscema story & part-c, 6(1981)-Kane-c/a						6.00
Annual 7-12: 7('82)-Based on novel "Conan of the Isles" (new-a). 8(1984). 9(1984). 10(1986). 11(1986). 12(1987)						4.00
Special Edition 1 (Red Nails)						4.00
The Chronicles of Conan Vol. 1: Tower of the Elephant and Other Stories (Dark Horse, 2003, $15.95) r/#1-8; afterword by Roy Thomas						16.00
The Chronicles of Conan Vol. 2: Rogues in the House and Other Stories (Dark Horse, 2003, $15.95) r/#9-13,16; afterword by Roy Thomas						16.00
The Chronicles of Conan Vol. 3: The Monster of the Monoliths and Other Stories (Dark Horse, 2003, $15.95) r/#14,15,17-21; afterword by Roy Thomas						16.00
The Chronicles of Conan Vol. 4: The Song of Red Sonja and Other Stories (Dark Horse, 2004, $15.95) r/#23-26 & "Red Nails" from Savage Tales; afterword by Roy Thomas						16.00
The Chronicles of Conan Vol. 5: The Shadow in the Tomb and Other Stories (Dark Horse, 2004, $15.95) r/#27-34; afterword by Roy Thomas						16.00
The Chronicles of Conan Vol. 6: The Curse of the Skull and Other Stories (Dark Horse, 2004, $15.95) r/#35-42; afterword by Roy Thomas						16.00
The Chronicles of Conan Vol. 7: The Dweller in the Pool and Other Stories (Dark Horse, 2005, $15.95) r/#43-51; afterword by Roy Thomas						16.00
The Chronicles of Conan Vol. 8: Brothers of the Blade and Other Stories (Dark Horse, 2005, $16.95) r/#52-59; afterword by Roy Thomas						17.00
The Chronicles of Conan Vol. 9: Riders of the River-Dragons and Other Stories (Dark Horse, 11/05, $16.95) r/#60-63,65,69-71; afterword by Roy Thomas						17.00
The Chronicles of Conan Vol. 10: When Giants Walk the Earth and Other Stories (Dark Horse, 3/06, $16.95) r/#72-77,79-82; afterword by Roy Thomas						17.00
The Chronicles of Conan Vol. 11: The Dance of the Skull and Other Stories (Dark Horse, 2/07, $16.95) r/#82-86,88-90; afterword by Roy Thomas						17.00
The Chronicles of Conan Vol. 12: The King Beast of Abombi and Other Stories (Dark Horse, 7/07, $16.95) r/#91,93-100; afterword by Roy Thomas						17.00
The Chronicles of Conan Vol. 13: Whispering Shadows and Other Stories (Dark Horse, 12/07, $16.95) r/#92,100-107; afterword by Roy Thomas						17.00
The Chronicles of Conan Vol. 14: Shadow of the Beast and Other Stories (Dark Horse, 3/08, $16.95) r/#92,108-115; afterword by Roy Thomas						17.00
The Chronicles of Conan Vol. 15: The Corridor of Mullah-Kajar and Other Stories (Dark Horse, 7/08, $16.95) r/#116-121 & Annual #2; afterword by Roy Thomas						17.00

NOTE: ***Arthur Adams*** *c-248, 249.* ***Neal Adams*** *a-116r(i); c-49i.* ***Austin*** *a-125, 126; c-125i, 126i.* ***Brunner*** *c-17i. c-40.* ***Buscema*** *a-25-36p, 38, 39, 41-56p, 58-63p, 65-67p, 68, 70-78p, 84-86p, 88-91p, 93-126p, 136p, 140, 141-144p, 146-158p, 159, 161, 162, 163p, 165-185p, 187-190p, Annual 2(3pgs.). 3-5p, 7p; c(p)-26, 36, 44, 46, 52, 56, 58, 59, 64, 65, 72, 78-80, 83-91, 93-103, 105-126, 136-151, 155-159, 161, 162, 168, 169, 171, 172, 174, 175, 178-185, 188, 189, Annual 4, 5, 7.* ***Chaykin*** *a-79-83.* ***Golden*** *c-152.* ***Kaluta*** *c-167.* ***Gil Kane*** *a-12p, 17p, 18p, 127-130, 131-134p; c-12p, 17p, 18p, 23, 25, 27-32, 34, 35, 38, 39, 41-43, 45-51, 53-55, 57, 60-63, 65-71, 73p, 76p, 127-134.* ***Jim Lee*** *c-242.* ***McFarlane*** *c-241p.* ***Ploog*** *a-57.* ***Russell*** *a-21; c-251i.* ***Simonson*** *c-135.* ***B. Smith*** *a-1-11p, 12, 13-15p, 16, 19-21, 23, 24; c-1-11, 13-16, 19-24p.* ***Starlin*** *a-64.* ***Wood*** *a-47r. Issue Nos. 3-5, 7-9, 11, 16-18, 21, 23, 25, 27-30, 35, 37, 38, 42, 45, 52, 57, 58, 65, 69-71, 73, 79-83, 99, 100, 104, 114, Annual 2 have original Robert E. Howard stories adapted. Issues #32-34 adapted from Norvell Page's novel* ***Flame Winds.***

CONAN THE BARBARIAN (Volume 2)
Marvel Comics: July, 1997 - No. 3, Oct, 1997 ($2.50, limited series)

1-3-Castellini-a 3.00

CONAN THE BARBARIAN
Dark Horse Comics: Feb, 2012 - No. 25, Feb, 2014 ($3.50)

1-25: 1-3-Brian Wood-s/Becky Cloonan-a. 1-Two covers by Carnevale & Cloonan 3.50
One for One: Conan the Barbarian #1 (1/14, $1.00) r/#1 3.00

CONAN THE BARBARIAN
Marvel Comics: Mar, 2019 - Present ($4.99/$3.99)

1-($4.99) Jason Aaron-s/Mahmud Asrar-a; part 1 of a bonus text novella 5.00
2-18-($3.99)-Bonus text novella continues: 2,3,5-7,9-12-Asrar-a. 4,8-Zaffino-a 4.00
...: Exodus 1 (10/19, $3.99) Esad Ribic-s/a; bonus thumbnails of layout sketches 4.00

CONAN THE BARBARIAN MOVIE SPECIAL (Movie)
Marvel Comics Group: Oct, 1982 - No. 2, Nov, 1982

1,2-Movie adaptation; Buscema-a 4.00

CONAN THE BARBARIAN: THE MASK OF ACHERON (Based on the 2011 movie)
Dark Horse Comics: Jul, 2011 ($6.99, one-shot)

1-Stuart Moore-s/Gabriel Guzman-a/c 7.00

CONAN THE BARBARIAN: THE USURPER
Marvel Comics: Dec, 1997 - No. 3, Feb, 1998 ($2.50, limited series)

1-3-Dixon-s 3.00

CONAN: THE BOOK OF THOTH
Dark Horse Comics: Mar, 2006 - No. 4, June, 2006 ($4.99, limited series)

1-4-Origin of Thoth-amon; Len Wein & Kurt Busiek-s/Kelley Jones-a/c 5.00
TPB (12/06, $17.95) r/#1-4 18.00

CONAN THE CIMMERIAN
Dark Horse Comics: No. 0, Jun, 2008 - No. 25, Nov, 2010 (99¢/$2.99)

0-Follows Conan #50; Truman-s/Giorello-a/c 3.00
1-(7/08, $2.99) Two covers by Joe Kubert and Cho; Giorello & Corben-a 3.00
2-25: 2-7-Cho-c; Giorello & Corben-a. 8-18-Linsner-c. 14-Joe Kubert-a (7 pgs.) 3.00

CONAN THE DESTROYER (Movie)
Marvel Comics Group: Jan, 1985 - No. 2, Mar, 1985

1,2-r/Marvel Super Special 4.00

CONAN THE FRAZETTA COVER SERIES
Dark Horse Comics: Dec, 2007 - No. 8 ($3.50/$5.99/$6.99)

1-($3.50) Reprints from Dark Horse series with Frazetta covers 6.00
2,3-($5.99) 6.00
4-8-($6.99) 7.00

CONAN THE KING (Formerly King Conan)
Marvel Comics Group: No. 20, Jan, 1984 - No. 55, Nov, 1989

	GD 2.0	VG 4.0	FN 6.0	VF 8.0	VF/NM 9.0	NM- 9.2
20-49						4.00
50-54						5.00
55-Last issue	2	4	6	8	10	12

NOTE: ***Kaluta*** *c-20-23, 24i, 26, 27, 30, 50, 52.* ***Williamson*** *a-37i; c-37i, 38i.*

CONAN: THE LEGEND (See Conan 2004 series)

CONAN: THE LORD OF THE SPIDERS
Marvel Comics: Mar, 1998 - No. 3, May, 1998 ($2.50, limited series)

1-3-Roy Thomas-s/Raffaele-a 3.00

CONAN THE SAVAGE
Marvel Comics: Aug, 1995 - No. 10, May, 1996 ($2.95, B&W, Magazine)

1-10: 1-Bisley-c. 4-vs. Malibu Comics' Rune. 5,10-Brereton-c 4.00

CONAN THE SLAYER
Dark Horse Comics: Jul, 2016 - No. 12, Aug, 2017 ($3.99)

1-12: 1-Bunn-s/Dávila-a/Bermejo-c. 11-Verma-a 4.00

CONAN 2099
Marvel Comics: Jan, 2020 ($4.99, one-shot)

1-Duggan-s/Antonio-a; Morgan Le Fay app. 5.00

CONAN VS. RUNE (Also See Conan #4)
Marvel Comics: Nov, 1995 ($2.95, one-shot)

1-Barry Smith-c/a/scripts 4.00

CONCRETE (Also see Dark Horse Presents & Within Our Reach)
Dark Horse Comics: March, 1987 - No. 10, Nov, 1988 ($1.50, B&W)

	GD 2.0	VG 4.0	FN 6.0	VF 8.0	VF/NM 9.0	NM- 9.2
1-Paul Chadwick-c/a in all	2	4	6	8	11	14
1-2nd print						3.00
2						6.00
3-Origin						5.00

Concrete: Killer Smile #1 © Paul Chadwick

Confessions of Romance #10 © STAR

Constantine: The Hellblazer #1 © DC

	GD 2.0	VG 4.0	FN 6.0	VF 8.0	VF/NM 9.0	NM- 9.2

4-10 4.00
A New Life 1 (1989, $2.95, B&W)-r/#3,4 plus new-a (11 pgs.) 4.00
Celebrates Earth Day 1990 ($3.50, 52 pgs.) 6.00
Color Special 1 (2/89, $2.95, 44 pgs.)-r/1st two Concrete apps. from Dark Horse Presents #1,2 plus new-a 6.00
Depths TPB (7/05, $12.95)-r/#1-5, stories from DHP #1,8,10,150; other short stories 13.00
Land And Sea 1 (2/89, $2.95, B&W)-r/#1,2 6.00
Odd Jobs 1 (7/90, $3.50)-r/5,6 plus new-a 4.00
...Vol. 1: Depths ('05, $12.95, 9"x6") r/#1-5 & short stories 13.00
...Vol. 2: Heights ('05, $12.95, 9"x6") r/#6-10 & short stories 13.00
...Vol. 3: Fragile Creatures (1/06, $12.95, 9"x6") r/mini-series & short stories from DHP 13.00
...Vol. 4: Killer Smile (3/06, $12.95, 9"x6") r/mini-series & short stories from various 13.00
...Vol. 5: Think Like a Mountain (5/06, $12.95, 9"x6") r/mini-series & short stories 13.00
...Vol. 6: Strange Armor (7/06, $12.95, 9"x6") r/mini-series & short stories 13.00
...Vol. 7: The Human Dilemma (4/06, $12.95, 9"x6") r/mini-series 13.00

CONCRETE: (Title series), **Dark Horse Comics**
--ECLECTICA, 4/93 - No. 2, 5/93 ($2.95) 1,2 4.00
--FRAGILE CREATURE, 6/91 - No. 4, 2/92 ($2.50) 1-4 4.00
--KILLER SMILE, (Legend), 7/94 - No. 4, 10/94 ($2.95) 1-4 4.00
--STRANGE ARMOR, 12/97 - No. 5, 5/98 ($2.95, color) 1-5-Chadwick-s/c/a; retells origin 4.00
--THE HUMAN DILEMMA, 12/04 - No. 6, 5/05 ($3.50)
1-6: Chadwick-a/c & scripts; Concrete has a child 3.50
--THINK LIKE A MOUNTAIN, (Legend), 3/96 - No. 6, 8/96 ($2.95)
1-6: Chadwick-a/scripts & Darrow-c in all 4.00

CONDORMAN (Walt Disney)
Whitman Publishing: Oct, 1981 - No. 3, Jan, 1982
1-3: 1,2-Movie adaptation; photo-c 1 3 4 6 8 10

CONEHEADS
Marvel Comics: June, 1994 - No. 4, 1994 ($1.75, limited series)
1-4 3.00

CONFESSIONS ILLUSTRATED (Magazine)
E. C. Comics: Jan-Feb, 1956 - No. 2, Spring, 1956
1-Craig, Kamen, Wood, Orlando-a 32 64 96 192 314 435
2-Craig, Crandall, Kamen, Orlando-a 24 48 72 142 234 325

CONFESSIONS OF LOVE
Artful Publ.: Apr, 1950 - No. 2, July, 1950 (25¢, 7-1/4x5-1/4", 132 pgs.)
1-Bakerish-a 84 168 252 538 919 1300
2-Art & text; Bakerish-a 53 106 159 334 567 800

CONFESSIONS OF LOVE (Formerly Startling Terror Tales #10; becomes Confessions of Romance No. 7 on)
Star Publications: No. 11, 7/52 - No. 14, 1/53; No. 4, 3/53- No. 6, 8/53
11-13: 12,13-Disbrow-a 30 60 90 177 289 400
14,5,6 20 40 60 117 189 260
4-Disbrow-a 22 44 66 132 216 300
NOTE: *All have **L. B. Cole** covers.*

CONFESSIONS OF ROMANCE (Formerly Confessions of Love)
Star Publications: No. 7, Nov, 1953 - No. 11, Nov, 1954
7 24 48 72 142 234 325
8 19 38 57 112 179 245
9-Wood-a 20 40 60 118 192 265
10,11-Disbrow-a 20 40 60 115 185 255
NOTE: *All have **L. B. Cole** covers.*

CONFESSIONS OF THE LOVELORN (Formerly Lovelorn)
American Comics Group (Regis Publ./Best Synd. Features): No. 52, Aug, 1954 - No. 114, June-July, 1960
52 (3-D effect) 47 94 141 296 498 700
53,55 18 36 54 103 162 220
54 (3-D effect) 40 80 120 246 411 575
56-Anti-communist propaganda story, 10 pgs; last pre-code (2/55) 20 40 60 115 185 255
57-90,100 12 24 36 69 97 125
91-Williamson-a 14 28 42 78 112 145
92-99,101-114 10 20 30 56 76 95
NOTE: ***Whitney** a-most issues; c-52, 53. Painted c-106, 107.*

CONFIDENTIAL DIARY (Formerly High School Confidential Diary; Three Nurses #18 on)
Charlton Comics: No. 12, May, 1962 - No. 17, Mar, 1963
12-17 3 6 9 16 23 30

CONGO BILL (See Action Comics & More Fun Comics #56)
National Periodical Publication: Aug-Sept, 1954 - No. 7, Aug-Sept, 1955
1 200 400 600 1600 -- --
2,7 125 250 375 1000 -- --
3-6: 4-Last pre-Code issue 100 200 300 800 -- --
NOTE: *(Rarely found in fine to mint condition.)* ***Nick Cardy** c-1-7.*

CONGO BILL
DC Comics (Vertigo): Oct, 1999 - No. 4, Jan, 2000 ($2.95, limited series)
1-4-Corben-c 3.00

CONGORILLA (Also see Action Comics #224)
DC Comics: Nov, 1992 - No. 4, Feb, 1993 ($1.75, limited series)
1-4: 1,2-Brian Bolland-c 3.00

CONJURORS
DC Comics: Apr, 1999 - No. 3, Jun, 1999 ($2.95, limited series)
1-3-Elseworlds; Phantom Stranger app.; Barreto-c/a 3.00

CONNECTICUT YANKEE, A (See King Classics)

CONNOR HAWKE: DRAGON'S BLOOD (Also see Green Arrow titles)
DC Comics: Jan, 2007 - No. 6, Jun, 2007 ($2.99, limited series)
1-6-Chuck Dixon-s/Derec Donovan-a/c 3.00
SC (2008, $19.99) r/#1-6 20.00

CONQUEROR, THE
Dell Publishing Co.: No., 690, Mar, 1956
Four Color 690-Movie, John Wayne photo-c 15 30 45 103 227 350

CONQUEROR COMICS
Albrecht Publishing Co.: Winter, 1945
nn 25 50 75 150 245 340

CONQUEROR OF THE BARREN EARTH (See The Warlord #63)
DC Comics: Feb, 1985 - No. 4, May, 1985 (Limited series)
1-4: Back-up series from Warlord 3.00

CONQUEST
Store Comics: 1953 (6¢)
1-Richard the Lion Hearted, Beowulf, Swamp Fox 8 16 24 42 54 65

CONQUEST
Famous Funnies: Spring, 1955
1-Crandall-a, 1 pg.; contains contents of 1953 ish. 7 14 21 37 46 55

CONSPIRACY
Marvel Comics: Feb, 1998 - No. 2, Mar, 1998 ($2.99, limited series)
1,2-Painted art by Korday/Abnett-s 3.00

CONSTANTINE (Also see Hellblazer)
DC Comics (Vertigo): 2005 (Based on the 2005 Keanu Reeves movie)
...: The Hellblazer Collection (2005, $14.95) Movie adaptation and r/#1, 27, 41; photo-c 15.00
...: The Official Movie Adaptation (2005, $6.95) Seagle-s/Randall-a/photo-c 7.00

CONSTANTINE (Also see Justice League Dark)
DC Comics: May, 2013 - No. 23, May, 2015 ($2.99)
1-Lemire & Fawkes-s/Guedes-a; two covers by Reis & Guedes 1 2 3 5 6 8
2-20: 2-The Spectre app. 5-Trinity War tie-in; Shazam app. 9-Forever Evil tie-in. 20-23-Constantine on Earth 2. 23-Darkseid app. 3.00
...: Futures End 1 (11/14, $2.99, regular-c) Five years later; Ferreyra-a/c 3.00
...: Futures End 1 (11/14, $3.99, 3-D cover) 4.00
.../Hellblazer Special Edition 1 (12/14, $1.00) Flipbook r/#1 and Hellblazer #1 3.00

CONSTANTINE: THE HELLBLAZER
DC Comics: Aug, 2015 - No. 13, Aug, 2016 ($2.99)
1-13: 1-Doyle & Tynion IV-s/Rossmo-a, covers by Rossmo & Doyle. 3,4-Doyle-a. 7-Swamp Thing app. 8-12-Neron app. 10,11-Foreman-a 3.00

CONSUMED
Platinum Studios: July, 2007 - No. 4, Oct, 2007 ($2.99, limited series)
1-4-Linsner-c/Budd-a/Shumskas-Tait-s 3.00

CONTACT COMICS
Aviation Press: July, 1944 - No. 12, May, 1946
nn-Black Venus, Flamingo, Golden Eagle, Tommy Tomahawk begin 84 168 252 538 919 1300
2-Classic sci-fi-c 76 152 228 486 831 1175
3-5: 3-Last Flamingo. 3,4-Black Venus by L. B. Cole. 5-The Phantom Flyer app. 54 108 162 343 574 825

Contest of Champions #2 © MAR

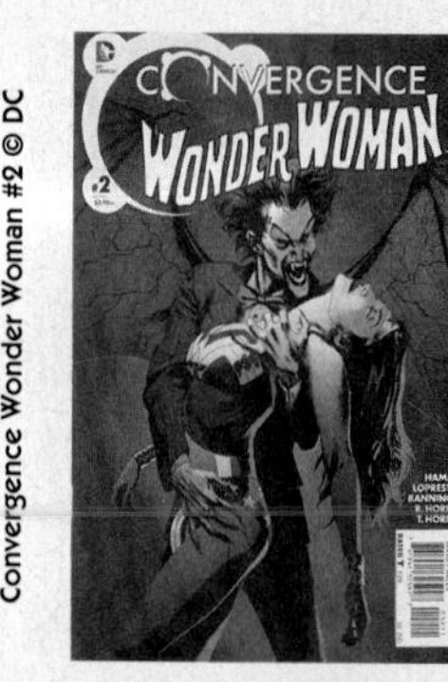

Convergence Wonder Woman #2 © DC

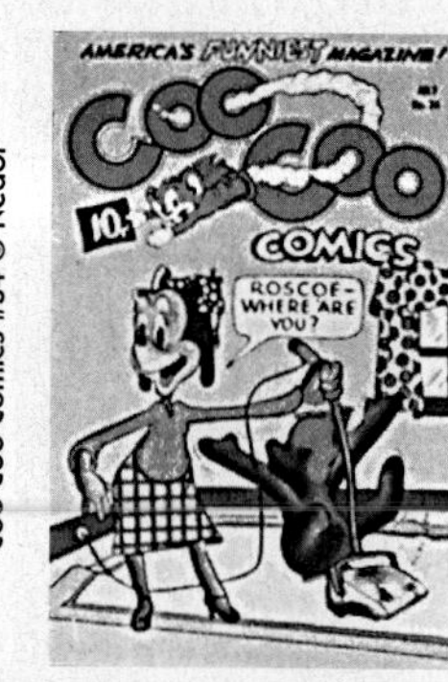

Coo Coo Comics #34 © Nedor

GD VG FN VF VF/NM NM-
2.0 4.0 6.0 8.0 9.0 9.2

6,11-Kurtzman's Black Venus; 11-Last Golden Eagle, last Tommy Tomahawk;
Feldstein-a 58 116 174 371 636 900
7-10 47 94 141 296 498 700
12-Sky Rangers, Air Kids, Ace Diamond app.; L.B. Cole sci-fi cover
343 686 1029 2400 4200 6000
NOTE: *L. B. Cole a-3, 9; c-1-12. Giunta a-3. Hollingsworth a-5, 7, 10. Palais a-11, 12.*

CONTAGION
Marvel Comics: Dec, 2019 - No. 5, Dec, 2019 ($3.99, weekly limited series)
1-5-Brisson-s; Fantastic Four, Iron Fist, Luke Cage, Avengers app. 4.00

CONTEMPORARY MOTIVATORS
Pendelum Press: 1977 - 1978 ($1.45, 5-3/8x8", 31 pgs., B&W)
14-3002 The Caine Mutiny; 14-3010 Banner in the Sky; 14-3029 God Is My Co-Pilot; 14-3037 Guadalcanal Diary; 14-3045 Hiroshima; 14-3053 Hot Rod; 14-3061 Just Dial a Number; 14-3088 The Diary of Anne Frank; 14-3096 Lost Horizon
2 4 6 8 10 12
NOTE: *Also see Pendulum Illustrated Classics. Above may have been distributed the same.*

CONTEST OF CHAMPIONS (See Marvel Super-Hero...)

CONTEST OF CHAMPIONS
Marvel Comics: Dec, 2015 - No. 10, Sept, 2016 ($4.99/$3.99, limited series)
1-($4.99) The Collector, Venom, Mr. Fixit, Iron Man, Gamora & Maestro app.; Medina-a 5.00
2-9-($3.99) 2-Ares and Punisher 2099 app. 3-5-The Sentry app. 7,8-Ultimates app. 9-Revisits Civil War 4.00
10-($4.99) Finale; Ewing-s/Marcellius-a 5.00

CONTEST OF CHAMPIONS II
Marvel Comics: Sept, 1999 - No. 5, Nov, 1999 ($2.50, limited series)
1-5-Claremont-s/Jimenez-a 3.00

CONTRACT WITH GOD, A
Baronet Publishing Co./Kitchen Sink Press: 1978 ($4.95/$7.95, B&W, graphic novel)
nn-Will Eisner-s/a 3 6 9 14 20 25
Reprint (DC Comics, 2000, $12.95) 13.00

CONVERGENCE
DC Comics: No. 0, Jun, 2015 - No. 8, July, 2015 ($4.99/$3.99, weekly limited series)
0-Superman & multiple Brainiacs app.; intro Telos; Van Sciver-a/Jurgens & King-s 5.00
1-($4.99) Earth-2 heroes vs. Telos; Pagulayan-a; wraparound-c by Reis 5.00
2-7-($3.99) 2-Intro. Deimos; Pagulayan-a. 4,5-Warlord app. 5-Andy Kubert-a 4.00
8-($4.99) Conclusion; art by Segovia, Pagulayan, Pansica & Van Sciver 5.00

CONVERGENCE
DC Comics: June, 2015 - July, 2015 ($3.99, 2-part tie-in miniseries, each issue has a variant cover designed by Chip Kidd)
... Action Comics 1,2 - Pre-Crisis Earth Two Superman & Power Girl; Red Son Superman, Wonder Woman & Lex Luthor app.; Conner-c. 2-Bonus preview of Sinestro #12 4.00
... Adventures of Superman 1,2 - Pre-Crisis Earth One Superman & Supergirl app.; Wolfman-s. 2-Kamandi app.; bonus preview of Martian Manhunter #1 4.00
... Aquaman 1,2 - Harpoon-hand Aquaman & Deathblow app.; Cloonan-c; Richards-a. 2-Bonus preview of Doctor Fate #1 4.00
... Atom 1,2 - Pre-Flashpoint Ray Palmer & Deathstroke app.; Dillon-c/Yeowell-a. 2-Ryan Choi app.; bonus preview of Green Lantern #41 4.00
... Batgirl 1,2 - Stephanie Brown, Cassadra Cain, Tim Drake & Catman app; Leonardi-a. 2-Grodd app.; bonus preview of Prez #1 4.00
... Batman and Robin 1,2 - Pre-Flashpoint Batman, Damian & Red Hood app.; Cowan & Janson-a. 2-Superman app.; bonus preview of Omega Men #1 4.00
... Batman and The Outsiders 1,2 - Pre-Crisis Outsiders and Omac app.; Andy Kubert-c. 2-Bonus preview of Batman Beyond #1 4.00
... Batman: Shadow of the Bat 1,2 - Pre-Zero Hour Batman & Azrael app. 1-Philip Tan-a/c. 2-Leonardi-a; bonus preview of Deathstroke #7 4.00
... Blue Beetle 1,2 - Charlton Blue Beetle, Captain Atom & The Question app.; Blevins-c. 2-Legion of Super-Heroes app.; bonus preview of Black Canary #1 4.00
... Booster Gold 1,2 - Rip Hunter & the Legion of Super-Heroes app.; Jurgens-c. 2-Blue Beetle app.; bonus preview of Earth-2: Society #1 4.00
... Catwoman 1,2 - Pre-Zero Hour purple suit Catwoman & Kingdom Come Batman app.; Ron Randall-a. Bonus preview of Gotham By Midnight #6 4.00
... Crime Syndicate 1,2 - Earth-Three villains & 853rd Century JLA app.; Winslade-a. 2-Bonus preview of Cyborg #1 4.00
... Detective Comics 1,2 - Earth-Two pre-Crisis Robin & Huntress vs. Red Son Superman; Cowan & Sienkiewicz-a. 2-Red Son Batman app.; bonus preview of Flash #41 4.00
... Flash 1,2 - Earth-One pre-Crisis Barry Allen vs. Tangent Superman; Abnett-s/Dallocchio-a; 2-Bonus preview of New Suicide Squad #9 4.00
... Green Arrow 1,2 - Pre-Zero Hour Oliver Queen & Connor Hawke vs. Kingdom Come Black Canary & Dinah Lance; Morales-a; 2-Bonus preview of G.L.C. Lost Army #1 4.00
... Green Lantern Corps 1,2 - Earth-One pre-Crisis Guy Gardner, John Stewart & Hal Jordan; Hercules from Durvale app. 2-Bonus preview of Gotham Academy #7 4.00
... Green Lantern/Parallax 1,2 - Pre-Zero Hour Hal Jordan & Kyle Rayner; Ron Wagner-a. Princess Fern of Electropolis app. 2-Bonus preview of Lobo #7 4.00
... Harley Quinn 1,2 - Pre-Flashpoint Harley, Poison Ivy & Catwoman; Winslade-a. 2-Harley battles Captain Carrot. 2-Bonus preview of Section Eight #1 4.00
... Hawkman 1,2 - Earth-One pre-Crisis Katar Hol & Shayera; Parker-s/Truman-a. 2-Bonus preview of Grayson #9 4.00
... Infinity Inc. 1,2 - Earth-Two pre-Crisis Infinity Inc. vs. Future Jonah Hex & The Dogs of War; Ordway-s, 1-Ben Caldwell-a. 2-Bonus preview of Batgirl #41 4.00
... Justice League 1,2 - Pre-Flashpoint female Justice League vs. Flashpoint Aquaman; Buckingham-c. 2-Bonus preview of Detective Comics #41 4.00
... Justice League International 1,2 - Pre-Zero Hour JLI vs. Kingdom Come; Manley-a. 2-Bonus preview of Justice League 3001 #1 4.00
... Justice League of America 1,2 - Earth-One pre-Crisis Detroit JLA vs. Tangent Secret Six; ChrisCross-a. 2-Bonus preview of Batman/Superman #21 4.00
... Justice Society of America 1,2 - Earth-Two pre-Crisis JSA vs. Weaponers of Qward; Derenick-a. 2-Bonus preview of Superman/Wonder Woman #18 4.00
... New Teen Titans 1,2 - Earth-One pre-Crisis Teen Titans vs. Tangent Doom Patrol; Nicola Scott-a. 2-Bonus preview of Robin: Son of Batman #1 4.00
... Nightwing and Oracle 1,2 - Pre-Flashpoint version vs. Flashpoint Hawkman; Duursema-a/Thompson-c. 2-Bonus preview of Midnighter #1 4.00
... Plastic Man and the Freedom Fighters 1,2 - Earth-X team vs. Futures End cyborgs; Silver Ghost app.; McCrea-a/Barta-c. 2-Bonus preview of Harley Quinn #17 4.00
... The Question 1,2 - Pre-Flashpoint Question (Renee Montoya); Huntress, Batwoman & Two-Face app.; Rucka-s/Hamner-a. 2-Bonus preview of Starfire #1 4.00
... Shazam! 1,2 - Earth-S Marvel Family vs. Gotham By Gaslight Batman; Shaner-a Sivana, Ibac, Mr. Atom app. 2-Bonus preview of Constantine The Hellblazer #1 4.00
... Speed Force 1,2 - Pre-Flashpoint Flash (Wally West) vs. Flashpoint Wonder Woman Grummett-a; Fastback (Zoo Crew) app. 2-Bonus preview of Green Arrow #41 4.00
... Suicide Squad 1,2 - Pre-Zero Hour vs. Kingdom Come Green Lantern Mandrake-a; Lex Luthor app. 2-Bonus preview of Aquaman #41 4.00
... Superboy 1,2 - Pre-Zero Hour Kon-El vs. Kingdom Come Superman, Flash & Red Robin; Moline-a/Tarr-c. 2-Bonus preview of Action Comics #41 4.00
... Superboy and the Legion of Super-Heroes 1,2 - Pre-Crisis Legion vs. The Atomic Knights; Storms-a/Guerra-c. 2-Bonus preview of Teen Titans #9 4.00
... Supergirl: Matrix 1,2 - Pre-Zero Hour Supergirl vs. Lady Quark (Electropolis); Ambush Bug app.; Giffen-s/Green II-a/Porter-c. 2-Bonus preview of Bat-Mite #1 4.00
... Superman 1,2 - Pre-Flashpoint Superman & Lois vs. Flashpoint heroes; Jurgens-s/Weeks-a; 2-Baby born (Jonathan Kent); bonus preview of Doomed #1 (See Superman: Lois & Clark series) 4.00
... Superman: Man of Steel 1,2 - Pre-Zero Hour Steel vs. Gen-13; Parasite app.; Louise Simonson-s/June Brigman-a/Walt Simonson-c. 2-Bonus preview of Bizarro #1 4.00
... Swamp Thing 1,2 - Earth-One pre-Crisis Swamp Thing vs. Red Rain vampire Batman; Len Wein-s/Kelley Jones-a. 2-Bonus preview of Catwoman #41 4.00
... Titans 1,2 - Pre-Flashpoint Titans vs. The Extremists; Nicieza-s/Wagner-a; 2-Bonus preview of Red Hood & Arsenal #1 4.00
... Wonder Woman 1,2 - Earth-One pre-Crisis Wonder Woman vs. Red Rain vampire Joker, Catwoman & Poison Ivy. 1-Middleton-a/c. 2-Lopresti-a; bonus preview of Secret Six 4.00
... World's Finest 1,2 - Earth-Two pre-Crisis Seven Soldiers of Victory vs. Weaponers of Qward; Scribbly Jibbet app.; Levitz-s. 2-Bonus preview of We Are Robin #1 4.00

CONVOCATIONS: A MAGIC THE GATHERING GALLERY
Acclaim Comics (Armada): Jan, 1996 ($2.50, one-shot)
1-pin-ups by various artists including Kaluta, Vess, and Dringenberg 4.00

COO COO COMICS (...the Bird Brain No. 57 on)
Nedor Publ. Co./Standard (Animated Cartoons): Oct, 1942 - No. 62, Apr, 1952
1-Origin/1st app. Super Mouse & begin series (cloned from Superman); the first funny animal super hero series (see Looney Tunes #5 for 1st funny animal super hero)
55 110 165 352 601 850
2 22 44 66 130 213 295
3-10: 10-(3/44) 16 32 48 94 147 200
11-33: 33-1 pg. Ingels-a 14 28 42 80 115 150
34-40,43-46,48-50Text illos by Frazetta in all. 36-Super Mouse covers begin
16 32 48 96 151 205
41-Frazetta-a (6-pg. story & 3 text illos) 28 56 84 165 270 375
42,47-Frazetta-a & text illos. 20 40 60 118 192 265
51-62: 56-58,61-Super Mouse app. 13 26 39 72 101 130

"COOKIE" (Also see Topsy-Turvy)
Michel Publ./American Comics Group(Regis Publ.): Apr, 1946 - No. 55, Aug-Sept, 1955
1-Teen-age humor 32 64 96 192 314 435
2-1st app. Tee-Pee Tim who takes over Ha Ha Comics later
17 34 51 100 158 215
3-10: 8-Bing Crosby app. 14 28 42 81 118 155
11-20: 12-Hedy Lamarr app. 13-Jackie Robinson mentioned. 15-Gregory Peck cover app.

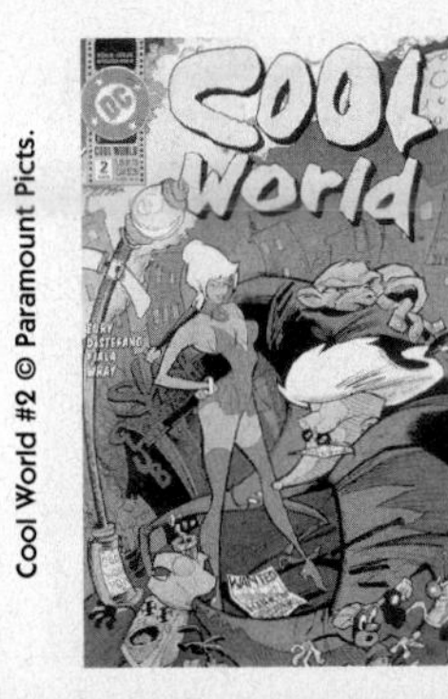

Cool World #2 © Paramount Picts.

Cosmic Ghost Rider #4 © MAR

Cosmo the Merry Martian #1 © ACP

	GD	VG	FN	VF	VF/NM	NM-
	2.0	4.0	6.0	8.0	9.0	9.2

16-Ub Iwerks (a creator of Mickey Mouse) name used. 18-Jane Russell-type Jane Bustle.
19-Cookie takes a dog to see Lassie movie 12 24 36 69 97 125
21-23,26,28-30: 26-Milt Gross & Starlett O'Hara stories. 28,30-Starlett O'Hara stories
10 20 30 58 79 100
24,25,27-Starlett O'Hara stories 11 22 33 60 83 105
31-34,37-48,52-55 9 18 27 52 69 85
35,36-Starlett O'Hara stories 10 20 30 56 76 95
49-51: 49-(6-7/54)-3-D effect-c/s. 50-3-D effect. 51-(10-11/54) 8pg. TrueVision 3-D effect story
15 30 45 86 133 180

COOL CAT (What's Cookin' With...) (Formerly Black Magic)
Prize Publications: V8#6, Mar-Apr, 1962 - V9#2, July-Aug, 1962
V8#6, nn(V9#1, 5-6/62), V9#2 3 6 9 21 33 45

COOL WORLD (Movie by Ralph Bakshi)
DC Comics: Apr, 1992 - No. 4, Sept, 1992 ($1.75, limited series)
1-4: Prequel to animated/live action movie. 1-Bakshi-c. Bill Wray inks in all 3.00
Movie Adaptation nn ('92, $3.50, 68pg.)-Bakshi-c 4.00

COPPER CANYON (See Fawcett Movie Comics)

COPPERHEAD
Image Comics: Sept, 2014 - No. 19, Jun, 2018 ($3.50/$3.99)
1-19: 1-Faerber-s/Godlewski-a; multiple covers. 11-$3.99-c begins. 11-18-Moss-a 4.00

COPS (TV)
DC Comics: Aug, 1988 - No. 15, Aug, 1989 ($1.00)
1 ($1.50, 52 pgs.)-Based on Hasbro Toys 4.00
2-15: 14-Orlando-c(p) 3.00

COPS: THE JOB
Marvel Comics: June, 1992 - No. 4, Sept, 1992 ($1.25, limited series)
1-4: All have Jusko scripts & Golden-c 3.00

CORBEN SPECIAL, A
Pacific Comics: May, 1984 (one-shot)
1-Corben-c/a; E.A. Poe adaptation 6.00

CORE, THE
Image Comics: July, 2008 ($3.99)
Pilot Season - Hickman-s/Rocafort-a 4.00

CORKY & WHITE SHADOW (Disney, TV)
Dell Publishing Co.: No. 707, May, 1956 (Mickey Mouse Club)
Four Color 707-Photo-c 6 12 18 42 79 115

CORLISS ARCHER (See Meet Corliss Archer)

CORMAC MAC ART (Robert E. Howard's...)
Dark Horse Comics: 1990 - No. 4, 1990 ($1.95, B&W, mini-series)
1-4: All have Bolton painted-c; Howard adapts. 3.00

CORPORAL RUSTY DUGAN (See Holyoke One-Shot #2)

CORPSES OF DR. SACOTTI, THE (See Ideal a Classical Comic)

CORSAIR, THE (See A-1 Comics No. 5, 7, 10 under Texas Slim)

CORUM: THE BULL AND THE SPEAR (See Chronicles Of Corum)
First Comics: Jan, 1989 - No. 4, July, 1989 ($1.95)
1-4: Adapts Michael Moorcock's novel 3.00

COSMIC BOOK, THE
Ace Comics: Dec, 1986 - No. 1, 1987 ($1.95)
1,2: 1-(44pgs.)-Wood, Toth-a. 2-(B&W) 4.00

COSMIC BOY (Also see The Legion of Super-Heroes)
DC Comics: Dec, 1986 - No. 4, Mar, 1987 (limited series)
1-4: Legends tie-ins all issues 4.00

COSMIC GHOST RIDER (See Thanos 2017 series #13 for debut)
Marvel Comics: Sept, 2018 - No. 5, Jan, 2019 ($3.99)
1-Cates-s/Burnett-a; Frank Castle as Ghost Rider; Odin and baby Thanos app. 4.00
2-5: 2,3-Galactus app. 5-Leads into Guardians of the Galaxy 2019 series 4.00

COSMIC GHOST RIDER DESTROYS MARVEL HISTORY
Marvel Comics: May, 2019 - No. 6, Oct, 2019 ($3.99, limited series)
1-6: 1-Scheer & Giovannetti-s/Sandoval-a: Uato the Watcher app. 2,4,6-Nauck-a 4.00

COSMIC GUARD
Devil's Due Publ.: Aug, 2004 - No. 6, Dec, 2005 ($2.99)
1-6-Jim Starlin-s/a 3.00

COSMIC HEROES
Eternity/Malibu Graphics: Oct, 1988 - No. 11, Dec, 1989 ($1.95, B&W)
1-11: Reprints 1934-1936's Buck Rogers newspaper strips #1-728 3.00

COSMIC ODYSSEY
DC Comics: 1988 - No. 4, 1988 ($3.50, limited series, squarebound)
1-4: Reintro. New Gods into DC continuity; Superman, Batman, Green Lantern (John Stewart) app; Starlin scripts, Mignola-c/a in all. 2-Darkseid merges Demon & Jason Blood (separated in Demon limited series #4) 5.00
TPB (1992,2009, $19.99) r/#1-4; Robert Greenberger intro. 20.00

COSMIC POWERS
Marvel Comics: Mar, 1994 - No. 6, Aug, 1994 ($2.50, limited series)
1,2-Thanos app. 1-Ron Lim-c/a(p). 2-Terrax 5.00
3-6: 3-Ganymede & Jack of Hearts app. 4.00

COSMIC POWERS UNLIMITED
Marvel Comics: May, 1995 - No. 5, May, 1996 ($3.95, quarterly)
1-5 4.00

COSMIC SLAM
Ultimate Sports Entertainment: 1999 ($3.95, one-shot)
1-McGwire, Sosa, Bagwell, Justice battle aliens; Sienkiewicz-c 4.00

COSMO (The Merry Martian)
Archie Comic Publications: Feb, 2018 - No. 5, Jul, 2018 ($2.99, limited series)
1-5-Cosmo, Astra, and Orbi app.; Ian Flynn-s/Tracy Yardley-a; multiple covers 3.00

COSMO CAT (Becomes Sunny #11 on; also see All Top & Wotalife Comics)
Fox Publications/Green Publ. Co./Norlen Mag.: July-Aug, 1946 - No. 10, Oct, 1947; 1957; 1959
1 32 64 96 192 314 435
2 16 32 48 94 147 200
3-Origin (11-12/46) 20 40 60 115 185 255
4-Robot-c 16 32 48 92 144 195
5-10 11 22 33 62 86 110
2-4(1957-Green Publ. Co.) 6 12 18 27 33 38
2-4(1959-Norlen Mag.) 5 10 15 23 28 32
I.W. Reprint #1 2 4 6 11 16 20

COSMO THE MERRY MARTIAN
Archie Publications (Radio Comics): Sept, 1958 - No. 6, Oct, 1959
1-Bob White-a in all 19 38 57 111 176 240
2-6 12 24 36 69 97 125

COSMO THE MIGHTY MARTIAN
Archie Comic Publications: Jan, 2020 - No. 5, Jun, 2020 ($3.99, limited series)
1-5-Ian Flynn-s/Tracy Yardley-a; multiple covers 4.00

COTTON WOODS (All-American athlete)
Dell Publishing Co.: No. 837, Sept, 1957
Four Color 837 5 10 15 30 50 70

COUGAR, THE (Cougar No. 2)
Seaboard Periodicals (Atlas): April, 1975 - No. 2, July, 1975
1,2: 1-Vampire; Adkins-a(p). 2-Cougar origin; werewolf-s; Buckler-c(p)
2 4 6 11 16 20

COUNT CROWLEY: RELUCTANT MIDNIGHT MONSTER HUNTER
Dark Horse Comics: Oct, 2019 - No. 4, Jan, 2020 ($3.99, limited series)
1-4-David Dastmalchian-s/Lukas Ketner-a 4.00

COUNTDOWN (See Movie Classics)

COUNTDOWN
DC Comics (WildStorm): June, 2000 - No. 8, Jan, 2001 ($2.95)
1-8-Mariotte-s/Lopresti-a 3.00

COUNTDOWN (Continued from 52 weekly series)
DC Comics: No. 51, July, 2007 - No. 1, June, 2008 ($2.99, weekly, limited series)
(issue #s go in reverse)
51-Gatefold wraparound-c by Andy Kubert; Duela Dent killed; the Monitors app. 3.00
50-1: 50-Joker-c. 48-Lightray dies. 47-Mary Marvel gains Black Adam's powers. 46-Intro. Forerunner. 43-Funeral for Bart Allen. 39-Karate Kid-c 3.00
Countdown to Final Crisis Vol. 1 TPB (2008, $19.99) r/#51-39 20.00
Countdown to Final Crisis Vol. 2 TPB (2008, $19.99) r/#38-26 20.00
Countdown to Final Crisis Vol. 3 TPB (2008, $19.99) r/#25-13 20.00
Countdown to Final Crisis Vol. 4 TPB (2008, $19.99) r/#12-1 20.00

COUNTDOWN: ARENA (Takes place during Countdown #21-18)
DC Comics: Feb, 2008 - No. 4, Feb, 2008 ($3.99, weekly, limited series)
1-4-Battles between alternate Earth heroes; McDaniel-a; Andy Kubert variant-c on each 4.00

Countdown to Mystery #1 © DC

Coup D'Etat: Sleeper #1 © WSP

Coven #4 © Awesome

TPB (2008, $17.99) r/#1-4; variant covers 18.00

COUNTDOWN PRESENTS: LORD HAVOK & THE EXTREMISTS
DC Comics: Dec, 2007 - No. 8 ($2.99, limited series)

1-6: 1-Tieri-s/Sharp-a/c; Challengers From Beyond app. 3.00
TPB (2008, $17.99) r/#1-6 18.00

COUNTDOWN PRESENTS THE SEARCH FOR RAY PALMER (Leads into Countdown #18)
DC Comics: Nov, 2007 - Feb, 2008 ($2.99, series of one-shots)

...: Wildstorm (11/07) Part 1; The Authority app.; Art Adams-c/Unzueta-a 3.00
...: Crime Society (12/07) Earth-3 Owlman & Jokester app.; Igle-a 3.00
...: Red Rain (1/08) Vampire Batman app.; Kelley Jones-c; Jones, Battle & Unzueta-a 3.00
...: Gotham By Gaslight (1/08) Victorian Batman app.; Tocchini-a/Nguyen-c 3.00
...: Red Son (2/08) Soviet Superman app.; Foreman-a 3.00
...: Superwoman/Batwoman (2/08) Conclusion; gender-reversed heroes; Sook-c 3.00
TPB (2008, $17.99) r/one-shots 18.00

COUNTDOWN SPECIAL
DC Comics: Dec, 2007 - Jun, 2008 ($4.99, collection of reprints related to Countdown)

...: Eclipso (5/08) r/Eclipso #10 & Spectre #17,18 (1994); Sook-c 5.00
...: Jimmy Olsen (1/08) r/Superman's Pal, Jimmy Olsen #136,147,148; Kirby-s/a; Sook-c 5.00
...: Kamandi (6/08) r/Kamandi: The Last Boy on Earth #1,10,29; Kirby-s/a; Sook-c 5.00
...: New Gods (3/08) r/Forever People #1, Mr. Miracle #1, New Gods #7; Kirby-s/a; Sook-c 5.00
...: Omac (4/08) r/Omac (1974) #1, Warlord #37-39, DC Comics Presents #61; Sook-c 5.00
...: The Atom 1,2 (2/08) r/stories from Super-Team Family #11-14; Sook-c on both 5.00
...: The Flash (12/07) r/Rogues Gallery in Flash (1st series) #106,113,155,174; Sook-c 5.00

COUNTDOWN TO ADVENTURE
DC Comics: Oct, 2007 - No. 8, May, 2008 ($3.99, limited series)

1-8: 1-Adam Strange, Animal Man and Starfire app.; origin of Forerunner 4.00
TPB (2008, $17.99) r/#1-8 18.00

COUNTDOWN TO INFINITE CRISIS (See DC Countdown)

COUNTDOWN TO MYSTERY (See Eclipso: The Music of the Spheres TPB for reprint)
DC Comics: Nov, 2007 - No. 8, Jun, 2008 ($3.99, limited series)

1-8: 1-Doctor Fate, Eclipso, The Spectre and Plastic Man app. 4.00
TPB (2008, $17.99) r/#1-8 18.00

COUNT DUCKULA (TV)
Marvel Comics: Nov, 1988 - No. 15, Jan, 1991 ($1.00)

1,8: 1-Dangermouse back-up. 8-Geraldo Rivera photo-c/& app.; Sienkiewicz-a(i) 7.00
2-7,9-15: Dangermouse back-ups in all 4.00

COUNT OF MONTE CRISTO, THE
Dell Publishing Co.: No. 794, May, 1957

Four Color 794-Movie, Buscema-a 8 16 24 51 96 140

COUP D'ETAT (Oneshots)
DC Comics (WildStorm): April, 2004 ($2.95, weekly limited series)

...: Sleeper 1 (part 1 of 4) Jim Lee-a; 2 covers by Lee and Bermejo 3.00
...: Stormwatch 1 (part 2 of 4) D'Anda-a; 2 covers by D'Anda and Bermejo 3.00
...: Wildcats Version 3.0 1 (part 3 of 4) Garza-a; 2 covers by Garza and Bermejo 3.00
...: The Authority 1 (part 4 of 4) Portacio-a; 2 covers by Portacio and Bermejo 3.00
...: Afterword 1 (5/04) Profile pages and prelude stories for Sleeper & Wetworks 3.00
TPB (2004, $12.95) r/series and profile pages from Afterword 13.00

COURAGE COMICS
J. Edward Slavin: 1945

1,2,77 17 34 51 98 154 210

COURTNEY CRUMRIN
Oni Press: Apr, 2012 - No. 10, Feb, 2013 ($3.99)

1-10-Ted Naifeh-s/a 4.00
#1 (5/14, Free Comic Book Day giveaway) r/#1 3.00

COURTNEY CRUMRIN...
Oni Press: July, 2005; July 2007; Dec, 2008 ($5.95, B&W, series of one-shots)

... And The Fire Thief's Tale (7/07) Naifeh-s/a 6.00
... And The Prince of Nowhere (12/08) Naifeh-s/a 6.00
... Tales (5/11) sequel to Tales Portrait of the Warlock...; Naifeh-s/a 6.00
... Tales Portrait of the Warlock as a Young Man (7/05) origin Uncle Aloysius; Naifeh-s/a 6.00

COURTNEY CRUMRIN & THE COVEN OF MYSTICS
Oni Press: Dec, 2002 - No. 4, March, 2003 ($2.95, B&W, limited series)

1-4-Ted Naifeh-s/a 3.00
TPB (9/03, $11.95, 8" x 5-1/2") r/#1-4 12.00

COURTNEY CRUMRIN & THE NIGHT THINGS
Oni Press: Mar, 2002 - No. 4, June, 2002 ($2.95, B&W, limited series)

1-4-Ted Naifeh-s/a 3.00
Free Comic Book Day Edition (5/03) Naifeh-s/a 3.00
TPB (12/02, $11.95) r/#1-4 12.00

COURTNEY CRUMRIN IN THE TWILIGHT KINGDOM
Oni Press: Dec, 2003 - No. 4, May, 2004 ($2.99, B&W, limited series)

1-4-Ted Naifeh-s/a 3.00
TPB (9/04, $11.95, digest-size) r/#1-4 12.00

COURTSHIP OF EDDIE'S FATHER (TV)
Dell Publishing Co.: Jan, 1970 - No. 2, May, 1970

1-Bill Bixby photo-c on both 5 10 15 34 60 85
2 4 8 12 23 37 50

COVEN
Awesome Entertainment: Aug, 1997 - No. 5, Mar, 1998 ($2.50)

Preview 1 2 3 5 6 8
1-Loeb-s/Churchill-a; three covers by Churchill, Liefeld, Pollina
1 2 3 5 6 8
1-Fan Appreciation Ed.(3/98); new Churchill-c 3.00
1+ :Includes B&W art from Kaboom 1 3 4 6 8 10
2-Regular-c w/leaping Fantom 6.00
2-Variant-c w/circle of candles 1 2 3 5 6 8
3-6-Contains flip book preview of ReGex 3.00
3-White variant-c 1 2 3 4 5 7
3,4: 3-Halloween wraparound-c. 4-Purple variant-c 3.00
...Black & White (9/98) Short stories 3.00
...Fantom Special (2/98) w/sketch pages 5.00

COVEN
Awesome Entertainment: Jan, 1999 - No. 3, June, 1999 ($2.50)

1-3: 1-Loeb-s/Churchill-a; 6 covers by various. 2-Supreme-c/app. 3-Flip book w/Kaboom preview 3.00
... Dark Origins (7/99, 2.50) w/Lionheart gallery 3.00

COVENANT, THE
Image Comics (Top Cow): 2005 ($9.99, squarebound, one-shot)

nn-Tone Rodriguez-a/Aron Coleite-s 10.00

COVENANT, THE
Image Comics: Jun, 2015 - No. 5, Dec, 2015 ($3.99)

1-5-Rob Liefeld-s/c; Matt Horak-a; story of the Ark of the Covenant 4.00

COVER
DC Comics (Jinxworld): Nov, 2018 - Present ($3.99)

1-6-Brian Michael Bendis-s/David Mack-a/c; comic creator as spy 4.00

COVERED WAGONS, HO (Disney, TV)
Dell Publishing Co.: No. 814, June, 1957 (Donald Duck)

Four Color 814-Mickey Mouse app. 6 12 18 37 66 95

COWBOY ACTION (Formerly Western Thrillers No. 1-4; Becomes Quick-Trigger Western No. 12 on)
Atlas Comics (ACI): No. 5, March, 1955 - No. 11, March, 1956

5 15 30 45 90 140 190
6-10: 6-8-Heath-c 12 24 36 67 94 120
11-Williamson-a (4 pgs.); Baker-a 14 28 42 76 108 140
NOTE: *Ayers a-8. Drucker a-6. Maneely c/a-5, 6. Severin c-10. Shores a-7.*

COWBOY COMICS (Star Ranger #12, Stories #14)(Star Ranger Funnies #15)
Centaur Publishing Co.: No. 13, July, 1938 - No. 14, Aug, 1938

13-(Rare)-Ace and Deuce, Lyin Lou, Air Patrol, Aces High, Lee Trent, Trouble Hunters begin
277 554 831 1759 3030 4300
14-(Rare)-Filchock-c 213 426 639 1363 2332 3300
NOTE: *Guardineer a-13, 14. Gustavson a-13, 14.*

COWBOY IN AFRICA (TV)
Gold Key: Mar, 1968

1(10219-803)-Chuck Connors photo-c 4 8 12 25 40 55

COWBOY LOVE (Becomes Range Busters?)
Fawcett Publications/Charlton Comics No. 28 on: 7/49 - V2#10, 6/50; No. 11, 1951; No. 28, 2/55 - No. 31, 8/55

V1#1-Rocky Lane photo back-c 18 36 54 103 162 220
2 9 18 27 50 65 80
V1#3,4,6 (12/49) 8 16 24 42 54 65
5-Bill Boyd photo back-c (11/49) 9 18 27 50 65 80
V2#7-Williamson/Evans-a 10 20 30 56 76 95
V2#8-11 7 14 21 37 46 55

Cowboys 'n' Injuns #1 © ME

Coyotes #8 © Lewis & Yarsky

Crackajack Funnies #20 © DELL

	GD 2.0	VG 4.0	FN 6.0	VF 8.0	VF/NM 9.0	NM- 9.2

V1#28 (Charlton)-Last precode (2/55) (Formerly Romantic Story?)
7 14 21 35 43 50
V1#29-31 (Charlton; becomes Sweetheart Diary #32 on)
6 12 18 31 38 45
NOTE: *Powell a-10. Marcus Swayze a-2, 3. Photo c-1-11. No. 1-3, 5-7, 9, 10 are 52 pgs.*

COWBOY ROMANCES (Young Men No. 4 on)
Marvel Comics (IPC): Oct, 1949 - No. 3, Mar, 1950 (All photo-c & 52 pgs.)
1-Photo-c 27 54 81 158 259 360
2-William Holden, Mona Freeman "Streets of Laredo" photo-c
18 36 54 107 169 230
3-Photo-c 15 30 45 90 140 190

COWBOYS 'N' INJUNS (...and Indians No. 6 on)
Compix No. 1-5/Magazine Enterprises No. 6 on: 1946 - No. 5, 1947; No. 6, 1949 - No. 8, 1952
1-Funny animal western 16 32 48 92 144 195
2-5-All funny animal western 10 20 30 56 76 95
6(A-1 23)-Half violent, half funny; Ayers-a 15 30 45 85 130 175
7(A-1 41, 1950), 8(A-1 48)-All funny 9 18 27 52 69 85
I.W. Reprint No. 1,7,10 (Reprinted in Canada by Superior, No. 7), 10('63)
2 4 6 11 16 20

COWBOY WESTERN COMICS (TV)(Formerly Jack In The Box; Becomes Space Western No. 40-45 & Wild Bill Hickok & Jingles No. 68 on; title: Cowboy Western Heroes No. 47 & 48; Cowboy Western No. 49 on)
Charlton (Capitol Stories): No. 17, 7/48 - No. 39, 8/52; No. 46, 10/53; No. 47, 12/53; No. 48, Spr, '54; No. 49, 5-6/54 - No. 67, 3/58 (nn 40-45)
17-Jesse James, Annie Oakley, Wild Bill Hickok begin; Texas Rangers app.
19 38 57 112 179 245
18,19-Orlando-c/a. 18-Paul Bunyan begins. 19-Wyatt Earp story
10 20 30 58 79 100
20-25: 21-Buffalo Bill story. 22-Texas Rangers-c/story. 24-Joel McCrea photo-c & adaptation from movie "Three Faces West". 25-James Craig photo-c & adaptation from movie "Northwest Stampede" 9 18 27 52 69 85
26-George Montgomery photo-c and adaptation from movie "Indian Scout"; 1 pg. bio on Will Rogers 10 20 30 58 79 100
27-Sunset Carson photo-c & adapts movie "Sunset Carson Rides Again" plus 1 other Sunset Carson story 39 78 117 240 395 550
28-Sunset Carson line drawn-c; adapts movies "Battling Marshal" & "Fighting Mustangs" starring Sunset Carson 20 40 60 114 182 250
29-Sunset Carson line drawn-c; adapts movies "Rio Grande" with Sunset Carson & "Winchester '73" w/James Stewart plus 5 pg. life history of Sunset Carson featuring Tom Mix 20 40 60 114 182 250
30-Sunset Carson photo-c; adapts movie "Deadline" starring Sunset Carson plus 1 other Sunset Carson story 39 78 117 240 395 550
31-34,38,39,47-50 (no #40-45): 50-Golden Arrow, Rocky Lane & Blackjack (r?) stories
9 18 27 47 61 75
35,36-Sunset Carson-c/stories (2 in each). 35-Inside front-c photo of Sunset Carson plus photo on-c 20 40 60 120 195 270
37-Sunset Carson stories (2) 15 30 45 94 147 200
46-(Formerly Space Western)-Space western story 15 30 45 94 147 200
51-57,59-66: 51-Golden Arrow(r?) & Monte Hale-r renamed Rusty Hall. 53,54-Tom Mix-r. 55-Monte Hale story(r?). 66-Young Eagle story. 67-Wild Bill Hickok and Jingles-c/story
7 14 21 35 43 50
58-(1/56)-Wild Bill Hickok, Annie Oakley & Jesse James stories; Forgione-a
8 16 24 44 57 70
67-(15¢, 68 pgs.)-Williamson/Torres-a, 5 pgs. 9 18 27 50 65 80
NOTE: *Many issues trimmed 1" shorter. Maneely a-67(5). Inside front/back photo c-29.*

COWGIRL ROMANCES
Marvel Comics (CCC): No. 28, Jan, 1950 (52 pgs.)
28(#1)-Photo-c 23 46 69 136 223 310

COWGIRL ROMANCES
Fiction House Magazines: 1950 - No. 12, Winter, 1952-53 (No. 1-3: 52 pgs.)
1-Kamen-a 55 110 165 352 601 850
2 31 62 93 186 303 420
3-5: 5-12-Whitman-c (most) 27 54 81 162 266 370
6-9,11,12 26 52 78 152 249 345
10-Frazetta?/Williamson?-a; Kamen?/Baker-a; r/Mitzi story from Movie Comics #4 w/all new dialogue 50 100 150 315 533 750

C.O.W.L.
Image Comics: May, 2014 - No. 11, Jul, 2015 ($3.50)
1-11: 1-Higgins & Siegel-s/Reis-a. 6-Origin of Grey Raven; Charretier-a 3.50

COW PUNCHER (...Comics)
Avon Periodicals: Jan, 1947; No. 2, Sept, 1947 - No. 7, 1949
1-Clint Cortland, Texas Ranger, Kit West, Pioneer Queen begin; Kubert-a; Alabam stories begin 61 122 183 390 670 950
2-Kubert, Kamen/Feldstein-a; Kamen-c 53 106 159 334 567 800
3-5,7: 3-Kiefer story 39 78 117 240 395 550
6-Opium drug mention story; bondage, headlight-c; Reinman-a
53 106 159 334 567 800

COWPUNCHER
Realistic Publications: 1953 (nn) (Reprints Avon's No. 2)
nn-Kubert-a 15 30 45 90 140 190

COWSILLS, THE (See Harvey Pop Comics)

COW SPECIAL, THE
Image Comics (Top Cow): Spring-Summer 2000; 2001 ($2.95)
1-Previews upcoming Top Cow projects; Yancy Butler photo-c 3.00
Vol. 2 #1-Witchblade-c; previews and interviews 3.00

COYOTE
Marvel Comics (Epic Comics): June, 1983 - No. 16, Mar, 1986
1-10,15: 7-10-Ditko-a 4.00
11-1st McFarlane-a. 3 6 9 17 25 34
12-14,16: 12-14-McFarlane-a. 14-Badger x-over. 16-Reagan c/app. 6.00
Coyote Collection Vol. 1 (2005, $14.99) reprints from Coyote #1-7 & Scorpio Rose #1,2 plus Rogers layout pages for unpublished #3; Englehart intro. 15.00
Coyote Collection Vol. 2 (2005, $12.99) reprints from Coyote #1-4 13.00
Coyote Collection Vol. 3 (2006, $12.99) reprints from Coyote #5-8 13.00
Coyote Collection Vol. 4 (2007, $14.99) reprints from Coyote #9-12 15.00
Coyote Collection Vol. 5 (2007, $12.99) reprints from Coyote #13-16 13.00

COYOTES
Image Comics: Nov, 2017 - No. 8, Nov, 2018 ($3.99, limited series)
1-8-Sean Lewis-s/Caitlin Yarsky-a 4.00

CRACKAJACK FUNNIES (Also see The Owl)
Dell Publishing Co.: June, 1938 - No. 43, Jan, 1942
1-Dan Dunn, Freckles, Myra North, Wash Tubbs, Apple Mary, The Nebbs, Don Winslow, Tom Mix, Buck Jones, Major Hoople, Clyde Beatty, Boots begin
194 388 582 1242 2121 3000
2 77 154 231 493 847 1200
3 58 116 174 371 636 900
4 48 96 144 302 514 725
5-Nude woman on cover (10/38) 57 114 171 362 619 875
6-8,10: 8-Speed Bolton begins (1st app.) 42 84 126 265 445 625
9-(3/39)-Red Ryder strip-r begin by Harman; 1st app. in comics & 1st cover app.
174 348 522 1114 1907 2700
11-14 36 72 108 216 351 485
15-Tarzan text feature begins by Burroughs (9/39); not in #26,35
39 78 117 234 385 535
16-24: 18-Stratosphere Jim begins (1st app., 12/39). 23-Ellery Queen begins plus-c (1st comic book app., 5/40) 32 64 96 188 307 425
25-The Owl begins (1st app., 7/40); in new costume #26 by Frank Thomas (also see Popular Comics #72) 90 180 270 576 988 1400
26,27,29,30 50 100 150 315 533 750
28-Part Owl-c 61 122 183 390 670 950
31-Owl covers begin, end #42 65 130 195 416 708 1000
32-Origin Owl Girl 68 136 204 435 743 1050
33-37: 36-Last Tarzan issue. 37-Cyclone & Midge begin (1st app.)
55 110 165 352 601 850
38-(scarce) Classic giant gorilla vs. Owl-c 87 174 261 553 952 1350
39-Andy Panda begins (intro/1st app., 9/41) 81 162 243 518 884 1250
40-42: 42-Last Owl-c. 53 106 159 334 567 800
43-Terry & the Pirates-r 26 52 78 154 252 350
NOTE: *McWilliams art in most issues.*

CRACK COMICS (Crack Western No. 63 on)
Quality Comics Group: May, 1940 - No. 62, Sept, 1949
1-Origin & 1st app. The Black Condor by Lou Fine, Madame Fatal, Red Torpedo, Rock Bradden & The Space Legion; The Clock, Alias the Spider (by Gustavson), Wizard Wells, & Ned Brant begin; Powell-a; Note: Madame Fatal is a man dressed as a woman
470 940 1410 3431 6066 8700
2 226 452 678 1446 2473 3500
3 168 336 504 1075 1838 2600
4 132 264 396 838 1444 2050
5-10: 5-Molly The Model begins. 10-Tor, the Magic Master begins
110 220 330 704 1202 1700
11-20: 13-1 pg. J. Cole-a. 15-1st app. Spitfire 92 184 276 584 1005 1425

Crackdown #1 © Microsoft

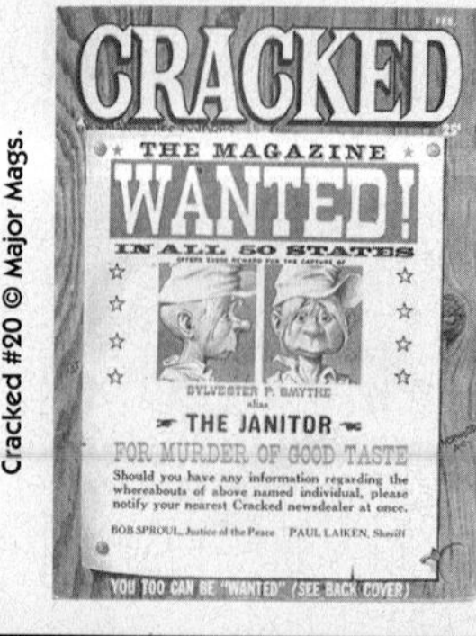

Cracked #20 © Major Mags.

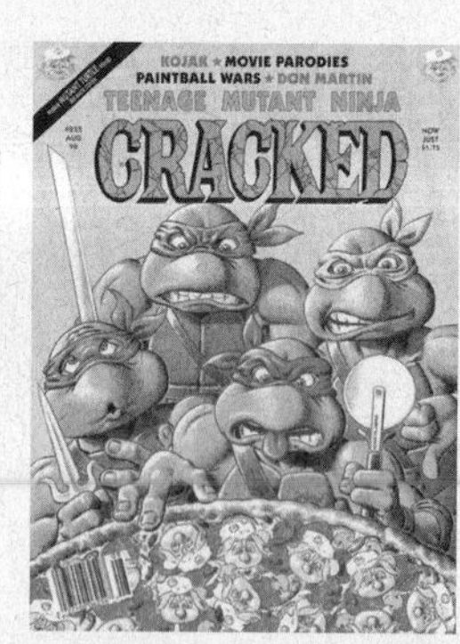

Cracked #255 © Globe Comms.

GD VG FN VF VF/NM NM-
2.0 4.0 6.0 8.0 9.0 9.2

21-24: 23-Pen Miller begins; continued from National Comics #22. 24-Last Fine Black Condor 71 142 213 454 777 1100
25 57 114 171 362 619 875
26-Flag-c 71 142 213 454 777 1100
27-(1/43)-Intro & origin Captain Triumph by Alfred Andriola (Kerry Drake artist) & begin series 118 236 354 749 1287 1825
28-30 43 86 129 271 461 650
31-39: 31-Last Black Condor 24 48 72 142 234 325
40-46 17 34 51 100 158 215
47-57,59,60-Capt. Triumph by Crandall 18 36 54 107 169 230
58,61,62-Last Captain Triumph 15 30 45 85 130 175

NOTE: *Black Condor by* **Fine**: *No. 1, 2, 5, 6, 8, 10-24; by* **Sultan**: *No. 3, 7; by* **Fugitani**: *No. 9.* **Cole** *a-34.* **Crandall** *a-61(unsigned); c-48, 49, 51-61.* **Guardineer** *a-17.* **Gustavson** *a-1, 2, 4, 7, 13, 17, 23.* **McWilliams** *a-15-27. Black Condor c-2, 4, 6, 8, 10, 12, 14, 16, 18, 20-26. Capt. Triumph c-27-62. The Clock c-1, 3, 5, 7, 9, 11, 13, 15, 17, 19.*

CRACK COMICS (Next Issue Project)
Image Comics: No. 63, Oct, 2011 ($4.99, one-shot)

63-Mimics style & format of a 1949 issue; Weiss-c; s/a by various; Capt. Triumph app. 5.00

CRACK COMICS
Quality Comics: May 1940

1-Ashcan comic, not distributed to newsstands, only for in-house use. Cover art is the same as published version of Crack Comics #1with exception of text panel on bottom left of cover. A CGC certified 4.0 copy sold for $1,495 in 2005.

CRACKDOWN (Based on the videogame)
Dynamite Entertainment: 2018 - No. 4, 2018 ($3.99)

1-4-Jonathan Goff-s/Ricardo Jaime-a 4.00

CRACKED (Magazine) (Satire) (Also see The 3-D Zone #19)
Major Magazines(#1-212)/Globe Communications(#213-346/American Media #347 on): Feb-Mar, 1958 - No. 365, Nov, 2004

1-One pg. Williamson-a; Everett-c; Gunsmoke-s 37 74 111 274 612 950
2-1st Shut-Ups & Bonus Cut-Outs; Superman parody-c by Severin (his 1st cover on the title) Frankenstein-s 17 34 51 117 259 400
3-5 12 24 36 81 176 270
6-10: 7-Reprints 1st 6 covers on-c. 8-Frankenstein-c. 10-Wolverton-a 10 20 30 64 132 200
11-12, 13(nn,3/60), 7 14 21 48 89 130
14-Kirby-a 8 16 24 54 102 150
15-17, 18(nn,2/61), 19,20 6 12 18 40 73 105
21-27(11/62), 27(No.28, 2/63; mis-#d), 29(5/63) 5 10 15 35 63 90
30-40(11/64): 37-Beatles and Superman cameos 4 8 12 27 44 60
41-45,47-56,59,60: 47,49,52-Munsters. 51-Beatles inside-c. 59-Laurel and Hardy photos 4 8 12 23 37 50
46,57,58: 46,58-Man From U.N.C.L.E. 46-Beatles. 57-Rolling Stones 4 8 12 25 40 55
61-80: 62-Beatles cameo. 69-Batman, Superman app. 70-(8/68) Elvis cameo. 71-Garrison's Gorillas; W.C. Fields photos 3 6 9 16 23 30
81-99: 99-Alfred E. Neuman on-c 3 6 9 14 20 25
100 3 6 9 17 26 35
101-119: 104-Godfather-c/s. 108-Archie Bunker-s. 112,119-Kung Fu (TV). 113-Tarzan-s. 115-MASH. 117-Cannon. 118-The Sting-c/s 2 4 6 10 14 18
120(12/74) Six Million Dollar Man-c/s; Ward-a 2 4 6 13 18 22
121,122,124-126,128-133,136-140: 121-American Graffiti. 122-Korak-c/s. 124,131-Godfather-c/s. 128-Capone-c. 129,131-Jaws. 132-Baretta-c/s. 133-Space 1999. 136-Laverne and Shirley/Fonz-c. 137-Travolta/Kotter-c/s. 138-Travolta/Laverne and Shirley/ Fonz-c. 139-Barney Miller-c/s. 140-King Kong-c/s; Fonz-s 2 4 6 10 14 18
123-Planet of the Apes-c/s; Six Million Dollar Man 3 6 9 14 20 25
127,134,135: 127-Star Trek-c/s; Ward-a. 134-Fonz-c/s; Starsky and Hutch. 135-Bionic Woman-c/s; Ward-a 2 4 6 13 18 22
141,151-Charlie's Angels-c/s. 151-Frankenstein 2 4 6 13 18 22
142,143,150,152-155,157: 142-MASH-c/s. 143-Rocky-c/s; King Kong-s. 150-(5/78) Close Encounters-c/s. 152-Close Enc./Star Wars-c/s. 153-Close Enc./Fonz-c/s. 154-Jaws II-c/s; Star Wars-s. 155-Star Wars/Fonz-c 2 4 6 9 13 16
144,149,156,158-160: 144-Fonz/Happy Days-c. 149-Star Wars/Six Mil.$ Man-c/s. 156-Grease/Travolta-c. 158-Mork & Mindy. 159-Battlestar Galactica-c/s; MASH-s. 160-Superman-c/s 2 4 6 11 16 20
145,147-Both have insert postcards: 145-Fonz/Rocky/L&S-c/s. 147-Star Wars-s; Farrah photo page (missing postcards-1/2 price) 3 6 9 15 22 28
146,148: 46-Star Wars-c/s with stickers insert (missing stickers-1/2 price). 148-Star Wars-c/s with inside-c color poster 3 6 9 17 26 35
161,170-Ward-a: 161-Mork & Mindy-c/s. 170-Dukes of Hazzard-c/s 2 4 6 8 11 14
162,165-168,171,172,175-178,180-Ward-a: 162-Sherlock Holmes-s. 165-Dracula-c/s. 167-Mork-c/s. 168,175-MASH-c/s. 168-Mork-s. 172-Dukes of Hazzard/CHiPs-c/s. 176-Barney Miller-c/s 2 4 6 8 10 12

GD VG FN VF VF/NM NM-
2.0 4.0 6.0 8.0 9.0 9.2

163,179:163-Postcard insert; Mork & Mindy-c/s. 179-Insult cards insert; Popeye, Dukes of Hazzard-c/s 3 6 9 14 19 24
164,169,173,174: 164-Alien movie-c/s; Mork & Mindy-s. 169-Star Trek. 173,174-Star Wars-Empire Strikes Back. 173-SW poster 2 4 6 9 13 16
181,182,185-191,193,194,196-198-most Ward-a: 182-MASH-c/s. 185-Dukes of Hazzard-c/s; Jefferson-s. 187-Love Boat. 188-Fall Guy-s. 189-Fonz/Happy Days-c. 190,194-MASH-c/s. 191-Magnum P.I./Rocky-c; Magnum-s. 193-Knight Rider-s. 196-Dukes of Hazzard/Knight Rider-c/s. 198-Jaws III-c/s; Fall Guy-s 1 2 3 5 7 9
183,184,192,195,199,200-Ward-a in all: 183-Superman-c/s. 184-Star Trek-c/s. 192-E.T.-c/s; Rocky-s. 195-E.T.-c/s. 199-Jabba-c; Star Wars-s. 200-(12/83) 1 3 4 6 8 10
201,203,210-A-Team-c/s 6.00
202,204-206,211-224,226,227,230-233: 202-Knight Rider-s. 204-Magnum P.I.; A-Team-s. 206-Michael Jackson/Mr. T-c/s. 212-Prince-s; Cosby-s. 213-Monsters issue-c/s. 215-Hulk Hogan/Mr. T-c/s. 216-Miami Vice-s; James Bond-s. 217-Rambo-s; Cosby-s; A-Team-s. 218-Rocky-c/s. 219-Arnold/Commando-c/s; Rocky-s; Godzilla. 220-Rocky-c/s. 221-Stephen King app. 223-Miami Vice-s. 224-Cosby-s. 226-29th Anniv.; Tarzan-s; Aliens-s; Family Ties-s. 227-Cosby, Family Ties, Miami Vice-s. 230-Monkees-c/s; Elvis on-c; 232-Alf, Cheers, StarTrek-s. 233-Superman/James Bond-c/s; Robocop, Predator-s 5.00
207-209,225,234: 207-Michael Jackson-c/s. 208-Indiana Jones-c/s. 209-MichaelJackson/ Gremlins-c/s; Star Trek III-s. 225-Schwarzenegger/Stallone/G.I. Joe-c/s. 234-Don Martin-a begins; Batman/Robocop/Clint Eastwood-c/s 6.00
228,229: 228-Star Trek-c/s; Alf, Pee Wee Herman-s. 229-Monsters issue-c/s; centerfold with many superheroes 6.00
235,239,243,249: 235-1st Martin-c; Star Trek:TNG-s; Alf-s. 239-Beetlejuice-c/s; Mike Tyson-s. 243-X-Men and other heroes app. 249-Batman/Indiana Jones/Ghostbusters-c/s 6.00
236,244,245,248: 236-Madonna/Stallone-c/s; Twilight Zone-s. 244-Elvis-c/s; Martin-c. 245-Roger Rabbit-c/s. 248-Batman issue 6.00
237,238,240-242,246,247,250: 237-Robocop-s. 238-Rambo-c/s; Star Trek-s. 242-Dirty Harry-s, Ward-a. 246-Alf-s; Star Trek-s., Ward-a. 247-Star Trek-s. 250-Batman/Ghostbusters-s 4.00
251-253,255,256,259,261-265,275-278,281,284,286-297,299: 252-Star Trek-s. 253-Back to the Future-c/s. 255-TMNT-c/s. 256-TMNT-c/s; Batman, Bart Simpson on-c. 259-Die Hard II, Robocop-s. 261-TMNT, Twin Peaks-s. 262-Rocky-c/s; Rocky Horror-s. 265-TMNT-s. 276-Aliens III, Batman-s. 277-Clinton-c. 284-Bart Simpson-c; 90210-s. 297-Van Damme-s/photo-c. 299-Dumb & Dumber-c/s 4.00
254,257,266,267,272,280,282,285,298,300: 254-Back to the Future, Punisher-s; Wolverton-a, Batman-s, Ward-a. 257-Batman, Simpsons-s; Spider-Man and other heroes app. 266-Terminator-c/s. 267-Toons-c/s. 272-Star Trek VI-s. 280-Swimsuit issue. 282-Cheers-c/s. 285-Jurassic Park-c/s. 298-Swimsuit issue; Martin-c. 300-(8/95) Brady Bunch-c/s 5.00
258,260,274,279,283: 258-Simpsons-c/s; Back to the Future-s. 260-Spider-Man-c/s; Simpsons-s. 274-Batman-c/s. 279-Madonna-c/s. 283-Jurassic Park-c/s; Wolverine app. inside back-c 5.00
301-305,307-365: 365-Freas-c 3.00
306-Toy Story-c/s 4.00
Biggest... (Winter, 1977) 2 4 6 13 18 22
Biggest, Greatest... nn('65) 5 10 15 30 50 70
Biggest, Greatest... 2('66/67) - #5('69/70) 3 6 9 19 30 40
Biggest, Greatest... 6('70) - #12(Wint. '77) 3 6 9 14 19 24
Biggest, Greatest...13(Fall '78) - #21(Fall/Wint. '86) 2 4 6 8 11 14
...Blockbuster 1(Sum '87), 2('88), 3(Sum. '89) 1 3 4 6 8 10
...Blockbuster 4 - 6(Sum. '92) 6.00
...Collectors' Edition 4 ('73; formerly ...Special) 2 4 6 13 18 22
5-9,10(10/75) 2 4 6 11 16 20
11-19,20(11/17) 2 4 6 8 11 14
21,22,23(5/78): 23-Ward-a 2 4 6 8 11 14
(#24-62,64 not numbered)
1978 (nn; July, Sept, Nov, Dec) (#24-27) 2 4 6 8 11 14
1979 (nn; May, July, Sept, Nov, Dec) (#28-33) 2 4 6 8 11 14
1980 (nn; Feb, May, July, Sept, Nov, Dec) (#34-39) 1 3 4 6 8 10
1981 (nn; Feb, May, July, Sept, Nov, Dec) (#40-45) 1 3 4 6 8 10
1982 (nn; Feb, May, July, Sept, Nov, Dec) (#46-51) 1 3 4 6 8 10
1983 (nn; Feb, May, Sept, Nov, Dec) (#52-56) 1 3 4 6 8 10
1984 (nn; Feb, May, July, Nov) (#57-60) 1 2 3 4 5 7
1985 (nn; Feb) (#61) 1 2 3 4 5 7
62(9/85), nn(#63,11/85), 64(12/85), 65-69, 70(4/87) 1 2 3 4 5 7
71,72,73(100 pgs., 1/88), 74-79, 80(9/89) 5.00
81-96, 97(two diff. issues), 98-115: 83-Elvis, Batman parodies 5.00
116('98)-Last issue? 6.00
...Digest 1(Fall, '86, 148 pgs.), 2(1/87) 1 2 3 6 8 10
...Digest 3-5 1 2 3 4 5 7
...Party Pack 1,2('88) - 4('90) 4.00
...Shut-Ups 1(2/72) 3 6 9 17 26 35
...Shut-Ups 2('72) becomes Cracked Spec. #3 3 6 9 14 19 24
...Special 3('73; formerly Cracked Shut-Ups; ...Collectors' Edition#4 on)

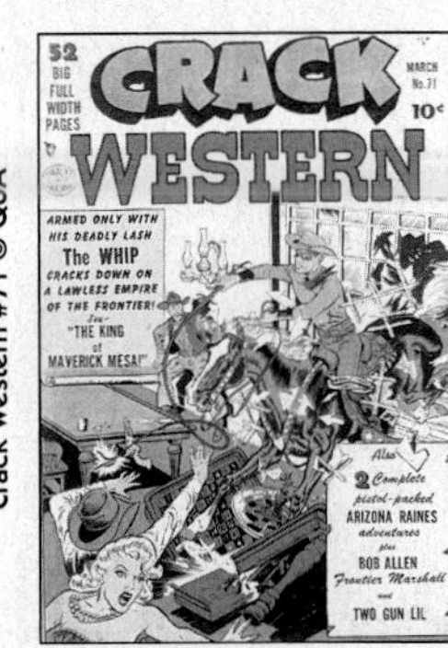

Crack Western #71 © QUA

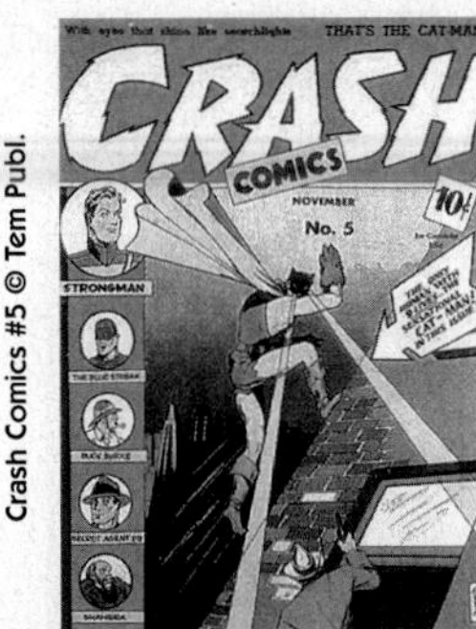

Crash Comics #5 © Tem Publ.

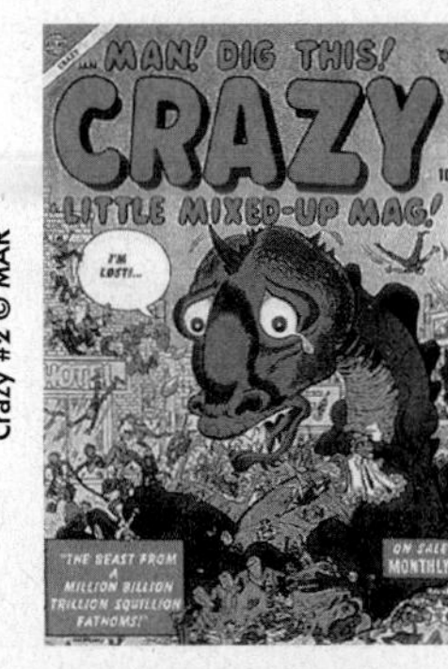

Crazy #2 © MAR

	GD 2.0	VG 4.0	FN 6.0	VF 8.0	VF/NM 9.0	NM- 9.2
	2	4	6	13	18	22
... Summer Special 1(Sum. '91), 2(Sum. '92)-Don Martin-a						4.00
... Summer Special 3(Sum. '93) - 8(Sum. '98)						3.00
... Super (Vol. 2, formerly Super Cracked) 5(Wint. '91/92) - 14(Wint.'97/98)						3.00
Extra Special... 1(Spr. '76)	2	4	6	11	16	20
Extra Special... 2(Spr./Sum. '77)	2	4	6	10	14	18
Extra Special... 3(Wint. '79) - 9(Wint. '86)	1	2	3	4	5	7
Giant... nn('65)	5	10	15	33	57	80
Giant... 2('66) - 5('69)	3	6	9	21	33	45
Giant...6('70) - 12('76)	3	6	9	16	24	32
Giant...nn(9/77, #13), nn(1/78, #14), nn(3/78, #15), nn(5/78, #16), nn(7/78, #17), nn(11/78, #18), nn(3/79, #19), nn(7/79, #20), nn(10/79, #21), nn(12/79, #22), nn(3/80, #23), nn(7/80, #24)	2	4	6	11	16	20
Giant...nn(10/80, #25), nn(12/80, #26), nn(3/81, #27), nn(7/81, #28), nn(10/81, #29), nn(12/81, #30), nn(7/82, #31), nn(10/82, #32), nn(12/82, #33), nn(7/83, #34),	2	4	6	8	11	14
Giant...nn(10/83, #35), nn(12/83, #36), nn(3/84, #37), nn(7/84, #38), nn(10/84, #39), nn(3/85, #40), nn(7/85, #41), nn(10/85, #42)	1	2	3	5	7	9
Giant...43(3/86) - 46(1/87), 47(Wint. '88), 48(Wint. '89)	1	2	3	4	5	7
King Sized... 1('67)	4	8	12	25	40	55
King Sized... 2('68) - 5('71)	3	6	9	17	26	35
King Sized... 6('72) - 11('77)	3	6	9	14	20	26
King Sized... 12(Fall '78) - 17(Sum. '83)	2	4	6	8	11	14
King Sized... 18-20 (Sum/'86) (#21,22 exist?)	1	3	4	6	8	10
Spaced Out... 1-4 ('93 - '94)						5.00
Super... 1('68)	4	8	12	25	40	55
Super... 2('69) - 6('73)	3	6	9	19	30	40
Super... 7('74), 8(Spr. '75) - 10(Spr. '77)	3	6	9	15	22	28
Super... 11(Sum. '78) - 16(Fall '81)	2	4	6	11	16	20
Super... 17(Spr. '82) - 22(Fall '83)	2	4	6	8	11	14
Super... 23(Sum. '84, mis-numbered as #24)	2	4	6	8	11	14
Super... 24(Fall '84, correctly numbered)	2	4	6	8	11	14
Super... 25(Wint. '85) - 32(Fall '86)	2	4	6	8	10	12
Super... (Vol. 2) 1('87, 100 pgs.)-Severin & Elder-a	1	3	4	6	8	10
Super... (Vol. 2) 2(Sum. '88), 3(Wint. '89), 4(exist?)(Becomes Cracked Super)						6.00

NOTE: ***Burgos** a-1-10. **Colan** a-257. **Davis** a-5, 11-17, 24, 40, 80; c-12-14, 16. **Elder** a-5, 6, 10-13; c-10. **Everett** a-1-10, 23-25, 61; c-1. **Heath** a-1-3, 6, 13, 14, 17, 110; c-6. **Jaffee** a-5, 6. **Don Martin** c-235, 244, 247, 259, 261, 264. **Morrow** a-8-10. **Reinman** a-1-4. **Severin** c/a-in most all issues. **Shores** a-3-7. **Torres** a-7-10. **Ward** a-22-24, 27, 35, 40, 120-193, 195, 197-205, 242, 244, 246, 247, 250, 252-257. **Williamson** a-1 (1 pg.). **Wolverton** a-10 (2 pgs.), Giant nn('65). **Wood** a-27, 35, 40. Alfred E. Neuman c-177, 200, 202. Batman c-234, 248, 249, 256, 274. Captain America c-256. Christmas c-234, 243. Spider-Man c-260. Star Trek c-127, 169, 207, 228. Star Wars c-145, 146, 148, 149, 152, 155, 173, 174, 199. Superman c-183, 233. #144, 146 have free full-color pre-glued stickers. #145, 147, 155, 163 have free full-color postcards. #123, 137, 154, 157 have free iron-ons.*

CRACKED MONSTER PARTY
Globe Communications: July, 1988 - No. 27, Wint. 1999/2000

	GD 2.0	VG 4.0	FN 6.0	VF 8.0	VF/NM 9.0	NM- 9.2
1	2	4	6	11	16	20
2-10	2	4	6	8	10	12
11-26	1	2	3	4	5	7
27-Interview with a Vampire-c/s	2	4	6	8	10	12

CRACKED'S FOR MONSTERS ONLY
Major Magazines: Sept, 1969 - No. 9, Sept, 1969; June, 1972

	GD 2.0	VG 4.0	FN 6.0	VF 8.0	VF/NM 9.0	NM- 9.2
1	4	8	12	28	47	65
2-9, nn(6/72)	3	6	9	19	30	40

CRACK WESTERN (Formerly Crack Comics; Jonesy No. 85 on)
Quality Comics Group: No. 63, Nov, 1949 - No. 84, May, 1953 (36 pgs., 63-68,74-on)

	GD 2.0	VG 4.0	FN 6.0	VF 8.0	VF/NM 9.0	NM- 9.2
63(#1)-Ward-c; Two-Gun Lil (origin & 1st app.)(ends #84), Arizona Ames, his horse Thunder (with sidekick Spurs & his horse Calico), Frontier Marshal (ends #70), & Dead Canyon Days (ends #69) begin; Crandall-a	18	36	54	107	169	230
64,65: 64-Ward-c. Crandall-a in both.	15	30	45	83	124	165
66,68-Photo-c. 66-Arizona Ames becomes A. Raines (ends #84)	13	26	39	72	101	130
67-Randolph Scott photo-c; Crandall-a	14	28	42	82	121	160
69(52pgs.)-Crandall-a	13	26	39	72	101	130
70(52pgs.)-The Whip (origin & 1st app.) & his horse Diablo begin (ends #84); Crandall-a	13	26	39	72	101	130
71(52pgs.)-Frontier Marshal becomes Bob Allen F. Marshal (ends #84); Crandall-c/a	14	28	42	80	115	150
72(52pgs.)-Tim Holt photo-c	12	24	36	67	94	120
73(52pgs.)-Photo-c	10	20	30	58	79	100
74-76,78,79,81,83-Crandall-c. 83-Crandall-a(p)	11	22	33	62	86	110
77,80,82	8	16	24	44	57	70
84-Crandall-c/a	12	24	36	67	94	120

NOTE: *Crandall c-71p, 74-81, 83p(w/**Cuidera**-i).*

CRASH COMICS (Cat-Man Comics No. 6 on)
Tem Publishing Co.: May, 1940 - No. 5, Nov, 1940

	GD 2.0	VG 4.0	FN 6.0	VF 8.0	VF/NM 9.0	NM- 9.2
1-The Blue Streak, Strongman (origin), The Perfect Human, Shangra begin (1st app. of each); Kirby-a	377	754	1131	2639	4620	6600
2-Simon & Kirby-a	219	438	657	1402	2401	3400
3-Simon & Kirby-a	194	388	582	1242	2121	3000
4-Origin & 1st app. The Cat-Man; S&K-a	476	952	1428	3475	6138	8800
5-1st Cat-Man-c & 2nd app.; Simon & Kirby-a	271	542	813	1734	2967	4200

NOTE: *Solar Legion by **Kirby** No. 1-5 (5 pgs. each). Strongman c-1-4. Catman c-5.*

CRASH DIVE (See Cinema Comics Herald)

CRASH METRO AND THE STAR SQUAD
Oni Press: May, 1999 ($2.95, B&W, one-shot)

	GD 2.0	VG 4.0	FN 6.0	VF 8.0	VF/NM 9.0	NM- 9.2
1-Allred-s/Ontiveros-a						3.00

CRASH RYAN (Also see Dark Horse Presents #44)
Marvel Comics (Epic): Oct, 1984 - No. 4, Jan, 1985 (Baxter paper, lim. series)

	GD 2.0	VG 4.0	FN 6.0	VF 8.0	VF/NM 9.0	NM- 9.2
1-4						3.00

CRAZY (Also see This Magazine is Crazy)
Atlas Comics (CSI): Dec, 1953 - No. 7, July, 1954

	GD 2.0	VG 4.0	FN 6.0	VF 8.0	VF/NM 9.0	NM- 9.2
1-Everett-c/a	65	130	195	416	708	1000
2	39	78	117	231	378	525
3-7: 4-I Love Lucy satire. 5-Satire on censorship	34	68	102	204	332	460

NOTE: ***Ayers** a-5. **Berg** a-1, 2. **Burgos** c-5, 6. **Drucker** a-6. **Everett** a-1-4. **Al Hartley** a-4. **Heath** a-3, 7; c-7. **Maneely** a-1-7, c-3, 4. **Post** a-3-6. Funny monster c-1-4.*

CRAZY (Satire)
Marvel Comics Group: Feb, 1973 - No. 3, June, 1973

	GD 2.0	VG 4.0	FN 6.0	VF 8.0	VF/NM 9.0	NM- 9.2
1-Not Brand Echh-r; Beatles cameo (r)	3	6	9	18	28	38
2,3-Not Brand Echh-r; Kirby-a	2	4	6	13	18	22

CRAZY MAGAZINE (Satire)
Oct, 1973 - No. 94, Apr, 1983 (40-90¢, B&W magazine)
Marvel Comics: (#1, 44 pgs; #2-90, reg. issues, 52 pgs; #92-95, 68 pgs)'

	GD 2.0	VG 4.0	FN 6.0	VF 8.0	VF/NM 9.0	NM- 9.2
1-Wolverton(1 pg.), Bode-a; 3 pg. photo story of Neal Adams & Dick Giordano; Harlan Ellison story; TV Kung Fu sty.	5	10	15	31	53	75
2-"Live & Let Die" c/s; 8pgs; Adams/Buscema-a; McCloud w5 pgs. Adams-a; Kurtzman's "Hey Look" 2 pg.-r	3	6	9	19	30	40
3-5: 3-"High Plains Drifter" w/Clint Eastwood c/s; Waltons app; Drucker, Reese-a. 4-Shaft-c/s; Ploog-a; Nixon 3 pg. app; Freas-a. 5-Michael Crichton's "Westworld" c/s; Nixon app.	3	6	9	16	24	32
6,7,18: 6-Exorcist c/s; Nixon app. 7-TV's Kung Fu c/s; Nixon app.; Ploog & Freas-a. 18-Six Million Dollar Man/Bionic Woman c/s; Welcome Back Kotter story	3	6	9	15	22	28
8-10: 8-Serpico c/s; Casper parody; TV's Police Story. 9-Joker cameo; Chinatown story; Eisner s/a begins; Has 1st 8 covers on-c. 10-Playboy Bunny-c; M. Severin-a; Lee Marrs-a begins; "Deathwish" story	3	6	9	14	20	26
11-17,19: 11-Towering Inferno. 12-Rhoda. 13-"Tommy" the Who Rock Opera. 14-Mandingo. 15-Jaws story. 16-Santa/Xmas-c; "Good Times" TV story; Jaws. 17-Bicentennial issue; Baretta; Woody Allen. 19-King Kong c/s; Reagan, J. Carter, Howard the Duck cameos, "Laverne & Shirley"	2	4	6	11	16	20
20,24,27: 20-Bicentennial-c; Space 1999 sty; Superheroes song sheet, 4pgs. 24-Charlie's Angels. 27-Charlie's Angels/Travolta/Fonz-c; Bionic Woman sty	3	6	9	14	19	24
21-23,25,26,28-30: 21-Starsky & Hutch. 22-Mount Rushmore/J. Carter-c; TV's Barney Miller; Superheroes spoof. 23-Santa/Xmas-c; "Happy Days" sty; "Omen" sty. 25-J. Carter-c/s; Grandenetti-a begins; TV's Alice; Logan's Run. 26-TV Stars-c; Mary Hartman, King Kong. 28-Donny & Marie Osmond-c/s; Marathon Man. 29-Travolta/Kotter-c; "One Day at a Time", Gong Show. 30-1977, 84 pgs. w/bonus; Jaws, Baretta, King Kong, Happy Days	2	4	6	9	12	15
31,33-35,38,40: 31-"Rocky"-c/s; TV game shows. 33-Peter Benchley's "Deep". 34-J. Carter-c; TV's "Fish". 35-Xmas-c with Fonz/Six Million Dollar Man/Wonder Woman/Darth Vader/ Travolta, TV's "Mash" & "Family Matters". 38-Close Encounters of the Third Kind-c/s. 40-"Three's Company-c/s	1	3	4	6	8	11
32-Star Wars/Darth Vader-c/s; "Black Sunday"	3	6	9	14	19	24
36,42,47,49: 36-Farrah Fawcett/Six Million Dollar Man-c; TV's Nancy Drew & Hardy Boys; 1st app. Howard The Duck in Crazy, 2 pgs. 42-84 pgs. w/bonus; TV Hulk/Spider-Man-c; Mash, Gong Show, One Day at a Time, Disco, Alice. 47-Battlestar Galactica xmas-c; movie "Foul Play". 49-1979, 84 pgs. w/bonus; Mork & Mindy-c; Jaws, Saturday Night Fever, Three's Company	2	4	6	9	12	15
37-1978, 84 pgs. w/bonus. Darth Vader-c; Barney Miller, Laverne & Shirley, Good Times, Rocky, Donny & Marie Osmond, Bionic Woman	2	4	6	13	18	22
39,44: 39-Saturday Night Fever-c/s. 44-"Grease"-c w/Travolta/O. Newton-John	2	4	6	11	16	20
41-Kiss-c & 1pg. photos; Disaster movies, TV's "Family", Annie Hall	4	8	12	28	47	65

Crazy #82 © MAR

Creator-Owned Heroes #1 © Paperfilms

Creature Commandos #3 © DC

GD VG FN VF VF/NM NM-
2.0 4.0 6.0 8.0 9.0 9.2

43,45,46,48,51: 43-Jaws-c; Saturday Night Fever. 43-E.C. swipe from Mad #131. 45-Travolta/O. Newton-John/J. Carter-c; Eight is Enough. 46-TV Hulk-c/s; Punk Rock. 48-"Wiz"-c, Battlestar Galactica-s. 51-Grease/Mork & Mindy/D&M Osmond-c, Mork & Mindy-sty. "Boys from Brazil" 1 3 4 6 8 11

50,58: 50-Superman movie-c/sty, Playboy Mag., TV Hulk, Fonz; Howard the Duck, 1 pg. 58-1980, 84 pgs. w/32 pg. color comic bonus insert-Full reprint of Crazy Comic #1, Battlestar Galactica, Charlie's Angels, Starsky & Hutch 2 4 6 11 16 20

52,59,60,64: 52-1979, 84 pgs. w/bonus. Marlon Brando-c; TV Hulk, Grease. Kiss, 1 pg. photos. 59-Santa Ptd-c by Larkin; "Alien", "Moonraker", Rocky-2, Howard the Duck, 1 pg. 60-Star Trek w/Muppets-c; Star Trek sty; 1st app/origin Teen Hulk; Severin-a. 64-84 pgs. w/bonus Monopoly game satire. "Empire Strikes Back", 8 pgs., One Day at a Time 2 4 6 11 16 20

53,54,65,67-70: 53-"Animal House"-c/sty; TV's "Vegas", Howard the Duck, 1 pg. 54-Love at First Bite-c/sty, Fantasy Island sty, Howard the Duck 1 pg. 65-(Has #66 on-c, Aug/'80). "Black Hole" w/Janson-a; Kirby,Wood/Severin-a(r), 5 pgs. Howard the Duck, 3 pgs.; Broderick-a; Buck Rogers, Mr. Rogers. 67-84 pgs. w/bonus; TV's Kung Fu, Exorcist; Ploog-a(r). 68-American Gigolo, Dukes of Hazzard, Teen Hulk; Howard the Duck, 3 pgs. Broderick-a; Monster sty/5 pg. Ditko-a(r). 69-Obnoxio the Clown-c/sty; Stephen King's "Shining", Teen Hulk, Richie Rich, Howard the Duck, 3pgs; Broderick-a. 70-84 pgs. Towering Inferno, Daytime TV; Trina Robbins-a 1 3 4 6 8 10

55-57,61,63: 55-84 pgs. w/bonus; Love Boat, Mork & Mindy, Fonz, TV Hulk. 56-Mork/Rocky/ J. Carter-c; China Syndrome. 57-TV Hulk with Miss Piggy-c, Dracula, Taxi, Muppets. 61-1980, 84 pgs. Adams-a(r), McCloud, Pro wrestling, Casper, TV's Police Story. 63-Apocalypse Now-Coppola's cult movie; 3rd app. Teen Hulk, Howard the Duck, 3 pgs. 2 4 6 8 11 14

62-Kiss-c & 2 pg. app; Quincy, 2nd app. Teen Hulk 4 8 12 25 40 55

66-Sept/'80, Empire Strikes Back-c/sty; Teen Hulk by Severin, Howard the Duck, 3pgs. by Broderick 2 4 6 11 16 20

71,72,75-77,79: 71-Blues Brothers parody, Teen Hulk, Superheroes parody, WKRP in Cincinnati, Howard the Duck, 3pgs. by Broderick. 72-Jackie Gleason/Smokey & the Bandit II-c/sty, Shogun, Teen Hulk. Howard the Duck, 3pgs. by Broderick. 75-Flash Gordon movie c/sty; Teen Hulk, Cat in the Hat, Howard the Duck 3pgs. by Broderick. 76-84 pgs. w/bonus; Monster-sty w/ Crandall-a(r), Monster-stys(2) w/Kirby-a(r), 5pgs. ea; Mash, TV Hulk, Chinatown. 77-Popeye movie/R. Williams-c/sty; Teen Hulk, Love Boat, Howard the Duck 3 pgs. 79-84 pgs. w/bonus color stickers; has new material; "9 to 5" w/Dolly Parton, Teen Hulk, Magnum P.I., Monster-sty w/5pgs, Ditko-a(r), "Rat" w/Sutton-a(r), Everett-a, 4 pgs.(r) 1 3 4 6 8 10

73,74,78,80: 73-84 pgs. w/bonus Hulk/Spiderman Finger Puppets-c & bonus; "Live & Let Die, Jaws, Fantasy Island. 74-Dallas/"Who Shot J.R."-c/sty; Elephant Man, Howard the Duck 3pgs. by Broderick. 78-Clint Eastwood-c/sty; Teen Hulk, Superheroes parody, Lou Grant. 80-Star Wars, 2 pg. app; "Howling", TV's "Greatest American Hero" 2 4 6 8 11 14

81,84,86,87,89: 81-.Superman Movie II-c/sty; Wolverine cameo, Mash, Teen Hulk. 84-American Werewolf in London, Johnny Carson app; Teen Hulk. 86-Time Bandits-c/sty; Private Benjamin. 87-Rubix Cube-c; Hill Street Blues, "Ragtime", Origin Obnoxio the Clown; Teen Hulk. 89-Burt Reynolds "Sharkey's Machine", Teen Hulk 1 3 4 6 8 10

82-X-Men-c w/new Byrne-a, 84 pgs. w/new material; Fantasy Island, Teen Hulk, "For Your Eyes Only", Spiderman/Human Torch-r by Kirby/Ditko; Sutton-a(r); Rogers-a; Hunchback of Notre Dame, 5 pgs. 2 4 6 11 16 20

83-Raiders of the Lost Ark-c/sty; Hart to Hart; Reese-a; Teen Hulk 2 4 6 9 13 20

85,88: 85-84 pgs; Escape from New York, Teen Hulk; Kirby-a(r), 5 pgs, Poseidon Adventure, Flintstones, Sesame Street. 88-84 pgs. w/bonus Dr. Strange Game; some new material; Jeffersons, X-Men/Wolverine, 10 pgs.; Byrne-a; Apocalypse Now, Teen Hulk 1 3 4 6 8 11

90-94: 90-Conan-c/sty; M. Severin-a; Teen Hulk. 91-84 pgs, some new material; Bladerunner-c/sty, "Deathwish-II, Teen Hulk, Black Knight, 10 pgs.-'50s-r w/Maneely-a. 92-Wrath of Khan Star Trek-c/sty; Joanie & Chachi, Teen Hulk. 93-"E.T."-c/sty, Teen Hulk, Archie Bunkers Place, Dr. Doom Game. 94-Poltergeist, Smurfs, Teen Hulk, Casper, Avengers parody-8pgs. Adams-a 2 4 6 10 14 18

Crazy Summer Special #1 (Sum, '75, 100 pgs.)-Nixon, TV Kung Fu, Babe Ruth, Joe Namath, Waltons, McCloud, Chariots of the Gods 3 6 9 14 20 26

NOTE: ***N. Adams*** *a-2, 61r, 94p.* ***Austin*** *a-82i.* ***Buscema*** *a-2, 82.* ***Byrne*** *c-82p.* ***Nick Cardy*** *c-7, 8, 10, 12-16, Super Special 1.* ***Crandall*** *a-76r.* ***Ditko*** *a-68r, 79r, 82r.* ***Drucker*** *a-3.* ***Eisner*** *a-9-16.* ***Kelly Freas*** *c-1-6, 9, 11; a-7.* ***Kirby/Wood*** *a-66r.* ***Ploog*** *a-1, 4, 7, 67r, 73r.* ***Rogers*** *a-82.* ***Sparling*** *a-92.* ***Wood*** *a-65r. Howard the Duck in 36, 50, 51, 53, 54, 59, 63, 65, 66, 68, 69, 71, 72, 74, 75, 77. Hulk in 46, c-42, 46, 57, 73. Star Wars in 32, 66; c-37.*

CRAZY (Homage to the humor magazine)
Marvel Comics: Dec, 2019 ($4.99, one-shot)

1-Short stories by various incl. Duggan, Macchio, Koblish, Simpson, Bill Morrison 5.00

CRAZYMAN
Continuity Comics: Apr, 1992 - No. 3, 1992 ($2.50, high quality paper)

1-($3.95, 52 pgs.)-Embossed-c; N. Adams part-i 4.00

GD VG FN VF VF/NM NM-
2.0 4.0 6.0 8.0 9.0 9.2

2,3 ($2.50): 2-N. Adams/Bolland-c 3.00

CRAZYMAN
Continuity Comics: V2#1, 5/93 - No. 4, 1/94 ($2.50, high quality paper)

V2#1-4: 1-Entire book is die-cut. 2-(12/93)-Adams-c(p) & part scripts. 3-(12/93). 4-Indicia says #3, Jan. 1993 3.00

CRAZY, MAN, CRAZY (Magazine) (Becomes This Magazine is...?) (Formerly From Here to Insanity)
Humor Magazines (Charlton): V2#1, Dec, 1955 - V2#2, June, 1956

V2#1,V2#2-Satire; Wolverton-a, 3 pgs. 20 40 60 117 189 260

CREATOR-OWNED HEROES
Image Comics: Jun, 2012 - No. 8, Jan, 2013 ($3.99)

1-8-Anthology of short stories by various and creator interviews 4.00

CREATURE, THE (See Movie Classics)

CREATURE COMMANDOS (See Weird War Tales #93 for 1st app.)
DC Comics: May, 2000 - No. 8, Dec, 2000 ($2.50, limited series)

1-8: Truman-s/Eaton-a 3.00

CREATURES OF THE ID
Caliber Press: 1990 ($2.95, B&W)

1-Frank Einstein (Madman) app.; Allred-a 7 14 21 49 92 135

CREATURES OF THE NIGHT
Dark Horse Books: Nov, 2004 ($12.95, hardcover graphic novel)

HC-Neil Gaiman-s/Michael Zulli-a/c 13.00

CREATURES ON THE LOOSE (Formerly Tower of Shadows No. 1-9)(See Kull)
Marvel Comics: No. 10, March, 1971 - No. 37, Sept, 1975 (New-a & reprints)

10-(15¢)-1st full app. King Kull; see Kull the Conqueror; Wrightson-a 8 16 24 54 102 150
11-Classic story about an underground comic artist going to Hell 4 8 12 27 44 60
12-15: 13-Last 15¢ issue 4 8 12 23 37 50
16-Origin Warrior of Mars (begins, ends #21) 3 6 9 15 22 28
17-20 2 4 6 9 13 16
21-Steranko-c 3 6 9 16 24 32
22-Steranko-c; Thongor stories begin 3 6 9 17 26 35
23-29-Thongor-c/stories 1 3 4 6 8 10
30-Manwolf begins 3 6 9 19 30 40
31-33 2 4 6 9 13 16
34-37 2 4 6 8 10 12

NOTE: ***Crandall*** *a-13.* ***Ditko*** *r-15, 17, 18, 20, 22, 24, 27, 28.* ***Everett*** *a-16i(new).* ***Matt Fox*** *r-21i.* ***Howard*** *a-26i.* ***Gil Kane*** *a-16p, 17p, 19i; c-16, 17, 19, 20, 25, 29, 33p, 35p, 36p.* ***Kirby*** *a-10-15r, 16(2)r, 17r, 19r.* ***Morrow*** *a-20, 21.* ***Perez*** *a-33-37; c-34p.* ***Shores a-11. innott*** *r-21.* ***Sutton*** *c-10.* ***Tuska*** *a-30-32p.*

CREECH, THE
Image Comics: Oct, 1997 - No. 3, Dec, 1997 ($1.95/$2.50, limited series)

1-3: 1-Capullo-s/c/a(p) 3.00
TPB (1999, $9.95) r/#1-3, McFarlane intro. 10.00
Out for Blood 1-3 (7/01 - No. 3, 11/01; $4.95) Capullo-s/c/a 5.00

CREED
Hall of Heroes Comics: Dec, 1994 - No. 2, Jan, 1995 ($2.50, B&W)

1-Trent Kaniuga-s/a 2 4 6 10 14 18
2 2 4 6 8 10 12

CREED
Lightning Comics: June, 1995 - No. 3 ($2.75/$3.00, B&W/color)

1-($2.75) 4.00
1-($3.00, color) 5.00
1-($9.95)-Commemorative Edition 10.00
1-TwinVariant Edition (1250? print run) 10.00
1-Special Edition; polybagged w/certificate 4.00
1 Gold Collectors Edition; polybagged w/certificate 3.00
2,3-($3.00, color)-Butt Naked Edition & regular-c 3.00
3-($9.95)-Commemorative Edition; polybagged w/certificate & card 10.00

CREED: CRANIAL DISORDER
Lightning Comics: Oct, 1996 ($3.00, limited series)

1-3-Two covers 3.00
1-($5.95)-Platinum Edition 6.00
2,3-($9.95) Ltd. Edition 10.00

CREED/TEENAGE MUTANT NINJA TURTLES
Lightning Comics: May, 1996 ($3.00, one-shot)

1-Kaniuga-a(p)/scripts; Laird-c; variant-c exists 6.00

The Creeper #7 © DC

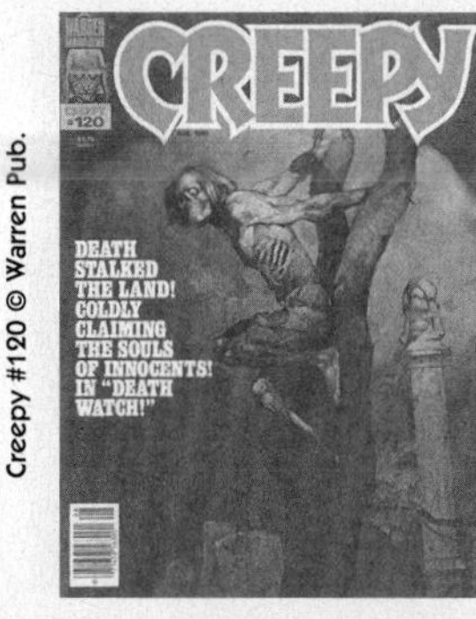

Creepy #120 © Warren Pub.

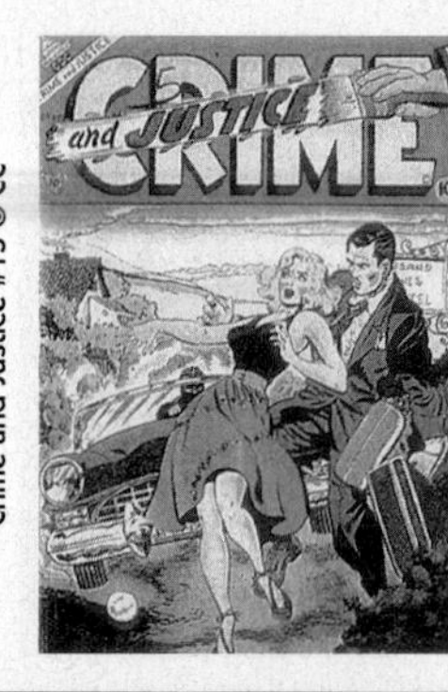

Crime and Justice #15 © CC

GD 2.0 | VG 4.0 | FN 6.0 | VF 8.0 | VF/NM 9.0 | NM- 9.2

1-($9.95)-Platinum Edition 12.00
1-Special Edition; polybagged w/certificate 6.00

CREEP, THE
Dark Horse Books: No. 0, Aug, 2012 - No. 4, Dec, 2012 ($2.99/$3.50)

0-Frank Miller-c; Arcudi-s/Case-a 4.00
1-4-($3.50): 1-Mignola-c. 2-Sook-c 4.00

CREEPER BY STEVE DITKO, THE
DC Comics: 2010 ($39.99, hardcover with dustjacket)

HC-Reprints Showcase #73, Beware the Creeper #1-6, First Issue Special #7 and apps. in World's Finest #249-255 and Cancelled Comic Cavalcade #2; intro. by Steve Niles 40.00

CREEPER, THE (See Beware… , Showcase #73 & 1st Issue Special #7)
DC Comics: Dec, 1997 - No. 11; #1,000,000 Nov, 1998 ($2.50)

1-11-Kaminski-s/Martinbrough-a(p). 7,8-Joker-c/app. 4.00
#1,000,000 (11/98) 853rd Century x-over 4.00

CREEPER, THE (See DCU Brave New World)
DC Comics: Oct, 2006 - No. 6, Mar, 2007 ($2.99, limited series)

1-6-Niles-s/Justiniano-a/c; Jack Ryder becomes the Creeper. 2-6-Batman app. 3.00
... - Welcome to Creepsville TPB ('07, $19.99) r/#1-6 & story from DCU Brave New World 20.00

CREEPS
Image Comics: Oct, 2001 - No. 4, May, 2002 ($2.95)

1-4-Mandrake-a/Mishkin-s 3.00

CREEPSHOW
Plume/New American Library Pub.: July, 1982 (softcover graphic novel)

1st edition-nn-(68 pgs.) Kamen-c/Wrightson-a; screenplay by Stephen King for the George Romero movie 8 16 24 54 102 150
2nd-7th printings 3 6 9 17 26 35

CREEPY (See Warren Presents)
Warren Publishing Co./Harris Publ. #146: 1964 - No. 145, Feb, 1983; No. 146, 1985 (B&W, magazine)

1-Frazetta-a (his last story in comics?); Jack Davis-c; 1st Warren all comics magazine; 1st app. Uncle Creepy 15 30 45 101 223 345
2-Frazetta-c & 1 pg. strip 11 22 33 73 157 240
3-8,11-13,15-17: 3-7,9-11,15-17-Frazetta-c. 7-Frazetta 1 pg. strip. 15,16-Adams-a. 16-Jeff Jones-a 6 12 18 37 66 95
9-Creepy fan club sketch by Wrightson (1st published-a); has 1/2 pg. anti-smoking strip by Frazetta; Frazetta-c; 1st Wood and Ditko art on this title; Toth-a (low print) 8 16 24 56 108 160
10-Brunner fan club sketch (1st published work) 6 12 18 41 76 110
14-Neal Adams 1st Warren work 7 14 21 44 82 120
18-28,30,31: 27-Frazetta-c 4 8 12 28 47 65
29,34: 29-Jones-a 5 10 15 30 50 70
32-(scarce) Frazetta-c; Harlan Ellison sty 8 16 24 58 108 160
33,35,37,39,40,42-47,49: 35-Hitler/Nazi-s. 39-1st Uncle Creepy solo-s, Cousin Eerie app.; early Brunner-a. 42-1st San Julian-c. 44-1st Ploog-a. 46-Corben-a 4 8 12 23 37 50
36-(11/70)1st Corben art at Warren 5 10 15 30 50 70
38,41-(scarce): 38-1st Kelly-c. 41-Corben-a 5 10 15 33 57 80
48,55,65-(1972, 1973, 1974 Annuals) #55 & 65 contain an 8 pg. slick comic insert. 48-(84 pgs.). 55-Color poster bonus (1/2 price if missing). 65-(100 pgs.) Summer Giant 5 10 15 30 50 70
50-Vampirella/Eerie/Creepy-c 5 10 15 35 63 90
51,54,56-61,64: All contain an 8 pg. slick comic insert in middle. 59-Xmas horror. 54,64-Chaykin-a 4 8 12 27 44 60
52,53,66,71,72,75,76,78-80: 71-All Bermejo-a; Space & Time issue. 72-Gual-a. 78-Fantasy issue. 79,80-Monsters issue 3 6 9 19 30 40
62,63-1st & 2nd full Wrightson story art; Corben-a; 8 pg. color comic insert 4 8 12 27 44 60
67,68,73 3 6 9 21 33 45
69,70-Edgar Allan Poe issues; Corben-a 4 8 12 23 37 50
74,77: 74-All Crandell-a. 77-Xmas Horror issue; Corben-a,Wrightson-a 4 8 12 23 37 50
81,84,85,88-90,92-94,96-99,102,104-112,114-118,120,122-130: 84,93-Sports issue. 85,97,102-Monster issue. 89-All war issue; Nino-a. 94-Weird Children issue. 96,109-Aliens issue. 99-Disasters. 103-Corben-a. 104-Robots issue. 106-Sword & Sorcery.107-Sci-fi. 116-End of Man. 125-Xmas Horror 2 4 6 10 14 18
82,100,101: 82-All Maroto issue. 100-(8/78) Anniversary. 101-Corben-a 3 6 9 14 20 26
83,95-Wrightson-a. 83-Corben-a. 95-Gorilla/Apes. 2 4 6 13 18 22
86,87,91,103-Wrightson-a. 86-Xmas Horror 2 4 6 13 18 22
113-All Wrightson-r issue 3 6 9 19 29 38
119,121: 119-All Nino issue.121-All Severin-r issue 2 4 6 13 18 22
131,133-136,138,140: 135-Xmas issue 2 4 6 13 18 22
132,137,139: 132-Corben. 137-All Williamson-r issue. 139-All Toth-r issue 3 6 9 14 20 26
141,143,144 (low dist.): 144-Giant, $2.25; Frazetta-c 3 6 9 17 26 35
142,145 (low dist.): 142-(10/82, 100 pgs.) All Torres issue. 145-(2/83) last Warren issue 3 6 9 19 30 40
146 ($2.95)-1st from Harris; resurrection issue 7 14 21 46 86 125
Year Book '68-'70: '70-Neal Adams, Ditko-a(r) 5 10 15 33 57 80
Annual 1971,1972 5 10 15 31 53 75
1993 Fearbook ($3.95)-Harris Publ.; Brereton-c; Vampirella by Busiek-s/Art Adams-a; David-s; Paquette-a 3 6 9 17 26 35
...:The Classic Years TPB (Harris/Dark Horse, '91, $12.95) Kaluta-c; art by Frazetta,Torres, Crandall, Ditko, Morrow, Williamson, Wrightson 25.00

NOTE: *All issues contain many good artists works:* ***Neal Adams, Brunner, Corben, Craig (Taycee), Crandall, Ditko, Evans, Frazetta, Heath, Jeff Jones, Krenkel, McWilliams, Morrow, Nino, Orlando, Ploog, Severin, Torres, Toth, Williamson, Wood, & Wrightson****; covers by* ***Crandall, Davis, Frazetta, Morrow, San Julian, Todd/Bode****; Otto Binder's "Adam Link" stories in No. 2, 4, 6, 8, 9, 12, 13, 15 with* ***Orlando*** *art.* ***Frazetta*** *c-2-7, 9-11, 15-17, 27, 32, 83r, 89r, 91r.* ***E.A. Poe*** *adaptations in 66, 69, 70.*

CREEPY (Mini-series)
Harris Comics/Dark Horse: 1992 - Book 4, 1992 (48 pgs, B&W, squarebound)

Book 1-4: Brereton painted-c on all. Stories and art by various incl. David (all), Busiek(2), Infantino(2), Guice(3), Colan(1) 2 4 6 8 10 12

CREEPY
Dark Horse Comics: July, 2009 - No. 24, Jun, 2016 ($4.99/$3.99, 48 pgs, B&W, quarterly)

1-13: 1-Powell-c; art by Wrightson, Toth, Alexander. 8,12-Corben-c. 5.00
14-24-($3.99) 18-Nguyen-c. 20,23,24-Corben-a 4.00

CREEPY THINGS
Charlton Comics: July, 1975 - No. 6, June, 1976

1-Sutton-c/a 3 6 9 14 19 24
2-6: Ditko-a in 3,5. Sutton c-3,4. 6-Zeck-c 2 4 6 8 10 12
Modern Comics Reprint 2-6(1977) 5.00

NOTE: ***Larson*** *a-2,6.* ***Sutton*** *a-1,2,4,6.* ***Zeck*** *a-2.*

CREW, THE
Marvel Comics: July, 2003 - No. 7, Jan, 2004 ($2.50)

1-7-Priest-s/Bennett-a; James Rhodes (War Machine) app. 3.00

CRIME AND JUSTICE (Badge Of Justice #22 on; Rookie Cop? No. 27 on)
Capitol Stories/Charlton Comics: March, 1951 - No. 21, Nov, 1954; No. 23, Mar, 1955 - No. 26, Sept, 1955 (No #22)

1 47 94 141 296 498 700
2 22 44 66 132 216 300
3-8,10-13: 6-Negligee panels 20 40 60 117 189 260
9-Classic story "Comics Vs. Crime" 39 78 117 236 388 540
14-Color illos in **POP**; story of murderer who beheads women 34 68 102 204 332 460
15-17,19-21,23,24: 15-Negligee panels. 23-Rookie Cop (1st app.) 15 30 45 84 127 170
18-Ditko-a 34 68 102 204 332 460
25,26: (scarce) 21 42 63 124 202 280

NOTE: ***Alascia*** *c-20.* ***Ayers*** *a-17.* ***Shuster*** *a-19-21; c-19. Bondage c-11, 12.*

CRIME AND PUNISHMENT (Title inspired by 1935 film)
Lev Gleason Publications: April, 1948 - No. 74, Aug, 1955

1-Mr. Crime app. on-c 47 94 141 296 498 700
2-Narrator, Officer Common Sense (a ghost) begins, ends #27? (see Crime Does Not Pay #41) 23 46 69 136 223 310
3-(6/48)-Used in **SOTI**, pg. 112; contains Biro & Gleason self censorship code of 12 listed restrictions 25 50 75 147 241 335
4,5 16 32 48 96 151 205
6-10 14 28 42 81 118 155
11-20 13 26 39 72 101 130
21-30 11 22 33 62 86 110
31-38,40-44,46: 46-One pg. Frazetta-a 10 20 30 56 76 95
39-Drug mention story "The Five Dopes" 17 34 51 98 154 210
45- "Hophead Killer" drug story 17 34 51 98 154 210
47-53,55,57,60-65,70-74: 10 20 30 54 72 90
54-Electric Chair-c 11 22 33 62 86 110
56-Classic dagger/torture-c 13 26 39 74 105 135
58-Used in **POP**, pg. 79 13 26 39 72 101 130
59-Used in **SOTI**, illo "What comic-book America stands for" 39 78 117 231 378 525
66-Toth-c/a(4); 3-D effect issue (3/54); 1st "Deep Dimension" process 42 84 126 265 445 625

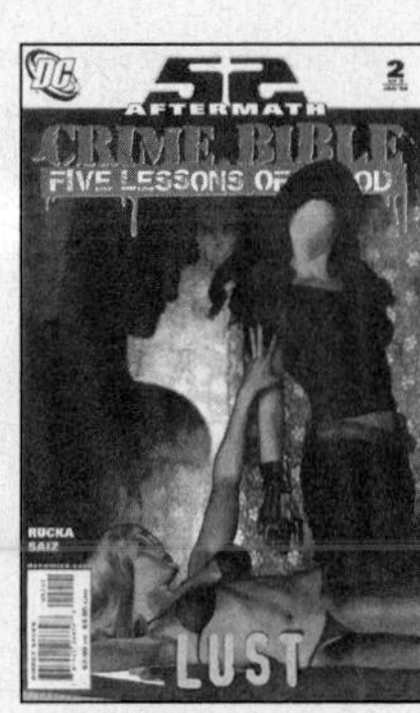

Crime Bible: The Five Lessons #2 © DC

Crime Clinic #11 (#2) © Z-D

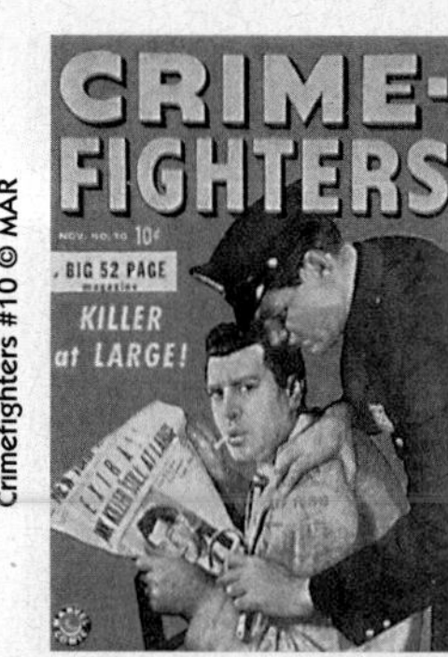

Crimefighters #10 © MAR

	GD 2.0	VG 4.0	FN 6.0	VF 8.0	VF/NM 9.0	NM- 9.2
67- "Monkey on His Back" heroin story; 3-D effect issue	39	78	117	240	395	550
68-3-D effect issue; Toth-c (7/54)	34	68	102	204	332	460
69- "The Hot Rod Gang" dope crazy kids	16	32	48	94	147	200

NOTE: ***Belfi** a- 2, 3, 5. **Biro** c-most. **Al Borth** a-9, 35. **Cooper** a-9. **Joe Certa** a-8. **Tony Dipreta** a-3, 5, 15, 34. **Everett** a-31. **Bob Fujitani (Fuje)** a-2-20, 26, 27. **Joseph Gaguardi** a-15, 18, 20. **Fred Guardineer** a-2-5, 10-12, 14, 15, 17, 18, 20, 26-28, 32, 34, 35, 38-44, 51, 54. **Jack Keller** a-18. **Kinstler** c-69. **Martinott** a-13. **Al McWilliams** a-36, 41, 48, 49. **William Overgard** a-36. **Dick Rockwell** a-35, 51. **Robert Q. Sale** a-43. **George Tuska** a-28, 30, 51, 64, 70. Painted-c-31.*

CRIME AND PUNISHMENT: MARSHALL LAW TAKES MANHATTAN
Marvel Comics (Epic Comics): 1989 ($4.95, 52 pgs., direct sales only, mature)

	GD	VG	FN	VF	VF/NM	NM-
nn-Graphic album featuring Marshall Law						5.00

CRIME BIBLE: THE FIVE LESSONS (Aftermath of DC's 52 series)
DC Comics: Dec, 2007 - No. 5, Apr, 2008 ($2.99, limited series)

	GD	VG	FN	VF	VF/NM	NM-
1-5-Rucka-s; The Question (Renee Montoya) app. 3-Batwoman app.						3.00
The Question: The Five Books of Blood HC (2008, $19.99) r/#1-5						20.00
The Question: The Five Books of Blood SC (2009, $14.99) r/#1-5						15.00

CRIME CAN'T WIN (Formerly Cindy Smith)
Marvel/Atlas Comics (TCI 41/CCC 42,43,4-12): No. 41, 9/50 - No. 43, 2/51; No. 4, 4/51 - No. 12, 9/53

	GD	VG	FN	VF	VF/NM	NM-
41(#1)-"The Girl Who Planned Her Own Murder"	34	68	102	204	332	460
42(#2)	20	40	60	117	189	260
43(#3)-Horror story	24	48	72	140	230	320
4(4/51),5-12: 10-Possible use in **SOTI**, pg. 161	16	32	48	94	147	200

NOTE: ***Robinson** a-9-11. **Tuska** a-43.*

CRIME CASES COMICS (Formerly Willie Comics)
Marvel/Atlas Comics(CnPC No.24-8/MJMC No.9-12): No. 24, 8/50 - No. 27, 3/51; No. 5, 5/51 - No. 12, 7/52

	GD	VG	FN	VF	VF/NM	NM-
24 (#1, 52 pgs.)-True police cases	26	52	78	154	252	350
25-27(#2-4): 27-Maneely & Morisi-a	20	40	60	114	182	250
5-12: 11-Robinson-a. 12-Tuska-a	17	34	51	98	154	210

CRIME CLINIC
Ziff-Davis Publishing Co.: No. 10, July-Aug, 1951 - No. 5, Summer, 1952

	GD	VG	FN	VF	VF/NM	NM-
10(#1)-Painted-c; origin Dr. Tom Rogers	37	74	111	222	361	500
11(#2),4,5: 4,5-Painted-c	24	48	72	144	237	330
3-Used in **SOTI**, pg. 18	26	52	78	154	252	350

NOTE: *All have painted covers by **Saunders**. **Starr** a-10.*

CRIME CLINIC
Slave Labor Graphics: May, 1995 - No. 2, Oct, 1995 ($2.95, B&W, limited series)

	GD	VG	FN	VF	VF/NM	NM-
1,2						3.00

CRIME DETECTIVE COMICS
Hillman Periodicals: Mar-Apr, 1948 - V3#8, May-June, 1953

	GD	VG	FN	VF	VF/NM	NM-
V1#1-The Invisible 6, costumed villains app; Fuje-c/a, 15 pgs.	41	82	123	256	428	600
2,5: 5-Krigstein-a	20	40	60	120	195	270
3,4,6,7,10-12: 6-McWilliams-a	18	36	54	103	162	220
8-Kirbyish-a by McCann	18	36	54	103	162	220
9-Used in **SOTI**, pg. 16 & "Caricature of the author in a position comic book publishers wish he were in permanently" illo.	48	96	144	302	514	725
V2#1,4,7-Krigstein-a: 1-Tuska-a	15	30	45	90	140	190
2,3,5,6,8-12 (1-2/52)	15	30	45	84	127	170
V3#1-Drug use-c	15	30	45	86	133	180
2-8	14	28	42	78	112	145

NOTE: ***Briefer** a-11, V3#1. **Kinstlerish**-a by **McCann**-V2#7, V3#2. **Powell** a-10, 11. **Starr** a-10.*

CRIME DETECTOR
Timor Publications: Jan, 1954 - No. 5, Sept, 1954

	GD	VG	FN	VF	VF/NM	NM-
1	30	60	90	177	289	400
2	18	36	54	103	162	220
3,4	15	30	45	88	137	185
5-Disbrow-a (classic)	28	56	84	168	274	380

CRIME DOES NOT PAY (Formerly Silver Streak Comics No. 1-21)
Comic House/Lev Gleason/Golfing: No. 22, June, 1942 - No. 147, July, 1955 (1st crime comic)(Title inspired by film)

	GD	VG	FN	VF	VF/NM	NM-
22 (23 on cover, 22 on indicia)-Origin The War Eagle & only app.; Chip Gardner begins; #22 was rebound in Complete Book of True Crime (Scarce)	757	1514	2271	5526	9763	14,000
23-(9/42) (Scarce)	320	640	960	2240	3920	5600
24-(11/42) Intro. & 1st app. Mr. Crime; classic Biro-c showing woman's head on fire being pushed onto hot stovetop burner	1300	2600	3900	6500	11,250	16,000
25-(1/43) 2nd app. Mr. Crime; classic '40s crime-c	148	296	444	947	1624	2300
26-(3/43) 3rd app. Mr. Crime	119	238	357	762	1306	1850
27-Classic Biro-c pushing man into hot oven	148	296	444	947	1624	2300
28-30: 30-Wood and Biro app.	86	172	258	546	936	1325
31,32,34-40	48	96	144	302	514	725
33-(5/44) Classic Biro hanging & hatchet-c	300	600	900	1950	3375	5000
41-(9/45) Origin & 1st app. Officer Common Sense	45	90	135	284	480	675
42-(11/45) Classic electrocution-c	84	168	252	538	919	1300
43-46,48-50: 44-50 are 68 pg. issues. 44-"Legs" Diamond story. 50-(3/47)-1st issue to advertise 5 million readers on front-c. 58-(12/47)-shows 6 million readers (these ads believed to have influenced the crime comic wave of 1948)	31	62	93	182	296	410
47-(9/46)-Electric chair-c	53	106	159	334	567	800
51-70: 58(12/47)-Thomas Dun, killer of thousands (1565) story. 63,64-Possible use in **SOTI**, pg. 306. 63-Contains Biro & Gleason self censorship code of 12 listed restrictions (5/48)	22	44	66	130	213	295
71-99: 87-Chip Gardner begins, ends #100. 87-99-Painted-c	17	34	51	100	158	215
100-Painted-c	19	38	57	111	176	240
101-104,107-110: 101,102-Painted-c. 102-Chip Gardner app.	14	28	42	82	121	160
105-Used in **POP**, pg. 84	15	30	45	90	140	190
106,114-Frazetta-a, 1 pg.	15	30	45	85	130	175
111-Used in **POP**, pgs. 80 & 81; injury-to-eye sty illo	18	36	54	103	162	220
112,113,115-130	12	24	36	69	97	125
131-140	11	22	33	62	86	110
141,142-Last pre-code issue; Kubert-a(1)	13	26	39	72	101	130
143-Kubert-a in one story	13	26	39	72	101	130
144-146	11	22	33	62	86	110
147-Last issue (scarce); Kubert-a	18	36	54	103	162	220
1(Golfing-1945)	10	20	30	58	79	100
The Best of...(1944, 128 pgs.)-Series contains 4 rebound issues	123	246	369	787	1344	1900
...1945 issue	81	162	243	518	884	1250
...1946-48 issues	61	122	183	390	670	950
...1949-50 issues	52	104	156	328	552	775
...1951-53 issues (25¢)	45	90	135	284	480	675

NOTE: *Many issues contain violent covers and stories. Who Dunit by **Guardineer**-39-42, 44-105, 108-110; Chip Gardner by **Bob Fujitani (Fuge)**-88-103. **Alderman** a-29, 41-44, 49. **Dan Barry** a-67, 75. **Charles Biro** c-1-76, 122, 142. **Dick Briefer** a-29(2), 30, 31, 33, 37, 39. **G. Colan** a-105. **Tony Dipreta** a-79, 90, 92. **Fuje** c-88, 89, 91-94, 96, 98, 99, 102, 103. **Fred Guardineer** a-51, 57, 58(2), 66-68, 71, 74, 79, 81, 90, 92. **Joe Kubert** c-143. **Landau** a-118. **Al Mandell** a-37. **Norman Maurer** a-29, 39, 41, 42. **McWilliams** a-91, 93, 95, 100-103. **Rudy Palais** a-30, 33, **Bob Powell** a-146, 147. **George Tuska** a-48-50(2ea.), 51, 52 56, 57(2), 58, 60-64, 66-68, 71, 74, 81. Painted c-87-103. Bondage c-43, 62, 98.*

CRIME EXPOSED
Marvel Comics (PPI)/Marvel Atlas Comics (PrPI): June, 1948; Dec, 1950 - No. 14, June, 1952

	GD	VG	FN	VF	VF/NM	NM-
1(6/48)	42	84	126	265	445	625
1(12/50)	28	56	84	168	274	380
2	18	36	54	107	169	230
3-9,11,14	16	32	48	92	144	195
10-Used in **POP**, pg. 81	17	34	51	98	154	210
12-Krigstein & Robinson-a	17	34	51	98	154	210
13-Used in **POP**, pg. 81; Krigstein-a	18	36	54	103	162	220

NOTE: ***Keller** a-8, 10. **Maneely** c-8. **Robinson** a-11, 12. **Sale** a-4. **Tuska** a-3, 4.*

CRIMEFIGHTERS
Marvel Comics (CmPS 1-3/CCC 4-10): Apr, 1948 - No. 10, Nov, 1949

	GD	VG	FN	VF	VF/NM	NM-
1-Some copies are undated & could be reprints	37	74	111	218	354	490
2,3: 3-Morphine addict story	19	38	57	111	176	240
4-10: 4-Early John Buscema-a. 6-Anti-Wertham editorial. 9,10-Photo-c	15	30	45	90	140	190

CRIME FIGHTERS (...Always Win)
Atlas Comics (CnPC): No. 11, Sept, 1954 - No. 13, Jan, 1955

	GD	VG	FN	VF	VF/NM	NM-
11-13: 11-Maneely-a,13-Pakula, Reinman, Severin-a	15	30	45	88	137	185

CRIME-FIGHTING DETECTIVE (Shock Detective Cases No. 20 on; formerly Criminals on the Run)
Star Publications: No. 11, Apr-May, 1950 - No. 19, June, 1952 (Based on true crime cases)

	GD	VG	FN	VF	VF/NM	NM-
11-L. B. Cole-c/a (2 pgs.); L. B. Cole-c on all	28	56	84	165	270	375
12,13,15-19: 17-Young King Cole & Dr. Doom app.	19	38	57	112	179	245
14-L. B. Cole-c/a, r/Law-Crime #2	20	40	60	120	195	270

CRIME FILES
Standard Comics: No. 5, Sept, 1952 - No. 6, Nov, 1952

	GD	VG	FN	VF	VF/NM	NM-
5-1pg. Alex Toth-a; used in **SOTI**, pg. 4 (text)	30	60	90	177	289	400
6-Sekowsky-a	16	32	48	92	144	195

Crime Must Pay the Penalty #23 © ACE

Crime Reporter #2 © STJ

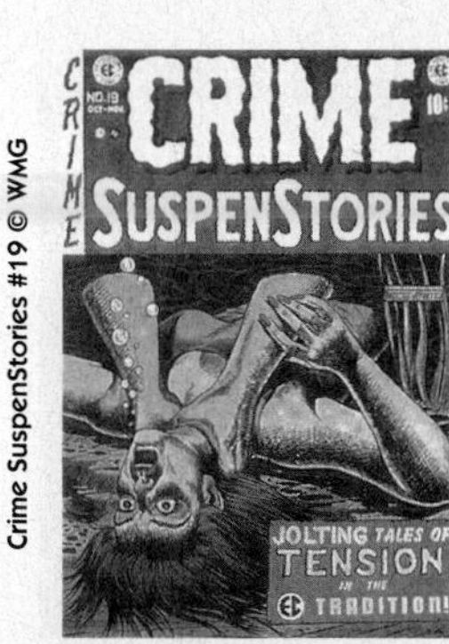

Crime SuspenStories #19 © WMG

	GD	VG	FN	VF	VF/NM	NM-
	2.0	4.0	6.0	8.0	9.0	9.2

CRIME ILLUSTRATED (Magazine)
E. C. Comics: Nov-Dec, 1955 - No. 2, Spring, 1956 (25¢, Adult Suspense Stories on-c)

1-Ingels & Crandall-a 25 50 75 150 245 340
2-Ingels & Crandall-a 17 34 51 98 154 210

NOTE: ***Craig** a-2. **Crandall** a-1, 2; c-2. **Evans** a-1. **Davis** a-2. **Ingels** a-1, 2. **Krigstein/Crandall** a-1. **Orlando** a-1, 2; c-1.*

CRIME INCORPORATED (Formerly Crimes Incorporated)
Fox Feature Syndicate: No. 2, Aug, 1950; No. 3, Aug, 1951

2 32 64 96 192 314 435
3(1951)-Hollingsworth-a 21 42 63 126 206 285

CRIME MACHINE (Magazine reprints pre-code crime and gangster comics)
Skywald Publications: Feb, 1971 - No. 2, May, 1971 (B&W, 68 pgs., roundbound)

1-Kubert-a(2)(r)(Avon); bikini girl in cake-c 6 12 18 40 73 105
2-Torres, Wildey-a; violent-c/a 4 8 12 28 47 65

CRIME MUST LOSE! (Formerly Sports Action?)
Sports Action (Atlas Comics): No. 4, Oct, 1950 - No. 12, April, 1952

4-Ann Brewster-a in all; c-used in N.Y. Legis. Comm. documents
26 52 78 152 249 345
5-10,12: 9-Robinson-a 18 36 54 105 165 225
11-Used in **POP**, pg. 89 19 38 57 109 172 235

CRIME MUST PAY THE PENALTY (Formerly Four Favorites; Penalty #47, 48)
Ace Magazines (Current Books): No. 33, Feb, 1948; No. 2, Jun, 1948 - No. 48, Jan, 1956

33(#1, 2/48)-Becomes Four Teeners #34? 50 100 150 315 533 750
2(6/48)-Extreme violence; Palais-a? 31 62 93 186 303 420
3,4,8: 3- "Frisco Mary" story used in Senate Investigation report, pg. 7. 4,8-Transvestism stories 23 46 69 136 223 310
5-7,9,10 18 36 54 107 169 230
11-19 17 34 51 98 154 210
20-Drug story "Dealers in White Death" 26 52 78 156 256 355
21-32,34-40,42-48: 44-Last pre-code 14 28 42 82 121 160
33(7/53)- "Dell Fabry-Junk King" drug story; mentioned in Love and Death
21 42 63 124 202 280
41-reprints "Dealers in White Death" 15 30 45 84 127 170

NOTE: ***Cameron** a-29-31, 34, 35, 39-41. **Colan** a-20, 31. **Kremer** a-3, 37r. **Larsen** a-32. **Palais** a-5?,37.*

CRIME MUST STOP
Hillman Periodicals: October, 1952 (52 pgs.)

V1#1(Scarce)-Similar to Monster Crime; Mort Lawrence, Krigstein-a
135 270 405 864 1482 2100

CRIME MYSTERIES (Secret Mysteries #16 on; combined with Crime Smashers #7 on)
Ribage Publ. Corp. (Trojan Magazines): May, 1952 - No. 15, Sept, 1954

1-Transvestism story; crime & terror stories begin 129 258 387 826 1413 2000
2-Marijuana story (7/52) 97 194 291 621 1061 1500
3-One pg. Frazetta-a 61 122 183 390 670 950
4-Cover shows girl in bondage having her blood drained; 1 pg. Frazetta-a
300 600 900 2010 3505 5000
5-10 50 100 150 315 533 750
11,12,14 43 86 129 271 461 650
13-(5/54)-Angelo Torres 1st comic work (inks over Check's pencils); Check-a
65 130 195 416 708 1000
15-Acid in face-c 71 142 213 454 777 1100

NOTE: ***Fass** a-13; c-4, 6, 10. **Hollingsworth** a-10-13, 15; c-2, 12, 13, 15. **Kiefer** a-4. **Woodbridge** a-13? Bondage-c-1, 8, 12.*

CRIME ON THE RUN (See Approved Comics #8)

CRIME ON THE WATERFRONT (Formerly Famous Gangsters)
Realistic Publications: No. 4, May, 1952 (Painted cover)

4 37 74 111 222 361 500

CRIME PATROL (Formerly International #1-5; International Crime Patrol #6; becomes Crypt of Terror #17 on)
E. C. Comics: No. 7, Summer, 1948 - No. 16, Feb-Mar, 1950

7-Intro. Captain Crime 103 206 309 659 1130 1600
8-14: 12-Ingels-a 87 174 261 553 952 1350
15-Intro. of Crypt Keeper (inspired by Witches Tales radio show) & Crypt of Terror (see Tales From the Crypt #33 for origin); used by N.Y. Legis. Comm.; last pg. Feldstein-a
389 778 1167 2723 4762 6800
16-2nd Crypt Keeper app.; Roussos-a 258 516 774 1651 2826 4000

NOTE: ***Craig** c/a in most issues. **Feldstein** a-9-16. **Kiefer** a-8, 10, 11. **Moldoff** a-7.*

CRIME PATROL
Gemstone Publishing: Apr, 2000 - No. 10, Jan, 2001 ($2.50)

1-10: E.C. reprints 4.00

Volume 1,2 (2000, $13.50) 1-r/#1-5. 2-r/#6-10 14.00

CRIME PHOTOGRAPHER (See Casey...)

CRIME REPORTER
St. John Publ. Co.: Aug, 1948 - No. 3, Dec, 1948 (Indicia shows Oct.)

1-Drug club story 94 188 282 597 1024 1450
2-Used in **SOTI**: illo- "Children told me what the man was going to do with the red-hot poker;" r/Dynamic #17 with editing; Baker-c; Tuska-a 258 516 774 1651 2826 4000
3-Baker-c; Tuska-a 100 200 300 635 1093 1550

CRIMES BY WOMEN
Fox Feature Syndicate: June, 1948 - No. 15, Aug, 1951; 1954 (True crime cases)

1-True story of Bonnie Parker 135 270 405 864 1482 2100
2 81 162 243 518 884 1250
3-Used in **SOTI**, pg. 234 119 238 357 762 1306 1850
4,5,7-9,11-15: 8-Used in **POP**. 14-Bondage-c 73 146 219 467 796 1125
6-Classic girl fight-c; acid-in-face panel 135 270 405 864 1482 2100
10-Used in **SOTI**, pg. 72; girl fight-c 90 180 270 576 988 1400
54(M.S. Publ.-'54)-Reprint; (formerly My Love Secret)
31 62 93 186 303 420

CRIMES INCORPORATED (Formerly My Past)
Fox Feature Syndicate: No. 12, June, 1950 (Crime Incorporated No. 2 on)

12 34 68 102 199 325 450

CRIMES INCORPORATED (See Fox Giants)

CRIME SMASHER (See Whiz #76)
Fawcett Publications: Summer, 1948 (one-shot)

1-Formerly Spy Smasher 45 90 135 284 480 675

CRIME SMASHERS (Becomes Secret Mysteries No. 16 on)
Ribage Publishing Corp.(Trojan Magazines): Oct, 1950 - No. 15, Mar, 1953

1-Used in **SOTI**, pg. 19,20, & illo "A girl raped and murdered;" Sally the Sleuth begins
100 200 300 635 1093 1550
2-Kubert-c 53 106 159 334 567 800
3,4 45 90 135 284 480 625
5-Wood-a 52 104 156 328 552 775
6,8-11: 8-Lingerie panel 34 68 102 204 332 460
7-Female heroin junkie story 39 78 117 240 395 550
12-Injury to eye panel; 1 pg. Frazetta-a 37 74 111 219 357 495
13-Used in **POP**, pgs. 79,80; 1 pg. Frazetta-a 37 74 111 219 357 495
14,15 29 58 87 174 285 395

NOTE: ***Hollingsworth** a-14. **Kiefer** a-15. Bondage c-7, 9.*

CRIME SUSPENSTORIES (Formerly Vault of Horror No. 12-14)
E. C. Comics: No. 15, Oct-Nov, 1950 - No. 27, Feb-Mar, 1955

15-Identical to #1 in content; #1 printed on outside front cover. #15 (formerly "The Vault of Horror") printed and blackened out on inside front cover with Vol. 1, No. 1 printed over it. Evidently, several of No. 15 were printed before a decision was made not to drop the Vault of Horror and Haunt of Fear series. The print run was stopped on No. 15 and continued on No. 1. All of the No. 15 issues were changed as described above.
217 434 651 1736 2768 3800
1 166 332 498 1328 2114 2900
2 80 160 240 640 1020 1400
3-5: 3-Poe adaptation. 3-Old Witch stories begin 60 120 180 480 765 1050
6-10: 9-Craig bio. 53 106 159 424 675 925
11,12,14,15: 15-The Old Witch guest stars 41 82 123 328 527 725
13,16-Williamson-a 43 86 129 344 547 750
17-Classic "bullet in the head" cover; Williamson/Frazetta-a (6 pgs.); Williamson bio.
89 178 267 712 1131 1550
18,19: 19-Used in **SOTI**, pg. 235 40 80 120 320 510 700
20-Classic hanging cover used in **SOTI**, illo "Cover of a children's comic book"; issue was on display at the 1954 Senate hearing 171 342 513 1368 2184 3000
21,24-26: 24- "Food For Thought" similar to "Cave In" in Amazing Detective Cases #13 (1952)
30 60 90 240 383 525
22-Classic ax decapitation-c; exhibited in the 1954 Senate Investigation on juvenile delinquency trial; decapitation story 1029 2058 3087 8232 13,116 18,000

NOTE: *Senator Kefauver questioning Bill Gaines: "Here is your May issue. This seems to be a man with a bloody ax holding a woman's head up which has been severed from her body. Do you think that's in good taste?" Gaines: "Yes I do - for the cover of a horror comic. A cover in bad taste, for example, might be defined as holding her head a little higher so that blood could be seen dripping from it and moving the body over a little further so that the neck of the body could be seen to be bloody." It was actually drawn this way first and Gaines had Craig change it to the published version.*

23-Used in Senate investigation on juvenile delinquency
46 92 138 368 584 800
27-Last issue (Low distribution) 51 102 153 408 654 900

NOTE: ***Craig** a-1-21; c-1-18, 20-22. **Crandall** a-18-26. **Davis** a-4, 5, 7, 9-12, 20. **Elder** a-17,18. **Evans** a-15, 19, 21, 23, 25, 27; c-23, 24. **Feldstein** c-19. **Ingels** a-1-12, 14, 15, 27. **Kamen** a-2, 4-18, 20-27; c-25-27. **Krigstein** a-22, 24, 25, 27. **Kurtzman** a-1, 3. **Orlando** a-16, 22, 24, 26. **Wood** a-1, 3. Issues No. 1-3 were printed in Canada as "Weird Suspenstories." Issues No. 11-15 have E. C. "quickie" stories. No. 25 contains the famous "Are You a Red Dupe?"*

Criminal V2 #1 © Brubaker & Phillips

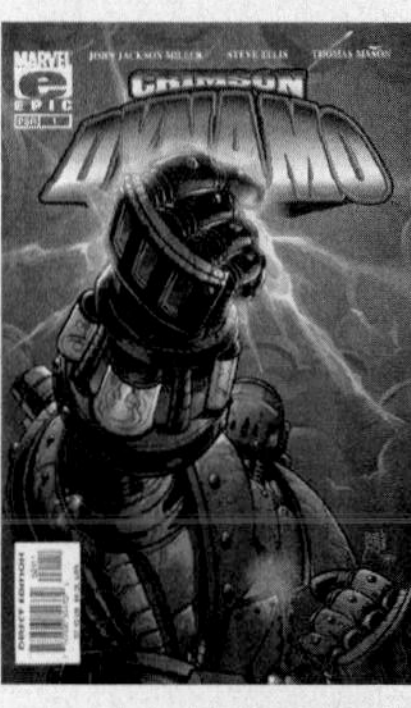

Crimson Dynamo #1 © MAR

Crisis on Infinite Earths Giant #2 © DC

	GD	VG	FN	VF	VF/NM	NM-
	2.0	4.0	6.0	8.0	9.0	9.2

editorial. Ray Bradbury adaptations-15, 17.

CRIME SUSPENSTORIES
Russ Cochran/Gemstone Publ.: Nov, 1992 - No. 27, May, 1999 ($1.50/$2.00/$2.50)

1-27: Reprints Crime SuspenStories series 4.00

CRIMINAL (Also see Criminal: The Sinners)
Marvel Comics (Icon): Oct, 2006 - No. 10, Oct, 2007 ($2.99)
Volume 2: Feb, 2008 - No. 7, Nov, 2008 ($3.50)

1-10-Ed Brubaker-s/Sean Phillips-a/c 3.00
Volume 2: 1-7-Brubaker-s/Phillips-a 3.50
...: Tenth Anniversary Special Edition (Image Comics, 4/16, $5.99) Brubaker-s/Phillips-a; 1970s Kung Fu magazine pastishe within story; intro. Fang the Kung Fu Werewolf 6.00
...: The Special Edition (Image Comics, 2/15, $4.99) Brubaker-s/Phillips-a; 1970s Conan B&W magazine pastishe within story 5.00
... Vol. 1: Coward TPB (2007, $14.99) r/#1-5; intro. by Tom Fontana 15.00
... Vol. 2: Lawless TPB (2007, $14.99) r/#6-10; intro. by Frank Miller 15.00
... Vol. 3: The Dead and the Dying TPB (2008, $11.99) r/V2#1-4; intro. by John Singleton 12.00

CRIMINAL
Image Comics: Jan, 2019 - No. 12, Jan, 2020 ($3.99)

1-12-Ed Brubaker-s/Sean Phillips-a/c 4.00

CRIMINAL MACABRE: (limited series and one-shots)
Dark Horse Comics: ($2.99)

...: Cellblock 666 (9/08 - No. 4, 5/09)(#25-28 in series) 1-4-Niles-s/Stakal-a/Bradstreet-c 3.00
...: Die, Die, My Darling (4/12, $3.50) reprints serial from DHP #4-6; Staples-c 3.50
...: Feat of Clay (6/06, $2.99) Niles-s/Hotz-a/c 3.00
Free Comic Book Day: Criminal Macabre - Call Me Monster (5/11) flip book w/Baltimore 3.00
...: My Demon Baby (9/07 - No. 4, 4/08)(#21-24 in the series) 1-4-Niles-s/Stakal-a 3.00
...: No Peace For Dead Men (9/11, $3.99) Niles-s/Mitten-a/Staples-c 4.00
...: The Big Bleed Out (12/19 - No. 4, 3/20 $3.99) 1-4-Niles-s/Németh-a 4.00
...: The Eyes of Frankenstein (9/13 - No. 4, 12/13 $3.99) 1-4-Niles-s/Mitten-a 4.00
...: The Goon (7/11, $3.99) Niles-s/Mitten-a; covers by Powell & Staples 4.00
...: They Fight By Night (11/12, $3.99) reprints serial from DHP #10-13; Staples-c 4.00
...: Two Red Eyes (12/06 - No. 4, 3/07) 1-4-Niles-s/Hotz-a/Bradstreet-c 3.00

CRIMINAL MACABRE: A CAL MCDONALD MYSTERY (Also see Last Train to Deadsville)
Dark Horse Comics: May, 2003 - No. 5, Sept, 2003 ($2.99)

1-5-Niles-s/Templesmith-a 3.00

CRIMINAL MACABRE: FINAL NIGHT - THE 30 DAYS OF NIGHT CROSSOVER
Dark Horse Comics: Dec, 2012 - No. 4, Mar, 2013 ($3.99, limited series)

1-4-Niles-s/Mitten-a/Erickson-c 4.00

CRIMINAL MACABRE:THE THIRD CHILD
Dark Horse Comics: Sept, 2014 - No. 4, Dec, 2014 ($3.99, limited series)

1-4-Niles-s/Mitten-a/Erickson-c 4.00

CRIMINALS ON THE RUN (Formerly Young King Cole) (Crime Fighting Detective No. 11 on)
Premium Group (Novelty Press): V4#1, Aug-Sep, 1948-#10, Dec-Jan, 1949-50

	GD	VG	FN	VF	VF/NM	NM-
V4#1-Young King Cole continues	34	68	102	204	332	460
2-6: 6-Dr. Doom app.	27	54	81	162	266	370
7-Classic "Fish in the Face" c by L. B. Cole	148	296	444	940	1620	2300
V5#1,2 (#8,9),10: 9,10-L. B. Cole-c	24	48	72	142	234	325

NOTE: *Most issues have* **L. B. Cole** *covers.* **McWilliams** *a-V4#6, 7, V5#2, 10; c-V4#5.*

CRIMINAL: THE LAST OF THE INNOCENT
Marvel Comics (Icon): Jun, 2011 - No. 4, Sept, 2011 ($3.50)

1-4-Ed Brubaker-s/Sean Phillips-a/c 3.50

CRIMINAL: THE SINNERS
Marvel Comics (Icon): Sept, 2009 - No. 5, Mar, 2010 ($3.50)

1-5-Ed Brubaker-s/Sean Phillips-a/c 3.50

CRIMSON (Also see Cliffhanger #0)
Image Comics (Cliffhanger Productions): May, 1998 - No. 7, Dec, 1998;
DC Comics (Cliffhanger Prod.): No. 8, Mar, 1999 - No. 24, Apr, 2001 ($2.50)

1-Humberto Ramos-a/Augustyn-s 5.00
1-Variant-c by Warren 8.00
1-Chromium-c 15.00
2-Ramos-c with street crowd, 2-Variant-c by Art Adams 4.00
2-Dynamic Forces CrimsonChrome cover 15.00
3-7: 3-Ramos Moon background-c. 7-Three covers by Ramos, Madureira, & Campbell 3.50
8-23: 8-First DC issue 3.00
24-($3.50) Final issue; wraparound-c 4.00
DF Premiere Ed. 1998 ($6.95) covers by Ramos and Jae Lee 7.00
Crimson: Scarlet X Blood on the Moon (10/99, $3.95) 4.00
Crimson Sourcebook (11/99, $2.95) Pin-ups and info 3.00
Earth Angel TPB (2001, $14.95) r/#13-18 15.00
Heaven and Earth TPB (1/00, $14.95) r/#7-12 15.00
Loyalty and Loss TPB ('99, $12.95) r/#1-6 15.00
Redemption TPB ('01, $14.95) r/#19-24 15.00

CRIMSON AVENGER, THE (See Detective Comics #20 for 1st app.)(Also see Leading Comics #1 & World's Best/Finest Comics)
DC Comics: June, 1988 - No. 4, Sept, 1988 ($1.00, limited series)

1-4 4.00

CRIMSON DYNAMO
Marvel Comics (Epic): Oct, 2003 - No. 6, Apr, 2004 ($2.50/$2.99)

1-4,6: 1-John Jackson Miller-s/Steve Ellis-a/c 3.00
5-($2.99) Iron Man-c/app. 4.00

CRIMSON LOTUS
Dark Horse Comics: Nov, 2018 - No. 5, Mar, 2019 ($3.99, limited series)

1-5-John Arcudi-s/Mindy Lee-a/Tonci Zonjic-c 4.00

CRIMSON PLAGUE
Event Comics: June, 1997 ($2.95, unfinished mini-series)

1-George Perez-a 3.00

CRIMSON PLAGUE (George Pérez's...)
Image Comics (Gorilla): June, 2000 - No. 2, Aug, 2000 ($2.95, mini-series)

1-George Pérez-a; reprints 6/97 issue with 16 new pages 3.00
2-($2.50) 3.00

CRISIS AFTERMATH: THE BATTLE FOR BLUDHAVEN (Also see Infinite Crisis)
DC Comics: Jun, 2006 - No. 6, Sept, 2006 ($2.99, limited series)

1-Atomic Knights return; Teen Titans app.; Jurgens-a/Acuna-c 4.00
1-2nd printing with pencil cover 3.00
2-6: 2-Intro S.H.A.D.E. (new Freedom Fighters) 3.00
TPB (2007, $12.99) r/#1-6 13.00

CRISIS AFTERMATH: THE SPECTRE (Also see Infinite Crisis, Gotham Central and Tales of the Unexpected)
DC Comics: Jul, 2006 - No. 3, Sept, 2006 ($2.99, limited series)

1-3-Crispus Allen becomes the Spectre; Pfeifer-s/Chiang-a/c 3.00
TPB (2007, $12.99) r/#1-3 and Tales of the Unexpected #1-3 13.00

CRISIS OF INFINITE CEREBI (Cerebus figures placed over original Gustave Doré artwork)
Aardvark-Vanaheim: Sept, 2018 ($4.00, B&W, one-shot)

1-Crisis on Infinite Earths #7-c swipe 4.00

CRISIS ON INFINITE EARTHS (Also see Official... Index and Legends of the DC Universe)
DC Comics: Apr, 1985 - No. 12, Mar, 1986 (maxi-series)

	GD	VG	FN	VF	VF/NM	NM-
1-1st DC app. Blue Beetle & Detective Karp from Charlton; Pérez-c on all	3	6	9	15	22	28
2-6: 6-Intro Charlton's Capt. Atom, Nightshade, Question, Judomaster, Peacemaker & Thunderbolt into DC Universe	2	4	6	8	11	14
7-Double size; death of Supergirl	3	6	9	17	26	35
8-Death of the Flash (Barry Allen)	3	6	9	17	25	34
8-Facsimile Edition (2019, $3.99) Reprints issue with original ads and letter column						4.00
9-11: 9-Intro. Charlton's Ghost into DC Universe. 10-Intro. Charlton's Banshee, Dr. Spectro, Image, Punch & Jewelee into DC Universe; Starman (Prince Gavyn) dies	2	4	6	8	10	12
12-(52 pgs.)-Deaths of Dove, Kole, Lori Lemaris, Sunburst, G.A. Robin & Huntress; Kid Flash becomes new Flash; 3rd & final DC app. of the 3 Lt. Marvels; Green Fury gets new look (becomes Green Flame in Infinity, Inc. #32)	2	4	6	9	13	16

Slipcased Hardcover (1998, $99.95) Wraparound dust-jacket cover pencilled by Pérez and painted by Alex Ross; sketch pages by Pérez; Wolfman intro.; afterword by Giordano 125.00
TPB (2000, $29.95) Wraparound-c by Pérez and Ross 30.00
NOTE: *Crossover issues: All Star Squadron 50-56,60; Amethyst 13; Blue Devil 17,18; DC Comics Presents 78,86-88,95; Detective Comics 558; Fury of Firestorm 41,42; G.I. Combat 274; Green Lantern 194-196,198; Infinity, Inc. 18-25 & Annual 1, Justice League of America 244,245 & Annual 3; Legion of Super-Heroes 16,18; Losers Special 1; New Teen Titans 13,14; Omega Men 31,33; Superman 413-415; Swamp Thing 44,46; Wonder Woman 327-329.*

CRISIS ON INFINITE EARTHS GIANT
DC Comics: 2019 - No. 2, 2020 ($4.99, 100 pgs., squarebound, Mass Market & Direct Market editions exist for each issue, with different covers)

1,2: 1-Two new stories tied to TV event plus reprints #1,7. 2-Include reprints #8,11 5.00

CRISIS ON MULTIPLE EARTHS
DC Comics: 2002 - 2010 ($14.95, trade paperbacks)

TPB-(2003) Reprints 1st 4 Silver Age JLA/JSA crossovers from J.L.ofA. #21,22; 29,30; 37,38; 46,47; new painted-c by Alex Ross; intro. by Mark Waid 15.00
Volume 2 (2003, $14.95) r/J.L.ofA. #55,56; 64,65; 73,74; 82,83; new Ordway-c 15.00
Volume 3 (2004, $14.95) r/J.L.ofA. #91,92; 100-102; 107,108; 113; Wein intro., Ross-c 15.00

Critical Role Vox Machina Origins #4 © CRP

Crossover #1 © Cates & Shaw

Crow: Hack/Slash #1 © O'Barr & H/S

GD VG FN VF VF/NM NM-
2.0 4.0 6.0 8.0 9.0 9.2

Volume 4 (2006, $14.99) r/J.L.ofA. #123-124 (Earth-Prime),135-137 (Fawcett's Shazam characters), 147-148 (Legion of Super-Heroes); Ross-c 15.00
Volume 5 (2010, $19.99) r/J.L.ofA. #159-160 (Jonah Hex, Enemy Ace), #171-172 (Murder of Mr. Terrific), 1#83-185 (New Gods & Darkseid); Pérez-c 20.00
... The Team-Ups Volume 1 (2005, $14.99) r/Flash #123,129,137,151; Showcase #55,56; Green Lantern #40, Brave and the Bold #61 and Spectre #7; new Ordway-c 15.00

CRITICAL MASS (See A Shadowline Saga: Critical Mass)

CRITICAL ROLE VOX MACHINA ORIGINS (Based on characters from the D&D web series)
Dark Horse Comics: Jul, 2019 - No. 6, Apr, 2020 ($3.99, limited series)
1-6-Matthew Mercer & Jody Houser-s/Olivia Samson 4.00
(Series) III 1-(2/21, $3.99) Mercer & Houser-s/Samson-a 4.00

CRITTER
Big Dog Press: Jul, 2011 - No. 4, 2011; Jun, 2012 - No. 20, Apr, 2014 ($3.50)
1-4-Multiple covers on all 3.50
Vol. 2 1-20-Multiple covers on all 3.50

CRITTER
Aspen MLT: Jul, 2015 - No. 4, Oct, 2015 ($3.99)
1-4-Reprints the 2011 series; multiple covers on all 4.00

CRITTERS (Also see Usagi Yojimbo Summer Special)
Fantagraphics Books: 1986 - No. 50, 1990 ($1.70/$2.00, B&W)
1-Cutey Bunny, Usagi Yojimbo app. 3 6 9 17 26 35
2,4,5,8,9 6.00
3,6,7,10-Usagi Yojimbo app. 1 3 4 6 8 10
11,14-Usagi Yojimbo app. 11-Christmas Special (68 pgs.) 6.00
12,13,15-22,24-37,39,40: 22-Watchmen parody; two diff. covers exist 3.00
23-With Alan Moore Flexi-disc ($3.95) 5.00
38-($2.75-c) Usagi Yojimbo app. 5.00
41-49 4.00
50 ($4.95, 84 pgs.)-Neil the Horse, Capt. Jack, Sam & Max & Usagi Yojimbo app.; Quagmire, Shaw-a 1 2 3 4 5 7
Special 1 (1/88, $2.00) 4.00

CRONE
Dark Horse Comics: Nov, 2019 - No. 5, Mar, 2020 ($3.99, limited series)
1-5-Dennis Culver-s/Justin Greenwood-a 4.00

CROSS
Dark Horse Comics: No. 0, Oct, 1995 - No. 6, Apr, 1995 ($2.95, limited series, mature)
0-6: Darrow-c & Vachss scripts in all 3.00

CROSS AND THE SWITCHBLADE, THE
Spire Christian Comics (Fleming H. Revell Co.): 1972 (35-49¢)
1-Some issues have nn 3 6 9 19 30 40

CROSS BRONX, THE
Image Comics: Sept, 2006 - No. 4, Dec, 2006 ($2.99, limited series)
1-4: 1-Oeming-a/c; Oeming & Brandon-s; Ribic var-c. 2-Johnson var-c. 4-Mack var-c 3.00

CROSSFIRE
Spire Christian Comics (Fleming H. Revell Co.): 1973 (39/49¢)
nn 2 4 6 13 18 22

CROSSFIRE (Also see DNAgents)
Eclipse Comics: 5/84 - No. 17, 3/86; No. 18, 1/87 - No. 26, 2/88 ($1.50, Baxter paper) (#18-26 are B&W)
1-11,14-26: 1-DNAgents x-over; Spiegle-c/a begins 4.00
12-Death of Marilyn Monroe; Dave Stevens-c 3 6 9 15 22 28
13-Death of Marilyn Monroe 1 2 3 5 6 8

CROSSFIRE AND RAINBOW (Also see DNAgents)
Eclipse Comics: June, 1986 - No. 4, Sept, 1986 ($1.25, deluxe format)
1-3: Spiegle-a 4.00
4-Elvis cover by Dave Stevens 6.00

CROSSGEN...
CrossGeneration Comics
CrossGenesis (1/00) Previews CrossGen universe; cover gallery 3.00
...Primer (1/00) Wizard supplement; intro. to the CrossGen universe 3.00
...Sampler (2/00) Retailer preview book 3.00

CROSSGEN CHRONICLES
CrossGeneration Comics: June, 2000 - No. 8, Jul, 2002 ($3.95)
1-Intro. to CrossGen characters & company 4.00
1-(no cover price) same contents, customer preview 4.00
2-8: 2-(3/01) George Pérez-c/a. 3-5-Pérez-a/Waid-s. 6,8-Maroto-c/a. 7-Nebres-c/a 4.00

CROSSING MIDNIGHT
DC Comics (Vertigo): Jan, 2007 - No. 19, Jul, 2008 ($2.99)
1-19: 1-Carey-s/Fern-a/Williams III-c. 10-12-Nguyen-a 3.00
...: Cut Here TPB (2007, $9.99) r/#1-5 10.00
...: A Map of Midnight TPB (2008, $14.99) r/#6-12; afterword by Carey 15.00
...: The Sword in the Soul TPB (2008, $14.99) r/#13-19 15.00

CROSSING THE ROCKIES (See Classics Illustrated Special Issue)

CROSSOVER
Image Comics: Nov, 2020 - Present ($3.99)
1-4-Donny Cates-s/Geoff Shaw-a. 3,4-Madman app. 4.00

CROSSOVERS, THE
CrossGeneration Comics: Feb, 2003 - No. 12 ($2.95)
1-12-Robert Rodi-s. 1-6-Mauricet & Ernie Colon-a. 7-Staton-a begins 3.00
Vol. 1: Cross Currents (2003, $9.95) digest-sized reprints #1-6 10.00

CROSSWIND
Image Comics: Jun, 2017 - No. 6, Jan, 2018 ($3.99)
1-6-Gail Simone-s/Cat Staggs-a 4.00

CROW, THE (Also see Caliber Presents)
Caliber Press: Feb, 1989 - No. 4, 1989 ($1.95, B&W, limited series)
1-James O'Barr-c/a/scripts 23 46 69 161 356 550
1-3-2nd printing 3 6 9 17 26 35
2 6 12 18 38 69 100
2-3rd printing 6.00
3,4 5 10 15 34 60 85

CROW, THE
Tundra Publishing, Ltd.: Jan, 1992 - No. 3, 1992 ($4.95, B&W, 68 pgs.)
1-r/#1,2 of Caliber series 3 6 9 15 22 28
2,3: 2-r/#3 of Caliber series w/new material. 3-All new material 2 4 6 8 11 14

CROW, THE
Kitchen Sink Press: 1/96 - No. 3, 3/96 ($2.95, B&W)
1-James O'Barr-c/scripts in all 1 3 4 6 8 10
2,3 6.00
#0-A Cycle of Shattered Lives (12/98, $3.50) new story by O'Barr 4.00

CROW, THE
Image Comics (Todd McFarlane Prod.): Feb, 1999 - No. 10, Nov, 1999 ($2.50)
1-Two covers by McFarlane and Kent Williams; Muth-s in all 1 3 4 6 8 10
2-10: 2-6,10-Paul Lee-a 4.00
Book 1 - Vengeance (2000, $10.95, TPB) r/#1-3,5,6 15.00
Book 2 - Evil Beyond Reach (2000, $10.95, TPB) r/#4,7-10 15.00
Todd McFarlane Presents The Crow Magazine 1 (3/00, $4.95) 1 2 3 5 6 8

CROW, THE: CITY OF ANGELS (Movie)
Kitchen Sink Press: July, 1996 - No. 3, Sept, 1996 ($2.95, limited series)
1-3: Adaptation of film; two-c (photo & illos.). 1-Vincent Perez interview 4.00

CROW, THE: CURARE
IDW Publishing: Jun, 2013 - No. 3, Aug, 2013 ($3.99, limited series)
1-3-James O'Barr-s/Antoine Dodé-a; multiple covers on each 4.00

CROW, THE: DEATH AND REBIRTH
IDW Publishing: Jul, 2012 - No. 5, Nov, 2012 ($3.99, limited series)
1-5-Shirley-s/Colden-a; multiple covers on each 4.00

CROW, THE: FLESH AND BLOOD
Kitchen Sink Press: May, 1996 - No. 3, July, 1996 ($2.95, limited series)
1-James O'Barr-c on all 1 2 3 5 6 8
2,3 4.00

CROW: HACK / SLASH
IDW Publishing: Jun, 2019 - No. 4, Sept, 2019 ($3.99, limited series)
1-4-Tim Seeley-s/Jim Terry-a; multiple covers on each 4.00

CROW: HARK THE HERALD
IDW Publishing: Nov, 2019 ($4.99, one-shot)
1-Tim Seeley-s/Meredith Laxton-a; four covers 5.00

CROW: LETHE
IDW Publishing: Feb, 2020 - Present ($3.99, limited series)
1-Tim Seeley-s/Ilias Kyriazis-a; four covers 4.00

Crown Comics #15 © Golfing/McCombs

The Crusades #17 © Seagle & Jones

Cryptocracy #5 © BCC & Woods

CROW, THE: MEMENTO MORI
IDW Publishing: Mar, 2018 - No. 4, Jun, 2018 ($3.99, limited series)

	GD 2.0	VG 4.0	FN 6.0	VF 8.0	VF/NM 9.0	NM- 9.2
1-4-Recchioni-s/Dell'edera-a in all; back-up short stories in each by various						4.00

CROW, THE: PESTILENCE
IDW Publishing: Mar, 2014 - No. 4, Jun, 2014 ($3.99, limited series)

	GD 2.0	VG 4.0	FN 6.0	VF 8.0	VF/NM 9.0	NM- 9.2
1-4-Frank Bill-s/Drew Moss-a; two covers						4.00

CROW, THE: RAZOR - KILL THE PAIN
London Night Studios: Apr, 1998 - No. 3, July, 1998 ($2.95, B&W, lim. series)

	GD 2.0	VG 4.0	FN 6.0	VF 8.0	VF/NM 9.0	NM- 9.2
1-Hartsoe-s/O'Barr-painted-c	1	2	3	5	6	8
2,3-Hartsoe-s/O'Barr-painted-c						4.00
0(10/98) Dorien painted-c, Finale (2/99)						4.00
The Lost Chapter (2/99, $4.95), Tour Book-(12/97) pin-ups; 4 diff.-c	1	2	3	5	6	8

CROW, THE: SKINNING THE WOLVES
IDW Publishing: Dec, 2012 - No. 3, Feb, 2013 ($3.99, limited series)

	GD 2.0	VG 4.0	FN 6.0	VF 8.0	VF/NM 9.0	NM- 9.2
1-3-James O'Barr-s/Jim Terry-s/a; multiple covers on each						4.00

CROW, THE: WAKING NIGHTMARES
Kitchen Sink Press: Jan, 1997 - No. 4, 1998 ($2.95, B&W, limited series)

	GD 2.0	VG 4.0	FN 6.0	VF 8.0	VF/NM 9.0	NM- 9.2
1-Miran Kim-c on all	1	3	4	6	8	10
2-4						5.00

CROW, THE: WILD JUSTICE
Kitchen Sink Press: Oct, 1996 - No. 3, Dec, 1996 ($2.95, B&W, limited series)

	GD 2.0	VG 4.0	FN 6.0	VF 8.0	VF/NM 9.0	NM- 9.2
1-Prosser-s/Adlard-a in all	1	3	4	6	8	10
2,3						5.00

CROWN COMICS (Also see Vooda)
Golfing/McCombs Publ.: Wint, 1944-45; No. 2, Sum, 1945 - No. 19, July, 1949

	GD 2.0	VG 4.0	FN 6.0	VF 8.0	VF/NM 9.0	NM- 9.2
1- "The Oblong Box" E.A. Poe adaptation	55	110	165	352	601	850
2-Baker-a	36	72	108	216	350	485
3-Baker-a; Voodah by Baker; racist-c	45	90	135	284	480	675
4-6-Baker-c/a; Voodah app. #4,5	41	82	123	256	428	600
7-Feldstein, Baker, Kamen-a; Baker-c	53	106	159	334	567	800
8-Baker-a; Voodah app.	32	64	96	188	307	425
9-11,13-19: Voodah in #10-19. 13-New logo	21	42	63	122	199	275
12-Master Marvin by Feldstein, Starr-a; Voodah-c	21	42	63	126	206	285

NOTE: ***Bolle*** *a-11, 13-16, 18, 19; c-11p, 15.* ***Powell*** *a-19.* ***Starr*** *a-11-13; c-11i.*

CRUCIBLE
DC Comics (Impact): Feb, 1993 - No. 6, July, 1993 ($1.25, limited series)

	GD 2.0	VG 4.0	FN 6.0	VF 8.0	VF/NM 9.0	NM- 9.2
1-6: 1-(99¢)-Neon ink-c. 1,2-Quesada-c(p). 1-4-Quesada layouts						3.00

CRUDE
Image Comics (Skybound): Apr, 2018 - No. 6, Sept, 2018 ($3.99, limited series)

	GD 2.0	VG 4.0	FN 6.0	VF 8.0	VF/NM 9.0	NM- 9.2
1-6-Steve Orlando-s/Garry Brown-a						4.00

CRUEL AND UNUSUAL
DC Comics (Vertigo): June, 1999 - No. 4, Sept, 1999 ($2.95, limited series)

	GD 2.0	VG 4.0	FN 6.0	VF 8.0	VF/NM 9.0	NM- 9.2
1-4-Delano & Peyer-s/McCrea-c/a						3.00

CRUSADER FROM MARS (See Tops in Adventure)
Ziff-Davis Publ. Co.: Jan-Mar, 1952 - No. 2, Fall, 1952 (Painted-c)

	GD 2.0	VG 4.0	FN 6.0	VF 8.0	VF/NM 9.0	NM- 9.2
1-Cover is dated Spring	87	174	261	553	952	1350
2-Bondage-c	61	122	183	390	670	950

CRUSADER RABBIT (TV)
Dell Publishing Co.: No. 735, Oct, 1956 - No. 805, May, 1957

	GD 2.0	VG 4.0	FN 6.0	VF 8.0	VF/NM 9.0	NM- 9.2
Four Color 735 (#1)	21	42	63	147	324	500
Four Color 805	16	32	48	111	246	380

CRUSADERS, THE (Religious)
Chick Publications: 1974 - Vol. 17, 1988 (39/69¢, 36 pgs.)

	GD 2.0	VG 4.0	FN 6.0	VF 8.0	VF/NM 9.0	NM- 9.2
Vol.1-Operation Bucharest ('74). Vol.2-The Broken Cross ('74). Vol.3-Scarface ('74). Vol.4-Exorcists ('75). Vol.5-Chaos ('75)	3	6	9	16	23	30
Vol.6-Primal Man? ('76)-(Disputes evolution theory). Vol.7-The Ark-(claims proof of existence, destroyed by Bolsheviks). Vol.8-The Gift-(Life story of Christ). Vol.9-Angel of Light-(Story of the Devil). Vol.10-Spellbound?-(Tells how rock music is Satanic & produced by witches). 11-Sabotage?. 12-Alberto. 13-Double Cross. 14-The Godfathers. (No. 6-14 low in distribution; loaded with religious propaganda.). 15-The Force. 16-The Four Horsemen	3	6	9	16	23	30
Vol. 17-The Prophet (low print run)	3	6	9	17	26	35

CRUSADERS (Southern Knights No. 2 on)
Guild Publications: 1982 (B&W, magazine size)

	GD 2.0	VG 4.0	FN 6.0	VF 8.0	VF/NM 9.0	NM- 9.2
1-1st app. Southern Knights	2	4	6	10	14	18

CRUSADERS, THE (Also see Black Hood, The Jaguar, The Comet, The Fly, Legend of the Shield, The Mighty... & The Web)
DC Comics (Impact): May, 1992 - No. 8, Dec, 1992 ($1.00/$1.25)

	GD 2.0	VG 4.0	FN 6.0	VF 8.0	VF/NM 9.0	NM- 9.2
1-8-Contains 3 Impact trading cards						4.00

CRUSADES, THE
DC Comics (Vertigo): 2001 - No. 20, Dec, 2002 ($3.95/$2.50)

	GD 2.0	VG 4.0	FN 6.0	VF 8.0	VF/NM 9.0	NM- 9.2
...: Urban Decree ('01, $3.95) Intro. the Knight; Seagle-s/Kelley Jones-c/a						4.00
1-(5/01, $2.50) Sienkiewicz-c						3.00
2-20: 2-Moeller-c. 18-Begin $2.95-c						3.00

CRUSH
Dark Horse Comics: Oct, 2003 - No. 4, Jan, 2004 ($2.99, limited series)

	GD 2.0	VG 4.0	FN 6.0	VF 8.0	VF/NM 9.0	NM- 9.2
1-4-Jason Hall-s/Sean Murphy-a						3.00

CRUSH, THE
Image Comics (Motown Machineworks): Jan, 1996 - No. 5, July, 1996 ($2.25, limited series)

	GD 2.0	VG 4.0	FN 6.0	VF 8.0	VF/NM 9.0	NM- 9.2
1-5: Baron scripts						3.00

CRUX
CrossGeneration Comics: May, 2001 - No. 33, Feb, 2004 ($2.95)

	GD 2.0	VG 4.0	FN 6.0	VF 8.0	VF/NM 9.0	NM- 9.2
1-33: 1-Waid-s/Epting & Magyar-a/c. 6-Pelletier-a. 13-Dixon-s begin. 25-Cover has fake creases and other aging						3.00
Atlantis Rising Vol. 1 TPB (2002, $15.95) r/#1-6						16.00
Test of Time Vol. 2 TPB (12/02, $15.95) r/#7-12						16.00
Vol. 3: Strangers in Atlantis (2003, $15.95) r/#13-18						16.00
Vol. 4: Chaos Reborn (2003, $15.95) r/#19-24						16.00

CRY FOR DAWN
Cry For Dawn Pub.: 1989 - No. 9 ($2.25, B&W, mature)

	GD 2.0	VG 4.0	FN 6.0	VF 8.0	VF/NM 9.0	NM- 9.2
1	8	16	24	54	102	150
1-2nd printing	3	6	9	21	33	45
1-3rd printing	3	6	9	14	20	25
2	4	8	12	23	37	50
2-2nd printing	2	4	6	11	16	20
3	3	6	9	16	23	30
3a-HorrorCon Edition (1990, less than 400 printed, signed inside-c)						200.00
4-6	2	4	6	11	16	20
5-2nd printing	1	2	3	5	6	8
7-9	2	4	6	9	12	15
4-9-Signed & numbered editions	3	6	9	14	20	25
Angry Christ Comix HC (4/03, $29.99) reprints various stories; and 30 pgs. new material						30.00
...Calendar (1993)						35.00

CRY HAVOC
Image Comics: Jan, 2016 - No. 6, Jun, 2016 ($3.99)

	GD 2.0	VG 4.0	FN 6.0	VF 8.0	VF/NM 9.0	NM- 9.2
1-6-Simon Spurrier-s/Ryan Kelly-a; 2 covers on each						4.00

CRYIN' LION COMICS
William H. Wise Co.: Fall, 1944 - No. 3, Spring, 1945

	GD 2.0	VG 4.0	FN 6.0	VF 8.0	VF/NM 9.0	NM- 9.2
1-Funny animal	18	36	54	107	169	230
2-Hitler and Tojo app.	15	30	45	84	127	170
3	11	22	33	62	86	110

CRYPT
Image Comics (Extreme): Aug, 1995 - No. 2, Oct. 1995 ($2.50, limited series)

	GD 2.0	VG 4.0	FN 6.0	VF 8.0	VF/NM 9.0	NM- 9.2
1,2-Prophet app.						3.00

CRYPTIC WRITINGS OF MEGADETH
Chaos! Comics: Sept, 1997 - No. 4, Jun, 1998 ($2.95, quarterly)

	GD 2.0	VG 4.0	FN 6.0	VF 8.0	VF/NM 9.0	NM- 9.2
1-4-Stories based on song lyrics by Dave Mustaine						3.00

CRYPTOCRACY
Dark Horse Comics: Jun, 2016 - No. 6, Nov, 2016 ($3.99)

	GD 2.0	VG 4.0	FN 6.0	VF 8.0	VF/NM 9.0	NM- 9.2
1-6: 1-Van Jensen-s/Pete Woods-a						4.00

CRYPT OF DAWN (see Dawn)
Sirius: 1996 ($2.95, B&W, limited series)

	GD 2.0	VG 4.0	FN 6.0	VF 8.0	VF/NM 9.0	NM- 9.2
1-Linsner-c/s; anthology.						6.00
2, 3 (2/98)						4.00
4,5: 4- (6/98), 5-(11/98)						3.00
Ltd. Edition						20.00

CRYPT OF SHADOWS
Marvel Comics Group: Jan, 1973 - No. 21, Nov, 1975 (#1-9 are 20¢)

	GD 2.0	VG 4.0	FN 6.0	VF 8.0	VF/NM 9.0	NM- 9.2
1-Wolverton-r/Advs. Into Terror #7	5	10	15	34	60	85
2-10: 2-Starlin/Everett-c	3	6	9	17	25	34
11-21: 18,20-Kirby-a	3	6	9	15	22	28

NOTE: ***Briefer*** *a-2r.* ***Ditko*** *a-13r, 18-20r.* ***Everett*** *a-6, 14r; c-2i.* ***Heath*** *a-1r.* ***Gil Kane*** *c-1, 6.* ***Mort Lawrence*** *a-1r, 8r.*

Cryptozoic Man #2 © Flanagan & Johnson

The Curse of Brimstone Annual #1 © DC

Curse Words #7 © Silent E Prods.

GD VG FN VF VF/NM NM-
2.0 4.0 6.0 8.0 9.0 9.2

Maneely a-2r. Moldoff a-8. Powell a-12r, 14r. Tuska a-2r.

CRYPT OF SHADOWS (Marvel 80th Anniversary salute to horror comics)
Marvel Comics: Mar, 2019 ($3.99, one-shot)
1-Al Ewing-s; art by Garry Brown, Stephen Green, Djibril Morissett-Phan; Kyle Hotz-c 4.00

CRYPT OF TERROR (Formerly Crime Patrol; Tales From the Crypt No. 20 on)
(Also see EC Archives • Tales From the Crypt)
E. C. Comics: No. 17, Apr-May, 1950 - No. 19, Aug-Sept, 1950
17-1st New Trend to hit stands 389 778 1167 3112 4956 6800
18,19 194 388 582 1552 2476 3400
NOTE: *Craig c/a-17-19. Feldstein a-17-19. Ingels a-19. Kurtzman a-18. Wood a-18. Canadian reprints known; see Table of Contents.*

CRYPTOZOIC MAN (Comic Book Men)
Dynamite Entertainment: 2013 - No. 4, 2014 ($3.99, limited series)
1-Bryan Johnson-s/Walt Flanagan-a/c 2 4 6 11 16 20
2-4 2 4 6 8 10 12

CRYSIS (Based on the EA videogame)
IDW Publishing: Jun, 2011 - No. 6, Oct, 2011 ($3.99, limited series)
1-6: 1-Richard K. Moran-s/Peter Bergting-a; two covers 4.00

CSI: CRIME SCENE INVESTIGATION (Based on TV series)
IDW Publishing: Jan, 2003 - No. 5, May, 2003 ($3.99, limited series)
1-Two covers (photo & Ashley Wood); Max Allan Collins-s 4.00
2-5 4.00
Free Comic Book Day edition (7/04) Previews CSI: Bad Rap; The Shield: Spotlight; 24: One Shot; and 30 Days of Night 3.00
...: Case Files Vol. 1 TPB (8/06, $19.99) B&W rep/Serial TPB, CSI - Bad Rap and CSI - Demon House limited series 20.00
...: Serial TPB (2003, $19.99) r/#1-5; bonus short story by Collins/Wood 20.00
...: Thicker Than Blood (7/03, $6.99) Mariotte-s/Rodriguez-a 7.00

CSI: CRIME SCENE INVESTIGATION - BAD RAP
IDW Publishing: Aug, 2003 - No. 5, Dec, 2003 ($3.99, limited series)
1-5-Two photo covers; Max Allan Collins-s/Rodriguez-a 4.00
TPB (3/04, $19.99) r/#1-5 20.00

CSI: CRIME SCENE INVESTIGATION - DEMON HOUSE
IDW Publishing: Feb, 2004 - No. 5, Jun, 2004 ($3.99, limited series)
1-5-Photo covers on all; Max Allan Collins-s/Rodriguez-a 4.00
TPB (10/04, $19.99) r/#1-5 20.00

CSI: CRIME SCENE INVESTIGATION - DOMINOS
IDW Publishing: Aug, 2004 - No. 5, Dec, 2004 ($3.99, limited series)
1-5-Photo covers on all; Oprisko-s/Rodriguez-a 4.00

CSI: CRIME SCENE INVESTIGATION - DYING IN THE GUTTERS
IDW Publishing: Aug, 2006 - No. 5, Dec, 2006 ($3.99, limited series)
1-5-"Rich Johnston" murdered; comic creators (Quesada, Rucka, David, Brubaker, Silvestri and others) appear as suspects; Stephen Mooney-a; photo-c 4.00

CSI: CRIME SCENE INVESTIGATION - SECRET IDENTITY
IDW Publishing: Feb, 2005 - No. 5, Jun, 2005 ($3.99, limited series)
1-5-Photo covers on all; Steven Grant-s/Gabriel Rodriguez-a 4.00

CSI: MIAMI
IDW Publishing: Oct, 2003; Apr, 2004 ($6.99, one-shots)
... - Blood Money (9/04)-Oprisko-s/Guedes & Perkins-a 7.00
... - Smoking Gun (10/03)-Mariotte-s/Avilés & Wood-a 7.00
... - Thou Shalt Not... (4/04)-Oprisko-s/Guedes & Wood-a 7.00
TPB (2/05, $19.99) reprints one-shots 20.00

CSI: NY - BLOODY MURDER
IDW Publishing: July, 2005 - No. 5, Nov, 2005 ($3.99, limited series)
1-5-Photo covers on all; Collins-s/Woodward-a 4.00

C•23 (Jim Lee's...) (Based on Wizards of the Coast card game)
Image Comics: Apr, 1998 - No. 8, Nov, 1998 ($2.50)
1-8: 1,2-Choi & Mariotte-s/ Charest-c. 2-Variant-c by Jim Lee. 4-Ryan Benjamin-c. 5,8-Corben var-c. 6-Flip book with Planetary preview; Corben-c 3.00

CUD
Fantagraphics Books: 8/92 - No. 8, 12/94 ($2.25-$2.75, B&W, mature)
1-8: Terry LaBan scripts & art in all. 6-1st Eno & Plum 3.00

CUD COMICS
Dark Horse Comics: Jan, 1995 - No. 8, Sept, 1997 ($2.95, B&W)
1-8: Terry LaBan-c/a/scripts. 5-Nudity; marijuana story 3.00
Eno and Plum TPB (1997, $12.95) r/#1-4, DHP #93-95 13.00

GD VG FN VF VF/NM NM-
2.0 4.0 6.0 8.0 9.0 9.2

CUPID
Marvel Comics (U.S.A.): Dec, 1949 - No. 2, Mar, 1950
1-Photo-c 26 52 78 154 252 350
2-Bettie Page ('50s pin-up queen) photo-c; Powell-a (see My Love #4) 81 162 243 518 884 1250

CURB STOMP
BOOM! Studios: Feb, 2015 - No. 4, May, 2015 ($3.99, limited series)
1-4-Ryan Ferrier-s/Devaki Neogi-a 4.00

CURIO
Harry 'A' Chesler: 1930's(?) (Tabloid size, 16-20 pgs.)
nn 22 44 66 132 216 300

CURLY KAYOE COMICS (Boxing)
United Features Syndicate/Dell Publ. Co.: 1946 - No. 8, 1950; Jan, 1958
1 (1946)-Strip-r (Fritzi Ritz); biography of Sam Leff, Kayoe's artist 25 50 75 150 245 340
2 17 34 51 98 154 210
3-8 14 28 42 80 115 150
United Presents...(Fall, 1948) 14 28 42 80 115 150
Four Color 871 (Dell, 1/58) 5 10 15 30 50 70

CURSED
Image Comics (Top Cow): Oct, 2003 - No. 4, Feb, 2004 ($2.99)
1-4-Avery & Blevins-s/Molenaar-a 3.00

CURSED COMICS CAVALCADE
DC Comics: Dec, 2018 ($9.99, square-bound one-shot)
1-Short stories of DC heroes facing ghosts and monsters by various; Mahnke-c 10.00

CURSE OF BRIMSTONE, THE
DC Comics: Jun, 2018 - No. 12, May, 2019 ($2.99)
1-12: 1-3-Justin Jordan-s/Philip Tan-a. 6,11,12-Cowan-a. 9-Dr. Fate app. 3.00
Annual 1 (3/19, $4.99) Swamp Thing & Constantine app.; Perkins-a 5.00

CURSE OF DRACULA, THE
Dark Horse Comics: July, 1998 - No. 3, Sept, 1998 ($2.95, limited series)
1-3-Marv Wolfman-s/Gene Colan-a 4.00
TPB (2005, $9.95) r/series; intro. by Marv Wolfman 10.00

CURSE OF RUNE (Becomes Rune, 2nd Series)
Malibu Comics (Ultraverse): May, 1995 - No. 4, Aug, 1995 ($2.50, lim. series)
1-4: 1-Two covers form one image 3.00

CURSE OF THE SPAWN
Image Comics (Todd McFarlane Prod.): Sept, 1996 - No. 29, Mar, 1999 ($1.95)
1-Dwayne Turner-a(p) 2 4 6 8 11 14
1-B&W Edition 3 6 9 14 20 26
2-3 1 2 3 5 6 8
4-29: 12-Movie photo-c of Melinda Clarke (Priest) 4.00
Blood and Sutures ('99, $9.95, TPB) r/#5-8 10.00
Lost Values ('00, $10.95, TPB) r/#12-14,22; Ashley Wood-c 11.00
Sacrifice of the Soul ('99, $9.95, TPB) r/#1-4 10.00
Shades of Gray ('00, $9.95, TPB) r/#9-11,29 10.00
The Best of the Curse of the Spawn (6/06, $16.99, TPB) B&W r/#1-8,12-16,20-29 17.00

CURSE OF THE WEIRD
Marvel Comics: Dec, 1993 - No. 4, Mar, 1994 ($1.25, limited series)
(Pre-code horror-r)
1-4: 1,3,4-Wolverton-r(1-Eye of Doom; 3-Where Monsters Dwell; 4-The End of the World). 2-Orlando-r. 4-Zombie-r by Everett; painted-c 1 2 3 5 6 8
NOTE: *Briefer r-2. Davis a-4r. Ditko a-1r, 2r, 4r; c-1r. Everett r-1. Heath r-1-3. Kubert r-3. Wolverton a-1r, 3r, 4r.*

CURSE WORDS
Image Comics: Jan, 2017 - Present ($3.99)
1-25-Charles Soule-s/Ryan Browne-a 4.00
Holiday Special (12/17, $3.99) Mike Norton-a 4.00
... Spring Special (4/19, $3.99) Norton-a; takes place after #20; Ascender #1 preview 4.00
... Summer Swimsuit Special (8/18, $3.99) Joe Quinones-a; takes place after #15 4.00

CUSTER'S LAST FIGHT
Avon Periodicals: 1950
nn-Partial reprint of Cowpuncher #1 20 40 60 115 185 255

CUTEY BUNNY (See Army Surplus Komikz Featuring...)

CUTIE PIE
Junior Reader's Guild (Lev Gleason): May, 1955 - No. 3, Dec, 1955; No. 4, Feb, 1956; No. 5, Aug, 1956

Cyber Force V5 #11 © TCOW

Cyberpunk 2077: Trauma Team #1 © CD Projekt

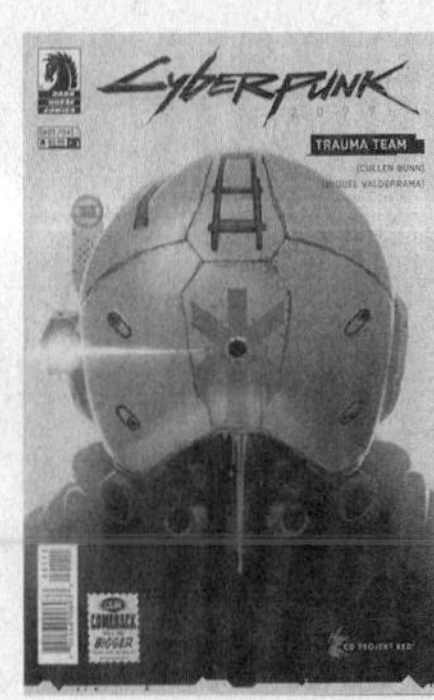

Cyborg #11 © DC

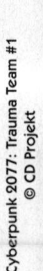

	GD 2.0	VG 4.0	FN 6.0	VF 8.0	VF/NM 9.0	NM- 9.2
1	10	20	30	56	76	95
2-5: 4-Misdated 2/55	7	14	21	35	43	50

CUTTING EDGE
Marvel Comics: Dec, 1995 ($2.95)
1-Hulk-c/story; Messner-Loebs scripts 3.00

CVO: COVERT VAMPIRIC OPERATIONS
IDW Publishing: June, 2003 ($5.99, one-shot)
1-Alex Garner-s/Mindy Lee-a(p) 6.00
... - Human Touch 1 (8/04, $3.99, one-shot) Hernandez & Garner-a 4.00
... - 100-Page Spectacular (4/11, $7.99) r/#1, African Blood #2 Rogue State #5 8.00
TPB (9/04, $19.99) r/#1 and ... - Artifact #1-3; intro. by Garner 20.00

CVO: COVERT VAMPIRIC OPERATIONS - AFRICAN BLOOD
IDW Publishing: Sept, 2006 - No. 4, May, 2007 ($3.99, limited series)
1-4-El Torres-s/Luis Czerniawski-a 4.00

CVO: COVERT VAMPIRIC OPERATIONS - ARTIFACT
IDW Publishing: Oct, 2003 - No. 3, Dec, 2003 ($3.99, limited series)
1-3-Jeff Mariotte-s/Gabriel Hernandez-a/Alex Garner-c 4.00

CVO: COVERT VAMPIRIC OPERATIONS - ROGUE STATE
IDW Publishing: Nov, 2004 - No. 5, Mar, 2005 ($3.99, limited series)
1-5-Jeff Mariotte-s/Vazquez-a 4.00
TPB (7/05, $19.99) r/#1-5; cover gallery 20.00

CYBERELLA
DC Comics (Helix): Sept, 1996 - No. 12, Aug, 1997 ($2.25/$2.50)(1st Helix series)
1-12: 1-5-Chaykin & Cameron-a. 1,2-Chaykin-c. 3-5-Cameron-c 3.00

CYBERFORCE
Image Comics (Top Cow Productions): Oct, 1992 - No. 4, 1993; No. 0, Sept, 1993 ($1.95, limited series)
1-Silvestri-c/a in all; coupon for Image Comics #0; 1st Top Cow Productions title 6.00
1-With coupon missing 2.00
2-4,0: 2-(3/93). 3-Pitt-c/story. 4-Codename: Stryke Force back-up (1st app.); foil-c. 0-(9/93)-Walt Simonson-c/a/scripts 3.00

CYBERFORCE
Image Comics (Top Cow Productions)/Top Cow Comics No. 28 on:
V2#1, Nov, 1993 - No. 35, Sept. 1997 ($1.95)
V2#1-24: 1-7-Marc Silvestri/Keith Williams-c/a. 8-McFarlane-c/a. 10-Painted variant-c exists. 18-Variant-c exists. 23-Velocity-c. 3.00
1-3: 1-Gold Logo-c. 2-Silver embossed-c. 3-Gold embossed-c 10.00
1-(99¢, 3/96, 2nd printing) 3.00
25-($3.95)-Wraparound, foil-c 4.00
26-35: 28-(11/96)-1st Top Cow Comics iss. Quesada & Palmiotti's Gabriel app. 27-Quesada & Palmiotti's Ash app. 3.00
Annual 1,2 (3/95, 8/96, $2.50, $2.95) 4.00
NOTE: *Annuals read Volume One in the indica.*

CYBERFORCE (Volume 3)
Image Comics (Top Cow): Apr, 2006 - No. 6, Nov, 2006 ($2.99)
1-6: 1-Pat Lee-a/Ron Marz-s; three covers by Pat Lee, Marc Silvestri and Dave Finch 3.00
#0-(6/06, $2.99) reprints origin story from Image Comics Hardcover Vol. 1 3.00
.../X-Men 1 (1/07, $3.99) Pat Lee-a/Ron Marz-s; 2 covers by Lee and Silvestri 4.00
Vol. 1 TPB (12/06, $14.99) r/#1-6, #0 & story from The Cow Quarterly; cover gallery 15.00

CYBER FORCE (Volume 4)
Image Comics (Top Cow): Dec, 2012 - No. 11 (no cover price/$2.99)
1-11: 1-Silvestri & Hawkins-s/Pham-a; multiple covers on each 3.00
...: Artifacts #0 (12/16, $3.99) Short stories by various; Khoi Pham-c 4.00

CYBER FORCE (Volume 5) (See Aphrodite IX and Ninth Generation)
Image Comics (Top Cow): Mar, 2018 - Present ($3.99)
1-11: 1-Matt Hawkins & Bryan Hill-s/Atilio Rojo-a; two covers; origin story 4.00

CYBERFORCE/HUNTER-KILLER
Image Comics (Top Cow Productions): July, 2009 - No. 5, Mar, 2010 ($2.99)
1-5-Waid-s/Rocafort-a; multiple covers on each 3.00

CYBERFORCE ORIGINS
Image Comics (Top Cow Productions): Jan, 1995 - No. 3, Nov, 1995 ($2.50)
1-Cyblade (1/95) 5.00
1-Cyblade (3/96, 99¢, 2nd printing) 3.00
1A-Exclusive Ed.; Tucci-c 4.00
2,3: 2-Stryker (2/95)-1st Mike Turner-a. 3-Impact 3.00
(#4) Misery (12/95, $2.95) 3.00

CYBERFORCE/STRYKEFORCE: OPPOSING FORCES (See Codename: Stryke Force #15)
Image Comics (Top Cow Productions): Sept, 1995 - No. 2, Oct, 1995 ($2.50, limited series)
1,2: 2-Stryker disbands Strykeforce. 3.00

CYBERFORCE UNIVERSE SOURCEBOOK
Image Comics (Top Cow Productions): Aug, 1994/Feb, 1995 ($2.50)
1,2-Silvestri-c 3.00

CYBERFROG
Hall of Heroes: June, 1994 - No. 2, Dec, 1994 ($2.50, B&W, limited series)

	GD	VG	FN	VF	VF/NM	NM-
1-Ethan Van Sciver-c/a/scripts	8	16	24	54	102	150
2	5	10	15	33	57	80

CYBERFROG
Harris Comics: Feb, 1996 - No. 3, Apr, 1996 ($2.95)

	GD	VG	FN	VF	VF/NM	NM-
0-3: Van Sciver-c/a/scripts. 2-Variant-c exists	2	4	6	8	10	12

CYBERFROG: (Title series), **Harris Comics**

	GD	VG	FN	VF	VF/NM	NM-
--RESERVOIR FROG, 9/96 - No. 2, 10/96 ($2.95) 1,2: Van Sciver-c/a/scripts; wraparound-c	1	2	3	5	6	8
--3RD ANNIVERSARY SPECIAL, 1/97 - #2, ($2.50, B&W) 1,2	1	2	3	5	6	8
--VS. CREED, 7/97 ($2.95, B&W)1	1	2	3	5	6	8

CYBERNARY (See Deathblow #1)
Image Comics (WildStorm Productions): Nov, 1995 - No.5, Mar, 1996 ($2.50)
1-5 3.00

CYBERNARY 2.0
DC Comics (WildStorm): Sept, 2001 - No. 6, Apr, 2002 ($2.95, limited series)
1-6: Joe Harris-s/Eric Canete-a. 6-The Authority app. 3.00

CYBERPUNK
Innovation Publishing: Sept, 1989 - No. 2, Oct, 1989 ($1.95, 28 pgs.) Book 2, #1, May, 1990 - No. 2, 1990 ($2.25, 28 pgs.)

	GD	VG	FN	VF	VF/NM	NM-
1-Ken Steacy painted-cover (Adults)	2	4	6	9	12	15

2, Book 2 #1,2: 2-Ken Steacy painted-covers (Adults) 6.00

CYBERPUNK: THE SERAPHIM FILES
Innovation Publishing: Nov, 1990 - No. 2, Dec, 1990 ($2.50, 28 pgs., mature)
1,2: 1-Painted-c; story cont'd from Seraphim 5.00

CYBERPUNK 2077: TRAUMA TEAM (Based on the video game Cyberpunk 2077)
Dark Horse Comics: Sept, 2020 - No. 4, Dec, 2020 ($3.99, limited series)
1-4-Cullen Bunn-s/Miguel Valderrama-a 4.00

CYBERRAD
Continuity Comics: 1991 - No. 7, 1992 ($2.00)(Direct sale & newsstand-c variations) V2#1, 1993 ($2.50)
1-7: 5-Glow-in-the-dark-c by N. Adams (direct sale only). 6-Contains 4 pg. fold-out poster; N. Adams layouts 4.00
V2#1-($2.95, direct sale ed.)-Die-cut-c w/B&W hologram on-c; Neal Adams sketches 4.00
V2#1-($2.50, newsstand ed.)-Without sketches 3.00

CYBERRAD DEATHWATCH 2000 (Becomes CyberRad w/#2, 7/93)
Continuity Comics: Apr, 1993 - No. 2, 1993 ($2.50)
1,2: 1-Bagged w/2 cards; Adams-c & layouts & plots. 2-Bagged w/card; Adams scripts 4.00

CYBER 7
Eclipse Comics: Mar, 1989 - #7, Sept, 1989; V2#1, Oct, 1989 - #10, 1990 ($2.00, B&W)
1-7, Book 2 #1-10: Stories translated from Japanese 3.00

CYBLADE
Image Comics (Top Cow Productions): Oct, 2008 - No. 4, Mar, 2009 ($2.99)
1-4: 1,2-Mays-a/Fialkov-s. 1-Two covers. 3,4-Ferguson-a 3.00
.../ Ghost Rider 1 (Marvel/Top Cow, 1/97, $2.95) Devil's Reign pt. 2 4.00
...: Pilot Season 1 (9/07, $2.99) Rick Mays-a 3.00

CYBLADE/SHI (Also see Battle For The Independents & Shi/Cyblade: The Battle For The Independents)
Image Comics (Top Cow Productions): 1995 ($2.95, one-shot)

	GD	VG	FN	VF	VF/NM	NM-
San Diego Preview	2	4	6	13	18	22
1-($2.95)-1st app. Witchblade	2	4	6	9	13	16

1-($2.95)-variant-c; Tucci-a 6.00

CYBORG (From Justice League)
DC Comics: Sept, 2015 - No. 12, Aug, 2016 ($2.99)
1-12: 1-Walker-s/Reis-a. 3-6-Metal Men app. 9,10-Shazam app. 3.00

CYBORG (DC Rebirth)

Cyclops #1 © MAR

Dagar, Desert Hawk #23 © FOX

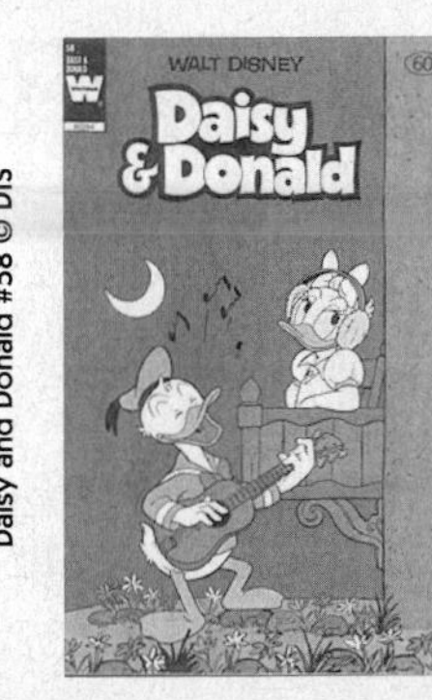

Daisy and Donald #58 © DIS

	GD	VG	FN	VF	VF/NM	NM-
	2.0	4.0	6.0	8.0	9.0	9.2

DC Comics: Nov, 2016 - No. 23, Aug, 2018 ($2.99/$3.99)

1-10: 1-Semper Jr.-s/Pelletier-a; Kilg%re app. 6-Intro. Variant 3.00
11-23: 11-Begin $3.99-c. 15-Metal Men app. 15-17-Beast Boy app. 4.00
...: Rebirth 1 (11/16, $2.99) Semper Jr.-s/Pelletier-a; origin retold 3.00

CYBRID
Maximum Press: July, 1995; No. 0, Jan, 1997 ($2.95/$3.50)

1-(7/95) 3.50
0-(1/97)-Liefeld-a/script; story cont'd in Avengelyne #4 3.50

CYCLONE COMICS (Also see Whirlwind Comics)
Bilbara Publishing Co.: June, 1940 - No. 5, Nov, 1940

1-Origin Tornado Tom; Volton (the human generator), Tornado Tom, Kingdom of the Moon, Mister Q begin (1st app. of each) 84 168 252 538 919 1300
2 65 130 195 416 708 1000
3-Classic-c (scarce) 132 264 396 838 1444 2050
4-(9/40) 71 142 213 454 777 1100
5-(Scarce) 97 194 291 621 1061 1500
Ashcan - (5/40) Not distributed to newsstands, only for in house use. Cover produced on green stock paper. A CGC certified FN (6.0) copy sold for $2,000 in 2006.

CYCLOPS (X-Men)
Marvel Comics: Oct, 2001 - No. 4, Jan, 2002 ($2.50, limited series)

1-4-Texeira-c/a. 1,2-Black Tom and Juggernaut app. 4.00
1-(5/11, $2.99, one-shot) Haspiel-a; Batroc and the Circus of Crime app. 4.00

CYCLOPS (All-New X-Men)
Marvel Comics: Jul, 2014 - No. 12, Jun, 2015 ($3.99)

1-10: 1-Rucka-s/Dauterman-a; Corsair app. 6-12-Layman-s. 12-Black Vortex x-over 4.00

CYCLOPS: RETRIBUTION
Marvel Comics: 1994 ($5.95, trade paperback)

nn-r/Marvel Comics Presents #17-24 1 3 4 6 8 10

CY-GOR (See Spawn #38 for 1st app.)
Image Comics (Todd McFarlane Prod.): July, 1999 - No. 6, Dec, 1999 ($2.50)

1-6-Veitch-s 3.00

CYNTHIA DOYLE, NURSE IN LOVE (Formerly Sweetheart Diary)
Charlton Publications: No. 66, Oct, 1962 - No. 74, Feb, 1964

66-74 3 6 9 15 22 28

DAFFODIL
Marvel Comics (Soleil): 2010 - No. 3, 2010 ($5.99, limited series)

1-3-English version of French comic; Brrémaud-s/Rigano-a 6.00

DAFFY (Daffy Duck No. 18 on)(See Looney Tunes)
Dell Publishing Co./Gold Key No. 31-127/Whitman No. 128 on: #457, 3/53 - #30, 7-9/62; #31, 10-12/62 - #145, 6/84 (No #132,133)

Four Color 457(#1)-Elmer Fudd x-overs begin 12 24 36 81 176 270
Four Color 536,615('55) 7 14 21 49 92 135
4(1-3/56)-11('57) 5 10 15 33 57 80
12-19(1958-59) 4 8 12 28 47 65
20-40(1960-64) 3 6 9 20 31 42
41-60(1964-68) 3 6 9 16 23 30
61-90(1969-74)-Road Runner in most. 76-82-"Daffy Duck and the Road Runner" on-c 2 4 6 11 16 20
90-Whitman variant 3 6 9 14 19 24
91-110 2 4 6 8 11 14
111-127 1 3 4 6 8 10
128,134-141: 139(2/82), 140(2-3/82), 141(4/82) 2 4 6 8 10 12
129(8/80),130,131 (pre-pack?) (scarce). 129-Sherlock Holmes parody-s 4 8 12 28 47 65
142-145(#90029 on-c; nd, nd code, pre-pack): 142(6/83), 143(8/83), 144(3/84), 145(6/84) 3 6 9 17 26 35
Mini-Comic 1 (1976; 3-1/4x6-1/2") 1 3 4 6 8 10
NOTE: *Reprint issues-No.41-46, 48, 50, 53-55, 58, 59, 65, 67, 69, 73, 81, 96, 103-108; 136-142, 144, 145(1/3-2/3-r). (See March of Comics No. 277, 288, 303, 313, 331, 347, 357,375, 387, 397, 402, 413, 425, 437, 460).*

DAFFY DUCK (Digest-size reprints from Looney Tunes)
DC Comics: 2005 ($6.99, digest)

Vol. 1: You're Despicable! - Reprints from Looney Tunes #38,43,45,47,51,53,54,58,61,62,66,70 7.00

DAFFY TUNES COMICS
Four-Star Publications: June, 1947; No. 12, Aug, 1947

nn 11 22 33 62 86 110
12-Al Fago-c/a; funny animal 10 20 30 56 76 95

DAGAR, DESERT HAWK (Captain Kidd No. 24 on; formerly All Great)
Fox Feature Syndicate: No. 14, Feb, 1948 - No. 23, Apr, 1949 (No #17,18)

14-Tangi & Safari Cary begin; Good bondage-c/a 123 246 369 787 1344 1900
15,16-E. Good-a; 15-Headlight-c 63 126 189 403 689 975
19,20,22: 19-Used in **SOTI**, pg. 180 (Tangi) 58 116 174 371 636 900
21,23: 21-Bondage-c; "Bombs & Bums Away" panel in "Flood of Death" story used in **SOTI.** 23-Bondage-c 65 130 195 416 708 1000
NOTE: *Tangi by **Kamen**-14-16, 19, 20; c-20, 21.*

DAGAR THE INVINCIBLE (Tales of Sword & Sorcery...) (Also see Dan Curtis Giveaways & Gold Key Spotlight)
Gold Key: Oct, 1972 - No. 18, Dec, 1976; No. 19, Apr, 1982

1-Origin; intro. Villains Olstellon & Scor 4 8 12 23 37 50
2-5: 3-Intro. Graylin, Dagar's woman; Jarn x-over 3 6 9 14 19 24
6-1st Dark Gods story 2 4 6 9 13 16
7-10: 9-Intro. Torgus. 10-1st Three Witches story 2 4 6 9 13 16
11-18: 13-Durak & Torgus x-over; story continues in Dr. Spektor #15. 14-Dagar's origin retold. 18-Origin retold 2 4 6 8 10 12
19(4/82)-Origin-r/#18 6.00
NOTE: *Durak app. in 7, 12, 13. Tragg app. in 5, 11.*

DAGWOOD (Chic Young's) (Also see Blondie Comics)
Harvey Publications: Sept, 1950 - No. 140, Nov, 1965

1 18 36 54 126 281 435
2 9 18 27 59 117 175
3-10 7 14 21 44 82 120
11-20 5 10 15 35 63 90
21-30 5 10 15 31 53 75
31-50: 33-Sci-Fi-c 4 8 12 28 47 65
51-70 3 6 9 21 33 45
71-100 3 6 9 17 26 35
101-121,123-128,130,135 3 6 9 16 23 30
122,129,131-134,136-140-All are 68-pg. issues 3 6 9 21 33 45
NOTE: *Popeye and other one page strips appeared in early issues.*

DAI KAMIKAZE!
Now Comics: June, 1987 - No. 12, Aug, 1988 ($1.75)

1-1st app. Speed Racer 5.00
1-Second printing 3.00
2-12 3.00

DAILY BUGLE (See Spider-Man)
Marvel Comics: Dec, 1996 - No. 3, Feb, 1997 ($2.50, B&W, limited series)

1-3-Paul Grist-s 4.00

DAISY AND DONALD (See Walt Disney Showcase No. 8)
Gold Key/Whitman No. 42 on: May, 1973 - No. 59, July, 1984 (no No. 48)

1-Barks-r/WDC&S #280,308 4 8 12 23 37 50
2-5: 4-Barks-r/WDC&S #224 2 4 6 11 16 20
6-10 2 4 6 9 12 15
11-20 1 3 4 6 8 10
21-41: 32-r/WDC&S #308 1 2 3 5 6 8
36,42-44 (Whitman) 2 4 6 8 11 14
45 (8/80),46-(pre-pack?)(scarce) 4 8 12 27 44 60
47-(12/80)-Only distr. in Whitman 3-pack (scarce) 5 10 15 35 63 90
48(3/81)-50(8/81): 50-r/#3 2 4 6 10 14 18
51-54: 51-Barks-r/4-Color #1150. 52-r/#2. 53(2/82), 54(4/82) 2 4 6 9 13 16
55-59-(all #90284 on-c, nd, nd code, pre-pack): 55(5/83), 56(7/83), 57(8/83), 58(8/83), 59(7/84) 3 6 9 19 30 40

DAISY & HER PUPS (Dagwood & Blondie's Dogs)(Formerly Blondie Comics #20)
Harvey Publications: No. 21, 7/51 - No. 27, 7/52; No. 8, 9/52 - No. 18, 5/54

21 (#1)-Blondie's dog Daisy and her 5 pups led by Elmer begin. Rags Rabbit app. 5 10 15 35 63 90
22-27 (#2-7): 26 has No. 6 on cover but No. 26 on inside. 23,25-The Little King app. 24-Bringing Up Father by McManus app. 25-27-Rags Rabbit app. 4 8 12 27 44 60
8-18: 8,9-Rags Rabbit app. 8,17-The Little King app. 11-The Flop Family Swan begins. 22-Cookie app. 11-Felix The Cat app. by 17,18-Popeye app. 4 8 12 25 40 55

DAISY DUCK & UNCLE SCROOGE PICNIC TIME (See Dell Giant #33)

DAISY DUCK & UNCLE SCROOGE SHOW BOAT (See Dell Giant #55)

DAISY DUCK'S DIARY (See Dynabrite Comics, & Walt Disney's C&S #298)
Dell Publishing Co.: No. 600, Nov, 1954 - No. 1247, Dec-Fef, 1961-62 (Disney)

Four Color 600 (#1) 8 16 24 51 96 140
Four Color 659, 743 (11/56) 6 12 18 40 73 105

Dale Evans Comics #20 © DC

Damage (2018 series) #16 © DC

Danger #10 © Comic Media

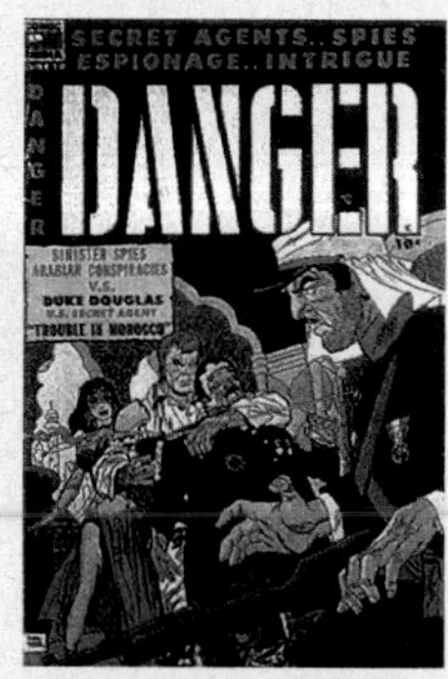

	GD 2.0	VG 4.0	FN 6.0	VF 8.0	VF/NM 9.0	NM- 9.2

Four Color 858 (11/57), 948 (11/58), 1247 (12-2/61-62)
5 10 15 35 63 90
Four Color 1055 (11-1/59-60), 1150 (12-1/60-61)-By Carl Barks)
8 16 24 56 108 160

DAISY HANDBOOK
Daisy Manufacturing Co.: 1946; No. 2, 1948 (10¢, pocket-size, 132 pgs.)
1-Buck Rogers, Red Ryder; Wolverton-a (2 pgs.) 24 48 72 142 234 325
2-Captain Marvel & Ibis the Invincible, Red Ryder, Boy Commandos & Robotman; Wolverton-a (2 pgs.); contains 8 pg. color catalog 24 48 72 142 234 325

DAISY MAE (See Oxydol-Dreft)

DAISY'S RED RYDER GUN BOOK
Daisy Manufacturing Co.: 1955 (25¢, pocket-size, 132 pgs.)
nn-Boy Commandos, Red Ryder; 1pg. Wolverton-a 15 30 45 90 140 190

DAKEN: DARK WOLVERINE
Marvel Comics: Nov, 2010 - No. 23, May, 2012 ($3.99/$2.99)
1-Camuncoli-a/c; Way & Liu-s; back-up history of the character 5.00
2-9, 9.1, 10-23-($2.99) 3,4-Fantastic Four app. 7-9-Crossover with X-23 #8,9; Gambit app. 9.1-Avengers app. 13-16-Moon Knight app. 17-19-Runaways app. 3.00

DAKKON BLACKBLADE ON THE WORLD OF MAGIC: THE GATHERING
Acclaim Comics (Armada): June, 1996 ($5.95, one-shot)
1-Jerry Prosser scripts; Rags Morales-c/a. 6.00

DAKOTA LIL (See Fawcett Movie Comics)

DAKTARI (Ivan Tors) (TV)
Dell Publishing Co.: July, 1967 - No. 3, Oct, 1968; No. 4, Oct, 1969
1-Marshall Thompson photo-c on all 4 8 12 23 37 50
2-4 3 6 9 17 26 35

DALE EVANS COMICS (Also see Queen of the West...)(See Boy Commandos #32)
National Periodical Publications: Sept-Oct, 1948 - No. 24, Jul-Aug, 1952 (No. 1-19: 52 pgs.)
1-Dale Evans & her horse Buttermilk begin; Sierra Smith begins by Alex Toth
58 116 174 371 636 900
2-Alex Toth-a 30 60 90 177 289 400
3-11-Alex Toth-a 20 40 60 114 182 250
12-20: 12-Target-c 14 28 42 80 115 150
21-24 14 28 42 82 121 160
NOTE: *Photo-c-1, 2, 4-14.*

DALGODA
Fantagraphics Books: Aug, 1984 - No. 8, Feb, 1986 (High quality paper)
1,8: 1- Fujitake-c/a in all. 8-Alan Moore story 4.00
2-7: 2,3-Debut Grimwood's Daughter. 3.00

DALTON BOYS, THE
Avon Periodicals: 1951
1-(Number on spine)-Kinstler-c 22 44 66 130 213 295

DAMAGE
DC Comics: Apr, 1994 - No. 20, Jan, 1996 ($1.75/$1.95/$2.25)
1-20: 6-(9/94)-Zero Hour. 0-(10/94). 7-(11/94). 14-Ray app. 3.00

DAMAGE
DC Comics: Mar, 2018 - No. 16, Jun, 2019 ($2.99/$3.99)
1-12: 1-Venditti-s/Daniel-a; intro. Ethan Avery. 2-Suicide Squad app. 2,3-Wonder Woman app. 4,5-Poison Ivy app. 4-Nord-a. 8,9-Unknown Soldier app. 10-12-Justice League app. 3.00
13-16-($3.99) 13-Batman app. 14-16-Congo Bill app. 4.00
Annual 1 (10/18, $4.99) Takes place between #8&9; Lopresti-a 5.00

DAMAGE CONTROL (See Marvel Comics Presents #19)
Marvel Comics: 5/89 - No. 4, 8/89; V2#1, 12/89 - No. 4, 2/90 ($1.00)
V3#1, 6/91 - No. 4, 9/91 ($1.25, all are limited series)
V1#1-4,V2#1-4,V3#1-4: V1#4-Wolverine app. V2#2,4-Punisher app. 1-Spider-Man app. 2-New Warriors app. 3,4-Silver Surfer app. 4-Infinity Gauntlet parody 3.00

DAMAGED
Radical Comics: Jul, 2011 - No. 6 ($3.99/$3.50, limited series)
1-($3.99) Lapham-s/Manco-a; covers by Maleev & Manco 4.00
2-4-($3.50) Maleev-c 3.50

DAMIAN: SON OF BATMAN
DC Comics: Dec, 2013 - No. 4, Mar, 2014 ($3.99, limited series)
1-4-Andy Kubert-s/c/a; near-future Damian; Ra's al Ghul & Talia app. 4.00
1-Variant-c by Tony Daniel 8.00

DAMNATION: JOHNNY BLAZE - GHOST RIDER
Marvel Comics: May, 2018 ($3.99, one-shot)
1-Part of x-over with Doctor Strange: Damnation; Sebela-s/Noto-a/Crain-c 4.00

DAMNED
Image Comics (Homage Comics): June, 1997 - No. 4, Sept, 1997 ($2.50, limited series)
1-4-Steven Grant-s/Mike Zeck-c/a in all 3.00

DAMN NATION
Dark Horse Comics: Feb, 2005 - No. 3, Apr, 2005 ($2.99, limited series)
1-3-J. Alexander-a/Andrew Cosby-s 3.00

DAMSELS
Dynamite Entertainment: 2012 - No. 13, 2014 ($3.99)
1-13: 1-Leah Moore & John Reppion-s/Aneke-a. 1-Campbell-c. 2-8-Linsner-c 4.00
... Giant Killer One Shot (2013, $4.99) Leah Moore & John Reppion-s/Dietrich Smith-a 5.00

DAMSELS IN EXCESS
Aspen MLT: Jul, 2014 - No. 5, May, 2015 ($3.99, limited series)
1-5-Vince Hernandez-s/Mirka Andolfo-a; multiple covers on each 4.00

DAMSELS: MERMAIDS
Dynamite Entertainment: No. 0, 2013 - No. 5, 2013 ($3.99)
0-Free Comic Book Day giveaway; Sturges-s/Deshong-a/Hans-c 3.00
1-5-($3.99) Sturges-s/Deshong-a. 1-Two covers by Anacleto & Renaud. 2-5-Renaud-c 4.00

DANCES WITH DEMONS (See Marvel Frontier Comics Unlimited)
Marvel Frontier Comics: Sept, 1993 - No. 4, Dec, 1993 ($1.95, limited series)
1-($2.95)-Foil embossed-c; Charlie Adlard & Rod Ramos-a 4.00
2-4 3.00

DAN DARE
Virgin Comics: Nov, 2007 - No. 7, July, 2008 ($2.99/$5.99)
1-6-Ennis-s/Erskine-a. 1-Two covers by Talbot and Horn. 2-6-Two covers on each 3.00
7-($5.99) Double sized finale with wraparound Erskine-c; Gibbons variant-c 6.00

DAN DARE
Titan Comics: Nov, 2017 - No. 4, Jan, 2018 ($3.99)
1-4-MIlligan-s/Foche-a; multiple covers on each 4.00

DANDEE: **Four Star Publications:** 1947 (Advertised, not published)

DAN DUNN (See Crackajack Funnies, Detective Dan, Famous Feature Stories & Red Ryder)

DANDY COMICS (Also see Happy Jack Howard)
E. C. Comics: Spring, 1947 - No. 7, Spring, 1948
1-Funny animal; Vince Fago-a in all; Dandy in all 52 104 156 328 552 775
2 35 70 105 208 339 470
3-7: 3-Intro Handy Andy who is c-feature #3 on 30 60 90 177 289 400

DANGER
Comic Media/Allen Hardy Assoc.: Jan, 1953 - No. 11, Aug, 1954
1-Heck-c/a 36 72 108 211 343 475
2,3,5,7,9-11: 20 40 60 114 182 250
4-Marijuana cover/story 22 44 66 132 216 300
6- "Narcotics" story; begin spy theme 20 40 60 120 195 270
8-Bondage/torture/headlights panels 26 52 78 154 252 350
NOTE: ***Morisi** a-2, 5, 6(3), 10; c-2. Contains some reprints from Danger & Dynamite.*

DANGER (Formerly Comic Media title)
Charlton Comics Group: No. 12, June, 1955 - No. 14, Oct, 1955
12(#1) 15 30 45 84 127 170
13,14: 14-r/#12 12 24 36 67 94 120

DANGER
Super Comics: 1964
Super Reprint #10-12 (Black Dwarf; #10-r/Great Comics #1 by Novack. #11-r/Johnny Danger #1. #12-r/Red Seal #14), #15-r/Spy Cases #26. #16-Unpublished Chesler material (Yankee Girl), #17-r/Scoop #8 (Capt. Courage & Enchanted Dagger), #18(nd)-r/Guns Against Gangsters #5 (Gun-Master, Annie Oakley, The Chameleon; L.B. Cole-r)
2 4 6 13 18 22

DANGER AND ADVENTURE (Formerly This Magazine Is Haunted; Robin Hood and His Merry Men No. 28 on)
Charlton Comics: No. 22, Feb, 1955 - No. 27, Feb, 1956
22-Ibis the Invincible-c/story (last G.A. app.); Nyoka app.; last pre-code issue
12 24 36 69 97 125
23-Lance O'Casey-c/sty; Nyoka app.; Ditko-a thru #27
14 28 42 78 112 145
24-27: 24-Mike Danger & Johnny Adventure begin 10 20 30 56 76 95

DANGER GIRL (Also see Cliffhanger #0)
Image Comics (Cliffhanger Productions): Mar, 1998 - No. 4, Dec, 1998;
DC Comics (Cliffhanger Prod.): No. 5, July, 1999 - No. 7, Feb, 2001

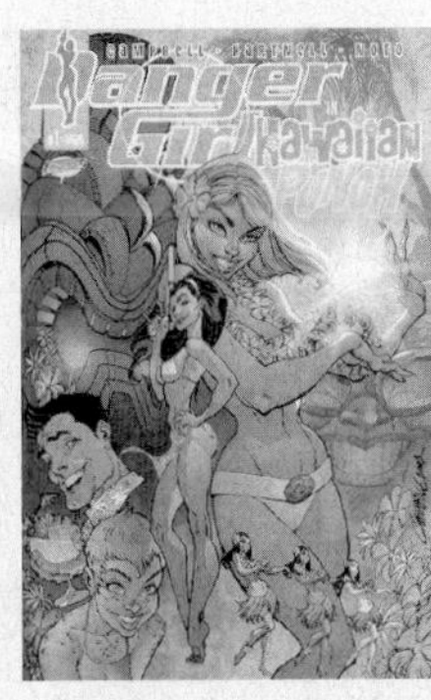
Danger Girl: Hawaiian Punch #1 © JSC

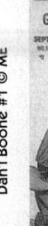

Dan'l Boone #1 © ME

Daphne Byrne #6 © Marks & Jones

	GD	VG	FN	VF	VF/NM	NM-
	2.0	4.0	6.0	8.0	9.0	9.2

Preview-Bagged in DV8 #14 Voyager Pack 5.00
Preview Gold Edition 10.00
1-($2.95) Hartnell & Campbell-s/Campbell/Garner-a 2 4 6 8 10 12
1-($4.95) Chromium cover 55.00
1-American Entertainment Ed. 8.00
1-American Entertainment Gold Ed., 1-Tourbook edition 14.00
1-"Danger-sized" ed.; over-sized format 3 6 9 16 24 32
2-($2.50) 1 2 3 5 6 8
2-Smoking Gun variant cover 6 12 18 38 69 100
2-Platinum Ed. 8 16 24 54 102 150
2-Dynamic Forces Omnichrome variant-c 3 6 9 16 23 30
2-Gold foil cover 2 4 6 11 16 20
2-Ruby red foil cover 13 26 39 86 188 290
3,4: 3-c by Campbell, Charest and Adam Hughes. 4-Big knife variant-c 4.00
3,5: 3-Gold foil cover. 5-DF Bikini variant-c 6.00
4-6 4.00
7-($5.95) Wraparound gatefold-c; Last issue 6.00
...: Dangerous Visions 3-D (IDW, 2/19, $6.99) r/#1 & Preview; bagged with glasses 7.00
...: Danger-Sized Treasury Edition #1 (IDW, 1/12, $9.99, 13" x 8-1/2") r/#1,2 & Preview 10.00
...: Hawaiian Punch (5/03, $4.95) Campbell-c; Phil Noto-a 5.00
...: Odd Jobs TPB (2004, $14.95) r/one-shots Hawaiian Punch, Viva Las Danger & Special; Campbell-c 15.00
San Diego Preview (8/98, B&W) flip book w/Wildcats preview 5.00
Sketchbook (2001, $6.95) Campbell-a; sketches for comics, toys, games 7.00
...Special (2/00, $3.50) art by Campbell, Chiodo, and Art Adams 3.50
... 3-D #1 (4/03, $4.95, bagged with 3-D glasses) r/ Preview & #1 in 3-D 5.00
...: Viva Las Danger (1/04, $4.95) Noto-a/Campbell-c 5.00
... :The Dangerous Collection nn (8/98; r-#1) 6.00
... :The Dangerous Collection 2,3: 2-(11/98, $5.95) r/#2,3. 3-('99) r/#4,5 6.00
... :The Dangerous Collection nn, 2-($10.00) Gold foil logo 10.00
... :The Ultimate Collection HC ($29.95) r/#1-7; intro by Bruce Campbell 30.00
... :The Ultimate Collection SC ($19.95) r/#1-7; intro by Bruce Campbell 20.00

DANGER GIRL AND THE ARMY OF DARKNESS
Dynamite Entertainment/ IDW Publ.: 2011 - No. 6, 2012 ($3.99, limited series)
1-6-Hartnell-s/Bolson-a. 1,2 Covers by Campbell, Bradshaw & Renaud 4.00

DANGER GIRL: BACK IN BLACK
DC Comics (Cliffhanger): Jan, 2006 - No. 4, Apr, 2006 ($2.99, limited series)
1-Hartnell-s/Bradshaw-a; Campbell-c 1 3 4 6 8 10
2-4-Hartnell-s/Bradshaw-a 3.00
TPB (2007, $12.99) r/series & covers 13.00

DANGER GIRL: BODY SHOTS
DC Comics (WildStorm): Jun, 2007 - No. 4, Sept, 2007 ($2.99, limited series)
1-4-Hartnell-s/Bradshaw-a 5.00
TPB (2007, $12.99) r/series & covers 13.00

DANGER GIRL/ G.I. JOE
IDW Publishing: Jul, 2012 - No. 5, Nov, 2012 ($3.99, limited series)
1-Hartnell-s/Royle-a; 2 covers by Campbell on each 1 2 3 5 6 8
2-5-Hartnell-s/Royle-a 5.00

DANGER GIRL KAMIKAZE
DC Comics (Cliffhanger): Nov, 2001 - No. 2, Dec., 2001 ($2.95, lim. series)
1,2-Tommy Yune-s/a 3.00

DANGER GIRL: MAYDAY
IDW Publishing: Apr, 2014 - No. 4, Aug, 2014 ($3.99, limited series)
1-4-Hartnell-s/Royle-a; 2 covers by Royle on each 4.00

DANGER GIRL: RENEGADE
IDW Publishing: Sept, 2015 - No. 4, Jan, 2016 ($3.99, limited series)
1-4-Hartnell-s/Molnar-a/Campbell-c 4.00

DANGER GIRL: REVOLVER
IDW Publishing: Jan, 2012 - No. 4, Apr, 2012 ($3.99, limited series)
1-4-Hartnell-s/Madden-a; covers by Campbell & Madden 4.00

DANGER GIRL: THE CHASE
IDW Publishing: Sept, 2013 - No. 4, Dec, 2013 ($3.99, limited series)
1-4-Hartnell-s/Tolibao-a. 1-Three covers (Panosian, Wallace & photo) 5.00

DANGER GIRL: TRINITY
IDW Publishing: Apr, 2013 - No. 4, Jul, 2013 ($3.99, limited series)
1-Hartnell-s/Campbell-c; art by Royle, Tolibao, & Molnar; variant-c by Garner 2 4 6 9 12 15
2-4 1 2 3 5 6 8

DANGER IS OUR BUSINESS!
Toby Press: 1953(Dec.) - No. 10, June, 1955
1-Captain Comet by Williamson/Frazetta-a, 6 pgs. (science fiction) 55 110 165 352 601 850
2 17 34 51 98 154 210
3-10 15 30 45 83 124 165
I.W. Reprint #9('64)-Williamson/Frazetta-r/#1; Kinstler-c 8 16 24 51 96 140

DANGER IS THEIR BUSINESS (Also see A-1 Comic)
Magazine Enterprises: No. 50, 1952
A-1 50-Powell-a 16 32 48 94 147 200

DANGER MAN (TV)
Dell Publishing Co.: No. 1231, Sept-Nov, 1961
Four Color 1231-Patrick McGoohan photo-c 10 20 30 68 144 220

DANGER TRAIL (Also see Showcase #50, 51)
National Periodical Publ.: July-Aug, 1950 - No. 5, Mar-Apr, 1951 (52 pgs.)
1-King Faraday begins, ends #4; Toth-a in all 148 296 444 947 1624 2300
2 103 206 309 659 1130 1600
3-(Rare) one of the rarest early '50s DCs 161 322 483 1030 1765 2500
4,5: 5-Johnny Peril-c/story (moves to Sensation Comics #107); new logo (also see Comic Cavalcade #15-29) 77 154 231 493 847 1200

DANGER TRAIL
DC Comics: Apr, 1993 - No. 4, July, 1993 ($1.50, limited series)
1-4: Gulacy-c on all 3.00

DANGER UNLIMITED (See San Diego Comic Con Comics #2 & Torch of Liberty Special)
Dark Horse (Legend): Feb, 1994 - No. 4, May, 1994 ($2.00, limited series)
1-4: Byrne-c/a/scripts in all; origin stories of both original team (Doc Danger, Thermal, Miss Mirage, & Hunk) & future team (Thermal, Belebet, & Caucus). 1-Intro Torch of Liberty & Golgotha (cameo) in back-up story. 4-Hellboy & Torch of Liberty cameo in lead story 3.00
TPB (1995, $14.95)-r/#1-4; includes last pg. originally cut from #4 15.00

DAN HASTINGS (See Syndicate Features)

DANIEL BOONE (See The Exploits of..., Fighting... Frontier Scout...,The Legends of... & March of Comics No. 306)
Dell Publishing Co.: No. 1163, Mar-May, 1961
Four Color 1163-Marsh-a 5 10 15 35 63 90

DANIEL BOONE (TV) (See March of Comics No. 306)
Gold Key: Jan, 1965 - No. 15, Apr, 1969 (All have Fess Parker photo-c)
1-Back-c and last eight pages fold in half to form "Official Handbook Fess Parker as Daniel Boone Trail Blazers Club" 8 16 24 54 102 150
2-Back-c pin-up 5 10 15 30 50 70
3-5-Back-c pin-ups 4 8 12 25 40 55
6-15: 7,8-Back-c pin-up 3 6 9 19 30 40

DAN'L BOONE
Sussex Publ. Co.: Sept, 1955 - No. 8, Sept, 1957
1 15 30 45 86 133 180
2 10 20 30 54 72 90
3-8 8 16 24 40 50 60

DANNY BLAZE (...Firefighter) (Nature Boy No. 3 on)
Charlton Comics: Aug, 1955 - No. 2, Oct, 1955
1-Authentic stories of fire fighting 15 30 45 83 124 165
2 10 20 30 56 76 95

DANNY DINGLE (See Sparkler Comics)
United Features Syndicate: No. 17, 1940
Single Series 17 31 62 93 182 296 410

DANNY THOMAS SHOW, THE (TV)
Dell Publishing Co.: No. 1180, Apr-June, 1961 - No. 1249, Dec-Feb, 1961-62
Four Color 1180-Toth-a, photo-c 14 28 42 96 211 325
Four Color 1249-Manning-a, photo-c 12 24 36 80 173 265

DANTE'S INFERNO (Based on the video game)
DC Comics (WildStorm): Feb, 2010 - No. 6, Jul, 2010 ($3.99, limited series)
1-6-Christos Gage-s/Diego Latorre-a 4.00
TPB (2010, $19.99) r/#1-6 20.00

DAOMU (Based on a novel series from China)
Image Comics: Feb, 2011 - No. 8, Dec, 2011 ($2.99)
1-8-Kennedy Xu-s/Ken Chou-a 3.00

Daredevil #9 © LEV

Daredevil #2 © MAR

Daredevil #54 © MAR

	GD	VG	FN	VF	VF/NM	NM-
	2.0	4.0	6.0	8.0	9.0	9.2

DAPHNE BYRNE
DC Comics (Hill House Comics): Mar, 2020 - No. 6, Sept, 2020 ($3.99)

1-6-Laura Marks-s/Kelley Jones-a; back-up Sea Dogs serial 4.00

DARBY O'GILL & THE LITTLE PEOPLE (Movie)(See Movie Comics)
Dell Publishing Co.: 1959 (Disney)

Four Color 1024-Toth-a; photo-c. 9 18 27 57 111 165

DAREDEVIL ("Daredevil Comics" on cover of #2) (See Silver Streak Comics)
Lev Gleason Publications (Funnies, Inc. No. 1): July, 1941 - No. 134, Sept, 1956
(52 pgs. #52-80; 64 pgs. #35-41)(Charles Biro stories)

1-No. 1 titled "Daredevil Battles Hitler," Classic battle issue as Daredevil teams up in each strip - The Silver Streak, Lance Hale, Cloud Curtis, Dickey Dean & Pirate Prince to battle Hitler; The Claw unites with Hitler and Japanese and battles Daredevil; Origin of Hitler feature story "The Man of Hate." Classic Hitler photo app. on-c
1300 2600 3900 9700 17,350 25,000

2-London (by Jerry Robinson), Pat Patriot (by Reed Crandall), Nightro, Real American No. 1 (by Briefer #2-11), Dash Dillon, Whirlwind begin; Dickie Dean, Pirate Prince end; intro. & only app. Pioneer, Champion of America & Times Square. The Claw continues #2-4 406 812 1218 2842 4971 7100

3-Intro./origin of 13. Newspaper editor has name "Roussos." Daredevil battles the Claw ill. text story 271 542 813 1734 2967 4200

4-The Claw captured and taken to New York Central Park Zoo. Whirlwind, the Blond Bomber begins, ends #6 235 470 705 1492 2571 3650

5-Ghost vs. Claw begins by Bob Wood, ends #20; 13 & Jinx begin; origin 13 retold in text; intro./origin Jinx, 13's sidekick; intro. Sniffer in Daredevil
200 400 600 1280 2190 3100

6-(12/41)-Classic horror-c; Daredevil battles wolf with human brain; Dash Dillon ends
184 368 552 1168 2009 2850

7,9: 7-(2/42), shows #6 on cover; delayed one month due to Pearl Harbor attack. 9-Daredevil vs. Daredevil-c; Sniffer strip begins, ends #69
126 252 378 806 1378 1950

8-Nazi WWII war-c. Nightro ends. Sniffer/Daredevil fight Nazi insurgents;
148 296 444 947 1624 2300

10-(5-42), "Remember Pearl Harbor" Japanese WWII-c; classic splash page w/American flag. Daredevil joins Air Corps. to fight Japanese. Ghost Battles Claw & Japanese. Last Whirlwind 190 380 570 1207 2079 2950

11-Classic Quasimodo (hunchback of Notre Dame) bondage/torture-c/sty. London, Pat Patriot, Real America #1 end 657 1314 1971 4205 6603 9000

12-Origin of The Claw; Scoop Scuttle by Wolverton begins (2-4 pgs.), ends #22, not in #21. Charles Biro biography. Dickey Dean, Pirate Prince return (both end #32)
145 290 435 921 1586 2250

13-Intro of Little Wise Guys (10/42)(also see Boy #4); Daredevil fights Nazi hooded cult; Ghost battles Claw, Hitler & Nazis in Britain; Bob Wood biography
108 216 324 686 1181 1675

14-Classic Daredevil facial portrait-c; Hitler app.; "Slap the Jap" game included
97 194 291 621 1061 1500

15-Death of Meatball 113 226 339 718 1234 1750

16-WWII-c w/freighter hit by German torpedo. Meatball is buried & Curly joins Little Wise Guys team 84 168 252 538 919 1300

17-Little Wise Guys hanging and beating Japanese soldiers on cover
219 438 657 1402 2401 3400

18-New origin of Daredevil (not same as Silver Streak #6). Hitler, Mussolini Tojo and Mickey Mouse app. on-c at carnival 140 280 420 889 1532 2175

19,20: Last Ghost vs. Claw 66 132 198 419 722 1025

21-Reprints cover of Silver Streak #6 (on inside) plus intro. of The Claw from Silver Streak #1. The Claw strip begins by Bob Q. Siege, ends #31 87 174 261 553 952 1350

22,23: 22-Daredevil fights the Tramp. 23-Dickie Dean by Bob Montana
46 92 138 290 488 685

24-Bloody puppet show-c; classic Claw splash pg. 55 110 165 352 601 850

25-1st Little Wise Guys-c without Daredevil 37 74 111 222 361 500

26,28-30 41 82 123 256 428 600

27-Bondage/torture-c 103 206 309 659 1130 1600

31-Death of The Claw 87 174 261 553 952 1350

32-34: 32,33-Egbert app. 33-Roger Wilco begins, ends #35
34 68 102 206 336 465

35-37,39-41: 35-Two Daredevil stories begin, end #68; Chauncey app. 37-39-Go Along Gallagher app. (#35-41 are 64 pgs.); 41-Dickie Dean ends
36 72 108 216 351 485

38-Origin Daredevil retold from #18 47 94 141 296 498 700

42-Intro. Kilroy in Daredevil who unveils Daredevil's I.D.-c/sty
31 62 93 182 296 410

43-45,47,48-All Daredevil-c. 43-Daredevil in costume on-c & 1 panel only inside; 44-DD back in costume; i.d. revealed on-c. 29 58 87 172 281 390

46,50: DD not on-c 24 48 72 142 234 325

49-Wise Guys fight secret hooded group c/sty. DD not on-c
29 58 87 172 281 390

51,52,56-60,63-66,68,69-Last Daredevil & Sniffer (12/50). 56-Wise Guys start their own circus. DD not on-c 20 40 60 115 185 255

53-Daredevil/Wise Guys find lost palace of Zanzarah, an underground Egyptian tomb w/mummy & treasure; classic c/story. DD-c 22 44 66 128 209 290

54,55-Daredevil-c 21 42 63 124 202 280

61-Daredevil & Wise Guys in haunted house classic c/story. Daredevil/Wise Guys fly rocket into stratosphere. DD not on-c 22 44 66 128 209 290

62-Wise Guys in medieval times, a dream by Peewee locked in a medieval museum; classic c/story. DD not on-c 22 44 66 128 209 290

67-Last Daredevil-c 21 42 63 124 202 280

70-Little Wise Guys take over book without Daredevil. Daredevil removed from-c & logo; Air Devils w/Hot Rock Flanagan begins, ends #80 14 28 42 80 115 150

71-78,81: 81-Dilly Duncan begins, ends #134 11 22 33 60 83 105

79,80: 79-(10/51)-Daredevil returns; Wise Guys go to Africa. 80-Daredevil & Wise Guys blast into space & land on Mars; last Daredevil app. in title
12 24 36 69 97 125

82,90: One pg. Frazetta ad in both 11 22 33 60 83 105

83-89,91-99,101-134 10 20 30 56 76 95

100-(7/53) 12 24 36 69 97 125

NOTE: ***Biro** a-1-22, 38; c-1-134; script-1-134. **Dan Barry** a(Daredevil) 40-48; **Roy Belft**-a (Daredevil) 49-55. **Bolle** a-125. **Al Borth**-a(Daredevil) #57-59. **Briefer** a-1-11 (Real American #1); Pirate Prince-#1, 2, 12-31. **Tony Dipreta**-a(Wise Guys) #108-110, 112-134. **R.W. Hall** a-22. **Carl Hubbell** a-9-21, 23-26, 27(Daredevil), 28-32. **Al Mandel** a-13. **Hy Mankin**-a(Wise Guys)-#80, 81. **Maurer**-a(Daredevil)-23, 31, 37, 38, 41, 43-51, 53-67, 69; (Little Wise Guys)-70-89. **McWilliams** a-70, 73-80. **Bob Montana** a-12, 23, 27, 28, 31-33. **Wm. Overgard**-a(Daredevil) #67, (Wise Guys) 74-79, 83-85, 87. **Jerry Robinson** a(London) #2-8. **Roussos** a(Nightro)-2-8. **Bob Q. Siege**-a(Claw) 27-31; (Daredevil)-#35. **Wolverton** a-12-22. **Bob Wood**-a(The Claw)-1-20; (The Ghost)-5-20. **Dick Wood** sty-2-10, 13-22, 27-32. **Daredevil** not on-c #46,49-52,56-66,68-134.*

DAREDEVIL (...& the Black Widow #92-107 on-c only; see Giant-Size...,Marvel Advs., Marvel Graphic Novel #24, Marvel Super Heroes, '66 & Spider-Man &...)
Marvel Comics Group: Apr, 1964 - No. 380, Oct, 1998

1-Origin/1st app. Daredevil; intro Foggy Nelson & Karen Page; death of Battling Murdock; Bill Everett-c/a; reprinted in Marvel Super Heroes #1 (1966)
667 1334 2000 4650 8825 13,000

2-Fantastic Four cameo; 2nd app. Electro (Spidey villain); Thing guest star
75 150 225 600 1350 2100

3-Origin & 1st app. The Owl (villain) 46 92 138 359 805 1250

4-Origin & 1st app. The Purple Man 40 80 120 296 673 1050

5-Minor costume change; Wally Wood-a begins 29 58 87 209 467 725

6-Mr. Fear app. 21 42 63 147 324 500

7-Daredevil battles Sub-Mariner & dons red costume for 1st time (4/65); Marvel Masterwork pin-up by Wood 100 200 300 800 1800 2800

8-10: 8-Origin/1st app. Stilt Man. 10-1st app. Cat Man, Bird Man, Ape Man & Frog Man
15 30 45 103 227 350

11-15: 11-Last Wally Wood. 12-1st app. Plunderer; Ka-Zar app. Kirby/Romita-a begins. 13-Facts about Ka-Zar's origin; vs. the Plunderer; Kirby/Romita-a. 14-Romita-a begins; Ka-Zar & the Plunderer app. 15-1st app. the Ox 10 20 30 66 138 210

16,17- Spider-Man x-over. 16-1st Romita-a on Spider-Man (5/66)
20 40 60 141 313 485

18-Origin & 1st app. Gladiator 11 22 33 77 166 255

19,20: 19-DD vs. the Gladiator. 20-DD vs. the Owl; 1st Gene Colan-a
9 18 27 58 114 170

21-26,28-30: 21-DD vs. the Owl. 22-DD vs. the Owl, Gladiator & and Masked Marauder; 1st app the Tri-Man. 23-Owl, Gladiator, Masked Marauder & Tri-Man app. 24-Ka-Zar app. 25-1st app. Leap-Frog; 1st app. 'Mike Murdock' Daredevil's fake twin brother. 26-Stilt-Man app. 30-Thor app. vs. Cobra and Mr. Hyde 6 12 18 41 76 110

27-Spider-Man x-over; Stilt-Man & the Masked Marauder app.
7 14 21 48 89 150

31-36,39,40: 31,32-DD vs. Cobra & Mr. Hyde. 33,34-DD vs. the Beetle. 35-DD vs. the Trapster. 36-DD vs. the Trapster; Dr. Doom cameo. 39-1st app. Exterminator (later becomes Death-Stalker); Ape Man, Cat Man & Bird Man app. as the Unholy Three. 40-DD vs. the Unholy Three 6 12 18 37 66 95

37,38: 37-Daredevil vs. Dr. Doom. 38-Dr. Doom app; Fantastic Four x-over; continued in Fantastic Four #73 7 14 21 49 92 135

41,42-44-49: 41- 'Death' of Mike Murdock; Daredevil drops the fake twin persona; DD vs. the Exterminator and the Unholy Three. 42-1st app. Jester. 44-46-DD vs. the Jester. 48-DD vs. Stilt-Man. 49-1st app. Star Saxon & the Plastoid
5 10 15 34 60 85

43-Daredevil vs. Captain America; origin partially retold; Kirby-c
9 18 27 58 114 170

50-51,53: 50-Barry Smith-a; last Stan Lee-s; vs. Star Saxon & the Plastoid. 51-1st Roy Thomas-s; Barry Smith-a; vs. Star Saxon & the Plastoid. 53-Gene Colan-a returns; origin retold 5 10 15 35 63 90

52-Barry Smith-a; Black Panther app.; learns Daredevil's secret identity
7 14 21 46 86 125

Daredevil #98 © MAR

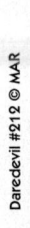

Daredevil #212 © MAR

Daredevil #272 © MAR

	GD 2.0	VG 4.0	FN 6.0	VF 8.0	VF/NM 9.0	NM- 9.2

54-56,58-60: 54-Spider-Man cameo; vs. Mr. Fear. 55-DD vs. Mr. Fear. 56-1st app. Death's Head (Star Saxon) (9/69); story continued in #57. 58-1st app. Stunt-Master. 59-1st app. Torpedo (dies this issue) 4 8 12 27 44 60

57-Reveals i.d. to Karen Page; Death's Head app. 6 12 18 41 76 110

61,63-68,70-72,74-76,78-80: 61-DD vs. the Jester, Cobra & Mr. Hyde. 63-vs. Gladiator. 64-Stunt-Master app. 67-Stilt-Man app. 71-Last Roy Thomas-s. 72-1st app Tagak 'Lord of Leopards'; 1st Gerry Conway-s. 75-1st app. El Condor. 76-Death El Condor. 78-1st app. Man-Bull. 79-DD vs. Man-Bull. 80-vs the Owl 4 8 12 23 37 50

62,69,73: 62-Origin of Nighthawk (Kyle Richmond). 69-Black Panther app. 73-Continued from Iron Man #35; Nick Fury app. vs. the Zodiac; concluded in Iron Man #36.
4 8 12 28 47 65

77-Spider-Man & Sub-Mariner app.; story continues in Sub-Mariner #40
5 10 15 34 60 85

81-(52 pgs.)-Black Widow becomes regular guest star (11/71); receives co-billing w/issue #92 through issue #107; vs. Mr. Kline and the Owl 7 14 21 49 92 135

82,84-87,89-98: 82-DD vs. Mr. Kline. 84-Conclusion of the Mr. Kline story; see Iron Man #41-45 & Sub-Mariner #42. 85-DD vs. Gladiator. 86-Death of the Ox. 87-Daredevil & the Black Widow relocate to San Francisco; Electro app. 89-Purple Man & Electro app. 90-Mr. Fear app. 91-Death of Mr. Fear. 92-Black Widow gets co-billing as of this issue. 93,94-DD vs. the Indestructible Man. 95,96-DD vs. the Man-Bull. 97-99-DD vs. the Dark Messiah; Steve Gerber co-script; 98-Last Conway-s
3 6 9 19 30 40

83,99: 83-Barry Smith layouts/Weiss-p. 99-Hawkeye app; Steve Gerber-s begin; plot continues in Avengers #111 3 6 9 21 33 45

88-Purple Man app; early life of Black Widow revealed
4 8 12 27 44 60

100-1st app. Angar the Screamer; origin retold; Jann Wenner, editor of Rolling Stone app.
5 10 15 34 60 85

101,102,104,106,108-110: 101-vs Angar the Screamer. 102-vs. Stilt Man. 104-Kraven the Hunter app. 106-Moondragon app; vs. Terrex. 108-Title returns to 'Daredevil'. Moondragon app.; 1st app. Black Spectre; Beetle app; Daredevil and Black Widow break-up. 109-Shanna the She-Devil app.; vs. Nekra & Black Spectre; story continues in Marvel Two-in-One #3. 110-Continued from Marvel Two-in-One #3; vs. the Mandrill, Nekra & Black Spectre; brief Thing app. 3 6 9 16 23 30

103-1st app. & origin of Ramrod; Spider-Man app. 4 8 12 25 40 55

105-Origin of Moondragon by Starlin (12/73) Thanos cameo in flashback (early app.)
6 12 18 42 79 115

107-Starlin-c; Thanos cameo; Moondragon & Captain Marvel app; death of Terrex
3 6 9 21 33 45

111-1st app. Silver Samurai; Shanna the She-Devil, Mandrill, Nekra & Black Spectre app.
6 12 18 41 76 110

112-114,116-120: 112-Conclusion of the Black Spectre story; Mandrill & Nekra app. 113-1st brief app. Death-Stalker; Gladiator app. 114-1st full Death-Stalker app; Man-Thing & Gladiator app. 116,117-DD vs. the Owl; 117-Last Gerber-s. 118-1st app. Blackwing; vs. the Circus of Crime. 119-Tony Isabella-s begin. 120-1st app. El Jaguar Agent of HYDRA
3 6 9 16 23 30

115-Death-Stalker app.; advertisement for Wolverine in Incredible Hulk #181 (on pg. 19)
5 10 15 33 57 80

121-123,125-130,137: 121-vs. HYDRA; El Jaguar and the Dreadnaught app; Nick Fury app. 122-Return of Silvermane as the new Supreme HYDRA. 123-Silvermane, El Jaguar, Dreadnaught, Mentallo & HYDRA app; Nick Fury and SHIELD app; last Isabella-s. 125-Death of Copperhead; Wolfman-s begin. 126-1st app. the second and third Torpedos; 1st app. Heather Glenn. 127-vs. the third Torpedo (Brock Jones). 128-Death-Stalker app. 129-vs the Man-Bull 3 6 9 14 20 25

124-1st app. Copperhead; Black Widow leaves; Len Wein & Marv Wolfman co-plot
3 6 9 21 33 45

131-Origin/1st app. Bullseye (see Nick Fury #15) 15 30 45 103 227 350

132-2nd Bullseye app. new Bullseye (regular 25c edition)
6 12 18 37 66 95

132-(30¢-c variant, limited distribution)(4/76) 10 20 30 66 138 210

133-136: 133-Uri Geller & the Jester app. 134-Torpedo app. vs. the Chameleon. 135,136-vs. the Jester 3 6 9 14 20 25

133-136-(30¢-c variants, limited distribution)(5-8/76) 5 10 15 30 50 70

138-Ghost Rider-c/story; Death's Head is reincarnated; Byrne-a
3 6 9 19 30 40

139,140,142-145,147-154: 140-vs the Beetle & Gladiator. 142-vs. Cobra & Hyde; Nova cameo. 143-Cobra & Hyde app; last Wolfman-s. 144-vs the Man-Bull & Owl. 145-vs the Owl. 147-Purple Man app. 148-Death-Stalker app. 149-1st app. the third Smasher. 150-1st app. Paladin. 151-Reveals i.d. to Heather Glenn. 152-vs Death-Stalker; Roger McKenzie-s begin. 153-vs Cobra & Hyde. 154-vs Purple Man, Cobra & Hyde & Jester
2 4 6 13 18 22

141,146-Bullseye app. 4 8 12 25 40 55

146-(35¢-c variant, limited distribution) 10 20 30 69 147 225

147,148-(35¢-c variants, limited distribution) 8 16 24 55 105 155

155-157-DD vs. Death-Stalker; Black Widow, Hercules, Captain America & the Beast app.
3 6 9 14 20 25

158-Frank Miller-a begins (5/79) origin/death of Death-Stalker (see Captain America #235 & Spectacular Spider-Man #27) 8 16 24 56 108 160

159-Brief Bullseye app. 5 10 15 30 50 70

160,161-Bullseye and Black Widow app. 4 8 12 25 40 55

162-Ditko-a; no Miller-a; origin retold 3 6 9 14 20 25

163,164: 163-vs. the Hulk. 164-Origin retold and expanded
3 6 9 20 31 42

165-167,170: 165-1st Miller co-plot w/McKenzie; Dr. Octopus app. 166-vs. Gladiator. 167-Last McKenzie co-plot; 1st app. Mauler. 170-Kingpin app.
3 6 9 16 24 32

168-(1/81) Origin/1st app. Elektra; 1st Miller scripts 12 24 36 80 173 265

169-2nd Elektra app; Bullseye app. 5 10 15 30 50 70

171-173: 171,172-vs. the Kingpin 3 6 9 17 16 35

174-1st app. the Hand (Ninjas who trained Elektra) 3 6 9 21 33 45

175-Elektra & Daredevil vs. the Hand 3 6 9 19 30 40

176-180-Elektra app: 176-1st app. Stick (Daredevil's mentor). 177-Kingpin & the Hand app. 178-Kingpin & Power Man & Iron Fist app. 179-Anti-smoking issue mentioned in the Congressional Record 3 6 9 16 24 32

181-(4/82, 52-pgs)-Death of Elektra; Punisher cameo out of costume
4 8 12 25 40 55

182-184: 182-Bullseye app. 183,184 -'Angel Dust' drug story; Punisher app.
3 6 9 16 23 30

185-191: 186-Stilt-Man app. 187-New Black Widow vs. the Hand. 188-Black Widow app. 189-Death of Stick; Black Widow app. 190-Elektra returns, part origin; 2 pin-ups. 191-Classic 'Russian Roulette' story with Bullseye; last Miller Daredevil
2 4 6 8 11 14

192-195,198,199: 192-Alan Brennert story; Klaus Janson (p)&(i) begin. 193-Larry Hama-s. 194-Denny O'Neil-s begin. 198-Bullseye receives Adamantium bones. 199-Bullseye app; death of Dark Wind 5.00

196-Wolverine-c/app; 1st app. Dark Wind. Bullseye app.
3 6 9 14 19 24

197-Bullseye-c/app; 1st app, Yuriko Oyama (becomes Lady Deathstrike in Alpha Flight #33)
2 4 6 11 16 20

200-Bulleye vs. Daredevil; Byrne-c 2 4 6 8 11 14

201-207,209-218: 201-Black Widow solo story. 202-1st app. Micah Synn. 203-1st app. the Trump; Byrne-c. 204-1st app. Crossbow (Green Arrow homage?) 205-1st app. Gael (Irish Republican Army hitman). 206-DD vs. Micah Synn; 1st Mazzucchelli-p on DD. Kingpin app. 207-HYDRA & Black Widow app. 209-Harlan Ellison plot. 210-Crossbow & Kingpin app. 211,212-DD & Kingpin team-up vs Micah Synn. 215-Two-Gun Kid flashback. 216-Gael app. 217-Gael app; 1st app. the Cossack; Barry-Windsor-Smith-c. 218-DD appears as the Jester 5.00

208,219: 208-Harlan Ellison and Arthur Byron Cover scripts borrowed from Avengers TV episode 'House that Jack Built'. 219-Miller-c/script 6.00

220-226,234-237: 220-Death of Heather Glenn. 222-Black Widow app. 223-Secret Wars II crossover; Beyonder gives DD his sight back; DD rejects the gift. 225-Vulture app. 226-Gladiator app.; last Denny O'Neil-s. 234-Madcap app. 235-DD vs. Mr. Hyde. 237-DD vs. Klaw; Black Widow app. 5.00

227-(2/86, 36 pgs.)-Miller scripts begin; classic 'Born Again' Pt.1 story begins; Kingpin learns DD's secret identity. 6.00

228-233: 'Born Again'; Kingpin ruins Matt Murdock's life. 232-1st app Nuke. 233-Last Miller script; Captain America app.; death of Nuke 5.00

238-Mutant massacre; Sabretooth app; 1st Ann Nocenti-s 6.00

239,240,242-247: 239-1st app. Rotgut. 243-1st app. Nameless One. 245-Black Panther app. 246-1st app. Chance. 247-Black Widow app. 4.00

241-Todd McFarlane-a(p) 5.00

248-Wolverine cameo; 1st app. Bushwacker. 249-DD vs. Wolverine; Bushwacker app. 6.00

250,251,253,258: 250-1st app. Bullet; Romita Jr-a begins. 251-vs. Bullet. 253-Kingpin app. 258-1st app. Bengal 4.00

252-(52 pgs)-Fall of the Mutants tie-in; 1st app. Ammo. 260-(52 pgs)-Bushwacker, Bullet, Ammo & Typhoid Mary vs. DD 5.00

254-Origin & 1st app. Typhoid Mary (5/88) 3 6 9 21 33 45

255,256: 2nd&3rd app. Typhoid Mary. 259-Typhoid Mary app. 5.00

257-Punisher app. (x-over w/Punisher #10) 2 4 6 9 13 16

261-269,271-281: 261-Typhoid Mary & Human Torch app. 262-Inferno tie-in. 263-Inferno tie-in; 1st new look 'monstrous' Mephisto. 264-vs the Owl. 265-Inferno tie-in; Mephisto app. 266-Mephisto app. 267-Bullet app. 269-Blob & Pyro (from Freedom Force) app. 272-1st app. Shotgun; Inhumans app. 273-DD vs. Shotgun; Inhumans app. 274-Black Bolt & the Inhumans app. 275,276-'Acts of Vengeance' x-over; Ultron app. 278-Mephisto & Blackheart app. 279-Mephisto app. 280-DD in Hell; Mephisto app. 281-Silver Surfer cameo; Mephisto & Blackheart app. 3.00

270-1st app. Blackheart (the son of Mephisto); Spider-Man app.
1 3 4 6 8 10

282-DD escapes Hell; Silver Surfer, Mephisto & Blackheart app. 4.00

283-287,289 294-299: 283-Captain America app. 284-287,289-Bullseye impersonates DD;

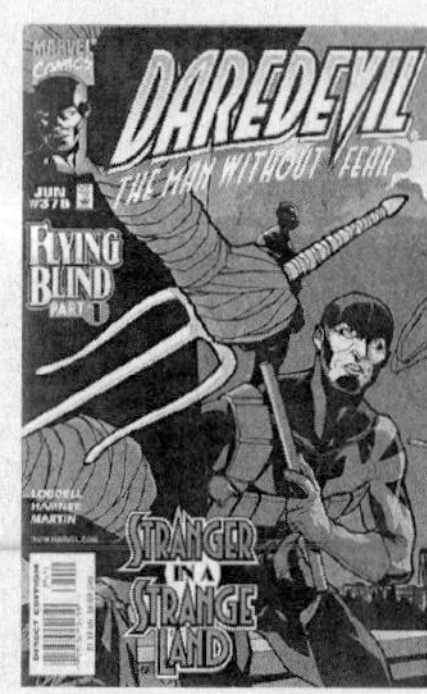

Daredevil #376 © MAR

Daredevil V2 #9 © MAR

Daredevil V2 #71 © MAR

GD 2.0 VG 4.0 FN 6.0 VF 8.0 VF/NM 9.0 NM- 9.2

284-1st Lee Weeks-a. 291-vs. Bullet; last Nocenti-s. 292,293-Punisher app. 295-Ghost Rider app. 297-'Last Rights' Pt.1; Typhoid Mary app. 298-Pt.2; Nick Fury & SHIELD app. 299-Pt. 3; Baron Strucker & Hydra vs. the Kingpin 3.00
287-Bulleye-c/s; Kingpin app; Elektra dream sequence 5.00
290-Bullseye vs. Daredevil 1 3 4 6 8 10
300-(52 pgs.)-'Last Rights' Pt.4; Kingpin loses criminal empire; last Weeks-a 4.00
301-318: 301-303-vs. the Owl. 305-306-Spider-Man app. 307-'Dead Man's Hand' Pt. 1; Nomad & Tombstone app.; continued in Nomad #4. 308-'Dead Man's Hand' Pt. 5; continued from Punisher War Journal #45; Punisher app; continues in Punisher War Journal #46. 309-'Dead Man's Hand' Pt. 7; continued from Nomad #5; continued in Punisher War Journal #47. 310-Infinity War tie-in; Calypso vs. DD doppelganger. 311-Calypso & Brother Voodoo app. 314,315-Shock & Mr. Fear app. 317,318-Taskmaster, Stilt-Man & Tatterdemalion app. 3.00
319-Prologue to Fall From Grace Pt. 1; Elektra returns; Silver Sable app. 6.00
319-2nd printing w/black-c 3.00
320-(9/93) Fall From Grace Pt. 1; Silver Sable app. 5.00
321-Fall From Grace regular ed; Pt. 2 new armored costume; Venom app. 3.00
321-($2.00)-Wraparound Glow-in-the-dark-c 5.00
322-325: 322-Fall From Grace Pt. 3; Eddie Brock app. 323,324: Fall From Grace Pts. 4,5. 323-vs. Venom-c/story. 324-Morbius-c/story. 325-($2.50, 52 pgs.) Fall From Grace ends; contains bound-in poster; Elektra app. 4.00
326-338: 326-New logo; Captain America app. 327-Captain America-c/story. 328-Captain America & Baron Strucker app. 329-Iron Fist app. 330-Gambit app. 331,332-vs. Baron Strucker. 334-336-Bushwacker app. 338-Kingpin app. 3.00
339-343: 339-342-Kingpin app. 4.00
344-(9/95)-Title becomes part of the 'Marvel Edge' imprint; story continued from Double Edge: Alpha; Punisher & Nick Fury app.; continued in Ghost Rider #65 5.00
345-Original red costume returns; Marvel Overpower card insert 6.00
346-350: 348-1st Cary Nord-a in DD (1/96) 'Dec' on-c. 350-($2.95)-Double-Sized 4.00
350-($3.50)-Variant gold ink-c 5.00
351-353,355-360,362-364: 351-Last 'Marvel Edge' imprint issue. 353-Karl Kessel scripts; Nord-c/a begins. 354-Bullseye (illusion)-c. 355-Pyro app. 357-Enforcers app. 358-Mysterio app. 360-Absorbing Man app. 363-Colan-c/a. 364-Mr. Fear app. 4.00
354-Spider-Man app.; $1.50-c begins 1 2 3 5 6 8
361,365-367: 361-Black Widow & DD vs. Grey Gargoyle. 365-367: 365-Molten Man & Mr. Fear app. 366-Mr. Fear app.; Colan-c/a. 367-Colan-c/a; Mr. Fear & Gladiator app. 5.00
368-Omega Red & Black Widow app. 1 3 4 6 8 10
369-Black Widow app. 6.00
370-374: 370-Darkstar, Vanguard & Ursa Major app; last Colan-a. 371-Black Widow app. 372-Ghost Rider (Daniel Ketch) app. 373,374-Mr. Fear app. 5.00
375-($2.99)-Wraparound-c; Mr. Fear-c/app. 5.00
376-379: "Flying Blind", DD goes undercover for SHIELD 3.00
380-($2.99) Final issue; flashback story; Kingpin, Bullseye & Bushwacker app. 1 3 4 6 8 10
#(-1) Flashback issue (7/97, $1.95); Gene Colan-c/a 3.00
No. 181 Facsimile Edition (11/19, $4.99) r/#181 with original 1982 ads and letter column 5.00
Special 1 (9/67, 25¢, 68-pgs)-New art/story by Lee/Colan; DD vs. the 'Emissaries of Evil' (Electro, Leapfrog, Stilt-Man, Matador & Gladiator) 8 16 24 51 96 140
Special 2,3: 2 (2/71, 25¢, 52 pgs.) Reprints issues #10-11 by Wood. 3-(1/72, 25¢, 52 pgs.) Reprints issues #16-17 4 8 12 23 37 50
Annual 4 (10/76, squarebound) Sub-Mariner & Black Panther app. 3 6 9 18 28 38
Annual 4 (#5, 1989) Atlantis Attacks; continued from Spectacular Spider-Man Annual #9; Spider-Man app.; continued in Avengers Annual #18 5.00
Annual 6-9: 6-('90) Lifeform Pt. 2; continued from Punisher Annual #3; continues in Silver Surfer Annual #3. 7-('91) The Von Strucker Gambit Pt. 1; continued in Punisher Annual #4. Guice-a (7 pgs.). 8-('92) System Bites Pt. 2; Deathlok & Bushwacker app; continued in Wonder Man Annual #1. 9-('93) Polybagged w/card; 1st app. Devourer 4.00
Annual 10-('94) Elektra, Nick Fury, Shang-Chi (Master of Kung-Fu) vs. Ghostmaker 5.00
...: Born Again TPB ($17.95)-r/#227-233; Miller-s/Mazzucchelli-a & new-c 20.00
... By Frank Miller and Klaus Janson Omnibus HC (2007, $99.99, dustjacket) r/#158-161, 163-191 and What If...? #28; intros by Miller and Janson; interviews, bonus art 100.00
... By Frank Miller and Klaus Janson Omnibus Companion HC (2007, $59.99, die-cut d.j.) r/#219,226-233, Daredevil: The Man Without Fear #1-5, Daredevil: Love and War, and Peter Parker, the Spect. Spider-Man #27-28; bonus materials 60.00
.../Deadpool (Annual '97, $2.99)-Wraparound-c 6.00
...: Fall From Grace TPB ($19.95)-r/#319-325 20.00
...: Gang War TPB ($15.95)-r/#169-172,180; Miller-s/a(p) 16.00
...Legends: (Vol. 4) Typhoid Mary TPB (2003, $19.95) r/#254-257,259-263 20.00
... :Love's Labors Lost TPB ($19.99)-r/#215-217,219-222,225,226; Mazzucchelli-c 20.00
.../Punisher TPB (1988, $4.95)-r/D.D. #182-184 (all printings) 6.00
...Visionaries: Frank Miller Vol. 1 TPB ($17.95) r/#158-161,163-167 18.00
...Visionaries: Frank Miller Vol. 2 TPB ($24.95) r/#168-182; new Miller-c 25.00
...Visionaries: Frank Miller Vol. 3 TPB ($24.95) r/#183-191, What If? #28,35 & Bizarre Adventures #28; new Miller-c 25.00

GD 2.0 VG 4.0 FN 6.0 VF 8.0 VF/NM 9.0 NM- 9.2

... Vs. Bullseye Vol. 1 TPB (2004, $15.99) r/#131-132,146,169,181,191 16.00
Wizard Ace Edition: Daredevil (Vol. 1) #1 (4/03, $13.99) Acetate Campbell-c 14.00
NOTE: ***Art Adams*** *c-238p, 239.* ***Austin*** *a-191i; c-151i, 200i.* ***John Buscema*** *a-136, 137p, 234p, 235p; c-86p, 136i, 137p, 142, 219.* ***Byrne*** *c-200p, 201, 203, 223.* ***Capullo*** *a-286p.* ***Colan*** *a(p)-20-49, 53-82, 84-98, 100, 110, 112, 124, 153, 154, 156, 157, 363, 366-370, Spec. 1p; c(p)-20-42, 44-49, 53-60, 71, 92, 98, 138, 153, 154, 156, 157, Annual 1.* ***Craig*** *a-50i, 52i.* ***Ditko*** *a-162, 234p, 235p, 264p; c-162.* ***Everett*** *c/a-1; inks-21, 83.* ***Garney*** *c/a-304.* ***Gil Kane*** *a-141p, 146-148p, 151p; c(p)-85, 90, 91, 93, 94, 115, 116, 119, 120, 125-128, 133, 139, 147, 152.* ***Kirby*** *c-2-4, 12p, 13p, 43.* ***Layton*** *c-202.* ***Miller*** *scripts-168-182, 183(part), 184-191, 219, 227-233; a-158-161p, 163-184p, 191p; c-158-161p, 163-184p, 185-189, 190p, 191.* ***Orlando*** *a-2-4p.* ***Powell*** *a-9p, 11p, Special 1r, 2r.* ***Simonson*** *c-199, 236p.* ***B. Smith*** *a-236p; c-51p, 52p, 217.* ***Starlin*** *a-105p.* ***Steranko*** *c-44i.* ***Tuska*** *a-39i, 145p.* ***Williamson*** *a(i)-237, 239, 240, 243, 248-257, 259-282, 283(part), 284, 285, 287, 288(part), 289(part), 293-300; c(i)-237, 243, 244, 248-257, 259-263, 265-278, 280-289, Annual 8.* ***Wood*** *a-5-8, 9i, 10, 11i, Spec. 2i; c-5-11, 164i.*

DAREDEVIL (Volume 2)(Marvel Knights)(Becomes Black Panther: The Man Without Fear #513)
Marvel Comics: Nov, 1998 - No. 512, Feb, 2011 ($2.50/$2.99)

1-Kevin Smith-s/Quesada & Palmiotti-a 12.00
1-($6.95) DF Edition w/Quesada & Palmiotti var.-c 15.00
1-($6.00) DF Sketch Ed. w/B&W-c 10.00
2-Two covers by Campbell and Quesada/Palmiotti 9.00
3-8: 4,5-Bullseye app. 5-Variant-c exists. 8-Spider-Man-c/app.; last Smith-s 6.00
9-15: 9-11-David Mack-s; intro Echo. 12-Begin $2.99-c; Haynes-a. 13,14-Quesada-a 4.00
16-19-Direct editions; Bendis-s/Mack-c/painted-a 4.00
18,19,21,22-Newsstand editions with variant cover logo "Marvel Unlimited Featuring... 4.00
20-($3.50) Gale-s/Winslade-a; back-up by Stan Lee-s/Colan-a; Mack-c 5.00
21-40: 21-25-Gale-s. 26-38-Bendis-s/Maleev-a. 32-Daredevil's ID revealed. 35-Spider-Man-c/app. 38-Iron Fist & Luke Cage app. 40-Dodson-a 3.50
41-(25¢-c) Begins "Lowlife" arc; Maleev-a; intro Milla Donovan 3.00
41-(Newsstand edition with 2.99¢-c) 3.00
42-45-"Lowlife" arc; Maleev-a 3.00
46-50-($2.99). 46-Typhoid Mary returns. 49-Bullseye app. 50-Art panels by various incl. Romita, Colan, Mack, Janson, Oeming, Quesada 3.00
51-64,66-74,76-81: 51-55-Mack-s/a; Echo app. 54-Wolverine-c/app. 61-64-Black Widow app. 71-Decalogue begins. 76-81-The Murdock Papers. 81-Last Bendis-s/Maleev-a 3.00
65-($3.99) 40th Anniversary issue; Land-c; art by Maleev, Horn, Bachalo and others 4.00
75-($3.99) Decalogue ends; Jester app. 4.00
82-99,101-119: 82-Brubaker-s/Lark-a begin; Foggy "killed". 84-86-Punisher app. 87-Other Daredevil ID revealed. 94-Romita-c. 111-Lady Bullseye debut 3.00
82-Variant-c by McNiven 4.00
100-($3.99) Three covers (Djurdjevic, Bermejo and Turner); art by Romita Sr., Colan, Lark, Sienkiewicz, Maleev, Bermejo & Djurdjevic; sketch art gallery; r/Daredevil #90 (1972) 4.00
(After Vol. 2 #119, Aug, 2009, numbering reverts to original Vol. 1 with #500)
500-(10/09, $4.99) Kingpin, Lady Bullseye app.; back-up stories, pin-up & cover galleries; r/#191; five covers by Djurdjevic, Darrow, Dell'Otto, Ross and Zircher 5.00
501-512: 501-Daredevil takes over The Hand; Diggle-s begins; Ribic-c. 508-Shadowland begins. 512-Black Panther app. 3.00
Annual #1 (12/07, $3.99) Brubaker-s/Fernandez-a/Djurdjevic-c; Black Tarantula app. 4.00
... & Captain America: Dead on Arrival (2008, $4.99) English version of Italian story 5.00
... Black & White 1 (10/10, $3.99) B&W short stories by various; Aja-c 4.00
... Blood of the Tarantula (6/08, $3.99) Parks & Brubaker-s/Samnee-a/Djurdjevic-c 4.00
... By Brian Michael Bendis Omnibus Vol. 1 HC (2008, $99.99) oversized r/#16-19,26-50, and 56-60 100.00
... By Ed Brubaker Saga (2008, giveaway) synopsis of issues #82-110, preview of #111 3.00
... Cage Match 1 (7/10, $2.99) flashback early Luke Cage team-up; Chen-a 3.00
... MGC #26 (8/10, $1.00) r/#26 with "Marvel's Greatest Comics" logo on cover 3.00
...2099 #1 (11/04, $2.99) Kirkman-s/Moline-a 3.00
TPB ($9.95) r/#1-3 10.00
...Vol. 1 HC (2001, $29.99, with dustjacket) r/#1-11,13-15 30.00
...Vol. 1 HC (2003, $29.99, with dustjacket) r/#1-11,13-15; larger page size 30.00
...Vol. 2 HC (2002, $29.99, with dustjacket) r/#26-37; afterword by Bendis 30.00
...Vol. 3 HC (2004, $29.99, with dustjacket) r/#38-50; Maleev sketch pages 30.00
...Vol. 4 HC (2005, $29.99, with dustjacket) r/#56-65; Vol. 1 #81 (1971) Black Widow 30.00
...Vol. 5 HC (2006, $29.99, with dustjacket) r/#66-75 30.00
...Vol. 6 HC (2006, $34.99, with dustjacket) r/#76-81 & What If Karen Page Had Lived? 35.00
(Vol. 1) Visionaries TPB ($19.95) r/#1-8; Ben Affleck intro. 20.00
(Vol. 2) Parts of a Hole TPB (1/02, $17.95) r/#9-15; David Mack intro. 18.00
(Vol. 3) Wake Up TPB (7/02, $9.99) r/#16-19 10.00
...Vol. 4: Underboss TPB (8/02, $14.99) r/#26-31 15.00
...Vol. 5: Out TPB (2003, $19.99) r/#32-40 20.00
...Vol. 6: Lowlife TPB (2003, $13.99) r/#41-45 14.00
...Vol. 7: Hardcore TPB (2003, $13.99) r/#46-50 14.00
...Vol. 8: Echo - Vision Quest TPB (2004, $13.99) r/#51-55; David Mack-s/a 14.00
...Vol. 9: King of Hell's Kitchen TPB (2004, $13.99) r/#56-60 14.00
...Vol. 10: The Widow TPB (2004, $16.99) r/#61-65 & Vol. 1 #81 17.00
...Vol. 11: Golden Age TPB (2005, $13.99) r/#66-70 14.00
...Vol. 12: Decalogue TPB (2005, $14.99) r/#71-75 15.00
...Vol. 13: The Murdock Papers TPB (2006, $14.99) r/#76-81 15.00
...: The Devil Inside and Out Vol. 1 (2006, $14.99) r/#82-87; Brubaker & Lark interview 15.00

Daredevil #596 © MAR

Daredevil: Dark Nights #5 © MAR

Daredevil: Yellow #2 © MAR

GD VG FN VF VF/NM NM-
2.0 4.0 6.0 8.0 9.0 9.2

...: The Devil Inside and Out Vol. 2 (2007, $14.99) r/#88-93; Bermejo cover sketches 15.00
...: Hell To Pay Vol. 1 TPB (2007, $14.99) r/#94-99; Djurdjevic cover sketches 15.00
...: Hell To Pay Vol. 2 TPB (2008, $15.99) r/#100-105 16.00

DAREDEVIL (Volume 3)
Marvel Comics: Sept, 2011 - No. 36, Apr, 2014 ($3.99/$2.99)

1-($3.99) Mark Waid-s/Paolo Rivera-a; back-up tale with Marcos Martin-a 4.00
1-Variant-c by Marcos Martin 8.00
1-Variant-c by Neal Adams 10.00
2-10,10.1,11-20,23,24,25,27-36-($2.99) 2-Capt. America app. 3-Klaw returns. 4-6-Marcos Martin-a. 8-X-over w/Amazing Spider-Man #677; Spider-Man and Black Cat app. 11-Spider-Man app. 17-Allred-a. 30-Silver Surfer app. 32,33-Satana & monsters app. 3.00
21,22: 21-1st Superior Spider-Man app. (cameo). 22-Superior Spider-Man app. 5.00
26-($3.99) Bullseye and Lady Bullseye app.; back-up "Fighting Cancer" story 4.00
Annual 1 (10/12, $4.99) Alan Davis-s/a/c; Dr. Strange & ClanDestine app. 5.00

DAREDEVIL (Volume 4)
Marvel Comics: May, 2014 - No. 18, Nov, 2015 ($3.99)

1-18-($3.99) Mark Waid-s/Chris Samnee-a; Murdock moves to San Francisco. 6,7-Original Sin tie-in. 8-10-Purple Man app. 14-Owl's daughter app. 15-18-Kingpin app. 4.00
#0.1-(9/14, $4.99) Waid-s/Krause-a/Samnee-c 5.00
#1.50-($4.99) 50th Anniversary issue; Murdock at 50; back-up Bendis-s/Maleev-a 5.00
#15.1-(7/15, $4.99) Waid-s/Samnee-a; Guggenheim-s/Krause-a 5.00

DAREDEVIL (Follows Secret Wars)
Marvel Comics: Feb, 2016 - No. 28, Dec, 2017; No. 595, Jan, 2018 - No. 612, Jan, 2019 ($3.99)

1-28: 1-Soule-s/Garney-a; Blindspot app. 2,3-The Hand app. 4-Steve Rogers app. 6,7-Elektra app.; Sienkiewicz-c. 9-Spider-Man app. 16-Bullseye app. 18,19-Purple Man app. 23-She-Hulk app. 28-Kingpin becomes mayor of New York 4.00

[Title switches to legacy numbering after #28 (12/17)]

595-599,601-611: 595-(1/18) Soule-s/Landini-a. 603,609-Elektra app. 4.00
600-(5/18, $5.99) Soule-s/Garney-a; Spider-Man and The Defenders app. 6.00
612-($4.99) Soule-s/Noto-a; leads into Man Without Fear 2019 series 5.00
Annual 1 (10/16, $4.99) Echo returns; Vanesa Del Ray-a 5.00
Annual 1 (10/18, $4.99) Schultz-s/Takara-a; flashback to 1st meeting with Misty Knight 5.00

DAREDEVIL (Follows Man Without Fear)
Marvel Comics: Apr, 2019 - Present ($4.99/$3.99)

1-($4.99) Zdarsky-s/Checchetto-a; Kingpin app.; intro Det. Cole North 5.00
2-24,26-($3.99) 3,4-Punisher app. 10-16-Elektra app. 19,20-Bullseye, Crossbones, Rhino app. 20,22,24,26-Typhoid Mary app. 23-Spider-Man app. 26-King in Black tie-in 4.00
25-Daredevil goes to jail; Elektra dons Daredevil costume 5.00
Annual 1 (10/20, $4.99) Zdarsky-s/Garcia-a; spotlight on Mike Murdock; The Hood app. 5.00

DAREDEVIL/ BATMAN (Also see Batman/Daredevil)
Marvel Comics/ DC Comics: 1997 ($5.99, one-shot)

nn-McDaniel-c/a 6.00

DAREDEVIL BATTLES HITLER (See Daredevil #1 [1941 series])

DAREDEVIL: BATTLIN' JACK MURDOCK
Marvel Comics: Aug, 2007 - No. 4, Nov, 2007 ($3.99, limited series)

1-4-Wells-s/DiGiandomenico-a; flashback to the fixed fight 4.00
TPB (2007, $12.99) r/#1-4; page layouts and cover inks 13.00

DAREDEVIL COMICS (Golden Age title) (See Daredevil)

DAREDEVIL: DARK NIGHTS
Marvel Comics: Aug, 2013 - No. 8, Mar, 2014 ($3.99, limited series)

1-8: 1-3-Lee Weeks-s/a. 4,5-David Lapham-s/a; The Shocker app. 6-8-Conner-c 4.00

DAREDEVIL/ ELEKTRA: LOVE AND WAR
Marvel Comics: 2003 ($29.99, hardcover with dust jacket)

HC-Larger-size reprints of Daredevil: Love and War (Marvel Graphic Novel #24) & Elektra: Assassin; Frank Miller-s; Bill Sienkiewicz-a 30.00

DAREDEVIL: END OF DAYS
Marvel Comics: Dec, 2012 - No. 8, Aug, 2013 ($3.99, limited series)

1-8-Bendis & Mack-s/Janson & Sienkiewicz-a; death of Daredevil in the future 4.00

DAREDEVIL: FATHER
Marvel Comics: June, 2004 - No. 6, Feb, 2007 ($3.50/$2.99, limited series)

1-Quesada-s/a; Isanove-painted color 3.50
1-Director's Cut ($2.99) cover and page development art; partial sketch-c 3.00
2-6: 2-($2.99,10/05). 3-Santerians app. 3.00
HC (2006, $24.99) r/series; Lindelof intro.; sketch pages, cover pencils and bonus art 25.00

DAREDEVIL: NINJA
Marvel Comics: Dec, 2000 - No. 3, Feb, 2001 ($2.99, limited series)

1-3: Bendis-s/Haynes-a 3.00
1-Dynamic Forces foil-c 10.00
TPB (7/01, $12.95) r/#1-3 with cover and sketch gallery 13.00

DAREDEVIL NOIR
Marvel Comics: June, 2009 - No. 4, Sept, 2009 ($3.99, limited series)

1-4-Irvine-s/Coker-a; covers by Coker and Calero 4.00

DAREDEVIL / PUNISHER: SEVENTH CIRCLE
Marvel Comics: Jul, 2016 - No. 4, Oct, 2016 ($4.99, limited series)

1-4-Soule-s/Kudranski-a; Blindspot app. 3,4-Crimson Dynamo app. 5.00

DAREDEVIL: REBORN (Follows Shadowland x-over)
Marvel Comics: Mar, 2011 - No. 4, Jul, 2011 ($3.99, limited series)

1-4-Diggle-s/Gianfelice-a 4.00

DAREDEVIL: REDEMPTION
Marvel Comics: Apr, 2005 - No. 6, Aug, 2005 ($2.99, limited series)

1-6-Hine-s/Gaydos-a/Sienkiewicz-c 3.00
TPB (2005, $14.99) r/#1-6 15.00

DAREDEVIL: SEASON ONE
Marvel Comics: 2012 ($24.99, hardcover graphic novel)

HC - Story of early career, yellow costume; Johnston-s/Alves-a/Tedesco painted-c 25.00

DAREDEVIL/ SHI (See Shi/ Daredevil)
Marvel Comics/ Crusade Comics: Feb,1997 ($2.95, one-shot)

1 3.00

DAREDEVIL/ SPIDER-MAN
Marvel Comics: Jan, 2001 - No. 4, Apr, 2001 ($2.99, limited series)

1-4-Jenkins-s/Winslade-a/Alex Ross-c; Stilt Man app. 3.00
TPB (8/01, $12.95) r/#1-4; Ross-c 13.00

DAREDEVIL THE MAN WITHOUT FEAR
Marvel Comics: Oct, 1993 - No. 5, Feb, 1994 ($2.95, limited series) (foil embossed covers)

1-Miller scripts; Romita, Jr./Williamson-c/a 6.00
2-5 5.00
Hardcover 100.00
Trade paperback 20.00

DAREDEVIL: THE MOVIE (2003 movie adaptation)
Marvel Comics: March, 2003 ($3.50/$12.95, one-shot)

1-Photo-c of Ben Affleck; Bruce Jones-s/Manuel Garcia-a 3.50
TPB ($12.95) r/movie adaptation; Daredevil #32; Ultimate Daredevil & Elektra #1 and Spider-Man's Tangled Web #4; photo-c of Ben Affleck 13.00

DAREDEVIL: THE TARGET (Daredevil Bullseye on cover)
Marvel Comics: Jan, 2003 ($3.50, unfinished limited series)

1-Kevin Smith-s/Glenn Fabry-c/a 3.50

DAREDEVIL VS. PUNISHER
Marvel Comics: Sept, 2005 - No. 6, Jan, 2006 ($2.99, limited series)

1-5-David Lapham-s/a 3.00
TPB (2005, $15.99) r/#1-6 16.00

DAREDEVIL: YELLOW
Marvel Comics: Aug, 2001 - No. 6, Jan, 2002 ($3.50, limited series)

1-6-Jeph Loeb-s/Tim Sale-a/c; origin & yellow costume days retold 3.50
HC (5/02, $29.95) r/#1-6 with dustjacket; intro by Stan Lee; sketch pages 30.00
Daredevil Legends Vol. 1: Daredevil Yellow (2002, $14.99, TPB) r/#1-6 15.00

DARING ADVENTURES (Also see Approved Comics)
St. John Publishing Co.: Nov, 1953 (25¢, 3-D, came w/glasses)

1 (3-D)-Reprints lead story from Son of Sinbad #1 by Kubert 27 54 81 158 259 360

DARING ADVENTURES
I.W. Enterprises/Super Comics: 1963 - 1964

I. W. Reprint #8-r/Fight Comics #53; Matt Baker-a 5 10 15 30 50 70
I.W. Reprint #9-r/Blue Bolt #115; Disbrow-a(3) 5 10 15 31 53 75
Super Reprint #10,11('63)-r/Dynamic #24,16; 11-Marijuana story; Yankee Boy app.; Mac Raboy-a 4 8 12 21 33 45
Super Reprint #12('64)-Phantom Lady from Fox (r/#14 only? w/splash pg. omitted); Matt Baker-a 9 18 27 58 114 170
Super Reprint #15('64)-r/Hooded Menace #1 6 12 18 37 66 95
Super Reprint #16('64)-r/Dynamic #12 3 6 9 19 30 40
Super Reprint #17('64)-r/Green Lama #3 by Raboy 4 8 12 25 40 55
Super Reprint #18-Origin Atlas from unpublished Atlas Comics #1 4 8 12 23 37 50

Daring Love #1 © Gilmore

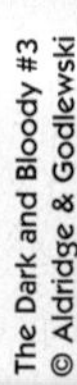

The Dark and Bloody #3 © Aldridge & Godlewski

Dark Ark #12 © Cullen Bunn

	GD 2.0	VG 4.0	FN 6.0	VF 8.0	VF/NM 9.0	NM- 9.2

DARING COMICS (Formerly Daring Mystery) (Jeanie Comics No. 13 on)
Timely Comics (HPC): No. 9, Fall, 1944 - No. 12, Fall, 1945

9-Human Torch, Toro & Sub-Mariner begin 219 438 657 1402 2401 3400
10-12: 10-The Angel only app. 11,12-The Destroyer app. 194 388 562 1242 2121 3000

NOTE: ***Schomburg** c-9-11. **Sekowsky** c-12? Human Torch, Toro & Sub-Mariner c-9-12.*

DARING CONFESSIONS (Formerly Youthful Hearts)
Youthful Magazines: No. 4, 11/52 - No. 7, 5/53; No. 8, 10/53

4-Doug Wildey-a; Tony Curtis story 23 46 69 134 220 305
5-8: 5-Ray Anthony photo on-c. 6,8-Wildey-a 16 32 48 98 154 210

DARING ESCAPES
Image Comics: Sept, 1998 - No. 4, Mar, 1999 ($2.95/$2.50, mini-series)

1-Houdini; following app. in Spawn #19,20 3.00
2-4-($2.50) 3.00

DARING LOVE (Radiant Love No. 2 on)
Gilmor Magazines: Sept-Oct, 1953

1–Steve Ditko's 1st published work (1st drawn was Fantastic Fears #5)(Also see Black Magic #27)(scarce) 354 708 1062 2478 4339 6200

DARING LOVE (Formerly Youthful Romances)
Ribage/Pix: No. 15, 12/52; No. 16, 2/53-c, 4/53-Indicia; No. 17-4/53-c & indicia

15 17 34 51 103 162 220
16,17: 17-Photo-c 15 30 45 88 137 185

NOTE: ***Colletta** a-15. **Wildey** a-17.*

DARING LOVE STORIES (See Fox Giants)

DARING MYSTERY COMICS (Comedy Comics No. 9 on; title changed to Daring Comics with No. 9)
Timely Comics (TPI 1-6/TCI 7,8): 1/40 - No. 5, 6/40; No. 6, 9/40; No. 7, 4/41 - No. 8, 1/42

1-Origin The Fiery Mask (1st app.) by Joe Simon; Monako, Prince of Magic (1st app.), John Steele, Soldier of Fortune (1st app.), Doc Denton (1st app.) begin; Flash Foster & Barney Mullen, Sea Rover only app; bondage-c 2280 4560 6840 17,700 35,850 54,000
2-(Rare)-Origin The Phantom Bullet (1st & only app.); The Laughing Mask & Mr. E only app.; Trojak the Tiger Man begins, ends #6; Zephyr Jones & K-4 & His Sky Devils app., also #4 1220 2440 3660 9200 17,850 26,500
3-The Phantom Reporter, Dale of FBI, Captain Strong only app.; Breeze Barton, Marvex the Super-Robot, The Purple Mask begin 703 1406 2109 5132 9086 13,000
4,5: 4-Last Purple Mask; Whirlwind Carter begins; Dan Gorman, G-Man app. 5-The Falcon begins (1st app.); The Fiery Mask, Little Hercules app. by Sagendorf in the Segar style; bondage-c 476 952 1428 3475 6138 8800
6-Origin & only app. Marvel Boy by S&K; Flying Flame, Dynaman, & Stuporman only app.; The Fiery Mask by S&K; S&K-c 530 1060 1590 3869 6835 9800
7-Origin and 1st app. The Blue Diamond, Captain Daring by S&K, The Fin by Everett, The Challenger, The Silver Scorpion & The Thunderer by Burgos; Mr. Millions app 423 846 1269 3154 5577 7800
8-Origin Citizen V; Last Fin, Silver Scorpion, Capt. Daring by Borth, Blue Diamond & The Thunderer; Kirby & part solo Simon-c; Rudy the Robot only app.; Citizen V, Fin & Silver Scorpion continue in Comedy #9 389 778 1167 2723 4762 6800

NOTE: ***Schomburg** c-1-4, 7. **Simon** a-2, 3, 5. Cover features: 1-Fiery Mask; 2-Phantom Bullet; 3-Purple Mask; 4-G-Man; 5-The Falcon; 6-Marvel Boy; 7, 8-Multiple characters.*

DARING MYSTERY COMICS 70th ANNIVERARY SPECIAL
Marvel Comics: Nov, 2009 ($3.99, one-shot)

1-New story of The Phantom Reporter; r/app. in Daring Mystery #3 (1940); 2 covers 5.00

DARING NEW ADVENTURES OF SUPERGIRL, THE
DC Comics: Nov, 1982 - No. 13, Nov, 1983 (Supergirl No. 14 on)

1-Origin retold; Lois Lane back-ups in #2-12 2 4 6 11 16 20
2-13: 8,9-Doom Patrol app. 13-New costume; flag-c 5.00

NOTE: ***Buckler** c-1p, 2p. **Giffen** c-3p, 4p. **Gil Kane** c-6,8, 9, 11-13.*

DARK, THE
Continum Comics: Nov, 1990 - No. 4, Feb, 1993; V2#1, May, 1993 - V2#7, Apr?, 1994 ($1.95)

1-4: 1-Bright-p; Panosian, Hanna-i; Stroman-c. 2-(1/92)-Stroman-c/a(p). 4-Perez-c & part-i 3.00
V2#1,V2#2-6: V2#1-Red foil Bart Sears-c. V2#1-Red non-foil variant-c. V2#1-2nd printing w/blue foil Bart Sears-c. V2#2-Stroman/Bryant-a. 3-Perez-c(i). 3-6-Foil-c. 4-Perez-c & part-i; bound-in trading cards. 5,6-(2,3/94)-Perez-c(i). 7-(B&W)-Perez-c(i) 3.00
Convention Book 1 ,2(Fall/94, 10/94)-Perez-c 3.00

DARK AGES
Dark Horse Comics: Aug, 2014 - No. 4, Nov, 2014 ($3.99, limited series)

1-4-Abnett-s/Culbard-a/c 4.00

DARK AGNES (Robert E. Howard character)
Marvel Comics: Apr, 2020 - No. 5 ($3.99, limited series)

1,2-Becky Cloonan-s/Luca Pizzari-a; set in 1521 France 4.00

DARK AND BLOODY, THE
DC Comics (Vertigo): Apr, 2016 - No. 6, Sept, 2016 ($3.99, limited series)

1-6-Aldridge-s/Godlewski-a 4.00

DARK ANGEL (Formerly Hell's Angel)
Marvel Comics UK, Ltd.: No. 6, Dec, 1992 - No. 16, Dec, 1993 ($1.75)

6-8,13-16: 6-Excalibur-c/story. 8-Psylocke app. 3.00
9-12-Wolverine/X-Men app. 3.50

DARK ANGEL: PHOENIX RESURRECTION (Kia Asamiya's...)
Image Comics: May, 2000 - No. 4, Oct, 2001 ($2.95)

1-4-Kia Asamiya-s/a. 3-Van Fleet variant-c 3.00

DARK ARK
AfterShock Comics: Sept, 2017 - No. 15, Mar, 2019 ($3.99)

1-15-Cullen Bunn-s/Juan Doe-a 4.00

DARK ARK: AFTER THE FLOOD
AfterShock Comics: Oct, 2019 - No. 5, Jul, 2020 ($3.99, limited series)

1-5: 1-Cullen Bunn-s/Juan Doe-a. 3-5-Jesus Hervas-a 4.00

DARK AVENGERS (See Secret Invasion and Dark Reign titles)
Marvel Comics: Mar, 2009 - No. 16, Jul, 2010 ($3.99)

1-Norman Osborn assembles his Avengers; Bendis-s/Deodato-a/c 4.00
1-Variant Iron Patriot armor cover by Djurdjevic 8.00
2-16: 2-6-Bendis-s/Deodato-a/c. 2-4 Dr. Doom app. 7,8-Utopia x-over; X-Men app. 9-Nick Fury app. 11,12-Deodato & Horn-a. 13-16-Siege. 13-Sentry origin 4.00
Annual 1 (2/10, $4.99) Bendis-s/Bachalo-a; Marvel Boy new costume; Siege preview 5.00
,,,/ Uncanny X-Men: Exodus (11/09, $3.99) Conclusion of x-over; Deodato & Dodson-a 4.00
,,,/ Uncanny X-Men: Utopia (8/09, $3.99) Part 1 of x-over w/Uncanny X-Men #513,514 4.00

DARK AVENGERS (Title continues from Thunderbolts #174)
Marvel Comics: No. 175, Aug, 2012 - No. 190, Jul, 2013 ($2.99)

175-190: 175-New team assembles; Parker-s/Shalvey-a/Deodato-c 3.00

DARK AVENGERS: ARES
Marvel Comics: Dec, 2009 - No. 3, Feb, 2010 ($3.99, limited series)

1-3-Garcia-a/Gillen-s. 1-Nord-c. 2-Tan-c. 3-McGuinness-c 4.00

DARKCHYLDE (Also see Dreams of the Darkchylde)
Maximum Press #1-3/ Image Comics #4 on: June, 1996 - No. 5, Sept, 1997 ($2.95/ $2.50)

1-Randy Queen-c/a/scripts; "Roses" cover 6.00
1-American Entertainment Edition-wraparound-c 6.00
1-"Fashion magazine-style" variant-c 1 2 3 4 5 7
1-Special Comicon Edition (contents of #1) Winged devil variant-c 5.00
1-($2.50)-Remastered Ed.-wraparound-c 4.00
2(Reg-c),2-Spiderweb and Moon variant-c 6.00
3(Reg-c),3-"Kalvin Clein" variant-c by Drew 4.00
4,5(Reg-c), 4-Variant-c 4.00
5-B&W Edition, 5-Dynamic Forces Gold Ed. 8.00
0-(3/98, $2.50) 3.00
0-Remastered (1/01, $2.95) includes Darkchylde: Redemption preview 3.00
1/2-WIzard offer 4.00
1/2 Variant-c 6.00
... The Descent TPB ('98, $19.95) r/#1-5; bagged with Darkchylde The Legacy Preview Special 1998; listed price is for TPB only 20.00

DARKCHYLDE LAST ISSUE SPECIAL
Darkchylde Entertainment: June, 2002 ($3.95)

1-Wraparound-c; cover gallery 4.00

DARKCHYLDE REDEMPTION
Darkchylde Entertainment: Feb, 2001 - No. 2, Dec, 2001 ($2.95)

1,2: 1-Wraparound-c 3.00
1-Dynamic Forces alternate-c 6.00
1-Dynamic Forces chrome-c 16.00

DARKCHYLDE SKETCH BOOK
Image Comics (Dynamic Forces): 1998

1-Regular-c 8.00
1-DarkChrome cover 16.00

DARKCHYLDE SUMMER SWIMSUIT SPECTACULAR
DC Comics (WildStorm): Aug, 1999 ($3.95, one-shot)

1-Pin-up art by various 4.00

DARKCHYLDE SWIMSUIT ILLUSTRATED

Darkdevil #2 © MAR

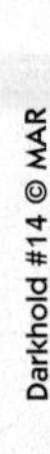
Darkhold #14 © MAR

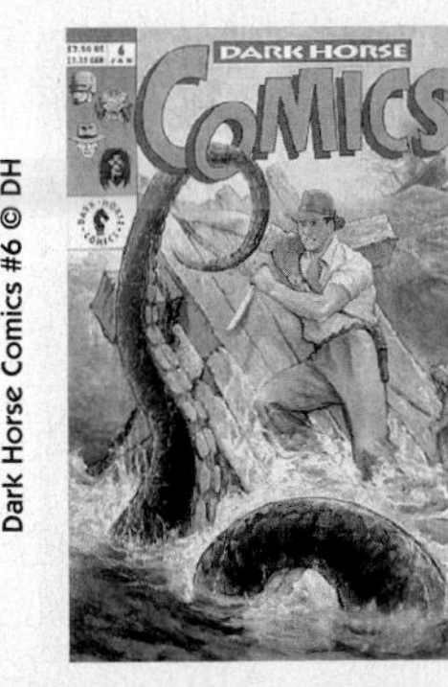

Dark Horse Comics #6 © DH

	GD	VG	FN	VF	VF/NM	NM-
	2.0	4.0	6.0	8.0	9.0	9.2

Image Comics: 1998 ($2.50, one-shot)
1-Pin-up art by various 3.00
1-(6.95) Variant cover 7.00
1-Chromium cover 15.00

DARKCHYLDE THE DIARY
Image Comics: June, 1997 ($2.50, one-shot)
1-Queen-c/s/ art by various 3.00
1-Variant-c 5.00
1-Holochrome variant-c 8.00

DARKCHYLDE THE LEGACY
Image Comics/DC (WildStorm) #3 on: Aug, 1998 - No. 3, June, 1999 ($2.50)
1-3: 1-Queen-c. 2-Two covers by Queen and Art Adams 3.00

DARK CLAW ADVENTURES
DC Comics (Amalgam): June, 1997 ($1.95, one-shot)
1-Templeton-c/s/a & Burchett-a 3.00

DARK CROSSINGS: DARK CLOUDS RISING
Image Comics (Top Cow): June, 2000; Oct, 2000 ($5.95, limited series)
1-Witchblade, Darkness, Tomb Raider crossover; Dwayne Turner-a 6.00
1-(Dark Clouds Overhead) 6.00

DARK CRYSTAL, THE (Movie)
Marvel Comics Group: April, 1983 - No. 2, May, 1983
1,2-Adaptation of film 5.00

DARK DAYS (See 30 Days of Night)
IDW Publishing: June, 2003 - No. 6, Dec, 2003 ($3.99, limited series)
1-6-Sequel to 30 Days of Night; Niles-s/Templesmith-a 4.00
1-Retailer variant (Diamond/Alliance Fort Wayne 5/03 summit) 15.00
TPB (2004, $19.99) r/#1-6; cover gallery; intro. by Eric Red 20.00

DARK DAYS (Tie-ins to Dark Nights: Metal series)
DC Comics: Aug, 2017 - Sept, 2017 ($4.99, one-shots)
...: The Casting 1 (9/17, $4.99) Snyder & Tynion IV-s; Jim Lee, Andy Kubert & Romita Jr.-a; Joker, Green Lantern & Hawkman app. 5.00
...: The Forge (8/17, $4.99) Lee, Kubert & Romita Jr.-a; Mister Miracle, Mr. Terrific app. 5.00
...: The Forge/The Casting Director's Cut (1/18, $7.99) reprints 2 issues with B&W pencil-a; original script for The Forge 8.00

DARKDEVIL (See Spider-Girl)
Marvel Comics: Nov, 2000 - No. 3, Jan, 2001 ($2.99, limited series)
1-3: 1-Origin of Darkdevil; Kingpin-c/app. 3.00

DARK DOMINION
Defiant: Oct, 1993 - No. 10, July, 1994 ($2.50)
1-10-Len Wein scripts begin. 1-Intro Chasm. 4-Free extra 16 pgs. 7-9-J.G. Jones-c/a (his 1st pro work). 10-Pre-Schism issue; Shooter/Wein script; John Ridgway-a 3.00

DARKER IMAGE (Also see Deathblow, The Maxx, & Bloodwulf)
Image Comics: Mar, 1993 ($1.95, one-shot)
1-The Maxx by Sam Kieth begins; Bloodwulf by Rob Liefeld & Deathblow by Jim Lee begin (both 1st app.); polybagged w/1 of 3 cards by Kieth, Lee or Liefeld 3.00
1-B&W interior pgs. w/silver foil logo 6.00

DARK FANG
Image Comics: Nov, 2017 - No. 5, Mar, 2018 ($3.99)
1-5-Gunter-s/Shannon-a 4.00

DARK FANTASIES
Dark Fantasy: 1994 - No. 8, 1995 ($2.95)
1-Test print Run (3,000)-Linsner-c 1 2 3 5 6 8
1-Linsner-c 5.00
2-8: 2-4 (Deluxe), 2-4 (Regular), 5-8 (Deluxe; $3.95) 4.00
5-8 (Regular; $3.50) 3.50

DARK GUARD
Marvel Comics UK: Oct, 1993 - No. 4, Jan, 1994 ($1.75)
1-($2.95)-Foil stamped-c 4.00
2-4 3.00

DARKHAWK (Also see War of Kings)
Marvel Comics: Mar, 1991 - No. 50, Apr, 1995 ($1.00/$1.25/$1.50)
1-Origin/1st app. Darkhawk; Hobgoblin cameo 3 6 9 16 23 30
2,3,13,14: 2-Spider-Man & Hobgoblin app. 3-Spider-Man & Hobgoblin app. 13,14-Venom-c/story 5.00
4-12,15-24,26-49: 6-Capt. America & Daredevil x-over. 9-Punisher app. 11,12-Tombstone app. 19-Spider-Man & Brotherhood of Evil Mutants-c/story. 20-Spider-Man app. 22-Ghost Rider-c/story. 23-Origin begins, ends #25. 27-New Warriors-c/story. 35-Begin 3 part Venom story. 39-Bound-in trading card sheet 4.00
25,50: (52 pgs.)-Red holo-grafx foil-c w/double gatefold poster; origin of Darkhawk armor 5.00
Annual 1-3 ('92-'94,68 pgs.)-1-Vs. Iron Man. 2 -Polybagged w/card 5.00

DARKHAWK (Marvel Legacy)
Marvel Comics: No. 51, Jan, 2018 ($3.99, one-shot)
51-Bowers & Sims-s/Kev Walker-a/Nakayama-c 4.00

DARKHOLD: PAGES FROM THE BOOK OF SINS (See Midnight Sons Unlimited)
Marvel Comics (Midnight Sons imprint #15 on): Oct, 1992 - No. 16, Jan, 1994
1-($2.75, 52 pgs.)-Polybagged w/poster by Andy & Adam Kubert; part 4 of Rise of the Midnight Sons storyline 4.00
2-10,12-16: 3-Reintro Modred the Mystic (see Marvel Chillers #1). 4-Sabertooth-c/sty. 5-Punisher & Ghost Rider app. 15-Spot varnish-c. 15,16-Siege of Darkness pt. 4&12 3.00
11-($2.25)-Outer-c is a Darkhold envelope made of black parchment w/gold ink 4.00

DARK HORSE BOOK OF..., THE
Dark Horse Comics: Aug, 2003 - Nov, 2006 ($14.95/$15.95, HC, 9 1/4" x 6 1/4")
... Hauntings (8/03, $14.95)-Short stories by various incl. Mignola (Hellboy), Thompson, Dorkin, Russell; Gianni-c 15.00
... Monsters (11/06, $15.95)-Short-s by Mignola, Thompson, Dorkin, Giffen, Busiek; Gianni-c 16.00
... The Dead (6/05, $14.95)-Short-s by Mignola, Thompson, Dorkin, Powell; Gianni-c 15.00
... Witchcraft (6/04, $14.95)-Short-s by Mignola, Thompson, Dorkin, Millionaire; Gianni-c 15.00

DARK HORSE CLASSICS (Title series), **Dark Horse Comics**
1992 ($3.95, B&W, 52 pgs. nn's): The Last of the Mohicans. 20,000 Leagues Under the Sea 4.00

DARK HORSE CLASSICS, 5/96 ($2.95) 1-r/Predator: Jungle Tales 4.00
--ALIENS VERSUS PREDATOR, 2/97 - No. 6, 7/97 ($2.95,) 1-6: r/Aliens Versus Predator 4.00
--GODZILLA: KING OF THE MONSTERS, 4/98 ($2.95) 1-6: 1-r/Godzilla: Color Special; Art Adams-a 4.00
--STAR WARS: DARK EMPIRE, 3/97 - No. 6, 8/97 ($2.95) 1-6: r/Star Wars: Dark Empire 4.00
--TERROR OF GODZILLA, 8/98 - No. 6, 1/99 ($2.95) 1-6-r/manga Godzilla in color; Art Adams-c 4.00

DARK HORSE COMICS
Dark Horse Comics: Aug, 1992 - No. 25, Sept, 1994 ($2.50)
1-Dorman double gategold painted-c; Predator, Robocop, Timecop (3-part) & Renegade stories begin 5.00
2-6,11-25: 2-Mignola-c. 3-Begin 3-part Aliens story; Aliens-c. 4-Predator-c. 6-Begin 4 part Robocop story. 12-Begin 2-part Aliens & 3-part Predator stories. 13-Thing From Another World begins w/Nino-a(i). 15-Begin 2-part Aliens: Cargo story. 16-Begin 3-part Predator story. 17-Begin 3-part Star Wars: Droids story & 3-part Aliens: Alien story; Droids-c. 19-Begin 2-part X story; X cover 4.00
7-Begin Star Wars: Tales of the Jedi 3-part story 1 3 4 6 8 10
8-1st app. X and begins; begin 4-part James Bond 1 2 3 5 6 8
9,10: 9-Star Wars ends. 10-X ends; Begin 3-part Predator & Godzilla stories 5.00
NOTE: *Art Adams c-11.*

DARK HORSE DAY SAMPLER 2016
Dark Horse Comics: Jun, 2016 (no price, promotional one-shot)
nn-New Buffy the Vampire Slayer story; reprint stories of Sin City, AvP, Umbrella Academy 3.00

DARK HORSE DOWN UNDER
Dark Horse Comics: Jun, 1994 - No. 3, Oct, 1994 ($2.50, B&W, limited series)
1-3 3.00

DARK HORSE MAVERICK
Dark Horse Comics: July, 2000; July, 2001; Sept, 2002 (B&W, annual)
2000-($3.95) Short stories by Miller, Chadwick, Sakai, Pearson 4.00
2001-($4.99) Short stories by Sakai, Wagner and others; Miller-c 5.00
...: Happy Endings (9/02, $9.95) Short stories by Bendis, Oeming, Mahfood, Mignola, Miller, Kieth and others; Miller-c 10.00

DARK HORSE MONSTERS
Dark Horse Comics: Feb, 1997 ($2.95, one-shot)
1-Reprints 3.00

DARK HORSE PRESENTS
Dark Horse Comics: July, 1986 - No. 157, Sept, 2000 ($1.50-$2.95, B&W)
1-1st app. Concrete by Paul Chadwick 3 6 9 15 21 26
1-2nd printing (1988, $1.50) 3.00
1-Silver ink 3rd printing (1992, $2.25)-Says 2nd printing inside 3.00
2-9: 2-6,9-Concrete app. 6.00
10-1st app. The Mask; Concrete app. 3 6 9 19 30 40

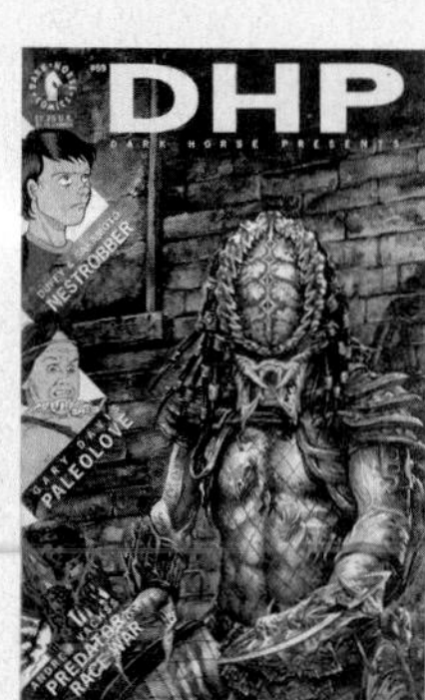

Dark Horse Presents #69 © DH

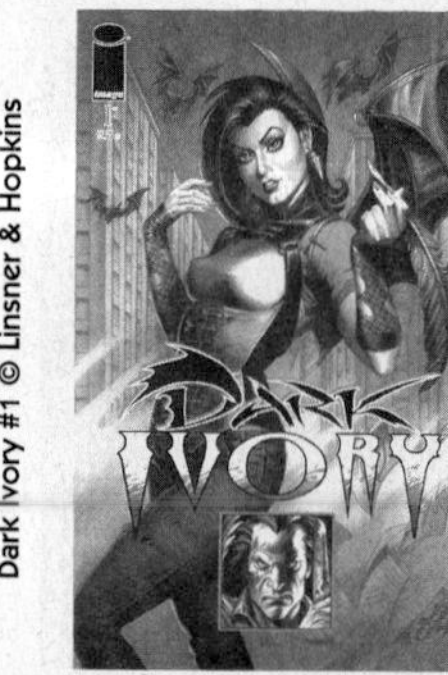

Dark Ivory #1 © Linsner & Hopkins

Darkminds #1 © Dreamwave

GD VG FN VF VF/NM NM-
2.0 4.0 6.0 8.0 9.0 9.2

11-19,21-23: 11-19,21-Mask stories. 12,14,16,18,22-Concrete app. 15(2/88). 17-All Roachmill issue 6.00
20-(68 pgs.)-Concrete, Flaming Carrot, Mask 1 3 4 6 8 10
24-Origin Aliens-c/story (11/88); Mr. Monster app. 3 6 9 16 23 30
25-27,29-31,37-39,41,44,45,47-49: 38-Concrete. 44-Crash Ryan. 48,49-Contain 2 trading cards 3.00
28,33,40: 28-(52 pgs.)-Concrete app.; Mr. Monster story (homage to Graham Ingels). 33-(44 pgs.). 40-(52 pgs.)-1st Argosy story 4.00
32,34,35: 32-(68 pgs.)-Annual; Concrete, American. 34-Aliens-c/story. 35-Predator-c/app. 4.00
36-1st Aliens Vs. Predator story; painted-c 3 6 9 14 19 24
36-Variant line drawn-c 3 6 9 17 26 35
42,43,46: 42,43-Aliens-c/stories. 46-Prequel to new Predator II mini-series 3.00
50-S/F story by Perez; contains 2 trading cards 4.00
51-53-Sin City by Frank Miller, parts 2-4; 51,53-Miller-c (see D.H.P. Fifth Anniversary Special for pt. 1) 1 2 3 4 6 8
54-61: 54-(9/91) The Next Men begins (1st app.) by Byrne; Miller-a/Morrow-c. Homocide by Morrow (also in #55). 55-2nd app. The Next Men; parts 5 & 6 of Sin City by Miller; Miller-c. 56-(68 pg. annual)-part 7 of Sin City by Miller; part prologue to Aliens: Genocide; Next Men by Byrne. 57-(52 pgs.)-Part 8 of Sin City by Miller; Next Men by Byrne; Byrne & Miller-c; Alien Fire story; swipes cover to Daredevil #1. 58,59-Alien Fire stories. 58-61- Part 9-12 Sin City by Miller 5.00
62-Last Sin City (entire book by Miller, c/a; 52 pgs.) 2 4 6 8 11 14
63-66,68-79,81-84-($2.25): 64-Dr. Giggles begins (1st app.), ends #66; Boris the Bear story. 66-New Concrete-c/story by Chadwick. 71-Begin 3 part Dominque story by Jim Balent; Balent-c. 72-(3/93)-Begin 3-part Eudaemon (1st app.) story by Nelson 3.00
67-($3.95, 68 pgs.)-Begin 3-part prelude to Predator: Race War mini-series; Oscar Wilde adapt. by Russell 4.00
80-Art Adams-c/a (Monkeyman & O'Brien) 4.00
85-87,92-99: 85-Begin $2.50-c. 92, 93, 95-Too Much Coffee Man 3.00
88-Hellboy by Mignola. 2 4 6 9 13 16
89-91-Hellboy by Mignola. 1 2 3 5 6 8
NOTE: *There are 5 different Dark Horse Presents #100 issues*
100-1-Intro Lance Blastoff by Miller; Milk & Cheese by Evan Dorkin 5.00
100-2-Hellboy-c by Wrightson; Hellboy story by Mignola; includes Roberta Gregory & Paul Pope stories 1 2 3 5 6 8
100-3-100-5: 100-3-Darrow-c, Concrete by Chadwick; Pekar story. 100-4-Gibbons-c: Miller story, Geary story/a. 100-5-Allred-c, Adams, Dorkin, Pope 3.00
101-125: 101-Aliens c/a by Wrightson, story by Pope. 103-Kirby gatefold-c. 106-Big Blown Baby by Bill Wray. 107-Mignola-c/a. 109-Begin $2.95-c; Paul Pope-c. 110-Ed Brubaker-a/s. 114-Flip books begin; Lance Blastoff by Miller; Star Slammers by Simonson. 115-Miller-c. 117-Aliens-c/app. 118-Evan Dorkin-c/a. 119-Monkeyman & O'Brien. 124-Predator. 125-Nocturnals 3.00
126-($3.95, 48 pgs.)-Flip book: Nocturnals, Starship Troopers 4.00
127-134,136-140: 127-Nocturnals. 129-The Hammer. 132-134-Warren-a 3.00
135-($3.50) The Mark 3.50
141-All Buffy the Vampire Slayer issue 4.00
142-149: 142-Mignola-c. 143-Tarzan. 146,147-Aliens vs. Predator. 148-Xena 3.00
150-($4.50) Buffy-c by Green; Buffy, Concrete, Fish Police app. 4.50
151-157: 151-Hellboy-c/app. 153-155-Angel flip-c. 156,157-Witch's Son 3.00
Annual 1997 ($4.95, 64 pgs.)-Flip book; Body Bags, Aliens. Pearson-c; stories by Allred & Stephens, Pope, Smith & Morrow 1 2 3 5 6 8
Annual 1998 ($4.95, 64 pgs.) 1st Buffy the Vampire Slayer comic app.; Hellboy story and cover by Mignola 3 6 9 14 20 25
Annual 1999 (7/99, $4.95) Stories of Xena, Hellboy, Ghost, Luke Skywalker, Groo, Concrete, the Mask and Usagi Yojimbo in their youth. 5.00
Annual 2000 ($4.95) Girl sidekicks; Chiodo-c and flip photo Buffy-c 5.00
...Aliens Platinum Edition (1992)-r/DHP #24,43,43,56 & Special 2 4 6 9 12 15
...Fifth Anniversary Special nn (4/91, $9.95)-Part 1 of Sin City by Frank Miller (c/a); Aliens, Aliens vs. Predator, Concrete, Roachmill, Give Me Liberty & The American stories 35.00
The One Trick Rip-off (1997, $12.95, TPB)-r/stories from #101-112 13.00
NOTE: ***Geary** a-59, 60. **Miller** a-Special, 51-53, 55-62; c-59-62, 100-1; c-51, 53, 55, 59-62, 100-1. **Moebius** a-63; c-63, 70. **Vess** a-78; c-75, 78.*

DARK HORSE PRESENTS
Dark Horse Comics: Apr, 2011 - No. 36, May, 2014 ($7.99, anthology)
1-36: 1-Frank Miller-c & Xerxes preview; Neal Adams-s/a. 1-3-Concrete by Chadwick. 1-8-Chaykin-s/a. 2,3,9-Corben-a. 3-Steranko interview. 7-Hellboy app. 10-Milk & Cheese. 12-17-Aliens; Kieth-a. 14-Flipbook. 18-Capt. Midnight. 23-26,29-34-Nexus. 25,26-Buffy. 28,29-Neal Adams-s/a. 31,32-Hellboy; McMahon-a 8.00

DARK HORSE PRESENTS (Volume 3)
Dark Horse Comics: Aug, 2014 - No. 33, Apr, 2017 ($4.99, anthology)
1-6: 1-Two covers. 1,2-Rusty & Big Guy by Darrow-s/a. 2-Aliens. 5-Alex Ross-c 5.00
7-(2/15) 200th Issue; Hellboy by Mignola & Bá, Groo, Mind Mgmt; Gibbons, Darrow-a 5.00
8-15,17-33: 8-10-Tarzan by Grell. 14,15-The Rook; Gulacy-a. 17,18-Levitz-s 5.00
16-($5.99) Flip book with Hellboy by Mignola; art by Calero, Ordway, McCarthy 6.00

DARK HORSE TWENTY YEARS
Dark Horse Comics: 2006 (25¢, one-shot)
nn-Pin-ups by Dark Horse artists of other artists' Dark Horse characters; Mignola-c 3.00

DARK IVORY
Image Comics: Mar, 2008 - No. 4, Jan, 2009 ($2.99, limited series)
1-4-Eva Hopkins & Joseph Michael Linsner-s/Linsner-a/c 3.00

DARK KNIGHT (See Batman: The Dark Knight Returns & Legends of the...)

DARK KNIGHT RETURNS: THE GOLDEN CHILD
DC Comics (Black Label): Feb, 2020 ($5.99, squarebound, one-shot)
1-Frank Miller-s/Rafael Grampá-a; Lara & Carrie from DK III vs. Joker & Darkseid 6.00
1-Retailer incentive-c (limited 1 for 100) 35.00

DARK KNIGHT RETURNS, THE: THE LAST CRUSADE
DC Comics: Aug, 2016 ($6.99, squarebound, one-shot)
1-Miller & Azzarello-s/Romita Jr.-a; Jason Todd Robin vs. The Joker; Poison Ivy app. 7.00

DARK KNIGHTS RISING: THE WILD HUNT (See Dark Nights: Metal series and other tie-ins)
DC Comics: Apr, 2018 ($4.99, one-shot)
1-Snyder & Morrison-s/Porter & Mahnke-a; Detective Chimp app.; foil-c 5.00

DARK KNIGHT STRIKES AGAIN, THE (Also see Batman: The Dark Knight Returns)
DC Comics: 2001 - No. 3, 2002 ($7.95, prestige format, limited series)
1-Frank Miller-s/a/c; sequel set 3 years after Dark Knight Returns; 2 covers 10.00
2,3 10.00
HC (2002, $29.95) intro. by Miller; sketch pages and exclusive artwork; cover has 3 1/4" tall partial dustjacket 30.00
SC (2002, $19.95) intro. by Miller; sketch pages 20.00

DARK KNIGHT III: THE MASTER RACE (Also see Batman: The Dark Knight Returns)
DC Comics: Jan, 2016 - No. 9, Jul, 2017 ($5.99, cardstock cover, limited series)
1-9: 1-Miller & Azzarello-s/Andy Kubert-a; Dark Knight Universe Presents: The Atom mini-comic attached at centerfold, Miller-a. 2-Wonder Woman mini-comic. 3-Superman returns; Green Lantern mini-comic. 4-Batgirl mini-comic. 5-Lara mini-comic. 6-World's Finest mini-comic. 7-Strange Adventures mini-comic. 8-Detective mini. 9-Action mini 6.00
1-8-Deluxe Edition ($12.99, HC) reprints story plus mini-comic at full size; cover gallery 13.00
9-Deluxe Edition ($12.99, HC) Sold with slipcase fitting all 9 Deluxe Edition HCs 13.00
... Book One - Director's Cut (11/16, $7.99) r/ #1 in B&W art; script, variant cover gallery 8.00

DARKLON THE MYSTIC (Also see Eerie Magazine #79,80)
Pacific Comics: Oct, 1983 (one-shot)
1-Starlin-c/a(r) 4.00

DARKMAN (Movie)
Marvel Comics: Sept, 1990; Oct, 1990 - No. 3, Dec, 1990 ($1.50)
1 (9/90, $2.25, B&W mag., 68 pgs.)-Adaptation of film 4.00
1-3: Reprints B&W magazine 3.00

DARKMAN
Marvel Comics: V2#1, Apr, 1993 -No. 6, Sept, 1993 ($2.95, limited series)
V2#1 ($3.95, 52 pgs.) 4.00
2-6 3.00

DARK MANSION OF FORBIDDEN LOVE, THE (Becomes Forbidden Tales of Dark Mansion No. 5 on)
National Periodical Publ.: Sept-Oct, 1971 - No. 4, Mar-Apr, 1972 (52 pgs.)
1-Greytone-c on all 17 34 51 119 265 410
2-4: 2-Adams-c. 3-Jeff Jones-c 9 18 27 60 120 180

DARKMAN VS. THE ARMY OF DARKNESS (Movie crossover)
Dynamite Entertainment: 2006 - No. 4, 2007 ($3.50)
1-4: 1-Busiek & Stern-s/Fry-a; photo-c and Perez and Bradshaw covers 3.50

DARK MATTER (Inspired 2015 TV series on SyFy channel)
Dark Horse Comics.: Jan, 2012 - No. 4, Apr, 2012 ($3.50, limited series)
1-4-Joseph Mallozzi & Paul Mullie-s/Garry Brown-a 4.00

DARKMINDS
Image Comics (Dreamwave Prod.): July, 1998 - No. 8, Apr, 1999 ($2.50)
1-Manga; Pat Lee-s/a; 2 covers 1 3 4 6 8 10
1-2nd printing 3.00
2, 0-(1/99, $5.00) Story and sketch pages 5.00
3-8, 1/2-(5/99, $2.50) Story and sketch pages 3.00
... Collected 1,2 (1/99,3/99; $7.95) 1-r/#1-3. 2-r/#4-6 8.00
... Collected 3 (5/99; $5.95) r/#7,8 6.00

DARKMINDS (Volume 2)

Dark Mysteries #1 © Merit

The Darkness #92 © TCOW

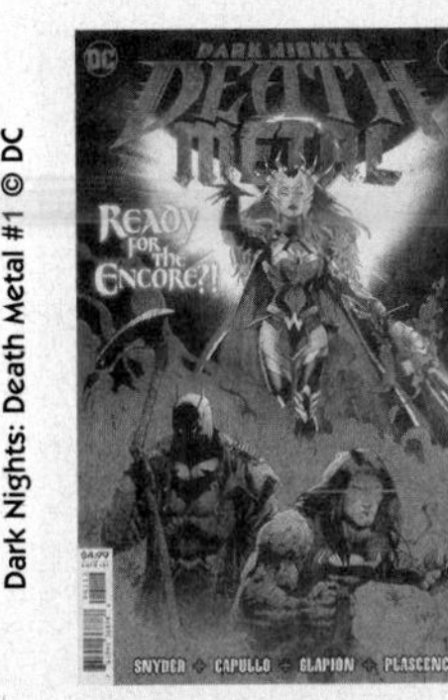

Dark Nights: Death Metal #1 © DC

GD 2.0 | VG 4.0 | FN 6.0 | VF 8.0 | VF/NM 9.0 | NM- 9.2

Image Comics (Dreamwave Prod.): Feb, 2000 - No. 10, Apr, 2001 ($2.50)
1-10-Pat Lee-c 3.00
0-(7/00) Origin of Mai Murasaki; sketchbook 3.00

DARKMINDS: MACROPOLIS
Image Comics (Dreamwave Prod.): Jan, 2002 - No. 4, Dec, 2002 ($2.95)
Preview (8/01) Flip book w/Banished Knights preview 3.00
1-4-Jo Chen-a 3.00

DARKMINDS: MACROPOLIS (Volume 2)
Dreamwave Prod.: Sept, 2003 - No. 4, Jul, 2004 ($2.95)
1-4-Chris Sarracini-s/Kwang Mook Lim-a 3.00

DARKMINDS / WITCHBLADE (Also see Witchblade/Dark Minds)
Image Comics (Top Cow/Dreamwave Prod.): Aug, 2000 ($5.95, one-shot)
1-Wohl-s/Pat Lee-a; two covers by Silvestri and Lee 6.00

DARK MYSTERIES (Thrilling Tales of Horror & Suspense)
"Master" - "Merit" Publications: June-July, 1951 - No. 24, July, 1955
1-Wood-c/a (8 pgs.) 161 322 483 1030 1765 2500
2-Classic skull-c; Wood/Harrison-c/a (8 pgs.) 165 330 495 1056 1803 2550
3-9: 7-Dismemberment, hypo blood drainage stys 68 136 204 435 743 1050
10-Cannibalism story; witch burning-c 161 322 483 1030 1765 2500
11-13,15-17: 11-Severed head panels. 13-Dismemberment-c/story. 17-The Old Gravedigger host 58 116 174 371 636 900
14-Several E.C. Craig swipes 63 126 189 403 689 975
18-Bondage, skeletons-c 100 200 300 635 1093 1550
19-Injury-to-eye panel; E.C. swipe; torture-c 354 708 1062 2478 4339 6200
20-Female bondage, blood drainage story 74 148 222 470 810 1150
21,22: 21-Devil-c. 22-Last pre-code issue, misdated 3/54 instead of 3/55 48 96 144 302 514 725
23,24 39 78 117 240 395 550
NOTE: ***Cameron*** *a-1, 2.* ***Myron Fass*** *c/a-21.* ***Harrison*** *a-3, 7; c-3.* ***Hollingsworth*** *a-7-17, 20, 21, 23.* ***Wildey*** *a-5. Woodish art by* ***Fleishman****-9; c-10, 14-17. Bondage c-10, 18, 19.*

DARK NEMESIS (VILLAINS) (See Teen Titans)
DC Comics: Feb, 1998 ($1.95, one-shot)
1-Jurgens-s/Pearson-c 4.00

DARKNESS, THE (See Witchblade #10)
Image Comics (Top Cow Productions): Dec, 1996 - No. 40, Aug, 2001 ($2.50)
Special Preview Edition-(7/96, B&W)-Ennis script; Silvestri-a(p) 2 4 6 9 13 16
0 2 4 6 8 10 12
0-Gold Edition 16.00
1/2 1 3 4 6 8 10
1/2-Christmas-c 3 6 9 14 19 24
1/2-(3/01, $2.95) r/#1/2 w/new 6 pg. story & Silvestri-c 3.00
1-Ennis-s/Silvestri-a, 1-Black variant-c 2 4 6 9 12 15
1-Platinum variant-c 20.00
1-DF Green variant-c 12.00
1-25th Anniversary Commemorative Edition (11/20, $4.99) r/#1 with creator interviews 5.00
1,2: 1-Fan Club Ed. 1 3 4 6 8 10
3-5 6.00
6-10: 9,10-Witchblade "Family Ties" x-over pt. 2,3 4.00
7-Variant-c w/concubine 1 2 3 5 7 9
8-American Entertainment 6.00
8-10-American Entertainment Gold Ed. 7.00
11-Regular Ed.; Ennis-s/Silverstri & D-Tron-c 3.00
11-Nine (non-chromium) variant-c (Benitez, Cabrera, the Hildebrandts, Finch, Keown, Peterson, Portacio, Tan, Turner 4.50
11-Chromium-c by Silvestri & Batt 20.00
12-19: 13-Begin Benitez-a(p) 3.00
20-24,26-40: 34-Ripclaw app. 3.00
25-($3.99) Two covers (Benitez, Silvestri) 4.00
25-Chromium-c variant by Silvestri 8.00
.../ Batman (8/99, $5.95) Silvestri, Finch, Lansing-a(p) 6.00
...Collected Editions #1-4 ($4.95,TPB) 1-r/#1,2. 2-r/#3,4. 3- r/#5,6. 4- r/#7,8 6.00
...Collected Editions #5,6 ($5.95, TPB)5- r/#11,12. 6-r/#13,14 6.00
Deluxe Collected Editions #1 (12/98, $14.95, TPB) r/#1-6 & Preview 15.00
...: Heart of Darkness (2001, $14.95, TPB) r/ #7,8, 11-14 15.00
Holiday Pin-up-American Entertainment 5.00
Holiday Pin-up Gold Ed.-American Entertainment 7.00
Image Firsts: Darkness #1 (9/10, $1.00) r/#1 with "Image Firsts" logo on cover 3.00
Infinity #1 (8/99, $3.50) Lobdell-s 3.50
Prelude-American Entertainment 4.00
Prelude Gold Ed.-American Entertainment 9.00
Volume 1 Compendium (2006, $59.99) r/#1-40, V2 #1, Tales of the Darkness #1-4; #1/2, Darkness/Witchblade #1/2, Darkness: Wanted Dead; cover and sketch gallery 60.00
...: Wanted Dead 1 (8/03, $2.99) Texiera-a/Tieri-s 3.00
Wizard ACE Ed.- Reprints #1 2 4 6 8 10 12

DARKNESS (Volume 2)
Image Comics (Top Cow Productions): Dec, 2002 - No. 24, Oct, 2004 ($2.99)
1-24: 1-6-Jenkins-s/Keown-a. 17-20-Lapham-s. 23,24-Magdalena app. 3.00
... Black Sails (3/05, $2.99) Marz-s/Cha-a; Hunter-Killer preview 3.00
... and Tomb Raider (4/05, $2.99) r/Darkness Prelude & Tomb Raider/Darkness Special 3.00
...: Resurrection TPB (2/04, $16.99) r/#1-6 & Vol. 1 #40 17.00
.../ The Incredible Hulk (7/04, $2.99) Keown-a/Jenkins-s 3.00
.../ Vampirella (7/05, $2.99) Terry Moore-s; two covers by Basaldua and Moore 3.00
... Vol. 5 TPB (2006, $19.99) r/#7-16 & The Darkness: Wanted Dead #1; cover gallery 20.00
... vs. Mr Hyde Monster War 2005 (9/05, $2.99) x-over w/Witchblade, Tomb Raider and Magdalena; two covers 3.00
.../ Wolverine (2006, $2.99) Kirkham-a/Tieri-s 3.00

DARKNESS (Volume 3) (Numbering jumps from #10 to #75)
Image Comics (Top Cow Productions): Dec, 2007 - No. 116, Dec, 2013 ($2.99)
1-10: 1-Hester-s/Broussard-a. 1-Three covers. 7-9-Lucas-a. 8-Aphrodite IV app. 3.00
75 (2/09, $4.99) Four covers; Hester-s/art by various 5.00
76-99,101-113,115-($2.99) 76-99,101-Multiple covers on each 3.00
100 (2/12, $4.99) Four covers; Hester-s/art by various; cover gallery; series timeline 5.00
114-($4.99) The Age of Reason Part 1; Hine-s/Haun-a; bonus Darkness timeline 5.00
116-($3.99) The Age of Reason Part 3; Hine-s/Haun-a 4.00
... : Butcher (4/08, $3.99) Story of Butcher Joyce; Levin-s/Broussard-a/c 4.00
... : Close Your Eyes (6/14, $3.99) Story of Adelmo Estacado in 1912; Kot-s/Oleksicki-a/c 4.00
...: Confession (5/11) Free Comic Boy Day giveaway; Broussard & Molnar-a 3.00
... / Darkchylde: Kingdom Pain 1 (5/10, $4.99) Randy Queen-s/a 5.00
... First Look (11/07, 99¢) Previews series; sketch pages 3.00
... : Hope (4/16, $3.99) Harmon-s/Dwyer-a/Linda Sejic-c 4.00
... : Lodbrok's Hand (12/08, $2.99) Hester-s/Oeming-a/c; variant-c by Carnevale 3.00
... : Shadows and Flame 1 (1/10, $2.99) Lucas-c/a 3.00
... : Vicious Traditions 1 (3/14, $3.99) Ales Kot-s/Dean Ormston-a/Dale Keown-c 4.00

DARKNESS: FOUR HORSEMEN
Image Comics (Top Cow): Aug, 2010 - No. 4, May, 2011 ($3.99, limited series)
1-4-Hine-s/Wamester-a 4.00

DARKNESS: LEVEL...
Image Comics (Top Cow): No. 0, Dec, 2006 - No. 5, Aug, 2007 ($2.99, limited series)
0-5: 0-Origin of The Darkness in WW1; Jenkins-s. 1-Jackie's origin retold; Sejic-a 3.00

DARKNESS/ PITT
Image Comics (Top Cow): Dec, 2006; Aug, 2009 - No. 3, Nov, 2009 ($2.99)
...: First Look (12/06) Jenkins script pages with Keown B&W and color art 3.00
1-3: 1-(8/09) Jenkins-s/Keown-a; covers by Keown and Sejic. 2,3-Two covers 3.00

DARKNESS/ SUPERMAN
Image Comics (Top Cow Productions): Jan, 2005 - No. 2, Feb, 2005 ($2.99, limited series)
1,2-Marz-s/Kirkham & Banning-a/Silvestri-c 3.00

DARKNESS VISIBLE
IDW Publishing: Feb, 2017 - No. 6, 2017 ($3.99)
1-6: 1-Mike Carey & Arvind David-s/Brendan Cahill-a. 3,6-Ramondelli-a 4.00

DARKNESS VS. EVA: DAUGHTER OF DRACULA
Dynamite Entertainment: 2008 - No. 4, 2008 ($3.50, limited series)
1-4-Leah Moore & John Reppion-s/Salazar-a; three covers on each 3.50

DARK NIGHT: A TRUE BATMAN STORY
DC Comics: 2016 ($22.99, HC Graphic Novel)
HC - Paul Dini-s/Eduardo Risso-a 23.00

DARK NIGHTS: DEATH METAL
DC Comics: Jul, 2020 - No. 7, Mar, 2021 ($4.99/$5.99, limited series)
1-6-Snyder-s/Capullo-a; sequel to Dark Nights: Metal; Batman Who Laughs app. 5.00
7-($5.99) Multiverse restored; leads into Future State titles 6.00
... - Guidebook 1 (10/20, $5.99) short s/a by various; Harley Quinn app. 6.00
... Infinite Hour Exxxtreme 1 (1/21, $5.99) Extremely violent stories hosted by Lobo 6.00
... Legends of the Dark Knights 1 (10/20, $5.99) Origin Robin King & other Batmen 6.00
... Multiverse's End 1 (11/20, $5.99) Capt. Carrot, Owlman. Pres. Superman & others 6.00
... Rise of the New God 1 (11/20, $5.99) Perpetua vs. The Batman Who Laughs 6.00
... Robin King 1 (11/20, $5.99) Robin King vs. the Robins; Rossmo & Sampere-a 6.00
... Speed Metal 1 (11/20, $5.99) Barrows-s; Wally West and other Flashes app. 6.00
... The Last 52: War of the Multiverses 1 (2/21, $8.99) Short stories by various 9.00
... The Last Stories of the DC Universe 1 (2/21, $8.99) Short stories by various 9.00

Dark Red #2 © Seeley, Howell & AS

Darkseid (Villains) #1 © DC

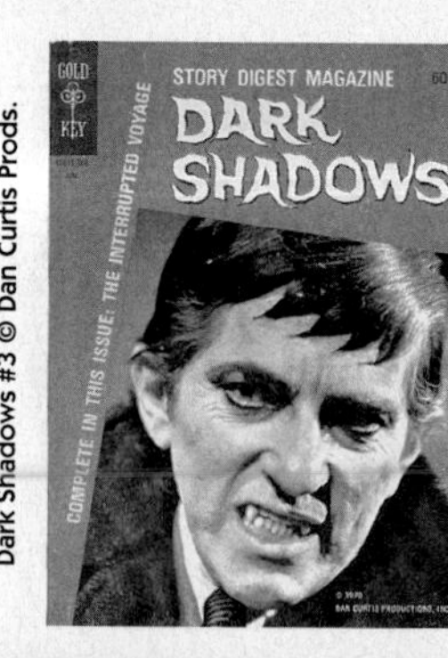

Dark Shadows #3 © Dan Curtis Prods.

	GD 2.0	VG 4.0	FN 6.0	VF 8.0	VF/NM 9.0	NM- 9.2
... The Multiverse That Laughs 1 (1/21, $5.99) Twisted humor short stories by various						6.00
... The Secret Origin 1 (2/21, $5.99) Origin/spotlight on Superboy-Prime						6.00
... Trinity Crisis 1 (11/20, $5.99) Snyder-s/Manapul-a; Batman, Superman, Wonder Woman						6.00

DARK NIGHTS: METAL (Also see Dark Days prelude one-shots)
DC Comics: Nov, 2017 - No. 6, May, 2018 ($4.99/$3.99)

	GD 2.0	VG 4.0	FN 6.0	VF 8.0	VF/NM 9.0	NM- 9.2
1-($4.99) Snyder-s/Capullo-a; Justice League & Dream of the Endless app.; foil logo-c						5.00
1-Second printing; red title logo on cover						5.00
2-5-($3.99) 2-Barbatos app.						4.00
6-($4.99) Finale; leads into Justice League: No Justice series						5.00
Director's Cut 1 (2/18, $6.99) r/#1 pencil art; gallery of variant covers						7.00

DARK NIGHTS: THE BATMAN WHO LAUGHS (Dark Nights: Metal) (Also see Teen Titans #12 [11/17])
DC Comics: Jan, 2018 ($3.99, one-shot)

1-Tynion IV-s/Rossmo-a; Fabok foil-c; Bruce Wayne as Dark Multiverse Joker 15.00

DARK RED
AfterShock Comics: Mar, 2019 - No. 10, Jul, 2020 ($3.99)

1-10-Vampire Nazis in North Dakota; Tim Seeley-s/Corin Howell-a 4.00
1-Special Edition; r/#1 with bonus creator interviews and sketch art 4.00

DARK REIGN (Follows Secret Invasion crossover)
Marvel Comics: 2009 ($3.99/$4.99, one-shots)

...: Files 1 (2009, $4.99) profile pages of villains tied in to Dark Reign x-over 5.00
...: Made Men 1 (11/09, $3.99) short stories by various incl. Pham, Leon, Oliver 4.00
...: New Nation 1 (2/09, $3.99) previews of various series tied in to Dark Reign x-over 4.00
...: The Cabal 1 (6/09, $3.99) Cabal members stories by various incl. Granov, Acuña 4.00
...: The Goblin Legacy 1 (2009, $3.99) r/ASM #39,40; Osborn history; Mayhew-a 4.00

DARK REIGN: ELEKTRA
Marvel Comics: May, 2009 - No. 5, Oct, 2009 ($3.99, limited series)

1-5-Mann-a/Bermejo-c; Elektra after the Skrull replacement. 2,3-Bullseye app. 4.00

DARK REIGN: FANTASTIC FOUR
Marvel Comics: May, 2009 - No. 5, Sept, 2009 ($2.99, limited series)

1-5-Chen-a 3.00

DARK REIGN: HAWKEYE
Marvel Comics: June, 2009 - No. 5, Mar, 2010 ($3.99, limited series)

1-5-Bullseye in the Dark Avengers; Raney-a/Langley-c. 5-Guinaldo-a 4.00

DARK REIGN: LETHAL LEGION
Marvel Comics: Aug, 2009 - No. 3, Nov, 2009 ($3.99, limited series)

1-3-Santolouco-a/Edwards-c; Grim Reaper and Wonder Man app. 4.00

DARK REIGN: MR. NEGATIVE (Also see Amazing Spider-Man #546)
Marvel Comics: Aug, 2009 - No. 3, Oct, 2009 ($3.99, limited series)

1-3-Jae Lee-c/Gugliotta-a; Spider-Man app. 4.00

DARK REIGN: SINISTER SPIDER-MAN
Marvel Comics: Aug, 2009 - No. 4, Nov, 2009 ($3.99, limited series)

1-4-Bachalo-c/a; Venom/Scorpion as Dark Avenger Spider-Man 4.00

DARK REIGN: THE HOOD
Marvel Comics: Jul, 2009 - No. 5, Nov, 2009 ($3.99, limited series)

1-5-Hotz-a/Djurdjevic-c 4.00

DARK REIGN: THE LIST
Marvel Comics: 2009 - 2010 ($3.99, one-shots)

... - Amazing Spider-Man (1/10, $3.99) Adam Kubert-c/a; back-up r/Pulse #5 4.00
... - Avengers (11/09, $3.99) Bendis-s/Djurdjevic-c/a; Ronin (Hawkeye) app. 4.00
... - Daredevil (11/09, $3.99) Diggle-s/Tan-c/a; Bullseye app.; leads into Daredevil #501 4.00
... - Hulk (12/09, $3.99) Pak-s/Oliver-a; Skaar app.; back-up r/Amaz. Spider-Man #14 4.00
... - Punisher (12/09, $3.99) Romita Jr.-a/c; Castle killed by Daken; preview of Franken-Castle in Punisher #11 6.00
... - Secret Warriors (12/09, $3.99) McGuinness-a/c; Nick Fury; back-up r/Steranko-a 4.00
... - Wolverine (12/09, $3.99) Ribic-a/c; Marvel Boy and Fantomex app. 4.00
... - X-Men (11/09, $3.99) Alan Davis-a/c; Namor app.; back-up r/Kieth-a 4.00

DARK REIGN: YOUNG AVENGERS
Marvel Comics: Jul, 2009 - No. 5, Dec, 2009 ($3.99, limited series)

1-5-Brooks-a; Osborn's Young Avengers vs. original Young Avengers 4.00

DARK REIGN: ZODIAC
Marvel Comics: Aug, 2009 - No. 3, Nov, 2009 ($3.99, limited series)

1-3-Casey-s/Fox-a. 1-Human Torch app. 4.00

DARKSEID SPECIAL (Jack Kirby 100th Birthday tribute)
DC Comics: Oct, 2017 ($4.99, one-shot)

1-Evanier-s/Kolins-a; Omac story with Levitz-s/Hester-a; r/Forever People #6 (4 pgs) 5.00

DARKSEID (VILLAINS) (See Jack Kirby's New Gods and New Gods)
DC Comics: Feb, 1998 ($1.95, one-shot)

1-Byrne-s/Pearson-c 5.00

DARKSEID VS. GALACTUS: THE HUNGER
DC Comics: 1995 ($4.95, one-shot) (1st DC/Marvel x-over by John Byrne)

	GD 2.0	VG 4.0	FN 6.0	VF 8.0	VF/NM 9.0	NM- 9.2
nn-John Byrne-c/a/script	2	4	6	8	11	14

DARK SHADOWS
Steinway Comic Publ. (Ajax)(America's Best): Oct, 1957 - No. 3, May, 1958

	GD 2.0	VG 4.0	FN 6.0	VF 8.0	VF/NM 9.0	NM- 9.2
1	33	66	99	201	323	445
2,3	21	42	63	125	206	285

DARK SHADOWS (TV) (See Dan Curtis Giveaways)
Gold Key: Mar, 1969 - No. 35, Feb, 1976 (Photo-c: 1-7)

	GD 2.0	VG 4.0	FN 6.0	VF 8.0	VF/NM 9.0	NM- 9.2
1(30039-903)-With pull-out poster (25¢)	22	44	66	154	340	525
1-With poster missing	7	14	21	48	89	130
2	8	16	24	54	102	150
3-With pull-out poster	9	18	27	60	120	180
3-With poster missing	5	10	15	35	63	90
4-7: 7-Last photo-c	6	12	18	38	69	100
8-10	5	10	15	30	50	70
11-20	4	8	12	27	44	60
21-35: 30-Last painted-c	4	8	12	23	37	50
Story Digest 1 (6/70, 148pp.)-Photo-c (low print)	7	14	21	46	86	125

DARK SHADOWS (TV) (See Nightmare on Elm Street)
Innovation Publishing: June, 1992 - No. 4, Spring, 1993 ($2.50, limited series, coated stock)

1-Based on 1991 NBC TV mini-series; painted-c 5.00
2-4 4.00

DARK SHADOWS: BOOK TWO
Innovation Publishing: 1993 - No. 4, July, 1993 ($2.50, limited series)

1-4-Painted-c. 4-Maggie Thompson scripts 4.00

DARK SHADOWS: BOOK THREE
Innovation Publishing: Nov, 1993 ($2.50)

1-(Whole #9) 4.00

DARK SHADOWS/VAMPIRELLA
Dynamite Entertainment: 2012 - No. 5, 2012 ($3.99, limited series)

1-5-Andreyko-s/Berkenkotter-a/Neves-c 4.00

DARK SHADOWS, VOLUME 1
Dynamite Entertainment: 2011 - No. 23, 2013 ($3.99)

1-23-Set in 1971. 1-Aaron Campbell-a; covers by Campbell & Francavilla 4.00

DARK SHADOWS: YEAR ONE
Dynamite Entertainment: 2013 - No. 6, 2013 ($3.99, limited series)

1-6-Origin of Barnabas Collins; Andreyko-s/Vilanova-a 4.00

DARK SOULS: LEGENDS OF THE FLAME (Based on the Bandai Namco video game)
Titan Comics: Sept, 2016 - No. 2, Nov, 2016 ($3.99, limited series)

1,2-Short stories by various; multiple covers on each 4.00

DARK SOULS: THE AGE OF FIRE (Based on the Bandai Namco video game)
Titan Comics: May, 2018 - No. 4, Oct, 2018 ($3.99, limited series)

1-4-O'Sullivan-s/Kokarev-a; multiple covers on each 4.00

DARK SOULS: THE BREATH OF ANDOLUS (Based on the Bandai Namco video game)
Titan Comics: May, 2016 - No. 4, Sept, 2016 ($3.99, limited series)

1-4-George Mann-s/Alan Quah-a; multiple covers on each 4.00

DARK SOULS: WINTER'S SPITE (Based on the Bandai Namco video game)
Titan Comics: Dec, 2016 - No. 4, Apr, 2017 ($3.99, limited series)

1-4-George Mann-s/Alan Quah-a; multiple covers on each 4.00

DARKSTAR AND THE WINTER GUARD
Marvel Comics: Aug, 2010 - No. 3, Oct, 2010 ($3.99, limited series)

1-3-Gallaher-s/Ellis-a/Henry-c; back-up reprint from X-Men Unlimited #28 4.00

DARKSTARS, THE
DC Comics: Oct, 1992 - No. 38, Jan, 1996 ($1.75/$1.95)

1-1st app. The Darkstars 4.00
2-24,0,25-38: 5-Hawkman & Hawkwoman app. 18-20-Flash app. 24-(9/94)-Zero Hour. 0-(10/94). 25-(11/94). 30-Green Lantern app. 31-...vs. Darkseid. 32-Green Lantern app. 3.00

NOTE: *Travis Charest a(p)-4-7; c(p)-2-5; c-6-11. Stroman a-1-3; c-1.*

Dark Tower: The Gunslinger Born #7 © Stephen King

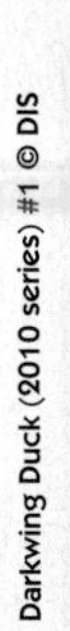

Darkwing Duck (2010 series) #1 © DIS

Darth Vader #25 © Lucasfilm

GD	VG	FN	VF	VF/NM	NM-
2.0	4.0	6.0	8.0	9.0	9.2

GD VG FN VF VF/NM NM-
2.0 4.0 6.0 8.0 9.0 9.2

DARK TALES FROM THE VOKESVERSE
American Mythology: 2016 ($4.99, B&W)

1-Short horror stories by Neil Vokes and various; 2 covers 5.00

DARK TOWER: THE BATTLE OF JERICHO HILL (Based on Stephen King's Dark Tower)
Marvel Comics: Feb, 2010 - No. 5, Jun, 2010 ($3.99, limited series)

1-5-Peter David & Robin Furth-s/Jae Lee & Richard Isanove-a/c; variant-c for each 4.00

DARK TOWER: THE DRAWING OF THE THREE - BITTER MEDICINE (Stephen King)
Marvel Comics: Jun, 2016 - No. 5, Oct, 2016 ($3.99, limited series)

1-5-Peter David & Robin Furth-s/Jonathan Marks-a/Nimit Malavia-c 4.00

DARK TOWER: THE DRAWING OF THE THREE - HOUSE OF CARDS (Stephen King)
Marvel Comics: May, 2015 - No. 5, Sept, 2015 ($3.99, limited series)

1-5-Peter David & Robin Furth-s/Piotr Kowalski-a/J.T. Tedesco-c 4.00

DARK TOWER: THE DRAWING OF THE THREE - LADY OF SHADOWS (Stephen King)
Marvel Comics: Nov, 2015 - No. 5, Mar, 2016 ($3.99, limited series)

1-5-Peter David & Robin Furth-s/Jonathan Marks-a/Nimit Malavia-c 4.00

DARK TOWER: THE DRAWING OF THE THREE - THE PRISONER (Stephen King)
Marvel Comics: Nov, 2014 - No. 5, Feb, 2015 ($3.99, limited series)

1-5-Peter David & Robin Furth-s/Piotr Kowalski-a/J.T. Tedesco-c 4.00

DARK TOWER: THE DRAWING OF THE THREE - THE SAILOR (Stephen King)
Marvel Comics: Dec, 2016 - No. 5, Apr, 2017 ($3.99, limited series)

1-5-Peter David & Robin Furth-s/Ramirez-a/Anacleto-c 4.00

DARK TOWER: THE FALL OF GILEAD (Based on Stephen King's Dark Tower)
Marvel Comics: July, 2009 - No. 6, Jan, 2010 ($3.99, limited series)

1-6-Peter David & Robin Furth-s/Richard Isanove-a/Jae Lee-c; variant-c for each 4.00
Dark Tower: Guide to Gilead (2009, $3.99) profile pages of people and places 4.00

DARK TOWER: THE GUNSLINGER BORN (Based on Stephen King's Dark Tower series)
Marvel Comics: Apr, 2007 - No. 7, Oct, 2007 ($3.99, limited series)

1-Peter David & Robin Furth-s/Jae Lee & Richard Isanove-a; boyhood of Roland Deschain; afterword by Ralph Macchio; map of New Canaan 6.00
1-Variant cover by Quesada 10.00
1-Second printing with variant-c by Quesada 5.00
1-Sketch cover variant by Jae Lee 30.00
2-6-Jae Lee-c 4.00
2-Second printing with variant-c by Immonen 4.00
2-7-Variant covers. 2-Finch-c. 3-Yu-c. 4-McNiven-c. 5-Land-c. 6-Campbell. 7-Coipel 6.00
2-7-B&W sketch-c by Jae Lee 20.00
... MGC #1 (5/11, $1.00) r/#1 with "Marvel's Greatest Comics" logo on cover 3.00
... Sketchbook (2006, no cover price) pencil art and designs by Lee; coloring process 5.00
Dark Tower: Gunslinger's Guidebook (2007, $3.99) profile pages with Jae Lee-a 4.00
HC (2007, $24.99) r/#1-7; variant covers and sketch pages; Macchio intro. 25.00

DARK TOWER: THE GUNSLINGER - EVIL GROUND (Stephen King's Dark Tower)
Marvel Comics: Jun, 2013 - No. 2, Aug, 2013 ($3.99, limited series)

1,2-Robin Furth & Peter David-s/Richard Isanove-a/c 4.00

DARK TOWER: THE GUNSLINGER - SHEEMIE'S TALE (Stephen King's Dark Tower)
Marvel Comics: Mar, 2013 - No. 2, Apr, 2013 ($3.99, limited series)

1,2-Robin Furth-s/Richard Isanove-a/c 4.00

DARK TOWER: THE GUNSLINGER - SO FELL LORD PERTH (Stephen King's Dark Tower)
Marvel Comics: Sept, 2013 ($3.99, one-shot)

1-Robin Furth & Peter David-s/Richard Isanove-a/c 4.00

DARK TOWER: THE GUNSLINGER - THE BATTLE OF TULL (Stephen King's Dark Tower)
Marvel Comics: Aug, 2011 - No. 5, Dec, 2011 ($3.99, limited series)

1-5-Peter David & Robin Furth-s/Michael Lark-a/c 4.00

DARK TOWER: THE GUNSLINGER - THE JOURNEY BEGINS (Stephen King's Dark Tower)
Marvel Comics: Jul, 2010 - No. 5, Nov, 2010 ($3.99, limited series)

1-5-Peter David & Robin Furth-s/Sean Phillips-a/c 4.00
1-Variant cover by Jae Lee 5.00

DARK TOWER: THE GUNSLINGER - THE LITTLE SISTERS OF ELURIA (Stephen King)
Marvel Comics: Feb, 2011 - No. 5, Jun, 2011 ($3.99, limited series)

1-5: 1-Peter David & Robin Furth-s/Luke Ross-a/c 4.00

DARK TOWER: THE GUNSLINGER - THE MAN IN BLACK (Stephen King)
Marvel Comics: Aug, 2012 - No. 5, Dec, 2012 ($3.99, limited series)

1-5-Peter David & Robin Furth-s/Maleev-a/c 4.00

DARK TOWER: THE GUNSLINGER - THE WAY STATION (Stephen King)
Marvel Comics: Feb, 2012 - No. 5, Jun, 2012 ($3.99, limited series)

1-5-Peter David & Robin Furth-s/Laurence Campbell-a/c 4.00

DARK TOWER: THE LONG ROAD HOME (Based on Stephen King's Dark Tower series)
Marvel Comics: May, 2008 - No. 5, Sept, 2008 ($3.99, limited series)

1-Peter David & Robin Furth-s/Jae Lee & Richard Isanove-a 4.00
1-Variant cover by Deodato 6.00
1-Sketch cover variant by Jae Lee 30.00
2-5-Jae Lee-c 4.00
2-5: 2-Variant-c by Quesada. 3-Djurdjevic var-c. 4-Garney var-c. 5-Bermejo var-c 6.00
2-5-B&W sketch-c by Jae Lee 20.00
2-Second printing with variant-c by Lee 4.00
Dark Tower: End-World Almanac (2008, $3.99) guide to locations and inhabitants 4.00

DARK TOWER: THE SORCEROR (Based on Stephen King's Dark Tower)
Marvel Comics: June, 2009 ($3.99, one-shot)

1-Robin Furth-s/Richard Isanove-a/c; the story of Marten Broadcloak 4.00

DARK TOWER: TREACHERY (Based on Stephen King's Dark Tower series)
Marvel Comics: Nov, 2008 - No. 6, Apr, 2009 ($3.99, limited series)

1-6-Peter David & Robin Furth-s/Jae Lee & Richard Isanove-a 4.00
1-Variant cover by Dell'otto 10.00

DARKWING DUCK (TV cartoon) (Also see Cartoon Tales)
Disney Comics: Nov, 1991 - No. 4, Feb, 1992 ($1.50, limited series)

1-4: Adapts hour-long premiere TV episode 4.00

DARKWING DUCK (TV cartoon)
BOOM! Studios (KABOOM!): Jun, 2010 - No. 18, Nov, 2011 ($3.99)

1-Brill-s/Silvani-a; Launchpad McQuack app.; 3 covers 5.00
2-18-Multiple covers on all. 7-Batman #1 cover swipe. 8-Detective #31 cover swipe 4.00
Annual 1 (3/11, $4.99) Three covers; Quackerjack app. 5.00
... Free Comic Book Day Edition (5/11) Flip book with Chip 'N' Dale Rescue Rangers 3.00

DARK WOLVERINE (See Wolverine 2003 series)

DARK X-MEN (See Dark Avengers and the Dark Reign mini-series)
Marvel Comics: Jan, 2010 - No. 5, May, 2010 ($3.99, limited series)

1-5-Cornell-s/Kirk-a. 1-3-Bianchi-c. 1-Nate Grey returns 4.00
...: The Confession (11/09, $3.99) Cansino-a; Paquette-c 4.00

DARK X-MEN: THE BEGINNING (See Dark Avengers and the Dark Reign mini-series)
Marvel Comics: Sept, 2009 - No. 3, Oct, 2009 ($3.99, limited series)

1-3: 1-Cornell-s/Kirk-a; Jae Lee-c on all. 2-Daken app. 3-Mystique app.; Jock-a 4.00

DARLING LOVE
Close Up/Archie Publ. (A Darling Magazine): Oct-Nov, 1949 - No. 11, 1952 (no month) (52 pgs.)(Most photo-c)

	GD	VG	FN	VF	VF/NM	NM-
1-Photo-c	28	56	84	165	270	375
2-Photo-c	15	30	45	90	140	190
3-8,10,11: 3-6-photo-c	14	28	42	81	118	155
9-Krigstein-a	15	30	45	83	124	165

DARLING ROMANCE
Close Up (MLJ Publications): Sept-Oct, 1949 - No. 7, 1951 (All photo-c)

	GD	VG	FN	VF	VF/NM	NM-
1-(52 pgs.)-Photo-c	31	62	93	186	303	420
2	15	30	45	90	140	190
3-7	14	28	42	82	121	160

DARQUE PASSAGES (See Master Darque)
Acclaim (Valiant): April, 1998 ($2.50)

1-Christina Z.-s/Manco-c/a 3.00

DART (Also see Freak Force & Savage Dragon)
Image Comics (Highbrow Entertainment): Feb, 1996 - No. 3, May, 1996 ($2.50, lim. series)

1-3 3.00

DARTH MAUL (See Star Wars: Darth Maul)

DARTH VADER (Follows after the end of Star Wars Episode IV)
Marvel Comics: Apr, 2015 - No. 25, Dec, 2016 ($4.99/$3.99)

	GD	VG	FN	VF	VF/NM	NM-
1-($4.99) Gillen-s/Larroca-a/Granov-c; Jabba the Hut & Boba Fett app.	1	2	3	5	6	8
2,4-12-($3.99) 6-Boba Fett app.						5.00
3-Intro. Doctor Aphra and Triple Zero	7	14	21	46	86	125
13-19,21-24: 13-15-Vader Down x-over pts. 2,4,6. 24-Flashbacks to Episode III						5.00
20-($4.99) The Emperor app.; back-up Triple-Zero & Beetee story w/Norton-a						7.00
25-($5.99) Gillen-s/Larroca-a; back-up story with Fiumara-a; bonus cover gallery						6.00
Annual 1 (2/16, $4.99) Gillen-s/Yu-a/c						5.00
...: Doctor Aphra No. 1 Halloween Comic Fest 2016 (12/16, giveaway) r/#3						4.00

DARTH VADER (Follows after the end of Star Wars Episode III)

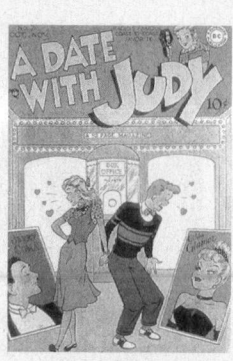

A Date With Judy #7 © DC

Dawn / Vampirella #3 © JM Linsner & DYN

Days of Hate #9 © Kot & Zezelj

	GD 2.0	VG 4.0	FN 6.0	VF 8.0	VF/NM 9.0	NM- 9.2
Marvel Comics: Aug, 2017 - No. 25, Feb, 2019 ($4.99/$3.99)						
1-($4.99) Soule-s/Camuncoli-a/Cheung-c; back-up by Eliopoulos-s/a						5.00
2-24-($3.99) Soule-s/Camuncoli-a. 5-Vader acquires the red light saber						4.00
25-($4.99) Soule-s/Camuncoli-a/c; recap of Vader's life						5.00
Annual 2 (9/18, $4.99) Wendig-s/Kirk-a/Deodato-c; Commander Krennic app.						5.00
DASTARDLY & MUTTLEY (See Fun-In No. 1-4, 6 and Kite Fun Book)						
DC Comics: Nov, 2017 - No. 6, Apr, 2018 ($3.99, limited series)						
1-6: 1-New origin for the pair; Ennis-s/Mauricet-a						4.00
DATE WITH DANGER						
Standard Comics: No. 5, Dec, 1952 - No. 6, Feb, 1953						
5-Secret agent stories in both	55	110	165	352	601	850
6-Atom bomb story	32	64	96	188	307	425
DATE WITH DEBBI (Also see Debbi's Dates)						
National Periodical Publ.: Jan-Feb, 1969 - No. 17, Sept-Oct, 1971; No. 18, Oct-Nov, 1972						
1-Teenage	9	18	27	57	111	165
2-5,17-(52 pgs) James Taylor sty.	4	8	12	28	47	65
6-12,18-Last issue	4	8	12	25	40	55
13-16-(68 pgs.): 14-1 pg. story on Jack Wild. 15-Marlo Thomas/"That Girl" story	4	8	12	28	47	65
DATE WITH JUDY, A (Radio/TV, and 1948 movie)						
National Periodical Publications: Oct-Nov, 1947 - No. 79, Oct-Nov, 1960 (No. 1-25: 52 pgs.)						
1-Teenage	39	78	117	240	395	550
2	19	38	57	112	179	245
3-10	15	30	45	85	130	175
11-20	12	24	36	69	97	125
21-40	11	22	33	64	90	115
41-45: 45-Last pre-code (2-3/55)	11	22	33	60	83	105
46-79: 79-Drucker-c/a	10	20	30	56	76	95
DATE WITH MILLIE, A (Life With Millie No. 8 on)(Teenage)						
Atlas/Marvel Comics (MPC): Oct, 1956 - No. 7, Aug, 1957; Oct, 1959 - No. 7, Oct, 1960						
1(10/56)-(1st Series)-Dan DeCarlo-a in #1-7	65	130	195	416	708	1000
2	41	82	123	256	428	600
3-7	25	50	75	150	245	340
1(10/59)-(2nd Series)	42	84	126	265	445	625
2-7	16	32	48	98	154	210
DATE WITH PATSY, A (Also see Patsy Walker)						
Atlas Comics: Sept, 1957 (One-shot)						
1-Starring Patsy Walker	26	52	78	154	252	350
DAUGHTERS OF THE DRAGON (See Heroes For Hire)						
Marvel Comics: 2005; Mar, 2006 - No. 6, Aug, 2006 ($2.99, limited series)						
1-6-Palmiotti & Gray-s/Evans-a. 1-Rhino app. 5,6-Iron Fist app.						3.00
... Deadly Hands Special (2005, $3.99) reprints app. from Deadly Hands of Kung Fu #32,33 & Bizarre Adventures #25; Claremont-s/Rogers-a; new Rogers-c & interview						4.00
...: Deep Cuts MPGN (2018, $19.99, SC) printing of digital-first story; MacKay-s						20.00
...: Samurai Bullets TPB (2006, $15.99) r/#1-6						16.00
DAVID AND GOLIATH (Movie)						
Dell Publishing Co.: No. 1205, July, 1961						
Four Color 1205-Photo-c	7	14	21	44	82	120
DAVID BORING (See Eightball)						
Pantheon Books: 2000 ($24.95, hardcover w/dust jacket)						
Hardcover - reprints David Boring stories from Eightball; Clowes-s/a						25.00
DAVID CASSIDY (TV)(See Partridge Family, Swing With Scooter #33 & Time For Love #30)						
Charlton Comics: Feb, 1972 - No. 14, Sept, 1973						
1-Most have photo covers	6	12	18	41	76	110
2-5	4	8	12	25	40	55
6-14	4	8	12	23	37	50
DAVID LADD'S LIFE STORY (See Movie Classics)						
DAVY CROCKETT (See Dell Giants, Fightin..., Frontier Fighters, It's Game Time, Power Record Comics, Western Tales & Wild Frontier)						
DAVY CROCKETT (Frontier Fighter...)						
Avon Periodicals: 1951						
nn-Tuska?, Reinman-a; Fawcette-c	25	50	75	147	241	335
DAVY CROCKETT (...King of the Wild Frontier No. 1,2)(TV)						
Dell Publishing Co./Gold Key: 5/55 - No. 671, 12/55; No. 1, 12/63; No. 2, 11/69 (Walt Disney)						
Four Color 631(#1)-Fess Parker photo-c	14	28	42	98	217	335
Four Color 639-Photo-c	11	22	33	76	163	260
Four Color 664,671(Marsh-a)-Photo-c	11	22	33	75	160	245
1(12/63-Gold Key)-Fess Parker photo-c; reprints	7	14	21	46	86	125
2(11/69)-Fess Parker photo-c; reprints	4	8	12	28	44	60
DAVY CROCKETT (...Frontier Fighter #1,2; Kid Montana #9 on)						
Charlton Comics: Aug, 1955 - No. 8, Jan, 1957						
1	10	20	30	58	79	100
2	7	14	21	37	46	55
3-8	6	12	18	28	34	40
DAWN						
Sirius Entertainment/Image Comics: June, 1995 - No. 6, 1996 ($2.95)						
1/2-w/certificate	1	2	3	5	6	8
1/2-Variant-c	2	4	6	10	14	18
1-Linsner-c/a	1	3	4	6	8	10
1-Black Light Edition	2	4	6	10	14	18
1-White Trash Edition	3	6	9	17	25	34
1-Look Sharp Edition	3	6	9	19	30	40
2-4: Linsner-c/a						4.50
2-Variant-c, 3-Limited Edition	2	4	6	13	18	22
4-6-Vibrato-c						3.50
4, 5-Limited Edition	2	4	6	8	10	12
6-Limited Edition	2	4	6	8	10	12
...Convention Sketchbook (Image Comics, 2002, $2.95) pin-ups						3.00
...2003 Convention Sketchbook (Image Comics, 3/03, $2.95) pin-ups						3.00
...2004 Convention Sketchbook (Image Comics, 4/04, $2.95) pin-ups						3.00
...2005 Convention Sketchbook (Image Comics, 5/05, $2.95) pin-ups						3.00
Genesis Edition ('99, Wizard supplement) previews Return of the Goddess						3.00
Lucifer's Halo TPB (11/97, $19.95) r/Drama, Dawn #1-6 plus 12 pages of new artwork						20.00
...: Not to Touch The Earth (9/10, $5.99) Linsner-s/c/a; pin-ups by various incl. Turner						6.00
...: Tenth Anniversary Special (9/99, $2.95) Interviews						3.00
The Portable Dawn ($9.95, 5"x4", 64 pgs.) Pocket-sized cover gallery						10.00
...: The Swordmaster's Daughter & Other Stories (2013, $3.99) Linsner-s/c/a						4.00
DAWN OF THE DEAD (George A. Romaro's...)						
IDW Publishing: Apr, 2004 - No. 3, Jun, 2004 ($3.99, limited series)						
1-3-Adaptation of the 2004 movie; Niles-s	1	3	4	6	8	10
TPB (9/04, $17.99) r/#1-3; intro. by George A. Romero						18.00
DAWN OF THE PLANET OF THE APES						
BOOM! Studios: Nov, 2014 - No. 6, Apr, 2015 ($3.99, limited series)						
1-6: 1-Takes place between the 2011 and 2014 movies; Moreci-s/McDaid-a						4.00
DAWN: THE RETURN OF THE GODDESS						
Sirius Entertainment: Apr, 1999 - No. 4, July, 2000 ($2.95, limited series)						
1-4-Linsner-s/a						3.00
TPB (4/02, $12.95) r/#1-4; intro. by Linsner						13.00
DAWN: THREE TIERS						
Image Comics: Jun, 2003 - No. 6, Aug, 2005 ($2.95, limited series)						
1-6-Linsner-s/a. 2-Preview of Vampire's Christmas						3.00
DAWN / VAMPIRELLA						
Dynamite Entertainment: 2014 - No. 5, 2015 ($3.99, limited series)						
1-5-Linsner-s/a/c. 3-Vampirella origin re-told						5.00
DAYDREAMERS (See Generation X)						
Marvel Comics: Aug, 1997 - No. 3, Oct, 1997 ($2.50, limited series)						
1-3-Franklin Richards, Howard the Duck, Man-Thing app.						3.00
DAY MEN						
BOOM! Studios: Jul, 2013 - No. 8, Oct, 2015 ($3.99)						
1-Stelfreeze-a/c; Gagnon & Nelson-s						5.00
2-8: 2-Covers by Stelfreeze & Pérez						4.00
...: Pen & Ink No. 1 (12/13, $9.99, 11"x17") Pen and ink art for #1&2 with commentary						10.00
DAY OF JUDGMENT						
DC Comics: Nov, 1999 - No. 5, Nov, 1999 ($2.95/$2.50, limited series)						
1-($2.95) Spectre possessed; Matt Smith-a						3.00
2-5: Parallax returns. 5-Hal Jordan becomes the Spectre						3.00
...Secret Files 1 (11/99, $4.95) Harris-c						5.00
DAY OF VENGEANCE (Prelude to Infinite Crisis)(Also see Birds of Prey #76 for 1st app. of Black Alice)						
DC Comics: June, 2005 - No. 6, Nov, 2005 ($2.50, limited series)						
1-6: 1-Jean Loring becomes Eclipso; Spectre, Ragman, Enchantress, Detective Chimp, Shazam app.; Justiniano-a. 2,3-Capt. Marvel app. 4-6-Black Alice app.						3.00
...: Infinite Crisis Special 1 (3/06, $4.99) Justiniano-a/Simonson-c						5.00

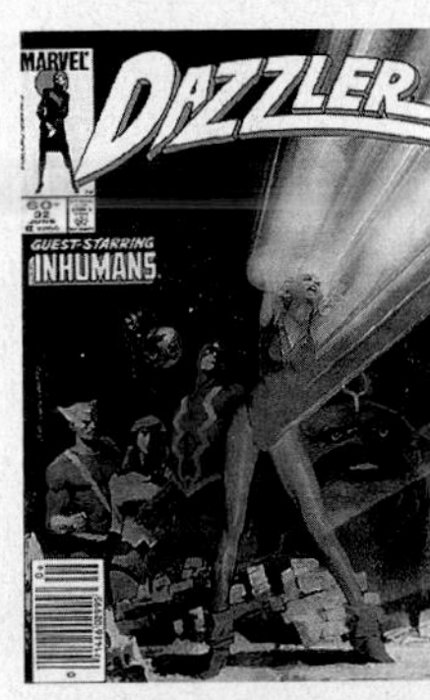
The Dazzler #32 © MAR

DC Comics: Bombshells #27 © DC

DC Comics Presents #1 © DC

GD VG FN VF VF/NM NM-
2.0 4.0 6.0 8.0 9.0 9.2

TPB (2005, $12.99) r/series & Action #826, Advs. of Superman #639, Superman #216 13.00

DAYS OF HATE
Image Comics: Jan, 2018 - No. 12, Jan, 2019 ($3.99)
1-12-Ales Kot-s/Danijel Zezelj-a 4.00

DAYS OF THE DEFENDERS (See Defenders, The)
Marvel Comics: Mar, 2001 ($3.50, one-shot)
1-Reprints early team-ups of members, incl. Marvel Feature #1; Larsen-c 3.50

DAYS OF THE MOB (See In the Days of the Mob)

DAYTRIPPER
DC Comics (Vertigo): Feb, 2010 - No. 10, Nov, 2010 ($2.99, limited series)
1-10-Gabriel Bá & Fábio Moon-s/a 3.00
TPB (2010, $19.99) r/#1-10; sketch art pages 20.00

DAZEY'S DIARY
Dell Publishing Co.: June-Aug, 1962
01-174-208: Bill Woggon-c/a 4 8 12 27 44 60

DAZZLER, THE (Also see Marvel Graphic Novel & X-Men #130)
Marvel Comics Group: Mar, 1981 - No. 42, Mar, 1986
1-X-Men app.; DeFalco-s/Romita Jr.-a 2 4 6 11 16 20
2-20,23,25,26,29-32,34-37,39-41: 2-X-Men app. 10,11-Galactus app. 23-Rogue/Mystique 1 pg. app. 26-Jusko-c. 40-Secret Wars II 4.00
21,22,24,27,28,38,42: 21-Double size; photo-c. 22 (12/82)-vs. Rogue Battle-c/sty. 24-Full app. Rogue w/Powerman (Iron Fist). 27-Rogue app. 28-Full app. Rogue; Mystique app. 38-Wolverine-c/app.; X-Men app. 42-Beast-c/app. 5.00
33-Michael Jackson "Thriller" swipe-c/sty 3 6 9 14 20 25
... No. 1 Facsimile Edition (4/19, $3.99) reprints #1 with original ads 4.00
One-shot (7/10, $3.99) Andrasofszky-a/c; Arcade app. 4.00
...: X-Song 1 (8/18, $3.99) Visaggio-s/Braga-a
NOTE: *No. 1 distributed only through comic shops.* ***Alcala*** *a-1i, 2i.* ***Chadwick*** *a-38-42p; c(p)-39, 41, 42.* ***Guice*** *a-38i, 42i; c-38, 40.*

DC CHALLENGE (Most DC superheroes appear)
DC Comics: Nov, 1985 - No. 12, Oct, 1986 ($1.25/$2.00, maxi-series)
1-11: 1-Colan-a. 2,8-Batman-c/app. 4-Gil Kane-c/a 4.00
12-($2.00-c) Giant; low print 5.00
NOTE: *Batman app. in 1-4, 6-12. Joker app. in 7.* ***Infantino*** *a-3.* ***Ordway*** *c-12.* ***Swan/Austin*** *c-10.*

DC CLASSICS: THE BATMAN ADVENTURES
DC Comics: Aug, 2020 - No. 7, Feb, 2021 ($1.99)
1-7-Reprints The Batman Adventures series. 2-Catwoman app. 3-Joker app. 3.00

DC COMICS: BOMBSHELLS (Continues in Bombshelss: United)
DC Comics: Oct, 2015 - No. 33, Oct, 2017 ($3.99, printings of digital-first stories)
1-Bennett-s/Sauvage-a/Lucia-a; set in 1940 WWII 1 3 4 6 8 10
2-24: 4,14-18-Harley Quinn-c/app. 5.00
25-($4.99) Suicide Squad app.; intro. Faora Hu-Ul; Aneke-a 6.00
26-33: 27,32,33-Harley Quinn/Poison Ivy-c. 29-Superman app. 5.00
Annual 1 (10/16, $4.99) Bennett-s/Charretier-a; origin of vampire Batgirl 8.00

DC COMICS CLASSICS LIBRARY (Hardcover collections of classic DC stories)
DC Comics: 2009 - 2010 ($39.99, hardcover with dustjacket)
Batman: A Death in the Family ('09)- r/Batman #426-429, 440-442, New Titans #60,61 40.00
Batman Annuals ('09)- r/Batman Annual #1-3; afterword by Richard Bruning 40.00
Batman Annuals Volume 2 ('10)- r/Batman Annual #4-7; intro. by Michael Uslan 40.00
Flash of Two Worlds ('09)- r/Flash #123,129,137,151,170&173 team-ups with G.A. Flash 40.00
Justice League of America by George Pérez ('09) r/J.L.of A. #184-186, 192-194 40.00
Justice League of America by George Pérez Vol. 2 ('10) r/J.L.of A. #195-197,200 40.00
Legion of Super-Heroes: The Life and Death of Ferro Lad ('09) - r/Adventure Comics # 346, 347,352-355,357; intro. by Paul Levitz; afterword by Jim Shooter 40.00
Roots of the Swamp Thing ('09)- r/House of Secrets #92 & Swamp Thing #1-13; Wein intro. 40.00
Superman: Kryptonite Nevermore ('09)- r/Superman #233-238,240-242; afterword by Denny O'Neil 40.00

DC COMICS ESSENTIALS
DC Comics: ($1.00, flipbooks with DC Graphic Novel catalog of recommended titles)
...: Action Comics #1 (2/14, $1.00) Reprints Action #1 (2011) with flipbook of DC GNs 3.00
...: Batman #1 (12/13, $1.00) Reprints Batman #1 (2011) with flipbook of DC GNs 3.00
...: Batman and Robin #1 (4/16, $1.00) Reprints Batman and Robin #1 (2011) with flipbook 3.00
...: Batman and Son Special Ed. ('14, $1.00) Reprints Batman #655 with flipbook 3.00
...: Batman: Death of the Family (6/16, $1.00) Reprints Batman #13 (2011) with flipbook 3.00
...: Batman: Hush Spec. Ed. ('14, $1.00) Reprints Batman #608 with flipbook of DC GNs 3.00
...: Batman: The Black Mirror Special Ed. ('14, $1.00) Reprints Detective #871 w/flipbook 3.00
...: Batman: The Dark Knight Returns #1 (5/16, $1.00) Reprints #1 with flipbook 3.00
...: Batman: The Dark Knight Returns Special Ed. ('14, $1.00) Reprints #1 with flipbook 3.00
...: Batman: Year One #1 ('14, $1.00) Reprints Batman #404 with flipbook of DC GNs 3.00
...: DC: The New Frontier #1 (3/16, $1.00) Reprints first issue with flipbook 3.00
...: Green Lantern #1 (1/14, $1.00) Reprints Green Lantern #1 (2011) with flipbook 3.00
...: JLA #1 (6/16, $1.00) Reprints JLA #1 with flipbook of DC GNs 3.00
...: Justice League #1 (1/14, $1.00) Reprints Justice League #1 (2011) with flipbook 3.00
...: Superman Unchained #1 (5/16, $1.00) Reprints Superman Unchained #1 with flipbook 3.00
...: Watchmen #1 (2/14, $1.00) Reprints Watchmen #1 (1986) with flipbook 3.00
...: Wonder Woman #1 (12/13, $1.00) Reprints Wonder Woman #1 (2011) with flipbook 3.00

DC COMICS MEGA SAMPLER
DC Comics: 2009; Jul, 2010 (6-1/4" x 9-1/2", FCBD giveaways)
1, 2010- Short stories of kid-friendly titles; Tiny Titans, Billy Batson, Super Friends app. 3.00

DC COMICS PRESENTS
DC Comics: July-Aug, 1978 - No. 97, Sept, 1986 (Superman team-ups in all)
1-4th Superman/Flash race 4 8 12 28 47 65
1-(Whitman variant) 5 10 15 35 63 90
2-Part 2 of Superman/Flash race 3 6 9 15 22 28
2-(Whitman variant) 3 6 9 17 26 35
3,4,9-12,14-16,19,21,22-(Whitman variants, low print run, none have issue # on cover) 3 6 9 14 20 25
3-10: 3-Adam Strange. 4-Metal Men. 5-Aquaman. 6-Green Lantern. 7-Red Tornado. 8-Swamp Thing. 9-Wonder Woman. 10-Sgt. Rock 2 4 6 8 10 12
11-25,28-40: 12-Mister Miracle. 13-Legion of Super-Heroes. 19-Batgirl. 21-Elongated Man. 23-Dr. Fate. 24-Deadman. 30-Black Canary. 31-Robin. 34-Marvel Family. 35-Man-Bat. 36-Starman. 37-Hawkgirl. 38-The Flash 6.00
26-(10/80)-Green Lantern; intro Cyborg, Starfire, Raven (1st app. New Teen Titans in 16 pg. preview); Starlin-c/a; Sargon the Sorcerer back-up 9 18 27 81 123 185
27-1st app. Mongul 4 8 12 27 44 60
41-Superman/Joker-c/story; 1st app. New Wonder Woman in 16 pg. preview; Colan-a 2 4 6 9 13 16
42-46,48,50,52-71,73-76,79-83: 42-Sandman. 43,80-Legion of Super-Heroes. 52-Doom Patrol; 1st app. Ambush Bug. 58-Robin. 64-Kamandi. 82-Adam Strange. 83-Batman & Outsiders 4.00
47-(7/82) He-Man-c/s (1st app. in comics) 10 20 30 94 147 200
49-Black Adam & Captain Marvel app. 4 8 12 23 37 50
51-Preview insert (16 pgs.) of He-Man (2nd app.) 2 4 6 10 14 18
72,77,78,97: 72-Joker/Phantom Stranger-c/story. 77,78-Animal Man app. (77-c also). 97-Phantom Zone 6.00
84-Challengers of the Unknown; Kirby-c/s. 6.00
85-Swamp Thing; Alan Moore scripts 6.00
86,88-96: 86-88-Crisis x-over. 88-Creeper 4.00
87-Origin/1st app. Superboy of Earth Prime 3 6 9 17 26 35
Annual 1(9/82)-G.A. Superman; 1st app. Alexander Luthor 2 4 6 8 10 12
Annual 2,3: 2(7/83)-Intro/origin Superwoman. 3(9/84)-Shazam 4.00
Annual 4(10/85)-Superwoman 4.00
NOTE: ***Adkins*** *a-2, 54; c-2.* ***Buckler*** *a-33, 34; c-30, 33, 34.* ***Giffen*** *a-39; c-59.* ***Gil Kane*** *a-28, 35, Annual 3; c-48p, 56, 58, 60, 62, 64, 68, Annual 2, 3.* ***Kirby*** *c/a-84.* ***Kubert*** *c/a-66.* ***Morrow*** *c/a-65.* ***Newton*** *c/a-54p.* ***Orlando*** *c-53i.* ***Perez*** *a-26p, 61p; c-38, 61, 94.* ***Starlin*** *a-26-29p, 36p, 37p; c-26-29, 36, 37, 93.* ***Toth*** *a-84.* ***Williamson*** *i-79, 85, 87.*

DC COMICS PRESENTS: ...(Julie Schwartz tribute series of one-shots based on classic covers)
DC Comics: Sept, 2004 - Oct, 2004 ($2.50)
The Atom -(Based on cover of Atom #10) Gibbons-s/Oliffe-a; Waid-s/Jurgens-a; Bolland-c 3.00
Batman -(Batman #183) Johns-s/Infantino-a; Wein-s/Kuhn-a; Hughes-c 3.00
The Flash -(Flash #163) Loeb-s/McGuinness-a; O'Neil-s/Mahnke-a; Ross-c 3.00
Green Lantern -(Green Lantern #31) Azzarello-s/Breyfogle-a; Pasko-s/McDaniel-a; Bolland-c 3.00
Hawkman -(Hawkman #6) Bates-s/Byrne-a; Busiek-s/Simonson-a; Garcia-Lopez-c 3.00
Justice League of America -(J.L. of A. #53) Ellison & David-s/Giella-a; Wolfman-s/Nguyen-a; Garcia-Lopez-c 3.00
Mystery in Space -(M.I.S. #82) Maggin-s/Williams-a; Morrison-s/Ordway-a; Ross-c 3.00
Superman -(Superman #264) Stan Lee-s/Cooke-a; Levitz-s/Giffen-a; Hughes-c 3.00

DC COMICS PRESENTS: ...
DC Comics: Dec, 2010 - Feb, 2016 ($7.99/$9.99, squarebound, one-shot reprints)
The Atom 1 (3/11) r/Legends of the DC Universe #28,29,40,41; Gil Kane-a 8.00
Batman 1 (12/10) r/Batman #582-585,600 8.00
Batman 2 (1/11) r/Batman #591-594 8.00
Batman 3 (2/11) r/Batman #595-598 8.00
Batman Adventures 1 (9/14) reprints; Burchett, Parobeck, Templeton, Timm-a 8.00
Batman: Arkham 1 (6/11) r/Batman Chronicles #6, Batman; Arkham Asylum - Tales of Madness #1, Batman Villains Secret Files #1 & Justice Leagues: J.L. of Arkham #1 8.00
Batman - Bad 1 (1/12) r/Batman: Legends of the D.K. #146-148 8.00
Batman Beyond 1 (2/11) r/Batman Beyond #13,14,21,22 8.00
Batman: Blaze of Glory 1 (2/12) r/Batman: Legends of the D.K. #197-199,212 8.00
Batman - Blink 1 (12/11) r/Batman: Legends of the D.K. #156-158 8.00
Batman/Catwoman 1 (12/10) r/Batman and Catwoman: Trail of the Gun 8.00
Batman - Conspiracy 1 (4/11) r/Batman: Legends of the D.K. #86-88; Detective #821 8.00

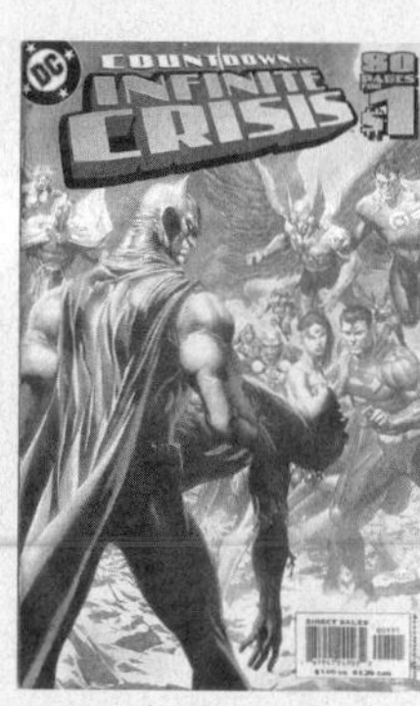
DC Countdown #1 © DC

DCeased #3 © DC

DC Graphic Novel #4 © DC

GD	VG	FN	VF	VF/NM	NM-
2.0	4.0	6.0	8.0	9.0	9.2

Batman - Dark Knight, Dark City 1 (7/11) r/Batman #452-454; Detective #633 8.00
Batman - Don't Blink 1 (1/12) r/Batman: Legends of the D.K. #164-167 8.00
Batman: Gotham Noir 1 (9/11) r/Batman: Gotham Noir #1 & Batman #604 8.00
Batman - Irresistible 1 (5/11) r/Batman: Legends of the D.K. #169-171; Hourman #22 8.00
Batman - The Demon Laughs 1 (12/11) r/Batman: Legends of the D.K. #142-145; Aparo-a 8.00
Batman: The Secret City 1 (2/12) r/Batman: Legends of the D.K. #180,181,190,191 8.00
Batman: Urban Legends 1 (2/12) r/Batman: Legends of the D.K. #168,177-179 8.00
Brightest Day 1 (12/10) r/Strange Advs. #205, Hawkman #27,34,36, Solo #8, DC Hol. '09 8.00
Brightest Day 2 (1/11) r/Firestorm #11-13 & Martian Manhuner #11,24 8.00
Brightest Day 3 (2/11) r/Legends of the DC Univ. #25-27 & Teen Titans #27,28 8.00
Captain Atom 1 (2/12) r/back-up stories from Action Comics #879-889 8.00
Catwoman - Guardian of Gotham 1 (12/11) r/Catwoman: Guardian of Gotham #1,2 8.00
Chase 1 (1/11) r/Chase #1,6-8 8.00
Darkseid War 1 (2/16, $7.99) r/New Gods #1,7, Mister Miracle #1 & Forever People #1 8.00
Demon Driven Out, The 1 (7/14, $9.99) r/The Demon: Driven Out #1-6 10.00
Elseworlds 80-Page Giant 1 (1/12) r/Elseworlds 80-Page Giant (pulled from distribution) 8.00
Flash 1 (7/11) r/Showcase #4,14 and Flash #125,130,139 8.00
Flash/Green Lantern: Faster Friends (1/11) r/G.L./Flash: Faster Friends & Flash/G.L.: FF 8.00
Green Lantern 1 (12/10) r/Green Lantern #137-140 (2001) 8.00
Green Lantern - Fear Itself 1 (4/11) r/Green Lantern: Fear Itself GN 8.00
Green Lantern - Willworld 1 (7/11) r/Green Lantern: Willworld GN 8.00
Harley Quinn 1 (4/14) r/Batman: Harley Quinn #1, Joker's Asylum II: HQ #1 and others 8.00
Impulse 1 (8/11) r/Impulse #50-53 8.00
Jack Kirby Omnibus Sampler 1 (12/11) r/Kirby art stories from 1957,1958 8.00
JLA 1 (2/11) r/JLA #90-93 8.00
JLA - Age of Wonder 1 (12/11) r/JLA: Age of Wonder 8.00
JLA: Black Baptism 1 (8/11) r/JLA: Black Baptism #1-4 8.00
JLA Heaven's Ladder 1 (10/11) comic-sized reprint; and r/Green Lantern #1,000,000 8.00
Legion of Super-Heroes 1 (6/11) r/Legion of Super-Heroes #122,123 & Legionnaires 79,80 8.00
Legion of Super-Heroes 2 (2/12) r/Adv. #247 and recent Legion short stories 8.00
Lobo 1 (3/11) r/Lobo #63,64 & DC First: Superman/Lobo #1 8.00
Metal Men 1 (4/11) r/Doom Patrol ('09) #1-7 and Silver Age: The Brave and the Bold #1 8.00
Night Force 1 (4/11) r/Night Force #1-4; Gene Colan-a 8.00
Ninja Boy 1 (6/11) r/Ninja Boy #1-4 8.00
Robin War 100-Page Super Spectacular 1 (2/16) Ryan Sook-c 8.00
Shazam! 1,2 (9/11,10/11) 1-r/Power of Shazam #38-41. 2-r/ #42-46 8.00
Son of Superman 1 (7/11) r/Son of Superman GN 8.00
Superboy's Legion 1 (12/11) r/Superboy's Legion #1,2 (Elseworlds) 8.00
Superman 1 (12/10) r/Superman: The Man of Steel #121 & Superman #179,180,185 8.00
Superman 2 (1/11) r/Action #798, Superman: The Man of Steel #133, Superman #189 & Advs. of Superman #611 8.00
Superman 3 (2/11) r/Superman #177,178,181,182 8.00
Superman 4 (9/11) r/Action #768,771-773 8.00
Superman Adventures 1 (8/12) r/Superman Adventures #16,19,22,23 8.00
Superman/Doomsday 1 (5/11) r/Doomsday Annual #1 & Superman #175 8.00
Superman - Infestation 1 (8/11) r/Action #778, Advs. of Superman #591, Superman #169 and Superman: The Man of Steel #113 8.00
Superman: Lois and Clark 100-Page S.S. 1 (1/16) r/Superman: The Wedding Album 8.00
Superman - Secret Identity 1 (12/11) r/Superman: Secret Identity #1,2 8.00
Superman - Secret Identity 2 (1/12) r/Superman: Secret Identity #3,4 8.00
Superman - Sole Survivor 1 (3/11) r/Legends of the DC Universe #1-3,39 8.00
Superman - The Kents 1,2 (1/12, 2/12) 1-r/The Kents #1-4. 2-The Kents #5-8 8.00
Teen Titans 1 (10/11) Teen Titans Lost Annual #1 and Solo #7; Allred-a 8.00
Titans Hunt 100-Page Super Spectacular 1 (1/16) r/Teen Titans early apps.; Sook-c 8.00
The Life Story of the Flash 1 (1/12) r/The Life Story of the Flash GN 8.00
T.H.U.N.D.E.R. Agents 1 (2/11) r/T.H.U.N.D.E.R. Agents #1,2,7 (1966) 8.00
Wonder Woman 1 (4/11) r/Wonder Woman #139-142 (1998) 8.00
Wonder Woman Adventures 1 (9/12) r/Advs. in the DC Universe #1,3,11,19 8.00
Young Justice 1 (12/10) r/JLA World Without Grownups #1,2 8.00
Young Justice 2 (1/11) r/Y.J: The Secret, Y.J. Secret Files #1, Y.J. In No Man's Land 8.00
Young Justice 3 (2/11) r/Young Justice #7 & Y.J Secret Origins 80-Page Giant #1 8.00

DC COMICS - THE NEW 52 FCBD SPECIAL EDITION
DC Comics: Jun, 2012 (giveaway one-shot)

1-Origin of The Trinity of Sin (Pandora, The Question, Phantom Stranger); Justice League app.; Jim Lee, Reis, Ha, Rocafort-a; previews Earth 2, G.I. Combat, Ravagers 3.00

DC COMICS THE NEW 52 PRESENTS: ...
DC Comics: Mar, 2012 ($7.99, squarebound, one-shot reprints)

The Dark 1 (3/12) r/Animal Man #1, Swamp Thing #1, I, Vampire #1, and J.L. Dark #1 8.00

DC COUNTDOWN (To Infinite Crisis)
DC Comics: May, 2005 ($1.00, 80 pages, one-shot)

1-Death of Blue Beetle; prelude to OMAC Project, Day of Vengeance, Rann/Thanagar War and Villains United mini-series; s/a by various; Jim Lee/Alex Ross-c 4.00

DCEASED
DC Comics: Jul, 2019 - No. 6, Dec, 2019 ($3.99, limited series)

1-5-Zombie apocalypse in DC universe; Taylor-s/Hairsine-a. 1-Darkseid app. 4.00
3,5-($4.99) 3-Variant zombie Wonder Woman-c by Mattina. 5-Zombie Harley Quinn-c 5.00
6-($4.99) Continues in DCeased: A Good Day to Die 5.00
6-($5.99) Variant Darkseid-c by Mattina 6.00
...: A Good Die to Die (11/19, $4.99) Taylor-s/Braga-a; Mr Miracle, Barda, Mr. Terrific app. 5.00

DCEASED: DEAD PLANET
DC Comics: Sept, 2020 - No. 7, Mar, 2021 ($4.99/$3.99, limited series)

1-($4.99)-Zombie apocalypse; Damian Wayne, Jon Kent, Cassie Sandsmark app. 5.00
2-6-($3.99) John Constantine, Swamp Thing, Zatanna app. 4.00
7-($4.99)-Justice League vs. Amazo army; Constantine & Zatanna vs. Trigon 5.00

DCEASED: UNKILLABLES
DC Comics: Apr, 2020 - No. 3, Jul, 2020 ($4.99, limited series)

1-3-Zombie apocalypse continues; Deathstroke with a team of villains; Red Hood app. 5.00

DC FIRST: ...(series of one-shots)
DC Comics: July, 2002 ($3.50)

Batgirl/Joker 1-Sienkiewicz & Terry Moore-a; Nowlan-c 3.50
Green Lantern/Green Lantern 1-Alan Scott & Hal Jordan vs. Krona 3.50
Flash/Superman 1-Superman races Jay Garrick; Abra Kadabra app. 3.50
Superman/Lobo 1-Giffen-s; Nowlan-c 3.50

DC GOES APE
DC Comics: 2008 ($19.99, trade paperback)

Vol. 1 - Reprints app. of Grodd, Beppo, Titano and other monkey tales; Art Adams-c 20.00

DC GRAPHIC NOVEL (Also see DC Science Fiction...)
DC Comics: Nov, 1983 - No. 7, 1986 ($5.95, 68 pgs.)

1-3,5,7: 1-Star Raiders; García-López-c/a; prequel to Atari Force #1. 2-Warlords; not from regular Warlord series. 3-The Medusa Chain; Ernie Colon story/a. 5-Me and Joe Priest; Chaykin-c. 7-Space Clusters; Nino-c/a 2 4 6 9 12 15
4-The Hunger Dogs by Kirby; Darkseid kills Himon from Mister Miracle & destroys New Genesis 5 10 15 33 57 80
6-Metalzoic; Sienkiewicz-c ($6.95) 2 4 6 9 12 15

DC HOLIDAY SPECIAL
DC Comics: Feb, 2010 ($5.99/$9.99, one-shots)

... '09 (2/10, $5.99) 1-Christmas short stories by various incl. Tucci, Chaykin; Nguyen-c 6.00
... 2017 (2/18, $9.99) 1-Story/art by various incl. Rucka, King, Francavilla; Andy Kubert-c 10.00

DC HOUSE OF HORROR
DC Comics: Dec, 2017 ($9.99, square-bound one-shot)

1-Horror short stories by various incl. Giffen, Porter, Baker, Raney, Chaykin; Kaluta-c 10.00

DC INFINITE HALLOWEEN SPECIAL
DC Comics: Dec, 2007 ($5.99, one-shot)

1-Halloween short stories by various incl. Dini, Waid, Hairsine, Kelley Jones; Gene Ha-c 6.00

DC LOVE IS A BATTLEFIELD
DC Comics: Apr, 2021 ($9.99, squarebound, 80 pgs., one-shot)

1-Romance short stories by various; Harley Quinn, Poison Ivy, Batman, Catwoman app. 10.00

DC/MARVEL: ALL ACCESS (Also see DC Versus Marvel & Marvel Versus DC)
DC Comics: 1996 - No. 4, 1997 ($2.95, limited series)

1-4: 1-Superman & Spider-Man app. 2-Robin & Jubilee app. 3-Dr. Strange & Batman-c/app., X-Men, JLA app. 4-X-Men vs. JLA-c/app. rebirth of Amalgam 3.00

DC/MARVEL: CROSSOVER CLASSICS
DC Comics: 1998; 2003 ($14.95, TPB)

Vol. II-Reprints Batman/Punisher: Lake of Fire, Punisher/Batman: Deadly Knights, Silver Surfer/Superman, Batman & Capt. America 15.00
Vol. 4 (2003, $14.95) Reprints Green Lantern/Silver Surfer: Unholy Alliances, Darkseid/Galactus: The Hunger, Batman & Spider-Man, and Superman/Fantastic Four 15.00

DC NATION
DC Comics: Jul, 2018 (25¢, one-shot)

0-Short stories; Joker by King-s/Mann-a; Superman by Bendis-s/García-López-a; prelude to Justice League: No Justice series; Jimenez-a 3.00

DC NATION FCBD SUPER SAMPLER
DC Comics: (Giveaway)

.../ Superman Adventures Flip Book (6/12) stories from Superman Family Adventures, Young Justice, Green Lantern: The Animated Series 3.00
... (7/13) Stories from Beware the Batman and Teen Titans Go! 3.00

DC NUCLEAR WINTER SPECIAL
DC Comics: Jan, 2019 ($9.99, square-bound, one-shot)

DC One Million #4 © DC

DC Special #22 © DC

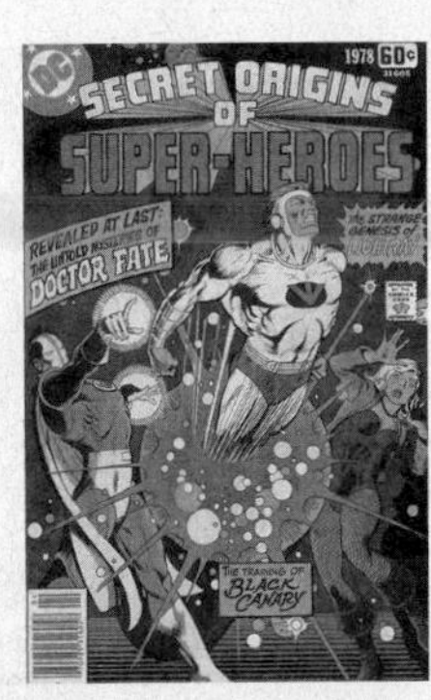

DC Special Series #10 © DC

	GD	VG	FN	VF	VF/NM	NM-
	2.0	4.0	6.0	8.0	9.0	9.2

	GD	VG	FN	VF	VF/NM	NM-
	2.0	4.0	6.0	8.0	9.0	9.2

1-Wasteland short stories by various incl. Russell, Duce, Ordway, Hester; Paquette-c 10.00

DC 100 PAGE SUPER SPECTACULAR
(Title is 100 Page… No. 14 on)(Square bound) (Reprints, 50¢)
National Periodical Publications: No. 4, Summer, 1971 - No. 13, 6/72; No. 14, 2/73 - No. 22, 11/73 (No #1-3)

4-Weird Mystery Tales; Johnny Peril & Phantom Stranger; cover & splashes by Wrightson; origin Jungle Boy of Jupiter 26 52 78 182 404 625
5-Love Stories; Wood inks (7 pgs.)(scarcer) 50 100 150 400 900 1400
6- "World's Greatest Super-Heroes"; JLA, JSA, Spectre, Johnny Quick, Vigilante & Hawkman; contains unpublished Wildcat story; N. Adams wrap-around-c; r/JLA #21,22 18 36 54 124 275 425
6-Replica Edition (2004, $6.95) complete reprint w/wraparound-c 7.00
7-(Also listed as Superman #245) Air Wave, Kid Eternity, Hawkman-r; Atom-r/Atom #3 9 18 27 62 126 190
8-(Also listed as Batman #238) Batman, Legion, Aquaman-r; G.A. Atom, Sargon (r/Sensation #57), Plastic Man (r/Police #14) stories; Doom Patrol origin-r; Neal Adams wraparound-c 15 30 45 103 227 350
9-(Also listed as Our Army at War #242) Kubert-c 9 18 27 58 114 170
10-(Also listed as Adventure Comics #416) Golden Age-reprints; r/1st app. Black Canary from Flash #86; no Zatanna 10 20 30 68 144 220
11-(Also listed as Flash #214) origin Metal Men-r/Showcase #37; never before published G.A. Flash story. 8 16 24 54 102 150
12,14: 12-(Also listed as Superboy #185) Legion-c/story; Teen Titans, Kid Eternity (r/Hit #46), Star Spangled Kid-r(S.S. #55). 14-Batman-r/Detective #31,32,156; Atom-r/Showcase #34 8 16 24 51 96 140
13-(Also listed as Superman #252) Ray(r/Smash #17), Black Condor, (r/Crack #18), Hawkman(r/Flash #24); Starman-r/Adv. #67; Dr. Fate & Spectre-r/More Fun #57; Neal Adams-c 10 20 30 66 138 210
15,16,18,19,21,22: 15-r/2nd Boy Commandos/Det. #64. 16-Sgt. Rock; r/Capt. Storm #1, 1st Johnny Cloud/All-American Men of War #82. 18-Superman. 21-Superboy; r/Brave & the Bold #54. 22-r/All-Flash #13 6 12 18 37 66 95
17,20: 17-JSA-r/All Star #37 (10-11/47, 38 pgs.), Sandman-r/Adv. #65 (8/41), JLA #23 (11/63) & JLA #43 (3/66). 20-Batman-r/Det. #66,68, Spectre; origin Two-Face 6 12 18 38 69 100
... : Love Stories Replica Edition (2000, $6.95) reprints #5 7.00

NOTE: ***Anderson*** *r-11, 14, 18i, 22.* ***B. Baily*** *r-18, 20.* ***Burnley*** *r-18, 20.* ***Crandall*** *r-14p, 20.* ***Drucker*** *r-4.* ***Grandenetti*** *a-22(2)r.* ***Heath*** *a-22r.* ***Infantino*** *r-17, 20, 22.* ***G. Kane*** *r-18.* ***Kirby*** *r-15.* ***Kubert*** *r-6, 7, 16, 17; c-16, 19.* ***Manning*** *a-19r.* ***Meskin*** *r-4, 22.* ***Mooney*** *r-15, 21.* ***Toth*** *r-17, 20.*

DC ONE MILLION (Also see crossover #1,000,000 issues and JLA One Million TPB)
DC Comics: Nov, 1998 - No. 4, Nov, 1998 ($2.95/$1.99, weekly lim. series)

1-($2.95) JLA travels to the 853rd century; Morrison-s 4.00
2-4-($1.99) 3.00
... Eighty-Page Giant (8/99, $4.95) 5.00
TPB ('99, $14.95) r/#1-4 and several x-over stories 15.00

DC REBIRTH HOLIDAY SPECIAL
DC Comics: Feb, 2017 ($9.99, one-shot)

1-Short stories by various; framing pages of Harley Quinn by Dini-s/Charretier-a 2 4 6 8 11 14

DC RETROACTIVE (New stories done in old style plus reprint from decade)
DC Comics: Sept, 2011 - Oct, 2011 ($4.99, series of one-shots)

...: Batman - The '70s (9/11, $4.99) Len Wein-s/Tom Mandrake-a; r/Batman #307 5.00
...: Batman - The '80s (10/11, $4.99) Mike Barr-s/Jerry Bingham-a; The Reaper app. 5.00
...: Batman - The '90s (10/11, $4.99) Grant-s/Breyfogle-a; Scarface & Ventriloquist app. 5.00
...: Flash - The '70s (9/11, $4.99) Bates-s/Gallego-a; r/DC Comics Presents #2 5.00
...: Flash - The '80s (10/11, $4.99) Messner-Loebs-s/LaRocque-a; r/Flash v2 #18 5.00
...: Flash - The '90s (10/11, $4.99) Augustyn-s/Bowden-a; r/Flash v2 #142 5.00
...: Green Lantern - The '70s (9/11, $4.99) O'Neil-s/Grell-a; r/Green Lantern #76 5.00
...: Green Lantern - The '80s (10/11, $4.99) Wein-s/Staton-a; r/Green Lantern #172 5.00
...: Green Lantern - The '90s (10/11, $4.99) Marz-s/Banks-a; r/Green Lantern v3 #78 5.00
...: JLA - The '70s (9/11, $4.99) Bates-s; Adam Strange app.; r/J.L. of A. #123 5.00
...: JLA - The '80s (10/11, $4.99) Conway-s/Randall-a; Felix Faust app.; r/J.L.of A. #239 5.00
...: JLA - The '90s (10/11, $4.99) Giffen & DeMatteis-s/Maguire-a; r/J.L.A. #6 5.00
...: Superman - The '70s (9/11, $4.99) Pasko-s/Barreto-a; r/Action Comics #484 5.00
...: Superman - The '80s (10/11, $4.99) Wolfman-s/Cariello-a; r/Superman #352 5.00
...: Superman - The '90s (10/11, $4.99) L. Simonson-s/Bogdanove-a; Guardian app. 5.00
...: Wonder Woman - The '70s (9/11, $4.99) O'Neil-s/J. Bone-a; r/Wonder Woman #201 5.00
...: Wonder Woman - The '80s (10/11, $4.99) Thomas-s/Buckler-a; r/W.W. #288 5.00
...: Wonder Woman - The '90s (10/11, $4.99) Messner-Loebs-s/Moder-a; r/W.W. v2 #66 5.00

DC'S BEACH BLANKET BAD GUYS SUMMER SPECIAL
DC Comics: Sept, 2018 ($9.99, 80 pgs, square-bound, one-shot)

1-Summer short stories by various; Conner-c; Joker, Mr. Freeze, Black Manta app. 10.00

DC SCIENCE FICTION GRAPHIC NOVEL
DC Comics: 1985 - No. 7, 1987 ($5.95)

SF1-SF7: SF1-Hell on Earth by Robert Bloch; Giffen-p. SF2-Nightwings by Robert Silverberg; G. Colan-p. SF3-Frost & Fire by Bradbury. SF4-Merchants of Venus. SF5-Demon With A Glass Hand by Ellison; M. Rogers-a. SF6-The Magic Goes Away by Niven. SF7-Sandkings by George R.R. Martin 2 4 6 8 11 14

DC'S CRIMES OF PASSION
DC Comics: Apr, 2020 ($9.99, 80 pgs, square-bound, one-shot)

1-Romance-themed short stories by various; Yasmine Putri-c 10.00

DC SILVER AGE CLASSICS
DC Comics: 1992 ($1.00, all reprints)

...Action Comics #252-r/1st Supergirl. Adventure Comics #247-r/1st Legion of Super-Heroes. The Brave and the Bold #28-r/1st JLA. Detective Comics #225-r/1st Martian Manhunter. Detective Comics #327-r/1st new look Batman. Green Lantern #76-r/1st Green Lantern/ Green Arrow. House of Secrets #92-r/1st Swamp Thing. Showcase #4-r/1st S.A. Flash. Showcase #22-r/1st S.A. Green Lantern 4.00
...Sugar and Spike #99; includes 2 unpublished stories 5.00

DC SPECIAL (Also see Super DC Giant)
National Per. Publ.: 10-12/68 - No. 15, 11-12/71; No. 16, Spr/75 - No. 29, 8-9/77

1-All Infantino issue; Flash, Batman, Adam Strange-r; begin 68 pg. issues, end #21 8 16 24 54 102 150
2-Teen humor; Binky, Buzzy, Harvey app. 9 18 27 62 126 190
3-All-Girl issue; unpubl. GA Wonder Woman story 9 18 27 57 111 165
4,11: 4-Horror (1st Abel, brief). 11-Monsters 5 10 15 33 57 80
5-10,12-15: 5-All Kubert issue; Viking Prince, Sgt. Rock-r. 6-Western. 7,9,13-Strangest Sports. 12-Viking Prince; Kubert-c/a (r/B&B almost entirely). 15-G.A. Plastic Man origin-r/ Police #1; origin Woozy by Cole; 14,15-(52 pgs.) 4 8 12 27 44 60
16-27: 16-Super Heroes Battle Super Gorillas. 17-Early S.A. Green Lantern-r. 22-Origin Robin Hood. 26-Enemy Ace. 27-Captain Comet story 3 6 9 16 23 30
28-Earth Shattering Disaster Stories; Legion of Super-Heroes story 3 6 9 17 25 34
29-New "The Untold Origin of the Justice Society"; Staton-a/Neal Adams-c; Hitler app. in story and on cover 5 10 15 34 60 85

NOTE: ***N. Adams*** *c-3, 4, 6, 11, 29.* ***Grell*** *a-20; c-17, 20.* ***Heath*** *a-12r.* ***G. Kane*** *a-6p, 13r, 17r, 19-21r.* ***Kirby*** *a-4,11.* ***Kubert*** *a-6r, 12r, 22.* ***Meskin*** *a-10.* ***Moreira*** *a-10.* ***Staton*** *a-29p.* ***Toth*** *a-13, 20r. #1-15: 25¢; 16-27: 50¢; 28, 29: 60¢. #1-13, 16-21: 68 pgs.; 14, 15: 52 pgs.; 25-27: oversized.*

DC SPECIAL BLUE RIBBON DIGEST
DC Comics: Mar-Apr, 1980 - No. 24, Aug, 1982

1,2,4,5: 1-Legion reprints. 2-Flash. 4-Green Lantern. 5-Secret Origins; new Zatara and Zatanna 2 4 6 9 13 16
3-Justice Society reprints; new Dr. Fate story 2 4 6 11 16 20
6,8-10: 6-Ghosts. 8-Legion. 9-Secret Origins. 10-Warlord-"The Deimos Saga"-Grell-s/c/a 2 4 6 9 13 16
7-Sgt. Rock's Prize Battle Tales 3 6 9 14 19 24
11,16: 11-Justice League. 16-Green Lantern/Green Arrow-r; all Adams-a 2 4 6 13 18 22
12-Haunted Tank; reprints 1st app. 3 6 9 14 19 24
13-15,17-19: 13-Strange Sports Stories. 14-UFO Invaders; Adam Strange app. 15-Secret Origins of Super Villains; JLA app. 17-Ghosts. 18-Sgt. Rock; Kubert front & back-c. 19-Doom Patrol; new Perez-c 2 4 6 10 14 18
20-Dark Mansion of Forbidden Love (scarce) 5 10 15 30 50 70
21-Our Army at War 3 6 9 16 23 30
22-24: 22-Secret Origins. 23-Green Arrow, w/new 7 pg. story (Spiegle-a). 24-House of Mystery; new Kubert wraparound-c 3 6 9 14 19 24

NOTE: ***N. Adams*** *a-16(6)r, 17r, 23r; c-16.* ***Aparo*** *a-6r, 24r; c-23.* ***Grell*** *a-8, 10; c-10.* ***Heath*** *a-14.* ***Infantino*** *a-15r.* ***Kaluta*** *a-17r.* ***Gil Kane*** *a-15r, 22r.* ***Kirby*** *a-5, 9, 23r.* ***Kubert*** *a-3, 18r, 21r; c-7, 12, 14, 17, 18, 21, 24.* ***Morrow*** *a-24r.* ***Orlando*** *a-17r, 22r; c-1, 20.* ***Toth*** *a-21r, 24r.* ***Wood*** *a-3, 17r, 24r.* ***Wrightson*** *a-16r, 17r, 24r.*

DC SPECIAL: CYBORG (From Teen Titans) (See Teen Titans 2003 series for TPB collection)
DC Comics: Jul, 2008 - No. 6, Dec, 2008 ($2.99, limited series)

1-6: 1-Sable-s/Lashley-a; origin re-told. 3-6-Magno-a 3.00

DC SPECIAL: RAVEN (From Teen Titans) (See Teen Titans 2003 series for TPB collection)
DC Comics: May, 2008 - No. 5, Sept, 2008 ($2.99, limited series)

1-5-Marv Wolfman-s/Damion Scott-a 3.00

DC SPECIAL SERIES
National Periodical Publications/DC Comics: 9/77 - No. 16, Fall, 1978; No. 17, 8/79 - No. 27, Fall, 1981 (No. 18, 19, 23, 24 - digest size, 100 pgs.; No. 25-27 - Treasury sized)

1-"5-Star Super-Hero Spectacular 1977"; Batman, Atom, Flash, Green Lantern, Aquaman, in solo stories, Kobra app.; 1st app. Patty Spivot in Flash story; N. Adams-c 5 10 15 34 60 85
2(#1)-"The Original Swamp Thing Saga 1977"-r/Swamp Thing #1&2 by Wrightson; new Wrightson wraparound-c. 3 6 9 14 19 24

DC Special: The Return of Donna Troy #1 © DC

DC Super-Stars #1 © DC

DC Universe Presents #10 © DC

GD	VG	FN	VF	VF/NM	NM-
2.0	4.0	6.0	8.0	9.0	9.2

3,4,6-8: 3-Sgt Rock. 4-Unexpected. 6-Secret Society of Super Villains, Jones-a. 7-Ghosts Special. 8-Brave and Bold w/ new Batman, Deadman & Sgt Rock team-up 2 4 6 13 18 22
5-"Superman Spectacular 1977"-(84 pg, $1.00)-Superman vs. Brainiac & Lex Luthor, new 63 pg. story 3 6 9 16 23 30
9-Wonder Woman; Ditko-a (11 pgs.) 3 6 9 18 28 38
10-"Secret Origins of Superheroes Special 1978"-(52 pgs.)-Dr. Fate, Lightray & Black Canary on-c/new origin stories; Staton, Newton-a 3 6 9 14 20 26
11-"Flash Spectacular 1978"-(84 pgs.) Flash, Kid Flash, GA Flash & Johnny Quick vs. Grodd; Wood-i on Kid Flash chapter 2 4 6 13 18 22
12-"Secrets of Haunted House Special Spring 1978" 2 4 6 13 18 22
13-"Sgt. Rock Special Spring 1978", 50 pg new story 3 6 9 14 19 24
14,17,20-"Original Swamp Thing Saga", Wrightson-a: 14-Sum '78, r/#3,4. 17-Sum '79 r/#5-7. 20-Jan/Feb '80, r/#8-10 2 4 6 9 13 16
15-"Batman Spectacular Summer 1978", Ra's Al Ghul-app.; Golden-a. Rogers-a/front & back-c 4 8 12 25 40 55
16-"Jonah Hex Spectacular Fall 1978"; death of Jonah Hex, Heath-a; Bat Lash and Scalphunter stories 6 12 18 40 73 105
18,19-Digest size: 18-"Sgt. Rock's Prize Battle Tales Fall 1979". 19-"Secret Origins of Super-Heroes Fall 1979"; origins Wonder Woman (new-a),r/Robin, Batman-Superman team, Aquaman, Hawkman and others 2 4 6 13 18 22
21-"Super-Star Holiday Special Spring 1980", Frank Miller-a in "Batman--Wanted Dead or Alive" (1st Batman story); Jonah Hex, Sgt. Rock, Superboy & LSH and House of Mystery/ Witching Hour-c/stories 5 10 15 31 53 75
22-"G.I. Combat Sept. 1980", Kubert-c. Haunted Tank-s 3 6 9 14 19 24
23,24-Digest size: 23-World's Finest-r. 24-Flash 2 4 6 11 16 20
V5#25-($2.95)-"Superman II, the Adventure Continues Summer 1981"; photos from movie & photo-c (see All-New Coll. Ed. C-62 for first Superman movie) 3 6 9 14 19 24
26-($2.50)-"Superman and His Incredible Fortress of Solitude Summer 1981" 3 6 9 14 19 24
27-($2.50)-"Batman vs. The Incredible Hulk Fall 1981" 4 8 12 25 40 55

NOTE: ***Aparo*** *c-8.* ***Heath*** *a-12i, 16.* ***Infantino*** *a-19r.* ***Kirby*** *a-23, 19r.* ***Kubert*** *c-13, 19r.* ***Nasser/Netzer*** *a-1, 10i, 15.* ***Newton*** *a-10.* ***Nino*** *a-4, 7.* ***Starlin*** *c-12.* ***Staton*** *a-1.* ***Tuska*** *a-19r. #25 & 26. were advertised as All-New Collectors' Edition C-63, C-64. #26 was originally planned as All-New Collectors' Ed. C-30?; has C-630 & A.N.C.E. on cover.*

DC SPECIAL: THE RETURN OF DONNA TROY
DC Comics: Aug, 2005 - No. 4, Late Oct, 2005 ($2.99, limited series)

1-4-Jimenez-s/Garcia-Lopez-a(p)/Pérez-i 3.00

DC SUPERHERO GIRLS
DC Comics: May, 2016; May, 2017; May 2018 (All-ages FCBD giveaway)

1 FCBD 2017 Special Edition (5/17); teenage girl heroes; Fontana-s/Labat-a 3.00
1 FCBD 2018 Special Edition (5/18); Date With Disaster; Fontana-s/Labat-a 3.00
1 Special Edition (5/16); teenage girl heroes at Super Hero High; Fontana-s/Labat-a 3.00
... 2017 Halloween Comic Fest Special Edition (11/17) Labat & Garbowska-a 3.00
... Halloween Fest Special Edition (12/16); teenage girl heroes at Super Hero High 3.00

DC SUPERHERO GIRLS GIANT
DC Comics: 2019 - No. 2, 2020 ($4.99, 100 pgs., squarebound, Mass Market & Direct Market editions exist for each issue, with different covers)

1,2-Direct Market Edition - New stories and reprints from graphic novels 5.00

DC SUPER-STARS
National Periodical Publ./DC Comics: March, 1976 - No. 18, Winter, 1978 (No. 3-18: 52 pgs.)

1-(68 pgs.)-Re-intro Teen Titans (predates T. T. #44 (11/76); tryout iss.) plus r/Teen Titans; W.W. as girl was original Wonder Girl 3 6 9 19 30 40
2-6,9,12,16: 2,4,6,8-Adam Strange; 2-(68 pgs.)-r/1st Adam Strange/Hawkman team-up from Mystery in Space #90 plus Atomic Knights origin-r. 3-Legion issue. 4-r/Tales/Unexpected #45. 2 4 6 8 11 14
7-Aquaman spotlight; Aqualad, Aquagirl, Ocean Master & Black Manta app.; Aparo-c 3 6 9 21 33 45
8-r/1st Space Ranger from Showcase #15, Adam Strange-r/Mystery in Space #89 & Star Rovers-r/M.I.S. #80 2 4 6 9 13 16
10-Strange Sports Stories; Batman/Joker-c/story 2 4 6 10 14 18
11-Magic; Zatanna-c/reprint from Adv. #413-415 with Morrow-a; Morrow-c; Flash vs. Abra Kadabra (r/Flash #128) 9 18 27 51 123 185
13-Sergio Aragonés Special 3 6 9 15 22 28
14,15,18: 15-Sgt. Rock 2 4 6 9 13 16
17-Secret Origins of Super-Heroes (origin of The Huntress); origin Green Arrow by Grell; Legion app.; Earth II Batman & Catwoman marry (1st revealed; also see B&B #197 & Superman Family #211) 9 18 27 60 120 180
#17 (Facsimile Edition) (2020, $4.99) Reprints #17 with original ads 5.00

NOTE: ***M. Anderson*** *r-2, 4, 6.* ***Aparo*** *c-7, 14, 18.* ***Austin*** *a-11i.* ***Buckler*** *a-14p; c-10.* ***Grell*** *a-17.* ***G. Kane*** *a-1r, 10r.* ***Kubert*** *c-15.* ***Layton*** *c/a-16i, 17i.* ***Mooney*** *a-4r, 6r.* ***Morrow*** *c/a-11r.* ***Nasser*** *a-11.* ***Newton*** *c/a-16p.* ***Staton*** *a-17; c-17. No. 10, 12-18 contain all new material; the rest are reprints. #1 contains new and reprint material.*

DC'S VERY MERRY MULTIVERSE
DC Comics: Feb, 2021 ($9.99, one-shot)

1-Short Holiday stories; Batman, Harley Quinn, Capt. Carrot, Lobo and others app. 10.00

DC'S YEAR OF THE VILLAIN SPECIAL
DC Comics: Jul, 2019 (25¢, one-shot)

1-Short preludes; Legion of Doom, Leviathan, Batman Who Laughs app.; Capullo-c 3.00

DC: THE DOOMED AND THE DAMNED
DC Comics: Dec, 2020 ($9.99, one-shot)

1-Short horror stories; Batman, Madame Xanadu, Man-Bat, Etrigan, Green Lantern app. 10.00

DC: THE NEW FRONTIER (Also see Justice League: The New Frontier Special)
DC Comics: Mar, 2004 - No. 6, Nov, 2004 ($6.95, limited series)

1-6-DCU in the 1940s-60s; Darwyn Cooke-c/s/a in all. 1-Hal Jordan and The Losers app. 2-Origin Martian Manhunter; Barry Allen app. 3-Challengers of the Unknown 7.00
...Volume One (2004, $19.95, TPB) r/#1-3; cover gallery & intro. by Paul Levitz 20.00
...Volume Two (2005, $19.99, TPB) r/#4-6; cover gallery & afterword by Cooke 20.00

DC TOP COW CROSSOVERS
DC Comics/Top Cow Productions: 2007 ($14.99, TPB)

SC-r/The Darkness/Batman; JLA/Witchblade; The Darkness/Superman; JLA/Cyberforce 15.00

DC 2000
DC Comics: 2000 - No. 2, 2000 ($6.95, limited series)

1,2-JLA visit 1941 JSA; Semeiks-a 7.00

DCU BRAVE NEW WORLD (See Infinite Crisis and tie-ins)
DC Comics: Aug, 2006 ($1.00, 80 pgs., one-shot)

1-Previews 2006 series Martian Manhunter, OMAC, The Creeper, The All-New Atom, The Trials of Shazam, and Uncle Sam and the Freedom Fighters; the Monitor app. 4.00

DCU (Halloween and Christmas one-shot anthologies)
DC Comics

... Halloween Special '09 (12/09, $5.99) Ha-c; art from Bagley, Tucci, K. Jones, Nguyen 6.00
... Halloween Special 2010 (12/10, $4.99) Ha-c; art from Tucci, Garbett; I...Vampire app. 5.00
... Holiday Special (2/09, $5.99) Christmas by various incl. Dini, Maguire, Reis; Quitely-c 6.00
... Holiday Special 2010 (2/11, $4.99) Jonah Hex, Spectre, Legion of S.H., Anthro app. 5.00
... Infinite Halloween Special (12/08, $5.99) Ralph & Sue Dibny app.; Gene Ha-c 6.00
... Infinite Holiday Special (2/07, $4.99) by various; Batwoman app.; Porter-c 5.00

DCU HEROES SECRET FILES
DC Comics: Feb, 1999 ($4.95, one-shot)

1-Origin-s and pin-ups; new Star Spangled Kid app. 5.00

DCU: LEGACIES
DC Comics: Jul, 2010 - No. 10, Apr, 2011 ($3.99, limited series)

1-10: 1,2-Andy Kubert-c; JSA app.; two covers on each. 3-JLA app.; Garcia-Lopez-a. 4-Sgt. Rock back-up; Joe Kubert-a. 5-Pérez-a. 8-Back-up Quitely-a 4.00

DC UNIVERSE CHRISTMAS, A
DC Comics: 2000 ($19.95)

TPB-Reprints DC Christmas stories by various 20.00

DC UNIVERSE: DECISIONS
DC Comics: Early Nov, 2008 - No. 4, Late Dec, 2008 ($2.99, limited series)

1-4-Assassination plot in the Presidential election; Winick & Willingham-s/Porter-a 3.00

DC UNIVERSE HOLIDAY BASH
DC Comics: 1997- 1999 ($3.95)

I,II-(X-mas '96,'97) Christmas stories by various 5.00
III (1999, for Christmas '98, $4.95) 5.00

DC UNIVERSE ILLUSTRATED BY NEAL ADAMS (Also see Batman Illustrated by Neal Adams HC Vol. 1-3)
DC Comics: 2008 ($39.99, hardcover with dustjacket)

Vol. 1 - Reprints Adams' non-Batman/non-Green Lantern work from 1967-1972; incl. Teen Titans, DC war, Enemy Ace, Superman and PSAs; promo art; Levitz foreword 40.00

DC UNIVERSE: LAST WILL AND TESTAMENT
DC Comics: Oct, 2008 ($3.99, one-shot)

1-Geo-Force vs. Deathstroke; DC heroes prepare for Final Crisis; Brad Meltzer-s; Adam Kubert & Joe Kubert-a; two covers 4.00

DC UNIVERSE ONLINE LEGENDS (Based on the online game)
DC Comics: Early Apr. 2011 - Late May, 2012 ($2.99)

1-26: 1-Wolfman & Bedard-s/Porter-a; DC heroes & Luthor vs. Brainiac. 1-Wraparound-c 3.00

DC UNIVERSE: ORIGINS
DC Comics: 2009 ($14.99, TPB)

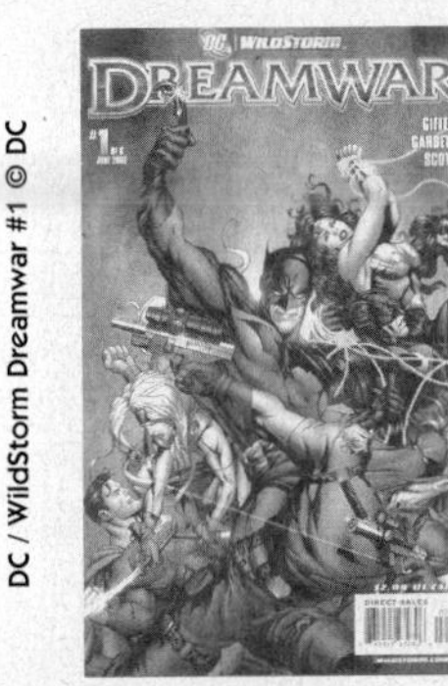

DC / WildStorm Dreamwar #1 © DC

Dead Boy Detectives #9 © DC

Deadly Class #7 © Remender & Craig

	GD	VG	FN	VF	VF/NM	NM-
	2.0	4.0	6.0	8.0	9.0	9.2

nn-Reprints 2-page origins of DC characters from back-ups in 52, Countdown and Justice League: Cry For Justice #1-3; s/a by various; Alex Ross-c 15.00

DC UNIVERSE PRESENTS (DC New 52)
DC Comics: Nov, 2011 - No. 19, Jun, 2013 ($2.99)

1-5-Deadman. 1-Deadman origin re-told; Jenkins-s/Chang-a/Sook-c 3.00
6-8-Challengers of the Unknown; DiDio-s/Ordway-a/Sook-c 3.00
9-19: 9-11-Savage; Chang-a. 12-Kid Flash. 13-16-Black Lightning & Blue Devil 3.00
#0 (11/12, $5.99) O.M.A.C., Mr. Terrific, Hawk & Dove, Blackhawks, Deadman origins 6.00

DC UNIVERSE: REBIRTH
DC Comics: Jul, 2016 ($2.99, one-shot)

1-($2.99) Wally West returns; Johns-s; art by Frank, Van Sciver, Reis & Jimenez; wraparound-c by Gary Frank 3.00
1-2nd printing ($5.99, squarebound) same wraparound-c by Gary Frank 6.00
1-3rd printing ($5.99, squarebound) variant Kid Flash cover by Gary Frank 6.00

DC UNIVERSE SPECIAL
DC Comics: July, 2008 - Aug, 2008 ($4.99, collection of reprints related to Final Crisis)

...: Justice League of America (7/08) r/J.L. of A. #111,166-168 & Detective #274; Sook-c 5.00
...: Reign in Hell (8/08) r/Blaze/Satanus War x-over; Sook-c 5.00
...: Superman (7/08) r/Mongul app. in Superman #32, Showcase '95 #7,8, Flash #102 5.00

DC UNIVERSE: THE STORIES OF ALAN MOORE (Also see Across the Universe:...)
DC Comics: 2006 ($19.99)

TPB-Reprints Batman: The Killing Joke, "Whatever Happened to the Man of Tomorrow", "For The Man Who Has Everything, and other classic Moore DC stories; Bolland-c 20.00

DC UNIVERSE: TRINITY
DC Comics: Aug, 1993 - No. 2, Sept, 1993 ($2.95, 52 pgs, limited series)

1,2-Foil-c; Green Lantern, Darkstars, Legion app. 4.00

DC UNIVERSE VS. MASTERS OF THE UNIVERSE
DC Comics: Oct, 2013 - No. 6, May, 2014 ($2.99, limited series)

1-6: 1-3-Giffen-s/Soy-a/Benes-c; Constantine app. 4-6-Mhan-a 3.00

DCU VILLAINS SECRET FILES
DC Comics: Apr, 1999 ($4.95, one-shot)

1-Origin-s and profile pages 5.00

DC VERSUS MARVEL (See Marvel Versus DC) (Also see Amazon, Assassins, Bruce Wayne: Agent of S.H.I.E.L.D., Bullets & Bracelets, Doctor Strangefate, JLX, Legend of the Dark Claw, Magneto & The Magnetic Men, Speed Demon, Spider-Boy, Super Soldier, X-Patrol)
DC Comics: No. 1, 1996, No. 4, 1996 ($3.95, limited series)

1,4: 1-Marz script, Jurgens-a(p); 1st app. of Access. 5.00
.../Marvel Versus DC ($12.95, trade paperback) r/1-4 13.00

DC/WILDSTORM DREAMWAR
DC Comics: Jun, 2008 - No. 6, Nov, 2008 ($2.99, limited series)

1-6-Giffen-s; Silver Age JLA, Teen Titans, JSA, Legion app. on WildStorm Earth 3.00
1-Variant-c of Superman & Midnighter by Garbett 6.00
TPB (2009, $19.99) r/series 20.00

DC: WORLD WAR III (See 52/WWIII)

D-DAY (Also see Special War Series)
Charlton Comics (no No. 3): Sum/63; No. 2, Fall/64; No. 4, 9/66; No. 5, 10/67; No. 6, 11/68

	GD	VG	FN	VF	VF/NM	NM-
1,2: 1(1963)-Montes/Bache-c. 2(Fall '64)-Wood-a(4)	4	8	12	23	37	50
4-6('66-'68)-Montes/Bache-a #5	3	6	9	14	20	25

DEAD AIR
Slave Labor Graphics: July, 1989 ($5.95, graphic novel)

	GD	VG	FN	VF	VF/NM	NM-
nn-Mike Allred's 1st published work	1	2	3	5	6	8

DEAD BODY ROAD: BAD BLOOD
Image Comics (Skybound): Jun, 2020 - No. 6, Dec, 2020 ($3.99)

1-6-Justin Jordan-s/Benjamin Tiesma-a/Matthew Scalera-c 4.00

DEAD BOY DETECTIVES
DC Comics (Vertigo): Feb, 2014 - No. 12, Feb, 2015 ($2.99, limited series)

1-12-Litt-s/Buckingham-a. 1-Covers by Buckingham & Chiang 3.00

DEAD CORPSE
DC Comics (Helix): Sept, 1998 - No. 4, Dec, 1998 ($2.50, limited series)

1-4-Pugh-a/Hinz-s 3.00

DEAD DAY
AfterShock Comics: May, 2020 - No. 5, Nov, 2020 ($3.99)

1-5-Ryan Parrott-s/Evgeniy Bornyakov-a 4.00

DEAD DROP
Valiant Entertainment: May, 2015 - No. 4, Aug, 2015 ($3.99, limited series)

1-4-Ales Kot-s/Adam Gorham-a; X-O Manowar app. 2-Archer app. 4.00

DEAD END CRIME STORIES
Kirby Publishing Co.: April, 1949 (52 pgs.)

	GD	VG	FN	VF	VF/NM	NM-
nn-(Scarce)-Powell, Roussos-a; painted-c	65	130	195	416	708	1000

DEAD ENDERS
DC Comics (Vertigo): Mar, 2000 - No. 16, June, 2001 ($2.50)

1-16-Brubaker-s/Pleece & Case-a 3.00
Stealing the Sun (2000, $9.95, TPB) r/#1-4, Vertigo Winter's Edge #3 10.00

DEAD EYES (Issues recalled due to trademark dispute, cancelled after #2)(See Dead Rabbit)
Image Comics: Oct, 2019 - Present ($3.99)

1-Duggan-s/McCrea-a 6.00

DEAD-EYE WESTERN COMICS
Hillman Periodicals: Nov-Dec, 1948 - V3#1, Apr-May, 1953

	GD	VG	FN	VF	VF/NM	NM-
V1#1-(52 pgs.)-Krigstein, Roussos-a	24	48	72	144	237	330
V1#2,3-(52 pgs.)	15	30	45	83	124	165
V1#4-12-(52 pgs.)	11	22	33	62	86	110
V2#1,2,5-8,10-12: 1-7-(52 pgs.)	9	18	27	50	65	80
3,4-Krigstein-a	10	20	30	54	72	90
9-One pg. Frazetta ad	9	18	27	50	65	80
V3#1	9	18	27	50	65	80

NOTE: *Briefer a-V1#8. Kinstleresque stories by* ***McCann****-12, V2#1, 2, V3#1.* ***McWilliams*** *a-V1#5.* ***Ed Moore*** *a-V1#4.*

DEADFACE: DOING THE ISLANDS WITH BACCHUS
Dark Horse Comics: July, 1991 - No. 3, Sept, 1991 ($2.95, B&W, lim. series)

1-3: By Eddie Campbell 3.00

DEADFACE: EARTH, WATER, AIR, AND FIRE
Dark Horse Comics: July, 1992 - No. 4, Oct, 1992 ($2.50, B&W, limited series; British-r)

1-4: By Eddie Campbell 3.00

DEAD HAND, THE
Image Comics: Apr, 2018 - No. 6, Sept, 2018 ($3.99)

1-6-Kyle Higgins-s/Stephen Mooney-a 4.00

DEAD INSIDE
Dark Horse Comics: Dec, 2016 - No. 5, May, 2017 ($3.99)

1-5-Arcudi-s/Fejzula-a/Dave Johnson-c 4.00

DEAD IN THE WEST
Dark Horse Comics: Oct, 1993 - No. 2, Mar, 1994 ($3.95, B&W, 52 pgs.)

1,2-Timothy Truman-c 4.00

DEAD IRONS
Dynamite Entertainment: 2009 - No. 4, 2009 ($3.99)

1-4-Kuhoric-s/Alexander-a/Jae Lee-c 4.00

DEAD KINGS
AfterShock Comics: Oct, 2018 - No. 5, May, 2019 ($3.99)

1-5-Steve Orlando-s/Matthew Dow Smith-a 4.00

DEADLANDER (Becomes Dead Rider for #2)
Dark Horse Comics: Oct, 2007 - No. 4, ($2.99, limited series)

1-2-Kevin Ferrara-s/a 3.00

DEADLANDS (Old West role playing game)
Image Comics: Jul, 2011; Aug, 2011; Jan, 2012 ($2.99, one-shots)

...: Black Water (1/12) Mariotte-s/Brook Turner-a 3.00
...: Death Was Silent (8/11) Marz-s/Sears-a/c 3.00
...: Massacre at Red Wing (7/11) Palmiotti & Gray-s/Moder-a/c 3.00

DEADLIEST HEROES OF KUNG FU (Magazine)
Marvel Comics Group: Summer, 1975 (B&W)(76 pgs.)

	GD	VG	FN	VF	VF/NM	NM-
1-Bruce Lee vs. Carradine painted-c; TV Kung Fu, 4pgs. photos/article; Enter the Dragon, 24 pgs. photos/article w/ Bruce Lee; Bruce Lee photo pinup	5	10	15	34	60	85

DEADLINE
Marvel Comics: June, 2002 - No. 4, Sept, 2002 ($2.99, limited series)

1-4: 1-Intro. Kat Farrell; Bill Rosemann-s/Guy Davis-a; Horn painted-c 3.00
TPB (2002, $9.99) r/#1-4 10.00

DEADLY CLASS (Inspired the 2018 SYFY Channel TV show)
Image Comics: Jan, 2014 - Present ($3.99)

1-Remender-s/Craig-a 20.00

The Deadly Hands of Kung Fu #3 © MAR

Deadman (2006 series) #1 © DC

Deadpool #23 © MAR

GD VG FN VF VF/NM NM-
2.0 4.0 6.0 8.0 9.0 9.2

2-6 6.00
7-44: 40-44-Bone Machine 4.00
...: Killer Set, FCBD Special (5/19, giveaway) New story by Remender-s/Craig-a 3.00

DEADLY DUO, THE
Image Comics (Highbrow Entertainment): Nov, 1994 - No. 3, Jan, 1995 ($2.50, lim. series)
1-3: 1-1st app. of Kill Cat 4.00

DEADLY DUO, THE
Image Comics (Highbrow Entertainment): June, 1995 - No. 4, Oct, 1995 ($2.50, lim. series)
1-4: 1-Spawn app. 2-Savage Dragon app. 3-Gen 13 app. 4.00

DEADLY FOES OF SPIDER-MAN (See Lethal Foes of...)
Marvel Comics: May, 1991 - No. 4, Aug, 1991 ($1.00, limited series)
1-4: 1-Punisher, Kingpin, Rhino app. 4.00

DEADLY HANDS OF KUNG FU, THE (See Master of Kung Fu)
Marvel Comics Group: April, 1974 - No. 33, Feb, 1977 (75¢) (B&W, magazine)
1(V1#4 listed in error)-Origin Sons of the Tiger; Shang-Chi, Master of Kung Fu begins (ties w/Master of Kung Fu #17 as 3rd app. Shang-Chi); Bruce Lee painted-c by Neal Adams; 2pg. memorial photo pinup w/8 pgs. photos/articles; TV Kung Fu, 9 pgs. photos/articles; 15 pgs. Starlin-a 7 14 21 49 92 135
2-Adams painted-c; 1st time origin of Shang-Chi, 34 pgs. by Starlin. TV Kung Fu, 6 pgs. photos & article w/2 pg. pinup. Bruce Lee, 11 pgs. ph/a 5 10 15 33 57 80
3,4,7,10: 3-Adams painted-c; Gulacy-a. Enter the Dragon, photos/articles, 8 pgs. 4-TV Kung Fu painted-c by Neal Adams; TV Kung Fu 7 pg. article/art; Fu Manchu; Enter the Dragon, 10 pg. photos/article w/Bruce Lee. 7-Bruce Lee painted-c & 9 pgs. photos/articles-Return of Dragon plus 1 pg. photo pinup. 10-(3/75)-Iron Fist painted-c & 34 pg. sty-Early app. 4 8 12 25 40 55
5,6: 5-1st app. Manchurian, 6 pgs. Gulacy-a. TV Kung Fu, 4 pg. article; reprints books w/Barry Smith-a. Capt. America-sty, 10 pgs. Kirby-a(r). 6-Bruce Lee photos/article, 6 pgs.; 15 pgs. early Perez-a 4 8 12 22 35 48
8,9,11: 9-Iron Fist, 2 pg. Preview pinup; Nebres-a. 11-Billy Jack painted-c by Adams; 17 pgs. photos/article 3 6 9 19 30 40
12,13: 12-James Bond painted-c by Adams; 14 pg. photos/article. 13-16 pgs. early Perez-a; Piers Anthony, 7 pgs. photos/article 3 6 9 17 26 35
14-Classic Bruce Lee painted-c by Adams. Lee pinup by Chaykin. Lee 16 pg. photos/article w/2 pgs. Green Hornet TV 7 14 21 46 86 125
15-Sum, '75 Giant Annual #1; 20pgs. Starlin-a. Bruce Lee photo pinup & 3 pg. photos/ article re book; Man-Thing app. Iron Fist-c/sty; Gulacy-a 18pgs. 4 8 12 22 35 48
16,18,20: 16-1st app. Corpse Rider, a Samurai w/Sanho Kim-a. 20-Chuck Norris painted-c & 16 pgs. interview w/photos/article; Bruce Lee vs. C. Norris pinup by Ken Barr. Origin The White Tiger, Perez-a 3 6 9 16 24 32
17-Bruce Lee painted-c by Adams; interview w/R. Clouse, director Enter Dragon 7 pgs. w/B. Lee app. 1st Giffen-a (1pg. 11/75) 5 10 15 31 53 75
19-Iron Fist painted-c & series begins; 1st White Tiger 7 14 21 46 86 125
21-Bruce Lee 1pg. photos/article 3 6 9 17 25 34
22-1st brief app. Jack of Hearts. 1st Giffen sty-a (along w/Amazing Adv. #35, 3/76) 4 8 12 26 47 65
23-1st full app. Jack of Hearts 5 10 15 30 50 70
24-26,29: 24-Iron Fist-c & centerfold pinup. early Zeck-a; Shang Chi pinup; 6 pgs. Piers Anthony text sty w/Pérez/Austin-a; Jack of Hearts app. early Giffen-a. 25-1st app. Shimuru, "Samurai", 20 pgs. Mantlo-sty/Broderick-a; "Swordquest"-c & begins 17 pg. sty by Sanho Kim; 11 pg. photos/article; partly Bruce Lee. 26-Bruce Lee painted-c & pinup; 16 pgs. interviews w/Kwon & Clouse; talk about Bruce Lee re-filming of Lee legend. 29-Ironfist vs. Shang Chi battle-c/sty; Jack of Hearts app. 3 6 9 18 28 38
27 3 6 9 15 22 28
28-All Bruce Lee Special Issue; (1st time in comics). Bruce Lee painted-c by Ken Barr & pinup. 36 pgs. comics chronicaling Bruce Lee's life; 15 pgs. B. Lee photos/article (Rare in high grade) 8 16 24 52 99 145
30-32: 30-Swordquest-c/sty & conclusion; Jack of Hearts app. 31-Jack of Hearts app; Staton-a. 32-1st Daughters of the Dragon-c/sty, 21 pgs. M. Rogers-a/Claremont-sty; Iron Fist pinup 3 6 9 16 23 30
33-Shang Chi-c/sty; Classic Daughters of the Dragon, 21 pgs. M. Rogers-a/Claremont-story with nudity; Bob Wall interview, photos/article, 14 pgs. 4 8 12 23 37 50
...Special Album Edition 1(Summer, '74)-Iron Fist-c/story (early app., 3rd?); 10 pgs. Adams-i; Shang Chi/Fu Manchu, 10 pgs.; Sons of Tiger, 11 pgs.; TV Kung Fu, 6 pgs. photos/article 5 10 15 30 50 70

NOTE: ***Bruce Lee:*** *1-7, 14, 15, 17, 25, 26, 28.* ***Kung Fu (TV):*** *1, 2, 4.* ***Jack of Hearts:*** *22, 23, 29-33.* ***Shang Chi Master of Kung Fu:*** *1-9, 11-18, 29, 31, 33.* ***Sons of Tiger:*** *1, 3, 4, 6-14, 16-19.* ***Swordquest:*** *25-27, 29-33.* ***White Tiger:*** *19-24, 26, 27, 29-33.* ***N. Adams*** *a-1i(part), 27i; c-1, 2-4, 11, 12, 14, 17.* ***Giffen*** *a-22p, 24p.* ***G. Kane*** *a-23p.* ***Kirby*** *a-5r.* ***Nasser*** *a-27p, 28.* ***Perez*** *a(p)-6-14, 16, 17, 19, 21.* ***Rogers*** *a-26, 32, 33.* ***Starlin*** *a-1, 2r, 15r.* ***Staton*** *a-28p, 31, 32.*

DEADLY HANDS OF KUNG FU
Marvel Comics: Jul, 2014 - No. 4, Oct, 2014 ($3.99, limited series)
1-4-Benson-s/Huat-a/Johnson-c. 2-4-Misty Knight & Colleen Wing app. 4.00

DEADMAN (See The Brave and the Bold & Phantom Stranger #39)
DC Comics: May, 1985 - No. 7, Nov, 1985 ($1.75, Baxter paper)
1-7: 1-Deadman-r by Infantino, N. Adams in all. 5-Batman-c/story-r/Strange Adventures. 7-Batman-r 4.00
... Book One TPB (2011, $19.99) r/apps. in Strange Adventures #205-213 20.00

DEADMAN
DC Comics: Mar, 1986 - No. 4, June, 1986 (75¢, limited series)
1-4: Lopez-c/a. 4-Byrne-c(p) 4.00

DEADMAN
DC Comics: Feb, 2002 - No. 9, Oct, 2002 ($2.50)
1-9: 1-4-Vance-s/Beroy-a. 3,4-Mignola-c. 5,6-Garcia-Lopez-a 3.00

DEADMAN
DC Comics (Vertigo): Oct, 2006 - No. 13, Oct, 2007 ($2.99)
1-13: 1-Bruce Jones-s/John Watkiss-a/c; intro Brandon Cayce 3.00
...: Deadman Walking TPB (2007, $9.99) r/#1-5 10.00

DEADMAN
DC Comics: Jan, 2018 - No. 6, Jun, 2018 ($3.99, limited series)
1-6-Neal Adams-s/a; Zatanna, The Spectre, Hook and Commissioner Gordon app. 4.00

DEADMAN: DARK MANSION OF FORBIDDEN LOVE
DC Comics: Dec, 2016 - No. 3, Apr, 2017 ($5.99, limited series, squarebound)
1-3-Sarah Vaughn-s/Lan Medina-a/Stephanie Hans-c 6.00

DEADMAN: DEAD AGAIN (Leads into 2002 series)
DC Comics: Oct, 2001 - No. 5, Oct, 2001 ($2.50, weekly limited series)
1-5: Deadman at the deaths of the Flash, Robin, Superman, Hal Jordan 3.00

DEADMAN: EXORCISM
DC Comics: 1992 - No. 2, 1992 ($4.95, limited series, 52 pgs.)
1,2: Kelley Jones-c/a in both 5.00

DEAD MAN LOGAN (Follows Old Man Logan series)
Marvel Comics: Jan, 2019 - No. 12, Dec, 2019 ($4.99/$3.99, limited series)
1-Ed Brisson-s/Mike Henderson-a; Mysterio, Miss Sinister & Hawkeye app. 5.00
2-12-($3.99) 2,3-Avengers app. 5-Mysterio app. 11-Dani Cage becomes Thor 4.00

DEADMAN: LOVE AFTER DEATH
DC Comics: 1989 - No. 2, 1990 ($3.95, 52 pgs., limited series, mature)
Book One, Two: Kelley Jones-c/a in both. 1-Contains nudity 5.00

DEAD MAN'S RUN
Aspen MLT: No. 0, Dec, 2011 - No. 6, Jul, 2013 ($2.50/$3.50)
0-($2.50) Greg Pak-s/Tony Parker-a; 3 covers; bonus design sketch art 3.00
1-6: 1-(2/12, $3.50) Greg Pak-s/Tony Parker-a; 2 covers 3.50

DEAD OF NIGHT
Marvel Comics Group: Dec, 1973 - No. 11, Aug, 1975
1-Horror reprints 5 10 15 34 60 85
2-10: 10-Kirby-a. 6-Jack the Ripper-c/s 3 6 9 17 26 35
11-Intro Scarecrow; Kane/Wrightson-c 5 10 15 31 53 75
NOTE: ***Ditko*** *r-7, 10.* ***Everett*** *c-2.* ***Sinnott*** *r-1.*

DEAD OF NIGHT FEATURING DEVIL-SLAYER
Marvel Comics (MAX): Nov, 2008 - No. 4, Feb, 2009 ($3.99, limited series)
1-4-Keene-s/Samnee-a/Andrews-c 4.00

DEAD OF NIGHT FEATURING MAN-THING
Marvel Comics (MAX): Apr, 2008 - No. 4, July, 2008 ($3.99, limited series)
1-4: 1-Man-Thing origin re-told; Kano-a. 2-4-Jennifer Kale app. 4.00

DEAD OF NIGHT FEATURING WEREWOLF BY NIGHT
Marvel Comics (MAX): Mar, 2009 - No. 4, Jun, 2009 ($3.99, limited series)
1-4: 1-Werewolf By Night origin re-told; Swierczynski-s/Suayan-a 4.00

DEADPOOL (See New Mutants #98 for 1st app.)
Marvel Comics: Aug, 1994 - No. 4, Nov, 1994 ($2.50, limited series)
1-Mark Waid's 1st Marvel work; Ian Churchill-c/a 3 6 9 14 20 26
2-4 1 2 3 5 6 8

DEADPOOL (... : Agent of Weapon X on cover #57-60) (title becomes Agent X)
Marvel Comics: Jan, 1997 - No. 69, Sept, 2002 ($2.95/$1.95/$1.99)
1-($2.95)-Wraparound-c; Kelly-s/McGuinness-a 6 12 18 37 66 95
2-Begin-$1.95-c. 2 4 6 9 12 15

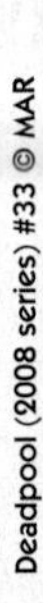
Deadpool (2008 series) #33 © MAR

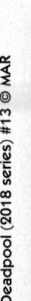

Deadpool (2018 series) #13 © MAR

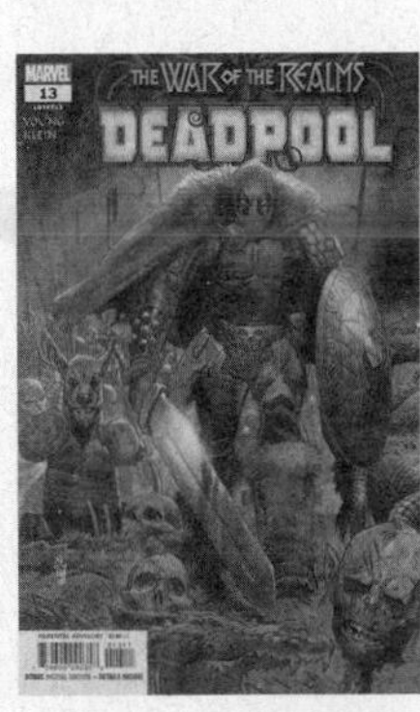

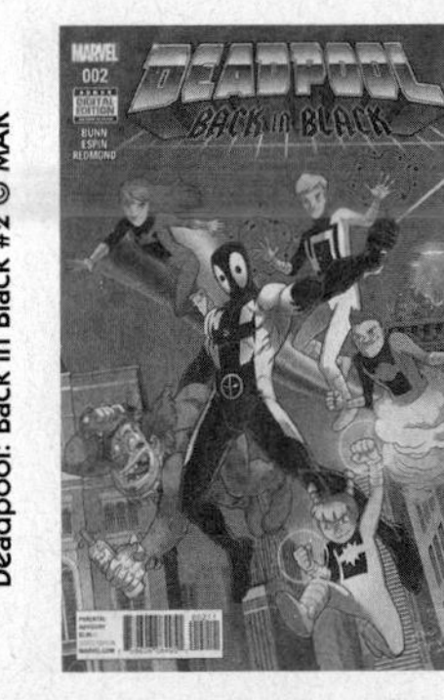

Deadpool: Back in Black #2 © MAR

GD 2.0 VG 4.0 FN 6.0 VF 8.0 VF/NM 9.0 NM- 9.2

3,5-10,12,13,15-22,24: 12-Variant-c. 22-Cable app. 6.00
4-Hulk-c/app. 3 6 9 14 20 25
11-($3.99)-Deadpool replaces Spider-Man from Amazing Spider-Man #47; Kraven, Gwen Stacy app. 3 6 9 18 28 38
14-1st Ajax; begin McDaniel-a 3 6 9 14 20 25
23,25-($2.99); 23-Dead Reckoning pt. 1; wraparound-c 1 2 3 4 5 7
26-40: 27-Wolverine-c/app. 37-Thor app. 5.00
41,43-49,51-53,56-60: 41-Begin $2.25-c. 44-Black Panther-c/app. 46-49-Chadwick-a 51-Cover swipe of Detective #38. 57-60-BWS-c 4.00
42-G.I. Joe #21 cover swipe; silent issue 2 4 6 11 16 20
50-1st Kid Deadpool 2 4 6 11 16 20
54,55-Punisher-c/app. 54-Dillon-c. 55-Bradstreet-c 3 6 9 14 20 25
61-64,66-68: 61-64-Funeral For a Freak on cover. 66-69-Udon Studios-a. 67-Dazzler-c/app. 1 3 4 6 8 10
65-Girl in bunny suit-c; Udon Studios-a 4 8 12 23 37 50
69-Udon Studios-a 2 4 6 9 12 15
#(-1) Flashback (7/97) Lopresti-a; Wade Wilson's early days 2 4 6 9 12 15
.../Death '98 Annual ($2.99) Kelly-s 3 6 9 16 23 30
... Team-Up (12/98, $2.99) Widdle Wade-c/app. 2 4 6 8 10 12
Baby's First Deadpool Book (12/98, $2.99) 3 6 9 16 23 30
Encyclopædia Deadpoolica (12/98, $2.99) Synopses 3 6 9 14 20 25
.../GLI - Summer Fun Spectacular #1 (9/07, $3.99) short stories; Pelletier-c 2 4 6 8 10 12
... Classic Vol. 1 TPB (2008, $29.99) r/#1, New Mutants #98, Deadpool: The Circle Chase #1-4 and Deadpool (1994 series) #1-4 30.00
Mission Improbable TPB (9/98, $14.95) r/#1-5 20.00
Wizard #0 ('98, bagged with Wizard #87) 6.00

DEADPOOL
Marvel Comics: Nov, 2008 - No. 63, Dec, 2012 ($3.99/$2.99)

1-($3.99) Medina-a; Secret Invasion x-over; Crain-c 3 6 9 16 24 32
1-Variant cover by Liefeld 4 8 12 27 44 60
2 1 3 4 6 8 10
3-10: 4-10-Pearson-c. 8,9-Thunderbolts x-over. 10-Dark Reign 6.00
11-24,26-33, 33.1, 34-44,46-49-($2.99): 11-20-Pearson-c. 16-18-X-Men app. 19-21-Spider-Man & Hit-Monkey app. 26-Ghost Rider app. 27-29-Secret Avengers app. 30,31-Curse of the Mutants. 37-39-Hulk app. 4.00
25-($3.99) 3-D cover, fake 3-D glasses on back-c; back-up story w/Bond-a 5.00
45-1st full app. of Evil Deadpool 2 4 6 11 16 20
49.1, 51-63 ($2.99) 49-McCrea-a. 51-Garza-a. 61-Hit-Monkey app. 4.00
50-($3.99) Uncanny X-Force & Kingpin app.; Barberi-a 1 2 3 5 6 8
900-(12/09, $4.99) Stories by various incl. Liefeld, Baker; wraparound-c by Johnson 6.00
1000-(10/10, $4.99) Stories by various; gallery of variant covers; Johnson-c 6.00
Annual 1 (7/11, $3.99) "Identity Wars" crossover; Spider-Man & Hulk app. 5.00
... & Cable #26 (4/11, $3.99) Swierczynski-s/Fernandez-a 4.00
... Family 1 (6/11, $3.99) short stories by various; Pearson-c 4.00
...: Games of Death 1 (5/09, $3.99) Benson-s/Crystal-a/Land-c 4.00
... MCG (7/10, $1.00) r/#1 with "Marvel's Greatest Comics" logo on cover 3.00

DEADPOOL
Marvel Comics: Jan, 2013 - No. 45, Jun, 2015 ($2.99)

1-Posehn & Duggan-s/Tony Moore-a/Darrow-c; Deadpool vs. Zombie ex-Presidents 2 4 6 9 13 16
2-5 6.00
6-26: 7-Iron Man app.; spoof in 1980s style; Koblish-a/Maguire-c. 10-Spider-Man app. 13-Spoof in 1970s style; Heroes For Hire app. 15-19-Wolverine & Capt. America app. 4.00
27-($9.99) Wedding of Deadpool & Shiklah; wraparound-c with 236 characters 15.00
28-33,35-44-($3.99): 30-32-Dazzler app. 36-39-AXIS tie-in. 40-Gracking issue 4.00
34-($4.99) Original Sin tie-in; flashback in 1990s style; Sabretooth & Alpha Flight app. 1 2 3 5 6 8
45-(#250 on cover, 5/15, $9.99) Death of Deadpool; back-up short stories by various 10.00
Annual 1 (1/14, $4.99) Madcap and Avengers app.; Acker & Blacker-s/Shaner-a 5.00
Annual 2 (7/14, $4.99) Spider-Man and The Chameleon app.; Camagni-a/Nakayama-c 5.00
Bi-Annual 1 (11/14, $4.99) Scheer & Giovannetti-s/Espin-a; Brute Force app. 5.00
...: The Gauntlet (3/14, giveaway) printing of Marvel digital comics content; Cho-c 3.00

DEADPOOL (Continues in Despicable Deadpool #287)
Marvel Comics: Jan, 2016 - No. 36, Nov, 2017 ($4.99/$3.99)

1-($4.99) Duggan-s/Hawthorne-a; Deadpool starts a Heroes For Hire 1 2 3 5 6 8
2-6,8-12-($3.99) 3,4-Steve Rogers app. 6-Intro. Deadpool 2099; Koblish-a. 8-11-Sabretooth app. 12-Deadpool 2099 app. 4.00
7-($9.99) 25th Anniversary issue; back-up short stories about the Mercs For Money 10.00
13-($9.99) Crossover with Daredevil & Power Man and Iron Fist 10.00
14-20,22-24,26-29: 14-17-Civil War II tie-ins. 14-Ulysses app. 15-Black Panther app. 4.00
21-($9.99) Duggan-s/Lolli-a; Shakespeare-style story by Doescher-s/Oliveira-a 10.00
25-($5.99) Duggan-s/Koblish-a; Deadpool 2099 story 6.00
30-($9.99) Duggan-s/Hawthorne-a; Deadpool in space; Agent Adsit & Rocket app. 10.00
31-36: 31-35-Secret Empire tie-ins 4.00
#3.1-(2/16, $3.99) All-Spanish issue about the Mexican Deadpool Masacre; Koblish-a 4.00
Annual 1 (11/16, $4.99) Spoof of Spider-Man and His Amazing Friends cartoon; Koblish-a 5.00
...: Last Days of Magic 1 (7/16, $4.99) Koblish-a/Ramos-c; Doctor Strange app. 5.00
...: Masacre 1 (7/16, $3.99) Reprints #3.1 in English 4.00

DEADPOOL
Marvel Comics: Aug, 2018 - No. 15, Sept, 2019 ($4.99/$3.99)

1-($4.99) Skottie Young-s/Nic Klein-a; Scott Hepburn-a; Guardians of the Galaxy app. 5.00
2-14-($3.99) 2-Avengers and Champions app. 13,14-War of The Realms tie-in 4.00
15-($4.99) Mephisto app.; Young-s/Klein & Hepburn-a 5.00
Annual 1 (10/19, $4.99) "Acts of Evil" tie-in; Nightmare & Dr. Strange app. 5.00

DEADPOOL
Marvel Comics: Jan, 2020 - Present ($4.99/$3.99)

1-($4.99) Kelly Thompson-s/Chris Bachalo-a; Elsa Bloodstone app. 5.00
2-10-($3.99) 2-4-Kraven The Hunter app. 2-Captain America app. 10-King in Black tie-in 4.00
...: The End 1 (3/20, $4.99) Various "endings" to Deadpool; Kelly-s/Hawthorne-a 5.00

DEADPOOL & CABLE: SPLIT SECOND
Marvel Comics: Feb, 2016 - No. 3, Apr, 2016 ($3.99, limited series)

1-3-Nicieza-s/Reilly Brown-a 4.00

DEADPOOL & THE MERCS FOR MONEY
Marvel Comics: Apr, 2016 - No. 5, Aug, 2016 ($3.99)

1-5: 1-Bunn-s/Espin-a; bonus reprint of Spidey #1 4.00

DEADPOOL & THE MERCS FOR MONEY
Marvel Comics: Sept, 2016 - No. 10, Jun, 2017 ($3.99)

1-10: 1-Bunn-s/Coello-a; Negasonic Teenage Warhead app. 10-Dracula app. 4.00

DEADPOOL: ASSASSIN
Marvel Comics: Aug, 2018 - No. 6, Oct, 2018 ($3.99)

1-($4.99) Bunn-s/Bagley-a; Weasel app. 5.00
2-6-($3.99) 4.00

DEADPOOL: BACK IN BLACK (Deadpool with the Venom symbiote right before ASM #300)
Marvel Comics: Dec, 2016 - No. 5, Feb, 2017 ($3.99, limited series)

1-5: 2-Power Pack app. 5-Spider-Man in black costume app.; Eddie Brock app. 4.00

DEADPOOL: BAD BLOOD
Marvel Comics: 2017 ($24.99, HC, original graphic novel)

1-Rob Liefeld-s/a/c; Cable, Domino and X-Force app. 25.00

DEADPOOL: DRACULA'S GAUNTLET (Printing of Marvel digital comic mini-series)
Marvel Comics: Sept, 2014 - No. 7, Oct, 2014 ($3.99, weekly limited series)

1-7-Duggan & Posehn-s; Deadpool meets Shiklah. 2,3,6-Blade app. 4-Frightful Four app. 4.00

DEADPOOL CORPS (Continues from Prelude to Deadpool Corps series)
Marvel Comics: Jun, 2010 - No. 12, May, 2011 ($3.99/$2.99)

1-($3.99) Liefeld-a/c; Gischler-s; 2 covers by Liefeld 1 2 3 5 6 8
2-12-($2.99) 2-5,7,9-Liefeld-a. 6-Mychaels-a 3.00
...: Rank and Foul 1 (5/10, $3.99) Handbook-style profile pages of allies and enemies 4.00

DEADPOOL KILLS DEADPOOL
Marvel Comics: Sept, 2013 - No. 4, Dec, 2013 ($2.99, limited series)

1-Bunn-s/Espin-a; Deadpool Corps app. 1 2 3 5 6 8
2-4 3.00

DEADPOOL KILLS THE MARVEL UNIVERSE
Marvel Comics: Oct, 2012 - No. 4, Oct, 2012 ($2.99, weekly limited series)

1-Bunn-s/Talajic-a/Andrews-c 3 6 9 18 28 38
2-4 2 4 6 8 10 12

DEADPOOL KILLS THE MARVEL UNIVERSE AGAIN
Marvel Comics: Sept, 2017 - No. 5, Nov, 2017 ($3.99, limited series)

1-5-Bunn-s/Talajic-a/Johnson-c. 3-Gwenpool app. 1,5-Red Skull app. 4.00

DEADPOOL KILLUSTRATED
Marvel Comics: Mar, 2013 - No. 4, Jun, 2013 ($2.99, limited series)

1-Bunn-s/Lolli-a/Del Mundo-c; stories/covers styled like Classics Illustrated 1 2 3 5 6 8
2-4 4.00

Deadpool the Duck #5 © MAR

Dead Rabbit #1 © Duggan & McCrea

Dear Beatrice Fairfax #5 © STD

GD 2.0 | VG 4.0 | FN 6.0 | VF 8.0 | VF/NM 9.0 | NM- 9.2

GD 2.0 | VG 4.0 | FN 6.0 | VF 8.0 | VF/NM 9.0 | NM- 9.2

DEADPOOL MAX
Marvel Comics (MAX): Dec, 2010 - No. 12, Nov, 2011 ($3.99)
1-12: 1-8,10-12-David Lapham-s/Kyle Baker-a/c. 6,7-Domino app. 9-Crystal-a 4.00
... X-Mas Special 1 (2/12, $4.99) Lapham-s; art by Lapham, Baker & Crystal; Baker-c 5.00

DEADPOOL MAX 2
Marvel Comics (MAX): Dec, 2011 - No. 6, May, 2012 ($3.99)
1-6: 1,2-David Lapham-s/Kyle Baker-a/c. 3-Crystal-a 4.00

DEADPOOL: MERC WITH A MOUTH
Marvel Comics: Sept, 2009 - No. 13, Sept, 2010 ($3.99/$2.99)
1-($3.99) Suydam-c/Dazo-a; Zombie-head Deadpool & Ka-Zar app.; r/Deadpool #4 ('97) 2 4 6 9 12 15
2-6,8-12-($2.99) Suydam-c on all. 8-Deadpool goes to Zombie dimension 4.00
7-($3.99) Covers by Suydam & Liefeld; art by Liefeld, Baker, Pastoras, Dazo; 1st app. Lady Deadpool 4 8 12 23 37 50
13-($3.99) Silence of the Lambs-c 2 4 6 10 14 18

DEADPOOL PULP
Marvel Comics: Nov, 2010 - No. 4, Feb, 2011 ($3.99, limited series)
1-4-Alternate Deadpool in 1955; Glass & Benson-s/Laurence Campbell-a/Jae Lee-c 4.00

DEADPOOL'S ART OF WAR
Marvel Comics: Dec, 2014 - No. 4, Mar, 2015 ($3.99, limited series)
1-4-David-s/Koblish-a; Loki and Thor app. 4.00

DEADPOOL'S SECRET SECRET WARS (Secret Wars tie-in)
Marvel Comics: Jul, 2015 - No. 4, Oct, 2015 ($4.99/$3.99, limited series)
1-($4.99) Deadpool inserts himself into the 1984 Secret Wars series; Bunn-s/Harris-c 5.00
2-4-($3.99) Spider-Man, Avengers & X-Men app. 3-Black costume created 4.00
2-Gwenpool variant-c by Bachalo; 1st app. of Gwenpool 20.00

DEADPOOL: SUICIDE KINGS
Marvel Comics: Jun, 2009 - No. 5, Oct, 2009 ($3.99, limited series)
1-Barberi-a; Punisher, Daredevil, & Spider-Man app. 2 4 6 8 10 12
2-5 5.00

DEADPOOL TEAM-UP
Marvel Comics: No. 899, Jan, 2010 - No. 883, May, 2011 ($2.99, numbering runs in reverse)
899-883: 899-Hercules app.; Ramos-c. 897-Ghost Rider app. 894-Franken-Castle app. 887-Thor app. 883-Galactus & Silver Surfer app. 3.00

DEADPOOL: THE CIRCLE CHASE (See New Mutants #98)
Marvel Comics: Aug, 1993 - No. 4, Nov, 1993 ($2.00, limited series)
1-($2.50)-Embossed-c 3 6 9 15 22 28
2-4 1 3 4 6 8 10

DEADPOOL: THE DUCK
Marvel Comics: Mar, 2017 - No. 5, May, 2017 ($3.99, limited series)
1-5-Deadpool & Howard the Duck merge; Rocket Raccoon app.; Camagni-a 4.00

DEADPOOL: TOO SOON
Marvel Comics: Dec, 2016 - No. 4, Mar, 2017 ($4.99, limited series)
1-4-Corin-s/Nauck-a; Squirrel Girl, Howard the Duck, Punisher, Forbush Man app. 5.00

DEADPOOL V GAMBIT
Marvel Comics: Aug, 2016 - No. 5, Nov, 2016 ($3.99, limited series)
1-5-Acker & Blacker-s/Beyruth-s. 1-Spider-Man & Daredevil app. 4.00

DEADPOOL VS. CARNAGE
Marvel Comics: Jun, 2014 - No. 4, Aug, 2014 ($3.99, limited series)
1-Bunn-s/Espin-a/Fabry-c 2 4 6 8 10 12
2-4 6.00

DEADPOOL VS. OLD MAN LOGAN
Marvel Comics: Dec, 2017 - No. 5, Apr, 2018 ($3.99, limited series)
1-5-Declan Shalvey-s/Mike Henderson-a 4.00

DEADPOOL VS. THANOS
Marvel Comics: Nov, 2015 - No. 4, Dec, 2015 ($3.99, limited series)
1-4-Seeley-s/Bondoc-a; Death app. 2-Guardians of the Galaxy app. 4.00

DEADPOOL VS. THE PUNISHER
Marvel Comics: Jun, 2017 - No. 5, Aug, 2017 ($3.99, limited series)
1-5-Van Lente-s/Pere Pérez-a/Shalvey-c 4.00

DEADPOOL VS. X-FORCE
Marvel Comics: Sept, 2014 - No. 4, Nov, 2014 ($3.99, limited series)
1-4-Swierczynski-s/Larraz-a/Shane Davis-c 4.00

DEADPOOL: WADE WILSON'S WAR
Marvel Comics: Aug, 2010 - No. 4, Nov, 2010 ($3.99, limited series)
1-4-Swierczynski-s/Pearson-a/c; Bullseye, Domino & Silver Sable app. 4.00

DEAD RABBIT (Issues recalled due to trademark dispute, cancelled after #2)(See Dead Eyes)
Image Comics: Oct, 2018 - No. 2, Nov, 2018 ($3.99)
1-Duggan-s/McCrea-a 6.00
2-Bonus preview of Self/Made #1 4.00

DEAD RIDER (See Deadlander)

DEAD ROMEO
DC Comics: June, 2009 - No. 6, Nov, 2009 ($2.99, limited series)
1-6-Ryan Benjamin-a/Jesse Snider-s 3.00
TPB (2010, $19.99) r/#1-6; cover gallery 20.00

DEAD, SHE SAID
IDW Publishing: May, 2008 - No. 3, Sept, 2008 ($3.99, limited series)
1-3-Bernie Wrightson-a/Steve Niles-s 4.00

DEADSHOT (See Batman #59, Detective Comics #474, & Showcase '93 #8)
DC Comics: Nov, 1988 - No. 4, Feb, 1989 ($1.00, limited series)
1-Ostrander & Yale-s/Luke McDonnell-a 1 2 3 5 6 8
2-4 5.00

DEADSHOT
DC Comics: Feb, 2005 - No. 5, June 2005 ($2.95, limited series)
1-5-Zeck-c/Gage-s/Cummings-a. 3-Green Arrow app. 4.00

DEAD SPACE (Based on the Electronics Arts videogame)
Image Comics: Mar, 2008 - No. 6, Sept, 2008 ($2.99, limited series)
1-6-Templesmith-a/Johnston-s 3.00
... Extraction (9/09, $3.50) Templesmith-a/Johnston-s 3.50

DEAD VENGEANCE
Dark Horse Comics: Oct, 2015 - No. 4, Jan, 2016 ($3.99, limited series)
1-4-Bill Morrison-s. 1-Morrison-a. 2-4-Tone Rodriguez-a 4.00

DEAD WHO WALK, THE (See Strange Mysteries-Super Reprint #15,16 {1963-64})
Realistic Comics: 1952 (one-shot)
nn 116 232 348 742 1271 1800

DEADWORLD (Also see The Realm)
Arrow Comics/Caliber Comics: Dec, 1986 - No. 26 ($1.50/$1.95/#15-28: $2.50, B&W)
1-4 4.00
5-26-Graphic cover version 4.00
5-26-Tame cover version 3.00
...Archives 1-3 (1992, $2.50) 3.00

DEAN KOONTZ'S FRANKENSTEIN: STORM SURGE
Dynamite Entertainment: 2015 - No. 6, 2016 ($3.99)
1-6-Chuck Dixon-s/Andres Ponce-a 4.00

DEAN MARTIN & JERRY LEWIS (See Adventures of...)

DEAR BEATRICE FAIRFAX
Best/Standard Comics (King Features): No. 5, Nov, 1950 - No. 9, Sept, 1951 (Vern Greene art)
5-All have Schomburg air brush-c 19 38 57 112 179 245
6-9 14 28 42 81 118 155

DEAR HEART (Formerly Lonely Heart)
Ajax: No. 15, July, 1956 - No. 16, Sept, 1956
15,16 10 20 30 58 78 100

DEAR LONELY HEART (...Illustrated No. 1-6)
Artful Publications: Mar, 1951; No. 2, Oct, 1951 - No. 8, Oct, 1952
1 22 44 66 130 213 295
2 14 28 42 76 108 140
3-Matt Baker Jungle Girl story 23 46 69 136 223 310
4-8 12 24 36 67 94 120

DEAR LONELY HEARTS (Lonely Heart #9 on)
Harwell Publ./Mystery Publ. Co. (Comic Media): Aug, 1953 -No. 8, Oct, 1954
1 16 32 48 95 151 205
2-8 13 26 39 74 105 135

DEARLY BELOVED
Ziff-Davis Publishing Co.: Fall, 1952
1-Photo-c 20 40 60 120 195 270

DEAR NANCY PARKER
Gold Key: June, 1963 - No. 2, Sept, 1963

Deathblow #13 © WSP

The Death-Defying Doctor Mirage #1 © VAL

Deathlok (1999 series) #1 © MAR

	GD 2.0	VG 4.0	FN 6.0	VF 8.0	VF/NM 9.0	NM- 9.2
1-Painted-c on both	4	8	12	23	37	50
2	3	6	9	17	26	35

DEATH, THE ABSOLUTE... (From Neil Gaiman's Sandman titles)
DC Comics (Vertigo): 2009 ($99.99, oversized hardcover in slipcase)
nn-Reprints 1st app. in Sandman #8, Sandman #20, Death: The High Cost of Living #1-3, Death: the Time of Your Life #1-3, Death Talks About Life; short stories and pin-ups; merchandise pics; script and sketch art for Sandman #8; Gaiman afterword 100.00

DEATH: AT DEATH'S DOOR (See Sandman: The Season of Mists)
DC Comics (Vertigo): 2003 ($9.95, graphic novel one-shot, B&W, 7-1/2" x 5")
1-Jill Thompson-s/a/c; manga-style; Morpheus and the Endless app. 10.00

DEATHBED
DC Comics (Vertigo): Apr, 2018 - No. 6, Sept, 2018 ($3.99)
1-6-Joshua Williamson-s/Riley Rossmo-a 4.00

DEATH BE DAMNED
BOOM! Studios: Feb, 2017 - No. 4, May, 2017 ($3.99, limited series)
1-4-Ben Acker, Ben Blacker & Andrew Miller-s/Hannah Christenson-a 4.00

DEATHBLOW (Also see Batman/Deathblow and Darker Image)
Image Comics (WildStorm Productions): May (Apr. inside), 1993 - No. 29, Aug, 1996 ($1.75/$1.95/$2.50)
0-(8/96, $2.95, 32 pgs.)-r/Darker Image w/new story & art; Jim Lee & Trevor Scott-a; new Jim Lee-c 4.00
1-($2.50)-Red foil stamped logo on black varnish-c; Jim Lee-c/a; flip-book side has Cybernary -c/story (#2 also) 4.00
1-($1.95)-Newsstand version w/o foil-c & varnish 3.00
2-29: 2-(8/93)-Lee-a; with bound-in poster. 2-($1.75)-Newsstand version w/o poster. 4-Jim Lee-c/Tim Sale-a begin. 13-W/pinup poster by Tim Sale & Jim Lee. 16-($1.95 Newsstand & $2.50 Direct Market editions)-Wildstorm Rising Pt. 6. 17-Variant "Chicago Comicon" edition exists. 20,21-Gen 13 app. 23-Backlash-c/app. 24,25-Grifter-c/app; Gen 13 & Dane from Wetworks app. 28-Deathblow dies. 29-Memorial issue 3.00
5-Alternate Portacio-c (Forms larger picture when combined with alternate-c for Gen 13 #5, Kindred #3, Stormwatch #10, Team 7 #1, Union #0, Wetworks #2 & WildC.A.T.S #11) 6.00
...:Sinners and Saints TPB ('99, $19.95) r/#1-12; Sale-c 20.00

DEATHBLOW (Volume 2)
DC Comics (WildStorm): Dec, 2006 - No. 9, Apr, 2008 ($2.99)
1-9: 1-Azzarello-s/D'Anda-a; two covers by D'Anda & Platt 3.00
...: And Then You Live! TPB (2008, $19.99) r/#1-9 20.00

DEATHBLOW BY BLOWS
DC Comics (WildStorm): Nov, 1999 - No. 3, Jan, 2000 ($2.95, limited series)
1-3-Alan Moore-s/Jim Baikie-a 3.00

DEATHBLOW/WOLVERINE
Image Comics (WildStorm Productions)/ Marvel Comics: Sept, 1996 - No. 2, Feb, 1997 ($2.50, limited series)
1,2: Wiesenfeld-s/Bennett-a 3.00
TPB (1997, $8.95) r/#1,2 9.00

DEATH DEALER (Also see Frank Frazetta's...)
Verotik: July, 1995 - No. 4, July, 1997 ($5.95)

	GD 2.0	VG 4.0	FN 6.0	VF 8.0	VF/NM 9.0	NM- 9.2
1-Frazetta-c; Bisley-a	2	4	6	11	16	20
1-2nd print, 2-4-($6.95)-Frazetta-c; embossed logo	1	2	3	4	5	7

DEATH-DEFYING 'DEVIL, THE (Also see Project Superpowers)
Dynamite Entertainment: 2008 - No. 4, 2009 ($3.50, limited series)
1-4-Casey & Ross-s/Salazar-a; multiple covers; the Dragon app. 3.50

DEATH-DEFYING 'DEVIL (Volume 2)
Dynamite Entertainment: 2019 - No. 5, 2020 ($3.99, limited series)
1-5-Gail Simone-s/Walter Giovani-a; multiple covers 4.00

DEATH-DEFYING DOCTOR MIRAGE, THE
Valiant Entertainment: Sept, 2014 - No. 5, Jan, 2015 ($3.99, limited series)
1-5-Van Meter-s/de la Torre-a. 1-3-Foreman-c. 4,5-Wada-c 4.00

DEATH-DEFYING DOCTOR MIRAGE, THE: SECOND LIVES
Valiant Entertainment: Dec, 2015 - No. 4, Mar, 2016 ($3.99, limited series)
1-4-Van Meter-s/de La Torre-a 4.00

DEATH HEAD
Dark Horse Comics: Jul, 2015 - No. 6, Feb, 2016 ($3.99, limited series)
1-6-Zach & Nick Keller-s/Joanna Estep-a 4.00

DEATH, JR.
Image Comics: Apr, 2005 - No. 3, Aug, 2005 ($4.99, squarebound, limited series)
1-3-Gary Whitta-s/Ted Naifeh-a 5.00
Vol. 1 TPB (2005, $14.99) r/series; concept and promotional art 15.00

DEATH, JR. (Volume 2)
Image Comics: Jul, 2006 - No. 3, May, 2007 ($4.99, squarebound, limited series)
1-3-Gary Whitta-s/Ted Naifeh-a. 1-Dan Brereton-c 5.00
... Halloween Special (10/06, 8-1/2"x 5-1/2", Halloween giveaway) Guy Davis-a 3.00
Vol. 2 TPB (2007, $14.99) r/series; Halloween story w/Guy Davis-a; promotional art 15.00

DEATHLOK (Also see Astonishing Tales #25)
Marvel Comics: July, 1990 - No. 4, Oct, 1990 ($3.95, limited series, 52 pgs.)
1-4: 1,2-Guice-a(p). 3,4-Denys Cowan-a, c-4 5.00

DEATHLOK
Marvel Comics: July, 1991 - No. 34, Apr, 1994 ($1.75)

	GD 2.0	VG 4.0	FN 6.0	VF 8.0	VF/NM 9.0	NM- 9.2
1-Silver ink cover; Denys Cowan-c/a(p) begins	1	2	3	5	6	8

2-18,20-24,26-34: 2-Forge (X-Men) app. 3-Vs. Dr. Doom. 5-X-Men & F.F. x-over. 6,7-Punisher x-over. 9,10-Ghost Rider-c/story. 16-Infinity War x-over. 17-Jae Lee-c. 22-Black Panther app. 27-Siege app. 3.00
19-($2.25)-Foil-c 4.00
25-($2.95, 52 pgs.)-Holo-grafx foil-c 4.00
Annual 1 (1992, $2.25, 68 pgs.)-Guice-p; Quesada-c(p) 5.00
Annual 2 (1993, $2.95, 68 pgs.)-Bagged w/card; intro Tracer 4.00
NOTE: *Denys Cowan a(p)-9-13, 15, Annual 1; c-9-12, 13p, 14. Guice/Cowan c-8.*

DEATHLOK
Marvel Comics: Sept, 1999 - No. 11, June, 2000 ($1.99)
1-11: 1-Casey-s/Manco-a. 2-Two covers. 4-Canete-a 3.00

DEATHLOK (... The Demolisher on cover)
Marvel Comics: Jan, 2010 - No. 7, Jul, 2010 ($3.99, limited series)
1-7-Huston-s/Medina-a/Peterson-c 4.00

DEATHLOK
Marvel Comics: Dec, 2014 - No. 10, Sept, 2015 ($3.99)
1-10: 1-Edmonson-s/Perkins-a; intro. Henry Hayes. 2-5,8-10-Domino app. 4.00

DEATHLOK SPECIAL
Marvel Comics: May, 1991 - No. 4, June, 1991 ($2.00, bi-weekly lim. series)
1-4: r/1-4(1990) w/new Guice-c #1,2; Cowan c-3,4 3.00
1-2nd printing w/white-c 3.00

DEATHMASK
Future Comics: Mar, 2003 - No. 3, June, 2003 ($2.99)
1-3-Giordano-a(p)/Michelinie & Layton-s 3.00

DEATHMATCH
BOOM! Studios: Dec, 2012 - No. 12, Nov, 2013 ($2.99)
1-($1.00) Jenkins-s/Magno-a; multiple covers 3.00
2-12 ($3.99) Multiple covers on each 4.00

DEATHMATE
Valiant (Prologue/Yellow/Blue)/Image Comics (Black/Red/Epilogue): Sept, 1993 - Epilogue (#6), Feb, 1994 ($2.95/$4.95, limited series)
Preview-(7/93, 8 pgs.) 3.00
Prologue (#1)–Silver foil; Jim Lee/Layton-c; B. Smith/Lee-a; Liefeld-a(p) 3.00
Prologue–Special gold foil ed. of silver ed. 4.00
Black (#2)-(9/93, $4.95, 52 pgs.)-Silvestri/Jim Lee-c; pencils by Peterson/Silvestri/Capullo/Jim Lee/Portacio; 1st story app. Gen 13 telling their rebellion against the Troika (see WildC.A.T.S. Trilogy) 6.00
Black-Special gold foil edition 7.00
Yellow (#3)-(10/93, $4.95, 52 pgs)-Yellow foil-c; Indicia says Prologue Sept 1993 by mistake; 3rd app. Ninjak; Thibert-c(i) 5.00
Yellow-Special gold foil edition 6.00
Blue (#4)-(10/93, $4.95, 52 pgs.)-Thibert blue foil-c(i); Reese-a(i) 5.00
Blue-Special gold foil edition 6.00
Red (#5), Epilogue (#6)-(2/94, $2.95)-Silver foil Quesada/Silvestri-c; Silvestri-a(p) 3.00

DEATH METAL
Marvel Comics UK: Jan, 1994 - No. 4, Apr, 1994 ($1.95, limited series)
1-4: 1-Silver ink-c. Alpha Flight app. 3.00

DEATH METAL VS. GENETIX
Marvel Comics UK: Dec, 1993 - No. 2, Jan, 1994 (Limited series)
1-($2.95)-Polybagged w/2 trading cards 3.00
2-($2.50)-Polybagged w/2 trading cards 3.00

DEATH OF CAPTAIN MARVEL (See Marvel Graphic Novel #1)

Death of Wolverine #4 © MAR

Death Sentence #1 © Montynero

Deathstroke (2014 series) #8 © DC

GD 2.0 | VG 4.0 | FN 6.0 | VF 8.0 | VF/NM 9.0 | NM- 9.2

DEATH OF DRACULA
Marvel Comics: Aug, 2010 ($3.99, one shot)
1-Gischler-s/Camuncoli-a/c 4.00

DEATH OF HAWKMAN, THE
DC Comics: Dec, 2016 - No. 6, May, 2017 ($3.99, limited series)
1-6-Andreyko-s/Lopresti-a; Adam Strange app. 2-6-Despero app. 4.00

DEATH OF MR. MONSTER, THE (See Mr. Monster #8)

DEATH OF SUPERMAN (See Superman, 2nd Series)

DEATH OF THE INHUMANS
Marvel Comics: Sept, 2018 - No. 5, Jan, 2019($4.99/$3.99, limited series)
1-($4.99) Cates-s/Olivetti-a; Vox app. 5.00
2-5-($3.99) Karnak app. 4-Beta Ray Bill app. 4.00

DEATH OF THE NEW GODS (Tie-in to the Countdown series)
DC Comics: Early Dec, 2007 - No. 8, Jun, 2008 ($3.50, limited series)
1-8-Jim Starlin-s/a/c. 1-Barda killed. 6-Orion dies. 7-Scott Free and Metron die 3.50
TPB (2009, $19.99) r/#1-8; Starlin intro.; cover gallery 20.00

DEATH OF WOLVERINE
Marvel Comics: Nov, 2014 - No. 4, Dec, 2014 ($4.99, limited series)
1-4-Soule-s/McNiven-a; multiple covers on each; bonus art & commentary in each 5.00
...: Deadpool & Captain America (12/14, $4.99) Duggan-s/Kolins-a 5.00
...: Life After Logan (1/15, $4.99) Short stories by various; Cyclops, Nightcrawler app. 5.00

DEATH OF WOLVERINE: THE LOGAN LEGACY (Continues in Wolverines #1)
Marvel Comics: Dec, 2014 - No. 7, Feb, 2015 ($3.99, bi-weekly limited series)
1-7: 1-Soule-s; X-23, Daken, Deathstrike, Mystique & Sabretooth app. 4.00

DEATH OF WOLVERINE: THE WEAPON X PROGRAM
Marvel Comics: Jan, 2015 - No. 5, Mar, 2015 ($3.99, bi-weekly limited series)
1-5-Soule-s. 1-3-Larroca-a. 3-Sabretooth app. 4.00

DEATH OF X (Leads into X-Men vs. Inhumans)
Marvel Comics: Dec, 2016 - No. 4, Jan, 2017 ($4.99/$3.99, limited series)
1-($4.99) Soule & Lemire-s; Kuder-a; X-Men, Inhumans & Hydra app. 5.00
2-4-($3.99) 2-Kuder-a. 3,4-Kuder & Garrón-a. 4-Death of Cyclops 4.00

DEATH ORB
Dark Horse Comics: Oct, 2018 - No. 5, Feb, 2019 ($3.99, limited series)
1-5-Ryan Ferrier-s/Alejandro Aragon-a 4.00

DEATH OR GLORY
Image Comics: May, 2018 - No. 11, Jul, 2020 ($4.99/$3.99)
1-Remender-s/Bengal-a; three covers by Bengal, Fegredo & Harren 5.00
2-11-($3.99) 2-Three covers. 3-11-Two covers 4.00

DEATH RACE 2020
Roger Corman's Cosmic Comics: Apr, 1995 - No. 8, Nov, 1995 ($2.50)
1-8: Sequel to the Movie 3.00

DEATH RATTLE (Formerly an Underground)
Kitchen Sink Press: V2#1, 10/85 - No. 18, 1988, 1994 ($1.95, Baxter paper, mature); V3#1, 11/95 - No. 5, 6/96 ($2.95, B&W)
V2#1-7,9-18: 1-Corben-c. 2-Unpubbed Spirit story by Eisner. 5-Robot Woman-r by Wolverton. 6-B&W issues begin. 10-Savage World-r by by Williamson/Torres/Krenkel/Frazetta from Witzend #1. 16-Wolverton Spacehawk-r 5.00
8-(12/86)-1st app. Mark Schultz's Xenozoic Tales/Cadillacs & Dinosaurs 3 6 9 17 26 35
8-(1994)-r plus interview w/Mark Schultz 3.50
V3#1-5 ($2.95-c): 1-Mark Schultz-c 3.50

DEATH SENTENCE
Titan Comics: Nov, 2003 - No. 6, Apr, 2014 ($3.99)
1-6-Montynero-s/c; Dowling-a 4.00

DEATH SENTENCE LONDON
Titan Comics: Jun, 2015 - No. 6, Jan, 2016 ($3.99)
1-6-Montynero-s/c; Simmonds-a 4.00

DEATH'S HEAD (See Daredevil #56, Dragon's Claws #5 & Incomplete...)(See Amazing Fantasy (2004) for Death's Head 3.0)
Marvel Comics: Dec, 1988 - No. 10, Sept, 1989 ($1.75)
1-Dragon's Claws spin-off 3.00
2-Fantastic Four app.; Dragon's Claws x-over 3.00
3-10: 8-Dr. Who app. 9-F. F. x-over; Simonson-c(p) 3.00

DEATH'S HEAD
Marvel Comics: Sept, 2019 - No. 4, Dec, 2019 ($3.99, limited series)
1-4-Tini Howard-s/Kei Zama-a; Wiccan, Hulkling & Hawkeye (Kate) app. 4.00

GD 2.0 | VG 4.0 | FN 6.0 | VF 8.0 | VF/NM 9.0 | NM- 9.2

DEATH'S HEAD II (Also see Battletide)
Marvel Comics UK, Ltd.: Mar, 1992 - No. 4, June (May inside), 1992 ($1.75, color, lim. series)
1-4: 2-Fantastic Four app. 4-Punisher, Spider-Man, Daredevil, Dr. Strange, Capt. America & Wolverine in the year 2020 4.00
1,2-Silver ink 2nd printiings 4.00

DEATH'S HEAD II (Also see Battletide)
Marvel Comics UK, Ltd.: Dec, 1992 - No. 16, Mar, 1994 ($1.75/$1.95)
V2#1-13,15,16: 1-Gatefold-c. 1-4-X-Men app. 15-Capt. America & Wolverine app. 4.00
V2# 14-($2.95)-Foil flip-c w/Death's Head II Gold #0 4.00
...Gold 1 (1/94, $3.95, 68 pgs.)-Gold foil-c 4.00

DEATH'S HEAD II & THE ORIGIN OF DIE CUT
Marvel Comics UK, Ltd.: Aug, 1993 - No. 2, Sept, 1993 (limited series)
1-($2.95)-Embossed-c 5.00
2 ($1.75) 4.00

DEATHSTROKE (DC New 52)
DC Comics: Nov, 2011 - No. 20, Jul, 2013 ($2.99)
1-Higgins-s/Bennett-a/Bisley-c 6.00
2-20: 4-Blackhawks app. 9-12-Liefeld-s/a/c; Lobo app. 3.00
#0 (11/12, $2.99) Origin story, Team 7 app.; Liefeld-s/a/c 3.00

DEATHSTROKE (DC New 52)
DC Comics: Dec, 2014 - No. 20, Sept, 2016 ($2.99)
1-20: 1-Tony Daniel-s/a; I Ching app. 3-6-Harley Quinn app. 7-10-Wonder Woman app. 11-13-Harley Quinn & Suicide Squad app. 3.00
Annual 1 (9/15, $4.99) Takes place between #8 & 9; Wonder Woman app.; Kirkham-a 5.00
Annual 1 (8/16, $4.99) Hester-s/Colak & Viacava-a 5.00

DEATHSTROKE (DC Rebirth)
DC Comics: Oct, 2016 - No. 50, Feb, 2020 ($2.99/$3.99)
1-19: 1-Priest-s/Pagulayan-a; Clock King app. 4,5-Batman & Robin (Damian) app. 8-Superman app. 11-The Creeper app.; Cowan & Sienkiewicz-a. 19-Lazarus Contract tie-in with Teen Titans and Titans 3.00
20-49-($3.99) 21-The Defiance team forms; Terra app. 22-Dr. Light app. 32-35-Vs. Batman. 37-40-Two-Face app. 42,43-Crossover with Teen Titans #28-30. 44-Funeral 4.00
50-($4.99) Pagulayan & Pasarin-a; Raven app. 5.00
Annual 1 (3/18, $4.99) Priest-s/Cowan & Sienkiewicz-a; Power Girl app. 5.00
... Rebirth 1 (10/16, $2.99) Priest-s/Pagulayan-a; Clock King app. 3.00
.../ Yogi Bear Special 1 (12/18, $4.99) Texeira-a; Kirkham-c; Secret Squirrel back-up 5.00

DEATHSTROKE: THE TERMINATOR (Deathstroke: The Hunted #0-47; Deathstroke #48-60) (Also see Marvel & DC Present, New Teen Titans #2, New Titans, Showcase '93 #7,9 & Tales of the Teen Titans #42-44)
DC Comics: Aug, 1991 - No. 60, June, 1996 ($1.75-$2.25)
1-New Titans spin-off; Mike Zeck c-1-28 2 4 6 13 18 24
1-Gold ink 2nd printing ($1.75) 1 2 3 5 6 8
2 5.00
3-40,0(10/94),41(11/94)-49,51-60: 6,8-Batman cameo. 7,9-Batman-c/story. 9-1st brief app. new Vigilante (female). 10-1st full app. new Vigilante; Perez-i. 13-Vs. Justice League; Team Titans cameo on last pg. 14-Total Chaos, part 1; Team Titans-c/story cont'd in New Titans #90. 15-1st app. Rose Wilson. 40-(9/94). 0-(10/94)-Begin Deathstroke, The Hunted, ends #47. 3.00
50 ($3.50) 4.00
Annual 1-4 ('92-'95, 68 pgs.): 1-Nightwing & Vigilante app.; minor Eclipso app. 2-Bloodlines Deathstorm; 1st app. Gunfire. 3-Elseworlds story. 4-Year One story 5.00
NOTE: *Golden a-12. Perez a-11i. Zeck c-Annual 1, 2.*

DEATH: THE HIGH COST OF LIVING (See Sandman #8) (Also see the Books of Magic limited & ongoing series)
DC Comics (Vertigo): Mar, 1993 - No. 3, May, 1993 ($1.95, limited series)
1-Bachalo/Buckingham-a; Dave McKean-c; Neil Gaiman scripts in all 6.00
1-Platinum edition 45.00
2 3.50
3-Pgs. 19 & 20 had wrong placement 3.00
3-Corrected version w/pgs. 19 & 20 facing each other 4.00
Death Talks About Life-giveaway about AIDS prevention 5.00
Hardcover (1994, $19.95)-r/#1-3 & Death Talks About Life; intro. by Tori Amos 20.00
Trade paperback (6/94, $12.95, Titan Books)-r/#1-3 & Death Talks About Life; prism-c 13.00

DEATH: THE TIME OF YOUR LIFE (See Sandman #8)
DC Comics (Vertigo): Apr, 1996 - No. 3, July, 1996 ($2.95, limited series)
1-3: Neil Gaiman story & Bachalo/Buckingham-a; Dave McKean-c. 2-(5/96) 3.00
Hardcover (1997, $19.95)-r/#1-3 w/3 new pages & gallery art by various 20.00

Deathwish #1 © Milestone Media

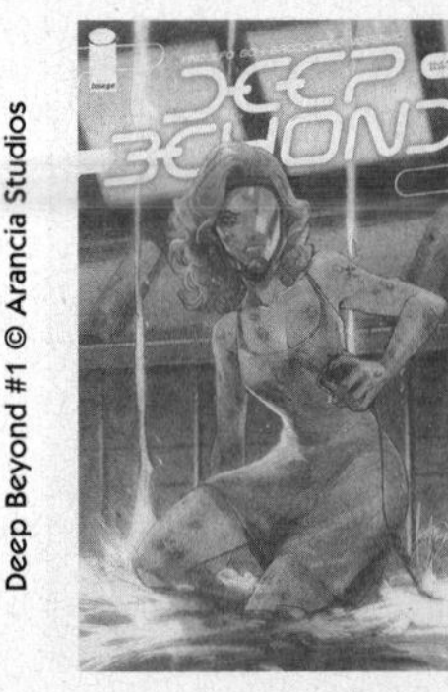

Deep Beyond #1 © Arancia Studios

The Defenders #15 © MAR

GD VG FN VF VF/NM NM-
2.0 4.0 6.0 8.0 9.0 9.2

TPB (1997, $12.95)-r/#1-3 & Visions of Death gallery; Intro. by Claire Danes 13.00

DEATH 3
Marvel Comics UK: Sept, 1993 - No. 4, Dec, 1993 ($1.75, limited series)
1-($2.95)-Embossed-c 4.00
2-4 3.00

DEATH TO THE ARMY OF DARKNESS
Dynamite Entertainment: 2020 - No. 5, 2020 ($3.99, limited series)
1-5-Ryan Parrott-s/Jacob Edgar-a; intro. Lady Ash, dog Ash, skeleton Ash, mini Ash 4.00

DEATH VALLEY (Cowboys and Indians)
Comic Media: Oct, 1953 - No. 6, Aug, 1954
1-Billy the Kid; Morisi-a; Andru/Esposito-c/a 26 52 78 152 249 345
2-Don Heck-c 15 30 45 92 144 195
3-6: 3,5-Morisi-a. 5-Discount-a 15 30 45 83 124 165

DEATH VALLEY (Becomes Frontier Scout, Daniel Boone No.10-13)
Charlton Comics: No. 7, 6/55 - No. 9, 10/55 (Cont'd from Comic Media series)
7-9: 8-Wolverton-a (half pg.) 11 22 33 62 86 120

DEATH VIGIL
Image Comics (Top Cow): Jul, 2014 - No. 8, Sept, 2015 ($3.99)
1-8-Stjepan Sejic-s/a/c 4.00

DEATHWISH
DC Comics (Milestone Media): Dec, 1994 - No. 4, Mar, 1995 ($2.50, lim. series)
1-4 3.00

DEATH WRECK
Marvel Comics UK: Jan, 1994 - No. 4, Apr, 1994 ($1.95, limited series)
1-4: 1-Metallic ink logo; Death's Head II app. 3.00

DEBBIE DEAN, CAREER GIRL
Civil Service Publ.: April, 1945 - No. 2, July, 1945
1,2-Newspaper reprints by Bert Whitman 15 30 45 92 144 195

DEBBI'S DATES (Also see Date With Debbi)
National Periodical Publications: Apr-May, 1969 - No. 11, Dec-Jan, 1970-71
1 8 16 24 52 99 145
2,3,5,7-11: 2-Last 12¢ issue 4 8 12 27 44 60
4-Neal Adams text illo 5 10 15 30 50 70
6-Superman cameo 6 12 18 37 66 95

DECADE OF DARK HORSE, A
Dark Horse Comics: Jul, 1996 - No. 4, Oct, 1996 ($2.95, B&W/color, lim. series)
1-4: 1-Sin City-c/story by Miller; Grendel by Wagner; Predator. 2-Star Wars wraparound-c. 3-Aliens-c/story; Nexus, Mask stories 3.00

DECAPITATOR (Randy Bowen's...)
Dark Horse Comics: Jun, 1998 - No. 4, ($2.95)
1-4-Bowen-s/art by various. 1-Mahnke-c. 3-Jones-c 4.00

DECEPTION, THE
Image Comics (Flypaper Press): 1999 - No. 3, 1999 ($2.95, B&W, mini-series)
1-3-Horley painted-c 3.00

DECIMATION: THE HOUSE OF M
Marvel Comics: Jan, 2006 ($3.99)
... - The Day After (one-shot) Claremont-s/Green-a 4.00

DECISION 2012 (Biographies of the main 2012 presidential candidates)
BOOM! Studios: Nov, 2011 ($3.99, series of one-shots)
...: Barack Obama 1 (11/11, $3.99) biography; Damian Couceiro-a; 2 covers 4.00
...: Michelle Bachman 1 (11/11) biography; Aaron McConnell-a; 2 covers 4.00
...: Ron Paul 1 (11/11) biography; Dean Kotz-a; 2 covers 4.00
...: Sarah Palin 1 (11/11) biography; Damian Couceiro-a; 2 covers 4.00

DECORUM
Image Comics: Mar, 2020 - Present ($4.99)
1-6-Hickman-s/Huddleston-a 5.00

DEEP, THE (Movie)
Marvel Comics Group: Nov, 1977 (Giant)
1-Infantino-c/a 1 3 4 6 8 10

DEEP BEYOND
Image Comics: Feb, 2021 - No. 12 ($3.99, limited series)
1-Andolfo & Goy-s/Broccardo-a 4.00

DEEP GRAVITY
Dark Horse Comics: Jul, 2014 - No. 4, Oct, 2014 ($3.99, limited series)
1-4-Hardman & Bechko-s/Baldó-a/Hardman-c 4.00

DEEP SLEEPER
Oni Press/Image Comics: Feb, 2004 - No. 4, Sept, 2004 ($3.50/$2.95, B&W, limited series)
1,2-(Oni Press, $3.50)-Hester-s/Huddleston-a 3.50
3,4-(Image Comics, $2.95) 3.00
... Omnibus (Image, 8/04, $5.95) r/#1,2 6.00
... Vol. 1 TPB (2005, $12.95) r/#1-4; cover gallery 13.00

DEEP STATE
BOOM! Studios: Nov, 2014 - No. 8, Jul, 2015 ($3.99)
1-8-Justin Jordan-s/Ariela Kristantina-a 4.00

DEFCON 4
Image Comics (WildStorm Productions): Feb, 1996 - No. 4, Sept, 1996 ($2.50, lim. series)
1/2 1 2 3 5 7 9
1/2 Gold-(1000 printed) 14.00
1-Main Cover by Mat Broome & Edwin Rosell 3.00
1-Hordes of Cymulants variant-c by Michael Golden 5.00
1-Backs to the Wall variant-c by Humberto Ramos & Alex Garner 5.00
1-Defcon 4-Way variant-c by Jim Lee 1 2 3 4 5 7
2-4 3.00

DEFEND COMICS (The CBLDF Presents...)
Comic Book Legal Defense Fund: May, 2015 - Present (giveaway)
FCBD Edition - (5/15) Short stories incl. Kevin Keller, Beanworld; art by Liew, Parent 3.00
...: FCBD 2016 Edition - Short stories by various incl. James Kochalka; Craig Thompson-c 3.00
...: FCBD 2017 Edition - Short stories by various incl. Ryan North; Jeffrey Brown-c 3.00
...: FCBD 2018 Edition - Reading Without Walls 3.00
...: FCBD 2019 Edition - Short stories by various incl. Bill Griffith; Derek Charm-c 3.00

DEFENDERS, THE (TV)
Dell Publishing Co.: Sept-Nov, 1962 - No. 2, Feb-Apr, 1963
12-176-211(#1) 4 8 12 25 40 55
12-176-304(#2) 3 6 9 20 31 42

DEFENDERS, THE (Also see Giant-Size..., Marvel Feature, Marvel Treasury Edition, Secret Defenders & Sub-Mariner #34, 35; The New...#140-on)
Marvel Comics Group: Aug, 1972 - No. 152, Feb, 1986
1-Englehart-s/Sal Buscema-a begins; The Hulk, Doctor Strange, Sub-Mariner app.; last app. as Defenders in Marvel Feature #3; 1st Necrodamus; plot continued from Incredible Hulk #126; minor Omegatron app. 13 26 39 90 198 305
2-Silver Surfer x-over; 1st Calizuma (a wizard in the service of the Nameless Ones) 8 16 24 51 96 140
3,5: 3-Silver Surfer x-over; vs. The Nameless Ones; Barbara Norris app. from Incredible Hulk #126. 5-vs. The Omegatron (destroyed) 5 10 15 31 53 75
4-Barbara Norris becomes the third incarnation of the Valkyrie (previously seen in Avengers #83 & Incredible Hulk #142; Enchantress, the Executioner & The Black Knight app (turned to stone); Valkyrie joins the Defenders 7 14 21 44 82 120
6,7: 6-Silver Surfer x-over. 7-Silver Surfer, Hawkeye app. vs. Red Ghost & Attuma 3 6 9 21 33 45
8,9: 8-Silver Surfer & Hawkeye app. vs. Red Ghost & Attuma; 4-pg story begins "Avengers/Defenders War"; Dormammu & Loki team-up; story continues in Avengers #116. 9-Continued from Avengers #116; Iron Man vs. Hawkeye, Dr. Strange vs. Mantis; continued in Avengers #117. 4 8 12 28 47 65
10-Hulk vs. Thor; continued in Avengers #118 8 16 24 56 108 160
11-"Avengers/Defenders War" concludes; Silver Surfer, Black Knight & King Richard app.; last Englehart-s 4 8 12 27 44 60
12-Last 20¢ issue; Wein-s begin; brief origin Valkyrie retold; vs. Xemnu the Titan; Defenders app. next in Giant-Size Defenders #1 3 6 9 14 20 25
13,14: 13-Nighthawk app. vs. The Squadron Sinister (Hyperion, Dr. Spectrum & the Whizzer; 1st app. Nebulon the Celestial Man. 14-vs. The Squadron Sinister & Nebulon; Sub-Mariner leaves; Nighthawk joins 3 6 9 14 20 25
15,16: 15-Magneto & Brotherhood of Evil Mutants app.; first Alpha the Ultimate Mutant; Professor X app. 16-Magneto & the Brotherhood of Evil mutants turned into children; Defenders app. next in Giant-Size Defenders #2 3 6 9 16 23 30
17-Power Man x-over (11/74); 1st app. of the Wrecking Crew (Thunderball, Bulldozer & Piledriver); Valkyrie leaves 3 6 9 21 33 45
18-20: 18-19-vs. the Wrecking Crew. 20-Continued from Marvel Two-in-one #7; Valkyrie returns (origin retold) 1st Gerber-s 2 4 6 9 12 15
21-25: 21-1st Headmen (Chondu the Mystic, Dr. Arthur Nagan, Jerold Morgan); Valkyrie origin continued from last issue; Hulk returns; story continued in Giant-Size Defenders #4. 22-25-vs. Sons of the Serpent. 23-Yellowjacket app. 24-25-Son of Satan, Daredevil, Yellowjacket & Power Man app; story continues in Giant-Size Defenders #5; 25-1st app. "Elf with a gun" 1 3 4 6 8 10
26-Continued from Giant-Size Defenders #5; Guardians of the Galaxy app. (pre-dates Marvel

The Defenders #101 © MAR

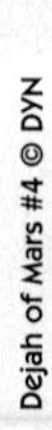

Dejah of Mars #4 © DYN

Delinquents #1 © VAL

	GD 2.0	VG 4.0	FN 6.0	VF 8.0	VF/NM 9.0	NM- 9.2

Presents #3); origin of Vance Astro; Killraven & Badoon x-over 3 6 9 14 20 25
27-1st brief app. Starhawk (unnamed); Guardians of the Galaxy & Defenders vs. the Badoon 3 6 9 21 33 45
28-1st full app. Starhawk; Guardians of the Galaxy & Badoon app. 6 12 18 38 69 100
29-Starhawk joins the Guardians of the Galaxy; 1st app. Aleta (Starhawks wife); Guardians story continues in Marvel Presents #3 2 4 6 10 14 18
30-Mantlo-s (fill-in issue) 1 2 3 5 6 8
31-40: 31-Headman app. 32-Origin of Nighthawk; Headmen & Son of Satan app; 1st app. Ruby Thursday; 2nd app. "Elf with a gun". 33-Origin Nighthawk continued; return of Nebulon. 34-38-(Regular 25¢ editions). 34-vs. Nebulon. 35-1st new Red Guardian (Dr. Tania Belinsky); Headmen & Nebulon app. 36-Red Guardian & Plant Man app. 37-Power Man guest app.; vs. Plant Man, Eel & Porcupine; Nebulon app. 38-Power Man app.; vs. Eel & Porcupine; "Elf with a gun" app. 39-Power Man app. 40-1st new Valkyrie (gold) costume; "Elf with a gun" app.; story continued in Defenders Annual #1 1 2 3 5 6 8
34-38 (30¢-c variants, limited distribution 4-8/76) 4 8 12 28 47 65
41-46: 41-Last Gerber-s/Sal Buscema-a. 42,43-Egg Head, Rhino, Solarr & Cobalt Man app.; Giffen-a; 43-1st Red Rajah; Power Man app. 44-Power Man & Hellcat app. 45-Power Man & Hellcat app. 46-Dr. Strange & Red Guardian leave; "Elf with a gun" app; vs. Scorpio 6.00
47-50-Moon Knight guest app. 47,48-Wonder Man app. 47-49-vs. Scorpio (Jacob Fury). 48-50-(Regular 30¢ editions). 50-Death Scorpio; SHIELD app. 6.00
48-52-(35c-c variants, limited distribution)(6-10/77) 7 14 21 48 89 130
51-60: 51,52-(Regular 30¢ editions). 51-Nighthawk vs. The Ringer. 52-Hulk vs. Sub-Mariner. 53-1st brief app. Lunatik (Lobo lookalike) created by Roger Slifer & Keith Giffen, six years before they create Lobo in Omega Men #3; 1st app. Sergie Krylov (The Presence). 54,55-vs. the Presence. 54-last Giffen-a. 55-Origin Red Guardian; Lunatik cameo. 56-Red Guardian leaves; Valkyrie vs. Lunatik. 57-Ms. Marvel (Carol Danvers) app. 58-60-Devil Slayer app. 6.00
61-vs. Lunatik; Spider-Man app. 5.00
62-"Defender for a day" issue; Jack of Hearts, Ms. Marvel (Carol Danvers), Hercules, Iron Man, White Tiger, Nova, Marvel Man (later Quasar), Son of Satan, Havok, Prowler, Paladin, Falcon, Torpedo, Black Goliath, Stingray, Polaris, Captain Ultra, Iron Fist, Captain Marvel (Mar-Vell), Tagak app. (all try to join Defenders) 5.00
63-93,97-99: 63-Various villains form their own Defenders team. 64-Villains defeated; the various new Defenders leave. 66-68-Defenders in Asgard. 66-Hulk returns. 68-Hela app. 69-Omegatron app. 70-vs. Lunatik. 71-Origin Lunatik; Dr. Strange returns. 72,73-Lunatik app. 73-Foolkiller app. 74-Nighthawk resigns as leader; Foolkiller app. 75-vs. Foolkiller. 76-Wasp, Omega the Unknown & Ruby Thursday app. 77-Origin Omega the Unknown; Moondragon & Wasp app. 78-Original Defenders return (Hulk, Dr. Strange & Namor; continue thru #101); Wasp, Yellowjacket & Moondragon app. 79,80-Mandrill app; Wasp & Yellowjacket app. 84-Atlantis vs. Wakanda; Namor vs. Black Panther. 85,86-Black Panther app. 87-Origin Hellcat retold. 90,91-vs. Mandrill; Daredevil app. 97,98-Devil Slayer & Man-Thing app. 98-Nighthawk leaves; Avengers app. 99-Mephisto app. 4.00
94-1st Gargoyle (Isaac Christians) 1 2 3 5 6 8
95,96: Ghost Rider app. 95-Dracula app. 4.00
100-(52-pgs.)-Hellcat (Patsy Walker) revealed as Satan's daughter; Silver Surfer app. 2 4 6 8 10 12
101-Silver Surfer app. 4.00
102-111,115-119-124: 104-Beast joins. 105-Son of Satan joins; Mr. Fantastic app. 106-Captain America app.; death of Nighthawk. 107-Daredevil & Captain America app. 109-Spider-Man app; Defenders app. next in Avengers Annual #11. 111-Overmind cameo. 120-122-Son of Satan-c/stories. 122-"Elf with a gun" returns; Silver Surfer & Iceman app. 123-"Elf with a Gun" app.; Moondragon cameo; 1st app. Cloud; Vision & Scarlet Witch app. 124-Origin of the "Elf with a gun" 4.00
112-114-Overmind & Squadron Supreme app. 4.00
125-(52 pgs)-Intro new Defenders (Angel, Beast, Iceman, Valkyrie, Gargoyle & Moondragon); Hulk, Dr. Strange, Namor & Silver Surfer resign; "Elf with a Gun" mystery resolved 6.00
126-149,151: 126-130-Secret Empire story. 129-New Mutants cameo (3/84, early x-over). 134-1st full app. Manslaughter. 139-Odin app. 140-New Moondragon costume. 145-Johnny Blaze (Ghost Rider) app. 147-1st app. Interloper; Sgt. Fury app. 151-Manslaughter app. 4.00
150-(52 pgs.)-Origin Cloud 5.00
152-(52 pgs.)-Continued from Secret Wars II #7; Beyonder app.; vs. The Dragon of the Moon; leads into X-Factor #1 6.00
Annual 1 (1976, 52 pgs-) Continued from Defenders #40; Power Man app.; vs. Nebulon, the Bozos and the Headmen 3 6 9 22 35 45
...: Marvel Feature No. 1 Facsimile Edition (7/19, $4.99) r/Marvel Feature #1 w/orig. ads 5.00

NOTE: ***Art Adams*** *c-142p.* ***Austin*** *a-53i; c-65i, 119i, 145i.* ***Frank Bolle*** *a-7i, 10i, 11i.* ***Buckler*** *c(p)-34, 38, 76, 77, 79-86, 90, 91.* ***J. Buscema*** *c-66.* ***Giffen*** *a-42-49p, 50, 51-54p.* ***Golden*** *a-53p, 54p; c-94, 96.* ***Guice*** *c-129.* ***G. Kane*** *c(p)-13, 16, 18, 19, 21-26, 31-33, 35-37, 40, 41, 52, 55.* ***Kirby*** *c-42-45.* ***Mooney*** *a-3i, 31-34i, 62i, 63i, 85i.* ***Nasser*** *c-88p.* ***Perez*** *c(p)-51, 53, 54.* ***Rogers*** *c-98.* ***Starlin*** *c-110.* ***Tuska*** *a-57p. Silver Surfer in No. 2, 3, 6, 8-11, 92, 98-101, 107, 112-115, 122-125.*

DEFENDERS, THE (Volume 2) (Continues in The Order)
Marvel Comics: Mar, 2001 - No. 12, Feb, 2002 ($2.99/$2.25)

	GD 2.0	VG 4.0	FN 6.0	VF 8.0	VF/NM 9.0	NM- 9.2

1-Busiek & Larsen-s/Larsen & Janson-a/c 3.00
2-11: 2-Two covers by Larsen & Art Adams; Valkyrie app. 4-Frenz-a 3.00
12-($3.50) 'Nuff Said issue; back-up-s Reis-a 4.00
...: From the Vault (9/11, $2.99) Previously unpublished story; Bagley-a 3.00

DEFENDERS, THE
Marvel Comics: Sept, 2005 - No. 5, Jan, 2006 ($2.99, limited series)

1-5-Giffen & DeMatteis-s/Maguire-a. 2-Dormammu app. 3.00
...: Indefensible HC (2006, $19.99, dust jacket) r/#1-5; Giffen & Maguire sketch page 20.00
...: Indefensible SC (2007, $13.99) r/#1-5; Giffen & Maguire sketch page 14.00

DEFENDERS, THE
Marvel Comics: Feb, 2012 - No. 12, Jan, 2013 ($3.99)

1-12: 1-Dr. Strange, Namor, Silver Surfer, Red She-Hulk, Iron Fist team; Dodson-a 4.00
...: Strange Heroes 1 (2/12, $4.99) Handbook-style profiles of team members and foes 5.00
...: The Coming of the Defenders 1 (2/12, $5.99) r/Marvel Feature #1-3; recolored-c of #1 6.00
...: Tournament of Heroes 1 (3/12, $5.99) r/Defenders #62-65 (1978); recolored-c of #62 6.00

DEFENDERS
Marvel Comics: Aug, 2017 - No. 10, Apr, 2018 ($4.99/$3.99)

1-($4.99) Luke Cage, Jessica Jones, Daredevil, Iron Fist team; Bendis-s/Marquez-a 5.00
2-10-($3.99) 3-Punisher app. 6-8-Deadpool app. 4.00

DEFENDERS OF DYNATRON CITY
Marvel Comics: Feb, 1992 - No. 6, July, 1992 ($1.25, limited series)

1-6-Lucasarts characters. 2-Origin 3.00

DEFENDERS OF THE EARTH (TV)
Marvel Comics (Star Comics): Jan, 1987 - No. 4, July, 1987

1-4: The Phantom, Mandrake The Magician, Flash Gordon begin. 3-Origin Phantom. 4-Origin Mandrake 4.00

DEFENDERS: THE BEST DEFENSE
Marvel Comics: Feb, 2019 ($4.99)

1-Doctor Strange, Immortal Hulk, Siler Surfer, Namor app.; Ewing-s/Bennett-a 5.00

DEFEX
Devil's Due Publ.: Oct, 2004 - No. 6, Apr, 2005 ($2.95)

1-6: 1-Wolfman-s/Caselli-a. 6-Pérez-c 3.00

DEFIANCE
Image Comics: Feb, 2002 - No. 8, Jun, 2003 ($2.95)

Preview Edition (12/01) 3.00
1-8-Barré-s/Kang & Suh-a 3.00

DEFINITIVE DIRECTORY OF THE DC UNIVERSE, THE (See Who's Who...)

DEJAH OF MARS (Warlord of Mars)
Dynamite Entertainment: 2014 - No. 4, 2014 ($3.99)

1-4-Rahner-s/Morales-a; multiple covers on each 4.00

DEJAH THORIS (Warlord of Mars)
Dynamite Entertainment: 2016 - No. 6, 2016 ($3.99)

1-6-Barbarie-s/Manna-a; multiple covers 4.00

DEJAH THORIS AND THE GREEN MEN OF MARS (Warlord of Mars)
Dynamite Entertainment: 2013 - No. 12, 2014 ($3.99)

1-12: 1-8-Rahner-s/Antonio-a; multiple covers on each. 9-12-Morales-a 4.00

DEJAH THORIS AND THE WHITE APES OF MARS (Warlord of Mars)
Dynamite Entertainment: 2012 - No. 3, 2012 ($3.99)

1-3-Rahner-s/Antonio-a; 2 covers by Peterson & Garza 4.00

DEJAH THORIS, VOLUME 2
Dynamite Entertainment: No. 0, 2018 - No. 10, 2018 ($3.99)

0-(25¢-c) Amy Chu-s/Pasquale Qualano-a; multiple covers 3.00
1-10-($3.99) Chu-s/Qualano-a; multiple covers 4.00

DEJAH THORIS, VOLUME 3
Dynamite Entertainment: 2019 - Present ($3.99)

1-10: 1-6-Dan Abnett-s/Vasco Georgiev-a; multiple covers on each. 7-10-Piriz-a 4.00

DELECTA OF THE PLANETS (See Don Fortune & Fawcett Miniatures)

DELETE
1First Comics: 2016 - No. 4, 2016 ($4.99, limited series)

1-4-Palmiotti & Gray-s/Timms-a/Conner-c 5.00

DELICATE CREATURES
Image Comics (Top Cow): 2001 ($16.95, hardcover with dust jacket)

nn-Fairy tale storybook; J. Michael Straczynski-s; Michael Zulli-a 17.00

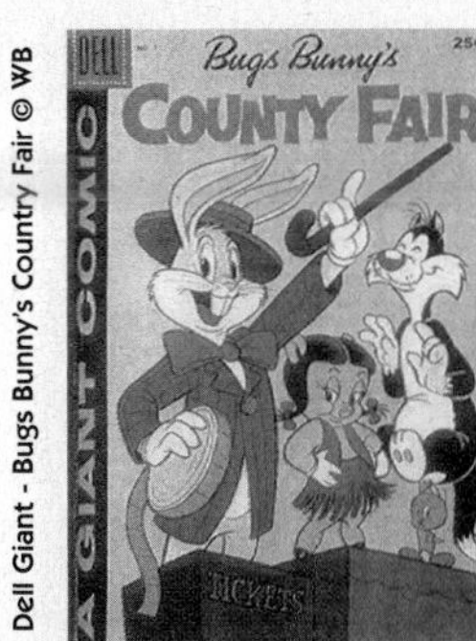

Dell Giant - Bugs Bunny's Country Fair © WB

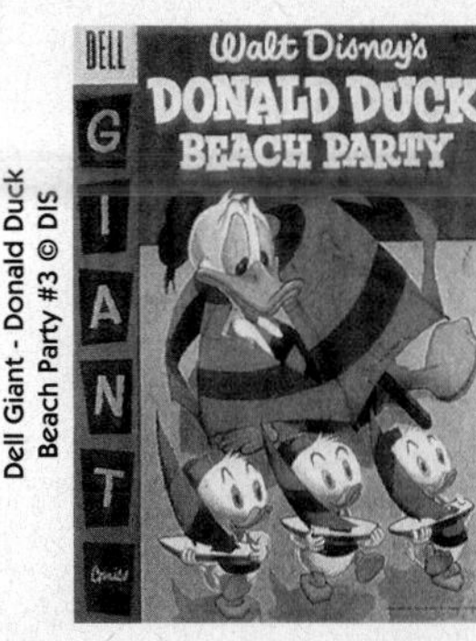

Dell Giant - Donald Duck Beach Party #3 © DIS

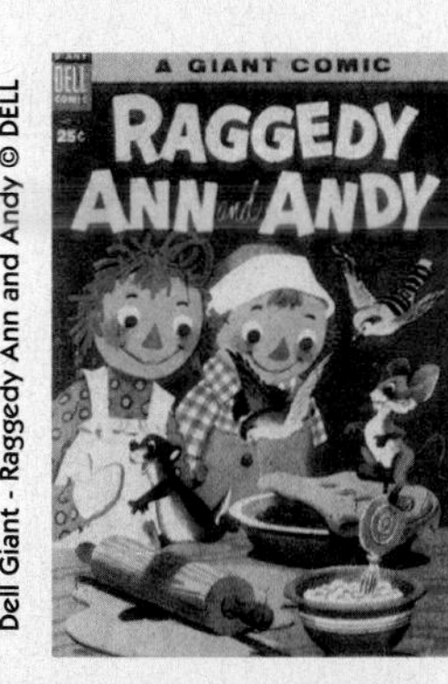

Dell Giant - Raggedy Ann and Andy © DELL

	GD	VG	FN	VF	VF/NM	NM-
	2.0	4.0	6.0	8.0	9.0	9.2

DELINQUENTS
Valiant Entertainment: Aug, 2014 - No. 4, Nov, 2014 ($3.99, limited series)
1-4-Quantum & Woody meet Archer & Armstrong; Asmus & Van Lente-s/Kano-a 4.00

DELIRIUM'S PARTY: A LITTLE ENDLESS STORYBOOK (Characters from The Sandman titles and The Little Endless Storybook)
DC Comics: 2011 ($14.99, hardcover, one-shot)
HC-Jill Thompson-s/painted-a/c; Little Delirium throws a party; watercolor page process 15.00

DELLA VISION (...The Television Queen) (Patty Powers #4 on)
Atlas Comics: April, 1955 - No. 3, Aug, 1955
1-Al Hartley-c 68 136 204 435 743 1050
2,3 40 80 120 246 411 575

DELLEC
Aspen MLT.: Aug, 2009 - No. 6, Oct, 2011 ($2.50)
1-6-Gunnell-a/c 3.00

DELLEC VOLUME 2
Aspen MLT.: Sept, 2018 - No. 4, Jan, 2019 ($3.99)
1-4-Frank Mastromauro & Vince Hernandez-s 4.00
... 2018 Primer 1 (9/18, 25¢) New short story and recap of Volume 1 3.00

DELL GIANT COMICS
Dell Publishing began to release square bound comics in 1949 with a 132-page issue called Christmas Parade #1. The covers were of a heavier stock to accommodate the increased number of pages. The books proved profitable at 25 cents, but the average number of pages was quickly reduced to 100. Ten years later they were converted to a numbering system similar to the Four Color Comics, for greater ease in distribution and the page counts cut back to mostly 84 pages. The label "Dell Giant" began to appear on the covers in 1954. Because of the size of the books and the heavier, less pliant cover stock, they are rarely found in high grade condition, and with the exception of a small quantity of copies released from Western Publishing's warehouse–are almost never found in near mint.

Abraham Lincoln Life Story 1(3/58) 8 16 24 56 108 160
Bugs Bunny Christmas Funnies 1(11/50, 116pp) 22 44 66 176 303 430
...Christmas Funnies 2(11/51, 116pp) 13 26 39 104 180 225
...Christmas Funnies 3-5(11/52-11/54,)-Becomes Christmas Party #6
10 20 30 80 140 200
...Christmas Funnies 7-9(12/56-12/58) 9 18 27 72 124 175
...Christmas Party 6(11/55)-Formerly Bugs Bunny Christmas Funnies
9 18 27 72 124 175
...County Fair 1(9/57) 11 22 33 88 149 210
...Halloween Parade 1(10/53) 12 24 36 96 171 245
...Halloween Parade 2(10/54)-Trick 'N' Treat Halloween Fun #3 on
10 20 30 80 135 190
...Trick 'N' Treat Halloween Fun 3,4(10/55-10/56)-Formerly Halloween Parade #2
9 18 27 72 129 185
...Vacation Funnies 1(7/51, 112pp) 20 40 60 160 280 400
...Vacation Funnies 2('52) 13 26 39 104 180 255
...Vacation Funnies 3-5('53-'55) 10 20 30 80 138 195
...Vacation Funnies 6,7,9('56-'59) 9 18 27 72 124 175
...Vacation Funnies 8('58) 1st app. Beep Beep the Road Runner, Wile E. Coyote (1st meeting), Mathilda (Mrs. Beep Beep) and their 3 children who hatch from eggs; one month before Four Color #918 11 22 33 88 157 225
Cadet Gray of West Point 1(4/58)-Williamson-a, 10pgs.; Buscema-a; photo-c
8 16 24 64 107 150
Christmas In Disneyland 1(12/57)-Barks-a, 18 pgs. 25 50 75 200 350 500
Christmas Parade 1(11/49)(132 pgs.)(1st Dell Giant)-Donald Duck (25 pgs. by Barks, r-in G.K. Christmas Parade #5); Mickey Mouse & other film oriented stories; Cinderella (prior to movie), 7 Dwarfs, Bambi & Thumper, So Dear To My Heart, Flying Mouse, Dumbo, Cookieland & others 65 130 195 520 910 1300
Christmas Parade 2('50)-Donald Duck (132 pgs.)(25 pgs. by Barks, r-in Gold Key's Christmas Parade #6). Mickey, Pluto, Chip & Dale, etc. Contents shift to a holiday expansion of W.D. C&S type format 43 86 129 344 597 850
Christmas Parade 3-7('51-'55, #3-116pgs; #4-7, 100 pgs.)
14 28 42 112 196 280
Christmas Parade 8(12/56)-Barks-a, 8 pgs. 22 44 66 176 306 435
Christmas Parade 9(12/58)-Barks-a, 20 pgs. 25 50 75 200 350 500
Christmas Treasury, A 1(11/54) 10 20 30 80 135 190
Davy Crockett, King Of The Wild Frontier 1(9/55)-Fess Parker photo-c; Marsh-a
19 38 57 152 269 385
Disneyland Birthday Party 1(10/58)-Barks-a, 16 pgs. r-by Gladstone
25 50 75 200 350 500
Donald and Mickey In Disneyland 1(5/58) 11 22 33 88 157 225
Donald Duck Beach Party 1(7/54)-Has an Uncle Scrooge story (not by Barks) that prefigures the later rivalry with Flintheart Glomgold and tells of Scrooge's wild rivalry with another millionaire 17 34 51 136 233 330
...Beach Party 2(1955)-Lady & Tramp 11 22 33 88 157 225
...Beach Party 3-5(1956-58) 11 22 33 88 152 215
...Beach Party 6(8/59, 84pp)-Stapled 8 16 24 64 115 165
Donald Duck Fun Book 1,2 (1953 & 10/54)-Games, puzzles, comics & cut-outs (very rare in unused condition)(most copies commonly have defaced interior pgs.)
63 126 189 504 877 1250
Donald Duck In Disneyland 1(9/55)-1st Disneyland Dell Giant
15 30 45 120 210 300
Golden West Rodeo Treasury 1(10/57) 10 20 30 80 135 190
Huey, Dewey and Louie Back To School 1(9/58) 9 18 27 72 126 180
Lady and The Tramp 1(6/55) 17 34 51 136 238 340
Life Stories of American Presidents 1(11/57)-Buscema-a
8 16 24 64 107 150
Lone Ranger Golden West 3(8/55)-Formerly Lone Ranger Western Treasury
18 36 54 144 255 365
Lone Ranger Movie Story nn(3/56)-Origin Lone Ranger in text; Clayton Moore photo-c
36 72 108 288 507 725
...Western Treasury 1(9/53)-Origin Lone Ranger, Silver, & Tonto; painted cover
23 46 69 184 325 465
...Western Treasury 2(8/54)-Becomes Lone Ranger Golden West #3
18 36 54 144 255 365
Marge's Little Lulu & Alvin Story Telling Time 1(3/59)-r/#2,5,3,11,30,10,21,17,8, 14,16; Stanley-a 14 28 42 112 196 280
...& Her Friends 4(3/56)-Tripp-a 14 28 42 112 191 270
...& Her Special Friends 3(3/55)-Tripp-a 15 30 45 120 210 300
...& Tubby At Summer Camp 5,2: 5(10/57)-Tripp-a. 2(10/58)-Tripp-a
13 26 39 104 182 260
...& Tubby Halloween Fun 6,2: 6(10/57)-Tripp-a. 2(10/58)-Tripp-a
13 26 39 104 182 260
...& Tubby In Alaska 1(7/59)-Tripp-a 13 26 39 104 177 250
...On Vacation 1(7/54)-r/4C-110,14,4C-146,5,4C-97,4,4C-158,3,1;Stanley-a
25 50 75 200 350 500
...& Tubby Annual 1(3/53)-r/4C-165,4C-74,4C-146,4C-97,4C-158, 4C-139, 4C-131; Stanley-a (1st Lulu Dell Giant) 30 60 90 240 420 600
...& Tubby Annual 2('54)-r/4C-139,6,4C-115,4C-74,5,4C-97,3,4C-146,18; Stanley-a
25 50 75 200 350 500
Marge's Tubby & His Clubhouse Pals 1(10/56)-1st app. Gran'pa Feeb;1st app. Janie; written by Stanley; Tripp-a 15 30 45 120 210 300
Mickey Mouse Almanac 1(12/57)-Barks-a, 8pgs. 27 54 81 216 378 540
...Birthday Party 1(9/53)-r/entire 48pgs. of Gottfredson's "Mickey Mouse in Love Trouble" from WDC&S 36-39. Quality equal to original. Also reprints one story each from Four Color 27, 79, & 181 plus 6 panels of highlights in the career of Mickey Mouse
31 62 93 248 434 620
...Club Parade 1(12/55)-r/4-Color 16 with some death trap scenes redrawn by Paul Murry & recolored with night turned into day; quality less than original
22 44 66 176 308 440
...In Fantasy Land 1(5/57) 13 26 39 104 180 255
...In Frontier Land 1(5/56)-Mickey Mouse Club iss. 13 26 39 104 180 255
...Summer Fun 1(8/58)-Mobile cut-outs on back-c; becomes Summer Fun with #2; Canadian version exists with 30¢-c price 13 26 39 104 180 255
Moses & The Ten Commandments 1(8/57)-Not based on movie; Dell's adaptation; Sekowsky-a; variant version has "Gods of Egypt" comic back-c 8 16 24 64 107 150
Nancy & Sluggo Travel Time 1(9/58) 8 16 24 64 115 165
Peter Pan Treasure Chest 1(1/53, 212pp)-Disney; contains 54-page movie adaptation & other Peter Pan stories; plus Donald & Mickey stories w/P. Pan; a 32-page retelling of "D. Duck Finds Pirate Gold" with yellow beak, called "Capt. Hook & the Buried Treasure"
140 280 420 1120 1960 2800
Picnic Party 6,7(7/55-6/56)(Formerly Vacation Parade)-Uncle Scrooge, Mickey & Donald
12 24 36 96 166 235
Picnic Party 8(7/57)-Barks-a, 6pgs 21 42 63 168 289 410
Pogo Parade 1(9/53)-Kelly-a(r-/Pogo from Animal Comics in this order: #11,13,21,14,27,16,23,9,18,15,17) 25 50 75 200 350 500
Raggedy Ann & Andy 1(2/55) 16 32 48 128 224 320
Santa Claus Funnies 1(11/52)-Dan Noonan -A Christmas Carol adaptation
10 20 30 80 140 200
Silly Symphonies 1(9/52)-Redrawing of Gotfredson's Mickey Mouse strip of "The Brave Little Tailor;" 2 Good Housekeeping pages (from 1943); Lady and the Two Siamese Cats, three years before "Lady & the Tramp;" a retelling of Donald Duck's first app. in "The Wise Little Hen" & other stories based on 1930's Silly Symphony cartoons
34 68 102 272 474 675
Silly Symphonies 2(9/53)-M. Mouse in "The Sorcerer's Apprentice", 2 Good Housekeeping pages (from 1944); The Pelican & the Snipe, Elmer Elephant, Peculiar Penguins, Little Hiawatha, & others 24 48 72 192 339 485
Silly Symphonies 3(2/54)-r/Mickey & The Beanstalk (4-Color #157, 39pgs.), Little Minnehaha,

Dell Giant - Vacation Parade #1 © DIS

Dell Giant #31 © H-B

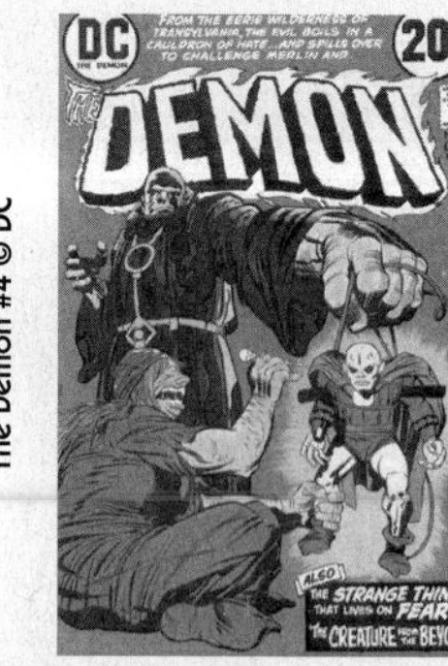

The Demon #4 © DC

GD VG FN VF VF/NM NM-
2.0 4.0 6.0 8.0 9.0 9.2

GD VG FN VF VF/NM NM-
2.0 4.0 6.0 8.0 9.0 9.2

Pablo, The Flying Gauchito, Pluto, & Bongo, & 2 Good Housekeeping pages (1944)
20 40 60 160 275 390
Silly Symphonies 4(8/54)-r/Dumbo (4-Color 234), Morris The Midget Moose, The Country Cousin, Bongo, & Clara Cluck 20 40 60 160 275 390
Silly Symphonies 5-8: 5(2/55)-r/Cinderella (4-Color 272), Bucky Bug, Pluto, Little Hiawatha, The 7 Dwarfs & Dumbo, Pinocchio. 6(8/55)-r/Pinocchio (WDC&S 63), The 7 Dwarfs & Thumper (WDC&S 45), M. Mouse "Adventures With Robin Hood" (40 pgs.), Johnny Appleseed, Pluto & Peter Pan, & Bucky Bug; Cut-out on back-c. 7(2/57)-r/Reluctant Dragon, Ugly Duckling, M. Mouse & Peter Pan, Jiminy Cricket, Peter & The Wolf, Brer Rabbit, Bucky Bug; Cut-out on back-c. 8(2/58)-r/Thumper Meets The 7 Dwarfs (4-Color #19), Jiminy Cricket, Niok, Brer Rabbit; Cut-out on back-c
16 32 48 128 224 320
Silly Symphonies 9(2/59)-r/Paul Bunyan, Humphrey Bear, Jiminy Cricket, The Social Lion, Goliath II; cut-out on back-c 15 30 45 120 210 300
Sleeping Beauty 1(4/59) 26 52 78 208 367 525
Summer Fun 2(8/59, 84pp, stapled binding)(Formerly Mickey Mouse...)-Barks-a(2), 24 pgs.
24 48 72 192 336 480
Tarzan's Jungle Annual 1(8/52)-Lex Barker photo on-c of #1,2
16 32 48 128 219 310
...Annual 2(8/53) 11 22 33 88 152 215
...Annual 3-7('54-9/58)(two No. 5s)-Manning-a-No. 3,5-7; Marsh-a in No. 1-7 plus painted-c 1-7 9 18 27 72 124 175
Tom And Jerry Back To School 1(9/56) 2 different back-c, variant has "Apple for the Teacher" cut-out 12 24 36 96 168 240
...Picnic Time 1(7/58) 10 20 30 80 135 190
...Summer Fun 1(7/54)-Droopy written by Barks 15 30 45 120 205 290
...Summer Fun 2-4(7/55-7/57) 8 16 24 64 107 150
...Toy Fair 1(6/58) 9 18 27 72 126 180
...Winter Carnival 1(12/52)-Droopy written by Barks 20 40 60 160 280 400
...Winter Carnival 2(12/53)-Droopy written by Barks 16 32 48 128 224 320
...Winter Fun 3(12/54) 8 16 24 64 115 165
...Winter Fun 4-7(12/55-11/58) 7 14 21 56 101 145
Treasury of Dogs, A 1(10/56) 8 16 24 64 107 150
Treasury of Horses, A (9/55) 8 16 24 64 107 150
Uncle Scrooge Goes To Disneyland 1(8/57p)-Barks-a, 20 pgs. r-by Gladstone; 2 different back-c; variant shows 6 snapshots of Scrooge 26 52 78 208 367 525
Vacation In Disneyland 1(8/58) 11 22 33 88 157 225
Vacation Parade 1(7/50, 132pp)-Donald Duck & Mickey Mouse; Barks-a, 55 pgs.
98 196 294 784 1367 1950
Vacation Parade 2(7/51,116pp) 26 52 78 208 367 525
Vacation Parade 3-5(7/52-7/54)-Becomes Picnic Party No. 6 on. #4-Robin Hood Advs.
14 28 42 112 194 275
Western Roundup 1(6/52)-Photo-c; Gene Autry, Roy Rogers, Johnny Mack Brown, Rex Allen, & Bill Elliott begin; photo back-c begin, end No. 14,16,18
25 50 75 200 350 500
Western Roundup 2(2/53)-Photo-c 14 28 42 112 196 280
Western Roundup 3-5(7-9/53 - 1-3/54)-Photo-c 11 22 33 88 157 225
Western Roundup 6-10(4-6/54 - 4-6/55)-Photo-c 11 22 33 88 149 210
Western Roundup 11-17,25: 11-17-Photo-c; 11-13,16,17-Manning-a. 11-Flying A's Range Rider, Dale Evans begin 9 18 27 72 129 185
Western Roundup 18-Toth-a; last photo-c; Gene Autry ends
11 22 33 88 149 210
Western Roundup 19-24-Manning-a. 19-Buffalo Bill Jr. begins (7-9/57; early app.). 19,20,22-Toth-a. 21-Rex Allen, Johnny Mack Brown end. 22-Jace Pearson's Texas Rangers, Rin Tin Tin, Tales of Wells Fargo (2nd app., 4-6/58) & Wagon Train (2nd app.) begin 9 18 27 72 129 185
Woody Woodpecker Back To School 1(10/52) 10 20 30 80 140 200
...Back To School 2-4,6('53-10/57)-County Fair No. 5 8 16 24 64 112 160
...County Fair 5(9/56)-Formerly Back To School 8 16 24 64 112 160
...County Fair 2(11/58) 7 14 21 56 101 145

DELL GIANTS (Consecutive numbering)
Dell Publishing Co.: No. 21, Sept, 1959 - No. 55, Sept, 1961 (Most 84 pgs., 25¢)

21-(#1)-M.G.M.'s Tom & Jerry Picnic Time (84pp, stapled binding)-Painted-c
11 22 33 88 157 225
22-Huey, Dewey & Louie Back to School (Disney; 10/59, 84pp, square binding begins)
9 18 27 72 129 185
23-Marge's Little Lulu & Tubby Halloween Fun (10/59)-Tripp-a
12 24 36 96 168 240
24-Woody Woodpecker's Family Fun (11/59)(Walter Lantz)
8 16 24 64 112 160
25-Tarzan's Jungle World(11/59)-Marsh-a; painted-c 11 22 33 88 152 215
26-Christmas Parade(Disney; 12/59)-Barks-a, 16pgs.; Barks draws himself on wanted poster on pg. 13 21 42 63 168 289 410
27-Walt Disney's Man in Space (10/59) r-/4-Color 716,866, & 954 (100 pgs., 35¢)(TV)
9 18 27 72 129 185
28-Bugs Bunny's Winter Fun (2/60) 9 18 27 72 126 180
29-Marge's Little Lulu & Tubby in Hawaii (4/60)-Tripp-a
12 24 36 96 166 235
30-Disneyland USA(Disney; 6/60) 9 18 27 72 124 175
31-Huckleberry Hound Summer Fun (7/60)(TV)(HannaBarbera)-Yogi Bear & Pixie & Dixie app. 12 24 36 96 173 250
32-Bugs Bunny Beach Party 7 14 21 56 101 145
33-Daisy Duck & Uncle Scrooge Picnic Time (Disney; 9/60)
9 18 27 72 124 175
34-Nancy & Sluggo Summer Camp (8/60) 7 14 21 56 101 145
35-Huey, Dewey & Louie Back to School (Disney; 10/60)-1st app. Daisy Duck's Nieces, April, May & June 12 24 36 96 163 230
36-Marge's Little Lulu & Witch Hazel Halloween Fun (10/60)-Tripp-a
11 22 33 88 157 225
37-Tarzan, King of the Jungle (11/60)-Marsh-a; painted-c
9 18 27 72 129 185
38-Uncle Donald & His Nephews Family Fun (Disney; 11/60)-Cover painting based on a pencil sketch by Barks 12 24 36 96 173 250
39-Walt Disney's Merry Christmas (Disney; 12/60)-Cover painting based on a pencil sketch by Barks 12 24 36 96 173 250
40-Woody Woodpecker Christmas Parade (12/60)(Walter Lantz)
6 12 18 48 87 125
41-Yogi Bear's Winter Sports (12/60)(TV)(Hanna-Barbera)-Huckleberry Hound, Pixie & Dixie, Augie Doggie app. 12 24 36 96 173 250
42-Marge's Little Lulu & Tubby in Australia (4/61) 12 24 36 96 166 235
43-Mighty Mouse in Outer Space (5/61) 18 36 54 144 252 360
44-Around the World with Huckleberry and His Friends (7/61)(TV)(Hanna-Barbera)-Yogi Bear, Pixie & Dixie, Quick Draw McGraw, Augie Doggie app.; 1st app. Yakky Doodle
13 26 39 104 182 260
45-Nancy & Sluggo Summer Camp (8/61) 7 14 21 56 96 135
46-Bugs Bunny Beach Party (8/61) 7 14 21 56 96 135
47-Mickey & Donald in Vacationland (Disney; 8/61) 8 16 24 64 115 165
48-The Flintstones (No. 1)(Bedrock Bedlam)(7/61)(TV)(Hanna-Barbera) 1st app. in comics 25 50 75 200 350 500
49-Huey, Dewey & Louie Back to School (Disney; 9/61)
9 18 27 72 124 175
50-Marge's Little Lulu & Witch Hazel Trick 'N' Treat (10/61)
11 22 33 88 157 225
51-Tarzan, King of the Jungle by Jesse Marsh (11/61)-Painted-c
8 16 24 64 110 155
52-Uncle Donald & His Nephews Dude Ranch (Disney; 11/61)
8 16 24 64 115 165
53-Donald Duck Merry Christmas (Disney; 12/61) 8 16 24 64 112 160
54-Woody Woodpecker's Christmas Party (12/61)-Issued after No. 55
7 14 21 56 98 140
55-Daisy Duck & Uncle Scrooge Showboat (Disney; 9/61)
8 16 24 64 117 170

NOTE: All issues printed with & without ad on back cover.

DELL JUNIOR TREASURY
Dell Publishing Co.: June, 1955 - No. 10, Oct, 1957 (15¢) (All painted-c)

1-Alice in Wonderland; r/4-Color #331 (52 pgs.) 8 16 24 54 102 150
2-Aladdin & the Wonderful Lamp 6 12 18 41 76 110
3-Gulliver's Travels (1/56) 6 12 18 37 66 95
4-Adventures of Mr. Frog & Miss Mouse 6 12 18 38 69 100
5-The Wizard of Oz (7/56) 6 12 18 41 76 110
6-10: 6-Heidi (10/56). 7-Santa and the Angel. 8-Raggedy Ann and the Camel with the Wrinkled Knees. 9-Clementina the Flying Pig. 10-Adventures of Tom Sawyer
6 12 18 37 66 95

DELTA 13
IDW Publishing: May, 2018 - No. 4, Aug, 2018 ($3.99, limited series)

1-4-Steve Niles-s/Nat Jones-a 4.00

DEMOLITION MAN
DC Comics: Nov, 1993 - No. 4, Feb, 1994 ($1.75, limited series)

1-4-Movie adaptation 4.00

DEMON, THE (See Detective Comics No. 482-485)
National Periodical Publications: Aug-Sept, 1972 - V3#16, Jan, 1974

1-Origin; Kirby-s/c/a in all; 1st Morgaine Le Fey 13 26 39 89 195 300
2-5 4 8 12 27 44 60
6-16: 7-1st app. Klarion the Witch Boy 3 6 9 19 30 40

DEMON, THE (1st limited series)(Also see Cosmic Odyssey #2)
DC Comics: Nov, 1986 - No. 4, Feb, 1987 (75¢, limited series)(#2 has #4 of 4 on-c)

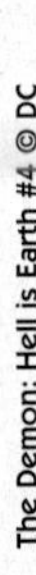
The Demon: Hell is Earth #4 © DC

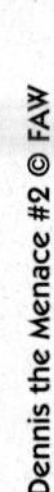
Dennis the Menace #2 © FAW

Dennis the Menace Bonus Magazine #86 © FAW

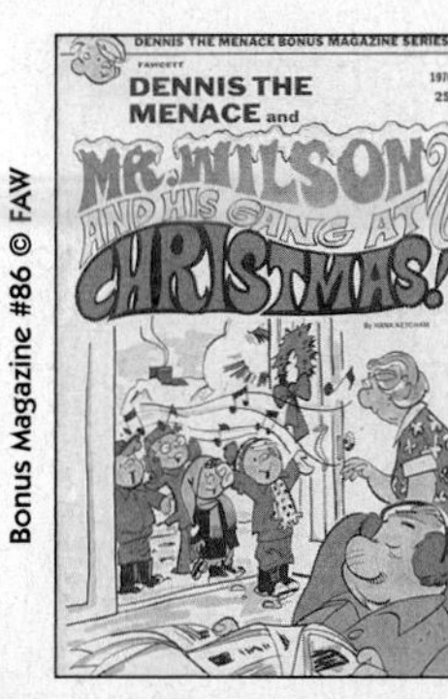

	GD 2.0	VG 4.0	FN 6.0	VF 8.0	VF/NM 9.0	NM- 9.2

1-4: Matt Wagner-a(p) & scripts in all. 4-Demon & Jason Blood become separate entities 4.00

DEMON, THE (2nd Series)
DC Comics: July, 1990 - No. 58, May, 1995 ($1.50/$1.75/$1.95)

1-Grant scripts begin, ends #39: 1-4-Painted-c 5.00
2-18,20-27,29-39,41,42: 3,8-Batman app. (cameo #4). 12-Bisley painted-c. 12-15,21-Lobo app. (1 pg. cameo #11). 23-Robin app. 29-Superman app. 31,33-39-Lobo app. 3.00
19-($2.50, 44 pgs.)-Lobo poster stapled inside 5.00
28,40: 28-Superman-c/story; begin $1.75-c. 40-Garth Ennis scripts begin 4.00
43-45-Hitman app. 1 2 3 5 7 10
46-48 Return of The Haunted Tank-c/s. 48-Begin $1.95-c. 5.00
49,51,0-(10/94),55-58: 51-(9/94) 3.00
50 ($2.95, 52 pgs.) 4.00
52-54-Hitman-s 5.00
Annual 1 (1992, $3.00, 68 pgs.)-Eclipso-c/story 5.00
Annual 2 (1993, $3.50, 68 pgs.)-1st app. of Hitman 3 6 9 18 27 36
NOTE: *Alan Grant scripts in #1-16, 20, 21, 23-25, 30-39, Annual 1.* ***Wagner*** *a/scripts-22.*

DEMON DREAMS
Pacific Comics: Feb, 1984 - No. 2, May, 1984

1,2-Mostly r-/Heavy Metal 3.00

DEMON: DRIVEN OUT
DC Comics: Nov, 2003 - No. 6, Apr, 2004 ($2.50, limited series)

1-6-Dysart-s/Mhan-a 3.00

DEMON, THE: HELL IS EARTH (Etrigan)
DC Comics: Jan, 2018 - No. 6, Jun, 2018 ($2.99, limited series)

1-6-Andrew Constant-s/Brad Walker-a; Xanadu app. 3.00

DEMON-HUNTER (See Marvel Spotlight #33)
Seaboard Periodicals (Atlas): Sept, 1975

1-Origin/1st app. Demon-Hunter; Buckler-c/a 3 6 9 14 20 25

DEMON KNIGHT: A GRIMJACK GRAPHIC NOVEL
First Publishing: 1990 ($8.95, 52 pgs.)

nn-Flint Henry-a 9.00

DEMON KNIGHTS (New DC 52) (Set in the Dark Ages)
DC Comics: Nov, 2011 - No. 23, Oct, 2013 ($2.99)

1-23: 1-Cornell-s/Neves-a/Daniel-c; Etrigan, Madame Xanadu & The Shining Knight app. 3.00
#0 (11/12, $2.99) Origin of Etrigan The Demon; Merlin app.; Cornell-s/Chang-a 3.00

DENNIS THE MENACE (TV with 1959 issues) (Becomes ...Fun Fest Series; See The Best of... & The Very Best of...)(...Fun Fest on-c only to #156-166)
Standard Comics/Pines No.15-31/Hallden (Fawcett) No.32 on: 8/53 - #14, 1/56; #15, 3/56 - #31, 11/58; #32, 1/59 - #166, 11/79

1-1st app. Dennis, Mr. & Mrs. Wilson, Ruff & Dennis' mom & dad; Wiseman-a, written by Fred Toole-most issues 271 542 813 1734 2967 4200
2 65 130 195 416 708 1000
3-5 40 80 120 244 402 560
6-10: 8-Last pre-code issue 32 64 96 192 314 435
11-20 21 42 63 122 199 275
21,23-30 14 28 42 76 108 140
22-1st app. Margaret w/blonde hair 16 32 48 94 147 200
31-1st app. Joey 16 32 48 98 154 210
32-38,40(1/60): 37-A-Bomb blast panel 9 18 27 52 69 85
39-1st app. Gina (11/59) 12 24 36 67 94 120
41-60(7/62) 4 8 12 22 34 45
61-80(9/65),100(1/69) 3 6 9 14 20 25
81-99 2 4 6 11 16 20
101-117: 102-Last 12¢ issue 2 4 6 9 12 15
118(1/72)-131 (All 52 pages) 2 4 6 10 14 18
132(1/74)-142,144-160 1 2 3 5 7 9
143(3/76) Olympic-c/s; low print 2 4 6 10 14 18
161-166 1 3 4 6 8 10
NOTE: ***Wiseman*** *c/a-1-46, 53, 68, 69.*

DENNIS THE MENACE (Giants) (No. 1 titled Giant Vacation Special; becomes Dennis the Menace Bonus Magazine No. 76 on)
(#1-8,18,23,25,30,38: 100 pgs.; rest to #41: 84 pgs.; #42-75: 68 pgs.)
Standard/Pines/Hallden(Fawcett): Summer, 1955 - No. 75, Dec, 1969

nn-Giant Vacation Special(Summ/55-Standard) 18 36 54 109 172 235
nn-Christmas issue (Winter '55) 15 30 45 94 147 200
2-Giant Vacation Special (Summer '56-Pines) 14 28 42 82 121 160
3-Giant Christmas issue (Winter '56-Pines) 13 26 39 74 105 135
4-Giant Vacation Special (Summer '57-Pines) 12 24 36 69 97 125
5-Giant Christmas issue (Winter '57-Pines) 12 24 36 69 97 125
6-In Hawaii (Giant Vacation Special)(Summer '58-Pines) 11 22 33 64 90 115
6-In Hawaii (Summer '59-Hallden)-2nd printing; says 3rd large printing on-c
6-In Hawaii (Summer '60)-3rd printing; says 4th large printing on-c
6-In Hawaii (Summer '62)-4th printing; says 5th large printing on-c each.... 8 16 24 44 57 70
6-Giant Christmas issue (Winter '58) 11 22 33 64 90 115
7-In Hollywood (Winter '59-Hallden) 5 10 15 31 53 75
7-In Hollywood (Summer '61)-2nd printing 3 6 9 20 31 42
8-In Mexico (Winter '60, 100 pgs.-Hallden/Fawcett) 5 10 15 31 53 75
8-In Mexico (Summer '62, 2nd printing) 3 6 9 20 31 42
9-Goes to Camp (Summer '61, 84 pgs.)-1st CCA approved issue 5 10 15 30 50 70
9-Goes to Camp (Summer '62)-2nd printing 3 6 9 20 31 42
10-12: 10-X-Mas issue (Winter '61), 11-Giant Christmas issue (Winter '62), 12-Triple Feature (Winter '62) 5 10 15 33 57 80
13-17: 13-Best of Dennis the Menace (Spring '63)-Reprints, 14-And His Dog Ruff (Summer '63), 15-In Washington, D.C. (Summer '63), 16-Goes to Camp (Summer '63)-Reprints No. 9, 17-& His Pal Joey (Winter '63) 4 8 12 23 37 50
18-In Hawaii (Reprints No. 6) 3 6 9 19 30 40
19-Giant Christmas issue (Winter '63) 4 8 12 23 37 50
20-Spring Special (Spring '64) 4 8 12 23 37 50
21-40 (Summer '66): 30-r/#6. #35-Xmas spec.Wint,'65 3 6 9 17 26 35
41-60 (Fall '68) 3 6 9 14 19 24
61-75 (12/69): 68-Partial-r/#6 2 4 6 11 16 20
NOTE: ***Wiseman*** *c/a-1-8, 12, 14, 15, 17, 20, 22, 27, 28, 31, 35, 36, 41, 49.*

DENNIS THE MENACE
Marvel Comics Group: Nov, 1981 - No. 13, Nov, 1982

1-New-a 2 4 6 9 12 15
2-13: 2-New art. 3-Part-r. 4,5-r. 5-X-Mas-c & issue, 7-Spider Kid-c/sty 1 2 3 4 5 7
NOTE: ***Hank Ketcham*** *c-most; a-3, 12.* ***Wiseman*** *a-4, 5.*

DENNIS THE MENACE AND HIS DOG RUFF
Hallden/Fawcett: Summer, 1961

1-Wiseman-c/a 6 12 18 37 66 95

DENNIS THE MENACE AND HIS FRIENDS
Fawcett Publ.: 1969; No. 5, Jan, 1970 - No. 46, April, 1980 (All reprints)

Dennis the Menace & Joey No. 2 (7/69) 2 4 6 13 18 22
Dennis the Menace & Ruff No. 2 (9/69) 2 4 6 13 18 22
Dennis the Menace & Mr. Wilson No. 1 (10/69) 3 6 9 15 22 28
Dennis & Margaret No. 1 (Winter '69) 3 6 9 15 22 28
5-12: 5-Dennis the Menace & Margaret. 6-...& Joey. 7-...& Ruff. 8-...& Mr. Wilson 2 4 6 8 11 14
13-21-(52 pg Giants): 13-(1/72). 21-(1/74) 2 4 6 10 14 18
22-37 1 3 4 6 8 10
38-46 (Digest size, 148 pgs., 4/78, 95¢) 2 4 6 8 11 14
NOTE: *Titles rotate every four issues, beginning with No. 5. Joey issues: #2(7/69),6,10,14,18,22,26,30,34. Ruff issues: #2(9/69), 7,11,15,19,23,27,31,35. Mr. Wilson issues: #1(10/69),8,12,16,20,24,28,32,36. Margaret issues: #1 (Wint./69),5,9,13,17,21,25,29,33,37.*

DENNIS THE MENACE AND HIS PAL JOEY
Fawcett Publ.: Summer, 1961 (10¢) (See Dennis the Menace Giants No. 45)

1-Wiseman-c/a 6 12 18 37 66 95

DENNIS THE MENACE AND THE BIBLE KIDS
Word Books: 1977 (36 pgs.)

1-6: 1-Jesus. 2-Joseph. 3-David. 4-The Bible Girls. 5-Moses. 6-More About Jesus 2 4 6 9 12 15
7-9-Low print run: 7-The Lord's Prayer. 8-Stories Jesus told. 9-Paul, God's Traveller 3 6 9 19 30 40
10-Low print run; In the Beginning 5 10 15 33 57 80
NOTE: ***Ketcham*** *c/a in all.*

DENNIS THE MENACE BIG BONUS SERIES
Fawcett Publications: No. 10, Feb, 1980 - No. 11, Apr, 1980

10,11 1 2 3 5 6 8

DENNIS THE MENACE BONUS MAGAZINE (Formerly Dennis the Menace Giants Nos. 1-75) (...Big Bonus Series on-c for #174-194)
Fawcett Publications: No. 76, 1/70 - No. 95, 7/71; No. 95, 7/71; No. 97, '71; No. 194, 10/79; (No. 76-124: 68 pgs.; No. 125-163: 52 pgs.; No. 164 on: 36 pgs.)

76-90(3/71) 2 4 6 10 14 18
91-95, 97-110(10/72): Two #95's with same date(7/71) A-Summer Games, and

Department of Truth #3 © Tynion IV & Simmonds

Descender #1 © 171 Studios & Nguyen

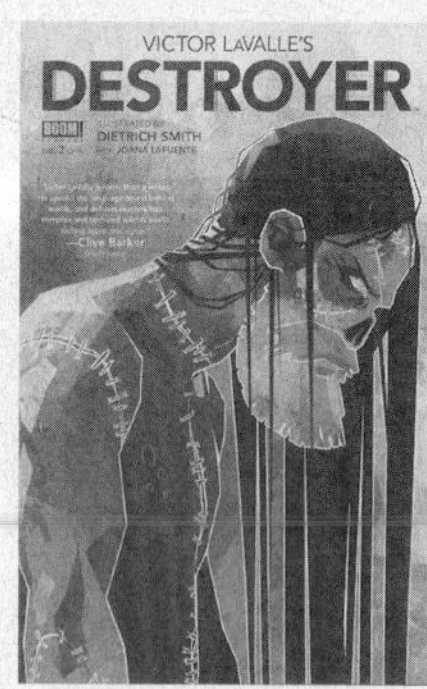

Destroyer #2 © Victor LaValle

	GD 2.0	VG 4.0	FN 6.0	VF 8.0	VF/NM 9.0	NM- 9.2

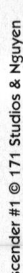

B-That's Our Boy. No #96 2 4 6 9 13 16
111-124 2 4 6 8 10 12
125-163-(52 pgs.) 2 4 6 8 10 12
164-194: 166-Indicia printed backwards 1 2 3 4 5 7

DENNIS THE MENACE COMICS DIGEST
Marvel Comics Group: April, 1982 - No. 3, Aug, 1982 ($1.25, digest-size)

1-3-Reprints 1 3 4 6 8 10
1-Mistakenly printed with DC emblem on cover 2 4 6 10 12 15
NOTE: *Ketcham* c-all. *Wiseman* a-all. A few thousand #1's were published with a DC emblem on cover.

DENNIS THE MENACE FUN BOOK
Fawcett Publications/Standard Comics: 1960 (100 pgs.)

1-Part Wiseman-a 5 10 15 35 63 90

DENNIS THE MENACE FUN FEST SERIES (Formerly Dennis the Menace #166)
Hallden (Fawcett): No. 16, Jan, 1980 - No. 17, Mar, 1980 (40¢)

16,17-By Hank Ketcham 1 2 3 4 5 7

DENNIS THE MENACE POCKET FULL OF FUN!
Fawcett Publications (Hallden): Spring, 1969 - No. 50, March, 1980 (196 pgs.) (Digest size)

1-Reprints in all issues 5 10 15 33 57 80
2-10 4 8 12 23 37 50
11-20 3 6 9 15 22 28
21-28 2 4 6 11 16 20
29-50: 35,40,46-Sunday strip-r 2 4 6 8 11 14
NOTE: *No. 1-28 are 196 pgs.; No. 29-36: 164 pgs.; No. 37: 148 pgs.; No. 38 on: 132 pgs. No. 8, 11, 15, 21, 25, 29 all contain strip reprints.*

DENNIS THE MENACE TELEVISION SPECIAL
Fawcett Publ. (Hallden Div.): Summer, 1961 - No. 2, Spring, 1962 (Giant)

1 6 12 18 37 66 95
2 3 6 9 21 33 45

DENNIS THE MENACE TRIPLE FEATURE
Fawcett Publications: Winter, 1961 (Giant)

1-Wiseman-c/a 6 12 18 37 66 95

DEPT. H
Dark Horse Comics: Apr, 2016 - No. 24, Mar, 2018 ($3.99)

1-24-Matt Kindt-s/a. 1-Two covers 4.00

DEPARTMENT OF TRUTH
Image Comics: Sept, 2020 - Present ($3.99)

1-6: 1-5-James Tynion IV-s/Martin Simmonds-a. 6-Elsa Charretier-a 4.00

DEPUTY, THE (TV)
Dell Publishing Co.: No. 1077, Feb-Apr, 1960 - No. 1225, Oct-Dec, 1961 (all-Henry Fonda photo-c)

Four Color 1077 (#1)-Buscema-a 10 20 30 64 132 200
Four Color 1130 (9-11/60)-Buscema-a,1225 8 16 24 54 102 150

DEPUTY DAWG (TV) (Also see New Terrytoons)
Dell Publishing Co./Gold Key: Oct-Dec, 1961 - No. 1299, 1962; No. 1, Aug, 1965

Four Color 1238,1299 9 18 27 63 129 195
1(10164-508)(8/65)-Gold Key 9 18 27 63 129 195

DEPUTY DAWG PRESENTS DINKY DUCK AND HASHIMOTO-SAN (TV)
Gold Key: August, 1965

1(10159-508) 9 18 27 57 111 165

DESCENDENT, THE
AfterShock Comics: May, 2019 - No. 5, Sept, 2019 ($3.99)

1-5-Stephanie Phillips-s/Evgeniv Bornyakov-a 4.00

DESCENDER (Also see Ascender)
Image Comics: Mar, 2015 - No. 32, Jul, 2018 ($2.99/$3.99)

1-Lemire-s/Nguyen-a/c in all; bonus concept-a 5.00
1-Variant-c by Lemire 6.00
2-18-Lemire-s/Nguyen-a/c 3.00
19-32-($3.99) 4.00

DESERT GOLD (See Zane Grey 4-Color 467)

DESIGN FOR SURVIVAL (Gen. Thomas S. Power's...)
American Security Council Press: 1968 (36 pgs. in color) (25¢)

nn-Propaganda against the Threat of Communism-Aircraft cover; H-Bomb panel
3 6 9 17 26 35
Twin Circle Edition-Cover shows panels from inside 2 4 6 13 18 22

DESOLATION JONES
DC Comics (WildStorm): July, 2005 - No. 8, Feb, 2007 ($2.95/$2.99)

1-8: 1-6-Warren Ellis-s/J.H. Williams-a. 7,8-Zezelj-a 3.00

DESPERADO (Becomes Black Diamond Western No. 9 on)
Lev Gleason Publications: June, 1948 - No. 8, Feb, 1949 (All 52 pgs.)

1-Biro-c on all; contains inside photo-c of Charles Biro, Lev Gleason & Bob Wood
18 36 54 109 172 235
2 11 22 33 62 86 110
3-Story with over 20 killings 11 22 33 64 90 115
4-8 9 18 27 47 61 75
NOTE: *Barry* a-2. *Fuje* a-4, 8. *Guardineer* a-5-7. *Kida* a-3-7. *Ed Moore* a-4, 6.

DESPERADO PRIMER
Image Comics (Desperado): Apr, 2005 ($1.99, one-shot)

1-Previews of Roundeye, World Traveler, A Mirror To The Soul; Bolland-c 3.00

DESPERADOES
Image Comics (Homage): Sept, 1997 - No. 5, June, 1998 ($2.50/$2.95)

1-5-Mariotte-s/Cassaday-c/a: 1-($2.50-c). 2-5-($2.95) 3.00
...: A Moment's Sunlight TPB ('98, $16.95) r/#1-5 17.00
...: Epidemic! (11/99, $5.95) Mariotte-s 6.00

DESPERADOES: BANNERS OF GOLD
IDW Publishing: Dec, 2004 - No. 5, Apr, 2005 ($3.99, limited series)

1-5: Mariotte-s/Haun-a. 1-Cassaday-c 4.00

DESPERADOES: BUFFALO DREAMS
IDW Publishing: Jan, 2007 - No. 4, Apr, 2007 ($3.99, limited series)

1-4: Mariotte-s/Dose-a/c 4.00

DESPERADOES: QUIET OF THE GRAVE
DC Comics (Homage): Jul, 2001 - No. 5, Nov, 2001 ($2.95)

1-5-Jeff Mariotte-s/John Severin-c/a 3.00
TPB (2002, $14.95) r/#1-5; intro. by Brian Keene 15.00

DESPERATE TIMES (See Savage Dragon)
Image Comics: Jun, 1998 - No. 4, Dec, 1998; Nov, 2000 - No. 4, July, 2001 ($2.95, B&W)

1-4-Chris Eliopoulos-s/a 3.00
(Vol. 2) 1-4 3.00
(Vol. 3) 0-(1/04, $3.50) Pages read sideways 3.50
(Vol. 3) 1-Pages read sideways 3.00

DESPICABLE DEADPOOL (Marvel Legacy)
Marvel Comics: No. 287, Dec, 2017 - No. 300, Jul, 2018 ($3.99)

287-299: 287-Duggan-s/Koblish-a; Cable app. 293-Rogue app. 296-Capt. America app. 4.00
300-($5.99) Avengers and Champions app. 6.00

DESTINATION MOON (See Fawcett Movie Comics, Space Adventures #20, 23, & Strange Adventures #1)

DESTINY: A CHRONICLE OF DEATHS FORETOLD (See Sandman)
DC Comics (Vertigo): 1997 - No. 3, 1998 ($5.95, limited series)

1-3-Alisa Kwitney-s in all: 1-Kent Williams & Michael Zulli-a, Williams painted-c. 2-Williams & Scott Hampton-painted-c/a. 3-Williams & Guay-a 6.00
TPB (2000, $14.95) r/series 15.00

DESTROY!!
Eclipse Comics: 1986 ($4.95, B&W, magazine-size, one-shot)

1-Scott McCloud-s/a 8.00
3-D Special 1-r-/#1 ($2.50) 5.00

DESTROYER
Marvel Comics: June, 2009 - No. 5, Oct, 2009 ($3.99, limited series)

1-5-Kirkman-s/Walker-a/Pearson-c 4.00

DESTROYER, THE
Marvel Comics (MAX): Nov, 1989 - No. 9, Jun, 1990 ($2.25, B&W, magazine, 52 pgs.)

1-Based on Remo Williams movie, paperbacks 6.00
2-9: 2-Williamson part inks. 4-Ditko-a 4.00

DESTROYER, THE
Marvel Comics: V2#1, March, 1991 ($1.95, 52 pgs.)
V3#1, Dec, 1991 - No. 4, Mar, 1992 ($1.95, mini-series)

V2#1,V3#1-4: Based on Remo Williams paperbacks. V3#1-4-Simonson-c. 3-Morrow-a 4.00

DESTROYER, THE (Also see Solar, Man of the Atom)
Valiant: Apr, 1995 ($2.95, color, one-shot)

0-Indicia indicates #1 3.00

DESTROYER (VICTOR LAVALLE'S...)
BOOM! Studios: May, 2017 - No. 6, Oct, 2017 ($3.99, limited series)

1-6-LaValle-s/Dietrich Smith-a; Frankenstein's monster app. 4.00

DESTROYER DUCK

Detective Comics #4 © DC

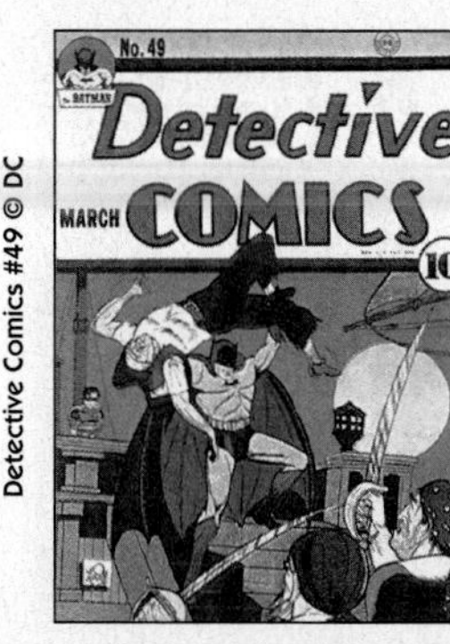

Detective Comics #49 © DC

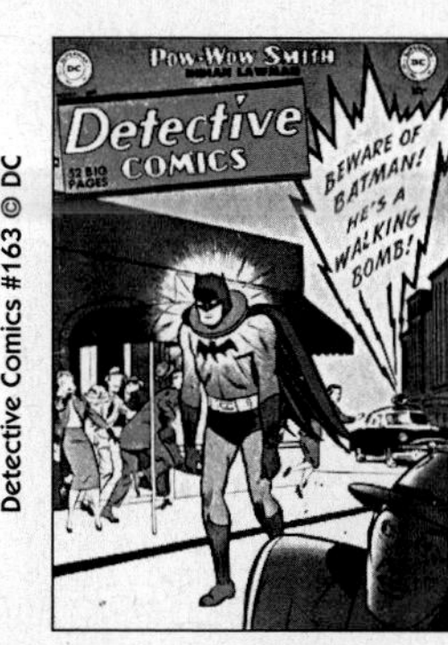

Detective Comics #163 © DC

Eclipse Comics: Feb, 1982 - No. 7, May, 1984 (#2-7: Baxter paper) ($1.50)

	GD 2.0	VG 4.0	FN 6.0	VF 8.0	VF/NM 9.0	NM- 9.2
1-Origin Destroyer Duck; 1st app. Groo; Kirby-c/a(p)	3	6	9	16	24	32
2-5: 2-Starling back-up begins; Kirby-c/a(p) thru #5						5.00
6,7						4.00

NOTE: ***Neal Adams*** *c-1i.* ***Kirby*** *c/a-1-5p.* ***Miller*** *c-7.*

DESTRUCTOR, THE
Atlas/Seaboard: February, 1975 - No. 4, Aug, 1975

	GD 2.0	VG 4.0	FN 6.0	VF 8.0	VF/NM 9.0	NM- 9.2
1-Origin/1st app.; Ditko/Wood-a; Wood-c(i)	3	6	9	14	20	26
2-4: 2-Ditko/Wood-a. 3,4-Ditko-a(p)	2	4	6	9	13	16

DETECTIVE COMICS (Also see other Batman titles)
National Periodical Publications/DC Comics: Mar, 1937 - No. 881, Oct, 2011

	GD 2.0	VG 4.0	FN 6.0	VF 8.0	VF/NM 9.0	NM- 9.2
1-(Scarce)-Slam Bradley & Spy by Siegel & Shuster, Speed Saunders by Stoner and Flessel, Cosmo, the Phantom of Disguise, Buck Marshall, Bruce Nelson begin; Chin Lung in 'Claws of the Red Dragon' serial begins; Vincent Sullivan-c	17,500	35,000	52,500	130,000	--	--
2 (Rare)-Creig Flessel-c begin; new logo	6460	12,920	19,380	42,000	--	--
3 (Rare)	4100	8200	12,300	30,000	--	--
4,5: 5-Larry Steele begins	2100	4200	6300	11,550	16,275	21,000
6,7,9,10	1550	3100	4650	8525	12,013	15,500
8-Mister Chang-c; classic-c	2650	5300	7950	14,575	20,538	26,500
11-14,17,19: 17-1st app. Fu Manchu in Detective	1350	2700	4050	7425	10,463	13,500
15,16-Have interior ad for Action Comics #1	1550	3100	4650	8525	12,013	15,500
18-Classic Fu Manchu-c; last Flessel-c	2100	4200	6300	11,550	16,275	21,000
20-The Crimson Avenger begins (1st app.)	1550	3100	4650	8525	12,013	15,500
21,23-25	1150	2300	3450	6325	8913	11,500
22-1st Crimson Avenger-c by Chambers (12/38)	1350	2700	4050	7425	10,463	13,500
26	1300	2600	3900	7150	10,075	13,000
27-The Bat-Man & Commissioner Gordon begin (1st app.), created by Bill Finger & Bob Kane (5/39); Batman-c (1st)(by Kane). Bat-Man's secret identity revealed as Bruce Wayne in six pg. story. Signed Rob't Kane (also see Det. PIcture Stories #5 & Funny Pages V3#1)	245,000	490,000	735,000	1,634,000	2,617,000	3,600,000

27-Reprint, Oversize 13-1/2x10". WARNING: This comic is an exact duplicate reprint of the original except for its size. DC published it in 1974 with a second cover titling it as Famous First Edition. There have been many reported cases of the outer cover being removed and the interior sold as the original edition. The reprint with the new outer cover removed is practically worthless; see Famous First Edition for value.

	GD 2.0	VG 4.0	FN 6.0	VF 8.0	VF/NM 9.0	NM- 9.2
28-2nd app. The Batman (6 pg. story); non-Bat-Man-c; signed Rob't Kane	9300	18,600	27,900	51,000	83,500	116,000
29-1st app. Doctor Death-c/story, Batman's 1st name villain. 1st 2 part story (10 pgs.). 2nd Batman-c by Kane	23,500	47,000	70,500	129,000	227,000	325,000
30-Dr. Death app. Story concludes from issue #29. Classic Batman splash panel by Kane.	2600	5200	7800	18,200	30,100	42,000
31-Classic Batman over castle cover; 1st app. The Monk & 1st Julie Madison (Bruce Wayne's 1st love interest); 1st Batplane (Bat-Gyro) and Batarang; 2nd 2-part Batman adventure. Gardner Fox takes over script from Bill Finger. 1st mention of locale (New York City) where Batman lives	37,200	74,400	111,600	208,000	304,000	400,000
32-Batman story concludes from issue #31. 1st app. Dala (Monk's assistant). Batman uses gun for 1st time to slay The Monk and Dala. This was the 1st time a costumed hero used a gun in comic books. 1st Batman head logo on cover	2050	4100	6150	14,000	25,000	36,000
33-Origin The Batman (2 pgs.)(1st told origin); Batman gun holster-c; Batman w/smoking gun panel at end of story. Batman story now 12 pgs. Classic Batman-c	15,600	31,200	46,800	97,500	173,750	250,000
34-2nd Crimson Avenger-c by Creig Flessel and last non Batman-c. Story from issue #32 x-over as Bruce Wayne sees Julie Madison off to America from Paris. Classic Batman splash panel used later in Batman #1 for origin story. Steve Malone begins	1800	3600	5400	13,000	22,000	31,000
35-Classic Batman hypodermic needle-c that reflects story in issue #34. Classic Batman with smoking .45 automatic splash panel. Batman-c begin	18,600	37,200	55,800	119,000	172,000	225,000
36-Batman-c that reflects adventure in issue #35. Origin/1st app. of Dr. Hugo Strange (1st major villain, 2/40). 1st finned-gloves worn by Batman	8100	16,200	24,300	58,700	88,350	118,000
37-Last solo Golden-Age Batman adventure in Detective Comics. Panel at end of story reflects solo Batman adventure in Batman #1 that was originally planned for Detective #38. Cliff Crosby begins	5000	10,000	15,000	35,500	56,750	78,000
38-Origin/1st app. Robin the Boy Wonder (4/40); Batman and Robin-c begin; cover by Kane	14,000	28,000	42,000	98,000	144,000	190,000
39-Opium story; Clayface app. in 1 panel ad at the end of the Batman story	1000	2000	3000	7600	13,800	20,000
40-Origin & 1st app. Clayface (Basil Karlo); 1st Joker cover app. (6/40); Joker story intended for this issue was used in Batman #1 instead; cover is similar to splash page in 2nd Joker story in Batman #1	2500	5000	7500	16,700	29,350	42,000
41-Robin's 1st solo	492	984	1476	3592	6346	9100
42-44: 44-Crimson Avenger-new costume	406	812	1218	2842	4971	7100
45-1st Joker story in Det. (3rd book app. & 4th story app. over all, 11/40)	541	1082	1623	3950	6975	10,000
46-50: 46-Death of Hugo Strange. 48-1st time car called Batmobile (2/41); Gotham City 1st mention in Detective (1st mentioned in Wow #1; also see Batman #4). 49-Last Clayface	371	742	1113	2600	4550	6500
51-53,55-57	300	600	900	1920	3310	4700
54-Cover mimics Detective #33 cover	300	600	900	1980	3440	4900
58-1st Penguin app. (12/41); last Speed Saunders; Fred Ray-c	2000	4000	6000	15,000	22,500	30,000
59-Last Steve Malone; 2nd Penguin; Wing becomes Crimson Avenger's aide.	295	590	885	1918	3259	4600
60-Intro. Air Wave; Joker app. (2nd in Det.)	303	606	909	2121	3711	5300
61,63: 63-Last Cliff Crosby; 1st app. Mr. Baffle	271	542	813	1734	2967	4200
62-Joker-c/story (2nd Joker-c, 4/42)	1000	2000	3000	7400	13,200	19,000
64-Origin & 1st app. Boy Commandos by Simon & Kirby (6/42); Joker app.	476	952	1428	3475	6138	8800
65-1st Boy Commandos-c (S&K-a on Boy Commandos & Ray/Robinson-a on Batman & Robin on-c; 4 artists on one-c)	314	628	951	2251	3976	5700
66-Origin & 1st app. Two-Face (originally named Harvey Kent)	1900	3800	5700	13,500	21,750	30,000
67-1st Penguin-c (9/42)	541	1082	1623	3950	6975	10,000
68-Two-Face-c/story; 1st Two-Face-c	530	1060	1590	3869	6835	9800
69-Classic Joker with 2 guns in his hands-c	1900	3800	5700	13,500	21,750	30,000
70	300	600	900	2040	3570	5100
71-Classic Joker black background calendar-c	1400	2800	4200	9300	16,650	24,000
72,74,75: 74-1st Tweedledum & Tweedledee plus-c; S&K-a	223	446	669	1427	2439	3450
73-Scarecrow-c/story (1st Scarecrow-c)	1400	2800	4200	9300	16,650	24,000
76-Newsboy Legion & The Sandman x-over in Boy Commandos; S&K-a; Joker-c/story	427	854	1281	3121	5511	7900
77-79: All S&K-a	190	380	570	1216	2083	2950
80-Two-Face-c/sty; S&K-a	277	554	831	1773	3037	4300
81,82,84,86-90: 81-1st Cavalier-c & app. 87-Penguin app. 89-Last Crimson Avenger; 2nd Cavalier-c & app.	158	316	474	1011	1731	2450
83-1st "skinny" Alfred (1/44)(see Batman #21; last S&K Boy Commandos (also #92,128); most issues #84 on signed S&K are not by them	171	342	513	1094	1872	2650
85-Joker-c/story; last Spy; Kirby/Klech Boy Commandos	343	686	1029	2400	4200	6000
91,102,109-Joker-c/stories	300	600	900	1920	3310	4700
92-98: 96-Alfred's last name 'Beagle' revealed, later changed to 'Pennyworth' in #214	126	252	378	806	1378	1950
99-Penguin-c/story	194	388	582	1242	2121	3000
100 (6/45)	158	316	474	1011	1731	2450
101,103-107,110-113,115-117,119	110	220	330	704	1202	1700
108-1st Bat-signal-c (2/46)	181	362	543	1158	1979	2800
114,118-Joker-c/stories. 114-1st small logo (8/46)	271	542	813	1734	2967	4200
120-Penguin-c/story	206	412	618	1318	2259	3200
121,123,125,127,129,130	106	212	318	678	1164	1650
122-1st Catwoman-c (4/47)	495	990	1785	4350	7675	11,000
124,128-Joker-c/stories	245	490	735	1568	2684	3800
126-Penguin-c	165	330	495	1056	1803	2550
131-134,136,139	100	200	300	635	1093	1550
135-Frankenstein-c/story	135	270	405	864	1482	2100
137-Joker-c/story; last Air Wave	295	590	885	1888	3244	4600
138-Origin Robotman (see Star Spangled #7 for 1st app.); series ends #202	161	322	483	1030	1765	2500
140-The Riddler-c/story (1st app., 10/48)	2800	5600	8400	18,700	31,850	45,000
141,143-148,150: 150-Last Boy Commandos	100	200	300	635	1093	1550
142-2nd Riddler-c/story	366	732	1098	2562	4481	6400
149-Joker-c/story	232	464	696	1485	2543	3600
151-Origin & 1st app. Pow Wow Smith, Indian lawman (9/49) & begins series	116	232	348	742	1271	1800
152,154,155,157-160: 152-Last Slam Bradley	100	200	300	635	1093	1550
153-1st app. Roy Raymond TV Detective (11/49); origin The Human Fly	113	263	339	723	1237	1750
156(2/50)-The new classic Batmobile	258	516	774	1651	2826	4000
161-167,169,170,172-176: Last 52 pg. issue	97	194	291	621	1061	1500
168-Origin the Joker	3500	7000	10,500	21,400	34,950	48,000
171-Penguin-c	161	322	483	1030	1765	2500
177-179,181-186,188,189,191,192,194-199,201,202,204,206-210,212,214-216: 184-1st app. Fire Fly. 185-Secret of Batman's utility belt. 202-Last Robotman & Pow Wow Smith. 215-1st app. of Batmen of all Nations. 216-Last precode (2/55)	94	188	282	597	1025	1450
180,193-Joker-c/story	187	374	561	1197	2049	2900

Detective Comics #254 © DC

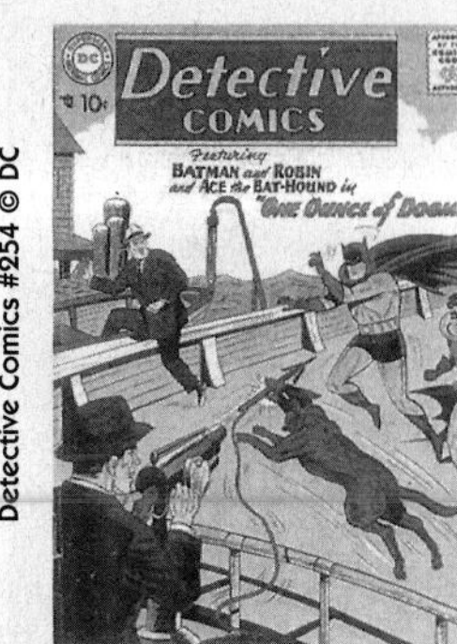

Detective Comics #400 © DC

Detective Comics #492 © DC

	GD 2.0	VG 4.0	FN 6.0	VF 8.0	VF/NM 9.0	NM- 9.2
187-Two-Face-c/story	258	516	774	1651	2826	4000
190-Origin Batman retold	116	232	348	742	1271	1800
200(10/53), 205: 205-Origin Batcave	110	220	330	704	1202	1700
203,211-Catwoman-c/stories	142	284	426	909	1555	2200
213-Origin & 1st app. Mirror Man	110	220	330	704	1202	1700
217-224: 218-Batman Jr. & Robin Sr. app.	77	154	231	493	847	1200
225-(11/55)-1st app. Martian Manhunter (J'onn J'onzz); origin begins; also see Batman #78	1400	2800	4200	10,400	25,200	40,000
226-Origin Martian Manhunter cont'd (2nd app.)	203	406	609	1299	2225	3150
227-229: Martian Manhunter stories in all	90	180	270	576	988	1400
230-1st app. Mad Hatter (imposter, not the one from Batman #49, this one's appearance inspired the 1966 TV version); brief recap origin of Martian Manhunter	142	284	426	909	1555	2200
231-Brief origin recap Martian Manhunter	68	136	204	435	743	1050
232,234,237,238,240	63	126	189	403	689	975
233-Origin & 1st app. Batwoman (7/56)	541	1082	1623	3950	6975	10,000
235-Origin Batman & his costume; tells how Bruce Wayne's father (Thomas Wayne) wore Bat costume & fought crime (reprinted in Batman #255)	123	246	369	787	1344	1900
236-1st S.A. issue; J'onn J'onzz talks to parents and Mars-1st since being stranded on Earth; 1st app. Bat-Tank?	73	146	219	467	796	1125
239-Early DC grey tone-c	100	200	300	635	1093	1550
241-Rainbow Batman cover and story	129	258	387	826	1413	2000
242-260: 246-Intro. Diane Meade, John Jones' girl. 249-Batwoman-c/app. 253-1st app. The Terrible Trio. 254-Bat-Hound-c/story. 257-Intro. & 1st app. Whirly Bats. 259-1st app. The Calendar Man	52	104	156	328	552	775
261-264,266,268-271: 261-J. Jones tie-in to sci/fi movie "Incredible Shrinking Man"; 1st app. Dr. Double X. 262-Origin Jackal. 268,271-Manhunter origin recap	40	80	120	246	411	575
265-Batman's origin retold with new facts	55	110	165	352	601	850
267-Origin & 1st app. Bat-Mite (5/59)	135	270	405	864	1482	2100
272,274,275,277-280	34	68	102	204	332	460
273-J'onn J'onzz i.d. revealed for 1st time	37	74	111	222	361	500
276-2nd app. Bat-Mite	52	104	156	328	552	775
281-292, 294-297: 286,292-Batwoman-c/app. 287-Origin J'onn J'onzz retold. 289-Bat-Mite-c/story. 292-Last Roy Raymond. 297-Last 10¢ issue (11/61)	27	54	81	158	259	360
293-(7/61)-Aquaman begins (pre #1); ends #300	32	64	96	192	314	435
298-(12/61)-1st modern Clayface (Matt Hagen)	57	114	171	456	1028	1600
299, 300-(2/62)-Aquaman ends	15	30	45	105	233	360
301-(3/62)-J'onn J'onzz returns to Mars (1st time since stranded on Earth six years before)	14	28	42	97	214	330
302-Batwoman-c/app.	15	30	45	103	227	350
303-306,308-310,312-317,319-321,323,324,326,329,330: 321-2nd Terrible Trio. 326-Last J'onn J'onzz, story cont'd in House of Mystery #143; intro. Idol-Head of Diabolu	10	20	30	66	138	210
307-Batwoman-c/app.	11	22	33	75	160	245
311-1st app. Cat-Man; intro. Zook in John Jones	25	50	75	175	388	600
318,322,325: 318,325-Cat-Man-c/story (2nd & 3rd app.); also 1st & 2nd app. Batwoman as the Cat-Woman. 322-Bat-Girl's 1st/only app. in Det. (6th in all); Batman cameo in J'onn J'onzz (only hero to app. in series)	12	24	36	84	185	285
327-(5/64)-Elongated Man begins, ends #383; 1st new look Batman with new costume; Infantino/Giella new look-a begins; Batman with gun	17	34	51	117	259	400
328-Death of Alfred; Bob Kane biog, 2 pgs.	13	26	39	89	195	300
331,333-340: 334-1st app. The Outsider	8	16	24	56	108	160
332,341,365-Joker-c/stories	11	22	33	76	163	250
342-358,360,361,366-368: 345-Intro Block Buster. 347-"What If" theme story (1/66). 350-Elongated Man new costume. 355-Zatanna x-over in Elongated Man. 356-Alfred brought back in Batman, early SA app.	8	16	24	52	99	145
359-Intro/origin Batgirl (Barbara Gordon)-c/story (1/67); 1st Silver Age app. Killer Moth; classic Batgirl-c	172	344	516	1419	3210	5000
359-Facsimile Edition (2020, $3.99) Reprints issue with original ads and letter column						4.00
362,364-S.A. Riddler app. (early)	9	18	27	60	120	180
363-2nd app. new Batgirl	16	32	48	112	249	385
369(11/67)-N. Adams-a (Elongated Man); 3rd app. S.A. Catwoman (cameo; leads into Batman #197); 4th app. new Batgirl	18	36	54	124	275	425
370-1st Neal Adams-a on Batman (cover only, 12/67)	10	20	30	68	144	220
371-(1/68) 1st new Batmobile from TV show; classic Batgirl-c	12	24	36	84	185	285
372-376,378-386,389,390: 375-New Batmobile-c	6	12	18	41	76	110
377-S.A. Riddler-c/sty	7	14	21	49	92	135
387-r/1st Batman story from #27 (30th anniversary, 5/69); Joker-c; last 12¢ issue	10	20	30	65	135	205
388-Joker-c/story	10	20	30	68	144	220
391-394,396,398,399,401,403,406,409: 392-1st app. Jason Bard. 401-2nd Batgirl/Robin team-up	6	12	18	40	73	105
395,397,402,404,407,408,410-Neal Adams-a. 402-Man-Bat-c/app. (2nd app.). 404-Tribute to Enemy Ace	11	22	33	75	160	245
400-(6/70)-Origin & 1st app. Man-Bat; 1st Batgirl/Robin team-up (cont'd in #401); Neal Adams-a	32	64	96	230	515	800
405-Debut League of Assassins	18	36	54	125	276	430
411-(5/71) Intro. Talia, daughter of Ra's al Ghul (Ra's mentioned, but doesn't appear until Batman #232 (6/71); Bob Brown-a	36	72	108	259	580	900
412-413: 413-Last 15¢ issue	6	12	18	40	73	105
414-424: All-25¢, 52 pgs. 418-Creeper x-over. 424-Last Batgirl.	6	12	18	41	76	110
425-436: 426,430,436-Elongated Man app. 428,434-Hawkman begins, ends #467	5	10	15	31	53	75
437-New Manhunter begins (10-11/73, 1st app.) by Simonson, ends #443	5	10	15	34	60	85
438-440,442-445 (All 100 Page Super Spectaculars): 438-Kubert Hawkman-r. 439-Origin Manhunter. 440-G.A. Manhunter(Adv. #79) by S&K, Hawkman, Dollman, Green Lantern; Toth-a. 442-G.A. Newsboy Legion, Black Canary, Elongated Man, Dr. Fate-r. 443-Origin The Creeper-r; death of Manhunter; G.A. Green Lantern, Spectre-r; Batman-r/Batman #18. 444-G.A. Kid Eternity-r. 445-G.A. Dr. Midnite-r	6	12	18	41	76	110
441-(6,7/74)(100 Page S.S.) 1st app. Lt. (Harvey) Bullock, first name not given, appears in only 3 panels; G.A. Plastic Man, Batman, Ibis-r	7	14	21	46	86	125
446-460: 457-Classic origin-c; origin retold & updated; 1st app. Leslie Thompkins	3	6	9	17	26	35
461-465,470,480: 480-(44 pgs.). 463-1st app. Black Spider. 464-2nd app. Black Spider 470-Intro. Silver St. Cloud.	3	6	9	16	23	30
466-468,471-473,478,479-Rogers-a in all: 466-1st app. Signalman since Batman #139. 470,471-1st modern app. Hugo Strange. 478-1st app. 3rd Clayface (Preston Payne). 479-(44 pgs.)	4	8	12	25	40	55
469-Intro/origin Dr. Phosphorous; Simonson-a	4	8	12	25	40	55
474-1st app. new Deadshot	6	12	18	42	79	115
475-Joker-c/story; Rogers-a	8	16	24	54	102	150
475-Facsimile Edition (2020, $3.99) Reprints issue with original ads and letter column						4.00
476-Joker-c/story; Rogers-a	6	12	18	37	66	95
477-Neal Adams-a(r); Rogers-a (3 pgs.)	4	8	12	23	37	50
481-(Combined with Batman Family, 12-1/78-79, begin $1.00, 68 pg. issues, ends #495); 481-495-Batgirl, Robin solo stories	4	8	12	23	37	50
482,483: 482-Starlin/Russell, Golden-a; The Demon begins (origin-r), ends #485 (by Ditko #483-485). 483-40th Anniversary issue; origin retold in brief; Newton Batman begins; Human Target with Chaykin-a; Batman Family pin-up on back-c	3	6	9	15	22	28
484-495 (68 pgs): 484-Origin Robin. 485-Death of Batwoman. 486-Killer Moth app. 487-The Odd Man by Ditko. 489-Robin/Batgirl team-up. 490-Black Lightning begins. 491-(#492 on inside). 493-Intro. The Swashbuckler	2	4	6	9	13	16
496-499: 496-Clayface app.	2	4	6	8	10	12
500-($1.50, 52 pgs.)-Batman/Deadman team-up with Infantino-a; new Hawkman story by Joe Kubert; incorrectly says 500th Anniv. of Det.	3	6	9	15	22	28
501-503,505-522: 509-Catman-c. 510-Mad Hatter-c. 512-2nd app. new Dr. Death. 513-Two-Face app. 519-Last Batgirl. 521-Green Arrow series begins	1	3	4	6	8	10
504-Joker-c/story	2	4	6	11	16	20
523-1st Killer Croc (cameo); Solomon Grundy app.	4	8	12	23	37	50
524-2nd app. Jason Todd (cameo)(3/83)	2	4	6	10	14	18
525-3rd app. Jason Todd (See Batman #357)	2	4	6	9	12	15
526-Batman's 500th app. in Detective Comics ($1.50, 68 pgs.); Death of Jason Todd's parents, Joker-c/story (55 pgs.); Bob Kane pin-up	3	6	9	16	24	32
527-531,533,534,536-553,555-568,571,573: 538-Cat-Man-c/story cont'd from Batman #371. 542-Jason Todd quits as Robin (becomes Robin again #547). 549,550-Alan Moore scripts (Green Arrow). 566-Batman villains profiled. 567-Harlan Ellison scripts	1	2	3	5	6	8
532,569,570-Joker-c/stories	3	6	9	14	19	24
535-Intro new Robin (Jason Todd)-1st appeared in Batman	1	3	4	6	8	10
554-1st new Black Canary (9/85)	1	3	4	6	8	10
572-(3/87, $1.25, 60 pgs.)-50th Anniv. of Det. Comics	1	3	4	6	8	10
574-Origin Batman & Jason Todd retold	2	4	6	8	10	12
575-Year 2 begins, ends #578	3	6	9	15	22	28
576-578: McFarlane-c/a; The Reaper app.	3	6	9	15	22	28
579-597,599,601-607,609,610: 579-New bat wing logo. 583-1st app. villains Scarface & Ventriloquist. 589,595-(52 pgs.)-Each contain free 16 pg. Batman stories. 604-607-Mudpack storyline; 604,607-Contain Batman mini-posters. 610-Faked death of Penguin; artists names app. on tombstone on-c						6.00
598-($2.95, 84 pgs.)- "Blind Justice" storyline begins by Batman movie writer Sam Hamm, ends #600	1	3	4	6	8	10

Detective Comics #743 © DC

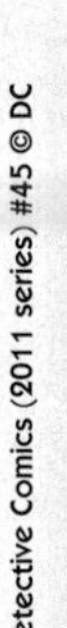
Detective Comics (2011 series) #45 © DC

Detective Comics #1027 © DC

GD VG FN VF VF/NM NM-
2.0 4.0 6.0 8.0 9.0 9.2

600-(5/89, $2.95, 84 pgs.)-50th Anniv. of Batman in Det.; 1 pg. Neal Adams pin-up, among other artists 2 4 6 8 10 12
608-1st app. Anarky 1 3 4 6 8 10
611-626,628-646,649-658: 612-1st new look Cat-Man; Catwoman app. 615- "The Penguin Affair" part 2 (See Batman #448,449). 617-Joker-c/story. 624-1st new Catwoman (w/death) & 1st new Batwoman. 626-Batman's 600th app. in Detective. 642-Return of Scarface, part 2. 644-Last $1.00-c. 644-646-The (2nd) Electrocutioner (Lester Buchinsky) app. 652,653-Huntress-c/story w/new costume plus Charest-c on both 6.00
627-($2.95, 84 pgs.)-Batman's 601st app. in Det.; reprints 1st story/#27 plus 3 versions (2 new) of same story 1 2 3 5 6 8
647-1st app. Stephanie Brown 2 4 6 13 18 22
648-1st full app. Spoiler (Stephanie Brown) 1 3 4 6 8 10
659-664: 659-Knightfall part 2; Kelley Jones-c. 660-Knightfall part 4; Bane-c by Sam Kieth. 661-Knightfall part 6; brief Joker & Riddler app. 662-Knightfall part 8; Riddler app.; Sam Kieth-c. 663-Knightfall part 10; Kelley Jones-c. 664-Knightfall part 12; Bane-c/story; Joker app.; continued in Showcase 93 #7 & 8; Jones-c 1 3 4 6 8 10
665-675: 665,666-Knightfall parts 16 & 18; 666-Bane-c/story. 667-Knightquest: The Crusade & new Batman begins (1st app. in Batman #500). 669-Begin $1.50-c; Knightquest, cont'd in Robin #1. 671,673-Joker app. 5.00
675-($2.95)-Collectors edition w/foil-c 6.00
676-($2.50, 52 pgs.)-KnightsEnd pt. 3 6.00
677,678: 677-KnightsEnd pt. 9. 678-(9/94)-Zero Hour tie-in. 5.00
679-685: 679-(11/94). 682-Troika pt. 3 4.00
682-($2.50) Embossed-c Troika pt. 3 5.00
686-699,701-719: 686-Begin $1.95-c. 693,694-Poison Ivy-c/app. 695-Contagion pt. 2; Catwoman, Penguin app. 696-Contagion pt. 8. 698-Two-Face-c/app. 701-Legacy pt. 6; Batman vs. Bane-c/app. 702-Legacy Epilogue. 703-Final Night x-over. 705-707-Riddler-app. 714,715-Martian Manhunter-app. 4.00
700-($4.95, Collectors Edition)-Legacy pt. 1; Ra's Al Ghul-c/app; Talia & Bane app; book displayed at shops in envelope 1 2 3 5 6 8
700-($2.95, Regular Edition)-Different-c 5.00
720-736,738,739: 720,721-Cataclysm pts. 5,14. 723-Green Arrow app. 730-740-No Man's Land stories. 735-1st app. Mercy Graves in regular DCU 4.00
737-Harley Quinn-c/app. (1st app. in Detective); No Man's Land 3 6 9 14 19 24
740-Joker, Bane-c/app.; Harley Quinn app.; No Man's Land 2 4 6 8 10 12
741-($2.50) Endgame; Joker-c/app.; Harley Quinn app. 1 2 3 5 6 8
742-749,751-765: 742-New look Batman begins; 1st app. Crispus Allen (who later becomes the Spectre). 751,752-Poison Ivy app. 756-Superman-c/app. 759-762-Catwoman back-up 4.00
750-($4.95, 64 pgs.) Ra's al Ghul-c 6.00
766-772: 766,767-Bruce Wayne: Murderer pt. 1,8. 769-772-Bruce Wayne: Fugitive pts. 4,8,12,16 4.00
773,774,776-782,784-799: 773-Begin $2.75-c; Sienkiewicz-c. 777-784-Sale-c. 784-786-Alan Scott app. 787-Mad Hatter app. 797-799-War Games 4.00
775-($3.50) Sienkiewicz-c 5.00
783-1st Nyssa 5.00
800-($3.50) Jock-c; aftermath of War Games; back-up by Lapham 5.00
801-830,832-836,838-849,851,852: 801-814-Lapham-s. 804-Mr. Freeze app. 809-War Crimes. 817-820: One Year Later 8-part x-over with Batman #651-654; Robinson-s/Bianchi-c. 819-Begin $2.99-c. 820-Dini-s/Williams III-a. 821-Harley Quinn app. 825-Dr. Phosphorus app. 827-Debut of new Scarface. 833,834-Zatanna & Joker app. 838,839-Resurrection of Ra's al Ghul x-over. 846-847-Batman R.I.P. x-over 4.00
817,818,838,839-2nd printings. 817-Combo-c of #817̳ cover images. 818-Combo-c of #818 and Batman #653 cover images. 838-Andy Kubert variant-c. 839-Red bkgd-c 4.00
831,837-Harley Quinn-c/app. 831-Dini-s 1 3 4 6 8 10
850-($3.99) Batman vs. Hush; Dini-s/Nguyen-a 6.00
853-($3.99) Gaiman-s/Andy Kubert-a; continued from Batman #686; Kubert sketch pgs. 4.00
853-Variant-c with red background by Andy Kubert 12.00
854-872-($3.99) 854-Batwoman features begin; Rucka-a/J.H. Williams-a/c; The Question back-ups begin. 858-860-Batwoman origin. 871-1st Scott Snyder Batman-s 5.00
854,858,859,860-Variant-c: 854-JG Jones. 858-Hughes. 859-Jock. 860-Alex Ross 6.00
854-Special Edition (8/10, $1.00) reprints issue with "What's Next?" logo on cover 3.00
873-879-($2.99) 874,875,879-Francavilla-a 4.00
880-Joker-c/app.; Jock-c/a 9 18 27 61 123 185
881-(10/11) Last issue of first volume; Snyder-s/Jock & Francavilla-a 4.00
#0-(10/94) Zero Hour tie-in, released between #678 & 679 4.00
#38-Facsimile Edition (2020, $3.99) Reprints issue with original ads and letter column 4.00
#1,000,000 (11/98) 853rd Century x-over 4.00
Annual 1 (1988, $1.50) 1 2 3 5 6 8
Annual 2-7,9 ('89-'94, '96, 68 pgs.)-4-Painted-c. 5-Joker-c/story (54 pgs.) continued in Robin Annual #1; Sam Kieth-c; Eclipso app. 6-Azrael as Batman in new costume; intro Geist the Twilight Man; Bloodlines storyline. 7-Elseworlds story. 9-Legends of the Dead Earth story 6.00
Annual 8 (1995, $3.95, 68 pgs.)-Year One story 5.00
Annual 10 (1997, $3.95)-Pulp Heroes story 5.00
Annual 11 (12/09, $4.99)-Azrael & The Question app.; continued from Batman Ann. #27 5.00
Annual 12 (2/11, $4.99)-Nightrunner & The Question app.; continued in Batman Ann. #28 5.00
NOTE: ***Neal Adams*** *c-370, 372, 385, 389, 391, 392, 394-422, 439.* ***Aparo*** *a-437, 438, 444-446, 500, 625-632p, 638-643p; c-430, 437, 440-446, 448, 468-470, 480, 484(back), 492-502,508, 509, 515, 518-522, 641, 716, 719, 722, 724.* ***Austin*** *a(i)-450, 451, 463-468, 471-476; c(i)-474-476, 478.* ***Baily*** *a-443r.* ***Buckler*** *a-434, 446p, 479p; c(p)-467, 482, 505-507, 511, 513-516, 518.* ***Burnley*** *a(Batman)-65, 75, 78, 83, 100, 103, 125; c-62i, 63i, 64, 73i, 78, 83p, 96p, 103p, 105p, 106, 108, 121p, 123p, 125p.* ***Chaykin*** *a-441.* ***Colan*** *a(p)-510, 512, 517, 523, 528-538, 540-546, 555-567; c(p)-510, 512, 528, 530-535, 537, 538, 540, 541, 543-545, 556-558, 560-564.* ***J. Craig*** *a-488.* ***Ditko*** *a-443r, 483-485, 487.* ***Golden*** *a-482p; c-625, 626, 628-631, 633, 644-646.* ***Alan Grant*** *scripts-584-597, 601-621, 641, 642, Annual 5.* ***Grell*** *a-445, 455, 463p, 464p; c-455.* ***Guardineer*** *c-23, 24, 26, 28, 30, 32.* ***Gustavson*** *a-441r.* ***Infantino*** *a-354, 442(2)r, 500, 572.* ***Infantino/Anderson*** *c-333, 337-340, 343, 344, 347, 351, 352, 359, 361-368, 371.* ***Kelley Jones*** *c-651, 657i, 658i, 659, 661, 663-675.* ***Kaluta*** *c-423, 424, 426-428, 431, 434, 438, 484, 486, 572.* ***Bob Kane*** *a-Most early issues #27 on, 297r, 356r, 438-440r, 442r, 443r.* ***Kane/Robinson*** *c-33.* ***Gil Kane*** *a(p)-368, 370-374, 384, 385, 388-407, 438r, 439r, 520.* ***Kane/Anderson*** *c-369.* ***Sam Kieth*** *c-654-656 (657, 658 w/**Kelley Jones**), 660, 662, Annual #5.* ***Kubert*** *a-438r, 439r, 500; c-348-350.* ***McFarlane*** *c/a(p)-576-578.* ***Meskin*** *a-420r.* ***Mignola*** *c-583.* ***Moldoff*** *c-233-354, 259, 266, 267, 275, 287, 289, 290, 297, 300.* ***Moldoff/Giella*** *a-328, 330, 332, 334, 336, 338, 340, 342, 344, 346, 348, 350, 352, 354, 356.* ***Mooney*** *a-444r.* ***Moreira*** *a-153-300, 419r, 444r, 445r.* ***Nasser/Netzer*** *a-654, 655, 657, 658.* ***Newton*** *a(p)-480, 481, 483-499, 501-509, 511, 513-516, 518-520, 524, 526, 539; c-526p.* ***Irv Novick*** *c-375-377, 383.* ***Robbins*** *a-426p, 429p.* ***Robinson*** *a-part: 66, 68, 71-73; all: 74-76, 79, 80; c-62, 64, 66, 68-74, 76, 79, 82, 86, 88, 442r, 443r.* ***Rogers*** *a-466-468, 471-479p, 481p; c-471p, 472p, 473, 474-479p.* ***Roussos*** *Airwave-76-105(most); c(i)-71, 72, 74-76, 79, 107.* ***Russell*** *a-481i, 482i.* ***Simon/Kirby*** *a-440r, 442r.* ***Simonson*** *a-437-443, 450, 469, 470, 500.* ***Dick Sprang*** *c-77, 82, 84, 85, 87, 89-93, 95-100, 102, 103i, 104i, 106, 108, 114, 117, 118, 122, 123, 128, 129, 131, 133, 135, 141, 148, 149, 168, 622-624.* ***Starlin*** *a-481p, 482p; c-503, 504, 567p.* ***Starr*** *a-444r.* ***Toth*** *a-442; r-414, 416, 418, 424, 440-441, 443, 444.* ***Tuska*** *a-486p, 490p.* ***Matt Wagner*** *c-647-649.* ***Wrightson*** *c-425.*

DETECTIVE COMICS (DC New 52)(Numbering reverts to original series #934 after #52)
DC Comics: Nov, 2011 - No. 52, Jul, 2016 ($2.99/$3.99)

1-Joker app.; Tony Daniel-s/a/c 3 6 9 15 22 28
2-7: 2-Intro of The Dollmaker. 5-7-Penguin app. 5.00
8,10-14,16-18: 8-($3.99) Catwoman & Scarecrow app.; back-up Two-Face story begins 4.00
9-Night of the Owls 5.00
15-Die-cut Joker cover; Death of the Family tie-in 8.00
19-(6/13, $7.99) 900th issue of Detective; bonus back-up stories and pin-up art 8.00
20-24,26: 21-23-Man-Bat back-up story. 26-Man-Bat app. 4.00
23.1, 23.2, 23.3, 23.4 (11/13, $2.99, regular covers) 3.00
23.1 (11/13, $3.99, 3-D cover) "Poison Ivy #1" on cover; Fridolfs-s/Pina-a 1 3 4 6 8 10
23.2 (11/13, $3.99, 3-D cover) "Harley Quinn #1" on cover; Googe-a/Kindt-s; origin 2 4 6 13 18 22
23.3 (11/13, $3.99, 3-D cover) "Scarecrow #1" on cover; Kudranski-a 5.00
23.4 (11/13, $3.99, 3-D cover) "Man-Bat #1" on cover; Tieri-s/Eaton-a 5.00
25-($3.99) Zero Year focus on Lt. Gordon; Fabok-a/c; Man-Bat back-up 4.00
27-($7.99) Start of Gothtopia; short stories by Meltzer, Hitch, Neal Adams, Francavilla, Murphy 8.00
28-49,51,52: 28,29-Gothtopia. 30-34,37-40-Manupul-a. 37-40-Anarky app. 43,44-Joker's Daughter. 45,46-Justice League app. 47-"Robin War" tie-in 4.00
50-($4.99) Bonus pin-up swipes of classic Detective covers by various 5.00
#0 (11/12, $3.99) Flashback to training and return to Alfred 4.00
Annual 1 (10/12, $4.99) Black Mask app.; Daniel-s/c; Molenaar-a 5.00
Annual 2 (9/13, $4.99) The Wrath app.; Eaton-a/Clarke-c 5.00
Annual 3 (9/14, $4.99) March-c 5.00
...: Endgame 1 (5/15, $2.99) Tie-in to Endgame story in Batman #35-40; Anarky app. 3.00
...: Futures End 1 (11/14, $2.99, regular-c) Five years later; Riddler app. 3.00
...: Futures End 1 (11/14, $3.99, 3-D cover) 4.00

DETECTIVE COMICS (Numbering reverts to original V1 #934 after #52 from 2011-2016 series)
DC Comics: No. 934, Aug, 2016 - Present ($2.99/$3.99)

934-Tynion IV-s/Barrows-a; Batwoman, Spoiler, Red Robin, Clayface app. 3.00
935-949,951-974: 936-938-Alvaro Martinez-a. 937-Intro. Ulysses Armstrong. 940-Apparent death of Tim Drake. 941,942-Night of the Monster Men x-over. 944-Batwing returns. 948,949-Batwoman begins. 951-956-"League of Shadows." 958-961-Zatanna app. 965-Tim Drake vs. Mr. Oz. 965-967-Future Batman (Tim Drake) app. 3.00
950-($3.99) Prologue to "League of Shadows"; Takara-a; Shiva & Azrael app. 4.00
975-($3.99) Trial of Batwoman; Tynion IV-s/Martinez-a 4.00
976-987: 976-Batmen Eternal begins. 983-987-Black Lightning app. 3.00
988-999-($3.99) 989-993-Two-Face app. 994-999-Mahnke-a 4.00
1000-(5/19, $9.99) Short stories and pin-ups by various incl. Snyder/Capullo, Kevin Smith/Jim Lee, Dini/Nguyen, Ellis/Cloonan, O'Neil/Epting, Priest/Adams, Bendis/Maleev; Johns/Kelley Jones, Tynion IV/Martinez-Bueno, Daniel/Joëlle Jones; Slam Bradley app.; intro. The Arkham Knight by Tomasi-s/Mahnke-a; 10 regular covers 15.00
1001-1023: 1001-1005-Arkham Knight app. 1004-Arkham Knight origin. 1006,1007-Spectre app.; Kyle Hotz-a 1008-Joker app. 1008-1016-Mr. Freeze app. 1009-1011-Deadshot app. 1013-Nora Fries revived. 1023-Joker War tie-in
1024-1026-Joker War tie-ins. 1026-KIller Croc app. 2 4 6 8 10 12
1027-(11/20, $9.99) Short stories by various incl. Bendis-s/Marquez-a, Fraction-s/Zdarsky-a, Rucka-s/Risso-a, King-s/Simonson-a, Snyder-s/Reis-a; Jurgens-s/a with 1930s Batman meets Kamandi (leads into Generations Shattered #1); bonus pin-ups; multiple covers 10.00
1028-1033: 1029-Debut The Mirror. 1131-1133-Hush app. 4.00

Detectives, Inc. #1 © McGregor & Rogers

Devil Dinosaur #2 © MAR

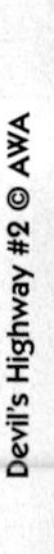
Devil's Highway #2 © AWA

	GD 2.0	VG 4.0	FN 6.0	VF 8.0	VF/NM 9.0	NM- 9.2
Annual 1 (3/18, $4.99) Tynion IV-s/Barrows-a; Clayface origin re-told						5.00
Annual 2 (7/19, $4.99) Tomasi-s/Travis Moore-a; The Reaper app.						5.00
Annual 3 (Late March/20, $4.99) Spotlight on Alfred; back-up with Risso-a; Rude-c						5.00

DETECTIVE COMICS: BATMAN 80TH ANNIVERSARY GIANT
DC Comics: 2019 ($4.99, 100 pgs., squarebound, Walmart exclusive)

	GD	VG	FN	VF	VF/NM	NM-
1-New story Venditti-s/Segovia-a; Two-Face app.; reprints 1st apps. of Batman, Robin, Batgirl, Leslie Thompkins, plus stories from Detective #500 and Batman Black and White #4	6	12	18	41	76	110

DETECTIVE DAN, SECRET OP. 48 (Also see Adventures of Detective Ace King and Bob Scully, The Two-Fisted Hick Detective)
Humor Publ. Co. (Norman Marsh): 1933 (10¢, 10x13", 36 pgs., B&W, one-shot) (3 color, cardboard-c)

	GD	VG	FN	VF	VF/NM	NM-
nn-By Norman Marsh, 1st comic w/ original-a; 1st newsstand-c; Dick Tracy look-alike; forerunner of Dan Dunn. (Title and Wu Fang character inspired Detective Comics #1 four years later.) (1st comic of a single theme)	2100	4200	6300	12,600	--	--

DETECTIVE EYE (See Keen Detective Funnies)
Centaur Publications: Nov, 1940 - No. 2, Dec, 1940

	GD	VG	FN	VF	VF/NM	NM-
1-Air Man (see Keen Detective) & The Eye Sees begins; The Masked Marvel & Dean Denton app.	300	600	900	1920	3310	4700
2-Origin Don Rance and the Mysticape; Binder-a; Frank Thomas-c	232	464	696	1485	2543	3600

DETECTIVE PICTURE STORIES (Keen Detective Funnies No. 8 on?)
Comics Magazine Company: Dec, 1936 - No. 5, Apr, 1937

	GD	VG	FN	VF	VF/NM	NM-
1 (All issues are very scarce)	667	1334	2000	3800	6250	8700
2-The Clock app. (1/37, early app.)	350	700	1050	2000	3250	4500
3,4: 4-Eisner-a	275	550	825	1550	2575	3600
5-The Clock-c/story (4/37); "The Case of the Missing Heir" 1st detective/adventure art by Bob Kane; Bruce Wayne prototype app. (story reprinted in Funny Pages V3 #1)	475	950	1425	2700	4450	6200

DETECTIVES, THE (TV)
Dell Publishing Co.: No. 1168, Mar-May, 1961 - No. 1240, Oct-Dec, 1961

	GD	VG	FN	VF	VF/NM	NM-
Four Color 1168 (#1)-Robert Taylor photo-c	9	18	27	61	123	185
Four Color 1219-Robert Taylor, Adam West photo-c	9	18	27	61	123	185
Four Color 1240-Tufts-a; Robert Taylor photo-c; 2 different back-c	8	16	24	51	96	140

DETECTIVES, INC. (See Eclipse Graphic Album Series)
Eclipse Comics: Apr, 1985 - No. 2, Apr, 1985 ($1.75, both w/April dates)

	GD	VG	FN	VF	VF/NM	NM-
1,2: 2-Nudity						4.00

DETECTIVES, INC.: A TERROR OF DYING DREAMS
Eclipse Comics: Jun, 1987 - No. 3, Dec, 1987 ($1.75, B&W& sepia)

	GD	VG	FN	VF	VF/NM	NM-
1-3: Colan-a						4.00
TPB ('99, $19.95) r/series						20.00

DETENTION COMICS
DC Comics: Oct, 1996 ($3.50, 56 pgs., one-shot)

	GD	VG	FN	VF	VF/NM	NM-
1-Robin story by Dennis O'Neil & Norm Breyfogle; Superboy story by Ron Marz & Ron Lim; Warrior story by Ruben Diaz & Joe Phillips; Phillips-c						5.00

DETHKLOK (Based on the animated series Metalocalypse)
Dark Horse Comics: Oct, 2010 - No. 3, Feb, 2011 ($3.99, limited series)

	GD	VG	FN	VF	VF/NM	NM-
1-3-Small & Schnepp-s; covers by Schnepp & Eric Powell						4.00
...: Versus the Goon 1-(7/09, $3.50) Powell-s/a/c; Dethklok visits the Goon universe						3.50
...: Versus the Goon 1-Variant cover by Jon Schnepp						5.00
HC (7/11, $19.99) r/#1-3 & Dethklok: Versus the Goon						20.00

DETONATOR (Mike Baron's...)
Image Comics: Nov, 2004 - No. 4 ($2.50/$2.95)

	GD	VG	FN	VF	VF/NM	NM-
1-4-Mike Baron-s/Mel Rubi-a						3.00

DEUS EX (Based on the Square Enix videogame)
DC Comics: Apr, 2011 - No. 6, Sept, 2011 ($2.99, limited series)

	GD	VG	FN	VF	VF/NM	NM-
1-6-Robbie Morrison-s/Trevor Hairsine-a						3.00

DEUS EX: CHILDREN'S CRUSADE (Based on the Square Enix videogame)
Titan Comics: Mar, 2016 - No. 5, Jul, 2016 ($3.99, limited series)

	GD	VG	FN	VF	VF/NM	NM-
1-5-Alex Irvine-s/John Aggs-a; 3 covers on each						4.00

DEVASTATOR
Image Comics/Halloween: 1998 - No. 3 ($2.95, B&W, limited series)

	GD	VG	FN	VF	VF/NM	NM-
1,2-Hudnall-s/Horn-c/a						3.00

DEVI (Shekhar Kapur's...)
Virgin Comics: July, 2006 - No. 20, Jun, 2008 ($2.99)

	GD	VG	FN	VF	VF/NM	NM-
1-20: 1-Mukesh Singh-a/Siddharth Kotian-s. 2-Greg Horn-c						3.00
.../Witchblade (4/08, $2.99) Singh-a/Land-c; continued from Witchblade/Devi						3.00
... Vol. 1 TPB (5/07, $14.99) r/#1-5 and Story from Virgin Comics Preview #0						15.00
... Vol. 2 TPB (9/07, $14.99) r/#6-10; character and cover sketches						15.00

DEVIL CHEF
Dark Horse Comics: July, 1994 ($2.50, B&W, one-shot)

	GD	VG	FN	VF	VF/NM	NM-
nn						3.00

DEVIL DINOSAUR
Marvel Comics Group: Apr, 1978 - No. 9, Dec, 1978

	GD	VG	FN	VF	VF/NM	NM-
1-Kirby/Royer-a in all; all have Kirby-c	4	8	12	23	37	50
2-9: 4-7-UFO/sci. fic. 8-Dinoriders-c/sty	2	4	6	10	14	18
... By Jack Kirby Omnibus HC (2007, $29.99, dustjacket) r/#1-9; intro. by Brevoort						30.00

DEVIL DINOSAUR SPRING FLING
Marvel Comics: June, 1997 ($2.99. one-shot)

	GD	VG	FN	VF	VF/NM	NM-
1-(48 pgs.) Moon-Boy-c/app.						4.00

DEVIL-DOG DUGAN (Tales of the Marines No. 4 on)
Atlas Comics (OPI): July, 1956 - No. 3, Nov, 1956

	GD	VG	FN	VF	VF/NM	NM-
1-Severin-c	21	42	63	122	199	275
2-Iron Mike McGraw x-over; Severin-c	14	28	42	78	112	145
3	13	26	39	74	105	135

DEVIL DOGS
Street & Smith Publishers: 1942

	GD	VG	FN	VF	VF/NM	NM-
1-Boy Rangers, U.S. Marines	48	96	144	302	514	725

DEVILERS
Dynamite Entertainment: 2014 - No. 7, 2015 ($2.99)

	GD	VG	FN	VF	VF/NM	NM-
1-7-Fialkov-s/Triano-a/Jock-c						3.00

DEVILINA (Magazine)
Atlas/Seaboard: Feb, 1975 - No. 2, May, 1975 (B&W)

	GD	VG	FN	VF	VF/NM	NM-
1-Art by Reese, Marcos; "The Tempest" adapt.	5	10	15	30	50	70
2 (Low printing)	5	10	15	31	53	75

DEVIL KIDS STARRING HOT STUFF
Harvey Publications (Illustrated Humor): July, 1962 - No. 107, Oct, 1981 (Giant-Size #41-55)

	GD	VG	FN	VF	VF/NM	NM-
1 (12¢ cover price #1-#41-9/69)	32	64	96	230	515	800
2	10	20	30	69	147	225
3-10 (1/64)	8	16	24	51	96	140
11-20	5	10	15	33	57	80
21-30	4	8	12	25	40	55
31-40: 40-(6/69)	3	6	9	19	30	40
41-50: All 68 pg. Giants	3	6	9	21	33	45
51-55: All 52 pg. Giants	3	6	9	19	30	40
56-70	2	4	6	11	16	20
71-90	2	4	6	8	11	14
91-107	1	2	3	5	6	8

DEVIL'S DUE FREE COMIC BOOK DAY
Devil's Due Publ.: May, 2005 (Free Comic Book Day giveaway)

	GD	VG	FN	VF	VF/NM	NM-
nn-Short stories of G.I. Joe, Defex and Darkstalkers; Darkstalkers flip cover						3.00

DEVIL'S FOOTPRINTS, THE
Dark Horse Comics: March, 2003 - No. 4, June, 2003 ($2.99, limited series)

	GD	VG	FN	VF	VF/NM	NM-
1-4-Paul Lee-c/a; Scott Allie-s						3.00

DEVIL'S HIGHWAY
AWA Studios: Jul, 2020 - No. 5, Nov, 2020 ($3.99, limited series)

	GD	VG	FN	VF	VF/NM	NM-
1-5-Benjamin Percy-s/Brent Schoonover-a						4.00

DEVI / WITCHBLADE
Graphic India Pte, Ltd.: Jan, 2016 ($4.99, one-shot)

	GD	VG	FN	VF	VF/NM	NM-
1-Ron Marz & Samit Basu-s/Eric & Rick Basuldua & Mukesh Singh-a; multiple covers						5.00

DEVOLUTION
Dynamite Entertainment: 2016 - No. 5, 2016 ($3.99)

	GD	VG	FN	VF	VF/NM	NM-
1-5-Remender-s/Wayshak-a/Jae Lee-c						4.00

DEXTER (Character from the novels and Showtime series)
Marvel Comics: Sept, 2013 - No. 5, Jan, 2014 ($3.99, limited series)

	GD	VG	FN	VF	VF/NM	NM-
1-Linsday-s/Talajic-a/Mike Del Mundo-c in all	2	4	6	8	10	12
2-5						5.00

DEXTER COMICS
Dearfield Publ.: Summer, 1948 - No. 5, July, 1949

	GD	VG	FN	VF	VF/NM	NM-
1-Teen-age humor	20	40	60	114	182	250

Diablo House #1 © Ted Adams & IDW

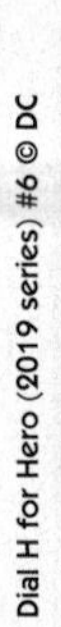

Dial H for Hero (2019 series) #6 © DC

Dick Tracy #16 © NYNS

	GD 2.0	VG 4.0	FN 6.0	VF 8.0	VF/NM 9.0	NM- 9.2
2-Junie Prom app.	14	28	42	78	112	145
3-5	11	22	33	62	85	110

DEXTER DOWN UNDER (Character from the novels and Showtime series)
Marvel Comics: Apr, 2014 - No. 5, Aug, 2014 ($3.99, limited series)

1-5-Jeff Linsday-s/Dalibor Talajic-a/Mike Del Mundo-c 4.00

DEXTER'S LABORATORY (Cartoon Network)
DC Comics: Sept, 1999 - No. 34, Apr, 2003 ($1.99/$2.25)

1 6.00
2-10: 2-McCracken-s 3.00
11-24, 26-34: 31-Begin $2.25-c. 32-34-Wray-c 3.00
25-(50¢-c) Tartakovsky-s/a; Action Hank-c/app. 3.00

DEXTER'S LABORATORY (Cartoon Network)
IDW Publishing: Apr, 2014 - No. 4, Jul, 2014 ($3.99)

1-4-Fridolfs-s/Jampole-a; three covers on each 4.00

DEXTER THE DEMON (Formerly Melvin The Monster)(See Cartoon Kids & Peter the Little Pest)
Atlas Comics (HPC): No. 7, Sept, 1957

	GD	VG	FN	VF	VF/NM	NM-
7	13	26	39	74	105	135

DHAMPIRE: STILLBORN
DC Comics (Vertigo): 1996 ($5.95, one-shot, mature)

1-Nancy Collins script; Paul Lee-c/a 6.00

DIABLO
DC Comics: Jan, 2012 - No. 5, Oct, 2012 ($2.99, limited series)

1-5-Aaron Williams-s/Joseph Lacroix-a/c 3.00

DIABLO HOUSE
IDW Publishing: Jul, 2017 - No. 4, Dec, 2017 ($3.99)

1-4-Horror anthology; Ted Adams-s/Santipérez-a 4.00

DIAL H (Dial H for HERO)(Also see Justice League #23.3)
DC Comics: Jul, 2012 - No. 15, Oct, 2013 ($2.99/$4.99)

1-14: 1-6-China Miéville-s/Mateus Santolouco-a/Brian Bolland-c. 1-Variant-c by Finch 3.00
15-($4.99) Mieville-s/Ponticelli-a/Bolland-c 5.00
#0 (11/12, $2.99) Origin of the dial; Miéville-s/Burchielli-a/Bolland-c 3.00

DIAL H FOR HERO
DC Comics: May, 2019 - No. 12, Apr, 2020 ($3.99)

1-12: 1-Intro. Miguel Montez; Humphries-s/Quinones-a. 3-Robby Reed returns 4.00

DIARY CONFESSIONS (Formerly Ideal Romance)
Stanmor/Key Publ.(Medal Comics): No. 9, May, 1955 - No. 14, Apr, 1955

	GD	VG	FN	VF	VF/NM	NM-
9	14	28	42	76	108	140
10-14	10	20	30	58	79	100

DIARY LOVES (Formerly Love Diary #1; G. I. Sweethearts #32 on)
Quality Comics Group: No. 2, Nov, 1949 - No. 31, April, 1953

	GD	VG	FN	VF	VF/NM	NM-
2-Ward-c/a, 9 pgs.	24	48	72	140	230	320
3 (1/50)-Photo-c begin, end #27?	14	28	42	80	115	150
4-Crandall-a	15	30	45	83	124	165
5-7,10	12	24	36	69	97	125
8,9-Ward-a 6,8 pgs. 8-Gustavson-a; Esther Williams photo-c	15	30	45	90	140	190
11,13,14,17-20	12	24	36	67	94	120
12,15,16-Ward-a 9,7,8 pgs.	15	30	45	85	130	175
21-Ward-a, 7 pgs.	14	28	42	82	121	160
22-31: 31-Whitney-a	11	22	33	64	90	115

NOTE: *Photo c-3-10, 12-28.*

DIARY OF HORROR
Avon Periodicals: December, 1952

	GD	VG	FN	VF	VF/NM	NM-
1-Hollingsworth-c/a; bondage-c	94	188	282	597	1025	1450

DIARY SECRETS (Formerly Teen-Age Diary Secrets)(See Giant Comics Ed.)
St. John Publishing Co.: No. 10, Feb, 1952 - No. 30, Sept, 1955

	GD	VG	FN	VF	VF/NM	NM-
10-Baker-c/a most issues	76	152	228	486	831	1175
11-16,18,19: 12,13,15-Baker-c	68	136	198	419	722	1025
17,20: Kubert-r/Hollywood Confessions #1. 17-r/Teen Age Romances #9	81	162	243	518	884	1250
21-30: 22,27-Signed stories by Estrada. 28-Last precode (3/55)	60	120	180	381	653	925
nn-(25¢ giant, nd (1950?)-Baker-c & rebound St. John comics	161	322	483	1030	1765	2500

DICK COLE (Sport Thrills No. 11 on)(See Blue Bolt & Four Most #1)
Curtis Publ./Star Publications: Dec-Jan, 1948-49 - No. 10, June-July, 1950

	GD	VG	FN	VF	VF/NM	NM-
1-Sgt. Spook; L. B. Cole-c; McWilliams-a; Curt Swan's 1st work	39	78	117	231	378	525
2,5	16	32	48	94	147	200
3,4,6-10: All-L.B. Cole-c. 10-Joe Louis story	22	44	66	132	216	300
Accepted Reprint #7(V1#6 on-c)(1950's)-Reprints #7; L.B. Cole-c	9	18	27	47	61	75
Accepted Reprint #9(nd)-(Reprints #9 & #8-c)	9	18	27	47	61	75

NOTE: ***L. B. Cole** c-1, 3, 4, 6-10. **Al McWilliams** a-6. Dick Cole in 1-9. Baseball c-10. Basketball c-9. Football c-8.*

DICKIE DARE
Eastern Color Printing Co.: 1941 - No. 4, 1942 (#3 on sale 6/15/42)

	GD	VG	FN	VF	VF/NM	NM-
1-Caniff-a, bondage-c by Everett	65	130	195	416	708	1000
2	31	62	93	182	296	410
3,4-Half Scorchy Smith by Noel Sickles who was very influential in Milton Caniff's development	32	64	96	192	314	435

DICK POWELL (Also see A-1 Comics)
Magazine Enterprises: No. 22, 1949 (one shot)

	GD	VG	FN	VF	VF/NM	NM-
A-1 22-Photo-c	22	44	66	132	216	300

DICK QUICK, ACE REPORTER (See Picture News #10)

DICKS
Caliber Comics: 1997 - No. 4, 1998 ($2.95, B&W)

1-4-Ennis-s/McCrea-c/a; r/Fleetway 4.00
TPB ('98, $12.95) r/series 13.00

DICK'S ADVENTURES
Dell Publishing Co.: No. 245, Sept, 1949

	GD	VG	FN	VF	VF/NM	NM-
Four Color 245	6	12	18	37	66	95

DICK TRACY (See Famous Feature Stories, Harvey Comics Library, Limited Collectors' Ed., Mammoth Comics, Merry Christmas, The Original..., Popular Comics, Super Book No. 1, 7, 13, 25, Super Comics & Tastee-Freez)

DICK TRACY
David McKay Publications: May, 1937 - Jan, 1938

	GD	VG	FN	VF	VF/NM	NM-
Feature Books nn - 100 pgs., partially reprinted as 4-Color No. 1 (appeared before Large Feature Comics, 1st Dick Tracy comic book) (Very Rare-five known copies; two incomplete)	1550	3100	4650	11,600	21,300	31,000
Feature Books 4 - Reprints nn issue w/new-c	155	310	465	992	1696	2400
Feature Books 6,9	107	214	321	680	1165	1650

DICK TRACY (...Monthly #1-24)
Dell Publishing Co.: 1939 - No. 24, Dec, 1949

	GD	VG	FN	VF	VF/NM	NM-
Large Feature Comic 1 (1939) -Dick Tracy Meets The Blank	239	478	717	1530	2615	3700
Large Feature Comic 4,8	116	232	348	742	1271	1800
Large Feature Comic 11,13,15	103	206	309	659	1130	1600
Four Color 1(1939)('35-r)	1100	2200	3300	8360	15,930	23,500
Four Color 6(1940)('37-r)-(Scarce)	277	554	831	1773	3037	4300
Four Color 8(1940)('38-'39-r)	148	396	444	947	1624	2300
Large Feature Comic 3(1941, Series II)	106	212	318	678	1164	1650
Four Color 21('41)('38-r)	95	190	285	603	1039	1475
Four Color 34('43)('39-'40-r)	39	78	114	289	657	1025
Four Color 56('44)('40-r)	34	68	102	247	554	860
Four Color 96('46)('40-r)	23	46	69	161	356	550
Four Color 133('47)('40-'41-r)	18	36	54	124	275	425
Four Color 163('47)('41-r)	16	32	48	110	243	375
1(1/48)('34-r)	47	94	141	364	820	1275
2,3	24	48	72	168	372	575
4-10	19	38	57	131	291	450
11-18: 13-Bondage-c	14	28	42	97	214	330
19-1st app. Sparkle Plenty, B.O. Plenty & Gravel Gertie in a 3-pg. strip not by Gould	15	30	45	103	227	350
20-1st app. Sam Catchem; c/a not by Gould	13	26	39	91	201	310
21-24-Only 2 pg. Gould-a in each	13	26	39	89	195	300

NOTE: *No. 19-24 have a 2 pg. biography of a famous villain illustrated by **Gould**: 19-Little Face; 20-Flattop; 21-Breathless Mahoney; 22-Measles; 23-Itchy; 24-The Brow.*

DICK TRACY (Continued from Dell series)(...Comics Monthly #25-140)
Harvey Publications: No. 25, Mar, 1950 - No. 145, April, 1961

	GD	VG	FN	VF	VF/NM	NM-
25-Flat Top-c/story (also #26,27)	11	22	33	76	163	250
26-28,30: 28-Bondage-c. 28,29-The Brow-c/stories	9	18	27	61	123	185
29-1st app. Gravel Gertie in a Gould-r	10	20	30	69	147	225
31,32,34,35,37-40: 40-Intro/origin 2-way wrist radio (6/51)	8	16	24	52	99	145
33- "Measles the Teen-Age Dope Pusher"	9	18	27	61	123	185
36-1st app. B.O. Plenty in a Gould-r	9	18	27	61	123	185
41-50	7	14	21	46	86	125

Dick Tracy Forever #3 © Tribune

Die!namite #1 © DYN

Dilly #1 © LEV

	GD	VG	FN	VF	VF/NM	NM-
	2.0	4.0	6.0	8.0	9.0	9.2

51-56,58-80: 51-2pgs Powell-a 6 12 18 40 73 105
57-1st app. Sam Catchem in a Gould-r 7 14 21 46 86 125
81-99,101-140: 99-109-Painted-c 6 12 18 37 66 95
100, 141-145 (25¢)(titled "Dick Tracy") 6 12 18 40 73 105
NOTE: *Powell a(1-2pgs.)-43, 44, 104, 108, 109, 145. No. 110-120, 141-145 are all reprints from earlier issues.*

DICK TRACY ("Reuben Award" series)
Blackthorne Publishing: 12/84 - No. 24, 6/89 (1-12: $5.95; 13-24: $6.95, B&W, 76 pgs.)
1-8-1st printings; hard-c ed. ($14.95) 20.00
1-3-2nd printings, 1986; hard-c ed. 20.00
1-12-1st & 2nd printings; squarebound. thick-c 12.00
13-24 ($6.95): 21,22-Regular-c & stapled 14.00
NOTE: *Gould daily & Sunday strip-r in all. 1-12 r-12/31/45-4/5/49; 13-24 r-7/13/41-2/20/44.*

DICK TRACY (Disney)
WD Publications: 1990 - No. 3, 1990 (color) (Book 3 adapts 1990 movie)
Book One ($3.95, 52pgs.)-Kyle Baker-c/a 6.00
Book Two, Three ($5.95, 68pgs.)-Direct sale 6.00
Book Two, Three ($2.95, 68pgs.)-Newsstand 4.00

DICK TRACY ADVENTURES
Gladstone Publishing: May, 1991 ($4.95, 76 pgs.)
1-Reprints strips 2/1/42-4/18/42 5.00

DICK TRACY: DEAD OR ALIVE
IDW Publishing: Sept, 2018 - No. 4, Dec, 2018 ($3.99, limited series)
1-4-Lee & Michael Allred-s/Rich Tommaso-a 4.00

DICK TRACY, EXPLOITS OF
Rosdon Books, Inc.: 1946 ($1.00, hard-c strip reprints)
1-Reprints the near complete case of "The Brow" from 6/12/44 to 9/24/44
(story starts a few weeks late) 25 50 75 147 241 335
with dust jacket... 39 78 117 240 395 550

DICK TRACY FOREVER
IDW Publishing: Apr, 2019 - No. 4, Jul, 2019 ($3.99, limited series)
1-4-Michael A. Oeming-s/a. 1-Set in 1931. 2-Set in 1951. 3-Set in 2021. 4-Set in 2031 4.00

DICK TRACY MONTHLY/WEEKLY
Blackthorne Publishing: May, 1986 - No. 99, 1989 ($2.00, B&W)
(Becomes Weekly #26 on)
1-60: Gould-r. 30,31-Mr. Crime app. 4.00
61-90 4.00
91-95 6.00
96-99-Low print 1 2 3 5 7 9
NOTE: *#1-10 reprint strips 3/10/40-7/13/41; #10(pg.8)-51 reprint strips 4/6/49-12/31/55; #52-99 reprint strips 12/26/56-4/26/64.*

DICK TRACY SPECIAL
Blackthorne Publ.: Jan, 1988 - No. 3, Aug. (no month), 1989 ($2.95, B&W)
1-3: 1-Origin D. Tracy; 4/strips 10/12/31-3/30/32 4.00

DICK TRACY: THE EARLY YEARS
Blackthorne Publishing: Aug, 1987 - No. 4, Aug (no month) 1989 ($6.95, B&W, 76 pgs.)
1-3: 1-4-r/strips 10/12/31(1st daily)-8/31/32 & Sunday strips 6/12/32-8/28/32;
Big Boy apps. in #1-3 1 2 3 4 5 7
4 ($2.95, 52pgs.) 4.00

DICK TRACY UNPRINTED STORIES
Blackthorne Publishing: Sept, 1987 - No. 4, June, 1988 ($2.95, B&W)
1-4: Reprints strips 1/1/56-12/25/56 4.00

DICK TURPIN (See Legend of Young...)

DIE (Singular of dice)
Image Comics: Dec, 2018 - Present ($3.99)
1-15-Kieron Gillen-s/Stephanie Hans-a; Dungeons & Dragons-themed story 4.00

DIE-CUT
Marvel Comics UK, Ltd: Nov, 1993 - No. 4, Feb, 1994 ($1.75, limited series)
1-4: 1-Die-cut-c; The Beast app. 3.00

DIE-CUT VS. G-FORCE
Marvel Comics UK, Ltd: Nov, 1993 - No. 2, Dec, 1993 ($2.75, limited series)
1,2-($2.75)-Gold foil-c on both 4.00

DIE!DIE!DIE!
Image Comics (Skybound): Jul, 2018 - Present ($3.99)
1-13: 1-Robert Kirkman-s/Chris Burnham-a 4.00

DIE HARD: YEAR ONE (Based on the John McClane character)
BOOM! Studios: Aug, 2009 - No. 8, Mar, 2010 ($3.99, limited series)
1-8-Chaykin-s; Officer McClane in 1976 NYC; multiple covers on each 4.00

DIE KITTY DIE!
Chapterhouse Comics: Oct, 2016 - Present ($3.99/$4.99)
1,3,4-($3.99) Fernando Ruiz-s/Dan Parent-a; Harvey-style spoof 4.00
2-($4.99) Bonus faux 1969 reprint; Li'l Satan app. 5.00
... Christmas Special 1 (12/07, $4.99) Christmas stories 5.00
... Summer Vacation 1 (7/17, $3.99) Parent, Ruiz & Lagace-a 4.00

DIE KITTY DIE! HEAVEN & HELL
Chapterhouse Comics: No. 0, May, 2018 - No. 4, Jan, 2019 ($3.99/$4.99)
0-4-($3.99) Fernando Ruiz-s/Dan Parent-a 4.00
...: 2018 Halloween Special (10/18, $3.99) Art by Parent, Lagace, Bone, Pepoy 4.00

DIE KITTY DIE! HOLLYWOOD OR BUST
Chapterhouse Comics: Jul, 2017 - No. 4, Sept, 2017 ($3.99/$4.99)
1,2-($3.99) Fernando Ruiz-s/Dan Parent-a 4.00
3,4-($4.99) 5.00

DIE, MONSTER, DIE (See Movie Classics)

DIE!NAMITE
Dynamite Entertainment: 2020 - No. 5, 2021 ($3.99, limited series)
1-5-Vampirella, Red Sonja, Dejah Thoris, Peter Cannon Thunderbolt vs. zombies 4.00
... Valentine's Special, Our Bloody Valentine (2021, $4.99) short stories by various 5.00

DIESEL (TYSON HESSE'S...)
Boom Entertainment (BOOM! Box): Sept, 2015 - No. 4, Dec, 2015 ($3.99, limited series)
1-4-Tyson Hesse-s/a in all. 1-Three covers 4.00

DIGIMON DIGITAL MONSTERS (TV)
Dark Horse Comics: May, 2000 - No. 12, Nov, 2000 ($2.95/$2.99)
1-12 3.00

DIGITEK
Marvel UK, Ltd: Dec, 1992 - No. 4, Mar, 1993 ($1.95/$2.25, mini-series)
1-4: 3-Deathlock-c/story 3.00

DILLY (Dilly Duncan from Daredevil Comics; see Boy Comics #57)
Lev Gleason Publications: May, 1953 - No. 3, Sept, 1953
1-Teenage; Biro-c 10 20 30 58 79 100
2,3-Biro-c 8 16 24 40 50 60

DILTON'S STRANGE SCIENCE (See Pep Comics #78)
Archie Comics: May, 1989 - No. 5, May, 1990 (75¢/$1.00)
1-5 3.00

DIME COMICS
Newsbook Publ. Corp.: 1945; 1951
1-(32 pgs.) Silver Streak/Green Dragon-c/sty; Japanese WWII-c by L. B. Cole (Rare)
216 432 648 1382 2366 3350
1(1951) 23 46 69 136 223 310

DINGBATS (See 1st Issue Special)

DING DONG
Compix/Magazine Enterprises: Summer?, 1946 - No. 5, 1947 (52 pgs.)
1-Funny animal 40 80 120 244 402 560
2 (9/46) 18 36 54 107 169 230
3 (Wint '46-'47) - 5 15 30 45 85 130 175

DINKY DUCK (Paul Terry's...) (See Approved Comics, Blue Ribbon, Giant Comics Edition #5A & New Terrytoons)
St. John Publishing Co./Pines No. 16 on: Nov, 1951 - No. 16, Sept, 1955; No. 16, Fall, 1956; No. 17, May, 1957 - No. 19, Summer, 1958
1-Funny animal 15 30 45 86 133 180
2 9 18 27 47 61 75
3-10 6 12 18 31 38 45
11-16(9/55) 6 12 18 28 34 40
16 (Fall, '56) - 19 5 10 15 23 28 32

DINKY DUCK & HASHIMOTO-SAN (See Deputy Dawg Presents...)

DINO (TV)(The Flintstones)
Charlton Publications: Aug, 1973 - No. 20, Jan, 1977 (Hanna-Barbera)
1 3 6 9 19 30 40
2-10 2 4 6 10 14 18
11-20 2 4 6 8 10 12
Digest nn (w/Xerox Pub., 1974) (low print run) 2 4 6 11 16 20

DINO ISLAND
Mirage Studios: Feb, 1994 - No. 2, Mar, 1994 ($2.75, limited series)

Dirty Pair #3 © Studio Proteus

Disaster Inc. #1 © Harris & AfterShock

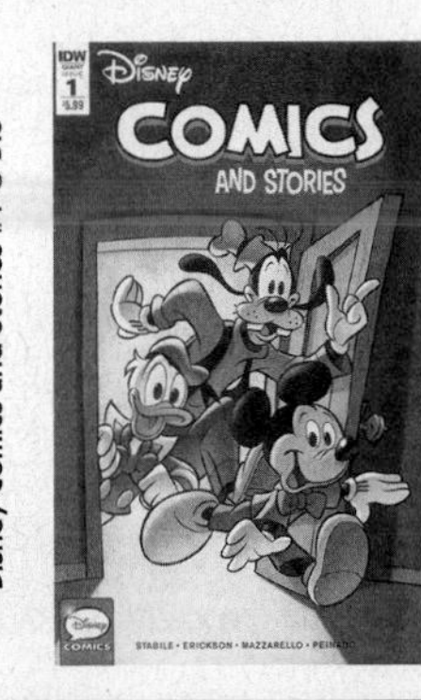

Disney Comics and Stories #1 © DIS

GD 2.0 | VG 4.0 | FN 6.0 | VF 8.0 | VF/NM 9.0 | NM- 9.2

1,2-By Jim Lawson 3.00

DINO RIDERS
Marvel Comics: Feb, 1989 - No. 3, 1989 ($1.00)
1-3: Based on toys 3.00

DINOSAUR REX
Upshot Graphics (Fantagraphics): 1986 - No. 3, 1986 ($2.00, limited series)
1-3 3.00

DINOSAURS, A CELEBRATION
Marvel Comics (Epic): Oct, 1992 - No. 4, Oct, 1992 ($4.95, lim. series, 52 pgs.)
1-4: 2-Bolton painted-c 5.00

DINOSAURS ATTACK! (Based on Topps trading card set)
IDW Publishing: Jul, 2013 - No. 5, Nov, 2013 ($3.99, limited series)
1-5: 1,2-Remastered version of 1991 graphic novel. 3-5-New continuation of story 4.00

DINOSAURS ATTACK! THE GRAPHIC NOVEL
Eclipse Comics: 1991 ($3.95, coated stock, stiff-c)
Book One- Based on Topps trading cards 5.00

DINOSAURS FOR HIRE
Malibu Comics: Feb, 1993 - No. 12, Feb, 1994 ($1.95/$2.50)
1-12: 1,10-Flip bk. 8-Bagged w/Skycap; Staton-c. 10-Flip book 3.00

DINOSAURS GRAPHIC NOVEL (TV)
Disney Comics: 1992 - No. 2, 1993 ($2.95, 52 pgs.)
1,2-Staton-a; based on Dinosaurs TV show 4.00

DINOSAURUS
Dell Publishing Co.: No. 1120, Aug, 1960
Four Color 1120-Movie, painted-c 8 16 24 51 96 140

DIPPY DUCK
Atlas Comics (OPI): October, 1957
1-Maneely-a; code approved 15 30 45 86 133 180

DIRECTORY TO A NONEXISTENT UNIVERSE
Eclipse Comics: Dec, 1987 ($2.00, B&W)
1 3.00

DIRK GENTLY'S HOLISTIC DETECTIVE AGENCY
IDW Publishing: May, 2015 - No. 5, Oct, 2015 ($3.99, limited series)
1-5: 1-Ryall-s/Kyriazis-a; multiple covers on each 4.00
...: A Spoon Too Short 1-5 (2/16 - No. 5, 6/16, $3.99) A.E. David-s/Kyriazis-a 4.00
...: The Salmon of Doubt 1-9 (10/16 - No. 9, 6/17, $3.99) A.E. David-s/Kyriazis-a 4.00

DIRTY DOZEN (See Movie Classics)

DIRTY PAIR (Manga)
Eclipse Comics: Dec, 1988 - No. 4, Apr, 1989 ($2.00, B&W, limited series)
1-4: Japanese manga with original stories 3.00
...: Start the Violence (Dark Horse, 9/99, $2.95) r/B&W stories in color from Dark Horse Presents #132-134; covers by Warren & Pearson 3.00

DIRTY PAIR: FATAL BUT NOT SERIOUS (Manga)
Dark Horse Comics: July, 1995 - No. 5, Nov, 1995 ($2.95, limited series)
1-5 3.00

DIRTY PAIR: RUN FROM THE FUTURE (Manga)
Dark Horse Comics: Jan, 2000 - No. 4, Mar, 2000 ($2.95, limited series)
1-4-Warren-s/c/a. Variant-c by Hughes(1), Stelfreeze(2), Timm(3), Ramos(4) 3.00

DIRTY PAIR: SIM HELL (Manga)
Dark Horse Comics: May, 1993 - No. 4, Aug, 1993 ($2.50, B&W, limited series)
1-4 3.00
...Remastered #1-4 (5/01 - 8/01) reprints in color, with pin-up gallery 3.00

DIRTY PAIR II (Manga)
Eclipse Comics: June, 1989 - No. 5, Mar, 1990 ($2.00, B&W, limited series)
1-5: 3-Cover is misnumbered as #1 3.00

DIRTY PAIR III, THE (A Plague of Angels) (Manga)
Eclipse Comics: Aug, 1990 - No. 5, Aug, 1991 ($2.00/$2.25, B&W, lim. series)
1-5 3.00

DISASTER INC.
AfterShock Comics: Apr, 2020 - No. 5, Dec, 2020 ($4.99/$3.99)
1-($4.99)-Joe Harris-s/Sebastian Piriz-a 5.00
2-5-($3.99) 4.00

GD 2.0 | VG 4.0 | FN 6.0 | VF 8.0 | VF/NM 9.0 | NM- 9.2

DISCIPLINE
Image Comics: Mar, 2016 - No. 6, Aug, 2016 ($2.99)
1-6-Peter Milligan-s/Leandro Fernández-a 3.00

DISNEY AFTERNOON, THE (TV)
Marvel Comics: Nov, 1994 - No. 10?, Aug, 1995 ($1.50)
1-10: 3-w/bound-in Power Ranger Barcode Card 4.00

DISNEY AFTERNOON GIANT
IDW Publishing: Oct, 2018 - No. 8, Dec, 2019 ($5.99)
1-8: 1-4-DuckTales and Chip 'n' Dale stories. 5-Darkwing Duck and Chip 'n' Dale 6.00

DISNEY COMIC ALBUM
Disney Comics: 1990(no month, year) - No. 8, 1991 ($6.95/$7.95)
1,2 ($6.95): 1-Donald Duck and Gyro Gearloose by Barks(r). 2-Uncle Scrooge by Barks(r); Jr. Woodchucks app. 9.00
3-8: 3-Donald Duck-r/F.C. 308 by Barks; begin $7.95-c. 4-Mickey Mouse Meets the Phantom Blot; r/M.M Club Parade (censored 1956 version of story). 5-Chip 'n' Dale Rescue Rangers; new-a. 6-Uncle Scrooge. 7-Donald Duck in Too Many Pets; Barks-r(4) including F.C. #29. 8-Super Goof; r/S.G. #1, D.D. #102 9.00

DISNEY COMIC HITS
Marvel Comics: Oct, 1995 - No. 16, Jan, 1997 ($1.50/$2.50)
1-16: 4-Toy Story. 6-Aladdin. 7-Pocahontas. 10-The Hunchback of Notre Dame (Same story in Disney's The Hunchback of Notre Dame). 13-Aladdin and the Forty Thieves 4.00

DISNEY COMICS
Disney Comics: June, 1990
Boxed set of #1 issues includes Donald Duck Advs., Ducktales, Chip 'n Dale Rescue Rangers, Roger Rabbit, Mickey Mouse Advs. & Goofy Advs.; limited to 10,000 sets 2 4 6 11 16 20

DISNEY COMICS AND STORIES
IDW Publishing: Sept, 2018 - No. 13, May, 2020 ($5.99)
1-13-Reprints of Danish and Italian stories 6.00

DISNEY GIANT HALLOWEEN HEX
IDW Publishing: Oct, 2016 ($6.99)
1-Halloween-themed reprints of U.S., Dutch and Italian stories; three covers 7.00

DISNEY KINGDOMS: FIGMENT 2 (Sequel to Figment series)
Marvel Comics: Nov, 2015 - No. 5, Mar, 2016 ($3.99)
1-5: 1-Jim Zub-s/Ramon Bachs-a/J. T. Christopher-c 4.00

DISNEY KINGDOMS: SEEKERS OF THE WEIRD
Marvel Comics: Mar, 2014 - No. 5, Jul, 2014 ($3.99)
1-5: 1-Seifert-s/Moline-a/Del Mundo-c. 3-Andrade-a 4.00

DISNEYLAND BIRTHDAY PARTY (Also see Dell Giants)
Gladstone Publishing Co.: Aug, 1985 ($2.50)
1-Reprints Dell Giant with new-photo-c 2 4 6 8 10 12
...Comics Digest #1-(Digest) 2 4 6 8 11 14

DISNEYLAND MAGAZINE
Fawcett Publications: Feb. 15, 1972 - ? (10-1/4"x12-5/8", 20 pgs, weekly)
1-One or two page painted art features on Dumbo, Snow White, Lady & the Tramp, the Aristocats, Brer Rabbit, Peter Pan, Cinderella, Jungle Book, Alice & Pinocchio. Most standard characters app. 3 6 9 16 23 30

DISNEYLAND, USA (See Dell Giant No. 30)

DISNEY MAGIC KINGDOM COMICS
IDW Publishing: May, 2016 - No. 2, Aug, 2016 ($6.99, squarebound, quarterly)
1,2-Reprints inspired by the theme parks; Barks-a 7.00

DISNEY MOVIE BOOK
Walt Disney Productions (Gladstone): 1990 ($7.95, 8-1/2"x11", 52 pgs.) (w/pull-out poster)
1-Roger Rabbit in Tummy Trouble; from the cartoon film strips adapted to the comic format. Ron Dias-c 2 4 6 8 10 12

DISNEY'S ACTION CLUB
Acclaim Books: 1997 - No. 4 ($4.50, digest size)
1-4: 1-Hercules. 4-Mighty Ducks 4.50

DISNEY'S ALADDIN (Movie)
Marvel Comics: no date (Oct, 1994) - No. 11, 1995 ($1.50)
1-11 3.00

DISNEY'S BEAUTY AND THE BEAST (Movie)
Marvel Comics: Sept, 1994 - No. 13, 1995 ($1.50)
1-13 3.00

Disney's The Little Mermaid: Underwater Engagements © DIS

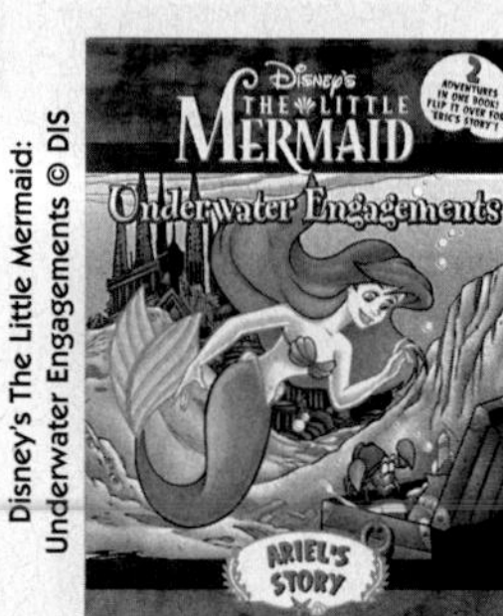

Dissension: War Eternal #3 © Gunderson

Divided States of Hysteria #4 © H. Chaykin

GD 2.0 | VG 4.0 | FN 6.0 | VF 8.0 | VF/NM 9.0 | NM- 9.2

DISNEY'S BEAUTY AND THE BEAST HOLIDAY SPECIAL
Acclaim Books: 1997 ($4.50, digest size, one-shot)

1-Based on The Enchanted Christmas video 4.50

DISNEY'S COLOSSAL COMICS COLLECTION
Disney Comics: 1991 - No. 10, 1993 ($1.95, digest-size, 96/132 pgs.)

1-10: Ducktales, Talespin, Chip 'n Dale's Rescue Rangers. 4-r/Darkwing Duck #1-4. 6-Goofy begins. 8-Little Mermaid 5.00

DISNEY'S COMICS IN 3-D
Disney Comics: 1992 ($2.95, w/glasses, polybagged)

1-Infinity-c; Barks, Rosa, Gottfredson-r 5.00

DISNEY'S ENCHANTING STORIES
Acclaim Books: 1997 - No. 5 ($4.50, digest size)

1-5: 1-Hercules. 2-Pocahontas 4.50

DISNEY'S HERO SQUAD
BOOM! Studios: Jan, 2010 - No. 8, Aug, 2010 ($2.99)

1-8: 1-3-Phantom Blot app. 1-Back-up reprint of Super Goof #1 3.00

DISNEY'S NEW ADVENTURES OF BEAUTY AND THE BEAST (Also see Beauty and the Beast & Disney's Beauty and the Beast)
Disney Comics: 1992 - No. 2, 1992 ($1.50, limited series)

1,2-New stories based on movie 3.00

DISNEY'S POCAHONTAS (Movie)
Marvel Comics: 1995 ($4.95, one-shot)

1-Movie adaptation 1 2 3 4 5 7

DISNEY'S TALESPIN LIMITED SERIES: "TAKE OFF" (TV) (See Talespin)
W. D. Publications (Disney Comics): Jan, 1991 - No. 4, Apr, 1991 ($1.50, lim. series, 52 pgs.)

1-4: Based on animated series; 4 part origin 4.00

DISNEY'S TARZAN (Movie)
Dark Horse Comics: June, 1999 - No. 2, July, 1999 ($2.95, limited series)

1,2: Movie adaptation 3.00

DISNEY'S THE LION KING (Movie)
Marvel Comics: July, 1994 - No. 2, July, 1994 ($1.50, limited series)

1,2: 2-part movie adaptation 3.00
1-($2.50, 52 pgs.)-Complete story 5.00

DISNEY'S THE LITTLE MERMAID (Movie)
Marvel Comics: Sept, 1994 - No. 12, 1995 ($1.50)

1-12 4.00

DISNEY'S THE LITTLE MERMAID LIMITED SERIES (Movie)
Disney Comics: Feb, 1992 - No. 4, May, 1992 ($1.50, limited series)

1-4: Peter David scripts; takes place before the movie 4.00
Set of #1-4 in unopened 4-issue Collector's Pack 65.00

DISNEY'S THE LITTLE MERMAID: UNDERWATER ENGAGEMENTS
Acclaim Books: 1997 ($4.50, digest size)

1-Flip book 4.50

DISNEY'S THE HUNCHBACK OF NOTRE DAME (Movie)(See Disney's Comic Hits #10)
Marvel Comics: July, 1996 ($4.95, squarebound, one-shot)

1-Movie adaptation. 1 2 3 4 5 9

NOTE: A different edition of this series was sold at Wal-Mart stores with new covers depicting scenes from the 1989 feature film. Inside contents and price were identical.

DISNEY'S THE PRINCE AND THE PAUPER
W. D. Publications: no date ($5.95, 68 pgs., squarebound)

nn-Movie adaptation 6.00

DISNEY'S THE THREE MUSKETEERS (Movie)
Marvel Comics: Jan, 1994 - No. 2, Feb, 1994 ($1.50, limited series)

1,2-Morrow-c; Spiegle-a; Movie adaptation 3.00

DISNEY'S TOY STORY (Movie)
Marvel Comics: Dec, 1995 ($4.95, one-shot)

nn-Adaptation of film 1 2 3 5 7 9

DISNEY TSUM TSUM KINGDOM ONE-SHOT (Based on the Japanese collectible stuffed toys)
IDW Publishing: Sept, 2018 ($7.99, squarebound, one-shot)

1-Short stories by various; Baldari-c 8.00

DISSENSION: WAR ETERNAL
Aspen MLT: Jul, 2018 - No. 5, Jan, 2019 ($3.99)

1-5-Fielder-s/Gunderson-a; Aspen Mascots bonus back-up story in each 4.00

GD 2.0 | VG 4.0 | FN 6.0 | VF 8.0 | VF/NM 9.0 | NM- 9.2

DISTANT SOIL, A (1st Series)
WaRP Graphics: Dec, 1983 - No. 9, Mar 1986 ($1.50, B&W)

1-Magazine size 6.00
2-9: 2-4 are magazine size 4.00

NOTE: Second printings exist of #1, 2, 3 & 6.

DISTANT SOIL, A
Donning (Star Blaze): Mar, 1989 ($12.95, trade paperback)

nn-new material 13.00

DISTANT SOIL, A (2nd Series)
Aria Press/Image Comics (Highbrow Entertainment) #15 on:
June, 1991 - No. 42, Oct, 2013 ($1.75/$2.50/$2.95/$3.50/$3.95, B&W)

1-27: 13-$2.95-c begins. 14-Sketchbook. 15-(8/96)-1st Image issue 4.00
29-33,35,37-($3.95) 4.00
34-($4.95, 64 pages) includes sketchbook pages 5.00
36,38-($4.50) 36-Back-up story by Darnall & Doran. 38-Includes sketch pages 4.50
39-42-($3.50) 3.50
The Aria ('01, $16.95,TPB) r/#26-31 17.00
The Ascendant ('98, $18.95,TPB) r/#13-25 19.00
The Gathering ('97, $18.95,TPB) r/#1-13; intro. Neil Gaiman 19.00
Vol. 4: Coda (2005, $17.99, TPB) r/#32-38 18.00

NOTE: Four separate printings exist for #1 and are clearly marked. Second printings exist of #2-4 and are also clearly marked.

DISTANT SOIL, A: IMMIGRANT SONG
Donning (Star Blaze): Aug, 1987 ($6.95, trade paperback)

nn-new material 7.00

DISTRICT X (Also see X-Men titles) (Also see Mutopia X)
Marvel Comics: July, 2004 - No. 14, Aug, 2005 ($2.99)

1-14: 1-3-Bishop app.; Yardin-a/Hine-s 3.00
...Vol. 1: Mr. M (2005, $14.99) r/#1-6; sketch page by Yardin 15.00
...Vol. 2: Underground (2005, $19.99) r/#7-14; prologue from X-Men Unlimited #2 20.00

DIVER DAN (TV)
Dell Publishing Co.: Feb-Apr, 1962 - No. 2, June-Aug, 1962

Four Color 1254(#1), 2 5 10 15 33 57 80

DIVERGENCE FCBD SPECIAL EDITION
DC Comics: Jun, 2015 (Free Comic Book Day giveaway)

1-Previews Batman #41, Superman #41, Justice League Darkseid War 1 3 4 6 8 10

DIVIDED STATES OF HYSTERIA
Image Comics: Jun, 2017 - No. 6, Nov, 2017 ($3.99)

1-6-Howard Chaykin-s/a 4.00

DIVINE RIGHT
Image Comics (WildStorm Prod.): Sept, 1997 - No. 12, Nov, 1999 ($2.50)

Preview 5.00
1,2: 1-Jim Lee-s/a(p)/c, 1-Variant-c by Charest 4.00
1-($3.50)-Voyager Pack w/Stormwatch preview 4.00
1-American Entertainment Ed. 6.00
2-Variant-c of Exotica & Blaze 5.00
3-Chromium-c by Jim Lee 5.00
3-12: 3-5-Fairchild & Lynch app. 4-American Entertainment Ed. 8-Two covers. 9-1st DC issue. 11,12-Divine Intervention pt. 1,4 3.00
5-Pacific Comicon Ed. 6.00
6-Glow in the dark variant-c, European Tour Edition 20.00
...Book One TPB (2002, $17.95) r/#1-7 18.00
...Book Two TPB (2002, $17.95) r/#8-12 & Divine Intervention Gen13, ...Wildcats 18.00
...Collected Edition #1-3 ($5.95, TPB) 1-r/#1,2. 2-r/#3,4. 3-r/#5,6 6.00
Divine Intervention/Gen 13 (11/99, $2.50) Part 3; D'Anda-a 3.00
Divine Intervention/Wildcats (11/99, $2.50) Part 2; D'Anda-a 3.00

DIVINITY
Valiant Entertainment: Feb, 2015 - No. 4, May, 2015 ($3.99, limited series)

1-4-Kindt-s/Hairsine-a 4.00
#0 (8/17, $3.99) Kindt-s/Guedes-a; bonus preview of Eternity #1 4.00

DIVINITY II
Valiant Entertainment: Apr, 2016 - No. 4, Jul, 2016 ($3.99, limited series)

1-4-Kindt-s/Hairsine-a; 1-Origin of Myshka 4.00

DIVINITY III: STALINVERSE
Valiant Entertainment: Dec, 2016 - No. 4, Mar, 2017 ($3.99, limited series)

1-4-Kindt-s/Hairsine-a 4.00
Divinity III: Aric, Son of the Revolution 1 (1/17, $3.99) Joe Harris-s/Cafu-a 4.00

Dizzy Dames #1 © ACG

DMZ #27 © Wood & Burchielli

Doc Savage (2013 series) #4 © Conde Nast

GD 2.0 | VG 4.0 | FN 6.0 | VF 8.0 | VF/NM 9.0 | NM- 9.2

Divinity III: Escape From Gulag 396 1 (3/17, $3.99) Eliot Rahal-s/Francis Portela-a 4.00
Divinity III: Komandar Bloodshot 1 (12/16, $3.99) Jeff Lemire-s/Clayton Crain-a 4.00
Divinity III: Shadowman and the Battle for New Stalingrad 1 (2/17, $3.99) Robert Gill-a 4.00

DIVISION 13 (See Comic's Greatest World)
Dark Horse Comics: Sept, 1994 - Jan, 1995 ($2.50, color)
1-4: Giffen story in all. 1-Art Adams-c 4.00

DIXIE DUGAN (See Big Shot, Columbia Comics & Feature Funnies)
McNaught Syndicate/Columbia/Publication Ent.: July, 1942 - No. 13, 1949
(Strip reprints in all)
1-Joe Palooka x-over by Ham Fisher 32 64 96 192 314 435
2 17 34 51 103 162 220
3(1943) 14 28 42 81 118 155
4,5(1945-46)-Bo strip-r 11 22 33 62 86 110
6-13(1/47-49): 6-Paperdoll cut-outs 10 20 30 56 76 95

DIXIE DUGAN
Prize Publications (Headline): V3#1, Nov, 1951 - V4#4, Feb, 1954
V3#1 12 24 36 69 97 125
2-4 8 16 24 42 54 65
V4#1-4(#5-8) 7 14 21 37 46 55

DIZZY DAMES
American Comics Group (B&M Distr. Co.): Sept-Oct, 1952 - No. 6, Jul-Aug, 1953
1-Whitney-c 71 142 213 454 777 1100
2 26 52 78 156 256 355
3-6 23 46 69 134 220 305

DIZZY DON COMICS
F. E. Howard Publications/Dizzy Don Ent. Ltd (Canada): 1942 - No. 22, Oct, 1946; No. 3, Apr, 1947 - No. 4, Sept./Oct., 1947 (Most B&W)
1 (B&W) 55 110 165 352 601 850
2 (B&W) 37 74 111 220 358 495
4-21 (B&W) 32 64 96 192 314 435
22-Full color, 52 pgs. 36 72 108 216 351 485
3 (4/47), 4 (9-10/47)-Full color, 52 pgs. 36 72 108 216 351 485

DIZZY DUCK (Formerly Barnyard Comics)
Standard Comics: No. 32, Nov, 1950 - No. 39, Mar, 1952
32-Funny animal 12 24 36 67 94 120
33-39 8 16 24 42 54 65

DJANGO UNCHAINED (Adaptation of the 2012 movie)
DC Comics (Vertigo): Feb, 2013 - No. 7, Oct, 2013 ($3.99, limited series)
1-Adaptation of Quentin Tarantino's script; Guéra-a; Tarantino foreword; sketch pages 20.00
1-Variant-c by Jim Lee 80.00
2-Cowan-c; bonus concept art and cover sketch art 8.00
2-Variant-c by Mark Chiarello 35.00
3-7: 5-Quitely-c. 7-Alex Ross-c 5.00

DJANGO / ZORRO (Django from the 2012 Taratino movie)
Dynamite Entertainment: 2014 - No. 7, 2015 ($3.99/$5.99, limited series)
1-6-Tarantino & Matt Wagner-s/Esteve Polls-a; multiple covers on each 4.00
7-($5.99) Covers by Jae Lee & Francesco Francavilla 6.00

DMZ
DC Comics (Vertigo): Jan, 2006 - No. 72, Feb, 2012 ($2.99)
1-Brian Wood-s/Riccardo Burchielli-a 4.00
1-(2008, no cover price) Convention Exclusive promotional edition 3.00
2-49,51-72: 2-10-Brian Wood-s/Riccardo Burchielli-a. 11-Donaldson-a. 12-Wood-s/a 3.00
50-($3.99) Short stories by various incl. Risso, Moon, Gibbons, Bermejo, Jim Lee 4.00
...: Blood in the Game TPB (2009, $12.99) r/#29-34; intro. by Greg Palast 13.00
...: Body of a Journalist TPB (2007, $12.99) r/#6-12; intro. by D. Randall Blythe 13.00
...: Collective Punishment TPB (2011, $14.99) r/#55-59 15.00
...: Friendly Fire TPB (2008, $12.99) r/#18-22; intro. by Sgt. John G. Ford 13.00
...: Hearts and Minds TPB (2010, $16.99) r/#42-49; intro. by Morgan Spurlock 17.00
...: M.I.A. TPB (2011, $14.99) r/#50-54 15.00
...: On the Ground TPB (2006, $9.99) r/#1-5; intro. by Brian Azzarello 10.00
...: Public Works TPB (2007, $12.99) r/#13-17; intro. by Cory Doctorow 13.00
...: The Hidden War TPB (2008, $12.99) r/#23-28 13.00
...: War Powers TPB (2009, $14.99) r/#35-41 15.00

DNAGENTS (The New DNAgents V2/1 on)(Also see Surge)
Eclipse Comics: March, 1983 - No. 24, July, 1985 ($1.50, Baxter paper)
1-Origin. 5.00
2-23: 4-Amber app. 8-Infinity-c 4.00
24-Dave Stevens-c 1 2 3 5 6 8

... Industrial Strength Edition TPB (Image, 2008, $24.99) B&W r/#1-14; Evanier intro. 25.00

DOBERMAN (See Sgt. Bilko's Private...)

DOBERMAN
IDW Publishing (Darby Pop): Jul, 2014 - No. 5, Jan, 2015 ($3.99)
1-5-Marder, Rosell, & Lambert-s/McKinney-a 4.00

DOBIE GILLIS (See The Many Loves of...)

DOC FRANKENSTEIN
Burlyman Entertainment: Nov, 2004 - No. 6 ($3.50)
1-6-Wachowski brothers-s/Skroce-a 3.50

DOCK WALLOPER (Ed Burns' ...)
Virgin Comics: Nov, 2007 - No. 5, Jun, 2008 ($2.99)
1-5-Burns & Palmiotti-s/Siju Thomas-a; Prohibition time 3.00

DOC MACABRE
IDW Publishing: Dec, 2010 - No. 3, Feb, 2011 ($3.99)
1-3-Steve Niles-s/Bernie Wrightson-a/c 4.00

DOC SAMSON (Also see Incredible Hulk)
Marvel Comics: Jan, 1996 - No. 4, Apr, 1996 ($1.95, limited series)
1-4: 1-Hulk c/app. 2-She-Hulk-c/app. 3-Punisher-c/app. 4-Polaris-c/app. 3.00

DOC SAMSON (Incredible Hulk)
Marvel Comics: Mar, 2006 - No. 5, July, 2006 ($2.99, limited series)
1-5: 1-DiFilippo-s/Fiorentino-a. 3-Conner-c 3.00

DOC SAVAGE
Gold Key: Nov, 1966
1-Adaptation of the Thousand-Headed Man; James Bama c-r/1964 Doc Savage paperback
12 24 36 84 185 285

DOC SAVAGE (Also see Giant-Size...)
Marvel Comics Group: Oct, 1972 - No. 8, Jan, 1974
1 5 10 15 31 53 75
2,3-Steranko-c 3 6 9 21 33 45
4-8 2 4 6 10 14 18
...: The Man of Bronze TPB (DC Comics, 2010, $17.99) r/#1-8 18.00
NOTE: *Gil Kane c-5, 6. Mooney a-1i.* No. 1, 2 adapts pulp story "The Man of Bronze"; No. 3, 4 adapts "Death in Silver"; No. 5, 6 adapts "The Monsters"; No. 7, 8 adapts "The Brand of The Werewolf".

DOC SAVAGE (Magazine) (See Showcase Presents for reprint)
Marvel Comics Group: Aug, 1975 - No. 8, Spring, 1977 ($1.00, B&W)
1-Cover from movie poster; Ron Ely photo-c 3 6 9 18 28 38
2-5: 3-Buscema-a. 5-Adams-a(1 pg.), Rogers-a(1 pg) 2 4 6 9 13 16
6-8 2 4 6 10 14 18

DOC SAVAGE
DC Comics: Nov, 1987 - No. 4, Feb, 1988 ($1.75, limited series)
1-4: Dennis O'Neil-s/Adam & Andy Kubert-a/c in all 4.00
...: The Silver Pyramid TPB (2009, $19.99) r/#1-4 20.00

DOC SAVAGE
DC Comics: Nov, 1988 - No. 24, Oct, 1990 ($1.75/$2.00: #13-24)
1-16,19-24 4.00
17,18-Shadow x-over 5.00
Annual 1 (1989, $3.50, 68 pgs.) 5.00

DOC SAVAGE (First Wave)
DC Comics: Jun, 2010 - No. 18, Nov, 2011 ($3.99/$2.99)
1-9: 1-4-Malmont-s/Porter-a/J.G. Jones-c. Justice Inc. back-up; S. Hampton-a 4.00
1-6-Variant covers by Cassaday 5.00
10-17-($2.99) 10,16,17-Winslade-a 3.00

DOC SAVAGE
Dynamite Entertainment: 2013 - No. 8, 2014 ($3.99)
1-8: 1-Roberson-s/Evely-a; covers by Ross & Cassaday 4.00
Annual 2014 ($5.99) Denton-s/Castro-a 6.00
Special 2014: Woman of Bronze ($7.99, squarebound) Walker-s/Baal-a; Patricia Savage 8.00

DOC SAVAGE COMICS (Also see Shadow Comics)
Street & Smith Publ.: May, 1940 - No. 20, Oct, 1943 (1st app. in Doc Savage pulp, 3/33)
1-Doc Savage, Cap Fury, Danny Garrett, Mark Mallory, The Whisperer, Captain Death, Billy the Kid, Sheriff Pete & Treasure Island begin; Norgil, the Magician app.
676 1352 2028 4935 8718 12,500
2-Origin & 1st app. Ajax, the Sun Man; Danny Garrett, The Whisperer end; classic sci-fi cover 252 504 756 1613 2757 3900
3 171 342 513 1094 1872 2650

Doctor Fate (2003 series) #1 © DC

Doctor Mirage #4 © VAL

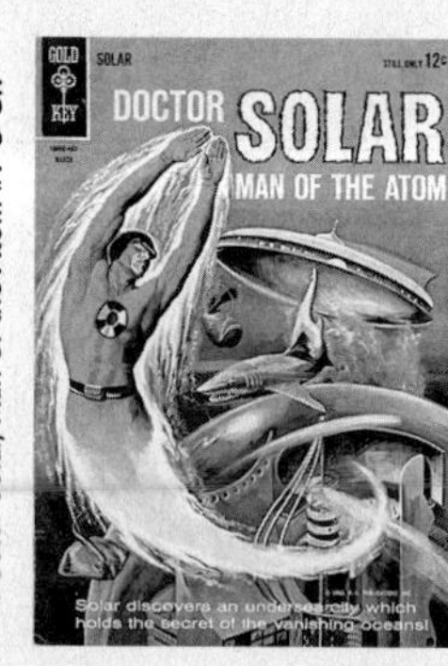

Doctor Solar, Man of the Atom #7 © GK

GD 2.0 | VG 4.0 | FN 6.0 | VF 8.0 | VF/NM 9.0 | NM- 9.2

4-Treasure Island ends; Tuska-a 135 270 405 864 1482 2100
5-Origin & 1st app. Astron, the Crocodile Queen, not in #9 & 11; Norgi the Magician app.; classic-c 119 238 357 762 1306 1850
6-10: 6-Cap Fury ends; origin & only app. Red Falcon in Astron story. 8-Mark Mallory ends; Charlie McCarthy app. on-c plus true life story. 9-Supersnipe app. 10-Origin & only app. The Thunderbolt 71 142 213 454 777 1100
11,12 58 116 174 371 636 900
V2#1-6,8(#13-18,20): 15-Origin of Ajax the Sun Man; Jack Benny on-c; Hitler app. 16-The Pulp Hero, The Avenger app.; Fanny Brice story. 17-Sun Man ends; Nick Carter begins; Duffy's Tavern part photo-c & story. 18-Huckleberry Finn part-c/story. 19-Henny Youngman part photo-c & life story. 20-Only all funny-c w/Huckleberry Finn 54 108 162 343 574 825
V2#7-Classic Devil-c 58 116 174 371 636 900

DOC SAVAGE: CURSE OF THE FIRE GOD
Dark Horse Comics: Sept, 1995 - No, 4, Dec, 1995 ($2.95, limited series)
1-4 4.00

DOC SAVAGE: THE MAN OF BRONZE
Skylark Pub: Mar, 1979, 68pgs. (B&W comic digest, 5-1/4x7-5/8")(low print)
15406-0: Whitman-a, 60 pgs., new comics 4 8 12 23 37 50

DOC SAVAGE: THE MAN OF BRONZE
Millennium Publications: 1991 - No. 4, 1991 ($2.50, limited series)
1-4: 1-Bronze logo 4.00
...: The Manual of Bronze 1 ($2.50, B&W, color, one-shot)-Unpublished proposed Doc Savage strip in color, B&W strip-r 4.00

DOC SAVAGE: THE MAN OF BRONZE, DOOM DYNASTY
Millennium Publ.: 1992 (Says 1991) - No. 2, 1992 ($2.50, limited series)
1,2 4.00

DOC SAVAGE: THE MAN OF BRONZE - REPEL
Innovation Publishing: 1992 ($2.50)
1-Dave Dorman painted-c 4.00

DOC SAVAGE: THE MAN OF BRONZE THE DEVIL'S THOUGHTS
Millennium Publ.: 1992 (Says 1991) - No. 3, 1992 ($2.50, limited series)
1-3 4.00

DOC SAVAGE: THE RING OF FIRE
Dynamite Entertainment: 2017 - No. 4, 2017 ($3.99, limited series)
1-4-Avallone-s/Acosta-a; multiple covers on each 4.00

DOC SAVAGE: THE SPIDER'S WEB
Dynamite Entertainment: 2015 - No. 5, 2016 ($3.99, limited series)
1-5-Roberson-s/Razek-a. 1-Multiple covers 4.00

DOC STEARN...MR. MONSTER (See Mr. Monster)

DR. ANTHONY KING, HOLLYWOOD LOVE DOCTOR
Minoan Publishing Corp./Harvey Publications No. 4: 1952(Jan) - No. 3, May, 1953; No. 4, May, 1954
1 20 40 60 114 182 250
2-4: 4-Powell-a 12 24 36 69 97 125

DR. ANTHONY'S LOVE CLINIC (See Mr. Anthony's...)

DOCTOR APHRA (Star Wars)(Title changes to Star Wars: Doctor Aphra with #7) (See Darth Vader #3 for debut)
Marvel Comics: Feb, 2017 - No. 6, Jun, 2017 ($4.99/$3.99)
1-Gillen-s/Walker-a; back-up with Larroca-a; BT-1, Triple-Zero and Black Krrsantan app. 5.00
2-6-($3.99) Walker-a 4.00

DOCTOR APHRA (Star Wars)(2nd series)(Listed under Star Wars: Doctor Aphra)

DR. BOBBS
Dell Publishing Co.: No. 212, Jan, 1949
Four Color 212 6 12 18 42 79 115

DOCTOR DOOM
Marvel Comics: Dec, 2019 - No. 10, Feb, 2021 ($4.99/$3.99)
1-($4.99) Cantwell-s/Larroca-a; Kang the Conqueror app. 5.00
2-10-($3.99) Blue Marvel, Morgan Le Fay, Mephisto app. 4.00

DOCTOR DOOM AND THE MASTERS OF EVIL (All ages title)
Marvel Comics: Mar, 2009 - No. 4, Jun, 2009 ($2.99)
1-4: 1-Sinister Six app. 4-Magneto app. 3.00

DR. DOOM'S REVENGE
Marvel Comics: 1989 (Came w/computer game from Paragon Software)
V1#1-Spider-Man & Captain America fight Dr. Doom 4 8 12 23 37 50

GD 2.0 | VG 4.0 | FN 6.0 | VF 8.0 | VF/NM 9.0 | NM- 9.2

DR. FATE (See 1st Issue Special, The Immortal..., Justice League, More Fun #55, & Showcase)

DOCTOR FATE
DC Comics: July, 1987 - No. 4, Oct, 1987 ($1.50, limited series, Baxter paper)
1-Giffen-c/a in all 1 2 3 5 6 8
2-4 5.00

DOCTOR FATE
DC Comics: Winter, 1988-'89 - No. 41, June, 1992 ($1.25/$1.50 #5 on)
1,15: 15-Justice League app. 5.00
2-14,16-41: 25-1st new Dr. Fate. 36-Original Dr. Fate returns 4.00
Annual 1(1989, $2.95, 68 pgs.)-Sutton-a 5.00

DOCTOR FATE
DC Comics: Oct, 2003 - No. 5, Feb, 2004 ($2.50, limited series)
1-5-Golden-s/Kramer-a 4.00

DOCTOR FATE
DC Comics: Aug, 2015 - No. 18, Jan, 2017 ($2.99)
1-18: 1-Levitz-s/Liew-a; Khalid Nassour chosen as new Doctor. 12-15-Kent Nelson app. 3.00

DR. FU MANCHU (See The Mask of...)
I.W. Enterprises: 1964
1-r/Avon's "Mask of Dr. Fu Manchu"; Wood-a 7 14 21 46 86 125

DR. GIGGLES (See Dark Horse Presents #64-66)
Dark Horse Comics: Oct, 1992 - No. 2, Oct, 1992 ($2.50, limited series)
1,2-Based on movie 4.00

DOCTOR GRAVES (Formerly The Many Ghosts of...)
Charlton Comics: No. 73, Sept, 1985 - No. 75, Jan, 1986
73-75-Low print run. 73,74-Ditko-a 2 4 6 8 10 12
... Magic Book nn (Charlton Press/Xerox Education, 1977, 68 pgs., digest) Ditko-c/a; Staton-a 4 8 12 23 37 50

DR. HORRIBLE (Based on Joss Whedon's internet feature)
Dark Horse Comics: Nov, 2009 ($3.50, one-shot)
1-Zack Whedon-s/Joëlle Jones-a; Captain Hammer pin-up by Gene Ha; 3 covers 3.50
... and other Horrible Stories TPB (9/10, $9.99) r/#1 and 3 stories from MySpace DHP 10.00
...: Best Friends Forever one-shot (11/18, $3.99) Whedon-s/Beroy & Soler-a/Fabio Moon-c 4.00

DR. JEKYLL AND MR. HYDE (See A Star Presentation & Supernatural Thrillers #4)

DR. KILDARE (TV)
Dell Publishing Co.: No. 1337, 4-6/62 - No. 9, 4-6/65 (All Richard Chamberlain photo-c)
Four Color 1337(#1, 1962) 9 18 27 59 117 175
2-9 6 12 18 37 66 95

DR. MASTERS (See The Adventures of Young...)

DOCTOR MID-NITE (Also see All-American #25)
DC Comics: 1999 - No. 3, 1999 ($5.95, square-bound, limited series)
1-3-Matt Wagner-s/John K. Snyder III-painted art 6.00
TPB (2000, $19.95) r/series 20.00

DOCTOR MIRAGE (Also see Death-Defying Doctor Mirage)
Valiant Entertainment: Aug, 2019 - No. 5, Dec, 2019 ($3.99, limited series)
1-5-Visaggio-s/Robles-a 4.00

DOCTOR OCTOPUS: NEGATIVE EXPOSURE
Marvel Comics: Dec, 2003 - No. 5, Apr, 2004 ($2.99, limited series)
1-5-Vaughan-s/Staz Johnson-a; Spider-Man app. 3.00
Spider-Man/Doctor Octopus: Negative Exposure TPB (2004, $13.99) r/series 14.00

DR. ROBOT SPECIAL
Dark Horse Comics: Apr, 2000 ($2.95, one-shot)
1-Bernie Mireault-s/a; some reprints from Madman Comics #12-15 3.00

DOCTOR SOLAR, MAN OF THE ATOM (See The Occult Files of Dr. Spektor #14 & Solar)
Gold Key/Whitman No. 28 on: 10/62 - No. 27, 4/69; No. 28, 4/81 - No. 31, 3/82 (1-27 have painted-c)
1-(#10000-210)-Origin/1st app. Dr. Solar (1st original Gold Key character) 57 114 171 456 1028 1600
2-Prof. Harbinger begins 13 26 39 90 198 305
3,4 8 16 24 55 105 155
5-Intro. Man of the Atom in costume 9 18 27 63 129 195
6-10 6 12 18 37 66 95
11-14,16-20 5 10 15 30 50 70
15-Origin retold 5 10 15 34 60 85
21-23: 23-Last 12¢ issue 4 8 12 27 44 60
24-27 4 8 12 23 37 50

Doctor Spectrum #1 © MAR

Doctor Strange #56 © MAR

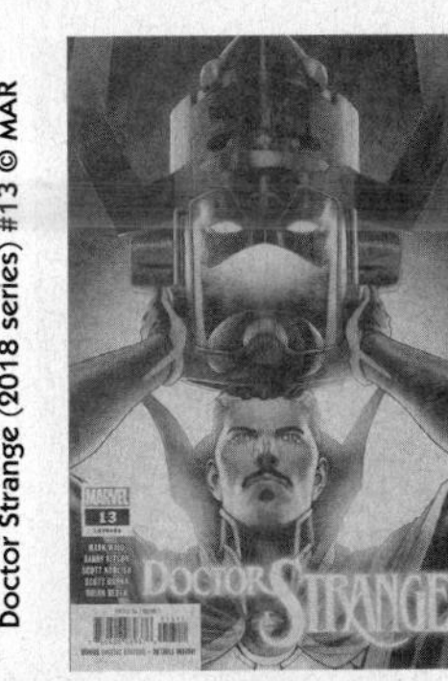
Doctor Strange (2018 series) #13 © MAR

GD	VG	FN	VF	VF/NM	NM-
2.0	4.0	6.0	8.0	9.0	9.2

GD VG FN VF VF/NM NM-
2.0 4.0 6.0 8.0 9.0 9.2

28-31: 29-Magnus Robot Fighter begins. 31-(3/82)The Sentinel app.
3 6 9 16 23 30
Hardcover Vol. One (Dark Horse Books, 2004, $49.95) r/#1-7; creator bios 50.00
Hardcover Vol. Two (Dark Horse Books, 6/05, $49.95) r/#8-14; Jim Shooter foreword 50.00
Hardcover Vol. Three (Dark Horse Books, 9/05, $49.95) r/#15-22; Mike Baron foreword 50.00
Hardcover Vol. Four (Dark Horse Books, 11/07, $49.95) r/#23-31 and The Occult Files of Dr. Spektor #14; Batton Lash foreword 50.00
NOTE: ***Frank Bolle** a-6-19, 29-31; c-29i, 30i. **Bob Fujitani** a-1-5. **Spiegle** a-29-31. **Al McWilliams** a-20-23.*

DOCTOR SOLAR, MAN OF THE ATOM
Valiant Comics: 1990 - No. 2, 1991 ($7.95, card stock-c, high quality, 96 pgs.)
1,2: Reprints Gold Key series 1 3 4 6 8 10

DOCTOR SOLAR, MAN OF THE ATOM
Dark Horse Comics: Jul, 2010 - No. 8, Sept, 2011 ($3.50)
1-(48 pgs.) Shooter-s/Calero-a; back-up reprint of origin/1st app. in D.S. #1 (1962) 4.00
2-8: 2-7-Roger Robinson-a 3.50
Free Comic Book Day Doctor Solar, Man of the Atom & Magnus, Robot Fighter (5/10, free) short story re-intros of Solar & Magnus; Shooter-s/Swanland-c; Calero & Reinhold-a 3.00

DOCTOR SPECTRUM (See Supreme Power)
Marvel Comics: Oct, 2004 - No. 6, Mar, 2005 ($2.99, limited series)
1-6-Origin; Sara Barnes-s/Travel Foreman-a 3.00
TPB (2005, $16.99) r/#1-6 17.00

DOCTOR SPEKTOR (See The Occult Files of..., & Spine-Tingling Tales)

DOCTOR SPEKTOR: MASTER OF THE OCCULT
Dynamite Entertainment: 2014 - No. 4, 2014 ($3.99)
1-4-Mark Waid-s; multiple covers on each 4.00

DOCTOR STAR AND THE KINGDOM OF LOST TOMORROW (Also see Black Hammer)
Dark Horse Comics: Mar, 2018 - No. 4, Jun, 2018 ($3.99, limited series)
1-4-Lemire-s/Fiumara-a 4.00

DOCTOR STRANGE (Formerly Strange Tales #1-168) (Also see The Defenders, Giant-Size..., Marvel Fanfare, Marvel Graphic Novel, Marvel Premiere, Marvel Treasury Edition, Strange & Strange Tales, 2nd Series)
Marvel Comics Group: No. 169, Jun, 1968 - No. 183, Nov, 1969
169(#1)-Origin retold; continued from Strange Tales #167; Roy Thomas-s/Dan Adkins-a; panel swipe/M.D. #1-c 36 72 108 259 580 900
170-176: 170-vs. Nightmare. 171-173-vs. Dormammu. 172-1st Colan-a. 174-1st Sons of Satanish 6 12 18 38 69 100
177-New masked costume 9 18 27 60 120 180
178-181: 178-Black Knight app.; continues in Avengers #61. 179-r/Spider-Man & Dr. Strange story from Amazing Spider-Man Annual #2. 180-Nightmare & Eternity app.; photo montage-c. 181-Brunner-c(part-i), last 12¢ issue 5 10 15 35 63 90
182-Juggernaut app. 6 12 18 42 79 115
183-Intro. The Undying Ones; cont'd in Sub-Mariner #22; concludes in Incredible Hulk #126; Dr. Strange returns in Marvel Feature #1 (second story)
6 12 18 42 79 115

DOCTOR STRANGE (2nd series)(Follows from Marvel Premiere #14)
Marvel Comics Group: Jun, 1974 - No. 81, Feb, 1987
1-Englehart-s/Brunner-c/a; 1st Silver Dagger 10 20 30 67 141 215
2-Silver Dagger app.; Defenders-c 5 10 15 35 63 90
3-5: 3-Mostly reprints; r-Strange Tales #126-127; 1 pg. original art. 4-5-Silver Dagger app. 5-Last Brunner-a 3 6 9 17 26 35
6-10: 6-Dormammu app; Colan-a begins. 7-Dormammu app.; story x-over with Giant-Size Avengers #4. 8-Dormammu app.; continued from Giant-Size Avengers #4. 9-Dormammu app.; Umar revealed as Clea's mother. 10-Baron Mordo & Eternity app.
2 4 6 10 14 18
11-13,15-20: 13,15-17-(Regular 25¢ editions). 13-Nightmare app; slight x-over with Tomb of Dracula #44. 15,16-Strange vs. Satan. 17-1st Stygyro. 18-vs. Stygyro; last Englehart-s. 19-Wolfman-s begin; 1st Xander & the Creators. 20-vs. Xander & the Creators; slight x-over w/Annual #1 1 3 4 6 8 10
13,15-17-(30¢-c variants, limited distribution) 5 10 15 31 53 75
14-(5/76) (Regular 25¢ edition) Dracula app.; story continues from Tomb of Dracula #44 and leads into Tomb of Dracula #45 2 4 6 10 14 18
14-(30¢-c variant, limited distribution) 5 10 15 35 63 90
21-25,30,32-40: 21-Reprints origin from Dr. Strange #169. 22-1st Apalla, Queen of the Sun. 23-25-(Regular 30¢ editions). 23-Starlin layouts; last Wolfman-s. 24-Starlin-s. 25-Starlin-c/s. 30-1st full app. Dweller in Darkness. 32-vs. Dweller in Darkness; 1st Dream Weaver. 33-Dweller in Darkness & Dream Weaver app. 34-vs. Cyrus Black & Nightmare. 35-Captain America & Iron Man app; Black Knight statue app. 36-Ningal app. (from Chamber of Chills #3). 37-Ningal, Dweller in Darkness & D'Spayre app. 38-Claremont-s begin. 40-Baron Mordo app.; continues in Man-Thing Vol. 2 #4 6.00
23-25-(35¢-c variants, limited distribution)(6,8,10/77) 8 16 24 56 108 160
26-29,31: 26-Starlin-a (p); Ancient One & In-Betweener app. 27-vs. Stygyro; Roger Stern-s begin; Ancient One & In-Betweener app. 28-vs. In-Betweener; Brunner-c/a. 29-vs. Deathstalker; Nighthawk app; Brunner-c/a. 31-Sub-Mariner app. 6.00
41-57,63-77,79-81: 41-Continued from Man-Thing Vol. 2 #4; Man-Thing & Baron Mordo app. 46-Miller-c/p. 48,49-Brother Voodoo app; 48-Marshall Rogers-p begin. 49-Baron Mordo app. 50-vs. Baron Mordo. 51-Dormammu app. 52-Nightmare. 53-Fantastic Four & Rama-Tut app.; takes place during FF #19. 55-D'Spayre app; Golden-c/a. 56-Paul Smith-a; origin retold. 67-Hannibal King, Blade & Frank Drake app. 68,69-Black Knight app. 71-73 vs. Umar. 74-Secret Wars II x-over; Beyonder app. 75-Mignola-c; continued from FF #277; vs. Mephisto; last Stern-s. 79-1st Urthona. 80-1st Rintrah. 81-Last issue; Rintrah app; story continued in Strange Tales Vol. 2 #1 4.00
58-62: 58-Re-intro Hannibal King (cameo). 59-Hannibal King full app. 59-62-Dracula app. (Darkhold storyline). 61,62-Doctor Strange, Blade, Hannibal King & Frank Drake team-up to battle. Dracula. 62-Death of Dracula & Lilith 6.00
78-New costume; Cloak (from Cloak & Dagger) app. 1 2 3 5 6 8
Annual 1 (1976, 52 pgs.)-New Russell-a (35 pgs.) 3 6 9 16 24 32
....: From the Marvel Vault (4/11, $2.99) Stern-s/Vokes-a 3.00
.../Silver Dagger Special Edition 1 (3/83, $2.50)-r/#1,2,4,5; Wrightson-c 4.00
... Vs. Dracula TPB (2006, $19.99) r/#14,58-62 and Tomb of Dracula #44 20.00
...What Is It That Disturbs You, Stephen? #1 (10/97, $5.99, 48 pgs.) Russell-a/Andreyko & Russell-s, retelling of Annual #1 story 6.00
NOTE: ***Adkins** a-169, 170, 171i; c-169-171, 172i, 173. **Adams** a-4i. **Austin** a(i)-48-60, 66, 68, 70, 73; c(i)-38, 47-53, 55, 58-60, 70. **Brunner** a-1-5p; c-1-6, 22, 28-30, 33. **Colan** a(p)-172-178, 180-183, 6-18, 36-45, 47; c(p)-172, 174-183, 11-21, 23, 27, 35, 36, 47. **Ditko** a-179r, 3r. **Everett** c-183i. **Golden** a-46p, 55p; c-42-44, 46, 55p. **G. Kane** c(p)-8-10. **Miller** c-46p. **Nebres** a-20, 22, 23, 24i, 26i, 32i; c-32i, 34. **Rogers** a-48-53p; c-47p-53p. **Russell** a-34i, 46i, Annual 1. **B. Smith** c-179. **Paul Smith** a-54p, 56p, 65, 66p, 68p, 69, 71-73; c-56, 65, 66, 68, 71. **Starlin** a-23p, 26; c-25, 26. **Sutton** a-27-29p, 31i, 33, 34p. Painted c-62, 63.*

DOCTOR STRANGE (Volume 2)
Marvel Comics: Feb, 1999 - No. 4, May, 1999 ($2.99, limited series)
1-4: 1,2-Tony Harris-a/painted cover. 3,4-Chadwick-a 4.00

DOCTOR STRANGE (Follows Secret Wars event)
Marvel Comics: Dec, 2015 - No. 26, Dec, 2017; No. 381, Jan, 2018 - No. 390, Jul, 2018 ($4.99/$3.99)
1-($4.99) Aaron-s/Bachalo-a; back-up with Nowlan-a 5.00
2-5,7-19-($3.99) Aaron-s/Bachalo-a. 7-10-The Last Days of Magic 4.00
6-($4.99) The Last Days of Magic 5.00
20-($4.99) Doctor Strange in Weirdworld; art by Bachalo & Nowlan; last Aaron-s 5.00
21-24,26: 21-24-Secret Empire tie-ins; Kingpin & Baron Mordo app.; Henrichon-a 4.00
25-($4.99) Barber-s/Nowlan-a/c 5.00
[Title switches to legacy numbering after #26 (12/17)]
381-390: 381-385-Walta-a; Loki as Sorceror Supreme. 383-385-The Sentry app. 386-Mephisto app.; Henrichon-a. 387-389-Damnation tie-ins. 390-Irving-a 4.00
#1.MU (4/17, $4.99) Monsters Unleashed tie-in; Chip Zdarsky-s/Julian Lopez-a 5.00
Annual 1 (11/16, $4.99) K. Immonen-s/Romero-a; Clea app. 5.00
...: Last Days of Magic 1 (6/16, $5.99) Story between #6 & 7; Doctor Voodoo & The Wu 6.00
...: Mystic Apprentice 1 (12/16, $3.99) New story w/Di Vito-a; r/Strange Tales #115. 1104.00

DOCTOR STRANGE
Marvel Comics: Aug, 2018 - No. 20, Dec, 2019 ($3.99)
1-9,11-20: 1-Waid-s/Saiz-a; Strange goes to space. 2-Intro. Kanna. 3-Super-Skrull app. 11-17-Galactus app. 19-Strange's hands healed 4.00
10-($5.99) 400th issue; The Ancient One app.; bonus flashback with Nowlan-a 6.00
Annual 1 (12/19, $4.99) Scarlet Witch, Talisman & Agatha Harkness app. 5.00
...: The Best Defense 1 (2/19, $4.99) Duggan-s/Smallwood-a; x-over with other Defenders 5.00
...: The End 1 (3/20, $4.99) Leah Williams-s/Filipe Andrade-a; Illyana Rasputin app. 5.00

DR. STRANGE (... Surgeon Supreme on cover)
Marvel Comics: Feb, 2020 - No. 6, Oct, 2020 ($3.99)
1-6: 1-Waid-s/Walker-a; The Wrecker app. 2-6-Dr. Druid app. 5,6-Madame Masque app. 4.00

DOCTOR STRANGE AND THE SORCERERS SUPREME (Prelude in Doctor Strange Annual #1)
Marvel Comics: Dec, 2016 - No. 12, Nov, 2017 ($3.99)
1-12: 1-9-Thompson-s/Rodriguez-a; The Ancient One, Wiccan & Merlin app. 5.00

DOCTOR STRANGE CLASSICS
Marvel Comics Group: Mar, 1984 - No. 4, June, 1984 ($1.50, Baxter paper)
1-4: Ditko-r; Byrne-c. 4-New Golden pin-up 4.00
NOTE: ***Byrne** c-1i, 2-4.*

DOCTOR STRANGE: DAMNATION
Marvel Comics: Apr, 2018 - No. 4, Jun, 2018 ($3.99, limited series)
1-4-Spencer & Cates-s; Las Vegas is restored; Mephisto app. 1,2,4-Rod Reis-a 4.00

DOCTOR STRANGEFATE (See Marvel Versus DC #3 & DC Versus Marvel #4)
DC Comics (Amalgam): Apr, 1996 ($1.95)
1-Ron Marz script w/José Garcia-Lopez-(p) & Kevin Nowlan-(i). Access & Charles Xavier app. 4.00

Doctor Tomorrow (2020 series) #4 © VAL

Doctor Voodoo: Avenger of the Supernatural #5 © MAR

Doctor Who (2020 series) #2 © BBC

	GD	VG	FN	VF	VF/NM	NM-
	2.0	4.0	6.0	8.0	9.0	9.2

DOCTOR STRANGE MASTER OF THE MYSTIC ARTS (See Fireside Book Series)

DOCTOR STRANGE/PUNISHER: MAGIC BULLETS
Marvel Comics: Feb, 2017 - No. 4, May, 2017 ($4.99, limited series)

1-4-Barber-s/Broccardo-a 5.00

DOCTOR STRANGE, SORCERER SUPREME
Marvel Comics (Midnight Sons imprint #60 on): Nov, 1988 - No. 90, June, 1996 ($1.25/$1.50/$1.75/$1.95, direct sales only, Mando paper)

1-Continued from Strange Tales Vol. 2 #19; Fantastic Four, Avengers, Spider-Man, Silver Surfer, Hulk, Daredevil app. (cameos); Dormammu app. 2 4 6 8 11 14

2-9: 2-Dormammu app. 3-New Defenders app. (Valkyrie, Andromeda, Interloper & Manslaughter.) 4-New Defenders becomes Dragoncircle; vs. Dragon of the Moon. 5-Roy & Dan Thomas-s & Guice-p begin; Rintrah app; vs. Baron Mordo. 6-1st Mephista (daughter of Mephisto); Satannish & Mephisto app; Rintrah appears as Howard the Duck this issue; origin of Baron Mordo Pt. 1 (in back-up). 7-Agamotto, Satannish, Mephisto app.; origin of Baron Mordo Pt. 2 (in back-up). 8-Mephisto vs. Satannish; origin of Baron Mordo Pt. 3 (in back-up). 9-History of Dr. Strange 6.00

10-49: 10-Re-intro Morbius w/new costume (11/89). 14-Origin Morbius. 15-Unauthorized Amy Grant photo-c. 16-vs. Baron Blood; Brother Voodoo app. also in back-up story (origin). 17-Morbius & Brother Voodoo app.; origin of Zombies in back-up. 19-Origin of the 1st Brother Voodoo in back-up. 20-Dormammu app. 21-24: Dormammu & Baron Mordo app.; last Guice-a. 26-Werewolf by Night app. 28-Ghost Rider story continued from Ghost Rider #12; published at the same time as Dr. Strange/Ghost Rider Special #1 (4/91). 31-Infinity Gauntlet x-over; continued from Infinity Gauntlet #1; Silver Surfer app. 33-Thanos app. 34-36-Infinity Gauntlet x-overs. 34-Dr. Doom app. 35-Scarlet Witch & Thor app. 41-Wolverine app. 42-47-Infinity War x-overs. 42-Galactus app.; continues in Silver Surfer #67. 43-Continued from Infinity War #2; Galactus vs. Agamotto. 44-Galactus, Silver Surfer & Juggernaut app. 45-Galactus, Silver Surfer & Death app. 46-Dr. Druid, Scarlet Witch & Agatha Harkness app. 5.00

50-($2.95, 52 pgs.)-Holo-grafx foil-c; Hulk, Ghost Rider & Silver Surfer app.; leads into new Secret Defenders series 1 3 4 6 8 10

51-74: 52,53-Nightmare & Morbius app. 54-56: Infinity Crusade x-overs. 61-Siege of Darkness Pt. 15; new Dr. Strange begins (cameo, 1st app. 'Strange'; continued from Marvel Comics Presents #146; continued in Ghost Rider/Blaze Spirits of Vengeance #18. 62-Dr. Doom vs. Strange. 64,65-Sub-Mariner app. 65-Begin $1.95-c; bound-in card sheet. 66-Midnight Sons app.; continued in Dr. Strange Annual #4. 67-Clea returns; continued from Dr. Strange Annual #4. 69-Polaris & Forge app.; story takes place between X-Factor #105,106. 70,71-Hulk app. 72-Silver ink-c; Last Rites Pt. 1. 73-Last Rites Pt. 2.; Salom app. 74-Last Rites Pt. 3; Salom app. 4.00

75-($3.50) Foil-c; Last Rites Pt. 4; death of 'Strange' 1 2 3 5 6 8

75-($2.50) Reg-c 4.00

76-90: 76-New look Dr. Strange. 80-Warren Ellis-s begin; another new look for Dr. Strange. 81-Begins "Over the Edge" branding. 82-Last Ellis-s. 84-DeMatteis-s begin; Baron Mordo app. 85-Baron Mordo revealed to have cancer. 86-Baron Mordo app. 87-'Death' of Baron Mordo. 90-Last issue; Chthon app. 4.00

Annual 1 (See Doctor Strange 2nd series)

Annual 2 ('92, $2.25, 68 pgs.) Return of the Defenders Pt. 4; continued from Silver Surfer Annual #5; Hulk, Sub-Mariner, Silver Surfer app.; vs. Wild One 5.00

Annual 3 ('93, $2.95, 68 pgs.) Polybagged w/card; 1st Kyllian 5.00

Annual 4 ('94, $2.95, 68 pgs.) Story occurs between Doctor Strange #66-67 5.00

Ashcan (1995, 75¢) 3.00

.../Ghost Rider Special 1 (4/91, $1.50)-Same book as Doctor Strange, Sorceror Supreme #28 4.00

...Vs. Dracula 1 (3/94, $1.75, 52 pgs.)-r/Tomb of Dracula #44 & Dr. Strange #14 4.00

NOTE: *Colan c/a-19.* ***Golden*** *c-28.* ***Guice*** *a-5-16, 18, 20-24; c-5-12, 20-24.*

DOCTOR STRANGE: THE OATH
Marvel Comics: Dec, 2006 - No. 5, Apr, 2007 ($2.99, limited series)

1-5-Vaughan-s/Martin-a; Night Nurse app. 1-Origin re-told 4.00
1-Halloween Comic Fest 2015 (12/15, giveaway) r/#1 with logo on cover 4.00
TPB (2007, $13.99) r/#1-5; sketch pages and promotional art 14.00

DR. TOM BRENT, YOUNG INTERN
Charlton Publications: Feb, 1963 - No. 5, Oct, 1963

1 3 6 9 16 23 30
2-5 2 4 6 11 16 20

DR. TOMORROW
Acclaim Comics (Valiant): Sept, 1997 - No. 12 ($2.50)

1-12: 1-Mignola-c 4.00

DOCTOR TOMORROW
Valiant Entertainment: Feb, 2020 - No. 5, Aug, 2020 ($3.99, limited series)

1-5-Arbona-s/Towe-a; intro. new Doctor Tomorrow 4.00

DR. VOLTZ (See Mighty Midget Comics)

	GD	VG	FN	VF	VF/NM	NM-
	2.0	4.0	6.0	8.0	9.0	9.2

DOCTOR VOODOO: AVENGER OF THE SUPERNATURAL
Marvel Comics: Dec, 2009 - No. 5, Apr, 2010 ($2.99, limited series)

1-5-Dr. Doom, Son of Satan & Ghost Rider app.; Palo-a 3.00
Doctor Voodoo: The Origin of Jericho Drumm (1/10, $4.99) r/Strange Tales #169,170 5.00

DR. WEIRD
Big Bang Comics: Oct, 1994 - No. 2, May, 1995 ($2.95, B&W)

1,2: 1-Frank Brunner-c 4.00
... Special (2/94, $3.95, B&W, 68 pgs.) Origin-r by Starlin; Starlin-c 4.00

DOCTOR WHO (Also see Marvel Premiere #57-60)
Marvel Comics Group: Oct, 1984 - No. 23, Aug, 1986 ($1.50, direct sales, Baxter paper)

1-British-r 2 4 6 10 14 18
2-15-British-r 5.00
16-23 6.00
Graphic Novel Voyager (1985, $8.95) color reprints of B&W comic pages from Doctor Who Magazine #88-99; Colin Baker afterword 15.00

DOCTOR WHO (Based on the 2005 TV series with David Tennant)
IDW Publishing: Jan, 2008 - No. 6, Jun, 2008 ($3.99)

1-6: 1-Nick Roche-a/Gary Russell-s; two covers 4.00

DOCTOR WHO (Based on the 2005 TV series with David Tennant)
IDW Publishing: Jul, 2009 - No. 16, Oct, 2010 ($3.99)

1-16-Grist-c on all. 3-5,13-16-Art by Matt Smith (not the actor) 4.00
... Annual 2010 (7/10, $7.99) short stories by various; Yates-c; cameo by 11th Doctor 8.00
...: Autopia (6/09, $3.99) Ostrander-s; Yates-a/c; variant photo-c 4.00
...: Black Death White Life (9/09, $3.99) Mandrake-a; Guy Davis- c; variant photo-c 4.00
...: Cold-Blooded War (8/09, $3.99) Salmon-a/c; variant photo-c 4.00
...: Room With a Déjà View (6/09, $3.99) Eric J-a; Mandrake-c; variant photo-c 4.00
...: The Whispering Gallery (2/09, $3.99) Moore & Reppion-s; Templesmith-a/2 covers 4.00
...: Time Machination (5/09, $3.99) Paul Grist-a/c; variant photo-c 4.00

DOCTOR WHO (Based on the 2010 TV series with Matt Smith)
IDW Publishing: Jan, 2011 - No. 12, Apr, 2012 ($3.99)

1-16: 1-Edwards & photo-c; Currie-a. 5-Buckingham-a. 12-Grist-a 4.00
Annual 2011 (8/11, $7.99) short stories by Fialkov, Shedd, Smith, McDaid and others 8.00
... Convention Special (7/11, no cover price, BBC America Shop Exclusive) The Doctor, Amy, and Rory at the San Diego Comic-Con; Matthew Dow Smith-s/Domingues-a 15.00
... 100 Page Spectacular 1 (7/12, $7.99) Short story reprints from various eras 8.00

DOCTOR WHO (Volume 3)(Based on the 2010 TV series with Matt Smith)
IDW Publishing: Sept, 2012 - No. 16, Dec, 2013 ($3.99)

1-16-Regular & photo-c on each: 1,2-Diggle-s/Buckingham-a. 3,4-Bond-a 4.00
...: 2016 Convention Exclusive (7/16, $10.00) Short stories of the various doctors 10.00
... Special 2012 (8/12, $7.99) Short stories by various incl. Wein, Diggle; Buckingham-c 8.00
... Special 2013 (12/13, $7.99) Cornell-s/Broxton-a; The Doctor visits the real world 8.00

DOCTOR WHO (Based on the TV series with Jodie Whittaker)
Titan Comics: Dec, 2020 - No. 4, Mar, 2021 ($3.99)

1-4-The 13th and 10th Doctors team up; Rose app. 4.00

DOCTOR WHO: A FAIRYTALE LIFE (Based on the 2010 TV series with Matt Smith)
IDW Publishing: Apr, 2011 - No. 4, Jul, 2011 ($3.99, limited series)

1-4: 1-Sturges-s/Yeates-a; covers by Buckingham & Mebberson. 3-Shearer-a 4.00

DR. WHO & THE DALEKS (See Movie Classics)

DOCTOR WHO CLASSICS
IDW Publishing: Nov, 2005 - Oct, 2013 ($3.99)

1-10: Reprints from Doctor Who Weekly (1979); art by Gibbons, Neary and others 4.00
Series 2 (12/08 - No. 12, 11/09, $3.99) 1-12 4.00
Series 3 (3/10 - No. 6, 8/10, $3.99) 1-6 4.00
Series 4 (2/12 - No. 6, 7/12, $3.99) 1-6: Colin Baker era 4.00
Series 5 (3/13 - No. 5, 10/13 $3.99) 1-5: Sylvester McCoy era 4.00
...: The Seventh Doctor (2/11, $3.99) 1-5: 1-Furman-s/Ridgway-a; Sylvester McCoy-era 4.00

DOCTOR WHO EVENT 2015: FOUR DOCTORS
Titan Comics: Sept, 2015 - No. 5, Oct, 2015 ($3.99, weekly limited series)

1-5-Paul Cornell-s/Neil Edwards-a; 10th, 11th, 12th and War Doctor app. 4.00

DOCTOR WHO EVENT 2016: SUPREMACY OF THE CYBERMEN
Titan Comics: Aug, 2016 - No. 5, Dec, 2016 ($3.99, limited series)

1-5-Mann & Scott-s; 9th, 10th, 11th, 12th Doctors app.; multiple covers on each 4.00

DOCTOR WHO: FREE COMIC BOOK DAY
Titan Comics: Jun, 2015; Jun, 2016; Jun, 2017, 2019 (giveaways)

1-Short stories with the 10th, 11th & 12th Doctors; Paul Cornell interview 3.00
2016 - (6/16) Short stories with the 9th, 10th, 11th & 12th Doctors 3.00

Doctor Who: The Tenth Doctor #1 © BBC

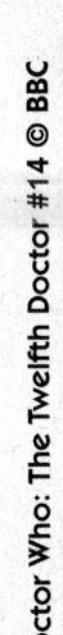
Doctor Who: The Twelfth Doctor #14 © BBC

Dollar Comics: Batman #608 © DC

	GD	VG	FN	VF	VF/NM	NM-
	2.0	4.0	6.0	8.0	9.0	9.2

2017 - (6/17) 12th Doctor and Bill; flashbacks with the 9th, 10th, 11th Doctors 3.00
2018 - (20189) 7th, 10th, 11th, 12th and 13th Doctors app.; photo-c 3.00
2019 - (2019) 13th Doctor and companions; Houser-s/Angiolini-c 3.00

DOCTOR WHO: GHOST STORIES (Sequel to the 2016 Christmas episode with The Ghost)
IDW Publishing: May, 2017 - No. 4, Aug, 2017 ($3.99, limited series)

1-4-George Mann-s; Grant and Lucy app.; multiple covers on each. 3-Calero-a 4.00

DOCTOR WHO: PRISONERS OF TIME
IDW Publishing: Feb, 2013 - No. 12, Nov, 2013 ($3.99, limited series)

1-50th Anniversary series with each issue spotlighting one Doctor; Francavilla-c 6.00
1-12-Photo covers 5.00
2-12: Francavilla-c on all. 5-12-Dave Sim variant-c. 8-Langridge-a 4.00

DOCTOR WHO: SPECIAL (Also see Doctor Who: The Lost Dimension)
IDW Publishing: Nov, 2017 - No. 2, Nov, 2017 ($4.99)

1,2-The Lost Dimension x-over parts 5 & 7; River Song and the 4th Doctor app. 5.00

DOCTOR WHO: THE EIGHTH DOCTOR (Based on the Paul McGann version)
Titan Comics: Nov, 2015 - No. 5, Apr, 2016 ($3.99, limited series)

1-5: 1-Intro. Josephine; Vieceli-a; multiple covers on each 4.00

DOCTOR WHO: THE ELEVENTH DOCTOR (Based on the Matt Smith version)
Titan Comics: Aug, 2014 - No. 15, Sept, 2015 ($3.99)

1-15: 1-Intro. Alice; Fraser-a; multiple covers on each 4.00

DOCTOR WHO: THE ELEVENTH DOCTOR YEAR TWO (Matt Smith version)
Titan Comics: Oct, 2015 - No. 15, Dec, 2016 ($3.99)

1-15: 1-War Doctor & Abslom Daak app.; multiple covers on each 4.00

DOCTOR WHO: THE ELEVENTH DOCTOR YEAR THREE (Matt Smith version)
Titan Comics: Feb, 2017 - No. 13, Feb, 2018 ($3.99)

1-13: 1-The Doctor and Alice; Rob Williams-s; multiple covers on each. 10-Lost Dimension x-over part 4 4.00

DOCTOR WHO: THE FORGOTTEN (Based on the 2005 TV series with David Tennant)
IDW Publishing: Aug, 2008 - No. 6, Jan, 2009 ($3.99)

1-6: 1,2-Pia Guerra-a/Tony Lee-s; two covers 4.00

DOCTOR WHO: THE FOURTH DOCTOR (Based on the Tom Baker version)
Titan Comics: Apr, 2016 - No. 5, Oct, 2016 ($3.99)

1-5: Sarah Jane app.; Brian Williamson-a; multiple covers on each 4.00

DOCTOR WHO: THE LOST DIMENSION (Eight part x-over with 2017 Doctor Who titles)
Titan Comics: Sept, 2017 - Nov, 2017 ($3.99)

... Alpha (9/17, $3.99) Part one; multiple doctors and Capt. Jack app.; Stott-a 4.00
... Omega (11/17, $3.99) Concluding Part eight; multiple doctors and Jenny app. 4.00

DOCTOR WHO: THE NINTH DOCTOR (Based on the Christopher Eccleston version)
Titan Comics: Apr, 2015 - No. 5, Dec, 2015 ($3.99)

1-5: 1-Rose & Capt. Jack app.; Cavan Scott-s; multiple covers on each 4.00

DOCTOR WHO: THE NINTH DOCTOR ONGOING (Christopher Eccleston version)
Titan Comics: May, 2016 - No. 15, Sept, 2017 ($3.99)

1-15: 1-Rose & Capt. Jack app.; Cavan Scott-s; multiple covers on each 4.00
Doctor Who: The Ninth Special (Lost Dimension Part 2) (10/17, $3.99) Vastra app. 4.00

DOCTOR WHO: THE ROAD TO THE THIRTEEN DOCTOR
Titan Comics: Aug, 2018 - No. 3, Oct, 2018 ($3.99, limited series)

1-3: 1-The Tenth Doctor & companions; Peaty-s/Zanfardino-a. 2-Eleventh. 3-Twelfth 4.00

DOCTOR WHO: THE SEVENTH DOCTOR: OPERATION VOLCANO (Sylvester McCoy)
Titan Comics: Jul, 2018 - No. 3, Sept, 2018 ($5.99/$3.99)

1-($5.99) Ace & Gilmore app.; Andrew Cartmel-s/Christopher Jones-a 6.00
2,3-($3.99) 4.00

DOCTOR WHO: THE TENTH DOCTOR (Based on the David Tennant version)
Titan Comics: Aug, 2014 - No. 15, Sept, 2015 ($3.99)

1-15: 1-5-Casagrande-a; multiple covers on each. 1-Intro. Gabby. 6,7-Weeping Angels 4.00

DOCTOR WHO: THE TENTH DOCTOR YEAR TWO (David Tennant version)
Titan Comics: Oct, 2015 - No. 17, Jan, 2017 ($3.99)

1-17: 1-Abadzis-s/Carlini-a; multiple covers on each. 3-Captain Jack app. 4.00

DOCTOR WHO: THE TENTH DOCTOR YEAR THREE (David Tennant version)
Titan Comics: Feb, 2017 - No. 14, Mar, 2018 ($3.99)

1-14: 1-The Doctor & Gabby; Abadzis-s; multiple covers on each. 9-Lost Dimension x-over part 3 4.00

DOCTOR WHO: THE THIRD DOCTOR (Based on the Jon Pertwee version)
Titan Comics: Oct, 2016 - No. 5, Mar, 2017 ($3.99)

1-5-Jo and The Brigadier app.; multiple covers on each 4.00

DOCTOR WHO: THE THIRTEEN DOCTOR (Jodie Whittaker version)
Titan Comics: No. 0, Oct, 2018; No. 1, Dec, 2018 - No. 12, Oct, 2019 ($3.99)

0 - The Many Lives of Doctor Who ($7.99); short stories of each of the previous Doctors 8.00
1-12: 1-Houser-s/Stott-a; Ryan, Yasmin & Graham app. 4.00
... Holiday Special #1, (12/19, 1/20, $5.99) Houser-s/Ingranata-a 6.00
(Season 2) 2.1-2.4: 2.1-(2/20) Tenth Doctor & Martha app. 4.00

DOCTOR WHO: THE TWELFTH DOCTOR (Based on the Peter Capaldi version)
Titan Comics: Nov, 2014 - No. 15, Jan, 2016 ($3.99)

1-15: 1-The Doctor and Clara; Dave Taylor-a; multiple covers on each 4.00

DOCTOR WHO: THE TWELFTH DOCTOR YEAR TWO (Based on the Peter Capaldi version)
Titan Comics: Feb, 2016 - No. 15, Apr, 2017 ($3.99)

1-15: 1-The Doctor and Clara. 6-Intro. Hattie 4.00

DOCTOR WHO: THE TWELFTH DOCTOR YEAR THREE (The Peter Capaldi version)
Titan Comics: May, 2017 - No. 13, Apr, 2018 ($3.99)

1-13: 5-Bill Potts comic debut. 8-Lost Dimension x-over part 6; 9th & 10th Doctors app. 4.00

DOCTOR WHO: TIME LORD VICTORIOUS
Titan Comics: Oct, 2020 - No. 2, Nov, 2020 ($5.99, limited series)

1,2-The 10th Doctor and the Daleks app.; Jody Houser-s 6.00

DR. WONDER
Old Town Publishing: June, 1996 - No. 5 ($2.95, B&W)

1-5: 1-Intro & origin of Dr. Wonder; Dick Ayers-c/a; Irwin Hasen-a 3.00

DOCTOR ZERO
Marvel Comics (Epic Comics): Apr, 1988 - No. 8, Aug, 1989 ($1.25/$1.50)

1-8: 1-Sienkiewicz-c. 6,7-Spiegle-a 3.00
NOTE: ***Sienkiewicz*** *a-3i, 4i; c-1.*

DO-DO (Funny Animal Circus Stories)
Nation-Wide Publishers: 1950 - No. 7, 1951 (5¢, 5x7-1/4" Miniature)

	GD	VG	FN	VF	VF/NM	NM-
1 (52 pgs.)	22	44	66	132	216	300
2-7	12	24	36	69	97	125

DODO & THE FROG, THE (Formerly Funny Stuff; also see It's Game Time #2)
National Periodical Publications: No. 80, 9-10/54 - No. 88, 1-2/56; No. 89, 8-9/56; No. 90, 10-11/56; No. 91, 9/57; No. 92, 11/57 (See Comic Cavalcade and Captain Carrot)

	GD	VG	FN	VF	VF/NM	NM-
80-1st app. Doodles Duck by Sheldon Mayer	20	40	60	114	182	250
81-91: Doodles Duck by Mayer in #81,83-90	11	22	33	62	86	110
92-(Scarce)-Doodles Duck by S. Mayer	18	36	54	105	165	225

DOG DAYS OF SUMMER
DC Comics: Jul, 2019 ($9.99, one-shot, squarebound)

1-Short stories by various; Krypto, Beast Boy, Batcow, Killer Croc, Animal Man app. 10.00

DOGFACE DOOLEY
Magazine Enterprises: 1951 - No. 5, 1953

	GD	VG	FN	VF	VF/NM	NM-
1(A-1 40)	28	56	84	165	270	375
2(A-1 43), 3(A-1 49), 4(A-1 53)	18	36	54	109	172	235
5(A-1 64) Classic good girl-c	45	90	135	264	480	675
I.W. Reprint #1('64), Super Reprint #17	2	4	6	11	16	20

DOG MOON
DC Comics (Vertigo): 1996 ($6.95, one-shot)

1-Robert Hunter-scripts; Tim Truman-c/a. 7.00

DOG OF FLANDERS, A
Dell Publishing Co.: No. 1088, Mar, 1960

	GD	VG	FN	VF	VF/NM	NM-
Four Color 1088-Movie, photo-c	5	10	15	31	53	75

DOGPATCH (See Al Capp's... & Mammy Yokum)

DOGS OF WAR (Also see Warriors of Plasm #13)
Defiant: Apr, 1994 - No. 5, Aug, 1994 ($2.50)

1-5: 5-Schism x-over 4.00

DOGS-O-WAR
Crusade Comics: June, 1996 - No. 3, Jan, 1997 ($2.95, B&W, limited series)

1-3: 1,2-Photo-c 4.00

DOLLAR COMICS
DC Comics: 2019 - Present ($1.00, reprints with new house ads)

...: Amethyst 1 - ('20) Reprints Amethyst, Princess of Gemworld #1; Estrada & Colón-a 3.00
...: Batman 386 - ('20) Reprints intro/origin of Black Mask; Moench-s/Mandrake-a 3.00
...: Batman 428 - ('20) Reprints Death of Jason Todd; Starlin-s/Aparo-a/Mignola-c 3.00
...: Batman 497 - ('19) Reprints Bane breaking Batman's back; Moench-s/Aparo-a/Jones-c 3.00

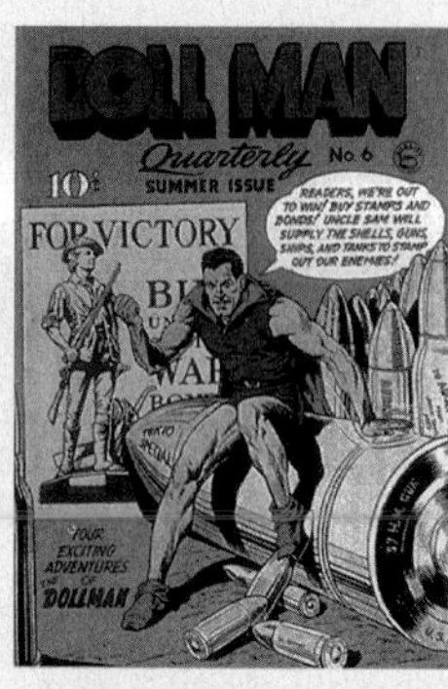

Doll Man Quarterly #6 © QUA

Dolly #10 © Z-D

Domino: Hotshots #2 © MAR

	GD 2.0	VG 4.0	FN 6.0	VF 8.0	VF/NM 9.0	NM- 9.2

...: Batman 567 - ('20) Reprints 1st app. of Cassandra Cain Batgirl; Damion Scott-a 3.00
...: Batman 608 - ('19) Reprints 1st issue of Hush storyline; Loeb-s/Jim Lee-a 3.00
...: Batman 613 - ('19) Reprint from Hush storyline; Harley Quinn & Catwoman app. 3.00
...: Batman 663 - ('20) Reprints Joker storybook issue; Morrison-s/Van Fleet-a 3.00
...: Batman Adventures 12 - ('19) Reprints comic book debut of Harley Quinn; Batgirl app. 3.00
...: Batman/Huntress: Cry For Blood 1 (3/20) - Rucka-s/Burchett-a; The Question app. 3.00
...: Batman: Shadow of the Bat 1 - ('20) The Last Arkham; Grant-s/Breyfogle-a 3.00
...: Birds of Prey 1 - ('19) Reprints 1st 1999 Black Canary/Oracle issue; Dixon-s/Land-a 3.00
...: Blackest Night 1 - ('19) Reprints 1st issue of series; Johns-s/Reis-a 3.00
...: Catwoman 1 - ('20) Reprints 1st issue of 2002 series; Darwyn Cooke & Mike Allred-a 3.00
...: Crisis of Infinite Earths 1 - ('19) 1st issue of series; Wolfman-s/Pérez-a; Alex Ross-c 3.00
...: Detective Comics 554 - ('20) Reprints 1st new look Black Canary 3.00
...: Detective Comics 854 - (11/19) Early Batwoman spotlight; Williams III-a; photo-c 3.00
...: Flashpoint 1 - (1/20) Reprints 1st issue of series; Johns-s/Andy Kubert-a/c 3.00
...: Green Lantern 1 - ('20) Reprints 2011 New 52 issue; Johns-s/Mahnke-a 3.00
...: Green Lantern: Rebirth 1 - ('20) Reprints 2004 issue; Johns-s/Van Sciver-a 3.00
...: Harley Quinn 1 - ('19) Reprints 1st issue of 2013 series; Conner-c 3.00
...: Infinite Crisis 1 - ('19) Reprints 1st issue of series; Johns-s/Jimenez-a/Jim Lee-c 3.00
...: JLA 1 - ('20) Reprints 1996 issue; Morrison-s/Porter-a 3.00
...: JLA: Year One 1 - ('20) Reprints 1998 issue; Waid & Augustyn-s/Kitson-a 3.00
...: Justice League 1 - ('20) Reprints 1987 issue; Giffen & DeMatteis-s/Maguire-a 3.00
...: Justice League 1 - ('20) Reprints 2011 New 52 issue; Geoff Johns-s/Jim Lee-a 3.00
...: Justice League of America 1 - ('20) Reprints 2006 issue; Meltzer-s/Benes-a 3.00
...: Luthor 1 - ('19) Reprints Lex Luthor: Man of Steel #1; Azzarello-s/Bermejo-a/c 3.00
...: New Teen Titans 2 - ('20) Reprints debut of Deathstroke; Wolfman-s/Pérez-a 3.00
...: Robin 1 - ('20) Reprints 1991 issue; Tim Drake; Dixon-s/Lyle-a 3.00
...: Sandman 23 - ('20) Lucifer loses his wings and leaves Hell; Gaiman-s/Kelley Jones-a 3.00
...: Superman 75 - ('19) Reprints Death of Superman issue from 1993 3.00
...: Swamp Thing 1 - ('19) Reprints 1st issue of 1972 series; Wein-s/Wrightson-a 3.00
...: Swamp Thing 57 - ('20) Reprints #57 from '82 series; Adam Strange app.; Moore-s 3.00
...: Tales of the Teen Titans 3 - ('19) Conclusion of The Judas Contract; Pérez-a 3.00
...: The Brave and the Bold 197 - (3/20) Golden Age Batman and Catwoman team-up 3.00
...: The Flash 1 - ('20) Reprints 1987 issue with Wally West as the Flash; Guice-a 3.00
...: The Flash 164 - ('19) Reprints 2000 issue; Johns-s/Unzueta-a/Bolland-c 3.00
...: The Flash: Rebirth 1 - ('20) Reprints 2009 issue; Johns-s/Van Sciver-a 3.00
...: The Joker 1 - ('19) Reprints 1st issue of 1975 series; O'Neil-s/Novick-a 3.00
...: Watchmen 1 - ('19) Reprints 1st issue of series; Alan Moore-s/Dave Gibbons-a 3.00

DOLLFACE & HER GANG (Betty Betz'...)
Dell Publishing Co.: No. 309, Jan, 1951

	GD	VG	FN	VF	VF/NM	NM-
Four Color 309	7	14	21	44	82	120

DOLLHOUSE
Dark Horse Comics: Mar, 2011; Jul, 2011 - No. 5, Nov, 2011 ($3.50, limited series)
1-5-Richards-a; two covers on each 4.00
...: Epitaphs (3/11, $3.50) reprints story from DVD collection; covers by Noto & Morris 4.00

DOLLHOUSE FAMILY, THE
DC Comics (Hill House Comics): Jan, 2020 - No. 6, Jun, 2020 ($3.99)
1-6-Carey-s/Gross-a; back-up serial Sea Dogs in each 4.00

DOLLMAN (Movie)
Eternity Comics: Sept, 1991 - No. 4, Dec, 1991 ($2.50, limited series)
1-4: Adaptation of film 4.00

DOLL MAN QUARTERLY, THE (Doll Man #17 on; also see Feature Comics #27 & Freedom Fighters)
Quality Comics: Fall, 1941 - No. 7, Fall, '43; No. 8, Spr, '46 - No. 47, Oct, 1953

	GD	VG	FN	VF	VF/NM	NM-
1-Dollman (by Cassone), Justin Wright begin	349	698	1047	2443	4272	6100
2-The Dragon begins; Crandall-a(5)	158	316	474	1003	1727	2450
3,4	97	194	291	621	1061	1500
5-Crandall-a	94	188	282	597	1024	1450
6,7(1943)	55	110	165	352	601	850
8(1946)-1st app. Torchy by Bill Ward	177	354	531	1133	1942	2750
9(Summer 1946)	55	110	165	352	601	850
10-20	42	84	126	265	445	625
21-26,28-30: 28-Vs. The Flame	39	78	117	240	395	550
27-Sci-fi bondage-c	43	86	129	271	461	650
31-(12/50)-Intro Elmo, the wonder dog (Dollman's faithful dog)	45	90	135	284	480	675
32-35,38,40: 32-34-Jeb Rivers app. 34-Crandall-a(p)	40	80	120	246	411	575
36-Giant shark-c	43	86	129	271	461	650
37-Origin & 1st app. Dollgirl; Dollgirl bondage-c	87	174	261	553	952	1350
39- "Narcotics...the Death Drug" c-/story	53	106	159	334	567	800
41-47	34	68	102	199	325	450
Super Reprint #11('64, r/#20),15(r/#23),17(r/#28): 15,17-Torchy app.; Andru/Esposito-c	3	6	9	20	30	40

NOTE: ***Ward*** *Torchy in 8, 9, 11, 12, 14-24, 27; by Fox-#26, 30, 35-47.* ***Crandall*** *a-2, 5, 10, 13 & Super #11, 17, 18.* ***Crandall/Cuidera*** *c-40-42.* ***Guardineer*** *a-3. Bondage c-27, 37, 38, 39.*

DOLLY
Ziff-Davis Publ. Co.: No. 10, July-Aug, 1951 (Funny animal)

	GD	VG	FN	VF	VF/NM	NM-
10-Painted-c	12	24	36	69	97	125

DOLLY DILL
Marvel Comics/Newsstand Publ.: 1945

	GD	VG	FN	VF	VF/NM	NM-
1	32	64	96	188	307	425

DOLLZ, THE
Image Comics: Apr, 2001 - No. 2, June, 2001 ($2.95)
1,2: 1-Four covers; Sniegoski & Green-s/Green-a 3.00

DOMINATION FACTOR
Marvel Comics: Nov, 1999 - 4.8, Feb, 2000 ($2.50, interconnected mini-series)
1.1, 2.3, 3.5, 4.7-Fantastic Four; Jurgens-s/a 3.00
1.2, 2.4, 3.6, 4.8-Avengers; Ordway-s/a 3.00

DOMINIC FORTUNE
Marvel Comics (MAX): Oct, 2009 - No. 4, Jan, 2010 ($3.99, limited series)
1-4-Howard Chaykin-s/a/c 4.00

DOMINION
Image Comics: Jan, 2003 - No. 2 ($2.95)
1,2-Keith Giffen-s/a 3.00

DOMINION (Manga)
Eclipse Comics: Dec, 1990 - No. 6., July, 1990 ($2.00, B&W, limited series)
1-6 3.00

DOMINION: CONFLICT 1 (Manga)
Dark Horse Comics: Mar, 1996 - No. 6, Aug, 1996 ($2.95, B&W, limited series)
1-6: Shirow-c/a/scripts 3.00

DOMINIQUE LAVEAU: VOODOO CHILD
DC Comics (Vertigo): May, 2012 - No. 7, Nov, 2012 ($2.99, limited series)
1-7-Selwyn Seyfu Hinds-s/Denys Cowan-a 3.00

DOMINO (See X-Force)
Marvel Comics: Jan, 1997 - No. 3, Mar, 1997 ($1.95, limited series)
1-3: 2-Deathstrike-c/app. 4.00

DOMINO (See X-Force)
Marvel Comics: Jun, 2003 - No. 4, Aug, 2003 ($2.50, limited series)
1-4-Stelfreeze-c/a; Pruett-s 3.00

DOMINO (X-Force)
Marvel Comics: Jun, 2018 - No. 10, Mar, 2019 ($3.99)
1-10-Simone-s/Baldeón-a. 4-6-Shang-Chi app. 8-Morbius app. 9,10-Longshot app. 4.00
Annual 1 (11/18, $4.99) Short flashback stories by various incl. Simone, Nicieza, Kirk 5.00

DOMINO CHANCE
Chance Enterprises: May-June, 1982 - No. 9, May, 1985 (B&W)
1-9: 7-1st app. Gizmo, 2 pgs. 8-1st full Gizmo story. 1-Reprint, May, 1985 4.00

DOMINO: HOTSHOTS (X-Force)
Marvel Comics: May, 2019 - No. 5, Sept, 2019 ($3.99, limited series)
1-5-Simone-s/Baldeón-a; Black Widow and Deadpool app. 4.00

DONALD AND MICKEY
IDW Publishing: Aug, 2017 - No. 4, May, 2018 ($5.99)
1-4-Reprints from European stories; 2 covers on each 6.00

DONALD AND MICKEY IN DISNEYLAND (See Dell Giants)

DONALD AND SCROOGE
Disney Comics: 1992 ($8.95, squarebound, 100 pgs.)

	GD	VG	FN	VF	VF/NM	NM-
nn-Don Rosa reprint special; r/U.S., D.D. Advs.	1	3	4	6	8	10

1-3 (1992, $1.50)-r/D.D. Advs. (Disney) #1,22,24 & U.S. #261-263,269 3.00

DONALD AND THE WHEEL (Disney)
Dell Publishing Co.: No. 1190, Nov, 1961

	GD	VG	FN	VF	VF/NM	NM-
Four Color 1190-Movie, Barks-c	8	16	24	54	102	150

DONALD DUCK (See Adventures of Mickey Mouse, Cheerios, Donald & Mickey, Ducktales, Dynabrite Comics, Gladstone Comic Album, Mickey & Donald, Mickey Mouse Mag., Story Hour Series, Uncle Scrooge, Walt Disney's Comics & Stories, W. D.'s Donald Duck, Wheaties & Whitman Comic Books, Wise Little Hen, The)

DONALD DUCK
Whitman Publishing Co./Grosset & Dunlap/K.K.: 1935, 1936 (All pages on heavy linen-like

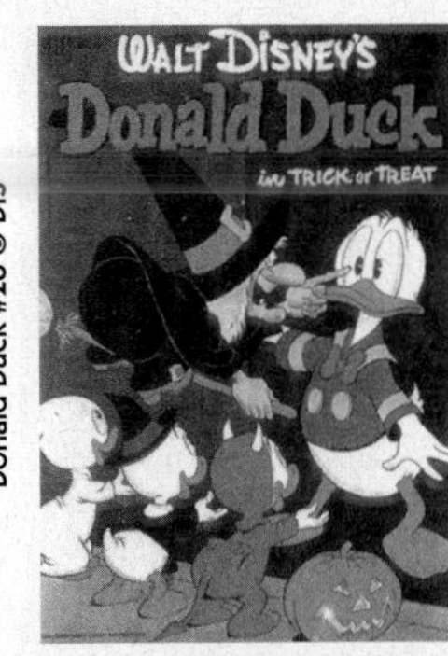

Donald Duck #26 © DIS

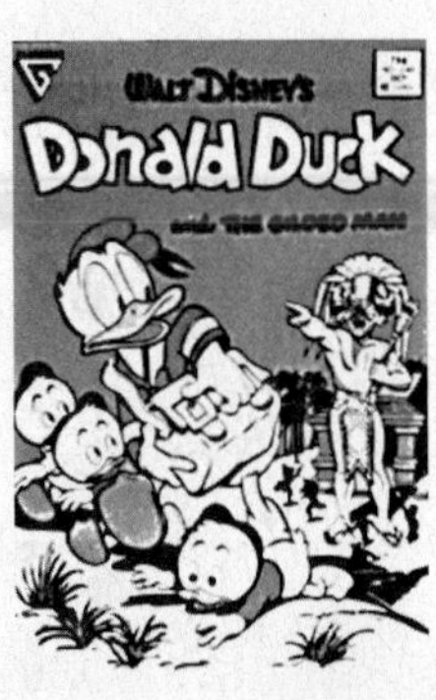

Donald Duck #246 © DIS

Donald Duck and Friends #356 © DIS

	GD	VG	FN	VF	VF/NM	NM-
	2.0	4.0	6.0	8.0	9.0	9.2

finish cover stock in color;1st book ever devoted to Donald Duck; see Advs. of Mickey Mouse for 1st app.) (9-1/2x13")

978(1935)-16 pgs.; Illustrated text story book 206 412 618 1318 2259 3200

nn(1936)-36 pgs.plus hard cover & dust jacket. Story completely rewritten with B&W illos added. Mickey appears and his nephews are named Morty & Monty

Book only 194 388 582 1242 2121 3000

Dust jacket only.... 39 78 117 240 395 550

DONALD DUCK (Walt Disney's) (10¢)
Whitman/K.K. Publications: 1938 (8-1/2x11-1/2", B&W, cardboard-c)
(Has D. Duck with bubble pipe on-c)

nn-The first Donald Duck & Walt Disney comic book; 1936 & 1937 Sunday strip-r(in B&W); same format as the Feature Books; 1st strips with Huey, Dewey & Louie from 10/17/37; classic bubble pipe cover 427 854 1281 3117 5509 7900

DONALD DUCK (Walt Disney's...#262 on; see 4-Color listings for titles & Four Color No. 1109 for origin story)
Dell Publ. Co./Gold Key #85-216/Whitman #217-245/Gladstone #246 on: 1940 - No. 84, Sept-Nov, 1962; No. 85, Dec, 1962 - No. 245, July, 1984; No. 246, Oct, 1986 - No. 279, May, 1990; No. 280, Sept, 1993 - No. 307, Mar,1998

Four Color 4(1940)-Daily 1939 strip-r by Al Taliaferro
2250 4500 6750 16,900 30,950 45,000

Large Feature Comic 16(1/41?)-1940 Sunday strips-r in B&W
919 1838 2757 6709 11,855 17,000

Large Feature Comic 20('41)-Comic Paint Book, r-single panels from Large Feature #16 at top of each pg. to color; daily strip-r across bottom of each pg. (Rare)
1025 2050 3075 7800 14,150 20,500

Four Color 9('42)- "Finds Pirate Gold"; 64 pgs. by Carl Barks & Jack Hannah (pgs. 1,2,5,12-40 are by Barks, his 1st Donald Duck comic book art work; © 8/17/42)
1000 2000 3000 7600 13,800 20,000

Four Color 29(9/43)- "Mummy's Ring" by Barks; reprinted in Uncle Scrooge & Donald Duck #1('65), W. D. Comics Digest #44('73) & Donald Duck Advs. #14
805 1610 2415 5877 10,389 14,900

Four Color 62(1/45)- "Frozen Gold"; 52 pgs. by Barks, reprinted in The Best of W.D. Comics & Donald Duck Advs. #4 231 462 693 1906 4303 6700

Four Color 108(1946)- "Terror of the River"; 52 pgs. by Carl Barks; reprinted in Gladstone Comic Album #2 148 296 444 1221 2761 4300

Four Color 147(5/47)-in "Volcano Valley" by Barks 104 208 312 832 1866 2900

Four Color 159(8/47)-in "The Ghost of the Grotto";52 pgs. by Carl Barks; reprinted in Best of Uncle Scrooge & Donald Duck #1 ('66) & The Best of W.D. Comics & D.D. Advs. #9; two Barks stories 93 186 279 744 1672 2600

Four Color 178(12/47)-1st app. Uncle Scrooge by Carl Barks; reprinted in Gold Key Christmas Parade #3 & The Best of Walt Disney Comics 145 290 435 1196 2698 4200

Four Color 189(6/48)-by Carl Barks; reprinted in Best of Donald Duck & Uncle Scrooge #1('64) & D.D. Advs. #19 91 182 273 728 1639 2550

Four Color 199(10/48)-by Carl Barks; mentioned in Love and Death; r/in Gladstone Comic Album #5 91 182 273 728 1639 2550

Four Color 203(12/48)-by Barks; reprinted as Gold Key Christmas Parade #4
63 126 189 504 1127 1750

Four Color 223(4/49)-by Barks; reprinted as Best of Donald Duck #1 & Donald Duck Advs. #3
82 164 246 656 1478 2300

Four Color 238(8/49)-in "Voodoo Hoodoo" by Barks 61 122 183 488 1094 1700

Four Color 256(12/49)-by Barks; reprinted in Best of Donald Duck & Uncle Scrooge #2('67), Gladstone Comic Album #16 & W.D. Comics Digest 44('73)
50 100 150 400 900 1400

Four Color 263(2/50)-Two Barks stories; r-in D.D. #278
46 92 138 368 834 1300

Four Color 275(5/50), 282(7/50), 291(9/50), 300(11/50)-All by Carl Barks; 275, 282 reprinted in W.D. Comics Digest #44('73). #275 r/in Gladstone Comic Album #10. #291 r/in D. Duck Advs. #16 47 94 141 367 821 1275

Four Color 308(1/51), 318(3/51)-by Barks; #318-reprinted in W.D. Comics Digest #34 & D.D. Advs. #2,19 46 92 138 340 770 1200

Four Color 328(5/51)-by Carl Barks 45 90 135 333 754 1175

Four Color 339(7-8/51), 379-2nd Uncle Scrooge-c; art not by Barks.
33 66 99 238 532 825

Four Color 348(9-10/51), 356,394-Barks-c only 24 48 72 168 372 575

Four Color 367(1-2/52)-by Barks; reprinted as Gold Key Christmas Parade #2 & #8
38 76 114 281 628 925

Four Color 408(7-8/52), 422(9-10/52)-All by Carl Barks. #408-r-in Best of Donald Duck & Uncle Scrooge #1('64) & Gladstone Comic Album #13
36 72 108 259 580 900

26(11-12/52)-In "Trick or Treat" (Barks-a, 36pgs.) 1st story r-in Walt Disney Digest #16 & Gladstone C.A. #23 36 72 108 259 580 900

27-30-Barks-c only 12 24 36 82 179 275

31-44,47-50 7 14 21 46 86 125

	GD	VG	FN	VF	VF/NM	NM-
	2.0	4.0	6.0	8.0	9.0	9.2

45-Barks-a (6 pgs.) 13 26 39 89 195 300

46- "Secret of Hondorica" by Barks, 24 pgs.; reprinted in Donald Duck #98 & 154
17 34 51 119 265 410

51-Barks-a,1/2 pg. 7 14 21 46 86 125

52- "Lost Peg-Leg Mine" by Barks, 10 pgs. 13 26 39 89 195 300

53,55-59 6 12 18 38 69 100

54- "Forbidden Valley" by Barks, 26 pgs. (10¢ & 15¢ versions exist)
14 28 42 98 217 335

60- "Donald Duck & the Titanic Ants" by Barks, 20 pgs. plus 6 more pgs.
14 28 42 98 217 335

61-67,69,70 5 10 15 34 60 85

68-Barks-a, 5 pgs. 9 18 27 62 126 190

71-Barks-r, 1/2 pg. 5 10 15 34 60 85

72-78,80,82-97,99,100: 96-Donald Duck Album 5 10 15 33 57 80

79,81-Barks-a, 1pg. 5 10 15 34 60 85

98-Reprints #46 (Barks) 5 10 15 34 60 85

101,103-111,113-135: 120-Last 12¢ issue. 134-Barks-r/#52 & WDC&S 194.
135-Barks-r/WDC&S 198, 19 pgs. 4 8 12 22 35 48

102-Super Goof. 112-1st Moby Duck 4 8 12 23 37 50

136-153,155,156,158: 149-20¢-c begin 3 6 9 14 20 26

154-Barks-r(#46) 3 6 9 16 24 32

157,159,160,164: 157-Barks-r(#45); 25¢-c begin. 159-Reprints/WDC&S #192 (10 pgs.).
160-Barks-r(#26). 164-Barks-r(#79) 3 6 9 14 20 26

161-163,165-173,175-187,189-191: 175-30¢-c begin. 187-Barks r/#68.
2 4 6 13 18 22

174,188: 174-r/4-Color #394. 3 6 9 14 19 24

175-177-Whitman variants 3 6 9 14 19 24

192-Barks-r(40 pgs.) from Donald Duck #60 & WDC&S #226,234 (52 pgs.)
3 6 9 15 22 28

193-200,202-207,209-211,213-216 2 4 6 9 13 16

201,208,212: 201-Barks-r/Christmas Parade #26, 16pgs. 208-Barks-r/#60 (6 pgs.).
212-Barks-r/WDC&S #130 2 4 6 9 13 16

217-219: 217 has 216 on-c. 219-Barks-r/WDC&S #106,107, 10 pgs. ea.
2 4 6 10 14 18

220,225-228: 228-Barks-r/F.C. #275 2 4 6 13 18 22

221,223,224: Scarce; only sold in pre-packs. 221(8/80), 223(11/80), 224(12/80)
5 10 15 35 63 90

222-(9-10/80)-(Very low distribution) 17 34 51 119 265 410

229-240: 229-Barks-r/F.C. #282. 230-Barks-r/ #52 & WDC&S #194. 236(2/82), 237(2-3/82), 238(3/82), 239(4/82), 240(5/82) 2 4 6 9 13 16

241-245: 241(4/83), 242(5/83), 243(3/84), 244(4/84), 245(7/84)(low print)
3 6 9 14 19 24

246-(1st Gladstone issue)-Barks-r/FC #422 3 6 9 15 21 26

247-249,251: 248,249-Barks-r/DD #54 & 26. 251-Barks-r/1945 Firestone
2 4 6 9 13 16

250-($1.50, 68 pgs.)-Barks-r/4-Color #9 2 4 6 10 14 18

252-277,280: 254-Barks-r/FC #328. 256-Barks-r/FC #147. 257-($1.50, 52 pgs.)-Barks-r/ Vacation Parade #1. 261-Barks-r/FC #300. 275-Kelly-r/FC #92. 280 (#1, 2nd Series)
1 2 3 5 6 8

278,279,286: 278,279 ($1.95, 68 pgs.): 278-Rosa-a; Barks-r/FC #263. 279-Rosa-c; Barks-r/MOC #4. 286-Rosa-a 1 2 3 5 7 9

281,282,284 1 2 3 4 5 7

283-Don Rosa-a, part-c & scripts 1 2 3 5 6 8

285,287-307 5.00

286 ($2.95, 68 pgs.)-Happy Birthday, Donald 6.00

Mini-Comic #1(1976)-(3-1/4x6-1/2"); r/D.D. #150 2 4 6 8 11 14

NOTE: ***Carl Barks** wrote all issues he illustrated, but #117, 126, 138 contain his script only. Issues 4-Color #189, 199, 203, 223, 238, 256, 263, 275, 282, 308, 348, 356, 367, 394, 408, 422, 26-30, 35, 44, 46, 52, 55, 57, 60, 65, 70-73, 77-80, 83, 101, 103, 105, 106, 111, 126, 246r, 266r, 268r, 271r, 275r, 278r(F.C. 263) all have **Barks** covers. **Barks** r-263-267, 269-278-282, 284, 285. #96 titled "Comic Album", #99-"Christmas Album". New art issues (not reprints)-106-46, 148-63, 167, 169, 170, 172, 173, 175, 178, 179, 196, 209, 223, 225, 236. **Taliaferro** daily newspaper strips #258-260, 264, 284, 285; Sunday strips #247, 280-283.*

DONALD DUCK (Numbering continues from Donald Duck and Friends #362)
BOOM! Studios (Kaboom!): No. 363, Feb, 2011 - No. 367, Jun, 2011 ($3.99)

363-367: 363-Barks reprints incl. "Mystery of the Loch". 364-Rosa-c 4.00

DONALD DUCK
IDW Publishing: May, 2015 - No. 21, Jun, 2017 ($3.99)

1-Legacy numbered #368; art by Scarpa and others; multiple covers 4.00

2-21-Reprints of Italian & Dutch stories; multiple covers on each. 8-Christmas issue 4.00

...'s Halloween Scream (10/15, Halloween giveaway) r/Donald Duck Advs. #7,8 (1990) 3.00

DONALD DUCK ADVENTURES (See Walt Disney's Donald Duck Adventures)

DONALD DUCK ALBUM (See Comic Album No. 1,3 & Duck Album)
Dell Publishing Co./Gold Key: 5-7/59 - F.C. No. 1239, 10-12/61; 1962; 8/63 - No. 2, Oct, 1963

Don Rosa's Comics and Stories #1 © Don Rosa

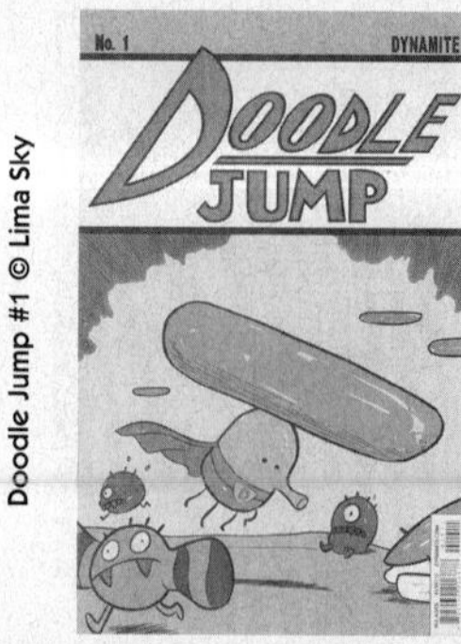

Doodle Jump #1 © Lima Sky

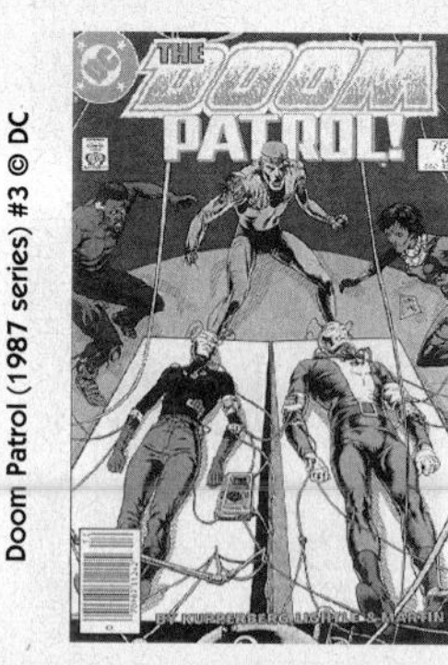

Doom Patrol (1987 series) #3 © DC

	GD 2.0	VG 4.0	FN 6.0	VF 8.0	VF/NM 9.0	NM- 9.2

Four Color 995 (#1) 7 14 21 44 82 120
Four Color 1099,1140,1239-Barks-c 7 14 21 44 82 120
Four Color 1182, 01204-207 (1962-Dell) 5 10 15 34 60 85
1(8/63-Gold Key)-Barks-c 5 10 15 34 60 85
2(10/63) 4 8 12 28 47 65

DONALD DUCK AND FRIENDS (Numbering continues from Walt Disney's ...)
BOOM! Studios: No. 347, Oct, 2009 - No. 362, Jan, 2011 ($2.99)
347-362: Two covers on most. Retitled "Donald Duck" with #363 3.00

DONALD DUCK AND THE BOYS (Also see Story Hour Series)
Whitman Publishing Co.: 1948 (5-1/4x5-1/2", 100pgs., hard-c; art & text)
845-(49) new illos by Barks based on his Donald Duck 10-pager in WDC&S #74, Expanded text not written by Barks; Cover not by Barks
50 100 150 350 600 850
(Prices vary widely on this book)

DONALD DUCK AND THE CHRISTMAS CAROL
Whitman Publishing Co.: 1960 (A Little Golden Book, 6-3/8"x7-5/8", 28 pgs.)
nn-Story book pencilled by Carl Barks with the intended title "Uncle Scrooge's Christmas Carol." Finished art adapted by Norman McGary. (Rare)-Reprinted in Uncle Scrooge in Color. 20 40 60 100 185 270

DONALD DUCK BEACH PARTY (Also see Dell Giants)
Gold Key: Sept, 1965 (12¢)
1(#10158-509)-Barks-r/WDC&S #45; painted-c 6 12 18 37 66 95

DONALD DUCK BOOK (See Story Hour Series)

DONALD DUCK COMICS DIGEST
Gladstone Publishing: Nov, 1986 - No. 5, July, 1987 ($1.25/$1.50, 96 pgs.)
1,3: 1-Barks-c/a-r 1 3 4 6 8 10
2,4,5: 4,5-$1.50-c 6.00

DONALD DUCK FUN BOOK (See Dell Giants)

DONALD DUCK IN DISNEYLAND (See Dell Giants)

DONALD DUCK MARCH OF COMICS (See March of Comics #4,20,41,56,69,263)

DONALD DUCK MERRY CHRISTMAS (See Dell Giant No. 53)

DONALD DUCK PICNIC PARTY (See Picnic Party listed under Dell Giants)

DONALD DUCK TELLS ABOUT KITES (See Kite Fun Book)

DONALD DUCK, THIS IS YOUR LIFE (Disney, TV)
Dell Publishing Co.: No. 1109, Aug-Oct, 1960
Four Color 1109-Gyro flashback to WDC&S #141; origin Donald Duck (1st told)
12 24 36 81 176 270

DONALD DUCK XMAS ALBUM (See regular Donald Duck No. 99)

DONALD IN MATHMAGIC LAND (Disney)
Dell Publishing Co.: No. 1051, Oct-Dec, 1959 - No. 1198, May-July, 1961
Four Color 1051 (#1)-Movie 8 16 24 56 108 160
Four Color 1198-Reprint of above 6 12 18 37 66 95

DONALD QUEST (Donald Duck in parallel universe of Feudarnia)
IDW Publishing: Nov, 2016 - No. 5, Mar, 2017 ($3.99, limited series)
1-5-English version of Italian story; multiple covers on each. 1-Ambrosio-s/Freccero-a4.00

DONATELLO, TEENAGE MUTANT NINJA TURTLE
Mirage Studios: Aug, 1986 ($1.50, B&W, one-shot, 44 pgs.)
1 3 6 9 15 22 28

DONDI
Dell Publishing Co.: No. 1176, Mar-May, 1961 - No. 1276, Dec, 1961
Four Color 1176 (#1)-Movie; origin, photo-c 6 12 18 37 66 95
Four Color 1276 4 8 12 28 47 65

DON FORTUNE MAGAZINE
Don Fortune Publishing Co.: Aug, 1946 - No. 6, Feb, 1947
1-Delecta of the Planets by C.C. Beck in all 32 64 96 192 314 435
2 15 30 45 90 140 190
3-6: 3-Bondage-c 14 28 42 81 118 155

DONG XOAI, VIETNAM 1965
DC Comics: 2010 ($19.95, B&W graphic novel)
SC-Joe Kubert-s/a/c; includes report of actual events that inspired the story 20.00

DONKEY KONG (See Blip #1)

DONNA MATRIX
Reactor, Inc.: Aug, 1993 ($2.95, 52 pgs.)
1-Computer generated-c/a by Mike Saenz; 3-D effects 4.00

DON NEWCOMBE
Fawcett Publications: 1950 (Baseball)
nn-Photo-c 54 108 162 343 574 825

DON ROSA'S COMICS AND STORIES
Fantagraphics Books (CX Comics): 1983 ($2.95)
1,2: 1-(68 pgs.) Reprints Rosa's The Pertwillaby Papers episodes #128-133.
2-(60 pgs.) Reprints episodes #134-138 2 4 6 11 16 20

DON SIMPSON'S BIZARRE HEROES (Also see Megaton Man)
Kitchen Sink Press/Fiasco Comics: May, 1990 - No. 17, Sept, 1996 ($2.50/$2.95, B&W)
1-(5/90, Kitchen Sink) Don Simpson-s/a 1 3 4 6 8 10
1-(5/94, Fiasco) Features Megaton Man 2 4 6 10 14 18
2-10: 9-Title changes to Bizarre Heroes 2 4 6 8 10 12
0,11-17: 0-(12/94)-Begin $2.95-c; r/Bizarre Heroes #1. 16-Indicia also reads Megaton Man vs. Forbidden Frankenstein #1. 17-(9/96)-Indicia also reads Megaton Man #0; intro Megaton Man and the Fiascoverse to new readers 1 2 3 5 6 8

DON'T GIVE UP THE SHIP
Dell Publishing Co.: No. 1049, Aug, 1959
Four Color 1049-Movie, Jerry Lewis photo-c 9 18 27 58 114 170

DON WINSLOW OF THE NAVY
Merwil Publishing Co.: Apr, 1937 - No. 2, May, 1937 (96 pgs.)(A pulp/comic book cross; stapled spine)
V1#1-Has 16 pgs. comics in color. Captain Colorful & Jupiter Jones by Sheldon Mayer; complete Don Winslow novel 680 1360 2040 5100 -- --
2-Sheldon Mayer-a 185 370 555 1400 -- --

DON WINSLOW OF THE NAVY (See Crackajack Funnies, Famous Feature Stories, Popular Comics & Super Book #5,6)
Dell Publishing Co.: No. 2, Nov, 1939 - No. 22, 1941
Four Color 2 (#1)-Rare 245 490 735 1568 2684 3800
Four Color 22 57 114 171 362 619 875

DON WINSLOW OF THE NAVY (See TV Teens; Movie, Radio, TV) (Fightin' Navy No. 74 on)
Fawcett Publications/Charlton No. 70 on: 2/43 - #64, 12/48; #65, 1/51 - #69, 9/51; #70, 3/55 - #73, 9/55
1-(68 pgs.)-Captain Marvel on cover 126 252 378 806 1378 1950
2 45 90 135 284 480 675
3 37 74 111 222 361 500
4-6: 6-Flag-c 30 60 90 177 289 400
7-10: 8-Last 68 pg. issue? 22 44 66 132 216 300
11-20 19 38 57 111 176 240
21-40 16 32 48 94 147 200
41-43,45-64: 51,60-Singapore Sal (villain) app. 64-(12/48)
15 30 45 85 130 175
44-Classic spider-c 40 80 120 246 471 575
65(1/51)-Flying Saucer attack; photo-c 23 46 69 136 223 310
66 - 69(9/51): All photo-c. 66-sci-fi story 15 30 45 85 130 175
70(3/55)-73: 70-73 r-/#26,58 & 59 10 20 30 56 76 95

DOODLE JUMP (Based on the game app)
Dynamite Entertainment: 2014 - No. 6, 2015 ($3.99, limited series)
1-6-Steve Uy-a; multiple covers on each 4.00

DOOM
Marvel Comics: Oct, 2000 - No. 3, Dec, 2000 ($2.99, limited series)
1-3-Dr. Doom; Dixon-s/Manco-a 4.00

DOOMED (Also see Teen Titans #14 (2016))
DC Comics: Aug, 2015 - No. 6, Jan, 2016 ($2.99, limited series)
1-6: 1-Lobdell-s/Fernandez-a. 3-Alpha Centurion app. 4-6-Superman app. 3.00

DOOM FORCE SPECIAL
DC Comics: July, 1992 ($2.95, 68 pgs., one-shot, mature) (X-Force parody)
1-Morrison scripts; Simonson, Steacy, & others-a; Giffen/Mignola-c 4.00

DOOM PATROL, THE (Formerly My Greatest Adventure No. 1-85; see Brave and the Bold, DC Special Blue Ribbon Digest 19, Official... Index & Showcase No. 94-96)
National Periodical Publ.: No. 86, 3/64 - No. 121, 9-10/68; No. 122, 2/73 - No. 124, 6-7/73
86-1 pg. origin (#86-121 are 12¢ issues) 26 52 78 182 404 625
87-98: 88-Origin The Chief. 91-Intro. Mento 9 18 27 60 120 180
99-Intro. Beast Boy (later becomes the Changeling in New Teen Titans)
59 118 177 413 619 825
100-Origin Beast Boy; Robot-Maniac series begins (12/65)
12 24 36 84 185 285
101-110: 102-Challengers of the Unknown app. 104-Wedding issue. 105-Robot-Maniac series

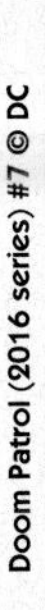

Doom Patrol (2016 series) #7 © DC

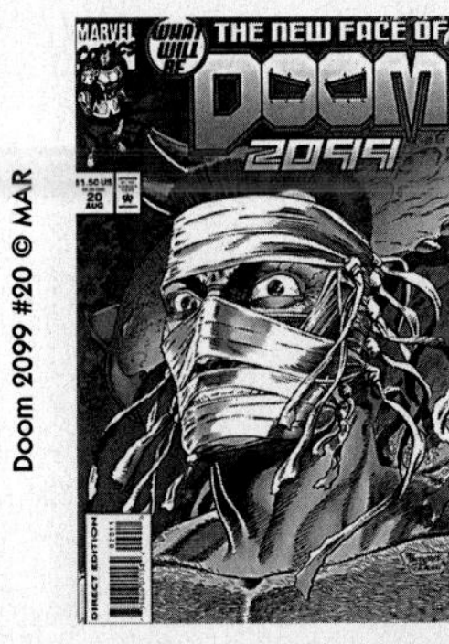

Doom 2099 #20 © MAR

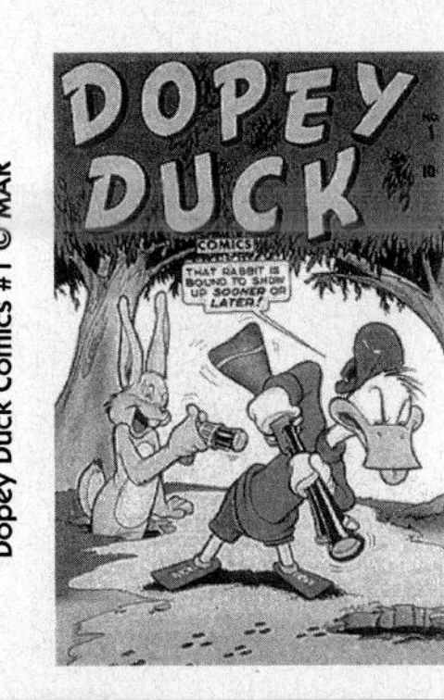

Dopey Duck Comics #1 © MAR

	GD	VG	FN	VF	VF/NM	NM-
	2.0	4.0	6.0	8.0	9.0	9.2
ends. 106-Negative Man begins (origin)	6	12	18	40	73	105
111-120	5	10	15	33	57	80
121-Death of Doom Patrol; Orlando-c.	12	24	36	81	176	270
122-124: All reprints	2	4	6	8	11	14

DOOM PATROL
DC Comics (Vertigo imprint #64 on): Oct, 1987 - No, 87, Feb, 1995 (75¢-$1.95, new format)

1-Wraparound-c; Lightle-a 2 4 6 9 12 15
2-18: 3-1st app. Lodestone. 4-1st app. Karma. 8,15,16-Art Adams-c(i). 18-Invasion tie-in 4.00
19-(2/89)-Grant Morrison scripts begin, ends #63; 1st app Crazy Jane; $1.50-c & new format begins. 2 4 6 9 12 15
20-30: 29-Superman app. 30-Night Breed fold-out 6.00
31-34,37-41,45-49,51-56,58-60: 39-World Without End preview 4.00
35-1st brief app. of Flex Mentallo 2 4 6 8 10 12
36-1st full app. of Flex Mentallo 2 4 6 8 10 12
42-44-Origin of Flex Mentallo. 4.00
50,57 ($2.50, 52 pgs.) 5.00
61-87: 61,70-Photo-c. 73-Death cameo (2 panels) 4.00
...And Suicide Squad 1 (3/88, $1.50, 52 pgs.)-Wraparound-c 5.00
Annual 1 (1988, $1.50, 52 pgs.) 5.00
Annual 2 (1994, $3.95, 68 pgs.)-Children's Crusade tie-in. 5.00
...: Crawling From the Wreckage TPB (2004, $19.95) r/#19-25; Morrison-s 20.00
...: Down Paradise Way TPB (2005, $19.99) r/#35-41; Morrison-s 20.00
...: Magic Bus TPB (2007, $19.99) r/#51-57; Morrison-s; new Bolland-c 20.00
...: Musclebound TPB (2006, $19.99) r/#42-50; Morrison-s; new Bolland-c 20.00
...: Planet Love TPB (2008, $19.99) r/#58-63 & Doom Force Special #1; Morrison-s 20.00
...: The Painting That Ate Paris TPB (2004, $19.95) r/#26-34; Morrison-s 20.00
NOTE: ***Bisley*** *painted c-26-48, 55-58.* ***Bolland*** *c-64, 75.* ***Dringenberg*** *a-42(p).* ***Steacy*** *a-53.*

DOOM PATROL
DC Comics: Dec, 2001 - No. 22, Sept, 2003 ($2.50)

1-Intro. new team with Robotman; Tan Eng Huat-c/a; John Arcudi-s 4.00
2-22: 4,5-Metamorpho & Elongated Man app. 13,14-Fisher-a. 20-Geary-a 3.00

DOOM PATROL (see JLA #94-99)
DC Comics: Aug, 2004 - No. 18, Jan, 2006 ($2.50)

1-18-John Byrne-s/a. 1-Green Lantern, Batman app. 3.00

DOOM PATROL
DC Comics: Oct, 2009 - No. 22, Jul, 2011 ($3.99/$2.99)

1-7: 1-Giffen-s/Clark-a; back-up Metal Men feature w/Maguire-a. 1-Two covers. 4-5-Blackest Night. 6-Negative Man origin re-told 4.00
8-22-($2.99) 11,12-Ambush Bug app. 16-Giffen-a. 21-Robotman origin retold 3.00
...: Brotherhood TPB (2011, $17.99) r/#7-13 18.00
...: We Who Are About to Die TPB (2010, $14.99) r/#1-6; cover gallery; design art 15.00

DOOM PATROL
DC Comics (Young Animal): Nov, 2016 - No. 12, Dec, 2018 ($3.99)

1-12: 1-Gerald Way-s/Nick Derington-a; main cover has peel-off gyro sticker. 8-Allred-a 4.00
1-Director's Cut (5/17, $5.99) Pencil/ink art; original script with thumbnails 6.00
.../ JLA Special 1 (4/18, $4.99) Part 5 of Milk Wars crossover; Eaglesham-a/Mann-c 5.00

DOOM PATROL (See Tangent Comics/ Doom Patrol)

DOOM PATROL: WEIGHT OF THE WORLDS
DC Comics (Young Animal): Sept, 2019 - No. 7, Sept, 2020 ($3.99)

1-7: 1-Gerald Way-s/James Harvey-a. 3-Shaner-a. 5-Cloonan-a 4.00

DOOMSDAY
DC Comics: 1995 ($3.95, one-shot)

1-Year One story by Jurgens, L. Simonson, Ordway, and Gil Kane; Superman app. 5.00

DOOMSDAY CLOCK (See Watchmen)
DC Comics: Jan, 2018 - No. 12, Feb, 2020 ($4.99/$5.99, limited series)

1-Follows end of Watchmen; intro new Rorschach; Johns-s/Frank-a; 2 covers by Frank 5.00
1-($5.99) Lenticular cover 6.00
2-11: Two covers on each. 2-Comedian returns; Nathaniel Dusk makes DCU return as fictional 1940s -'50s film noir detective. 5-7-Joker app.; origin of Marionette 5.00
12-($5.99) Superman vs. Dr. Manhattan; intro of the Metaverse 6.00

DOOMSDAY + 1 (Also see Charlton Bullseye)
Charlton Comics: July, 1975 - No. 6, June, 1976; No. 7, June, 1978 - No. 12, May, 1979

1: #1-5 are 25¢ issues 3 6 9 19 30 40
2-6: 4-Intro Lor. 5-Ditko-a(1 pg.) 6-Begin 30¢-c 2 4 6 10 14 18
V3#7-12 (reprints #1-6) 6.00
5 (Modern Comics reprint, 1977) 6.00
NOTE: ***Byrne*** *c/a-1-12; Painted covers-2-7.*

DOOMSDAY.1
IDW Publishing: May, 2013 - No. 4, Aug, 2013 ($3.99)

1-4-John Byrne-s/a/c 4.00

DOOMSDAY SQUAD, THE
Fantagraphics Books: Aug, 1986 - No. 7, 1987 ($2.00)

1,2,4-7: Byrne-a in all. 1,2-New Byrne-c. 4-Neal Adams-c. 5-7-Gil Kane-c 4.00
3-Usagi Yojimbo app. (1st in color); new Byrne-c 6.00

DOOM'S IV
Image Comics (Extreme): July, 1994 - No.4, Oct, 1994 ($2.50, limited series)

1-4-Liefeld story 4.00
1,2-Two alternate Liefeld-c each, 4 covers form 1 picture 5.00

DOOM: THE EMPEROR RETURNS
Marvel Comics: Jan, 2002 - No. 3, Mar, 2002 ($2.50, limited series)

1-3-Dixon-s/Manco-a; Franklin Richards app. 4.00

DOOM 2099 (See Marvel Comics Presents #118 & 2099: World of Tomorrow)
Marvel Comics: Jan, 1993 - No. 44, Aug, 1996 ($1.25/$1.50/$1.95)

1-Metallic foil stamped-c 6.00
1-2nd printing 3.00
2-24,26-44: 4-Ron Lim-c(p). 17-bound-in trading card sheet. 40-Namor & Doctor Strange app. 41-Daredevil app., Namor-c/app. 44-Intro The Emissary; story contin'd in 2099: World of Tomorrow 4.00
18-Variant polybagged with Sega Sub-Terrania poster 5.00
25 ($2.25, 52 pgs.) 5.00
25 ($2.95, 52pgs.) Foil embossed cover 6.00
29 ($3.50)-acetate-c. 5.00
No. 1 (2/20, $4.99) Zdarsky-s/Castiello-a; tie-in to 2099 specials and ASM #33-36 (2020) 5.00

DOOMWAR
Marvel Comics: Apr, 2010 - No. 6, Sept, 2010 ($3.99, limited series)

1-6-Doctor Doom invades Wakanda; Black Panther & X-Men app.; Romita Jr.-c/Eaton-a 4.00

DOORWAY TO NIGHTMARE (See Cancelled Comic Cavalcade and Madame Xanadu)
DC Comics: Jan-Feb, 1978 - No. 5, Sept-Oct, 1978

1-Madame Xanadu in all 3 6 9 21 33 45
2-5: 4-Craig-a 2 4 6 8 11 14
NOTE: ***Kaluta*** *covers on all. Merged into The Unexpected with No. 190.*

DOPEY DUCK COMICS (Wacky Duck No. 3) (See Super Funnies)
Timely Comics (NPP): Fall, 1945 - No. 2, Apr, 1946

1-Casper Cat, Krazy Krow 45 90 135 284 480 675
2-Casper Cat, Krazy Krow 34 68 102 199 325 450

DORK
Slave Labor: June, 1993 - No. 11 ($2.50-$3.50, B&W, mature)

1-7,9-11: Evan Dorkin-c/a/scripts in all. 1(8/95),2(1/96)-(2nd printings). 1(3/97) (3rd printing). 1-Milk & Cheese app. 3-Eltingville Club starts. 6-Reprints 1st Eltingville Club app. from Instant Piano #1 4.00
8-($3.50) 4.00
Who's Laughing Now? TPB (2001, $11.95) reprints most of #1-5 12.00
The Collected Dork, Vol. 2: Circling the Drain (6/03, $13.95) r/most of #7-10 & other-s 14.00

DOROTHY & THE WIZARD IN OZ (Adaptation of the original 1908 L. Frank Baum book) (Also see Wonderful Wizard of Oz, Marvelous Land of Oz, and Ozma of Oz)
Marvel Comics: Nov, 2011 - No. 8, Aug, 2012 ($3.99, limited series)

1-8-Eric Shanower-a/Skottie Young-a/c 4.00

DOROTHY LAMOUR (Formerly Jungle Lil)(Stage, screen, radio)
Fox Feature Syndicate: No. 2, June, 1950 - No. 3, Aug, 1950

2-Wood-a(3), photo-c 40 80 120 244 402 560
3-Wood-a(3), photo-c 32 64 96 192 314 435

DOROTHY OF OZ PREQUEL
IDW Publishing: Mar, 2012 - No. 4, Aug, 2012 ($3.99, limited series)

1-4-Tipton-s/Shedd-a 4.00

DOT DOTLAND (Formerly Little Dot Dotland)
Harvey Publications: No. 62, Sept, 1974 - No. 63, Nov, 1974

62,63 2 4 6 11 16 20

DOTTY (...& Her Boy Friends)(Formerly Four Teeners; Glamorous Romances No. 41 on)
Ace Magazines (A. A. Wyn): No. 35, June, 1948 - No. 40, May, 1949

35-Teen-age 14 28 42 81 118 155
36-40: 37-Transvestism story 10 20 30 56 76 95

DOTTY DRIPPLE (Horace & Dotty Dripple No. 25 on)
Magazine Ent.(Life's Romances)/Harvey No. 3 on: 1946 - No. 24, June, 1952 (Also see A-1 No. 1, 3-8, 10)

1 (nd) (10¢) 15 30 45 85 130 175

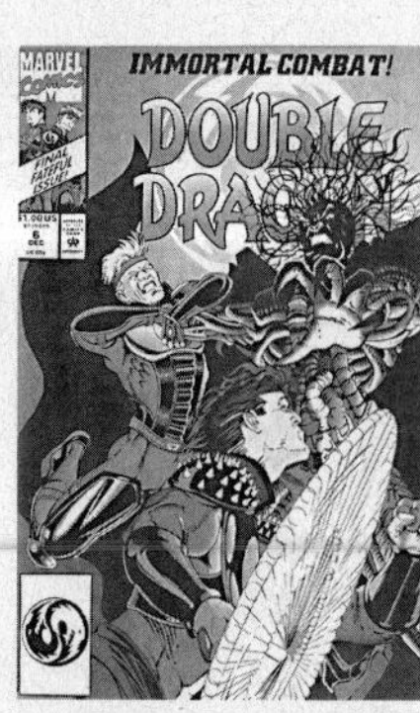

Double Dragon #6 © Technos Japan

Down With Crime #6 © FAW

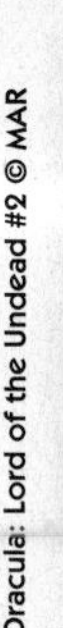

Dracula: Lord of the Undead #2 © MAR

	GD 2.0	VG 4.0	FN 6.0	VF 8.0	VF/NM 9.0	NM- 9.2
2	10	20	30	56	76	95
3-10: 3,4-Powell-a	7	14	21	35	43	50
11-24	6	12	18	28	34	40

DOTTY DRIPPLE AND TAFFY
Dell Publishing Co.: No. 646, Sept, 1955 - No. 903, May, 1958

	GD 2.0	VG 4.0	FN 6.0	VF 8.0	VF/NM 9.0	NM- 9.2
Four Color 646 (#1)	6	12	18	37	66	95
Four Color 691,718,746,801,903	4	8	12	28	47	65

DOUBLE ACTION COMICS
National Periodical Publications: No. 2, Jan, 1940 (68 pgs., B&W)

	GD 2.0	VG 4.0	FN 6.0	VF 8.0	VF/NM 9.0	NM- 9.2
2-Contains original stories(?); pre-hero DC contents; same cover as Adventure No. 37. (seven known copies, four in high grade) (not an ashcan)	4000	8000	12,000	24,000	32,000	40,000

NOTE: *The cover to this book was probably reprinted from Adventure #37. #1 exists as an ash can copy with B&W cover; contains a coverless comic on inside with 1st & last page missing. There is proof of at least limited newsstand distribution. #2 cover proof only sold in 2005 for $4,000.*

DOUBLE COMICS
Elliot Publications: 1940 - 1944 (132 pgs.)

	GD 2.0	VG 4.0	FN 6.0	VF 8.0	VF/NM 9.0	NM- 9.2
1940 issues; Masked Marvel-c & The Mad Mong vs. The White Flash covers known	309	618	927	2163	3782	5400
1941 issues; Tornado Tim-c, Nordac-c, & Green Light covers known	226	452	678	1446	2473	3500
1942 issues	161	322	483	1030	1765	2500
1943,1944 issues	135	270	405	864	1482	2100

NOTE: *Double Comics consisted of an almost endless combination of pairs of remaindered, unsold issues of comics representing most publishers and usually mixed publishers in the same book; e.g., a Captain America with a Silver Streak, or a Feature with a Detective, etc., could appear inside the same cover. The actual contents would have to determine its price. Prices listed are for average contents. Any containing rare origin or first issues are worth much more. Covers also vary in same year. Value would be approximately 50 percent of contents.*

DOUBLE-CROSS (See The Crusaders)

DOUBLE-DARE ADVENTURES
Harvey Publications: Dec, 1966 - No. 2, Mar, 1967 (35¢/25¢, 68 pgs.)

	GD 2.0	VG 4.0	FN 6.0	VF 8.0	VF/NM 9.0	NM- 9.2
1-Origin Bee-Man, Glowing Gladiator, & Magic-Master; Simon/Kirby-a	6	12	18	40	73	105
2-Torres-a; r/Alarming Adv. #3('63)	5	10	15	31	53	75

NOTE: ***Powell** a-1. **Simon/Sparling** c-1, 2.*

DOUBLE DRAGON
Marvel Comics: July, 1991 - No. 6, Dec, 1991 ($1.00, limited series)

	GD 2.0	VG 4.0	FN 6.0	VF 8.0	VF/NM 9.0	NM- 9.2
1-6: Based on video game. 2-Art Adams-c						4.00

DOUBLE EDGE
Marvel Comics: Alpha, 1995; Omega, 1995 ($4.95, limited series)

	GD 2.0	VG 4.0	FN 6.0	VF 8.0	VF/NM 9.0	NM- 9.2
Alpha ($4.95)- Punisher story, Nick Fury app.						5.00
Omega ($4.95)-Punisher, Daredevil, Ghost Rider app. Death of Nick Fury						5.00

DOUBLE IMAGE
Image Comics: Feb, 2001 - No. 5, July, 2001 ($2.95)

	GD 2.0	VG 4.0	FN 6.0	VF 8.0	VF/NM 9.0	NM- 9.2
1-5: 1-Flip covers of Codeflesh (Casey-s/Adlard-a) and The Bod (Young-s). 2-Two covers. 5-"Trust in Me" begins; Chaudhary-a						3.00

DOUBLE LIFE OF PRIVATE STRONG, THE
Archie Publications/Radio Comics: June, 1959 - No. 2, Aug, 1959

	GD 2.0	VG 4.0	FN 6.0	VF 8.0	VF/NM 9.0	NM- 9.2
1-Origin & re-intro The Shield; Simon & Kirby-c/a, their re-entry into the super-hero genre; intro./1st app. The Fly; 1st S.A. super-hero for Archie Publ.	34	68	102	245	548	850
2-S&K-c/a; Tuska-a; The Fly app. (2nd or 3rd?)	18	36	54	126	281	435

DOUBLE TROUBLE
St. John Publishing Co.: Nov, 1957 - No. 2, Jan-Feb, 1958

	GD 2.0	VG 4.0	FN 6.0	VF 8.0	VF/NM 9.0	NM- 9.2
1,2: Tuffy & Snuffy by Frank Johnson; dubbed "World's Funniest Kids"	8	16	24	44	57	70

DOUBLE TROUBLE WITH GOOBER
Dell Publishing Co.: No. 417, Aug, 1952 - No. 556, May, 1954

	GD 2.0	VG 4.0	FN 6.0	VF 8.0	VF/NM 9.0	NM- 9.2
Four Color 417	5	10	15	33	57	80
Four Color 471,516,556	4	8	12	27	44	60

DOUBLE UP COMICS
Elliott Publications: 1941 (Pocket size, 192 pgs., 10¢)

	GD 2.0	VG 4.0	FN 6.0	VF 8.0	VF/NM 9.0	NM- 9.2
1-Contains rebound copies of digest sized issues of Pocket Comics, Speed Comics, & Spitfire Comics; Japanese WWII-c	271	542	813	1734	2967	4200

DOVER & CLOVER (See All Funny & More Fun Comics #93)

DOVER BOYS (See Adventures of the...)

DOVER THE BIRD
Famous Funnies Publishing Co.: Spring, 1955

	GD 2.0	VG 4.0	FN 6.0	VF 8.0	VF/NM 9.0	NM- 9.2
1-Funny animal; code approved (10¢-c)	10	20	30	56	76	95
1-Same cover; not code approved (6¢-c, 3 for 15¢)	9	18	27	52	69	85

DOWN
Image Comics (Top Cow): Dec, 2005 - No. 4, Mar, 2006 ($2.99)

	GD 2.0	VG 4.0	FN 6.0	VF 8.0	VF/NM 9.0	NM- 9.2
1-4-Warren Ellis-s. 1-Tony Harris-a/c. 2-4-Cully Hamner-a						3.00
Down & Top Cow's Best of Warren Ellis TPB (6/06, $15.99) r/#1-4 & Tales of the Witchblade #3,4; Ellis-s; script for Down #1 with Harris sketch pages						16.00

DOWN WITH CRIME
Fawcett Publications: Nov, 1952 - No. 7, Nov, 1953

	GD 2.0	VG 4.0	FN 6.0	VF 8.0	VF/NM 9.0	NM- 9.2
1	43	86	129	271	461	650
2,4,5: 2,4-Powell-a in each. 5-Bondage-c	24	48	72	142	234	325
3-Used in **POP**, pg. 106; "H is for Heroin" drug story	28	56	84	165	270	375
6,7: 6-Used in **POP**, pg. 80	24	48	72	142	234	325

DO YOU BELIEVE IN NIGHTMARES?
St. John Publishing Co.: Nov, 1957 - No. 2, Jan, 1958

	GD 2.0	VG 4.0	FN 6.0	VF 8.0	VF/NM 9.0	NM- 9.2
1-Mostly Ditko-c/a	71	142	213	454	777	1100
2-Ayers-a	41	82	123	256	428	600

D.P. 7
Marvel Comics Group (New Universe): Nov, 1986 - No. 32, June, 1989

	GD 2.0	VG 4.0	FN 6.0	VF 8.0	VF/NM 9.0	NM- 9.2
1-20,						3.00
21-32-Low print						4.00
Annual #1 (11/87)-Intro. The Witness						4.00
... Classic Vol. 1 TPB (2007, $24.99) r/#1-9; Mark Gruenwald-s/Paul Ryan-a in all						25.00

NOTE: ***Williamson** a-9i, 11i; c-9i.*

DRACULA (See Bram Stoker's Dracula, Giant-Size..., Little Dracula, Marvel Graphic Novel, Requiem for Dracula, Spider-Man Vs...., Stoker's..., Tomb of... & Wedding of...; also see Movie Classics under Universal Presents as well as Dracula)

DRACULA (See Movie Classics for #1)(Also see Frankenstein & Werewolf)
Dell Publ. Co.: No. 2, 11/66 - No. 4, 3/67; No. 6, 7/72 - No. 8, 7/73 (No #5)

	GD 2.0	VG 4.0	FN 6.0	VF 8.0	VF/NM 9.0	NM- 9.2
2-Origin & 1st app. Dracula (11/66) (super hero)	5	10	15	31	53	75
3,4: 4-Intro. Fleeta ('67)	3	6	9	21	33	45
6-('72)-r/#2 w/origin	3	6	9	15	22	28
7,8-r/#3, #4	2	4	6	13	18	22

DRACULA (Magazine)
Warren Publishing Co.: 1979 (120 pgs., full color)

	GD 2.0	VG 4.0	FN 6.0	VF 8.0	VF/NM 9.0	NM- 9.2
Book 1-Maroto art; Spanish material translated into English (mail order only)	6	12	18	37	66	95

DRACULA
Marvel Comics: Jul, 2010 - No. 4, Sept, 2010 ($3.99, limited series)

	GD 2.0	VG 4.0	FN 6.0	VF 8.0	VF/NM 9.0	NM- 9.2
1-4-Colored reprint of Bram Stoker's Classic Dracula adapt. from Dracula Lives!, Legion of Monsters and Stoker's Dracula; Thomas-s/Giordano-a; J. Djurdjevic-c						4.00

DRACULA CHRONICLES
Topps Comics: Apr, 1995 - No. 3, June, 1995 ($2.50, limited series)

	GD 2.0	VG 4.0	FN 6.0	VF 8.0	VF/NM 9.0	NM- 9.2
1-3-Linsner-c						4.00

DRACULA LIVES! (Magazine)(Also see Tomb of Dracula) (Reprinted in Stoker's Dracula)
Marvel Comics Group: 1973(no month) - No. 13, July, 1975 (75¢, B&W) (76 pgs.)

	GD 2.0	VG 4.0	FN 6.0	VF 8.0	VF/NM 9.0	NM- 9.2
1-Boris painted-c	8	16	24	54	102	150
2 (7/73)-1st time origin Dracula; Adams, Starlin-a	5	10	15	33	57	80
3-1st app. Robert E. Howard's Soloman Kane; Adams-c/a	5	10	15	31	53	75
4,5: 4-Ploog-a. 5(V2#1)-Bram Stoker's Classic Dracula adapt. begins	4	8	12	23	37	50
6-9: 6-8-Bram Stoker adapt. 9-Bondage-c	4	8	12	23	37	50
10 (1/75)-16 pg. Lilith solo (1st?)	4	8	12	27	44	60
11-13: 11-21 pg. Lilith solo sty. 12-31 pg. Dracula sty	4	8	12	23	37	50
Annual 1(Summer, 1975, $1.25, 92 pgs.)-Morrow painted-c; 6 Dracula stys. 25 pgs. Adams-a(r)	4	8	12	25	40	55

NOTE: ***N. Adams** a-2, 3i, 10i, Annual 1r(2, 3i). **Alcala** a-9. **Buscema** a-3p, 6p, Annual 1p. **Colan** a(p)-1, 2, 5, 6, 8. **Evans** a-7. **Gulacy** a-9. **Heath** a-1r, 13. **Pakula** a-6r. Sutton a-13.**Weiss** r-Annual 1p. 4 **Dracula** stories each in 1, 609; 3 **Dracula** stories each in 2, 4, 5,, 13.*

DRACULA: LORD OF THE UNDEAD
Marvel Comics: Dec, 1998 - No. 3, Dec, 1998 ($2.99, limited series)

	GD 2.0	VG 4.0	FN 6.0	VF 8.0	VF/NM 9.0	NM- 9.2
1-3-Olliffe & Palmer-a						4.00

DRACULA: RETURN OF THE IMPALER
Slave Labor Graphics: July, 1993 - No. 4, Oct, 1994 ($2.95, limited series)

	GD 2.0	VG 4.0	FN 6.0	VF 8.0	VF/NM 9.0	NM- 9.2
1-4						4.00

DRACULA'S REVENGE

The Dragon #2 © Erik Larsen

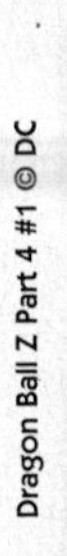
Dragon Ball Z Part 4 #1 © DC

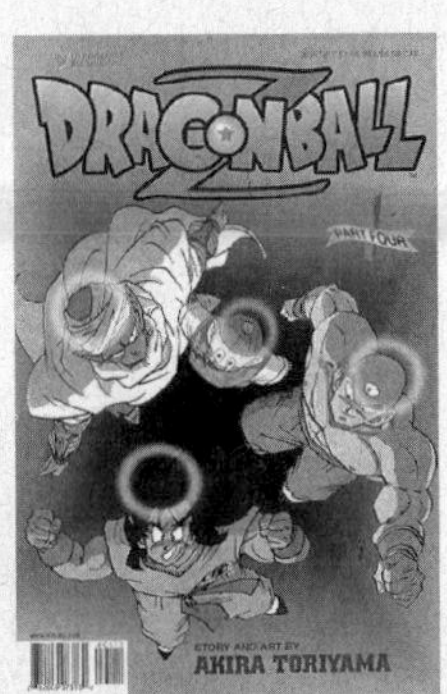

The Dragon: Blood & Guts #3 © Erik Larsen

	GD	VG	FN	VF	VF/NM	NM-
	2.0	4.0	6.0	8.0	9.0	9.2

IDW Publishing: Apr, 2004 - No. 3 ($3.99, limited series)
1,2-Forbeck-s/Kudranski-a 4.00

DRACULA: THE COMPANY OF MONSTERS
BOOM! Studios: Aug, 2010 - No. 12, Jul, 2011 ($3.99)
1-12: 1-5-Busiek & Gregory-s/Godlewski-a. 1-Two covers by Brereton and Salas 4.00

DRACULA VERSUS ZORRO
Topps Comics: Oct, 1993 - No. 2, Nov, 1993 ($2.95, limited series)
1,2: 1-Spot varnish & red foil-c. 2-Polybagged w/16 pg. Zorro #0 4.00

DRACULA VERSUS ZORRO
Dark Horse Comics: Sept, 1998 - No. 2, Oct, 1998 ($2.95, limited series)
1,2 4.00

DRACULA: VLAD THE IMPALER (Also see Bram Stoker's Dracula)
Topps Comics: Feb, 1993 - No. 3, Apr, 1993 ($2.95, limited series)
1-3-Polybagged with 3 trading cards each; Maroto-c/a 4.00

DRAFT, THE
Marvel Comics: 1988 ($3.50, one-shot, squarebound)
1-Sequel to "The Pitt" 4.00

DRAFTED: ONE HUNDRED DAYS
Devil's Due Publishing: June, 2009 ($5.99, one-shot)
1-Barack Obama on a post-galactic-war Earth; Powers-s 6.00

DRAG 'N' WHEELS (Formerly Top Eliminator)
Charlton Comics: No. 30, Sept, 1968 - No. 59, May, 1973

	GD	VG	FN	VF	VF/NM	NM-
30	4	8	12	27	44	60
31-40-Scot Jackson begins	3	6	9	18	28	38
41-50	3	6	9	16	24	32
51-59: Scot Jackson	2	4	6	13	18	22
Modern Comics Reprint 58('78)						5.00

DRAGON, THE (Also see The Savage Dragon)
Image Comics (Highbrow Ent.): Mar, 1996 - No. 5, July, 1996 (99¢, lim. series)
1-5: Reprints Savage Dragon limited series w/new story & art. 5-Youngblood app; includes 5 pg. Savage Dragon story from 1984 4.00

DRAGON AGE (Based on the EA videogame)
IDW Publishing (EA Comics): Mar, 2010 - No. 6, Nov, 2010 ($3.99)
1-6-Orson Scott Card & Aaron Johnston-s; Ramos-c 4.00

DRAGON AGE: BLUE WRAITH (Based on the EA videogame)
Dark Horse Comics: Jan, 2020 - No. 3, Mar, 2020 ($3.99, limited series)
1-3-DeFilippis & Weir-s/Furukawa-a/Teng-c 4.00

DRAGON AGE: DECEPTION (Based on the EA videogame)
Dark Horse Comics: Oct, 2018 - No. 3, Dec, 2018 ($3.99, limited series)
1-3-DeFilippis & Weir-s/Furukawa-a/Teng-c 4.00

DRAGON AGE: KNIGHT ERRANT (Based on the EA videogame)
Dark Horse Comics: May, 2017 - No. 5, Sept, 2017 ($3.99, limited series)
1-5-DeFilippis & Weir-s/Furukawa-a/Teng-c 4.00

DRAGON AGE: MAGEKILLER (Based on the EA videogame)
Dark Horse Comics: Dec, 2015 - No. 5, Apr, 2016 ($3.99, limited series)
1-3-Rucka-s/Carnero-a/Teng-c 4.00

DRAGON AGE: THOSE WHO SPEAK (Based on the EA videogame)
Dark Horse Comics: Aug, 2012 - No. 3, Nov, 2012 ($3.50, limited series)
1-3-Gaider-s/Hardin-a/Palumbo-c 3.50

DRAGON ARCHIVES, THE (Also see The Savage Dragon)
Image Comics: Jun, 1998 - No. 4, Jan, 1999 ($2.95, B&W)
1-4: Reprints early Savage Dragon app. 4.00

DRAGON BALL
Viz Comics: Mar, 1998 - Part 6: #2, Feb, 2003($2.95, B&W, Manga reprints read right to left)

	GD	VG	FN	VF	VF/NM	NM-
Part 1: 1-Akira Toriyama-s/a	4	8	12	23	37	50
2-12						6.00
1-12 (2nd & 3rd printings)						4.00
Part 2: 1-15: 15-($3.50-c)						5.00
Part 3: 1-14						4.00
Part 4: 1-10						4.00
Part 5: 1-7						4.00
Part 6: 1,2						4.00

DRAGON BALL Z
Viz Comics: Mar, 1998 - Part 5: #10, Oct, 2002 ($2.95, B&W, Manga reprints read right to left)

	GD	VG	FN	VF	VF/NM	NM-
Part 1: 1-Akira Toriyama-s/a	3	6	9	14	19	24
2-9						6.00
1-9 (2nd & 3rd printings)						4.00
Part 2: 1-14						5.00
Part 3: 1-10						4.00
Part 4: 1-15						4.00
Part 5: 1-10						4.00

DRAGON, THE: BLOOD & GUTS (Also see The Savage Dragon)
Image Comics (Highbrow Entertainment): Mar, 1995 - No. 3, May, 1995 ($2.50, lim. series)
1-3: Jason Pearson-c/a/scripts 4.00

DRAGON CHIANG
Eclipse Books: 1991 ($3.95, B&W, squarebound, 52 pgs.)
nn-Timothy Truman-c/a(p) 4.00

DRAGONFLIGHT
Eclipse Books: Feb, 1991 - No. 3, 1991 ($4.95, 52 pgs.)
Book One - Three: Adapts 1968 novel 5.00

DRAGONFLY (See Americomics #4)
Americomics: Sum, 1985 - No. 8, 1986 ($1.75/$1.95)
1 5.00
2-8 4.00

DRAGONFLY & DRAGONFLYMAN (See The Wrong Earth)
AHOY Comics: 2019 - No. 5, 2020 ($3.99, limited series)
1-5-Each hero versus Devil Man; Peyer-s/Krause-a 4.00
1-Free Comic Book Day 2019 Edition; Russ Braun-a; back-up Captain Ginger story 3.00

DRAGONFORCE
Aircel Publishing: 1988 - No. 13, 1989 ($2.00)
1-Dale Keown-c/a/scripts in #1-12 4.00
2-13: 13-No Keown-a 3.00
...Chronicles Book 1-5 ($2.95, B&W, 60 pgs.): Dale Keown-r/Dragonring & Dragonforce 4.00

DRAGONHEART (Movie)
Topps Comics: May, 1996 - No. 2, June, 1996 ($2.95/$4.95, limited series)
1-($2.95, 24 pgs.)-Adaptation of the film; Hildebrandt Bros-c; Lim-a. 3.00
2-($4.95, 64 pgs.) 5.00

DRAGONLANCE (Also see TSR Worlds)
DC Comics: Dec, 1988 - No. 34, Sept, 1991 ($1.25/$1.50, Mando paper)
1-Based on TSR game 4.00
2-34: Based on TSR game. 30-32-Kaluta-c 3.00

DRAGONLANCE: CHRONICLES
Devil's Due Publ.: Aug, 2005 - No. 8, Mar, 2006 ($2.95)
1-8-Dabb-s/Kurth-a 3.00
...: Dragons of Autumn Twilight TPB (2006, $17.95) r/#1-8 18.00

DRAGONLANCE: CHRONICLES (Volume 2)
Devil's Due Publ.: July, 2006 - No. 4, Jan, 2007 ($4.95/$4.99, 48 pgs.)
1-4-Dragons of Winter Night; Dabb-s/Kurth-a 5.00
...: Dragons of Winter Night TPB (3/07, $18.99) r/#1-4; cover gallery 19.00

DRAGONLANCE: CHRONICLES (Volume 3)
Devil's Due Publ.: Mar, 2007 - No. 12, ($3.50)
1-11-Dragons of Spring Dawning; Dabb-s/Cope-a 3.50

DRAGONLANCE: THE LEGEND OF HUMA
Devil's Due Publ.: Jan, 2004 - No. 6, Oct, 2005 ($2.95)
1-6-Mike Miller & Rael-a 3.00

DRAGON LINES
Marvel Comics (Epic Comics/Heavy Hitters): May, 1993 - No. 4, Aug, 1993 ($1.95, lim. series)
1-($2.50)-Embossed-c; Ron Lim-c/a in all 4.00
2-4 3.00

DRAGON LINES: WAY OF THE WARRIOR
Marvel Comics (Epic Comics/ Heavy Hitters): Nov, 1993 - No. 2, Jan, 1994 ($2.25, limited series)
1,2-Ron Lim-c/a(p) 3.00

DRAGONQUEST
Silverwolf Comics: Dec, 1986 - No. 2, 1987 ($1.50, B&W, 28 pgs.)
1,2-Tim Vigil-c/a in all 5.00

DRAGON'S CLAWS
Marvel UK, Ltd.: July, 1988 - No. 10, Apr, 1989 ($1.25/$1.50/$1.75, British)

Drawing Blood #2 © Eastman & Avallone

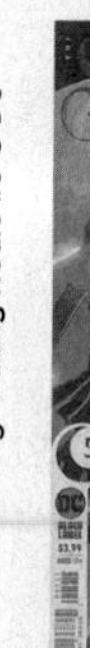
Dreadstar #56 © FC

The Dreaming: Waking Hours #5 © DC

	GD 2.0	VG 4.0	FN 6.0	VF 8.0	VF/NM 9.0	NM- 9.2

1-10: 3-Death's Head 1 pg. strip on back-c (1st app.). 4-Silhouette of Death's Head on last pg. 5-1st full app. new Death's Head — 4.00

DRAGON'S LAIR: SINGE'S REVENGE (Based on the Don Bluth video game)
CrossGen Comics: Sept, 2003 - No. 3 ($2.95, limited series)

1-3-Mangels-s/Laguna-a — 3.00

DRAGONSLAYER (Movie)
Marvel Comics Group: October, 1981 - No. 2, Nov, 1981

1,2-Paramount Disney movie adaptation — 4.00

DRAGOON WELLS MASSACRE
Dell Publishing Co.: No. 815, June, 1957

	GD	VG	FN	VF	VF/NM	NM-
Four Color 815-Movie, photo-c	7	14	21	49	92	135

DRAGSTRIP HOTRODDERS (World of Wheels No. 17 on)
Charlton Comics: Sum, 1963; No. 2, Jan, 1965 - No. 16, Aug, 1967

	GD	VG	FN	VF	VF/NM	NM-
1	6	12	18	42	79	115
2-5	4	8	12	25	40	55
6-16	3	6	9	21	33	45

DRAIN
Image Comics: Nov, 2006 - No. 6, Mar, 2008 ($2.99)

1-6: 1-Cebulski-s/Takeda-a; two covers by Takeda and Finch — 3.00
Vol. 1 TPB (2008, $16.99) r/#1-6; cover gallery and Takeda sketch art gallery — 17.00

DRAKUUN
Dark Horse Comics: Feb, 1997 - No. 25, Mar, 1999 ($2.95, B&W, manga)

1-25; 1-6- Johji Manabe-s/a in all. Rise of the Dragon Princess series. 7-12-Revenge of Gustav. 13-18-Shadow of the Warlock. 19-25-The Hidden War — 3.00

DRAMA
Sirius: June, 1994 ($2.95, mature)

	GD	VG	FN	VF	VF/NM	NM-
1-1st full color Dawn app. in comics	2	4	6	8	10	12
1-Limited edition (1400 copies); signed & numbered; fingerprint authenticity	3	6	9	19	30	40

NOTE: *Dawn's 1st full color app. was a pin-up in Amazing Heroes' Swimsuit Special #5.*

DRAMA OF AMERICA, THE
Action Text: 1973 ($1.95, 224 pgs.)

	GD	VG	FN	VF	VF/NM	NM-
1- "Students' Supplement to History"	2	4	6	8	10	12

DRAWING BLOOD
Kevin Eastman Studios: May, 2019 - No. 4, Aug, 2019 ($3.99, limited series)

1-4-Avallone-s/Bishop & Eastman-a — 4.00

DRAWING ON YOUR NIGHTMARES
Dark Horse Comics: Oct, 2003 ($2.99, one-shot)

1-Short stories; The Goon, Criminal Macabre, Tales of the Vampires; Templesmith-c — 3.00

DRAX (Guardians of the Galaxy)
Marvel Comics: Jan, 2016 - No. 11, Nov, 2016 ($3.99)

1-11-CM Punk & Cullen Bunn-s/Hepburn-a. 1-Guardians app. 4,5-Fin Fang Foom app. — 4.00

DRAX THE DESTROYER (Guardians of the Galaxy)
Marvel Comics: Nov, 2005 - No. 4, Feb, 2006 ($2.99, limited series)

1-4-Giffen-s/Breitweiser-a — 5.00
...: Earthfall TPB (2006, $10.99) r/#1-4; character design page — 11.00

DREAD GODS
IDW Publishing: Jul, 2017 - No. 4, Oct, 2018 ($3.99)

1-4-Marz-s/Raney-a — 4.00

DREADLANDS (Also see Epic)
Marvel Comics (Epic Comics): 1992 - No. 4, 1992 ($3.95, lim. series, 52 pgs.)

1-4: Stiff-c — 4.00

DREADSTAR (See Epic Illustrated #3 for 1st app. and Eclipse Graphic Album Series #5)
Marvel Comics (Epic Comics)/First Comics No. 27 on: Nov, 1982 - No. 64, Mar, 1991

	GD	VG	FN	VF	VF/NM	NM-
1	2	4	6	11	16	20
2-5,8-49						4.00
6,7,51-64: 6,7-1st app. Interstellar Toybox; 8pgs. ea.; Wrightson-a. 51-64-Lower print run						5.00
50						6.00
Annual 1 (12/83)-r/The Price (Eclipse Graphic Album Series #5)						5.00

DREADSTAR
Malibu Comics (Bravura): Apr, 1994 - No. 6, Jan, 1995 ($2.50, limited series)

1-6-Peter David scripts: 1,2-Starlin-c — 4.00

NOTE: *Issues 1-6 contain Bravura stamps.*

DREADSTAR AND COMPANY
Marvel Comics (Epic Comics): July, 1985 - No. 6, Dec, 1985

1-6: 1,3,6-New Starlin-a: 2-New Wrightson-c; reprints of Dreadstar series — 4.00

DREAM BOOK OF LOVE (Also see A-1 Comics)
Magazine Enterprises: No. 106, June-July, 1954 - No. 123, Oct-Nov, 1954

	GD	VG	FN	VF	VF/NM	NM-
A-1 106 (#1)-Powell, Bolle-a; Montgomery Clift, Donna Reed photo-c	20	40	60	118	192	265
A-1-114 (#2)-Guardineer, Bolle-a; Piper Laurie, Victor Mature photo-c	15	30	45	85	130	175
A-1 123 (#3)-Movie photo-c	14	28	42	82	121	160

DREAM BOOK OF ROMANCE (Also see A-1 Comics)
Magazine Enterprises: No. 92, 1954 - No. 124, Oct-Nov, 1954

	GD	VG	FN	VF	VF/NM	NM-
A-1 92 (#5)-Guardineer-a; photo-c	18	36	54	109	172	235
A-1 101 (#6)(4-6/54)-Marlon Brando photo-c; Powell, Bolle, Guardineer-a	36	72	108	216	351	485
A-1 109,110,124: 109 (#7)(7-8/54)-Powell-a; movie photo-c. 110 (#8)(1/54)-Movie photo-c. 124 (#9)(10-11/54)	14	28	42	82	121	160

DREAMER, THE
Kitchen Sink Press: 1986 ($6.95, B&W, graphic novel)

nn-Will Eisner-s/a — 20.00
DC Comics Reprint ($7.95, 6/00) — 8.00

DREAMERY, THE
Eclipse Comics: Dec, 1986 - No. 14, Feb, 1989 ($2.00, B&W, Baxter paper)

1-14: 2-7-Alice In Wonderland adapt. — 4.00

DREAMING, THE (See Sandman, 2nd Series)
DC Comics (Vertigo): June, 1996 - No. 60, May, 2001 ($2.50)

1-McKean-c on all.; LaBan scripts & Snejbjerg-a — 4.00
2-30,32-60: 2,3-LaBan scripts & Snejbjerg-a. 4-7-Hogan scripts; Parkhouse-a. 8-Zulli-a. 9-11-Talbot-s/Taylor-a(p). 41-Previews Sandman: The Dream Hunters. 50-Hempel, Fegredo, McManus, Totleben-a — 3.00
31-($3.95) Art by various — 4.00
...Beyond The Shores of Night TPB ('97, $19.95) r/#1-8 — 20.00
...Special (7/98, $5.95, one-shot) Trial of Cain — 6.00
...Through The Gates of Horn and Ivory TPB ('99, $19.95) r/#15-19,22-25 — 20.00

DREAMING, THE (The Sandman Universe)
DC Comics (Vertigo): Nov, 2018 - No. 20, Jun, 2020 ($3.99)

1-20: 1-Spurrier-s/Evely-a/Jae Lee-c; Lucien & Merv Pumpkinhead app. 7,8-Larson-a — 4.00

DREAMING EAGLES
AfterShock Comics: Dec, 2015 - No. 6, Jun, 2016 ($3.99)

1-6-Ennis-s/Coleby-a; Tuskegee Airmen in WWII — 4.00

DREAMING, THE: WAKING HOURS (The Sandman Universe)
DC Comics (Vertigo): Oct, 2020 - No. 12 ($3.99)

1-7: 1-G. Willow Wilson-s/Nick Robles-a; intro Ruin — 4.00

DREAM OF LOVE
I. W. Enterprises: 1958 (Reprints)

	GD	VG	FN	VF	VF/NM	NM-
1,2,8: 1-r/Dream Book of Love #1; Bob Powell-a. 2-r/Great Lover's Romances #10. 8-Great Lover's Romances #1; also contains 2 Jon Juan stories by Siegel & Schomburg; Kinstler-c.	3	6	9	15	22	28
9-Kinstler-c; 1pg. John Wayne interview & Frazetta illo from John Wayne Adv. Comics #2	3	6	9	15	22	28

DREAM POLICE
Marvel Comics (Icon): Aug, 2005 ($3.99)

1-Straczynski-s/Deodato-a/c — 4.00

DREAM POLICE
Image Comics (Joe's Comics): Apr, 2014 - No. 12, Sept, 2016 ($2.99)

1-12-Straczynski-s/Kotian-a — 3.00

DREAMS OF THE DARKCHYLDE
Darkchylde Entertainment: Oct, 2000 - No. 6, Sept, 2001 ($2.95)

1-6-Randy Queen-s in all. 1-Brandon Peterson-c/a — 3.00

DREAM TEAM (See Battlezones: Dream Team 2)
Malibu Comics (Ultraverse): July, 1995 ($4.95, one-shot)

1-Pin-ups teaming up Marvel & Ultraverse characters by various artists including Allred, Romita, Darrow, Balent, Quesada & Palmiotti — 5.00

DREAM THIEF
Dark Horse Comics: May, 2013 - No. 5, Sept, 2013 ($3.99, limited series)

1-5-Nitz-s/Smallwood-a. 1-Alex Ross-c. 2-Ryan Sook-c. 4-Dan Brereton-c — 4.00

Droids #4 © Lucasfilm

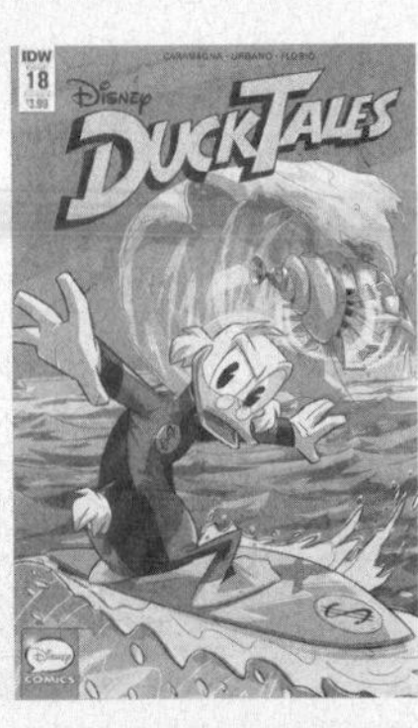

Ducktales (2017 series) #18 © DIS

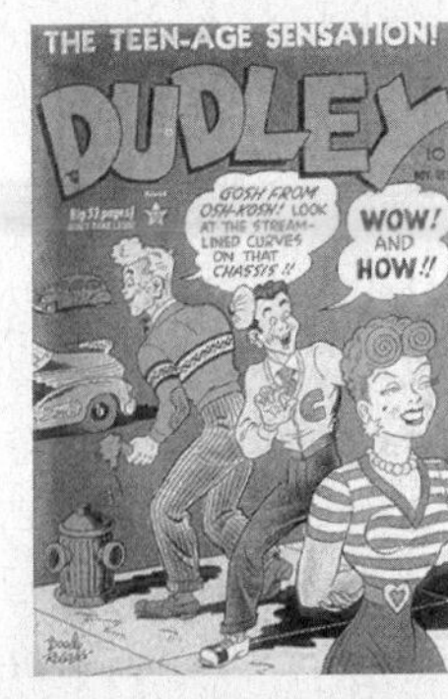

Dudley #1 © Prize

	GD 2.0	VG 4.0	FN 6.0	VF 8.0	VF/NM 9.0	NM- 9.2

DREAM THIEF: ESCAPE
Dark Horse Comics: Jun, 2014 - No. 4, Sept, 2014 ($3.99, limited series)
1-4-Nitz-s/Smallwood-c. 1,2-Smallwood-a. 3,4-Galusha-a 4.00

DREAMWAVE PRODUCTIONS PREVIEW
Dreamwave Productions: May, 2002 ($1.00, one-shot)
nn-Previews Arkanium, Transformers: The War Within and other series 3.00

DRESDEN FILES (See Jim Butcher's...)

DRIFTER
Image Comics: Nov, 2014 - No. 19, Jun, 2017 ($3.50/$3.99)
1-19-Ivan Brandon-s/Nic Klein-a; multiple covers on each. 15-Start $3.99-c 4.00

DRIFT FENCE (See Zane Grey 4-Color 270)

DRIFT MARLO
Dell Publishing Co.: May-July, 1962 - No. 2, Oct-Dec, 1962 (Painted-c)
01-232-207 (#1) 5 10 15 30 50 70
2 (12-232-212) 4 8 12 27 44 60

DRISCOLL'S BOOK OF PIRATES
David McKay Publ. (Not reprints): 1934 (B&W, hardcover; 124 pgs, 7x9")
nn-"Pieces of Eight" strip by Montford Amory 27 54 81 158 259 360

DRIVER: CROSSING THE LINE (Based on the Ubisoft videogame)
DC Comics: Oct, 2011 ($2.99, one-shot)
1-David Lapham-s/Greg Scott-a/ Jock-c; bonus character design art 3.00

DROIDS (Based on Saturday morning cartoon) (Also see Dark Horse Comics)
Marvel Comics (Star Comics): April, 1986 - No. 8, June, 1987
1-R2D2 & C-3PO from Star Wars app. in all 3 6 9 16 23 30
2-8: 2,5,7,8-Williamson-a(i) 2 4 6 8 10 12
NOTE: ***Romita** a-3p. **Sinnott** a-3i.*

DRONES
IDW Publishing: Apr, 2015 - No. 5, Aug, 2015 ($3.99, limited series)
1-5-Chris Lewis-s/Bruno Oliveira-a 4.00

DROOPY (see Tom & Jerry #60)

DROOPY (Tex Avery's...)
Dark Horse Comics: Oct, 1995 - No. 3, Dec, 1995 ($2.50, limited series)
1-Characters created by Tex Avery; painted-c on all 1 3 4 6 8 10
2 4.00
3-Headlights Christmas-c 1 3 4 6 8 10

DROPSIE AVENUE: THE NEIGHBORHOOD
Kitchen Sink Press: June, 1995 ($15.95/$24.95, B&W)
nn-Will Eisner (softcover) 18.00
nn-Will Eisner (hardcover) 30.00

DROWNED GIRL, THE
DC Comics (Piranha Press): 1990 ($5.95, 52 pgs, mature)
nn 1 2 3 5 6 8

DRUG WARS
Pioneer Comics: 1989 ($1.95)
1-Grell-c 4.00

DRUID
Marvel Comics: May, 1995 - No. 4, Aug, 1995 ($2.50, limited series)
1-4: Warren Ellis scripts. 4.00

DRUM BEAT
Dell Publishing Co.: No. 610, Jan, 1955
Four Color 610-Movie, Alan Ladd photo-c 8 16 24 55 105 155

DRUMS OF DOOM
United Features Syndicate: 1937 (25¢)(Indian)(Text w/color illos.)
nn-By Lt. F.A. Methot; Golden Thunder app.; Tip Top Comics ad in comic; nice-c
45 90 135 284 480 675

DRUNKEN FIST
Jademan Comics: Aug, 1988 - No. 54, Jan, 1993 ($1.50/$1.95, 68 pgs.)
1 5.00
2-50 4.00
51-54 4.00

DUCK ALBUM (See Donald Duck Album)
Dell Publishing Co.: No. 353, Oct, 1951 - No. 840, Sept, 1957
Four Color 353 (#1)-Barks-c; 1st Uncle Scrooge-c (also appears on back-c).
12 24 36 84 185 285
Four Color 450-Barks-c 9 18 27 59 117 175
Four Color 492,531,560,586,611,649,686, 7 14 21 46 86 125
Four Color 726,782,840 6 12 18 37 66 95

DUCK AVENGER
IDW Publishing: No. 0, Aug, 2016; Oct, 2016 - No. 5, Jun, 2017 ($4.99/$5.99/$6.99)
0-Reprints of Italian Donald Duck costumed super-hero stories 6.00
1,3-($5.99) Three covers. 1-(10/16) Red Raider app. 1 2 3 5 6 8
2-($4.99) Three covers; Xadhoom app. 6.00
4,5-($6.99) 1 2 3 5 6 8

DUCKMAN
Dark Horse Comics: Sept, 1990 ($1.95, B&W, one-shot)
1-Story & art by Everett Peck 2 4 6 9 12 15

DUCKMAN
Topps Comics: Nov, 1994 - No. 5, May, 1995; No. 0, Feb, 1996 ($2.50)
0 (2/96, $2.95, B&W)-r/Duckman #1 from Dark Horse Comics 4.00
1-5: 1-w/ coupon #A for Duckman trading card. 2-w/Duckman 1st season episode guide 4.00

DUCKMAN: THE MOB FROG SAGA
Topps Comics: Nov, 1994 - No. 3, Feb, 1995 ($2.50, limited series)
1-3: 1-w/coupon #B for Duckman trading card, S. Shaw!-c 4.00

DUCKTALES
Gladstone Publ.: Oct, 1988 - No. 13, May, 1990 (1,2,9-11: $1.50; 3-8: 95¢)
1-Barks-r 1 3 4 6 8 10
2-11: 2-7,9-11-Barks-r 5.00
12,13 ($1.95, 68 pgs.)-Barks-r; 12-r/F.C. #495 6.00
Disney Presents Carl Barks' Greatest DuckTales Stories Vol. 1 (Gemstone Publ., 2006, $10.95)
r/stories adapted for the animated TV series including "Back to the Klondike" 11.00
Disney Presents Carl Barks' Greatest DuckTales Stories Vol. 2 (Gemstone Publ., 2006, $10.95)
r/stories adapted for the animated TV series; "Robot Robbers" app. 11.00

DUCKTALES (TV)
Disney Comics: June, 1990 - No. 18, Nov, 1991 ($1.50)
1-All new stories; Marv Wolfman-s 6.00
2-18 4.00
Disney's DuckTales by Marv Wolfman: Scrooge's Quest TPB (Gemstone, 9/07, $15.99)
r/#1-7; intro. by Wolfman 16.00
Disney's DuckTales: The Gold Odyssey TPB (Gemstone, 10/08, $15.99) 16.00
The Movie nn (1990, $7.95, 68 pgs.)-Graphic novel adapting animated movie 8.00

DUCKTALES (TV)
Boom Entertainment (KABOOM!): May, 2011 - No. 6, Nov, 2011 ($3.99)
1-6: 1-4-Three covers on each; Spector-s/Massaroli-a. 5,6-Two covers; Crossover with Darkwing Duck #17,18 4.00

DUCKTALES (Based on the 2017 TV series)
IDW Publishing: No. 0, Jul, 2017; No. 1, Sept, 2017 - No. 20, Apr, 2019 ($3.99)
0-20: 0,1-Caramagna-s; multiple covers 4.00

DUCKTALES: FAIRES AND SCARES
IDW Publishing: Dec, 2019 - No. 3, Feb, 2020 ($3.99, limited series)
1-3: 1,2-Behling-s. 3-Caramagna-s 4.00

DUCKTALES: SCIENCE AND SILENCE
IDW Publishing: Aug, 2019 - No. 3, Oct, 2019 ($3.99, limited series)
1-3-Behling-s 4.00

DUDLEY (Teen-age)
Feature/Prize Publications: Nov-Dec, 1949 - No. 3, Mar-Apr, 1950
1-By Boody Rogers 21 42 63 126 206 285
2,3 14 28 42 81 118 155

DUDLEY DO-RIGHT (TV)
Charlton Comics: Aug, 1970 - No. 7, Aug, 1971 (Jay Ward)
1 8 16 24 52 99 145
2-7 6 12 18 37 66 95

DUEL MASTERS (Based on a trading card game)
Dreamwave Productions: Nov, 2003 - No. 8, Sept, 2004 ($2.95)
1-8: 1-Bagged with card; Augustyn-s 3.00

DUKE NUKEM: GLORIOUS BASTARD (Based on the video game)
IDW Publishing: Jul, 2011 - No. 4, Nov, 2011 ($3.99)
1-4: 1-Three covers; Waltz-s/Xermanico-a 4.00

DUKE OF THE K-9 PATROL

Dune: House of Atreides #1 © Herbert Props.

The Durango Kid #8 © ME

Dying is Easy #1 © Hill, Simmonds, & IDW

	GD 2.0	VG 4.0	FN 6.0	VF 8.0	VF/NM 9.0	NM- 9.2
Gold Key: Apr, 1963						
1 (10052-304)	4	8	12	25	40	55

DUMBO (Disney; see Movie Comics, & Walt Disney Showcase #12)
Dell Publishing Co.: No. 17, 1941 - No. 668, Jan, 1958

	GD 2.0	VG 4.0	FN 6.0	VF 8.0	VF/NM 9.0	NM- 9.2
Four Color 17 (#1)-Mickey Mouse, Donald Duck, Pluto app.	274	548	822	1740	2995	4250
Large Feature Comic 19 ('41)-Part-r 4-Color 17	300	600	900	1950	3375	4800
Four Color 234 ('49)	13	26	39	89	195	310
Four Color 668 (12/55)-1st of two printings. Dumbo on-c with starry sky. Same-c as #234	10	20	30	66	138	210
Four Color 668 (1/58)-2nd printing. Same cover altered with Timothy Mouse added. Same contents	7	14	21	44	82	120

DUMBO COMIC PAINT BOOK (See Dumbo, Large Feature Comic No. 19)

DUNC AND LOO (#1-3 titled "Around the Block with Dunc and Loo")
Dell Publishing Co.: Oct-Dec, 1961 - No. 8, Oct-Dec, 1963

	GD 2.0	VG 4.0	FN 6.0	VF 8.0	VF/NM 9.0	NM- 9.2
1	5	10	15	35	63	90
2	4	8	12	27	44	60
3-8	3	6	9	21	33	45

NOTE: *Written by* **John Stanley**; **Bill Williams** *art.*

DUNE (Movie)
Marvel Comics: Apr, 1985 - No. 3, June, 1985

	GD 2.0	VG 4.0	FN 6.0	VF 8.0	VF/NM 9.0	NM- 9.2
1-r/Marvel Super Special; movie adaptation	2	4	6	11	16	20
2,3-Adaptation continues	1	2	3	5	6	8

DUNE: HOUSE ATREIDES
BOOM! Studios: Oct, 2020 - No. 12, ($4.99)
1-4-Prequel to the original novel; Brian Herbert & Kevin J. Anderson-s/Dev Pramanik-a 4.00

DUNGEONS & DRAGONS
IDW Publishing: No. 0, Aug, 2010 - No. 15, Jan, 2012 ($1.00/$3.99)
0-(8/10, $1.00) Five covers; previews D&D series and Dark Sun mini-series 3.00
1-15: 1-(11/10, $3.99) Di Vito-a/Rogers-s; two covers. 2-Two covers 4.00
Annual 2012: Eberron (3/12, $7.99) Crilley-s/Diaz & Rojo-a 8.00
... 100 Page Giant (9/19, $5.99) Reprints by various incl. Zub & Dunbar 6.00
... 100 Page Spectacular (1/12, $7.99) Reprints by various incl. Duursema & Morales 8.00

DUNGEONS & DRAGONS: A DARKENED WISH
IDW Publishing: Feb, 2019 - No. 5, Aug, 2019 ($3.99, limited series)
1-5-B. Dave Walters-s/Tess Fowler-a; multiple covers on each 4.00

DUNGEONS & DRAGONS: AT THE SPINE OF THE WORLD
IDW Publishing: Oct, 2020 - Present ($3.99, limited series)
1-3-Garcia & Mendez-s/Coccolo-a; multiple covers on each 4.00

DUNGEONS & DRAGONS: CUTTER
IDW Publishing: Apr, 2013 - No. 5, Sept, 2013 ($3.99, limited series)
1-5-R.A. & Geno Salvatore-s/Baldeon-a; 2 covers on each 4.00

DUNGEONS & DRAGONS: EVIL AT BALDUR'S GATE
IDW Publishing: Apr, 2018 - No. 5, Aug, 2018 ($3.99, limited series)
1-5: 1-Jim Zub-s/Dean Kotz-a 4.00

DUNGEONS & DRAGONS: FORGOTTEN REALMS
IDW Publishing: Apr, 2012 - No. 5, Sept, 2012 ($3.99, limited series)
1-5-Greenwood-s/Ferguson-a 4.00
... 100 Page Spectacular (4/12, $7.99) Reprints by various incl. Rags Morales 8.00

DUNGEONS & DRAGONS: FROST GIANT'S FURY
IDW Publishing: Dec, 2016 - No. 5, Apr, 2017 ($3.99, limited series)
1-5-Jim Zub-s/Netho Diaz-a 4.00

DUNGEONS & DRAGONS: INFERNAL TIDES
IDW Publishing: Nov, 2019 - No. 5 ($3.99, limited series)
1,2-Jim Zub-s/Max Dunbar-a; multiple covers on each 4.00

DUNGEONS & DRAGONS: LEGENDS OF BALDUR'S GATE
IDW Publishing: Oct, 2014 - No. 5, Feb, 2016 ($3.99, limited series)
1-5-Jim Zub-s/Max Dunbar-a 4.00
... #1 Greatest Hits Collection (4/16, $1.00) reprints #1 3.00

DUNGEONS & DRAGONS: SHADOWS OF THE VAMPIRE
IDW Publishing: Apr, 2016 - No. 5, Aug, 2016 ($4.99/$3.99, limited series)
1-($4.99) Jim Zub-s/Nelson Dániel-a; 4 covers 5.00
2-5-($3.99) Three covers on each 4.00

DUNGEONS & DRAGONS: THE LEGEND OF DRIZZT: NEVERWINTER TALES
IDW Publishing: Aug, 2011 - No. 5, Dec, 2011 ($3.99, limited series)
1-5-R.A. & Geno Salvatore-s/Agustin Padilla-a 4.00

DURANGO KID, THE (Also see Best of the West, Great Western & White Indian)
(Charles Starrett starred in Columbia's Durango Kid movies)
Magazine Enterprises: Oct-Nov, 1949 - No. 41, Oct-Nov, 1955 (All 36 pgs.)

	GD 2.0	VG 4.0	FN 6.0	VF 8.0	VF/NM 9.0	NM- 9.2
1-Charles Starrett photo-c; Durango Kid & his horse Raider begin; Dan Brand & Tipi (origin) begin by Frazetta & continue through #16	74	148	222	470	810	1150
2-Starrett photo-c.	34	68	102	199	325	450
3-5-All have Starrett photo-c.	29	58	87	172	281	390
6-10: 7-Atomic weapon-c/story	16	32	48	94	147	200
11-16-Last Frazetta issue	14	28	42	80	115	150
17-Origin Durango Kid	16	32	48	94	147	200
18-30: 18-Fred Meagher-a on Dan Brand begins.19-Guardineer-c/a(3) begins, end #41. 23-Intro. The Red Scorpion	10	20	30	54	72	90
31-Red Scorpion returns	9	18	27	52	69	85
32-41-Bolle/Frazetta*ish*-a (Dan Brand; true in later issues?)	9	18	27	50	65	80

NOTE: *#6, 8, 14, 15 contain* **Frazetta** *art not reprinted in White Indian.* **Ayers** *c-18.* **Guardineer** *a(3)-19-41; c-19-41.* **Fred Meagher** *a-18-29 at least.*

DURANGO KID, THE
AC Comics: 1990 - #2, 1990 ($2.50,$2.75, half-color)
1,2: 1-Starrett photo front/back-c; Guardineer-r. 2-B&W)-Starrett photo-c; White Indian-r by Frazetta; Guardineer-r (50th anniversary of films) 4.00

DUSTCOVERS: THE COLLECTED SANDMAN COVERS 1989-1997
DC Comics (Vertigo): 1997 ($39.95, Hardcover)
Reprints Dave McKean's Sandman covers with Gaiman text 40.00
Softcover (1998, $24.95) 25.00

DUSTY STAR
Image Comics (Desperado Studios): No. 0, Apr, 1997 - No. 1 ($2.95, B&W)
0,1-Pruett-s/Robinson-a 3.00

DUSTY STAR
Image Comics (Desperado Publishing): June, 2006 ($3.50)
1-Pruett-s/Robinson-s/a 3.50

DV8 (See Gen 13)
Image Comics (WildStorm Productions): Aug, 1996 - No. 25, Dec, 1998;
DC Comics (WildStorm Prod.): No. 0, Apr, 1999 - No. 32, Nov, 1999 ($2.50)
1/2 6.00
1-Warren Ellis scripts & Humberto Ramos-c/a(p) 4.00
1-(7-variant covers, w/1 by Jim Lee) ...each 4.00
2-4: 3-No Ramos-a 3.00
5-32: 14-Regular-c, 14-Variant-c by Charest. 26-(5/99)-McGuinness-c 3.00
14-($3.50) Voyager Pack w/Danger Girl preview 5.00
0-(4/99, $2.95) Two covers (Rio and McGuinness) 3.00
Annual 1 (1/98, $2.95) 4.00
Annual 1999 ($3.50) Slipstream x-over with Gen13 4.00
Rave-(7/96, $1.75)-Ramos-c; pinups & interviews 3.00
...: Neighborhood Threat TPB (2002, $14.95) r/#1-6 & #1/2; Ellis intro.; Ramos-c 15.00

DV8: GODS AND MONSTERS
DC Comics (WildStorm): June, 2010 - No. 8, Jan, 2011 ($2.99, limited series)
1-8-Wood-s/Issacs-a 3.00
TPB (2011, $17.99) r/#1-8 18.00

DV8 VS. BLACK OPS
Image Comics (WildStorm): Oct, 1997 - No. 3, Dec, 1997 ($2.50, limited series)
1-3-Bury-s/Norton-a 3.00

DWIGHT D. EISENHOWER
Dell Publishing Co.: December, 1969

	GD 2.0	VG 4.0	FN 6.0	VF 8.0	VF/NM 9.0	NM- 9.2
01-237-912 - Life story	5	10	15	31	53	75

DYING IS EASY
IDW Publishing: Dec, 2019 - Present ($3.99)
1-3-Joe Hill-s/Martin Simmonds-a/c 4.00

DYNABRITE COMICS
Whitman Publishing Co.: 1978 - 1979 (69¢, 10x7-1/8", 48 pgs., cardboard-c)
(Blank inside covers)
11350 - Walt Disney's Mickey Mouse & the Beanstalk (4-C 157). 11350-1 - Mickey Mouse Album (4-C 1057, 1151,1246). 11351 - Mickey Mouse & His Sky Adventure (4-C 214, 343). 11354 - Goofy: A Gaggle of Giggles. 11354-1 - Super Goof Meets Super Thief. 11356 - (?). 11359 - Bugs Bunny-r. 11360 - Winnie the Pooh Fun and Fantasy (Disney-r).

	GD 2.0	VG 4.0	FN 6.0	VF 8.0	VF/NM 9.0	NM- 9.2
each....	2	4	6	10	14	18

11352 - Donald Duck (4-C 408, Donald Duck 45,52)-Barks-a. 11352-1 - Donald Duck (4-C 318, 10 pg. Barks/WDC&S 125,128)-Barks-c(r). 11353 - Daisy Duck's Diary (4-C 1055,1150) Barks-a. 11355 - Uncle Scrooge (Barks-

Dynamo 5 #1 © Faerber & Asrar

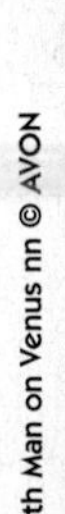

Earth Man on Venus nn © AVON

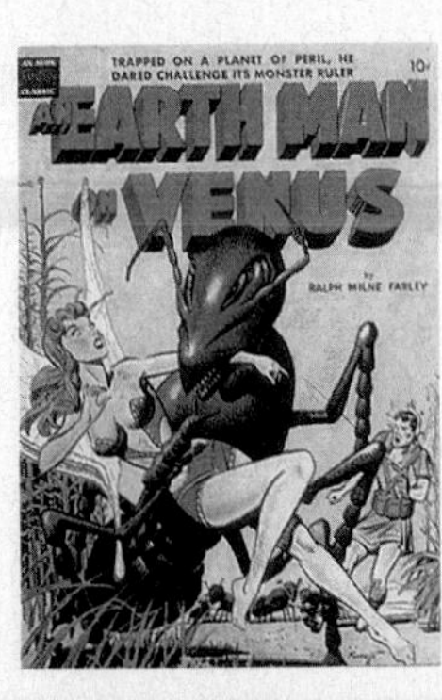

Earth 2: Society #22 © DC

GD 2.0 | VG 4.0 | FN 6.0 | VF 8.0 | VF/NM 9.0 | NM- 9.2

GD 2.0 | VG 4.0 | FN 6.0 | VF 8.0 | VF/NM 9.0 | NM- 9.2

a/U.S. 12,33). 11355-1 - Uncle Scrooge (Barks-a/U.S. 13,16) - Barks-c(r). 11357 - Star Trek (r/-Star Trek 33,41). 11358 - Star Trek (r/-Star Trek 34,36). 11361 - Gyro Gearloose & the Disney Ducks (r/4-C 1047,1184)-Barks-c(r)
each.... 2 4 6 11 16 20

DYNAMIC ADVENTURES
I. W. Enterprises: No. 8, 1964 - No. 9, 1964

8-Kayo Kirby-r by Baker?/Fight Comics 53. 3 6 9 15 22 28
9-Reprints Avon's "Escape From Devil's Island"; Kinstler-c
3 6 9 16 24 32

DYNAMIC CLASSICS (See Cancelled Comic Cavalcade)
DC Comics: Sept-Oct, 1978 (44 pgs.)

1-Neal Adams Batman, Simonson Manhunter-r 2 4 6 8 10 12

DYNAMIC COMICS (No #4-7)
Harry 'A' Chesler: Oct, 1941 - No. 3, Feb, 1942; No. 8, Mar, 1944 - No. 25, May, 1948

1-Origin Major Victory by Charles Sultan (reprinted in Major Victory #1), Dynamic Man & Hale the Magician; The Black Cobra only app.; Major Victory & Dynamic Man begin
271 542 813 1734 2967 4200
2-Origin Dynamic Boy & Lady Satan; intro. The Green Knight & sidekick Lance Cooper
168 336 504 1075 1838 2600
3-1st small logo, resumes with #10 142 284 426 909 1555 2200
8-Classic-c; Dan Hastings, The Echo, The Master Key, Yankee Boy begin; Yankee Doodle Jones app.; hypo story 1025 2050 3075 6800 10,900 15,000
9-Mr. E begins; Mac Raboy-c 134 268 402 858 1467 2075
10-Small logo begins 121 242 363 774 1325 1875
11-Classic-c 306 612 918 2142 3821 5500
12-16: 15-The Sky Chief app. 16-Marijuana story 84 168 252 538 919 1300
17(1/46)-Illustrated in **SOTI**, "The children told me what the man was going to do with the hot poker," but Wertham saw this in Crime Reporter #2
87 174 261 553 952 1350
18-Classic Airplanehead monster-c 87 174 261 553 952 1350
19-Classic puppeteer-c by Gattuso 84 168 252 538 919 1300
20-Bare-breasted woman-c 152 304 456 973 1662 2350
21-Dinosaur-c; new logo 60 120 180 381 653 925
22,25 53 106 159 334 567 800
23,24-(68 pgs.): 23-Yankee Girl app. 50 100 150 315 533 750
I.W. Reprint #1,8('64): 1-r/#23. 8-Exist? 3 6 9 17 26 35
NOTE: ***Kinstler** c-IW #1. **Tuska** art in many issues, #3, 9, 11, 12, 16, 19. Bondage c-16.*

DYNAMITE (Becomes Johnny Dynamite No. 10 on)
Comic Media/Allen Hardy Publ.: May, 1953 - No. 9, Sept, 1954

1-Pete Morisi-a; Don Heck-c; r-as Danger #6 43 86 129 271 461 650
2 24 48 72 142 234 325
3-Marijuana story; Johnny Dynamite (1st app.) begins by Pete Morisi(c/a); Heck text-a; man shot in face at close range 31 62 93 182 296 410
4-Injury-to-eye, prostitution; Morisi-c/a 29 58 87 174 285 395
5-9-Morisi-c/a in all. 7-Prostitute story & reprints 23 46 69 134 220 305

DYNAMO (Also see Tales of Thunder & T.H.U.N.D.E.R. Agents)
Tower Comics: Aug, 1966 - No. 4, June, 1967 (25¢)

1-Crandall/Wood, Ditko/Wood-a; Weed series begins; NoMan & Lightning cameos; Wood-c/a 8 16 24 54 105 150
2-4: Wood-c/a in all 5 10 15 34 60 85
NOTE: ***Adkins/Wood** a-2. **Ditko** a-4?. **Tuska** a-2, 3.*

DYNAMO 5 (See Noble Causes: Extended Family #2 for debut of Captain Dynamo)
Image Comics: Jan, 2007 - No. 25, Oct, 2009 ($3.50/$2.99)

1-Intro. the offspring of Captain Dynamo; Faerber-s/Asrar-a 8.00
2 5.00
3-7,11-24 : 5-Intro. Synergy. 13-Origin of Myriad. 21-Firebird app. 3.50
8-10-($2.99) 3.50
25-($4.99) Back-up short stories of team members 5.00
Annual #1 (4/08, $5.99) r/Captain Dynamo app. in Nobel Causes: Extended Family #2 and three new stories by Faerber & various; pin-up gallery 6.00
#0 (2/09, 99¢) short story leading into #20; text synopsis of story so far 3.00
...: Holiday Special 2010 (12/10, $3.99) Faerber-s/Takara-a 4.00
... Vol. 1: Post-Nuclear Family TPB (2007, $9.99) r/#1-7; Kirkman intro. 10.00
... Vol. 2: Moments of Truth TPB (2008, $14.99) r/#8-13 15.00

DYNAMO 5: SINS OF THE FATHER
Image Comics: Jun, 2010 - No. 5, Oct, 2010 ($3.99, limited series)

1-5-Faerber-s/Brilha-a. 2-4-Invincible app. 4.00

DYNAMO JOE (Also see First Adventures & Mars)
First Comics: May, 1986 - No. 15, Jan, 1988 (#12-15: $1.75)

1-15: 4-Cargonauts begin, Special 1(1/87)-Mostly-r/Mars 3.00

DYNOMUTT (TV)(See Scooby-Doo (3rd series))
Marvel Comics Group: Nov, 1977 - No. 6, Sept, 1978 (Hanna-Barbera)

1-The Blue Falcon, Scooby Doo in all 4 8 12 27 44 60
2-6-All newsstand only 3 6 9 17 26 35

EAGLE, THE (1st Series) (See Science Comics & Weird Comics #8)
Fox Feature Syndicate: July, 1941 - No. 4, Jan, 1942

1-The Eagle begins; Rex Dexter of Mars app. by Briefer; all issues feature German war covers 245 490 735 1568 2684 3800
2-The Spider Queen begins (origin) 155 310 465 992 1696 2400
3,4: 3-Joe Spook begins (origin) 148 296 444 947 1624 2300

EAGLE COMICS (2nd Series)
Rural Home Publ.: Feb-Mar, 1945 - No. 2, Apr-May, 1945

1-Aviation stories 100 200 300 635 1093 1550
2-Lucky Aces 47 94 141 296 498 700
NOTE: ***L. B. Cole** c/a in each.*

EARTH 4 (Also see Urth 4)
Continuity Comics: Dec, 1993 - No. 4, Jan, 1994 ($2.50)

1-4: 1-3 all listed as Dec, 1993 in indicia 3.00

EARTH 4 DEATHWATCH 2000
Continuity Comics: Apr, 1993 - No. 3, Aug, 1993 ($2.50)

1-3 3.00

EARTH MAN ON VENUS (An...) (Also see Strange Planets)
Avon Periodicals: 1951

nn-Wood-a (26 pgs.); Fawcette-c 181 362 543 1158 1979 2800

EARTH 2
DC Comics: Jul, 2012 - No. 32, May, 2015 ($3.99/$2.99)

1-($3.99) James Robinson-s/Nicola Scott-a/Ivan Reis-c; 4.00
1-Variant-c by Hitch 6.00
2-15-($2.99) 2-New Flash. 3-New Green Lantern. 4-New Atom 3.00
15.1, 15.2 (11/13, $2.99, regular covers) 3.00
15.1 (11/13, $3.99, 3-D cover) "Desaad #1" on cover; Levitz-s/Cinar-a 5.00
15.2 (11/13, $3.99, 3-D cover) "Solomon Grundy #1" on cover; Kindt-s/Lopresti-a 5.00
16-24,26-30: 16-Superman returns. 17-Batman returns. 20-Jae Lee-c. 28-Lobo app. 3.00
25-($3.99) New Superman revealed 4.00
#0 (11/12, $2.99) Superman, Batman, Wonder Woman, Terry Sloan app.; Giorello-a 3.00
Annual 1 (7/13, $4.99) Robinson-s/Cafu-a; new Batman app. 5.00
Annual 2 (3/14, $4.99) Taylor-s/Rocha-a; origin of new Batman 5.00
...: Futures End 1 (11/14, $2.99, regular-c) Five years later; Barrows-a 3.00
...: Futures End 1 (11/14, $3.99, 3-D cover) 4.00

EARTH 2: SOCIETY
DC Comics: Aug, 2015 - No. 22, May, 2017 ($2.99)

1-22: 1-Johnny Sorrow app.; Dick Grayson as Batman. 4-Anarky app. 6-Intro. Hourman. 15-Tony Harris-a (8 pgs.) 3.00
Annual 1 (10/16, $4.99) Abnett-s/Redondo & Neves-a; The Ultra-Humanite app. 5.00

EARTH 2: WORLD'S END
DC Comics: Dec, 2014 - No. 26, Jun, 2015 ($2.99, weekly series)

1-25: 1-Prelude to Darkseid's first attack. 3,7,8,10-Constantine app. 3.00
26-($3.99) Andy Kubert-c; leads into Convergence #1 4.00

EARTHWORM JIM (TV, cartoon)
Marvel Comics: Dec, 1995 - No. 3, Feb, 1996 ($2.25)

1-Based on video game and toys 4 8 12 23 37 50
2,3 1 3 4 6 8 10

EARTH X
Marvel Comics: No. 0, Mar, 1999 - No. 12, Apr, 2000 ($3.99/$2.99, lim. series)

nn- (Wizard supplement) Alex Ross sketchbook; painted-c 6.00
Sketchbook (2/99) New sketches and previews 6.00
0-(3/99)-Prelude; Leon-a(p)/Ross-c 1 2 3 4 5 7
1-(4/99)-Leon-a(p)/Ross-c 1 2 3 4 5 7
1-2nd printing 4.00
2-12 4.00
#1/2 (Wizard) Nick Fury on cover; Reinhold-a 6.00
#X (6/00, $3.99) 4.00
... Trilogy Companion TPB (2008, $29.99) r/#1/2; artwork and content from the Earth X, Paradise X and Universe X series; gallery of variant covers and promotional art 30.00
HC (2005, $49.99) r/#0,1-12, #1/2, X; foreward by Joss Whedon; Ross sketch pages 50.00
TPB (12/00, $24.95) r/#0,1-12, X; foreward by Joss Whedon 25.00

EASTER BONNET SHOP (See March of Comics No. 29)

EASTER WITH MOTHER GOOSE
Dell Publishing Co.: No. 103, 1946 - No. 220, Mar, 1949

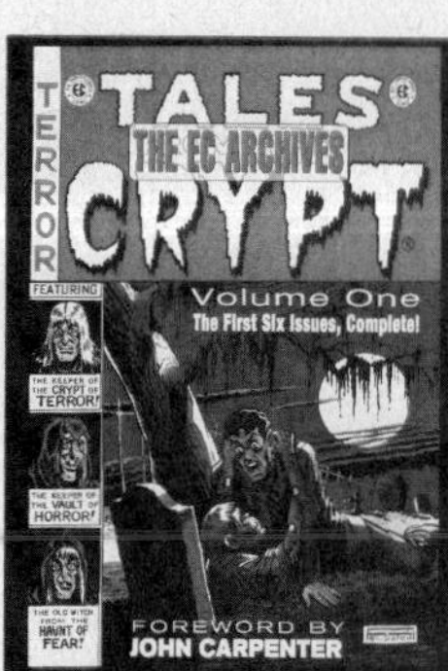

EC Archives Tales From the Crypt Vol. 1 © WMG

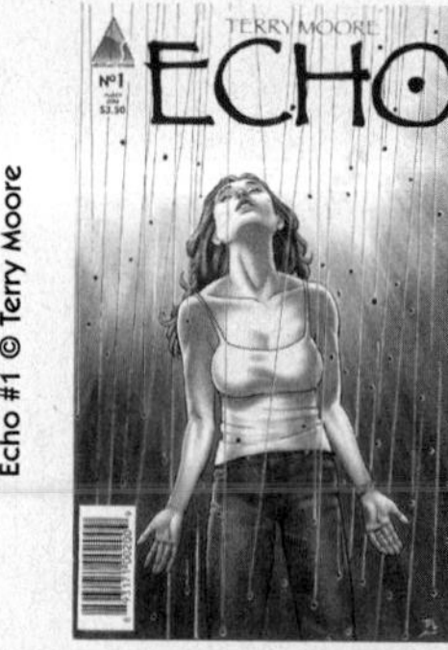

Echo #1 © Terry Moore

Eclipso #6 © DC

GD VG FN VF VF/NM NM-
2.0 4.0 6.0 8.0 9.0 9.2

Four Color 103 (#1)-Walt Kelly-a 19 38 57 129 287 445
Four Color 140 ('47)-Kelly-a 14 28 42 97 214 330
Four Color 185 ('48), 220-Kelly-a 13 26 39 87 191 295

EAST MEETS WEST
Innovation Publishing: Apr, 1990 - No. 2, 1990 ($2.50, limited series, mature)

1,2: 1-Stevens part-i; Redondo-c(i). 2-Stevens-c(i); 1st app. Cheech & Chong in comics 4.00

EAST OF WEST
Image Comics: Mar, 2013 - Present ($3.50/$3.99)

1-Hickman-s/Dragotta-a 6.00
2-26-Hickman-s/Dragotta-a 3.50
27-44-($3.99) 4.00
45-($4.99) 5.00
...: The World (12/14, $3.99) Source book for characters, events, settings, timelines 4.00

EC ARCHIVES
Gemstone Publishing/Dark Horse Books: 2006 - Present ($49.95/$49.99, hardcover with dustjacket)

Crime SuspenStories Vol. 1 - Recolored reprints of #1-6; foreward by Max Allan Collins 50.00
Frontline Combat Vol. 1 - Recolored reprints of #1-6; foreward by Henry G. Franke III 50.00
Haunt of Fear Vol. 1 - Recolored reprints of #15-17,4-6; foreward by Robert Englund 50.00
Haunt of Fear Vol. 2 - Recolored reprints of #7-12; foreward by Tim Sullivan 50.00
Panic Vol. 1 - Recolored reprints of #1-6; foreward by Bob Fingerman 50.00
Shock SuspenStories Vol. 1 - Recolored reprints of #1-6; foreward by Steven Spielberg 50.00
Shock SuspenStories Vol. 2 - Recolored reprints of #7-12; foreward by Dean Kamen 50.00
Shock SuspenStories Vol. 3 - Recolored reprints of #13-18; foreward by Brian Bendis 50.00
Tales From the Crypt Vol. 1 - Recolored reprints of Crypt of Terror #17-19 and Tales From the Crypt #20-22; foreward by John Carpenter; Al Feldstein behind-the-scenes info 100.00
Tales From the Crypt Vol. 2 - Recolored reprints of #23-28; foreward by Joe Dante 50.00
Tales From the Crypt Vol. 3 - Recolored reprints of #29-34; foreward by Bob Overstreet 50.00
Tales From the Crypt Vol. 4 - (DH) Recolored reprints of #35-40; foreward by Russ Cochran 50.00
Tales From the Crypt Vol. 5 - (DH) Recolored reprints of #41-46; foreward by Bruce Campbell 50.00
Two-Fisted Tales Vol. 1 - Recolored reprints of #18-23; foreward by Stephen Geppi 50.00
Two-Fisted Tales Vol. 2 - Recolored reprints of #24-29; foreward by Rocco Versaci, Ph.D. 50.00
Two-Fisted Tales Vol. 3 - (DH) Recolored reprints of #30-35; foreward by Joe Kubert 50.00
Vault of Horror Vol. 1 - Recolored reprints of #12-17; foreward by R.L. Stine 50.00
Vault of Horror Vol. 2 - Recolored reprints of #18-23; foreward by John Landis 80.00
Vault of Horror Vol. 3 - (DH) Recolored reprints of #24-29; foreward by Mike Richardson 50.00
Vault of Horror Vol. 4 - (DH) Recolored reprints of #30-35; foreward by Jonathan Maberry 50.00
Weird Fantasy Vol. 1 - (DH) Recolored reprints of #13-17; foreward by Walt Simonson 50.00
Weird Science Vol. 1 - Recolored reprints of #1-6; foreward by George Lucas 75.00
Weird Science Vol. 2 - Recolored reprints of #7-12; foreward by Paul Levitz 50.00
Weird Science Vol. 3 - Recolored reprints of #13-18; foreward by Jerry Weist 50.00

E. C. CLASSIC REPRINTS
East Coast Comix Co.: May, 1973 - No. 12, 1976 (E.C. Comics reprinted in color minus ads)

1-The Crypt of Terror #1 (Tales from the Crypt #46) 2 4 6 11 16 20
2-12: 2-Weird Science #15('52). 3-Shock SuspenStories #12. 4-Haunt of Fear #12. 5-Weird Fantasy #13('52). 6-Crime SuspenStories #25. 7-Vault of Horror #26. 8-Shock SuspenStories #6. 9-Two-Fisted Tales #34. 10-Haunt of Fear #23. 11-Weird Science 12(#1). 12-Shock SuspenStories #2 2 4 6 8 11 14

EC CLASSICS
Russ Cochran: Aug, 1985 - No. 12, 1986? (High quality paper; each-r 8 stories in color) (#2-12 were resolicited in 1990)($4.95, 56 pgs., 8x11")

1-12: 1-Tales From the Crypt. 2-Weird Science. 3-Two-Fisted Tales (r/31); Frontline Combat (r/9). 4-Shock SuspenStories. 5-Weird Fantasy. 6-Vault of Horror. 7-Weird Science-Fantasy (r/23,24). 8-Crime SuspenStories (r/17,18). 9-Haunt of Fear (r/14,15). 10-Panic (r/1,2). 11-Tales From the Crypt (r/23,24). 12-Weird Science (r/20,22) 1 2 3 4 5 7

ECHO
Abstract Studio: Mar, 2008 - No. 30, May, 2011 ($3.50)

1-Terry Moore-s/a/c 8.00
2-30 3.50
Terry Moore's Echo: Moon Lake TPB (2008, $15.95) r/#1-5; Moore sketch pages 16.00

ECHO OF FUTUREPAST
Pacific Comics/Continuity Com.: May, 1984 - No. 9, Jan, 1986 ($2.95, 52 pgs.)

1-9: Neal Adams-c/a in all? 6.00
NOTE: ***N. Adams** a-1-6,7i,9i; c-1-3, 5p,7i,8,9i. **Golden** a-1-6 (Bucky O'Hare); c-6. **Toth** a-6,7.*

ECLIPSE GRAPHIC ALBUM SERIES
Eclipse Comics: Oct, 1978 - 1989 (8-1/2x11") (B&W #1-5)

1-Sabre (10/78, B&W, 1st print.); Gulacy-a; 1st direct sale graphic novel 16.00
1-Sabre (2nd printing, 1/79) 8.00
1-Sabre (3rd printing, $5.95) 6.00
1-Sabre 30th Anniversary Edition (2008, $14.99, 9x6" HC) new McGregor & Gulacy intros. original script with sketch art 15.00
2,6,7: 2-Night Music (11/79, B&W)-Russell-a. 6-I Am Coyote (11/84, color)-Rogers-c/a. 7-The Rocketeer (2nd print, $7.95). 7-The Rocketeer (3rd print, 1991, $8.95) 10.00
3,4: 3-Detectives, Inc. (5/80, B&W, $6.95)-Rogers-a. 4-Stewart The Rat (1980, B&W) -G. Colan-a 10.00
5-The Price (10/81, B&W)-Starlin-a 20.00
7-The Rocketeer (9/85, color)-Dave Stevens-a (r/chapters 1-5)(see Pacific Presents & Starslayer); has 7 pgs. new-a 25.00
7-The Rocketeer, signed & limited HC 90.00
7-The Rocketeer, hardcover (1986, $19.95) 40.00
7-The Rocketeer, unsigned HC (3rd, $32.95) 33.00
8-Zorro In Old California ('86, color) 14.00
8,12-Hardcover 18.00
9,10: 9-Sacred And The Profane ('86)-Steacy-a. 10-Somerset Holmes ('86, $15.95)-Adults, soft-c 16.00
9,10,12-Hardcover ($24.95). 12-signed & #'d 25.00
11-Floyd Farland, Citizen of the Future ('87, $2.95, B&W) Chris Ware-s/a 15.00
12,28,31,35: 12-Silverheels ('87, $7.95, color). 28-Miracleman Book I ($5.95). 31-Pigeons From Hell by R. E. Howard (11/88). 35-Rael: Into The Shadow of the Sun ('88, $7.95) 10.00
13-The Sisterhood of Steel ('87, $8.95, color) 10.00
14,16,18,20,23,24: 14-Samurai, Son of Death ('87, $4.95, B&W). 16,18,20,23-See Airfighters Classics #1-4. 24-Heartbreak ($4.95, B&W) 7.00
14 (2nd pr.),17,21: 14-Samurai, Son of Death ($3.95, 2nd printing). 17-Valkyrie, Prisoner of the Past SC ('88, $3.95, color). 21-XYR-Multiple ending comic (`88, $3.95, B&W) 6.00
15,22,27: 15-Twisted Tales (11/87, color)-Dave Stevens-c. 22-Alien Worlds #1 (5/88, $3.95, 52 pgs.)-Nudity. 27-Fast Fiction (She) ($5.95, B&W) 8.00
17-Valkyrie, Prisoner of the Past S&N Hardcover ('88, $19.95) 25.00
19-Scout: The Four Monsters ('88, $14.95, color)-r/Scout #1-7; soft-c 15.00
25,30,32-34: 25-Alex Toth's Zorro Vol. 1 ,2($10.95, B&W). 30-Brought To Light; Alan Moore scripts ('89). 32-Teenaged Dope Slaves and Reform School Girls. 33-Bogie. 34-Air Fighters Classics #5 12.00
29-Real Love: Best of Simon & Kirby Romance Comics (10/88, $12.95) 15.00
30,31: Limited hardcover ed. ($29.95). 31-signed 30.00
36-Dr. Watchstop: Adventures in Time and Space ('89, $8.95) 10.00

ECLIPSE MAGAZINE (Becomes Eclipse Monthly)
Eclipse Publishing: May, 1981 - No. 8, Jan, 1983 ($2.95, B&W, magazine)

1-8: 1-1st app. Cap'n Quick and a Foozle by Rogers, Ms. Tree by Beatty, and Dope by Trina Robbins. 2-1st app. I Am Coyote by Rogers. 7-1st app. Masked Man by Boyer 4.00
NOTE: ***Colan** a-3, 5, 8. **Golden** c/a-2. **Gulacy** a-6, c-1, 6. **Kaluta** c/a-5. **Mayerik** a-2, 3. **Rogers** a-1-8. **Starlin** a-1. **Sutton** a-6.*

ECLIPSE MONTHLY
Eclipse Comics: Aug, 1983 - No. 10, Jul, 1984 (Baxter paper, $2.00/$1.50/$1.75)

1-10: ($2.00, 52 pgs.)-Cap'n Quick and a Foozle by Rogers, Static by Ditko, Dope by Trina Robbins, Rio by Wildey, The Masked Man by Boyer begin. 3-Ragamuffins begins 4.00
NOTE: ***Boyer** c-6. **Ditko** a-1-3. **Rogers** a-1-4; c-2, 4, 7. **Wildey** a-1, 2, 5, 9, 10; c-5, 10.*

ECLIPSO (See Brave and the Bold #64, House of Secrets #61 & Phantom Stranger, 1987)
DC Comics: Nov, 1992 - No. 18, Apr, 1994 ($1.25)

1-18: 1-Giffen plots/breakdowns begin. 10-Darkseid app. Creeper in #3-6,9,11-13. 18-Spectre-c/s 4.00
Annual 1 (1993, $2.50, 68 pgs.)-Intro Prism 5.00
...: The Music of the Spheres TPB (2009, $19.99) r/stories from Countdown to Mystery #1-8 20.00

ECLIPSO: THE DARKNESS WITHIN
DC Comics: July, 1992 - No. 2, Oct, 1992 ($2.50, 68 pgs.)

1,2: 1-With purple gem attached to-c, 1-Without gem; Superman, Creeper app., 2-Concludes Eclipso storyline from annuals 4.00

EC SAMPLER - FREE COMIC BOOK DAY
Gemstone Publishing: May, 2008

Reprinted stories with restored color from Weird Science #6, Two-Fisted Tales #22, Crypt of Terror #17, Shock Suspenstories #6 3.00

E. C. 3-D CLASSICS (See Three Dimensional...)

ECTOKID (See Razorline)
Marvel Comics: Sept, 1993 - No. 9, May, 1994 ($1.75/$1.95)

1-($2.50)-Foil embossed-c; created by C. Barker 5.00
2-9: 2-Origin. 5-Saint Sinner x-over 4.00
...: Unleashed! 1 (10/94, $2.95, 52 pgs.) 5.00

ED "BIG DADDY" ROTH'S RATFINK COMIX (Also see Ratfink)
World of Fandom/ Ed Roth: 1991 - No. 3, 1991 ($2.50)

1-3: Regular Ed., 1-Limited double cover 2 4 6 9 12 15

EDDIE CAMPBELL'S BACCHUS

Edge #2 © Grant & Kane

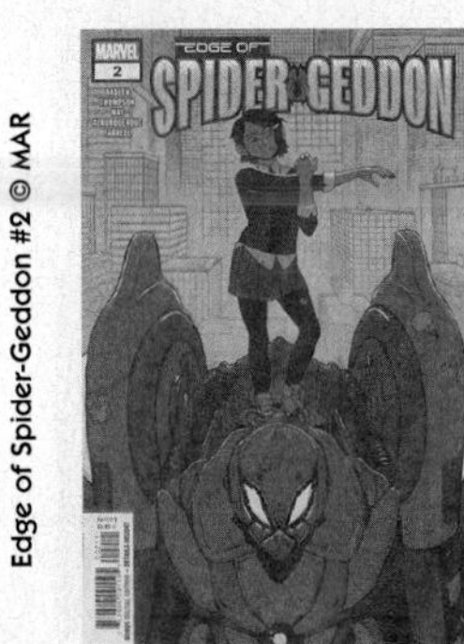

Edge of Spider-Geddon #2 © MAR

Eerie #3 © AVON

	GD	VG	FN	VF	VF/NM	NM-
	2.0	4.0	6.0	8.0	9.0	9.2

Eddie Campbell Comics: May, 1995 - No. 60, May, 2001 ($2.95, B&W)

1-Cerebus app.	1	2	3	5	6	8
1-2nd printing (5/97)						3.00
2-10: 9-Alex Ross back-c						5.00
11-60						3.00
Doing The Islands With Bacchus ('97, $17.95)						18.00
Earth, Water, Air & Fire ('98, $9.95)						10.00
King Bacchus ('99, $12.95)						13.00
The Eyeball Kid ('98, $8.50)						8.50

EDDIE STANKY (Baseball Hero)
Fawcett Publications: 1951 (New York Giants)

nn-Photo-c	40	80	120	246	411	575

EDEN'S FALL (Characters from Postal, The Tithe, and Think Tank)
Image Comics (Top Cow): Aug, 2016 - No. 3 ($3.99)

1-3-Matt Hawkins & Bryan Hill-s/Atilio Rojo-a 4.00

EDEN'S TRAIL
Marvel Comics: Jan, 2003 - No. 5, May 2003 ($2.99, unfinished lim. series, printed sideways)

1-5-Chuck Austen-s/Steve Uy-a 3.00

EDGAR ALLAN POE'S MORELLA AND THE MURDERS IN THE RUE MORGUE
Dark Horse Comics: Jun, 2015 ($3.99, one-shot)

1-Adaptation of Poe's poems; story and art by Richard Corben 4.00

EDGAR ALLAN POE'S SNIFTER OF BLOOD
AHOY Comics: 2020 - Present ($4.99)

1-5-Short stories; adaptations and paradies of Poe by various. 2-Monster Serials 5.00

EDGAR ALLAN POE'S SNIFTER OF TERROR
AHOY Comics: 2018 - 2020 ($3.99)

1-6-Short stories; adaptations and paradies of Poe by various 4.00
Season Two 1-6: 2-Action Comics #1 cover spoof; Russell-s. 3-Medley-s/a 4.00

EDGAR ALLAN POE'S THE CONQUEROR WORM
Dark Horse Comics: Nov, 2012 ($3.99, one-shot)

1-Adaptation of Poe's poem; story and art by Richard Corben; Corben sketch pages 4.00

EDGAR ALLAN POE'S THE FALL OF THE HOUSE OF USHER
Dark Horse Comics: May, 2013 - No. 2, Jun, 2013 ($3.99, limited series)

1,2-Adaptation of Poe's poem; story and art by Richard Corben; Corben sketch pages4.00

EDGAR ALLAN POE'S - THE FALL OF THE HOUSE OF USHER AND OTHER TALES OF HORROR
Catlan Communications Pub.: Sept. 1985 (hardcover graphic novel)

nn-Reprints of Poe story issues from Warren comic mags; all Richard Corben-a; numbered edition of 350 signed by Corben; 60 pgs. 130.00
nn-Softcover edition 60.00

EDGAR ALLAN POE'S THE PREMATURE BURIAL
Dark Horse Comics: Apr, 2014 ($3.99, one-shot)

1-Adaptation of The Premature Burial and The Cask of Amontillado; Corben-s/a/c 4.00

EDGAR ALLAN POE'S THE RAVEN AND THE RED DEATH
Dark Horse Comics: Oct, 2013 ($3.99, one-shot)

1-Adaptation of The Raven and The Masque of the Red Death; Corben-s/a/c 4.00

EDGAR BERGEN PRESENTS CHARLIE McCARTHY
Whitman Publishing Co. (Charlie McCarthy Co.): No. 764, 1938 (36 pgs.; 15x10-1/2"; color)

764	87	174	261	553	952	1350

EDGAR RICE BURROUGHS' CARSON OF VENUS
American Mythology Prods.: 2018 - Present ($3.99)

...Fear on Four Worlds 1 - part 1 of crossover; Mills-s/Mesarcia-a 4.00
...: Pirates of Venus 1,2 - Reprints from Korak, Son of Tarzan #46-53; Wein-s/Kaluta-a 4.00
...: The Flames Beyond 1-3: 1-Kaluta-c/Carey-s/Mesarcia-a 4.00
.../ Warlord of Mars 1-Kaluta-c/Avallone-s/Mesarcia-a 4.00

EDGAR RICE BURROUGHS' PELLUCIDAR
American Mythology Prods.: 2018 - 2019 ($3.99)

1-At the Earth's Core; Wolfer-s/Rearte-a 4.00
1-Fear on Four Worlds; part 3 of crossover; Wolfer-s/Mesarcia-a 4.00
1-Wings of Death; Wolfer-s/Büll-a 4.00

EDGAR RICE BURROUGHS' TARZAN: A TALE OF MUGAMBI
Dark Horse Comics: 1995 ($2.95, one-shot)

1 3.00

EDGAR RICE BURROUGHS' TARZAN: IN THE LAND THAT TIME FORGOT AND THE POOL OF TIME
Dark Horse Comics: 1996 ($12.95, trade paperback)

nn-r/Russ Manning-a 13.00

EDGAR RICE BURROUGHS' TARZAN OF THE APES
Dark Horse Comics: May, 1999 ($12.95, trade paperback)

nn-reprints 13.00

EDGAR RICE BURROUGHS' TARZAN: THE LOST ADVENTURE
Dark Horse Comics: Jan, 1995 - No. 4, Apr, 1995 ($2.95, B&W, limited series)

1-4: ERB's last Tarzan story, adapted by Joe Lansdale 3.00
Hardcover (12/95, $19.95) 20.00
Limited Edition Hardcover ($99.95)-signed & numbered 100.00

EDGAR RICE BURROUGHS' TARZAN: THE RETURN OF TARZAN
Dark Horse Comics: May, 1997 - No. 3, July, 1997 ($2.95, limited series)

1-3 3.00

EDGAR RICE BURROUGHS' TARZAN: THE RIVERS OF BLOOD
Dark Horse Comics: Nov, 1999 - No. 4, Feb, 2000 ($2.95, limited series)

1-4-Kordey-c/a 3.00

EDGAR RICE BURROUGHS' THE LAND THAT TIME FORGOT
American Mythology Prods.: 2016 - No. 3, 2016 ($3.99, limited series)

1-3-Wolfer-s/Caracuzzo-a
1-Fear on Four Worlds; part 4 of crossover; Wolfer-s/Büll-a 4.00
.../ Pellucidar: Terror From the Earth's Core 1-3 ('17, $3.99) Wolfer-s/Magora & Cuesta-a 4.00
... See-Ta The Savage 1,2 (2017, $3.99) Wolfer-s/a 4.00

EDGAR RICE BURROUGHS' THE MOON MAID
American Mythology Prods.: 2018 - 2019 ($3.99)

1-3-Catacombs of the Moon 4.00
1-Fear on Four Worlds; part 2 of x-over; Mills-s/Rearte-a 4.00

EDGE
Malibu Comics (Bravura): July, 1994 - No. 3, Apr, 1995 ($2.50/$2.95, unfinished lim.series)

1-3-S. Grant-story & Gil Kane-c/a; w/Bravura stamp. 3-($2.95-c) 3.00

EDGE (Re-titled as Vector starting with #13)
CrossGeneration Comics: May, 2002 - No. 12, Apr, 2003 ($9.95/$11.95/$7.95, TPB)

1-3: Reprints from various CrossGen titles 10.00
4-8-($11.95) 12.00
9-12-($7.95, 8-1/4" x 5-1/2") digest-sized reprints 8.00

EDGE OF CHAOS
Pacific Comics: July, 1983 - No. 3, Jan, 1984 (Limited series)

1-3-Morrow c/a; all contain nudity 3.00

EDGE OF DOOM (Horror anthology)
IDW Publishing: Oct, 2010 - No. 5, Mar, 2011 ($3.99)

1-5-Steve Niles-s/Kelley Jones-a 4.00

EDGE OF SPIDER-GEDDON (Leads into Spider-Geddon #0)
Marvel Comics: Oct, 2018 - No. 4, Dec, 2018 ($3.99, limited series)

1-4: 1-Anarchic Spider-Man app.; Sandoval-a. 2-Peni Parker, SP//dr app. 4-Kuder-s/a 4.00

EDGE OF SPIDER-VERSE (See Amazing Spider-Man 2014 series #7-14)
Marvel Comics: Nov, 2014 - No. 5, Dec, 2014 ($3.99, limited series)

1-Spider-Man Noir; Isanove-a.	2	4	6	8	10	12
2-Gwen Stacy Spider-Woman 1st app.; Robbi Rodriguez-a/c	13	26	39	89	195	300
3,4: 3-Weaver-s/a	1	3	4	6	8	10
5-1st app. Sp//dr & Peni Parker; Gerard Way-s	3	6	9	16	23	30

EDGE OF VENOMVERSE (Leads into Venomverse series)
Marvel Comics: Aug, 2017 - No. 5, Oct, 2017 ($3.99, limited series)

1-5: 1-Venom merges with X-23; Boschi-a. 2-Gwenpool/Venom; Daredevil app. 3-Ghost Rider. 4-Old Man Logan. 5-Deadpool; Stokoe-a 4.00

EDWARD SCISSORHANDS (Based on the movie)
IDW Publishing: Oct, 2014 - No. 10, Jul, 2015 ($3.99)

1-10-Kate Leth-s/Drew Rausch-a; multiple covers on each 4.00

ED WHEELAN'S JOKE BOOK STARRING FAT & SLAT (See Fat & Slat)

EERIE (Strange Worlds No. 18 on)
Avon Per.: No. 1, Jan, 1947; No. 1, May-June, 1951 - No. 17, Aug-Sept, 1954

1(1947)-1st supernatural comic; Kubert, Fugitani-a; bondage-c	861	1722	2583	6285	10,893	15,500
1(1951)-Reprints story from 1947 #1	148	296	444	947	1624	2300
2-Wood-c/a; bondage-c	161	322	483	1030	1765	2500
3-Wood-c; Kubert, Wood/Orlando-a	119	238	357	762	1306	1850

Eerie #6 © Warren Pub.

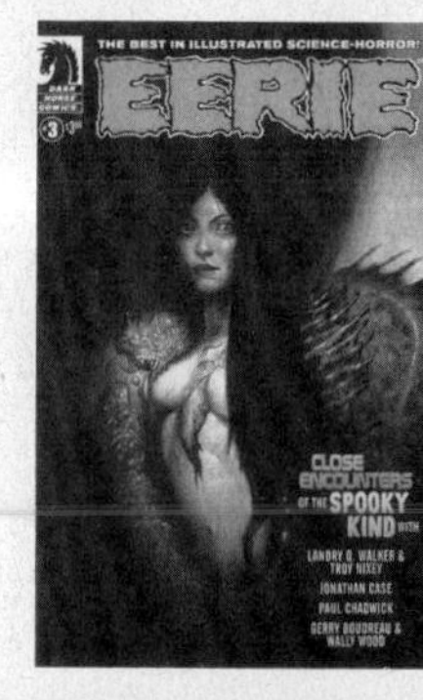

Eerie (2012 series) #3 © NCC

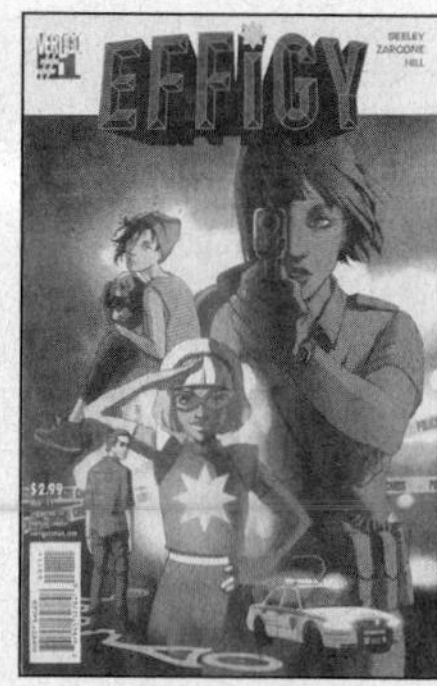

Effigy #1 © Seeley & Zarcone

	GD 2.0	VG 4.0	FN 6.0	VF 8.0	VF/NM 9.0	NM- 9.2

4,5-Wood-c 90 180 270 576 988 1400
6,8,13,14: 8-Kinstler-a; bondage-c; Phantom Witch Doctor story 53 106 159 334 567 800
7-Wood/Orlando-c; Kubert-a 77 154 231 493 847 1200
9-Kubert-a; Check-c 58 116 174 371 636 900
10,11: 10-Kinstler-a. 11-Kinstlerish-a by McCann 55 110 165 352 601 850
12-Dracula story from novel, 25 pgs. 58 116 174 371 636 900
15-Reprints No. 1('51) minus-c(bondage) 41 82 123 256 428 600
16-Wood-a r-/No. 2 41 82 123 256 428 600
17-Wood/Orlando & Kubert-a; reprints #3 minus inside & outside Wood-c 42 84 126 265 445 625

NOTE: *Hollingsworth a-9-11; c-10, 11.*

EERIE
I. W. Enterprises: 1964

I.W. Reprint #1('64)-Wood-c(r); r-story/Spook #1 4 8 12 25 40 55
I.W. Reprint #2,6,8: 8-Dr. Drew by Grandenetti from Ghost #9 3 6 9 21 33 45
I.W. Reprint #9-r/Tales of Terror #1(Toby); Wood-c 4 8 12 27 44 60

EERIE (Magazine)(See Warren Presents)
Warren Publ. Co.: No. 1, Sept, 1965; No. 2, Mar, 1966 - No. 139, Feb, 1983

1-24 pgs., black & white, small size (5-1/4x7-1/4"), low distribution; cover from inside back cover of Creepy No. 2; stories reprinted from Creepy No. 7, 8. At least three different versions exist.
First Printing - B&W, 5-1/4" wide x 7-1/4" high, evenly trimmed. On page 18, panel 5, in the upper left-hand corner, the large rear view of a bald headed man blends into solid black and is unrecognizable. Overall printing quality is poor. 57 114 171 456 1028 1600
Second Printing - B&W, 5-1/4x7-1/4", with uneven, untrimmed edges (if one of these were trimmed evenly, the size would be less than as indicated). The figure of the bald headed man on page 18, panel 5 is clear and discernible. The staples have a 1/4" blue stripe. 15 30 45 103 227 350
Other unauthorized reproductions for comparison's sake would be practically worthless. One known version was probably shot off a first printing copy with some loss of detail; the finer lines tend to disappear in this version which can be determined by looking at the lower right-hand corner of page one, first story. The roof of the house is shaded with straight lines. These lines are sharp and distinct on original, but broken on this version.

NOTE: ***The Overstreet Comic Book Price Guide** recommends that, before buying a 1st issue, you consult an expert.*

2-Frazetta-c; Toth-a; 1st app. host Cousin Eerie 11 22 33 73 157 240
3-Frazetta-c & half pg. ad (rerun in #4); Toth, Williamson, Ditko-a 9 18 27 60 120 180
4,6: 4-Frazetta-a (1/2 pg. ad) 6 12 18 38 69 100
5,7-Frazetta-c. Ditko-a in all 7 14 21 46 86 125
8-Frazetta-c; Ditko-a 8 16 24 52 99 145
9-11,25: 9,10-Neal Adams-a, Ditko-a. 11-Karloff Mummy adapt.-Wood-s/a. 25-Steranko-c 6 12 18 38 69 100
12-16,18-22,24,32-35,40,45: 12,13,20-Poe-s. 12-Bloch-s. 12,15-Jones-a. 13-Lovecraft-s. 14,16-Toth-a. 16,19,24-Stoker-s. 16,32,33,43-Corben-a. 34-Early Boris-c. 35-Early Brunner-a. 35,40-Early Ploog-a. 40-Frankenstein; Ploog-a (6/72, 6 months before Marvel's series) 4 8 12 28 47 65
17-(low distribution) 20 40 60 141 313 485
23-Classic Frazetta-c; Adams-a(reprint) 17 34 57 117 259 400
26-31,36-38,43,44 4 8 12 25 40 55
39,41: 39-1st Dax the Warrior; Maroto-a. 41-(low distribution) 5 10 15 33 57 80
42,51: 42-('73 Annual, 84 pgs.) Spooktacular; Williamson-a. 51-('74 Annual, 76 pgs.) Color poster insert; Toth-a 4 8 12 28 47 65
46,48: 46-Dracula series by Sutton begins; 2pgs. Vampirella. 48-Begin "Mummy Walks" and "Curse of the Werewolf" series (both continue in #49,50,52,53) 4 8 12 25 40 55
47,49,50,52,53: 47-Lilith. 49-Marvin the Dead Thing. 50-Satanna, Daughter of Satan. 52-Hunter by Neary begins. 53-Adams-a 4 8 12 23 37 50
54,55-Color insert Spirit story by Eisner, reprints sections 12/21/47 & 6/16/46 54-Dr. Archaeus series begins 3 6 9 19 30 40
56,57,59,63,69,77,78: All have 8 pg. slick color insert. 56,57,77-Corben-a. 59-(100 pgs.) Summer Special, all Dax issue. 69-Summer Special, all Hunter issue, Neary-a. 78-All Mummy issue 3 6 9 19 30 40
58,60,62,68,72,: 8 pg. slick color insert & Wrightson-a in all. 58,60,62-Corben-a. 60-Summer Giant (9/74, $1.25) 1st Exterminator One; Wood-a. 62-Mummies Walk. 68-Summer Special (84 pgs.) 3 6 9 21 33 45
61,64-67,71: 61-Mummies Walk-s, Wood-a. 64-Corben-a. 64,65,67-Toth-a. 65,66-El Cid. 67-Hunter II. 71-Goblin-c/1st app. 3 6 9 17 26 35
70,73-75 3 6 9 14 20 26
76-1st app. Darklon the Mystic by Starlin-s/a 3 6 9 20 31 42
79,80-Origin Darklon the Mystic by Starlin 3 6 9 17 26 35
81,86,97: 81-Frazetta-c, King Kong; Corben-a. 86-(92 pgs.) All Corben issue. 97-Time Travel/ Dinosaur issue; Corben,Adams-a 3 6 9 16 23 30
82-Origin/1st app. The Rook 3 6 9 18 28 38
83,85,88,89,91-93,98,99: 98-Rook (31 pgs.). 99-1st Horizon Seekers. 2 4 6 10 14 18
84,87,90,96,100: 84,100-Starlin-a. 87-Hunter 3; Nino-a. 87,90-Corben-a. 96-Summer Special (92 pgs.). 100-(92 pgs.) Anniversary issue; Rook (30 pgs.) 2 4 6 13 18 22
94,95-The Rook & Vampirella team-up. 95-Vampirella-c; 1st MacTavish 3 6 9 16 24 32
101,106,112,115,118,120,121,128: 101-Return of Hunter II, Starlin-a. 106-Hard John Nuclear Hit Parade Special, Corben-a. 112-All Maroto issue, Luana-s. 115-All José Ortiz issues. 118-1st Haggarth. 120-1st Zud Kamish. 121-Hunter/Darklon. 128-Starlin-a, Hsu-a 2 4 6 10 14 18
102-105,107-111,113,114,116,117,119,122-124,126,127,129: 103-105,109-111-Gulacy-a. 104-Beast World. 2 4 6 9 13 16
125-(10/81, 84 pgs.) all Neal Adams issue 3 6 9 14 19 24
130-(76 pgs.) Vampirella-c/sty (54 pgs.); Pantha, Van Helsing, Huntress, Dax, Schreck, Hunter, Exterminator One, Rook app. 3 6 9 16 23 30
131-(Lower distr.); all Wood issue 3 6 9 14 20 26
132-134,136: 132-Rook returns. 133-All Ramon Torrents-a issue. 134,136-Color comic insert 2 4 6 10 14 18
135-(Lower distr., 10/82, 100 pgs.) All Ditko issue 3 6 9 14 20 26
137-139 (lower distr.):137-All Super-Hero issue. 138-Sherlock Holmes. 138,139-Color comic insert 2 4 6 13 18 22
Yearbook '70-Frazetta-c 5 10 15 33 57 80
Annual '71, '72-Reprints in both 4 8 12 25 40 55
... Archives - Volume One HC (Dark Horse, 3/09, $49.95, dustjacket) r/#1-5 50.00
... Archives - Volume Two HC (Dark Horse, 9/09, $49.95, dustjacket) r/#6-10; interview with Frank Frazetta from 1985 50.00

NOTE: *The above books contain art by many good artists:* ***N. Adams, Brunner, Corben, Craig (Taycee), Crandall, Ditko, Eisner, Evans, Jeff Jones, Krenkel, McWilliams, Morrow, Orlando, Ploog, Severin, Starlin, Torres, Toth, Williamson, Wood,*** *and* ***Wrightson;*** *covers by* ***Bode', Corben, Davis, Frazetta, Morrow,*** *and* ***Orlando. Frazetta*** *c-2, 3, 7, 8, 23. Annuals from 1973-on are included in regular numbering. 1970-74 Annuals are complete reprints. Annuals from 1975-on are in the format of the regular issues.*

EERIE
Dark Horse Comics: Jul, 2012 - No. 8, Dec, 2015 ($2.99, B&W)

1-8-Sci-fi anthology by various. 2-Allred-a. 3-Wood-a(r). 4,6-Kelley Jones-a 3.00

EERIE ADVENTURES (Also see Weird Adventures)
Ziff-Davis Publ. Co.: Winter, 1951 (Painted-c)

1-Powell-a(2), McCann-a; used in **SOTI**; bondage-c; Krigstein back-c 100 200 300 635 1093 1550

NOTE: *Title dropped due to similarity to Avon's Eerie & legal action.*

EERIE TALES (Magazine)
Hastings Associates: 1959 (Black & White)

1-Williamson, Torres, Tuska-a, Powell(2), & Morrow(2)-a 24 48 72 142 234 325

EERIE TALES
Super Comics: 1963-1964

Super Reprint No. 10,11,12,18: 10('63)-r/Spook #27. Purple Claw in #11,12 ('63); #12-r/Avon's Eerie #1('51)-Kida-r 3 6 9 16 24 32
15-Wolverton-a, Spacehawk-r/Blue Bolt Weird Tales #113; Disbrow-a 4 8 12 28 47 65

EFFIGY
DC Comics (Vertigo): Mar, 2015 - No. 7, Sept, 2015 ($2.99/$3.99)

1-5: 1-Tim Seeley-s/Marley Zarcone-a 3.00
6,7-($3.99) 4.00

EGBERT
Arnold Publications/Quality Comics Group: Spring, 1946 - No. 20, Aug, 1950

1-Funny animal; intro Egbert & The Count 23 46 69 136 223 310
2 13 26 39 74 105 135
3-10 9 18 27 52 69 85
11-20 8 16 24 42 54 65

EGYPT
DC Comics (Vertigo): Aug, 1995 - No.7, Feb, 1996 ($2.50, lim. series, mature)

1-7: Milligan scripts in all. 3.00

EH! (...Dig This Crazy Comic) (From Here to Insanity No. 8 on)
Charlton Comics: Dec, 1953 - No. 7, Nov-Dec, 1954 (Satire)

1-Davis-*ish*-c/a by Ayers, Wood-*ish*-a by Giordano; Atomic Mouse app. 43 86 129 271 461 650
2-Ayers-c/a 26 52 78 154 252 350
3,5,7 24 48 72 140 230 320
4,6: Sexual innuendo-c. 6-Ayers-a 29 58 87 170 278 385

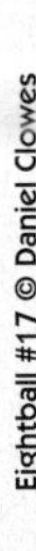
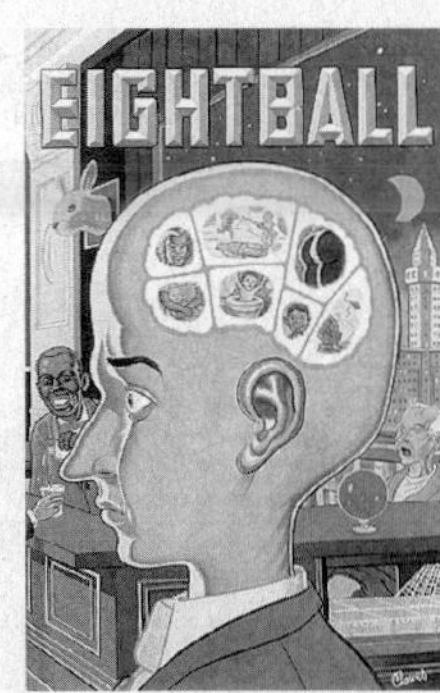

Eightball #17 © Daniel Clowes

El Diablo (2001 series) #1 © DC

Elektra #16 © MAR

	GD	VG	FN	VF	VF/NM	NM-
	2.0	4.0	6.0	8.0	9.0	9.2

EI8GT
Dark Horse Comics: Feb, 2015 - No. 5, Jun, 2015 ($3.50)

1-Rafael Albuquerque-a/c; Mike Johnson-s 3.50

EIGHTBALL (Also see David Boring)
Fantagraphics Books: Oct, 1989 - Present ($2.75/$2.95/$3.95, semi-annually, mature)

	GD	VG	FN	VF	VF/NM	NM-
1 (1st printing) Daniel Clowes-s/a in all	10	20	30	67	141	215
2,3	3	6	9	14	19	24
4-19: 17-(8/96)	2	4	6	8	11	14
20,21: 21-($4.95) Concludes David Boring 3-parter	2	4	6	8	10	12
22-($5.95) 29 short stories	2	4	6	8	10	12
23-($7.00, 9" x 12") The Death Ray	2	4	6	9	12	15

Twentieth Century Eightball (2002, $19.00) r/Clowes strips 20.00

EIGHTH WONDER, THE
Dark Horse Comics: Nov, 1997 ($2.95, one-shot)

nn-Reprints stories from Dark Horse Presents #85-87 3.00

EIGHT IS ENOUGH KITE FUN BOOK (See Kite Fun Book 1979 in the Promotional Comics section)

EIGHT LEGGED FREAKS
DC Comics (WildStorm): 2002 ($6.95, one-shot, squarebound)

nn-Adaptation of 2002 mutant spider movie; Joe Phillips-a; intro by Dean Devlin 7.00

1872 (Secret Wars tie-in)
Marvel Comics: Sept, 2015 - No. 4, Dec, 2015 ($3.99, limited series)

1-4-Red Wolf in the western town of Timely in 1872. 4-Avengers of the West 4.00

80 PAGE GIANT (...Magazine No. 2-15)
National Periodical Publications: 8/64 - No. 15, 10/65; No. 16, 11/65 - No. 89, 7/71 (25¢)
(All reprints) (#1-56: 84 pgs.; #57-89: 68 pgs.)

	GD	VG	FN	VF	VF/NM	NM-
1-Superman Annual; originally planned as Superman Annual #9 (8/64)	34	68	102	245	548	850
2-Jimmy Olsen	18	36	54	125	276	430
3,4: 3-Lois Lane. 4-Flash-G.A.-r; Infantino-a	15	30	45	103	227	350
5-Batman; has Sunday newspaper strip; Catwoman-r; Batman's Life Story-r (25th anniversary special)	15	30	45	103	227	350
6-Superman	13	26	39	91	201	310
7-Sgt. Rock's Prize Battle Tales; Kubert-c/a	26	52	78	182	404	625
8-More Secret Origins-origins of JLA, Aquaman, Robin, Atom, & Superman; Infantino-a	26	52	78	182	404	625
9-15: 9-Flash (r/Flash #106,117,123 & Showcase #14); Infantino-a. 10-Superboy. 11-Superman; all Luthor issue. 12-Batman; has Sunday newspaper strip. 13-Jimmy Olsen. 14-Lois Lane. 15-Superman and Batman; Joker-c/story	12	24	36	82	179	275

Continued as part of regular series under each title in which that particular book came out, a Giant being published instead of the regular size. Issues No. 16 to No. 89 are listed for your information. See individual titles for prices. 16-JLA #39 (11/65), 17-Batman #176, 18-Superman #183, 19-Our Army at War #164, 20-Action #334, 21-Flash #160, 22-Superboy #129, 23-Superman #187, 24-Batman #182, 25-Jimmy Olsen #95, 26-Lois Lane #68, 27-Batman #185, 28-World's Finest #161, 29-JLA #48, 30-Batman #187, 31-Superman #193, 32-Our Army at War #177, 33-Action #347, 34-Flash #169, 35-Superboy #138, 36-Superman #197, 37-Batman #193, 38-Jimmy Olsen #104, 39-Lois Lane #77, 40-World's Finest #170, 41-JLA #58, 42-Superman #202, 43-Batman #198, 44-Our Army at War #190, 45-Action #360, 46-Flash #178, 47-Superboy #147, 48-Superman #207, 49-Batman #203, 50-Jimmy Olsen #113, 51-Lois Lane #86, 52-World's Finest #179, 53-JLA #67, 54-Superman #212, 55-Batman #208, 56-Our Army at War #203, 57-Action #373, 58-Flash #187, 59-Superboy #156, 60-Superman #217, 61-Batman #213, 62-Jimmy Olsen #122, 63-Lois Lane #95, 64-World's Finest #188, 65-JLA #76, 66-Superman #222, 67-Batman #218, 68-Our Army at War #216, 69-Adventure #390, 70-Flash #196, 71-Superboy #165, 72-Superman #227, 73-Batman #223, 74-Jimmy Olsen #131, 75-Lois Lane #104, 76-World's Finest #197, 77-JLA #85, 78-Superman #232, 79-Batman #228, 80-Our Army at War #229, 81-Adventure #403, 82-Flash #205, 83-Superboy #174, 84-Superman #239, 85-Batman #233, 86-Jimmy Olsen #140, 87-Lois Lane #113, 88-World's Finest #206, 89-JLA #93.

87TH PRECINCT (TV) (Based on the Ed McBain novels)
Dell Publishing Co.: Apr-June, 1962 - No. 2, July-Sept, 1962

	GD	VG	FN	VF	VF/NM	NM-
Four Color 1309(#1)-Krigstein-a	9	18	27	60	120	180
2-Photo-c	7	14	21	43	89	130

E IS FOR EXTINCTION (Secret Wars tie-in)
Marvel Comics: Aug, 2015 - No. 4, Nov, 2015 ($4.99/$3.99, limited series)

1-($4.99) New X-Men in Mutopia; Burnham-s/Villalobos-a 5.00
2-4-($3.99) Cassandra Nova returns 4.00

EL BOMBO COMICS
Standard Comics/Frances M. McQueeny: 1946

	GD	VG	FN	VF	VF/NM	NM-
nn(1946), 1(no date)	19	38	57	111	176	240

EL CAZADOR
CrossGen Comics: Oct, 2003 - No. 6, Jun, 2004 ($2.95)

1-Dixon-s/Epting-a 5.00
2-6: 5-Lady Death preview 3.00
...: The Bloody Ballad of Blackjack Tom 1 (4/04, $2.95, one-shot) Cariello-a 3.00

EL CID
Dell Publishing Co.: No. 1259, 1961

	GD	VG	FN	VF	VF/NM	NM-
Four Color 1259-Movie, photo-c	7	14	21	46	86	125

EL DIABLO (See All-Star Western #2 & Weird Western Tales #12)
DC Comics: Aug, 1989 - No. 16, Jan, 1991 ($1.50-$1.75, color)

1 ($2.50, 52pgs.)-Masked hero 4.00
2-16 3.00

EL DIABLO
DC Comics (Vertigo): Mar, 2001 - No. 4, Jun, 2001 ($2.50, limited series)

1-4-Azzarello-s/Zezelj-a/Sale-c 3.00
TPB (2008, $12.99) r/#1-4 13.00

EL DIABLO
DC Comics: Nov, 2008 - No. 6, Apr, 2009 ($2.99, limited series)

1-6-Nitz-s/Hester-a/c. 4,5-Freedom Fighters app. 3.00

EL DORADO (See Movie Classics)

ELEANOR & THE EGRET
AfterShock Comics: Apr, 2017 - No. 5, Nov, 2017 ($3.99)

1-5-John Layman-s/Sam Kieth-a/c 4.00

ELECTRIC ANT
Marvel Comics: Jun, 2010 - No. 5, Oct, 2010 ($3.99, Baxter paper)

1-5-Based on a Philip K. Dick story; David Mack-s/Pascal Alixe-a; Paul Pope-c 4.00

ELECTRIC SUBLIME
IDW Publishing: Oct, 2016 - No. 4, Jan, 2017 ($3.99, limited series)

1-4-W. Maxwell Prince-s/Martin Morazzo-a; two covers on each 4.00

ELECTRIC UNDERTOW (See Strikeforce Morituri: Electric Undertow)

ELECTRIC WARRIOR
DC Comics: May, 1986 - No. 18, Oct, 1987 ($1.50, Baxter paper)

1-18 3.00

ELECTRIC WARRIORS
DC Comics: Jan, 2019 - No. 6, Jun, 2019 ($3.99, limited series)

1-6-Steve Orlando-s/Travel Foreman-a 4.00

ELECTROPOLIS
Image Comics: May, 2001 - No. 4, Jan, 2003 ($2.95/$5.95)

1-3-Dean Motter-s/a. 3-(12/01) 3.00
4-(1/03, $5.95, 72 pages) The Infernal Machine pts. 4-6 6.00

ELEKTRA (Also see Daredevil #319-325)
Marvel Comics: Mar, 1995 - No. 4, June, 1995 ($2.95, limited series)

1-4-Embossed-c; Scott McDaniel-a 5.00

ELEKTRA (Also see Daredevil)
Marvel Comics: Nov, 1996 - No. 19, Jun, 1998 ($1.95)

1-Peter Milligan scripts; Deodato-c/a 4.00
1-Variant-c 6.00
2-19: 4-Dr. Strange-c/app. 10-Logan-c/app. 3.00
#(-1) Flashback (7/97) Matt Murdock-c/app.; Deodato-c/a 3.00
.../Cyblade (Image, 3/97,$2.95) Devil's Reign pt. 7 3.00

ELEKTRA (Vol. 2) (Marvel Knights)
Marvel Comics: Sept, 2001 - No. 35, Jun, 2004 ($3.50/$2.99)

1-Bendis-s/Austen-a/Horn-c 4.00
2-6: 2-Two covers (Sienkiewicz and Horn) 3,4-Silver Samurai app. 3.00
3-Initial printing with panel of nudity; most copies pulped 55.00
7-35: 7-Rucka-s begin. 9,10,17-Bennett-a. 19-Meglia-a. 23-25-Chen-a; Sienkiewicz-c 3.00
...Vol. 1: Introspect TPB (2002, $16.99) r/#10-15; Marvel Knights: Double Shot #3 17.00
...Vol. 2: Everything Old is New Again TPB (2003, $16.99) r/#16-22 17.00
...Vol. 3: Relentless TPB (2004, $14.99) r/#23-28 15.00
...Vol. 4: Frenzy TPB (2004, $17.99) r/#29-35 18.00

ELEKTRA (All-New Marvel Now!)
Marvel Comics: Jun, 2014 - No. 11, May, 2015 ($3.99)

1-11: 1-Blackman-s/Del Mundo-a; multiple covers. 2,6,7-Lady Bullseye app. 4.00

ELEKTRA
Marvel Comics: Apr, 2017 - No. 5, Aug, 2017 ($3.99, limited series)

1-5: Matt Owens-s/Juann Cabal-a; Arcade app. 4.00

ELEKTRA & WOLVERINE: THE REDEEMER
Marvel Comics: Jan, 2002 - No. 3, Mar, 2002 ($5.95, square-bound, lim. series)

1-3-Greg Rucka-s/Yoshitaka Amano-a/c 6.00

Elektra: Glimpse & Echo #1 © MAR

Elephantmen #54 © Active Images

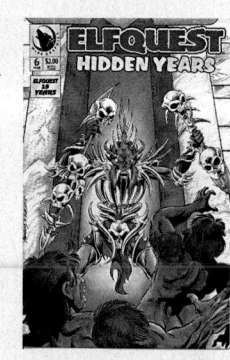

Elfquest Hidden Years #6 © Warp

	GD 2.0	VG 4.0	FN 6.0	VF 8.0	VF/NM 9.0	NM- 9.2

HC (5/02, $29.95, with dustjacket) r/#1-3, interview with Greg Rucka 30.00

ELEKTRA: ASSASSIN (Also see Daredevil)
Marvel Comics (Epic Comics): Aug, 1986 - No. 8, June, 1987 (Limited series, mature)
1,8-Miller scripts in all; Sienkiewicz-c/a 1 2 3 5 6 8
2-7 5.00
Signed & numbered hardcover (Graphitti Designs, $39.95, 2000 print run)- reprints 1-8 60.00
TPB (2000, $24.95) 25.00

ELEKTRA: GLIMPSE & ECHO
Marvel Comics: Sept, 2002 - No. 4, Dec, 2002 ($2.99, limited series)
1-4-Scott Morse-s/painted-a 3.00

ELEKTRA LIVES AGAIN (Also see Daredevil)
Marvel Comics (Epic Comics): 1990 ($24.95, oversize, hardcover, 76 pgs.)(Produced by Graphitti Designs)
nn-Frank Miller-c/a/scripts; Lynn Varley painted-a; Matt Murdock & Bullseye app. 40.00
2nd printing (9/02, $24.99) 25.00

ELEKTRA MEGAZINE
Marvel Comics: Nov, 1996 - No. 2, Dec, 1996 ($3.95, 96 pgs., reprints, limited series)
1,2: Reprints Frank Miller's Elektra stories in Daredevil 4.00

ELEKTRA SAGA, THE
Marvel Comics Group: Feb, 1984 - No. 4, June, 1984 ($2.00, limited series, Baxter paper)
1-4-r/Daredevil #168-190; Miller-c/a 5.00

ELEKTRA: THE HAND
Marvel Comics: Nov, 2004 - No. 5, Feb, 2005 ($2.99, limited series)
1-5-Gossett-a/Sienkiewicz-c/Yoshida-s; origin of the Hand in the 16th century 3.00

ELEKTRA: THE MOVIE
Marvel Comics: Feb, 2005 ($5.99)
1-Movie adaptation; McKeever-s/Perkins-a; photo-c 6.00
TPB (2005, $12.95) r/movie adaptation, Daredevil #168, 181 & Elektra #(-1) 13.00

ELEMENTALS, THE (See The Justice Machine & Morningstar Spec.)
Comico The Comic Co. : June, 1984 - No. 29, Sept, 1988; V2#1, Mar, 1989 - No. 28, 1994? ($1.50/$2.50, Baxter paper); V3#1, Dec, 1995 - No. 3 ($2.95)
1-Willingham-c/a, 1-8 5.00
2-29, V2#1-28: 9-Bissette-a(p). 10-Photo-c. V2#6-1st app. Strike Force America. 18-Prelude to Avalon mini-series. 27-Prequel to Strike Force America series 3.00
V3#1-3: 1-Daniel-a(p), bagged w/gaming card 3.00
Lingerie (5/96, $2.95) 3.00
Special 1,2 (3/86, 1/89)-1-Willingham-a(p) 3.00

ELEMENTALS: (Title series), **Comico**
--GHOST OF A CHANCE, 12/95 ($5.95)-graphic novel, nn-Ross-c. 6.00
--HOW THE WAR WAS WON, 6/96 - No. 2, 8/96 ($2.95) 1,2-Tony Daniel-a, & 1-Variant-c; no logo 3.00
--SEX SPECIAL, 1991 - No. 4, Feb, 1993 ($2.95, color) 2 covers for each 3.00
--SEX SPECIAL, 5/97 - No. 2, 6/97 ($2.95, B&W) 1-Tony Daniel, Jeff Moy-a, 2-Robb Phipps, Adam McDaniel-a 3.00
--SWIMSUIT SPECTACULAR 1996, 6/96 ($2.95), 1-pin-ups, 1-Variant-c; no logo 3.00
--THE VAMPIRE'S REVENGE, 6/96 - No. 2 8/96 ($2.95) 1,2-Willingham-s, 1-Variant-c; no logo 3.00

ELEPHANTMEN
Image Comics: July, 2006 - No. 80, Jan, 2018 ($2.99/$3.50/$3.99) (Flip covers on most)
1-16: 1-Starkings-s/Moritat-a/Ladronn-c. 6-Campbell flip-c. 15-Sale flip-c 4.00
17-30-($3.50) 25-Flip book preview of Marineman 4.00
31-49,51-80-($3.99) 32-Conan/Red Sonja homage. 42-44-Dave Sim-a (5 pgs.) 4.00
50-($5.99) Flip book with reprint of #1; cover gallery 6.00
...: Man and Elephantman 1 (3/11, $3.99) Three covers 4.00
... Shots (5/15, $5.99) Reprints short stories from anthologies; art by Sim, Sale, & others 6.00
...: The Pilot (5/07, $2.99) short stories and pin-ups by various incl. Sale, Jim Lee, Jae Lee 4.00
...: War Toys (11/07 - No. 3, 4/08, $2.99) 1-3-Mappo war; Starkings-s/Moritat-a/Ladronn-c 4.00
... War Toys: Yvette (7/09, $3.50) Starkings-s/Moritat-a 4.00
Giant-Size Elephantmen 1 (10/11, $5.99) r/#31,32 & Man and Elephantman; Campbell-c 6.00

1111 (ELEVEN ELEVEN)
Crusade Entertainment: Oct, 1996 ($2.95, B&W, one-shot)
1-Wrightson-c/a 4.00

ELEVEN OR ONE
Sirius: Apr, 1995 ($2.95)
1-Linsner-c/a 1 3 4 6 8 10

	GD 2.0	VG 4.0	FN 6.0	VF 8.0	VF/NM 9.0	NM- 9.2

1-(6/96) 2nd printing 3.50

ELFLORD
Nightwind Productions: Jun, 1980 - Vol. 2 #1, 1982 (B&W, magazine-size)
1-1st Barry Blair-s/c/a in comics; B&W-c; limited print run for all 10 20 30 64 132 200
2-5-B&W-c 5 10 15 31 53 75
6-14: 9-14-Color-c 4 8 12 27 44 60
Vol. 2 #1 (1982) 4 8 12 23 37 50

ELFLORD
Aircel Publ.: 1986 - No. 6, Oct, 1989 ($1.70, B&W); V2#1- V2#31, 1995 ($2.00)
1 4.00
2-4,V2#1-20,22-30: 4-6: Last B&W. V2#1-Color-a begin. 22-New cast. 25-Begin B&W 3.00
1,2-2nd printings 3.00
21-Double size ($4.95) 5.00

ELFLORD
Warp Graphics: Jan, 1997-No.4, Apr, 1997 ($2.95, B&W, mini-series)
1-4 3.00

ELFLORD (CUTS LOOSE) (Vol. 2)
Warp Graphics: Sept, 1997 - No. 7, Apr, 1998 ($2.95, B&W, mini-series)
1-7 3.00

ELFLORD: DRAGON'S EYE
Night Wynd Enterprises: 1993 ($2.50, B&W)
1 3.00

ELFLORD: THE RETURN
Mad Monkey Press: 1996 ($6.95, magazine size)
1 7.00

ELFQUEST (Also see Fantasy Quarterly & Warp Graphics Annual)
Warp Graphics, Inc.: No. 2, Aug, 1978 - No. 21, Feb, 1985 (All magazine size)
No. 1, Apr, 1979
NOTE: **Elfquest** was originally published as one of the stories in **Fantasy Quarterly** #1. When the publisher went out of business, the creative team, Wendy and Richard Pini, formed WaRP Graphics and continued the series, beginning with **Elfquest** #2. **Elfquest** #1, which reprinted the story from **Fantasy Quarterly**, was published about the same time **Elfquest** #4 was released. Thereafter, most issues were reprinted as demand warranted, until Marvel announced it would reprint the entire series under its Epic imprint (Aug., 1985).
1(4/79)-Reprints Elfquest story from Fantasy Quarterly No. 1
1st printing ($1.00-c) 7 14 21 46 86 125
2nd printing ($1.25-c) 2 4 6 9 12 15
3rd printings ($1.50-c) 1 2 3 5 6 8
4th printing; different-c ($1.50-c) 5.00
2(8/78) 1st printing ($1.00-c) 4 8 12 28 47 65
2nd printings ($1.25-c) 6.00
3rd & 4th printings ($1.50-c)(all 4th prints 1989) 5.00
3-5: 1st printings ($1.00-c) 3 6 9 16 23 30
6-9: 1st printings ($1.25-c) 3 6 9 14 20 25
2nd & 3rd printings ($1.50-c) 5.00
10-21: ($1.50-c); 16-8pg. preview of A Distant Soil 2 4 6 11 16 20
10-14: 2nd printings ($1.50) 5.00

ELFQUEST
Marvel Comics (Epic Comics): Aug, 1985 - No. 32, Mar, 1988
1-Reprints in color the Elfquest epic by Warp Graphics 1 2 3 5 6 8
2-32 4.00

ELFQUEST
DC Comics: 2003 - 2005
Archives Vol. 1 (2003, $49.95, HC) r/#1-5 50.00
Archives Vol. 2 (2005, $49.95, HC) r/#6-10 & Epic Illustrated #1 50.00
25th Anniversary Special (2003, $2.95) r/Elfquest #1 (Apr, 1979); interview w/Pinis 4.00

ELFQUEST (Title series), Warp Graphics
'89 - No. 4, '89 ($1.50, B&W) 1-4: R-original Elfquest series 4.00

ELFQUEST (Volume 2),**Warp Graphics:** V2#1, 5/96 - No. 33, 2/99 ($4.95/$2.95, B&W)
V2#1-31: 1,3,5,8,10,12,13,18,21,23,25-Wendy Pini-c 6.00
32,33-($2.95-c) 4.00
--BLOOD OF TEN CHIEFS, 7/93 - No. 20, 9/95 ($2.00/$2.50)
1-20-By Richard & Wendy Pini 4.00
--HIDDEN YEARS, 5/92 - No. 29, 3/96 ($2.00/$2.25)1-9,9 1/2, 10-29 4.00
--JINK, 11/94 - No. 12, 2/6 ($2.25/$2.50) 1-12-W. Pini/John Byrne-back-c 4.00
--KAHVI, 10/95 - No. 6,3/96 ($2.25, B&W) 1-6 4.00
--KINGS CROSS, 11/97 - No. 2, 12/97 ($2.95, B&W) 1,2 4.00

Elfquest: The Final Quest #17 © Warp

Ellery Queen #3 © SUPR

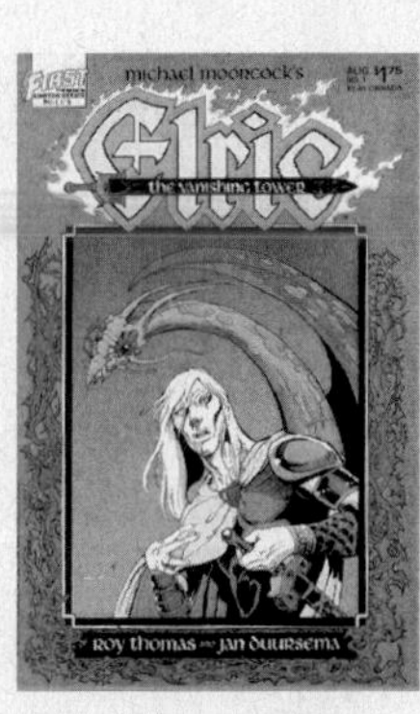

Elric: The Vanishing Tower #1 © FC

	GD 2.0	VG 4.0	FN 6.0	VF 8.0	VF/NM 9.0	NM- 9.2

--KINGS OF THE BROKEN WHEEL, 6/90 - No. 9, 2/92 ($2.00, B&W) (3rd Elfquest saga)
1-9: By R. & W. Pini; 1-Color insert 5.00
1-2nd printing 4.00

--METAMORPHOSIS, 4/96 ($2.95, B&W) 1 4.00

--NEW BLOOD (...Summer Special on-c #1 only), 8/92 - No. 35, 1/96 ($2.00-$2.50, color/B&W) 1-($3.95, 68 pgs.,...Summer Special on-c)-Byrne-a/scripts (16 pgs.) 5.00
2-35: Barry Blair-a in all 4.00
1993 Summer Special ($3.95) Byrne-a/scripts 5.00

--SHARDS, 8/94 - No. 16, 3/96 ($2.25/$2.50) 1-16 4.00

--SIEGE AT BLUE MOUNTAIN, WaRP Graphics/Apple 3/87 - No. 8, 12/88 (1.75/ $1.95, B&W)

	GD	VG	FN	VF	VF/NM	NM-
1-Staton-a(i) in all; 2nd Elfquest saga	1	2	3	5	6	8
1-3-2nd printing						4.00
2-8						5.00

--THE REBELS, 11/94 - No. 12, 3/96 ($2.25/$2.50, B&W/color) 1-12 4.00

--TWO-SPEAR, 10/95 - No. 5, 2/96 ($2.25, B&W) 1-5 4.00

--WAVE DANCERS, 12/93 - No. 6, 3/96, 1-6: 1-Foil-c & poster 4.00
Special 1 ($2.95) 4.00

--WORLDPOOL, 7/97 ($2.95, B&W) 1-Richard Pini-s/Barry Blair-a 4.00

ELFQUEST: STARGAZER'S HUNT
Dark Horse Comics: Nov, 2019 - No. 4, Oct, 2020 ($3.99)
1-4-Wendy & Richard Pini-s/Sonny Strait-a 4.00

ELFQUEST: THE DISCOVERY
DC Comics: Mar, 2006 - No. 4, Sept, 2006 ($3.99, limited series)
1-4-Wendy Pini-a/Wendy & Richard Pini-s 5.00
TPB (2006, $14.99) r/#1-4 15.00

ELFQUEST: THE FINAL QUEST
Dark Horse Comics: Oct, 2013; No. 1, Jan, 2014 - No. 24, Feb, 2018 ($3.50/$3.99)
1-14-Wendy Pini-a/Wendy & Richard Pini-s 3.50
15-24-($3.99) 4.00
... Special (10/13, $5.99) Wendy Pini-a/Wendy & Richard Pini-s; prologue to series 6.00

ELFQUEST: THE GRAND QUEST
DC Comics: 2004 - No. 14, 2006 ($9.95/$9.99, B&W, digest-size)
Vol. 1-6 ('04)1-r/Elfquest #1-5; new W. Pini-c. 2-r/#5-8. 3-r/#8-11. 4-r/#11-15. 5-r/#15-18 6-r/#18-20 10.00
Vol. 7-9 ('05) 1-r/Siege At Blue Mountain #1-3. 8-r/SABM #3-5. 9-r/SABM #6-8 10.00
Vol. 10-14 ('05) 10-r/Kings of the Broken Wheel #1-3. 11-KotBW #5-7 & Frazetta Fant. Ill. 12-r/Kings of the Broken Wheel #8&9. 13-r/Elfquest V2 #4-18. 14-r/Hidden Years #4-91/2 10.00

ELFQUEST: THE SEARCHER AND THE SWORD
DC Comics: 2004 ($24.95/$14.99, graphic novel)
HC (2004, $24.95, with dust jacket)-Wendy and Richard Pini-s/a/c 25.00
SC (2004, $14.99) 15.00

ELFQUEST: WOLFRIDER
DC Comics: 2003 - No. 2, 2003 ($9.95, digest-size)
Volume 1 ('03, $9.95, digest-size) r/Elfquest V2#19,21,23,25,27,29,31; Blood of Ten Chiefs #2; Hidden Years #5; New Blood Special #1; New Blood 1993 Special #1; new W. Pini-c 10.00
Volume 2 ('03, $9.95, digest-size) r/Elfquest V2#33; Blood of Ten Chiefs #10,11,19; Warp Graphics Annual #1 10.00

ELIMINATOR (Also see The Solution #16 & The Night Man #16)
Malibu Comics (Ultraverse): Apr, 1995 - No. 3, Jul, 1995 ($2.95/$2.50, lim. series)
0-Mike Zeck-a in all 3.00
1-3-($2.50): 1-1st app. Siren 3.00
1-($3.95)-Black cover edition 4.00

ELIMINATOR FULL COLOR SPECIAL
Eternity Comics: Oct, 1991 ($2.95, one-shot)
1-Dave Dorman painted-c 4.00

ELLA CINDERS (See Comics On Parade, Comics Revue #1,4, Famous Comics Cartoon Book, Giant Comics Editions, Sparkler Comics, Tip Top & Treasury of Comics)

ELLA CINDERS
United Features Syndicate: 1938 - 1940

	GD	VG	FN	VF	VF/NM	NM-
Single Series 3(1938)	45	90	135	284	480	675
Single Series 21(#2 on-c, #21 on inside), 28('40)	39	78	117	231	378	525

ELLA CINDERS
United Features Syndicate: Mar, 1948 - No. 5, Mar, 1949

	GD	VG	FN	VF	VF/NM	NM-
1-(#2 on cover)	15	30	45	94	147	200
2	11	22	33	62	86	110
3-5	9	18	27	47	61	75

ELLERY QUEEN
Superior Comics Ltd.: May, 1949 - No. 4, Nov, 1949

	GD	VG	FN	VF	VF/NM	NM-
1-Kamen-c; L.B. Cole-a; r-in Haunted Thrills	55	110	165	352	601	850
2-4: 3-Drug use stories(2)	41	82	123	256	428	600

NOTE: *Iger shop art in all issues.*

ELLERY QUEEN (TV)
Ziff-Davis Publishing Co.: 1-3/52 (Spring on-c) - No. 2, Summer/52 (Saunders painted-c)

	GD	VG	FN	VF	VF/NM	NM-
1-Saunders-c	50	100	150	315	533	750
2-Saunders bondage, torture-c	39	78	117	240	395	550

ELLERY QUEEN (Also see Crackajack Funnies No. 23)
Dell Publishing Co.: No. 1165, Mar-May, 1961 - No.1289, Apr, 1962

	GD	VG	FN	VF	VF/NM	NM-
Four Color 1165 (#1)	9	18	27	58	114	175
Four Color 1243 (11/61-1/62), 1289	7	14	21	48	89	130

ELMER FUDD (Also see Camp Comics, Daffy, Looney Tunes #1 & Super Book #10, 22)
Dell Publishing Co.: No. 470, May, 1953 - No. 1293, Mar-May, 1962

	GD	VG	FN	VF	VF/NM	NM-
Four Color 470 (#1)	10	20	30	64	132	200
Four Color 558,628,689('56)	6	12	18	38	69	100
Four Color 725,783,841,888,938,977,1032,1081,1131,1171,1222,1293('62)	5	10	15	33	57	80

ELMO COMICS
St. John Publishing Co.: Jan, 1948 (Daily strip-r)

	GD	VG	FN	VF	VF/NM	NM-
1-By Cecil Jensen	14	28	42	78	112	145

ELONGATED MAN (See Flash #112 & Justice League of America #105)
DC Comics: Jan, 1992 - No. 4, Apr, 1992 ($1.00, limited series)
1-4: 3-The Flash app. 3.00

ELRIC (Of Melnibone)(See First Comics Graphic Novel #6 & Marvel Graphic Novel #2)
Pacific Comics: Apr, 1983 - No. 6, Apr, 1984 ($1.50, Baxter paper)
1-6: Russell-c/a(i) in all 3.00

ELRIC
Topps Comics: 1996 ($2.95, one-shot)
0-One Life: Russell-c/a; adapts Neil Gaiman's short story "One Life--Furnished in Early Moorcock." 3.00

ELRIC, SAILOR ON THE SEAS OF FATE
First Comics: June, 1985 - No. 7, June, 1986 ($1.75, limited series)
1-7: Adapts Michael Moorcock's novel 3.00

ELRIC, STORMBRINGER
Dark Horse Comics/Topps Comics: 1997 - No. 7, 1997 ($2.95, limited series)
1-7: Russell-c/s/a; adapts Michael Moorcock's novel 3.00

ELRIC: THE BALANCE LOST
BOOM! Studios: Jul, 2011 - No. 12, Jun, 2012 ($3.99)
1-12: 1-Roberson-s/Biagini-a; four covers. 2-11-Three covers 4.00

ELRIC: THE BANE OF THE BLACK SWORD
First Comics: Aug, 1988 - No. 6, June, 1989 ($1.75/$1.95, limited series)
1-6: Adapts Michael Moorcock's novel 3.00

ELRIC: THE VANISHING TOWER
First Comics: Aug, 1987 - No. 6, June, 1988 ($1.75, limited series)
1-6: Adapts Michael Moorcock's novel 3.00

ELRIC: WEIRD OF THE WHITE WOLF
First Comics: Oct, 1986 - No. 5, June, 1987 ($1.75, limited series)
1-5: Adapts Michael Moorcock's novel 3.00

EL SALVADOR - A HOUSE DIVIDED
Eclipse Comics: March, 1989 ($2.50, B&W, Baxter paper, stiff-c, 52 pgs.)
1-Gives history of El Salvador 4.00

ELSEWHERE
Image Comics: Aug, 2017 - No. 8, Jul, 2018 ($3.99)
1-8: 1-Jay Faerber-s/Sumeyye Kesgin-a; Amelia Earhart & DB Cooper app. 4.00

ELSEWHERE PRINCE, THE (Moebius' Airtight Garage)
Marvel Comics (Epic): May, 1990 - No. 6, Oct, 1990 ($1.95, limited series)
1-6: Moebius scripts & back-up-a in all 3.00

ELSEWORLDS 80-PAGE GIANT (See DC Comics Presents: ... for reprint)
DC Comics: Aug, 1999 ($5.95, one-shot)
1-Most copies destroyed by DC over content of the "Superman's Babysitter" story; some UK

Elvira Mistress of the Dark (2018 series) #4 © Queen B Prods.

E-Man #3 © FC

Emma #5 © MAR

	GD 2.0	VG 4.0	FN 6.0	VF 8.0	VF/NM 9.0	NM- 9.2
shipments sold before recall	12	24	36	83	182	280

ELSEWORLD'S FINEST
DC Comics: 1997 - No. 2, 1997 ($4.95, limited series)
1,2: Elseworld's story-Superman & Batman in the 1920's 5.00

ELSEWORLD'S FINEST: SUPERGIRL & BATGIRL
DC Comics: 1998 ($5.95, one-shot)
1-Haley-a 6.00

ELSIE THE COW
D. S. Publishing Co.: Oct-Nov, 1949 - No. 3, July-Aug, 1950

	GD	VG	FN	VF	VF/NM	NM-
1-(36 pgs.)	31	62	93	186	303	420
2,3	21	42	63	122	199	275

ELSON'S PRESENTS
DC Comics: 1981 (100 pgs., no cover price)
Series 1-6: Repackaged 1981 DC comics; 1-DC Comics Presents #29, Flash #303, Batman #331. 2-Superman #335, Ghosts #96, Justice League of America #186. 3-New Teen Titans #3, Secrets of Haunted House #32, Wonder Woman #275. 4-Secrets of the LSH #1, Brave & the Bold #170, New Adv. of Superboy #13. 5-LSH #271, Green Lantern #136, Super Friends #40. 6-Action #515, Mystery in Space #115, Detective #498
2 4 6 11 16 20

ELTINGVILLE CLUB, THE (Characters from Dork)
Dark Horse Comics: Apr, 2014 - No. 2, Aug, 2015 ($3.99, B&W, limited series)
1,2-Evan Dorkin-s/a 4.00
HC-(2/16, $19.99) Reprints #1,2 and stories from Dork, Instant Piano, DHP 20.00

ELVEN (Also see Prime)
Malibu Comics (Ultraverse): Oct, 1994 - No. 4, Feb, 1995 ($2.50, lim. series)
0 ($2.95)-Prime app. 3.00
1-4: 2,4-Prime app. 3-Primevil app. 3.00
1-Limited Foil Edition- no price on cover 4.00

ELVIRA MISTRESS OF THE DARK
Marvel Comics: Oct, 1988 ($2.00, B&W, magazine size)
1-Movie adaptation 3 6 9 16 23 30

ELVIRA MISTRESS OF THE DARK
Claypool Comics (Eclipse): May, 1993 - No. 166, Feb, 2007 ($2.50, B&W)
1-Austin-a(i). Spiegle-a 2 4 6 8 10 12
2-6: Spiegle-a 4.00
7-99,101-166-Photo-c: 3.00
100-(8/01) Kurt Busiek back-up-s; art by DeCarlo and others 4.00
TPB ($12.95) 13.00

ELVIRA MISTRESS OF THE DARK
Dynamite Entertainment: 2018 - No. 12, 2020 ($3.99)
1-12: 1-Avallone-s/Acosta-a; multiple covers; Mary Wollstonecraft app. 2-E.A. Poe app. 4.00
... Spring Special One-Shot (2019, $4.99) Ruiz & Parent-s/a

ELVIRA'S HOUSE OF MYSTERY
DC Comics: Jan, 1986 - No. 11, Jan, 1987
1,11: 11-Dave Stevens-c 3 6 9 16 23 30
2-10: 9-Photo-c, Special 1 (3/87, $1.25) 6.00

ELVIRA THE SHAPE OF ELVIRA
Dynamite Entertainment: 2019 - No. 4, 2019 ($3.99, limited series)
1-4: 1-3-Avallone-s/Strukan-a; multiple covers. 4-Qualano-a 4.00

ELVIS MANDIBLE, THE
DC Comics (Piranha Press): 1990 ($3.50, 52 pgs., B&W, mature)
nn 4.00

ELVIS PRESLEY (See Career Girl Romances #32, Go-Go, Howard Chaykin's American Flagg #10, Humbug #8, I Love You #60 & Young Lovers #18)

EL ZOMBO FANTASMA
Dark Horse Comics (Rocket Comics): Apr, 2004 - No. 3, June, 2004 ($2.99)
1-3-Wilkins-s&a/Munroe-s 3.00

E-MAN
Charlton Comics: Oct, 1973 - No. 10, Sept, 1975 (Painted-c No. 7-10)
1-Origin & 1st app. E-Man; Staton c/a in all 3 6 9 17 25 34
2-5: 2,4,5-Ditko-a. 3-Howard-a. 5-Miss Liberty Belle app. by Ditko
2 4 6 9 12 15
6-10: 6,7,9,10-Early Byrne-a (#6 is 1/75). 6-Disney parody. 8-Full-length story; Nova begins as E-Man's partner 2 4 6 11 16 20
1-4,9,10 (Modern Comics reprints, '77) 5.00
NOTE: *Killjoy app.-No. 2, 4. Liberty Belle app.-No. 5. Rog 2000 app.-No. 6, 7, 9, 10. Travis app.-No. 3.* ***Sutton*** *a-1.*

E-MAN
Comico: Sept, 1989 ($2.75, one-shot, no ads, high quality paper)
1-Staton-c/a; Michael Mauser story 4.00

E-MAN
Comico: V4#1, Jan, 1990 - No. 3, Mar, 1990 ($2.50, limited series)
1-3: Staton-c/a 4.00

E-MAN
Alpha Productions: Oct, 1993 ($2.75)
V5#1-Staton-c/a; 20th anniversary issue 4.00

E-MAN COMICS (Also see Michael Mauser & The Original E-Man)
First Comics: Apr, 1983 - No. 25, Aug, 1985 ($1.00/$1.25, direct sales only)
1-25: 2-X-Men satire. 3-X-Men/Phoenix satire. 6-Origin retold. 8-Cutey Bunny app. 10-Origin Nova Kane. 24-Origin Michael Mauser 4.00
NOTE: ***Staton*** *a-1-5, 6-25p; c-1-25.*

E-MAN RETURNS
Alpha Productions: 1994 ($2.75, B&W)
1-Joe Staton-c/a(p) 4.00

EMERALD CITY OF OZ, THE (Dorothy Gale from Wonderful Wizard of Oz)
Marvel Comics: Sept, 2013 - No. 5, Feb, 2014 ($3.99, limited series)
1-5-Eric Shanower-s/Skottie Young-a/c 4.00

EMERALD DAWN
DC Comics: 1991 ($4.95, trade paperback)
nn-Reprints Green Lantern: Emerald Dawn #1-6 1 2 3 5 6 8

EMERALD DAWN II (See Green Lantern...)

EMERGENCY (Magazine)
Charlton Comics: June, 1976 - No. 4, Jan, 1977 (B&W)

	GD	VG	FN	VF	VF/NM	NM-
1-Neal Adams-c/a; Heath, Austin-a	4	8	12	23	37	50
2,3: 2-N. Adams-c. 3-N. Adams-a.	3	6	9	18	28	38
4-Alcala-a	3	6	9	14	20	25

EMERGENCY (TV)
Charlton Comics: June, 1976 - No. 4, Dec, 1976

	GD	VG	FN	VF	VF/NM	NM-
1-Staton-c; early Byrne-a (22 pages)	3	6	9	19	30	40
2-4: 2-Staton-c. 2,3-Byrne text illos.	3	6	9	14	20	25

EMERGENCY DOCTOR
Charlton Comics: Summer, 1963 (one-shot)
1 3 6 9 20 31 42

EMIL & THE DETECTIVES (See Movie Comics)

EMISSARY (Jim Valentino's...)
Image Comics (Shadowline): May, 2006 - No. 6 ($3.50)
1-6: 1-Rand-s/Ferreyra-a. 4-6-Long-s 3.50

EMMA (Adaptation of the Jane Austen novel)
Marvel Comics: May, 2011 - No. 5, Sept, 2011 ($3.99)
1-5-Nancy Butler-s/Janet K. Lee-a 4.00

EMMA FROST
Marvel Comics: Aug, 2003 - No. 18, Feb, 2005 ($2.50/$2.99)
1-7-Emma in high school; Bollers-s/Green-a/Horn-c 3.00
8-18-($2.99) 3.00
... Vol. 1: Higher Learning TPB (2004, $7.99, digest size) r/#1-6 8.00
... Vol. 2: Mind Games TPB (2005, $7.99, digest size) r/#7-12 8.00
... Vol. 3: Bloom TPB (2005, $7.99, digest size) r/#13-18 8.00

EMMA PEEL & JOHN STEED (See The Avengers)

EMPEROR'S NEW CLOTHES, THE
Dell Publishing Co.: 1950 (10¢, 68 pgs., 1/2 size, oblong)
nn - (Surprise Books series) 7 14 21 37 46 55

EMPIRE
Image Comics (Gorilla): May, 2000 - No. 2, Sept, 2000 ($2.50)
DC Comics: No. 0, Aug, 2003; Sept, 2003 - No. 6, Feb, 2004 ($4.95/$2.50, limited series)
1,2: 1 (5/00)-Waid-s/Kitson-a; w/Crimson Plague prologue 3.00
0-(8/03) reprints #1,2 5.00
1-6: 1-(9/03) new Waid-s/Kitson-a/c 3.00
TPB (DC, 2004, $14.95) r/series; Kitson sketch pages; Waid intro. 15.00

EMPIRE OF THE DEAD: ACT ONE (George Romero's...)
Marvel Comics: Mar, 2014 - No. 5, Aug, 2014 ($3.99)
1-5-George Romero-s/Alex Maleev-a/c; zombies & vampires 4.00

Empyre #1 © MAR

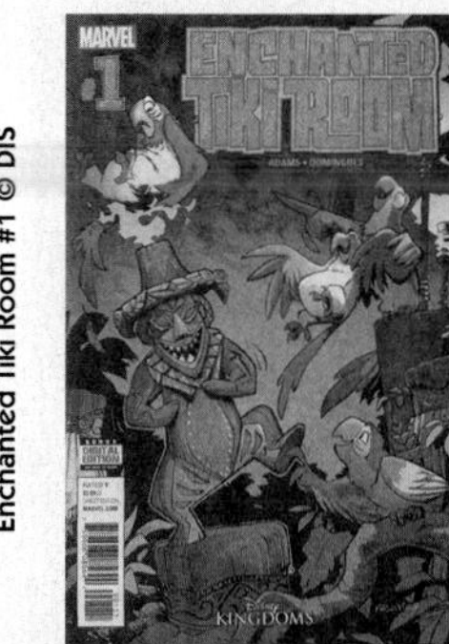

Enchanted Tiki Room #1 © DIS

Enigma #2 © DC

	GD 2.0	VG 4.0	FN 6.0	VF 8.0	VF/NM 9.0	NM- 9.2

EMPIRE OF THE DEAD: ACT TWO (George Romero's...)
Marvel Comics: Nov, 2014 - No. 5, Mar, 2015 ($3.99)

1-5-George Romero-s/Dalibor Talajic-a; zombies & vampires 4.00

EMPIRE OF THE DEAD: ACT THREE (George Romero's...)
Marvel Comics: Jun, 2015 - No. 5, Nov, 2015 ($3.99)

1-5-George Romero-s/Andrea Mutti-a; zombies & vampires 4.00

EMPIRE STRIKES BACK, THE (See Marvel Comics Super Special #16 & Marvel Special Edition)

EMPIRE: UPRISING
IDW Publishing: Apr, 2015 - No. 4, Jul, 2015 ($3.99)

1-4: Sequel to the 2003-2004 series; Waid-s/Kitson-a; two covers on each 4.00

EMPRESS
Marvel Comics (Icon): Jun, 2016 - No. 7, Jan, 2017 ($3.99/$5.99)

1-6-Millar-s/Immonen-a 4.00
7-($5.99) 6.00

EMPTY, THE
Image Comics: Feb, 2015 - No. 6, Sept, 2015 ($3.50/$3.99)

1-3-Jimmie Robinson-s/a 3.50
4-6-($3.99) 4.00

EMPTY LOVE STORIES
Slave Labor #1 & 2/Funny Valentine Press: Nov, 1994 - No. 2 ($2.95, B&W)

1,2: Steve Darnall scripts in all. 1-Alex Ross-c. 2-(8/96)-Mike Allred-c 4.00
1,2-2nd printing (Funny Valentine Press) 3.00
... 1999-Jeff Smith-c; Doran-a 4.00
..."Special" (2.95) Ty Templeton-c 4.00

EMPTY ZONE
Image Comics: Jun, 2015 - No. 10, Jul, 2016 ($3.50/$3.99)

1-8-Jason Shawn Alexander-s/a 3.50
9,10-($3.99) 4.00

EMPYRE (Also see Road to Empyre)
Marvel Comics: Sept, 2020 - No. 6 ($5.99/$4.99, weekly limited series)

1-($5.99) Ewing & Slott-s/Schiti-a; multiple covers; Fantastic Four & the Avengers app. 6.00
2-5-($4.99) 2-Carol Danvers gains the Accuser hammer. 3-Black Panther app. 5.00
6-($5.99) Ewing & Slott-s/Schiti-a; FF, Avengers, Spider-Man, Wolverine app. 6.00
...: Aftermath Avengers #1 (11/20, $4.99) Wedding of Hulkling and Wiccan 5.00
...: Fallout Fantastic Four #1 (11/20, $3.99) Slott-s/Izaakse-a; Uatu returns 4.00
...: Fantastic Four #0 (6/20, $4.99) Slott-s/Silva-a; leads into Empyre #1; The Profiteer app. 5.00
... Handbook 1 (6/20, $4.99) Profile pages of participants, teams, alien races 5.00
...: Savage Avengers 1 (9/20, $4.99) Duggan-s/Smallwood-a; Conan & Venom app. 5.00

EMPYRE: AVENGERS
Marvel Comics: No. 0, Jul, 2020; Sept, 2020 - No. 3 Oct, 2020 ($4.99/$3.99 limited series)

0-($4.99) Ewing-s/Larraz-a 5.00
1-3-($3.99) Zub-s/Magno-a; Avengers & Ka-Zar app. 4.00

EMPYRE: CAPTAIN AMERICA
Marvel Comics: Sept, 2020 - No. 3, Oct, 2020 ($3.99 limited series)

1-3-P.K. Johnson-s/Olivetti-a 4.00

EMPYRE: X-MEN
Marvel Comics: Sept, 2020 - No. 4, Oct, 2020 ($4.99 limited series)

1-4: 1-Hickman & Howard-s/Buffagni-a. 2-Werneck-a; Hordeculture app. 5.00

ENCHANTED APPLES OF OZ, THE (See First Comics Graphic Novel #5)

ENCHANTED TIKI ROOM
Marvel Comics (Disney Kingdoms): Dec, 2016 - No. 5, Apr, 2017 ($3.99)

1-5-Jon Adams-s/Horacio Domingues-a 4.00

ENCHANTER
Eclipse Comics: Apr, 1987 - No. 3, Aug. 1987 ($2.00, B&W, limited series)

1-3 3.00

ENCHANTING LOVE
Kirby Publishing Co.: Oct, 1949 - No. 6, July, 1950 (All 52 pgs.)

	GD	VG	FN	VF	VF/NM	NM-
1-Photo-c	23	46	69	136	223	310
2-Photo-c; Powell-a	14	28	42	82	121	160
3,4,6: 3-Jimmy Stewart photo-c. 4-Photo-c	14	28	42	81	118	155
5-Ingels-a, 9 pgs.; photo-c	20	40	60	114	182	250

ENCHANTMENT VISUALETTES (Magazine)
World Editions: Dec, 1949 - No. 5, Apr, 1950 (Painted c-1)

	GD	VG	FN	VF	VF/NM	NM-
1-Contains two romance comic strips each	26	52	78	154	252	350
2	17	34	51	103	162	220
3-5	15	30	45	88	137	185

ENDER IN EXILE (Orson Scott Card's...)
Marvel Comics: Aug, 2010 - No. 5, Dec, 2010 ($3.99, limited series)

1-5-Sequel to Ender's Game; Johnston-s/Mhan-a/Fiumara-c 4.00

ENDER'S GAME: BATTLE SCHOOL
Marvel Comics: Dec, 2008 - No. 5, Jun, 2009 ($3.99, limited series)

1-5-Adaptation of Orson Scott Card novel Ender's Game; Yost-s/Ferry-a. 1-Two covers 4.00
Ender's Game: Mazer in Prison Special (4/10, $3.99) Johnston-s/Mhan-a 4.00
Ender's Game: Recruiting Valentine (8/09, $3.99) Timothy Green-a 4.00
Ender's Game: The League War (6/10, $3.99) Aaron Johnston-s/Timothy Green-a 4.00
Ender's Game: War of Gifts Special (2/10, $4.99) Timothy Green-a 5.00

ENDER'S GAME: COMMAND SCHOOL
Marvel Comics: Nov, 2009 - No. 5, Apr, 2010 ($3.99, limited series)

1-5-Adaptation of Orson Scott Card novel Ender's Game; Yost-s/Ferry-a 4.00

ENDER'S SHADOW: BATTLE SCHOOL
Marvel Comics: Feb, 2009 - No. 5, Jun, 2009 ($3.99, limited series)

1-5-Adaptation of O.S. Card novel Ender's Shadow; Carey-s/Fiumara-a. 1-Two covers 4.00

ENDER'S SHADOW: COMMAND SCHOOL
Marvel Comics: Nov, 2009 - No. 5, Apr, 2010 ($3.99, limited series)

1-5-Adaptation of O.S. Card novel Ender's Shadow; Carey-s/Fiumara-a 4.00

END LEAGUE, THE
Dark Horse Comics: Dec, 2007 - No. 9, Nov, 2009 ($2.99/$3.99)

1-8: 1-Broome-c/a; Remender-s. 5,6-Canete-a 3.00
9-($3.99) MacDonald-a/Canete-c 4.00

END OF NATIONS
DC Comics: Jan, 2012 - No. 4, Apr, 2012 ($2.99, limited series)

1-4-Based on the Trion Worlds videogame; Sanchez-s/Guichet-a/Sprouse-c 3.00

END TIMES OF BRAM AND BEN
Image Comics: Jan, 2013 - No. 4, Apr, 2013 ($2.99, limited series)

1-4: 1-Rapture parody; Asmus & Festante-s/Broo-a. 1-Mahfood-c 3.00

ENEMY ACE SPECIAL (Also see Our Army at War #151, Showcase #57, 58 & Star Spangled War Stories #138)
DC Comics: 1990 ($1.00, one-shot)

1-Kubert-r/Our Army #151,153; c-r/Showcase 57 5.00

ENEMY ACE: WAR IDYLL
DC Comics: 1990 (Graphic novel)

Hardcover-George Pratt-s/painted-a/c 30.00
Softcover (1991, $14.95) 15.00

ENEMY ACE: WAR IN HEAVEN
DC Comics: 2001 - No. 2, 2001 ($5.95, squarebound, limited series)

1,2-Ennis-s; Von Hammer in WW2. 1-Weston & Alamy-a. 2-Heath-a 6.00
TPB (2003, $14.95) r/#1,2 & Star Spangled War Stories #139; Jim Dietz-painted-c 15.00

ENGINEHEAD
DC Comics: June, 2004 - No. 6, Nov, 2004 ($2.50, limited series)

1-6-Joe Kelly-s/Ted McKeever-a/c. 6-Metal Men app. 3.00

ENIGMA
DC Comics (Vertigo): Mar, 1993 - No. 8, Oct, 1993 ($2.50, limited series)

1-8: Milligan scripts 3.00
Trade paperback ($19.95)-reprints 20.00

ENO AND PLUM (Also see Cud Comics)
Oni Press: Mar, 1998 ($2.95, B&W)

1-Terry LaBan-s/c/a 3.00

ENSIGN O'TOOLE (TV)
Dell Publishing Co.: Aug-Oct, 1963

	GD	VG	FN	VF	VF/NM	NM-
1	3	6	9	21	33	45

ENSIGN PULVER (See Movie Classics)

ENTER THE HEROIC AGE
Marvel Comics: July, 2010 ($3.99, one-shot)

1-Short stories of Avengers Academy, Atlas, Black Widow, Thunderbolts; Hitch-c 4.00

EPIC
Marvel Comics (Epic Comics): 1992 - Book 4, 1992 ($4.95, lim. series, 52 pgs.)

Book One-Four: 2-Dorman painted-c 5.00
NOTE: *Alien Legion in #3. Cholly & Flytrap by* **Burden**(*scripts*) & **Suydam**(*art*) *in 3, 4. Dinosaurs in #4. Dreadlands in #1. Hellraiser in #1. Nightbreed in #2. Sleeze Brothers in #2. Stalkers in #1-4. Wild Cards in #1-4.*

Epic Illustrated #14 © MAR

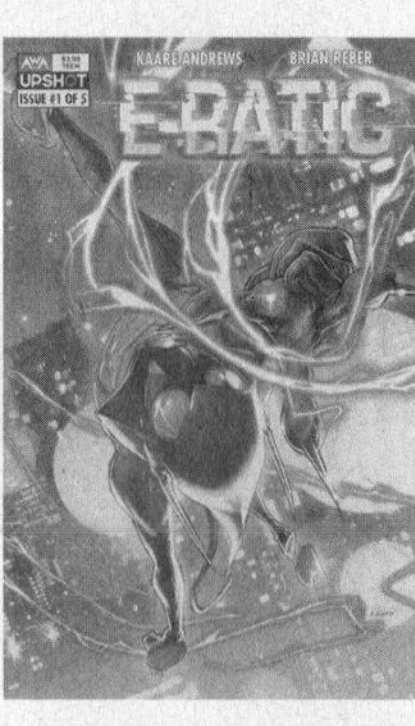

E-Ratic #1 © AWA

Essential Fantastic Four Vol. 1 © MAR

GD 2.0 | VG 4.0 | FN 6.0 | VF 8.0 | VF/NM 9.0 | NM- 9.2

GD 2.0 | VG 4.0 | FN 6.0 | VF 8.0 | VF/NM 9.0 | NM- 9.2

EPIC ANTHOLOGY
Marvel Comics (Epic Comics): Apr, 2004 ($5.99)

1-Short stories by various; debut 2nd Sleepwalker by Kirkman-s 6.00

EPIC ILLUSTRATED (Magazine)
Marvel Comics Group: Spring, 1980 - No. 34, Feb, 1986 ($2.00/$2.50, B&W/color, mature)

1-Frazetta-c; Silver Surfer/Galactus-sty; Wendy Pini-s/a; Suydam-s/a; Metamorphosis Odyssey begins (thru #9) Starlin-a 3 6 9 19 33 45
2,4-10: 2-Bissette/Veitch-a; Goodwin-s. 4-Ellison 15 pg. story w/Steacy-a; Hempel-s/a; Veitch-s/a. 5-Hildebrandts-c/interview; Jusko-a; Vess-s/a. 6-Ellison-s (26 pgs). 7-Adams-s/a(16 pgs.); BWS interview. 8-Suydam-s/a; Vess-s/a. 9-Conrad-c. 10-Marada the She-Wolf-c/sty(21 pgs.) by Claremont/Bolton 2 4 6 8 10 12
3-1st app. Dreadstar (face apps. in 1 panel in #2) 5 10 15 31 53 75
11-20: 11-Wood-a; Jusko-a. 12-Wolverton Spacehawk-r edited & recolored w/article on him; Muth-a. 13-Blade Runner preview by Williamson. 14-Elric of Melnibone by Russell; Revenge of the Jedi preview. 15-Vallejo-c & interview; 1st Dreadstar solo story (cont'd in Dreadstar #1). 16-B. Smith-c/a(2); Sim-s/a. 17-Starslammers preview. 18-Go Nagai; Williams-a. 19-Jabberwocky w/Hampton-a; Cheech Wizard-s. 20-The Sacred & the Profane begins by Ken Steacy; Elric by Gould; Williams-a 1 3 4 6 8 10
21-30: 21-Vess-s/a. 22-Frankenstein w/Wrightson-a. 26-Galactus series begins (thru #34); Cerebus the Aardvark story by Dave Sim. 27-Groo. 28-Cerebus. 29-1st Sheeva. 30-Cerebus; History of Dreadstar, Starlin-s/a; Williams-a; Vess-a
2 4 6 8 10 12
31-33: 31-Bolton-c/a. 32-Cerebus portfolio. 2 4 6 8 11 14
34-R.E.Howard tribute by Thomas-s/Plunkett-a; Moore-s/Veitch-a; Cerebus; Cholly & Flytrap w/Suydam-a; BWS-a 2 4 6 11 16 20
Sampler (early 1980 8 pg. preview giveaway) same cover as #1 with "Sampler" text 6.00

NOTE: ***N. Adams** a-7; c-6. **Austin** a-15-20i. **Bode** a-19, 23, 27r. **Bolton** a-7, 10-12, 15, 18, 22-25; c-10, 18, 22, 23. **Boris** c/a-15. **Brunner** c-12. **Buscema** a-1p, 9p, 11-13p. **Byrne/Austin** a-26-34. **Chaykin** a-2; c-8. **Conrad** a-2-5, 7-9, 25-34; c-17. **Corben** a-15; c-2. **Frazetta** c-1. **Golden** a-3r. **Gulacy** c/a-3. **Jeff Jones** c-25. **Kaluta** a-17r, 21, 24r, 26; c-4, 28. **Nebres** a-1. **Reese** a-12. **Russell** a-2-4, 9, 14, 33; c-14. **Simonson** a-17. **B. Smith** c/a-7, 16. **Starlin** a-1-9, 14, 15, 34. **Steranko** c-19. **Williamson** a-13, 27, 34. **Wrightson** a-13p, 22, 25, 27, 34; c-30.*

EPIC LITE
Marvel Comics (Epic Comics): Sept, 1991 ($3.95, 52 pgs., one-shot)

1-Bob the Alien, Normalman by Valentino 4.00

EPICURUS THE SAGE
DC Comics (Piranha Press): Vol. 1, 1991 - Vol. 2, 1991 ($9.95, 8-1/8x10-7/8")

Volume 1,2-Sam Kieth-c/a; Messner-Loebs-s 12.00
TPB (2003, $19.95) r/ #1,2, Fast Forward Rising the Sun; new story 20.00

EPILOGUE
IDW Publishing: Sept, 2008 - No. 4, Dec, 2008 ($3.99)

1-4-Steve Niles-s/Kyle Hotz-a/c 4.00

EQUILIBRIUM (Based on the 2002 movie)
American Mythology Prods.: 2016 - No. 3, 2017 ($3.99)

1-3-Pat Shand-s/Jason Craig-a; multiple covers 4.00
...: Deconstruction 1 (2017, $3.99) Moroney-s/Dela Cuesta-a 4.00
...: Gunkata Casebook 1 (2018, $3.99) Mell-s/Hilinski-a 4.00

ERADICATOR
DC Comics: Aug, 1996 - No. 3, Oct, 1996 ($1.75, limited series)

1-3: Superman app. 3.00

E-RATIC
AWA Studios: Dec, 2020 - No. 5 ($3.99, limited series)

1-3-Kaare Andrews-s/a/c. 1-Variant-c by Mike Deodato 4.00

ERNIE COMICS (Formerly Andy Comics #21; All Love Romances #26 on)
Current Books/Ace Periodicals: No. 22, Sept, 1948 - No. 25, Mar, 1949

nn (9/48,11/48; #22,23)-Teenage humor 13 26 39 72 101 130
24,25 10 20 30 56 76 95

ERRAND BOYS
Image Comics: Oct, 2018 - No. 5, Feb, 2019 ($3.99, limited series)

1-5-Kirkbridge-s/Koutsis-a 4.00

ESCAPADE IN FLORENCE (See Movie Comics)

ESCAPE FROM DEVIL'S ISLAND
Avon Periodicals: 1952

1-Kinstler-c; r/as Dynamic Adventures #9 45 90 135 284 480 675

ESCAPE FROM NEW YORK (Based on the Kurt Russell movie)
BOOM! Studios: Dec, 2014 - No. 16, Apr, 2016 ($3.99)

1-16: 1-8-Christopher Sebela-s/Diego Barreto-a; multiple covers on each. 9-16-Simic-a 4.00

ESCAPE FROM THE PLANET OF THE APES (See Power Record Comics)

ESCAPE TO WITCH MOUNTAIN (See Walt Disney Showcase No. 29)

ESCAPISTS, THE (See Michael Chabon Presents The Amazing Adventures of the Escapist)
Dark Horse Comics: July, 2006 - No. 6, Dec, 2006 ($1.00/$2.99, limited series)

1-($1.00) Frank Miller-c; r/Vaughan story from Michael Chabon... #8 3.00
2-6($2.99) Vaughan-s/Rolston & Alexander-a. 2-James Jean-c. 3-Cassaday-c 3.00

ESPERS (Also see Interface)
Eclipse Comics: July, 1986 - No. 5, Apr, 1987 ($1.25/$1.75, Mando paper)

1-5-James Hudnall story & David Lloyd-a. 3.00

ESPERS
Halloween Comics: V2#1, 1996 - No. 6, 1997 ($2.95, B&W) (1st Halloween Comics series)

V2#1-6: James D. Hudnall scripts 3.00
Undertow TPB ('98, $14.95) r/#1-6 15.00

ESPERS
Image Comics: V3#1, 1997 - No. 7, 1998 ($2.95, B&W, limited series)

V3#1-7: James D. Hudnall scripts 3.00
Black Magic TPB ('98, $14.95) r/#1-4 15.00

ESPIONAGE (TV)
Dell Publishing Co.: May-July, 1964

1 3 6 9 20 31 42

ESSENTIAL (Title series), **Marvel Comics**

--ANT-MAN, '02 (B&W- r) V1-Reprints app. from Tales To Astonish #27, #35-69; Kirby-c 15.00

--AVENGERS, '98 (B&W- r) V1-R-Avengers #1-24; new Immonen-c 15.00
V2(6/00)-Reprints Avengers #25-46, King-Size Special #1; Immonen-c 15.00
V3(3/01)-Reprints Avengers #47-68, Annual #2; Immonen-c 15.00
V4('04)-Reprints Avengers #69-97, Incredible Hulk #140; Neal Adams-c 17.00
V5('06)-Reprints Avengers #98-119, Daredevil #99, Defenders #8-11 17.00
V6('08)-Reprints Avengers #120-140, Giant Size #1-4, Capt. Marvel #33 & FF #150 17.00

--CAPTAIN AMERICA, '00 (B&W- r) V1-Reprints stories from Tales of Suspense #59-99, Captain America #100-102; new Romita & Milgrom-c 15.00
V2(1/02)-Reprints #103-126; Steranko-c 15.00
V3('06)-Reprints #127-153 17.00
V4('07)-Reprints #157-186 17.00

--CLASSIC X-MEN, '06 (B&W- r) (See Essential Uncanny X-Men for V1)
V2-($16.99) R-X-Men #25-53 & Avengers #53; Gil Kane-c 17.00

--CONAN, '00 (B&W- r) V1-R-Conan the Barbarian#1-25; new Buscema-c 15.00

--DAREDEVIL, '02 - V4 (B&W-r)
V1-R-Daredevil #1-25 15.00
V2-($16.99) R-Daredevil #26-48, Special #1, Fantastic Four #73 17.00
V3-($16.99) R-Daredevil #49-74, Iron Man #35-38 17.00
V4-($16.99) R-Daredevil #75-101, Avengers #111 17.00

--DAZZLER, '07 (B&W- r) V1-R/#1-21, X-Men #130-131, Amaz. Spider-Man #203 17.00

--DEFENDERS, '05 (B&W-r) V1-Reprints Doctor Strange #183, Sub-Mariner #22,34,35, Incredible Hulk #126, Marvel Feature #1-3, Defenders #1-14, Avengers #115-118 17.00
V2-($16.99) R- Defenders #15-30, Giant-Size Defenders #1-4, Marvel Two-In-One #6,7, Marvel Team-Up #33-35 and Marvel Treasury Edition #12 17.00
V3-($16.99) R- Defenders #31-60 and Annual #1 17.00

--DOCTOR STRANGE, '04 - V3 (B&W-r)
V1-($15.95) Reprints Strange Tales #110,111,114-168 17.00
V1 (2nd printing)-(2006, $16.99) Reprints Strange Tales #110,111,114-168 17.00
V2-($16.99) R-Doctor Strange #169-178,180-183; Avengers #61, Sub-Mariner #22 Marvel Feature #1, Incredible Hulk #126 and Marvel Premiere #3-14 17.00
V3-($16.99) R-Doctor Strange #1-29 & Annual #1;Tomb of Dracula #44,45 17.00

--FANTASTIC FOUR, '98 - V6 (B&W-r)
V1-Reprints FF #1-20, Annual #1; new Alan Davis-c; multiple printings exist 17.00
V2-Reprints FF #21-40, Annual #2; Davis and Farmer-c 15.00
V3-Reprints FF #41-63, Annual #3,4; Davis-c 15.00
V4-Reprints FF #64-83, Annual #5,6 17.00
V5-Reprints FF #84-110 17.00
V6-Reprints FF #111-137 17.00

--GHOST RIDER, '05 (B&W-r) V1-Reprints Marvel Spotlight #5-12, Ghost Rider #1-20 and Daredevil #138 17.00
V2-Reprints Ghost Rider #21-50 17.00

--GODZILLA, '06 (B&W-r) V1-Godzilla #1-24 20.00

--HOWARD THE DUCK, '02 (B&W- r) V1-Reprints #1-27, Annual #1; plus stories from Marvel Treasury Ed. #12, Man-Thing #1, Giant-Size Man-Thing #4,5, Fear #19; Bolland-c 15.00

--HULK, '99 (B&W-r) V1-R-Incred. Hulk #1-6, Tales To Astonish stories; new Timm-c 15.00
V2-Reprints Tales To Astonish #102-117, Annual #1 15.00

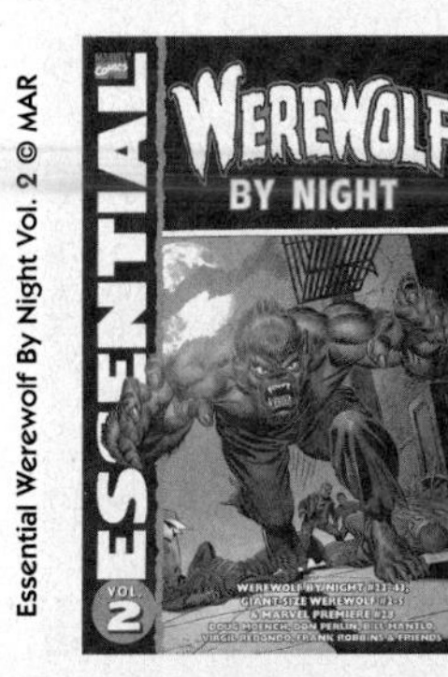

Essential Werewolf By Night Vol. 2 © MAR

The Establishment #8 © DC

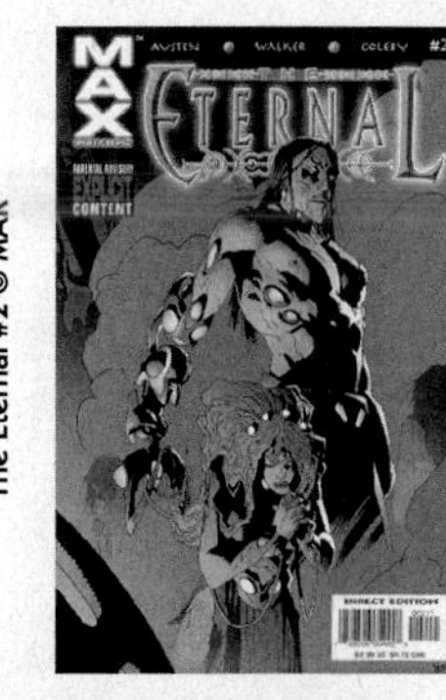

The Eternal #2 © MAR

GD 2.0 | VG 4.0 | FN 6.0 | VF 8.0 | VF/NM 9.0 | NM- 9.2

V3-Reprints Incredible Hulk #118-142, Capt. Marvel #20&21, Avengers #88 17.00
V4-Reprints Incredible Hulk #143-170 17.00
V5-Reprints Incredible Hulk #171-200, Annual #5 17.00

--**HUMAN TORCH,** '03 (B&W-r) V1-Strange Tales #101-134 & Ann. 2; Kirby-c 15.00

--**IRON MAN,** '00 - V3 (B&W-r)
V1-Reprints Tales Of Suspense #39-72; new Timm-c and back-c 15.00
V2-Reprints Tales Of Suspense #73-99, Tales To Astonish #82 & Iron Man #1-11 17.00
V3-Reprints Iron Man #12-38 & Daredevil #73 17.00

--**KILLRAVEN,** '05 (B&W-r) V1-Reprints Amazing Adventures V2 #18-39, Marvel Team-Up #45, Marvel Graphic Novel #7, Killraven #1 (2001) 17.00

--**LUKE CAGE, POWER MAN,** '05 (B&W-r) V1-Hero For Hire #1-16 & Power Man #17-27 17.00
V2-Reprints Power Man #28-49 & Annual #1 17.00

--**MAN-THING,** '06 (B&W-r) V1-Reprints Savage Tales #1, Astonishing Tales #12-13, Adventure Into Fear #10-19, Man-Thing #1-14, Giant-Size Man-Thing #1-2 & Monsters Unleashed #5,8,9 17.00
V2-R/Man-Thing #15-22 & #1-11 ('79 series), Giant-Size Man-Thing #3-5, Rampaging Hulk #7, Marvel Team-Up #68, Marvel Two-In-One #43 & Doctor Strange #41 17.00

--**MARVEL HORROR,** '06 (B&W-r) V1-R/#Ghost Rider #1-2, Marvel Spotlight #12-24, Son of Satan #1-8, Marvel Two-In-One #14, Marvel Team-Up #32,80,81, Vampire Tales #2-3, Haunt of Horror #2,4,5, Marvel Premiere #27, & Marvel Preview #7 17.00

--**MARVEL SAGA,** '08 (B&W-r) V1-R/#1-12 17.00

--**MARVEL TEAM-UP,** '02 - V2 (B&W-r) V1('02, '06)-R/#1-24 17.00
V2-R/#25-51 and Marvel Two-In-One #17 17.00

--**MARVEL TWO-IN-ONE,** '05 - V2 (B&W-r)
V1-Reprints Marvel Feature #11&12, Marvel Two-In-One #1-20,22-25 & Annual #1, Marvel Team-Up #47 and Fantastic Four Ann. #11 17.00
V2-R/#26-52 & Annual #2,3 17.00

--**MONSTER OF FRANKENSTEIN,** '04 (B&W-r) V1-Reprints Monster of Frankenstein #1-5, Frankenstein Monster #6-18, Giant-Size Werewolf #2, Monsters Unleashed #2,4-10 & Legion of Monsters #1 17.00

--**MOON KNIGHT,** '06 (B&W-r) V1-Reprints Moon Knight #1-10 and early apps. 17.00
V2-R/#11-30 17.00

--**MS. MARVEL,** '07 (B&W-r) V1-Reprints Ms. Marvel #1-23, Marvel Super-Heroes Magazine #10,11, and Avengers Annual #10 17.00

--**NOVA,** '06 (B&W-r) V1-Reprints Nova #1-25, AS-M #171, Marvel Two-In-One Ann. #3 17.00

--**OFFICIAL HANDBOOK OF THE MARVEL UNIVERSE,** '06 (B&W-r) V1-Reprints #1-15 profiling Abomination through Zzzax; dead and inactive characters; weapons & hardware; wraparound-c by Byrne 17.00

--**OFFICIAL HANDBOOK OF THE MARVEL UNIVERSE - DELUXE EDITION,** '06 (B&W-r)
V1-Reprints #1-7 profiling Abomination through Magneto; wraparound-c by Byrne 17.00
V2-Reprints #8-14 profiling Magus through Wolverine; wraparound-c by Byrne 17.00
V3-Reprints #15-20 profiling Wonder Man through Zzzax & Book of the Dead 17.00

--**OFFICIAL HANDBOOK OF THE MARVEL UNIVERSE - MASTER EDITION,** '08 (B&W-r)
V1-Reprints profiling Abomination through Gargoyle 17.00
V2-Reprints profiles 17.00

--**OFFICIAL HANDBOOK OF THE MARVEL UNIVERSE - UPDATE '89,** '06 (B&W-r)
V1-Reprints #1-8; wraparound-c by Frenz 17.00

--**PETER PARKER, THE SPECTACULAR SPIDER-MAN,** '05 (B&W-r) V1-Reprints #1-31 17.00
V2-Reprints #32-53 & Annual #1,2; Amazing Spider-Man Annual #13 17.00
V3-Reprints #54-74 & Annual #3; Frank Miller-c 17.00

--**POWER MAN AND IRON FIST,** '07 (B&W-r) V1-R/#50-72,74-75 17.00

--**PUNISHER,** '04, '06 - '12 (B&W-r) V1-Reprints early app. in Amazing Spider-Man, Captain America, Daredevil, Marvel Preview and Punisher #1-5 (2 printings) 17.00
V2-Punisher #1-20, Annual #1 and Daredevil #257 17.00
V3-Punisher #21-40, Annual #2,3 17.00
V4-Punisher #41-59 17.00

--**RAMPAGING HULK,** '08 (B&W-r) V1-R/#1-9, The Hulk! #10-15 & Incredible Hulk #269 17.00

--**SAVAGE SHE-HULK,** '06 (B&W-r) V1-R/#1-25 17.00

--**SILVER SURFER,** '98 - Present (B&W-r)
V1-R-material from SS#1-18 and Fantastic Four Ann. #5 15.00
V2-R-SS#1(1982), SS#1-18 & Ann#1(1987), Epic Illustrated #1, Marvel Fanfare #51 17.00

--**SPIDER-MAN,** '96 - V8 (B&W-r)
V1-R-AF #15, Amaz. S-M #1-20, Ann. #1 (2 printings) 15.00
V2-R-Amaz. Spider-Man #21-43, Annual #2,3 15.00
V3-R-Amaz. Spider-Man #44-68 15.00
V4-R-Amaz. Spider-Man #69-89; Annual #4,5; new Timm-f&b-c 15.00
V5-R-Amaz. Spider-Man #90-113; new Romita-c 15.00
V6-R-Amaz. Spider-Man #114-137, Giant-Size Super-Heroes #1 G-S S-M #1,2 17.00
V7-R-Amaz. Spider-Man #138-160, Annual #10; Giant-Size Spider-Man #3-5 17.00
V8-R-Amaz. Spider-Man #161-185, Annual #11; G-S Spider-Man #6; Nova #12 17.00

--**SPIDER-WOMAN,** '05 (B&W-r) V1-Reprints Marvel Spotlight #32, Marvel Two-In-One #29-33, Spider-Woman #1-25 17.00
V2-R-Spider-Woman #26-50, Marvel Team-Up #97 & Uncanny X-Men #148 17.00

--**SUPER-VILLAIN TEAM-UP,** '04 (B&W-r) V1-r/S-V T-U #1-14 & 16-17, Giant-Size S-V T-U #1,2; Avengers #154-156; Champions #16, & Astonishing Tales #1-8 17.00

--**TALES OF THE ZOMBIE,** '06 (B&W-r) V1-($16.99) r/#1-10 & Dracula Lives #1,2 17.00

--**THOR,** '01 (B&W-r) V1-R-Journey Into Mystery #83-112 15.00
V2-($16.99) R-Thor #113-136 & Annual #1,2 17.00
V3-($16.99) R-Thor #137-166 17.00

--**TOMB OF DRACULA,** '03 - V4 (B&W-r) V1-R-Tomb of Dracula #1-25, Werewolf By Night #15, Giant-Size Chillers #1 15.00
V2-($16.99) R-Tomb of Dracula #26-49, Giant-Size Dracula #2-5, Dr. Strange #14 17.00
V3-($16.99) R-Tomb of Dracula #50-70, Tomb of Dracula Magazine #1-4 17.00
V4-($16.99) R/Stories from Tomb of Dracula Magazine #2-6, Dracula Lives! #1-13, and Frankenstein Monster #7-9 17.00

--**UNCANNY X-MEN,** '99 (B&W reprints) (See Essential Classic X-Men for V2)
V1-Reprints X-Men (1st series) #1-24; Timm-c 15.00

ESSENTIAL VERTIGO: THE SANDMAN
DC Comics (Vertigo): Aug, 1996 - No. 32, Mar, 1999 ($1.95/$2.25, reprints)

1-13,15-31: Reprints Sandman, 2nd series 4.00
14-($2.95) 4.00
32-($4.50) Reprints Sandman Special #1 4.50

ESSENTIAL VERTIGO: SWAMP THING
DC Comics: Nov, 1996 - No. 24, Oct, 1998 ($1.95/$2.25,B&W, reprints)

1-11,13-24: 1-9-Reprints Alan Moore's Swamp Thing stories 4.00
12-($3.50) r/Annual #2 4.00

ESSENTIAL WEREWOLF BY NIGHT
Marvel Comics: 2005 - V2 (B&W reprints)

V1-($16.99) r/Marvel Spotlight #2-4, Werewolf By Night 1-23, Marvel Team-Up #12, Tomb of Dracula #18, Giant-Size Creatures #1 17.00
V2-R/#22-43, Giant-Size Werewolf #2-5 and Marvel Premiere #28 17.00

ESSENTIAL WOLVERINE
Marvel Comics: 1999 - V4 (B&W reprints)

V1-r/#1-23, V2-r/#24-47, V3-R/#48-69, V4-R/#70-90 17.00

ESSENTIAL X-FACTOR
Marvel Comics: 2005 - V2 (B&W reprints)

V1-($16.99) r/X-Factor #1-16 & Annual #1, Avengers #262, Fantastic Four #286, Thor #373&374 and Power Pack #27 17.00
V2-Reprints X-Factor #17-35 & Annual #2, Thor #378 17.00

ESSENTIAL X-MEN
Marvel Comics: 1996 - V8 (B&W reprints)

V1-V4: V1-R/Giant Size X-Men #1, X-Men #94-119. V2-R-X-Men #120-144. V3-R-Uncanny X-Men #145-161, Ann. #3-5. V4-Uncanny X-Men #162-179, Ann. #6 15.00
V5-($16.99) R/Uncanny X-Men #180-198, Ann. #7-8 17.00
V6-($16.99) R/Uncanny X-Men #199-213, Ann. #9, New Mutants Special Edition #1, X-Factor #9-11, New Mutants #46, Thor #373-374 and Power Pack #27 17.00
V7-($16.99) R/Uncanny X-Men #214-228, Ann. #10,11, and F.F. vs. The X-Men #1-4 17.00
V8-($16.99) R/Uncanny X-Men #229-243, Ann. #12 & X-Factor #36-39 17.00

ESTABLISHMENT, THE (Also see The Authority and The Monarchy)
DC Comics (WildStorm): Nov, 2001 - No. 13, Nov, 2002 ($2.50)

1-13-Edginton-s/Adlard-a 3.00

ETERNAL
BOOM! Studios: Dec, 2014 - No. 4, Apr, 2015 ($3.99)

1-4: 1-Harms-s/Valletta-a/Irving-c 4.00

ETERNAL, THE
Marvel Comics (MAX): Aug, 2003 - No. 6, Jan, 2004 ($2.99, mature)

1-6-Austen-s/Walker-a 3.00

ETERNAL BIBLE, THE
Authentic Publications: 1946 (Large size) (16 pgs. in color)

1 16 32 48 94 147 200

ETERNAL EMPIRE
Image Comics: May, 2017 - No. 10, Aug, 2018 ($3.99)

1-9-Sarah Vaughn & Jonathan Luna-s/Luna-a/c 4.00

The Eternals #11 © MAR

Eternal Warrior #16 © VAL

Event Leviathan #4 © DC

	GD	VG	FN	VF	VF/NM	NM-
	2.0	4.0	6.0	8.0	9.0	9.2

10-($4.99) Conclusion 5.00

ETERNALS, THE
Marvel Comics Group: July, 1976 - No. 19, Jan, 1978

	GD	VG	FN	VF	VF/NM	NM-
1-(Regular 25¢ edition)-Origin & 1st app. Ikaris & The Eternals	10	20	30	64	132	200
1-(30¢-c variant, limited distribution)	36	72	108	259	580	900
2-(Reg. 25¢ edition)-1st app. Ajak & The Celestials	5	10	15	34	60	85
2-(30¢-c variant, limited distribution)	13	26	39	89	195	300
3-19: 3-1st app. Sersi. 5-1st app. Makarri, Domo, Zuras, & Thena. 11-1st app. Kingo. 14,15-Cosmic powered Hulk-c/story	3	6	9	14	19	24
12-16-(35¢-c variants, limited distribution)	9	18	27	59	117	175
Annual 1(10/77)	3	6	9	14	20	25

... No. 1 Facsimile Edition (2/20, $3.99) Reprints #1 with original 1976 ads 4.00
...: Secrets From the Marvel Universe 1 (2/20, $4.99) Reprints from What If? #23-30 5.00
Eternals by Jack Kirby HC (2006, $75.00, dust jacket) r/#1-19 & Annual #1; intro by Royer; letter pages from #1,2,Annual #1; afterwords by Robert Greenberger 75.00
NOTE: *Kirby c/a(p) in all.*

ETERNALS, THE
Marvel Comics: Oct, 1985 - No. 12, Sept, 1986 (Maxi-series, mando paper)

1,12 (52 pgs.): 12-Williamson-a(i) 5.00
2-11 4.00

ETERNALS
Marvel Comics: Aug, 2006 - No. 7, Mar, 2007 ($3.99, limited series)

1-7-Neil Gaiman-s/John Romita Jr.-a/Rick Berry-c 4.00
1-7-Variant covers by Romita Jr. 4.00
1-Variant cover by Coipel 4.00
... Sketchbook (2006, $1.99, B&W) character sketches and sketch pages from #1 4.00
HC (2007, $29.99, dustjacket) r/#1-7; gallery of variant covers; sketches, Gaiman interview, Gaiman's original proposal; background essay on Kirby's Eternals 30.00

ETERNALS
Marvel Comics: Aug, 2008 - No. 9, May, 2009 ($2.99)

1-9: 1-6-Acuña-a/c; Knauf-s. 2,4-Iron Man app. 7,8-Nguyen-a; X-Men app. 3.00
Annual 1 (1/09, $3.99) Alixe-a/McGuinness-c; & reprint from Eternals #7 ('77) Kirby-s/a 4.00

ETERNALS
Marvel Comics: Mar, 2021 - Present ($4.99/$3.99)

1-($4.99) Kieron Gillen-s/Esad Ribic-a; Ikaris returns; Iron Man & Thanos app. 5.00
2-($3.99) Ikaris battles Thanos 4.00

ETERNAL SOULFIRE (Also see Soulfire)
Aspen MLT, Inc.: Jul, 2015 - No. 6, Feb, 2016 ($3.99, limited series)

1-6-Multiple covers on each. 1-Krul-s/Konat-a. 3-Tovar & Konat-a 4.00

ETERNALS: THE HEROD FACTOR
Marvel Comics: Nov, 1991 ($2.50, 68 pgs.)

1 4.00

ETERNAL WARRIOR (See Solar #10 & 11)
Valiant/Acclaim Comics (Valiant): Aug, 1992 - No. 50, Mar, 1996 ($2.25/$2.50)

	GD	VG	FN	VF	VF/NM	NM-
1-Unity x-over; Miller-c; origin Eternal Warrior & Aram (Armstrong)	2	4	6	8	10	12
1-($2.25-c) Gold logo	3	6	9	14	19	24
1-Gold foil logo on embossed cover; no cover price	4	8	12	23	37	50
2,3,5-8: 2-Unity x-over; Simonson-c. 3-Archer & Armstrong x-over. 5-2nd full app. Bloodshot (12/92; see Rai #0). 6,7: 6-2nd app. Master Darque. 8-Flip book w/Archer & Armstrong #8						4.00
4-1st brief app. Bloodshot (last pg.); see Rai #0 for 1st full app.; Cowan-c	3	6	9	18	28	38
9-25,27-34: 9-1st Book of Geomancer. 14-16-Bloodshot app. 18-Doctor Mirage cameo. 19-Doctor Mirage app. 22-W/bound-in trading card. 25-Archer & Armstrong app.; cont'd from A&A #25						3.00
26-($2.75, 44 pgs.)-Flip book w/Archer & Armstrong						4.00
35-50: 35-Double-c; $2.50-c begins. 50-Geomancer app.						3.00
Special 1 (2/96, $2.50)-Wings of Justice; Art Holcomb script						3.00
Yearbook 1 (1993, $3.95), 2(1994, $3.95)						4.00

ETERNAL WARRIOR (Also see Wrath of the Eternal Warrior)
Valiant Entertainment: Sept, 2013 - No. 8, Apr, 2014 ($3.99)

1-8: 1-Pak-s/Hairsine-a; 2 covers. 2-Hairsine & Crain-a 4.00
...: Awakening 1 (5/17, $3.99) Venditti-s/Guedes-a 4.00

ETERNAL WARRIORS: BLACKWORKS
Acclaim Comics (Valiant Heroes): Mar, 1998 ($3.50, one-shot)

1 3.50

	GD	VG	FN	VF	VF/NM	NM-
	2.0	4.0	6.0	8.0	9.0	9.2

ETERNAL WARRIOR: DAYS OF STEEL
Valiant Entertainment: Nov, 2014 - No. 3, Jan, 2015 ($3.99)

1-3-Milligan-s/Nord-a 4.00

ETERNAL WARRIORS: DIGITAL ALCHEMY
Acclaim Comics (Valiant Heroes): Vol. 2, Sep, 1997 ($3.95, one-shot, 64 pgs.)

Vol. 2-Holcomb-s/Eaglesham-a(p) 4.00

ETERNAL WARRIORS: FIST AND STEEL
Acclaim Comics (Valiant): May, 1996 - No. 2, June, 1996 ($2.50, lim. series)

1,2: Geomancer app. in both. 1-Indicia reads "June." 2-Bo Hampton-a 4.00

ETERNAL WARRIORS: TIME AND TREACHERY
Acclaim Comics (Valiant Heroes): Vol. 1, Jun, 1997 ($3.95, one-shot, 48 pgs.)

Vol. 1-Reintro Aram, Archer, Ivar the Timewalker, & Gilad the Warmaster; 1st app. Shalla Redburn; Art Holcomb script 4.00

ETERNITY (Also see Divinity)
Valiant Entertainment: Oct, 2017 - No. 4, Jan, 2018 ($3.99, limited series)

1-4: 1-Kindt-s/Hairsine-a; 5 covers 4.00

ETERNITY GIRL
DC Comics (Young Animal): May, 2018 - No. 6, Oct, 2018 ($3.99)

1-6-Visaggio-s/Liew-a. 1-Intro. Caroline Sharp 4.00

ETERNITY SMITH
Renegade Press: Sept, 1986 - No. 5, May, 1987 ($1.25/$1.50, 36 pgs.)

1-5: 1st app. Eternity Smith. 5-Death of Jasmine 4.00

ETERNITY SMITH
Hero Comics: Sept, 1987 - No. 9, 1988 ($1.95)

V2#1-9: 8-Indigo begins 4.00

ETHER
Dark Horse Comics: Nov, 2016 - No. 5, Mar, 2017 ($3.99)

1-5-Matt Kindt-s/David Rubin-a 4.00

ETHER ("The Copper Golems" on cover)
Dark Horse Comics: May, 2018 - No. 5, Sept, 2018 ($3.99)

1-5-Matt Kindt-s/David Rubin-a 4.00

ETHER: THE DISAPPEARANCE OF VIOLET BELL
Dark Horse Comics: Sept, 2019 - No. 5, Jan, 2020 ($3.99)

1-5-Matt Kindt-s/David Rubin-a 4.00

ETTA KETT
King Features Syndicate/Standard: No. 11, Dec, 1948 - No. 14, Sept, 1949

	GD	VG	FN	VF	VF/NM	NM-
11-Teenage	15	30	45	85	130	175
12-14	12	24	36	67	94	120

EUTHANAUTS
IDW Publishing (Black Crown): Jul, 2018 - No. 5, Nov, 2018 ($3.99)

1-5-Tini Howard-s/Nick Robles-a 4.00

EVA: DAUGHTER OF THE DRAGON
Dynamite Entertainment: 2007 ($4.99, one-shot)

1-Two covers by Jo Chen and Edgar Salazar; Jerwa-s/Salazar-a 5.00

EVANGELINE (Also see Primer)
Comico/First Comics V2#1 on/Lodestone Publ.: 1984 - #2, 6/84; V2#1, 5/87 - V2#12, Mar, 1989 (Baxter paper)

1,2, V2#1 (5/87) - 12, Special #1 (1986, $2.00)-Lodestone Publ. 4.00

EVA THE IMP
Red Top Comic/Decker: 1957 - No. 2, Nov, 1957

	GD	VG	FN	VF	VF/NM	NM-
1,2	6	12	18	31	38	45

EVEN MORE FUND COMICS (Benefit book for the Comic Book Legal Defense Fund) (Also see More Fund Comics)
Sky Dog Press: Sept, 2004 ($10.00, B&W, trade paperback)

nn-Anthology of short stories and pin-ups by various; Spider-Man-c by Cho 10.00

EVENT LEVIATHAN (See Action Comics #1007-1012 and Leviathan Dawn one-shot)
DC Comics: Aug, 2019 - No. 6, Jan, 2020 ($3.99, limited series)

1-6-Bendis-s/Maleev-a; Batman, Lois Lane, The Question, Green Arrow, Manhunter app. 4.00

E.V.E. PROTOMECHA
Image Comics (Top Cow): Mar, 2000 - No. 6, Sept, 2000 ($2.50)

	GD	VG	FN	VF	VF/NM	NM-
Preview ($5.95) Flip book w/Soul Saga preview	2	4	6	8	10	12
1-6: 1-Covers by Finch, Madureira, Garza. 2-Turner var-c						3.00
1-Another Universe variant-c						5.00

Ever The Way Out GN © Terry Moore

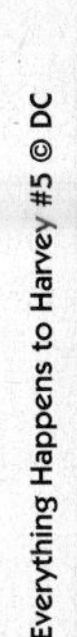

Everything Happens to Harvey #5 © DC

Evil Ernie (2012 series) #1 © DYN

	GD 2.0	VG 4.0	FN 6.0	VF 8.0	VF/NM 9.0	NM- 9.2

TPB (5/01, $17.95) r/#1-6 plus cover galley and sketch pages 18.00

EVERAFTER (See Fables)
DC Comics (Vertigo): Nov, 2016 - No. 12, Oct, 2017 ($3.99)
1-12: 1-Justus & Sturges-s/Travis Moore-a; Snow & Bigby app. 7-Buckingham-a 4.00

EVERQUEST: ... (Based on online role-playing game)
DC Comics (WildStorm): 2002 ($5.95, one-shots)
The Ruins of Kunark - Jim Lee & Dan Norton-a; McQuaid & Lee-s; Lee-c 6.00
Transformations - Philip Tan-a; Devin Grayson-s; Portacio-c 6.00

EVER THE WAY OUT
Abstract Studio: 2020 ($17.99, B&W, graphic novel)
GN - Terry Moore-s/a; intro. Everly; Rachel & Lilith app. 18.00

EVERYBODY'S COMICS (See Fox Giants)

EVERYMAN, THE
Marvel Comics (Epic Comics): Nov, 1991 ($4.50, one-shot, 52 pgs.)

	GD	VG	FN	VF	VF/NM	NM-
1-Mike Allred-a	1	2	3	4	5	7

EVERYTHING
Dark Horse Comics (Berger Books): Sept, 2019 - No. 5, Jan, 2020 ($3.99)
1-5-Christopher Cantwell-s/I.N.J. Culbard-a 4.00

EVERYTHING HAPPENS TO HARVEY
National Periodical Publications: Sept-Oct, 1953 - No. 7, Sept-Oct, 1954

	GD	VG	FN	VF	VF/NM	NM-
1	40	80	120	246	411	575
2	21	42	63	122	199	275
3-7	16	32	48	98	154	210

EVERYTHING'S ARCHIE
Archie Publications: May, 1969 - No. 157, Sept, 1991 (Giant issues No. 1-20)

	GD	VG	FN	VF	VF/NM	NM-
1-(68 pages)	9	18	27	57	111	165
2-(68 pages)	4	8	12	28	47	65
3-5-(68 pages)	4	8	12	25	40	55
6-13-(68 pages)	3	6	9	17	26	35
14-31-(52 pages)	2	4	6	13	18	22
32 (7/74)-50 (8/76)	2	4	6	8	10	12
51-80 (12/79),100 (4/82)	1	2	3	5	6	8
81-99						6.00
101-103,105,106,108-120						5.00
104,107-Cheryl Blossom app.	1	2	3	4	5	7
121-156: 142,148-Gene Colan-a						4.00
157-Last issue						5.00

EVERYTHING'S DUCKY (Movie)
Dell Publishing Co.: No. 1251, 1961

	GD	VG	FN	VF	VF/NM	NM-
Four Color 1251-Mickey Rooney & Buddy Hackett photo-c	6	12	18	37	66	95

EVE STRANGER
IDW Publishing (Black Crown): Apr, 2019 - No. 5, Aug, 2019 ($3.99)
1-5-David Barnett-s/Philip Bond-a/c 4.00

EVE: VALKYRIE (Based on the video game)
Dark Horse Comics: Oct, 2015 - No. 4, Jan, 2016 ($3.99, limited series)
1-4-Brian Wood-s/Eduardo Francisco-a 4.00

EVIL DEAD, THE (Movie)
Dark Horse Comics: Jan, 2008 - No. 4, Apr, 2008 ($2.99, limited series)
1-4-Adaptation of the Sam Raimi/Bruce Campbell movie; Bolton painted-a/c 4.00

EVIL DEAD 2 (Movie)
Space Goat Productions: 2016 ($3.99, one-shots)
...: Revenge of Hitler 1 - Edginton-s/Watts-a 4.00
...: Revenge of Jack the Ripper 1 - Ball-s/Mauriz-a 4.00
...: Revenge of Krampus 1 - Edginton-s/Youkovich-a 4.00

EVIL DEAD 2: BEYOND DEAD BY DAWN (Movie)
Space Goat Productions: 2015 - No. 3, 2015 ($3.99, limited series)
1-3-Sequel to the Sam Raimi/Bruce Campbell movie; Hannah-s/Bagenda & Bazaldua-a 4.00

EVIL DEAD 2: CRADLE OF THE DAMNED (Movie)
Space Goat Productions: 2016 - No. 3, 2016 ($3.99, limited series)
1-3-Hannah-s/Bagenda & Bazaldua-a 4.00

EVIL DEAD 2: DARK ONES RISING (Movie)
Space Goat Productions: 2016 - No. 3, 2016 ($3.99, limited series)
1-3-Sequel to the Sam Raimi/Bruce Campbell movie; Hannah-s/Valdes-a 4.00

EVIL DEAD 2: REVENGE OF EVIL ED (Movie)
Space Goat Productions: 2017 - No. 2, 2017 ($3.99, limited series)
1,2-Edginton-s/Riccardi-a; Hitler, Rasputin, Bin Laden & Dracula app. 4.00

EVIL ERNIE
Eternity Comics: Dec, 1991 - No. 5, 1992 ($2.50, B&W, limited series)

	GD	VG	FN	VF	VF/NM	NM-
1-1st app. Lady Death by Steven Hughes (12,000 print run); Lady Death app. in all issues	13	26	39	89	195	300
2-1st Lady Death-c (7,000 print run)	8	16	24	54	102	150
3-(7,000 print run)	5	10	15	30	50	70
4-(8,000 print run)	4	8	12	25	40	55
5	3	6	9	21	33	45
Special Edition 1	3	6	9	19	30	40
Youth Gone Wild! ($9.95, trade paperback)-r/#1-5	2	4	6	8	10	12
Youth Gone Wild! Director's Cut ($4.95)-Limited to 15,000, shows the making of the comic						6.00

EVIL ERNIE (Monthly series)
Chaos! Comics: July, 1998 - No. 10, Apr, 1999 ($2.95)
1-10-Pulido & Nutman-s/Brewer-a 4.00
1-($10.00) Premium Ed. 10.00
... Baddest Battles (1/97, $1.50) Pin-ups; 2 covers 4.00
... Pieces of Me (11/00, $2.95, B&W) Flashback story; Pulido-s/Beck-a 3.00
... Relentless (5/02, $4.99, B&W) Pulido-s/Beck, Bonk, & Brewer-a 5.00
... Returns (10/01, $3.99, B&W) Pulido-s/Beck-a 4.00

EVIL ERNIE
Dynamite Entertainment: 2012 - No. 6, 2013 ($3.99)
1-6: 1-Origin re-told; Snider-s/Craig-a; covers by Brereton, Seeley, Syaf & Bradshaw 4.00

EVIL ERNIE (Volume 2)
Dynamite Entertainment: 2014 - No. 6, 2015 ($3.99)
1-6-Tim & Steve Seeley-s/Rafael Lanhellas-a; multiple covers 4.00

EVIL ERNIE: DEPRAVED
Chaos! Comics: Jul, 1999 - No. 3, Sept, 1999 ($2.95, limited series)
1-3-Pulido-s/Brewer-a 4.00

EVIL ERNIE: DESTROYER
Chaos! Comics: Oct, 1997 - No. 9, Jun, 1998 ($2.95, limited series)
Preview ($2.50), 1-9-Flip cover 4.00

EVIL ERNIE: GODEATER
Dynamite Entertainment: 2016 - No. 5, 2016 ($3.99)
1-5-Jordan-s/Worley-a; Davidsen-s/Razek-a; multiple covers 4.00

EVIL ERNIE: IN SANTA FE
Devil's Due Publ.: Sept, 2005 - No. 4, Mar, 2006 ($2.95, limited series)
1-4-Alan Grant-s/Tommy Castillo-a/Alex Horley-c 4.00

EVIL ERNIE: REVENGE
Chaos! Comics: Oct, 1994 - No. 4, Feb, 1995 ($2.95, limited series)

	GD	VG	FN	VF	VF/NM	NM-
1-Glow-in-the-dark-c; Lady Death app. 1-3-flip book w. Kilzone Preview (series of 3)						6.00
1-Commemorative-(4000 print run)	1	3	4	6	8	10
2-4						4.00
Trade paperback (10/95, $12.95)						13.00

EVIL ERNIE: STRAIGHT TO HELL
Chaos! Comics: Oct, 1995 - No. 5, May, 1996 ($2.95, limited series)
1-5: 1-fold-out-c 4.00
1,3:1-($19.95) Chromium Ed. 3-Chastity Chase-c-(4000 printed) 20.00
Special Edition (10,000) 20.00

EVIL ERNIE: THE RESURRECTION
Chaos! Comics: 1993 - No. 4, 1994 (Limited series)

	GD	VG	FN	VF	VF/NM	NM-
0						5.00
1	2	4	6	8	10	12
1A-Gold	3	6	9	16	23	30
2-4	1	2	3	5	6	8

EVIL ERNIE VS. THE MOVIE MONSTERS
Chaos! Comics: Mar, 1997 ($2.95, one-shot)
1 4.00
1-Variant-"Chaos-Scope•Terror Vision" card stock-c 6.00

EVIL ERNIE VS. THE SUPER HEROES
Chaos! Comics: Aug, 1995; Sept, 1998 ($2.95)

	GD	VG	FN	VF	VF/NM	NM-
1-Lady Death poster						4.00
1-Foil-c variant (limited to 10,000)	2	4	6	11	16	20
1-Limited Edition (1000)	2	4	6	11	16	20

Evil Eye #4 © Richard Sala

Excalibur (2019 series) #10 © MAR

Exciting Comics #9 © Nedor

	GD 2.0	VG 4.0	FN 6.0	VF 8.0	VF/NM 9.0	NM- 9.2
2-(9/98) Ernie vs. JLA and Marvel parodies						4.00

EVIL ERNIE: WAR OF THE DEAD
Chaos! Comics: Nov, 1999 - No. 3, Jan, 2000 ($2.95, limited series)

	GD 2.0	VG 4.0	FN 6.0	VF 8.0	VF/NM 9.0	NM- 9.2
1-3-Pulido & Kaminski-s/Brewer-a. 3-End of Evil Ernie						4.00

EVIL EYE
Fantagraphics Books: June, 1998 - No. 12, Jun, 2004 ($2.95/$3.50/$3.95, B&W)

	GD 2.0	VG 4.0	FN 6.0	VF 8.0	VF/NM 9.0	NM- 9.2
1-7-Richard Sala-s/a						4.00
8-10-($3.50)						4.00
11,12-($3.95)						4.00

EVO (Crossover from Tomb Raider #25 & Witchblade #60)
Image Comics (Top Cow): Feb, 2003 ($2.99, one-shot)

	GD 2.0	VG 4.0	FN 6.0	VF 8.0	VF/NM 9.0	NM- 9.2
1-Silvestri-c/a(p); Endgame x-over pt. 3; Sara Pezzini & Lara Croft app.						3.00

EWOKS (Star Wars) (TV) (See Star Comics Magazine)
Marvel Comics (Star Comics): June, 1985 - No. 14, Jul, 1987 (75¢/$1.00)

	GD 2.0	VG 4.0	FN 6.0	VF 8.0	VF/NM 9.0	NM- 9.2
1	3	6	9	17	26	35
2-9	2	4	6	9	12	15
10-Williamson-a (From Star Wars)	3	6	9	21	33	45
11-14: 14-($1.00-c)	2	4	6	11	16	20

EXCALIBUR (Also see Marvel Comics Presents #31)
Marvel Comics: Apr, 1988; Oct, 1988 - No. 125, Oct, 1998 ($1.50/$1.75/$1.99)

	GD 2.0	VG 4.0	FN 6.0	VF 8.0	VF/NM 9.0	NM- 9.2
Special Edition nn (The Sword is Drawn)(4/88, $3.25)-1st Excalibur comic	1	2	3	5	6	8
Special Edition nn (4/88)-no price on-c	2	4	6	8	10	12
Special Edition nn (2nd & 3rd print, 10/88, 12/89)						5.00
...The Sword is Drawn (Apr, 1992, $4.50)						5.00
1($1.50, 10/88)-X-Men spin-off; Nightcrawler, Shadowcat (Kitty Pryde), Capt. Britain, Phoenix & Meggan begin						6.00
2-4						5.00
5-10						4.00
11-49,51-70,72-74,76: 10,11-Rogers/Austin-a. 21-Intro Crusader X. 22-Iron Man x-over. 24-John Byrne app. in story. 26-Ron Lim-c/a. 27-B. Smith-a(p). 37-Dr. Doom & Iron Man app. 41-X-Men (Wolverine) app.; Cable cameo. 49-Neal Adams c-swipe. 52,57-X-Men (Cyclops, Wolverine) app. 53-Spider-Man-c/story. 58-X-Men (Wolverine, Gambit, Cyclops, etc.)-c/story. 61-Phoenix returns. 68-Starjammers-c/story						3.00
50-($2.75, 56 pgs.)-New logo						4.00
71-($3.95, 52 pgs.)-Hologram on-c; 30th anniversary						5.00
75-($3.50, 52 pgs.)-Holo-grafx foil-c						5.00
75-($2.25, 52 pgs.)-Regular edition						4.00
77-81,83-86: 77-Begin $1.95-c; bound-in trading card sheet. 83-86-Deluxe Editions and Standard Editions. 86-1st app. Pete Wisdom						3.00
82-($2.50)-Newsstand edition						4.00
82-($3.50)-Enhanced edition						5.00
87-89,91-99,101-110: 87-Return from Age of Apocalypse. 92-Colossus-c/app. 94-Days of Future Tense 95-X-Man-c/app. 96-Sebastian Shaw & the Hellfire Club app. 99-Onslaught app. 101-Onslaught tie-in. 102-w/card insert. 103-Last Warren Ellis scripts; Belasco app. 104,105-Hitch & Neary-c/a. 109-Spiral-c/app.						3.00
90,100-($2.95)-double-sized. 100-Onslaught tie-in; wraparound-c						4.00
111-124: 111-Begin $1.99-c, wraparound-c. 119-Calafiore-a						3.00
125-($2.99) Wedding of Capt. Britain and Meggan						4.00
Annual 1,2 ('93, '94, 68 pgs.)-1st app. Khaos. 2-X-Men & Psylocke app.						4.00
#(-1) Flashback (7/97)						3.00
...Air Apparent nn (12/91, $4.95)-Simonson-c						6.00
...Mojo Mayhem nn (12/89, $4.50)-Art Adams/Austin-c/a						6.00
...: The Possession nn (7/91, $2.95, 52 pgs.)						4.00
...: XX Crossing (7/92, 5/92-inside, $2.50)-vs. The X-Men						4.00
...Classic Vol. 1: The Sword is Drawn TPB (2005, $19.99) r/#1-5 & Special Edition nn (The Sword is Drawn)						20.00
...Classic Vol. 2: Two-Edged Sword TPB (2006, $24.99) r/#6-11						25.00
...Classic Vol. 3: Cross-Time Caper Book 1 TPB (2007, $24.99) r/#12-20						25.00
...Classic Vol. 4: Cross-Time Caper Book 2 TPB (2007, $24.99) r/#21-28						25.00
...Classic Vol. 5 TPB (2008, $24.99) r/#29-34 & Marvel GN Excalibur: Weird War III						25.00

EXCALIBUR
Marvel Comics: Feb, 2001 - No. 4, May, 2001 ($2.99)

	GD 2.0	VG 4.0	FN 6.0	VF 8.0	VF/NM 9.0	NM- 9.2
1-4-Return of Captain Britain; Raimondi-a						3.00

EXCALIBUR (X-Men Reloaded title) (Leads into House of M series, then New Excalibur)
Marvel Comics: July, 2004 - No. 14, July, 2005 ($2.99)

	GD 2.0	VG 4.0	FN 6.0	VF 8.0	VF/NM 9.0	NM- 9.2
1-14: 1-Claremont-s/Lopresti-a/Park-c; Magneto returns. 6-11-Beast app. 13,14-Prelude to House of M; Dr. Strange app.						3.00
House of M Prelude: Excalibur TPB (2005, $11.99) r/#11-14						12.00
... Vol. 1: Forging the Sword (2004, $9.99) r/#1-4						10.00
... Vol. 2: Saturday Night Fever (2005, $14.99) r/#5-10						15.00

EXCALIBUR (Follows from House of X & Powers of X series)
Marvel Comics: Dec, 2019 - Present ($4.99/$3.99)

	GD 2.0	VG 4.0	FN 6.0	VF 8.0	VF/NM 9.0	NM- 9.2
1-($4.99) Tini Howard-s/Marcus To-a; Betsy Braddock, Rogue, Gambit, Jubilee app.						5.00
2-17-($3.99): 10,11-Kitty Pryde app. 12-15-"X of Swords" tie-ins. 14-Noto-a						4.00

EXCELLENCE
Image Comics (Skybound): May, 2019 - No. 6, Oct, 2019 ($3.99)

	GD 2.0	VG 4.0	FN 6.0	VF 8.0	VF/NM 9.0	NM- 9.2
1-10-Brandon Thomas-s/Khary Randolph-a						4.00

EXCITING COMICS
Nedor/Better Publications/Standard Comics: Apr, 1940 - No. 69, Sept, 1949

	GD 2.0	VG 4.0	FN 6.0	VF 8.0	VF/NM 9.0	NM- 9.2
1-Origin & 1st app. The Mask, Jim Hatfield, Sgt. Bill King, Dan Williams begin; early Robot-c (see Smash #1)	511	1022	1533	3730	6465	9200
2-The Sphinx begins; The Masked Rider app.; Son of the Gods begins, ends #8	255	310	765	1632	2791	3950
3-Classic Science Fiction Robot-c	252	504	756	1613	2757	3900
4-6: All have Sci-Fi covers by Max Plaisted	190	380	570	1216	2083	2950
7,8-Schomburg jungle covers	135	270	405	864	1482	2100
9-Origin/1st app. of The Black Terror & sidekick Tim, begin series (5/41) (Black Terror c-9-21,23-52,54,55)	1500	3000	4500	11,200	21,100	31,000
10-2nd app. Black Terror (6/41)	406	812	1218	2842	4871	6900
11-3rd app. Black Terror (7/41)	248	496	744	1587	2719	3850
12,13-Bondage covers	184	368	552	1178	2014	2850
14-Last Sphinx, Dan Williams	148	296	444	947	1624	2300
15-The Liberator begins (origin); WWII-c	190	380	570	1216	2083	2950
16,19,20: 20-The Mask ends	123	246	369	787	1344	1900
17,18-WWII-c	148	296	444	947	1624	2300
21,23,24	97	194	291	621	1061	1500
22-Origin The Eaglet; The American Eagle begins	123	246	369	787	1344	1900
25-Robot-c	177	354	531	1133	1942	2750
26-Schomburg-c begin; Nazi WWII-c	223	446	669	1427	2439	3450
27,30-Japanese WWII-c	203	406	609	1299	2225	3150
28-(Scarce) Crime Crusader begins, ends #58; Nazi WWII-c	750	1500	2250	4500	7500	10,500
29-Nazi WWII-c	203	406	609	1299	2225	3150
31,35,36-Japanese WWII-c. 35-Liberator ends, not in 31-33	168	336	504	1075	1838	2600
32-34,37-Nazi WWII-c	168	336	504	1075	1838	2600
38 Gangster-c	119	238	357	762	1306	1850
39-WWII-c; Nazis giving poison candy to kids on cover; origin Kara, Jungle Princess	1250	2500	3750	7800	11,650	15,500
40,41-Last WWII covers in this title; Japanese WWII-c	161	322	483	1030	1765	2500
42-50: 42-The Scarab begins. 45-Schomburg Robot-c. 49-Last Kara, Jungle Princess. 50-Last American Eagle	87	174	261	553	952	1350
51-Miss Masque begins (1st app.)	116	232	348	742	1271	1800
52,54: 54-Miss Masque ends	81	162	243	518	884	1250
53-Miss Masque-c	194	388	582	1242	2121	3000
55-58: 55-Judy of the Jungle begins (origin), ends #69; 1 pg. Ingels-a; Judy of the Jungle c-56-66. 57,58-Airbrush-c	81	162	243	518	884	1250
59-Frazetta art in Caniff style; signed Frank Frazeta (one t), 9 pgs.	90	180	270	576	988	1400
60-66: 60-Rick Howard, the Mystery Rider begins. 66-Robinson/Meskin-a	73	146	219	457	796	1125
67-69-All western covers	27	54	81	162	266	370

NOTE: *Schomburg (Xela) c-26-68; airbrush c-57-66. Black Terror by **R. Moreira**-#65. **Roussos** a-62. Bondage-c 9, 12, 13, 20, 23, 25, 30, 59.*

EXCITING ROMANCES
Fawcett Publications: 1949 (nd); No. 2, Spring, 1950 - No. 5, 10/50; No. 6 (1951, nd); No. 7, 9/51 -No. 12, 1/53 (Photo-c on #1-3)

	GD 2.0	VG 4.0	FN 6.0	VF 8.0	VF/NM 9.0	NM- 9.2
1,3: 1(1949). 3-Wood-a	15	30	45	86	133	180
2,4,5-(1950)	10	20	30	58	79	100
6-12	9	18	27	52	69	85

NOTE: ***Powell** a-8-10. **Marcus Swayze** a-5, 6, 9. Photo c-1-7, 10-12.*

EXCITING ROMANCE STORIES (See Fox Giants)

EXCITING WAR (Korean War)
Standard Comics (Better Publ.): No. 5, Sept, 1952 - No. 8, May, 1953; No. 9, Nov, 1953

	GD 2.0	VG 4.0	FN 6.0	VF 8.0	VF/NM 9.0	NM- 9.2
5	15	30	45	94	147	200
6-Flame thrower/burning body-c	41	82	123	256	428	600
7,9	14	28	42	82	121	160
8-Toth-a	15	30	45	86	133	180

EXCITING X-PATROL

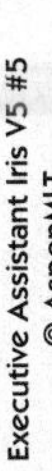

Executive Assistant Iris V5 #5 © AspenMLT

Exiles #22 © MAR

Ex Machina #42 © Vaughan & Harris

GD VG FN VF VF/NM NM-
2.0 4.0 6.0 8.0 9.0 9.2

Marvel Comics (Amalgam): June, 1997 ($1.95, one-shot)
1-Barbara Kesel-s/Bryan Hitch-a 4.00

EX-CON
Dynamite Entertainment: 2014 - No. 5, 2015 ($2.99, limited series)
1-5-Swierczynski-s/Burns-a/Bradstreet-c 3.00

EXECUTIONER, THE (Don Pendleton's...)
IDW Publishing: Apr, 2008 - No. 5, Aug, 2008 ($3.99)
1-5-Mack Bolan origin re-told; Gallant-a/Wojtowicz-s 4.00

EXECUTIVE ASSISTANT: ASSASSINS
Aspen MLT: Jul, 2012 - No. 18, Feb, 2014 ($3.99)
1-18: 1-Five covers; Hernandez-s/Gunderson-a 4.00

EXECUTIVE ASSISTANT: IRIS (Also see All New Executive Assistant: Iris)
Aspen MLT: No. 0, Apr, 2009 - No. 6, Nov, 2010 ($2.50/$2.99)
0-($2.50) Wohl-s/Francisco-a; 3 covers 3.00
1-6-($2.99) Multiple covers on each 3.00
Annual 2015 (3/15, $5.99) Three stories by various; Benitez-c 6.00
... Sourcebook 1 (1/16, $4.99) Character profiles & storyline summaries 5.00

EXECUTIVE ASSISTANT: IRIS (Volume 2) (The Hit List Agenda x-over)
Aspen MLT: No. 0, Jul, 2011 - No. 5, Dec, 2011 ($2.50/$2.99/$3.50)
0-($2.50) Wohl-s/Francisco-a; sketch page art; 3 covers 3.00
1-4-($2.99) Multiple covers on each. 1-Francisco-a. 2-4-Odagawa-a 3.00
5-($3.50) Odagawa-a 3.50

EXECUTIVE ASSISTANT: IRIS (Volume 3) (See All New Executive Assistant: Iris for Vol. 4)
Aspen MLT: Dec, 2012 - No. 5, Sept, 2013 ($3.99)
1-5-Multiple covers on each. 1-Wohl-s/Lei-a 4.00

EXECUTIVE ASSISTANT: IRIS (Volume 5)
Aspen MLT: May, 2018 - No. 5, Sept, 2018 ($3.99)
1-5-Multiple covers on each. 1-Northcott-s/Tran-a 4.00
... Primer 1 (5/18, 25¢) Origin re-told; recaps of previous volumes 3.00

EXECUTIVE ASSISTANT: LOTUS (The Hit List Agenda x-over)
Aspen MLT: Aug, 2011 - No. 3, Oct, 2011 ($2.99, limited series)
1-3-Multiple covers on each. Hernandez-s/Nome-a 3.00

EXECUTIVE ASSISTANT: ORCHID (The Hit List Agenda x-over)
Aspen MLT: Aug, 2011 - No. 3, Oct, 2011 ($2.99, limited series)
1-3: 1-Lobdell-s/Gunnell-a; multiple covers 3.00

EXECUTIVE ASSISTANT: VIOLET (The Hit List Agenda x-over)
Aspen MLT: Aug, 2011 - No. 3, Oct, 2011 ($2.99, limited series)
1-3: 1-Andreyko-s/Mhan-a; multiple covers 3.00

EXILED (Part 1 of x-over with Journey Into Mystery #637,638 & New Mutants #42,43)
Marvel Comics: July, 2012 ($2.99, one-shot)
1-Thor, Loki and New Mutants app.; DiGiandomenico-a 3.00

EXILE ON THE PLANET OF THE APES
BOOM! Studios: Mar, 2012 - No. 4 ($3.99, limited series)
1-3-Bechko & Hardman-s/Laming-a 4.00

EXILES (Also see Break-Thru)
Malibu Comics (Ultraverse): Aug, 1993 - No. 4, Nov, 1993 ($1.95)
1,2,4: 1,2-Bagged copies of each exist. 4-Team dies; story cont'd in Break-Thru #1 3.00
3-($2.50, 40 pgs.)-Rune flip-c/story by B. Smith (3 pgs.) 4.00
1-Holographic-c edition 1 2 3 5 6 8

EXILES (All New, The) (2nd Series) (Also see Black September)
Malibu Comics (Ultraverse): Sept, 1995 - V2#11, Aug, 1996 ($1.50)
Infinity (9/95, $1.50)-Intro new team including Marvel's Juggernaut & Reaper 3.00
Infinity (2000 signed), V2#1 (2000 signed) 1 3 4 6 8 10
V2 #1-(10/95, 64 pgs.)-Reprint of Ultraforce V2#1 follows lead story 4.00
V2#2-4,6-11: 2-1st app. Hellblade. 8-Intro Maxis. 11-Vs. Maxis; Ripfire app.; cont'd in Ultraforce #12 3.00
V2#5-($2.50) Juggernaut returns to the Marvel Universe. 4.00

EXILES (Also see X-Men titles) (Leads into New Exiles series)
Marvel Comics: Aug, 2001 - No. 100, Feb, 2008 ($2.99/$2.25)
1-($2.99) Blink and parallel world X-Men; Winick-s/McKone & McKenna-a
1 2 3 4 5 7
2-10-($2.25) 2-Two covers (McKone & JH Williams III). 5-Alpha Flight app. 4.00
11-24: 22-Blink leaves; Magik joins. 23,24-Walker-a; alternate Weapon-X app. 3.00
25-99: 25-Begin $2.99-c; Inhumans app.; Walker-a. 26-30-Austen-s. 33-Wolverine app. 35-37-Fantastic Four app. 37-Sunfire dies, Blink returns. 38-40-Hyperion app. 69-71-House of M. 77,78-Squadron Supreme app. 85,86-Multiple Wolverines. 90-Claremont-s begin; Psylocke app. 97-Shadowcat joins 3.00
100-($3.99) Last issue; Blink leaves; continues in Exiles (Days of Then and Now); r/#1 4.00
Annual 1 (2/07, $3.99) Bedard-s/Raney-a/c 4.00
Exiles #1 (Days of Then and Now) (3/08, $3.99) short stories by various 4.00

EXILES
Marvel Comics: Jun, 2009 - No. 6, Nov, 2009 ($2.99/$3.99)
1,6-($3.99) Blink and parallel world Scarlet Witch, Beast and others; Bullock-c 4.00
2-5-($2.99) 3.00

EXILES
Marvel Comics: Jun, 2018 - No. 12, Mar, 2019 ($3.99)
1-12-Blink and parallel world Ms. Marvel, Iron Lad, Valkyrie & Wolvie; Nick Fury app. 3-Peggy Carter (Capt. America) app. 4-The Thing & Falcon app. 8-Quinones-a 4.00

EXILES VS. THE X-MEN
Malibu Comics (Ultraverse): Oct, 1995 (one-shot)
0-Limited Super Premium Edition; signed w/certificate; gold foil logo,
0-Limited Premium Edition 1 3 4 6 8 10

EXIT STAGE LEFT: THE SNAGGLEPUSS CHRONICLES
DC Comics: Mar, 2018 - No. 6, Aug, 2018 ($3.99)
1-6-Russell-s/Feehan-a; Snagglepuss as a 1950s playwright; Huckleberry Hound app. 4.00

EX MACHINA
DC Comics: Aug, 2004 - No. 50, Sept, 2010 ($2.95/$2.99)
1-Intro. Mitchell Hundred; Vaughan-s/Harris-a/c 4.00
1-Special Edition (6/10, $1.00) Reprints #1 with "What's Next?" logo on cover 3.00
2-49: 12-Intro. Automaton. 33-Mitchell meets the Pope 3.00
50-($4.99) Wraparound-c 5.00
...: The Deluxe Edition Book One HC (2008, $29.99, dustjacket) r/#1-11; Vaughan's original proposal, Harris sketch pages; Brad Meltzer intro. 30.00
...: The Deluxe Edition Book Two HC (2009, $29.99, dustjacket) r/#12-20; Special #1,2; script and pencil art for #20; Wachowski Bros. intro. 30.00
...: The Deluxe Edition Book Three HC (2010, $29.99, dustjacket) r/#21-29; Special #3 and Ex Machina: Inside the Machine 30.00
...: The Deluxe Edition Book Four HC (2010, $29.99, dustjacket) r/#30-40; cover gallery 30.00
...: The Deluxe Edition Book Five HC (2011, $29.99, dustjacket) r/#41-50; Special #4 30.00
...: Inside the Machine (4/07, $2.99) script pages and Harris art and cover process 3.00
...: Masquerade Special (#3) (10/07, $3.50) John Paul Leon-a; Harris-c 3.50
... Special 1,2 (6/06 - No. 2, 8/06, $2.99) Sprouse-a; flashback to the Great Machine 3.00
... Special 4 (5/09, $3.99) Leon-a; Great Machine flashback; covers by Harris & Leon 4.00
...: Dirty Tricks TPB (2009, $12.99) r/#35-39 and Masquerade Special #3 13.00
...: Ex Cathedra TPB (2008, $12.99) r/#30-34 13.00
...: March To War TPB (2006, $12.99) r/#17-20 and Special #1,2 13.00
...: Power Down TPB (2008, $12.99) r/#26-29 & ...: Inside the Machine 13.00
...: Ring Out the Old TPB (2010, $14.99) r/#40-44 and Special #4 15.00
...: Smoke Smoke TPB (2007, $12.99) r/#21-25 13.00
...: The First Hundred Days TPB ('05, $9.95) r/#1-5; photo reference and sketch pages 10.00
...: Tag TPB (2005, $12.99) r/#6-10; Harris sketch pages 13.00
...: Term Limits TPB (2010, $14.99) r/#45-50 15.00

EX-MUTANTS
Malibu Comics: Nov, 1992 - No. 18, Apr, 1994 ($1.95/$2.25/$2.50)
1-18: 1-Polybagged w/Skycap; prismatic cover 3.00

EXORCISTS (See The Crusaders)

EXORSISTERS
Image Comics: Oct, 2018 - Present ($3.99)
1-6-Ian Boothby-s/Gisele Lagacé-a. 1-Four covers. 2-6-Two covers 4.00

EXOSQUAD (TV)
Topps Comics: No. 0, Jan, 1994 ($1.00)
0-($1.00, 20 pgs.)-1st app.; Staton-a(p); wraparound-c 3.00

EXOTIC ROMANCES (Formerly True War Romances)
Quality Comics Group (Comic Magazines): No. 22, Oct, 1955 - No. 31, Nov, 1956

	GD 2.0	VG 4.0	FN 6.0	VF 8.0	VF/NM 9.0	NM- 9.2
22	15	30	45	94	147	200
23-26,29	13	26	39	72	101	130
27,31-Baker-c/a	26	52	78	154	252	350
28,30-Baker-a	18	36	54	109	172	235

EXPANSE, THE (Based on the books of James S.A. Corey)
BOOM! Studios: Dec, 2020 - No. 4 ($3.99, limited series)
1-3-Bechko-s/Aragon-a 4.00

EXPENDABLES, THE (Movie)
Dynamite Entertainment: 2010 - No. 4, 2010 ($3.99, limited series)

Explorers of the Unknown #5 © ACP

Extreme Justice #17 © DC

Fables #94 © Bill Willingham & DC

	GD 2.0	VG 4.0	FN 6.0	VF 8.0	VF/NM 9.0	NM- 9.2
1-4-Chuck Dixon-s/Esteve Polls-a/Lucio Parrillo-c; prelude to the 2010 movie						4.00

EXPLOITS OF DANIEL BOONE
Quality Comics Group: Nov, 1955 - No. 6, Oct, 1956

	GD	VG	FN	VF	VF/NM	NM-
1-All have Cuidera-c(i)	20	40	60	114	182	250
2 (1/56)	14	28	42	82	121	160
3-6	13	26	39	74	105	135

EXPLOITS OF DICK TRACY (See Dick Tracy)

EXPLORER JOE
Ziff-Davis Comic Group (Approved Comics): Win, 1951 - No. 2, Oct-Nov, 1952

	GD	VG	FN	VF	VF/NM	NM-
1-2: Saunders painted covers; 2-Krigstein-a	15	30	45	92	144	195

EXPLORERS OF THE UNKNOWN (See Archie Giant Series #587, 599)
Archie Comics: June, 1990 - No. 6, Apr, 1991 ($1.00)

1-6: Featuring Archie and the gang 4.00

EXPOSED (...True Crime Cases; ...Cases in the Crusade Against Crime #5-9)
D. S. Publishing Co.: Mar-Apr, 1948 - No. 9, July-Aug, 1949

	GD	VG	FN	VF	VF/NM	NM-
1	103	206	309	659	1130	1600
2-Giggling killer story with excessive blood; two injury-to-eye panels; electrocution panel	42	84	126	265	445	625
3,8,9	19	38	57	111	176	240
4-Orlando-a	20	40	60	114	182	250
5-Breeze Lawson, Sky Sheriff by E. Good	20	40	60	114	182	250
6,7: 6-Ingels-a; used in **SOTI**, illo. "How to prepare an alibi" 7-Illo. in **SOTI**, "Diagram for housebreakers;" used by N.Y. Legis. Committee	42	84	126	265	445	625

EXTERMINATION
BOOM! Studios: Jun, 2012 - No. 8, Jan, 2013 ($1.00/$3.99)

1-($1.00) Nine covers; Spurrier-s/Jeffrey Edwards-a 3.00
2-8-($3.99) 4.00

EXTERMINATION
Marvel Comics: Oct, 2018 - No. 5, Feb, 2019 ($4.99, limited series)

1-($4.99)-Brisson-s/Larraz-a; the original five X-Men and Cable app.; Bloodstorm killed 5.00
2-4-($3.99) 4.00
5-($4.99) Brisson-s/Larraz-a; original X-Men return to their past 5.00

EXTERMINATORS, THE
DC Comics (Vertigo): Mar, 2006 - No. 30, Aug, 2008 ($2.99)

1-30: Simon Oliver-s/Tony Moore-a in most. 11,12-Hawthorne-a 3.00
...: Bug Brothers TPB (2006, $9.99) r/#1-5; intro. by screenwriter Josh Olson 10.00
...: Bug Brothers Forever TPB (2008, $14.99) r/#24-30; intro. by Simon Oliver 15.00
...: Crossfire and Collateral TPB (2008, $14.99) r/#17-23 15.00
...: Insurgency TPB (2007, $12.99) r/#6-10 13.00
...: Lies of Our Fathers TPB (2007, $14.99) r/#11-16 15.00

EXTINCT!
New England Comics Press: Wint, 1991-92 - No. 2, Fall, 1992 ($3.50, B&W)

1,2-Reprints and background info of "perfectly awful" Golden Age stories 4.00

EXTINCTION EVENT
DC Comics (WildStorm): Sept, 2003 - No. 5, Jan, 2004 ($2.50, limited series)

1-5-Booth-a/Weinberg-s 3.00

EXTRA!
E. C. Comics: Mar-Apr, 1955 - No. 5, Nov-Dec, 1955

	GD	VG	FN	VF	VF/NM	NM-
1-Not code approved	25	50	75	200	318	435
2-5: 3-1st EC Picto-Fiction story	15	30	45	120	190	260

NOTE: ***Craig, Crandall, Severin** art in all.*

EXTRA!
Gemstone Publishing: Jan, 2000 - No. 5, May, 2000 ($2.50)

1-5-Reprints E.C. series 4.00

EXTRA COMICS
Magazine Enterprises: 1948 (25¢, 3 comics in one)

	GD	VG	FN	VF	VF/NM	NM-
1-Giant; consisting of rebound ME comics. Two versions known; (1)-Funnyman by Siegel & Shuster, Space Ace, Undercover Girl, Red Fox by L.B. Cole, Trail Colt & (2)-All Funnyman	71	142	213	454	777	1100

EXTRAORDINARY X-MEN
Marvel Comics: Jan, 2016 - No. 20, May, 2017 ($4.99/$3.99)

1-($4.99) Team of Old Man Logan, Storm, Jean Grey & others; Lemire-s/Ramos-a 5.00
2-7,9-20-($3.99) 2-Mister Sinister returns. 6,7,13-16-Ibanez-a. 9-12-Apocalypse Wars 4.00
8-($4.99) Apocalypse Wars x-over; Ramos-a; back-up story with Doctor Strange 5.00
Annual 1 (11/16, $4.99) Masters-s/Barberi-a; Montclare-s/Kämpe-a; Moon Girl app. 5.00

EXTREME
Image Comics (Extreme Studios): Aug, 1993 (Giveaway)

0 3.00

EXTREME DESTROYER
Image Comics (Extreme Studios): Jan, 1996 ($2.50)

Prologue 1-Polybagged w/card; Liefeld-c, Epilogue 1-Liefeld-c 3.00

EXTREME JUSTICE
DC Comics: No. 0, Jan, 1995 - No. 18, July, 1996 ($1.50/$1.75)

0-18 3.00

EXTREMELY YOUNGBLOOD
Image Comics (Extreme Studios): Sept, 1996 ($3.50, one-shot)

1 3.50

EXTREME SACRIFICE
Image Comics (Extreme Studios): Jan, 1995 ($2.50, limited series)

Prelude (#1)-Liefeld wraparound-c; polybagged w/ trading card 3.00
Epilogue (#2)-Liefeld wraparound-c; polybagged w/trading card 3.00
Trade paperback (6/95, $16.95)-Platt-a 17.00

EXTREME SUPER CHRISTMAS SPECIAL
Image Comics (Extreme Studios): Dec, 1994 ($2.95, one-shot)

1 3.00

EXTREMIST, THE
DC Comics (Vertigo): Sept, 1993 - No. 4, Dec, 1993 ($1.95, limited series)

1-4-Peter Milligan scripts; McKeever-c/a 3.00
1-Platinum Edition 5.00

EYE OF NEWT
Dark Horse Comics: Jun, 2014 - No. 4, Sept, 2014 ($3.99, limited series)

1-4-Michael Hague-s/a/c 4.00

EYE OF THE STORM
DC Comics (WildStorm): Sept, 2003 ($4.95)

Annual 1-Short stories by various incl. Portacio, Johns, Coker, Pearson, Arcudi 5.00

FABLES
DC Comics (Vertigo): July, 2002 - No. 149, Apr, 2015 ($2.50/$2.75/$2.99)

1-Willingham-s/Medina-a; two covers by Maleev & Jean 65.00
1: Special Edition (12/06, 25¢) r/#1 with preview of 1001 Nights of Snowfall 3.00
1: Special Edition (9/09, $1.00) r/#1 with preview of Peter & Max 3.00
1-Special Edition (8/10, $1.00) Reprints #1 with "What's Next?" logo on cover 3.00
1-Special Edition (3/16, $3.99) Reprints #1 with new cover by Dave McKean 4.00
2-Medina-a 15.00
3-5 10.00
6-37: 6-10-Buckingham-a. 11-Talbot-a. 18-Medley-a. 26-Preview of The Witching 5.00
6-RRP Edition wraparound variant-c; promotional giveaway for retailers (200 printed) 215.00
38-49,51-74,76-99,101-149: 38-Begin $2.75-c. 49-Begin $2.99-c. 57,58,76-Allred-a. 83-85-X-over with Jack of Fables & The Literals. 101-Shanower-a. 107-Terry Moore-a 113-Back-up art by Russell, Cannon, Hughes. 147-Terry Moore-a (3 pgs.) 3.00
50-($3.99) Wedding of Snow White and Bigby Wolf; preview of Jack of Fables series 5.00
75-($4.99) Geppetto surrenders; pin-up gallery by Powell, Nowlan, Cooke & others 5.00
100-(1/11, $9.99, squarebound) Buckingham-a; short stories art by Hughes & others 10.00
Animal Farm (2003, $12.95, TPB) r/#6-10; sketch pages by Buckingham & Jean 13.00
...: Arabian Nights (And Days) (2006, $14.99, TPB) r/#42-47 15.00
...: Homelands (2005, $14.99, TPB) r/#34-41 15.00
Legends in Exile (2002, $9.95, TPB) r/#1-5; new short story Willingham-s/a 15.00
...: March of the Wooden Soldiers (2004, $17.95, TPB) r/#19-21 & ...: The Last Castle 18.00
...: 1001 Nights of Snowfall HC (2006, $19.99) short stories by Willingham with art by various incl. Bolton, Kaluta, Jean, McPherson, Thompson, Vess, Wheatley, Buckingham 20.00
...: 1001 Nights of Snowfall (2008, $14.99, TPB) short stories with art by various 15.00
...: Rose Red (2011, $17.99, TPB) r/#94-100; Buckingham design and sketch pages 18.00
...: Sons of Empire (2007, $17.99, TPB) r/#52-59 18.00
...: Storybook Love (2004, $14.95, TPB) r/#11-18 15.00
...: The Dark Ages (2009, $17.99, TPB) r/#76-82 18.00
...: The Deluxe Edition Book One HC (2009, $29.99, DJ) r/#1-10; character sketch-a 30.00
...: The Deluxe Edition Book Two HC (2010, $29.99, DJ) r/#11-18 & ...: The Last Castle 30.00
...: The Good Prince (2008, $17.99, TPB) r/#60-69 18.00
...: The Great Fables Crossover (2010, $17.99, TPB) r/#83-85, Jack of Fables #33-35 and The Literals #1-3; sneak preview of Peter & Max: A Fables Novel 18.00
...: The Last Castle (2003, $5.95) Hamilton-a/Willingham-s; prequel to title 6.00
...: The Mean Seasons (2005, $14.99, TPB) r/#22,28-33 15.00
...: War and Pieces (2008, $17.99, TPB) r/#70-75; sketch and pin-up pages 18.00
...: Witches (2010, $17.99, TPB) r/#86-93 18.00
...: Wolves (2006, $17.99, TPB) r/#48-51; script to #50 18.00

Fairest #3 © Bill Willingham & DC

Faith #4 © VAL

Falcon & Winter Soldier #1 © MAR

	GD 2.0	VG 4.0	FN 6.0	VF 8.0	VF/NM 9.0	NM- 9.2

FABLES: THE WOLF AMONG US (Based on the Telltale Games video game)
DC Comics (Vertigo): Mar, 2015 - No. 16, Jun, 2016 ($3.99, printing of digital first stories)

1-16-Prequel to Fables; Sturges & Justus-s 4.00

FACE, THE (Tony Trent, the Face No. 3 on) (See Big Shot Comics)
Columbia Comics Group: 1941 - No. 2, 1943

	GD	VG	FN	VF	VF/NM	NM-
1-The Face; Mart Bailey WWII-c	106	212	318	678	1164	1650
2-Bailey WWII-c	71	142	213	454	777	1100

FACES OF EVIL
DC Comics: Mar, 2009 ($2.99, series of one-shots)

...: Deathstroke 1 - Jeanty-a/Ladronn-c; Ravager app. 3.00
...: Kobra 1 - Jason Burr returns; Julian Lopez-a 3.00
...: Prometheus 1 - Gates-s/Dallacchio-a; origin re-told; Anima killed 3.00
...: Solomon Grundy 1 - Johns-s/Kolins-a; leads into Solomon Grundy mini-series 3.00

FACTOR X
Marvel Comics: Mar, 1995 - No. 4, July, 1995 ($1.95, limited series)

1-Age of Apocalypse 5.00
2-4 4.00

FACULTY FUNNIES
Archie Comics: June, 1989 - No. 5, May, 1990 (75¢/95¢ #2 on)

1-5: 1,2,4,5-The Awesome Foursome app. 3.00

FADE FROM GRACE
Beckett Comics: Aug, 2004 - No. 5, Mar, 2005 (99¢/$1.99)

1-(99¢) Jeff Amano-a/c; Gabriel Benson-s; origin of Fade 3.00
2-5-($1.99) 3.00
TPB (2005, $14.99) r/#1-5; cover gallery, afterword by David Mack 15.00

FADE OUT, THE
Image Comics: Aug, 2014 - No. 12, Jan, 2016 ($3.50/$3.99)

1-12-Ed Brubaker-s/Sean Phillips-a/c. 12-($3.99) 4.00

FAFHRD AND THE GREY MOUSER (Also see Sword of Sorcery & Wonder Woman #202)
Marvel Comics: Oct, 1990 - No. 4, 1991 ($4.50, 52 pgs., squarebound)

1-4: Mignola/Williamson-a; Chaykin scripts 5.00

FAGIN THE JEW
Doubleday: Oct, 2003 ($15.95, softcover graphic novel)

nn-Will Eisner-s/a; story of Fagin from Dickens' Oliver Twist 16.00

FAIREST (Characters from Fables)
DC Comics (Vertigo): May, 2012 - No. 33, Mar, 2015 ($2.99)

1-33: 1-6-Willingham-s/Jimenez-a. 1-Wraparound-c by Hughes & variant-c by Jimenez 3.00
...: In All The Land HC (2013, $24.99, dustjacket) New short stories by various; Hughes-c 25.00

FAIRLADY
Image Comics: Apr, 2019 - No. 5, Aug, 2019 ($3.99)

1-5-Brian Schirmer-s/Claudio Balboni-a 4.00

FAIRY QUEST: OUTCASTS
BOOM! Studios: Nov, 2014 - No. 2, Dec, 2014 ($3.99, limited series)

1,2-Jenkins-s/Ramos-a/c 4.00

FAIRY QUEST: OUTLAWS
BOOM! Studios: Feb, 2013 - No. 2, Mar, 2013 ($3.99, limited series)

1,2-Jenkins-s/Ramos-a/c 4.00

FAIRY TALE PARADE (See Famous Fairy Tales)
Dell Publishing Co.: June-July, 1942 - No. 121, Oct, 1946 (Most by Walt Kelly)

	GD	VG	FN	VF	VF/NM	NM-
1-Kelly-a begins	86	172	258	688	1544	2400
2(8-9/42)	38	76	114	285	641	1000
3-5 (10-11/42 - 2-4/43)	29	58	87	196	441	685
6-9 (5-7/43 - 11-1/43-44)	22	44	66	154	340	525
Four Color 50('44), 69('45), 87('45)	21	42	63	147	324	500
Four Color 104, 114('46)-Last Kelly issue	16	32	48	112	249	385
Four Color 121('46)-Not by Kelly	10	20	30	69	147	225

NOTE: #1-9, 4-Color #50, 69 have ***Kelly*** *c/a; 4-Color #87, 104, 114-**Kelly** art only. #9 has a redrawn version of The Reluctant Dragon. This series contains all the classic fairy tales from Jack In The Beanstalk to Cinderella.*

FAIRY TALES
Ziff-Davis Publ. Co. (Approved Comics): No. 10, Apr-May, 1951 - No. 11, June-July, 1951

	GD	VG	FN	VF	VF/NM	NM-
10,11-Painted-c	23	46	69	136	223	310

FAITH
DC Comics (Vertigo): Nov, 1999 - No. 5, Mar, 2000 ($2.50, limited series)

1-5-Ted McKeever-s/c/a 3.00

FAITH (Zephyr from Harbinger)
Valiant Entertainment: Jan, 2016 - No. 4, Apr, 2016 ($3.99, limited series)

1-4-Houser-s/Portela-a. 3,4-Torque app. 4.00

FAITH (Harbinger)
Valiant Entertainment: Jul, 2016 - No. 12, Jun, 2017 ($3.99)

1-12: 1-4-Houser-s/Pere Pérez-a. 5-Hillary Clinton app. 7-12-Eisma-a 4.00
Faith's Winter Wonderland Special 1 (12/17, $3.99) Sauvage-s/Portela & Kim-a 4.00

FAITH AND THE FUTURE FORCE (Harbinger)
Valiant Entertainment: Jul, 2017 - No. 4, Oct, 2017 ($3.99, limited series)

1-4-Houser-s. 1-Segovia & Kitson-a. 2-Kitson & Bernard-a. 3-Most Valiant heroes app. 4.00

FAITH DREAMSIDE (Harbinger)
Valiant Entertainment: Sept, 2018 - No. 4, Jan, 2019 ($3.99, limited series)

1-4-Houser-s/MJ Kim-a; Doctor Mirage app. 4.00

FAITHFUL
Marvel Comics/Lovers' Magazine: Nov, 1949 - No. 2, Feb, 1950 (52 pgs.)

	GD	VG	FN	VF	VF/NM	NM-
1,2-Photo-c	16	32	48	98	154	210

FAITHLESS (Also see Heartbeat)
BOOM! Studios: Apr, 2019 - No. 6, Sept, 2019 ($3.99, limited series)

1-6-Brian Azzarello-s/Marie Llovet-a 4.00

FAITHLESS II
BOOM! Studios: Apr, 2020 - Present ($3.99, limited series)

1-6-Brian Azzarello-s/Marie Llovet-a 4.00

FAKER
DC Comics (Vertigo): Sept, 2007 - No. 6, Feb, 2008 ($2.99, limited series)

1-6-Mike Carey-s/Jock-a/c 3.00
TPB (2008, $14.99) r/#1-6; Jock sketch pages 15.00

FALCON (See Marvel Premiere #49, Avengers #181 & Captain America #117 & 133)
Marvel Comics Group: Nov, 1983 - No. 4, Feb, 1984 (Mini-series)

	GD	VG	FN	VF	VF/NM	NM-
1-Paul Smith-c/a(p)	2	4	6	9	13	16
2-4: 2-Paul Smith-c/Mark Bright-a. 3-Kupperberg-c						6.00

FALCON (Marvel Legacy)
Marvel Comics: Dec, 2017 - No. 8, Jul, 2018 ($3.99)

1-8: 1-Sam Wilson back as the Falcon after Secret Empire; Barnes-s/Cassara-a. 6-8-Misty Knight app. 7,8-Blade app. 4.00

FALCON & WINTER SOLDIER
Marvel Comics: Apr, 2020 - No. 5, Jan, 2021 ($3.99, limited series)

1-5-Derek Landy-s/Federico Vicentini-a; intro. The Natural 4.00

FALL AND RISE OF CAPTAIN ATOM, THE
DC Comics: Mar, 2017 - No. 6, Aug, 2017 ($2.99, limited series)

1-6-Bates-s/Conrad-a 3.00

FALLEN ANGEL
DC Comics: Sept, 2003 - No. 20, July, 2005 ($2.50/$2.95)

1-9-Peter David-s/David Lopez-a/Stelfreeze-c; intro. Lee 3.00
10-20: 10-Begin $2.95-c. 13,17-Kaluta-c. 20-Last issue; Pérez-c 3.00
TPB (2004, $12.95) r/#1-6; intro. by Harlan Ellison 13.00
Down to Earth TPB (2007, $14.99) r/#7-12 15.00

FALLEN ANGEL
IDW Publ.: Dec, 2005 - No. 33, Dec, 2008 ($3.99)

1-33: 1-14-Peter David-s/J.K Woodward-a. Retailer variant-c for each. 15-Donaldson-a. 17-Flip cover with Shi story; Tucci-a. 25-Wraparound-c; character gallery 4.00
... Reborn 1-4 (7/09 - No. 4, 10/09, $3.99) David-s/Woodward-a; Illyria (from Angel) app. 4.00
... Return of the Son 1-4 (1/11 - No. 4, 4/11, $3.99) David-s/Woodward-a; 4.00
...: To Serve in Heaven TPB (8/06, $19.99) r/#1-5; gallery of reg & variant covers 20.00

FALLEN ANGEL ON THE WORLD OF MAGIC: THE GATHERING
Acclaim (Armada): May, 1996 ($5.95, one-shot)

1-Nancy Collins story 6.00

FALLEN ANGELS
Marvel Comics Group: April, 1987 - No. 8, Nov, 1987 (Limited series)

1-8 4.00

FALLEN ANGELS (Follows from House of X & Powers of X series)
Marvel Comics: Jan, 2020 - No. 6, Mar, 2020 ($4.99/$3.99, limited series)

1-($4.99) Bryan Hill-s/Szymon Kudranski-a; Psylocke, Magneto, Cable, X-23 app. 5.00
2-6-($3.99) 5,6-Bling! and Husk app. 4.00

FALLEN SON: THE DEATH OF CAPTAIN AMERICA
Marvel Comics: June, 2007 - No. 5, Aug, 2007 ($2.99, limited series)

Falling In Love #1 © DC

Family Tree #3 © 171 Studios & Hester

Famous First Edition C-26 © DC

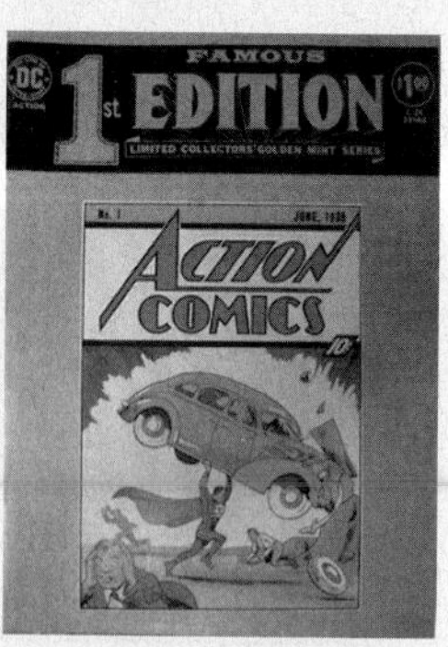

	GD 2.0	VG 4.0	FN 6.0	VF 8.0	VF/NM 9.0	NM- 9.2
1-5: Loeb-s in all. 1-Wolverine; Yu-a/c. 2-Avengers; McGuinness-a/c. 3-Captain America; Romita Jr.-a/c; Hawkeye app. 4-Spider-Man; Finch-c/a. 5-Cassaday-c/a						3.00
1-5-Variant covers by Turner						3.00
HC (2007, $19.99, dustjacket) r/#1-5						20.00
TPB (2008, $13.99) r/#1-5						14.00

FALLEN WORLD
Valiant Entertainment: May, 2019 - No. 5, Sept, 2019 ($3.99, limited series)

	GD	VG	FN	VF	VF/NM	NM-
1-5-Abnett-s/Pollina-a; cyborg samurai Rai in New Japan in 4002 AD						4.00

FALLING IN LOVE
Arleigh Pub. Co./National Per. Pub.: Sept-Oct, 1955 - No. 143, Oct-Nov, 1973

	GD	VG	FN	VF	VF/NM	NM-
1	52	104	156	328	552	775
2	28	56	84	168	274	380
3-10	18	36	54	107	169	230
11-20	15	30	45	86	133	180
21-40	14	28	42	76	108	140
41-47: 47-Last 10¢ issue	12	24	36	69	97	125
48-70	6	12	18	37	66	95
71-99,108: 108-Wood-a (4 pgs., 7/69)	4	8	12	28	47	65
100 (7/68)	5	10	15	30	50	70
101-107,109-124	3	6	9	19	30	40
125-133: 52 pgs.	4	8	12	25	40	55
134-143	3	6	9	15	22	28

NOTE: *Colan c/a-75, 81. 52 pgs.-#125-133.*

FALLING MAN, THE
Image Comics: Feb, 1998 ($2.95)

	GD	VG	FN	VF	VF/NM	NM-
1-McCorkindale-s/Hester-a						3.00

FALL OF THE HOUSE OF USHER, THE (See A Corben Special & Spirit section 8/22/48)

FALL OF THE HULKS (Also see Hulk and Incredible Hulk)
Marvel Comics: Feb, 2010 - July, 2010 ($3.99, one-shots & limited series)

	GD	VG	FN	VF	VF/NM	NM-
Alpha (2/10) Pelletier-a; The Leader, Dr. Doom, MODOK and The Thinker app.						4.00
Gamma (2/10) Romita Jr. -a; funeral for General Ross						4.00
Red Hulk (3/10 - No. 4, 6/10) 1-4: 1-A-Bomb app.						4.00
Savage She-Hulks (5/10 - No. 3, 7/10) 1-3: Cover tryptich by Campbell; Espin-a						4.00

FALL OF THE ROMAN EMPIRE (See Movie Comics)

FALL OUT TOY WORKS
Image Comics: Sept, 2009 - No. 5, Jun, 2010 ($3.99)

	GD	VG	FN	VF	VF/NM	NM-
1-5-Co-created by Pete Wentz of the band Fall Out Boy; Basri-a. 5-Lau-c						4.00

FAMILY AFFAIR (TV)
Gold Key: Feb, 1970 - No. 4, Oct, 1970 (25¢)

	GD	VG	FN	VF	VF/NM	NM-
1-With pull-out poster; photo-c	5	10	15	34	60	85
1-With poster missing	3	6	9	17	26	35
2-4-Photo-c	3	6	9	20	31	42

FAMILY DYNAMIC, THE
DC Comics: Oct, 2008 - No. 3, Dec, 2008 ($2.25)

	GD	VG	FN	VF	VF/NM	NM-
1-3-J. Torres-s/Tim Levins-a						3.00

FAMILY FUNNIES
Parents' Magazine Institute: No. 9, Aug-Sept, 1946

	GD	VG	FN	VF	VF/NM	NM-
9	6	12	18	31	38	45

FAMILY FUNNIES (Tiny Tot Funnies No. 9)
Harvey Publications: Sept, 1950 - No. 8, Apr, 1951

	GD	VG	FN	VF	VF/NM	NM-
1-Mandrake (has over 30 King Feature strips)	11	22	33	62	86	110
2-Flash Gordon, 1 pg.	8	16	24	42	54	65
3-8: 4,5,7-Flash Gordon, 1 pg.	7	14	21	35	43	50

FAMILY GUY (TV)
Devil's Due Publ.: 2006 ($6.95)

	GD	VG	FN	VF	VF/NM	NM-
nn-101 Ways to Kill Lois; 2-Peter Griffin's Guide to Parenting; 3-Books Don't Taste Very Good						7.00
... A Big Book o' Crap TPB (10/06, $16.95) r/nn,2,3						17.00

FAMILY MATTER
Kitchen Sink Press: 1998 ($24.95/$15.95, graphic novel)

	GD	VG	FN	VF	VF/NM	NM-
Hardcover ($24.95) Will Eisner-s/a						25.00
Softcover ($15.95)						16.00

FAMILY TREE
Image Comics: Nov, 2019 - No. 12 ($3.99)

	GD	VG	FN	VF	VF/NM	NM-
1-11-Jeff Lemire-s/Phil Hester-a/c						4.00

FAMOUS AUTHORS ILLUSTRATED (See Stories by...)

FAMOUS CRIMES
Fox Feature Syndicate/M.S. Dist. No. 51,52: June, 1948 - No. 19, Sept, 1950; No. 20, Aug, 1951; No. 51, 52, 1953

	GD 2.0	VG 4.0	FN 6.0	VF 8.0	VF/NM 9.0	NM- 9.2
1-Blue Beetle app. & crime story-r/Phantom Lady #16	148	296	444	947	1624	2300
2-Has woman dissolved in acid; lingerie-c/panels	65	130	195	416	708	1000
3-Injury-to-eye story used in **SOTI**, pg. 112; has two electrocution stories	71	142	213	454	777	1100
4-6	30	60	90	177	289	400
7- "Tarzan, the Wyoming Killer" (**SOTI**, pg. 44)	48	96	144	302	514	725
8-20: 17-Morisi-a. 20-Same cover as #15	22	44	66	130	213	295
51 (nd, 1953)	18	36	54	109	172	235
52 (Exist?)	18	36	54	109	172	235

FAMOUS FEATURE STORIES
Dell Publishing Co.: 1938 (7-1/2x11", 68 pgs.)

	GD	VG	FN	VF	VF/NM	NM-
1-Tarzan, Terry & the Pirates, King of the Royal Mtd., Buck Jones, Dick Tracy, Smilin' Jack, Dan Dunn, Don Winslow, G-Man, Tailspin Tommy, Mutt & Jeff, Little Orphan Annie reprints - all illustrated text	71	142	213	454	777	1100

FAMOUS FIRST EDITION (See Limited Collectors' Edition)
National Periodical Publications/DC Comics: ($1.00, 10x13-1/2", 72 pgs.) (No.6-8, 68 pgs.) 1974 - No. 8, Aug-Sept, 1975; C-61, 1979
(Hardbound editions with dust jackets are from Lyle Stuart, Inc.)

	GD	VG	FN	VF	VF/NM	NM-
C-26-Action Comics #1; gold ink outer-c	6	12	18	37	66	95
C-26-Hardbound edition w/dust jacket	15	30	45	105	233	360
C-28-Detective #27; silver ink outer-c	6	12	18	37	66	95
C-28-Hardbound edition w/dust jacket	15	30	45	105	233	360
C-30-Sensation #1(1974); bronze ink outer-c	5	10	15	30	50	70
C-30-Hardbound edition w/dust jacket	13	26	39	89	195	300
F-4-Whiz Comics #2(#1)(10-11/74)-Cover not identical to original (dropped "Gangway for Captain Marvel" from cover); gold ink on outer-c	5	10	15	30	50	70
F-4-Hardbound edition w/dust jacket	13	26	39	89	195	300
F-5-Batman #1(F-6 inside); silver ink on outer-c	5	10	15	33	57	80
F-5-Hardbound edition w/dust jacket (exist?)	13	26	39	89	195	300
V2#F-6-Wonder Woman #1	5	10	15	30	50	70
F-6-Wonder Woman #1 Hardbound w/dust jacket	13	26	39	89	195	300
F-7-All-Star Comics #3	5	10	15	30	50	70
F-8-Flash Comics #1(8-9/75)	5	10	15	30	50	70
V8#C-61-Superman #1(1979, $2.00)	4	8	12	27	44	60
V8#C-61 (Whitman variant)	4	8	12	28	47	65
V8#C-61 (Softcover in plain grey slipcase, edition of 250 copies) Each signed by Jerry Siegel and Joe Shuster at the bottom of the inside front cover						550.00

Warning: The above books are almost **exact** reprints of the originals that they represent except for the Giant-Size format. None of the originals are Giant-Size. The first five issues and C-61 were printed with two covers. Reprint information can be found on the outside cover, but not on the inside cover which was reprinted exactly like the original (inside and out).

FAMOUS FUNNIES
Eastern Color: 1934; July, 1934 - No. 218, July, 1955

A Carnival of Comics (See Promotional Comics section)

	GD	VG	FN	VF	VF/NM	NM-
Series 1-(Very rare)(nd-early 1934)(68 pgs.) No publisher given (Eastern Color PrintingCo.); sold in chain stores for 10¢. 35,000 print run. Contains Sunday strip reprints of Mutt & Jeff, Reg'lar Fellers, Nipper, Hairbreadth Harry, Strange As It Seems, Joe Palooka, Dixie Dugan, The Nebbs, Keeping Up With the Jones, and others. Inside front and back covers and pages 1-16 of Famous Funnies Series 1, #s 49-64 reprinted from **Famous Funnies, A Carnival of Comics**, and most of pages 17-48 reprinted from **Funnies on Parade**.	7400	14,800	22,200	44,500	--	--
No. 1 (Rare)(7/34-on stands 5/34) - Eastern Color Printing Co. First monthly newsstand comic book. Contains Sunday strip reprints of Toonerville Folks, Mutt & Jeff, Hairbreadth Harry, S'Matter Pop, Nipper, Dixie Dugan, The Bungle Family, Connie, Ben Webster, Tailspin Tommy, The Nebbs, Joe Palooka, & others.	3300	6600	9900	24,800	--	--
2 (Rare, 9/34)	812	1624	2436	6100	--	--
3-Buck Rogers Sunday strip-r by Rick Yager begins, ends #218; not in #191-208; 1st comic book app. of Buck Rogers; the number of the 1st strip reprinted is pg. 190, Series No. 1	960	1920	2880	7200	--	--
4	340	680	1020	2550	--	--
5-1st Christmas-c on a newsstand comic	375	750	1125	2800	--	--
6-10	250	500	750	1875	--	--
11,12,18-Four pgs. of Buck Rogers in each issue, completes stories in Buck Rogers #1 which lacks these pages. 18-Two pgs. of Buck Rogers reprinted in Daisy Comics #1	123	246	369	787	1344	1900
13-17,19,20: 14-Has two Buck Rogers panels missing. 17-2nd Christmas-c on a newsstand comic (12/35)	92	184	276	593	1009	1425
21,23-30: 27-(10/36)-War on Crime begins (4 pgs.); 1st true crime in comics (reprints); part photo-c. 29-X-Mas-c (12/36)	68	136	204	435	743	1050
22-Four pgs. of Buck Rogers needed to complete stories in Buck Rogers #1	82	164	246	528	902	1275

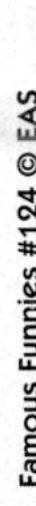
Famous Funnies #124 © EAS

Famous Stars #4 © Z-D

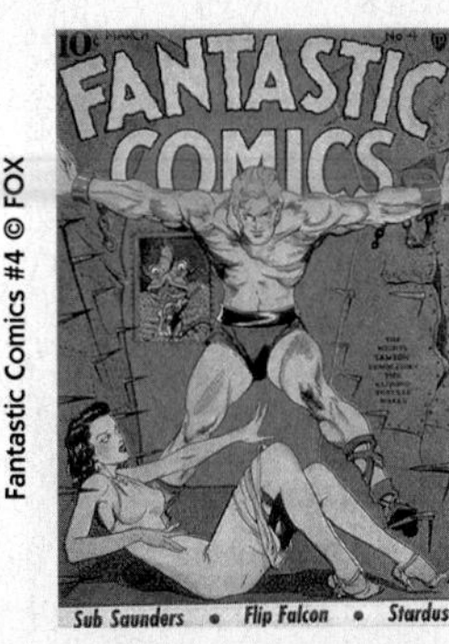

Fantastic Comics #4 © FOX

GD VG FN VF VF/NM NM-
2.0 4.0 6.0 8.0 9.0 9.2

31,33,34,36,37,39,40: 33-Careers of Baby Face Nelson & John Dillinger traced
50 100 150 315 533 750
32-(3/37) 1st app. the Phantom Magician (costume hero) in Advs. of Patsy
55 110 165 352 601 850
35-Two pgs. Buck Rogers omitted in Buck Rogers #2
55 110 165 352 601 850
38-Full color portrait of Buck Rogers 48 96 144 288 532 775
41-60: 41,53-X-Mas-c. 55-Last bottom panel, pg. 4 in Buck Rogers redrawn in Buck Rogers #3 39 78 117 231 378 525
61,63,64,66,67,69,70 27 54 81 158 259 360
62,65,68,73-78-Two pgs. Kirby-a "Lightnin' & the Lone Rider". 65,77-X-Mas-c
29 58 87 170 278 385
71,79,80: 80-(3/41)-Buck Rogers story continues from Buck Rogers #5
24 48 72 142 234 325
72-Speed Spaulding begins by Marvin Bradley (artist), ends #88. This series was written by Edwin Balmer & Philip Wylie (later appeared as film & book "When Worlds Collide")
25 50 75 147 241 335
81-Origin & 1st app. Invisible Scarlet O'Neil (4/41); strip begins #82, ends #167; 1st non-funny-c (Scarlet O'Neil) 39 78 117 231 378 525
82-Buck Rogers-c 36 72 108 216 351 485
83-87,90: 86-Connie vs. Monsters on the Moon-c (sci/fi). 87 has last Buck Rogers full page-r. 90-Bondage-c 21 42 63 122 199 275
88,89: 88-Buck Rogers in "Moon's End" by Calkins, 2 pgs.(not reprints). Beginning with #88, all Buck Rogers pgs. have rearranged panels. 89-Origin & 1st app. Fearless Flint, the Flint Man 23 46 69 136 223 310
91-93,95,96,98-99,101,103-110: 98-Hitler, Tojo and Mussolini on inside back-c. 101-Christmas cover. 105-Series 2 begins (Strip Page #1) 17 34 51 98 154 210
94-Buck Rogers in "Solar Holocaust" by Calkins, 3 pgs.(not reprints)
18 36 54 107 169 230
97-War Bond promotion, Buck Rogers by Calkins, 2 pgs.(not reprints)
18 36 54 107 169 230
100-1st comic to reach #100; 100th Anniversary cover features 11 major Famous Funnies characters, including Buck Rogers 23 46 69 136 223 310
102-Chief Wahoo vs. Hitler,Tojo & Mussolini-c (1/43) 82 164 246 528 902 1275
111-130 (5/45): 113-X-Mas-c 14 28 42 76 108 140
131-150 (1/47): 137-Strip page No. 110 omitted; Christmas-c. 144-(7/46) 12th Anniversary cover 12 24 36 69 97 125
151-162,164-168: 162-New Year's Eve-c 11 22 33 64 90 115
163-St. Valentine's Day-c (2/48) 14 28 42 76 108 140
169,170-Two text illos. by Al Williamson, his 1st comic book work
14 28 42 80 115 150
171-190: 171-Strip pgs. 227,229,230, Series 2 omitted. 172-Strip Pg. 232 omitted. 173-Christmas-c. 190-Buck Rogers ends with start of strip pg. 302, Series 2; Oaky Doaks-c/story 11 22 33 60 83 105
191-197,199,201,203,206-208: No Buck Rogers. 191-Barney Carr, Space detective begins, ends #192. 10 20 30 58 79 100
198,200,202,205-One pg. Frazetta ads; no B. Rogers 11 22 33 60 83 105
204-Used in **POP**, pg. 79,99; war-c begin, end #208 11 22 33 64 90 115
209-216: Frazetta-c. 209-Buck Rogers begins (12/53) with strip pg. 480, Series 2; 211-Buck Rogers ads by Anderson begins, ends #217. #215-Contains B. Rogers strip pg. 515-518, series 2 followed by pgs.179-181, Series 3 200 400 600 1280 2190 3100
217-Buck Rogers-c 18 36 54 109 172 235
218-Buck Rogers ends with pg. 199, Series 3; Wee Three-c/story
11 22 33 60 83 105

NOTE: ***Rick Yager*** *did the Buck Rogers Sunday strips reprinted in Famous Funnies. The Sundays were formerly done by Russ Keaton and Lt. Dick Calkins did the dailies, but would sometimes assist Yager on a panel or two from time to time. Strip No. 169 is Yager's first full Buck Rogers page. Yager did the strip until 1958 when* ***Murphy Anderson*** *took over.* ***Tuska*** *art from 4/26/59 - 1965. Virtually every panel was rewritten for Famous Funnies. Not identical to the original Sunday page. The Buck Rogers reprints run continuously through Famous Funnies issue No. 190 (Strip No. 302) with no break in story line. The story line has no continuity after No. 190. The Buck Rogers newspaper strips came out in four series: Series 1, 3/30/30 - 9/21/41 (No. 1 - 600); Series 2, 9/28/41 -10/21/51 (No. 1 -525)(Strip No. 110-1/2 (1/2 pg.) published in only a few newspapers); Series 3, 10/28/51 -2/9/58 (No. 100-428) (No No.1-99); Series 4, 2/16/58 - 6/13/65 (No numbers, dates only).* ***Everett*** *c-85, 86.* ***Moulton*** *a-100. Chief Wahoo c-93, 97, 102, 116, 136, 139, 151. Dickie Dare c-83, 88. Fearless Flint c-89. Invisible Scarlet O'Neil c-81, 87, 95, 121(part), 132. Scorchy Smith c-84, 90.*

FAMOUS FUNNIES
Eastern Color: 1936

nn-2-color cvr/reprint of #10 w/issue #21(4/36) on inside. Blank back & interior cvrs. A CGC 5.5 copy sold in 2018 for $1920

FAMOUS FUNNIES
Super Comics: 1964

Super Reprint Nos. 15-18:17-r/Double Trouble #1. 18-Space Comics #?
2 4 6 9 12 15

FAMOUS GANGSTERS (Crime on the Waterfront No. 4)
Avon Periodicals/Realistic No. 3: Apr, 1951 - No. 3, Feb, 1952

1-3: 1-Capone, Dillinger; c-/Avon paperback #329. 2-Dillinger Machine Gun Killer; Wood-c/a (1 pg.); r/Saint #7 & retitled "Mike Strong". 3-Lucky Luciano & Murder, Inc; c-/Avon paperback #66 42 84 126 265 445 625

FAMOUS INDIAN TRIBES
Dell Publishing Co.: July-Sept, 1962; No. 2, July, 1972

12-264-209(#1) (The Sioux) 3 6 9 15 21 26
2(7/72)-Reprints above 1 3 4 6 8 10

FAMOUS STARS
Ziff-Davis Publ. Co.: Nov-Dec, 1950 - No. 6, Spring, 1952 (All have photo-c)

1-Shelley Winters, Susan Peters, Ava Gardner, Shirley Temple; Jimmy Stewart & Shelley Winters photo-c; Whitney-a 41 82 123 250 418 585
2-Betty Hutton, Bing Crosby, Colleen Townsend, Gloria Swanson; Betty Hutton photo-c; Everett-a(2) 30 60 90 177 289 400
3-Farley Granger, Judy Garland's ordeal (life story; she died 6/22/69 at the age of 47), Alan Ladd; Farley Granger photo-c; Whitney-a 36 72 108 216 351 485
4-Al Jolson, Bob Mitchum, Ella Raines, Richard Conte, Vic Damone; Jane Russell and Bob Mitchum photo-c; Crandall-a, 6pgs. 25 50 75 150 245 340
5-Liz Taylor, Betty Grable, Esther Williams, George Brent, Mario Lanza; Liz Taylor photo-c; Krigstein-a 57 114 171 362 619 875
6-Gene Kelly, Hedy Lamarr, June Allyson, William Boyd, Janet Leigh, Gary Cooper; Gene Kelly photo-c 24 48 72 140 230 320

FAMOUS STORIES (...Book No. 2)
Dell Publishing Co.: 1942 - No. 2, 1942

1,2: 1-Treasure Island. 2-Tom Sawyer 31 62 93 182 296 410

FAMOUS TV FUNDAY FUNNIES
Harvey Publications: Sept, 1961 (25¢ Giant)

1-Casper the Ghost, Baby Huey, Little Audrey 5 10 15 34 60 85

FAMOUS WESTERN BADMEN (Formerly Redskin)
Youthful Magazines: No. 13, Dec, 1952 - No. 15, Apr, 1953

13-Redskin story 15 30 45 88 137 185
14,15: 15-The Dalton Boys story 11 22 33 64 90 115

FAN BOY
DC Comics: Mar, 1999 - No. 6, Aug, 1999 ($2.50, limited series)

1-6: 1-Art by Aragonés and various in all. 2-Green Lantern-c/a by Gil Kane. 3-JLA. 4-Sgt. Rock art by Heath, Marie Severin. 5-Batman art by Sprang, Adams, Miller, Timm. 6-Wonder Woman; art by Rude, Grell 3.00
TPB (2001, $12.95) r/#1-6 13.00

FANBOYS VS. ZOMBIES
BOOM! Studios: Apr, 2012 - No. 20, Nov, 2013 ($1.00/$3.99)

1-($1.00) Eight covers; Humphries-s/Gaylord-a; zombies at San Diego Comic-Con 3.00
2-20-($3.99) 2-12-Multiple covers on each. 17-Bryan Turner-a 4.00

FANTASTIC (Formerly Captain Science; Beware No. 10 on)
Youthful Magazines: No. 8, Feb, 1952 - No. 9, Apr, 1952

8-Capt. Science by Harrison 58 116 174 371 636 900
9-Harrison-a; decapitation, shrunken head panels 43 86 129 271 461 650

FANTASTIC ADVENTURES
Super Comics: 1963 - 1964 (Reprints)

9,10,12,15,16,18: 9-r/? 10-r/He-Man #2(Toby). 11-Disbrow-a. 12-Unpublished Chesler material? 15-r/Spook #23. 16-r/Dark Shadows #2(Steinway); Briefer-a.18-r/Superior Stories #1 3 6 9 17 26 35
11-Wood-a; r/Blue Bolt #118 4 8 12 23 37 50
17-Baker-a(2) r/Seven Seas #6 4 8 12 23 37 50

FANTASTIC COMICS
Fox Feature Syndicate: Dec, 1939 - No. 23, Nov, 1941

1-Intro/origin Samson; Stardust, The Super Wizard, Sub Saunders (by Kiefer), Space Smith, Capt. Kidd begin 861 1722 2583 6285 10,893 15,500
2-Powell text illos 354 708 1062 2478 4339 6200
3-Classic Lou Fine Robot-c; Powell text illos 6900 13,800 20,700 30,400 40,200 50,000
4-Lou Fine-c 331 662 993 2317 4059 5800
5-Classic Lou Fine-c 427 854 1281 3117 5509 7900
6,7-Simon-c. 6-Bondage/torture-c 300 600 900 1990 3495 5000
8-Bondage/torture-c 226 452 678 1446 2473 3500
9,10: 9-Bondage-c. 10-Intro/origin David, Samson's aide
168 336 504 1075 1838 2600
11-16,18-20: 11-Bondage/torture on a bed of nails-c. 16-Stardust ends
139 278 417 890 1520 2150
17,23: 17-1st app. Black Fury & sidekick Chuck; ends #23. 23-Origin The Gladiator
148 296 444 947 1624 2300

Fantastic Fears #5 © AJAX

Fantastic Four #15 © MAR

Fantastic Four #94 © MAR

GD VG FN VF VF/NM NM-
2.0 4.0 6.0 8.0 9.0 9.2

21-The Banshee begins(origin); ends #23; Hitler-c 290 580 870 1856 3178 4500
22-WWII Holocaust bondage torture-c (likeness of Hitler as furnace on-c)
541 1082 1623 3950 6975 10,000

NOTE: *Lou Fine c-1-5. Tuska a-3-5, 8. Issue #11 has indicia to Mystery Men Comics #15. All issues feature Samson covers.*

FANTASTIC COMICS (Imagining of a 1941 issue by modern creators in Golden Age style)
Image Comics: No. 24, Jan, 2008 ($5.99, Golden Age sized, one-shot)

24-Samson, Yank Wilson, Stardust, Sub Saunders, Space Smith, Capt. Kidd app.; Larsen-c/a; art by Allred, Sienkiewicz, Yeates, Scioli, Hembeck, Ashley Wood & others 6.00

FANTASTIC COMICS (Fantastic Fears #1-9; Becomes Samson #12)
Ajax/Farrell Publ.: No. 10, Nov-Dec, 1954 - No. 11, Jan-Feb, 1955

10 (#1) 30 60 90 177 289 400
11-Robot-c 36 72 108 214 347 480

FANTASTIC FABLES
Silverwolf Comics: Feb, 1987 - No. 2, 1987 ($1.50, 28 pgs., B&W)

1,2: 1-Tim Vigil-a (6 pgs.). 2-Tim Vigil-a (7 pgs.) 4.00

FANTASTIC FEARS (Formerly Captain Jet) (Fantastic Comics #10 on)
Ajax/Farrell Publ.: No. 7, May, 1953 - No. 9, Sept-Oct, 1954

7(#1, 5/53)-Tales of Stalking Terror 90 180 270 576 988 1400
8(#2, 7/53) 53 106 159 334 567 800
3,4 47 94 141 296 498 700
5-(1-2/54)-Ditko story (1st drawn) is written by Bruce Hamilton; r-in Weird V2#8 (1st pro work for Ditko but Daring Love #1 was published 1st) 206 412 618 1318 2259 3200
6-Decapitation-girl's head w/paper cutter (classic) 123 246 369 787 1344 1900
7(5-6/54), 9(9-10/54) 41 82 123 256 428 600
8(7-8/54)-Contains story intended for Jo-Jo; name changed to Kaza; decapitation story
43 86 129 271 461 650

FANTASTIC FIVE
Marvel Comics: Oct, 1999 - No. 5, Feb, 2000 ($1.99)

1-5: 1-M2 Universe; recaps origin; Ryan-a. 2-Two covers 3.00
Spider-Girl Presents Fantastic Five: In Search of Doom (2006, $7.99, digest) r/#1-5 8.00

FANTASTIC FIVE
Marvel Comics: Sept, 2007 - No. 5, Nov, 2007 ($2.99, limited series)

1-5-DeFalco-s/Lim-a; Dr. Doom returns vs. the future Fantastic Five 3.00
...: The Final Doom TPB (2007, $13.99) r/#1-5; cover sketches with inks 14.00

FANTASTIC FORCE
Marvel Comics: Nov, 1994 - No. 18, Apr, 1996 ($1.75)

1-($2.50)-Foil wraparound-c; intro Fantastic Force w/Huntara, Devlor, Psi-Lord & Vibraxas 5.00
2-18: 13-She-Hulk app. 4.00

FANTASTIC FORCE (See Fantastic Four #558, Nu-World heroes from 500 years in the future)
Marvel Comics: Jun, 2009 - No. 4, Sept, 2009 ($3.99/$2.99, limited series)

1-($3.99)-Ahearne-s/Kurth-a/Hitch-c; Fantastic Four app. 4.00
2-4-($2.99) 3,4-Ego the Living Planet app. 3.00

FANTASTIC FOUR (See America's Best TV..., Fireside Book Series, Giant-Size..., Giant Size Super-Stars, Marvel Age..., Marvel Collectors Item Classics, Marvel Knights 4, Marvel Milestone Edition, Marvel's Greatest, Marvel Treasury Edition, Marvel Triple Action, Official Marvel Index to..., Power Record Comics & Ultimate...)

FANTASTIC FOUR (See Volume Three for issues #500-611)
Marvel Comics Group: Nov, 1961 - No. 416, Sept, 1996 (Created by Stan Lee & Jack Kirby)

1-Origin & 1st app. The Fantastic Four (Reed Richards: Mr. Fantastic, Johnny Storm: The Human Torch, Sue Storm: The Invisible Girl, & Ben Grimm: The Thing–Marvel's 1st super-hero group since the G.A.; 1st app. S.A. Human Torch); origin/1st app. The Mole Man.
4650 9300 18,600 46,000 128,000 210,000
1-Golden Record Comic Set Reprint (1966)-cover not identical to original
27 54 81 189 420 650
with Golden Record 33 66 99 238 532 850
2-Vs. The Skrulls (last 10¢ issue); (should have a pin-up of The Thing which many copies are missing) 540 1080 1620 4450 11,225 18,000
3-Fantastic Four don costumes & establish Headquarters; brief 1pg. origin; intro. The Fantasti-Car; Human Torch drawn w/two left hands on-c
450 900 1350 4150 10,325 16,500
4-1st S. A. Sub-Mariner app. (5/62) 540 1080 1620 4450 11,225 18,000
5-Origin & 1st app. Doctor Doom 2000 4000 6000 16,000 33,000 50,000
6-Sub-Mariner, Dr. Doom team up; 1st Marvel villain team-up (2nd S.A. Sub-Mariner app.
241 482 723 1988 4494 7000
7,9,10: 7-1st app. Kurrgo. 9-3rd Sub-Mariner app. 10-Stan Lee & Jack Kirby app. in story
159 318 477 1336 2893 4450
8-1st app. Puppet-Master & Alicia Masters 166 332 498 1370 3085 4800
11-Origin/1st app. The Impossible Man (2/63) 152 304 456 1254 2827 4400
12-Fantastic Four vs. The Hulk (1st meeting); 1st Hulk x-over & ties w/Amazing Spider-Man #1 as 1st Marvel x-over; (3/63) 375 750 1125 3400 8950 14,500
13-Intro. The Watcher; 1st app. The Red Ghost 172 344 516 1419 3210 5000
14,15,17,19: 14-Sub-Mariner x-over. 15-1st app. Mad Thinker. 19-Intro. Rama-Tut (Kang)
61 122 183 488 1094 1700
16-1st Ant-Man x-over (7/63); Wasp cameo 84 168 252 672 1511 2350
18-Origin/1st app. The Super Skrull 96 192 288 768 1734 2700
20-Origin/1st app. The Molecule Man 63 126 189 510 1130 1750
21-Intro. The Hate Monger; 1st Sgt. Fury x-over (12/63)
46 92 138 359 805 1250
22-24: 22-Sue Storm gains more powers 37 74 111 274 612 950
25-The Hulk vs. The Thing (their 1st battle); 3rd Avengers x-over (1st time w/Captain America)(cameo, 4/64); 2nd S.A. app. Cap (takes place between Avengers #4 & 5)
89 178 267 712 1606 2500
26-The Hulk vs. The Thing (continued); 4th Avengers x-over
64 128 192 512 1156 1800
27-1st Doctor Strange x-over (6/64) 46 92 138 340 770 1200
28-Early X-Men x-over (7/64); same date as X-Men #6
53 106 159 424 950 1475
29,30: 30-Intro. Diablo 28 56 84 202 451 700
31-35,37-40: 31-Early Avengers x-over (10/64). 33-1st app. Attuma; part photo-c. 35-Intro/1st app. Dragon Man. 39-Wood inks on Daredevil (early x-over)
22 44 66 154 340 525
36-Intro/1st app. Madam Medusa & the Frightful Four (Sandman, Wizard, Paste Pot Pete)
54 108 162 432 966 1500
41-44: 41-43-Frightful Four app. 44-Intro. Gorgon 14 28 42 96 211 325
45-Intro/1st app. The Inhumans (c/story, 12/65); also see Incredible Hulk Special #1 & Thor #146, & 147 125 250 375 1000 2250 3500
46-1st Black Bolt-c (Kirby) & 1st full app. 46 92 138 368 834 1300
47-3rd app. The Inhumans 20 40 60 135 300 465
48-Partial origin/1st app. The Silver Surfer & Galactus (3/66) by Lee & Kirby; Galactus brief app. in last panel; 1st of 3 part story 207 414 621 1708 3854 6000
49-2nd app./1st cover Silver Surfer & Galactus 141 282 423 1142 2571 4000
50-Silver Surfer battles Galactus; full S.S.-c 107 214 321 856 1928 3000
51-Classic "This Man...This Monster" story 28 56 84 202 451 700
52-1st app. The Black Panther (7/66) 300 600 900 2550 5775 9000
53-Origin & 2nd app. The Black Panther; origin/1st app. of Klaw
28 56 84 202 451 700
54-Inhumans cameo 12 24 36 84 185 285
55-Thing battles Silver Surfer; 4th app. Silver Surfer 28 56 84 202 451 700
56-Silver Surfer cameo 13 26 39 87 191 295
57-60: Dr. Doom steals Silver Surfer's powers (also see Silver Surfer: Loftier Than Mortals). 59,60-Inhumans cameo 10 20 30 67 141 215
61-63,68-71: 61-Silver Surfer cameo; Sandman app. (new costume). 62-1st Blastaar; Sandman app. 63-Sandman & Blastaar team-up 8 16 24 55 105 155
64-1st Kree Sentry #459 9 18 27 63 129 195
65-1st app. Ronan the Accuser; 1st Kree Supreme Intelligence
20 40 60 141 313 485
66-Begin 2 part origin of Him (Warlock); does not app. (9/67)
25 50 75 175 388 600
66,67-2nd printings (1994) 2 4 6 11 16 20
67-Origin/1st brief app. Him (Warlock); 1 page; see Thor #165,166 for 1st full app.; white cover scarcer in true high grade 46 92 138 340 770 1200
72-Silver Surfer-c/story (pre-dates Silver Surfer #1) 19 38 57 131 291 450
73-Spider-Man, D.D., Thor x-over; cont'd from Daredevil #38
11 22 33 72 154 235
74-Silver Surfer app. 12 24 36 82 179 275
75-77: Silver Surfer app.(#77 is same date/S.S. #1) 10 20 30 65 135 205
78-80: 78-Wizard app. 80-1st Tomazooma, the Living Totem
6 12 18 42 79 115
81,84-88: 81-Crystal joins & dons costume; vs. the Wizard. 84-87-Dr. Doom app. 88-Mole Man app. 6 12 18 40 73 105
82,83-Black Bolt & the Inhumans app.; vs. Maximus 6 12 18 41 80 125
89-93,95-98,101: 89-Mole Man app. 91-Skrulls disguised as 1930s era gangsters; 1st app. Torgo. 92-The Thing app. as a space gladiator. 93-Thing vs. Torgo. 95-1st app. the Monocle. 96-Mad-Thinker app. 98-Neil Armstrong Moon landing issue. 101-Last Kirby-a issue
6 12 18 37 66 95
94-(1/70) Intro Agatha Harkness; Frightful Four app. 7 14 21 48 89 130
99-Black Bolt & the Inhumans app. 6 12 18 40 73 105
100 (7/70) F.F. vs Thinker and Puppet-Master 9 18 27 62 126 190
102-104: 102-Romita Sr-a; 102-104-Sub-Mariner & Magneto app.
6 12 18 37 66 95
105,106,108,109,111: 108-Features Kirby & Buscema-a; Kirby material produced after issue #101, his last official issue before leaving Marvel. 109-Annihilus app. 111-Hulk cameo 5 10 15 35 63 90

Fantastic Four #197 © MAR

Fantastic Four #257 © MAR

Fantastic Four #307 © MAR

	GD	VG	FN	VF	VF/NM	NM-
	2.0	4.0	6.0	8.0	9.0	9.2

107-Classic Thing transformation-c; 1st John Buscema-a on FF (2/71); 1st app. Janus
6 12 18 40 73 105

110-Initial version w/green Thing and blue faces and pink uniforms on-c
24 48 72 168 372 575

110-Corrected-c w/accurately colored faces and uniforms and orange Thing
6 12 18 41 76 110

112-Hulk Vs. Thing (7/71) 23 46 69 156 348 540

113-115: 113-1st app. The Overmind; Watcher app. 114-vs the Overmind. 115-Origin of the Overmind; plot by Stan Lee, Archie Goodwin script; last 15¢ issue
5 10 15 30 50 70

116 (52 pgs.) FF and Dr. Doom vs. the Overmind; the Stranger app.; Goodwin story
6 12 18 41 76 110

117-119: 117,118-Diablo app; Goodwin-s 119-Black Panther app. vs Klaw; 1st Roy Thomas FF story 4 8 12 28 47 65

120-1st app. Gabriel the Air-Walker (new herald of Galactus); Stan Lee story
8 16 24 54 102 150

121,123: 121-Silver Surfer vs. Gabriel; Galactus app. 123-Silver Surfer & Galactus app.
6 12 18 37 65 95

122-Silver Surfer & Galactus app; black cover, scarcer in higher grade
6 12 18 41 76 110

124,125,127,130,134-140: 125-Last Stan Lee-s. 127-Mole Man & Tyrannus app. 130-vs the new Frightful Four (Thundra, Sandman, Trapster and Wizard; Black Bolt & Inhumans app.). 134,135-Dragon Man app. 134-1st full Gerry Conway issue. 136-Shaper of Worlds app; Dragon Man cameo. 137-Shaper of Worlds app. 138-Return of the Miracle Man. 139-vs. Miracle Man. 140-Annihilus app. 4 8 12 23 37 50

126-Origin FF retold; cover swipe of FF #1; Roy Thomas scripts begin
4 8 12 27 44 60

128-Four page glossy insert of FF Friends & Foes; Mole Man app.
4 8 12 25 40 55

129,131-133: 1st app. Thundra (super-strong Femizon) joins new Frightful Four; Medusa app. 131-Black Bolt, Medusa, Crystal, Quicksilver app; New Frightful Four app; Ross Andru-a; Steranko-c. 132-Black Bolt & Inhumans app.; vs. Maximus; last Roy Thomas-s (returns in issue #158). 133-Thing vs Thundra battle issue; Ramona Fradon-a; Gerry Conway script
5 10 15 31 53 75

141-Franklin Richards 'depowered'; Annihilus app.; FF break-up; last Buscema-a
4 8 12 23 37 50

142-146,148-149: 142-1st Darkoth the Demon; Dr. Doom app; Kirbyish-a by Buckler begins. 143,144-vs. Dr. Doom. 145,146-vs. Ternak the Abominable Snowman. 148-vs. Wizard, Sandman, Trapster. 149-Sub-Mariner app. 3 6 9 21 33 45

147-Thing vs. Sub-Mariner-c/s 4 8 12 27 44 60

150-Crystal & Quicksilver's wedding; Avengers, Ultron-7 and Black Bolt & the Inhumans app; story continued from Avengers #127 5 10 15 31 53 75

151-154,158-160: 151-1st Mahkizmo the Nuclear Man; origin Thundra. 152,153-Thundra & Mahkizmo app. 154-Nick Fury app; part-r issue (Strange Tales #127). 158,159 vs. Xemu; Black Bolt & Inhumans app. 160-Arkon app. 3 6 9 15 22 28

155-157: Silver Surfer & Dr. Doom in all 3 6 9 19 30 40

161-163,168-171: 162,163-Arkon app. 168-Luke Cage, Power Man joins the FF (to replace the Thing). 169-Luke Cage app; 1st app. Thing exoskeleton. 170-Luke Cage leaves the FF; Puppet Master app. 171-1st Gorr the Golden Gorilla; Pérez-a
2 4 6 10 14 18

164,165: 164-Re-intro Marvel Boy (as the Crusader); 1st George Pérez-a on FF. 165-Origin of Marvel Boy & the Crusader; 1st app. Frankie Ray. Pérez-a; death of the Crusader (a new Marvel Boy appears in Captain America #217) 3 6 9 16 23 30

166,167-vs the Hulk; Pérez-a. 167-The Thing loses his powers
3 6 9 17 26 35

169-173-(30¢-c, limited distribution)(4-8/76) 5 10 15 33 57 80

172-175: 172-Galactus & High Evolutionary app. 175-Galactus vs. High Evolutionary; the Thing regains his powers 2 4 6 10 15 20

176-180: 176-Re-intro Impossible Man; Marvel artists app. 177-1st app. the Texas Twister & Captain Ultra; Impossible Man & Brute app. 178-179-Impossible Man, Tigra & Thundra app; Reed loses his stretching ability. 180-r/#101 by Kirby
2 4 6 10 14 18

181-199: 181-183-The Brute, Mad Thinker & Annihilus app; last Roy Thomas-s. 184-1st Eliminator; Len Wein-s begin. (co-plotter in #183-182) 185,186-New Salem Witches app.; part origin Agatha Harkness. 187,188-vs. Klaw & the Molecule Man. 189-G.A Human Torch app.; r-FF Annual #4. 190-1st Marv Wolfman FF. 191-FF break-up; Wolfman/Wein-s. 192-Last Pérez-a; Texas Twister app. 193,194-Diablo & Darkoth the Death Demon app. 195-Sub-Mariner app.; Wolfman begins as full plotter & scripter. 196-1st full app. of the clone of Dr. Doom. 197-vs. the Red Ghost; Reed regains his stretching ability. 198-vs Dr. Doom. 199-Origin & death of the clone of Doom; Dr. Doom app. 2 4 6 8 10 12

200-(11/78 52 pgs)-FF reunited vs. Dr. Doom 3 6 9 16 23 30

201-203,219,222-231: 202-vs. Quasimodo. 219-Sub-Mariner app.; Moench & Sienkiewicz 1st FF work. 222-Agatha Harkness & Gabriel the Devil Hunter app. 224-Contains unused alternate-c for #3 and pin-ups. 225-Thor & Odin app. 226-1st Samurai Destroyer. 229-1st Ebon-Seeker. 230-vs. Ebon Seeker; Avengers app. 231-1st Stygorr of the Negative Zone 6.00

204-1st Nova Corps (cameo); 1st app. Queen Adora of Xandar; 1st app. of Xandar; FF vs. the Skrulls 2 4 6 11 16 20

205-208: 205-1st full app. Nova Corps; Xandarian/Skrull war. 206-Nova app.; story continued from Nova #25; Sphinx & Skrulls app. 207-Spider-Man app. 208-Nova & and the New Champions app. (Powerhouse, Diamondhead, the Comet & Crimebuster); Sphinx app.
1 2 3 5 6 8

209-210,213,214: 209-1st Byrne-a on FF; 1st Herbie the Robot. 210-Galactus app. 213-Galactus vs. the Sphinx; Terrax app. 1 3 4 6 8 10

211-1st app. Terrax (new Herald of Galactus) 5 10 15 33 57 80

212-Byrne-a; Galactus vs. the High Evolutionary 2 4 6 11 16 20

215-218,220-221: Byrne-a in all. 215-Blastaar app; 1st app. the Futurist. 216-Blastaar & Futurist app; last Wolfman-s. 217-Early app. Dazzler (4/80); by Byrne; vs Herbie the Robot (destroyed). 218-Spider-Man app; vs. Frightful Four; continued from Spectacular Spider-Man #42. 220-1st Byrne story on FF; origin retold; Avengers and Vindicator app.
1 2 3 5 6 8

232-Byrne story & art begins (7/81); vs. Diablo; brief Dr. Strange app; re-intro Frankie Raye
2 4 6 9 12 15

233-235,237-241,245-249,251,253-256: 233-Hammerhead app. 234,235-Ego the Living Planet. 238-Origin & 1st app. of Frankie Raye's flame powers, joins the FF. The Thing is 'devolved' into an 'uglier' version. 239-1st app. Aunt Petunia. 240-Black Bolt & the Inhumans app; Attilan (home of the Inhumans) relocated to the Moon. 241-Black Panther app. 245-Thing returns to his rocky-look. 246-Dr. Doom returns. 247-Doom and FF team-up vs. Prince Zorba; Doom regains rule of Latveria; 1st app. Kristoff. 248-Black Bolt & and the Inhumans app. 249-vs Gladiator (of the Sh'iar). 251-FF explore the Negative Zone; Annihilus app. 254-1st Mantracora. 255-Brief Daredevil app; Annihilus app. 256-FF return from the Negative Zone; vs Annihilus; Avengers, Galactus and Nova (Frankie Raye) app. 6.00

236-20th Anniversary issue (11/81, 68 pgs, $1.00)-brief origin FF; Byrne-c(p)/a; new Kirby-a; Marvel Super-Heroes & Stan Lee app. on cover; Dr. Doom and Puppet Master app.; 1st 'Liddleville' 1 2 3 5 6 8

242-vs. Terrax; Thor, Iron Man & Daredevil cameos 1 2 3 5 6 8

243-Classic Galactus-c by Byrne; Thor, Captain America, Dr. Strange, Spider-Man & Daredevil app. 2 4 6 13 18 22

244-Frankie Raye becomes Nova – the new Herald of Galactus
3 6 9 17 26 35

250,257-260: 250-(52 pgs)-Spider-Man x-over; Byrne-a; Skrulls impersonate New X-Men; Gladiator app. 257-Galactus devours the Skrull homeworld; Sue announces pregnancy; Vision & Scarlet Witch cameo. 258-Dr. Doom team-up with Terrax; Kristoff app. 259-Dr. Doom & Terrax. vs FF; Silver Surfer cameo. 260-Terrax, Silver Surfer & Sub-Mariner app.; 'death' of Dr. Doom 1 2 3 5 6 8

252-Reads sideways; Annihilus app. Contains skin 'Tattooz' decals (no 'Tattooz' were included in Canadian editions, also in Amazing Spider-Man #238)
with Tattooz 1 2 3 5 6 8
without Tattooz 6.00

261-262: The Trial of Reed Richards. 261-Silver Surfer & the Watcher app. 262-Origin Galactus; John Byrne writes himself into story; the Watcher, Odin, Eternity app. 6.00

263-285: 263-Mole Man app. Vision cameo. 264-vs Mole Man; swipes-c of FF #1. 265-Secret Wars x-over; She-Hulk replaces the Thing; Vision & Scarlet Witch app. 267-Dr. Octopus, Michael Morbius, Donald Blake & Bruce Banner app; Sue loses her baby. 268-Origin She-Hulk retold; Hulk and Dr. Octopus app. 269-1st app. Terminus; re-intro. Wyatt Wingfoot. 270-vs Terminus. 271-1st Gormuu (flashback story pre-FF #1). 272-1st app. Nathaniel Richards – the Warlord (Reed's father). 273-Nathaniel Richards app. 274-Spider-Man's alien costume app; (4th app. 1/85, 2 pgs.) the Thing app. on Battleworld. 275-She-Hulk solo story. 276-Mephisto & Dr. Strange app. 277-Split story format - the Thing returns to Earth and battles Dire Wraiths; FF battle Mephisto; Dr. Strange app. 278-Origin Dr. Doom retold; Kristoff becomes new Dr. Doom. 279-Baxter Building destroyed by Kristoff; new Hate Monger app. 280-New Hate Monger & Psycho Man app.; 1st app. Sue as Malice. 281-New Hate Monger, Malice & Psycho Man app. 282-Power Pack cameo; Secret Wars II x-over; Psycho Man app.; infinity cover. 283,284-vs. Psycho Man. 285-Secret Wars II x-over; Beyonder app. 4.00

286-2nd app. X-Factor 2 4 6 9 13 16

287-295: 287-Return of Dr. Doom. 288-Secret Wars II x-over; Dr. Doom vs. the Beyonder. 289-Blastaar app; Basilisk killed by Scourge; Nick Fury app; Annihilus returns. 290-Blastaar, Annihilus & Nick Fury app. 291-Action Comics #1 cover swipe; Nick Fury app. 292-Hitler-c; Nick Fury app. 293-West Coast Avengers app; last Byrne-a. 294-Byrne plot only (last); Ordway-a; Roger Stern script. 295-Stern-s begin (over brief Byrne plot) 4.00

296-($1.50, 64-pgs)-Barry Smith-c/a (pgs 1-10); Shooter plot; Stan Lee script; Gammil, Frenz, Milgrom, John Buscema, Silvestri and Ordway-p; Sinnott & Colletta-inks; Mole Man app; the Thing returns to the FF 5.00

297-318,321-330: 297-Roger Stern-s begins; John Buscema-a returns. 299-Black costume Spider-Man app. 300-Wedding of Johnny Storm and 'Alicia'- see issue #358. 301-Wizard & Mad-Thinker app. 303-Thundra app. 304-Steve Englehart-s begins; vs. Quicksilver; the Thing becomes leader of the FF. 305-Quicksilver & Kristoff app ; Crystal rejoins FF; Dr. Doom app; leads into FF Annual #20. 306-v.s Diablo; Black Bolt & the Inhumans app;

Fantastic Four #360 © MAR

Fantastic Four #401 © MAR

Fantastic Four Annual #14 © MAR

GD	VG	FN	VF	VF/NM	NM-
2.0	4.0	6.0	8.0	9.0	9.2

Captain America cameo; Ms. Marvel (Sharon Ventura) app. 307-Ms. Marvel joins the FF. vs. Diablo; Reed and Sue leave the FF. 308-1st Fasaud. 309-vs Fasaud; last Buscema-a. 310-Keith Pollard-a begins; 1st mutated Thing; Ms. Marvel becomes 'She-Thing'. 311-Black Panther & Dr. Doom app. 312-Dr. Doom, Black Panther & X-Factor app. 313-Mole Man app. 314-Belasco & Master Pandemonium app. 315-Master Pandemonium & Comet Man app; Morbius the Living Vampire cameo. 316-Ka-Zar & Shanna the She-Devil app.; origin of the Savage Land. 317-Comet Man app. 318-Molecule Man & Dr. Doom app. 322-Ron Lim guest-a; She-Hulk vs. Ms. Marvel; Dragon Man app; Aron the Renegade Watcher app. 322-Inferno x-over; Graviton, Aron & Dragon Man app. 323-Inferno x-over; Mantis & Kang app. 324-Kang, Mantis & Necrodamus app; Silver Surfer cameo. 325-Mantis, Kang & Silver Surfer app. 326-vs new Frightful Four (Wizard, Hydroman, Klaw and Titania); Reed & Sue return; the Thing becomes human; Englehart-s as 'John Harkness'. 327-vs Frightful Four; Aron the Renegade Watcher & Dragon Man app. 328-1st app. Aron's evil version of the FF; Frightful Four & Dragon Man app. 329-Evil FF vs. Mole Man; Aron app. 4.00

319,320: 319-(Double-size, 39 pgs); Secret Wars III; origin of the Beyonder; Dr. Doom, Molecule Man, Shaper of Worlds, Kubik app. 320-Grey Hulk vs. Thing; Dr. Doom app; x-over w/Incredible Hulk #350 6.00

331-346, 351-357,359,360: 331-Ultron app. in dream sequence; Aron the Renegade Watcher app. 333-Avengers & Dr. Strange app. Evil FF vs real FF; Aron the Renegade Watcher app. 334-Acts of Vengeance x-over; Simonson-s begin; Buckler-a; Thor & Captain America app. 335-Acts of Vengeance x-over; Apocalypse cameo. 336-Acts of Vengeance x-over. 337-Simonson-s and art begin; Thor & Iron Man join FF's mission. 338-Iron Man & Thor app. Death's Head app. Galactus cameo. 339-Thor vs. Gladiator; Galactus & the Black Celestial app. 340-Iron Man, Thor & Galactus app; death of the Black Celestial. 341-Thor, Iron Man & Galactus app. 342-Spider-Man cameo; no Simonson-s or art. 343-President Dan Quale app. 346-T.V.A (Time Variance Authority) app. 351-Kubik & Kosmos app; Mark Bagley-a. 352-Reed vs Dr. Doom; Kristof app; Justice Peace & the T.V.A app. 353,354-FF on trial by the T.V.A; Justice Peace and Mark Gruenwald (as Mr. Chairman) app; 354-Last Simonson issue. 355-vs. the Wrecker. 356-1st Tom Defalco-s & Paul Ryan-a (begin four-year run); Puppet Master & New Warriors app. 357-Alicia Masters revealed to be a Skrull (since issue #265); Puppet Master app. 4.00

347-Ghost Rider, Wolverine, Spider-Man, Hulk-c/stories thru #349; Arthur Adams-c/a(p) in each 5.00

347,348-Gold second printings 5.00

348-350: 348-349-Arthur Adams-c/a(p). 350-($1.50, 52 pgs)-The 'real' Dr. Doom returns; Kristoff app. Sharon Ventura becomes human again. Ben becomes the Thing again 5.00

358-(11/91, $2.25, 88 pgs)-30th anniversary issue; gives history of the FF; die-cut-c; Art Adams back-up story-a; origin of Lyja the Skrull as Alicia Masters; 1st app. Paibok the Power Skrull 5.00

361-368, 372-373: 361-Dr. Doom & the Yancy Street gang app. 362-Spider-Man app; 1st app. of the Innerverse. 363-1st app. Occulus. 364,365-vs. Occulus; 365-Sharon Ventura returns. 366-Infinity War x-over; Magus app; Paibok & Devos team-up. 367-Infinity War x-over; Magus app. numerous super-heroes app. 368-Infinity War x-over; Magus app. Human Torch vs. X-Men doppelgangers. 372-Spider-Man, Molecule Man, Puppet Master & Aron the Renegade Watcher app.; Silver Sable & the Wild Pack cameo; Devos, Paibok & Lyja app. 373-Human Torch vs. Silver Sable & the Wild Pack; Molecule Man vs. Aron the Rogue Watcher; Dr. Doom app. (steals the power of Aron) 4.00

369,370-Infinity War x-over. 369-Thanos & Warlock and the Infinity Watch app; Aron the Renegade Watcher app.; the Magus gains the Infinity Gauntlet. 370-Warlock vs. the Magus for the Infinity Gauntlet; 1st app. Lyja the Lazer-fist. 5.00

371-All-white embossed-c ($2.00); 1st new (revealing) Invisible Woman costume; Paibok, Devos & Lyja vs. Human Torch; Aron the Renegade Watcher app; Ms. Marvel (Sharon Ventura) rejoins the FF 5.00

371-All-red 2nd printing ($2.00) 3.00

374,375: 374-vs Wolverine, Dr. Strange, Ghost Rider, the Hulk and Spider-Man (as the Secret Defenders); Thing's face injured by Wolverine; Dr. Doom app; Black Bolt & the Inhumans cameo; Uatu the Watcher app. 375-($2.95, 52 pgs)-Holo-Grafx foil-c; Secret Defenders app.; Black Bolt & the Inhumans app; cosmic powered Dr. Doom app. Uatu app.; re-intro Nathaniel Richards (from issue #273); Lyja changes allegiance to the FF 4.00

376-($2.95)-Variant polybagged w/Dirt Magazine #4 and music tape; harder to find in true NM- 9.2 due to being packaged with a tape cassette 5.00

376-380,382-386: 376-Nathaniel Richards and Dr. Doom app; Franklin becomes an adult (Psi-Lord). 377-1st app. Huntara; origin Devos; Paibok, Dr. Doom & Klaw app. 378-vs. Devos, Paibok & Huntara; Avengers, Spider-Man & Daredevil app. 379-Devos, Paibok, Huntara & Dr. Doom app. 380-Dr. Doom app. 382-Contains a coupon from Kaybee Toys for an exclusive Ghost Rider issue; also has 16-pg Midnight Sons 'Siege of Darkness' insert; Devos vs. the Skrull Empire. 383-Paibok vs. Devos. 384-Scott Lang app. as Ant-Man; Psi-Lord vs. Invisible Woman. 385-Starblast x-over; Ant-Man & Sub-Mariner app.; continues in Namor the Sub-Mariner #48. 386-Starblast x-over; Ant-Man & Sub-Mariner app. 4.00

381-'Death' of Reed Richards (Mr. Fantastic) & Dr. Doom 4.00

387-Newstand ed. ($1.25) 4.00

387-($2.95)-Collectors Ed. w/die-cut foil-c; Ant-Man app; Invisible Woman returns to her regular costume 5.00

GD	VG	FN	VF	VF/NM	NM-
2.0	4.0	6.0	8.0	9.0	9.2

388-393,396,397: 388-Bound in trading card sheet; Ant-Man, Sub-Mariner & Avengers app; 1st app. the Dark Raider. 389-Ant-Man, Sub-Mariner and the Collector app. 390- Ant-Man & Sub-Mariner app. Galactus & Silver Surfer app. in flashback to FF #48-50. 391-Ant-Man, Sub-Mariner, Galactus & Silver Surfer app. 392-vs. the Dark Raider. 396-Power Rangers card insert. 397-Aron the Renegade Watcher & the Dark Raider app; return of Kristoff; Ant-Man app. 4.00

394-($2.95)-Collectors Edition-polybagged w/16-pg. Marvel; Action Hour book and acetate print; pink logo; Ant-Man, Wyatt Wingfoot & She-Hulk app. 5.00

394-(Newstand Edition-$1.50; white logo 4.00

395,398,399: 395-Wolverine-c/story; Ant-Man app. 398,399-($2.50)-Rainbow foil-c; Ant-Man, Uatu, Aron & the Dark Raider app. 5.00

400-($3.95, 64-pgs)-Rainbow foil-c; Stan Lee introduction; Celestials vs. the Watchers; Kristoff joins the FF. Ant-Man app.; Avengers & Spider-Man app. in back-up story; origin of the FF retold; Uatu vs. Aron (dies) 5.00

401-404: 401-Atlantis Rising x-over; Sub-Mariner & Thor app; Black Bolt cameo. 402-Atlantis Rising x-over; Sub-Mariner vs. Black Bolt; Thor vs. the FF. 404-1st brief app. Hyperstorm (arm only) 4.00

405-Overpower card insert; scarcer in higher grades due to card indentation; new Ant-Man costume; Zarko the Tomorrow Man app; Conan cameo; 2nd app. Hyperstorm (cameo) 5.00

406-414: 406-Return of Dr. Doom; Hyperstorm revealed, battles FF. 407-Return of Mr. Fantastic; x-over w/FF Unlimited #12; Hyperstorm app. 408-vs Hyperstorm; Dr. Doom app. 409-Dr. Doom & FF vs. Hyperstorm; Thing's facial injury cured (since #374). 410-Gorgon of the Inhumans app. 411-Black Bolt & the Inhumans app. 412-Mr. Fantastic vs. Sub-Mariner. 413-Silver Surfer cameo; x-over w/Doom 2099 #42; Doom 2099 & Hyperstorm app; Franklin returns to being a child (Psi-Lord since #376). 414-Galactus vs. Hyperstorm; last Paul Ryan-a (since #356) 5.00

415-Onslaught tie-in; Pacheco-a; Professor X & Avengers app.; Apocalypse cameo; story continued in X-Men #55 5.00

416-($2.50, 48 pgs)-Onslaught tie-in; Pacheco-a; Dr. Doom app; last issue; story continues in Onslaught Marvel Universe #1; Reed, Ben & Victor Von Doom app. in flashback in back-up story; Uatu the Watcher app. 6.00

#500-up (See Fantastic Four Vol. 3; series resumed original numbering after Vol. 3 #70)

Annual 1('63)-Origin of Sub-Mariner & 1st modern app. of Atlantis & the Atlanteans incl. Lady Dorma; FF origin retold; Spider-Man app. in detailed retelling of his app. from Amazing Spider-Man #1 71 142 213 568 1284 2000

Annual 2('64)-Dr. Doom origin & c/story; FF #5-r in 2nd story; Pharaoh Rama-Tut app. in 3rd story 46 92 138 359 805 1250

Annual 3('65)-Reed & Sue wed; r/#6,11 20 40 60 138 307 475

Special 4(11/66)-G.A. Torch x-over (1st S.A. app.) & origin retold; r/#25,26 (Hulk vs. Thing); Torch vs. Torch battle; Mad-Thinker app; 1st app Quasimodo 12 24 36 82 179 275

Special 5(11/67)-New art; Intro. Psycho-Man; early Black Panther, Inhumans & Silver Surfer (1st solo story); Black Bolt & the Inhumans app; Sue is revealed to be pregnant; Quasimodo app. 13 26 39 86 188 290

Special 6(11/68)-Intro. Annihilus; birth of Franklin Richards; new 48 pg. movie length epic; last non-reprint annual 54 108 162 432 966 1500

Annual No. 6 Facsimile Edition (3/20, $4.99) Reprints Special #6 with original 1968 ads5.00

Special 7(11/69)-all reprint issue; r/FF #1; r/origin of Dr. Doom from FF #5 & Dr. Doom story from FF Annual #2; Marvel staff photos seen in 'Because you Demanded it' featurette; new-c by Kirby 6 12 18 37 66 95

Special 8-10: All reprints. 8(12/70)-F.F. vs. Sub-Mariner plus gallery of F.F. foes. Special 9(12/71)-r/FF #43, Strange Tales #131 & FF Annual #3. Special 10('73)-r/FF Annual #3,4; new-c by John Buscema 3 6 9 21 33 45

Annual 11-14: 11-('76)-New story & art begins; alternate Earth versions of the Invaders app; story continues into Marvel Two-in-One Annual #1; Kirby-c. Annual 12 ('78)-Black Bolt & the Inhumans app; vs. the Sphinx. Annual 13 ('78)-vs the Mole Man; Daredevil app. Annual 14 ('79)-Pérez-a; Avengers cameo; Sandman & Salem's Seven app. 2 4 6 8 11 14

Annual 15-17: 15-(80, 68 pgs.); Perez-a; Captain Marvel & Dr. Doom app. Annual 16-('81)-Ditko-a/c; 1st Dragon lord. Annual 17-('83)-Byrne-c/a; Skrulls app. 6.00

Annual 18-23: 18-('84)-Minor x-over w/X-Men #137; Wolverine cameo; wedding of Black Bolt & Medusa; the Watcher app. Annual 19-('85)-vs the Skrulls; x-over w/Avengers Annual #14. Annual 20-('87)-Dr. Doom & Mephisto app; continued from FF #305. Annual 21-('88, 64 pgs.)-Square bound; Evolutionary War x-over; Black Bolt & the Inhumans app. Aron the Watcher app. (unnamed). Annual 22-('89, 64 pgs.)-Square bound; Atlantis Attacks x-over; Avengers & Dr. Strange app. Annual 23-('90, 64 pgs.)-Squarebound; 'Days of Future Present' Pt. 1; 1st Ahab; story continues in New Mutants Annual #6 (not X-Factor Annual #5 as noted); Dr. Doom app. in back-up feature; Byrne-c 5.00

Annual 24-27 (all square bound editions): Annual 24-('91, 64 pgs.); Korvac Quest Pt.1; Guardians of the Galaxy app; story continues in Thor Annual #16; Molecule Man & Super-Skrull app. in back-up features. Annual 25-('92, 64 pgs.)-Citizen Kang Pt.3; continued from Thor Annual #17; Avengers app.; story continues in Avengers Annual #21; Moondragon vs. Mantis solo story & Kang retrospective. Annual 26-('93, 64 pgs.)-Bagged w/card featuring a new character 'Wildstreak'; vs. Dreadface; Kubik & Kosmos app. in solo story featuring the Celestials. Annual 27-('94, 64 pgs.)-Justice Peace & the T.V.A (Time

Fantastic Four V2 #4 © MAR

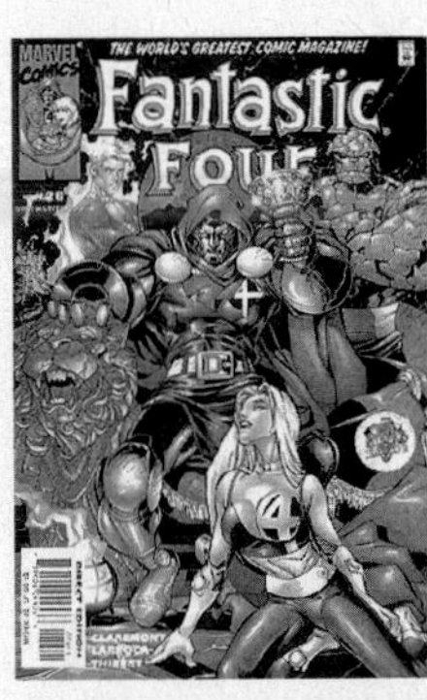

Fantastic Four V3 #26 © MAR

Fantastic Four (2013 series) #1 © MAR

GD 2.0 VG 4.0 FN 6.0 VF 8.0 VF/NM 9.0 NM- 9.2

Variance Authority) app.; featuring the chairman (Mark Gruenwald); Molecule Man vs. Beyonder solo story 5.00
... #1 Facsimile Edition (10/2018, $3.99) reprints #1 with original 1961 ads; bonus essays and gallery of FF #1 cover swipes and homages 4.00
Best of the Fantastic Four Vol. 1 HC (2005, $29.99) oversized reprints of classic stories from FF#1,39,40,51,100,116,176,236,267, Ann.2, V3#56,60 and more; Brevoort intro. 30.00
Maximum Fantastic Four HC (2005, $49.99, dust jacket) r/Fantastic Four #1 with super-sized art; historical background from Walter Mosley and Mark Evanier; dust jacket unfolds to a poster: giant FF#1 cover on one side, gallery of interior pages on other 50.00
...: Monsters Unleashed nn (1992, $5.95)-r/F.F. #347-349 w/new Arthur Adams-c 1 2 3 5 6 8
...: Nobody Gets Out Alive (1994, $15.95) TPB r/ #387-392 16.00
... Omnibus Vol. 1 HC (2005, $99.99) r/#1-30 & Annual 1 plus letter pages; 3 intros. and a 1974 essay by Stan Lee; original plot synopsis for FF #1; essays and Kirby art 100.00
... Omnibus Vol. 2 HC (2007, $99.99) r/#31-60, Annual 2-4 and Not Brand Echh #1 plus letter pages and essays by Stan Lee, Reginald Hudlin, Roy Thomas and others 100.00
Special Edition 1(5/84)-r/Annual #1; Byrne-c/a 5.00
...: The Lost Adventure (4/08, $4.99) Lee & Kirby story partially used in flashback in FF #108 completed with additional art by Frenz & Sinnott; plus reprint of FF #108 5.00
... Visionaries: George Pérez Vol. 1 (2005, $19.99) r/#164-167,170,176-178,184-186 20.00
... Visionaries: George Pérez Vol. 2 (2006, $19.99) r/#187-188,191-192, Annual #14-15, Marvel Two-In-One #60 and back-up story from Adventures of the Thing #3 20.00
... Visionaries (11/01, $19.95) r/#232-240 by John Byrne 20.00
... Visionaries Vol. 2 (2004, $24.99) r/#241-250 by John Byrne 25.00
... Visionaries John Byrne Vol. 3 (2004, $24.99) r/#251-257; Annual #17; Avengers #233 and Thing #2 25.00
... Visionaries John Byrne Vol. 4 (2005, $24.99) r/#258-267; Alpha Flight #4 & Thing #10 25.00
... Visionaries John Byrne Vol. 5 (2005, $24.99) r/#268-275; Annual #18 & Thing #19 25.00
... Visionaries John Byrne Vol. 6 ('06, $24.99) r/#276-284; Secret Wars II #2 & Thing #23 25.00
... Visionaries John Byrne Vol. 7 ('07, $24.99) r/#285,286, Ann. #19, Avengers #263 & Ann. #14, and X-Factor #1 25.00
... Visionaries John Byrne Vol. 8 ('07, $24.99) r/#287-295 25.00
... Visionaries: Walter Simonson Vol. 1 (2007, $19.99) r/#334-341 20.00

*NOTE: **Arthur Adams** c/a-347-349p. **Austin** c(i)-232-236, 238, 240-242, 250i, 286i. **Buckler** c-151, 168. **John Buscema** a(p)-107, 108(w/**Kirby, Sinnott** & **Romita**),109-130, 132, 134-141, 160, 173-175, 202, 296-309p, Annual 11, 13; c(p)-107-122, 124-129, 133-139, 202, Annual 12p, Special 10. **Byrne** a-209-218p, 220p, 221p, 232-265, 266i, 267-273, 274-293p, Annual 17, 19; c-211-214p, 220p, 232-236p, 237, 238p, 239, 240-242p, 243-249, 250p, 251-267, 269-277, 278-281p, 283p, 284, 285, 286p, 288-293, Annual 17, 18. **Ditko** a-13i, 14i(w/**Kirby-p**), Annual 16. **G. Kane** c-145p, 146p, 150p, 160p. **Kirby** a-1-102p, 108p, 180r, 189r, 236p, Special 1-10; c-1-101, 164, 167, 171-177, 180, 181, 190, 200, Annual 11, Special 1-7, 9. **Marcos** a-Annual 14i. **Mooney** a-118i, 152i. **Perez** a(p)-164-167, 170-172, 176-178, 184-188, 191p, 192p. Annual 14p, 15p; c(p)-183-188, 191, 192, 194-197. **Simonson** a-337-341, 343, 344p, 345p, 346, 350p, 352-354; c-212, 334-341, 342p, 343-346, 350, 353, 354. **Steranko** c-130-132p. **Williamson** c-357i.*

FANTASTIC FOUR (Volume Two)
Marvel Comics: V2#1, Nov, 1996 - No. 13, Nov, 1997 ($2.95/$1.95/$1.99) (Produced by WildStorm Productions)

1-($2.95)-Reintro Fantastic Four; Jim Lee-c/a; Brandon Choi scripts; Mole Man app. 5.00
1-($2.95)-Variant-c 1 2 3 4 5 7
2-9: 2-Namor-c/app. 3-Avengers-c/app. 4-Two covers; Dr. Doom cameo 3.00
10,11,13: All $1.99-c. 13-"World War 3"-pt. 1, x-over w/Image 3.00
12-($2.99) "Heroes Reunited"-pt. 1 4.00
...: Heroes Reborn (7/00, $17.95, TPB) r/#1-6 18.00
Heroes Reborn: Fantastic Four (2006, $29.99, TPB) r/#1-12; Jim Lee intro.; pin-ups 30.00

FANTASTIC FOUR (Volume Three)
Marvel Comics: V3#1, Jan, 1998 - No. 588, Apr, 2011 ($2.99/$1.99/$2.25)
No. 600, Jan, 2012 - No. 611, Dec, 2012 (Issues #589-#599 do not exist, see FF series)

1-($2.99)-Heroes Return; Lobdell-s/Davis & Farmer-a1 2 3 5 6 8
1-Alternate Heroes Return-c 1 3 4 6 8 10
2-4,12: 2-2-covers. 4-Claremont-s/Larroca-a begin; Silver Surfer c/app. 12-($2.99) Wraparound-c by Larroca 5.00
5-11: 6-Heroes For Hire app. 9-Spider-Man-c/app. 11-1st app. Ayesha 4.00
13-25: 13,14-Ronan-c/app. 25-($2.99) Dr. Doom returns 4.00
26-49: 27-Dr. Doom marries Sue. 30-Begin $2.25-c. 32,42-Namor-c/app. 35-Regular cover; Pacheco-s/a begins. 37-Super-Skrull-c/app. 38-New Baxter Building 3.00
35-($3.25) Variant foil enhanced-c; Pacheco-s/a begins 4.00
50-($3.99, 64 pgs.) BWS-c; Grummett, Pacheco, Rude, Udon-a 4.00
51-53,55-59: 51-53-Bagley-a(p)/Wieringo-c; Inhumans app. 55,56-Immonen-a 57-59-Warren-s/Grant-a 3.00
54-($3.50, 100 pgs.) Birth of Valeria; r/Annual #6 birth of Franklin 4.00
60-(9¢-c) Waid-s/Wieringo-a begin 3.00
60-($2.25 newsstand edition)(also see Promotional Comics section) 3.00
61-70: 62-64-FF vs. Modulus. 65,66-Buckingham-a. 68-70-Dr. Doom app. 3.00

(After #70 [Aug, 2003] numbering reverted back to original Vol. 1 with #500, Sept, 2003)

500-($3.50) Regular edition; concludes Dr. Doom app.; Dr. Strange app.; Rivera painted-c 4.00
500-($4.99) Director's Cut Edition; chromium-c by Wieringo; sketch and script pages 8.00
501-516: 501,502-Casey Jones-a. 503-508-Porter-a. 509-Wieringo-c/a resumes. 512,513-Spider-Man app. 514-516-Ha-c/Medina-a 3.00
517-537: 517-Begin $2.99-c. 519-523-Galactus app. 527-Straczynski-s begins. 537-Dr. Doom. 3.00
527-Variant Edition with different McKone-c 3.00
527-Wizard World Philadelphia Edition with B&W McKone sketch-c 3.00
536-Variant cover by Bryan Hitch 5.00
537-B&W variant cover 5.00
538-542-Civil War. 538-Don Blake reclaims Thor's hammer 4.00
543-45th Anniversary; Black Panther and Storm replace Reed and Sue; Granov-c 4.00
544-553: 544-546-Silver Surfer app.; Turner-c 3.00
554-568-Millar-s/Hitch-a/c. 558-561-Doctor Doom-c/app. 562-Funeral & proposal 3.00
554-Variant-c by Bianchi 6.00
554-Variant Skrull-c by Suydam 30.00
569-($3.99) Wraparound-c; Immonen-a; Dr. Doom app. 4.00
570-586: 570-572,575-578-Eaglesham-a. 574-Spider-Man app. 584-586-Galactus app. 3.00
587-(3/11, $3.99) Death of Human Torch; Epting-a; issue is in black polybag; Davis-c 4.00
587-Variant-c by Cassaday 10.00
588-($3.99) Last issue; Dragotta-a; preview of FF #1; back-up w/Spider-Man; Davis-c 4.00
589-599-**Do not exist**; story continues in FF series
600-(1/12, $7.99) Avengers app.; Human Torch returns, back-up short stories; Dell'Otto-c 8.00
600-Variant-c by John Romita, Jr. 10.00
600-Variant-c by Art Adams 15.00
601-603,605,605.1, 606-611: 601-603-Johnny Storm & Avengers app. 602,603-Galactus app. 605.1-Alternate origin; Choi-a. 607,608-Black Panther app. 611-Doctor Doom app. 3.00
604-($3.99) Future Franklin and Valeria app. 4.00
...'98 Annual ($3.50) Immonen-a 4.00
...'99 Annual ($3.50) Ladronn-a 4.00
...'00 Annual ($3.50) Larocca-a; Marvel Girl back-up story 4.00
...'01 Annual ($2.99) Maguire-a; Thing back-up w/Yu-a 4.00
... Annual 32 (8/10, $4.99) Hitch-a/c 5.00
... Annual 33 (9/12, $4.99) Alan Davis-s/a/c; Dr. Strange & Clan Destine app. 5.00
... : A Death in the Family (7/06, $3.99, one-shot) Weeks-a/c; and r/F.F. #245 4.00
... By J. Michael Straczynski Vol. 1 (2005, $19.99, HC) r/#527-532 20.00
Civil War: Fantastic Four TPB (2007, $17.99) r/#538-543; 45th Anniversary Toasts 18.00
... Cosmic-Size Special 1 (2/09, $4.99) Cary Bates-s/Bing Cansino-a; r/F.F. #237 5.00
Fantastic 4th Voyage of Sinbad (9/01, $5.95) Claremont-s/Ferry-a 6.00
Flesh and Stone (8/01, $12.95, TPB) r/#35-39 13.00
... Giant-Size Adventures 1 (8/09, $3.99) Cifuentes & Coover-a; Egghead app. 4.00
... In...Ataque del M.O.D.O.K.! (11/10, $3.99) English & Spanish editions; Beland-s/Doe-a 4.00
... /Inhumans TPB (2007, $19.99) r/#51-54 and Inhumans ('00) #1-4 20.00
...: Isla De La Muerte! (2/08, $3.99) English & Spanish editions; Beland-s/Doe-a 4.00
... MGC #570 (7/11, $1.00) r/#570 with "Marvel's Greatest Comics" cover banner 3.00
... Presents: Franklin Richards 1 (11/05, $2.99) r/back-up stories from Power Pack #1-4 plus new 5 pg. story; Sumerak-s/Eliopoulos-a (Also see Franklin Richards) 3.00
...Special (2/06, $2.99) McDuffie-s/Casey Jones-a; dinner with Dr. Doom 3.00
...Tales Vol. 1 (2005, $7.99, digest) r/Marvel Age: FF Tales #1, Tales of the Thing #1-3, and Spider-Man Team-Up Special 8.00
...: The Last Stand (8/11, $4.99) r/#574, 587 & 588 (death of Johnny Storm) 5.00
...: The New Fantastic Four HC (2007, $19.99) r/#544-550; variant covers & sketch pgs. 20.00
...: The New Fantastic Four SC (2008, $15.99) r/#544-550; variant covers & sketch pgs. 16.00
... : The Wedding Special 1 (1/06, $5.00) 40th Anniversary new story & r/FF Annual #3 5.00
... Vol. 1 HC (2004, $29.99, dust jacket) oversized reprint /#60-70, 500-502; Mark Waid intro and series proposal; cover gallery 30.00
... Vol. 2 HC (2005, $29.99, d.j.) oversized r/#503-513; Waid intro.; deleted scenes 30.00
... Vol. 3 HC (2005, $29.99, d.j.) oversized r/#514-524; Waid commentaries; cover sketches 30.00
... Vol. 1: Imaginauts (2003, $17.99, TPB) r/#56,60-66; Mark Waid's series proposal 18.00
... Vol. 2: Unthinkable (2003, $17.99, TPB) r/#67-70,500-502; #500 Director's Cut extras 18.00
... Vol. 3: Authoritative Action (2004, $12.99, TPB) r/#503-508 13.00
... Vol. 4: Hereafter (2004, $11.99, TPB) r/#509-513 12.00
... Vol. 5: Disassembled (2004, $14.99, TPB) r/#514-519 15.00
... Vol. 6: Rising Storm (2005, $13.99, TPB) r/#520-524 14.00
...: The Beginning of the End TPB (2008, $14.99) r/#525,526,551-553 & Fantastic Four: Isla De La Muerte! one-shot 15.00
...: The Life Fantastic TPB (2006, $16.99) r/#533-535; The Wedding Special, Special (2/06) and A Death in the Family one-shots 17.00
Wizard #1/2 -Lim-a 10.00

FANTASTIC FOUR (Volume Four) (Marvel NOW!) (Also see FF)
Marvel Comics: Jan, 2013 - No. 16, Mar, 2014 ($2.99)

1-5-Fraction-s/Bagley-a/c 3.00
5AU-(5/13, $3.99) Age of Ultron tie-in; Fraction-s/Araújo-a/Bagley-c 4.00
6-15: 6,7-Blastaar app. 9,13-15-Dr. Doom app. 14,15-Ienco-a 3.00
16-($3.99) Fantastic Four vs. Doom, The Annihilating Conqueror; back-up w/Quinones-a 4.00

FANTASTIC FOUR (Volume Five) (All-New Marvel NOW!)
Marvel Comics: Apr, 2014 - No. 14, Feb, 2015; No. 642, Mar, 2015 - No. 645, Jun, 2015 ($3.99)

Fantastic Four (2018 series) #28 © MAR

Fantastic Four: Antithesis #2 © MAR

Fantastic Four: The Movie #1 © MAR

	GD	VG	FN	VF	VF/NM	NM-
	2.0	4.0	6.0	8.0	9.0	9.2

1-4-Robinson-s/Kirk-a. 3,4-Frightful Four app. 4.00
5-($4.99) Trial of the Fantastic Four; flashback-a by various incl. Starlin, Allred, Samnee 5.00
6-14: 6-8-Original Sin tie-in. 10,11-Scarlet Witch app. 11,12-Spider-Man app. 4.00
642-(3/15)-644: Heroes Reborn Avengers app. 643,644-Sleepwalker app. 4.00
645-($5.99) Psycho Man & the Frightful Four app.; Kirk-a; bonus back-up stories 6.00
Annual 1 (11/14, $4.99) Sue vs. Doctor Doom in Latveria; Grummett-a 5.00
100th Anniversary Special: Fantastic Four 1 (9/14, $3.99) Van Meter-s/Estep-a 4.00

FANTASTIC FOUR (Volume Six)
Marvel Comics: Oct, 2018 - Present ($5.99/$3.99)

1-($5.99) Slott-s/Pichelli & Bianchi-a; Ben proposes to Alicia 6.00
2-4,6-11,13-20-($3.99) 4-Wrecking Crew app.; intro The Fantastix. 6-9-Doom vs. Galactus. 10-War of The Realms tie-in; Moon Girl app. 13-Thing vs. Hulk. 15-Intro. Sky 4.00
5-($7.99) Wedding of Ben and Alicia; art by Kuder, Allred (origin re-telling) and Hughes 8.00
12-($4.99) Thing battles the Immortal Hulk; Izaakse-a; Future Foundation back-up 5.00
21-24,26-28: 21-23-Tie-in to Empyre event; Wolverine and Spider-Man app. 24-Iceman app. 28-Silver Surfer app. 4.00
25-($5.99) She-Hulk & Doctor Doom app.; back-up story with Uatu & Nick Fury 6.00
...: 4 Yancy Street 1 (10/19, $4.99) Duggan-s; the Terrible Trio app. 5.00
...: Grimm Noir 1 (4/20, $4.99) Duggan-s/Garney-a 5.00
...: Marvels Snapshots 1 (5/20, $4.99) Dorkin & Dyer-s/Dewey-a 5.00
...: Negative Zone 1 (1/20, $4.99) Carey-s/Caselli-a; Blastaar app. 5.00
...: Road Trip 1 (2/21, $4.99) Cantwell-s/Andrade-a 5.00
...: The Prodigal Sun 1 (9/19, $4.99) Davis-s/Manna-a; Ka-Zar app. 5.00
...: Wedding Special 1 (2/19, $4.99) Simone-s/Braga-a; Slott-a/Buckingham-a; Hembeck-s/a 5.00

FANTASTIC FOUR AND POWER PACK
Marvel Comics: Sept, 2007 - No. 4, Dec, 2007 ($2.99, limited series)

1-4-Gurihiru-a/Van Lente-s; the Wizard app. 3.00
...: Favorite Son TPB (2008, $7.99, digest size) r/#1-4 8.00

FANTASTIC FOUR: ANTITHESIS
Marvel Comics: Oct, 2020 - No. 4, Jan, 2021 ($4.99, limited series)

1-4-Neal Adams-a/Mark Waid-s; Silver Surfer & Galactus app. 5.00

FANTASTIC FOUR: ATLANTIS RISING
Marvel Comics: June, 1995 - No. 2, July, 1995 ($3.95, limited series)

1,2: Acetate-c 5.00
Collector's Preview (5/95, $2.25, 52 pgs.) 4.00

FANTASTIC FOUR: BIG TOWN
Marvel Comics: Jan, 2001 - No. 4, Apr, 2001 ($2.99, limited series)

1-4:"What If?" story; McKone-a/Englehart-s 3.00

FANTASTIC FOUR: FIREWORKS
Marvel Comics: Jan, 1999 - No. 3, Mar, 1999 ($2.99, limited series)

1-3-Remix; Jeff Johnson-a 4.00

FANTASTIC FOUR: FIRST FAMILY
Marvel Comics: May, 2006 - No. 6, Oct, 2006 ($2.99, limited series)

1-6-Casey-s/Weston-a; flashback to the days after the accident 3.00
TPB (2006, $15.99) r/#1-6 16.00

FANTASTIC FOUR: FOES
Marvel Comics: Mar, 2005 - No. 6, Aug, 2005 ($2.99, limited series)

1-6-Kirkman-s/Rathburn-a. 1-Puppet Master app. 3-Super-Skrull app. 4-Mole Man app. 3.00
TPB (2005, $16.99) r/#1-6 17.00

FANTASTIC FOUR: GRAND DESIGN
Marvel Comics: Dec, 2019 - No. 2, Jan, 2020 ($5.99, limited series)

1,2-History of the Fantastic Four retold; Tom Scioli-s/a/c; bonus background text info 6.00

FANTASTIC FOUR: HOUSE OF M (Reprinted in House of M: Fantastic Four/ Iron Man TPB)
Marvel Comics: Sept, 2005 - No. 3, Nov, 2005 ($2.99, limited series)

1-3: Fearsome Four, led by Doom; Scot Eaton-a 3.00

FANTASTIC FOUR INDEX (See Official...)

FANTASTIC FOUR/ IRON MAN: BIG IN JAPAN
Marvel Comics: Dec, 2005 - No. 4, Mar, 2006 ($3.50, limited series)

1-4-Seth Fisher-a/c; Zeb Wells-s; wraparound-c on each 3.50
TPB (2006, $12.99) r/#1-4 and Seth Fisher illustrated story from Spider-Man Unlimited #8 13.00

FANTASTIC FOUR: 1 2 3 4
Marvel Comics: Oct, 2001 - No. 4, Jan, 2002 ($2.99, limited series)

1-4-Morrison-s/Jae Lee-a. 2-4-Namor-c/app. 3.00
TPB (2002, $9.99) r/#1-4 10.00

FANTASTIC FOUR ROAST
Marvel Comics Group: May, 1982 (75¢, one-shot, direct sales)

1-Celebrates 20th anniversary of F.F.#1; X-Men, Ghost Rider & many others cameo; Golden, Miller, Buscema, Rogers, Byrne, Anderson art; Hembeck/Austin-c 5.00

FANTASTIC FOUR: THE END
Marvel Comics: Jan, 2007 - No. 6, May, 2007 ($2.99, limited series)

1-6-Alan Davis-s/a; last adventure of the future FF. 1-Dr. Doom-c/app. 3.00
Roughcut #1 ($3.99) B&W pencil art for full story and text script; B&W sketch cover 4.00
HC (2007, $19.99, dustjacket) r/#1-6 20.00
SC (2008, $14.99) r/#1-6 15.00

FANTASTIC FOUR: THE LEGEND
Marvel Comics: Oct, 1996 ($3.95, one-shot)

1-Tribute issue 4.00

FANTASTIC FOUR: THE MOVIE
Marvel Comics: Aug, 2005 ($4.99/$12.99, one-shot)

1-($4.99) Movie adaptation; Jurgens-a; behind the scenes feature; Doom origin; photo-c 5.00
TPB-($12.99) Movie adaptation, r/Fantastic Four #5 & 190, and FF Vol. 3 #60, photo-c 13.00

FANTASTIC FOUR: TRUE STORY
Marvel Comics: Sept, 2008 - No. 4, Jan, 2009 ($2.99, limited series)

1-4-Cornell-s/Domingues-a/Henrichon-c 3.00

FANTASTIC FOUR 2099
Marvel Comics: Jan, 1996 - No. 8, Aug, 1996 ($3.95/$1.95)

1-($3.95)-Chromium-c; X-Nation preview 5.00
2-8: 4-Spider-Man 2099-c/app. 5-Doctor Strange app. 7-Thibert-c 4.00
... No. 1 (1/20, $4.99) Karla Pacheco-s/Steven Cummings-a; H.E.R.B.I.E. app. 5.00
NOTE: *Williamson a-1i; c-1i.*

FANTASTIC FOUR UNLIMITED
Marvel Comics: Mar, 1993 - No. 12, Dec, 1995 ($3.95, 68 pgs.)

1-12: 1-Black Panther app. 4-Thing vs. Hulk. 5-Vs. The Frightful Four. 6-Vs. Namor. 7, 9-12-Wraparound-c 4.00

FANTASTIC FOUR UNPLUGGED
Marvel Comics: Sept, 1995 - No. 6, Aug 1996 (99¢, bi-monthly)

1-6 4.00

FANTASTIC FOUR - UNSTABLE MOLECULES
(Indicia for #1 reads STARTLING STORIES: ... ; #2 reads UNSTABLE MOLECULES)
Marvel Comics: Mar, 2003 - No. 4, June, 2003 ($2.99, limited series)

1-4-Guy Davis-c/a 3.00
Fantastic Four Legends Vol. 1 TPB (2003, $13.99) r/#1-4, origin from FF #1 (1963) 14.00
TPB (2005, $13.99) r/#1-4 14.00

FANTASTIC FOUR VS. X-MEN
Marvel Comics: Feb, 1987 - No. 4, June, 1987 (Limited series)

1-4: 4-Austin-a(i) 5.00

FANTASTIC FOUR: WORLD'S GREATEST COMICS MAGAZINE
Marvel Comics: Feb, 2001 - No. 12 (Limited series)

1-12: Homage to Lee & Kirby era of F.F.; s/a by Larsen & various. 5-Hulk-c/app. 10-Thor app. 3.00

FANTASTIC GIANTS (Formerly Konga #1-23)
Charlton Comics: V2#24, Sept, 1966 (25¢, 68 pgs.)

V2#24-Special Ditko issue; origin Konga & Gorgo reprinted plus two new Ditko stories 7 14 21 49 92 135

FANTASTIC TALES
I. W. Enterprises: 1958 (no date) (Reprint, one-shot)

1-Reprints Avon's "City of the Living Dead" 4 8 12 23 37 50

FANTASTIC VOYAGE (See Movie Comics)
Gold Key: Aug, 1969 - No. 2, Dec, 1969

1 (TV) 4 8 12 27 44 60
2-Cover has the text "Civilian Miniaturized Defense Force" in yellow bar at top; back cover has painted art 3 6 9 19 30 40
2-Variant cover has text "In This Issue Sweepstakes..." along top; ad on back-c 4 8 12 23 37 50

FANTASTIC VOYAGES OF SINDBAD, THE
Gold Key: Oct, 1965 - No. 2, June, 1967

1-Painted-c on both 6 12 18 38 69 100
2 5 10 15 30 50 70

FANTASTIC WORLDS
Standard Comics: No. 5, Sept, 1952 - No. 7, Jan, 1953

5-Toth, Anderson-a 41 82 123 256 428 600

Fantomex MAX #1 © MAR

Far Sector #3 © DC

Fatale #6 © Basement Gang

	GD 2.0	VG 4.0	FN 6.0	VF 8.0	VF/NM 9.0	NM- 9.2
6-Toth-c/a	33	66	99	194	317	440
7	25	50	75	150	245	340

FANTASY ILLUSTRATED
New Media Publ.: Spring 1982 ($2.95, B&W magazine)

	GD	VG	FN	VF	VF/NM	NM-
1-P. Craig Russell-c/a; art by Ditko, Sekowsky, Sutton; Englehart-s	1	3	4	6	8	10

FANTASY MASTERPIECES (Marvel Super Heroes No. 12 on)
Marvel Comics Group: Feb, 1966 - No. 11, Oct, 1967; V2#1, Dec, 1979 - No. 14, Jan, 1981

	GD	VG	FN	VF	VF/NM	NM-
1-Photo of Stan Lee (12¢-c #1,2)	9	18	27	58	114	170
2-r/1st Fin Fang Foom from Strange Tales #89	5	10	15	35	63	90
3-8: 3-G.A. Capt. America-r begin, end #11; 1st 25¢ Giant; Colan-r. 3-6-Kirby-c(p). 4-Kirby-c(p)(i). 7-Begin G.A. Sub-Mariner, Torch-r/M. Mystery. 8-Torch battles the Sub-Mariner-r/Marvel Mystery #9	6	12	18	40	73	105
9-Origin Human Torch-r/Marvel Comics #1	6	12	18	37	66	95
10,11: 10-r/origin & 1st app. All Winners Squad from All Winners #19. 11-r/origin of Toro (H.T. #1) & Black Knight #1	5	10	15	34	60	85
V2#1(12/79, 75¢, 52 pgs.)-r/origin Silver Surfer from Silver Surfer #1 with editing plus reprints cover; J. Buscema-a	2	4	6	9	12	15
2-14-Reprints Silver Surfer #2-14 w/covers						6.00

NOTE: ***Buscema** c-V2#7-9(in part). **Ditko** r-1-3, 7, 9. **Everett** r-1,7-9. **Matt Fox** r-9i. **Kirby** r-1-11; c(p)-3, 4i, 5, 6. **Starlin** r-8-13. Some direct sale V2#14's had a 50¢ cover price. #3-11 contain Capt. America-r/Capt. America #3-10. #7-11 contain G.A.Human Torch & Sub-Mariner-r.*

FANTASY QUARTERLY (Also see Elfquest)
Independent Publishers Syndicate: Spring, 1978 (B&W)

	GD	VG	FN	VF	VF/NM	NM-
1-1st app. Elfquest; Dave Sim-a (6 pgs.)	9	18	27	59	117	175

FANTOMAN (Formerly Amazing Adventure Funnies)
Centaur Publications: No. 2, Aug, 1940 - No. 4, Dec, 1940

	GD	VG	FN	VF	VF/NM	NM-
2-The Fantom of the Fair, The Arrow, Little Dynamite-r begin; origin The Ermine by Filchock; Burgos, J. Cole, Ernst, Gustavson-a	168	336	504	1075	1838	2600
3,4: Gustavson-r. 4-Red Blaze story	135	270	405	864	1482	2100

FANTOMEX MAX
Marvel Comics: Dec, 2013 - No. 4, Mar, 2014 ($3.99)

1-4-Hope-s/Crystal-a/Francavilla-c — 4.00

FAREWELL MOONSHADOW (See Moonshadow)
DC Comics (Vertigo): Jan, 1997 ($7.95, one-shot)

nn-DeMatteis-s/Muth-c/a — 8.00

FARGO KID (Formerly Justice Traps the Guilty)(See Feature Comics #47)
Prize Publications: V11#3(#1), June-July, 1958 - V11#5, Oct-Nov, 1958

	GD	VG	FN	VF	VF/NM	NM-
V11#3(#1)-Origin Fargo Kid, Severin-c/a; Williamson-a(2); Heath-a	18	36	54	105	165	225
V11#4,5-Severin-c/a	13	26	39	74	105	135

FARMER'S DAUGHTER, THE
Stanhall Publ./Trojan Magazines: Feb-Mar, 1954 - No. 3, June-July, 1954; No. 4, Oct, 1954

	GD	VG	FN	VF	VF/NM	NM-
1-Lingerie, nudity panel	142	284	426	909	1555	2200
2-4(Stanhall)	103	206	309	659	1130	1600

FARMHAND
Image Comics: Jul, 2018 - Present ($3.99)

1-15-Rob Guillory-s/a — 4.00

FARSCAPE (Based on TV series)
BOOM! Studios: Nov, 2008 - No. 4, Feb, 2009 ($3.99)

1-4-O'Bannon-s/Patterson-a; multiple covers — 4.00

FARSCAPE (Based on TV series)
BOOM! Studios: Nov, 2009 - No. 24, Oct, 2011 ($3.99)

1-24-O'Bannon-s/Sliney-a; multiple covers — 4.00
...: D'Argo's Lament 1-4 (4/09 - No. 4, 7/09, $3.99) Edwards-a; three covers on each — 4.00
...: D'Argo's Quest 1-4 (12/09 - No. 4, 3/10, $3.99) Cleveland-a; three covers on each — 4.00
...: D'Argo's Trial 1-4 (8/09 - No. 4, 11/09, $3.99) Cleveland-a; multiple covers on each — 4.00
...: Gone and Back 1-4 (7/09 - No. 4, 10/09, $3.99) Patterson-a; multiple covers on each — 4.00
...: Scorpius 0-7 (4/10 - No. 7, 2010, $3.99) 0-3-Ruiz-a; multiple-c. 4-7-Purcell-a — 4.00
...: Strange Detractors 1-4 (3/09 - No. 4, 6/09, $3.99) Sliney-a; three covers on each — 4.00

FARSCAPE: WAR TORN (Based on TV series)
DC Comics (WildStorm): Apr, 2002 - No. 2, May, 2002 ($4.95, limited series)

1,2-Teranishi-a/Wolfman-s; photo-c — 5.00

FAR SECTOR
DC Comics (Young Animal): Jan, 2020 - No. 12 ($3.99)

1-10: 1-Intro Green Lantern Sojourner Mullein; N.K. Jemisin-s/Jamal Campbell-a — 4.00

FASHION IN ACTION
Eclipse Comics: Aug, 1986 - Feb, 1987 (Baxter paper)

Summer Special 1, Winter Special 1, each Snyder III-c/a — 3.00

FASTBALL EXPRESS (Major League Baseball)
Ultimate Sports Force: 2000 ($3.95, one-shot)

1-Polybagged with poster; Johnson, Maddux, Park, Nomo, Clemens app. — 4.00

FASTER THAN LIGHT
Image Comics (Shadowline): Sept, 2015 - No. 10, Sept, 2016 ($2.99)

1-10-Brian Haberlin-s/a — 3.00

FASTEST GUN ALIVE, THE (Movie)
Dell Publishing Co.: No. 741, Sept, 1956 (one-shot)

	GD	VG	FN	VF	VF/NM	NM-
Four Color 741-Photo-c	7	14	21	44	82	120

FAST FICTION (...Action) (Stories by Famous Authors Illustrated #6 on)
Seaboard Publ./Famous Authors Ill.: Oct, 1949 - No. 5, Mar, 1950
(All have Kiefer-c)(48 pgs.)

	GD	VG	FN	VF	VF/NM	NM-
1-Scarlet Pimpernel; Jim Lavery-c/a	33	66	99	194	317	440
2-Captain Blood; H. C. Kiefer-c/a	25	50	75	147	241	335
3-She, by Rider Haggard; Vincent Napoli-a	31	62	93	186	303	420
4-(1/50, 52 pgs.)-The 39 Steps; Lavery-c/a	19	38	57	112	176	240
5-Beau Geste; Kiefer-c/a	19	38	57	112	176	240

NOTE: ***Kiefer** a-2, 5; c-2, 3,5. **Lavery** c/a-1, 4. **Napoli** a-3.*

FAST FORWARD
DC Comics (Piranha Press): 1992 - No. 3, 1993 ($4.95, 68 pgs.)

1-3: 1-Morrison scripts; McKean-c/a. 3-Sam Kieth-a — 5.00

FAST WILLIE JACKSON
Fitzgerald Periodicals, Inc.: Oct, 1976 - No. 7, 1977

	GD	VG	FN	VF	VF/NM	NM-
1	5	10	15	35	63	90
2-7	3	6	9	21	33	45

FAT ALBERT (...& the Cosby Kids) (TV)
Gold Key: Mar, 1974 - No. 29, Feb, 1979

	GD	VG	FN	VF	VF/NM	NM-
1	4	8	12	28	47	65
2-10	3	6	9	15	22	28
11-29	2	4	6	10	14	18

FATALE (Also see Powers That Be #1 & Shadow State #1,2)
Broadway Comics: Jan, 1996 - No. 6, Aug, 1996 ($2.50)

1-6: J.G. Jones-c/a in all, Preview Edition 1 (11/95, B&W) — 3.00

FATALE
Image Comics: Jan, 2012 - No. 24, Jul, 2014 ($3.50)

1-Brubaker-s/Phillips-a/c — 5.00
1-Variant-c of Demon with machine gun — 8.00
1-Second through Fifth printings — 4.00
2-23-Brubaker-s/Phillips-a/c in all — 3.50
24-($4.99) Story conclusion; bonus preview of The Fade Out series — 5.00

FAT AND SLAT (Ed Wheelan) (Becomes Gunfighter No. 5 on)
E. C. Comics: Summer, 1947 - No. 4, Spring, 1948

	GD	VG	FN	VF	VF/NM	NM-
1-Intro/origin Voltage, Man of Lightning; "Comics" McCormick, the World's No. 1 Comic Book Fan begins, ends #4	45	90	135	284	480	675
2-4: 4-Comics McCormick-c feature	31	62	93	186	303	420

FAT AND SLAT JOKE BOOK
All-American Comics (William H. Wise): Summer, 1944 (52 pgs., one-shot)

	GD	VG	FN	VF	VF/NM	NM-
nn-by Ed Wheelan	37	74	111	218	354	490

FATE (See Hand of Fate & Thrill-O-Rama)

FATE
DC Comics: Oct, 1994 - No. 22, Sept, 1996 ($1.95/$2.25)

0,1-22: 8-Begin $2.25-c. 11-14-Alan Scott (Sentinel) app. 10,14-Zatanna app. 21-Phantom Stranger app. 22-Spectre app. — 3.00

FATHER'S DAY
Dark Horse Comics: Oct, 2014 - No. 4, Jan, 2015 ($3.99, limited series)

1-4-Mike Richardson-s/Gabriel Guzmán-a — 4.00

FATHOM
Comico: May, 1987 - No. 3, July, 1987 ($1.50, limited series)

1-3 — 3.00

FATHOM
Image Comics (Top Cow Prod.): Aug, 1998 - No. 14, May, 2002 ($2.50)

Fathom V3 #3 © AspenMLT

Fatman, The Human Flying Saucer #3 © Milson

Fawcett Movie Comic #9 © FAW

GD VG FN VF VF/NM NM-
2.0 4.0 6.0 8.0 9.0 9.2

Preview 12.00
0-Wizard supplement 7.00
0-($6.95) DF Alternate 7.00
1/2 (Wizard) origin of Cannon; Turner-a 6.00
1/2 (3/03, $2.99) origin of Cannon 3.00
1-Turner-s/a; three covers; alternate story pages 6.00
1-Wizard World Ed. 9.00
2-14: 12-14-Witchblade app. 13,14-Tomb Raider app. 3.00
9-Green foil-c edition 15.00
9,12-Holofoil editions 18.00
12,13-DFE alternate-c 6.00
13,14-DFE Gold edition 8.00
14-DFE Blue 15.00
... Collected Edition 1 (3/99, $5.95) r/Preview & all three #1's 6.00
... Collected Edition 2-4 (3-12/99, $5.95) 2-r/#2,3. 3-r/#4,5. 4-r/#6,7 6.00
... Collected Edition 5 (4/00, $5.95) 5-r/#8,9 6.00
... Primer (6/11, $1.00) Comic style summary of Volume 1; text summaries of Vol. 2 & 3 3.00
... Swimsuit Special (5/99, $2.95) Pin-ups by various 3.00
... Swimsuit Special 2000 (12/00, $2.95) Pin-ups by various; Turner-c 3.00
Michael Turner's Fathom HC ('01, $39.95) r/#1-9, black-c w/silver foil 40.00
Michael Turner's Fathom SC ('01, $24.95) r/#1-9, new Turner-c 25.00
Michael Turner's Fathom The Definitive Edition ('08, $49.95) r/Preview, #0,1/2,1-14, Swimsuit Special 1999 & 2000; cover gallery; foreword by Geoff Johns 50.00

FATHOM (MICHAEL TURNER'S...) (Volume 2)
Aspen MLT, Inc.: No. 0, Apr, 2005 - No. 11, Dec, 2006 ($2.50/$2.99)

0-($2.50) Turnbull-a/Turner-c 3.00
1-11-($2.99) 1-Five covers. 2-Two covers. 4-Six covers 3.00
... Beginnings (2005, $1.99) Two covers; Turnbull-a 3.00
...: Killian's Vessel 1 (7/07, $2.99) 3 covers; Odagawa-a 3.00
... Prelude (6/05, $2.99) Seven covers; Garza-a 3.00

FATHOM (MICHAEL TURNER'S...) (Volume 3)
Aspen MLT, Inc.: No. 0, Jun, 2008 - No. 10, Feb, 2010 ($2.50/$2.99)

0-($2.50) Garza-a/c 3.00
1-10-($2.99) Garza-a; multiple covers on each 3.00

FATHOM (MICHAEL TURNER'S...) (Volume 4)
Aspen MLT, Inc.: No. 0, Jun, 2011 - No. 9, May, 2013 ($2.50/$2.99/$3.50)

0-($2.50) Lobdell-s/Konat-a/c; interview with Lobdell; sketch art 3.00
1-3-($2.99) 1-Five covers 3.00
4-9-($3.50) 3.50

FATHOM (MICHAEL TURNER'S...) (Volume 5)
Aspen MLT, Inc.: Jul, 2013 - No. 8, Sept, 2014 ($1.00/$3.99)

1-($1.00) Wohl-s/Konat-a; multiple covers 3.00
2-8-($3.99) Multiple covers on all 4.00
Annual 1 (6/14, $5.99) Turner-c; short stories by Turner, Wohl/Calero, Ruffino & others 6.00

FATHOM (ALL NEW MICHAEL TURNER'S...) (Volume 6)
Aspen MLT, Inc.: Feb, 2017 - No. 8, Sept, 2017 ($3.99)

1-8-Northcott-s/Renna-a; multiple covers 4.00

FATHOM (ALL NEW MICHAEL TURNER'S...) (Volume 7)
Aspen MLT: Jun, 2018 - No. 8, Apr, 2019 ($3.99)

1-8-Multiple covers on each; Ron Marz-s/Siya Oum-a 4.00
... Primer 1 (6/18, 25¢) Origin re-told; recaps of previous volumes 3.00

FATHOM (ALL NEW MICHAEL TURNER'S...) (Volume 8)
Aspen MLT: May, 2019 - No. 6, Oct, 2019 ($3.99)

1-6-Multiple covers on each; Hernandez-s/Campetella-a 4.00

FATHOM BLUE (MICHAEL TURNER'S...)
Aspen MLT, Inc.: Jun, 2015 - No. 6, Dec, 2015 ($3.99, limited series)

1-6-Hernandez-s/Avella-a; multiple covers on all 4.00

FATHOM: BLUE DESCENT (MICHAEL TURNER'S...)
Aspen MLT, Inc.: Jun, 2010 - No. 4, Feb, 2012 ($2.50/$2.99, limited series)

0-($2.50) Scott Clark-a; covers by Clark & Benitez 3.00
1-4-($2.99) Alex Sanchez-a. 1-Covers by Clark & Finch 3.00

FATHOM: CANNON HAWKE (MICHAEL TURNER'S...)
Aspen MLT, Inc.: Nov, 2005 - No. 5, Feb, 2006 ($2.99)

1-5-To-a/Turner-c 3.00
... Prelude (11/05, $2.50) Turner-c 3.00

FATHOM: DAWN OF WAR (MICHAEL TURNER'S...)
Aspen MLT, Inc.: Oct, 2004 - No. 3, Dec, 2004 ($2.99, limited series)

0-Caldwell-a 3.00
1-3-Caldwell-a 3.00
...: Cannon Hawke #0 ('04, $2.50) Turner-c 3.00
... The Complete Saga Vol. 1 (2005, $9.99) r/series with cover gallery 10.00

FATHOM: KIANI (MICHAEL TURNER'S...)
Aspen MLT, Inc.: No. 0, Feb, 2007 - No. 4, Dec, 2007 ($2.99, limited series)

0-4-Marcus To-a. 1-Six covers 3.00
Vol. 2 (4/12, $2.50) 0-Four covers 3.00
Vol. 2 (5/12 - No. 4, 11/12, $3.50) 1-4-Hernandez-s/Nome-a; multiple covers on each 3.50
Vol. 3 (3/14 - No. 4, 6/14, $3.99) 1-4-Hernandez-s/Cafaro-a; multiple covers on each 4.00
Vol. 4 (2/15 - No. 4, 5/15, $3.99) 1-4-Hernandez-s/Cafaro-a; multiple covers on each 4.00

FATHOM: KILLIAN'S TIDE
Image Comics (Top Cow Prod.): Apr, 2001 - No. 4, Nov, 2001 ($2.95)

1-4-Caldwell-a(p); two covers by Caldwell and Turner. 2-Flip-book preview of Universe 3.00
1-DFE Blue, 1-Holographic logo 12.00
4-Foil-c 12.00

FATHOM: THE ELITE SAGA (MICHAEL TURNER'S...)
Aspen MLT, Inc.: Jun, 2013 - No. 5, Jul, 2013 ($3.99, weekly limited series)

1-5-Hernandez-s/Marion-a; multiple covers; leads into Fathom Volume 5 4.00

FATIMA...CHALLENGE TO THE WORLD (Also see Our Lady of Fatima)
Catechetical Guild: 1951, 36 pgs. (15¢)

nn (not same as 'Challenge to the World') 7 14 21 37 46 55

FATMAN, THE HUMAN FLYING SAUCER
Lightning Comics (Milson Publ. Co.): April, 1967 - No. 3, Aug-Sept, 1967 (68 pgs.) (Written by Otto Binder)

1-Origin/1st app. Fatman & Tinman by C.C. Beck; 1st app. Anti-Man; 2-pg. Fatman pin-up by Beck 6 12 18 42 79 115
2-C. C. Beck-a 4 8 12 28 47 65
3-(Scarce)-Beck-a 6 12 18 38 69 100

FAUNTLEROY COMICS (Super Duck Presents...)
Close-Up/Archie Publications: 1950; No. 2, 1951; No. 3, 1952

1-Super Duck-c/stories by Al Fagaly in all 11 22 33 62 86 110
2,3 7 14 21 37 46 55

FAUST
Northstar Publishing/Rebel Studios #7 on: 1989 - No 13, 1997 ($2.00/$2.25, B&W, mature themes)

1-Decapitation-c; Tim Vigil-c/a in all 3 6 9 16 23 30
1-2nd - 4th printings 4.00
2 2 4 6 8 11 14
2-2nd & 3rd printings, 3,5-2nd printing 4.00
3 2 4 6 8 10 12
4-10: 7-Begin Rebel Studios series 5.00
11-13-Scarce 2 4 6 8 11 14

FAWCETT MOTION PICTURE COMICS (See Motion Picture Comics)

FAWCETT MOVIE COMIC
Fawcett Publications: 1949 - No. 20, Dec, 1952 (All photo-c)

nn- "Dakota Lil"; George Montgomery & Rod Cameron (1949) 20 40 60 120 195 270
nn- "Copper Canyon"; Ray Milland & Hedy Lamarr (1950) 15 30 45 90 140 190
nn- "Destination Moon" (1950) 65 130 195 416 708 1000
nn- "Montana"; Errol Flynn & Alexis Smith (1950) 15 30 45 90 140 190
nn- "Pioneer Marshal"; Monte Hale (1950) 15 30 45 90 140 190
nn- "Powder River Rustlers"; Rocky Lane (1950) 20 40 60 117 189 260
nn- "Singing Guns"; Vaughn Monroe, Ella Raines & Walter Brennan (1950) 14 28 42 82 121 160
7- "Gunmen of Abilene"; Rocky Lane; Bob Powell-a (1950) 16 32 48 92 144 195
8- "King of the Bullwhip"; Lash LaRue; Bob Powell-a (1950) 21 42 63 126 206 285
9- "The Old Frontier"; Monte Hale; Bob Powell-a (2/51; mis-dated 2/50) 15 30 45 90 140 190
10- "The Missourians"; Monte Hale (4/51) 15 30 45 90 140 190
11- "The Thundering Trail"; Lash LaRue (6/51) 19 38 57 111 176 240
12- "Rustlers on Horseback"; Rocky Lane (8/51) 15 30 45 90 140 190
13- "Warpath"; Edmond O'Brien & Forrest Tucker (10/51) 14 28 42 80 115 150
14- "Last Outpost"; Ronald Reagan (12/51) 32 64 96 188 307 425
15-(Scarce)- "The Man From Planet X"; Robert Clark; Schaffenberger-a (2/52) 252 504 758 1613 2757 3900

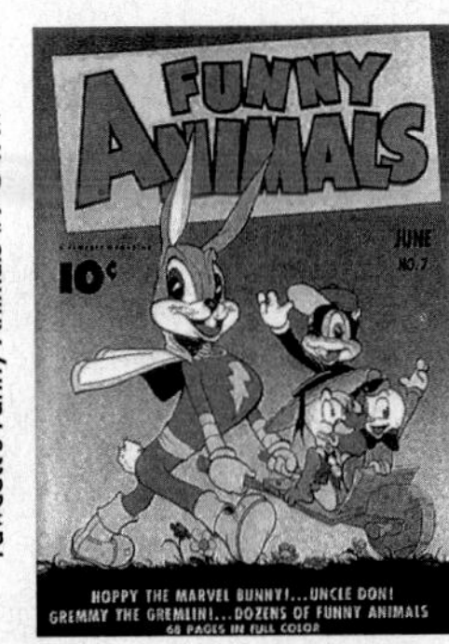

Fawcett's Funny Animals #7 © FAW

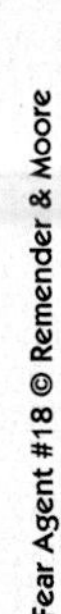
Fear Agent #18 © Remender & Moore

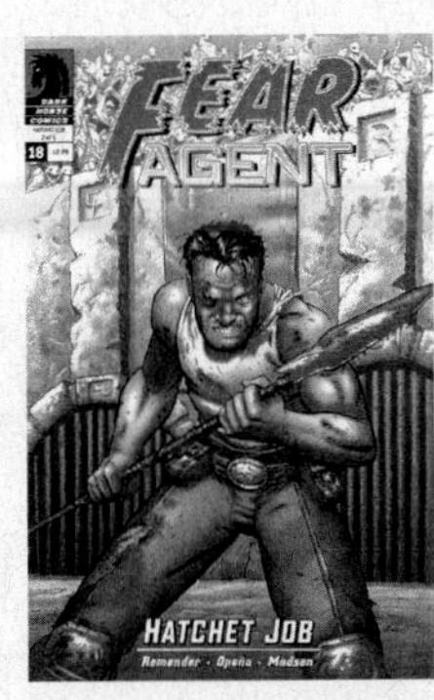

Fearless #4 © MAR

	GD 2.0	VG 4.0	FN 6.0	VF 8.0	VF/NM 9.0	NM- 9.2
16- "Ten Tall Men"; Burt Lancaster	13	26	39	74	105	135
17- "Rose of Cimarron"; Jack Buetel & Mala Powers	10	20	30	58	79	100
18- "The Brigand"; Anthony Dexter & Anthony Quinn; Schaffenberger-a	10	20	30	58	79	100
19- "Carbine Williams"; James Stewart; Costanza-a; James Stewart photo-c	11	22	33	62	86	110
20- "Ivanhoe"; Robert Taylor & Liz Taylor photo-c	18	36	54	105	165	225

FAWCETT'S FUNNY ANIMALS (No. 1-26, 80-on titled "Funny Animals"; becomes Li'l Tomboy No. 92 on?)
Fawcett Publications/Charlton Comics No. 84 on: 12/42 - #79, 4/53; #80, 6/53 - #83, 12?/53; #84, 4/54 - #91, 2/56

	GD	VG	FN	VF	VF/NM	NM-
1-Capt. Marvel on cover; intro. Hoppy The Captain Marvel Bunny, cloned from Capt. Marvel; Billy the Kid & Willie the Worm begin	60	120	180	381	653	925
2-Xmas-c	36	72	108	216	351	485
3-5: 3(2/43)-Spirit of '43-c	26	52	78	154	252	350
6,7,9,10	15	30	45	88	137	185
8-Flag-c	16	32	48	92	144	195
11-20: 14-Cover is a 1944 calendar	12	24	36	69	97	125
21-40: 25-Xmas-c. 26-St. Valentine's Day-c	10	20	30	54	72	90
41-86,90,91	9	18	27	47	61	75
87-89(10-54-2/55)-Merry Mailman ish (TV/Radio)-part photo-c	10	20	30	54	72	90

NOTE: *Marvel Bunny in all issues to at least No. 68 (not in 49-54).*

FAZE ONE FAZERS
AC Comics: 1986 - No. 4, Sept, 1986 (Limited series)

1-4 3.00

F.B.I., THE
Dell Publishing Co.: Apr-June, 1965

1-Sinnott-a 4 8 12 23 37 50

F.B.I. STORY, THE (Movie)
Dell Publishing Co.: No. 1069, Jan-Mar, 1960

Four Color 1069-Toth-a; James Stewart photo-c 9 18 27 59 117 175

FBP: FEDERAL BUREAU OF PHYSICS (Titled Collider for issue #1)
DC Comics (Vertigo): Sept, 2013 - No. 24, Nov, 2015 ($2.99/$3.99)

Collider #1- Simon Oliver-s/Robbi Rodriguez-a/Nathan Fox-c 3.00
2-20: 2-(10/13) 3.00
21-24-($3.99) 4.00

FEAR (Adventure into...)
Marvel Comics Group: Nov, 1970 - No. 31, Dec, 1975

	GD	VG	FN	VF	VF/NM	NM-
1-Fantasy & Sci-Fi-r in early issues; 68 pg. Giant size; Kirby-a(r)	8	16	24	56	108	160
2-6: 2-4-(68 pgs.). 5,6-(52 pgs.) Kirby-a(r)	4	8	12	28	47	65
7-9-Kirby-a(r)	3	6	9	18	28	38
10-Man-Thing begins (10/72, 4th app.), ends #19; see Savage Tales #1 for 1st app.; 1st solo series; Chaykin/Morrow-c/a;	6	12	18	41	76	110
11,12: 11-N. Adams-c. 12-Starlin/Buckler-a	3	6	9	16	24	32
13,14,16-18: 17-Origin/1st app. Wundarr	3	6	9	16	23	30
15-1st full-length Man-Thing story (8/73)	3	6	9	18	27	36
19-Intro. Howard the Duck; Val Mayerik-a (12/73)	11	22	33	76	163	250
20-Morbius, the Living Vampire begins, ends #31; has history recap of Morbius with X-Men & Spider-Man	6	12	18	41	76	110
21-23,25	3	6	9	16	23	30
24-Blade-c/sty	6	12	18	42	79	115
26-31	2	4	6	11	16	20

NOTE: ***Bolle** a-13i. **Brunner** c-15-17. **Buckler** a-11p, 12i. **Chaykin** a-10i. **Colan** a-23r. **Craig** a-10p. **Ditko** a-6-8r. **Evans** a-30. **Everett** a-9, 10i, 21r. **Gulacy** a-20p. **Heath** a-12r. **Heck** a-8r, 13r. **Gil Kane** a-21p; c(p)-20, 21, 23-28, 31. **Kirby** a-1-9r. **Maneely** a-24r. **Mooney** a-11i, 26r. **Morrow** a-11i. **Paul Reinman** a-14r. **Robbins** a(p)-25-27, 31. **Russell** a-23p, 24p. **Severin** c-8. **Starlin** c-12p.*

FEAR AGENT
Image Comics (#1-11)/Dark Horse Comics.: Oct, 2005 - No. 32, Nov, 2011 ($2.99/$3.50)

1-11: 1-Remender-s/Moore-a. 5-Opeña-a begins. 11-Francavilla-a 3.00
... The Last Goodbye 1-4 (Dark Horse, 6/07 - No. 4, 9/07) (#12-15) 3.00
Tales of the Fear Agent: Twelve Steps in One (#16), 17-27 3.00
28-32-($3.50) Hawthorne & Moore-a/Moore-c 3.50
... Vol 1.: Re-Ignition TPB (2006, $9.99) r/#1-4 10.00
... Vol 2.: My War TPB (Dark Horse Books, 2007, $14.95) r/#5-10; Opeña sketch pages 15.00

FEARBOOK
Eclipse Comics: April, 1986 ($1.75, one-shot, mature)

1-Scholastic Mag-r; Bissette-a 4.00

FEAR CASE
Dark Horse Comics: Feb, 2021 - Present ($3.99)

1-Matt Kindt-s/Tyler Jenkins-a 4.00

FEAR EFFECT (Based on the video game)
Image Comics (Top Cow): May, 2000; March, 2001 ($2.95)

Retro Helix 1 (3/01), Special 1 (5/00) 3.00

FEAR IN THE NIGHT (See Complete Mystery No. 3)

FEAR ITSELF
Marvel Comics: Jun, 2011 - No. 7, Dec, 2011 ($3.99/$4.99, limited series)

1-6-Fraction-s/Immonen-a/McNiven-c. 3-Bucky apparently killed 4.00
1-Blank cover 4.00
7-($4.99) Thor perishes; previews of ...: The Fearless, Incredible Hulk #1, Defenders #1 5.00
7.1 Captain America (1/12, $3.99) Brubaker-s/Guice-a; Bucky's fate 4.00
7.2 Thor (1/12, $3.99) Fraction-s/Adam Kubert-a/c; Thor's funeral; Tanarus returns 4.00
7.3 Iron Man (1/12, $3.99) Fraction-s/Larroca-a/c; Odin app. 4.00
...: Black Widow (8/11, $3.99) Peter Nguyen-a; Peregrine app. 4.00
...: Book of the Skull (5/11, $3.99) prequel to series; WWII flashback, Red Skull app. 4.00
...: Fellowship of Fear (10/11, $3.99) profiles of hammer-wielders and fear thrivers 4.00
...: FF (9/11, $2.99) Reed & Sue vs. Ben Grimm; Grummett-a/Dell'Otto-c 3.00
...: Sin's Past (6/11, $4.99) r/Captain America #355-357; Sisters of Sin app. 5.00
... Spotlight (6/11, $3.99) Interviews with Fraction and Immonen; feature articles 4.00
...: The Monkey King (11/11, $2.99) Joshua Fialkov-s/Juan Doe-a 3.00
...: The Worthy (9/11, $3.99) Origins of the hammer wielders; s/a by various 4.00

FEAR ITSELF: DEADPOOL
Marvel Comics: Aug, 2011 - No. 3, Oct, 2011 ($2.99, limited series)

1-3-Hastings-s/Dazo-a 3.00

FEAR ITSELF: FEARSOME FOUR
Marvel Comics: Aug, 2011 - No. 4, Nov, 2011 ($2.99, limited series)

1-4-Art by Bisley and others; Man-Thing, She-Hulk & Howard the Duck app. 3.00

FEAR ITSELF: HULK VS. DRACULA
Marvel Comics: Nov, 2011 - No. 3, Dec, 2011 ($2.99, limited series)

1-3-Gischler-s/Stegman-a; Dell'Otto-c 3.00

FEAR ITSELF: SPIDER-MAN
Marvel Comics: Jul, 2011 - No. 3, Sept, 2011 ($2.99, limited series)

1-3-Yost-s/McKone-a; Vermin app. 3.00

FEAR ITSELF: THE DEEP
Marvel Comics: Aug, 2011 - No. 4, Nov, 2011 ($2.99, limited series)

1-4-Bunn-s/Garbett-a; Sub-Mariner vs. Attuma; Doctor Strange & Silver Surfer app. 3.00

FEAR ITSELF: THE FEARLESS (Follows Fear Itself #7)
Marvel Comics: Dec, 2011 - No. 12, Jun, 2012 ($2.99, limited series)

1-12: 1-Fate of the Hammers; Bagley & Pelletier-a; Art Adams-c. 7-Wolverine app. 3.00

FEAR ITSELF: THE HOME FRONT
Marvel Comics: Jun, 2011 - No. 7, Dec, 2011 ($3.99, limited series)

1-7-Short story anthology; Speedball w/Mayhew-a in all; Chaykin-a; Djurdjevic-c 4.00

FEAR ITSELF: UNCANNY X-FORCE
Marvel Comics: Sept, 2011 - No. 3, Nov, 2011 ($2.99, limited series)

1-3-Bianchi-a/c 3.00

FEAR ITSELF: WOLVERINE
Marvel Comics: Sept, 2011 - No. 3, Nov, 2011 ($2.99, limited series)

1-3-Boschi-a; Wolverine vs. S.T.R.I.K.E. 1-Acuña-c. 2,3-Molina-c 3.00

FEAR ITSELF: YOUTH IN REVOLT
Marvel Comics: Jul, 2011 - No. 6, Dec, 2011 ($2.99, limited series)

1-6-Firestar and The Initiative app.; McKeever-s/Norton-a 3.00

FEARLESS
Marvel Comics: Sept, 2019 - No. 4, Dec, 2019 ($4.99, limited series)

1-4 Stories of Captain Marvel, Storm, Invisible Woman and other female heroes 5.00

FEARLESS DAWN MEETS HELLBOY
Albatross Funnybooks: 2020 ($3.99, one-shot)

1-Mike Mignola & Steve Mannion-s/a 4.00

FEARLESS DEFENDERS (Marvel NOW!)
Marvel Comics: Apr, 2013 - No. 12, Feb, 2014 ($2.99/3.99)

1-4,5-7: 1-Valkyrie & Misty Knight team-up; Bunn-s/Sliney-a. 2-Dani Moonstar app. 3.00
4AU-(7/13, $3.99) Age of Ultron tie-in; Dr. Doom & Ares app. 4.00
8-12-($3.99) 4.00

FEARLESS FAGAN

Feature Comics #54 © QUA

Feature Presentation #5 (#1) © FOX

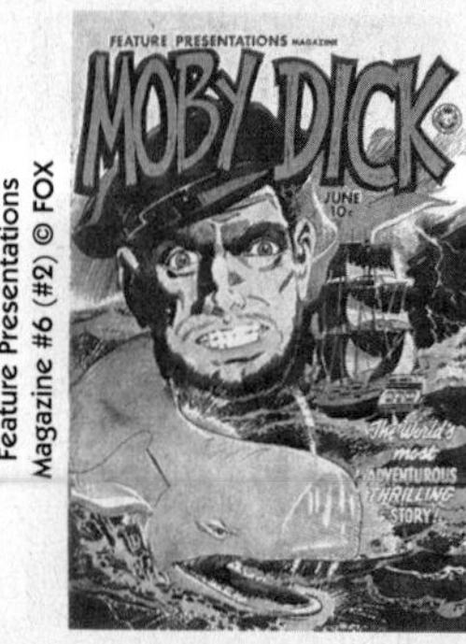
Feature Presentations Magazine #6 (#2) © FOX

	GD 2.0	VG 4.0	FN 6.0	VF 8.0	VF/NM 9.0	NM- 9.2
Dell Publishing Co.: No. 441, Dec, 1952 (one-shot)						
Four Color 441	5	10	15	31	53	75

FEATHERS
Archaia (BOOM! Studios): Jan, 2015 - No. 6, Jun, 2015 ($3.99, limited series)

1-6-Jorge Corona-s/a						4.00

FEATURE BOOK (Dell) (See Large Feature Comic)

FEATURE BOOKS (Newspaper-r, early issues)
David McKay Publications: May, 1937 - No. 57, 1948 (B&W)
(Full color, 68 pgs. begin #26 on)

Note: See individual alphabetical listings for prices

nn-Popeye & the Jeep (#1, 100 pgs.); reprinted as Feature Books #3(Very Rare; only 3 known copies, 1-VF, 2-in low grade)
nn-Dick Tracy (#1)-Reprinted as Feature Book #4 (100 pgs.) & in part as 4-Color #1 (Rare, less than 10 known copies)

NOTE: *Above books were advertised together with different covers from Feat. Books #3 & 4.*

1-King of the Royal Mtd. (#1)
3-Popeye (7/37) by Segar;
4-Dick Tracy (8/37)-Same as nn issue but a new cover added
6-Dick Tracy (10/37)
8-Secret Agent X-9 (12/37) -Not by Raymond
9-Dick Tracy (1/38)
11-Little Annie Rooney (#1, 3/38)
13-Inspector Wade (5/38)
15-Barney Baxter (#1) (7/38)
17-Gangbusters (#1, 9/38) (1st app.)
20-Phantom (#1, 12/38)
22-Phantom
24-Lone Ranger (1941)
26-Prince Valiant (1941)-Hal Foster-c/a; newspaper strips reprinted, pgs. 1-28,30-63; color & 68 pg. issues begin; Foster cover is only original comic book artwork by him
36('43),38,40('44),42,43, 45,47-Blondie
39-Phantom
46-Mandrake in the Fire World-(58 pgs.)
48-Maltese Falcon by Dashiell Hammett('46)
51,54-Rip Kirby; Raymond-c/s; origin-#51
53,56,57-Phantom
2-Popeye (6/37) by Segar same as nn issue but a new cover added
5-Popeye (9/37) by Segar
7-Little Orphan Annie (#1, 11/37) (Rare)-Reprints strips from 12/31/34 to 7/17/35
10-Popeye (2/38)
12-Blondie (#1) (4/38) (Rare)
14-Popeye (6/38) by Segar
16-Red Eagle (8/38)
18,19-Mandrake
21-Lone Ranger
23-Mandrake
25-Flash Gordon (#1)-Reprints not by Raymond
27-29,31,34-Blondie
30-Katzenjammer Kids (#1, 1942)
32,35,41,44-Katzenjammer Kids
33(nn)-Romance of Flying; World War II photos
37-Katzenjammer Kids; has photo & biog. of Harold H. Knerr (1883-1949) who took over strip from Rudolph Dirks in 1914
49,50-Perry Mason; based on Gardner novels
52,55-Mandrake

NOTE: *All Feature Books through #25 are over-sized 8-1/2x11-3/8" comics with color covers and black and white interiors. The covers are rough, heavy stock. The page counts, including covers, are as follows: nn, #3, 4-100 pgs.; #1, 2-52 pgs.; #5-25 are all 76 pgs. #33 was found in bound set from publisher. Reprints from 1980s exist.*

FEATURE COMICS (Formerly Feature Funnies)
Quality Comics Group: No. 21, June, 1939 - No. 144, May, 1950

	GD 2.0	VG 4.0	FN 6.0	VF 8.0	VF/NM 9.0	NM- 9.2
21-The Clock, Jane Arden & Mickey Finn continue from Feature Funnies	65	130	195	416	708	1000
22-26: 23-Charlie Chan begins (8/39, 1st app.)	47	94	141	296	498	700
26-(nn, nd)-Cover in one color, (10¢, 36 pgs.; issue No. blanked out. Two variations exist, each contain half of the regular #26)	50	100	150	315	533	750
27-(12/39, Rare)-Origin/1st app. Doll Man by Eisner (scripts) & Lou Fine (art); Doll Man begins, ends #139	757	1514	2271	5526	9763	14,000
28-(1/40, Rare)-2nd app. Doll Man by Lou Fine	248	496	744	1587	2719	3850
29-Clock-c	129	258	387	826	1413	2000
30-1st Doll Man-c	219	438	657	1402	2401	3400
31-Last Clock & Charlie Chan issue (4/40); Charlie Chan moves to Big Shot #1 following month (5/40)	84	168	252	538	919	1300
32,34,36: Dollman covers. 32-Rusty Ryan & Samar begin. 34-Captain Fortune app.	84	168	252	538	919	1300
33,35,37: 37-Last Fine Doll Man	52	104	156	328	552	775
NOTE: *A 15¢ Canadian version of Feature Comics #37, made in the US, exists.*						
38,40-Dollman covers. 38-Origin the Ace of Space. 40-Bruce Blackburn in costume	57	114	171	362	619	875
39,41: 39-Origin The Destroying Demon, ends #40; X-Mas-c.	40	80	120	242	401	560
42,46,48,50-Dollman covers. 42-USA, the Spirit of Old Glory begins. 46-Intro. Boyville Brigadiers in Rusty Ryan. 48-USA ends	43	86	129	271	461	650
43,45,47,49: 47-Fargo Kid begins	30	60	90	177	289	400
44-Doll Man by Crandall begins, ends #63; Crandall-a(2)	57	114	171	362	619	875
51,53,55,57,59: 57-Spider Widow begins	22	44	66	128	209	290
52,54,56,58,60-Dollman covers. 56-Marijuana story in Swing Sisson strip. 60-Raven begins, ends #71	32	64	96	188	307	425
61,63,65,67	20	40	60	114	182	250
62,64,66,68-Dollman covers. 68-(5/43)	28	56	84	165	270	375
69,71-Phantom Lady x-over in Spider Widow	22	44	66	128	209	290
70-Dollman-c; Phantom Lady x-over	32	64	96	188	307	425
72,74,77-80,100-Dollman covers. 72-Spider Widow ends	23	46	69	136	223	310
73,75,76	17	34	51	98	154	210
81-99-All Dollman covers	19	38	57	111	176	240
101-144: 139-Last Doll Man & last Doll Man cover. 140-Intro. Stuntman Stetson (Stuntman Stetson c-140-144)	16	32	48	94	147	200

NOTE: ***Celardo** a-37-43. **Crandall** a-44-60, 62, 63-on(most). **Gustavson** a-(Rusty Ryan)- 32-134. **Powell** a-34, 64-73. The Clock c-25, 28, 29. Doll Man c-30, 32, 34, 36, 38, 40, 42, 44, 46, 48, 50, 52, 54, 56, 58, 60, 62, 64, 66, 68, 70, 72, 74, 77-139. Joe Palooka c-21, 24, 27.*

FEATURE FILMS
National Periodical Publ.: Mar-Apr, 1950 - No. 4, Sept-Oct, 1950 (All photo-c)

	GD 2.0	VG 4.0	FN 6.0	VF 8.0	VF/NM 9.0	NM- 9.2
1- "Captain China" with John Payne, Gail Russell, Lon Chaney & Edgar Bergen	65	130	195	416	708	1000
2- "Riding High" with Bing Crosby	69	138	207	435	735	1035
3- "The Eagle & the Hawk" with John Payne, Rhonda Fleming & D. O'Keefe	66	132	198	416	701	985
4- "Fancy Pants"; Bob Hope & Lucille Ball	72	144	216	454	770	1085

FEATURE FUNNIES (Feature Comics No. 21 on)(Earliest Quality Comics title)
Comic Favorites Inc./Quality Comics Group: Oct, 1937 - No. 20, May, 1939

	GD 2.0	VG 4.0	FN 6.0	VF 8.0	VF/NM 9.0	NM- 9.2
1(V9#1-indicia)-Joe Palooka, Mickey Finn (1st app.), The Bungles, Jane Arden, Dixie Dugan (1st app.), Big Top, Ned Brant, Strange As It Seems, & Off the Record strip reprints begin	280	560	840	1540	2520	3500
2-The Hawk app. (11/37); Goldberg-c	123	246	369	787	1344	1900
3-Hawks of Seas begins by Eisner, ends #12; The Clock begins; Christmas-c	97	194	291	621	1061	1500
4,5	69	138	207	442	759	1075
6-12: 11-Archie O'Toole by Bud Thomas begins, ends #22	53	106	159	334	567	800
13-Espionage, Starring Black X begins by Eisner, ends #20	57	114	171	362	619	875
14-20	42	84	126	265	445	625

NOTE: *Joe Palooka covers 1, 6, 9, 12, 15, 18.*

FEATURE PRESENTATION, A (Feature Presentations Magazine #6)
(Formerly Women in Love) (Also see Startling Terror Tales #11)
Fox Feature Syndicate: No. 5, April, 1950

	GD 2.0	VG 4.0	FN 6.0	VF 8.0	VF/NM 9.0	NM- 9.2
5(#1)-Black Tarantula (scarce)	68	136	204	435	743	1050

FEATURE PRESENTATIONS MAGAZINE (Formerly A Feature Presentation #5; becomes Feature Stories Magazine #3 on)
Fox Feature Syndicate: No. 6, July, 1950

	GD 2.0	VG 4.0	FN 6.0	VF 8.0	VF/NM 9.0	NM- 9.2
6(#2)-Moby Dick; Wood-c	34	68	102	199	325	450

FEATURE STORIES MAGAZINE (Formerly Feature Presentations Mag. #6)
Fox Feature Syndicate: No. 3, Aug, 1950

	GD 2.0	VG 4.0	FN 6.0	VF 8.0	VF/NM 9.0	NM- 9.2
3-Jungle Lil, Zegra stories; bondage-c	41	82	123	256	428	600

FEDERAL MEN COMICS
DC Comics: 1936

nn-Ashcan comic, not distributed to newsstands, only for in house use (no known sales)

FEDERAL MEN COMICS (See Adventure Comics #32, The Comics Magazine, New Adventure Comics, New Book of Comics, New Comics & Star Spangled Comics #91)
Gerard Publ. Co.: No. 2, 1945 (DC reprints from 1930's)

	GD 2.0	VG 4.0	FN 6.0	VF 8.0	VF/NM 9.0	NM- 9.2
2-Siegel/Shuster-a; cover redrawn from Det. #9	40	80	120	246	411	575

FELICIA HARDY: THE BLACK CAT
Marvel Comics: July, 1994 - No. 4, Oct, 1994 ($1.50, limited series)

1-4: 1,4-Spider-Man app.						4.00

FELIX'S NEPHEWS INKY & DINKY
Harvey Publications: Sept, 1957 - No. 7, Oct, 1958

	GD 2.0	VG 4.0	FN 6.0	VF 8.0	VF/NM 9.0	NM- 9.2
1-Cover shows Inky's left eye with 2 pupils	11	22	33	64	90	115
2-7	8	16	24	40	50	60

NOTE: ***Messmer** art in 1-6. **Oriolo** a-1-7.*

FELIX THE CAT (See Cat Tales 3-D, The Funnies, March of Comics #24,36,51, New Funnies & Popular Comics)
Dell Publ. No. 1-19/Toby No. 20-61/Harvey No. 62-118/Dell No. 1-12:

Felix The Cat #19 © KING

Felon #1 © Rucka & TCOW

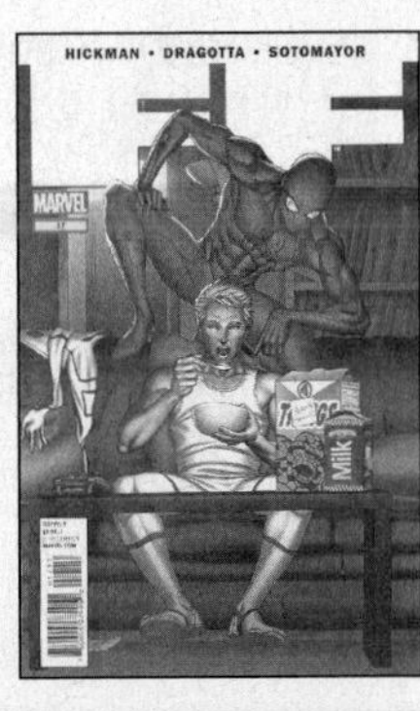

FF #17 © MAR

GD VG FN VF VF/NM NM-
2.0 4.0 6.0 8.0 9.0 9.2

1943 - No. 118, Nov, 1961; Sept-Nov, 1962 - No. 12, July-Sept, 1965

Four Color 15 82 164 246 656 1478 2300
Four Color 46('44) 42 84 126 311 706 1100
Four Color 77('45) 38 76 114 281 628 975
Four Color 119('46)-All new stories begin 34 68 102 245 548 850
Four Color 135('46) 21 42 63 147 324 500
Four Color 162(9/47) 16 32 48 110 243 375
1(2-3/48)(Dell) 27 54 81 189 420 650
2 12 24 36 81 176 270
3-5 9 18 27 62 126 190
6-19(2-3/51-Dell) 8 16 24 51 96 140
20-30,32,33,36,38-61(6/55)-All Messmer issues.(Toby): 28-(2/52)-Some copies have #29 on cover, #28 on inside (Rare in high grade) 14 28 42 96 211 325
31,34,35-No Messmer-a; Messmer-c only 31,34 8 16 24 51 96 140
37-(100 pgs., 25 ¢, 1/15/53, X-Mas-c, Toby; daily & Sunday-r (rare)
35 70 105 252 564 875
62(8/55)-80,100 (Harvey) 4 8 12 27 44 60
81-99 4 8 12 23 37 50
101-118(11/61): 101-117-Reprints. 118-All new-a 3 6 9 17 26 35
12-269-211(#1, 9-11/62)(Dell)-No Messmer 4 8 12 28 47 65
2-12(7-9/65)(Dell, TV)-No Messmer 4 8 12 23 37 50
3-D Comic Book 1(1953-One Shot, 25¢)-w/glasses 35 70 105 208 339 470
Summer Annual nn ('53, 25¢, 100 pgs., Toby)-Daily & Sunday-r
47 94 141 296 498 700
Winter Annual 2 ('54, 25¢, 100 pgs., Toby)-Daily & Sunday-r
43 86 129 271 461 650

(Special note: Despite the covers on Toby 37 and the Summer Annual above proclaiming "all new stories," they were actually reformatted newspaper strips)

NOTE: ***Otto Messmer*** *went to work for Universal Film as an animator in 1915 and then worked for the Pat Sullivan animation studio in 1916. He created a black cat in the cartoon short, Feline Follies in 1919 that became known as Felix in the early 1920s. The Felix Sunday strip began Aug. 14, 1923 and continued until Sept. 19, 1943 whjen* ***Messmer*** *took the character to Dell (Western Publishing) and began doing Felix comic books, first adapting strips to the comic format. The first all new Felix comic was Four Color #119 in 1946 (#4 in the Dell run). The daily Felix was begun on May 9, 1927 by another artist, but by the following year,* ***Messmer*** *did it too. King Features took the daily away from* ***Messmer*** *in 1954 and he began to do some of his most dynamic art for Toby Press. The daily was continued by* ***Joe Oriolo*** *who drew it until it was discontinued Jan. 9, 1967.* ***Oriolo*** *was* ***Messmer's*** *assistant for many years and inked some of* ***Messmer's*** *pencils through the Toby run, as well as doing some of the stories by himself. Though* ***Messmer*** *continued to work for Harvey, his contirubitons were limited, and no all* ***Messmer*** *stories appeared after the Toby run until some early Toby reprints were published in the 1990s Harvey revival of the title. 4-Color No. 15, 46, 77 and the Toby Annuals are all daily or Sunday newspaper reprints from the 1930's-1940's drawn by* ***Otto Messmer****. #101-r/#64; 102-r/#65; 103-r/#67; 104-117-r/#68-81.* ***Messmer****-a in all Dell/Toby/Harvey issues except #31, 34, 35, 97, 98, 100, 118.* ***Oriolo*** *a-20, 31-on.*

FELIX THE CAT (Also see The Nine Lives of...)
Harvey Comics/Gladstone: Sept, 1991 - No. 7, Jan, 1993 ($1.25/$1.50, bi-monthly)

1: 1950s-r/Toby issues by Messmer begins. 1-Inky and Dinky back-up story (produced by Gladstone) 4.00
2-7, Big Book, V2#1 (9/92, $1.95, 52 pgs.) 4.00

FELIX THE CAT AND FRIENDS
Felix Comics: 1992 - No. 5, 1993 ($1.95)

1-5: 1-Contains Felix trading cards 4.00

FELIX THE CAT & HIS FRIENDS (Pat Sullivan's...)
Toby Press: Dec, 1953 - No. 3, 1954 (Indicia title for #2&3 as listed)

1 (Indicia title, "Felix and His Friends," #1 only) 31 62 93 182 296 410
2-3 19 38 57 111 176 240

FELIX THE CAT DIGEST MAGAZINE
Harvey Comics: July, 1992 ($1.75, digest-size, 98 pgs.)

1-Felix, Richie Rich stories 6.00

FELIX THE CAT KEEPS ON WALKIN'
Hamilton Comics: 1991 ($15.95, 8-1/2"x11", 132 pgs.)

nn-Reprints 15 Toby Press Felix the Cat and Felix and His Friends stories in new color 16.00

FELL
Image Comics: Sept, 2005 - No. 9, Jan, 2008 ($1.99)

1-9-Warren Ellis-s/Ben Templesmith-a 3.00
..., Vol. 1: Feral City TPB (2007, $14.99) r/#1-8 15.00

FELON
Image Comics (Minotaur Press): Nov, 2001 - No. 4, Apr, 2002 ($2.95, B&W)

1-4-Rucka-s/Clark-a/c 3.00

FEMALE FURIES (See New Gods titles)
DC Comics: Apr, 2019 - No. 6, Sept, 2019 ($3.99, limited series)

1-6-Origin of the Granny Goodness & the Furies; Castellucci-s/Melo-a. 4-Simonson-c 4.00

FEM FANTASTIQUE
AC Comics: Aug, 1988 ($1.95, B&W)

GD VG FN VF VF/NM NM-
2.0 4.0 6.0 8.0 9.0 9.2

V2#1-By Bill Black; Bettie Page pin-up 4.00

FEMFORCE (Also see Untold Origin of the Femforce)
Americomics: Apr, 1985 - No. 109 (1.75-/2.95, B&W #16-56)

1-Black-a in most; Nightveil, Ms. Victory begin 1 3 4 6 8 10
2-10 4.00
11-43: 25-Origin/1st app. new Ms. Victory. 28-Colt leaves. 29,30-Camilla-r by Mayo from Jungle Comics. 36-(2.95, 52 pgs.) 4.00
44,64: 44-W/mini-comic, Catman & Kitten #0. 64-Re-intro Black Phantom 5.00
45-49,51-63,65-99: 51-Photo-c from movie. 57-Begin color issues. 95-Photo-c 3.00
50 ($2.95, 52 pgs.)-Contains flexi-disc; origin retold; most AC characters app. 4.00
100-($3.95) 5.00
100-($6.90)-Polybagged 1 2 3 5 6 8
101-109-($4.95) 5.00
Special 1 (Fall, '84)(B&W, 52pgs.)-1st app. Ms. Victory, She-Cat, Blue Bulleteer, Rio Rita & Lady Luger 4.00
Bad Girl Backlash-(12/95, $5.00) 5.00
Frightbook 1 ('92, $2.95, B&W)-Halloween special, In the House of Horror 1 ('89, 2.50, B&W), Night of the Demon 1 ('90, 2.75, B&W), Out of the Asylum Special 1 ('87, B&W, $1.95), Pin-Up Portfolio 4.00
Pin-Up Portfolio (5 issues) 4.00

FEMFORCE UP CLOSE
AC Comics: Apr, 1992 - No. 11, 1995 ($2.75, quarterly)

1-11: 1-Stars Nightveil; inside f/c photo from Femforce movie. 2-Stars Stardust. 3-Stars Dragonfly. 4-Stars She-Cat 4.00

FENCE
BOOM! Studios (Boom! Box): Nov, 2017 - No. 12, Nov, 2018 ($3.99)

1-12-C.S. Pacat-s/Johanna the Mad-a 4.00

FERDINAND THE BULL (See Mickey Mouse Magazine V4#3)(Walt Disney's)
Dell Publishing Co.: 1938 (10¢, large size (9-1/2" x 10"), some color w/rest B&W)

nn 22 44 66 128 209 290

FERRET
Malibu Comics: Sept, 1992; May, 1993 - No. 10, Feb, 1994 ($1.95)

1-(1992, one-shot) 3.00
1-10: 1-Die-cut-c. 2-4-Collector's Ed. w/poster. 5-Polybagged w/Skycap 3.00
2-4-($1.95)-Newsstand Edition w/different-c 3.00

FERRYMAN
DC Comics (WildStorm): Early Dec, 2008 - No. 5, Mar, 2009 ($3.50)

1-5-Andreyko-s/Wayshak-a 3.50

FEVER RIDGE: A TALE OF MACARTHUR'S JUNGLE WAR
IDW Publishing: Feb, 2013 - No. 4, Oct, 2013 ($3.99)

1-4-Heimos-s/Runge-a/DeStefano-I; 1940s War stories on New Guinea 4.00

FF (Fantastic Four after Human Torch's death)
Marvel Comics: May, 2011 - No. 23, Dec, 2012 ($3.99)

1-Hickman-s/Epting-a; Spider-Man joins 4.00
1-Blank variant cover 4.00
1-Variant-c by Daniel Acuña 8.00
1-Variant-c by Stan Goldberg 6.00
2-23-($2.99) 2-Dr. Doom joins. 4,5-Kitson-a. 5-7-Black Bolt returns. 10,11-Avengers app. 3.00
...: Fifty Fantastic Years 1 (11/11, $4.99) Handbook format profiles of heroes and foes 5.00

FF (Marvel NOW!)
Marvel Comics: Jan, 2013 - No. 16, Mar, 2014 ($2.99)

1-15: 1-Fraction-s/Allred-a; new team forms (Ant-Man, She-Hulk, Medusa, Ms. Thing) 6,9-Quinones-a. 7,8,12-15-Dr. Doom app. 11-Impossible Man app. 3.00
16-($3.99) Ant-Man vs. Doom; back-up w/Quinones-a; Uatu & Silver Surfer app. 4.00

F5
Image Comics/Dark Horse: Jan, 2000 - No. 4, Oct, 2000 ($2.50/$2.95)

Preview (1/00, $2.50) Character bios and b&w pages; Daniel-s/a 3.00
1-($2.95, 48 pages) Tony Daniel-s/a 4.00
1-($20.00) Variant bikini-c 20.00
2-4-($2.50) 3.00
F5 Origin (Dark Horse Comics, 11/01, $2.99) w/cover gallery & sketches 3.00

FIBBER McGEE & MOLLY (Radio)(Also see A-1 Comics)
Magazine Enterprises: No. 25, 1949 (one-shot)

A-1 25 14 28 42 80 115 150

FICTION ILLUSTRATED
Byron Preiss Visual Publ./Pyramid: No. 1, Jan, 1975 - No. 4, Jan, 1977 ($1.00, #1,2 are digest size, 132 pgs.; #3,4 are graphic novels for mail order and specialty bookstores only)

Fiction Squad #4 © Fiction Farm

52 #20 © DC

Fight Comics #49 © FH

	GD 2.0	VG 4.0	FN 6.0	VF 8.0	VF/NM 9.0	NM- 9.2

1,2: 1-Schlomo Raven; Sutton-a. 2-Starfawn; Stephen Fabian-a. 2 4 6 13 18 22
3-($1.00-c, 4 3/4 x 6 1/2" digest size) Chandler; new Steranko-a 3 6 9 14 20 26
3-($4.95-c, 8 1/2 x 11" graphic novel; low print) same contents and indicia, but "Chandler" is the cover feature title 5 10 15 31 53 75
4-($4.95-c, 8 1/2 x 11" graphic novel; low print) Son of Sherlock Holmes; Reese-a 4 8 12 27 44 60

FICTION SQUAD
BOOM! Studios: Oct, 2014 - No. 6, Mar, 2015 ($3.99, limited series)
1-6-Jenkins-s/Bachs-a 4.00

FIELD, THE
Image Comics: Apr, 2014 - No. 4, Sept, 2014 ($3.50, limited series)
1-4-Brisson-s/Roy-a 3.50

FIERCE
Dark Horse Comics (Rocket Comics): July, 2004 - No. 4, Dec, 2004 ($2.99, limited series)
1-4-Jeremy Love-s/Robert Love-a 3.00

15-LOVE
Marvel Comics: Aug, 2011 - No. 3, Oct, 2011 ($4.99, limited series)
1-3-Tennis academy story; Andi Watson-s/Tommy Ohtsuka-a/c; Sho Murase-c 5.00

50 GIRLS 50
Image Comics: Jun, 2011 - No. 4, Sept, 2011 ($2.99, limited series)
1-4-Frank Cho-c; Cho & Murray-s/Medellin-a 3.00

52 (Leads into Countdown series)
DC Comics: Week One, July, 2006 - Week Fifty-Two, Jul, 2007 ($2.50, weekly series)
1-Chronicles the year after Infinite Crisis; Johns, Morrison, Rucka & Waid-s; JG Jones-c 4.00
2-10: 2-History of the DC Universe back-up thru #11. 6-1st app. The Great Ten. 7-Intro. Kate Kane. 10-Supernova 3.00
11-Batwoman debut (single panel cameo in #9) 4.00
12-52: 12-Isis gains powers; back-up 2 pg. origins begin. 15-Booster Gold killed. 17-Lobo returns. 30-Batman-c/Robin & Nightwing app. 37-Booster Gold returns. 38-The Question dies. 42-Ralph Dibny dies. 44-Isis dies. 48-Renee becomes The Question. 50-World War III. 51-Mister Mind evolves. 52-The Multiverse is re-formed; wraparound-c 3.00
...: The Companion TPB (2007, $19.99) r/solo stories of series' prominent characters 20.00
...: Volume One TPB (2007, $19.99) r/#1-13; sample of page development; cover gallery 20.00
...: Volume Two TPB (2007, $19.99) r/#14-26; creator notes and sketches; cover gallery 20.00
...: Volume Three TPB (2007, $19.99) r/#27-39; notes and sketches; cover gallery 20.00
...: Volume Four TPB (2007, $19.99) r/#40-52; creator commentary; cover gallery 20.00

52 AFTERMATH: THE FOUR HORSEMEN (Takes place during 52 Week Fifty)
DC Comics: Oct, 2007 - No. 6, Mar, 2008 ($2.99, limited series)
1-6-Giffen-s/Olliffe-a; Superman, Batman & Wonder Woman app. 2-4,6-Van Sciver-c 3.00
TPB (2008, $19.99) r/#1-6 20.00

52/WWIII (Takes place during 52 Week Fifty)
DC Comics: Part One, Jun, 2007 - Part Four, Jun, 2007 ($2.50, 4 issues came out same day)
Part One - Part Four: Van Sciver-c; heroes vs. Black Adam. 3-Terra dies 3.00
DC: World War III TPB (2007, $17.99) r/Part One - Four and 52 Week 50 18.00

55 DAYS AT PEKING (See Movie Comics)

FIGHT AGAINST CRIME (Fight Against the Guilty #22, 23)
Story Comics: May, 1951 - No. 21, Sept, 1954
1-True crime stories #1-4 61 122 183 390 870 950
2 37 74 111 218 354 490
3,5: 5-Frazetta-a, 1 pg.; content chan.ge to horror & suspense 36 72 108 216 351 485
4-Drug story "Hopped Up Killers" 40 80 120 246 411 575
6,7: 6-Used in **POP**, pgs. 83,84 39 78 117 240 395 550
8-Last crime format issue 34 68 102 204 332 460
NOTE: *No. 9-21 contain violent, gruesome stories with blood, dismemberment, decapitation, E.C. style plot twists and several E.C. swipes. Bondage c-4, 6, 18, 19.*
9-11,13 60 120 180 381 653 925
12-Morphine drug story "The Big Dope" 71 142 213 454 777 1100
14-Tothish art by Ross Andru; electrocution-c 97 194 291 621 1061 1500
15-B&W & color illos in **POP** 63 126 189 403 689 975
16-E.C. story swipe/Haunt of Fear #19; Tothish-a by Ross Andru; bondage-c 77 154 231 493 847 1200
17-Wildey E.C. story swipe/Shock SuspenStories #9; knife through neck-c (1/54) 90 180 270 576 988 1400
18,19: 19-Bondage/torture-c 60 120 180 381 653 925
20-Decapitation cover; contains hanging, ax murder, blood & violence 1000 2000 3000 7600 13,800 20,000
21-E.C. swipe 65 130 195 416 708 1000
NOTE: ***Cameron** a-4, 5, 8. **Hollingsworth** a-3-7, 9, 10, 13. **Wildey** a-6, 15, 16.*

FIGHT AGAINST THE GUILTY (Formerly Fight Against Crime)
Story Comics: No. 22, Dec, 1954 - No. 23, Mar, 1955
22-Toth styled art by Ross Andru; Ditko-a; E.C. story swipe; electrocution-c (Last pre-code) 52 104 156 328 552 775
23-Hollingsworth-a 33 66 99 196 321 445

FIGHT CLUB 2 (Sequel to the movie)(Also see Free Comic Book Day 2015)
Dark Horse Comics: May, 2015 - No. 10, Mar, 2016 ($3.99)
1-10-Chuck Palahniuk-s/Cameron Stewart-a 4.00

FIGHT CLUB 3 (Sequel to the movie)
Dark Horse Comics: Jan, 2019 - No. 12, Dec, 2019 ($3.99)
1-12-Chuck Palahniuk-s/Cameron Stewart-a/David Mack-c 4.00

FIGHT COMICS
Fiction House Magazines: Jan, 1940 - No. 83, 11/52; No. 84, Wint, 1952-53; No. 85, Spring, 1953; No. 86, Summer, 1954
1-Origin Spy Fighter, Starring Saber; Jack Dempsey life story; Shark Brodie & Chip Collins begin; Fine-c; Eisner-a 400 800 1200 2800 4900 7000
2-Joe Louis life story; Fine/Eisner-c 181 362 543 1158 1979 2800
3-Rip Regan, the Power Man begins (3/40); classic-c 219 438 657 1402 2401 3400
4,5: 4-Fine-c 135 270 405 864 1482 2100
6-10: 6,7-Powell-c 119 238 357 762 1306 1850
11-14: Rip Regan ends 113 226 339 723 1237 1750
15-1st app. Super American plus-c (10/41) 148 296 444 947 1624 2300
16-Captain Fight begins (12/41); Spy Fighter ends 135 270 405 864 1482 2100
17,18: Super American ends 97 194 291 621 1061 1500
19-Japanese WWII-c; Captain Fight ends; Senorita Rio begins (6/42, origin & 1st app.); Rip Carson, Chute Trooper begins 116 232 348 742 1271 1800
20-Classic female decapitation-c 123 246 369 787 1344 1900
21-27,29,30: 21-24,26,27-Japanese WWII-c 90 180 270 576 988 1400
28-Classic Japanese WWII torture-c 135 270 405 864 1482 2100
31-Classic Japanese WWII decapitation-c 432 864 1296 3154 5577 8000
32-Tiger Girl begins (6/44, 1st app.?); Nazi WWII-c 226 452 678 1446 2473 3500
33,35-39,41,42: 42-Last WWII-c (2/46) 71 142 213 454 777 1100
34-Classic Japanese WWII bondage-c 126 252 378 806 1376 1950
40-Classic Nazi vulture bondage-c 126 252 378 806 1376 1950
43,45-50: 48-Used in Love and Death by Legman. 49-Jungle-c begin, end #81 41 82 123 256 428 600
44-Classic bondage/torture-c; Capt. Fight returns 181 362 543 1158 1979 2800
51-Origin Tiger Girl; Patsy Pin-Up app. 42 84 126 265 445 625
52-60,62-64-Last Baker issue 28 56 84 168 274 380
61-Origin Tiger Girl retold 29 58 87 172 281 390
65-78: 78-Used in **POP**, pg. 99 24 48 72 140 230 320
79-The Space Rangers app. 25 50 75 150 245 340
80-85: 81-Last jungle-c. 82-85-War-c/stories 21 42 63 124 202 280
86-Two Tigerman stories by Evans-r/Rangers Comics #40,41; Moreira-r/Rangers Comics #45 21 42 63 126 206 285
NOTE: *Bondage covers, Lingerie, headlights panels are common. Captain Fight by **Kamen**-51-66. Kayo Kirby by **Baker**-#43-64, 67(not by Baker). Senorita Rio by **Kamen**-#57-64; by **Grandenetti**-#65, 66. Tiger Girl by **Baker**-#36-60, 62-64; **Eisner** c-1-3, 5, 10, 11. **Kamen** a-54?, 57? **Tuska** a-1, 5, 8, 10, 21, 29, 34. **Whitman** c-73-84. **Zolnerwich** c-16, 17, 22. Power Man c-5, 6, 9. Super American c-15-17. Tiger Girl c-49-81.*

FIGHT FOR LOVE
United Features Syndicate: 1952 (no month)
nn-Abbie & Slats newspaper-r 11 22 33 62 86 110

FIGHT FOR TOMORROW
DC Comics (Vertigo): Nov, 2002 - No. 6, Apr, 2003 ($2.50, limited series)
1-6-Denys Cowan-a/Brian Wood-s. 1-Jim Lee-c. 5-Jo Chen-c 3.00
TPB (2008, $14.99) r/#1-6 15.00

FIGHTING AIR FORCE (See United States Fighting Air Force)

FIGHTIN' AIR FORCE (Formerly Sherlock Holmes?; Never Again? War and Attack #54 on)
Charlton Comics: No. 3, Feb, 1956 - No. 53, Feb-Mar, 1966
V1#3 10 20 30 56 76 95
4-10 7 14 21 37 46 55
11(3/58, 68 pgs.) 9 18 27 50 65 80
12 (100 pgs.)-U.S. Nukes Russia 15 30 45 84 127 170
13-30: 13,24-Glanzman-a. 24-Glanzman-c. 27-Area 51, UFO story 3 6 9 21 33 45
31-53: 50-American Eagle begins 3 6 9 16 23 30

FIGHTING AMERICAN

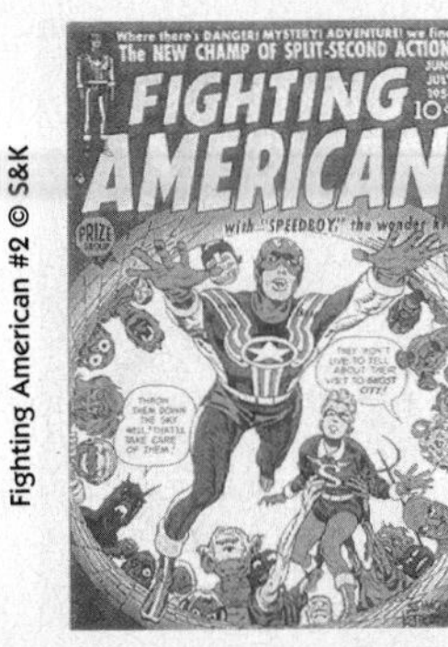

Fighting American #2 © S&K

Fighting Fronts! #1 © HARV

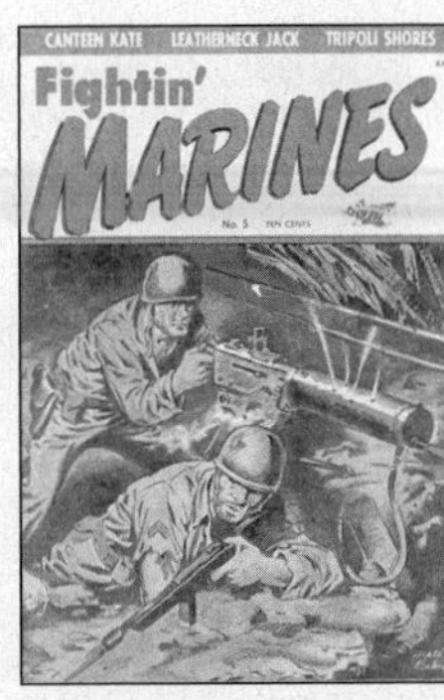

Fightin' Marines #5 © STJ

	GD 2.0	VG 4.0	FN 6.0	VF 8.0	VF/NM 9.0	NM- 9.2

Headline Publ./Prize (Crestwood): Apr-May, 1954 - No. 7, Apr-May, 1955

	GD	VG	FN	VF	VF/NM	NM-
1-Origin & 1st app. Fighting American & Speedboy (Capt. America & Bucky clones); S&K-c/a(3); 1st super hero satire series	210	420	630	1334	2292	3250
2-S&K-a(3)	102	204	306	648	1112	1575
3-5: 3,4-S&K-a(3). 5-S&K-a(2); Kirby/?-a	89	178	267	565	970	1375
6-Origin-r (4 pgs.) plus 2 pgs. by S&K	82	164	246	528	902	1275
7-Kirby-a	76	152	228	486	831	1175

NOTE: *Simon & Kirby covers on all. 6 is last pre-code issue.*

FIGHTING AMERICAN
Harvey Publications: Oct, 1966 (25¢)

	GD	VG	FN	VF	VF/NM	NM-
1-Origin Fighting American & Speedboy by S&K-r; S&K-c/a(3); 1 pg. Neal Adams ad	6	12	18	37	66	95

FIGHTING AMERICAN
DC Comics: Feb, 1994 - No. 6, 1994 ($1.50, limited series)

	GD	VG	FN	VF	VF/NM	NM-
1-6						4.00

FIGHTING AMERICAN (Vol. 3)
Awesome Entertainment: Aug, 1997 - No. 2, Oct, 1997 ($2.50)

	GD	VG	FN	VF	VF/NM	NM-
Preview-Agent America (pre-lawsuit)	1	2	3	5	6	7
1-Four covers by Liefeld, Churchill, Platt, McGuinness						4.00
1-Platinum Edition, 1-Gold foil Edition						10.00
1-Comic Cavalcade Edition, 2-American Ent. Spice Ed.						4.00
2-Platt-c, 2-Liefeld variant-c						4.00

FIGHTING AMERICAN
Titan Comics: Oct, 2017 - No. 4, Jan, 2018 ($3.99)

	GD	VG	FN	VF	VF/NM	NM-
1-4-Rennie-s/Mighten-a; multiple covers; Fighting American & Speedboy trapped in 2017						4.00

FIGHTING AMERICAN: DOGS OF WAR
Awesome-Hyperwerks: Sept, 1998 - No. 3, May, 1999 ($2.50)

	GD	VG	FN	VF	VF/NM	NM-
Limited Convention Special (7/98, B&W) Platt-a						4.00
1-3-Starlin-s/Platt-a/c						4.00

FIGHTING AMERICAN: RULES OF THE GAME
Awesome Entertainment: Nov, 1997 - No. 3, Mar, 1998 ($2.50, lim. series)

	GD	VG	FN	VF	VF/NM	NM-
1-3: 1-Loeb-s/McGuinness-a/c. 2-Flip book with Swat! preview						4.00
1-Liefeld SPICE variant-c, 1-Dynamic Forces Ed.; McGuinness-c						4.00
1-Liefeld Fighting American & cast variant-c						4.00

FIGHTING AMERICAN: THE TIES THAT BIND
Titan Comics: Apr, 2018 - No. 4, Jul, 2018 ($3.99, limited series)

	GD	VG	FN	VF	VF/NM	NM-
1-4-Rennie-s/Andie Tong-a; multiple covers						4.00

FIGHTIN' ARMY (Formerly Soldier and Marine Comics) (See Captain Willy Schultz)
Charlton Comics: No. 16, 1/56 - No. 127, 12/76; No. 128, 9/77 - No. 172, 11/84

	GD	VG	FN	VF	VF/NM	NM-
16	10	20	30	54	72	90
17-19,21-23,25-30	7	14	21	35	43	50
20-Ditko-a	9	18	27	50	65	80
24 (3/58, 68 pgs.)	9	18	27	47	61	75
31-45	3	6	9	18	28	38
46-50,52-60	3	6	9	16	23	30
51-Hitler-c	3	6	9	18	28	38
61-75	3	6	9	14	19	24
76-1st The Lonely War of Willy Schultz	3	6	9	17	26	35
77-80: 77-92-The Lonely War of Willy Schultz. 79-Devil Brigade	3	6	9	14	19	24
81-88,91,93-99: 82,83-Devil Brigade	2	4	6	10	14	18
89,90,92-Ditko-a	3	6	9	14	20	26
100	2	4	6	13	18	22
101-127	2	4	6	8	11	14
128-140	1	2	3	5	7	9
141-165	1	2	3	4	5	7
166-172-Low print run	1	2	3	5	6	8
108 (Modern Comics-1977)-Reprint						5.00

NOTE: *Aparo c-154.* ***Glanzman*** *a-77-88.* ***Montes/Bache*** *a-48, 49, 51, 69, 75, 76, 170r.*

FIGHTING CARAVANS (See Zane Grey 4-Color 632)

FIGHTING DANIEL BOONE
Avon Periodicals: 1953

	GD	VG	FN	VF	VF/NM	NM-
nn-Kinstler-c/a, 22 pgs.	21	42	63	122	199	275
I.W. Reprint #1-Reprints #1 above; Kinstler-c/a; Lawrence/Alascia-a	3	6	9	14	19	24

FIGHTING DAVY CROCKETT (Formerly Kit Carson)
Avon Periodicals: No. 9, Oct-Nov, 1955

	GD	VG	FN	VF	VF/NM	NM-
9-Kinstler-c	11	22	33	62	86	110

FIGHTIN' FIVE, THE (Formerly Space War) (Also see The Peacemaker)
Charlton Comics: July, 1964 - No. 41, Jan, 1967; No. 42, Oct, 1981 - No. 49, Dec, 1982

	GD	VG	FN	VF	VF/NM	NM-
V2#28-Origin/1st app. Fightin' Five; Montes/Bache-a	5	10	15	35	63	90
29-39-Montes/Bache-a in all	3	6	9	21	33	45
40-Peacemaker begins (1st app.)	42	84	126	311	706	1100
41-Peacemaker (2nd app.); Montes/Bache-a	10	20	30	64	132	200
42-49: Reprints						5.00

FIGHTING FRONTS!
Harvey Publications: Aug, 1952 - No. 5, Jan, 1953

	GD	VG	FN	VF	VF/NM	NM-
1	11	22	33	62	86	110
2-Extreme violence; Nostrand/Powell-a	11	22	33	64	90	115
3-5: 3-Powell-a	8	16	24	40	50	60

FIGHTING INDIAN STORIES (See Midget Comics)

FIGHTING INDIANS OF THE WILD WEST!
Avon Periodicals: Mar, 1952 - No. 2, Nov, 1952

	GD	VG	FN	VF	VF/NM	NM-
1-Geronimo, Chief Crazy Horse, Chief Victorio, Black Hawk begin; Larsen-a; McCann-a(2)	22	44	66	128	209	290
2-Kinstler-c & inside-c only; Larsen, McCann-a	15	30	45	85	130	175
100 Pg. Annual (1952, 25¢)-Contains three comics rebound; Geronimo, Chief Crazy Horse, Chief Victorio; Kinstler-c	42	84	126	265	445	625

FIGHTING LEATHERNECKS
Toby Press: Feb, 1952 - No. 6, Dec, 1952

	GD	VG	FN	VF	VF/NM	NM-
1- "Duke's Diary"; full pg. pin-ups by Sparling	21	42	63	124	202	280
2-5: 2- "Duke's Diary" full pg. pin-ups. 3-5- "Gil's Gals"; full pg. pin-ups	13	26	39	72	101	130
6-(Same as No. 3-5?)	13	26	39	72	101	130

FIGHTING MAN, THE (War)
Ajax/Farrell Publications(Excellent Publ.): May, 1952 - No. 8, July, 1953

	GD	VG	FN	VF	VF/NM	NM-
1	18	36	54	109	172	235
2	13	26	39	74	105	135
3-8	10	20	30	56	76	95
Annual 1 (1952, 25¢, 100 pgs.)	42	84	126	265	445	625

FIGHTIN' MARINES (Formerly The Texan; also see Approved Comics)
St. John(Approved Comics)/Charlton Comics No. 14 on: No. 15, 8/51 - No. 12, 3/53; No. 14, 5/55 - No. 132, 11/76; No. 133, 10/77 - No. 176, 9/84 (No #13?) (Korean War #1-3)

	GD	VG	FN	VF	VF/NM	NM-
15(#1)-Matt Baker c/a "Leatherneck Jack"; slightly large size; Fightin' Texan No. 16 & 17?	58	116	174	371	636	900
2-1st Canteen Kate by Baker; slightly large size; partial Baker-c	77	154	231	493	847	1200
3-9,11-Canteen Kate by Baker; Baker c-#2,3,5-11; 4-Partial Baker-c	41	82	123	256	428	600
10-Matt Baker-c	37	74	111	222	361	500
12-No Baker-a; Last St. John issue?	12	24	36	69	97	125
14 (5/55; 1st Charlton issue; formerly?)-Canteen Kate by Baker; all stories reprinted from #2	23	46	69	136	223	310
15-Baker-c	15	30	45	86	133	180
16,18-20-Not Baker-c. 16-Grey-tone-c	9	18	27	47	61	75
17-Canteen Kate by Baker	18	36	54	109	172	235
21-24	8	16	24	40	50	60
25-(68 pgs.)(3/58)-Check-a?	11	22	33	62	86	110
26-(100 pgs.)(8/58)-Check-a(5)	15	30	45	85	130	175
27-50	3	6	9	18	28	38
51-81: 78-Shotgun Harker & the Chicken series begin	3	6	9	15	22	28
82-85: 85-Last 12¢ issue	3	6	9	14	20	25
86-94: 94-Last 15¢ issue	2	4	6	10	14	18
95-100,122: 122-(1975) Pilot issue for "War" title (Fightin' Marines Presents War)	2	4	6	9	13	16
101-121	2	4	6	8	10	12
123-140: 132 Hitler-c	1	2	3	5	7	9
141-170						6.00
171-176-Low print run	1	2	3	5	6	8
120(Modern Comics reprint, 1977)						5.00

NOTE: *No. 14 & 16 (CC) reprint St. John issues; No. 16 reprints St. John insignia on cover.* ***Colan*** *a-3, 7.* ***Glanzman*** *c/a-92, 94.* ***Montes/Bache*** *a-48, 53, 55, 64, 65, 72-74, 77-83, 176r.*

FIGHTING MARSHAL OF THE WILD WEST (See The Hawk)

FIGHTIN' NAVY (Formerly Don Winslow)
Charlton Comics: No. 74, 1/56 - No. 125, 4-5/66; No. 126, 8/83 - No. 133, 10/84

	GD	VG	FN	VF	VF/NM	NM-
74	5	10	15	34	60	85

Fighting Yank #13 © Nedor

Fight The Enemy #3 © Tower

Final Crisis #7 © DC

	GD 2.0	VG 4.0	FN 6.0	VF 8.0	VF/NM 9.0	NM- 9.2
75-81	4	8	12	23	37	50
82-Sam Glanzman-a (68 pg. Giant)	5	10	15	31	53	75
83-(100 pgs.)	6	12	18	41	76	110
84-99,101: 101-UFO-c/story	3	6	9	17	26	35
100	3	6	9	18	28	38
102-105,106-125('66)	3	6	9	14	21	26
126-133 (1984)-Low print run	1	2	3	5	6	8

NOTE: ***Montes/Bache*** *a-109.* ***Glanzman*** *a-82, 92, 96, 98, 100, 131r.*

FIGHTING PRINCE OF DONEGAL, THE (See Movie Comics)

FIGHTIN' TEXAN (Formerly The Texan & Fightin' Marines?)
St. John Publishing Co.: No. 16, Sept, 1952 - No. 17, Dec, 1952

	GD 2.0	VG 4.0	FN 6.0	VF 8.0	VF/NM 9.0	NM- 9.2
16,17: Tuska-a each. 17-Cameron-c/a	11	22	33	64	90	115

FIGHTING UNDERSEA COMMANDOS (See Undersea Fighting...)
Avon Periodicals: May, 1952 - No. 5, April, 1953 (U.S. Navy frogmen)

	GD 2.0	VG 4.0	FN 6.0	VF 8.0	VF/NM 9.0	NM- 9.2
1-Cover title is Undersea Fighting... #1 only	19	38	57	111	176	240
2	13	26	39	72	101	130
3-5: 1,3-Ravielli-c. 4-Kinstler-c	11	22	33	62	86	110

FIGHTING WAR STORIES
Men's Publications/Story Comics: Aug, 1952 - No. 5, 1953

	GD 2.0	VG 4.0	FN 6.0	VF 8.0	VF/NM 9.0	NM- 9.2
1	15	30	45	94	147	200
2-5	11	22	33	62	86	110

FIGHTING YANK (See America's Best Comics & Startling Comics)
Nedor/Better Publ./Standard: Sept, 1942 - No. 29, Aug, 1949

	GD 2.0	VG 4.0	FN 6.0	VF 8.0	VF/NM 9.0	NM- 9.2
1-The Fighting Yank begins; Mystico, the Wonder Man app; bondage-c	371	742	1113	2600	4550	6500
2	206	412	618	1318	2259	3200
3,4: Nazi WWII-c. 4-Schomburg-c begin	168	336	504	1075	1838	2600
5,8,9: 5-Nazi-c. 8,9-Japan War-c	168	336	504	1075	1838	2600
6-Classic Japanese WWII-c	343	686	1029	2400	4200	6000
7-Classic Hitler special bomb-c; Grim Reaper app.	343	686	1029	2400	4200	6000
10-Nazi bondage/torture/hypo-c	245	490	735	1588	2684	3800
11,14,15: 11-The Oracle app. 15-Bondage/torture-c	90	180	270	576	988	1400
12-Hirohito bondage Japanese WWII-c	189	374	561	1197	2049	2900
13-Last War-c (Japanese)	194	388	562	1242	2121	3000
16-20: 18-The American Eagle app.	68	136	204	435	743	1050
21-Kara, Jungle Princess app.; lingerie-c	181	362	543	1158	1979	2800
22-Schomburg Miss Masque dinosaur-c	106	212	318	678	1164	1650
23-Classic Schomburg hooded vigilante-c	258	516	774	1651	2826	4000
24-Miss Masque app.	74	148	222	470	810	1150
25-Robinson/Meskin-a; strangulation, lingerie panel; The Cavalier app.	74	148	222	470	810	1150
26-29: All-Robinson/Meskin-a. 28-One pg. Williamson-a	55	110	165	352	601	850

NOTE: ***Schomburg (Xela)*** *c-4-29; airbrush-c 28, 29. Bondage c-1, 4, 8, 10, 11, 12, 15, 17.*

FIGHTMAN
Marvel Comics: June, 1993 ($2.00, one-shot, 52 pgs.)

	GD 2.0	VG 4.0	FN 6.0	VF 8.0	VF/NM 9.0	NM- 9.2
1						4.00

FIGHT THE ENEMY
Tower Comics: Aug, 1966 - No. 3, Mar, 1967 (25¢, 68 pgs.)

	GD 2.0	VG 4.0	FN 6.0	VF 8.0	VF/NM 9.0	NM- 9.2
1-Lucky 7 & Mike Manly begin	5	10	15	33	57	80
2-1st Boris Vallejo comic art; McWilliams-a	4	8	12	23	37	50
3-Wood-a (1/2 pg.); McWilliams, Bolle-a	4	8	12	23	37	50

FIGMENT (Disney Kingdoms) (See Disney Kingdoms: Figment 2 for sequel)
Marvel Comics: Aug, 2014 - No. 5, Dec, 2014 ($3.99, limited series)

	GD 2.0	VG 4.0	FN 6.0	VF 8.0	VF/NM 9.0	NM- 9.2
1-5-Jim Zub-s/Filipe Andrade-a						4.00

FILM FUNNIES
Marvel Comics (CPC): Nov, 1949 - No. 2, Feb, 1950 (52 pgs.)

	GD 2.0	VG 4.0	FN 6.0	VF 8.0	VF/NM 9.0	NM- 9.2
1-Krazy Krow, Wacky Duck	25	50	75	150	245	340
2-Wacky Duck	18	36	54	107	169	230

FILM STARS ROMANCES
Star Publications: Jan-Feb, 1950 - No. 3, May-June, 1950 (True life stories of movie stars)

	GD 2.0	VG 4.0	FN 6.0	VF 8.0	VF/NM 9.0	NM- 9.2
1-Rudy Valentino & Gregory Peck stories; L. B. Cole-c; lingerie panels	50	100	150	315	533	750
2-Liz Taylor/Robert Taylor photo-c & true life story	63	126	189	403	689	975
3-Douglas Fairbanks story; photo-c	30	60	90	177	289	400

FILTH, THE
DC Comics (Vertigo): Aug, 2002 - No. 13, Oct, 2003 ($2.95, limited series)

	GD 2.0	VG 4.0	FN 6.0	VF 8.0	VF/NM 9.0	NM- 9.2
1-13-Morrison-s/Weston & Erskine-a						3.00
TPB (2004, $19.95) r/#1-13						20.00

FINAL CRISIS
DC Comics: July, 2008 - No. 7, Mar, 2009 ($3.99, limited series)

	NM- 9.2
1-Grant Morrison-s/J.G. Jones-a/c; Martian Manhunter killed; 2 covers	4.00
1-Director's Cut (10/08, $4.99) B&W printing of #1 with creator commentary	5.00
2-7: 2-Barry Allen-c/cameo; intro Big Science Action; two covers. 6-Batman zapped	4.00
SC (2010, $19.99) r/#1-7, FC: Superman Beyond #1,2, FC: Submit & FC Sketchbook	20.00
...: Rage of the Red Lanterns (12/08, $3.99) Atrocitus app.; intro. Blue Lantern; 3 covers	4.00
...: Requiem (9/08, $3.99) History, death and funeral of the Martian Manhunter; 2 covers	4.00
...: Resist (12/08, $3.99) Checkmate app; Rucka & Trautman-s/Sook-a; 2 covers	4.00
...: Secret Files (2/09, $3.99) origin of Libra; Wein-s/Shasteen-a; JG Jones sketch-a	4.00
... Sketchbook (7/08, $2.99) Jones development sketches with Morrison commentary	3.00
...: Submit (12/08, $3.99) Black Lightning & Tattooed Man team up; Morrison-s; 2 covers	4.00

FINAL CRISIS: DANCE (Final Crisis Aftermath)
DC Comics: Jul, 2009 - No. 6, Dec, 2009 ($2.99, limited series)

	NM- 9.2
1-6-Super Young Team; Joe Casey-s/Chriscross-a/Stanley Lau-c	3.00
TPB (2009, $17.99) r/#1-6	18.00

FINAL CRISIS: ESCAPE (Final Crisis Aftermath)
DC Comics: Jul, 2009 - No. 6, Dec, 2009 ($2.99, limited series)

	NM- 9.2
1-6-Nemesis & Cameron Chase app.; Ivan Brandon-s/Marco Rudy-a/Scott Hampton-c	3.00
TPB (2010, $17.99) r/#1-6	18.00

FINAL CRISIS: INK (Final Crisis Aftermath)
DC Comics: Jul, 2009 - No. 6, Dec, 2009 ($2.99, limited series)

	NM- 9.2
1-6-The Tattooed Man; Eric Wallace-s/Fabrizio Florentino-a/Brian Stelfreeze-c	3.00
TPB (2010, $17.99) r/#1-6	18.00

FINAL CRISIS: LEGION OF THREE WORLDS
DC Comics: Oct, 2008 - No. 5, Sept, 2009 ($3.99, limited series)

	NM- 9.2
1-Johns-s/Pérez-a; R.J. Brande killed; Time Trapper app.; two covers on each issue	5.00
2-5-Three Legions meet; two covers. 3-Bart Allen returns. 4-Superboy (Conner) returns	4.00
HC (2009, $19.99) r/#1-5; variant covers	20.00
SC (2010, $14.99) r/#1-5; variant covers	15.00

FINAL CRISIS: REVELATIONS
DC Comics: Oct, 2008 - No. 5, Feb, 2009 ($3.99, limited series)

	NM- 9.2
1-5-Spectre and The Question; 2 covers on each. 1-Dr. Light killed; Rucka-s/Tan-a	4.00
HC (2009, $19.99, d.j.) r/#1-5; variant covers	20.00
SC (2010, $14.99) r/#1-5; variant covers	15.00

FINAL CRISIS: ROGUE'S REVENGE
DC Comics: Sept, 2008 - No. 3, Nov, 2008 ($3.99, limited series)

	NM- 9.2
1-3-Johns-s/Kolins-a; Flash's Rogues, Zoom and Inertia app.	4.00
HC (2009, $19.99, d.j.) r/#1-3 & Flash #182,197; variant covers	20.00
SC (2010, $14.99) r/#1-3 & Flash #182,197; variant covers	15.00

FINAL CRISIS: RUN (Final Crisis Aftermath)
DC Comics: Jul, 2009 - No. 6, Dec, 2009 ($2.99, limited series)

	NM- 9.2
1-6-The Human Flame on the run; Sturges-s/Williams-a/Kako-c	3.00
TPB (2010, $17.99) r/#1-6	18.00

FINAL CRISIS: SUPERMAN BEYOND
DC Comics: Oct, 2008 - No. 2, Mar, 2009 ($4.50, limited series)

	NM- 9.2
1,2-Morrison-s/Mahnke-a; parallel-Earth Supermen app.; 3-D pages and glasses	4.50

FINAL NIGHT, THE (See DC related titles and Parallax: Emerald Night)
DC Comics: Nov, 1996 - No. 4, Nov, 1996 ($1.95, weekly limited series)

	NM- 9.2
1-4: Kesel-s/Immonen-a(p) in all. 4-Parallax's final acts	4.00
Preview	3.00
TPB-(1998, $12.95) r/#1-4, Parallax: Emerald Night #1, and preview	13.00

FINALS (See Vertigo Resurrected:... for collected reprint)
DC Comics (Vertigo): Sept, 1999 - No. 4, Dec, 1999 ($2.95, limited series)

	NM- 9.2
1-4-Will Pfeifer-s/Jill Thompson-a	4.00

FINDING NEMO (Based on the Pixar movie)
BOOM! Studios: Jul, 2010 - No. 4, Oct, 2010 ($2.99, limited series)

	NM- 9.2
1-4-Michael Raicht & Brian Smith-s/Jake Myler-a. 1-Three covers	4.00

FINDING NEMO: REEF RESCUE (Based on the Pixar movie)
BOOM! Studios: May, 2009 - No. 4, Aug, 2009 ($2.99, limited series)

	NM- 9.2
1-4-Marie Croall-s/Erica Leigh Currey-a; 2 covers	3.00

FIN FANG FOUR RETURN!
Marvel Comics: Jul, 2009 ($3.99, one-shot)

	NM- 9.2
1-Fin Fang Foom, Googam, Elektro, Gorgilla and Doc Samson app.	5.00

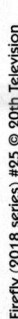

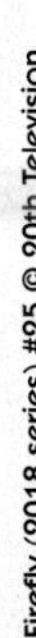
Firefly (2018 series) #25 © 20th Television

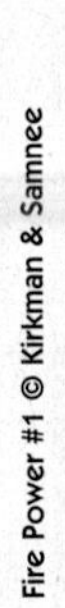
Fire Power #1 © Kirkman & Samnee

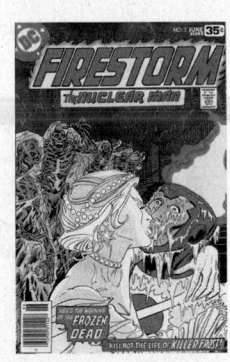

Firestorm #3 © DC

	GD	VG	FN	VF	VF/NM	NM-
	2.0	4.0	6.0	8.0	9.0	9.2

FIRE
Caliber Press: 1993 - No. 2, 1993 ($2.95, B&W, limited series, 52 pgs.)
1,2-Brian Michael Bendis-s/a 4.00
TPB (1999, 2001, $9.95) Restored reprints of series 10.00

FIREARM (Also see Codename: Firearm, Freex #15, Night Man #4 & Prime #10)
Malibu Comics (Ultraverse): Sept, 1993 - No. 18, Mar, 1995 ($1.95/$2.50)
0 ($14.95)-Came w/ video containing 1st half of story (comic contains 2nd half); 1st app. Duet 15.00
1,3-6: 1-James Robinson scripts begin; Cully Hamner-a; Chaykin-c; 1st app. Alec Swan. 3-Intro The Sportsmen; Chaykin-c. 4-Break-Thru x-over; Chaykin-c. 5-1st app. Ellen (Swan's girlfriend); 2 pg. origin of Prime. 6-Prime app. (story cont'd in Prime #10); Brereton-c 3.00
1-($2.50)-Newsstand edition polybagged w/card 3.50
1-Ultra Limited silver foil-c 1 2 3 5 6 8
2 ($2.50, 44 pgs.)-Hardcase app.;Chaykin-c; Rune flip-c/story by B. Smith (3 pgs.) 4.00
7-10,12-17: 12-The Rafferty Saga begins, ends #18; 1st app. Rafferty. 15-Night Man & Freex app. 17-Swan marries Ellen 3.00
11-($3.50, 68 pgs.)-Flip book w/Ultraverse Premiere #5 4.00
18-Death of Rafferty; Chaykin-c 4.00
NOTE: ***Brereton** c-6. **Chaykin** c-1-4, 14, 16, 18. **Hamner** a-1-4. **Herrera** a-12. **James Robinson** scripts-0-18.*

FIRE BALL XL5 (See Steve Zodiac & The ...)

FIREBIRDS (See Noble Causes)
Image Comics: Nov, 2004 ($5.95)
1-Faerber-s/Ponce-a/c; intro. Firebird 6.00

FIREBRAND (Also see Showcase '96 #4)
DC Comics: Feb, 1996 - No. 9, Oct, 1996 ($1.75)
1-9: Brian Augustyn scripts; Velluto-c/a in all. 9-Daredevil #319-c/swipe 3.00

FIREBREATHER
Image Comics: Jan, 2003 - No. 4, Apr, 2003 ($2.95)
1-4-Hester-s/Kuhn-a 3.00
...: The Iron Saint (12/04, $6.95, squarebound) Hester-s/Kuhn-a 7.00
TPB (7/04, $13.95) r/#1-4; foreword by Brad Meltzer; gallery and sketch pages 14.00

FIREBREATHER
Image Comics: Jun, 2008 - No. 4, Feb, 2009 ($2.99)
1-4-Hester-s/Kuhn-a 3.00

FIREBREATHER (Vol.3): HOLMGANG
Image Comics: Nov, 2010 - No. 4, ($3.99, limited series)
1,2-Hester-s/Kuhn-a 4.00

FIREFLY (Based on the 2002 TV series)(Also see Serenity)
BOOM! Studios: Nov, 2018 - Present ($3.99)
1-24,26: 1-Greg Pak-s/Dan McDaid-a. 20-24-Blue Sun Rising 4.00
25-($4.99) Pius Bak-a; time-jumps to after the movie 5.00
...: Bad Company 1 (3/19, $7.99) Back story on Saffron; Gordon-s/Mortarino-a 8.00
...: Blue Sun Rising 0 (9/20, $7.99) Leads into Firefly #21; Greg Pak-s/Dan McDaid-a 8.00
...: Blue Sun Rising 1 (12/20, $7.99) Follows Firefly #24; Greg Pak-s/Dan McDaid-a 8.00
...: The Outlaw Ma Reynolds 1 (1/20, $7.99) Takes place after #12; Pak-s/Gianfelice-a 8.00
...: The Sting (11/19, $19.99, HC) Saffron returns; Delilah S. Dawson-s; art by various 20.00

FIRE FROM HEAVEN
Image Comics (WildStorm Productions): Mar, 1996 ($2.50)
1,2-Moore-s 3.00

FIREHAIR COMICS (Formerly Pioneer West Romances #3-6; also see Rangers Comics)
Fiction House Magazines (Flying Stories): Winter/48-49; No. 2, Wint/49-50; No. 7, Spr/51 - No. 11, Spr/52
1-Origin Firehair 39 78 117 236 388 540
2-Continues as Pioneer West Romances for #3-6 20 40 60 115 185 255
7-11 15 30 45 86 133 180
I.W. Reprint 8-(nd)-Kinstler-c; reprints Rangers #57; Dr. Drew story by Grandenetti 3 6 9 16 23 30

FIRE POWER
Image Comics: Aug, 2020 - Present ($3.99)
1-8-Robert Kirkman-s/Chris Samnee-a 4.00

FIRESIDE BOOK SERIES (Hard and soft cover editions)
Simon and Schuster: 1974 - 1980 (130-260 pgs.), Square bound, color
Amazing Spider-Man, The, 1979, 130 pgs., $3.95, Bob Larkin-c HC 7 14 21 48 89 130; SC 5 10 15 33 57 80
America At War–The Best of DC War Comics, 1979, $6.95, 260 pgs, Kubert-c HC 10 20 30 64 132 200; SC 6 12 18 42 79 115
Best of Spidey Super Stories (Electric Company) 1978, $3.95, HC 9 18 27 57 111 165; SC 6 12 18 37 66 95
Bring On The Bad Guys (Origins of the Marvel Comics Villains) 1976, $6.95, 260 pgs.; Romita-c HC 7 14 21 46 86 125; SC 5 10 15 31 53 75
Captain America, Sentinel of Liberty,1979, 130 pgs., $12.95, Cockrum-c HC 7 14 21 48 89 130; SC 5 10 15 33 57 80
Doctor Strange Master of the Mystic Arts, 1980, 130 pgs. HC 7 14 21 48 89 130; SC 5 10 15 33 57 80
Fantastic Four, The, 1979, 130 pgs. HC 7 14 21 46 86 125; SC 5 10 15 31 53 75
Heart Throbs–The Best of DC Romance Comics, 1979, 260 pgs., $6.95 HC 13 26 39 86 188 290; SC 8 16 24 56 108 160
Incredible Hulk, The, 1978, 260 pgs. (8 1/4" x 11") HC 7 14 21 46 86 125; SC 5 10 15 31 53 75
Marvel's Greatest Superhero Battles, 1978, 260 pgs., $6.95, Romita-c HC 9 18 27 57 111 165; SC 6 12 18 37 66 95
Mysteries in Space, 1980, $7,95, Anderson-c. r-DC sci/fi stories HC 8 16 24 52 99 145; SC 5 10 15 34 60 85
Origins of Marvel Comics, 1974, 260 pgs., $5.95. r-covers & origins of Fantastic Four, Hulk, Spider-Man, Thor, & Doctor Strange HC 7 14 21 46 86 125; SC 5 10 15 31 53 75
Silver Surfer, The, 1978, 130 pgs., $4.95, Norem-c HC 7 14 21 48 89 130; SC 5 10 15 34 60 85
Son of Origins of Marvel Comics, 1975, 260 pgs., $6.95, Romita-c. Reprints covers & origins of X-Men, Iron Man, Avengers, Daredevil, Silver Surfer HC 7 14 21 46 86 125; SC 5 10 15 31 53 75
Superhero Women, The–Featuring the Fabulous Females of Marvel Comics, 1977, 260 pgs., $6.95, Romita-c HC 9 18 27 57 111 165; SC 6 12 18 37 66 95
Note: *Prices listed are for 1st printings. Later printings have lesser value.*

FIRESTAR
Marvel Comics Group: Mar, 1986 - No. 4, June, 1986 (75¢)(From Spider-Man TV series)
1,2: 1-X-Men & New Mutants app. 2-Wolverine-c (not real Wolverine?); Art Adams-a(p) 6.00
3,4: 3-Art Adams/Sienkiewicz-c. 4-B. Smith-c 4.00
X-Men: Firestar Digest (2006, $7.99, digest-size) r/#1-4; profile pages 8.00
1 (Jun, 2010, $3.99) Sean McKeever-s/Emma Rios-a 4.00

FIRESTONE (See Donald And Mickey Merry Christmas)

FIRESTORM (Also see The Fury of Firestorm, Cancelled Comic Cavalcade, DC Comics Presents, Flash #289, & Justice League of America #179)
DC Comics: March, 1978 - No. 5, Oct-Nov, 1978
1-Origin & 1st app. 6 12 18 28 69 100
2,4,5: 2-Origin Multiplex. 4-1st app. Hyena 2 4 6 10 14 18
3-Origin & 1st app. Killer Frost (Crystal Frost) 4 8 12 27 44 60
...: The Nuclear Man TPB (2011, $17.99) r/#1-5 and stories from Flash #289-293, plus story from Cancelled Comic Cavalcade (uncolored) 18.00

FIRESTORM
DC Comics: July, 2004 - No. 35, June, 2007 ($2.50/$2.99)
1-24: 1-Intro. Jason Rusch; Jolley-s/ChrisCross-a. 6-Identity Crisis tie-in. 7-Bloodhound x-over. 8-Killer Frost returns. 9-Ronnie Raymond returns. 17-Villains United tie-in. 21-Infinite Crisis. 24-One Year Later; Killer Frost app. 3.00
25-35: 25-Begin $2.99-c; Mr. Freeze app. 33-35-Mister Miracle & Orion app. 3.00
...: Reborn TPB (2007, $14.99) r/#23-27 15.00

FIRESTORM, THE NUCLEAR MAN (Formerly Fury of Firestorm)
DC Comics: No. 65, Nov, 1987 - No. 100, Aug, 1990
65-99: 66-1st app. Zuggernaut; Firestorm vs. Green Lantern. 67,68-Millennium tie-ins. 71-Death of Capt. X. 83-1st new look 4.00
100-($2.95, 68 pgs.) 5.00
Annual 5 (10/87)-1st app. new Firestorm 5.00

FIRST, THE
CrossGeneration Comics: Jan, 2001 - No. 37, Jan, 2004 ($2.95)
1-3: 1-Barbara Kesel-s/Bart Sears & Andy Smith-a 5.00
4-10 4.00
11-37 3.00
Preview (11/00, free) 8 pg. intro 3.00
Two Houses Divided Vol. 1 TPB (11/01, $19.95) r/#1-7; new Moeller-c 20.00
Magnificent Tension Vol. 2 TPB (2002, $19.95) r/#8-13 20.00

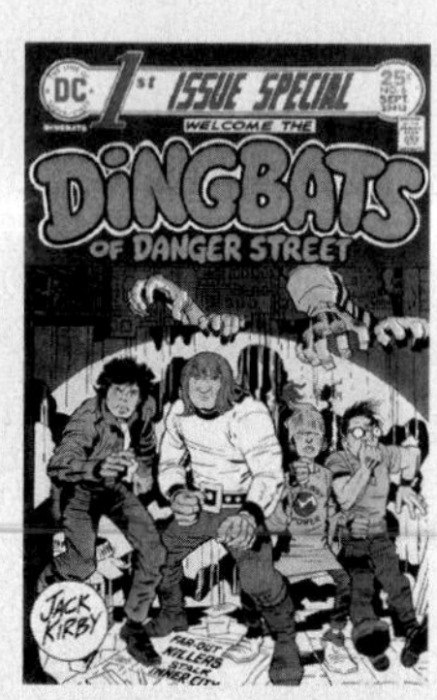

First Issue Special #6 © DC

First Love Illustrated #2 © HARV

The First X-Men #1 © MAR

GD 2.0 | VG 4.0 | FN 6.0 | VF 8.0 | VF/NM 9.0 | NM- 9.2

Sinister Motives Vol. 3 TPB (2003, $15.95) r/#14-19 16.00
Vol. 4 Futile Endeavors (2003, $15.95) r/#20-25 16.00
Vol. 5 Liquid Alliances (2003, $15.95) r/#26-31 16.00
Vol. 6 Ragnarok (2004, $15.95) r/#32-37 16.00

FIRST AMERICANS, THE
Dell Publishing Co.: No. 843, Sept, 1957

Four Color 843-Marsh-a 8 16 24 51 96 140

FIRST BORN (See Witchblade and Darkness titles)
Image Comics (Top Cow): Aug, 2007 - No. 3 ($2.99, limited series)

... First Look (6/07, 99¢) Preview; The Darkness app.; Sejic-a; 2 covers (color & B&W) 3.00
1-3-($2.99) Two covers; Marz-s/Sejic-a. 3-Sara's baby is born 3.00
1-B&W variant Sejic cover 5.00
...: Aftermath (5/08, $3.99) short stories; Magdalena app.; two covers by Sook & Sejic 4.00

FIRST CHRISTMAS, THE (3-D)
Fiction House Magazines (Real Adv. Publ. Co.): 1953 (25¢, 8-1/4x10-1/4", oversize)(Came w/glasses)

nn-(Scarce)-Kelly Freas painted-c; Biblical theme, birth of Christ; Nativity-c
37 74 111 222 361 500

FIRST COMICS GRAPHIC NOVEL
First Comics: Jan, 1984 - No. 21? (52 pgs./176 pgs., high quality paper)

1,2: 1-Beowulf ($5.95)(both printings). 2-Time Beavers 10.00
3($11.95, 100 pgs.)-American Flagg! Hard Times (2nd printing exists) 15.00
4-Nexus ($6.95)-r/B&W 1-3 15.00
5,7: 5-The Enchanted Apples of Oz ($7.95, 52 pgs.)-Intro by Harlan Ellison (1986). 7-The Secret Island Of Oz ($7.95) 10.00
6-Elric of Melnibone ($14.95, 176 pgs.)-Reprints with new color 18.00
8,10,14,18: Teenage Mutant Ninja Turtles Book I -IV ($9.95, 132 pgs.)-8-r/TMNT #1-3 in color w/12 pgs. new-a; origin. 10-r/TMNT #4-6 in color. 14-r/TMNT #7,8 in color plus new 12 pg. story. 18-r/TMNT #10,11 plus 3 pg. fold-out 11.00
9-Time 2: The Epiphany by Chaykin (11/86, $7.95, 52 pgs. - indicia says #8) 15.00
11-Sailor On The Sea of Fate ($14.95) 16.00
nn-Time 2: The Satisfaction of Black Mariah (9/87) 10.00
12-American Flagg! Southern Comfort (10/87, $11.95) 15.00
13,16,17,21: 13-The Ice King Of Oz. 16-The Forgotten Forest of Oz ($8.95). 17-Mazinger (68 pgs., $8.95). 21-Elric, The Weird of the White Wolf; r/#1-5 10.00
15,19: 15-Hex Breaker: Badger ($7.95). 19-The Original Nexus Graphic Novel ($7.95, 104 pgs.)-Reprints First Comics Graphic Novel #4 12.00
20-American Flagg!: State of the Union ($11.95, 96 pgs.); r/A.F. #7-9 15.00
NOTE: *Most or all issues have been reprinted.*

1ST FOLIO (The Joe Kubert School Presents...)
Pacific Comics: Mar, 1984 ($1.50, one-shot)

1-Joe Kubert-c/a(2 pgs.); Adam & Andy Kubert-a 4.00

1ST ISSUE SPECIAL
National Periodical Publications: Apr, 1975 - No. 13, Apr, 1976 (Tryout series)

1,6: 1-Intro. Atlas; Kirby-c/a/script. 6-Dingbats 3 6 9 16 24 32
2,12: 2-Green Team (see Cancelled Comic Cavalcade). 12-Origin/1st app. "Blue" Starman (2nd app. in Starman, 2nd Series #3); Kubert-c 2 4 6 8 11 14
3-Metamorpho by Ramona Fradon 2 4 6 10 14 18
4,10,11: 4-Lady Cop. 10-The Outsiders. 11-Code Name: Assassin; Grell-c
1 3 4 6 8 10
5-Manhunter; Kirby-c/a/script 3 6 9 16 24 32
7,9: 7-The Creeper by Ditko (c/a). 9-Dr. Fate; Kubert-c/Simonson-a.
2 4 6 11 16 20
8-Origin/1st app. The Warlord; Grell-c/a (11/75) 5 10 15 34 60 85
13-Return of the New Gods; Darkseid app.; 1st new costume Orion; predates New Gods #12 by more than a year 3 6 9 21 33 45

FIRST KISS
Charlton Comics: Dec, 1957 - No. 40, Jan, 1965

V1#1 5 10 15 33 57 80
V1#2-10 3 6 9 19 30 40
11-40 3 6 9 14 20 26

FIRST LOVE ILLUSTRATED
Harvey Publications(Home Comics)(True Love): 2/49 - No. 9, 6/50; No. 10, 1/51 - No. 86, 3/58; No. 87, 9/58 - No. 88, 11/58; No. 89, 11/62, No. 90, 2/63

1-Powell-a(2) 21 42 63 124 202 280
2-Powell-a 13 26 39 72 104 130
3-"Was I Too Fat To Be Loved" story 15 30 45 88 137 185
4-10 10 20 30 56 76 95
11,12,14-30: 30-Lingerie panel 9 18 27 47 61 75
13-"I Joined a Teen-age Sex Club" story 37 74 111 222 361 500
31-34,37,39-49: 49-Last pre-code (2/55) 8 16 24 42 54 65
35-Used in **SOTI**, illo "The title of this comic book is First Love"
21 42 63 126 206 285
36-Communism story, "Love Slaves" 14 28 42 76 108 140
38-Nostrand-a 9 18 27 52 69 85
50-66,71-90 7 14 21 37 46 55
67-70-Kirby-c 9 18 27 47 61 75
NOTE: ***Disbrow** a-13. **Orlando** c-87. **Powell** a-1, 3-5, 7, 10, 11, 13-17, 19-24, 26-29, 33,35-41, 43, 45, 46, 50, 54, 55, 57, 58, 61-63, 65, 71-73, 76, 79r, 82, 84, 88.*

FIRST MEN IN THE MOON (See Movie Comics)

FIRST ROMANCE MAGAZINE
Home Comics(Harvey Publ.)/True Love: 8/49 - #6, 6/50; #7, 6/51 - #50, 2/58; #51, 9/58 - #52, 11/58

1 19 38 57 111 176 240
2 11 22 33 62 86 110
3-5 9 18 27 52 69 85
6-10,28: 28-Nostrand-a(Powell swipe) 8 16 24 42 54 65
11-20 7 14 21 37 46 55
21-27,29-32: 32-Last pre-code issue (2/55) 7 14 21 35 43 50
33-40,44-52 6 12 18 31 38 45
41-43-Kirby-c 8 16 24 42 54 65
NOTE: ***Powell** a-1-5, 8-10, 14, 18, 20-22, 24, 25, 28, 36, 46, 48, 51.*

FIRST STRIKE (Hasbro heroes)
IDW Publishing: Aug, 2017 - No. 6, Oct, 2017 ($3.99, limited series)

1-6-Transformers, G.I. Joe, Rom, Micronauts and MASK app.; multiple covers on each 4.00

FIRST TRIP TO THE MOON (See Space Adventures No. 20)

FIRST WAVE (Based on Sci-Fi Channel TV series)
Andromeda Entertainment: Dec, 2000 - No. 4, Jun, 2001 ($2.99)

1-4-Kuhoric-s/Parsons-a/Busch-c 3.00

FIRST WAVE (Also see Batman/Doc Savage Special #1)
DC Comics: May, 2010 - No. 6, Mar, 2011 ($3.99, limited series)

1-6-Batman, Doc Savage and The Spirit app.; Azzarello-s/Morales-a/JG Jones-c 4.00
... Special 1 (6/11, $3.99) Winslade-a/Jones-c 4.00
HC (2011, $29.99, dustjacket) r/#1-6 & Batman/Doc Savage Special #1; sketch art 30.00

FIRST X-MEN
Marvel Comics: Oct, 2012 - No. 5, Mar, 2013 ($3.99, limited series)

1-5: 1-Neal Adams-a/c; Adams & Gage-s; Wolverine & Sabretooth 1st meet Xavier 4.00

FISH POLICE (Inspector Gill of the...#2, 3)
Fishwrap Productions/Comico V2#5-17/Apple Comics #18 on: Dec, 1985 - No. 11, Nov, 1987 ($1.50, B&W); V2#5, April, 1988 - V2#17, May, 1989 ($1.75, color) No. 18, Aug, 1989 - No. 26, Dec, 1990 ($2.25, B&W)

1-11, 1(5/86),2-2nd print, V2#5-17-(Color): V2#5-11. 12-17, new-a, 18-26 ($2.25-c, B&W). 18-Origin Inspector Gill 3.00
Special 1($2.50, 7/87, Comico) 3.00
Graphic Novel: Hairballs (1987, $9.95, TPB) r/#1-4 in color 10.00

FISH POLICE
Marvel Comics: V2#1, Oct, 1992 - No. 6, Mar, 1993 ($1.25)

V2#1-6: 1-Hairballs Saga begins; r/#1 (1985) 3.00

FISTFUL OF BLOOD
IDW Publishing: Oct, 2015 - No. 4, Jan, 2016 ($4.99, limited series)

1-4-Eastman-s/Bisley-a; remastering of series from Heavy Metal magazine 5.00

5 CENT COMICS (Also see Whiz Comics)
Fawcett Publ.: Feb, 1940 (8 pgs., reg. size, B&W)

nn - 1st app. Dan Dare. Ashcan comic, not distributed to newsstands, only for in-house use. A CGC certified 9.6 copy sold for $10,800 in 2003, and a CGC 9.4 sold for $11,500 in 2005.

5 RONIN (Marvel characters in Samurai setting)
Marvel Comics: May, 2011 - No. 5, May, 2011 ($2.99, weekly limited series)

1-Wolverine. 2-Hulk. 3-Punisher. 4-Psylocke; Mack-c. 5-Deadpool 5.00

5-STAR SUPER-HERO SPECTACULAR (See DC Special Series No. 1)

FIVE WEAPONS
Image Comics: Feb, 2013 - No. 10, Jul, 2014 ($3.50)

1-10-Jimmie Robinson-s/a/c 3.50

FIVE YEARS
Abstract Studio: 2019 - No. 10, 2020 ($3.99, B&W)

1-10-Terry Moore-s/a; characters from Strangers in Paradise, Rachel Rising, Echo app. 7-David-c/app. 4.00

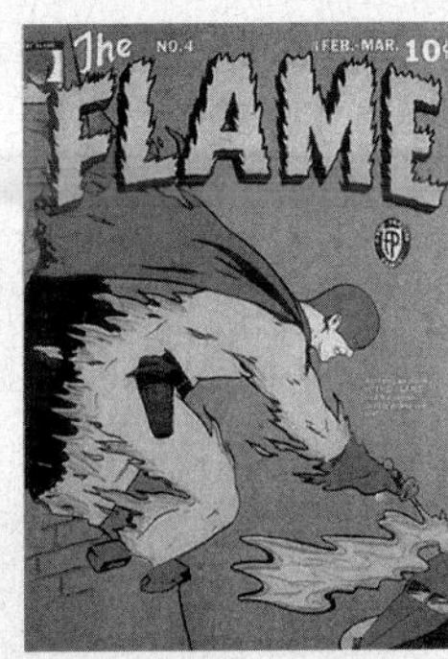

The Flame #4 © FOX

Flaming Love #1 © QUA

The Flash #159 © DC

GD	VG	FN	VF	VF/NM	NM-
2.0	4.0	6.0	8.0	9.0	9.2

FIX, THE
Image Comics: Apr, 2016 - No. 12, Jun, 2018 ($3.99)

1-12-Nick Spencer-s/Steve Lieber-a 4.00

FLAME, THE (See Big 3 & Wonderworld Comics)
Fox Feature Synd.: Sum, 1940 - No. 8, Jan, 1942 (#1,2: 68 pgs; #3-8: 44 pgs.)

1-Flame stories reprinted from Wonderworld #5-9; origin The Flame; Lou Fine-a (36 pgs.), 406 812 1218 2842 4971 7100
2-Fine-a(2); Wing Turner by Tuska; r/Wonderworld #3,10 168 336 504 1075 1838 2600
3-8: 3-Powell-a 123 246 369 787 1344 1900

FLAME, THE (Formerly Lone Eagle)
Ajax/Farrell Publications (Excellent Publ.): No. 5, Dec-Jan, 1954-55 - No. 3, April-May, 1955

5(#1)-1st app. new Flame 63 126 188 403 689 975
2,3 43 86 129 271 461 650

FLAMING CARROT COMICS (Also see Junior Carrot Patrol)
Killian Barracks Press: Summer-Fall, 1981 ($1.95, one shot) (Lg size, 8-1/2x11")

1-Bob Burden-c/a/scripts; serially #'ed to 6500 6 12 18 38 69 100

FLAMING CARROT COMICS (See Anything Goes, Cerebus, Teenage Mutant Ninja Turtles/Flaming Carrot Crossover & Visions)
Aardvark-Vanaheim/Renegade Press #6-17/Dark Horse #18-31:
May, 1984 - No. 5, Jan, 1985; No. 6, Mar, 1985 - No. 31, Oct, 1994 ($1.70/$2.00, B&W)

1-Bob Burden story/art 5 10 15 30 50 70
2 3 6 9 16 23 30
3 2 4 6 10 16 20
4-6 2 4 6 9 12 15
7-9 1 3 4 6 8 10
10-12 6.50
13-15 4.00
15-Variant without cover price 6.00
16-(6/87) 1st app. Mystery Men 1 2 3 6 8 10
17-23,25: 18-1st Dark Horse issue. 25-Contains trading cards; TMNT app. 4.00
24-(2.50, 52 pgs.)-10th anniversary issue 5.00
26,27-Teenage Mutant Ninja Turtles x-over. 26-Begin $2.25-c. 27-McFarlane-c 6.00
28-31: 29-Begin $2.50-c 4.00
Annual 1(1/97, $5.00) 5.00
... & Reid Fleming, World's Toughest Milkman (12/02, $3.99) listed as #32 in indicia 4.00
... :Fortune Favors the Bold (1998, $16.95, TPB) r/#19-24 17.00
... :Men of Mystery (7/97, $12.95, TPB) r/#1-3, + new material 13.00
... 's Greatest Hits (4/98, $17.95, TPB) r/#12-18, + new material 18.00
... :The Wild Shall Wild Remain (1997, $17.95, TPB) r/#4-11, + new s/a 18.00

FLAMING CARROT COMICS
Image Comics (Desperado): Dec, 2004 - 2006 ($2.95/$3.50, B&W)

1-3-Bob Burden story/art 3.00
4-($3.50-c) 3.50
... Special #1 (3/06, $3.50) All Photo comic 3.50
... Vol. 6 (2006, $14.99) r/1-4 & Special #1; intro. by Brian Bolland 15.00

FLAMING LOVE
Quality Comics Group (Comic Magazines): Dec, 1949 - No. 6, Oct, 1950 (Photo covers #2-6) (52 pgs.)

1-Ward-c/a (9 pgs.) 52 104 156 328 552 775
2 26 52 78 152 249 345
3-Ward-a (9 pgs.); Crandall-a 36 72 108 211 343 475
4-6: 4-Gustavson-a 22 44 66 132 216 300

FLAMING WESTERN ROMANCES (Formerly Target Western Romances)
Star Publications: No. 3, Mar-Apr, 1950

3-Robert Taylor, Arlene Dahl photo on-c with biographies inside; L. B. Cole-c 54 108 162 343 574 825

FLARE (Also see Champions for 1st app. & League of Champions)
Hero Comics/Hero Graphics Vol. 2 on: Nov, 1988 - No. 3, Jan, 1989 ($2.75, color, 52 pgs); V2#1, Nov, 1990 - No. 7, Nov, 1991 ($2.95/$3.50, color, mature, 52 pgs.);V2#8, Oct, 1992 - No. 16, Feb, 1994 ($3.50/$3.95, B&W, 36 pgs.)

V1#1-3, V2#1-16: 5-Eternity Smith returns. 6-Intro The Tigress 4.00
Annual 1(1992, $4.50, B&W, 52 pgs.)-Champions-r 4.50

FLARE ADVENTURES
Hero Graphics: Feb, 1992 - No. 12, 1993? ($3.50/$3.95)

1 (90¢, color, 20 pgs.) 4.00
2-12-Flip books w/Champions Classics 4.00

FLASH, THE (See Adventure Comics, The Brave and the Bold, Crisis On Infinite Earths, DC Comics Presents, DC Special, DC Special Series, DC Super-Stars, The Greatest Flash Stories Ever Told, Green Lantern, Impulse, JLA, Justice League of America, Showcase, Speed Force, Super Team Family, Titans & World's Finest)

FLASH, THE (1st Series)(Formerly Flash Comics)(See Showcase #4,8,13,14)
National Periodical Publ./DC: No. 105, Feb-Mar, 1959 - No. 350, Oct, 1985

105-(2-3/59)-Origin Flash(retold), & Mirror Master (1st app.) 730 1460 2555 9100 21,550 34,000
106-Origin Grodd & Pied Piper; Flash's 1st visit to Gorilla City; begin Grodd the Super Gorilla trilogy (Scarce) 338 676 1014 2941 6371 9800
107-Grodd trilogy, part 2 136 272 408 1088 2444 3800
108-Grodd trilogy ends 121 242 363 972 2186 3400
109-2nd app. Mirror Master 89 178 267 712 1606 2500
110-Intro/origin Kid Flash who later becomes Flash in Crisis On Infinite Earths #12; begin Kid Flash trilogy, ends #112 (also in #114,116,118); 1st app. & origin of The Weather Wizard 279 358 837 2305 5253 8200
111-2nd Kid Flash tryout; Cloud Creatures 89 178 267 712 1606 2500
112-Origin & 1st app. Elongated Man (4-5/60); also apps. in #115,119,130 93 186 279 744 1672 2600
113-Origin & 1st app. Trickster 69 138 207 555 1253 1950
114-Captain Cold app. (see Showcase #8) 59 118 177 472 1061 1650
115,116,118-120: 119-Elongated Man marries Sue Dearborn. 120-Flash & Kid Flash team-up for 1st time 44 88 132 326 738 1150
117-Origin & 1st app. Capt. Boomerang; 1st & only S.A. app. Winky Blinky & Noddy 50 100 150 400 900 1400
121,122: 122-Origin & 1st app. The Top 32 64 96 230 515 800
123-(9/61)-Re-intro. Golden Age Flash; origins of both Flashes; 1st mention of an Earth II where DC G. A. heroes live 287 574 861 2440 5520 8600
123-(Facsimile Edition)(2020, $3.99) Reprints issue with original 1961 ads and letters 4.00
124-Last 10¢ issue 28 56 84 202 451 700
125-128,130: 127-Return of Grodd-c/story. 128-Origin & 1st app. Abra Kadabra. 130-(7/62)-1st Gauntlet of Super-Villains (Mirror Master, Capt. Cold, The Top, Capt. Boomerang & Trickster) 26 52 78 182 404 625
129-2nd G.A. Flash x-over; J.S.A. cameo in flashback (1st S.A. app. G.A. Green Lantern, Hawkman, Atom, Black Canary & Dr. Mid-Nite. Wonder Woman (1st S.A. app.?) appears) 27 54 81 194 435 675
131-134,136,138: 131-Early Green Lantern x-over (9/62). 136-1st Dexter Miles 17 34 51 117 259 400
135-1st app. of Kid Flash's yellow costume (3/63) 23 46 69 161 356 550
137-G.A. Flash x-over; J.S.A. cameo (1st S.A. app.)(1st real app. since 2-3/51); 1st S.A. app. Vandal Savage & Johnny Thunder; JSA team decides to re-form 44 82 123 303 689 1075
139-Origin & 1st app. Prof. Zoom 148 296 444 947 2174 3400
140-Origin & 1st app. Heat Wave 22 44 66 154 340 525
141-146,148-150: 142-Trickster app. 12 24 36 84 185 285
147-2nd Prof. Zoom 19 38 57 129 287 445
151-Engagement of Barry Allen & Iris West; G.A. Flash vs. The Shade. 11 22 33 76 163 250
152-159: 159-Dr. Mid-Nite cameo 10 20 30 64 132 200
160-(80-Pg. Giant G-21); G.A. Flash & Johnny Quick-r 11 22 33 73 157 240
161-164,166,167: 167-New facts about Flash's origin 8 16 24 54 102 150
165-Barry Allen weds Iris West 8 16 24 56 108 160
168,170: 168-Green Lantern-c/app. 170-Dr. Mid-Nite, Dr. Fate, G.A. Flash x-over 8 16 24 54 102 150
169-(80-Pg. Giant G-34)-New facts about origin 9 18 27 57 111 165
171,172,174,176,177,179,180: 171-JLA, Green Lantern, Atom flashbacks. 174-Barry Allen reveals I.D. to wife. 179-(5/68)-Flash travels to Earth-Prime and meets DC editor Julie Schwartz; 1st unnamed app. Earth-Prime (See Justice League of America #123 for 1st named app. & 3rd app. overall) 7 14 21 46 86 125
173-G.A. Flash x-over 8 16 24 54 102 150
175-2nd Superman/Flash race (12/67) (See Superman #199 & World's Finest #198,199); JLA cameo; gold kryptonite used (on J'onn J'onzz impersonating Superman) 18 36 54 124 275 425
178-(80-Pg. Giant G-46) 8 16 24 52 99 145
181-186,188,189: 186-Re-intro. Sargon. 189-Last 12¢-c 5 10 15 34 60 85
187,196: (68-Pg. Giants G-58, G-70) 6 12 18 40 73 105
190-195,197-199: 198-Zatanna 1st solo story 4 8 12 27 44 60
200-(9/70) 5 10 15 31 53 75
201-204,206,207: 201-New G.A. Flash story. 206-Elongated Man begins 207-Last 15¢ issue 3 6 9 21 33 45
205-(68-Pg. Giant G-82) 6 12 18 41 76 110
208-213-(52 pg.): 211-G.A. Flash origin-r/#104; Roller Derby-c. 213-Reprints #137 4 8 12 25 40 55
214-DC 100 Page Super Spectacular DC-11; origin Metal Men-r/Showcase #37; never before published G.A. Flash story 8 16 24 54 102 150

The Flash #233 © DC

Flash #145 © DC

The Flash (2010 series) #1 © DC

GD 2.0 | VG 4.0 | FN 6.0 | VF 8.0 | VF/NM 9.0 | NM- 9.2

215 (52 pgs.)-Flash-r/Showcase #4; G.A. Flash x-over, continued in #216 5 10 15 30 50 70
216,220: 220-1st app. Turtle since Showcase #4 3 6 9 17 26 35
217-219: Neal Adams-a in all. 217-Green Lantern/Green Arrow series begins (9/72); 2nd G.L. & G.A. team-up series (see Green Lantern #76). 219-Last Green Arrow 5 10 15 34 60 85
221-224,227,228,230,231: 222-G. Lantern x-over. 228-(7-8/74)-Flash writer Cary Bates travels to Earth-One & meets Flash, Iris Allen & Trickster; 2nd unnamed app. Earth-Prime (See Justice League of America #123 for 1st named app. & 3rd app. overall) 3 6 9 14 19 24
225-Professor Zoom-c/app. 5 10 15 35 63 90
226-Neal Adams-p 3 6 9 17 26 35
229,232-(100 pg. issues)-G.A. Flash-r & new-a. 229-G.A. Flash & Rag Doll app. in new story 5 10 15 30 50 70
233-Professor Zoom-c/app. 3 6 9 21 33 45
234-236,238-250: 235-Green Lantern x-over. 243-Death of The Top. 245-Origin The Floronic Man in Green Lantern back-up, ends #246. 246-Last Green Lantern. 247-Jay Garrick app. 250-Intro Golden Glider 2 4 6 10 14 18
237-Professor Zoom-c/app. 3 6 9 18 28 38
251-274: 256-Death of The Top retold. 265-267-(44 pgs.). 267-Origin of Flash's uniform. 270-Intro The Clown 2 4 6 8 10 12
268,273,274,278,283,286-(Whitman variants; low print run; no issue #s shown on covers) 2 4 6 8 11 14
275,276-Iris Allen dies 2 4 6 13 18 22
275,276-(Whitman variants; low print run; no issue #s shown on covers) 3 6 9 16 23 30
277-288,290: 286-Intro/origin Rainbow Raider 1 2 3 5 6 8
289-1st Pérez DC art (Firestorm); new Firestorm back-up series begins (9/80), ends #304 2 3 4 6 8 10
291-299,301-305: 291-1st app. Saber-Tooth (villain). 295-Gorilla Grodd-c/story. 298-Intro & origin new Shade. 301-Atomic bomb-c. 303-The Top returns. 304-Intro/origin Colonel Computron; 305-G.A. Flash x-over 6.00
300-(8/81, 52 pgs.)-25th Anniversary issue; Flash's origin and life story retold; wraparound-c by Infantino; no ads 1 3 4 6 8 10
306-313-Dr. Fate by Giffen. 309-Origin Flash retold 6.00
314-322,325-340: 318-322-Creeper back-ups. 319-Origin of Eradicator. 328-Iris West Allen's death retold. 329-JLA app. 340-Trial of the Flash begins 5.00
323,324-Two part Flash vs. Flash story. 323-Creeper back-up. 324-Death of Reverse Flash (Professor Zoom) 3 6 9 21 32 44
341-349: 344-Origin Kid Flash 6.00
350-Double size ($1.25) Final issue 1 2 3 5 6 8
Annual 1 (10-12/63, 84 pgs.)-Origin Elongated Man & Kid Flash-r; origin Grodd; G.A. Flash-r 34 68 102 245 548 850
Annual 1 Replica Edition (2001, $6.95)-Reprints the entire 1963 Annual 7.00
...Chronicles SC Vol. 1 (2009, $14.99)-r/Showcase #4,8,13,14 and Flash #105,106 15.00
...Chronicles SC Vol. 2 (2010, $14.99)-r/Flash #107-112 15.00
The Flash Spectacular (See DC Special Series No. 11)
The Flash vs. The Rogues TPB (2009, $14.99) r/1st app. of classic rogues in Showcase #8 and Flash #105,106,110,113,117,122,140,155; new Van Sciver-c 15.00
The Life Story of the Flash (1997, $19.95, Hardcover) "Iris Allen's" chronicle of Barry Allen's life; comic panels w/additional text; Waid & Augustyn-s/ Kane & Staton-a/Orbik painted-c 20.00
The Life Story of the Flash (1998, $12.95, Softcover) New Orbik-c 13.00

NOTE: ***N. Adams*** *c-194, 195, 203, 204, 206-208, 211, 213, 215, 226p, 246.* ***M. Anderson*** *c-165, a(i)-195, 200-204, 206-208.* ***Austin*** *a-233i, 234i, 246i.* ***Buckler*** *a-271p, 272p; c(p)-247-250, 252, 253p, 255, 256p, 258, 262, 265-267, 269-271.* ***Giffen*** *a-306-313p; c-310p, 315.* ***Giordano*** *a-226i.* ***Sid Greene*** *a-167-174i, 229i(r).* ***Grell*** *a-237p, 238p, 240-243p; c-236.* ***Heck*** *a-198p.* ***Infantino/Anderson*** *a-135. c-135, 170-174, 192, 200, 201, 328-330.* ***Infantino/Giella*** *c-105-112, 163, 164, 166-168.* ***G. Kane*** *a-195p, 197-199p, 229r, 232r; c-197-199, 312p.* ***Kubert*** *a-108p, 215i(r); c-189-191.* ***Lopez*** *c-272.* ***Meskin*** *a-229r, 232r.* ***Perez*** *a-289-293p; c-293.* ***Starlin*** *a-294-296p.* ***Staton*** *c-263p, 264p. Green Lantern x-over-131, 143, 168, 171, 191.*

FLASH (2nd Series)(See Crisis on Infinite Earths #12 and All Flash #1)
DC Comics: June, 1987 - No. 230, Mar, 2006; No. 231, Oct, 2007 - No. 247, Feb, 2009

1-Guice-c/a begins; New Teen Titans app. 3 6 9 14 20 26
2-10: 3-Intro. Kilgore. 5-Intro. Speed McGee. 7-1st app. Blue Trinity. 8,9-Millennium tie-ins. 9-1st app. The Chunk 5.00
11-78,80: 12-Free extra 16 pg. Dr. Light story. 19-Free extra 16 pg. Flash story. 28-Capt. Cold app. 29-New Phantom Lady app. 40-Dr. Alchemy app. 50-($1.75, 52 pgs.). 62-Flash: Year One begins, ends #65. 65-Last $1.00-c. 66-Aquaman app. 69,70-Green Lantern app. 70-Gorilla Grodd story ends. 73-Re-intro Barry Allen & begin saga ("Barry Allen's" true ID revealed in #78). 76-Re-intro of Max Mercury (Quality Comics' Quicksilver), not in uniform until #77. 80-($1.25-c) Regular Edition 4.00
79,80 ($2.50): 79-(68 pgs.) Barry Allen saga ends. 80-Foil-c 5.00
81-91,93,94,0,95-99,101: 81,82-Nightwing & Starfire app. 84-Razer app. 94-Zero Hour. 0-(10/94). 95-"Terminal Velocity" begins, ends #100. 96,98,99-Kobra app. 97-Origin Max Mercury; Chillblaine app. 4.00
92-1st Impulse 3 6 9 19 30 40
100 ($2.50)-Newstand edition; Kobra & JLA app. 4.00
100 ($3.50)-Foil-c edition; Kobra & JLA app. 5.00
102-131: 102-Mongul app.; begin-$1.75-c. 105-Mirror Master app. 107-Shazam app. 108-"Dead Heat" begins; 1st app. Savitar. 109-"Dead Heat" Pt. 2 (cont'd in Impulse #10). 110-"Dead Heat" Pt. 4 (cont'd in Impulse #11). 111-"Dead Heat" finale; Savitar disappears into the Speed Force; John Fox cameo (2nd app.). 112-"Race Against Time" begins, ends #118; re-intro John Fox. 113-Tornado Twins app. 119-Final Night x-over. 127-129-Rogue's Gallery & Neron. 128,129-JLA-app.130-Morrison & Millar-s begin 3.50
132-149: 135-GL & GA app. 138,140-Black Flash cameos. 141-1st full app. Black Flash. 142-Wally almost marries Linda; Waid-s return. 144-Cobalt Blue origin. 145-Chain Lightning begins. 147-Professor Zoom app. 149-Barry Allen app. 3.00
150-($2.95) Final showdown with Cobalt Blue 4.00
151-162: 151-Casey-s. 152-New Flash-c. 154-New Flash ID revealed. 159-Wally marries Linda. 162-Last Waid-s. 3.00
163-169,171-187,189-196,201-206: 163-Begin $2.25-c. 164-186-Bolland-c. 183-1st app of 2nd Trickster (Axel Walker). 196-Winslade-a. 201-Dose-a begins. 205-Batman-c/app. 3.00
170-1st app. Cicada; Bolland-c 5.00
188-($2.95) Mirror Master, Weather Wizard, Trickster app. 4.00
197-Origin of Zoom (Hunter Zolomon) (6/03) 4 8 12 28 47 65
198,199-Zoom app. 1 2 3 5 6 8
200-($3.50) Flash vs. Zoom; Barry Allen & Hal Jordan app.; wraparound-c 1 2 3 5 6 8
207-230: 207-211-Turner-c/Porter-a. 209-JLA app. 210-Nightwing app. 212-Origin Mirror Master. 214-216-Identity Crisis x-over. 219-Wonder Woman app. 220-Rogue War 224-Zoom & Prof. Zoom app. 225-Twins born; Barry Allen app.; last Johns-s 3.00
231-247: 231-(10/07) Waid-s/Acuña-a. 240-Grodd app.; "Dark Side Club" 3.00
#1,000,000 (11/98) 853rd Century x-over 3.00
Annual 1-7,9: 2-('87-'94,'96, 68 pgs), 3-Gives history of G.A.,S.A., & Modern Age Flash in text. 4-Armaggedon 2001. 5-Eclipso-c/story. 7-Elseworlds story. 9-Legends of the Dead Earth story; J.H. Williams-a(p); Mick Gray-a(i) 4.00
Annual 8 (1995, $3.50)-Year One story 4.00
Annual 10 (1997, $3.95)-Pulp Heroes stories 4.00
Annual 11,12 ('98, '99)-11-Ghosts; Wrightson-c. 12-JLApe; Art Adams-c 4.00
Annual 13 ('00, $3.50) Planet DC; Alcatena-c/a 4.00
...: Blitz (2004, $19.95, TPB)-r/#192-200; Kolins-c 20.00
...: Blood Will Run (2002, 2008; $17.95, TPB)-r/#170-176, Secret Files #3, Iron Heights 18.00
...: Crossfire (2004, $17.95, TPB)-r/#183-191 & parts of Flash Secret Files #3 18.00
Dead Heat (2000, $14.95, TPB)-r/#108-111, Impulse #10,11 15.00
...80-Page Giant (8/98, $4.95) Flash family stories by Waid, Millar and others; Mhan-c 5.00
...80-Page Giant 2 (4/99, $4.95) Stories of Flash family, future Kid Flash, original Teen Titans and XS 5.00
...: Emergency Stop (2008, $12.99, TPB)-r/#130-135; Morrison & Millar-s 13.00
...: Ignition (2005, $14.95, TPB)-r/#201-206 15.00
...: Iron Heights (2001, $5.95)-Van Sciver-c/a; 1st app. of the prison; intro. Girder, Murmur, Double Down and Blacksmith 6.00
...: Mercury Falling (2009, $14.99, TPB)-r/Impulse #62-67 15.00
...: Our Worlds at War 1 (10/01, $2.95)-Jae Lee-c; Black Racer app. 3.00
...Plus 1 (1/1997, $2.95)-Nightwing-c/app. 4.00
Race Against Time (2001, $14.95, TPB)-r/#112-118 15.00
...: Rogues (2003, $14.95, TPB)-r/#177-182 15.00
...: Rogue War (2006, $17.99, TPB)-r/#1/2,212,218,220-225; cover gallery 18.00
...Secret Files 1 (11/97, $4.95) Origin-s & pin-ups 5.00
...Secret Files 2 (11/99, $4.95) Origin of Replicant 5.00
...Secret Files 3 (11/01; $4.95) Intro. Hunter Zolomon (who later becomes Zoom) 15.00
Special 1 (1990, $2.95, 84 pgs.)-50th anniversary issue; Kubert-c; 1st Flash story by Mark Waid; 1st app. John Fox (27th Century Flash) 5.00
Terminal Velocity (1996, $12.95, TPB)-r/#95-100. 13.00
...: The Greatest Stories Ever Told (2007, $19.99, TPB) reprints; Ross-c/Waid intro. 20.00
The Return of Barry Allen (1996, $12.95, TPB)-r/#74-79 13.00
The Secret of Barry Allen (2005, $19.99, TPB)-r/#207-211,213-217; Turner sketch page 20.00
...: The Wild Wests HC (2008, $24.99, dustjacket)-r/#231-237 25.00
...: Time Flies (2002, $5.95)-Seth Fisher-c/a; Rozum-s 6.00
TV Special 1 (1991, $3.95, 76 pgs.)-Photo-c plus behind the scenes photos of TV show; Saltares-a, Byrne scripts 5.00
Wizard #1/2 (2005) prelude to Rogue Wars; Justiano-a 10.00
...: Wonderland TPB (2007, $12.99, TPB)-r/#164-169 13.00

NOTE: ***Guice*** *a-1-9p, 11p, Annual 1p; c-1-9p, Annual 1p.* ***Perez*** *c-15-17, Annual 2i.* ***Charest*** *c/a-Annual 5p.*

FLASH, THE (Brightest Day)(Leads into Flashpoint series)
DC Comics: Jun, 2010 - No. 12, Jul, 2011 ($3.99/$2.99)

1-($3.99) Barry Allen vs. the 25th Century Rogues; Johns-s/Manapul-a/c 4.00
1-Variant-c by Tony Harris 10.00
2-12-($2.99) Capt. Boomerang app. 8-Reverse Flash origin retold 3.00
2-12-Variant covers. 2-Sook. 3-Horn. 4-Kolins. 5-Sook. 6-Garza. 7-Cooke 5.00

Flash (2011 series) #41 © DC

The Flash (2016 series) #73 © DC

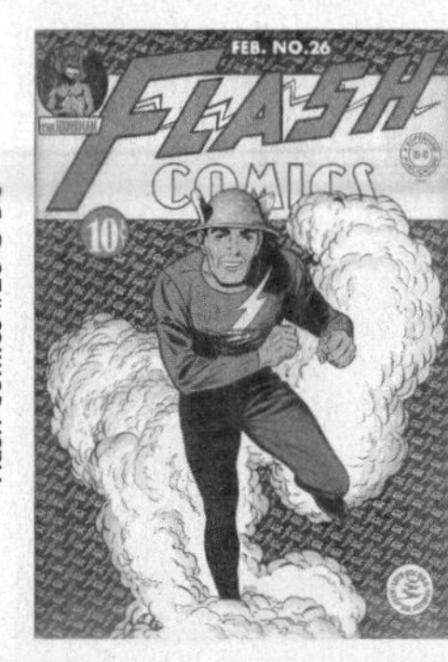

Flash Comics #26 © DC

	GD 2.0	VG 4.0	FN 6.0	VF 8.0	VF/NM 9.0	NM- 9.2

...: Secret Files and Origins 1 (5/10, $3.99) Johns-s/Kolins-a; profiles of the Rogues 4.00
...: The Dastardly Death of the Rogues HC (2011, $19.99, dj) r/#1-7 & Secret Files 20.00

FLASH (New DC 52)
DC Comics: Nov, 2011 - No. 52, Jul, 2016 ($2.99/$3.99)

1-Manapul & Buccellato-s; Manapul-a/c 1 3 4 6 8 10
1-Special Edition (12/14, $1.00) reprints #1 with Flash TV image above cover logo 3.00
2-24: 6,7-Captain Cold app. 8,9,13-17-Grodd app. 17-24-Reverse Flash app. 18-Takara-a. 21-Kid Flash app. 3.00
23.1, 23.2, 23.3 (11/13, $2.99, regular-c) 3.00
23.1 (11/13, $3.99, 3-D cover) "Grodd #1" on cover; Batista-a/Manapul-c 1 2 3 5 6 8
23.2 (11/13, $3.99, 3-D cover) "Reverse Flash #1" on cover; origin; Hepburn-a/Manapul-c 1 2 3 5 6 8
23.3 (11/13, $3.99, 3-D cover) "The Rogues #1" on cover; Zircher-a/Manapul-c 1 2 3 5 6 8
25-($3.99) Zero Year; Sprouse & Manapul-a; first meeting of Barry and Iris 4.00
26-39: 26-Googe-a. 27-Buccellato-s begin. 28-Deadman app. 3.00
40-49,51,52: 40-($3.99) Professor Zoom cameo. 41-47-Prof. Zoom app. 4.00
50-($4.99) The Rogues and The Riddler app.; back-up Kid Flash story 5.00
#0 (11/12, $2.99) Barry's childhood and origin re-told; Manapul-a/c 3.00
Annual #1 (10/12, $4.99) Continued from #12; origin of Glider; Kolins-a 5.00
Annual #2 (9/13, $4.99) Green Lantern app.; Basri-a 5.00
Annual #3 (6/14, $4.99) Intro. Wally West; Grodd app.; leads into Flash #31 5.00
Annual #4 (9/15, $4.99) Jensen-s/Dazo-a; background on Eobard Thawne; cont'd in #43 5.00
...: Futures End 1 (11/14, $2.99, reg.-c) Five years later; Wally West gains speed power 3.00
...: Futures End 1 (11/14, $3.99, 3-D cover) 4.00

FLASH, THE (DC Rebirth)(Reverts to legacy numbering with #750)
DC Comics: Aug, 2016 - No. 88, Early Apr, 2020; No. 750, Late Apr, 2020 - Present ($2.99/$3.99)

1-20: 1-3-Williamson-s/Di Giandomenico-a. 3-Intro Godspeed. 8-Wally becomes the new Kid Flash in costume. 9-Flash of Two Worlds cover swipe; both Wallys app. 10-12-The Shade app. 14-17-Rogues Reloaded 3.00
21,22-The Button x-over with Batman #21,22. 21-Flashpoint Thomas Wayne app.; Porter-a. 22-Reverse Flash app; Jay Garrick app.; leads into Doomsday Clock series 3.00
23,24,26-49: 23-Reverse Flash & Hal Jordan app. 28-Intro. Negative Flash. 33-Dark Nights: Metal tie-in. 36-Preview of Damage #1. 39-44-Grodd app. 42-Panosian-a. 46-Zoom app. 47-49-Flash War; the Renegades app.; Porter-a 3.00
25-($3.99) Reverse Flash origin re-told; art by Di Giandomenico, Sook & Googe 4.00
50-74-($3.99) 50-Flash War concl.; Zoom app.; Impulse returns. 59-Intro. Fuerza. 64,65-X-over with Batman #64,65; Gotham Girl app. 70-74-Year One; origin re-told 4.00
75-($4.99) Year of the Villain tie-in; Turtle app.; art by Porter, Duce & Kolins 5.00
76-88: 76-83-Year of the Villain tie-ins. 82-Acetate-c 4.00
750-($7.99, 80 pages) The Flash Age pt. 1; short stories and pin-ups by various incl. Johns, Wolfman, & Manapul; Flash Forward epilogue; multiple covers 10.00
751-767: 758-760-Tornado Twins app.; Jesse Quick & Max Mercury return. 759-762-Reverse Flash app. 763-766-Dr. Alchemy app. 767-Endless Winter pt. 2; Black Adam app. 4.00
Annual 1 (3/18, $4.99) Porter & Duce-a; leads into Flash War in Flash #47 5.00
Annual 2 (3/19, $4.99) Kolins-a; Godspeed & Impulse app. 5.00
Annual 3 (8/20, $4.99) Suicide Squad app.; Segovia, Peterson & Pagulayan-a 5.00
...: Rebirth (8/16) Williamson-s/Di Giandomenico-a; Wally West & Batman app. 3.00
.../ Speed Buggy Special 1 (7/18, $4.99) Lobdell-s/Booth-a; Wally West & Savitar app. 5.00

FLASH, THE (See Tangent Comics/ The Flash)

FLASH AND GREEN LANTERN: THE BRAVE AND THE BOLD
DC Comics: Oct, 1999 - No. 6, Mar, 2000 ($2.50, limited series)

1-6-Waid & Peyer-s/Kitson-a. 4-Green Arrow app.; Grindberg-a(p) 4.00
TPB (2001, $12.95) r/#1-6 13.00

FLASH COMICS
DC Comics: Dec. 1939

1-Ashcan comic, not distributed to newsstands, only for in-house use. Cover art is Adventure Comics #41 and interior from All-American Comics #8. A CGC certified 9.6 sold for $11,500 in 2004. A CGC certified 9.4 sold for $6,572.50 in 2008. A CGC certified 9.6 sold for $8,513 in 2013. A CGC certified 9.4 sold for $20,315 in 2018.

FLASH COMICS (Whiz Comics No. 2 on)
Fawcett Publications: Jan, 1940 (12 pgs., B&W, regular size)
(Not distributed to newsstands; printed for in-house use)

NOTE: ***Whiz Comics** #2 was preceded by two books, **Flash Comics** and **Thrill Comics**, both dated Jan, 1940, (12 pgs, B&W, regular size) and were not distributed. These two books are identical except for the title, and were sent out to major distributors as ad copies to promote sales. It is believed that the complete 68 page issue of Fawcett's **Flash** and **Thrill Comics** #1 was finished and ready for publication with the January date. Since DC Comics was also about to publish a book with the same date and title, Fawcett hurriedly printed up the black and white version of **Flash Comics** to secure copyright before DC. The inside covers are blank, with the covers and inside pages printed on a high quality uncoated paper stock. The eight page origin story of Captain Thunder is composed of pages 1-7 and 13 of the Captain Marvel story essentially as they appeared in the first issue of **Whiz Comics**. The balloon dialogue on page thirteen was relettered to tie the story into the end of page seven in **Flash** and **Thrill Comics** to produce a shorter version of the origin story for copyright purposes. Obviously, DC acquired the copyright and Fawcett dropped **Flash** as well as **Thrill** and came out with **Whiz Comics** a month later. Fawcett never used the cover to **Flash** and **Thrill** #1, designing a new cover for **Whiz Comics**. Fawcett also must have discovered that Captain Thunder had already been used by another publisher (Captain Terry Thunder by Fiction House). All references to Captain Thunder were relettered to Captain Marvel before appearing in **Whiz**.*

1-(nn on-c, #1 on inside)-Origin & 1st app. Captain Thunder. Cover by C.C. Beck. Eight copies of Flash and three copies of Thrill exist. All 3 copies of Thrill sold in 1986 for between $4,000-$10,000 each. A NM copy of Thrill sold in 1987 for $12,000. A VG copy of Thrill sold in 1987 for $9000 cash. A CGC certified 9.0 copy of the Flash Comics version sold for $10,117.50 in 2006. A CGC certified 9.4 copy of the Flash Comics version sold for $14,340 in 2008. A CGC certified 9.0 copy of the Thrill Comics version sold for $20,315 in 2008. A CGC certified 8.0 copy sold for $12,999 in 2012. A CGC certified 4.5 copy sold for $19,750 in 2017. A CGC certified 9.0 copy of Thrill Comics sold for $41,040 in 2017. A CGC certified 9.4 copy of Flash Comics sold for $85,000 in 2019.

FLASH COMICS (The Flash No. 105 on) (Also see All-Flash)
National Periodical Publ./All-American: Jan, 1940 - No. 104, Feb, 1949

1-The Flash (origin/1st app.) by Harry Lampert, Hawkman (origin/1st app.) by Gardner Fox, The Whip, & Johnny Thunder (origin/1st app.) by Stan Asch; Cliff Cornwall by Moldoff, Flash Picture Novelets (later Minute Movies w/#12) begin; Moldoff (Shelly) cover; 1st app. Shiera Sanders who later becomes Hawkgirl, #24; reprinted in Famous First Edition (on sale 11/10/39); The Flash-c 21,400 42,800 64,200 156,000 228,000 300,000

1-Reprint, Oversize 13-1/2x10". **WARNING:** This comic is an exact reprint of the original except for its size. DC published it in 1974 with a second cover titling it as a Famous First Edition. There have been many reported cases of the outer cover being removed and the interior sold as the original edition. The reprint with the new outer cover removed is practically worthless. See Famous First Edition for value.

2-Rod Rian begins, ends #11; Hawkman-c 1625 3250 4875 10,400 18,200 26,000
3-King Standish begins (1st app.), ends #41 (called The King #16-37,39-41); E.E. Hibbard-a begins on Flash 481 962 1443 3511 6206 8900
4-Moldoff (Shelly) Hawkman begins; The Whip-c 343 686 1029 2400 4200 6000
5-The King-c 295 590 885 1888 3244 4600
6-2nd Flash-c (alternates w/Hawkman #6 on) 784 1568 2352 5723 10,112 14,500
7-2nd Hawkman-c; 1st Moldoff Hawkman-c 649 1298 1947 4738 8369 12,000
8-New logo begins; classic Moldoff Flash-c 406 812 1218 2842 4971 7100
9,10: 9-Moldoff Hawkman-c; 10-Classic Moldoff Flash-c 411 822 1233 2877 5039 7200
11-13,15-20: 12-Les Watts begins; "Sparks" #16 on. 13-Has full page ad for All Star Comics #3. 17-Last Cliff Cornwall 258 516 774 1651 2826 4000
14-World War II cover 300 600 900 1950 3375 4800
21-Classic Hawkman-c 265 530 795 1694 2897 4100
22,23 232 464 696 1485 2543 3600
24-Shiera becomes Hawkgirl (12/41); see All-Star Comics #5 for 1st app. 274 548 822 1754 3002 4250
25-28,30: 28-Last Les Sparks. 152 304 456 965 1658 2350
29-Ghost Patrol begins (origin/1st app.), ends #104 174 348 522 1114 1907 2700
31-Classic Hawkman dragon-c 184 368 552 1178 2014 2850
32,34,35,37-40: 145 290 435 921 1586 2250
33-Classic Hawkman WWII-c; origin The Shade 300 600 900 1950 3375 4800
36-1st app. Rag Doll (see Flash #229) 165 330 495 1056 1803 2550
41-50 129 258 387 826 1413 2000
51-61: 52-1st computer in comics, c/s (4/44). 59-Last Minute Movies. 61-Last Moldoff Hawkman 103 206 309 659 1130 1600
62-Hawkman by Kubert begins 132 264 396 845 1448 2050
63-66,68-85: 66,68-Hop Harrigan app. 70-Mutt & Jeff app. 80-Atom begins, ends #104 97 194 291 621 1061 1500
67-Hawkman dinosaur-c; Hop Harrigan app. 132 264 396 845 1448 2050
86-Intro. The Black Canary in Johnny Thunder (8/47); see All-Star #38. 2850 5700 8550 17,000 22,750 28,500
87,88,90: 87-Intro. The Foil. 88-Origin Ghost. 142 284 426 909 1555 2200
89-Intro villain The Thorn (scarce) 277 554 831 1773 3037 4350
91,93-99: 98-Atom & Hawkman don new costumes 148 296 444 947 1624 2300
92-1st solo Black Canary plus-c; rare in Mint due to black ink smearing on white-c 649 1298 1947 4738 8369 12,000
100 (10/48),103(Scarce)-52 pgs. each 300 600 900 2010 3505 5000
101,102(Scarce) 295 590 885 1888 3244 4600
104-Origin The Flash retold (Scarce) 892 1784 2676 6512 11,506 16,500

NOTE: ***Irwin Hasen** a-Wheaties Giveaway. c-97, Wheaties Giveaway. **E.E. Hibbard** c-6, 12, 20, 24, 26, 28, 30, 44, 46, 48, 50, 52, 54, 56, 58, 60, 66, 68, 69, 72, 74, 76, 78, 80, 82. **Infantino** a-86p, 90, 93-95, 99-104; c-90, 92, 93, 97, 99, 101, 103. **Kinstler** a-87, 89(Hawkman); c-87. **Chet Kozlak** c-77, 79, 81. **Krigstein** a-94. **Kubert** a-62-76, 83, 85, 86, 88-104; c-63, 65, 67, 70, 71, 73, 75, 83, 85, 86, 88, 89, 91, 94, 96, 98, 100, 104. **Moldoff** a-3; c-3, 7-11, 13-17, plus odd #'s 19-61. **Martin Naydell** c-52, 54, 56, 58, 60, 64, 84.*

FLASH DIGEST, THE (See DC Special Series #24)

FLASH FORCE 2000
DC Comics: 1984

Flash Gordon (2014 series) #4 © KING

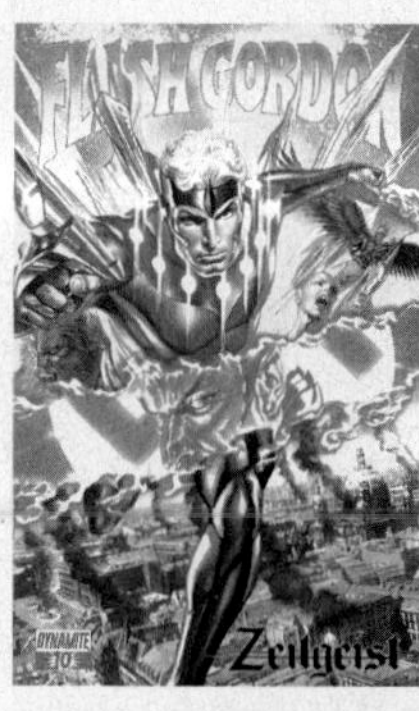

Flash Gordon: Zeitgeist #10 © KING

Flashpoint #1 © DC

	GD 2.0	VG 4.0	FN 6.0	VF 8.0	VF/NM 9.0	NM- 9.2

1-5 6.00

FLASH FORWARD (See Heroes in Crisis series)
DC Comics: Nov, 2019 - No. 6, Apr, 2020 ($3.99, limited series)

1-6-Follows Wally West after Heroes in Crisis; Lobdell-s/Booth-a. 2-Jai & Iris app. 4.00

FLASH GIANT (Barry Allen)
DC Comics: 2019 - No. 7, 2019 ($4.99, 100 pgs., squarebound, Walmart exclusive)

1-New story Simone-s/Henry-a; reprints from Flash #8 ('11), Adam Strange #1 ('04), and Shazam from Justice League #7 & 8('11) 8.00
2-7: 2-New story plus Flash, Adam Strange and Shazam reprints continue 5.00

FLASH GIANT
DC Comics: 2019 - No. 4, 2020 ($4.99, 100 pgs., squarebound, Mass Market & Direct Market editions exist for each issue, with different covers)

1-4: 1-New stories vs. King Shark and Grodd; reprints. 3-The Atom app. 5.00

FLASH GORDON (See Defenders Of The Earth, Eat Right to Work..., Giant Comic Album, King Classics, King Comics, March of Comics #118, 133, 142, The Phantom #18, Street Comix & Wow Comics, 1st series)

FLASH GORDON
Dell Publishing Co.: No. 25, 1941; No. 10, 1943 - No. 512, Nov, 1953

Issue	GD	VG	FN	VF	VF/NM	NM-
Feature Books 25 (#1)(1941))-r-not by Raymond	174	348	522	1114	1907	2700
Four Color 10(1942)-by Alex Raymond; reprints "The Ice Kingdom"	89	178	267	712	1606	2500
Four Color 84(1945)-by Alex Raymond; reprints "The Fiery Desert"	42	84	126	311	698	1085
Four Color 173	23	46	69	168	382	560
Four Color 190-Bondage-c; "The Adventures of the Flying Saucers"; 5th Flying Saucer story (6/48)- see The Spirit 9/28/47(1st), Shadow Comics V7#10 (2nd, 1/48), Captain Midnight #60 (3rd, 2/48) & Boy Commandos #26 (4th, 3-4/48)	28	56	84	202	451	700
Four Color 204,247	17	34	51	117	259	400
Four Color 424-Painted-c	12	24	36	81	176	270
2(5-7/53-Dell)-Painted-c; Evans-a?	9	18	27	63	129	195
Four Color 512-Painted-c	9	18	27	62	126	190

FLASH GORDON (See Tiny Tot Funnies)
Harvey Publications: Oct, 1950 - No. 4, April, 1951

Issue	GD	VG	FN	VF	VF/NM	NM-
1-Alex Raymond-a; bondage-c; reprints strips from 7/14/40 to 12/8/40	50	100	150	315	533	750
2-Alex Raymond-a; r/strips 12/15/40-4/27/41	31	62	93	186	303	420
3,4-Alex Raymond-a; 3-bondage-c; r/strips 5/4/41-9/21/41. 4-r/strips 10/24/37-3/27/38	30	60	90	177	289	400
5-(Rare)-Small size-5-1/2x8-1/2"; B&W; 32 pgs.; Distributed to some mail subscribers only	94	188	282	597	1025	1450

(Also see All-New No. 15, Boy Explorers No. 2, and Stuntman No. 3)

FLASH GORDON
Gold Key: June, 1965

Issue	GD	VG	FN	VF	VF/NM	NM-
1 (1947 reprint)-Painted-c	8	16	24	52	99	145

FLASH GORDON (Also see Comics Reading Libraries in the Promotional Comics section)
King #1-11/Charlton #12-18/Gold Key #19-23/Whitman #28 on:
9/66 - #11, 12/67; #12, 2/69 - #18, 1/70; #19, 9/78 - #37, 3/82 (Painted covers No. 19-30, 34)

Issue	GD	VG	FN	VF	VF/NM	NM-
1-1st S.A. app Flash Gordon; Williamson c/a(2); E.C. swipe/Incredible S.F. #32; Mandrake story	8	16	24	51	96	140
1-Army giveaway(1968)("Complimentary" on cover)(Same as regular #1 minus Mandrake story & back-c)	4	8	12	28	47	65
2-8: 2-Bolle, Gil Kane-c; Mandrake story. 3-Williamson-c. 4-Secret Agent X-9 begins, Williamson-c/a(3). 5-Williamson-c/a(2). 6,8-Crandall-a. 7-Raboy-a (last in comics?). 8-Secret Agent X-9-r	4	8	12	28	47	65
9-13: 9,10-Raymond-r. 10-Buckler's 1st pro work (11/67). 11-Crandall-a. 12-Crandall-c/a. 13-Jeff Jones-a (15 pgs.)	4	8	12	27	44	60
14,15: 15-Last 12¢ issue	3	6	9	19	30	40
16,17: 17-Brick Bradford story	3	6	9	16	24	32
18-Kaluta-a (3rd pro work?)(see Teen Confessions)	3	6	9	21	33	45
19(9/78, G.K.), 20-26	2	4	6	8	10	12
27-29,34-37: 34-37-Movie adaptation	2	4	6	8	11	14
30 (10/80) (scarce, from Whitman 3-pack only, 40¢-c)	4	8	12	27	44	60
30 (7/81; re-issue, 50¢-c), 31-33-single issues	2	4	6	11	16	20
31-33 (Bagged 3-pack): Movie adaptation; Williamson-a.						60.00

NOTE: ***Aparo** a-8. **Bolle** a-21, 22. **Boyette** a-14-18. **Briggs** c-10. **Buckler** a-10. **Crandall** c-6. **Estrada** a-3. **Gene Fawcette** a-29, 30, 34, 37. **McWilliams** a-31-33, 36.*

FLASH GORDON
DC Comics: June, 1988 - No. 9, Holiday, 1988-'89 ($1.25, mini-series)

1-9: 1,5-Painted-c 4.00

	GD 2.0	VG 4.0	FN 6.0	VF 8.0	VF/NM 9.0	NM- 9.2

FLASH GORDON
Marvel Comics: June, 1995 - No. 2, July, 1995 ($2.95, limited series)

1,2: Schultz scripts; Williamson-a 4.00

FLASH GORDON (The Mercy Wars)
Ardden Entertainment: Aug, 2008 - No. 6, Jul, 2009 ($3.99)

1-6: 1-Deneen-s/Green-a; two covers 4.00
...: The Mercy Wars #0 (4/09, $2.99) 3.00

FLASH GORDON
Dynamite Entertainment: 2014 ($3.99)

1-8: 1-Parker-s/Shaner-a; six covers. 2-8-Multiple covers on each 4.00
Annual 2014 ($7.99, squarebound) Short stories of the characters' pasts 8.00
Holiday Special 2014 ($5.99) Christmas-themed short stories by various 6.00

FLASH GORDON: INVASION OF THE RED SWORD
Ardden Entertainment: Jan, 2011 - No. 6, Nov, 2011 ($3.99)

1-6-Deneen-s/Garcia-a. 1-Two covers 4.00

FLASH GORDON: KINGS CROSS
Dynamite Entertainment: 2016 - No. 5, 2017 ($3.99)

1-5-Jeff Parker-s/Jesse Hamm-a; multiple covers on each; Mandrake & Phantom app. 4.00

FLASH GORDON THE MOVIE
Western Publishing Co.: 1980 (8-1/4 x 11", $1.95, 68 pgs.)

Issue	GD	VG	FN	VF	VF/NM	NM-
11294-Williamson-c/a; adapts movie	2	4	6	10	14	18
13743-Hardback edition	3	6	9	15	21	26

FLASH GORDON: ZEITGEIST
Dynamite Entertainment: 2011 - No. 10, 2013 ($1.00/$3.99)

1-($1.00) Flash, Dale and Zarkov head to Mongo; 4 covers by Ross, Renaud & others 4.00
2-10-($3.99) 2-8-Three covers. 9,10-Ross-c 4.00

FLASH/ GREEN LANTERN: FASTER FRIENDS (See Green Lantern/Flash...)
DC Comics: No. 2, 1997 ($4.95, continuation of Green Lantern/Flash: Faster Friends #1)

2-Waid/Augustyn-s 5.00

FLASHPOINT (Elseworlds Flash)
DC Comics: Dec, 1999 - No. 3, Feb, 2000 ($2.95, limited series)

1-3-Paralyzed Barry Allen; Breyfogle-a/McGreal-s 3.00

FLASHPOINT (Leads into DC New 52 relaunches)
DC Comics: Jul, 2011 - No. 5, Late Oct, 2011 ($3.99, limited series)

Issue	GD	VG	FN	VF	VF/NM	NM-
1-Johns-s/Andy Kubert-a; 2 covers on each	2	4	6	11	16	20

2-5-Johns-s/Andy Kubert-a. 2-4-Bonus design art. 5-New timeline 6.00
...: Abin Sur - The Green Lantern 1-3 (8/11 - No. 3, 10/11, $2.99) Massaferra-a/c 3.00
...: Batman Knight of Vengeance 1-3 (8/11 - No. 3, 10/11, $2.99) Risso-a/Johnson-c 5.00
...: Canterbury Cricket, The (8/11, $2.99, one-shot) Carlin-s/Morales-a 3.00
...: Citizen Cold 1-3 (8/11 - No. 3, 10/11, $2.99) Scott Kolins-s/a/c 3.00
...: Deadman and the Flying Grayson 1-3 (8/11 - No. 3, 10/11, $2.99) Chiang-c 3.00
...: Deathstroke & The Curse of the Ravager 1-3 (8/11 - No. 3, 10/11, $2.99) Bennett-a 3.00
...: Emperor Aquaman 1-3 (8/11 - No. 3, 10/11, $2.99) Bedard-s/Syaf-c 3.00
...: Frankenstein and the Creatures of the Unknown 1-3 (8/11 - No. 3, 10/11, $2.99) 3.00
...: Green Arrow Industries (8/11, $2.99, one-shot) Kalvachev-c 3.00
...: Grodd of War (8/11, $2.99, one-shot) Manapul-c 3.00
...: Hal Jordan 1-3 (8/11 - No. 3, 10/11, $2.99) 1-Oliver-a. 2,3-Richards-a 3.00
...: Kid Flash Lost 1-3 (8/11 - No. 3, 10/11, $2.99) Gates-s/Manapul-c; Brainiac app. 3.00
...: Legion of Doom 1-3 (8/11 - No. 3, 10/11, $2.99) Glass-s/Sepulveda-c 3.00
...: Lois Lane and the Resistance 1-3 (8/11 - No. 3, 10/11, $2.99) Abnett & Lanning-s 3.00
...: Outsider, The 1-3 (8/11 - No. 3, 10/11, $2.99) Robinson-s/Nowlan-c 3.00
...: Project Superman 1-3 (8/11 - No. 3, 10/11, $2.99) Gene Ha-c/a 3.00
...: Reverse Flash (8/11, $2.99, one-shot) Kolins-s/Gomez-a 5.00
...: Secret Seven 1-3 (8/11 - No. 3, 10/11, $2.99) Pérez-c on all. 1-Pérez-a. 3.00
...: Wonder Woman and The Furies 1-3 (8/11 - No. 3, 10/11, $2.99) Aquaman app. 4.00
...: World of Flashpoint 1-3 (8/11 - No. 3, 10/11, $2.99) Traci 13 app. 3.00

FLASH: REBIRTH
DC Comics: Jun, 2009 - No. 6, Apr, 2010 ($3.99/$2.99, limited series)

1-($3.99) Barry Allen's return; Johns-s/Van Sciver-a; Flash-c by Van Sciver 5.00
1-Variant Barry Allen-c by Van Sciver 10.00
1-Second thru fourth printings 4.00
1-Special Edition (8/10, $1.00) reprints #1 with "What's Next?" logo on cover 3.00
2-6-($2.99) 3-Max Mercury returns 3.00
2-6-Variant covers by Van Sciver 8.00
HC (2010, $19.99, dustjacket) r/#1-6; Johns original proposal; sketch art; cover gallery 20.00
SC (2011, $14.99) r/#1-6; Johns original proposal; sketch art; cover gallery 15.00

FLASH: SEASON ZERO (Based on the 2014 TV series)
DC Comics: Dec, 2014 - No. 12, Nov, 2015 ($2.99, printings of digital-first stories)

Flash: The Fastest Man Alive #13 © DC

The Flintstones (1995 series) #7 © H-B

Flippity & Flop #7 © DC

	GD 2.0	VG 4.0	FN 6.0	VF 8.0	VF/NM 9.0	NM- 9.2
1-12-Photo-c on #1-8. 1-4,6-9-Hester-a. 5-Felicity Smoak app. 7-9-Intro. Suicide Squad						3.00

FLASH: THE FASTEST MAN ALIVE (3rd Series)(See Infinite Crisis)
DC Comics: Aug, 2006 - No. 13, Aug, 2007 ($2.99)

	GD 2.0	VG 4.0	FN 6.0	VF 8.0	VF/NM 9.0	NM- 9.2
1-Bart Allen becomes the Flash; Lashley-a/Bilson & Demeo-s						3.00
1-Variant-c by Joe and Andy Kubert						5.00
2-12: 5-Cyborg app. 7-Inertia returns. 10-Zoom app.						3.00
13-Bart Allen dies; 2 covers						3.00
13-DC Nation Edition from the 2007 San Diego Comic-Con						8.00
...: Full Throttle TPB (2007, $12.99) r/#7-13, All-Flash #1, DCU Infinite Holiday Spec. story						13.00
...: Lightning in a Bottle TPB (2007, $12.99) r/#1-6						13.00

FLAT-TOP
Mazie Comics/Harvey Publ.(Magazine Publ.) No. 4 on: 11/53 - No. 3, 5/54; No. 4, 3/55 - No. 7, 9/55

	GD 2.0	VG 4.0	FN 6.0	VF 8.0	VF/NM 9.0	NM- 9.2
1-Teenage; Flat-Top, Mazie, Mortie & Stevie begin	13	26	39	72	101	130
2,3	8	16	24	44	57	70
4-7	7	14	21	35	43	50

FLAVOR
Image Comics: May, 2018 - No. 6, Oct, 2018 ($3.99)

	GD 2.0	VG 4.0	FN 6.0	VF 8.0	VF/NM 9.0	NM- 9.2
1-6-Joseph Keatinge-s/Wook Jin Clark-a						4.00

FLESH AND BONES
Upshot Graphics (Fantagraphics Books): June, 1986 - No. 4, Dec, 1986 (Limited series)

	GD 2.0	VG 4.0	FN 6.0	VF 8.0	VF/NM 9.0	NM- 9.2
1-4: Alan Moore scripts (r) & Dalgoda by Fujitake						4.00

FLESH CRAWLERS
Kitchen Sink Press: Aug, 1993 - No. 3, 1995 ($2.50, B&W, limited series, mature)

	GD 2.0	VG 4.0	FN 6.0	VF 8.0	VF/NM 9.0	NM- 9.2
1-3						4.00

FLEX MENTALLO (Man of Muscle Mystery) (See Doom Patrol, 2nd Series)
DC Comics (Vertigo): Jun, 1996 - No. 4, Sept, 1996 ($2.50, lim. series, mature)

	GD 2.0	VG 4.0	FN 6.0	VF 8.0	VF/NM 9.0	NM- 9.2
1-4: Grant Morrison scripts & Frank Quitely-c/a in all; banned from reprints due to Charles Atlas legal action	2	4	6	9	13	16

FLINCH (Horror anthology)
DC Comics (Vertigo): Jun, 1999 - No. 16, Jan, 2001 ($2.50)

	GD 2.0	VG 4.0	FN 6.0	VF 8.0	VF/NM 9.0	NM- 9.2
1-16: 1-Art by Jim Lee, Quitely, and Corben. 5-Sale-c. 11-Timm-a						3.00

FLINTSTONE KIDS, THE (TV) (See Star Comics Digest)
Star Comics/Marvel Comics #5 on: Aug, 1987 - No. 11, Apr, 1989

	GD 2.0	VG 4.0	FN 6.0	VF 8.0	VF/NM 9.0	NM- 9.2
1	1	2	3	5	6	8
2-11						5.00

FLINTSTONES, THE (TV)(See Dell Giant #48 for No. 1)
Dell Publ. Co./Gold Key No. 7 (10/62) on: No. 2, Nov-Dec, 1961 - No. 60, Sept, 1970 (Hanna-Barbera)

	GD 2.0	VG 4.0	FN 6.0	VF 8.0	VF/NM 9.0	NM- 9.2
2-2nd app. (TV show debuted on 9/30/60); 1st app. of Cave Kids; 15¢-c thru #5	11	22	33	76	163	250
3-6(7-8/62): 3-Perry Gunnite begins. 6-1st 12¢-c	6	12	18	42	79	115
7 (10/62; 1st GK)	7	14	21	48	89	130
8-10	5	10	15	34	60	85
11-1st app. Pebbles (6/63)	8	16	24	54	102	150
12-15,17-20	4	8	12	28	47	65
16-1st app. Bamm-Bamm (1/64)	8	16	24	56	108	160
21-23,25-30,33: 26,27-2nd & 3rd app. The Grusomes. 30-1st app. Martian Mopheads (10/65). 33-Meet Frankenstein & Dracula	4	8	12	27	44	60
24-1st app. The Grusomes	6	12	18	38	69	100
31,32,35-40: 31-Xmas-c. 36-Adaptation of "the Man Called Flintstone" movie. 39-Reprints	4	8	12	23	37	50
34-1st app. The Great Gazoo	6	12	18	38	69	100
41-60: 46-Last 12¢ issue	3	6	9	20	31	42
At N. Y. World's Fair ('64)-J.W. Books (25¢)-1st printing; no date on-c (29¢ version exists, 2nd print?) Most H-B characters app.; including Yogi Bear, Top Cat, Snagglepuss and the Jetsons	5	10	15	35	63	90
At N. Y. World's Fair (1965 on-c; re-issue; Warren Pub.) NOTE: *Warehouse find in 1984.*	2	4	6	11	16	20
Bigger & Boulder 1(#30013-211) (Gold Key Giant, 11/62, 25¢, 84 pgs.)	7	14	21	49	92	135
Bigger & Boulder 2-(1966, 25¢)-Reprints B&B No. 1	4	8	12	25	40	55
...On the Rocks (9/61, $1.00, 6-1/4x9", cardboard-c, high quality paper,116 pgs.) B&W new material	8	16	24	56	108	160
...With Pebbles & Bamm Bamm (100 pgs., G.K.)-30028-511 (paper-c, 25¢) (11/65)	6	12	18	42	79	115

NOTE: *(See Comic Album #16, Bamm-Bamm & Pebbles Flintstone, Dell Giant 48, Golden Comics Digest, March of Comics #229, 243, 271, 289, 299, 317, 327, 341, Pebbles Flintstone, Top Comics #2-4, and Whitman Comic Book.)*

FLINTSTONES, THE (TV)(...& Pebbles)
Charlton Comics: Nov, 1970 - No. 50, Feb, 1977 (Hanna-Barbera)

	GD 2.0	VG 4.0	FN 6.0	VF 8.0	VF/NM 9.0	NM- 9.2
1	7	14	21	44	82	120
2	4	8	12	27	44	60
3-7,9,10	3	6	9	19	30	40
8- "Flintstones Summer Vacation" (Summer, 1971, 52 pgs.)	5	10	15	31	53	75
11-20,36: 36-Mike Zeck illos (early work)	3	6	9	16	23	30
21-35,38-41,43-45	3	6	9	14	19	24
37-Byrne text illos (early work; see Nightmare #20)	3	6	9	16	23	30
42-Byrne-a (2 pgs.)	3	6	9	16	23	30
46-50	2	4	6	13	18	22
Digest nn (1972, B&W, 100 pgs.) (low print run)	3	6	9	19	30	40

(Also see Barney & Betty Rubble, Dino, The Great Gazoo, & Pebbles & Bamm-Bamm)

FLINTSTONES, THE (TV)(See Yogi Bear, 3rd series) (Newsstand sales only)
Marvel Comics Group: October, 1977 - No. 9, Feb, 1979 (Hanna-Barbera)

	GD 2.0	VG 4.0	FN 6.0	VF 8.0	VF/NM 9.0	NM- 9.2
1,7-9: 1-(30¢-c). 7-9-Yogi Bear app.	3	6	9	19	30	40
1-(35¢-c variant, limited distribution)	9	18	27	59	117	175
2,3,5,6: Yogi Bear app.	3	6	9	15	22	28
4-The Jetsons app.	3	6	9	16	24	32

FLINTSTONES, THE (TV)
Harvey Comics: Sept, 1992 - No. 13, Jun, 1994 ($1.25/$1.50) (Hanna-Barbera)

	GD 2.0	VG 4.0	FN 6.0	VF 8.0	VF/NM 9.0	NM- 9.2
V2#1-13						4.00
...Big Book 1,2 (11/92, 3/93; both $1.95, 52 pgs.)						5.00
...Giant Size 1-3 (10/92, 4/93, 11/93; $2.25, 68 pgs.)						5.00

FLINTSTONES, THE (TV)
Archie Publications: Sept, 1995 - No. 22, June, 1997 ($1.50)

	GD 2.0	VG 4.0	FN 6.0	VF 8.0	VF/NM 9.0	NM- 9.2
1-22						3.00

FLINTSTONES, THE (TV)
DC Comics: Sept, 2016 - No. 12, Aug, 2017 ($3.99)

	GD 2.0	VG 4.0	FN 6.0	VF 8.0	VF/NM 9.0	NM- 9.2
1-12: 1-6,8-12-Mark Russell-s/Steve Pugh-a; multiple covers. 2-Intro. Dino. 7-Leonardi-a; Great Gazoo app. 11-Jill Thompson-c. 11,12-Great Gazoo app.						4.00

FLINTSTONES AND THE JETSONS, THE (TV)
DC Comics: Aug, 1997 - No. 21, May, 1999 ($1.75/$1.95/$1.99)

	GD 2.0	VG 4.0	FN 6.0	VF 8.0	VF/NM 9.0	NM- 9.2
1						6.00
2-21: 19-Bizarro Elroy-c						3.00

FLINTSTONES CHRISTMAS PARTY, THE (See The Funtastic World of Hanna-Barbera No. 1)

FLIP
Harvey Publications: April, 1954 - No. 2, June, 1954 (Satire)

	GD 2.0	VG 4.0	FN 6.0	VF 8.0	VF/NM 9.0	NM- 9.2
1-Nostrand-a	23	46	69	161	356	550
2-Nostrand & Powell-a	15	30	45	105	233	360

FLIPPER (TV)
Gold Key: Apr, 1966 - No. 3, Nov, 1967 (All have photo-c)

	GD 2.0	VG 4.0	FN 6.0	VF 8.0	VF/NM 9.0	NM- 9.2
1	6	12	18	38	69	100
2,3	4	8	12	28	47	65

FLIPPITY & FLOP
National Per. Publ. (Signal Publ. Co.): 12-1/51-52 - No. 46, 8-10/59; No. 47, 9-11/60

	GD 2.0	VG 4.0	FN 6.0	VF 8.0	VF/NM 9.0	NM- 9.2
1-Sam dog & his pets Flippity The Bird and Flop The Cat begin; Twiddle and Twaddle begin	39	78	117	240	395	550
2	18	36	54	107	169	230
3-5	15	30	45	83	124	165
6-10	14	28	42	76	108	140
11-20: 20-Last precode (3/55)	11	22	33	60	83	105
21-47	10	20	30	54	72	90

FLOYD FARLAND (See Eclipse Graphic Album Series #11)

FLY, THE (Also see Adventures of..., Blue Ribbon Comics & Flyman)
Archie Enterprises, Inc.: May, 1983 - No. 9, Oct, 1984

	GD 2.0	VG 4.0	FN 6.0	VF 8.0	VF/NM 9.0	NM- 9.2
1,2: 1-Mr. Justice app; origin Shield; Kirby-a; Steranko-c. 2-Ditko-a; Flygirl app.						6.00
3-5: Ditko-a in all. 4,5-Ditko-c(p)						5.00
6-9: Ditko-a in all. 6-8-Ditko-c(p)						6.00

NOTE: *Ayers c-9. Buckler a-1, 2. Kirby a-1. Nebres c-3, 4, 5i, 6, 7i. Steranko c-1, 2.*

FLY, THE
Impact Comics (DC): Aug, 1991 - No. 17, Dec, 1992 ($1.00)

	GD 2.0	VG 4.0	FN 6.0	VF 8.0	VF/NM 9.0	NM- 9.2
1						5.00
2-17: 4-Vs. The Black Hood. 9-Trading card inside						4.00
Annual 1 ('92, $2.50, 68 pgs.)-Impact trading card						5.00

FLYBOY (Flying Cadets)(Also see Approved Comics #5)
Ziff-Davis Publ. Co. (Approved): Spring, 1952 - No. 2, Oct-Nov, 1952

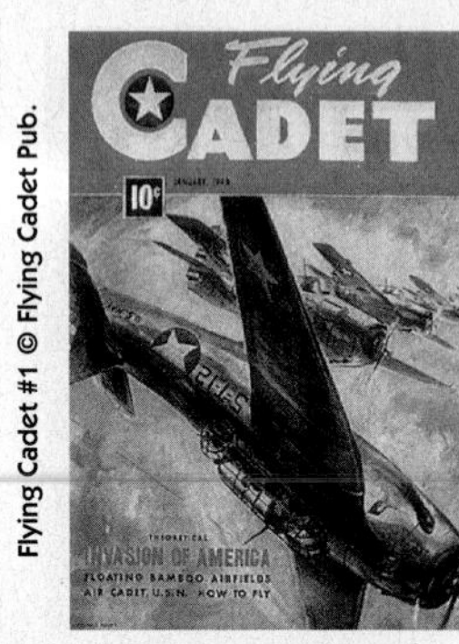

Flying Cadet #1 © Flying Cadet Pub.

Foodini #2 © HOKE

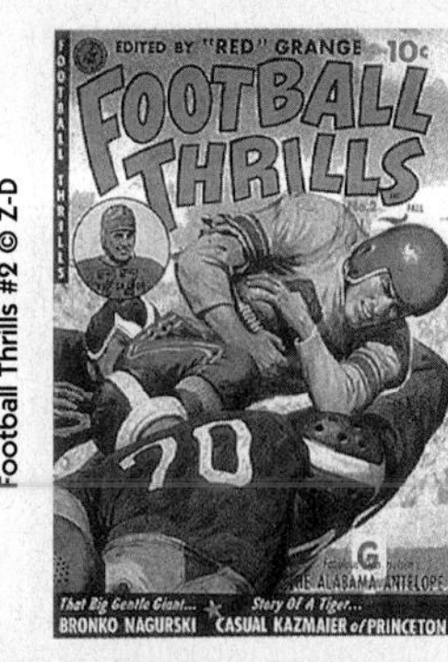

Football Thrills #2 © Z-D

	GD 2.0	VG 4.0	FN 6.0	VF 8.0	VF/NM 9.0	NM- 9.2
1-Saunders painted-c	22	44	66	130	213	295
2-(10-11/52)-Saunders painted-c	15	30	45	86	133	180
FLYING ACES (Aviation stories)						
Key Publications: July, 1955 - No. 5, Mar, 1956						
1	12	24	36	67	94	120
2-5: 2-Trapani-a	8	16	24	42	54	65
FLYING A'S RANGE RIDER, THE (TV)(See Western Roundup under Dell Giants)						
Dell Publishing Co.: #404, 6-7/52; #2, June-Aug, 1953 - #24, Aug, 1959 (All photo-c)						
Four Color 404(#1)-Titled "The Range Rider"	9	18	27	62	126	190
2	6	12	18	37	66	95
3-10	5	10	15	33	57	80
11-16,18-24	4	8	12	28	47	65
17-Toth-a	5	10	15	33	57	80
FLYING CADET (WW II Plane Photos)						
Flying Cadet Publ. Co.; Jan, 1943 - V2#8, Nov, 1944 (Half photos, half comics)						
V1#1-Painted-c	21	42	63	124	202	280
2-Photo-c, P-47 Thunderbolt	13	26	39	72	101	130
3-9 (Two #6's, Sept. & Oct.): 4,5,6a,6b-Photo-c	12	24	36	67	94	120
V2#1-7 (1/44-9/44)(#10-16): 1,2,4-7-Photo-c	11	22	33	62	86	110
7 (#17 on cover)-Bare-breasted woman-c	52	104	156	328	552	775
FLYING COLORS 10th ANNIVERSARY SPECIAL						
Flying Colors Comics: Fall 1998 ($2.95, one-shot)						
1-Dan Brereton-c; pin-ups by Jim Lee and Jeff Johnson						3.00
FLYIN' JENNY						
Pentagon Publ. Co./Leader Enterprises #2: 1946 - No. 2, 1947 (1945 strip-r)						
nn-Marcus Swayze strip-r (entire insides)	24	48	72	142	234	325
2-Baker-c; Swayze strip reprints	53	106	159	334	587	800
FLYING MODELS						
H-K Publ. (Health-Knowledge Publs.): V61#3, May, 1954 (5¢, 16 pgs.)						
V61#3 (Rare)	14	28	42	80	115	150
FLYING NUN (TV)						
Dell Publishing Co.: Feb, 1968 - No. 4, Nov, 1968						
1-Sally Field photo-c	8	16	24	51	96	140
2-4: 2-Sally Field photo-c	4	8	12	28	47	65
FLYING NURSES (See Sue & Sally Smith...)						
FLYING SAUCERS (See The Spirit 9/28/47(1st app.), Shadow Comics V7#10 (2nd, 1/48), Captain Midnight #60 (3rd, 2/48), Boy Commandos #26 (4th, 3-4/48) & Flash Gordon Four Color 190 (5th, 6/48))						
FLYING SAUCERS (See Out of This World Adventures #2)						
Avon Periodicals/Realistic: 1950; 1952; 1953						
1(1950)-Wood-a, 21 pgs.; Fawcette-c	129	258	387	826	1413	2000
nn(1952)-Cover altered plus 2 pgs. of Wood-a not in original	65	130	195	416	708	1000
nn(1953)-Reprints above (exist?)	61	122	183	390	670	950
FLYING SAUCERS (Comics)						
Dell Publishing Co.: April, 1967 - No. 4, Nov, 1967; No. 5, Oct, 1969						
1-(12¢-c)	10	20	30	64	132	200
2-5: 5-Has same cover as #1, but with 15¢ price	4	8	12	28	47	65
FLY MAN (Formerly Adventures of The Fly; Mighty Comics #40 on)						
Mighty Comics Group (Radio Comics) (Archie): No. 32, July, 1965 - No. 39, Sept, 1966 (Also see Mighty Crusaders)						
32,33-Comet, Shield, Black Hood, The Fly & Flygirl x-over. 33-Re-intro Wizard, Hangman (1st S.A. appearances)	5	10	15	34	60	85
34-39: 34-Shield begins. 35-Origin Black Hood. 36-Hangman x-over in Shield; re-intro. & origin of Web (1st S.A. app.). 37-Hangman, Wizard x-over in Flyman; last Shield issue. 38-Web story. 39-Steel Sterling (1st S.A. app.)	4	8	12	27	44	60
FLY, THE ; OUTBREAK (Sequel to the 1986 and 1989 movies)						
IDW Publishing: Mar, 2015 - No. 5, Aug, 2015 ($3.99)						
1-5-Martin Brundle's story continues; Brandon Seifert-s/Menton3-a; multiple covers						4.00
FOLKLORDS						
BOOM! Studios: Nov, 2019 - No. 5 ($3.99, limited series)						
1-5-Matt Kindt-s/Matt Smith-a						4.00
FOLLOW THE SUN (TV)						
Dell Publishing Co.: May-July, 1962 - No. 2, Sept-Nov, 1962 (Photo-c)						
01-280-207(No.1)	5	10	15	30	50	70
12-280-211(No.2)	4	8	12	27	44	60
FOODINI (TV)(The Great...; see Jingle Dingle & Pinhead &...)						
Continental Publ. (Holyoke): March, 1950 - No. 4, Aug, 1950 (All have 52 pgs.)						
1-Based on TV puppet show (very early TV comic)	24	48	72	144	237	330
2-Jingle Dingle begins	15	30	45	84	127	170
3,4	12	24	36	67	94	120
FOOEY (Magazine) (Satire)						
Scoff Publishing Co.: Feb, 1961 - No. 4, May, 1961						
1	5	10	15	33	57	80
2-4	3	6	9	21	33	45
FOOFUR (TV)						
Marvel Comics (Star Comics)/Marvel No. 5 on: Aug, 1987 - No. 6, Jun, 1988						
1-6						5.00
FOOLKILLER (Also see The Amazing Spider-Man #225, The Defenders #73, Man-Thing #3 & Omega the Unknown #8)						
Marvel Comics: Oct, 1990 - No. 10, Oct, 1991 ($1.75, limited series)						
1-10: 1-Origin 3rd Foolkiller; Greg Salinger app; DeZuniga-a(i) in 1-4. 8-Spider-Man x-over						3.00
FOOLKILLER						
Marvel Comics: Dec, 2007 - No. 5, Jul, 2008 ($3.99, limited series)						
1-5-Hurwitz-s/Medina-a. 2-Origin						4.00
FOOLKILLER						
Marvel Comics: Jan, 2017 - No. 5, May, 2017 ($3.99, limited series)						
1-5-Max Bemis-s/Dalibor Talajic-a. 4-Deadpool app. 5-The Hood app.						4.00
FOOLKILLER: WHITE ANGELS						
Marvel Comics: Sept, 2008 - No. 5, Jan, 2009 ($3.99, limited series)						
1-5-Hurwitz-s/Azaceta-a						4.00
FOOM (Friends Of Ol' Marvel)						
Marvel Comics: 1973 - No. 22, 1979 (Marvel fan magazine)						
1	9	18	27	63	129	195
2-Hulk-c by Steranko; Wolverine prototype	11	22	33	76	163	250
3,4	6	12	18	37	66	95
5-9,11: 5-Deathlok preview. 11-Kirby-a & interview	5	10	15	34	60	85
10-Article on new X-Men that came out before Giant-Size X-Men #1; new X-Men cover by Dave Cockrum	28	56	84	202	451	700
12-15: 11-Star-Lord preview. 12-Vision-c. 13-Daredevil-c. 14-Conan. 15-Howard the Duck; preview of Ms. Marvel & Capt. Britain	5	10	15	34	60	85
16-20: 16-Marvel bullpen. 17-Stan Lee issue. 19-Defenders	5	10	15	31	53	75
21-Star Wars	6	12	18	37	66	95
22-Spider-Man-c; low print run final issue	6	12	18	41	76	110
FOOTBALL THRILLS (See Tops In Adventure)						
Ziff-Davis Publ. Co.: Fall-Winter, 1951-52 - No. 2, Fall, 1952 (Edited by "Red" Grange)						
1-Powell a(2); Saunders painted-c; Red Grange, Jim Thorpe stories	31	62	93	182	296	410
2-Saunders painted-c	20	40	60	115	185	255
FOOT SOLDIERS, THE						
Dark Horse Comics: Jan, 1996 - No. 4, Apr, 1996 ($2.95, limited series)						
1-4: Krueger story & Avon Oeming-a. in all. 1-Alex Ross-c. 4-John K. Snyder, III-c						4.00
FOOT SOLDIERS, THE (Volume Two)						
Image Comics: Sept, 1997 - No. 5, May, 1998 ($2.95, limited series)						
1-5: 1-Yeowell-a. 2-McDaniel, Hester, Sienkiewicz, Giffen-a						3.00
FOR A NIGHT OF LOVE						
Avon Periodicals: 1951						
nn-Two stories adapted from the works of Emile Zola; Astarita, Ravielli-a; Kinstler-c	39	78	117	240	395	550
FORBIDDEN BRIDES OF THE FACELESS SLAVES IN THE SECRET HOUSE OF THE NIGHT OF DREAD DESIRE (Neil Gaiman's...)						
Dark Horse Books: 2017 ($17.99, HC graphic novel)						
HC-Neil Gaiman-s/Shane Oakley-a						18.00
FORBIDDEN KNOWLEDGE: ADVENTURE BEYOND THE DOORWAY TO SOULS WITH RADICAL DREAMER (Also see Radical Dreamer)						
Mark's Giant Economy Size Comics: 1996 ($3.50, B&W, one-shot, 48 pgs.)						
nn-Max Wrighter app.; Wheatley-c/a/script; painted infinity-c						4.00
FORBIDDEN LOVE						
Quality Comics Group: Mar, 1950 - No. 4, Sept, 1950 (52 pgs.)						
1-(Scarce)-Classic photo-c; Crandall-a	142	284	426	909	1555	2200

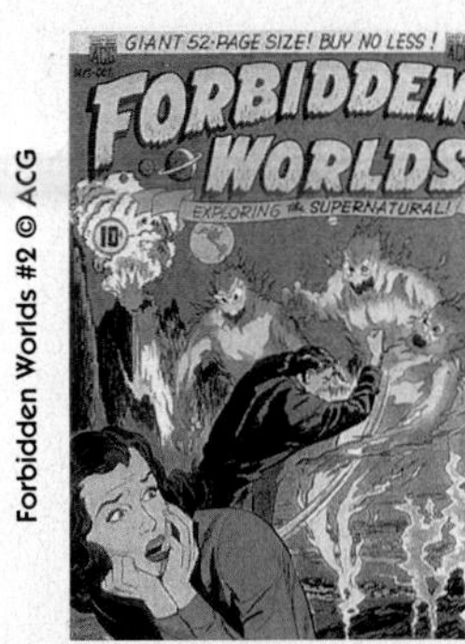

Forbidden Worlds #2 © ACG

Force Works #11 © MAR

Forever Evil #4 © DC

	GD 2.0	VG 4.0	FN 6.0	VF 8.0	VF/NM 9.0	NM- 9.2
2-(Scarce)-Classic photo-c	97	194	291	621	1061	1500
3-(Scarce)-Photo-c	77	154	231	493	847	1200
4-(Scarce)-Ward/Cuidera-a; photo-c	84	168	252	538	919	1300

FORBIDDEN LOVE (See Dark Mansion of...)

FORBIDDEN PLANET
Innovation Publishing: May, 1992 - No. 4, 1992 ($2.50, limited series)

	GD 2.0	VG 4.0	FN 6.0	VF 8.0	VF/NM 9.0	NM- 9.2
1-4: Adapts movie; painted-c						4.00

FORBIDDEN TALES OF DARK MANSION (Formerly Dark Mansion of Forbidden Love #1-4)
National Periodical Publ.: No. 5, May-June, 1972 - No. 15, Feb-Mar, 1974

	GD 2.0	VG 4.0	FN 6.0	VF 8.0	VF/NM 9.0	NM- 9.2
5-(52 pgs.)	6	12	18	38	69	100
6-15: 13-Kane/Howard-a	3	6	9	17	26	35

NOTE: ***N. Adams*** *c-9.* ***Alcala*** *a-9-11, 13.* ***Chaykin*** *a-7,15.* ***Evans*** *a-14.* ***Heck*** *a-5.* ***Kaluta*** *a-7i, 8-12; c-7, 8, 13.* ***G. Kane*** *a-13.* ***Kirby*** *a-6.* ***Nino*** *a-8, 12, 15.* ***Redondo*** *a-14.*

FORBIDDEN WORLDS
American Comics Group: 7-8/51 - No. 34, 10-11/54; No. 35, 8/55 - No. 145, 8/67 (No. 1-5: 52 pgs.; No. 6-8: 44 pgs.)

	GD 2.0	VG 4.0	FN 6.0	VF 8.0	VF/NM 9.0	NM- 9.2
1-Williamson/Frazetta-a (10 pgs.)	190	380	570	1216	2083	2950
2	74	148	222	470	810	1150
3-Williamson/Wood-a (7 pgs.); Frazetta (1 panel)	74	148	222	470	810	1150
4	47	94	141	296	498	700
5-Krenkel/Williamson-a (8 pgs.)	57	114	171	362	619	875
6-Harrison/Williamson-a (8 pgs.)	52	104	156	328	552	775
7,8,10: 7-1st monthly issue	37	74	111	222	361	500
9-A-Bomb explosion story	39	78	117	234	385	535
11-20	26	52	78	154	252	350
21-33: 24-E.C. swipe by Landau	21	42	63	122	199	275
34(10-11/54)(Scarce)(becomes Young Heroes #35 on)-Last pre-code issue; A-Bomb explosion story	24	48	72	142	234	325
35(8/55)-Scarce	22	44	66	128	209	290
36-62	14	28	42	82	121	160
63,69,76,78-Williamson-a in all; w/Krenkel #69	15	30	45	83	124	165
64,66-68,70-72,74,75,77,79-85,87-90	11	22	33	60	83	105
65- "There's a New Moon Tonight" listed in #114 as holding 1st record fan mail response	15	30	45	85	130	175
73-1st app. Herbie by Ogden Whitney	60	120	180	381	653	925
86-Flying saucer-c by Schaffenberger	12	24	36	67	94	120
91-93,95-100	5	10	15	34	60	85
94-Herbie (2nd app.)	12	24	36	82	179	275
101-109,111-113,115,117-120	4	8	12	28	44	60
110,116-Herbie app. 116-Herbie goes to Hell; Elizabeth Tayor-c	8	16	24	54	102	150
114-1st Herbie-c; contains list of editor's top 20 ACG stories	10	20	30	70	150	230
121-123	3	6	9	21	33	45
124,127-130: 124-Magic Agent app.	4	8	12	23	37	50
125-Magic Agent app.; intro. & origin Magicman series, ends #141; Herbie app.	5	10	15	31	53	75
126-Herbie app.	4	8	12	27	44	60
131-139: 133-Origin/1st app. Dragonia in Magicman (1-2/66); returns in #138. 136-Nemesis x-over in Magicman	3	6	9	21	33	45
140-Mark Midnight app. by Ditko	4	8	12	23	37	50
141-145	3	6	9	19	30	40

NOTE: ***Buscema*** *a-75, 79, 81, 82, 140r.* ***Cameron*** *a-5.* ***Disbrow*** *a-10.* ***Ditko*** *a-137p, 138, 140.* ***Landau*** *a-24, 27-29, 31-34, 48, 86r, 96, 143-45.* ***Lazarus*** *a-18, 23, 24, 57.* ***Moldoff*** *a-27, 31, 139r.* ***Reinman*** *a-93.* ***Whitney*** *a-70, 115, 116, 137; c-40, 46, 57, 60, 68, 70, 78, 79, 90, 93, 94, 100, 102, 103, 106-108, 114, 129.*

FORCE, THE (See The Crusaders)

FORCE MAJEURE: PRAIRIE BAY (Also see Wild Stars)
Little Rocket Publications: May, 2002 ($2.95, B&W)

	GD 2.0	VG 4.0	FN 6.0	VF 8.0	VF/NM 9.0	NM- 9.2
1-Tierney-s/Gil-c/a						3.00

FORCE OF BUDDHA'S PALM THE
Jademan Comics: Aug, 1988 - No. 55, Feb, 1993 ($1.50/$1.95, 68 pgs.)

	GD 2.0	VG 4.0	FN 6.0	VF 8.0	VF/NM 9.0	NM- 9.2
1,55-Kung Fu stories in all						5.00
2-54						4.00

FORCE WORKS
Marvel Comics: July, 1994 - No. 22, Apr, 1996 ($1.50)

	GD 2.0	VG 4.0	FN 6.0	VF 8.0	VF/NM 9.0	NM- 9.2
1-($3.95)-Fold-out pop-up-c; Iron Man, Wonder Man, Spider-Woman, U.S. Agent & Scarlet Witch (new costume)						4.00
2-11, 13-22: 5-Blue logo & pink logo versions. 9-Intro Dreamguard. 13-Avengers app.						3.00
5-Pink logo ($2.95)-polybagged w/ 16pg. Marvel Action Hour Preview & acetate print						4.00
12 ($2.50)-Flip book w/War Machine.						4.00

FORD ROTUNDA CHRISTMAS BOOK (See Christmas at the Rotunda)

FOREIGN INTRIGUES (Formerly Johnny Dynamite; becomes Battlefield Action #16 on)
Charlton Comics: No. 14, 1956 - No. 15, Aug, 1956

	GD 2.0	VG 4.0	FN 6.0	VF 8.0	VF/NM 9.0	NM- 9.2
14,15-Johnny Dynamite continues	9	18	27	47	61	75

FOREMOST BOYS (See 4Most)

FOREVER DARLING (Movie)
Dell Publishing Co.: No. 681, Feb, 1956

	GD 2.0	VG 4.0	FN 6.0	VF 8.0	VF/NM 9.0	NM- 9.2
Four Color 681-w/Lucille Ball & Desi Arnaz; photo-c	10	20	30	69	147	225

FOREVER EVIL (See Justice League #23 (2013))
DC Comics: Nov, 2013 - No. 7, Jul, 2014 ($3.99, limited series)

	GD 2.0	VG 4.0	FN 6.0	VF 8.0	VF/NM 9.0	NM- 9.2
1-Earth Three Crime Syndicate takes over; Nightwing unmasked; Johns-s/Finch-a						4.00
1-Director's Cut 1 (12/13, $5.99) Pencil artwork with full script						6.00
2-6: 2-Luthor dons the green battlesuit. 4-Sinestro returns						4.00
7-($4.99)						5.00
... Aftermath: Batman vs. Bane 1 (6/14, $3.99) Tomasi-s/Eaton-a						4.00

FOREVER EVIL: A.R.G.U.S.
DC Comics: Dec, 2013 - No. 6, May, 2014 ($2.99, limited series)

	GD 2.0	VG 4.0	FN 6.0	VF 8.0	VF/NM 9.0	NM- 9.2
1-6-Gates-s. Steve Trevor in search of missing heroes. 1,2-Deathstroke app.						3.00

FOREVER EVIL: ARKHAM WAR
DC Comics: Dec, 2013 - No. 6, May, 2014 ($2.99, limited series)

	GD 2.0	VG 4.0	FN 6.0	VF 8.0	VF/NM 9.0	NM- 9.2
1-6-Tomasi-s/Eaton-a; Bane and the Arkham inmates. 4-6-The Talons app.						4.00

FOREVER EVIL: ROGUES REBELLION
DC Comics: Dec, 2013 - No. 6, May, 2014 ($2.99, limited series)

	GD 2.0	VG 4.0	FN 6.0	VF 8.0	VF/NM 9.0	NM- 9.2
1-6-Buccellato-s/Hepburn-a/Shalvey-c. 2-Deathstorm & Power Ring app. 6-Grodd app.						3.00

FOREVER MAELSTROM
DC Comics: Jan, 2003 - No. 6, Jun, 2003 ($2.95, limited series)

	GD 2.0	VG 4.0	FN 6.0	VF 8.0	VF/NM 9.0	NM- 9.2
1-6-Chaykin & Tischman-s/Lucas & Barreto-a						3.00

FOREVER PEOPLE, THE
National Periodical Publications: Feb-Mar, 1971 - No. 11, Oct-Nov, 1972 (Fourth World) (#1-3, 10-11 are 36 pgs; #4-9 are 52 pgs.)

	GD 2.0	VG 4.0	FN 6.0	VF 8.0	VF/NM 9.0	NM- 9.2
1-1st app. Forever People; Superman x-over; Kirby-c/a begins; 1st full app. Darkseid (3rd anywhere, 3 weeks before New Gods #1); Darkseid storyline begins, ends #8 (app. in 1-4,6,8; cameos in 5,11)	16	32	48	110	243	375
2-9: 4-G.A. reprints thru #9. 9,10-Deadman app.	4	8	12	25	40	55
10,11	3	6	9	19	30	40
Jack Kirby's Forever People TPB (1999, $14.95, B&W&Grey) r/#1-11 plus bonus cover gallery						15.00

NOTE: ***Kirby*** *c/a(p)-1-11; #4-9 contain Sandman reprints from Adventure #85, 84, 75, 80, 77, 74 in that order.*

FOREVER PEOPLE
DC Comics: Feb, 1988 - No. 6, July, 1988 ($1.25, limited series)

	GD 2.0	VG 4.0	FN 6.0	VF 8.0	VF/NM 9.0	NM- 9.2
1-6						4.00

FORGE
CrossGeneration Comics: Feb, 2002 - No. 13, May, 2003 ($9.95/$11.95/$7.95, TPB)

	GD 2.0	VG 4.0	FN 6.0	VF 8.0	VF/NM 9.0	NM- 9.2
1-3: Reprints from various CrossGen titles						10.00
4-8-($11.95)						12.00
9-13-($7.95, 8-1/4" x 5-1/2") digest-sized reprints						8.00

FOR GIRLS ONLY
Bernard Baily Enterprises: 11/53 - No. 2, 6/54 (100 pgs., digest size, 25¢)

	GD 2.0	VG 4.0	FN 6.0	VF 8.0	VF/NM 9.0	NM- 9.2
1-25% comic book, 75% articles, illos, games	40	80	120	246	411	575
2-Eddie Fisher photo & story.	33	66	99	196	321	445

FORGOTTEN FOREST OF OZ, THE (See First Comics Graphic Novel #16)

FORGOTTEN QUEEN, THE
Valiant Entertainment: Feb, 2019 - No. 4, May, 2019 ($3.99, limited series)

	GD 2.0	VG 4.0	FN 6.0	VF 8.0	VF/NM 9.0	NM- 9.2
1-4-Tini Howard-s/Amilcar Pinna-a						4.00

FORGOTTEN REALMS (Also see Avatar & TSR Worlds)
DC Comics: Sept, 1989 - No. 25, Sept, 1991 ($1.50/$1.75)

	GD 2.0	VG 4.0	FN 6.0	VF 8.0	VF/NM 9.0	NM- 9.2
1, Annual 1 (1990, $2.95, 68 pgs.)						4.00
2-25: Based on TSR role-playing game. 18-Avatar story						3.00

FORGOTTEN REALMS (Based on Wizards of the Coast game)
Devil's Due Publ.: June, 2005 - No. 3, Aug, 2005 ($4.95)

	GD 2.0	VG 4.0	FN 6.0	VF 8.0	VF/NM 9.0	NM- 9.2
1-3-Salvatore-s/Seeley-a						5.00
...Exile (11/05 - No. 3, 1/06, $4.95) 1-3-Daab-s/Seeley-a. 1-Flip cover						5.00
...: Legacy (2/08 - No. 3, 6/08, $5.50) 1-3-Daab-s/Atkins-a						5.50
The Legend of Drizzt Book II: Exile (2006, $14.95, TPB) r/#1-3						15.00
...Sojourn (3/06 - No. 3, 6/06, $4.95) 1-3-Daab-s/Seeley-a						5.00
...: Streams of Silver (12/06 - No. 3, $5.50) 1-3-Daab-s/Semeiks-a						5.50

Formic Wars: Burning Earth #6 © OSC

Four Color Comics Series 1 #14 © DELL

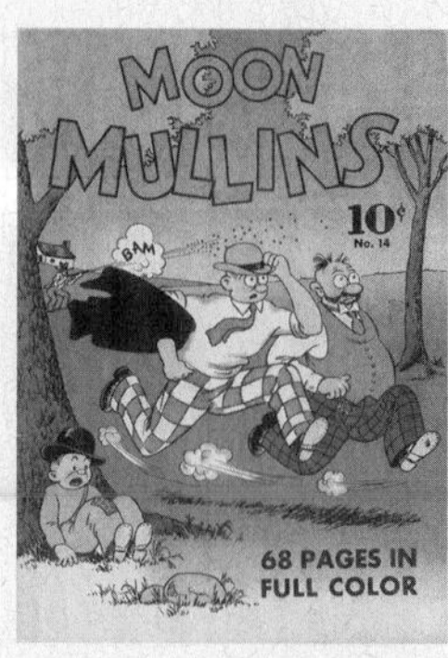

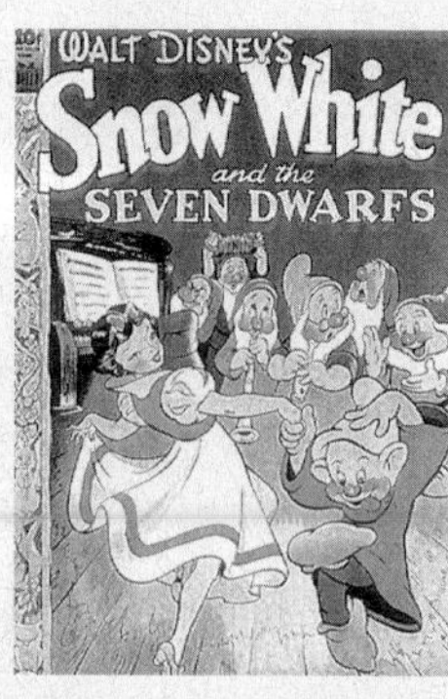

Four Color Comics Series 2 #49 © DIS

GD VG FN VF VF/NM NM-
2.0 4.0 6.0 8.0 9.0 9.2

...The Crystal Shard (8/06 - No. 3, 12/06, $4.95) 1-3-Daab-s/Semeiks-a 5.00
...The Halfling's Gem (8/07 - No. 3, 12/07, $5.50) 1-3-Daab-s/Seeley-a; two covers 5.50

FORLORN RIVER (See Zane Grey Four Color 395)

FOR LOVERS ONLY (Formerly Hollywood Romances)
Charlton Comics: No. 60, Aug, 1971 - No. 87, Nov, 1976

	GD 2.0	VG 4.0	FN 6.0	VF 8.0	VF/NM 9.0	NM- 9.2
60	3	6	9	19	30	40
61-80,82-87: 67-Morisi-a	2	4	6	11	16	20
81-Psychedelic cover	3	6	9	16	23	30

FORMERLY KNOWN AS THE JUSTICE LEAGUE
DC Comics: Sept, 2003 - No. 6, Feb, 2004 ($2.50, limited series)

1-Giffen & DeMatteis-s/Maguire-a; Booster Gold, Blue Beetle, Captain Atom, Mary Marvel, Fire, and Elongated Man app. 4.00
2-6: 3,4-Roulette app. 6-JLA app. 3.00
TPB (2004, $12.95) r/#1-6 13.00

FORMIC WARS: BURNING EARTH
Marvel Comics: Apr, 2011 - No. 7, Sept, 2011 ($3.99, limited series)

1-7-Prequel to Orson Scott Card's novel Ender's Game. 1-Covers by Larroca & Hitch 4.00

FORMIC WARS: SILENT STRIKE (Follows Burning Earth limited series)
Marvel Comics: Feb, 2012 - No. 5, Jun, 2012 ($3.99, limited series)

1-5-Johnston-s/Caracuzzo-a/Camuncoli-c 4.00

FORT: PROPHET OF THE UNEXPLAINED
Dark Horse Comics: June, 2002 - No. 4, Sept, 2002 ($2.99, B&W, limited series)

1-4-Peter Lenkov-s/Frazer Irving-c/a 3.00
TPB (2003, $9.95) r/#1-4 10.00

FORTUNE AND GLORY
Oni Press: Dec, 1999 - No. 3, Apr, 2000 ($4.95, B&W, limited series)

1-3-Brian Michael Bendis in Hollywood 5.00
TPB ($14.95) 15.00

40 BIG PAGES OF MICKEY MOUSE
Whitman Publ. Co.: No. 945, Jan, 1936 (10-1/4x12-1/2", 44 pgs., cardboard-c)

945-Reprints Mickey Mouse Magazine #1, but with a different cover; ads were eliminated and some illustrated stories had expanded text. The book is 3/4" shorter than Mickey Mouse Mag. #1, but the reprints are same size (Rare) 174 348 522 1114 1907 2700

47 RONIN
Dark Horse Comics: Nov, 2012 - No. 5, Jul, 2013 ($3.99, limited series)

1-5-Mike Richardson-s/Stan Sakai-a/c; 18th century samurai legend 4.00

FOR YOUR EYES ONLY (See James Bond...)

FOUNTAIN, THE (Companion graphic novel to the Darren Aronofsky film)
DC Comics (Vertigo): 2005 ($39.99, hardcover with dust jacket)

1-Darren Aronofsky-s/Kent Williams-a 40.00

FOUR (Fantastic Four; See Marvel Knights 4 #28-30)

FOUR COLOR
Dell Publishing Co.: Sept?, 1939 - No. 1354, Apr-June, 1962
(Series I are all 68 pgs.)

NOTE: *Four Color only appears on issues #19-25, 1-99,101. Dell Publishing Co. filed these as Series I, #1-25, and Series II, #1-1354. Issues beginning with #710? were printed with and without ads on back cover. Issues without ads are worth more.*

SERIES I:

	GD 2.0	VG 4.0	FN 6.0	VF 8.0	VF/NM 9.0	NM- 9.2
1(nn)-Dick Tracy	1100	2200	3300	8360	15,930	23,500
2(nn)-Don Winslow of the Navy (#1) (Rare) (11/39?)	245	490	735	1568	2684	3800
3(nn)-Myra North (1/40)	116	232	348	742	1271	1800
4-Donald Duck by Al Taliaferro (1940)(Disney)(3/40?)	2250	4500	6750	16,900	30,950	45,000
(Prices vary widely on this book)						
5-Smilin' Jack (#1) (5/40?)	94	188	282	597	1025	1450
6-Dick Tracy (Scarce)	277	554	831	1773	3037	4300
7-Gang Busters	65	130	195	416	708	1000
8-Dick Tracy	148	396	444	947	1624	2300
9-Terry and the Pirates-r/Super #9-29	81	162	243	518	884	1250
10-Smilin' Jack	77	154	231	493	847	1200
11-Smitty (#1)	57	114	171	362	619	875
12-Little Orphan Annie; reprints strips from 12/19/37 to 6/4/38	74	148	222	470	810	1150
13-Walt Disney's Reluctant Dragon('41)-Contains 2 pgs. of photos from film; 2 pg. foreword to Fantasia by Leopold Stokowski; Donald Duck, Goofy, Baby Weems & Mickey Mouse (as the Sorcerer's Apprentice) app. (Disney)	226	452	678	1446	2473	3500
14-Moon Mullins (#1)	50	100	150	315	533	750
15-Tillie the Toiler (#1)	61	122	183	390	670	950
16-Mickey Mouse (#1) (Disney) by Gottfredson	1350	2700	4050	17,500	--	--
17-Walt Disney's Dumbo, the Flying Elephant (#1)(1941)-Mickey Mouse, Donald Duck, & Pluto app. (Disney)	274	548	822	1740	2995	4250
18-Jiggs and Maggie (#1)(1936-38-r)	57	114	171	362	619	875
19-Barney Google and Snuffy Smith (#1)-(1st issue with Four Color on the cover)	52	104	156	323	549	775
20-Tiny Tim	43	86	129	271	461	650
21-Dick Tracy	95	190	285	603	1039	1475
22-Don Winslow	57	114	171	362	619	875
23-Gang Busters	52	104	156	328	552	775
24-Captain Easy	57	114	171	362	619	875
25-Popeye (1942)	113	226	339	718	1234	1750

SERIES II:

	GD 2.0	VG 4.0	FN 6.0	VF 8.0	VF/NM 9.0	NM- 9.2
1-Little Joe (1942)	70	140	210	567	1259	1950
2-Harold Teen	34	68	102	245	548	850
3-Alley Oop (#1)	49	98	147	382	866	1350
4-Smilin' Jack	71	142	213	454	777	1100
5-Raggedy Ann and Andy (#1)	48	96	144	362	831	1300
6-Smitty	25	50	75	175	388	600
7-Smokey Stover (#1)	25	50	75	175	388	600
8-Tillie the Toiler	25	50	75	182	404	625
9-Donald Duck Finds Pirate Gold, by Carl Barks & Jack Hannah (Disney) (© 8/17/42)	1000	2000	3000	7600	13,800	20,000
10-Flash Gordon by Alex Raymond; reprinted from "The Ice Kingdom"	89	178	267	712	1606	2500
11-Wash Tubbs	27	514	81	189	420	650
12-Walt Disney's Bambi (#1)	46	92	138	359	805	1250
13-Mr. District Attorney (#1)-See The Funnies #35 for 1st app.	29	58	87	209	467	725
14-Smilin' Jack	32	64	96	230	515	800
15-Felix the Cat (#1)	82	164	246	656	1478	2300
16-Porky Pig (#1)(1942)- "Secret of the Haunted House"	100	200	300	800	1800	2800
17-Popeye	49	98	147	382	866	1350
18-Little Orphan Annie's Junior Commandos; Flag-c; reprints strips from 6/14/42 to 11/21/42	61	122	183	390	670	950
19-Walt Disney's Thumper Meets the Seven Dwarfs (Disney); reprinted in Silly Symphonies	46	92	138	359	805	1250
20-Barney Baxter	25	50	75	175	388	600
21-Oswald the Rabbit (#1)(1943)	40	80	120	296	673	1050
22-Tillie the Toiler	18	36	54	121	268	415
23-Raggedy Ann and Andy	34	68	102	245	548	850
24-Gang Busters	30	60	90	216	483	750
25-Andy Panda (#1) (Walter Lantz)	50	100	150	390	870	1350
26-Popeye	49	98	147	382	866	1350
27-Walt Disney's Mickey Mouse and the Seven Colored Terror	73	146	219	584	1317	2050
28-Wash Tubbs	17	34	51	119	265	410
29-Donald Duck and the Mummy's Ring, by Carl Barks (Disney) (9/43)	805	1610	2415	5877	10,389	14,900
30-Bambi's Children (1943)-Disney	41	82	123	303	689	1075
31-Moon Mullins	16	32	48	110	243	375
32-Smitty	16	32	48	112	249	385
33-Bugs Bunny "Public Nuisance #1"	118	236	354	944	2122	3300
34-Dick Tracy	39	78	114	289	657	1025
35-Smokey Stover	15	30	45	105	233	360
36-Smilin' Jack	22	44	66	154	340	525
37-Bringing Up Father	19	38	57	129	287	445
38-Roy Rogers (#1, © 4/44)-1st western comic with photo-c (see Movie Comics #3)	155	310	465	1279	2890	4500
39-Oswald the Rabbit (1944)	27	54	81	194	435	675
40-Barney Google and Snuffy Smith	20	40	60	135	300	465
41-Mother Goose and Nursery Rhyme Comics (#1)-All by Walt Kelly	23	46	69	161	356	550
42-Tiny Tim (1934-r)	17	34	51	117	259	400
43-Popeye (1938-'42-r)	30	60	90	216	483	750
44-Terry and the Pirates (1938-r)	31	62	93	223	499	775
45-Raggedy Ann	26	52	78	182	404	625
46-Felix the Cat and the Haunted Castle	42	84	126	311	706	1100
47-Gene Autry (copyright 6/16/44)	35	70	105	252	564	875
48-Porky Pig of the Mounties by Carl Barks (7/44)	98	196	294	794	1772	2750
49-Snow White and the Seven Dwarfs (Disney)	50	100	150	400	900	1400

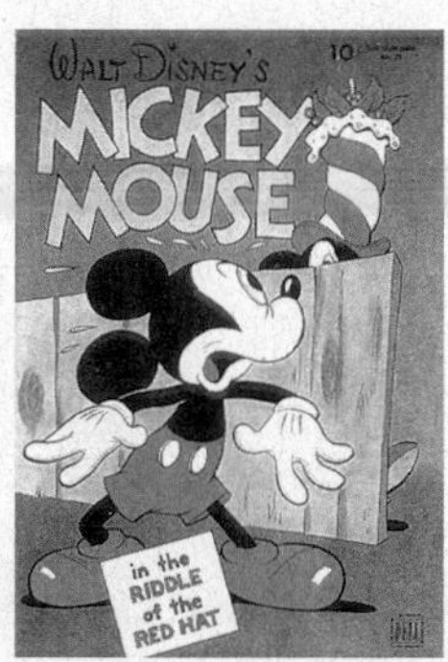

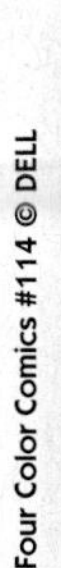
Four Color Comics #79 © DIS

Four Color Comics #114 © DELL

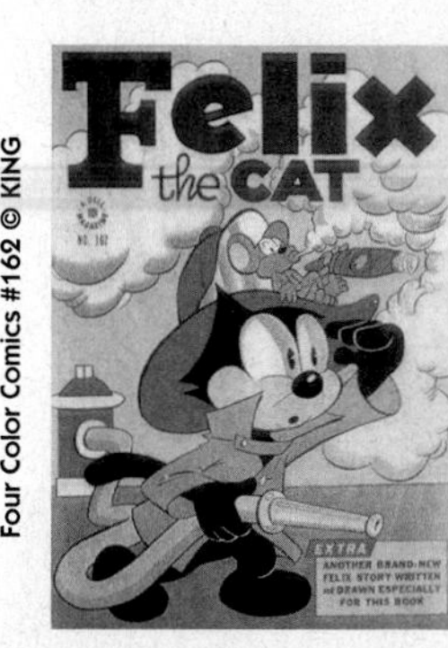

Four Color Comics #162 © KING

	GD 2.0	VG 4.0	FN 6.0	VF 8.0	VF/NM 9.0	NM- 9.2
50-Fairy Tale Parade-Walt Kelly art (1944)	21	42	63	147	324	500
51-Bugs Bunny Finds the Lost Treasure	37	74	111	274	612	950
52-Little Orphan Annie; reprints strips from 6/18/38 to 11/19/38	25	50	75	175	388	600
53-Wash Tubbs	13	26	39	91	201	310
54-Andy Panda	25	50	75	175	388	600
55-Tillie the Toiler	13	26	39	87	191	295
56-Dick Tracy	34	68	102	247	554	860
57-Gene Autry	30	60	90	216	483	750
58-Smilin' Jack	22	44	66	154	340	525
59-Mother Goose and Nursery Rhyme Comics-Kelly-c/a	18	36	54	125	276	430
60-Tiny Folks Funnies	15	30	45	103	227	350
61-Santa Claus Funnies(11/44)-Kelly art	23	46	69	161	356	550
62-Donald Duck in Frozen Gold, by Carl Barks (Disney) (1/45)	231	462	693	1906	4303	6700
63-Roy Rogers; color photo-all 4 covers	40	80	120	296	673	1050
64-Smokey Stover	12	24	36	84	185	285
65-Smitty	13	26	39	87	191	295
66-Gene Autry	30	60	90	216	483	750
67-Oswald the Rabbit	16	32	48	112	249	385
68-Mother Goose and Nursery Rhyme Comics, by Walt Kelly	18	36	54	125	276	430
69-Fairy Tale Parade, by Walt Kelly	21	42	63	147	324	500
70-Popeye and Wimpy	23	46	69	156	348	540
71-Walt Disney's Three Caballeros, by Walt Kelly (© 4/45)-(Disney)	64	128	192	512	1156	1800
72-Raggedy Ann	20	40	60	141	313	485
73-The Gumps (#1)	12	24	36	82	179	275
74-Marge's Little Lulu (#1)	186	372	558	1535	3468	5400
75-Gene Autry and the Wildcat	23	46	69	164	362	560
76-Little Orphan Annie; reprints strips from 2/28/40 to 6/24/40	20	40	60	138	307	475
77-Felix the Cat	38	76	114	281	628	975
78-Porky Pig and the Bandit Twins	28	56	84	202	451	700
79-Walt Disney's Mickey Mouse in The Riddle of the Red Hat by Carl Barks (8/45)	94	188	282	752	1651	2550
80-Smilin' Jack	13	26	39	89	195	300
81-Moon Mullins	10	20	30	68	144	220
82-Lone Ranger	38	76	114	285	641	1000
83-Gene Autry in Outlaw Trail	23	46	69	164	362	560
84-Flash Gordon by Alex Raymond-Reprints from "The Fiery Desert"	42	84	126	311	698	1085
85-Andy Panda and the Mad Dog Mystery	15	30	45	103	227	350
86-Roy Rogers; photo-c	29	58	87	209	467	725
87-Fairy Tale Parade by Walt Kelly; Dan Noonan-c	21	42	63	147	324	500
88-Bugs Bunny's Great Adventure (Sci/fi)	23	46	69	164	362	560
89-Tillie the Toiler	13	26	39	87	191	295
90-Christmas with Mother Goose by Walt Kelly (11/45)	15	30	45	103	227	350
91-Santa Claus Funnies by Walt Kelly (11/45)	17	34	51	117	259	400
92-Walt Disney's The Wonderful Adventures Of Pinocchio (1945); Donald Duck by Kelly, 16 pgs. (Disney)	49	98	147	382	866	1350
93-Gene Autry in The Bandit of Black Rock	19	38	57	133	297	460
94-Winnie Winkle (1945)	12	24	36	81	176	270
95-Roy Rogers Comics; photo-c	29	58	87	209	467	725
96-Dick Tracy	23	46	69	161	356	550
97-Marge's Little Lulu (1946)	70	140	210	560	1255	1950
98-Lone Ranger, The	27	54	81	194	435	675
99-Smitty	10	20	30	66	138	210
100-Gene Autry Comics; 1st Gene Autry photo-c	22	44	66	155	345	535
101-Terry and the Pirates	20	40	60	135	300	465
NOTE: *No. 101 is last issue to carry "Four Color" logo on cover; all issues beginning with No. 100 are marked "...O. S." (One Shot) which can be found in the bottom left-hand panel on the first page; the numbers following "O. S." relate to the year/month issued.*						
102-Oswald the Rabbit-Walt Kelly art, 1 pg.	14	28	42	94	207	320
103-Easter with Mother Goose by Walt Kelly	19	38	57	129	287	445
104-Fairy Tale Parade by Walt Kelly	16	32	48	112	249	385
105-Albert the Alligator and Pogo Possum (#1) by Kelly (4/46)	57	114	171	456	1028	1600
106-Tillie the Toiler (5/46)	10	20	30	65	135	205
107-Little Orphan Annie; reprints strips from 11/16/42 to 3/24/43	18	36	54	122	271	420
108-Donald Duck in The Terror of the River, by Carl Barks (Disney) (© 4/16/46)	148	296	444	1221	2761	4300
109-Roy Rogers Comics; photo-c	22	44	66	154	340	525
110-Marge's Little Lulu	44	88	132	326	738	1150
111-Captain Easy	13	26	39	86	188	290
112-Porky Pig's Adventure in Gopher Gulch	16	32	48	111	246	380
113-Popeye; all new Popeye stories begin	14	28	42	94	207	320
114-Fairy Tale Parade by Walt Kelly	16	32	48	112	249	385
115-Marge's Little Lulu	41	82	123	303	689	1075
116-Mickey Mouse and the House of Many Mysteries (Disney)	27	54	81	184	410	635
117-Roy Rogers Comics; photo-c	17	34	51	119	265	410
118-Lone Ranger, The	27	54	81	194	435	675
119-Felix the Cat; all new Felix stories begin	34	68	102	245	548	850
120-Marge's Little Lulu	36	72	108	259	580	900
121-Fairy Tale Parade-(not Kelly)	10	20	30	69	147	225
122-Henry (#1) (10/46)	16	32	48	110	243	375
123-Bugs Bunny's Dangerous Venture	16	32	48	110	243	375
124-Roy Rogers Comics; photo-c	17	34	51	119	265	410
125-Lone Ranger, The	19	38	57	131	291	450
126-Christmas with Mother Goose by Walt Kelly (1946)	11	22	33	76	163	250
127-Popeye	14	28	42	94	207	320
128-Santa Claus Funnies- "Santa & the Angel" by Gollub; "A Mouse in the House" by Kelly	14	28	42	94	207	320
129-Walt Disney's Uncle Remus and His Tales of Brer Rabbit (#1) (1946)-Adapted from Disney movie "Song of the South"	25	50	75	175	388	600
130-Andy Panda (Walter Lantz)	10	20	30	70	150	230
131-Marge's Little Lulu	36	72	108	259	580	900
132-Tillie the Toiler (1947)	10	20	30	65	135	205
133-Dick Tracy	18	36	54	124	275	425
134-Tarzan and the Devil Ogre; Marsh-c/a	57	114	171	456	1028	1600
135-Felix the Cat	21	42	63	147	324	500
136-Lone Ranger, The	19	38	57	131	291	450
137-Roy Rogers Comics; photo-c	17	34	51	119	265	410
138-Smitty	9	18	27	59	117	175
139-Marge's Little Lulu (1947)	34	68	102	245	548	850
140-Easter with Mother Goose by Walt Kelly	14	28	42	97	214	330
141-Mickey Mouse and the Submarine Pirates (Disney)	22	44	66	155	345	535
142-Bugs Bunny and the Haunted Mountain	16	32	48	110	243	375
143-Oswald the Rabbit & the Prehistoric Egg	9	18	27	59	117	175
144-Roy Rogers Comics (1947)-Photo-c	17	34	51	119	265	410
145-Popeye	14	28	42	94	207	320
146-Marge's Little Lulu	34	68	102	245	548	850
147-Donald Duck in Volcano Valley, by Carl Barks (Disney) (5/47)	104	208	312	832	1866	2900
148-Albert the Alligator and Pogo Possum by Walt Kelly (5/47)	40	80	120	296	673	1050
149-Smilin' Jack	9	18	27	62	126	190
150-Tillie the Toiler (6/47)	9	18	27	61	123	185
151-Lone Ranger, The	16	32	48	112	249	385
152-Little Orphan Annie; reprints strips from 1/2/44 to 5/6/44	12	24	36	79	170	260
153-Roy Rogers Comics; photo-c	15	30	45	105	233	360
154-Walter Lantz Andy Panda	10	20	30	70	150	230
155-Henry (7/47)	10	20	30	70	150	230
156-Porky Pig and the Phantom	11	22	33	75	160	245
157-Mickey Mouse & the Beanstalk (Disney)	22	44	66	155	345	535
158-Marge's Little Lulu	34	68	102	245	548	850
159-Donald Duck in the Ghost of the Grotto, by Carl Barks (Disney) (8/47)	93	186	279	744	1672	2600
160-Roy Rogers Comics; photo-c	15	30	45	105	233	360
161-Tarzan and the Fires Of Tohr; Marsh-c/a	46	92	138	359	805	1250
162-Felix the Cat (9/47)	16	32	48	110	243	375
163-Dick Tracy	16	32	48	110	243	375
164-Bugs Bunny Finds the Frozen Kingdom	16	32	48	110	243	375
165-Marge's Little Lulu	36	72	108	259	580	900
166-Roy Rogers Comics (52 pgs.)-Photo-c	15	30	45	105	233	360
167-Lone Ranger, The	16	32	48	112	249	385
168-Popeye (10/47)	14	28	42	94	207	320
169-Woody Woodpecker (#1)- "Manhunter in the North"; drug use story	19	38	57	131	291	450
170-Mickey Mouse on Spook's Island (11/47)(Disney)-reprinted in Mickey Mouse #103	19	38	57	133	297	460
171-Charlie McCarthy (#1) and the Twenty Thieves	26	52	78	182	404	625
172-Christmas with Mother Goose by Walt Kelly (11/47)						

Four Color Comics #193 © Loews Inc.

Four Color Comics #212 © KING

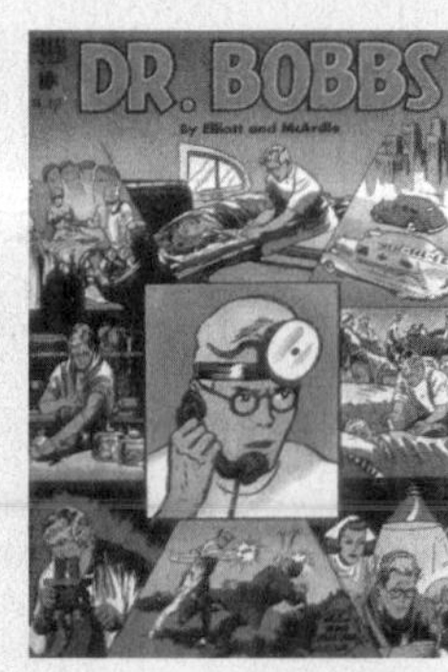

Four Color Comics #235 © News Synd.

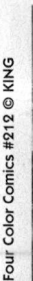

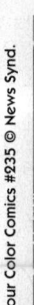

	GD 2.0	VG 4.0	FN 6.0	VF 8.0	VF/NM 9.0	NM- 9.2
	11	22	33	76	163	250
173-Flash Gordon	23	46	69	168	382	560
174-Winnie Winkle	8	16	24	56	108	160
175-Santa Claus Funnies by Walt Kelly (1947)	14	28	42	94	207	320
176-Tillie the Toiler (12/47)	9	18	27	61	123	185
177-Roy Rogers Comics-(36 pgs.); Photo-c	15	30	45	100	220	340
178-Donald Duck "Christmas on Bear Mountain" by Carl Barks; 1st app. Uncle Scrooge (Disney)(12/47)	145	290	435	1196	2698	4200
179-Uncle Wiggily (#1)-Walt Kelly-c	14	28	42	97	214	330
180-Ozark Ike (#1)	11	22	33	73	157	240
181-Walt Disney's Mickey Mouse in Jungle Magic	19	38	57	133	297	460
182-Porky Pig in Never-Never Land (2/48)	11	22	33	75	160	245
183-Oswald the Rabbit (Lantz)	9	18	27	59	117	175
184-Tillie the Toiler	9	18	27	61	123	185
185-Easter with Mother Goose by Walt Kelly (1948)	13	26	39	87	191	295
186-Walt Disney's Bambi (4/48)-Reprinted as Movie Classic Bambi #3 (1956)	14	28	42	98	217	335
187-Bugs Bunny and the Dreadful Dragon	12	24	36	79	170	260
188-Woody Woodpecker (Lantz, 5/48)	11	22	33	76	163	250
189-Donald Duck in The Old Castle's Secret, by Carl Barks (Disney) (6/48)	91	182	273	728	1639	2550
190-Flash Gordon (6/48); bondage-c; "The Adventures of the Flying Saucers"; 5th Flying Saucer story- see The Spirit 9/28/47(1st), Shadow Comics V7#10 (2nd, 1/48),Captain Midnight #60 (3rd, 2/48) & Boy Commandos #26 (4th, 3-4/48)	28	56	84	202	451	700
191-Porky Pig to the Rescue	11	22	33	75	160	245
192-The Brownies (#1)-by Walt Kelly (7/48)	13	26	39	91	201	310
193-M.G.M. Presents Tom and Jerry (#1)(1948)	26	52	78	182	404	625
194-Mickey Mouse in The World Under the Sea (Disney)-Reprinted in Mickey Mouse #101	19	38	57	133	297	460
195-Tillie the Toiler	8	16	24	52	99	145
196-Charlie McCarthy in The Haunted Hide-Out; part photo-c	16	32	48	111	246	380
197-Spirit of the Border (#1) (Zane Grey) (1948)	11	22	33	76	163	250
198-Andy Panda	10	20	30	70	150	230
199-Donald Duck in Sheriff of Bullet Valley, by Carl Barks; Barks draws himself on wanted poster, last page; used in Love & Death (Disney) (10/48)	91	182	273	728	1639	2550
200-Bugs Bunny, Super Sleuth (10/48)	12	24	36	79	170	260
201-Christmas with Mother Goose by W. Kelly	10	20	30	64	132	200
202-Woody Woodpecker	8	16	24	56	108	160
203-Donald Duck in the Golden Christmas Tree, by Carl Barks (Disney) (12/48)	63	126	189	504	1127	1750
204-Flash Gordon (12/48)	17	34	51	117	259	400
205-Santa Claus Funnies by Walt Kelly	12	24	36	84	185	285
206-Little Orphan Annie; reprints strips from 11/10/40 to 1/11/41	8	16	24	52	99	145
207-King of the Royal Mounted (#1) (12/48)	13	26	39	89	195	300
208-Brer Rabbit Does It Again (Disney) (1/49)	10	20	30	70	150	230
209-Harold Teen	6	12	18	41	76	110
210-Tippie and Cap Stubbs	7	14	21	48	89	130
211-Little Beaver (#1)	10	20	30	67	141	215
212-Dr. Bobbs	6	12	18	42	79	115
213-Tillie the Toiler	8	16	24	52	99	145
214-Mickey Mouse and His Sky Adventure (2/49)(Disney)-Reprinted in Mickey Mouse #105	15	30	45	105	233	360
215-Sparkle Plenty (Dick Tracy-r by Gould)	11	22	33	75	160	245
216-Andy Panda and the Police Pup (Lantz)	8	16	24	55	105	155
217-Bugs Bunny in Court Jester	12	24	36	79	170	260
218-Three Little Pigs and the Wonderful Magic Lamp (Disney) (3/49)(#1)	10	20	30	68	144	220
219-Swee'pea	9	18	27	59	117	175
220-Easter with Mother Goose by Walt Kelly	13	26	39	87	191	295
221-Uncle Wiggily-Walt Kelly cover in part	9	18	27	60	120	180
222-West of the Pecos (Zane Grey)	7	14	21	49	92	135
223-Donald Duck "Lost in the Andes" by Carl Barks (Disney-4/49) (square egg story)	82	164	246	656	1478	2300
224-Little Iodine (#1), by Hatlo (4/49)	12	24	36	81	176	270
225-Oswald the Rabbit (Lantz)	7	14	21	46	86	125
226-Porky Pig and Spoofy, the Spook	9	18	27	61	123	185
227-Seven Dwarfs (Disney)	10	20	30	69	147	225
228-Mark of Zorro, The (#1) (1949)	21	42	63	147	324	500
229-Smokey Stover	6	12	18	42	79	115
230-Sunset Pass (Zane Grey)	7	14	21	49	92	135
231-Mickey Mouse and the Rajah's Treasure (Disney)						

	GD 2.0	VG 4.0	FN 6.0	VF 8.0	VF/NM 9.0	NM- 9.2
	15	30	45	105	233	360
232-Woody Woodpecker (Lantz, 6/49)	8	16	24	56	108	160
233-Bugs Bunny, Sleepwalking Sleuth	12	24	36	79	170	260
234-Dumbo in Sky Voyage (Disney)	13	26	39	89	195	310
235-Tiny Tim	6	12	18	42	79	115
236-Heritage of the Desert (Zane Grey) (1949)	7	14	21	49	92	135
237-Tillie the Toiler	8	16	24	52	99	145
238-Donald Duck in Voodoo Hoodoo, by Carl Barks (Disney) (8/49)	61	122	183	488	1094	1700
239-Adventure Bound (8/49)	6	12	18	38	69	100
240-Andy Panda (Lantz)	8	16	24	55	105	155
241-Porky Pig, Mighty Hunter	9	18	27	61	123	185
242-Tippie and Cap Stubbs	5	10	15	31	53	75
243-Thumper Follows His Nose (Disney)	12	24	36	80	173	265
244-The Brownies by Walt Kelly	10	20	30	64	132	200
245-Dick's Adventures (9/49)	6	12	18	37	66	95
246-Thunder Mountain (Zane Grey)	6	12	18	37	66	95
247-Flash Gordon	17	34	51	117	259	400
248-Mickey Mouse and the Black Sorcerer (Disney)	15	30	45	105	233	360
249-Woody Woodpecker in the "Globetrotter" (10/49)	8	16	24	56	108	160
250-Bugs Bunny in Diamond Daze; used in **SOTI**, pg. 309	12	24	36	81	176	270
251-Hubert at Camp Moonbeam	9	18	27	61	123	185
252-Pinocchio (Disney)-not by Kelly; origin	12	24	36	79	170	260
253-Christmas with Mother Goose by W. Kelly	10	20	30	64	132	200
254-Santa Claus Funnies by Walt Kelly; Pogo & Albert story by Kelly (11/49)	12	24	36	84	185	285
255-The Ranger (Zane Grey) (1949)	6	12	18	37	66	95
256-Donald Duck in "Luck of the North" by Carl Barks (Disney) (12/49)-Shows #257 on inside	50	100	150	400	900	1400
257-Little Iodine	8	16	24	55	105	155
258-Andy Panda and the Balloon Race (Lantz)	8	16	24	55	105	155
259-Santa and the Angel (Gollub art-condensed from #128) & Santa at the Zoo (12/49) -two books in one	7	14	21	49	92	135
260-Porky Pig, Hero of the Wild West (12/49)	9	18	27	61	123	185
261-Mickey Mouse and the Missing Key (Disney)	15	30	45	105	233	360
262-Raggedy Ann and Andy	9	18	27	57	111	165
263-Donald Duck in "Land of the Totem Poles" by Carl Barks (Disney) (2/50)-Has two Barks stories	46	92	138	368	834	1300
264-Woody Woodpecker in the Magic Lantern (Lantz)	8	16	24	56	108	160
265-King of the Royal Mounted (Zane Grey)	9	18	27	60	120	180
266-Bugs Bunny on the "Isle of Hercules" (2/50)-Reprinted in Best of Bugs Bunny #1	9	18	27	62	126	190
267-Little Beaver; Harmon-c/a	7	14	21	44	82	120
268-Mickey Mouse's Surprise Visitor (1950)(Disney)	14	28	42	98	217	335
269-Johnny Mack Brown (#1)-Photo-c	18	36	54	124	275	425
270-Drift Fence (Zane Grey) (3/50)	6	12	18	37	66	95
271-Porky Pig in Phantom of the Plains	9	18	27	61	123	185
272-Cinderella (Disney) (4/50)	12	24	36	84	185	285
273-Oswald the Rabbit (Lantz)	7	14	21	46	86	125
274-Bugs Bunny, Hare-brained Reporter	9	18	27	62	126	190
275-Donald Duck in "Ancient Persia" by Carl Barks (Disney) (5/50)	47	94	141	367	821	1275
276-Uncle Wiggily	7	14	21	49	92	135
277-Porky Pig in Desert Adventure (5/50)	9	18	27	61	123	185
278-(Wild) Bill Elliott Comics (#1)-Photo-c	12	24	36	82	179	275
279-Mickey Mouse and Pluto Battle the Giant Ants (Disney); reprinted in Mickey Mouse #102 & 245	12	24	36	79	170	260
280-Andy Panda in The Isle Of Mechanical Men (Lantz)	8	16	24	55	105	155
281-Bugs Bunny in The Great Circus Mystery	9	18	27	62	126	190
282-Donald Duck and the Pixilated Parrot by Carl Barks (Disney) (© 5/23/50)	47	94	141	367	821	1275
283-King of the Royal Mounted (7/50)	9	18	27	60	120	180
284-Porky Pig in The Kingdom of Nowhere	9	18	27	61	123	185
285-Bozo the Clown & His Minikin Circus (#1) (TV)	18	36	54	122	271	420
286-Mickey Mouse in The Uninvited Guest (Disney	12	24	36	79	170	260
287-Gene Autry's Champion in The Ghost Of Black Mountain; photo-c	11	22	33	76	163	250
288-Woody Woodpecker in Klondike Gold (Lantz)	8	16	24	56	108	160
289-Bugs Bunny in "Indian Trouble"	9	18	27	62	126	190
290-The Chief (#1) (8/50)	8	16	24	54	102	150
291-Donald Duck in "The Magic Hourglass" by Carl Barks (Disney) (9/50)	47	94	141	367	821	1275

Four Color Comics #336 © W. Lantz

Four Color Comics #358 © W. Lantz

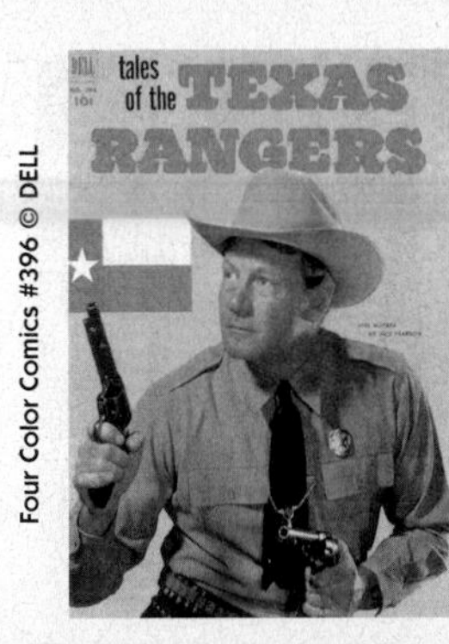

Four Color Comics #396 © DELL

	GD 2.0	VG 4.0	FN 6.0	VF 8.0	VF/NM 9.0	NM- 9.2
292-The Cisco Kid Comics (#1)	21	42	63	147	324	500
293-The Brownies-Kelly-c/a	10	20	30	64	132	200
294-Little Beaver	7	14	21	44	82	120
295-Porky Pig in President Porky (9/50)	9	18	27	61	123	185
296-Mickey Mouse in Private Eye for Hire (Disney)	12	24	36	79	170	260
297-Andy Panda in The Haunted Inn (Lantz, 10/50)	8	16	24	55	105	155
298-Bugs Bunny in Sheik for a Day	9	18	27	62	126	190
299-Buck Jones & the Iron Horse Trail (#1)	13	26	39	86	188	290
300-Donald Duck in "Big-Top Bedlam" by Carl Barks (Disney) (11/50)	47	94	141	367	821	1275
301-The Mysterious Rider (Zane Grey)	6	12	18	37	66	95
302-Santa Claus Funnies (11/50)	8	16	24	51	96	140
303-Porky Pig in The Land of the Monstrous Flies	8	16	24	51	96	140
304-Mickey Mouse in Tom-Tom Island (Disney) (12/50)	11	22	33	72	154	235
305-Woody Woodpecker (Lantz)	6	12	18	41	76	110
306-Raggedy Ann	7	14	21	46	86	125
307-Bugs Bunny in Lumber Jack Rabbit	8	16	24	55	105	155
308-Donald Duck in "Dangerous Disguise" by Carl Barks (Disney) (1/51)	46	92	138	340	770	1200
309-Betty Betz' Dollface and Her Gang (1951)	7	14	21	44	82	120
310-King of the Royal Mounted (1/51)	7	14	21	46	86	125
311-Porky Pig in Midget Horses of Hidden Valley	8	16	24	51	96	140
312-Tonto (#1)	11	22	33	75	160	245
313-Mickey Mouse in The Mystery of the Double-Cross Ranch (#1) (Disney) (2/51)	11	22	33	72	154	235

Note: Beginning with the above comic in 1951 Dell/Western began adding #1 in small print on the covers of several long running titles with the evident intention of switching these titles to their own monthly numbers, but when the conversions were made, there was no connection. It is thought that the post office may have stepped in and decreed the sequences should commence as though the first four colors printed had each begun with number one, or the first issues sold by subscription. Since the regular series' numbers don't correctly match to the numbers of earlier issues published, it's not known whether or not the numbering was in error.

	GD 2.0	VG 4.0	FN 6.0	VF 8.0	VF/NM 9.0	NM- 9.2
314-Ambush (Zane Grey)	6	12	18	37	66	95
315-Oswald the Rabbit (Lantz)	6	12	18	40	73	105
316-Rex Allen (#1)-Photo-c; Marsh-a	13	26	39	86	188	290
317-Bugs Bunny in Hair Today Gone Tomorrow (#1)	8	16	24	55	105	155
318-Donald Duck in "No Such Varmint" by Carl Barks (#1)-Indicia shows #317 (Disney, © 1/23/51)	46	92	138	340	770	1200
319-Gene Autry's Champion; painted-c	6	12	18	41	76	110
320-Uncle Wiggily (#1)	7	14	21	49	92	135
321-Little Scouts (#1) (3/51)	6	12	18	37	66	95
322-Porky Pig in Roaring Rockets (#1 on-c)	8	16	24	51	96	140
323-Susie Q. Smith (#1) (3/51)	6	12	18	38	69	100
324-I Met a Handsome Cowboy (3/51)	7	14	21	49	92	135
325-Mickey Mouse in The Haunted Castle (#2) (Disney) (4/51)	11	22	33	72	154	235
326-Andy Panda (#1) (Lantz)	6	12	18	41	76	110
327-Bugs Bunny and the Rajah's Treasure (#2)	8	16	24	55	105	155
328-Donald Duck in Old California (#2) by Carl Barks-Peyote drug use issue (Disney) (5/51)	45	90	135	333	754	1175
329-Roy Roger's Trigger (#1)(5/51)-Painted-c	14	28	42	97	214	330
330-Porky Pig Meets the Bristled Bruiser (#2)	8	16	24	51	96	140
331-Alice in Wonderland (Disney) (1951)	16	32	48	112	249	385
332-Little Beaver	7	14	21	44	82	120
333-Wilderness Trek (Zane Grey) (5/51)	6	12	18	37	66	95
334-Mickey Mouse and Yukon Gold (Disney) (6/51)	11	22	33	72	154	235
335-Francis the Famous Talking Mule (#1, 6/51)-1st Dell non animated movie comic (all issues based on movie)	10	20	30	68	144	220
336-Woody Woodpecker (Lantz)	6	12	18	41	76	110
337-The Brownies-not by Walt Kelly	6	12	18	38	69	100
338-Bugs Bunny and the Rocking Horse Thieves	8	16	24	55	105	155
339-Donald Duck and the Magic Fountain-not by Carl Barks (Disney) (7-8/51)	33	66	99	238	532	825
340-King of the Royal Mounted (7/51)	7	14	21	46	86	125
341-Unbirthday Party with Alice in Wonderland (Disney) (7/51)	16	32	48	112	249	385
342-Porky Pig the Lucky Peppermint Mine; r/in Porky Pig #3	6	12	18	40	73	105
343-Mickey Mouse in The Ruby Eye of Homar-Guy-Am (Disney)-Reprinted in Mickey Mouse #104	9	18	27	62	126	190
344-Sergeant Preston from Challenge of The Yukon (#1) (TV)	12	24	36	83	182	280
345-Andy Panda in Scotland Yard (8-10/51) (Lantz)	6	12	18	41	76	110
346-Hideout (Zane Grey)	6	12	18	37	66	95

	GD 2.0	VG 4.0	FN 6.0	VF 8.0	VF/NM 9.0	NM- 9.2
347-Bugs Bunny the Frigid Hare (8-9/51)	8	16	24	55	105	155
348-Donald Duck "The Crocodile Collector"; Barks-c only (Disney) (9-10/51)	24	48	72	168	372	575
349-Uncle Wiggily	6	12	18	41	76	110
350-Woody Woodpecker (Lantz)	6	12	18	41	76	110
351-Porky Pig & the Grand Canyon Giant (9-10/51)	6	12	18	40	73	105
352-Mickey Mouse in The Mystery of Painted Valley (Disney)	9	18	27	62	126	190
353-Duck Album (#1)-Barks-c (Disney)	12	24	36	84	185	285
354-Raggedy Ann & Andy	7	14	21	46	86	125
355-Bugs Bunny Hot-Rod Hare	8	16	24	55	105	155
356-Donald Duck in "Rags to Riches"; Barks-c only	24	48	72	168	372	575
357-Comeback (Zane Grey)	5	10	15	33	57	80
358-Andy Panda (Lantz) (11-1/52)	6	12	18	41	76	110
359-Frosty the Snowman (#1)	10	20	30	68	144	220
360-Porky Pig in Tree of Fortune (11-12/51)	6	12	18	40	73	105
361-Santa Claus Funnies	8	16	24	51	96	140
362-Mickey Mouse and the Smuggled Diamonds (Disney)	9	18	27	62	126	190
363-King of the Royal Mounted	6	12	18	40	73	105
364-Woody Woodpecker (Lantz)	6	12	18	37	66	95
365-The Brownies-not by Kelly	6	12	18	38	69	100
366-Bugs Bunny Uncle Buckskin Comes to Town (12-1/52)	8	16	24	55	105	155
367-Donald Duck in "A Christmas for Shacktown" by Carl Barks (Disney) (1-2/52)	38	76	114	281	628	925
368-Bob Clampett's Beany and Cecil (#1)	24	48	72	168	372	575
369-The Lone Ranger's Famous Horse Hi-Yo Silver (#1); Silver's origin	11	22	33	72	154	235
370-Porky Pig in Trouble in the Big Trees	6	12	18	40	73	105
371-Mickey Mouse in The Inca Idol Case (1952) (Disney)	9	18	27	62	126	190
372-Riders of the Purple Sage (Zane Grey)	5	10	15	33	57	80
373-Sergeant Preston (TV)	8	16	24	56	108	160
374-Woody Woodpecker (Lantz)	6	12	18	37	66	95
375-John Carter of Mars (E. R. Burroughs)-Jesse Marsh-a; origin	32	64	96	230	515	800
376-Bugs Bunny, "The Magic Sneeze"	8	16	24	55	105	155
377-Susie Q. Smith	5	10	15	31	53	75
378-Tom Corbett, Space Cadet (#1) (TV)-McWilliams-a	17	34	51	117	259	400
379-Donald Duck in "Southern Hospitality"; 2nd Uncle Scrooge-c; not by Barks (Disney)	33	66	99	238	532	825
380-Raggedy Ann & Andy	7	14	21	46	86	125
381-Marge's Tubby (#1)	19	38	57	129	287	445
382-Snow White and the Seven Dwarfs (Disney)-origin; partial reprint of Four Color #49 (Movie)	11	22	33	73	157	240
383-Andy Panda (Lantz)	5	10	15	35	63	90
384-King of the Royal Mounted (3/52)(Zane Grey)	6	12	18	40	73	105
385-Porky Pig in The Isle of Missing Ships (3-4/52)	6	12	18	40	73	105
386-Uncle Scrooge (#1)-by Carl Barks (Disney) in "Only a Poor Old Man" (3/52)	185	370	555	1500	4000	6500
387-Mickey Mouse in High Tibet (Disney) (4-5/52)	9	18	27	62	126	190
388-Oswald the Rabbit (Lantz)	6	12	18	40	73	105
389-Andy Hardy Comics (#1)	6	12	18	40	73	105
390-Woody Woodpecker (Lantz)	6	12	18	37	66	95
391-Uncle Wiggily	6	12	18	41	76	110
392-Hi-Yo Silver	7	14	21	44	82	120
393-Bugs Bunny	8	16	24	55	105	155
394-Donald Duck in Malayalaya-Barks-c only (Disney)	24	48	72	168	372	575
395-Forlorn River(Zane Grey)-First Nevada (5/52)	5	10	15	33	57	80
396-Tales of the Texas Rangers(#1)(TV)-Photo-c	10	20	30	67	141	215
397-Sergeant Preston of the Yukon (TV) (5/52)	8	16	24	56	108	160
398-The Brownies-not by Kelly	6	12	18	38	69	100
399-Porky Pig in The Lost Gold Mine	6	12	18	40	73	105
400-Tom Corbett, Space Cadet (TV)-McWilliams-c/a	10	20	30	66	138	210
401-Mickey Mouse and Goofy's Mechanical Wizard (Disney) (6-7/52)	8	16	24	56	108	160
402-Mary Jane and Sniffles	9	18	27	59	117	175
403-Li'l Bad Wolf (Disney) (6/52)(#1)	8	16	24	56	108	160
404-The Range Rider (#1) (Flying A's...)(TV)-Photo-c	9	18	27	62	126	190
405-Woody Woodpecker (Lantz) (6-7/52)	6	12	18	37	66	95
406-Tweety and Sylvester (#1)	13	26	39	89	195	300
407-Bugs Bunny, Foreign-Legion Hare	7	14	21	48	89	130

Four Color Comics #468 © DIS

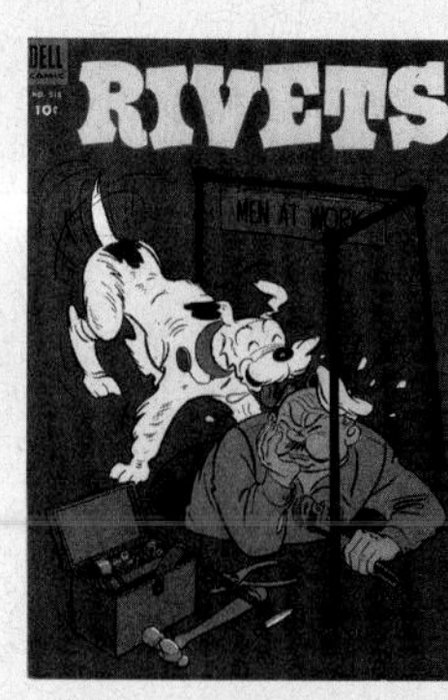

Four Color Comics #518 © DELL

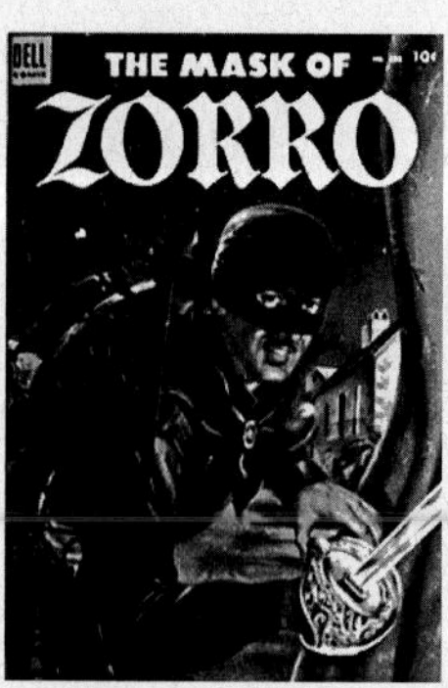

Four Color Comics #538 © J. McCulley

	GD 2.0	VG 4.0	FN 6.0	VF 8.0	VF/NM 9.0	NM- 9.2
408-Donald Duck and the Golden Helmet by Carl Barks (Disney) (7-8/52)	36	72	108	259	580	900
409-Andy Panda (7-9/52)	5	10	15	35	63	90
410-Porky Pig in The Water Wizard (7/52)	6	12	18	40	73	105
411-Mickey Mouse and the Old Sea Dog (Disney) (8-9/52)	8	16	24	56	108	160
412-Nevada (Zane Grey)	5	10	15	33	57	80
413-Robin Hood (Disney-Movie) (8/52)-Photo-c (1st Disney movie Four Color book)	9	18	27	60	120	180
414-Bob Clampett's Beany and Cecil (TV)	13	26	39	87	191	295
415-Rootie Kazootie (#1) (TV)	9	18	27	61	123	185
416-Woody Woodpecker (Lantz)	6	12	18	37	66	95
417-Double Trouble with Goober (#1) (8/52)	5	10	15	33	57	80
418-Rusty Riley, a Boy, a Horse, and a Dog (#1)-Frank Godwin-a (strip reprints) (8/52)	7	14	21	44	82	120
419-Sergeant Preston (TV)	8	16	24	56	108	160
420-Bugs Bunny in The Mysterious Buckaroo (8-9/52)	7	14	21	48	89	130
421-Tom Corbett, Space Cadet(TV)-McWilliams-a	10	20	30	66	138	210
422-Donald Duck and the Gilded Man, by Carl Barks (Disney) (9-10/52) (#423 on inside)	36	72	108	259	580	900
423-Rhubarb, Owner of the Brooklyn Ball Club (The Millionaire Cat) (#1)-Painted cover	7	14	21	44	82	120
424-Flash Gordon-Test Flight in Space (9/52)	12	24	36	81	176	270
425-Zorro, the Return of	11	22	33	75	160	245
426-Porky Pig in The Scalawag Leprechaun	6	12	18	40	73	105
427-Mickey Mouse and the Wonderful Whizzix (Disney) (10-11/52)-Reprinted in Mickey Mouse #100	8	16	24	56	108	160
428-Uncle Wiggily	5	10	15	34	63	90
429-Pluto in "Why Dogs Leave Home" (Disney) (10/52)(#1)	11	22	33	73	157	240
430-Marge's Tubby, the Shadow of a Man-Eater	11	22	33	73	157	240
431-Woody Woodpecker (10/52) (Lantz)	6	12	18	37	66	95
432-Bugs Bunny and the Rabbit Olympics	7	14	21	48	89	130
433-Wildfire (Zane Grey) (11-1/52-53)	5	10	15	33	57	80
434-Rin Tin Tin "In Dark Danger" (#1) (TV) (11/52)-Photo-c	15	30	45	103	227	350
435-Frosty the Snowman (11/52)	7	14	21	44	82	120
436-The Brownies-not by Kelly (11/52)	5	10	15	35	63	90
437-John Carter of Mars (E.R. Burroughs)-Marsh-a	17	34	51	119	265	410
438-Annie Oakley (#1) (TV)	13	26	39	89	195	300
439-Little Hiawatha (Disney) (12/52)j(#1)	7	14	21	46	86	125
440-Black Beauty (12/52)	5	10	15	35	63	90
441-Fearless Fagan	5	10	15	31	53	75
442-Peter Pan (Disney) (Movie)	10	20	30	70	150	230
443-Ben Bowie and His Mountain Men (#1)	9	18	27	63	129	195
444-Marge's Tubby	11	22	33	73	157	240
445-Charlie McCarthy	6	12	18	41	76	110
446-Captain Hook and Peter Pan (Disney)(Movie)(1/53)	9	18	27	61	123	185
447-Andy Hardy Comics	4	8	12	27	44	60
448-Bob Clampett's Beany and Cecil (TV)	13	26	39	87	191	295
449-Tappan's Burro (Zane Grey) (2-4/53)	5	10	15	33	57	80
450-Duck Album; Barks-c (Disney)	9	18	27	59	117	175
451-Rusty Riley-Frank Godwin-a (strip-r) (2/53)	5	10	15	30	50	70
452-Raggedy Ann & Andy (1953)	7	14	21	46	86	125
453-Susie Q. Smith (2/53)	5	10	15	31	53	75
454-Krazy Kat Comics; not by Herriman	6	12	18	37	66	95
455-Johnny Mack Brown Comics(3/53)-Photo-c	6	12	18	40	73	105
456-Uncle Scrooge Back to the Klondike (#2) by Barks (3/53) (Disney)	90	180	270	720	1860	3000
457-Daffy (#1)	12	24	36	81	176	270
458-Oswald the Rabbit (Lantz)	5	10	15	35	63	90
459-Rootie Kazootie (TV)	6	12	18	41	76	110
460-Buck Jones (4/53)	6	12	18	42	79	115
461-Marge's Tubby	10	20	30	68	144	220
462-Little Scouts	5	10	15	30	50	70
463-Petunia (4/53)	5	10	15	33	57	80
464-Bozo (4/53)	9	18	27	58	114	170
465-Francis the Famous Talking Mule	6	12	18	41	76	110
466-Rhubarb, the Millionaire Cat; painted-c	6	12	18	37	66	95
467-Desert Gold (Zane Grey) (5-7/53)	5	10	15	33	57	80
468-Goofy (#1) (Disney)	12	24	36	79	170	260
469-Beetle Bailey (#1) (5/53	13	26	39	86	188	290
470-Elmer Fudd	10	20	30	64	132	200
471-Double Trouble with Goober	4	8	12	27	44	60

	GD 2.0	VG 4.0	FN 6.0	VF 8.0	VF/NM 9.0	NM- 9.2
472-Wild Bill Elliott (6/53)-Photo-c	5	10	15	35	63	90
473-Li'l Bad Wolf (Disney) (6/53)(#2)	6	12	18	37	66	95
474-Mary Jane and Sniffles	7	14	21	44	82	120
475-M.G.M.'s The Two Mouseketeers (#1)	9	18	27	57	111	165
476-Rin Tin Tin (TV)-Photo-c	9	18	27	59	117	175
477-Bob Clampett's Beany and Cecil (TV)	13	26	39	87	191	295
478-Charlie McCarthy	6	12	18	41	76	110
479-Queen of the West Dale Evans (#1)-Photo-c	16	32	48	110	243	375
480-Andy Hardy Comics	4	8	12	27	44	60
481-Annie Oakley And Tagg (TV)	9	18	27	59	117	175
482-Brownies-not by Kelly	5	10	15	35	63	90
483-Little Beaver (7/53)	5	10	15	35	63	90
484-River Feud (Zane Grey) (8-10/53)	5	10	15	33	57	80
485-The Little People-Walt Scott (#1)	8	16	24	54	102	150
486-Rusty Riley-Frank Godwin strip-r	5	10	15	30	50	70
487-Mowgli, the Jungle Book (Rudyard Kipling's)	7	14	21	46	86	125
488-John Carter of Mars (Burroughs)-Marsh-a; painted-c	17	34	51	119	265	410
489-Tweety and Sylvester	8	16	24	54	102	150
490-Jungle Jim (#1)	9	18	27	58	114	170
491-Silvertip (#1) (Max Brand)-Kinstler-a (8/53)	8	16	24	52	99	145
492-Duck Album (Disney)	7	14	21	46	86	125
493-Johnny Mack Brown; photo-c	6	12	18	40	73	105
494-The Little King (#1)	8	16	24	56	108	160
495-Uncle Scrooge (#3) (Disney)-by Carl Barks (9/53)	60	120	180	480	1240	2000
496-The Green Hornet; painted-c	25	50	75	175	388	600
497-Zorro (Sword of...)-Kinstler-a	12	24	36	79	170	260
498-Bugs Bunny's Album (9/53)	6	12	18	38	69	100
499-M.G.M.'s Spike and Tyke (#1) (9/53)	7	14	21	49	92	135
500-Buck Jones	6	12	18	42	79	115
501-Francis the Famous Talking Mule	5	10	15	35	63	90
502-Rootie Kazootie (TV)	6	12	18	41	76	110
503-Uncle Wiggily (10/53)	5	10	15	34	63	90
504-Krazy Kat; not by Herriman	6	12	18	37	66	95
505-The Sword and the Rose (Disney) (10/53)(Movie)-Photo-c	8	16	24	55	105	155
506-The Little Scouts	5	10	15	30	50	70
507-Oswald the Rabbit (Lantz)	5	10	15	35	63	90
508-Bozo (10/53)	9	18	27	58	114	170
509-Pluto (Disney) (10/53)	7	14	21	46	86	125
510-Son of Black Beauty	5	10	15	31	53	75
511-Outlaw Trail (Zane Grey)-Kinstler-a	5	10	15	35	63	90
512-Flash Gordon (11/53)	9	18	27	62	126	190
513-Ben Bowie and His Mountain Men	5	10	15	34	60	85
514-Frosty the Snowman (11/53)	7	14	21	44	82	120
515-Andy Hardy	4	8	12	27	44	60
516-Double Trouble With Goober	4	8	12	27	44	60
517-Chip 'N' Dale (#1) (Disney)	11	22	33	76	163	250
518-Rivets (11/53)	5	10	15	31	53	75
519-Steve Canyon (#1)-Not by Milton Caniff	8	16	24	56	108	160
520-Wild Bill Elliott-Photo-c	5	10	15	35	63	90
521-Beetle Bailey (12/53)	7	14	21	49	92	135
522-The Brownies	5	10	15	35	63	90
523-Rin Tin Tin (TV)-Photo-c (12/53)	9	18	27	59	117	175
524-Tweety and Sylvester	8	16	24	54	102	150
525-Santa Claus Funnies	8	16	24	51	96	140
526-Napoleon	5	10	15	30	50	70
527-Charlie McCarthy	6	12	18	41	76	110
528-Queen of the West Dale Evans; photo-c	9	18	27	60	120	180
529-Little Beaver	5	10	15	35	63	90
530-Bob Clampett's Beany and Cecil (TV) (1/54)	13	26	39	87	191	295
531-Duck Album (Disney)	7	14	21	46	86	125
532-The Rustlers (Zane Grey) (2-4/54)	5	10	15	33	57	80
533-Raggedy Ann and Andy	7	14	21	46	86	125
534-Western Marshal (Ernest Haycox's)-Kinstler-a	6	12	18	41	76	110
535-I Love Lucy (#1) (TV) (2/54)-Photo-c	46	92	138	359	805	1250
536-Daffy (3/54)	7	14	21	49	92	135
537-Stormy, the Thoroughbred... (Disney-Movie) on top 2/3 of each page; Pluto story on bottom 1/3 of each page (2/54)	5	10	15	34	60	85
538-The Mask of Zorro; Kinstler-a	12	24	36	79	170	260
539-Ben and Me (Disney) (3/54)	5	10	15	30	50	70
540-Knights of the Round Table (3/54) (Movie)-Photo-c	6	12	18	41	76	110
541-Johnny Mack Brown; photo-c	6	12	18	40	73	105

Four Color Comics #589 © Buck Jones

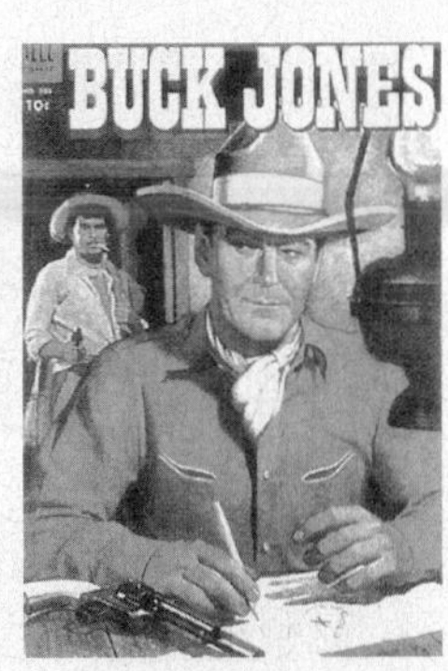

Four Color Comics #615 © WB

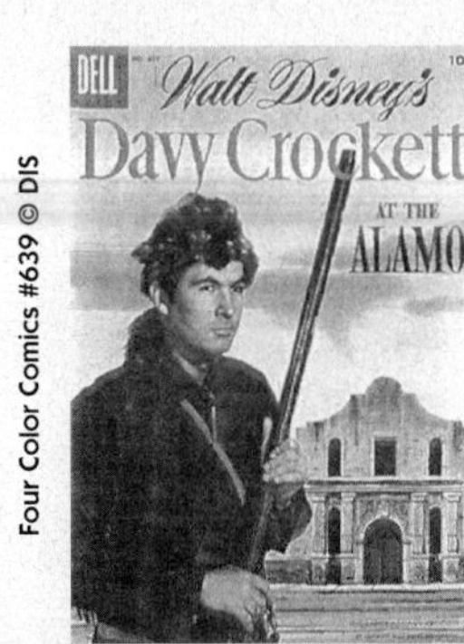

Four Color Comics #639 © DIS

	GD 2.0	VG 4.0	FN 6.0	VF 8.0	VF/NM 9.0	NM- 9.2
542-Super Circus Featuring Mary Hartline (TV) (3/54)	7	14	21	49	92	135
543-Uncle Wiggily (3/54)	5	10	15	34	63	90
544-Rob Roy (Disney-Movie)-Manning-a; photo-c	8	16	24	52	99	145
545-The Wonderful Adventures of Pinocchio-Partial reprint of Four Color #92 (Disney-Movie)	8	16	24	56	108	160
546-Buck Jones	6	12	18	42	79	115
547-Francis the Famous Talking Mule	5	10	15	35	63	90
548-Krazy Kat; not by Herriman (4/54)	5	10	15	31	53	75
549-Oswald the Rabbit (Lantz)	5	10	15	35	63	90
550-The Little Scouts	5	10	15	30	50	70
551-Bozo (4/54)	9	18	27	58	114	170
552-Beetle Bailey	7	14	21	49	92	135
553-Susie Q. Smith	5	10	15	31	53	75
554-Rusty Riley (Frank Godwin strip-r)	5	10	15	30	50	70
555-Range War (Zane Grey)	5	10	15	33	57	80
556-Double Trouble With Goober (5/54)	4	8	12	27	44	60
557-Ben Bowie and His Mountain Men	5	10	15	34	60	85
558-Elmer Fudd (5/54)	6	12	18	38	69	100
559-I Love Lucy (#2) (TV)-Photo-c	28	56	84	202	451	700
560-Duck Album (Disney) (5/54)	7	14	21	46	86	125
561-Mr. Magoo (5/54)	9	18	27	58	114	170
562-Goofy (Disney)(#2)	7	14	21	46	86	125
563-Rhubarb, the Millionaire Cat (6/54)	6	12	18	37	66	95
564-Li'l Bad Wolf (Disney)(#3)	6	12	18	37	66	95
565-Jungle Jim	5	10	15	34	60	85
566-Son of Black Beauty	5	10	15	31	53	75
567-Prince Valiant (#1)-By Bob Fuje (Movie)-Photo-c	10	20	30	66	138	210
568-Gypsy Colt (Movie) (6/54)	5	10	15	35	63	90
569-Priscilla's Pop	6	12	18	37	66	95
570-Bob Clampett's Beany and Cecil (TV)	13	26	39	87	191	295
571-Charlie McCarthy	6	12	18	41	76	110
572-Silvertip (Max Brand) (7/54); Kinstler-a	5	10	15	34	60	85
573-The Little People by Walt Scott	5	10	15	35	63	90
574-The Hand of Zorro; Kinstler-a	12	24	36	79	170	260
575-Annie Oakley and Tagg (TV)-Photo-c	9	18	27	59	117	175
576-Angel (#1) (8/54)	5	10	15	31	53	75
577-M.G.M.'s Spike and Tyke	5	10	15	35	63	90
578-Steve Canyon (8/54)	5	10	15	35	63	90
579-Francis the Famous Talking Mule	5	10	15	35	63	90
580-Six Gun Ranch (Luke Short-8/54)	5	10	15	33	57	80
581-Chip 'N' Dale (#2) (Disney)	6	12	18	42	79	115
582-Mowgli Jungle Book (Kipling) (8/54)	5	10	15	33	57	80
583-The Lost Wagon Train (Zane Grey)	5	10	15	33	57	80
584-Johnny Mack Brown-Photo-c	6	12	18	40	73	105
585-Bugs Bunny's Album	6	12	18	38	69	100
586-Duck Album (Disney)	7	14	21	46	86	125
587-The Little Scouts	5	10	15	30	50	70
588-King Richard and the Crusaders (Movie) (10/54) Matt Baker-a; photo-c	9	18	27	60	120	180
589-Buck Jones	6	12	18	42	79	115
590-Hansel and Gretel; partial photo-c	7	14	21	46	86	125
591-Western Marshal (Ernest Haycox's)-Kinstler-a	5	10	15	34	60	85
592-Super Circus (TV)	6	12	18	38	69	100
593-Oswald the Rabbit (Lantz)	5	10	15	35	63	90
594-Bozo (10/54)	9	18	27	58	114	170
595-Pluto (Disney)	6	12	18	40	73	105
596-Turok, Son of Stone (#1)	89	178	267	712	1606	2500
597-The Little King	5	10	15	34	60	85
598-Captain Davy Jones	6	12	18	37	66	95
599-Ben Bowie and His Mountain Men	5	10	15	34	60	85
600-Daisy Duck's Diary (#1) (Disney) (11/54)	8	16	24	51	96	140
601-Frosty the Snowman	7	14	21	44	82	120
602-Mr. Magoo and Gerald McBoing-Boing	9	18	27	58	114	170
603-M.G.M.'s The Two Mouseketeers	6	12	18	41	76	110
604-Shadow on the Trail (Zane Grey)	5	10	15	33	57	80
605-The Brownies-not by Kelly (12/54)	5	10	15	35	63	90
606-Sir Lancelot (not TV)	6	12	18	42	79	115
607-Santa Claus Funnies	8	16	24	51	96	140
608-Silvertip- "Valley of Vanishing Men" (Max Brand)-Kinstler-a	5	10	15	34	60	85
609-The Littlest Outlaw (Disney-Movie) (1/55)-Photo-c	6	12	18	41	76	110
610-Drum Beat (Movie); Alan Ladd photo-c	8	16	24	55	105	155

	GD 2.0	VG 4.0	FN 6.0	VF 8.0	VF/NM 9.0	NM- 9.2
611-Duck Album (Disney)	7	14	21	46	86	125
612-Little Beaver (1/55)	5	10	15	34	60	85
613-Western Marshal (Ernest Haycox's) (2/55)-Kinstler-a	5	10	15	34	60	85
614-20,000 Leagues Under the Sea (Disney) (Movie) (2/55)-Painted-c	9	18	27	59	117	175
615-Daffy	7	14	21	49	92	135
616-To the Last Man (Zane Grey)	5	10	15	33	57	80
617-The Quest of Zorro	11	22	33	75	160	245
618-Johnny Mack Brown; photo-c	6	12	18	40	73	105
619-Krazy Kat; not by Herriman	5	10	15	31	53	75
620-Mowgli Jungle Book (Kipling)	5	10	15	33	57	80
621-Francis the Famous Talking Mule (4/55)	5	10	15	33	57	80
622-Beetle Bailey	7	14	21	49	92	135
623-Oswald the Rabbit (Lantz)	5	10	15	33	57	80
624-Treasure Island(Disney-Movie)(4/55)-Photo-c	8	16	24	51	96	140
625-Beaver Valley (Disney-Movie)	6	12	18	37	66	95
626-Ben Bowie and His Mountain Men	5	10	15	34	60	85
627-Goofy (Disney) (5/55)	7	14	21	46	86	125
628-Elmer Fudd	6	12	18	38	69	100
629-Lady and the Tramp with Jock (Disney)	8	16	24	55	105	155
630-Priscilla's Pop	6	12	18	37	66	95
631-Davy Crockett, Indian Fighter (#1) (Disney) (5/55) (TV)-Fess Parker photo-c	14	28	42	98	217	335
632-Fighting Caravans (Zane Grey)	5	10	15	33	57	80
633-The Little People by Walt Scott (6/55)	5	10	15	35	63	90
634-Lady and the Tramp Album (Disney) (6/55)	6	12	18	41	76	110
635-Bob Clampett's Beany and Cecil (TV)	13	26	39	87	191	295
636-Chip 'N' Dale (Disney)	6	12	18	42	79	115
637-Silvertip (Max Brand)-Kinstler-a	5	10	15	34	60	85
638-M.G.M.'s Spike and Tyke (8/55)	5	10	15	35	63	90
639-Davy Crockett at the Alamo (Disney) (7/55) (TV)-Fess Parker photo-c	11	22	33	76	163	260
640-Western Marshal (Ernest Haycox's)-Kinstler-a	5	10	15	34	60	85
641-Steve Canyon (1955)-by Caniff	5	10	15	35	63	90
642-M.G.M.'s The Two Mouseketeers	6	12	18	41	76	110
643-Wild Bill Elliott; photo-c	5	10	15	33	57	80
644-Sir Walter Raleigh (5/55)-Based on movie "The Virgin Queen"; photo-c	6	12	18	42	79	115
645-Johnny Mack Brown; photo-c	6	12	18	40	73	105
646-Dotty Dripple and Taffy (#1)	6	12	18	37	66	95
647-Bugs Bunny's Album (9/55)	6	12	18	38	69	100
648-Jace Pearson of the Texas Rangers (TV)-Photo-c	6	12	18	40	73	105
649-Duck Album (Disney)	7	14	21	46	86	125
650-Prince Valiant; by Bob Fuje	8	16	24	51	96	140
651-King Colt (Luke Short) (9/55)-Kinstler-a	5	10	15	33	57	80
652-Buck Jones	5	10	15	35	63	90
653-Smokey the Bear (#1) (10/55)	10	20	30	67	141	215
654-Pluto (Disney)	6	12	18	40	73	105
655-Francis the Famous Talking Mule	5	10	15	33	57	80
656-Turok, Son of Stone (#2) (10/55)	37	74	111	274	612	950
657-Ben Bowie and His Mountain Men	5	10	15	34	60	85
658-Goofy (Disney)	7	14	21	46	86	125
659-Daisy Duck's Diary (Disney)(#2)	6	12	18	40	73	105
660-Little Beaver	5	10	15	34	60	85
661-Frosty the Snowman	7	14	21	44	82	120
662-Zoo Parade (TV)-Marlin Perkins (11/55)	5	10	15	34	60	85
663-Winky Dink (TV)	8	16	24	54	102	150
664-Davy Crockett in the Great Keelboat Race (TV) (Disney) (11/55)-Fess Parker photo-c	11	22	33	75	160	245
665-The African Lion (Disney-Movie) (11/55)	5	10	15	34	60	85
666-Santa Claus Funnies	8	16	24	51	96	140
667-Silvertip and the Stolen Stallion (Max Brand) (12/55)-Kinstler-a	5	10	15	34	60	85
668-Dumbo (Disney) (12/55)-First of two printings. Dumbo on cover with starry sky. Reprints 4-Color #234?; same-c as #234	10	20	30	66	138	210
668-Dumbo (Disney) (1/58)-Second printing. Same cover altered, with Timothy Mouse added. Same contents as above	7	14	21	44	82	120
669-Robin Hood (Disney-Movie) (12/55)-Reprints #413 plus-c; photo-c	5	10	15	35	63	90
670-M.G.M's Mouse Musketeers (#1) (1/56)-Formerly the Two Mouseketeers	6	12	18	38	69	100
671-Davy Crockett and the River Pirates (TV) (Disney) (12/55)-Jesse Marsh-a; Fess Parker photo-c	11	22	33	75	160	245

Four Color Comics #700 © DIS

Four Color Comics #748 © DELL

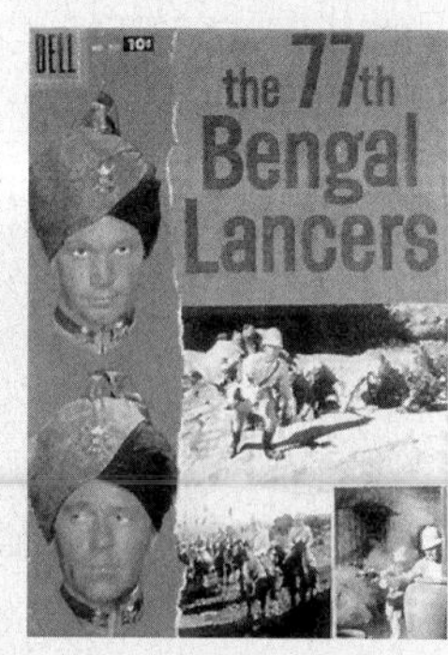

Four Color Comics #791 © DELL

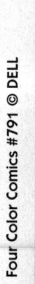

	GD 2.0	VG 4.0	FN 6.0	VF 8.0	VF/NM 9.0	NM- 9.2
672-Quentin Durward (1/56) (Movie)-Photo-c	6	12	18	42	79	115
673-Buffalo Bill, Jr. (#1) (TV)-James Arness photo-c	9	18	27	57	111	165
674-The Little Rascals (#1) (TV)	9	18	27	59	117	175
675-Steve Donovan, Western Marshal (#1) (TV)-Kinstler-a; photo-c	7	14	21	48	89	130
676-Will-Yum!	4	8	12	28	47	65
677-Little King	5	10	15	34	60	85
678-The Last Hunt (Movie)-Photo-c	6	12	18	42	79	115
679-Gunsmoke (#1) (TV)-Photo-c	17	34	51	119	265	410
680-Out Our Way with the Worry Wart (2/56)	5	10	15	31	53	75
681-Forever Darling (Movie) with Lucille Ball & Desi Arnaz (2/56)-; photo-c	10	20	30	69	147	225
682-The Sword & the Rose (Disney-Movie)-Reprint of #505; Renamed When Knighthood Was in Flower for the novel; photo-c	6	12	18	40	73	105
683-Hi and Lois (3/56)	5	10	15	35	63	90
684-Helen of Troy (Movie)-Buscema-a; photo-c	9	18	27	60	120	180
685-Johnny Mack Brown; photo-c	6	12	18	40	73	105
686-Duck Album (Disney)	7	14	21	46	86	125
687-The Indian Fighter (Movie)-Kirk Douglas photo-c	7	14	21	48	89	130
688-Alexander the Great (Movie) (5/56)-Buscema-a; photo-c	6	12	18	42	79	115
689-Elmer Fudd (3/56)	6	12	18	38	69	100
690-The Conqueror (Movie) - John Wayne photo-c	15	30	45	103	227	350
691-Dotty Dripple and Taffy	4	8	12	28	47	65
692-The Little People-Walt Scott	5	10	15	33	57	80
693-Song of the South (Disney) (1956)-Partial reprint of #129	8	16	24	51	96	140
694-Super Circus (TV)-Photo-c	6	12	18	38	69	100
695-Little Beaver	5	10	15	34	60	85
696-Krazy Kat; not by Herriman (4/56)	5	10	15	31	53	75
697-Oswald the Rabbit (Lantz)	5	10	15	33	57	80
698-Francis the Famous Talking Mule (4/56)	5	10	15	33	57	80
699-Prince Valiant-by Bob Fuje	8	16	24	51	96	140
700-Water Birds and the Olympic Elk (Disney-Movie) (4/56)	5	10	15	33	57	80
701-Jiminy Cricket (#1) (Disney) (5/56)	8	16	24	51	96	140
702-The Goofy Success Story (Disney)	7	14	21	46	86	125
703-Scamp (#1) (Disney)	9	18	27	59	117	175
704-Priscilla's Pop (5/56)	6	12	18	37	66	95
705-Brave Eagle (#1) (TV)-Photo-c	6	12	18	42	79	115
706-Bongo and Lumpjaw (Disney) (6/56)	6	12	18	41	76	110
707-Corky and White Shadow (Disney) (5/56)-Mickey Mouse Club (TV); photo-c	6	12	18	42	79	115
708-Smokey the Bear	6	12	18	40	73	105
709-The Searchers (Movie) - John Wayne photo-c	26	52	78	182	404	625
710-Francis the Famous Talking Mule	5	10	15	33	57	80
711-M.G.M's Mouse Musketeers	5	10	15	31	53	75
712-The Great Locomotive Chase (Disney-Movie) (9/56)-Photo-c	6	12	18	42	79	115
713-The Animal World (Movie) (8/56)	5	10	15	33	57	80
714-Spin and Marty (#1) (TV) (Disney)-Mickey Mouse Club (6/56); photo-c	11	22	33	75	160	245
715-Timmy (8/56)	6	12	18	37	66	95
716-Man in Space (Disney)(A science feature from Tomorrowland)	7	14	21	49	92	135
717-Moby Dick (Movie)-Gregory Peck photo-c	8	16	24	52	99	145
718-Dotty Dripple and Taffy	4	8	12	28	47	65
719-Prince Valiant; by Bob Fuje (8/56)	8	16	24	51	96	140
720-Gunsmoke (TV)-James Arness photo-c	9	18	27	59	117	175
721-Captain Kangaroo (TV)-Photo-c	13	26	39	91	201	310
722-Johnny Mack Brown-Photo-c	6	12	18	40	73	105
723-Santiago (Movie)-Kinstler-a (9/56); Alan Ladd photo-c	9	18	27	60	120	180
724-Bugs Bunny's Album	5	10	15	34	60	85
725-Elmer Fudd (9/56)	5	10	15	33	57	80
726-Duck Album (Disney) (9/56)	6	12	18	37	66	95
727-The Nature of Things (TV) (Disney)-Jesse Marsh-a	5	10	15	33	57	80
728-M.G.M's Mouse Musketeers	5	10	15	31	53	75
729-Bob Son of Battle (11/56)	4	8	12	28	47	65
730-Smokey Stover	5	10	15	34	60	85
731-Silvertip and The Fighting Four (Max Brand)-Kinstler-a	5	10	15	34	60	85
732-Zorro, the Challenge of (10/56)	11	22	33	75	160	245
733-Buck Jones	5	10	15	35	63	90

	GD 2.0	VG 4.0	FN 6.0	VF 8.0	VF/NM 9.0	NM- 9.2
734-Cheyenne (#1) (TV) (10/56)-Clint Walker photo-c	13	26	39	86	188	290
735-Crusader Rabbit (#1) (TV)	21	42	63	147	324	500
736-Pluto (Disney)	6	12	18	40	73	105
737-Steve Canyon-Caniff-a	5	10	15	35	63	90
738-Westward Ho, the Wagons (Disney-Movie)-Fess Parker photo-c	8	16	24	54	102	150
739-Bounty Guns (Luke Short)-Drucker-a	5	10	15	30	50	70
740-Chilly Willy (#1) (Walter Lantz)	8	16	24	54	102	150
741-The Fastest Gun Alive (Movie)(9/56)-Photo-c	7	14	21	44	82	120
742-Buffalo Bill, Jr. (TV)-Photo-c	6	12	18	37	66	95
743-Daisy Duck's Diary (Disney) (11/56)	6	12	18	40	73	105
744-Little Beaver	5	10	15	34	60	85
745-Francis the Famous Talking Mule	5	10	15	33	57	80
746-Dotty Dripple and Taffy	4	8	12	28	47	65
747-Goofy (Disney)	7	14	21	46	86	125
748-Frosty the Snowman (11/56)	5	10	15	35	63	90
749-Secrets of Life (Disney-Movie)-Photo-c	5	10	15	31	53	75
750-The Great Cat Family (Disney-TV/Movie)-Pinocchio & Alice app.	6	12	18	40	73	105
751-Our Miss Brooks (TV)-Photo-c	8	16	24	52	99	145
752-Mandrake, the Magician	10	20	30	70	150	230
753-Walt Scott's Little People (11/56)	5	10	15	33	57	80
754-Smokey the Bear	6	12	18	40	73	105
755-The Littlest Snowman (12/56)	5	10	15	35	63	90
756-Santa Claus Funnies	8	16	24	51	96	140
757-The True Story of Jesse James (Movie)-Photo-c	9	18	27	58	114	170
758-Bear Country (Disney-Movie)	5	10	15	34	60	85
759-Circus Boy (TV)-The Monkees' Mickey Dolenz photo-c (12/56)	12	24	36	81	176	270
760-The Hardy Boys (#1) (TV) (Disney)-Mickey Mouse Club; photo-c	10	20	30	65	165	205
761-Howdy Doody (TV) (1/57)	9	18	27	61	123	185
762-The Sharkfighters (Movie) (1/57); Buscema-a; photo-c	8	16	24	52	99	145
763-Grandma Duck's Farm Friends (#1) (Disney)	8	16	24	51	96	140
764-M.G.M's Mouse Musketeers	5	10	15	31	53	75
765-Will-Yum!	4	8	12	28	47	65
766-Buffalo Bill, Jr. (TV)-Photo-c	6	12	18	37	66	95
767-Spin and Marty (TV) (Disney)-Mickey Mouse Club (2/57)	9	18	27	58	114	170
768-Steve Donovan, Western Marshal (TV)-Kinstler-a; photo-c	6	12	18	38	69	100
769-Gunsmoke (TV)-James Arness photo-c	9	18	27	59	117	175
770-Brave Eagle (TV)-Photo-c	5	10	15	31	53	75
771-Brand of Empire (Luke Short)(3/57)-Drucker-a	5	10	15	30	50	70
772-Cheyenne (TV)-Clint Walker photo-c	8	16	24	51	96	140
773-The Brave One (Movie)-Photo-c	5	10	15	34	60	85
774-Hi and Lois (3/57)	4	8	12	28	47	65
775-Sir Lancelot and Brian (TV)-Buscema-a; photo-c	9	18	27	59	117	175
776-Johnny Mack Brown; photo-c	6	12	18	40	73	105
777-Scamp (Disney) (3/57)	6	12	18	40	73	105
778-The Little Rascals (TV)	6	12	18	38	69	100
779-Lee Hunter, Indian Fighter (3/57)	6	12	18	37	66	95
780-Captain Kangaroo (TV)-Photo-c	12	24	36	79	170	260
781-Fury (#1) (TV) (3/57)-Photo-c	7	14	21	49	92	135
782-Duck Album (Disney)	6	12	18	37	66	95
783-Elmer Fudd	5	10	15	33	57	80
784-Around the World in 80 Days (Movie) (2/57)-Photo-c	7	14	21	46	86	125
785-Circus Boy (TV) (4/57)-The Monkees' Mickey Dolenz photo-c	9	18	27	62	126	190
786-Cinderella (Disney) (3/57)-Partial-r of #272	6	12	18	42	79	115
787-Little Hiawatha (Disney) (4/57)(#2)	5	10	15	34	60	85
788-Prince Valiant; by Bob Fuje	7	14	21	44	82	120
789-Silvertip-Valley Thieves (Max Brand) (4/57)-Kinstler-a	5	10	15	34	60	85
790-The Wings of Eagles (Movie) (John Wayne)-Toth-a; John Wayne photo-c; 10¢ & 15¢ editions exist	13	26	39	89	195	300
791-The 77th Bengal Lancers (TV)-Photo-c	7	14	21	44	82	120
792-Oswald the Rabbit (Lantz)	5	10	15	33	57	80
793-Morty Meekle	5	10	15	30	50	70
794-The Count of Monte Cristo (5/57) (Movie)-Buscema-a	8	16	24	51	96	140
795-Jiminy Cricket (Disney)(#2)	6	12	18	38	69	100

Four Color Comics #823 © DELL

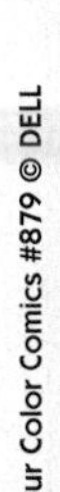
Four Color Comics #879 © DELL

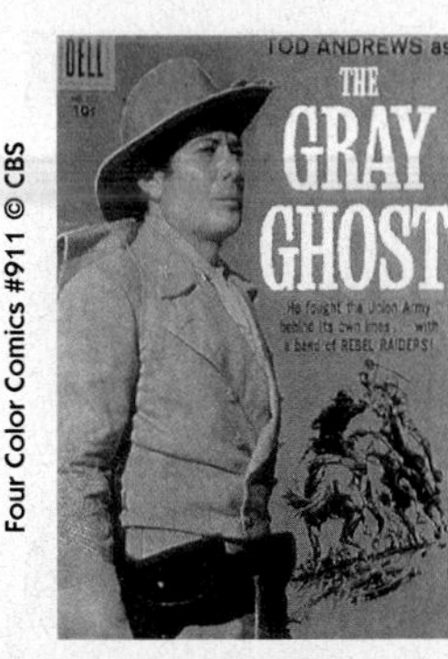

Four Color Comics #911 © CBS

	GD 2.0	VG 4.0	FN 6.0	VF 8.0	VF/NM 9.0	NM- 9.2
796-Ludwig Bemelman's Madeleine and Genevieve	5	10	15	31	53	75
797-Gunsmoke (TV)-Photo-c	9	18	27	59	117	175
798-Buffalo Bill, Jr. (TV)-Photo-c	6	12	18	37	66	95
799-Priscilla's Pop	6	12	18	37	66	95
800-The Buccaneers (TV)-Photo-c	6	12	18	42	79	115
801-Dotty Dripple and Taffy	4	8	12	28	47	65
802-Goofy (Disney) (5/57)	7	14	21	46	86	125
803-Cheyenne (TV)-Clint Walker photo-c	8	16	24	51	96	140
804-Steve Canyon-Caniff-a (1957)	5	10	15	35	63	90
805-Crusader Rabbit (TV)	16	32	48	111	246	380
806-Scamp (Disney) (6/57)	6	12	18	40	73	105
807-Savage Range (Luke Short)-Drucker-a	5	10	15	30	50	70
808-Spin and Marty (TV)(Disney)-Mickey Mouse Club; photo-c	9	18	27	58	114	170
809-The Little People (Walt Scott)	5	10	15	33	57	80
810-Francis the Famous Talking Mule	5	10	15	31	53	75
811-Howdy Doody (TV) (7/57)	9	18	27	61	123	185
812-The Big Land (Movie); Alan Ladd photo-c	8	16	24	52	99	145
813-Circus Boy (TV)-The Monkees' Mickey Dolenz photo-c	9	18	27	62	126	190
814-Covered Wagons, Ho! (Disney)-Donald Duck (TV) (6/57); Mickey Mouse app.	6	12	18	37	66	95
815-Dragoon Wells Massacre (Movie)-photo-c	7	14	21	49	92	135
816-Brave Eagle (TV)-photo-c	5	10	15	31	53	75
817-Little Beaver	5	10	15	34	60	85
818-Smokey the Bear (6/57)	6	12	18	40	73	105
819-Mickey Mouse in Magicland (Disney) (7/57)	6	12	18	41	76	110
820-The Oklahoman (Movie)-Photo-c	8	16	24	54	102	150
821-Wringle Wrangle (Disney)-Based on movie "Westward Ho, the Wagons"; Marsh-a; Fess Parker photo-c	7	14	21	46	86	125
822-Paul Revere's Ride with Johnny Tremain (TV) (Disney)-Toth-a	7	14	21	49	92	135
823-Timmy	5	10	15	33	57	80
824-The Pride and the Passion (Movie) (8/57)-Frank Sinatra & Cary Grant photo-c	9	18	27	61	123	185
825-The Little Rascals (TV)	6	12	18	38	69	100
826-Spin and Marty and Annette (TV) (Disney)-Mickey Mouse Club; Annette Funicello photo-c	18	36	54	126	281	435
827-Smokey Stover (8/57)	5	10	15	34	60	85
828-Buffalo Bill, Jr. (TV)-Photo-c	6	12	18	37	66	95
829-Tales of the Pony Express (TV) (8/57)-Painted-c	5	10	15	35	63	90
830-The Hardy Boys (TV) (Disney)-Mickey Mouse Club (8/57); photo-c	8	16	24	56	108	160
831-No Sleep 'Til Dawn (Movie)-Karl Malden photo-c	6	12	18	42	79	115
832-Lolly and Pepper (#1)	6	12	18	40	73	105
833-Scamp (Disney) (9/57)	6	12	18	40	73	105
834-Johnny Mack Brown; photo-c	6	12	18	40	73	105
835-Silvertip-The False Rider (Max Brand)	5	10	15	34	60	85
836-Man in Flight (Disney) (TV) (9/57)	6	12	18	41	76	110
837-Cotton Woods, (All-American Athlete...)	5	10	15	30	50	70
838-Bugs Bunny's Life Story Album (9/57)	5	10	15	34	60	85
839-The Vigilantes (Movie)	8	16	24	51	96	140
840-Duck Album (Disney) (9/57)	6	12	18	37	66	95
841-Elmer Fudd	5	10	15	33	57	80
842-The Nature of Things (Disney-Movie) ('57)-Jesse Marsh-a (TV series)	5	10	15	33	57	80
843-The First Americans (Disney) (TV)-Marsh-a	8	16	24	51	96	140
844-Gunsmoke (TV)-Photo-c	9	18	27	59	117	175
845-The Land Unknown (Movie)-Alex Toth-a	11	22	33	76	163	250
846-Gun Glory (Movie)-by Alex Toth; photo-c	8	16	24	51	96	140
847-Perri (squirrels) (Disney-Movie)-Two different covers published	6	12	18	37	66	95
848-Marauder's Moon (Luke Short)	5	10	15	30	50	70
849-Prince Valiant; by Bob Fuje	7	14	21	44	82	120
850-Buck Jones	5	10	15	35	63	90
851-The Story of Mankind (Movie) (1/58)-Hedy Lamarr & Vincent Price photo-c	7	14	21	48	89	130
852-Chilly Willy (2/58) (Lantz)	5	10	15	34	60	85
853-Pluto (Disney) (10/57)	6	12	18	40	73	105
854-The Hunchback of Notre Dame (Movie)-Photo-c	11	22	33	76	163	250
855-Broken Arrow (TV)-Photo-c	6	12	18	38	69	100
856-Buffalo Bill, Jr. (TV)-Photo-c	6	12	18	37	66	95
857-The Goofy Adventure Story (Disney) (11/57)	7	14	21	46	86	125
858-Daisy Duck's Diary (Disney) (11/57)	5	10	15	35	63	90
859-Topper and Neil (TV) (11/57)	6	12	18	38	69	100
860-Wyatt Earp (#1) (TV)-Manning-a; photo-c	10	20	30	65	135	205
861-Frosty the Snowman	5	10	15	35	63	90
862-The Truth About Mother Goose (Disney-Movie) (11/57)	7	14	21	44	82	120
863-Francis the Famous Talking Mule	5	10	15	31	53	75
864-The Littlest Snowman	5	10	15	35	63	90
865-Andy Burnett (TV) (Disney) (12/57)-Photo-c	8	16	24	54	102	150
866-Mars and Beyond (Disney-TV)(A science feature from Tomorrowland)	8	16	24	52	99	145
867-Santa Claus Funnies	8	16	24	51	96	140
868-The Little People (12/57)	5	10	15	33	57	80
869-Old Yeller (Disney-Movie)-Photo-c	6	12	18	38	69	100
870-Little Beaver (1/58)	5	10	15	34	60	85
871-Curly Kayoe	5	10	15	30	50	70
872-Captain Kangaroo (TV)-Photo-c	12	24	36	79	170	260
873-Grandma Duck's Farm Friends (Disney)	6	12	18	37	66	95
874-Old Ironsides (Disney-Movie with Johnny Tremain) (1/58)	6	12	18	42	79	115
875-Trumpets West (Luke Short) (2/58)	5	10	15	30	50	70
876-Tales of Wells Fargo (#1)(TV)(2/58)-Photo-c	8	16	24	52	99	145
877-Frontier Doctor with Rex Allen (TV)-Alex Toth-a; Rex Allen photo-c	9	18	27	57	111	165
878-Peanuts (#1)-Schulz-c only (2/58)	148	296	444	1243	2697	4150
879-Brave Eagle (TV) (2/58)-Photo-c	5	10	15	31	53	75
880-Steve Donovan, Western Marshal-Drucker-a (TV)-Photo-c	5	10	15	31	53	75
881-The Captain and the Kids (2/58)	5	10	15	30	50	70
882-Zorro (Disney)-1st Disney issue; by Alex Toth (TV) (2/58); photo-c	13	26	39	91	201	310
883-The Little Rascals (TV)	5	10	15	35	63	90
884-Hawkeye and the Last of the Mohicans (TV) (3/58); photo-c	7	14	21	44	82	120
885-Fury (TV) (3/58)-Photo-c	5	10	15	35	63	90
886-Bongo and Lumpjaw (Disney) (3/58)	5	10	15	31	53	75
887-The Hardy Boys (Disney) (TV)-Mickey Mouse Club (1/58)-Photo-c	8	16	24	56	108	160
888-Elmer Fudd (3/58)	5	10	15	33	57	80
889-Clint and Mac (Disney) (TV) (3/58)-Alex Toth-a; photo-c	10	20	30	64	132	200
890-Wyatt Earp (TV)-by Russ Manning; photo-c	7	14	21	46	86	125
891-Light in the Forest (Disney-Movie) (3/58)-Fess Parker photo-c	6	12	18	42	79	115
892-Maverick (#1) (TV) (4/58)-James Garner photo-c	19	38	57	131	291	450
893-Jim Bowie (TV)-Photo-c	6	12	18	41	76	110
894-Oswald the Rabbit (Lantz)	5	10	15	33	57	80
895-Wagon Train (#1) (TV) (3/58)-Photo-c	9	18	27	62	126	190
896-The Adventures of Tinker Bell (Disney)	10	20	30	66	138	210
897-Jiminy Cricket (Disney)	6	12	18	38	69	100
898-Silvertip (Max Brand)-Kinstler-a (5/58)	5	10	15	34	60	85
899-Goofy (Disney) (5/58)	5	10	15	35	63	90
900-Prince Valiant; by Bob Fuje	7	14	21	44	82	120
901-Little Hiawatha (Disney)	5	10	15	34	60	85
902-Will-Yum!	4	8	12	28	47	65
903-Dotty Dripple and Taffy	4	8	12	28	47	65
904-Lee Hunter, Indian Fighter	5	10	15	30	50	70
905-Annette (Disney) (TV) (5/58)-Mickey Mouse Club; Annette Funicello photo-c	23	46	69	156	348	540
906-Francis the Famous Talking Mule	5	10	15	31	53	75
907-Sugarfoot (#1) (TV)Toth-a; photo-c	10	20	30	67	141	215
908-The Little People and the Giant-Walt Scott (5/58)	5	10	15	33	57	80
909-Smitty	4	8	12	23	37	50
910-The Vikings (Movie)-Buscema-a; Kirk Douglas photo-c	8	16	24	56	108	160
911-The Gray Ghost (TV)-Photo-c	7	14	21	49	92	135
912-Leave It to Beaver (#1) (TV)-Photo-c	15	30	45	100	220	340
913-The Left-Handed Gun (Movie) (7/58); Paul Newman photo-c	9	18	27	57	111	165
914-No Time for Sergeants (Movie)-Andy Griffith photo-c; Toth-a	9	18	27	60	120	180
915-Casey Jones (TV)-Alan Hale photo-c	6	12	18	37	66	95
916-Red Ryder Ranch Comics (7/58)	4	8	12	28	47	65
917-The Life of Riley (TV)-Photo-c	10	20	30	66	138	210
918-Beep Beep, the Roadrunner (#1) (7/58)-Published with two different back covers	12	24	36	84	185	285

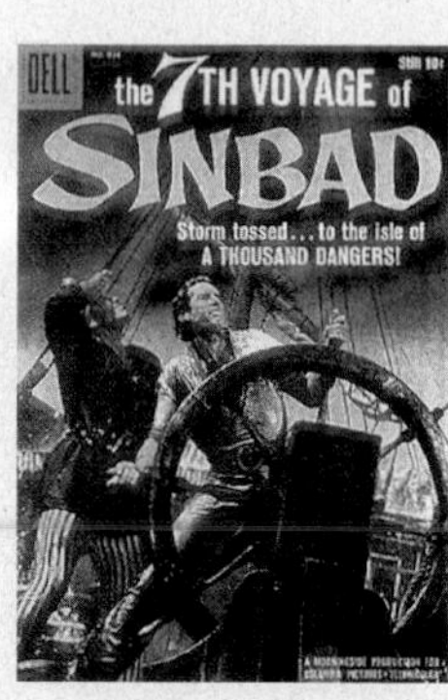

Four Color Comics #944 © Columbia Pict.

Four Color Comics #978 © Chicago Tribune

Four Color Comics #1016 © DELL

	GD 2.0	VG 4.0	FN 6.0	VF 8.0	VF/NM 9.0	NM- 9.2
919-Boots and Saddles (#1) (TV)-Photo-c	7	14	21	48	89	130
920-Zorro (Disney) (TV) (6/58)Toth-a; photo-c	10	20	30	66	138	210
921-Wyatt Earp (TV)-Manning-a; photo-c	7	14	21	46	86	125
922-Johnny Mack Brown by Russ Manning; photo-c	6	12	18	41	76	110
923-Timmy	5	10	15	33	57	80
924-Colt .45 (#1) (TV) (8/58)-W. Preston photo-c	9	18	27	62	126	190
925-Last of the Fast Guns (Movie) (8/58)-Photo-c	6	12	18	41	76	110
926-Peter Pan (Disney)-Reprint of #442	5	10	15	35	63	90
927-Top Gun (Luke Short) Buscema-a	5	10	15	30	50	70
928-Sea Hunt (#1) (9/58) (TV)-Lloyd Bridges photo-c	10	20	30	68	144	220
929-Brave Eagle (TV)-Photo-c	5	10	15	31	53	75
930-Maverick (TV) (7/58)-James Garner photo-c	10	20	30	65	135	205
931-Have Gun, Will Travel (#1) (TV)-Photo-c	12	24	36	84	185	285
932-Smokey the Bear (His Life Story)	6	12	18	40	73	105
933-Zorro (Disney, 9/58) (TV)-Alex Toth-a; photo-c	10	20	30	66	138	210
934-Restless Gun (#1) (TV)-Photo-c	9	18	27	61	123	185
935-King of the Royal Mounted	5	10	15	31	53	75
936-The Little Rascals (TV)	5	10	15	35	63	90
937-Ruff and Reddy (#1) (9/58) (TV) (1st Hanna-Barbera comic book)	10	20	30	69	147	225
938-Elmer Fudd (9/58)	5	10	15	33	57	80
939-Steve Canyon - not by Caniff	5	10	15	35	63	90
940-Lolly and Pepper (10/58)	4	8	12	28	47	65
941-Pluto (Disney) (10/58)	5	10	15	33	57	80
942-Pony Express (Tales of the ...) (TV)	5	10	15	31	53	75
943-White Wilderness (Disney-Movie) (10/58)	6	12	18	37	66	95
944-The 7th Voyage of Sinbad (Movie) (9/58)-Buscema-a; photo-c	11	22	33	77	166	255
945-Maverick (TV)-James Garner/Jack Kelly photo-c	10	20	30	65	135	205
946-The Big Country (Movie)-Photo-c	6	12	18	42	79	115
947-Broken Arrow (TV)-Photo-c (11/58)	5	10	15	31	53	75
948-Daisy Duck's Diary (Disney) (11/58)	5	10	15	35	63	90
949-High Adventure(Lowell Thomas')(TV)-Photo-c	5	10	15	34	60	85
950-Frosty the Snowman	5	10	15	35	63	90
951-The Lennon Sisters Life Story (TV)-Toth-a, 32 pgs.; photo-c	11	22	33	73	157	240
952-Goofy (Disney) (11/58)	5	10	15	35	63	90
953-Francis the Famous Talking Mule	5	10	15	31	53	75
954-Man in Space-Satellites (TV)	6	12	18	41	76	110
955-Hi and Lois (11/58)	4	8	12	28	47	65
956-Ricky Nelson (#1) (TV)-Photo-c	15	30	45	103	227	350
957-Buffalo Bee (#1) (TV)	8	16	24	54	102	150
958-Santa Claus Funnies	6	12	18	41	76	110
959-Christmas Stories-(Walt Scott's Little People) (1951-56 strip reprints)	5	10	15	33	57	80
960-Zorro (Disney) (TV) (12/58)-Toth art; photo-c	10	20	30	66	138	210
961-Jace Pearson's Tales of the Texas Rangers (TV)-Spiegle-a; photo-c	5	10	15	34	60	85
962-Maverick (TV) (1/59)-James Garner/Jack Kelly photo-c	10	20	30	65	135	205
963-Johnny Mack Brown; photo-c	6	12	18	40	73	105
964-The Hardy Boys (TV) (Disney) (1/59)-Mickey Mouse Club; photo-c	8	16	24	56	108	160
965-Grandma Duck's Farm Friends (Disney)(1/59)	5	10	15	34	60	85
966-Tonka (starring Sal Mineo; Disney-Movie)-Photo-c	8	16	24	54	102	150
967-Chilly Willy (2/59) (Lantz)	5	10	15	34	60	85
968-Tales of Wells Fargo (TV)-Photo-c	7	14	21	48	89	130
969-Peanuts (2/59)	34	68	102	245	548	850
970-Lawman (#1) (TV)-Photo-c	10	20	30	69	147	225
971-Wagon Train (TV)-Photo-c	6	12	18	41	76	110
972-Tom Thumb (Movie)-George Pal (1/59)	8	16	24	52	99	145
973-Sleeping Beauty and the Prince(Disney)(5/59)	11	22	33	76	163	250
974-The Little Rascals (TV) (3/59)	5	10	15	35	63	90
975-Fury (TV)-Photo-c	5	10	15	35	63	90
976-Zorro (Disney) (TV)-Toth-a; photo-c	10	20	30	66	138	210
977-Elmer Fudd (3/59)	5	10	15	33	57	80
978-Lolly and Pepper	4	8	12	28	47	65
979-Oswald the Rabbit (Lantz)	5	10	15	33	57	80
980-Maverick (TV) (4-6/59)-James Garner/Jack Kelly photo-c	10	20	30	65	135	205
981-Ruff and Reddy (TV) (Hanna-Barbera)	7	14	21	44	82	120
982-The New Adventures of Tinker Bell (TV) (Disney)	9	18	27	58	114	170
983-Have Gun, Will Travel (TV) (4-6/59)-Photo-c	9	18	27	60	120	180
984-Sleeping Beauty's Fairy Godmothers (Disney)	9	18	27	62	126	190
985-Shaggy Dog (Disney-Movie)-Photo-all four covers; Annette on back-c(5/59)	7	14	21	49	92	135
986-Restless Gun (TV)-Photo-c	7	14	21	46	86	125
987-Goofy (Disney) (7/59)	5	10	15	35	63	90
988-Little Hiawatha (Disney)	5	10	15	34	60	85
989-Jiminy Cricket (Disney) (5-7/59)	6	12	18	38	69	100
990-Huckleberry Hound (#1)(TV)(Hanna-Barbera); 1st app. Huck, Yogi Bear, & Pixie & Dixie & Mr. Jinks	17	34	51	117	259	400
991-Francis the Famous Talking Mule	5	10	15	31	53	75
992-Sugarfoot (TV)-Toth-a; photo-c	9	18	27	63	129	195
993-Jim Bowie (TV)-Photo-c	5	10	15	35	63	90
994-Sea Hunt (TV)-Lloyd Bridges photo-c	8	16	24	51	96	140
995-Donald Duck Album (Disney) (5-7/59)(#1)	7	14	21	44	82	120
996-Nevada (Zane Grey)	5	10	15	33	57	80
997-Walt Disney Presents-Tales of Texas John Slaughter (#1) (TV) (Disney)-Photo-c; photo of W. Disney inside-c	6	12	18	42	79	115
998-Ricky Nelson (TV)-Photo-c	15	30	45	103	227	350
999-Leave It to Beaver (TV)-Photo-c	12	24	36	83	182	280
1000-The Gray Ghost (TV) (6-8/59)-Photo-c	7	14	21	49	92	135
1001-Lowell Thomas' High Adventure (TV) (8-10/59)-Photo-c	5	10	15	33	57	80
1002-Buffalo Bee (TV)	6	12	18	41	76	110
1003-Zorro (TV) (Disney)-Toth-a; photo-c	10	20	30	66	138	210
1004-Colt .45 (TV) (6-8/59)-Photo-c	7	14	21	48	89	130
1005-Maverick (TV)-James Garner/Jack Kelly photo-c	10	20	30	65	135	205
1006-Hercules (Movie)-Buscema-a; photo-c	9	18	27	61	123	185
1007-John Paul Jones (Movie)-Robert Stack photo-c	6	12	18	37	66	95
1008-Beep Beep, the Road Runner (7-9/59)	8	16	24	51	96	140
1009-The Rifleman (#1) (TV)-Photo-c	23	46	69	156	348	540
1010-Grandma Duck's Farm Friends (Disney)-by Carl Barks	11	22	33	73	157	240
1011-Buckskin (#1) (TV)-Photo-c	7	14	21	44	82	120
1012-Last Train from Gun Hill (Movie) (7/59)-Photo-c	8	16	24	52	99	145
1013-Bat Masterson (#1) (TV) (8/59)-Gene Barry photo-c	10	20	30	69	147	225
1014-The Lennon Sisters (TV)-Toth-a; photo-c	10	20	30	69	147	225
1015-Peanuts-Schulz-c	34	68	102	245	548	850
1016-Smokey the Bear Nature Stories	5	10	15	31	53	75
1017-Chilly Willy (Lantz)	5	10	15	34	60	85
1018-Rio Bravo (Movie)(6/59)-John Wayne; Toth-a; John Wayne, Dean Martin & Ricky Nelson photo-c	27	54	81	189	420	650
1019-Wagon Train (TV)-Photo-c	6	12	18	41	76	110
1020-Jungle Jim-McWilliams-a	5	10	15	33	57	80
1021-Jace Pearson's Tales of the Texas Rangers (TV)-Photo-c	5	10	15	34	60	85
1022-Timmy	5	10	15	33	57	80
1023-Tales of Wells Fargo (TV)-Photo-c	7	14	21	48	89	130
1024-Darby O'Gill and the Little People (Disney-Movie)-Toth-a; photo-c	9	18	27	57	111	165
1025-Vacation in Disneyland (8-10/59)-Carl Barks-a(24pgs.) (Disney)	14	28	42	93	204	315
1026-Spin and Marty (TV) (Disney) (9-11/59)-Mickey Mouse Club; photo-c	7	14	21	44	82	120
1027-The Texan (#1)(TV)-Photo-c	8	16	24	55	105	155
1028-Rawhide (#1) (TV) (9-11/59)-Clint Eastwood photo-c; Tufts-a	23	46	69	161	356	550
1029-Boots and Saddles (TV) (9/59)-Photo-c	5	10	15	34	60	85
1030-Spanky and Alfalfa, the Little Rascals (TV)	5	10	15	35	63	90
1031-Fury (TV)-Photo-c	5	10	15	35	63	90
1032-Elmer Fudd	5	10	15	33	57	80
1033-Steve Canyon-not by Caniff; photo-c	5	10	15	35	63	90
1034-Nancy and Sluggo Summer Camp (9-11/59)	5	10	15	30	50	70
1035-Lawman (TV)-Photo-c	7	14	21	46	86	125
1036-The Big Circus (Movie)-Photo-c	6	12	18	40	73	105
1037-Zorro (Disney) (TV)-Tufts-a; Annette Funicello photo-c	12	24	36	81	176	270
1038-Ruff and Reddy (TV)(Hanna-Barbera)(1959)	7	14	21	44	82	120
1039-Pluto (Disney) (11-1/60)	5	10	15	33	57	80
1040-Quick Draw McGraw (#1) (TV) (Hanna-Barbera) (12-2/60)	12	24	36	83	182	280
1041-Sea Hunt (TV) (10-12/59)-Toth-a; Lloyd Bridges photo-c	8	16	24	51	96	140

Four Color Comics #1047 © DIS

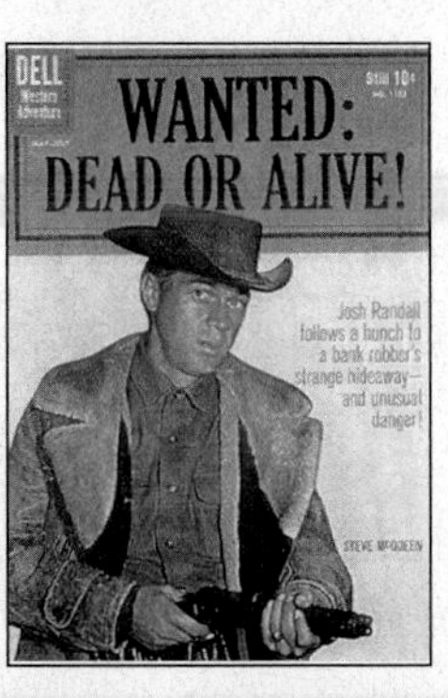

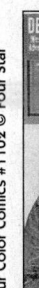

Four Color Comics #1102 © Four Star

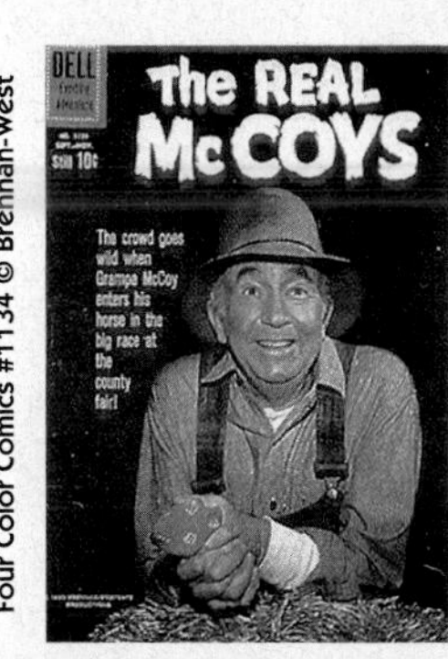

Four Color Comics #1134 © Brennan-West

	GD 2.0	VG 4.0	FN 6.0	VF 8.0	VF/NM 9.0	NM- 9.2
1042-The Three Chipmunks (Alvin, Simon & Theodore) (#1) (TV) (10-12/59)	9	18	27	62	126	190
1043-The Three Stooges (#1)-Photo-c	23	46	69	161	356	550
1044-Have Gun, Will Travel (TV)-Photo-c	9	18	27	60	120	180
1045-Restless Gun (TV)-Photo-c	7	14	21	46	86	125
1046-Beep Beep, the Road Runner (11-1/60)	8	16	24	51	96	140
1047-Gyro Gearloose (#1) (Disney)-All Barks-c/a	15	30	45	103	227	350
1048-The Horse Soldiers (Movie) (John Wayne)-Sekowsky-a; painted cover featuring John Wayne	11	22	33	76	163	250
1049-Don't Give Up the Ship (Movie) (8/59)-Jerry Lewis photo-c	9	18	27	58	114	170
1050-Huckleberry Hound (TV) (Hanna-Barbera) (10-12/59)	11	22	33	73	157	240
1051-Donald in Mathmagic Land (Disney-Movie)	8	16	24	56	108	160
1052-Ben-Hur (Movie) (11/59)-Manning-a	9	18	27	61	123	185
1053-Goofy (Disney) (11-1/60)	5	10	15	35	63	90
1054-Huckleberry Hound Winter Fun (TV) (Hanna-Barbera) (12/59)	11	22	33	73	157	240
1055-Daisy Duck's Diary (Disney)-by Carl Barks (11-1/60)	8	16	24	56	108	160
1056-Yellowstone Kelly (Movie)-Clint Walker photo-c	6	12	18	37	66	95
1057-Mickey Mouse Album (Disney)	6	12	18	37	66	95
1058-Colt .45 (TV)-Photo-c	7	14	21	48	89	130
1059-Sugarfoot (TV)-Photo-c	7	14	21	49	92	135
1060-Journey to the Center of the Earth (Movie)-Pat Boone & James Mason photo-c	11	22	33	75	160	245
1061-Buffalo Bee (TV)	6	12	18	41	76	110
1062-Christmas Stories (Walt Scott's Little People strip-r)	5	10	15	33	57	80
1063-Santa Claus Funnies	6	12	18	41	76	110
1064-Bugs Bunny's Merry Christmas (12/59)	5	10	15	34	60	85
1065-Frosty the Snowman	5	10	15	35	63	90
1066-77 Sunset Strip (#1) (TV)-Toth-a (1-3/60)-Efrem Zimbalist, Jr. & Edd "Kookie" Byrnes photo-c	9	18	27	61	123	185
1067-Yogi Bear (#1) (TV) (Hanna-Barbera)	12	24	36	84	185	285
1068-Francis the Famous Talking Mule	5	10	15	31	53	75
1069-The FBI Story (Movie)-Toth-a; James Stewart photo on-c	9	18	27	59	117	175
1070-Solomon and Sheba (Movie)-Sekowsky-a; photo-c	9	18	27	60	120	180
1071-The Real McCoys (#1) (TV) (1-3/60)-Toth-a; Walter Brennan photo-c	8	16	24	54	102	150
1072-Blythe (Marge's)	5	10	15	34	60	85
1073-Grandma Duck's Farm Friends-Barks-c/a (Disney)	11	22	33	73	157	240
1074-Chilly Willy (Lantz)	5	10	15	34	60	85
1075-Tales of Wells Fargo (TV)-Photo-c	7	14	21	48	89	130
1076-The Rebel (#1) (TV)-Sekowsky-a; photo-c	10	20	30	66	138	210
1077-The Deputy (#1) (TV)-Buscema-a; Henry Fonda photo-c	10	20	30	64	132	200
1078-The Three Stooges (2-4/60)-Photo-c	11	22	33	76	163	250
1079-The Little Rascals (TV) (Spanky & Alfalfa)	5	10	15	35	63	90
1080-Fury (TV) (2-4/60)-Photo-c	5	10	15	35	63	90
1081-Elmer Fudd	5	10	15	33	57	80
1082-Spin and Marty (Disney) (TV)-Photo-c	7	14	21	44	82	120
1083-Men into Space (TV)-Anderson-a; photo-c	6	12	18	38	69	100
1084-Speedy Gonzales	6	12	18	41	76	110
1085-The Time Machine (H.G. Wells) (Movie) (3/60)-Alex Toth-a; Rod Taylor photo-c	14	28	42	94	207	320
1086-Lolly and Pepper	4	8	12	28	47	65
1087-Peter Gunn (TV)-Photo-c	8	16	24	52	99	145
1088-A Dog of Flanders (Movie)-Photo-c	5	10	15	31	53	75
1089-Restless Gun (TV)-Photo-c	7	14	21	46	86	125
1090-Francis the Famous Talking Mule	5	10	15	31	53	75
1091-Jacky's Diary (4-6/60)	5	10	15	33	57	80
1092-Toby Tyler (Disney-Movie)-Photo-c	6	12	18	38	69	100
1093-MacKenzie's Raiders (Movie/TV)-Richard Carlson photo-c from TV show	6	12	18	37	66	95
1094-Goofy (Disney)	5	10	15	35	63	90
1095-Gyro Gearloose (Disney)-All Barks-c/a	9	18	27	59	117	175
1096-The Texan (TV)-Rory Calhoun photo-c	7	14	21	46	86	125
1097-Rawhide (TV)-Manning-a; Clint Eastwood photo-c	13	26	39	91	201	310
1098-Sugarfoot (TV)-Photo-c	7	14	21	49	92	135
1099-Donald Duck Album (Disney) (5-7/60)-Barks-c	7	14	21	44	82	120
1100-Annette's Life Story (Disney-Movie) (5/60)-Annette Funicello photo-c	18	36	54	122	271	420
1101-Robert Louis Stevenson's Kidnapped (Disney-Movie) (5/60); photo-c	6	12	18	37	66	95
1102-Wanted: Dead or Alive (#1) (TV) (5-7/60); Steve McQueen photo-c	11	22	33	76	163	250
1103-Leave It to Beaver (TV)-Photo-c	12	24	36	83	182	280
1104-Yogi Bear Goes to College (TV) (Hanna-Barbera) (6-8/60)	8	16	24	56	108	160
1105-Gale Storm (Oh! Susanna) (TV)-Toth-a; photo-c	10	20	30	66	138	210
1106-77 Sunset Strip(TV)(6-8/60)-Toth-a; photo-c	7	14	21	49	92	135
1107-Buckskin (TV)-Photo-c	6	12	18	40	73	105
1108-The Troubleshooters (TV)-Keenan Wynn photo-c	6	12	18	40	73	105
1109-This Is Your Life, Donald Duck (Disney) (TV) (8-10/60)-Gyro flashback to WDC&S #141; origin Donald Duck (1st told)	12	24	36	81	176	270
1110-Bonanza (#1) (TV) (6-8/60)-Photo-c	30	60	90	216	483	750
1111-Shotgun Slade (TV)-Photo-c	6	12	18	37	66	95
1112-Pixie and Dixie and Mr. Jinks (#1) (TV) (Hanna-Barbera) (7-9/60)	7	14	21	49	92	135
1113-Tales of Wells Fargo (TV)-Photo-c	7	14	21	48	89	130
1114-Huckleberry Finn (Movie) (7/60)-Photo-c	6	12	18	40	73	105
1115-Ricky Nelson (TV)-Manning-a; photo-c	12	24	36	80	173	265
1116-Boots and Saddles (TV) (8/60)-Photo-c	5	10	15	34	60	85
1117-Boy and the Pirates (Movie)-Photo-c	6	12	18	37	66	95
1118-The Sword and the Dragon (Movie) (6/60)-Photo-c	8	16	24	51	96	140
1119-Smokey the Bear Nature Stories	5	10	15	31	53	75
1120-Dinosaurus (Movie)-Painted-c	8	16	24	51	96	140
1121-Hercules Unchained (Movie) (8/60)-Crandall/Evans-a	9	18	27	57	111	165
1122-Chilly Willy (Lantz)	5	10	15	34	60	85
1123-Tombstone Territory (TV)-Photo-c	7	14	21	49	92	135
1124-Whirlybirds (#1) (TV)-Photo-c	7	14	21	49	92	135
1125-Laramie (#1) (TV)-Photo-c; G. Kane/Heath-a	8	16	24	54	102	150
1126-Hotel Deparee - Sundance (TV) (8-10/60)-Earl Holliman photo-c	6	12	18	40	73	105
1127-The Three Stooges-Photo-c (8-10/60)	11	22	33	76	163	250
1128-Rocky and His Friends (#1) (TV) (Jay Ward) (8-10/60)	26	52	78	182	404	625
1129-Pollyanna (Disney-Movie)-Hayley Mills photo-c	7	14	21	49	92	135
1130-The Deputy (TV)-Buscema-a; Henry Fonda photo-c	8	16	24	54	102	150
1131-Elmer Fudd (9-11/60)	5	10	15	33	57	80
1132-Space Mouse (Lantz) (8-10/60)	5	10	15	33	57	80
1133-Fury (TV)-Photo-c	5	10	15	35	63	90
1134-Real McCoys (TV)-Toth-a; photo-c	8	16	24	54	102	150
1135-M.G.M.'s Mouse Musketeers (9-11/60)	4	8	12	28	47	65
1136-Jungle Cat (Disney-Movie)-Photo-c	6	12	18	37	66	95
1137-The Little Rascals (TV)	5	10	15	35	63	90
1138-The Rebel (TV)-Photo-c	8	16	24	55	105	155
1139-Spartacus (Movie) (11/60)-Buscema-a; Kirk Douglas photo-c	11	22	33	75	160	245
1140-Donald Duck Album (Disney)-Barks-c	7	14	21	44	82	120
1141-Huckleberry Hound for President (TV) (Hanna-Barbera) (10/60)	7	14	21	46	86	125
1142-Johnny Ringo (TV)-Photo-c	6	12	18	41	76	110
1143-Pluto (Disney) (11-1/61)	5	10	15	33	57	80
1144-The Story of Ruth (Movie)-Photo-c	9	18	27	57	111	165
1145-The Lost World (Movie)-Gil Kane-a; photo-c; 1 pg. Conan Doyle biography by Torres	9	18	27	59	117	175
1146-Restless Gun (TV)-Photo-c; Wildey-a	7	14	21	46	86	125
1147-Sugarfoot (TV)-Photo-c	7	14	21	49	92	135
1148-I Aim at the Stars-the Werner Von Braun Story (Movie) (11-1/61)-Photo-c	6	12	18	41	76	110
1149-Goofy (Disney) (11-1/61)	5	10	15	35	63	90
1150-Daisy Duck's Diary (Disney) (12-1/61) by Carl Barks	8	16	24	56	108	160
1151-Mickey Mouse Album (Disney) (11-1/61)	6	12	18	37	66	95
1152-Rocky and His Friends (TV) (Jay Ward) (12-2/61)	16	32	48	107	236	365
1153-Frosty the Snowman	5	10	15	35	63	90
1154-Santa Claus Funnies	6	12	18	41	76	110
1155-North to Alaska (Movie)-John Wayne photo-c	15	30	45	100	220	340

Four Color Comics #1180 © Danny Thomas

Four Color Comics #1195 © DELL

Four Color Comics #1216 © DELL

	GD 2.0	VG 4.0	FN 6.0	VF 8.0	VF/NM 9.0	NM- 9.2
1156-Walt Disney Swiss Family Robinson (Movie) (12/60)-Photo-c	8	16	24	51	96	140
1157-Master of the World (Movie) (7/61)	8	16	24	52	99	145
1158-Three Worlds of Gulliver (2 issues exist with different covers) (Movie)-Photo-c	6	12	18	42	79	115
1159-77 Sunset Strip (TV)-Toth-a; photo-c	7	14	21	49	92	135
1160-Rawhide (TV)-Clint Eastwood photo-c	13	26	39	91	201	310
1161-Grandma Duck's Farm Friends (Disney) by Carl Barks (2-4/61)	11	22	33	73	157	240
1162-Yogi Bear Joins the Marines (TV) (Hanna-Barbera) (5-7/61)	8	16	24	56	108	160
1163-Daniel Boone (3-5/61); Marsh-a	5	10	15	35	63	90
1164-Wanted: Dead or Alive (TV)-Steve McQueen photo-c	9	18	27	58	114	170
1165-Ellery Queen (#1) (3-5/61)	9	18	27	58	114	175
1166-Rocky and His Friends (TV) (Jay Ward)	16	32	48	107	236	365
1167-Tales of Wells Fargo (TV)-Photo-c	7	14	21	44	82	120
1168-The Detectives (TV)-Robert Taylor photo-c	9	18	27	61	123	185
1169-New Adventures of Sherlock Holmes	12	24	36	79	170	260
1170-The Three Stooges (3-5/61)-Photo-c	11	22	33	76	163	250
1171-Elmer Fudd	5	10	15	33	57	80
1172-Fury (TV)-Photo-c	5	10	15	35	63	90
1173-The Twilight Zone (#1) (TV) (5/61)-Crandall/Evans-c/a; Crandall tribute to Ingles	20	40	60	138	307	475
1174-The Little Rascals (TV)	5	10	15	33	57	80
1175-M.G.M.'s Mouse Musketeers (3-5/61)	4	8	12	28	47	65
1176-Dondi (Movie)-Origin; photo-c	6	12	18	37	66	95
1177-Chilly Willy (Lantz) (4-6/61)	5	10	15	34	60	85
1178-Ten Who Dared (Disney-Movie) (12/60)-Painted-c; cast member photo on back-c	7	14	21	46	86	125
1179-The Swamp Fox (TV) (Disney)-Leslie Nielsen photo-c	8	16	24	56	108	160
1180-The Danny Thomas Show (TV)-Toth-a; photo-c	14	28	42	96	211	325
1181-Texas John Slaughter (TV) (Walt Disney Presents...) (4-6/61)-Photo-c	5	10	15	35	63	90
1182-Donald Duck Album (Disney) (5-7/61)	5	10	15	34	60	85
1183-101 Dalmatians (Disney-Movie) (3/61)	10	20	30	66	138	210
1184-Gyro Gearloose; All Barks-c/a (Disney) (5-7/61) Two variations exist	9	18	27	59	117	175
1185-Sweetie Pie	6	12	18	37	66	95
1186-Yak Yak (#1) by Jack Davis (2 versions - one minus 3-pg. Davis-c/a)	8	16	24	54	102	150
1187-The Three Stooges (6-8/61)-Photo-c	11	22	33	76	163	250
1188-Atlantis, the Lost Continent (Movie) (5/61)-Photo-c	9	18	27	60	120	180
1189-Greyfriars Bobby (Disney-Movie) (11/61)-Photo-c (scarce)	6	12	18	41	76	110
1190-Donald and the Wheel (Disney-Movie) (11/61); Barks-c	8	16	24	54	102	150
1191-Leave It to Beaver (TV)-Photo-c	12	24	36	83	182	280
1192-Ricky Nelson (TV)-Manning-a; photo-c	12	24	36	80	173	265
1193-The Real McCoys (TV) (6-8/61)-Photo-c	7	14	21	48	89	130
1194-Pepe (Movie) (4/61)-Photo-c	5	10	15	30	50	70
1195-National Velvet (#1) (TV)-Photo-c	6	12	18	41	76	110
1196-Pixie and Dixie and Mr. Jinks (TV) (Hanna-Barbera) (7-9/61)	5	10	15	35	63	90
1197-The Aquanauts (TV) (5-7/61)-Photo-c	6	12	18	41	76	110
1198-Donald in Mathmagic Land (Disney-Movie)-Reprint of #1051	6	12	18	37	66	95
1199-The Absent-Minded Professor (Disney-Movie) (4/61)-Photo-c	7	14	21	49	92	135
1199-Shaggy Dog & The Absent-Minded Professor (Disney-Movie) (8/67)-Photo-c	7	14	21	49	92	135
1200-Hennessey (TV) (8-10/61)-Gil Kane-a; photo-c	7	14	21	48	89	130
1201-Goofy (Disney) (8-10/61)	5	10	15	35	63	90
1202-Rawhide (TV)-Clint Eastwood photo-c	13	26	39	91	201	310
1203-Pinocchio (Disney) (3/62)	6	12	18	42	79	115
1204-Scamp (Disney)	4	8	12	27	44	60
1205-David and Goliath (Movie) (7/61)-Photo-c	7	14	21	44	82	120
1206-Lolly and Pepper (9-11/61)	4	8	12	28	47	65
1207-The Rebel (TV)-Sekowsky-a; photo-c	8	16	24	55	105	155
1208-Rocky and His Friends (Jay Ward) (TV)	16	32	48	107	236	365
1209-Sugarfoot (TV)-Photo-c (10-12/61)	7	14	21	49	92	135
1210-The Parent Trap (Disney-Movie) (8/61)-Hayley Mills photo-c	9	18	27	58	114	170
1211-77 Sunset Strip (TV)-Manning-a; photo-c	7	14	21	46	86	125
1212-Chilly Willy (Lantz) (7-9/61)	5	10	15	34	60	85
1213-Mysterious Island (Movie)-Photo-c	8	16	24	52	99	145
1214-Smokey the Bear	5	10	15	31	53	75
1215-Tales of Wells Fargo (TV) (10-12/61)-Photo-c	7	14	21	44	82	120
1216-Whirlybirds (TV)-Photo-c	7	14	21	46	86	125
1218-Fury (TV)-Photo-c	5	10	15	35	63	90
1219-The Detectives (TV)-Robert Taylor & Adam West photo-c	9	18	27	61	123	185
1220-Gunslinger (TV)-Photo-c	8	16	24	52	99	145
1221-Bonanza (TV) (9-11/61)-Photo-c	15	30	45	100	220	340
1222-Elmer Fudd (9-11/61)	5	10	15	33	57	80
1223-Laramie (TV)-Gil Kane-a; photo-c	6	12	18	37	66	95
1224-The Little Rascals (TV) (10-12/61)	5	10	15	33	57	80
1225-The Deputy (TV)-Henry Fonda photo-c	8	16	24	54	102	150
1226-Nikki, Wild Dog of the North (Disney-Movie) (9/61)-Photo-c	5	10	15	33	57	80
1227-Morgan the Pirate (Movie)-Photo-c	7	14	21	46	86	125
1229-Thief of Baghdad (Movie)-Crandall/Evans-a; photo-c	6	12	18	41	76	110
1230-Voyage to the Bottom of the Sea (#1) (Movie)-Photo insert on-c	10	20	30	70	150	230
1231-Danger Man (TV) (9-11/61)-Patrick McGoohan photo-c	10	20	30	68	144	220
1232-On the Double (Movie)	5	10	15	34	60	85
1233-Tammy Tell Me True (Movie) (1961)	7	14	21	44	82	120
1234-The Phantom Planet (Movie) (1961)	7	14	21	49	92	135
1235-Mister Magoo (#1) (12-2/62)	7	14	21	48	89	130
1235-Mister Magoo (3-5/65) 2nd printing; reprint of 12-2/62 issue	5	10	15	35	63	90
1236-King of Kings (Movie)-Photo-c	7	14	21	46	86	125
1237-The Untouchables (#1) (TV)-Not by Toth; photo-c	17	34	51	117	259	400
1238-Deputy Dawg (TV)	9	18	27	63	129	195
1239-Donald Duck Album (Disney) (10-12/61)-Barks-c	7	14	21	44	82	120
1240-The Detectives (TV)-Tufts-a; Robert Taylor photo-c	8	16	24	51	96	140
1241-Sweetie Pie	5	10	15	30	50	70
1242-King Leonardo and His Short Subjects (#1) (TV) (11-1/62)	10	20	30	67	141	215
1243-Ellery Queen	7	14	21	48	89	130
1244-Space Mouse (Lantz) (11-1/62)	5	10	15	33	57	80
1245-New Adventures of Sherlock Holmes	10	20	30	70	150	230
1246-Mickey Mouse Album (Disney)	6	12	18	37	66	95
1247-Daisy Duck's Diary (Disney) (12-2/62)	5	10	15	35	63	90
1248-Pluto (Disney)	5	10	15	33	57	80
1249-The Danny Thomas Show (TV)-Manning-a; photo-c	12	24	36	80	173	265
1250-The Four Horsemen of the Apocalypse (Movie)-Photo-c	7	14	21	49	92	135
1251-Everything's Ducky (Movie) (1961)	6	12	18	37	66	95
1252-The Andy Griffith Show (TV)-Photo-c; 1st show aired 10/3/60	38	76	114	285	641	1000
1253-Space Man (#1) (1-3/62)	8	16	24	51	96	140
1254- "Diver Dan" (#1) (TV) (2-4/62)-Photo-c	5	10	15	33	57	80
1255-The Wonders of Aladdin (Movie) (1961)	6	12	18	40	73	105
1256-Kona, Monarch of Monster Isle (#1) (2-4/62)-Glanzman-a	9	18	27	61	123	185
1257-Car 54, Where Are You? (#1) (TV) (3-5/62)-Photo-c	8	16	24	56	108	160
1258-The Frogmen (#1)-Evans-a	8	16	24	54	102	150
1259-El Cid (Movie) (1961)-Photo-c	7	14	21	46	86	125
1260-The Horsemasters (TV, Movie) (Disney) (12-2/62)-Annette Funicello photo-c	10	20	30	69	147	225
1261-Rawhide (TV)-Clint Eastwood photo-c	13	26	39	91	201	310
1262-The Rebel (TV)-Photo-c	8	16	24	55	105	155
1263-77 Sunset Strip (TV) (12-2/62)-Manning-a; photo-c	7	14	21	46	86	125
1264-Pixie and Dixie and Mr. Jinks (TV) (Hanna-Barbera)	5	10	15	35	63	90
1265-The Real McCoys (TV)-Photo-c	7	14	21	48	89	130
1266-M.G.M.'s Spike and Tyke (12-2/62)	4	8	12	28	47	65
1267-Gyro Gearloose; Barks-c/a, 4 pgs. (Disney) (12-2/62)						

Four Color Comics #1307 © DELL

Four Favorites #12 © ACE

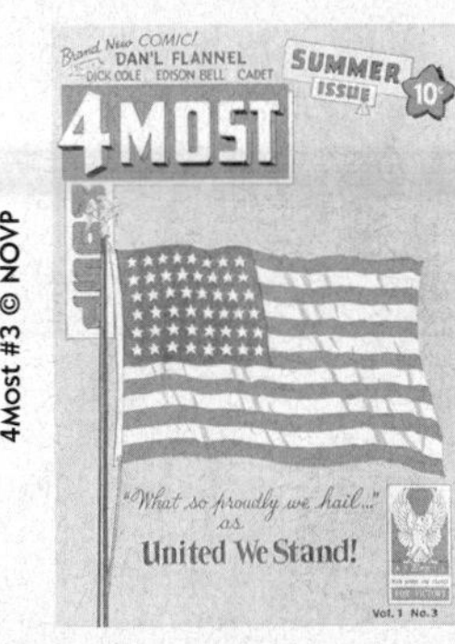

4Most #3 © NOVP

	GD 2.0	VG 4.0	FN 6.0	VF 8.0	VF/NM 9.0	NM- 9.2
	7	14	21	48	89	130
1268-Oswald the Rabbit (Lantz)	5	10	15	33	57	80
1269-Rawhide (TV)-Clint Eastwood photo-c	13	26	39	91	201	310
1270-Bullwinkle and Rocky (#1) (TV) (Jay Ward) (3-5/62)	16	32	48	112	249	385
1271-Yogi Bear Birthday Party (TV) (Hanna-Barbera) (11/61) (Given away for 1 box top from Kellogg's Corn Flakes)	6	12	18	40	73	105
1272-Frosty the Snowman	5	10	15	35	63	90
1273-Hans Brinker (Disney-Movie)-Photo-c (2/62)	6	12	18	37	66	95
1274-Santa Claus Funnies (12/61)	6	12	18	41	76	110
1275-Rocky and His Friends (TV) (Jay Ward)	16	32	48	107	236	365
1276-Dondi	4	8	12	28	47	65
1278-King Leonardo and His Short Subjects (TV)	10	20	30	67	141	215
1279-Grandma Duck's Farm Friends (Disney)	5	10	15	34	60	85
1280-Hennesey (TV)-Photo-c	6	12	18	40	73	105
1281-Chilly Willy (Lantz) (4-6/62)	5	10	15	34	60	85
1282-Babes in Toyland (Disney-Movie) (1/62); Annette Funicello photo-c	13	26	39	86	188	290
1283-Bonanza (TV) (2-4/62)-Photo-c	15	30	45	100	220	340
1284-Laramie (TV)-Heath-a; photo-c	6	12	18	37	66	95
1285-Leave It to Beaver (TV)-Photo-c	12	24	36	83	182	280
1286-The Untouchables (TV)-Photo-c	12	24	36	82	179	275
1287-Man from Wells Fargo (TV)-Photo-c	6	12	18	40	73	105
1288-Twilight Zone (TV) (4/62)-Crandall/Evans-c/a	11	22	33	72	154	235
1289-Ellery Queen	7	14	21	48	89	130
1290-M.G.M.'s Mouse Musketeers	4	8	12	28	47	65
1291-77 Sunset Strip (TV)-Manning-a; photo-c	7	14	21	46	86	125
1293-Elmer Fudd (3-5/62)	5	10	15	33	57	80
1294-Ripcord (TV)	6	12	18	40	73	105
1295-Mister Ed, the Talking Horse (#1) (TV) (3-5/62)-Photo-c	12	24	36	80	173	265
1296-Fury (TV) (3-5/62)-Photo-c	5	10	15	35	63	90
1297-Spanky, Alfalfa and the Little Rascals (TV)	5	10	15	33	57	80
1298-The Hathaways (TV)-Photo-c	5	10	15	31	53	75
1299-Deputy Dawg (TV)	9	18	27	63	129	195
1300-The Comancheros (Movie) (1961)-John Wayne photo-c	14	28	42	94	207	320
1301-Adventures in Paradise (TV) (2-4/62)	6	12	18	37	66	95
1302-Johnny Jason, Teen Reporter (2-4/62)	4	8	12	23	37	50
1303-Lad: A Dog (Movie)-Photo-c	5	10	15	33	57	80
1304-Nellie the Nurse (3-5/62)-Stanley-a	9	18	27	57	111	165
1305-Mister Magoo (3-5/62)	7	14	21	48	89	130
1306-Target: The Corruptors (#1) (TV) (3-5/62)-Photo-c	5	10	15	33	57	80
1307-Margie (TV) (3-5/62)	6	12	18	42	79	115
1308-Tales of the Wizard of Oz (TV) (3-5/62)	12	24	36	83	182	280
1309-87th Precinct (#1) (TV) (4-6/62)-Krigstein-a; photo-c	9	18	27	60	120	180
1310-Huck and Yogi Winter Sports (TV) (Hanna-Barbera) (3/62)	8	16	24	51	96	140
1311-Rocky and His Friends (TV) (Jay Ward)	16	32	48	107	236	365
1312-National Velvet (TV)-Photo-c	4	8	12	27	44	60
1313-Moon Pilot (Disney-Movie)-Photo-c	6	12	18	41	76	110
1328-The Underwater City (Movie) (1961)-Evans-a; photo-c	7	14	21	46	86	125
1329-See Gyro Gearloose #01329-207						
1330-Brain Boy (#1)-Gil Kane-a	10	20	30	66	138	210
1332-Bachelor Father (TV)	7	14	21	46	86	125
1333-Short Ribs (4-6/62)	5	10	15	35	63	90
1335-Aggie Mack (4-6/62)	5	10	15	33	57	80
1336-On Stage; not by Leonard Starr	5	10	15	34	60	85
1337-Dr. Kildare (#1) (TV) (4-6/62)-Photo-c	9	18	27	59	117	175
1341-The Andy Griffith Show (TV) (4-6/62)-Photo-c	35	70	105	252	564	875
1348-Yak Yak (#2)-Jack Davis-c/a	7	14	21	46	86	125
1349-Yogi Bear Visits the U.N. (TV) (Hanna-Barbera) (1/62)-Photo-c	8	16	24	54	102	150
1350-Comanche (Disney-Movie)(1962)-Reprints 4-Color #966 (title change from "Tonka" to "Comanche") (4-6/62)-Sal Mineo photo-c	5	10	15	33	57	80
1354-Calvin & the Colonel (#1) (TV) (4-6/62)	9	18	27	58	114	170

NOTE: *Missing numbers probably do not exist.*

4-D MONKEY, THE (Adventures of... #? on)
Leung's Publications: 1988 - No. 11, 1990 ($1.80/$2.00, 52 pgs.)

	GD 2.0	VG 4.0	FN 6.0	VF 8.0	VF/NM 9.0	NM- 9.2
1-11: 1-Karate Pig, Ninja Flounder & 4-D Monkey (48 pgs., centerfold is a Christmas card).						
2-4 (52 pgs.)						4.00

FOUR FAVORITES (Crime Must Pay the Penalty No. 33 on)
Ace Magazines: Sept, 1941 - No. 32, Dec, 1947

	GD 2.0	VG 4.0	FN 6.0	VF 8.0	VF/NM 9.0	NM- 9.2
1-Vulcan, Lash Lightning (formerly Flash Lightning in Sure-Fire), Magno the Magnetic Man & The Raven begin; flag/Hitler-c	300	600	900	2010	3505	5000
2-The Black Ace only app.; WWII flag-c	148	296	444	947	1624	2300
3-Last Vulcan; V For Victory WWII-c	142	284	426	909	1555	2200
4,5: 4-The Raven & Vulcan end; Unknown Soldier begins (see Our Flag), ends #28. 5-Captain Courageous begins (5/42), ends #28 (moves over from Captain Courageous #6); not in #6. 5,6-Bondage/torture-c	148	296	444	947	1624	2300
6-8: 6-The Flag app.; Mr. Risk begins (7/42)	129	258	387	826	1413	2000
9-Kurtzman-a (Lash Lightning); robot-c	132	264	396	845	1448	2050
10-Classic Kurtzman-c/a (Magno & Davey)	300	600	900	2010	3505	5000
11-Kurtzman-a; Hitler, Mussolini, Hirohito-c; L.B. Cole-a; Unknown Soldier by Kurtzman	306	612	918	2198	3849	5500
12-L.B. Cole-a; Japanese WWII-c	135	270	405	864	1482	2100
13-L.B. Cole-c (his first cover?); WWII-c	135	270	405	864	1482	2100
14,16-18,20: 18,20-Palais-c/a	71	142	213	454	777	1100
15-Japanese WWII-c	74	148	222	470	810	1150
19-Nazi WWII bondage-c	103	206	309	659	1130	1600
21-No Unknown Soldier; The Unknown app.	65	130	195	416	708	1000
22-27: 22-Captain Courageous drops costume. 23-Unknown Soldier drops costume. 25-29-Hap Hazard app. 26-Last Magno	55	110	165	352	601	850
28,29: Hap Hazard app. in all	39	78	117	240	395	550
30-32: 30-Funny-c begin (teen humor), end #32	20	40	60	115	188	260

NOTE: ***Dave Berg** c-5. **Jim Mooney** a-6; c-1-3. **Palais** a-18-20; c-18-25.*

FOUR HORSEMEN, THE (See The Crusaders)

FOUR HORSEMEN
DC Comics (Vertigo): Feb, 2000 - No. 4, May, 2000 ($2.50, limited series)

	GD 2.0	VG 4.0	FN 6.0	VF 8.0	VF/NM 9.0	NM- 9.2
1-4-Esad Ribic-c/a; Robert Rodi-s						3.00

FOUR HORSEMEN OF THE APOCALYPSE, THE (Movie)
Dell Publishing Co.: No. 1250, Jan-Mar, 1962 (one-shot)

	GD 2.0	VG 4.0	FN 6.0	VF 8.0	VF/NM 9.0	NM- 9.2
Four Color 1250-Photo-c	7	14	21	49	92	135

4MOST (Foremost Boys No. 32-40; becomes Thrilling Crime Cases #41 on)
Novelty Publications/Star Publications No. 37-on:
Winter, 1941-42 - V8#5(#36), 9-10/49; #37, 11-12/49 - #40, 4-5/50

	GD 2.0	VG 4.0	FN 6.0	VF 8.0	VF/NM 9.0	NM- 9.2
V1#1-The Target by Sid Greene, The Cadet & Dick Cole begin with origins retold; produced by Funnies Inc.; quarterly issues begin, end V6#3; German WWII-c	219	438	657	1402	2401	3400
2-Last Target (Spr/42); WWII cover	74	148	222	470	810	1150
3-Dan'l Flannel begins; flag-c	52	104	156	328	552	775
4-1pg. Dr. Seuss (signed) (Aut/42); fish in the face-c	53	106	159	334	567	800
V2#1-3	28	56	84	165	270	375
4-Hitler, Tojo & Mussolini app. as pumpkins on-c	68	136	204	435	743	1050
V3#1-4	20	40	60	114	182	250
V4#1-4: 2-Walter Johnson-c	15	30	45	83	124	165
V5#1-4: 1-The Target & Targeteers app.	14	28	42	76	108	140
V6#1-4	11	22	33	62	86	110
5-L.B. Cole-c	22	44	66	132	216	300
V7#1,3,5, V8#1, 37	11	22	33	60	83	105
2,4,6-L.B. Cole-c. 6-Last Dick Cole	20	40	60	115	188	260
V8#2,3,5-L.B. Cole-c/a	23	46	69	136	223	310
4-L.B. Cole-a	15	30	45	85	130	175
38-40: 38-Johnny Weismuller (Tarzan) life story & Jim Braddock (boxer) life story. 38-40-L.B. Cole-c. 40-Last White Rider	17	34	51	98	154	210
Accepted Reprint 38-40 (nd): 40-r/Johnny Weismuller life story; all have L.B. Cole-c	10	20	30	56	76	95

411
Marvel Comics: June, 2003 - No. 3 ($3.50, limited series)

	GD 2.0	VG 4.0	FN 6.0	VF 8.0	VF/NM 9.0	NM- 9.2
1,2-Tributes to peacemakers; s/a by various. 1-Millar, Quitely, Mack, Winslade & others-s/a. 2-Harris, Phillips, Manco, Bruce Jones.						3.50

FOUR POINTS, THE
Aspen MLT Inc.: Apr, 2015 - No. 5, Aug, 2015 ($3.99)

	GD 2.0	VG 4.0	FN 6.0	VF 8.0	VF/NM 9.0	NM- 9.2
1-5-Lobdell-s/Gunderson-a; multiple covers						4.00

FOUR-STAR BATTLE TALES
National Periodical Publications: Feb-Mar, 1973 - No. 5, Nov-Dec, 1973

	GD 2.0	VG 4.0	FN 6.0	VF 8.0	VF/NM 9.0	NM- 9.2
1-Reprints begin	3	6	9	16	24	32
2-5	2	4	6	11	16	20

NOTE: ***Drucker** r-1, 3-5. **Heath** r-2, 5; c-1. **Krigstein** r-5. **Kubert** r-4; c-2.*

Fox and the Crow #78 © DC

Fox Giant - Book of Love nn © FOX

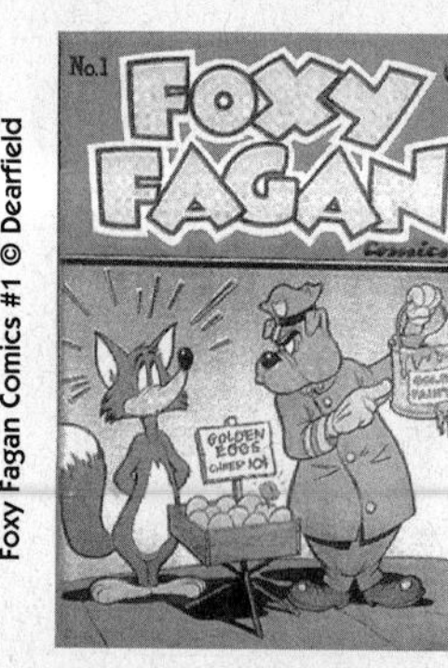

Foxy Fagan Comics #1 © Dearfield

	GD 2.0	VG 4.0	FN 6.0	VF 8.0	VF/NM 9.0	NM- 9.2

FOUR STAR SPECTACULAR
National Periodical Publications: Mar-Apr, 1976 - No. 6, Jan-Feb, 1977

1-Includes G.A. Flash story with new art 2 4 6 13 18 22
2-6: Reprints in all. 2-Infinity cover 2 4 6 8 10 12

NOTE: *All contain DC Superhero reprints. #1 has 68 pgs.; #2-6, 52 pgs.. #1, 4-Hawkman app.; #2-Kid Flash app.; #3-Green Lantern app; #2, 4, 5-Wonder Woman, Superboy app; #5-Green Arrow, Vigilante app; #6-Blackhawk G.A.-r.*

FOUR TEENERS (Formerly Crime Must Pay The Penalty; Dotty No. 35 on)
A. A. Wyn: No. 34, April, 1948 (52 pgs.)

34-Teen-age comic; Dotty app.; Curly & Jerry continue from Four Favorites
15 30 45 94 147 200

4001 A.D. (See Valiant 2016 FCBD edition for prelude)
Valiant Entertainment: May, 2016 - No. 4, Aug, 2016 ($3.99, limited series)

1-4-Matt Kindt-s/Clayton Crain-a. 1-David Mack-a (3 pages) 4.00
...: Bloodshot 1 (6/16, $3.99) Lemire-s/Braithwaite-a; Bloodshot reforms in 4001 A.D. 4.00
...: Shadowman 1 (7/16, $3.99) Houser & Roberts-s/Gill-a 4.00
...: War Mother 1 (8/16, $3.99) Van Lente-s/Giorello-a 4.00
...: X-O Manowar 1 (5/16, $3.99) Venditti-s/Henry-a; prelude to main series 4.00

FOURTH WORLD GALLERY, THE (Jack Kirby's...)
DC Comics: 1996 (9/96) ($3.50, one-shot)

nn-Pin-ups of Jack Kirby's Fourth World characters (New Gods, Forever People & Mister Miracle) by John Byrne, Rick Burchett, Dan Jurgens, Walt Simonson & others 4.00

FOUR WOMEN
DC Comics (Homage): Dec, 2001 - No. 5, Apr, 2002 ($2.95, limited series)

1-5-Sam Kieth-s/a 3.00
TPB (2002, $17.95) r/series; foreward by Kieth 18.00

FOX, THE
Archie Comic Publications (Red Circle Comics): Dec, 2013 - No. 5, Apr, 2014 ($2.99)

1-5-Dean Haspiel-a/Haspiel and Mark Waid-s. 1-Three covers. 2-Two covers 3.00

FOX, THE
Archie Comic Publications (Dark Circle Comics): Jun, 2015 - No. 5, Oct, 2015 ($3.99)

1-5-Dean Haspiel-a/Haspiel and Mark Waid-s; multiple covers on each 4.00

FOX AND THE CROW (Stanley & His Monster No. 109 on) (See Comic Cavalcade & Real Screen Comics)
National Periodical Publications: Dec-Jan, 1951-52 - No. 108, Feb-Mar, 1968

1 129 258 387 826 1413 2000
2(Scarce) 57 114 171 362 619 875
3-5 37 74 111 222 361 500
6-10 (6-7/53) 26 52 78 154 252 350
11-20 (10/54) 20 40 60 114 182 250
21-30: 22-Last precode issue (2/55) 15 30 45 83 124 165
31-40 12 24 36 69 97 125
41-60 6 12 18 37 66 95
61-80 5 10 15 31 53 75
81-94: 94-(11/65)-The Brat Finks begin 4 8 12 25 40 55
95-Stanley & His Monster begins (origin & 1st app) 8 16 24 54 102 150
96-99,101-108 3 6 9 19 30 40
100 (10-11/66) 3 6 9 21 33 45

NOTE: *Many later covers by* ***Mort Drucker.***

FOX AND THE HOUND, THE (Disney)(Movie)
Whitman Publishing Co.: Aug, 1981 - No. 3, Oct, 1981

11292- Golden Press Graphic Novel 2 4 6 8 10 12
1-3-Based on animated movie 1 2 3 5 7 9

FOXFIRE (See The Phoenix Resurrection)
Malibu Comics (Ultraverse): Feb, 1996 - No. 4, May, 1996 ($1.50)

1-4: Sludge, Ultraforce app. 4-Punisher app. 3.00

FOX GIANTS (Also see Giant Comics Edition)
Fox Feature Syndicate: 1944 - 1950 (25¢, 132 - 196 pgs.)

Album of Crime nn(1949, 132p) 68 136 204 435 743 1050
Album of Love nn(1949, 132p) 74 148 222 470 810 1150
All Famous Crime Stories nn('49, 132p) 68 136 204 435 743 1050
All Good Comics 1(1944, 132p)(R.W. Voigt)-The Bouncer, Purple Tigress,Rick Evans, Puppeteer, Green Mask; Infinity-c 84 168 252 538 919 1300
All Great nn(1944, 132p)-Capt. Jack Terry, Rick Evans, Jaguar Man
57 114 171 362 619 875
All Great nn(Chicago Nite Life News)(1945, 132p)-Green Mask, Bouncer, Puppeteer, Rick Evans, Rocket Kelly 55 110 165 352 601 850
All-Great Confession Magazine nn(1949, 132p) 71 142 213 454 777 1100
All-Great Confessions nn(1949, 132p) 71 142 213 454 777 1100
All Great Crime Stories nn('49, 132p) 68 136 204 435 743 1050
All Great Jungle Adventures nn('49, 132p) 87 174 261 553 952 1350
All Real Confession Magazine 3 (3/49, 132p) 71 142 213 454 777 1100
All Real Confession Magazine 4 (4/49, 132p) 71 142 213 454 777 1100
All Your Comics 1(1944, 132p)-The Puppeteer, Red Robbins, & Merciless the Sorcerer
58 116 174 371 636 900
Almanac Of Crime nn(1948, 148p)-Phantom Lady 77 154 231 493 847 1200
Almanac Of Crime 1(1950, 132p) 65 130 195 416 708 1000
Book Of Love nn(1950, 132p) 68 136 204 435 743 1050
Burning Romances 1(1949, 132p) 81 162 243 518 884 1250
Crimes Incorporated nn(1950, 132p) 61 122 183 390 670 950
Daring Love Stories nn(1950, 132p) 68 136 204 435 743 1050
Everybody's Comics 1(1944, 50¢, 196p)-The Green Mask, The Puppeteer, The Bouncer, Rocket Kelly, Rick Evans 69 138 207 442 759 1075
Everybody's Comics 1(1946, 196p)-Green Lama, The Puppeteer
57 114 171 362 619 875
Everybody's Comics 1(1946, 196p)-Same as 1945 Ribtickler
45 90 135 284 480 675
Everybody's Comics nn(1947, 132p)-Jo-Jo, Purple Tigress, Cosmo Cat, Bronze Man
57 114 171 362 619 875
Exciting Romance Stories nn(1949, 132p) 71 142 213 454 777 1100
Famous Love nn(1950, 132p)-Photo-c 69 138 207 442 759 1075
Intimate Confessions nn(1950, 132p) 68 136 204 435 743 1050
Journal Of Crime nn(1949, 132p) 68 136 204 435 743 1050
Love Problems nn(1949, 132p) 71 142 213 454 777 1100
Love Thrills nn(1950, 132p) 68 136 204 435 743 1050
March of Crime nn('48, 132p)-Female w/rifle-c 68 136 204 435 743 1050
March of Crime nn('49, 132p)-Cop w/pistol-c 63 126 189 403 689 975
March of Crime nn(1949, 132p)-Coffin & man w/machine-gun-c
63 126 189 403 689 975
Revealing Love Stories nn(1950, 132p) 68 136 204 435 743 1050
Ribtickler nn(1945, 50¢, 196p)-Chicago Nite Life News; Marvel Mutt, Cosmo Cat, Flash Rabbit, The Nebbs app. 53 106 159 334 557 800
Romantic Thrills nn(1950, 132p) 68 136 204 435 743 1050
Secret Love Stories nn(1949, 132p) 71 142 213 454 777 1100
Strange Love nn(1950, 132p)-Photo-c 94 188 282 597 1025 1450
Sweetheart Scandals nn(1950, 132p) 68 136 204 435 743 1050
Teen-Age Love nn(1950, 132p) 68 136 204 435 743 1050
Throbbing Love nn(1950, 132p)-Photo-c; used in **POP**, pg. 107
94 188 282 597 1025 1450
Truth About Crime nn(1949, 132p) 68 136 204 435 743 1050
Variety Comics 1(1946, 132p)-Blue Beetle, Jungle Jo
58 116 174 371 636 900
Variety Comics nn(1950, 132p)-Jungle Jo, My Secret Affair (w/Harrison/Wood-a), Crimes by Women & My Story 55 110 165 352 601 850
Western Roundup nn('50, 132p)-Hoot Gibson; Cody of the Pony Express app.
43 86 129 271 461 650

NOTE: *Each of the above usually contain four remaindered Fox books minus covers. Since these missing covers often had the first page of the first story, most Giants therefore are incomplete. Approximate values are listed. Books with appearances of Phantom Lady, Rulah, Jo-Jo, etc. could bring more.*

FOXHOLE (Becomes Never Again #8?)
Mainline/Charlton No. 5 on: 9-10/54 - No. 4, 3-4/55; No. 5, 7/55 - No. 7, 3/56

1-Classic Kirby-c 74 148 222 470 810 1150
2-Kirby-c/a(2); Kirby scripts based on his war time experiences
43 86 129 271 461 650
3-5-Simon/Kirby-c only 31 62 93 186 303 420
6-Kirby-c/a(2) 39 78 117 240 395 550
7-Simon & Kirby-c 17 34 51 103 162 220
Super Reprints #10,15-17: 10-r/? 15,16-r/United States Marines #5,8. 17-r/Monty Hall #? 2 4 6 11 16 20
11,12,18-r/Foxhole #1,2,3; Kirby-c 3 6 9 17 26 35

NOTE: ***Kirby*** *a(r)-Super #11, 12.* ***Powell*** *a(r)-Super #15, 16. Stories by actual veterans.*

FOXY FAGAN COMICS (Funny Animal)
Dearfield Publishing Co.: Dec, 1946 - No. 7, Summer, 1948

1-Foxy Fagan & Little Buck begin 15 30 45 83 124 165
2 9 18 27 47 61 75
3-7: 6-Rocket ship-c 8 16 24 42 54 65

FRACTION
DC Comics (Focus): June, 2004 - No. 6, Nov, 2004 ($2.50, limited series)

1-6-David Tischman-s/Timothy Green II-a 3.00
SC (2011, $17.99) r/#1-6; cover gallery 18.00

FRACTURED FAIRY TALES (TV)
Gold Key: Oct, 1962 (Jay Ward)

Frankenstein #2 © MAR

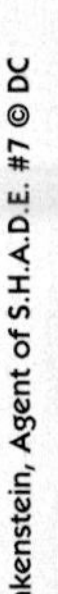

Frankenstein, Agent of S.H.A.D.E. #7 © DC

Frankenstein Underground #5 © Mike Mignola

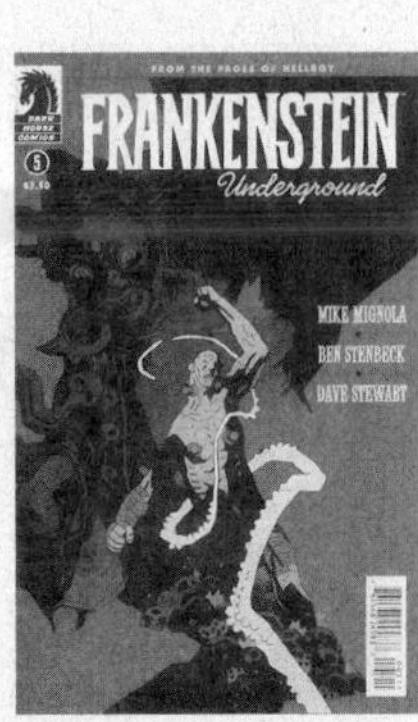

	GD 2.0	VG 4.0	FN 6.0	VF 8.0	VF/NM 9.0	NM- 9.2
1 (10022-210)-From Bullwinkle TV show	10	20	30	64	132	200

FRAGGLE ROCK (TV)
Marvel Comics (Star Comics)/Marvel V2#1 on: Apr, 1985 - No. 8, Sept, 1986; V2#1, Apr, 1988 - No. 5, Aug, 1988

	GD	VG	FN	VF	VF/NM	NM-
1-6 (75¢-c)						5.00
7,8						6.00
V2#1-5-($1.00): Reprints 1st series						3.00

FRAGGLE ROCK: JOURNEY TO THE EVERSPRING, (JIM HENSON'S...)
Archaia: Oct, 2014 - No. 4, Jan, 2015 ($3.99, limited series)

	GD	VG	FN	VF	VF/NM	NM-
1-4-Kate Leth-s/Jake Myler-a. 1-Multiple covers						4.00

FRANCIS, BROTHER OF THE UNIVERSE
Marvel Comics Group: 1980 (75¢, 52 pgs., one-shot)

	GD	VG	FN	VF	VF/NM	NM-
1-John Buscema/Marie Severin-a; story of Francis Bernadone, celebrating his 800th birthday in 1982						6.00

FRANCIS THE FAMOUS TALKING MULE (All based on movie)
Dell Publishing Co.: No. 335 (#1), June, 1951 - No. 1090, March, 1960

	GD	VG	FN	VF	VF/NM	NM-
Four Color 335 (#1)	10	20	30	68	144	220
Four Color 465	6	12	18	41	76	110
Four Color 501,547,579	5	10	15	35	63	90
Four Color 621,655,698,710,745	5	10	15	33	57	80
Four Color 810,863,906,953,991,1068,1090	5	10	15	31	53	75

FRANK
Nemesis Comics (Harvey): Apr (Mar inside), 1994 - No. 4, 1994 ($1.75/$2.50, limited series)

	GD	VG	FN	VF	VF/NM	NM-
1-4-($2.50, direct sale): 1-Foil-c Edition						3.50
1-4-($1.75)-Newsstand Editions; Cowan-a in all						3.00

FRANK
Fantagraphics Books: Sept, 1996 ($2.95, B&W)

	GD	VG	FN	VF	VF/NM	NM-
1-Woodring-c/a/scripts						3.00

FRANK BUCK (Formerly My True Love)
Fox Feature Syndicate: No. 70, May, 1950 - No. 3, Sept, 1950

	GD	VG	FN	VF	VF/NM	NM-
70-Wood a(p)(3 stories)-Photo-c	39	78	117	234	385	535
71-Wood-a (9 pgs.); photo/painted-c	20	40	60	118	192	265
3: 3-Photo/painted-c	15	30	45	85	130	175

NOTE: *Based on "Bring 'Em Back Alive" TV show.*

FRANKEN-CASTLE (See The Punisher, 2009 series)

FRANKENSTEIN (See Dracula, Movie Classics & Werewolf)
Dell Publishing Co.: Aug-Oct, 1964; No. 2, Sept, 1966 - No. 4, Mar, 1967

	GD	VG	FN	VF	VF/NM	NM-
1(12-283-410)(1964)(2nd printing; see Movie Classics for 1st printing)	6	12	18	42	79	115
2-Intro. & origin super-hero character (9/66)	5	10	15	34	60	85
3,4	4	8	12	25	40	55

FRANKENSTEIN (The Monster of...; also see Monsters Unleashed #2, Power Record Comics, Psycho & Silver Surfer #7)
Marvel Comics Group: Jan, 1973 - No. 18, Sept, 1975

	GD	VG	FN	VF	VF/NM	NM-
1-Ploog-c/a begins, ends #6	8	16	24	52	99	145
2	5	10	15	30	50	70
3-5	3	6	9	21	33	45
6,7,10: 7-Dracula cameo	3	6	9	17	26	35
8,9-Dracula c/sty. 9-Death of Dracula	4	8	12	28	47	65
11-17	3	6	9	15	22	28
18-Wrighston-c(i)	3	6	9	16	24	32

NOTE: ***Adkins** c-17i. **Buscema** a-7-10p. **Ditko** a-12r. **G. Kane** c-15p. **Orlando** a-8r. **Ploog** a-1-3, 4p, 5p, 6; c-1-6. **Wrightson** c-18i.*

FRANKENSTEIN (Mary Wollstonecraft Shelley's...; A Marvel Illustrated Novel)
Marvel Pub.: 1983 ($8.95, B&W, 196 pgs., 8x11" TPB)

	GD	VG	FN	VF	VF/NM	NM-
nn-Wrightson-a; 4 pg. intro. by Stephen King	5	10	15	30	50	70
Limited HC Edition						175.00

FRANKENSTEIN, AGENT OF S.H.A.D.E. (New DC 52)
DC Comics: Nov, 2011 - No. 16, Mar, 2013 ($2.99)

	GD	VG	FN	VF	VF/NM	NM-
1-16: 1-Lemire-s/Ponticelli-a/J.G. Jones-c; Ray Palmer & The Creature Commandos app. 5-Crossover with OMAC #5. 13-15-Rotworld						3.00
#0 (11/12, $2.99) Kindt-s/Ponticelli-a; Frankenstein's origin						3.00

FRANKENSTEIN ALIVE, ALIVE
IDW Publishing: May, 2012 - No. 4, Jan, 2018 ($3.99, B&W)

	GD	VG	FN	VF	VF/NM	NM-
1-3-Niles-s/Wrightson-a; interview with creators; excerpt from M.W. Shelley writings						4.00
4-($4.99) Art by Wrightson and Kelley Jones						5.00
... Reanimated Edition (4/14, $5.99) r/#1,2; silver foil cover logo						6.00
... Trio (1/18, $7.99) r/#1-3; silver foil cover logo						8.00

FRANKENSTEIN COMICS (Also See Prize Comics)
Prize Publ. (Crestwood/Feature): Sum, 1945 - V5#5(#33), Oct-Nov, 1954

	GD	VG	FN	VF	VF/NM	NM-
1-Frankenstein begins by Dick Briefer (origin); Frank Sinatra parody	320	640	960	2240	3970	5700
2	100	200	300	635	1093	1550
3-5	77	154	231	493	847	1200
6-10: 7-S&K a(r)/Headline Comics. 8(7-8/47)-Superman satire	65	130	195	416	708	1000
11-17(1-2/49)-11-Boris Karloff parody-c/story. 17-Last humor issue	55	110	165	352	601	850
18(3/52)-New origin, horror series begins	123	246	369	787	1344	1900
19,20(V3#4, 8-9/52)	87	174	261	553	952	1350
21(V3#5), 22(V3#6), 23(V4#1) - #28(V4#6)	65	130	195	416	708	1000
29(V5#1) - #33(V5#5)	58	116	174	371	636	900

NOTE: ***Briefer** c/a-all. **Meskin** a-21, 29.*

FRANKENSTEIN/DRACULA WAR, THE
Topps Comics: Feb, 1995 - No. 3, May, 1995 ($2.50, limited series)

	GD	VG	FN	VF	VF/NM	NM-
1-3						4.00

FRANKENSTEIN, JR. (...& the Impossibles) (TV)
Gold Key: Jan, 1966 (Hanna-Barbera)

	GD	VG	FN	VF	VF/NM	NM-
1-Super hero (scarce)	11	22	33	73	157	240

FRANKENSTEIN MOBSTER
Image Comics: No. 0, Oct, 2003 - No. 7, Dec, 2004 ($2.95)

	GD	VG	FN	VF	VF/NM	NM-
0-7: 0-Two covers by Wheatley and Hughes; Wheatley-s/a. 1-Variant-c by Wieringo						3.00

FRANKENSTEIN: OR THE MODERN PROMETHEUS
Caliber Press: 1994 ($2.95, one-shot)

	GD	VG	FN	VF	VF/NM	NM-
1						4.00

FRANKENSTEIN UNDERGROUND (From Hellboy)
Dark Horse Comics: Mar, 2015 - No. 5, Jul, 2015 ($3.50, limited series)

	GD	VG	FN	VF	VF/NM	NM-
1-5-Mike Mignola-s/c; Ben Stenbeck-a						3.50

FRANKENSTEIN UNDONE (From Hellboy)
Dark Horse Comics: Jan, 2020 - No. 5 ($3.99, limited series)

	GD	VG	FN	VF	VF/NM	NM-
1,2-Mike Mignola & Scott Allie-s/Ben Stenbeck-a/c						4.00

FRANK FRAZETTA FANTASY ILLUSTRATED (Magazine)
Quantum Cat Entertainment: Spring 1998 - No. 8 ($5.95, quarterly)

	GD	VG	FN	VF	VF/NM	NM-
1-Anthology; art by Corben, Horley, Jusko	1	3	4	6	8	10
1-Linsner variant-c						15.00
2-Battle Chasers by Madureira; Harris-a						8.00
2-Madureira Battle Chasers variant-c						12.00
3-8-Frazetta-c						6.00
3-Tony Daniel variant-c						15.00
5,6-Portacio variant-c, 7,8-Alex Nino variant-c						10.00
8-Alex Ross Chicago Comicon variant-c						10.00

FRANK FRAZETTA'S DEATH DEALER
Image Comics: Mar, 2007 - No. 6, Jan, 2008 ($3.99)

	GD	VG	FN	VF	VF/NM	NM-
1-6-Nat Jones-a; 3 covers (Frazetta, Jones, Jones sketch)						4.00

FRANK FRAZETTA'S...
Fantagraphics Books/Image Comics: one-shots

	GD	VG	FN	VF	VF/NM	NM-
... Creatures 1 (Image Comics, 7/08, $3.99) Bergting-a; covers by Frazetta & Bergting						4.00
... Dark Kingdom 1-4 (Image, 4/08 - No. 4, 1/10, $3.99) Vigil-a; covers by Frazetta & Vigil						4.00
... Dracula Meets the Wolfman 1 (Image, 8/08, $3.99) Francavilla-a; 2 covers						4.00
... Moon Maid 1 (Image, 1/09, $3.99) Tim Vigil-a; covers by Frazetta & Vigil						4.00
... Neanderthal 1 (Image, 4/09, $3.99) Fotos & Vigil-a; covers by Frazetta & Fotos						4.00
... Sorcerer 1 (Image, 8/09, $3.99) Medors-a; covers by Frazetta & Medors						4.00
... Swamp Demon 1 (Image, 7/08, $3.99) Medors-a; covers by Frazetta & Medors						4.00
... Thun'da Tales 1 (Fantagraphics Books, 1987, $2.00) Frazetta-r						6.00
... Untamed Love 1 (Fantagraphics Books, 11/87, $2.00) r/1950's romance comics						6.00

FRANKIE COMICS (...& Lana No. 13-15) (Formerly Movie Tunes; becomes Frankie Fuddle No. 16 on)
Marvel Comics (MgPC): No. 4, Wint, 1946-47 - No. 15, June, 1949

	GD	VG	FN	VF	VF/NM	NM-
4-Mitzi, Margie, Daisy app.	28	56	84	165	270	375
5-9	17	34	51	105	165	225
10-15: 13-Anti-Wertham editorial	15	30	45	88	137	185

FRANKIE DOODLE (See Sparkler, both series)
United Features Syndicate: No. 7, 1939

	GD	VG	FN	VF	VF/NM	NM-
Single Series 7	34	68	102	204	332	460

Fray #4 © Joss Whedon

Freckles and His Friends #11 © STD

Free Comic Book Day 2019 © DH

GD VG FN VF VF/NM NM-
2.0 4.0 6.0 8.0 9.0 9.2

GD VG FN VF VF/NM NM-
2.0 4.0 6.0 8.0 9.0 9.2

FRANKIE FUDDLE (Formerly Frankie & Lana)
Marvel Comics: No. 16, Aug, 1949 - No. 17, Nov, 1949

16,17 15 30 45 84 127 170

FRANKLIN RICHARDS (Fantastic Four)
Marvel Comics: April, 2006 - Jun, 2009 ($2.99/$3.99, one-shots)

...: A Fantastic Year 1 (2018, $7.99) reprints various one-shots; Eliopoulos-s/a 8.00
...: April Fools (6/09, $3.99) Eliopoulos-s/a 4.00
...: Collected Chaos (2008, $8.99, digest) reprints various one-shots 9.00
...: Fall Football Fiasco (1/08, $2.99) Eliopoulos-a/Sumerak-s 3.00
...: Happy Franksgiving (1/07, $2.99) Thanksgiving stories by Eliopoulos-a/Sumerak-s 3.00
...: It's Dark Reigning Cats & Dogs (4/09, $3.99) Eliopoulos-s/a 4.00
...: Lab Brat (2007, $7.99, digest) reprints one-shots and Masked Marvel back-ups 8.00
...: March Madness (5/07, $2.99) More science gone wrong by Eliopoulos-a/Sumerak-s 3.00
...: Monster Mash (11/07, $2.99) Science mishaps by Eliopoulos-a/Sumerak-s 3.00
...: Not-So-Secret Invasion (7/08, $2.99) Skrull cover; The Wizard app. 3.00
... One Shot (4/06, $2.99) short stories by Eliopoulos-a/Sumerak-s 3.00
...: School's Out (4/09, $3.99) Eliopoulos-s/a; Katie Power app. 4.00
...: Sons of Geniuses (1/09, $3.99) parallel dimension alternate version hijinks 4.00
...: Spring Break (5/08, $2.99) short stories by Eliopoulos-a/Sumerak-s 3.00
...: Summer Smackdown (10/08, $2.99) short stories by Eliopoulos-a/Sumerak-s 3.00
...: Super Summer Spectacular (9/06, $2.99) short stories by Eliopoulos-a/Sumerak-s 3.00
...: World Be Warned (8/07, $2.99) short stories by Eliopoulos-a/Sumerak-s; Hulk app. 3.00

FRANK LUTHER'S SILLY PILLY COMICS (See Jingle Dingle...)
Children's Comics (Maltex Cereal): 1950 (10¢)

1-Characters from radio, records, & TV 13 26 39 72 101 130

NOTE: *Also printed as a promotional comic for Maltex cereal.*

FRANK MERRIWELL AT YALE (Speed Demons No. 5 on?)
Charlton Comics: June, 1955 - No. 4, Jan, 1956 (Also see Shadow Comics)

1 8 16 24 44 57 70
2-4 6 12 18 31 38 45

FRANTIC (Magazine) (See Ratfink & Zany)
Pierce Publishing Co.: Oct, 1958 - V2#2, Apr, 1959 (Satire)

V1#1 37 74 111 222 361 500
2 14 28 42 80 115 150
V2#1,2: 1-Burgos-a, Severin-c/a; Powell-a? 10 20 30 58 79 100

FRAY (Also see Buffy the Vampire Slayer "season eight" #16-19)
Dark Horse Comics: June, 2001 - No. 8, July, 2003 ($2.99, limited series)

1-Joss Whedon-s/Moline & Owens-a 1 2 3 5 6 8
1-DF Gold edition 2 4 6 9 12 15
2-8: 6-(3/02). 7-(4/03) 4.00
TPB (11/03, $19.95) r/#1-8; intros by Whedon & Loeb; Moline sketch pages 20.00

FREAK FORCE (Also see Savage Dragon)
Image Comics (Highbrow Ent.): Dec, 1993 - No. 18, July, 1995 ($1.95/$2.50)

1-18-Superpatriot & Mighty Man in all; Erik Larsen scripts in all. 4-Vanguard app. 8-Begin $2.50-c. 9-Cyberforce-c & app. 13-Variant-c 3.00

FREAK FORCE (Also see Savage Dragon)
Image Comics: Apr, 1997 - No. 3, July, 1997 ($2.95)

1-3-Larsen-s 3.00

FREAK OUT, USA (See On the Scene Presents...)

FREAK SHOW
Image Comics (Desperado): 2006 ($5.99, B&W, one-shot)

nn-Bruce Jones-s/Bernie Wrightson-c/a 6.00

FREAKS OF THE HEARTLAND
Dark Horse Comics: Jan, 2004 - No. 6, Nov, 2004 ($2.99)

1-6-Steve Niles-s/Greg Ruth-a 3.00

FRECKLES AND HIS FRIENDS (See Crackajack Funnies, Famous Comics Cartoon Book, Honeybee Birdwhistle... & Red Ryder)

FRECKLES AND HIS FRIENDS
Standard Comics/Argo: No. 5, 11/47 - No. 12, 8/49; 11/55 - No. 4, 6/56

5-Reprints 15 30 45 92 144 195
6-12-Reprints. 7-9-Airbrush-c (by Schomburg?). 11-Lingerie panels
10 20 30 56 76 95

NOTE: *Some copies of No. 8 & 9 contain a printing oddity. The negatives were elongated in the engraving process, probably to conform to page dimensions on the filler pages. Those pages only look normal when viewed at a 45 degree angle.*

1(Argo,'55)-Reprints (NEA Service) 7 14 21 35 43 50
2-4 4 8 12 18 22 25

FREDDY (Formerly My Little Margie's Boy Friends) (Also see Blue Bird)
Charlton Comics: V2#12, June, 1958 - No. 47, Feb, 1965

V2#12-Teenage 4 8 12 28 47 65
13-15 3 6 9 16 23 30
16-47 2 4 6 11 16 20

FREDDY
Dell Publishing Co.: May-July, 1963 - No. 3, Oct-Dec, 1964

1 3 6 9 18 28 38
2,3 3 6 9 14 20 26

FREDDY KRUEGER'S A NIGHTMARE ON ELM STREET
Marvel Comics: Oct, 1989 - No. 2, Dec, 1989 ($2.25, B&W, movie adaptation, magazine)

1,2: Origin Freddy Krueger; Buckler/Alcala-a 3 6 9 14 20 25

FREDDY'S DEAD: THE FINAL NIGHTMARE
Innovation Publishing: Oct, 1991 - No. 3, Dec 1991 ($2.50, color mini-series, adapts movie)

1-3: Dismukes (film poster artist) painted-c 4.00

FREDDY VS. JASON VS. ASH (Freddy Krueger, Friday the 13th, Army of Darkness)
DC Comics (WildStorm): Early Jan, 2008 - No. 6, May, 2008 ($2.99, limited series)

1-Three covers by J. Scott Campbell; Kuhoric-s/Craig-a 5.00
1-Second printing with 3 covers combined sideways 4.00
2-6: 2-4-Eric Powell-c. 5,6-Richard Friend-c 4.00
2-4-Second printings with B&W covers 3.00
TPB (2008, $17.99) r/#1-6; creators' interview afterword 18.00

FREDDY VS. JASON VS. ASH: THE NIGHTMARE WARRIORS
DC Comics (WildStorm): Aug, 2009 - No. 6, Jan, 2010 ($3.99, limited series)

1-6-Katz & Kuhoric-s/Craig-a. 1-Suydam-c 4.00
TPB (2010, $17.99) r/#1-6; cover gallery 18.00

FRED HEMBECK DESTROYS THE MARVEL UNIVERSE
Marvel Comics: July, 1989 ($1.50, one-shot)

1-Punisher app.; Staton-i (5 pgs.) 4.00

FRED HEMBECK SELLS THE MARVEL UNIVERSE
Marvel Comics: Oct, 1990 ($1.25, one-shot)

1-Punisher, Wolverine parodies; Hembeck/Austin-c 4.00

FREE COMIC BOOK DAY
Various publishers

2013 (Avengers/Hulk)(Marvel, 5/13) Hulk and Avengers Assemble animated series 3.00
2014 (Guardians of the Galaxy)(Marvel, 5/14) r/#1; Thanos & Spider-Verse back-ups 3.00
2015 (Avengers)(Marvel, 6/15) All-New Avengers and Uncanny Humans 3.00
2015 (Dark Horse, 5/15) Previews Fight Club 2, The Goon, and The Strain 3.00
2015 (Secret Wars #1)(Marvel, 6/15) Prelude to Secret Wars series (#0 on cover); back-up with Avengers/Attack on Titan x-over; Alex Ross wraparound-c 3.00
2016 (Captain America #1)(Marvel, 5/16) Preview of Captain America: Steve Rogers #1 and Amazing Spider-Man "Dead No More" storyline 3.00
2016 (Civil War II #1)(Marvel, 5/16) Preview of Civil War II #1 and All-New All-Different Avengers #9; Nadia Pym (The Wasp) app. 3.00
2016 (Dark Horse, 5/16) Previews Serenity, Hellboy and Aliens: Defiance 3.00
2017 (Dark Horse, 5/17) Avatar (movie) w/Doug Wheatley-a; Briggs Land story - Wood-s/ Dell'Edera-a 3.00
2017 (All-New Guardians of the Galaxy)(Marvel, 7/17) 1-Duggan-s/Kuder-a; preview of Defenders #1; Bendis-s/Marquez-a 3.00
2017 (Secret Empire)(Marvel, 7/17) 1-Spencer-s/Sorrentino-a/Brooks-c; Steve Rogers vs. the Avengers; back-up prelude to Peter Parker: The Spectacular Spider-Man #1; Zdarsky-s/Siqueira-a; Vulture app. 3.00
2018 (Amazing Spider-Man/Guardians of the Galaxy)(Marvel, 5/18) Ottley-c 3.00
2018 (Avengers/Captain America)(Marvel, 5/18) Aaron-s/Pichelli-a & Coates-s/Yu-a 3.00
2018 (Dark Horse, 5/18) Previews Overwatch and Black Hammer; Niemczyk-c 3.00
2019 (Dark Horse, 5/19) Previews Minecraft and Incredibles 2; Cassie Anderson-c 3.00
2019 (Dark Horse, 5/19) Stranger Things and Black Hammer; Chun Lo-c 3.00
2019 (Avengers/Savage Avengers)(Marvel, 7/19) Aaron-s/Caselli-a; McGuinness-c 3.00
2019 (Spider-Man/Venom)(Marvel, 7/19) Stegman-c; previews Absolute Carnage 3.00
...: Dark Circle 1 (Archie Comic Pub., 6-7/15) Previews Black Hood, The Fox, The Shield 3.00
...: R.I.P.D. and The True Lives of the Fabulous Killjoys (Dark Horse, 5/13) Flipbook with Mass Effect 3.00

FREEDOM AGENT (Also see John Steele)
Gold Key: Apr, 1963 (12¢)

1 (10054-304)-Painted-c 4 8 12 27 44 60

FREEDOM FIGHTERS (See Justice League of America #107,108)
National Periodical Publ./DC Comics: Mar-Apr, 1976 - No. 15, July-Aug, 1978

1-Uncle Sam, The Ray, Black Condor, Doll Man, Human Bomb, & Phantom Lady begin (all former Quality characters) 3 6 9 17 26 35

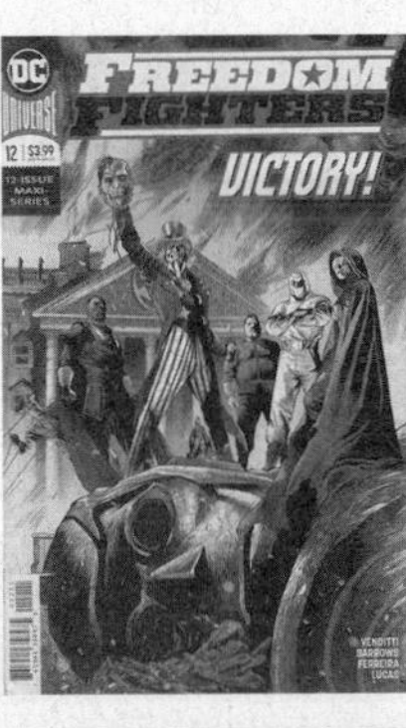

Freedom Fighters (2019 series) #12 © DC

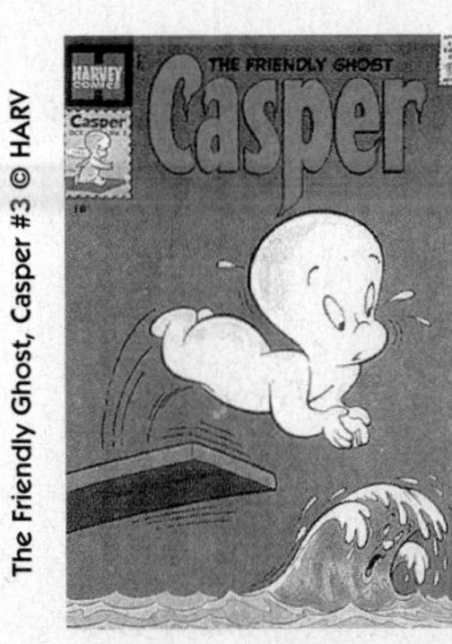

The Friendly Ghost, Casper #3 © HARV

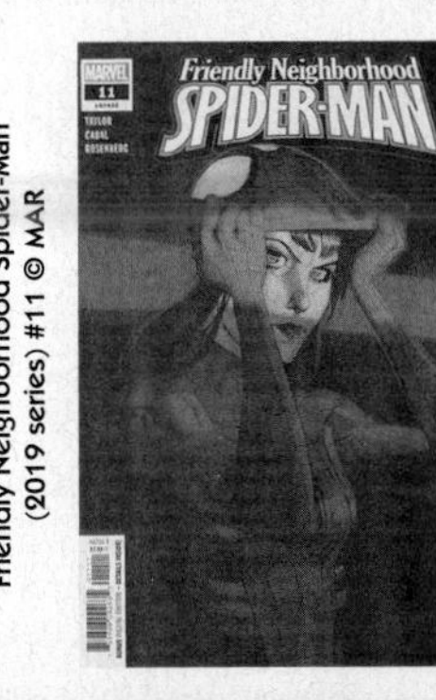

Friendly Neighborhood Spider-Man (2019 series) #11 © MAR

	GD 2.0	VG 4.0	FN 6.0	VF 8.0	VF/NM 9.0	NM- 9.2
2-9: 4,5-Wonder Woman x-over. 7-1st app. Crusaders	2	4	6	9	12	15
10-15: 10-Origin Doll Man; Cat-Man-c/story (4th app; 1st revival since Detective #325). 11-Origin The Ray. 12-Origin Firebrand. 13-Origin Black Condor. 14-Batgirl & Batwoman app. 15-Batgirl & Batwoman app.; origin Phantom Lady	2	4	6	9	13	16

NOTE: *Buckler c-5-11p, 13p, 14p.*

FREEDOM FIGHTERS (Also see "Uncle Sam and the Freedom Fighters")
DC Comics: Nov, 2010 - No. 9, Jul, 2011 ($2.99)

1-9-Travis Moore-a. 1-6-Dave Johnson-c 3.00

FREEDOM FIGHTERS
DC Comics: Feb, 2019 - No. 12, Mar, 2020 ($3.99, limited series)

1-12: 1-Venditti-s/Barrows-a; intro. new Freedom Fighters on present day Earth-X 4.00

FREEDOM FORCE
Image Comics: Jan, 2005 - No. 6, June, 2005 ($2.95)

1-6-Eric Dieter-s/Tom Scioli-a 3.00

FREELANCERS
BOOM! Studios: Oct, 2012 - No. 6, Mar, 2013 ($1.00/$3.99)

1-($1.00) Brill-s/Covey-a; eight covers; back-up origin of Valerie & Cassie 3.00
2-6-($3.99) Multiple covers on each 4.00

FREEMIND
Future Comics: No. 0, Aug, 2002; Nov, 2002 - No. 7, June, 2003 ($3.50)

0-($2.25) Two covers by Giordano & Layton 3.00
1-7 ($3.50) 1-Two covers by Giordano & Layton; Giordano-a thru #3. 4,5-Leeke-a 3.50

FREEREALMS
DC Comics (WildStorm): Sept, 2009 - No. 12, Oct, 2010 ($3.99, limited series)

1-12-Based on the online game; Jon Buran-a 4.00
... Book One TPB (2010, $19.99) r/#1-6 20.00
... Book Two TPB (2010, $19.99) r/#7-12 20.00

FREEX
Malibu Comics (Ultraverse): July, 1993 - No. 18, Mar, 1995 ($1.95)

1-3,5-14,16-18: 1-Polybagged w/trading card. 2-Some were polybagged w/card. 6-Nightman-c/story. 7-2 pg. origin Hardcase by Zeck. 17-Rune app. 3.00
1-Holographic-c edition 8.00
1-Ultra 5,000 limited silver ink-c 5.00
4-($2.50, 48 pgs.)-Rune flip-c/story by B. Smith (3 pgs.); 3 pg. Night Man preview 4.00
15 ($3.50)-w/Ultraverse Premiere #9 flip book; Alec Swan & Rafferty app. 4.00
Giant Size 1 (1994, $2.50)-Prime app. 4.00
NOTE: *Simonson c-1.*

FRENEMY OF THE STATE
Oni Press: May, 2010 - No. 5, Dec, 2011 ($3.99)

1-5-Rashida Jones, Christina Weir & Nunzio DeFilippis-s 4.00

FRENZY (Magazine) (Satire)
Picture Magazine: Apr, 1958 - No. 7, Jun, 1959

	GD 2.0	VG 4.0	FN 6.0	VF 8.0	VF/NM 9.0	NM- 9.2
1-Painted-c	15	30	45	84	127	170
2-7	9	18	27	47	61	75

FRESHMEN
Image Comics: Jul, 2005 - No. 6, Mar, 2006 ($2.99)

1-Sterbakov-s/Kirk-a; co-created by Seth Green; covers by Pérez, Migliari, Linsner 3.00
2-6-Migliari-c 3.00
... Yearbook (1/06, $2.99) profile pages of characters; art by various incl. Chaykin, Kirk 3.00
... Vol. 1 (3/06, $16.99, TPB) r/#1-6 & Yearbook; cover gallery with concept art 17.00

FRESHMEN (Volume 2)
Image Comics: Nov, 2006 - No. 6, Aug, 2007 ($2.99)

1-6: 1-Sterbakov-s/Conrad-a; 4 covers 3.00
...: Summer Vacation Special (7/08, $4.99) Sterbakov-s; bonus pin-ups by various 5.00
... Vol. 2 Fundamentals of Fear (6/07, $16.99, TPB) r/#1-6; cover gallery, journals 17.00

FREEZE, THE
Image Comics: Dec, 2018 - No. 4, Mar, 2019 ($3.99)

1-4-Dan Wickline-s/Phillip Sevy-a 4.00

FRIDAY FOSTER
Dell Publishing Co.: October, 1972

	GD 2.0	VG 4.0	FN 6.0	VF 8.0	VF/NM 9.0	NM- 9.2
1-Black heroine; Jack Sparling-a	7	14	21	44	82	120

FRIDAY THE 13TH (Based on the horror movie franchise)
DC Comics (WildStorm): Feb, 2007 - No. 6, July, 2007 ($2.99, mature)

1-6: 1-Two covers by Sook and Bradstreet; Gray & Palmiotti-s 3.00
...: Abuser and The Abused (6/08, $3.50) Fialkov-s/Andy B. -a 3.50
...: Bad Land 1,2 (3/08 - No. 2, 4/08, $2.99) Marz-s/Huddleston-a/McKone-c 3.00
...: How I Spent My Summer Vacation 1,2 (11/07 - No. 2, 12/07, $2.99) Aaron-s/Archer-a 3.00
...: Pamela's Tale 1,2 (9/07 - No. 2, 10/07, $2.99) Andreyko-s/Moll-a/Nguyen-c 3.00

FRIENDLY GHOST, CASPER, THE (Becomes Casper... #254 on)
Harvey Publications: Aug, 1958 - No. 224, Oct, 1982; No. 225, Oct, 1986 - No. 253, June, 1990

	GD 2.0	VG 4.0	FN 6.0	VF 8.0	VF/NM 9.0	NM- 9.2
1-Infinity-c	68	136	204	544	1222	1900
2	23	46	69	161	356	550
3-6: 6-X-Mas-c	10	20	30	69	147	225
7-10	9	18	27	58	114	170
11-20: 18-X-Mas-c	7	14	21	48	89	130
21-30	5	10	15	33	57	80
31-50	4	8	12	25	40	55
51-70,100: 54-X-Mas-c	3	6	9	19	30	40
71-99	3	6	9	16	23	30
101-131: 131-Last 12¢ issue	3	6	9	14	20	26
132-159	2	4	6	11	16	20
160-163: All 52 pg. Giants	3	6	9	14	20	26
164-199: 173,179,185-Cub Scout Specials	2	4	6	8	10	12
200	2	4	6	8	11	14
201-224	1	2	3	5	7	9
225-237: 230-X-mas-c. 232-Valentine's-c						5.00
238-253: 238-Begin $1.00-c. 238,244-Halloween-c. 243-Last new material						4.00

FRIENDLY NEIGHBORHOOD SPIDER-MAN
Marvel Comics: Dec, 2005 - No. 24, Nov, 2007 ($2.99)

1-Evolve or Die pt. 1; Peter David-s/Mike Wieringo-a; Morlun app. 4.00
1-Variant Wieringo-c with regular costume 5.00
2-4: 2-New Avengers app. 3-Spider-Man dies 3.00
2-4-var-c: 2-Bag-Head Fantastic Four costume. 3-Captain Universe. 4-Wrestler 5.00
5-10: 6-Red & gold costume. 8-10-Uncle Ben app. 3.00
11-23: 17-Black costume; Sandman app. 3.00
24-($3.99) "One More Day" part 2; Quesada-a; covers by Quesada & Djurdjevic 4.00
Annual 1 (7/07, $3.99) Origin of The Sandman; back-up w/Doran-a 4.00
... Vol. 1: Derailed (2006, $14.99) r/#5-10; Wieringo sketch pages 15.00
... Vol. 2: Mystery Date (2007, $13.99) r/#11-16 14.00

FRIENDLY NEIGHBORHOOD SPIDER-MAN
Marvel Comics: Mar, 2019 - No. 14, Feb, 2020 ($4.99/$3.99)

1-($4.99) Taylor-s/Cabal-a; Aunt May's diagnosis; Ferreira-a 5.00
2-14-($3.99) 2-Intro. The Rumor. 7-10-Lashley-a; Prowler app. 12,13-Fantastic Four app. 4.00

FRIENDS OF MAXX (Also see Maxx)
Image Comics (I Before E): Apr, 1996 - No. 3, Mar, 1997 ($2.95)

1-3: Sam Kieth-c/a/scripts. 1-Featuring Dude Japan 3.00

FRIGHT
Atlas/Seaboard Periodicals: June, 1975 (Aug. on inside)

	GD 2.0	VG 4.0	FN 6.0	VF 8.0	VF/NM 9.0	NM- 9.2
1-Origin/1st app. The Son of Dracula; Frank Thorne-c/a	3	6	9	16	23	30

FRIGHT NIGHT
Now Comics: Oct, 1988 - No. 22, 1990 ($1.75)

1-22: 1,2 Adapts movie. 8, 9-Evil Ed horror photo-c from movie 3.00

FRIGHT NIGHT II
Now Comics: 1989 ($3.95, 52 pgs.)

1-Adapts movie sequel 4.00

FRINGE (Based on the 2008 FOX television series)
DC Comics (WildStorm): Oct, 2008 - No. 6, Aug, 2009 ($2.99, limited series)

1-6-Anthology by various. 1-Mandrake & Coleby-a 3.00
TPB (2009, $19.99) r/#1-6; intro. by TV series co-creators Kurtzman & Orci 20.00

FRINGE: TALES FROM THE FRINGE (Based on the 2008 FOX television series)
DC Comics (WildStorm): Aug, 2010 - No. 6, Jan, 2011 ($3.99, limited series)

1-6-Anthology by various; LaTorre-c. 1-Reg & photo-c 4.00
2-6-Variant covers from parallel world. 2-Death of Batman. 3-Superman/Dark Knight Returns. 4-Crisis #7 Supergirl holding dead Superman. 5-Justice League #1 w/Jonah Hex. 6-Red Lantern/Red Arrow #76 10.00
TPB (2011, $14.99) r/#1-6 with variant cover gallery and sketch art 15.00

FRISKY ANIMALS (Formerly Frisky Fables; Super Cat #56 on)
Star Publications: No. 44, Jan, 1951 - No. 55, Sept, 1953

	GD 2.0	VG 4.0	FN 6.0	VF 8.0	VF/NM 9.0	NM- 9.2
44-Super Cat; L.B. Cole	23	46	69	136	223	310
45-Classic L. B. Cole-c	34	687	102	199	325	450
46-51,53-55: Super Cat. 54-Super Cat-c begin	21	42	63	122	199	275
52-L. B. Cole-c/a, 3 1/2 pgs.; X-Mas-c	22	44	66	128	209	290

Frisky Fables V2 #4 © STAR

Fritzi Ritz Comics #6 © UFS

Frontier Doctor FC #877 © Studio City

	GD 2.0	VG 4.0	FN 6.0	VF 8.0	VF/NM 9.0	NM- 9.2

NOTE: *All have* ***L. B. Cole****-c. No. 47-No Super Cat.* ***Disbrow*** *a-49, 52.* ***Fago*** *a-51.*

FRISKY ANIMALS ON PARADE (Formerly Parade Comics; becomes Superspook)
Ajax-Farrell Publ. (Four Star Comic Corp.): Sept, 1957 - No. 3, Dec-Jan, 1957-1958

	GD	VG	FN	VF	VF/NM	NM-
1-L. B. Cole-c	18	36	54	109	172	235
2-No L. B. Cole-c	10	20	30	56	76	95
3-L. B. Cole-c	15	30	45	88	137	185

FRISKY FABLES (Frisky Animals No. 44 on)
Premium Group/Novelty Publ./Star Publ. V5#4 on: Spring, 1945 - No. 43, Oct, 1950

	GD	VG	FN	VF	VF/NM	NM-
V1#1-Funny animal; Al Fago-c/a #1-38	26	52	78	152	249	345
2,3(Fall & Winter, 1945)	15	30	45	86	133	180
V2#1(#4, 4/46) - 9,11,12(#15, 3/47): 4-Flag-c	12	24	36	67	94	120
10-Christmas-c. 12-Valentine's-c	12	24	36	69	97	125
V3#1(#16, 4/47) - 12(#27, 3/48): 4-Flag-c. 7,9-Infinity-c. 10-X-Mas-c. 12-Washington crossing the Delaware parody-c	11	22	33	60	83	105
V4#1(#28, 4/48) - 7(#34, 2-3/49)	10	20	30	56	76	95
V5#1(#35, 4-5/49) - 4(#38, 10-11/49)	10	20	30	54	72	90
39-43-L. B. Cole-c; 40-Xmas-c	21	42	63	126	206	285
Accepted Reprint No. 43 (nd); L.B. Cole-c; classic story "The Mad Artist"	10	20	30	58	79	100

FRITZI RITZ (See Comics On Parade, Single Series #5, 1(reprint), Tip Top & United Comics)

FRITZI RITZ (United Comics No. 8-26) (Also see Tip Topper for early Peanuts by Schulz)
United Features Synd./St. John No. 37-55/Dell No. 56 on:
1939; Fall, 1948; No. 3, 1949 - No. 7, 1949; No. 27, 3-4/53 - No. 36, 9-10/54; No. 37 - No. 55, 9-11/57; No. 56, 12-2/57-58 - No. 59, 9-11/58

	GD	VG	FN	VF	VF/NM	NM-
Single Series #5 (1939)	42	84	126	265	445	625
nn(1948)-Special Fall issue; by Ernie Bushmiller	24	48	72	142	234	325
3(#1)	20	40	60	114	182	250
4-7(1949): 6-Abbie & Slats app.	14	28	42	76	108	140
27(1953)-33,37-50,57-59-Early Peanuts (1-4 pgs.) by Schulz. 29-Five pg. Abbie & Slats; 1 pg. Mamie by Russell Patterson. 38(9/55)-41(4/56)-Low print run	20	40	60	114	182	250
34-36,51-56: 36-1 pg. Mamie by Patterson	11	22	33	60	83	105

NOTE: *Abbie & Slats in #6,7, 27-31. Li'l Abner in #32-36.*

FROGMAN COMICS
Hillman Periodicals: Jan-Feb, 1952 - No. 11, May, 1953

	GD	VG	FN	VF	VF/NM	NM-
1	19	38	57	111	176	240
2	11	22	33	64	90	115
3,4,6-11: 4-Meskin-a	10	20	30	56	79	95
5-Krigstein-a	11	22	33	60	83	105

FROGMEN, THE
Dell Publishing Co.: No. 1258, Feb-Apr, 1962 - No. 11, Nov-Jan, 1964-65 (Painted-c)

	GD	VG	FN	VF	VF/NM	NM-
Four Color 1258(#1)-Evans-a	8	16	24	54	102	150
2,3-Evans-a; part Frazetta inks in #2,3	5	10	15	33	57	80
4,6-11	4	8	12	23	37	50
5-Toth-a	4	8	12	27	44	60

FROM BEYOND THE UNKNOWN
National Periodical Publications: 10-11/69 - No. 25, 11-12/73

	GD	VG	FN	VF	VF/NM	NM-
1	5	10	15	33	57	80
2-6	3	6	9	19	30	40
7-11: (64 pgs.) 7-Intro Col. Glenn Merrit	3	6	9	21	33	45
12-17: (52 pgs.) 13-Wood-a(i)(r). 17-Pres. Nixon-c	3	6	9	17	26	35
18-25: Star Rovers-r begin #18,19. Space Museum in #23-25	2	4	6	13	18	22

NOTE: ***N. Adams*** *c-3, 6, 8, 9.* ***Anderson*** *c-2, 4, 5, 10, 11i, 15-17, 22; reprints-3, 4, 6-8, 10, 11, 13-16, 24, 25.* ***Infantino*** *r-1-5, 7-19, 23-25; c-11p.* ***Kaluta*** *c-18, 19.* ***Gil Kane*** *a-9r.* ***Kubert*** *c-1, 7, 12-14.* ***Toth*** *a-2r.* ***Wood*** *a-13i. Photo c-22.*

FROM BEYOND THE UNKNOWN GIANT
DC Comics: 2020 ($4.99, one-shot, 100 pgs., squarebound, Mass Market & Direct Market editions exist with different covers)

	GD	VG	FN	VF	VF/NM	NM-
1-New stories of Green Lantern, Kamandi & Legion of Super-Heroes and reprints						5.00

FROM DUSK TILL DAWN (Movie)
Big Entertainment: 1996 ($4.95, one-shot)

	GD	VG	FN	VF	VF/NM	NM-
nn-Adaptation of the film; Brereton-c						5.00
nn-($9.95)Deluxe Ed. w/ new material						10.00

FROM HELL
Mad Love/Tundra Publishing/Kitchen Sink: 1991 - No. 11, Sept, 1998 (B&W)

	GD	VG	FN	VF	VF/NM	NM-
1-Alan Moore and Eddie Campbell's Jack The Ripper story collected from the Taboo anthology series	3	6	9	16	23	30
1-(2nd printing)	2	4	6	8	10	12
1-(3rd printing)	1	2	3	4	5	7
2	1	3	4	6	8	10
2-(2nd printing)						6.00
2-(3rd printing)						4.00
3-1st Kitchen Sink Press issue	1	3	4	6	8	10
3-(2nd printing)						5.00
4-10: 10-(8/96)	1	2	3	5	6	8
11-Dance of the Gull Catchers (9/98, $4.95) Epilogue	2	4	6	10	14	18
Tundra Publishing reprintings 1-5 ('92)	1	2	3	4	5	7
HC						125.00
HC Ltd. Edition of 1,000 (signed and numbered)						230.00
TPB-1st printing (11/99)						60.00
TPB-2nd printing (3/00)						50.00
TPB-3rd printing (11/00)						40.00
TPB-4th printing (7/01) Regular and movie covers						35.00
TPB-5th printing - Regular and movie covers						35.00

FROM HERE TO INSANITY (Satire) (Formerly Eh! #1-7) (See Frantic & Frenzy)
Charlton Comics: No. 8, Feb, 1955 - V3#1, 1956

	GD	VG	FN	VF	VF/NM	NM-
8	23	46	69	136	223	310
9	21	42	63	124	202	280
10-Ditko-c/a (3 pgs.)	32	64	96	192	314	435
11-All Kirby except 4 pgs.	41	82	123	256	428	600
12-(Mag. size) Marilyn Monroe, Jackie Gleason-c; all Kirby except 4 pgs.	43	86	129	271	461	650
V3#1(1956)-Ward-c/a(2) (signed McCartney); 5 pgs. Wolverton-a; 3 pgs. Ditko-a; magazine format (cover says "Crazy, Man, Crazy" and becomes Crazy, Man, Crazy with V2#2)	65	130	195	416	708	1000

FROM THE PIT
Fantagor Press: 1994 ($4.95, one-shot, mature)

	GD	VG	FN	VF	VF/NM	NM-
1-R. Corben-a; HP Lovecraft back-up story	1	3	4	6	8	10

FRONTIER DOCTOR (TV)
Dell Publishing Co.: No. 877, Feb, 1958 (one-shot)

	GD	VG	FN	VF	VF/NM	NM-
Four Color 877-Toth-a, Rex Allen photo-c	9	18	27	57	111	165

FRONTIER FIGHTERS
National Periodical Publications: Sept-Oct, 1955 - No. 8, Nov-Dec, 1956

	GD	VG	FN	VF	VF/NM	NM-
1-Davy Crockett, Buffalo Bill (by Kubert), Kit Carson begin (Scarce)	60	120	180	381	653	925
2	40	80	120	246	411	575
3-8	37	74	111	222	361	500

NOTE: *Buffalo Bill by* ***Kubert*** *in all.*

FRONTIER ROMANCES
Avon Periodicals/I. W.: Nov-Dec, 1949 - No. 2, Feb-Mar, 1950 (Painted-c)

	GD	VG	FN	VF	VF/NM	NM-
1-Used in **SOTI**, pg. 180 (General reference) & illo. "Erotic spanking in a western comic book"	77	154	231	493	847	1200
2 (Scarce)-Woodish-a by Stallman	47	94	141	296	498	700
I.W. Reprint #1-Reprints Avon's #1	3	6	9	21	33	45
I.W. Reprint #9-Reprints ?	3	6	9	15	22	28

FRONTIER SCOUT: DAN'L BOONE (Formerly Death Valley; The Masked Raider No. 14 on)
Charlton Comics: No. 10, Jan, 1956 - No. 13, Aug, 1956; V2#14, Mar, 1965

	GD	VG	FN	VF	VF/NM	NM-
10	10	20	30	54	72	90
11-13(1956)	6	12	18	31	38	45
V2#14(3/65)	3	6	9	15	22	28

FRONTIER TRAIL (The Rider No. 1-5)
Ajax/Farrell Publ.: No. 6, May, 1958

	GD	VG	FN	VF	VF/NM	NM-
6	6	12	18	31	38	45

FRONTIER WESTERN
Atlas Comics (PrPI): Feb, 1956 - No. 10, Aug, 1957

	GD	VG	FN	VF	VF/NM	NM-
1-The Pecos Kid rides	24	48	72	144	237	330
2,3,6-Williamson-a, 4 pgs. each	15	30	45	90	140	190
4,7,9,10: 10-Check-a	12	24	36	69	97	125
5-Crandall, Baker, Davis-a; Williamson text illos	15	30	45	84	127	170
8-Crandall, Morrow, & Wildey-a	13	26	39	72	101	130

NOTE: ***Baker*** *a-9.* ***Colan*** *a-2, 6.* ***Drucker*** *a-3, 4.* ***Heath*** *c-5.* ***Maneely*** *c/a-2, 7, 9.* ***Maurera*** *a-2.* ***Romita*** *a-7.* ***Severin*** *c-6, 8, 10.* ***Tuska*** *a-2.* ***Wildey*** *a-5, 8. Ringo Kid in No. 4.*

FRONTLINE COMBAT
E. C. Comics: July-Aug, 1951 - No. 15, Jan, 1954

	GD	VG	FN	VF	VF/NM	NM-
1-Severin/Kurtzman-a	97	194	291	776	1238	1700
2	46	92	138	368	584	800
3	36	72	108	288	456	625

Front Page Comic Book #1 © HARV

Fu Jitsu #3 © Nitz & St. Claire

The Funnies #9 © DELL

	GD 2.0	VG 4.0	FN 6.0	VF 8.0	VF/NM 9.0	NM- 9.2
4-Used in **SOTI**, pg. 257; contains "Air Burst" by Kurtzman which is his personal all-time favorite story; "Light Brigade!" story based on Tennyson's "Charge of the Light Brigade"	36	72	108	288	456	625
5-John Severin and Bill Elder bios.	29	58	87	232	366	500
6-10: 6-Kurtzman bio. 9-Civil War issue	23	46	69	184	297	410
11-15	19	38	57	152	241	330

NOTE: ***Davis*** *a-in all; c-11, 12.* ***Evans*** *a-10-15.* ***Heath*** *a-1.* ***Kubert*** *a-14.* ***Kurtzman*** *a-1-5; c-1-9.* ***Severin*** *a-5-7, 9, 13, 15.* ***Severin/Elder*** *a-2-11; c-10.* ***Toth*** *a-8, 12.* ***Wood*** *a-1-4, 6-10, 12-15; c-13-15. Special issues: No. 7 (Iwo Jima), No. 9 (Civil War), No. 12 (Air Force).*

(Canadian reprints known; see Table of Contents.)

FRONTLINE COMBAT
Russ Cochran/Gemstone Publishing: Aug, 1995 - No. 14 ($2.00/$2.50)

	GD 2.0	VG 4.0	FN 6.0	VF 8.0	VF/NM 9.0	NM- 9.2
1-14-E.C. reprints in all						4.00

FRONT PAGE COMIC BOOK
Front Page Comics (Harvey): 1945

	GD 2.0	VG 4.0	FN 6.0	VF 8.0	VF/NM 9.0	NM- 9.2
1-Kubert-a; intro. & 1st app. Man in Black by Powell; Fuje-c	58	116	174	371	636	900

FROST AND FIRE (See DC Science Fiction Graphic Novel)

FROSTBITE
DC Comics (Vertigo): Nov, 2016 - No. 6, Apr, 2017 ($3.99)

	GD 2.0	VG 4.0	FN 6.0	VF 8.0	VF/NM 9.0	NM- 9.2
1-6-Joshua Williamson-s/Jason Shawn Alexander-a						4.00

FROSTY THE SNOWMAN
Dell Publishing Co.: No. 359, Nov, 1951 - No. 1272, Dec-Feb?/1961-62

	GD 2.0	VG 4.0	FN 6.0	VF 8.0	VF/NM 9.0	NM- 9.2
Four Color 359 (#1)	10	20	30	68	144	220
Four Color 435,514,601,661	7	14	21	44	82	120
Four Color 748,861,950,1065,1153,1272	5	10	15	35	63	90

FROZEN (Disney movie)
Joe Books Ltd.: Jul, 2016 - No. 5 ($2.99)

	GD 2.0	VG 4.0	FN 6.0	VF 8.0	VF/NM 9.0	NM- 9.2
1-5-Georgia Ball-s/Benedetta Barone-a						4.00

FROZEN... (Disney movie)
Dark Horse Comics: 2018 - Present ($3.99, limited series)

	GD 2.0	VG 4.0	FN 6.0	VF 8.0	VF/NM 9.0	NM- 9.2
...: Breaking Boundaries (8/18 - No. 3, 10/18) 1-3: 1-Caranagna & Nitz-s						4.00
...: Reunion Road (3/19 - No. 3, 5/19) 1-3-Caranagna-s/Francisco-a						4.00
...: The Hero Within (6/19 - No. 3, 9/19) 1-3-Caranagna-s						4.00
...: True Treasure (11/19 - No. 3, 1/20) 1-3-Caranagna-s; leads up to Frozen 2 movie						4.00

FRUITMAN SPECIAL (See Bunny #2 for 1st app.)
Harvey Publications: Dec, 1969 (68 pgs.)

	GD 2.0	VG 4.0	FN 6.0	VF 8.0	VF/NM 9.0	NM- 9.2
1-Funny super hero	4	8	12	25	40	55

F-TROOP (TV)
Dell Publishing Co.: Aug, 1966 - No. 7, Aug, 1967 (All have photo-c)

	GD 2.0	VG 4.0	FN 6.0	VF 8.0	VF/NM 9.0	NM- 9.2
1	13	26	39	87	191	295
2-7	5	10	15	34	60	85

FUGITIVES FROM JUSTICE (True Crime Stories)
St. John Publishing Co.: Feb, 1952 - No. 5, Oct, 1952

	GD 2.0	VG 4.0	FN 6.0	VF 8.0	VF/NM 9.0	NM- 9.2
1	31	62	93	182	296	410
2-Matt Baker-r/Northwest Mounties #2; Vic Flint strip reprints begin	27	54	81	158	259	360
3-Reprints panel from Authentic Police Cases that was used in **SOTI** with changes; Tuska-a	26	52	78	154	252	350
4	15	30	45	85	133	180
5-Last Vic Flint-r; bondage-c	20	40	60	114	182	250

FUGITOID
Mirage Studios: 1985 (B&W, magazine size, one-shot)

	GD 2.0	VG 4.0	FN 6.0	VF 8.0	VF/NM 9.0	NM- 9.2
1-Ties into Teenage Mutant Ninja Turtles #5	4	8	12	27	44	60

FU JITSU
AfterShock Comics: Sept, 2017 - No. 5, Feb, 2018 ($3.99)

	GD 2.0	VG 4.0	FN 6.0	VF 8.0	VF/NM 9.0	NM- 9.2
1-5-Jai Nitz-s/Wesley St. Claire-a						4.00

FULL OF FUN
Red Top (Decker Publ.)(Farrell)/I. W. Enterprises: Aug, 1957 - No. 2, Nov, 1957; 1964

	GD 2.0	VG 4.0	FN 6.0	VF 8.0	VF/NM 9.0	NM- 9.2
1(1957)-Funny animal; Dave Berg-a	8	16	24	44	57	70
2-Reprints Bingo, the Monkey Doodle Boy	5	10	15	23	28	32
8-I.W. Reprint('64)	2	4	6	9	12	15

FUN AT CHRISTMAS (See March of Comics No. 138)

FUN CLUB COMICS (See Interstate Theatres...)

FUN COMICS (Formerly Holiday Comics #1-8; Mighty Bear #13 on)
Star Publications: No. 9, Jan, 1953 - No. 12, Oct, 1953

	GD 2.0	VG 4.0	FN 6.0	VF 8.0	VF/NM 9.0	NM- 9.2
9-(25¢ Giant)-L. B. Cole X-Mas-c; X-Mas issue	25	50	75	147	241	335
10-12-L. B. Cole-c. 12-Mighty Bear-c/story	20	40	60	114	182	250

FUNDAY FUNNIES (See Famous TV..., and Harvey Hits No. 35,40)

FUN-IN (TV)(Hanna-Barbera)
Gold Key: Feb, 1970 - No. 10, Jan, 1972; No. 11, 4/74 - No. 15, 12/74

	GD 2.0	VG 4.0	FN 6.0	VF 8.0	VF/NM 9.0	NM- 9.2
1-Dastardly & Muttley in Their Flying Machines; Perils of Penelope Pitstop in #1-4; It's the Wolf in all	6	12	18	41	76	110
2-4,6-Cattanooga Cats in 2-4	3	6	9	21	33	45
5,7-Motormouse & Autocat, Dastardly & Muttley in both; It's the Wolf in #7	4	8	12	23	37	50
8,10-The Harlem Globetrotters, Dastardly & Muttley in #10	4	8	12	23	37	50
9-Where's Huddles?, Dastardly & Muttley, Motormouse & Autocat app.	4	8	12	23	37	50
11-Butch Cassidy	3	6	9	19	30	40
12-15: 12,15-Speed Buggy. 13-Hair Bear Bunch. 14-Inch High Private Eye	3	6	9	19	30	40

FUNKY PHANTOM, THE (TV)
Gold Key: Mar, 1972 - No. 13, Mar, 1975 (Hanna-Barbera)

	GD 2.0	VG 4.0	FN 6.0	VF 8.0	VF/NM 9.0	NM- 9.2
1	5	10	15	31	53	75
2-5	3	6	9	18	28	38
6-13	3	6	9	15	22	28

FUNLAND
Ziff-Davis (Approved Comics): No date (1940s) (25¢)

	GD 2.0	VG 4.0	FN 6.0	VF 8.0	VF/NM 9.0	NM- 9.2
nn-Contains games, puzzles, cut-outs, etc.	23	46	69	138	227	315

FUNLAND COMICS
Croyden Publishers: 1945

	GD 2.0	VG 4.0	FN 6.0	VF 8.0	VF/NM 9.0	NM- 9.2
1-Funny animal	19	38	57	112	179	245

FUNNIES, THE (New Funnies No. 65 on)
Dell Publishing Co.: Oct, 1936 - No. 64, May, 1942

	GD 2.0	VG 4.0	FN 6.0	VF 8.0	VF/NM 9.0	NM- 9.2
1-Tailspin Tommy, Mutt & Jeff, Alley Oop (1st app?), Capt. Easy (1st app.), Don Dixon begin	350	700	1050	2100	3635	5200
2 (11/36)-Scribbly by Mayer begins (see Popular Comics #6 for 1st app.)	160	320	480	960	1636	2350
3	110	220	330	660	1165	1650
4,5: 4(1/37)-Christmas-c	85	170	255	510	847	1200
6-10	70	140	210	403	646	900
11-20: 16-Christmas-c	65	130	195	374	619	875
21-29: 25-Crime Busters by McWilliams(4pgs.)	52	104	156	299	480	675
30-John Carter of Mars (origin/1st app.) begins by Edgar Rice Burroughs; Jim Gary-a Warner Bros.' Bosko-c (4/39)	258	516	774	1651	2826	4000
31-34,36-44: 31,32-Gary-a. 33-John Coleman Burroughs art begins on John Carter. 34-Last funny-c. 40-John Carter of Mars-c	103	206	309	659	1130	1600
35-(9/39)-Mr. District Attorney begins; based on radio show; 1st cover app. John Carter of Mars	194	388	582	1242	2121	3000
45-Origin/1st app. Phantasmo, the Master of the World (Dell's 1st super-hero, 7/40) & his sidekick Whizzer McGee	116	232	346	742	1271	1800
46-50: 46-The Black Knight begins, ends #62	61	122	183	390	670	950
51-56-Last ERB John Carter of Mars	50	100	150	315	533	750
57-Intro. & origin Captain Midnight (7/41)	377	754	1131	2639	4620	6600
58-60: 58-Captain Midnight-c begin, end #63	94	188	282	597	1024	1450
61-Andy Panda begins by Walter Lantz; WWII-c	142	284	426	909	1555	2200
62,63: 63-Last Captain Midnight-c; bondage-c	77	154	231	493	847	1200
64-Format change; Oswald the Rabbit, Felix the Cat, Li'l Eight Ball app.; origin & 1st app. Woody Woodpecker in Oswald; last Capt. Midnight; Oswald, Andy Panda, Li'l Eight Ball-c	271	542	813	1734	2967	4200

NOTE: ***Mayer*** *c-26, 48.* ***McWilliams*** *art in many issues on "Rex King of the Deep". Alley Oop c-17, 20. Captain Midnight c-57(i/2), 58-63. John Carter c-35-37, 40. Phantasmo c-45-56, 57(1/2), 58-61(part). Rex King c-38, 39, 42. Tailspin Tommy c-41.*

FUNNIES ANNUAL, THE
Avon Periodicals: 1959 ($1.00, approx. 7x10", B&W; tabloid-size)

	GD 2.0	VG 4.0	FN 6.0	VF 8.0	VF/NM 9.0	NM- 9.2
1-(Rare)-Features the best newspaper comic strips of the year: Archie, Snuffy Smith, Beetle Bailey, Henry, Blondie, Steve Canyon, Buz Sawyer, The Little King, Hi & Lois, Popeye, & others. Also has a chronological history of the comics from 2000 B.C. to 1959.	57	114	171	362	619	875

FUNNIES ON PARADE (See Promotional Comics section)

FUNNY ANIMALS (See Fawcett's Funny Animals)
Charlton Comics: Sept, 1984 - No. 2, Nov, 1984

	GD 2.0	VG 4.0	FN 6.0	VF 8.0	VF/NM 9.0	NM- 9.2
1,2-Atomic Mouse-r; low print						6.00

FUNNYBONE (... The Laugh-Book of Comical Comics)

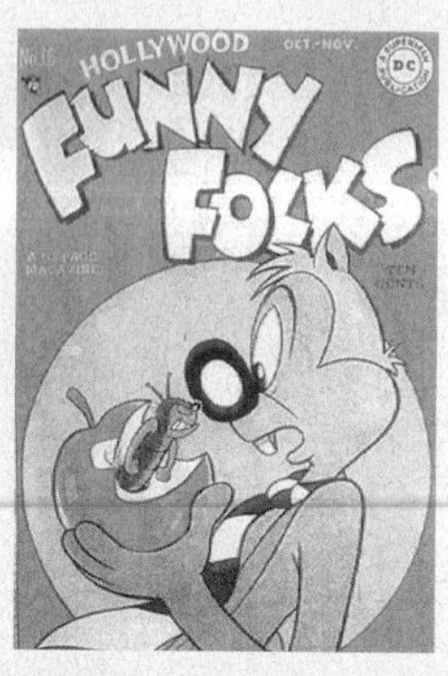

Funny Folks #16 © DC

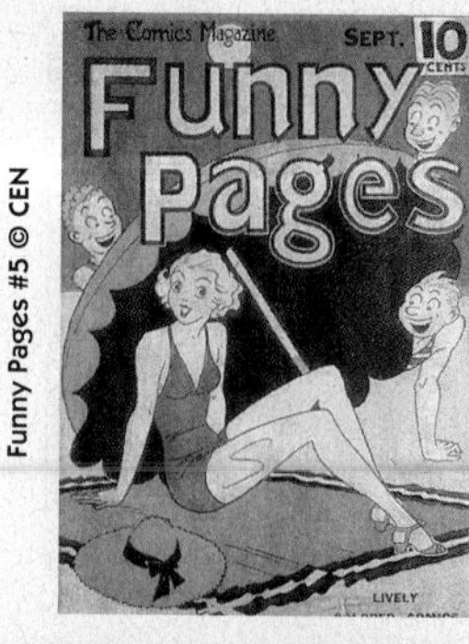

Funny Pages #5 © CEN

Funny Tunes #3 © AVON

	GD 2.0	VG 4.0	FN 6.0	VF 8.0	VF/NM 9.0	NM- 9.2

La Salle Publishing Co.: 1944 (25¢, 132 pgs.)

	GD	VG	FN	VF	VF/NM	NM-
nn	37	74	111	222	361	500

FUNNY BOOK (...Magazine for Young Folks) (Hocus Pocus No. 9)
Parents' Magazine Press (Funny Book Publishing Corp.): Dec, 1942 - No. 9, Aug-Sept, 1946 (Comics, stories, puzzles, games)

	GD	VG	FN	VF	VF/NM	NM-
1-Funny animal; Alice In Wonderland app.	19	38	57	111	176	240
2-Gulliver in Giant-Land	12	24	36	69	97	125
3-9: 4-Advs. of Robin Hood. 9-Hocus-Pocus strip	10	20	30	56	76	95

FUNNY COMICS
Modern Store Publ.: 1955 (7¢, 5x7", 36 pgs.)

	GD	VG	FN	VF	VF/NM	NM-
1-Funny animal	5	10	15	33	57	90

FUNNY COMIC TUNES (See Funny Tunes)

FUNNY FABLES
Decker Publications (Red Top Comics): Aug, 1957 - V2#2, Nov, 1957

	GD	VG	FN	VF	VF/NM	NM-
V1#1	7	14	21	37	46	55
V1#2,V2#1,2: V1#2 (11/57)-Reissue of V1#1	5	10	15	24	30	35

FUNNY FILMS (Features funny animal characters from films)
American Comics Group(Michel Publ./Titan Publ.): Sept-Oct, 1949 - No. 29, May-June, 1954 (No. 1-4: 52 pgs.)

	GD	VG	FN	VF	VF/NM	NM-
1-Puss An' Boots, Blunderbunny begin	19	38	57	111	176	240
2	11	22	33	64	90	115
3-10: 3-X-Mas-c	9	18	27	47	61	75
11-20	7	14	21	35	43	50
21-29	6	12	18	28	34	40

FUNNY FOLKS
DC Comics: Feb, 1946

nn-Ashcan comic, not distributed to newsstands, only for in house use (no known sales)

FUNNY FOLKS (Hollywood... on cover only No. 16-26; becomes Hollywood Funny Folks No. 27 on)
National Periodical Publ.: April-May, 1946 - No. 26, June-July, 1950 (52 pgs., #15 on)

	GD	VG	FN	VF	VF/NM	NM-
1-Nutsy Squirrel begins (1st app.) by Rube Grossman; Grossman-a in most issues	43	86	129	271	461	650
2	21	42	63	126	206	285
3-5: 4-1st Nutsy Squirrel-c	15	30	45	86	133	180
6-10: 6,9-Nutsy Squirrel-c begin	11	22	33	62	86	110
11-26: 15-Begin 52 pg. issues (8-9/48)	10	20	30	54	72	90

NOTE: ***Sheldon Mayer*** *a-in some issues.* ***Post*** *a-18. Christmas c-12.*

FUNNY FROLICS
Timely/Marvel Comics (SPI): Summer, 1945 - No. 5, Dec, 1946

	GD	VG	FN	VF	VF/NM	NM-
1-Sharpy Fox, Puffy Pig, Krazy Krow	33	66	99	196	321	445
2-(Fall 1945)	18	36	54	109	172	235
3,4: 3-(Spring 1946)	15	30	45	86	133	180
5-Kurtzman-a	15	30	45	92	144	195

FUNNY FUNNIES
Nedor Publishing Co.: April, 1943 (68 pgs.)

	GD	VG	FN	VF	VF/NM	NM-
1-Funny animals; Peter Porker app.	24	48	72	140	230	320

FUNNYMAN (Also see Cisco Kid Comics & Extra Comics)
Magazine Enterprises: Dec, 1947; No. 1, Jan, 1948 - No. 6, Aug, 1948

nn(12/47)-Prepublication B&W undistributed copy by Siegel & Shuster-(5-3/4x8"), 16 pgs.; Sold at auction in 1997 for $575.00

	GD	VG	FN	VF	VF/NM	NM-
1-Siegel & Shuster-a in all; Dick Ayers 1st pro work (as assistant) on 1st few issues	54	108	162	343	574	825
2	33	66	99	196	321	445
3-6	29	58	87	170	278	385

FUNNY MOVIES (See 3-D Funny Movies)

FUNNY PAGES (Formerly The Comics Magazine)
Comics Magazine Co./Ultem Publ.(Chesler)/Centaur Publications: No. 6, Nov, 1936 - No. 42, Oct, 1940

	GD	VG	FN	VF	VF/NM	NM-
V1#6 (nn, nd)-The Clock begins (2 pgs., 1st app.), ends #11; The Clock is the 1st masked comic book hero	423	846	1269	3088	5444	7800
7-11: 11-(6/37)	181	362	543	1158	1979	2800
V2#1-V2#5: V2#1 (9/37)(V2#2 on-c; V2#1 in indicia). V2#2 (10/37)(V2#3 on-c; V2#2 in indicia). V2#3(11/37) - 5	148	296	444	947	1624	2300
6(1st Centaur, 3/38)	168	336	504	1075	1838	2600
7-9	139	278	417	890	1520	2150
10(Scarce, 9/38)-1st app. of The Arrow by Gustavson (Blue costume)	486	972	1458	3550	6275	9000
11,12	174	348	522	1114	1907	2700
V3#1-Bruce Wayne prototype in "Case of the Missing Heir," by Bob Kane, 3 months before app. Batman (See Det. Pic. Stories #5)	295	590	885	1888	3244	4600
2-6,8: 6,8-Last funny covers	168	336	504	1075	1838	2600
7-1st Arrow-c (9/39)	449	898	1347	3278	5789	8300
9-Tarpe Mills jungle-c	181	362	543	1158	1979	2800
10-2nd Arrow-c (Rare)	438	876	1314	3197	5649	8100
V4#1(1/40, Arrow-c)-(Rare)-The Owl & The Phantom Rider app.; origin Mantoka, Maker of Magic by Jack Cole. Mad Ming begins, ends #42; Tarpe Mills-a	449	898	1347	3278	5789	8300
35-Classic Arrow-c (Scarce)	459	918	1377	3350	5925	8500
36-38-Mad Ming-c	284	568	852	1818	3109	4400
39-41-Arrow-c	306	612	942	2198	3849	5500
42 (Scarce,10/40)-Arrow-c	371	742	1113	2600	4550	6500

NOTE: ***Biro*** *c-V2#9.* ***Burgos*** *c-V3#10.* ***Jack Cole*** *a-V2#3, 7, 8, 10, 11, V3#2, 6, 9, 10, V4#1, 37; c-V3#2, 4.* ***Eisner*** *a-V1#7, 8?, 10.* ***Ken Ernst*** *a-V1#7, 8.* ***Everett*** *a-V2#11 (illos).* ***Filchock*** *c-V2#10, V3#6.* ***Gill Fox*** *a-V2#11.* ***Sid Greene*** *a-39.* ***Guardineer*** *a-V2#2, 3, 5.* ***Gustavson*** *a-V2#5, 11, 12, V3#1-10, 35, 38-42; c-V3#7, 35, 39-42.* ***Bob Kane*** *a-V3#1.* ***McWilliams*** *a-V2#12, V3#1, 3-6.* ***Tarpe Mills*** *a-V3#8-10, V4#1; c-V3#9.* ***Ed Moore Jr.*** *a-V2#12.* ***Schwab*** *c-V3#1.* ***Bob Wood*** *a-V2#2, 3, 8, 11, V3#6, 9, 10; c-V2#6, 7. Arrow c-V3#7, 10, V4#1, 35, 40-42.*

FUNNY PICTURE STORIES (Comic Pages V3#4 on)
Comics Magazine Co./Centaur Publications: Nov, 1936 - V3#3, May, 1939

	GD	VG	FN	VF	VF/NM	NM-
V1#1-The Clock begins (c-feature)(see Funny Pages for 1st app.)	508	1016	1524	3708	6554	9400
2	239	478	717	1530	2615	3700
3-6(4/37): 4-Eisner-a	181	362	543	1158	1979	2800
7-(6/37) (Rare) Racial humor-c	420	840	1260	2940	5170	7400
V2#1 (9/37; V1#10 on-c; V2#1 in indicia)-Jack Strand begins	129	258	387	826	1413	2000
2 (10/37; V1#11 on-c; V2#2 in indicia)	129	258	387	826	1413	2000
3-5,7-11(11/38): 4-Christmas-c	119	238	357	762	1306	1850
6-(1st Centaur, 3/38)	129	258	387	826	1413	2000
V3#1(1/39)-3	113	226	339	723	1237	1750

NOTE: ***Biro*** *c-V2#1, 8, 9, 11.* ***Guardineer*** *a-V1#11; c-V2#6, V3#5.* ***Bob Wood*** *c/a-V1#11, V2#2; c-V2#3, 5.*

FUNNY STUFF (Becomes The Dodo & the Frog No. 80)
All-American/National Periodical Publications No. 7 on: Summer, 1944 - No. 79, July-Aug, 1954 (#1-7 are quarterly)

	GD	VG	FN	VF	VF/NM	NM-
1-The Three Mouseketeers (ends #28) & The "Terrific Whatzit" begin; Sheldon Mayer-a; Grossman-a in most issues	100	200	300	635	1093	1550
2-Sheldon Mayer-a	45	90	135	284	480	675
3-5: 3-Flash parody. 5-All Mayer-a/scripts issue	32	64	96	188	307	425
6-10 10-(6/46)	20	40	60	117	189	260
11-17,19	15	30	45	90	140	190
18-The Dodo & the Frog (2/47, 1st app?) begin?; X-Mas-c	28	56	84	165	270	375
19-1st Dodo & the Frog-c (3/47)	20	40	60	117	189	260
20-2nd Dodo & the Frog-c (4/47)	15	30	45	84	127	170
21,23-30: 24-Infinity-c. 30-Christmas-c	11	22	33	62	86	110
22-Superman cameo	39	78	117	240	395	550
31-79: 62-Bo Bunny app. by Mayer. 70-Bo Bunny series begins	10	20	30	56	76	95

NOTE: ***Mayer*** *a-1-8, 55, ,57, 58, 61, 62, 64, 65, 68, 70, 72, 74-79; c-2, 5, 6, 8.*

FUNNY STUFF STOCKING STUFFER
DC Comics: Mar, 1985 ($1.25, 52 pgs.)

	GD	VG	FN	VF	VF/NM	NM-
1-Almost every DC funny animal featured						4.00

FUNNY 3-D
Harvey Publications: December, 1953 (25¢, came with 2 pair of glasses)

	GD	VG	FN	VF	VF/NM	NM-
1-Shows cover in 3-D on inside	12	24	36	69	97	125

FUNNY TUNES (Animated Funny Comic Tunes No. 16-22; Funny Comic Tunes No. 23, on covers only; Oscar No. 24 on)
U.S.A. Comics Magazine Corp. (Timely): No. 16, Summer, 1944 - No. 23, Fall, 1946

	GD	VG	FN	VF	VF/NM	NM-
16-Silly Seal, Ziggy Pig, Krazy Krow begin	27	54	81	158	259	360
17 (Fall/44)-Becomes Gay Comics #18 on?	21	42	63	126	206	285
18-22: 21-Super Rabbit app.	20	40	60	115	188	260
23-Kurtzman-a	20	40	60	120	195	270

FUNNY TUNES (Becomes Space Comics #4 on)
Avon Periodicals: July, 1953 - No. 3, Dec-Jan, 1953-54

	GD	VG	FN	VF	VF/NM	NM-
1-Space Mouse, Peter Rabbit, Merry Mouse, Spotty the Pup, Cicero the Cat begin; all continue in Space Comics	14	28	42	78	112	145
2,3	9	18	27	47	61	75

FUNNY WORLD
Marbak Press: 1947 - No. 3, 1948

Furious #1 © Glass & Santos

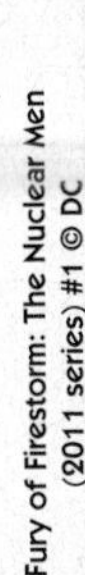
Fury of Firestorm: The Nuclear Men (2011 series) #1 © DC

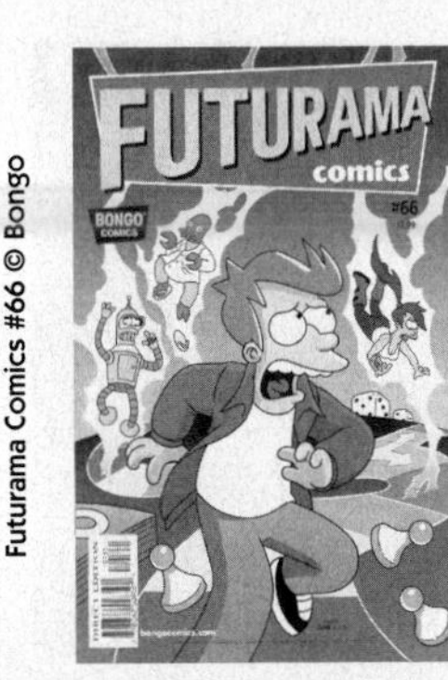
Futurama Comics #66 © Bongo

	GD 2.0	VG 4.0	FN 6.0	VF 8.0	VF/NM 9.0	NM- 9.2
1-The Berrys, The Toodles & other strip-r begin	9	18	27	52	69	85
2,3	7	14	21	35	43	50

FUNTASTIC WORLD OF HANNA-BARBERA, THE (TV)
Marvel Comics Group: Dec, 1977 - No. 3, June, 1978 ($1.25, oversized)

1-3: 1-The Flintstones Christmas Party(12/77). 2-Yogi Bear's Easter Parade(3/78). 3-Laff-a-lympics(6/78) 4 8 12 25 40 55

FUN TIME
Ace Periodicals: Spring, 1953; No. 2, Sum, 1953; No. 3(nn), Fall, 1953; No. 4, Wint, 1953-54

	GD	VG	FN	VF	VF/NM	NM-
1-(25¢, 100 pgs.)-Funny animal	22	44	66	128	209	290
2-4 (All 25¢, 100 pgs.)	16	32	48	98	154	210

FUN WITH SANTA CLAUS (See March of Comics No. 11, 108, 325)

FURIOUS
Dark Horse Comics: Jan, 2014 - No. 5, May, 2014 ($3.99)

1-5-Glass-s/Santos-a 4.00

FURTHER ADVENTURES OF CYCLOPS AND PHOENIX (Also see Adventures of Cyclops and Phoenix, Uncanny X-Men & X-Men)
Marvel Comics: June, 1996 - No. 4, Sept, 1996 ($1.95, limited series)

1-4: Origin of Mr. Sinister; Milligan scripts; John Paul Leon-c/a(p). 2-4-Apocalypse app. 4.00
Trade Paperback (1997, $14.99) r/1-4 15.00

FURTHER ADVENTURES OF INDIANA JONES, THE (Movie) (Also see Indiana Jones and the Last Crusade & Indiana Jones and the Temple of Doom)
Marvel Comics Group: Jan, 1983 - No. 34, Mar, 1986

	GD	VG	FN	VF	VF/NM	NM-
1-Byrne/Austin-a; Austin-c	2	4	6	8	10	12
2-34: 2-Byrne/Austin-c/a						4.00

NOTE: ***Austin** a-1i, 2i, 6i, 9i; c-1, 2i, 6i, 9i. **Byrne** a-1p, 2p; c-2p. **Chaykin** a-6p; c-6p, 8p-10p. **Ditko** a-21p, 25-28, 34. **Golden** c-24, 25. **Simonson** c-9. Painted c-14.*

FURTHER ADVENTURES OF NICK WILSON, THE
Image Comics: Jan, 2018 - No. 5, May 2018 ($3.99)

1-5-Gorodetsky & Andreyko-s/Sadowski-a 4.00

FURTHER ADVENTURES OF NYOKA, THE JUNGLE GIRL, THE (See Nyoka)
AC Comics: 1988 - No. 5, 1989 ($1.95, color; $2.25/$2.50, B&W)

1-5 : 1,2-Bill Black-a plus reprints. 3-Photo-c. 5-(B&W)-Reprints plus movie photos 4.00

FURY (Straight Arrow's Horse...) (See A-1 No. 119)

FURY (TV) (See March Of Comics #200)
Dell Publishing Co./Gold Key: No. 781, Mar, 1957 - Nov, 1962 (All photo-c)

	GD	VG	FN	VF	VF/NM	NM-
Four Color 781	7	14	21	49	92	135
Four Color 885,975,1031,1080,1133,1172,1218,1296	5	10	15	35	63	90
01292-208(#1-'62), 10020-211(11/62-G.K.)	5	10	15	33	57	80

FURY
Marvel Comics: May, 1994 ($2.95, one-shot)

1-Iron Man, Red Skull, FF, Hatemonger, Logan app.; origin Nick Fury 4.00

FURY (Volume 3)
Marvel Comics (MAX): Nov, 2001 - No. 6, Apr, 2002 ($2.99, mature content)

1-6-Ennis-s/Robertson-a 4.00

FURY/ AGENT 13
Marvel Comics: June, 1998 - No. 2, July, 1998 ($2.99, limited series)

1,2-Nick Fury returns 4.00

FURY MAX (Nick Fury)("My War Gone By" on cover)
Marvel Comics (MAX): Jul, 2012 - No. 13, Aug, 2013 ($3.99, mature content)

1-13: 1-Ennis-s/Parlov-a/Johnson-c; Nick Fury in 1954 Indochina. 7-9-Frank Castle app. 4.00

FURY OF FIRESTORM, THE (Becomes Firestorm The Nuclear Man on cover with #50, in indicia with #65) (Also see Firestorm)
DC Comics: June, 1982 - No. 64, Oct, 1987 (75¢ on)

	GD	VG	FN	VF	VF/NM	NM-
1-Intro The Black Bison; brief origin	3	6	9	17	26	35
2-6,8-22,25-40,43-64: 4-JLA x-over. 6-Masters of the Universe preview insert. 17-1st app. Firehawk. 21-Death of Killer Frost. 22-Origin. 27-Firestorm pin-up by Gil Kane. 34-1st app./origin Killer Frost II. 39-Weasel's ID revealed. 48-Intro. Moonbow. 53-Origin & 1st app. Silver Shade. 55,56-Legends x-over. 58-1st app./origin new Parasite						4.00
7-1st app. Plastique	2	4	6	9	12	15
23-(5/84) 1st app. Felicity Smoak (Byte)	3	6	9	14	20	26
24-(6/84)-1st app. Bug (origin); origin Byte; 1st app. Blue Devil in a prevue pull-out	3	6	9	14	20	26
41,42-Crisis x-over. 41-Harbinger, Psycho Pirate-c/app.						5.00
61-Test cover variant; Superman logo	4	8	12	27	44	60
Annual 1-4: 1(1983), 2(1984), 3(1985), 4(1986)						5.00

NOTE: ***Colan** a-19p, Annual 4p. **Giffen** a-Annual 4p. **Gil Kane** c-30. **Nino** a-37. **Tuska** a-(p)-17, 18, 32, 45.*

FURY OF FIRESTORM: THE NUCLEAR MEN (New DC 52)
DC Comics: Nov, 2011 - No. 20, Jul, 2013 ($2.99)

1-18: 1-Van Sciver & Simone-s/Cinar-a/Van Sciver-c. 7,8-Van Sciver-a. 9-JLI app. 3.00
19,20-Killer Frost app. 5.00
#0 (11/12, #2.99) Cinar-a/c 3.00

FURY OF SHIELD
Marvel Comics: Apr, 1995 - No. 4, July, 1995 ($2.50/$1.95, limited series)

1 ($2.50)-Foil-c 5.00
2-4: 4-Bagged w/ decoder 4.00

FURY: PEACEMAKER
Marvel Comics: Apr, 2006 - No. 6, Sept, 2006 ($3.50, limited series)

1-6-Flashback to WW2; Ennis-s/Robertson-a. 1-Deodato-c. 2-Texeira-c. 5-Dillon-c 3.50
TPB (2006, $17.99) r/#1-6 18.00

FURY: S.H.I.E.L.D. 50TH ANNIVERSARY
Marvel Comics: Nov, 2015 ($3.99, one-shot)

1-Walker-s/Ferguson-a/Deodato-c; Nick Fury Jr. time travels to meet 1965 Nick Fury 4.00

FUSED
Image Comics: Mar, 2002 - No. 4, Jan, 2003 ($2.95)

1-4-Steve Niles-s. 1,2-Paul Lee-a. 3-Brad Rader-a. 4-Templesmith-a 3.00

FUSED
Dark Horse Comics: Dec, 2003 - No. 4, Mar, 2004 ($2.95)

1-4-Steve Niles-s/Josh Medors-a. 1-Powell-c 3.00

FUSION
Eclipse Comics: Jan, 1987 - No. 17, Oct, 1989 ($2.00, B&W, Baxter paper)

1-17: 11-The Weasel Patrol begins (1st app.?) 3.00

FUSION
Image Comics (Top Cow): May, 2009 - No. 3, Jul, 2009 ($2.99, limited series)

1-3-Avengers, Thunderbolts, Cyberforce and Hunter-Killer meet; Kirkham-a 3.00

FUTURAMA (TV)
Bongo Comics: 2000 - No. 81, 2016 ($2.50/$2.99/$3.99, bi-monthly)

	GD	VG	FN	VF	VF/NM	NM-
1-Based on the FOX-TV animated series; Groening/Morrison-c	3	6	9	21	33	45
1-San Diego Comic-Con Premiere Edition	6	12	18	38	69	100
2-10: 8-CGC cover spoof; X-Men parody	2	4	6	8	10	12
11-30						6.00
31-81: 40,64-Santa app. 50-55-Poster included						4.00
Annual 1 (2018, $4.99) Wacky Races spoof; Pinocchio homage						5.00
Futurama Adventures TPB (2004, $14.95) r/#5-9						15.00
Futurama Conquers the Universe TPB (2007, $14.95) r/#10-13						15.00
Futurama-O-Rama TPB (2002, $12.95) r/#1-4; sketch pages of Fry's development						15.00
...: The Time Bender Trilogy TPB (2006, $14.95) r/#16-19; cover gallery						15.00

FUTURAMA/SIMPSONS INFINITELY SECRET CROSSOVER CRISIS (TV) (See Simpsons/ Futurama Crossover Crisis II for sequel)
Bongo Comics: 2002 - No. 2, 2002 ($2.50, limited series)

	GD	VG	FN	VF	VF/NM	NM-
1-Evil Brain Spawns put Futurama crew into the Simpsons' Springfield	2	4	6	11	16	20
2	1	2	3	5	6	8

FUTURE COMICS
David McKay Publications: June, 1940 - No. 4, Sept, 1940

	GD	VG	FN	VF	VF/NM	NM-
1-(6/40, 64 pgs.)-Origin The Phantom (1st in comics) (4 pgs.); The Lone Ranger (8 pgs.) & Saturn Against the Earth (4 pgs.) begin	309	618	927	2163	3782	5400
2	155	310	465	992	1696	2400
3,4	116	232	348	742	1271	1800

FUTURE COP L.A.P.D. (Electronic Arts video game) (Also see Promotional Comics section)
DC Comics (WildStorm): Jan, 1999 ($4.95, magazine sized)

1-Stories & art by various 5.00

FUTURE FIGHT FIRSTS (Also see Agents of Atlas 2019 series)
Marvel Comics: Dec, 2019 - Jan, 2020 ($4.99, limited series of one-shots)

...: Crescent and Io 1 (1/20) Origin stories; Alyssa Wong-s/Jon Lam-a 5.00
...: Luna Snow 1 (12/19) Origin story; Alyssa Wong-s/Gang Hyuk Lim-a 5.00
...: White Fox 1 (12/19) Origin story; Alyssa Wong-s/Kevin Libranda & Geoffo-a 5.00

FUTURE FOUNDATION (From Fantastic Four)
Marvel Comics: Oct, 2019 - No. 5, Feb, 2020 ($3.99, limited series)

1-5-Whitley-s; Alex & Julie Power, Dragon Man, Onome, Bentley-23 app. 1-3-Robson-a 4.00

FUTURE IMPERFECT (Secret Wars tie-in)

Future Quest #12 © H-B

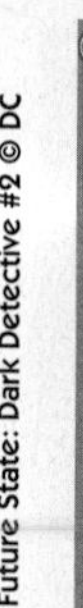

Future State: Dark Detective #2 © DC

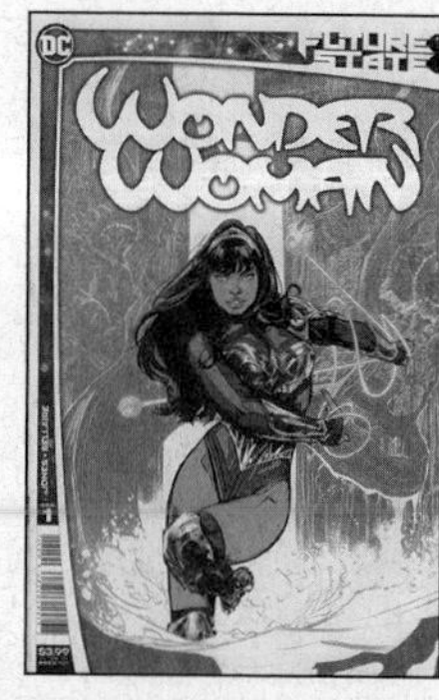
Future State: Wonder Woman #1 © DC

	GD 2.0	VG 4.0	FN 6.0	VF 8.0	VF/NM 9.0	NM- 9.2

Marvel Comics: Aug, 2015 - No. 5, Nov, 2015 ($3.99, limited series)
1-5-Peter David-s/Greg Land-a; Maestro (Hulk) and The Thing (Thaddeus Ross) app. 4.00

FUTURE QUEST
DC Comics: Jul, 2016 - No. 12, Jul, 2017 ($3.99)
1-12: 1-Jonny Quest, Space Ghost, Birdman and Dr. Zin app.; Shaner & Rude-a. 8-Olivetti-a; The Impossibles app. 4.00

FUTURE QUEST PRESENTS
DC Comics: Oct, 2017 - No. 12, Sept, 2018 ($3.99)
1-4: 1-3-Space Ghost and the Herculoids; Parker-s/Olivetti-a/c. 4-Galaxy Trio; Randall-a 4.00
5-12: 5-7-Birdman; Hester-s/Rude-a; Mentok app. 8-Mightor. 9-11-Herculoids 4.00

FUTURE SHOCK
Image Comics: 2006 (Free Comic Book Day giveaway)
...: FCBD 2006 Edition; Spawn, Invincible, Savage Dragon & others short stories 3.00

FUTURE STATE: AQUAMAN
DC Comics: Mar, 2021 - No. 2, Apr, 2021 ($3.99, limited series)
1,2-Aquaman (Jackson Hyde) & Aquawoman (Andy Curry) app.; Thomas-s/Sampere-a 4.00

FUTURE STATE: BATMAN / SUPERMAN
DC Comics: Mar, 2021 - No. 2, Apr, 2021 ($3.99, limited series)
1,2-Batman & Superman vs. False Face Society in the near future; Yang-s/Oliver-a 4.00

FUTURE STATE: CATWOMAN
DC Comics: Mar, 2021 - No. 2, Apr, 2021 ($3.99, limited series)
1,2-Catwoman (Selina Kyle) in the near future; Talia app.; Ram V-s/Schmidt-a 4.00

FUTURE STATE: DARK DETECTIVE
DC Comics: Mar, 2021 - No. 4, Late Apr, 2021 ($5.99, limited series)
1-4-Bruce Wayne in the near future; Tamaki-s/Mora-a. 1,3-Back-up with Grifter and Huntress. 2,4-Back-up with Red Hood & Ravager. 4-White Rabbit app. 6.00

FUTURE STATE: GREEN LANTERN
DC Comics: Mar, 2021 - No. 2, Apr, 2021 ($5.99, limited series)
1,2-The Corps without rings. 1-Back-up with Jessica Cruz vs. Lyssa Drak; Guy Gardner. 2-Back-ups with Hal Jordan, Mogo, Keli Quintela, & Jo Mullein 6.00

FUTURE STATE: HARLEY QUINN
DC Comics: Mar, 2021 - No. 2, Apr, 2021 ($3.99, limited series)
1,2-Harley in the near future; Black Mask app.; Stephanie Phillips-s/Simone DiMeo-a 4.00

FUTURE STATE: IMMORTAL WONDER WOMAN
DC Comics: Mar, 2021 - No. 2, Apr, 2021 ($5.99, limited series)
1,2-Diana in the far future; Darkseid app.; Bartel-a; back-up with Nubia 6.00

FUTURE STATE: JUSTICE LEAGUE
DC Comics: Mar, 2021 - No. 2, Apr, 2021 ($5.99, limited series)
1,2-Superman (Jon Kent), Batman (Tim Fox), WW (Yara Flor), Aquawoman, G.L. (Jo Mullein), and Flash team; Hyperclan app.; back-up with J.L. Dark; Doctor Fate app. 6.00

FUTURE STATE: KARA ZOR-EL, SUPERWOMAN
DC Comics: Mar, 2021 - No. 2, Apr, 2021 ($3.99, limited series)
1,2-Kara on the Moon colony; intro. Lynari; Bennett-s/Sauvage-a 4.00

FUTURE STATE: LEGION OF SUPER-HEROES
DC Comics: Mar, 2021 - No. 2, Apr, 2021 ($3.99, limited series)
1,2-Bendis-s/Rossmo-a; Legion reunites in the farther future 4.00

FUTURE STATE: NIGHTWING
DC Comics: Mar, 2021 - No. 2, Apr, 2021 ($3.99, limited series)
1,2-Nightwing & Batman (Tim Fox) vs. Peacekeepers; Nicola Scott-a/Andrew Constant-s 4.00

FUTURE STATE: ROBIN ETERNAL
DC Comics: Mar, 2021 - No. 2, Apr, 2021 ($3.99, limited series)
1,2-Tim Drake and Spoiler; Fitzmartin-s/Barrows-a 4.00

FUTURE STATE: SHAZAM! (Continues in Future State: Black Adam)
DC Comics: Mar, 2021 - No. 2, Apr, 2021 ($3.99, limited series)
1,2-Vixen, Question, Miss Martian, Powerhouse, Creeper, Giganta app.; Pansica-a 4.00

FUTURE STATE: SUICIDE SQUAD
DC Comics: Mar, 2021 - No. 2, Apr, 2021 ($5.99, limited series)
1,2-Team with Superman (Conner Kent), Batman (Talon), Martian Manhunter (Clayface), Aquaman (Fisherman), Flash (Bolt); back-up with Black Adam & Justice Legion-A 6.00

FUTURE STATE: SUPERMAN: HOUSE OF EL
DC Comics: Apr, 2021 ($5.99, one-shot)
1-P.K. Johnson-s/Scott Godlewski-a; set in the far future with Kal-El's descendants 6.00

FUTURE STATE: SUPERMAN OF METROPOLIS
DC Comics: Mar, 2021 - No. 2, Apr, 2021 ($5.99, limited series)
1,2-Jon Kent vs. Supergirl; Timms-a; back-ups with Mister Miracle and The Guardian 6.00

FUTURE STATE: SUPERMAN VS. IMPERIOUS LEX
DC Comics: Mar, 2021 - No. 3, May, 2021 ($3.99, limited series)
1-Lexor joining the United Planets; Mark Russell-s/Steve Pugh-a 4.00

FUTURE STATE: SUPERMAN / WONDER WOMAN
DC Comics: Mar, 2021 - No. 2, Apr, 2021 ($3.99, limited series)
1,2-Jon Kent & Yara Flor vs. Solaris; Watters-s/Del Duca-a 4.00

FUTURE STATE: SUPERMAN: WORLDS OF WAR (Continues in Superman: House of El)
DC Comics: Mar, 2021 - No. 2, Apr, 2021 ($7.99, limited series)
1,2-Janin-a; back-ups with Mr. Miracle, Midnighter and Black Racer 8.00

FUTURE STATE: SWAMP THING
DC Comics: Mar, 2021 - No. 2, Apr, 2021 ($3.99, limited series)
1,2-Ram V-s/Mike Perkins-a; Jason Woodrue & Obsidian app. 4.00

FUTURE STATE: TEEN TITANS (Leads into Teen Titans Academy)
DC Comics: Mar, 2021 - No. 2, Apr, 2021 ($3.99, limited series)
1,2-Sheridan-s/Sandoval-a; Red X app.; Dick Grayson as Death-Wing 4.00

FUTURE STATE: THE FLASH (Prelude to Future State: Teen Titans)
DC Comics: Mar, 2021 - No. 2, Apr, 2021 ($3.99, limited series)
1,2-Vietti-s. 1-Eaglesham-a; Flashes vs. Wally West as Famine. 2-Peterson-a 4.00

FUTURE STATE: THE NEXT BATMAN
DC Comics: Mar, 2021 - No. 4, Apr, 2021 ($7.99, limited series)
1-4-Tim Fox as Batman; Ridley-s. 1-Derington-a. 1,3-Back-ups with Outsiders, Arkham Knights. 2,4-Back-ups with Batgirls & Gotham City Sirens 8.00

FUTURE STATE: THE FLASH (Prelude to Future State: Teen Titans)
DC Comics: Mar, 2021 - No. 2, Apr, 2021 ($3.99, limited series)
1,2-Yara Flor from the Amazon Rainforest; Jöelle Jones-s/a 4.00

FUTURE WORLD COMICS
George W. Dougherty: Summer, 1946 - No. 2, Fall, 1946

	GD	VG	FN	VF	VF/NM	NM-
1,2: H.C. Kiefer-c; preview of the World of Tomorrow	34	68	102	204	332	460

FUTURE WORLD COMIX (Warren Presents...)
Warren Publications: Sept, 1978 (B&W magazine, 84 pgs.)

	GD	VG	FN	VF	VF/NM	NM-
1-Corben, Maroto, Morrow, Nino, Sutton-a; Todd-c/a; contains nudity panels	2	4	6	8	11	14

FUTURIANS, THE (See Marvel Graphic Novel #9)
Lodestone Publishing/Eternity Comics: Sept, 1985 - No. 3, 1985 ($1.50)
1-3: Indicia title "Dave Cockrum's..." 4.00
Graphic Novel 1 ($9.95, Eternity)-r/#1-3, plus never published #4 issue 10.00

FX
IDW Publishing: Mar, 2008 - No. 6, Aug, 2008 ($3.99)
1-6-John Byrne-a/c; Wayne Osborne-s 4.00

G-8 (Listed at G-Eight)

GABBY (Formerly Ken Shannon) (Teen humor)
Quality Comics Group: No. 11, Jul, 1953; No. 2, Sep, 1953 - No. 9, Sep, 1954

	GD	VG	FN	VF	VF/NM	NM-
11(#1)(7/53)	12	24	36	67	94	120
2	9	18	27	47	61	75
3-9	8	16	24	42	54	65

GABBY GOB (See Harvey Hits No. 85, 90, 94, 97, 100, 103, 106, 109)

GABBY HAYES ADVENTURE COMICS
Toby Press: Dec, 1953

	GD	VG	FN	VF	VF/NM	NM-
1-Photo-c	15	30	45	90	140	190

GABBY HAYES WESTERN (Movie star)(See Monte Hale, Real Western Hero & Western Hero)
Fawcett Publications/Charlton Comics No. 51 on: Nov, 1948 - No. 50, Jan, 1953; No. 51, Dec, 1954 - No. 59, Jan, 1957

	GD	VG	FN	VF	VF/NM	NM-
1-Gabby & his horse Corker begin; photo front/back-c begin	42	84	126	265	445	625
2	21	42	63	124	202	280
3-5	15	30	45	88	137	185
6-10: 9-Young Falcon begins	14	28	42	78	112	145
11-20: 19-Last photo back-c	11	22	33	64	90	115
21-49: 20,22,24,26,28,29-(52 pgs.)	9	18	27	52	69	85
50-(1/53)-Last Fawcett issue; last photo-c?	10	20	30	58	79	100
51-(12/54)-1st Charlton issue; photo-c	11	22	33	60	83	105

Galacta: Daughter of Galactus #1 © MAR

Gambit V2 #16 © MAR

A Game of Thrones #18 © G.R.R. Martin

GD 2.0 | VG 4.0 | FN 6.0 | VF 8.0 | VF/NM 9.0 | NM- 9.2

52-59(1955-57): 53,55-Photo-c. 58-Swayze-a 8 16 24 42 54 65

GAGS
United Features Synd./Triangle Publ. No. 9 on: Jul, 1937 - V3#10, Oct, 1944 (13-3/4x10-3/4")
1(7/37)-52 pgs.; 20 pgs. Grin & Bear It, Fellow Citizen 26 52 78 154 252 350
V1#9 (36 pgs.) (7/42) 12 24 36 67 94 120
V3#10 10 20 30 54 72 90

GALACTA: DAUGHTER OF GALACTUS
Marvel Comics: July, 2010 ($3.99, one-shot)
1-Adam Warren-s/Hector Sevilla-a; Warren & Sevilla-c : Wolverine and the FF app. 4.00

GALACTICA 1980 (Based on the Battlestar Galactica TV series)
Dynamite Entertainment: 2009 - No. 4, 2009 ($3.50)
1-4-Guggenheim-s/Razek-a 3.50

GALACTICA: THE NEW MILLENNIUM
Realm Press: Sept, 1999 ($2.99)
1-Stories by Shooter, Braden, Kuhoric 3.00

GALACTIC GUARDIANS
Marvel Comics: July, 1994 - No. 4, Oct, 1994 ($1.50, limited series)
1-4 4.00

GALACTIC WARS COMIX (Warren Presents... on cover)
Warren Publications: Dec, 1978 (B&W magazine, 84 pgs.)
nn-Wood, Williamson-r; Battlestar Galactica/Flash Gordon photo/text stories 2 4 6 8 11 14

GALACTUS THE DEVOURER
Marvel Comics: Sept, 1999 - No. 6, Mar, 2000 ($3.50/$2.50, limited series)
1-($3.50) L. Simonson-s/Muth & Sienkiewicz-a 4.00
2-5-($2.50) Buscema & Sienkiewicz-a 3.00
6-($3.50) Death of Galactus; Buscema & Sienkiewicz-a 4.00

GALAKTIKON
Albatross Funnybooks: 2017 - No. 6, 2018 ($3.99, limited series)
1-6-Brendon Small-s/Steve Mannion-a. 1-5-Eric Powell-c. 6-Mannion-c 4.00

GALAXIA (Magazine)
Astral Publ.: 1981 ($2.50, B&W, 52 pgs.)
1-Buckler/Giordano-c; Texeira/Guice-a; 1st app. Astron, Sojourner, Bloodwing, Warlords; Buckler-s/a 2 4 6 10 14 18

GALAXY QUEST: GLOBAL WARNING! (Based on the 1999 movie)
IDW Publishing: Aug, 2008 - No. 5, Dec, 2008 ($3.99)
1-5-Lobdell-s/Kyriazis-a 4.00

GALAXY QUEST: THE JOURNEY CONTINUES (Based on the 1999 movie)
IDW Publishing: Jan, 2015 - No. 4, Apr, 2015 ($3.99)
1-4-Erik Burnham-s/Nacho Arranz-a 4.00

GALLANT MEN, THE (TV)
Gold Key: Oct, 1963 (Photo-c)
1(1008-310)-Manning-a 3 6 9 21 33 45

GALLEGHER, BOY REPORTER (Disney, TV)
Gold Key: May, 1965
1(10149-505)-Photo-c 3 6 9 17 26 35

GAMBIT (See X-Men #266 & X-Men Annual #14)
Marvel Comics: Dec, 1993 - No. 4, Mar, 1994 ($2.00, limited series)
1-($2.50)-Lee Weeks-c/a in all; gold foil stamped-c 3 6 9 15 22 28
1 (Gold) 4 8 12 28 47 65
2-4 6.00

GAMBIT
Marvel Comics: Sept, 1997 - No. 4, Dec, 1997 ($2.50, limited series)
1-4-Janson-a/Mackie & Kavanagh-s 1 2 3 5 6 8

GAMBIT
Marvel Comics: Feb, 1999 - No. 25, Feb, 2001 ($2.99/$1.99)
1-($2.99) Five covers; Nicieza-a/Skroce-a 1 2 3 5 6 8
2-11,13-16-($1.99): 2-Two covers (Skroce & Adam Kubert) 3.00
12-($2.99) 4.00
17-24: 17-Begin $2.25-c. 21-Mystique-c/app. 3.00
25-($2.99) Leads into "Gambit & Bishop" 4.00
...1999 Annual ($3.50) Nicieza-s/McDaniel-a 4.00
...2000 Annual ($3.50) Nicieza-s/Derenick & Smith-a 4.00

GAMBIT
Marvel Comics: Nov, 2004 - No. 12, Aug, 2005 ($2.99)
1-12: 1-Jeanty-a/Land-c/Layman-s. 5-Wolverine-c/app. 9-Brother Voodoo-c/app. 3.00
... and the Champions: From the Marvel Vault 1 (10/11, $2.99) George Tuska's last art 3.00
...: Hath No Fury TPB (2005, $14.99) r/#7-12 15.00
...: House of Cards TPB (2005, $14.99) r/#1-6; Land cover sketches; unused covers 15.00

GAMBIT
Marvel Comics: Oct, 2012 - No. 17, Nov, 2013 ($2.99)
1-17: 1-Asmus-s/Mann-a; covers by Mann & Bachalo. 6,7-Pete Wisdom app. 3.00

GAMBIT & BISHOP (... : Sons of the Atom on cover)
Marvel Comics: Feb, 2001 - No. 6, May, 2001 ($2.25, bi-weekly limited series)
Alpha (2/01) Prelude to series; Nord-a 3.00
1-6-Jeanty-a/Williams-c 3.00
Genesis (3/01, $3.50) reprints their first apps. and first meeting 4.00

GAMBIT AND THE X-TERNALS
Marvel Comics: Mar, 1995 - No. 4, July, 1995 ($1.95, limited series)
1-4-Age of Apocalypse 4.00

GAMEBOY (Super Mario covers on all)
Valiant: 1990 - No. 5 ($1.95, coated-c)
1-5: 3,4-Layton-c. 4-Morrow-a. 5-Layton-c(i) 2 4 6 9 12 15

GAMEKEEPER (Guy Ritchie's...)
Virgin Comics: Mar, 2007 - No. 5, Sept, 2007; Mar, 2008 - No. 5, Jul, 2008 ($2.99)
1-5-Andy Diggle-s/Mukesh Singh-a; 2 covers on each 3.00
1-Extended Edition (6/07, $2.99) r/#1 with script excerpt and sketch art 3.00
Series 2 (3/08 - No. 5, 7/08) 1-5-Parker-s/Randle-a 3.00
Vol. 1 TPB (10/07, $14.99) r/#1-5; script and sketch pages; Guy Ritchie intro. 15.00

GAME OF THRONES, A (George R.R. Martin's...) (Based on A Song of Ice and Fire)
Dynamite Entertainment: 2011 - No. 24, 2014 ($3.99)
1-Covers by Alex Ross and Mike Miller 3 6 9 16 23 30
2-24: 2-Covers by Alex Ross and Mike Miller 6.00

GAMERA
Dark Horse Comics: Aug, 1996 - No. 4, Nov, 1996 ($2.95, limited series)
1-4 3.00

GAMMARAUDERS
DC Comics: Jan, 1989 - No. 10, Dec, 1989 ($1.25/$1.50/$2.00)
1-10-Based on TSR game 3.00

GAMORA (Guardians of the Galaxy)
Marvel Comics: Feb, 2017 - No. 5, Jul, 2017 ($3.99, limited series)
1-5-Perlman-s/Checchetto-a. 1,5-Thanos & Nebula app. 4.00

GAMORRA SWIMSUIT SPECIAL
Image Comics (WildStorm Productions): June, 1996 ($2.50, one-shot)
1-Campbell wraparound-c; pinups 4.00

GANDY GOOSE (Movies/TV)(See All Surprise, Giant Comics Edition #5A &10, Paul Terry's Comics & Terry-Toons)
St. John Publ. Co./Pines No. 5,6: Mar, 1953 - No. 5, Nov, 1953; No. 5, Fall, 1956 - No. 6, Sum/58
1-All St. John issues are pre-code 14 28 42 80 115 150
2 8 16 24 44 57 70
3-5(1953)(St. John) 7 14 21 35 43 50
5,6(1956-58)(Pines)-CBS Television Presents... 5 10 15 24 30 35

GANG BUSTERS (See Popular Comics #38)
David McKay/Dell Publishing Co.: 1938 - 1943
Feature Books 17(McKay)('38)-1st app. 87 174 261 553 952 1350
Large Feature Comic 10('39)-(Scarce) 87 174 261 553 952 1350
Large Feature Comic 17('41) 58 116 174 371 636 900
Four Color 7(1940) 65 130 195 416 708 1000
Four Color 23('42) 52 104 156 328 552 775
Four Color 24('43) 30 60 90 216 483 750

GANG BUSTERS (Radio/TV)(Gangbusters #14 on)
National Periodical Publ.: Dec-Jan, 1947-48 - No. 67, Dec-Jan, 1958-59 (No. 1-23: 52 pgs.)
1 94 188 282 597 1025 1450
2 41 82 123 256 428 600
3-5 28 56 84 165 270 375
6-10: 9-Dan Barry-a. 9,10-Photo-c 21 42 63 122 199 275
11-13-Photo-c 17 34 51 100 158 215

Garfield #1 © PAWS, Inc

Gasolina #8 © Skybound

Gay Comics #32 © MAR

GD VG FN VF VF/NM NM-
2.0 4.0 6.0 8.0 9.0 9.2

14,17-Frazetta-a, 8 pgs. each. 14-Photo-c 36 72 108 211 343 475
15,16,18-20,26: 26-Kirby-a 15 30 45 85 130 175
21-25,27-30 14 28 42 76 108 140
31-44: 44-Last Pre-code (2-3/55) 12 24 36 67 94 120
45-67 10 20 30 54 72 90
NOTE: ***Barry** a-6, 8, 10. **Drucker** a-51. **Moreira** a-48, 50, 59. **Roussos** a-8.*

GANGLAND
DC Comics (Vertigo): Jun, 1998 - No. 4, Sept, 1998 ($2.95, limited series)
1-4: Crime anthology by various. 2-Corben-a 3.00
TPB-(2000, $12.95) r/#1-4; Bradstreet-c 13.00

GANGSTERS AND GUN MOLLS
Avon Per./Realistic Comics: Sept, 1951 - No. 4, June, 1952 (Painted c-1-3)
1-Wood-a, 1 pg; c-/Avon paperback #292 68 136 204 435 743 1050
2-Check-a, 8 pgs.; Kamen-a; Bonnie Parker story 63 126 189 403 689 975
3-Marijuana mentioned; used in **POP**, pg. 84,85 53 106 159 334 567 800
4-Syd Shores-c 50 100 150 315 533 750

GANGSTERS CAN'T WIN
D. S. Publishing Co.: Feb-Mar, 1948 - No. 9, June-July, 1949 (All 52 pgs?)
1-True crime stories 43 86 129 271 461 650
2-Skull-c 34 68 102 204 332 460
3,5,6 23 46 69 136 223 310
4-Acid in face story 29 58 87 174 285 395
7-9 19 38 57 111 176 240
NOTE: ***Ingles** a-5, 6. **McWilliams** a-5, 7, 8. **Reinman** c-6.*

GANG WORLD
Standard Comics: No. 5, Nov, 1952 - No. 6, Jan, 1953
5-Bondage-c 24 48 72 142 234 325
6 17 34 51 105 165 225

GARBAGE PAIL KIDS COMIC BOOK (Based on the tranding cards)
IDW Publishing: Dec, 2014 - Feb, 2015 ($3.99, series of one-shots)
... Love Stinks (2/15) short stories by various incl. Haspiel, Wheeler, Bagge; 3 covers 4.00
... Puke-tacular (12/14) short stories by various incl. Bagge, Wray, Barta; 3 covers 4.00

GARFIELD (Newspaper/cartoon cat)(Also see Grumpy Cat)
Boom Entertainment (KaBOOM!): May, 2012 - No. 36, Apr, 2015 ($3.99)
1-24-Evanier-s. 1-Two covers by Barker. 8-Christmas-c. 13,20-Pet Force app. 4.00
1-4-First Appearance Variants by Jim Davis. 1-Garfield. 2-Odie. 3-Jon. 4-Nermal 10.00
25-($4.99) Covers by George Pérez and Barker; bonus pin-ups 5.00
26-36: 30-EC-style horror cover. 33-36-His 9 Lives 4.00
... 2016 Summer Special 1 (7/16, $7.99) Evanier & Nickel-s; Batman spoof
1 2 3 5 6 8
... 2018 Vacation Times Blues 1 (5/18, $7.99) Evanier & Nickel-s; Hirsch-c
1 2 3 5 6 8
... Cheesy Holiday Special 1 (12/15, $4.99) Christmas stories; Evanier & Nickel-s 5.00
...: Pet Force Special 1 (8/13, $4.99) Cover swipe of Amazing Spider-Man #50 5.00
...: Pet Force 2014 Special (4/14, $4.99) The Pet Force multiverse; bonus sketch art 5.00
... TV or Not TV? 1 (10/18, $7.99) Halloween stories; Evanier & Nickel-s; Hirsch-c 8.00

GARFIELD: HOMECOMING (Newspaper/cartoon cat)
Boom Entertainment (KaBOOM!): Jun, 2018 - No. 4, Sept, 2018 ($3.99, limited series)
1-4-Scott Nickel-s. 1-Talmadge & Alfaro-a. 2-Paroline, Lamb & Alfaro-a 4.00

GARGOYLE (See The Defenders #94)
Marvel Comics Group: June, 1985 - No. 4, Sept, 1985 (75¢, limited series)
1-Wrightson-c; character from Defenders 5.00
2-4 4.00

GARGOYLES (TV cartoon)
Marvel Comics: Feb, 1995 - No. 11, Dec, 1995 ($2.50)
1-11: Based on animated series 3.00

GARRISON
DC Comics (WildStorm): Jun, 2010 - No. 6, Nov, 2010 ($2.99)
1-6-Mariotte-s/Francavilla-a/c 3.00

GARRISON'S GORILLAS (TV)
Dell Publishing Co.: Jan, 1968 - No. 4, Oct, 1968; No. 5, Oct, 1969 (Photo-c)
1 4 8 12 28 47 65
2-5: 5-Reprints #1 3 6 9 19 30 40

GARY GIANNI'S THE MONSTERMEN
Dark Horse Comics: Aug, 1999 ($2.95, one-shot)
1-Gianni-s/c/a; back-up Hellboy story by Mignola 4.00

GASM (Sci-Fi, Horror, Fantasy comics magazine)(Mature content)
Stories, Layouts & Press, Inc.: Nov, 1977 - nn (No. 5), Jun, 1978 (B&W/color)

GD VG FN VF VF/NM NM-
2.0 4.0 6.0 8.0 9.0 9.2

1-Mark Wheatley-s/a; Gene Day-s/a; Workman-a 3 6 9 14 20 26
2 (12/77) Wheatley-a; Winnick-s/a; Workman-a 2 4 6 11 16 20
nn(#3, 2/78) Day-s/a; Wheatley-a; Workman-a 2 4 6 10 14 18
nn(#4, 4/78) Day-s/a; Wheatley-a; Corben-a 3 6 9 14 20 26
nn(#5, 6/78) Hempel-a; Howarth-a; Corben-a 3 6 9 16 23 30

GASOLINA
Image Comics (Skybound): Sept, 2017 - No. 18, May, 2019 ($3.99)
1-18-Sean Mackiewicz-s/Niko Walter-a 4.00

GASOLINE ALLEY (Top Love Stories No. 3 on?)
Star Publications: Sept-Oct, 1950 - No. 2, Dec, 1950 (Newspaper-r)
1-Contains 1 pg. intro. history of the strip (The Life of Skeezix); reprints 15 scenes of highlights from 1921-1935, plus an adventure from 1935 and 1936 strips; a 2-pg. filler is included on the life of the creator Frank King, with photo of the cartoonist.
22 44 66 132 216 300
2-(1936-37 reprints)-L. B. Cole-c 25 50 75 150 245 340
(See Super Book No. 21)

GASP!
American Comics Group: Mar, 1967 - No. 4, Aug, 1967 (12¢)
1 5 10 15 33 57 80
2-4 3 6 9 21 33 45

GATECRASHER
Black Bull Entertainment: Mar, 2000 - No. 4, Jun, 2000 ($2.50, limited series)
1,2-Waid-s/Conner & Palmiotti-c/a; 1,2-variant-c by J.G. Jones 3.00
3,4: 3-Jusko var-c. 4-Linsner-c 3.00
... Ring of Fire TPB (11/00, $12.95) r/#1-4; Hughes-c; Ennis intro. 13.00

GATECRASHER (Regular series)
Black Bull Entertainment: Aug, 2000 - No. 6, Jan, 2001 ($2.50, limited series)
1-6-Waid-s/Conner & Palmiotti-c/a; 1-3-Variant-c by Fabry. 4-Hildebrandts variant-c. 5-Art Adams var-c. 6-Texeira var-c 3.00

GAY COMICS (Honeymoon No. 41)
Timely Comics/USA Comic Mag. Co. No. 18-24: Mar, 1944 (no month); No. 18, Fall, 1944 - No. 40, Oct, 1949
1-Wolverton's Powerhouse Pepper; Tessie the Typist begins; 1st app. Willie (one shot)
103 206 309 659 1130 1600
18-(Formerly Funny Tunes #17?)-Wolverton-a 63 126 189 403 689 975
19-29: Wolverton-a in all. 21,24-6 pg., 7 pg. Powerhouse Pepper; additional 2 pg. story in 24). 23-7 pg Wolverton story & 2 two pg stories (total of 11pgs.).
24,29-Kurtzman-a (24-"Hey Look"(2)) 53 106 159 234 567 800
30,33,36,37-Kurtzman's "Hey Look" 27 54 81 162 266 370
31-Kurtzman's "Hey Look" (1), Giggles 'N' Grins (1-1/2)
27 54 81 162 266 370
32,35,38-40: 35-Nellie The Nurse begins? 25 50 75 147 241 335
34-Three Kurtzman's "Hey Look" 27 54 81 162 266 370

GAY COMICS (Also see Smile, Tickle, & Whee Comics)
Modern Store Publ.: 1955 (7¢, 5x7-1/4", 52 pgs.)
1 6 12 18 40 73 105

GAY PURR-EE (See Movie Comics)

GEARS OF WAR (Based on the video game)
DC Comics (WildStorm): Dec, 2008 - No. 24, Aug, 2012 ($3.99/$2.99)
1-15: 1-Liam Sharp-a/Joshua Ortega-s. 1-Two covers 4.00
16-24-($2.99) 16-Traviss-s/Gopez-a. 18-20-Mhan-a. 19-24-Prelude to Gears of War 3 3.00
... Reader (4/09, $3.99) r/#1 & 2 in flipbook 4.00
... Sourcebook (8/09, $3.99) character pin-ups by various; Platt-c 4.00
Book One HC (2009, $19.99, dustjacket) r/#1-6 & Sourcebook 20.00
Book One SC (2010, $14.99) r/#1-6 & Sourcebook 15.00
Book Two HC (2011, $24.99, dustjacket) r/#7-13 25.00

GEARS OF WAR: HIVEBUSTERS (Based on the video game)
IDW Publishing: Mar, 2019 - No. 4, Jun, 2019 ($3.99)
1-4-Kurtis Wiebe-s, 1,2-Alan Quah-a. 3-Quah & Coccolo-a. 4-Padilla & Wagner Reis-a 4.00
Gears Pop One-Shot (7/19, $4.99) Art in the style of Funko Pop figures 5.00

GEARS OF WAR: THE RISE OF RAAM (Based on the video game)
IDW Publishing: Jan, 2018 - No. 4, Apr, 2018 ($3.99)
1-4-Kurtis Wiebe-s/Max Dunbar-a 4.00

GEAR STATION, THE
Image Comics: Mar, 2000 - No. 5, Nov, 2000 ($2.50)
1-Four covers by Ross, Turner, Pat Lee, Fraga 3.00

Gene Autry Comics #73 © DELL

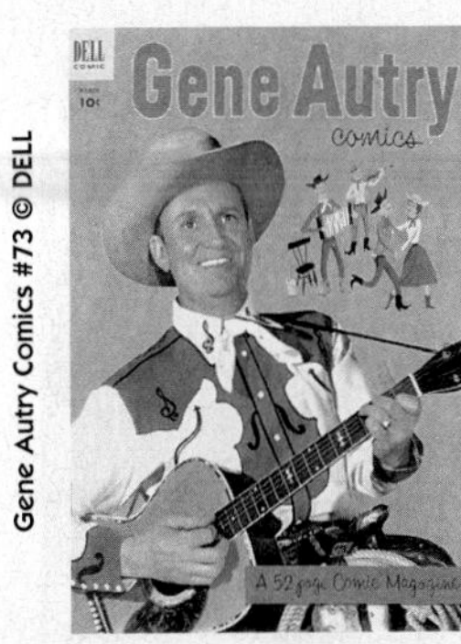

Generation M #1 © MAR

Generations Shattered #1 © DC

	GD 2.0	VG 4.0	FN 6.0	VF 8.0	VF/NM 9.0	NM- 9.2
1-($6.95) DF Cover						7.00
2-5: 2-Two covers by Fraga and Art Adams						3.00

GEEK, THE (See Brother Power... & Vertigo Visions)

GEEKSVILLE (Also see 3 Geeks, The)
3 Finger Prints/ Image: Aug, 1999 - No. 6, Mar, 2001 ($2.75/$2.95, B&W)

	GD 2.0	VG 4.0	FN 6.0	VF 8.0	VF/NM 9.0	NM- 9.2
1,2,4-6-The 3 Geeks by Koslowski; Innocent Bystander by Sassaman						3.00
3-Includes "Babes & Blades" mini-comic						5.00
0-(3/00) First Image issue						3.00
(Vol. 2) 1-4-($2.95) 3-Mini-comic insert by the Geeks. 4-Steve Borock app.						3.00

G-8 AND HIS BATTLE ACES (Based on pulps)
Gold Key: Oct, 1966

	GD 2.0	VG 4.0	FN 6.0	VF 8.0	VF/NM 9.0	NM- 9.2
1 (10184-610)-Painted-c	4	8	12	25	40	55

G-8 AND HIS BATTLE ACES
Blazing Comics: 1991 ($1.50, one-shot)

	GD 2.0	VG 4.0	FN 6.0	VF 8.0	VF/NM 9.0	NM- 9.2
1-Glanzman-a; Truman-c						3.00

NOTE: *Flip book format with "The Spider's Web" #1 on other side w/****Glanzman****-a,* ***Truman****-c.*

GEM COMICS
Spotlight Publishers: Apr, 1945 (52 pgs)

	GD 2.0	VG 4.0	FN 6.0	VF 8.0	VF/NM 9.0	NM- 9.2
1-Little Mohee, Steve Strong app.; Jungle bondage-c	71	142	213	454	777	1100

GEMINI BLOOD
DC Comics (Helix): Sept, 1996 - No. 9, May, 1997 ($2.25, limited series)

	GD 2.0	VG 4.0	FN 6.0	VF 8.0	VF/NM 9.0	NM- 9.2
1-9: 5-Simonson-c						3.00

GEN ACTIVE
DC Comics (WildStorm): May, 2000 - No. 6, Aug, 2001 ($3.95)

	GD 2.0	VG 4.0	FN 6.0	VF 8.0	VF/NM 9.0	NM- 9.2
1-6: 1-Covers by Campbell and Madureira; Gen 13 & DV8 app. 5-Mahfood-a; Quitely and Stelfreeze-c. 6-Portacio-a/c						4.00

GENE AUTRY (See March of Comics No. 25, 28, 39, 54, 78, 90, 104, 120, 135, 150 in the Promotional Comics section & Western Roundup under Dell Giants)

GENE AUTRY COMICS (Movie, Radio star; singing cowboy)
Fawcett Publications: Jan, 1942 (On sale 12/17/41) - No. 10, 1943 (68 pgs.)
(Dell takes over with No. 11)

	GD 2.0	VG 4.0	FN 6.0	VF 8.0	VF/NM 9.0	NM- 9.2
1 (Scarce)-Gene Autry & his horse Champion begin; photo back-c	423	846	1269	3000	5250	7500
2-(1942)	90	180	270	576	988	1400
3-5: 3-(11/1/42)	50	100	150	315	533	750
6-10	41	82	123	256	428	600

GENE AUTRY COMICS (...& Champion No. 102 on)
Dell Publishing Co.: No. 11, 1943 - No. 121, Jan-Mar, 1959 (TV - later issues)

	GD 2.0	VG 4.0	FN 6.0	VF 8.0	VF/NM 9.0	NM- 9.2
11 (1943, 60 pgs.)-Continuation of Fawcett series; photo back-c; first Dell issue	32	64	96	230	515	800
12 (2/44, 60 pgs.)	28	56	84	202	451	700
Four Color 47 (1944, 60 pgs.)	35	70	105	252	564	875
Four Color 57 (11/44), 66 ('45)(52 pgs. each)	30	60	90	216	483	750
Four Color 75, 83 ('45, 36 pgs. each)	23	46	69	164	362	560
Four Color 93 ('45, 36 pgs.)	19	38	57	133	297	460
Four Color 100 ('46, 36 pgs.) First Gene Autry photo-c	22	44	66	155	345	535
1 (5-6/46, 52 pgs.)	33	66	99	238	532	825
2 (7-8/46)-Photo-c begin, end #111	14	28	42	96	211	325
3-5: 4-Intro Flapjack Hobbs	11	22	33	76	163	250
6-10	10	20	30	64	132	200
11-20: 20-Panhandle Pete begins	9	18	27	60	120	180
21-29 (36 pgs.)	8	16	24	52	99	145
30-40 (52 pgs.)	7	14	21	44	82	120
41-56 (52 pgs.)	6	12	18	38	69	100
57-66 (36 pgs.): 58-X-mas-c	5	10	15	34	60	85
67-80 (52 pgs.): 70-X-mas-c	5	10	15	34	60	85
81-90 (52 pgs.): 82-X-mas-c. 87-Blank inside-c	5	10	15	31	53	75
91-99 (36 pgs. No. 91-on). 94-X-mas-c	4	8	12	28	47	65
100	5	10	15	30	50	70
101-111-Last Gene Autry photo-c	4	8	12	27	44	60
112-121-All Champion painted-c, most by Savitt	4	8	12	25	40	55

NOTE: *Photo back covers 4-18, 20-45, 48-65.* ***Manning*** *a-118.* ***Jesse Marsh*** *art: 4-Color No. 66, 75, 93, 100, No. 1-25, 27-37, 39, 40.*

GENE AUTRY'S CHAMPION (TV)
Dell Publ. Co.: No. 287, 8/50; No. 319, 2/51; No. 3, 8-10/51 - No. 19, 8-10/55

	GD 2.0	VG 4.0	FN 6.0	VF 8.0	VF/NM 9.0	NM- 9.2
Four Color 287(#1)('50, 52 pgs.)-Photo-c	11	22	33	76	163	250
Four Color 319(#2, '51), 3: 2-Painted-c begin, most by Sam Savitt	6	12	18	41	76	110
4-19: 19-Last painted-c	4	8	12	28	47	65

GENE COLAN TRIBUTE BOOK (Produced for The Hero Initiative)
Marvel Comics: 2008 ($9.99, one-shot)

	GD 2.0	VG 4.0	FN 6.0	VF 8.0	VF/NM 9.0	NM- 9.2
1-Spotlighted stories from Tales of Suspense #89,90, Doctor Strange #174 and others						10.00

GENE DOGS
Marvel Comics UK: Oct, 1993 - No. 4, Jan, 1994 ($1.75, limited series)

	GD 2.0	VG 4.0	FN 6.0	VF 8.0	VF/NM 9.0	NM- 9.2
1-($2.75)-Polybagged w/4 trading cards						5.00
2-4: 2-Vs. Genetix						4.00

GENE POOL
IDW Publishing: Oct, 2003 ($6.99, squarebound)

	GD 2.0	VG 4.0	FN 6.0	VF 8.0	VF/NM 9.0	NM- 9.2
nn-Wein & Wolfman-s/Cummings-a						7.00

GENERAL DOUGLAS MACARTHUR
Fox Feature Syndicate: 1951

	GD 2.0	VG 4.0	FN 6.0	VF 8.0	VF/NM 9.0	NM- 9.2
nn-True life story	20	40	60	115	188	260

GENERATION HEX
DC Comics (Amalgam): June, 1997 ($1.95, one-shot)

	GD 2.0	VG 4.0	FN 6.0	VF 8.0	VF/NM 9.0	NM- 9.2
1-Milligan-s/ Pollina & Morales-a						4.00

GENERATION HOPE (See X-Men titles and Cable)
Marvel Comics: Jan, 2011 - No. 17, May, 2012 ($3.99/$2.99)

	GD 2.0	VG 4.0	FN 6.0	VF 8.0	VF/NM 9.0	NM- 9.2
1-($3.99) Gillen-s/Espin-a; Coipel-c; back-up bio of Hope Summers						4.00
1-Variant-c by Greg Land						8.00
2-17-($2.99) 5,9-McKelvie-a. 10,11-Seeley-a. 11-X-Men: Schism tie-in						3.00

GENERATION M (Follows House of M x-over)
Marvel Comics: Jan, 2006 - No. 5, May, 2006 ($2.99, limited series)

	GD 2.0	VG 4.0	FN 6.0	VF 8.0	VF/NM 9.0	NM- 9.2
1-5-Jenkins-s/Bachs-a. 1-Chamber app. 2-Jubilee app. 3-Blob-c. 4-Angel-c						3.00
Decimation: Generation M TPB (2006, $13.99) r/#1-5						14.00

GENERATION NEXT
Marvel Comics: Mar, 1995 - No. 4, June, 1995 ($1.95, limited series)

	GD 2.0	VG 4.0	FN 6.0	VF 8.0	VF/NM 9.0	NM- 9.2
1-4-Age of Apocalypse; Scott Lobdell scripts & Chris Bachalo-c/a						4.00

GENERATIONS: (Team-ups of legacy characters after Secret Empire)
Marvel Comics: Oct, 2017 - Nov, 2017 ($4.99, series of one-shots)

	GD 2.0	VG 4.0	FN 6.0	VF 8.0	VF/NM 9.0	NM- 9.2
... Banner Hulk & The Totally Awesome Hulk 1 (10/17) Pak-s/Buffagni-a						5.00
... Captain Marvel & Captain Mar-Vell 1 (11/17) Stohl-s/Schoonover-a; Annihilus app.						5.00
... Hawkeye & Hawkeye 1 (10/17) Thompson-s/Raffaele-a; Swordsman app.						5.00
... Iron Man & Ironheart 1 (11/17) Bendis-s; future Tony Stark as Sorceror Supreme app.						5.00
... Miles Morales Spider-Man & Peter Parker Spider-Man 1 (11/17) Bendis-s						5.00
... Ms. Marvel & Ms. Marvel 1 (11/17) Kamala meets younger Carol; Nightscream app.						5.00
... Phoenix & Jean Grey 1 (10/17) Bunn-s/Silva-a; Galactus app.						5.00
... Sam Wilson Captain America & Steve Rogers Captain America 1 (11/17) Spencer-s						5.00
... The Unworthy Thor & The Mighty Thor 1 (10/17) Aaron-s/Asrar-a; Apocalypse app.						5.00
... Wolverine & All-New Wolverine 1 (10/17) Taylor-s/Rosanas-a; Sabretooth app.						5.00

GENERATIONS... (Follows events in Dark Nights: Death Metal)
DC Comics: Mar, 2021 - Apr, 2021 ($9.99, limited series)

	GD 2.0	VG 4.0	FN 6.0	VF 8.0	VF/NM 9.0	NM- 9.2
... Forged 1 (4/21, $9.99) Conclusion vs. Dominus; Jor-El, O.M.A.C. app.; art by various						10.00
... Shattered 1 (3/21, $9.99) Kamandi teams with Booster Gold, 1939 Batman, Steel, Slnestro, Starfire, Silver Age Superboy and Dr. Light; intro Dominus; art by various						10.00

GENERATION X (See Gen [13]/ Generation X)
Marvel Comics: Oct, 1994 - No. 75, June, 2001 ($1.50/$1.95/$1.99/$2.25)

	GD 2.0	VG 4.0	FN 6.0	VF 8.0	VF/NM 9.0	NM- 9.2
Collectors Preview ($1.75), "Ashcan" Edition						3.00
-1(7/97) Flashback story						3.00
1/2 (San Diego giveaway)	2	4	6	8	10	12
1-($3.95)-Wraparound chromium-c; Scott Lobdell scripts & Chris Bachalo-a begins						6.00
2-($1.95)-Deluxe edition, Bachalo-a						4.00
3,4-($1.95)-Deluxe Edition; Bachalo-a						4.00
2-10: 2-4-Standard Edition. 5-Returns from "Age of Apocalypse," begin $1.95-c. 6-Bachalo-a(p) ends, returns #17. 7-Roger Cruz-a(p). 10-Omega Red-c/app.						3.00
11-24, 26-28: 13,14-Bishop-app. 17-Stan Lee app. (Stan Lee scripts own dialogue); Bachalo/Buckingham-a; Onslaught update. 18-Toad cameo. 20-Franklin Richards app; Howard the Duck cameo. 21-Howard the Duck app. 22-Nightmare app.						3.00
25-($2.99)-Wraparound-c. Black Tom, Howard the Duck app.						4.00
29-37: 29-Begin $1.99-c, "Operation Zero Tolerance". 33-Hama-s						3.00
38-49: 38-Dodson-a begins. 40-Penance ID revealed. 49-Maggott app.						3.00
50,57-($2.99): 50-Crossover w/X-Man #50						4.00
51-56, 58-62: 59-Avengers & Spider-Man app.						3.00
63-74: 63-Ellis-s begin. 64-Begin $2.25-c. 69-71-Art Adams-c						3.00
75-($2.99) Final issue; Chamber joins the X-Men; Lim-a						4.00
'95 Special-($3.95)						4.00

GeNext #1 © MAR

Gen13 #13A © WSP

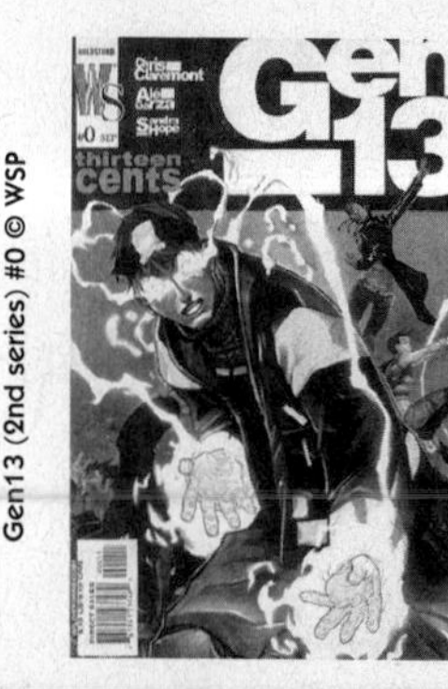

Gen13 (2nd series) #0 © WSP

GD VG FN VF VF/NM NM-
2.0 4.0 6.0 8.0 9.0 9.2

'96 Special-($2.95)-Wraparound-c; Jeff Johnson-c/a 4.00
'97 Special-($2.99)-Wraparound-c; 4.00
'98 Annual-($3.50)-vs. Dracula 4.00
'99 Annual-($3.50)-Monet leaves 4.00
75¢ Ashcan Edition 3.00
...Holiday Special 1 (2/99, $3.50) Pollina-a 4.00
...Underground Special 1 (5/98, $2.50, B&W) Mahfood-a 3.00

GENERATION X
Marvel Comics: Jul, 2017 - No. 9, Jan, 2018; No. 85, Feb, 2018 - No. 87, Apr, 2018 ($3.99)
1-9: 1-Strain-s/Pinna-a 4.00
[Title switches to legacy numbering after #9 (1/18)]
85-87: 85-(2/18) Monet app.; Dodson-c 4.00

GENERATION X/ GEN 13 (Also see Gen 13/ Generation X)
Marvel Comics: 1997 ($3.99, one-shot)
1-Robinson-s/Larroca-a(p) 4.00

GENERATION ZERO (see Harbinger Wars)
Valiant Entertainment: Aug, 2016 - No. 9, Apr, 2017 ($3.99)
1-9: 1-Van Lente-s/Portela-a; multiple covers. 3-Archie-style art by Derek Charm 4.00

GENERIC COMIC, THE
Marvel Comics Group: Apr, 1984 (one-shot)
1 3.00

GENE RODDENBERRY'S LOST UNIVERSE
Tekno Comix: Apr, 1995 - No. 7, Oct, 1995 ($1.95)
1-7: 1-3-w/ bound-in game piece & trading card. 4-w/bound-in trading card 3.00

GENE RODDENBERRY'S XANDER IN LOST UNIVERSE
Tekno Comix: No. 0, Nov, 1995; No. 1, Dec, 1995 - No. 8, July, 1996 ($2.25)
0,1-8: 1-5-Jae Lee-c. 4-Polybagged. 8-Pt. 5 of The Big Bang x-over 3.00

GENESIS (See DC related titles)
DC Comics: Oct, 1997 - No. 4, Oct, 1997 ($1.95, weekly limited series)
1-4: Byrne-s/Wagner-a(p) in all. 4.00

GENESIS: THE #1 COLLECTION (WildStorm Archives)
WildStorm Productions: 1998 ($9.99, TPB, B&W)
nn-Reprints #1 issues of WildStorm titles and pin-ups 10.00

GENETIX
Marvel Comics UK: Oct, 1993 - No. 6, Mar, 1994 ($1.75, limited series)
1-($2.75)-Polybagged w/4 cards; Dark Guard app. 4.00
2-6: 2-Intro Tektos. 4-Vs. Gene Dogs 3.00

GENEXT (Next generation of X-Men)
Marvel Comics: July, 2008 - No. 5, Nov, 2008 ($3.99, limited series)
1-5: 1-Claremont-s/Scherberger-a; character profile pages 4.00

GENEXT: UNITED
Marvel Comics: July, 2009 - No. 5, Dec, 2009 ($3.99, limited series)
1-5: 1-Claremont-s/Meyers-a; Beast app. 4.00

GENIUS
Image Comics (Top Cow): Aug, 2014 - No. 5, Aug, 2014 ($3.99, limited series)
1-5-Bernardin & Freeman-s/Afua Richardson-a 4.00

GEN:LOCK (Based on the animated series) (Printings of stories that first appeared online) (Issues #6 & #7 were solicited but not printed)
DC Comics (Rooster Teeth Productions): Jan, 2020 - No. 5, May, 2020 ($3.99)
1-5: 1,2,5-Kelly & Lanzing-s/Barberi-a. 3,4-Prasetya-a 4.00

GEN 12 (Also see Gen 13 and Team 7)
Image Comics (WildStorm Productions): Feb, 1998 - No. 5, June, 1998 ($2.50, lim. series)
1-5: 1-Team 7 & Gen 13 app.; wraparound-c 3.00

GEN 13 (Also see Wild C.A.T.S. #1 & Deathmate Black #2)
Image Comics (WildStorm Productions): Feb, 1994 - No. 5, July 1994 ($1.95, limited series)
0 (8/95, $2.50)-Ch. 1 w/Jim Lee-p; Ch. 4 w/Charest-p 4.00
1/2 1 2 3 4 5 7
1-($2.50)-Created by Jim Lee 1 3 4 6 8 10
1-2nd printing 3.00
1-"3-D" Edition (9/97, $4.95)-w/glasses 5.00
2-($2.50) 1 2 3 4 5 7
3-Pitt-c & story 4.00
4-Pitt-c & story; wraparound-c 4.00
5 4.00
5-Alternate Portacio-c; see Deathblow #5 6.00
...Collected Edition ('94, $12.95)-r/#1-5 13.00
...Rave ($1.50, 3/95)-wraparound-c 4.00
...: Who They Are And How They Came To Be... (2006, $14.99) r/#1-5; sketch gallery 15.00
NOTE: *Issues 1-4 contain coupons redeemable for the ashcan edition of Gen 13 #0. Price listed is for a complete book.*

GEN 13
Image Comics (WildStorm Productions): Mar, 1995 - No. 36, Dec, 1998;
DC Comics (WildStorm): No. 37, Mar, 1999 - No. 77, Jul, 2002 ($2.95/$2.50)
1-A (Charge)-Campbell/Garner-c 1 2 3 5 6 8
1-B (Thumbs Up)-Campbell/Garner-c 1 2 3 5 6 8
1-C-1-F,1-I-1-M: 1-C (Lil' GEN 13)-Art Adams-c. 1-D (Barbari-GEN)-Simon Bisley-c. 1-E (Your Friendly Neighborhood Grunge)-Cleary-c. 1-F (GEN 13 Goes Madison Ave.)-Golden-c. 1-I (That's the way we became GEN 13)-Campbell/Gibson-c. 1-J (All Dolled Up)-Campbell/McWeeney-c. 1-K (Verti-GEN)-Dunn-c. 1-L (Picto-Fiction). 1-M (Do it Yourself Cover) 1 2 3 4 5 7
1-G (Lin-GEN-re)-Michael Lopez-c 3 6 9 16 24 32
1-H (GEN-et Jackson)-Jason Pearson-c 2 4 6 9 16 20
1-Chromium-c by Campbell 4 8 12 27 44 60
1-Chromium-c by Jim Lee 5 10 15 33 57 80
1-"3-D" Edition (2/98, $4.95)-w/glasses 5.00
2 ($1.95, Newsstand)-WildStorm Rising Pt. 4; bound-in card 4.00
2-12: 2-($2.50, Direct Market)-WildStorm Rising Pt. 4, bound-in card. 6,7-Jim Lee-c/a(p). 9-Ramos-a. 10,11-Fire From Heaven Pt. 3. & Pt.9 4.00
11-($4.95)-Special European Tour Edition; chromium-c 3 6 9 14 20 25
13A,13B,13C-($1.30, 13 pgs.): 13A-Archie & Friends app. 13B-Bone-c/app.; Teenage Mutant Ninja Turtles, Madman, Spawn & Jim Lee app. 5.00
14-24: 20-Last Campbell-a 4.00
25-($3.50)-Two covers by Campbell and Charest 4.00
25-($3.50)-Voyager Pack w/Danger Girl preview 5.00
25-Foil-c 10.00
26-32,34: 26-Arcudi-s/Frank-a begins. 34-Back-up story by Art Adams 3.00
33-Flip book w/Planetary preview 4.00
35-49: 36,38,40-Two covers. 37-First DC issue. 41-Last Frank-a 3.00
50-($3.95) Two covers by Lee and Benes; art by various 4.00
51-76: 51-Moy-a; Fairchild loses her powers. 60-Warren-s/a. 66-Art by various incl. Campbell (3 pgs.). 70,75,76-Mays-a. 76-Original team dies 3.00
77-($3.50) Mays, Andrews, Warren-a 4.00
Annual 1 (1997, $2.95) Ellis-s/ Dillon-c/a. 5.00
Annual 1999 ($3.50, DC) Slipstream x-over w/ DV8 5.00
Annual 2000 ($3.50) Devil's Night x-over w/WildStorm titles; Bermejo-c 4.00
...: A Christmas Caper (1/00, $5.95, one-shot) McWeeney-s/a 6.00
... Archives (4/98, $12.99) B&W reprints of mini-series, #0,1/2,1-13ABC; includes cover gallery and sourcebook 13.00
...: Carny Folk (2/00, $3.50) Collect back-up stories 3.50
... European Vacation TPB ($6.95) r/#6,7 7.00
.../ Fantastic Four (2001, $5.95) Maguire-s/c/a(p) 6.00
...: Going West (6/99, $2.50, one-shot) Pruett-s 3.00
...: Grunge Saves the World (5/99, $5.95, one-shot) Altieri-c/a 6.00
... I Love New York TPB ($9.95) r/part #25, 26-29; Frank-c 10.00
... London, New York, Hell TPB ($6.95) r/Annual #1 & Bootleg Ann. #1 7.00
... Lost in Paradise TPB ($6.95) r/#3-5 7.00
.../ Maxx (12/95, $3.50, one-shot) Messner-Loebs-s, 1st Coker-c/a. 4.00
...: Meanwhile (2003, $17.95) r/#43,44,66-70; all Warren-s; art by various 18.00
...: Medicine Song (2001, $5.95) Brent Anderson-c/a(p)/Raab-s 6.00
... Science Friction (2001, $5.95) Haley & Lopresti-a 6.00
... Starting Over TPB ($14.95) r/#1-7 15.00
... Superhuman Like You TPB ($12.95) r/#60-65; Warren-c 13.00
... #13 A,B&C Collected Edition ($6.95, TPB) r/#13A,B&C 7.00
... 3-D Special (1997, $4.95, one-shot) Art Adams-s/a(p) 5.00
...: The Unreal World (7/96, $2.95, one-shot) Humberto Ramos-c/a 3.00
... We'll Take Manhattan TPB ($14.95) r/#45-50; new Benes-c 15.00
...: Wired (4/99, $2.50, one-shot) Richard Bennett-c/a 3.00
... Yearbook 1997 (6/97, $2.50) College-themed stories and pin-ups by various 3.00
...: 'Zine (12/96, $1.95, B&W, digest size) Campbell/Garner-c 3.00
Variant Collection-Four editions (all 13 variants w/Chromium variant-limited, signed) 100.00

GEN 13
DC Comics (WildStorm): No. 0, Sept, 2002 - No. 16, Feb, 2004 ($2.95)
0-(13¢-c) Intro. new team; includes previews of 21 Down & The Resistance 3.00
1-Claremont-s/Garza-c/a; Fairchild app. 3.00
2-16: 8-13-Bachs-a. 16-Original team returns 3.00
...: September Song TPB (2003, $19.95) r/#0-6; Garza sketch pages 20.00

GEN 13 (Volume 4)
DC Comics (WildStorm): Dec, 2006 - No. 39, Feb, 2011 ($2.99)

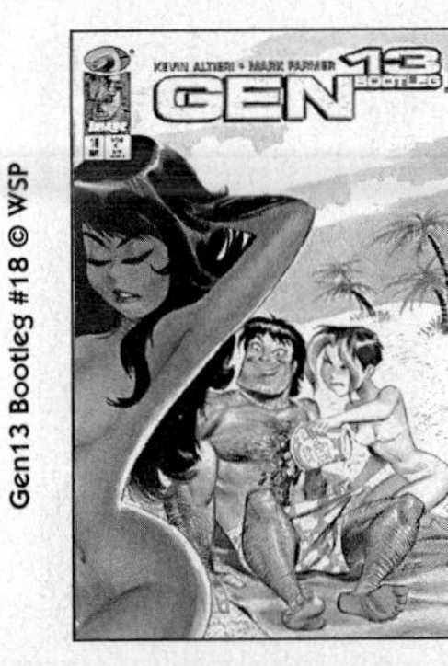

Gen13 Bootleg #18 © WSP

Georgie Comics #9 © MAR

Get Smart #8 © Talent Associates

	GD	VG	FN	VF	VF/NM	NM-
	2.0	4.0	6.0	8.0	9.0	9.2

1-39: 1-Simone-s/Caldwell-a; re-intro the original team; Caldwell-c. 8-The Authority app. 3.00
1-Variant-c by J. Scott Campbell 5.00
...: Armageddon (1/08, $2.99) Gage-s/Meyers-a; future Gen13 app. 3.00
...: Best of a Bad Lot TPB (2007, $14.99) r/#1-6 15.00
...: 15 Minutes TPB (2008, $14.99) r/#14-20 15.00
...: Road Trip TPB (2008, $14.99) r/#7-13 15.00
...: World's End TPB (2009, $17.99) r/#21-26 18.00

GEN 13 BOOTLEG
Image Comics (WildStorm): Nov, 1996 - No. 20, Jul, 1998 ($2.50)
1-Alan Davis-a; alternate costumes-c 4.00
1-Team falling variant-c 5.00
2-7: 2-Alan Davis-a. 5,6-Terry Moore-s. 7-Robinson-s/Scott Hampton-a 4.00
8-10-Adam Warren-s/a 4.00
11-20: 11,12-Lopresti-s/a & Simonson-s. 13-Wieringo-s/a. 14-Mariotte-s/Phillips-a. 15,16-Strnad-s/Shaw-a. 18-Altieri-s/a(p)/c, 18-Variant-c by Bruce Timm 4.00
Annual 1 (2/98, $2.95) Ellis-s/Dillon-c/a 5.00
... Grunge: The Movie (12/97, $9.95) r/#8-10, Warren-c 10.00
...Vol. 1 TPB (10/98, $11.95) r/#1-4 12.00

GEN 13/ GENERATION X (Also see Generation X / Gen 13)
Image Comics (WildStorm Publications): July, 1997 ($2.95, one-shot)
1-Choi-s/ Art Adams-p/Garner-i. Variant covers by Adams/Garner and Campbell/McWeeney 4.00
1-($4.95) 3-D Edition w/glasses; Campbell-c 5.00

GEN 13 INTERACTIVE
Image Comics (WildStorm): Oct, 1997 - No. 3, Dec, 1997 ($2.50, lim. series)
1-3-Internet voting used to determine storyline 4.00
... Plus! (7/98, $11.95) r/series & 3-D Special (in 2-D) 12.00

GEN 13: MAGICAL DRAMA QUEEN ROXY
Image Comics (WildStorm): Oct, 1998 - No. 3, Dec, 1998 ($3.50, lim. series)
1-3-Adam Warren-s/c/a; manga style, 2-Variant-c by Hiroyuki Utatane 4.00
1-($6.95) Dynamic Forces Ed. w/Variant Warren-c 7.00

GEN 13/MONKEYMAN & O'BRIEN
Image Comics (WildStorm): Jun, 1998 - No. 2, July, 1998 ($2.50, lim. series)
1,2-Art Adams-s/a(p); 1-Two covers 4.00
1-($4.95) Chromium-c 5.00
1-($6.95) Dynamic Forces Ed. 7.00

GEN 13: ORDINARY HEROES
Image Comics (WildStorm Publications): Feb, 1996 - No. 2, July, 1996 ($2.50, lim. series)
1,2-Adam Hughes-c/a/scripts 4.00
TPB (2004, $14.95) r/series, Gen13 Bootleg #1&2 and Wildstorm Thunderbook; new Hughes-c and art pages 15.00

GENTLE BEN (TV)
Dell Publishing Co.: Feb, 1968 - No. 5, Oct, 1969 (All photo-c)
1 4 8 12 25 40 55
2-5: 5-Reprints #1 3 6 9 16 23 30

GEOMANCER (Also see Eternal Warrior: Fist & Steel)
Valiant: Nov, 1994 - No. 8, June, 1995 ($3.75/$2.25)
1 ($3.75)-Chromium wraparound-c; Eternal Warrior app. 5.00
2-8 4.00

GEORGE OF THE JUNGLE (TV)(See America's Best TV Comics)
Gold Key: Feb, 1969 - No. 2, Oct, 1969 (Jay Ward)
1 8 16 24 56 108 160
2 5 10 15 35 63 90

GEORGE PAL'S PUPPETOONS (Funny animal puppets)
Fawcett Publications: Dec, 1945 - No. 18, Dec, 1947; No. 19, 1950
1-Captain Marvel-c 47 94 141 296 498 700
2 24 48 72 140 230 320
3-10 15 30 45 90 140 190
11-19 14 28 42 78 112 145

GEORGE PEREZ'S SIRENS
BOOM! Studios: Sept, 2014 - No. 6, Dec, 2016 ($3.99, limited series)
1-6-George Pérez-s/a; multiple covers 4.00

GEORGE R.R. MARTIN'S A CLASH OF KINGS (Based on A Song of Ice and Fire, Book 2)
Dynamite Entertainment: 2017 - No. 16, 2019; 2020 - Present ($3.99)
1-16: 1-Landry Q. Walker-s/Mel Rubi-a; multiple covers 4.00
Volume 2 (2020 - Present) 1-11-Landry Q.Walker-s/Mel Rubi-a 4.00

GEORGIE COMICS (...& Judy Comics #20-35?; see All Teen & Teen Comics)
Timely Comics/GPI No. 1-34: Spr, 1945 - No. 39, Oct, 1952 (#1-3 are quarterly)
1-Dave Berg-a 53 106 159 334 567 800
2 31 62 93 186 303 420
3-5,7,8(11/46) 24 48 72 140 230 320
6-Georgie visits Timely Comics 30 60 90 177 289 400
9,10-Kurtzman's "Hey Look" (1 & ?); Millie the Model & Margie app. 27 54 81 162 266 370
11,12: 11-Margie, Millie app. 20 40 60 118 192 265
13-Kurtzman's "Hey Look", 3 pgs. 20 40 60 120 195 270
14-Wolverton-a(1 pg.); Kurtzman's "Hey Look" 21 42 63 124 202 280
15,16,18-20 19 38 57 111 176 240
17,29-Kurtzman's "Hey Look", 1 pg. 20 40 60 115 188 260
21-24,27,28,30-39: 21-Anti-Wertham editorial. 33-38-Hy Rosen-c 19 38 57 111 176 240
25-Painted-c by classic pin-up artist Peter Driben 110 220 330 704 1202 1700
26-Logo design swipe from Archie Comics 39 78 117 231 378 525

GERALD McBOING-BOING AND THE NEARSIGHTED MR. MAGOO (TV)
(Mr. Magoo No. 6 on)
Dell Publishing Co.: Aug-Oct, 1952 - No. 5, Aug-Oct, 1953
1 9 18 27 62 126 190
2-5 8 16 24 54 102 150

GERONIMO (See Fighting Indians of the Wild West!)
Avon Periodicals: 1950 - No. 4, Feb, 1952
1-Indian Fighter; Maneely-a; Texas Rangers-r/Cowpuncher #1; Fawcette-c 23 46 69 138 227 315
2-On the Warpath; Kit West app.; Kinstler-c/a 15 30 45 90 140 190
3-And His Apache Murderers; Kinstler-c/a(2); Kit West-r/Cowpuncher #6 15 30 45 90 140 190
4-Savage Raids of; Kinstler-c & inside front-c; Kinstlerish-a by McCann(3) 15 30 45 86 133 180

GERONIMO JONES
Charlton Comics: Sept, 1971 - No. 9, Jan, 1973
1 3 6 9 15 22 28
2-9 2 4 6 8 10 12
Modern Comics Reprint #7('78) 5.00

GETALONG GANG, THE (TV)
Marvel Comics (Star Comics): May, 1985 - No. 6, Mar, 1986
1-6: Saturday morning TV stars 5.00

GET JIRO!
DC Comics (Vertigo): 2012 ($24.99, hardcover graphic novel with dust jacket)
HC - Anthony Bourdain & Joel Rose-s/Langdon Foss-a 25.00
SC - (2013, $14.99) Anthony Bourdain & Joel Rose-s/Langdon Foss-a 15.00

GET JIRO: BLOOD AND SUSHI
DC Comics (Vertigo): 2015 ($22.99, hardcover graphic novel with dust jacket)
HC - Prequel to Get Jiro!; Anthony Bourdain & Joel Rose-s/Alé Garza-a/Dave Johnson-c 23.00

GET LOST
Mikeross Publications/New Comics: Feb-Mar, 1954 - No. 3, June-July, 1954 (Satire)
1-Andru/Esposito-a in all? 41 82 123 256 428 600
2-Andru/Esposito-c; has 4 pg. E.C. parody featuring "The Sewer Keeper" 28 56 84 168 274 380
3-John Wayne 'Hondo' parody 24 48 72 140 230 320
1,2 (10,12/87-New Comics)-B&W r-original 4.00

GET SMART (TV)
Dell Publ. Co.: June, 1966 - No. 8, Sept, 1967 (All have Don Adams photo-c)
1 9 18 27 59 117 175
2,3-Ditko-a 6 12 18 40 73 105
4-8: 8-Reprints #1 (cover and insides) 5 10 15 33 57 80

GHOST (...Comics #9)
Fiction House Magazines: 1951(Winter) - No. 11, Summer, 1954
1-Most covers by Whitman 232 464 696 1485 2543 3600
2-Ghost Gallery & Werewolf Hunter stories; classic-c 161 322 483 1030 1765 2500
3-9: 3,6,7,9-Bondage-c. 9-Abel, Discount-a 129 258 387 826 1413 2000
10,11-Dr. Drew by Grandenetti in each, reprinted from Rangers; 11-Evans-r/Rangers #39; Grandenetti-r/Rangers #49 97 194 291 621 1061 1500

GHOST (See Comic's Greatest World)
Dark Horse Comics: Apr, 1995 - No. 36, Apr, 1998 ($2.50/$2.95)
1-Adam Hughes-a 1 3 4 6 8 10

Ghost (2012 series) #12 © DH

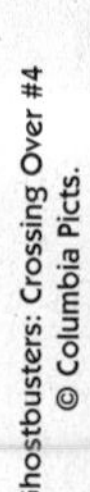

Ghostbusters: Crossing Over #4 © Columbia Picts.

Ghosted #5 © Skybound

	GD 2.0	VG 4.0	FN 6.0	VF 8.0	VF/NM 9.0	NM- 9.2

2,3-Hughes-a 5.00
4-24: 4-Barb Wire app. 5,6-Hughes-c. 12-Ghost/Hellboy preview. 15,21-X app. 18,19-Barb Wire app. 4.00
25-($3.50)-48 pgs. special 5.00
26-36: 26-Begin $2.95-c. 29-Flip book w/Timecop. 33-36-Jade Cathedral; Harris painted-c 4.00

	GD	VG	FN	VF	VF/NM	NM-
Special 1 (7/94, $3.95, 48 pgs.)	1	2	3	4	5	7

Special 2 (6/98, $3.95) Barb Wire app. 5.00
... Black October (1/99, $14.95, trade paperback)-r/#6-9,26,27 15.00
... Nocturnes (1996, $9.95, trade paperback)-r/#1-3 & 5 10.00
... Omnibus Vol. 1 (10/08, $24.95, 9x6") r/#1-12; Special 1 and Decade of Dark Horse #2 25.00
... Stories (1995, $9.95, trade paperback)-r/Early Ghost app. 10.00

GHOST (Volume 2)
Dark Horse Comics: Sept, 1998 - No. 22, Aug, 2000 ($2.95)

1-22: 1-4-Ryan Benjamin-c/Zanier-a 3.00
Handbook (8/99, $2.95) guide to issues and characters 3.00
Special 3 (12/98, $3.95) 4.00

GHOST (3rd series)
Dark Horse Comics: No. 0, Sept, 2012 - No. 4, Mar, 2013 ($2.99)

0-4-DeConnick-s/Noto-a. 0-Frison-c. 1,2-Covers by Noto & Alex Ross 3.00

GHOST (4th series)
Dark Horse Comics: Dec, 2013 - No. 12, Feb, 2015 ($2.99)

1-12: 1,2-DeConnick & Sebela-s/Sook-a/Dodson-c. 3,4-Borges-a 3.00

GHOST AND THE SHADOW
Dark Horse Comics: Dec, 1995 ($2.95, one-shot)

1-Moench scripts 3.00

GHOST/BATGIRL
Dark Horse Comics: Aug, 2000 - No. 4, Dec, 2000 ($2.95, limited series)

1-4-Cassandra Cain Batgirl; Oracle & Bruce Wayne app.; Benjamin-c/a 4.00

GHOST/HELLBOY
Dark Horse Comics: May, 1996 - No. 2, June, 1996 ($2.50, limited series)

1,2: Mike Mignola-c/scripts & breakdowns; Scott Benefiel finished-a 5.00

GHOST BREAKERS (Also see Racket Squad in Action, Red Dragon & (CC) Sherlock Holmes Comics)
Street & Smith Publications: Sept, 1948 - No. 2, Dec, 1948 (52 pgs.)

	GD	VG	FN	VF	VF/NM	NM-
1-Powell-c/a(3); Dr. Neff (magician) app.	48	96	144	302	514	725
2-Powell-c/a(2); Maneely-a	39	78	117	240	395	550

GHOSTBUSTERS (TV) (Also, see Real...and Slimer)
First Comics: Feb, 1987 - No. 6, Aug, 1987 ($1.25)

1-6: Based on new animated TV series 5.00

GHOSTBUSTERS
IDW Publishing: Sept, 2011 - No. 16, Dec, 2012 ($3.99)

1-16-Burnham-s/Schoening-a; multiple covers 4.00
...: 100-Page Spooktacular (10/12, $7.99) reprints of IDW stories 8.00

GHOSTBUSTERS
IDW Publishing: (one-shots)

Annual 2017 (1/17, $7.99) Burnham-s/Schoening-a and short stories by various 8.00
Annual 2018 (2/18, $7.99) Burnham-s/Schoening-a; Ghostbusters: Crossing Over prelude 8.00
Answer the Call Ghostbusters 35th Anniversary One-Shot (4/19, $3.99) Female team 4.00
...: Con-Volution (6/10, $3.99) Josh Howard-a 4.00
...: Deviations (3/16, $4.99) What If.. Ghostbusters never crossed the streams 5.00
... Funko Universe One Shot (5/17, $4.99) Story with Funko Pop-styled characters 5.00
... Halloween Comicfest 2017 (10/17, giveaway) Burnham-s/Schoening-a 3.00
...: Tainted Love (2/10, $3.99) Salgood Sam-a 4.00
... 35th Anniversary: Extreme: One Shot (4/20, $3.99) Comic team 4.00
... 35th Anniversary: Ghostbusters: One Shot (4/20, $3.99) Movie team; Schoening-a 4.00
... 35th Anniversary: Tthe Real Ghostbusters: One Shot (4/20, $3.99) Cartoon team 4.00
... 20/20 (1/19, $4.99) Set 20 years in the future; Sanctum of Slime team app. 5.00
...: What in Samhain Just Happened? (10/10, $3.99) Peter David-s/Dan Schoening-a 4.00

GHOSTBUSTERS
IDW Publishing: Feb, 2013 - No. 20, Sept, 2014 ($3.99)

1-20-Janine & the female Ghostbuster crew; Burnham-s/Schoening-a; multiple covers4.00
Annual 2015 (11/15, $7.99) Burnham-s/Schoening-a and bonus 1-pagers by various 8.00

GHOSTBUSTERS: ANSWER THE CALL
IDW Publishing: Oct, 2017 - No. 5, Feb, 2018 ($3.99)

1-5-Female crew; Thompson-s/Howell-a 4.00

GHOSTBUSTERS: CROSSING OVER
IDW Publishing: Mar, 2018 - No. 8, Oct, 2018 ($3.99)

1-8-Meeting of movie, cartoon, comic Ghostbusters teams; Burnham-s/Schoening-a 4.00

GHOSTBUSTERS: DISPLACED AGGRESSION
IDW Publishing: Sept, 2009 - No. 4, Dec, 2009 ($3.99)

1-3-Lobdell-s/Kyriazis-a 4.00
Hundred Penny Press: Ghostbusters: Displaced Aggression (3/11, $1.00) r/#1 3.00

GHOSTBUSTERS: GET REAL
IDW Publishing: Jun, 2015 - No. 4, Sept, 2015 ($3.99)

1-4-Burnham-s/Schoening-a; multiple-c; Real Ghostbusters meet comic Ghostbusters4.00

GHOSTBUSTERS: INFESTATION (Zombie x-over with Star Trek, G.I. Joe & Transformers)
IDW Publishing: Mar, 2011 - No. 2, Mar, 2011 ($3.99, limited series)

1,2-Kyle Hotz-a; covers by Hotz and Snyder III 4.00

GHOSTBUSTERS: INTERNATIONAL
IDW Publishing: Jan, 2016 - No. 11, Nov, 2016 ($3.99)

1-11-Burnham-s/Schoening-a; 2 covers on each 4.00

GHOSTBUSTERS: LEGION (Movie)
88 MPH Studios: Feb, 2004 - No. 4, May, 2004 ($2.95/$3.50)

1-4-Steve Kurth-a/Andrew Dabb-s 3.00
1-3-($3.50) Brereton variant-c 3.50

GHOSTBUSTERS 101
IDW Publishing: Mar, 2017 - No. 6, Aug, 2017 ($3.99, limited series)

1-6-Burnham-s/Schoening-a; multiple covers on each; original and female teams meet 4.00

GHOSTBUSTERS: THE OTHER SIDE
IDW Publishing: Oct, 2008 - No. 4, Jan, 2009 ($3.99)

1-4-Champagne-s/Nguyen-a 4.00

GHOSTBUSTERS II
Now Comics: Oct, 1989 - No. 3, Dec, 1989 ($1.95, mini-series)

1-3: Movie Adaptation 5.00

GHOSTBUSTERS: YEAR ONE
IDW Publishing: Jan, 2020 - No. 4, ($3.99, limited series)

1,2-Burnham-s/Schoening-a; multiple-c; first year after the events of the first movie 4.00

GHOST CASTLE (See Tales of...)

GHOSTED
Image Comics (Skybound): Jul, 2013 - No. 20, May, 2015 ($2.99)

1-20: 1-Williamson-s/Sudzuka-a/Phillips-c. 6-10-Gianfelice-a. 16-Ryp-a 3.00

GHOSTED IN L.A.
BOOM! Studios (BOOM! Box): Jul, 2019 - No. 12, Aug, 2020 ($3.99)

1-12-Sina Grace-s/Siobhan Keenan-a. 10-Grace-a 4.00

GHOST IN THE SHELL (Manga)
Dark Horse: Mar, 1995 - No. 8, Oct, 1995 ($3.95, B&W/color, lim. series)

	GD	VG	FN	VF	VF/NM	NM-
1	5	10	15	35	63	90
2	3	6	9	18	27	36
3	3	6	9	14	20	26
4-8	2	4	6	8	10	12

GHOST IN THE SHELL 2: MAN-MACHINE INTERFACE (Manga)
Dark Horse Comics: Jan, 2003 - No. 11, Dec, 2003 ($3.50, color/B&W, lim. series)

1-11-Masamune Shirow-s/a. 5-B&W 5.00

GHOSTLY HAUNTS (Formerly Ghost Manor)
Charlton Comics: #20, 9/71 - #53, 12/76; #54, 9/77 - #55, 10/77; #56, 1/78 - #58, 4/78

	GD	VG	FN	VF	VF/NM	NM-
20	3	6	9	21	33	45
21	2	4	6	13	18	22
22-25,27,31-34,36-Ditko-c/a. 27-Dr. Graves x-over. 32-New logo. 33-Back to old logo	3	6	9	15	22	28
26,29,30,35-Ditko-c	2	4	6	13	18	22
28,37-40-Ditko-a. 39-Origin & 1st app. Destiny Fox	2	4	6	11	16	20
41,42: 41-Sutton-c; Ditko-a. 42-Newton-c/a	2	4	6	13	18	22
43-46,48,50,52-Ditko-a	2	4	6	10	14	18
47,54,56-Ditko-c/a. 56-Ditko-a(r).	3	6	9	14	19	24
49,51,53,55,57	2	4	6	8	10	12
58 (4/78) Last issue	3	6	9	14	19	24
40,41(Modern Comics-r, 1977, 1978)						6.00

NOTE: ***Ditko** a-22-25, 27, 28, 31-34, 36-41, 43-48, 50, 52, 54, 56r; c-22-27, 29, 30, 33-36, 47, 54, 56. **Glanzman** a-20. **Howard** a-27, 30, 35, 40-43, 48, 54, 57. **Kim** a-38, 41, 57. **Larson** a-48, 50. **Newton** c/a-42. **Staton** a-32, 35; c-28, 46. **Sutton** c-33, 37, 39, 41.*

GHOSTLY TALES (Formerly Blue Beetle No. 50-54)
Charlton Comics: No. 55, 4-5/66 - No. 124, 12/76; No. 125, 9/77 - No. 169, 10/84

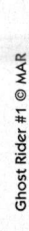

Ghost Manor #57 © CC

Ghost Rider #1 © MAR

Ghost Rider #11 © MAR

	GD 2.0	VG 4.0	FN 6.0	VF 8.0	VF/NM 9.0	NM- 9.2
55-Intro. & origin Dr. Graves; Ditko-a	9	18	27	61	123	185
56-58,60,61,70,71,72,75-Ditko-a. 70-Dr. Graves ends. 75-Last 12¢ issue	5	10	15	30	50	70
59,62-66,68	4	8	12	23	37	50
67,69,73-Ditko-c/a	5	10	15	33	57	80
74,91,98,119,123,124,127-130: 127,130-Sutton-a	2	4	6	13	18	22
76,79-82,85-Ditko-a	3	6	9	16	24	32
77,78,83,84,86-90,92-95,97,99-Ditko-c/a	4	8	12	23	37	50
96-Ditko-c	3	6	9	16	24	32
100-Ditko-c; Sutton-a	3	6	9	17	26	35
101,103-105-Ditko-a	3	6	9	14	19	24
102,109-Ditko-c/a	3	6	9	16	23	30
110,113-Sutton-c; Ditko-a	3	6	9	14	19	24
106-Ditko & Sutton-a; Sutton-c	3	6	9	14	19	24
107-Ditko, Wood, Sutton-a	3	6	9	14	20	26
108,116,117,126-Ditko-a	3	6	9	14	19	24
111,118,120-122,125-Ditko-c/a	3	6	9	16	23	30
112,114,115: 112,114-Ditko, Sutton-a. 114-Newton-a. 115-Newton, Ditko-a.	3	6	9	14	19	24
131-134,151,157,163-Ditko-c/a	2	4	6	13	18	22
135,142,145-150,153,154,156,158-160	1	2	3	5	7	9
136-141,143,144,152,155-Ditko-a	2	4	6	8	10	12
161,162,164-168-Lower print run. 162-Nudity panel	2	4	6	9	12	15
169 (10/84) Last issue; lower print run	2	4	6	11	16	20

NOTE: ***Aparo*** *a-65, 66, 68, 72, 137, 141r, 142r; c-71, 72, 74-76, 81, 146r, 149.* ***Ditko*** *a-55-58, 60, 61, 67, 69-73, 75-90, 92-95, 97, 99-118, 120-122, 125r, 126r, 131-141r, 143r, 144r, 146, 147, 149-152, 154-157, 159-161, 163; c-67, 69, 73, 77, 78, 83, 84, 86-90, 92-97, 99, 102, 109, 111, 118, 120-122, 125, 131-133, 147, 148, 151, 157-160, 163.* ***Glanzman*** *a-167.* ***Howard*** *a-95, 98, 99, 108, 117, 129, 131; c-98, 107, 120, 121, 161.* ***Larson*** *a-117, 119, 136, 159; c-136.* ***Morisi*** *a-83, 84, 86.* ***Newton*** *a-114; c-115(painted).* ***Palais*** *a-61.* ***Staton*** *a-161; c-117.* ***Sutton*** *a-106, 107, 111-114, 127, 130, 162; c-100, 106, 110, 113(painted).* ***Wood*** *a-107.*

GHOSTLY WEIRD STORIES (Formerly Blue Bolt Weird)
Star Publications: No. 120, Sept, 1953 - No. 124, Sept, 1954

	GD	VG	FN	VF	VF/NM	NM-
120-Jo-Jo-r	129	258	387	826	1413	2000
121-124: 121-Jo-Jo-r. 122-The Mask-r/Capt. Flight #5; Rulah-r; has 1pg. story 'Death and the Devil Pills'-r/Western Outlaws #17. 123-Jo-Jo; Disbrow-a(2). 124-Torpedo Man	97	194	291	621	1061	1500

NOTE: ***Disbrow*** *a-120-124.* ***L. B. Cole*** *covers-all issues (#122 is a sci-fi cover).*

GHOST MANOR (Ghostly Haunts No. 20 on)
Charlton Comics: July, 1968 - No. 19, July, 1971

	GD	VG	FN	VF	VF/NM	NM-
1	8	16	24	52	99	145
2-7: 7-Last 12¢ issue	4	8	12	27	44	60
8-12,17: 17-Morisi-a	3	6	9	19	30	40
13,14,16-Ditko-a	4	8	12	22	35	48
15,18,19-Ditko-c/a	4	8	12	28	47	65

GHOST MANOR (2nd Series)
Charlton Comics: Oct, 1971-No. 32, Dec, 1976; No. 33, Sept, 1977-No. 77, 11/84

	GD	VG	FN	VF	VF/NM	NM-
1	5	10	15	36	63	90
2,3,5-7,9-Ditko-c	3	6	9	17	26	35
4,10-Ditko-c/a	3	6	9	21	33	45
8-Wood, Ditko-a; Sutton-c	3	6	9	19	30	40
11,14-Ditko-c/a	3	6	9	16	24	32
12,17,27,30	2	4	6	9	13	16
13,15,16,23-26,29: 13-Ditko-a. 15,16-Ditko-c. 23-Sutton-a. 24-26,29-Ditko-a. 26-Early Zeck-a; Boyette-c	2	4	6	13	18	22
18-(3/74) Newton 1st pro art; Ditko-a; Sutton-c	3	6	9	15	22	28
19-21: 19-Newton, Sutton-a; nudity panels. 20-Ditko-a. 21-E-Man, Blue Beetle, Capt. Atom cameos; Ditko-a.	2	4	6	13	18	22
22-Newton-c/a; Ditko-a	3	6	9	14	19	24
25,28,31,37,38-Ditko-c/a: 28-Nudity panels	3	6	9	14	19	24
32-36,39,41,45,48-50,53: 34-Black Cat by Kim	2	4	6	8	10	12
40-Ditko-a; torture & drug use	2	4	6	13	18	22
42,43,46,47,51,52,60,62,69-Ditko-c/a	2	4	6	11	16	20
44,54,71-Ditko-a	2	4	6	8	11	14
55,56,58,59,61,63,65-68,70	1	2	3	5	7	9
57-Wood, Ditko, Howard-a	2	4	6	9	12	15
64-Ditko & Newton-a	2	4	6	8	11	14
71-76 (low print)	2	3	4	6	8	10
77-(11/84) Last issue Aparo-r/Space Adventures V3#60 (Paul Mann)	2	4	6	9	13	16
19 (Modern Comics reprint, 1977)						6.00

NOTE: ***Ditko*** *a-4, 8, 10, 11(2), 13, 14, 18, 20-22, 24-26, 28, 29, 31, 37r, 38r, 40r, 42-44r, 46r, 47, 51r, 52r, 54r, 57, 60, 62(4), 64r, 69, 71; c-2-7, 9-11, 14-16, 28, 31, 37, 38, 42, 43, 46, 47, 51, 52, 60, 62, 64.* ***Howard*** *a-4, 8, 12, 17, 19-21, 31, 41, 45, 57.* ***Newton*** *a-18-20, 22, 64; c-22.* ***Staton*** *a-13, 38, 44, 45.* ***Sutton*** *a-19, 23, 25, 45; c-8, 18.*

GHOST RACERS (Secret Wars Battleworld tie-in)
Marvel Comics: Aug, 2015 - No. 4, Nov, 2015 ($3.99, limited series)

	GD	VG	FN	VF	VF/NM	NM-
1-4-Johnny Blaze, Danny Ketch, Robbie Reyes, Carter Slade app.; Francavilla-c						4.00

GHOST RIDER (See A-1 Comics, Best of the West, Black Phantom, Bobby Benson, Great Western, Red Mask & Tim Holt)
Magazine Enterprises: 1950 - No. 14, 1954

NOTE: *The character was inspired by Vaughn Monroe's "Ghost Riders in the Sky", and Disney's movie "The Headless Horseman".*

	GD	VG	FN	VF	VF/NM	NM-
1(A-1 #27)-Origin Ghost Rider	129	258	387	826	1413	2000
2-5: 2(A-1 #29), 3(A-1 #31), 4(A-1 #34), 5(A-1 #37)-All Frazetta-c only	103	206	309	659	1130	1600
6,7: 6(A-1 #44)-Loco weed story, 7(A-1 #51)	47	94	141	296	498	700
8,9: 8(A-1 #57)-Drug use story, 9(A-1 #69)	39	78	117	231	378	525
10(A-1 #71)-Vs. Frankenstein	40	80	120	246	411	525
11-14: 11(A-1 #75). 12(A-1 #80)-Bondage-c; one-eyed Devil-c. 13(A-1 #84). 14(A-1 #112)	34	68	102	204	332	460

NOTE: ***Dick Ayers*** *art in all; c-1, 6-14.*

GHOST RIDER, THE (See Night Rider & Western Gunfighters)
Marvel Comics Group: Feb, 1967 - No. 7, Nov, 1967 (Western hero)(12¢)

	GD	VG	FN	VF	VF/NM	NM-
1-Origin & 1st app. Ghost Rider; Kid Colt-reprints begin	32	64	96	230	515	800
2	8	16	24	52	99	145
3-7: 6-Last Kid Colt-r; All Ayers-c/a(p)	7	12	21	48	89	130

GHOST RIDER (See The Champions, Marvel Spotlight #5, Marvel Team-Up #15, 58, Marvel Treasury Edition #18, Marvel Two-In-One #8, The Original Ghost Rider & The Original Ghost Rider Rides Again)
Marvel Comics Group: Sept, 1973 - No. 81, June, 1983 (Super-hero)

	GD	VG	FN	VF	VF/NM	NM-
1-Johnny Blaze, the Ghost Rider begins; 1st brief app. Daimon Hellstrom (Son of Satan)	36	72	108	259	580	900
2-1st full app. Daimon Hellstrom; gives glimpse of costume (1 panel); story continues in Marvel Spotlight #12	12	24	36	83	182	280
3-5: 3-Ghost Rider gains power to make cycle of fire; Son of Satan app.	5	10	15	35	63	90
6-10: 10-Hulk on cover; reprints origin/1st app. from Marvel Spotlight #5; Ploog-a	4	8	12	23	37	50
11-16: 11-Hulk app.	3	6	9	14	20	25
17,19-(Reg. 25¢ editions)(4,8/76)	3	6	9	14	20	25
17,19-(30¢-c variants, limited distribution)	5	10	15	35	63	90
18-(Reg. 25¢ edition)(6/76). Spider-Man-c & app.	3	6	9	16	23	30
18-(30¢-c variant, limited distribution)	6	12	18	37	66	95
20-Daredevil x-over; ties into D.D. #138; Byrne-a	3	6	9	17	26	35
21-30: 22-1st app. Enforcer. 29,30-Vs. Dr. Strange	2	4	6	9	12	15
24-26-(35¢-c variants, limited distribution)	5	10	15	35	63	90
31-34,36-49: 40-Nuclear explosion-c	2	3	4	6	8	10
35-Death Race classic; Starlin-c/a/sty	2	4	6	11	16	20
50-Double size	2	4	6	10	14	18
51-76: 55-Werewolf by Night app. 68-Origin retold						6.00
77-80: 77-Origin retold. 80-Brief origin recap	1	2	3	5	6	8
81-Death of Ghost Rider (Demon leaves Blaze)	3	6	9	19	30	40
... Team Up TPB (2007, $15.99) r/#27, 50, Marvel Team-Up #91, Marvel Two-In-One #80, Avengers #214 and Marvel Premiere #28; Night Rider app.; cover gallery						16.00

NOTE: ***Anderson*** *c-64p.* ***Infantino*** *a(p)-43, 44, 51.* ***G. Kane*** *a-21p; c(p)-1, 2, 4, 5, 8, 9, 11-13, 19, 20, 24, 25.* ***Kirby*** *c-21-23.* ***Mooney*** *a-2-9p, 30i.* ***Nebres*** *c-26i.* ***Newton*** *a-23i.* ***Perez*** *c-26p.* ***Shores*** *a-2i. J.* ***Sparling*** *a-62p, 64p, 65p.* ***Starlin*** *a(p)-35.* ***Sutton*** *a-1p, 44i, 64i, 65i, 66, 67i.* ***Tuska*** *a-13p, 14p, 16p.*

GHOST RIDER (Volume 2) (Also see Doctor Strange/Ghost Rider Special, Marvel Comics Presents & Midnight Sons Unlimited)
Marvel Comics (Midnight Sons imprint #44 on): V2#1, May, 1990 - No. 93, Feb, 1998 ($1.50/$1.75/$1.95)

	GD	VG	FN	VF	VF/NM	NM-
1-($1.95, 52 pgs.)-Origin/1st app. new Ghost Rider; Kingpin app.	3	6	9	19	30	40
1-2nd printing (not gold)						5.00
2-5: 3-Kingpin app. 5-Punisher app.; Jim Lee-c						6.00
5-Gold background 2nd printing						4.00
6-14,16-24,29,30,32-39: 6-Punisher app. 6,17-Spider-Man/Hobgoblin-c/story. 9-X-Factor app. 10-Reintro Johnny Blaze on the last pg. 11-Stroman-c/a(p). 12,13-Dr. Strange x-over cont'd in D.S. #28. 13-Painted-c. 14-Johnny Blaze vs. Ghost Rider; origin recap 1st Ghost Rider (Blaze). 18-Painted-c by Nelson. 29-Wolverine-c/story. 32-Dr. Strange x-over; Johnny Blaze app. 34-Williamson-a(i). 36-Daredevil app. 37-Archangel app.						4.00
15-Glow in the dark-c	1	3	4	6	8	10
25-27: 25-($2.75)-Double-size; contains pop-up scene insert. 26,27-X-Men x-over; Lee/Williams-c on both						5.00
28,31-($2.50, 52 pgs.)-Polybagged w/poster; part 1 & part 6 of Rise of the Midnight Sons storyline (see Ghost Rider/Blaze #1)						5.00
40-Outer-c is Darkhold envelope made of black parchment w/gold ink; Midnight Massacre;						

Ghost Rider (2008 series) #21 © MAR

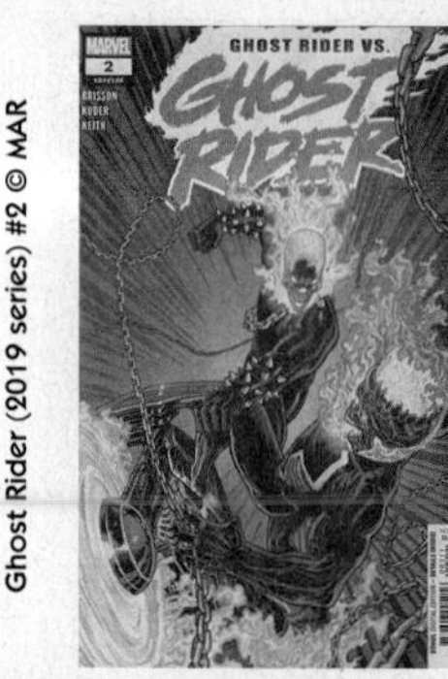

Ghost Rider (2019 series) #2 © MAR

Ghost-Spider #6 © MAR

	GD	VG	FN	VF	VF/NM	NM-
	2.0	4.0	6.0	8.0	9.0	9.2

Demogoblin app. 6.00
41-48: 41-Lilith & Centurious app.; begin $1.75-c. 41-43-Neon ink-c. 43-Has free extra 16 pg. insert on Siege of Darkness. 44,45-Siege of Darkness parts 2 & 10. 44-Spot varnish-c. 46-Intro new Ghost Rider. 48-Spider-Man app. 4.00
49,51-60,62-74: 49-Begin $1.95-c; bound-in trading card sheet; Hulk app. 55-Werewolf by Night app. 65-Punisher app. 67,68-Gambit app. 68-Wolverine app. 73,74-Blaze, Vengeance app. 4.00
50,61: 50-($2.50, 52 pgs.)-Regular edition 5.00
50-($2.95, 52 pgs.)-Collectors Ed. die cut foil-c 5.00
75-89: 76-Vs. Vengeance. 77,78-Dr. Strange-app. 78-New costume 4.00
90-92 6.00
93-($2.99)-Last issue; Saltares & Texeira-a 2 4 6 8 10 12
(#94, see Ghost Rider Finale for unpublished story)
#(-1) Flashback (7/97) Saltares-a 4.00
Annual 1,2 ('93, '94, $2.95, 68 pgs.) 1-Bagged w/card 5.00
...And Cable 1 (9/92, $3.95, stiff-c, 68 pgs.)-Reprints Marvel Comics Presents #90-98 w/new Kieth-c 4.00
...:Crossroads (11/95, $3.95) Die cut cover; Nord-a 5.00
... Cycle of Vengeance 1 (3/12, $5.99) r/Marvel Spotlight #5, Ghost Rider (1990) #1 and Ghost Rider (2006) #1; Leinil Yu-c 6.00
... Finale (2007, $3.99) r/#93 and the story meant for the unpublished #94; Saltares-a 4.00
Highway to Hell (2001, $3.50) Reprints origin from Marvel Spotlight #5 3.50
...: Resurrected TPB (2001, $12.95) r/#1-7 13.00
NOTE: ***Andy & Joe Kubert*** *c/a-28-31.* ***Quesada*** *c-21.* ***Williamson*** *a(i)-33-35; c-33i.*

GHOST RIDER (Volume 3)
Marvel Comics: Aug, 2001 - No. 6, Jan, 2002 ($2.99, limited series)

1-6-Grayson-s/Kaniuga-a/c 3.00
...: The Hammer Lane TPB (6/02, $15.95) r/#1-6 16.00

GHOST RIDER
Marvel Comics: Nov, 2005 - No. 6, Apr, 2006 ($2.99, limited series)

1-6-Garth Ennis-s/Clayton Crain-a/c. 1-Origin retold 3.00
1 (Director's Cut) (2005, $3.99) r/#1 with Ennis pitch and script and Crain art process 4.00
...: Road to Damnation HC (2006, $19.99, dust jacket) r/#1-6; variant covers & concept-a 20.00
...: Road to Damnation SC (2007, $14.99) r/#1-6; variant covers & concept-a 15.00

GHOST RIDER
Marvel Comics: Sept, 2006 - No. 35, Jul, 2009 ($2.99)

1-11: 1-Daniel Way-s/Saltares & Texeira-a. 2-4-Dr. Strange app. 6,7-Corben-a 3.00
12-27,29-35: 12,13-World War Hulk; Saltares-a/Dell'Otto-c. 23-Danny Ketch returns 3.00
28-($3.99) Silvestri-c/Huat-a; back-up history of Danny Ketch 4.00
Annual 1 (1/08, $3.99) Ben Oliver-a/c/Stuart Moore-s 4.00
Annual 2 (10/08, $3.99) Spurrier-s/Robinson-a; r/Ghost Rider #35 (1979) 4.00
... Vol. 1: Vicious Cycle TPB (2007, $13.99) r/#1-5 14.00
... Vol. 2: The Life and Death of Johnny Blaze TPB (2007, $13.99) r/#6-11 14.00
... Vol. 3: Apocalypse Soon TPB (2008, $10.99) r/#12,13 & Annual #1 11.00
... Vol. 4: Revelations TPB (2008, $14.99) r/#14-19 15.00

GHOST RIDER
Marvel Comics: No. 0.1, Aug, 2011 - No. 9, May 2012 ($2.99/$3.99)

0.1-($2.99) Johnny Blaze gets rid of the Spirit of Vengeance; Matthew Clark-a 3.00
1-($3.99) Adam Kubert-c; Fear Itself tie-in; new female Ghost Rider; Mephisto app. 4.00
2-9: 2-4-($2.99) Fear Itself tie-in. 5-Garbett-a. 7,8-Hawkeye app. 3.00

GHOST RIDER (Robbie Reyes) (Also see All-New Ghost Rider)
Marvel Comics: Jan, 2017 - No. 5, May, 2017 ($3.99)

1-5-Felipe Smith-s; Hulk (Amadeus Cho) and X-23 app. 1-Intro. Pyston Nitro. 3-5-Silk app.4.00

GHOST RIDER (Danny Ketch)
Marvel Comics: Dec, 2019 - No. 7, Sept, 2020 ($4.99/$3.99)

1-($4.99) Brisson-s/Kuder-a; Johnny Blaze, Lilith & Mephisto app. 5.00
2-7-($3.99) 2-Johnny becomes the Rider. 5-7-Punisher & Wolverine app. 6,7-Dr. Strange 4.00
...: Return of Vengeance 1 (2/21, $4.99) Howard Mackie-s/Javier Saltares-a 5.00

GHOST RIDER/BALLISTIC
Marvel Comics: Feb, 1997 ($2.95, one-shot)

1-Devil's Reign pt. 3 4.00

GHOST RIDER/BLAZE: SPIRITS OF VENGEANCE (Also see Blaze)
Marvel Comics (Midnight Sons imprint #17 on): Aug, 1992 - No. 23, June, 1994 ($1.75)

1-($2.75, 52 pgs.)-Polybagged w/poster; part 2 of Rise of the Midnight Sons storyline; Adam Kubert-c/a begins 5.00
2-11,14-21: 4-Art Adams & Joe Kubert-p. 5,6-Spirits of Venom parts 2 & 4 cont'd from Web of Spider-Man #95,96 w/Demogoblin. 14-17-Neon ink-c. 15-Intro Blaze's new costume & power. 17,18-Siege of Darkness parts 8 & 13. 17-Spot varnish-c 4.00
12-($2.95)-Glow-in-the-dark-c 6.00
13-($2.25)-Outer-c is Darkhold envelope made of black parchment w/gold ink; Midnight Massacre x-over 6.00
22,23: 22-Begin $1.95-c; bound-in trading card sheet 4.00
NOTE: ***Adam & Joe Kubert*** *c-7, 8.* ***Adam Kubert/Steacy*** *c-6.* ***J. Kubert*** *a-13p(6 pgs.)*

GHOST RIDER/CAPTAIN AMERICA: FEAR
Marvel Comics: Oct, 1992 ($5.95, 52 pgs.)

nn-Wraparound gatefold-c; Williamson inks 6.00

GHOST RIDER: DANNY KETCH
Marvel Comics: Dec, 2008 - No. 5, Apr, 2009 ($3.99, limited series)

1-5-Saltares-a 4.00

GHOST RIDER: HEAVEN'S ON FIRE
Marvel Comics: Oct, 2009 - No. 6, Mar, 2010 ($3.99, limited series)

1-6: 1-Jae Lee-c/Boschi-a/Aaron-s; Hellstorm app.; r/pages from Ghost Rider #1 ('73) 4.00

GHOST RIDER: TRAIL OF TEARS
Marvel Comics: Apr, 2007 - No. 6, Sept, 2007 ($2.99, limited series)

1-6-Garth Ennis-s/Clayton Crain-a/c; Civil War era tale 3.00
HC (2007, $19.99) r/series 20.00
SC (2008, $14.99) r/series 15.00

GHOST RIDER 2099
Marvel Comics: May, 1994 - No. 25, May, 1996 ($1.50/$1.95)

1 ($2.25)-Collector's Edition w/prismatic foil-c 5.00
1 ($1.50)-Regular Edition; bound-in trading card sheet 4.00
2-24: 7-Spider-Man 2099 app. 4.00
2-(Variant; polybagged with Sega Sub-Terrania poster) 5.00
25 ($2.95) 4.00
... No. 1 (2/20, $4.99) Brisson-s/Couceiro-a; tie-in with 2099 one-shots 5.00

GHOST RIDER, WOLVERINE, PUNISHER: THE DARK DESIGN
Marvel Comics: Dec, 1994 ($5.95, one-shot)

nn-Gatefold-c 6.00

GHOST RIDER; WOLVERINE; PUNISHER: HEARTS OF DARKNESS
Marvel Comics: Dec, 1991 ($4.95, one-shot, 52 pgs.)

1-Double gatefold-c; John Romita, Jr.-c/a(p) 6.00

GHOSTS (See The World Around Us #24)

GHOSTS (Ghost No. 1)
National Periodical Publications/DC Comics: Sept-Oct, 1971 - No. 112, May, 1982 (No. 1-5: 52 pgs.)

	GD 2.0	VG 4.0	FN 6.0	VF 8.0	VF/NM 9.0	NM- 9.2
1-Aparo-a	12	24	36	82	179	275
2-Wood-a(i)	7	14	21	44	82	120
3-5-(52 pgs.)	6	12	18	38	69	100
6-10	4	8	12	27	44	60
11-20	3	6	9	14	20	25
21-39	2	4	6	9	13	16
40-(68 pgs.)	3	6	9	16	23	30
41-60	2	4	6	8	10	12
61-96	1	2	3	5	6	8
97-99-The Spectre vs. Dr. 13 by Aparo. 97,98-Spectre-c by Aparo.	2	4	6	10	14	18
100-Infinity-c	2	4	6	8	10	12
101-112	1	2	3	5	6	8

NOTE: ***B. Baily*** *a-77.* ***Buckler*** *c-99, 100.* ***J. Craig*** *a-108.* ***Ditko*** *a-77, 111.* ***Giffen*** *a-104p, 106p, 111p.* ***Glanzman*** *a-2.* ***Golden*** *a-88.* ***Infantino*** *a-8.* ***Kaluta*** *c-7, 93, 101.* ***Kubert*** *a-8; c-89, 105-108, 111.* ***Mayer*** *a-111.* ***McWilliams*** *a-99.* ***Win Mortimer*** *a-89, 91, 94.* ***Nasser/Netzer*** *a-97.* ***Newton*** *a-92p, 94p.* ***Nino*** *a-35, 37, 57.* ***Orlando*** *a-74i; c-80.* ***Redondo*** *a-8, 13, 45.* ***Sparling*** *a(p)-90, 93, 94.* ***Spiegle*** *a-103, 105.* ***Tuska*** *a-2i. Dr. 13, the Ghostbreaker back-ups in 95-99, 101.*

GHOSTS
DC Comics (Vertigo): Dec, 2012 ($7.99, one-shot)

1-Short stories by various incl. Johns, Lemire, Pope, Lapham; Joe Kubert's last work 8.00

GHOSTS GIANT
DC Comics: 2019 ($4.99, 100-page, squarebound)

1-Short stories; new Spectre, Constantine and Gentleman Ghost plus reprints 8.00

GHOST-SPIDER (Also see Spider-Gwen)
Marvel Comics: Oct, 2019 - No. 10, Oct, 2020 ($3.99)

1-10: 1-McGuire-s/Miyazawa-a; Gwen goes to college on Earth-616; Jackal app. 4.00
Annual 1 (11/19, $4.99) Vita Ayala-a/Pere Pérez-a; Arcade app. 5.00

GHOSTS SPECIAL (See DC Special Series No. 7)

GHOST STATION ZERO (See Codename: Baboushka)
Image Comics: Aug, 2017 - No. 4, Nov, 2017 ($3.99)

1-4-Johnston-s/Chankhamma-a 4.00

Ghost Whisperer: The Muse #4 © CBS

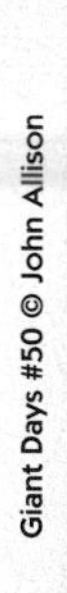
Giant Days #50 © John Allison

Giant-Man #1 © MAR

	GD 2.0	VG 4.0	FN 6.0	VF 8.0	VF/NM 9.0	NM- 9.2

GHOST STORIES (See Amazing Ghost Stories)

GHOST STORIES
Dell Publ. Co.: Sept-Nov, 1962; No. 2, Apr-June, 1963 - No. 37, Oct, 1973

12-295-211(#1)-Written by John Stanley 7 14 21 46 86 125
2 4 8 12 27 44 60
3-10: Two No. 6's exist with different c/a(12-295-406 & 12-295-503)
#12-295-503 is actually #9 with indicia to #6 3 6 9 19 30 40
11-21: 21-Last 12¢ issue 3 6 9 16 23 30
22-37 2 4 6 13 18 22
NOTE: *#21-34, 36, 37 all reprint earlier issues.*

GHOST WHISPERER (Based on the CBS television series)
IDW Publishing: Mar, 2008 - No. 5, July, 2008 ($3.99)

1-5: 1-Two covers by Casagrande & Ho; Casagrande-a 4.00

GHOST WHISPERER: THE MUSE
IDW Publishing: Dec, 2008 - No. 4, Mar, 2009 ($3.99)

1-4-Two covers (photo & art) for each; Barbara Kesel-s/ Adriano Loyola-a 4.00

GHOUL, THE
IDW Publishing: Nov, 2009 - No. 3, Mar, 2010 ($3.99, limited series)

1-3-Niles-s/Wrightson-a 4.00

GHOUL TALES (Magazine)
Stanley Publications: Nov, 1970 - No. 5, July, 1971 (52 pgs.) (B&W)

1-Aragon pre-code reprints; Mr. Mystery as host; bondage-c
8 16 24 55 105 155
2,3: 2-(1/71)Reprint/Climax #1. 3-(3/71) 5 10 15 31 53 75
4-(5/71)Reprints story "The Way to a Man's Heart" used in **SOTI**
5 10 15 34 60 85
5-ACG reprints 4 8 12 27 44 60
NOTE: *No. 1-4 contain pre-code Aragon reprints.*

GIANT BOY BOOK OF COMICS (Also see Boy Comics)
Newsbook Publications (Gleason): 1945 (240 pgs., hard-c)

1-Crimebuster & Young Robin Hood; Biro-c 119 238 357 762 1306 1850

GIANT COMIC ALBUM
King Features Syndicate: 1972 (59¢, 11x14", 52 pgs., B&W, cardboard-c)

Newspaper reprints: Barney Google, Little Iodine, Katzenjammer Kids, Henry, Beetle Bailey,
Blondie, & Snuffy Smith each... 3 6 9 19 30 40
Flash Gordon ('68-69 Dan Barry) 4 8 12 25 40 55
Mandrake the Magician ('59 Falk), Popeye 4 8 12 23 37 50

GIANT COMICS
Charlton Comics: Summer, 1957 - No. 3, Winter, 1957 (25¢, 96 pgs., not rebound material)

1-Atomic Mouse, Lil Genius, Lil Tomboy app. 28 56 84 165 270 375
2-(Fall '57) Romance 31 62 93 182 296 410
3-Christmas Book; Atomic Mouse, Atomic Rabbit, Li'l Genius, Li'l Tomboy & Atom the Cat
stories 20 40 60 120 195 270

GIANT COMICS (See Wham-O Giant Comics)

GIANT COMICS EDITION (See Terry-Toons) (Also see Fox Giants)
St. John Publishing Co.: 1947 - No. 17, 1950 (25¢, 100-164 pgs.)

1-Mighty Mouse 63 126 189 403 689 975
2-Abbie & Slats 39 78 117 231 378 525
3-Terry-Toons Album; 100 pgs. 50 100 150 315 533 750
4-Crime comics; contains Red Seal No. 16, used & illo. in **SOTI**
87 174 261 553 952 1350
5-Police Case Book (4/49, 132 pgs.)-Contents varies; contains remaindered St. John books
- some volumes contain 5 copies rather than 4, with 160 pages; Matt Baker-c
81 162 243 518 884 1250
5A-Terry-Toons Album (132 pgs.)-Mighty Mouse, Heckle & Jeckle, Gandy Goose &
Dinky stories 42 84 126 265 445 625
6-Western Picture Stories; Baker-c/a(3); Tuska-a; The Sky Chief, Blue Monk, Ventrilo app.,
132 pgs. 63 126 189 403 689 975
7-Contains a teen-age romance plus 3 Mopsy comics
84 168 252 538 919 1300
8-The Adventures of Mighty Mouse (10/49) 42 84 126 265 445 625
9-Romance and Confession Stories; Kubert-a(4); Baker-a; photo-c (132 pgs.)
174 348 522 1114 1907 2700
10-Terry-Toons Album (132 pgs.)-Mighty Mouse, Heckle & Jeckle, Gandy Goose stories
42 84 126 265 445 625
11-Western Picture Stories-Baker-c/a(4); The Sky Chief, Desperado, & Blue Monk app.;
another version with Son of Sinbad by Kubert (132 pgs.)
68 136 204 435 743 1050
12-Diary Secrets; Baker prostitute-c; 4 St. John romance comics; Baker-a
1400 2800 4200 8400 12,700 17,000
13-Romances; Baker, Kubert-a 187 374 561 1197 2049 2900
14-Mighty Mouse Album (132 pgs.) 42 84 126 265 445 625
15-Romances (4 love comics)-Baker-c 232 464 696 1485 2543 3600
16-Little Audrey; Abbott & Costello, Casper 58 116 174 371 636 900
17(nn)-Mighty Mouse Album (nn, no date, but did follow No. 16); 100 pgs.
on cover but has 148 pgs. 43 86 129 271 461 650
NOTE: *The above books contain remaindered comics and contents could vary with each issue. No. 11, 12 have part photo magazine insides.*

GIANT COMICS EDITIONS
United Features Syndicate: 1940's (132 pgs.)

1-Abbie & Slats, Abbott & Costello, Jim Hardy, Ella Cinders, Iron Vic, Gordo,
& Bill Bumlin 52 104 156 328 552 775
2-Jim Hardy, Ella Cinders, Elmo & Gordo 39 78 117 231 378 525
NOTE: *Above books contain rebound copies; contents can vary.*

GIANT DAYS
BOOM! Studios (BOOM! Box): Mar, 2015 - No. 54, Sept, 2019 ($3.99)

1-24,26-49,51-54: 1-6-John Allison-s/Lissa Treiman-a/c. 7-Max Sarin-a begins. 38-Madrigal-a.
Allison-a. 54-Esther & Daisy's graduations 4.00
25,50-($4.99) 25-Christmas story 5.00
...: As Time Goes By 1 (10/19, $7.99) Final issue; takes place a year after #54 8.00
... 2016 Holiday Special #1 (10/16, $7.99) Treiman-a/c; back-up w/Caanan Grall-a 8.00
... 2017 Holiday Special #1 (10/16, $7.99) St-Onge-a/c 8.00
... : Where Women Glow and Men Plunder 1 (12/18, $7.99) Ed visits Australia; Allison-s/a 8.00

GIANT GRAB BAG OF COMICS (See Archie All-Star Specials under Archie Comics)

GIANTKILLER
DC Comics: Aug, 1999 - No. 6, Jan, 2000 ($2.50, limited series)

1-6-Story and painted art by Dan Brereton 3.00
...A to Z: A Field Guide to Big Monsters (8/99) 3.00
...Vol. 1 TPB (Image Comics, 2006, $14.99) r/#1-6 & A-Z; gallery of concept art 15.00

GIANTKILLERS
IDW Publishing: No. 0, Nov, 2017 ($3.99)

0-Bart Sears-s/a; Ron Marz-s/Tom Raney-a 4.00
... One-Shot (3/19, $7.99) Sears-s; art by Leonardi/Pennington & Hetrick 8.00

GIANT-MAN (Tie-in to War of the Realms event)
Marvel Comics: Jul, 2019 - No. 3, Aug, 2019 ($3.99, limited series)

1-3-Williams-s/Castiello-a; Ant-Man, Giant-Man, Goliath & Atlas app. 3-Moonstone app. 4.00

GIANTS (See Thrilling True Story of the Baseball...)

GIANTS
Dark Horse Comics: Dec, 2017 - No. 5, Apr, 2018 ($3.99)

1-5-Carlos & Miguel Valderrama-s/a 4.00

GIANT-SIZE ATOM
DC Comics: May, 2011 ($4.99, one-shot)

1-Gary Frank-c; Hawkman app.; Lemire-s/Asrar-a 5.00

GIANT-SIZE...
Marvel Comics Group: May, 1974 - Dec, 1975 (35/50¢, 52/68 pgs.)
(Some titles quarterly) (Scarce in strict NM or better due to defective cutting, gluing and binding; warping, splitting and off-center pages are common)

Avengers 1(8/74)-New-a plus G.A. H. Torch-r; 1st modern app. The Whizzer;
1st modern app. Miss America; 2nd app. Invaders; Kang, Rama-Tut, Mantis app.
6 12 18 41 76 110
Avengers 2,3,5: 2(11/74)-Death of the Swordsman; origin of Rama-Tut. 3(2/75).
5(12/75)-Reprints Avengers Special #1 4 8 12 27 44 60
Avengers 4 (6/75)-Vision marries Scarlet Witch. 6 12 18 38 69 100
Captain America 1(12/75)-r/stories T.O.S. 59-63 by Kirby (#63 reprints origin)
4 8 12 28 47 65
Captain Marvel 1(12/75)-r/Capt. Marvel #17, 20, 21 by Gil Kane (p)
4 8 12 27 44 60
Chillers 1(6/74, 52 pgs)-Curse of Dracula; origin/1st app. Lilith, Dracula's daughter; Heath-r,
Colan-c/a(p); becomes Giant-Size Dracula #2 on 10 20 30 64 132 200
Chillers 1(2/75, 50¢, 68 pgs.)-Alcala-a 5 10 15 31 53 75
Chillers 2(5/75)-All-r; Everett-r from Advs. into Weird Worlds
3 6 9 18 28 38
Chillers 3(8/75)-Wrightson-c(new)/a(r); Colan, Kirby, Smith-r
4 8 12 23 37 50
Conan 1(9/74)-B. Smith-r/#3; start adaptation of Howard's "Hour of the
Dragon" (ends #4); 1st app. Belit; new-a begins 5 10 15 30 50 70
Conan 2(12/74)-B. Smith-r/#5; Sutton-a(i)(#1 also); Buscema-c
3 6 9 19 30 40

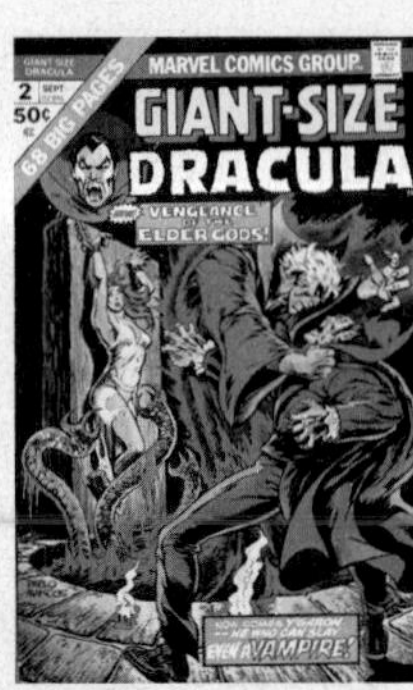

Giant-Size Dracula #2 © MAR

Giant-Size Avengers (2008) #1 © MAR

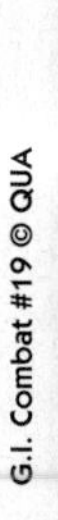
G.I. Combat #19 © QUA

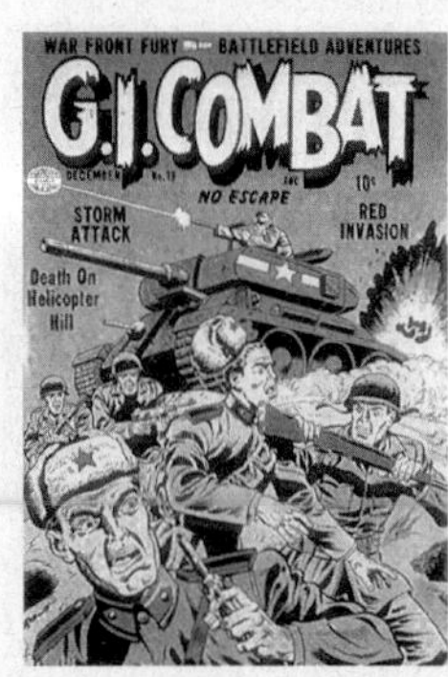

	GD	VG	FN	VF	VF/NM	NM-
	2.0	4.0	6.0	8.0	9.0	9.2

GD VG FN VF VF/NM NM-
2.0 4.0 6.0 8.0 9.0 9.2

Conan 3-5: 3(4/75)-B. Smith-r/#6; Sutton-a(i). 4(6/75)-B. Smith-r/#7.
5(1975)-B. Smith-r/#14,15; Kirby-c 3 6 9 16 24 32
Creatures 1(5/74, 52 pgs.)-Werewolf app; 1st app. Tigra (formerly Cat);
Crandall-r; becomes Giant-Size Werewolf w/#2 10 20 30 64 132 200
Daredevil 1(1975)-Reprints Daredevil Annual #1 4 8 12 27 44 60
Defenders 1(7/74, 68-pgs.)-Dr. Strange, Hulk, Namor & Valkyrie app; continued from Defenders #12; mostly reprint stories, with a few pages of new material by Jim Starlin; Hulk-r from Incredible Hulk #3; Sub-Mariner-r from Sub-Mariner (Golden Age) #41; Dr. Strange-r from Strange Tales #145; Silver Surfer-r from Fantastic Four Annual #5
5 10 15 33 57 80
Defenders 2(10/74, 68-pgs.)-New G. Kane-c/a/p; Son of Satan app. vs. Asmodeus; Sub-Mariner-r from Young Men #25; Black Knight-r from Black Knight #4 (1955); Dr. Strange-r from Strange Tales #119 4 8 12 23 37 50
Defenders 3(1/75, 68-pgs.)-1st app. Korvac; Grandmaster vs. The Prime Mover; Daredevil app.; G.A. Sub-Mariner-r from Sub-Mariner #38; Dr. Strange-r from Strange Tales #120
17 34 51 117 259 400
Defenders No. 3 Facsimile Edition (2/20, $4.99) Reprints issue with original ads 5.00
Defenders 4(4/75, 68-pgs.)-Continued from Defenders #21; Yellowjacket & Wasp app; vs. Egghead, Squadron Sinister (Hyperion, Dr. Spectrum and the Whizzer; Sub-Mariner-r from Human Torch Comics #4 (technically 3rd issue); Dr. Strange-r from Strange Tales #121
3 6 9 21 33 45
Defenders 5(7/75, 68-pgs.)-Continued from Defenders #25; Guardians of the Galaxy app; (3rd app); continued from Marvel Two-in-One #5; story continued in Defenders #26; Nighthawk-r from Daredevil #62 3 6 9 21 33 45
Doc Savage 1(1975, 68 pgs.)-r/#1,2; Mooney-r 3 6 9 18 28 38
Doctor Strange 1(11/75)-Reprints stories from Strange Tales #164-168;
Lawrence, Tuska-r 4 8 12 25 40 55
Dracula 2(9/74, 50¢)-Formerly Giant-Size Chillers 4 8 12 23 37 50
Dracula 3(12/74)-Fox-r/Uncanny Tales #6 3 6 9 20 31 42
Dracula 4(3/75)-Ditko-r(2) 3 6 9 20 31 42
Dracula 5(6/75)-1st Byrne art at Marvel 5 10 15 33 57 80
Fantastic Four 2,3: 2(8/74)-Formerly Giant-Size Super-Stars; Ditko-r. 2-Buscema-a.
3(11/74)-Buckler-a 4 8 12 25 40 55
Fantastic Four 4(2/75)-1st Madrox; Buscema-a 10 20 30 69 147 225
Fantastic Four 5,6: 5(5/75)-All-r; Kirby, G. Kane-r. 6(10/75)-All-r; Kirby-r
4 8 12 22 35 48
Hulk 1(1975) r/Hulk Special #1 4 8 12 27 44 60
Invaders 1(6/75, 50¢, 68 pgs.)-Origin; G.A. Sub-Mariner-r/Sub-Mariner #1; intro Master Man
6 12 18 38 69 100
Iron Man 1(1975)-Ditko reprint 5 10 15 30 53 75
Kid Colt 1-3: 1(1/75). 2(4/75). 3(7/75)-new Ayers-a 7 14 21 48 89 130
Man-Thing 1(8/74)-New Ploog-c/a (25 pgs.); Ditko-r/Amazing Adv. #11; Kirby-r/ Strange Tales Ann. #2 & T.O.S. #15; (#1-5 all have new Man-Thing stories, pre-hero-r & are 68 pgs.) 5 10 15 31 53 75
Man-Thing 2,3: 2(11/74)-Buscema-c/a(p); Kirby, Powell-r. 3(2/75)-Alcala-a;
Ditko, Kirby, Sutton-r; Gil Kane-c 3 6 9 20 31 42
Man-Thing 4,5: 4(5/75)-Howard the Duck by Brunner-c/a; Ditko-r. 5(8/75)-Howard the Duck by Brunner (p); Dracula cameo in Howard the Duck; Buscema-a(p); Sutton-a(i); G. Kane-c
4 8 12 28 47 65
Marvel Triple Action 1,2: 1(5/75). 2(7/75) 3 6 9 18 27 36
Master of Kung Fu 1(9/74)-Russell-a; Yellow Claw-r in #1-4; Gulacy-a in #1,2
5 10 15 31 53 75
Master of Kung Fu 2-4: 2-(12/74)-r/Yellow Claw #1. 3(3/75)-Gulacy-a; Kirby-a. 4(6/75)-Kirby-a
3 6 9 21 33 46
Power Man 1(1975) 4 8 12 23 37 50
Spider-Man 1(7/74)-Spider-Man /Human Torch-r by Kirby/Ditko; Byrne-r plus new-a
(Dracula-c/story) 7 14 21 44 82 120
Spider-Man 2,3: 2(10/74)-Shang-Chi-c/app. 3(1/75)-Doc Savage-c/app.; Daredevil/ Spider-Man-r w/Ditko-a 4 8 12 28 47 65
Spider-Man 4(4/75)-3rd Punisher app.; Byrne, Ditko-r
10 20 30 66 138 210
Spider-Man 5,6: 5(7/75)-Man-Thing/Lizard-c. 6(9/75) 4 8 12 23 37 50
Super-Heroes Featuring Spider-Man 1(6/74, 35¢, 52 pgs.)-Spider-Man vs. Man-Wolf; Morbius, the Living Vampire app.; Ditko-r; G. Kane-a(p); Spidey villains app.
8 16 24 54 102 150
Super-Stars 1(5/74, 35¢, 52 pgs.)-Fantastic Four; Thing vs. Hulk; Kirbyish-c/a by Buckler/Sinnott; F.F. villains profiled; becomes Giant-Size Fantastic Four #2 on
6 12 18 41 76 110
Super-Villain Team-Up 1(3/75, 68 pgs.)-Craig-r(i) (Also see Fantastic Four #6 for 1st super-villain team-up) 4 8 12 25 40 55
Super-Villain Team-Up 2(6/75, 68 pgs.)-Dr. Doom, Sub-Mariner app.; Spider-Man-r from Amazing Spider-Man #8 by Ditko; Sekowsky-a(p) 3 6 9 19 30 40
Thor 1(7/75) 5 10 15 30 50 70
Werewolf 2(10/74, 68 pgs.)-Formerly Giant-Size Creatures; Ditko-r; Frankenstein app.
3 6 9 21 33 45
Werewolf 3,5: 3(1/75, 68 pgs.). 5(7/75, 68 pgs.) 3 6 9 19 30 40
Werewolf 4(4/75, 68 pgs.)-Morbius the Living Vampire app.
4 8 12 23 37 50
X-Men 1(Summer, 1975, 50¢, 68 pgs.)-1st app. new X-Men; intro. Nightcrawler, Storm, Colossus & Thunderbird; 2nd full app. Wolverine after Incredible Hulk #181
500 1000 1500 2500 3750 5000
X-Men No. 1 Facsimile Edition (9/19, $4.99) Reprints issue with original ads 5.00
X-Men 2 (11/75)-N. Adams-r (51 pgs) 8 16 24 56 108 160
Giant Size Marvel TPB (2005, $24.99) reprints stories from Giant-Size Avengers #1, G-S Fantastic Four #4, G-S Defenders #4, G-S Super-Heroes #1, G-S Invaders #1, G-S X-Men #1 and Giant-Size Creatures #1 25.00

GIANT-SIZE...
Marvel Comics: 2005 - 2020 ($4.99/$3.99)

Astonishing X-Men 1 (7/08, $4.99) Concludes story from Astonishing X-Men #24; Whedon-s/ Cassaday-a/wraparound-c; Spider-Man, FF, Dr. Strange app.; variant cover gallery 5.00
Astonishing X-Men 1 (7/08, $4.99) Variant B&W cover 5.00
Avengers 1 (2/08, $4.99) new short stories and r/Avengers #58, 201; Hitch-c 5.00
Avengers/Invaders 1 ('08, $3.99) r/Avengers #71; Invaders #10, Ann. 1 & G-S #2 4.00
Hulk 1 (8/06, $4.99)-2 new stories; Planet Hulk (David-s/Santacruz-a) & Hulk vs. The Champions (Pak-s/Lopresti-a; r/Incredible Hulk: The End) 5.00
Incredible Hulk 1 (7/08, $3.99)-1 new story; r/Incredible Hulk Annual #7; Frank-c 4.00
Invaders 2 ('05, $4.99)-new Thomas-s/Weeks-a; r/Invaders #1&2 & All-Winners #1&2 5.00
Marvel Adventures The Avengers (9/07, $3.99) Agents of Atlas and Kang app.; Kirk-a: reprint of 1st Namora app. from Marvel Mystery Comics #82; reprint from Venus #1 4.00
Spider-Man (7/14, $4.99) origin retold, other short stories; Scherberger-c 5.00
Spider-Woman ('05, $4.99)-new Bendis-s/Mays-a; r/Marvel Spotlight #32 & S-W #1,37,38 5.00
Wolverine (12/06, $4.99)-new Lapham-s/Aja-a; r/X-Men #6,7 5.00
X-Men 3 ('05, $4.99)-new Whedon-s/N. Adams-a; r/team-ups; Cockrum & Cassaday-c 5.00
X-Men: Fantomex 1 (10/20, $4.99) Hickman-s/Rod Reis-a; history revealed 5.00
X-Men: Jean Grey and Emma Frost 1 (4/20, $4.99) Hickman-s/Dauterman-a 5.00
X-Men: Magneto 1 (9/20, $4.99) Hickman-s/Ramón Pérez-a; Namor app. 5.00
X-Men: Nightcrawler 1 (5/20, $4.99) Hickman-s/Alan Davis-a; Magik & Lockheed app. 5.00
X-Men: Storm 1 (11/20, $4.99) Hickman-s/Dauterman-a; Cypher & Fantomex app. 5.00
X-Men: Tribute to Wein & Cockrum 1 (11/20, $5.99) Wein's original script re-drawn by modern artists (1 page each); bonus profiles of Wein, Cockrum & Claremont; Granov-c 6.00
X-Statix 1 (9/19, $4.99) Milligan-s/Allred-a; intro new team members 5.00

GIANT-SIZE JINGLES (Cerebus figures placed over original Gustave Doré artwork)
Aardvark-Vanaheim: 2019 ($4.00, B&W)

1-"Three Giant-Size Firsts worth noting" according to the cover; G.S X-Men #1-c swipe 4.00

GIANT-SIZE LITTLE MARVEL: AVX (Secret Wars tie-in)
Marvel Comics: Aug, 2015 - No. 4, Nov, 2015 ($3.99, limited series)

1-4-Skottie Young-s/a; all ages kid-version Avengers vs. X-Men spoof. 4-GOTG app. 4.00

GIANT SPECTACULAR COMICS (See Archie All-Star Special under Archie Comics)

GIANT SUMMER FUN BOOK (See Terry-Toons...)

G. I. COMBAT
Quality Comics Group: Oct, 1952 - No. 43, Dec, 1956

	GD	VG	FN	VF	VF/NM	NM-
1-Crandall-c; Cuidera a-1-43i	226	452	678	1446	2473	3500
2	54	108	162	343	574	825
3-5,10-Crandall-c/a	48	96	144	302	514	725
6-Crandall-a	43	86	129	271	461	650
7-9	41	82	123	256	428	600
11-20	32	64	96	190	310	430
21-31,33,35-43: 41-1st S.A. issue	31	62	93	182	296	410
32-Nuclear attack-c/story "Atomic Rocket Assault"	41	82	123	256	428	600
34-Crandall-a	34	68	102	199	325	450

G. I. COMBAT (See DC Special Series #22)
National Periodical Publ./DC Comics: No. 44, Jan, 1957 - No. 288, Mar, 1987

	GD	VG	FN	VF	VF/NM	NM-
44-Grey tone-c	96	192	288	768	1734	2700
45	42	84	126	311	706	1100
46-50	36	72	108	259	580	900
51-Grey tone-c	40	80	120	296	673	1050
52-54,59,60	30	60	90	216	483	750
55-Minor Sgt. Rock prototype by Finger	34	68	102	245	548	850
56-Sgt. Rock prototype by Kanigher/Kubert	46	92	138	340	770	1200
57,58-Pre-Sgt. Rock Easy Co. stories	36	72	108	266	596	925
61-65,70-73	23	46	69	161	356	550
66-Pre-Sgt. Rock Easy Co. story	34	68	102	245	548	850
67-1st Tank Killer	44	88	132	326	738	1150

68-(1/59) "The Rock" - Sgt. Rock prototype. Part of lead-up trio to 1st definitive Sgt. Rock. Character named Jimmy referred to as "The Rock" appears as a sergeant on the cover and as a private in the story. In reprint (Our Army at War #242) DC edits Jimmy's name out;

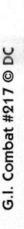

G.I. Combat #217 © DC

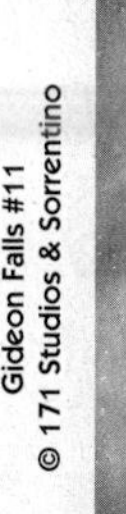
Gideon Falls #11 © 171 Studios & Sorrentino

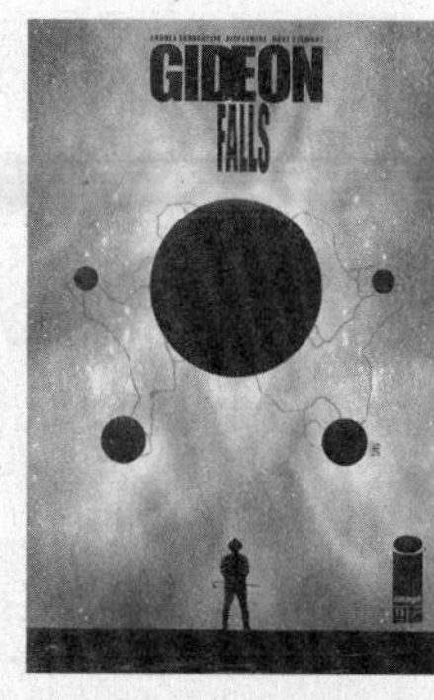

Giggle Comics #32 © ACG

GD VG FN VF VF/NM NM-
2.0 4.0 6.0 8.0 9.0 9.2

GD VG FN VF VF/NM NM-
2.0 4.0 6.0 8.0 9.0 9.2

also see Our Army at War #81-84 159 318 477 1312 2956 4600
69-Grey tone-c 38 76 114 285 641 1000
74-American flag-c 28 56 84 202 451 700
75-80: 75-Grey tone-c begin, end #109 36 72 108 259 580 900
81,82,84-86-Grey tone-c 32 64 96 230 515 800
83-1st Big Al, Little Al, & Charlie Cigar; grey tone-c 42 84 126 311 706 1100
87-(4-5/61) 1st Haunted Tank; series begins; classic Heath washtone-c
186 372 558 1535 3468 5400
88-(6-7/61) 2nd Haunted Tank; Grey tone-c 50 100 150 400 900 1400
89,90: 90-Last 10¢ issue; Grey tone-c 31 62 93 223 499 775
91-(12/61-1/62)1st Haunted Tank-c; Grey tone-c 68 136 204 544 1222 1900
92-95,99-Grey tone-c. 94-Panel inspired a famous Roy Lichtenstein painting
27 54 81 189 420 650
96-98-Grey tone-c 21 42 63 144 317 490
100,108: 100-(6-7/63). 108-1st Sgt. Rock x-over; Grey tone-c
22 44 66 154 340 525
101-103,105-107-Grey tone-c 16 32 48 112 249 385
104,109-Grey tone-c 20 40 60 141 313 485
110-112,115-118,120 12 24 36 84 185 285
113-Grey tone-c 16 32 48 112 249 385
114-Origin Haunted Tank 37 74 111 274 612 950
119-Grey tone-c 15 30 45 105 233 360
121-136: 121-1st app. Sgt. Rock's father. 125-Sgt. Rock app. 136-Last 12¢ issue
8 16 24 56 108 160
137,139,140 5 10 15 35 63 90
138-Intro. The Losers (Capt. Storm, Gunner/Sarge, Johnny Cloud) in Haunted Tank (10-11/69)
12 24 36 84 185 285
141-143 4 8 12 25 40 55
144-148 (68 pgs.) 5 10 15 30 50 70
149,151-154 (52 pgs.): 151-Capt. Storm story. 151,153-Medal of Honor series by Maurer
4 8 12 25 40 55
150- (52 pgs.) Ice Cream Soldier story (tells how he got his name); Death of Haunted Tank-c/s
5 10 15 30 50 70
155-167,169,170 3 6 9 14 20 25
168-Neal Adams-c 3 6 9 19 30 40
171-194,196-199 2 4 6 11 16 20
195-(10/76) Haunted Tank meets War That Time Forgot; Dinosaur-c/s; Kubert-a
3 6 9 14 20 25
200-(3/77) Haunted Tank-c/s; Sgt. Rock and the Losers app.; Kubert-c
3 6 9 16 23 30
201,202 ($1.00 size) Neal Adams-c 3 6 9 16 23 30
203-210 ($1.00 size) 3 6 9 14 20 25
211-230 ($1.00 size) 2 4 6 11 16 20
231-259 ($1.00 size).232-Origin Kana the Ninja. 244-Death of Slim Stryker; 1st app. The Mercenaries. 246-(76 pgs., $1.50)-30th Anniversary issue. 257-Intro. Stuart's Raiders
2 4 6 9 13 16
260-281: 260-Begin $1.25, 52 pg. issues, end #281. 264-Intro Sgt. Bullet; origin Kana. 269-Intro. The Bravos of Vietnam. 274-Cameo of Monitor from Crisis on Infinite Earths
2 4 6 8 10 12
282-288 (75¢): 282-New advs. begin 1 2 3 5 7 9

NOTE: ***N. Adams*** *c-168, 201, 202.* ***Check*** *a-168, 173.* ***Drucker*** *a-48, 61, 63, 66, 71, 72, 76, 134, 140, 141, 144, 147, 148, 153.* ***Evans*** *a-135, 138, 158, 164, 166, 201, 202, 204, 205, 215, 256. Giffen a-267.* ***Glanzman*** *a-most issues.* ***Kubert/Heath*** *a-most issues;* ***Kubert*** *covers most issues.* ***Morrow*** *a-159-161(2 pgs.).* ***Redondo*** *a-189, 240i, 243i.* ***Sekowsky*** *a-162p.* ***Severin*** *a-147, 152, 154.* ***Simonson*** *c-169.* ***Thorne*** *a-152, 156.* ***Wildey*** *a-153. Johnny Cloud app.-112, 115, 120. Mlle. Marie app.-123, 132, 200. Sgt. Rock app.-111-113, 115, 120, 125, 141, 146, 147, 149, 200. USS Stevens by* ***Glanzman****-145, 150-153, 157.* ***Grandenetti*** *c-44-48.*

G. I. COMBAT
DC Comics: Nov, 2010 ($3.99, one-shot)

1-Haunted Tank and General J.E.B. Stuart app.; Sturges-s/Winslade-a/Darrow-c 4.00

G. I. COMBAT
DC Comics: Jul, 2012 - No. 7, Feb, 2013 ($3.99)

1-7: 1-War That Time Forgot; Olivetti-a; Unknown Soldier; Panosian-a; two covers 4.00
#0 (11/12, $3.99) Unknown Soldiers through history; War That Time Forgot; Olivetti-a 4.00

GIDEON FALLS
Image Comics: Mar, 2018 - No. 27, Dec, 2020 ($3.99)

1-26-Lemire-s/Sorrentino-a 4.00
#1 Director's Cut (9/18, $4.99) r/#1 in B&W with original script 5.00
27-($7.99, 80 pgs.) Last issue; Lemire-s/Sorrentino-a 8.00

GIDGET (TV)
Dell Publishing Co.: Apr, 1966 - No. 2, Dec, 1966

1-Sally Field photo-c 9 18 27 58 114 170
2 6 12 18 42 79 115

GIFT COMICS
Fawcett Publications: 1942 - No. 4, 1949 (50¢/25¢, 324 pgs./152 pgs.)

1-Captain Marvel, Bulletman, Golden Arrow, Ibis the Invincible, Mr. Scarlet, & Spy Smasher begin; not rebound, remaindered comics, printed at same time as originals; 50¢-c & 324 pgs. begin, end #3. 320 640 960 2240 3920 5600
2-Commando Yank, Phantom Eagle, others app. 200 400 600 1280 2190 3100
3-(50¢, 324 pgs.) 148 296 444 947 1624 2300
4-(25¢, 152 pgs.)-The Marvel Family, Captain Marvel, etc.; each issue can vary in contents
90 180 270 576 988 1400

GIFTS FROM SANTA (See March of Comics No. 137)

GIFTS OF THE NIGHT
DC Comics (Vertigo): Feb, 1999 - No. 4, May, 1999 ($2.95, limited series)

1-4-Bolton-c/a; Chadwick-s 3.00

GIGANTIC
Dark Horse Comics: Nov, 2008 - No. 5, Jan, 2010 ($3.50, limited series)

1-5-Remender-s/Nguyen-a; Earth as a reality show 3.50

GIGGLE COMICS (Spencer Spook No. 100) (Also see Ha Ha Comics)
Creston No.1-63/American Comics Group No. 64 on; Oct, 1943 - No. 99, Jan-Feb, 1955

1-Funny animal 47 94 141 296 498 700
2 23 46 69 136 223 310
3-5: Ken Hultgren-a begins? 16 32 48 92 144 195
6-9: 9-1st Superkatt (6/44) 14 28 42 81 118 155
10-Superkatt shoots Japanese plane & fights Nazi robot
15 30 45 88 137 185
11-20 12 24 36 69 97 125
21-40: 22-Spencer Spook 2nd app. 32-Patriotic-c. 37-X-Mas-c. 39-St. Valentine-c
11 22 33 62 86 110
41-54,56-59,62-99: Spencer Spook app. in many. 44-Mussel-Man app. (Superman parody). 45-Witch Hazel 1st app. 46-Bob Hope & Bing Crosby app. 49,69-X-Mas-c.
13 26 39 74 105 135
55,60,61-Milt Gross-a. 61-X-Mas-c 12 24 36 69 97 125

G-I IN BATTLE (G-I No. 1 only)
Ajax-Farrell Publ./Four Star: Aug, 1952 - No. 9, July, 1953; Mar, 1957 - No. 6, May, 1958

1 20 40 60 115 185 255
2 13 26 39 72 101 130
3-9 10 20 30 56 76 95
Annual 1(1952, 25¢, 100 pgs.) 37 74 111 222 361 500
1(1957-Ajax) 9 18 27 52 69 85
2-6 6 12 18 28 34 40

G. I. JANE
Stanhall/Merit No. 11: May, 1953 - No. 11, Mar, 1955 (Misdated 3/54)

1-PX Pete begins; Bill Williams-c/a 48 96 144 302 514 725
2-7(5/54) 37 74 111 222 361 500
8-10(12/54, Stanhall) 26 52 78 154 252 350
11 (3/55, Merit) 26 52 78 154 252 350

G. I. JOE (Also see Advs. of..., Showcase #53, 54 & The Yardbirds)
Ziff-Davis Publ. Co. (Korean War): No. 10, Feb/Mar, 1951; No. 11, Apr/May, 1951 - No. 51, Jun, 1957 (52 pgs.: #10-14, V2 #6-17?)

10(#1)-Saunders painted-c begin 27 54 81 158 259 360
11-14(#2-5, 10/51): 11-New logo. 12-New logo 15 30 45 84 127 170
V2#6(12/51)-17-(11/52; Last 52 pgs.?) 14 28 42 78 112 145
18-(25¢, 100 pg. Giant, 12-1/52-53) 34 68 102 199 325 450
19-30: 20-22,24,28-31-The Yardbirds app. 12 24 36 69 97 125
31-47,49-51 11 22 33 62 86 110
48-Atom bomb story 11 22 33 64 90 115

NOTE: ***Powell*** *a-V2#7, 8, 11.* ***Norman Saunders*** *painted c-10-14, V2#6-14, 26, 30, 31, 35, 38, 39.* ***Tuska*** *a-7. Bondage c-29, 35, 38.*

G. I. JOE (America's Movable Fighting Man)
Custom Comics: 1967 (5-1/8x8-3/8", 36 pgs.)

nn-Schaffenberger-a; based on Hasbro toy 4 8 12 27 44 60

G.I. JOE
Dark Horse Comics: Dec, 1995 - No. 4, Apr, 1996 ($1.95, limited series)

1-4: Mike W. Barr scripts. 1-Three Frank Miller covers with title logos in red, white and blue. 2-Breyfogle-c. 3-Simonson-c 4.00

G.I. JOE
Dark Horse Comics: V2#1, June, 1996 - V2#4, Sept, 1996 ($2.50)

V2#1-4: Mike W. Barr scripts. 4-Painted-c 5.00

G.I. JOE
Image Comics/Devil's Due Publishing: 2001 - No. 43, May, 2005 ($2.95)

G.I. Joe #8 © Hasbro

G.I. Joe V2 #28 © Hasbro

G.I. Joe, A Real American Hero #152 © Hasbro

	GD	VG	FN	VF	VF/NM	NM-
	2.0	4.0	6.0	8.0	9.0	9.2

1-Campbell-c; back-c painted by Beck; Blaylock-s 2 4 6 8 10 12
1-2nd printing with front & back covers switched 6.00
2,3 5.00
4-($3.50) 5.00
5-20,22-41: 6-SuperPatriot preview. 18-Brereton-c. 31-33-Wraith back-up; Caldwell-a 3.00
21-Silent issue; Zeck-a; two covers by Campbell and Zeck 4.00
42,43-($4.50)-Dawn of the Red Shadows; leads into G.I. Joe Vol. 2 4.50
...: Cobra Reborn (1/04, $4.95) Bradstreet-c/Jenkins-s 5.00
...: G.I. Joe Reborn (2/04, $4.95) Bradstreet-c/Bennett & Saltares-a 5.00
...: Malfunction (2003, $15.95) r/#11-15 16.00
... M. I. A. (2002, $4.95) r/#1&2; Beck back-c from #1 on cover 5.00
...: Players & Pawns (11/04, $12.95) r/#28-33; cover gallery 13.00
...: Reborn (2004, $9.95) r/Cobra Reborn & G.I. Joe Reborn 10.00
...: Reckonings (2002, $12.95) r/#6-9; Zeck-c 13.00
...: Reinstated (2002, $14.95) r/#1-4 15.00
...: The Return of Serpentor (9/04, $12.95) r/#16,22-25; cover gallery 13.00
...Vol. 8: The Rise of the Red Shadows (1/06, $14.95) r/#42,43 & prologue pgs. from #37-41 15.00

G.I. JOE (Volume 2) (Also see Snake Eyes: Declassified)
Devil's Due Publishing: No. 0, June, 2005 - No. 36, June, 2008 (25¢/$2.95/$3.50/$4.50)

0-(25¢-c) Casey-s/Caselli-a 3.00
1-4,7-19 ($2.95): 1-Four covers; Casey-s/Caselli-a. 4-R. Black-c 3.00
5,6-($4.50) 6-Wraparound-c 4.50
20-29,31-35-($3.50) 25-Wraparound-c World War III part 1 3.50
30,36-($5.50) 30-Double-sized World War III part 6. 36-Double-sized WW III part 12 5.50
...America's Elite Vol. 1: The Newest War TPB ('06, $14.95) r/#0-5; cover gallery 15.00
...America's Elite Vol. 2: The Ties That Bind TPB (8/06, $15.95) r/#6-12; cover gallery 16.00
...America's Elite Vol. 3: In Sheep's Clothing TPB (2007, $18.99) r/#13-18; cover gallery 19.00
...America's Elite Vol. 4: Truth and Consequences TPB (9/07, $18.99) r/#19-24; covers 19.00
... Data Desk Handbook (10/05, $2.95) character profile pages 3.00
... Data Desk Handbook A-M (10/07, $5.50) character profile pages 5.50
... Data Desk Handbook N-Z (11/07, $3.50) character profile pages 3.50
...: Scarlett: Declassified (7/06, $4.95) Scarlett's childhood and training; Noto-c/a 5.00
... Special Missions (2/06, $4.95) short stories and profile pages by various 5.00
... Special Missions Antarctica (12/06, $4.95) short stories and profile pages by various 5.00
... Special Missions Brazil (4/07, $5.50) short stories and profile pages by various 5.50
... Special Missions: The Enemy (9/07, $5.50) two stories and profile pages by various 5.50
... Special Missions Tokyo (9/06, $4.95) short stories and profile pages by various 5.00
...: The Hunt For Cobra Commander (5/06, 25¢) short story and character profiles 3.00

G.I. JOE
IDW Publishing: No. 0, Oct, 2008; No. 1, Jan, 2009 - No. 27, Feb, 2011 ($1.00/$3.99)

0-($1.00) Short stories by Dixon & Hama; creator interviews and character sketches 3.00
1-27-($3.99) 1-Dixon-s/Atkins-a; covers by Johnson, Atkins and Dell'Otto 4.00
...: Cobra Commander Tribute - 100-Page Spectacular 1 (4/11, $7.99) reprints 8.00
...: Special - Helix (8/09, $3.99) Reed-s/Suitor-a 4.00

G.I. JOE, VOLUME 2 (Prelude in G.I. Joe: Cobra Civil War #0) (Season 2 in indicia)
IDW Publishing: May, 2011 - No. 21, Jan, 2013 ($3.99)

1-21: 1-Dixon-s/Saltares-a; three covers by Howard. 9-Cobra Command Part 1 4.00

G.I. JOE VOLUME 3
IDW Publishing: Feb, 2013 - No. 15, Apr, 2014 ($3.99)

1-15-Van Lente-s/Kurth-a in most; multiple covers. 6-Igle-a. 12-15-Allor-s 4.00

G.I. JOE VOLUME 4
IDW Publishing: Sept, 2014 - No. 8, Apr, 2015 ($3.99)

1-4-The Fall of G.I. Joe; Karen Traviss-s/Steve Kurth-a; multiple covers 4.00

G.I. JOE (Follows the Revolution x-over)
IDW Publishing: Jan, 2017 - No. 9, Oct, 2017 ($3.99)

1-9: 1-4-Reconstruction; Dreadnoks app.; Milonogiannis-a; multiple covers 4.00
... First Strike 1 (9/17, $3.99) Tie-in to First Strike x-over series; Kyriazis-a; 3 covers 4.00
...: Revolution 1 (10/16, $3.99) Tie-in to Revolution x-over; Sitterson-s/Milonogiannis-a 4.00

G.I. JOE
IDW Publishing: Sept, 2019 - Present ($3.99)

1-5: 1-Intro. Tiger; Allor-s/Evenhuis-a; multiple covers. 4-Walter-a 4.00

G.I. JOE AND THE TRANSFORMERS
Marvel Comics Group: Jan, 1987 - No. 4, Apr, 1987 (Limited series)

1 2 4 6 11 16 20
2-4 1 2 3 5 6 8

G.I. JOE, A REAL AMERICAN HERO (...Starring Snake-Eyes on-c #135 on)
Marvel Comics Group: June, 1982 - No. 155, Dec, 1994

1-Printed on Baxter paper; based on Hasbro toy 10 20 30 64 132 200
2-Printed on regular paper; 1st app. Kwinn 4 8 12 25 40 55
3-10: 6-1st app. Oktober Guard 3 6 9 15 22 28
11-20: 11-Intro Airborne. 13-1st Destro (cameo). 14-1st full app. Destro. 15-1st app. Major Blood. 16-1st app. Cover Girl and Trip-Wire 2 4 6 11 16 20
21-1st app. Storm Shadow; silent issue 7 14 21 44 82 120
22-1st app. Duke and Roadblock 3 6 9 16 24 32
23,24,28-30,60: 60-Todd McFarlane-a 2 4 6 8 10 12
25-1st full app. Zartan, 1st app of Cutter, Deep Six, Mutt and Junkyard, and The Dreadnoks 3 6 9 21 33 45
26,27-Origin Snake-Eyes parts 1 & 2 3 6 9 16 23 30
31-50: 31-1st Spirit Iron-Knife. 32-1st Blowtorch, Lady J, Recondo, Ripcord. 33-New headquarters. 40-1st app. of Shipwreck, Barbecue. 48-1st app. Sgt. Slaughter. 49-1st app. of Lift-Ticket, Slipstream, Leatherneck, Serpentor 6.00
51-59,61-90 5.00
91,92,94-99: 94-96-Snake Eyes Trilogy 6.00
93-Snake-Eyes' face first revealed 3 6 9 14 19 24
100,135-138: 135-138-($1.75)-Bagged w/trading card. 138-Transformers app. 2 4 6 9 13 16
101-134: 101-New Oktober Guard app. 110-1st Garney-a. 117- Debut G.I. Joe Ninja Force 2 3 4 6 8 10
139-142-New Transformers app. 2 4 6 13 18 22
143,145-149: 145-Intro. G.I. Joe Star Brigade 2 4 6 9 13 16
144-Origin Snake-Eyes 3 6 9 14 19 24
150-Low print thru #155 3 6 9 19 30 40
151-154: 152-30th Anniversary (of doll) issue, original G.I. Joe General Joseph Colton app. (also app. in #151) 3 6 9 18 28 38
155-Last issue 12 24 36 67 94 120
All 2nd printings 4.00
Special #1 (2/95, $1.50) r/#60 w/McFarlane-a. Cover swipe from Spider-Man #1 14 28 42 60 115 150
Special Treasury Edition (1982)-r/#1 3 6 9 19 30 40
Volume 1 TPB (4/02, $24.95) r/#1-10; new cover by Michael Golden 25.00
Volume 2 TPB (6/02, $24.95) r/#11-20; new cover by J. Scott Campbell 25.00
Volume 3 TPB (2002, $24.99) r/#21-30; new cover by J. Scott Campbell 25.00
Volume 4 TPB (2002, $25.99) r/#31-40; new cover by J. Scott Campbell 26.00
Volume 5 TPB (2002, $24.99) r/#42-50; new cover by J. Scott Campbell 25.00
Yearbook 1-4: (3/85-3/88)-r/#1; Golden-c/back-c. 2-Golden-c/a. 3-Zeck-c; silent story 5.00
Yearbook #1 Reprint (1/21, $3.99) Reprints #1 with new cover by Netho Diaz 4.00
NOTE: ***Garney*** *a(p)-110.* ***Golden*** *c-23, 29, 34, 36.* ***Heath*** *a-24.* ***Rogers*** *a(p)-75, 77-82, 84, 86; c-77.*

G. I. JOE, A REAL AMERICAN HERO
IDW Publishing: No. 156, Jul, 2010 - Present ($3.99)

156-199-Continuation of story from Marvel series #155 (1994); Hama-s 4.00
200-(3/14, $5.99) Multiple covers; bonus interview with artist SL Gallant 6.00
201-249,251-254,256-278: 201-214-Hama-s/Gallant-a. 213-Death of Snake Eyes. 216-218-Villanelli-a. 219-225-Cobra World Order 4.00
250-($4.99) Hama-s/Diaz-a; Dawn of the Arashikage conclusion 5.00
255-($4.99) Hama-s/Tolibao-a; IDW's 100th issue; Snake Eyes origin 5.00
Annual 2012 (2/12, $7.99) Hama-s; Frenz, Wagner & Trimpe-a 8.00
... #1 Anniversary Edition (3/18, $3.99) r/#1(1982); silver foil cover logo 4.00
...: Cobra World Order Prelude (10/15, $3.99) Starts seven-part bi-weekly event 4.00
Hundred Penny Press: G.I. Joe: Real American Hero #1 (3/11, $1.00) r/#1 (1982) 3.00
... Yearbook 2019 (1/19, $4.99) Dawn Moreno, new Snake Eyes app.; Hama-s 5.00

G. I. JOE, A REAL AMERICAN HERO: SILENT OPTION
IDW Publishing: Sept, 2018 - No. 4, Dec, 2018 ($4.99, limited series)

1-4-Hama-s/Diaz-a; spotlight on Snake Eyes (Dawn Moreno); Agent Helix back-up story 5.00

G. I. JOE, A REAL AMERICAN HERO VS. THE SIX MILLION DOLLAR MAN
IDW Publishing: Feb, 2018 - No. 4, May, 2018 ($3.99, limited series)

1-4-Ferrier-s/Gallant-a; 5 covers 4.00

G.I. JOE: BATTLE FILES
Image Comics: 2002 - No. 3, 2002 ($5.95)

1-3-Profile pages of characters and history; Beck-c 6.00

G.I. JOE: COBRA (#5-on is continuation of G.I. Joe: Cobra II #4, not G.I. Joe: Cobra #4)
IDW Publishing: Mar, 2009 - No. 13, Feb, 2011 ($3.99)

1-4,5-13: 1-4-Gage & Costa-s/Fuso-a/covers by Chaykin & Fuso. 5-8-Carrera-a 4.00
Hundred Penny Press: G.I. Joe: Cobra #1 (4/11, $1.00) r/#1 with Chaykin-c 3.00
... Special (9/09, $3.99) Costa-s/Fuso-a 4.00
... Special 2 - Chameleon (9/10, $3.99) Costa-s/Fuso-a 4.00
... II (1/10 - No. 4, 4/10, $3.99) 1-4-Gage & Costa-s/Fuso-a/covers by Chaykin & Fuso 4.00

G.I. JOE: COBRA CIVIL WAR
IDW Publishing: No. 0, Apr, 2011 ($3.99)

0-Prelude to G.I. Joe, Cobra & Snake Eyes Civil War series; four covers 4.00
0-Muzzle Flash Edition (6/11, price not shown) r/#0 in B&W and partial color 4.00

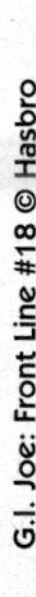
G.I. Joe: Front Line #18 © Hasbro

G.I. Joe Special Missions #26 © Hasbro

Ginger #8 © ACP

	GD 2.0	VG 4.0	FN 6.0	VF 8.0	VF/NM 9.0	NM- 9.2

G.I. JOE: COBRA VOLUME 2 (Prelude in G.I. Joe: Cobra Civil War #0)
IDW Publishing: May, 2011 - No. 9, Jan, 2012 ($3.99)(Re-named Cobra with #10)

1-9: Multiple covers on all. 1-4-Costa-s/Fuso-a 4.00

G. I. JOE COMICS MAGAZINE
Marvel Comics Group: Dec, 1986 - No. 13, 1988 ($1.50, digest-size)

	GD	VG	FN	VF	VF/NM	NM-
1-G.I. Joe reprints	2	4	6	11	16	20
2-13: G.I. Joe-r	2	4	6	8	10	12

G.I. JOE DECLASSIFIED
Devil's Due Publishing: June, 2006 - No. 3 ($4.95, bi-monthly)

1-3-New "early" adventures of the team; Hama-s; Quinn & DeLandro-a; var-c for each 5.00
TPB (1/07, $18.99) r/#1-3; cover gallery 19.00

G.I. JOE: DEVIATIONS
IDW Publishing: Mar, 2016 ($4.99, one-shot)

1-Paul Allor-s/Corey Lewis-a; What If Cobra defeated G.I. Joe and ruled the world 5.00

G.I. JOE DREADNOKS: DECLASSIFIED
Devil's Due Publishing: Nov, 2006 - No. 3, Mar, 2007 ($4.95/$4.99/$5.50, bi-monthly)

1,2-Secret history of the team; Blaylock-s; var-c for each 5.00
3-($5.50) 5.50

G.I. JOE EUROPEAN MISSIONS (Action Force in indicia) (Series reprints Action Force)
Marvel Comics Ltd. (British): Jun, 1988 - No. 15, Dec, 1989 ($1.50/$1.75)

	GD	VG	FN	VF	VF/NM	NM-
1,3-Snake Eyes & Storm Shadow-c/s	2	4	6	10	14	18
2,4-15						6.00

G.I. JOE: FRONT LINE
Image Comics: 2002 - No. 18, Dec, 2003 ($2.95)

1-18: 1-Jurgens-a/Hama-s. 1-Two covers by Dorman & Sharpe. 7,8-Harris-c 3.00
...Vol. 1 - The Mission That Never Was TPB (2003, $14.95) r/ #1-4; script pages 15.00
...Vol. 2 - Icebound TPB (3/04, $12.95) r/ #5-8 13.00
...Vol. 3 - History Repeating TPB (4/04, $9.95) r/#11-14 10.00
...Vol. 4 - One-Shots TPB (5/04, $15.95) r/#9,10,15-18 16.00

G.I. JOE: FUTURE NOIR SPECIAL
IDW Publishing: Nov, 2010 - No. 2, Dec, 2010 ($3.99, limited series, greytone art)

1,2-Schmidt-s/Bevilacqua-a 4.00

G. I. JOE: HEARTS & MINDS
IDW Publishing: May, 2010 - No. 5, Sept, 2010 ($3.99)

1-5: Short origin stories; Brooks-s; Chaykin & Fuso-a 4.00

G. I. JOE: INFESTATION (Zombie x-over with Star Trek, Ghostbusters & Transformers)
IDW Publishing: Mar, 2011 - No. 2, Mar, 2011 ($3.99, limited series)

1,2-Timpano-a; covers by Timpano and Snyder III 4.00

G.I. JOE: MASTER & APPRENTICE
Image Comics: May, 2004 - No. 4, Aug, 2004 ($2.95)

1-4-Caselli-a/Jerwa-s 3.00

G.I. JOE: MASTER & APPRENTICE 2
Image Comics: Feb, 2005 - No. 4, May, 2005 ($2.95, limited series)

1-4: Stevens & Vedder-a/Jerwa-s 3.00

G.I. JOE MOVIE PREQUEL...
IDW Publishing: Mar, 2009 - No. 4, June, 2009 ($3.99, limited series)

1-4-Two covers on each: 1-Duke. 2-Destro. 3-The Baroness. 4-SnakeEyes 4.00

G.I. JOE: OPERATION HISS
IDW Publishing: Feb, 2010 - No. 5, Jun, 2010 ($3.99, limited series)

1-5: 1-4-Reed-s/Padilla-a; covers by Corroney & Padilla. 5-Guglotta-a 4.00

G. I. JOE ORDER OF BATTLE, THE
Marvel Comics Group: Dec, 1986 - No. 4, Mar, 1987 (limited series)

1-4 6.00

G.I. JOE: ORIGINS
IDW Publishing: Feb, 2009 - No. 23, Jan, 2011 ($3.99)

1-23: 1-Origin of Snake Eyes; Hama-s. 12-Templesmith-a. 19-Benitez-a 4.00

G.I. JOE: RELOADED
Image Comics: Mar, 2004 -No. 14, Apr, 2005 ($2.95)

1-14: 1-3-Granov-c/Ney Rieber-s. 5,6-Rieber-s/Saltares-a. 8-Origin of the Baroness 4.00
Vol. 1 In the Name of Patriotism (11/04, $12.95) r/#1-6; cover gallery 13.00

G.I. JOE: RISE OF COBRA MOVIE ADAPTATION
IDW Publishing: July, 2009 - No. 4, July, 2009 ($3.99, weekly limited series)

1-4-Tipton-s/Maloney-a; two covers 4.00

G.I. JOE: SIERRA MUERTE
IDW Publishing: Feb, 2019 - No. 3, Apr, 2019 ($4.99, limited series)

1-3-Michel Fiffe-s/a 5.00

G.I. JOE SIGMA 6 (Based on the cartoon TV series)
Devil's Due Publishing: Dec, 2005 - No. 6, May, 2006 ($2.95, limited series)

1-6-Andrew Daab-s 3.00
TPB Vol. 1 (10/06, $10.95, 8-1/4" x 5-3/4") r/#1-6; cover gallery 11.00

G.I. JOE: SNAKE EYES
IDW Publishing: Oct, 2009 - No. 4, Jan, 2010 ($3.99, limited series)

1-4-Ray Park & Kevin VanHook-s/Lee Ferguson-a; two covers 4.00

G.I. JOE: SNAKE EYES, AGENT OF COBRA
IDW Publishing: Jan, 2015 - No. 5, May, 2015 ($3.99, limited series)

1-5-Costa-s/Villanelli-a 4.00

G.I. JOE: SNAKE EYES, VOLUME 2 (Continues as Snake Eyes #8)
IDW Publishing: May, 2011 - No. 7, Nov, 2011 ($3.99)

1-7: 1-Dixon-s/Atkins & Padilla-a; two covers 4.00

G. I. JOE SPECIAL MISSIONS (Indicia title: Special Missions)
Marvel Comics Group: Oct, 1986 - No. 28, Dec, 1989 ($1.00)

1-20 5.00
21-28 6.00

G. I. JOE: SPECIAL MISSIONS
IDW Publishing: Mar, 2013 - No. 14, Apr, 2014($3.99)

1-14: 1-4-Dixon-s/Gulacy-a; covers by Chen and Gulacy. 5-7-Rosado-a. 10-13-Gulacy-a 4.00

G. I. JOE: THE COBRA FILES
IDW Publishing: Apr, 2013 - No. 9, Dec, 2013 ($3.99)

1-9: 1-Costa-s/Fuso-a; multiple covers. 5,6-Dell'edera-a 4.00

G.I. JOE 2 MOVIE PREQUEL...
IDW Publishing: Feb, 2012 - No. 4, Apr, 2012 ($3.99, limited series)

1-4-Barber-s/Navarro & Rojo-a 4.00

G.I. JOE VS. THE TRANSFORMERS
Image Comics: Jun, 2003 - No. 6, Nov, 2003 ($2.95, limited series)

1-Blaylock-s/Mike Miller-a; three covers by Miller, Campbell & Andrews 4.00
1-2nd printing; black cover with logo; back-c by Campbell 3.00
2-6: 2-Two covers by Miller & Brooks 3.00
TPB (3/04, $15.95) r/series; sketch pages 16.00

G.I. JOE VS. THE TRANSFORMERS (Volume 2)
Devil's Due Publ.: Sept, 2004 - No. 4, Dec, 2004 ($4.95/$2.95, limited series)

1-($4.95) Three covers; Jolley-s/Su & Seeley-a 5.00
2-4-($2.95) Two covers by Su & Pollina 3.00
Vol. 2 TPB (4/05, $14.95) r/series; interview with creators; sketch pages and covers 15.00

G.I. JOE VS. THE TRANSFORMERS (Volume 3) THE ART OF WAR
Devil's Due Publ.: Mar, 2006 - No. 5, July, 2006 ($2.95, limited series)

1-5: 1-Three covers; Seeley-s/Ng-a 3.00
TPB (8/06, $14.95) r/series; cover gallery 15.00

G.I. JOE VS. THE TRANSFORMERS (Volume 4) BLACK HORIZON
Devil's Due Publ.: Jan, 2007 - No. 2, Feb, 2007 ($5.50, limited series)

1,2: 1-Three covers; Seeley-s/Wildman-a. 2-Two covers 5.50

G. I. JUNIORS (See Harvey Hits No. 86,91,95,98,101,104,107,110,112,114,116,118,120,122)

GILES SEASON 11 (From Buffy the Vampire Slayer)
Dark Horse Comics: Feb, 2018 - No. 4, May, 2018 ($3.99, limited series)

1-4-Whedon & Alexander-s/Jon Lam-a 5.00

GILGAMESH II
DC Comics: 1989 - No. 4, 1989 ($3.95, limited series, prestige format, mature)

1-4: Starlin-c/a/scripts 5.00

GIL THORP
Dell Publishing Co.: May-July, 1963

	GD	VG	FN	VF	VF/NM	NM-
1-Caniff-*ish* art	4	8	12	23	37	50

GINGER
Archie Publications: 1951 - No. 10, Summer, 1954

	GD	VG	FN	VF	VF/NM	NM-
1-Teenage humor; headlights-c	226	452	678	1446	2473	3500
2-(1952)	30	60	90	177	289	400
3-6: 6-(Sum/53)	20	40	60	114	182	250
7-10-Katy Keene app.	37	74	111	222	361	500

Girl Comics #12 © MAR

Girls' Life #1 © MAR

Girls' Romances #5 © DC

	GD	VG	FN	VF	VF/NM	NM-
	2.0	4.0	6.0	8.0	9.0	9.2

GINGER FOX (Also see The World of Ginger Fox)
Comico: Sept, 1988 - No. 4, Dec, 1988 ($1.75, limited series)

1-4: Part photo-c on all 3.00

GIRL
DC Comics (Vertigo Verite): Jul, 1996 - No. 3, 1996 ($2.50, lim. series, mature)

1-3: Peter Milligan scripts; Fegredo-c/a 3.00

GIRL COMICS (Becomes Girl Confessions No. 13 on)
Marvel/Atlas Comics(CnPC): Oct, 1949 - No. 12, Jan, 1952 (#1-4: 52 pgs.)

	GD	VG	FN	VF	VF/NM	NM-
1-Photo-c	34	68	102	199	325	450
2-Kubert-a; photo-c	17	34	51	105	165	225
3-Everett-a; Liz Taylor photo-c	40	80	120	244	402	560
4-11: 4-Photo-c. 10-12-Sol Brodsky-c	15	30	45	88	137	185
12-Krigstein-a; Al Hartley-c	15	30	45	92	144	195

GIRL COMICS
Marvel Comics: May, 2010 - No. 3, Sept, 2010 ($4.99, limited series)

1-3-Anthology of short stories by women creators. 1-Conner-c. 2-Thompson-c. 3-Chen-c 5.00

GIRL CONFESSIONS (Formerly Girl Comics)
Atlas Comics (CnPC/ZPC): No. 13, Mar, 1952 - No. 35, Aug, 1954

	GD	VG	FN	VF	VF/NM	NM-
13-Everett-a	17	34	51	103	162	220
14,15,19,20	15	30	45	84	127	170
16-18-Everett-a	15	30	45	90	140	190
21-35: Robinson-a	14	28	42	78	112	145

GIRL CRAZY
Dark Horse Comics: May, 1996 - No. 3, July, 1996 ($2.95, B&W, limited series)

1-3: Gilbert Hernandez-a/scripts. 3.00

GIRL FROM U.N.C.L.E., THE (TV) (Also see The Man From...)
Gold Key: Jan, 1967 - No. 5, Oct, 1967

	GD	VG	FN	VF	VF/NM	NM-
1-McWilliams-a; Stephanie Powers photo front/back-c & pin-ups (no ads, 12¢)	7	14	21	46	86	125
2-5-Leonard Swift-Courier No. 5. 4-Back-c pin-up	5	10	15	33	57	80

GIRL IN THE BAY, THE
Dark Horse Comics (Berger Books): Feb, 2019 - No. 4, May, 2019 ($3.99)

1-4-J.M. DeMatteis-s/Corin Howell-a 4.00

GIRLS
Image Comics: May, 2005 - No. 24, Apr, 2007 ($2.95/$2.99)

1-Luna Brothers-s/a/c 4.00
2-24 3.00
Image Firsts: Girls #1 (4/10, $1.00) r/#1 with "Image Firsts" cover logo 3.00
... Vol. 1: Conception TPB (2005, $14.99) r/#1-6 15.00
... Vol. 2: Emergence TPB (2006, $14.99) r/#7-12 15.00
... Vol. 3: Survival TPB (2006, $14.99) r/#13-18 15.00
... Vol. 4: Extinction TPB (2007, $14.99) r/#19-24 15.00

GIRLS' FUN & FASHION MAGAZINE (Formerly Polly Pigtails)
Parents' Magazine Institute: V5#44, Jan, 1950 - V5#48, Sept., 1950

	GD	VG	FN	VF	VF/NM	NM-
V5#44	9	18	27	47	61	75
45-48	7	14	21	37	46	55

GIRLS IN LOVE
Fawcett Publications: May, 1950 - No. 2, July, 1950

	GD	VG	FN	VF	VF/NM	NM-
1-Photo-c	14	28	42	78	112	145
2-Photo-c	10	20	30	58	79	100

GIRLS IN LOVE (Formerly G. I. Sweethearts No. 45)
Quality Comics Group: No. 46, Sept, 1955 - No. 57, Dec, 1956

	GD	VG	FN	VF	VF/NM	NM-
46	14	28	42	80	115	150
47-53,55,56	11	22	33	62	86	110
54- 'Commie' story	13	26	39	74	105	135
57-Matt Baker-c/a	17	34	51	105	165	225

GIRLS IN WHITE (See Harvey Comics Hits No. 58)

GIRLS' LIFE (Patsy Walker's Own Magazine For Girls!)
Atlas Comics (BFP): Jan, 1954 - No. 6, Nov, 1954

	GD	VG	FN	VF	VF/NM	NM-
1	22	44	66	128	209	290
2-Al Hartley-c	14	28	42	81	118	155
3-6	14	28	42	78	112	145

GIRLS' LOVE STORIES
National Comics (Signal Publ. No. 9-65/Arleigh No. 83-117): Aug-Sept, 1949 - No. 180, Nov-Dec, 1973 (No. 1-13: 52 pgs.)

	GD	VG	FN	VF	VF/NM	NM-
1-Toth, Kinstler-a, 8 pgs. each; photo-c	81	162	243	518	884	1250
2-Kinstler-a?	39	78	117	231	378	525
3-10: 1-9-Photo-c	25	50	75	147	241	335
11-20	20	40	60	114	182	250
21-33: 21-Kinstler-a. 33-Last pre-code (1-2/55)	14	28	42	82	121	160
34-50	11	22	33	62	86	110
51-70	10	20	30	56	76	95
71-99: 83-Last 10¢ issue	5	10	15	31	53	75
100	5	10	15	33	57	80
101-146: 113-117-April O'Day app.	3	6	9	20	31	42
147-151- "Confessions" serial. 150-Wood-a	3	6	9	21	33	45
152-160,171-179	3	6	9	16	23	30
161-170 (52 pgs.)	4	8	12	22	35	48
180 Last issue	3	6	9	20	31	42

Ashcan (8-9/49) not distributed to newsstands (a FN/VF copy sold for $836.50 in 2012)

GIRLS' ROMANCES
National Periodical Publ.(Signal Publ. No. 7-79/Arleigh No. 84): Feb-Mar, 1950 - No. 160, Oct, 1971 (No. 1-11: 52 pgs.)

	GD	VG	FN	VF	VF/NM	NM-
1-Photo-c	68	136	204	435	743	1050
2-Photo-c; Toth-a	37	74	111	222	361	500
3-10: 3-6-Photo-c	24	48	72	140	230	320
11,12,14-20	17	34	51	98	154	210
13-Toth-c	19	38	57	109	172	235
21-31: 31-Last pre-code (2-3/55)	14	28	42	80	115	150
32-50	6	12	18	40	73	105
51-99: 78-Panel inspired a famous Roy Lichtenstein painting. 80-Last 10¢ issue	5	10	15	31	53	75
100	5	10	15	33	57	80
101-108,110-120: 105-Panel inspired a famous Roy Lichtenstein painting	3	6	9	20	31	42
109-Beatles-c/story	17	34	51	117	259	400
121-133,135-140	3	6	9	18	28	38
134-Neal Adams-c (splash pg. is same as-c)	5	10	15	35	63	90
141-158	3	6	9	16	23	30
159,160-52 pgs.	4	8	12	27	44	60

GIRL WHO KICKED THE HORNETS NEST, THE
DC Comics (Vertigo): 2015 ($29.99, HC graphic novel, dustjacket)

HC-Adaptation of the novel; Mina-s/Mutti & Fuso-a/Bermejo-c 30.00

GIRL WHO WOULD BE DEATH, THE
DC Comics (Vertigo): Dec, 1998 - No. 4, March, 1999 ($2.50, lim. series)

1-4-Kiernan-s/Ormston-a 3.00

GIRL WITH THE DRAGON TATTOO, THE
DC Comics (Vertigo): Book One, 2012; Book Two, 2013 ($19.99, HC graphic novels)

Book One HC-First part of the adaptation of the novel; Mina-s/Manco-a/Bermejo-c 20.00
Book Two HC-Second part of the adaptation; Mina-s/Manco-a/Bermejo-c 20.00

G. I. SWEETHEARTS (Formerly Diary Loves; Girls In Love #46 on)
Quality Comics Group: No. 32, June, 1953 - No. 45, May, 1955

	GD	VG	FN	VF	VF/NM	NM-
32	14	28	42	82	121	160
33-45: 44-Last pre-code (3/55)	11	22	33	64	90	110

G.I. TALES (Formerly Sgt. Barney Barker No. 1-3)
Atlas Comics (MCI): No. 4, Feb, 1957 - No. 6, July, 1957

	GD	VG	FN	VF	VF/NM	NM-
4-Severin-a(4)	14	28	42	82	121	160
5	11	22	33	62	86	110
6-Orlando, Powell, & Woodbridge-a	11	22	33	64	90	115

GIVE ME LIBERTY (Also see Dark Horse Presents Fifth Anniversary Special, Dark Horse Presents #100-4, Happy Birthday Martha Washington, Martha Washington Goes to War, Martha Washington Stranded In Space & San Diego Comicon Comics #2)
Dark Horse Comics: June, 1990 - No. 4, 1991 ($4.95, limited series, 52 pgs.)

1-4: 1st app. Martha Washington; Frank Miller scripts, Dave Gibbons-c/a in all 6.00

G. I. WAR BRIDES
Superior Publishers Ltd.: Apr, 1954 - No. 8, June, 1955

	GD	VG	FN	VF	VF/NM	NM-
1	15	30	45	94	147	200
2	11	22	33	62	86	110
3-8: 4-Kamenesque-a; lingerie panels	10	20	30	58	79	100

G. I. WAR TALES
National Periodical Publications: Mar-Apr, 1973 - No. 4, Oct-Nov, 1973

	GD	VG	FN	VF	VF/NM	NM-
1-Reprints in all; dinosaur-c/s	3	6	9	21	33	45
2-N. Adams-a(r)	3	6	9	14	20	26
3,4: 4-Krigstein-a(r)	3	6	9	14	19	24

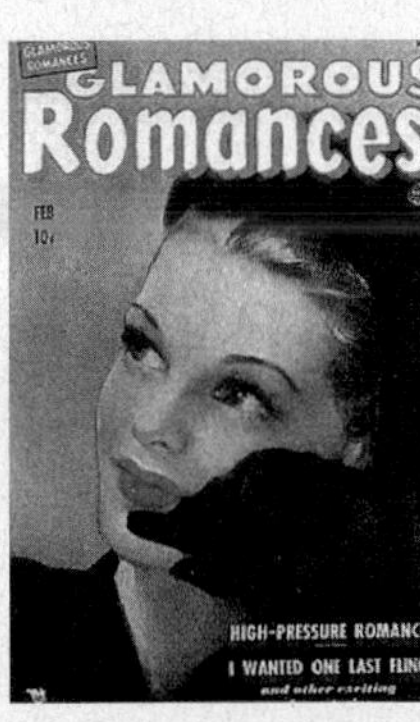

Glamorous Romances #50 © ACE

GLOW #4 © Netflix

Go-Bots #4 © Hasbro

	GD	VG	FN	VF	VF/NM	NM-
	2.0	4.0	6.0	8.0	9.0	9.2

NOTE: ***Drucker*** *a-3r, 4r.* ***Heath*** *a-4r.* ***Kubert*** *a-2, 3; c-4r.*

GIZMO
Mirage Studios: 1986 - No. 6, July, 1987 ($1.50, B&W)
1-6 4.00

G.L.A. (Great Lakes Avengers)(Also see GLX-Mas Special)
Marvel Comics: June, 2005 - No. 4, Sept, 2005 ($2.99, limited series)
1-4-Slott-s/Pelletier-a 3.00
...: Misassembled TPB (2005, $14.99) r/#1-4, West Coast Avengers #46 (1st app.) and Marvel Super-Heroes #8 (1st app. Squirrel Girl; Ditko-a) 15.00

GLADSTONE COMIC ALBUM
Gladstone: 1987 - No. 28, 1990 ($5.95/$9.95, 8-1/2x11")(All Mickey Mouse albums are by Gottfredson)
1-25: 1-Uncle Scrooge; Barks-r; Beck-c. 2-Donald Duck; r/F.C. #108 by Barks. 3-Mickey Mouse-r by Gottfredson. 4-Uncle Scrooge; r/F.C. #456 by Barks w/unedited story. 5-Donald Duck Advs.; r/F.C. #199. 6-Uncle Scrooge-r by Barks. 7-Donald Duck-r by Barks. 8-Mickey Mouse-r. 9-Bambi; r/F.C. #186? 10-Donald Duck Advs.; r/F.C. #275. 11-Uncle Scrooge; r/U.S. #4. 12-Donald And Daisy; r/F.C. #1055, WDC&S. 13-Donald Duck Advs.; r/F.C. #408. 14-Uncle Scrooge; Barks-r/U.S #21. 15-Donald And Gladstone; Barks-r. 16-Donald Duck Advs.; r/F.C. #238. 17-Mickey Mouse strip-r (The World of Tomorrow, The Pirate Ghost Ship). 18-Donald Duck and the Junior Woodchucks; Barks-r. 19-Uncle Scrooge; r/U.S. #12; Rosa-c. 20-Uncle Scrooge; r/F.C. #386; Barks-c/a(r). 21-Donald Duck Family; Barks-c/a(r). 22-Mickey Mouse strip-r. 23-Donald Duck; Barks-r/D.D. #26 w/unedited story. 24-Uncle Scrooge; Barks-r; Rosa-c. 25-D. Duck; Barks-c/a-r/F.C. #367 1 3 4 6 8 10
26-28: All have $9.95-c. 26-Mickey & Donald; Gottfredson-c/a(r). 27-Donald Duck; r/WDC&S by Barks; Barks painted-c. 28-Uncle Scrooge & Donald Duck; Rosa-c/a (4 stories) 1 3 4 6 8 10
Special 1-7: 1 ('89-'90, $9.95/13.95)-1-Donald Duck Finds Pirate Gold; r/F.C. #9. 2 ('89, $8.95)-Uncle Scrooge and Donald Duck; Barks-r/Uncle Scrooge #5; Rosa-c. 3 ('89, $8.95)-Mickey Mouse strip-r. 4 ('89, $11.95)-Uncle Scrooge; Rosa-c/a-r/Son of the Sun from U.S. #219 plus Barks-r/U.S. 5 ('90, $11.95)-Donald Duck Advs.; Barks-r/F.C. #282 & 422 plus Barks painted-c. 6 ('90, $12.95)-Uncle Scrooge; Barks-c/a-r/Uncle Scrooge. 7 ('90, $13.95)-Mickey Mouse; Gottfredson strip-r 2 4 6 9 11 14

GLADSTONE COMIC ALBUM (2nd Series)(Also see The Original Dick Tracy)
Gladstone Publishing: 1990 ($5.95, 8-1/2 x 11," stiff-c, 52 pgs.)
1,2-The Original Dick Tracy. 2-Origin of the 2-way wrist radio 6.00
3-D Tracy Meets the Mole-r by Gould ($6.95). 1 2 3 5 6 8

GLAMOROUS ROMANCES (Formerly Dotty)
Ace Magazines (A. A. Wyn): No. 41, July, 1949 - No. 90, Oct, 1956 (Photo-c 68-90)
41-Dotty app. 15 30 45 94 147 200
42-72,74-80: 44-Begin 52 pg. issues. 45,50-61-Painted-c. 80-Last pre-code (2/55) 13 26 39 72 101 130
73-L.B. Cole-r/All Love #27 13 26 39 74 105 135
81-90 11 22 33 62 86 110

GLAMOURPUSS
Aardvark-Vanaheim Inc.: Apr, 2008 - No. 26, Jul, 2012 ($3.00, B&W)
1-26: 1-Two covers; Dave Sim-s/a/c. 9,10-Gene Colan-c. 11-Heath-c. 19-Allred-c 3.00
1-Comics Industry Preview Edition (Diamond Dateline supplement) 4.00

GLOBAL FREQUENCY
DC Comics (WildStorm): Dec, 2002 - No. 12, Aug, 2004 ($2.95, limited series)
1-12-Warren Ellis-s. 1-Leach-a. 2-Fabry-a. 3-Dillon-a. 5-Muth-a. 7-Bisley-a. 12-Ha-a 3.00
1-RRP Edition variant-c; promotional giveaway for retailers (200 printed) 10.00
...: Detonation Radio TPB (2005, $14.95) r/#7-12 15.00
...: Planet Ablaze TPB (2003, $14.95) r/#1-6 15.00

GLORY
Image Comics (Extreme Studios)/Maximum Press: Mar, 1995 - No. 22, Apr, 1997 ($2.50)
0-Deodato-c/a, 1-(3/95)-Deodato-a 4.00
1A-Variant-c 5.00
2-11,13-22: 4-Variant-c by Quesada & Palmiotti. 5-Bagged w/Youngblood gaming card. 7,8-Deodato-c/a(p). 8-Babewatch x-over. 9-Cruz-c; Extreme Destroyer Pt. 5; polybagged w/card. 10-Angela-c/app. 11-Deodato-c. 3.00
12-($3.50)-Photo-c 4.00
... & Friends Christmas Special (12/95, $2.50) Deodato-c 3.00
... & Friends Lingerie Special (9/95, $2.95) Pin-ups w/photos; photo-c; variant-c exists 3.00
... /Angela: Angels in Hell (4/96, $2.50) Flip book w/Darkchylde #1 4.00
... /Avengelyne (10/95, $3.95) 1-Chromium-c, 1-Regular-c 4.00
Trade Paperback (1995, $9.95)-r/#1-4 10.00

GLORY (Continues numbering from the 1995-1997 series)
Image Comics: Feb, 2012 - No. 34, Apr, 2013 ($2.99/$3.99)
23-28-Joe Keatinge-s/Ross Campbell-a. 23-Supreme app. 3.00
29-34-($3.99) 4.00

GLORY
Awesome Comics: Mar, 1999 ($2.50)
0-Liefeld-c; story and sketch pages 3.00

GLORY (ALAN MOORE'S...)
Avatar Press: Dec, 2001 - No. 2 ($3.50)
Preview-(9/01, $1.99) B&W pages and cover art; Alan Moore-s 3.00
0-Four regular covers 3.50
1,2: 1-Alan Moore-s/Mychaels & Gebbie-a; nine covers by various. 2-Five covers 3.50

GLORY & FRIENDS BIKINI FEST
Image Comics (Extreme): Sept, 1995 - No. 2, Oct, 1995 ($2.50, limited series)
1,2: 1-Photo-c; centerfold photo; pin-ups 4.00

GLORY/CELESTINE: DARK ANGEL
Image Comics/Maximum Press (Extreme Studios): Sept, 1996 - No. 3, Nov, 1996 ($2.50)
1-3 3.00

GLOW (Gorgeous Ladies of Wrestling)(Based on the Netflix series)
IDW Publishing: Mar, 2019 - No. 4, Jun, 2019 ($3.99, limited series)
1-4-Tini Howard-s/Hannah Templer-a; multiple covers on each 4.00
...: Summer Special (7/19, $3.99) Devin Grayson-s/Lisa Sterle-a 4.00

GLOW VS THE BABYFACE (Gorgeous Ladies of Wrestling)(Based on the Netflix series)
IDW Publishing: Nov, 2019 - No. 4, Feb, 2020 ($3.99, limited series)
1-4-Garcia & Mendez-s/Templer-a; multiple covers on each 4.00

GLX-MAS SPECIAL (Great Lakes Avengers)
Marvel Comics: Feb, 2006 ($3.99, one-shot)
1-Christmas themed stories by various incl. Haley, Templeton, Grist, Wieringo 4.00

G-MAN: CAPE CRISIS
Image Comics: Aug, 2009 - No. 5, Jan, 2010 ($2.99, limited series)
1-5-Chris Giarrusso-s/a; back-up short strips by various 3.00

GNOME MOBILE, THE (See Movie Comics)

GOBBLEDYGOOK
Mirage Studios: 1984 - No. 2, 1984 (B&W)(1st Mirage comics, published at same time)
1-(24 pgs.)-(distribution of approx. 50) Teenage Mutant Ninja Turtles app. on full page back-c ad; Teenage Mutant Ninja Turtles do not appear inside. 1st app of Fugitoid 333 666 1000 2831 6416 10,000
2-(24 pgs.)-Teenage Mutant Ninja Turtles on full page back-c ad 141 282 423 1142 2571 4000
NOTE: *Counterfeit copies exist. Originals feature both black & white covers and interiors. Signed and numbered copies do not exist.*

GOBBLEDYGOOK
Mirage Studios: Dec, 1986 ($3.50, B&W, one-shot, 100 pgs.)
1-New 8 pg. TMNT story plus a Donatello/Michaelangelo 7 pg. story & a Gizmo story; Corben-i(r)/TMNT #7 5 10 15 33 57 80

GOBLIN, THE
Warren Publishing Co.: June, 1982 - No. 3, Dec, 1982 ($2.25, B&W magazine with 8 pg. color insert comic in all)
1-The Gremlin app. Philo Photon & the Troll Patrol, Micro-Buccaneers & Wizard Wormglow begin & app. in all. Tin Man app. Golden-a(p). Nebres-c/a in all 3 6 9 14 19 24
2,3: 2-1st Hobgoblin. 3-Tin Man app. 2 4 6 10 14 18
NOTE: ***Bermejo*** *a-1-3.* ***Elias*** *a-1-3.* ***Laxamana*** *a-1-3.* ***Nino*** *a-3.*

GO-BOTS (Based on the Hasbro toys)
IDW Publishing: Nov, 2018 - No. 5, Mar, 2019 ($3.99, limited series)
1-5-Tom Scioli-s/a/c 3.00

GOD COMPLEX
Image Comics: Dec, 2009 - No. 7, Jun, 2010 ($2.99)
1-7-Oeming & Berman-s/Broglia-a/Oeming-c 3.00

GOD COMPLEX: DOGMA
Image Comics (Top Cow): Oct, 2017 - No. 6, Jun, 2018 ($3.99)
1-6-Jenkins-s/Prasetya-a 4.00

GOD COUNTRY
Image Comics: Jan, 2017 - No. 6, Jun, 2017 ($3.99, limited series)
1-Donny Cates-s/Geoff Shaw-a 3 6 9 21 33 45
2-6 6.00

Gods Hates Astronauts #8 © Ryan Browne

God of War #1 © Sony

Godzilla: Kingdom of Monsters #9 © Toho

	GD 2.0	VG 4.0	FN 6.0	VF 8.0	VF/NM 9.0	NM- 9.2

GODDAMNED, THE
Image Comics: Nov, 2015 - No. 5, Nov, 2016 ($3.99)
1-5-Jason Aaron-s/r.m. Guéra-a; story of Cain and Noah 4.00

GODDAMNED, THE: THE VIRGIN BRIDES
Image Comics: Jul, 2020 - Present ($3.99)
1-4-Jason Aaron-s/r.m. Guéra-a 4.00

GODDESS
DC Comics (Vertigo): Jun, 1995 - No. 8, Jan, 1996 ($2.95, limited series)
1-Garth Ennis scripts; Phil Winslade-c/a in all 5.00
2-8 4.00

GODDESS MODE
DC Comics (Vertigo): Feb, 2019 - No. 6, Jul, 2019 ($3.99)
1-6-Zoë Quinn-s/Robbi Rodriguez-a 4.00

GODFATHERS, THE (See The Crusaders)

GOD HATES ASTRONAUTS
Image Comics: Sept, 2014 - No. 10, Jul, 2015 ($3.50)
1-10-Ryan Browne-s/a. 1-Covers by Browne & Darrow 3.50

GOD IS
Spire Christian Comics (Fleming H. Revell Co.): 1973, 1975 (35-49¢)

	GD	VG	FN	VF	VF/NM	NM-
nn-(1973) By Al Hartley	3	6	9	14	19	24
nn-(1975)	2	4	6	10	14	18

GOD IS DEAD
Avatar Press: Aug, 2013 - No. 48, Feb, 2016 ($3.99)
1-24,26-46: 1-5-Hickman & Costa-s/Amorim-a 4.00
25,48-($5.99) 25-Costa-s/DiPascale, Nobile & Urdinola-a. 48-Last issue; cover gallery 6.00
...Book of Acts Alpha (7/14, $5.99) Short stories by Alan Moore and others 6.00
...Book of Acts Omega (7/14, $5.99) Short stories by various 6.00

GODKILLERS
AfterShock Comics: Feb, 2020 - No. 5, Aug, 2020 ($3.99, limited series)
1-5-Mark Sable-s/Maan House-a 4.00

GODLAND
Image Comics: July, 2005 - Finale, Dec, 2013 ($2.99)
1-35-Joe Casey-s; Kirby-esque art by Tom Scioli. 13-Var-c by Giffen & Larsen. 33-"Dogland" on cover 3.00
16-(60¢-c) Re-cap/origin issue 3.00
36-($3.99) 4.00
... Finale (12/13, $6.99) Final issue 7.00
Image Firsts: Godland #1 (9/10, $1.00) r/#1 with "Image Firsts" cover logo 3.00
...: Celestial Edition One HC (2007, $34.99) r/#1-12 and story from Image Holiday Special; intro. by Grant Morrison; cover gallery, developmental art and original story pitches 35.00

GOD OF WAR (Based on the Sony videogame)
DC Comics (WildStorm): May, 2010 - No. 6, Mar, 2011 ($3.99/$2.99, limited series)
1-6-Wolfman-s/Sorrentino-a/Park-c. 6-($2.99) 4.00

GOD OF WAR (Based on the Sony videogame)
Dark Horse Comics: Nov, 2018 - No. 4, Feb, 2019 ($3.99, limited series)
1-4-Chris Roberson-s/Tony Parker-a/E.M. Gist-c 4.00

GOD SAVE THE QUEEN
DC Comics (Vertigo): 2007 ($19.99, hardcover with dustjacket, graphic novel)
HC-Mike Carey-s/John Bolton-painted art 20.00
SC-(2008, $12.99) Different painted-c by Bolton 13.00

GOD'S COUNTRY (Also see Marvel Comics Presents)
Marvel Comics: 1994 ($6.95)
nn-P. Craig Russell-a; Colossus story; r/Marvel Comics Presents #10-17 7.00

GOD'S HEROES IN AMERICA
Catechetical Guild Educational Society: 1956 (nn) (25¢/35¢, 68 pgs.)

	GD	VG	FN	VF	VF/NM	NM-
307	3	6	9	18	27	36

GOD'S SMUGGLER (Religious)
Spire Christian Comics/Fleming H. Revell Co.: 1972 (35¢/39¢/40¢)

	GD	VG	FN	VF	VF/NM	NM-
1-Three variations exist	3	6	9	14	19	24

GODWHEEL
Malibu Comics (Ultraverse): No. 0, Jan, 1995 - No. 3, Feb, 1995 ($2.50, limited series)
0-3: 0-Flip-c. 1-1st app. Primevil; Thor cameo (1 panel). 3-Pérez-a in Ch. 3, Thor app. 3.00

GODZILLA (Movie)
Marvel Comics : August, 1977 - No. 24, July, 1979 (Based on movie series)

	GD	VG	FN	VF	VF/NM	NM-
1-(Regular 30¢ edition)-Moench-s/Trimpe-a/Mooney-i	5	10	15	30	50	70
1-(35¢-c variant, limited distribution)	17	34	51	117	259	400
2-(Regular 30¢ edition)-Tuska-i.	3	6	9	15	22	28
2,3-(35¢-c variant, limited distribution)	10	20	30	64	132	200
3-(30¢-c) Champions app.(w/o Ghost Rider)	3	6	9	16	23	30
4-10: 4,5-Sutton-a	2	4	6	10	14	18
11-23: 14-Shield app. 20-F.F. app. 21,22-Devil Dinosaur app.	2	4	6	8	11	14
24-Last issue	3	6	9	15	22	28

GODZILLA (Movie)
Dark Horse Comics: May, 1988 - No. 6, 1988 ($1.95, B&W, limited series) (Based on movie series)

	GD	VG	FN	VF	VF/NM	NM-
1	2	4	6	8	11	14
2-6	1	2	3	5	6	8
...Collection (1990, $10.95)-r/1-6 with new-c						14.00
...Color Special 1 (Sum, 1992, $3.50, color, 44 pgs.)-Arthur Adams wraparound-c/a & part scripts	1	2	3	5	6	8
...King Of The Monsters Special (8/87, $1.50)-Origin; Bissette-c/a	1	2	3	5	6	8
...Vs. Barkley nn (12/93, $2.95, color)-Dorman painted-c	1	2	3	5	6	8

GODZILLA (King of the Monsters) (Movie)
Dark Horse Comics: May, 1995 - No. 16, Sept, 1996 ($2.50) (Based on movies)
0-16: 0-r/Dark Horse Comics #10,11. 1-3-Kevin Maguire scripts. 3-8-Art Adams-c 5.00
...Vs. Hero Zero ($2.50) 5.00

GODZILLA
IDW Publishing: May, 2012 - May, 2013 ($3.99)
1-13: 1-5,7,8,10-Swierczynski-s/Gane-a; multiple covers on each. 6-Wachter-a 4.00
...: The IDW Era (5/14, $3.99) Plot synopses of mini-series and cover galleries 4.00

GODZILLA: CATACLYSM
IDW Publishing: Aug, 2014 - No. 5, Dec, 2014 ($3.99, limited series)
1-5-Bunn-s/Wachter-a; multiple covers on each 4.00

GODZILLA: GANGSTERS AND GOLIATHS
IDW Publishing: Jun, 2011 - No. 5, Oct, 2011 ($3.99, limited series)
1-5-Layman-s/Ponticelli-a; Mothra app. 1-Darrow-c 4.00

GODZILLA IN HELL
IDW Publishing: Jul, 2015 - No. 5, Nov, 2015 ($3.99, limited series)
1-5: Two covers on each. 1-Stokoe-s/a. 5-Wachter-s/a 4.00

GODZILLA: KINGDOM OF MONSTERS
IDW Publishing: Mar, 2011 - No. 12, Feb, 2012 ($3.99)
1-12: 1-Hester-a; covers by Ross & Powell. 2,3-Covers by Hester & Powell 4.00
...: 100 Cover Charity Spectacular (8/11, $7.99) Variant covers for Japan Disaster Relief 8.00

GODZILLA LEGENDS (Spotlight on other monsters)
IDW Publishing: Nov, 2011 - No. 5, Mar, 2012 ($3.99, limited series)
1-5-Art Adams-c. 1-Anguirus. 2-Rodan. 3-Titanosaurus. 4-Hedorah. 5-Kumonga 4.00

GODZILLA: OBLIVION
IDW Publishing: Mar, 2016 - No. 5, Jul, 2016 ($3.99, limited series)
1-5-Fialkov-s/Churilla-a; Mechagodzilla & Ghidorah app. 4.00

GODZILLA: RAGE ACROSS TIME
IDW Publishing: Aug, 2016 - No. 5, Nov, 2016 ($3.99, limited series)
1-5-Story & art by various 4.00

GODZILLA: RULERS OF EARTH
IDW Publishing: Jun, 2013 - No. 25, Jun, 2015 ($3.99, limited series)
1-24: 1-8-Chris Mowry-s/Matt Frank-a 4.00
25-($7.99) Mowry-s/Frank & Zornow-a 8.00

GODZILLA: THE HALF-CENTURY WAR
IDW Publishing: Aug, 2012 - No. 5, Feb, 2013 ($3.99, limited series)
1-5-James Stokoe-s/a 4.00

GOG (VILLAINS) (See Kingdom Come)
DC Comics: Feb, 1998 ($1.95, one-shot)
1-Waid-s/Ordway-a(p)/Pearson-c 3.00

GO GIRL!
Image Comics: Aug, 2000 - No. 5 ($3.50, B&W, quarterly)
1-5-Trina Robbins-s/Anne Timmons-a; pin-up gallery 3.50

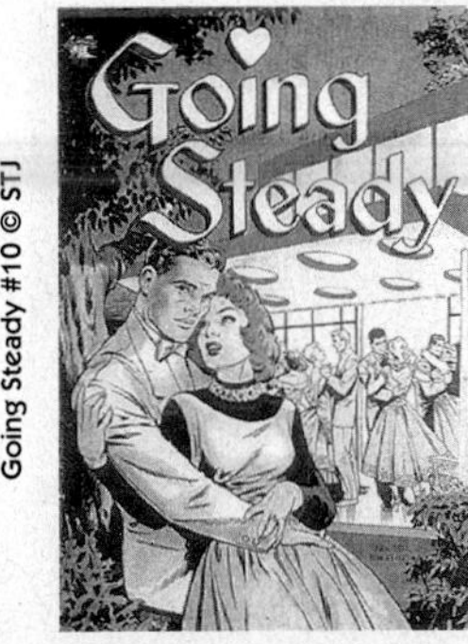

Going Steady #10 © STJ

Golden Comics Digest #23 © GK

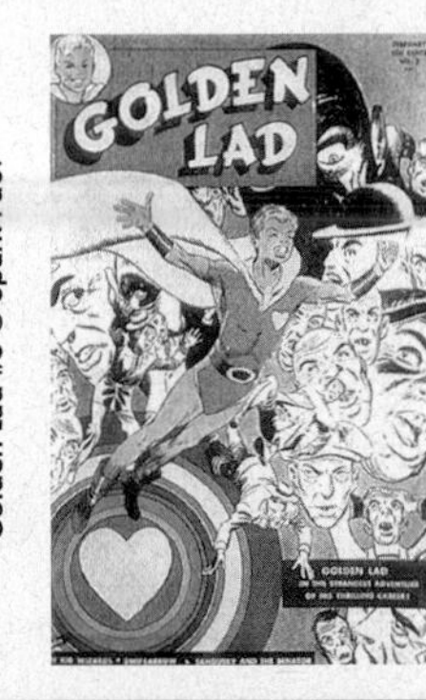

Golden Lad #3 © Spark Pub.

GD VG FN VF VF/NM NM-
2.0 4.0 6.0 8.0 9.0 9.2

GO-GO
Charlton Comics: June, 1966 - No. 9, Oct, 1967
1-Miss Bikini Luv begins; Rolling Stones, Beatles, Elvis, Sonny & Cher, Bob Dylan, Sinatra, parody; Herman's Hermits pin-ups; D'Agostino-c/a in #1-8 8 16 24 52 99 145
2-Ringo Starr, David McCallum & Beatles photos on cover; Beatles story and photos; Blooperman & parody of JLA heroes 8 16 24 52 99 145
3,4: 3-Blooperman, ends #6; 1 pg. Batman & Robin satire; full pg. photo pin-ups Lovin' Spoonful & The Byrds 5 10 15 31 53 75
5,7,9: 5 (2/67)-Super Hero & TV satire by Jim Aparo & Grass Green begins. 6-8-Aparo-a. 7-Photo of Brian Wilson of Beach Boys on-c & Beach Boys photo inside f/b-c. 9-Aparo-c/a 5 10 15 35 55 75
6-Parody of JLA & DC heroes vs. Marvel heroes; Aparo-a; Elvis parody; Petula Clark photo-c; first signed work by Jim Aparo 5 10 15 34 60 85
8-Monkees photo on-c & photo inside f/b-c 6 12 18 38 69 100

GO-GO AND ANIMAL (See Tippy's Friends...)

GOING STEADY (Formerly Teen-Age Temptations)
St. John Publ. Co.: No. 10, Dec, 1954 - No. 13, June, 1955; No. 14, Oct, 1955
10(1954)-Matt Baker-c/a 168 336 504 1075 1838 2600
11(2/55, last precode), 12(4/55)-Baker-c 68 136 204 435 743 1050
13(6/55)-Baker-c/a 84 168 262 538 919 1300
14(10/55)-Matt Baker-c/a, 25 pgs. 110 220 330 704 1202 1700

GOING STEADY (Formerly Personal Love)
Prize Publications/Headline: V3#3, Feb, 1960 - V3#6, Aug, 1960; V4#1, Sept-Oct, 1960
V3#3-6, V4#1 6 12 18 38 69 100

GOING STEADY WITH BETTY (Becomes Betty & Her Steady No. 2)
Avon Periodicals: Nov-Dec, 1949 (Teen-age)
1-Partial photo-c 41 82 123 256 428 600

GOLDEN AGE, THE (TPB also reprinted in 2005 as JSA: The Golden Age)
DC Comics (Elseworlds): 1993 - No. 4, 1994 ($4.95, limited series)
1-4: James Robinson scripts; Paul Smith-c/a; gold foil embossed-c 6.00
Trade Paperback (1995, $19.95) intro by Howard Chaykin 20.00

GOLDEN AGE SECRET FILES
DC Comics: Feb, 2001 ($4.95, one-shot)
1-Origins and profiles of JSA members and other G.A. heroes; Lark-c 5.00

GOLDEN ARROW (See Fawcett Miniatures, Mighty Midget & Whiz Comics)

GOLDEN ARROW (...Western No. 6)
Fawcett Publications: Spring, 1942 - No. 6, Spring, 1947 (68 pgs.)
1-Golden Arrow begins 48 96 144 302 514 725
2-(1943) 22 44 66 132 216 300
3-5: 3-(Win/45-46). 4-(Spr/46). 5-(Fall/46) 15 30 45 90 140 190
6-Krigstein-a 16 32 48 94 147 200
Ashcan (1942) not distributed to newsstands, only for in house use. A CGC certified 9.0 sold for $3,734.38 in 2008.

GOLDEN COMICS DIGEST
Gold Key: May, 1969 - No. 48, Jan, 1976
NOTE: *Whitman editions exist of many titles and are generally valued the same.*
1-Tom & Jerry, Woody Woodpecker, Bugs Bunny 5 10 15 33 57 80
2-Hanna-Barbera TV Fun Favorites; Space Ghost, Flintstones, Atom Ant, Jetsons, Yogi Bear, Banana Splits, others app. 6 12 18 41 76 110
3-Tom & Jerry, Woody Woodpecker 3 6 9 16 24 32
4-Tarzan; Manning & Marsh-a 4 8 12 28 47 65
5,8-Tom & Jerry, W. Woodpecker, Bugs Bunny 3 6 9 16 23 30
6-Bugs Bunny 3 6 9 16 23 30
7-Hanna-Barbera TV Fun Favorites 5 10 15 33 57 80
9-Tarzan 4 8 12 28 47 65
10,12-17: 10-Bugs Bunny. 12-Tom & Jerry, Bugs Bunny, W. Woodpecker Journey to the Sun. 13-Tom & Jerry. 14-Bugs Bunny Fun Packed Funnies. 15-Tom & Jerry, Woody Woodpecker, Bugs Bunny. 16-Woody Woodpecker Cartoon Special. 17-Bugs Bunny 3 6 9 16 23 30
11-Hanna-Barbera TV Fun Favorites 5 10 15 34 60 85
18-Tom & Jerry; Barney Bear-r by Barks 3 6 9 16 24 32
19-Little Lulu 4 8 12 25 40 55
20-22: 20-Woody Woodpecker Falltime Funtime. 21-Bugs Bunny Showtime. 22-Tom & Jerry Winter Wingding 3 6 9 16 23 30
23-Little Lulu & Tubby Fun Fling 4 8 12 25 40 55
24-26,28: 24-Woody Woodpecker Fun Festival. 25-Tom & Jerry. 26-Bugs Bunny Halloween Hulla-Boo-Loo; Dr. Spektor article, also #25. 28-Tom & Jerry 3 6 9 14 20 26
27-Little Lulu & Tubby in Hawaii 4 8 12 24 38 52
29-Little Lulu & Tubby 4 8 12 24 38 52
30-Bugs Bunny Vacation Funnies 3 6 9 14 20 26
31-Turok, Son of Stone; r/4-Color #596,656; c-r/#9 4 8 12 27 44 60
32-Woody Woodpecker Summer Fun 3 6 9 14 20 26
33,36: 33-Little Lulu & Tubby Halloween Fun; Dr. Spektor app. 36-Little Lulu & Her Friends 4 8 12 24 38 52
34,35,37-39: 34-Bugs Bunny Winter Funnies. 35-Tom & Jerry Snowtime Funtime. 37-Woody Woodpecker County Fair. 39-Bugs Bunny Summer Fun 3 6 9 14 20 26
38-The Pink Panther 3 6 9 16 24 32
40,43: 40-Little Lulu & Tubby Trick or Treat; all by Stanley. 43-Little Lulu in Paris 4 8 12 24 38 52
41,42,44,47: 41-Tom & Jerry Winter Carnival. 42-Bugs Bunny. 44-Woody Woodpecker Family Fun Festival. 47-Bugs Bunny 3 6 9 14 20 25
45-The Pink Panther 3 6 9 16 24 32
46-Little Lulu & Tubby 4 8 12 21 33 45
48-The Lone Ranger 3 6 9 17 26 35
NOTE: *#1-30, 164 pgs.; #31 on, 132 pgs..*

GOLDEN LAD
Spark/Fact & Fiction Publ.: July, 1945 - No. 5, June, 1946 (#4, 5: 52 pgs.)
1-Origin & 1st app. Golden Lad & Swift Arrow; Sandusky and the Senator begins 65 130 195 416 708 1000
2-Mort Meskin-c/a 31 62 93 182 296 410
3,4-Mort Meskin-c/a 27 54 81 162 266 370
5-Origin & 1st app. Golden Girl; Shaman & Flame app. 39 78 117 240 395 550
NOTE: *All have* ***Robinson,*** *and* ***Roussos*** *art plus* ***Meskin*** *covers and art.*

GOLDEN LEGACY
Fitzgerald Publishing Co.: 1966 - 1972 (Black History) (25¢)
1-12,14-16: 1-Toussaint L'Ouverture (1966), 2-Harriet Tubman (1967), 3-Crispus Attucks & the Minutemen (1967), 4-Benjamin Banneker (1968), 5-Matthew Henson (1969), 6-Alexander Dumas & Family (1969), 7-Frederick Douglass, Part 1 (1969), 8-Frederick Douglass, Part 2 (1970), 9-Robert Smalls (1970), 10-J. Cinque & the Amistad Mutiny (1970), 11-Men in Action: White, Marshall J. Wilkins (1970), 12-Black Cowboys (1972), 14-The Life of Alexander Pushkin (1971), 15-Ancient African Kingdoms (1972), 16-Black Inventors (1972) each.... 4 8 12 23 37 50
13-The Life of Martin Luther King, Jr. (1972) 5 10 15 30 50 70
1-10,12,13,15,16(1976)-Reprints 2 4 6 9 12 15

GOLDEN LOVE STORIES (Formerly Golden West Love)
Kirby Publishing Co.: No. 4, April, 1950
4-Powell-a; Glenn Ford/Janet Leigh photo-c 17 34 51 103 162 220

GOLDEN PICTURE CLASSIC, A
Western Printing Co. (Simon & Shuster): 1956-1957 (Text stories w/illustrations in color; 100 pgs. each)
CL-401: Treasure Island 11 22 33 64 90 115
CL-402,403: 402: Tom Sawyer. 403: Black Beauty 10 20 30 54 72 90
CL-404, 405: CL-404: Little Women. CL-405: Heidi 10 20 30 54 72 90
CL-406: Ben Hur 8 16 24 44 57 70
CL-407: Around the World in 80 Days 8 16 24 44 57 70
CL-408: Sherlock Holmes 9 18 27 50 65 80
CL-409: The Three Musketeers 8 16 24 44 57 70
CL-410: The Merry Advs. of Robin Hood 8 16 24 44 57 70
CL-411,412: 411: Hans Brinker. 412: The Count of Monte Cristo 9 18 27 50 65 80
(Both soft & hardcover editions are valued the same)
NOTE: *Recent research has uncovered new information. Apparently #s 1-6 were issued in 1956 and #7-12 in 1957. But they can be found in five different series listings: CL-1 to CL-12 (softbound); CL-401 to CL-412 (also softbound); CL-101 to CL-112 (hardbound); plus two new series discoveries: A Golden Reading Adventure, publ. by Golden Press; edited down to 60 pages and reduced in size to 6x9"; only #s discovered so far are #381 (CL-4), #382 (CL-6) & #387 (CL-3). They have no reorder list and some have covers different from GPC. There have also been found British hardbound editions of GPC with dust jackets. Copies of all five listed series vary from scarce to very rare. Some editions of some series have not yet been found at all.*

GOLDEN PICTURE STORY BOOK
Racine Press (Western): Dec, 1961 (50¢, Treasury size, 52 pgs.) (All are scarce)
ST-1-Huckleberry Hound (TV); Hokey Wolf, Pixie & Dixie, Quick Draw McGraw, Snooper and Blabber, Augie Doggie app. 15 30 45 103 227 350
ST-2-Yogi Bear (TV); Snagglepuss, Yakky Doodle, Quick Draw McGraw, Snooper and Blabber, Augie Doggie app. 15 30 45 103 227 350
ST-3-Babes in Toyland (Walt Disney's...)-Annette Funicello photo-c 19 38 57 131 291 450
ST-4-(...of Disney Ducks)-Walt Disney's Wonderful World of Ducks (Donald Duck, Uncle Scrooge, Donald's Nephews, Grandma Duck, Ludwig Von Drake, & Gyro Gearloose

Gomer Pyle #1 © GK

Goofy Comics #9 © STD

The Goon #24 © Eric Powell

GD 2.0 | VG 4.0 | FN 6.0 | VF 8.0 | VF/NM 9.0 | NM- 9.2

stories) 19 38 57 131 291 450

GOLDEN RECORD COMIC (See Amazing Spider-Man #1, Avengers #4, Fantastic Four #1, Journey Into Mystery #83) (Also see Superman Record Comic and Batman Record Comic in the Promotional section)

GOLDEN STORY BOOKS
Western Printing Co. (Simon & Shuster): 1949-1950 (Heavy covers, digest size, 128 pgs.) (Illustrated text in color)

7-Walt Disney's Mystery in Disneyville, a book-length adventure starring Donald and Nephews, Mickey and Nephews, and with Minnie, Daisy and Goofy. Art by Dick Moores & Manuel Gonzales (scarce) 31 62 93 182 296 410
10-Bugs Bunny's Treasure Hunt, a book-length adventure starring Bugs & Porky Pig, with Petunia Pig & Nephew, Cicero. Art by Tom McKimson (scarce) 21 42 63 122 199 275
11,12 ('50): 11-M-G-M's Tom & Jerry. 12-Walt Disney's "So Dear My Heart" 20 40 60 114 182 250

GOLDEN WEST LOVE (Golden Love Stories No. 4)
Kirby Publishing Co.: Sept-Oct, 1949 - No. 3, Feb, 1950 (All 52 pgs.)

1-Powell-a in all; Roussos-a; painted-c 23 46 69 136 223 310
2,3: Photo-c 17 34 51 100 158 215

GOLDEN WEST RODEO TREASURY (See Dell Giants)

GOLDFISH (See A.K.A. Goldfish)

GOLDIE VANCE
Boom Entertainment (BOOM! Box): Apr, 2016 - No. 12, May, 2017 ($3.99)

1-12: 1-8-Hope Larson-s/Brittney Williams-a. 1-Five covers. 2-4-Two covers. 9-12-Hayes-a4.00

GOLDILOCKS (See March of Comics No. 1)

GOLD KEY: ALLIANCE
Dynamite Entertainment: 2016 - No. 5, 2016 ($3.99, limited series)

1-5: 1-Team up of Magnus, Turok, Solar & Samson; Hester-s/Peeples-a 4.00

GOLD KEY CHAMPION
Gold Key: Mar, 1978 - No. 2, May, 1978 (50¢, 52 pgs.)

1,2: 1-Space Family Robinson; half-r. 2-Mighty Samson; half-r 1 3 4 6 8 10

GOLD KEY SPOTLIGHT
Gold Key: May, 1976 - No. 11, Feb, 1978

1-Tom, Dick & Harriet 2 4 6 8 11 14
2-11: 2-Wacky Advs. of Cracky. 3-Wacky Witch. 4-Tom, Dick & Harriet. 5-Wacky Advs. of Cracky. 6-Dagar the Invincible; Santos-a; origin Demonomicon. 7-Wacky Witch & Greta Ghost. 8-The Occult Files of Dr. Spektor, Simbar, Lu-sai; Santos-a. 9-Tragg. 10-O. G. Whiz. 11-Tom, Dick & Harriet 2 4 6 8 10 12

GOLD MEDAL COMICS
Cambridge House: 1945 (25¢, one-shot, 132 pgs.)

nn-Captain Truth by Fujitani as well as Stallman and Howie Post, Crime Detector, The Witch of Salem, Luckyman, others app. 40 80 120 246 411 575

GOMER PYLE (TV)
Gold Key: July, 1966 - No. 3, Oct, 1967

1-Photo front/back-c 9 18 27 61 123 185
2,3-Photo-c 5 10 15 35 63 90

GON
DC Comics (Paradox Press): July, 1996 - No. 4, Oct, 1996; No. 5, 1997 ($5.95, B&W, digest-size, limited series)

1-5: Misadventures of baby dinosaur; 1-Gon. 2-Gon Again. 3-Gon: Here Today, Gone Tomorrow. 4-Gon: Going, Going...Gon. 5-Gon Swimmin'. Tanaka-c/a/scripts in all 1 2 3 5 6 8

GON COLOR SPECTACULAR
DC Comics (Paradox Press): 1998 ($5.95, square-bound)

nn-Tanaka-c/a/scripts 1 2 3 5 6 8

GONERS
Image Comics: Oct, 2014 - No. 6, Mar, 2015 ($2.99)

1-6-Semahn-s/Corona-a 3.00

GON ON SAFARI
DC Comics (Paradox Press): 2000 ($7.95, B&W, digest-size)

nn-Tanaka-c/a/scripts 1 2 3 5 6 8

GON UNDERGROUND
DC Comics (Paradox Press): 1999 ($7.95, B&W, digest-size)

nn-Tanaka-c/a/scripts 1 2 3 5 6 8

GON WILD

GD 2.0 | VG 4.0 | FN 6.0 | VF 8.0 | VF/NM 9.0 | NM- 9.2

DC Comics (Paradox Press): 1997 ($9.95, B&W, digest-size)

nn-Tanaka-c/a/scripts in all. (Rep. Gon #3,4) 1 3 4 6 8 10

GOODBYE, MR. CHIPS (See Movie Comics)

GOOD GIRL ART QUARTERLY
AC Comics: Summer, 1990 - No. 15, Spring, 1994, No. 19, 2001 (B&W/color, 52 pgs.)

1,3-15 ($3.50)-All have one new story (often FemForce) & rest reprints by Baker, Ward & other "good girl" artists 4.00
2 ($3.95), 19 (2001) FX Convention Exclusive 4.00

GOOD GIRL COMICS (Formerly Good Girl Art Quarterly)
AC Comics: No. 16, Summer, 1994 - No. 18, 1995 (B&W)

16-18 4.00

GOOD GUYS, THE
Defiant: Nov, 1993 - No. 9, July, 1994 ($2.50/$3.25/$3.50)

1-($3.50, 52 pgs.)-Glory x-over from Plasm 4.00
2,3,5-9: 3-Chasm app. 9-Pre-Schism issue 3.00
4-($3.25, 52 pgs.) Nudge sends Chasm to Plasm 4.00

GOOD, THE BAD AND THE UGLY, THE (Also see Man With No Name)
Dynamite Entertainment: 2009 - No. 8 ($3.50)

1-8: 1-Character from the 1966 Clint Eastwood movie; Dixon-s/Polls-a; three covers 3.50

GOOD TRIUMPHS OVER EVIL! (Also see Narrative Illustration)
M.C. Gaines: 1943 (12 pgs., 7-1/4"x10", B&W) (not a comic book) (Rare)

nn-A pamphlet, sequel to Narrative Illustration 161 322 483 1030 1765 2500
NOTE: ***Print, A Quarterly Journal of the Graphic Arts*** *Vol. 3 No. 3 (64 pg. square bound) features 1st printing of Good Triumphs Over Evil! A VG copy sold for $350 in 2005.*

GOOFY (Disney)(See Dynabrite Comics, Mickey Mouse Magazine V4#7, Walt Disney Showcase #35 & Wheaties)
Dell Publishing Co.: No. 468, May, 1953 - Sept-Nov, 1962

Four Color 468 (#1) 12 24 36 79 170 260
Four Color 562,627,658,702,747,802,857 7 14 21 46 86 125
Four Color 899,952,987,1053,1094,1149,1201 5 10 15 35 63 90
12-308-211(Dell, 9-11/62) 5 10 15 31 53 75

GOOFY ADVENTURES
Disney Comics: June, 1990 - No. 17, 1991 ($1.50)

1-17: Most new stories. 2-Joshua Quagmire-a w/free poster. 7-WDC&S-r plus new-a. 9-Gottfredson-r. 14-Super Goof story. 15-All Super Goof issue. 17-Gene Colan-a(p) 3.00

GOOFY ADVENTURE STORY (See Goofy No. 857)

GOOFY COMICS (Companion to Happy Comics)(Not Disney)
Nedor Publ. Co. No. 1-14/Standard No. 14-48: June, 1943 - No. 48, 1953 (Animated Cartoons)

1-Funny animal; Oriolo-c 39 78 117 240 395 550
2 20 40 60 115 188 260
3-10 15 30 45 85 130 175
11-19 13 26 39 72 101 130
20-35-Frazetta text illos in all 14 28 42 78 112 145
36-48 11 22 33 60 83 105

GOOFY SUCCESS STORY (See Goofy No. 702)

GOON, THE
Avatar Press: Mar, 1999 - No. 3, July, 1999 ($3.00, B&W)

1-Eric Powell-s/a 17 34 51 117 259 400
2 6 12 18 42 79 115
3 5 10 15 35 63 90
...: Rough Stuff (Albatross, 1/03, $15.95) r/Avatar Press series #1-3 20.00
...: Rough Stuff (Dark Horse, 2/04, $12.95) r/Avatar Press series #1-3 newly colored 15.00

GOON, THE (2nd series)
Albatross Exploding Funny Books: Oct, 2002 - No. 4, Feb, 2003 ($2.95)

1-Eric Powell-s/a 5 10 15 35 63 90
2-4 3 6 9 14 20 25
...Color Special 1 (8/02) 3 6 9 16 23 30
...: Nothin' But Misery Vol. 1 (Dark Horse, 7/03, $15.95, TPB) - Reprints The Goon #1-4 (Albatross series), Color Special, and story from DHP #157 18.00

GOON, THE (3rd series) (Also see Dethklok Versus the Goon)
Dark Horse Comics: June, 2003 - No. 44, Nov, 2013 ($2.99/$3.50)

1-Eric Powell-s/a in all 3 6 9 19 30 40
2-4 2 4 6 8 10 12
5-31: 7-Hellboy-c/app; framing seq. by Mignola 14-Two covers 4.00
32-($3.99, 3/09) Tenth Anniversary issue; with sketch pages and pin-ups 5.00
33-44-($3.50) 33-Silent issue. 35-Dorkin-s. 39-Gimmick issue. 41-43-Buckingham-a.

Goosebumps: Download and Die #1 © Scholastic

Gotham Academy: Second Semester #1 © DC

Gotham City Garage #1 © DC

GD VG FN VF VF/NM NM-
2.0 4.0 6.0 8.0 9.0 9.2

44-Spanish issue 3.50
... 25¢ Edition (9/05, 25¢) 3.00
...: Chinatown and the Mystery of Mr. Wicker HC (11/07, $19.95) original GN; Powell-s/a 20.00
...: Fancy Pants Edition HC (10/05, $24.95, dust jacket) r/#1,2 of 2nd series & #1,3,5,9 of 3rd series; Powell intro.; sketch pages and cover gallery 25.00
...: Heaps of Ruination (5/05, $12.95, TPB) r/#5-8; intro. by Frank Darabont 13.00
...: My Murderous Childhood (And Other Grievous Yarns) (5/04, $13.95, TPB) r/#1-4 and short story from Drawing on Your Nightmares one-shot; intro. by Frank Cho 14.00
...: One For One (8/10, $1.00) r/#1 with red cover frame 3.00
...: One For The Road (6/14, $3.50) Jack Davis-c; EC horror hosts app. 3.50
...: Theater Bizarre (10/15, $3.99) Prelude to The Lords of Misery; Zombo app. 4.00
...: Virtue and the Grim Consequences Thereof (2/06, $16.95) r/#9-13 17.00
...: Wicked Inclinations (12/06, $14.95) r/#14-18; intro. by Mike Allred 15.00

GOON, THE (4th series)
Albatross Funnybooks: 2019 - Present ($3.99)
1-12: 1-4-Eric Powell-s/a. 5-8-Powell & Sniegoski-s/Parson-a. 9-12-Langridge-s/Norton-a 4.00

GOON NOIR, THE (Dwight T. Albatross's...)
Dark Horse Comics: Sept, 2006 - No. 3, Jan, 2007 ($2.99, B&W, limited series)
1-3-Anthology 1-Oswalt-s/Ploog-a; Sniegoski-s/Powell-a; Morrison-s/a; Niles-s/Sook-a 4.00

GOON: OCCASION OF REVENGE, THE
Dark Horse Comics: Jul, 2014 - No. 4, Dec, 2014 ($3.50, limited series)
1-4-Powell-s/a. 3-Origin of Kid Gargantuan 3.50

GOON: ONCE UPON A HARD TIME, THE
Dark Horse Comics: Feb, 2015 - No. 4, Oct, 2015 ($3.50, limited series)
1-4-Powell-s/a 3.50

GOOSE (Humor magazine)
Cousins Publ. (Fawcett): Sept, 1976 - No. 3, 1976 (75¢, 52 pgs., B&W)
1-Nudity in all 3 6 9 18 28 38
2,3: 2-(10/76) Fonz-c/s; Lone Ranger story. 3-Wonder Woman, King Kong, Six Million Dollar Man stories 3 6 9 14 20 26

GOOSEBUMPS: DOWNLOAD AND DIE!
IDW Publishing: Feb, 2018 - No. 3, Apr, 2018 ($3.99, limited series)
1-3-Jen Vaughn-s/Michelle Wong-a 4.00

GOOSEBUMPS: HORRORS OF THE WITCH HOUSE
IDW Publishing: Mar, 2019 - No. 3, May, 2019 ($3.99, limited series)
1-3-Denton J. Tipton & Matthew Dow Smith-s/Chris Fenoglio-a 4.00

GOOSEBUMPS: MONSTERS AT MIDNIGHT
IDW Publishing: Oct, 2017 - No. 3, Dec, 2017 ($3.99, limited series)
1-3-Lambert-s/Fenoglio-a 4.00

GOOSEBUMPS: SECRETS OF THE SWAMP
IDW Publishing: Sept, 2020 - No. 5, Jan, 2021 ($3.99, limited series)
1-5-Nijkamp-s/Montanez-a 4.00

GORDO (See Comics Revue No. 5 & Giant Comics Edition)

GORGO (Based on M.G.M. movie) (See Return of...)
Charlton Comics: May, 1961 - No. 23, Sept, 1965
1-Ditko-a, 22 pgs. 27 54 81 189 420 650
2,3-Ditko-c/a 13 26 39 89 195 300
4-Ditko-c 9 18 27 62 126 190
5-11,13-16: 11,13-16-Ditko-a. 11-Ditko-c 8 16 24 51 96 140
12,17-23: 12-Reptisaurus x-over. 17-23-Montes/Bache-a. 20-Giordano-c 5 10 15 35 63 90
Gorgo's Revenge('62)-Becomes Return of... 7 14 21 44 82 120

GORILLA MAN (From Agents of Atlas)
Marvel Comics: Sept, 2010 - No. 3, Nov, 2010 ($3.99, limited series)
1-3-Parker-s/Caracuzzo-a. 1-Johnson-c. 3-Dell'Otto-c 4.00

GOSPEL BLIMP, THE
Spire Christian Comics (Fleming H. Revell Co.): 1974, 1975 (35¢/39¢, 36 pgs.)
nn-(1974) 3 6 9 14 19 24
nn-(1975) 2 4 6 9 13 16

GOTHAM ACADEMY
DC Comics: Dec, 2014 - No. 18, Jul, 2016 ($2.99)
1-18: 1-Cloonan & Fletcher-s/Kerschl-a. 4-6-Killer Croc. 6,7-Damian Wayne app. 3.00
Annual 1 (10/16, $4.99) Art by Archer, Wildgoose, Dialynas, Msassyk; Blight app. 5.00
...: Endgame 1 (5/15, $2.99) Tie-in to Joker story in Batman titles 3.00

GOTHAM ACADEMY: SECOND SEMESTER
DC Comics: Nov, 2016 - No. 12, Oct, 2017 ($2.99)
1-12: 1-3-Cloonan, Fletcher & Kerschl-s/Archer-a. 4-Jon Lam-a. 11-Damian app. 3.00

GOTHAM BY GASLIGHT (A Tale of the Batman)(See Batman: Master of...)
DC Comics: 1989 ($3.95, one-shot, squarebound, 52 pgs.)
nn-Mignola/Russell-a; intro by Robert Bloch 2 4 6 9 12 15

GOTHAM BY MIDNIGHT
DC Comics: Jan, 2015 - No. 12, Feb, 2016 ($2.99)
1-12: 1-5-Fawkes-s/Templesmith-a/c. 4,5,7-11-The Spectre app. 6-12-Ferreyra-a 3.00
Annual 1 (9/15, $4.99) Fawkes-s/Duce-a; The Gentleman Ghost origin 5.00

GOTHAM CENTRAL
DC Comics: Early Feb, 2003 - No. 40, Apr, 2006 ($2.50)
1-40-Stories of Gotham City Police. 1-Brubaker & Rucka-s/Lark-c/a. 10-Two-Face app. 13,15-Joker-c. 18-Huntress app. 27-Catwoman-c. 32-Poison Ivy app. 34-Teen Titans-c/app. 38-Crispus Allen killed (becomes The Spectre in Infinite Crisis #5) 3.00
... Special Edition 1 (11/14, $1.00) r/#1 with Gotham TV show banner on cover 3.00
... Book One: In the Line of Duty HC (2008, $29.99, dustjacket) r/#1-10; sketch pages 30.00
... Book One: In the Line of Duty SC (2008, $19.99) r/#1-10; sketch pages 20.00
... Book Two: Jokers and Madmen HC (2009, $29.99, dustjacket) r/#11-22 30.00
... Book Two: Jokers and Madmen SC (2011, $19.99) r/#11-22 20.00
... Book Three: On the Freak Beat HC (2010, $29.99, dustjacket) r/#23-31 30.00
... Book Four: Corrigan HC (2011, $29.99, dustjacket) r/#32-40 30.00
...: Dead Robin (2007, $17.99, TPB) r/#33-40; cover gallery 18.00
...: Half a Life (2005, $14.99, TPB) r/#6-10, Batman Chronicles #16 and Detective #747 15.00
...: In The Line of Duty (2004, $9.95, TPB) r/#1-5, cover gallery & sketch pages 10.00
...: The Quick and the Dead TPB (2006, $14.99) r/#23-25,28-31 15.00
...: Unresolved Targets (2006, $14.99, TPB) r/#12-15,19-22, cover gallery 15.00

GOTHAM CITY GARAGE
DC Comics: Dec, 2017 - No. 12, May, 2018 ($2.99, printings of stories that first appeared online)
1-12: 1-Female heroes as a biker gang; Kelly & Lanzing-s/Ching-a/Albuquerque-c 3.00

GOTHAM CITY MONSTERS
DC Comics: Nov, 2019 - No. 6, Apr, 2020 ($3.99, limited series)
1-6-Orlando-s/Nahuelpan-a; Frankenstein, Killer Croc, Orca app. 3-6-Batwoman app. 4.00

GOTHAM CITY SIRENS (Batman: Reborn)
DC Comics: Aug, 2009 - No. 26, Oct, 2011 ($2.99)
1-Catwoman, Harley Quinn and Poison Ivy; Dini-s/March-a/c 5 10 15 30 50 70
1-Variant-c by JG Jones 12 24 36 79 170 260
2-4 2 4 6 10 14 18
5-Full Harley Quinn cover 3 6 9 14 20 25
6-10 2 4 6 8 10 12
11-19 1 3 4 6 8 10
20,23-Joker, Harley Quinn cover 2 4 6 9 12 15
21-Full Harley Quinn cover 2 4 6 9 12 15
22,24-26 5.00
...: Song of the Sirens HC (2010, $19.99, dustjacket) r/#8-13 & Catwoman #83 20.00
...: Union HC (2010, $19.99, dustjacket) r/#1-7 20.00
...: Union SC (2011, $17.99) r/#1-7 18.00

GOTHAM GAZETTE (Battle For The Cowl crossover in Batman titles)
DC Comics: May, 2009; Jul, 2009 ($2.99, one-shots)
1-Short stories of Gotham without Batman; Nguyen, March, ChrisCross & others-a 3.00
...: Batman Alive? (7/09) Vicki Vale app.; Nguyen, March, ChrisCross & others-a 3.00

GOTHAM GIRLS
DC Comics: Oct, 2002 - No. 5, Feb, 2003 ($2.25, limited series)
1-Catwoman, Batgirl, Poison Ivy, Harley Quinn from animated series; Catwoman-c 3 6 9 14 19 24
2,4,5: 2-Poison Ivy-c. 4-Montoya-c. 5-Batgirl-c 2 4 6 9 13 16
3-Harley Quinn-c 4 8 12 27 44 60

GOTHAM NIGHTS (See Batman: Gotham Nights II)
DC Comics: Mar, 1992 - No. 4, June, 1992 ($1.25, limited series)
1-4: Featuring Batman 4.00

GOTHAM UNDERGROUND
DC Comics: Dec, 2007 - No. 9, Aug, 2008 ($2.99, limited series)
1-9-Nine covers interlock for single image; Tieri-s/Calafiore-a/c. 7,8-Vigilante app. 4.00
Batman: Gotham Underground TPB (2008, $19.99) r/#1-9; interlocked image cover 20.00

GOTHIC ROMANCES (Also see My Secrets)
Atlas/Seaboard Publ.: Dec, 1974 (75¢, B&W, magazine, 76 pgs.)
1-Text w/ illos by N. Adams, Chaykin, Heath (2 pgs. ea.); painted cover from Ravenwood Gothic paperback "The Conservatory"(scarce) 31 62 93 223 499 775

The Grackle #1 © Acclaim

Grass Kings #7 © Kindt & Jenkins

Grayson #4 © DC

	GD 2.0	VG 4.0	FN 6.0	VF 8.0	VF/NM 9.0	NM- 9.2
GOTHIC TALES OF LOVE (Magazine)						
Marvel Comics: Apr, 1975 - No. 3, 1975 (B&W, 76 pgs.)						
1-3-Painted-c/a (scarce)	30	60	90	216	483	750
GOVERNOR & J. J., THE (TV)						
Gold Key: Feb, 1970 - No. 3, Aug, 1970 (Photo-c)						
1	4	8	12	25	40	55
2,3	3	6	9	18	28	38
GRACKLE, THE						
Acclaim Comics: Jan, 1997 - No. 4, Apr, 1997 ($2.95, B&W)						
1-4: Mike Baron scripts & Paul Gulacy-c/a. 1-4-Doublecross						3.00
GRAFIK MUSIK						
Caliber Press: Nov, 1990 - No. 4, Aug, 1991 ($3.50/$2.50)						
1-($3.50, 48 pgs., color) Mike Allred-c/a/scripts-1st app. in color of Frank Einstein (Madman)	3	6	9	15	22	28
2-($2.50, 24 pgs., color)	2	4	6	9	12	15
3,4-($2.50, 24 pgs., B&W)	2	4	6	8	10	12
GRANDMA DUCK'S FARM FRIENDS(See Walt Disney's C&S 293 & Wheaties)						
Dell Publishing Co.: No. 763, Jan, 1957 - No. 1279, Feb, 1962 (Disney)						
Four Color 763 (#1)	8	16	24	51	96	140
Four Color 873	6	12	18	37	66	95
Four Color 965,1279	5	10	15	34	60	85
Four Color 1010,1073,1161-Barks-a; 1073,1161-Barks-c/a	11	22	33	73	157	240
GRAND PASSION						
Dynamite Entertainment: 2016 - No. 5, 2017 ($3.99, limited series)						
1-5-James Robinson-s/Tom Feister-a/John Cassaday-c						4.00
GRAND PRIX (Formerly Hot Rod Racers)						
Charlton Comics: No. 16, Sept, 1967 - No. 31, May, 1970						
16-Features Rick Roberts	3	6	9	21	33	45
17-20	3	6	9	17	26	35
21-31	3	6	9	16	23	30
GRAPHIC FANTASY						
Image Comics: Feb, 2021 - No. 2, Feb, 2021 ($9.99/$5.99, B&W)						
1-Reprint of 1982 fanzine with the 1st app. of Savage Dragon by Erik Larsen						10.00
2-($5.99) Reprint of 1982 fanzine with the 2nd app. of Savage Dragon						6.00
GRAPHIQUE MUSIQUE						
Slave Labor Graphics: Dec, 1989 - No. 3, May, 1990 ($2.95, 52 pgs.)						
1-Mike Allred-c/a/scripts	3	6	9	21	33	45
2,3	3	6	9	17	26	35
GRASS KINGS						
BOOM! Studios: Mar, 2017 - No. 15, May, 2018 ($3.99)						
1-14-Matt Kindt-s/Tyler Jenkins-a						4.00
15-($4.99) Last issue; Kindt-s/Jenkins-a						5.00
GRAVESLINGER						
Image Comics (Shadowline): Oct, 2007 - No. 4, Mar, 2008 ($3.50, limited series)						
1-4-Denton & Mariotte-s/Cboins-a						3.50
GRAVE TALES						
Hamilton Comics: Oct, 1991 - No. 3, Feb, 1992 ($3.95, B&W, mag., 52 pgs.)						
1-Staton-c/a	2	3	4	6	8	10
2,3: 2-Staton-a; Morrow-c	1	2	3	5	6	8
GRAVEYARD SHIFT						
Image Comics: Dec, 2014 - No. 4, Apr, 2015 ($3.50)						
1-4: 1-Jay Faerber-s/Fran Bueno-a; wraparound-c						3.50
GRAVITY (Also see Beyond! limited series)						
Marvel Comics: Aug, 2005 - No. 5, Dec, 2005 ($2.99, limited series)						
1-5: 1-Intro. Gravity; McKeever-s/Norton-a. 2-Rhino-c/app. 5-Spider-Man app.						3.00
...: Big-City Super Hero (2005, $7.99, digest) r/#1-5						8.00
GRAY AREA, THE						
Image Comics: Jun, 2004 - No. 3, Oct, 2004 ($5.95/$3.95, limited series)						
1,3-($5.95) Romita, Jr.-a/Brunswick-s; sketch pages and script pages. 3-Pin-up pages						6.00
2-($3.95)						4.00
...Vol. 1: All Of This Can Be Yours (2005, $14.95) r/series & sketch,script & pin-up pages						15.00
GRAY GHOST, THE						
Dell Publishing Co.: No. 911, July, 1958; No. 1000, June-Aug, 1959						
Four Color 911 (#1), 1000-Photo-c each	7	14	21	49	92	135

	GD 2.0	VG 4.0	FN 6.0	VF 8.0	VF/NM 9.0	NM- 9.2
GRAYSON (See Forever Evil) (Leads into Nightwing: Rebirth)						
DC Comics: Sept, 2014 - No. 20, Jul, 2016 ($2.99/$3.99)						
1-8-Dick Grayson as secret agent; Seeley & King-s/Janin-a. 1,2,6,7-Midnighter app.						3.00
9-20-($3.99): 10-Lex Luthor app. 12-Return to Gotham; Batgirl, Red Robin app. 15-"Robin War" tie-in						4.00
Annual 1 (2/15, $4.99) Mooney-a						5.00
Annual 2 (11/15, $4.99) Superman and Blockbuster app.; Alvaro Martinez-a						5.00
Annual 3 (8/16, $4.99) Harley Quinn, Constantine, Azrael, Simon Baz app.						5.00
...: Futures End 1 (11/14, $2.99, regular-c) Five years later; Mooney-a						3.00
...: Futures End 1 (11/14, $3.99, 3-D cover)						4.00
GREAT ACTION COMICS						
I. W. Enterprises: 1958 (Reprints with new covers)						
1-Captain Truth reprinted from Gold Medal #1	3	6	9	16	23	30
8,9-Reprints Phantom Lady #15 & 23	7	14	21	44	82	120
GREAT AMERICAN COMICS PRESENTS - THE SECRET VOICE						
Peter George 4-Star Publ./American Features Syndicate: 1945 (10¢)						
1-Anti-Nazi; "What Really Happened to Hitler"	71	142	213	454	777	1100
GREAT AMERICAN WESTERN, THE						
AC Comics: 1987 - No. 4, 1990? ($1.75/$2.95/$3.50, B&W with some color)						
1-4: 1-Western-r plus Bill Black-a. 2-Tribute to ME comics; Durango Kid photo-c 3-Tribute to Tom Mix plus Roy Rogers, Durango Kid; Billy the Kid-r by Severin; photo-c. 4- ($3.50, 52 pgs., 16 pgs. color)-Tribute to Lash LaRue; photo-c & interior photos; Fawcett-r						4.00
...Presents 1 (1991, $5.00) New Sunset Carson; film history						5.00
GREAT CAT FAMILY, THE (Disney-TV/Movie)						
Dell Publishing Co.: No. 750, Nov, 1956 (one-shot)						
Four Color 750-Pinocchio & Alice app.	6	12	18	40	73	105
GREAT COMICS						
Great Comics Publications: Nov, 1941 - No. 3, Jan, 1942						
1-Origin/1st app. The Great Zarro; Madame Strange & Guy Gorham, Wizard of Science & The Great Zarro begin	148	296	444	947	1624	2300
2-Buck Johnson, Jungle Explorer app.; X-Mas-c	74	148	222	470	810	1150
3-Futuro Takes Hitler to Hell-c/s; "The Lost City" movie story (starring William Boyd); continues in Choice Comics #3 (scarce)	1900	3800	5700	9500	14,250	19,000
GREAT COMICS						
Novack Publishing Co./Jubilee Comics/Knockout/Barrel O' Fun: 1945						
1-(Four publ. variations: Barrel O-Fun, Jubilee, Knockout & Novack)-The Defenders, Capt. Power app.; L. B. Cole-c	37	74	111	222	361	500
1-(Jubilee)-Same cover; Boogey Man, Satanas, & The Sorcerer & His Apprentice	32	64	96	188	307	425
1-(Barrel O' Fun)-L. B. Cole-c; Barrel O' Fun overprinted in indicia; Li'l Cactus, Cuckoo Sheriff (humorous)	24	48	72	142	234	325
GREAT DOGPATCH MYSTERY (See Mammy Yokum & the...)						
GREATEST ADVENTURE, THE (Edgar Rice Burroughs characters)						
Dynamite Entertainment: 2017 - No. 9, 2018 ($3.99)						
1-9: 1-Tarzan & Jane, Korak, Jason Gridley, John Carter & Dejah Thoris app.; Razek-a						4.00
GREATEST AMERICAN HERO (Based on the 1981-1986 TV series)						
Catastrophic Comics: Dec, 2008 - No. 3, May, 2009 ($3.50/$3.95)						
1-3-Origin re-told; William Katt and others-s. 3-Obama-c/app.						4.00
GREATEST BATMAN STORIES EVER TOLD, THE						
DC Comics						
Hardcover ($24.95)						50.00
Softcover ($15.95) "Greatest DC Stories Vol. 2" on spine						20.00
Vol. 2 softcover (1992, $16.95) "Greatest DC Stories Vol. 7" on spine						20.00
GREATEST FLASH STORIES EVER TOLD, THE						
DC Comics: 1991						
nn-Hardcover ($29.95); Infantino-c						45.00
nn-Softcover ($14.95)						20.00
GREATEST GOLDEN AGE STORIES EVER TOLD, THE						
DC Comics: 1990 ($24.95, hardcover)						
nn-Ordway-c						60.00
GREATEST HITS						
DC Comics (Vertigo): Dec, 2008 - No. 6, Apr, 2009 ($2.99, limited series)						
1-6-Intro. The Mates superhero team in 1967 England; Tischman-s/Fabry-a/c						3.00
GREATEST JOKER STORIES EVER TOLD, THE (See Batman)						
DC Comics: 1983						
Hardcover ($19.95)-Kyle Baker painted-c						50.00

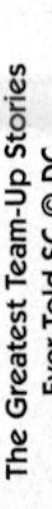

The Greatest Team-Up Stories Ever Told SC © DC

Greek Street #10 © Milligan & Gianfelice

Green Arrow #55 © DC

	GD 2.0	VG 4.0	FN 6.0	VF 8.0	VF/NM 9.0	NM- 9.2

Softcover ($14.95) 20.00
Stacked Deck...Expanded Edition (1992, $29.95)-Longmeadow Press Publ. 35.00

GREATEST 1950s STORIES EVER TOLD, THE
DC Comics: 1990

Hardcover ($29.95)-Kubert-c 55.00
Softcover ($14.95) "Greatest DC Stories Vol. 5" on spine 22.00

GREATEST TEAM-UP STORIES EVER TOLD, THE
DC Comics: 1989

Hardcover ($24.95)-DeVries and Infantino painted-c 55.00
Softcover ($14.95) "Greatest DC Stories Vol. 4" on spine; Adams-c 22.00

GREATEST SUPERMAN STORIES EVER TOLD, THE
DC Comics: 1987

Hardcover ($24.95) 50.00
Softcover ($15.95) 22.00

GREAT EXPLOITS
Decker Publ./Red Top: Oct, 1957

1-Krigstein-a(2) (re-issue on cover); reprints Daring Advs. #6 by Approved Comics
7 14 21 37 46 55

GREAT FOODINI, THE (See Foodini)

GREAT GAZOO, THE (The Flintstones)(TV)
Charlton Comics: Aug, 1973 - No. 20, Jan, 1977 (Hanna-Barbera)

1 4 8 12 23 37 50
2-10 3 6 9 14 19 24
11-20 2 4 6 10 14 18

GREAT GRAPE APE, THE (TV)(See TV Stars #1)
Charlton Comics: Sept, 1976 - No. 2, Nov, 1976 (Hanna-Barbera)

1 3 6 9 21 33 45
2 3 6 9 14 20 25

GREAT GRIMMAX, THE
Defiant: Aug. 1994 (8 pgs.)

0-Hero Illustrated giveaway, Polgardy/Shooter story, J.G. Jones-c, Cockrum-a 4.00

GREAT LAKES AVENGERS (Also see G.L.A.)
Marvel Comics: Dec, 2016 - No. 7, Jun, 2017 ($3.99)

1-7: 1-Team reunites; Squirrel Girl cameo; Gorman-s/Robson-a. 7-Deadpool app. 4.00

GREAT LOCOMOTIVE CHASE, THE (Disney)
Dell Publishing Co.: No. 712, Sept, 1956 (one-shot)

Four Color 712-Movie, photo-c 6 12 18 42 79 115

GREAT LOVER ROMANCES (Young Lover Romances #4,5)
Toby Press: 3/51; #2, 1951(nd); #3, 1952 (nd); #6, Oct?, 1952 - No. 22, May, 1955 (Photo-c #1-5, 10 ,13, 15, 17) (no #4, 5)

1-Jon Juan story-r/Jon Juan #1 by Schomburg; Dr. Anthony King app.
26 52 78 152 249 345
2-Jon Juan, Dr. Anthony King app. 15 30 45 85 130 175
3,7,9-14,16-22: 10-Rita Hayworth photo-c. 17-Rita Hayworth & Aldo Ray photo-c
12 24 36 69 97 125
6-Kurtzman-a (10/52) 14 28 42 82 121 160
8-Five pgs. of "Pin-Up Pete" by Sparling 14 28 42 81 118 155
15-Liz Taylor photo-c (scarce) 54 108 162 343 574 825

GREAT RACE, THE (See Movie Classics)

GREAT SCOTT SHOE STORE (See Bulls-Eye)

GREAT SOCIETY COMIC BOOK, THE (Political parody)
Pocket Books Inc./Parallax Pub.: 1966 ($1.00, 36 pgs., 7"x10", one-shot)

nn-Super-LBJ-c/story; 60s politicians app. as super-heroes; Tallarico-a
3 6 9 17 26 35

GREAT TEN, THE (Characters from Final Crisis)
DC Comics: Jan, 2010 - No. 9, Sept, 2010 ($2.99, limited series)

1-9-Super team of China; Bedard-s/McDaniel-a/Stanley Lau-c 3.00

GREAT WEST (Magazine)
M. F. Enterprises: 1969 (B&W, 52 pgs.)

V1#1 2 4 6 10 14 18

GREAT WESTERN
Magazine Enterprises: No. 8, Jan-Mar, 1954 - No. 11, Oct-Dec, 1954

8(A-1 93)-Trail Colt by Guardineer; Powell Red Hawk-r/Straight Arrow begins, ends #11; Durango Kid story 18 36 54 103 162 220
9(A-1 105), 11(A-1 127)-Ghost Rider, Durango Kid app. in each. 9-Red Mask-c, but no app.
15 30 45 83 124 165
10(A-1 113)-The Calico Kid by Guardineer-r/Tim Holt #8; Straight Arrow, Durango Kid app.
12 24 36 69 97 125
I.W. Reprint #1,2 9: 1,2-r/Straight Arrow #36,42. 9-r/Straight Arrow #?
3 6 9 15 22 28
I.W. Reprint #8-Origin Ghost Rider(r/Tim Holt #11); Tim Holt app.; Bolle-a
3 6 9 16 24 32

NOTE: *Guardineer c-8. **Powell** a(r)-8-11 (from Straight Arrow).*

GREEK STREET
DC Comics (Vertigo): Sept, 2009 - No. 16, Dec, 2010 ($1.00/$2.99)

1-16: 1-($1.00) Milligan-s/Gianfelice-a. 2: Begin $2.99-c 3.00
...: Blood Calls For Blood SC (2010, $9.99) r/#1-5; Mike Carey intro.; sketch art 10.00
...: Cassandra Complex SC (2010, $14.99) r/#6-11 15.00

GREEN ARROW (See Action #440, Adventure, Brave & the Bold, DC Super Stars #17, Detective #521, Flash #217, Green Lantern #76, Justice League of America #4, Leading Comics, More Fun #73 (1st app.), Showcase '95 #9 & World's Finest Comics)

GREEN ARROW
DC Comics: May, 1983 - No. 4, Aug, 1983 (limited series)

1-Origin; Speedy cameo; Mike W. Barr scripts, Trevor Von Eeden-c/a
3 6 9 17 26 35
2-4 1 3 4 6 8 10

GREEN ARROW
DC Comics: Feb, 1988 - No. 137, Oct, 1998 ($1.00-$2.50) (Painted-c #1-3)

1-Mike Grell scripts begin, ends #80 2 4 6 9 12 15
2-49,51-74,76-86: 27,28-Warlord app. 35-38-Co-stars Black Canary; Bill Wray-i. 40-Grell-a. 47-Begin $1.50-c. 63-No longer has mature readers on-c. 63-66-Shado app. 81-Aparo-a begins, ends #100; Nuklon app. 82-Intro & death of Rival. 83-Huntress-c/story. 84, 85-Deathstroke app. 86-Catwoman-c/story w/Jim Balent layouts 4.00
50,75-($2.50, 52 pgs.): Anniversary issues. 75-Arsenal (Roy Harper) & Shado app. 5.00
0,87-96: 87-$1.95-c begins. 88-Guy Gardner, Martian Manhunter, & Wonder Woman-c/app.; Flash-c. 89-Anarky app. 90-(9/94)-Zero Hour tie-in. 0-(10/94)-1st app. Connor Hawke; Aparo-a(p). 91-(11/94). 93-1st app. Camorouge. 95-Hal Jordan cameo. 96-Intro new Force of July; Hal Jordan (Parallax) app; Oliver Queen learns that Connor Hawke is his son 3.00
97-99,102-109: 97-Begin $2.25-c; no Aparo-a. 97-99-Arsenal app. 102,103-Underworld Unleashed x-over. 104-GL(Kyle Rayner)-c/app. 105-Robin-c/app. 107-109-Thorn app. 109-Lois Lane cameo; Weeks-c. 3.00
100-($3.95)-Foil-c; Superman app. 1 3 4 6 8 10
101-Death of Oliver Queen; Superman app. 3 6 9 16 23 30
110,111-124: 110,111-GL x-over. 110-Intro Hatchet. 114-Final Night. 115-117-Black Canary & Oracle app. 3.00
125-($3.50, 48 pgs)-GL x-over cont. in GL #92 4.00
126-136: 126-Begin $2.50-c. 130-GL & Flash x-over. 132,133-JLA app. 134,135-Brotherhood of the Fist pts. 1,5. 136-Hal Jordan-c/app. 3.00
137-Last issue; Superman app.; last panel cameo of Oliver Queen
2 4 6 9 12 15
#1,000,000 (11/98) 853rd Century x-over 3.00
Annual 1-6 ('88-'94, 68 pgs.)-1-No Grell scripts. 2-No Grell scripts; recaps origin Green Arrow, Speedy, Black Canary & others. 3-Bill Wray-a. 4-50th anniversary issue. 5-Batman, Eclipso app. 6-Bloodlines; Hook app. 4.00
Annual 7-('95, $3.95)-Year One story 4.00

NOTE: ***Aparo** a-0, 81-85, 86 (partial),87p, 88p, 91-95, 96i, 98-100p, 109p; c-81,98-100p. **Austin** c-96i. **Balent** layouts-86. **Burchett** c-91-95. **Campanella** a-100-108i, 110-113i; c-99i, 101-108i,110-113i. **Denys Cowan** a-39p, 41-43p, 47p, 48p, 60p; c-41-43. **Damaggio** a(p)-97p, 100-108p, 110-112p; c-97-99p, 101-108p, 110-113p. **Mike Grell** c-1-4, 10p, 11, 39, 40, 44, 45, 47-80, Annual 4, 5. **Nasser/Netzer** a-89, 96. **Sienkiewicz** a-109i. **Springer** a-67, 68. **Weeks** c-109.*

GREEN ARROW
DC Comics: Apr, 2001 - No. 75, Aug, 2007 ($2.50/$2.99)

1-Oliver Queen returns; Kevin Smith-s/Hester-a/Wagner-painted-c
2 4 6 10 14 18
1-2nd-4th printings 3.00
2-Batman cameo 1 2 3 4 5 7
2-2nd printing 3.00
3-5: 4-JLA app. 5.00
6-15: 7-Barry Allen & Hal Jordan app. 9,10-Stanley & his Monster app. 10-Oliver regains his soul. 12-Hawkman-c/app. 4.00
16-25: 16-Brad Meltzer-s begin; The Shade app. 18-Solomon Grundy-c/app. 19-JLA app. 22-Beatty-s; Count Vertigo app. 23-25-Green Lantern app.; Raab-s/Adlard-a 3.00
26-49: 26-Winick-s begin. 35-37-Riddler app. 43-Mia learns she's HIV+. 45-Mia becomes the new Speedy. 46-Teen Titans app. 49-The Outsiders app. 3.00
50-($3.50) Green Arrow's team and the Outsiders vs. The Riddler and Drakon 4.00
51-59: 51-Anarky app. 52-Zatanna-c/app. 55-59-Dr. Light app. 3.00
60-74: 60-One Year Later starts. 62-Begin $2.99-c; Deathstroke app. 69-Batman app. 3.00
75-($3.50) Ollie proposes to Dinah (see Black Canary mini-series); JLA app. 4.00

Green Arrow (2016 series) #49 © DC

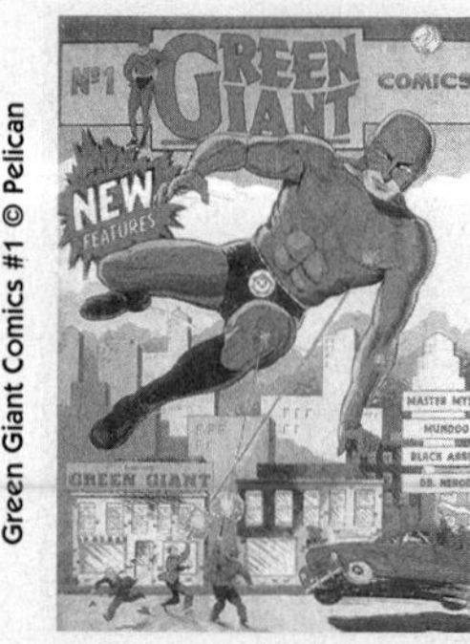

Green Giant Comics #1 © Pelican

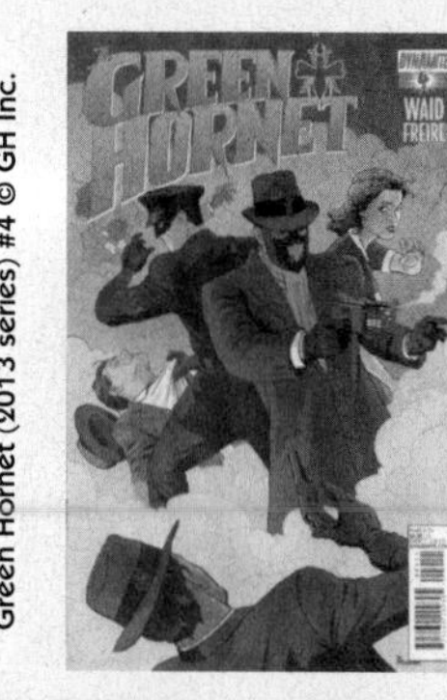

Green Hornet (2013 series) #4 © GH Inc.

	GD	VG	FN	VF	VF/NM	NM-
	2.0	4.0	6.0	8.0	9.0	9.2

... By Jack Kirby (2001, $5.95) Collects Green Arrow stories by Kirby from the 1950s; introduction by Evanier 6.00
...: City Walls SC (2005, $17.95) r/#32, 34-39 18.00
...: Crawling Through the Wreckage SC (2007, $12.99) r/#60-65 13.00
...: Heading Into the Light SC (2006, $12.99) r/#52,54-59 13.00
...: Moving Targets SC (2006, $17.99) r/#40-50 18.00
...: Quiver HC (2002, $24.95) r/#1-10; Smith intro. 25.00
...: Quiver SC (2003, $17.95) r/#1-10; Smith intro. 18.00
...: Road to Jericho SC (2007, $17.99) r/#66-75 18.00
...Secret Files & Origins 1-(12/02, $4.95) Origin stories & profiles; Wagner-c 5.00
...: Sounds of Violence HC (2003, $19.95) r/#11-15; Hester intro. & sketch pages 20.00
...: Sounds of Violence SC (2003, $12.95) r/#11-15; Hester intro. & sketch pages 13.00
...: Straight Shooter SC (2004, $12.95) r/#26-31 13.00
...: The Archer's Quest HC (2003, $19.95) r/#16-21; pitch, script and sketch pages 20.00
...: The Archer's Quest SC (2004, $14.95) r/#16-21; pitch, script and sketch pages 15.00

GREEN ARROW (Brightest Day)
DC Comics: Aug, 2010 - No. 15, Oct, 2011 ($3.99/$2.99)

1-Oliver Queen in the Star City forest; Green Lantern app.; Neves-a/Cascioli-c 5.00
1-Variant-c by Van Sciver 8.00
2-15-($2.99) 2-Green Lantern app. 7-Mayhew-a. 8-11-The Demon app. 12-Swamp Thing 3.00
...: Into the Woods HC (2011, $22.99) r/#1-7; variant cover gallery 23.00

GREEN ARROW (DC New 52)
DC Comics: Nov, 2011 - No. 52, Jul, 2016 ($2.99)

1-Krul-s/Jurgens & Pérez-a/Wilkins-c 1 3 4 6 8 10
2-24: 4,5-Giffen-s. 13,14-Hawkman app. 17-24-Lemire-s/Sorrentino-a/c. 22-Count Vertigo app. 23,24-Richard Dragon app. 3.00
23.1 (11/13, $2.99, regular cover) "Count Vertigo #1" on cover; Sorrentino-a/c 3.00
23.1 (11/13, $3.99, 3-D cover) "Count Vertigo #1" on cover; Sorrentino-a/c 5.00
25-($3.99) Zero Year tie-in; Batman app.; back-up with Cowan-a 4.00
26-49: 26-31-Outsiders War; Lemire-s/Sorrentino-a/c. 35-40-Hitch-c; Felicity Smoak app. 3.00
50-($4.99) Kudranski-a; Deathstroke app. 5.00
51,52-Deathstroke app. 3.00
#0 (11/12) Origin story re-told; Nocenti-s/Williams II-a 3.00
Annual 1 (11/15, $4.99) Percy-s/Kudranski-a/Edwards-c 5.00
...: Futures End 1 (11/14, $2.99, regular-c) Five years later; Lemire-s/Sorrentino-a 3.00
...: Futures End 1 (11/14, $3.99, 3-D cover) 4.00

GREEN ARROW (DC Rebirth)
DC Comics: Aug, 2016 - No. 50, May, 2019 ($2.99/$3.99)

1-24: 1,2-Percy-s/Schmidt-a; Black Canary & Shado app. 3-5-Ferreyra-a. 14-Malcolm Merlyn returns. 21-24-Cheshire app. 3.00
25-($3.99) Schmidt-a; Kate Spencer app.; Moira Queen returns 4.00
26-33: 26,27-Flash app. 27-Wonder Woman app. 28-Superman app. 29-Batman app. 30,31-Green Lantern app. 32-Dark Nights: Metal tie-in 3.00
34-49-($3.99) 41,42-The Parasite app. 45-Roy Harper's funeral 4.00
50-($4.99) Nowlan-c 5.00
Annual 1 (1/18, $4.99) Count Vertigo app.; Percy-s/Carlini-a 5.00
Annual 2 (7/18, $4.99) Justice League: No Justice tie-in; Carnero-a 5.00
...: Rebirth 1 (8/16, $2.99) Percy-a/Schmidt-a; Black Canary app. 3.00

GREEN ARROW/BLACK CANARY (Titled Green Arrow for #30-32)
DC Comics: Dec, 2007 - No. 32, Jun, 2010 ($3.50/$2.99)

1-($3.50) Connor Hawke & Black Canary; follows Wedding Special; Winick-s/Chang-a 4.00
2-21-($2.99) 3-Two covers; Connor shot. 5-Dinah & Ollie's real wedding 3.00
22-30-($3.99) Back-up stories begin. 28-Origin of Cupid. 30-Blackest Night 4.00
30-Variant cover by Mike Grell 8.00
31-32-($2.99) Rise and Fall; Dallocchio-a 3.00
...: A League of Their Own TPB (2009, $17.99) r/#11-14 & G.A. Secret Files & Origins 18.00
...: Big Game TPB (2010, $19.99) r/#21-26 20.00
...: Enemies List TPB (2009, $17.99) r/#15-20 18.00
...: Family Business TPB (2008, $17.99) r/#5-10 18.00
...: Five Stages TPB (2010, $17.99) r/#27-30 18.00
...: Road To The Altar TPB (2008, $17.99) r/proposal pages from Green Arrow #75, Birds of Prey #109, Black Canary #1-4 and Black Canary Wedding Planner #1 18.00
...: The Wedding Album HC (2008, $19.99, dustjacket) r/#1-5 & Wedding Special #1 20.00
...: The Wedding Album SC (2009, $17.99) r/#1-5 & Wedding Special #1 18.00
... Wedding Special 1 (11/07, $3.99) Winick-s/Conner-a/c; Dinah & Ollie's "wedding" 5.00
... Wedding Special 1 (11/07, $3.99) 2nd printing with Ryan Sook variant-c 4.00

GREEN ARROW: THE LONG BOW HUNTERS
DC Comics: Aug, 1987 - No. 3, Oct, 1987 ($2.95, limited series, mature)

1-Grell-c/a in all 2 4 6 8 10 12
1,2-2nd printings 4.00
2,3 6.00
Trade paperback (1989, $12.95)-r/#1-3 15.00

GREEN ARROW: THE WONDER YEAR
DC Comics: Feb, 1993 - No. 4, May, 1993 ($1.75, limited series)

1-4: Mike Grell-a(p)/scripts & Gray Morrow-a(i) 4.00

GREEN ARROW: YEAR ONE
DC Comics: Early Sept, 2007 - No. 6, Late Nov, 2007 ($2.99, bi-weekly limited series)

1-6-Origin re-told; Diggle-s/Jock-a 3.00
1-Special Edition (12/14, $1.00) Reprints #1; Arrow TV show banner atop cover 3.00
HC (2008, $24.99) r/#1-6; intro. by Brian K. Vaughan; script and sketch pages 25.00
SC (2009, $14.99) r/#1-6; intro. by Brian K. Vaughan; script and sketch pages 15.00

GREEN BERET, THE (See Tales of...)

GREEN DANTE / GREEN VIRGIL
Aardvark-Vanaheim: Apr, 2020 ($4.00, B&W)

1-Cerebus figures with original Gustave Doré artwork; Green Lantern #76-c swipe 4.00

GREEN GIANT COMICS (Also see Colossus Comics)
Pelican Publ. (Funnies, Inc.): 1940 (No price on cover; distributed in New York City only)

1-Dr. Nerod, Green Giant, Black Arrow, Mundoo & Master Mystic app.; origin Colossus (Rare) 1500 3000 4500 11,700 22,100 33,000

NOTE: The idea for this book came from George Kapitan. Printed by Moreau Publ. of Orange, N.J. as an experiment to see if they could profitably use the idle time of their 40-page Hoe color press. The experiment failed due to the difficulty of obtaining good quality color registration and Mr. Moreau believes the book never reached the stands. The book has no price or date which lends credence to this. Contains five pages reprinted from Motion Picture Funnies Weekly.

GREEN GOBLIN
Marvel Comics: Oct, 1995 - No. 13, Oct, 1996 ($2.95/$1.95)

1-($2.95)-Scott McDaniel-c/a begins, ends #7; foil-c 4.00
2-13: 2-Begin $1.95-c. 4-Hobgoblin-c/app; Thing app. 6-Daredevil-c/app. 8-Robertson-a; McDaniel-c. 12,13-Onslaught x-over. 13-Green Goblin quits; Spider-Man app. 3.00

GREENHAVEN
Aircel Publishing: 1988 - No. 3, 1988 ($2.00, limited series, 28 pgs.)

1-3 3.00

GREEN HORNET, THE (TV)
Dell Publishing Co./Gold Key: Sept, 1953; Feb, 1967 - No. 3, Aug, 1967

Four Color 496-Painted-c. 25 50 75 175 388 600
1-Bruce Lee photo-c and back-c pin-up 18 36 54 125 276 430
2,3-Bruce Lee photo-c 11 22 33 73 157 240

GREEN HORNET, THE (Also see Kato of the... & Tales of the...)
Now Comics: Nov, 1989 - No. 14, Feb, 1991 ($1.75)
V2#1, Sept, 1991 - V2#40, Jan, 1995 ($1.95)

1 ($2.95, double-size)-Steranko painted-c; G.A. Green Hornet 6.00
1,2: 1-2nd printing ('90, $3.95)-New Butler-c 4.00
3-14: 5-Death of original ('30s) Green Hornet. 6-Dave Dorman painted-c. 11-Snyder-c 4.00
V2#1-11,13-21,24-26,28-30,32-37: 1-Butler painted-c. 9-Mayerik-c 4.00
12-($2.50)-Color Green Hornet button polybagged inside 4.00
22,23-($2.95)-Bagged w/color hologravure card 5.00
27-($2.95)-Newsstand ed. polybagged w/multi-dimensional card (1993 Anniversary Special on cover), 27-($2.95)-Direct Sale ed. polybagged w/multi-dimensional card; cover variations 4.00
31,38: 31-($2.50)-Polybagged w/trading card 4.00
39,40-Low print run 6.00
1-($2.50)-Polybagged w/button (same as #12) 5.00
2,3-($1.95)-Same as #13 & 14 4.00
Annual 1 (12/92, $2.50), Annual 1994 (10/94, $2.95) 5.00

GREEN HORNET (Becomes Green Hornet: Legacy with #34)
Dynamite Entertainment: 2010 - No. 33, 2013 ($3.99)

1-Kevin Smith-s/Jonathan Lau-a; multiple covers by Alex Ross, Cassaday, Campbell and Segovia 4.00
2-33-Multiple covers by Ross and others on each. 11-Hester-s begins 4.00
Annual 1 (2010, $5.99) Hester-s/Netzer & Rafael-a 6.00
Annual 2 (2012, $4.99) Hester-c/Rahner-s/Cliquet-a; back-up r/G.H. Comics #1 (1940) 5.00
... FCBD Edition; 5 previews of various new Green Hornet series; Cassaday-c 3.00

GREEN HORNET
Dynamite Entertainment: 2013 - No. 13, 2014 ($3.99)

1-13: 1-Set in 1941; Mark Waid-s/Daniel Indro-a; 2 covers by Alex Ross & Paolo Rivera 4.00

GREEN HORNET: AFTERMATH
Dynamite Entertainment: 2011 - No. 4, 2011 ($1.99/$3.99, limited series)

1-Nitz-s/Raynor-a; Green Hornet & Kato after the 2011 movie 3.00
2-4-($3.99) 4.00

GREEN HORNET: BLOOD TIES

Green Hornet Comics #13 © HARV

Green Hornet V3 #1 © GH Inc.

Green Lantern #31 © DC

	GD 2.0	VG 4.0	FN 6.0	VF 8.0	VF/NM 9.0	NM- 9.2

Dynamite Entertainment: 2010 - No. 4, 2011 ($3.99)

1-4-Ande Parks-s/Johnny Desjardins-a; original Green Hornet & Kato 4.00

GREEN HORNET COMICS (...Racket Buster #44) (Radio, movies)
Helnit Publ. Co.(Holyoke) No. 1-6/Family Comics(Harvey) No. 7-on:
Dec, 1940 - No. 47, Sept, 1949 (See All New #13,14)(Early issues: 68 pgs.)

Issue	GD 2.0	VG 4.0	FN 6.0	VF 8.0	VF/NM 9.0	NM- 9.2
1-1st app. Green Hornet & Kato; text origin of Green Hornet on inside front-c; intro the Black Beauty (Green Hornet's car); painted-c	850	1700	2550	6200	12,100	18,000
2-(3/41) Early issues based on radio adventures	277	554	831	1759	3030	4300
3	181	362	543	1158	1979	2800
4-6: 6-(8/41)	161	322	483	1030	1765	2500
7 (6/42)-1st app. of the Green Hornet villain The Murdering Clown; origin The Zebra & begins; Robin Hood, Spirit of '76, Blonde Bomber & Mighty Midgets begin; new logo	168	336	504	1075	1838	2600
8-Classic horror bondage killer dwarf-c	200	400	600	1280	2190	3100
9-Kirby-c	181	362	543	1158	1979	2800
10-(12/42) Hornet vs. The Murdering Clown-c/sty	135	270	405	864	1482	2100
11-Mr. Q app.	123	246	369	787	1344	1900
12-1st WWII cover for this title; Mr. Q app.	123	246	369	787	1344	1900
13-1st Nazi-c; shows Hitler poster on-c	258	516	774	1651	2826	4000
14-Bondage-c; Mr. Q app.	110	220	330	704	1202	1700
15-Nazi WWII-c	132	264	396	845	1448	2050
16-Nazi WWII prisoner of war cable car cover	135	270	405	864	1482	2100
17-Nazi WWII-c	129	258	387	826	1413	2000
18,19-Japanese WWII-c	129	258	387	826	1413	2000
20-Classic Japanese WWII-c	135	270	405	869	1482	2100
21-23-Japanese WWII-c	97	194	291	621	1061	1500
24-Classic Japanese poison rockets Sci-Fi-c	129	258	387	826	1413	2000
25,27,28,30	52	104	156	328	552	775
26-(9/45) Japanese WWII-c	57	114	171	362	619	875
29-Jerry Robinson skull-c	53	106	159	334	567	800
31-The Man in Black Called Fate begins (11-12/45, early app.)	54	108	162	343	574	825
32-36	36	72	108	216	351	485
37,38: Shock Gibson app. by Powell. 37-S&K Kid Adonis reprinted from Stuntman #3. 38-Kid Adonis app.	36	72	108	211	343	475
39-Stuntman story by S&K	39	78	117	240	395	550
40-47: 42-47-Kerry Drake in all. 45-Boy Explorers on-c only. 46- "Case of the Marijuana Racket" cover/story; Kerry Drake app.	27	54	81	160	263	365

NOTE: ***Fuje*** *a-23, 24, 26.* ***Henkle*** *c-7-9.* ***Kubert*** *a-20, 30.* ***Powell*** *a-7-10, 12, 14, 16-21, 30, 31(2), 32(3), 33, 34(3), 35, 36, 37(2), 38.* ***Robinson*** *a-27.* ***Schomburg*** *c-17-23. Kirbyish c-7, 15. Bondage c-8, 11, 14, 18, 26, 36.*

GREEN HORNET: DARK TOMORROW
Now Comics: Jun, 1993 - No. 3, Aug, 1993 ($2.50, limited series)

1-3: Future Green Hornet 4.00

GREEN HORNET: GOLDEN AGE RE-MASTERED
Dynamite Entertainment: 2010 - No. 8, 2011 ($3.99)

1-8-Re-colored reprints of 1940's Green Hornet Comics; new Rubenstein-c 4.00

GREEN HORNET: LEGACY (Numbering continues from Green Hornet 2010-2013 series)
Dynamite Entertainment: No. 34, 2013 - No. 42, 2013 ($3.99)

34-42: 34-Jai Nitz-s/Jethro Morales-a 4.00

GREEN HORNET: PARALLEL LIVES
Dynamite Entertainment: 2010 - No. 5, 2010 ($3.99, limited series)

1-5-Jai Nitz-s/Nigel Raynor-a; semi-prequel to the 2011 movie; Kato's origin 4.00

GREEN HORNET: REIGN OF THE DEMON
Dynamite Entertainment: 2016 - No. 4, 2017 ($3.99, limited series)

1-4-David Liss-s/Kewber Baal-a 4.00

GREEN HORNET '66 MEETS THE SPIRIT: VOLUME 1
Dynamite Entertainment: 2017 - No. 5, 2017 ($3.99, limited series)

1-5-Fred VanLente-s/Bob Q-a; The Octopus app. 4.00

GREEN HORNET: SOLITARY SENTINEL, THE
Now Comics: Dec, 1992 - No. 3, 1993 ($2.50, limited series)

1-3 4.00

GREEN HORNET STRIKES!
Dynamite Entertainment: 2010 - No. 10, 2012 ($3.99, limited series)

1-10: 1-Matthews-s/Padilla-a/Cassaday-c; future Green Hornet 4.00

GREEN HORNET, VOLUME 2
Dynamite Entertainment: 2018 - No. 5, 2018 ($3.99)

1-5-Amy Chu-s/German Erramouspe-a; new female Green Hornet 4.00

GREEN HORNET, VOLUME 3
Dynamite Entertainment: 2020 - No. 5, 2020 ($3.99, B&W & green tint)

1-5-Lobdell-s/Marques & Bone-a; regular Green Hornet & Kato 4.00

GREEN HORNET: YEAR ONE
Dynamite Entertainment: 2010 - No. 12, 2011 ($3.99, limited series)

1-12-Matt Wagner-s/Aaron Campbell-a; 1940s' Green Hornet & Kato. 1-5-Cassaday-c4.00
...: Special 1 (2013, $4.99) Crosby-s/Menna-a/Chen-c 5.00

GREEN JET COMICS, THE (See Comic Books, Series 1 in the Promotional Comics section)

GREEN LAMA (Also see Comic Books, Series 1, Daring Adventures #17 & Prize Comics #7)
Spark Publications/Prize No. 7 on: Dec, 1944 - No. 8, Mar, 1946

Issue	GD 2.0	VG 4.0	FN 6.0	VF 8.0	VF/NM 9.0	NM- 9.2
1-Intro. Lt. Hercules & The Boy Champions; Mac Raboy-c/a #1-8	139	278	417	883	1517	2150
2-Lt. Hercules borrows the Human Torch's powers for one panel	81	162	243	518	884	1250
3-5,8: 4-Dick Tracy take-off in Lt. Hercules story by H. L. Gold (science fiction writer); Japanese WWII-c; Emperor Hirohito app. 5-Nazi WWII-c; Hitler story; Lt. Hercules story; Little Orphan Annie, Smilin' Jack & Snuffy Smith take-off (5/45)	55	110	165	352	601	850
6-Classic Raboy swastika-c	84	168	252	538	919	1300
7-Christmas-c; Raboy craft tint-c/a (note: a small quantity of NM copies surfaced)	34	68	102	199	325	450

... Archives Featuring the Art of Mac Raboy Vol. 1 HC (Dark Horse Books, 4/08, $49.95) r/#1-4 including back-up features; foreward by Chuck Rozanski 50.00
... Archives Featuring the Art of Mac Raboy Vol. 2 HC (Dark Horse Books, 1/09, $49.95) r/#5-8; foreward by Chuck Rozanski 50.00

NOTE: ***Robinson*** *a-3-5, 8. Roussos a-8. Formerly a pulp hero who began in 1940.*

GREEN LANTERN (1st Series) (See All-American, All Flash Quarterly, All Star Comics, The Big All-American & Comic Cavalcade)
National Periodical Publications/All-American: Fall, 1941 - No. 38, May-June, 1949 (#1-18 are quarterly)

Issue	GD 2.0	VG 4.0	FN 6.0	VF 8.0	VF/NM 9.0	NM- 9.2
1-Origin retold; classic Purcell-c	2900	5800	8700	23,200	42,400	77,000
2-1st book-length story	750	1500	2250	5475	9488	13,500
3-Classic German war-c by Mart Nodell	750	1500	2250	5475	9488	13,500
4-Green Lantern & Doiby Dickles join the Army	400	800	1200	2800	4900	7000
5-WWII-c	337	674	1011	2359	4130	5900
6,8: 8-Hop Harrigan begins; classic-c	300	600	900	1920	3310	4700
7-Classic robot-c	309	618	927	2163	3782	5400
9-School for Vandals-s	245	490	735	1568	2684	3800
10-Origin/1st app. Vandal Savage	309	618	927	2163	3782	5400
11,13-15	194	388	582	1242	2121	3000
12-Origin/1st app. Gambler	190	380	570	1207	2079	2950
16-Classic jungle-c (scarce in high grade)	190	380	570	1207	2079	2950
17,19,20	145	290	435	921	1586	2250
18-Christmas-c	190	380	570	1207	2079	2950
21-26	142	284	426	909	1555	2200
27-Origin/1st app. Sky Pirate	174	348	522	1114	1907	2700
28-1st Sportsmaster (Crusher Crock)	161	322	483	1030	1765	2500
29-All Harlequin issue; classic Harlequin-c	232	464	696	1485	2543	3600
30-Origin/1st app. Streak the Wonder Dog by Toth (2-3/48) (Rare)	423	846	1269	3088	5444	7800
31-Harlequin-c/app.	155	310	465	992	1696	2400
32-35: 35-Kubert-c. 35-38-New logo	126	252	378	806	1378	1950
36-38: 37-Sargon the Sorcerer app.	148	296	444	947	1624	2300

NOTE: *Book-length stories #2-7.* ***Mayer/Moldoff*** *c-9.* ***Mayer/Purcell*** *c-8.* ***Purcell*** *c-1.* ***Mart Nodell*** *c-2, 3, 7.* ***Paul Reinman*** *c-11, 12, 15-22.* ***Toth*** *a-28, 30, 31, 34-38; c-28, 30, 34p, 36-38p. Cover to #8 says Fall while the indicia says Summer Issue. Streak the Wonder Dog c-30 (w/Green Lantern), 34, 36, 38.*

GREEN LANTERN (See Action Comics Weekly, Adventure Comics, Brave & the Bold, Day of Judgment, DC Special, DC Special Series, Flash, Guy Gardner, Guy Gardner Reborn, JLA, JSA, Justice League of America, Parallax: Emerald Night, Showcase, Showcase '93 #12 & Tales of The...Corps)

GREEN LANTERN (2nd Series)(Green Lantern Corps #206 on) (See Showcase #22-24)
National Periodical Publ./DC Comics: Jul/Aug. 1960 - No. 89, Apr/May 1972;
No. 90, Aug/Sept. 1976 - No. 205, Oct, 1986

Issue	GD 2.0	VG 4.0	FN 6.0	VF 8.0	VF/NM 9.0	NM- 9.2
1-(7-8/60)-Origin retold; Gil Kane-c/a continues; 1st app. Guardians of the Universe	470	940	1410	4370	11,185	18,000
2-1st Pieface	93	186	279	744	1672	2600
3-Contains readers poll	54	108	162	432	966	1500
4,5: 5-Origin/1st app. Hector Hammond	45	90	135	333	754	1175
6-Intro Tomar-Re the alien G.L.	43	86	129	318	722	1125
7-Origin/1st app. Sinestro (7-8/61)	114	228	342	923	2062	3200
8-1st 5700 A.D. story; grey tone-c	42	84	126	311	706	1100
9-1st Sinestro-c; 1st Jordan Brothers; last 10¢-c	37	74	111	274	612	950
10	34	68	102	245	548	850
11,12	21	42	63	147	324	500

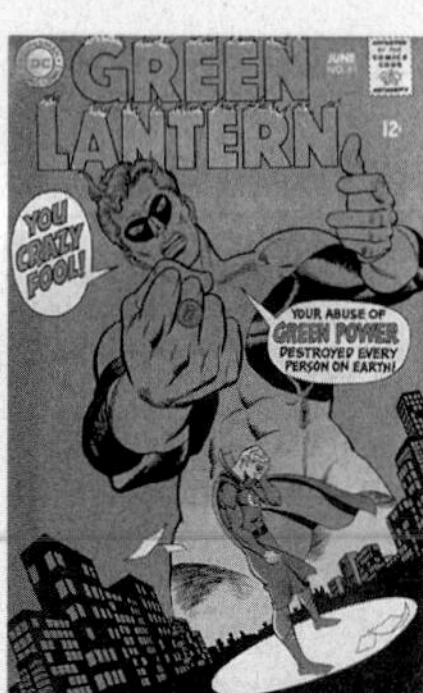

Green Lantern (2nd series) #61 © DC

Green Lantern (2nd series) #110 © DC

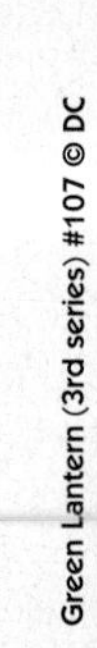
Green Lantern (3rd series) #107 © DC

GD VG FN VF VF/NM NM-
2.0 4.0 6.0 8.0 9.0 9.2

13-Flash x-over 34 68 102 245 548 850
14,15,17-20: 14-Origin/1st app. Sonar. 20-Flash x-over
17 34 51 117 259 400
16-Origin & 1st app. (Silver Age) Star Sapphire 42 84 126 311 706 1100
21,22,25-28,30: 21-Origin & 1st app. Dr. Polaris 12 24 36 81 176 270
23-1st Tattooed Man 15 30 45 101 223 345
24-Origin & 1st app. Shark 26 52 78 182 404 625
29-JLA cameo; 1st Blackhand 17 34 51 117 259 400
31-39: 37-1st app. Evil Star (villain) 10 20 30 69 147 225
40-Origin of Infinite Earths (10/65); 2nd solo G.A. Green Lantern in Silver Age (see Showcase #55); origin The Guardians; Doiby Dickles app. 46 92 138 335 760 1185
41-44,46-50: 42-Zatanna x-over. 43-Flash x-over 9 18 27 60 120 180
45-2nd S.A. app. G.A. Green Lantern in title (6/66) 13 26 39 91 201 310
51,53-58 8 16 24 51 96 140
52-G.A. Green Lantern x-over; Sinestro app. 11 22 33 72 154 235
59-1st app. Guy Gardner (3/68) 32 64 96 230 515 800
60,62-69: 69-Wood inks; last 12¢ issue 6 12 18 38 69 100
61-G.A. Green Lantern x-over 7 14 21 46 86 125
70-75 5 10 15 34 60 85
76-(4/70)-Begin Green Lantern/Green Arrow series (by Neal Adams #76-89) ends #122 (see Flash #217 for 2nd series) 96 192 288 768 1734 2700
77-Neal Adams-c/a 12 24 36 82 179 275
78-80-Neal Adams-c/a 10 20 30 67 141 215
81-84: 82-Wrightson-i(1 pg.). 83-G.L. reveals i.d. to Carol Ferris. 84-N. Adams/Wrightson-a (22 pgs.); last 15¢-c; partial photo-c 9 18 27 59 117 175
85,86-(52 pgs.) Classic anti-drug covers/stories; Speedy as a heroin junkie. 86-G.A. Green Lantern-r; Toth-a 11 22 33 76 163 250
87-(52 pgs.) 1st app. John Stewart (12-1/71-72) (becomes 3rd Green Lantern in #182); 2nd app. Guy Gardner (cameo) 28 56 84 202 451 700
88-(2-3/72, 52 pgs.)-Unpubbed G.A. Green Lantern story; Green Lantern-r/Showcase #23. N. Adams-c/a (1 pg.) 8 16 24 56 108 160
89-(4-5/72, 52 pgs.)-G.A. Green Lantern-r; Green Lantern & Green Arrow move to Flash #217 (2nd team-up series) 8 16 24 56 108 160
90 (8-9/76)-Begin 3rd Green Lantern/Green Arrow team-up series; Mike Grell-c/a begins, ends #111 3 6 9 19 30 40
91-99 2 4 6 10 16 20
100-(1/78, Giant)-1st app. Air Wave II 3 6 9 19 30 40
101-107,111,113-115,117-119: 107-1st Tales of the G.L. Corps story
2 4 6 8 11 14
108-110-(44 pgs)-G.A. Green Lantern back-ups in each. 111-Origin retold; G.A. Green Lantern app. 2 4 6 10 14 18
112-G.A. Green Lantern origin retold 2 4 6 13 18 22
116-1st app. Guy Gardner as a G.L. (5/79) 4 8 12 27 44 60
116-Whitman variant; issue # on cover 5 10 15 31 53 75
117-119,121-(Whitman variants; low print run; none have issue # on cover)
2 4 6 10 14 18
120,121,123-140,142-150: 123-Last Green Lantern/Green Arrow team-up. 130-132-Tales of the G.L. Corps. 132-Adam Strange series begins, ends147. 136,137-1st app. Citadel; Space Ranger app. 142,143-Omega Men app.;Perez-c. 144-Omega Men cameo. 148-Tales of the G.L. Corps begins, ends #173. 150-Anniversary issue, 52 pgs.; no G.L. Corps 1 2 3 5 7 9
122-2nd app. Guy Gardner as Green Lantern; Flash & Hawkman brief app.
3 6 9 14 20 25
141-1st app. Omega Men (6/81) 4 8 12 25 40 55
151-180,183,184,186,187: 159-Origin Evil Star. 160,161-Omega Men app. 172-Gibbons-c/a begins. 175-No issue number shown on cover 6.00
181,182,185,188,191: 181-Hal Jordan resigns as G.L. 182-John Stewart becomes new G.L.; origin recap of Hal Jordan as G.L. 185-Origin new G.L. (John Stewart).188-I.D. revealed; 1st app. Mogo; Alan Moore back-up scripts. 191-Re-intro Star Sapphire (cameo)
1 2 3 5 6 8
189,190,193,196-199,202-205: 194,198-Crisis x-over. 199-Hal Jordan returns as a member of G.L. Corps (3 G.L.s now). 5.00
192-Re-intro & origin of Star Sapphire (1st full app.) 2 4 6 9 13 16
194-Hal Jordan/Guy Gardner battle; Guardians choose Guy Gardner to become new Green Lantern 1 2 3 5 6 8
195-Guy Gardner becomes Green Lantern; Crisis on Infinite Earths x-over
2 4 6 10 13 18
200-Double-size 1 2 3 5 6 8
201-Green Lantern Corps begins (is cover title, says premiere issue); intro. Kilowog
3 6 9 18 27 36
Annual 1 (Listed as Tales Of The Green Lantern Corps Annual 1)
Annual 2,3 (See Green Lantern Corps Annual #2,3) 5.00
... No. 1 (Facsimile Edition)(2020, $3.99) r/#1 with original 1960 ads and letter column 4.00
... No. 85 (Facsimile Edition)(2019, $3.99) r/#85 with original ads and letter column 4.00
Special 1 (1988), 2 (1989)-(Both $1.50, 52 pgs.) 5.00

GD VG FN VF VF/NM NM-
2.0 4.0 6.0 8.0 9.0 9.2

... Chronicles TPB (2009, $14.99) r/Showcase #22-24 & Green Lantern #1-3 15.00
... Chronicles Vol. 2 TPB (2009, $14.99) r/Green Lantern #4-9 15.00
... Chronicles Vol. 3 TPB (2010, $14.99) r/Green Lantern #10-14 and Flash #131 15.00
NOTE: ***N. Adams** a-76, 77-87p, 89; c-63, 76-89. **M. Anderson** a-137i. **Austin** a-93i, 94i, 171i. **Chaykin** c-196. **Greene** a-39-49i, 58-63i; c-54-58i. **Grell** a-90-100, 106, 108-111; c-90-106, 108-112. **Heck** a-120-122p. **Infantino** a-137p, 145-147p, 151, 152p. **Gil Kane** a-1-49p, 50-57, 58-61p, 68-75p, 85p(r), 87p(r), 88p(r), 156, 177, 184p; c-1-52, 54-61p, 67-75, 123, 154, 156, 165-171, 177, 184. **Newton** a-148p, 149p, 181. **Perez** c-132p, 141-144. **Sekowsky** a-65p, 170p. **Simonson** c-200. **Sparling** a-63p. **Starlin** c-129, 133. **Staton** a-117p, 123-127p, 128, 129-131p, 132-139, 140p, 141-146, 147p, 148-150, 151-155p; c-107p, 117p, 135(i), 136p, 145p, 146, 147, 148-152p, 155p. **Toth** a-86r, 171p. **Tuska** a-166-168p, 170p.*

GREEN LANTERN (3rd Series)
DC Comics: June, 1990 - No. 181, Nov, 2004 ($1.00/$1.25/$1.50/$1.75/$1.95/$1.99/$2.25)
1-Hal Jordan, John Stewart & Guy Gardner return; Batman & JLA app.
1 3 4 6 8 10
2-18,20-26: 9-12-Guy Gardner solo story. 13-(52 pgs.). 18-Guy Gardner solo story. 25-($1.75, 52 pgs.)-Hal Jordan/Guy Gardner battle 5.00
19-($1.75, 52 pgs.)-50th anniversary issue; Mart Nodell (original G.A. artist) part-p on G.A. Green Lantern; G. Kane-c 6.00
27-45,47: 30,31-Gorilla Grodd-c/story(see Flash #69). 38,39-Adam Strange-c/story. 42-Deathstroke-c/s. 47-Green Arrow x-over 4.00
46,48,49,50: 46-Superman app. cont'd in Superman #82. 48-Emerald Twilight part 1. 50-($2.95, 52 pgs.)-Glow-in-the-dark-c 6.00
0, 51-62: 51-1st app. New Green Lantern (Kyle Rayner) with new costume. 53-Superman-c/story. 55-(9/94)-Zero Hour. 0-(10/94). 56-(11/94) 4.00
63,64-Kyle Rayner vs. Hal Jordan. 4.00
65-80,82-92: 63-Begin $1.75-c. 65-New Titans app. 66,67-Flash app. 71-Batman & Robin app. 72-Shazam!-c/app. 73-Wonder Woman-c/app. 73-75-Adam Strange app. 76,77-Green Arrow x-over. 80-Final Night. 87-JLA app. 91-Genesis x-over. 92-Green Arrow x-over 4.00
81-(Regular Ed.)-Memorial for Hal Jordan (Parallax); most DC heroes app. 5.00
81-($3.95, Deluxe Edition)-Embossed prism-c 6.00
93-99: 93-Begin $1.95-c; Deadman app. 94-Superboy app. 95-Starlin-a(p). 98,99-Legion of Super-Heroes-c/app. 4.00
100-($2.95) Two covers (Jordan & Rayner); vs. Sinestro 6.00
101-106: 101-106-Hal Jordan-c/app. 103-JLA-c/app. 104-Green Arrow app. 105,106-Parallax app. 4.00
107-126: 107-Jade becomes a Green Lantern. 119-Hal Jordan/Spectre app. 125-JLA app. 3.00
127-149: 127-Begin $2.25-c. 129-Winick-s begin. 134-136-JLA-c/app. 143-Joker: Last Laugh; Lee-c. 145-Kyle becomes The Ion. 149-Superman-c/app. 3.00
150-($3.50) Jim Lee-c; Kyle becomes Green Lantern again; new costume 4.00
151-181: 151-155-Jim Lee-c: 154-Terry attacked. 155-Spectre-c/app. 162-164-Crossover with Green Arrow #23-25. 165-Raab-s begin. 169-Kilowog returns 3.00
#1,000,000 (11/98) 853rd Century x-over; Hitch & Neary-a/c 3.00
Annual 1-3: ('92-'94, 68 pgs.)-1-Eclipso app. 2 -Intro Nightblade. 3-Elseworlds story 5.00
Annual 4 (1995, $3.50)-Year One story 5.00
Annual 5,7,8 ('96, '98, '99, $2.95): 5-Legends of the Dead Earth. 7-Ghosts; Wrightson-c. 8-JLApe; Art Adams-c 5.00
Annual 6 (1997, $3.95)-Pulp Heroes story 5.00
Annual 9 (2000, $3.50) Planet DC 4.00
...80 Page Giant (12/98, $4.95) Stories by various 5.00
...80 Page Giant 2 (6/99, $4.95) Team-ups 5.00
...80 Page Giant 3 (8/00, $5.95) Darkseid vs. the GL Corps 6.00
...: 1001 Emerald Nights (2001, $6.95) Elseworlds; Guay-a/c; LaBan-s 7.00
...3-D #1 (12/98, $3.95) Jeanty-a 4.00
...: A New Dawn TPB (1998, $9.95)-r/#50-55 10.00
...: Baptism of Fire TPB (1999, $12.95)-r/#59,66,67,70-75 13.00
...: Brother's Keeper (2003, $12.95)-r/#151-155; Green Lantern Secret Files #3 13.00
...: Emerald Allies TPB (2000, $14.95)-r/GL/GA team-ups 15.00
...: Emerald Knights TPB (1998, $12.95)-r/Hal Jordan's return 13.00
...: Emerald Twilight nn (1994, $5.95)-r/#48-50 6.00
...: Emerald Twilight/New Dawn TPB (2003, $19.95)-r/#48-55 20.00
...: Ganthet's Tale nn (1992, $5.95, 68 pgs.)-Silver foil logo; Niven scripts; Byrne-c/a 6.00
.../Green Arrow Vol. 1 (2004, $12.95) -r/GL #76-82; intro. by O'Neil 13.00
.../Green Arrow Vol. 2 (2004, $12.95) -r/GL #83-87,89 & Flash #217-219, 226; cover gallery with 1983-84 GL/GA covers #1-7; intro. by Giordano 13.00
.../Green Arrow Collection, Vol. 2-r/GL #84-87,89 & Flash #217-219 & GL/GA #5-7 by O'Neil/Adams/Wrightson 13.00
...: New Journey, Old Path TPB (2001, $12.95)-r/#129-136 13.00
...: Our Worlds at War (8/01, $2.95) Jae Lee-c; prelude to x-over 3.00
...: Passing The Torch (2004, $12.95, TPB) r/#156,158-161 & GL Secret Files #2 13.00
...Plus 1 (12/1996, $2.95)-The Ray & Polaris-c/app. 4.00
...Secret Files 1-3 (7/98-7/02, $4.95)1-Origin stories & profiles. 2-Grell-c 5.00
.../Superman: Legend of the Green Flame (2000, $5.95) 1988 unpub. Neil Gaiman story of Hal Jordan with new art by various; Frank Miller-c 6.00
...: The Power of Ion (2003, $14.95, TPB) r/#142-150 15.00
...The Road Back nn (1992, $8.95)-r/1-8 w/covers 9.00
...: Traitor TPB (2001, $12.95) r/Legends of the DCU #20,21,28,29,37,38 13.00

Green Lantern (2005 series) #29 © DC

Green Lantern (2011 series) #40 © DC

Green Lantern Corps #19 © DC

GD VG FN VF VF/NM NM-
2.0 4.0 6.0 8.0 9.0 9.2

...: Willworld (2001, $24.95, HC) Seth Fisher-a/J.M. DeMatteis-s; Hal Jordan 25.00
...: Willworld (2003, $17.95, SC) Seth Fisher-a/J.M. DeMatteis-s; Hal Jordan 18.00
NOTE: *Staton a(p)-9-12; c-9-12.*

GREEN LANTERN (See Tangent Comics/ Green Lantern)

GREEN LANTERN (4th Series) (Follows Hal Jordan's return in Green Lantern: Rebirth)
DC Comics: July, 2005 - No. 67, Aug, 2011 ($3.50/$2.99)

1-($3.50) Two covers by Pacheco and Ross; Johns-s/Van Sciver and Pacheco-a 5.00
2-20-($2.99) 2-4-Manhunters app. 6-Bianchi-a. 7,8-Green Arrow app. 8-Bianchi-c. 9-Batman app.; two covers by Bianchi and Van Sciver. 10,11-Reis-a. 17-19-Star Sapphire returns. 18-Acuna-a; Sinestro Corps back-ups begin 3.00
8-Variant-c by Neal Adams 8.00
21-Sinestro Corps War pt. 2 5.00
21-2nd printing with variant green hued background-c 3.00
22-24: 22-Sinestro Corps War pt. 4; green hued-c. 23-Part 6. 24-Part 8 4.00
22,23-2nd printings. 22-Yellow hued-c. 23-B&W Hal Jordan with colored rings 3.00
25-($4.99) Sinestro Corps War conclusion; Ivan Reis-c 6.00
25-($4.99) Variant cover by Gary Frank; Sinestro Corps War conclusion 8.00
26-28,30-43: 26-Alpha Lanterns. 30-35-Childhood & origin re-told; Sinestro app. 41-Origin Larfleeze. 43-Prologue to Blackest Night, origin of Black Hand; Mahnke-a 3.00
29-Childhood & origin re-told 5.00
29-Special Edition (6/10, $1.00) reprints #29 with "What's Next?" logo on cover 3.00
29-Special Edition (2010 San Diego Comic-Con giveaway) reprints #29 with new Van Sciver cover and Geoff Johns intro on inside front cover 3.00
39-43-Variant covers: 39,40-Migliari. 41-42-Barrows 12.00
44-49,51,52-Blackest Night. 44-Flash app. 46-Sinestro vs. Mongul. 47-Black Lantern Abin Sur. 49-Art by Benes & Ordway; Atom and Mera app. 51-Nekron app. 3.00
44-49,51-Variant covers: 44-Tan. 45-Manapul. 46. Andy Kubert. 47-Benes. 48-Morales. 49-Migliari. 51-Horn. 52-Shane Davis 8.00
50-($3.99)-Black Lantern Spectre & Parallax app.; Mahnke-a/c 4.00
50-Variant-c by Jim Lee 12.00
53-67: 53-62-Brightest Day. 54,55-Lobo app. 58-60-Flash app. 60-Krona returns. 64-67-War of the Green Lanterns x-over. 67-Sinestro becomes a Green Lantern 3.00
FCBD 2011 Green Lantern Flashpoint Special Edition (6/11, giveaway) r/#30 and previews Flashpoint x-over; Andy Kubert-a 3.00
...: Larfleeze Christmas Special 1 (2/11, $3.99) Johns-s/Booth-a/Ha-c 4.00
.../Plastic Man: Weapons of Mass Deception (2/11, $4.99) Brent Anderson-a 5.00
...Secret Files and Origins 2005 (6/05, $4.99) Johns-s/Cooke & Van Sciver-a; profiles with art by various incl. Chaykin, Gibbons, Gleason, Igle; Pacheco-c 5.00
.../Sinestro Corps: Secret Files 1 (2/08, $4.99) Profiles of Green Lanterns and Corps info 5.00
...: Agent Orange HC (2009, $19.99) r/#38-42 & Blackest Night #0; sketch art 20.00
...: Agent Orange SC (2010, $14.99) r/#38-42 & Blackest Night #0; sketch art 15.00
Blackest Night: Green Lantern HC (2010, $24.99) r/#43-52; variant covers; sketch art 25.00
Blackest Night: Green Lantern SC (2011, $19.99) r/#43-52; variant covers; sketch art 20.00
...: Brightest Day HC (2011, $22.99) r/#53-62; variant cover gallery 23.00
...: In Brightest Day SC (2008, $19.99) r/stories selected by Geoff Johns w/commentary 20.00
...: No Fear HC (2006, $24.99) r/#1-6 & Secret Files and Origins 25.00
...: No Fear SC (2008, $12.99) r/#1-6 & Secret Files and Origins 13.00
...: Rage of the Red Lanterns HC (2009, $24.99) r/#26-28,36-38 & Final Crisis: Rage... 25.00
...: Rage of the Red Lanterns SC (2010, $14.99) r/#26-28,36-38 & Final Crisis: Rage... 15.00
...: Revenge of the Green Lanterns HC (2006, $19.99) r/#7-13; variant cover gallery 20.00
...: Revenge of the Green Lanterns SC (2008, $12.99) r/#7-13; variant cover gallery 13.00
...: Secret Origin HC (2008, $19.99) r/#29-35 20.00
...: Secret Origin (New Edition) HC (2010, $19.99) r/#29-35; intro. by Ryan Reynolds 20.00
...: Secret Origin SC (2008, $14.99) r/#29-35 15.00
...: Secret Origin (New Edition) SC (2011, $14.99) r/#29-35; intro. by Ryan Reynolds; photo-c of Reynolds from movie; movie preview photo gallery 15.00
... Super Spectacular (1/12, $7.99, magazine-size) r/Blackest Night #0,1, Green Lantern #76 from 1970 and Brave and the Bold #30 from 2009 8.00
...: Tales of the Sinestro Corps HC (2008, $29.99, d.j.) r/back-up stories from #18-20, Tales of the Sinestro Corps series, Green Lantern: Sinestro Corps Special and Sinestro Corps: Secret Files 30.00
...: Tales of the Sinestro Corps SC (2009, $14.99) same contents as HC 15.00
...: The Sinestro Corps War Vol. 1 HC (2008, $24.99, d.j.) r/#21-23, Green Lantern Corps #14-15 and Green Lantern: Sinestro Corps Special 25.00
...: The Sinestro Corps War Vol. 1 SC (2009, $14.99) same contents as HC 15.00
...: The Sinestro Corps War Vol. 2 HC (2008, $24.99, d.j.) r/#24,25, Green Lantern Corps #16-19; interview with the creators and sketch art 25.00
... - Wanted: Hal Jordan HC (2007, $19.99) r/#14-20 without Sinestro Corps back-ups 20.00
... - Wanted: Hal Jordan SC (2008, $14.99) r/#14-20 without Sinestro Corps back-ups 15.00

GREEN LANTERN (DC New 52)
DC Comics: Nov, 2011 - No. 52, Jul, 2016 ($2.99/$3.99)

1-19: 1-Sinestro as Green Lantern; Johns-s/Mahnke-a/Reis-c (1st & 2nd print). 6-Choi-a. 9-Origin of the Indigo tribe. 14-Justice League app. 17-19-Wrath of the First Lantern 3.00
1-9-Variant-c. 1-Capullo. 2-Finch. 3-Van Sciver. 4-Manapul. 5-Choi. 6-Reis. 8-Keown 4.00
8-Combo pack ($3.99) polybagged with digital code 4.00
20-($7.99, squarebound) Conclusion of "Wrath of the First Lantern"; last Johns-s 8.00
21-23: 21-Venditti-s/Tan-a begin 3.00
23.1, 23.2, 23.3, 23.4 (11/13, $2.99, regular covers) 3.00
23.1 (11/13, $3.99, 3-D cover) "Relic #1" on cover; origin of Relic; Morales-a 6.00
23.2 (11/13, $3.99, 3-D cover) "Mongul #1" on cover; origin; Starlin-s/Porter-a 5.00
23.3 (11/13, $3.99, 3-D cover) "Black Hand #1" on cover; Soule-s/Ponticelli-a 5.00
23.4 (11/13, $3.99, 3-D cover) "Sinestro #1" on cover; origin; Kindt-s/Eaglesham-a 5.00
24-27,29-34: 24-Lights Out pt. 1; Relic app.; Central Battery destroyed 3.00
28-Flip-book with Red Lanterns #28; Red Lantern Supergirl app. 3.00
35-40: 35-37-Godhead x-over; New Gods, Orion & Metron app. 36,37-Black Hand app. 3.00
41-49,51,52-($3.99) 42,43,45,46-Black Hand app. 43-Relic returns. 47-Parallax app. 4.00
50-($4.99) Parallax app.; Sienkiewicz-c 5.00
#0 (11/12, $2.99) Simon Baz becomes a Green Lantern; Mahnke-a 3.00
Annual 1 (10/12, $4.99) 1st print w/black-c; Rise of the Third Army prologue 5.00
Annual 2 (12/13, $4.99) Lights Out pt. 5; Sean Chen-a 5.00
Annual 3 (2/15, $4.99) Godhead conclusion; Van Sciver-c 5.00
Annual 4 (11/15, $4.99) Venditti-s/Alixe-a 5.00
...: Futures End 1 (11/14, $2.99, regular-c) Five years later; Relic app. 3.00
...: Futures End 1 (11/14, $3.99, 3-D cover) 4.00
.../New Gods: Godhead 1 (12/14, $4.99) Part 1 to Godhead x-over; Highfather app. 5.00

GREEN LANTERN, THE
DC Comics: Jan, 2019 - No. 12, Dec, 2019 ($4.99/$3.99)

1-($4.99) Grant Morrison-s/Liam Sharp-a 5.00
2-11-($3.99) 2-Evil Star app. 5,6-Adam Strange app. 8-Green Arrow app. 4.00
12-($4.99) Leads into Green Lantern: Blackstars #1 5.00
Annual 1 (9/19, $4.99) Air Wave app.; Morrison-s/Camuncoli-a 5.00

GREEN LANTERN ANNUAL NO. 1, 1963
DC Comics: 1998 ($4.95, one-shot)

1-Reprints Golden Age & Silver Age stories in 1963-style 80 pg. Giant format; new Gil Kane sketch art 5.00

GREEN LANTERN: BLACKSTARS
DC Comics: Jan, 2020 - No. 3, Mar, 2020 ($3.99, limited series)

1-3-Morrison-s/Xermanico-a; Mongul app. 4.00

GREEN LANTERN: BRIGHTEST DAY; BLACKEST NIGHT
DC Comics: 2002 ($5.95, squarebound, one-shot)

nn-Alan Scott vs. Solomon Grundy in 1944; Snyder III-c/a; Seagle-s
1 2 3 5 6 8

GREEN LANTERN: CIRCLE OF FIRE
DC Comics: Early Oct, 2000 - No. 2, Late Oct, 2000 (limited series)

1-($4.95) Intro. other Green Lanterns 5.00
2-($3.75) 4.00
Green Lantern (x-overs)- .../Adam Strange; .../Atom; .../Firestorm; ... /Green Lantern, Winick-s; .../Power Girl (all $2.50-c) 3.00
TPB (2002, $17.95) r/#1,2 & x-overs 18.00

GREEN LANTERN CORPS, THE (Formerly Green Lantern; see Tales of...)
DC Comics: No. 206, Nov, 1986 - No. 224, May, 1988

206-223: 212-John Stewart marries Katma Tui. 220,221-Millennium tie-ins 4.00
224-Double-size last issue 5.00
...Corps Annual 2,3- (12/86,8/87) 1-Formerly Tales of ...Annual #1; Alan Moore scripts. 3-Indicia says Green Lantern Annual #3; Moore scripts; Byrne-a 5.00
NOTE: ***Austin** a-Annual 3i. **Gil Kane** a-223, 224p; c-223, 224, Annual 2. **Russell** a-Annual 3i. **Staton** a-207-213p, 217p, 221p, 222p, Annual 3; c-207-213p, 217p, 221p, 222p. **Willingham** a-213p, 219p, 220p, 218p, 219p, Annual 2, 3p; c-218p, 219p.*

GREEN LANTERN CORPS
DC Comics: Aug, 2006 - No. 63, Oct, 2011 ($2.99)

1,14-19: 1-Gibbons-s. 14-19-Sinestro Corps War pts. 3,5,7,9,10, Epilogue 4.00
2-13: 2-6,10,11-Gibbons-s. 9-Darkseid app. 3.00
20-38: 20-Mongul app. 3.00
20-Second printing with sketch-c 3.00
34-38: 34-37-Variant covers by Migliari. 38-Fabry var-c 10.00
39-45-Blackest Night. 43-45-Red Lantern Guy Gardner 3.00
39-45-Variant covers: 39-Jusko. 40-Tucci. 41,42,44-Horn. 43-Ladronn. 45 Bolland 8.00
46,47-($3.99) 46-Blackest Night. 47-Brightest Day 4.00
48-61-($2.99) 48-Migliari-c; Ganthet joins the Corps. 49-52-Cyborg Superman app. 58-60-War of the Green Lanterns x-over. 60-Mogo destroyed 3.00
Blackest Night: Green Lantern Corps HC (2010, $24.99, d.j.) r/#39-47, cover gallery 25.00
Blackest Night: Green Lantern Corps SC (2011, $19.99) r/#39-47, cover gallery 20.00
...: Emerald Eclipse HC (2009, $24.99) r/#33-39; gallery of variant covers 25.00
...: Emerald Eclipse SC (2010, $14.99) r/#33-39; gallery of variant covers 15.00
...: Revolt of the Alpha-Lanterns HC (2011, $22.99) r/#21,22,48-52 23.00

Green Lantern Corps (2001 series) #18 © DC

Green Lantern: Rebirth #5 © DC

The Green Lantern: Season Two #1 © DC

	GD	VG	FN	VF	VF/NM	NM-
	2.0	4.0	6.0	8.0	9.0	9.2

...: Ring Quest TPB (2008, $14.99) r/#19,20,23-26 15.00
...: The Dark Side of Green TPB (2007, $12.99) r/#7-13 13.00
...: To Be a Lantern TPB (2007, $12.99) r/#1-6 13.00

GREEN LANTERN CORPS (DC New 52)
DC Comics: Nov, 2011 - No. 40, May, 2015 ($2.99)

1-23: 1-Tomasi-s/Pasarin-a/Mahnke-c; John Stewart & Guy Gardner. 4-6-Andy Kubert-c 3.00
24-39: 24-Lights Out pt. 2; Oa destroyed. 25-Year Zero. 35-37-Godhead x-over 3.00
40-($3.99) Chang-a 4.00
#0 (11/12, $2.99) Origin of Guy Gardner; Tomasi-s/Pasarin-a 3.00
Annual 1 (3/13, $4.99) Rise of the Third Army conclusion; Mogo returns 5.00
Annual 2 (3/14, $4.99) Villains United; Evil Star, Bolphunga, Kanjar Ro app. 5.00
...: Futures End 1 (11/14, $2.99, regular-c) Five years later; Indigo Tribe app. 3.00
...: Futures End 1 (11/14, $3.99, 3-D cover) 4.00

GREEN LANTERN CORPS: EDGE OF OBLIVION
DC Comics: Mar, 2016 - No. 6, Aug, 2016 ($2.99, limited series)

1-6: 1-3-Taylor-s/Van Sciver-a. 4,5-Syaf-a 3.00

GREEN LANTERN CORPS QUARTERLY
DC Comics: Summer, 1992 - No. 8, Spring, 1994 ($2.50/$2.95, 68 pgs.)

1-G.A. Green Lantern story; Staton-a(p) 5.00
2-8: 2-G.A. G.L.-c/story; Austin-c(i); Gulacy-a(p). 3-G.A. G.L. story. 4-Austin-i. 7-Painted-c; Tim Vigil-a. 8-Lobo-c/s 4.00

GREEN LANTERN CORPS: RECHARGE
DC Comics: Nov, 2005 - No. 5, Mar, 2006 ($3.50/$2.99, limited series)

1-($3.50) Kyle Rayner, Guy Gardner & Kilowog app.; Gleason-a 4.00
2-5-($2.99) 3.00
TPB (2006, $12.99) r/series 13.00

GREEN LANTERN: DRAGON LORD
DC Comics: 2001 - No. 3, 2001 ($4.95, squarebound, limited series)

1-3: A G.L. in ancient China; Moench-s/Gulacy-c/a 5.00

GREEN LANTERN: EARTH ONE
DC Comics: Mar, 2018 (Graphic novel)

Volume One HC ($24.95) Hardman & Bechko-s/Hardman-a; re-imagined origin 25.00

GREEN LANTERN 80TH ANNIVERSARY 100-PAGE SUPER SPECTACULAR
DC Comics: Aug, 2020 ($9.99, squarebound, one-shot)

1-Short stories and pin-ups by various incl. Johns, O'Neil, Grell, Reis; multiple covers 10.00

GREEN LANTERN: EMERALD DAWN (Also see Emerald Dawn)
DC Comics: Dec, 1989 - No. 6, May, 1990 ($1.00, limited series)

1-Origin retold; Giffen plots in all 6.00
2-6: 4-Re-intro. Tomar-Re 4.00

GREEN LANTERN: EMERALD DAWN II (Emerald Dawn II #1 & 2)
DC Comics: Apr, 1991 - No. 6, Sept, 1991 ($1.00, limited series)

1-6 4.00
TPB (2003, $12.95) r/#1-6; Alan Davis-c 13.00

GREEN LANTERN: EMERALD WARRIORS
DC Comics: Oct, 2010 - No. 13, Oct, 2011 ($3.99/$2.99)

1-5-($3.99) Guy Gardner's exploits; Migliari-c. 1-Bermejo variant-c. 2-5-Massaferra var-c 4.00
6-13-($2.99) 6,7-Covers by Migliari & Massaferra. 8-10-War of the Green Lanterns x-over 3.00

GREEN LANTERN: EVIL'S MIGHT (Elseworlds)
DC Comics: 2002 - No. 3 ($5.95, squarebound, limited series)

1-3-Kyle Rayner in 19th century NYC; Rogers-a; Chaykin & Tischman-s 6.00

GREEN LANTERN: FEAR ITSELF
DC Comics: 1999 (Graphic novel)

Hardcover ($24.95) Ron Marz-s/Brad Parker painted-a 25.00
Softcover ($14.95) 15.00

GREEN LANTERN/FLASH: FASTER FRIENDS (See Flash/Green Lantern...)
DC Comics: 1997 ($4.95, limited series)

1-Marz-s 5.00

GREEN LANTERN GALLERY
DC Comics: Dec, 1996 ($3.50, one-shot)

1-Wraparound-c; pin-ups by various 4.00

GREEN LANTERN/GREEN ARROW (Also see The Flash #217)
DC Comics: Oct, 1983 - No. 7, April, 1984 (52-60 pgs.)

1-7- r-Green Lantern #76-89 2 4 6 8 10 12
NOTE: ***Neal Adams** r-1-7; c-1-4.* ***Wrightson** r-4, 5.*

GREEN LANTERN/HUCKLEBERRY HOUND SPECIAL
DC Comics: Dec, 2018 ($4.99, one-shot)

1-John Stewart and Huckleberry Hound meet in 1972; Russell-s/Leonardi-a 5.00

GREEN LANTERN • LEGACY: THE LAST WILL & TESTAMENT OF HAL JORDAN
DC Comics: 2002 ($24.95, hardcover graphic novel)

Hardcover-Anderson & Sienkiewicz-a/c; Kelly-s; Return of Oa 25.00
Softcover (2004, $17.95) 18.00

GREEN LANTERN: LOST ARMY
DC Comics: Aug, 2015 - No. 6, Jan, 2016 ($2.99)

1-6: 1-Bunn-s/Saiz-a; featuring John Stewart, Guy Gardner, Kilowog, Arisia, Krona 3.00

GREEN LANTERN: MOSAIC (Also see Cosmic Odyssey #2)
DC Comics: June, 1992 - No. 18, Nov, 1993 ($1.25)

1-18: Featuring John Stewart. 1-Painted-c by Cully Hamner 3.00

GREEN LANTERN MOVIE PREQUEL (2011 movie)
DC Comics: July, 2011; Oct, 2011 ($2.99, one-shots)

...: Abin Sur 1 - Green-s/Gleason-a; movie photo-c 3.00
...: Hal Jordan 1 - Johns & Berlanti-s/Ordway-a; movie photo-c; Sinestro & Tomar-Re app. 3.00
...: Kilowog 1 - Tomasi-s/Ferreira-a; movie photo-c 3.00
...: Sinestro 1 (10/11) - Johns-s/Tolibao, Richards & Ordway-a; movie photo-c 3.00
...: Tomar-Re 1 - Guggenheim-s/Richards-a; movie photo-c 3.00

GREEN LANTERN: NEW GUARDIANS (DC New 52)
DC Comics: Nov, 2011 - No. 40, May, 2015 ($2.99)

1-Bedard-s/Kirkham-a/c; Kyle origin flashback; Fatality app. 6.00
2-23: 13-16-Third Army. 21-Relic freed. 22,23-Kyle vs. Relic. 23-Blue Lanterns destroyed 3.00
24-34: 24-Lights Out pt. 3. 3.00
35-39: 35-37-Godhead x-over; Highfather app. 38,39-Oblivion returns 3.00
40-($3.99) Oblivion app.; the start of the White Lantern Corps 4.00
#0 (11/12, $2.99) Bedard-s/Kuder-a; Zamarons app. 3.00
Annual 1 (3/13, $4.99) Giffen-s/Kolins-a/c 5.00
Annual 2 (6/14, $4.99) Segovia-a; takes place between #30 & #31 5.00
...: Futures End 1 (11/14, $2.99, regular-c) Five years later; intro. Saysoran 3.00
...: Futures End 1 (11/14, $3.99, 3-D cover) 4.00

GREEN LANTERN: REBIRTH
DC Comics: Dec, 2004 - No. 6, May, 2005 ($2.95, limited series)

1-Johns-s/Van Sciver-a; Hal Jordan as The Spectre on-c 8.00
1-2nd printing; Hal Jordan as Green Lantern on-c 4.00
1-3rd printing; B&W-c version of 1st printing 3.00
1 Special Edition (9/09, $1.00) r/#1 with "After Watchmen" cover frame 3.00
2-Guy Gardner becomes a Green Lantern again; JLA app. 5.00
2-2nd & 3rd printings 3.00
3-6: 3-Sinestro returns. 4-6-JLA & JSA app. 3.00
HC (2005, $24.99, dust jacket) r/series & Wizard preview; intro. by Brad Meltzer 25.00
SC (2007, 2010, $14.99) r/series & Wizard preview; intro. by Brad Meltzer 15.00

GREEN LANTERNS (DC Rebirth) (Also see Hal Jordan and the Green Lantern Corps)
DC Comics: Aug, 2016 - No. 57, Dec, 2018 ($2.99/$3.99)

1-24: 1-Simon Baz and Jessica Cruz team up; Humphries-s/Rocha-a. 6-1st app. the Phantom Ring. 8-Dominators app.; Benes-a. 9-14-Phantom Lantern. 16,17-Batman app. 3.00
25-($3.99) Lanterns vs. Volthoom; Rocha-a 4.00
26-49: 28-31-The Ancient Lanterns app. 35-Intro. Singularity Jain. 35,36-Bolphunga app. 3.00
50-57-($3.99) 50,51,55-57-Perkins-a. 53-57-Cyborg Superman app. 4.00
Annual 1 (7/18, $4.99) Diggle-s/Perkins-a 5.00
...: Rebirth 1 (8/16, $2.99) Van Sciver & Benes-a; Hal Jordan & Atrocitus app. 3.00

GREEN LANTERN SEASON TWO, THE (Follows Green Lantern: Blackstars series)
DC Comics: Apr, 2020 - Present ($4.99/$3.99)

1-($4.99) Grant Morrison-s/Liam Sharp-a; intro Young Guardians; Hal returns to Earth 5.00
2-11-($3.99) 4-The Flash app. 11-Hector Hammond app. 4.00

GREEN LANTERN/SENTINEL: HEART OF DARKNESS
DC Comics: Mar, 1998 - No. 3, May, 1998 ($1.95, limited series)

1-3-Marz-s/Pelletier-a 4.00

GREEN LANTERN/SILVER SURFER: UNHOLY ALLIANCES
DC Comics: 1995 ($4.95, one-shot)(Prelude to DC Versus Marvel)

nn-Hal Jordan app. 2 4 6 8 10 12

GREEN LANTERN SINESTRO CORPS SPECIAL (Continues in Green Lantern #21)
DC Comics: Aug, 2007 ($4.99, one-shot)

1-Kyle Rayner becomes Parallax; Cyborg Superman & Earth-Prime Superboy app.; Johns-s; Van Sciver-a/c; back-up story origin of Sinestro; Gibbons-a; Sinestro on cover 2 4 6 8 10 12
1-(2nd printing) Kyle Rayner as Parallax on cover 6.00

Green Lantern: The Animated Series #1 © DC

Green Mask #2 © FOX

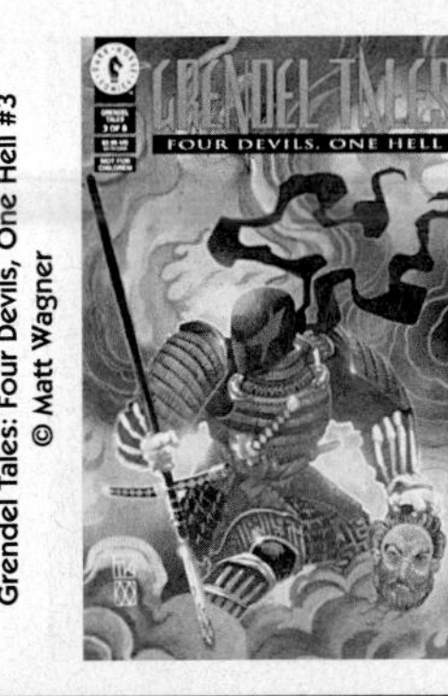

Grendel Tales: Four Devils, One Hell #3 © Matt Wagner

	GD	VG	FN	VF	VF/NM	NM-
	2.0	4.0	6.0	8.0	9.0	9.2

1-(3rd printing) Sinestro cover with muted colors 5.00

GREEN LANTERN/ SPACE GHOST SPECIAL
DC Comics: May, 2017 ($4.99, one-shot)
1-Tynion IV-s/Olivetti-a/c; back-up Ruff 'n' Ready re-intro. by Chaykin-s/a 5.00

GREEN LANTERN: THE ANIMATED SERIES (Based on the Cartoon Network series)
DC Comics: No. 0, Jan, 2012 - No. 14, Sept, 2013 ($2.99)
0,1: 0-Baltazar & Franco-s/Brizuela-a; Kilowog and Red Lanterns app. 5.00
2-14: 13-Lobo app. 4.00

GREEN LANTERN: THE GREATEST STORIES EVER TOLD
DC Comics: 2006 ($19.99, TPB)
SC-Reprints Showcase #22; G.L. #1,31,74,87,172; ('90 series) #3, and others; Ross-c 20.00

GREEN LANTERN: THE NEW CORPS
DC Comics: 1999 - No. 2, 1999 ($4.95, limited series)
1,2-Kyle recruits new GLs; Eaton-a 5.00

GREEN LANTERN VS. ALIENS
Dark Horse Comics: Sept, 2000 - No. 4, Dec, 2000 ($2.95, limited series)
1-4: 1-Hal Jordan and GL Corps vs. Aliens; Leonardi-p. 2-4-Kyle Rayner 3.00

GREEN MASK, THE (See Mystery Men)
Summer, 1940 - No. 9, 2/42; No. 10, 8/44 - No. 11, 11/44;
Fox Feature Syndicate: V2#1, Spring, 1945 - No. 6, 10-11/46

	GD	VG	FN	VF	VF/NM	NM-
V1#1-Origin The Green Mask & Domino; reprints/Mystery Men #1-3,5-7; Lou Fine-c	300	600	900	1980	3415	4850
2-Zanzibar The Magician by Tuska	126	252	378	806	1378	1950
3-Powell-a; Marijuana story	97	194	291	621	1061	1500
4-Navy Jones begins, ends #6	77	154	231	493	847	1200
5	61	122	183	390	670	950
6-The Nightbird begins, ends #9; Good Girl bondage/torture-c	132	264	396	845	1448	2050
7,9: 9(2/42)-Becomes The Bouncer #10(nn) on? & Green Mask #10 on	50	100	150	315	533	750
8-Classic Good Girl torture/bondage-c	206	412	618	1318	2251	3200
10,11: 10-Origin One Round Hogan & Rocket Kelly	37	74	111	222	361	525
V2#1	27	54	81	158	259	375
2-6	22	44	66	130	213	310

GREEN PLANET, THE
Charlton Comics: 1962 (one-shot) (12¢)

	GD	VG	FN	VF	VF/NM	NM-
nn-Giordano-c; sci-fi	9	18	27	63	129	195

GREEN TEAM (See Cancelled Comic Cavalcade & 1st Issue Special)

GREEN TEAM: TEEN TRILLIONAIRES
DC Comics: Jul, 2013 - No. 8, Mar, 2014 ($2.99)
1-8-Baltazar & Franco-s/Guara-a. 1-3-Conner-c. 3-Deathstroke app. 8-Teen Titans app. 3.00
1-Variant-c by Chiang 3.00

GREEN VALLEY
Image Comics (Skybound): Oct, 2016 - No. 9, Jun, 2017 ($2.99/$3.99)
1-8-Max Landis-s/Giuseppe Camuncoli-a 3.00
9-($3.99) 4.00

GREEN WOMAN, THE
DC Comics (Vertigo): 2010 ($24.99, HC graphic novel)
HC-John Bolton-a/Peter Straub & Michael Easton-s 25.00

GREETINGS FROM SANTA (See March of Comics No. 48)

GRENDEL (Also see Primer #2, Mage and Comico Collection)
Comico: Mar, 1983 - No. 3, Feb, 1984 ($1.50, B&W)(#1 has indicia to Skrog #1)

	GD	VG	FN	VF	VF/NM	NM-
1-Origin Hunter Rose	9	18	27	62	126	190
2,3: 2-Origin Argent	7	14	21	46	86	125

GRENDEL
Comico: Oct, 1986 - No. 40, Feb, 1990 ($1.50/$1.95/$2.50, mature)

	GD	VG	FN	VF	VF/NM	NM-
1	2	4	6	8	10	12
1,2: 2nd printings						3.00
2,3,5-15: 13-15-Ken Steacy-c.						4.00
4,16: 4-Dave Stevens-c(i). 16-Re-intro Mage (series begins, ends #19)						6.00
17-40: 24-25,27-28,30-31-Snyder-c/a						3.00
Devil by the Deed (Graphic Novel, 10/86, $5.95, 52 pgs.)-r/Grendel back-ups/ Mage 6-14; Alan Moore intro.	1	3	4	6	8	10
Devil's Legacy ($14.95, 1988, Graphic Novel)	2	4	6	9	12	15

Devil's Vagary (10/87, B&W & red)-No price; included in Comico Collection

	GD	VG	FN	VF	VF/NM	NM-
	2.0	4.0	6.0	8.0	9.0	9.2
	2	4	6	8	10	12

GRENDEL (Title series): **Dark Horse Comics**
--ARCHIVES, 5/07 ($14.95, HC) r/1st apps. in Primer #2 and Grendel #1-3; Wagner intro. 15.00
--BEHOLD THE DEVIL, No. 0, 7/07 - No. 8, 6/08 ($3.50/50¢, B&W&Red)
0-(50¢-c) Prelude to series; Matt Wagner-s/a; interview with Wagner 3.00
1-8-Matt Wagner-s/a/c in all 3.50
--BLACK, WHITE, AND RED, 11/98 - No. 4, 2/99 ($3.95, anthology)
1-Wagner-s in all. Art by Sale, Leon and others 5.00
2-4: 2-Mack, Chadwick-a. 3-Allred, Kristensen-a. 4-Pearson, Sprouse-a 4.00
--CLASSICS, 7/95 - 8/95 ($3.95, mature) 1,2-reprints; new Wagner-c 4.00
--CYCLE, 10/95 ($5.95) 1-nn-history of Grendel by M. Wagner & others 6.00
--DEVIL BY THE DEED, 7/93 ($3.95, varnish-c) 1-nn-M. Wagner-c/a/scripts; r/Grendel back-ups from Mage #6-14 6.00
Reprint (12/97, $3.95) w/pin-ups by various 4.00
Hardcover (2007, $12.95) reprint recolored to B&W&red; includes covers and intros from previously reprinted editions 13.00
--DEVIL CHILD, 6/99 - No. 2, 7/99 ($2.95, mature) 1,2-Sale & Kristiansen-a/Schutz-s 3.00
--DEVIL QUEST, 11/95 ($4.95) 1-nn-Prequel to Batman/Grendel II; M. Wagner story & art; r/back-up story from Grendel Tales series. 5.00
--DEVILS AND DEATHS, 10/94 - 11/94 ($2.95, mature) 1,2 3.00
: DEVIL'S LEGACY, 3/00 - No. 12, 2/01 ($2.95, reprints 1986 series, recolored)
1-12-Wagner-s/c; Pander Bros.-a 3.00
: DEVIL'S ODYSSEY, 10/9 - No. 8 ($3.99) 1-4-Wagner-s/a; Grendel Prime returns 4.00
: DEVIL'S REIGN, 5/04 - No. 7, 12/04 ($3.50, repr. 1989 series #34-40, recolored)
1-7-Sale-c/a. 3.50
: GOD AND THE DEVIL, No. 0, 1/03 - No. 10, 12/03 ($3.50/$4.99, repr. 1986 series, recolored)
0-9: 0-Sale-c/a; r/#23. 1-9-Snyder-c 3.50
10-($4.99) Double-sized; Snyder-c 5.00
--RED, WHITE & BLACK, 9/02 - No. 4, 12/02 ($4.99, anthology)
1-4-Wagner-s in all. 1-Art by Thompson, Sakai, Mahfood and others. 2-Kelley Jones, Watson, Brereton, Hester & Parks-a. 3-Oeming, Noto, Cannon, Ashley Wood, Huddleston-a 4-Chiang, Dalrymple, Robertson, Snyder III and Zulli-a 5.00
TPB (2005, $19.95) r/#1-4; cover gallery, artist bios 20.00
--TALES: DEVIL'S CHOICES, 3/95 - 6/95 ($2.95, mature) 1-4 3.00
--TALES: FOUR DEVILS, ONE HELL, 8/93 - 1/94 ($2.95, mature)
1-6-Wagner painted-c 3.00
TPB (12/94, $17.95) r/#1-6 18.00
--TALES: HOMECOMING, 12/94 - 2/95 ($2.95, mature) 1-3 3.00
--TALES: THE DEVIL IN OUR MIDST, 5/94 - 9/95 ($2.95, mature) 1-5-Wagner painted-c 3.00
--TALES: THE DEVIL MAY CARE, 12/95 - No. 6, 5/96 ($2.95, mature)
1-6-Terry LaBan scripts. 5-Batman/Grendel II preview 3.00
--TALES: THE DEVIL'S APPRENTICE, 9/97 - No. 3, 11/97 ($2.95, mature)
1-3 3.00
--TALES: THE DEVIL'S HAMMER, 2/94 - No. 3, 4/94 ($2.95, mature)
1-3-Rob Walton-s/a; back-up stories by Wagner 3.00
: THE DEVIL INSIDE, 9/01 - No. 3, 11/01 ($2.99)
1-3-r/#13-15 with new Wagner-c 3.00
VS. THE SHADOW, 9/14 - No. 3, 11/14 ($5.99, squarebound)
Matt Wagner-s/a/c; Grendel time-travels to The Shadow's era 6.00
: WAR CHILD, 8/92 - No. 10, 6/93 ($2.50, lim. series, mature)
1-9: 1-4-Bisley painted-c; Wagner-i & scripts in all 3.00
10-($3.50, 52 pgs.) Wagner-c 4.00
Limited Edition Hardcover ($99.95) 100.00

GRENDEL, KENTUCKY
AWA Studios: Sept, 2020 - No. 4, Dec, 2020 ($3.99, limited series)
1-4-Jeff McComsey-s/Tommy Lee Edwards-a 4.00

GREYFRIARS BOBBY (Disney)(Movie)
Dell Publishing Co.: No. 1189, Nov, 1961 (one-shot)

	GD	VG	FN	VF	VF/NM	NM-
Four Color 1189-Photo-c	6	12	18	41	76	110

GREYLORE
Sirius: 12/85 - No. 5, Sept, 1986 ($1.50/$1.75, high quality paper)
1-5: Bo Hampton-a in all 3.00

GREYSHIRT: INDIGO SUNSET (Also see Tomorrow Stories)
America's Best Comics: Dec, 2001 - No. 6, Aug, 2002 ($3.50, limited series)

Grifter V2 #4 © WSP

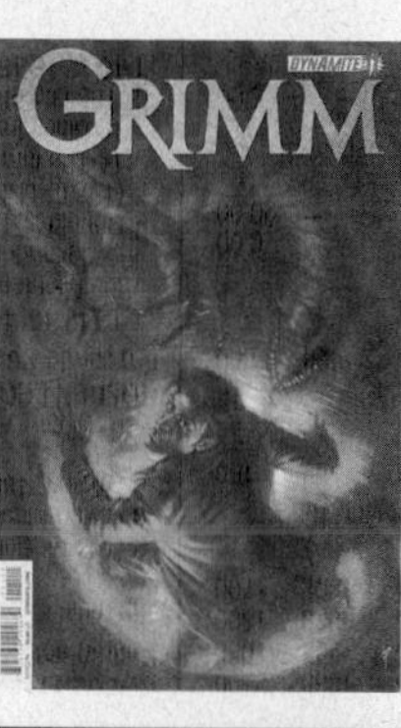

Grimm #11 © Universal TV

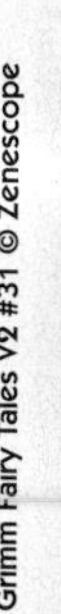

Grimm Fairy Tales V2 #31 © Zenescope

GD 2.0 | VG 4.0 | FN 6.0 | VF 8.0 | VF/NM 9.0 | NM- 9.2

1-6-Veitch-s/a. 4-Back-up w/John Severin-a. 6-Cho-a 3.50
TPB (2002, $19.95) r/#1-6; preface by Alan Moore 20.00

GRIDIRON GIANTS
Ultimate Sports Ent.: 2000 - No. 2 ($3.95, cardstock covers)
1,2-NFL players Sanders, Marino, Plummer, T. Davis battle evil 4.00

GRIFFIN, THE
DC Comics: 1991 - No. 6, 1991 ($4.95, limited series, 52 pgs.)
Book 1-6: Matt Wagner painted-c 5.00

GRIFTER (Also see Team 7 & WildC.A.T.S)
Image Comics (WildStorm Prod.): May, 1995 - No. 10, Mar, 1996 ($1.95)
1 ($1.95, Newsstand)-WildStorm Rising Pt. 5 3.00
1-10:1 ($2.50, Direct)-WildStorm Rising Pt. 5, bound-in trading card 3.00
...: One Shot (1/95, $4.95) Flip-c 5.00

GRIFTER
Image Comics (WildStorm Prod.): V2#1, July, 1996 - No. 14, Aug, 1997 ($2.50)
V2#1-14: Steven Grant scripts 3.00

GRIFTER (DC New 52)
DC Comics: Nov, 2011 - No. 16, Mar, 2013 ($2.99)
1-16: 1-Grifter in the new DC universe; Edmonson-s/Cafu-a/c. 4-Green Arrow app. 3.00
#0 (11/12, $2.99) Liefeld-s/c; Clark-a 3.00

GRIFTER & MIDNIGHTER
DC Comics (WildStorm Prod.): May, 2007 - No. 6, Oct, 2007 ($2.99, limited series)
1-6-Dixon-s/Benjamin-a/c. 1,3-The Authority app. 3.00
TPB (2008, $17.99) r/#1-6 18.00

GRIFTER AND THE MASK
Dark Horse Comics: Sept, 1996 - No. 2, Oct, 1996 ($2.50, limited series)
(1st Dark Horse Comics/Image x-over)
1,2: Steve Seagle scripts 3.00

GRIFTER/BADROCK (Also see WildC.A.T.S & Youngblood)
Image Comics (Extreme Studios): Oct, 1995 - No.2, Nov, 1995 ($2.50, unfinished lim. series)
1,2: 2-Flip book w/Badrock #2 3.00

GRIFTER/SHI
Image Comics (WildStorm Productions): Apr, 1996 - No. 2, May, 1996 ($2.95, limited series)
1,2: 1-Jim Lee-c/a(p); Travis Charest-a(p). 2-Billy Tucci-c/a(p); Travis Charest-a(p) 3.00

GRIM GHOST, THE
Atlas/Seaboard Publ.: Jan, 1975 - No. 3, July, 1975
1-3: Fleisher-s in all. 1-Origin. 2-Son of Satan; Colan-a. 3-Heath-c
2 4 6 13 18 22

GRIM GHOST
Ardden Entertainment (Atlas Comics): Mar, 2011 - No. 5 ($2.99)
1-5-Isabella & Susco-s/Kelley Jones-a. 1-Re-intro. Matthew Dunsinane 3.00
... Issue Zero - NY Comicon Edtion (10/10, $2.99) Qing Ping Mui-a; prequel to #1 3.00

GRIMJACK (Also see Demon Knight & Starslayer)
First Comics: Aug, 1984 - No. 81, Apr, 1991 ($1.00/$1.95/$2.25)
1-John Ostrander scripts & Tim Truman-c/a begins 1 2 3 5 6 8
2-25: 20-Sutton-c/a begins. 22-Bolland-a. 3.00
26-2nd color Teenage Mutant Ninja Turtles 2 4 6 8 10 12
27-74,76-81 (Later issues $1.95, $2.25): 30-Dynamo Joe x-over; 31-Mandrake-c/a begins. 73,74-Kelley Jones-a 3.00
75-($5.95, 52 pgs.)-Fold-out map; coated stock 6.00
The Legend of Grimjack Vol. 1 (IDW Publishing, 2004, $19.99) r/Starslayer #10-18; 8 new pages & art 20.00
The Legend of Grimjack Vol. 2 (IDW, 2005, $19.99) r/#1-7; unpublished art 20.00
The Legend of Grimjack Vol. 3 (IDW, 2005, $19.99) r/#8-14; cover gallery 20.00
The Legend of Grimjack Vol. 4 (IDW, 2005, $24.99) r/#15-21; cover gallery 25.00
The Legend of Grimjack Vol. 5 (IDW, 5/06, $24.99) r/#22-30; cover gallery 25.00
The Legend of Grimjack Vol. 6 (IDW, 1/07, $24.99) r/#31-37; cover gallery 25.00
The Legend of Grimjack Vol. 7 (IDW, 4/07, $24.99) r/#38-46; covers; "Rough Trade" 25.00
NOTE: *Truman c/a-1-17.*

GRIMJACK CASEFILES
First Comics: Nov, 1990 - No. 5, Mar, 1991 ($1.95, limited series)
1-5 Reprints 1st stories from Starslayer #10 on 3.00

GRIMJACK: KILLER INSTINCT
IDW Publ.: Jan, 2005 - No. 6, June, 2005 ($3.99, limited series)
1-6-Ostrander-s/Truman-a 4.00

GRIMJACK: THE MANX CAT
IDW Publ.: Aug, 2009 - No. 6, Jan, 2010 ($3.99, limited series)
1-6-Ostrander-s/Truman-a 4.00

GRIMM (Based on the NBC TV series)
Dynamite Entertainment.: 2013 - No. 12, 2014 ($3.99)
1-11: 1-Two covers (Alex Ross & photo). 2-11-Pararillo & photo-c on each 4.00
12-($4.99) Gaffen & McVey-s/Rodolfo-a; Pararillo & photo-c 5.00
#0 (2013, Free Comic Book Day giveaway) Prequel to issue #1; Portacio-c 3.00
... Portland, WU (2014, $7.99) Gaffen & McVey-s/Govar-a/c 8.00
...: The Warlock 1-4 (2013 - No. 4, 2014, $3.99) Nitz-s/Malaga-a 4.00

GRIMM VOLUME 2 (Based on the NBC TV series)
Dynamite Entertainment.: 2016 - No. 5, 2017 ($3.99)
1-5-Kittredge-s/Sanapo-a; two covers 4.00

GRIMM FAIRY TALES
Zenescope Entertainment: Jun, 2005 - No. 125, Aug, 2016 ($2.99/$3.99)
1-Al Rio-c; Little Red Riding Hood app.; multiple variant covers
6 12 18 37 66 95
2-Multiple variant covers 3 6 9 19 30 40
3-6-Multiple variant covers 2 4 6 10 14 18
7-12: Multiple covers on each 6.00
13-74,76-84,86-99,101,102: Multiple covers on each 3.00
75-(7/12, $5.99) Covers by Campbell, Sejic, Michaels and others 6.00
85-(5/13, $5.99) Unleashed part 2 6.00
100-(7/14, $5.99) Age of Darkness; covers by Neal Adams and others 6.00
103-124-($3.99) 4.00
125-(8/16, $9.99) Five covers 10.00
#0 Free Comic Book Day Special Edition (4/14, giveaway) Age of Darkness tie-in 3.00
2016 Annual (10/16, $5.99) Spotlight on Skylar; art by various; 4 covers 6.00
... Animated One Shot (10/12, $3.99) Schnepp-c; bonus design art 4.00
Grimm Tales of Terror 2016 Holiday Special (11/16, $5.99) 4 covers 6.00
Grimm Tales of Terror 2019 Halloween Special (10/19, $5.99) 5 covers 6.00
Grimm Universe Presents Fall 2019 (8/19, $7.99) 5 covers 8.00
... Halloween Special 1,2, 2013, 2014, 2015, 2016 (10/09, 10/10, 10/13, 10/14, 9/15, 10/16, $5.99) Multiple covers on each 6.00
... Holiday Edition (11/14, $5.99) The story of Krampus; multiple covers 6.00
... Presents Wounded Warriors (7/13, $6.99) Multiple military-themes covers 7.00
... The Dark Queen One Shot (1/14, $5.99) Sharma-a; 4 covers 6.00

GRIMM FAIRY TALES (Volume 2)
Zenescope Entertainment: Dec, 2016 - Present ($3.99)
1-24,26-45: 1-3-Brusha-s/Silva-a; multiple covers on each. 37-Leads into 2020 Annual 4.00
25-($5.99) The War of the Grail; continues in Annual 2019; Goetten-a 6.00
... 2017 Halloween Special (10/17, $5.99) Short stories by various; 4 covers 6.00
...: 2019 Annual (1/19, $5.99) Casallos-a; 4 covers 6.00
...: 2019 Giant-Size (2/19, $5.99) Casallos-a; 5 covers; continues in #26 6.00
...: 2019 Holiday Special (11/19, $5.99) Short stories by various; 5 covers 6.00
...: 2020 Annual (6/20, $5.99) Abrera-a; 4 covers; Skye vs. Merlin; follows #37 6.00
...: 2020 Holiday Special (12/20, $5.99) Short stories by various; 5 covers 6.00
...: Universus One-Shot (3/20, $4.99) Franchini-s/Garcia-a; two covers; includes cards 5.00

GRIMM FAIRY TALES PRESENTS ALICE IN WONDERLAND
Zenescope Entertainment: Jan, 2012 - No. 6, May, 2012 ($2.99)
1-Multiple variant covers 3 6 9 14 20 26
2-6: Multiple covers on each 1 2 3 5 6 8

GRIMM FAIRY TALES MYTHS & LEGENDS
Zenescope Entertainment: Jan, 2011 - No. 25, Feb, 2013 ($2.99)
1-Campbell-c; multiple variant covers 2 4 6 8 10 12
2-5 5.00
6-24 3.00
25-(2/13, $5.99) Multiple variant covers 6.00

GRIMM FAIRY TALES PRESENTS WONDERLAND (Title changes to Wonderland with #43)
Zenescope Entertainment: Jul, 2012 - Finale, Sept, 2016 ($2.99)
1-Campbell-c; multiple variant covers 2 4 6 8 10 12
2,3 5.00
4-18 3.00
19-24,26-49-($3.99) 4.00
25-(7/14, $5.99) Multiple variant covers 6.00
50-(8/16, $5.99) Multiple variant covers 6.00
... Finale (9/16, $5.99) Last issue; 4 covers; Shand-s/Follini-a 6.00
Free Comic Book Day 2015 Special Edition (5/15, giveaway) Brescini-a 3.00

GRIMMISS ISLAND (Issue #1 titled Itty Bitty Comics #5: Grimmiss Island)

Grip: The Strange World of Men #1 © G. Hernandez

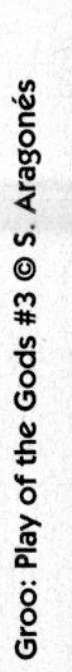
Groo: Play of the Gods #3 © S. Aragonés

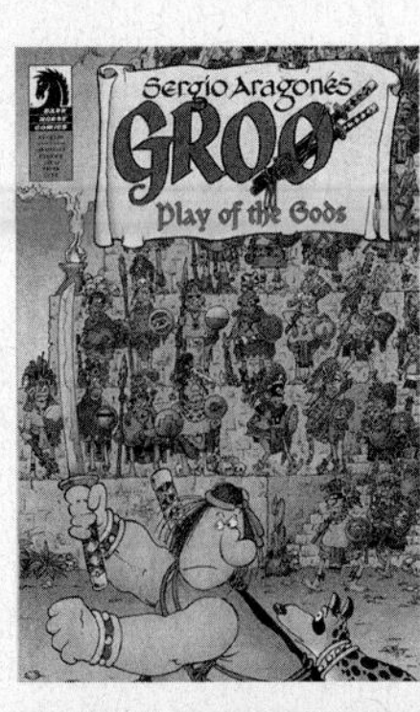

Grumble #4 © Roberts & Norton

GD 2.0 | VG 4.0 | FN 6.0 | VF 8.0 | VF/NM 9.0 | NM- 9.2

Dark Horse Comics: Mar, 2015 - No. 4, Jun, 2015 ($2.99, limited series)
1-4-All-ages humor story by Art Baltazar & Franco 3.00

GRIMM'S GHOST STORIES (See Dan Curtis)
Gold Key/Whitman No. 55 on: Jan, 1972 - No. 60, June, 1982 (Painted-c #1-42,44,46-56)
1 4 8 12 27 44 60
2-5,8: 5,8-Williamson-a 2 4 6 13 18 22
6,7,9,10 2 4 6 11 16 20
11-20 2 4 6 8 11 14
21-42,45-54: 32,34-Reprints. 45-Photo-c 1 3 4 6 8 10
43,44,55-60: 43,44-(52 pgs.). 43-Photo-c. 58(2/82). 59(4/82)-Williamson-a(r/#8). 60(6/82)
2 4 6 8 11 14
Mini-Comic No. 1 (3-1/4x6-1/2", 1976) 1 3 4 6 8 10
NOTE: *Reprints-#32?, 34?, 39, 43, 44, 47?, 53; 56-60(1/3).* ***Bolle*** *a-8, 17, 22-25, 27, 29(2), 33, 35, 41, 43r, 45(2), 48(2), 50, 52, 57.* ***Celardo*** *a-17, 26, 28p, 30, 31, 43(2), 45.* ***Lopez*** *a-24, 25.* ***McWilliams*** *a-33, 44r, 48, 54(2), 57, 58.* ***Win Mortimer*** *a-31, 33, 49, 51, 55, 56, 58(2), 59, 60.* ***Roussos*** *a-25, 30.* ***Sparling*** *a-23, 24, 28, 30, 31, 33, 43r, 44, 45, 51(2), 52, 56-58, 59(2), 60.* ***Spiegle*** *a-44.*

GRIN (The American Funny Book) (Satire)
APAG House Pubs: Nov, 1972 - No. 3, April, 1973 (Magazine, 52 pgs.)
1-Parodies-Godfather, All in the Family 3 6 9 16 24 32
2,3 2 4 6 11 16 20

GRIN & BEAR IT (See Gags)
Dell Publishing Co.: No. 28, 1941
Large Feature Comic 28 20 40 60 118 192 265

GRINDHOUSE: DOORS OPEN AT MIDNIGHT
Dark Horse Comics: Oct, 2013 - No. 8, May, 2014 ($3.99)
1-8: 1-Francavilla-c/DeCampi-s. 1,2-Bee Vixens From Mars. 3,4-Prison Ship Antares 4.00

GRINDHOUSE: DRIVE IN, BLEED OUT
Dark Horse Comics: Nov, 2014 - No. 8, Aug, 2015 ($3.99)
1-8: 1,2-Slay Ride; DeCampi-s/Guéra-a. 7,8-Nebulina. 8-Manara-c 4.00

GRIPS (Extreme violence)
Silverwolf Comics: Sept, 1986 - No. 4, Dec, 1986 ($1.50, B&W, mature)
1-Tim Vigil-c/a in all 6.00
2-4 4.00

GRIP: THE STRANGE WORLD OF MEN
DC Comics (Vertigo): Jan, 2002 - No. 5, May, 2002 ($2.50, limited series)
1-4-Gilbert Hernandez-s/a 3.00

GRIT GRADY (See Holyoke One-Shot No. 1)

GROO (Also see Sergio Aragonés' Groo...)

GROO (Sergio Aragonés'...)
Image Comics: Dec, 1994 - No. 12, Dec, 1995 ($1.95)
1-12: 2-Indicia reads #1, Jan, 1995; Aragonés-c/a in all 4.00

GROO (Sergio Aragonés'...)
Dark Horse Comics: Jan, 1998 - No. 4, Apr, 1998 ($2.95)
1-4: Aragonés-c/a in all 4.00
...: One For One (9/10, $1.00) reprints #1 with red cover frame 3.00

GROO CHRONICLES, THE (Sergio Aragonés)
Marvel Comics (Epic Comics): June, 1989 - No. 6, Feb, 1990 ($3.50)
Book 1-6: Reprints early Pacific issues 5.00

GROO: FRAY OF THE GODS (Sergio Aragonés'...)
Dark Horse Comics: Jul, 2016 - No. 4, Jan, 2017 ($3.99, limited series)
1-4-Aragonés-c/a; Evanier-s 4.00

GROO: FRIENDS AND FOES (Sergio Aragonés'...)
Dark Horse Comics: Jan, 2015 - No. 12, Jan, 2016 ($3.99)
1-12-Aragonés-c/a in all; spotlights on various characters. 1-Spotlight on Captain Ahax 4.00

GROO: PLAY OF THE GODS (Sergio Aragonés'...)
Dark Horse Comics: Jul, 2017 - No. 4, Oct, 2017 ($3.99, limited series)
1-4-Aragonés-c/a; Evanier-s 4.00

GROO SPECIAL
Eclipse Comics: Oct, 1984 ($2.00, 52 pgs., Baxter paper)
1-Aragonés-c/a 3 6 9 16 23 30

GROOT (Guardians of the Galaxy)
Marvel Comics: Aug, 2015 - No. 6, Jan, 2016 ($3.99)
1-6: 1-Loveness-s/Kesinger-a; Rocket Raccoon app. 2-Flashback to Groot meeting Rocket. 3-Silver Surfer app. 4.00

GROO THE WANDERER (See Destroyer Duck #1 & Starslayer #5)
Pacific Comics: Dec, 1982 - No. 8, Apr, 1984
1-Aragonés-c/a(p)/Evanier-s in all; Aragonés bio. 3 6 9 17 26 35
2-5: 5-Deluxe paper (1.00-c) 2 4 6 9 13 16
6-8 2 4 6 10 14 18

GROO THE WANDERER (Sergio Aragonés'...) (See Marvel Graphic Novel #32)
Marvel Comics (Epic Comics): March, 1985 - No. 120, Jan, 1995
1-Aragonés-c/a in all 3 6 9 14 20 26
2-10 1 2 3 5 6 8
11-20,50-($1.50, double size) 5.00
21-49,51-99: 87-direct sale only, high quality paper 4.00
100-($2.95, 52 pgs.) 5.00
101-120 4.00
Groo Carnival, The (12/91, $8.95)-r/#9-12 11.00
Groo Garden, The (4/94, $10.95)-r/#25-28 11.00

GROO VS. CONAN (Sergio Aragonés'...)
Dark Horse Comics: Jul, 2014 - No. 4, Oct, 2014 ($3.50, limited series)
1-4: Aragonés & Evanier-s/Aragonés-c/a in all; Thomas Yeates on Conan art 3.50

GROOVY (Cartoon Comics - not CCA approved)
Marvel Comics Group: March, 1968 - No. 3, July, 1968
1-Monkees, Ringo Starr, Sonny & Cher, Mamas & Papas photos
8 16 24 56 108 160
2,3 6 12 18 37 66 95

GROSS POINT
DC Comics: Aug, 1997 - No. 14, Aug, 1998 ($2.50)
1-14: 1-Waid/Augustyn-s 3.00

GROUNDED
Image Comics: July, 2005 - No. 6, May, 2006 ($2.95/$2.99, limited series)
1-6-Mark Sable-s/Paul Azaceta-a. 1-Mike Oeming-c 3.00
Vol. 1: Powerless TPB (2006, $14.99) r/#1-6; sketch pages and creator bios 15.00

GRRL SCOUTS (Jim Mahfood's...) (Also see 40 oz. Collected)
Oni Press: Mar,1999 - No. 4, Dec, 1999 ($2.95, B&W, limited series)
1-4-Mahfood-s/c/a 3.00
TPB (2003, $12.95) r/#1-4; pin-ups by Warren, Winick, Allred, Fegredo and others 13.00

GRRL SCOUTS: MAGIC SOCKS
Image Comics: May, 2017 - No. 6, Oct, 2017 ($3.99, limited series)
1-6-Mahfood-s/c/a 4.00

GRRL SCOUTS: WORK SUCKS
Image Comics: Feb, 2003 - No. 4, May, 2003 ($2.95, B&W, limited series)
1-4-Mahfood-s/c/a 3.00
TPB (2004, $12.95) r/#1-4; pin-ups by Oeming, Dwyer, Tennapel and others 13.00

GRUMBLE
Albatross Funnybooks: 2018 - Present ($3.99)
1-10-Rafer Roberts-s/Mike Norton-a 4.00
...: Memphis & Beyond the Infinite 1-5 (2020 - No 5, 2020, $3.99) Roberts-s/Norton-a 4.00
... vs. The Goon (2019, Free Comic Book Day giveaway) Mike Norton & Eric Powell-a 3.00

GRUMPY CAT
Dynamite Entertainment: 2015 - No. 3, 2015 ($3.99, limited series)
1-3-Short stories; Ben McCool & Ben Fisher-s/Steve Uy & Michelle Nguyen-a 4.00
..., Free Comic Book Day 2016 (giveaway) Short stories by various 3.00

GRUMPY CAT AND POKEY
Dynamite Entertainment: 2016 - No. 6, 2016 ($3.99, limited series)
1-6-Short stories. 1-McCool & Fisher-s/Uy, Haeser & Garbowska-a; multiple covers 4.00

GRUMPY CAT / GARFIELD
Dynamite Entertainment: 2017 - No. 3, 2017 ($3.99, limited series)
1-3-Mark Evanier-s/Steve Uy-a; multiple covers 4.00

GUADALCANAL DIARY (See American Library)

GUARDIAN ANGEL
Image Comics: May, 2002 - No. 2, July, 2002 ($2.95)
1,2-Peterson-s/Wiesenfeld-a 3.00

GUARDIANS
Marvel Comics: Sept, 2004 - No. 5, Dec, 2004 ($2.99, limited series)
1-5-Sumerak-s/Casey Jones-a 3.00

GUARDIANS OF INFINITY
Marvel Comics: Feb, 2016 - No. 8, Sept, 2016 ($4.99)

Guardians of the Galaxy #24 © MAR

Guardians of the Galaxy (2013 series) #23 © MAR

Guardians of the Galaxy (2019 series) #4 © MAR

	GD 2.0	VG 4.0	FN 6.0	VF 8.0	VF/NM 9.0	NM- 9.2

1-8-Guardians of the Galaxy & 31st century Guardians. 1-Back-up story with The Thing 5.00

GUARDIANS OF KNOWHERE (Secret Wars tie-in)
Marvel Comics: Sept, 2015 - No. 4, Nov, 2015 ($3.99, limited series)

1-4-Bendis-s/Deodato-a; Guardians of the Galaxy, Angela & Mantis app. 4.00
1-Variant Gwenom (Gwen/Venom) cover by Guillory 8.00

GUARDIANS OF METROPOLIS
DC Comics: Nov, 1995 - Feb, 1995 ($1.50, limited series)

1-4: 1-Superman & Granny Goodness app. 4.00

GUARDIANS OF THE GALAXY (Also see The Defenders #26, Marvel Presents #3, Marvel Super-Heroes #18, Marvel Two-In-One #5)
Marvel Comics: June, 1990 - No. 62, July, 1995 ($1.00/$1.25)

1-Valentino-c/a(p) begin; 1st app. Taserface 3 6 9 19 30 40
2-5: 2-Zeck-c(i). 5-McFarlane-c(i) 1 3 4 6 8 10
6-15: 7-Intro Malevolence (Mephisto's daughter); Perez-c(i). 8-Intro Rancor (descendant of Wolverine) in cameo. 9-1st full app. Rancor; Rob Liefeld-c(i). 10-Jim Lee-c(i). 13,14-1st app. Spirit of Vengeance (futuristic Ghost Rider). 14-Spirit of Vengeance vs. The Guardians. 15-Starlin-c(i) 4.00
16-($1.50, 52 pgs.)-Starlin-c(i) 5.00
17-24,26-38,40-47: 17-20-31st century Punishers storyline. 20-Last $1.00-c. 21-Rancor app. 22-Reintro Starhawk. 24-Silver Surfer-c/story; Ron Lim-c. 26-Origin retold. 27-28-Infinity War x-over; 27-Inhumans app. 43-Intro Wooden (son of Thor) 4.00
25-($2.50)-Prism foil-c; Silver Surfer/Galactus-c/s 5.00
25-($2.50)-Without foil-c; newsstand edition 4.00
39-($2.95, 52 pgs.)-Embossed & holo-grafx foil-c; Dr. Doom vs. Rancor 5.00
48,49,51-56: 48-bound-in trading card sheet 4.00
50-($2.00, 52 pgs.)-Newsstand edition 5.00
50-($2.95, 52 pgs.)-Collectors ed. w/foil embossed-c 6.00
57-61 1 2 3 5 6 8
62 2 4 6 9 12 15
Annual 1-4: ('91-'94, 68 pgs.)-1-Origin. 2-Spirit of Vengeance-c/story. 3,4-Bagged w/card 5.00

GUARDIANS OF THE GALAXY (See Annihilation series)
Marvel Comics: July, 2008 - No. 25, Jun, 2010 ($2.99)

1-Continued from Annihilation Conquest #6; origin of the new Guardians: Star-Lord, Drax, Warlock, Rocket Raccoon, Quasar (female version: Phyla-Vell) and Gamora; Mantis and Groot appear but not official members; Cosmo the talking dog and Nova (Richard Rider) app.; Abnett & Lanning-s/Pelletier-a 5 10 15 35 63 90
1-Second printing; variant-c 3 6 9 14 20 25
2,3: 2-Vance Astro (Major Victory) app.; full-size Groot on the cover but still growing (potted plant-size) in story. 3-Starhawk app; Guardians vs. the Universal Church of Truth 2 4 6 10 14 18
3-Variant cover 2 4 6 11 16 20
4,5-Secret Invasion x-overs; Skrulls app. 1 3 4 6 8 10
5-Monkey variant-c by Nic Klein 2 4 6 9 12 15
6-Secret Invasion x-over; Warlock, Gamora, Quasar and Star-Lord leave the team 1 3 4 6 8 10
7-Original Guardians app: Vance Astro, Charlie-27, Martinex & Yondu app; Groot, Mantis and Bug (from the Micronauts) join Rocket Raccoon, Vance Astro (Major Victory) and a re-grown Groot as the Guardians; Blastaar app. 2 4 6 8 10 12
7-Variant-c by Jim Valentino 2 4 6 11 16 20
8-War of Kings x-over; Blastaar & Ronan the Accuser app. 1 3 4 6 8 10
8-Variant-c; Thanos with the Infinity Gauntlet by Brandon Peterson 3 6 9 19 30 40
9-12: 9-War of Kings x-over; Star-Lord and Jack Flagg vs. Blastaar at the super-villain prison in the Negative Zone. 10-War of Kings x-over; Blastaar & Reed Richards app. Star-Lord reunited with the Guardians. 11-Drax and Quasar (Phyla-Vell) story; Maelstrom & Dragon of the Moon app. 12-Moondragon returns; Quasar (Wendell Vaughn) regains the Quantum-bands becomes Protector of the Universe; Maelstrom & Oblivion app; Phyla-Vell becomes new Avatar of Death 1 3 4 6 8 10
13-War of Kings x-over; Phyla-Vell changes name to 'Martyr'; Moondragon & Jack Flagg join the Guardians; Warlock, Drax & Gamora return to Guardians; Black Bolt & the Inhumans, Vulcan, ruler of the Shi'ar Empire and the Starjammers app.; story continues on War of Kings #3 2 4 6 8 10 12
14-20: 14-War of Kings x-over; Warlock vs. Vulcan; Guardians vs. the Inhumans. 15-War of Kings x-over; Guardians vs. the Sh'iar; Black Bolt & the Inhumans app. 16-War of Kings x-over; Star-Lord, Bug, Jack Flagg, Mantis & Cosmo vs. the Badoon; original Guardians: Martinex, Youndu, Charlie-27, Starhawk and Major Victory app. 17-War of Kings x-over; 'death' of Warlock & Martyr; return of the Magus. 18-Star-Lord, Mantis, Cosmo, Bug & Jack Flagg in alternate future 3000AD; Killraven & Hollywood (Wonder Man) app.; vs. the Martians; original Guardians app.; Starhawk, Charlie-27 & Nikki. 19-Kang app.; 'death' of Martyr & Warlock again; 'death' of Major Victory, Gamora, Cosmo & Mantis. 20-Realm of Kings x-over; Star-Lord, Groot, Rocket Raccoon, Bug, Jack Flagg, Drax & Moondragon appear as the Guardians 1 3 4 6 8 10
17-Variant 70th Anniversary Frame-c by Perkins 2 4 6 11 16 20
21-Realm of Kings x-over; brief appearance of the Cancerverse 2 4 6 8 10 12
22,23: 23-Realm of Kings x-over; the Magus returns. 23-Martyr, Gamora, Cosmo, Mantis & Major Victory return to life; Magus app. 2 4 6 9 12 15
23-Deadpool Variant-c by Alex Garner 3 6 9 17 26 35
24-Realm of Kings x-over; Thanos returns, kills Martyr; Maelstrom app. 3 6 9 14 20 25
25-Last issue; Guardians vs. Thanos; leads into Thanos Imperative #1 3 6 9 16 23 30
25-Variant-c by Skottie Young 2 4 6 11 16 20

GUARDIANS OF THE GALAXY (Marvel NOW!) (Also see the 2013 Nova series) (See Incredible Hulk #271, Iron Man #55, Marvel Preview #4,7, Strange Tales #180 and Tales to Astonish #13 for 1st app. of 2014 movie characters)
Marvel Comics: No. 0.1, Apr, 2013; No. 1, May, 2013 - No. 27, Jul, 2015 ($3.99)

0.1-(4/13) Origin of Star-Lord; Bendis-s/McNiven-a 5.00
1-Bendis-s/McNiven-a; Iron Man app.; at least 15 variant covers exist 2 4 6 8 10 12
2-4: Iron Man app. 1 2 3 5 6 8
5-Angela & Thanos app. 5.00
6-13: 8,9-Infinity tie-in; Francavilla-a/c. 10-Maguire-a. 11-13-Trial of Jean Grey 4.00
14-($4.99) Venom and Captain Marvel app.; Bradshaw-a; Guardians of 3014 app. 5.00
15-24,26,27: 16,17-Angela app. 18-20-Original Sin tie-in; Thanos app. 23-Origin of the Symbiotes. 24-Black Vortex crossover 4.00
25-($4.99)-Black Vortex crossover; Kree homeworld destroyed 5.00
Annual 1 (2/15, $4.99) Bendis-s/Cho-a; Nick Fury, Dum Dum, Skrulls app. 5.00
...: Best Story Ever 1 (6/15, $3.99) Tim Seeley-s; Nebula & Thanos app. 4.00
...: Galaxy's Most Wanted 1 (9/14, $3.99) Rocket & Groot; DiVito-a; r/Thor #314 Drax app. 4.00
100th Anniversary Special: Guardians of the Galaxy (9/14, $3.99) Future Guardians 4.00
...: Tomorrow's Avengers 1 (9/13, $4.99) Short stories; art by various 5.00
Marvel's Guardians of the Galaxy Prelude 1,2 (6/14 - No. 2, 7/14, $2.99) 1-Gamora & Nebula app. 2-Rocket & Groot 3.00

GUARDIANS OF THE GALAXY
Marvel Comics: Dec, 2015 - No. 19, Jun, 2017 ($3.99)

1-18: 1-Rocket, Groot, Drax, Venom, The Thing and Kitty Pryde team; Bendis-s. 12,13-Civil War II tie-ins. 12-Avengers app. 14-Spider-Man app.; Maguire-a 4.00
19-($4.99) Thanos and Annihilus app.; Schiti, Noto, Pichelli, Bagley & others-a 5.00
1.MU (Monsters Unleashed) (5/17, $4.99) Baldeón-a/Walsh-c 5.00
... Dream On 1 (6/17, $3.99) Death's Head app.; r/1st Taserface from GOTG #1 (1990) 4.00
... Mission Breakout 1 (7/17, $4.99) Hastings-s/Salazar-a; The Collector app. 5.00

GUARDIANS OF THE GALAXY (Marvel Legacy)
Marvel Comics: No. 146, Jan, 2018 - No. 150, Mar, 2018 ($3.99)

146-149: 146-Ant-Man joins; Nova Corps app.; Duggan-s/To-a 4.00
150-($4.99) Lenticular-c by Ross; Adam Warlock returns 5.00

GUARDIANS OF THE GALAXY
Marvel Comics: Mar, 2019 - No. 12, Feb, 2020 ($4.99/$3.99)

1-($4.99) Cates-s/Shaw-a; Cosmic Ghost Rider, Silver Surfer, Beta Ray Bill & others join 5.00
2-11-($3.99) 2-Hela & The Collector app. 4.00
12-($4.99) Donny Cates-s/Cory Smith-a 5.00
Annual 1 (8/19, $4.99) Takes place before issue #7; Cosmo, Quasar, Adam Warlock app. 5.00
...: Marvel Presents No. 3 Facsimile Ed. (3/19, $3.99) r/Marvel Presents #3 w/original ads 4.00
...: The Prodigal Sun 1 (11/19, $4.99) Peter David-s/Francesco Manna-a 5.00

GUARDIANS OF THE GALAXY
Marvel Comics: Mar, 2020 - Present ($4.99/$3.99)

1-($4.99) Al Ewing-s/Juann Cabal-a; Nova (Richard Rider) and Marvel Boy app. 5.00
2-10-($3.99) 3-5-Blackjack O'Hare app. 10-King in Black tie-in 4.00

GUARDIANS OF THE GALAXY ADAPTATION ("... Vol. 2 Prelude" on cover)
Marvel Comics: Mar, 2017 - No. 2, Apr, 2017 ($3.99, limited series)

1,2-Adaptation of the 2014 movie; Corona Pilgrim-s/Chris Allen-a 4.00

GUARDIANS OF THE GALAXY & X-MEN: THE BLACK VORTEX
Marvel Comics: Alpha, Apr, 2015 - Omega, Jun, 2015 ($4.99, bookends for crossover)

... Alpha (4/15) Part 1 of crossover; McGuinness-a 5.00
... Omega (6/15) Part 13 of crossover; Ronan app.; McGuinness-a 5.00

GUARDIANS OF THE GALAXY: MOTHER ENTROPY
Marvel Comics: Jul, 2017 - No. 5, Jul, 2017 ($3.99, weekly limited series)

1-5-Starlin-s/Alan Davis-a; Pip the Troll app. 4-Gladiator app. 4.00

GUARDIANS TEAM-UP
Marvel Comics: May, 2015 - No. 10, Oct, 2015 ($3.99)

1-10: 1-Bendis-s/Art Adams-a. 1,2-The Avengers & Nebula app. 3-Black Vortex crossover.

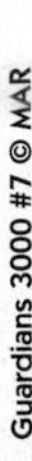

Guardians 3000 #7 © MAR

The Gumps #5 © News Synd.

Guns Against Gangsters #6 © NOVP

	GD	VG	FN	VF	VF/NM	NM-
	2.0	4.0	6.0	8.0	9.0	9.2

4-Gamora & She-Hulk. 7-Drax & Ant-Man. 9-Spider-Man & Star-Lord; Pulido-s/a. 10-Deadpool & Rocket 4.00

GUARDIANS OF THE GALAXY: TELLTALE GAMES (Based on the videogame)
Marvel Comics: Sept, 2017 - No. 5, Jan, 2018 ($3.99, limited series)
1-5: 1-Van Lente-s/Espin-a. 2-5-Cosmo app. 5-Thanos app. 4.00

GUARDIANS 3000
Marvel Comics: Dec, 2014 - No. 8, Jul, 2015 ($3.99)
1-8: 1-Abnett-s/Sandoval-a; Alex Ross-c; Guardians vs. Badoon in 3014 A.D. 1-6-Ross-c. 6-Guardians meet the 2015 Guardians 4.00

GUARDING THE GLOBE (See Invincible)
Image Comics: Aug, 2010 - No. 6, Oct, 2011 ($3.50)
1-6-Kirkman & Cereno-s/Getty-a. 1-Back-c swipe of Avengers #4 w/Obama 3.50

GUARDING THE GLOBE (2nd series) (See Invincible Universe)
Image Comics: Sept, 2012 - No. 6, Feb, 2013 ($2.99)
1-6: 1-Wraparound-c; Hester-s/Nauck-a 3.00

GUERRILLA WAR (Formerly Jungle War Stories)
Dell Publishing Co.: No. 12, July-Sept, 1965 - No. 14, Mar, 1966
12-14 3 6 9 15 22 28

GUIDEBOOK TO THE MARVEL CINEMATIC UNIVERSE
Marvel Comics: Dec, 2015 - Feb, 2017 ($3.99)
... - Marvel's Agents of S.H.I.E.L.D. Season One (8/16, $3.99) Profile pages 4.00
... - Marvel's Agents of S.H.I.E.L.D. Season Two/Marvel's Agent Carter Season One (12/16, $3.99) Flipbook with character profile pages; both covers by Marcos Martin 4.00
... - Marvel's Agents of S.H.I.E.L.D. Season Three/Marvel's Agent Carter Season Two (2/17, $3.99) Flipbook with character profile pages; covers by Del Mundo & Johnson 4.00
... - Marvel's Avengers: Age of Ultron (11/16, $3.99) Profile pages of characters 4.00
... - Marvel's Captain America: Civil War (3/17, $3.99) Profile pages 4.00
... - Marvel's Captain America: The First Avenger (3/16, $3.99) Profile pages 4.00
... - Marvel's Captain America: The Winter Soldier/Marvel's Ant-Man (7/16, $3.99) Flipbook 4.00
... - Marvel's Doctor Strange (5/17, $3.99) Profile pages of characters, weapons, locations 4.00
... - Marvel's Guardians of the Galaxy (9/16, $3.99) Profile pages of characters, locations 4.00
... - Marvel's Incredible Hulk/Marvel's Iron Man 2 (1/16, $3.99) Flipbook; profile pages 4.00
... - Marvel's Iron Man (12/15, $3.99) Profile pages of characters, weapons, locations 4.00
... - Marvel's Iron Man 3/Marvel's Thor: The Dark World (6/16, $3.99) Flipbook profiles 4.00
... - Marvel's The Avengers (4/16, $3.99) Profile pages of characters, weapons 4.00
... - Marvel's Thor (2/16, $3.99) Profile pages of characters, weapons, locations 4.00

GUILD, THE (Based on the web-series)
Dark Horse Comics: Mar, 2010 - No. 3, May, 2010 ($3.50, limited series)
1-3-Felicia Day-s/Jim Rugg-a; two covers on each 3.50
... Bladezz 1 (6/11, $3.50) Currie-a/Kerschl-c; variant-c by Dalrymple 3.50
... Clara 1 (9/11, $3.50) Chan-a/Chaykin-c; variant-c by Aronowitz 3.50
... Fawkes 1 (5/12, $3.50) Day & Wheaton-s/McKelvie-a; variant-c by Rios 3.50
... Tink 1 (3/11, $3.50) art by Donaldson, Warren, Seeley & others; variant-c by Bagge 3.50
... Vork 1 (12/10, $3.50) Robertson-a/c; variant-c by Hernandez 3.50
... Zaboo 1 (12/11, $3.50) Cloonan-a/Dorkin-c; variant-c by Jeanty 3.50

GUILTY (See Justice Traps the Guilty)

GULLIVER'S TRAVELS (See Dell Jr. Treasury No. 3)
Dell Publishing Co.: Sept-Nov, 1965
1 5 10 15 31 53 75

GUMBY
Wildcard Ink: July, 2006 - No. 3 ($3.99)
1-3-Bob Burden & Rick Geary-s&a 4.00

GUMBY'S SUMMER FUN SPECIAL
Comico: July, 1987 ($2.50)
1-Art Adams-c/a; B. Burden scripts 5.00

GUMBY'S WINTER FUN SPECIAL
Comico: Dec, 1988 ($2.50, 44 pgs.)
1-Art Adams-c/a 5.00

GUMPS, THE (See Merry Christmas..., Popular & Super Comics)
Dell Publ. Co./Bridgeport Herald Corp.: No. 73, 1945; Mar-Apr, 1947 - No. 5, Nov-Dec, 1947
Four Color 73 (Dell)(1945) 12 24 36 82 179 275
1 (3-4/47) 17 34 51 103 162 220
2-5 11 22 33 62 86 110

GUN CANDY (Also see The Ride)
Image Comics: July, 2005 - No. 2 ($5.99)
1,2-Stelfreeze-c/a; flip book with The Ride (1-Pearson-c. 2-Noto-c) 6.00

GUNFIGHTER (Fat & Slat #1-4) (Becomes Haunt of Fear #15 on)
E. C. Comics (Fables Publ. Co.): No. 5, Sum, 1948 - No. 14, Mar-Apr, 1950
5,6-Moon Girl in each 68 136 204 435 743 1050
7-14: 13,14-Bondage-c 48 96 144 302 514 725
NOTE: ***Craig & H. C. Kiefer*** *art in most issues.* ***Craig*** *c-5, 6, 13, 14.* ***Feldstein/Craig*** *a-10.* ***Feldstein*** *a-7-11.* ***Harrison/Wood*** *a-13, 14.* ***Ingels*** *a-5-14; c-7-12.*

GUNFIGHTERS, THE
Super Comics (Reprints): 1963 - 1964
10-12,15,16,18: 10,11-r/Billy the Kid #s? 12-r/The Rider #5(Swift Arrow). 15-r/Straight Arrow #42; Powell-r. 16-r/Billy the Kid #?(Toby). 18-r/The Rider #3; Severin-c
2 4 6 10 14 18

GUNFIGHTERS, THE (Formerly Kid Montana)
Charlton Comics: No. 51, 10/66 - No. 52, 10/67; No. 53, 6/79 - No. 85, 7/84
51,52 2 4 6 11 16 20
53,54,56:53,54-Williamson/Torres-r/Six Gun Heroes #47,49. 56-Williamson/Severin-c; Severin-r/Sheriff of Tombstone #1 1 3 4 6 8 10
55,57-80 6.00
81-84-Lower print run 1 2 3 5 6 8
85-S&K-r/1955 Bullseye 1 3 4 6 8 10

GUNFIRE (See Deathstroke Annual #2 & Showcase 94 #1,2)
DC Comics: May, 1994 - No. 13, June, 1995 ($1.75/$2.25)
1-5,0,6-13: 2-Ricochet-c/story. 5-(9/94). 0-(10/94). 6-(11/94) 3.00

GUN GLORY (Movie)
Dell Publishing Co.: No. 846, Oct, 1957 (one-shot)
Four Color 846-Toth-a, photo-c. 8 16 24 51 96 140

GUNHAWK, THE (Formerly Whip Wilson)(See Wild Western and Two-Gun Western #5)
Marvel Comics/Atlas (MCI): No. 12, Nov, 1950 - No. 18, Dec, 1951
12 22 44 66 132 216 300
13-18: 13-Tuska-a. 16-Colan-a. 18-Maneely-c 15 30 45 92 144 195

GUNHAWKS (Gunhawk No. 7)
Marvel Comics Group: Oct, 1972 - No. 7, October, 1973
1,6: 1-Reno Jones, Kid Cassidy; Shores-c/a(p). 6-Kid Cassidy dies
4 8 12 23 37 50
2-5,7: 7-Reno Jones solo 2 4 6 13 18 22

GUNHAWKS, THE (Marvel 80th Anniversary salute to western comics)
Marvel Comics: Apr, 2019 ($3.99, one shot)
1-David & Maria Lapham-s/Luca Pizzari-a 4.00

GUNMASTER (Becomes Judo Master #89 on)
Charlton Comics: 9/64 - No. 4, 1965; No. 84, 7/65 - No. 88, 3-4/66; No. 89, 10/67
V1#1 4 8 12 27 44 60
2-4, V5#84-86: 84-Formerly Six-Gun Heroes 3 6 9 15 22 28
V5#87-89 2 4 6 11 16 20
NOTE: *Vol. 5 was originally cancelled with #88 (3-4/66). #89 on, became Judo Master, then later in 1967, Charlton issued #89 as a Gunmaster one-shot.*

GUNNING FOR HITS
Image Comics: Jan, 2019 - No. 6, Jun, 2019 ($3.99)
1-6-Jeff Rougvie-s/Moritat-a 4.00

GUN RUNNER
Marvel Comics UK: Oct, 1993 - No. 6, Mar, 1994 ($1.75, limited series)
1-($2.75)-Polybagged w/4 trading cards; Spirits of Vengeance app. 5.00
2-6: 2-Ghost Rider & Blaze app. 4.00

GUNS AGAINST GANGSTERS (True-To-Life Romances #8 on)
Curtis Publications/Novelty Press: Sept-Oct, 1948 - No. 6, July-Aug, 1949; V2#1, Sept-Oct, 1949
1-Toni & Greg Gayle begins by Schomburg; L.B. Cole-c
52 104 156 328 552 775
2-L.B. Cole-c 37 74 111 222 361 500
3-5 33 66 99 196 321 445
6-Giant shark and Toni Gayle-c by Cole 110 220 330 704 1202 1700
V2#1 31 62 93 186 303 420
NOTE: ***L. B. Cole*** *c-1-6, V2#1, 2; a-1, 2, 3(2), 4-6.*

GUNSLINGER
Dell Publishing Co.: No. 1220, Oct-Dec, 1961 (one-shot)
Four Color 1220-Photo-c 8 16 24 52 99 145

GUNSLINGER (Formerly Tex Dawson...)
Marvel Comics Group: No. 2, Apr, 1973 - No. 3, June, 1973
2,3 2 4 6 13 18 22

Gunsmoke Western #68 © MAR

Gwenpool Strikes Back #1 © MAR

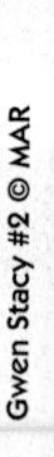

Gwen Stacy #2 © MAR

	GD 2.0	VG 4.0	FN 6.0	VF 8.0	VF/NM 9.0	NM- 9.2

GUNSLINGERS
Marvel Comics: Feb, 2000 ($2.99)

1-Reprints stories of Two-Gun Kid, Rawhide Kid and Caleb Hammer 3.00

GUNSMITH CATS: (Title series), **Dark Horse Comics**

--**BAD TRIP** (Manga), 6/98 - No. 6, 11/98 ($2.95, B&W) 1-6 3.00
--**BEAN BANDIT** (Manga), 1/99 - No. 9 ($2.95, B&W, limited series) 1-9 3.00
--**GOLDIE VS. MISTY** (Manga), 11/97 - No. 7, 5/98 ($2.95, B&W) 1-7 3.00
--**KIDNAPPED** (Manga), 11/99 - No. 10, 8/00 ($2.95, B&W) 1-10 3.00
--**MISTER V** (Manga), 10/00 - No. 11, 8/01 ($3.50/$2.99), B&W) 1-11 3.50
--**THE RETURN OF GRAY** (Manga), 8/96 - No. 7, 2/97 ($2.95, B&W) 1-7 3.00
--**SHADES OF GRAY** (Manga), 5/97 - No. 5, 9/97 ($2.95, B&W) 1-5 3.00
--**SPECIAL** (Manga) Nov, 2001 ($2.99, B&W, one-shot) 3.00

GUNSMOKE (Blazing Stories of the West)
Western Comics (Youthful Magazines): Apr-May, 1949 - No. 16, Jan, 1952

	GD	VG	FN	VF	VF/NM	NM-
1-Gunsmoke & Masked Marvel begin by Ingels; Ingels bondage-c	55	110	165	352	601	850
2-Ingels-c/a(2)	35	70	105	208	339	470
3-Ingels bondage-c/a	30	60	90	177	289	400
4-6: Ingels-c	24	48	72	142	234	325
7-10	15	30	45	94	147	200
11-16: 15,16-Western/horror stories	15	30	45	90	140	190

NOTE: ***Stallman** a-11, 14. **Wildey** a-15, 16.*

GUNSMOKE (TV)
Dell Publishing Co./Gold Key (All have James Arness photo-c): No. 679, Feb, 1956 - No. 27, Feb, 1969 - No. 6, Feb, 1970

	GD	VG	FN	VF	VF/NM	NM-
Four Color 679(#1)	17	34	51	119	265	410
Four Color 720,769,797,844 (#2-5),6(11-1/57-58)	9	18	27	59	117	175
7,8,9,11,12-Williamson-a in all, 4 pgs. each	8	16	24	54	102	150
10-Williamson/Crandall-a, 4 pgs.	8	16	24	54	102	150
13-27	7	14	21	44	82	120
1 (Gold Key)	7	14	21	44	82	120
2-6('69-70)	4	8	12	23	37	50

GUNSMOKE TRAIL
Ajax-Farrell Publ./Four Star Comic Corp.: June, 1957 - No. 4, Dec, 1957

	GD	VG	FN	VF	VF/NM	NM-
1	11	22	33	60	83	105
2-4	7	14	21	35	43	50

GUNSMOKE WESTERN (Formerly Western Tales of Black Rider)
Atlas Comics No. 32-35(CPS/NPI); Marvel No. 36 on: No. 32, Dec, 1955 - No. 77, July, 1963

	GD	VG	FN	VF	VF/NM	NM-
32-Baker & Drucker-a	27	54	81	158	259	360
33,35,36-Williamson-a in each: 5,6 & 4 pgs. plus Drucker-a #33. 33-Kinstler-a?	19	38	57	111	176	240
34-Baker-a, 4 pgs.; Severin-c	20	40	60	114	182	250
37-Davis-a(2); Williamson text illo	15	30	45	90	140	190
38,39: 39-Williamson text illo (unsigned)	14	28	42	82	121	160
40-Williamson/Mayo-a (4 pgs.)	15	30	45	84	127	170
41,42,45,46,48,49,52-54,57,58,60: 49,52-Kid from Texas story. 57-1st Two Gun Kid by Severin. 60-Sam Hawk app. in Kid Colt	13	26	39	74	105	135
43,44-Torres-a	13	26	39	74	105	135
47,51,59,61: 47,51,59-Kirby-a. 61-Crandall-a	14	28	42	80	115	150
50-Kirby, Crandall-a	15	30	45	84	127	170
55,56-Matt Baker-a	15	30	45	86	133	180
62-67,69,71-73,77-Kirby-a. 72-Origin Kid Colt	8	16	24	51	96	140
68,70,74-76: 68-(10¢-c)	7	14	21	46	86	125
68-(10¢ cover price blacked out, 12¢ printed on)	13	26	39	89	195	310

NOTE: ***Colan** a-35-37, 39, 72, 76. **Davis** a-37, 52, 54, 55; c-50, 54. **Ditko** a-66; c-56p. **Drucker** a-.32-34. **Heath** c-33. **Jack Keller** a-34, 35, 40, 51, 53, 55, 56, 60, 61, 65, 68, 69, 71, 72, 74, 75, 77; c-72. **Kirby** a-47, 50, 51, 59, 62(3), 63-67, 69, 71, 73, 77; c-56(w/**Ditko**), 57, 58, 60, 61(w/**Ayers**), 62, 63, 65, 66, 68, 69, 71-77. **Maneely** a-53; c-45. **Robinson** a-35. **Severin** a-35, 59-61; c-34, 35, 39, 42, 43. **Tuska** a-34. **Wildey** a-10, 37, 42, 56, 57. Kid Colt in all. Two-Gun Kid in No. 57, 59, 60-63. Wyatt Earp in No. 45, 48, 49, 51-56, 58.*

GUNS OF FACT & FICTION (Also see A-1 Comics)
Magazine Enterprises: No. 13, 1948 (one-shot)

	GD	VG	FN	VF	VF/NM	NM-
A-1 13-Used in **SOTI**, pg. 19; Ingels & J. Craig-a	31	62	93	186	303	420

GUNS OF THE DRAGON
DC Comics: Oct, 1998 - No. 4, Jan, 1999 ($2.50, limited series)

1-4-DCU in the 1920's; Enemy Ace & Bat Lash app. 3.00

GUNWITCH, THE : OUTSKIRTS OF DOOM (See The Nocturnals)
Oni Press: June, 2001 - No. 3, Oct, 2001 ($2.95, B&W, limited series)

1-3-Brereton-s/painted-c/Naifeh-s 3.00

GUY GARDNER (Guy Gardner: Warrior #17 on)(Also see Green Lantern #59)
DC Comics: Oct, 1992 - No. 44, July, 1996 ($1.25/$1.50/$1.75)

1-Staton-c/a(p) begins 4.00
2-24,0,26-30: 6-Guy vs. Hal Jordan. 8-Vs. Lobo-c/story. 15-JLA x-over, begin $1.50-c. 18-Begin 4-part Emerald Fallout story; splash page x-over GL #50. 18-21-Vs. Hal Jordan. 24-(9/94)-Zero Hour. 0-(10/94) 3.00
25 (11/94, $2.50, 52 pgs.) 4.00
29 ($2.95)-Gatefold-c 4.00
29-Variant-c (Edward Hopper's Nighthawks) 3.00
31-44: 31-$1.75-c begins. 40-Gorilla Grodd-c/app. 44-Parallax-app. (1 pg.) 3.00
Annual 1 (1995, $3.50)-Year One story 4.00
Annual 2 (1996, $2.95)-Legends of the Dead Earth story 4.00

GUY GARDNER: COLLATERAL DAMAGE
DC Comics: 2006 - No. 2 ($5.99, square-bound, limited series)

1,2-Howard Chaykin-s/a 6.00

GUY GARDNER REBORN
DC Comics: 1992 - Book 3, 1992 ($4.95, limited series)

1-3: Staton-c/a(p). 1-Lobo-c/cameo. 2,3-Lobo-c/s 6.00

GWAR: ORGASMAGEDDON (Based on the band GWAR)
Dynamite Entertainment: 2017 - No. 4, 2017 ($3.99, limited series)

1-4-Matt Maguire & Matt Miner-s/Sawyer & Maguire-a; multiple covers 4.00

GWENPOOL (Also see Unbelievable Gwenpool)
Marvel Comics: Feb, 2016; Feb, 2017 ($5.99, one-shots)

... Holiday Special: Merry Mix-Up (2/17, $5.99) 1-Deadpool, Squirrel Girl, Punisher app. 6.00
... Special (2/16, $5.99) 1-Christmas-themed short stories; She-Hulk, Deadpool app. 6.00

GWENPOOL STRIKES BACK
Marvel Comics: Oct, 2019 - No. 5, Feb, 2020 ($3.99, limited series)

1-5-Leah Williams-s/David Baldeón-a. 1-Spider-Man app. 3-5-Ms. Marvel app. 5-Photo-c 4.00

GWEN STACY
Marvel Comics: Apr, 2020 - Present ($4.99/$3.99)

1-($4.99) Gage-s/Nauck-a; main cover by Adam Hughes; Gwen in high school 5.00
2-($3.99) Norman Osborn app. 4.00

GYPSY COLT
Dell Publishing Co.: No. 568, June, 1954 (one-shot)

	GD	VG	FN	VF	VF/NM	NM-
Four Color 568-Movie	5	10	15	35	63	90

GYRO GEARLOOSE (See Dynabrite Comics, Walt Disney's C&S #140 & Walt Disney Showcase #18)
Dell Publishing Co.: No. 1047, Nov-Jan/1959-60 - May-July, 1962 (Disney)

	GD	VG	FN	VF	VF/NM	NM-
Four Color 1047 (No. 1)-All Barks-c/a	15	30	45	103	227	350
Four Color 1095,1184-All by Carl Barks	9	18	27	59	117	175
Four Color 1267-Barks c/a, 4 pgs.	7	14	21	48	89	130
01329-207 (#1, 5-7/62)-Barks-c only (intended as 4-Color 1329?)	5	10	15	35	63	90

HACKER FILES, THE
DC Comics: Aug, 1992 - No. 12, July, 1993 ($1.95)

1-12: 1-Sutton-a(p) begins; computer generated-c 3.00

HACK/SLASH
Devil's Due Publishing: Apr. 2004 - No. 32, Mar, 2010 ($3.25/$4.95)

	GD	VG	FN	VF	VF/NM	NM-
1-Seeley-s/Caselli-a/c	4	8	12	27	44	60
...: (The Series) 1-5,7-24,26,27,29-32 (5/07-No. 32, 3/10, $3.50) Flashack to Cassie's childhood and origin. 12-Milk & Cheese cameo. 15-Re-Animator app.						5.00
6,28-Archie parodies	2	4	6	11	16	20
25-($5.50) Double sized issue; Baugh-a; two covers						5.50
...: Comic Book Carnage (3/05) Manfredi-a/Seeley-s; Robert Kirkman & Steve Niles app.						5.00
...: First Cut TPB (10/05, $14.95) r/one-shots with sketch pages, designs, interviews						15.00
...: Girls Gone Dead (10/04, $4.95) Manfredi-a	1	2	3	5	6	8
...: Land of Lost Toys 1-3 (11/05 - No. 3, 1/06, $3.25) Crossland-a/Seeley-s						4.00
...: New Reader Halloween Treat #1 (10/08, $3.50) origin retold; Cassie's diary pages						5.00
...: The Final Revenge of Evil Ernie (6/05, $4.95) Salman-a/Seeley-s; two covers						5.00
...: Trailers (2/05, $3.25) short stories by Seeley; art by various; three covers						4.00
...: Slice Hard (12/05, $4.95) Seeley-s						5.00
...: Slice Hard Pre-Sliced 25¢ Special (2/06, 25¢) origin story by Seeley; sketch pages						3.00
...: Vs Chucky (3/07, $5.50) Seeley-s/Merhoff-a; 3 covers						5.50
...: Vol. 2 Death By Sequel TPB (1/07, $18.99) r/Land of Lost Toys #1-3, Trailers, Slice Hard						19.00
...: Vol. 3 Friday the 31st TPB (10/07, $18.99) r/The Series #1-4 & ... Vs Chucky						19.00

HACK/SLASH
Image Comics: Jun, 2010 - No. 25, Mar, 2013 ($3.50)

Hack/Slash #19 © Hack/Slash Inc.

Ha Ha Comics #10 © ACG

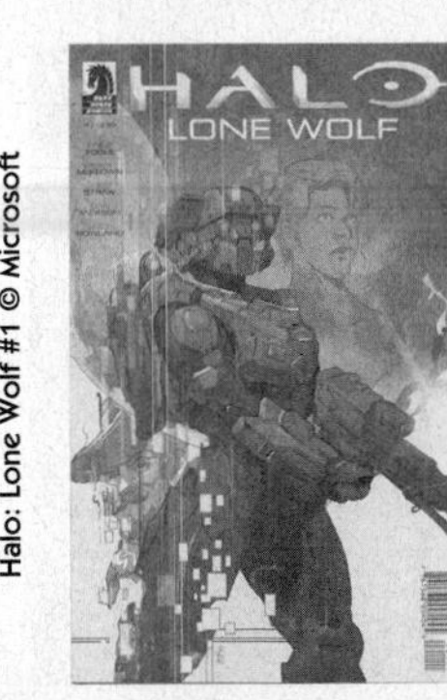

Halo: Lone Wolf #1 © Microsoft

	GD 2.0	VG 4.0	FN 6.0	VF 8.0	VF/NM 9.0	NM- 9.2
1-25: 1-(2/11, $3.50) Seeley-s/Leister-a. 5-Esquejo-c. 9-11-Bomb Queen app.						5.00
... Annual 2010: Murder Messiah (10/10, $5.99) Seeley-s/Morales-a						6.00
... Annual 2011: Hatchet/Slash (11/11, $5.99)						6.00
.../ Eva: Monster's Ball 1-4 (Dynamite Ent., 2011 - No. 4, 2011, $3.99) Jerwa-s/Razek-a						4.00
... 15th Anniversary Celebration (12/19, $5.99) Cassie appears in the real world; pin-ups						6.00
...: Me Without You (1/11, $3.50) Leister-a/Seeley-s; 2 covers						4.00
.../ Nailbiter 1 (3/15, $4.99) Flip book with Nailbiter / Hack/Slash 1						5.00
...: Son of Samhain 1-5 (7/14- No. 5, 11/14) Laiso-a/Moreci & Seeley-s	2	4	6	10	14	18
...: Trailers #2 (11/10, $6.99) short stories; story & art by various; Seeley-c						7.00
Image Firsts: Hack/Slash #1 (10/10, $1.00) r/#1 (2004) with "Image Firsts" cover frame						4.00

HACK SLASH: MY FIRST MANIAC
Image Comics: Jun, 2010 - No. 4, Sept, 2010 ($3.99)

1-Leister-a/Seeley-s	1	2	3	5	6	8
2-4						5.00

HACK SLASH: RESURRECTION
Image Comics: Oct, 2017 - No. 12, Oct, 2018 ($3.99)

1-12-Tini Howard-s/Celor-a. 3-Vlad returns. 8-11-Vampirella app. 4.00

HACK/SLASH VS. CHAOS
Dynamite Entertainment: 2018 - No. 5, 2019 ($3.99)

1-5-Seeley-s; multiple covers; Evil Ernie, Chastity, Purgatori app. 1-Lobosco-a 4.00

HACK/SLASH VS. VAMPIRELLA
Dynamite Entertainment: 2017 - No. 5, 2018 ($3.99)

1-5-Aldridge-s/Lobosco-a; multiple covers 4.00

HACKTIVIST
Archaia Black Label: Jan, 2014 - No. 4, Apr, 2014 ($3.99)

1-4-Kelly & Lanzing-s/To-a; created by Alyssa Milano 4.00
... Volume 2 (BOOM! Ent.; 7/15 - No. 6, 12/15, $3.99) 1-6-Kelly & Lanzing-s/To-a 4.00

HAGAR THE HORRIBLE (See Comics Reading Libraries in the Promotional Comics section)

HA HA COMICS (Teepee Tim No. 100 on; also see Giggle Comics)
Scope Mag.(Creston Publ.) No. 1-80/American Comics Group: Oct, 1943 - No. 99, Jan, 1955

1-Funny animal	41	82	123	256	428	600
2	22	44	66	130	213	295
3-5: Ken Hultgren-a begins?	17	34	51	98	154	210
6-10	14	28	42	81	118	155
11-20: 14-Infinity-c	13	26	39	72	101	130
21-40	11	22	33	62	86	110
41-43,45-94,97-99: 49,61-X-Mas-c	10	20	30	56	76	95
44-1st Tee-Pee Tim app.; begin series; Little Black Sambo app.	11	22	33	62	86	110
95,96-3-D effect-c/story	18	36	54	105	165	225

HAIL HYDRA (Secret Wars tie-in)
Marvel Comics: Sept, 2015 - No. 4, Jan, 2016 ($3.99, limited series)

1-4-Nomad (Ian Rogers) vs. Hydra; Remender-s/Boschi-a; Venom app. 4.00

HAIR BEAR BUNCH, THE (TV) (See Fun-In No. 13)
Gold Key: Feb, 1972 - No. 9, Feb, 1974 (Hanna-Barbera)

1	4	8	12	23	37	50
2-9	3	6	9	16	24	32

HALCYON
Image Comics: Nov, 2010 - No. 5, May, 2011 ($2.99)

1-5-Guggenheim & Butters-s/Bodenheim-a 3.00

HALF PAST DANGER
IDW Publishing: May, 2013 - No. 6, Oct, 2013 ($3.99, limited series)

1-6: Dinosaurs and Nazis in 1943; Stephen Mooney-s/a/c 4.00

HALF PAST DANGER 2
IDW Publishing: Sept, 2017 - No. 5, Jan, 2018 ($3.99, limited series)

1-5-Nazis in 1943; Stephen Mooney-s/a/c 4.00

HAL JORDAN AND THE GREEN LANTERN CORPS (DC Rebirth) (Also see Green Lanterns)
DC Comics: Sept, 2016 - No. 50, Early Oct, 2018 ($2.99)

1-24: 1-Venditti-s/Sandoval-a; Sinestro app.; GL Corps returns. 4,5,17,22-24-Van Sciver-a. 10-12-Larfleeze app. Kyle becomes a Green Lantern again 3.00
25-($3.99) Van Sciver-a 4.00
26-49: 26,27-Orion of the New Gods app. 30,31-Superman app. 32-Dark Nights: Metal. 37-41-Zod app. 42-Darkstars return. 42,45-Van Sciver-a 3.00
50-($3.99) Sandoval-a; Zod app.

	GD 2.0	VG 4.0	FN 6.0	VF 8.0	VF/NM 9.0	NM- 9.2
...: Rebirth 1 (9/16, $2.99) Venditti-s/Van Sciver-a; Sinestro & Lyssa app.						3.00

HALLELUJAH TRAIL, THE (See Movie Classics)

HALL OF FAME FEATURING THE T.H.U.N.D.E.R. AGENTS
JC Productions(Archie Comics Group): May, 1983 - No. 3, Dec, 1983

1-3: Thunder Agents-r(Crandall, Kane, Tuska, Wood-a). 2-New Ditko-c 4.00

HALLOWEEN (Movie)
Chaos! Comics: Nov, 2000; Apr, 2001 ($2.95/$2.99, one-shots)

1-Brewer-a; Michael Myers childhood at the Sanitarium 4.00
...II: The Blackest Eyes (4/01, $2.99) Beck-a 4.00
...III: The Devil's Eyes (11/01, $2.99) Justiniano-a 4.00

HALLOWEEN (Halloween Nightdance on cover)(Movie)
Devils Due Publishing: Mar, 2008 - No. 4, May, 2008 ($3.50, limited series)

1-4-Seeley-a/Hutchinson-s; multiple covers on each 3.50
...: 30 Years of Terror (8/08, $5.50) short stories by various incl. Seeley 5.50

HALLOWEEN EVE
Image Comics: Oct, 2012 ($3.99, one-shot)

One-Shot - Brandon Montclare-s/Amy Reeder-a; two covers by Reeder 4.00

HALLOWEEN HORROR
Eclipse Comics: Oct, 1987 (Seduction of the Innocent #7)($1.75)

1-Pre-code horror-r 5.00

HALLOWEEN MEGAZINE
Marvel Comics: Dec, 1996 ($3.95, one-shot, 96 pgs.)

1-Reprints Tomb of Dracula 4.00

HALO GRAPHIC NOVEL (Based on video game)
Marvel Publishing Inc.: 2006 ($24.99, hardcover with dust jacket)

HC-Anthology set in the Halo universe; art by Bisley, Moebius and others; pin-up gallery by various incl. Darrow, Pratt, Williams and Van Fleet; Phil Hale painted-c 25.00

HALO: BLOOD LINE (Based on video game)
Marvel Comics: Feb, 2010 - No. 5, Jul, 2010 ($3.99, limited series)

1-5-Van Lente-s/Portela-a 4.00

HALO: COLLATERAL DAMAGE (Based on video game)
Dark Horse Comics: Jun, 2018 - No. 3, Aug, 2018 ($3.99)

1-3-Alex Irvine-s/Dave Crossland-a 4.00

HALO: ESCALATION (Based on video game)
Dark Horse Comics: Dec, 2013 - No. 24, Nov, 2015 ($3.99)

1-24: 1-4-Chris Schlerf-s/Sergio Ariño-a 4.00

HALO: FALL OF REACH - BOOT CAMP (Based on video game)
Marvel Comics: Nov, 2010 - No. 4, Apr, 2011 ($3.99, limited series)

1-4-Reed-s/Ruiz-a 4.00

HALO: FALL OF REACH - COVENANT (Based on video game)
Marvel Comics: Jun, 2011 - No. 4, Dec, 2011 ($3.99, limited series)

1-4-Reed-s/Ruiz-a 4.00

HALO: FALL OF REACH - INVASION (Based on video game)
Marvel Comics: Mar, 2012 - No. 4, Aug, 2012 ($3.99, limited series)

1-4-Reed-s/Ruiz-a 4.00

HALO: HELLJUMPER (Based on video game)
Marvel Comics: Sept, 2009 - No. 5, Jan, 2010 ($3.99, limited series)

1-5-Peter David-s/Eric Nguyen-a 4.00

HALO: INITIATION (Based on video game)
Dark Horse Comics: Aug, 2013 - No. 3, Oct, 2013 ($3.99, limited series)

1-3-Brian Reed-s/Marco Castiello-a 4.00

HALO: LONE WOLF (Based on video game)
Dark Horse Comics: Jan, 2019 - No. 4, Apr, 2019 ($3.99, limited series)

1-4-Toole-s/McKeown-a; spotlight on Linda-058 4.00

HALO: RISE OF ATRIOX (Based on video game)
Marvel Comics: Aug, 2017 - No. 5, Jan, 2018 ($3.99, limited series)

1-5: 1-Cullen Bunn-s/Eric Nguyen-a. 2-Houser-s/Gonzalez-a. 3-John Jackson Miller-s 4.00

HALO: UPRISING (Based on video game) (Also see Marvel Spotlight: Halo)
Marvel Comics: Oct, 2007 - No. 4, Jun, 2009 ($3.99, limited series)

1-4-Bendis-s/Maleev-a; takes place between the *Halo 2* and *Halo 3* video games 4.00

HALO JONES (See The Ballad of...)

HAMMER, THE

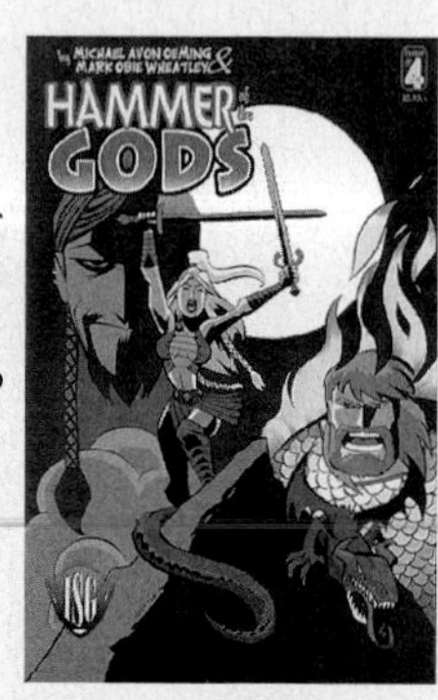

Hammer of the Gods #3 © Oeming & Wheatley

Hangman Comics #7 © MLJ

Hanna-Barbera All-Stars #3 © H-B

	GD	VG	FN	VF	VF/NM	NM-
	2.0	4.0	6.0	8.0	9.0	9.2

Dark Horse Comics: Oct, 1997 - No. 4, Jan, 1998 ($2.95, limited series)
1-4-Kelley Jones-s/c/a, ...: Uncle Alex (8/98, $2.95) 3.00

HAMMER, THE: THE OUTSIDER
Dark Horse Comics: Feb, 1999 - No. 3, Apr, 1999 ($2.95, limited series)
1-3-Kelley Jones-s/c/a 3.00

HAMMERLOCKE
DC Comics: Sept, 1992 - No. 9, May, 1993 ($1.75, limited series)
1-($2.50, 52 pgs.)-Chris Sprouse-c/a in all 4.00
2-9 3.00

HAMMER OF GOD (Also see Nexus)
First Comics: Feb, 1990 - No. 4, May, 1990 ($1.95, limited series)
1-4 3.00

HAMMER OF GOD: BUTCH
Dark Horse Comics: May, 1994 - No. 4, Aug, 1994 ($2.50, limited series)
1-3 3.00

HAMMER OF GOD: PENTATHLON
Dark Horse Comics: Jan, 1994 ($2.50, one shot)
1-Character from Nexus 3.00

HAMMER OF GOD: SWORD OF JUSTICE
First Comics: Feb 1991 - Mar 1991 ($4.95, lim. series, squarebound, 52 pgs.)
V2#1,2 5.00

HAMMER OF THE GODS
Insight Studio Groups: 2001 - No. 5, 2001 ($2.95, limited series)
1-Michael Oeming & Mark Wheatley-s/a; Frank Cho-c 6.00
1-(IDW, 7/11, $1.00) reprints #1 with "Hundred Penny Press" logo on Oeming cover 3.00
2-5: 3-Hughes-c. 5-Dave Johnson-c 3.00
The Color Saga (2002, $4.95) r/"Enemy of the Gods" internet strip 5.00
Mortal Enemy TPB (2002, $18.95) r/#1-5; intro. by Peter David; afterword by Raven 19.00

HAMMER OF THE GODS: HAMMER HITS CHINA
Image Comics: Feb, 2003 - No. 3, Sept, 2003 ($2.95, limited series)
1-3-Oeming & Wheatley-s/a; Oeming-c. 2-Frankenstein Mobster by Wheatley 3.00

HANDBOOK OF THE CONAN UNIVERSE, THE (Reprinted in The Official... Anniversary Ed.)
Marvel Comics: June, 1985; Jan, 1986 ($1.25, one-shot)
1-(6/85) Kaluta-c (2 printings) 6.00
1-(1/86) Kaluta-c 6.00
nn-(no date, circa '87-88, B&W, 36 pgs.) reprints '86 with changes; new painted cover 1 2 3 5 6 8

HAND OF FATE (Formerly Men Against Crime)
Ace Magazines: No. 8, Dec, 1951 - No. 25, Dec, 1954 (Weird/horror stories) (Two #25's)
8-Surrealistic text story 57 114 171 362 619 875
9,10,21-Necronomicon sty; drug belladonna used 39 78 117 240 395 550
11-18,20,22,23 33 66 99 196 321 445
19-Bondage, hypo needle scenes 37 74 111 222 361 500
24-Electric chair-c 43 86 129 271 461 650
25a(11/54), 25b(12/54)-Both have Cameron-a 32 64 96 192 314 435
NOTE: *Cameron a-9, 10, 19-25a, 25b; c-13. Sekowsky a-8, 9, 13, 14.*

HAND OF FATE
Eclipse Comics: Feb, 1988 - No. 3, Apr, 1988 ($1.75/$2.00, Baxter paper)
1-3; 3-B&W 4.00

HANDS OF THE DRAGON
Seaboard Periodicals (Atlas): June, 1975
1-Origin/1st app.; Craig-a(p)/Mooney inks 3 6 9 14 19 24

HANGMAN, THE
Archie Comic Publications: Dec, 2015 - No. 4, Dec, 2016 ($3.99)
1-4-Tieri-s/Ruiz-a; new Hangman recruited; multiple covers 4.00

HANGMAN COMICS (Special Comics No. 1; Black Hood No. 9 on)
(Also see Flyman, Mighty Comics, Mighty Crusaders & Pep Comics)
MLJ Magazines: No. 2, Spring, 1942 - No. 8, Fall, 1943
2-The Hangman, Boy Buddies begin 377 754 1131 2639 4620 6600
3-Beheading splash pg.; 1st Nazi war-c 423 846 1269 3000 5250 7500
4-Classic Nazi WWII hunchback torture-c 329 658 987 2303 4027 5750
5-1st Japan war-c 271 542 813 1734 2967 4200
6-8: 8-2nd app. Super Duck (ties w/Jolly Jingles #11) 245 490 735 1568 2684 3800
NOTE: *Fuje a-7(3), 8(3); c-3. Reinman c/a-3. Bondage c-3. Sahle c-6.*

HANK
Pentagon Publishing Co.: 1946
nn-Coulton Waugh's newspaper reprint 10 20 30 58 79 100

HANK JOHNSON, AGENT OF HYDRA (Secret Wars tie-in)
Marvel Comics: Oct, 2015 ($3.99, one-shot)
1-Mandel-s/Walsh-a; Steranko cover swipe by Conner 4.00

HANNA-BARBERA (See Golden Comics Digest No. 2, 7, 11)

HANNA-BARBERA ALL-STARS
Archie Publications: Oct, 1995 - No. 4, Apr, 1996 ($1.50, bi-monthly)
1-4 4.00

HANNA-BARBERA BANDWAGON (TV)
Gold Key: Oct, 1962 - No. 3, Apr, 1963
1-Giant, 84 pgs. 1-Augie Doggie app.; 1st app. Lippy the Lion, Touché Turtle & Dum Dum, Wally Gator, Loopy de Loop, 10 20 30 69 147 225
2-Giant, 84 pgs.; Mr. & Mrs. J. Evil Scientist (1st app.) in Snagglepuss story; Yakky Doodle, Ruff and Reddy and others app. 8 16 24 51 96 140
3-Regular size; Mr. & Mrs. J. Evil Scientist app. (pre-#1), Snagglepuss, Wally Gator and others app. 6 12 18 40 73 105

HANNA-BARBERA GIANT SIZE
Harvey Comics: Oct, 1992 - No. 3 ($2.25, 68 pgs.)
V2#1-3:Flintstones, Yogi Bear, Magilla Gorilla, Huckleberry Hound, Quick Draw McGraw, Yakky Doodle & Chopper, Jetsons & others 6.00

HANNA-BARBERA HI-ADVENTURE HEROES (See Hi-Adventure...)

HANNA-BARBERA PARADE (TV)
Charlton Comics: Sept, 1971 - No. 10, Dec, 1972
1 6 12 18 41 76 110
2,4-10 4 8 12 25 40 55
3-(52 pgs.)- "Summer Picnic" 5 10 15 33 57 80
NOTE: *No. 4 (1/72) went on sale late in 1972 with the January 1973 issues.*

HANNA-BARBERA PRESENTS
Archie Publications: Nov, 1995 - No. 8 ($1.50, bi-monthly)
1-8: 1-Atom Ant & Secret Squirrel. 2-Wacky Races. 3-Yogi Bear. 4-Quick Draw McGraw & Magilla Gorilla. 5-A Pup Named Scooby-Doo. 6-Superstar Olympics. 7-Wacky Races. 8-Frankenstein Jr. & the Impossibles 4.00

HANNA-BARBERA SPOTLIGHT (See Spotlight)

HANNA-BARBERA SUPER TV HEROES (TV)
Gold Key: Apr, 1968 - No. 7, Oct, 1969 (Hanna-Barbera)
1-The Birdman, The Herculoids (ends #6; not in #3), Moby Dick, Young Samson & Goliath (ends #2,4), and The Mighty Mightor begin; Spiegle-a in all 12 24 36 81 176 270
2-The Galaxy Trio app.; Shazzan begins; 12¢ & 15¢ versions exist 8 16 24 56 108 160
3,6,7-The Space Ghost app. 8 16 24 51 96 140
4,5 7 14 21 44 82 120
NOTE: *Birdman in #1,2,4,5. Herculoids in #2,4-7. Mighty Mightor in #1,2,4-7. Moby Dick in all. Shazzan in #2-5. Young Samson & Goliath in #1,3.*

HANNA-BARBERA TV FUN FAVORITES (See Golden Comics Digest #2,7,11)

HANNA-BARBERA (TV STARS) (See TV Stars)

HANS BRINKER (Disney)
Dell Publishing Co.: No. 1273, Feb, 1962 (one-shot)
Four Color 1273-Movie, photo-c 6 12 18 37 66 95

HANS CHRISTIAN ANDERSEN
Ziff-Davis Publ. Co.: 1953 (100 pgs., Special Issue)
nn-Danny Kaye (movie)-Photo-c; fairy tales 18 36 54 109 172 235

HANSEL & GRETEL
Dell Publishing Co.: No. 590, Oct, 1954 (one-shot)
Four Color 590-Partial photo-c 7 14 21 46 86 125

HANSI, THE GIRL WHO LOVED THE SWASTIKA
Spire Christian Comics (Fleming H. Revell Co.): 1973, 1976 (39¢/49¢)
1973 edition with 39¢-c 10 20 30 69 147 225
1976 edition with 39¢-c 8 16 24 56 108 160
1976 edition with 49¢-c 10 20 30 64 132 200

HAN SOLO (Star Wars)
Marvel Comics: Aug, 2016 - No. 5, Jan, 2017 ($3.99, limited series)
1-5-Marjorie Liu-s/Mark Brooks-a/Lee Bermejo-c; takes place between Episodes 4 & 5 4.00

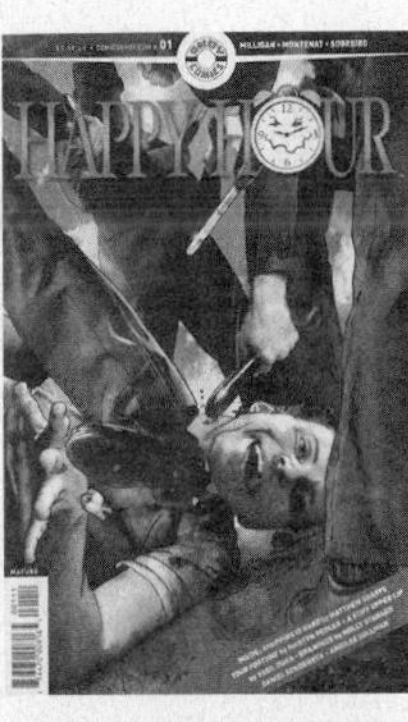

Happy Hour #1 © Milligan & Montenat

Harbinger #35 © VAL

Hardcore #4 © Skybound

	GD	VG	FN	VF	VF/NM	NM-
	2.0	4.0	6.0	8.0	9.0	9.2

HAP HAZARD COMICS (Real Love No. 25 on)
Ace Magazines (Readers' Research): Summer, 1944 - No. 24, Feb, 1949
(#1-6 are quarterly issues)

	GD	VG	FN	VF	VF/NM	NM-
1	17	34	51	103	162	220
2	10	20	30	58	79	100
3-10	9	18	27	52	69	85
11,12,15,16,20-24	9	18	27	47	61	75
13,17-19-Good Girl covers	34	68	102	199	325	450
14-(4/47) Feldstein-c; Cary Grant, Frank Sinatra, Van Johnson, Guy Madison, Alan Ladd and Robert Taylor app.	37	74	111	222	361	500

HAP HOPPER (See Comics Revue No. 2)

HAPPIEST MILLIONAIRE, THE (See Movie Comics)

HAPPI TIM (See March of Comics No. 182)

HAPPY
Image Comics: Sept, 2012 - No. 4, Feb, 2013 ($2.99, limited series)

1-4-Grant Morrison-s/Darick Robertson-a. 1-Covers by Robertson & Allred 5.00

HAPPY BIRTHDAY MARTHA WASHINGTON (Also see Give Me Liberty, Martha Washington Goes To War, & Martha Washington Stranded In Space)
Dark Horse Comics: Mar, 1995 ($2.95, one-shot)

1-Miller script; Gibbons-c/a 4.00

HAPPY COMICS (Happy Rabbit No. 41 on)
Nedor Publ./Standard Comics (Animated Cartoons): Aug, 1943 - No. 40, Dec, 1950
(Companion to Goofy Comics)

	GD	VG	FN	VF	VF/NM	NM-
1-Funny animal	37	74	111	222	361	500
2	19	38	57	109	172	235
3-10	14	28	42	81	118	155
11-19	12	24	36	69	97	125
20-31,34-37-Frazetta text illos in all (2 in #34&35, 3 in #27,28,30). 27-Al Fago-a	14	28	42	78	112	145
32-Frazetta-a, 7 pgs. plus 2 text illos; Roussos-a	24	48	72	140	230	320
33-Frazetta-a(2), 6 pgs. each (Scarce)	33	66	99	194	317	440
38-40	11	22	33	60	83	105

HAPPYDALE: DEVILS IN THE DESERT
DC Comics (Vertigo): 1999 - No. 2, 1999 ($6.95, limited series)

1,2-Andrew Dabb-s/Seth Fisher-a 7.00

HAPPY DAYS (TV)(See Kite Fun Book)
Gold Key: Mar, 1979 - No. 6, Feb, 1980

	GD	VG	FN	VF	VF/NM	NM-
1-Photo-c of TV cast; 35¢-c	3	6	9	21	33	45
2-6-(40¢-c)	2	4	6	9	12	15

HAPPY HOLIDAY (See March of Comics No. 181)

HAPPY HOULIHANS (Saddle Justice No. 3 on; see Blackstone, The Magician Detective)
E. C. Comics: Fall, 1947 - No. 2, Winter, 1947-48

	GD	VG	FN	VF	VF/NM	NM-
1-Origin Moon Girl (same date as Moon Girl #1)	71	142	213	454	777	1100
2	39	78	117	231	378	525

HAPPY HOUR
AHOY Comics: 2020 - Present ($3.99, limited series)

1-4-Peter Milligan-s/Michael Montenat-a 4.00

HAPPY JACK
Red Top (Decker): Aug, 1957 - No. 2, Nov, 1957

	GD	VG	FN	VF	VF/NM	NM-
V1#1,2	6	12	18	31	38	45

HAPPY JACK HOWARD
Red Top (Farrell)/Decker: 1957

	GD	VG	FN	VF	VF/NM	NM-
nn-Reprints Handy Andy story from E. C. Dandy Comics #5, renamed "Happy Jack"	6	12	18	28	34	40

HAPPY RABBIT (Formerly Happy Comics)
Standard Comics (Animated Cartoons): No. 41, Feb, 1951 - No. 48, Apr, 1952

	GD	VG	FN	VF	VF/NM	NM-
41-Funny animal	10	20	30	56	76	95
42-48	8	16	24	44	57	70

HARBINGER (Also see Unity)
Valiant: Jan, 1992 - No. 41, June, 1995 ($1.95/$2.50)

	GD	VG	FN	VF	VF/NM	NM-
0-Prequel to the series; available by redeeming coupons in #1-6; cover image has pink sky; title logo is blue	5	10	15	30	50	70
0-(2nd printing) cover has blue sky & red logo	1	3	4	6	8	10
1-1st app.	6	12	18	41	76	110
2-4: 4-Low print run	2	4	6	13	18	22
5,6: 5-Solar app. 6-Torque dies	2	4	6	9	12	15
7-10: 8,9-Unity x-overs. 8-Miller-c. 9-Simonson-c. 10-1st app. H.A.R.D Corps (10/92)	1	2	3	5	6	8

11-24,26-41: 14-1st app. Stronghold. 18-Intro Screen. 19-1st app. Stunner. 22-Archer & Armstrong app. 24-Cover similar to #1. 26-Intro New Harbingers. 29-Bound-in trading card. 30-H.A.R.D. Corps app. 32-Eternal Warrior app. 33-Dr. Eclipse app. 4.00
25-($3.50, 52 pgs.)-Harada vs. Sting 5.00
...Files 1,2 (8/94,2/95 $2.50) 4.00
...: The Beginning HC (2007, $24.95) recolored reprints #0-7 and Story of Harada from coupons from #1-6; new "Origin of Harada" story by Shooter and Bob Hall 30.00
Trade paperback nn (11/92, $9.95)-Reprints #1-4 & comes polybagged with a copy of Harbinger #0 w/new-c. Price for TPB only 15.00
NOTE: *Issues 1-6 have coupons with origin of Harada and are redeemable for Harbinger #0.*

HARBINGER
Valiant Entertainment: Jun, 2012 - No. 25, Jul, 2014 ($3.99)(#0 released between #8 & #9)

1-Dysart-s/Khari Evans-a; covers by Lozzi and Suayan (Pullbox variant) 4.00
1-Variant cover by Braithwaite 10.00
1-QR voice variant cover by Jelena Djurdjevic 40.00
2-24-Two covers on each (standard & pullbox). 2-Origin continues. 11-14-Harbinger Wars tie-in. 23-Flamingo dies 4.00
25-($4.99) Back-up story by Tiwary & Larosa; bonus features and cover gallery 5.00
#0 (2/13, $3.99) Origin of Harada; Suayan & Pere Pérez-a; covers by Crain & Suayan 4.00
#0-Variant gatefold-c by Lewis Larosa 15.00
... Bleeding Monk #0 (3/14, $3.99) Dysart-s; art by Evans, Suayan, Segovia & LaRosa 4.00
... Faith #0 (12/14, $3.99) Dysart-s; Robert Gill-a 4.00

HARBINGER: OMEGAS
Valiant Entertainment: Jul, 2014 - No. 3, Oct, 2014 ($3.99, limited series)

1-3-Dysart-s/Sandoval-a 4.00

HARBINGER RENEGADE
Valiant Entertainment: Nov, 2016 - No. 8, Oct, 2017; No. 0 Nov, 2017 ($3.99, limited series)

1-8: 1-Rafer Roberts-s/Darick Robertson-a; intro Alexander Solomon. 6-Ryp-a 4.00
#0-(11/17) Follows #8; Ryp-a; H.A.R.D. Corps app. 4.00

HARBINGER WARS
Valiant Entertainment: Apr, 2013 - No. 4, Jul, 2013 ($3.99, limited series)

1-4: 1-Dysart-s/Henry, Crain & Suayan-a; covers by Larosa & Henry (Pullbox) 4.00
1-Variant cover by Crain 10.00
1-Variant cover by Zircher 50.00

HARBINGER WARS 2
Valiant Entertainment: May, 2018 - No. 4, Aug, 2018 ($3.99, limited series)

1-4-Kindt-s/Giorello-a; Bloodshot, Ninjak, X-O Manowar, Live Wire app. 4.00
...: Aftermath 1 (9/18, $3.99) Kindt-s/Pollina-a; X-O Manowar & Live Wire app. 4.00
...: Prelude (5/18, $3.99) Heisserer-s/Allén-a 4.00

HARD BOILED
Dark Horse Comics: Sept, 1990 - No. 3, Mar, 1992 ($4.95/$5.95, 8 1/2x11", lim. series)

	GD	VG	FN	VF	VF/NM	NM-
1-Frank Miller-s/Darrow-c/a in all; sexually explicit & violent	2	4	6	11	16	20
2,3	2	4	6	8	10	12

TPB (5/93, $15.95) 20.00
Big Damn Hard Boiled (12/97, $29.95, B&W) r/#1-3 30.00

HARDCASE (See Break Thru, Flood Relief & Ultraforce, 1st Series)
Malibu Comics (Ultraverse): June, 1993 - No. 26, Aug, 1995 ($1.95/$2.50)

1-Intro Hardcase; Dave Gibbons-c; has coupon for Ultraverse Premiere #0; Jim Callahan-a(p) begin, ends #3 4.00
1-With coupon missing 2.00
1-Platinum Edition 6.00
1-Holographic Cover Edition; 1st full-c holograph tied w/Prime 1 & Strangers 1 8.00
1-Ultra Limited silver foil-c 6.00
2,3-Callahan-a, 2-($2.50)-Newsstand edition bagged w/trading card 3.00
4,6-15, 17-19: 4-Strangers app. 7-Break-Thru x-over. 8-Solution app. 9-Vs. Turf. 12-Silver foil logo, wraparound-c. 17-Prime app. 3.00
5-($2.50, 48 pgs.)-Rune flip-c/story by B. Smith (3 pgs.) 4.00
16 ($3.50, 68 pgs.)-Rune pin-up 4.00
20-26: 23-Loki app. 3.00
NOTE: *Perez a-8(2); c-20i.*

HARDCORE
Image Comics: May, 2012 ($2.99)

1-Kirkman-s/Stelfreeze-a/Silvestri-c 3.00

HARDCORE
Image Comics (Skybound): Dec, 2018 - No. 5, Apr, 2019 ($3.99)

1-5-Diggle-s/Vitti-a/Panosian-c 4.00

Hardware #21 © Milestone

Harleen #3 © DC

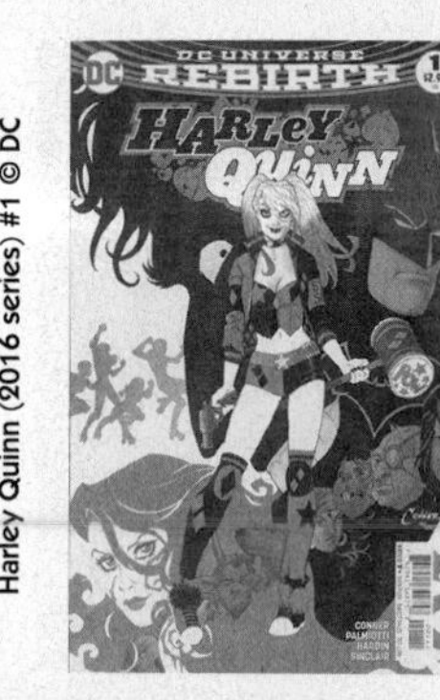

Harley Quinn (2016 series) #1 © DC

	GD	VG	FN	VF	VF/NM	NM-
	2.0	4.0	6.0	8.0	9.0	9.2

HARDCORE: RELOADED
Image Comics (Skybound): Dec, 2019 - No. 5, Jun, 2020 ($3.99)
1-5-Brandon Thomas-s/Francis Portela-a/Nic Klein-c 4.00

HARDCORE STATION
DC Comics: July, 1998 - No. 6, Dec, 1998 ($2.50, limited series)
1-6-Starlin-s/a(p). 3-Green Lantern-c/app. 5,6-JLA-c/app. 3.00

H.A.R.D. CORPS, THE (See Harbinger #10)
Valiant: Dec, 1992 - No. 30, Feb, 1995 ($2.25) (Harbinger spin-off)
1-($2.50)-Gatefold-c by Jim Lee & Bob Layton 5.00
1-Gold variant 15.00
2-30: 5-Bloodshot-c/story cont'd from Bloodshot #3. 5-Variant edition; came w/Comic Defense System. 10-Turok app. 17-vs. Armorines. 18-Bound-in trading card. 20-Harbinger app. 3.00

HARD TIME
DC Comics (Focus): Apr, 2004 - No. 12, Mar, 2005 ($2.50)
1-12-Gerber-s/Hurtt-a; 1-Includes previews of other DC Focus series 3.00
...: 50 to Life (2004, $9.95, TPB) r/#1-6; cover gallery with sketches 10.00

HARD TIME: SEASON TWO
DC Comics: Feb, 2006 - No. 7, Aug, 2006 ($2.50/$2.99)
1-5-Gerber-s/Hurtt-a 3.00
6,7-($2.99) 7-Ethan paroled in 2053 3.00

HARDWARE
DC Comics (Milestone): Apr, 1993 - No. 50, Apr, 1997 ($1.50/$1.75/$2.50)
1-($2.95)-Collector's Edition polybagged w/poster & trading card (direct sale only) 4.00
1-Platinum Edition 6.00
1-15,17-19: 11-Shadow War x-over. 11,14-Simonson-c. 12-Buckler-a(p). 17-Worlds Collide Pt. 2. 18-Simonson-c; Worlds Collide Pt. 9. 15-1st Humberto Ramos DC work 3.00
16,25: 16-($2.50, 52 pgs.)-Newsstand Ed. 25-($2.95, 52 pgs.) 4.00
16,50-($3.95, 52 pgs.)-16-Collector's Edition w/gatefold 2nd cover by Byrne; new armor; Icon app. 5.00
20-24,26-49: 49-Moebius-c 3.00
...: The Man in the Machine TPB (2010, $19.99) r/#1-8 20.00

HARDY BOYS, THE (Disney
Dell Publ. Co.: No. 760, Dec, 1956 - No. 964, Jan, 1959 (Mickey Mouse Club)

	GD	VG	FN	VF	VF/NM	NM-
Four Color 760 (#1)-Photo-c	10	20	30	65	165	205
Four Color 830(8/57), 887(1/58), 964-Photo-c	8	16	24	56	108	160

HARDY BOYS, THE (TV)
Gold Key: Apr, 1970 - No. 4, Jan, 1971

	GD	VG	FN	VF	VF/NM	NM-
1	4	8	12	27	44	60
2-4	3	6	9	17	26	35

HARLAN ELLISON'S DREAM CORRIDOR
Dark Horse Comics: Mar, 1995 - No. 5, July, 1995 ($2.95, anthology)
1-5: Adaptation of Ellison stories. 1-4-Byrne-a. 4.00
Special (1/95, $4.95) 6.00
Trade paperback-(1996, $18.95, 192 pgs)-r/#1-5 & Special #1 19.00

HARLAN ELLISON'S DREAM CORRIDOR QUARTERLY
Dark Horse Comics: V2#1, Aug, 1996 ($5.95, anthology, squarebound)
V2#1-Adaptations of Ellison's stories w/new material; Neal Adams-a 6.00
Volume 2 TPB (3/07, $19.95) r/V2#1 and unpublished material incl. last Swan-a 20.00

HARLEEN
DC Comics (Black Label): Nov, 2019 - No. 3, Feb, 2020 ($7.99, 10-3/4" x 8-1/2", lim. series)
1-3-Retelling of Harley Quinn's origin with the Joker; Stjepan Sejic-s/a 8.00

HARLEM GLOBETROTTERS (TV) (See Fun-In No. 8, 10)
Gold Key: Apr, 1972 - No. 12, Jan, 1975 (Hanna-Barbera)

	GD	VG	FN	VF	VF/NM	NM-
1	4	8	12	28	47	65
2-5	3	6	9	15	22	28
6-12	2	4	6	13	18	22

NOTE: *#4, 8, and 12 contain 16 extra pages of advertising.*

HARLEQUIN ROMANCE
Dark Horse Comics: Nov, 2001 ($10.95, hardcover, one-shot)
nn-Neil Gaiman-s; painted-a/c by John Bolton 11.00

HARLEY & IVY MEET BETTY & VERONICA (Archie Comics)
DC Comics: Dec, 2017 - No. 6, May, 2018 ($3.99, limited series)
1-6: 1-Harvey & Ivy go to Riverdale; Dini & Andreyko-s/Braga-a. 1-Conner-c. 2-Zatanna app. 3,4-The Joker app. 4.00
1-Variant-c by Adam Hughes 4.00

HARLEY QUINN (See Batman Adventures #12 for 1st app.)(Also see Gotham City Sirens, Old Lady Harley, and Suicide Squad)
DC Comics: Dec, 2000 - No. 38, Jan, 2004 ($2.95/$2.25/$2.50)

	GD	VG	FN	VF	VF/NM	NM-
1-Joker and Poison Ivy app.; Terry & Rachel Dodson-a/c	5	10	15	30	50	70
2,3-($2.25): 2-Two-Face-c/app. 3-Slumber party	2	4	6	10	14	18
4-9,11-($2.25). 6,7-Riddler app.	1	2	3	5	6	8
10-Batgirl-c/s	2	4	6	10	14	18
12-($2.95) Batman app.	2	4	6	10	14	18
13,17-19: 13-Joker: Last Laugh. 17,18-Bizarro-c/app. 19-Superman-c	2	4	6	10	14	18
14-16,20-24,26-31,33-37: 23-Begin $2.50-c. 23,24-Martian Manhunter app.	1	2	3	5	6	8
25-Classic Joker-c/s	3	6	9	16	23	30
32-Joker-c/app.	2	4	6	11	16	20
38-Last issue; Adlard-a/Morse-c	3	6	9	14	20	25
Harley & Ivy: Love on the Lam (2001, $5.95) Winick-s/Chiodo-c/a	3	6	9	14	19	24
...: Our Worlds at War (10/01, $2.95) Jae Lee-c; art by various	3	6	9	14	19	24

HARLEY QUINN (DC New 52)
DC Comics: No. 0, Jan, 2014 - No. 30, Sept, 2016 ($2.99/$3.99)

	GD	VG	FN	VF	VF/NM	NM-
0-Conner & Palmiotti-s; art by Conner & various; Conner-c	2	4	6	10	14	18
0-Variant-c by Stephane Roux	2	4	6	13	18	22
1-(2/14) Chad Hardin-a; Conner-c	3	6	9	16	23	30
1-Variant-c by Adam Hughes	12	24	36	84	185	285

1-Halloween Fest Special Edition (12/15, free) r/#1 with "Halloween ComicFest" logo 3.00

	GD	VG	FN	VF	VF/NM	NM-
2-Poison Ivy app.	2	4	6	9	12	15
3-5: 4-Roux-a	1	2	3	5	6	8

6-16: 6,7-Poison Ivy app. 11-13-Power Girl app. 16-Intro. of The Gang of Harleys 4.00
17-30-($3.99) 17-19-Capt Strong app. 20,21-Deadshot app. 25-Joker app. 26-28-Red Tool app. 30-Charretier-a; Poison Ivy app. 4.00
Annual 1 (12/14, $5.99) Polybagged with "Rub 'N Smell" pages 6.00
... & The Suicide Squad April Fools' Special 1 (6/16, $4.99) Rob Williams-s/Jim Lee-a 5.00
...Director's Cut #0 (8/14, $4.99) With commentary by Conner & Palmiotti; cover gallery 5.00
...: Futures End 1 (11/14, $2.99, regular-c) Five years later; Joker app. 3.00
...: Futures End 1 (11/14, $3.99, 3-D cover) 4.00
... Holiday Special (2/15, $4.99) Christmas-themed stories; back-up Darwyn Cooke-a 5.00
... Invades Comic-Con International: San Diego 1 (9/14, $4.99) Wraparound-c 5.00
... Road Trip Special (11/15, $5.99) Harley, Catwoman & Poison Ivy road trip; Conner-c 6.00
... Valentine's Day Special (4/15, $4.99) Bruce Wayne and Poison Ivy app. 5.00

HARLEY QUINN (DC Rebirth)
DC Comics: Oct, 2016 - No. 75, Oct, 2020 ($2.99/$3.99)
1-Conner & Palmiotti-s/Hardin-a; Poison Ivy & Red Tool app. 5.00
2-6: 4-Linsner-a. 6-Joker flashback w/Jill Thompson-a (4 pgs.) 4.00
7-24: 9-Kaluta-a (4 pgs.). 10-Linsner & Moritat-a. 15,16-Power Girl & Atlee app. 17-Back-up stories by Dini & Palmiotti-s/Blevins-a begin, thru #25; Joker app. 3.00
25-($3.99) Back-up story w/Joker continues in Harley Loves Joker #1 4.00
26-46: 27-Tieri-s/Carlini-a/Thompson-c. 29-Kaluta-a (5 pgs.) 34-Last Palmiotti & Conner-s. 35-39-Tieri-s. 36,37-Penguin app. 42-Old Lady Harley. 45,46-Granny Goodness & Female Furies app. 3.00
47-49,51-74 ($3.99) 47-Harley on Apokolips. 48,49-Lord Death Man app. 51,52-Capt. Triumph app. 57,58-Batman app. 71-74-Booster Gold app. 4.00
50-($4.99) Jonni DC app.; art by various; Conner infinity-c; Captain Triumph returns 5.00
63-($4.99) Variant Year of the Villain painted-c by Frank Cho 5.00
75-($5.99) Roast of Harley Quinn; back up story tie-in to Joker War; Punchline app. 6.00
... Batman Day Special Edition (10/17, giveaway) r/#7; Joker app. 3.00
...: Be Careful What You Wish For Special Edition 1 (3/18, $4.99) Reprints story from Loot Crate edition plus 18 new pages; art by Conner, Hardin, Schmidt & Caldwell 5.00
.../Gossamer 1 (10/18, $4.99) Looney Tunes monster; Conner-c/Brito-a 5.00
... 25th Anniversary Special 1 (11/17, $4.99) Short stories by various incl. Dini, Conner, Palmiotti, Zdarsky, Quinones, Hardin; 2 covers by Conner & Dodson 5.00
Harley Quinn's Greatest Hits TPB (2016, $9.99) r/Batman Advs. #12 & other stories 10.00
Harley Quinn's Villain of the Year (2019, $4.99) Russell-s/Norton-a/Conner-c 5.00

HARLEY QUINN AND HER GANG OF HARLEYS
DC Comics: Jun, 2016 - No. 6, Nov, 2016 ($3.99, limited series)
1-6-Palmiotti & Tieri-s/Mauricet-a/Conner-c; intro. Harley Sinn. 5-Origin of Harley Sinn 4.00

HARLEY QUINN & POISON IVY
DC Comics: Nov, 2019 - No. 6, Apr, 2020 ($3.99, limited series)
1-6-Houser-s/Melo-a. 1,2-Floronic Man app. 2,3-Mad Hatter app. 5-Batwoman app. 4.00

HARLEY QUINN AND POWER GIRL
DC Comics: Aug, 2015 - No. 6, Feb, 2016 ($3.99, limited series)

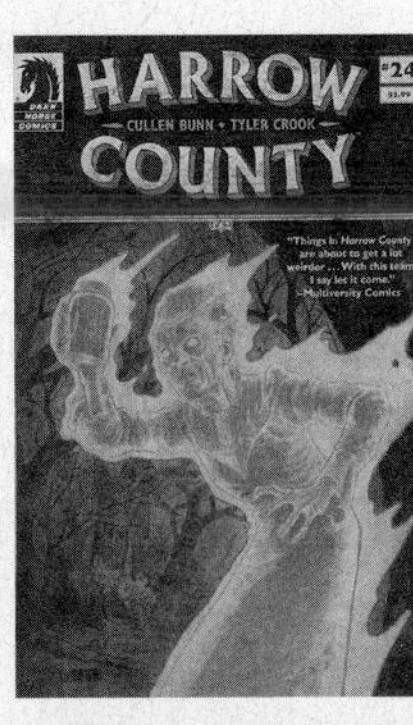

Harrow County #24 © Bunn & Crook

Harvey Comics Hits #48 © HARV

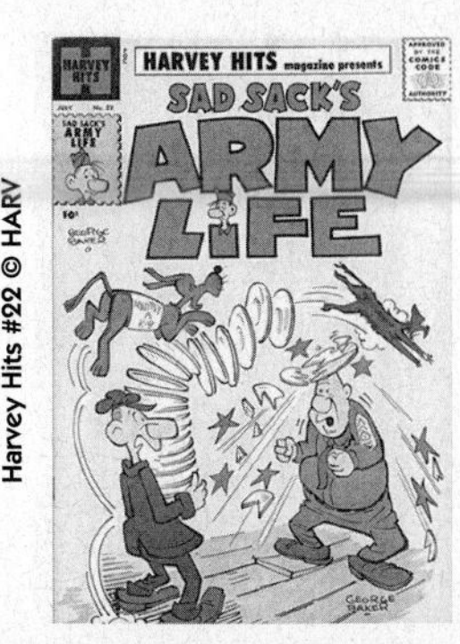

Harvey Hits #22 © HARV

	GD 2.0	VG 4.0	FN 6.0	VF 8.0	VF/NM 9.0	NM- 9.2

1-6-Takes place during Harley Quinn #11-13; Vartox app.; Roux-a 4.00

HARLEY QUINN & THE BIRDS OF PREY
DC Comics (Black Label): Apr, 2020 - No. 4, Mar, 2021 ($5.99, 10-3/4" x 8-1/2", lim. series)

1-4-Conner & Palmiotti-s/Conner-a; Power Girl, Huntress & Cassandra Cain app. 6.00

HARLEY QUINN: HARLEY LOVES JOKER
DC Comics: Early Jul, 2018 - No. 2, Jul, 2018 ($3.99, limited series)

1,2-Dini-s/Blevins-a; covers by Conner & Cho; original costume Harley; intro The Grison 4.00

HARLEY'S LITTLE BLACK BOOK (Harley Quinn team-up book)
DC Comics: Feb, 2016 - No. 6, May, 2017 ($4.99, bi-monthly)

1-4,6: 1-Palmiotti & Conner-s; Wonder Woman app.; Conner-c. 2-Green Lantern app. 3-Zatanna app.; Linsner-a. 4-DC Bombshells app.; Tucci-a. 6-Lobo app.; Bisley-a 5.00

1-Polybagged variant-c by Campbell (3 versions: sketch, B&W, and color) 1 2 3 5 6 8

5-Neal Adams-a; homage to "Superman vs. Muhammad Ali" 5.00

HAROLD TEEN (See Popular Comics, & Super Comics)
Dell Publishing Co.: No. 2, 1942 - No. 209, Jan, 1949

	GD	VG	FN	VF	VF/NM	NM-
Four Color 2	34	68	102	245	548	850
Four Color 209	6	12	18	41	76	110

HARROW COUNTY (Also see Tales From Harrow County)
Dark Horse Comics: May, 2015 - No. 32, Jun, 2018 ($3.99)

1-31: 1-8-Cullen Bunn-s/Tyler Crook-a. 9,17-Carla Speed McNeil-a 4.00
1-Halloween ComicFest Edition (10/16, no price) r/#1 3.00
32-($4.99) Last issue; Bunn-s/Crook-a 5.00

HARROWERS, THE (See Clive Barker's...)

HARSH REALM (Inspired 1999 TV series)
Harris Comics: 1993- No. 6, 1994 ($2.95, limited series)

1-6: Painted-c. Hudnall-s/Paquette & Ridgway-a 4.00
TPB (2000, $14.95) r/series 15.00

HARVESTER, THE
Legendary Comics: Feb, 2015 - No. 6, Jul, 2015 ($3.99)

1-6-Brandon Seifert-s/Eric Battle-a/c 4.00

HARVEY
Marvel Comics: Oct, 1970; No. 2, 12/70; No. 3, 6/72 - No. 6, 12/72

	GD	VG	FN	VF	VF/NM	NM-
1-Teenage	10	20	30	66	138	210
2-6	7	14	21	46	86	125

HARVEY COLLECTORS COMICS (Titled Richie Rich Collectors Comics on cover of #6-on)
Harvey Publ.: Sept, 1975 - No. 15, Jan, 1978; No. 16, Oct, 1979 (52 pgs.)

	GD	VG	FN	VF	VF/NM	NM-
1-Reprints Richie Rich #1,2	2	4	6	13	18	22
2-10: 7-Splash pg. shows cover to Friendly Ghost Casper #1	2	4	6	8	11	14
11-16: 16-Sad Sack-r	1	2	3	5	7	9

NOTE: *All reprints: Casper-#2, 7, Richie Rich-#1, 3, 5, 6, 8-15, Sad Sack-#16. Wendy-#4.*

HARVEY COMICS HITS (Formerly Joe Palooka #50)
Harvey Publications: No. 51, Oct, 1951 - No. 62, Apr, 1953

	GD	VG	FN	VF	VF/NM	NM-
51-The Phantom	39	78	117	240	395	550
52-Steve Canyon's Air Power(Air Force sponsored)	13	26	39	72	101	130
53-Mandrake the Magician	20	40	60	114	182	250
54-Tim Tyler's Tales of Jungle Terror	13	26	39	74	105	135
55-Love Stories of Mary Worth	12	24	36	69	97	125
56-The Phantom; bondage-c	31	62	93	182	296	410
57-Rip Kirby Exposes the Kidnap Racket; entire book by Alex Raymond	16	32	48	98	154	210
58-Girls in White (nurses stories)	13	26	39	72	101	130
59-Tales of the Invisible featuring Scarlet O'Neil	15	30	45	83	124	165
60-Paramount Animated Comics #1 (9/52) (3rd app. Baby Huey); 2nd Harvey app. Baby Huey & Casper the Friendly Ghost (1st in Little Audrey #25 (8/52)); 1st app. Herman & Catnip (c/story) & Buzzy the Crow	65	130	195	416	708	1000
61-Casper the Friendly Ghost #6 (3rd Harvey Casper, 10/52)-Casper-c	57	114	171	362	619	875
62-Paramount Animated Comics #2; Herman & Catnip, Baby Huey & Buzzy the Crow	19	38	57	111	176	240

HARVEY COMICS LIBRARY
Harvey Publications: Apr, 1952 - No. 2, 1952

	GD	VG	FN	VF	VF/NM	NM-
1-Teen-Age Dope Slaves as exposed by Rex Morgan, M.D.; drug propaganda story; used in **SOTI**, pg. 27	310	620	930	2224	3912	5600
2-Dick Tracy Presents Sparkle Plenty in "Blackmail Terror"	21	42	63	122	199	275

HARVEY COMICS SPOTLIGHT
Harvey Comics: Sept, 1987 - No. 4, Mar, 1988 (75¢/$1.00)

1-New material; begin 75¢, ends #3; Sad Sack 5.00
2-4: 2,4-All new material. 2-Baby Huey. 3-Little Dot; contains reprints w/5 pg. new story. 4-$1.00-c; Little Audrey 4.00
NOTE: No. 5 was advertised but not published.

HARVEY HITS (Also see Tastee-Freez Comics in the Promotional Comics section)
Harvey Publications: Sept, 1957 - No. 122, Nov, 1967

	GD	VG	FN	VF	VF/NM	NM-
1-The Phantom	30	60	90	216	483	750
2-Rags Rabbit (10/57)	6	12	18	41	76	110
3-Richie Rich (11/57)-r/Little Dot; 1st book devoted to Richie Rich; see Little Dot for 1st app.	152	304	456	1254	2827	4400
4-Little Dot's Uncles (12/57)	16	32	48	112	249	385
5-Stevie Mazie's Boy Friend (1/58)	5	10	15	30	50	70
6-The Phantom (2/58); 2pg. Powell-a	18	36	54	128	284	440
7-Wendy the Good Little Witch (3/58, pre-dates Wendy #1; 1st book devoted to Wendy)	50	100	150	400	900	1400
8-Sad Sack's Army Life; George Baker-c	8	16	24	56	108	160
9-Richie Rich's Golden Deeds; (2nd book devoted to Richie Rich) reprints Richie Rich story from Tastee-Freez #1	80	160	240	640	1445	2250
10-Little Lotta's Lunch Box	12	24	36	79	170	260
11-Little Audrey Summer Fun (7/58)	9	18	27	57	111	165
12-The Phantom; 2pg. Powell-a (8/58)	15	30	45	103	227	350
13-Little Dot's Uncles (9/58); Richie Rich 1pg.	10	20	30	69	147	225
14-Herman & Katnip (10/58, TV/movies)	5	10	15	30	50	70
15-The Phantom (12/58)-1 pg. origin	16	32	48	108	239	370
16-Wendy the Good Little Witch (1/59); Casper app.	13	26	39	86	188	290
17-Sad Sack's Army Life (2/59)	5	10	15	34	66	85
18-Buzzy & the Crow	4	8	12	25	40	55
19-Little Audrey (4/59)	5	10	15	33	57	80
20-Casper & Spooky	7	14	21	44	82	120
21-Wendy the Witch	7	14	21	44	82	120
22-Sad Sack's Army Life	4	8	12	28	47	65
23-Wendy the Witch (8/59)	7	14	21	44	82	120
24-Little Dot's Uncles (9/59); Richie Rich 1pg.	8	16	24	54	102	150
25-Herman & Katnip (10/59)	3	6	9	21	33	45
26-The Phantom (11/59)	11	22	33	76	163	250
27-Wendy the Good Little Witch (12/59)	6	12	18	42	79	115
28-Sad Sack's Army Life (1/60)	4	8	12	25	40	55
29-Harvey-Toon (No.1)('60); Casper, Buzzy	5	10	15	31	53	75
30-Wendy the Witch (3/60)	7	14	21	44	82	120
31-Herman & Katnip (4/60)	3	6	9	19	30	40
32-Sad Sack's Army Life (5/60)	3	6	9	21	33	45
33-Wendy the Witch (6/60)	6	12	18	40	73	105
34-Harvey-Toon (7/60)	4	8	12	23	37	50
35-Funday Funnies (8/60)	3	6	9	19	30	40
36-The Phantom (1960)	11	22	33	73	157	240
37-Casper & Nightmare	6	12	18	37	66	95
38-Harvey-Toon	4	8	12	23	37	50
39-Sad Sack's Army Life (12/60)	3	6	9	20	31	42
40-Funday Funnies (1/61)	3	6	9	16	24	32
41-Herman & Katnip	3	6	9	16	24	32
42-Harvey-Toon (3/61)	3	6	9	18	28	38
43-Sad Sack's Army Life (4/61)	3	6	9	18	28	38
44-The Phantom (5/61)	10	20	30	69	147	225
45-Casper & Nightmare	5	10	15	30	50	70
46-Harvey-Toon (7/61)	3	6	9	16	24	32
47-Sad Sack's Army Life (8/61)	3	6	9	16	24	32
48-The Phantom (9/61)	10	20	30	69	147	225
49-Stumbo the Giant (1st app. in Hot Stuff)	8	16	24	56	108	160
50-Harvey-Toon (11/61)	3	6	9	16	23	30
51-Sad Sack's Army Life (12/61)	3	6	9	16	23	30
52-Casper & Nightmare	4	8	12	28	47	65
53-Harvey-Toons (2/62)	3	6	9	16	23	30
54-Stumbo the Giant	5	10	15	33	57	80
55-Sad Sack's Army Life (4/62)	3	6	9	16	23	30
56-Casper & Nightmare	4	8	12	25	40	55
57-Stumbo the Giant	5	10	15	33	57	80
58-Sad Sack's Army Life	3	6	9	16	23	30
59-Casper & Nightmare (7/62)	4	8	12	25	40	55
60-Stumbo the Giant (9/62)	5	10	15	31	53	75
61-Sad Sack's Army Life	3	6	9	15	22	28
62-Casper & Nightmare	4	8	12	22	35	48
63-Stumbo the Giant	4	8	12	27	44	60

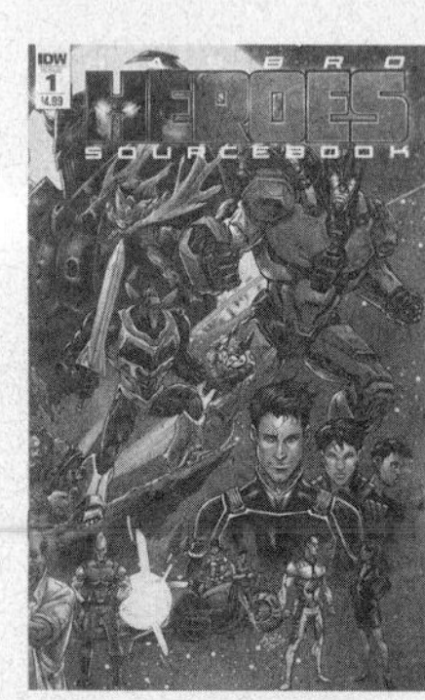

Hasbro Heroes Sourcebook 2017 #1 © Hasbro

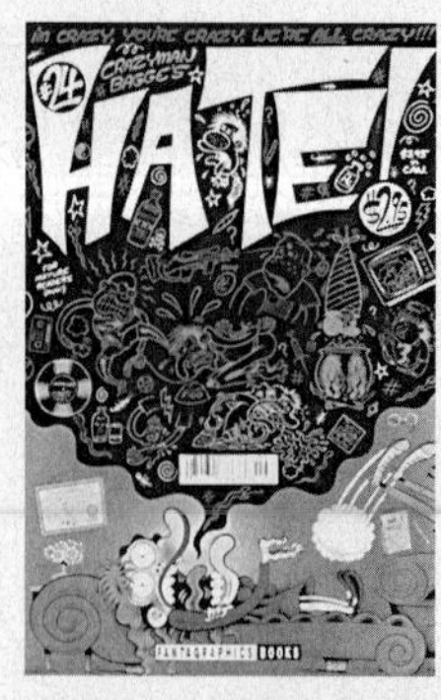

Hate #24 © Peter Bagge

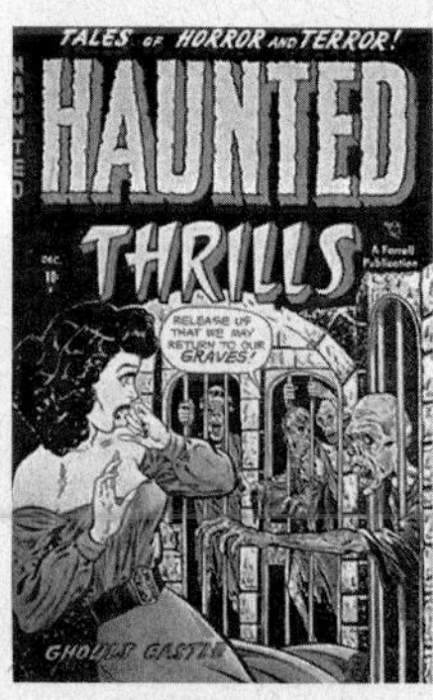

Haunted Thrills #4 © AJAX

	GD 2.0	VG 4.0	FN 6.0	VF 8.0	VF/NM 9.0	NM- 9.2
64-Sad Sack's Army Life (1/63)	3	6	9	15	22	28
65-Casper & Nightmare	4	8	12	22	35	48
66-Stumbo The Giant (3/63)	4	8	12	27	44	60
67-Sad Sack's Army Life (4/63)	3	6	9	15	22	28
68-Casper & Nightmare	4	8	12	22	35	48
69-Stumbo the Giant (6/63)	4	8	12	27	44	60
70-Sad Sack's Army Life (7/63)	3	6	9	15	22	28
71-Casper & Nightmare (8/63)	3	6	9	20	31	42
72-Stumbo the Giant	4	8	12	27	44	60
73-Little Sad Sack (10/63)	3	6	9	15	22	28
74-Sad Sack's Muttsy... (11/63)	3	6	9	15	22	28
75-Casper & Nightmare	3	6	9	18	28	38
76-Little Sad Sack	3	6	9	15	22	28
77-Sad Sack's Muttsy...	3	6	9	15	22	28
78-Stumbo the Giant (3/64); JFK caricature	4	8	12	28	44	60
79-87: 79-Little Sad Sack (4/64). 80-Sad Sack's Muttsy... (5/64). 81-Little Sad Sack. 82-Sad Sack's Muttsy... 83-Little Sad Sack(8/64). 84-Sad Sack's Muttsy... 85-Gabby Gob (#1) (10/64). 86-G. I. Juniors (#1)(11/64). 87-Sad Sack's Muttsy... (12/64)	3	6	9	15	22	28
88-Stumbo the Giant (1/65)	4	8	12	27	44	60
89-122: 89-Sad Sack's Muttsy... 90-Gabby Gob. 91-G. I. Juniors. 92-Sad Sack's Muttsy... (5/65). 93-Sadie Sack (6/65). 94-Gabby Gob. 95-G. I. Juniors (8/65). 96-Sad Sack's Muttsy... (9/65). 97-Gabby Gob (10/65). 98-G. I. Juniors (11/65). 99-Sad Sack's Muttsy... (12/65). 100-Gabby Gob(1/66). 101-G. I. Juniors (2/66). 102-Sad Sack's Muttsy... (3/66). 103-Gabby Gob. 104- G. I. Juniors. 105-Sad Sack's Muttsy... 106-Gabby Gob (7/66). 107-G. I. Juniors (8/66). 108-Sad Sack's Muttsy...109-Gabby Gob. 110-G. I. Juniors (11/66). 111-Sad Sack's Muttsy... (12/66). 112-G. I. Juniors. 113-Sad Sack's Muttsy... 114-G. I. Juniors. 115-Sad Sack's Muttsy... 116-G. I. Juniors (5/67). 117-Sad Sack's Muttsy... 118-G. I. Juniors. 119-Sad Sack's Muttsy... (8/67). 120-G. I. Juniors (9/67). 121-Sad Sack's Muttsy... (10/67). 122-G. I. Juniors (11/67)	2	4	6	10	14	18

HARVEY HITS COMICS
Harvey Publications: Nov, 1986 - No. 6, Oct, 1987

	GD 2.0	VG 4.0	FN 6.0	VF 8.0	VF/NM 9.0	NM- 9.2
1-Little Lotta, Little Dot, Wendy & Baby Huey	1	2	3	4	5	7
2-6: 3-Xmas-c						4.50

HARVEY POP COMICS (Rock Happening) (Teen Humor)
Harvey Publications: Oct, 1968 - No. 2, Nov, 1969 (Both are 68 pg. Giants)

	GD 2.0	VG 4.0	FN 6.0	VF 8.0	VF/NM 9.0	NM- 9.2
1-The Cowsills	5	10	15	34	60	85
2-Bunny	5	10	15	31	53	75

HARVEY 3-D HITS (See Sad Sack)

HARVEY-TOON (...S) (See Harvey Hits No. 29, 34, 38, 42, 46, 50, 53)

HARVEY WISEGUYS (...Digest #? on)
Harvey Comics: Nov, 1987; #2, Nov, 1988; #3, Apr, 1989 - No. 4, Nov, 1989 (98 pgs., digest-size, $1.25/$1.75)

	GD 2.0	VG 4.0	FN 6.0	VF 8.0	VF/NM 9.0	NM- 9.2
1-Hot Stuff, Spooky, etc.	2	3	4	6	8	10
2-4: 2 (68 pgs.)	1	2	3	4	5	7

HASBRO HEROES SOURCEBOOK 2017
IDW Publishing: May, 2017 - No. 3, Jul, 2017 ($4.99, limited series)

	NM- 9.2
1-3-Profile pages of characters from Transformers, G.I. Joe, Micronauts, Rom, M.A.S.K.	5.00

HASBRO TOYBOX QUARTERLY
IDW Publishing: Dec, 2017 ($5.99, one-shot)

	NM- 9.2
1-Short stories of My Little Pony, Equestria Girls and Hanazuki by various; pin-ups	6.00

HASHTAG: DANGER (Also see back-ups in High Heaven and Captain Ginger)
IDW Publishing: 2019 - No. 5, 2019 ($3.99, limited series)

	NM- 9.2
1-5-Peyer-s/Giarrusso-a; Snelson back-ups by Constant-s/Harper-a	4.00

HATARI (See Movie Classics)

HATCHET (Based on the 2007 movie)(Also see Victor Crowley's ...)
American Mythology Productions: No. 0, 2017 - No. 3, 2018 ($3.99)

	NM- 9.2
0-3-Kuhoric-s/Mangum-a; Victor Crowley app.	4.00

HATCHET: VENGEANCE (Based on the 2007 movie)
American Mythology Productions: 2018 - No. 3, 2019 ($3.99)

	NM- 9.2
1-3-Kuhoric-s/Calzada-a; prelude to the first movie	4.00

HATE
Fantagraphics Books: Spr, 1990 - No. 30, 1998 ($2.50/$2.95, B&W/color)

	GD 2.0	VG 4.0	FN 6.0	VF 8.0	VF/NM 9.0	NM- 9.2
1	2	4	6	11	16	20
2-3	1	2	3	5	6	8
4-10						5.00
11-20: 16- color begins						4.00
21-29						3.00
30-($3.95) Last issue						4.00
Annual 1 (2/01, $3.95) Peter Bagge-s/a						5.00
Annual 2-9 (12/01 - No. 9, Spr, 2011; $4.95) Peter Bagge-s/a						5.00
Buddy Bites the Bullet! (2001, $16.95) r/Buddy stories in color						17.00
Buddy Go Home! (1997, $16.95) r/Buddy stories in color						17.00
Hate-Ball Special Edition ($3.95, giveaway)-reprints						4.00
Hate Jamboree (10/98, $4.50) old & new cartoons						4.50

HATHAWAYS, THE (TV)
Dell Publishing Co.: No. 1298, Feb-Apr, 1962 (one-shot)

	GD 2.0	VG 4.0	FN 6.0	VF 8.0	VF/NM 9.0	NM- 9.2
Four Color 1298-Photo-c	5	10	15	31	53	75

HAUNT
Image Comics: Oct, 2009 - No. 28, Dec, 2012 ($2.99)

	NM- 9.2
1-McFarlane & Kirkman-s/Capullo & Ottley-a/McFarlane-a(i)/c; two variant-c	6.00
2-28: 2-Two covers. 13-($1.99). 19-Casey-s/Fox-a begins	3.00
Image Firsts: Haunt #1 (10/10, $1.00) r/#1 with "Image First" cover logo	3.00

HAUNTED (See This Magazine Is Haunted)

HAUNTED (Baron Weirwulf's Haunted Library on-c #21 on)
Charlton Comics: 9/71 - No. 30, 11/76; No. 31, 9/77 - No. 75, 9/84

	GD 2.0	VG 4.0	FN 6.0	VF 8.0	VF/NM 9.0	NM- 9.2
1-All Ditko issue	6	12	18	41	76	110
2-7-Ditko-c/a	3	6	9	21	33	45
8,12,28-Ditko-a	2	4	6	13	18	22
9,19	2	4	6	8	11	14
10,20,15,18: 10,20-Sutton-a. 15-Sutton-c	2	4	6	8	11	14
11,13,14,16-Ditko-c/a	3	6	9	16	23	30
17-Sutton-c/a; Newton-a	2	4	6	9	12	15
21-Newton-c/a; Sutton-a; 1st Baron Weirwulf	3	6	9	16	24	32
22-Newton-c/a; Sutton-a	2	4	6	9	13	16
23,24-Sutton-c; Ditko-a	2	4	6	9	13	16
25-27,29,32,33	1	3	4	6	8	10
30,41,47,49-52,60,74-Ditko-c/a: 51-Reprints #1	2	4	6	11	16	20
31,35,37,38-Sutton-a	1	3	4	6	8	10
34,36,39,40,42,57-Ditko-a	2	4	6	8	10	12
43-46,48,53-56,58,59,61-73: 59-Newton-a. 64-Sutton-c. 71-73-Low print	1	2	3	5	6	8
75-(9/84) Last issue; low print	2	4	6	9	13	16

NOTE: *Aparo c-45. Ditko a-1-8, 11-16, 18, 23, 24, 28, 30, 34r, 36r, 39-42r, 47r, 49-52r, 57, 60, 74. c-1-7, 11, 13, 14, 16, 30, 41, 47, 49-52, 74. Howard a-6, 9, 18, 22, 25, 32. Kim a-9, 19. Morisi a-13. Newton a-17, 21, 59r; c-21, 22(painted). Staton a-11, 12, 18, 21, 22, 30, 33, 35, 38; c-18, 33, 38. Sutton a-10, 17, 20-22, 31, 35, 37, 38; c-15, 17, 18, 23(painted), 24(painted), 27, 64r. #49 reprints Tales of the Mysterious Traveler #4.*

HAUNTED, THE
Chaos! Comics: Jan, 2002 - No. 4, Apr, 2002 ($2.99, limited series)

	NM- 9.2
1-4-Peter David-s/Nat Jones-a	3.00
...: Gray Matters (7/02, $2.99) David-s/Jones-a	3.00

HAUNTED CITY
Aspen MLT: No. 0, Aug, 2011 - No. 2 ($2.50/$3.50)

	NM- 9.2
0-($2.50)-Taylor & Johnson-s/Michael Ryan-a; four covers	3.00
1,2-($3.50) 1-Taylor & Johnson-s/Michael Ryan-a; four covers	3.50

HAUNTED LOVE
Charlton Comics: Apr, 1973 - No. 11, Sept, 1975

	GD 2.0	VG 4.0	FN 6.0	VF 8.0	VF/NM 9.0	NM- 9.2
1-Tom Sutton-a (16 pgs.)	6	12	18	40	73	105
2,3,6,7,10,11	3	6	9	19	30	40
4,5-Ditko-a	3	6	9	23	37	50
8,9-Newton-c	3	6	9	20	31	42
Modern Comics #1(1978)	2	3	4	6	8	10

NOTE: *Howard a-8i. Kim a-7-9. Newton c-8, 9. Staton a-1-6. Sutton a-1, 3-5, 10, 11.*

HAUNTED MANSION, THE (Disney Kingdoms)
Marvel Comics: May, 2016 - No. 5, Sept, 2016 ($3.99, limited series)

	NM- 9.2
1-5-Joshua Williamson-s/Jorge Coelho-a/E.M. Gist-c	4.00
... No. 1 Halloween Comic Fest 2016 (giveaway, 12/16) r/#1	3.00

HAUNTED TANK, THE
DC Comics (Vertigo): Feb, 2009 - No. 5, June, 2009 ($2.99, limited series)

	NM- 9.2
1-5-Marraffino-s/Flint-a. 1-Two covers by Flint and Joe Kubert	3.00
TPB (2010, $14.99) r/#1-5	15.00

HAUNTED THRILLS (Tales of Horror and Terror)
Ajax/Farrell Publications: June, 1952 - No. 18, Nov-Dec, 1954

	GD 2.0	VG 4.0	FN 6.0	VF 8.0	VF/NM 9.0	NM- 9.2
1-r/Ellery Queen #1	97	194	291	621	1061	1500
2-L. B. Cole-a r-/Ellery Queen #1	55	110	165	352	601	850
3,4: 3-Drug use story	50	100	150	315	533	750
5-Classic skull-c	168	336	504	1075	1838	2600
6-8,10,12: 7-Hitler story.	54	108	162	343	574	825

Haunt of Fear #21 © WMG

The Hawk #10 © Z-D

Hawk and the Dove #6 © DC

	GD	VG	FN	VF	VF/NM	NM-
	2.0	4.0	6.0	8.0	9.0	9.2

9-Classic decapitated heads-c 110 220 330 704 1202 1700
11-Nazi death camp story 97 194 291 621 1061 1500
13-18: 14-Jesus Christ apps. in story by Webb. 15-Jo-Jo-r. 18-Lingerie panels; skull-c
48 96 144 302 514 725

NOTE: ***Kamenish*** *art in most issues.* ***Webb*** *a-12.*

HAUNT OF FEAR (Formerly Gunfighter)
E. C. Comics: No. 15, May-June, 1950 - No. 28, Nov-Dec, 1954

15(#1, 1950)(Scarce) 343 686 1029 2744 4372 6000
16-1st app. "The Witches Cauldron" & the Old Witch (by Kamen); begin series as hostess of Haunt of Fear (also see Yellowjacket #7-10) 149 298 447 1192 1896 2600
17-Origin of Crypt of Terror, Vault of Horror, & Haunt of Fear; used in **SOTI**, pg. 43; last pg. Ingels-a used by N.Y. Legis. Comm.; story "Monster Maker" based on Frankenstein. Old Witch by Feldstein 143 286 429 1144 1822 2500
4-Ingels becomes regular artist for Old Witch. 1st Vault Keeper & Crypt Keeper app. in HOF; begin series 94 188 282 752 1201 1650
5-Injury-to-eye panel, pg. 4 of Wood story 86 172 258 688 1094 1500
6,7,9,10: 6-Crypt Keeper by Feldstein begins. 9-Crypt Keeper by Davis begins. 10-Ingels biog. 66 132 198 528 839 1150
8-Classic Feldstein Shrunken Head-c 91 182 273 728 1164 1600
11,12: Classic Ingels-c; 11-Kamen biog. 12-Feldstein biog.; "Poetic Justice" story adapted for the 1972 Tales From the Crypt film 57 114 171 456 728 1000
13,15,16,20: 16-Ray Bradbury adaptation. 20-Feldstein-r/Vault of Horror #12
51 102 153 408 654 900
14-Origin Old Witch by Ingels; classic-Ingels-c 77 154 231 616 983 1350
17-Classic Ingels-c and "Horror We? How's Bayou?" story, considered ECs best horror story
77 154 231 616 983 1350
18-Old Witch-c; Ray Bradbury adaptation & biography
74 148 222 592 946 1300
19-Used in **SOTI**, ill. "A comic book baseball game" & Senate investigation on juvenile delinq. bondage/decapitation-c 63 126 189 504 802 1100
21-27: 22-"Wish You Were Here" story inspired by "The Monkey's Paw" by W.W. Jacobs, which is referenced in story; adapted for the 1972 Tales From the Crypt film; Snow White satire. 23-EC version of the Hansel and Gretel story; **SOTI**, pg. 241 discusses the original Grimm tale in relation to comics. 24-Used in Senate Investigative Report, pg.8. 26-Contains anti-censorship editorial, 'Are you a Red Dupe?' 27-Cannibalism story; Vault Keeper shown reading **SOTI;** brief text reference to unpublished 4th EC horror title The Crypt of Terror
39 78 117 312 494 675
28-Low distribution 60 120 180 480 765 1050

NOTE: *(Canadian reprints known; see Table of Contents).* ***Craig*** *a-15-17, 5, 7, 10, 12, 13; c-15-17, 5-7.* ***Crandall*** *a-20, 21, 26, 27.* ***Davis*** *a-4-26, 28.* ***Evans*** *a-15-19, 22-25, 27.* ***Feldstein*** *a-15-17, 20; c-4, 8-10.* ***Ingels*** *a-16, 17, 4-28; c-11-28.* ***Kamen*** *a-16, 4, 6, 7, 9-11, 13-19, 21-28.* ***Krigstein*** *a-28.* ***Kurtzman*** *a-15(#1), 17(#3).* ***Orlando*** *a-9, 12.* ***Wood*** *a-15, 16, 4-6.*

HAUNT OF FEAR, THE
Gladstone Publishing: May, 1991 - No. 2, July, 1991 ($2.00, 68 pgs.)

1,2: 1-Ghastly Ingels-c(r); 2-Craig-c(r) 4.00

HAUNT OF FEAR
Russ Cochran/Gemstone Publ.: Sept, 1991 - No. 5, 1992 ($2.00, 68 pgs.); Nov, 1992 - No. 28, Aug, 1998 ($1.50/$2.00/$2.50)

1-28: 1-Ingels-c(r). 1-3-r/HOF #15-17 with original-c. 4,5-r/HOF #4,5 with original-c 4.00
Annual 1-5: 1- r/#1-5. 2- r/#6-10. 3- r/#11-15. 4- r/#16-20. 5- r/#21-25 14.00
Annual 6-r/#26-28 9.00

HAUNT OF HORROR, THE (Digest)
Marvel Comics: Jun, 1973 - No. 2, Aug, 1973 (164 pgs.; text and art)

1-Morrow painted skull-c; stories by Ellison, Howard, and Leiber; Brunner-a
4 8 12 25 40 55
2-Kelly Freas painted bondage-c; stories by McCaffrey, Goulart, Leiber, Ellison; art by Simonson, Brunner, and Buscema 3 6 9 16 24 32

HAUNT OF HORROR, THE (Magazine)
Cadence Comics Publ. (Marvel): May, 1974 - No. 5, Jan, 1975 (75¢) (B&W)

1,2: 2-Origin & 1st app. Gabriel the Devil Hunter; Satana begins
3 6 9 17 26 35
3-5: 4-Neal Adams-a. 5-Evans-a(2) 3 6 9 19 30 40

NOTE: ***Alcala*** *a-2.* ***Colan*** *a-2p.* ***Heath*** *r-1.* ***Krigstein*** *r-3.* ***Reese*** *a-1.* ***Simonson*** *a-1.*

HAUNT OF HORROR: EDGAR ALLAN POE
Marvel Comics (MAX): July, 2006 - No. 3, Sept, 2006 ($3.99, B&W, limited series)

1-3- Poe-inspired/adapted stories with Richard Corben-a 4.00
HC (2006, $19.99) r/series; cover sketches 20.00

HAUNT OF HORROR: LOVECRAFT
Marvel Comics (MAX): Aug, 2008 - No. 3, Oct, 2008 ($3.99, B&W, limited series)

1-3-Lovecraft-inspired/adapted stories with Richard Corben-a 4.00

HAVE GUN, WILL TRAVEL (TV)
Dell Publishing Co.: No. 931, 8/58 - No. 14, 7-9/62 (All Richard Boone photo-c)

Four Color 931 (#1) 12 24 36 84 185 285
Four Color 983,1044 (#2,3) 9 18 27 60 120 180
4 (1-3/60) - 10 7 14 21 46 86 125
11-14 7 14 21 44 82 120

HAVEN: THE BROKEN CITY (See JLA/Haven: Arrival and JLA/Haven: Anathema)
DC Comics: Feb, 2002 - No. 9, Oct, 2002 ($2.50, limited series)

1-9-Olivetti-c/a: 1- JLA app. Series concludes in JLA/Haven: Anathema 3.00

HAVOK & WOLVERINE - MELTDOWN (See Marvel Comics Presents #24)
Marvel Comics (Epic Comics): Mar, 1989 - No. 4, Oct, 1989 ($3.50, mini-series, squarebound, mature)

1-4: Art by Kent Williams & Jon J. Muth; story by Walt & Louise Simonson 6.00

HAWAIIAN DICK (Also see Aloha, Hawaiian Dick)
Image Comics: Dec, 2002 - No. 3, Feb, 2003 ($2.95, limited series)

1-3-B. Clay Moore-s/Steven Griffin-a 3.00
...: Byrd of Paradise TPB (8/03, $14.95) r/#1-3, script & sketch pages 15.00

HAWAIIAN DICK: SCREAMING BLACK THUNDER
Image Comics: Nov, 2007 - No. 5, Oct, 2008 ($2.99, limited series)

1-5-B. Clay Moore-s/Scott Chantler-a 3.00

HAWAIIAN DICK: THE LAST RESORT
Image Comics: Aug, 2004 - No. 4, June, 2006 ($2.95/$2.99, limited series)

1-4-B. Clay Moore-s/Steven Griffin-a 3.00
Vol. 2 TPB (10/06, $14.99) r/#1-4 & the original series pitch 15.00

HAWAIIAN EYE (TV)
Gold Key: July, 1963 (Troy Donahue, Connie Stevens photo-c)

1 (10073-307) 5 10 15 31 53 75

HAWAIIAN ILLUSTRATED LEGENDS SERIES
Hogarth Press: 1975 (B&W)(Cover printed w/blue, yellow, and green)

1-Kalelealuaka, the Mysterious Warrior 5.00

HAWK, THE (Also see Approved Comics #1, 7 & Tops In Adventure)
Ziff-Davis/St. John Publ. Co. No. 4 on: Wint/51 - No. 3, 11-12/52; No. 4, 1-2/53; No. 8, 9/54 - No. 12, 5/55 (Painted c-1-4)(#5-7 don't exist)

1-Anderson-a 30 60 90 177 289 400
2 (Sum, '52)-Kubert, Infantino-a 15 30 45 94 147 200
3-4 14 28 42 76 108 140
8-12: 8(9/54)-Reprints #3 w/different-c by Baker. 9-Baker-c/a; Kubert-a(r)/#2. 10-Baker-c/a; r/one story from #2. 11-Baker-c; Buckskin Belle & The Texan app. 12-Baker-c/a; Buckskin Belle app. 37 74 111 222 361 500
3-D 1(11/53, 25¢)-Came w/glasses; Baker-c 37 74 111 222 361 500

NOTE: ***Baker*** *c-8-12.* ***Larsen*** *a-10.* ***Tuska*** *a-1, 9, 12. Painted c-1, 4, 7.*

HAWK AND THE DOVE, THE (See Showcase #75 & Teen Titans) (1st series)
National Periodical Publications: Aug-Sept, 1968 - No. 6, June-July, 1969

1-Ditko-c/a 8 16 24 51 96 140
2-6: 5-Teen Titans cameo 5 10 15 32 51 70

NOTE: ***Ditko*** *c/a-1, 2.* ***Gil Kane*** *a-3p, 4p, 5, 6p; c-3-6.*

HAWK AND DOVE (2nd Series)
DC Comics: Oct, 1988 - No. 5, Feb, 1989 ($1.00, limited series)

1-Rob Liefeld-c/a(p) in all; 1st app. Dawn Granger as Dove 6.00
2-5 3.00
Trade paperback ('93, $9.95)-Reprints #1-5 12.00

HAWK AND DOVE
DC Comics: June, 1989 - No. 28, Oct, 1991 ($1.00)

1-28 4.00
Annual 1,2 ('90, '91; $2.00) 1-Liefeld pin-up. 2-Armageddon 2001 x-over 5.00

HAWK AND DOVE
DC Comics: Nov, 1997 - No. 5, Mar, 1998 ($2.50, limited series)

1-5-Baron-s/Zachary & Giordano-a 4.00

HAWK AND DOVE (DC New 52)
DC Comics: Nov, 2011 - No. 8, Jun, 2012 ($2.99)

1-8: 1-Gates-s/Liefeld-a/c; Deadman app. 6-Batman & Robin app.; Liefeld-s/a/c 3.00

HAWK AND WINDBLADE (See Elflord)
Warp Graphics: Aug, 1997 - No.2, Sept, 1997 ($2.95, limited series)

1,2-Blair-s/Chan-c/a 3.00

HAWKEN: MELEE (Based on the computer game Hawken)
Archaia Black Label: Dec, 2013 - No. 5 ($3.99, limited series)

Hawkeye (2012 series) #1 © DC

Hawkman (2018 series) #6 © DC

Hawkmoon: The Runestaff #1 © FC

	GD 2.0	VG 4.0	FN 6.0	VF 8.0	VF/NM 9.0	NM- 9.2

1,2: 1-Abnett-s/Dallocchio-a. 2-Jim Mahfood-s/a 4.00

HAWKEYE (See The Avengers #16 & Tales Of Suspense #57)
Marvel Comics Group: Sept, 1983 - No. 4, Dec, 1983 (limited series)

1-Mark Gruenwald-a/scripts in all; origin Hawkeye	3	6	9	14	20	26
2-4: 3-Origin Mockingbird. 4-Hawkeye & Mockingbird elope	1	3	4	6	8	10

HAWKEYE
Marvel Comics: Jan, 1994 - No. 4, Apr, 1994 ($1.75, limited series)

1-4 5.00

HAWKEYE (Volume 2)
Marvel Comics: Dec, 2003 - No. 8, Aug, 2004 ($2.99)

1-8: 1-6-Nicieza-s/Raffaele-a. 7,8-Bennett-a; Black Widow app. 4.00

HAWKEYE (Also see All-New Hawkeye)
Marvel Comics: Oct, 2012 - No. 22, Sept, 2015 ($2.99)

1-Fraction-s/Aja-a; Kate Bishop app.	3	6	9	16	23	30
2,3	1	3	4	6	8	10

4-8: 7-Lieber & Hamm-a 6.00
9-21: 10,12-Francavilla-a. 11-Dog issue. 16-Released before #15 4.00
22-($4.99) Aja-a 5.00
Annual 1 (9/13, $4.99) Pulido-a; Kate Bishop in L.A.; Madame Mask app. 5.00

HAWKEYE (Kate Bishop as Hawkeye)
Marvel Comics: Feb, 2017 - No. 16, May, 2018 ($3.99)

1-16: 1-5,7-11-Thompson-s/Romero-a. 5,6-Jessica Jones app. 4.00

HAWKEYE AND MOCKINGBIRD (Avengers) (Leads into Widowmaker mini-series)
Marvel Comics: Aug, 2010 - No. 6, Jan, 2011 ($3.99/$2.99)

1-($3.99) Heroic Age; Jim McCann-s/David Lopez-a; history of the characters 4.00
2-6-($2.99) Phantom Rider, Dominic Fortune & Crossfire app. 3.00

HAWKEYE & THE LAST OF THE MOHICANS (TV)
Dell Publishing Co.: No. 884, Mar, 1958 (one-shot)

Four Color 884-Lon Chaney Jr. photo-c	7	14	21	44	82	120

HAWKEYE: BLINDSPOT (Avengers)
Marvel Comics: Apr, 2011 - No. 4, Jul, 2011 ($2.99, limited series)

1-4: 1-McCann-s/Diaz-a; Zemo app. 2-Diaz & Dragotta-a 3.00

HAWKEYE: EARTH'S MIGHTIEST MARKSMAN
Marvel Comics: Oct, 1998 ($2.99, one-shot)

1-Justice and Firestar app.; DeFalco-s 5.00

HAWKEYE: FREEFALL
Marvel Comics: Mar, 2020 - No. 6, Nov, 2020 ($3.99, limited series)

1-6-Rosenberg-s/Schmidt-a; The Hood app. 4-Daredevil app. 4.00

HAWKEYE VS. DEADPOOL
Marvel Comics: No. 0, Nov, 2014 - No. 4, Mar, 2015 ($4.99/$3.99, limited series)

0-($4.99) Duggan-s/Lolli-a; Black Cat app. 5.00
1-4-($3.99) 1-Covers by Harren & Pearson; Kate Bishop & Typhoid Mary app. 4.00

HAWKGIRL (Title continued from Hawkman #49, Apr, 2006)
DC Comics: No. 50, May, 2006 - No. 66, Sept, 2007 ($2.50/$2.99)

50-66: 50-Chaykin-a/Simonson-s begin; One Year Later. 52-Begin $2.99-c. 57,58-Bennett-a. 59-Blackfire app. 63-Batman app. 64-Superman app. 3.00
...: Hath-Set TPB (2008, $17.99) r/#61-66 18.00
...: Hawkman Returns TPB (2007, $17.99) r/#57-60 & JSA Classified #21,22 18.00
...: The Maw TPB (2007, $17.99) r/#50-56 18.00

HAWKMAN (See Atom & Hawkman, The Brave & the Bold, DC Comics Presents, Detective Comics, Flash Comics, Hawkworld, JSA, Justice League of America #31, Legend of the Hawkman, Mystery in Space, Savage Hawkman, Shadow War Of..., Showcase, & World's Finest #256)

HAWKMAN (1st Series) (Also see The Atom #7 & Brave & the Bold #34-36, 42-44, 51)
National Periodical Publications: Apr-May, 1964 - No. 27, Aug-Sept, 1968

1-(4-5/64)-Anderson-c/a begins, ends #21	57	114	171	456	1028	1600
2	20	40	60	141	313	485
3,5: 5-2nd app. Shadow Thief	13	26	39	89	195	300
4-Origin & 1st app. Zatanna (10-11/64)	125	250	375	1000	1900	2800
6	10	20	30	66	138	210
7	9	18	27	62	126	190
8-10: 9-Atom cameo; Hawkman & Atom learn each other's I.D.; 3rd app. Shadow Thief	8	16	24	54	102	150
11-15	6	12	18	40	73	105
16-27: 18-Adam Strange x-over (cameo #19). 25-G.A. Hawkman-r by Moldoff. 26-Kirby-a(r). 27-Kubert-c	5	10	15	34	60	85

HAWKMAN (2nd Series)
DC Comics: Aug, 1986 - No. 17, Dec, 1987

1-17: 10-Byrne-c, Special #1 (1986, $1.25) 4.00
Trade paperback (1989, $19.95)-r/Brave and the Bold #34-36,42-44 by Kubert; Kubert-c 20.00

HAWKMAN (4th Series)(See both Hawkworld limited & ongoing series)
DC Comics: Sept, 1993 - No. 33, July, 1996 ($1.75/$1.95/$2.25)

1-($2.50)-Gold foil embossed-c; storyline cont'd from Hawkworld ongoing series; new costume & powers. 5.00
2-13,0,14-33: 2-Green Lantern x-over. 3-Airstryke app. 4,6-Wonder Woman app. 13-(9/94)-Zero Hour. 0-(10/94). 14-(11/94). 15-Aquaman-c & app. 23-Wonder Woman app. 25-Kent Williams-c. 29,30-Chaykin-c. 32-Breyfogle-c 4.00
Annual 1 (1993, $2.50, 68 pgs.)-Bloodlines Earthplague 5.00
Annual 2 (1995, $3.95)-Year One story 5.00

HAWKMAN (Title continues as Hawkgirl #50-on) (See JSA #23 for return)
DC Comics: May, 2002 - No. 49, Apr, 2006 ($2.50)

1-Johns & Robinson-s/Morales-a 5.00
1-2nd printing 3.00
2-40: 2-4-Shadow Thief app. 5,6-Green Arrow-c/app. 8-Atom-c/app. 13-Van Sciver-a. 14-Gentleman Ghost app. 15-Hawkwoman app. 16-Byth returns. 23-25-Black Reign x-over with JSA #56-58. 26-Byrne-c/a. 29,30-Land-c. 37-Golden Eagle returns 3.00
41-49: 41-Hawkman killed. 43-Golden Eagle origin. 46-49-Adam Kubert-c 3.00
...: Allies & Enemies TPB (2004, $14.95) r/#7-14 & pages from Secret Files and Origins 15.00
...: Endless Flight TPB (2003, $12.95) r/#1-6 & Secret Files and Origins 13.00
...: Rise of the Golden Eagle TPB (2006, $17.99) r/#37-45 18.00
... Secret Files and Origins (10/02, $4.95) profiles and pin-ups by various 5.00
... Special 1 (10/08, $3.50) Tie-in to Rann-Thanagar Holy War series; Starlin-s/a(p) 3.50
...: Wings of Fury TPB (2005, $17.99) r/#15-22 18.00

HAWKMAN
DC Comics: Aug, 2018 - No. 29, Jan, 2021 ($3.99)

1-29: 1-12-Venditti-s/Hitch-a. 1,9-12-Madame Xanadu app. 4-6-The Atom app. 13-Conrad-a 14-18-Year of the Villain tie-in. 14-17-Shadow Thief app. 18-22-The Infected. 27-Justice Society app. 4.00

HAWKMAN: FOUND (See Dark Nights: Metal series and other tie-ins)
DC Comics: Feb, 2018 ($3.99, one-shot)

1-Lemire-s/Hitch-a; foil-c 4.00

HAWKMOON: THE JEWEL IN THE SKULL
First Comics: May, 1986 - No. 4, Nov, 1986 ($1.75, limited series, Baxter paper)

1-4: Adapts novel by Michael Moorcock 3.00

HAWKMOON: THE MAD GOD'S AMULET
First Comics: Jan, 1987 - No. 4, July, 1987 ($1.75, limited series, Baxter paper)

1-4: Adapts novel by Michael Moorcock 3.00

HAWKMOON: THE RUNESTAFF
First Comics: Jun, 1988 -No. 4, Dec, 1988 ($1.75-$1.95, lim. series, Baxter paper)

1-4: ($1.75) Adapts novel by Michael Moorcock. 3,4 ($1.95) 3.00

HAWKMOON: THE SWORD OF DAWN
First Comics: Sept, 1987 - No. 4, Mar, 1988 ($1.75, lim. series, Baxter paper)

1-4: Dorman painted-c; adapts Moorcock novel 3.00

HAWKS OF THE SEAS (WILL EISNER'S...)
Dark Horse Comics: July, 2003 ($19.95, B&W, hardcover)

nn-Reprints 1937-1939 weekly Pirate serial by Will Eisner; Williamson intro. 20.00

HAWKWORLD
DC Comics: 1989 - No. 3, 1989 ($3.95, prestige format, limited series)

Book 1-3: 1-Tim Truman story & art in all; Hawkman dons new costume; reintro Byth 5.00
TPB (1991, $16.95) r/#1-3 17.00

HAWKWORLD (3rd Series)
DC Comics: June, 1990 - No. 32, Mar, 1993 ($1.50/$1.75)

1-Hawkman spin-off; story cont'd from limited series. 4.00
2-32: 15,16-War of the Gods x-over. 22-J'onn J'onzz app. 3.00
Annual 1-3 ('90-'92, $2.95, 68 pgs.), 2-2nd printing with silver ink-c 4.00
NOTE: *Truman a-30-32; c-27-32, Annual 1.*

HAYWIRE
DC Comics: Oct, 1988 - No. 13, Sept, 1989 ($1.25, mature)

1-13 3.00

HAZARD
Image Comics (WildStorm Prod.): June, 1996 - No. 7, Nov, 1996 ($1.75)

1-7: 1-Intro Hazard; Jeff Mariotte scripts begin; Jim Lee-c(p) 3.00

Headline Comics #5 © Prize

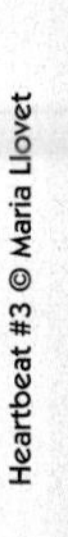
Heartbeat #3 © Maria Llovet

Heart Throbs #5 © QUA

HAZEL & CHA CHA SAVE CHRISTMAS: TALES FROM THE UMBRELLA ACADEMY
Dark Horse Comics: Nov, 2019 ($4.99, one-shot)

	GD 2.0	VG 4.0	FN 6.0	VF 8.0	VF/NM 9.0	NM- 9.2
1-Gerald Way & Scott Allie-s/Tommy Lee Edwards-a; covers by Edwards & Mahfood						5.00

HEADLINE COMICS
DC Comics: Jan. 1942

nn - Ashcan comic, not distributed to newsstands, only for in-house use. Cover art is More Fun Comics #73, interior being Star Spangled Comics #2 (a FN copy sold for $2270.50 in 2012)

HEADLINE COMICS (...For the American Boy) (...Crime No. 32-39)
Prize Publ./American Boys' Comics: Feb, 1943 - No. 22, Nov-Dec, 1946; No. 23, 1947 - No. 77, Oct, 1956

	GD 2.0	VG 4.0	FN 6.0	VF 8.0	VF/NM 9.0	NM- 9.2
1-WWII-c/sty.; Junior Rangers-c/stories begin; Yank & Doodle x-over in Junior Rangers (Junior Rangers are Uncle Sam's nephews)	110	220	330	704	1202	1700
2-Japanese WWII-c; Junior Rangers "Nip the Nippons!"-c	65	130	195	416	708	1000
3-Junior Rangers vs. Hitler sty.; 1st app. Invisible Boy; German WWII-c; used in **POP**, pg. 84 (scarce)	61	122	183	390	670	950
4-Junior Rangers vs. Hitler, Mussolini, Hirohito & Dr. Schmutz (1st app.); German WWII-c; (scarce)	58	116	174	371	636	900
5-7,9: 5-Junior Rangers invade Italy; WWII-c/sty. 6,7-Nazi WWII-c/sty. 7-1st app. Kinker Kinkaid (ends #12). 9-WWII Halloween-c/sty	57	114	171	362	619	875
8-Classic Hitler-c	1725	3450	5175	10,400	14,700	19,000
10-Hitler story	57	114	171	362	619	875
11-Classic Mad Japanese scientist WWII-c	161	322	483	1030	1765	2500
12,13,15: 13,15-Blue Streak app.	27	54	81	162	266	370
14-Japanese WWII-c	31	62	93	186	303	420
16-Origin & 1st app. Atomic Man (11-12/45)	39	78	117	231	378	525
17,18-Atomic Man-c/sty.	27	54	81	162	266	370
19-Atomic Man-c/sty.; S&K-a	39	78	117	231	378	525
20,21: 21-Atomic Man ends (9-10/46)	22	44	66	128	209	290
22-Last Junior Rangers; Kiefer-c	20	40	60	115	185	255
23,24: (All S&K-a). 23-Valentine's Day Massacre story; content changes to true crime. 24-Dope-crazy killer story	36	72	108	216	351	485
25-35-S&K-c/a. 25-Powell-a	31	62	93	186	303	420
36-S&K-a; photo-c begin	27	54	81	158	259	360
37-1 pg. S&K, Severin-a; rare Kirby photo-c app.	47	94	141	296	498	700
38,40-Meskin-a	15	30	45	88	137	185
39,41-43,46-56: 41-J. Edgar Hoover 26th Anniversary Issue with photo on-c. 43,49-Meskin-a. 48-Meskin-c	14	28	42	82	121	160
44,45-S&K-c; Severin/Elder, Meskin-a	20	40	60	114	182	250
57-77: 70-Roller Derby-c. 72-Meskin-c/a(i)	14	28	42	76	108	140

NOTE: ***Hollingsworth** a-30. Photo c-36-43. **H. C. Kiefer** c-12-16, 22. Atomic Man c-17-19.*

HEAP, THE
Skywald Publications: Sept, 1971 (52 pgs.)

	GD 2.0	VG 4.0	FN 6.0	VF 8.0	VF/NM 9.0	NM- 9.2
1-Kinstler-r/Strange Worlds #8; new-s w/Sutton-a	5	10	15	31	53	75

HEART AND SOUL
Mikeross Publications: April-May, 1954 - No. 2, June-July, 1954

	GD 2.0	VG 4.0	FN 6.0	VF 8.0	VF/NM 9.0	NM- 9.2
1,2	12	24	36	67	94	120

HEART ATTACK
Image Comics (Skybound): Nov, 2019 - No. 6, Jun, 2020 ($3.99)

	GD 2.0	VG 4.0	FN 6.0	VF 8.0	VF/NM 9.0	NM- 9.2
1-6-Shawn Kittelsen-s/Eric Zawadzki-a						4.00

HEARTBEAT (Also see Faithless)
BOOM! Studios: Nov, 2019 - No 5, Mar, 2020 ($3.99, limited series)

	GD 2.0	VG 4.0	FN 6.0	VF 8.0	VF/NM 9.0	NM- 9.2
1-5-Maria Llovet-s/a						4.00

HEARTBREAKERS (Also see Dark Horse Presents)
Dark Horse Comics: Apr, 1996 - No. 4, July, 1996 ($2.95, limited series)

	GD 2.0	VG 4.0	FN 6.0	VF 8.0	VF/NM 9.0	NM- 9.2
1-4: 1-With paper doll & pin-up. 2-Alex Ross pin-up. 3-Evan Dorkin pin-ups. 4-Brereton-c; Matt Wagner pin-up						3.00
...Superdigest (7/98, $9.95, digest-size) new stories						10.00

HEARTLAND (See Hellblazer)
DC Comics (Vertigo): Mar, 1997 ($4.95, one-shot, mature)

	GD 2.0	VG 4.0	FN 6.0	VF 8.0	VF/NM 9.0	NM- 9.2
1-Garth Ennis-s/Steve Dillon-c/a						5.00

HEART OF EMPIRE
Dark Horse Comics: Apr, 1999 - No. 9, Dec, 1999 ($2.95, limited series)

	GD 2.0	VG 4.0	FN 6.0	VF 8.0	VF/NM 9.0	NM- 9.2
1-9-Bryan Talbot-s/a						3.00

HEART OF THE BEAST, THE
DC Comics (Vertigo): 1994 ($19.95, hardcover, mature)

	GD 2.0	VG 4.0	FN 6.0	VF 8.0	VF/NM 9.0	NM- 9.2
1-Dean Motter scripts						20.00

HEARTS OF DARKNESS (See Ghost Rider; Wolverine; Punisher: Hearts of...)

HEART THROBS (Love Stories No. 147 on)
Quality Comics/National Periodical #47(4-5/57) on (Arleigh #48-101): 8/49 - No. 8, 10/50; No. 9, 3/52 - No. 146, Oct, 1972

	GD 2.0	VG 4.0	FN 6.0	VF 8.0	VF/NM 9.0	NM- 9.2
1-Classic Ward-c, Gustavson-a, 9 pgs.	54	108	162	343	574	825
2-Ward-c/a (9 pgs); Gustavson-a	33	66	100	196	321	445
3-Gustavson-a	17	34	51	103	162	220
4,6,8-Ward-a, 8-9 pgs.	21	42	63	124	202	280
5,7	15	30	45	86	133	180
9-Robert Mitchum, Jane Russell photo-c	17	34	51	103	162	220
10,15-Ward-a	17	34	51	103	162	220
11-14,16-20: 12 (7/52)	14	28	42	75	108	140
21-Ward-c	16	32	48	98	154	210
22,23-Ward-a(p)	14	28	42	80	115	150
24-33: 33-Last pre-code (3/55)	13	26	39	74	105	135
34-39,41-44,46 (12/56; last Quality issue)	12	24	36	69	97	125
40-Ward-a; r-7 pgs./#21	14	28	42	76	108	140
45-Baker-a	8	16	24	55	105	155
47-(4-5/57; 1st DC issue)	23	46	69	161	356	550
48-60, 100	9	18	27	62	126	190
61-70	7	14	21	46	86	125
71-99: 74-Last 10 cent issue	6	12	18	41	76	110
101-The Beatles app. on-c	17	34	51	119	265	410
102-119: 102-123-(Serial)-Three Girls, Their Lives, Their Loves	5	10	15	31	53	75
120-(6-7/69) Neal Adams-c	5	10	15	34	60	85
121-132,143-146	4	8	12	28	47	55
133-142-(52 pgs.)	5	10	15	30	50	70

NOTE: ***Gustavson** a-8. **Tuska** a-128. Photo c-4, 5, 8-10, 15, 17.*

HEART THROBS - THE BEST OF DC ROMANCE COMICS (See Fireside Book Series)

HEART THROBS
DC Comics (Vertigo): Jan, 1999 - No. 4, Apr, 1999 ($2.95, lim. series)

	GD 2.0	VG 4.0	FN 6.0	VF 8.0	VF/NM 9.0	NM- 9.2
1-4-Romance anthology. 1-Timm-c. 3-Corben-a						4.00

HEATHCLIFF (See Star Comics Magazine)
Marvel Comics (Star Comics)/Marvel Comics No. 23 on: Apr, 1985 - No. 56, Feb, 1991 (#16-on, $1.00)

	GD 2.0	VG 4.0	FN 6.0	VF 8.0	VF/NM 9.0	NM- 9.2
1-Post-a most issues	1	2	3	4	5	7
2-10,47: 47-Batman parody (Catman vs. the Soaker)						5.00
11-46,48-56: 43-X-Mas issue						4.00
Annual 1 ('87)						5.00

HEATHCLIFF'S FUNHOUSE
Marvel Comics (Star Comics)/Marvel No. 6 on: May, 1987 - No. 10, 1988

	GD 2.0	VG 4.0	FN 6.0	VF 8.0	VF/NM 9.0	NM- 9.2
1						5.00
2-10						4.00

HEAVY HITTERS
Marvel Comics (Epic Comics): 1993 ($3.75, 68 pgs.)

	GD 2.0	VG 4.0	FN 6.0	VF 8.0	VF/NM 9.0	NM- 9.2
1-Bound w/trading card; Lawdog, Feud, Alien Legion, Trouble With Girls, & Spyke						4.00

HEAVY LIQUID
DC Comics (Vertigo): Oct, 1999 - No. 5, Feb, 2000 ($5.95, limited series)

	GD 2.0	VG 4.0	FN 6.0	VF 8.0	VF/NM 9.0	NM- 9.2
1-5-Paul Pope-s/a; flip covers						6.00
TPB (2001, $29.95) r/#1-5						30.00
TPB (2009, $24.95) r/#1-5; development sketches and cover gallery; new cover						25.00
HC (2008, $39.99, dustjacket) r/#1-5; development sketches and cover gallery						40.00

HEAVY VINYL (Title changed from Hi-Fi Fight Club after #3)
Boom Entertainment (BOOM! Box): No. 4, Nov, 2017 ($3.99)

	GD 2.0	VG 4.0	FN 6.0	VF 8.0	VF/NM 9.0	NM- 9.2
4-Carly Usdin-s/Nina Vakueva-a						4.00

HECKLE AND JECKLE (Paul Terry's...)(See Blue Ribbon, Giant Comics Edition #5A & 10, Paul Terry's, Terry-Toons Comics)
St. John Publ. Co. No. 1-24/Pines No. 25 on: No. 3, 2/52 - No. 24, 10/55; No. 25, Fall/56 - No. 34, 6/59

	GD 2.0	VG 4.0	FN 6.0	VF 8.0	VF/NM 9.0	NM- 9.2
3(#1)-Funny animal	27	54	81	158	259	360
4(6/52), 5	14	28	42	80	115	150
6-10(4/53)	10	20	30	54	72	90
11-20	8	16	24	40	50	60
21-34: 25-Begin CBS Television Presents on-c	7	14	21	35	43	50

HECKLE AND JECKLE (TV) (See New Terrytoons)
Gold Key/Dell Publ. Co.: 11/62 - No. 4, 8/63; 5/66; No. 2, 10/66; No. 3, 8/67

	GD 2.0	VG 4.0	FN 6.0	VF 8.0	VF/NM 9.0	NM- 9.2
1 (11/62; Gold Key)	6	12	18	37	66	95
2-4	3	6	9	21	33	45
1 (5/66; Dell)	4	8	12	25	40	55

Hedy De Vine Comics #34 © MAR

Hellblazer #3 © DC

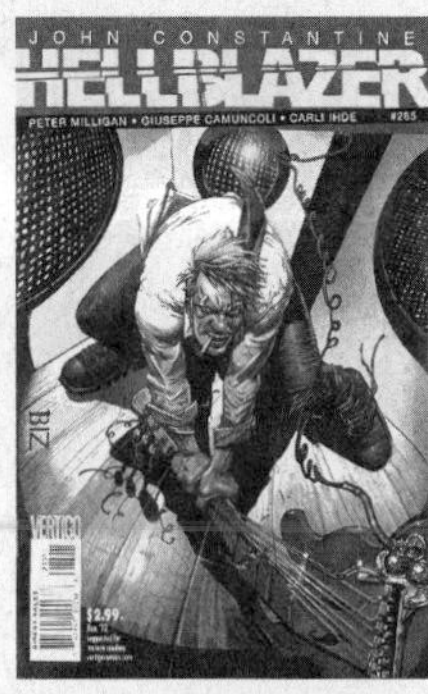

Hellblazer #285 © DC

	GD 2.0	VG 4.0	FN 6.0	VF 8.0	VF/NM 9.0	NM- 9.2

2,3 — 3 6 9 18 28 38

(See March of Comics No. 379, 472, 484)

HECKLE AND JECKLE 3-D
Spotlight Comics: 1987 - No. 2?, 1987 ($2.50)

1,2 — 5.00

HECKLER, THE
DC Comics: Sept, 1992 - No. 6, Feb, 1993 ($1.25)

1-6-T&M Bierbaum-s/Keith Giffen-c/a — 4.00

HECTIC PLANET
Slave Labor Graphics 1998 ($12.95/$14.95)

Book 1,2-r-Dorkin-s/a from Pirate Corp$ Vol. 1 & 2 — 15.00

HECTOR COMICS (The Keenest Teen in Town)
Key Publications: Nov, 1953 - No. 3, 1954

1-Teen humor — 10 20 30 56 76 95
2,3 — 7 14 21 37 46 55

HECTOR HEATHCOTE (TV)
Gold Key: Mar, 1964

1 (10111-403) — 6 12 18 41 76 110

HECTOR THE INSPECTOR (See Top Flight Comics)

HEDGE KNIGHT, THE
Image Comics: Aug, 2003 - No. 6, Apr, 2004 ($2.95, limited series)

1-6-George R.R. Martin-s/Mike S. Miller-a. 1-Two covers by Kaluta and Miller — 3.00
George R.R. Martin's The Hedge Knight HC (Marvel, 2006, $19.99) r/series; 2 covers — 20.00
George R.R. Martin's The Hedge Knight SC (Marvel, 2007, $14.99) r/series — 15.00
TPB (2004, $14.95) r/series plus new short story — 15.00

HEDGE KNIGHT II: SWORN SWORD
Marvel Comics (Dabel Brothers): Jun, 2007 - No. 6, Jun, 2008 ($2.99, limited series)

1-6-George R.R. Martin-s/Mike Miller-a. 1-Two covers by Yu & Miller, plus Miller B&W-c — 3.00
... HC (2008, $19.99) r/series; 2 covers — 20.00

HEDY DE VINE COMICS (Formerly All Winners #21? or Teen #22?(6/47); Hedy of Hollywood #36 on; also see Annie Oakley & Venus)
Marvel Comics (RCM): No. 22, Aug, 1947 - No. 35, Oct, 1949

22-1st app. Hedy De Vine (also see Joker #32) — 87 174 261 553 952 1350
23,24,27-30: 23-Wolverton-a, 1 pg; Kurtzman's "Hey Look", 2 pgs. 24,27-30- "Hey Look" by Kurtzman, 1-3 pgs. — 50 100 150 315 533 750
25-Classic "Hey Look" by Kurtzman, "Optical Illusion" — 52 104 156 328 552 775
26- "Giggles 'n' Grins" by Kurtzman — 41 82 123 256 428 600
31-34: 32-Anti-Wertham editorial — 32 64 96 188 307 425
35-Four pgs. "Rusty" by Kurtzman — 36 72 108 211 343 475

HEDY-MILLIE-TESSIE COMEDY (See Comedy Comics)

HEDY OF HOLLYWOOD (Formerly Hedy Devine Comics)
Marvel Comics (RCM)/Atlas #50: No. 36, Feb, 1950 - No. 50, Sept, 1952

36(#1) — 43 86 129 271 461 650
37-50 — 33 66 99 194 317 440

HEDY WOLFE (Also see Patsy & Hedy & Miss America Magazine V1#2)
Atlas Publishing Co. (Emgee): Aug, 1957

1-Patsy Walker's rival; Al Hartley-c — 33 66 100 196 321 445

HEE HAW (TV)
Charlton Press: July, 1970 - No. 7, Aug, 1971

1 — 5 10 15 30 50 70
2-7 — 3 6 9 21 33 45

HEIDI (See Dell Jr. Treasury No. 6)

HEIDI SAHA (AN ILLUSTRATED HISTORY OF...)
Warren Publishing: 1973 (500 printed)

nn-Photo-c; an early Vampirella model for Warren (a FN/VF copy sold in 2011 for $776.75)

HELEN OF TROY (Movie)
Dell Publishing Co.: No. 684, Mar, 1956 (one-shot)

Four Color 684-Buscema-a, photo-c — 9 18 27 60 120 180

HELL
Dark Horse Comics: July, 2003 - No. 4, Mar, 2004 ($2.99, limited series)

1-4-Augustyn-s/Demong-a/Meglia-c — 3.00

HELLBLAZER (John Constantine) (See Saga of Swamp Thing #37 & 2013 Constantine title) (Also see Books of Magic limited series and Sandman Universe Presents)
DC Comics (Vertigo #63 on): Jan, 1988 - No. 300, Apr, 2013 ($1.25-$2.99)

1-(44 pgs.)-John Constantine; McKean-c thru #21; 1st app. Papa Midnite — 4 8 12 28 47 65
1-Special Edition (7/10, $1.00) r/#1 with "What's Next?" cover logo — 3.00
2-5 — 1 2 3 5 7 9
6-8,10: 10-Swamp Thing cameo — 6.00
9,19: 9-X-over w/Swamp Thing #76. 19-Sandman app. — 1 2 3 5 6 8
11-18,20 — 6.00
21-26,28-30: 22-Williams-c. 24-Contains bound-in Shocker movie poster. 25,26-Grant Morrison scripts. — 5.00
27-Neil Gaiman scripts; Dave McKean-a; low print run — 3 6 9 14 19 24
31-39: 36-Preview of World Without End. — 5.00
40-($2.25, 52 pgs.)-Dave McKean-a & colors; preview of Kid Eternity — 6.00
41-Ennis scripts begin; ends #83 — 5.00
42-49,51-74,76-99,101-119: 44,45-Sutton-a(i). 52-Glenn Fabry painted-c begin. 62-Special Death insert by McKean. 63-Silver metallic ink on-c. 77-Totleben-c. 84-Sean Phillips-c/a begins; Delano story. 85-88-Eddie Campbell story. 89-Paul Jenkins scripts begin — 4.00
50,75,100,120: 50-($3.00, 52 pgs.). 75-($2.95, 52 pgs.). 100,120 ($3.50,48 pgs.) — 5.00
121-199, 201-249, 251-274,276-299: 129-Ennis-s. 141-Bradstreet-a. 146-150-Corben-a. 151-Azzarello-s begin. 175-Carey-s begin; Dillon-a. 176-Begin $2.75-c. 182,183-Bermejo-a. 216-Mina-s begins. 220-Begin $2.99-c. 229-Carey-s/Leon-a. 234-Initial printing (white title logo) has missing text; corrected printing has lt. blue title logo. 265,266,271-274-Bisley-a. 268-271-Shade the Changing Man app. — 4.00
200-($4.50) Carey-s/Dillon, Frusin, Manco-a — 5.00
250-($3.99) Short stories by various; art by Lloyd, Phillips, Milligan; Bermejo-c — 4.00
275-($4.99) Constantine's wedding; Bisley-c — 5.00
300-($4.99) Last issue; Bisley-c — 5.00
Annual 1 (1989, $2.95, 68 pgs.)-Bryan Talbot's 1st work in American comics — 6.00
Annual 1 (Annual 2011 on cover, 2/12, $4.99)-Milligan-s/Bisley-a/c — 5.00
Special 1 (1993, $3.95, 68 pgs.)-Ennis story; w/pin-ups. — 5.00
...Black Flowers (2005, $14.99, TPB) r/#181-186 — 15.00
...Bloodlines (2007, $19.99, TPB) r/#47-50,52-55,59-61 — 20.00
...Damnation's Flame (1999, $16.95, TPB) r/#72-77 — 17.00
...Dangerous Habits (1997, $14.95, TPB) r/#41-46 — 15.00
...Fear and Loathing (1997, $14.95, TPB) r/#62-67 — 18.00
...Fear and Loathing (2nd printing, $17.95) — 18.00
...: Freezes Over (2003, $14.95, TPB) r/#157-163 — 15.00
...Good Intentions (2002, $12.95, TPB) r/#151-156 — 13.00
...Hard Time (2001, $9.95, TPB) r/#146-150 — 10.00
...Haunting (2003, $12.95, TPB) r/#134-139 — 13.00
...Highwater (2004, $19.95, TPB) r/#164-174 — 20.00
John Constantine Hellblazer: All His Engines HC (2005, $24.95, with dustjacket) new graphic novel; Mike Carey-s/Leonardo Manco-a — 25.00
John Constantine Hellblazer: All His Engines SC (2006, $14.99) new graphic novel — 15.00
John Constantine Hellblazer: Bloody Carnations SC (2011, $19.99) r/#267-275 — 20.00
John Constantine Hellblazer: Empathy is the Enemy SC (2006, $14.99) r/#216-222 — 15.00
John Constantine Hellblazer: Hooked SC (2010, $14.99) r/#256-260 — 15.00
John Constantine Hellblazer: India SC (2010, $14.99) r/#261-266 — 15.00
John Constantine Hellblazer: Joyride SC (2008, $14.99) r/#230-237 — 15.00
John Constantine Hellblazer: Pandemonium HC (2010, $24.99, with dustjacket) new graphic novel; Jamie Delano-s/Jock-a — 25.00
John Constantine Hellblazer: Pandemonium SC (2011, $17.99) new graphic novel — 18.00
John Constantine Hellblazer: Scab SC (2009, $14.99) r/#250-255 — 15.00
John Constantine Hellblazer: The Devil You Know SC (2007, $19.99) r/#10-13, Annual #1 and The Horrorist miniseries #1,2 — 20.00
John Constantine Hellblazer: The Family Man SC (2008, $19.99, TPB) r/#23,24,28-33 — 20.00
John Constantine Hellblazer: The Fear Machine SC (2008, $19.99, TPB) r/#14-22 — 20.00
John Constantine Hellblazer: The Red Right Hand SC (2007, $14.99) r/#223-228 — 15.00
John Const. Hellblazer: The Roots of Coincidence SC ('09, $14.99) r/#243,244,247-249 — 15.00
...Original Sins (1993, $19.95, TPB) r/#1-9 — 20.00
...Original Sins (2011, $19.99, TPB) r/#1-9 — 20.00
...Rake at the Gates of Hell (2003, $19.95, TPB) r/#78-83; Heartland #1 — 20.00
...: Rare Cuts (2005, $14.95, TPB) r/#11,25,26,35,56,84 & Vertigo Secret Files: Hellblazer — 15.00
...: Reasons To Be Cheerful (2007, $14.99, TPB) r/#201-206 — 15.00
...: Red Sepulchre (2005, $12.99, TPB) r/#175-180 — 13.00
...: Setting Sun (2004, $12.95, TPB) r/#140-143 — 13.00
...: Son of Man (2004, $12.95, TPB) r/#129-133 — 13.00
...: Stations of the Cross (2006, $14.99, TPB) r/#194-200 — 15.00
...: Staring At The Wall (2005, $14.99, TPB) r/#187-193 — 15.00
...Tainted Love (1998, $16.95, TPB) r/#68-71, Vertigo Jam #1 and Hellblazer Special #1 — 17.00

NOTE: ***Alcala** a-8i, 9i, 18-22i. **Gaiman** scripts-27. **McKean** a-27,40; c-1-21. **Sutton** a-44i, 45i. **Talbot** a-Annual 1.*

HELLBLAZER (DC Rebirth)
DC Comics: Oct, 2016 - No. 24, Sept, 2018 ($2.99/$3.99)

Hellboy and the B.P.R.D.: The Seven Wives Club © Mike Mignola

Hellboy in Hell #6 © Mike Mignola

Hellboy: Seed of Destruction #1 © Mike Mignola

GD VG FN VF VF/NM NM-
2.0 4.0 6.0 8.0 9.0 9.2

1-8: 1-4-Simon Oliver-s/Moritat-a; Swamp Thing app. 5-7-Cassaday-c 3.00
9-24-($3.99): 9-12-Fabbri-a. 11,12-Lotay-c. 15-Justice League app. 20-24-Huntress app. 4.00
...: Rebirth 1 (9/16, $2.99) Oliver-s/Moritat-a; Swamp Thing, Wonder Woman app. 3.00

HELLBLAZER: CITY OF DEMONS
DC Comics (Vertigo): Early Dec, 2010 - No. 5, Feb, 2011 ($2.99, limited series)

1-5-Si Spencer-s/Sean Murphy-a/c 3.00
TPB (2011, $14.99) r/#1-5 & story from Vertigo Winter's Edge #3 15.00

HELLBLAZER: RISE AND FALL
DC Comics (Black Label): Nov, 2020 - No. 2, Jan, 2021 ($6.99, limited series, over-sized 10-7/8" x 8-1/2")

1,2-Tom Taylor-s/Darick Robertson-a; 2 covers on each 7.00

HELLBLAZER SPECIAL: BAD BLOOD
DC Comics (Vertigo): Sept, 2000 - No. 4, Dec, 2000 ($2.95, limited series)

1-4-Delano-s/Bond-a; Constantine in 2025 London 3.00

HELLBLAZER SPECIAL: CHAS
DC Comics (Vertigo): Sept, 2008 - No. 5, Jan, 2009 ($2.99, limited series)

1-5-Story of Constantine's cab driver; Oliver-s/Sudzuka-a/Fabry-c 3.00
... - The Knowledge TPB (2009, $14.99) r/#1-5 15.00

HELLBLAZER SPECIAL: LADY CONSTANTINE
DC Comics (Vertigo): Feb, 2003 - No. 4, May, 2003 ($2.95, limited series)

1-4-Story of Johanna Constantine in 1785; Diggle-s/Sudzuka-a/Noto-c 3.00

HELLBLAZER/THE BOOKS OF MAGIC
DC Comics (Vertigo): Dec, 1997 - No. 2, Jan, 1998 ($2.50, limited series)

1,2-John Constantine and Tim Hunter 4.00

HELLBOY (Also see Batman/Hellboy/Starman, Danger Unlimited #4, Dark Horse Presents, Gen[13] #13B, Ghost/Hellboy, John Byrne's Next Men, San Diego Comic Con #2, Savage Dragon, & Young Hellboy)

HELLBOY
Dark Horse Comics: Apr, 2008

... : Free Comic Book Day; Three short stories; Mignola-c; art by Fegredo, Davis, Azaceta 3.00

HELLBOY: ALMOST COLOSSUS
Dark Horse Comics (Legend): Jun, 1997 - No. 2, Jul, 1997 ($2.95, lim. series)

1,2-Mignola-s/a 1 3 4 6 8 10

HELLBOY AND THE B.P.R.D.
Dark Horse Comics: Dec, 2014 - No. 5, Apr, 2015 ($3.50, limited series)

1-5-Mignola & Arcudi-s/Maleev-a/c; Hellboy's first mission; set in 1952 3.50
...: Her Fatal Hour and The Sending (12/20, $3.99) Mignola-s/Trevallion-a 4.00
...: Long Night at Goloski Station (10/19, $3.99) Mignola-s/Matt Smith-a/Mignola-c 4.00
...: 1953 - Beyond the Fences 1-3 (2/16 - No. 3, 4/16, $3.50) Paolo Rivera-a/c 3.50
...: 1953 - The Phantom Hand & The Kelpie (10/15, $3.50) Mignola-s/c; Stenbeck-a 3.50
...: 1953 - The Witch Tree & Rawhead and Bloody Bones (11/15, $3.50) Mignola-s/c; Stenbeck-a 3.50
...: 1953 - The Witch Tree & Rawhead and Bloody Bones, Halloween Comics Fest (10/17, giveaway) Mignola-s/c; Stenbeck-a 3.00
...: 1954 - Black Sun 1,2 (9/16 - No. 2, 10/16, $3.99) Stephen Green-a/c 4.00
...: 1954 - Ghost Moon 1,2 (3/17 - No. 2, 4/17, $3.99) Mignola & Roberson-s/Churilla-a 4.00
...: 1954 - The Unreasoning Beast (11/16, $3.99) Mignola & Roberson-s/Reynolds-a 4.00
...: 1955 - Burning Season (2/18, $3.99) Mignola & Roberson-s/Rivera-a 4.00
...: 1955 - Occult Intelligence 1-3 (9/17 - No. 3, 11/17, $3.99) Churilla-a 4.00
...: 1955 - Secret Nature (8/16, $3.99) Mignola & Roberson-s/Martinbrough-a 4.00
...: 1956 1-5 (11/18 - No. 5, 3/19, $3.99) Mignola & Roberson-s/Norton, Li & Oeming-a 4.00
...: Saturn Returns 1-3 (8/19 - No. 3, 10/19, $3.99) Mignola & Allie-s/Mitten-a 4.00
...: The Beast of Vargu (6/19, $3.99) Mignola-s/Fegredo-a/c 4.00
...: The Return of Effie Kolb 1,2 (2/20 - No. 2, 10/20, $3.99) Mignola-s/Zach Howard-a 4.00
...: The Seven Wives Club (11/20, $4.99) Mignola-s/Hughes-a; covers by Mignola & Hughes 4.00

HELLBOY/BEASTS OF BURDEN
Dark Horse Comics: Oct, 2010 ($3.50, one-shot)

... Sacrifice - Dorkin & Mignola-s/Jill Thompson-a 1 2 3 5 6 8

HELLBOY: BEING HUMAN
Dark Horse Comics: May, 2011 ($3.50, one-shot)

nn-Mignola-s; Richard Corben-a/c; Roger app. 1 2 3 5 6 8

HELLBOY: BOX FULL OF EVIL
Dark Horse Comics: Aug, 1999 - No. 2, Sept, 1999 ($2.95, lim. series)

1,2-Mignola-s/a; back-up story w/ Matt Smith-a 1 3 4 6 8 10

HELLBOY: BUSTER OAKLEY GETS HIS WISH
Dark Horse Comics: Apr, 2011 ($3.50, one-shot)

nn-Mignola-s; Kevin Nowlan-a; two covers by Mignola & Nowlan
1 2 3 5 6 8

HELLBOY CHRISTMAS SPECIAL
Dark Horse Comics: Dec, 1997 ($3.95, one-shot)

nn-Christmas stories by Mignola, Gianni, Darrow 3 6 9 14 19 24

HELLBOY: CONQUEROR WORM
Dark Horse Comics: May, 2001 - No. 4, Aug, 2001 ($2.99, limited series)

1-4-Mignola-s/a/c 2 4 6 8 10 12

HELLBOY: DARKNESS CALLS
Dark Horse Comics: Apr, 2007 - No. 6, Nov, 2007 ($2.99, limited series)

1-6-Mignola-s/Fegredo-a 1 3 4 6 8 10

HELLBOY: DOUBLE FEATURE OF EVIL
Dark Horse Comics: Nov, 2010 ($3.50, one-shot)

1-Mignola-s; Corben-a/c 1 2 3 5 6 8

HELLBOY: HOUSE OF THE LIVING DEAD
Dark Horse Comics: Nov, 2011 ($14.99, hardcover graphic novel)

1-Mignola-s; Corben-a/c; Hellboy and Lucha Libre 15.00

HELLBOY IN HELL (Follows Hellboy's death in Hellboy: The Fury)
Dark Horse Comics: Dec, 2012 - No. 10, Jun, 2016 ($2.99)

1-Mignola-s/a/c in all 1 3 4 6 8 10
1-Variant "Year in Monsters" cover 12.00
2-6 5.00
7-10 3.00

HELLBOY IN MEXICO
Dark Horse Comics: May, 2010 ($3.50, one-shot)

1-Mignola-s; Corben-a/c; Mexican wrestlers vs. monsters
1 3 4 6 8 10

HELLBOY: IN THE CHAPEL OF MOLOCH
Dark Horse Comics: Oct, 2008 ($2.99, one-shot)

nn-Mignola-s/a/c 1 2 3 5 6 8

HELLBOY: INTO THE SILENT SEA
Dark Horse Comics: Apr, 2017 ($14.99, HC graphic novel)

nn-Mignola-s/c; Gianni-a 15.00

HELLBOY, JR.
Dark Horse Comics: Oct, 1999 - No. 2, Nov, 1999 ($2.95, limited series)

1,2-Stories and art by various 6.00
TPB (1/04, $14.95) r/#1&2, Halloween; sketch pages; intro. by Steve Niles; Bill Wray-c 15.00

HELLBOY, JR., HALLOWEEN SPECIAL
Dark Horse Comics: Oct, 1997 ($3.95, one-shot)

nn-"Harvey" style renditions of Hellboy characters; Bill Wray, Mike Mignola & various-s/a; wraparound-c by Wray 1 3 4 6 8 10

HELLBOY: KRAMPUSNACHT
Dark Horse Comics: Dec, 2017 ($3.99, one-shot)

nn-Krampus app.; Mike Mignola-s/Adam Hughes-a; covers by Mignola & Hughes 4.00

HELLBOY: MAKOMA, OR A TALE TOLD...
Dark Horse Comics: Feb, 2006 - No. 2, Mar, 2006 ($2.99, lim. series)

1,2-Mignola-s/c; Mignola & Corben-a 6.00

HELLBOY PREMIERE EDITION
Dark Horse Comics (Wizard): 2004 (no price, one-shot)

nn- Two covers by Mignola & Davis; Mignola-s/a; BPRD story w/Arcudi-s/Davis-a
2 4 6 9 12 15
Wizard World Los Angeles-Movie photo-c; Mignola-s/a; BPRD story w/Arcudi-s/Davis-a
2 4 6 9 13 16

HELLBOY: SEED OF DESTRUCTION (First Hellboy series)
Dark Horse Comics (Legend): Mar, 1994 - No. 4, Jun, 1994 ($2.50, lim. series)

1-Mignola-c/a w/Byrne scripts; Monkeyman & O'Brien back-up story (origin) by Art Adams. 4 8 12 25 40 55
2-1st app. Abe Sapien & Liz Sherman 3 6 9 14 20 25
3,4 2 4 6 8 11 14
Hellboy: One for One (8/10, $1.00) r/#1 Hellboy story with red cover frame 6.00
Trade paperback (1994, $17.95)-collects all four issues plus r/Hellboy's 1st app. in San Diego Comic Con #2 & pin-ups 18.00
Limited edition hardcover (1995, $99.95)-includes everything in trade paperback plus additional material. 100.00

HELLBOY STRANGE PLACES
Dark Horse Books: Apr, 2006 ($17.95, TPB)

Hellboy: The Crooked Man #1 © Mike Mignola

Hellcat #1 © MAR

Hellions #1 © MAR

	GD 2.0	VG 4.0	FN 6.0	VF 8.0	VF/NM 9.0	NM- 9.2

SC - Reprints Hellboy: The Third Wish #1,2 and Hellboy: The Island #1,2; sketch pages 18.00

HELLBOY: THE BRIDE OF HELL
Dark Horse Comics: Dec, 2009 ($3.50, one-shot)
1-Mignola-s/c; Corben-a; preview of The Marquis: Inferno 1 2 3 5 6 8

HELLBOY: THE CHAINED COFFIN AND OTHERS
Dark Horse Comics (Legend): Aug, 1998 ($17.95, TPB)
nn-Mignola-c/a/s; reprints out-of-print one shots; pin-up gallery 18.00

HELLBOY: THE COMPANION
Dark Horse Books: May, 2008 ($14.95, 9"x6", TPB)
nn-Overview of Hellboy history, characters, stories, mythology; text with Mignola panels 15.00

HELLBOY: THE CORPSE
Dark Horse Comics: Mar, 2004 (25¢, one-shot)
nn-Mignola-c/a/scripts; reprints "The Corpse" serial from Capitol City's Advance Comics catalog; development sketches and photos of the Corpse from the Hellboy movie 5.00

HELLBOY: THE CORPSE AND THE IRON SHOES
Dark Horse Comics (Legend): Jan, 1996 ($2.95, one-shot)
nn-Mignola-c/a/scripts; reprints "The Corpse" serial w/new story 1 3 4 6 8 10

HELLBOY: THE CROOKED MAN
Dark Horse Comics: Jul, 2008 - No. 3, Sept, 2008 ($2.99, lim. series)
1-3-Mignola-s/Corben-a/c 1 2 3 5 6 8

HELLBOY: THE FURY
Dark Horse Comics: Jun, 2011 - No. 3, Aug, 2011 ($2.99, lim. series)
1-3-Mignola-s/c; Fegredo-a. 1-Variant-c by Fegredo. 3-Hellboy dies 1 2 3 5 6 8
3-Retailer Incentive Variant 35 70 105 175 263 350

HELLBOY: THE GOLDEN ARMY
Dark Horse Comics: Jan, 2008 (no cover price)
nn-Prelude to the 2008 movie; Del Toro & Mignola-s/Velasco-a; 3 photo covers 1 3 4 6 8 10

HELLBOY: THE ISLAND
Dark Horse Comics: June, 2005 - No. 2, July, 2005 ($2.99, lim. series)
1,2: Mignola-c/a & scripts 1 2 3 5 6 8

HELLBOY: THE MIDNIGHT CIRCUS
Dark Horse Books: Oct, 2013 ($14.99, hardcover graphic novel)
nn-Mignola-s/c; Fegredo-a; young Hellboy runs away from BPRD in 1948 15.00

HELLBOY: THE RIGHT HAND OF DOOM
Dark Horse Comics (Legend): Apr, 2000 ($17.95, TPB)
nn-Mignola-c/a/s; reprints 18.00

HELLBOY: THE SLEEPING AND THE DEAD
Dark Horse Comics: Dec, 2010 - No. 2, Feb, 2011 ($3.50, lim. series)
1,2-Mignola-s/Scott Hampton-a 1 2 3 5 6 8

HELLBOY: THE STORM
Dark Horse Comics: Jul, 2010 - No. 3, Sept, 2010 ($2.99, lim. series)
1-3-Mignola-s/Fegredo-a 1 2 3 5 6 8

HELLBOY: THE THIRD WISH
Dark Horse Comics (Maverick): July, 2002 - No. 2, Aug, 2002 ($2.99, limited series)
1,2-Mignola-c/a/s 1 3 4 6 8 10

HELLBOY THE TROLL WITCH AND OTHERS
Dark Horse Books: Nov, 2007 ($17.95, TPB)
SC - Reprints Hellboy: Makoma, Hellboy Premiere Edition and stories from Dark Horse Book of Hauntings, DHB of Witchcraft, DHB of the Dead, DHB of Monsters 18.00

HELLBOY: THE WILD HUNT
Dark Horse Comics: Dec, 2008 - No. 8, Nov, 2009 ($2.99, lim. series)
1-8: Mignola-c/s; Fegredo-a 1 2 3 5 6 8

HELLBOY: THE WOLVES OF ST. AUGUST
Dark Horse Comics (Legend): 1995 ($4.95, squarebound, one-shot)
nn-Mignola--c/a/scripts; r/Dark Horse Presents #88-91 with additional story 2 4 6 8 10 12

HELLBOY VS. LOBSTER JOHNSON: THE RING OF DEATH
Dark Horse Comics: May, 2019 ($3.99, one-shot)
1-Mignola & Roberson-s; art by Norton & Grist; Paolo Rivera-c 4.00

HELLBOY: WAKE THE DEVIL (Sequel to Seed of Destruction)
Dark Horse Comics (Legend): Jun, 1996 - No. 5, Oct, 1996 ($2.95, lim. series)
1-5: Mignola-c/a & scripts; The Monstermen back-up story by Gary Gianni 2 4 6 8 10 12
TPB (1997, $17.95) r/#1-5 18.00

HELLBOY: WEIRD TALES
Dark Horse Comics: Feb, 2003 - No. 8, Apr, 2004 ($2.99, limited series, anthology)
1-8-Hellboy stories from other creators. 1-Cassaday-c/s/a; Watson-s/a. 6-Cho-c 1 2 3 5 6 8
... Vol. 1 (2004, 17.95) r/#1-4 18.00
... Vol. 2 (2004, 17.95) r/#5-8 and Lobster Johnson serial from #1-8 18.00

HELLBOY WINTER SPECIAL
Dark Horse Comics: Jan, 2016; Jan, 2017; Dec, 2018; Jan, 2020 ($3.99, one-shots)
1-Short stories by Mignola, Sale, Oeming, Allie, Roberson and others; Sale-c 4.00
nn (1/17)-Short stories; Mignola & Roberson-s, Mitten, Grist & Fiumara-a; Fiumara-c 4.00
... 2018 (12/18) Short stories; Mignola-s/Stenbeck-a; Bá & Moon-s/a; Zonjic-s/a 4.00
... 2019 (1/20) Short stories; Mignola-s/László-a; Roberson-s/Del Duca-a; Mutti-a 4.00

HELLCAT
Marvel Comics: Sept, 2000 - No. 3, Nov, 2000 ($2.99)
1-3-Englehart-s/Breyfogle-a; Hedy Wolfe app. 3.00

HELLCOP
Image Comics (Avalon Studios): Aug, 1998 - No. 4, Mar, 1999 ($2.50)
1-4: 1-(Oct. on-c) Casey-s 3.00

HELL ETERNAL
DC Comics (Vertigo Verité): 1998 ($6.95, squarebound, one-shot)
1-Delano-s/Phillips-a 7.00

HELLGATE: LONDON (Based on the video game)
Dark Horse Comics: No. 0, May 2006 - No. 3, Mar, 2007 ($2.99)
0-3-Edginton-s/Pugh-a/Briclot-c 3.00

HELLHOUNDS (...: Panzer Cops #3-6)
Dark Horse Comics: 1994 - No. 6, July, 1994 ($2.50, B&W, limited series)
1-6: 1-Hamner-c. 2-Joe Phillips-c. 3-(4/94) 4.00

HELLHOUND, THE REDEMPTION QUEST
Marvel Comics (Epic Comics): Dec, 1993 - No. 4, Mar, 1994 ($2.25, lim. series, coated stock)
1-4 4.00

HELLIONS (See 2020 X-Men titles)
Marvel Comics: May, 2020 - Present ($4.99/$3.99)
1-($4.99) Havok, Mr. Sinister, Psylocke, Scalphunter app.; Wells-s/Segovia-a 5.00
2-8-($3.99) 2-Scalphunter renamed Greycrow. 5,6-"X of Swords" tie-in 4.00

HELLMOUTH (Crossover with Buffy the Vampire Slayer and Angel)
BOOM! Studios: Oct, 2019 - No. 5, Feb, 2020 ($3.99, limited series)
1-5-Bellaire & Lambert-s/Carlini-a 4.00

HELLO BUDDIES
Harvey Publications: 1953 (25¢, small size)
1 4 8 12 27 44 60

HELLO, I'M JOHNNY CASH
Spire Christian Comics (Fleming H. Revell Co.): 1976 (39¢/49¢)
nn-(39¢-c) 3 6 9 16 23 30
nn-(49¢-c) 2 4 6 11 16 20

HELL ON EARTH (See DC Science Fiction Graphic Novel)

HELLO PAL COMICS (Short Story Comics)
Harvey Publications: Jan, 1943 - No. 3, May, 1943 (Photo-c)
1-Rocketman & Rocketgirl begin; Yankee Doodle Jones app.; Mickey Rooney photo-c 68 136 204 435 743 1050
2-Charlie McCarthy photo-c (scarce) 56 112 168 349 595 840
3-Bob Hope photo-c (scarce) 60 120 180 384 660 935

HELLRAISER (See Clive Barker's...)

HELLRAISER/NIGHTBREED – JIHAD (Also see Clive Barker's...)
Epic Comics (Marvel Comics): 1991 - Book 2, 1991 ($4.50, 52 pgs.)
Book 1,2 1 3 4 6 8 10

HELL-RIDER (Motorcycle themed magazine)
Skywald Publications: Aug, 1971 - No. 2, Oct, 1971 (B&W, 68 pgs.)
1-Origin & 1st app.; Butterfly & the Wild Bunch begin; 1st Hell-Rider by Andru, Esposito and Friedrich 7 14 21 44 82 120

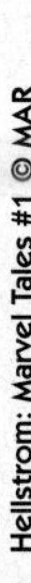
Hellstrom: Marvel Tales #1 © MAR

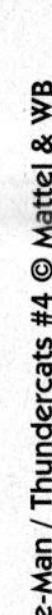
He-Man / Thundercats #4 © Mattel & WB

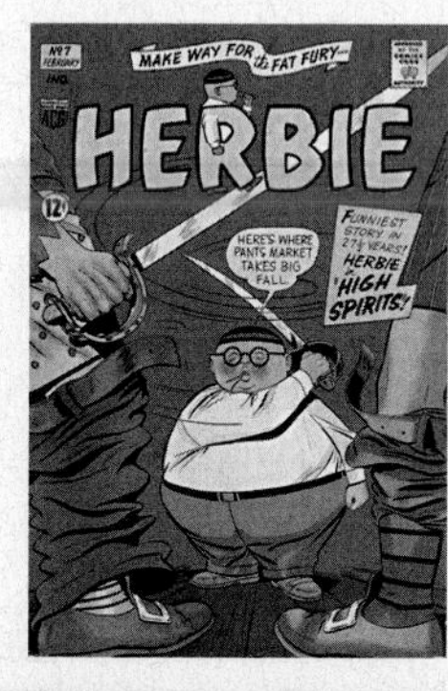

Herbie #7 © ACG

	GD	VG	FN	VF	VF/NM	NM-
	2.0	4.0	6.0	8.0	9.0	9.2

2-Andru, Ayers, Buckler, Shores-a 5 10 15 33 57 80
NOTE: *#3 advertised in Psycho #5 but did not come out.* ***Buckler*** *a-1, 2.* ***Rosenbaum*** *c-1,2.*

HELL'S ANGEL (Becomes Dark Angel #6 on)
Marvel Comics UK: July, 1992 - No. 5, Nov, 1993 ($1.75)
1-5: X-Men (Wolverine, Cyclops)-c/stories. 1-Origin. 3-Jim Lee cover swipe 4.00

HELLSHOCK
Image Comics: July, 1994 - No. 4, Nov, 1994 ($1.95, limited series)
1-4-Jae Lee-c/a & scripts. 4-Variant-c. 4.00

HELLSHOCK
Image Comics: Jan, 1997 - No. 3, Jan, 1998 ($2.95/$2.50, limited series)
1-($2.95)-Jae Lee-c/s/a, Villarrubia-painted-a 5.00
2-($2.50) 4.00
Book 3: The Science of Faith (1/98, $2.50) Jae Lee-c/s/a, Villarrubia-painted-a 4.00
Vol. 1 HC (2006, $49.99) r/#1-3 re-colored, with unpublished 22 pg. conclusion; cover gallery and sketches; alternate opening art; intro. by Jim Lee 50.00

HELLSPAWN
Image Comics: Aug, 2000 - No. 16, Apr, 2003 ($2.50)
1-Bendis-s/Ashley Wood-c/a; Spawn and Clown app. 5.00
2-9: 6-Last Bendis-s; Mike Moran (Miracleman app.). 7-Niles-s 3.00
10-16-Templesmith-a 3.00
...: The Ashley Wood Collection Vol. 1 (4/06, $24.95, TPB) r/#1-10; sketch & cover gallery 25.00

HELLSTORM: PRINCE OF LIES (See Ghost Rider #1 & Marvel Spotlight #12)
Marvel Comics: Apr, 1993 - No. 21, Dec, 1994 ($2.00)
1-($2.95)-Parchment-c w/red thermographic ink 4.00
2-21: 14-Bound-in trading card sheet. 18-P. Craig Russell-c 3.00

HELLSTORM: SON OF SATAN
Marvel Comics (MAX): Dec, 2006 - No. 5, Apr, 2007 ($3.99, limited series)
1-5-Suydam-c/Irvine-s/Braun & Janson-a 4.00
... - Equinox TPB (2007, $17.99) r/#1-5; interviews with the creators 18.00

HELLSTROM: MARVEL TALES
Marvel Comics: Jan, 2021 ($7.99, one-shot)
1-Reprints notable apps. in Ghost Rider #1, Son of Satan #1, Marvel Fanfare #59 and Hellstorm, Prince of Lies #1; Ralph Macchio intro. 8.00

HELMET OF FATE, THE (Series of one-shots following Doctor Fate's helmet)
DC Comics: Mar, 2007 - May 2007 ($2.99, one-shots)
...: Black Alice (5/07) Simone-s/Rouleau-a/c 3.00
...: Detective Chimp (3/07) Willingham-s/McManus-a/Bolland-c 3.00
...: Ibis the Invincible (3/07) Williams-s/Winslade-a; the Ibistick returns 3.00
...: Sargon the Sorcerer (4/07) Niles-s/Scott Hampton-s; debut new Sargon 3.00
...: Zauriel (4/07) Gerber-s/Snejbjerg-a/Kaluta-c; leads into new Doctor Fate series 3.00
TPB (2007, $14.99) r/one-shots 15.00

HELP US! GREAT WARRIOR
BOOM! Studios (BOOM! Box): Feb, 2015 - No. 6, Jul, 2015 ($3.99)
1-6-Madeleine Flores-s/a 4.00

HE-MAN (See Masters Of The Universe)

HE-MAN (Also see Tops In Adventure)
Ziff-Davis Publ. Co. (Approved Comics): Fall, 1952
1-Kinstler painted-c; Powell-a 18 36 54 109 172 235

HE-MAN
Toby Press: May, 1954 - No. 2, July, 1954 (Painted-c by B. Safran)
1-Gorilla-c 16 32 48 96 151 205
2-Shark-c 15 30 45 90 140 190

HE-MAN AND THE MASTERS OF THE UNIVERSE
DC Comics: Sept, 2012 - No. 6, Mar, 2013 ($2.99)
1-6: 1-James Robinson-s/Philip Tan-a/c; Skeletor app. 5-Adam gets the sword 3.00

HE-MAN AND THE MASTERS OF THE UNIVERSE
DC Comics: Jun, 2013 - No. 19, Jan, 2015 ($2.99)
1-19: 1-Giffen-s/Mhan-a/Benes-c. 7,8-Abnett-s/Kayanan-a. 13-18-Origin of She-Ra 3.00

HE-MAN AND THE MASTERS OF THE MULTIVERSE
DC Comics: Jan, 2020 - No. 6, Jul, 2020 ($3.99, limited series)
1-6: 1-3-Seeley-s/Fraga-a; He-Man of Hellskull app. 4-6-Derenick-a 4.00

HE-MAN: THE ETERNITY WAR
DC Comics: Feb, 2015 - No. 15, Apr, 2016 ($2.99)
1-15: 1-Abnett-s/Mhan-a; Hordak invades; origin of Grayskull 3.00

HE-MAN / THUNDERCATS
DC Comics: Dec, 2016 - No. 6, May, 2017 ($3.99, limited series)
1-6-Freddie Williams II-a; Mumm-Ra & Skeletor app. 4.00

HENNESSEY (TV)
Dell Publishing Co.: No. 1200, Aug-Oct, 1961 - No. 1280, Mar-May, 1962
Four Color 1200-Gil Kane-a, photo-c 7 14 21 48 89 130
Four Color 1280-Photo-c 6 12 18 40 73 105

HENRY (Also see Little Annie Rooney)
David McKay Publications: 1935 (52 pgs.) (Daily B&W strip reprints)(10"x10" cardboard-c)
1-By Carl Anderson 41 82 123 256 428 600

HENRY (See King Comics & Magic Comics)
Dell Publishing Co.: No. 122, Oct, 1946 - No. 65, Apr-June, 1961
Four Color 122-All new stories begin 16 32 48 110 243 375
Four Color 155 (7/47), 1 (1-3/48)-All new stories 10 20 30 70 150 230
2 6 12 18 40 73 105
3-10 5 10 15 34 60 85
11-20: 20-Infinity-c 5 10 15 30 50 70
21-30 4 8 12 25 40 55
31-40 3 6 9 21 33 45
41-65 3 6 9 17 26 35

HENRY (See Giant Comic Album and March of Comics No. 43, 58, 84, 101, 112, 129, 147, 162, 178, 189)

HENRY ALDRICH COMICS (TV)
Dell Publishing Co.: Aug-Sept, 1950 - No. 22, Sept-Nov, 1954
1-Part series written by John Stanley; Bill Williams-a
9 18 27 60 120 180
2 5 10 15 35 63 90
3-5 5 10 15 31 53 75
6-10 4 8 12 27 44 60
11-22 4 8 12 23 37 50

HENRY BREWSTER
Country Wide (M.F. Ent.): Feb, 1966 - V2#7, Sept, 1967 (All 25¢ Giants)
1 3 6 9 19 30 40
2-6(12/66), V2#7-Powell-a in most 3 6 9 14 20 25

HEPCATS
Antarctic Press: Nov, 1996 - No. 12 ($2.95, B&W)
0-12-Martin Wagner-c/s/a: 0-color 3.00
0-($9.95) CD Edition 10.00

HERALDS
Marvel Comics: Aug, 2010 - No. 5, Aug, 2010 ($2.99, weelky limited series)
1-5-Kathryn Immonen-s/Zonjic & Harren-a; She-Hulk, Hellcat, Emma Frost, Photon app. 3.00

HERBIE (See Forbidden Worlds #73,94,110,114,116 & Unknown Worlds #20)
American Comics Group: April-May, 1964 - No. 23, Feb, 1967 (All 12¢)
1-Whitney-c/a in most issues 18 36 54 126 281 435
2-4 8 16 24 56 108 160
5-Beatles parody (10 pgs.), Dean Martin, Frank Sinatra app. (10-11/64)
9 18 27 61 123 185
6,7,9,10 7 14 21 48 89 130
8-Origin & 1st app. The Fat Fury 8 16 24 55 105 155
11-23: 14-Nemesis & Magicman app. 17-r/2nd Herbie from Forbidden Worlds #94. 23-r/1st Herbie from F.W. #73 6 12 18 37 66 95
... Archives Volume One HC (Dark Horse, 8/08, $49.95, dust jacket) r/earliest apps. in Forbidden Worlds, Unknown Worlds, and Herbie #1-5; Scott Shaw intro. 50.00

HERBIE
Dark Horse Comics: Oct, 1992 - No. 12, 1993 ($2.50, limited series)
1-Whitney-r plus new-c/a in all; Byrne-c/a & scripts 4.00
2-6: 3-Bob Burden-c/a. 4-Art Adams-c 3.00

HERBIE GOES TO MONTE CARLO, HERBIE RIDES AGAIN (See Walt Disney Showcase No. 24, 41)

HERC (Hercules from the Avengers)
Marvel Comics: Jun, 2011 - No. 10, Jan, 2012 ($2.99)
1-6, (6.1), 7-10: 1-Pak & Van Lente-s; Hobgoblin app. 3-6-Fear Itself tie-in. 6.1-Grell-a 7,8-Spider-Island tie-in; Herc gets Spider-powers. 10-Elektra app. 3.00

HERCULES (See Hit Comics #1-21, Journey Into Mystery Annual, Marvel Graphic Novel #37, Marvel Premiere #26 & The Mighty...)

HERCULES (See Charlton Classics)
Charlton Comics: Oct, 1967 - No. 13, Sept, 1969; Dec, 1968
1-Thane of Bagarth begins; Glanzman-a in all 4 8 12 28 47 65
2-13: 1-5,7-10-Aparo-a. 8-(12¢-c) 4 8 12 23 37 50
4-Magazine format (low distribution) 8 16 24 54 102 150

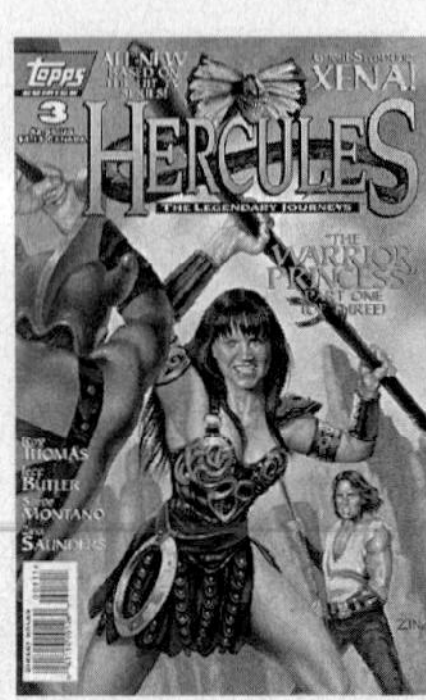

Hercules: The Legendary Journeys #3 © MCA TV

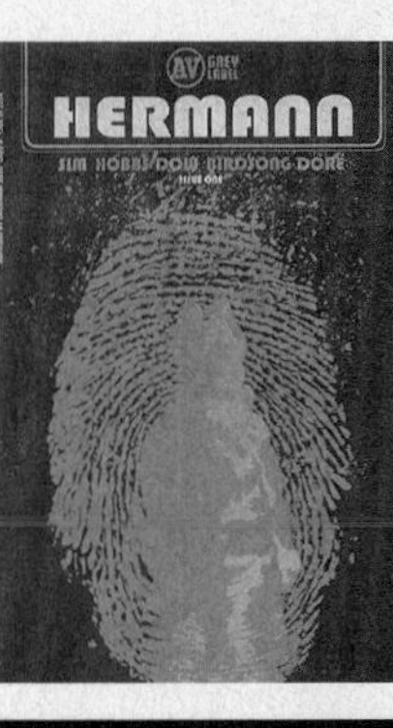

Hermann #1 © A-V

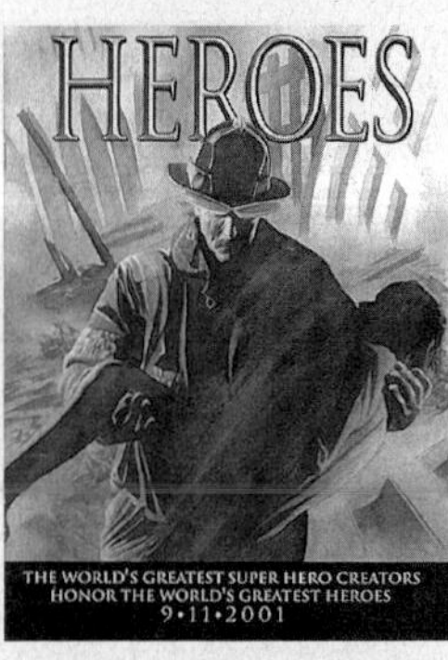

HEROES
THE WORLD'S GREATEST SUPER HERO CREATORS
HONOR THE WORLD'S GREATEST HEROES
9•11•2001

Heroes © MAR

	GD	VG	FN	VF	VF/NM	NM-
	2.0	4.0	6.0	8.0	9.0	9.2

8-Magazine format (low distribution)(12/68, 35¢, B&W); new Hercules story plus-r story/#1; Thane-r/#1-3	5	10	15	33	57	80
Modern Comics reprint 10('77), 11('78)						6.00

HERCULES (Prince of Power) (Also see The Champions)
Marvel Comics Group: V1#1, Sept, 1982 - V1#4, Dec, 1982; V2#1, Mar, 1984 - V2#4, Jun, 1984 (color, both limited series)

1-4, V2#1-4: Layton-c/a. 4-Death of Zeus. 4.00
NOTE: *Layton a-1, 2, 3p, 4p, V2#1-4; c-1-4, V2#1-4.*

HERCULES
Marvel Comics: Jun, 2005 - No. 5, Sept, 2005 ($2.99, limited series)

1-5-Texeira-a/c; Tieri-s. 4-Capt. America, Wolverine and New Avengers app. 3.00
...: New Labors of Hercules TPB (2005, $13.99) r/#1-5 14.00

HERCULES
Marvel Comics: Jan, 2016 - No. 6, Jun, 2016 ($3.99)

1-6: 1-Dan Abnett-s/Luke Ross-a; Gilgamesh app. 4.00

HERCULES: FALL OF AN AVENGER (Continues in Heroic Age: Prince of Power)
Marvel Comics: May, 2010 - No. 2, June, 2010 ($3.99, limited series)

1,2-Follows Hercules' demise in Incredible Hercules #141; Olivetti-c/a 4.00

HERCULES: HEART OF CHAOS
Marvel Comics: Aug, 1997 - No. 3, Oct, 1997 ($2.50, limited series)

1-3-DeFalco-s, Frenz-a 3.00

HERCULES: OFFICIAL COMICS MOVIE ADAPTION
Acclaim Books: 1997 ($4.50, digest size)

nn-Adaptation of the Disney animated movie 4.50

HERCULES: THE LEGENDARY JOURNEYS (TV)
Topps Comics: June, 1996 - No. 5, Oct, 1996 ($2.95)

1-2: 1-Golden-c						4.00
3-Xena-c/app.	1	2	3	5	6	8
3-Variant-c	2	4	6	10	14	18
4,5: Xena-c/app.						5.00

HERCULES UNBOUND
National Periodical Publications: Oct-Nov, 1975 - No. 12, Aug-Sept, 1977

1-García-López-a/Wood-i begins	2	4	6	10	14	18
2-12: 2-6-García-López-a. 7-Adams ad. 10-Atomic Knights x-over	2	3	4	6	8	10

NOTE: ***Buckler** c-7p. **Layton** inks-No. 9, 10. **Simonson** a-7-10p, 11, 12; c- 8p, 9-12. **Wood** a-1-8i; c-7i, 8i.*

HERCULES (...Unchained #1121) (Movie)
Dell Publishing Co.: No. 1006, June-Aug, 1959 - No.1121, Aug, 1960

Four Color 1006-Buscema-a, photo-c	9	18	27	61	123	185
Four Color 1121-Crandall/Evans-a	9	18	27	57	111	165

HERCULES: TWILIGHT OF A GOD
Marvel Comics: Aug, 2010 - No. 4, Nov, 2010 ($3.99, limited series)

1-4-Layton-s/a(i); Lim-a; Galactus app. 4.00

HERCULIAN
Image Comics: Mar, 2011 ($4.99, oversized, one-shot)

1-Golden Age style superhero stories and humor pages; Erik Larsen-s/a/c 5.00

HERE COMES SANTA (See March of Comics No. 30, 213, 340)

HERE'S HOWIE COMICS
National Periodical Publications: Jan-Feb, 1952 - No. 18, Nov-Dec, 1954

1	39	78	117	240	395	550
2	20	40	60	115	188	260
3-5: 5-Howie in the Army issues begin (9-10/52)	15	30	45	92	144	195
6-10	15	30	45	84	127	170
11-18	14	28	42	82	121	160

Ashcan (1,2/51) not distributed to newsstands (a FN copy sold for $836.50 in 2012)

HERETIC, THE
Dark Horse (Blanc Noir): Nov, 1996 - No. 4, Mar, 1997 ($2.95, lim. series)

1-4:-w/back-up story 3.00

HERITAGE OF THE DESERT (See Zane Grey, 4-Color 236)

HERMAN & KATNIP (See Harvey Comics Hits #60 & 62, Harvey Hits #14,25,31,41 & Paramount Animated Comics #1)

HERMANN
Aardvark-Vanaheim: Dec, 2020 ($4.00, B&W)

1-Cerebus figures with original Gustave Doré artwork; homage to Watchmen's Rorschach 4.00

HERMES VS. THE EYEBALL KID
Dark Horse Comics: Dec, 1994 - No. 3,Feb, 1995 ($2.95, B&W, limited series)

1-3: Eddie Campbell-c/a/scripts 3.00

H-E-R-O (Dial H For HERO)
DC Comics: Apr, 2003 - No. 22, Jan, 2005 ($2.50)

1-Will Pfeiffer-s/Kano-a/Van Fleet-c 3.50
2-22: 2-6-Kano-a. 7,8-Gleason-a. 12-14-Kirk-a. 15-22-Robby Reed app. 3.00
...: Double Feature (6/03, $4.95) r/#1&2 5.00
...: Powers and Abilities (2003, $9.95) r/#1-6; intro. by Geoff Johns 10.00

HERO (Warrior of the Mystic Realms)
Marvel Comics: May, 1990 - No. 6, Oct, 1990 ($1.50, limited series)

1-6: 1-Portacio-i 3.00

HERO ALLIANCE, THE
Sirius Comics: Dec, 1985 - No. 2, Sept, 1986 (B&W)

1,2: 2-($1.50), Special Edition 1 (7/86, color) 3.00

HERO ALLIANCE
Wonder Color Comics: May, 1987 ($1.95)

1-Ron Lim-a 3.00

HERO ALLIANCE
Innovation Publishing: V2#1, Sept, 1989 - V2#17, Nov, 1991 ($1.95, 28 pgs.)

V2#1-17: 1,2-Ron Lim-a 3.00
Annual 1 (1990, $2.75, 36 pgs.)-Paul Smith-c/a 3.00
Special 1 (1992, $2.50, 32 pgs.)-Stuart Immonen-a (10 pgs.) 3.00

HERO ALLIANCE: END OF THE GOLDEN AGE
Innovation Publ.: July, 1989 - No. 3, Aug, 1989 ($1.75, bi-weekly lim. series)

1-3: Bart Sears & Ron Lim-c/a; reprints & new-a 3.00

HEROBEAR AND THE KID
Boom Entertainment (KaBOOM!)

... 2013 Annual 1 (10/13, $3.99) Halloween-themed story 4.00
... 2016 Fall Special 1 (10/16, $5.99) Saving Time: Part Two 6.00
... Special (6/13, $3.99) Mike Kunkel-s/a/c 4.00
...: The Inheritance (8/13 - No. 5, 12/13, $3.99) 1-5-Mike Kunkel-s/a/c; origin re-told 4.00

HERO COMICS (Hero Initiative benefit book)
IDW Publishing: 2009 - Present ($3.99)

1-Short story anthology by various incl. Colan, Chaykin; covers by Wagner & Campbell 4.00
2011-Covers by Campbell & Hughes; Gaiman-s/Kieth-a; Chew & Elephantmen app. 4.00
2012-Cover by Campbell; TMNT by Eastman; art by Heath, Sim, Kupperberg, & others 4.00
2014-Covers by Campbell & Kieth; Sable by Grell; art by Kieth, Goldberg & others 4.00
...: A Hero Initiative Benefit Book SC (5/16, $19.99) reprints from previous editions 20.00

HEROES
Marvel Comics: Dec, 2001 ($3.50, magazine-size, one-shot)

1-Pin-up tributes to the rescue workers of the Sept. 11 tragedy; art and text by various; cover by Alex Ross 6.00
1-2nd and 3rd printings 4.00

HEROES (Also see Shadow Cabinet & Static)
DC Comics (Milestone): May, 1996 - No. 6, Nov, 1996 ($2.50, limited series)

1-6: 1-Intro Heroes (Iota, Donner, Blitzen, Starlight, Payback & Static) 3.00

HEROES (Based on the NBC TV series)
DC Comics (WildStorm): 2007; 2009 ($29.99, hardcover with dustjacket)

Vol. 1 - Collects 34 installments of the online graphic novel; art by various; two covers by Jim Lee and Alex Ross; intro. by Masi Oka; Jeph Loeb interview 30.00
Vol. 2 - (2009) Collects 46 installments of the online graphic novel; art by various incl. Gaydos, Grummett, Gunnell, Odagawa; two covers by Tim Sale and Gene Ha 30.00

HER-OES
Marvel Comics: Jun, 2010 - No. 4, Sept, 2010 ($2.99, limited series)

1-4-Randolph-s/Rousseau-a; Wasp, She-Hulk, Namora as teenagers 3.00

HEROES AGAINST HUNGER
DC Comics: 1986 ($1.50; one-shot for famine relief)

1-Superman, Batman app.; Neal Adams-c(p); includes many artists work; Jeff Jones assist (2 pg.) on B. Smith-a; Kirby-a 6.00

HEROES ALL CATHOLIC ACTION ILLUSTRATED
Heroes All Co.: 1943 - V6#5, Mar 10, 1948 (paper covers)

V1#1-(16 pgs., 8x11")	24	48	72	142	234	325
V1#2-(16 pgs., 8x11")	19	38	57	111	176	240
V2#1(1/44)-3(3/44)-(16 pgs., 8x11")	15	30	45	94	147	200
V3#1(1/45)-10(12/45)-(16 pgs., 8x11")	15	30	45	85	130	175

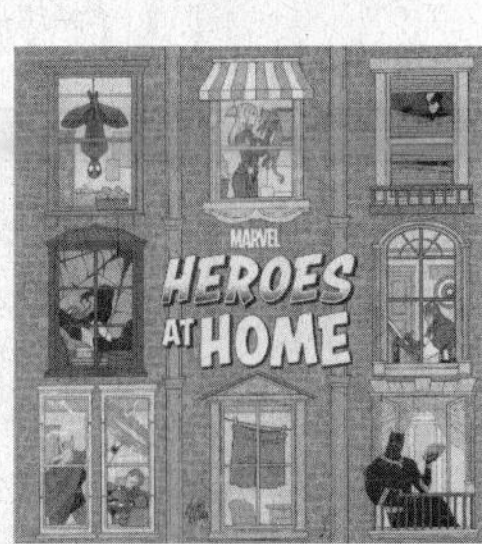

Heroes at Home #1 © MAR

Heroes Reborn: The Return #3 © MAR

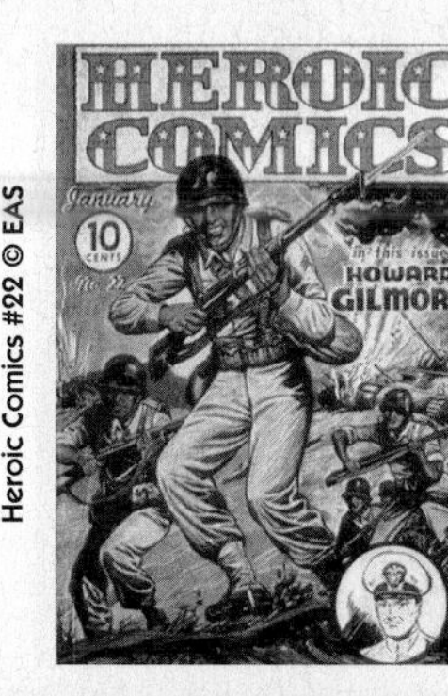

Heroic Comics #22 © EAS

GD 2.0 | VG 4.0 | FN 6.0 | VF 8.0 | VF/NM 9.0 | NM- 9.2

V4#1-35 (12/20/46)-(16 pgs.) 14 28 42 80 115 150
V5#1(1/10/47)-8(2/28/47)-(16 pgs.), V5#9(3/7/47)-20(11/25/47)-(32 pgs.), V6#1(1/10/48)-5(3/10/48)-(32 pgs.) 12 24 36 69 97 125

HEROES ANONYMOUS
Bongo Comics: 2003 - No. 6, 2004 ($2.99, limited series)

1-6-($2.99)-Bill Morrison-c. 2-Guerra-a. 3-Pepoy-a 3.00

HEROES AT HOME
Marvel Comics: 2020 ($9.99, 5" x 5", one-shot)

1-Zeb Wells-s/Gurihiru-a; humor strips of Marvel heroes quarantined at home 10.00

HEROES FOR HIRE
Marvel Comics: July, 1997 - No. 19, Jan, 1999 ($2.99/$1.99)

1-($2.99)-Wraparound cover 6.00
2-19: 2-Variant cover. 7-Thunderbolts app. 9-Punisher-c/app. 10,11-Deadpool-c/app. 18,19-Wolverine-c/app. 4.00
.../Quicksilver '98 Annual ($2.99) Siege of Wundagore pt.5 5.00

HEROES FOR HIRE
Marvel Comics: Oct, 2006 - No. 15, Dec, 2007 ($2.99)

1-5-Tucci-a/c; Black Cat, Shang-Chi, Tarantula, Humbug & Daughters of the Dragon app. 3.00
6-15: 6-8-Sparacio-c. 9,10-Golden-c. 11-13-World War Hulk x-over. 13-Takeda-c 3.00
... Vol. 1: Civil War (2007, $13.99) r/#1-5 14.00
... Vol. 2: Ahead of the Curve (2007, $13.99) r/#6-10 14.00
... Vol. 3: World War Hulk (2008, $13.99) r/#11-15 14.00

HEROES FOR HIRE
Marvel Comics: Feb, 2011 - No. 12, Nov, 2011 ($3.99/$2.99)

1-($3.99) Abnett & Lanning-s/Walker-a; back-up history of the various teams 4.00
2-12-($2.99) 2-Silver Sable & Ghost Rider app. 5-Punisher app. 9-11-Fear Itself tie-in 3.00

HEROES FOR HOPE STARRING THE X-MEN
Marvel Comics Group: Dec, 1985 ($1.50, one-shot, 52 pgs., proceeds donated to famine relief)

1-Stephen King scripts; Byrne, Miller, Corben-a; Wrightson/J. Jones-a (3 pgs.); Art Adams-c; Starlin back-c 1 3 4 6 8 10

HEROES: GODSEND (Based on the NBC TV series)(Prelude to the 2015 revival)
Titan Comics: Apr, 2016 - No. 5, Aug, 2016 ($3.99, limited series)

1-5: 1-Origin of Farah Nazan; Roy Allan Martinez-a; multiple covers on each 4.00

HEROES, INC. PRESENTS CANNON
Wally Wood/CPL/Gang Publ.: 1969 - No. 2, 1976 (Sold at Army PXs)

nn-Ditko, Wood-a; Wood-c; Reese-a(p) 2 4 6 11 16 20
2-Wood-c; Ditko, Byrne, Wood-a; 8-1/2x10-1/2"; B&W; $2.00 3 6 9 17 26 35

NOTE: *First issue not distributed by publisher; 1,800 copies were stored and 900 copies were stolen from warehouse. Many copies have surfaced in recent years.*

HEROES IN CRISIS
DC Comics: Nov, 2018 - No. 9, Jul, 2019 ($3.99, limited series)

1-9: 1-Tom King-s/Clay Mann-a; murder of Wally West, Arsenal and others 4.00

HEROES OF THE WILD FRONTIER (Formerly Baffling Mysteries)
Ace Periodicals: No. 27, Jan, 1956 - No. 2, Apr, 1956

27(#1),2-Davy Crockett, Daniel Boone, Buffalo Bill 6 12 18 29 36 42

HEROES REBORN (one-shots)
Marvel Comics: Jan, 2000 ($1.99)

...:Ashema; ...:Doom; ...:Doomsday; ...:Masters of Evil; ...:Rebel; ...:Remnants; ...:Young Allies 3.00

HEROES REBORN: THE RETURN (Also see Avengers, Fantastic Four, Iron Man & Captain America titles for issues and TPBs)
Marvel Comics: Dec, 1997 - No. 4 ($2.50, weekly mini-series)

1-4-Avengers, Fantastic Four, Iron Man & Captain America rejoin regular Marvel Universe; Peter David-s/Larocca-c/a 4.00
1-4-Variant-c for each 6.00
Wizard 1/2 1 2 3 5 7 9
Return of the Heroes TPB ('98, $14.95) r/#1-4 15.00

HEROES: VENGEANCE (Based on the NBC TV series)(Prelude to the 2015 revival)
Titan Comics: Nov, 2015 - No. 5, Mar, 2016 ($3.99, limited series)

1-5: 1-Origin of El Vengador; Rubine-a; multiple covers on each 4.00

HERO FOR HIRE (Power Man No. 17 on; also see Cage)
Marvel Comics Group: June, 1972 - No. 16, Dec, 1973

1-Origin & 1st app. Luke Cage; Tuska-a(p) 57 114 171 456 1028 1600
2-Tuska-a(p); 1st app. Claire Temple 6 12 18 42 79 115
3,4: 3-1st app. Mace. 4-1st app. Phil Fox of the Bugle 5 10 15 31 53 75
5-1st app. Black Mariah 5 10 15 34 60 85
6-10: 8,9-Dr. Doom app. 9-F.F. app. 10-1st app. Mr. Death 4 8 12 23 37 50
11-16: 14-Origin retold. 15-Everett Sub-Mariner-r('53). 16-Origin Stilletto; death of Rackham 3 6 9 19 30 40

HERO HOTLINE (1st app. in Action Comics Weekly #637)
DC Comics: April, 1989 - No. 6, Sept, 1989 ($1.75, limited series)

1-6: Super-hero humor; Schaffenberger-i 3.00

HEROIC ADVENTURES (See Adventures)

HEROIC AGE
Marvel Comics: Nov, 2010 ($3.99, limited series)

... Heroes 1 (11/10, $3.99) profile of heroes, bios, pros, cons, "power grid"; Raney-c 4.00
... Villains 1 (1/11, $3.99) profile of villains, bios, pros, cons, "power grid"; Jae Lee-c 4.00
... X-Men 1 (2/11, $3.99) profile of members in Steve Rogers journal entries,; Jae Lee-c4.00

HEROIC AGE: PRINCE OF POWER (Continued from Hercules: Fall of an Avenger)
Marvel Comics: Jul, 2010 - No. 4, Oct, 2010 ($3.99, limited series)

1-4-Van Lente & Pak-s; Thor app.; leads into Chaos War #1 4.00

HEROIC COMICS (Reg'lar Fellers...#1-15; New Heroic #41 on)
Eastern Color Printing Co./Famous Funnies (Funnies, Inc. No. 1): Aug, 1940 - No. 97, June, 1955

1-Hydroman (origin) by Bill Everett, The Purple Zombie (origin) & Mann of India by Tarpe Mills begins (all 1st apps.) 245 490 735 1568 2684 3800
2 103 206 309 659 1130 1600
3,4 57 114 171 362 619 875
5,6 50 100 150 315 533 750
7-Origin & 1st app. Man O'Metal (1 pg.) 52 104 156 328 552 775
8-10: 10-Lingerie panels 39 78 117 234 385 535
11,13 37 74 111 222 361 500
12-Music Master (origin/1st app.) begins by Everett, ends No. 31; last Purple Zombie & Mann of India 41 82 123 256 428 600
14,15-Hydroman x-over in Rainbow Boy. 14-Origin & 1st app. Rainbow Boy (super hero). 15-1st app. Downbeat 37 74 111 222 361 500
16-20: 16-New logo. 17-Rainbow Boy x-over in Hydroman. 19-Rainbow Boy x-over in Hydroman & vice versa 26 52 78 154 252 350
21-30:25-Rainbow Boy x-over in Hydroman. 28-Last Man O'Metal. 29-Last Hydroman 20 40 60 114 182 250
31,34,38 9 18 27 50 65 80
32,36,37-Toth-a (3-4 pgs. each) 10 20 30 56 76 95
33,35-Toth-a (8 & 9 pgs.) 10 20 30 58 79 100
39-42-Toth, Ingels-a 10 20 30 58 79 100
43,46,47,49-Toth-a (2-4 pgs.). 47-Ingels-a 10 20 30 54 72 90
44,45,50-Toth-a (6-9 pgs.) 10 20 30 56 76 95
48,53,54 9 18 27 47 61 75
51-Williamson-a 10 20 30 56 76 95
52-Williamson-a (3 pg. story) 9 18 27 50 65 80
55-Toth-a 10 20 30 54 72 90
56-60: 60-Everett-a 9 18 27 50 65 80
61-Everett-a 9 18 27 47 61 75
62,64-Everett-c/a 10 20 30 54 72 90
63-Everett-c 9 18 27 52 69 85
65-Williamson/Frazetta-a; Evans-a (2 pgs.) 13 26 39 72 101 130
66,75,94-Frazetta-a (2 pgs. each) 9 18 27 52 69 85
67,73-Frazetta-a (4 pgs. each) 11 22 33 60 83 105
68,74,76-80,84,85,88-93,95-97: 95-Last pre-code 9 18 27 47 61 75
69,72-Frazetta-a (6 & 8 pgs. each); 1st (?) app. Frazetta Red Cross ad 13 26 39 72 101 130
70,71,86,87-Frazetta, 3-4 pgs. each; 1 pg. ad by Frazetta in #70 10 20 30 56 76 95
81,82-Frazetta art (1 pg. each): 81-1st (?) app. Frazetta Boy Scout ad (tied w/ Buster Crabbe #9 9 18 27 50 65 80
83-Frazetta-a (1/2 pg.) 9 18 27 50 65 80

NOTE: ***Evans** a-64, 65. **Everett** a-(Hydroman-c/a-No. 1-9), 44, 60-64; c-1-9, 62-64. **Harvey Fuller** c-28-35. **Sid Greene** a-38-43, 46. **Guardineer** a-42(3), 43, 44, 45(2), 49(3), 50, 60, 61(2), 65, 67(2) 70-72. **Ingels** c-41. **Kiefer** a-46, 48; c-19-22, 24, 44, 46, 48, 51-53, 65, 67-69, 71-74, 76, 77, 79, 80, 82, 85, 86, 88, 89, 94, 95. **Mort Lawrence** a-45. **Tarpe Mills** a-2(2), 3(2), 10. **Ed Moore** a-49, 52-54, 56-63, 65-69, 72-74, 76, 77. **H.G. Peter** a-58-74, 76, 77, 87. **Paul Reinman** a-49. **Rico** a-31. Captain Tootsie by **Beck**-31, 32. Painted-c #16 on. Hydroman c-1-11. Music Master c-12, 13, 15. Rainbow Boy c-14.*

HERO INITIATIVE: MIKE WIERINGO BOOK (Also see Hero Comics)
Marvel Comics: Aug, 2008 ($4.99)

1-The "What If" Fantastic Four story with Wieringo-a (7 pgs.) finished by other artists after

Hex Wives #6 © Ben Blacker

Hickory #2 © QUA

Hi-Ho Comics #1 © Four Star

	GD	VG	FN	VF	VF/NM	NM-
	2.0	4.0	6.0	8.0	9.0	9.2

his passing; art by Davis, Immonen, Ramos, Kitson and others; written tributes 5.00

HERO WORSHIP
Avatar Press: Jun, 2012 - No. 6, Nov, 2012 ($3.99)
1-6: 1-Zak Penn & Scott Murphy-s/Michael DiPascale-a; 2 covers 4.00

HERO ZERO (Also see Comics' Greatest World & Godzilla Versus Hero Zero)
Dark Horse Comics: Sept, 1994 ($2.50)
0 3.00

HEX (Replaces Jonah Hex)
DC Comics: Sept, 1985 - No. 18, Feb, 1987 (Story cont'd from Jonah Hex # 92)
1-Hex in post-atomic war world; origin 2 4 6 8 10 12
2-10,14-18: 6-Origin Stiletta 1 2 3 4 5 7
11-13: All contain future Batman storyline. 13-Intro The Dogs of War (origin #15) 1 3 4 6 8 10
NOTE: *Giffen a(p)-15-18; c(p)-15,17,18.* ***Texeira*** *a-1, 2p, 3p, 5-7p, 9p, 11-14p; c(p)-1, 2, 4-7, 12.*

HEXBREAKER (See First Comics Graphic Novel #15)

HEXED
BOOM! Studios: Aug, 2014 - No. 12, Aug, 2015 ($3.99)
1-12: 1-Michael Alan Nelson-s/Dan Mora-s; 3 covers 4.00

HEX WIVES
DC Comics (Vertigo): Dec, 2018 - No. 6, May, 2019 ($3.99)
1-6: 1-Ben Blacker-s/Mirka Andolfo-a/Joëlle Jones-c. 5-Lotay-c 4.00

HEY KIDS! COMICS!
Image Comics: Aug, 2018 - No. 5, Dec, 2018 ($3.99, limited series)
1-5-Howard Chaykin-s/a 4.00

HEY THERE, IT'S YOGI BEAR (See Movie Comics)

HI-ADVENTURE HEROES (TV)
Gold Key: May, 1969 - No. 2, Aug, 1969 (Hanna-Barbera)
1-Three Musketeers, Gulliver, Arabian Knights 5 10 15 30 50 70
2-Three Musketeers, Micro-Venture, Arabian Knights 4 8 12 27 44 60

HI AND LOIS
Dell Publishing Co.: No. 683, Mar, 1956 - No. 955, Nov, 1958
Four Color 683 (#1) 5 10 15 35 63 90
Four Color 774(3/57),955 4 8 12 28 47 65

HI AND LOIS
Charlton Comics: Nov, 1969 - No. 11, July, 1971
1 3 6 9 14 20 25
2-11 2 4 6 9 12 15

HICKORY (See All Humor Comics)
Quality Comics Group: Oct, 1949 - No. 6, Aug, 1950
1-Sahl-c/a in all; Feldstein?-a 30 60 90 177 289 400
2 19 38 57 112 179 245
3-6-Good Girl covers 37 74 111 222 361 500

HIDDEN CREW, THE (See The United States Air Force Presents:...)

HIDDEN SOCIETY
Dark Horse Comics: Feb, 2020 - No. 4, Oct, 2020 ($3.99, limited series)
1-4-Rafael Scavone-s/Rafael Albuquerque-a; two covers 4.00

HIDE-OUT (See Zane Grey, Four Color No. 346)

HIDING PLACE, THE
Spire Christian Comics (Fleming H. Revell Co.): 1973 (39¢/49¢)
nn 3 6 9 17 26 35

HI-FI FIGHT CLUB (Title changes to Heavy Vinyl for #4)
Boom Entertainment (BOOM! Box): Aug, 2017 - No. 3, Oct, 2017 ($3.99)
1-3-Carly Usdin-s/Nina Vakueva-a 4.00

HIGH ADVENTURE
Red Top(Decker) Comics (Farrell): Oct, 1957
1-Krigstein-r from Explorer Joe (re-issue on-c) 5 10 15 23 28 32

HIGH ADVENTURE (TV)
Dell Publishing Co.: No. 949, Nov, 1958 - No. 1001, Aug-Oct, 1959 (Lowell Thomas)
Four Color 949 (#1)-Photo-c 5 10 15 34 60 85
Four Color 1001-Lowell Thomas'...(#2) 5 10 15 33 57 80

HIGH CHAPPARAL (TV)
Gold Key: Aug, 1968 (Photo-c)
1 (10226-808)-Tufts-a 6 12 18 38 69 100

HIGH HEAVEN
Ahoy Comics: 2018 - No. 5, 2019 ($3.99)
1-5-Tom Peyer-s/Greg Scott-a; back-up w/Giarusso-a 4.00

HIGHLANDER
Dynamite Entertainment: No. 0, 2006 - No. 12, 2007 (25¢/$2.99)
0-(25¢-c) Takes place after the first movie; photo-c and Dell'Otto painted-c 3.00
1-12: 1-($2.99) Three covers; Moder-a/Jerwa & Oeming-s. 2-Three covers 3.00
... Origins: The Kurgan 1,2 (2009 - No. 2, 2009, $4.99) Three covers; Rafael-a 5.00
...: Way of the Sword (2007 - No. 4, 2008, $3.50) Two interlocking covers for each 3.50

HIGHLANDER: THE AMERICAN DREAM
IDW Publishing: Feb, 2017 - No. 5, Jun, 2017 ($3.99)
1-5-Brian Ruckley-s/Andrea Mutti-a; multiple covers; MacLeod in 1985 New York 4.00

HIGH LEVEL
DC Comics (Vertigo): Apr, 2019 - No. 6, Nov, 2019 ($3.99)
1-6-Sheridan-s/Bagenda-a 4.00

HIGH ROADS
DC Comics (Cliffhanger): June, 2002 - No. 6, Nov, 2002 ($2.95, limited series)
1-6-Leinil Yu-c/a; Lobdell-s 3.00
TPB (2003, $14.95) r/#1-6; sketch pages 15.00

HIGH SCHOOL CONFIDENTIAL DIARY (Confidential Diary #12 on)
Charlton Comics: June, 1960 - No. 11, Mar, 1962
1 5 10 15 31 53 75
2-11 3 6 9 19 30 40

HIGHWAYMEN
DC Comics (WildStorm): Aug, 2007 - No. 5, Dec, 2007 ($2.99)
1-5-Bernardin & Freeman-s/Garbett-a 3.00
TPB (2008, $17.99) r/#1-5 18.00

HIGH WAYS, THE
IDW Publishing: Dec, 2012 - No. 4, Apr, 2013 ($3.99, limited series)
1-4-John Byrne-s/a/c 4.00

HI HI PUFFY AMIYUMI (Based on Cartoon Network animated series)
DC Comics: Apr, 2006 - No. 3, June, 2006 ($2.25, limited series)
1-3-Phil Moy-a 3.00

HI-HO COMICS
Four Star Publications: nd (2/46?) - No. 3, 1946
1-Funny Animal; L.B. Cole-c 41 82 123 256 428 600
2,3: 2-L. B. Cole-c 29 58 87 170 278 385

HI-JINX (Teen-age Animal Funnies)
La Salle Publ. Co./B&I Publ. Co. (American Comics Group)/Creston: 1945; July-Aug, 1947 - No. 7, July-Aug, 1948
nn-(© 1945, 25 cents, 132 Pgs.)(La Salle) 32 64 96 192 314 435
1-Teen-age, funny animal 21 42 63 124 202 280
2,3 14 28 42 82 121 160
4-7-Milt Gross. 4-X-Mas-c 20 40 60 117 189 260

HI-LITE COMICS
E. R. Ross Publishing Co.: Fall, 1945
1-Miss Shady 24 48 72 140 230 320

HILLBILLY
Albatross Funnybooks: 2016 - No. 12, 2018 ($3.99)
1-12-Eric Powell-s/c; Powell-a in #1-7. 2-The Buzzard app. 5-Back-up with Mannion-a. 8-Di Meo-a 4.00

HILLBILLY (Red Eyed Witchery From Beyond on cover)
Albatross Funnybooks: 2018 - No. 4, 2019 ($3.99)
1-4-Eric Powell-s/c; Simone Di Meo-a 4.00

HILLBILLY COMICS
Charlton Comics: Aug, 1955 - No. 4, July, 1956 (Satire)
1-By Art Gates 14 28 42 82 121 160
2-4 11 22 33 60 83 105

HILL HOUSE COMICS 2019 SAMPLER
DC Comics (Hill House Comics): Oct, 2019 (no price, promotional giveaway)
nn-Previews Basketful of Heads, The Dollhouse Family, and The Low, Low Woods 3.00

HILLY ROSE'S SPACE ADVENTURES
Astro Comics: May, 1995 - No. 9 ($2.95, B&W)

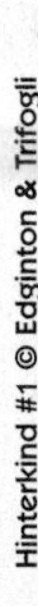
Hinterkind #1 © Edginton & Trifogli

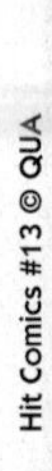
Hit Comics #13 © QUA

Hit Girl Season 2 #4 © D&E & JRJr.

	GD 2.0	VG 4.0	FN 6.0	VF 8.0	VF/NM 9.0	NM- 9.2

1 1 2 3 5 7 9
2-9 5.00
Trade Paperback (1996, $12.95)-r/#1-5 13.00

HINTERKIND
DC Comics (Vertigo): Dec, 2013 - No. 18, Jul, 2015 ($2.99)
1-18: 1-Ian Edginton-s/Francesco Trifogli-a/Greg Tocchini-c 3.00

HIP FLASK (Also see Elephantmen)
Active Images/Image Comics
...: Ouroborous (12/12, $4.99) Starkings-s/Ladronn-a 5.00
... Unnatural Selection (9/02, $2.99) Casey & Starkings-s/Ladronn-a; var.-c by Madureira, Campbell, Churchill 3.00

HIP-IT-TY HOP (See March of Comics No. 15)

HIRE, THE (BMWfilms.com's...)
Dark Horse Comics: July, 2004 - No. 6 ($2.99)
1-4: 1-Matt Wagner-s/Wagner & Velasco-a. 2-Bruce Campbell-s/Plunkett-a. 3-Waid-s 3.00
TPB (4/06, $17.95) r/#1-4 18.00

HI-SCHOOL ROMANCE (...Romances No. 41 on)
Harvey Publ./True Love(Home Comics): Oct, 1949 - No. 5, June, 1950; No. 6, Dec, 1950 - No. 73, Mar, 1958; No. 74, Sept, 1958 - No. 75, Nov, 1958

	GD	VG	FN	VF	VF/NM	NM-
1-Photo-c	16	32	48	98	154	210
2-Photo-c	11	22	33	60	83	105
3-9: 3-5-Photo-c	9	18	27	50	65	80
10-Rape story	14	28	42	82	121	160
11-20	8	16	24	42	54	65
21-31	7	14	21	35	43	50
32- "Unholy passion" story	10	20	30	54	72	90
33-36: 36-Last pre-code (2/55)	6	12	18	31	38	45
37-53,59-72,74,75	6	12	18	28	34	40
54-58,73-Kirby-c	7	14	21	35	43	50

NOTE: ***Powell** a-1-3, 5, 8, 12-16, 18, 21-23, 25-27, 30-34, 36, 37, 39, 45-48, 50-52, 57, 58, 60, 64, 65, 67, 69.*

HI-SCHOOL ROMANCE DATE BOOK
Harvey Publications: Nov, 1962 - No. 3, Mar, 1963 (25¢ Giants)

	GD	VG	FN	VF	VF/NM	NM-
1-Powell, Baker-a	6	12	18	41	76	110
2,3	3	6	9	21	33	45

HIS NAME IS SAVAGE (Magazine format)
Adventure House Press: June, 1968 (35¢, 52 pgs.)

	GD	VG	FN	VF	VF/NM	NM-
1-Gil Kane-a	5	10	15	31	53	75

HI-SPOT COMICS (Red Ryder No. 1 & No. 3 on)
Hawley Publications: No. 2, Nov, 1940

	GD	VG	FN	VF	VF/NM	NM-
2-David Innes of Pellucidar; art by J. C. Burroughs; written by Edgar Rice Burroughs	194	388	582	1242	2121	3000

HISTORY OF THE DC UNIVERSE (Also see Crisis on Infinite Earths)
DC Comics: Sept, 1986 - No. 2, Nov, 1986 ($2.95, limited series)
1,2: 1-Perez-c/a 5.00
Limited Edition hardcover 4 8 12 26 41 55
Softcover (2002, $9.95) new Alex Ross wraparound-c 13.00
Softcover (2009, $12.99) Alex Ross wraparound-c 13.00

HISTORY OF THE MARVEL UNIVERSE
Marvel Comics: Sept, 2019 - No. 6, Feb, 2020 ($4.99, limited series)
1-6-Mark Waid-s/Javier Rodríguez-a chronological Marvel history & bonus annotations 5.00

HISTORY OF VIOLENCE, A (Inspired the 2005 movie)
DC Comics (Paradox Press) 1997 ($9.95, B&W graphic novel)
nn-Paperback ($9.95) John Wagner-s/Vince Locke-a 18.00

HIT
BOOM! Studios: Sept, 2013 - No. 4, Dec, 2013 ($3.99, limited series)
1-4-Bryce Carlson-s/Vanesa R. Del Ray-a/Ryan Sook-c 4.00
...: 1957 (3/15 - No. 4, 7/15, $3.99) 1-4-Bryce Carlson-s/Vanesa R. Del Ray-a/c 4.00

HITCHHIKERS GUIDE TO THE GALAXY (See Life, the Universe and Everything & Restaurant at the End of the Universe)
DC Comics: 1993 - No. 3, 1993 ($4.95, limited series)
1-3: Adaptation of Douglas Adams book 5.00
TPB (1997, $14.95) r/#1-3 15.00

HIT COMICS
Quality Comics Group: July, 1940 - No. 65, July, 1950

	GD	VG	FN	VF	VF/NM	NM-
1-Origin/1st app. Neon, the Unknown & Hercules; intro. The Red Bee; Bob & Swab, Blaze Barton, the Strange Twins, X-5 Super Agent, Casey Jones & Jack & Jill (ends #7) begin	919	1838	2757	6709	11,855	17,000
2-The Old Witch begins, ends #14 (scarce)	360	720	1080	2520	4410	6300
3-Casey Jones ends; transvestism story "Jack & Jill"	354	708	1062	2478	4339	6200
4-Super Agent (ends #17), & Betty Bates (ends #65) begin; X-5 ends	300	600	900	2040	3570	5100
5-Classic Lou Fine cover	975	1950	2919	7100	12,550	18,000
6,8-10: 10-Old Witch by Crandall (4 pgs.); 1st work in comics (4/41)	271	542	813	1734	2967	4200
7-Skull bondage-c	360	720	1080	2520	4410	6300
11-Classic cover	337	674	1011	2359	4130	5900
12-16: 13-Blaze Barton ends	177	354	531	1124	1937	2750
17-Last Neon; Crandall Hercules in all; last Lou Fine-c; skeleton-c	252	504	756	1613	2757	3900
18-Origin & 1st app. Stormy Foster, the Great Defender (12/41); The Ghost of Flanders begins; Crandall-c	200	400	600	1280	2190	3100
19,20	139	278	417	883	1517	2150
21-24: 21-Last Hercules. 24-Last Red Bee & Strange Twins	126	252	378	806	1378	1950
25-Origin & 1st app. Kid Eternity and begins by Moldoff (12/42); 1st app. The Keeper (Kid Eternity's aide)	239	478	717	1530	2615	3700
26-Blackhawk x-over in Kid Eternity	113	226	339	718	1234	1750
27-29	52	104	156	328	552	775
30,31- "Bill the Magnificent" by Kurtzman, 11 pgs. in each	47	94	141	296	498	700
32-40: 32-Plastic Man x-over. 34-Last Stormy Foster	31	62	93	182	296	410
41-50	22	44	66	128	209	290
51-60-Last Kid Eternity	21	42	63	122	199	275
61-63-Crandall-c/a; 61-Jeb Rivers begins	21	42	63	126	206	285
64,65-Crandall-a	21	42	63	122	199	275

NOTE: ***Crandall** a-11-17(Hercules), 23, 24(Stormy Foster); c-18-20, 23, 24. **Fine** c-1-14, 16, 17(most). **Ward** c-33. Bondage c-7, 64. Hercules c-3, 10-17. Jeb Rivers c-61-65. Kid Eternity c-25-60 (w/ Keeper-28-34, 36, 39-43, 45-55). Neon the Unknown c-2, 4, 8, 9. Red Bee c-1, 5-7. Stormy Foster c-18-24.*

HIT-GIRL (Also see Kick-Ass)
Marvel Comics (Icon): Aug, 2012 - No. 5, Apr, 2013 ($2.99, limited series)
1-Takes place between Kick-Ass & Kick Ass 2 series; Millar-s/Romita Jr.-a/c 1 2 3 5 6 8
2-5 3.00

HIT-GIRL (Also see Kick-Ass)
Image Comics: Feb, 2018 - No. 12, Jan, 2019 ($3.99)
1-12: 1-4-Millar-s/Ortiz-a. 5-8-In Canada; Lemire-s/Risso-a. 9-12-Albuquerque-s/a 4.00

HIT-GIRL SEASON TWO (Also see Kick-Ass)
Image Comics: Feb, 2019 - No. 12, Jan, 2020 ($3.99)
1-12: 1-4-Kevin Smith-s/Pernille Orum-a. 5-8-Hong Kong; Parlov-a. 9-12-India 4.00

HITLER'S ASTROLOGER (See Marvel Graphic Novel #35)

HITMAN (Also see Bloodbath #2, Batman Chronicles #4, Demon #43-45 & Demon Annual #2)
DC Comics: May, 1996 - No. 60, Apr, 2001 ($2.25/$2.50)
1-Garth Ennis-s & John McCrea-c/a begin; Batman app. 2 4 6 10 14 18
2-Joker-c;Two Face, Mad Hatter, Batman app. 1 2 3 5 6 8
3-5: 3-Batman-c/app.; Joker app. 4-1st app. Nightfist 5.00
6-20: 8-Final Night x-over. 10-GL cameo. 11-20: 11,12-GL-c/app. 15-20-"Ace of Killers". 16-18-Catwoman app. 17-19-Demon-app. 4.00
21-59: 34-Superman-c/app. 3.00
60-($3.95) Final issue; includes pin-ups by various 4.00
#1,000,000 (11/98) Hitman goes to the 853rd Century 3.00
Annual 1 (1997, $3.95) Pulp Heroes 5.00
.../Lobo: That Stupid Bastich (7/00, $3.95) Ennis-s/Mahnke-a 4.00
TPB-(1997, $9.95) r/#1-3, Demon Ann. #2, Batman Chronicles #4 10.00
Ace of Killers TPB ('00/'11, $17.95/$17.99) r/#15-22 18.00
Local Heroes TPB ('99, $17.95) r/#9-14 & Annual #1 18.00
10,000 Bullets TPB ('98, $9.95) r/#4-8 10.00
Ten Thousand Bullets TPB ('10, $17.99) r/#4-8 & Annual #1; intro, by Kevin Smith 18.00
Who Dares Wins TPB ('01, $12.95) r/#23-28 13.00

HIT-MONKEY (See Deadpool)
Marvel Comics: Apr, 2010; Sept, 2010 - No. 3, Nov, 2010 ($3.99/$2.99)
1-(4/10, $3.99) Printing of story from Marvel Digital Comics; Frank Cho-c; origin revealed 4.00
1-3-Daniel Way-s/Talajic-a/Johnson-c; Bullseye app. 3.00

HI-YO SILVER (See Lone Ranger's Famous Horse... and The Lone Ranger; and March of Comics No. 215 in the Promotional Comics section)

Holiday Comics #5 © STAR

Hollywood Diary #3 © QUA

Holyoke One-Shot #9 © HOKE

	GD 2.0	VG 4.0	FN 6.0	VF 8.0	VF/NM 9.0	NM- 9.2

HOBBIT, THE
Eclipse Comics: 1989 - No. 3, 1990 ($4.95, squarebound, 52 pgs.)

	GD	VG	FN	VF	VF/NM	NM-
Book 1-3: Adapts novel; Wenzel-a	2	4	6	8	10	12
Book 1-Second printing						5.00
Graphic Novel (1990, Ballantine)-r/#1-3						25.00

HOCUS POCUS (See Funny Book #9)

HOGAN'S HEROES (TV) (Also see Wild!)
Dell Publishing Co.: June, 1966 - No. 8, Sept, 1967; No. 9, Oct, 1969

	GD	VG	FN	VF	VF/NM	NM-
1: Photo-c on #1-7	8	16	24	51	96	140
2,3-Ditko-a(p)	5	10	15	35	63	90
4-9: 9-Reprints #1	5	10	15	30	50	70

HOKUM & HEX (See Razorline)
Marvel Comics (Razorline): Sept, 1993 - No. 9, May, 1994 ($1.75/$1.95)

	GD	VG	FN	VF	VF/NM	NM-
1-($2.50)-Foil embossed-c; by Clive Barker						5.00
2-9: 5-Hyperkind x-over						4.00

HOLIDAY COMICS
Fawcett Publications: 1942 (25¢, 196 pgs.)

	GD	VG	FN	VF	VF/NM	NM-
1-Contains three Fawcett comics plus two page portrait of Captain Marvel; Capt. Marvel, Jungle Girl #1, & Whiz. Not rebound, remaindered comics; printed at the same time as originals (scarce in high grade)	325	650	975	2300	4563	6825

HOLIDAY COMICS (Becomes Fun Comics #9-12)
Star Publications: Jan, 1951 - No. 8, Oct, 1952

	GD	VG	FN	VF	VF/NM	NM-
1-Funny animal contents (Frisky Fables) in all; L. B. Cole X-Mas-c	41	82	123	256	428	600
2-Classic L. B. Cole-c	39	78	117	231	378	525
3-8: 5,8-X-Mas-c; all L.B. Cole-c	22	44	66	128	209	290
Accepted Reprint 4 (nd)-L.B. Cole-c	11	22	33	62	86	110

HOLIDAY DIGEST
Harvey Comics: 1988 ($1.25, digest-size)

	GD	VG	FN	VF	VF/NM	NM-
1	1	2	3	5	7	9

HOLIDAY PARADE (Walt Disney's...)
W. D. Publications (Disney): Winter, 1990-91(no year given) - No. 2, Winter, 1990-91 ($2.95, 68 pgs.)

	GD	VG	FN	VF	VF/NM	NM-
1-Reprints 1947 Firestone by Barks plus new-a						5.00
2-Barks-r plus other stories						4.00

HOLI-DAY SURPRISE (Formerly Summer Fun)
Charlton Comics: V2#55, Mar, 1967 (25¢ Giant)

	GD	VG	FN	VF	VF/NM	NM-
V2#55	4	8	12	23	37	50

HOLLYWOOD COMICS
New Age Publishers: Winter, 1944 (52 pgs.)

	GD	VG	FN	VF	VF/NM	NM-
1-Funny animal	22	44	66	128	209	290

HOLLYWOOD CONFESSIONS
St. John Publishing Co.: Oct, 1949 - No. 2, Dec, 1949

	GD	VG	FN	VF	VF/NM	NM-
1-Kubert-c/a (entire book)	47	94	141	296	498	700
2-Kubert-c/a (entire book) (Scarce)	48	96	144	302	514	725

HOLLYWOOD DIARY
Quality Comics Group: Dec, 1949 - No. 5, July-Aug, 1950

	GD	VG	FN	VF	VF/NM	NM-
1-No photo-c	31	62	93	186	303	420
2-Photo-c	19	38	57	112	179	245
3-5-Photo-c. 3-Betty Carlin photo-c. 5-June Allyson/Peter Lawford photo-c	16	32	48	98	154	210

HOLLYWOOD FILM STORIES
Feature Publications/Prize: April, 1950 - No. 4, Oct, 1950 (All photo-c; "Fumetti" type movie comic)

	GD	VG	FN	VF	VF/NM	NM-
1-June Allyson photo-c	24	48	72	140	230	320
2-4: 2-Lizabeth Scott photo-c. 3-Barbara Stanwick photo-c. 4-Betty Hutton photo-c	16	32	48	98	154	210

HOLLYWOOD FUNNY FOLKS (Formerly Funny Folks; Becomes Nutsy Squirrel #61 on)
National Periodical Publ.: No. 27, Aug-Sept, 1950 - No. 60, July-Aug, 1954

	GD	VG	FN	VF	VF/NM	NM-
27-Nutsy Squirrel continues	14	28	42	78	112	145
28-40	10	20	30	56	76	95
41-60	9	18	27	50	65	80

NOTE: ***Rube Grossman** a-most issues. **Sheldon Mayer** a-27-35, 37-40, 43-46, 48-51, 53, 56, 57, 60.*

HOLLYWOOD LOVE DOCTOR (See Doctor Anthony King...)

HOLLYWOOD PICTORIAL (...Romances on cover)
St. John Publishing Co.: No. 3, Jan, 1950

	GD	VG	FN	VF	VF/NM	NM-
3-Matt Baker-a; photo-c	40	80	120	246	411	575

(Becomes a movie magazine - Hollywood Pictorial Western with No. 4.)

HOLLYWOOD ROMANCES (Formerly Brides In Love; becomes For Lovers Only #60 on)
Charlton Comics: V2#46, 11/66; #47, 10/67; #48, 11/68;V3#49,11/69-V3#59, 6/71

	GD	VG	FN	VF	VF/NM	NM-
V2#46-Rolling Stones-c/story	9	18	27	60	120	180
V2#47-V3#59: 56- "Born to Heart Break" begins	3	6	9	15	22	28

HOLLYWOOD SECRETS
Quality Comics Group: Nov, 1949 - No. 6, Sept, 1950

	GD	VG	FN	VF	VF/NM	NM-
1-Ward-c/a (9 pgs.)	47	94	141	296	498	700
2-Crandall-a, Ward-c/a (9 pgs.)	37	74	111	222	361	500
3-6: All photo-c. 5-Lex Barker (Tarzan)-c	18	36	54	109	175	235
...of Romance, I.W. Reprint #9; r/#2 above w/Kinstler-c	2	4	6	11	16	20

HOLLYWOOD SUPERSTARS
Marvel Comics (Epic Comics): Nov, 1990 - No. 5, Apr, 1991 ($2.25)

	GD	VG	FN	VF	VF/NM	NM-
1-($2.95, 52 pgs.)-Spiegle-c/a in all; Aragonés-a, inside front-c plus 2-4 pgs.						4.00
2-5 ($2.25)						3.00

HOLO-MAN (See Power Record Comics)

HOLYOKE ONE-SHOT
Holyoke Publishing Co. (Tem Publ.): 1944 - No. 10, 1945 (All reprints)

	GD	VG	FN	VF	VF/NM	NM-
1,2: 1-Grit Grady (on cover only), Miss Victory, Alias X (origin)-All reprints from Captain Fearless. 2-Rusty Dugan (Corporal); Capt. Fearless (origin), Mr. Miracle (origin) app.	36	72	108	211	343	475
3-Miss Victory; r/Crash #4; Cat Man (origin), Solar Legion by Kirby app.; Miss Victory on cover only (1945)	54	108	162	343	574	825
4,6,8: 4-Mr. Miracle; The Blue Streak app.; reprints early Cat-Man story. 6-Capt. Fearless, Alias X, Capt. Stone (splash used as-c to #10); Diamond Jim & Rusty Dugan (splash from cover of #2). 8-Blue Streak, Strong Man (story matches cover to #7)-Crash reprints	29	58	87	174	285	395
5,7: 5-U.S. Border Patrol Comics (Sgt. Dick Carter of the...), Miss Victory (story matches cover to #3), Citizen Smith, & Mr. Miracle app. 7-Secret Agent Z-2, Strong Man, Blue Streak (story matches cover to #8); Reprints from Crash #2	31	62	93	182	296	410
9-Citizen Smith, The Blue Streak, Solar Legion by Kirby & Strongman, the Perfect Human app.; reprints from Crash #4 & 5; Citizen Smith on cover only-from story in #5 (1944-before #3)	33	66	100	196	321	445
10-Captain Stone; r/Crash; Solar Legion by S&K	33	66	100	196	321	445

HOLY TERROR
Legendary Comics: Sept, 2011 ($29.95, HC graphic novel, 12-1/4" wide x 9-1/4" tall)

	GD	VG	FN	VF	VF/NM	NM-
HC-Frank Miller-s/a/c; B&W art with spot color; The Fixer vs. Al-Qaeda in Empire City						30.00

HOME (Based on the DreamWorks movie)
Titan Comics: Aug, 2015 - No. 4, Nov, 2015 ($3.99)

	GD	VG	FN	VF	VF/NM	NM-
1-4: 1-Davison-s/Hebb-a						4.00

HOMECOMING
Aspen MLT: Aug, 2012 - No. 4, Sept, 2013 ($3.99)

	GD	VG	FN	VF	VF/NM	NM-
1-4: 1-Wohl-s/Laiso-a; covers by Michael Turner and Mike DeBalfo						4.00

HOMER COBB (See Adventures of...)

HOMER HOOPER
Atlas Comics: July, 1953 - No. 4, Dec, 1953

	GD	VG	FN	VF	VF/NM	NM-
1-Teenage humor	15	30	45	90	140	190
2-4	12	24	36	67	94	120

HOMER, THE HAPPY GHOST (See Adventures of...)
Atlas(ACI/PPI/WPI)/Marvel: 3/55 - No. 22, 11/58; V2#1, 11/69 - V2#4, 5/70

	GD	VG	FN	VF	VF/NM	NM-
V1#1-Dan DeCarlo-c/a begins, ends #22	37	74	111	222	361	500
2-1st code approved issue	20	40	60	115	188	260
3-10	19	38	57	111	176	240
11-20,22	17	34	51	100	158	215
21-Sci-fi cover	35	70	105	208	339	470
V2#1 (11/69)	12	24	36	80	173	265
2-4	8	16	24	51	96	140

HOME RUN (Also see A-1 Comics)
Magazine Enterprises: No. 89, 1953 (one-shot)

	GD	VG	FN	VF	VF/NM	NM-
A-1 89 (#3)-Powell-a; Stan Musial photo-c	18	36	54	109	172	235

HOMICIDE (Also see Dark Horse Presents)
Dark Horse Comics: Apr, 1990 ($1.95, B&W, one-shot)

	GD	VG	FN	VF	VF/NM	NM-
1-Detective story						3.00

HOMIES

Honeymoon Romance #2 © Artful

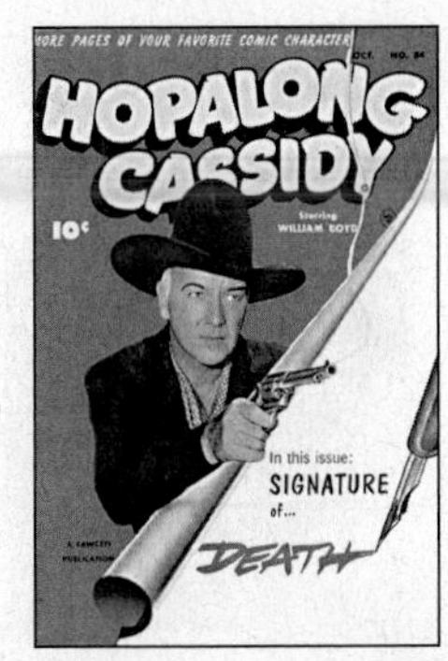

Hopalong Cassidy #84 © FAW

Horizon Zero Dawn #1 © Guerrilla Games

	GD 2.0	VG 4.0	FN 6.0	VF 8.0	VF/NM 9.0	NM- 9.2
Dynamite Entertainment: 2016 - No. 4, 2017 ($3.99)						
1-4-Gonzales & Serrano-s/Huerta-a						4.00
HONEYMOON (Formerly Gay Comics)						
A Lover's Magazine(USA) (Marvel): No. 41, Jan, 1950						
41-Photo-c; article by Betty Grable	16	32	48	98	154	210
HONEYMOONERS, THE (TV)						
Lodestone: Oct, 1986 ($1.50)						
1-Photo-c						6.00
HONEYMOONERS, THE (TV)						
Triad Publications: Sept, 1987 - No. 13? ($2.00)						
1-13						5.00
HONEYMOON ROMANCE						
Artful Publications (Canadian): Apr, 1950 - No. 2, July, 1950 (25¢, digest size)						
1,2-(Rare)	240	480	720	1200	1800	2400
HONEY WEST (TV)						
Gold Key: Sept, 1966 (Photo-c)						
1 (10186-609)	9	18	27	59	117	175
HONEY WEST (TV)						
Moonstone: 2010 - No. 4 ($5.99/$3.99)						
1-($5.99) Trina Robbins-s/Cynthia Martin-a; two art covers & two photo covers						6.00
2-4-($3.99)						4.00
HONG KONG PHOOEY (TV)						
Charlton Comics: June, 1975 - No. 9, Nov, 1976 (Hanna-Barbera)						
1	6	12	18	37	66	95
2	3	6	9	19	30	40
3-9	3	6	9	15	22	28
HONG ON THE RANGE						
Image/Flypaper Press: Dec, 1997 - No. 3, Feb, 1998 ($2.50, lim. series)						
1-3: Wu-s/Lafferty-a						3.00
HOOD, THE						
Marvel Comics (MAX): Jul, 2002 - No. 6, Dec, 2002 ($2.99, limited series)						
1-6-Vaughan-s/Hotz-c/a						3.00
Vol. 1 Blood From Stones HC (2007, $19.99, dustjacket) r/#1-6; production sketch art						20.00
Vol. 1 Blood From Stones TPB (2003, $14.99) r/#1-6						15.00
HOODED HORSEMAN, THE (Formerly Blazing West)						
American Comics Group (Michel Publ.): No. 21, 1-2/52 - No. 27, 1-2/54; No. 18, 12-1/54-55 - No. 22, 8-9/55						
21(1-2/52)-Hooded Horseman, Injun Jones cont.	15	30	45	94	147	200
22	11	22	33	64	90	115
23,24,27(1-2/54)	10	20	30	56	76	95
25 (9-10/53)-Cowboy Sahib on cover only; Hooded Horseman i.d. revealed	10	20	30	58	79	100
26-Origin/1st app. Cowboy Sahib by L. Starr	12	24	36	69	97	125
18(12-1/54-55)(Formerly Out of the Night)	10	20	30	58	79	100
19,21,22: 19-Last precode (1-2/55)	9	18	27	47	61	75
20-Origin Johnny Injun	9	18	27	52	69	85
NOTE: *Whitney c/a-21('52), 20-22.*						
HOODED MENACE, THE (Also see Daring Adventures)						
Realistic/Avon Periodicals: 1951 (one-shot)						
nn-Based on a band of hooded outlaws in the Pacific Northwest, 1900-1906; reprinted in Daring Advs. #15	129	258	387	826	1413	2000
HOODS UP (See the Promotional Comics section)						
HOOK (Movie)						
Marvel Comics: Early Feb, 1992 - No. 4, Late Mar, 1992 ($1.00, limited series)						
1-4: Adapts movie; Vess-c; 1-Morrow-a(p)						3.00
nn (1991, $5.95, 84 pgs.)-Contains #1-4; Vess-c						6.00
1 (1991, $2.95, magazine, 84 pgs.)-Contains #1-4; Vess-c (same cover as nn issue)						4.00
HOOK JAW						
Titan Comics: Jan, 2017 - No. 5, May, 2017 ($3.99)						
1-5-Inspired by a 1976 British comic strip; Si Spurrier-s/Conor Boyle-a; multiple covers						4.00
HOOT GIBSON'S WESTERN ROUNDUP (See Western Roundup under Fox Giants)						
HOOT GIBSON WESTERN (Formerly My Love Story)						
Fox Feature Syndicate: No. 5, May, 1950 - No. 3, Sept, 1950						
5,6(#1,2): 5-Photo-c. 6-Photo/painted-c	21	42	63	123	197	270
3-Wood-a; painted-c	22	44	66	131	211	290

	GD 2.0	VG 4.0	FN 6.0	VF 8.0	VF/NM 9.0	NM- 9.2
HOPALONG CASSIDY (Also see Bill Boyd Western, Master Comics, Real Western Hero, Six Gun Heroes & Western Hero; Bill Boyd starred as Hopalong Cassidy in movies, radio & TV)						
Fawcett Publications: Feb, 1943; No. 2, Summer, 1946 - No. 85, Nov, 1953						
1 (1943, 68 pgs.)-H. Cassidy & his horse Topper begin (on sale 1/8/43)-Captain Marvel app. on-c	194	388	582	1242	2121	3000
2-(Sum, '46)	41	82	123	256	428	600
3,4: 3-(Fall, '46, 52 pgs. begin)	20	40	60	114	182	250
5- "Mad Barber" story mentioned in **SOTI**, pgs. 308,309; photo-c	20	40	60	115	188	260
6-10: 8-Photo-c	16	32	48	94	147	200
11-19: 11,13-19-Photo-c	14	28	42	80	115	150
20-29 (52 pgs.)-Painted/photo-c	12	24	36	69	97	125
30,31,33,34,37-39,41 (52 pgs.)-Painted-c	11	22	33	60	83	105
32,40 (36pgs.)-Painted-c	10	20	30	54	72	90
35,42,43,45-47,49-51,53,54,56 (52 pgs.)-Photo-c	10	20	30	56	76	95
36,44,48 (36 pgs.)-Photo-c	9	18	27	52	69	85
52,55,57-70 (36 pgs.)-Photo-c	9	18	27	47	61	75
71-84-Photo-c	8	16	24	42	54	65
85-Last Fawcett issue; photo-c	9	18	27	52	69	85
NOTE: *Line-drawn c-1-4, 6, 7, 9, 10, 12.*						
... & The 5 Men of Evil (AC Comics, 1991, $12.95) r/newspaper strips and Fawcett story "Signature of Death"						13.00
HOPALONG CASSIDY						
National Periodical Publications: No. 86, Feb, 1954 - No. 135, May-June, 1959 (All-36 pgs.)						
86-Gene Colan-a begins, ends #117; photo covers continue	36	72	108	216	351	485
87	20	40	60	118	189	260
88-91: 91-1 pg. Superboy-sty (7/54)	15	30	45	83	124	165
92-99 (98 has #93 on-c; last precode issue, 2/55). 95-Reversed photo-c to #52. 98-Reversed photo-c to #61. 99-Reversed photo-c to #60	14	28	42	76	108	140
100-Same cover as #50	15	30	45	83	124	165
101-108: 105-Same photo-c as #54. 107-Same photo-c as #51. 108-Last photo-c	6	12	18	38	69	100
109-130: 118-Gil Kane-a begins. 123-Kubert-a (2 pgs.). 124-Grey tone-c	5	10	15	35	63	90
131-135	6	12	18	37	66	95
HOPELESS SAVAGES (Also see Too Much Hopeless Savages)						
Oni Press: Aug, 2001 - No. 4, Nov, 2001 ($2.95, B&W, limited series)						
1-4-Van Meter-s/Norrie-a/Clugston-Major-a/Watson-c						3.00
Free Comic Book Day giveaway (5/02) r/#1 with "Free Comic Book Day" banner on-c						3.00
TPB (2002, $13.95, 8" x 5.75") r/#1-4; plus color stories; Watson-c						14.00
HOPELESS SAVAGES: GROUND ZERO						
Oni Press: June, 2002 - No. 4, Oct, 2002 ($2.95, B&W, limited series)						
1-4-Van Meter-s/O'Malley-a/Dodson-c. 1-Watson-a						3.00
TPB (2003, $11.95, 8" x 5.75") r/#1-4; Dodson-c						12.00
HOPE SHIP						
Dell Publishing Co.: June-Aug, 1963						
1	3	6	9	15	22	28
HOPPY THE MARVEL BUNNY (See Fawcett's Funny Animals)						
Fawcett Publications: Dec, 1945 - No. 15, Sept, 1947						
1	30	60	90	177	289	400
2	15	30	45	84	127	170
3-15: 7-Xmas-c	12	24	36	67	94	120
HORACE & DOTTY DRIPPLE (Dotty Dripple No. 1-24)						
Harvey Publications: No. 25, Aug, 1952 - No. 43, Oct, 1955						
25-43	5	10	14	20	24	28
HORIZONTAL LIEUTENANT, THE (See Movie Classics)						
HORIZON ZERO DAWN (Based on the Guerrilla Games videogame)						
Titan Comics: Sept, 2020 - Present ($3.99)						
1-4-Anne Toole-s/Ann Maulina-a; multiple covers						4.00
HOROBI						
Viz Premiere Comics: 1990 - No. 8, 1990 ($3.75, B&W, mature readers, 84 pgs.) V2#1, 1990 - No. 7, 1991 ($4.25, B&W, 68 pgs.)						
1-8: Japanese manga, Part Two, #1-7						5.00
HORRIFIC (Terrific No. 14 on)						
Artful/Comic Media/Harwell/Mystery: Sept, 1952 - No. 13, Sept, 1954						
1	116	232	348	742	1271	1800
2	77	154	231	493	847	1200
3-Bullet in head-c	300	600	900	1950	3375	4800

Horror Tales V8 #2 © Eerie Publ.

Hot Rod Comics #1 © FAW

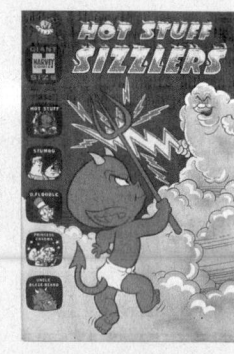

Hot Stuff Sizzlers #36 © HARV

	GD 2.0	VG 4.0	FN 6.0	VF 8.0	VF/NM 9.0	NM- 9.2
4,5,7,9,10: 4-Shrunken head-c. 7-Guillotine-c	58	116	174	371	636	900
6-Jack The Ripper story	65	130	195	416	708	1000
8-Origin & 1st app. The Teller (E.C. parody)	65	130	195	416	708	1000
11-13: 11-Swipe/Witches Tales #6,27; Devil-c	50	100	150	315	533	750

NOTE: ***Don Heck** a-8; c-3-13. **Hollingsworth** a-4. **Morisi** a-8. **Palais** a-5, 7-12.*

HORRORCIDE
IDW Publishing: Sept, 2004 ($6.99)

	GD	VG	FN	VF	VF/NM	NM-
1-Steve Niles short stories; art by Templesmith, Medors and Chee						7.00

HORROR FROM THE TOMB (Mysterious Stories No. 2 on)
Premier Magazine Co.: Sept, 1954

	GD	VG	FN	VF	VF/NM	NM-
1-Woodbridge/Torres, Check-a; The Keeper of the Graveyard is host	194	388	582	1242	2121	3000

HORRORIST, THE (Also see Hellblazer)
DC Comics (Vertigo): Dec, 1995 - No. 2, Jan, 1996 ($5.95, lim. series, mature)

	GD	VG	FN	VF	VF/NM	NM-
1,2: Jamie Delano scripts, David Lloyd-c/a; John Constantine (Hellblazer) app.						6.00

HORROR OF COLLIER COUNTY
Dark Horse Comics: Oct, 1999 - No. 5, Feb, 2000 ($2.95, B&W, limited series)

	GD	VG	FN	VF	VF/NM	NM-
1-5-Rich Tommaso-s/a						3.00

HORRORS, THE (Formerly Startling Terror Tales #10)
Star Publications: No. 11, Jan, 1953 - No. 15, Apr, 1954

	GD	VG	FN	VF	VF/NM	NM-
11-Horrors of War; Disbrow-a(2)	52	104	156	328	552	775
12-Horrors of War; color illo in **POP**	50	100	150	315	533	750
13-Horrors of Mystery; crime stories	103	206	309	659	1130	1600
14,15-Horrors of the Underworld; crime stories	50	100	150	315	533	750

NOTE: *All have **L. B. Cole** covers; a-12. **Hollingsworth** a-13. **Palais** a-13r.*

HORROR TALES (Magazine)
Eerie Publications: V1#7, 6/69 - V6#6, 12/74; V7#1, 2/75; V7#2, 5/76 - V8#5, 1977; V9#1-3, 8/78; V10#1(2/79) (V1-V6: 52 pgs.; V7, V8#2: 112 pgs.; V8#4 on: 68 pgs.) (No V5#3, V8#1,3)

	GD	VG	FN	VF	VF/NM	NM-
V1#7	8	16	24	56	108	160
V1#8,9	6	12	18	41	76	110
V2#1-6('70), V3#1-6('71), V4#1-3,5-7('72)	6	12	18	37	66	95
V4#4-LSD story reprint/Weird V3#5	6	12	18	42	79	115
V5#1,2,4,5(6/73),5(10/73),6(12/73),V6#1-6('74),V7#1,2,4('76),V7#3('76)-Giant issue, V8#2,4,5('77)	5	10	15	35	63	90
V9#1-3(11/78, $1.50), V10#1(2/79)	6	12	18	37	66	95

NOTE: *Bondage-c-V6#1, 3, V7#2.*

HORSE FEATHERS COMICS
Lev Gleason Publ.: Nov, 1945 - No. 4, July(Summer on-c), 1948 (52 pgs.) (#2,3 are oversized)

	GD	VG	FN	VF	VF/NM	NM-
1-Wolverton's Scoop Scuttle, 2 pgs.	20	40	60	120	195	270
2	12	24	36	69	97	125
3,4: 3-(5/48)	9	18	27	52	69	85

HORSEMAN
Crusade Comics/Kevlar Studios: Mar, 1996 - No. 3, Nov, 1997 ($2.95)

	GD	VG	FN	VF	VF/NM	NM-
0-1st Kevlar Studios issue, 1-(3/96)-Crusade issue; Shi-c/app., 1-(11/96)-3-(11/97)-Kevlar Studios						4.00

HORSEMASTERS, THE (Disney)(TV, Movie)
Dell Publishing Co.: No. 1260, Dec-Feb, 1961/62

	GD	VG	FN	VF	VF/NM	NM-
Four Color 1260-Annette Funicello photo-c	10	20	30	69	147	225

HORSE SOLDIERS, THE
Dell Publishing Co.: No. 1048, Nov-Jan, 1959/60 (John Wayne movie)

	GD	VG	FN	VF	VF/NM	NM-
Four Color 1048-Painted-c, Sekowsky-a	11	22	33	76	163	250

HORSE WITHOUT A HEAD, THE (See Movie Comics)

HOT DOG
Magazine Enterprises: June-July, 1954 - No. 4, Dec-Jan, 1954-55

	GD	VG	FN	VF	VF/NM	NM-
1(A-1 #107)	10	20	30	56	76	95
2,3(A-1 #115),4(A-1 #136)	8	16	24	40	50	60

HOT DOG (See Jughead's Pal, Hotdog)

HOTEL DEPAREE - SUNDANCE (TV)
Dell Publishing Co.: No. 1126, Aug-Oct, 1960 (one-shot)

	GD	VG	FN	VF	VF/NM	NM-
Four Color 1126-Earl Holliman photo-c	6	12	18	40	73	105

HOTELL
AWA Studios: Mar, 2020 - No. 4, Aug, 2020 ($3.99, limited series)

	GD	VG	FN	VF	VF/NM	NM-
1-4-John Lees-s/Dalibor Talajic-a						4.00

HOT ROD AND SPEEDWAY COMICS
Hillman Periodicals: Feb-Mar, 1952 - No. 5, Apr-May, 1953

	GD	VG	FN	VF	VF/NM	NM-
1	31	62	93	182	296	410
2-Krigstein-a	20	40	60	115	185	255
3-5	13	26	39	74	105	135

HOT ROD COMICS (...Featuring Clint Curtis) (See XMas Comics)
Fawcett Publications: Nov, 1951 (no month given) - V2#7, Feb, 1953

	GD	VG	FN	VF	VF/NM	NM-
nn (V1#1)-Powell-c/a in all	33	66	99	194	317	440
2 (4/52)	17	34	51	105	165	225
3-6, V2#7	14	28	42	76	112	145

HOT ROD KING (Also see Speed Smith the Hot Rod King)
Ziff-Davis Publ. Co.: Fall, 1952

	GD	VG	FN	VF	VF/NM	NM-
1-Giacoia-a; Saunders painted-c	33	66	99	194	317	440

HOT ROD RACERS (Grand Prix No. 16 on)
Charlton Comics: Dec, 1964 - No. 15, July, 1967

	GD	VG	FN	VF	VF/NM	NM-
1	8	16	24	52	99	145
2-5	5	10	15	30	50	70
6-15	4	8	12	23	37	50

HOT RODS AND RACING CARS
Charlton Comics (Motor Mag. No. 1): Nov, 1951 - No. 120, June, 1973

	GD	VG	FN	VF	VF/NM	NM-
1-Speed Davis begins; Indianapolis 500 story	33	66	99	196	321	445
2	17	34	51	100	158	215
3-10	12	24	36	69	97	125
11-20	10	20	30	54	72	90
21-33,36-40	8	16	24	44	57	70
34, 35 (? & 6/58, 68 pgs.)	11	22	33	60	83	105
41-60	7	14	21	37	46	55
61-80	3	6	9	19	30	40
81-100	3	6	9	16	23	30
101-120	3	6	9	14	19	24

HOT SHOT CHARLIE
Hillman Periodicals: 1947 (Lee Elias)

	GD	VG	FN	VF	VF/NM	NM-
1	16	32	48	86	133	180

HOT SHOTS: AVENGERS
Marvel Comics: Oct, 1995 ($2.95, one-shot)

	GD	VG	FN	VF	VF/NM	NM-
nn-pin-ups						4.00

HOTSPUR
Eclipse Comics: Jun, 1987 - No. 3, Sep, 1987 ($1.75, lim. series, Baxter paper)

	GD	VG	FN	VF	VF/NM	NM-
1-3						3.00

HOT STUFF (See Stumbo Tinytown)
Harvey Comics: V2#1, Sept, 1991 - No. 12, June, 1994 ($1.00)

	GD	VG	FN	VF	VF/NM	NM-
V2#1-Stumbo back-up story						5.00
2-12 ($1.50)						4.00
...Big Book 1 (11/92), 2 (6/93) (Both $1.95, 52 pgs.)						5.00

HOT STUFF CREEPY CAVES
Harvey Publications: Nov, 1974 - No. 7, Nov, 1975

	GD	VG	FN	VF	VF/NM	NM-
1	3	6	9	21	33	45
2-7	3	6	9	15	21	26

HOT STUFF DIGEST
Harvey Comics: July, 1992 - No. 5, Nov, 1993 ($1.75, digest-size)

	GD	VG	FN	VF	VF/NM	NM-
V2#1-Hot Stuff, Stumbo, Richie Rich stories						6.00
2-5						4.00

HOT STUFF GIANT SIZE
Harvey Comics: Oct, 1992 - No. 3, Oct, 1993 ($2.25, 68 pgs.)

	GD	VG	FN	VF	VF/NM	NM-
V2#1-Hot Stuff & Stumbo stories						5.00
2,3						4.00

HOT STUFF SIZZLERS
Harvey Publications: July, 1960 - No. 59, Mar, 1974; V2#1, Aug, 1992

	GD	VG	FN	VF	VF/NM	NM-
1- 84 pgs. begin, ends #5; Hot Stuff, Stumbo begin	14	28	42	96	211	325
2-5	7	14	21	49	92	135
6-10: 6-68 pgs. begin, ends #45	5	10	15	35	63	90
11-20	4	8	12	27	44	60
21-45	3	6	9	19	30	40
46-52: 52 pgs. begin	3	6	9	16	23	30
53-59	2	4	6	10	14	18
V2#1-(8/92, $1.25)-Stumbo back-up						5.00

HOT STUFF, THE LITTLE DEVIL (Also see Devil Kids & Harvey Hits)
Harvey Publications (Illustrated Humor): 10/57 - No. 141, 7/77; No. 142, 2/78 - No. 164, 8/82; No. 165, 10/86 - No. 171, 11/87; No. 172, 11/88; No. 173, Sept, 1990 - No. 177, 1/91

Hot Wheels #1 © DC

House of Fun #1 © Evan Dorkin

House of Mystery #143 © DC

	GD 2.0	VG 4.0	FN 6.0	VF 8.0	VF/NM 9.0	NM- 9.2
1-1st app. Hot Stuff; UFO story	159	318	477	1312	2956	4600
2-Stumbo-like giant 1st app. (12/57)	37	74	111	274	612	950
3-Stumbo the Giant debut (2/58)	19	38	57	133	297	460
4,5	17	34	51	117	259	400
6-10	10	20	30	66	138	210
11-20	8	16	24	51	96	140
21-40	5	10	15	34	60	85
41-60	4	8	12	25	40	55
61-80	3	6	9	19	30	40
81-105	3	6	9	15	22	28
106-112: All 52 pg. Giants	3	6	9	17	26	35
113-125	2	4	6	9	12	15
126-141	1	2	3	5	7	9
142-177: 172-177-($1.00)						6.00
Harvey Comics Classics Vol. 3 TPB (Dark Horse Books, 3/08, $19.95) Reprints Hot Stuff's earliest appearances in this title and Devil Kids, mostly B&W with some color stories; history, early concept drawings; foreword by Mark Arnold						20.00

HOT WHEELS (TV)
National Periodical Publications: Mar-Apr, 1970 - No. 6, Jan-Feb, 1971

	GD 2.0	VG 4.0	FN 6.0	VF 8.0	VF/NM 9.0	NM- 9.2
1	11	22	33	66	138	210
2,4,5	5	10	15	34	60	85
3-Neal Adams-c	6	12	18	41	76	110
6-Neal Adams-c/a	7	14	21	49	92	135

NOTE: ***Toth** a-1p, 2-5; c-1p, 5.*

HOURMAN (Justice Society member, see Adventure Comics #48)

HOURMAN (See JLA and DC One Million)
DC Comics: Apr, 1999 - No. 25, Apr, 2001 ($2.50)

	NM- 9.2
1-25: 1-JLA app.; McDaniel-c. 2-Tomorrow Woman-c/app. 6,7-Amazo app. 11-13-Justice Legion A app. 16-Silver Age flashback. 18,19-JSA-c/app. 22-Harris-c/a. 24-Hourman Vs. Rex Tyler	4.00

HOUSE OF CEREBUS
Aardvark-Vanaheim: Jan, 2020 ($4.00, B&W)

	NM- 9.2
1-Swamp Thing parady; Dave Sim-s/a; House of Secrets #92-c swipe	4.00

HOUSE OF FUN
Dark Horse Comics: Dec, 2012 ($3.50)

	NM- 9.2
0-Reprints Evan Dorkin humor strips from Dark Horse Presents #10-12	3.50

HOUSE OF GOLD AND BONES
Dark Horse Comics: Apr, 2013 - No. 4, Jul, 2013 ($3.99, limited series)

	NM- 9.2
1-4-Corey Taylor-s/Richard Clark-a; 2 covers on each	4.00

HOUSE OF HEM
Marvel Comics: 2015 ($7.99, one-shot)

	NM- 9.2
1-Reprints Fred Hembeck's Marvel highlights incl. Fantastic Four Roast; wraparound-c	8.00

HOUSE OF M (Also see miniseries with Fantastic Four, Iron Man and Spider-Man)
Marvel Comics: Aug, 2005 - No. 8, Dec, 2005 ($2.99, limited series)

	NM- 9.2
1-Bendis-s/Coipel-a/Ribic-c; Scarlet Witch changes reality; Quesada variant-c	5.00
2-8-Variant covers for each. 3-Hawkeye returns	3.00
... MGC #1 (6/11, $1.00) r/#1 with "Marvel's Greatest Comics" logo on cover	3.00
Secrets Of The House Of M (2005, $3.99, one-shot) profile pages and background info	4.00
... Sketchbook (6/05) B&W preview sketches by Coipel, Davis, Hairsine, Quesada	3.00
TPB (2006, $24.99) r/#1-8 and The Pulse: House of M Special Edition newspaper	25.00
...: Fantastic Four/ Iron Man TPB (2006, $13.99) r/ both House of M mini-series	14.00
...: World of M Featuring Wolverine TPB (2006, $13.99) r/2005 x-over issues Wolverine #33-35, Black Panther #7, Captain America #10 and The Pulse #10	14.00
HC (2008, $29.99, oversized with d.j.) r/#1-8, The Pulse: House of M Special Edition newspaper and Secrets Of The House Of M one-shot; script pages; cover gallery	30.00

HOUSE OF M (Secret Wars tie-in)
Marvel Comics: Oct, 2015 - No. 4, Dec, 2015 ($3.99, limited series)

	NM- 9.2
1-4: 1,2-Hopeless & Bunn-s/Failla-a; Magneto & the House of Magnus. 3,4-Anindito-a	4.00

HOUSE OF M: AVENGERS
Marvel Comics: Jan, 2008 - No. 5, Apr, 2008 ($2.99, limited series)

	NM- 9.2
1-5-Gage-s/Perkins-a; Luke Cage, Iron Fist, Hawkeye, Tigra, Misty Knight, Shang-Chi	3.00

HOUSE OF M: MASTERS OF EVIL
Marvel Comics: Oct, 2009 - No. 4, Jan, 2010 ($3.99, limited series)

	NM- 9.2
1-4-Gage-s/Garcia-a/Perkins-c; The Hood app.	4.00

HOUSE OF MYSTERY
DC Comics: Dec/Jan. 1951

nn - Ashcan comic, not distributed to newsstands, only for in-house use. Cover art is Danger Trail #3 with interior being Star Spangled Comics #109. A VG+ copy sold for $2,357.50 in 2002.

HOUSE OF MYSTERY (See Brave and the Bold #93, Elvira's House of Mystery, Limited Collectors' Edition & Super DC Giant)

HOUSE OF MYSTERY, THE
National Periodical Publications/DC Comics: Dec-Jan, 1951-52 - No. 321, Oct, 1983 (No. 194-203: 52 pgs.)

	GD 2.0	VG 4.0	FN 6.0	VF 8.0	VF/NM 9.0	NM- 9.2
1-DC's first horror comic	297	594	891	1901	3276	4650
2	129	258	387	826	1413	2000
3	76	152	228	486	831	1175
4,5	63	126	189	403	689	975
6-10	57	114	171	362	619	875
11-15	48	96	144	302	514	725
16(7/53)-25	39	78	117	240	395	550
26-35(2/55)-Last pre-code issue; 30-Woodish-a	33	66	99	194	317	440
36-50: 50-Text story of Orson Welles' War of the Worlds broadcast	17	34	51	117	259	400
51-60: 55-1st S.A. issue	15	30	45	100	220	340
61,63,65,66,69,70,72,76,79,85-Kirby-a	16	32	48	112	249	385
62,64,67,68,71,73-75,77,78,80-83,86-99: 92-Grey tone-c	14	28	42	94	207	320
84-Prototype of Negative Man (Doom Patrol)	23	46	69	161	356	550
100 (7/60)	15	30	45	100	220	340
101-116: 109-Toth, Kubert-a. 116-Last 10¢ issue	11	22	33	75	160	245
117-130: 117-Swipes-c to HOS #20. 120-Toth-a	10	20	30	64	132	200
131-142	9	18	27	58	114	170
143-J'onn J'onzz, Manhunter begins (6/64), ends #173; story continues from Detective #326; intro. Idol-Head of Diabolu	18	36	54	126	281	435
144	8	16	24	54	102	150
145-155,157-159: 149-Toth-a. 155-The Human Hurricane app. (12/65), Red Tornado prototype. 158-Origin Diabolu Idol-Head	5	10	15	35	63	90
156-Robby Reed begins (origin/1st app.), ends #173	8	16	24	54	102	150
160-(7/66)-Robby Reed becomes Plastic Man in this issue only; 1st S.A. app. Plastic Man; intro Marco Xavier (Martian Manhunter) & Vulture Crime Organization; ends #173	10	20	30	69	147	225
161-173: 169-Origin/1st app. Gem Girl	4	8	12	28	47	65
174-Mystery format begins.	16	32	48	107	236	365
175-1st app. Cain (House of Mystery host); Adams-c	14	28	42	98	217	335
176,177-Neal Adams-c	9	18	27	62	126	190
178-Neal Adams-c/a (2/69)	10	20	30	65	135	205
179-Neal Adams/Orlando, Wrightson-a (1st pro work, 3 pgs.); Adams-c	17	34	51	117	259	400
180,181,183: Wrightson-a (3,10, & 3 pgs.); Adams-c. 180-Last 12¢ issue; Kane/Wood-a(2). 183-Wood-a	8	16	24	56	108	160
182,184-Adams-c. 182-Toth-a. 184-Kane/Wood, Toth-a	6	12	18	41	76	110
185-Williamson/Kaluta-a; Howard-a (3 pgs.); Adams-c	7	14	21	44	82	120
186-N. Adams-c/a; Wrightson-a (10 pgs.)	9	18	27	59	117	175
187,190: Adams-c. 187-Toth-a. 190-Toth-a(r)	6	12	18	40	73	105
188-Wrightson-a (8 & 3pgs.); Adams-c	7	14	21	49	92	135
189,192,197: Adams-c on all. 189-Wood-a(i). 192-Last 15¢-c	6	12	18	40	73	105
191-Wrightson-a (8 & 3pgs.); Adams-c	7	14	21	49	92	135
193-Wrightson-c	6	12	18	40	73	105
194-Wrightson-c; 52 pgs begin, end #203; Toth,Kirby-a	8	16	24	51	96	140
195: Wrightson-c. Swamp creature story by Wrightson similar to Swamp Thing (10 pgs.)(10/71)	9	18	27	61	123	185
196,198	5	10	15	35	63	90
199-Adams-c; Wood-a(8pgs.); Kirby-a	6	12	18	42	79	115
200-(25¢, 52 pgs.)-One third-r (3/72)	6	12	18	41	76	110
201-203-(25¢, 52 pgs.)-One third-r	5	10	15	33	57	80
204-Wrightson-c/a, 9 pgs.	6	12	18	38	69	100
205,206,208,210,212,215,216,218	4	8	12	23	37	50
207-Wrightson-c/a; Starlin, Redondo-a	6	12	18	38	69	100
209,211,213,214,217,219-Wrightson-c	5	10	15	31	53	75
220,222,223	3	6	9	21	33	45
221-Wrightson/Kaluta-a(8 pgs.); Wrightson-c	6	12	18	37	66	95
224-229: 224-Wrightson-r from Spectre #9; Dillin/Adams-r from House of Secrets #82; begin 100 pg. issues; Phantom Stranger-r. 225,227-(100 pgs.): 225-Spectre app. 226-Wrightson/Redondo-a Phantom Stranger-r. 228-N. Adams inks; Wrightson-r. 229-Wrightson-a(r); Toth-r; last 100 pg. issue	5	10	15	35	63	90
230,232-235,237-250: 230-UFO-c	3	6	9	15	22	28
231-Classic Wrightson-c	6	12	18	37	66	95
236-Wrightson-c; Ditko-a(p); N. Adams-i	5	10	15	35	63	90
251-254-(84 pgs.)-Adams-c. 251-Wood-a	4	8	12	27	44	60

House of Night #5 © PC Cast

House of Whispers #4 © DC

House of X #2 © MAR

	GD 2.0	VG 4.0	FN 6.0	VF 8.0	VF/NM 9.0	NM- 9.2
255,256-(84 pgs.)-Wrightson-c	4	8	12	27	44	60
257-259-(84 pgs.)	3	6	9	18	28	38
260-289: 282-(68 pgs.)-Has extra story "The Computers That Saved Metropolis" Radio Shack giveaway by Jim Starlin	2	4	6	8	10	12
290-1st "I, Vampire"	6	12	18	41	76	110
291-299: 291,293,295-299- "I, Vampire"	2	4	6	10	14	18
300,319-"I, Vampire"	2	4	6	11	16	20
301-318,320: 301-318-"I, Vampire"	2	4	6	10	14	18
321-Death of "I, Vampire"	3	6	9	16	23	30

Welcome to the House of Mystery (7/98, $5.95) reprints stories with new framing story by Gaiman and Aragonés 6.00

NOTE: **Neal Adams** *a-236i; c-175-192, 197, 199, 251-254.* **Alcala** *a-209, 217, 219, 224, 227.* **M. Anderson** *a-212; c/a-37.* **Aparo** *a-209.* **Aragones** *a-185, 186, 194, 196, 200, 202, 229, 251.* **Baily** *a-279p.* **Cameron** *a-76, 79.* **Colan** *a-202r.* **Craig** *a-263, 275, 295, 300.* **Dillin/Adams** *r-224.* **Ditko** *a-236p, 247, 254, 258, 276; c-277.* **Drucker** *a-37.* **Evans** *c-218.* **Fradon** *a-251.* **Giffen** *a-284.* **Giunta** *a-199, 227r.* **Golden** *a-257, 259.* **Heath** *a-194r; c-203.* **Howard** *a-182, 185, 187, 196, 229r, 247i, 254, 279i.* **Kaluta** *a-195, 200, 250r; c-200-202, 210, 212, 233, 260, 261, 263, 265, 267, 268, 273, 276, 284, 287, 288, 293-295, 300, 302, 304, 305, 309-319, 321.* **Bob Kane** *a-84.* **Gil Kane** *a-196p, 253p, 300p.* **Kirby** *a-194r, 199r; c-65, 76, 78, 79, 85.* **Kubert** *c-282, 283, 285, 286, 289-292, 297-299, 301, 303, 306-308.* **Maneely** *a-68, 227r.* **Mayer** *a-317p.* **Meskin** *a-52-144 (most), 195r, 224r, 229r; c-63, 66, 124, 127.* **Mooney** *a-24, 159, 160.* **Moreira** *a-3, 4, 20-50, 58, 59, 62, 68, 77, 79, 90, 108, 113, 123, 201r, 228; c-4-28, 44, 47, 50, 54, 59, 62, 64, 68, 70, 73.* **Morrow** *a-192, 196, 255, 320i.* **Mortimer** *a-204(3 pgs.).* **Nasser** *a-276.* **Newton** *a-259, 272.* **Nino** *a-204, 212, 213, 220, 224, 225, 245, 250, 252-256, 283.* **Orlando** *a-175(2 pgs.), 178, 240i; c-240, 258p, 262, 264p, 270p, 271, 272, 274, 275, 278, 296i.* **Redondo** *a-194, 195, 197, 202, 203, 207, 211, 214, 217, 219, 226, 227, 229, 235, 241, 287(layout), 302p, 303i, 308; c-229.* **Reese** *a-195, 200, 205i.* **Rogers** *a-254, 274, 277.* **Roussos** *a-65, 84, 224i.* **Sekowsky** *a-282p.* **Sparling** *a-203.* **Starlin** *a-207(2 pgs.), 282p; c-281.* **Leonard Starr** *a-9.* **Staton** *a-300p.* **Sutton** *a-189, 271, 290, 291, 293, 295, 297-299, 302, 303, 306-309, 310-313i, 314.* **Tuska** *a-293p, 294p, 316p.* **Wrightson** *c-193-195, 204, 207, 209, 211, 213, 214, 217, 219, 221, 231, 236, 255, 256; r-224.*

HOUSE OF MYSTERY
DC Comics (Vertigo): Jul, 2008 - No. 42, Dec, 2011 ($2.99)

1-12,14-42: 1-Cain & Abel app.; Rossi-a/Weber-c. 9-Wrightson-a (6 pgs.). 16-Corben-a 3.00
1-Variant-c by Bernie Wrightson 5.00
13-Art by Neal Adams, Ralph Reese, Eric Powell, Sergio Aragonés 3.00
13-Variant-c by Neal Adams 5.00
... Halloween Annual #1 (12/09, $4.99) 1st app. I, Zombie in 7 pg. preview; short stories by various incl. Nowlan, Wagner, Willingham 3 6 9 14 20 25
... Halloween Annual #2 (12/10, $4.99) short stories by various incl. Carey, Allred, Gross 5.00
...: Love Stories for Dead People TPB (2009, $14.99) r/#6-10 15.00
...: Room and Boredom TPB (2008, $9.99) r/#1-5 10.00
...: Safe as Houses TPB (2011, $14.99) r/#26-30 15.00
...: The Beauty of Decay TPB (2010, $17.99) r/#16-20 & Halloween Annual #1 18.00
...: The Space Between TPB (2010, $14.99) r/#11-15; sketch pages 15.00
...: Under New Management TPB (2011, $14.99) r/#20-25 15.00

HOUSE OF NIGHT (Based on the series of novels by P.C. Cast and Kristin Cast)
Dark Horse Comics: Nov, 2011 - No. 5, Mar, 2012 ($1.00/$2.99, limited series)

1-($1.00) Cast, Cast & Dalian-s/Joëlle Jones & Kerschl-a; Frison-c 3.00
1-($1.00) Variant-c by Steve Morris 4.00
2-5-($2.99) Jones-a; two covers by Jones & Ryan Hill on each 3.00

HOUSE OF PENANCE
Dark Horse Comics: Apr, 2016 - No. 5, Aug, 2016 ($3.99)

1-5: 1-Peter J. Tomasi-s/Ian Bertram-a 4.00

HOUSE OF SECRETS (Combined with The Unexpected after #154)
National Periodical Publications/DC Comics: 11-12/56 - No. 80, 9-10/66; No. 81, 8-9/69 - No. 140, 2-3/76; No. 141, 8-9/76 - No. 154, 10-11/78

	GD 2.0	VG 4.0	FN 6.0	VF 8.0	VF/NM 9.0	NM- 9.2
1-Drucker-a; Moreira-c	141	282	423	1163	2632	4100
2-Moreira-a	46	92	138	359	805	1250
3-Kirby-c/a	42	84	126	311	706	1100
4-Kirby-a	31	62	93	223	499	775
5-7	23	46	69	168	382	560
8-Kirby-a	25	50	75	175	388	600
9-11: 11-Lou Cameron-a (unsigned); Kirby-a	21	42	63	147	324	500
12-Kirby-c/a; Lou Cameron-a	23	46	69	161	356	550
13-15: 14-Flying saucer-c	16	32	48	110	243	375
16-20	15	30	45	101	223	345
21,22,24-30	13	26	39	89	195	300
23-1st app. Mark Merlin & begin series (8/59)	16	32	48	107	236	365
31-50: 48-Toth-a. 50-Last 10¢ issue	11	22	33	77	166	255
51-60: 58-Origin Mark Merlin	9	18	27	59	117	175
61-First Eclipso (7-8/63) and begin series	59	118	177	472	1061	1650
62	8	16	24	54	102	150
63-65-Toth-a on Eclipso (see Brave and the Bold #64)	6	12	18	41	76	110
66-1st Eclipso-c (also #67,70,78,79); Toth-a	9	18	27	62	126	190
67,73: 67-Toth-a on Eclipso. 73-Mark Merlin becomes Prince Ra-Man (1st app.)	6	12	18	41	76	110
68-72,74-80: 76-Prince Ra-Man vs. Eclipso. 80-Eclipso, Prince Ra-Man end	6	12	18	37	66	95
81-Mystery format begins; 1st app. Abel (House Of Secrets host); (cameo in DC Special #4)	18	36	54	124	275	425
82-84: 82-Neal Adams-c(i)	8	16	24	51	96	140
85,90: 85-N. Adams-a(i). 90-Buckler (early work)/N. Adams-a(i)	8	16	24	52	99	145
86,88,89,91	7	14	21	44	82	120
87-Wrightson & Kaluta-a	8	16	24	52	99	145
92-1st app. Swamp Thing-c/story (8 pgs.)(6-7/71) by Berni Wrightson(p) w/JeffJones/Kaluta/Weiss ink assists; classic-c	280	560	1120	2240	3370	4500
92 (Facsimile Edition)(2019, $3.99) r/#92 w/original ads and letter column						4.00
93,94,96-(52 pgs.)-Wrightson-c. 94-Wrightson-a(i); 96-Wood-a	7	14	21	49	92	135
95,97,98-(52 pgs.)	5	10	15	35	63	90
99-Wrightson splash pg.	5	10	15	34	60	85
100-Classic Wrightson-c	8	16	24	52	99	145
101,102,104,105,108-111,113-120	3	6	9	19	30	40
103,106,107-Wrightson-c	5	10	15	33	57	80
112-Grey tone-c	4	8	12	23	37	50
121-133	2	4	6	11	16	20
134-Wrightson-a	3	6	9	17	26	35
135,136,139-Wrightson-a/c	3	6	9	20	31	42
137,138,141-153	2	4	6	8	10	12
140-1st solo origin of the Patchworkman (see Swamp Thing #3)	3	6	9	16	23	30
154 (10-11/78, 44 pgs.) Last issue	2	4	6	9	13	16

NOTE: **Neal Adams** *c-81, 82, 84-88, 90, 91.* **Alcala** *a-104-107.* **Anderson** *a-91.* Aparo *a-93, 97, 105.* **B. Bailey** *a-107.* **Cameron** *a-13, 15.* **Colan** *a-63.* **Ditko** *a-139p, 148.* **Elias** *a-58.* **Evans** *a-118.* **Finlay** *a-7r(Real Fact?).* **Glanzman** *a-91.* **Golden** *a-151.* **Heath** *a-31.* **Heck** *a-85.* **Kaluta** *a-87, 98, 99; c-98, 99, 101, 102, 105, 149, 151, 154.* **Bob Kane** *a-18, 21.* **G. Kane** *a-85p.* **Kirby** *c-3, 11, 12.* **Kubert** *a-39.* **Meskin** *a-2-68 (most), 94r; c-55-60.* **Moreira** *a-7, 8, 51, 54, 102-104, 106, 108, 113, 116, 118, 121, 123, 127; c-1, 2, 4-10, 13-20.* **Morrow** *a-86, 89, 90; c-89, 146-148.* **Nino** *a-101, 103, 106, 109, 115, 117, 126, 128, 131, 147, 153.* **Redondo** *a-95, 99, 102, 104p, 113, 116, 134, 136, 139, 140.* **Reese** *a-85.* **Severin** *a-91.* **Starlin** *c-150.* **Sutton** *a-154.* **Toth** *a-63-67, 83, 93r, 94r, 96r-98r, 123.* **Tuska** *a-90, 104.* **Wrightson** *a-134; c-92-94, 96, 100, 103, 106, 107, 135, 136, 139.*

HOUSE OF SECRETS
DC Comics (Vertigo): Oct, 1996 - No. 25, Dec, 1998 ($2.50) (Creator-owned series)

1-Steven Seagle-s/Kristiansen-c/a. 5.00
2-25: 5,7-Kristiansen-c/a. 6-Fegrado-a 4.00
TPB-(1997, $14.95) r/1-5 15.00

HOUSE OF SECRETS: FACADE
DC Comics (Vertigo): 2001 - No. 2, 2001 ($5.95, limited series)

1,2-Steven Seagle-s/Teddy Kristiansen-c/a. 6.00

HOUSE OF TERROR (3-D)
St. John Publishing Co.: Oct, 1953 (25¢, came w/glasses)

1-Kubert, Baker-a 30 60 90 177 289 400

HOUSE OF WHISPERS (The Sandman Universe)(Issues #21 & #22 were only released digitally)
DC Comics (Vertigo): Nov, 2018 - No. 20, Jun, 2020 ($3.99)

1-20: 1-Hopkinson-s/Stanton-a; Abel & Goldie app. 4.00

HOUSE OF X (Weekly series alternating with Powers of X #1-6)
Marvel Comics: Sept, 2019 - No. 6, Dec, 2019 ($5.99/$4.99)

1-($5.99) Hickman-s/Larraz-a; Fantastic Four app. 6.00
2-6-($4.99) 2-Moira MacTaggart new origin. 3-Bonus Krakoan alphabet translation guide 5.00

HOUSE OF YANG, THE (See Yang)
Charlton Comics: July, 1975 - No. 6, June, 1976; 1978

1-Sanho Kim-a in all 2 4 6 13 18 22
2-6 2 4 6 8 10 12
Modern Comics #1,2(1978) 6.00

HOUSE ON THE BORDERLAND
DC Comics (Vertigo): 2000 ($29.95, hardcover, one-shot)

HC-Adaptation of William Hope Hodgson book; Corben-a 30.00
SC (2003, $19.95) 20.00

HOUSE II: THE SECOND STORY
Marvel Comics: Oct, 1987 (One-shot)

1-Adapts movie 4.00

HOWARD CHAYKIN'S AMERICAN FLAGG (See American Flagg!)
First Comics: V2#1, May, 1988 - V2#12, Apr, 1989 ($1.75/$1.95, Baxter paper)

V2#1-9,11,12-Chaykin-c(p) in all 3.00
10-Elvis Presley photo-c 4.00

HOWARD THE DUCK (See Bizarre Adventures #34, Crazy Magazine, Fear, Man-Thing,

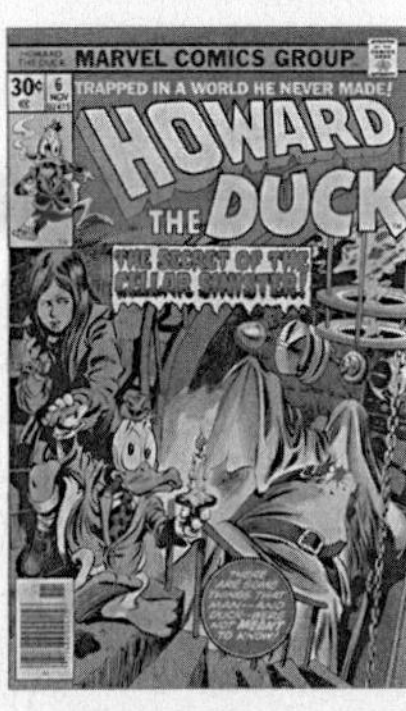

Howard the Duck #6 © MAR

Howdy Doody #10 © CNP

Huckleberry Hound #16 © H-B

GD VG FN VF VF/NM NM-
2.0 4.0 6.0 8.0 9.0 9.2

Marvel Treasury Edition & Sensational She-Hulk #14-17)
Marvel Comics Group: Jan, 1976 - No. 31, May, 1979; No. 32, Jan, 1986; No. 33, Sept, 1986

1-Brunner-c/a; Spider-Man x-over (low distr.) 6 12 18 38 69 100
2-Brunner-c/a 3 6 9 14 19 24
3,4-(Regular 25¢ edition). 3-Buscema-a(p), (7/76) 2 4 6 10 14 18
3,4-(30¢-c, limited distribution) 5 10 15 30 50 70
5 2 4 6 9 13 16
6-11: 8-Howard The Duck for president. 9-1st Sgt. Preston Dudley of RCMP. 10-Spider-Man-c/sty 1 2 3 5 7 9
12-1st brief app. Kiss (3/77) 4 8 12 23 37 50
13-(30¢-c) 1st full app. Kiss (6/77); Daimon Hellstrom app. plus cameo of Howard as Son of Satan 4 8 12 27 44 60
13-(35¢-c, limited distribution) 10 20 30 64 132 200
14-32: 14-17-(Regular 30¢-c). 14-Howard as Son of Satan-c/story; Son of Satan app. 16-Album issue; 3 pgs. comics. 22,23-Man-Thing-c/stories; Star Wars parody. 30,32-P. Smith-a 6.00
14-17-(35¢-c, limited distribution) 6 12 18 38 69 100
33-Last issue; low print run 1 2 3 5 6 8
Annual 1(1977, 52 pgs.)-Mayerik-a 2 4 6 8 10 12
... No. 1 Facsimile Ed. (8/19, $3.99) r/#1 w/original ads 4.00
... Omnibus HC (2008, $99.99, dustjacket) r/#1-33 & Annual #1, Adventure Into Fear #19, Man-Thing #1, Giant-Size Man-Thing #4&5, Marvel Treasury Ed. #12, Marvel Team-Up #96 and FOOM #15; Gerber foreword; creator interviews; bonus art; 2 covers 100.00

NOTE: ***Austin*** *c-29i.* ***Bolland*** *c-33.* ***Brunner*** *a-1p, 2p; c-1, 2.* ***Buckler*** *c-3p.* ***Buscema*** *a-3p.* ***Colan*** *a(p)-4-15, 17-20, 24-27, 30, 31; c(p)-4-31, Annual 1p.* ***Leialoha*** *a-1-13i; c(i)-3-5, 8-11.* ***Mayerik*** *a-22, 23, 33.* ***Paul Smith*** *a-30p, 32. Man-Thing app. in #22, 23.*

HOWARD THE DUCK (Magazine)
Marvel Comics Group: Oct, 1979 - No. 9, Mar, 1981 (B&W, 68 pgs.)

1-Art by Colan, Janson, Golden. Kidney Lady app. 2 4 6 11 16 20
2,3,6-9 (nudity in most): 2-Mayerick-c. 3-Xmas issue; Jack Davis-c; Duck World flashback. 6-1st Street People back-up story. 7-Has pin-up by Byrne; Man-Thing-c/s (46 pgs.). 8-Batman parody w/Marshall Rogers-a; Dave Sim-a (1 pg.). 9-Marie Severin-a; John Pound painted-c 1 3 4 6 8 10
4,5: 4-Beatles, John Lennon, Elvis, Kiss & Devo cameos; Hitler app. 5-Undead Duck, Dracula app. 2 4 6 9 12 15

NOTE: ***Buscema*** *a-4p.* ***Colan*** *a-1-5p, 7-9p.* ***Jack Davis*** *c-3.* ***Golden*** *a(p)-1, 5, 6(51pgs.).* ***Rogers*** *a-7, 8.* ***Simonson*** *a-7.*

HOWARD THE DUCK (Volume 2)
Marvel Comics: Mar, 2002 - No. 6, Aug, 2002 ($2.99)

1-Gerber-s/Winslade-a/Fabry-c 5.00
2-6: 2,4-6-Gerber-s/Winslade-a/Fabry-c. 3-Fabry-a/c 3.00
TPB (9/02, $14.99) r/#1-6 15.00

HOWARD THE DUCK (Volume 3)
Marvel Comics: Dec, 2007 - No. 4, Feb, 2008 ($2.99, limited series)

1-4-Templeton-s/Bobillo-a/c; She-Hulk app. 3.00
...: Media Duckling TPB (2008, $11.99) r/#1-4; Howard the Duck #1 (1/76) and pages from Civil War: Choosing Sides 12.00

HOWARD THE DUCK (Volume 4)
Marvel Comics: May 2015 - No. 5, Oct, 2015 ($3.99)

1-5-Zdarsky-s/Quinones-a. 1-Spider-Man app. 2-Guardians of the Galaxy app. 4.00

HOWARD THE DUCK (Volume 5)
Marvel Comics: Jan, 2016 - No. 11, Dec, 2016 ($4.99/$3.99)

1-($4.99) Zdarsky-s/Quinones-a; back-up with Gwenpool in #1-3 2 4 6 11 16 20
2-3-($4.99): 2-Fish-a 6.00
4-11-($3.99) 4,5-Silver Surfer, Galactus & the Guardians of the Galaxy app. 6-Squirrel Girl x-over. 7-Maguire-a. 8-Beverly app. 9-Lea Thompson app. 9-11-Mojo app. 4.00

HOWARD THE DUCK HOLIDAY SPECIAL
Marvel Comics: Feb, 1997 ($2.50, one-shot)

1-Wraparound-c; Hama-s 6.00

HOWARD THE DUCK: THE MOVIE
Marvel Comics Group: Dec, 1986 - No. 3, Feb, 1987 (Limited series)

1-3: Movie adaptation; r/Marvel Super Special 4.00

HOWARD THE HUMAN (Secret Wars tie-in)
Marvel Comics: Oct, 2015 ($3.99, one-shot)

1-Howard the Duck as human in an all-animal world; Skottie Young-s/Jim Mahfood-a 4.00

HOW BOYS AND GIRLS CAN HELP WIN THE WAR
The Parents' Magazine Institute: 1942 (10¢, one-shot)

1-All proceeds used to buy war bonds 39 78 117 240 395 550

GD VG FN VF VF/NM NM-
2.0 4.0 6.0 8.0 9.0 9.2

HOWDY DOODY (TV)(See Jackpot of Fun-- & Poll Parrot)(Some have stories by John Stanley)
Dell Publishing Co.: 1/50 - No. 38, 7-9/56; No. 761, 1/57; No. 811, 7/57

1-(Scarce)-Photo-c; 1st TV comic 75 150 225 600 1350 2100
2-Photo-c 34 68 102 241 541 840
3-5: All photo-c 19 38 57 133 297 460
6-Used in **SOTI**, pg. 309; classic-c; painted covers begin 23 46 69 161 356 550
7-10 12 24 36 84 185 285
11-20: 13-X-Mas-c 10 20 30 70 150 230
21-38, Four Color 761,811 9 18 27 61 123 185

HOW IT BEGAN
United Features Syndicate: No. 15, 1939 (one-shot)

Single Series 15 37 74 111 222 361 500

HOWLING COMMANDOS OF S.H.I.E.L.D.
Marvel Comics: Dec, 2015 - No. 6, May, 2016 ($3.99)

1-6: 1-Barbiere-s/Schoonover-a; Dum Dum Dugan, Orrgo, Man-Thing, Hit-Monkey app. 4.00

HOW SANTA GOT HIS RED SUIT (See March of Comics No. 2)

HOW THE WEST WAS WON (See Movie Comics)

HOW TO DRAW FOR THE COMICS
Street and Smith: No date (1942?) (10¢, 64 pgs., B&W & color, no ads)

nn-Art by Robert Winsor McCay (recreating his father's art), George Marcoux (Supersnipe artist), Vernon Greene (The Shadow artist), Jack Binder (with biog.), Thorton Fisher, Jon Small, & Jack Farr; has biographies of each artist 40 80 120 246 411 575

H. P. LOVECRAFT'S CTHULHU
Millennium Publications: Dec, 1991 - No. 3, May, 1992 ($2.50, limited series)

1-3: 1-Contains trading cards on thin stock 4.00

H. R. PUFNSTUF (TV) (See March of Comics #360)
Gold Key: Oct, 1970 - No. 8, July, 1972

1-Photo-c 10 20 30 64 132 200
2-8-Photo-c on all. 6-8-Both Gold Key and Whitman editions exist 7 14 21 46 86 125

HUBERT AT CAMP MOONBEAM
Dell Publishing Co.: No. 251, Oct, 1949 (one shot)

Four Color 251 9 18 27 61 123 185

HUCK
Image Comics: Nov, 2015 - No. 6, Apr, 2016($3.50/$3.99)

1-5-Millar-s/Albuquerque-a; 2 covers on each 3.50
6-($3.99) 4.00

HUCK & YOGI JAMBOREE (TV)
Dell Publishing Co.: Mar, 1961 ($1.00, 6-1/4x9", 116 pgs., cardboard-c, high quality paper) (B&W original material)

nn (scarce) 8 16 24 54 102 150

HUCK & YOGI WINTER SPORTS (TV)
Dell Publishing Co.: No. 1310, Mar, 1962 (Hanna-Barbara) (one-shot)

Four Color 1310 8 16 24 51 96 140

HUCK FINN (See The New Adventures of... & Power Record Comics)

HUCKLEBERRY FINN (Movie)
Dell Publishing Co.: No. 1114, July, 1960

Four Color 1114-Photo-c 6 12 18 40 73 105

HUCKLEBERRY HOUND (See Dell Giant #31,44, Golden Picture Story Book, Kite Fun Book, March of Comics #199, 214, 235, Spotlight #1 & Whitman Comic Books)

HUCKLEBERRY HOUND (TV)
Dell/Gold Key No. 18 (10/62) on: No. 990, 5-7/59 - No. 43, 10/70 (Hanna-Barbera)

Four Color 990(#1)-1st app. Huckleberry Hound, Yogi Bear, & Pixie & Dixie & Mr. Jinks 17 34 51 117 259 400
Four Color 1050,1054 (12/59) 11 22 33 73 157 240
3(1-2/60) - 7 (9-10/60), Four Color 1141 (10/60) 7 14 21 46 86 125
8-10 6 12 18 37 66 95
11,13-17 (6-8/62) 5 10 15 30 50 70
12-1st Hokey Wolf & Ding-a-Ling 5 10 15 33 57 80
18,19 (84pgs.; 18-20 titled ...Chuckleberry Tales) 7 14 21 44 82 120
20-Titled Chuckleberry Tales 4 8 12 28 47 65
21-30: 28-30-Reprints 4 8 12 23 37 50
31-43: 31,32,35,37-43-Reprints 3 6 9 19 30 40

HUCKLEBERRY HOUND (TV)

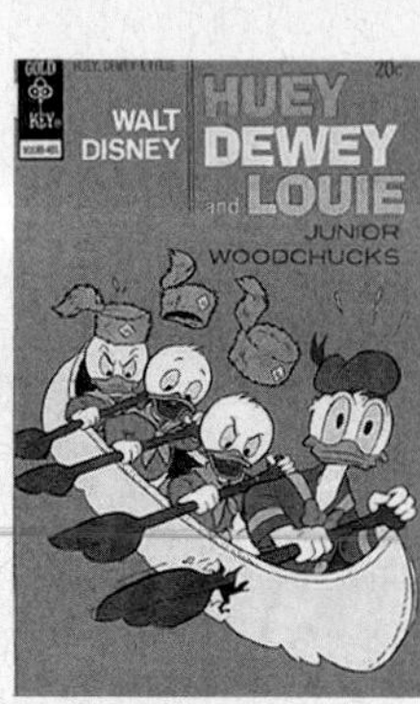

Huey, Dewey, and Louie Junior Woodchucks #24 © DIS

Hulk #26 © MAR

Hulk Smash #1 © MAR

	GD 2.0	VG 4.0	FN 6.0	VF 8.0	VF/NM 9.0	NM- 9.2

Charlton Comics: Nov, 1970 - No. 8, Jan, 1972 (Hanna-Barbera)

	GD	VG	FN	VF	VF/NM	NM-
1	5	10	15	31	53	75
2-8	3	6	9	17	26	35

HUEY, DEWEY, & LOUIE (See Donald Duck, 1938 for 1st app. Also see Mickey Mouse Magazine V4#2, V5#7 & Walt Disney's Junior Woodchucks Limited Series)

HUEY, DEWEY, & LOUIE BACK TO SCHOOL (See Dell Giant #22, 35, 49 & Dell Giants)

HUEY, DEWEY, AND LOUIE JUNIOR WOODCHUCKS (Disney)
Gold Key No. 1-61/Whitman No. 62 on: Aug, 1966 - No. 81, July, 1984
(See Walt Disney's Comics & Stories #125)

	GD	VG	FN	VF	VF/NM	NM-
1	7	14	21	44	82	120
2,3(12/68)	4	8	12	23	37	50
4,5(4/70)-r/two WDC&S D.Duck stories by Barks	3	6	9	19	30	40
6-17	3	6	9	17	26	35
18,27-30	3	6	9	15	21	26
19-23,25-New storyboarded scripts by Barks, 13-25 pgs. per issue	3	6	9	18	28	38
24,26: 26-r/Barks Donald Duck WDC&S stories	3	6	9	16	23	30
31-57,60,61: 35,41-r/Barks J.W. scripts	2	4	6	8	11	14
58,59: 58-r/Barks Donald Duck WDC&S stories	2	4	6	9	13	16
62-64 (Whitman)	2	4	6	9	13	16
65-(9/80), 66 (Pre-pack? scarce)	4	8	12	25	40	55
67 (1/81),68	2	4	6	9	13	16
67-40¢ cover variant	4	8	12	17	21	24
69-74: 72(2/82), 73(2-3/82), 74(3/82)	2	4	6	8	11	14
75-81 (all #90183; pre-pack; nd, nd code; scarce): 75(4/83), 76(5/83), 77(7/83), 78(8/83), 79(4/84), 80(5/84), 81(7/84)	3	6	9	16	23	30

HUGGA BUNCH (TV)
Marvel Comics (Star Comics): Oct, 1986 - No. 6, Aug, 1987

	GD	VG	FN	VF	VF/NM	NM-
1-6						5.00

HULK (Magazine)(Formerly The Rampaging Hulk)(Also see The Incredible Hulk)
Marvel Comics: No. 10, Aug., 1978 - No. 27, June, 1981 ($1.50)

	GD	VG	FN	VF	VF/NM	NM-
10-18: 10-Bill Bixby interview. 11-Moon Knight begins. 12-15,17,18-Moon Knight stories. 12-Lou Ferrigno interview.	2	4	6	10	14	18
19-27: 20-Moon Knight story. 23-Last full color issue; Banner is attacked. 24-Part color, Lou Ferrigno interview. 25-Part color. 26,27-are B&W	2	4	6	9	12	15

NOTE: #10-20 have fragile spines which split easily. ***Alcala*** *a(i)-15, 17-20, 22, 24-27.* ***Buscema*** *a-23; c-26.* ***Chaykin*** *a-21-25.* ***Colan*** *a(p)-11, 19, 24-27.* ***Jusko*** *painted c-12.* ***Nebres*** *a-16.* ***Severin*** *a-19i. Moon Knight by* ***Sienkiewicz*** *in 13-15, 17, 18, 20.* ***Simonson*** *a-27; c-23. Dominic Fortune appears in #21-24.*

HULK (Becomes Incredible Hulk Vol. 2 with issue #12) (Also see Marvel Age Hulk)
Marvel Comics: Apr, 1999 - No. 11, Feb, 2000 ($2.99/$1.99)

	GD	VG	FN	VF	VF/NM	NM-
1-($2.99) Byrne-s/Garney-a	1	2	3	5	6	8
1-Variant-c	2	4	6	8	10	12
1-DFE Remarked-c						50.00
1-Gold foil variant						10.00
2-7-($1.99): 2-Two covers. 5-Art by Jurgens, Buscema & Texeira. 7-Avengers app.						4.00
8-Hulk battles Wolverine	2	4	6	8	10	12
9-11: 11-She-Hulk app.						3.00
1999 Annual ($3.50) Chapter One story; Byrne-s/Weeks-a						4.00
Hulk Vs. The Thing (12/99, $3.99, TPB) reprints their notable battles						4.00

HULK (Also see Fall of the Hulks and King-Size Hulk) (Becomes Red She-Hulk with #58)
Marvel Comics: Mar, 2008 - No. 57, Oct, 2012 ($2.99/$3.99)

	GD	VG	FN	VF	VF/NM	NM-
1-Red Hulk app.; Abomination killed; Loeb-s/McGuinness-a/c	3	6	9	21	33	45
1-Variant-c by Acuña	3	6	9	19	30	40
1-Variant-c with Incredible Hulk #1 cover swipe by McGuinness						55.00
1,2-2nd printings with wraparound McGuinness variant-c						3.00
2-22: 2-Iron Man app.; Rick Jones becomes the new Abomination. 4,6-Red Hulk vs. green Hulk; two covers (each Hulk); Thor app. 7-9-Art Adams & Cho-a (2 covers) 10-Defenders re-form. 14,15-X-Force, Elektra & Deadpool app. 15-Red She-Hulk app. 19-21-Fall of the Hulks x-over. 19-FF app. 22-World War Hulks						4.00
2-9: 2-Variant-c by Djurdjevic. 3-Var-c by Finch. 5-Var-c by Coipel. 6,7-Var-c by Turner 8-Var-c by Sal Buscema. 9-Two covers w/Hulks as Santa						6.00
23-($4.99) Origin of the Red Hulk; art by Sale, Romita, Deodato, Trimpe, Yu, others						5.00
24-31-($3.99): 24-World war Hulks. 25,26-Iron Man app. 26-Thor app.						4.00
30.1, 32-49 ($2.99): 34-Planet Red Hulk begins. 37-38-Fear Itself tie-in						3.00
50-($3.99) Haunted Hulk; Dr. Strange app.; back-up w/Brereton-a; Pagulayan-c						4.00
50-Variant covers by Art Adams, Humberto Ramos & Walt Simonson						10.00
51-57: 53-57-Eaglesham-a; Alpha Flight app.						3.00
... Family: Green Genes 1 (2/09, $4.99) new She-Hulk, Scorpion, Skaar & Mr. Fixit stories						5.00
... Let the Battle Begin 1 (5/10, $3.99) Snider-s/Kurth-a; Del Mundo-c; McGuinness-a						4.00
... MGC #1 (6/10, $1.00) r/#1 with "Marvel's Greatest Comics" logo on cover						3.00
... Monster-Size Special (12/08, $3.99) monster-themed stories by Niles, David & others						4.00
...: Raging Thunder 1 (8/08, $3.99) Hulk vs. Thundra; Breitweiser-a; r/FF #133; Land-c						4.00
Hulk-Sized Mini-Hulks ('11, $2.99) Red, Green & Blue Hulks all-ages humor; Giarrusso-a						3.00
... Vs. Fin Fang Foom (2/08, $3.99) new re-telling of first meeting; r/Strange Tales #89						4.00
... Vs. Hercules (6/08, $3.99) Djurdjevic-c; new story w/art by various; r/Tales To Ast. #79						4.00
...: Winter Guard (2/10, $3.99) Darkstar, Crimson Dynamo app. Steve Ellis-a/c						4.00
Hulk 100 Project (2008, $10.00, SC, charity book for the HERO Initiative) collection of 100 variant covers by Adams, Romita Sr. & Jr., Cho, McGuinness and more						10.00

HULK (Follows Indestructible Hulk series)
Marvel Comics: Jun, 2014 - No. 16, Jul, 2015 ($3.99)

	GD	VG	FN	VF	VF/NM	NM-
1-15: 1-4-Waid-s/Bagley-a. 3,4-Avengers app. 5-Alex Ross-c. 6-15-Duggan-s. 13,14-Deadpool app. 14-15-Hulk vs. Red Hulk						4.00
16-($4.99) Avengers app.; Duggan-s/Bagley-a; leads into Secret Wars						5.00
Annual 1 (11/14, $4.99) Monty Nero-s; art by Luke Ross, Goddard & Laming						5.00

HULK (Jennifer Walters as Hulk; follows events of Civil War II)(Continues as She-Hulk #159)
Marvel Comics: Feb, 2017 - No. 11, Dec, 2017 ($3.99)

	GD	VG	FN	VF	VF/NM	NM-
1-11: 1-6-Mariko Tamaki-s/Nico Leon-a. 3,11-Hellcat app.						4.00

HULK AND POWER PACK (All ages series)
Marvel Comics: May, 2007 - No. 4, Aug, 2007 ($2.99, limited series)

	GD	VG	FN	VF	VF/NM	NM-
1-4-Sumerak-s. 1,2,4-Williams-a. 1-Absorbing Man app. 3-Kuhn-a; Abomination app.						3.00
...: Pack Smash! (2007, $6.99, digest) r/#1-4						7.00

HULK & THING: HARD KNOCKS
Marvel Comics: Nov, 2004 - No. 4, Feb, 2005 ($3.50, limited series)

	GD	VG	FN	VF	VF/NM	NM-
1-4-Bruce Jones-s/Jae Lee-a/c						3.50
TPB (2005, $13.99) r/#1-4 and Giant-Size Super-Stars #1						14.00

HULK: BROKEN WORLDS
Marvel Comics: May, 2009 -No. 2, July, 2009 ($3.99, limited series)

	GD	VG	FN	VF	VF/NM	NM-
1,2-Short stories of alternate world Hulks by various, incl. Trimpe, David, Warren						4.00

HULK CHRONICLES: WWH
Marvel Comics: Oct, 2008 - No. 6, Mar, 2009 ($4.99, limited series)

	GD	VG	FN	VF	VF/NM	NM-
1-6-Reprints stories from World War Hulk x-over. 1-R/Inc. Hulk #106 & WWH Prologue						5.00

HULK: DESTRUCTION
Marvel Comics: Sept, 2005 - No. 4, Dec, 2005 ($2.99, limited series)

	GD	VG	FN	VF	VF/NM	NM-
1-4-Origin of the Abomination; Peter David-s/Jim Muniz-a						3.00

HULKED-OUT HEROES
Marvel Comics: Jun, 2010 - No. 2, Jun, 2010 ($3.99, limited series)

	GD	VG	FN	VF	VF/NM	NM-
1,2-World War Hulks tie-in; Deadpool app.; Ramos-a						4.00

HULK: FUTURE IMPERFECT
Marvel Comics: Jan, 1993 - No. 2, Dec, 1992 (In error) ($5.95, 52 pgs., squarebound, limited series)

	GD	VG	FN	VF	VF/NM	NM-
1,2: Embossed-c; Peter David story & George Perez-c/a. 1-1st app. Maestro.	2	4	6	11	16	20

HULK: GRAY
Marvel Comics: Dec, 2003 - No. 6, Apr, 2004 ($3.50, limited series)

	GD	VG	FN	VF	VF/NM	NM-
1-6-Hulk's origin & early days; Loeb-s/Sale-a/c						3.50
HC (2004, $21.99, with dust jacket) oversized r/#1-6						22.00
SC (2005, $19.99) r/#1-6						20.00

HULK: NIGHTMERICA
Marvel Comics: Aug, 2003 - No. 6, May, 2004 ($2.99, limited series)

	GD	VG	FN	VF	VF/NM	NM-
1-6-Brian Ashmore painted-a/c						3.00

HULK/ PITT
Marvel Comics: 1997 ($5.99, one-shot)

	GD	VG	FN	VF	VF/NM	NM-
1-David-s/Keown-c/a						6.00

HULK: SEASON ONE
Marvel Comics: 2012 ($24.99, hardcover graphic novel)

	GD	VG	FN	VF	VF/NM	NM-
HC - Origin and early days; Van Lente-s/Fowler-a/Tedesco painted-c						25.00

HULK SMASH
Marvel Comics: Mar, 2001 - No. 2, Apr, 2001 ($2.99, limited series)

	GD	VG	FN	VF	VF/NM	NM-
1,2-Ennis-s/McCrea & Janson-a/Nowlan painted-c						3.00

HULK SMASH AVENGERS
Marvel Comics: Jul, 2012 - No. 5, July, 2012 ($2.99, weekly limited series)

	GD	VG	FN	VF	VF/NM	NM-
1-5-Hulk vs. Avengers from various points in Marvel History. 1-Frenz-a. 5-Oeming-a						3.00

HULK: THE MOVIE
Marvel Comics

Human Bomb #1 © DC

The Human Fly #9 © MAR

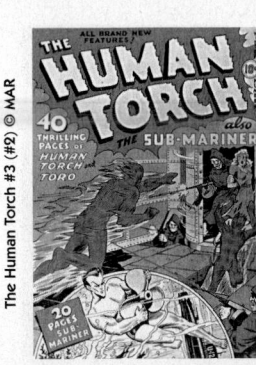

The Human Torch #3 (#2) © MAR

	GD 2.0	VG 4.0	FN 6.0	VF 8.0	VF/NM 9.0	NM- 9.2
...Adaptation (8/03, $3.50) Bruce Jones-s/Bagley-a/Keown-c						3.50
TPB (2003, $12.99) r/Adaptation, Ultimates #5, Inc. Hulk #34, Ult. Marvel Team-Up #2&3						13.00
HULK 2099						
Marvel Comics: Dec, 1994 - No. 10, Sept, 1995 ($1.50/$1.95)						
1-($2.50)-Green foil-c						6.00
2-10: 2-A. Kubert-c						4.00
HULKVERINES						
Marvel Comics: Apr, 2019 - No. 3, Jun, 2019 ($4.99)						
1-3-Hulk, Weapon H, Wolverine and The Leader app.; Pak-s/Anindito-a						4.00
HULK/WOLVERINE: 6 HOURS						
Marvel Comics: Mar, 2003 - No. 4, May, 2003 ($2.99, limited series)						
1-4-Bruce Jones-s/Scott Kolins-a; Bisley-c						3.00
Hulk Legends Vol. 1: Hulk/Wolverine: 6 Hours (2003, $13.99, TPB) r/#1-4 & 1st Wolverine app. from Incredible Hulk #181						14.00
HUMAN BOMB						
DC Comics: Feb, 2013 - No. 4, May, 2013 ($2.99, limited series)						
1-4: 1-Re-intro/origin; Gray & Palmiotti-s/Ordway-a/c						3.00
HUMAN DEFENSE CORPS						
DC Comics: Jul, 2003 - No. 6, Dec, 2003 ($2.50, limited series)						
1-6-Ty Templeton-s/Sauve, Jr & Vlasco-a. 1-Lois Lane app.						3.00
HUMAN FLY						
I.W. Enterprises/Super: 1963 - 1964 (Reprints)						
I.W. Reprint #1-Reprints Blue Beetle #44('46)	2	4	6	13	18	22
Super Reprint #10-R/Blue Beetle #46('47)	2	4	6	13	18	22
HUMAN FLY, THE						
Marvel Comics Group: Sept, 1977 - No. 19, Mar, 1979						
1-(Regular 30¢-c) Origin; Spider-Man x-over	3	6	9	16	23	30
1-(35¢-c, limited distribution)	9	18	27	59	117	175
2,9,19: 2-(Regular 30¢-c). 2-Ghost Rider app. 9-Daredevil x-over; Byrne-c(p). 19-Last issue	2	3	4	6	8	10
2-(35¢-c, limited distribution)	6	12	18	41	76	110
3-8,10-18						5.00

NOTE: ***Austin** c-4i, 9i. **Elias** a-1, 3p, 4p, 7p, 10-12p, 15p, 18p, 19p. **Layton** c-19.*

	GD 2.0	VG 4.0	FN 6.0	VF 8.0	VF/NM 9.0	NM- 9.2
HUMANKIND						
Image Comics (Top Cow): Sept, 2004 - No. 5, Mar, 2005 ($2.99, limited series)						
1-5-Tony Daniel-a. 1-Three covers by Daniel, Silvestri, and Land						3.00
HUMAN RACE, THE						
DC Comics: May, 2005 - No. 7, Nov, 2005 ($2.99, limited series)						
1-7-Raab-s/Justiniano-a/c						3.00
HUMAN TARGET						
DC Comics (Vertigo): Apr, 1999 - No. 4, July, 1999 ($2.95, limited series)						
1-4-Milligan-s/Bradstreet-c/Biukoviˊc-a						3.00
1-Special Edition (6/10, $1.00) r/#1 with "What's Next?" logo on cover						3.00
TPB (2000, $12.95) new Bradstreet-c						13.00
...: Chance Meetings TPB (2010, $14.99) r/#1-4 and Human Target: Final Cut GN						15.00
HUMAN TARGET						
DC Comics (Vertigo): Oct, 2003 - No. 21, June, 2005 ($2.95)						
1-21: 1-5-Milligan-s/Pulido-a/c. 6-Chiang-a						3.00
...: Living in Amerika TPB (2004, $14.95) r/#6-10; Chiang sketch pages						15.00
...: Second Chances TPB (2011, $19.99) r/#1-10; Chiang sketch pages						20.00
...: Strike Zones TPB (2004, $9.95) r/#1-5						10.00
HUMAN TARGET (Based on the Fox TV series)						
DC Comics: Apr, 2010 - No. 6, Sept, 2010 ($2.99, limited series)						
1-6-Wein-s/Redondo-a; back-up stories by various. 1-Bermejo-c. 5-Sook-c						3.00
TPB (2010, $17.99) r/#1-6						18.00
HUMAN TARGET: FINAL CUT						
DC Comics (Vertigo): 2002 ($29.95/$19.95, graphic novel)						
Hardcover (2002, $29.95) Milligan-s/Pulido-a/c						30.00
Softcover (2003, $19.95)						20.00
HUMAN TARGET SPECIAL (TV)						
DC Comics: Nov, 1991 ($2.00, 52 pgs., one-shot)						
1						4.00
HUMAN TORCH, THE (Red Raven #1)(See All-Select, All Winners, Marvel Mystery, Men's Adventures, Mystic Comics (2nd series), Sub-Mariner, USA & Young Men)						
Timely/Marvel Comics (TP 2,3/TCI 4-9/SePI 10/SnPC 11-25/CnPC 26-35/Atlas Comics (CPC 36-38)): No. 2, Fall, 1940 - No. 15, Spring, 1944; No. 16, Fall, 1944 - No. 35, Mar, 1949						
(Becomes Love Tales #36 on); No. 36, April, 1954 - No. 38, Aug, 1954						
2(#1)-Intro & Origin Toro; The Falcon, The Fiery Mask, Mantor the Magician, & Microman only app.; Human Torch by Burgos, Sub-Mariner by Everett begin (origin of each in text); WWII-c	2740	5480	8220	19,180	45,200	73,000
3(#2)-40 pg. H.T. story; H.T. & S.M. battle over who is best artist in text-Everett or Burgos	730	1460	2190	5329	9415	13,500
4(#3)-Origin The Patriot in text; last Everett Sub-Mariner; Sid Greene-a	533	1066	1599	3891	6746	9600
5(#4)-The Patriot app; Angel x-over in Sub-Mariner (Summer, 1941); 1st Nazi war-c this title; back-c ad for Young Allies #1 with diff. cover-a	443	886	1329	3234	5717	8200
5-Human Torch battles Sub-Mariner (Fall, '41); 60 pg. story	703	1406	2109	5132	9066	13,000
6-Schomburg hooded villain bondage-c	389	778	1167	2723	4762	6800
7-1st Japanese war-c	418	836	1254	2926	5163	7400
8-Human Torch battles Sub-Mariner; 52 pg. story; Wolverton-a, 1 pg.; Nazi WWII-c	541	1082	1623	3950	6975	10,000
9-Classic Human Torch vs. Gen. Rommel, "The Desert Rat"; Nazi WWII-c	423	846	1269	3000	5250	7500
10-Human Torch battles Sub-Mariner, 45 pg. story; Wolverton-a, 1 pg.; Nazi WWII-c	438	876	1314	3197	5649	8100
11,14,15: 11-Nazi WWII-c. 14-Nazi WWII-c; 1st Atlas Globe logo (Winter, 1943-44; see All Winners #11 also)	322	644	966	2254	4027	5800
12-Classic Japanese WWII-c, Torch melts Japanese soldier's arm	1000	2000	3000	7500	13,500	19,500
13-Classic Schomburg Japanese WWII bondage-c	371	742	1113	2600	4550	6500
16-20: 16-18,20-Japanese WWII-c. 19-Bondage-c. 20-Last War issue	265	530	795	1694	2897	4100
21,22,24-30: 27-2nd app. (1st-c) Asbestos Lady (see Capt. America Comics #63 for 1st app.)	200	400	600	1280	2190	3100
23 (Sum/46)-Becomes Junior Miss 24? Classic Schomburg Robot-c	306	612	918	2198	3849	5500
31,32: 31-Namora x-over in Sub-Mariner (also #30); last Toro. 32-Sungirl, Namora app.; Sungirl-c	181	362	543	1158	1979	2800
33-Capt. America x-over	187	374	561	1197	2049	2900
34-Sungirl solo	171	342	513	1094	1873	2650
35-Captain America & Sungirl app. (1949)	171	342	513	1094	1873	2650
36-38(1954)-Sub-Mariner in all	135	270	405	864	1482	2100

NOTE: *Ayers Human Torch in 36(3). **Brodsky** c-25, 31-33?, 37, 38. **Burgos** c-36. **Everett** a-1-3, 27, 28, 30, 37, 38. **Powell** a-36(Sub-Mariner). **Schomburg** c-1-3, 5-8, 10-23. **Sekowsky** c-28, 34?, 35? **Shores** c-24, 26, 27, 29, 30. **Mickey Spillane** text 4-6. Bondage c-2, 12, 19.*

	GD 2.0	VG 4.0	FN 6.0	VF 8.0	VF/NM 9.0	NM- 9.2
HUMAN TORCH, THE (Also see Avengers West Coast, Fantastic Four, The Invaders, Saga of the Original... & Strange Tales #101)						
Marvel Comics Group: Sept, 1974 - No. 8, Nov, 1975						
1: 1-8-r/stories from Strange Tales #101-108	5	10	15	35	63	90
2-8: 1st H.T. title since G.A. 7-vs. Sub-Mariner	3	6	9	15	22	28

NOTE: *Golden Age & Silver Age Human Torch-r #1-8. **Ayers** r-6, 7. **Kirby/Ayers** r-1-5, 8.*

	GD 2.0	VG 4.0	FN 6.0	VF 8.0	VF/NM 9.0	NM- 9.2
HUMAN TORCH (From the Fantastic Four)						
Marvel Comics: June, 2003 - No. 12, Jun, 2004 ($2.50/$2.99)						
1-7-Skottie Young-c/a; Karl Kesel-s						3.00
8-12-($2.99) 8,10-Dodd-a. 9-Young-a. 11-Porter-a. 12-Medina-a						3.00
... Vol. 1: Burn TPB (2005, $7.99, digest size) r/#1-6						8.00
HUMAN TORCH COMICS 70TH ANNIVERSARY SPECIAL						
Marvel Comics: July, 2009 ($3.99, one-shot)						
1-Covers by Granov and Martin; new story and r/1st app Toro from Human Torch #2						5.00
HUMBUG (Satire by Harvey Kurtzman)						
Humbug Publications: Aug, 1957 - No. 9, May, 1958; No. 10, June, 1958; No. 11, Oct, 1958						
1-Wood-a (intro pgs. only)	28	56	84	165	270	375
2	15	30	45	85	130	175
3-9: 8-Elvis in Jailbreak Rock	14	28	42	76	108	140
10,11-Magazine format. 10-Photo-c	15	30	45	90	140	190
Bound Volume(#1-9)(extremely rare)	65	130	195	416	708	1000

NOTE: ***Davis** a-1-11. **Elder** a-2-4, 6-9, 11. **Heath** a-2, 4-8, 10. **Jaffee** a-2, 4-9. **Kurtzman** a-11.*

	GD 2.0	VG 4.0	FN 6.0	VF 8.0	VF/NM 9.0	NM- 9.2
HUMDINGER (Becomes White Rider and Super Horse #3 on?)						
Novelty Press/Premium Group: May-June, 1946 - V2#2, July-Aug, 1947						
1-Jerkwater Line, Mickey Starlight by Don Rico, Dink begin	37	74	111	222	361	500
2	16	32	48	94	147	200
3-6, V2#1,2	12	24	36	69	97	125
HUMONGOUS MAN						
Alternative Press (Ikon Press): Sept, 1997 -No. 3 ($2.25, B&W)						
1-3-Stepp & Harrison-c/s/a.						3.00

Hunger #1 © MAR

Huntress: Year One #1 © DC

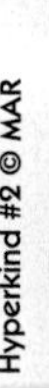
Hyperkind #2 © MAR

	GD 2.0	VG 4.0	FN 6.0	VF 8.0	VF/NM 9.0	NM- 9.2

HUMOR (See All Humor Comics)

HUMPHREY COMICS (Joe Palooka Presents...; also see Joe Palooka)
Harvey Publications: Oct, 1948 - No. 22, Apr, 1952

	GD	VG	FN	VF	VF/NM	NM-
1-Joe Palooka's pal (r); (52 pgs.)-Powell-a	15	30	45	86	133	180
2,3: Powell-a	9	18	27	50	65	80
4-Boy Heroes app.; Powell-a	9	18	27	52	69	85
5-8,10: 5,6-Powell-a. 7-Little Dot app.	8	16	24	40	50	60
9-Origin Humphrey	9	18	27	47	61	75
11-22	7	14	21	37	46	55

HUNCHBACK OF NOTRE DAME, THE
Dell Publishing Co.: No. 854, Oct, 1957 (one shot)

	GD	VG	FN	VF	VF/NM	NM-
Four Color 854-Movie, photo-c	11	22	33	76	163	250

HUNGER (See Age of Ultron and Cataclysm titles)
Marvel Comics: Sept, 2013 - No. 4, Dec, 2013 ($3.99, limited series)

1-4-Fialkov-s/Kirk-a/Granov-c; Galactus in the Ultimate Universe. 2-4-Silver Surfer app. 4.00
1-Variant-c by Neal Adams 18.00

HUNGER, THE
Speakeasy Comics: May, 2005 ($2.99)

1-Andy Bradshaw-s/a; Eric Powell-c 3.00

HUNGER DOGS, THE (See DC Graphic Novel #4)

HUNGRY GHOSTS
Dark Horse Comics (Berger Books): Jan, 2018 - No. 4, Apr, 2018 ($3.99, limited series)

1-4-Anthony Bourdain & Joel Rose-s/Paul Pope-c. 1-Ponticelli & Del Rey-a. 2-Manco & Santolouco-a. 3-Cabrol & Paul Pope-a. 4-Francavilla & Koh-a 4.00

HUNK
Charlton Comics: Aug, 1961 - No. 11, 1963

	GD	VG	FN	VF	VF/NM	NM-
1	4	8	12	23	37	50
2-11	3	6	9	14	20	25

HUNT, THE
Image Comics (Shadowline): Jul, 2016 - No. 5, Dec, 2016 ($3.99)

1-5-Colin Lorimer-s/a 4.00

HUNTED (Formerly My Love Memoirs)
Fox Feature Syndicate: No. 13, July, 1950; No. 2, Sept, 1950

	GD	VG	FN	VF	VF/NM	NM-
13(#1)-Used in **SOTI**, pg. 42 & illo. "Treating police contemptuously" (lower left); Hollingsworth bondage-c	58	116	174	371	636	900
2	23	46	69	136	223	310

HUNTER-KILLER
Image Comics (Top Cow): Nov, 2004 - No. 12, Mar, 2007 ($2.99)

0-(11/04, 25¢) Prelude with Silvestri sketch page and Waid afterword 3.00
1-12: 1-(3/05, $2.99) Waid-s/Silvestri-a; four covers. 2-Linsner variant-c 3.00
... Collected Edition Vol. 1 (9/05, $4.99) r/#0-3 5.00
...Dossier 1 (9/05, $2.99) character profiles with art by various; Migliari-c 3.00
... Volume 1 TPB (1/08, $24.99) r/#0-12; Dossier and Script Book; variant covers 25.00

HUNTER: THE AGE OF MAGIC (See Books of Magic)
DC Comics (Vertigo): Sept, 2001 - No. 25, Sept, 2003 ($2.50/$2.75)

1-25: Horrocks-s/Case-a. 1-8-Bolton-c. 14-Begin $2.75-c. 19-Bachalo-c 3.00

HUNT FOR WOLVERINE (Leads into Return of Wolverine series)
Marvel Comics: Jun, 2018 ($5.99)

1-Soule-s; Logan's removal from the statue; X-Men, Tony Stark, Daredevil app. 6.00
...: Dead Ends 1 (10/18, $4.99) Soule-s/Rosanas-a; conclusion to story 5.00

HUNT FOR WOLVERINE: ADAMANTIUM AGENGA
Marvel Comics: Jul, 2018 - No. 4, Oct, 2018 ($3.99, limited series)

1-4-Iron Man, Spider-Man, Jessica Jones & Luke Cage app.; Taylor-s/Silva-a 4.00

HUNT FOR WOLVERINE: CLAWS OF A KILLER
Marvel Comics: Jul, 2018 - No. 4, Oct, 2018 ($3.99, limited series)

1-4-Sabretooth, Daken & Lady Deathstrike app.; Tamaki-s/Guice-a 4.00

HUNT FOR WOLVERINE: MYSTERY IN MADRIPOOR
Marvel Comics: Jul, 2018 - No. 4, Oct, 2018 ($3.99, limited series)

1-4-Psylocke, Storm, Rogue, Jubilee, Kitty Pryde & Domino app.; Zub-s/Silas-a 4.00

HUNT FOR WOLVERINE: WEAPON LOST
Marvel Comics: Jul, 2018 - No. 4, Oct, 2018 ($3.99, limited series)

1-4-Daredevil, Misty Knight & Cypher app.; Soule-s/Buffagni-a 4.00

HUNTRESS, THE (See All-Star Comics #69, Batman Family, DC Super Stars #17, Detective #652, Infinity, Inc. #1 & Wonder Woman #271)
DC Comics: Apr, 1989 - No. 19, Oct, 1990 ($1.00, mature)

1-Staton-c/a(p) in all 6.00
2-19: 17-19-Batman-c/stories 4.00
...: Darknight Daughter TPB (2006, $19.99) r/origin & early apps. in DC Super Stars #17, Batman Family #18-20 & Wonder Woman #271-287,289,290,294,295; Bolland-c 20.00

HUNTRESS, THE
DC Comics: June, 1994 - No. 4, Sept, 1994 ($1.50, limited series)

1-4-Netzer-c/a: 2-Batman app. 4.00

HUNTRESS (Leads into 2012 World's Finest series)
DC Comics: Dec, 2011 - No. 6, May, 2012 ($2.99, limited series)

1-6-Levitz-s/To-a/March-c 3.00

HUNTRESS: YEAR ONE
DC Comics: Early July, 2008 - No. 6, Late Sept, 2008 ($2.99, limited series)

1-6-Origin re-told; Cliff Richards-a/Ivory Madison-s 3.00
TPB (2009, $17.99) r/#1-6; intro. by Paul Levitz 18.00

HURRICANE COMICS
Cambridge House: 1945 (52 pgs.)

	GD	VG	FN	VF	VF/NM	NM-
1-(Humor, funny animal)	32	64	96	188	307	425

HYBRIDS
Continuity Comics: Jan, 1994 ($2.50, one-shot)

1-Neal Adams-c(p) & part-a(i); embossed-c. 4.00

HYBRIDS DEATHWATCH 2000
Continuity Comics: Apr, 1993 - No. 3, Aug, 1993 ($2.50)

0-(Giveaway)-Foil-c; Neal Adams-c(i) & plots (also #1,2) 4.00
1-3: 1-Polybagged w/card; die-cut-c. 2-Thermal-c. 3-Polybagged w/card; indestructible-c; Adams plot 4.00

HYBRIDS ORIGIN
Continuity Comics: 1993 - No. 5, Jan, 1994 ($2.50)

1-5: 2,3-Neal Adams-c. 4,5-Valeria the She-Bat app. Adams-c(i) 4.00

HYDE
IDW Publ.: Oct, 2004 ($7.49, one-shot)

1-Steve Niles-s/Nick Stakal 7.50

HYDE-25
Harris Publications: Apr, 1995 ($2.95, one-shot)

0-Coupon for poster; r/Vampirella's 1st app. 3.00

HYDROMAN (See Heroic Comics)

HYPERION (Squadron Supreme)
Marvel Comics: May, 2016 - No. 6, Oct, 2016 ($3.99)

1-6: 1-4,6-Wendig-s/Virella-a. 5-Anindito-a. 5,6-Iron Man & Thundra app. 4.00

HYPERKIND (See Razorline)
Marvel Comics: Sept, 1993 - No. 9, May, 1994 ($1.75/$1.95)

1-($2.50)-Foil embossed-c; by Clive Barker 4.00
2-9 3.00
...Unleashed 1 (8/94, $2.95, 52 pgs., one-shot) 4.00

HYPER MYSTERY COMICS
Hyper Publications: May, 1940 - No. 2, June, 1940 (68 pgs.)

	GD	VG	FN	VF	VF/NM	NM-
1-Hyper, the Phenomenal begins; Calkins-a	273	546	819	1747	3024	4300
2-H.G. Peter-a	158	316	474	1011	1731	2450

HYPERNATURALS
BOOM! Studios: Jul, 2012 - No. 12, Jun, 2013 ($3.99)

1-12: 1-Abnett & Lanning-s/Walker & Guinaldo-a; at least eight covers. 2-Two printings 4.00
... Free Comic Book Day Edition (5/12) Prelude to issue #1 3.00

HYPERSONIC
Dark Horse Comics: Nov, 1997 - No. 4, Feb, 1998 ($2.95, limited series)

1-4: Abnett & White-s/Erskine-a 3.00

I AIM AT THE STARS (Movie)
Dell Publishing Co.: No. 1148, Nov-Jan/1960-61 (one-shot)

	GD	VG	FN	VF	VF/NM	NM-
Four Color 1148-The Werner Von Braun Sty-photo-c	6	12	18	41	76	110

I AM AN AVENGER (See Avengers, Young Avengers and Pet Avengers)
Marvel Comics: Nov, 2010 - No. 5, Mar, 2011 ($3.99, limited series)

1-5-Short stories by various. 1-Yu-c. 2-Land-c. 2-4-Mayhew-a. 3-Noto-c. 4-Acuña-c 4.00

I AM CAPTAIN AMERICA
Marvel Comics: Jan, 2012 ($3.99, one-shot)

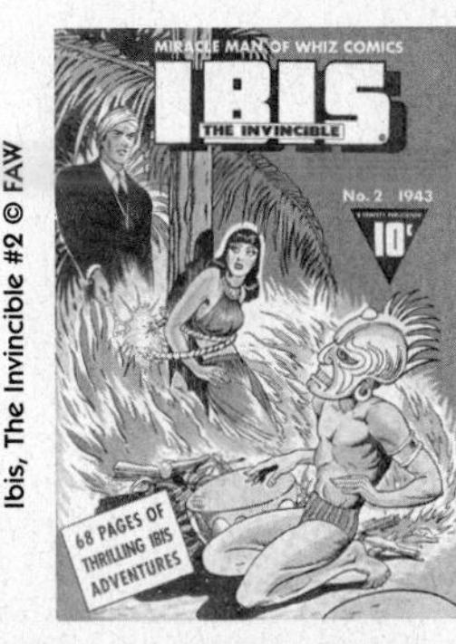

Ibis, The Invincible #2 © FAW

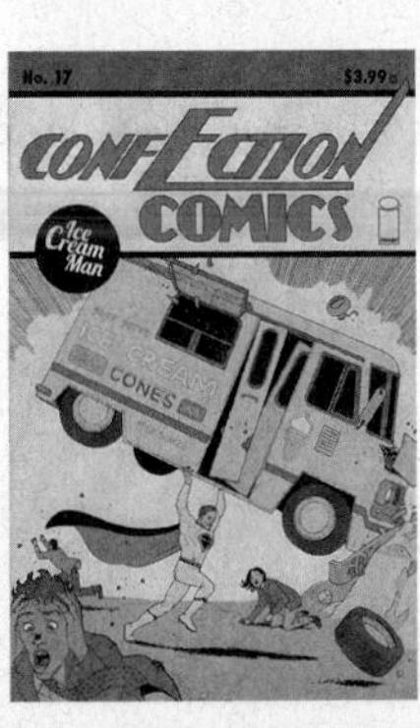

Ice Cream Man #17 © Prince & Morazzo

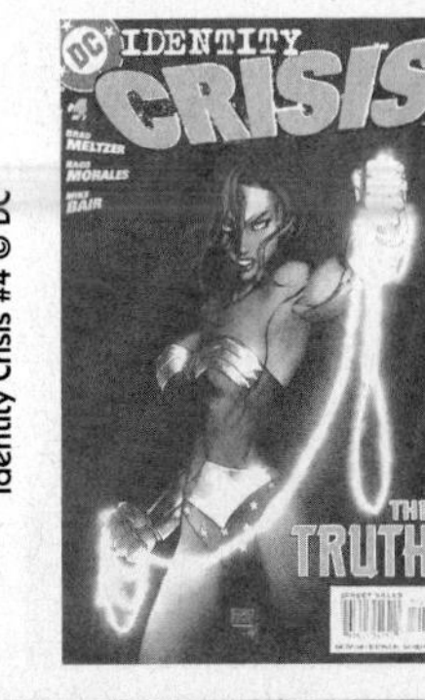

Identity Crisis #4 © DC

	GD	VG	FN	VF	VF/NM	NM-
	2.0	4.0	6.0	8.0	9.0	9.2

1-Collection of Captain America-themed 70th Anniversary covers with artist profiles 4.00

I AM COYOTE (See Eclipse Graphic Album Series & Eclipse Magazine #2)

I AM GROOT (Guardians of the Galaxy)
Marvel Comics: Jul, 2017 - No. 5, Nov, 2017 ($3.99, limited series)

1-5-Hastings-s/Flaviano-a. 1,5-Guardians of the Galaxy app. 4.00

I AM LEGEND
Eclipse Books: 1991 - No. 4, 1991 ($5.95, B&W, squarebound, 68 pgs.)

	GD	VG	FN	VF	VF/NM	NM-
1-4: Based on 1954 novel by Richard Matheson	1	2	3	5	6	8

I AM LEGION (English version of French graphic novel Je Suis Légion)
Devils Due Publishing: Jan, 2009 - No. 6, July, 2009 ($3.50)

1-6-John Cassaday-a/Fabien Nury-s; two covers 3.50

IBIS, THE INVINCIBLE (See Fawcett Miniatures, Mighty Midget & Whiz)
Fawcett Publications: 1942 (Fall?); #2, Mar.,1943; #3, Wint, 1945 - #5, Fall, 1946; #6, Spring, 1948

	GD	VG	FN	VF	VF/NM	NM-
1-Origin Ibis; Raboy-c; on sale 1/2/43	271	542	813	1734	2967	4200
2-Bondage-c (on sale 2/5/43)	113	226	339	718	1234	1750
3-Wolverton-a #3-6 (4 pgs. each)	77	154	231	493	847	1200
4-6: 5-Bondage-c	53	106	159	334	567	800

NOTE: ***Mac Raboy c(p)-3-5. Schaffenberger c-6.***

I-BOTS (See Isaac Asimov's I-BOTS)

I CAN SELL YOU A BODY
IDW Publ.: Dec, 2019 - No. 4, Mar, 2020 ($3.99)

1-4-Ryan Ferrier-s/George Kambadais-a 4.00

ICE AGE ON THE WORLD OF MAGIC: THE GATHERING (See Magic The Gathering)

ICE CREAM MAN (Horror anthology)
Image Comics: Jan, 2018 - Present ($3.99)

	GD	VG	FN	VF	VF/NM	NM-
1-Prince-s/Morazzo-a; 1st app. of the Ice Cream Man	8	16	24	54	102	150
1-2nd printing	5	10	15	33	57	80
2	3	6	9	21	33	45
3-15	2	4	6	10	14	18
16-23: 17-Action Comics #1 cover swipe. 20-Dr. Seuss homage (10 pgs.)						4.00
... Presents Quarantine Comix Special 1 (9/20, $5.99) Printing of online mini-comics	2	4	6	10	14	18

ICE KING OF OZ, THE (See First Comics Graphic Novel #13)

ICEMAN (Also see The Champions & X-Men #94)
Marvel Comics Group: Dec, 1984 - No. 4, June, 1985 (Limited series)

1,2,4: Zeck covers on all 4.00
3-The Defenders, Champions (Ghost Rider) & the original X-Men x-over 5.00

ICEMAN (X-Men)
Marvel Comics: Dec, 2001 - No. 4, Mar, 2002 ($2.50, limited series)

1-4-Abnett & Lanning-s/Kerschl-a 3.00

ICEMAN (X-Men)
Marvel Comics: Aug, 2017 - No. 11, May, 2018 ($3.99)

1-11: 1-Grace-s/Vitti-a. 2-Kitty Pryde app. 5-Juggernaut app. 4.00

ICEMAN (X-Men)
Marvel Comics: Nov, 2018 - No. 5, Mar, 2019 ($3.99, limited series)

1-5: 1-Grace-s/Stockman-a. 2-White Queen app. 4,5-Mr. Sinister app. 4.00

ICEMAN AND ANGEL (X-Men)
Marvel Comics: May, 2011 ($2.99, one-shot)

1-Brian Clevinger-s/Juan Doe-a; Goom & Googam app. 3.00

ICON
DC Comics (Milestone): May, 1993 - No. 42, Feb, 1997($1.50/$1.75/$2.50)

1-($2.95)-Collector's Edition polybagged w/poster & trading card (direct sale only) 4.00
1-24,30-42: 9-Simonson-c. 15,16-Worlds Collide Pt. 4 & 11. 15-Superboy app. 16-Superman-c/story. 40-Vs. Blood Syndicate 3.00
25-($2.95, 52 pgs.) 4.00
... A Hero's Welcome SC (2009, $19.99) r/#1-8; intro. by Reginald Hudlin 20.00
...: Mothership Connection SC (2010, $24.99) r/#13,19-22,24-27,30 25.00

IDAHO
Dell Publishing Co.: June-Aug, 1963 - No. 8, July-Sept, 1965

	GD	VG	FN	VF	VF/NM	NM-
1	3	6	9	16	24	32
2-8: 5-7-Painted-c	2	4	6	9	13	16

IDEAL (... a Classical Comic) (2nd Series) (Love Romances No. 6 on)
Timely Comics: July, 1948 - No. 5, March, 1949 (Feature length stories)

	GD	VG	FN	VF	VF/NM	NM-
1-Antony & Cleopatra	39	78	117	231	378	525
2-The Corpses of Dr. Sacotti	32	64	96	190	310	430
3-Joan of Arc; used in **SOTI**, pg. 310 'Boer War'	30	60	90	177	289	400
4-Richard the Lion-hearted; titled "...the World's Greatest Comics"; The Witness story	41	82	123	256	428	600
5-Ideal Love & Romance; change to love; photo-c	20	40	60	120	195	270

IDEAL COMICS (1st Series) (Willie Comics No. 5 on)
Timely Comics (MgPC): Fall, 1944 - No. 4, Spring, 1946

	GD	VG	FN	VF	VF/NM	NM-
1-Funny animal; Super Rabbit in all	43	86	129	271	461	650
2	22	44	66	130	213	295
3,4	20	40	60	115	188	260

IDEAL LOVE & ROMANCE (See Ideal, A Classical Comic)

IDEAL ROMANCE (Formerly Tender Romance)
Key Publ.: No. 3, April, 1954 - No. 8, Feb, 1955 (Diary Confessions No. 9 on)

	GD	VG	FN	VF	VF/NM	NM-
3-Bernard Baily-c	12	24	36	69	97	125
4-8: 4-6-B. Baily-c	9	18	27	52	69	85

IDEALS (Secret Stories)
Ideals Publ., USA: 1981 (68 pgs, graphic novels, 7x10", stiff-c)

	GD	VG	FN	VF	VF/NM	NM-
Captain America - Star Spangled Super Hero	3	6	9	19	30	40
Fantastic Four - Cosmic Quartet	3	6	9	19	30	40
Incredible Hulk - Gamma Powered Goliath	3	6	9	19	30	40
Spider-Man - World Famous Wall Crawler	4	8	12	23	37	50

IDENTITY CRISIS
DC Comics: Aug, 2004 - No. 7, Feb, 2005 ($3.95, limited series)

1-Meltzer-s/Morales-a/Turner-c in all; Sue Dibny murdered 5.00
1-(Second printing) black-c with white sketch lines 5.00
1-(3rd & 4th) 3rd-Bloody broken photo glass image-c by Morales. 4th-Turner red-c 4.00
1-Diamond Retailer Summit Edition with sketch-c 30.00
1-Special Edition (6/09, $1.00) r/#1 with "After Watchmen" cover frame 3.00
2-7: 2-4-Deathstroke app. 5-Firestorm, Jack Drake, Capt. Boomerang killed 4.00
2-(Second printing) new Morales sketch-c 4.00
Final printings for all issues with red background variant covers 4.00
HC (2005, $24.99, dust jacket) r/series; Director's Cut extras; cover gallery; Whedon intro.; 2 covers: Direct Market-c by Turner, Bookstore-c with Morales-a 25.00
SC (2006, $14.99) r/series; Director's Cut extras; cover gallery; Whedon intro 15.00

IDENTITY DISC
Marvel Comics: Aug, 2004 - No. 5, Dec, 2004 ($2.99, limited series)

1-5-Sabretooth, Bullseye, Sandman, Vulture, Deadpool, Juggernaut app.; Higgins-a 4.00
TPB (2004, $13.99) r/#1-5 14.00

IDES OF BLOOD
DC Comics (WildStorm): Oct, 2010 - No. 6, Mar, 2011 ($3.99/$2.99, limited series)

1-6-Stuart Paul-s/Christian Duce-a/Michael Geiger-c; Roman Empire vampires 4.00

I DIE AT MIDNIGHT (Vertigo V2K)
DC Comics (Vertigo): 2000 ($6.95, prestige format, one-shot)

1-Kyle Baker-s/a 7.00

IDOL
Marvel Comics (Epic Comics): 1992 - No. 3, 1992 ($2.95, mini-series, 52 pgs.)

Book 1-3 4.00

IDOLIZED
Aspen MLT: No. 0, Jun, 2012 - No. 5, Apr, 2013 ($2.50/$3.99)

0-($2.50) Schwartz-s/Gunnell-a; regular & photo covers; Superhero Idol background 3.00
1-5-($3.99) 1-Art Adams & photo covers; origin of Joule 4.00

I DREAM OF JEANNIE (TV)
Dell Publishing Co.: Apr, 1965 - No. 2, Dec, 1966 (Photo-c)

	GD	VG	FN	VF	VF/NM	NM-
1-Barbara Eden photo-c, each	15	30	45	103	227	350
2	10	20	30	66	138	210

I FEEL SICK
Slave Labor Graphics: Aug, 1999 - No. 2, May, 2000 ($3.95, limited series)

1,2-Jhonen Vasquez-s/a 4.00

IGNITED
Humanoids, Inc.: 2019 - Present ($3.99)

1-8: 1-Waid & Osajvefo-s/Briones-a 4.00

I HATE FAIRYLAND (Also see I Hate Image, FCBD Special)
Image Comics: Oct, 2015 - No. 20, Jul, 2018 ($3.50/$3.99)

1-10-Skottie Young-s/a/c; each has variant cover with "F*** Fairyland" title 3.50

I Hate Image, FCBD Special © Image

I Love Lucy #10 © Desilu

I, Lusiphur #2 © Drew Hayes

GD VG FN VF VF/NM NM-
2.0 4.0 6.0 8.0 9.0 9.2

11-20-($3.99) 12-Lone Wolf & Cub homage-c. 13-Rankine-a. 20-Finale 4.00
...: I Hate Image Special Edition (10/17, $5.99) r/I Hate Image FCBD Special with 4 new pages; bonus script and sketch art; 2 covers 6.00

I HATE GALLANT GIRL
Image Comics (Shadowline): Nov, 2008 - No. 3, Jan, 2009 ($3.50, limited series)
1-3-Kat Cahill-s/Seth Damoose-a 3.50

I HATE IMAGE, FCBD SPECIAL
Image Comics: May, 2017 (free giveaway)
1-Gert from I Hate Fairyland vs. Image characters from Walking Dead, Bitch Planet, Saga, Paper Girls, Chew, Spawn and others; Skottie Young-s/a/c 3.00

I (heart) MARVEL
Marvel Comics: Apr, 2006; May, 2006 ($2.99, one-shots)
...: Marvel AI 1 (4/06) Cebulski-s; manga art by various; Vision, Daredevil, Elektra app. 3.00
...: Masked Intentions 1 (5/06) Squirrel Girl, Speedball, Firestar, Justice app.; Nicieza-s 4.00
...: My Mutant Heart 1 (4/06) Wolverine, Cannonball, Doop app. 3.00
...: Outlaw Love 1 (4/06) Bullseye, The Answer, Ruby Thursday app.; Nicieza-s 3.00
...: Web of Romance 1 (4/06) Spider-Man, Mary Jane, The Avengers app. 3.00

ILLEGITIMATES, THE
IDW Publishing: Dec, 2013 - No. 6, May, 2014 ($3.99)
1-6: 1-Taran Killam & Marc Andreyko-a/Kevin Sharpe-a; covers by Ordway & Willingham 4.00

ILLUMUNATI
Marvel Comics: Jan, 2016 - No. 7, Jul, 2016 ($3.99)
1-7: 1-Williamson-s/Crystal-a; The Hood, Titania and others team. 4-Thor app. 4.00

ILLUMINATOR
Marvel Comics/Nelson Publ.: 1993 - No. 4, 1993 ($4.99/$2.95, 52 pgs.)
1,2-($4.99) Religious themed 5.00
3,4 4.00

ILLUSTRATED GAGS
United Features Syndicate: No. 16, 1940
Single Series 16 21 42 63 122 199 275

ILLUSTRATED LIBRARY OF..., AN (See Classics Illustrated Giants)

ILLUSTRATED STORIES OF THE OPERAS
Baily (Bernard) Publ. Co.: 1943 (16 pgs.; B&W) (25 cents) (covers are black & red ink on white or yellow paper, with scarcer editions having B&W with red)
nn-(Rare)(4 diff. issues)-Faust (part-r in Cisco Kid #1, 2 cover versions: 25¢ & no price)
nn-Aida, nn-Carmen; Baily-a, nn-Rigoletto 81 162 243 518 864 1250

ILLUSTRATED STORY OF ROBIN HOOD & HIS MERRY MEN, THE (See Classics Giveaways, 12/44)

ILLUSTRATED TARZAN BOOK, THE (See Tarzan Book)

I LOVED (Formerly Rulah; Colossal Features Magazine No. 33 on)
Fox Feature Syndicate: No. 28, July, 1949 - No. 32, Mar, 1950
28 23 46 69 136 223 310
29-32 16 32 48 98 154 210

I LOVE LUCY
Eternity Comics : 6/90 - No. 6, 1990;V2#1, 11/90 - No. 6, 1991 ($2.95, B&W, mini-series)
1-6: Reprints 1950s comic strip; photo-c 4.00
Book II #1-6: Reprints comic strip; photo-c 4.00
...In Full Color 1 (1991, $5.95, 52 pgs.)-Reprints I Love Lucy Comics #4,5,8,16; photo-c with embossed logo (2 versions exist, one with pgs. 18 & 19 reversed, the other corrected)
1 2 3 5 6 8
...In 3-D 1 (1991, $3.95, w/glasses)-Reprints I Love Lucy Comics; photo-c; bagged 6.00

I LOVE LUCY COMICS (TV) (Also see The Lucy Show)
Dell Publishing Co.: No. 535, Feb, 1954 - No. 35, Apr-June, 1962 (Lucille Ball photo-c on all)
Four Color 535(#1) 46 92 138 359 805 1250
Four Color 559(#2, 5/54) 28 56 84 202 451 700
3 (8-10/54) - 5 16 32 48 111 246 380
6-10 12 24 36 84 185 285
11-20 10 20 30 66 138 210
21-35 9 18 27 57 111 165

I LOVE NEW YORK
Linsner.com: 2002 ($2.95, B&W, one-shot)
1-Linsner-s/a; benefit book for the Sept. 11 charities 3.00

I LOVE YOU
Fawcett Publications: June, 1950 (one-shot)
1-Photo-c 16 32 48 98 154 210

I LOVE YOU (Formerly In Love)
Charlton Comics: No. 7, 9/55 - No. 121, 12/76; No. 122, 3/79 - No. 130, 5/80
7-Kirby-c; Powell-a 9 18 27 58 114 170
8-10 5 10 15 31 53 75
11-16,18-20 4 8 12 28 47 65
17-(68 pg. Giant) 6 12 18 42 79 115
21-50: 26-No Torres-a 3 6 9 21 33 45
51-59 3 6 9 17 26 35
60-(1/66)-Elvis Presley line drawn c/story 15 30 45 104 230 355
61-85 3 6 9 14 20 25
86-90,92-98,100-110 2 4 6 8 10 12
91-(5/71) Ditko-a (5 pgs.) 2 4 6 13 18 22
99-David Cassidy pin-up 2 4 6 10 14 18
111-113,115-130 1 3 4 6 8 10
114-Psychedelic cover 3 6 9 17 26 35

I, LUSIPHUR (Becomes Poison Elves, 1st series #8 on)
Mulehide Graphics: 1991 - No. 7, 1992 (B&W, magazine size)
1-Drew Hayes-c/a/scripts 6 12 18 38 69 100
2,4,5 3 6 9 14 20 25
3-Low print run 4 8 12 27 44 60
6,7 2 4 6 8 11 14
Poison Elves: Requiem For An Elf (Sirius Ent., 6/96, $14.95, trade paperback)
-Reprints I, Lusiphur #1,2 as text, and 3-6 15.00

I'M A COP
Magazine Enterprises: 1954 - No. 3, 1954
1(A-1 #111)-Powell-c/a in all 17 34 51 100 158 215
2(A-1 #126), 3(A-1 #128) 11 22 33 62 86 110

IMAGE COMICS HARDCOVER
Image Comics: 2005 ($24.99, hardcover with dust jacket)
Vol. 1-New Spawn by McFarlane-s/a; Savage Dragon origin by Larsen; CyberForce by Silvestri; ShadowHawk by Valentino; intro by Marder; Image timeline 25.00

IMAGE COMICS SUMMER SPECIAL
Image Comics: July, 2004 (Free Comic Book Day giveaway)
1-New short stories of Spawn, Invincible, Savage Dragon and Witchblade 3.00

IMAGE FIRST
Image Comics: 2005 ($6.99, TPB)
Vol. 1 (2005) r/Strange Girl #1, Sea of Red #1, The Walking Dead #1 and Girls #1
3 6 9 14 20 25

IMAGE FIRSTS (Reprints of first issues)
Image Comics: Feb, 2021 ($1.00, series of one-shots)
...: Ascender #1 - Lemire-s/Nguyen-a 3.00
...: Bitter Root #1 - Walker & Brown-s/Greene-a 3.00
...: Die #1 - Gillen-s/Hans-a 3.00
...: Killadelphia #1 - Barnes-s/Alexander-a 3.00
...: Mercy #1 - Mirka Andolfo-a 3.00
...: The Old Guard #1 - Rucka-s/Fernández-a 3.00
...: Undiscovered Country #1 - Snyder & Soule-s/Camuncoli-a 3.00

IMAGE GRAPHIC NOVEL
Image Int.: 1984 ($6.95)(Advertised as Pacific Comics Graphic Novel #1)
1-The Seven Samuroid; Brunner-c/a 12.00

IMAGE HOLIDAY SPECIAL 2005
Image Comics: 2005 ($9.99, TPB)
nn-Holiday-themed short stories by various incl. Walking Dead by Kirkman; Larsen, Kurtz, Valentino; Frank Cho-c 3 6 9 14 20 25

IMAGE INTRODUCES...
Image Comics: Oct, 2001 - June, 2002 ($2.95, anthology)
Believer #1-Schamberger-s/Thurman & Molder-a; Legend of Isis preview 3.00
Cryptopia #1-Raab-s/Quinn-a 3.00
Dog Soldiers #1-Hunter-s/Pachoumis-a 3.00
Legend of Isis #1-Valdez-a 3.00
Primate #1-Two covers; Beau Smith & Bernhardt-s/Byrd-a 3.00

IMAGES OF A DISTANT SOIL
Image Comics: Feb, 1997 ($2.95, B&W, one-shot)
1-Sketches by various 3.00

IMAGES OF SHADOWHAWK (Also see Shadowhawk)
Image Comics: Sept, 1993 - No. 3, 1994 ($1.95, limited series)
1-3: Keith Giffen-c/a; Trencher app. 3.00

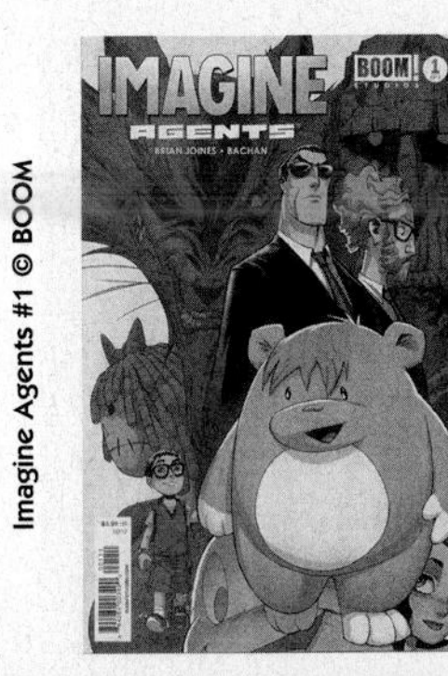

Imagine Agents #1 © BOOM

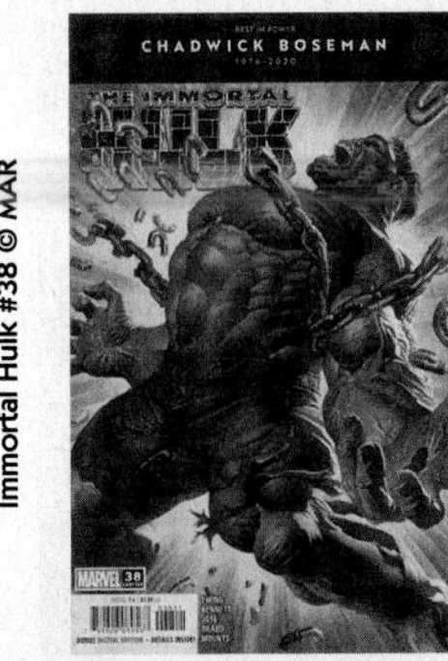

Immortal Hulk #38 © MAR

Impulse #50 © DC

	GD	VG	FN	VF	VF/NM	NM-
	2.0	4.0	6.0	8.0	9.0	9.2

IMAGE 20 (FREE COMIC BOOK DAY 2012...)
Image Comics: May, 2012 (giveaway, one-shot)

nn-Previews of Revival, Guarding the Globe, It-Girl and the Atomics, Near Death 3.00

IMAGE TWO-IN-ONE
Image Comics: Mar, 2001 ($2.95, 48 pgs., B&W, one-shot)

1-Two stories; 24 pages produced in 24 hrs. by Larsen and Eliopoulos 4.00

IMAGE UNITED
Image Comics: No. 0, Mar, 2010; Nov, 2009 - No. 6 ($3.99, limited series)

0-(3/10, $2.99) Fortress and Savage Dragon app. 3.00
1-3-($3.99) Image character crossover; Kirkman-s; art by Larsen, Liefeld, McFarlane, Portacio, Silvestri and Valentino; Spawn, Witchblade, Savage Dragon, Youngblood, Cyberforce and Shadowhawk app. Multiple covers on each 4.00
1-Jim Lee variant-c 8.00

IMAGE ZERO
Image Comics: 1993 (Received through mail w/coupons from Image books)

0-Savage Dragon, StormWatch, Shadowhawk, Strykeforce; 1st app. Troll; 1st app. McFarlane's Freak, Blotch, Sweat and Bludd 5.00

IMAGINARIES, THE
Image Comics: Mar, 2005 - No. 4, June, 2005 ($2.95, limited series)

1-4-Mike S. Miller & Ben Avery-s; Miller & Titus-a 3.00

IMAGINARY FIENDS
DC Comics (Vertigo): Jan, 2018 - No. 6, Jun, 2016 ($3.99, limited series)

1-6-Tim Seeley-s/Stephen Molnar-a/Richard Pace-c 4.00

IMAGINE AGENTS
BOOM! Studios: Oct, 2013 - No. 4, Jan, 2014 ($3.99, limited series)

1-4-Brian Joines-s/Bachan-a 4.00

I'M DICKENS - HE'S FENSTER (TV)
Dell Publishing Co.: May-July, 1963 - No. 2, Aug-Oct, 1963 (Photo-c)

	GD	VG	FN	VF	VF/NM	NM-
1	5	10	15	33	57	80
2	5	10	15	30	50	70

I MET A HANDSOME COWBOY
Dell Publishing Co.: No. 324, Mar, 1951

	GD	VG	FN	VF	VF/NM	NM-
Four Color 324	7	14	21	49	92	135

IMMORTAL BROTHERS: THE TALE OF THE GREEN KNIGHT
Valiant Entertainment: Apr, 2017 ($4.99, one-shot)

1-Van Lente-s/Nord & Henry-a; Archer & Faith app.; bonus preview of Rapture 5.00

IMMORTAL DOCTOR FATE, THE
DC Comics: Jan, 1985 - No. 3, Mar, 1985 ($1.25, limited series)

1-3: 1-Reprints; Simonson-c/a. 2-R/back-ups from Flash #306-313; Giffen-c/a(p) 4.00

IMMORTAL HULK
Marvel Comics: Aug, 2018 - Present ($4.99/$3.99)

	GD	VG	FN	VF	VF/NM	NM-
1-($4.99) Bruce Banner returns; intro Jackie McGee; Ewing-s/Bennett-a	3	6	9	14	20	25
2-($3.99) Intro Dr. Frye	3	6	9	21	33	45
3-15: 4,5-Sasquatch app. 6,7-Avengers app. 9-13-Absorbing Man app. 13,14-Betty app. 14-Kyle Hotz-a	2	4	6	11	16	20
16-Joe Fixit returns	1	3	4	6	8	10

17-24-($3.99) 4.00
25-($5.99) Hulk as the Breaker of Worlds; Germán García-a 6.00
26-32,34-43: 26-Amadeus Cho app. 30-32-Xemnu app. 34-The Leader's origin retold 4.00
33-($5.99) 750th Legacy issue; Xemnu app.; art by Bennett & Pitarra 6.00
#0-(11/20, $4.99) Reprints Incredible Hulk #312 & #(-1) with new framing story; De Iulis-a 5.00
...: Flatline 1 (4/21, $4.99) Declan Shalvey-s/a 5.00
...: Great Power 1 (4/20, $4.99) Spider-Man gets Hulk powers; Fantastic Four app. 5.00
...: The Best Defense 1 (2/19, $4.99) Ewing-s/Di Meo-a; see Defenders: The Best Defense 5.00
...: The Threshing Place 1 (11/19, $4.99) Lemire-s/Del Mundo-a/c 5.00

IMMORTAL HULK DIRECTOR'S CUT
Marvel Comics: Oct, 2019 - No. 6, Dec, 2019 ($5.99/$4.99)

1-($5.99) Reprints #1 with bonus pencil art, variant cover gallery; creator interviews 6.00
2-6-($4.99) Reprints with bonus pencil art and/or scripts and interviews 5.00

IMMORTAL IRON FIST, THE (Also see Iron Fist)
Marvel Comics: Jan, 2007 - No. 27, Aug, 2009 ($2.99/$3.99)

	GD	VG	FN	VF	VF/NM	NM-
1-Brubaker & Fraction-s/Aja-c/a; origin retold; intro. Orson Randall	1	3	4	6	8	10
1-Variant-c by Dell'Otto	3	6	9	17	26	35

1-Director's Cut ($3.99) r/#1 and 8-page story from Civil War: Choosing Sides; script excerpt; character designs; sketch and inks art; cover variant and concepts 4.00

	GD	VG	FN	VF	VF/NM	NM-
2,3	1	2	3	5	6	8

4-13,15-26: 6,17-20-Flashback-a by Heath. 8-1st Immortal weapons. 21-Green-a 3.00
14,27: 14-($3.99) Heroes For Hire app. 27-Last issue; 2 covers; Foreman & Lapham-a 4.00
Annual 1 (11/07, $3.99) Brubaker & Fraction-s/Chaykin, Brereton & J. Djurdjevic-a 4.00
... Orson Randall and the Death Queen of California (11/08, $3.99) art by Camuncoli 4.00
... Orson Randall and the Green Mist of Death (4/08, $3.99) art by Heath and various 4.00
...: The Origin of Danny Rand (2008, $3.99) r/Marvel Premiere #15-16 recolored 4.00
... Vol. 1: The Last Iron Fist Story HC (2007, $19.99, dustjacket) r/#1-6, story from Civil War: Choosing Sides; sketch pages 20.00
... Vol. 1: The Last Iron Fist Story SC (2007, $14.99) same content as HC 15.00
... Vol. 2: The Seven Capital Cities HC (2008, $24.99, dustjacket) r/#8-14 & Annual #1 25.00

IMMORTALIS (See Mortigan Goth: Immortalis)

IMMORTAL MEN, THE (Follows events of Dark Nights: Metal)
DC Comics: Jun, 2018 - No. 6, Nov, 2018 ($2.99)

1-6: 1-Jim Lee & Ryan Benjamin-a/Tynion IV-s; Batman Who Laughs cameo 4.00

IMMORTAL SHE-HULK
Marvel Comics: Nov, 2020 ($4.99, one-shot)

1-Ewing-s/Davis-Hunt-a; origin re-told, Wolverine, Thor, The Leader app. 5.00

IMMORTAL WEAPONS (Also see Immortal Iron Fist)
Marvel Comics: Sept, 2009 - No. 5, Jan, 2010 ($3.99, limited series)

1-5: Back-up Iron Fist stories in all. 1-Origin of Fat Cobra. 2-Brereton-a 4.00

IMPACT
E. C. Comics: Mar-Apr, 1955 - No. 5, Nov-Dec, 1955

	GD	VG	FN	VF	VF/NM	NM-
1-Not code approved; classic Holocaust story	34	68	102	272	436	600
1-Variant printed by Charlton. Title logo is white instead of yellow and print quality is inferior. Distributed to newsstands before being destroyed & reprinted (scarce)	37	74	111	296	473	650
2	16	32	48	128	202	275
3-5: 4-Crandall-a	14	28	42	112	179	245

NOTE: *Crandall* a-1-4. *Davis* a-2-4; c-1-5. *Evans* a-1, 4, 5. *Ingels* a-in all. *Kamen* a-3. *Krigstein* a-1, 5. *Orlando* a-2, 5.

IMPACT
Gemstone Publishing: Apr, 1999 - No. 5, Aug, 1999 ($2.50)

1-5-Reprints E.C. series 4.00

IMPACT CHRISTMAS SPECIAL
DC Comics (Impact Comics): 1991 ($2.50, 68 pgs.)

1-Gift of the Magi by Infantino/Rogers; The Black Hood, The Fly, The Jaguar, & The Shield stories 4.00

IMPERIAL GUARD
Marvel Comics: Jan, 1997 - No. 3, Mar, 1997 ($1.95, limited series)

1-3: Augustyn-s in all; 1-Wraparound-c 3.00

IMPERIUM
Valiant Entertainment: Mar, 2015 - No. 16, May, 2016 ($3.99)

1-16: 1-4-Dysart-s/Braithwaite-a. 5-8-Eaton-a. 9-12-The Vine Imperative; Cafu-a 4.00

IMPOSSIBLE MAN SUMMER VACATION SPECTACULAR, THE
Marvel Comics: Aug, 1990; No. 2, Sept, 1991 ($2.00, 68 pgs.) (See Fantastic Four#11)

1-Spider Man, Quasar, Dr. Strange, She-Hulk, Punisher & Dr. Doom stories; Barry Crain, Guice-a; Art Adams-c(i) 4.00
2-Ka Zar & Thor app.; Cable Wolverine-c app. 4.00

IMPULSE (See Flash #92, 2nd Series for 1st app.) (Also see Young Justice)
DC Comics: Apr, 1995 - No. 89, Oct, 2002 ($1.50/$1.75/$1.95/$2.25/$2.50)

1-Mark Waid scripts & Humberto Ramos-c/a(p) begin; brief retelling of origin 6.00
2-12: 9-XS from Legion (Impulse's cousin) comes to the 20th Century, returns to the 30th Century in #12. 10-Dead Heat Pt. 3 (cont'd in Flash #110). 11-Dead Heat Pt. 4 (cont'd in Flash #111); Johnny Quick dies. 4.00
13-25: 14-Trickster app. 17-Zatanna-c/app. 21-Legion-c/app. 22-Jesse Quick-c/app. 24-Origin; Flash app. 25-Last Ramos-a. 3.00
26-55: 26-Rousseau-a begins. 28-1st new Arrowette (see World's Finest #113). 30-Genesis x-over. 47-Superman-c/app. 50-Batman & Joker-c/app. Van Sciver-a begins 3.00
56-62: 56-Young Justice app. 3.00
63-89: 63-Begin $2.50-c. 66-JLA,JSA-c/app. 68,69-Adam Strange, GL app. 77-Our Worlds at War x-over; Young Justice-c/app. 85-World Without Young Justice x-over pt. 2. 3.00
#1,000,000 (11/98) John Fox app. 3.00
Annual 1 (1996, $2.95)-Legends of the Dead Earth; Parobeck-a 4.00
Annual 2 (1997, $3.95)-Pulp Heroes stories; Orbik painted-c 4.00
.../Atom Double-Shot 1(2/98, $1.95) Jurgens-s/Mhan-a 3.00
...: Bart Saves the Universe (4/99, $5.95) JSA app. 6.00

Incognegro: Renaissance #1 © Johnson & Pleece

Incredible Hercules #132 © MAR

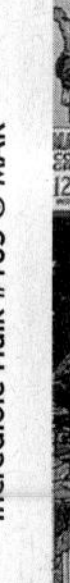
Incredible Hulk #105 © MAR

	GD	VG	FN	VF	VF/NM	NM-
	2.0	4.0	6.0	8.0	9.0	9.2

...Plus (9/97, $2.95) w/Gross Out (Scare Tactics)-c/app. 4.00
...Reckless Youth (1997, $14.95, TPB) r/Flash #92-94, Impulse #1-6 15.00

INCAL, THE
Marvel Comics (Epic): Nov, 1988 - No. 3, Jan, 1989 ($10.95/$12.95, mature)

1-Moebius-c/a in all; sexual content 3 6 9 14 20 25
2,3 2 4 6 10 14 18

INCOGNEGRO
DC Comics (Vertigo): 2008 ($19.99, B&W, hardcover graphic novel with dustjacket)

HC-Mat Johnson-s/Warren Pleece-a 20.00

INCOGNEGRO: RENAISSANCE
Dark Horse Comics (Berger Books): Feb, 2018 - No. 5, Jun, 2018 ($3.99, B&W, lim. series)

1-5-Mat Johnson-s/Warren Pleece-a 20.00

INCOGNITO
Marvel Comics (Icon): Dec, 2008 - No. 6, Aug, 2009 ($3.50/$3.99, limited series)

1-5-Brubaker-s/Phillips-a/c; pulp noir-style 3.50
6-($3.99) Bonus history of the Zeppelin pulps 4.00
...: Bad Influences (10/10 - No. 5, 4/11, $3.50) 1-5 Brubaker-s/Phillips-a/c 3.50

INCOMING
Marvel Comics: Feb, 2020 ($9.99, one-shot)

1-Leads into the Empyre event; Masked Raider app.; connecting short stories by various 10.00

INCOMPLETE DEATH'S HEAD (Also see Death's Head)
Marvel Comics UK: Jan, 1993 - No. 12, Dec, 1993 ($1.75, limited series)

1-($2.95, 56 pgs.)-Die-cut cover 4.00
2-11: 2-Re-intro original Death's Head. 3-Original Death's Head vs. Dragon's Claws 3.00
12-($2.50, 52 pgs.)-She Hulk app. 4.00

INCORRUPTIBLE (Also see Irredeemable)
BOOM! Studios: Dec, 2000 - No. 30, May, 2012 ($3.99)

1-30: 1-Waid-s/Diaz-a; 3 covers 4.00
1-Artist Edition (12/11, $3.99) r/#1 in B&W with bonus sketch and design art 4.00

INCREDIBLE HERCULES (Continued from Incredible Hulk #112, Jan, 2008)
Marvel Comics: No. 113, Feb, 2008 - No. 141, Apr, 2010 ($2.99/$3.99)

113-125: 113-Ares and Wonder Man app.; Art Adams-c. 116-Romita Jr-c; Eternals app. 3.00
113-Variant-c by Pham 5.00
126-($3.99) Hercules origin retold; back-up story w/Miyazawa-a 4.00
127-137: 128-Dark Avengers app. 132-Replacement Thor. 136-Thor app. 3.00
138-141-($3.99) Assault on New Olympus; Avengers app. 4.00

INCREDIBLE HULK, THE (See Aurora, The Avengers #1, The Defenders #1, Giant-Size..., Hulk, Marvel Collectors Item Classics, Marvel Comics Presents #26, Marvel Fanfare, Marvel Treasury Edition, Power Record Comics, Rampaging Hulk, She-Hulk, 2099 Unlimited & World War Hulk)

INCREDIBLE HULK, THE
Marvel Comics: May, 1962 - No. 6, Mar, 1963; No. 102, Apr, 1968 - No. 474, Mar, 1999

1-Origin & 1st app. (skin is grey colored); Kirby pencils begin, end #5
5500 11,000 19,250 58,600 184,300 310,000
2-1st green skinned Hulk; Kirby/Ditko-a 500 1000 1500 4250 9625 15,000
3-Origin retold; 1st app. Ringmaster (9/62) 266 532 798 2195 4948 7700
4-Brief origin retold 200 400 600 1650 3725 5800
5-1st app of Tyrannus 214 428 642 1766 3983 6200
6-(3/63) Intro. Teen Brigade; all Ditko-a 190 380 570 1568 3534 5500
102-(4/68) (Continued from Tales to Astonish #101)-Origin retold; Hulk in Asgard; Enchantress & Executioner app; Gary Friedrich-s begin 26 52 78 182 404 625
103-1st Space Parasite 11 22 33 76 163 250
104-Hulk vs. the Rhino 10 20 30 67 141 215
105-1st Missing Link 10 20 30 64 132 200
106-110: 106-vs. Missing Link; Nick Fury & SHIELD app; Trimpe pencils begin (continues through issue #193). 107,108-vs. the Mandarin. 108-Nick Fury & SHIELD app.; Stan Lee-s (continues through issue #120). 109,110-Ka-Zar app.
7 14 21 49 92 135
111-117: 111-Ka-Zar app.; 1st Galaxy Master. 112-Origin of the Galaxy Master. 113-vs. Sandman. 114-Sandman & Mandarin vs. the Hulk. 115-117-vs. the Leader
5 10 15 33 57 80
118-Hulk vs. Sub-Mariner 8 16 24 54 102 150
119,120,123-125: 119-Maximus (of the Inhumans) app. 120-Last Stan Lee plot, Roy Thomas script; Maximus app. 123,124-vs. The Leader. 124-1st Sal Buscema-p (as a fill-in). 125-vs. the Absorbing Man 4 8 12 27 44 60
121-Roy Thomas-s begin; 1st app. and origin of the Glob
6 12 18 37 66 95
122-Hulk battles Thing (12/69); Fantastic Four app. 9 18 27 59 117 175
126-1st Barbara Norriss (becomes Valkyrie in Defenders #4); story continued from Sub-Mariner #22 (see Dr. Strange #183 for pt.1); Dr. Strange gives up being Sorcerer Supreme 6 12 18 38 69 100
127,129,130,132-139: 127-Tryannus & the Mole Man app; 1st app. Mogol. 129-Leader revives the Glob. 130-(story continues from Captain Marvel #21); 132-HYDRA app. 134-1st Golem. 135-Kang & Phantom Eagle app. 136-1st Xeron the Starslayer; Abomination cameo. 137-Xeron app. Hulk vs. Abomination. 138-Sandman app. 139-Leader app; Hulk story continues in Avengers #88 4 8 12 23 37 50
128-Avengers app. 5 10 15 31 53 75
131-1st Jim Wilson; Iron Man app. 5 10 15 34 60 85
140-Writtem by Harlan Ellison; 1st Jarella (Hulk's love); story continues from Avengers #88; battles Psyklop 4 8 12 27 44 60
140-2nd printing 2 4 6 8 10 12
141-1st app. Doc Samson (7/71) 12 24 36 80 173 265
142-2nd Valkyrie app. (Samantha Parrington) (see Avengers #82 for 1st Marvel Valkyrie); Enchantress app. 5 10 15 35 63 90
143,144-Doctor Doom app. 4 8 12 23 37 50
145-(52-pgs)-Origin retold 5 10 15 31 53 75
146-151: 146,147-Richard Nixon & The Leader app. 148-Jarella app. 149-1st app. The Inheritor. 150-Havok app. 151-Has minor Ant-Man app.
3 6 9 19 30 40
152,153: Hulk on trial; Daredevil, Fantastic Four, Avengers app.
4 8 12 23 37 50
154-Ant-Man app; story coincides with Ant-Man's re-intro in Marvel Feature #4; Hydra & the Chameleon app. 3 6 9 21 33 45
155-160: 155-1st Shaper of Worlds. 156-Jarella app. 157,158-the Leader & Rhino app. 158-Counter-Earth & the High Evolutionary app. 159-Steve Englehart-s begin; Hulk vs. Abomination. 160-vs. Tiger Shark app. 3 6 9 17 26 35
161-The Mimic dies; Beast app. 5 10 15 33 57 80
162-1st app. The Wendigo (4/73) Beast app. 10 20 30 66 138 210
163-165,170,173,174,179: 163-1st app. The Gremlin. 164-1st Capt. Omen & Colonel John D. Armbuster. 165-Capt. Omen app; 1st Aquon. 173,174-vs the Cobalt Man. 179-Return of the Missing Link; 1st Len Wein-s 3 6 9 15 22 28
166-169,171: 166-1st Zzzax; Hawkeye app.; story continues into Defenders #7. 167-Hulk vs. MODOK. 168-1st Harpy (transformed Betty Ross; also seen briefly in nudity panels) 169-1st Bi-Beast; MODOK and A.I.M app; Harpy transformed back into Betty. 171-vs. Abomination; last Englehart-s 3 6 9 16 24 32
172-X-Men cameo; origin Juggernaut retold 5 10 15 30 50 70
175-Black Bolt/Inhumans c/story 3 6 9 21 33 45
176-Hulk on Counter-Earth; Man-Beast app; Warlock cameo (2 panels only)
3 6 9 19 30 40
177-1st actual death of Warlock (last panel only); Man-Beast app.
5 10 15 30 50 70
178-Rebirth of Warlock (story continues in Strange Tales #178)
5 10 15 30 50 70
180-(10/74)-1st brief app. Wolverine (last pg.) 50 100 150 400 900 1400
181-(11/74)-1st full Wolverine story; Trimpe-a 800 1600 2400 4000 6000 8000
182-Wolverine cameo; see Giant-Size X-Men #1 for next app.; 1st Crackajack Jackson
16 32 48 110 243 375
183-192,194-196,199: 183-Zzzax app. 184-vs. Warlord Kraa. 185-Death of Col. Armbuster. 186-1st Devastator. 187-188-vs. the Gremlin, Nick Fury app. 189-Mole Man app. 190-1st Glorian; Shaper of Worlds app. 191-vs. the Toad Men; Glorian & Shaper of Worlds app. 194-vs. the Locust; 1st Sal Buscema-p (through #309). 195-Abomination & Hulk team-up. 196-Hulk vs. Abomination. 199-Hulk vs. SHIELD & Doc Samson; Nick Fury app.
3 6 9 14 19 24
193-vs. Doc Samson c/story; last regular Trimpe-p 3 6 9 15 22 28
197-Collector, Man-Thing & Glob app; Wrightson-c 4 8 12 28 47 65
198-Collector, Man-Thing & Glob app. 3 6 9 17 25 34
198,199, 201,202-(30¢-c variants, lim. distribution) 7 14 21 46 86 125
200-(25¢-c) Silver Surfer app. (illusion only); anniversary issue
3 6 9 21 33 45
200-(30¢-c variant, limited distribution)(6/76) 7 14 21 46 86 125
201-205,208-211,213,215-220: 201-Conan swipe-c/sty (vs. Bronak the Barbarian). 202-Jarella app.; Psyklop cameo. 203-Jarella app.; death of Psyklop. 204-Trimpe-p; alternate Hulk origin. 205-Death of Jarella; vs. the Crypto Man. 208-Absorbing Man app. 209-Hulk vs. Absorbing Man. 210,211-Hulk team-up with Dr. Druid vs. the Maha Yogi. 213-1st Quintronic Man. 215,216-vs. the second Bi-Beast. 218-Doc Samson vs. the Rhino (no Hulk in story). 219-220-vs. Captain Barracuda 2 4 6 8 11 14
206,207-Defenders app. 2 4 6 9 13 16
212,214: 212-1st app. The Constrictor. 214-Hulk vs. Jack of Hearts (1st app. outside of B&W magazines) 2 4 6 9 13 16
212-216-(35¢-c variant, limited distribution) 11 22 33 73 157 240
221-227,230-231: 221-Stingray app. 222-Last Wein-s; Jim Starlin co-plot and (p). 223-The Leader returns; Roger Stern-s begin. 224-225-vs. The Leader. 227-Original Avengers app. (in dream sequence) 1 3 4 6 8 10
228-1st female Moonstone (Karla Sofen) (10/78) 3 6 9 21 33 45
229-2nd app. new Moonstone 2 4 6 8 11 14

Incredible Hulk #257 © MAR

Incredible Hulk #366 © MAR

Incredible Hulk #404 © MAR

	GD 2.0	VG 4.0	FN 6.0	VF 8.0	VF/NM 9.0	NM- 9.2
232,233: 232-Captain America x-over from Captain America #230; vs. Moonstone, Vamp and 'the Corporation'; Marvel Man (Quasar) app. 233-Marvel Man app. (Quasar)	2	4	6	8	10	12
234-(4/79)-Marvel Man formally changes his name to Quasar	4	8	12	27	44	60
235-249: 235-237-Machine Man app. 238-President Jimmy Carter app. 241-243-vs. Tyrannus. 243-Last Stern-s. 244-vs. It the Living Colossus. 245-1st Mantlo-s (through #313); 1st app. The Super-Mandroid (Col. Talbot); Captain Mar-Vell cameo. 246-Captain Mar-Vell app.; Hulk vs. Super-Mandroid. 247-Minor Captain Mar-Vell app. 248-vs. the Gardener. 249-Steve Ditko-p	1	3	4	6	8	10
250-Giant-Size (square-bound, 48-pgs)-Silver Surfer app.	3	6	9	21	33	45
251-254,256-270: 251-3-D Man app. 252,253-Woodgod app. 254-1st app. the U-Foes (evil versions of the Fantastic Four). 256-1st Sabra (Israeli super-hero). 257-1st Arabian Knight. 258,259-Soviet Super-Soldiers, Red Guardian & the Presence app. 260-Death of Col. Talbot. 261-Absorbing Man app. 263-Landslide & Avalanche app. 264-Death of the Night Flyer; Corruptor app. 265-1st app. The Rangers (Firebird, Shooting Star, Night Rider, Red Wolf & Lobo, Texas Tornado); Corruptor app. 266-High Evolutionary app. 267-Glorian & the Shaper of Worlds app. 268-Pariah-c/s; origin of Rick Jones retold. 269-1st Marvel Universe app. of Bereet; 1st Hulk-Hunters (Amphibion, Torgo, Dark Crawler). 270-Hulk Hunters, Bereet & Galaxy Master app.	1	2	3	5	6	8
255-Hulk vs. Thor	2	4	6	10	14	18
271-(5/82)-2nd app. & 1st full app. Rocket Raccoon (see Marvel Preview #7 for debut)	10	20	30	64	132	200
272-3rd app Rocket Raccoon; Sasquatch & Wendigo app; Wolverine & Alpha Flight cameo in flashback; Bruce Banner's mind takes control of the Hulk	3	6	9	16	23	30
273-277,280-299: 273-Sasquatch app. 275-vs. Megalith; U-Foes app. 276,277-U-foes app. 280,281-The Leader returns. 282-She-Hulk app. 283,284-Avengers app; vs. the Leader. 285-Zzzax app. 287-290-MODOK & Abomination app. 292-Circus of Crime & Dragon Man app. 293-Fantastic Four app. (in a dream). 294,295-Boomerang app. 296-Rom app. 297-299-Dr. Strange & Nightmare app.	1	2	3	5	6	8
278,279-Most Marvel characters app. (Wolverine in both). 279-X-Men & Alpha Flight cameos	1	2	3	5	6	8
300-(11/84, 52 pgs)-Spider-Man app. in new black costume on-c & 2 pg. cameo; Hulk reverts to savagery; Thor, Daredevil, Power Man & Iron Fist, Human Torch app; Dr. Strange banishes the Hulk from Earth	2	4	6	11	16	20
301-313: 301-Hulk banished to the 'Crossroads' (through #313); Dr. Strange app. 302-Mignola-c. 304-U-Foes cameo; Mignola-c (through issue #309). 305-vs the U-Foes. 306-Return of Xeron the Starslayer. 307-Death of Xeron. 308-vs N'Garia demons. 309-Last Sal Buscema-a. 310-Blevins-a. 311-Mignola-c/a. 312-Secret Wars II x-over; Mignola-c/a; origin retold w/further details regarding physical abuse at the hands of his father. 313-Crossover w/Alpha Flight #29; Mignola-c/a						6.00
314-Byrne-c/a begins; ends #319; Hulk returns to Earth; vs. Doc Samson	1	2	3	5	6	8
315-319: 315-Hulk & Banner separated. 316-vs Hercules, Sub-Mariner, Wonder Man & Iron Man of the Avengers. 317-1st app. the new Hulkbusters; Hulk vs. Doc Samson. 318-Doc Samson vs. Hulkbusters. 319-Banner and Betty Ross wed						6.00
320,325,327-329: 320-Al Milgrom story & art begin. 325-vs. Zzzax. 327-Zzzax app. 328-1st Peter David-s. 329-1st app. The Outcasts						5.00
321-323: 321-Avengers vs. Hulk. 322-Avengers & West Coast Avengers app. 323-East & West Coast Avengers app.						6.00
324-Return of the Grey Hulk (Banner & Hulk rejoined) first since #1 (c-swipe of #1)	3	6	9	17	26	35
326-Grey vs. Green (Rick Jones) Hulk	2	4	6	8	10	12
330-1st McFarlane-c/p; last Milgrom-s; Thunderbolt Ross 'dies'	3	6	9	19	30	40
331-Peter David begins as regular plotter; McFarlane-p	3	6	9	17	25	34
332-Grey Hulk & Leader vs. Green Hulk (Rick Jones)	2	4	6	8	11	14
333-334,338-339: 338-1st app. Mercy. 339-The Leader app.	1	2	3	4	8	10
335-No McFarlane-a						6.00
336,337-X-Factor app.	1	3	4	6	8	10
340-Classic Hulk vs. Wolverine-c by McFarlane	8	16	24	51	96	140
341-344,346: 341-vs. The Man-Bull; McFarlane begins pencils and inks. 342-The Leader app. 343-1st app. Rock & Redeemer. 344-McFarlane (p) only; vs. The Leader, Rock & Redeemer; Betty revealed to be pregnant. 346-The Leader app. Last McFarlane-p (co-penciled with Erik Larsen)	1	2	3	4	8	12
345-($1.50, 52 pgs) vs. The Leader; Gamma-Bomb explosion; World thinks the Hulk is dead; McFarlane (p) only	3	6	9	18	27	36
347-349,351-366: 347-1st app. The Hulk as 'Mr. Fixit'; relocated to Las Vegas; 1st app. Marlo; Absorbing Man app. 348-vs. Absorbing Man. 349-Spider-Man app; Dr. Doom cameo. 351-How the Hulk survived the Gamma-Bomb is revealed. 355-Glorian app. 356-Glorian & Shaper of Worlds app. 359-Wolverine-c (illusion) by John Byrne. 360-Nightmare & D'spayre app; Betty loses her baby. 361-Iron Man app. 362-Werewolf by Night app. 363-Acts of Vengeance tie-in; Dr. Doom & Grey Gargoyle app. 364-vs Abomination; 1st app. Madman. 365-Fantastic Four app. 366-Leader & Madman app.						5.00
350-Hulk/Thing battle	1	3	4	6	8	10
367-1st Dale Keown-a on Hulk (3/90) Leader & Madman app.	1	2	3	5	6	8
368-371,373-375: 368-Sam Kieth-c/a; 1st app. Pantheon. 369-Keown-a (becomes regular artist through #398); vs. the Freedom Force. 370,371-Dr. Strange & Namor app. (Defenders reunion). 374,375-vs. the Super-Skrull.						5.00
372-Green Hulk returns	1	2	3	5	6	8
376-Green vs. Grey Hulk; 1st app. Agamemnon of the Pantheon	2	4	6	9	12	15
377-(1/91, $1.00) 1st all new Hulk; fluorescent green background-c	3	6	9	17	26	35
377-($1.00) 2nd printing; black background-c	3	6	9	14	20	25
377-($1.75) 3rd printing from 1994; low print run; muted green background-c	12	24	36	82	179	275
378-392,394-399: 378,380,389-No Keown-a. 379-Contined from issue #377; new direction for the Hulk; 1st app. of Delphi, Ajax, Achilles, Paris & Hector of the Pantheon. 380-Doc Samson app. 381,382-Pantheon app. 383-Infinity Gauntlet x-over; Abomination app. 384-Infinity Gauntlet tie-in; Abomination app. 385-Infinity Gauntlet tie-in. 386,387-Sabra app. 388-1st app. Speedfreak. 390-X-Factor cameo. 391,392-X-Factor app.394-1st app. Trauma; no Keown-a. 395,396-Punisher app. 397-399; Leader & U-Foes app. 398-Last Keown-a.						4.00
393-($2.50, 72 pgs)						5.00
393-2nd print; silver-ink background						4.00
400-($2.50, 68-pgs)-Holo-grafx foil-c & r/TTA #63						4.00
400-2nd print; yellow logo						4.00
401-403,405-416: 401-U-Foes app. 402-Return of Doc Samson; Juggernaut & Red Skull app. 403-Gary Frank-a begins; Juggernaut & Red Skull app. 405-1st app. Piecemeal. 406-Captain America app. 407-vs. Piecemeal & Madman. 408-vs. Piecemeal & Madman; Motormouth & Killpower (Marvel UK characters) app. 409-vs. Madman; Motormouth & Killpower app. 410-Nick Fury & SHIELD app. 411-Pantheon vs. SHIELD; Nick Fury app. 412-Hulk & She-Hulk vs. Bi-Beast. 413-Trauma app; Pt. 1 (of 4) of the Troyjan War. 414-vs. Trauma; Silver Surfer app. 415-Silver Surfer & Starjammers app. 416-Final of the Troyjan War; death of Trauma.						4.00
404-Avengers vs. Juggernaut & the Hulk; Red Skull app.						5.00
417,419-424: 417-Begins $1.50-c; Rick Jones Bachelor party; many heroes from Avengers & Fantastic Four app; Hulk returns from "Future Imperfect". 419-No Frank-a. 420-Special AIDS awareness issue; death of Jim Wilson. 421-Hulk & the Pantheon in Asgard. 423-Hela app.						4.00
418-($2.50)-Collectors Edition w/Gatefold die-cut-c; the wedding of Rick Jones & Marlo; includes cameo apps. of various Marvel characters as well as DC"s Death & Peter David						5.00
418-($1.50, Regular Edition)						4.00
425-($2.25, 52 pgs); Last Frank-a; Liam Sharp-a begins; death of Achilles						5.00
425-($3.50, 52 pgs)-Holographic-c						5.00
426-433,441,442: 426-Nick Fury app. 427,428-Man-Thing app. 430-Speedfreak app. 431,432-Abomination app. 432-Last Sharp-a. 433-Punisher app; title becomes part of the 'Marvel Edge' titles (through #439) 441-She-Hulk-c/s; "Pulp Fiction" parody-c. 442-She-Hulk & Doc Samson team-up; no Hulk app.						4.00
434-Funeral for Nick Fury; Wolverine, Dr. Strange, Avengers app; Marvel Overpower card insert (harder to find above 9.2 due to card indentations)						5.00
435-($2.50)-Rhino app; excerpt from "What Savage Beast"						5.00
436-439: 436-"Ghosts of the Future" Pt.1 (of 5); Leader app. 439-Maestro app.						5.00
440-"Ghosts of the Future" Pt. 5; Hulk vs. Thor						5.00
443,446-448: 443-Begin $1.50-c; re-app. of Hulk. 446-w/card insert. 447-Begin Deodato-c/a						4.00
444,445: 444-Cable-c/app; Onslaught x-over. 445-Onslaught x-over; Avengers app.						5.00
447-Variant-c						5.00
449-1st app. Thunderbolts (1/97); Citizen V, Songbird, Mach-1, Techno, Atlas & Meteorite	5	10	15	35	63	90
450-($2.95)-Thunderbolts app. 2 stories; Heroes Reborn versions of Hulk, Dr. Strange, Mr. Fantastic & Iron Man app.						6.00
451-453, 458-470: 452-Heroes Reborn Hulk app. 453-Hulk vs. Heroes Reborn Hulk. 458-Mr. Hyde app. 459-Abomination app. 461-Maestro app. 463-Silver Surfer cameo. 464-Silver Surfer app. 465-Mr. Fantastic & Tony Stark app. 466-'Death' of Betty Banner. 467-Last Peter David issue. 468-Casey-s/Puilido-a begin. 469-Super-Adaptoid & Ringmaster app. 470-Ringmaster & the Circus of Crime app.						4.00
454-Wolverine & Ka-Zar app; Adam Kubert-a						5.00
455-Wolverine, Storm, Cannonball & Cyclops of the X-Men app.; Adam Kubert-a						5.00
456-Apocalypse enlists the Hulk as 'War'; Juggernaut app.						6.00
457-Hulk (as Horseman of the Apocalypse 'War' vs. Juggernaut. Apocalypse app.	1	2	3	4	6	8
471-473: 471-Circus of Crime app. 473-Watcher app; Abomination revealed as Betty's killer.						

Incredible Hulk V2 #34 © MAR

Incredible Hulks #612 © MAR

The Incredibles #1 © DIS & Pixar

	GD	VG	FN	VF	VF/NM	NM-
	2.0	4.0	6.0	8.0	9.0	9.2

474-($2.99) Last issue; Abomination app; c-homage to issue #1 5.00
1 3 4 6 8 10
#(-1) Flashback (7/97) Kubert-a 3.00
Special 1 (10/68, 25¢, 68 pg.)-New 51 pg. story; Hulk battles the Inhumans (early app)
27 54 81 189 420 650
Special 2 (10/69, 25¢, 68 pg.)-Origin retold (from issue #3) r-TTA #62-66
6 12 18 41 76 110
Special 3,4: 3-(1/71, 25¢, 68 pg.)-r/TTA #70-74. 4-(1/72, 52 pg.)-r/TTA 75-77 & Not Brand Echh #5 4 8 12 25 40 55
Annual 5 (1976) 2nd app. Groot 5 10 15 35 63 90
Annual 6 (1977)-1st app. Paragon (later becomes Her, then later Ayesha); Dr. Strange app.
3 6 9 19 30 40
Annual 7 ('78)-Byrne/Layton-c/a; Iceman & Angel app; vs. the Mastermold
3 6 9 16 23 30
Annual 8 ('79)-Byrne/Stern-s; Hulk vs. Sasquatch 2 4 6 8 10 12
Annual 9,10: 9-('80)-Ditko-p. 10-('81)-Captain Universe app. 6.00
Annual 11 ('82)-Doc Samson back-up by Miller-(p)(5 pg); Spider-Man & Avengers app.
1 2 3 5 6 8
Annual 12-14: 12-('83)-Trimpe-a. 13-('84)-Story takes place at the 'Crossroads' (after Hulk was banished from Earth); takes place between Incredible Hulk #301-302. 14-Byrne-s; takes place between pages of Incredible Hulk #314 5.00
Annual 15-('86)-Zeck-c; Abomination & Tryannus app. 5.00
Annual 16-20: 16-('90, $2.00, 68 pgs. "Lifeform" Pt. 3; continued from Daredevil Annual #6, continued in Silver Surfer Annual #3; She-Hulk app. in back-up story. 17-('91, $2.00)-"Subterranean Wars" Pt. 2; continued from Avengers Annual #20; continued in Namor the Sub-Mariner Annual #1. 18-('92)-"Return of the Defenders" Pt.1; continued in Namor the Sub-Mariner Annual #1. 19-('93)-Bagged w/card; 1st app. Lazarus 5.00
...'97 ($2.99) Pollina-c 5.00
...And Wolverine 1 (10/86, $2.50)-r/1st app. (#180-181) 3 6 9 15 22 28
...: Beauty and the Behemoth ('98, $19.95, TPB) r/Bruce & Betty stories 20.00
...Ground Zero ('95, $12.95) r/#340-346 13.00
...Hercules Unleashed (10/96, $2.50) David-s/Deodato-c/a 4.00
... No. 1 Facsimile Edition (12/19, $3.99) r/#1 with original 1962 ads 4.00
... No. 180 Facsimile Edition (3/20, $3.99) r/#180 with original ads and letter column 4.00
... No. 181 Facsimile Edition (5/19, $3.99) r/#181 with original ads and letter column 4.00
... No. 182 Facsimile Edition (5/19, $3.99) r/#182 with original ads and letter column 4.00
... Omnibus Vol. 1 HC (2008, $99.99, dustjacket) r/#1-6 & 102, Tales To Astonish #59-101 bonus art, cover reprints; afterword by Peter David; Kirby cover from #1 160.00
... Omnibus Vol. 1 HC (2008, $99.99, dustjacket) Variant-c swipe of #1 by Alex Ross 140.00
.../Sub-Mariner '98 Annual ($2.99) 4.00
...Versus Quasimodo 1 (3/83, one-shot)-Based on Saturday morning cartoon 4.00
...Vs. Superman 1 (7/99, $5.95, one-shot)-painted-c by Rude 6.00
...Versus Venom 1 (4/94, $2.50, one-shot)-Embossed-c; red foil logo 4.00
... Visionaries: Peter David Vol. 1 (2005, $19.99) r/#331-339 written by Peter David 20.00
... Visionaries: Peter David Vol. 2 (2005, $19.99) r/#340-348 20.00
... Visionaries: Peter David Vol. 3 (2006, $19.99) r/#349-354, Web of Spider-Man #44, and Fantastic Four #320 20.00
... Visionaries: Peter David Vol. 4 (2007, $19.99) r/#355-363 and Marvel Comics Presents #26,45 20.00
... Visionaries: Peter David Vol. 5 (2008, $19.99) r/#364-372 and Annual #16 20.00
Wizard #1 Ace Edition - Reprints #1 with new Andy Kubert-c 14.00
Wizard #181 Ace Edition - Reprints #181 with new Chen-c 14.00
(Also see titles listed under **Hulk**)

NOTE: ***Adkins*** *a-111-116i.* ***Austin*** *a(i)-350, 351, 353, 354; c-302i, 350i.* ***Ayers*** *a-3-5i.* ***Buckler*** *a-Annual 5; c-252.* ***John Buscema*** *c-202p.* ***Byrne*** *a-314-319p; c-314-316, 318, 319, 359, Annual 14i.* ***Colan*** *c-363.* ***Ditko*** *a-2i, 6, 249, Annual 2r(5), 3r, 9p; c-2i, 6, 235, 249.* ***Everett*** *c-133i.* ***Golden*** *c-248, 251.* ***Kane*** *c(p)-193, 194, 196, 198.* ***Dale Keown*** *a(p)-367, 369-377, 379, 381-388, 390-393, 395-398; c-369-377p, 381, 382p, 384, 385, 386, 387p, 388, 390p, 391-393, 395p, 396, 397p, 398.* ***Kirby*** *a-1-5p, Special 2, 3p, Annual 5p; c-1-5, Annual 5.* ***McFarlane*** *a-330-334p, 336-339p, 340-343, 344-346p; c-330p, 340p, 341-343, 344p, 345, 346p.* ***Mignola*** *c-302, 305, 313.* ***Miller*** *c-258p, 261, 264, 268.* ***Mooney*** *a-230p, 287i, 288i.* ***Powell*** *a-Special 3r(2).* ***Romita*** *a-Annual 17p.* ***Severin*** *a(i)-108-110, 131-133, 141-151, 153-155; c(i)-109, 110, 132, 142, 144-155.* ***Simonson*** *c-283, 364-367.* ***Starlin*** *a-222p; c-217.* ***Staton*** *a(i)-187-189, 191-209.* ***Tuska*** *a-102i, 105i, 106i, 218p.* ***Williamson*** *a-310i; c-310i, 311i.* ***Wrightson*** *c-197.*

INCREDIBLE HULK (Vol. 2) (Formerly Hulk #1-11; becomes Incredible Hercules with #113) (Re-titled Incredible Hulks #612-on)(Also see World War Hulk)
Marvel Comics: No. 12, Mar, 2000 - No. 112, Jan, 2008 ($1.99-$3.50)
No. 600, Sept, 2009 - No. 625, Oct, 2011 ($3.99/$4.99)

12-Jenkins-s/Garney & McKone-a 4.00
13,14-($1.99) Garney & Buscema-a 3.00
15-24,26-32: 15-Begin $2.25-c. 21-Maximum Security x-over. 24-($1.99-c) 3.00
25-($2.99) Hulk vs. The Abomination; Romita Jr.-a 4.00
33-($3.50, 100 pgs.) new Bogdanove-a/Priest-s; reprints 4.00
34-Bruce Jones-s begin; Romita Jr.-a 5.00
35-49,51-54: 35-39-Jones-s/Romita Jr.-a. 40-43-Weeks-a. 44-49-Immonen-a 3.00
50-($3.50) Deodato-a begins; Abomination app. thru #54 4.00
55-74,77-91: 55(25¢-c) Absorbing Man returns; Fernandez-a. 60-65,70-72-Deodato-a. 66-69-Braithwaite-a. 71-74-Iron Man app. 77-($2.99-c) Peter David-s begin/Weeks-a. 80-Wolverine-c. 82-Jae Lee-c/a. 83-86-House of M x-over. 87-Scorpion app. 3.00
75,76-($3.50) The Leader app. 75-Robertson-a/Frank-c. 76-Braithwaite-a 4.00
92-Planet Hulk begins; Ladronn-c 5.00
92-2nd printing with variant-c by Bryan Hitch 4.00
93-99,101-105 Planet Hulk; Ladronn-c 3.00
100-($3.99) Planet Hulk continues; back-up w/Frank-a; r/#152,153; Ladronn-c 5.00
100-($3.99) Green Hulk variant-c by Michael Turner 10.00
100-($3.99) Gray Hulk variant-c by Michael Turner 30.00
106-World War Hulk begins; Gary Frank-a/c 6.00
106-2nd printing with new cover of Hercules and Angel 3.00
107-112: 107-Hercules vs. Hulk. 108-Rick Jones app. 112-Art Adams-c 3.00
600-(9/09, $4.99) Covers by Ross, Sale and wraparound-c by McGuinness; back-up with Stan Lee-s; r/Hulk: Gray #1; cover gallery 5.00
601-611-($3.99): 601-605-Olivetti-a. 603-Wolverine app. 606-608-Fall of the Hulks 4.00
(Title becomes Incredible Hulks with #612, Nov, 2010)
612-621: 612-617-Dark Son. 618-620-Chaos War. 621-Hercules app. 4.00
622-634-($2.99) 623-625-Ka-Zar app.; Eaglesham-a. 626-629-Grummett-a 3.00
635-($3.99) Fin Fang Foom & Dr. Strange app.; Greg Pak interview 4.00
Annual 2000 ($3.50) Texeira-a/Jenkins-s; Avengers app. 4.00
Annual 2001 ($2.99) Thor-c/app.; Larsen-s/Williams III-c 4.00
Annual 1 (8/11, $3.99) Identity Wars; Spider-Man and Deadpool app.; Barrionuevo-a 4.00
... & The Human Torch: From the Marvel Vault 1 (8/11, $2.99) unpublished story w/Ditko-a 3.00
... : Boiling Point (Volume 2, 2002, $8.99, TPB) r/#40-43; Andrews-c 9.00
Dogs of War (6/01, $19.95, TPB) r/#12-20 20.00
House of M (2006, $13.99) r/House of M tie-in issues Incredible Hulk #83-87 14.00
Hulk: Planet Hulk HC (2007, $39.99, dustjacket) oversized r/#92-105, Planet Hulk: Gladiator Guidebook, stories from Amazing Fantasy (2004) #15 and Giant-Size Hulk #1 40.00
Hulk: Planet Hulk SC (2008, $34.99) same content as HC 35.00
Planet Hulk: Gladiator Guidebook (2006, $3.99) bios of combatants and planet history 4.00
...: Prelude to Planet Hulk (2006, $13.99, TPB) r/#88-91 & Official Handbook: Hulk 2004 14.00
...: Return of the Monster (7/02, $12.99, TPB) r/#34-39 13.00
...: The End (8/02, $5.95) David-s/Keown-a; Hulk in the far future 6.00
...: The End HC (2008, $19.99, dustjacket) r/The End and Hulk: Future Imperfect #1-2 20.00
...Volume 1 HC (2002, $29.99, oversized) r/#34-43 & Startling Stories: Banner #1-4 30.00
...Volume 2 HC (2003, $29.99, oversized) r/#44-54; sketch pages and cover gallery 30.00
Volume 3: Transfer of Power (2003, $12.99, TPB) r/#44-49 13.00
Volume 4: Abominable (2003, $11.99, TPB) r/#50-54; Abomination app.; Deodato-a 12.00
Volume 5: Hide in Plain Sight (2003, $11.99, TPB) r/#55-59; Fernandez-a 12.00
Volume 6: Split Decisions (2004, $12.99, TPB) r/#60-65; Deodato-a 13.00
Volume 7: Dead Like Me (2004, $12.99, TPB) r/#66-69 & Hulk Smash #1&2 13.00
Volume 8: Big Things (2004, $17.99, TPB) r/#70-76; Iron Man app. 18.00
Volume 9: Tempest Fugit (2005, $14.99, TPB) r/#77-82 15.00

INCREDIBLE HULK (Also see Indestructible Hulk)
Marvel Comics: Dec, 2011 - No. 15, Dec, 2012 ($3.99)

1-Aaron-s/Silvestri-a; bonus interview with Aaron; cover by Silvestri 4.00
1-Variant covers by Neal Adams, Whilce Portacio & Ladronn 8.00
2-7: 2-Silvestri, Portacio & Tan-a. 7-Hulk & Banner merge; Portacio-a 4.00
7.1-(7/12, $2.99) Palo-a/Komarck-c; Red She-Hulk app. 3.00
8-15: 8-Punisher app.; Dillon-a. 12-Wolverine & The Thing app. 4.00

INCREDIBLE HULK (Marvel Legacy)(Continued from Totally Awesome Hulk #23)
Marvel Comics: No. 709, Dec, 2017 - No. 717, Jul, 2018 ($3.99)

709-717: 709-713-"Return to Planet Hulk"; Hulk goes to Sakaar; Pak-s/Land-a. 717-Cho-c 4.00
...: Last Call 1 (8/19, $4.99) Peter David-s/Dale Keown-a; Mister Hyde app. 5.00

INCREDIBLE HULKS: ENIGMA FORCE
Marvel Comics: Nov, 2010 - No. 3, Jan, 2011 ($3.99, limited series)

1-3-Reed-s/Munera-a/Pagulayan-c; Bug app. 4.00

INCREDIBLE MR. LIMPET, THE (See Movie Classics)

INCREDIBLES, THE
Image Comics: Nov, 2004 - No. 4, Feb, 2005 ($2.99, limited series)

1-4-Adaptation of 2004 Pixar movie; Ricardo Curtis-a 3.00
TPB (2005, $12.95) r/#1-4; cover gallery 13.00

INCREDIBLES, THE (Pixar characters)
BOOM! Studios: No. 0, Jul, 2009 - No. 15, Oct, 2010 ($2.99)

0-15: 0-3-City of Incredibles; Waid & Walker-s. 0,1-Wagner-c. 8-15-Walker-s 3.00
...: Family Matters 1-4 (3/09 - No. 4, 6/09) Waid-s/Takara-a. 1-Five covers 3.00

INCREDIBLES 2: CRISIS IN MID-LIFE! & OTHER STORIES (Pixar characters)
Dark Horse Comics: Jul, 2018 - No. 3, Sept, 2018 ($3.99, limited series)

1-3-Short stories by Gage, Gurihiru, Bone, Walker and Greppi 4.00

Incursion #3 © VAL

Indestructible Hulk #1 © MAR

Indians #3 © FH

	GD 2.0	VG 4.0	FN 6.0	VF 8.0	VF/NM 9.0	NM- 9.2

INCREDIBLES 2: SECRET IDENTITIES (Pixar characters)
Dark Horse Comics: Apr, 2019 - No. 3, Jun, 2019 ($3.99, limited series)

	GD	VG	FN	VF	VF/NM	NM-
1-3-Christos Gage-s/Jean-Claudio Vinci-a						4.00

INCREDIBLES 2: SLOW BURN (Pixar characters)
Dark Horse Comics: Feb, 2020 - No. 3 ($3.99, limited series)

	GD	VG	FN	VF	VF/NM	NM-
1-3-Christos Gage-s/Jean-Claudio Vinci-a; Jack loses his speed powers						4.00

INCREDIBLE SCIENCE FICTION (Formerly Weird Science-Fantasy)
E. C. Comics: No. 30, July-Aug, 1955 - No. 33, Jan-Feb, 1956

	GD	VG	FN	VF	VF/NM	NM-
30-Davis-c begin, end #32	50	100	150	400	638	875
31-Williamson/Krenkel-a, Wood-a(2)	44	88	132	352	564	775
32-"Food For Thought" by Williamson/Krenkel	44	88	132	352	564	775
33-Classic Wood-c; "Judgment Day" story-r/Weird Fantasy #18; final issue & last E.C. comic book	54	108	162	432	691	950

NOTE: ***Davis** a-30, 32, 33; c-30-32. **Krigstein** a-in all. **Orlando** a-30, 32, 33. **Wood** a-30, 31, 33; c-33.*

INCREDIBLE SCIENCE FICTION (Formerly Weird Science-Fantasy)
Russ Cochran/Gemstone Publ.: No. 8, Aug, 1994 - No. 11, May, 1995 ($2.00)

	GD	VG	FN	VF	VF/NM	NM-
8-11: Reprints #30-33 of E.C. series						4.00

INCURSION
Valiant Entertainment: Feb, 2019 - No. 4, May, 2019 ($3.99, limited series)

	GD	VG	FN	VF	VF/NM	NM-
1-4: 1-Diggle & Paknadel-s/Braithwaite-a; Geomancer app.; Punk Mambo preview						4.00

INDEPENDENCE DAY (Movie)
Marvel Comics: No. 0, June, 1996 - No. 2, Aug, 1996 ($1.95, limited series)

	GD	VG	FN	VF	VF/NM	NM-
0-Special Edition; photo-c						5.00
0-2						3.00

INDEPENDENCE DAY (Movie)
Titan Comics: Mar, 2016 - No. 5, Jul, 2016 ($3.99, limited series)

	GD	VG	FN	VF	VF/NM	NM-
1-5: 1-Victor Gischler-s/Steve Scott-a; four covers. 2-5-Two covers						4.00

INDESTRUCTIBLE
IDW (Darby Pop): Dec, 2013 - No. 10, Dec, 2014 ($3.99)

	GD	VG	FN	VF	VF/NM	NM-
1-10: 1-Kline-s/Garron & Garcia-a						4.00
...: Stingray One Shot (5/15, $3.99) Marsick-s/Reguzzoni-a						4.00

INDESTRUCTIBLE HULK (Marvel NOW!)(Follows Incredible Hulk 2011-2012 series)
Marvel Comics: Jan, 2013 - No. 20, May, 2014 ($3.99)

	GD	VG	FN	VF	VF/NM	NM-
1-Waid-s/Yu-a; Banner hired by SHIELD; Maria Hill app.						4.00
2-20: 2-Iron Man app. 4,5-Attuma app. 6-8-Thor app.; Simonson-a/c. 9,10-Daredevil app. 12-Two-Gun Kid, Kid Colt, and Rawhide Kid app. 17,18-Iron Man app.						4.00
Annual 1 (2/14, $4.99) Parker-s/Asrar-a; Iron Man app.						5.00
... Special 1 (12/13, $4.99) Original X-Men and Superior Spider-Man app.						5.00

INDIANA JONES (Title series), **Dark Horse Comics**

	GD	VG	FN	VF	VF/NM	NM-
--ADVENTURES, 6/08 ($6.95, digest-sized) Vol. 1 - new all-ages adventures; Beavers-a						7.00
--AND THE ARMS OF GOLD, 2/94 - 5/94 ($2.50) 1-4						3.00
--AND THE FATE OF ATLANTIS, 3/91 - 9/91 ($2.50) 1-4-Dorman painted-c on all; contain trading cards (#1 has a 2nd printing, 10/91)						3.00
--AND THE GOLDEN FLEECE, 6/94 - 7/94 ($2.50) 1,2						3.00
--AND THE IRON PHOENIX, 12/94 - 3/95 ($2.50) 1-4						3.00

INDIANA JONES AND THE KINGDOM OF THE CRYSTAL SKULL
Dark Horse Comics: May, 2008 - No. 2, May, 2008 ($5.99, limited series, movie adaptation)

	GD	VG	FN	VF	VF/NM	NM-
1,2-Luke Ross-a/John Jackson Miller-adapted-s; two covers by Struzan & Fleming						6.00
TPB (5/08, $12.95) r/#1,2; Struzan-c						13.00

INDIANA JONES AND THE LAST CRUSADE
Marvel Comics: 1989 - No. 4, 1989 ($1.00, limited series, movie adaptation)

	GD	VG	FN	VF	VF/NM	NM-
1-4: Williamson-i assist						3.00
1-(1989, $2.95, B&W mag., 80 pgs.)						4.00
--AND THE SHRINE OF THE SEA DEVIL: Dark Horse, 9/94 ($2.50, one shot) 1-Gary Gianni-a						3.00
--AND THE SARGASSO PIRATES: Dark Horse, 12/95 - 3/96 ($2.50) 1-4: 1,2-Ross-c						3.00
--AND THE SPEAR OF DESTINY: Dark Horse, 4/95 - 8/95 ($2.50) 1-4						3.00
--AND THE TOMB OF THE GODS, 6/08 - No. 4, 3/09 ($2.99) 1-4: 1-Tony Harris-c						3.00
--THUNDER IN THE ORIENT: Dark Horse, 9/93 - '94 ($2.50) 1-6: Dan Barry story & art in all; 1-Dorman painted-c						3.00

INDIANA JONES AND THE TEMPLE OF DOOM
Marvel Comics Group: Sept, 1984 - No. 3, Nov, 1984 (Movie adaptation)

	GD	VG	FN	VF	VF/NM	NM-
1-3-r/Marvel Super Special; Guice-a						5.00

INDIANA JONES OMNIBUS
Dark Horse Books: Feb, 2008; June 2008; Feb, 2009 ($24.95, digest-size)

	GD	VG	FN	VF	VF/NM	NM-
Volume One - Reprints Indiana Jones and the Fate of Atlantis, Indiana Jones: Thunder in the Orient; and Indiana Jones and the Arms of Gold mini-series						25.00
Volume Two - Reprints I.J. and the Golden Fleece, I.J. and the Shrine of the Sea Devil, I.J. and the Iron Phoenix, I.J. and the Spear of Destiny, I.J. and the Sargasso Pirates						25.00
The Further Adventures Volume One - (2/09) r/Raiders of the Lost Ark #1-3 & The Further Adventures of Indiana Jones #1-12						25.00

INDIAN BRAVES (Baffling Mysteries No. 5 on)
Ace Magazines: March, 1951 - No. 4, Sept, 1951

	GD	VG	FN	VF	VF/NM	NM-
1-Green Arrowhead begins, apps. in all	26	52	78	152	249	345
2	10	20	30	56	76	95
3,4	9	18	27	47	61	75
I.W. Reprint #1 (nd)-r/Indian Braves #4	2	4	6	9	13	16

INDIAN CHIEF (White Eagle...) (Formerly The Chief, Four Color 290)
Dell Publ. Co.: No. 3, July-Sept, 1951 - No. 33, Jan-Mar, 1959 (All painted-c)

	GD	VG	FN	VF	VF/NM	NM-
3	5	10	15	33	57	80
4-11: 6-White Eagle app.	4	8	12	28	47	65
12-1st White Eagle (10-12/53)-Not same as earlier character	5	10	15	33	57	80
13-29	4	8	12	23	37	50
30-33-Buscema-a	4	8	12	25	40	55

INDIAN CHIEF (See March of Comics No. 94, 110, 127, 140, 159, 170, 187)

INDIAN FIGHTER, THE (Movie)
Dell Publishing Co.: No. 687, May, 1956 (one-shot)

	GD	VG	FN	VF	VF/NM	NM-
Four Color 687-Kirk Douglas photo-c	7	14	21	48	89	130

INDIAN FIGHTER
Youthful Magazines: May, 1950 - No. 11, Jan, 1952

	GD	VG	FN	VF	VF/NM	NM-
1	20	40	60	117	189	260
2-Wildey-a/c(bondage)	14	28	42	80	115	150
3-11: 3,4-Wildey-a. 6-Davy Crockett story	11	22	33	62	86	110

NOTE: ***Hollingsworth** a-5. **Walter Johnson** c-1, 3, 4, 6. **Palais** a-10. **Stallman** a-5-8. **Wildey** a-2-4; c-2, 5.*

INDIAN LEGENDS OF THE NIAGARA (See American Graphics)

INDIANS
Fiction House Magazines (Wings Publ. Co.): Spring, 1950 - No. 17, Spr, 1953 (1-8: 52 pgs.)

	GD	VG	FN	VF	VF/NM	NM-
1-Manzar The White Indian, Long Bow & Orphan of the Storm begin	32	64	96	192	314	435
2-Starlight begins	16	32	48	96	151	205
3-5: 5-17-Most-c by Whitman	15	30	45	83	124	165
6-10	14	28	42	76	108	140
11-17	12	24	36	69	97	125

INDIANS OF THE WILD WEST
I. W. Enterprises: Circa 1958? (no date) (Reprints)

	GD	VG	FN	VF	VF/NM	NM-
9-Kinstler-c; Whitman-a; r/Indians #?	2	4	6	10	14	18

INDIANS ON THE WARPATH
St. John Publishing Co.: 1950 (no month) (132 pgs.)

	GD	VG	FN	VF	VF/NM	NM-
nn-Matt Baker-c; contains St. John comics rebound. Many combinations possible	48	96	144	302	514	725

INDIAN TRIBES (See Famous Indian Tribes)

INDIAN WARRIORS (Formerly White Rider and Super Horse; becomes Western Crime Cases #9)
Star Publications: No. 7, June, 1951 - No. 8, Sept, 1951

	GD	VG	FN	VF	VF/NM	NM-
7-White Rider & Superhorse continue; "Last of the Mohicans" serial begins; L.B. Cole-c	20	40	60	118	192	265
8-L.B. Cole-c	19	38	57	112	179	245
3-D 1(12/53, 25¢)-Came w/glasses; L.B. Cole-c	34	68	102	204	332	460
Accepted Reprint(nn)(inside cover shows White Rider & Superhorse #11)-r/cover to #7; origin White Rider &...; L.B. Cole-c	8	16	24	40	50	60
Accepted Reprint #8 (nd); L.B. Cole-c (r-cover to #8)	8	16	24	40	50	60

INDOORS-OUTDOORS (See Wisco)

INDUSTRIAL GOTHIC
DC Comics (Vertigo): Dec, 1995 - No. 5, Apr, 1996 ($2.50, limited series)

	GD	VG	FN	VF	VF/NM	NM-
1-5: Ted McKeever-c/a/scripts						3.00

INFAMOUS (Based on the Sony videogame)
DC Comics: Early May, 2011 - No. 6, Late July, 2011 ($2.99, limited series)

	GD	VG	FN	VF	VF/NM	NM-
1-6: 1-William Harms-s/Eric Nguyen-a/Doug Mahnke-c. 3-6-Benes-c						3.00

INFAMOUS IRON MAN (Doctor Doom as Iron Man)
Marvel Comics: Dec, 2016 - No. 12, Nov, 2017 ($3.99)

Inferior Five #7 © DC

Infinite Crisis #4 © DC

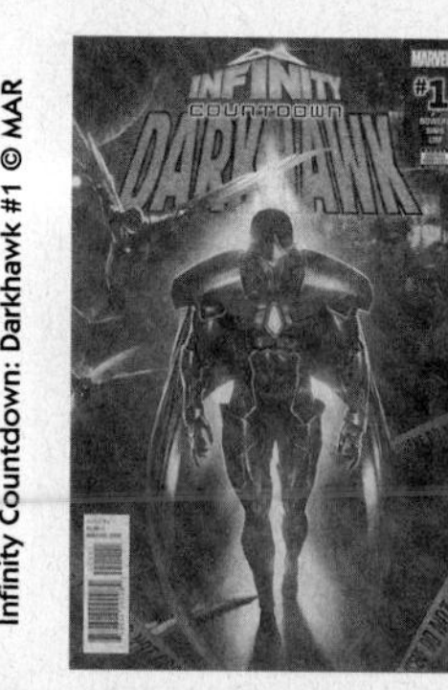

Infinity Countdown: Darkhawk #1 © MAR

	GD	VG	FN	VF	VF/NM	NM-
	2.0	4.0	6.0	8.0	9.0	9.2

1-12: 1-Bendis-s/Maleev-a; Diablo app. 1-9-The Thing app. 5-Doom's mother returns 4.00

INFECTED, THE (Year of the Villain tie-ins)
DC Comics: Feb, 2020 ($3.99, series of one-shots)

...: Deathbringer (2/20) Donna Troy corrupted by The Batman That Laughs; Teen Titans app. 4.00
...: King Shazam (1/20) Billy Batson corrupted; Marvel Family app.; Bennett-a 4.00
...: Scarab (2019) Jaime Reyes Blue Beetle corrupted; Williams II-a 4.00
...: The Commissioner (2/20) Jim Gordon corrupted; Batgirl app.; Herbert-a 4.00

INFERIOR FIVE, THE (Inferior 5 #11, 12) (See Showcase #62, 63, 65)
National Periodical Publications (#1-10: 12¢): 3-4/67 - No. 10, 9-10/68; No. 11, 8-9/72 - No. 12, 10-11/72

	GD	VG	FN	VF	VF/NM	NM-
1-(3-4/67)-Sekowsky-a(p); 4th app.	5	10	15	35	63	90
2-5: 2-Plastic Man, F.F. app. 4-Thor app.	3	6	9	21	33	45
6-9: 6-Stars DC staff	3	6	9	16	23	30
10-Superman x-over; F.F., Spider-Man & Sub-Mariner app.	3	6	9	21	33	45
11,12: Orlando-c/a; both r/Showcase #62,63	2	4	6	11	16	20

INFERIOR FIVE
DC Comics: Nov, 2019 - No. 6 ($3.99, limited series originally planned for 12 issues)

1-4-Giffen & Lemire-s&a; back-up with Peacemaker 4.00

INFERNAL MAN-THING (Sequel to story in Man-Thing #12 [1974])
Marvel Comics: Sept, 2012 - No. 3, Oct, 2012 ($3.99, limited series)

1-3-Gerber-s; painted-a by Nowlan; Art Adams-c. 1,2-Bonus reprint of Man-Thing #12 4.00

INFERNO (See Legion of Super-Heroes)
DC Comics: Oct, 1997 - No. 4, Feb, 1998 ($2.50, limited series)

1-Immonen-s/c/a in all 4.00
2-4 3.00

INFERNO (Secret Wars tie-in)
Marvel Comics: Jul, 2015 - No. 5, Nov, 2015 ($3.99, limited series)

1-5-Hopeless-s/Garrón-a; Magik, Colossus, Nightcrawler, Madelyne Pryor app. 4.00

INFERNO: HELLBOUND
Image Comics (Top Cow): Jan, 2002 - No. 3 ($2.50/$2.99)

1,2: 1-Seven covers; Silvestri-a/Silvestri and Wohl-s 3.00
3-($2.99) Tan-a 3.00
#0 (7/02, $3.00) Tan-a 3.00
Wizard #0- Previews series; bagged with Wizard Top Cow Special mag 3.00

INFESTATION (Zombie crossover with G.I. Joe, Star Trek, Transformers and Ghostbusters)
IDW Publishing: Jan, 2011 - No. 2, Apr, 2011 ($3.99, limited series)

1,2-Abnett & Lanning-s/Messina-a; two covers by Messina & Snyder III 4.00
...: Outbreak 1-4 (6/11 - No. 4, 9/11, $3.99) Messina-a; Covert Vampiric Operations app. 4.00

INFESTATION 2 (IDW characters vs. H.P. Lovecraft's Elder Gods)
IDW Publishing: Jan, 2012 - No. 2, Apr, 2012 ($3.99, limited series)

1,2-Swierczynski-s/Messina-a; three covers by Garner, Ramondelli & Messina 4.00
...: Dungeons & Dragons 1,2 (2/12 - No. 2, 2/12, $3.99) 3 covers 4.00
...: G.I. Joe 1,2 (3/12 - No. 2, 3/12, $3.99) Raicht-s/De Landro-a; 3 covers 4.00
...: Team-Up 1 (2/12, $3.99) Ryall-s/Robinson-a; covers by Powell & Morrison 4.00
...: Teenage Mutant Ninja Turtles 1,2 (3/12 - No. 2, 3/12, $3.99) Mark Torres-a; 3 covers 4.00
...: 30 Days of Night 1 (4/12, $3.99) Swierczynski-s/Sayger-a; 3 covers 4.00
...: Transformers 1,2 (2/12 - No. 2, 2/12, $3.99) Dixon-s/Guidi-a; 3 covers 4.00

INFIDEL
Image Comics: Mar, 2018 - No. 5, Jul, 2018 ($3.99, limited series)

1-5-Pornsak Pichetshote-s/Aaron Campbell-a 4.00

INFINITE, THE
Image Comics (SkyBound): Aug, 2011 - No. 4, Nov, 2011 ($2.99)

1-4: 1-Robert Kirkman-s/Rob Liefeld-a; at least 11 covers. 2-Six covers 3.00

INFINITE CRISIS
DC Comics: Dec, 2005 - No. 7, Jun, 2006 ($3.99, limited series)

	GD	VG	FN	VF	VF/NM	NM-
1-Johns-s/Jimenez-a; two covers by Jim Lee and George Pérez	1	2	3	5	6	8
1-RRP Edition with Jim Lee sketch-c						100.00
2,4,6,7: 4-New Spectre; Earth-2 returns. 6-Superboy killed, new Earth formed. 7-Earth-2 Superman dies						5.00
3-1st app. Jaime Reyes	1	3	4	6	8	10
5-1st Jaime Reyes as new Blue Beetle; Earth-2 Lois Lane dies	3	6	9	17	26	35

HC (2006, $24.99, dustjacket) r/#1-7; DiDio intro.; sketch cover gallery; interview/commentary with Johns, Jimenez and editors; sketch art 25.00
... Companion TPB (2006, $14.99) r/Day of Vengeance: Infinite Crisis Special #1, Rann-Thanagar War: ICS #1, The Omac Project: ICS #1, Villains United: ICS #1 15.00
... Secret Files 2006 (4/06, $5.99) tie-in story with Earth-2 Lois and Superman, Earth-Prime Superboy and Alexander Luthor; art by various; profile pages 6.00

INFINITE CRISIS AFTERMATH (See Crisis Aftermath:...)

INFINITE CRISIS: FIGHT FOR THE MULTIVERSE (Based on the video game)
DC Comics: Sept, 2014 - No. 12, Aug, 2015 ($3.99, limited series)

1-12: 1-Abnett-s; art by various. 2-6-Polybagged 4.00

INFINITE DARK
Image Comics: Oct, 2018 - No. 8, Jul, 2019 ($3.99)

1-8-Ryan Cady-s/Andrea Mutti-a 4.00

INFINITE LOOP
IDW Publishing: Apr, 2015 - No. 6, Sept, 2015 ($3.99)

1-6-Pierrick Colinet-s/Elsa Charretier-a 4.00

INFINITE LOOP, VOLUME 2
IDW Publishing: Sept, 2017 - No. 4, Dec, 2017 ($3.99)

1-4-Colinet & Charretier-s/Di Nicuolo-a 4.00

INFINITE VACATION
Image Comics (Shadowline): Jan, 2011 - No. 5, Jan, 2013 ($3.50/$5.99)

1-4-Nick Spencer-s/Christian Ward-a/c 3.50
5-($5.99) Conclusion; gatefold centerfold 6.00

INFINITY (Crossover with the Avengers titles)
Marvel Comics: Oct, 2013 - No. 6, Jan, 2014 ($4.99/$3.99/$5.99, limited series)

1-($4.99) Avengers, Inhumans and Thanos app.; Hickman-s/Cheung-a/Adam Kubert-c 5.00
2-5-($3.99) Opeña-a. 3-Terragen bomb triggered 4.00
6-($5.99) Cheung-a 6.00
Free Comic Book Day 2013 (Infinity) 1 (5/13, giveaway) Previews series; Cheung-a 3.00

INFINITY ABYSS (Also see Marvel Universe: The End)
Marvel Comics: Aug, 2002 - No. 6, Oct, 2002 ($2.99, limited series)

1-5-Starlin-s/a; Thanos, Captain Marvel, Spider-Man, Dr. Strange app. 4.00
6-($3.50) 4.00
Thanos Vol. 2: Infinity Abyss TPB (2003, $17.99) r/ #1-6 25.00

INFINITY COUNTDOWN
Marvel Comics: May, 2018 - No. 5, Sept, 2018 ($4.99, limited series with one-shots)

1-5-Duggan-s/Kuder-a; Guardians of the Galaxy app.; Groot restored 5.00
... Adam Warlock 1 (4/18, $4.99) Prelude to series; Duggan-s/Allred-a 5.00
... Black Widow 1 (8/18, $4.99) Duggan-s/Virella-a; Jamie Braddock app. 5.00
... Captain Marvel 1 (7/18, $4.99) McCann-s/Olortegui-a; alternate Capt. Marvels app. 5.00
... Champions 1,2 (8/18, 9/18, $4.99) 1-Zub-s/Laiso-a; Warbringer & Thanos app. 5.00
... Daredevil 1 (7/18, $4.99) Duggan-s/Sprouse, Noto & Ferguson-a 5.00
... Darkhawk 1-4 (7/18 - No. 4, 9/18, $4.99) Bowers & Sims-s/Gang Lim-a 5.00
... Prime 1 (4/18, $4.99) Prelude; Duggan-s/Deodato-a; Wolverine, Magus, Ultron app. 5.00

INFINITY CRUSADE
Marvel Comics: June, 1993 - No. 6, Nov, 1993 ($3.50/$2.50, limited series, 52 pgs.)

1-6: By Jim Starlin & Ron Lim. 1-($3.50). 2-6-($2.99) 6.00

INFINITY ENTITY, THE (Concludes in Thanos: The Infinity Entity GN)
Marvel Comics: May, 2016 - No. 4, Jun, 2016 ($3.99, limited series)

1-4: Jim Starlin-s/Alan Davis-a. 1-Rebirth of Adam Warlock. 4-Mephisto app. 4.00

INFINITY GAUNTLET (The... #2 on; see Infinity Crusade, The Infinity War & Warlock & the Infinity Watch)
Marvel Comics: July, 1991 - No. 6, Dec, 1991 ($2.50, limited series)

	GD	VG	FN	VF	VF/NM	NM-
1-Thanos-c/stories in all; Starlin scripts in all	4	8	12	25	40	55
2-6: 5,6-Ron Lim-c/a	2	4	6	11	16	20
TPB (4/99, $24.95) r/#1-6						30.00

NOTE: *Lim a-3p(part), 5p, 6p; c-5i, 6i.* ***Perez*** *a-1-3p, 4p(part); c-1(painted), 2-4, 5i, 6i.*

INFINITY GAUNTLET (Secret Wars tie-in)
Marvel Comics: Jul, 2015 - No. 5, Jan, 2016 ($3.99, limited series)

1-5-Duggan & Weaver-s/Weaver-a; Thanos & The Guardians of the Galaxy app. 4.00

INFINITY: HEIST (Tie-in to the Infinity crossover)
Marvel Comics: Nov, 2013 - No. 4, Feb, 2014 ($3.99, limited series)

1-4-Tieri-s/Barrionuevo-a; Spymaster, Titanium Man, Whirlwind app. 4.00

INFINITY, INC. (See All-Star Squadron #25)
DC Comics: Mar, 1984 - No. 53, Aug, 1988 ($1.25, Baxter paper, 36 pgs.)

1-Brainwave, Jr., Fury, The Huntress, Jade, Northwind, Nuklon, Obsidian, Power Girl, Silver Scarab & Star Spangled Kid begin 5.00
2-13,38-49,51-53: 2-Dr. Midnite, G.A. Flash, W. Woman, Dr. Fate, Hourman, Green Lantern, Wildcat app. 5-Nudity panels. 13-Re-intro Rose and Thorn. 46,47-Millennium tie-ins.

Infinity Wars: Sleepwalker #4 © MAR

Inhuman #3 © MAR

Injection #6 © Ellis & Shalvey

	GD	VG	FN	VF	VF/NM	NM-
	2.0	4.0	6.0	8.0	9.0	9.2

49-Hector Hall becomes The Sandman (1970s Kirby) 3.00
14-Todd McFarlane-a (5/85, 2nd full story) 2 4 6 9 12 15
15-37-McFarlane-a (20,23,24: 5 pgs. only; 33: 2 pgs.); 18-24-Crisis x-over. 21-Intro new Hourman & Dr. Midnight. 26-New Wildcat app. 31-Star Spangled Kid becomes Skyman. 32-Green Fury becomes Green Flame. 33-Origin Obsidian. 35-1st modern app. G.A. Fury 4.00
50 ($2.50, 52 pgs.) 4.00
Annual 1,2: 1(12/85)-Crisis x-over. 2('88, $2.00), Special 1 ('87, $1.50) 4.00
...: The Generations Saga Volume One HC (2011, $39.99) r/#1-4, All-Star Squadron #25,26 & All-Star Squadron Annual #2 40.00

NOTE: ***Kubert** r-4. **McFarlane** a-14-37p, Annual 1p; c(p)-14-19, 22, 25, 26, 31-33, 37, Annual 1. **Newton** a-12p, 13p(last work 4/85). **Tuska** a-11p. JSA app. 3-10.*

INFINITY, INC. (See 52)
DC Comics: Nov, 2007 - No. 12, Oct, 2008 ($2.99)

1-12: 1-Milligan-s; Steel app. 3.00
...: Luthor's Monsters TPB (2008, $14.99) r/#1-5 15.00
...: The Bogeyman TPB (2008, $14.99) r/#6-10 15.00

INFINITY MAN AND THE FOREVER PEOPLE
DC Comics: Aug, 2014 - No. 9, May, 2015 ($2.99)

1-9: 1-DiDio-s/Giffen-a. 2,5,6-Grummett-a. 3-Starlin-a. 4-6-Guy Gardner app. 9-Giffen-a 3.00
...: Futures End 1 (11/14, $2.99, regular-c) Five years later; Philip Tan-a 3.00
...: Futures End 1 (11/14, $3.99, 3-D cover) 4.00

INFINITY: THE HUNT (Tie-in to the Infinity crossover)
Marvel Comics: Nov, 2013 - No. 4, Jan, 2014 ($3.99, limited series)

1-4-Kindt-s/Sanders-a; Avengers Academy, Wolverine & She-Hulk app. 4.00

INFINITY WAR, THE (Also see Infinity Gauntlet & Warlock and the Infinity...)
Marvel Comics: June, 1992 - No. 6, Nov, 1992 ($2.50, mini-series)

1-Starlin scripts, Lim-c/a(p), Thanos app. in all 1 3 4 6 8 10
2-6: All have wraparound gatefold covers 6.00
TPB (2006, $29.99) r/#1-6, Marvel Comics Presents #108-111, Warlock and the Infinity Watch #7-10; cover gallery and synopses of Infinity War crossovers 30.00

INFINITY WARS (Also see Infinity Countdown)
Marvel Comics: Oct, 2018 - No. 6 ($5.99/$4.99, limited series)

1-($5.99) Duggan-s/Deodato-a; Guardians of the Galaxy, Dr. Strange, Loki app. 6.00
2-5-($4.99) 3-Infinity Warps created; Deodato-a 5.00
6-($5.99) Duggan-s/Deodato-a; Adam Warlock app. 6.00
...: Fallen Guardian 1 (2/19, $4.99) MacDonald-a; takes place after #6 5.00
... Infinity 1 (3/19, $3.99) Duggan-s/Bagley-a; The fate of the Time Stone; Loki app. 4.00
... Prime 1 (9/18, $4.99) Duggan-s/Deodato-a; prelude to series; Thanos killed 5.00

INFINITY WARS: ARACHKNIGHT
Marvel Comics: Dec, 2018 - No. 2, Jan, 2019 ($3.99, limited series)

1,2-Origin of Spider-Man/Moon Knight combo; Hopeless-s/Garza-a 4.00

INFINITY WARS: GHOST PANTHER
Marvel Comics: Jan, 2019 - No. 2, Feb, 2019 ($3.99, limited series)

1,2-Origin of Ghost Rider/Black Panther combo; MacKay-s/Palo-a; Killraven app. 4.00

INFINITY WARS: INFINITY WARPS
Marvel Comics: Jan, 2019 - No. 2, Feb, 2019 ($3.99, limited series)

1,2-Short stories of Observer-X, Moon Squirrel and Tippysaur, Green Widow and others 4.00

INFINITY WARS: IRON HAMMER
Marvel Comics: Nov, 2018 - No. 2, Dec, 2018 ($3.99, limited series)

1,2-Origin of Iron Man/Thor combo; Ewing-s/Rosanas-a 4.00

INFINITY WARS: SLEEPWALKER
Marvel Comics: Dec, 2018 - No. 4, Feb, 2019 ($3.99, limited series)

1-4-Bowers & Sims-s/Nauck-a 4.00

INFINITY WARS: SOLDIER SUPREME
Marvel Comics: Nov, 2018 - No. 2, Dec, 2018 ($3.99, limited series)

1,2: 1-Origin of Captain America/Doctor Strange combo; Duggan-s/Adam Kubert-a 4.00

INFINITY WARS: WEAPON HEX
Marvel Comics: Dec, 2018 - No. 2, Jan, 2019 ($3.99, limited series)

1,2-Origin of X-23/Scarlet Witch combo; Acker & Blacker-s/Sandoval-a 4.00

INFORMER, THE
Feature Television Productions: April, 1954 - No. 5, Dec, 1954

1-Sekowsky-a begins 15 30 45 88 137 185
2 10 20 30 54 72 90
3-5 8 16 24 44 57 70

IN HIS STEPS

Spire Christian Comics (Fleming H. Revell Co.): 1973, 1977 (39/49¢)

nn 2 4 6 11 16 20

INHUMAN (Also see Uncanny Inhumans)
Marvel Comics: Jun, 2014 - No. 14, Jun, 2015 ($3.99)

1-14: 1-3-Soule-s/Madureira-a; Medusa app. 4-7,9-11-Stegman-a. 10-Spider-Man app. 4.00
Annual 1 (7/15, $4.99) Soule-s/Stegman-a; continues from #14; Ms. Marvel app. 5.00
... Special 1 (6/15, $4.99) Crossover with Amaz. Spider-Man & All-New Capt. America 5.00

INHUMANITY
Marvel Comics: Feb, 2014 - No. 2, Mar, 2014 ($3.99)

1,2: 1-After the fall of Attilan, origin of the Inhumans retold; Fraction-s/Coipel-a 4.00
...: Superior Spider-Man 1 (3/14, $3.99) Gage-s/Hans-a/c 4.00
...: The Awakening 1,2 (2/14 - No. 2, 3/14, $3.99) Kindt-s/Davidson-a 4.00

INHUMANOIDS, THE (TV)
Marvel Comics (Star Comics): Jan, 1987 - No. 4, July 1987

1-4: Based on Hasbro toys 4.00

INHUMANS, THE (See Amazing Adventures, Fantastic Four #54 & Special #5, Incredible Hulk Special #1, Marvel Graphic Novel & Thor #146)
Marvel Comics Group: Oct, 1975 - No. 12, Aug, 1977

1: #1-4,6 are 25¢ issues 6 12 18 41 76 110
2-4-Peréz-a 3 6 9 14 20 25
5-12: 9-Reprints Amazing Adventures #1,2('70). 12-Hulk app. 2 4 6 10 14 18
4-(30¢-c variant, limited distribution)(4/76) Pérez-a 4 8 12 27 44 60
6-(30¢-c variant, limited distribution)(8/76) 4 8 12 27 44 60
11,12-(35¢-c variants, limited distribution) 6 12 18 41 76 110
Special 1(4/90, $1.50, 52 pgs.)-F.F. cameo 5.00
...: The Great Refuge (5/95, $2.95) 4.00

NOTE: ***Buckler** c-2-4p, 5. **Gil Kane** a-5-7p; c-1p, 7p, 8p. **Kirby** a-9r. **Mooney** a-11i. **Perez** a-1-4p, 8p.*

INHUMANS (Marvel Knights)
Marvel Comics: Nov, 1998 - No. 12, Oct, 1999 ($2.99, limited series)

1-Jae Lee-c/a; Paul Jenkins-s 3 6 9 14 20 25
1-($6.95) DF Edition; Jae Lee variant-c 3 6 9 19 30 40
2-Two covers by Lee and Darrow 6.00
3,4,6-12 4.00
5-1st app. Yelena Belova (Black Widow) 5 10 15 33 57 80
TPB (10/00, $24.95) r/#1-12 25.00

INHUMANS (Volume 3)
Marvel Comics: Jun, 2000 - No. 4, Oct, 2000 ($2.99, limited series)

1-4-Ladronn-c/Pacheco & Marin-s. 1-3-Ladronn-a. 4-Lucas-a 3.00

INHUMANS (Volume 6)
Marvel Comics: Jun, 2003 - No. 12, Jun, 2004 ($2.50/$2.99)

1-12: 1-6-McKeever-s/Clark-a/JH Williams III-c. 7-Begin $2.99-c. 7,8-Teranishi-a 3.00
Vol. 1: Culture Shock (2005, $7.99, digest) r/#1-6; story pitch and sketch pages 8.00

INHUMANS: ATTILAN RISING (Secret Wars tie-in)
Marvel Comics: Jul, 2015 - No. 5, Nov, 2015 ($3.99, limited series)

1-5-Soule-s/Timms-a/Johnson-c 4.00

INHUMANS: JUDGMENT DAY
Marvel Comics: Mar, 2018 ($4.99, one-shot)

1-Follows from Royals #12; Al Ewing-s/Del Mundo & Libranda-a; Acuna-c 5.00

INHUMANS: ONCE AND FUTURE KINGS
Marvel Comics: Oct, 2017 - No. 5, Feb, 2018 ($3.99, limited series)

1-5: 1-Priest-s/Noto-a; young Black Bolt, Maximus & Medusa. 4-Spider-Man app. 4.00

INHUMANS PRIME
Marvel Comics: May, 2017 ($4.99, one-shot)

1-Follows IVX series; leads into Royals #1; Al Ewing-s/Ryan Sook & Chris Allen-a 5.00

INHUMANS 2099
Marvel Comics: Nov, 2004 ($2.99, one-shot)

1-Kirkman-s/Rathburn-a/Pat Lee-c 3.00

INHUMANS VS. X-MEN (See IVX)

INJECTION
Image Comics: May, 2015 - No. 15, Nov, 2017 ($2.99/$3.99)

1-10-Warren Ellis-s/Declan Shalvey-a 3.00
11-15-($3.99) 4.00

INJUSTICE: GODS AMONG US (Based on the video game)
DC Comics: Mar, 2013 - No. 12, Feb, 2014 ($3.99)

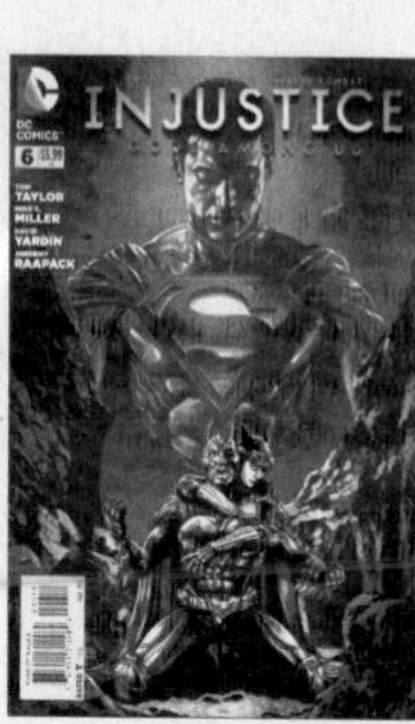
Injustice: Gods Among Us #6 © DC

Inkblot #1 © Kubert & Gladd

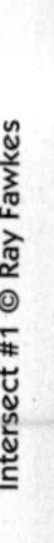
Intersect #1 © Ray Fawkes

	GD 2.0	VG 4.0	FN 6.0	VF 8.0	VF/NM 9.0	NM- 9.2
1-Lois Lane dies; Joker app.	3	6	9	19	30	40
1-Variant-c	4	8	12	23	37	50
1-Second printing						6.00
2-Joker killed						10.00
3-12: 6-Nightwing dies						4.00
Annual 1 (1/14, $4.99) Harley Quinn & Lobo app.; Ryp-c						5.00

INJUSTICE (Gods Among Us:) **YEAR TWO** (Based on the video game)
DC Comics: Mar, 2014 - No. 12, Late Nov, 2014 ($2.99)

	GD	VG	FN	VF	VF/NM	NM-
1-Sinestro app.	1	2	3	5	6	8
2-12: 2-6,9-12-Sinestro app. 7-11-Harley Quinn app.						4.00
Annual 1 (12/14, $4.99) Stories of Oracle, Green Lantern & Sinestro; Raapack-c						5.00

INJUSTICE: GODS AMONG US: YEAR THREE (Based on the video game)
DC Comics: Early Dec, 2014 - No. 12, Late May, 2015 ($2.99, printings of digital-first stories)

	NM-
1-12: 1-Constantine joins the fight. 5-New Deadman app.	3.00
Annual 1 (6/15, $4.99) Prequel to Year Three; Constantine app.; Titans vs. Superman	5.00

INJUSTICE: GODS AMONG US: YEAR FOUR (Based on the video game)
DC Comics: Early Jul, 2015 - No. 12, Late Dec, 2015 ($2.99, printings of digital-first stories)

	NM-
1-12: 1-The Olympus Gods join the fight. 10-Harley Quinn cover	3.00

INJUSTICE: GODS AMONG US: YEAR FIVE (Based on the video game)
DC Comics: Early Mar, 2016 - No. 20, Late Dec, 2016 ($2.99, printings of digital-first stories)

	NM-
1-20: 1-Doomsday & Bane app. 6-Solomon Grundy app. 7-Damian becomes Nightwing. 12-Alfred killed by Zsasz. 18-Deathstroke app.	3.00
Annual 1 (1/17, $4.99) Harley Quinn app.; leads into Injustice: Ground Zero	5.00

INJUSTICE: GROUND ZERO (Follows Year Five)
DC Comics: Early Feb, 2016 - No. 12, Jul, 2017 ($2.99, printings of digital-first stories)

	NM-
1-12: 1-Mhan & Derenick-a; Harley & Joker app. 12-Superman vs. Superman	3.00

INJUSTICE 2 (Follows Ground Zero)(Prequel to the Injustice 2 video game)
DC Comics: Early Jul, 2017 - No. 36, Dec, 2018 ($2.99, printings of digital-first stories)

	NM-
1-36: 1-Taylor-s/Redondo-a; Harley joins the Suicide Squad. 3-Intro. Athanasia. 6-Intro/origin Supergirl	3.00
Annual 1 (1/18, $4.99) Origin of Wonder Woman; back-up with Harley Quinn; Mhan-a	5.00
Annual 2 (1/19, $4.99) Follows #36; Ma & Pa Kent app.; Redondo-a	5.00

INJUSTICE VS. MASTERS OF THE UNIVERSE (Injustice: Gods Among Us)
DC Comics: Sept, 2018 - No. 6, Mar, 2019 ($3.99, limited series)

	NM-
1-6-Seeley-s/Williams II-a; Justice Leaguers & He-Man vs. Darkseid & Skeletor	4.00

INKBLOT
Image Comics: Sept, 2020 - Present ($3.99)

	NM-
1-6-Emma Kubert & Rusty Gladd-s/a	4.00

INKY & DINKY (See Felix's Nephews...)

IN LOVE (...Magazine on-c; I Love You No. 7 on)
Mainline/Charlton No. 5 (5/55)-on: Aug-Sept, 1954 - No. 6, July, 1955 ('Adult Reading' on-c)

	GD	VG	FN	VF	VF/NM	NM-
1-Simon & Kirby-a; book-length novel in all issues	61	122	183	390	670	950
2,3-S&K-a. 3-Last pre-code (12-1/54-55)	37	74	111	222	351	500
4-S&K-a.(Rare)	39	78	117	240	395	550
5-S&K-c only	21	42	63	126	206	285
6-No S&K-a	14	28	42	80	115	150

IN SEARCH OF THE CASTAWAYS (See Movie Comics)

INSEXTS
AfterShock Comics: Dec, 2015 - No. 13, Sept, 2017 ($3.99, mature)

	NM-
1-13-Marguerite Bennett-s/Ariela Kristantina-a	4.00

INSIDE CRIME (Formerly My Intimate Affair)
Fox Feature Syndicate (Hero Books): No. 3, July, 1950 - No. 2, Sept, 1950

	GD	VG	FN	VF	VF/NM	NM-
3-Wood-a (10 pgs.); L. B. Cole-c	37	74	111	220	358	495
2-Used in **SOTI**, pg. 182,183; r/Spook #24	26	52	78	156	256	355
nn (nd, M.S. Dist. Pub.) Wally Wood-c	13	26	39	72	101	130

INSPECTOR, THE (TV) (Also see The Pink Panther)
Gold Key: July, 1974 - No. 19, Feb, 1978

	GD	VG	FN	VF	VF/NM	NM-
1	3	6	9	18	28	38
2-5	2	4	6	13	18	22
6-9	2	4	6	10	14	18
10-19: 11-Reprints	2	4	6	8	10	12

INSPECTOR, THE Volume 2 (The Pink Panther)
American Mythology: 2016 ($3.99, one-shot)

	NM-
1-The Pink Files; new stories by Fridolfs & Gallagher; reprints	4.00

INSPECTOR GILL OF THE FISH POLICE (See Fish Police)

INSPECTOR WADE
David McKay Publications: No. 13, May, 1938

	GD	VG	FN	VF	VF/NM	NM-
Feature Books 13	37	74	111	222	361	500

INSTANT PIANO
Dark Horse Comics: Aug, 1994 - No. 4, Feb, 1995 ($3.95, B&W, bimonthly, mature)

	NM-
1-4	4.00

INSUFFERABLE
IDW Publishing: May, 2015 - No. 8, Dec, 2015 ($3.99)

	NM-
1-8-Waid-s/Krause-a	4.00

INSUFFERABLE: HOME FIELD ADVANTAGE
IDW Publishing: Oct, 2016 - No. 4, Jan, 2017 ($3.99)

	NM-
1-4-Waid-s/Krause-a	4.00

INSUFFERABLE: ON THE ROAD
IDW Publishing: Feb, 2016 - No. 6, Jul, 2016 ($3.99)

	NM-
1-6-Waid-s/Krause-a	4.00

INSURGENT
DC Comics: Mar, 2013 - No. 3, May, 2013 ($2.99, limited series)

	NM-
1-3-DeSanto & Farmer-s/Dallocchio-a	3.00

INTERFACE
Marvel Comics (Epic Comics): Dec, 1989 - No. 8, Dec, 1990 ($1.95, mature, coated paper)

	NM-
1-8: Cont. from 1st ESPers series; painted-c/a	3.00
Espers: Interface TPB ('98, $16.95) r/#1-6	17.00

INTERNATIONAL COMICS (...Crime Patrol No. 6)
E. C. Comics: Spring, 1947 - No. 5, Nov-Dec, 1947

	GD	VG	FN	VF	VF/NM	NM-
1-Schaffenberger-a begins, ends #4	113	226	339	723	1237	1750
2	60	120	180	381	653	925
3-5	53	106	159	334	567	800

INTERNATIONAL CRIME PATROL (Formerly International Comics #1-5; becomes Crime Patrol No. 7 on)
E. C. Comics: No. 6, Spring, 1948

	GD	VG	FN	VF	VF/NM	NM-
6-Moon Girl app.	129	258	387	826	1413	2000

INTERNATIONAL IRON MAN
Marvel Comics: May, 2016 - No. 7, Nov, 2016 ($3.99)

	NM-
1-7-Bendis-s/Maleev-a. 1-4-Flashback to college years in London. 5-Intro. Amanda Armstrong. 6,7-Flashback to Stark's real parents meeting	4.00

INTERSECT
Image Comics: Nov, 2014 - No. 6, Apr, 2015 ($3.50)

	NM-
1-6-Ray Fawkes-s/a. 1-Lemire-c. 2-Kindt-c	3.50

IN THE DAYS OF THE MOB (Magazine)
Hampshire Dist. Ltd. (National): Fall, 1971 (B&W)

	GD	VG	FN	VF	VF/NM	NM-
1-Kirby-a; John Dillinger wanted poster inside (1/2 value if poster is missing)	7	14	21	48	89	130

IN THE PRESENCE OF MINE ENEMIES
Spire Christian Comics/Fleming H. Revell Co.: 1973 (35/49¢)

	GD	VG	FN	VF	VF/NM	NM-
nn	2	4	6	11	16	20

IN THE SHADOW OF EDGAR ALLAN POE
DC Comics (Vertigo): 2002 (Graphic novel)

	NM-
Hardcover (2002, $24.95) Fuqua-s/Phillips and Parke photo-a	25.00
Softcover (2003, $17.95)	18.00

INTIMATE
Charlton Comics: Dec, 1957 - No. 3, May, 1958

	GD	VG	FN	VF	VF/NM	NM-
1	6	12	18	31	38	45
2,3	5	10	14	20	24	28

INTIMATE CONFESSIONS (See Fox Giants)

INTIMATE CONFESSIONS
Country Press Inc.: 1942

nn-Ashcan comic, not distributed to newsstands, only for in house use. A VF copy sold for $1,000 in 2007, and a VF+ copy sold for $1,525 in 2007.

INTIMATE CONFESSIONS
Realistic Comics: July-Aug, 1951 - No. 7, Aug, 1952; No. 8, Mar, 1953 (All painted-c)

	GD	VG	FN	VF	VF/NM	NM-
1-Kinstler-a; c/Avon paperback #222	219	438	657	1402	2401	3400
2	54	108	162	343	574	825
3-c/Avon paperback #250; Kinstler-c/a	55	110	165	352	601	850

4-8: 4-c/Avon paperback #304; Kinstler-c. 6-c/Avon paperback #120.

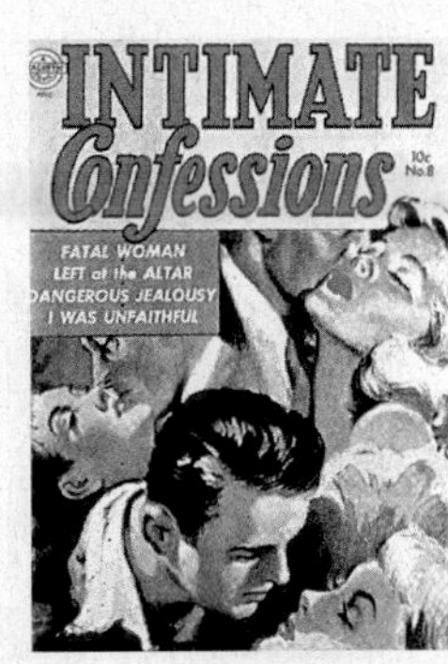

Intimate Confessions #8 © Realistic

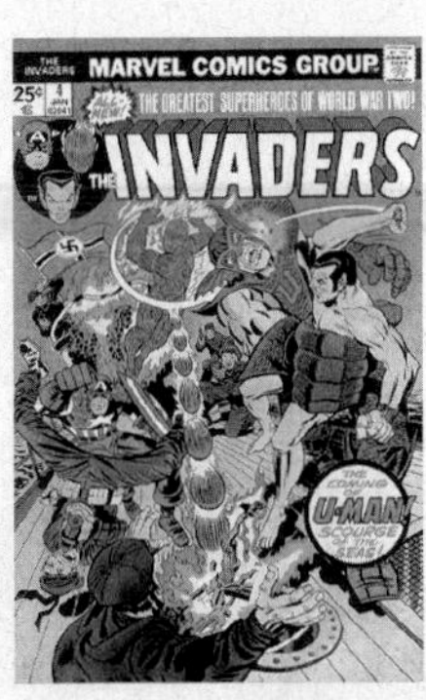

Invaders #4 © MAR

Invincible #60 © Kirkman & Walker

	GD 2.0	VG 4.0	FN 6.0	VF 8.0	VF/NM 9.0	NM- 9.2
8-c/Avon paperback #375; Kinstler-a	47	94	141	296	498	700

INTIMATE CONFESSIONS
I. W. Enterprises/Super Comics: 1964

	GD	VG	FN	VF	VF/NM	NM-
I.W. Reprint #9,10, Super Reprint #10,12,18	2	4	6	13	18	22

INTIMATE LOVE
Standard Comics: No. 5, 1950 - No. 28, Aug, 1954

	GD	VG	FN	VF	VF/NM	NM-
5-8: 6-8-Severin/Elder-a	14	28	42	81	118	155
9	11	22	33	62	86	110
10-Jane Russell, Robert Mitchum photo-c	15	30	45	94	147	200
11-18,20,23,25,27,28	10	20	30	58	79	100
19,21,22,24,26-Toth-a	11	22	33	64	90	115

NOTE: ***Celardo** a-8, 10. **Colletta** a-23. **Moreira** a-13(2). Photo-c-6, 7, 10, 12, 14, 15, 18-20, 24, 26, 27.*

INTIMATES, THE
DC Comics (WildStorm): Jan, 2005 - No. 12, Dec, 2005 ($2.95/$2.99)

1-12: 1-Joe Casey-s/Jim Lee-c/Lee and Giuseppe Camuncoli-a 3.00

INTIMATE SECRETS OF ROMANCE
Star Publications: Sept, 1953 - No. 2, Apr, 1954

	GD	VG	FN	VF	VF/NM	NM-
1,2-L. B. Cole-c	23	46	69	136	223	310

INTRIGUE
Quality Comics Group: Jan, 1955

	GD	VG	FN	VF	VF/NM	NM-
1-Horror; Jack Cole reprint/Web of Evil	41	82	123	256	428	600

INTRIGUE
Image Comics: Aug, 1999 - No. 3, Feb, 2000 ($2.50/$2.95)

1,2: 1-Two covers (Andrews, Wieringo); Shum-s/Andrews-a 3.00
3-($2.95) 3.00

INTRUDER
TSR, Inc.: 1990 - No. 10, 1991 ($2.95, 44 pgs.)

1-10 4.00

INVADERS, THE (TV)(Aliens From a Dying Planet)
Gold Key: Oct, 1967 - No. 4, Oct, 1968 (All have photo-c)

	GD	VG	FN	VF	VF/NM	NM-
1-Spiegle-a in all	9	18	27	60	120	180
2-4: 2-Pin-up on back-c. 3-Has variant 15¢-c with photo back-c	6	12	18	37	66	95

INVADERS, THE (Also see The Avengers #71, Giant-Size Invaders, and All-New Invaders)
Marvel Comics Group: August, 1975 - No. 40, May, 1979; No. 41, Sept, 1979

	GD	VG	FN	VF	VF/NM	NM-
1-Captain America & Bucky, Human Torch & Toro, & Sub-Mariner begin; cont'd. from Giant Size Invaders #1; #1-7 are 25¢ issues	6	12	18	41	76	110
2-5: 2-1st app. Brain-Drain. 3-Battle issue; Cap vs. Namor vs. Torch; intro U-Man	3	6	9	19	30	40
6-10: 6,7-(Regular 25¢ edition). 6-(7/76) Liberty Legion app. 7-Intro Baron Blood & intro/1st app. Union Jack; Human Torch origin retold. 8-Union Jack-c/story. 9-Origin Baron Blood. 10-G.A. Capt. America-r/C.A #22	2	4	6	11	16	20
6-(30¢-c variant, limited distribution)	5	10	15	35	63	90
7-(30¢-c variant, limited distribution)	10	20	30	64	132	200
11-19: 11-Origin Spitfire; intro The Blue Bullet. 14-1st app. The Crusaders. 16-Re-intro The Destroyer. 17-Intro Warrior Woman. 18-Re-intro The Destroyer w/new origin. 19-Hitler-c/story	2	4	6	8	11	14
17-19,21-(35¢-c variants, limited distribution)	10	20	30	65	135	205
20-(Regular 30¢-c) Reprints origin/1st app. Sub-Mariner from Motion Picture Funnies Weekly with color added & brief write-up about MPFW; 1st app. new Union Jack II	3	6	9	14	20	26
20-(35¢-c variant, limited distribution)	11	22	33	76	163	250
21-(Regular 30¢ edition)-r/Marvel Mystery #10 (battle issue)	2	4	6	9	13	16
22-30,34-40: 22-New origin Toro. 24-r/Marvel Mystery #17 (team-up issue; all-r). 25-All new-a begins. 28-Intro new Human Top & Golden Girl. 29-Intro Teutonic Knight. 34-Mighty Destroyer joins. 35-The Whizzer app.	1	2	3	5	7	9
31-33: 31-Frankenstein-c/sty. 32,33-Thor app.	2	4	6	8	11	14
41-Double size last issue	3	6	9	15	22	28
Annual 1 (9/77)-Schomburg, Rico stories (new); Schomburg-c/a (1st for Marvel in 30 years); Avengers app.; re-intro The Shark & The Hyena	5	10	15	33	57	80

... Classic Vol. 1 TPB (2007, $24.99) r/#1-9, Giant-Size Invaders #1 and Marvel Premiere #29,30; cover pencils and cover inks 25.00

NOTE: ***Buckler** a-5. **Everett** r-20('39), 21(1940), 24, Annual 1. **Gil Kane** c(p)-13, 17, 18, 20-27. **Kirby** c(p)-3-12, 14-16, 32, 33. **Mooney** a-5i, 16, 22. **Robbins** a-1-4, 6-9, 10(3 pg.), 11-15, 17-21, 23, 25-28; c-28.*

INVADERS (See Namor, the Sub-Mariner #12)
Marvel Comics Group: May, 1993 - No. 4, Aug, 1993 ($1.75, limited series)

1-4 4.00

INVADERS (2004 title - see New Invaders)

INVADERS
Marvel Comics: Mar, 2019 - No. 12, Feb, 2020 ($4.99/$3.99)

1-($4.99) Zdarsky-s/Magno & Guice-a; Captain America, Namor & Winter Soldier 5.00
2-12-($3.99) 2-Hydro-Man app. 5-7-Avengers app. 4.00

INVADERS FROM HOME
DC Comics (Piranha Press): 1990 - No. 6, 1990 ($2.50, mature)

1-6 3.00

INVADERS NOW! (See Avengers/Invaders and The Torch series)
Marvel Comics: Nov, 2010 - No. 5, Mar, 2011 ($3.99, limited series)

1-5-Alex Ross-c; Steve Rogers, Bucky, Human Torch & Toro, Sub-Mariner app. 4.00

INVADER ZIM
Oni Press: Jul, 2015 - Present ($3.99)

1-Jhonen Vasquez-s/Aaron Alexovich-a; multiple covers 4.00
2-49: 40-Multiverse Zims; short stories by various 4.00
50-($6.99) Vasquez & Trueheart-s/Wucinich-a 7.00
... #1 Square One Edition (2/17, $1.00) r/#1 3.00
...: Free Comic Book Day Edition (5/18, giveaway) r/#20; Floopsy & Shmoopsy app. 3.00;

INVADER ZIM QUARTERLY
Oni Press: Jun, 2020 - Present ($5.99)

...Dib's Dilemma 1 (9/20, $5.99) Logan-s/Wucinich-a; multiple covers 6.00
...Gir's Big Day 1 (6/20, $5.99) Eric Trueheart-s/Aaron Alexovich-a; multiple covers 6.00

INVASION
DC Comics: Holiday, 1988-'89 - No. 3, Jan, 1989 ($2.95, lim. series, 84 pgs.)

1-3: 1-McFarlane/Russell-a. 2-McFarlane/Russell & Giffen/Gordon-a 5.00
Invasion! TPB (2008, $24.99) r/#1-3 25.00

INVINCIBLE (Also see The Pact #4)
Image Comics: Jan, 2003 - No. 144, Feb, 2018 ($2.95/$2.99)

	GD	VG	FN	VF	VF/NM	NM-
1-Kirkman-s/Walker-a	25	50	75	175	388	600
2-Kirkman-s/Walker-a	5	10	15	35	63	90
3-Kirkman-s/Walker-a	3	6	9	21	33	45
4-8: 4-Preview of The Moth	2	4	6	10	14	18
9-14: 11-Origin of Omni-Man. 14-Cho-c	1	2	3	5	6	8
15-24,26-41,43-49: 33-Tie-in w/Marvel Team-Up #14						5.00
25-($4.95) Science Dog app.; back-up stories w/origins of Science Dog and teammates						6.00
42-($1.99) Includes re-cap of the entire series						5.00
50-(6/08, $4.99) Two covers; back-up origin of Cecil Stedman; Science Dog app.	1	3	4	6	8	10
51-59,61-74: 51-Jim Lee-c; new costumes. 57-Continues in Astounding Wolf-Man #11. 71-74-Viltrumite War						4.00
76-99,101-109,111-117: 89-Intro. Zandale. 97-Origin of Bulletproof. 112-Baby born						3.00
60-($3.99) Invincible War; Witchblade, Savage Dragon, Spawn, Youngblood app.	1	2	3	5	6	8
75-($5.99) Viltrumite War; Science Dog back-up; 2 covers	1	3	4	6	8	10
100-(1/13, $3.99) "The Death of Everyone" conclusion; multiple covers						5.00
110-Rape issue						6.00
118-141: 118-(25¢-c). 124-126-Reboot. 132-Oliver dies. 133-(25¢-c) Mark & Eve wedding						3.00
142-143-($3.99)						4.00
144-($5.99) Last issue; art by Ottley & Walker						6.00
#0-(4/05, 50¢) Origin of Invincible; Ottley-a						3.00
Image Firsts: Invincible #1 (4/10, $1.00) r/#1 with "Image Firsts" cover logo						3.00
Official Handbook of the Invincible Universe 1,2 (11/06, 1/07, $4.99) profile pages						5.00
Official Handbook of the Invincible Universe Vol. 1 (2007, $12.99) r/#1-2; sketch pages						13.00
... Presents Atom Eve 1,2 (12/07, 3/08, $2.99) origin of Atom Eve; Bellegarde-a						3.00
... Presents Atom Eve & Rex Splode 1-3 (10/09 - 2/10, $2.99) origin of Rex						3.00
... Returns (4/10, $3.99) Leads into Viltrumite War in #71; 4 covers						4.00
... Universe Primer 1 (5/08, $5.99) r/Invincible #1, Brit #1, Astounding Wolf-Man #1						6.00
The Complete Invincible Library Vol. 1 Slipcase HC (2006, $125.00) oversized r/#1-24, #0 and story from Image Comics Summer Special (FCBD 2004); sketch pages; script for #1						125.00
..., Ultimate Collection Vol. 1 HC (2005, $34.95) oversized r/#1-13; sketch pages						35.00
..., Ultimate Collection Vol. 2 HC (2006, $34.99) oversized r/#14-24, #0 and story from Image Comics Summer Special (FCBD 2004); sketch pages and script for #23; intro by Damon Lindelof; afterword by Robert Kirkman						35.00
..., Ultimate Collection Vol. 3 HC (2007, $34.95) oversized r/#25-35 & The Pact #4; sketch pages and script for #28; afterword by Robert Kirkman						35.00
..., Ultimate Collection Vol. 4 HC (2008, $34.99) oversized r/#36-47; sketch & script pgs.						35.00
Vol. 1: Family Matters TPB (8/03, $12.95) r/#1-4; intro. by Busiek; sketch pages						13.00
Vol. 2: Eight in Enough TPB (3/04, $12.95) r/#5-8; intro. by Larsen; sketch pages						13.00
Vol. 3: Perfect Strangers TPB (2004, $12.95) r/#9-12; intro. by Brevoort; sketch pages						13.00
Vol. 4: Head of the Class TPB (1/05, $14.95) r/#14-19; intro. by Waid; sketch pages						15.00
Vol. 5: The Facts of Life TPB (2005, $14.99) r/#0,20-24; intro. by Wieringo; sketch pages						15.00

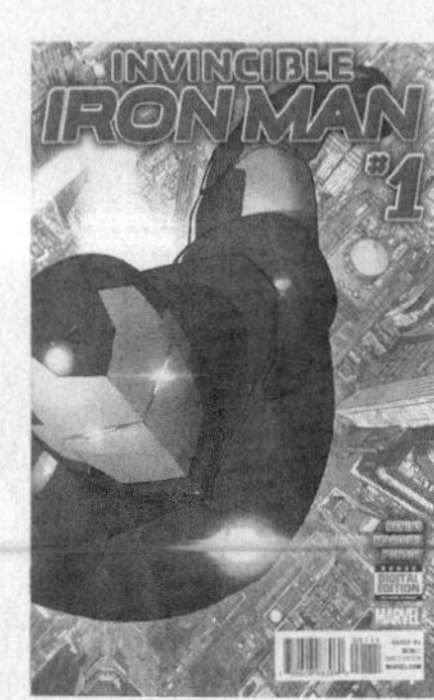

Invincible Iron Man #1 © MAR

The Invisibles #9 © Grant Morrison

Iron Fist #10 © MAR

GD VG FN VF VF/NM NM-
2.0 4.0 6.0 8.0 9.0 9.2

Vol. 6: A Different World TPB (2006, $14.99) r/#25-30; intro. by Brubaker; sketch pages 15.00
Vol. 7: Three's Company TPB (2006, $14.99) r/#31-35 & The Pact #4; sketch pages 15.00
Vol. 8: My Favorite Martian TPB (2007, $14.99) r/#36-41; sketch pages 15.00
Vol. 9: Out of This World TPB (2008, $14.99) r/#42-47; sketch pages 15.00

INVINCIBLE FOUR OF KUNG FU & NINJA
Leung Publications: April, 1988 - No. 6, 1989 ($2.00)

1-($2.75) 4.00
2-6: 2-Begin $2.00-c 3.00

INVINCIBLE IRON MAN
Marvel Comics: July, 2008 - No. 33, Feb, 2011;
No. 500, Mar, 2011 - No. 527, Dec, 2012 ($2.99/$3.99)

1-Fraction-s/Larroca-a; covers by Larroca & Quesada 5.00
1-Downey movie photo wraparound 6.00
1-Secret Movie Variant white-c with movie cast 30.00
2-18: 2-War Machine and Thor app. 7-Spider-Man app. 8-10-Dark Reign. 11-War Machine app.; Pepper gets her armor suit. 12-Namor app. 3.00
19,20-($3.99) 20-Stark Disassembled starts; back-up synopsis of recent storylines 4.00
21-24-Covers by Larocca and Zircher: 21-Thor & Capt. America app. 22-Dr. Strange app. 3.00
25-($3.99) Fraction-s/Larroca-a; new armor 4.00
26-31-($2.99) 29-New Rescue armor 3.00
32,33-($3.99)-War Machine app.; back-up w/McKelvie-a 4.00

(After #33, numbering reverts to original Vol. 1 as #500)

500-(3/11, $4.99) Two covers by Larroca; Mandarin & Spider-Man app.; cover gallery 5.00
500-Variant-c by Romita Jr. 10.00
500.1 (4/11, $2.99) History re-told; Fraction-s/Larroca-a/c 3.00
501-527-($3.99) 501-503-Doctor Octopus app. 503-Back-up w/Chaykin-a. 504-509-Fear Itself tie-in; Grey Gargoyle app. 517-New War Machine armor 4.00
Annual 1 (8/10, $4.99) Larroca-c; history of the Mandarin; Di Giandomenico-a 5.00
...MGC #1 (4/10, free) r/#1 with "Marvel's Greatest Comics" cover logo 3.00

INVINCIBLE IRON MAN
Marvel Comics: Dec, 2015 - No. 14, Dec, 2016 ($3.99)

1-6,8,10-14: 1-Bendis-s/Marquez-a; Doctor Doom & Madame Masque app. 6-14-Deodato-a. 8-Spider-Man app. 11-14-Civil War II tie-in 4.00
7-1st app. Riri Williams (cameo); Spider-Man app. 6 12 18 38 69 100
9-1st full app. of Riri Williams 7 14 21 46 86 125

INVINCIBLE IRON MAN (Riri Williams as Ironheart)
Marvel Comics: Jan, 2017 - No. 11, Nov, 2017 ($3.99)

1-11: 1-Bendis-s/Caselli-a; Riri Williams childhood origin; Animax app. 4.00

INVINCIBLE IRON MAN (Marvel Legacy)(Also continued from Infamous Iron Man)
Marvel Comics: No. 593, Dec, 2017 - No. 600, Jul, 2018 ($3.99)

593-599-Bendis-s/Caselli & Maleev-a; Ironheart & Doctor Doom app. 4.00
600-($5.99) James Rhodes returns; leads into Tony Stark: Iron Man series 6.00

INVINCIBLE UNIVERSE (Characters from Invincible)
Image Comics: Apr, 2013 - No. 12, Apr, 2014 ($2.99)

1-12-Hester-s/Nauck-a. 1-Wraparound-c 3.00

INVISIBLE BOY (See Approved Comics)

INVISIBLE KINGDOM
Dark Horse Comics (Berger Books): Mar, 2019 - Present ($3.99)

1-10-G. Willow Wilson-s/Christian Ward-a 4.00

INVISIBLE MAN, THE (See Superior Stories #1 & Supernatural Thrillers #2)

INVISIBLE PEOPLE
Kitchen Sink Press: 1992 (B&W, lim. series)

Book One: Sanctum; Book Two: "The Power": Will Eisner-s/a in all 4.00
Book Three: "Mortal Combat" 4.00
Hardcover ($34.95) 35.00
TPB (DC Comics, 9/00, $12.95) reprints series 13.00

INVISIBLE REPUBLIC
Image Comics: Feb, 2015 - No. 15, Mar, 2017 ($2.99/$3.99)

1-10-Hardman & Bechko-s/Hardman-a 3.00
11-15-($3.99) 4.00

INVISIBLES, THE (1st Series)
DC Comics (Vertigo): Sept, 1994 - No. 25, Oct, 1996 ($1.95/$2.50, mature)

1-($2.95, 52 pgs.)-Intro King Mob, Ragged Robin, Boy, Lord Fanny & Dane (Jack Frost); Grant Morrison scripts in all 1 3 4 6 8 10
2-8: 4-Includes bound-in trading cards. 5-1st app. Orlando; brown paper-c 4.00
9-25: 10-Intro Jim Crow. 13-15-Origin Lord Fanny. 19-Origin King Mob; polybagged. 20-Origin Boy. 21-Mister Six revealed. 25-Intro Division X 3.00
Apocalipstick (2001, $19.95, TPB)-r/#9-16; Bolland-c 20.00

GD VG FN VF VF/NM NM-
2.0 4.0 6.0 8.0 9.0 9.2

Entropy in the U.K. (2001, $19.95, TPB)-r/#17-25; Bolland-c 20.00
Say You Want A Revolution (1996, $17.50, TPB)-r/#1-8 18.00
NOTE: ***Buckingham** a-25p. **Rian Hughes** c-1, 5. **Phil Jimenez** a-17p-19p. **Paul Johnson** a-16, 21. **Sean Phillips** c-2-4, 6-25. **Weston** a-10p. **Yeowell** a-1p-4p, 22p-24p.*

INVISIBLES, THE (2nd Series)
DC Comics (Vertigo): V2#1, Feb, 1997 - No. 22, Feb, 1999 ($2.50, mature)

1-Intro Jolly Roger; Grant Morrison scripts, Phil Jimenez-a, & Brian Bolland-c begins 6.00
2-22: 9,14-Weston-a 4.00
Bloody Hell in America TPB ('98, $12.95) r/#1-4 13.00
Counting to None TPB ('99, $19.95) r/#5-13 20.00
Kissing Mr. Quimper TPB ('00, $19.95) r/#14-22 20.00

INVISIBLES, THE (3rd Series) (Issue #'s go in reverse from #12 to #1)
DC Comics (Vertigo): V3#12, Apr, 1999 - No. 1, June, 2000 ($2.95, mature)

1-12-Bolland-c; Morrison-s on all. 1-Quitely-a. 2-4-Art by various. 5-8-Phillips-a. 9-12-Phillip Bond-a. 4.00
The Invisible Kingdom TPB ('02, $19.95) r/#12-1; new Bolland-c 20.00

INVISIBLE SCARLET O'NEIL (Also see Famous Funnies #81 & Harvey Comics Hits #59)
Famous Funnies (Harvey): Dec, 1950 - No. 3, Apr, 1951 (2-3 pgs. of Powell-a in each issue.)

1 24 48 72 142 234 325
2,3 17 34 51 105 165 225

INVISIBLE WOMAN (Fantastic Four)
Marvel Comics: Sept, 2019 - No. 5, Jan, 2020 ($3.99, limited series)

1-5-Mark Waid-s/Mattia De Iulis-a; main cover by Adam Hughes; Black Widow app. 4.00

ION (Green Lantern Kyle Rayner) (See Countdown)
DC Comics: Jun, 2006 - No. 12, May, 2007 ($2.99)

1-12: 1-Marz-s/Tocchini-a. 3-Mogo app. 9,10-Tangent Green Lantern app. 12-Monitor app. 3.00
...: The Torchbearer TPB (2007, $14.99) r/#1-6 15.00

I, PAPARAZZI
DC Comics (Vertigo): 2001 ($29.95, HC, digitally manipulated photographic art)

nn-Pat McGreal-s/Steven Parke-digital-a/Stephen John Phillips-photos 30.00

IRON AGE
Marvel Comics: Aug, 2011 - No. 3, Oct, 2011 ($4.99, limited series)

1-3-Iron Man time travels. 1-Avengers. 2-Fantastic Four. 3-Dazzler & X-Men 5.00
...: Alpha (8/11, $2.99) First part of the series; Dark Phoenix app.; Issacs-a 3.00
...: Omega (10/11, $2.99) Conclusion of the series; Olivetti-c/Issacs-a 3.00

IRON AND THE MAIDEN
Aspen MLT: Sept, 2007 - No. 4, Dec, 2007 ($3.99)

1-4: 1-Two covers by Manapul and Madureira/Matsuda; Jason Rubin-s 4.00
...: Brutes, Bims and the City (2/08, $2.99) character backgrounds/development art 3.00

IRON CORPORAL, THE (See Army War Heroes #22)
Charlton Comics: No. 23, Oct, 1985 - No. 25, Feb, 1986

23-25: Glanzman-a(r); low print 6.00

IRON FIST (See Immortal Iron Fist, Deadly Hands of Kung Fu, Marvel Premiere & Power Man)
Marvel Comics: Nov, 1975 - No. 15, Sept, 1977

	GD 2.0	VG 4.0	FN 6.0	VF 8.0	VF/NM 9.0	NM- 9.2
1-Iron Fist battles Iron Man (#1-6: 25¢)	9	18	27	60	120	180
2	4	8	12	28	47	65
3-10: 4-6-(Regular 25¢ edition)(4-6/76). 8-Origin retold	3	6	9	19	30	40
4-6-(30¢-c variant, limited distribution)	6	12	18	41	76	100
11,13: 13-(30¢-c)	3	6	9	16	24	32
12-Capt. America app.	5	10	15	35	63	90
13-(35¢-c variant, limited distribution)	16	32	48	107	236	365
14-1st app. Sabretooth (8/77)(see Power Man)	20	40	60	140	310	480
14-(35¢-c variant, limited distribution)	159	318	477	1312	2956	4600
15-(Regular 30¢ ed.) X-Men app., Byrne-a	6	12	18	41	76	110
15-(35¢-c variant, limited distribution)	57	114	171	456	1028	1600

NOTE: ***Adkins** a-8p, 10i, 13i; c-8i. **Byrne** a-1-15p; c-8p, 15p. **G. Kane** c-4-6p. **McWilliams** a-1i.*

IRON FIST
Marvel Comics: Sept, 1996 - No. 2, Oct, 1996 ($1.50, limited series)

1,2 4.00

IRON FIST
Marvel Comics: Jul, 1998 - No. 3, Sept, 1998 ($2.50, limited series)

1-3: Jurgens-s/Guice-a 4.00

IRON FIST (Also see Immortal Iron Fist)
Marvel Comics: May, 2004 - No. 6, Oct, 2004 ($2.99)

1-6: 1-4,6-Kevin Lau-c/a. 5-Mays-c/a 4.00

IRON FIST

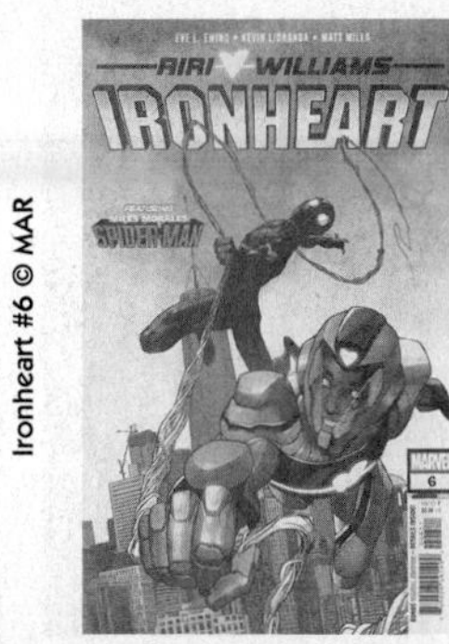

Ironheart #6 © MAR

Iron Man #10 © MAR

Iron Man #110 © MAR

	GD	VG	FN	VF	VF/NM	NM-
	2.0	4.0	6.0	8.0	9.0	9.2

Marvel Comics: May, 2017 - No. 7, Nov, 2017; No. 73, Dec, 2017 - No. 80, Jun, 2018 ($3.99)

1-7: 1-Brisson-s/Perkins-a. 4.00

[Title switches to legacy numbering after #7 (11/17)]

73-80: 73-77-Sabretooth app. 78-80-Damnation x-over; Orson Randall app. 4.00

IRON FIST: HEART OF THE DRAGON
Marvel Comics: Mar, 2021 - No. 6 ($3.99)

1,2-Hama-s/Wachter-a; Luke Cage, Taskmaster, and Lady Bullseye app. 4.00

IRON FIST: PHANTOM LIMB (Printing of digital-first story)
Marvel Comics: 2018 ($19.99, square-bound TPB)

nn-Chapman-s/Sanna-a; Luke Cage app. 20.00

IRON FIST: THE LIVING WEAPON
Marvel Comics: Jun, 2014 - No. 12, Jul, 2015 ($3.99)

1-12-Kaare Andrews-s/a/c; origin re-told in flashbacks 4.00

IRON FIST: WOLVERINE
Marvel Comics: Nov, 2000 - No. 4, Feb, 2001 ($2.99, limited series)

1-4-Igle-c/a; Kingpin app. 2-Iron Man app. 3,4-Capt. America app. 4.00

IRON GHOST
Image Comics: Apr, 2005 - No. 6, Mar, 2006 ($2.95/$2.99, limited series)

1-6-Chuck Dixon-s/Sergio Cariello-a; flip cover on each 3.00

IRONHAND OF ALMURIC (Robert E. Howard's...)
Dark Horse Comics: Aug, 1991 - No. 4, 1991 ($2.00, B&W, mini-series)

1-4: 1-Conrad painted-c 3.00

IRONHEART (Riri Williams) (See Invincible Iron Man #7)
Marvel Comics: Jan, 2019 - No. 12, Jan, 2020 ($4.99/$3.99)

1-($4.99) Eve L. Ewing-s/Libranda & Vecchio-a; Clash app. 5.00
2-12-($3.99) 6-Miles (Spider-Man) app. 7,8-Nadia (Wasp) app. 8-Dr. Strange app. 4.00

IRON HORSE (TV)
Dell Publishing Co.: March, 1967 - No. 2, June, 1967

1-Dale Robertson photo covers on both 3 6 9 17 26 35
2 3 6 9 15 21 26

IRONJAW (Also see The Barbarians)
Atlas/Seaboard Publ.: Jan, 1975 - No. 4, July, 1975

1,2-Neal Adams-c. 1-1st app. Iron Jaw; Sekowsky-a(p); Fleisher-s
3 6 9 15 22 28
3,4-Marcos. 4-Origin 2 4 6 9 13 16

IRON LANTERN
Marvel Comics (Amalgam): June, 1997 ($1.95, one-shot)

1-Kurt Busiek-s/Paul Smith & Al Williamson-a 4.00

IRON MAIDEN LEGACY OF THE BEAST
Heavy Metal Inc.: Oct, 2017 - No. 5 ($3.99, limited series)

1-Llexi Leon & Edginton-s/West-a/Casas-c; Eddie app. 4.00

IRON MAN (Also see The Avengers #1, Giant-Size..., Marvel Collectors Item Classics, Marvel Double Feature, Marvel Fanfare, Tales of Suspense #39 & Uncanny Tales #52)
Marvel Comics: May, 1968 - No. 332, Sept, 1996

1-Origin; Colan-c/a(p); story continued from Iron Man & Sub-Mariner #1
160 320 480 960 1480 2000
2 13 26 39 91 201 310
3-Iron Man vs. The Freak 10 20 30 70 150 230
4,5: 4-Unicorn app. 9 18 27 57 111 165
6-10: 7,8-Gladiator app. 9-Iron Man battles green Hulk-like android. 9,10-The Mandarin app.
7 14 21 46 86 125
11-15: 10,11-Mandarin app. 12-1st app. Controller. 15-Last 12¢ issue; vs Unicorn and the Red Ghost 6 12 18 38 69 100
16,18-20: 16-Vs. Unicorn and the Red Ghost. 18-Avengers app. 19-Captain America app. 5 10 15 31 53 75
17-1st Madame Masque & Midas (Mordecai Midas) 7 14 21 46 86 125
21-24,26-30: 21-Crimson Dynamo app. 22-Death of Janice Cord; Crimson Dynamo app. 27-Intro Firebrand. 28-Controller app. 4 8 12 25 40 55
25-Iron Man battles Sub-Mariner 5 10 15 34 60 85
31-42: 33-1st app. Spymaster. 35-Daredevil & Nick Fury vs. Zodiak; x-over w/Daredevil #73. 36-Daredevil & Nick Fury vs Zodiak. 39-Avengers app. 42-Last 15¢ issue
3 6 9 21 33 45
43-Intro the Guardsman (25¢ Giant, 52 pgs); Giant-Man back-up (r) from TTA #52
6 12 18 38 69 100
44-46,48-53: 44-Capt. America app; back-up Ant-Man w/Andru-a. 46-The Guardsman dies. 48-Firebrand app. 49-Super-Adaptoid app. 50-Princess Python app. 53-1st Black Lama; Starlin part pencils 3 6 9 18 30 40
47-Origin retold; Barry Smith-a(p) 10 20 30 64 132 200
54-Iron Man battles Sub-Mariner; 1st app. Moondragon (1/73) as Madame MacEvil; Everett part-c 14 28 42 94 207 320
55-1st app. Thanos, Drax the Destroyer, Mentor, Starfox & Kronos (2/73); Starlin-c/a
125 250 375 750 1175 1600
56-Starlin-a 5 10 15 33 57 80
57-63: 57,58-Mandarin and Unicorn app. 59-Firebrand app. 60,61-Vs. the Masked Marauder. 62-Whiplash app. 63-Vs. Dr. Spectrum 3 6 9 16 24 32
64,65,67-70: 64,65-Dr. Spectrum app; origin is #65; Thor brief app. 67-Last 20¢ issue. 68-Sunfire, Mandarin and Unicorn app. 69,70-Mandarin, Yellow Claw & Ultimo app.
3 6 9 14 20 25
66-Iron Man vs. Thor. 5 10 15 31 53 75
71-84: 71-Yellow Claw & Black Lama app. 72-Black Lama app; Iron Man at the San Diego Comic Con. 73-Vs. Crimson Dynamo & Radioactive Man; Stark Industries renamed Stark International. 74-Modok vs. Mad-Thinker; Black Lama app in "War of the Super-Villains". 75-Black Lama & Yellow Claw app. 76-r/#9. 77-Conclusion of the "War of the Super-Villains"; Black Lama app. 80-Origin of Black Lama. 81-Black Lama & Firebrand app. 82,83-Red Ghost app. 2 4 6 10 14 18
85-89-(Regular 25¢ editions): 86-1st app. Blizzard. 87-Origin Blizzard. 88-Brief Thanos cameo. 89-Daredevil app.; last 25¢-c 2 4 6 10 14 18
85-89-(30¢-c variants, limited distribution)(4-8/76) 6 12 18 37 66 95
90-99: 90,91-Blood Brothers & Controller app. 92-Vs. Melter. 95-Ultimo app. 96-1st new Guardsman (Michael O' Brien). 98,99-Mandarin & Sunfire app.
2 4 6 9 12 15
99,101-103-(35¢-c variants, limited dist.) 12 24 36 82 179 275
100-(7/77)-Starlin-c; Iron Man vs. The Mandarin 4 8 12 27 44 60
100-(35¢-c variant, limited dist.) 27 54 81 189 420 650
101-117: 101-Intro DreadKnight; Frankenstein app. 103-Jack of Hearts app; guest stars through issue #113. 104-107-Vs. Midas. 109-1st app. New Crimson Dynamo; 1st app. Vanguard. 110-Origin Jack of Hearts retold; death of Count Nefaria. 113,114-Unicorn and Titanium Man app. 114,115-Avengers app; 1st John Romita Jr. pencils on Iron Man (10/78). 116-1st David Michelinie & Bob Layton issue 2 4 6 8 10 12
118-Byrne-a(p); 1st app. Jim Rhodes 5 10 15 33 57 80
119,122-124,127: 122-Origin. 123-128-Tony treated for alcohol problem. 123,124-Vs. Blizzard, Melter & Whiplash; Justin Hammer app. 127-Vs. Justin Hammer's "Super-Villain army"
2 4 6 11 16 20
120,121,126: 120,121-Sub-Mariner app. 126-Classic Tony becoming Iron Man-c
2 4 6 13 19 25
125-Avengers & Ant-Man (Scott Lang) app. 3 6 9 16 23 30
128-(11/79) Classic Tony Stark alcoholism cover 6 12 18 41 76 110
129,130,134-149: 134,135-Titanium Man app. 137-139-Spymaster app. 142-Intro. Space Armor. 143-1st app. Sunturion. 146 Backlash app. (formally Whiplash). 148-Captain America app. 149-Dr. Doom app. 1 2 3 5 7 9
131-133: 131,132-Hulk x-over. 133-Hulk/Ant Man-c 2 4 6 9 12 15
150-Double size; Dr. Doom; Merlin & Camelot 3 6 9 14 20 26
151-168: 151-Ant-Man (Scott Lang) app. 152-1st app stealth armor. 153-Living Laser app; last Layton co-plot (returns in #215). 154-Unicorn app. 156-Intro the Mauler; last Michelinie plot (returns in issue #215); last Romita Jr. art (p). 159-Paul Smith-a(p); Fantastic Four app. 160-Serpent Squad app. 161-Moon Knight app. 163-Intro. Obadiah Stane (hand only). 166-1st full app. Obadiah Stane. 167-Tony Stark alcohol problem resurfaces. 168-Machine Man app. 1 2 3 5 6 8
169-New Iron Man (Jim Rhodes replaces Tony Stark) 2 4 6 9 12 15
170-199: 172-Captain America x-over. 180-181-Vs. Mandarin. 191-198-Tony Stark returns as original Iron Man. 197-Secret Wars II x-over; Byrne-c 6.00
200-(11/85, $1.25, 52 pgs.)-Tony Stark returns as new Iron Man (red & white armor) thru #230 2 4 6 13 18 22
201-213,215-224: 206-Hawkeye & Mockingbird app. 219-Intro. The Ghost. 220-Spymaster & Ghost app. 224-Vs. Beetle, Backlash, Blizzard & Justin Hammer 5.00
214-Spider-Woman (Julia Carpenter) app. in new black costume (1/87) 6.00
225-(12/87, $1.25, 40 pgs)- Armor Wars begins; Ant-Man app.
2 4 6 8 10 12
226-227,229-230: Armor Wars in all. 226-West Coast Avengers app. 227-Beetle app.; Iron Man vs SHIELD Mandroids. 229-Vs. Crimson Dynamo & Titanium Man. 230-Armor Wars conclusion; vs Firepower 5.00
228-Armor Wars; Iron Man vs. Captain America (as the Captain) 6.00
231,234,247: 231-Intro. new Iron Man armor. 234-Spider-Man x-over. 247-Hulk x-over 5.00
232,233,235-243,245,246,248,249: 232-Barry Windsor Smith co-plot and (p). 233-Ant-Man app. 235,236-Vs. Grey Gargoyle. 238-Rhino & Capt. America app. 239,240-Vs. Justin Hammer. 241,242-Mandarin app. 243-Tony Stark loses use of legs. 249-Dr. Doom app. 4.00
244-($1.50, 52 pgs.)-New Armor makes him walk 5.00
250-($1.50, 52 pgs.)-Dr. Doom-c/story; Acts of Vengeance x-over; last Michelinie/Layton issue
5.00
251-274,276-281,283,285-287,289,292-299: 255-Intro new Crimson Dynamo (Valenyine Shatalov). 258-Byrne script & Romita Jr.-a(p) begins. 261-264-Mandarin & Fin Fang Foom app. 290-James Rhodes retains the War Machine armor. 292-Capt. America app.

Iron Man #308 © MAR

Iron Man V3 #17 © MAR

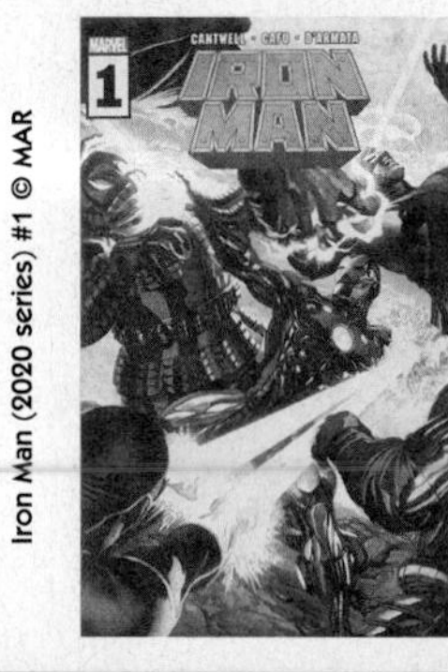

Iron Man (2020 series) #1 © MAR

GD 2.0 | VG 4.0 | FN 6.0 | VF 8.0 | VF/NM 9.0 | NM- 9.2

295-Infinity Crusade x-over. 296,297-Omega Red app. 298,299-Return of Ultimo 4.00
275-($1.50, 52 pgs.) Mandarin & Fin Fang Foom app. 5.00
282-1st full app. War Machine (7/92) 6 12 18 38 69 100
284-Death of Iron Man (Tony Stark); James Rhodes becomes War Machine 1 2 3 5 6 8
288-($2.50, 52pg.)-Silver foil stamped-c; Iron Man's 350th app. in comics 5.00
290-($2.95, 52pg.)-Gold foil stamped-c; 30th ann. 5.00
291-Iron Man & War Machine team-up 5.00
300-($3.95, 68 pgs.)-Collector's Edition w/embossed foil-c; anniversary issue; War Machine-c/story 5.00
300-($2.50, 68 pgs.)-Newsstand Edition 5.00
301,303: 301-Venom cameo. 303-Captain America app. 5.00
302-Venom-c/story; Captain America app. 2 4 6 8 10 12
304-Thunderstrike app; begin $1.50-c; bound-in-trading card sheet 3 6 9 16 24 32
305-Hulk-c/story 3 6 9 14 20 25
306-309-Mandarin app. 309-War Machine app. 4.00
310-($2.95) Polybagged w/16 pg Marvel Action Hour preview & acetate print 6.00
310-($1.50) Regular edition; white logo; "Hands of the Mandarin" x-over w/Force Works and War Machine 5.00
311,312- "Hands of the Mandarin" x-over w/Force Works and War Machine. 312-w/bound-in Power Ranger card 4.00
313,315,316,318: 315-316-Black Widow app. 316-Crimson Dynamo & Titanium Man app. 5.00
314-Crossover w/Captain America; Henry Pym app. 6.00
317-($2.50)-Flip book; Black Widow app; death of Titanium Man; Hawkeye, War Machine & USAgent app. 6.00
319-Intro. new Iron Man armor; Force Works app; prologue to "The Crossing" story 6.00
320-325: 321-w/Overpower card insert. 322-324-Avengers app; x-over w/Avengers and Force Works. 325-($2.95)-Wraparound-c; Tony Stark Iron Man vs "Teen" Tony Iron Man; Avengers & Force Works x-over; continued in Avengers #395 5.00
326- "Teen" Tony app. as Iron Man thru #332; Avengers, Thor & Cap America x-over 6.00
327-330: 330-War Machine & Stockpile app; return of Morgan Stark 4.00
331-War Machine app; leads into the "Onslaught" x-over 5.00
332-(9/96) Onslaught x-over; last issue 6.00
Special 1 (8/70)-Sub-Mariner x-over; Everett-c 6 12 18 37 66 95
Special 2 (11/71, 52 pgs.)-r/TOS #81,82,91 (all-r) 3 6 9 19 30 40
Annual 3 (1976)-Man-Thing app. 3 6 9 14 20 25
King Size 4 (8/77)-The Champions (w/Ghost Rider) app.; Newton-a(i) 3 6 9 14 19 24
Annual 5 ('82) Black Panther & Mandarin app. 2 4 6 9 12 15
Annual 6-9: ('83-'86) 6-New Iron Man (J. Rhodes) app. 8-X-Factor app. 5.00
Annual 10 ('89) Atlantis Attacks x-over; P. Smith-a; Layton/Guice-a; Sub-Mariner app. 5.00
Annual 11-15 ('90-'94): 11-Terminus Factor pt. 2; origin of Mrs. Arbogast by Ditko (p&i). 12-1 pg. origin recap; Ant-Man back-up-s; Subterranean Wars Pt. 4. 13-Darkhawk & Avengers West Coast app.; Colan/Williamson-a. 14-Bagged w/card; 1st app. Face Thief 15- Iron Man vs. the Controller 5.00
....: Armor Wars TPB (2007, $24.99) r/#225-232; Michelinie intro. 25.00
Manual 1 (1993, $1.75)-Operations handbook 3.00
Graphic Novel: Crash (1988, $12.95, Adults, 72 pgs.)-Computer generated art & color; violence & nudity 13.00
...Collector's Preview 1(11/94, $1.95)-wraparound-c; text & illos-no comics 3.00
....: Demon in a Bottle HC (2008, $24.99) r/#120-128; two covers 25.00
....: Demon in a Bottle TPB (2006, $24.99) r/#120-128 25.00
....: Many Armors of Iron Man (2008, $24.99) r/#47, 142-144, 152-153, 200, 218 25.00
...Vs. Dr. Doom (12/94, $12.95)-r/#149-150, 249,250. Julie Bell-c 13.00
...Vs. Dr. Doom: Doomquest HC (2008, $19.99, dustjacket)-r/#149-150, 249,250; new Michelinie intro.; bonus art 20.00
....: War Machine TPB (2008, $29.99) r/#280-291 30.00
The Invincible Iron Man Omnibus Vol. 1 HC (2008, $99.99, dustjacket) r/Iron Man stories from Tales of Suspense #39-83 & Tales To Astonish #82; 1992 intro. by Stan Lee; 1975 essay by Lee; 2008 essay by Layton; gallery of original art and covers; creator bios 100.00

NOTE: **Austin** *c-105i, 109-111i, 151i.* **Byrne** *a-118p; c-109p, 197, 253.* **Colan** *a-1p, 253, Special 1p(3); c-1p.* **Craig** *a-1i, 2-4, 5-13i, 14, 15-19i, 24p, 25p, 26-28i; c-2-4.* **Ditko** *a-160p.* **Everett** *c-29.* **Guice** *a-233-241p.* **G. Kane** *c(p)-52-54, 63, 67, 72-75, 77-79, 88, 98.* **Kirby** *a-Special 1p; 80p, 90, 92-95.* **Mooney** *a-40i, 43i, 47i.* **Perez** *c-103p.* **Simonson** *c-Annual 8.* **B. Smith** *a-232p, 243i; c-232.* **P. Smith** *a-159p, 245p, Annual 10p; c-159.* **Starlin** *a-53p(part), 55p, 56p; c-55p, 160, 163.* **Tuska** *a-5-13p, 15-23p, 24i, 32p, 38-46p, 48-54p, 57-61p, 63-69p, 70-72p, 78p, 86-92p, 95-106p, Annual 4p.* **Wood** *a-Special 1i.*

IRON MAN (The Invincible...) (Volume Two)
Marvel Comics: Nov, 1996 - No. 13, Nov, 1997 ($2.95/$1.95/$1.99)
(Produced by WildStorm Productions)

V2#1-3-Heroes Reborn begins; Scott Lobdell scripts & Whilce Portacio-c/a begin; new origin Iron Man & Hulk. 2-Hulk app. 3-Fantastic Four app. 5.00
1-Variant-c 6.00
4-11: 4-Two covers. 6-Fantastic Four app.; Industrial Revolution; Hulk app. 7-Return of Rebel. 11-($1.99) Dr. Doom-c/app. 4.00
12-($2.99) "Heroes Reunited"-pt. 3; Hulk-c/app. 5.00
13-($1.99) "World War 3"-pt. 3, x-over w/Image 4.00
Heroes Reborn: Iron Man (2006, $29.99, TPB) r/#1-12; Heroes Reborn #1/2; pin-ups 30.00

IRON MAN (The Invincible...) (Volume Three)
Marvel Comics: Feb, 1998 - No. 89, Dec, 2004 ($2.99/$1.99/$2.25)

V3#1-($2.99)-Follows Heroes Return; Busiek scripts & Chen-c/a begin; Deathsquad app. 6.00
1-Alternate Ed. 1 2 3 5 7 9
2-12: 2-Two covers. 6-Black Widow-c/app. 7-Warbird-c/app. 8-Black Widow app. 9-Mandarin returns 4.00
13-($2.99) battles the Controller 5.00
14-24: 14-Fantastic Four-c/app. 3.00
25-($2.99) Iron Man and Warbird battle Ultimo; Avengers app. 4.00
26-30-Quesada-s. 28-Whiplash killed. 29-Begin $2.25-c. 3.00
31-45,47-49,51-54: 35-Maximum Security x-over; FF-c/app. 41-Grant-a begins. 44-New armor debut. 48-Ultron-c/app. 3.00
46-($3.50, 100 pgs.) Sentient armor returns; r/V1#78,140,141 4.00
50-($3.50) Grell-s begin; Black Widow app. 4.00
55-($3.50) 400th issue; Asamiya-c; back-up story Stark reveals ID; Grell-a 4.00
56-66: 56-Reis-a. 57,58-Ryan-a. 59-61-Grell-c/a. 62,63-Ryan-a. 64-Davis-a; Thor-c/app. 3.00
67-89: 67-Begin $2.99-c; Gene Ha-c. 75-83-Granov-c. 84-Avengers Disassembled prologue 85-89-Avengers Disassembled. 85-88-Harris-a. 86-89-Pat Lee-c. 87-Rumiko killed 3.00
.../Captain America '98 Annual ($3.50) vs. Modok 4.00
1999, 2000 Annual ($3.50) 4.00
2001 Annual ($2.99) Claremont-s/Ryan-a 4.00
Avengers Disassembled: Iron Man TPB (2004, $14.99) r/#84-89 15.00
Mask in the Iron Man (5/01, $14.95, TPB) r/#26-30, #1/2 15.00

IRON MAN (The Invincible...)
Marvel Comics: Jan, 2005 - No. 35, Jan, 2009 ($3.50/$2.99)

1-($3.50-c) Warren Ellis-s/Adi Granov-c/a; start of Extremis storyline 5.00
2-6-($2.99): 5-Flashback to origin; Stark gets new abilities 4.00
7-14: 7-Knauf-s/Zircher-a. 13,14-Civil War 3.00
15-24,26,27,29-35: 15-Stark becomes Director of S.H.I.E.L.D. 19,20-World War Hulk. 33-Secret Invasion; War Machine app. 34,35-War Machine title logo 3.00
25,28-($3.99) 25-Includes movie preview & armor showcase. 28-Red & white armor 4.00
All-New Iron Manual (2/08, $4.99) Handbook-style guide to characters & armor suits 5.00
... By Design 1 (11/10, $3.99) Gallery of 2010 variant covers with artist commentary 4.00
.../Captain America: Casualities of War (2/07, $3.99) two covers; flashbacks 4.00
...: Director of S.H.I.E.L.D. Annual 1 (1/08, $3.99) Madame Hydra app.; Cheung-c 4.00
Free Comic Book Day 2010 (Iron Man: Supernova) #1 (5/10, 9-1/2" x 6-1/4") Nova app. 3.00
Free Comic Book Day 2010 (Iron Man/Thor) #1 (5/10, 9-1/2" x 6-1/4") Romita Jr.-a/c 3.00
...Golden Avenger 1 (11/08, $2.99) Santacruz-a; movie photo-c 3.00
.../Hulk/Fury 1 (2/09, $3.99) crossover of movie-version characters 4.00
Indomitable Iron Man (4/10, $3.99) B&W stories; Chaykin-s/a; Rosado-a; Parrillo-c 4.00
Iron Manual Mark 3 (6/10, $3.99) Handbook-format profiles of characters 4.00
...: Iron Protocols (12/09, $3.99) Olivetti-c/Nelson-a 4.00
...: Kiss and Kill (8/10, $3.99) Black Widow and Wolverine app. 4.00
Marvel Halloween Ashcan 2007 (8-1/2" x 5-3/8") updated origin; Michael Golden-c 3.00
...: Requiem (2009, $4.99) r/TOS #39, Iron Man #144 (1981); armor profiles 5.00
...: The End (1/09, $4.99) future Tony Stark retires; Michelinie-s/Chang & Layton-a 5.00
...: Titanium! 1 (12/10, $4.99) short stories by various; Yardin-c 5.00
Civil War: Iron Man TPB (2007, $11.99) r/#13,14, .../Captain America: Casualities of War, and Civil War: The Confession 12.00
HC (2006, $19.99, dust jacket) r/#1-6 and Granov covers from Iron Man V3 #75-83 20.00
...: Director of S.H.I.E.L.D. TPB (2007, $14.99) r/#15-18; Strange Tales #135 (1965) and Iron Man #129; profile pages for Iron Man and S.H.I.E.L.D.; creator interviews 15.00
...: Extremis SC (2007, $14.99) r/#1-6 and Granov covers from Iron Man V3 #75-83 15.00
...: Execute Program SC (2007, $14.99) r/#7-12; cover layouts and sketches 15.00

IRON MAN (Marvel Now!)(Leads into Superior Iron Man)
Marvel Comics: Jan, 2013 - No. 28, Aug, 2014 ($3.99)

1-28: 1-8-Gillen-s/Land-c/a. 5-Stark heads out to space. 9-17-Secret Origin of Tony Stark. 9-12-Eaglesham-a. 17-Arno Stark revealed. 23-26-Malekith app. 4.00
20.INH (3/12, $3.99) Inhumanity tie-in; origin The Exile; Padilla-a 4.00
Annual 1 (4/14, $4.99) Gillen-s/Martinez, Padilla & Marz-a 5.00
... Special 1 (9/14, $4.99) Cont'd from Uncanny X-Men Special #1; Ryan-s/Handoko-a 5.00

IRON MAN (The Armor Wars)
Marvel Comics: No. 258.1, Jul, 2013 - No. 258.4, Jul, 2013 ($3.99, weekly limited series)

258.1-258.4 - Set after Iron Man #258 (1990); Michelinie-s/Dave Ross & Bob Layton-a 4.00

IRON MAN (Follows the Iron Man 2020 series)
Marvel Comics: Nov, 2020 - Present ($4.99/$3.99)

1-($4.99) Cantwell-s/Cafu-a; main wraparound cover by Alex Ross; Patsy Walker app. 5.00
2-5-($3.99) Hellcat app. 2-Crusher Creel app. 4.00

Iron Man: Enter the Mandarin #1 © MAR

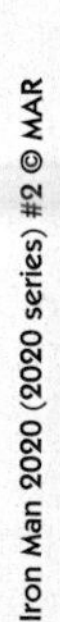
Iron Man 2020 (2020 series) #2 © MAR

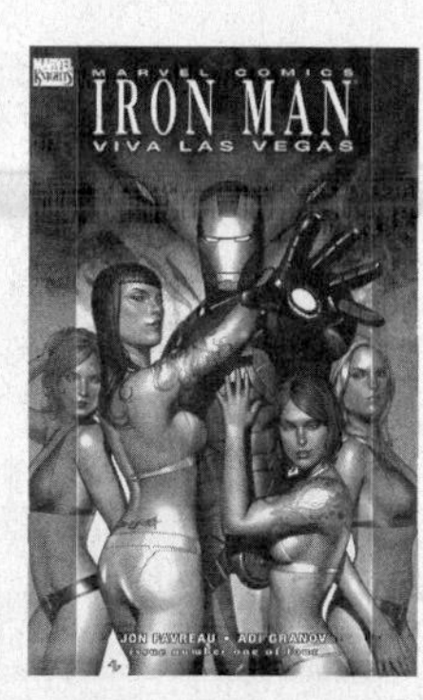

Iron Man: Viva Las Vegas #1 © MAR

	GD 2.0	VG 4.0	FN 6.0	VF 8.0	VF/NM 9.0	NM- 9.2

IRON MAN AND POWER PACK
Marvel Comics: Jan, 2008 - No. 4, Apr, 2008 ($2.99, limited series)
1-4-Gurihiru-c/Sumerak-s; Puppet Master app.; Mini Marvels back-ups in each 3.00
...: Armored and Dangerous TPB (2008, $7.99, digest size) r/series 8.00

IRON MAN & SUB-MARINER
Marvel Comics Group: Apr, 1968 (12¢, one-shot) (Pre-dates Iron Man #1 & Sub-Mariner #1)
1-Iron Man story by Colan/Craig continued from Tales of Suspense #99 & continued in Iron Man #1; Sub-Mariner story by Colan continued from Tales to Astonish #101 & continued in Sub-Mariner #1; Colan/Everett-c 25 50 75 175 388 600

IRON MAN AND THE ARMOR WARS
Marvel Comics: Oct, 2009 - No. 4, Jan, 2010 ($2.99, limited series)
1-4-Rousseau-a; Crimson Dynamo & Omega Red app. 3.00

IRON MAN: ARMORED ADVENTURES
Marvel Comics: Sept, 2009 ($3.99, one-shot)
1-Based on the 2009 cartoon; Brizuela-a; Nick Fury & Living Laser app. 4.00

IRON MAN: BAD BLOOD
Marvel Comics: Sept, 2000 - No. 4, Dec, 2000 ($2.99, limited series)
1-4-Micheline-s/Layton-a 3.00

IRON MAN: ENTER THE MANDARIN
Marvel Comics: Nov, 2007 - No. 6, Apr, 2008 ($2.99, limited series)
1-6-Casey-s/Canete-a; retells first meeting 3.00
TPB (2008, $14.99) r/#1-6 15.00

IRON MAN: EXTREMIS DIRECTOR'S CUT
Marvel Comics: Jun, 2010 - No. 6, Sept, 2010 ($3.99, limited series)
1-6-Reprints Iron Man #1-6 (2005 series) with script pages and design art 4.00

IRON MAN: FATAL FRONTIER
Marvel Comics: 2014 ($34.99, hardcover)
HC - Printing of digital comic #1-13 and r/Iron Man Annual #1 (4/14) 35.00

IRON MAN: HONG KONG HEROES
Marvel Comics: May, 2018 ($3.99, one-shot)
1-Howard Wong-s/Justice Wong-a; Hulk & Black Panther app.; intro Arwyn Wong 4.00

IRON MAN: HOUSE OF M (Also see House of M and related x-overs)
(Reprinted in House of M: Fantastic Four/ Iron Man TPB)
Marvel Comics: Sept, 2005 - No. 3, Nov, 2005 ($2.99, limited series)
1-3-Pat Lee-a/c; Greg Pak-s 3.00

IRON MAN: HYPERVELOCITY
Marvel Comics: Mar, 2007 - No. 6, Aug, 2007 ($2.99, limited series)
1-6-Adam Warren-s/Brian Denham-a/c 3.00
TPB (2007, $14.99) r/#1-6; layout pages and armor design sketches 15.00

IRON MAN: I AM IRON MAN
Marvel Comics: Mar, 2010 - No. 2, Apr, 2010 ($3.99, limited series)
1,2-Adaptation of the first movie; Peter David-s/Sean Chen-a/Adi Granov-c 4.00

IRON MAN: INEVITABLE
Marvel Comics: Feb, 2006 - No. 6, July, 2006 ($2.99, limited series)
1-6-Joe Casey-s/Frazer Irving; Spymaster and the Living Laser app. 3.00
TPB (2006, $14.99) r/#1-6; cover sketches 15.00

IRON MAN: LEGACY
Marvel Comics: Jun, 2010 - No. 11, Apr, 2011 ($3.99/$2.99)
1-Van Lente-s/Kurth-a; Dr. Doom app.; back-up r/debut in Tales of Suspense #39 4.00
2-11-($2.99) 4-Titanium Man & Crimson Dynamo app. 6-The Pride app. 3.00

IRON MAN: LEGACY OF DOOM
Marvel Comics: Jun, 2008 - No. 4, Sept, 2008 ($2.99, limited series)
1-4-Michelinie-s/Lim & Layton-a; Dr. Doom app. 3.00

IRON MAN NOIR
Marvel Comics: Jun, 2010 - No. 4, Sept, 2010 ($3.99, limited series)
1-4-Pulp-style set in 1939; Snyder-s/Garcia-a 4.00

IRON MAN: RAPTURE
Marvel Comics: Jan, 2011 - No. 4, Feb, 2011 ($3.99, limited series)
1-4-Irvine-s/Medina-a/Bradstreet-c. 3,4-War Machine app. 4.00

IRON MAN: SEASON ONE
Marvel Comics: 2013 ($24.99, hardcover graphic novel)
HC - Origin story and early days; Chaykin-s/Parel-a/Tedesco painted-c 25.00

IRON MAN: THE COMING OF THE MELTER
Marvel Comics: Jul, 2013 ($3.99, one-shot)
1-Movie version; Ron Lim-a; back-up reprint of Iron Man #72 (1/75); 3 covers 4.00

IRON MAN: THE IRON AGE
Marvel Comics: Aug, 1998 - No. 2, Sept, 1998 ($5.99, limited series)
1,2-Busiek-s; flashback story from gold armor days 6.00

IRON MAN: THE LEGEND
Marvel Comics: Sept, 1996 ($3.95, one-shot)
1-Tribute issue 5.00

IRON MAN/ THOR
Marvel Comics: Jan, 2011 - No. 4, Apr, 2011 ($3.99, limited series)
1-4-Eaton-a; Crimson Dynamo & Diablo app. 4.00

IRON MANTICORE (Reprints from Cerebus in Hell)
Aardvark-Vanaheim: Sept, 2019 ($4.00, B&W)
1-Cerebus figures placed over original Doré artwork of Hell; Iron Man #128-c swipe 4.00

IRON MAN 2: ... (Follows the first movie)
Marvel Comics: Jun, 2010 - Nov, 2010 ($3.99, limited series)
Agents of S.H.I.E.L.D. 1 (11/10, $3.99) Nick Fury, Agent Coulson & Black Widow app. 4.00
Public Identity (6/10 - No. 3, 7/10, $3.99) 1-3-Kitson & Lim-a/Granov-c 4.00
Spotlight (4/10, $3.99) Interviews with Granov, Guggenheim, Fraction, Ellis, Michelinie 4.00

IRON MAN 2 ADAPTATION, (MARVEL'S...)
Marvel Comics: Jan, 2013 - No. 2, Feb, 2013 ($2.99, limited series)
1,2-Photo-c; Rosanas-a 3.00

IRON MAN 2.0
Marvel Comics: Apr, 2011 - No. 12, Feb, 2012 ($3.99/$2.99)
1-($3.99) Spencer-s/Kitson-c; back-up history of War Machine 4.00
1-Variant-c by Djurdjevic 6.00
2-7,(7.1),8-12-($2.99) 2,3-Kitson, Kano & Di Giandomenico-a. 5-7-Fear Itself tie-in 3.00
...: Modern Warfare 1 (10/11, $4.99) r/#1-3 with variant covers 5.00

IRON MAN 3 PRELUDE, (MARVEL'S...)
Marvel Comics: Mar, 2013 - No. 2, Apr, 2013 ($2.99, limited series)
1,2-Photo-c; Gage-s/Kurth-a; War Machine app. 3.00

IRON MAN 2020 (Also see Machine Man limited series)
Marvel Comics: June, 1994 ($5.95, one-shot)
nn 6.00

IRON MAN 2020
Marvel Comics: Mar, 2020 - No. 6, Oct, 2020 ($4.99, limited series)
1-6-Slott & Gage-s/Woods-a; Arno Stark as Iron Man; Machine Man app. 5.00

IRON MAN: VIVA LAS VEGAS
Marvel Comics: Jul, 2008 - No. 2 ($3.99, unfinished limited series)
1,2-Jon Favreau-s/Adi Granov-a/c 4.00

IRON MAN VS WHIPLASH
Marvel Comics: Jan, 2010 - No. 4, Apr, 2010 ($3.99, limited series)
1-4-Briones-a/Peterson-c; origin of new Whiplash 4.00

IRON MAN/X-O MANOWAR: HEAVY METAL (See X-O Manowar/Iron Man: In Heavy Metal)
Marvel Comics: Sept, 1996 ($2.50, one-shot) (1st Marvel/Valiant x-over)
1-Pt. II of Iron Man/X-O Manowar x-over; Fabian Nicieza scripts; 1st app. Rand Banion 4.00

IRON MARSHALL
Jademan Comics: July, 1990 - No. 32, Feb, 1993 ($1.75, plastic coated-c)
1,32: Kung Fu stories. 1-Poster centerfold 5.00
2-31-Kung Fu stories in all 4.00

IRON PATRIOT (Marvel Now!)
Marvel Comics: May, 2014 - No. 5, Sept, 2014 ($3.99)
1-5-James Rhodes in the armor; Ales Kot-s/Garry Brown-a/c 4.00

IRON VIC (See Comics Revue No. 3 & Giant Comics Editions)
United Features Syndicate/St. John Publ. Co.: 1940
Single Series 22 39 78 117 231 378 525

IRONWOLF
DC Comics: 1986 ($2.00, one shot)
1-r/Weird Worlds #8-10; Chaykin story & art 4.00

IRONWOLF: FIRES OF THE REVOLUTION (See Weird Worlds #8-10)
DC Comics: 1992 ($29.95, hardcover)
nn-Chaykin/Moore story, Mignola-a w/Russell inks. 30.00

Irredeemable #8 © BOOM

It's Gametime #2 © DC

I, Zombie #3 © Monkeybrain & Allred

	GD 2.0	VG 4.0	FN 6.0	VF 8.0	VF/NM 9.0	NM- 9.2

IRREDEEMABLE (Also see Incorruptible)
BOOM! Studios: Apr, 2009 - No. 37, May, 2012 ($3.99)

1-37: 1-Waid-s/Krause-a; 3 covers; Grant Morrison afterword. 2-32-Three covers 4.00
1-Artist Edition (12/11, $3.99) r/#1 in B&W with bonus sketch and design art 4.00
... Special 1 (4/10, $3.99) Art by Azaceta, Rios & Chaykin; three covers 4.00

IRREDEEMABLE ANT-MAN, THE
Marvel Comics: Dec, 2006 - No. 12, Nov, 2007 ($2.99)

1-12-Kirkman-s/Hester-a/c; intro. Eric O'Grady as the new Ant-Man. 7-Ms. Marvel app. 10-World War Hulk x-over 3.00
... Vol. 1: Lowlife (2007, $9.99, digest) r/#1-6 10.00
... Vol. 2: Small-Minded (2007, $9.99, digest) r/#7-12 10.00

ISAAC ASIMOV'S I-BOTS
Tekno Comix: Dec, 1995 - No. 7, May, 1996 ($1.95)

1-7: 1-6-Perez-c/a. 2-Chaykin variant-c exists. 3-Polybagged. 7-Lady Justice-c/app. 4.00

ISAAC ASIMOV'S I-BOTS
BIG Entertainment: V2#1, June, 1996 - No. 9, Feb, 1997 ($2.25)

V2#1-9: 1-Lady Justice-c/app. 6-Gil Kane-c 4.00

ISIS (TV) (Also see Shazam)
National Per.l Publ./DC Comics: Oct-Nov, 1976 - No. 8, Dec-Jan, 1977-78

	GD	VG	FN	VF	VF/NM	NM-
1-Wood inks	3	6	9	21	33	45
2-8: 5-Isis new look. 7-Origin	2	4	6	8	11	14

ISLAND AT THE TOP OF THE WORLD (See Walt Disney Showcase #27)

ISLAND OF DR. MOREAU, THE (Movie)
Marvel Comics Group: Oct, 1977 (52 pgs.)

	GD	VG	FN	VF	VF/NM	NM-
1-Gil Kane-c	1	2	3	5	6	8

ISLAND OF DR. MOREAU, THE (Adaptation of the novel)
IDW Publishing: Jul, 2019 - No. 2, Aug, 2019 ($4.99, limited series)

1,2-Ted Adams & Gabriel Rodríguez-s/Rodríguez-a 5.00

ISOLA
Image Comics: Apr, 2018 - Present ($3.99)

1-10-Brenden Fletcher & Karl Kerschl-s/Kerschl & Msassyk-a 4.00
... Prologue (1/19, no cover price) reprints pages from Motor Crush #1-5 3.00

I SPY (TV)
Gold Key: Aug, 1966 - No. 6, Sept, 1968 (All have photo-c)

	GD	VG	FN	VF	VF/NM	NM-
1-Bill Cosby, Robert Culp photo covers	11	22	33	72	154	235
2-6: 3,4-McWilliams-a. 5-Last 12¢-c	6	12	18	38	69	100

IT! (See Astonishing Tales No. 21-24 & Supernatural Thrillers No. 1)

ITCHY & SCRATCHY COMICS (The Simpsons TV show)
Bongo Comics: 1993 - No. 3, 1993 ($1.95)

	GD	VG	FN	VF	VF/NM	NM-
1-3: 1-Bound-in jumbo poster. 3-w/decoder screen trading card	2	4	6	9	13	16
Holiday Special ('94, $1.95)	1	3	4	6	8	10

IT GIRL (Also see Atomics, and Madman Comics)
Oni Press: May, 2002 ($2.95, one-shot)

1-Allred-s/Clugston-Major-c/a; Atomics and Madman app. 3.00

IT GIRL! AND THE ATOMICS (Also see Atomics, and Madman Comics)
Image Comics: Aug, 2012 - No. 12, Jul, 2013 ($2.99)

1-12: 1-Rich-s/Norton-a/Allred-c. 2-Two covers (Allred & Cooke). 6-Clugston Flores-a 3.00

IT REALLY HAPPENED
William H. Wise No. 1,2/Standard (Visual Editions): 1944 - No. 11, Oct, 1947

	GD	VG	FN	VF	VF/NM	NM-
1-Kit Carson & Ben Franklin stories	32	64	96	188	307	425
2,3-Nazi WWII-c	15	30	45	92	144	195
4,6,9,11: 4-D-Day story. 6-Ernie Pyle WWII-c; Joan of Arc story. 9-Captain Kidd & Frank Buck stories	14	28	42	76	108	140
5-Lou Gehrig & Lewis Carroll stories	19	38	57	111	176	240
7-Teddy Roosevelt story	15	30	45	83	124	165
8-Story of Roy Rogers	17	34	51	98	154	210
10-Honus Wagner & Mark Twain stories	15	30	45	90	140	190

NOTE: ***Guardineer** a-7(2), 8(2), 10, 11. **Schomburg** c-1-7, 9-11.*

IT RHYMES WITH LUST (Also see Bold Stories & Candid Tales)
St. John Publishing Co.: 1950 (Digest size, 128 pgs., 25¢)

	GD	VG	FN	VF	VF/NM	NM-
nn (Rare)-Matt Baker & Ray Osrin-a	322	644	966	2254	4027	5800

IT'S A BIRD...
DC Comics: 2004 ($24.95, hardcover with dust jacket)

HC-Semi-autobiographical story of Steven Seagle writing Superman; Kristiansen-a 25.00
SC-($17.95) 18.00

IT'S ABOUT TIME (TV)
Gold Key: Jan, 1967

	GD	VG	FN	VF	VF/NM	NM-
1 (10195-701)-Photo-c	4	8	12	28	47	65

IT'S A DUCK'S LIFE
Marvel Comics/Atlas(MMC): Feb, 1950 - No. 11, Feb, 1952

	GD	VG	FN	VF	VF/NM	NM-
1-Buck Duck, Super Rabbit begin	20	40	60	115	168	260
2	13	26	39	72	101	130
3-11	11	22	33	62	86	110

IT'S GAMETIME
National Periodical Publications: Sept-Oct, 1955 - No. 4, Mar-Apr, 1956

	GD	VG	FN	VF	VF/NM	NM-
1-(Scarce)-Infinity-c; Davy Crockett app. in puzzle	106	212	318	678	1164	1650
2,3 (Scarce): 2-Dodo & The Frog	73	146	219	467	796	1125
4 (Rare)	76	152	228	486	831	1175

IT'S LOVE, LOVE, LOVE
St. John Publishing Co.: Nov, 1957 - No. 2, Jan, 1958 (10¢)

	GD	VG	FN	VF	VF/NM	NM-
1,2	9	18	27	50	65	80

IT! THE TERROR FROM BEYOND SPACE
IDW Publishing: Jul, 2010 - No. 3, Sept, 2010 ($3.99, limited series)

1-3-Naraghi-s/Dos Santos-a/Mannion-c 4.00

ITTY BITTY COMICS (Issue #5, see Grimmiss Island; title changes to Grimmiss Island)
Dark Horse Comics: Nov, 2014 - No. 4, Feb, 2015 ($2.99, limited series)

1-4-All-ages humor stories of kid-version Mask by Art Baltazar & Franco 3.00

ITTY BITTY COMICS: THE MASK
Dark Horse Comics: Nov, 2014 - No. 4, Feb, 2015 ($2.99, limited series)

1-4-All-ages humor stories of kid-version Mask by Art Baltazar & Franco 3.00

ITTY BITTY HELLBOY
Dark Horse Comics: Aug, 2013 - No. 5, Dec, 2013 ($2.99, limited series)

1-5-All-ages humor stories of kid-version Hellboy characters by Art Baltazar & Franco 3.00

ITTY BITTY HELLBOY: THE SEARCH FOR THE WERE-JAGUAR
Dark Horse Comics: Nov, 2015 - No. 4, Feb, 2016 ($2.99, limited series)

1-4-All-ages humor stories of kid-version Hellboy characters by Art Baltazar & Franco 3.00

I, VAMPIRE (DC New 52)
DC Comics: Nov, 2011 - No. 19, Jun, 2013 ($2.99)

1-Fialkov-s/Sorrentino-a/Frison-c 6.00
2-19: 4-Constantine app. 5-7-Batman app. 7,8-Crossover with Justice League Dark #7,8. 12-Stormwatch app. 16-19-Constantine app. 4.00
#0-(11/12, $2.99) Origin of Andrew Bennett; Fialkov-s/Sorrentino-a/Crain-c 3.00

IVANHOE (See Fawcett Movie Comics No. 20)

IVANHOE
Dell Publishing Co.: July-Sept, 1963

	GD	VG	FN	VF	VF/NM	NM-
1 (12-372-309)	3	6	9	20	31	42

IVAR, TIMEWALKER
Valiant Entertainment: Jan, 2015 - No. 12, Dec, 2015 ($3.99)

1-12: 1-4-Fred Van Lente-s/Clayton Henry-a. 5-8-Portela-a. 9-Pere Perez-a 4.00

IVX (Inhumans vs X-Men) (Also see Death of X)
Marvel Comics: No. 0, Jan, 2017 - No. 6, May, 2017 ($3.99/$4.99/$5.99)

0-($4.99) Soule-s/Rocafort-a; Beast, Medusa, Emma Frost, Magneto app. 5.00
1-($5.99) Soule & Lemire-s/Yu-a; multiple covers 6.00
2-5-($3.99) 2-Yu-a. 3-5-Garrón-a 4.00
6-($4.99) Yu-a; leads into Inhumans Prime #1, X-Men Prime #1 & Unc. Inhumans #20 5.00

IWO JIMA (See Spectacular Features Magazine)

IXTH GENERATION (See Ninth Generation)

I, ZOMBIE (Inspired the 2015 TV show)(See House of Mystery Halloween Annual #1 for 1st app.)
DC Comics (Vertigo): July, 2010 - No. 28, Oct, 2012 ($1.00/$2.99)

	GD	VG	FN	VF	VF/NM	NM-
1-($1.00) Allred-a/Roberson-s; 2 covers by Allred & Cooke	3	6	9	16	23	30

2-28-($2.99) Allred-c/a in most. 12-Gilbert Hernandez-a. 18-Jay Stephens-a. 25-Rugg-a 4.00
... Special Edition 1 (5/15, $1.00) r/#1; new inteview with Allred 4.00
...: Dead to the World TPB (2011, $14.99) r/#1-5 & House of Mystery Hall. Ann. #1 15.00

JACE PEARSON OF THE TEXAS RANGERS (Radio/TV)(4-Color #396 is titled Tales of the Texas Rangers; ...'s Tales of ... #11-on)(See Western Roundup under Dell Giants)
Dell Publishing Co.: No. 396, 5/52 - No. 1021, 8-10/59 (No #10) (All-Photo-c)

	GD	VG	FN	VF	VF/NM	NM-
Four Color 396 (#1)	10	20	30	67	141	215

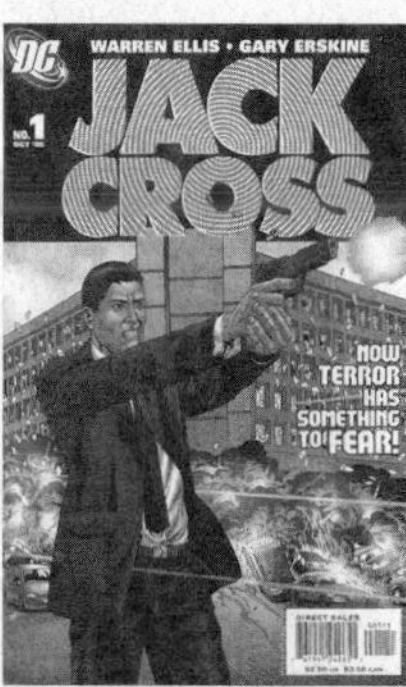

Jack Cross #1 © Ellis & DC

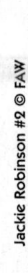

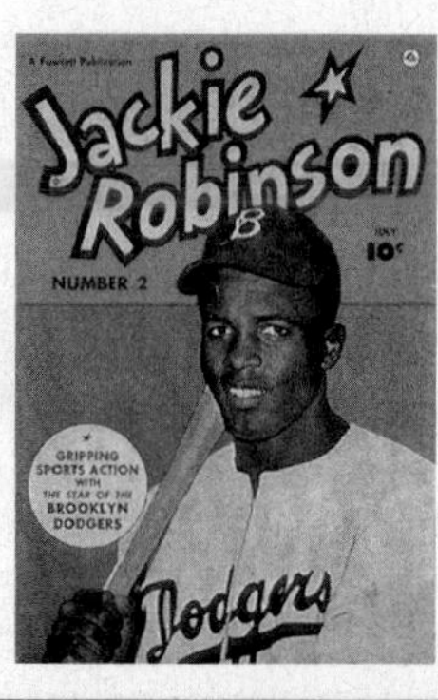

Jackie Robinson #2 © FAW

Jackpot #4 © Ray Fawkes

	GD	VG	FN	VF	VF/NM	NM-
	2.0	4.0	6.0	8.0	9.0	9.2
2(5-7/53) - 9(2-4/55)	6	12	18	40	73	105
Four Color 648(#10, 9/55)	6	12	18	40	73	105
11(11-2/55-56) - 14,17-20(6-8/58)	5	10	15	33	57	80
15,16-Toth-a	5	10	15	34	60	85
Four Color 961,1021: 961-Spiegle-a	5	10	15	34	60	85

NOTE: *Joel McCrea photo c-1-9, F.C. 648 (starred on radio show only); Willard Parker photo c-11-on (starred on TV series).*

JACK ARMSTRONG (Radio)(See True Comics)
Parents' Institute: Nov, 1947 - No. 9, Sept, 1948; No. 10, Mar, 1949 - No. 13, Sept, 1949

nn (6/47) Ashcan edition; full color slick cover (a FN/VF sold for $485 in 2011)
1-(Scarce) (odd size) Cast intro. inside front-c; Vic Hardy's Crime Lab begins

	GD	VG	FN	VF	VF/NM	NM-
1	50	100	150	315	533	750
2	21	42	63	126	206	285
3-5	15	30	45	90	140	190
6-13	14	28	42	81	118	155

JACK CROSS
DC Comics: Oct, 2005 - No. 4, Jan, 2006 ($2.50)

1-4-Warren Ellis-s/Gary Erskine-a 3.00
DC Comics Presents: Jack Cross #1 (12/10, $7.99, squarebound) r/#1-4 8.00

JACKED
DC Comics (Vertigo): Jan, 2016 - No. 6, Jun, 2016 ($3.99)

1-6-Eric Kripke-s/John Higgins-a/Glenn Fabry-c 4.00

JACKIE CHAN'S SPARTAN X
Topps Comics: May, 1997 - No. 3 ($2.95, limited series)

1-3-Michael Golden-s/a; variant photo-c 3.00

JACKIE CHAN'S SPARTAN X: HELL BENT HERO FOR HIRE
Image Comics (Little Eva Ink): Mar, 1998 - No. 3 ($2.95, B&W)

1-3-Michael Golden-s/a: 1-variant photo-c 3.00

JACKIE GLEASON (TV) (Also see The Honeymooners)
St. John Publishing Co.: Sept, 1955 - No. 4, Dec, 1955?

	GD	VG	FN	VF	VF/NM	NM-
1(1955)(TV)-Photo-c	84	168	252	538	919	1300
2-4	53	106	159	334	567	800

JACKIE GLEASON AND THE HONEYMOONERS (TV)
National Periodical Publications: June-July, 1956 - No. 12, Apr-May, 1958

	GD	VG	FN	VF	VF/NM	NM-
1-1st app. Ralph Kramden	148	296	444	947	1624	2300
2	77	154	231	493	847	1200
3-11: 8-Statue of Liberty-c	54	108	162	343	574	825
12 (Scarce)	74	148	222	470	810	1150

JACKIE JOKERS (Became Richie Rich &...)
Harvey Publications: March, 1973 - No. 4, Sept, 1973 (#5 was advertised, but not published)

	GD	VG	FN	VF	VF/NM	NM-
1-1st app.	3	6	9	16	23	30
2-4: 2-President Nixon app.	2	4	6	8	11	14

JACKIE ROBINSON (Famous Plays of...) (Also see Negro Heroes #2 & Picture News #4)
Fawcett Publications: May, 1950 - No. 6, 1952 (Baseball hero) (All photo-c)

	GD	VG	FN	VF	VF/NM	NM-
nn	103	206	309	659	1130	1600
2	55	110	165	352	601	850
3-6	47	94	141	296	498	700

JACK IN THE BOX (Formerly Yellowjacket Comics #1-10; becomes Cowboy Western Comics #17 on)
Frank Comunale/Charlton Comics No. 11 on: Feb, 1946; No. 11, Oct, 1946 - No. 16, Nov-Dec, 1947

	GD	VG	FN	VF	VF/NM	NM-
1-Stitches, Marty Mouse & Nutsy McKrow	24	48	72	142	234	325
11-Yellowjacket (early Charlton comic)	26	52	78	156	256	355
12,14,15	15	30	45	94	147	200
13-Wolverton-a	31	62	93	182	296	410
16-12 pg. adapt. of Silas Marner; Kiefer-a	16	32	48	98	154	210

JACK KIRBY OMNIBUS, THE
DC Comics: 2011; 2013 ($49.99, hardcover with dustjacket)

Vol. 1 ('11) Recolored reprints of Kirby's DC work from 1946, 1957-1959; Evanier intro. 50.00
Vol. 2 ('13) Recolored reprints of Kirby's DC work from 1973-1987; Morrow intro. 50.00

JACK KIRBY'S FOURTH WORLD (See Mister Miracle & New Gods, 3rd Series)
DC Comics: Mar, 1997 - No. 20, Oct, 1998 ($1.95/$2.25)

1-20: 1-Byrne-a/scripts & Simonson-c begin; story cont'd from New Gods, 3rd Series #15; retells "The Pact" (New Gods, 1st Series #7); 1st brief DC app. Thor. 2-Thor vs. Big Barda; "Apokolips Then" back-up begins; Kirby-c/swipe (Thor #126) 8-Genesis x-over. 10-Simonson-s/a 13-Simonson back-up story. 20-Superman-c/app. 4.00

JACK KIRBY'S FOURTH WORLD OMNIBUS
DC Comics: 2007 - Vol. 4, 2008 ($49.99, hardcovers with dustjackets)

Vol. 1 ('07) Recolored reprints in chronological order of Superman's Pal, Jimmy Olsen #133-139, Forever People #1-3, New Gods #1-3, and Mister Miracle #1-3; Morrison intro, bonus art 150.00
Vol. 2 ('07) r/Jimmy Olsen #141-145, F.P. #4-6, N.G. #4-6 & M.M. #4-6; bonus art 80.00
Vol. 3 ('07) r/Jimmy Olsen #146-148, F.P. #7-10, N.G. #7-10 & M.M. #7-9; bonus art 50.00
Vol. 4 ('08) r/F.P. #11, M.M. #10-18, N.G. #11 & reprint series #6, & DC Graphic Novel #6 (The Hunger Dogs); Levitz intro.; Evanier afterword; character profile pages 50.00

JACK KIRBY'S GALACTIC BOUNTY HUNTERS
Marvel Comics (Icon): July, 2006 - No. 6, Nov, 2007 ($3.99)

1-6-Based on a Kirby concept; Mike Thibodeaux-a; Lisa Kirby, Thibodeaux and others-s 4.00
HC (2007, $24.99) r/series; pin-ups and supplemental art and interviews 25.00

JACK KIRBY'S SECRET CITY SAGA
Topps Comics (Kirbyverse): No. 0, Apr, 1993; No. 1, May, 1993 - No. 4, Aug, 1993 ($2.95, limited series)

0-(No cover price, 20 pgs.)-Simonson-c/a 4.00
0-Red embossed-c (limited ed.) 5.00
1-4-Bagged w/3 trading cards; Ditko-c/a: 1-Ditko/Art Adams-c. 2-Ditko/Byrne-c; has coupon for Pres. Clinton holo-foil trading card. 3-Dorman poster; has coupon for Gore holo-foil trading card. 4-Ditko/Perez-c 4.00

NOTE: *Issues #1-4 contain coupons redeemable for Kirbychrome version of #1*

JACK KIRBY'S SILVER STAR (Also see Silver Star)
Topps Comics (Kirbyverse): Oct, 1993 ($2.95)(Intended as a 4-issue limited series)

1-Silver ink-c; Austin-c/a(i); polybagged w/3 cards 4.00

JACK KIRBY'S TEENAGENTS (See Satan's Six)
Topps Comics (Kirbyverse): Aug, 1993 - No. 4, Nov, 1993 ($2.95, limited series)

1-4: Bagged with/3 trading cards; Busiek-s/Austin-c(i): 3-Liberty Project app. 4.00

JACK KRAKEN
Dark Horse Comics: May, 2014 ($3.99, one-shot)

1-Tim Seeley-s; art by Ross Campbell & Jim Terry 4.00

JACK OF FABLES (See Fables)
DC Comics (Vertigo): Sept, 2006 - No. 50, Apr, 2011 ($2.99)

1-49: 1-Willingham & Sturges-s/Akins-a. 33-35-Crossover with Fables and The Literals 3.00
50-($4.99) Akins & Braun-a; Bolland-c 5.00
1-Special Edition (8/10, $1.00) r/#1 with "What's Next?" logo on cover 3.00
...: Americana TPB (2008, $14.99) r/#17-21 15.00
...: Jack of Hearts TPB (2007, $14.99) r/#6-11 15.00
...: The Bad Prince TPB (2008, $14.99) r/#12-16 15.00
...: The Big Book of War TPB (2009, $14.99) r/#28-32 15.00
...: The End TPB (2011, $17.99) r/#46-50 18.00
...: The Fulminate Blade TPB (2011, $14.99) r/#41-45 15.00
...: The (Nearly) Great Escape TPB (2007, $14.99) r/#1-5; Akins sketch pages 15.00
...: The New Adventures of Jack and Jack TPB (2010, $14.99) r/#36-40 15.00
...: Turning Pages TPB (2009, $14.99) r/#22-27 15.00

JACK OF HEARTS (Also see The Deadly Hands of Kung Fu #22 & Marvel Premiere #44)
Marvel Comics Group: Jan, 1984 - No. 4, Apr, 1984 (60¢, limited series)

1-4 4.00

JACKPOT!
AfterShock Comics: Apr, 2016 - No. 6, Jun, 2017 ($3.99)

1-6-Ray Fawkes-s/Brian Stelfreeze-c. 1-4-Marco Failla-a. 5,6-Georges Duarte-a 4.00

JACKPOT COMICS (Jolly Jingles #10 on)
MLJ Magazines: Spring, 1941 - No. 9, Spring, 1943

1-The Black Hood, Mr. Justice, Steel Sterling & Sgt. Boyle begin; Biro-c

	GD	VG	FN	VF	VF/NM	NM-
1	343	686	1029	2400	4200	6000
2-S. Cooper-c	171	342	513	1094	1872	2650
3-Hubbell-c	139	278	417	883	1517	2200

4-Archie begins; (his face appears on cover in small circle) (Win/41; on sale 12/41)-(also see Pep Comics #22); 1st app. Mrs. Grundy, the principal; Novick-c

	GD	VG	FN	VF	VF/NM	NM-
4	3900	7800	11,700	22,200	29,100	36,000

5-Hitler, Tojo, Mussolini-c by Montana; 1st definitive Mr. Weatherbee; 1st brief app. Reggie in 1 panel

	GD	VG	FN	VF	VF/NM	NM-
5	676	1352	2028	4935	8718	12,500
6,7-Bondage-c by Novick	274	548	822	1754	3027	4300
8,9-Sahle-c	252	504	756	1613	2757	3900

JACK Q FROST (See Unearthly Spectaculars)

JACK STAFF (Vol. 2; previously published in Britain)
Image Comics: Feb, 2003 - No. 20, May, 2009 ($2.95/$3.50)

1-5-Paul Grist-s/a 3.50
6-20-($3.50) 6-Flashback to the WW2 Freedom Fighters 3.50
... Special 1 (1/08, $3.50) Molachi the Immortal app. 3.50

Jamboree Comics #2 © Round Pub.

James Bond: Kill Chain #3 © Ian Fleming Pub.

Jane Arden #2 © UFS

	GD 2.0	VG 4.0	FN 6.0	VF 8.0	VF/NM 9.0	NM- 9.2

The Weird World of Jack Staff King Size Special 1 (7/07, $5.99, B&W) r/story serialized in Comics International magazine; afterword by Grist 6.00
Vol. 1: Everything Used to Be Black and White TPB (12/03, $19.95) r/British issues 20.00
Vol. 2: Soldiers TPB (2005, $15.95) r/#1-5; cover gallery 16.00
Vol. 3: Echoes of Tomorrow TPB (2006, $16.99) r/#6-12; cover gallery 17.00

JACK THE GIANT KILLER (See Movie Classics)

JACK THE GIANT KILLER (New Adventures of...)
Bimfort & Co.: Aug-Sept, 1953

	GD	VG	FN	VF	VF/NM	NM-
V1#1-H. C. Kiefer-c/a	30	60	90	177	289	400

JACKY'S DIARY
Dell Publishing Co.: No. 1091, Apr-June, 1960 (one-shot)

	GD	VG	FN	VF	VF/NM	NM-
Four Color 1091	5	10	15	33	57	80

JADEMAN COLLECTION
Jademan Comics: Dec, 1989 - No. 3, 1990 ($2.50, plastic coated-c, 68 pgs.)
1-3: 1-Wraparound-c w/fold-out poster 4.00

JADEMAN KUNG FU SPECIAL
Jademan Comics: 1988 ($1.50, 64 pgs.)
1 4.00

JADE WARRIORS (Mike Deodato's...)
Image Comics (Glass House Graphics): Nov, 1999 - No. 3, 2000 ($2.50)
1-3-Deodato-a 3.00
1-Variant-c 3.00

JAGUAR, THE (Also see The Adventures of...)
Impact Comics (DC): Aug, 1991 - No. 14, Oct, 1992 ($1.00)
1-14: 4-The Black Hood x-over. 7-Sienkiewicz-c. 9-Contains Crusaders trading card 4.00
Annual 1 (1992, $2.50, 68 pgs.)-With trading card 5.00

JAGUAR GOD
Verotik: Mar, 1995 - No. 7, June, 1997 ($2.95, mature)
0 (2/96, $3.50)-Embossed Frazetta-c; Bisley-a; w/pin-ups. 5.00
1-Frazetta-c. 5.00
2-7: 2-Frazetta-c. 3-Bisley-c. 4-Emond-c. 7-($2.95)-Frazetta-c 4.00

JAKE THRASH
Aircel Publishing: 1988 - No. 3, 1988 ($2.00)
1-3 3.00

JAM, THE (...Urban Adventure)
Slave Labor Nos. 1-5/Dark Horse Comics Nos. 6-8/Caliber Comics No. 9 on: Nov, 1989 - No. 14, 1997 ($1.95/$2.50/$2.95, B&W)
1-14: Bernie Mireault-c/a/scripts. 6-1st Dark Horse issue. 9-1st Caliber issue 3.00

JAMBOREE COMICS
Round Publishing Co.: Feb, 1946(no month given) - No. 3, Apr, 1946

	GD	VG	FN	VF	VF/NM	NM-
1-Funny animal	21	42	63	122	199	275
2,3	15	30	45	85	130	175

JAMES BOND
Dynamite Entertainment: 2015 - No. 12, 2016 ($3.99)
1-12-Warren Ellis-s/Jason Masters-a; multiple covers on each. 1-6-Vargr. 7-12-Eidolon 4.00
...: M (2018, $4.99) Shalvey-s/c; Holden-a 5.00
...: Moneypenny (2016, $4.99) Houser-s/Edgar-a/Lotay-c 5.00
...: Service (2017, $7.99) Kieron Gillen-s/Antonio Fuso-a/Jamie McKelvie-c 8.00
...: Solstice (2017, $4.99) Ibrahim Moustafa-s/a 5.00

JAMES BOND (Volume 2)
Dynamite Entertainment: 2017 - No. 6, 2017 ($3.99)
1-6-Black Box; Percy-s/Lobosco-a. 1-Five covers. 2-6-Multiple covers on each 4.00

JAMES BOND (Volume 3)
Dynamite Entertainment: 2019 - No. 6, 2020 ($3.99)
1-6: 1-Ayala & Lore-s/Gapstur-a 4.00

JAMES BOND 007
Dynamite Entertainment: 2018 - No. 12, 2019 ($3.99, limited series)
1-12: 1-3-Greg Pak-s/Marc Laming-a; Oddjob app. 4-6-Stephen Mooney-a; Goldfinger app. 4.00

JAMES BOND 007: A SILENT ARMAGEDDON
Dark Horse Comics/Acme Press: Mar, 1993 - Apr 1993 (limited series)
1,2 4.00

JAMES BOND 007: GOLDENEYE (Movie)
Topps Comics: Jan, 1996 ($2.95, unfinished limited series of 3)
1-Movie adaptation; Stelfreeze-c 4.00

JAMES BOND 007: SERPENT'S TOOTH
Dark Horse Comics/Acme Press: July 1992 - Aug 1992 ($4.95, limited series)
1-3-Paul Gulacy-c/a 5.00

JAMES BOND 007: SHATTERED HELIX
Dark Horse Comics: Jun 1994 - July 1994 ($2.50, limited series)
1,2 4.00

JAMES BOND 007: THE QUASIMODO GAMBIT
Dark Horse Comics: Jan 1995 - May 1995 ($3.95, limited series)
1-3 4.50

JAMES BOND: FELIX LEITER
Dynamite Entertainment: 2017 - No. 6, 2017 ($3.99)
1-6-James Robinson-s/Aaron Campbell-a 4.00

JAMES BOND FOR YOUR EYES ONLY
Marvel Comics Group: Oct, 1981 - No. 2, Nov, 1981
1,2-Movie adapt.; r/Marvel Super Special #19 6.00

JAMES BOND: HAMMERHEAD
Dynamite Entertainment: 2016 - No. 6, 2016 ($3.99)
1-6-Diggle-s/Casalanguida-a. 1-Three covers 4.00

JAMES BOND JR. (TV)
Marvel Comics: Jan, 1992 - No. 12, Dec, 1992 (#1: $1.00, #2-on: $1.25)
1-12: Based on animated TV show 4.00

JAMES BOND: KILL CHAIN
Dynamite Entertainment: 2017 - No. 6, 2017 ($3.99)
1-6-Diggle-s/Casalanguida-a. 1-Three covers. 2-Felix Leiter app. 4.00

JAMES BOND: LICENCE TO KILL (See Licence To Kill)

JAMES BOND: ORIGIN
Dynamite Entertainment: 2018 - No. 12, 2019 ($3.99)
1-12: 1-Parker-s/Bob Q-a; multiple covers; young James Bond in 1941 WWII England 4.00

JAMES BOND: PERMISSION TO DIE
Eclipse Comics/ACME Press: 1989 - No. 3, 1991 ($3.95, lim. series, squarebound, 52 pgs.)
1-3: Mike Grell-c/a/scripts in all. 3-($4.95) 5.00

JAMES BOND: THE BODY
Dynamite Entertainment: 2018 - No. 6, 2018 ($3.99)
1-6: 1-Kot-s/Casalanguida-a. 2-Fuso-a 4.00

JAM, THE: SUPER COOL COLOR INJECTED TURBO ADVENTURE #1 FROM HELL!
Comico: May, 1988 ($2.50, 44 pgs., one-shot)
1 4.00

JANE ARDEN (See Feature Funnies & Pageant of Comics)
St. John (United Features Syndicate): Mar, 1948 - No. 2, June, 1948

	GD	VG	FN	VF	VF/NM	NM-
1-Newspaper reprints	16	32	48	96	151	205
2	13	26	39	74	105	135

JANE WIEDLIN'S LADY ROBOTIKA
Image Comics: Jul, 2010 - No. 2, Aug, 2010 ($3.50, unfinished limited series)
1,2-Wiedlin & Bill Morrison-s. 1-Morrison & Rodriguez-a. 2-Moy-a 3.50

JANN OF THE JUNGLE (Jungle Tales No. 1-7)
Atlas Comics (CSI): No. 8, Nov, 1955 - No. 17, June, 1957

	GD	VG	FN	VF	VF/NM	NM-
8(#1)	47	94	141	296	498	700
9,11-15	28	56	84	168	274	380
10-Williamson/Colletta-c	30	60	90	177	289	400
16,17-Williamson/Mayo-a(3), 5 pgs. each	31	62	93	182	296	410

NOTE: *Everett c-15-17. Heck a-8, 15, 17. Maneely c-11. Shores a-8.*

JASON & THE ARGOBOTS
Oni Press: Aug, 2002 - No. 4, Dec, 2002 ($2.95, B&W, limited series)
1-4-Torres-s/Norton-c/a 3.00
Vol. 1 Birthquake TPB (6/03, $11.95, digest size) r/#1-4, Sunday comic strips 12.00
Vol. 2 Machina Ex Deus TPB (9/03, $11.95, digest size) new story 12.00

JASON & THE ARGONAUTS (See Movie Classics)

JASON GOES TO HELL: THE FINAL FRIDAY (Movie)
Topps Comics: July, 1993 - No. 3, Sept, 1993 ($2.95, limited series)

	GD	VG	FN	VF	VF/NM	NM-
1-Adaptation of film. 1-Glow-in-the-dark-c	3	6	9	14	19	24
2,3-Adaptation continues	2	4	6	9	12	15

JASON'S QUEST (See Showcase #88-90)

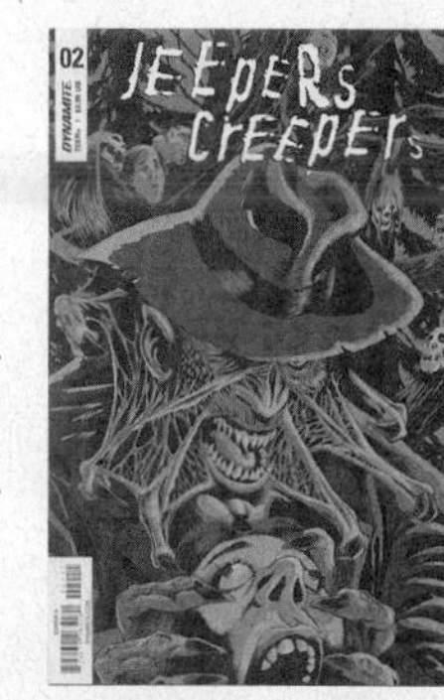

Jeepers Creepers #2 © UA

Jennifer Blood #3 © Spitfire

Jesse James #6 © AVON

GD VG FN VF VF/NM NM-
2.0 4.0 6.0 8.0 9.0 9.2

JASON VS. LEATHERFACE
Topps Comics: Oct, 1995 - No. 3, Jan, 1996 ($2.95, limited series)
1-Collins scripts; Bisley-c on all 2 4 6 13 18 22
2,3 2 4 6 8 11 14

JAWS 2 (See Marvel Comics Super Special, A)

JAY & SILENT BOB (See Clerks, Oni Double Feature, and Tales From the Clerks)
Oni Press: July, 1998 - No. 4, Oct, 1999 ($2.95, B&W, limited series)
1-Kevin Smith-s/Fegredo-a; photo-c & Quesada/Palmiotti-c 8.00
1-San Diego Comic Con variant covers (2 different covers, came packaged with action figures) 10.00
1-2nd & 3rd printings, 2-4: 2-Allred-c. 3-Flip-c by Jaime Hernandez 3.00
Chasing Dogma TPB (1999, $11.95) r/#1-4; Alanis Morissette intro. 13.00
Chasing Dogma TPB (2001, $12.95) r/#1-4 in color; Morissette intro. 13.00
Chasing Dogma HC (1999, $69.95, S&N) r/#1-4 in color; Morissette intro. 70.00

JCP FEATURES
J.C. Productions (Archie): Feb, 1982-c; Dec, 1981-indicia ($2.00, one-shot, B&W magazine)
1-T.H.U.N.D.E.R. Agents; Black Hood by Morrow & Neal Adams; Texeira-a; 2 pgs. S&K-a from Fly #1 2 4 6 10 14 18

JEAN GREY (X-Men) (Also see Phoenix Resurrection: The Return of Jean Grey)
Marvel Comics: Jul, 2017 - No. 11, Mar, 2018 ($3.99)
1-10: 1-Hopeless-s/Ibáñez-a. 4-Thor app. 6-Dr. Strange app. 7-Scarlet Witch app. 4.00
11-($4.99) Follows Phoenix Resurrection #5; leads into X-Men: Red #1 5.00

JEANIE COMICS (Formerly All Surprise; Cowgirl Romances #28)
Marvel Comics/Atlas(CPC): No. 13, April, 1947 - No. 27, Oct, 1949
13-Mitzi, Willie begin 39 78 117 231 378 525
14,15 26 52 78 152 249 345
16-Used in Love and Death by Legman; Kurtzman's "Hey Look" 30 60 90 177 289 400
17-19,21,22-Kurtzman's "Hey Look" (1-3 pgs. each) 21 42 63 124 202 280
20,23-27 20 40 60 115 185 255

JEEP COMICS (Also see G.I. Comics and Overseas Comics)
R. B. Leffingwell & Co.: Winter, 1944, No. 2, Spring, 1945 - No. 3, Mar-Apr, 1948
1-Capt. Power, Criss Cross & Jeep & Peep (costumed) begin 81 162 243 518 884 1250
2- Jeep & Peep-c 48 96 144 302 514 725
3-L. B. Cole dinosaur-c 61 122 183 390 670 950

JEEPERS CREEPERS (Based on the 2001 horror movie)
Dynamite Entertainment: 2018 - No. 5, 2018 ($3.99, limited series)
1-5-Marc Andreyko-s/Kewber Baal-a; multiple covers on each 4.00

JEFF JORDAN, U.S. AGENT
D. S. Publishing Co.: Dec, 1947 - Jan, 1948
1 20 40 60 115 185 255

JEFF STEINBERG: CHAMPION OF EARTH
Oni Press: Aug, 2016 - No. 6, Mar, 2017 ($4.99)
1-6: 1-Fialkov-s/Fleecs-a; covers by Fleecs & Burnham 5.00

JEM & THE HOLOGRAMS
IDW Publishing: Mar, 2015 - No. 26, Apr, 2017 ($3.99)
1-25: 1-Origin re-told; multiple covers 4.00
26-($4.99) Thompson-s/Lagace-a; previews Infinite x-over series; cover gallery 5.00
Annual 2017 (1/17, $7.99) Thompson-s; art by Lagace and others; 2 covers 8.00
... Holiday Special (12/15, $3.99) Mebberson-a 4.00
IDW Greatest Hits: Jem and the Holograms #1 (7/16, $1.00) r/#1 3.00
... 20/20 #1 (1/19, $4.99) Set 20 years in the future; Sina Grace-s/Siobhan Keenan-a 5.00
... Valentine Special (2/16, $3.99) Thompson-s/Bartel-a 4.00

JEM AND THE HOLOGRAMS: DIMENSIONS
IDW Publishing: Nov, 2017 - No. 4, Feb, 2018 ($3.99, limited series)
1-4-Anthology by various; multiple covers on each. 1-Leth-s/Ford-a 4.00

JEM AND THE HOLOGRAMS: INFINITE
IDW Publishing: Jun, 2017 - No. 3, Aug, 2017 ($3.99, limited series)
1-3-Part 1,3,5 of the x-over with Jem and the Holograms: The Misfits: Infinite 4.00

JEM AND THE HOLOGRAMS: THE MISFITS: INFINITE
IDW Publishing: Jun, 2017 - No. 3, Aug, 2017 ($3.99, limited series)
1-3-Part 2,4,6 of the x-over with Jem and the Holograms: Infinite 4.00

JEMM, SON OF SATURN
DC Comics: Sept, 1984 - No. 12, Aug, 1985 (Maxi-series, mando paper)
1-12: 3-Origin. 4-Superman app. 4.00
NOTE: ***Colan** a-1-12p; c-1-5, 7-12p.*

JEM: THE MISFITS (From Jem and the Holograms)
IDW Publishing: Dec, 2016 - No. 5, Apr, 2017 ($3.99)
1-5-Kelly Thompson-s/Jenn St-Onge-a 4.00

JENNIFER BLOOD
Dynamite Entertainment: 2011 - No. 36, 2014 ($3.99)
1-36: 1-3-Garth Ennis-s/Adriano Batista-a; four covers on each. 4-The Ninjettes app. 4.00
Annual 1 (2012, $4.99) Al Ewing-s/Igor Vitorino-a/Sean Chen-c; origin 5.00

JENNIFER BLOOD: BORN AGAIN
Dynamite Entertainment: 2014 - No. 5, 2014 ($3.99)
1-5-Steven Grant-s/Kewber Baal-a/Stephen Segovia-c 4.00

JENNIFER BLOOD: FIRST BLOOD
Dynamite Entertainment: 2011 - No. 6, 2013 ($3.99)
1-6-Mike Carroll-s/Igor Vitorino-a/Mike Mayhew-c; origin & training 4.00

JENNIFER'S BODY (Based on the 2009 movie)
BOOM! Studios: Aug, 2009 ($24.99, hardcover graphic novel)
HC-Short stories of Jennifer and her victims; Spears-s/art by various; pin-up art 25.00

JENNY FINN
Oni Press: June, 1999 - No. 2, Sept, 1999 ($2.95, B&W, unfinished lim. series)
1,2-Mignola & Nixey-s/Nixey-a/Mignola-c 3.00
...: Doom (Atomeka, 2005, $6.99, TPB) r/#1 & 2 with new supplemental material 7.00

JENNY SPARKS: THE SECRET HISTORY OF THE AUTHORITY
DC Comics (WildStorm): Aug, 2000 - No. 5, Mar, 2001 ($2.50, limited series)
1-Millar-s/McCrea & Hodgkins-a/Hitch & Neary-c 4.00
1-Variant-c by McCrea 1 3 4 6 8 10
2-5: 2-Apollo & Midnighter. 3-Jack Hawksmoor. 4-Shen. 5-Engineer 3.00
TPB (2001, $14.95) r/#1-5; Ellis intro. 15.00

JERICHO (Based on the TV series)
Devil's Due Publishing/IDW Publishing: Oct, 2009 - Jan, 2014 ($3.99)
... Redux (IDW, 2/11, $7.99) r/Season 3: Civil War #1-3 8.00
... Season 3: Civil War 1-4: 1-Story by the show's writing staff 4.00
... Season 4: 1-5: 1-(7/12) Photo-c & Bradstreet-c 4.00

JERRY DRUMMER (Boy Heroes of the Revolutionary War) (Formerly Soldier & Marine V2#9)
Charlton Comics: V3#10, Apr, 1957 - V3#12, Oct, 1957
V3#10-12: 11-Whitman-c/a 6 12 18 29 36 42

JERRY IGER'S... (All titles, Blackthorne/First)(Value: cover or less)

JERRY LEWIS (See The Adventures of...)

JERSEY GODS
Image Comics: Feb, 2009 - No. 12, May, 2010 ($3.50)
1-11: 1-Brunswick-s/McDaid-a; two covers by McDaid and Allred 3.50
12-($4.99) Wraparound cover swipe of Superman #252 by Allred 5.00

JESSE JAMES (The True Story Of..., also seeThe Legend of...)
Dell Publishing Co.: No. 757, Dec, 1956 (one shot)
Four Color 757-Movie, photo-c 9 18 27 58 114 170

JESSE JAMES (See Badmen of the West & Blazing Sixguns)
Avon Periodicals: 8/50 - No. 9, 11/52; No. 15, 10/53 - No. 29, 8-9/56
1-Kubert Alabam-r/Cowpuncher #1 23 46 69 136 223 310
2-Kubert-a(3) 17 34 51 103 162 220
3-Kubert Alabam-r/Cowpuncher #2 16 32 48 96 151 205
4,9-No Kubert 13 26 39 72 101 130
5,6-Kubert Jesse James-a(3); 5-Wood-a(1pg.) 16 32 48 96 151 205
7-Kubert Jesse James-a(2) 15 30 45 86 133 180
8-Kinstler-a(3) 14 28 42 76 108 140
15-Kinstler-r/#3 11 22 33 64 90 115
16-Kinstler-r/#3 & story-r/Butch Cassidy #1 12 24 36 67 94 120
17-19,21: 17-Jesse James-r/#4; Kinstler-c idea from Kubert splash in #6. 18-Kubert Jesse James-r/#5. 19-Kubert Jesse James-r/#6. 21-Two Jesse James-r/#4, Kinstler-r/#4 11 22 33 60 83 105
20-Williamson/Frazetta-a; r/Chief Vic. Apache Massacre; Kubert Jesse James-r/#6; Kit West story by Larsen 17 34 51 100 158 215
22-29: 22,23-No Kubert. 24-New McCarty strip by Kinstler; Kinstler-r. 25-New McCarty Jesse James strip by Kinstler; Jesse James-r/#7,9. 26,27-New McCarty Jesse James strip plus a Kinstler/McCann Jesse James-r. 28-Reprints most of Red Mountain, Featuring Quantrells Raiders 11 22 33 60 83 105
Annual nn (1952; 25¢, 100 pgs.)- "...Brings Six-Gun Justice to the West"- 3 earlier issues rebound; Kubert, Kinstler-a(3) 36 72 108 214 347 480
NOTE: *Mostly reprints #10 on. **Fawcette** c-1, 2. **Kida** a-5. **Kinstler** a-3, 4, 7-9, 15r, 16r(2), 21-27; c-3, 4, 9, 17-27.*

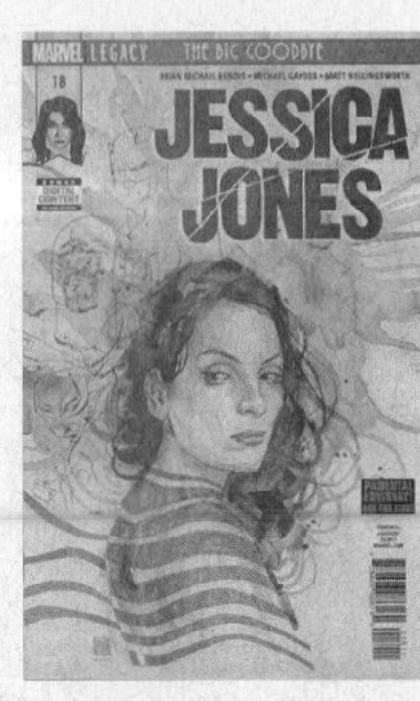

Jessica Jones #18 © MAR

The Jetsons #8 © H-B

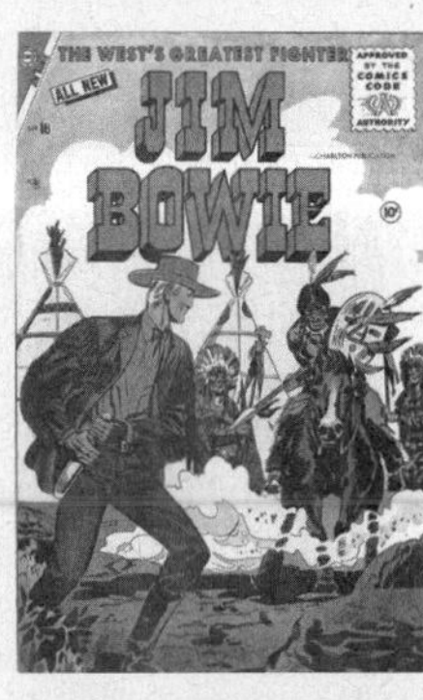

Jim Bowie #16 © CC

	GD 2.0	VG 4.0	FN 6.0	VF 8.0	VF/NM 9.0	NM- 9.2

Painted c-5-8. 22 has 2 stories r/Sheriff Bob Dixon's Chuck Wagon #1 with name changed to Sheriff Bob Trent.

JESSE JAMES
Realistic Publications: July, 1953

nn-Reprints Avon's #1; same-c, colors different	11	22	33	60	83	105

JESSICA JONES (Also see Alias)
Marvel Comics: Dec, 2016 - No. 18, May, 2018 ($3.99)

1-18-Bendis-s/Gaydos-a; Luke Cage app. 1-Misty Knight app. 13-17-Purple Man app. 4.00
...: Purple Daughter (2019, $19.99, square-bound) Printing of digital-first story; De Julis-a 20.00

JESSICA JONES: BLIND SPOT
Marvel Comics: Mar, 2020 - No. 6, May, 2020 ($3.99, printing of digital-first story)

1-6-Kelly Thompson-s/Mattia De Iulis-a. 2,3-Elsa Bloodstone app. 4-Spider-Man app. 4.00

JEST (Formerly Snap; becomes Kayo #12)
Harry 'A' Chesler: No. 10, 1944; No. 11, 1944

10-Johnny Rebel & Yankee Boy app. in text	26	52	78	154	252	350
11-Little Nemo in Adventure Land	23	46	69	136	223	310

JESTER
Harry 'A' Chesler: No. 10, 1945

10	22	44	66	128	209	290

JESUS
Spire Christian Comics (Fleming H. Revell Co.): 1979 (49¢)

nn	2	4	6	11	16	20

JET (See Jet Powers)

JET (Crimson from Wildcore & Backlash)
DC Comics (WildStorm): Nov, 2000 - No. 4, Feb, 2001 ($2.50, limited series)

1-4-Nguyen-a/Abnett & Lanning-s 3.00

JET ACES
Fiction House Magazines: 1952 - No. 4, 1953

1- Sky Advs. of American War Aces (on sale 6/20/52)	22	44	66	128	209	290
2-4	14	28	42	80	115	150

JETCAT CLUBHOUSE (Also see Land of Nod, The)
Oni Press: Apr, 2001 - No. 3, Aug, 2001 ($3.25)

1-3-Jay Stephens-s/a. 1-Wraparound-c 3.25
TPB (8/02, $10.95, 8 3/4" x 5 3/4") r/#1-3 & stories from Nickelodeon mag. & other 11.00

JET DREAM (...and Her Stunt-Girl Counterspies)(See The Man from Uncle #7)
Gold Key: June, 1968 (12¢)

1-Painted-c	4	8	12	23	37	50

JET FIGHTERS (Korean War)
Standard Magazines: No. 5, Nov, 1952 - No. 7, Mar, 1953

5,7-Toth-a. 5-Toth-c	15	30	45	92	144	195
6-Celardo-a	13	26	39	74	105	135

JET POWER
I.W. Enterprises: 1963

I.W. Reprint 1,2-r/Jet Powers #1,2	3	6	9	16	24	32

JET POWERS (American Air Forces No. 5 on)
Magazine Enterprises: 1950 - No. 4, 1951

1(A-1 #30)-Powell-c/a begins	41	82	123	256	428	600
2(A-1 #32) Classic Powell dinosaur-c/a	41	82	123	256	428	600
3(A-1 #35)-Williamson/Evans-a	42	84	126	265	445	625
4(A-1 #38)-Williamson/Wood-a; "The Rain of Sleep" drug story	43	86	129	271	461	650

JET PUP (See 3-D Features)

JETSONS, THE (TV) (See March of Comics #276, 330, 348 & Spotlight #3)
Gold Key: Jan, 1963 - No. 36, Oct, 1970 (Hanna-Barbera)

1-1st comic book app.	28	56	84	202	451	700
2	10	20	30	67	141	215
3-10: 9-Flintstones x-over	8	16	24	51	96	140
11-22	6	12	18	40	73	105
23-36-Reprints: 23-(7/67)	4	8	12	27	44	60

JETSONS, THE (TV) (Also see Golden Comics Digest)
Charlton Comics: Nov, 1970 - No. 20, Dec, 1973 (Hanna-Barbera)

1	9	18	27	61	123	185
2	4	8	12	28	47	65
3-10: Flintstones x-over	3	6	9	20	31	42
11-20	3	6	9	16	24	32
nn (1973, digest, 60¢, 100 pgs.) B&W one page gags	4	8	12	23	37	50

JETSONS, THE (TV)
Harvey Comics: V2#1, Sept, 1992 - No. 5, Nov, 1993 ($1.25/$1.50) (Hanna-Barbera)

V2#1-5 5.00
...Big Book V2#1,2,3 ($1.95, 52 pgs.): 1-(11/92). 2-(4/93). 3-(7/93) 5.00
...Giant Size 1,2,3 ($2.25, 68 pgs): 1-(10/92). 2-(4/93). 3-(10/93) 5.00

JETSONS, THE (TV)
Archie Comics: Sept, 1995 - No. 8, Apr, 1996 ($1.50)

1-8 4.00

JETSONS, THE (TV)
DC Comics: Jan, 2018 - No. 6, Mar, 2018 ($3.99, limited series)

1-6: 1-Palmiotti-s/Brito-a; covers by Conner & Dave Johnson 4.00

JETTA OF THE 21ST CENTURY
Standard Comics: No. 5, Dec, 1952 - No. 7, Apr, 1953 (Teen-age Archie type)

5-Dan DeCarlo-a	81	162	243	518	884	1250
6-Robot-c	57	114	171	362	619	875
7	45	90	135	284	480	675

TPB (Airwave Publ., 2006, $9.99) B&W reprint of series; Bill Morrison intro./back-c 10.00

JEW GANGSTER
DC Comics: 2005 ($14.99, SC graphic novel)

SC-Joe Kubert-s/a 15.00

JEZEBEL JADE (Hanna-Barbara)
Comico: Oct, 1988 - No. 3, Dec, 1988 ($2.00, mini-series)

1-3: Johnny Quest spin-off; early Adam Kubert-a 3.00

JEZEBELLE (See Wildstorm 2000 Annuals)
DC Comics (WildStorm): Mar, 2001 - No. 6, Aug, 2001 ($2.50, limited series)

1-6-Ben Raab-s/Steve Ellis-a 3.00

JIGGS & MAGGIE
Dell Publishing Co.: No. 18, 1941 (one shot)

Four Color 18 (#1)-(1936-38-r)	57	114	171	362	619	875

JIGGS & MAGGIE
Standard Comics/Harvey Publications No. 22 on: No. 11, 1949 (June) - No. 21, 2/53; No. 22, 4/53 - No. 27, 2-3/54

11	20	40	60	114	182	250
12-15,17-21	14	28	42	76	108	140
16-Wood text illos.	14	28	42	78	112	145
22-24-Little Dot app.	12	24	36	69	97	125
25,27	11	22	33	60	83	105
26-Four pgs. partially in 3-D	15	30	45	83	124	165

NOTE: *Sunday page reprints by McManus loosely blended into story continuity. Based on Bringing Up Father strip. Advertised on covers as "All New."*

JIGSAW (Big Hero Adventures)
Harvey Publ. (Funday Funnies): Sept, 1966 - No. 2, Dec, 1966 (36 pgs.)

1-Origin & 1st app.; Crandall-a (5 pgs.)	3	6	9	21	33	45
2-Man From S.R.A.M.	3	6	9	15	22	28

JIGSAW OF DOOM (See Complete Mystery No. 2)

JIM BOWIE (Formerly Danger?; Black Jack No. 20 on)
Charlton Comics: No. 16, Mar, 1956 - No. 19, Apr, 1957

16	8	16	24	42	54	65
17-19: 18-Giordano-c	6	12	18	29	36	42

JIM BOWIE (TV, see Western Tales)
Dell Publishing Co.: No. 893, Mar, 1958 - No. 993, May-July, 1959

Four Color 893 (#1)	6	12	18	41	76	110
Four Color 993-Photo-c	5	10	15	35	63	90

JIM BUTCHER'S THE DRESDEN FILES: DOG MEN (Based on the Dresden Files novels)
Dynamite Entertainment: 2017 - No. 6, 2017 ($3.99, limited series)

1-6: 1-Jim Butcher & Mark Powers-s/Diego Galindo-a/c 4.00

JIM BUTCHER'S THE DRESDEN FILES: DOWN TOWN (Based on the Dresden Files novels)
Dynamite Entertainment: 2015 - No. 6, 2015 ($3.99, limited series)

1-6: 1-Jim Butcher & Mark Powers-s/Carlos Gomez-a/Stjepan Sejic-c 4.00

JIM BUTCHER'S THE DRESDEN FILES: FOOL MOON
Dynamite Entertainment: 2011 - No. 8, 2012 ($3.99, limited series)

1-8: 1-Jim Butcher & Mark Powers-s/Chase Conley-a/Brett Booth-c 4.00

JIM BUTCHER'S THE DRESDEN FILES: GHOUL GOBLIN
Dynamite Entertainment: 2012 - No. 6, 2013 ($3.99, limited series)

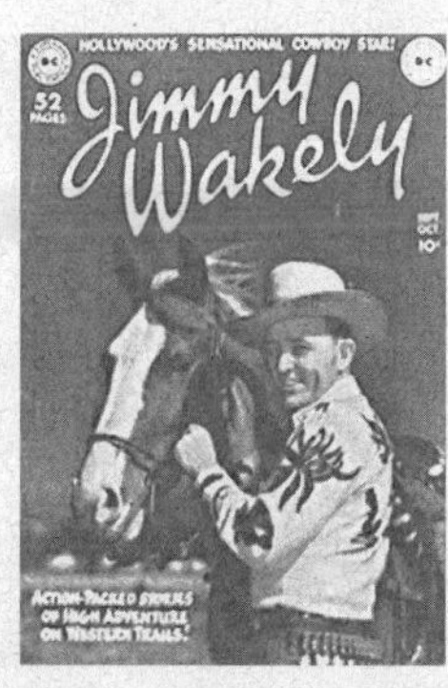

Jimmy Wakely #1 © DC

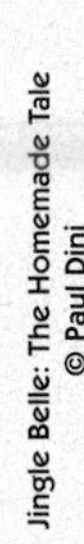
Jingle Belle: The Homemade Tale © Paul Dini

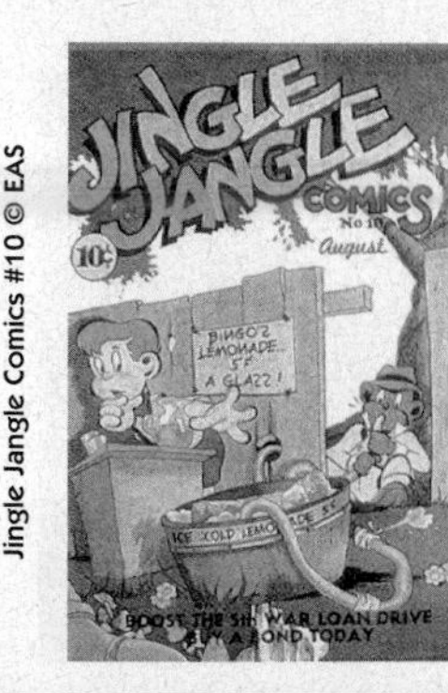

Jingle Jangle Comics #10 © EAS

	GD 2.0	VG 4.0	FN 6.0	VF 8.0	VF/NM 9.0	NM- 9.2

1-6: 1-Jim Butcher & Mark Powers-s/Joseph Cooper-a; Syaf-c 4.00

JIM BUTCHER'S THE DRESDEN FILES: STORM FRONT (Based on the Dresden Files novels)
Dabel Bros. Productions: Oct, 2008 (Nov. on-c) - No. 4, Apr, 2009 ($3.99, limited series)

1-4-Jim Butcher & Mark Powers-s/Ardian Syaf-a; covers by Syaf & Tsai 4.00
Vol. 2: 1,2 (7/09 - No. 4) 4.00

JIM BUTCHER'S THE DRESDEN FILES: WAR CRY
Dynamite Entertainment: 2014 - No. 5, 2014 ($3.99/$4.99, limited series)

1-4: 1-Jim Butcher & Mark Powers-s/Carlos Gomez-a; Sejic-c 4.00
5-($4.99) Wraparound-c by Sejic 5.00

JIM BUTCHER'S THE DRESDEN FILES: WELCOME TO THE JUNGLE
Dabel Bros. Productions: Mar, 2008 (Apr. on-c) - No. 4, Jul, 2008 ($3.99, limited series)

1-Jim Butcher-s/Ardian Syaf-a; Ardian Syaf-c 5.00
1-Variant-c by Chris McGrath 8.00
1-New York Comic-Con 2008 variant-c 15.00
1-Second printing 4.00
2-4-Two covers on each 4.00
HC (2008, $19.95, dustjacket) r/#1-4; Butcher intro.; concept art pages 20.00

JIM BUTCHER'S THE DRESDEN FILES: WILD CARD
Dynamite Entertainment: 2016 - No. 6, 2016 ($3.99, limited series)

1-6-Jim Butcher & Mark Powers-s/Carlos Gomez-a/c 4.00

JIM DANDY
Dandy Magazine (Lev Gleason): May, 1956 - No. 3, Sept, 1956 (Charles Biro)

1-Jim Dandy adventures w/Cup, an alien & his flying saucer (both invisible) from the planet Zikalug begins; ends #3. Biro-c. 1,2-Bammy Boozle app.
14 28 42 80 115 150
2,3: 2-Two pg. actual flying saucer reports 10 20 30 54 72 90

JIM HARDY (See Giant Comics Eds., Sparkler & Treasury of Comics #2 & 5)
United Features Syndicate/Spotlight Publ.: 1939; 1942; 1947 - No. 2, 1947

Single Series 6 ('39) 48 96 144 302 514 725
Single Series 27('42) 39 78 117 231 378 525
1('47)-Spotlight Publ. 16 32 48 96 151 205
2 10 20 30 58 79 100

JIM HARDY
Spotlight/United Features Synd.: 1944 (25¢, 132 pgs.) (Tip Top, Sparkler-r)

nn-Origin Mirror Man; Triple Terror app. 41 82 123 256 428 600

JIM HENSON'S BENEATH THE DARK CRYSTAL
BOOM! Studios (Archaia): Jul, 2018 - No. 12, Aug, 2019 ($3.99, limited series)

1-12-Adam Smith-s/Alexandria Huntington-a 4.00

JIM HENSON'S LABYRINTH: CORONATION
BOOM! Studios (Archaia): Feb, 2018 - No. 12, Mar, 2019 ($3.99, limited series)

1-12: 1-Spurrier-s/Bayliss-a/Staples-c; Jareth before becoming the Goblin King 4.00

JIM HENSON'S LABYRINTH: UNDER THE SPELL
BOOM! Studios (Archaia): Nov, 2018 ($7.99, one-shot)

1-Short stories; Vidaurri-s/Webb-a; Grace-s/Sun-a; Dialynas-s/a; Issacs-c 8.00

JIM HENSON'S THE DARK CRYSTAL: AGE OF RESISTANCE
BOOM! Studios (Archaia): Sept, 2019 - No. 12, Oct, 2020 ($3.99, limited series)

1-12: 1-6,8-Addis & Matthews-s/Andelfinger-a. 7-Carlomagno-a. 9-12-Migyeong-a 4.00

JIM HENSON'S THE STORYTELLER: DRAGONS (Also see The Storyteller)
BOOM! Studios (Archaia): Dec, 2015 - No. 4, Mar, 2016 ($3.99, limited series)

1-4: 2-Pride-s/a 4.00

JIM HENSON'S THE STORYTELLER: GHOSTS
BOOM! Studios (Archaia): Mar, 2019 - No. 4, Aug, 2020 ($3.99, limited series)

1-4: 1-Márk László-s/a. 2-Jennifer Rostowsky-s/a. 3-Michael Walsh-s/a 4-VER-s/a 4.00

JIM HENSON'S THE STORYTELLER: WITCHES
BOOM! Studios (Archaia): Sept, 2014 - No. 4, Dec, 2014 ($3.99, limited series)

1-4: 1-Vidaurri-s/a. 2-Vanderklugt-s/a. 3-Matthew Dow Smith-s/a. 4-Stokely-s/a 4.00

JIMINY CRICKET (Disney,, see Mickey Mouse Mag. V5#3 & Walt Disney Showcase #37)
Dell Publishing Co.: No. 701, May, 1956 - No. 989, May-July, 1959

Four Color 701 8 16 24 51 96 140
Four Color 795, 897, 989 6 12 18 38 69 100

JIM LEE SKETCHBOOK
DC Comics (WildStorm): 2002 (no price, 16 pgs.)

nn-Various DC and WildStorm character sketches by Lee 8.00

JIMMY CORRIGAN (See Acme Novelty Library)

JIMMY DURANTE (Also see A-1 Comics)
Magazine Enterprises: No. 18, Oct, 1949 - No. 20, Winter 1949-50

A-1 18,20-Photo-c (scarce) 52 104 156 328 552 775

JIMMY OLSEN (See Superman's Pal...)

JIMMY OLSEN
DC Comics: May, 2011 ($5.99, one-shot)

1-Reprints back-up feature from Action Comics #893-896 plus new material; Conner-c 6.00

JIMMY OLSEN: ADVENTURES BY JACK KIRBY
DC Comics: 2003, 2004 ($19.95, TPB)

nn-(2003) Reprints Jack Kirby's early issues of Superman's Pal Jimmy Olsen #133-139,141; Mark Evanier intro.; cover by Kirby and Steve Rude 20.00
Vol. 2 (2004) Reprints #142-148; Evanier intro.; cover gallery and sketch pages 20.00

JIMMY'S BASTARDS
AfterShock Comics: Jun, 2017 - No. 9, Jul, 2018 ($3.99)

1-9: 1-Garth Ennis-s/Russ Braun-a/Dave Johnson-c; intro. Secret Agent Jimmy Regent 4.00

JIMMY WAKELY (Cowboy movie star)
National Per. Publ.: Sept-Oct, 1949 - No. 18, July-Aug, 1952 (1-13: 52pgs.)

1-Photo-c, 52 pgs. begin; Alex Toth-a; Kit Colby Girl Sheriff begins
42 84 126 265 445 625
2-Toth-a 18 36 54 107 169 230
3,4,6,7-Frazetta-a in all, 3 pgs. each; Toth-a in all. 7-Last photo-c. 4-Kurtzman "Pot-Shot Pete", 1 pg; Toth-a 21 42 63 122 199 275
5,8-15-Toth-a; 12,14-Kubert-a (3 & 2 pgs.) 16 32 48 94 147 200
16-18 15 30 45 83 124 165
NOTE: *Gil Kane c-10-18p.*

JIM RAY'S AVIATION SKETCH BOOK
Vital Publishers: Mar-Apr, 1946 - No. 2, May-June, 1946 (15¢)

1-Picture stories of planes and pilots; atomic explosion panel
40 80 120 246 411 575
2-Story of General "Nap" Arnold 27 54 81 160 263 365

JIM SOLAR (See Wisco/Klarer in the Promotional Comics section)

JINGLE BELLE (Paul Dini's...)
Oni Press/Top Cow: Nov, 1999 - No. 2, Dec, 1999 ($2.95, B&W, limited series)

1,2-Paul Dini-s. 2-Alex Ross flip-c 4.00
Jingle Belle: Dash Away All (12/03, $11.95, digest-size) Dini-s/Garibaldi-a 12.00
Jingle Belle: Gift-Wrapped (Top Cow, 12/11, $3.99) Dini-s/Gladden-a 4.00
Jingle Belle: Santa Claus vs. Frankenstein (Top Cow, 12/08, $2.99) Dini-s/Gladden-a 3.00
Jingle Belle's Cool Yule (11/02, $13.95,TPB) r/All-Star Holiday Hullabaloo, The Mighty Elves, and Jubilee; internet strips and a color section w/DeStefano-a 14.00
Jingle Belle: The Homemade's Tale (IDW, 11/18, $4.99) Dini-s/Baldari-a/Buscema-c 5.00
Paul Dini's Jingle Belle Jubilee (11/01, $2.95) Dini-s; art by Rolston, DeCarlo, Morrison and Bone; pin-ups by Thompson and Aragonés 3.00
Paul Dini's Jingle Belle's All-Star Holiday Hullabaloo (11/00, $4.95) stories by various including Dini, Aragonés, Jeff Smith, Bill Morrison; Frank Cho-c 5.00
Paul Dini's Jingle Belle: The Fight Before Christmas (12/05, $2.99) Dini-s/Bone & others-a 3.00
Paul Dini's Jingle Belle: The Mighty Elves (7/01, $2.95) Dini-s/Bone-a 3.00
Paul Dini's Jingle Belle Winter Wingding (11/02, $2.95) Dini-s/Clugston-Major-c 3.00
The Bakers Meet Jingle Belle (12/06, $2.99) Dini-s/Kyle Baker-a 3.00
TPB (10/00, $8.95) r/#1&2, and app. from Oni Double Feature #13 9.00

JINGLE BELLE (Paul Dini's...)
Dark Horse Comics: Nov, 2004 - No. 4, Apr, 2005 ($2.99, limited series)

1-4-Paul Dini-s/Jose Garibaldi-a 3.00
TPB (9/05, $12.95) r/#1-4 13.00

JINGLE BELLS (See March of Comics No. 65)

JINGLE DINGLE CHRISTMAS STOCKING COMICS (See Foodini #2)
Stanhall Publications: V2#1, 1951 (no date listed) (25¢, 100 pgs.; giant-size) (Publ. annually)

V2#1-Foodini & Pinhead, Silly Pilly plus games & puzzles
26 52 78 152 249 345

JINGLE JANGLE COMICS (Also see Puzzle Fun Comics)
Eastern Color Printing Co.: Feb, 1942 - No. 42, Dec, 1949

1-Pie-Face Prince of Old Pretzleburg, Jingle Jangle Tales by George Carlson, Hortense, & Benny Bear begin 52 104 156 328 552 775
2-4: 2,3-No Pie-Face Prince. 4-Pie-Face Prince-c 23 46 69 136 223 310
5 (10/42) 20 40 60 115 188 260
6-10: 8-No Pie-Face Prince 15 30 45 86 133 180
11-15 13 26 39 72 101 130
16-30: 17,18-No Pie-Face Prince. 24,30-XMas-c 10 20 30 56 76 95
31-42: 36,42-Xmas-c 9 18 27 52 69 85

Jinny Hex Special #1 © DC

Jinx V2 #5 © Bendis

JLA #72 © DC

	GD	VG	FN	VF	VF/NM	NM-
	2.0	4.0	6.0	8.0	9.0	9.2

	GD	VG	FN	VF	VF/NM	NM-
	2.0	4.0	6.0	8.0	9.0	9.2

NOTE: ***George Carlson** a-(2) in all except No. 2, 3, 8; c-1-6. **Carlson** 1 pg. puzzles in 9, 10, 12-15, 18, 20. **Carlson** illustrated a series of Uncle Wiggily books in 1930's.*

JING PALS
Victory Publishing Corp.: Feb, 1946 - No. 4, Aug?, 1946 (Funny animal)

	GD	VG	FN	VF	VF/NM	NM-
1-Wishing Willie, Puggy Panda & Johnny Rabbit begin	19	38	57	114	176	240
2-4	13	26	39	72	101	130

JINKS, PIXIE, AND DIXIE (See Kite Fun Book & Whitman Comic Books)

JINNY HEX SPECIAL (From Young Justice 2019 series)
DC Comics: Feb, 2021 ($4.99, one shot)
1-Visaggio-s/Melnikov-a/Derington-c; Jonah Hex and Superman cameos 5.00

JINX
Caliber Press: 1996 - No. 7, 1996 ($2.95, B&W, 32 pgs.)
1-7: Brian Michael Bendis-c/a/scripts. 2-Photo-c 3.00

JINX (Volume 2)
Image Comics: 1997 - No. 5, 1998 ($2.95, B&W, bi-monthly)
1-4: Brian Michael Bendis-c/a/scripts. 3.00
5-($3.95) Brereton-c 4.00
...Buried Treasures ('98, $3.95) short stories, ...Confessions ('98, $3.95) short stories, ...Pop Culture Hoo-Hah ('98, $3.95) humor shorts 4.00
TPB (1997, $10.95) r/Vol 1,#1-4 11.00
...: The Definitive Collection ('01, $24.95) remastered #1-5, sketch pages, art gallery, script excerpts, Mack intro. 25.00

JINX: TORSO
Image Comics: 1998 - No. 6, 1999 ($3.95/$4.95, B&W)
1-6-Based on Eliot Ness' pursuit of America's first serial killer; Brian Michael Bendis & Marc Andreyko-s/Bendis-a. 3-6-($4.95) 5.00
Softcover (2000, $24.95) r/#1-6; intro. by Greg Rucka; photo essay of the actual murders and police documents 25.00
Hardcover (2000, $49.95) signed & numbered 50.00

JINXWORLD SAMPLER
DC Comics: 2018 ($1.00)
nn-Reprints Scarlet #1, United States of Murder, Inc. #1 & Powers #1; Bendis-s 3.00

JIRNI
Aspen MLT: Apr, 2013 - No. 5, Oct, 2013 ($1.00/$3.99)
1-($1.00) J.T. Krul-s/Paolo Pantalena-a; multiple covers 3.00
2-5-($3.99) Multiple covers on each 4.00
Vol. 2 #1 (6/14, $3.99) Krul-s/Pantalena-a 4.00
Vol. 2 #1-5 (8/15 - No. 5, 12/15, $3.99) Krul-s/Marion-a; multiple covers on each 4.00
Vol. 3 #1-5 (3/18 - No. 5, 7/18, $3.99) Krul-s/Maria-a; multiple covers on each 4.00
... Primer (3/18, 25¢) Origin re-told with re-cap of Vol. 1 & 2; sketch art 4.00

JLA (See Justice League of America and Justice Leagues)
DC Comics: Jan, 1997 - No. 125, Apr, 2006 ($1.95/$1.99/$2.25/$2.50)

	GD	VG	FN	VF	VF/NM	NM-
1-Morrison-s/Porter & Dell-a. The Hyperclan app.	2	4	6	9	12	15
2	1	3	4	6	8	10
3,4	1	2	3	5	7	9

5-Membership drive; Tomorrow Woman app. 6.00
6-9: 6-1st app. Zauriel. 8-Green Arrow joins. 6.00
10-21: 10-Rock of Ages begins. 11-Joker and Luthor-c/app. 12-Intro. Hourman from the 853rd century. 14-Darkseid app. 15-($2.95) Rock of Ages concludes; intro. Superman One Million. 16-New members join; Prometheus app. 17,20-Jorgensen-a. 18-21-Waid-s. 20,21-Adam Strange c/app. 5.00
22-40: 22-Begin $1.99-c; Sandman (Daniel) app. 23-1st app. Justice Legion A. 27-Amazo app. 28-31-JSA app. 35-Hal Jordan/Spectre app. 36-40-World War 3 4.00
41-($2.99) Conclusion of World War 3; last Morrison-s 5.00
42-49,51-74: 43-Waid-s; Ra's al Ghul app. 44-Begin $2.25-c. 46-Batman leaves. 47-Hitch & Neary-a begins; JLA battles Queen of Fables. 52-55-Hitch-a. 59-Joker: Last Laugh. 61-68-Kelly-s/Mahnke-a. 69-73-Hunt for Aquaman; bi-monthly with alternating art by Mahnke and Guichet 4.00
50-($3.75) JLA vs. Dr. Destiny; art by Hitch & various 5.00
75-(1/03, $3.95) leads into Aquaman (4th series) #1 5.00
76-99: 76-Firestorm app. 77-Banks-a. 79-Kanjar Ro app. 91-93-O'Neil-s/Huat-a. 94-99-Byrne & Ordway-a/Claremont-s; Doom Patrol app. 4.00
100-($3.50) Intro. Vera Black; leads into Justice League Elite #1 5.00
101-125: 101-106-Austen-s/Garney-a/c. 107-114-Crime Syndicate app.; Busiek-s. 115-Begin $2.50-c; Johns & Heinberg-s; Secret Society of Super-Villains app. 4.00
#1,000,000 (11/98) 853rd Century x-over 4.00
Annual 1 (1997, $3.95) Pulp Heroes; Augustyn-s/Olivetti & Ha-a 5.00
Annual 2 (1998, $2.95) Ghosts; Wrightson-c 5.00
Annual 3 (1999, $2.95) JLApe; Art Adams-c 5.00
Annual 4 (2000, $3.50) Planet DC x-over; Steve Scott-c/a 5.00
... American Dreams (1998, $7.95, TPB) r/#5-9 8.00
...: Crisis of Conscience TPB (2006, $12.99) r/#115-119 13.00
.../ Cyberforce (DC/Top Cow, 2005, $5.99) Kelly-s/Mahnke-a/Silvestri-c 6.00
Divided We Fall (2001, $17.95, TPB) r/#47-54 18.00
...80-Page Giant 1 (7/98, $4.95) stories & art by various 6.00
...80-Page Giant 2 (11/99, $4.95) Green Arrow & Hawkman app. Hitch-c 6.00
...80-Page Giant 3 (10/00, $5.95) Pariah & Harbinger; intro. Moon Maiden 6.00
...Foreign Bodies (1999, $5.95, one-shot) Kobra app.; Semeiks-a 6.00
...Gallery (1997, $2.95) pin-ups by various; Quitely-c 4.00
...God & Monsters (2001, $6.95, one-shot) Benefiel-a/c 7.00
Golden Perfect (2003, $12.95, TPB) r/#61-65 13.00
.../ Haven: Anathema (2002, $6.95) Concludes the Haven: The Broken City series 7.00
.../ Haven: Arrival (2001, $6.95) Leads into the Haven: The Broken City series 7.00
...In Crisis Secret Files 1 (11/98, $4.95) recap of JLA in DC x-overs 5.00
...: Island of Dr. Moreau, The (2002, $6.95, one-shot) Elseworlds; Pugh-c/a; Thomas-s 7.00
.../ JSA Secret Files & Origins (1/03, $4.95) prelude to JLA/JSA: Virtue & Vice; short stories and pin-ups by various; Pacheco-c 5.00
.../ JSA: Virtue and Vice HC (2002, $24.95) Teams battle Despero & Johnny Sorrow; Goyer & Johns-s/Pacheco-a/c 25.00
.../ JSA: Virtue and Vice SC (2003, $17.95) 18.00
Justice For All (1999, $14.95, TPB) r/#24-33 15.00
New World Order (1997, $5.95, TPB) r/#1-4 6.00
...: Obsidian Age Book One, The (2003, $12.95) r/#66-71 13.00
...: Obsidian Age Book Two, The (2003, $12.95) r/#72-76 13.00
One Million (2004, $19.95, TPB) r/#DC One Million #1-4 and other #1,000,000 x-overs 20.00
...: Our Worlds at War (9/01, $2.95) Jae Lee-c; Aquaman presumed dead 4.00
...: Pain of the Gods (2005, $12.99) r/#101-106 13.00
...Primeval (1999, $5.95, one-shot) Abnett & Lanning-s/Olivetti-a 6.00
...: Riddle of the Beast HC (2001, $24.95) Grant-s/painted-a by various; Sweet-c 25.00
...: Riddle of the Beast SC (2003, $14.95) Grant-s/painted-a by various; Kaluta-c 15.00
Rock of Ages (1998, $9.95, TPB) r/#10-15 10.00
Rules of Engagement (2004, $12.95, TPB) r/#77-82 13.00
...: Seven Caskets (2000, $5.95, one-shot) Brereton-s/painted-c/a 6.00
...: Shogun of Steel (2002, $6.95, one-shot) Elseworlds; Justiniano-c/a 7.00
...Showcase 80-Page Giant (2/00, $4.95) Hitch-c 5.00
Strength in Numbers (1998, $12.95, TPB) r/#16-23, Secret Files #2 and Prometheus #1 13.00
...Superpower (1999, $5.95, one-shot) Arcudi-s/Eaton-a; Mark Antaeus joins 6.00
Syndicate Rules (2005, $17.99, TPB) r/#107-114, Secret Files #4 18.00
Terror Incognita (2002, $12.95, TPB) r/#55-60 13.00
...: The Deluxe Edition Vol. 1 HC (2008, $29.99, dustjacket) oversized r/#1-9 and JLA Secret Files #1 30.00
...: The Deluxe Edition Vol. 2 HC (2009, $29.99, dustjacket) oversized r/#10-17, JLA/Wildcats, and Prometheus #1 30.00
...: The Deluxe Edition Vol. 3 HC (2010, $29.99, dustjacket) oversized r/#22-26, 28-31 & #1,000,000 30.00
...: The Deluxe Edition Vol. 4 HC (2010, $34.99, dustjacket) oversized r/#34, 36-41, JLA Classified #1-3 and JLA: Earth 2 GN 35.00
The Tenth Circle (2004, $12.95, TPB) r/#94-99 13.00
...: The Greatest Stories Ever Told TPB (2006, $19.99) r/Justice League of America #19,71, 122,166-168,200, Justice League #1, JLA Secret Files #1 and JLA #61; Alex Ross-c 20.00
Tower of Babel (2001, $12.95, TPB) r/#42-46, Secret Files #3, 80-Page Giant #1 13.00
Trial By Fire (2004, $12.95, TPB) r/#84-89 13.00
...Vs. Predator (DC/Dark Horse, 2000, $5.95, one-shot) Nolan-c/a 6.00
...: Welcome to the Working Week (2003, $6.95, one-shot) Patton Oswalt-s 7.00
...: World War III (2000, $12.95, TPB) r/#34-41 13.00
...: World Without a Justice League (2006, $12.99, TPB) r/#120-125 13.00
...: Zatanna's Search (2003, $12.95, TPB) rep. Zatanna's early app. & origin; Bolland-c 13.00

JLA: ACT OF GOD
DC Comics: 2000 - No. 3, 2001 ($4.95, limited series)
1-3-Elseworlds; metahumans lose their powers; Moench-s/Dave Ross-a 5.00

JLA: AGE OF WONDER
DC Comics: 2003 - No. 2, 2003 ($5.95, limited series)
1,2-Elseworlds; Superman and the League of Science during the Industrial Revolution 6.00

JLA: A LEAGUE OF ONE
DC Comics: 2000 (Graphic novel)
Hardcover ($24.95) Christopher Moeller-s/painted-a 25.00
Softcover (2002, $14.95) 15.00

JLA/AVENGERS (See Avengers/JLA for #2 & #4)
Marvel Comics: Sept, 2003; No. 3, Dec, 2003 ($5.95, limited series)
1-Busiek-s/Pérez-a; wraparound-c; Krona, Starro, Grandmaster, Terminus app. 6.00
3-Busiek-s/Pérez-a; wraparound-c; Phantom Stranger app. 6.00

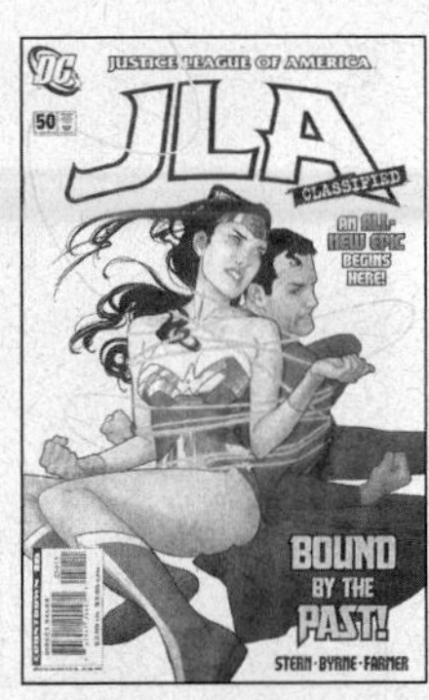

JLA Classified #50 © DC

JLA: Incarnations #2 © DC

JLA: Year One #5 © DC

	GD 2.0	VG 4.0	FN 6.0	VF 8.0	VF/NM 9.0	NM- 9.2

SC (2008, $19.99) r/4-issue series; cover gallery; intros by Stan Lee & Julius Schwartz 20.00

JLA: BLACK BAPTISM
DC Comics: May, 2001 - No. 4, Aug, 2001 ($2.50, limited series)

1-4-Saiz-a(p)/Bradstreet-c; Zatanna app. 4.00

JLA: CLASSIFIED
DC Comics: Jan, 2005 - No. 54, May, 2008 ($2.95/$2.99)

1-3-Morrison-s/McGuinness-a/c; Ultramarines app. 3.00
4-9-"I Can't Believe It's Not The Justice League," Giffen & DeMatteis-s/Maguire-a 3.00
10-31,33-54: 10-15-New Maps of Hell; Ellis-s/Guice-a. 16-21-Garcia-Lopez-a. 22-25-Detroit League & Royal Flush Gang app.; Englehart-s. 26-28-Chaykin-s. 37-41-Kid Amazo. 50-54-Byrne-a/Middleston-c 3.00
32-($3.99) Dr. Destiny app.; Jurgens-a 4.00
I Can't Believe It's Not The Justice League TPB (2005, $12.99) r/#4-9 13.00
...: Kid Amazo TPB (2007, $12.99) r/#37-41 13.00
...: New Maps of Hell TPB (2006, $12.99) r/#10-15 13.00
...: That Was Now, This Is Then TPB (2008, $14.99) r/#50-54 15.00
...: The Hypothetical Woman TPB (2008, $12.99) r/#16-21 13.00
...: Ultramarine Corps TPB (2007, $14.99) r/#1-3, JLA/WildC.A.T.s #1 and JLA Secret Files 2004 #1 15.00

JLA CLASSIFIED: COLD STEEL
DC Comics: 2005 - No. 2, 2006 ($5.99, limited series, prestige format)

1,2-Chris Moeller-s/a; giant robot Justice League 6.00

JLA: CREATED EQUAL
DC Comics: 2000 - No. 2, 2000 ($5.95, limited series, prestige format)

1,2-Nicieza-s/Maguire-a; Elseworlds-Superman as the last man on Earth 6.00

JLA: DESTINY
DC Comics: 2002 - No. 4, 2002 ($5.95, prestige format, limited series)

1-4-Elseworlds; Arcudi-s/Mandrake-a 6.00

JLA / DOOM PATROL SPECIAL (Milk Wars DC/Young Animal crossover)
DC Comics: Mar, 2018 ($4.99, one-shot)

1-Part 1 of crossover; Orlando & Way-s/Aco-a/Quitely-c; Lord Manga Khan app. 5.00

JLA: EARTH 2
DC Comics: 2000 (Graphic novel)

Hardcover ($24.95) Morrison-s/Quitely-a; Crime Syndicate app. 25.00
Softcover ($14.95) 15.00

JLA: GATEKEEPER
DC Comics: 2001 - No. 3, 2001 ($4.95, prestige format, limited series)

1-3-Truman-s/a 5.00

JLA: HEAVEN'S LADDER
DC Comics: 2000 ($9.95, Treasury-size one-shot)

nn-Bryan Hitch & Paul Neary-c/a; Mark Waid-s 10.00

JLA/HITMAN (Justice League/Hitman in indicia)
DC Comics: Nov, 2007 - No. 2, Dec, 2007 ($3.99, limited series)

1,2-Ennis-s/McCrea-a; Bloodlines creatures return 4.00

JLA: INCARNATIONS
DC Comics: Jul, 2001 - No. 7, Feb, 2002 ($3.50, limited series)

1-7-Ostrander-s/Semeiks-a; different eras of the Justice League 4.00

JLA: LIBERTY AND JUSTICE
DC Comics: Nov, 2003 ($9.95, Treasury-size one-shot)

nn-Alex Ross-c/a; Paul Dini-s; story of the classic Justice League 10.00

JLA PARADISE LOST
DC Comics: Jan, 1998 - No. 3, Mar, 1998 ($1.95, limited series)

1-3-Millar-s/Olivetti-a 4.00

JLA: SCARY MONSTERS
DC Comics: May, 2003 - No. 6, Oct, 2003 ($2.50, limited series)

1-6-Claremont-s/Art Adams-c 4.00

JLA SECRET FILES
DC Comics: Sept, 1997 - 2004 ($4.95)

1-Standard Ed. w/origin-s & pin-ups 5.00
1-Collector's Ed. w/origin-s & pin-ups; cardstock-c 6.00
2,3: 2-(8/98) origin-s of JLA #16's newer members. 3-(12/00) 5.00
... 2004 (11/04) Justice League Elite app.; Mahnke & Byrne-a; Crime Syndicate app. 5.00

JLA: SECRET ORIGINS
DC Comics: Nov, 2002 ($7.95, Treasury-size one-shot)

nn-Alex Ross 2-page origins of Justice League members; text by Paul Dini 8.00

JLA: SECRET SOCIETY OF SUPER-HEROES
DC Comics: 2000 - No. 2, 2000 ($5.95, limited series, prestige format)

1,2-Elseworlds JLA; Chaykin and Tischman-s/McKone-a 6.00

JLA /SPECTRE: SOUL WAR
DC Comics: 2003 - No. 2, 2003 ($5.95, limited series, prestige format)

1,2-DeMatteis-s/Banks & Neary-a 6.00

JLA: THE NAIL (Elseworlds) (Also see Justice League of America: Another Nail)
DC Comics: Aug, 1998 - No. 3, Oct, 1998 ($4.95, prestige format)

1-3-JLA in a world without Superman; Alan Davis-s/a(p) 5.00
TPB ('98, $12.95) r/series w/new Davis-c 13.00

JLA / TITANS
DC Comics: Dec, 1998 - No. 3, Feb, 1999 ($2.95, limited series)

1-3-Grayson-s; P. Jimenez-c/a 3.00
...:The Technis Imperative ('99, $12.95, TPB) r/#1-3; Titans Secret Files 13.00

JLA: TOMORROW WOMAN (Girlfrenzy)
DC Comics: June, 1998 ($1.95, one-shot)

1-Peyer-s; story takes place during JLA #5 3.00

JLA / WILDC.A.T.S
DC Comics: 1997 ($5.95, one-shot, prestige format)

1-Morrison-s/Semeiks & Conrad-a 6.00

JLA /WITCHBLADE
DC Comics/Top Cow: 2000 ($5.95, prestige format, one-shot)

1-Pararillo-c/a 6.00

JLA / WORLD WITHOUT GROWN-UPS (See Young Justice)
DC Comics: Aug, 1998 - No. 2, Sept, 1998 ($4.95, prestige format)

1,2-JLA, Robin, Impulse & Superboy app.; Ramos & McKone-a 6.00
TPB ('98, $9.95) r/series & Young Justice: The Secret #1 10.00

JLA: YEAR ONE
DC Comics: Jan, 1998 - No. 12, Dec, 1998 ($2.95/$1.95, limited series)

1-($2.95)-Waid & Augustyn-s/Kitson-a 5.00
1-Platinum Edition 12.00
2-12-($1.95): 5-Doom Patrol-c/app. 7-Superman app. 4.00
TPB ('99,'09; $19.95/$19.99) r/#1-12; Busiek intro. 20.00

JLA-Z
DC Comics: Nov, 2003 - No. 3, Jan, 2004 ($2.50, limited series)

1-3-Pin-ups and info on current and former JLA members and villains; art by various 4.00

JLX
DC Comics (Amalgam): Apr, 1996 ($1.95, one-shot)

1-Mark Waid scripts 5.00

JLX UNLEASHED
DC Comics (Amalgam): June, 1997 ($1.95, one-shot)

1-Priest-s/Oscar Jimenez & Rodriguez-a 4.00

JOAN OF ARC (Also see A-1 Comics, Classics Illustrated #78, and Ideal a Classical Comic)
Magazine Enterprises: No. 21, 1949 (one shot)

	GD 2.0	VG 4.0	FN 6.0	VF 8.0	VF/NM 9.0	NM- 9.2
A-1 21-Movie adaptation; Ingrid Bergman photo-covers & interior photos; Whitney-a	31	62	93	182	296	410

JOE COLLEGE
Hillman Periodicals: Fall, 1949 - No. 2, Wint, 1950 (Teen-age humor, 52 pgs.)

	GD 2.0	VG 4.0	FN 6.0	VF 8.0	VF/NM 9.0	NM- 9.2
1-Powell-a; Briefer-a	15	30	45	92	144	195
2-Powell-a	11	22	33	62	86	110

JOE FRANKENSTEIN
IDW Publishing: Feb, 2015 - No. 4, May, 2015 ($3.99)

1-4-Chuck Dixon & Graham Nolan-s/Graham Nolan-a 4.00

JOE GOLEM
Dark Horse Comics: Nov, 2015 - No. 5, Mar, 2016 ($3.50)

1-5-Mignola & Golden-s/Reynolds-a 4.00

JOE GOLEM: THE CONJURORS
Dark Horse Comics: May, 2019 - No. 5, Oct, 2019 ($3.99)

1-5-Mignola & Golden-s/Bergting-a 4.00

JOE GOLEM: THE DROWNING CITY
Dark Horse Comics: Sept, 2018 - No. 5, Jan, 2019 ($3.99)

1-5-Mignola & Golden-s/Bergting-a 4.00

Joe Kubert Presents #1 © DC

John Byrne's Next Men #5 © John Byrne

John Carter: The World of Mars #1 © DIS

GD 2.0 VG 4.0 FN 6.0 VF 8.0 VF/NM 9.0 NM- 9.2

JOE GOLEM: THE OUTER DARK
Dark Horse Comics: May, 2017 - No. 5, Jan, 2018 ($3.99)
1-5-Mignola & Golden-s/Reynolds-a. 4,5-Titled Joe Golem: Flesh and Blood #1,2 4.00

JOE JINKS
United Features Syndicate: No. 12, 1939
Single Series 12 33 66 99 196 321 445

JOE KUBERT PRESENTS
DC Comics: Dec, 2012 - No. 6, May, 2013 ($4.99, limited series)
1-6: Anthology of short stories by Kubert, Buniak & Glanzman. 1-Hawkman app. 5.00

JOE LOUIS (See Fight Comics #2, Picture News #6 & True Comics #5)
Fawcett Publications: Sept, 1950 - No. 2, Nov, 1950 (Photo-c) (Boxing champ) (See Dick Cole #10)
1-Photo-c; life story 60 120 180 381 653 925
2-Photo-c 42 84 126 265 445 625

JOE PALOOKA (1st Series)(Also see Big Shot Comics, Columbia Comics & Feature Funnies)
Columbia Comic Corp. (Publication Enterprises): 1942 - No. 4, 1944
1-1st to portray American president; gov't permission required
134 268 402 851 1463 2075
2 (1943)-Hitler-c 116 232 348 742 1271 1800
3-Nazi Sub-c 53 106 159 334 567 800
4 41 82 123 256 428 600

JOE PALOOKA (2nd Series) (Battle Adv. #68-74; ...Advs. #75, 77-81, 83-85, 87; Champ of the Comics #76, 82, 86, 89-93) (See All-New)
Harvey Publications: Nov, 1945 - No. 118, Mar, 1961
1-By Ham Fisher 58 116 174 371 636 900
2 30 60 90 177 289 400
3,4,6,7-1st Flyin' Fool, ends #25 17 34 51 98 154 210
5-Boy Explorers by S&K (7-8/46) 21 42 63 122 199 275
8-10 14 28 42 80 115 150
11-14,16,18-20: 14-Black Cat text-s(2). 18-Powell-a.; Little Max app. 19-Freedom Train-c
11 22 33 64 90 115
15-Origin & 1st app. Humphrey (12/47); Super-heroine Atoma app. by Powell
15 30 45 90 140 190
17-Humphrey vs. Palooka-c/s; 1st app. Little Max 15 30 45 90 140 190
21-26,29,30: 22-Powell-a. 30-Nude female painting 10 20 30 56 76 95
27-Little Max app.; Howie Morenz-s 10 20 30 58 79 100
28-Babe Ruth 4 pg. sty. 10 20 30 58 79 100
31,39,51: 31-Dizzy Dean 4 pg. sty. 39-(12/49) Humphrey & Little Max begin; Sonny Baugh football-s; Sherlock Max-s. 51-Babe Ruth 2 pg. sty; Jake Lamotta 1/2 pg. sty
9 18 27 50 65 80
32-38,40-50,52-61: 35-Little Max-c/story(4 pgs.); Joe Louis 1 pg. sty. 36-Humphrey story. 41-Bing Crosby photo on-c. 44-Palooka marries Ann Howe. 50-(11/51)-Becomes Harvey Comics Hits #51 8 16 24 44 57 70
62-S&K Boy Explorers-r 9 18 27 50 65 80
63-65,73-80,100: 79-Story of 1st meeting with Ann 8 16 24 40 50 60
66,67-'Commie' torture story "Drug-Diet Horror" 13 26 39 72 101 130
68,70-72: 68,70-Joe vs. "Gooks"-c. 71-Bloody bayonets-c. 72-Tank-c
12 24 36 69 97 125
69-1st "Battle Adventures" issue; torture & bondage 14 28 42 78 112 145
81-99,101-115: 104,107-Humphrey & Little Max-s 7 14 21 37 46 55
116-S&K Boy Explorers-r (Giant, '60) 9 18 27 47 61 75
117-(84 pg. Giant) r/Commie issues #66,67; Powell-a 9 18 27 52 69 85
118-(84 pg. Giant) Jack Dempsey 2 pg. sty, Powell-a 9 18 27 47 61 75
...**Visits the Lost City** nn (1945)(One Shot)(50¢)-164 page continuous story strip reprint. Has biography & photo of Ham Fisher; possibly the single longest comic book story published in that era (159 pgs.?) (scarce) 242 484 726 1537 2644 3750
NOTE: ***Nostrand/Powell** a-73. **Powell** a-7, 8, 10, 12, 14, 17, 19, 26-45, 47-53, 70, 73 at least. Black Cat text stories #8, 12, 13, 19.*

JOE PALOOKA
IDW Publishing: Dec, 2012 - No. 6, May, 2013 ($3.99, limited series)
1-6: 1-Bullock-s/Peniche-a; Joe Palooka updated as a MMA fighter 4.00

JOE PSYCHO & MOO FROG
Goblin Studios: 1996 - No. 5, 1997 ($2.50, B&W)
1-5: 4-Two covers 3.00
...Full Color Extravagarbonzo ($2.95, color) 3.00

JOE THE BARBARIAN
DC Comics (Vertigo): Mar, 2010 - No. 8, May, 2011 ($1.00/$2.99/$3.99)
1-($1.00) Grant Morrison-s/Sean Murphy-a 3.00
2-7-($2.99) 3.00
8-($3.99) 4.00

GD 2.0 VG 4.0 FN 6.0 VF 8.0 VF/NM 9.0 NM- 9.2

JOE YANK (Korean War)
Standard Comics (Visual Editions): No. 5, Mar, 1952 - No. 16, 1954
5-Toth, Celardo, Tuska-a 14 28 42 76 108 140
6-Toth, Severin/Elder-a 12 24 36 69 97 125
7-Pinhead Perkins by Dan DeCarlo (in all?) 10 20 30 54 72 90
8-Toth-c 11 22 33 62 86 110
9-16: 9-Andru-c. 12-Andru-a 10 20 30 56 76 95

JOHN BOLTON'S HALLS OF HORROR
Eclipse Comics: June, 1985 - No. 2, June, 1985 ($1.75, limited series)
1,2-British-r; Bolton-c/a 4.00

JOHN BOLTON'S STRANGE WINK
Dark Horse Comics: Mar, 1998 - No. 3, May, 1998 ($2.95, B&W, limited series)
1-3-Anthology; Bolton-s/c/a 4.00

JOHN BYRNE'S NEXT MEN (See Dark Horse Presents #54)
Dark Horse Comics (Legend imprint #19 on): Jan, 1992 - No. 30, Dec, 1994 ($2.50, mature)
1-Silver foil embossed-c; Byrne-c/a/scripts in all 1 2 3 5 6 8
1-4: 1-2nd printing with gold ink logo 3.00
0-(2/92)-r/chapters 1-4 from DHP w/new Byrne-c 4.00
5-20,22-30: 7-10-MA #1-4 mini-series on flip side. 16-Origin of Mark IV. 17-Miller-c. 19-22-Faith storyline. 23-26-Power storyline. 27-30-Lies storyline Pt. 1-4 4.00
21-(12/93) 2nd Hellboy; cover and Hellboy pages by Mike Mignola; Byrne other pages (see San Diego Comic Con Comics #2 for 1st app.) 7 14 21 44 82 120
...Parallel, Book 2 ($16.95)-TPB; r/#7-12 17.00
...Fame, Book 3($16.95)-TPB r/#13-18 17.00
...Faith, Book 4($14.95)-TPB r/#19-22 15.00
NOTE: *Issues 1 through 6 contain certificates redeemable for an exclusive Next Men trading card set by Byrne. Prices are for complete books. **Cody** painted c-23-26. **Mignola** a-21(part); c-21.*

JOHN BYRNE'S NEXT MEN (Continues in Next Men: Aftermath #40)
IDW Publishing: Dec, 2010 - No. 9, Aug, 2011 ($3.99)
1-9-John Byrne-s/a/c in all. 1-Origin retold. 6,7-Abraham Lincoln app. 4.00

JOHN BYRNE'S 2112
Dark Horse Comics (Legend): Oct, 1991 ($9.95, TPB)
1-Byrne-c/a/s 10.00

JOHN CARTER OF MARS (See The Funnies & Tarzan #207)
Dell Publishing Co.: No. 375, Mar-May, 1952 - No. 488, Aug-Oct, 1953 (Edgar Rice Burroughs)
Four Color 375 (#1)-Origin; Jesse Marsh-a 32 64 96 230 515 800
Four Color 437, 488-Painted-c 17 34 51 119 265 410

JOHN CARTER OF MARS
Gold Key: Apr, 1964 - No. 3, Oct, 1964
1(10104-404)-r/4-Color #375; Jesse Marsh-a 7 14 21 44 82 120
2(407), 3(410)-r/4-Color #437 & 488; Marsh-a 5 10 15 33 57 80

JOHN CARTER OF MARS
House of Greystroke: 1970 (10-1/2x16-1/2", 72 pgs., B&W, paper-c)
1941-42 Sunday strip-r; John Coleman Burroughs-a 4 8 12 23 37 50

JOHN CARTER OF MARS: A PRINCESS OF MARS
Marvel Comics: Nov, 2011 - No. 5, Mar, 2012 ($2.99, limited series)
1-5: 1-Langridge-s/Andrade-a; covers by Young and Andrade. 2-4-Young-c 3.00

JOHN CARTER: THE END
Dynamite Entertainment: 2017 - No. 5, 2017 ($3.99)
1-5-Brian Wood-s/Alex Cox-a; multiple covers 4.00

JOHN CARTER: THE GODS OF MARS
Marvel Comics: May, 2012 - No. 5, Sept, 2012 ($3.99, limited series)
1-5-Sam Humphries-s/Ramón Pérez-a; Carter's 2nd trip to Mars 4.00

JOHN CARTER: THE WORLD OF MARS
Marvel Comics: Dec, 2011 - No. 4, Mar, 2012 ($3.99, limited series)
1-4-Movie prequel; Peter David-s/Luke Ross-a. 1-Ribic-c. 4-Olivetti-c 4.00

JOHN CARTER, WARLORD OF MARS (Also see Tarzan #207-209 and Weird Worlds)
Marvel Comics: June, 1977 - No. 28, Oct, 1979
1,18: 1-Origin. 18-Frank Miller-a(p)(1st publ. Marvel work)
3 6 9 19 30 40
1-(35¢-c variant, limited dist.) 9 18 27 63 129 195
2-5-(35¢-c variants, limited dist.) 6 12 18 42 79 115
2-17,19-28: 11-Origin Dejah Thoris 2 4 6 8 10 12
Annuals 1-3: 1(1977). 2(1978). 3(1979)-All 52 pgs. with new book-length stories
1 3 4 6 8 10

John Carter, Warlord of Mars #2 © DYN

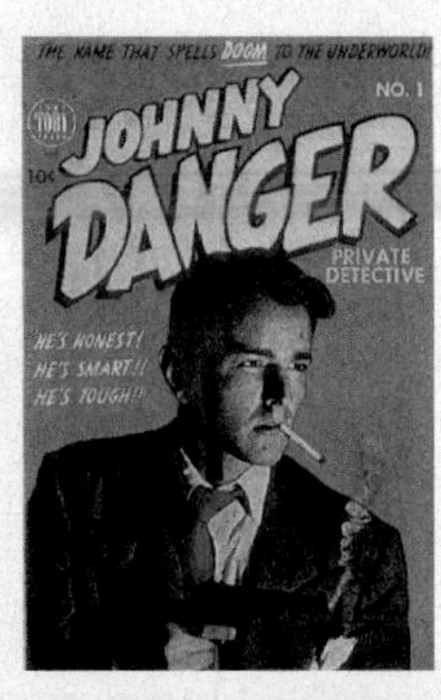

Johnny Danger #1 © TOBY

John Wayne Adventure Comics #3 © TOBY

	GD 2.0	VG 4.0	FN 6.0	VF 8.0	VF/NM 9.0	NM- 9.2

Edgar Rice Burroughs' John Carter of Mars: Weird Worlds TPB (Dark Horse Books, Jan. 2011, $14.99) r/stories from Tarzan #207-209 and Weird Worlds #1-7; Marv Wolfman intro. 15.00
NOTE: ***Austin** c-24i. **Gil Kane** a-1-10p; c-1p, 2p, 3, 4-9p, 10, 15p, Annual 1p. **Layton** a-17i. **Miller** c-25, 26p. **Nebres** a-2-4i, 8-16i; c(i)-6-9, 11-22, 25, Annual 1. **Perez** c-24p. **Simonson** a-15p. **Sutton** a-7i.*

JOHN CARTER, WARLORD OF MARS
Dynamite Entertainment: 2014 - No. 14, 2015 ($3.99)
1-14: 1-5-Marz-s/Malsuni-a; multiple covers on all 4.00
... 2015 Special ($4.99) Napton-s/Rodolfo-a/Parillo-c 5.00

JOHN CONSTANTINE: HELLBLAZER
DC Comics (Black Label): Jan, 2020 - No. 12, Jan, 2021 ($3.99)
1-12: Simon Spurrier-s. 1-3,6-8-Aaron Campbell-a. 4,5,9-Matias Bergara-a 4.00

JOHN CONSTANTINE - HELLBLAZER SPECIAL: PAPA MIDNITE
DC Comics (Vertigo): April, 2005 - No. 5, Aug, 2005 ($2.95/$2.99, limited series)
1-5-Origin of Papa Midnite; Akins-a/Johnson-s 3.00

JOHN F. KENNEDY, CHAMPION OF FREEDOM
Worden & Childs: 1964 (no month) (25¢)
nn-Photo-c 9 18 27 57 111 165

JOHN F. KENNEDY LIFE STORY
Dell Publishing Co.: Aug-Oct, 1964; Nov, 1965; June, 1966 (12¢)
12-378-410-Photo-c 8 16 24 54 102 150
12-378-511 (reprint, 11/65) 3 6 9 21 33 45
12-378-606 (reprint, 6/66) 3 6 9 19 30 40

JOHN FORCE (See Magic Agent)

JOHN HIX SCRAP BOOK, THE
Eastern Color Printing Co. (McNaught Synd.): Late 1930's (no date) (10¢, 68 pgs., regular size)
1-Strange As It Seems (resembles Single Series books) 45 90 135 284 480 675
2-Strange As It Seems 32 64 96 188 307 425

JOHN JAKES' MULLKON EMPIRE
Tekno Comix: Sept, 1995 - No. 6, Feb, 1996 ($1.95)
1-6 3.00

JOHN LAW DETECTIVE (See Smash Comics #3)
Eclipse Comics: April, 1983 ($1.50, Baxter paper)
1-Three Eisner stories originally drawn in 1948 for the never published John Law #1; original cover pencilled in 1948 & inked in 1982 by Eisner 4.00

JOHN McCAIN (See Presidential Material: John McCain)

JOHNNY APPLESEED (See Story Hour Series)

JOHNNY CASH (See Hello, I'm...)

JOHNNY DANGER (See Movie Comics, 1946)
Toby Press: 1950 (Based on movie serial)
1-Photo-c; Sparling-a 24 48 72 144 237 330

JOHNNY DANGER PRIVATE DETECTIVE
Toby Press: Aug, 1954 (Reprinted in Danger #11 by Super)
1-Photo-c; Opium den story 21 42 63 124 202 280

JOHNNY DYNAMITE (Formerly Dynamite #1-9; Foreign Intrigues #14 on)
Charlton Comics: No. 10, June, 1955 - No. 12, Oct, 1955
10-12 14 28 42 82 121 160

JOHNNY DYNAMITE
Dark Horse Comics: Sept, 1994 - Dec, 1994 ($2.95, B&W & red, limited series)
1-4: Max Allan Collins scripts in all; Terry Beatty-a 3.00
...: Underworld GN (AiT/Planet Lar, 3/03, $12.95, B&W) r/#1-4 in B&W without red 13.00

JOHNNY HAZARD
Best Books (Standard Comics) (King Features): No. 5, Aug, 1948 - No. 8, May, 1949; No. 35, date?
5-Strip reprints by Frank Robbins (c/a) 20 40 60 118 192 265
6,8-Strip reprints by Frank Robbins 17 34 51 103 162 220
7,35: 7-New art, not Robbins 14 28 42 78 112 145

JOHNNY JASON (...Teen Reporter)
Dell Publishing Co.: Feb-Apr, 1962 - No. 2, June-Aug, 1962
Four Color 1302, 2(01380-208) 4 8 12 23 37 50

JOHNNY LAW, SKY RANGER
Good Comics (Lev Gleason): Apr, 1955 - No. 3, Aug, 1955; No. 4, Nov, 1955
1-Edmond Good-c/a 12 24 36 69 97 125
2-4 9 18 27 50 65 80

JOHNNY MACK BROWN (Western star; see Western Roundup under Dell Giants)
Dell Publishing Co.: No. 269, Mar, 1950 - No. 963, Feb, 1959 (All Photo-c)
Four Color 269(#1)(3/50, 52pgs.)-Johnny Mack Brown & his horse Rebel begin; photo front/back-c begin; Marsh-a in #1-9 18 36 54 124 275 425
2(10-12/50, 52pgs.) 10 20 30 64 132 200
3(1-3/51, 52pgs.) 8 16 24 54 102 150
4-10 (9-11/52)(36pgs.), Four Color 455,493,541,584,618,645,685,722,776,834,963 6 12 18 40 73 105
Four Color 922-Manning-a 6 12 18 41 76 110

JOHNNY PERIL (See Comic Cavalcade #15, Danger Trail #5, Sensation Comics #107 & Sensation Mystery)

JOHNNY RINGO (TV)
Dell Publishing Co.: No. 1142, Nov-Jan, 1960/61 (one shot)
Four Color 1142-Photo-c 6 12 18 41 76 110

JOHNNY STARBOARD (See Wisco)

JOHNNY THE HOMICIDAL MANIAC (Also see Squee)
Slave Labor Graphics: Aug, 1995 - No. 7, Jan, 1997 ($2.95, B&W, lim. series)
1-Jhonen Vasquez-c/s/a (1995) 8 16 24 54 102 150
1-Special Signed & numbered edition of 2,000 (1996) 4 8 12 27 44 60
2,3: 2-(11/95). 3-(2/96) 1 3 4 6 8 10
4-7: 4-(5-96). 5-(8/96) 5.00
Hardcover-($29.95) r/#1-7 35.00
TPB-($19.95) 25.00

JOHNNY THUNDER
National Periodical Publications: Feb-Mar, 1973 - No. 3, July-Aug, 1973
1-Johnny Thunder & Nighthawk-r. in all 3 6 9 15 22 28
2,3: 2-Trigger Twins app. 2 4 6 8 11 14
NOTE: *All contain 1950s DC reprints from All-American Western. **Drucker** r-2, 3. **G. Kane** r-2, 3. **Moreira** r-1. **Toth** r-1, 3; c-1r, 3r. Also see All-American, All-Star Western, Flash Comics, Western Comics, World's Best & World's Finest.*

JOHN PAUL JONES
Dell Publishing Co.: No. 1007, July-Sept, 1959 (one-shot)
Four Color 1007-Movie, Robert Stack photo-c 6 12 18 37 66 95

JOHN ROMITA JR. 30TH ANNIVERSARY SPECIAL
Marvel Comics: 2006 ($3.99, one-shot)
nn-r/1st story in Amazing Spider-Man Annual #11; timeline, sketch pages, interviews 4.00

JOHN STEED & EMMA PEEL (See The Avengers, Gold Key series)

JOHN STEELE SECRET AGENT (Also see Freedom Agent)
Gold Key: Dec, 1964
1-Freedom Agent 5 10 15 35 63 100

JOHN WAYNE ADVENTURE COMICS (Movie star; See Big Tex, Oxydol-Dreft, Tim McCoy, & With The Marines...#1)
Toby Press: Winter, 1949-50 - No. 31, May, 1955 (Photo-c: 1-12,17,25-on)
1 (36pgs.)-Photo-c begin (1st time in comics on-c) 258 516 774 1651 2826 4000
2-4: 2-(4/50, 36pgs.)-Williamson/Frazetta-a(2) 6 & 2 pgs. (one story-r/Billy the Kid #1); photo back-c. 3-(36pgs.)-Williamson/Frazetta-a(2), 16 pgs. total; photo back-c. 4-(52pgs.)-Williamson/Frazetta-a(2), 16 pgs. total 84 168 252 538 919 1300
5 (52pgs.)-Kurtzman-a-(Alfred "L" Newman in Potshot Pete) 65 130 195 416 708 1050
6 (52pgs.)-Williamson/Frazetta-a (10 pgs.); Kurtzman-a "Pot-Shot Pete", (5 pgs.); & "Genius Jones", (1 pg.) 76 152 228 486 831 1175
7 (52pgs.)-Williamson/Frazetta-a (10 pgs.) 66 132 198 419 722 1025
8 (36pgs.)-Williamson/Frazetta-a(2) (12 & 9 pgs.) 77 154 231 493 847 1200
9-11: Photo western-c 43 86 129 268 454 640
12,14-Photo war-c. 12-Kurtzman-a(2 pg.) "Genius" 43 86 129 271 461 650
13,15: 13,15-Line-drawn-c begin, end #24 39 78 117 236 388 540
16-Williamson/Frazetta-r/Billy the Kid #1 40 80 120 248 414 580
17-Photo-c 40 80 120 248 414 580
18-Williamson/Frazetta-a (r/#4 & 8, 19 pgs.) 43 86 129 268 454 640
19-24: 23-Evans-a? 36 72 108 214 347 480
25-Photo-c resume; end #31; Williamson/Frazetta-r/Billy the Kid #3 43 86 129 268 454 640
26-28,30-Photo-c 39 78 117 236 388 540
29,31-Williamson/Frazetta-a in each (r/#4, 2) 41 82 123 256 428 600
NOTE: *Williamsonish art in later issues by **Gerald McCann.***

JOHN WICK (Based on the Keanu Reeves movies)
Dynamite Entertainment: 2018 - No. 5, 2019 ($3.99)
1-Pak-s/Valletta-a; four covers 3 6 9 19 30 40

Join the Future #1 © Kaplan & AS

Joker: Killer Smile #1 © DC

Jonah Hex #39 © DC

	GD 2.0	VG 4.0	FN 6.0	VF 8.0	VF/NM 9.0	NM- 9.2
2-Three covers	2	4	6	9	12	15
3-5-Gaudio-a; three covers						5.00

JOIN THE FUTURE
AfterShock Comics: Mar, 2020 - No. 5, Sept, 2020 ($4.99/$3.99)

	GD	VG	FN	VF	VF/NM	NM-
1-($4.99) Zack Kaplan-s/Piotr Kowalski-a						5.00
2-5-($3.99)						4.00

JO-JO COMICS (...Congo King #7-29; My Desire #30 on)(Also see Fantastic Fears and Jungle Jo)
Fox Feature Syndicate: 1945 - No. 29, July, 1949 (Two No.7's; no #13)

	GD	VG	FN	VF	VF/NM	NM-
nn(1945)-Funny animal, humor	27	54	81	158	259	360
2(Sum,'46)-6(4-5/47): Funny animal. 2-Ten pg. Electro story (Fall/46)	17	34	51	98	154	210
7(7/47)-Jo-Jo, Congo King begins (1st app.); Bronze Man & Purple Tigress app.	103	206	309	659	1130	1600
7(#8) (9/47)	77	154	231	493	847	1200
8(#9) Classic Kamen mountain of skulls-c; Tanee begins	110	220	330	704	1202	1700
9,10(#10,11)	66	132	198	419	722	1025
11,12(#12,13),14,16: 11,16-Kamen bondage-c	57	114	171	362	619	875
15-Cited by Dr. Wertham in 5/47 Saturday Review of Literature	58	116	174	371	636	900
17-Kamen bondage-c	77	154	231	493	847	1200
18-20	55	110	165	352	601	850
21-24,26-29: 21-Hollingsworth-a (4 pgs.; 23-1 pg.)	47	94	141	295	498	700
25-Bondage-c	113	226	339	723	1237	1750

NOTE: *Many bondage-c/a by* ***Baker/Kamen/Feldstein/Good.*** *No. 7's have Princesses Gwenna, Geesa, Yolda, & Safra before settling down on Tanee.*

JOKEBOOK COMICS DIGEST ANNUAL (...Magazine No. 5 on)
Archie Publications: Oct, 1977 - No. 13, Oct, 1983 (Digest Size)

	GD	VG	FN	VF	VF/NM	NM-
1(10/77)-Reprints; Neal Adams-a	2	4	6	13	18	22
2(4/78)-5	2	4	6	9	12	15
6-13	1	3	4	6	8	10

JOKER
DC Comics: 2008 ($19.99, hardcover graphic novel with dustjacket)

	GD	VG	FN	VF	VF/NM	NM-
HC-Joker is released from Arkham; Azzarello-s/Bermejo-a						20.00

JOKER, THE (See Batman #1, Batman: The Killing Joke, Brave & the Bold, Detective, Greatest Joker Stories & Justice League Annual #2)
National Periodical Publications: May, 1975 - No. 9, Sept-Oct, 1976

	GD	VG	FN	VF	VF/NM	NM-
1-Two-Face app.	9	18	27	61	123	185
2-Willie the Weeper app.	5	10	15	35	63	90
3,4: 3-The Creeper app. 4-Green Arrow-c/sty	4	8	12	28	47	65
5-9: 6-Sherlock Holmes-c/sty. 7-Lex Luthor-c/story. 8-Scarecrow-c/story. 9-Catwoman-c/story	4	8	12	25	40	55
...: The Greatest Stories Ever Told TPB (2008, $19.99) r/Batman #1 and other apps.						20.00

JOKER, THE (See Tangent Comics/ The Joker)

JOKER COMICS (Adventures Into Terror No. 43 on)
Timely/Marvel Comics No. 36 on (TCI/CDS): Apr, 1942 - No. 42, Aug, 1950

	GD	VG	FN	VF	VF/NM	NM-
1-(Rare)-Powerhouse Pepper (1st app.) begins by Wolverton; Stuporman app. from Daring Comics	337	674	1011	2359	4130	5900
2-Wolverton-a; 1st app. Tessie the Typist & begin series	148	296	444	947	1624	2300
3-5-Wolverton-a	90	180	270	576	988	1400
6-10-Wolverton-a. 6-Tessie-c begin	55	110	165	352	601	850
11-20-Wolverton-a	52	104	156	326	552	775
21,22,24-27,29,30-Wolverton cont'd. & Kurtzman's "Hey Look" in #23-27	45	90	135	284	480	675
23-1st "Hey Look" by Kurtzman; Wolverton-a	48	96	144	302	514	725
28,32,34,37-41: 28-Millie the Model begins. 32-Hedy begins. 41-Nellie the Nurse app.	25	50	75	150	245	340
31-Last Powerhouse Pepper; not in #28	40	80	120	246	411	575
33,35,36-Kurtzman's "Hey Look"	26	52	78	152	249	345
42-Only app. 'Patty Pinup,' clone of Millie the Model	26	52	78	152	249	345

JOKER / DAFFY DUCK
DC Comics: Oct, 2018 ($4.99, one-shot)

	GD	VG	FN	VF	VF/NM	NM-
1-Lobdell-s/Booth-a/c; Daffy Duck as a Joker henchman; Batman app.						5.00
1-Variant-c by Sanford Greene	1	3	4	6	8	10

JOKER: DEVIL'S ADVOCATE
DC Comics: 1996 ($24.95/$12.95, one-shot)

	GD	VG	FN	VF	VF/NM	NM-
nn-(Hardcover)-Dixon scripts/Nolan & Hanna-a						30.00
nn-(Softcover)						15.00

JOKER 80TH ANNIVERSARY 100-PAGE SUPER SPECTACULAR
DC Comics: Jun, 2020 ($9.99, squarebound, one-shot)

	GD	VG	FN	VF	VF/NM	NM-
1-Short stories and pin-ups by various; origin Punchline; multiple covers						10.00

JOKER / HARLEY: CRIMINAL SANITY
DC Comics (Black Label): Dec, 2019 - No. 9 ($5.99, 10-3/4" x 8-1/2", lim. series)

	GD	VG	FN	VF	VF/NM	NM-
1-7: 1,2-Kami Garcia-s/Mico Suayan & Mike Mayhew-a. 1-Three covers. 2-7-Two covers						6.00
... Secret Files 1 (9/20, $5.99) Covers by Mack & Sienkiewicz; art by Mack and others						6.00

JOKER: KILLER SMILE (See Batman: The Smile Killer one-shot for epilogue)
DC Comics (Black Label): Dec, 2019 - No. 3, Apr, 2020 ($5.99, 10-3/4" x 8-1/2", lim. series)

	GD	VG	FN	VF	VF/NM	NM-
1-3-Jeff Lemire-s/Andrea Sorrentino-a; two covers by Sorrentino & Kaare Andrews						6.00

JOKER: LAST LAUGH (See Batman: The Joker's Last Laugh for TPB)
DC Comics: Dec, 2001 - No. 6, Jan, 2002 ($2.95, weekly limited series)

	GD	VG	FN	VF	VF/NM	NM-
1-6: 1,6-Bolland-c						3.00
...Secret Files (12/01, $5.95) Short stories by various; Simonson-c						6.00

JOKER / MASK
Dark Horse Comics: May, 2000 - No. 4, Aug, 2000 ($2.95, limited series)

	GD	VG	FN	VF	VF/NM	NM-
1-4-Batman, Harley Quinn, Poison Ivy app.	2	4	6	9	12	15

JOKER'S ASYLUM
DC Comics: Sept, 2008 ($2.99, weekly limited series of one-shots)

	GD	VG	FN	VF	VF/NM	NM-
...: Joker - Andy Kubert-c, Sanchez-a; ...: Penguin - Pearson-c/a; ...: Poison Ivy - Guillem March-c/a; ...: Scarecrow - Juan Doe-c/a; ...: Two-Face - Andy Clarke-c/a						4.00
Batman: The Joker's Asylum TPB (2008, $14.99) r/one-shots						15.00

JOKER'S ASYLUM II
DC Comics: Aug, 2010 ($2.99, weekly limited series of one-shots)

	GD	VG	FN	VF	VF/NM	NM-
...: Clayface - Kelley Jones-c/a; ; ...: Killer Croc - Mattina-c; Mad Hatter - Giffen & Sienkiewicz-a, Sienkiewicz-c; ...: Riddler - Van Sciver-c						4.00
...: Harley Quinn - Quinones-a	3	6	9	15	22	28
Batman: The Joker's Asylum Volume 2 TPB (2011, $14.99) r/one-shots						15.00

JOKER, THE: YEAR OF THE VILLAIN
DC Comics: 2019 ($4.99, one-shot)

	GD	VG	FN	VF	VF/NM	NM-
1-John Carpenter & Anthony Burch-s/Philip Tan-a; Enchantress app.						5.00

JOLLY CHRISTMAS, A (See March of Comics No. 269)

JOLLY COMICS: **Four Star Publishing Co.:** 1947 (Advertised, not published)

JOLLY COMICS
No publisher: No date (1930s-40s)(10¢, cover is black/red ink on yellow paper, blank inside-c)

	GD	VG	FN	VF	VF/NM	NM-
nn-Snuffy Smith & Katzenjamer Kids on-c only. Buck Rogers, Dickey Dare, Napoleon & others app. Reprints Ace Comics #8-c. A GD copy sold in 2014 for $358.50	232	464	696	1485	2543	3600

JOLLY JINGLES (Formerly Jackpot Comics)
MLJ Magazines: No. 10, Sum, 1943 - No. 16, Wint, 1944/45

	GD	VG	FN	VF	VF/NM	NM-
10-Super Duck begins (origin & 1st app.); Woody The Woodpecker begins (not same as Lantz character)	65	130	195	416	708	1000
11 (Fall, '43)-2nd Super Duck (see Hangman #8)	34	68	102	204	332	460
12-Hitler-c	110	220	330	704	1202	1700
13-16: 13-Sahle-c. 15,16-Vigoda-c	24	48	72	142	234	325

JONAH HEX (See All-Star Western, Hex and Weird Western Tales)
National Periodical Pub./DC Comics: Mar-Apr, 1977 - No. 92, Aug, 1985

	GD	VG	FN	VF	VF/NM	NM-
1-Garcia-Lopez-c/a	10	20	30	69	147	225
2-1st app. El Papagayo	6	12	18	38	69	100
3,4,9: 9-Wrightson-c.	5	10	15	33	57	80
5,6,10: 5-Rep 1st app. from All-Star Western #10	5	10	15	30	50	70
7,8-Explains Hex's face disfigurement (origin)	5	10	15	35	63	90
11-20: 12-Starlin-c	3	6	9	19	30	40
21-32: 23-Intro. Mei Ling. 31,32-Origin retold	2	4	6	13	18	22
33-50	2	4	6	8	11	14
51-80	1	2	3	5	7	9
81-91: 89-Mark Texeira-a. 91-Cover swipe from Superman #243 (hugging a mystery woman)	2	4	6	8	10	12
92-Story cont'd in Hex #1	3	6	9	19	30	40

NOTE: ***Ayers*** *a(p)-35-37, 40, 41, 44-53, 56, 58-82.* ***Buckler*** *a-11; c-11, 13-16.* ***Kubert*** *c-43-46.* ***Morrow*** *a-90-92; c-10.* ***Spiegle(Tothish)*** *a-34, 38, 40, 49, 52.* ***Texeira*** *a-89p. Batlash back-ups in 49, 52. El Diablo back-ups in 48, 56-60, 73-75. Scalphunter back-ups in 40, 41, 45-47.*

JONAH HEX (Also see All Star Western [2011 DC New 52 title])
DC Comics: Jan, 2006 - No. 70, Oct, 2011 ($2.99)

	GD	VG	FN	VF	VF/NM	NM-
1-Justin Gray & Jimmy Palmiotti-s/Luke Ross-a/Quitely-c						5.00
1-Special Edition (7/10, $1.00) r/#1 with "What's Next?" logo on cover						3.00
2-49,51-70: 3-Bat Lash app. 10,16,17,19,20,22-Noto-a. 11-El Diablo app.; Beck-a.						

Jonesy #3 © QUA

Jonny Quest #5 © H-B

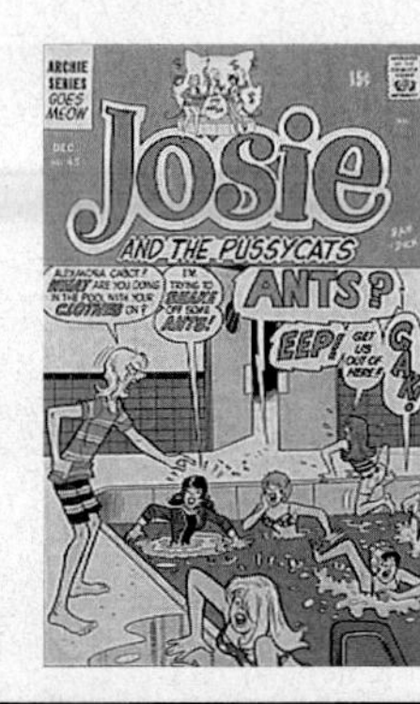

Josie and the Pussycats #45 © ACP

GD	VG	FN	VF	VF/NM	NM-
2.0	4.0	6.0	8.0	9.0	9.2

GD VG FN VF VF/NM NM-
2.0 4.0 6.0 8.0 9.0 9.2

13-15-Origin retold. 21,23,27,30,32,37,38,42,52,54,57,59,61,63,67-Bernet-a. 33-Darwyn Cooke-a/c. 34-Sparacio-a. 51-Giordano-c. 53-Tucci-c/a. 62-Risso-a 3.00
50-($3.99) Darwyn Cooke-a/c 4.00
...: Bullets Don't Lie TPB (2009, $14.99) r/#31-36 15.00
...: Counting Corpses TPB (2010, $14.99) r/#43,50-54 15.00
...: Face Full of Violence TPB (2006, $12.99) r/#1-6 13.00
...: Guns of Vengeance TPB (2007, $12.99) r/#7-12 13.00
...: Lead Poisoning TPB (2009, $14.99) r/#37-42 15.00
...: Luck Runs Out TPB (2008, $12.99) r/#25-30 13.00
...: No Way Back HC (2010, $19.99) new GN; Gray & Palmiotti-s/DeZuniga-a 20.00
...: No Way Back SC (2011, $14.99) new GN; Gray & Palmiotti-s/DeZuniga-a 15.00
...: Only the Good Die Young TPB (2008, $12.99) r/#19-24 13.00
...: Origins TPB (2007, $12.99) r/#13-18 13.00
...: Tall Tales TPB (2011, $14.99) r/#55-60 15.00
...: The Six Gun War TPB (2010, $14.99) r/#44-49 15.00
...: Welcome to Paradise TPB (2010, $17.99) r/debut in All-Star Western #10 plus early apps. in Weird Western Tales and Jonah Hex #2,4 (1977 series) 18.00

JONAH HEX AND OTHER WESTERN TALES (Blue Ribbon Digest)
DC Comics: Sept-Oct, 1979 - No. 3, Jan-Feb, 1980 (100 pgs.)

1-3: 1-Origin Scalphunter-r, Ayers/Evans, Neal Adams-a.; painted-c. 2-Weird Western Tales-r; Neal Adams, Toth, Aragonés-a. 3-Outlaw-r, Scalphunter-r; Gil Kane, Wildey-a 2 4 6 11 16 20

JONAH HEX: RIDERS OF THE WORM AND SUCH
DC Comics (Vertigo): Mar, 1995 - No. 5, July, 1995 ($2.95, limited series)

1-5-Lansdale story, Truman-a 4.00

JONAH HEX: SHADOWS WEST
DC Comics (Vertigo): Feb, 1999 - No. 3, Apr, 1999 ($2.95, limited series)

1-3-Lansdale-s/Truman-a 4.00

JONAH HEX SPECTACULAR (See DC Special Series No. 16)

JONAH HEX: TWO-GUN MOJO
DC Comics (Vertigo): Aug, 1993 - No. 5, Dec, 1993 ($2.95, limited series)

1-Lansdale scripts in all; Truman/Glanzman-a in all w/Truman-c 6.00
1-Platinum edition with no price on cover 20.00
2-5 4.00
TPB-(1994, $12.95) r/#1-5 13.00

JONAH HEX/ YOSEMITE SAM
DC Comics: Aug, 2017 ($4.99, one-shot)

1-Palmiotti-s/Teixeira-a; Foghorn Leghorn app. 5.00

JONESY (Formerly Crack Western)
Comic Favorite/Quality Comics Group: No. 85, Aug, 1953; No. 2, Oct, 1953 - No. 8, Oct, 1954

	GD	VG	FN	VF	VF/NM	NM-
85(#1)-Teen-age humor	11	22	33	64	90	115
2	8	16	24	40	50	60
3-8	6	12	18	31	38	45

JONESY
BOOM! Studios (BOOM! Box): Feb, 2016 - No. 12, Apr, 2017 ($3.99, originally a 4-part series)

1-12-Sam Humphries-s/Caitlin Rose Boyle-a. 1-Multiple covers 4.00

JON JUAN (Also see Great Lover Romances)
Toby Press: Spring, 1950

1-All Schomburg-a (signed Al Reid on-c); written by Siegel; used in **SOTI**, pg. 38 (Scarce) 86 172 248 546 936 1325

JONNI THUNDER (...A.K.A. Thunderbolt)
DC Comics: Feb, 1985 - No. 4, Aug, 1985 (75¢, limited series)

1-4: 1-Origin & 1st app. 4.00

JONNY DOUBLE
DC Comics (Vertigo): Sept, 1998 - No. 4, Dec, 1998 ($2.95, limited series)

1-4-Azzarello-s 3.00
TPB (2002, $12.95) r/#1-4; Chiarello-c 13.00

JONNY QUEST (TV)
Gold Key: Dec, 1964 (Hanna-Barbera)

1 (10139-412) 36 72 108 259 580 900

JONNY QUEST (TV)
Comico: June 1986 - No. 31, Dec, 1988 ($1.50/$1.75)(Hanna-Barbera)

1,3,5: 3,5-Dave Stevens-c 6.00
2,4,6-31: 30-Adapts TV episode 4.00
Special 1(9/88, $1.75), 2(10/88, $1.75) 4.00

NOTE: ***M. Anderson*** *a-9.* ***Mooney*** *a-Special 1.* ***Pini*** *a-2.* ***Quagmire*** *a-31p.* ***Rude*** *a-1; c-2i.* ***Sienkiewicz*** *c-11.* ***Spiegle*** *a-7, 12, 21; c-21* ***Staton*** *a-2i, 11p.* ***Steacy*** *c-8.* ***Stevens*** *a-4i; c-3,5.* ***Wildey*** *a-1, c-1, 7, 12.* ***Williamson*** *a-4i; c-4i.*

JONNY QUEST CLASSICS (TV)
Comico: May, 1987 - No. 3, July, 1987 ($2.00) (Hanna-Barbera)

1-3: Wildey-c/a; 3-Based on TV episode 4.00

JON SABLE, FREELANCE (Also see Mike Grell's Sable & Sable)
First Comics: 6/83 - No. 56, 2/88 (#1-17, $1; #18-33, $1.25, #34-on, $1.75)

1-Mike Grell-c/a/scripts 5.00
2-56: 3-5-Origin, parts 1-3. 6-Origin, part 4. 11-1st app. of Maggie the Cat. 14-Mando paper begins. 16-Maggie the Cat. app. 25-30-Shatter app. 34-Deluxe format begins ($1.75) 3.00
The Complete Jon Sable, Freelance: Vol. 1 (IDW, 2005, $19.99) r/#1-6 20.00
The Complete Jon Sable, Freelance: Vol. 2 (IDW, 2005, $19.99) r/#7-11 20.00
The Complete Jon Sable, Freelance: Vol. 3 (IDW, 2005, $19.99) r/#12-16 20.00
The Complete Jon Sable, Freelance: Vol. 4 (IDW, 2005, $19.99) r/#17-21 20.00

NOTE: ***Aragones*** *a-33; c-33(part).* ***Grell*** *a-1-43;c-1-52, 53p, 54-56.*

JON SABLE, FREELANCE
IDW Publ.: (Limited series)

...: Ashes of Eden 1-5 (2009 - No. 5, 2/10, $3.99) Mike Grell-c/a/scripts 4.00
...: Bloodtrail 1-6 (4/05 - No. 6, 11/05, $3.99) Mike Grell-c/a/scripts 4.00
...: Bloodtrail TPB (4/06, $19.99) r/#1-6; cover gallery 20.00

JOOK JOINT
Image Comics: Oct, 2018 - No. 5 ($3.99, limited series)

1,2-Tee Franklin-s/Alitha Martinez-a 4.00

JOSEPH & HIS BRETHREN (See The Living Bible)

JOSIE (She's... #1-16) (...& the Pussycats #45 on) (See Archie's Pals 'n' Gals #23 for 1st app.) (Also see Archie Giant Series Magazine #528, 540, 551, 562, 571, 584, 597, 610, 622)
Archie Publ./Radio Comics: Feb, 1963; No. 2, Aug, 1963 - No. 106, Oct, 1982

	GD	VG	FN	VF	VF/NM	NM-
1	57	114	171	456	1028	1600
2	15	30	45	105	233	360
3-5	10	20	30	64	132	200
6-10: 6-(5/64) Book length Haunted Mansion-c/s. 7-(8/64) 1st app. Alexandra Cabot?	6	12	18	41	76	110
11-20	5	10	15	31	53	75
21, 23-30	4	8	12	27	44	60
22 (9/66)-Mighty Man & Mighty (Josie Girl) app.	5	10	15	30	50	70
31-44	3	6	9	21	33	45
45 (12/69)-Josie and the Pussycats begins (Hanna Barbera TV cartoon); 1st app. of the Pussycats	34	68	102	245	548	850
46-2nd app./1st cover Pussycats	11	22	33	73	157	240
47-3rd app. of the Pussycats	7	14	21	48	89	130
48,49-Pussycats band-c/s	8	16	24	51	96	140
50-J&P-c; go to Hollywood, meet Hanna & Barbera	6	12	18	52	99	145
51-54	3	6	9	21	33	45
55-74 (2/74)(52 pg. issues). 73-Pussycats band-c	3	6	9	21	33	45
75-90(8/76)	3	6	9	14	19	24
91-99	2	4	6	10	14	18
100 (10/79)	2	4	6	13	18	22
101-106: 103-Pussycats band-c	2	4	6	11	16	20

JOSIE & THE PUSSYCATS (TV)
Archie Comics: 1993 - No. 2, 1994 ($2.00, 52 pgs.)(Published annually)

1,2-Bound-in pull-out poster in each. 2-(Spr/94) 5.00

JOSIE AND THE PUSSYCATS
Archie Comic Publications: Nov, 2016 - No. 9, Oct, 2017 ($3.99)

1-9: 1-Bennett & Deordio-s/Audrey Mok-a; multiple covers; back-up classic reprints. 5,6-Riverdale TV previews. 9-Shannon-a 4.00

JOURNAL OF CRIME (See Fox Giants)

JOURNEY
Aardvark-Vanaheim #1-14/Fantagraphics Books #15-on: 1983 - No. 14, Sept, 1984; No. 15, Apr, 1985 - No. 27, July, 1986 (B&W)

1 4.00
2-27: 20-Sam Kieth-a 3.00

JOURNEY INTO FEAR
Superior-Dynamic Publications: May, 1951 - No. 21, Sept, 1954

	GD	VG	FN	VF	VF/NM	NM-
1-Baker-r(2)	129	258	387	826	1413	2000
2	58	116	174	371	636	900
3,4	52	104	156	328	552	775
5-10,15: 15-Used in **SOTI**, pg. 389	43	86	129	271	461	650
11-14,16-21	41	82	123	256	428	600

NOTE: Kamenish 'headlight'-a most issues. ***Robinson*** *a-10.*

Journey Into Mystery #5 © MAR

Journey Into Mystery #112 © MAR

Journey Into Unknown Worlds #14 © MAR

GD VG FN VF VF/NM NM-
2.0 4.0 6.0 8.0 9.0 9.2

JOURNEY INTO MYSTERY (1st Series) (Thor Nos. 126-502)
Atlas(CPS No. 1-48/AMI No. 49-68/Marvel No. 69 (6/61) on): 6/52 - No. 48, 8/57; No. 49, 11/58 - No. 125, 2/66; 503, 11/96 - No. 521, June, 1998

1-Weird/horror stories begin 1350 2700 4050 9500 14,250 19,000
2 229 458 687 1466 2508 3550
3,4 187 374 561 1197 2049 2900
5,7-11 174 348 522 1114 1907 2700
6-Classic Everett-c 232 464 696 1485 2543 3600
12-20,22: 15-Atomic explosion panel. 22-Davis*esque*-a; last pre-code issue (2/55)
113 226 339 723 1237 1750
21-Kubert-a; Tothish-a by Andru 119 238 357 762 1306 1850
23-32,35-38,40: 24-Torres?-a. 38-Ditko-a 85 170 258 546 936 1325
33-Williamson-a; Ditko-a (his 1st for Atlas?) 97 194 291 621 1061 1500
34,39: 34-Krigstein-a. 39-1st S.A. issue; Wood-a 87 174 261 553 952 1350
41-Crandall-a; Frazetta*esque*-a by Morrow 43 86 129 318 722 1125
42,46,48: 42,48-Torres-a. 46-Torres & Krigstein-a 41 82 123 328 702 1075
43,44-Williamson/Mayo-a in both. 43-Invisible Woman prototype
46 92 138 340 770 1200
45,47 40 80 120 296 673 1050
49-Matt Fox, Check-a 45 90 135 333 754 1175
50,52-54: Ditko/Kirby-a. 50-Davis-a. 54-Williamson-a
48 96 144 375 850 1325
51-Kirby/Wood-a 54 108 162 432 966 1500
55-61,63-65,67-69,71,72,74,75: 74-Contents change to Fantasy. 75-Last 10¢ issue
40 80 120 296 673 1050
62-Prototype ish. (The Hulk); 1st app. Xemnu (Titan) called "The Hulk"
86 172 258 688 1544 2400
66-Prototype ish. (The Hulk)-Return of Xemnu "The Hulk"
64 128 192 512 1156 1800
70-Prototype ish. (The Sandman)(7/61); similar to Spidey villain
46 92 138 340 770 1200
73-Story titled "The Spider" where a spider is exposed to radiation & gets powers of a human and shoots webbing; a reverse prototype of Spider-Man's origin
68 136 204 544 1222 1900
76,77,80,81: 80-Anti-communist propaganda story 35 70 105 252 564 875
76-(10¢ cover price blacked out, 12¢ printed on) 50 100 150 400 900 1400
78-The Sorceror (Dr. Strange prototype) app. (3/62) 46 92 138 368 834 1300
79-Prototype issue. (Mr. Hyde) 42 84 126 311 706 1100
82-Prototype ish. (Scorpion) 38 76 114 285 641 1000
83-Origin & 1st app. The Mighty Thor by Kirby (8/62) and begin series; Thor-c also begin
2000 4000 7000 20,000 57,500 95,000
83-Reprint from the Golden Record Comic Set 19 38 57 131 291 450
With the record (1966) 28 56 84 202 451 700
84-2nd app. Thor 287 574 861 2440 5520 8600
85-1st app. Loki & Heimdall; 1st brief app. Odin (1 panel); 1st app. Asgard
287 574 861 2440 5520 8600
86-1st full app. Odin 107 214 321 856 1928 3000
87-89: 88-2nd Loki-c. 89-Origin Thor retold 87 174 261 705 1578 2450
90-No Kirby-a 65 130 195 527 1176 1825
91,92,94,96-Sinnott-a 47 94 141 375 850 1325
93,97-Kirby-a; Tales of Asgard series begins #97 (origin which concludes in #99); origin & 1st app. Lava Man. 97-1st app. Surtur (1 panel) 50 100 150 400 900 1400
95-Sinnott-a; Thor vs. Thor 57 114 171 456 1028 1600
98,99-Kirby/Heck-a. 98-Origin/1st app. The Human Cobra. 99-1st app. Mr. Hyde; Surtur app.
39 78 117 289 657 1025
100-Kirby/Heck-a; Thor battles Mr. Hyde 38 76 114 281 628 975
101,108: 101-(2/64)-2nd Avengers x-over (w/o Capt. America); see Tales Of Suspense #49 for 1st x-over. 108-(9/64)-Early Dr. Strange & Avengers x-over; ten extra pgs. Kirby-a
27 54 81 189 420 650
102-(3/64) 1st app. Sif, Balder and Hela 44 88 132 326 738 1150
103-1st app. Enchantress 89 178 267 712 1606 2500
104-107,110: 105-109-Ten extra pgs. Kirby-a in each. 107-1st app. Grey Gargoyle. 110,111-Two part battle vs. The Human Cobra & Mr. Hyde
26 52 78 182 404 625
109-Magneto-c & app. (1st x-over, 10/64) 46 92 138 340 770 1200
111,113: 113-Origin Loki 19 38 57 131 291 450
112-Thor Vs. Hulk (1/65); Origin Loki 62 124 186 502 1126 1750
114-Origin/1st app. Absorbing Man 32 64 96 230 515 800
115-Detailed origin of Loki 20 40 60 138 307 475
116,117,120-123,125 15 30 45 100 220 340
118-1st app. Destroyer 28 56 84 202 451 700
119-Intro Hogun, Fandral, Volstagg; 2nd Destroyer 22 44 66 154 340 525
124-Hercules-c/story 15 30 45 105 233 360
503-521: 503-(11/96, $1.50)-The Lost Gods begin; Tom DeFalco scripts & Deodato Studios-c/a. 505-Spider-Man-c/app. 509-Loki-c/app. 514-516-Shang-Chi 3.00

GD VG FN VF VF/NM NM-
2.0 4.0 6.0 8.0 9.0 9.2

#(-1) Flashback (7/97) Tales of Asgard Donald Blake app. 3.00
Annual 1(1965, 25¢, 72 pgs.)-New Thor vs. Hercules(1st app.)-c/story (see Incredible Hulk #3); Kirby-c/a; r/#85,93,95,97 57 114 171 456 1028 1600
NOTE: ***Ayers*** *a-14, 39, 64i, 71i, 74i, 80i.* ***Bailey*** *a-43.* ***Briefer*** *a-5, 12.* ***Cameron*** *a-35.* ***Check*** *a-17.* ***Colan*** *a-23, 81; c-14.* ***Ditko*** *a-33, 38, 50-96; c-58, 67, 71, 88i.* ***Kirby/Ditko*** *a-50-83.* ***Everett*** *a-20, 48; c-4-7, 9, 36, 37, 39-42, 44, 45, 47.* ***Forte*** *a-19, 35, 40, 53.* ***Heath*** *a-4-6, 11, 14; c-1, 8, 11, 15, 51.* ***Heck*** *a-53, 58, 73.* ***Kirby*** *a(p)-51, 52, 56, 57-60, 62-64, 66, 67, 69-89, 93, 97, 98, 100(w/**Heck**), 101-125; c-50-57, 59-66, 68-70, 72-82, 88(w/**Ditko**), 83 & 84 (w/**Sinnott**), 85-96(w/**Ayers**), 97-125p.* ***Leiber/Fox*** *a-93, 98-102.* ***Maneely*** *c-20-22.* ***Morisi*** *a-42.* ***Morrow*** *a-41, 42.* ***Orlando*** *a-30, 45, 57.* ***Mac Pakula*** *(Tothish) a-9, 35, 41.* ***Powell*** *a-20, 27, 34.* ***Reinman*** *a-39, 70, 87, 92, 96i.* ***Robinson*** *a-9.* ***Roussos*** *a-39.* ***Robert Sale*** *a-14.* ***Severin*** *a-27; c-30.* ***Sinnott*** *a-41; c-50.* ***Tuska*** *a-11.* ***Wildey*** *a-16.*

JOURNEY INTO MYSTERY (Series and numbering continue from Thor #621)
Marvel Comics: No. 622, Jun, 2011 - No. 655, Oct, 2013 ($3.99/$2.99)

622-Reincarnated young Loki; Thor app.; Braithwaite-a; Hans-c 4.00
622-Variant covers by Art Adams and Lee Weeks 6.00
623-626, 626.1, 627-630-($2.99) Fear Itself tie-in. 628,629-Portacio-a 3.00
631-655: 631-Portacio-a; Aftermath. 632-Hellstrom app. 637,638-Exiled x-over with New Mutants #41-43. 642-644-Crossover with Mighty Thor #19-21. 646-Features Sif 3.00

JOURNEY INTO MYSTERY (2nd Series)
Marvel Comics: Oct, 1972 - No. 19, Oct, 1975

1-Robert Howard adaptation; Starlin/Ploog-a 5 10 15 33 57 80
2-5: 2,3,5-Bloch adapt. 4-H. P. Lovecraft adapt. 3 6 9 17 26 35
6-19: Reprints 3 6 9 16 23 30
NOTE: ***N. Adams*** *a-2i.* ***Ditko*** *r-7, 10, 12, 14, 15, 19; c-10.* ***Everett*** *r-9, 14.* ***G. Kane*** *a-1p, 2p; c-1-3p.* ***Kirby*** *r-7, 13, 15, 18, 19; c-7.* ***Mort Lawrence*** *r-2.* ***Maneely*** *r-3.* ***Orlando*** *r-16.* ***Reese*** *a-1, 2i.* ***Starlin*** *a-1p, 3p.* ***Torres*** *r-16.* ***Wildey*** *r-9, 14.*

JOURNEY INTO MYSTERY: THE BIRTH OF KRAKOA
Marvel Comics: Nov, 2018 ($4.99, one-shot)

1-Nick Fury and the Howling Commandos app.; Hopeless-s/Morissette-Phan-a 5.00

JOURNEY INTO UNKNOWN WORLDS (Formerly Teen)
Atlas Comics (WFP): No. 36, Sept, 1950 - No. 38, Feb, 1951; No. 4, Apr, 1951 - No. 59, Aug, 1957

36(#1)-Science fiction/weird; "End Of The Earth" c/story
275 550 825 1750 3275 4800
37(#2)-Science fiction; "When Worlds Collide" c/story; Everett-c/a; Hitler story
135 270 405 864 1482 2100
38(#3)-Science fiction 110 220 330 704 1202 1700
4-6,8,10-Science fiction/weird 69 138 207 442 759 1075
7-Wolverton-a "Planet of Terror", 6 pgs; electric chair c-inset/story
105 210 315 667 1146 1625
9-Giant eyeball story 92 184 276 584 1005 1425
11,12-Krigstein-a 50 100 150 315 533 750
13,16,17,20 43 86 129 271 461 650
14-Wolverton-a "One of Our Graveyards Is Missing", 4 pgs; Tuska-a
82 164 246 528 902 1275
15-Wolverton-a "They Crawl by Night", 5 pgs.; 2 pg. Maneely s/f story
82 164 246 528 902 1275
18,19-Matt Fox-a 52 104 156 328 552 775
21-33: 21-Decapitation-c. 24-Sci/fic story. 26-Atom bomb panel. 27-Sid Check-a. 33-Last pre-code (2/55) 39 78 117 236 388 540
34-Kubert, Torres-a 34 68 102 199 325 450
35-Torres-a 31 62 93 182 296 410
36-45,48,50,53,55,59: 43-Krigstein-a. 44-Davis-a. 45,55,59-Williamson-a in all; with Mayo #55,59. 55-Crandall-a. 48,53-Crandall-a (4 pgs. #48). 48-Check-a. 50-Davis, Crandall-a
29 58 87 170 278 385
46,47,49,52,54,56-58: 54-Torres-a 27 54 81 158 259 360
51-Ditko, Wood-a 32 64 96 188 307 425
NOTE: ***Ayers*** *a-24, 43,* ***Berg*** *a-38(#3), 43.* ***Lou Cameron*** *a-33.* ***Colan*** *a-37(#2), 6, 17, 19, 20, 23, 39.* ***Ditko*** *a-45, 51.* ***Drucker*** *a-35, 58.* ***Everett*** *a-37(#2), 11, 14, 41, 55, 56; c-37(#2), 11, 13, 14, 17, 22, 47, 48, 50, 53-55, 59.* ***Forte*** *a-49.* ***Fox*** *a-21i.* ***Heath*** *a-36(#1), 4, 6-8, 17, 20, 22, 36i; c-18.* ***Keller*** *a-15.* ***Mort Lawrence*** *a-38, 39.* ***Maneely*** *a-7, 8, 15, 16, 22, 49, 58; c-8, 19, 25, 52.* ***Morrow*** *a-48.* ***Orlando*** *a-44, 57.* ***Pakula*** *a-36.* ***Powell*** *a-42, 53, 54.* ***Reinman*** *a-8.* ***Rico*** *a-21.* ***Robert Sale*** *a-24, 49.* ***Sekowsky*** *a-4, 5, 9.* ***Severin*** *a-38, 51; c-38, 48i, 56.* ***Sinnott*** *a-9, 21, 24.* ***Tuska*** *a-38(#3), 14.* ***Wildey*** *a-25, 43, 44.*

JOURNEY INTO UNKNOWN WORLDS (Marvel 80th Anniversary salute to science fiction)
Marvel Comics: Mar, 2019 ($3.99, one-shot)

1-Bunn-s/Sanna-a; Chapman-s/Manna-a; McKone-c 4.00

JOURNEY TO STAR WARS: THE FORCE AWAKENS - SHATTERED EMPIRE
Marvel Comics: Nov, 2015 - No. 4, Dec, 2015 ($3.99, weekly limited series)

1-4-Rucka-s; takes place just after Episode 6 Battle of Endor; multiple covers on each 4.00

JOURNEY TO STAR WARS: THE LAST JEDI - CAPTAIN PHASMA
Marvel Comics: Nov, 2017 - No. 4, Dec, 2017 ($3.99, weekly limited series)

1-4-Checchetto-a/Renaud-c; takes place at the end of Episode 7 and just after 4.00

JOURNEY TO STAR WARS: THE RISE OF SKYWALKER - ALLEGIANCE

JSA #7 © DC

JSA: All Stars #2 © DC

Judge Dredd (1994 series) #2 © DC

GD 2.0 | VG 4.0 | FN 6.0 | VF 8.0 | VF/NM 9.0 | NM- 9.2

Marvel Comics: Dec, 2019 - No. 4, Dec, 2020 ($4.99/$3.99, weekly limited series)
1-($4.99) Ethan Sacks-s/Luke Ross-a; follows events after Episode 8 5.00
2-4-($3.99) Sacks-s/Ross-a; interlocking covers with #1 4.00

JOURNEY TO THE CENTER OF THE EARTH (Movie)
Dell Publishing Co.: No. 1060, Nov-Jan, 1959/60 (one-shot)
Four Color 1060-Pat Boone & James Mason photo-c 11 22 33 75 160 245

JOYRIDE
BOOM! Studios: Apr, 2016 - No. 12, Apr, 2017 ($3.99, originally planned as a 4-part series)
1-12-Jackson Lanzing & Collin Kelly-s/Marcus To-a. 1-Multiple covers 4.00

JSA (Justice Society of America) (Also see All Star Comics)
DC Comics: Aug, 1999 - No. 87, Sept, 2006 ($2.50/$2.99)
1-Robinson and Goyer-s; funeral of Wesley Dodds 2 4 6 8 10 12
2-5: 4-Return of Dr. Fate 6.00
6-24: 6-Black Adam-c/app. 11,12-Kobra. 16-20-JSA vs. Johnny Sorrow. 19,20-Spectre app. 22-Hawkgirl origin. 23-Hawkman returns 4.00
25-($3.75) Hawkman rejoins the JSA 1 2 3 5 7 9
26-36, 38-49: 27-Capt. Marvel app. 29-Joker: Last Laugh. 31,32-Snejbjerg-a. 33-Ultra-Humanite. 34-Intro. new Crimson Avenger and Hourman. 42-G.A. Mr. Terrific and the Freedom Fighters app. 46-Eclipso returns 3.00
37-($3.50) Johnny Thunder merges with the Thunderbolt; origin new Crimson Avenger4.00
50-($3.95) Wraparound-c by Pacheco; Sentinel becomes Green Lantern again 4.00
51-74,76-82: 51-Kobra killed. 54-JLA app. 55-Ma Hunkle (Red Tornado) app. 56-58-Black Reign x-over with Hawkman #23-25. 64-Sand returns. 67-Identity Crisis tie-in; Gibbons-a. 68,69,72-81-Ross-c. 73,74-Day of Vengeance tie-in. 76-OMAC tie-in. 82-Infinite Crisis x-over; Levitz-s/Pérez-a 3.00
75-($2.99) Day of Vengeance tie-in; Alex Ross Spectre-c 4.00
83-87: One Year Later; Pérez-c. 83-85,87-Morales-a; Gentleman Ghost app. 85-Begin $2.99-c; Earth-2 Batman, Atom, Sandman, Mr. Terrific app. 86,87-Ordway-a. 3.00
Annual 1 (10/00, $3.50) Planet DC; intro. Nemesis 4.00
...: Black Reign TPB (2005, $12.99) r/#56-58, Hawkman #23-25; Watson cover gallery 13.00
...: Black Vengeance TPB (2006, $19.99) r/#66-75 20.00
...: Darkness Falls TPB (2002, $19.95) r/#6-15 20.00
...: Fair Play TPB (2003, $14.95) r/#26-31 & Secret Files #2 15.00
...: Ghost Stories TPB (2006, $14.99) r/#82-87 15.00
...: Justice Be Done TPB (2000, $14.95) r/Secret Files & #1-5 15.00
...: Lost TPB (2005, $19.99) r/#59-67 20.00
...: Mixed Signals TPB (2006, $14.99) r/#76-81 15.00
...: Our Worlds at War 1 (9/01, $2.95) Jae Lee-c; Saltares-a 3.00
... Presents Green Lantern TPB (2008, $14.99) r/JSA Classified #25,32,33 and Green Lantern: Brightest Day, Blackest Night 15.00
...: Princes of Darkness TPB (2005, $19.95) r/#46-55 20.00
...: Savage Times TPB (2004, $14.95) r/#39-45 15.00
... Secret Files 1 (8/99, $4.95) Origin stories and pin-ups; death of Wesley Dodds (G.A. Sandman); intro new Hawkgirl 5.00
... Secret Files 2 (9/01, $4.95) Short stories and profile pages 5.00
...: Stealing Thunder TPB (2003, $14.95) r/#32-38; JSA vs. The Ultra-Humanite 15.00
...: The Golden Age TPB (2005, $19.99) r/"The Golden Age" Elseworlds mini-series 20.00
...: The Return of Hawkman TPB (2002, $19.95) r/#16-26 & Secret Files #1 20.00

JSA: ALL STARS
DC Comics: July, 2003 - No. 8, Feb, 2004 ($2.50/$3.50, limited series, back-up stories in Golden Age style)
1-3,5,6,8-Goyer & Johns-s/Cassaday-c. 1-Velluto-a; intro. Legacy. 2-Hawkman by Loeb/Sale 3-Dr. Fate by Cooke. 5-Hourman by Chaykin. 6-Dr. Mid-nite by Azzarello/Risso 3.00
4-Starman by Robinson/Harris; 1st app. Courtney Whitmore as Stargirl 3.00
7-($3.50) Mr. Terrific back-up story by Chabon; Lark-a 4.00
TPB (2004, $14.95) r/#1-8 15.00

JSA: ALL STARS
DC Comics: Feb, 2010 - No. 18, Jul, 2011 ($3.99/$2.99)
1-13-Younger JSA members form team. 1-Covers by Williams and Sook 4.00
14-18-($2.99) 3.00
...: Constellations TPB (2010, $14.99) r/#1-6 and sketch art 15.00
...: Glory Days TPB (2011, $17.99) r/#7-13 18.00

JSA: CLASSIFIED (Issues #1-4 reprinted in Power Girl TPB)
DC Comics: Sept, 2005 - No. 39, Aug, 2008 ($2.50/$2.99)
1-(1st printing) Conner-c/a; origin of Power Girl 1 3 4 6 8 10
1-(1st printing) Adam Hughes variant-c 3 6 9 14 20 25
1-(2nd & 3rd printings) 2nd-Hughes B&W sketch-c. 3rd-Close-up of Conner-c 6.00
2-11: 2-LSH app. 4-Leads into Infinite Crisis #2. 5-7-Injustice Society app. 10-13-Vandal Savage origin retold; Gulacy-a/c 3.00
12-39: 12-Begin $2.99-c. 17,18-Bane app. 19,20-Morales-a. 21,22-Simonson-s/a 3.00
...: Honor Among Thieves TPB (2007, $14.99) r/#5-9 15.00

JSA LIBERTY FILES: THE WHISTLING SKULL
DC Comics: Feb, 2013 - No. 6, Jul, 2013 ($2.99, limited series)
1-6-Dr. Mid-Nite and Hourman in 1940; B. Clay Moore-s/Tony Harris-c/a 3.00

JSA STRANGE ADVENTURES
DC Comics: Oct, 2004 - No. 6, Mar, 2005 ($3.50, limited series)
1-6-Johnny Thunder as pulp writer; Kitson-a/Watson-c/ Kevin Anderson-s 3.50
TPB (2010, $14.99) r/#1-6 15.00

JSA: THE LIBERTY FILE (Elseworlds)
DC Comics: Feb, 2000 - No. 2, Mar, 2000 ($6.95, limited series)
1,2-Batman, Dr. Mid-Nite and Hourman vs. WW2 Joker; Tony Harris-c/a 7.00
JSA: The Liberty Files TPB (2004, $19.95) r/The Liberty File and The Unholy Three series 20.00

JSA: THE UNHOLY THREE (Elseworlds)(Sequel to JSA: The Liberty File)
DC Comics: 2003 - No. 2, 2003 ($6.95, limited series)
1,2-Batman, Superman and Hourman; Tony Harris-c/a 7.00

JSA VS. KOBRA
DC Comics: Aug, 2009 - No. 6, Jan, 2010 ($2.99, limited series)
1-6-Kramer-a/Ha-c; Jason Burr app. 3.00
TPB (2010, $14.99) r/#1-6; cover gallery 15.00

J2 (Also see A-Next and Juggernaut)
Marvel Comics: Oct, 1998 - No. 12, Sept, 1999 ($1.99)
1-12:1-Juggernaut's son; Lim-a. 2-Two covers; X-People app. 3-J2 battles the Hulk 3.00
Spider-Girl Presents Juggernaut Jr. Vol.1: Secrets & Lies (2006, $7.99, digest) r/#1-6 8.00

JUBILEE (X-Men)
Marvel Comics: Nov, 2004 - No. 6, Apr, 2005 ($2.99)
1-6: 1-Jubilee in a Los Angeles high school; Kirkman-s; Casey Jones-c 3.00

JUDAS
BOOM! Studios: Dec, 2017 - No. 4, Mar, 2018 ($3.99, limited series)
1-4-Judas' time with Jesus and in the Afterlife; Lucifer app.; Loveness-s/Rebelka-a 4.00

JUDAS COIN, THE
DC Comics: 2012 ($22.99, hardcover graphic novel with dust jacket)
HC-Walt Simonson-s/a/c; Batman, Two-Face, Golden Gladiator, Viking Prince, Captain Fear, Bat Lash, Manhunter 2070 app.; bonus sketch gallery 23.00

JUDENHASS
Aardvark-Vanaheim Press: 2008 ($4.00, B&W, squarebound)
nn-Dave Sim-writer/artist; The Shoah and Jewish persecution through history 4.00

JUDE, THE FORGOTTEN SAINT
Catechetical Guild Education Soc.: 1954 (16 pgs.; 8x11"; full color; paper-c)
nn 6 12 18 28 34 40

JUDGE COLT
Gold Key: Oct, 1969 - No. 4, Sept, 1970 (Painted cover)
1 3 6 9 16 23 30
2-4 2 4 6 9 13 16

JUDGE DREDD (...Classics #62 on; also see Batman - Judge Dredd, The Law of Dredd & 2000 A.D. Monthly)
Eagle Comics/IPC Magazines Ltd./Quality Comics #34-35, V2#1-37/ Fleetway #38 on: Nov, 1983 - No. 35, 1986; V2#1, Oct, 1986 - No. 77, 1993
1-Bolland-c/a 4 8 12 27 44 60
2-5 2 4 6 8 10 12
6-35 6.00
V2#1-('86)-New look begins 6.00
2-10 5.00
11-77: 20-Begin $1.50-c. 21/22, 23/24-Two issue numbers in one. 28-1st app. Megaman (super-hero). 39-Begin $1.75-c. 51-Begin $1.95-c. 53-Bolland-a. 57-Reprints 1st published Judge Dredd story 4.00
Special 1 5.00
NOTE: ***Bolland** a-1-6, 8, 10; c-1-10, 15. **Guice** c-V2#23/24, 26, 27.*

JUDGE DREDD (3rd Series)
DC Comics: Aug, 1994 - No. 18, Jan, 1996 ($1.95)
1-18: 12-Begin $2.25-c 4.00
nn ($5.95)-Movie adaptation, Sienkiewicz-c 6.00

JUDGE DREDD
IDW Publishing: Nov, 2012 - No. 30, May, 2015 ($3.99)
1-30: 1-Swierczynski-s; six covers 4.00

JUDGE DREDD
IDW Publishing: Dec, 2015 - No. 12, Nov, 2016 ($3.99)

Judge Dredd: Toxic #1 © Rebellion

Juggernaut (2020 series) #1 © MAR

Jughead #241 © ACP

	GD 2.0	VG 4.0	FN 6.0	VF 8.0	VF/NM 9.0	NM- 9.2
1-12: 1-Farinas & Freitas-s/McDaid-a; multiple covers						4.00
Annual 1 (2/17, $7.99) Farinas & Freitas-s/McDaid-a; two covers						8.00
...: Cry of the Werewolf (3/17, $5.99) Reprint from 2000 AD; Steve Dillon-a/c; new pin-ups						6.00
...: Deviations (3/17, $4.99) McCrea-s/a; What If Dredd stayed a werewolf; bonus pin-ups						5.00
... Funko Universe (4/17, $4.99) Short stories w/characters styled like Pop! Vinyl figures						5.00
...: Mega-City Zero 1 (5/18, $1.00) reprints #1						3.00
...: 100-Page Giant (2/20, $5.99) Reprints stories from recent mini-series						6.00

JUDGE DREDD: ANDERSON, PSI-DIVISION
IDW Publishing: Aug, 2014 - No. 4, Dec, 2014 ($3.99)

1-4-Matt Smith-s/Carl Critchlow-a; three covers on each 4.00

JUDGE DREDD CLASSICS (Reprints)
IDW Publishing: Jul, 2013 - No. 6 ($3.99)

1-6-Wagner & Grant-s 4.00
Free Comic Book Day 2013 (5/13, free) Judge Death app.; Walter the Wobot back-ups 3.00
...: The Dark Judges 1-5 (1/15 - No. 5, 5/15, $3.99) Wagner & Grant-s/Bolland-a 4.00

JUDGE DREDD: LEGENDS OF THE LAW
DC Comics: Dec, 1994 - No. 13, Dec, 1995 ($1.95)

1-13: 1-5-Dorman-c 4.00

JUDGE DREDD: MEGA-CITY TWO
IDW Publishing: Jan, 2014 - No. 5, May, 2014 ($3.99)

1-5-Wolk-s/Farinas-a 4.00

JUDGE DREDD'S CRIME FILE
Eagle Comics: Aug, 1985 - No. 6, Feb, 1986 ($1.25, limited series)

1-6: 1-Byrne-a 5.00

JUDGE DREDD: THE BLESSED EARTH
IDW Publishing: Apr, 2017 - No. 8, Nov, 2017 ($3.99)

1-8-Farinas & Freitas-a; multiple covers on each 4.00

JUDGE DREDD: THE EARLY CASES
Eagle Comics: Feb, 1986 - No. 6, Jul, 1986 ($1.25, Mega-series, Mando paper)

1-6: 2000 A.D.-r 5.00

JUDGE DREDD: THE JUDGE CHILD QUEST (Judge Child in indicia)
Eagle Comics: Aug, 1984 - No. 5, Oct, 1984 ($1.25, Lim. series, Baxter paper)

1-5: 2000A.D.-r; Bolland-c/a 6.00

JUDGE DREDD: THE MEGAZINE
Fleetway/Quality: 1991 - No. 3 ($4.95, stiff-c, squarebound, 52 pgs.)

1-3 5.00

JUDGE DREDD: TOXIC
IDW Publishing: Oct, 2018 - No. 4, Jan, 2019 ($3.99)

1-4-Paul Jenkins-s/Marco Castiello-a 4.00

JUDGE DREDD: UNDER SIEGE
IDW Publishing: May, 2018 - No. 4, Aug, 2018 ($3.99)

1-4-Mark Russell-s/Max Dunbar-a 4.00

JUDGE DREDD VS. ALIENS: INCUBUS
Dark Horse Comics: March, 2003 - No. 4, June, 2003 ($2.99, limited series)

1-4-Flint-a/Wagner & Diggle-s 3.00

JUDGE DREDD: YEAR ONE
IDW Publishing: Mar, 2013 - No. 4, Jul, 2013 ($3.99)

1-4-Matt Smith-s/Simon Coleby-a 4.00

JUDGE PARKER
Argo: Feb, 1956 - No. 2, 1956

	GD 2.0	VG 4.0	FN 6.0	VF 8.0	VF/NM 9.0	NM- 9.2
1-Newspaper strip reprints	7	14	21	37	46	55
2	6	12	18	27	33	38

JUDGMENT DAY
Awesome Entertainment: June, 1997 - No. 3, Oct, 1997 ($2.50, limited series)

1-3: 1 Alpha-Moore-s/Liefeld-c/a(p) flashback art by various in all. 2 Omega. 3 Final Judgment. All have a variant cover by Dave Gibbons 4.00
...Aftermath-($3.50) Moore-s/Kane-a; Youngblood, Glory, New Men, Maximage, Allies and Spacehunter short stories. Also has a variant cover by Dave Gibbons 4.00
TPB (Checker Books, 2003, $16.95) r/series 17.00

JUDO JOE
Jay-Jay Corp.: Aug, 1953 - No. 3, Dec, 1953 (Judo lessons in each issue)

	GD 2.0	VG 4.0	FN 6.0	VF 8.0	VF/NM 9.0	NM- 9.2
1-Drug ring story	15	30	45	86	133	180
2,3: 3-Hypo needle story	10	20	30	56	76	95

JUDOMASTER (Gun Master #84-89) (Also see Crisis on Infinite Earths, Sarge Steel #6, Special War Series, & Thunderbolt)
Charlton Comics: No. 89, May-June, 1966 - No. 98, Dec, 1967 (Two No. 89's)

	GD 2.0	VG 4.0	FN 6.0	VF 8.0	VF/NM 9.0	NM- 9.2
89-3rd app. Judomaster	4	8	12	25	40	55
90-Origin of Thunderbolt	4	8	12	23	37	50
91-Sarge Steel begins	3	6	9	21	33	45
92-98: 93-Intro. Tiger	3	6	9	20	31	42
93,94,96,98 (Modern Comics reprint, 1977)						6.00

NOTE: *Morisi Thunderbolt #90. #91 has 1 pg. biography on writer/artist Frank McLaughlin.*

JUDY CANOVA (Formerly My Experience) (Stage, screen, radio)
Fox Feature Syndicate: No. 23, May, 1950 - No. 3, Sept, 1950

	GD 2.0	VG 4.0	FN 6.0	VF 8.0	VF/NM 9.0	NM- 9.2
23(#1)-Wood-c,a(p)?	28	56	84	165	270	375
24-Wood-a(p)	26	52	78	154	252	350
3-Wood-c; Wood/Orlando-a	28	56	84	168	274	380

JUDY GARLAND (See Famous Stars)

JUDY JOINS THE WAVES
Toby Press: 1951 (For U.S. Navy)

	GD 2.0	VG 4.0	FN 6.0	VF 8.0	VF/NM 9.0	NM- 9.2
nn	9	18	27	47	61	75

JUGGERNAUT (See X-Men)
Marvel Comics: Apr, 1997, Nov, 1999 ($2.99, one-shots)

1-(4/97) Kelly-s/ Rouleau-a 4.00
1-(11/99) Casey-s; Eighth Day x-over; Thor, Iron Man, Spidey app. 4.00

JUGGERNAUT (X-Men)
Marvel Comics: Nov, 2020 - Present ($3.99)

1-5-Nicieza-s/Garney-a. 2-Hulk app. 4,5-Arnim Zola app. 4.00

JUGHEAD (Formerly Archie's Pal...)
Archie Publications: No. 127, Dec, 1965 - No. 352, June, 1987

	GD 2.0	VG 4.0	FN 6.0	VF 8.0	VF/NM 9.0	NM- 9.2
127-130: 129-LBJ on cover	3	6	9	17	26	35
131,133,135-160(9/68)	3	6	9	15	22	28
132,134: 132-Shield-c; The Fly & Black Hood app.; Shield cameo. 134-Shield-c	4	8	12	28	47	65
161-180	2	4	6	13	18	22
181-199	2	4	6	9	13	16
200(1/'72)	2	4	6	11	16	20
201-240(5/75)	2	4	6	8	10	12
241-270(11/77)	1	2	3	5	7	9
271-299	1	2	3	4	5	7
300(5/80)-Anniversary issue; infinity-c	1	2	3	5	6	8
301-320(1/82)						5.00
321-324,326-352						4.00
325-(10/82) Cheryl Blossom app. (not on cover); same month as intro. (cover & story) in Archie's Girls, Betty & Veronica #320; Jason Blossom app.; DeCarlo-a	9	18	27	60	120	180

JUGHEAD (2nd Series)(Becomes Archie's Pal Jughead Comics #46 on)
Archie Enterprises: Aug, 1987 - No. 45, May, 1993 (.75/$1.00/$1.25)

	GD 2.0	VG 4.0	FN 6.0	VF 8.0	VF/NM 9.0	NM- 9.2
1	1	2	3	4	5	7
2-10						4.00
11-45: 4-X-Mas issue. 17-Colan-c/a						3.00

JUGHEAD (Volume 3)
Archie Comic Publications: Nov, 2015 - No. 16, Aug, 2017 ($3.99)

1-16-Multiple covers and classic back-up reprints. 1-6-Chip Zdarsky-s/Erica Henderson-a. 5,6-Jughead as Captain Hero. 7-13-Derek Charm-a. 9-13-Ryan North-s; Sabrina app. 4.00

JUGHEAD AND ARCHIE DOUBLE DIGEST (Becomes Jughead & Archie Comics Digest)
Archie Comic Publ.: Jun, 2014 - No. 27, Oct, 2017 ($3.99-$6.99, digest-size)

1-3: 1-Reprints; That Wilkin Boy app. 4.00
4,7-9,11-14,16,19,26-($4.99) 5.00
5,10,15,21,23,25-($6.99, 320 pgs.) Titled Jughead & Archie Jumbo Comics Digest 7.00
6,17,18,20,22,24,27-($5.99, 192 pgs.) Titled Jughead & Archie Comics Annual. 24-Winter Annual 6.00

JUGHEAD & FRIENDS DIGEST MAGAZINE
Archie Publ.: Jun, 2005 - No. 38, Aug, 2010 ($2.39/$2.49/$2.69, digest-size)

1-38: 1-That Wilkin Boy app. 3.00

JUGHEAD AS CAPTAIN HERO (See Archie as Pureheart the Powerful, Archie Giant Series Magazine #142 & Life With Archie)
Archie Publications: Oct, 1966 - No. 7, Nov, 1967

	GD 2.0	VG 4.0	FN 6.0	VF 8.0	VF/NM 9.0	NM- 9.2
1-Super hero parody	8	16	24	51	96	140
2	5	10	15	31	53	75
3-7	4	8	12	27	44	60

JUGHEAD COMICS, NIGHT AT GEPPI'S ENTERTAINMENT MUSEUM

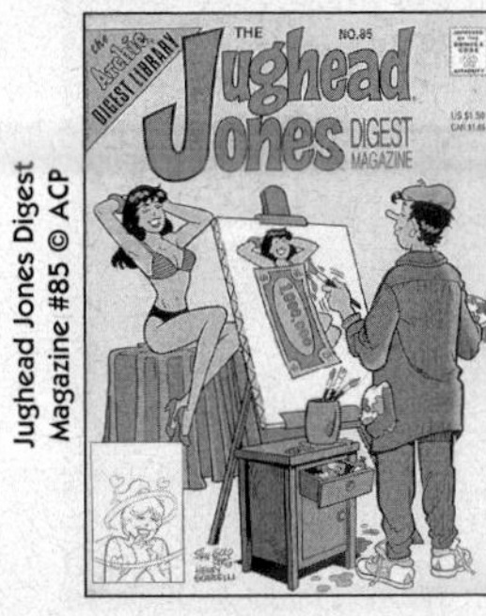

Jughead Jones Digest Magazine #85 © ACP

Jughead The Hunger One Shot © ACP

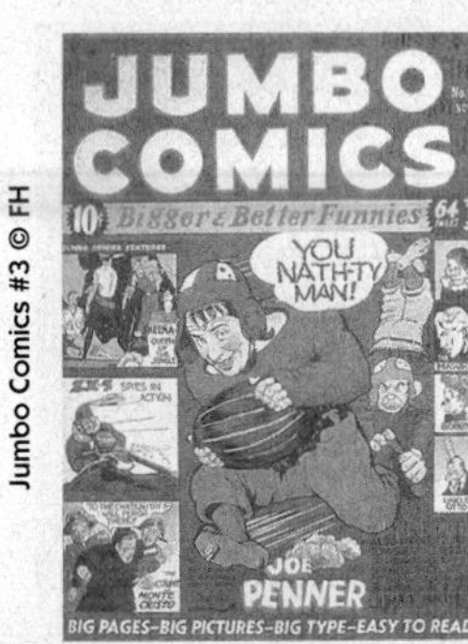

Jumbo Comics #3 © FH

	GD 2.0	VG 4.0	FN 6.0	VF 8.0	VF/NM 9.0	NM- 9.2

Archie Comic Publ. Inc: 2008

Free Comic Book Day giveaway - New story; Archie gang visits GEM; Steve Geppi app.						3.00

JUGHEAD JONES COMICS DIGEST, THE (...Magazine No. 10-64; Jughead Jones Digest Magazine #65)
Archie Publ.: June, 1977 - No. 100, May, 1996 ($1.35/$1.50/$1.75, digest-size, 128 pgs.)

	GD	VG	FN	VF	VF/NM	NM-
1-Neal Adams-a; Capt. Hero-r	3	6	9	20	31	42
2(9/77)-Neal Adams-a	3	6	9	15	22	28
3-6,8-10	2	4	6	11	16	20
7-Origin Jaguar-r; N. Adams-a.	2	4	6	13	18	22
11-20: 13-r/1957 Jughead's Folly	2	4	6	8	10	12
21-50	1	2	3	4	5	7
51-70						5.00
71-100						3.00

JUGHEAD'S BABY TALES
Archie Comics: Spring, 1994 - No. 2, Wint. 1994 ($2.00, 52 pgs.)

1,2: 1-Bound-in pull-out poster						4.00

JUGHEAD'S DINER
Archie Comics: Apr, 1990 - No. 7, Apr, 1991 ($1.00)

1						5.00
2-7						4.00

JUGHEAD'S DOUBLE DIGEST (...Magazine #5)
Archie Comics: Oct, 1989 - No. 200, Apr, 2014 ($2.25 - $3.99/$5.99)

	GD	VG	FN	VF	VF/NM	NM-
1	2	4	6	8	10	12
2-10: 2,5-Capt. Hero stories	1	2	3	5	6	8
11-25						5.00
26-195: 58-Begin $2.99-c. 66-Begin $3.19-c. 91-Begin $3.59-c. 138-Reprints entire Jughead #1 (1949). 139-142-"New Look" Jughead; Staton-a. 148-Begin $3.99-c						4.00
196-200-($5.99) Titled "Jughead's Double Double Digest"						6.00
Archie New Look Series Book 2, Jughead "The Matchmakers" TPB (2009, $10.95) r/new look series in #139-142; new cover by Staton & Milgrom						11.00

JUGHEAD'S EAT-OUT COMIC BOOK MAGAZINE (See Archie Giant Series Magazine No. 170)

JUGHEAD'S FANTASY
Archie Publications: Aug, 1960 - No. 3, Dec, 1960

	GD	VG	FN	VF	VF/NM	NM-
1	20	40	60	141	313	485
2	13	26	39	87	191	295
3	11	22	33	72	154	235

JUGHEAD'S FOLLY
Archie Publications (Close-Up): 1957 (36 pgs.)(one-shot)

	GD	VG	FN	VF	VF/NM	NM-
1-Jughead a la Elvis (Rare) (1st reference to Elvis in comics?)	81	162	243	518	884	1250

JUGHEAD'S JOKES
Archie Publications: Aug, 1967 - No. 78, Sept, 1982
(No. 1-8, 38 on: reg. size; No. 9-23: 68 pgs.; No. 24-37: 52 pgs.)

	GD	VG	FN	VF	VF/NM	NM-
1	7	14	21	46	86	125
2	4	8	12	28	47	65
3-8	3	6	9	16	24	32
9,10 (68 pgs.)	3	6	9	18	28	38
11-23(4/71) (68 pgs.)	3	6	9	16	23	30
24-37(1/74) (52 pgs.)	2	4	6	11	16	20
38-50(9/76)	1	3	4	6	8	10
51-78						6.00

JUGHEAD'S PAL HOT DOG (See Laugh #14 for 1st app.)
Archie Comics: Jan, 1990 - No. 5, Oct, 1990 ($1.00)

1						5.00
2-5						4.00

JUGHEAD'S SOUL FOOD
Spire Christian Comics (Fleming H. Revell Co.): 1979 (49¢/59¢)

	GD	VG	FN	VF	VF/NM	NM-
nn-Low print run	3	6	9	15	22	28

JUGHEAD'S TIME POLICE
Archie Comics: July, 1990 - No. 6, May, 1991 ($1.00, bi-monthly)

1						5.00
2-6: Colan-a-3-6p; c-3-6						4.00

JUGHEAD'S TIME POLICE
Archie Comic Publications: Aug, 2019 - No. 5, Dec, 2019 ($3.99, limited series)

1-5-Sina Grace-s/Derek Charm-a; multiple covers on each; January McAndrews app.						4.00

JUGHEAD: THE HUNGER (Continues in Jughead The Hunger vs Vampironica)
Archie Comic Publications: Dec, 2017 - No. 13, May, 2019 ($3.99)

1-13-Tieri-s; Jughead as a werewolf. 1-8-Pat & Tim Kennedy-a; 2-13-Eisma-a (partial)						4.00
Jughead The Hunger, One-Shot (5/17, $4.99) Tieri-s/Walsh-a; prelude to issue #1						5.00

JUGHEAD: THE HUNGER VS VAMPIRONICA
Archie Comic Publications: Jun, 2019 - No. 5, Dec, 2019 ($3.99, limited series)

1-5-Tieri-s/Pat & Tim Kennedy-a; Eisma-a (partial); multiple covers. 3-5 Sabrina app.						4.00

JUGHEAD WITH ARCHIE DIGEST (...Plus Betty & Veronica & Reggie Too No. 1,2; ...Magazine #33-?, 101-on; ...Comics Digest Mag.)
Archie Pub.: Mar, 1974 - No. 200, May, 2005 ($1.00-$2.39)

	GD	VG	FN	VF	VF/NM	NM-
1	5	10	15	31	53	75
2	3	6	9	21	33	45
3-10	3	6	9	17	26	35
11-13,15-17,19,20: Capt. Hero-r in #14-16; Capt. Pureheart #17,19	2	4	6	10	14	18
14,18,21,22-Pureheart the Powerful in #18,21,22	2	4	6	11	16	20
23-30: 29-The Shield-r. 30-The Fly-r	1	3	4	6	8	10
31-50,100	1	2	3	5	6	8
51-99	1	2	3	4	5	7
101-121						4.00
122-200: 156-Begin $2.19-c. 180-Begin $2.39-c						3.00

JUICE SQUEEZERS
Dark Horse Comics: Jan, 2014 - No. 4, Apr, 2014 ($3.99, limited series)

1-4-David Lapham-s/a/c						4.00

JUKE BOX COMICS
Famous Funnies: Mar, 1948 - No. 6, Jan, 1949

	GD	VG	FN	VF	VF/NM	NM-
1-Toth-c/a; Hollingsworth-a	39	78	117	240	395	550
2-Transvestism story	24	48	72	140	230	320
3-6: 3-Peggy Lee story. 4-Jimmy Durante line drawn-c. 6-Features Desi Arnaz plus Arnaz line drawn-c	19	38	57	109	172	235

JUMBO COMICS (Created by S.M. Iger)
Fiction House Magazines (Real Adv. Publ. Co.): Sept, 1938 - No. 167, Mar, 1953 (No. 1-3: 68 pgs.; No. 4-8: 52 pgs.)(No. 1-8 oversized-10-1/2x14-1/2"; black & white)

	GD	VG	FN	VF	VF/NM	NM-
1-(Rare)-Sheena Queen of the Jungle(1st app.) by Meskin, Hawks of the Seas (The Hawk #10 on; see Feature Funnies #3) by Eisner, The Hunchback by Dick Briefer (ends #8), Wilton of the West (ends #24), Inspector Dayton (ends #67) & ZX-5 (ends #140) begin; 1st comic art by Jack Kirby (Count of Monte Cristo & Wilton of the West); Mickey Mouse appears (1 panel) with brief biography of Walt Disney; 1st app. Peter Pupp by Bob Kane. Note: Sheena was created by Iger for publication in England as a newspaper strip. The early issues of Jumbo contain Sheena strip-r; multiple panel-c 1,2,7	4250	8500	12,750	34,000	--	--
2-(Rare)-Origin Sheena. Diary of Dr. Hayward by Kirby (also #3) plus 2 other stories; contains strip from Universal Film featuring Edgar Bergen & Charlie McCarthy plus-c (preview of film)	1375	2750	4125	11,000	--	--
3-Last Kirby issue	988	1976	2964	7900	--	--
4-(Scarce)-Origin The Hawk by Eisner; Wilton of the West by Fine (ends #14)(1st comic work); Count of Monte Cristo by Fine (ends #15); The Diary of Dr. Hayward by Fine (cont'd #8,9)	938	1876	2814	7500	--	--
5-Christmas-c	863	1926	2589	6900	--	--
6-8-Last B&W issue. #8 was a 1939 N. Y. World's Fair Special Edition; Frank Buck's Jungleland story	763	1526	2289	6100	--	--
9-Stuart Taylor begins by Fine (ends #140); Fine-c; 1st color issue (8-9/39)-1st Sheena (jungle) cover; 8-1/4x10-1/4" (oversized in width only)	1025	2050	3075	8200	--	--
10-Regular size 68 pg. issues begin; Sheena dons new costume w/origin costume; Stuart Taylor sci/fi-c; classic Lou Fine-c.	492	984	1476	3592	6346	9100
11-13: 12-The Hawk-c by Eisner. 13-Eisner-c	239	478	717	1530	2615	3700
14-Intro. Lightning (super-hero) on-c only	245	490	735	1568	2684	3800
15-1st Lightning story and begins, ends #41	165	330	495	1056	1803	2550
16-Lightning-c	181	362	543	1158	1979	2800
17,18,20: 17-Lightning part-c	135	270	405	864	1482	2100
19-Classic Sheena Giant Ape-c by Powell	168	336	504	1075	1838	2600
21-30: 22-1st Tom, Dick & Harry; origin The Hawk retold. 25-Midnight the Black Stallion begins, ends #65	97	194	291	621	1061	1500
31-(9/41)-1st app. Mars God of War in Stuart Taylor story (see Planet Comics #15.) (scarce)	300	600	900	1950	3375	4800
32-40: 35-Shows V2#11 (correct number does not appear)	77	154	231	493	847	1200
41-50: 42-Ghost Gallery begins, ends #167	52	104	156	328	552	775
51-60: 52-Last Tom, Dick & Harry	41	82	123	256	428	600
61-70: 68-Sky Girl begins, ends #130; not in #79	36	72	109	216	351	485
71-93,95-99: 89-ZX5 becomes a private eye.	29	58	87	170	278	385
94-Used in Love and Death by Legman	31	62	93	182	296	410
100	31	62	93	182	296	410

Jungle Action #12 © MAR

Jungle Comics #75 © FH

Jungle Girl #1 © Jungle Girl LLC

GD 2.0 VG 4.0 FN 6.0 VF 8.0 VF/NM 9.0 NM- 9.2

101-121 25 50 75 147 241 335
121-140,150-158: 155-Used in **POP**, pg. 98 22 44 66 132 216 300
141-149-Two Sheena stories. 141-Long Bow, Indian Boy begins, ends #160
23 46 69 136 223 310
159-163: Space Scouts serial in all. 160-Last jungle-c (6/52). 161-Ghost Gallery covers begin, end #167. 163-Suicide Smith app. 26 52 78 152 249 345
164-The Star Pirate begins, ends #165 36 72 108 211 343 475
165-167: 165,167-Space Rangers app. 33 66 99 196 321 445
NOTE: *Bondage covers, negligee panels, torture, etc. are common in this series. Hawks of the Seas, Inspector Dayton, Spies in Action, Sports Shorts, & Uncle Otto by Eisner, #1-7. Hawk by* **Eisner**-*#10-15.* **Eisner** *c-1-8, 12-14. 1pg. Patsy pin-ups in 92-97, 99-101. Sheena by* **Meskin**-*#1, 4; by* **Powell**-*#2, 3, 5-28;* **Powell** *c-14, 16, 17, 19.* **Powell/Eisner** *c-15. Sky Girl by* **Matt Baker**-*#69-78, 80-130. ZX-5 & Ghost Gallery by* **Kamen**-*#90-130.* **Bailey** *a-3-8.* **Briefer** *a-1-8, 10.* **Fine** *a-14; c-9-11.* **Kamen** *a-101, 105, 123, 132; c-105, 121-145.* **Bob Kane** *a-1-8.* **Whitman** *c-146-167(most). Jungle c-9, 13, 15, 17 on.*

JUMPER: JUMPSCARS
Oni Press: Jan, 2008 ($14.95, graphic novel)
SC-Prelude to 2008 movie Jumper; Brian Hurtt-a/c 15.00

JUNGLE ACTION
Atlas Comics (IPC): Oct, 1954 - No. 6, Aug, 1955
1-Leopard Girl begins by Al Hartley (#1,3); Jungle Boy by Forte; Maneely-a in all
54 108 162 343 574 825
2-(3-D effect cover) 45 90 135 284 480 675
3-6: 3-Last precode (2/55) 31 62 93 186 303 420
NOTE: **Maneely** *c-1, 2, 5, 6.* **Romita** *a-3, 6.* **Shores** *a-3, 6; c-3, 4?.*

JUNGLE ACTION (...& Black Panther #18-21?)
Marvel Comics Group: Oct, 1972 - No. 24, Nov, 1976
1-Lorna, Jann-r (All reprints in 1-4) 4 8 12 28 47 65
2-4 3 6 9 16 23 30
5-Black Panther begins (r/Avengers #62) 12 24 36 84 185 285
6-New solo Black Panther stories begin; 1st app. Erik Killmonger
17 34 51 117 259 400
7,9,10: 9-Contains pull-out centerfold ad by Mark Jewelers
4 8 12 23 37 50
8-Origin Black Panther 6 12 18 38 69 100
11-20,23,24: 18-1st app. Madame Slay (Erik Killmonger's girlfriend). 19-23-KKK x-over. 23-r/#22. 24-1st Wind Eagle; story contd in Marvel Premiere #51-#53
3 6 9 16 23 30
21(Regular 25¢ edition)(5/76) The Klan app. 4 8 12 28 47 65
21,22-(30¢-c variant, limited distribution) 10 20 30 66 138 210
22-(Regular 25¢ edition)(7/76) 3 6 9 16 23 30
NOTE: **Buckler** *a-6-9p, 22; c-8p, 12p.* **Buscema** *a-5p; c-22.* **Byrne** *c-23.* **Gil Kane** *a-8p; c-2, 4, 10p, 11p, 13-17, 19, 24.* **Kirby** *c-18.* **Maneely** *r-1.* **Russell** *a-13i.* **Starlin** *c-3p.*

JUNGLE ADVENTURES
Super Comics: 1963 - 1964 (Reprints)
10,12,15,17,18: 10-r/Terrors of the Jungle #4 & #10(Rulah). 12-r/Zoot #14(Rulah).15-r/Kaanga from Jungle #152 & Tiger Girl. 17-All Jo-Jo-r. 18-Reprints/White Princess of the Jungle #1; no Kinstler-a; origin of both White Princess & Cap'n Courage
3 6 9 18 28 38

JUNGLE ADVENTURES
Skywald Comics: Mar, 1971 - No. 3, June, 1971 (25¢, 52 pgs.) (Pre-code reprints & new-s)
1-Zangar origin; reprints of Jo-Jo, Blue Gorilla(origin)/White Princess #3, Kinstler-r/White Princess #2 3 6 9 19 30 40
2,3: 2-Zangar, Sheena-r/Sheena #17 & Jumbo #162, Jo-Jo, origin Slave Girl-r. 3-Zangar, Jo-Jo, White Princess, Rulah-r 3 6 9 15 22 28

JUNGLE BOOK (See King Louie and Mowgli, Movie Comics, Mowgli..., Walt Disney Showcase #45 & Walt Disney's The Jungle Book)

JUNGLE CAT (Disney)
Dell Publishing Co.: No. 1136, Sept-Nov, 1960 (one shot)
Four Color 1136-Movie, photo-c 6 12 18 37 66 95

JUNGLE COMICS
Fiction House Magazines: 1/40 - No. 157, 3/53; No. 158, Spr, 1953 - No. 163, Summer, 1954
1-Origin The White Panther, Kaanga, Lord of the Jungle, Tabu, Wizard of the Jungle; Wambi, the Jungle Boy, Camilla & Capt. Terry Thunder begin (all 1st app.). Lou Fine-c
622 1244 1866 4541 8021 11,500
2-Fantomah, Mystery Woman of the Jungle begins, ends #51; The Red Panther begins, ends #26 226 452 678 1446 2473 3500
3,4 168 336 504 1075 1838 2600
5-Classic Eisner-c 200 400 600 1280 2190 3100
6-10: 7,8-Powell-c 97 194 291 621 1061 1500
11-Classic dinosaur-c 135 270 405 864 1482 2100
12-20: 13-Tuska-c 68 136 204 435 743 1050
21-30: 25-Shows V2#1 (correct number does not appear). #27-New origin Fantomah, Daughter of the Pharoahs; Camilla dons new costume
54 108 162 343 574 825
31-40 42 84 126 265 445 625
41,43-50 39 78 117 240 395 550
42-Kaanga by Crandall, 12 pgs. 43 86 129 271 461 650
51-60 36 72 108 211 343 475
61-70: 67-Cover swipes Crandall splash pg. in #42 30 60 90 177 289 400
71-80: 79-New origin Tabu 26 52 78 152 249 345
81-97,99 24 48 72 144 237 330
98-Used in **SOTI**, pg. 185 & illo "In ordinary comic books, there are pictures within pictures for children who know how to look;" used by N.Y. Legis. Comm.
40 80 120 244 402 560
100 29 58 87 170 278 385
101-110: 104-In Camilla story, villain is Dr. Wertham 24 48 72 140 230 320
111-120: 118-Clyde Beatty app. 22 44 66 132 216 300
121-130 21 42 63 126 206 285
131-163: 135-Desert Panther begins in Terry Thunder (origin), not in #137; ends (dies) #138. 139-Last 52 pg. issue. 141-Last Tabu. 143,145-Used in **POP**, pg. 99. 151-Last Camilla & Terry Thunder. 152-Tiger Girl begins. 158-Last Wambi; Sheena app.
20 40 60 115 188 260
I.W. Reprint #1,9: 1-r/? 9-r/#151 3 6 9 16 24 32
NOTE: *Bondage covers, negligee panels, torture, etc. are common to this series. Camilla by* **Fran Hopper**-*#70-92; by* **Baker**-*#69, 100-113, 115, 116; by* **Lubbers**-*#97-99 by* **Tuska**-*#63, 65. Kaanga by* **John Celardo**-*#80-113; by* **Larsen**-*#71, 75-79; by* **Moreira**-*#58, 60, 61, 63-70, 72-74; by* **Tuska**-*#37, 62; by* **Whitman**-*#114-163. Tabu by* **Larsen**-*#59-75, 82-92; by* **Whitman**-*#93-115. Terry Thunder by* **Hopper**-*#71, 72; by* **Celardo**-*#78, 79; by* **Lubbers**-*#80-85. Tiger Girl-r by* **Baker**-*#152, 153, 155-157, 159. Wambi by* **Baker**-*#62-67, 74.* **Astarita** *c-45, 46.* **Celardo** *a-78; c-98-113.* **Crandall** *c-67 from splash pg.* **Eisner** *c-2, 5, 6.* **Fine** *c-1.* **Larsen** *a-65, 66, 71, 72, 74, 75, 79, 83, 84, 87-90.* **Moreira** *c-43, 44.* **Morisi** *a-51.* **Powell** *c-7, 8.* **Sultan** *c-3, 4.* **Tuska** *c-13.* **Whitman** *c-132-163(most).* **Zolnerowich** *c-11, 12, 18-41.*

JUNGLE COMICS
Blackthorne Publishing: May, 1988 - No. 4 ($2.00, B&W/color)
1-Dave Stevens-c; B. Jones scripts in all 2 4 6 13 18 22
2-4: 2-B&W-a begins 5.00

JUNGLE GIRL (See Lorna, the...)

JUNGLE GIRL (Nyoka, Jungle Girl No. 2 on)
Fawcett Publications: Fall, 1942 (one-shot)(No month listed)
1-Bondage-c; photo of Kay Aldridge who played Nyoka in movie serial app. on-c. Adaptation of the classic Republic movie serial Perils of Nyoka. 1st comic to devote entire contents to a movie serial adaptation 139 278 417 883 1517 2150

JUNGLE GIRL
Dynamite Entertainment: No. 0, 2007 - 2009 (25¢/$2.99/$3.50)
0-(25¢-c) Eight page preview; preview of Superpowers w/Alex Ross-a 3.00
1-5-Frank Cho-plot/cover; Batista-a/variant-c 3.00
... Season 2 ($3.50) 1-5-Two covers by Cho & Batista 3.50
... Season 3 ($3.99) 1-4-Cho-c/Jadson-a/Murray-s 4.00

JUNGLE JIM (Also see Ace Comics)
Standard Comics (Best Books): No. 11, Jan, 1949 - No. 20, Apr, 1951
11 15 30 45 83 124 165
12-20 11 22 33 60 83 105

JUNGLE JIM
Dell Publishing Co.: No. 490, 8/53 - No. 1020, 8-10/59 (Painted-c)
Four Color 490(#1) 9 18 27 58 114 170
Four Color 565(#2, 6/54) 5 10 15 34 60 85
3(10-12/54)-5 4 8 12 27 44 60
6-19(1-3/59) 4 8 12 25 40 55
Four Color 1020(#20) 5 10 15 33 57 80

JUNGLE JIM
King Features Syndicate: No. 5, Dec, 1967
5-Reprints Dell #5; Wood-c 2 4 6 10 14 18

JUNGLE JIM (Continued from Dell series)
Charlton Comics: No. 22, Feb, 1969 - No. 28, Feb, 1970 (#21 was an overseas edition only)
22-Dan Flagg begins; Ditko/Wood-a 3 6 9 21 33 45
23-26: 23-Last Dan Flagg; Howard-c. 24-Jungle People begin
3 6 9 15 21 26
27,28: 27-Ditko/Howard-a. 28-Ditko-a 3 6 9 16 24 32
NOTE: *Ditko cover of #22 reprints story panels*

JUNGLE JO
Fox Feature Syndicate (Hero Books): Mar, 1950 - No. 3, Sept, 1950
nn-Jo-Jo blanked out in titles of interior stories, leaving Congo King; came out after Jo-Jo #29 (intended as Jo-Jo #30?) 63 126 189 403 689 975
1-Tangi begins; part Wood-a 65 130 195 416 708 1000

Junie Prom #1 © Dearfield

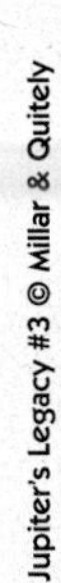
Jupiter's Legacy #3 © Millar & Quitely

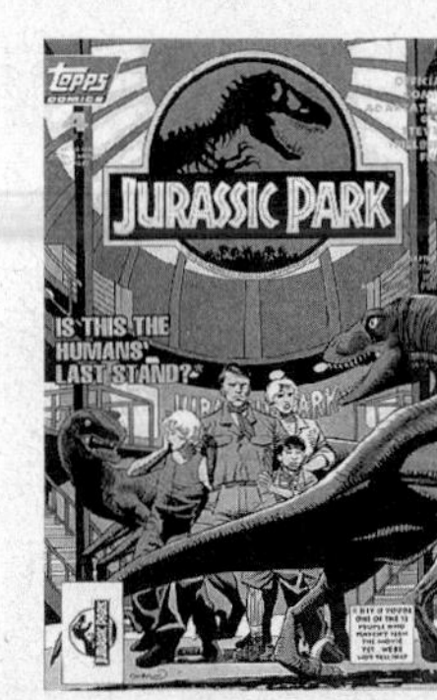

Jurassic Park #4 © Universal

	GD 2.0	VG 4.0	FN 6.0	VF 8.0	VF/NM 9.0	NM- 9.2
2,3	50	100	150	315	533	750

JUNGLE LIL (Dorothy Lamour #2 on; also see Feature Stories Magazine)
Fox Feature Syndicate (Hero Books): April, 1950

	GD 2.0	VG 4.0	FN 6.0	VF 8.0	VF/NM 9.0	NM- 9.2
1	57	114	171	362	619	875

JUNGLE TALES (Jann of the Jungle No. 8 on)
Atlas Comics (CSI): Sept, 1954 - No. 7, Sept, 1955

	GD 2.0	VG 4.0	FN 6.0	VF 8.0	VF/NM 9.0	NM- 9.2
1-Jann of the Jungle	47	94	141	296	498	700
2-7: 3-Last precode (1/55)	34	68	102	204	332	460

NOTE: ***Heath** c-5. **Heck** a-6, 7. **Maneely** a-2; c-1, 3. **Shores** a-5-7; c-4, 6. **Tuska** a-2.*

JUNGLE TALES OF TARZAN
Charlton Comics: Dec, 1964 - No. 4, July, 1965

	GD 2.0	VG 4.0	FN 6.0	VF 8.0	VF/NM 9.0	NM- 9.2
1	5	10	15	35	63	90
2-4	4	8	12	25	40	55

NOTE: ***Giordano** c-3p. **Glanzman** a-1-3. **Montes/Bache** a-4.*

JUNGLE TERROR (See Harvey Comics Hits No. 54)

JUNGLE THRILLS (Formerly Sports Thrills; Terrors of the Jungle #17 on)
Star Publications: No. 16, Feb, 1952; Dec, 1953; No. 7, 1954

	GD 2.0	VG 4.0	FN 6.0	VF 8.0	VF/NM 9.0	NM- 9.2
16-Phantom Lady & Rulah story-reprint/All Top No. 15; used in **POP**, pg. 98,99; L. B. Cole-c	61	122	183	390	670	950
3-D 1(12/53, 25¢)-Came w/glasses; Jungle Lil & Jungle Jo appear; L. B. Cole-c	53	106	159	334	567	800
7-Titled 'Picture Scope Jungle Adventures;' (1954, 36 pgs, 15¢)-3-D effect c/stories; story & coloring book; Disbrow-a/script; L.B. Cole-c	54	108	162	343	574	825

JUNGLE TWINS, THE (Tono & Kono)
Gold Key/Whitman No. 18: Apr, 1972 - No. 17, Nov, 1975; No. 18, May, 1982

	GD 2.0	VG 4.0	FN 6.0	VF 8.0	VF/NM 9.0	NM- 9.2
1-All painted covers	3	6	9	16	23	30
2-5	2	4	6	9	12	15
6-18: 18(Whitman, 5/82)-Reprints	1	3	4	6	8	10

NOTE: *UFO c/story No. 13. Painted-c No. 1-17. **Spiegle** c-18.*

JUNGLE WAR STORIES (Guerrilla War No. 12 on)
Dell Publishing Co.: July-Sept, 1962 - No. 11, Apr-June, 1965 (Painted-c)

	GD 2.0	VG 4.0	FN 6.0	VF 8.0	VF/NM 9.0	NM- 9.2
01-384-209 (#1)	4	8	12	25	40	55
2-11	3	6	9	16	24	32

JUNIE PROM (Also see Dexter Comics)
Dearfield Publishing Co.: Winter, 1947-48 - No. 7, Aug, 1949

	GD 2.0	VG 4.0	FN 6.0	VF 8.0	VF/NM 9.0	NM- 9.2
1-Teen-age	39	78	117	240	395	550
2	26	52	78	154	252	350
3-7	22	44	66	132	216	300

JUNIOR
Fantagraphics Books: June, 2000 - No. 5, Jan, 2001 ($2.95, B&W)

	GD 2.0	VG 4.0	FN 6.0	VF 8.0	VF/NM 9.0	NM- 9.2
1-5-Peter Bagge-s/a						3.00

JUNIOR CARROT PATROL (Jr. Carrot Patrol #2)
Dark Horse Comics: May, 1989; No. 2, Nov, 1990 ($2.00, B&W)

	GD 2.0	VG 4.0	FN 6.0	VF 8.0	VF/NM 9.0	NM- 9.2
1,2-Flaming Carrot spin-off. 1-Bob Burden-c(i)						4.00

JUNIOR COMICS (Formerly Li'l Pan; becomes Western Outlaws with #17)
Fox Feature Syndicate: No. 9, Sept, 1947 - No. 16, July, 1948

	GD 2.0	VG 4.0	FN 6.0	VF 8.0	VF/NM 9.0	NM- 9.2
9-Feldstein-c/a; headlights-c	194	388	582	1242	2121	3000
10-16: 10-12,14-16-Feldstein-c/a; headlights-c	177	354	531	1133	1942	2750

JUNIOR FUNNIES (Formerly Tiny Tot Funnies No. 9)
Harvey Publ. (King Features Synd.): No. 10, Aug, 1951 - No. 13, Feb, 1952

	GD 2.0	VG 4.0	FN 6.0	VF 8.0	VF/NM 9.0	NM- 9.2
10-Partial reprints in all; Blondie, Dagwood, Daisy, Henry, Popeye, Felix, Katzenjammer Kids	7	14	21	37	46	55
11-13	6	12	18	31	38	45

JUNIOR HOPP COMICS
Stanmor Publ.: Feb, 1952 - No. 3, July, 1952

	GD 2.0	VG 4.0	FN 6.0	VF 8.0	VF/NM 9.0	NM- 9.2
1-Teenage humor	21	42	63	122	199	275
2,3: 3-Dave Berg-a	15	30	45	84	127	170

JUNIOR MEDICS OF AMERICA, THE
E. R. Squire & Sons: No. 1359, 1957 (15¢)

	GD 2.0	VG 4.0	FN 6.0	VF 8.0	VF/NM 9.0	NM- 9.2
1359	6	12	18	27	33	36

JUNIOR MISS
Timely/Marvel (CnPC): Wint, 1944; No. 24, Apr, 1947 - No. 39, Aug, 1950

	GD 2.0	VG 4.0	FN 6.0	VF 8.0	VF/NM 9.0	NM- 9.2
1-Frank Sinatra & June Allyson life story	45	90	135	284	480	675
24-Formerly The Human Torch #23?	23	46	69	136	223	310
25-38: 29,31,32,34-Cindy-c/stories (others?)	15	30	45	90	140	190
39-Kurtzman-a	17	34	51	100	158	215

NOTE: *Painted-c 35-37. 35, 37-all romance. 36, 38-mostly teen humor. **Louise Alston** c-36.*

JUNIOR PARTNERS (Formerly Oral Roberts' True Stories)
Oral Roberts Evangelistic Assn.: No. 120, Aug, 1959 - V3#12, Dec, 1961

	GD 2.0	VG 4.0	FN 6.0	VF 8.0	VF/NM 9.0	NM- 9.2
120(#1)	4	8	12	25	40	55
2(9/59)	3	6	9	17	26	35
3-12(7/60)	2	4	6	13	18	22
V2#1(8/60)-5(12/60)	2	4	6	9	13	16
V3#1(1/61)-12	2	4	6	8	10	12

JUNIOR TREASURY (See Dell Junior...)

JUNIOR WOODCHUCKS GUIDE (Walt Disney's...)
Danbury Press: 1973 (8-3/4"x5-3/4", 214 pgs., hardcover)

	GD 2.0	VG 4.0	FN 6.0	VF 8.0	VF/NM 9.0	NM- 9.2
nn-Illustrated text based on the long-standing J.W. Guide used by Donald Duck's nephews Huey, Dewey & Louie by Carl Barks. The guidebook was a popular plot device to enable the nephews to solve problems facing their uncle or Scrooge McDuck (scarce)	5	10	15	31	53	75

JUNIOR WOODCHUCKS LIMITED SERIES (Walt Disney's...)
W. D. Publications (Disney): July, 1991 - No. 4, Oct, 1991 ($1.50, limited series; new & reprint-a)

	GD 2.0	VG 4.0	FN 6.0	VF 8.0	VF/NM 9.0	NM- 9.2
1-4: 1-The Beagle Boys app.; Barks-r						3.00

JUNIOR WOODCHUCKS (See Huey, Dewey & Louie...)

JUPITER'S CIRCLE (Prequel to Jupiter's Legacy)
Image Comics: Apr, 2015 - No. 6, Sept, 2015 ($3.50/$3.99)

	GD 2.0	VG 4.0	FN 6.0	VF 8.0	VF/NM 9.0	NM- 9.2
1-6-Mark Millar-s/Frank Quitely-a/c. 1-Three covers. 1-3,6-Torres-a. 4,5-Gianfelice-a						4.00
Volume 2 (11/15 - No. 6, 5/16) 1-6-Covers by Quitely & Sienkiewicz. 1,2,6-Torres-a. 3-5-Spouse-a						4.00

JUPITER'S LEGACY
Image Comics: Apr, 2013 - No. 5, Jan, 2015 ($2.99/$4.99)

	GD 2.0	VG 4.0	FN 6.0	VF 8.0	VF/NM 9.0	NM- 9.2
1-4-Mark Millar-s/Frank Quitely-a/c						3.00
1-Variant-c by Hitch						4.00
5-($4.99) Covers by Hitch and Fegredo; bonus pin-ups and cosplay photos						5.00
1-Studio Edition (12/13, $4.99) Quitely's B&W art and Millar's script; design art						5.00

JUPITER'S LEGACY 2
Image Comics: Jan, 2016 - No. 5, Jul, 2017 ($3.99)

	GD 2.0	VG 4.0	FN 6.0	VF 8.0	VF/NM 9.0	NM- 9.2
1-5-Mark Millar-s/Frank Quitely-a/c						4.00

JURASSIC PARK
Topps Comics: June, 1993 - No. 4, Aug, 1993; No. 5, Oct, 1994 - No. 10, Feb, 1995

	GD 2.0	VG 4.0	FN 6.0	VF 8.0	VF/NM 9.0	NM- 9.2
1-($2.50)-Newsstand Edition; Kane/Perez-a in all; 1-4: movie adaptation	2	4	6	8	10	12
1-($2.95)-Collector's Ed.; polybagged w/3 cards						5.00
1-Amberchrome Edition w/no price or ads	4	8	12	27	44	60
2-4-($2.50)-Newsstand Edition						4.00
2,3-($2.95)-Collector's Ed.; polybagged w/3 cards						5.00
4-10: 4-($2.95)-Collector's Ed.; polybagged w/1 of 4 different action hologram trading card; Gil Kane/Pérez-a. 5-becomes Advs. of						4.00
Annual 1 ($3.95, 5/95)						5.00
Trade paperback (1993, $9.95)-r/#1-4; bagged w/#0						10.00

JURASSIC PARK
IDW Publishing: Jun, 2010 - No. 5, Oct, 2010 ($3.99, limited series)

	GD 2.0	VG 4.0	FN 6.0	VF 8.0	VF/NM 9.0	NM- 9.2
1-5: Takes place 13 years after the first movie; Schreck-s. 1-Covers by Yeates & Miller						4.00

JURASSIC PARK: DANGEROUS GAMES
IDW Publishing: Sept, 2011 - No. 5, Jan, 2012 ($3.99, limited series)

	GD 2.0	VG 4.0	FN 6.0	VF 8.0	VF/NM 9.0	NM- 9.2
1-5-Erik Bear-s/Jorge Jimenez-a, 1-Covers by Darrow & Zornow						4.00

JURASSIC PARK: RAPTOR
Topps Comics: Nov, 1993 - No. 2, Dec, 1993 ($2.95, limited series)

	GD 2.0	VG 4.0	FN 6.0	VF 8.0	VF/NM 9.0	NM- 9.2
1,2: 1-Bagged w/3 trading cards & Zorro #0; Golden c-1,2						4.00

JURASSIC PARK: RAPTORS ATTACK
Topps Comics: Mar, 1994 - No. 4, June, 1994 ($2.50, limited series)

	GD 2.0	VG 4.0	FN 6.0	VF 8.0	VF/NM 9.0	NM- 9.2
1-4-Michael Golden-c/frontispiece						6.00

JURASSIC PARK: RAPTORS HIJACK
Topps Comics: July, 1994 - No. 4, Oct, 1994 ($2.50, limited series)

	GD 2.0	VG 4.0	FN 6.0	VF 8.0	VF/NM 9.0	NM- 9.2
1-4: Michael Golden-c/frontispiece						4.00

JURASSIC PARK: THE DEVILS IN THE DESERT
IDW Publishing: Jan, 2011 - No. 4, Apr, 2011 ($3.99, limited series)

	GD 2.0	VG 4.0	FN 6.0	VF 8.0	VF/NM 9.0	NM- 9.2
1-4-John Byrne-s/a/c						4.00

JUST A PILGRIM
Black Bull Entertainment: May, 2001 - No. 5, Sept, 2001 ($2.99)

Justice #1 © DC

Justice League #6 © DC

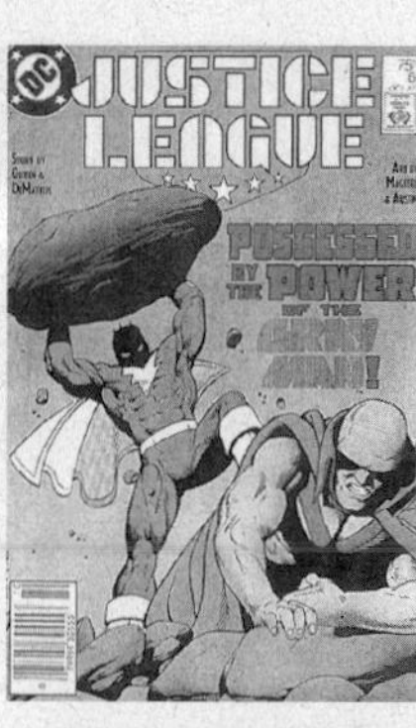

Justice League (2011 series) #34 © DC

	GD 2.0	VG 4.0	FN 6.0	VF 8.0	VF/NM 9.0	NM- 9.2

Limited Preview Edition (12/00, $7.00) Ennis & Ezquerra interviews 7.00
1-Ennis-s/Ezquerra-a; two covers by Texeira & JG Jones 3.00
2-5: 2-Fabry-c. 3-Nowlan-c. 4-Sienkiewicz-c 3.00
TPB (11/01, $12.99) r/#1-5; Waid intro. 13.00

JUST A PILGRIM: GARDEN OF EDEN
Black Bull Entertainment: May, 2002 - No. 4, Aug, 2002 ($2.99, limited series)

Limited Preview Ed. (1/02, $7.00) Ennis & Ezquerra interviews; Jones-c 7.00
1-4-Ennis-s/Ezquerra-a 3.00
TPB (11/02, $12.99) r/#1-4; Gareb Shamus intro. 13.00

JUSTICE
Marvel Comics Group (New Universe): Nov, 1986 - No. 32, June, 1989

1-32: 26-32-$1.50-c (low print run) 3.00

JUSTICE
DC Comics: Oct, 2005 - No. 12, Aug, 2007 ($2.99/$3.50/$3.99, bi-monthly maxi-series)

1-Classic Justice League vs. The Legion of Doom; Alex Ross & Doug Braithwaite-a; Jim Krueger-s; two covers by Ross; Ross sketch pages 5.00
1-2nd & 3rd printings 4.00
2-($3.50) 4.00
2 (2nd printing), 3-11-($3.50) 3.50
12-($3.99) Two covers (Heroes & Villains) 4.00
Absolute Justice HC (2009, $99.99, slipcased book with dustjacket) oversized r/#1-12; afterwords by creators; Ross sketch and design art; photo gallery of action figures 100.00
HC (2011, $39.99, dustjacket) r/#1-12 40.00
... Volume One HC (2006, $19.99, dustjacket) r/#1-4; Krueger intro.; sketch pages 20.00
... Volume One SC (2008, $14.99) r/#1-4; Krueger intro.; sketch pages 15.00
... Volume Two HC (2007, $19.99, dustjacket) r/#5-8; Krueger intro.; sketch pages 20.00
... Volume Two SC (2008, $14.99) r/#5-8; Krueger intro.; sketch pages 15.00
... Volume Three HC (2007, $19.99, dustjacket) r/#9-12; Ross intro.; sketch pages 20.00
... Volume Three SC (2007, $14.99) r/#9-12; Ross intro.; sketch pages 15.00

JUSTICE COMICS (Formerly Wacky Duck; Tales of Justice #53 on)
Marvel/Atlas Comics (NPP 7-9,4-19/CnPC 20-23/MjMC 24-38/Male 39-52:
No. 7, Fall/47 - No. 9, 6/48; No. 4, 8/48 - No. 52, 3/55

	GD	VG	FN	VF	VF/NM	NM-
7(#1, 1947)	39	78	117	231	378	525
8(#2)-Kurtzman-a "Giggles 'n' Grins" (3)	25	50	75	150	245	340
9(#3, 6/48)	22	44	66	128	209	290
4	20	40	60	114	182	250
5(9/48)-9: 8-Anti-Wertham editorial	17	34	51	100	158	215
10-15-Photo-c	15	30	45	85	130	175
16-30	14	28	42	82	121	160
31-40,42-52: 35-Gene Colan-a. 48-Last precode; Pakula & Tuska-a. 50-Ayers-a	14	28	42	80	115	150
41-Electrocution-c	21	42	63	126	206	285

NOTE: *Hartley a-48.* ***Heath*** *a-24.* ***Maneely*** *c-44, 52.* ***Pakula*** *a-43, 45, 47, 48.* ***Louis Ravielli*** *a-39, 47.* ***Robinson*** *a-22, 25, 28, 41.* ***Sale*** *c-45.* ***Shores*** *c-7(#1), 8(#2)?* ***Tuska*** *a-41, 48.* ***Wildey*** *a-52.*

JUSTICE: FOUR BALANCE
Marvel Comics: Sept, 1994 - No. 4, Dec, 1994 ($1.75, limited series)

1-4: 1-Thing & Firestar app. 3.00

JUSTICE, INC. (The Avenger) (Pulp)
National Periodical Publications: May-June, 1975 - No. 4, Nov-Dec, 1975

	GD	VG	FN	VF	VF/NM	NM-
1-McWilliams-a, Kubert-c; origin	2	4	6	11	16	20
2-4: 2-4-Kirby-a(p), c-2,3p. 4-Kubert-c	2	4	6	11	16	20

NOTE: *Adapted from Kenneth Robeson novel, creator of Doc Savage.*

JUSTICE, INC. (Pulp)
DC Comics: 1989 - No. 2, 1989 ($3.95, 52 pgs., squarebound, mature)

1,2: Re-intro The Avenger; Andrew Helfer scripts & Kyle Baker-c/a 5.00

JUSTICE, INC. (Pulp)
Dynamite Entertainment: 2014 - No. 6, 2015 ($3.99/$5.99)

1-5-The Shadow, Doc Savage and The Avenger app; Uslan-s/Timpano-a; multiple covers 4.00
6-($5.99) Covers by Ross, Francavilla, Hardman and Syaf 6.00

JUSTICE, INC.: THE AVENGER (Pulp)
Dynamite Entertainment: 2015 - No. 6, 2015 ($3.99)

1-6: 1-Waid-s/Freire-a; multiple covers incl. 1975 series #1 cover swipe by Ross 4.00

JUSTICE, INC.: THE AVENGER VOLUME 1 (Pulp)
Dynamite Entertainment: 2017 - No. 4, 2017 ($3.99)

1-4-Higgins & Gentile-s/Shibao-a. 1-Covers by Mandrake & Shibao 4.00

JUSTICE LEAGUE (...International #7-25; ...America #26 on)
DC Comics: May, 1987 - No. 113, Aug, 1996 (Also see Legends #6)

	GD	VG	FN	VF	VF/NM	NM-
1-Batman, Green Lantern (Guy Gardner), Blue Beetle, Mr. Miracle, Capt. Marvel & Martian Manhunter begin; 1st app. Maxwell Lord	3	6	9	15	22	28
2,3: 3-Regular-c (white background)						6.00
3-Limited-c (yellow background, Superman logo)	4	8	12	28	47	65

4-6,8-10: 4-Booster Gold joins. 5-Origin Gray Man; Batman vs. Guy Gardner; Creeper app. 9,10-Millennium x-over 5.00
7-($1.25, 52 pgs.)-Capt. Marvel & Dr. Fate resign; Capt. Atom & Rocket Red join 6.00
11-17,22,23,25-49,51-68,71-82: 16-Bruce Wayne-c/story. 31,32-J. L. Europe x-over. 58-Lobo app. 61-New team begins; swipes-c to J.L. of A. #1('60). 70-Newsstand version w/o outer-c. 71-Direct sales version w/black outer-c. 71-Newsstand version w/o outer-c. 80-Intro new Booster Gold. 82,83-Guy Gardner-c/stories 4.00
18-21,24,50: 18-21-Lobo app. 24-($1.50)-1st app. Justice League Europe. 50-($1.75, 52 pgs.) 5.00

	GD	VG	FN	VF	VF/NM	NM-
69-Doomsday tie-in; takes place between Superman: The Man of Steel #18 & Superman #74	2	4	6	9	13	16

69,70-2nd printings 3.00
70-Funeral for a Friend part 1; red 3/4 outer-c 5.00
83-99,101-113: 92-(9/94)-Zero Hour x-over; Triumph app. 113-Green Lantern, Flash & Hawkman app. 4.00
100 ($3.95)-Foil-c; 52 pgs. 5.00
100 ($2.95)-Newstand 4.00
#0-(10/94) Zero Hour (publ between #92 & #93); new team begins (Hawkman, Flash, Wonder Woman, Metamorpho, Nuklon, Crimson Fox, Obsidian & Fire) 4.00
Annual 1-8,10 ('87-'94, '96, 68 pgs.): 2-Joker-c/story; Batman cameo. 5-Armageddon 2001 x-over; Silver ink 2nd print. 7-Bloodlines x-over. 8-Elseworlds story. 10-Legends of the Dead Earth 5.00
Annual 9 (1995, $3.50)-Year One story 5.00
Special 1,2 ('90,'91, 52 pgs.): 1-Giffen plots. 2-Staton-a(p) 5.00
Spectacular 1 (1992, $1.50, 52 pgs.)-Intro new JLI & JLE teams; ties into JLI #61 & JLE #37; two interlocking covers by Jurgens 5.00
A New Beginning Trade Paperback (1989, $12.95)-r/#1-7 13.00
... International Vol. 1 HC (2008, $24.99) r/#1-7; new intro. by Giffen 25.00
... International Vol. 1 SC (2009, $17.99) r/#1-7; new intro. by Giffen 18.00
... International Vol. 2 HC (2008, $24.99) r/#8-13, Annual #1 and Suicide Squad #13 25.00
... International Vol. 2 SC (2009, $17.99) r/#8-13, Annual #1 and Suicide Squad #13 18.00
... International Vol. 3 SC (2009, $19.99) r/#14-22 20.00
... International Vol. 4 SC (2010, $17.99) r/#23-30 18.00
... International Vol. 5 SC (2011, $19.99) r/#Annual #2,3 & Justice League Europe #1-6 20.00
... International Vol. 6 SC (2011, $24.99) r/#31-35 & Justice League Europe #7-11 25.00

NOTE: ***Anderson*** *c-61i.* ***Austin*** *a-1i, 60i; c-1i.* ***Giffen*** *a-13; c-21p.* ***Guice*** *a-62i.* ***Maguire*** *a-1-12, 16-19, 22, 23.* ***Russell*** *a-Annual 1i; c-54i.* ***Willingham*** *a-30p, Annual 2.*

JUSTICE LEAGUE (DC New 52)
DC Comics: Oct, 2011 - No. 52, Aug, 2016 ($3.99)

	GD	VG	FN	VF	VF/NM	NM-
1-Johns-s/Jim Lee-a/c; Batman, Green Lantern & Superman app.; orange background-c	2	4	6	13	18	22
1-Combo-Pack edition ($4.99) polybagged with digital download code; blue background-c	1	3	4	6	8	10

1-Variant-c by Finch 25.00
1-Second printing 25.00
2-11,13-23: 3-Wonder Woman & Aquaman arrive. 4-Darkseid arrives. 6-Pandora back-up. 7-Gene Ha-a; back-up Shazam origin begins; Frank-a. 8-D'Anda-a. 13,14-Cheetah app. 15-17-Throne of Atlantis. 22,23-Trinity War. 23-Crime Syndicate arrives 4.00
12-Superman/Wonder Woman kiss-c 4.00
23.1, 23.2, 23.3, 23.4 (11/13, $2.99, regular-c) 3.00
23.1 (11/13, $3.99, 3-D cover) "Darkseid #1" on cover; origin; Kaiyo app.; Reis-c 5.00
23.2 (11/13, $3.99, 3-D cover) "Lobo #1" on cover; Bennett-s/Oliver-a/Kuder-c 5.00
23.3 (11/13, $3.99, 3-D cover) "Dial E #1" on cover; Miéville-s; art by various 5.00
23.4 (11/13, $3.99, 3-D cover) "Secret Society #1" on cover; Owlman app.; Kudranski-a 5.00
24-29-Forever Evil. 24-Origin of Ultraman. 25-Origin of Owlman. 27-Cyborg upgraded. 28,29-Metal Men return 4.00
30-39: 30-Lex Luthor app.; intro Jessica Cruz. 31-33-Doom Patrol app. 33-Luthor joins. 35-Amazo virus unleashed; intro Lena Luthor 4.00
40-Darkseid War prologue, continues in DC's 2015 FCBD edition; intro. Grail (cameo) 4.00
41-($4.99) Darkseid War pt 1; Mister Miracle & the Anti-Monitor app.; intro Myrina Black 5.00
42-49-Darkseid War; Darkseid vs. the Anti-Monitor. 45,46-Manapul-a 4.00
48-Coloring Book variant-c by Kolins 4.00

	GD	VG	FN	VF	VF/NM	NM-
50-($5.99) Conclusion to Darkseid War; Jessica Cruz becomes a Green Lantern; first mention of the "3 Jokers"	3	6	9	14	20	25

51,52: 51-Flashback with Robin; Pelletier-a. Lex Luthor as Superman; Grummett-a 4.00
#0-(11/12, $3.99) Origin of Shazam; back-up with Pandora 4.00
...: Darkseid War: Batman (12/15, $3.99) Pasarin-a; Batman on Mobius chair; Joe Chill app. 4.00
...: Darkseid War: Flash (1/16, $3.99) Merino-a; Flash vs. the Black Racer 4.00
...: Darkseid War: Green Lantern (1/16, $3.99) Shaner-a; Hal Jordan becomes God of Light 4.00
...: Darkseid War: Lex Luthor (2/16, $3.99) Dazo-a; The God of Apocalypse 4.00
...: Darkseid War: Shazam (1/16, $3.99) Kolins-a 4.00
...: Darkseid War Special (6/16, $3.99) Reis, Jimenez & Pelletier-a; Grail's origin 4.00

Justice League (2016 series) #1 © DC

Justice League Dark #19 © DC

Justice League of America #9 © DC

	GD	VG	FN	VF	VF/NM	NM-
	2.0	4.0	6.0	8.0	9.0	9.2

...: Darkseid War: Superman (1/16, $3.99) Dazo-a; The God of Steel 4.00
...: Futures End 1 (11/14, $2.99, regular-c) Cont'd from Justice League United: FE #1 3.00
...: Futures End 1 (11/14, $3.99, 3-D cover) 4.00
...: Trinity War Director's Cut 1 (10/13, $5.99) r/#22 pencil art and script 6.00

JUSTICE LEAGUE (DC Rebirth)
DC Comics: Sept, 2016 - No. 43, Jun, 2018 ($2.99)

1-11: 1-Hitch-s/Daniel-a. 4-Merino-a. 6-Clark & Derenick-a. 11-Amazo app. 3.00
1 Director's Cut (12/16, $5.99) r/#1 with B&W art; original script; variant cover gallery 6.00
12-24,26-43: 12,13: Justice League vs. Suicide Squad tie-ins. 12-Max Lord returns. 20,21-Hitch-a. 24-Mera app. 26-Intro. Justice League's children. 32,33-Dark Nights: Metal 41-43-Deathstroke app. 3.00
25-($3.99) HItch-s/Derenick-a; Mera app. 4.00
... Day Special Edition 1 (1/18, giveaway) r/Justice League #1 (2011) new Reis-c 3.00
...: Rebirth 1 (9/16, $2.99) Hitch-s/a; pre-New 52 Superman joins 3.00

JUSTICE LEAGUE (Follows Justice League: No Justice series)
DC Comics: Early Aug, 2018 - Present ($3.99)

1-24: 1-Snyder-s/Cheung-a; Legion of Doom app. 2-4-Jimenez-a. 5-Tynion IV-s/Mahnke-a. 7,8-Batman Who Laughs and Starman (Will Payton) app. 10,11-Manapul-a. 11,12-Drowned Earth x-over with Aquaman. 19-24-Mr. Mxyzptlk app. 4.00
25-($4.99) Year of the Villain prelude 5.00
26-49,51-58: 27-Amazo app. 30-37-Kamandi and the JSA app. 40-42-Madame Xanadu app. 45-The Spectre app. 48,49-Spurrier-s. 53-57-Death Metal tie-ins. 58-Endless Winter 4.00
50-($5.99) Conclusion of "The Rule of War"; Lopresti-a 6.00
Annual 1 (3/19, $4.99) New Gods & Green Lantern Corps app.; Sampere-a/Paquette-c 5.00
Annual 2 (11/20, $4.99) JLA vs. The Hall of Justice; Venditti-s/Lopresti-a 5.00
... /Aquaman: Drowned Earth 1 (12/18, $4.99) Porter-a; continues in Justice League #11 5.00

JUSTICE LEAGUE ADVENTURES (Based on Cartoon Network series)
DC Comics: Jan, 2002 - No. 34, Oct, 2004 ($1.99/$2.25)

1-Timm & Ross-c 4.00
2-32: 3-Nicieza-s. 5-Starro app. 10-Begin $2.25-c. 14-Includes 16 pg. insert for VERB with Haberlin CG-art. 15,29-Amancio-a. 16-McCloud-s. 20-Psycho Pirate app. 25,26-Adam Strange-c/app. 28-Legion of Super-Heroes app. 30-Kamandi app. 3.00
Free Comic Book Day giveaway - (5/02) r/#1 with "Free Comic Book Day" banner on-c 3.00
TPB (2003, $9.95) r/#1,3,6,10-13; Timm/Ross-c from #1 10.00
...Vol. 1: The Magnificent Seven (2004, $6.95) digest-size reprints #3,6,10-12 7.00
...Vol. 2: Friends and Foes (2004, $6.95) digest-size reprints #13,14,16,19,20 7.00

JUSTICE LEAGUE: A MIDSUMMER'S NIGHTMARE
DC Comics: Sept, 1996 - No. 3, Nov, 1996 ($2.95, limited series, 38 pgs.)

1-3: Re-establishes Superman, Batman, Green Lantern, The Martian Manhunter, Flash, Aquaman & Wonder Woman as the Justice League; Mark Waid & Fabian Nicieza co-scripts; Jeff Johnson & Darick Robertson-a(p); Kevin Maguire-c 5.00
TPB-(1997, $8.95) r/1-3 9.00

JUSTICE LEAGUE: CRY FOR JUSTICE
DC Comics: Sept, 2009 - No. 7, Apr, 2010 ($3.99, limited series)

1-7-James Robinson-s/Mauro Cascioli-a/c. 1-Two covers; Congorilla origin 4.00
HC (2010, $24.99, d.j.) r/#1-7, Face of Evil: Prometheus 25.00
SC (2011, $19.99) r/#1-7, Face of Evil: Prometheus 20.00

JUSTICE LEAGUE DARK (DC New 52)
DC Comics: Nov, 2011 - No. 40, May, 2015 ($2.99/$3.99)

1-23: 1-Milligan-s; Deadman, Madame Xanadu, Zatanna, Shade, John Constantine app. 7,8-Crossover with I,Vampire #6,7. 7-Batgirl app. 9-Black Orchid joins. 11,12-Tim Hunter app. 13-Leads into J.L. Dark Annual #1. 19-21-Flash app. 22,23-Trinity War 3.00
23.1, 23.2 (11/13, $2.99, regular-c) 3.00
23.1 (11/13, $3.99, 3-D cover) "The Creeper #1" on cover; origin; Nocenti-s/Janin-c 5.00
23.2 (11/13, $3.99, 3-D cover) "Eclipso #1" on cover; origin; Tan-a/Janin-c 5.00
24-40: 24-29-Forever Evil tie-ins. 40-Constantine returns 4.00
#0-(11/12, $2.99) Constantine and Zatanna's 1st meeting; Garbett-a/Sook-c 3.00
Annual #1 (12/12, $4.99) Continued from #13; Frankenstein & Amethyst app. 5.00
Annual #2 (12/14, $4.99) Janson-a/March-c; House of Wonders app. 5.00
...: Futures End 1 (11/14, $2.99, regular-c) Five years later; Etrigan app. 3.00
...: Futures End 1 (11/14, $3.99, 3-D cover) 4.00

JUSTICE LEAGUE DARK
DC Comics: Sept, 2018 - No. 29, Feb, 2021 ($3.99)

1-12: 1-Tynion IV-s; Wonder Woman, Zatanna, Swamp Thing, Detective Chimp app. 4.00
13-27: 13-18-Year of The Villain tie-ins. 13-Buckingham-a; origin Dr. Fate. 20-23-Animal Man app. 20,23-Hotz-a. 29-Endless Winter part 7 4.00
Annual 1 (9/19, $4.99) Jason Woodrue and Circe app. 5.00
... and Wonder Woman: The Witching Hour 1 (12/18, $4.99) Black Orchid app.; Merino-a 5.00

JUSTICE LEAGUE ELITE (See JLA #100 and JLA Secret Files 2004)
DC Comics: Sept, 2004 - No. 12, Aug, 2005 ($2.50)

1-12-Flash, Green Arrow, Vera Black and others; Kelly-s/Mahnke-a. 5,6-JSA app. 3.00
JL Elite TPB (2005, $19.99) r/#1-4, Action #775, JLA #100, JLA Secret Files 2004 20.00
... Vol. 2 TPB (2007, $19.99) r/#5-12 20.00

JUSTICE LEAGUE EUROPE (Justice League International #51 on)
DC Comics: Apr, 1989 - No. 68, Sept., 1994 (75¢/ $1.00/$1.25/$1.50)

1-Giffen plots in all, breakdowns in #1-8,13-30; Justice League #1-c/swipe 5.00
2-10: 7-9-Batman app. 7,8-JLA x-over. 8,9-Superman app. 4.00
11-49: 12-Metal Men app. 20-22-Rogers-c/a(p). 33,34-Lobo vs. Despero. 37-New team begins; swipes-c to JLA #9; see JLA Spectacular 4.00
50-($2.50, 68 pgs.)-Battles Sonar 4.00
51-68: 68-Zero Hour x-over; Triumph joins Justice League Task Force (See JLTF #17) 3.00
Annual 1-5 ('90-'94, 68 pgs.)-1-Return of the Global Guardians; Giffen plots/breakdowns. 2-Armageddon 2001; Giffen-a(p); Rogers-a(p); Golden-a(i). 5-Elseworlds story 5.00
NOTE: ***Phil Jimenez** a-68p. **Rogers** c/a-20-22. **Sears** a-1-12, 14-19, 23-29; c-1-10, 12, 14-19, 23-29.*

JUSTICE LEAGUE: GENERATION LOST (Brightest Day)
DC Comics: Early July, 2010 - No. 24, Early Jun, 2011 ($2.99, bi-weekly limited series)

1-23: 1-Maxwell Lord's return; Winick & Giffen-s. 1-5,7-Harris-c. 13-Magog killed 3.00
24-($4.99) Wonder Woman vs. Omac Prime; Lopresti-a/Nguyen-c 5.00
... Volume One HC (2010, $39.99, dustjacket) r/#1-12; cover gallery 40.00

JUSTICE LEAGUE GIANT (See Wonder Woman Giant #1 for continued JL & Aquaman) (See reprint of new stories in Wonder Woman: Come Back to Me)
DC Comics: 2018 - No. 7, 2019 ($4.99, 100 pgs., squarebound, Walmart exclusive)

1-New Wonder Woman story Seeley-s/Leonardi-a; reprints Justice League ('11), The Flash ('11), and Aquaman ('11) in all 8.00
2-7: 2-New WW by Seeley-s/Watanabe-a. 3-New WW by Palmiotti & Conner-s/Hardin-a begins. 4-7-Jonah Hex app. in new WW story 5.00

JUSTICE LEAGUE: GODS & MONSTERS (Tie-in to 2015 animated film)
DC Comics: Oct, 2015 - No. 3, Oct, 2015 ($3.99, weekly limited series)

1-3-DeMatteis & Timm-s/Silas-a; alternate Superman, Batman & Wonder Woman 4.00
... - Batman 1 (9/15, $3.99) origin of the Kirk Langstrom Batman; Matthew Dow Smith-a 4.00
... - Superman 1 (9/15, $3.99) origin of the Hernan Guerra Superman; Moritat-a 4.00
... - Wonder Woman 1 (9/15, $3.99) origin of Bekka of New Genesis; Leonardi-a 4.00

JUSTICE LEAGUE INTERNATIONAL (See Justice League Europe)

JUSTICE LEAGUE INTERNATIONAL (DC New 52)
DC Comics: Nov, 2011 - No. 12, Oct, 2012 ($2.99)

1-12: 1-Jurgens-s/Lopresti-a/c; Batman, Booster Gold, Guy Gardner, Vixen, Fire, Ice. 8-Batwing joins; OMAC app. 3.00
Annual 1 (10/12, $4.99) Fabok-a/c; JLI vs. OMAC; Blue Beetle joins 5.00

JUSTICE LEAGUE: NO JUSTICE
DC Comics: Jul, 2018 - No. 4, Jul, 2018 ($3.99, weekly limited series)

1-4: 1-Brainiac app.; Justice League, Teen Titans, Titans, Suicide Squad team ups. 1,2,4-Manapul-a. 2-Vril Dox app. 3-Rossmo-a 4.00

JUSTICE LEAGUE ODYSSEY
DC Comics: Nov, 2018 - No. 25, Dec, 2020 ($3.99)

1-10: 1-Williamson-s/Sejic-a; Cyborg, Starfire, Jessica Cruz and Azrael vs. Darkseid 4.00
11-25: 11-15-Year of The Villain tie-ins. 16-Intro Gamma Knife 4.00

JUSTICE LEAGUE OF AMERICA (See Brave & the Bold #28-30, Mystery In Space #75 & Official... Index) (See Crisis on Multiple Earths TPBs for reprints of JLA/JSA crossovers)
National Periodical Publ./DC Comics: Oct-Nov, 1960 - No. 261, Apr, 1987 (#91-99,139-157: 52 pgs.)

1-(10-11/60)-Origin & 1st app. Despero; Aquaman, Batman, Flash, Green Lantern, J'onn J'onzz, Superman & Wonder Woman continue from Brave and the Bold
590 1180 2360 7700 18,850 30,000
2 118 236 354 944 2122 3300
3-Origin/1st app. Kanjar Ro (see Mystery in Space #75)(scarce in high grade due to black-c)
120 240 360 972 2111 3250
4-Green Arrow joins JLA 77 154 231 616 1383 2150
5-Origin & 1st app. Dr. Destiny 59 118 177 472 1061 1650
6-8,10: 6-Origin & 1st app. Prof. Amos Fortune. 7-(10-11/61)-Last 10¢ issue. 10-(3/62)-Origin & 1st app. Felix Faust; 1st app. Lord of Time 45 90 135 333 754 1175
9-(2/62)-Origin JLA (1st origin) 53 106 159 424 950 1475
11-15: 12-(6/62)-Origin & 1st app. Dr. Light. 13-(8/62)-Speedy app. 14-(9/62)-Atom joins JLA. 28 56 84 202 451 700
16-20: 17-Adam Strange flashback 23 46 69 164 362 560
21-(8/63)-"Crisis on Earth-One"; re-intro. of JSA in this title (see Flash #129) (1st S.A. app. Hourman & Dr. Fate) 49 98 147 382 866 1350
22- "Crisis on Earth-Two"; JSA x-over (story continued from #21)
37 74 111 274 612 950
23-28: 24-Adam Strange app. 27-Robin app. 16 32 48 112 249 385
29-"Crisis on Earth-Three"; JSA x-over; 1st app. Crime Syndicate of America (Ultraman,

Justice League of America #75 © DC

Justice League of America #138 © DC

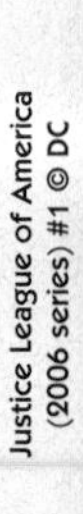

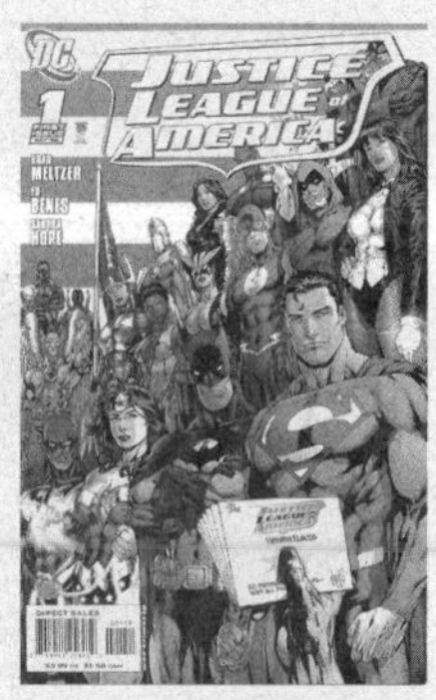

Justice League of America (2006 series) #1 © DC

	GD 2.0	VG 4.0	FN 6.0	VF 8.0	VF/NM 9.0	NM- 9.2
Owlman, Superwoman, Power Ring, Johnny Quick); 1st S.A. app. Starman	27	54	81	189	420	650
30-JSA x-over; Crime Syndicate app.	19	38	57	131	291	450
31-Hawkman joins JLA, Hawkgirl cameo (11/64)	14	28	42	97	214	330
32,34: 32-Intro & Origin Brain Storm. 34-Joker-c/sty	10	20	30	69	147	225
33,35,36,40,41: 40-3rd S.A. Penguin app. 41-Intro & origin The Key	10	20	30	66	138	210
37-39: 37,38-JSA x-over. 37-1st S.A. app. Mr. Terrific; Batman cameo. 38-"Crisis on Earth-A". 39-Giant G-16; r/B&B #28,30 & JLA #5	12	24	36	81	176	270
42-45: 42-Metamorpho app. 43-Intro. Royal Flush Gang	8	16	24	56	108	160
46-JSA x-over; 1st S.A. app. Sandman; 3rd S.A. app. of G.A. Spectre (8/66)	13	26	39	87	191	295
47-JSA x-over; 4th S.A. app of G.A. Spectre.	10	20	30	66	138	210
48-Giant G-29; r/JLA #2,3 & B&B #29	9	18	27	59	117	175
49,50,52-54,57,59,60	7	14	21	46	86	125
51-Zatanna app.	9	18	27	59	117	175
55-Intro. Earth 2 Robin (1st G.A. Robin in S.A.)	9	18	27	61	123	185
56-JLA vs. JSA (1st G.A. Wonder Woman in S.A.)	8	16	24	56	108	160
58-Giant G-41; r/JLA #6,8,1	8	16	24	55	105	155
61-63,66,68-72: 69-Wonder Woman quits. 71-Manhunter leaves. 72-Last 12¢ issue	5	10	15	35	63	90
64-(8/68)-JSA story; origin/1st app. S.A. Red Tornado	9	18	27	62	126	190
65-JSA story continues	6	12	18	38	69	100
67-Giant G-53; r/JLA #4,14,31	8	16	24	52	99	145
73-1st S.A. app. of G.A. Superman	7	14	21	44	82	120
74-Black Canary joins; Larry Lance dies; 1st meeting of G.A. & S.A. Superman; Neal Adams-c	8	16	24	56	108	160
75-2nd app. Green Arrow in new costume (see Brave & the Bold #85)	35	70	105	252	564	875
76-Giant G-65	6	12	18	42	79	115
77-80: 78-Re-intro Vigilante (1st S.A. app?)	4	8	12	28	47	65
81-90: 82-1st S.A. app. of G.A. Batman (cameo). 83-Apparent death of The Spectre. 87-Zatanna app. 90-Last 15¢ issue	4	8	12	27	44	60
91,92: 91-1st meeting of the G.A. & S.A. Robin; begin 25¢, 52 pgs. issues, ends #99. 92-S.A. Robin tries on costume that is similar to that of G.A. Robin in All Star Comics #58	4	8	12	28	47	65
93-(Giant G-77,G-89; 68 pgs.)	6	12	18	41	76	110
94-1st app. Merlyn (Green Arrow villain); reprints 1st Sandman story (Adv. #40) & origin/1st app. Starman (Adv. #61); Deadman x-over; N. Adams-a (4 pgs.)	8	16	24	54	102	150
95,96: 95-Origin Dr. Fate & Dr. Midnight -r/ More Fun #67, All-American #25). 96-Origin Hourman (Adv. #48); Wildcat-r	5	10	15	30	50	70
97-99: 97-Origin JLA retold; Sargon, Starman-r. 98-G.A. Sargon, Starman-r. 99-G.A. Sandman, Atom-r; last 52 pg. issue	4	8	12	27	44	60
100-(8/72)-1st meeting of G.A. & S.A. W. Woman	6	12	18	41	76	110
101,102: JSA x-overs. 102-Red Tornado destroyed	4	8	12	28	47	65
103-106,109: 103-Rutland Vermont Halloween x-over; Phantom Stranger joins. 105-Elongated Man joins. 106-New Red Tornado joins. 109-Hawkman resigns	3	6	9	19	30	40
107,108-JSA x-over; 1st revival app. of G.A. Uncle Sam, Black Condor, The Ray, Dollman, Phantom Lady & The Human Bomb	4	8	12	28	47	65
110,112-116: All 100 pgs. 112-Amazo app; Crimson Avenger, Vigilante-r; origin Starman-r/ Adv. #81. 115-Martian Manhunter app.	5	10	15	33	57	80
111-JLA vs. Injustice Gang; intro. Libra (re-appears in 2008's Final Crisis); Shining Knight, Green Arrow-r	5	10	15	34	60	85
117-122,125-134: 117-Hawkman rejoins. 120,121-Adam Strange app. 125,126-Two-Face-app. 128-Wonder Woman rejoins. 129-Destruction of Red Tornado	3	6	9	16	23	30
123-(10/75),124: JLA/JSA x-over. DC editor Julie Schwartz & JLA writers Cary Bates & Elliot S! Maggin appear in story as themselves. 1st named app. Earth-Prime (3rd app. after Flash; 1st Series #179 & 228)	3	6	9	17	26	35
135-136: 135-137-G.A. Bulletman, Bulletgirl, Spy Smasher, Mr. Scarlet, Pinky & Ibis x-over, 1st appearances since G.A.	3	6	9	17	26	35
137-(12/76) Superman battles G.A. Captain Marvel	4	8	12	27	44	60
138-Adam Strange app. w/c by Neal Adams; 1st app. Green Lantern of the 73rd Century	3	6	9	21	33	45
139-157: 139-157-(52 pgs.): 139-Adam Strange app. 144-Origin retold; origin J'onn J'onzz. 145-Red Tornado resurrected. 147,148-Legion of Super-Heroes x-over	2	4	6	10	14	18
158-160-(44 pgs.)	2	4	6	8	11	14
158,160-162,169,171,172,173,176,179,181-(Whitman variants; low print run, none show issue # on cover)	2	4	6	10	14	18
161-165,169-182: 161-Zatanna joins & new costume. 171,172-JSA x-over. 171-Mr. Terrific murdered. 178-Cover similar to #1; J'onn J'onzz app. 179-Firestorm joins. 181-Green Arrow leaves JLA	1	2	3	5	6	8
166-168- "Identity Crisis (2004)" precursor; JSA app. vs. Secret Society of Super-Villains	3	6	9	16	23	30
166-168-Whitman variants (no issue # on covers)	4	8	12	23	37	50
183-185-JSA/New Gods/Darkseid/Mr. Miracle x-over	2	4	6	10	14	18
186-194,198,199: 192,193-Real origin Red Tornado. 193-1st app. All-Star Squadron as free 16 pg. insert	1	2	3	5	6	8
195-197-JSA app. vs. Secret Society of Super-Villains	1	3	4	6	8	10
200 ($1.50, Anniversary issue, 76 pgs.)-JLA origin retold; Green Arrow rejoins; Bolland, Aparo, Giordano, Gil Kane, Infantino, Kubert-a; Pérez-c/a	2	4	6	8	10	12
201-206,209-243,246-259: 203-Intro/origin new Royal Flush Gang. 219,220-True origin Black Canary. 228-Re-intro Martian Manhunter. 228-230-War of the Worlds storyline; JLA Satellite destroyed by Martians. 233-Story cont'd from Annual #2. 243-Aquaman leaves. 250-Batman rejoins. 253-Origin Despero. 258-Death of Vibe. 258-261-Legends x-over						6.00
207,208-JSA, JLA, & All-Star Squadron team-up	1	2	3	5	6	8
244,245-Crisis x-over						6.00
260-Death of Steel	1	2	3	5	6	8
261-Last issue	1	3	4	6	8	10
Annual 1-3 ('83-'85), 2-Intro new J.L.A. (Aquaman, Martian Manhunter, Steel, Gypsy, Vixen, Vibe, Elongated Man & Zatanna). 3-Crisis x-over						6.00
... Hereby Elects (2006, $14.99, TPB) reprints issues where new members joined; JLofA #4,75,105,106,146,161,173 &174; roster of various incarnations; Ordway-c						15.00

NOTE: ***Neal Adams*** *c-63, 66, 67, 70, 74, 79, 81, 82, 86-89, 91, 92, 94, 96-98, 138, 139.* ***M. Anderson*** *c-1-4, 6, 7, 10, 12-14.* ***Aparo*** *a-200.* ***Austin*** *a-200i.* ***Baily*** *a-96r.* ***Bolland*** *a-200.* ***Buckler*** *c-158, 163, 164.* ***Burnley*** *r-94, 98, 99.* ***Greene*** *a-46-61i, 64-73i, 110i(r).* ***Grell*** *c-117, 122.* ***Kaluta*** *c-154p.* ***Gil Kane*** *a-200.* ***Krigstein*** *a-96(r/Sensation #84).* ***Kubert*** *a-200; c-72, 73.* ***Nino*** *a-228i, 230i.* ***Orlando*** *c-151i.* ***Perez*** *a-184-186p, 192-197p, 200p; c-184p, 186, 192-195, 196p, 197p, 199, 200, 201p, 202, 203-205p, 207-209, 212-215, 217, 219, 220.* ***Reinman*** *r-97.* ***Roussos*** *a-62i.* ***Sekowsky*** *a-37, 38, 44-63p, 110-112p(r); c-46-48p, 51p.* ***Sekowsky/Anderson*** *c-5, 8, 9, 11, 15.* ***B. Smith*** *c-185i.* ***Starlin*** *c-178-180, 183, 185p.* ***Staton*** *a-244p; c-157p, 244p.* ***Toth*** *r-110.* ***Tuska*** *a-153, 228p, 241-243p. JSA x-overs-21, 22, 29, 30, 37, 38, 46, 47, 55, 56, 64, 65, 73, 74, 82, 83, 91, 92, 100, 101, 102, 107, 108, 110, 113, 115, 123, 124, 135-137, 147, 148, 159, 160, 171, 172, 183-185, 195-197, 207-209, 219, 220, 231, 232, 244.*

JUSTICE LEAGUE OF AMERICA

DC Comics: No. 0, Sept, 2006 - No. 60, Oct, 2011 ($2.99/$3.99)

	NM- 9.2
0-Meltzer-s; history of the JLA; art by various incl. Lee, Giordano, Benes; Turner-c	5.00
0-Variant-c by Campbell	15.00
1-($3.99) Two interlocking covers by Benes; Benes-a	5.00
1-Variant-c by Turner	8.00
1-RRP Edition; sideways composite of both Benes covers	50.00
1-Second printing; Benes cover image between black bars	4.00
2-5-($2.99) Turner-c	4.00
2-5: Variant-c: 2-Jimenez. 3-Sprouse. 4-JG Jones. 5-Art Adams	5.00
6,7-($3.50) 6-JLA vs. Amazo; covers by Turner and Hughes. 7-Roster picked, new HQs; two Benes covers and Turner cover.	4.00
8-11,13-24,26-38-($2.99) 8-11-JLA/JSA team-up; covers by Turner & Jimenez. 10-Wally West returns. 13-Two covers. 13-15-Injustice Gang. 16-Tangent Flash. 20-Queen Bee app. 21-Libra app.; leads into Final Crisis #1. 35,36-Royal Flush Gang app. 38-Bagley-a begins	3.00
12-($3.50) Two Ross covers; origin retold with Wight-a; Benes-a	4.00
25-($3.99) McDuffie-s/art by various; Benes-c	4.00
39-49,51,52-($3.99) 39,40-Blackest Night. 41-New team; 2 covers. 44-48-Justice Society app. 44-Jade returns.	4.00
50-($4.99) Crime Syndicate app.; Bagley-a; wraparound-c by Van Sciver	5.00
50-Variant-c by Bagley, swipe of Quitely's JLA: Earth 2 cover	8.00
50-Variant-c by Jim Lee; swipe of Brave and the Bold #28 Starro cover	120.00
53-60-($2.99) 54-Booth-a; Eclipso returns. 55-Doomsday app.	3.00
... 80 Page Giant (11/09, $5.99) Anacleto-c; short stories by various; Ra's al Ghul app.	6.00
... 80 Page Giant 2011 (6/11, $5.99) Lau-c; chapters by various; JLA goes to Hell	6.00
Free Comic Book Day giveaway - (2007) r/#0 with "Free Comic Book Day" banner on-c	3.00
Justice League Wedding Special 1 (11/07, $3.99) McKone-a; Injustice League forms	4.00
...: Dark Things HC (2011, $24.99, dustjacket) r/#44-48 & J.S.A. #41,42	25.00
...: The Injustice Gang HC (2008, $19.99, dustjacket) r/#13-16; Wedding Special	20.00
...: The Lightning Saga HC (2008, $24.99, dustjacket) r/#0,8-12 & Justice Society of America #5,6; intro. by Patton Oswalt	25.00
...: The Lightning Saga SC (2008, $17.99) r/#0,8-12 & J.S.A. #5,6; intro. by Oswalt	18.00
...: Sanctuary SC (2009, $14.99) r/#17-21	15.00
...: Second Coming HC (2009, $19.99, dustjacket) r/#22-26	20.00
...: Second Coming SC (2010, $17.99) r/#22-26	18.00
...: Team History HC (2010, $19.99, dustjacket) r/#38-43	20.00
...: The Tornado's Path HC (2007, $24.99, dustjacket) r/#1-7; variant cover gallery; Lindelof intro.; commentary by Meltzer & Benes	25.00
...: The Tornado's Path SC (2008, $17.99) r/#1-7; variant cover gallery; Lindelof intro.; commentary by Meltzer & Benes	18.00
...: When Worlds Collide HC (2009, $24.99, dustjacket) r/#27,28,30-34	25.00
...: When Worlds Collide SC (2010, $14.99) r/#27,28,30-34	15.00

Justice League of America (2015 series) #1 © DC

Justice League Task Force #26 © DC

Justice League vs. Suicide Squad #1 © DC

	GD 2.0	VG 4.0	FN 6.0	VF 8.0	VF/NM 9.0	NM- 9.2

JUSTICE LEAGUE OF AMERICA (DC New 52)(Leads into Justice League United)
DC Comics: Apr, 2013 - No. 14, Jul, 2014 ($3.99)

1-14: 1-Johns-s/Finch-a/c; Green Arrow, Catwoman, Martian Manhunter, Katana & others team; variant covers with U.S. flag and each of the 50 state flags plus DC and Puerto Rico. 2-Covers by Finch and Ryp. 3-7: 3-5-Martian Manhunter back-up. 4,5-Shaggy Man app. 6,7-Trinity War. 8-14-Forever Evil. 10-Stargirl origin. 11,12-Despero app. 4.00
7.1, 7.2, 7.3, 7.4 (11/13, $2.99, regular-c) 3.00
7.1 (11/13, $3.99, 3-D cover) "Deadshot #1" on cover; origin; Kindt-s/Daniel-c 5.00
7.2 (11/13, $3.99, 3-D cover) "Killer Frost #1" on cover; origin; Gates-s/Santacruz-a 5.00
7.3 (11/13, $3.99, 3-D cover) "Shadow Thief #1" on cover; origin; Hardin-a/Daniel-c 5.00
7.4 (11/13, $3.99, 3-D cover) "Black Adam #1" on cover; Black Adam returns 5.00

JUSTICE LEAGUE OF AMERICA
DC Comics: Aug, 2015 - No. 10, Jan, 2017 ($5.99/$3.99)

1-($5.99) Bryan Hitch-s/a; the Parasite app. 6.00
2-10-($3.99) 2-4-Hitch-s/a. 5-Martian Manhunter spotlight; Kindt & Williams-s/Tan-a 4.00

JUSTICE LEAGUE OF AMERICA (DC Rebirth)
DC Comics: Apr, 2017 - No. 29, Jun, 2018 ($2.99)

1-24,26-29: 1-Orlando-s/Reis-a; team of Batman, Black Canary, Lobo, Vixen, Killer Frost, The Atom & The Ray; Lord Havok app. 14-17-Ray Palmer app. 18-20-Prometheus app. 21-Intro new Aztek. 22-24-Queen of Fables app. 23,24-Promethea app. 3.00
25-($3.99) Lord Havok app. 4.00
Annual 1 (1/18, $4.99) Lobo & Black Canary team-up; Kelley Jones-a 5.00
...: Killer Frost - Rebirth 1 (3/17, $2.99) Orlando-s/Andolfo-a; Amanda Waller app. 3.00
...: Rebirth 1 (4/17, $2.99) Orlando-s/Reis-a; team assembles 3.00
...: The Atom - Rebirth 1 (3/17, $2.99) Orlando-s; Ryan Choi as the new Atom 3.00
...: The Ray - Rebirth 1 (3/17, $2.99) Orlando-s; Stephen Byrne-a; origin 3.00
...: Vixen - Rebirth 1 (3/17, $2.99) Orlando & Houser-s; Jamal Campbell-a; origin retold 3.00

JUSTICE LEAGUE OF AMERICA : ANOTHER NAIL (Elseworlds) (Also see JLA: The Nail)
DC Comics: 2004 - No. 3, 2004 ($5.95, prestige format)

1-3-Sequel to JLA: The Nail; Alan Davis-s/a(p) 6.00
TPB (2004, $12.95) r/series 13.00

JUSTICE LEAGUE OF AMERICA SUPER SPECTACULAR
DC Comics: 1999 ($5.95, mimics format of DC 100 Page Super Spectaculars)

1-Reprints Silver Age JLA and Golden Age JSA 6.00

JUSTICE LEAGUE OF AMERICA'S VIBE (DC New 52)
DC Comics: Apr, 2013 - No. 10, Feb, 2014 ($2.99)

1-10: 1,2-Johns & Kreisberg-s/Woods-a/Finch-c; origin. 5-Suicide Squad app. 3.00

JUSTICE LEAGUE OF AMERICA/ THE 99
DC Comics: Dec, 2010 - No. 6, May, 2011 ($3.99/$2/99, limited series)

1-3-($3.99) Derenick-a/Massaferra-c; JLA meets Teshkeel Comics characters 4.00
4-6-($2.99) Starro app. 3.00

JUSTICE LEAGUE/ POWER RANGERS
DC Comics: Mar, 2017 - No. 6, Nov, 2017 ($3.99, limited series)

1-6-Tom Taylor-s/Stephen Byrne-a; Lord Zedd app.; Power Rangers in JLA dimension 4.00

JUSTICE LEAGUE QUARTERLY (...International Quarterly #6 on)
DC Comics: Winter, 1990-91 - No. 17, Winter, 1994 ($2.95/$3.50, 84 pgs.)

1-12,14-17: 1-Intro The Conglomerate (Booster Gold, Praxis, Gypsy, Vapor, Echo, Maxi-Man, & Reverb); Justice League #1-c/swipe. 1,2-Keith Giffen plots/breakdowns. 3-Giffen plot; 72 pg. story. 4-Rogers/Russell-a in back-up. 5,6-Mark Waid scripts. 8,17-Global Guardians app. 4.00
13-Linsner-c 6.00
NOTE: ***Phil Jimenez*** *a-17p.* ***Sprouse*** *a-1p.*

JUSTICE LEAGUE: RISE AND FALL
DC Comics: 2010, 2011

Justice League: The Rise and Fall Special #1 (5/10, $3.99) Hunt for Green Arrow 4.00
HC-(2011, $24.99) Reprints Justice League of America #43, Justice League: The Rise and Fall Special #1, Green Arrow #31,32 and Justice League: The Rise of Arsenal #1-4 25.00

JUSTICE LEAGUES...
DC Comics: Mar, 2001 ($2.50, limited series)

JL?, Justice League of Amazons, Justice League of Atlantis, Justice League of Arkham, Justice League of Aliens, JLA: JLA split by the Advance Man; Perez-c in all; s&a by various 3.00

JUSTICE LEAGUE TASK FORCE
DC Comics: June, 1993 - No. 37, Aug, 1996 ($1.25/$1.50/$1.75)

1-16,0,17-37: Aquaman, Nightwing, Flash, J'onn J'onzz, & Gypsy form team. 5,6-Knight-quest tie-ins (new Batman cameo #5, 1 pg.). 15-Triumph cameo. 16-(9/94)-Zero Hour x-over; Triumph app. 0-(10/94). 17-(11/94)-Triumph becomes part of Justice League Task Force (See JLE #68). 26-Impulse app. 35-Warlord app. 37-Triumph quits team 4.00

JUSTICE LEAGUE: THE NEW FRONTIER SPECIAL (Also see DC: The New Frontier)
DC Comics: May, 2008 ($4.99, one-shot)

1-Short stories by Darwyn Cooke, J. Bone and Dave Bullock; bonus storyboards from the movie 5.00

JUSTICE LEAGUE: THE RISE OF ARSENAL (Follows Justice League: Cry For Justice)
DC Comics: May, 2010 - No. 4, Aug, 2010 ($3.99, limited series)

1-4-Horn-c/Borges-a/Krul-s. 2,3-Cheshire app. 4.00

JUSTICE LEAGUE 3000
DC Comics: Feb, 2014 - No. 15, May, 2015 ($2.99)

1-15-Justice League of the 31st century. 1-Giffen & DeMatteis-s/Porter-a/c. 10-Etrigan app. 11-Blue Beetle and Booster Gold cameo. 12-14-Blue Beetle and Booster Gold app. 14-Kamandi app.; Kuhn-a 14,15-Etrigan app. 15-Fire returns 3.00

JUSTICE LEAGUE 3001
DC Comics: Aug, 2015 - No. 12, Jul, 2016 ($2.99)

1-12: 1-Giffen & DeMatteis-s/Porter-a/c; Supergirl app. 4-Kolins-a. 5,6-Harley Quinn app. 3.00

JUSTICE LEAGUE UNITED (DC New 52)
DC Comics: No. 0, Jun, 2014 - No. 16, Feb, 2016 ($3.99)

0-16: 0-Lemire-s/McKone-a; Adam Strange, Lobo & Byth app. 3-Hawkman killed. 6-10-Legion of Super-Heroes app. 11-13,15-Harris-c. 13-15-Sgt Rock app. 4.00
Annual #1 (12/14, $4.99) Legion of Super-Heroes app.; continued in #6 5.00
...: Futures End 1 (11/14, $2.99, reg-c) 5 years later; 2-parter with Justice League: FE #1 3.00
...: Futures End 1 (11/14, $3.99, 3-D cover) 4.00

JUSTICE LEAGUE UNLIMITED (Based on Cartoon Network animated series)
DC Comics: Nov, 2004 - No. 46, Aug, 2008 ($2.25)

1-46: 1-Zatanna app. 2,23,42-Royal Flush Gang app. 4-Adam Strange app. 10-Creeper app. 17-Freedom Fighters app. 18-Space Cabby app. 27-Black Lightning app. 34-Zod app. 41-Harley Quinn-c/app. 3.00
Free Comic Book Day giveaway (5/06) r/#1 with "Free Comic Book Day" banner on-c 3.00
Jam Packed Action (2005, $7.99, digest) adaptations of two TV episodes 8.00
... Vol. 1: United They Stand (2005, $6.99, digest) r/#1-5 7.00
... Vol. 2: World's Greatest Heroes (2006, $6.99, digest) r/#6-10 7.00
... Vol. 3: Champions of Justice (2006, $6.99, digest) r/#11-15 7.00
...: Heroes (2009, $12.99, full-size) r/#23-29 13.00
...: The Ties That Bind (2008, $12.99, full-size) r/#16-22 13.00

JUSTICE LEAGUE VS. SUICIDE SQUAD (Leads into Justice League of America '17 series)
DC Comics: Feb, 2017 - No. 6, Mar, 2017 ($3.99, weekly limited series)

1-6: 1-Max Lord & Lobo app.; Fabok-a. 2-Daniel-a. 4-6-Eclipso app. 6-Porter-a 4.00

JUSTICE MACHINE, THE
Noble Comics: June, 1981 - No. 5, Nov, 1983 ($2.00, nos. 1-3 are mag. size)

	GD 2.0	VG 4.0	FN 6.0	VF 8.0	VF/NM 9.0	NM- 9.2
1-Byrne-c(p)	3	6	9	15	21	26
2-Austin-c(i)	2	4	6	9	12	15
3	1	3	4	6	8	10

4,5, Annual 1: Ann. 1-(1/84, 68 pgs.)(published by Texas Comics); 1st app. The Elementals; Golden-c(p); new Thunder Agents story (43 pgs.) 6.00

JUSTICE MACHINE (Also see The New Justice Machine)
Comico/Innovation Publishing: Jan, 1987 - No. 29, May 1989 ($1.50/$1.75)

1-29 3.00
Annual 1(6/89, $2.50, 36 pgs.)-Last Comico ish. 3.00
Summer Spectacular 1 ('89, $2.75)-Innovation Publ.; Byrne/Gustovich-c 3.00

JUSTICE MACHINE, THE
Innovation Publishing: 1990 - No. 4, 1990 ($1.95/$2.25, deluxe format, mature)

1-4: Gustovich-c/a in all 3.00

JUSTICE MACHINE FEATURING THE ELEMENTALS
Comico: May, 1986 - No. 4, Aug, 1986 ($1.50, limited series)

1-4 3.00

JUSTICE RIDERS
DC Comics: 1997 ($5.95, one-shot, prestige format)

1-Elseworlds; Dixon-s/Williams & Gray-a 6.00

JUSTICE SOCIETY
DC Comics: 2006; 2007 ($14.99, TPB)

Vol. 1 - Rep. from 1976 revival in All Star Comics #58-67 & DC Special #29; Bolland-c 15.00
Vol. 2 - R/All Star Comics #68-74 & Adventure Comics #461-466; new Bolland-c 15.00

JUSTICE SOCIETY OF AMERICA (See Adventure #461 & All-Star #3)
DC Comics: April, 1991 - No. 8, Nov, 1991 ($1.00, limited series)

Justice Society of America (2008 series) #10 © DC

Justice Traps the Guilty #2 © Prize

Ka'a'nga Comics #2 © FH

GD VG FN VF VF/NM NM-
2.0 4.0 6.0 8.0 9.0 9.2

GD VG FN VF VF/NM NM-
2.0 4.0 6.0 8.0 9.0 9.2

1-8: 1-Flash. 2-Black Canary. 3-Green Lantern. 4-Hawkman. 5-Flash/Hawkman. 6-Green Lantern/Black Canary. 7-JSA 4.00

JUSTICE SOCIETY OF AMERICA (Also see Last Days of the... Special)
DC Comics: Aug, 1992 - No. 10, May, 1993 ($1.25)

1-10: 1-1st app. Jesse Quick 4.00

JUSTICE SOCIETY OF AMERICA (Follows JSA series)
DC Comics: Feb, 2007 - No. 54, Oct, 2011 ($3.99/$2.99)

1-($3.99) New team selected; intro. Maxine Hunkle; Alex Ross-c 4.00
1-Variant-c by Eaglesham 6.00
2-22,24-49,51-54: 1-Covers by Ross & Eaglesham. 3,4-Vandal Savage app. 5,6-JLA/JSA team-up. 9-22-Kingdom Come Superman app.18-Magog app. 22-Superman returns to Kingdom Come Earth; Ross partial art. 23-25-Ordway-a. 26-Triptych cover by Ross. 33-Team splits. 34,35-Mordru app. 41,42-Justice League x-over. 52-54-Challengers of the Unknown app. 54-Darwyn Cooke-c 3.00
23-Black Adam-c/app. 6.00
50-($4.99) Degaton app.; art by Derenick, Chaykin, Williams II, and Pérez; Massafera-c 5.00
JSA Annual 1 (9/08, $3.99) Power Girl on Earth-2; Ross-c/Ordway-a 5.00
JSA Annual 2 (4/10, $4.99) All Star team app.; Magog quits; Williams-a 5.00
... 80 Page Giant (1/10, $5.99) short stories by various incl. Ordway, S. Hampton 6.00
... 80 Page Giant 2010 (12/10, $5.99) short stories by various 6.00
... 80 Page Giant 2011 (8/11, $5.99) short stories by various incl. Chaykin, Hampton 6.00
... Special (11/10, $4.99) Scott Kolins-s/a; spotlight on Magog 5.00
...: Axis of Evil SC (2010, $14.99) r/#34-40 15.00
...: Black Adam and Isis HC (2009, $19.99, d.j.) r/#23-28 20.00
...: Black Adam and Isis SC (2010, $14.99) r/#23-28 15.00
... Kingdom Come Special: Magog (1/09, $3.99) Pasarin-a; origin re-told; 2 covers 4.00
... Kingdom Come Special: Superman (1/09, $3.99) Lois' death re-told; Alex Ross-s/a/c; thumbnails, photo references, sketch art 4.00
... Kingdom Come Special: Superman (1/09, $3.99) Eaglesham variant cover 8.00
... Kingdom Come Special: The Kingdom (1/09, $3.99) Pasarin-a; 2 covers 4.00
...: The Bad Seed SC (2010, $14.99) r/#29-33 15.00
...: The Next Age SC (2008, $14.99) r/#1-4; Ross and Eaglesham sketch pages 15.00
...: Thy Kingdom Come Part One HC (2008, $19.99, d.j.) r/#7-12; Ross sketch pages 20.00
...: Thy Kingdom Come Part One SC (2009, $14.99) r/#7-12; Ross sketch pages 15.00
...: Thy Kingdom Come Part Two HC (2008, $24.99, d.j.) r/#13-18 & Annual #1; Ross sketch pages 25.00
...: Thy Kingdom Come Part Two SC (2009, $19.99) r/#13-18 & Ann. #1; Ross sketch-a 20.00
...: Thy Kingdom Come Part Three HC (2009, $24.99, d.j.) r/#19-22 & K.C. Specials - Superman, Magog and The Kingdom; Ross sketch pages 25.00
...: Thy Kingdom Come Part Three SC (2010, $19.99) same contents as HC 20.00

JUSTICE SOCIETY OF AMERICA 100-PAGE SUPER SPECTACULAR
DC Comics: 2000 ($6.95, mimics format of DC 100 Page Super Spectaculars)

1-"1975 Issue" reprints Flash team-up and Golden Age JSA 7.00

JUSTICE SOCIETY RETURNS, THE (See All Star Comics (1999) for related titles)
DC Comics: 2003 ($19.95, TPB)

TPB-Reprints 1999 JSA x-over from All-Star Comics #1,2 and related one-shots 20.00

JUSTICE TRAPS THE GUILTY (Fargo Kid V11#3 on)
Prize/Headline Publications: Oct-Nov, 1947 - V11#2(#92), Apr-May, 1958 (True FBI Cases)

	GD	VG	FN	VF	VF/NM	NM-
V2#1-S&K-c/a; electrocution-c	77	154	231	493	847	1200
2-S&K-c/a	40	80	120	244	402	560
3-5-S&K-c/a	37	74	111	218	354	490
6-S&K-c/a; Feldstein-a	39	78	117	236	388	540
7,9-S&K-c/a. 7-9-V2#1-3 in indicia; #7-9 on-c	32	64	96	188	307	425
8-Krigstein-a; S&K-c; electric chair-c	29	58	87	172	281	390
10-Krigstein-a; S&K-c/a	32	64	96	188	307	425
11,18,19-S&K-c	18	36	54	109	172	235
12,14-17,20-No S&K. 14-Severin/Elder-a (8pg.)	13	26	39	72	101	130
13-Used in **SOTI**, pg. 110-111	14	28	42	81	118	165
21,30-S&K-c/a	19	38	57	112	179	245
22,23-S&K-c	15	30	45	84	127	170
24-26,27,29,31-50: 32-Meskin story	12	24	36	67	94	120
28-Kirby-c	14	28	42	80	115	150
51-55,57,59-70	10	20	30	58	79	100
56-Ben Oda, Joe Simon, Joe Genola, Mort Meskin & Jack Kirby app. in police line-up on classic-c	22	44	66	130	213	295
58-Illo. in **SOTI**, "Treating police contemptuously" (top left); text on heroin	31	62	93	182	296	410
71-92: 76-Orlando-a	9	18	27	50	65	80

NOTE: ***Bailey** a-12, 13. **Elder** a-8. **Kirby** a-19p. **Meskin** a-22, 27, 63, 64; c-45, 46. **Robinson/Meskin** a-5, 19. **Severin** a-8, 11p. Photo c-12, 15-17.*

JUST IMAGINE STAN LEE WITH... (Stan Lee re-invents DC icons)
DC Comics: 2001 - 2002 ($5.95, prestige format, one-shots)

(Adam Hughes back-c on all)(Michael Uslan back-up stories in all, diff. artists)

Scott McDaniel Creating **Aquaman**- Back-up w/Ramona Fradon-a 6.00
Joe Kubert Creating **Batman**- Back-up w/Michael Kaluta-a 6.00
Chris Bachalo Creating **Catwoman**- Back-up w/Darwyn Cooke & Mike Allred-a 2 4 6 8 10 12
John Cassaday Creating **Crisis**- no back-up story 6.00
Kevin Maguire Creating **The Flash**- Back-up w/Sergio Aragonés-a 6.00
Dave Gibbons Creating **Green Lantern**- Back-up w/Dick Giordano-a 6.00
Jerry Ordway Creating **JLA** 6.00
John Byrne Creating **Robin**- Back-up w/John Severin-a 6.00
Walter Simonson Creating **Sandman**- Back-up w/Richard Corben-a 6.00
Gary Frank Creating **Shazam!**- Back-up w/Kano-a 1 2 3 5 6 8
John Buscema Creating **Superman**- Back-up w/Kyle Baker-a 2 4 6 8 10 12
Jim Lee Creating **Wonder Woman**- Back-up w/Gene Colan-a 1 2 3 5 6 8
Secret Files and Origins #1 (3/02, $4.95) Crisis prologue; Jurgens-a 5.00
TPB -Just Imagine Stan Lee Creating the DC Universe: Book One (2002, $19.95) r/Batman, Wonder Woman, Superman, Green Lantern 20.00
TPB -Just Imagine Stan Lee Creating the DC Universe: Book Two (2003, $19.95) r/Flash, JLA, Secret Files and Origins, Robin, Shazam; sketch pages 20.00
TPB -Just Imagine Stan Lee Creating the DC Universe: Book Three (2004, $19.95) r/Aquaman, Catwoman, Sandman, Crisis; profile pages 20.00

JUST MARRIED
Charlton Comics: January, 1958 - No. 114, Dec, 1976

	GD	VG	FN	VF	VF/NM	NM-
1	8	16	24	51	96	140
2	4	8	12	27	44	60
3-10	3	6	9	19	30	40
11-30	3	6	9	16	23	30
31-50	2	4	6	11	16	20
51-70	2	4	6	9	13	16
71-78,80-89	2	4	6	8	11	14
79-Ditko-a (7 pages)	2	4	6	10	14	18
90-Susan Dey and David Cassidy full page poster	2	4	6	11	16	20
91-114	2	4	6	8	10	12

KA'A'NGA COMICS (...Jungle King)(See Jungle Comics)
Fiction House Magazines (Glen-Kel Publ. Co.): Spring, 1949 - No. 20, Summer, 1954

	GD	VG	FN	VF	VF/NM	NM-
1-Ka'a'nga, Lord of the Jungle begins	63	126	189	403	689	975
2 (Winter, '49-'50)	33	66	99	196	321	445
3,4	26	52	78	156	256	355
5-Camilla app.	25	50	75	147	241	335
6-10: 7-Tuska-a. 9-Tabu, Wizard of the Jungle app. 10-Used in **POP**, pg. 99	17	34	51	103	162	220
11-15: 15-Camilla-r by Baker/Jungle #106	15	30	45	83	124	165
16-Sheena app.	15	30	45	85	130	175
17-20	14	28	42	80	115	150
I.W. Reprint #1,8: 1-r/#18; Kinstler-c. 8-r/#10	3	6	9	14	20	25

NOTE: ***Celardo** c-1. **Whitman** c-8-20(most).*

KABOOM
Awesome Entertainment: Sept, 1997 - No. 3, Nov, 1997 ($2.50)

1-3: 1-Matsuda-a/Loeb-s; 4 covers exist (Matsuda, Sale, Pollina and McGuinness), 1-Dynamic Forces Edition, 2-Regular, 2-Alicia Watcher variant-c, 2-Gold logo variant-c, 3-Two covers by Liefeld & Matsuda, 3-Dynamic Forces Ed., Prelude Ed. 3.00
Prelude Gold Edition 4.00

KABOOM (2nd series)
Awesome Entertainment: July, 1999 - No. 3, Dec, 1999 ($2.50)

1-3: 1-Grant-a(p); at least 4 variant covers 3.00

KABOOM! SUMMER BLAST FREE COMIC BOOK DAY EDITION
Boom Entertainment (KaBOOM!): May 2013; May 2014 (free giveaways)

nn-(5/13) Short stories of Adventure Time, Regular Show, Herobear, Garfield, Peanuts 3.00
nn-(5/14) Adventure TIme, Regular Show, Steven Universe, Uncle Grandpa and others 3.00

KABUKI
Caliber: Nov, 1994 ($3.50, B&W, one-shot)

nn-(Fear The Reaper) 1st app.; David Mack-c/a/s 1 2 3 5 6 8
Color Special (1/96, $2.95)-Mack-c/a/scripts; pin-ups by Tucci, Harris & Quesada 4.00
Gallery (8/95, $2.95)- pinups from Mack, Bradstreet, Paul Pope & others 3.00

KABUKI
Image Comics: Oct, 1997 - No. 9, Mar, 2000 ($2.95, color)

1-David Mack-c/s/a 5.00
1-($10.00)-Dynamic Forces Edition 1 3 4 6 8 10

Kabuki: Skin Deep #3 © David Mack

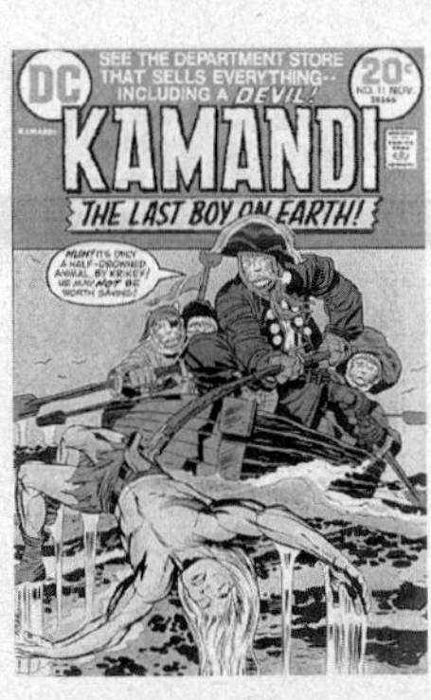

Kamandi, The Last Boy on Earth #11 © DC

Kathy #1 © MAR

GD 2.0 | VG 4.0 | FN 6.0 | VF 8.0 | VF/NM 9.0 | NM- 9.2

2-5 4.00
6-9 3.00
#1/2 (9/01, $2.95) r/Wizard 1/2; Eklipse Mag. article; bio 3.00
...Classics (2/99, $3.95) Reprints Fear the Reaper 4.00
...Classics 2 (3/99, $3.95) Reprints Dance of Dance 4.00
...Classics 3-5 (3-6/99, $4.95) Reprints Circle of Blood-Acts 1-3 5.00
...Classics 6-12 (7/99-3/00, $3.25) Various reprints 3.25
...Images (6/98, $4.95) r/#1 with new pin-ups 5.00
...Images 2 (1/99, $4.95) r/#1 with new pin-ups 5.00
...Metamorphosis TPB (10/00, $24.95) r/#1-9; Sienkiewicz intro.; 2nd printing exists 25.00
...Reflections 1-4 (7/98-5/02; $4.95) new story plus art techniques 5.00
... The Ghost Play (11/02, $2.95) new story plus interview 3.00

KABUKI
Marvel Comics (Icon): July, 2004 - No. 9, Sept, 2007 ($2.99, color)
1-9: 1-David Mack-c/s/a in all; variant-c by Alex Maleev. 4-Variant-c by Adam Hughes. 6-Variant-c by Mignola. 8-Variant-c by Kent Williams. 9-Allred var-c 3.00
...: The Alchemy HC (2008, $29.99, dust jacket) oversized r/#1-9; bonus art & content 30.00
... Reflections 5-15 (7/05-10/09, $5.99) paintings & sketches of recent work; photos 6.00

KABUKI AGENTS (SCARAB)
Image Comics: Aug, 1999 - No. 8, Aug, 2001 ($2.95, B&W)
1-8-David Mack-s/Rick Mays-a 3.00

KABUKI: CIRCLE OF BLOOD
Caliber Press: Jan, 1995 - No. 6, Nov, 1995 ($2.95, B&W)
1-David Mack story/a in all 5.00
2-6: 3-#1 on inside indicia. 3.00
6-Variant-c 3.00
TPB ($16.95) r/#1-6, intro. by Steranko 17.00
TPB (1997, $17.95) Image Edition-r/#1-6, intro. by Steranko 18.00
TPB ($24.95) Deluxe Edition 25.00

KABUKI: DANCE OF DEATH
London Night Studios: Jan, 1995 ($3.00, B&W, one-shot)
1-David Mack-c/a/scripts 1 2 3 5 6 8

KABUKI: DREAMS
Image Comics: Jan, 1998 ($4.95, TPB)
nn-Reprints Color Special & Dreams of the Dead 5.00

KABUKI: DREAMS OF THE DEAD
Caliber: July, 1996 ($2.95, one-shot)
nn-David Mack-c/a/scripts 3.00

KABUKI FAN EDITION
Gemstone Publ./Caliber: Feb, 1997 (mail-in offer, one-shot)
nn-David Mack-c/a/scripts 4.00

KABUKI: MASKS OF THE NOH
Caliber: May, 1996 - No. 4, Feb, 1997 ($2.95, limited series)
1-4: 1-Three-c (1A-Quesada, 1B-Buzz, &1C-Mack). 3-Terry Moore pin-up 3.00
TPB-(4/98, $10.95) r/#1-4; intro by Terry Moore 11.00

KABUKI: SKIN DEEP
Caliber Comics: Oct, 1996 - No. 3, May, 1997 ($2.95)
1-3:David Mack-c/a/scripts. 2-Two-c (1-Mack, 1-Ross) 3.00
TPB-(5/98, $9.95) r/#1-3; intro by Alex Ross 10.00

KAMANDI: AT EARTH'S END
DC Comics: June, 1993 - No. 6, Nov, 1993 ($1.75, limited series)
1-6: Elseworlds storyline 3.00

KAMANDI CHALLENGE, THE (Commemoration for Jack Kirby's 100th birthday)
DC Comics: Mar, 2017 - No. 12, Feb, 2018 ($4.99/$3.99, limited series)
1-($4.99) DiDio-s/Giffen-a; Abnett-s/Eaglesham-a; Timm-c 5.00
2-11-($3.99) 2-Neal Adams-a; Tomasi-s; covers by Adams & Rocafort. 3-Palmiotti-s/Conner-a. 8-Giffen-s/Rude-a; Jim Lee-c. 10-Shane Davis-a. 11-Simonson-a 4.00
12-($4.99) Gail Simone-s; art by Jill Thompson and Ryan Sook; afterword by Paul Levitz 5.00
... Special 1 (3/17, $7.99) r/#1,32 and unpubl'd #60,61 from Cancelled Comic Cavalcade 8.00

KAMANDI, THE LAST BOY ON EARTH (Also see Alarming Tales #1, Brave and the Bold #120 & 157, Cancelled Comic Cavalcade & Wednesday Comics)
National Periodical Publ./DC Comics: Oct-Nov, 1972 - No. 59, Sept-Oct, 1978
1-Origin & 1st app. Kamandi; intro Ben Boxer 7 14 21 46 86 125
2,3 4 8 12 28 47 65
4,5: 4-Intro. Prince Tuftan of the Tigers. 5-Intro. Flower 4 8 12 25 40 55
6-10 3 6 9 18 28 38
11-20 3 6 9 15 22 28
21-28,30,31,33-40: 24-Last 20¢ issue. 31-Intro Pyra. 2 4 6 13 18 22
29,32: 29-Superman x-over. 32-(68 pgs.)-r/origin from #1 plus one new story; 4 pg. biog. of Jack Kirby with B&W photos 3 6 9 14 20 26
41-57: 50 Kamandi becomes an OMAC 2 4 6 10 14 18
58-Karate Kid x-over from LSH (see Karate Kid #15) 3 6 9 14 19 24
59-(44 pgs.)-Story cont'd in Brave and the Bold #157; The Return of Omac back-up by Starlin-c/a(p) cont'd in Warlord #37 3 6 9 16 23 30
NOTE: *Ayers a(p)-48-59 (most).* ***Giffen*** *a-44p, 45p.* ***Kirby*** *a-1-40p; c-1-33.* ***Kubert*** *c-34-41.* ***Nasser*** *a-45p, 46p.* ***Starlin*** *a-59p; c-57, 59p.*

KAMUI (Legend Of...#2 on)
Eclipse Comics/Viz Comics: May 12, 1987 - No. 37, Nov. 15, 1988 ($1.50, B&W, bi-weekly)
1-37: 1-3 have 2nd printings 3.00

KANAN - THE LAST PADAWAN (Star Wars)
Marvel Comics: Jun, 2015 - No. 12, May, 2016 ($3.99)
1-12: 1-Weisman-s/Larraz-a; takes place after Episode 3; flashbacks to the Clone Wars. 9-11-General Grievous app. 4.00

KANE & LYNCH (Based on the video games)
DC Comics (WildStorm): Oct, 2010 - No. 6, Apr, 2011 ($3.99/$2.99, limited series)
1-4-($3.99) Templesmith-c/Edginton-s/Mitten-a 4.00
5,6-($2.99) 3.00
TPB (2011, $17.99) r/#1-6; cover gallery 18.00

KAOS MOON (Also see Negative Burn #34)
Caliber Comics: 1996 - No. 4, 1997 ($2.95, B&W)
1-4-David Boller-s/a 3.00
3,4-Limited Alternate-c 4.00
3,4-Gold Alternate-c, Full Circle TPB ($5.95) r/#1,2 6.00

KAPTARA
Image Comics: Apr, 2015 - No. 5, Nov, 2015 ($3.50)
1-5-Chip Zdarsky-s/Kagan McLeod-a 3.50

KARATE KID (See Action, Adventure, Legion of Super-Heroes, & Superboy)
National Periodical Publications/DC Comics: Mar-Apr, 1976 - No. 15, July-Aug, 1978 (Legion of Super-Heroes spin-off)
1-Meets Iris Jacobs; Estrada/Staton-a 3 6 9 19 30 40
2-14: 2-Major Disaster app. 14-Robin x-over 2 3 4 6 8 10
15-Continued into Kamandi #58 2 4 6 11 16 20
NOTE: ***Grell*** *c-1-4, 7, 8, 5p, 6p,* ***Staton*** *a-1-9i. Legion x-over-No. 1, 2, 4, 6, 10, 12, 13. Princess Projectra x-over-#8, 9.*

KARNAK (Inhumans)
Marvel Comics: Dec, 2015 - No. 6, Apr, 2017 ($3.99)
1-6: 1,2-Warren Ellis-s/Gerardo Zaffino-a. 3-6-Roland Boschi-a 4.00

KATANA (DC New 52) (From Justice League Of America 2013 series)
DC Comics: Apr, 2013 - No. 10, Feb, 2014 ($2.99)
1-10: 1,2-Nocenti-s/Sanchez-a/Finch-c; origin. 2-Steve Trevor app. 3-6-Creeper app. 3.00

KATHY
Standard Comics: Sept, 1949 - No. 17, Sept, 1955
1-Teen-age 34 68 102 199 325 450
2-Schomburg-c 17 34 51 103 162 220
3-5 14 28 42 78 112 145
6-17: 17-Code approved 14 28 42 76 108 140

KATHY (The Teenage Tornado)
Atlas Comics/Marvel (ZPC): Oct, 1959 - No. 27, Feb, 1964 (most issues contain paper dolls and pin-up pages)
1-The Teen-age Tornado; Goldberg-c/a in all 34 68 102 199 325 450
2 17 34 51 105 165 225
3-15 15 30 45 92 144 195
16-23,25,27 14 28 42 81 118 155
24-(8/63) Frank Sinatra, Cary Grant, Ed Sullivan & Liz Taylor-c 19 38 57 111 176 240
26-(12/63) Kathy becomes a model; Millie app. 15 30 45 84 127 170

KAT KARSON
I. W. Enterprises: No date (Reprint)
1-Funny animals 2 4 6 10 12 15

KATO (Also see The Green Hornet)
Dynamite Entertainment: 2010 - No. 14, 2011 ($3.99)
1-14: 1-Kato and daughter origin; Garza-a/Parks-s. 2-10 Bernard-a 4.00
Annual 1 (2011, $4.99) Parks-s/Salazar-a 5.00

Kato Origins #1 © GH Inc.

Katzenjammer Kids #16 © UFS

Ka-Zar V2 #6 © MAR

KATO OF THE GREEN HORNET (Also see The Green Hornet)
Now Comics: Nov, 1991 - No. 4, Feb, 1992 ($2.50, mini-series)

Issue	GD 2.0	VG 4.0	FN 6.0	VF 8.0	VF/NM 9.0	NM- 9.2
1-4: Brent Anderson-c/a						4.00

KATO OF THE GREEN HORNET II (Also see The Green Hornet)
Now Comics: Nov, 1992 - No. 2, Dec, 1993 ($2.50, mini-series)

Issue	GD 2.0	VG 4.0	FN 6.0	VF 8.0	VF/NM 9.0	NM- 9.2
1,2-Baron-s/Mayerik & Sherman-a						4.00

KATO ORIGINS (Also see The Green Hornet: Year One)
Dynamite Entertainment: 2010 - No. 11, 2011 ($3.99)

Issue	GD 2.0	VG 4.0	FN 6.0	VF 8.0	VF/NM 9.0	NM- 9.2
1-11-Kato in 1942; Jai Nitz-s/Colton Worley-a; covers by Worley & Francavilla						4.00

KATY KEENE (Also see Kasco Komics, Laugh, Pep, Suzie, & Wilbur)
Archie Publ./Close-Up/Radio Comics: 1949 - No. 4, 1951; No. 5, 3/52 - No. 62, Oct, 1961 (50-53-Adventures of...on-c) (Cut and missing pages are common)

Issue	GD 2.0	VG 4.0	FN 6.0	VF 8.0	VF/NM 9.0	NM- 9.2
1-Bill Woggon-c/a begins; swipes-c to Mopsy #1	245	490	735	1568	2684	3800
2-(1950)	77	154	231	493	847	1200
3-5: 3-(1951). 4-(1951). 5-(3/52)	60	120	180	381	653	925
6-10	42	84	126	265	445	625
11,13-21: 21-Last pre-code issue (3/55)	37	74	111	218	354	490
12-(Scarce)	42	84	126	265	445	625
22-40	26	52	78	152	249	345
41-60: 54-Wedding Album plus wedding pin-up	20	40	60	115	188	260
61-Sci-fi-c	26	52	78	156	256	355
62-Classic Robot-c	48	76	144	302	514	725
Annual 1('54, 25¢)-All new stories; last pre-code	61	122	183	390	670	950
Annual 2-6('55-59, 25¢)-All new stories	35	70	105	208	339	470
3-D 1(1953, 25¢, large size)-Came w/glasses	41	82	123	256	428	600
Charm 1(9/58)-Woggon-c/a; new stories, and cut-outs	34	68	102	204	332	450
Glamour 1(1957)-Puzzles, games, cut-outs	34	68	102	204	332	450
Spectacular 1('56)	34	68	102	206	334	455

NOTE: *Debby's Diary in #45, 47-49, 52, 57.*

KATY KEENE COMICS DIGEST MAGAZINE
Close-Up, Inc. (Archie Ent.): 1987 - No. 10, July, 1990 ($1.25/$1.35/$1.50, digest size)

Issue	GD 2.0	VG 4.0	FN 6.0	VF 8.0	VF/NM 9.0	NM- 9.2
1	2	4	6	10	14	18
2-10	1	3	4	6	8	10

NOTE: *Many used copies are cut-up inside.*

KATY KEENE FASHION BOOK MAGAZINE
Radio Comics/Archie Publications: 1955 - No. 13, Sum, '56 - N. 23, Wint, '58-59 (nn 3-10) (no #11,12)

Issue	GD 2.0	VG 4.0	FN 6.0	VF 8.0	VF/NM 9.0	NM- 9.2
1-Bill Woggon-c/a	61	122	183	390	670	950
2	34	68	102	204	332	460
13-18: 18-Photo Bill Woggon	26	52	78	154	252	350
19-23	22	44	66	128	209	290

KATY KEENE HOLIDAY FUN (See Archie Giant Series Magazine No. 7, 12)

KATY KEENE MODEL BEHAVIOR
Archie Comic Publications: 2008 ($10.95, TPB)

Issue	GD 2.0	VG 4.0	FN 6.0	VF 8.0	VF/NM 9.0	NM- 9.2
Vol. 1 - New story and reprinted apps./pin-ups from Archie & Friends #101-112						11.00

KATY KEENE PINUP PARADE
Radio Comics/Archie Publications: 1955 - No. 15, Summer, 1961 (25¢) (Cut-out & missing pages are common)

Issue	GD 2.0	VG 4.0	FN 6.0	VF 8.0	VF/NM 9.0	NM- 9.2
1-Cut-outs in all?; last pre-code issue	61	122	183	390	670	950
2-(1956)	33	66	99	194	317	440
3-5: 3-(1957). 5-(1959)	27	54	81	162	266	370
6-10,12-14: 8-Mad parody. 10-Bill Woggon photo	23	46	69	136	223	310
11-Story of how comics get CCA approved, narrated by Katy	29	58	87	174	285	395
15(Rare)-Photo artist & family	43	86	129	271	461	650

KATY KEENE SPECIAL (Katy Keene #7 on; see Laugh Comics Digest)
Archie Ent.: Sept, 1983 - No. 33, 1990 (Later issues published quarterly)

Issue	GD 2.0	VG 4.0	FN 6.0	VF 8.0	VF/NM 9.0	NM- 9.2
1-10: 1-Woggon-r; new Woggon-c. 3-Woggon-r	1	3	4	6	8	10
11-25: 12-Spider-Man parody	1	2	3	5	6	8
26-32-(Low print run)	2	4	6	8	10	12
33	2	4	6	8	11	14

KATZENJAMMER KIDS, THE (See Captain & the Kids & Giant Comic Album)
David McKay Publ./Standard No. 12-21(Spring/'50 - 53)/Harvey No. 22, 4/53 on: 1945-1946; Summer, 1947 - No. 27, Feb-Mar, 1954

Issue	GD 2.0	VG 4.0	FN 6.0	VF 8.0	VF/NM 9.0	NM- 9.2
Feature Books 30	21	42	63	122	199	275
Feature Books 32,35('45),41,44('46)	19	38	57	109	172	235
Feature Book 37-Has photos & biography of Harold Knerr	20	40	60	114	182	250
1(1947)-All new stories begin	20	40	60	114	182	250
2-5	12	24	36	69	97	125
6-11	10	20	30	56	76	95
12-14(Standard)	9	18	27	47	61	75
15-21(Standard)	8	16	24	44	57	70
22-25,27(Harvey): 22-24-Henry app.	7	14	21	35	43	50
26-Half in 3-D	16	32	48	94	147	200

KAYO (Formerly Bullseye & Jest; becomes Carnival Comics)
Harry 'A' Chesler: No. 12, Mar, 1945

Issue	GD 2.0	VG 4.0	FN 6.0	VF 8.0	VF/NM 9.0	NM- 9.2
12-Green Knight, Capt. Glory, Little Nemo (not by McCay)	30	60	90	177	289	400

KA-ZAR (Also see Marvel Comics #1, Savage Tales #6 & X-Men #10)
Marvel Comics Group: Aug, 1970 - No. 3, Mar, 1971 (Giant-Size, 68 pgs.)

Issue	GD 2.0	VG 4.0	FN 6.0	VF 8.0	VF/NM 9.0	NM- 9.2
1-Reprints earlier Ka-Zar stories; Avengers x-over in Hercules; Daredevil, X-Men app.; hidden profanity-c	5	10	15	31	53	75
2,3-Daredevil-r. 2-r/Daredevil #13 w/Kirby layouts; Ka-Zar origin, Angel-r from X-Men by Tuska. 3-Romita & Heck-a (no Kirby)	3	6	9	19	30	40

NOTE: ***Buscema** r-2. **Colan** a-1p(r). **Kirby** c/a-1, 2. #1-Reprints X-Men #10 & Daredevil #24.*

KA-ZAR
Marvel Comics Group: Jan, 1974 - No. 20, Feb, 1977 (Regular Size)

Issue	GD 2.0	VG 4.0	FN 6.0	VF 8.0	VF/NM 9.0	NM- 9.2
1	3	6	9	19	30	40
2-10	2	4	6	8	10	12
11-14,16,18-20: 16-Only a 30 ¢ edition exists	1	2	3	5	6	8
15,17-(Regular 25¢ edition)(8/76)	1	2	3	5	6	8
15,17-(30¢-c variants, limited distribution)	4	8	12	23	37	50

NOTE: ***Alcala** a-6i, 8i. **Brunner** c-4. **J. Buscema** a-6-10p; c-1, 5, 7. **Heath** a-12. **G. Kane** c(p)-3, 5, 8-11, 15, 20. **Kirby** c-12p. **Reinman** a-1p.*

KA-ZAR (Volume 2)
Marvel Comics: May, 1997 - No. 20, Dec, 1998 ($1.95/$1.99)

Issue	GD 2.0	VG 4.0	FN 6.0	VF 8.0	VF/NM 9.0	NM- 9.2
1-Waid-s/Andy Kubert-c/a. thru #4						5.00
1-2nd printing; new cover						4.00
2,4: 2-Two-c						4.00
3-Alpha Flight #1 preview						5.00
5-13,15-20: 8-Includes Spider-Man Cybercomic CD-ROM. 9-11-Thanos app. 15-Priest-s/Martinez & Rodriguez-a begin; Punisher app.						4.00
14-($2.99) Last Waid/Kubert issue; flip book with 2nd story previewing new creative team of Priest-s/Martinez & Rodriguez-a						5.00
'97 Annual ($2.99)-Wraparound-c						5.00

KA-ZAR
Marvel Comics: Aug, 2011 - No. 5, Dec, 2011 ($2.99, limited series)

Issue	GD 2.0	VG 4.0	FN 6.0	VF 8.0	VF/NM 9.0	NM- 9.2
1-5-Jenkins-s/Alixe-a/c						3.00

KA-ZAR OF THE SAVAGE LAND
Marvel Comics: Feb, 1997 ($2.50, one-shot)

Issue	GD 2.0	VG 4.0	FN 6.0	VF 8.0	VF/NM 9.0	NM- 9.2
1-Wraparound-c						4.00

KA-ZAR: SIBLING RIVALRY
Marvel Comics: July, 1997 ($1.95, one-shot)

Issue	GD 2.0	VG 4.0	FN 6.0	VF 8.0	VF/NM 9.0	NM- 9.2
(# -1) Flashback story w/Alpha Flight #1 preview						4.00

KA-ZAR THE SAVAGE (See Marvel Fanfare)
Marvel Comics Group: Apr, 1981 - No. 34, Oct, 1984 (Regular size)(Mando paper #10 on)

Issue	GD 2.0	VG 4.0	FN 6.0	VF 8.0	VF/NM 9.0	NM- 9.2
1-Bruce Jones-s begin	1	3	4	6	8	10
2-20,24,27,28,30-34: 11-Origin Zabu. 12-One of two versions with panel missing on pg. 10. 20-Kraven the Hunter-c/story (also apps. in #21)						4.00
12-Version with panel on pg. 10 (1600 printed)	1	3	4	6	8	10
21-23, 25,26-Spider-Man app. 26-Photo-c.						4.00
29-Double size; Ka-Zar & Shanna wed						5.00

NOTE: ***B. Anderson** a-1-15p, 18, 19; c-1-17, 18p, 20(back). **G. Kane** a(back-up)-11, 12, 14.*

KEEN DETECTIVE FUNNIES (Formerly Detective Picture Stories?)
Centaur Publications: No. 8, July, 1938 - No. 24, Sept, 1940

Issue	GD 2.0	VG 4.0	FN 6.0	VF 8.0	VF/NM 9.0	NM- 9.2
V1#8-The Clock continues-r/Funny Picture Stories #1; Roy Crane-a (1st?)	371	742	1113	2600	4550	6500
9-Tex Martin by Eisner; The Gang Buster app.	300	600	900	1950	3375	4800
10,11: 11-Dean Denton story (begins?)	275	550	825	1760	3030	4300
V2#1,2-The Eye Sees by Frank Thomas begins; ends #23(Not in V2#3&5). 2-Jack Cole-a	161	322	483	1030	1765	2500
3-6: 3-TNT Todd begins. 4-Gabby Flynn begins. 5,6-Dean Denton story	155	310	465	992	1696	2400
7-The Masked Marvel by Ben Thompson begins (7/39, 1st app.)(scarce)	309	618	927	2198	3849	5500
8-Nudist ranch panel w/four girls	194	388	582	1242	2121	3000
9-11	142	284	426	909	1555	2200

Keen Teens nn (#1) © ME

Kevin Keller #15 © ACP

MARK MILLAR • JOHN ROMITA JR.
KICK-ASS
RECESSION-PROOF!
ICON

Kick-Ass #4 © Millar & Romita Jr.

	GD	VG	FN	VF	VF/NM	NM-
	2.0	4.0	6.0	8.0	9.0	9.2

12(12/39)-Origin The Eye Sees by Frank Thomas; death of Masked Marvel's sidekick ZL 181 362 543 1158 1979 2800
V3#1 135 270 405 864 1482 2100
18-Bondage/torture-c 194 388 582 1242 2121 3000
19,21,22 135 270 405 864 1482 2100
20-Classic Eye Sees-c by Thomas 300 600 900 1950 3375 4800
23-Air Man begins (intro); Air Man-c 187 374 561 1197 2049 2900
24-(scarce) Air Man-c 219 438 657 1402 2401 3400
NOTE: ***Burgos*** *a-V2#2.* ***Jack Cole*** *a-V2#2.* ***Eisner*** *a-10, V2#6r.* ***Ken Ernst*** *a-V2#4-7, 9, 10, 19, 21; c-V2#4.* ***Everett*** *a-V2#6, 7, 9, 11, 12, 20.* ***Guardineer*** *a-V2#5, 66.* ***Gustavson*** *a-V2#4-6.* ***Simon*** *c-V3#1.* ***Thompson*** *c-V2#7, 9, 10, 22.*

KEEN KOMICS
Centaur Publications: V2#1, May, 1939 - V2#3, Nov, 1939

V2#1(Large size)-Dan Hastings (s/f), The Big Top, Bob Phantom the Magician, The Mad Goddess app. 300 600 900 2070 3635 5200
V2#2(Reg. size)-The Forbidden Idol of Machu Picchu; Cut Carson by Burgos begins 129 258 387 826 1413 2000
V2#3-Saddle Sniffl by Jack Cole, Circus Pays, Kings Revenge app. 116 232 348 742 1271 1800
NOTE: ***Binder*** *a-V2#2.* ***Burgos*** *a-V2#2, 3.* ***Ken Ernst*** *a-V2#3.* ***Gustavson*** *a-V2#2.* ***Jack Cole*** *a-V2#3.*

KEEN TEENS (Girls magazine)
Life's Romances Publ./Leader/Magazine Ent.: 1945; nn, 1946; No. 3, Feb-Mar, 1947 - No. 6, Aug-Sept, 1947

nn (#1)-14 pgs. Claire Voyant (cont'd. in other nn issue) movie photos, Dotty Dripple, Gertie O'Grady & Sissy; Van Johnson, Sinatra photo-c 55 110 165 352 601 850
nn (#2, 1946)-16 pgs. Claire Voyant & 16 pgs. movie photos 39 78 117 231 378 525
3-6: 4-Glenn Ford photo-c. 5-Perry Como-c 19 38 57 112 179 245

KELLYS, THE (Formerly Rusty Comics; Spy Cases No. 26 on)
Marvel Comics (HPC): No. 23, Jan, 1950 - No. 25, June, 1950 (52 pgs.)

23-Teenage 20 40 60 114 182 250
24,25: 24-Margie app. 14 28 42 82 121 160

KEN MAYNARD WESTERN (Movie star)(See Wow Comics, 1936)
Fawcett Publ.: Sept, 1950 - No. 8, Feb, 1952 (All 36 pgs; photo front/back-c)

1-Ken Maynard & his horse Tarzan begin 28 56 84 165 270 375
2 17 34 51 98 154 210
3-8: 6-Atomic bomb explosion panel 14 28 42 76 108 140

KENNEL BLOCK BLUES
BOOM! Studios: Feb, 2016 - No. 4, May, 2016 ($3.99, limited series)

1-4-Ryan Ferrier-s/Daniel Bayliss-a 4.00

KEN SHANNON (Becomes Gabby #11 on) (Also see Police Comics #103)
Quality Comics Group: Oct, 1951 - No. 10, Apr, 1953 (A private eye)

1-Crandall-a 52 104 156 328 552 775
2-Crandall c/a(2) 39 78 117 240 395 550
3-Horror-c; Crandall-a 43 86 129 271 461 650
4,5-Crandall-a 30 60 90 177 289 400
6-Crandall-c/a; "The Weird Vampire Mob"-c/s 47 94 141 296 498 700
7-"The Ugliest Man Alive"-c; Crandall-a 40 80 120 246 411 575
8,9: 8-Opium den drug use story 24 48 72 144 237 330
10-Crandall-c 25 50 75 150 245 340
NOTE: ***Crandall/Cuidera*** *c-1-10.* ***Jack Cole*** *a-1-9. #1-15 published after title change to Gabby.*

KEN STUART
Publication Enterprises: Jan, 1949 (Sea Adventures)

1-Frank Borth-c/a 14 28 42 80 115 150

KENT BLAKE OF THE SECRET SERVICE (Spy)
Marvel/Atlas Comics (20CC): May, 1951 - No. 14, July, 1953

1-Injury to eye, bondage, torture; Brodsky-c 32 64 96 188 307 425
2-Drug use w/hypo scenes; Brodsky-c 20 40 60 118 192 265
3-14: 8-R.Q. Sale-a (2 pgs.) 15 30 45 83 124 165
NOTE: ***Heath*** *c-5, 7, 8.* ***Infantino*** *c-12.* ***Maneely*** *c-3.* ***Sinnott*** *a-2(3).* ***Tuska*** *a-8(3pg.).*

KENTS, THE
DC Comics: Aug, 1997 - No. 12, July, 1998 ($2.50, limited series)

1-12-Ostrander-s/art by Truman and Bair (#1-8), Mandrake (#9-12) 4.00
TPB ($19.95) r/#1-12 20.00

KERRY DRAKE (Also see A-1 Comics)
Argo: Jan, 1956 - No. 2, March, 1956

1,2-Newspaper-r 8 16 24 44 57 70

KERRY DRAKE DETECTIVE CASES (...Racket Buster No. 32,33)
(Also see Chamber of Clues & Green Hornet Comics #42-47)
Life's Romances/Com/Magazine Ent. No.1-5/Harvey No.6 on: 1944 - No. 5, 1944; No. 6, Jan, 1948 - No. 33, Aug, 1952

nn(1944)(A-1 Comics)(slightly over-size) 37 74 111 218 354 490
2 21 42 63 124 202 280
3,4(1944) 17 34 51 103 162 220
5(1944)-Bondage headlight-c 54 108 162 343 574 825
6,8(1948): Lady Crime by Powell. 8-Bondage-c 14 28 42 80 115 150
7-Kubert-a; biog of Andriola (artist) 14 28 42 82 121 160
9,10-Two-part marijuana story; Kerry smokes marijuana in #10 16 32 48 96 151 215
11-15 11 22 33 60 83 115
16-33 9 18 27 52 69 85
NOTE: ***Andiola*** *c-6-9.* ***Berg*** *a-5.* ***Powell*** *a-10-23, 28, 29.*

KEVIN KELLER (Also see Veronica #202 for 1st app. & #207-210 for first mini-series)
Archie Comics Publications: Apr, 2012 - No. 15, Nov, 2014 ($2.99)

1-14-Two covers on each. 5-Action #1 swipe-c. 6-George Takei app. 3.00
15-($3.99) The Equalizer app.; 3 covers incl. Sensation #1 and X-Men #141 swipes 4.00

KEWPIES
Will Eisner Publications: Spring, 1949

1-Feiffer-a; Kewpie Doll ad on back cover; used in **SOTI**, pg. 35 68 136 204 435 743 1050

KEY COMICS
Consolidated Magazines: Jan, 1944 - No. 5, Aug, 1946

1-The Key, Will-O-The-Wisp begin 55 110 165 352 601 850
2 (3/44) 31 62 93 186 303 420
3,4: 3 (Winter 45/46). 4-(5/46)-Origin John Quincy The Atom (begins); Walter Johnson c-3-5 27 54 81 162 266 370
5-4pg. Faust Opera adaptation; Kiefer-a; back-c advertises "Masterpieces Illustrated" by Lloyd Jacquet after he left Classic Comics (no copies of Masterpieces Illustrated known) 35 70 105 208 339 470

KEY OF Z
BOOM! Studios: Oct, 2011 - No. 4, Jan, 2012 ($3.99, limited series)

1-4: 1-Claudio Sanchez & Chondra Echert-s/Aaron Kuder-a; covers by Fox & Moore 4.00

KEY RING COMICS
Dell Publishing Co.: 1941 (16 pgs.; two colors) (sold 5 for 10¢)

1-Sky Hawk, 1-Features Sleepy Samson, 1-Origin Greg Gilday; r/War Comics #2 16 32 48 98 154 210
1-Radior (Super hero) 19 38 57 111 176 240
1-Viking Carter (WWII Nazi-c) 19 38 57 111 176 240
NOTE: *Each book has two holes in spine to put in binder.*

KICK-ASS
Marvel Comics (Icon): April, 2008 - No. 8, Mar, 2010 ($2.99)

1-Mark Millar-s/John Romita Jr.-a/c 24.00
1-Red variant cover by McNiven 25.00
1-2nd printing 4.00
1-Director's Cut (8/08, $3.99) r/#1 with script and sketch pages; Millar afterword 5.00
2 8.00
3-8: 3-1st app. Hit-Girl. 5-Intro. Red Mist 4.00
NOTE: *Multiple printings exist for most issues.*

KICK-ASS
Image Comics: Feb, 2018 - No. 18, Oct, 2019 ($3.99)

1-18: 1-6-Mark Millar-s/John Romita Jr.-a/c. 1-Intro. Patience Lee. 7-18-Niles-s/Frusin-a 4.00

KICK-ASS 2
Marvel Comics (Icon): Dec, 2010 - No. 7, May, 2012 ($2.99/$4.99)

1-6-Mark Millar-s/John Romita Jr.-a/c. 1-Five printings 3.00
1-6-Variant covers. 1-Edwards. 2-Yu. 5-Photo & Hitch. 6-Photo-c 5.00
7-($4.99) Extra-sized finale; bonus preview of Secret Service #1 5.00
7-($4.99) Variant photo-c 7.00

KICK-ASS 3
Marvel Comics (Icon): Jul, 2013 - No. 8, Oct, 2014 ($2.99/$3.99/$4.99/$5.99)

1-5-($2.99) Mark Millar-s/John Romita Jr.-a/c 3.00
1-5-Variant covers. 1-Hughes. 2-Fegredo. 3-Mack. 5-Bond 5.00
6-($4.99) Secret origin of Hit-Girl 5.00
7-($3.99) 4.00
8-($5.99) 6.00

KICK-ASS VS. HIT-GIRL
Image Comics: Nov, 2020 - Present ($3.99)

1-4-Patience Lee vs. Mindy McCready; Niles-s/Frusin-a 4.00

Kid Colt Outlaw #6 © Z-D

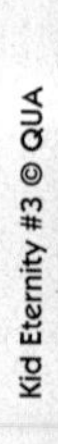
Kid Eternity #3 © QUA

Kid Komics #7 © MAR

KID CARROTS
St. John Publishing Co.: September, 1953

	GD 2.0	VG 4.0	FN 6.0	VF 8.0	VF/NM 9.0	NM- 9.2
1-Funny animal	11	22	33	62	86	110

KID COLT ONE-SHOT
Marvel Comics: Sept, 2009 ($3.99)

	GD 2.0	VG 4.0	FN 6.0	VF 8.0	VF/NM 9.0	NM- 9.2
1-DeFalco-s/Burchett-a/Luke Ross-c						4.00

KID COLT OUTLAW (Kid Colt #1-4; ...Outlaw #5-on)(Also see All Western Winners, Best Western, Black Rider, Giant-Size..., Two-Gun Kid, Two-Gun Western, Western Winners, Wild Western, Wisco)
Marvel Comics(LCC) 1-16; Atlas(LMC) 17-102; Marvel 103-on: 8/48 - No. 139, 3/68; No. 140, 11/69 - No. 229, 4/79

	GD 2.0	VG 4.0	FN 6.0	VF 8.0	VF/NM 9.0	NM- 9.2
1-Kid Colt & his horse Steel begin.	239	478	717	1530	2615	3700
2	97	194	291	621	1061	1500
3-5: 4-Anti-Wertham editorial; Tex Taylor app. 5-Blaze Carson app.	63	126	189	403	689	975
6-8: 6-Tex Taylor app; 7-Nimo the Lion begins, ends #10	41	82	123	256	428	600
9,10 (52 pgs.)	43	86	129	271	461	650
11-Origin (10/50)	45	90	135	284	480	675
12-20	28	56	84	165	270	375
21-32	23	46	69	136	223	310
33-45: Black Rider in all	20	40	60	115	188	260
46,47,49,50	18	36	54	109	172	235
48-Kubert-a	19	38	57	112	179	245
51-53,55,56	16	32	48	98	154	210
54-Williamson/Maneely-c	18	36	54	107	169	230
57-60,66: 4-pg. Williamson-a in all	10	20	30	68	144	220
61-63,67-78,80-86: 70-Severin-c. 69,73-Maneely-c. 86-Kirby-a(r).	10	20	30	68	138	210
64,65-Crandall-a	11	22	33	73	157	240
79,87: 79-Origin retold. 87-Davis-a(r)	10	20	30	68	144	220
88,89-Williamson-a in both (4 pgs.). 89-Redrawn Matt Slade #2	10	20	30	68	144	220
90-99,101-106,108,109: 91-Kirby/Ayers-c. 95-Kirby/Ayers-c/story. 102-Last 10¢ issue	12	24	36	81	176	270
100	15	30	45	105	233	360
107-Only Kirby sci-fi cover of title	38	76	114	285	641	1000
110-(5/63)-1st app. Iron Mask (Iron Man type villain)	15	30	45	105	233	360
111-113,115-120	9	18	27	60	120	180
114-(1/64)-2nd app. Iron Mask	12	24	36	79	170	260
121-129,133-139: 121-Rawhide Kid x-over. 125-Two-Gun Kid x-over. 139-Last 12¢ issue	6	12	18	40	73	105
130-132 (68 pgs.)-one new story each. 130-Origin	7	14	21	48	89	130
140-155: 140-Reprints begin (later issues mostly-r). 155-Last 15¢ issue	3	6	9	16	23	30
156-Giant; reprints (52 pgs.)	3	6	9	21	33	45
157-180,200: 170-Origin retold.	3	6	9	14	20	25
181-199	2	4	6	11	16	20
201-229: 201-New material w/Rawhide Kid app; Kane-c. 229-Rawhide Kid-r	2	4	6	10	14	18
205-209-(30¢-c variants, limited dist.)	12	24	36	79	170	260
218-220-(35¢-c variants, limited dist.)	21	42	63	147	324	500
...Album (no date; 1950's; Atlas Comics)-132 pgs.; cardboard cover, B&W stories; (Rare)	171	342	513	1094	1872	2650

NOTE: ***Ayers** a-many. **Colan** a-52, 53, 84, 112, 114; c(p)-223, 228, 229. **Crandall** a-140r, 167r. **Everett** a-90, 137i, 225i(r). **Heath** a-8(2); c-34, 35, 39, 44, 46, 48, 49, 57, 64. **Heck** a-135, 139. **Jack Keller** a-25(2), 26-68(3-4), 73, 78, 82, 84, 85, 88, 92, 94p, 98, 99, 101, 102, 106-130, 132, 140-150r. **Kirby** a-86r, 93, 96, 119, 176(part); c-87, 92-95, 97, 99-112, 114-117, 121-123, 197r; w/**Ditko** c-89. **Maneely** a-12, 68, 81; c-9, 17, 19, 40-43, 47, 52, 53, 62, 65, 68, 73, 78, 81, 142r, 150r. **Morrow** a-173r, 216r. **Rico** a-13, 18. **Severin** c-55, 58, 59, 84, 143, 148, 149i. **Shores** a-39, 41-43, 143r; c-1-10(most), 24. **Sutton** a-136, 137p, 225p(r). **Wildey** a-47, 54, 82, 144r. **Williamson** r-147, 170, 172, 216. **Woodbridge** a-64, 81. Black Rider in #33-45, 74, 86. Iron Mask in #110, 114, 121, 127. Sam Hawk in #80, 84, 101, 111, 121, 146, 174, 181, 188.*

KID COWBOY (Also see Approved Comics #4 & Boy Cowboy)
Ziff-Davis Publ./St. John (Approved Comics) #11,14: 1950 - No. 11, Wint, '52-'53; No. 13, April 1953; No. 14, June, 1954 (No #12) (Painted covers #1-10,13,14)

	GD 2.0	VG 4.0	FN 6.0	VF 8.0	VF/NM 9.0	NM- 9.2
1-Lucy Belle & Red Feather begin	22	44	66	128	209	290
2-Maneely-c	14	28	42	82	121	160
3-11,13,14: (#3, spr. '51). 5-Berg-a. 14-Code approved	14	28	42	76	108	140

KID DEATH & FLUFFY HALLOWEEN SPECIAL
Event Comics: Oct, 1997 ($2.95, B&W, one-shot)

	GD 2.0	VG 4.0	FN 6.0	VF 8.0	VF/NM 9.0	NM- 9.2
1-Variant-c by Cebollero & Quesada/Palmiotti						4.00

KID DEATH & FLUFFY SPRING BREAK SPECIAL
Event Comics: July, 1996 ($2.50, B&W, one-shot)

	GD 2.0	VG 4.0	FN 6.0	VF 8.0	VF/NM 9.0	NM- 9.2
1-Quesada & Palmiotti-c/scripts						4.00

KIDDIE KAPERS
Kiddie Kapers Co., 1945/Decker Publ. (Red Top-Farrell): 1945?(nd); Oct, 1957; 1963 - 1964

	GD 2.0	VG 4.0	FN 6.0	VF 8.0	VF/NM 9.0	NM- 9.2
1(nd, 1945-46?, 36 pgs.)-Infinity-c; funny animal	12	24	36	67	94	120
1(10/57)(Decker)-Little Bit-r from Kiddie Karnival	5	10	15	22	26	30
Super Reprint #7, 10('63), 12, 14('63), 15,17('64), 18('64): 10, 14-r/Animal Adventures #1. 15-Animal Advs. #? 17-Cowboys 'N' Injuns #?	2	4	6	8	11	14

KIDDIE KARNIVAL
Ziff-Davis Publ. Co. (Approved Comics): 1952 (25¢, 100 pgs.) (One Shot)

	GD 2.0	VG 4.0	FN 6.0	VF 8.0	VF/NM 9.0	NM- 9.2
nn-Rebound Little Bit #1,2; painted-c	39	78	117	236	388	540

KID ETERNITY (Becomes Buccaneers) (See Hit Comics)
Quality Comics Group: Spring, 1946 - No. 18, Nov, 1949

	GD 2.0	VG 4.0	FN 6.0	VF 8.0	VF/NM 9.0	NM- 9.2
1	90	180	270	576	988	1400
2	39	78	117	240	395	550
3-Mac Raboy-a	40	80	120	246	411	575
4-10	25	50	75	147	241	335
11-18	19	38	57	112	179	245

KID ETERNITY
DC Comics: 1991 - No. 3, Nov, 1991 ($4.95, limited series)

	GD 2.0	VG 4.0	FN 6.0	VF 8.0	VF/NM 9.0	NM- 9.2
1-3: Grant Morrison scripts/Duncan Fegredo-a/c						6.00
TPB (2006, $14.99) r/#1-3						15.00

KID ETERNITY
DC Comics (Vertigo): May, 1993 - No. 16, Sept, 1994 ($1.95, mature)

	GD 2.0	VG 4.0	FN 6.0	VF 8.0	VF/NM 9.0	NM- 9.2
1-16: 1-Gold ink-c. 6-Photo-c. All Sean Phillips-c/a except #15 (Phillips-c/i only)						3.00

KID FROM DODGE CITY, THE
Atlas Comics (MMC): July, 1957 - No. 2, Sept, 1957

	GD 2.0	VG 4.0	FN 6.0	VF 8.0	VF/NM 9.0	NM- 9.2
1-Don Heck-c	15	30	45	90	140	190
2-Everett-c	12	24	36	69	97	125

KID FROM TEXAS, THE (A Texas Ranger)
Atlas Comics (CSI): June, 1957 - No. 2, Aug, 1957

	GD 2.0	VG 4.0	FN 6.0	VF 8.0	VF/NM 9.0	NM- 9.2
1-Powell-a; Severin-c	15	30	45	85	130	175
2	11	22	33	60	83	105

KID KOKO
I. W. Enterprises: 1958

	GD 2.0	VG 4.0	FN 6.0	VF 8.0	VF/NM 9.0	NM- 9.2
Reprint #1,2-(r/M.E.'s Koko & Kola #4, 1947)	2	4	6	8	11	14

KID KOMICS (Kid Movie Komics No. 11)
Timely Comics (USA 1,2/FCI 3-10): Feb, 1943 - No. 10, Spring, 1946

	GD 2.0	VG 4.0	FN 6.0	VF 8.0	VF/NM 9.0	NM- 9.2
1-Origin Captain Wonder & sidekick Tim Mullrooney, & Subbie; intro the Sea-Going Lad, Pinto Pete, & Trixie Trouble; Knuckles & Whitewash Jones (from Young Allies) app.; Wolverton-a (7 pgs.)	625	1250	1875	4500	8250	12,000
2-The Young Allies, Red Hawk, & Tommy Tyme begin; last Captain Wonder & Subbie; Schomburg Japanese WWII bondage-c	300	600	900	1920	3310	4700
3-The Vision, Daredevils & Red Hawk app.	206	412	618	1318	2259	3200
4-The Destroyer begins; Sub-Mariner app.; Red Hawk & Tommy Tyme end; classic Schomburg WWII human meat grinder-c	271	542	813	1734	2967	4200
5,6: 5-Tommy Tyme begins, ends #10	129	258	387	826	1413	2000
7-10: 7,10-The Whizzer app. Destroyer not in #7,8. 10-Last Destroyer, Young Allies & Whizzer	113	226	339	723	1237	1750

NOTE: ***Brodsky** c-5. **Schomburg** c-2-4, 6-10. **Shores** c-1. Captain Wonder c-1, 2. The Young Allies c-3-10.*

KID LOBOTOMY
IDW Publishing (Black Crown): Oct, 2017 - No. 6, Mar, 2018 ($3.99)

	GD 2.0	VG 4.0	FN 6.0	VF 8.0	VF/NM 9.0	NM- 9.2
1-6: 1-Milligan-s/Fowler-a; covers by Fowler & Quitely						4.00

KID MONTANA (Formerly Davy Crockett Frontier Fighter; The Gunfighters No. 51 on)
Charlton Comics: V2#9, Nov, 1957 - No. 50, Mar, 1965

	GD 2.0	VG 4.0	FN 6.0	VF 8.0	VF/NM 9.0	NM- 9.2
V2#9 (#1)	4	8	12	27	44	60
10	3	6	9	19	30	40
11,12,14-20	3	6	9	15	22	28
13-Williamson-a	3	6	9	19	30	40
21-35: 25,31-Giordano-c. 32-Origin Kid Montana. 34-Geronimo-c/s. 35-Snow Monster-c/s	2	4	6	11	16	20
36-50: 36-Dinosaur-c/s. 37,48-Giordano-c	2	4	6	9	12	15

NOTE: *Title change to Montana Kid on cover only #44 & 45; remained Kid Montana on inside. **Chasal** a-29,30. **Giordano** c-25,31,37,48. **Giordano/Alascia** c-12. **Mastroserio** a-9,11,13,14,22; c-11,14. **Masulli/Mastroserio** c-13. **Montes/Bache** c-42. **Morisi** c-16,32-34,36?,40,41,44,46; a-13,15;16,31-50. **Nicholas/Alascia** a-44,48.*

KID MOVIE KOMICS (Formerly Kid Komics; Rusty Comics #12 on)
Timely Comics: No. 11, Summer, 1946

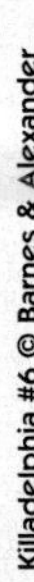
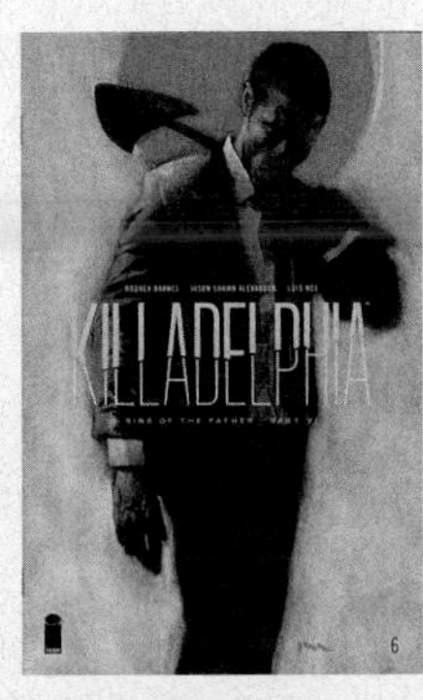

Killadelphia #6 © Barnes & Alexander

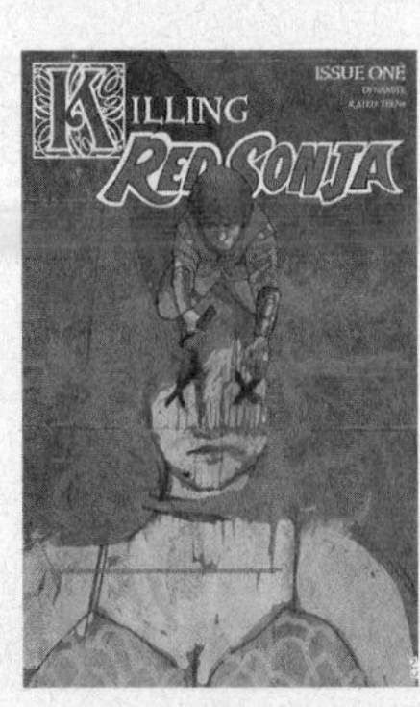

Killing Red Sonja #1 © RS LLC

Kin #6 © Gary Frank

	GD	VG	FN	VF	VF/NM	NM-
	2.0	4.0	6.0	8.0	9.0	9.2

11-Silly Seal & Ziggy Pig; 2 pgs. Kurtzman "Hey Look" plus 6 pg. "Pigtales" story 34 68 102 199 325 450

KIDNAPPED (See Marvel Illustrated: Kidnapped)

KIDNAPPED (Robert Louis Stevenson's...also see Movie Comics)(Disney)
Dell Publishing Co.: No. 1101, May, 1960

Four Color 1101-Movie, photo-c 6 12 18 37 66 95

KIDNAP RACKET (See Harvey Comics Hits No. 57)

KID SLADE, GUNFIGHTER (Formerly Matt Slade...)
Atlas Comics (SPI): No. 5, Jan, 1957 - No. 8, July, 1957

5-Maneely, Roth, Severin-a in all; Maneely-c 15 30 45 84 127 170
6,8-Severin-c 11 22 33 60 83 105
7-Williamson/Mayo-a, 4 pgs.; Maneely-c 13 26 39 72 101 130

KID SUPREME (See Supreme)
Image Comics (Extreme Studios): Mar, 1996 - No. 3, July, 1996 ($2.50)

1-3: Fraga-a/scripts. 3-Glory-c/app. 3.00

KID ZOO COMICS
Street & Smith Publications: July, 1948 (52 pgs.)

1-Funny Animal 34 68 102 199 325 450

KILLADELPHIA
Image Comics: Nov, 2019 - Present ($3.99)

1-12-Philadelphia vampires; Rodney Barnes-s/Jason Shawn Alexander-a/c 4.00

KILL ALL PARENTS
Image Comics: June, 2008 ($3.99, one-shot)

1-Marcelo Di Chiara-a/Mark Andrew Smith-s 4.00

KILLAPALOOZA
DC Comics (WildStorm): July, 2009 - No. 6, Dec, 2009 ($2.99, limited series)

1-6: 1-Beechen-s/Hairsine-a/c 3.00
TPB (2010, $19.99) r/#1-6 20.00

KILLER (...Tales By Timothy Truman)
Eclipse Comics: March, 1985 ($1.75, one-shot, Baxter paper)

1-Timothy Truman-c/a 4.00

KILLER INSTINCT (Video game)
Acclaim Comics: June, 1996 - No. 6 ($2.50, limited series)

1-6: 1-Bart Sears-a(p). 4-Special #1. 5-Special #2. 6-Special #3 4.00

KILLER INSTINCT (Video game)
Dynamite Entertainment: 2017 - No. 6, 2018 ($3.99, limited series)

1-6: 1,2-Ian Edginton-s/Cam Adams-a; multiple covers. 3-6-Ediano Silva-a 4.00

KILLERS
Valiant Entertainment: Jul, 2019 - No. 5, Nov, 2019 ($3.99, limited series)

1-5-B. Clay Moore-s/Fernando Dagnino-a; origin of KI-6 4.00

KILLERS, THE
Magazine Enterprises: 1947 - No. 2, 1948 (No month)

1-Mr. Zin, the Hatchet Killer; mentioned in **SOTI**, pgs. 179,180; used by N.Y. Legis. Comm.; L. B. Cole-c 168 336 504 1075 1838 2600
2-(Scarce)-Hashish smoking story; "Dying, Dying, Dead" drug story; Whitney, Ingels-a; Whitney hanging-c 135 270 405 864 1482 2100

KILLING GIRL
Image Comics: Aug, 2007 - No. 5, Dec, 2007 ($2.99, limited series)

1-5: 1-Frank Espinosa-a/Glen Brunswick-s; covers by Espinosa and Frank Cho 3.00

KILLING JOKE, THE (See Batman: The Killing Joke under Batman one-shots)

KILLING RED SONJA, VOLUME 1 (Follows Red Sonja Volume 5 #12)
Dynamite Entertainment: 2020 - No. 5, 2020 ($3.99)

1-5-Russell & Ingman-s/Rousseau-a. 4-Sorcerors of Wigur-Nomadene app. 4.00

KILL LOCK, THE
IDW Publishing: Dec, 2019 - Present ($3.99)

1-3-Livio Ramondelli-s/a 4.00

KILLMONGER (From Black Panther)
Marvel Comics: Feb, 2019 - No. 5, May, 2019 ($4.99/$3.99, limited series)

1-($4.99) Bryan Hill-s/Juan Ferreyra-a; N'Jadaka's rise to Killmonger; Kingpin app. 5.00
2-5-($3.99) 2,3-Bullseye app. 3-5-Black Widow app. 4.00

KILL OR BE KILLED
Image Comics: Aug, 2016 - No. 20, Jun, 2018 ($3.99)

1-20-Ed Brubaker-s/Sean Phillips-a 4.00

KILLPOWER: THE EARLY YEARS
Marvel Comics UK: Sept, 1993 - No. 4, Dec, 1993 ($1.75, mini-series)

1-($2.95)-Foil embossed-c 4.00
2-4: 2-Genetix app. 3-Punisher app. 3.00

KILLRAVEN (See Amazing Adventures #18 (5/73))
Marvel Comics: Feb, 2001 ($2.99, one-shot)

1-Linsner-s/a/c 3.00

KILLRAVEN
Marvel Comics: Dec, 2002 - No. 6, May, 2003 ($2.99, limited series)

1-6-Alan Davis-s/a(p)/Mark Farmer-i 3.00
HC (2007, $19.99) r/#1-6; cover gallery, pencil art; foreward by Alan Davis 20.00

KILLRAZOR
Image Comics (Top Cow Productions): Aug, 1995 ($2.50, one-shot)

1 3.00

KILL WHITEY DONOVAN
Dark Horse Comics: Dec, 2019 - No. 5, Apr, 2020 ($3.99, limited series)

1-5-Sydney Duncan-s/Natalie Barahona-a; 2 covers by Pearson and Barahona 4.00

KILL YOUR BOYFRIEND
DC Comics (Vertigo): June, 1995 ($4.95, one-shot)

1-Grant Morrison story 6.00
1 ($5.95, 1998) 2nd printing 6.00

KILROY (Volume 2)
Caliber Press: 1998 ($2.95, B&W)

1-Pruett-s 3.00

KILROY IS HERE
Caliber Press: 1995 ($2.95, B&W)

1-10 3.00

KILROYS, THE
B&I Publ. Co. No. 1-19/American Comics Group: June-July, 1947 - No. 54, June-July, 1955

1 28 56 84 168 274 380
2 15 30 45 92 144 195
3-5: 5-Gross-a 15 30 45 83 124 165
6-10: 8-Milt Gross's Moronica (1st app.) 12 24 36 69 97 125
11-20: 14-Gross-a 10 20 30 56 76 95
21-30 9 18 27 52 69 85
31-47,50-54 9 18 27 47 61 75
48,49-(3-D effect-c/stories) 19 38 57 112 179 245

KILROY: THE SHORT STORIES
Caliber Press: 1995 ($2.95, B&W)

1 3.00

KIM REAPER
Oni Press: Apr, 2017 - No. 4, Jul, 2017 ($3.99, limited series)

1-4-Sarah Graley-s/a/c 4.00

KIM REAPER: VAMPIRE ISLAND
Oni Press: Sept, 2018 - No. 4, Nov, 2018 ($3.99, limited series)

1-4-Sarah Graley-s/a/c 4.00

KIN
Image Comics (Top Cow): Mar, 2000 - No. 6, Sept, 2000 ($2.95)

1-5-Gary Frank-s/c/a 3.00
1-($6.95) DF Alternate footprint cover 7.00
6-($3.95) 4.00
... Descent of Man TPB (2002, $19.95) r/ #1-6 20.00

KINDRED, THE
Image Comics (WildStorm Productions): Mar, 1994 - No. 4, July, 1995 ($1.95, lim. series)

1-($2.50)-Grifter & Backlash app. in all; bound-in trading card 4.00
2-4 3.00
2,3: 2-Variant-c. 3-Alternate-c by Portacio, see Deathblow #5 4.00
Trade paperback (2/95, $9.95) 10.00
NOTE: *Booth c/a-1-4. The first four issues contain coupons redeemable for a Jim Lee Grifter/Backlash print.*

KINDRED II, THE
DC Comics (WildStorm): Mar, 2002 - No. 4, June, 2002 ($2.50, limited series)

1-4-Booth-s/Booth & Regla-a 3.00

KINETIC
DC Comics (Focus): May, 2004 - No. 8, Dec, 2004 ($2.50)

1-8-Puckett-s/Pleece-a/c 3.00

King Comics #23 © DMP

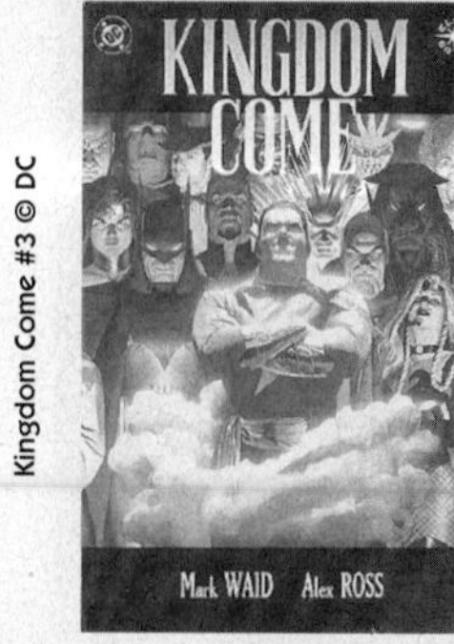

Kingdom Come #3 © DC

King in Black #1 © MAR

	GD 2.0	VG 4.0	FN 6.0	VF 8.0	VF/NM 9.0	NM- 9.2
TPB (2005, $9.99) r/#1-8; cover gallery and sketch pages						10.00

KING (Magazine)
Skywald Publ.: Mar, 1971 - No. 2, July, 1971

	GD	VG	FN	VF	VF/NM	NM-
1-Violence; semi-nudity; Boris Vallejo-a (2 pgs.)	5	10	15	31	53	75
2-Photo-c	3	6	9	21	33	45

KING ARTHUR AND THE KNIGHTS OF JUSTICE
Marvel Comics UK: Dec, 1993 - No. 3, Feb, 1994 ($1.25, limited series)

	GD	VG	FN	VF	VF/NM	NM-
1-3: TV adaptation						3.00

KING CLASSICS
King Features : 1977 (36 pgs., cardboard-c) (Printed in Spain for U.S. distr.)

1-Connecticut Yankee, 2-Last of the Mohicans, 3-Moby Dick, 4-Robin Hood, 5-Swiss Family Robinson, 6-Robinson Crusoe, 7-Treasure Island, 8-20,000 Leagues, 9-Christmas Carol, 10-Huck Finn, 11-Around the World in 80 Days, 12-Davy Crockett, 13-Don Quixote, 14-Gold Bug, 15-Ivanhoe, 16-Three Musketeers, 17-Baron Munchausen, 18-Alice in Wonderland, 19-Black Arrow, 20-Five Weeks in a Balloon, 21-Great Expectations, 22-Gulliver's Travels, 23-Prince & Pauper, 24-Lawrence of Arabia (Originals, 1977-78)

	GD	VG	FN	VF	VF/NM	NM-
each....	2	4	6	10	14	18
Reprints (1979; HRN-24)	2	4	6	8	10	12

NOTE: *The first eight issues were not numbered. Issues No. 25-32 were advertised but not published. The 1977 originals have HRN 32a; the 1978 originals have HRN 32b.*

KING COLT (See Luke Short's Western Stories)

KING COMICS (Strip reprints)
David McKay Publications/Standard #156-on: 4/36 - No. 155, 11-12/49; No. 156, Spr/50 - No. 159, 2/52 (Winter on-c)

	GD	VG	FN	VF	VF/NM	NM-
1-1st app. Flash Gordon by Alex Raymond; Brick Bradford (1st app.), Popeye, Henry (1st app.) & Mandrake the Magician (1st app.) begin; Popeye-c begin	1550	3100	4650	12,400	--	--
2	360	720	1080	1980	3040	4100
3	248	496	744	1364	2132	2900
4	196	392	588	1078	1689	2300
5	141	282	423	776	1213	1650
6-10: 9-X-Mas-c	98	196	294	539	845	1150
11-20	75	150	225	413	644	875
21-30: 21-X-Mas-c	55	110	165	303	477	650
31-40: 33-Last Segar Popeye	45	90	135	248	404	560
41-50: 46-Text illos by Marge Buell contain characters similar to Lulu, Alvin & Tubby. 50-The Lone Ranger begins	36	72	108	211	343	475
51-60: 52-Barney Baxter begins?	34	68	102	199	325	450
61-The Phantom begins	34	68	102	204	332	460
62-80: 76-Flag-c. 79-Blondie begins	20	40	60	114	182	250
81-99	15	30	45	85	130	175
100	18	36	54	103	162	220
101-114: 114-Last Raymond issue (1 pg.); Flash Gordon by Austin Briggs begins, ends #155	14	28	42	76	108	140
115-145: 117-Phantom origin retold	10	20	30	56	76	95
146,147-Prince Valiant in both	9	18	27	50	65	80
148-155: 155-Flash Gordon ends (11-12/49)	9	18	27	50	65	80
156-159: 156-New logo begins (Standard)	9	18	27	47	61	75

NOTE: *Marge Buell text illos in No. 24-46 at least.*

KING CONAN (Conan The King No. 20 on)
Marvel Comics Group: Mar, 1980 - No. 19, Nov, 1983 (52 pgs.)

	GD	VG	FN	VF	VF/NM	NM-
1	2	4	6	11	16	20
2-19: 4-Death of Thoth Amon. 7-1st Paul Smith-a, 1 pg. pin-up (9/81)						5.00

NOTE: ***J. Buscema** a-1-9p, 17p; c(p)-1-5, 7-9, 14, 17. **Kaluta** c-19. **Nebres** a-17i, 18, 19i. **Severin** c-18. **Simonson** c-6.*

KING CONAN: THE CONQUEROR
Dark Horse Comics: Feb, 2014 - No. 6, Jul, 2014 ($3.50, limited series)

	GD	VG	FN	VF	VF/NM	NM-
1-6-Truman-s/Giorello-a/c						3.50

KING CONAN: THE HOUR OF THE DRAGON
Dark Horse Comics: May, 2013 - No. 6, Oct, 2013 ($3.50, limited series)

	GD	VG	FN	VF	VF/NM	NM-
1-6-Truman-s/Giorello-a/Parel-c						3.50

KING CONAN: THE PHOENIX ON THE SWORD
Dark Horse Comics: Jan, 2012 - No. 4, Apr, 2012 ($3.50, limited series)

	GD	VG	FN	VF	VF/NM	NM-
1-4-Truman-s/Giorello-a/Robinson-c. 1-Variant-c by Parel						3.50

KING CONAN: THE SCARLET CITADEL
Dark Horse Comics: Feb, 2011 - No. 4, May, 2011 ($3.50, limited series)

	GD	VG	FN	VF	VF/NM	NM-
1-4-Truman-s/Giorello-a/Robertson-c. 1-Variant-c by Parel						3.50

KING CONAN: WOLVES BEYOND THE BORDER
Dark Horse Comics: Dec, 2015 - No. 4, Mar, 2016 ($3.99, limited series)

	GD	VG	FN	VF	VF/NM	NM-
1-4-Truman-s/Giorello-a/c. 1-Kull app. 4-Bran Mak Morn app.						4.00

KING DAVID
DC Comics (Vertigo): 2002 ($19.95, 8 1/2" x 11")

	GD	VG	FN	VF	VF/NM	NM-
nn-Story of King David; Kyle Baker-s/a						20.00

KINGDOM, THE
DC Comics: Feb, 1999 - No. 2, Feb, 1999 ($2.95/$1.99, limited series)

	GD	VG	FN	VF	VF/NM	NM-
1,2-Waid-s; sequel to Kingdom Come; introduces Hypertime						4.00
...: Kid Flash 1 (2/99, $1.99) Waid-s/Pararillo-a, ...: Nightstar 1 (2/99, $1.99) Waid-s/Haley-a, ...: Offspring 1 (2/99, $1.99) Waid-s/Quitely-a, ...: Planet Krypton 1 (2/99, $1.99) Waid-s/ Kitson-a, ...: Son of the Bat 1 (2/99, $1.99) Waid-s/Apthorp-a						3.00

KINGDOM COME (Also see Justice Society of America #9-22)
DC Comics: 1996 - No. 4, 1996 ($4.95, painted limited series)

	GD	VG	FN	VF	VF/NM	NM-
1-Mark Waid scripts & Alex Ross-painted c/a in all; tells the last days of the DC Universe; 1st app. Magog	2	4	6	10	14	18
2-Superman forms new Justice League	2	4	6	9	13	16
3-Return of Captain Marvel	2	4	6	8	10	12
4-Final battle of Superman and Captain Marvel	2	4	6	8	11	14
Deluxe Slipcase Edition-($89.95) w/Revelations companion book, 12 new story pages, foil stamped covers, signed and numbered						120.00
Hardcover Edition-($29.95)-Includes 12 new story pages and artwork from Revelations, new cover artwork with gold foil inlay						40.00
Hardcover 2nd printing						30.00
Softcover Ed.-($14.95)-Includes 12 new story pgs. & artwork from Revelations, new c-artwork						20.00
Softcover Ed.-(2008, $17.99)-New wraparound gatefold cover by Ross						18.00

KING: FLASH GORDON
Dynamite Entertainment: 2015 - No. 4, 2015 ($3.99)

	GD	VG	FN	VF	VF/NM	NM-
1-4: 1-Acker & Blacker-s/Ferguson-a/Cooke-c; variant-c by Liefeld. 2-Zdarsky-c						4.00

KING IN BLACK (See Venom and Knull: Marvel Tales)
Marvel Comics: Feb, 2021 - No. 5 ($5.99/$4.99)

	GD	VG	FN	VF	VF/NM	NM-
1-($5.99) Cates-s/Stegman-a; Knull arrives on Earth; Venom & the Avengers app.						6.00
2-4-($4.99) 2-Namor & Spider-Man app. 3-Thor returns. 4-Enigma Force app.						5.00
...: Black Panther 1 (4/21, $4.99) Thorne-s/Peralta-a; Shuri & Storm app.						5.00
...: Immortal Hulk 1 (2/21, $4.99) Ewing-s/Kuder-a; Savage Hulk vs. symbiotes						5.00
...: Iron Man/Doom 1 (2/21, $3.99) Cantwell-s/Larroca-a; battle a symbiote Santa Claus						4.00

KING IN BLACK: GWENOM VS. CARNAGE
Marvel Comics: Mar, 2021 - No. 3 ($3.99, limited series)

	GD	VG	FN	VF	VF/NM	NM-
1-McGuire-s/Flaviano-a; Ghost-Spider & Mary Jane Watson app.						4.00

KING IN BLACK: NAMOR
Marvel Comics: Feb, 2021 - No. 5 ($3.99, limited series)

	GD	VG	FN	VF	VF/NM	NM-
1-4-Busiek-s/Dewey-a; flashback to Namor's youth						4.00

KING IN BLACK: PLANET OF THE SYMBIOTES
Marvel Comics: Mar, 2021 - No. 3 ($3.99, limited series)

	GD	VG	FN	VF	VF/NM	NM-
1,2-Scream app.; Knull attacks Ravencroft; Misty Knight & John Jameson app.						4.00

KING IN BLACK: RETURN OF THE VALKYRIES
Marvel Comics: Feb, 2021 - No. 4 ($3.99, limited series)

	GD	VG	FN	VF	VF/NM	NM-
1-3-Aaron & Gronbekk-s/Vakueva-a; Jane Foster, The Sentry & Dani Moonstar app.						4.00

KING IN BLACK: THUNDERBOLTS
Marvel Comics: Mar, 2021 - No. 3 ($3.99, limited series)

	GD	VG	FN	VF	VF/NM	NM-
1,2-Rosenberg-s/Ferreyra-a; Star, Rhino, Batroc, Taskmaster app.						4.00

KING: JUNGLE JIM
Dynamite Entertainment: 2015 - No. 4, 2015 ($3.99)

	GD	VG	FN	VF	VF/NM	NM-
1-4: 1-Tobin-s/Jarrell-a/Cooke-c; variant-c by Liefeld. 2-Zdarsky-c						4.00

KING KONG (See Movie Comics)

KING KONG: THE 8TH WONDER OF THE WORLD (Adaptation of 2005 movie)
Dark Horse Comics: Dec, 2005 ($3.99, planned limited series completed in TPB)

	GD	VG	FN	VF	VF/NM	NM-
1-Photo-c; Dustin Weaver-a/Christian Gossett-s						4.00
TPB (11/06, $12.95) r/#1 and unpublished parts 2&3; photo-c; Dorman paintings						13.00

KING LEONARDO & HIS SHORT SUBJECTS (TV)
Dell Publishing Co./Gold Key: Nov-Jan, 1961-62 - No. 4, Sept, 1963

	GD	VG	FN	VF	VF/NM	NM-
Four Color 1242,1278	10	20	30	67	141	215
01390-207(5-7/62)(Dell)	8	16	24	52	99	145
1 (10/62)	9	18	27	60	120	180
2-4	7	14	21	48	89	130

KING LOUIE & MOWGLI (See Jungle Book under Movie Comics)
Gold Key: May, 1968 (Disney)

	GD	VG	FN	VF	VF/NM	NM-
1 (#10223-805)-Characters from Jungle Book	3	6	9	21	33	45

Kingpin #1 © MAR

King Thor #1 © MAR

KISS, Blood and Stardust #1 © KISS Catalog

	GD 2.0	VG 4.0	FN 6.0	VF 8.0	VF/NM 9.0	NM- 9.2

KING: MANDRAKE THE MAGICIAN
Dynamite Entertainment: 2015 - No. 4, 2015 ($3.99)
1-4: 1-Langridge-s/Treece-a/Cooke-c; variant-c by Liefeld. 2-Zdarsky-c 4.00

KING OF DIAMONDS (TV)
Dell Publishing Co.: July-Sept, 1962
01-391-209-Photo-c 4 8 12 25 40 55

KING OF KINGS (Movie)
Dell Publishing Co.: No. 1236, Oct-Nov, 1961
Four Color 1236-Photo-c 7 14 21 46 86 125

KING OF NOWHERE
BOOM! Studios: Mar, 2020 - No. 5, Sept, 2020 ($3.99, limited series)
1-5-W. Maxwell Prince-s/Tyler Jenkins-a 4.00

KING OF THE BAD MEN OF DEADWOOD
Avon Periodicals: 1950 (See Wild Bill Hickok #16)
nn-Kinstler-c; Kamen/Feldstein-r/Cowpuncher #2 21 42 63 122 199 275

KING OF THE ROYAL MOUNTED (See Famous Feature Stories, King Comics, Red Ryder #3 & Super Book #2, 6)

KING OF THE ROYAL MOUNTED (Zane Grey's...)
David McKay/Dell Publishing Co.: No. 1, May, 1937; No. 9, 1940; No. 207, Dec, 1948 - No. 935, Sept-Nov, 1958

	GD	VG	FN	VF	VF/NM	NM-
Feature Books 1 (5/37)(McKay)	110	220	330	704	1202	1700
Large Feature Comic 9 (1940)	54	108	162	343	574	825
Four Color 207(#1, 12/48)	13	26	39	89	195	300
Four Color 265,283	9	18	27	60	120	180
Four Color 310,340	7	14	21	46	86	125
Four Color 363,384, 8(6-8/52)-10	6	12	18	40	73	105
11-20	5	10	15	31	53	75
21-28(3-5/58)	4	8	12	27	44	60
Four Color 935(9-11/58)	5	10	15	31	53	75

NOTE: *4-Color No. 207, 265, 283, 310, 340, 363, 384 are all newspaper reprints with* ***Jim Gary*** *art. No. 8 on are all Dell originals. Painted c-No. 9-on.*

KINGPIN
Marvel Comics: Nov, 1997 ($5.99, squarebound, one-shot)
nn-Spider-Man & Daredevil vs. Kingpin; Stan Lee-s/ John Romita Sr.-a 6.00

KINGPIN
Marvel Comics: Aug, 2003 - No. 7, Jan, 2004 ($2.50/$2.99, limited series)
1-6-Bruce Jones-s/Sean Phillips & Klaus Janson-a 3.00
7-($2.99) 3.00

KINGPIN
Marvel Comics: Apr, 2017 - No. 5, Aug, 2017 ($3.99, limited series)
1-Wilson Fisk goes legit; Matthew Rosenberg-s/Ben Torres-a. 2-5-Tombstone app. 4.00

KING: PRINCE VALIANT
Dynamite Entertainment: 2015 - No. 4, 2015 ($3.99)
1-4: 1-Cosby-s/Salasl-a/Cooke-c; variant-c by Liefeld. 2-Zdarsky-c 4.00

KING RICHARD & THE CRUSADERS
Dell Publishing Co.: No. 588, Oct, 1954
Four Color 588-Movie, Matt Baker-a, photo-c 9 18 27 60 120 180

KING-SIZE CABLE SPECTACULAR (Takes place between Cable (2008 series) #6 & #7)
Marvel Comics: Nov, 2008 ($4.99, one-shot)
1-Lashley-a; Deadpool #1 preview; cover gallery of variants from 2008 series 5.00

KING-SIZE CONAN
Marvel Comics: Feb, 2021 ($6.99, one-shot)
1-Short stories by various incl. Roy Thomas, Eastman, Busiek, McNiven, Woods 7.00

KING-SIZE HULK (Takes place between Hulk (2008 series) #3 & #4)
Marvel Comics: July, 2008 ($4.99, one-shot)
1-Art Adams, Frank Cho, & Herb Trimpe-a; double-c by Cho & Adams; Red Hulk, She-Hulk & Wendigo app.; origin Abomination; r/Incr. Hulk #180,181 & Avengers #83 5.00

KING-SIZE SPIDER-MAN SUMMER SPECIAL
Marvel Comics: Oct, 2008 ($4.99, one-shot)
1-Short stories by various; Falcon app.; Burchett, Giarrusso & Coover-a 5.00

KINGSMEN: THE RED DIAMOND (Sequel to Secret Service)(Inspired Kingsmen movies)
Image Comics: Sept, 2017 - No. 6, Feb, 2018 ($3.99, limited series)
1-6-Rob Willliams-s/Simon Fraser-a. 1-Multiple covers 4.00

KINGS OF THE NIGHT
Dark Horse Comics: 1990 - No. 2, 1990 ($2.25, limited series)
1,2-Robert E. Howard adaptation; Bolton-c 3.00

KING SOLOMON'S MINES (Movie)
Avon Periodicals: 1951
nn (#1 on 1st page) 50 100 150 215 533 750

KINGS QUEST
Dynamite Entertainment: 2016 - No. 5, 2016 ($3.99, limited series)
1-5-Flash Gordon, Mandrake, Prince Valiant, The Phantom team; multiple-c on each 4.00

KING'S ROAD
Dark Horse Comics: Feb, 2016 - No. 3, Apr, 2016 ($3.99, limited series)
1-3-Peter Hogan-s/Phil Winslade & Staz Johnson-a; Johnson-c 4.00

KINGS WATCH
Dynamite Entertainment: 2013 - No. 5, 2014 ($3.99)
1-5-Flash Gordon, Mandrake and The Phantom team up; Parker-s/Laming-a 4.00

KINGSWAY WEST
Dark Horse Comics: Aug, 2016 - No. 4, Feb, 2017 ($3.99)
1-4-Greg Pak-s/Mirko Colak-a/c 4.00

KING TANK GIRL
Albatross Funnybooks: 2020 - No. 5 ($3.99, limited series)
1-3-Alan Martin-s/Brett Parson-a; Tank Girl and crew go to England 4.00

KING: THE PHANTOM
Dynamite Entertainment: 2015 - No. 4, 2015 ($3.99)
1-4: 1-Clevinger-s/Schoonover-a/Cooke-c; var-c by Liefeld; Mandrake app. 2-Zdarsky-c 4.00

KING THOR
Marvel Comics: Nov, 2019 - No. 4, Feb, 2020 ($3.99/$5.99, limited series)
1-3-($3.99) Jason Aaron-s/Esad Ribic-a; set in the far future; Frigg, Ellisiv & Atli app. 4.00
4-($5.99) Leads into 2020 Thor series; art by Ribic, Del Mundo, Coipel & others 6.00

KING TIGER
Dark Horse Comics: Aug, 2015 - No. 4, Nov, 2015 ($3.99, limited series)
1-4-Randy Stradley-s/Doug Wheatley-a/c 4.00

KIPLING, RUDYARD (See Mowgli, The Jungle Book)

KIRBY: GENESIS
Dynamite Entertainment: No. 0, 2011 - No. 8, 2012 ($1.00/$3.99)
0-($1.00) Busiek-s; art by Alex Ross & Jack Herbert; series preview, sketch-a 3.00
1-8-($3.99) Ross & Herbert-a. 1-Seven covers. 2-8-Covers by Ross & Sook 4.00

KIRBY: GENESIS - CAPTAIN VICTORY
Dynamite Entertainment: 2011 - No. 6, 2012 ($3.99)
1-6: 1-Origin retold; four covers; Sterling Gates-s/Wagner Reis-a 4.00

KIRBY: GENESIS - DRAGONSBANE
Dynamite Entertainment: 2012 - No. 4, 2013 ($3.99, unfinished limited series)
1-4-Rodi & Ross-s/Casas-a; covers by Ross and Herbert 4.00

KIRBY: GENESIS - SILVER STAR
Dynamite Entertainment: 2011 - No. 6, 2012 ($3.99)
1-6-Jai Nitz-s/Johnny Desjardins-a. 1-Four covers. 2-6-Three covers 4.00

KISS (See Crazy Magazine, Howard the Duck #12, 13, Marvel Comics Super Special #1, 5, Rock Fantasy Comics #10 & Rock N' Roll Comics #9)

KISS
Dark Horse Comics: June, 2002 - No. 13, Sept, 2003 ($2.99, limited series)
1-Photo-c and J. Scott Campbell-c; Casey-s 5.00
2-13: 2-Photo-c and J. Scott Campbell-c. 3-Photo-c and Leinil Yu-c 4.00
...: Men and Monsters TPB (9/03, $12.95) r/#7-10 13.00
...: Rediscovery TPB (2003, $9.95) r/#1-3 10.00
...: Return of the Phantom TPB (2003, $9.95) r/#4-6 10.00
...: Unholy War TPB (2004, $9.95) r/#11-13 10.00

KISS
IDW Publishing: June, 2012 - No. 8, Jan, 2013 ($3.99)
1-8-Multiple covers on each. 1,2-Ryall-s/Igle-a 4.00

KISS (Volume 1)
Dynamite Entertainment: 2016 - No. 10, 2017 ($3.99)
1-10-Amy Chu-s/Kewber Baal-a; multiple covers 4.00
...: Blood and Stardust 1-5 (2018 - No. 5, 2019, $3.99) Bryan Hill-s/Rodney Buscemi-a 4.00
...: Forever (2017, $7.99, squarebound) Burnham-s/Daniel HDR-a/Cinar-c 8.00
...: The Demon 1-4 (2017, $3.99) prequel to 2016 series; Chu & Burnham-s/Casallos-a 4.00

KISS 4K
Platinum Studios Comics: May, 2007 - No. 6, Apr, 2008 ($3.99/$2.99)

Kiss Kiss Bang Bang #2 © CRO

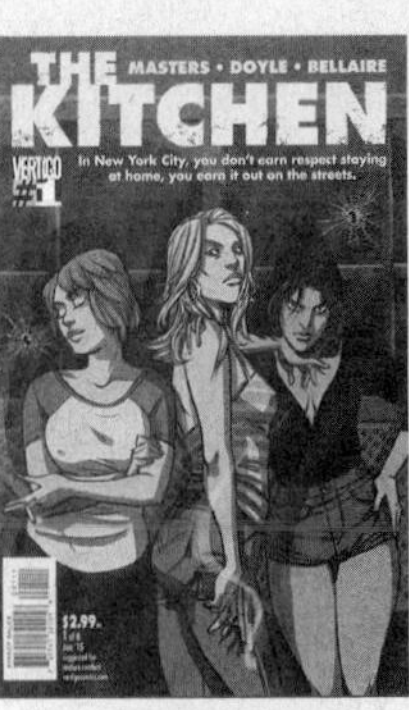

The Kitchen #1 © Masters & Doyle

Klaws of the Panther #4 © MAR

GD 2.0 | VG 4.0 | FN 6.0 | VF 8.0 | VF/NM 9.0 | NM- 9.2

1-Sprague-s/Crossley & Campos-a/Migliari-c 4.00
1-B&W sketch-c 6.00
1-Destroyer Edition ($50.00, 30"x18", edition of 5000) 50.00
2-6-($2.99) 3.00
KISSMAS (12/07, $4.99) Christmas-themed issue; re-cap of issues #1-4 5.00

KISSING CHAOS
Oni Press: Sept, 2001 - No. 8, Mar, 2002 ($2.25, B&W, 6" x 9", limited series)
1-8-Arthur Dela Cruz-s/a 3.00
...: Nine Lives (12/03, $2.99, regular comic-sized) 3.00
...: 1000 Words (7/03, $2.99, regular comic-sized) 3.00
TPB (9/02, $17.95) r/#1-8 18.00

KISSING CHAOS: NONSTOP BEAUTY
Oni Press: Oct, 2002 - No. 4, March, 2003 ($2.95, B&W, 6" x 9", limited series)
1-4-Arthur Dela Cruz-s/a 3.00
TPB (9/03, $11.95) r/#1-4 12.00

KISS KIDS
IDW Publishing: Aug, 2013 - No. 4, Nov, 2013 ($3.99, limited series)
1-4-Short stories of KISS members as grade-school kids; Ryall & Waltz-s 4.00

KISS KISS BANG BANG
CrossGen Comics: Feb, 2004 - No. 5, Jun, 2004 ($2.95)
1-5-Bedard-s/Perkins-a 3.00

KISS ME, SATAN
Dark Horse Comics: Sept, 2013 - No. 5, Jan, 2014 ($3.99, limited series)
1-5-Gischler-s/Ferreyra-a; Dave Johnson-c 4.00

KISS SOLO
IDW Publishing: Mar, 2013 - No. 4, Jun, 2013 ($3.99, limited series)
1-4-Multiple covers on each. 1-Ryall-s/Medina-a. 2-Waltz-s/Rodriguez-a 4.00

KISS THE ARMY OF DARKNESS
Dynamite Entertainment: 2018 ($3.99, one-shot)
1-Bowers & Sims-s/Coleman-a; multiple covers; KISS meets Ash 4.00

KISS: THE END
Dynamite Entertainment: 2019 - No. 5, 2019 ($3.99, limited series)
1-5-Amy Chu-s/Edu Menna-a; multiple covers. 2-Flashback to 1973 4.00

KISS: THE PSYCHO CIRCUS
Image Comics: Aug, 1997 - No. 31, June, 2000 ($1.95/$2.25/$2.50)
1-Holguin-s/Medina-a(p) 1 3 4 6 8 10
1-2nd & 3rd printings 3.00
2 6.00
3,4: 4-Photo-c 5.00
5-8: 5-Begin $2.25-c 4.00
9-29 4.00
30,31: 30-Begin $2.50-c 4.00
Book 1 TPB ('98, $12.95) r/#1-6 13.00
Book 2 Destroyer TPB (8/99, $9.95) r/#10-13 10.00
Book 3 Whispered Scream TPB ('00, $9.95) r/#7-9,18 10.00
...Magazine 1 ($6.95) r/#1-3 plus interviews 7.00
...Magazine 2-5 ($4.95) 2-r/#4,5 plus interviews. 3-r/#6,7. 4-r/#8,9 5.00
Wizard Edition ('98, supplement) Bios, tour preview and interviews 3.00

KISS / VAMPIRELLA
Dynamite Entertainment: 2017 - No. 5, 2017 ($3.99)
1-5-Sebela-s/Martello-a; multiple covers; Vampirella meets KISS in 1974 4.00

KISSYFUR (TV)
DC Comics: 1989 (Sept.) ($2.00, 52 pgs., one-shot)
1-Based on Saturday morning cartoon 4.00

KISS: ZOMBIES
Dynamite Entertainment: 2019 - No. 5, 2020 ($3.99, limited series)
1-5-Ethan Sacks-s/Rodney Buchemi-a; multiple covers; KISS in the zombie future 4.00

KIT CARSON (Formerly All True Detective Cases No. 4; Fighting Davy Crockett No. 9; see Blazing Sixguns & Frontier Fighters)
Avon Periodicals: 1950; No. 2, 8/51 - No. 3, 12/51; No. 5, 11-12/54 - No. 8, 9/55 (No #4)
nn(#1) (1950)- "...Indian Scout" ; r-Cowboys 'N' Injuns #? 16 32 48 92 144 195
2(8/51) 12 24 36 74 105 135
3(12/51)- "...Fights the Comanche Raiders" 11 22 33 64 90 115
5-6,8(11-12/54-9/55): 5-Formerly All True Detective Cases (last pre-code); titled "...and the Trail of Doom" 11 22 33 60 83 105
7-McCann-a? 11 22 33 60 83 105
I.W. Reprint #10('63)-r/Kit Carson #1; Severin-c 2 4 6 11 16 20
NOTE: *Kinstler c-1-3, 5-8.*

KIT CARSON & THE BLACKFEET WARRIORS
Realistic: 1953
nn-Reprint; Kinstler-c 12 24 36 67 94 120

KITCHEN, THE
DC Comics (Vertigo): Jan, 2015 - No. 8, Aug, 2015 ($2.99, limited series)
1-8-Masters-s/Doyle-a/Cloonan-c 3.00

KIT KARTER
Dell Publishing Co.: May-July, 1962
1 3 6 9 19 30 40

KITTY
St. John Publishing Co.: Oct, 1948
1-Teenage; Lily Renee-c/a 23 46 69 136 223 310

KITTY PRYDE, AGENT OF S.H.I.E.L.D. (Also see Excalibur and Mekanix)
Marvel Comics: Dec, 1997 - No. 3, Feb, 1998 ($2.50, limited series)
1-3-Hama-s 4.00

KITTY PRYDE AND WOLVERINE (Also see Uncanny X-Men & X-Men)
Marvel Comics Group: Nov, 1984 - No. 6, Apr, 1985 (Limited series)
1-6: Characters from X-Men 5.00
X-Men: Kitty Pryde and Wolverine HC (2008, $19.99) r/series 20.00

KLARER GIVEAWAYS (See Wisco in the Promotional Comics section)

KLARION (The Witchboy)
DC Comics: Dec, 2014 - No. 6, May, 2015 ($2.99)
1-6: 1-3-Nocenti-s/McCarthy-a. 4-Fiorentino-a 3.00

KLAUS
BOOM! Studios: Nov, 2015 - No. 7, Aug, 2016 ($3.99)
1-7: 1-Origin of Santa Claus; Grant Morrison-s/Dan Mora-a; multiple covers 4.00
... and the Crisis in Xmasville 1 (12/17, $7.99) Morrison-s/Mora-a; Snowmaiden app. 8.00
... and the Crying Snowman 1 (12/18, $7.99) Morrison-s/Mora-a; 8.00
... and the Life & Times of Joe Christmas 1 (12/19, $7.99) Morrison-s/Mora-a; calendar printed sideways showing Joe Christmas from 1930-2001 8.00
... and the Witch of Winter 1 (12/16, $7.99) Morrison-s/Mora-a; Geppetto app. 8.00

KLAWS OF THE PANTHER (Also see Black Panther)
Marvel Comics: Dec, 2010 - No. 4, Feb, 2011 ($3.99, limited series)
1-Maberry-s/Gugliotta-a/Del Mundo-c; Ka-Zar & Shanna app. 3 6 9 14 20 25
2-4: 3-Spider-Man app. 1 2 3 5 6 8

KNIGHT AND SQUIRE (Also see Batman #667-669)
DC Comics: Dec, 2010 - No. 6, May, 2011 ($2.99, limited series)
1-6-Cornell-s/Broxton-a. 1-Two covers by Paquette & Tucci. 5,6-Joker app. 3.00
TPB (2011, $14.99) r/#1-6; sketch and design art 15.00

KNIGHTHAWK
Acclaim Comics (Windjammer): Sept, 1995 - No. 6, Nov, 1995 ($2.50, lim. series)
1-6: 6-origin 3.00

KNIGHTMARE
Image Comics (Extreme Studios): Feb, 1995 - No. 5, June, 1995 ($2.50)
0 ($3.50) 4.00
1-5: 4-Quesada & Palmiotti variant-c, 5-Flip book w/Warcry 3.00

KNIGHTS 4 (See Marvel Knights 4)

KNIGHTS OF PENDRAGON, THE (Also see Pendragon)
Marvel Comics Ltd.: July, 1990 - No. 18, Dec, 1991 ($1.95)
1-18: 1-Capt. Britain app. 2,8-Free poster inside. 9,10-Bolton-c. 11,18-Iron Man app. 3.00

KNIGHTS OF THE ROUND TABLE
Dell Publishing Co.: No. 540, Mar, 1954
Four Color 540-Movie, photo-c 6 12 18 41 76 110

KNIGHTS OF THE ROUND TABLE
Pines Comics: No. 10, April, 1957
10-Features Sir Lancelot 5 10 15 24 30 35

KNIGHTS OF THE ROUND TABLE
Dell Publishing Co.: Nov-Jan, 1963-64
1 (12-397-401)-Painted-c 3 6 9 20 31 42

KNIGHTS TEMPORAL

Knull #1 © MAR

Koko and Kola #3 © ME

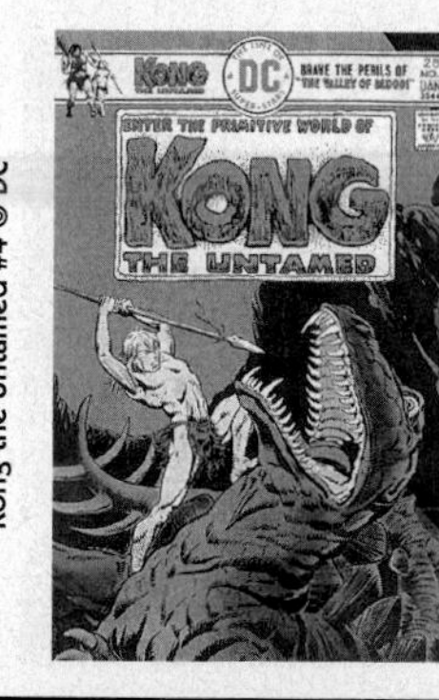

Kong the Untamed #4 © DC

	GD	VG	FN	VF	VF/NM	NM-
	2.0	4.0	6.0	8.0	9.0	9.2

AfterShock Comics: Jul, 2019 - No. 5, Jan, 2020 ($3.99, limited series)
1-5-Cullen Bunn-s/Fran Galán-a 4.00

KNIGHTSTRIKE (Also see Operation: Knightstrike)
Image Comics (Extreme Studios): Jan, 1996 ($2.50)
1-Rob Liefeld & Eric Stephenson story; Extreme Destroyer Part 6. 3.00

KNIGHT WATCHMAN (See Big Bang Comics & Dr. Weird)
Image Comics: June, 1998 - No. 4, Oct, 1998 ($2.95/$3.50, B&W, lim. series)
1-4-Ben Torres-c/a in all. 4-($3.50) 4.00

KNIGHT WATCHMAN: GRAVEYARD SHIFT
Caliber Press: 1994 ($2.95, B&W)
1,2-Ben Torres-a 4.00

KNOCK EM DEAD
AfterShock Comics: Dec, 2020 - Present ($4.99/$3.99)
1-($4.99) Eliot Rahal-s/Mattia Monaco-a 5.00
2,3-($3.99) 4.00

KNOCK KNOCK (...Who's There?)
Dell Publ./Gerona Publications: No. 801, 1936 (52 pgs.) (8x9", B&W)
801-Joke book; Bob Dunn-a 15 30 45 86 133 180

KNOCKOUT ADVENTURES
Fiction House Magazines: Winter, 1953-54
1-Reprints Fight Comics #53 w/Rip Carson-c/s 14 28 42 82 121 160

KNUCKLES (Spin-off of Sonic the Hedgehog)
Archie Publications: Apr, 1997 - No. 32, Feb, 2000 ($1.50/$1.75/$1.79)
1-32 4.00

KNUCKLES' CHAOTIX
Archie Publications: Jan, 1996 ($2.00, annual)
1 5.00

KNULL
Marvel Comics: Feb, 2021 ($7.99, one-host)
1-Reprints Venom (2018) #3,4,25 & Web of Venom: Carnage Born #1 8.00

KOBALT
DC Comics (Milestone): June, 1994 - No. 16, Sept, 1995 ($1.75/$2.50)
1-16: 1-Byrne-c. 4-Intro Page. 16-Kent Williams-c 3.00

KOBRA (Unpublished #8 appears in DC Special Series No. 1)
National Periodical Publications: Feb-Mar, 1976 - No. 7, Mar-Apr, 1977
1-1st app.; Kirby-a redrawn by Marcos; only 25¢-c 3 6 9 16 23 30
2-7: (All 30¢ issues) 3-Giffen-a 1 3 4 6 8 10
...: Resurrection TPB (2010, $19.99) r/#1, DC Special Series No. 1 and later apps. in Checkmate #23-25, Faces of Evil: Kobra #1 and various Who's Who issues 20.00
NOTE: *Austin a-3i. Buckler a-5p; c-5p. Kubert c-4. Nasser a-6p, 7; c-7.*

KOKEY KOALA (...and the Magic Button)
Toby Press: May, 1952
1-Funny animal 15 30 45 90 140 190

KOKO AND KOLA (Also see A-1 Comics #16 & Tick Tock Tales)
Com/Magazine Enterprises: Fall, 1946 - No. 5, May, 1947; No. 6, 1950
1-Funny animal 16 32 48 98 154 210
2-X-Mas-c 12 24 36 67 94 120
3-6: 6(A-1 28) 10 20 30 56 76 95

KO KOMICS
Gerona Publications: Oct, 1945 (scarce)
1-The Duke of Darkness & The Menace (hero); Kirby-c 106 212 318 678 1164 1650

KOLCHAK: THE NIGHT STALKER (TV)
Moonstone: 2002 - 2007 ($6.50/$6.95)
1-($6.50) Jeff Rice-s/Gordon Purcell-a 6.50
... Black & White & Read All Over (2005, $4.95) short stories by various; 2 covers 5.00
... Devil in the Details (2003, $6.95) Trevor Von Eeden-a 7.00
... Eve of Terror (2005, $5.95) Gentile-s/Figueroa-a/Beck-c 6.00
... Fever Pitch (2002, $6.95) Christopher Jones-a 7.00
... Get of Belial (2002, $6.95) Art Nichols-a 7.00
... Lambs to the Slaughter (2003, $6.95) Trevor Von Eeden-a 7.00
... Pain Most Human (2004, $6.95) Greg Scott-a 7.00
... Tales: The Frankenstein Agenda 1 (2007 - No. 3, $3.50) Michelinie-s 3.50
... Tales of the Night Stalker 1-7 (2003 - No. 7, $3.50) two covers by Moore & Ulanski 3.50
TPB (2004, $17.95) r/#1, Get of Belial & Fever Pitch 18.00
Vol. 2: Terror Within TPB (2006, $16.95) r/Pain Most Human, Pain Without Tears & Devil in the Details 17.00

KOMIC KARTOONS
Timely Comics (EPC): Fall, 1945 - No. 2, Winter, 1945
1,2-Andy Wolf, Bertie Mouse 33 66 99 194 317 440

KOMIK PAGES (Formerly Snap; becomes Bullseye #11)
Harry 'A' Chesler, Jr. (Our Army, Inc.): Apr, 1945 (All reprints)
10(#1 on inside)-Land O' Nod by Rick Yager (2 pgs.), Animal Crackers, Foxy GrandPa, Tom, Dick & Mary, Cheerio Minstrels, Red Starr plus other 1-2 pg. strips; Cole-a 28 56 84 168 274 380

KONA (...Monarch of Monster Isle)
Dell Publishing Co.: Feb-Apr, 1962 - No. 21, Jan-Mar, 1967 (Painted-c)
Four Color 1256 (#1) 9 18 27 61 123 185
2-10: 4-Anak begins. 6-Gil Kane-c 5 10 15 33 57 80
11-21 4 8 12 28 47 65
NOTE: *Glanzman a-all issues.*

KONGA (Fantastic Giants No. 24) (See Return of...)
Charlton Comics: 1960; No. 2, Aug, 1961 - No. 23, Nov, 1965
1(1960)-Based on movie; Giordano-c 26 52 78 182 404 625
2-5: 2-Giordano-c; no Ditko-a 10 20 30 67 141 215
6-9-Ditko-c/a 9 18 27 58 114 170
10-15 8 16 24 54 102 150
16-23 5 10 15 35 63 90
NOTE: *Ditko a-1, 3-15; c-4, 6-9, 11. Glanzman a-12. Montes & Bache a-16-23.*

KONGA'S REVENGE (Formerly Return of...)
Charlton Comics: No. 2, Summer, 1963 - No. 3, Fall, 1964; Dec, 1968
2,3: 2-Ditko-c/a 7 14 21 49 92 135
1(12/68)-Reprints Konga's Revenge #3 3 6 9 16 24 32

KONG: GODS OF SKULL ISLAND
BOOM! Studios: Oct, 2017 ($7.99, one-shot)
1-Phillip Kennedy Johnson-s/Chad Lewis-a 8.00

KONG OF SKULL ISLAND
BOOM! Studios: Jul, 2016 - No. 12, Jun, 2017 ($3.99, limited series)
1-12-James Asmus-s/Carlos Magno-a; multiple covers on each 4.00
... 2018 Special 1 (5/18, $7.99) Paul Allor-s/Carlos Magno-a 8.00

KONG ON THE PLANET OF THE APES
BOOM! Studios: Nov, 2017 - No. 6, Apr, 2018 ($3.99, limited series)
1-6-Ryan Ferrier-s/Carlos Magno-a; multiple covers on each 4.00

KONG THE UNTAMED
National Periodical Publications: June-July, 1975 - V2#5, Feb-Mar, 1976
1-1st app. Kong; Wrightson-c; Alcala-a 2 4 6 14 19 24
2-Wrightson-c; Alcala-a 2 4 6 10 14 18
3-5: 3-Alcala-a 1 3 4 6 8 10

KOOKABURRA K
Marvel Comics (Soleil): 2009 - No. 3, 2010 ($5.99, limited series)
1-3-Humberto Ramos-a/c 6.00

KOOKIE
Dell Publishing Co.: Feb-Apr, 1962 - No. 2, May-July, 1962 (15 cents)
1-Written by John Stanley; Bill Williams-a 7 14 21 46 86 125
2 6 12 18 41 76 110

KOOSH KINS
Archie Comics: Oct, 1991 - No. 3, Feb, 1992 ($1.00, bi-monthly, limited series)
1-3 4.00
NOTE: *No. 4 was planned, but cancelled.*

KORAK, SON OF TARZAN (Edgar Rice Burroughs)(See Tarzan #139)
Gold Key: Jan, 1964 - No. 45, Jan, 1972 (Painted-c No. 1-?)
1-Russ Manning-a 9 18 27 58 114 170
2-5-Russ Manning-a 5 10 15 33 57 80
6-11-Russ Manning-a 5 10 15 30 50 70
12-23: 12,13-Warren Tufts-a. 14-Jon of the Kalahari ends. 15-Mabu, Jungle Boy begins. 21-Manning-a. 23-Last 12¢ issue 4 8 12 27 44 60
24-30 3 6 9 21 33 45
31-45 3 6 9 17 26 35

KORAK, SON OF TARZAN (Tarzan Family #60 on; see Tarzan #230)
National Periodical Publications: V9#46, May-June, 1972 - V12#56, Feb-Mar, 1974; No. 57, May-June, 1975 - No. 59, Sept-Oct, 1975 (Edgar Rice Burroughs)

Krampus #1 © Joines & Kotz

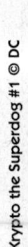

Krypto the Superdog #1 © DC

Kull the Conqueror #1 © REH

	GD 2.0	VG 4.0	FN 6.0	VF 8.0	VF/NM 9.0	NM- 9.2

46-(52 pgs.)-Carson of Venus begins (origin), ends #56; Pellucidar feature; Weiss-a 3 6 9 15 22 28
47-59: 49-Origin Korak retold 2 4 6 8 11 14
NOTE: *All have covers by* ***Joe Kubert. Manning*** *strip reprints-No. 57-59.* ***Murphy Anderson*** *a-52,56.* ***Michael Kaluta*** *a-46-56.* ***Frank Thorne*** *a-46-51.*

KORE
Image Comics: Apr, 2003 - No. 5, Sept, 2003 ($2.95)
1-5: 1-Two covers by Capullo and Seeley; Seeley-a (p) 3.00

KORG: 70,000 B. C. (TV)
Charlton Publications: May, 1975 - No. 9, Nov, 1976 (Hanna-Barbera)
1,2: 1-Boyette-c/a. 2-Painted-c; Byrne text illos 2 4 6 13 18 22
3-9 2 4 6 8 11 14

KORNER KID COMICS: Four Star Publications: 1947 (Advertised, not pub.)

KORVAC SAGA (Secret Wars tie-in)
Marvel Comics: Aug, 2015 - No. 4, Nov, 2015 ($3.99, limited series)
1-4-Guardians 3000, Avengers and Wonder Man app.; Abnett-s/Schmidt-a 4.00

KOSHCHEI THE DEATHLESS
Dark Horse Comics: Dec, 2017 - No. 6, Jun, 2018 ($3.99, limited series)
1-6-Mignola-s/c; Stenbeck-a; Hellboy app. 4.00

KRAMPUS
Image Comics: Dec, 2013 - No. 5, May, 2014 ($2.99)
1-5-Sinterklaas' assistant; Joines-s/Kotz-a 3.00

KRAZY KAT
Holt: 1946 (Hardcover)
Reprints daily & Sunday strips by Herriman 55 110 165 352 601 850
dust jacket only 42 84 126 265 450 635

KRAZY KAT (See Ace Comics & March of Comics No. 72, 87)

KRAZY KAT COMICS (...& Ignatz the Mouse early issues)
Dell Publ. Co./Gold Key: May-June, 1951 - F.C. #696, Apr, 1956; Jan, 1964 (None by Herriman)
1(1951) 9 18 27 62 126 190
2-5 (#5, 8-10/52) 5 10 15 34 60 85
Four Color 454,504 6 12 18 37 66 95
Four Color 548,619,696 (4/56) 5 10 15 31 53 75
1(10098-401)(1/64-Gold Key)(TV) 4 8 12 25 40 55

KRAZY KOMICS (1st Series) (Cindy Comics No. 27 on) (Also see Ziggy Pig)
Timely Comics (USA No. 1-21/JPC No. 22-26): July, 1942 - No. 26, Spr, 1947
1-Toughy Tomcat, Ziggy Pig (by Jaffee) & Silly Seal begin 142 284 426 909 1555 2200
2 52 104 156 328 552 775
3-8,10 37 74 111 222 361 500
9-Hitler parody-c 132 264 396 845 1448 2050
11,13,14 26 52 78 154 252 350
12-Timely's entire art staff drew themselves into a Creeper story 40 80 120 246 411 575
15-(8-9/44)-Has "Super Soldier" by Pfc. Stan Lee 27 54 81 162 266 370
16-24,26: 16-(10-11/44). 26-Super Rabbit-c/story 21 42 63 126 206 285
25-Wacky Duck-c/story & begin; Kurtzman-a (6pgs.) 27 54 81 162 266 370

KRAZY KOMICS (2nd Series)
Timely/Marvel Comics: Aug, 1948 - No. 2, Nov, 1948
1-Wolverton (10 pgs.) & Kurtzman (8 pgs.)-a; Eustice Hayseed begins (Li'l Abner swipe) 61 122 183 390 670 950
2-Wolverton-a (10 pgs.); Powerhouse Pepper cameo 42 84 126 265 445 625

KRAZY KROW (Also see Dopey Duck, Film Funnies, Funny Frolics & Movie Tunes)
Marvel Comics (ZPC): Summer, 1945 - No. 3, Wint, 1945/46
1 34 68 102 204 332 460
2,3 21 42 63 124 202 280
I.W. Reprint #1('57), 2('58), 7 2 4 6 11 16 20

KRAZYLIFE (Becomes Nutty Life #2)
Fox Feature Syndicate: 1945 (no month)
1-Funny animal 29 58 87 170 278 385

KREE/SKRULL WAR STARRING THE AVENGERS, THE
Marvel Comics: Sept, 1983 - No. 2, Oct, 1983 ($2.50, 68 pgs., Baxter paper)
1,2 6.00
NOTE: ***Neal Adams*** *p-1r, 2.* ***Buscema*** *a-1r, 2r.* ***Simonson*** *a-1p; c-1p.*

KROFFT SUPERSHOW (TV)
Gold Key: Apr, 1978 - No. 6, Jan, 1979
1-Photo-c 3 6 9 17 26 35
2-6: 6-Photo-c 3 6 9 14 19 24

KRULL
Marvel Comics Group: Nov, 1983 - No. 2, Dec, 1983
1,2-Adaptation of film; r/Marvel Super Special. 1-Photo-c from movie 4.00

KRUSTY COMICS (TV)(See Simpsons Comics)
Bongo Comics: 1995 - No. 3, 1995 ($2.25, limited series)
1-3 4.00

KRYPTON CHRONICLES
DC Comics: Sept, 1981 - No. 3, Nov, 1981
1-3: 1-Buckler-c(p) 4.00

KRYPTO THE SUPERDOG (TV)
DC Comics: Nov, 2006 - No. 6, Apr, 2007 ($2.25)
1-6-Based on Cartoon Network series. 1-Origin retold 3.00

KULL
Dark Horse Comics: Nov, 2008 - No. 6, May, 2009 ($2.99)
1-6: 1-Nelson-s/Conrad-a; two covers by Andy Brase and Joe Kubert 3.00

KULL AND THE BARBARIANS
Marvel Comics: May, 1975 - No. 3, Sept, 1975 ($1.00, B&W, magazine)
1-(84 pgs.) Andru/Wood-r/Kull #1; 2 pgs. Neal Adams; Gil Kane(p), Marie & John Severin-a(r); Krenkel text illo. 3 6 9 18 28 38
2,3: 2-(84 pgs.) Red Sonja by Chaykin begins; Solomon Kane by Weiss/Adams; Gil Kane-a; Solomon Kane pin-up by Wrightson. 3-(76 pgs.) Origin Red Sonja by Chaykin; Adams-a; Solomon Kane app. 3 6 9 16 24 32

KULL: ETERNAL
IDW Publsihing: Jun, 2017 - No. 3, Apr, 2018 ($3.99, limited series)
1-3-Waltz-s/Pizzari-a; multiple covers on each; Kull travels through history 4.00

KULL: THE CAT AND THE SKULL
Dark Horse Comics: Oct, 2011 - No. 4, Jan, 2012 ($3.50, limited series)
1-4-Lapham-s/Guzman-a/Chen-c. 1-Variant-c by Hans 3.50

KULL THE CONQUEROR (...the Destroyer #11 on; see Conan #1, Creatures on the Loose #10, Marvel Preview, Monsters on the Prowl)
Marvel Comics Group: June, 1971 - No. 2, Sept, 1971; No. 3, July, 1972 - No. 15, Aug, 1974; No. 16, Aug, 1976 - No. 29, Oct, 1978
1-Andru/Wood-a; 2nd app. & origin Kull; 15¢ issue 6 12 18 41 76 110
2-5: 2-3rd Kull app. Last 15¢ iss. 3-13: 20¢ issues. 3-Thulsa Doom-c/app. 3 6 9 19 30 40
6-10: 7-Thulsa Doom-c/app 2 4 6 10 14 18
11-15: 11-15-Ploog-a. 14,15: 25¢ issues 2 4 6 8 11 14
16-(Regular 25¢ edition)(8/76) 2 3 4 6 8 10
16-(30¢-c variant, limited distribution) 3 6 9 19 30 40
17-29: 21-23-(Reg. 30¢ editions) 2 3 4 6 8 10
21-23-(35¢-c variants, limited distribution) 10 20 30 68 144 220
NOTE: *No. 1, 2, 7-9, 11 are based on Robert E. Howard stories.* ***Alcala*** *a-17p, 18-20i; c-24.* ***Ditko*** *a-12r, 15r.* ***Gil Kane*** *c-15p, 21.* ***Nebres*** *a-22i-27i; c-25i, 27i.* ***Ploog*** *c-11, 12p, 13.* ***Severin*** *a-2-9i; c-2-10i, 19.* ***Starlin*** *c-14.*

KULL THE CONQUEROR
Marvel Comics Group: Dec, 1982 - No. 2, Mar, 1983 (52 pgs., Baxter paper)
1,2: 1-Buscema-a(p) 4.00

KULL THE CONQUEROR (No. 9,10 titled "Kull")
Marvel Comics Group: 5/83 - No. 10, 6/85 (52 pgs., Baxter paper)
V3#1-10: Buscema-a in #1-3,5-10 4.00
NOTE: Bolton a-4. Golden painted c-3-8. Guice a-4p. Sienkiewicz a-4; c-2.

KULL: THE HATE WITCH
Dark Horse Comics: Nov, 2010 - No. 4, Feb, 2011 ($3.50)
1-4-Lapham-s/Guzman-a/Fleming-c 3.50

KUNG FU (See Deadly Hands of..., & Master of...)

KUNG FU FIGHTER (See Richard Dragon...)

KUNG FU PANDA
Titan Comics: Nov, 2015 -No. 4, Jan, 2016 ($3.99, limited series)
1-4-Simon Furman-s. 1,2-Lee Robinson-a 4.00

KUNG FU PANDA 2
Ape Entertainment: 2011 - No. 6, 2012 ($3.95/$3.99, limited series)
1-6-Short stories by various 4.00

KURT BUSIEK'S ASTRO CITY (Limited series) (Also see Astro City: Local Heroes)

Kurt Busiek's Astro City V2 #2 © Jukebox

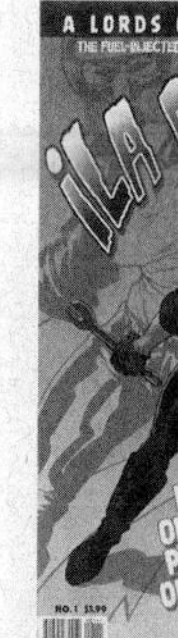
La Diabla #1 © Eric Powell

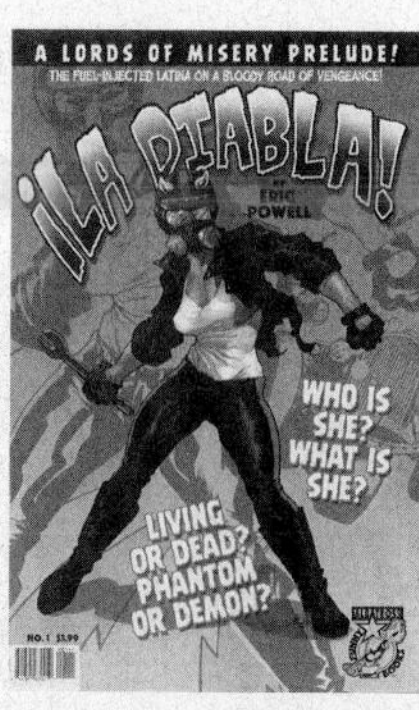

Lady Death #13 © Chaos!

	GD	VG	FN	VF	VF/NM	NM-
	2.0	4.0	6.0	8.0	9.0	9.2

Image Comics (Juke Box Productions): Aug, 1995 - No. 6, Jan, 1996 ($2.25)

1-Kurt Busiek scripts, Brent Anderson-a & Alex Ross front & back-c begins; 1st app. Samaritan & Honor Guard (Cleopatra, MHP, Beautie, The Black Rapier, Quarrel & N-Forcer) 3 6 9 14 19 24
2-6: 2-1st app. The Silver Agent, The Old Soldier, & the "original" Honor Guard (Max O'Millions, Starwoman, the "original" Cleopatra, the "original" N-Forcer, the Bouncing Beatnik, Leopardman & Kitkat). 3-1st app. Jack-in-the-Box & The Deacon. 4-1st app. Winged Victory (cameo), The Hanged Man & The First Family. 5-1st app. Crackerjack, The Astro City Irregulars, Nightingale & Sunbird. 6-Origin Samaritan; 1st full app. Winged Victory 1 3 4 6 8 10
Life In The Big City-(8/96, $19.95, trade paperback)-r/Image Comics limited series w/sketchbook & cover gallery; Ross-c 20.00
Life In The Big City-(8/96, $49.95, hardcover, 1000 print run)-r/Image Comics limited series w/sketchbook & cover gallery; Ross-c 50.00

KURT BUSIEK'S ASTRO CITY (1st Homage Comics series)
Image Comics (Homage Comics): V2#1, Sept, 1996 - No. 15, Dec, 1998;
DC Comics (Homage Comics): No. 16, Mar, 1999 - No. 22, Aug, 2000 ($2.50)

1/2-(10/96)-The Hanged Man story; 1st app. The All-American & Slugger, The Lamplighter, The Time-Keeper & Eterneon 1 3 4 6 8 10
1/2-(1/98) 2nd printing w/new cover 3.00
1- Kurt Busiek scripts, Alex Ross-c, Brent Anderson-p & Will Blyberg-i begin; intro The Gentleman, Thunderhead & Helia. 1 2 3 5 6 8
1-(12/97, $4.95) "3-D Edition" w/glasses 5.00
2-Origin The First Family; Astra story 1 2 3 4 5 7
3-5: 4-1st app. The Crossbreed, Ironhorse, Glue Gun & The Confessor (cameo) 6.00
6-10 5.00
11-22: 14-20-Steeljack story arc. 16-(3/99) First DC issue 3.00
TPB-($19.95) Ross-c, r/#4-9, #1/2 w/sketchbook 20.00
Family Album TPB ($19.95) r/#1-3,10-13 20.00
The Tarnished Angel HC ($29.95) r/#14-20; new Ross dust jacket; sketch pages by Anderson & Ross; cover gallery with reference photos 30.00
The Tarnished Angel SC ($19.95) r/#14-20; new Ross-c 20.00

LABMAN
Image Comics: Nov, 1996 ($3.50, one-shot)

1-Allred-c 4.00

LAB RATS
DC Comics: June, 2002 - No. 8, Jan, 2003 ($2.50)

1-8-John Byrne-s/a. 5,6-Superman app. 3.00

LABYRINTH
Marvel Comics Group: Nov, 1986 - No. 3, Jan, 1987 (Limited series)

1-3: David Bowie movie adaptation; r/Marvel Super Special #40 3 6 9 16 23 30

LABYRINTH (Jim Henson's...)
Boom Entertainment (Archaia): (one-shots)

... Masquerade 1 (12/21, $7.99)-Donnelly-s/Bak, Dodge, & Carlomagno-a 8.00
... 30th Anniversary Special 1 (8/16, $9.99)-Short stories by various; multiple covers 2 4 6 13 18 22
... 2017 Special 1 (11/17, $7.99) Short stories by various incl. Katie Cook & Landridge 8.00

LA COSA NOSTROID (See Scud: The Disposible Assassin)
Fireman Press: Mar, 1996 - No. 9, 1998 ($2.95, B&W)

1-9-Dan Harmon-s/Rob Schrab-c/a 3.00

LAD: A DOG (Movie)
Dell Publishing Co.: 1961 - No. 2, July-Sept, 1962

Four Color 1303 5 10 15 33 57 80
2 4 8 12 23 37 50

LA DIABLA (Prelude to The Lords of Misery)
Albatross Funnybooks: 2020 ($3.99, one-shot)

1-Eric Powell-s/a; various origins of La Diabla 4.00

LADY AND THE TRAMP (Disney, See Dell Giants & Movie Comics)
Dell Publishing Co.: No. 629, May, 1955 - No. 634, June, 1955

Four Color 629 (#1)-..with Jock 8 16 24 55 105 155
Four Color 634-...Album 6 12 18 41 76 110

LADY CASTLE
BOOM! Studios: Jan, 2017 - No. 4, May, 2017 ($3.99, limited series)

1-4: 1-Delilah Dawson-s/Ashley Woods-a. 2-4-Farrow-a 4.00

LADY COP (See 1st Issue Special)

LADY DEADPOOL
Marvel Comics: Sept, 2010 ($3.99, one-shot)

1-Land-c/Lashley-a 2 4 6 10 14 18

LADY DEATH (See Evil Ernie)
Chaos! Comics: Jan, 1994 - No. 3, Mar, 1994 ($2.75, limited series)

1/2-S. Hughes-c/a in all, 1/2 Velvet 1 2 3 4 5 7
1/2 Gold 1 3 4 6 8 10
1/2 Signed Limited Edition 2 4 6 8 10 12
1-($3.50)-Chromium-c 2 4 6 11 16 20
1-Commemorative 2 4 6 10 14 18
1-(9/96, $2.95) "Encore Presentation"; r/#1 3.00
2 1 3 4 6 8 10
3 5.00
... And Jade (4/02, $2.99) Augustyn-s/Reis-a 3.00
...And The Women of Chaos! Gallery #1 (11/96, $2.25) pin-ups by various 3.00
.../Bad Kitty (9/01, $2.99) Mota-c/a 3.00
.../Bedlam (6/02, $2.99) Augustyn-s/Reis-c 3.00
...By Steven Hughes (6/00, $2.95) Tribute issue to Steven Hughes 3.00
...By Steven Hughes Deluxe Edition(6/00, $15.95) 16.00
.../Chastity (1/02, $2.99) Mota-c/a; Augustyn-s 3.00
...Death Becomes Her #0 (11/97, $2.95) Hughes-c/a 3.00
...FAN Edition: All Hallow's Eve #1 (1/97, mail-in) 5.00
...In Lingerie #1 (8/95, $2.95) pin-ups, wraparound-c 3.00
...In Lingerie #1-Leather Edition (10,000) 12.00
...In Lingerie #1-Micro Premium Edition; Lady Demon-c (2,000) 35.00
...: Love Bites (3/01, $2.99) Kaminski-s/Luke Ross-a 3.00
.../Medieval Witchblade (8/01, $3.50) covers by Molenaar and Silvestri 3.50
.../Medieval Witchblade Preview Ed. (8/01, $1.99) Molenaar-c 3.00
...: Mischief Night (11/01, $2.99) Ostrander-s/Reis-a 3.00
...: Re-Imagined (7/02, $2.99) Gossett-c 3.00
...: River of Fear (4/01, $2.99) Bennett-a(p)/Cleavenger-c 3.00
...Swimsuit Special #1-($2.50)-Wraparound-c 3.00
...Swimsuit Special #1-Red velvet-c 14.00
...Swimsuit 2001 #1-(2/01, $2.99)-Reis-c; art by various 3.00
...: The Reckoning (7/94, $6.95)-r/#1-3 7.00
...: The Reckoning (8/95, $12.95)- new printing including Lady Death 1/2 & Swimsuit Special #1 13.00
.../Vampirella (3/99, $3.50) Hughes-c/a 3.50
.../Vampirella 2 (3/00, $3.50) Deodato-c/a 3.50
... Vs. Purgatori (12/99, $3.50) Deodato-a 3.50
... Vs. Vampirella Preview (2/00, $1.00) Deodato-a/c 3.00

LADY DEATH (Ongoing series)
Chaos! Comics: Feb, 1998 - No. 16, May, 1999 ($2.95)

1-16: 1-4: Pulido-s/Hughes-c/a. 5-8,13-16-Deodato-a. 9-11-Hughes-a 4.00
...Retribution (8/98, $2.95) Jadsen-a 4.00
...Retribution Premium Ed. 6.00

LADY DEATH
Boundless Comics: No. 0, Nov, 2010 - No. 26 ($3.99)

0-26-Pulido & Wolfer-s/Mueller-a on most; multiple covers on all. 25-Borstel-a 4.00
... Free Comic Book Day 2012 (5/12, free) "The Beginning" on cover; Mueller-a 3.00
... Origins Annual 1 (8/11, $4.99) Martin-a/Pulido-s 5.00
... Premiere (7/10, free) previews series; five covers 3.00

LADY DEATH...
Coffin Comics (One-shots)

... #1 - 25th Anniversary Edition (2/19, $4.99) remastered reprint of Lady Death #1 ('94) 5.00
... Chaos Rules 1 (5/16, $7.99) Pulido & Augustyn-s/Verma-a 8.00
... Hellraiders 1 (1/19, $4.99) Pulido & Maclean-s/Verma-a; multiple covers 5.00
... Merciless Onslaught 1 (8/17, $7.99) Pulido & Maclean-s/Verma-a; multiple covers 8.00
... Oblivion Kiss 1 (4/17, $7.99) Pulido & Maclean-s/Verma-a; multiple covers 8.00
... Revelations 1 (2/17, $3.99) Pin-up gallery of covers 4.00
... Zodiac 1 (12/16, $3.99) 12 pin-up images of the 12 zodiac signs by Nei Ruffino 4.00

LADY DEATH: ALIVE
Chaos! Comics: May, 2001 - No. 4, Aug, 2001 ($2.99, limited series)

1-4-Ivan Reis-a; Lady Death becomes mortal 3.00

LADY DEATH: A MEDIEVAL TALE (Brian Pulido's...)
CG Entertainment: Mar, 2003 - No. 12, Apr, 2004 ($2.95)

1-12: 1-Brian Pulido-s/Ivan Reis-a; Lady Death in the CrossGen Universe 3.00
Vol.1 TPB (2003, $9.95) digest-sized reprint of #1-6 10.00

LADY DEATH: APOCALYPSE
Boundless Comics: Jan, 2015 - No. 6, Jun, 2015 ($4.99)

1-6: 1-4-Wolfer-s/Borstel-a; multiple covers. 5,6-Wickline-s/Mueller-a 5.00

Lady Killer #1 © Jones & Rich

Lady Mechanika: Sangre #2 © Joe Benitez

Lady Pendragon V2 #1 © Matt Hawkins

GD VG FN VF VF/NM NM-
2.0 4.0 6.0 8.0 9.0 9.2

#0 (8/15, $6.99) Pulido-s/Valenzuela-a; bonus art gallery 7.00

LADY DEATH: APOCALYPTIC ABYSS
Coffin Comics: Feb, 2019 - No. 2, Apr, 2019 ($4.99, limited series)
1,2-Pulido & Maclean-s/Verma-a 5.00

LADY DEATH: BLASPHEMY ANTHEM
Coffin Comics: Dec, 2020 - No. 2, Feb, 2021 ($4.99, limited series)
1,2-Pulido & Maclean-s/Bernard-a; The Trinity app. 5.00

LADY DEATH: DARK ALLIANCE
Chaos! Comics: July, 2002 - No. 5, ($2.99, limited series)
1-3-Reis-a/Ostrander-s 3.00

LADY DEATH: DARK MILLENNIUM
Chaos! Comics: Feb, 2000 - No. 3, Apr, 2000 ($2.95, limited series)
Preview (6/00, $5.00) 5.00
1-3-Ivan Reis-a 3.00

LADY DEATH: GODDESS RETURNS
Chaos! Comics: Jun, 2002 - No. 2, Aug, 2002 ($2.99, limited series)
1,2-Mota-a/Ostrander-s 3.00

LADY DEATH: HEARTBREAKER
Chaos! Comics: Mar, 2002 - No. 4, ($2.99, limited series)
1-Molenaar-a/Ostrander-s 3.00

LADY DEATH: JUDGEMENT WAR
Chaos! Comics: Nov, 1999 - No. 3, Jan, 2000 ($2.95, limited series)
Prelude (10/99) two covers 4.00
1-3-Ivan Reis-a 4.00

LADY DEATH: LAST RITES
Chaos! Comics: Oct, 2001 - No. 4, Feb, 2001 ($2.99, limited series)
1-4-Ivan Reis-a/Ostrander-s 3.00

LADY DEATH: NIGHTMARE SYMPHONY
Coffin Comics: Nov, 2018 - No. 2, Dec, 2019 ($4.99, limited series)
1,2-Pulido & Maclean-s/Spay-a 5.00

LADY DEATH ORIGINS: CURSED
Boundless Comics: Mar, 2012 - No. 3, May, 2012 ($4.99/$3.99, limited series)
1-($4.99)-Pulido-s/Guzman-a; multiple covers 5.00
2,3-($3.99) 4.00

LADY DEATH: SCORCHED EARTH
Coffin Comics: Feb, 2020 - No. 2, Nov, 2020 ($4.99, limited series)
1,2-Pulido & Maclean-s/Bernard-a 5.00

LADY DEATH: THE CRUCIBLE
Chaos! Comics: Nov, 1996 - No. 6, Oct, 1997 ($3.50/$2.95, limited series)
1/2 4.00
1/2 Cloth Edition 8.00
1-Wraparound silver foil embossed-c 5.00
2-6-($2.95) 4.00

LADY DEATH: THE GAUNTLET
Chaos! Comics: Apr, 2002 - No. 2, May, 2002 ($2.99, limited series)
1,2: 1-J. Scott Campbell-c/redesign of Lady Death's outfit; Mota-a 4.00

LADY DEATH: THE ODYSSEY
Chaos! Comics: Apr, 1996 - No. 4, Aug, 1996 ($3.50/$2.95)
1-($1.50)-Sneak Peek Preview 3.00
1-($1.50)-Sneak Peek Preview Micro Premium Edition (2500 print run) 2 4 6 8 10 12
1-($3.50)-Embossed, wraparound goil foil-c 5.00
1-Black Onyx Edition (200 print run) 5 10 15 33 57 80
1-($19.95)-Premium Edition (10,000 print run) 20.00
2-4-($2.95) 3.00

LADY DEATH: THE RAPTURE
Chaos! Comics: Jun, 1999 - No. 4, Sept, 1999 ($2.95, limited series)
1-4-Ivan Reis-c/a; Pulido-s 4.00

LADY DEATH: THE WILD HUNT (Brian Pulido's...)
CG Entertainment: Apr, 2004 - No. 2, May, 2005 ($2.95)
1-2: 1-Brian Pulido-s/Jim Cheung-a 3.00

LADY DEATH: TRIBULATION
Chaos! Comics: Dec, 2000 - No. 4, Mar, 2001 ($2.95, limited series)
1-4-Ivan Reis-a; Kaminski-s 3.00

GD VG FN VF VF/NM NM-
2.0 4.0 6.0 8.0 9.0 9.2

LADY DEATH II: BETWEEN HEAVEN & HELL
Chaos! Comics: Mar, 1995 - No. 4, July, 1995 ($3.50, limited series)
1-Chromium wraparound-c; Evil Ernie cameo 5.00
1-Commemorative (4,000), 1-Black Velvet-c 2 4 6 10 14 18
1-Gold 1 3 4 6 8 10
1-"Refractor" edition (5,000) 2 4 6 11 16 20
2-4 3.50
4-Lady Demon variant-c 1 2 3 5 7 9
Trade paperback-($12.95)-r/#1-4 13.00

LADY DEATH: UNHOLY RUIN
Coffin Comics: Apr, 2018 - No. 2, Jun, 2018 ($4.99, limited series)
1,2-Pulido & Maclean-s/Verma-a 5.00

LADY DEMON
Chaos! Comics: Mar, 2000 - No. 3, May, 2000 ($2.95, limited series)
1-3-Kaminski-s/Brewer-a 3.00

LADY DEMON
Dynamite Entertainment: 2014 - No. 4, 2015 ($3.99)
1-4: 1-3-Gillespie-s/Andolfo-a; multiple covers. 1-Origin retold. 4-Ramirez-a 4.00

LADY FOR A NIGHT (See Cinema Comics Herald)

LADY JUSTICE (See Neil Gaiman's...)

LADY KILLER
Dark Horse Comics: Jan, 2015 - No. 5, May, 2015 ($3.50)
1-5-Joëlle Jones-a/Jones and Jamie Rich-s 3.50

LADY KILLER 2
Dark Horse Comics: Aug, 2016 - No. 5, Sept, 2017 ($3.99)
1-5-Joëlle Jones-s/a 4.00

LADY LUCK (Formerly Smash #1-85) (Also see Spirit Sections #1)
Quality Comics Group: No. 86, Dec, 1949 - No. 90, Aug, 1950
86(#1) 123 246 369 787 1344 1900
87-90 81 162 243 518 884 1250

LADY MECHANIKA
Aspen MLT: No. 0, Oct, 2010 - No. 5, Mar, 2015 ($2.50/$2.99)
0-Joe Benitez-s/a; two covers; Benitez interview and sketch pages 3.00
0-(Benitez Productions, 8/15, $1.00) 3.00
1-(1/11, $2.99) Multiple covers 10.00
2-5-Multiple covers on each. 5-($4.99) 5.00
... FCBD Vol. 1 Issue 1 (5/16, giveaway) r/#0; excerpt from mini-series 3.00
... FCBD 2019 Vol. 1 Issue 1 (5/19, giveaway) r/#0; excerpts from mini-series 3.00

LADY MECHANIKA: LA BELLE DAME SANS MERCI
Benitez Productions: Jul, 2018 - No. 3, Oct, 2018 ($3.99, limited series)
1-3-Joe Benitez-a/s; M.M. Chen-s; multiple covers on each 4.00

LADY MECHANIKA: LA DAMA DE LA MUERTE
Benitez Productions: Sept, 2016 - No. 3, Dec, 2016 ($3.99, limited series)
1-3-Joe Benitez-a/s; M.M. Chen-s; multiple covers on each 4.00

LADY MECHANIKA: SANGRE
Benitez Productions: Jun, 2019 - No. 5, Jan, 2020 ($3.99, limited series)
1-5-Joe Benitez-a/s; M.M. Chen-s; Brian Ching-a; multiple covers on each 4.00

LADY MECHANIKA: THE CLOCKWORK ASSASSIN
Benitez Productions: Jul, 2017 - No. 3, Oct, 2017 ($3.99, limited series)
1-3-Joe Benitez-a/M.M. Chen-s; multiple covers on each 4.00

LADY MECHANIKA: THE LOST BOYS OF WEST ABBEY
Benitez Productions: May, 2016 - No. 2, Jun, 2016 ($3.99, limited series)
1,2-Joe Benitez-a/M.M. Chen-s; multiple covers on each 4.00

LADY MECHANIKA: THE TABLET OF DESTINIES
Benitez Productions: Apr, 2015 - No. 6, Oct, 2015 ($3.99, limited series)
1-6-Joe Benitez-s/a; multiple covers on each 4.00

LADY PENDRAGON
Maximum Press: Mar, 1996 ($2.50)
1-Matt Hawkins script 3.00

LADY PENDRAGON
Image Comics: Nov, 1998 - No. 3, Jan, 1999 ($2.50, mini-series)
Preview (6/98) Flip book w/ Deity preview 3.00
1-3: 1-Matt Hawkins-s/Stinsman-a 3.00
1-($6.95) DF Ed. with variant-c by Jusko 7.00

Lady Rawhide (2013 series) #1 © Zorro Prods

Lake of Fire #1 © Fairbairn & Smith

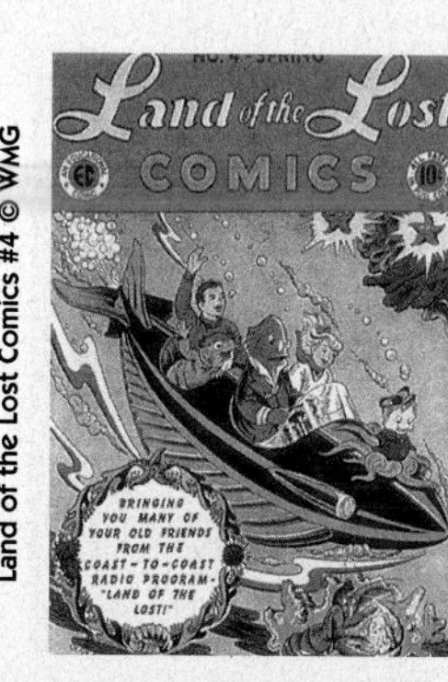

Land of the Lost Comics #4 © WMG

	GD	VG	FN	VF	VF/NM	NM-
	2.0	4.0	6.0	8.0	9.0	9.2

2-($4.95)Variant edition 5.00
0-(3/99) Origin; flip book 3.00

LADY PENDRAGON (Volume 3)
Image Comics: Apr, 1999 - No. 9, Mar, 2000 ($2.50, mini-series)
1,2,4-6,8-10: 1-Matt Hawkins-s/Stinsman-a. 2-Peterson-c 3.00
3-Flip book w/Alley Cat preview (1st app.) 4.00
7-($3.95) Flip book; Stinsman-a/Cleavenger painted-a 4.00
Gallery Edition (10/99, $2.95) pin-ups 3.00
...Merlin (1/00, $2.95) Stinsman-a 3.00
.../ More Than Mortal (5/99, $2.50) Scott-s/Norton-a; 2 covers by Norton & Finch 3.00
.../ More Than Mortal Preview (2/99) Diamond Dateline supplement 3.00
Pilot Season: Lady Pendragon (5/08, $3.99) Hawkins-s/Eru-a; wraparound-c by Struzan 4.00

LADY RAWHIDE
Topps Comics: July, 1995 - No. 5, Mar, 1996 ($2.95, bi-monthly, limited series)
1-5: Don McGregor scripts & Mayhew-a. in all. 2-Stelfreeze-c. 3-Hughes-c. 4-Golden-c. 5-Julie Bell-c. 3.00
It Can't Happen Here TPB (8/99, $16.95) r/#1-5 17.00
Mini Comic 1 (7/95) Maroto-a; Zorro app. 3.00
Special Edition 1 (6/95, $3.95)-Reprints 4.00

LADY RAWHIDE (Volume 2)
Topps Comics: Oct, 1996 - No. 5, June, 1997 ($2.95, limited series)
1-5: 1-Julie Bell-c. 3.00

LADY RAWHIDE (Volume 1)
Dynamite Entertainment: 2013 - No. 5, 2014 ($3.99)
1-5-Trautmann-s/Estevam-a/Linsner-c 4.00

LADY RAWHIDE / LADY ZORRO
Dynamite Entertainment: 2015 - No. 4, 2015 ($3.99, limited series)
1-4-Denton-s/Villegas-a. 1-Mayhew-c. 2-4-Chin-c 4.00

LADY RAWHIDE OTHER PEOPLE'S BLOOD (ZORRO'S ...)
Image Comics: Mar, 1999 - No. 5, July, 1999 ($2.95, B&W)
1-5-Reprints Lady Rawhide series in B&W 3.00

LADY SUPREME (See Asylum)(Also see Supreme & Kid Supreme)
Image Comics (Extreme): May, 1996 - No. 2, June, 1996 ($2.50, limited series)
1,2-Terry Moore -s: 1-Terry Moore-c. 2-Flip book w/Newmen preview 3.00

LADY ZORRO
Dynamite Entertainment: 2014 - No. 4, 2014 ($3.99, limited series)
1-4-de Campi-s/Villegas-a/Linsner-c 4.00

LADY ZORRO (Also see Zorro: Galleon of the Dead)
American Mythology Prods.: 2020 ($3.99, one-shot)
1-Pat Shand-s/Vincenzo Carratu-a; origin of Muat 4.00

LAFF-A-LYMPICS (TV)(See The Funtastic World of Hanna-Barbera)
Marvel Comics: Mar, 1978 - No. 13, Mar, 1979 (Newsstand sales only)
1-Yogi Bear, Scooby Doo, Pixie & Dixie, etc. 3 6 9 19 30 40
2-8 3 6 9 14 19 24
9-13: 11-Jetsons x-over; 1 pg. illustrated bio of Mighty Mightor, Herculoids, Shazzan, Galaxy Trio & Space Ghost 3 6 9 16 23 30

LAFFY-DAFFY COMICS
Rural Home Publ. Co.: Feb, 1945 - No. 2, Mar, 1945
1-Funny animal 14 28 42 80 115 150
2-Funny animal 11 22 33 64 90 115

LAGUARDIA
Dark Horse Comics (Berger Books): Dec, 2018 - No. 4, Mar, 2019 ($4.99, limited series)
1-4-Nnedi Okorafor-s/Tana Ford-a 5.00

LAKE OF FIRE
Image Comics: Aug, 2016 - No. 5, Dec, 2016 ($3.99)
1-5-Nathan Fairbairn-s/Matt Smith-a 4.00

LA MUERTA...
Coffin Comics (One-shots)
...: Ascension 1 (1019 $7.99) Maclean-s/Gomez-a 8.00
...: Descent 1 (7/16, $7.99) Maclean-s/Gomez-a; origin 8.00
...: Last Rites 1 (9/16, $7.99) Maclean-s/Gomez-a 8.00
...: Vengeance 1 (9/17, $7.99) Maclean-s/Gomez-a 8.00

LA MUERTA: RETRIBUTION
Coffin Comics: Sept, 2018 - No. 2, Sept, 2018 ($4.99, limited series)
1,2-Mike Maclean-s/Joel Gomez-a 5.00

LANA (Little Lana No. 8 on)
Marvel Comics (MjMC): Aug, 1948 - No. 7, Aug, 1949 (Also see Annie Oakley)
1-Rusty, Millie begin 61 122 183 390 670 950
2-Kurtzman's "Hey Look" (1); last Rusty 32 64 96 188 307 425
3-7: 3-Nellie begins 23 46 69 138 237 315

LANCELOT & GUINEVERE (See Movie Classics)

LANCELOT LINK, SECRET CHIMP (TV)
Gold Key: Apr, 1971 - No. 8, Feb, 1973 (All photo-c)
1 5 10 15 35 63 90
2-8 4 8 12 23 37 50

LANCELOT STRONG (See The Shield)

LANCE O'CASEY (See Mighty Midget & Whiz Comics)
Fawcett Publications: Spring, 1946 - No. 3, Fall, 1946; No. 4, Summer, 1948
1-Captain Marvel app. on-c 28 56 84 165 270 375
2 17 34 51 98 154 210
3,4 14 28 42 81 118 155
NOTE: *The cover for the 1st issue was done in 1942 but was not published until 1946. The cover shows 68 pages but actually has only 36 pages.*

LANCER (TV)(Western)
Gold Key: Feb, 1969 - No. 3, Sept, 1969 (All photo-c)
1 4 8 12 23 37 50
2,3 3 6 9 17 26 35

LANDO (Star Wars)
Marvel Comics: Sept, 2015 - No. 5, Dec, 2015 ($3.99, limited series)
1-5-Soule-s/Maleev-a; Lobot & Emperor Palpatine app. 4.00

LAND OF NOD, THE
Dark Horse Comics: July, 1997 - No. 3, Feb, 1998 ($2.95, B&W)
1-3-Jetcat; Jay Stephens-s/a 3.00

LAND OF OZ
Arrow Comics: 1998 - No. 9 ($2.95, B&W)
1-9-Bishop-s/Bryan-s/a 3.00

LAND OF THE DEAD (George A. Romaro's...)
IDW Publishing: Aug, 2005 - No. 5 ($3.99, limited series)
1-4-Adaptation of 2005 movie; Ryall-s/Rodriguez-a 4.00
TPB (3/06, $19.99) r/#1-5; cover gallery 20.00

LAND OF THE GIANTS (TV)
Gold Key: Nov, 1968 - No. 5, Sept, 1969 (All have photo-c)
1 6 12 18 40 73 105
2-5 4 8 12 27 44 60

LAND OF THE LOST COMICS (Radio)
E. C. Comics: July-Aug, 1946 - No. 9, Spring, 1948
1 43 86 129 271 461 650
2 28 56 84 165 270 375
3-9 24 48 72 140 230 320

LAND THAT TIME FORGOT, THE (Movie)
Amercan Mythology Productions: 2019 - No. 2, 2019 ($3.99, B&W)
1,2-Reprints movie adaptation from Marvel Movie Premiere #1; Wolfman-s/Cardy-c 4.00

LAND THAT TIME FORGOT, THE : FEARLESS
Amercan Mythology Productions: 2020 ($3.99)
1-Wolfer-s/Casas-a 4.00

LAND UNKNOWN, THE (Movie)
Dell Publishing Co.: No. 845, Sept, 1957
Four Color 845-Alex Toth-a 11 22 33 76 163 250

LANTERN CITY (TV)
BOOM! Studios (Archaia): May, 2015 - No. 12, Apr, 2016 ($3.99)
1-12: 1-Jenkins & Daley-s/Magno-a. 3-Daley & Scott-s 4.00

LA PACIFICA
DC Comics (Paradox Press): 1994/1995 ($4.95, B&W, limited series, digest size, mature)
1-3 5.00

LARA CROFT AND THE FROZEN OMEN (Also see Tomb Raider titles)
Dark Horse Comics: Oct, 2015 - No. 5, Feb, 2016 ($3.99)
1-5: 1-Corinna Bechko-s/Randy Green-a 4.00

LARAMIE (TV)
Dell Publishing Co.: Aug, 1960 - July, 1962 (All photo-c)

Larfleeze #8 © DC

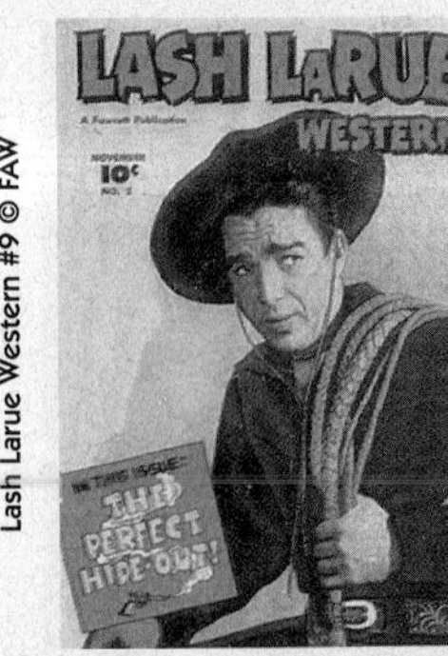

Lash Larue Western #9 © FAW

Lassie #3 © MGM

	GD 2.0	VG 4.0	FN 6.0	VF 8.0	VF/NM 9.0	NM- 9.2
Four Color 1125-Gil Kane/Heath-a	8	16	24	54	102	150
Four Color 1223,1284, 01-418-207 (7/62)	6	12	18	37	66	95

LAREDO (TV)
Gold Key: June, 1966

1 (10179-606)-Photo-c	3	6	9	21	33	45

LARFLEEZE (Orange Lantern) (Story continued from back-ups in Threshold #1-5)
DC Comics: Aug, 2013 - No. 12, Aug, 2014 ($2.99)

1-12: 1-Giffen & DeMatteis-s/Kolins-a/Porter-c; origin told 3.00

LARGE FEATURE COMIC (Formerly called Black & White in previous guides)
Dell Publishing Co.: 1939 - No. 13, 1943

Note: See individual alphabetical listings for prices

1 (Series I)-Dick Tracy Meets the Blank
3-Heigh-Yo Silver! The Lone Ranger (text & ill.)(76 pgs.); also exists as a Whitman #710; based on radio
6-Terry & the Pirates & The Dragon Lady; reprints dailies from 1936
8-Dick Tracy the Racket Buster
9-King of the Royal Mounted (Zane Grey's...)
10-(Scarce)-Gang Busters (No. appears on inside front cover); first slick cover (based on radio program)
13-Dick Tracy and Scottie of Scotland Yard
15-Dick Tracy and the Kidnapped Princes
17-Gang Busters (1941)
18-Phantasmo (see The Funnies #45)
20-Donald Duck Comic Paint Book (rarer than #16) (Disney)
21,22: 21-Private Buck. 22-Nuts & Jolts
24-Popeye in "Thimble Theatre" by Segar
26-Smitty
28-Grin and Bear It
30-Tillie the Toiler
2-Winnie Winkle (#1)
3-Dick Tracy
4-Tiny Tim (#1)
6-Terry and the Pirates; Caniff-a
8-Bugs Bunny (#1)('42)
9-Bringing Up Father
10-Popeye (Thimble Theatre)
11-Barney Google and Snuffy Smith
13-(nn)-1001 Hours Of Fun; puzzles & games; by A. W. Nugent. This book was bound as #13 with Large Feature Comics in publisher's files
2-Terry and the Pirates (#1)
4-Dick Tracy Gets His Man
5-Tarzan of the Apes (#1) by Harold Foster (origin); reprints 1st Tarzan dailies from 1929
7-(Scarce, 52 pgs.)-Hi-Yo Silver the Lone Ranger to the Rescue; also exists as a Whitman #715, based on radio program
11-Dick Tracy Foils the Mad Doc Hump
12-Smilin' Jack; no number on-c
14-Smilin' Jack Helps G-Men Solve a Case!
16-Donald Duck; 1st app. Daisy Duck on back cover (6/41-Disney)
19-Dumbo Comic Paint Book (Disney); partial-r from 4-Color #17
23-The Nebbs
25-Smilin' Jack-1st issue to show title on-c
27-Terry and the Pirates; Caniff-c/a
29-Moon Mullins
1 (Series II)-Peter Rabbit by Harrison Cady; arrival date-3/27/42
5-Toots and Casper
7-Pluto Saves the Ship (#1) (Disney)-Written by Carl Barks, Jack Hannah, & Nick George (Barks' 1st comic book work)
12-Private Buck

NOTE: *The Black & White Feature Books are oversized 8-1/2x11-3/8" comics with color covers and black and white interiors. The first nine issues all have rough, heavy stock covers and, except for #7, all have 76 pages, including covers. #7 and #10-on all have 52 pages. Beginning with #10 the covers are slick and thin and, because of their size, are difficult to handle without damaging. For this reason, they are seldom found in fine to mint condition. The paper stock, unlike Wow #1 and Capt. Marvel #1, is itself not unstable ...just thin. Many issues were reprinted in the early 1980s, identical except for the copyright notice on the first page.*

LARRY DOBY, BASEBALL HERO
Fawcett Publications: 1950 (Cleveland Indians)

nn-Bill Ward-a; photo-c	81	162	243	518	884	1250

LARRY HARMON'S LAUREL AND HARDY (...Comics)
National Periodical Publ.: July-Aug, 1972 (Digest advertised, not published)

1-Low print run	9	18	27	59	117	175

LARS OF MARS
Ziff-Davis Publishing Co.: No. 10, Apr-May, 1951 - No. 11, July-Aug, 1951 (Painted-c) (Created by Jerry Siegel, editor)

10-Origin; Anderson-a(3) in each; classic robot-c	123	246	369	787	1344	1900
11-Gene Colan-a; classic-c	94	188	282	597	1025	1450

LARS OF MARS 3-D
Eclipse Comics: Apr, 1987 ($2.50)

1-r/Lars of Mars #10,11 in 3-D plus new story 5.00
2-D limited edition (B&W, 100 copies) 20.00

LASER ERASER & PRESSBUTTON (See Axel Pressbutton & Miracle Man 9)
Eclipse Comics: Nov, 1985 - No. 6, 1987 (95¢/$2.50, limited series)

1-6: 5,6-(95¢) 3.00
...In 3-D 1 (8/86, $2.50) 4.00
2-D 1 (B&W, limited to 100 copies signed & numbered) 20.00

LASH LARUE WESTERN (Movie star; King of the bullwhip)(See Fawcett Movie Comic, Motion Picture Comics & Six-Gun Heroes)
Fawcett Publications: Sum, 1949 - No. 46, Jan, 1954 (36 pgs., 1-6,9,13,16-on)

	GD 2.0	VG 4.0	FN 6.0	VF 8.0	VF/NM 9.0	NM- 9.2
1-Lash & his horse Black Diamond begin; photo front/back-c begin	58	116	174	371	636	900
2(11/49)	28	56	84	165	270	375
3-5	21	42	63	126	206	285
6,9: 6-Last photo back-c; intro. Frontier Phantom (Lash's twin brother)	19	38	57	109	172	235
7,8,10 (52pgs.)	20	40	60	114	182	250
11,12,14,15 (52pgs.)	15	30	45	84	127	170
13,16-20 (36pgs.)	14	28	42	80	115	150
21-30: 21-The Frontier Phantom app.	12	24	36	69	97	125
31-45	11	22	33	60	83	105
46-Last Fawcett issue & photo-c	11	22	33	64	90	115

LASH LARUE WESTERN (Continues from Fawcett series)
Charlton Comics: No. 47, Mar-Apr, 1954 - No. 84, June, 1961

47-Photo-c	14	28	42	80	115	150
48	11	22	33	60	83	105
49-60, 67,68-(68 pgs.). 68-Check-a	9	18	27	52	69	85
61-66,69,70: 52-r/#8; 53-r/#22	9	18	27	47	61	75
71-83	8	16	24	40	50	60
84-Last issue	9	18	27	47	61	75

LASH LARUE WESTERN
AC Comics: 1990 ($3.50, 44 pgs) (24 pgs. of color, 16 pgs. of B&W)

1-Photo covers; r/Lash #6; r/old movie posters 4.00
Annual 1 (1990, $2.95, B&W, 44 pgs.)-Photo covers 4.00

LASSIE (TV)(M-G-M's... #1-36; see Kite Fun Book)
Dell Publ. Co./Gold Key No. 59 (10/62) on: June, 1950 - No. 70, July, 1969

1 (52 pgs.)-Photo-c; inside lists One Shot #282 in error	26	52	78	182	404	625
2-Painted-c begin	8	16	24	56	108	160
3-10	6	12	18	37	66	95
11-19: 12-Rocky Langford (Lassie's master) marries Gerry Lawrence. 15-1st app. Timbu	5	10	15	30	50	70
20-22-Matt Baker-a	5	10	15	33	57	80
23-38: 33-Robinson-a.	4	8	12	28	47	65
39-1st app. Timmy as Lassie picks up her TV family; photo-c	5	10	15	35	63	90
40-50-Photo-c on all	4	8	12	28	47	65
51-58-Photo-c on all	4	8	12	27	44	60
59 (10/62)-1st Gold Key	4	8	12	28	47	65
60-70: 63-Last Timmy (10/63). 64-r/#19. 65-Forest Ranger Corey Stuart begins, ends #69. 70-Forest Rangers Bob Ericson & Scott Turner app. (Lassie's new masters)	4	8	12	25	40	55
11193(1978, $1.95, 224 pgs., Golden Press)-Baker-r (92 pgs.)	4	8	12	25	40	55

NOTE: *Also see March of Comics #210, 217, 230, 254, 266, 278, 296, 308, 324,334, 346, 358, 370, 381, 394, 411, 432.*

LAST AMERICAN, THE
Marvel Comics (Epic): Dec, 1990 - No. 4, March, 1991 ($2.25, mini-series)

1-4: Alan Grant scripts 3.00

LAST AVENGERS STORY, THE (Last Avengers #1)
Marvel Comics: Nov, 1995 - No. 2, Dec, 1995 ($5.95, painted, limited series) (Alterniverse)

1,2: Peter David story; acetate-c in all. 1-New team (Hank Pym, Wasp, Human Torch, Cannonball, She-Hulk, Hotshot, Bombshell, Tommy Maximoff, Hawkeye & Mockingbird) forms to battle Ultron 59, Kang the Conqueror, The Grim Reaper & Oddball 6.00

LAST BATTLE, THE
Image Comics: Dec, 2011 ($7.99, square-bound, one-shot)

1-Facari-s/Brereton-painted art/c; Roman gladiator story; bonus Brereton sketch pages 8.00

LAST CHRISTMAS, THE
Image Comics: May, 2006 - No. 5, Oct, 2006 ($2.99, limited series)

1-5-Gerry Duggan & Brian Posehn-s/Rick Remender & Hilary Barta-a 3.00
TPB (2006, $14.99) r/#1-5; Patton Oswalt intro.; sketch pages and art 15.00

LAST CONTRACT, THE
BOOM! Studios: Jan, 2016 - No. 4, Apr, 2016 ($3.99, limited series)

The Last Defenders #1 © MAR

Last Sons of America #1 © PK Johnson

Laugh #14 © ACP

GD VG FN VF VF/NM NM-
2.0 4.0 6.0 8.0 9.0 9.2

1-4-Brisson-s/Estherren-a/c 4.00

LAST DAY IN VIETNAM
Dark Horse Books: July, 2000 ($10.95, graphic novel)

nn-Will Eisner-s/a/c 11.00

LAST DAYS OF ANIMAL MAN, THE
DC Comics: July, 2009 - No. 6, Dec, 2009 ($2.99, limited series)

1-6: 1-Conway-s/Batista-a/Bolland-c. 3,4-Starfire app. 5,6-Future Justice League app.3.00
TPB (2010, $17.99) r/#1-6 18.00

LAST DAYS OF THE JUSTICE SOCIETY SPECIAL
DC Comics: 1986 ($2.50, one-shot, 68 pgs.)

1-62 pg. JSA story plus unpubbed G.A. pg. 2 4 6 8 10 12

LAST DEFENDERS, THE
Marvel Comics: May, 2008 - No. 6, Oct, 2008 ($2.99, limited series)

1-6-Nighthawk, She-Hulk, Colossus, and Blazing Skull; Muniz-a. 2-Deodato-c 3.00

LAST FANTASTIC FOUR STORY, THE
Marvel Comics: Oct, 2007 ($4.99, one-shot)

1-Stan Lee-s/John Romita, Jr.-a/c; Galactus app. 5.00

LAST GANG IN TOWN
DC Comics (Vertigo): Feb, 2016 - No. 6, Aug, 2016 ($3.99, limited series)

1-6: 1-Simon Oliver-s/Rufus Dayglo-a/Rob Davis-c 4.00

LAST GENERATION, THE
Black Tie Studios: 1986 - No. 5, 1989 ($1.95, B&W, high quality paper)

1-5 3.00
Book 1 (1989, $6.95)-By Caliber Press 7.00

LAST GOD, THE
DC Comics (Black Label): Dec, 2019 - No. 12, Mar, 2021 ($4.99)

1-12-Phillip Kennedy Johnson-s/Riccardo Federici-a 5.00
...: Songs of Lost Children 1 (12/20, $4.99) Dan Watters-s/Steve Beach-a 5.00
...: Tales From the Book of Ages 1 (8/20, $4.99) Roleplaying sourcebook 5.00

LAST HERO STANDING (Characters from Spider-Girl's M2 universe)
Marvel Comics: Aug, 2005 - No. 5, Aug, 2005 ($2.99, weekly limited series)

1-5: 1-DeFalco-s/Olliffe-a. 4-Thor app. 5-Capt. America dies 3.00
TPB (2005, $13.99) r/#1-5 14.00

LAST HUNT, THE
Dell Publishing Co.: No. 678, Feb, 1956

Four Color 678-Movie, photo-c 6 12 18 42 79 115

LAST KISS
ACME Press (Eclipse): 1988 ($3.95, B&W, squarebound, 52 pgs.)

1-One story adapts E.A. Poe's The Black Cat 4.00

LAST OF THE COMANCHES (Movie) (See Wild Bill Hickok #28)
Avon Periodicals: 1953

nn-Kinstler-c/a, 21pgs.; Ravielli-a 20 40 60 117 189 260

LAST OF THE ERIES, THE (See American Graphics)

LAST OF THE FAST GUNS, THE
Dell Publishing Co.: No. 925, Aug, 1958

Four Color 925-Movie, photo-c 6 12 18 41 76 110

LAST OF THE MOHICANS (See King Classics & White Rider and...)

LAST OF THE VIKING HEROES, THE (Also see Silver Star #1)
Genesis West Comics: Mar, 1987 - No. 12 ($1.50/$1.95)

1-4,5A,5B,6-12: 4-Intro The Phantom Force, 1-Signed edition ($1.50), 5A-Kirby/Stevens-c. 5B,6 ($1.95). 7-Art Adams-c. 8-Kirby back-c. 4.00
Summer Special 1-3: 1-(1988)-Frazetta-c & illos. 2 (1990, $2.50)-A TMNT app. 3 (1991, $2.50)-Teenage Mutant Ninja Turtles 4.00
Summer Special 1-Signed edition (sold for $1.95) 4.00
NOTE: ***Art Adams** c-7. **Byrne** c-3. **Kirby** c-1p, 5p. **Perez** c-2i. **Stevens** c-5Ai.*

LAST ONE, THE
DC Comics (Vertigo): July, 1993 - No. 6, Dec, 1993 ($2.50, lim. series, mature)

1-6 3.00

LAST PHANTOM, THE (Lee Falk's Phantom)
Dynamite Entertainment: 2010 - No. 12, 2012 ($3.99)

1-12-Beatty-s/Ferigato-a; 1-Two covers by Alex Ross; Neves & Prado var. covers 4.00
Annual 1 (2011, $4.99) Beatty-s/Desjardins-a; two covers by Desjardins & Ross 5.00

LAST PLANET STANDING
Marvel Comics: July, 2006 - No. 5, Sept, 2006 ($2.99, limited series)

GD VG FN VF VF/NM NM-
2.0 4.0 6.0 8.0 9.0 9.2

1-5-Galactus threatens Spider-Girl & Fantastic Five's M2 Earth; Avengers app.; Olliffe-a 3.00
TPB (2006, $13.99) r/series 14.00

LAST RONIN, THE (See TMNT: The Last Ronin)

LAST SHOT
Image Comics: Aug, 2001 - No. 4, Mar, 2002 ($2.95, limited series)

1-4: 1-Wraparound-c; by Studio XD 3.00
...: First Draw (5/01, $2.95) Introductory one-shot 3.00

LAST SIEGE, THE
Image Comics: May, 2018 - No. 8, Jan, 2019 ($3.99)

1-8-Landry Q. Walker-s/Justin Greenwood-a 4.00

LAST SONS OF AMERICA
BOOM! Studios: Nov, 2015 - No. 4, Apr, 2016 ($3.99, limited series)

1-4-Phillip Johnson-s/Matthew Dow Smith-a 4.00

LAST SPACE RACE, THE
AfterShock Comics: Oct, 2018 - No. 5, Jul, 2019 ($3.99, limited series)

1-5-Peter Calloway-s/Alex Shibao-a 4.00

LAST STARFIGHTER, THE
Marvel Comics Group: Oct, 1984 - No. 3, Dec, 1984 (75¢, movie adaptation)

1-3: r/Marvel Super Special; Guice-c 4.00

LAST STOP ON THE RED LINE
Dark Horse Comics: May, 2019 - No. 4, Oct, 2019 ($3.99, limited series)

1-4-Paul Maybury-s/Sam Lotfi-a 4.00

LAST TEMPTATION, THE
Marvel Comics: 1994 - No. 3, 1994 ($4.95, limited series)

1-3-Alice Cooper story; Neil Gaiman scripts; McKean-c; Zulli-a: 1-Two covers 5.00
HC (Dark Horse Comics, 2005, $14.95) r/#1-3; Gaiman intro. 15.00

LAST TRAIN FROM GUN HILL
Dell Publishing Co.: No. 1012, July, 1959

Four Color 1012-Movie, photo-c 8 16 24 52 99 145

LAST TRAIN TO DEADSVILLE: A CAL McDONALD MYSTERY (See Criminal Macabre)
Dark Horse Comics: May, 2004 - No. 4, Sept, 2004 ($2.99, limited series)

1-4-Steve Niles-s/Kelley Jones-a/c 3.00
TPB (2005, $14.95) r/series 15.00

LATEST ADVENTURES OF FOXY GRANDPA (See Foxy Grandpa)

LATEST COMICS (Super Duper No. 3?)
Spotlight Publ./Palace Promotions (Jubilee): Mar, 1945 - No. 2, 1945?

1-Super Duper 20 40 60 120 195 270
2-Bee-29 (nd); Jubilee in indicia blacked out 15 30 45 86 133 180

LAUGH
Archie Enterprises: June, 1987 - No. 29, Aug, 1991 (75¢/$1.00)

V2#1 5.00
2-10,14,24: 5-X-Mas issue. 14-1st app. Hot Dog. 24-Re-intro Super Duck 4.00
11-13,15-23,25-29: 19-X-Mas issue 3.00

LAUGH COMICS (Teenage) (Formerly Black Hood #9-19) (Laugh #226 on)
Archie Publications (Close-Up): No. 20, Fall, 1946 - No. 400, Apr, 1987

	GD	VG	FN	VF	VF/NM	NM-
20-Archie begins; Katy Keene & Taffy begin by Woggon; Suzie & Wilbur also begin; Archie covers begin	174	348	522	1114	1907	2700
21-23,25	66	132	198	419	722	1025
24- "Pipsy" by Kirby (6 pgs.)	68	136	204	435	743	1050
26-30	43	86	129	271	461	650
31-40	35	70	105	208	339	470
41-60: 41,54-Debbi by Woggon	24	48	72	144	237	330
61-80: 67-Debbi by Woggon	16	32	48	98	154	210
81-99	9	18	27	60	120	180
100	9	18	27	61	123	185
101-105,110,112,114-126: 125-Debbi app.	7	14	21	46	86	125
106-109,111,113-Neal Adams-a (1 pg.) in each	7	14	21	48	89	130
127-144: Super-hero app. in all (see note)	8	16	24	54	102	150
145-(4/63) Josie by DeCarlo begins	8	16	24	54	102	150
146-149-early Josie app. by DeCarlo	6	12	18	37	66	95
150,162,163,165,167,169,170-No Josie	4	8	12	27	44	60
151-161,164,168-Josie app. by DeCarlo	5	10	15	31	53	75
166-Beatles-c (1/65)	7	14	21	49	92	135
171-180, 200 (11/67)	3	6	9	21	33	45
181-199	3	6	9	15	22	28
201-240(3/71)	2	4	6	11	16	20

Laurel and Hardy #1 © STJ

The L.A.W. #1 © DC

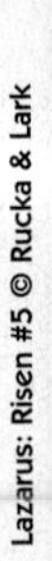

Lazarus: Risen #5 © Rucka & Lark

	GD 2.0	VG 4.0	FN 6.0	VF 8.0	VF/NM 9.0	NM- 9.2
241-280(7/74)	2	4	6	9	13	16
281-299	2	4	6	8	10	12
300(3/76)	2	4	6	8	11	14
301-340 (7/79)	1	2	3	5	7	9
341-370 (1/82)	1	2	3	4	5	7
371-379,385-399						5.00
380-Cheryl Blossom app.	2	4	6	9	12	15
381-384,400: 381-384-Katy Keene app.; by Woggon-381,382						6.00

NOTE: *The Fly app. in 128, 129, 132, 134, 138, 139. Flygirl app. in 136, 137, 143. Flyman app. in 137. The Jaguar app. in 127, 130, 131, 133, 135, 140-142, 144. Josie app. in 145-149, 151-161, 164, 168. Katy Keene app. in 20-125, 129, 130, 133. Horror/Sci-Fi covers on 128-135, 137, 139. Many issues contain paper dolls.* ***Al Fagaly*** *c-20-29.* ***Montana*** *c-33, 36, 37, 42.* ***Bill Vigoda*** *c-30, 50.*

LAUGH COMICS DIGEST (...Magazine #23-89; Laugh Digest Mag. #90 on)
Archie Publ. (Close-Up No. 1, 3 on): 8/74; No. 2, 9/75; No. 3, 3/76 - No. 200, Apr, 2005 (Digest-size) (Josie and Sabrina app. in most issues)

	GD 2.0	VG 4.0	FN 6.0	VF 8.0	VF/NM 9.0	NM- 9.2
1-Neal Adams-a	5	10	15	31	53	75
2,7,8,19-Neal Adams-a	3	6	9	19	30	40
3-6,9,10	3	6	9	15	22	28
11-18,20	2	4	6	11	16	20
21-40	2	4	6	9	13	16
41-60	1	3	4	6	8	10
61-80	1	2	3	5	6	8
81-99						5.00
100						6.00
101-138						4.00
139-200: 139-Begin $1.95-c. 148-Begin $1.99-c. 156-Begin $2.19-c. 180-Begin $2.39-c						3.00

NOTE: *Katy Keene in 23, 25, 27, 32-38, 40, 45-48, 50. The Fly-r in 19, 20. The Jaguar-r in 25, 27. Mr. Justice-r in 21. The Web-r in 23.*

LAUGH COMIX (Laugh Comics inside)(Formerly Top Notch Laugh; Suzie Comics No. 49 on)
MLJ Magazines: No. 46, Summer, 1944 - No. 48, Winter, 1944-45

	GD 2.0	VG 4.0	FN 6.0	VF 8.0	VF/NM 9.0	NM- 9.2
46-Wilbur & Suzie in all; Harry Sahle-c	39	78	117	240	395	550
47,48: 47-Sahle-c. 48-Bill Vigoda-c	27	54	81	158	259	360

LAUGH-IN MAGAZINE (TV)(Magazine)
Laufer Publ. Co.: Oct, 1968 - No. 12, Oct, 1969 (50¢) (Satire)

	GD 2.0	VG 4.0	FN 6.0	VF 8.0	VF/NM 9.0	NM- 9.2
V1#1	5	10	15	30	50	70
2-12	3	6	9	21	33	45

LAUREL & HARDY (See Larry Harmon's... & March of Comics No. 302, 314)

LAUREL AND HARDY (...Comics)
St. John Publ. Co.: 3/49 - No. 3, 9/49; No. 26, 11/55 - No. 28, 3/56 (No #4-25)

	GD 2.0	VG 4.0	FN 6.0	VF 8.0	VF/NM 9.0	NM- 9.2
1	103	206	309	659	1130	1600
2	45	90	135	284	480	675
3	39	78	117	231	378	525
26-28 (Reprints)	18	36	54	107	169	230

LAUREL AND HARDY (TV)
Dell Publishing Co.: Oct, 1962 - No. 4, Sept-Nov, 1963

	GD 2.0	VG 4.0	FN 6.0	VF 8.0	VF/NM 9.0	NM- 9.2
12-423-210 (8-10/62)	6	12	18	42	79	115
2-4 (Dell)	4	8	12	28	47	65

LAUREL AND HARDY (Larry Harmon's...)
Gold Key: Jan, 1967 - No. 2, Oct, 1967

	GD 2.0	VG 4.0	FN 6.0	VF 8.0	VF/NM 9.0	NM- 9.2
1-Photo back-c	5	10	15	30	50	70
2	4	8	12	21	33	45

LAUREL AND HARDY
American Mythology Productions: 2019 - No. 2, 2019 ($3.99)

	GD 2.0	VG 4.0	FN 6.0	VF 8.0	VF/NM 9.0	NM- 9.2
1,2-New stories and reprints						4.00
... Christmas Follies 1 (2020, $3.99) New stories; Check-s/Tapié-a; Pacheco-s/a						4.00
... Gold Key Edition #1 (2019, $3.99) Reprints #1 from Jan, 1967						4.00
.../ The Three Stooges 1 (2020, $3.99) New story; Check & Kuhoric-s/Tapié-a						4.00

L.A.W., THE (LIVING ASSAULT WEAPONS)
DC Comics: Sept, 1999 - No. 6, Feb, 2000 ($2.50, limited series)

	GD 2.0	VG 4.0	FN 6.0	VF 8.0	VF/NM 9.0	NM- 9.2
1-6-Blue Beetle, Question, Judomaster, Capt. Atom app.; Giordano-a. 5-JLA app.						3.00

LAW AGAINST CRIME (Law-Crime on cover)
Essenkay Publishing Co.: April, 1948 - No. 3, Aug, 1948 (Real Stories from Police Files)

	GD 2.0	VG 4.0	FN 6.0	VF 8.0	VF/NM 9.0	NM- 9.2
1-(#1-3 are half funny animal, half crime stories)-L. B. Cole-c/a in all; electrocution-c	123	246	369	787	1344	1900
2-L. B. Cole-c/a	71	142	213	454	777	1100
3-Used in **SOTI**, pg. 180,181 & illo "The wish to hurt or kill couples in lovers' lanes;" reprinted in All-Famous Crime #9	90	180	270	576	988	1400

LAW AND ORDER
Maximum Press: Sept, 1995 - No. 2, 1995 ($2.50, unfinished limited series)

	GD 2.0	VG 4.0	FN 6.0	VF 8.0	VF/NM 9.0	NM- 9.2
1,2						3.00

LAWBREAKERS (...Suspense Stories No. 10 on)
Law and Order Magazines (Charlton): Mar, 1951 - No. 9, Oct-Nov, 1952

	GD 2.0	VG 4.0	FN 6.0	VF 8.0	VF/NM 9.0	NM- 9.2
1	47	94	141	296	498	700
2	28	56	84	165	270	375
3,5,6,8,9: 6-Anti-Wertham editorial	23	46	69	136	223	310
4- "White Death" junkie story	34	68	102	204	332	460
7- "The Deadly Dopesters" drug story	37	74	111	222	361	500

LAWBREAKERS ALWAYS LOSE!
Marvel Comics (CBS): Spring, 1948 - No. 10, Oct, 1949

	GD 2.0	VG 4.0	FN 6.0	VF 8.0	VF/NM 9.0	NM- 9.2
1-2pg. Kurtzman-a, "Giggles 'n' Grins"	43	86	129	271	461	650
2	24	48	72	142	234	325
3-5: 4-Vampire story	19	38	57	111	176	240
6(2/49)-Has editorial defense against charges of Dr. Wertham	20	40	60	115	188	260
7-Used in **SOTI**, illo "Comic-book philosophy"	37	74	111	222	361	500
8-10: 9,10-Photo-c	16	32	48	98	154	210

NOTE: ***Brodsky*** *c-4, 5.* ***Shores*** *c-1-3, 6-8.*

LAWBREAKERS SUSPENSE STORIES (Formerly Lawbreakers; Strange Suspense Stories No. 16 on)
Capitol Stories/Charlton Comics: No. 10, Jan, 1953 - No. 15, Nov, 1953

	GD 2.0	VG 4.0	FN 6.0	VF 8.0	VF/NM 9.0	NM- 9.2
10	54	108	162	343	574	825
11 (3/53)-Severed tongues-c/story & woman negligee scene	423	846	1269	3000	5250	7500
12-14: 13-Giordano-c begin, end #15	40	80	120	246	411	575
15-Acid-in-face-c/story; hands dissolved in acid story	97	194	291	621	1061	1500

LAW-CRIME (See Law Against Crime)

LAWDOG
Marvel Comics (Epic Comics): May, 1993 - No. 10, Feb, 1993

	GD 2.0	VG 4.0	FN 6.0	VF 8.0	VF/NM 9.0	NM- 9.2
1-10						3.00

LAWDOG/GRIMROD: TERROR AT THE CROSSROADS
Marvel Comics (Epic Comics): Sept, 1993 ($3.50)

	GD 2.0	VG 4.0	FN 6.0	VF 8.0	VF/NM 9.0	NM- 9.2
1						4.00

LAWMAN (TV)
Dell Publishing Co.: No. 970, Feb, 1959 - No. 11, Apr-June, 1962 (All photo-c)

	GD 2.0	VG 4.0	FN 6.0	VF 8.0	VF/NM 9.0	NM- 9.2
Four Color 970(#1) John Russell, Peter Brown photo-c	10	20	30	69	147	225
Four Color 1035('60), 3(2-4/60)-Toth-a	7	14	21	46	86	125
4-11	6	12	18	37	66	95

LAW OF DREDD, THE (Also see Judge Dredd)
Quality Comics/Fleetway #8 on: 1989 - No. 33, 1992 ($1.50/$1.75)

	GD 2.0	VG 4.0	FN 6.0	VF 8.0	VF/NM 9.0	NM- 9.2
1-33: Bolland a-1-6,8,10-12,14(2 pg),15,19						3.00

LAWRENCE (See Movie Classics)

LAZARUS (Also see Lazarus: X +66)
Image Comics: Jun, 2013 - Present ($2.99/$3.50/$3.99)

	GD 2.0	VG 4.0	FN 6.0	VF 8.0	VF/NM 9.0	NM- 9.2
1-9-Rucka-s/Lark-a/c						3.50
10-21-($3.50) 19-Bonus preview of Black Magic #1						3.50
22-28-($3.99)						4.00
Image Firsts Lazarus #1 (11/15, $1.00) reprints #1; afterword by Rucka; Lark sketch art						3.00
... Sourcebook, Volume 1: Carlyle (4/16, $3.99) Dossier of politics, locations, weapons						4.00
... Sourcebook, Volume 2: Hock (5/17, $3.99) Dossier of politics, locations, weapons						4.00
... Sourcebook, Volume 3: Vassalovka (2/18, $3.99) Dossier of politics, locations						4.00

LAZARUS CHURCHYARD
Tundra Publishing: June, 1992 - No. 3, 1992 ($3.95/$4.50, 44 pgs., coated stock)

	GD 2.0	VG 4.0	FN 6.0	VF 8.0	VF/NM 9.0	NM- 9.2
1-3						5.00
The Final Cut (Image, 1/01, $14.95, TPB) Reprints Ellis/D'Israeli strips						15.00

LAZARUS FIVE
DC Comics: July, 2000 - No. 5, Nov, 2000 ($2.50, limited series)

	GD 2.0	VG 4.0	FN 6.0	VF 8.0	VF/NM 9.0	NM- 9.2
1-5-Harris-c/Abell-a(p)						3.00

LAZARUS: RISEN (Characters from Lazarus)
Image Comics: Mar, 2019 - Present ($7.99, squarebound, limited series)

	GD 2.0	VG 4.0	FN 6.0	VF 8.0	VF/NM 9.0	NM- 9.2
1-5-Rucka-s/Lark-a; takes place in the year X +68						4.00

LAZARUS: X +66 (Characters from Lazarus)
Image Comics: Jul, 2017 - No. 6, Feb, 2018 ($3.99, limited series)

	GD 2.0	VG 4.0	FN 6.0	VF 8.0	VF/NM 9.0	NM- 9.2
1-6: 1-Lieber-a; how Casey became a Dagger. 2-Chater-a. 5-Evely-a						4.00

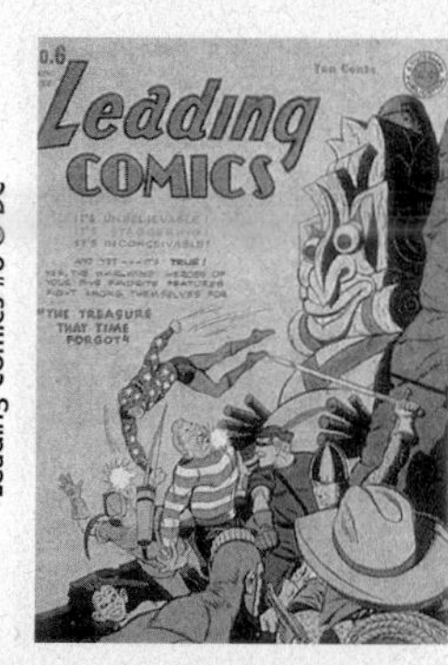

Leading Comics #6 © DC

Leave It to Chance #11 © Robinson & Smith

Legendary Star-Lord #1 © MAR

LEADING COMICS
DC Comics: Jan. 1942

nn - Ashcan comic, not distributed to newsstands, only for in-house use. Cover art is Detective Comics #57, interior of Star Spangled Comics #2 (a FN+ copy sold for $1015.75 in 2012)

LEADING COMICS (...Screen Comics No. 42 on)
National Periodical Publications: Winter, 1941-42 - No. 41, Feb-Mar, 1950

	GD 2.0	VG 4.0	FN 6.0	VF 8.0	VF/NM 9.0	NM- 9.2
1-Origin The Seven Soldiers of Victory; Green Arrow & Speedy, Crimson Avenger, Shining Knight, The Vigilante, Star Spangled Kid & Stripesy begin; The Dummy (Vigilante villain) 1st app.; 1st Green Arrow-c	448	896	1344	3270	5785	8300
2-Meskin-a; Fred Ray-c	135	270	405	864	1482	2100
3	106	212	318	678	1164	1650
4,5	71	142	213	454	777	1100
6-10	53	106	159	334	567	800
11,12,14(Spring, 1945)	41	82	123	256	428	600
13-Classic robot-c	110	220	330	704	1202	1700
15-(Sum,'45)-Contents change to funny animal	27	54	81	158	259	360
16-22,24-30: 16-Nero Fox-c begin, end #22	14	28	42	82	121	160
23-1st app. Peter Porkchops by Otto Feuer & begins	27	54	81	158	259	360
31,32,34-41: 34-41-Leading Screen... on-c only	13	26	39	72	101	130
33-(Scarce)	20	40	60	115	188	260

NOTE: *Otto Feuer-a most #15-on; **Rube Grossman**-a most #15-on;c-15-41. **Post** a-23-37, 39, 41.*

LEADING MAN
Image Comics: June, 2006 - No. 5, Feb, 2007 ($3.50, limited series)

	GD 2.0	VG 4.0	FN 6.0	VF 8.0	VF/NM 9.0	NM- 9.2
1-5-B. Clay Moore-s/Jeremy Haun-a						3.50
TPB (2/07, $14.95) r/#1-5; sketch gallery						15.00

LEADING SCREEN COMICS (Formerly Leading Comics)
National Periodical Publ.: No. 42, Apr-May, 1950 - No. 77, Aug-Sept, 1955

	GD 2.0	VG 4.0	FN 6.0	VF 8.0	VF/NM 9.0	NM- 9.2
42-Peter Porkchops-c/stories continue	12	24	36	67	94	120
43-77	11	22	33	60	83	105

NOTE: ***Grossman** a-most. **Mayer** a-45-48, 50, 54-57, 60, 62-74, 75(3), 76, 77.*

LEAGUE OF CHAMPIONS, THE (Also see The Champions)
Hero Graphics: Dec, 1990 - No. 12, 1992 ($2.95, 52 pgs.)

	GD 2.0	VG 4.0	FN 6.0	VF 8.0	VF/NM 9.0	NM- 9.2
1-12: 1-Flare app. 2-Origin Malice						4.00

LEAGUE OF EXTRAORDINARY CEREBI, THE (Reprints from Cerebus in Hell)
Aardvark-Vanaheim: Oct, 2018 ($4.00, B&W)

	GD 2.0	VG 4.0	FN 6.0	VF 8.0	VF/NM 9.0	NM- 9.2
1-Cerebus figures placed over original Gustave Doré artwork of Hell						4.00

LEAGUE OF EXTRAORDINARY GENTLEMEN, THE
America's Best Comics: Mar, 1999 - No. 6, Sept, 2000 ($2.95, limited series)

	GD 2.0	VG 4.0	FN 6.0	VF 8.0	VF/NM 9.0	NM- 9.2
1-Alan Moore-s/Kevin O'Neill-a	3	6	9	16	23	30
1-DF Edition ($10.00) O'Neill-c	3	6	9	15	22	28
2,3						6.00
4-6: 5-Revised printing with "Amaze 'Whirling Spray' Syringe" parody ad						4.00
5-Initial printing recalled because of "Marvel Co. Syringe" parody ad	14	28	42	93	204	315
... Compendium 1,2: 1-r/#1,2. 2-r/#3,4						6.00
Hardcover (2000, $24.95) r/#1-6 plus cover gallery						25.00

LEAGUE OF EXTRAORDINARY GENTLEMEN, THE (Volume 2)
America's Best Comics: Sept, 2002 - No. 6, Nov, 2003 ($3.50, limited series)

	GD 2.0	VG 4.0	FN 6.0	VF 8.0	VF/NM 9.0	NM- 9.2
1-6-Alan Moore-s/Kevin O'Neill-a						5.00
... Bumper Compendium 1,2: 1-r/#1,2. 2-r/#3,4						6.00
... Black Dossier (HC, 2007, $29.99) new graphic novel; 3-D section with glasses; extras						30.00

LEAGUE OF EXTRAORDINARY GENTLEMEN
Top Shelf Productions/Knockabout Comics: 2009; 2011; 2012 ($7.95/$9.95, squarebound)

	GD 2.0	VG 4.0	FN 6.0	VF 8.0	VF/NM 9.0	NM- 9.2
... Century: 1910 (2009, $7.95) Alan Moore-s/Kevin O'Neill-a						8.00
... Century #2 "1969" (2011, $9.95) Alan Moore-s/Kevin O'Neill-a						10.00
... Century #3 "2009" (2012, $9.95) Alan Moore-s/Kevin O'Neill-a						10.00

LEAGUE OF EXTRAORDINARY GENTLEMEN VOLUME 4: THE TEMPEST
Top Shelf Productions: Jun, 2018 - No. 6, Jun, 2019 ($4.99, limited series)

	GD 2.0	VG 4.0	FN 6.0	VF 8.0	VF/NM 9.0	NM- 9.2
1-6-Alan Moore-s/Kevin O'Neill-a. 3-Includes 3-D pages and glasses						5.00

LEAGUE OF JUSTICE
DC Comics (Elseworlds): 1996 - No. 2, 1996 ($5.95, 48 pgs., squarebound)

	GD 2.0	VG 4.0	FN 6.0	VF 8.0	VF/NM 9.0	NM- 9.2
1,2: Magic-based alternate DC Universe story; Giordano-i						6.00

LEATHERFACE
Arpad Publishing: May (April on-c), 1991 - No. 4, May, 1992 ($2.75, painted-c)

	GD 2.0	VG 4.0	FN 6.0	VF 8.0	VF/NM 9.0	NM- 9.2
1-Based on Texas Chainsaw movie; Dorman-c	2	4	6	11	16	20
2-4-Dorman-c on all	2	4	6	8	10	12

LEATHERNECK THE MARINE (See Mighty Midget Comics)

LEAVE IT TO BEAVER (TV)
Dell Publishing Co.: No. 912, June, 1958; May-July, 1962 (All photo-c)

	GD 2.0	VG 4.0	FN 6.0	VF 8.0	VF/NM 9.0	NM- 9.2
Four Color 912	15	30	45	100	220	340
Four Color 999,1103,1191,1285, 01-428-207	12	24	36	83	182	280

LEAVE IT TO BINKY (Binky No. 72 on) (Super DC Giant) (No. 1-22: 52 pgs.)
National Periodical Publs.: 2-3/48 - #60, 10/58; #61, 6-7/68 - #71, 2-3/70 (Teen-age humor)

	GD 2.0	VG 4.0	FN 6.0	VF 8.0	VF/NM 9.0	NM- 9.2
1-Lucy wears Superman costume	50	100	150	315	533	750
2	23	46	69	136	223	310
3,4	16	32	48	98	154	210
5-Superman cameo	20	40	60	120	195	270
6-10	14	28	42	80	115	150
11-14,16-22: Last 52 pg. issue	12	24	36	67	94	120
15-Scribbly story by Mayer	14	28	42	76	108	140
23-28,30-45: 45-Last pre-code (2/55)	10	20	30	56	76	95
29-Used in **POP**, pg. 78	10	20	30	58	79	100
46-60: 60-(10/58)	5	10	15	35	63	90
61 (6-7/68) 1950's reprints with art changes	5	10	15	34	60	85
62-69: 67-Last 12¢ issue	4	8	12	27	44	60
70-7pg. app. Bus Driver who looks like Ralph from Honeymooners	5	10	15	30	50	70
71-Last issue	4	8	12	28	47	65

NOTE: ***Aragones**-a-61, 62, 67. **Drucker** a-28. **Mayer** a-1, 2, 15. Created by **Mayer**.*

LEAVE IT TO CHANCE
Image Comics (Homage Comics): Sept, 1996 - No. 11, Sept, 1998; No. 13, July, 2002
DC Comics (Homage Comics): No. 12, Jun, 1999 ($2.50/$2.95/$4.95)

	GD 2.0	VG 4.0	FN 6.0	VF 8.0	VF/NM 9.0	NM- 9.2
1-3: 1-Intro Chance Falconer & St. George; James Robinson scripts & Paul Smith-c/a						5.00
4-12: 12-(6/99)						3.00
13-(7/02, $4.95) includes sketch pages and pin-ups						5.00
Free Comic Book Day Edition (2003) - James Robinson-s/Paul Smith-a						3.00
Shaman's Rain TPB (1997, $9.95) r/#1-4						10.00
Shaman's Rain HC (2002, $14.95, over-sized 8 1/4" x 12") r/#1-4						15.00
Trick or Threat TPB (1997, $12.95) r/#5-8						13.00
Trick or Threat HC (2002, $14.95, over-sized 8 1/4" x 12") r/#5-8						15.00
Vol. 3: Monster Madness and Other Stories HC (2003, $14.95, 8 1/4" x 12") r/#9-11						15.00

LEAVING MEGALOPOLIS: SURVIVING MEGALOPOLIS
Dark Horse Comics: Jan, 2016 - No. 6, Sept, 2016 ($3.99)

	GD 2.0	VG 4.0	FN 6.0	VF 8.0	VF/NM 9.0	NM- 9.2
1-6-Gail Simone-s/Jim Calafiore-a						4.00

LEE HUNTER, INDIAN FIGHTER
Dell Publishing Co.: No. 779, Mar, 1957; No. 904, May, 1958

	GD 2.0	VG 4.0	FN 6.0	VF 8.0	VF/NM 9.0	NM- 9.2
Four Color 779 (#1)	6	12	18	37	66	95
Four Color 904	5	10	15	30	50	70

LEFT-HANDED GUN, THE (Movie)
Dell Publishing Co.: No. 913, July, 1958

	GD 2.0	VG 4.0	FN 6.0	VF 8.0	VF/NM 9.0	NM- 9.2
Four Color 913-Paul Newman photo-c	9	18	27	57	111	165

LEGACY
Majestic Entertainment: Oct, 1993 - No. 2, Nov, 1993; No. 0, 1994 ($2.25)

	GD 2.0	VG 4.0	FN 6.0	VF 8.0	VF/NM 9.0	NM- 9.2
1-2,0: 1-Glow-in-the-dark-c. 0-Platinum						3.00

LEGACY
Image Comics: May, 2003 - No. 4, Feb, 2004 ($2.95)

	GD 2.0	VG 4.0	FN 6.0	VF 8.0	VF/NM 9.0	NM- 9.2
1-4: 1-Francisco-a/Treffiletti-s						3.00

LEGACY OF KAIN (Based on the Eidos video game)
Top Cow Productions: Oct, 1999; Jan, 2004 ($2.99)

	GD 2.0	VG 4.0	FN 6.0	VF 8.0	VF/NM 9.0	NM- 9.2
...Defiance 1 (1/04, $2.99) Cha-c; Kirkham-a						3.00
...Soul Reaver 1 (10/99, Diamond Dateline supplement) Benitez-c						3.00

LEGACY OF LUTHER STRODE, THE (Also see Legend of Luther Strode)
Image Comics: Apr, 2015 - No. 6, May, 2016 ($3.99/$3.50)

	GD 2.0	VG 4.0	FN 6.0	VF 8.0	VF/NM 9.0	NM- 9.2
1-($3.99) Justin Jordan-s/Tradd Moore-a						4.00
2-6-($3.50)						3.50

LEGEND
DC Comics (WildStorm): Apr, 2005 - No. 4, July, 2005 ($5.95/$5.99, limited series)

	GD 2.0	VG 4.0	FN 6.0	VF 8.0	VF/NM 9.0	NM- 9.2
1-4-Howard Chaykin-s/Russ Heath-a; inspired by Philip Wylie's novel "Gladiator"						6.00

LEGENDARY STAR-LORD (Guardians of the Galaxy)
Marvel Comics: Sept, 2014 - No. 12, Jul, 2015 ($3.99)

	GD 2.0	VG 4.0	FN 6.0	VF 8.0	VF/NM 9.0	NM- 9.2
1-12: 1-Humphries-s/Medina-a. 4-Thanos app. 9-11-Black Vortex x-over						4.00

LEGENDARY TALESPINNERS
Dynamite Entertainment: 2010 - No. 3, 2010 ($3.99)

	GD 2.0	VG 4.0	FN 6.0	VF 8.0	VF/NM 9.0	NM- 9.2
1-3-Kuhoric-s/Bond-a; two covers						4.00

Legenderry Vampirella #5 © DYN

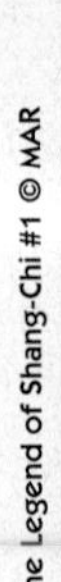
The Legend of Shang-Chi #1 © MAR

Legends of Red Sonja #1 © RS LLC

GD VG FN VF VF/NM NM-
2.0 4.0 6.0 8.0 9.0 9.2

LEGENDERRY: A STEAMPUNK ADVENTURE
Dynamite Entertainment: 2014 - No. 7, 2014 ($3.99)
1-7-Willingham-s/Davila-a/Benitez-c. 4.00

LEGENDERRY: GREEN HORNET
Dynamite Entertainment: 2015 - No. 5, 2015 ($3.99)
1-5-Gregory-s/Peeples-a; multiple covers 4.00

LEGENDERRY: RED SONJA
Dynamite Entertainment: 2015 - No. 5, 2015 ($3.99)
1-5: 1-Andreyko-s/Aneke-a; multiple covers; Steampunk Sonja; Bride of Frankenstein app. 4.00

LEGENDERRY: RED SONJA (Volume 2)
Dynamite Entertainment: 2018 - No. 5, 2018 ($3.99)
1-5-Andreyko-s/Lima-a; multiple covers; Kulan Gath app. 4.00

LEGENDERRY: VAMPIRELLA
Dynamite Entertainment: 2015 - No. 5, 2015 ($3.99)
1-5-Avallone-s/Cabrera-a; Steampunk Vampirella 4.00

LEGEND OF CUSTER, THE (TV)
Dell Publishing Co.: Jan, 1968
1-Wayne Maunder photo-c 3 6 9 17 26 35

LEGEND OF ISIS
Alias Entertainment: May, 2005 - No. 5 ($2.99)
1-5: 1-Three covers; Ottney-s/Fontana-a 3.00
...: Beginnings TPB (5/05, $9.99) Ottney-s 10.00

LEGEND OF JESSE JAMES, THE (TV)
Gold Key: Feb, 1966
10172-602-Photo-c 3 6 9 18 28 38

LEGEND OF KAMUI, THE (See Kamui)

LEGEND OF LOBO, THE (See Movie Comics)

LEGEND OF LUTHER STRODE, THE (Sequel to Strange Talent of Luther Strode)
Image Comics: Dec, 2012 - No. 6, Aug, 2013 ($3.50, limited series)
1-5: Justin Jordan-s/Tradd Moore-a 3.50

LEGEND OF OZ: TIK-TOK AND THE KALIDAH
Aspen MLT: Apr, 2016 - No. 3, Jul, 2016 ($3.99)
1-3-Rob Anderson-s/Renato Rei-a. 1-Three covers. 2,3-Two covers 4.00

LEGEND OF OZ: THE WICKED WEST
Big Dog Press: Oct, 2011 - No. 6, Aug, 2012; Oct, 2012 - No. 18, May 2014 ($3.50)
1-6-Multiple covers on all 3.50
Vol. 2 1-18-Multiple covers on all 3.50

LEGEND OF OZ: THE WICKED WEST
Aspen MLT: Oct, 2015 - No. 6, Mar, 2016 ($3.99)
1-6-Reprints 2011 series 4.00

LEGEND OF SHANG-CHI, THE
Marvel Comics: Apr, 2021 ($3.99, one-shot)
1-Alyssa Wong-s/Andie Tong-a; Lady Deathstrike app. 4.00

LEGEND OF SUPREME
Image Comics (Extreme): Dec, 1994 - No. 3, Feb, 1995 ($2.50, limited series)
1-3 3.00

LEGEND OF THE ELFLORD
DavDez Arts: July, 1998 - No. 2, Sept, 1998 ($2.95)
1,2-Barry Blair & Colin Chin-s/a 3.00

LEGEND OF THE HAWKMAN
DC Comics: 2000 - No. 3, 2000 ($4.95, limited series)
1-3-Raab-s/Lark-c/a 5.00

LEGEND OF THE SHADOW CLAN
Aspen MLT: Feb, 2013 - No. 5, Jul, 2013 ($1.00/$3.99)
1-($1.00) David Wohl-s/Cory Smith-a; mutiple covers 3.00
2-5-($3.99) 4.00

LEGEND OF THE SHIELD, THE
DC Comics (Impact Comics): July, 1991 - No. 16, Oct, 1992 ($1.00)
1-16: 6,7-The Fly x-over. 12-Contains trading card 4.00
Annual 1 (1992, $2.50, 68 pgs.)-Snyder-a; w/trading card 4.00

LEGEND OF THE SWAMP THING HALLOWEEN SPECTACULAR
DC Comics: Dec, 2020 ($5.99, one-shot)
1-Six short stories by various; art by Perkins, Timms, Stanton, Ward, Rios; Perkins-c 6.00

GD VG FN VF VF/NM NM-
2.0 4.0 6.0 8.0 9.0 9.2

LEGEND OF WONDER WOMAN, THE
DC Comics: May, 1986 - No. 4, Aug, 1986 (75¢, limited series)
1-4 1 3 4 6 8 10

LEGEND OF WONDER WOMAN, THE (Printing of digital-first stories)
DC Comics: Mar, 2016 - No. 9, Oct, 2016 ($3.99)
1-9: Childhood/origin flashbacks of Diana; Renae de Liz-s/a. 2-Steve Trevor app. 4.00

LEGEND OF YOUNG DICK TURPIN, THE (Disney)(TV)
Gold Key: May, 1966
1 (10176-605)-Photo/painted-c 3 6 9 17 26 35

LEGEND OF ZELDA, THE (Link: The Legend... in indicia)
Valiant Comics: 1990 - No. 4, 1990 ($1.95, coated stiff-c) V2#1, 1990 - No. 5, 1990 ($1.50)
1 5 10 15 34 60 85
2-4: 4-Layton-c(i) 3 6 9 16 24 32
V2#1-5 2 4 6 8 10 12

LEGENDS
DC Comics: Nov, 1986 - No. 6, Apr, 1987 (75¢, limited series)
1-Byrne-c/a(p) in all; 1st app. Amanda Waller and the new Captain Marvel 2 4 6 13 18 22
2,4,5 6.00
3-1st app. new Suicide Squad; death of Blockbuster 3 6 9 17 26 35
6-1st app. new Justice League 2 4 6 9 13 16

LEGENDS OF DANIEL BOONE, THE (...Frontier Scout)
National Periodical Publications: Oct-Nov, 1955 - No. 8, Dec-Jan, 1956-57
1 (Scarce)-Nick Cardy c-1-8 58 116 174 371 636 900
2 (Scarce) 42 84 126 265 445 625
3-8 (Scarce) 36 72 108 214 347 480

LEGENDS OF NASCAR, THE
Vortex Comics: Nov, 1990 - No. 14, 1992? (#1 3rd printing (1/91) says 2nd printing inside)
1-Bill Elliott biog.; Trimpe-a ($1.50) 5.00
1-2nd printing (11/90, $2.00) 3.00
1-3rd print; contains Maxx racecards ($3.00) 3.00
2-14: 2-Richard Petty. 3-Ken Schrader (7/91). 4-Bobby Allison; Spiegle-a(p); Adkins part-i. 5-Sterling Marlin. 6-Bill Elliott. 7-Junior Johnson; Spiegle-c/a. 8-Benny Parsons; Heck-a 3.00
1-13-Hologram cover versions. 2-Hologram shows Bill Elliott's car by mistake (all are numbered & limited) 5.00
2-Hologram corrected version 5.00
Christmas Special ($5.95) 6.00

LEGENDS OF RED SONJA
Dynamite Entertainment: 2013 - No. 5, 2014 ($3.99)
1-5-Short stories by various incl. Simone, Grayson; covers by Anacleto & Thorne 4.00

LEGENDS OF THE DARK CLAW
DC Comics (Amalgam): Apr, 1996 ($1.95)
1-Jim Balent-c/a 3.00

LEGENDS OF THE DARK KNIGHT (See Batman: ...)

LEGENDS OF THE DARK KNIGHT
DC Comics: Dec, 2012 - No. 13, Dec, 2013 ($3.99, printings of stories first released online)
1-13: 1-Lindelof-s. 2-4-Joker app. 5-Hester-a 4.00
... 100 Page Super Spectacular 1-5 (2/14 - No. 5, 3/15, quarterly, $9.99) 1-(2/14) 10.00

LEGENDS OF THE DC UNIVERSE
DC Comics: Feb, 1998 - No. 41, June, 2001 ($1.95/$1.99/$2.50)
1-13,15-21: 1-3-Superman; Robinson-s/Semeiks-a/Orbik-painted-c. 4,5-Wonder Woman; Deodato-a/Rude painted-c. 8-GL/GA, O'Neil-s. 10,11-Batgirl; Dodson-a. 12,13-Justice League. 15-17-Flash. 18-Kid Flash; Guice-a. 19-Impulse; prelude to JLApe Annuals. 20,21-Abin Sur 4.00
14-($3.95) Jimmy Olsen; Kirby-esque-c by Rude 5.00
22-27,30: 22,23-Superman; Rude-c/Ladronn-a. 26,27-Aquaman/Joker 3.00
28,29: Green Lantern & the Atom; Gil Kane-a; covers by Kane and Ross 3.00
31,32: 32-Begin $2.50-c; Wonder Woman; Texeira-c 3.00
33-36-Hal Jordan as The Spectre; DeMatteis-s/Zulli-a; Hale painted-c 3.00
37-41: 37,38-Kyle Rayner. 39-Superman. 40,41-Atom; Harris-c 3.00
... Crisis on Infinite Earths 1 (2/99, $4.95) Untold story during and after Crisis on Infinite Earths #4; Wolfman-s/Ryan-a/Orbik-c 5.00
... 80 Page Giant 1 (9/98, $4.95) Stories and art by various incl. Ditko, Perez, Gibbons, Mumy; Joe Kubert-c 5.00
... 80 Page Giant 2 (1/00, $4.95) Stories and art by various incl. Challengers by Art Adams; Sean Phillips-c 5.00

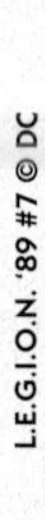
L.E.G.I.O.N. '89 #7 © DC

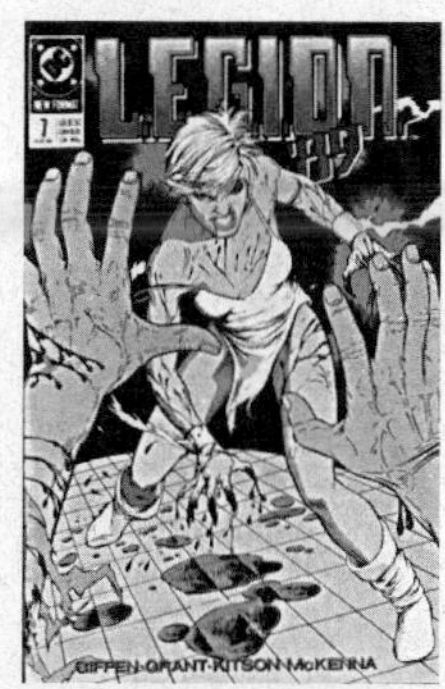

Legionnaires #80 © DC

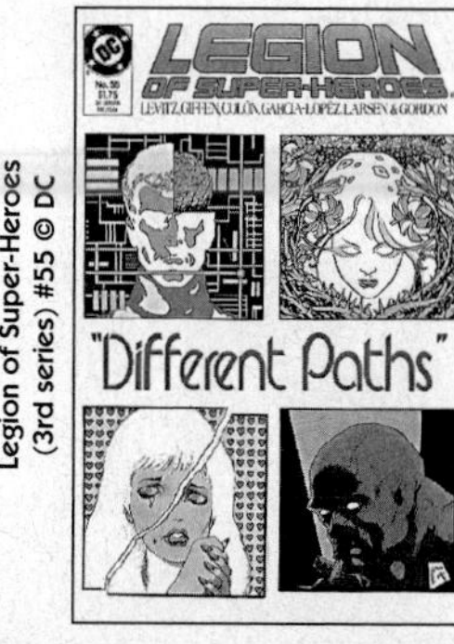

Legion of Super-Heroes (3rd series) #55 © DC

GD 2.0 | VG 4.0 | FN 6.0 | VF 8.0 | VF/NM 9.0 | NM- 9.2

... 3-D Gallery (12/98, $2.95) Pin-ups w/glasses 4.00

LEGENDS OF THE LEGION (See Legion of Super-Heroes)
DC Comics: Feb, 1998 - No. 4, May, 1998 ($2.25, limited series)
1-4:1-Origin-s of Ultra Boy. 2-Spark. 3-Umbra. 4-Star Boy 4.00

LEGENDS OF THE STARGRAZERS (See Vanguard Illustrated #2)
Innovation Publishing: Aug, 1989 - No. 6, 1990 ($1.95, limited series, mature)
1-6: 1-Redondo part inks 3.00

LEGENDS OF THE WORLD'S FINEST (See World's Finest)
DC Comics: 1994 - No. 3, 1994 ($4.95, squarebound, limited series)
1-3: Simonson scripts; Brereton-c/a; embossed foil logos 6.00
TPB-(1995, $14.95) r/#1-3 15.00

LEGENDS OF TOMORROW
DC Comics: May, 2016 - No. 6, Oct, 2016 ($7.99, squarebound)
1-6: Short stories of Firestorm, Metal Men, Metamorpho and Sugar & Spike. 6-Legion of Super-Heroes app. 8.00

LEGION (David Haller from X-Men)
Marvel Comics: Mar, 2018 - No. 5, Jul, 2018 ($3.99)
1-5: 1-3-MIlligan-s/Torres-a. 4-Ferguson-a 4.00

L.E.G.I.O.N. (The # to right of title represents year of print)(Also see Lobo & R.E.B.E.L.S.)
DC Comics: Feb, 1989 - No. 70, Sept, 1994 ($1.50/$1.75)
1-Giffen plots/breakdowns in #1-12,28 6.00
2-22,24-47: 3-Lobo app. #3 on. 4-1st Lobo-c this title. 5-Lobo joins L.E.G.I.O.N. 13-Lar Gand app. 16-Lar Gand joins L.E.G.I.O.N., leaves #19. 31-Capt. Marvel app. 35-L.E.G.I.O.N. '92 begins 4.00
23,70-($2.50, 52 pgs.)-L.E.G.I.O.N. '91 begins. 70-Zero Hour 5.00
48,49,51-69: 48-Begin $1.75-c. 63-L.E.G.I.O.N. '94 begins; Superman x-over 4.00
50-($3.50, 68 pgs.) 5.00
Annual 1-5 ('90-94, 68 pgs.): 1-Lobo, Superman app. 2-Alan Grant scripts. 5-Elseworlds story; Lobo app. 5.00
NOTE: ***Alan Grant** scripts in #1-39, 51, Annual 1, 2.*

LEGION, THE (Continued from Legion Lost & Legion Worlds)
DC Comics: Dec, 2001 - No. 38, Oct, 2004 ($2.50)
1-Abnett & Lanning-s; Coipel & Lanning-c/a 4.00
2-24: 3-8-Ra's al Ghul app. 5-Snejbjerg-a. 9-DeStefano-a. 12-Legion vs. JLA. 16-Fatal Five app.; Walker-a 17,18-Ra's al Ghul app. 20-23-Universo app. 3.00
25-($3.95) Art by Harris, Cockrum, Rivoche; teenage Clark Kent app.; Harris-c 4.00
26-38-Superboy in classic costume. 26-30-Darkseid app. 31-Giffen-a. 35-38-Jurgens-a 3.00
...Secret Files 3003 (1/04, $4.95) Kirk-a, Harris-c/a; Superboy app. 5.00
...Foundations TPB (2004, $19.95) r/#25-30 & Secret Files 3003; Harris-c 20.00

LEGION LOST (Continued from Legion of Super-Heroes [4th series] #125)
DC Comics: May, 2000 - No. 12, Apr, 2001 ($2.50, limited series)
1-Abnett & Lanning-s. Coipel & Lanning-c/a 1 2 3 4 5 7
2-12-Abnett & Lanning-s. Coipel & Lanning-c/a in most. 4,9-Alixe-a 3.00
HC (2011, $39.99, dustjacket) r/#1-12 40.00

LEGION LOST (DC New 52)
DC Comics: Nov, 2011 - No. 16, Mar, 2013 ($2.99)
1-16: 1-Nicieza-s/Woods/a/c; Legionnaires trapped in the 21st century. 7,8-DeFalco-s. 8-Prelude to The Culling; Ravagers app. 9-The Culling x-over with Teen Titans. 14-16-Superboy & the Ravagers app. 3.00
#0 (11/12, $2.99) Origin of Timber Wolf; DeFalco-s/Woods-a 3.00

LEGIONNAIRES (See Legion of Super-Heroes #40, 41 & Showcase 95 #6)
DC Comics: Apr, 1992 - No. 81, Mar, 2000 ($1.25/$1.50/$2.25)
0-(10/94)-Zero Hour restart of Legion; released between #18 & #19 3.00
1-49,51-77: 1-(4/92)-Chris Sprouse-c/a; polybagged w/SkyBox trading card. 11-Kid Quantum joins. 18-(9/94)-Zero Hour. 19(11/94). 37-Valor (Lar Gand) becomes M'onel (5/96). 43-Legion tryouts; reintro Princess Projectra, Shadow Lass & others. 47-Forms one cover image with LSH #91. 60-Karate Kid & Kid Quantum join. 61-Silver Age & 70's Legion app. 76-Return of Wildfire. 79,80-Coipel-c/a; Legion vs. the Blight 3.00
50-($3.95) Pullout poster by Davis/Farmer 4.00
#1,000,000 (11/98) Sean Phillips-a 3.00
Annual 1,3 ('94,'96 $2.95)-1-Elseworlds-s. 3-Legends of the Dead Earth-s 4.00
Annual 2 (1995, $3.95)-Year One-s 4.50

LEGIONNAIRES THREE
DC Comics: Jan, 1986 - No. 4, May, 1986 (75¢, limited series)
1-4 4.00

LEGION OF MONSTERS (Also see Marvel Premiere #28 & Marvel Preview #8)
Marvel Comics Group: Sept, 1975 ($1.00, B&W, magazine, 76 pgs.)
1-Origin & 1st app. Legion of Monsters; Neal Adams-c; Morrow-a; origin & only app. The Manphibian; Frankenstein by Mayerik; Bram Stoker's Dracula adaptation; Reese-a; painted-c (#2 was advertised with Morbius & Satana, but was never published) 11 22 33 72 154 235

GD 2.0 | VG 4.0 | FN 6.0 | VF 8.0 | VF/NM 9.0 | NM- 9.2

LEGION OF MONSTERS (One-shots)
Marvel Comics: Apr, 2007 - Sept, 2007 ($2.99)
... Man-Thing (5/07) Huston-s/Janson-a/Land-c; Simon Garth: Zombie by Ted McKeever 3.00
... Morbius (9/07) Cahill-s/Gaydos-a/Land-c; Dracula w/Finch-a/Cebulski-s 3.00
... Satana (8/07) Furth-s/Andrasofszky-a/Land-c; Living Mummy by Hickman 3.00
... Werewolf By Night (4/07) Carey-s/Land-a/c; Monster of Frankenstein by Skottie Young 3.00
HC (2007, $24.99, dustjacket) oversized r/series and classic stories; sketch pages 25.00

LEGION OF MONSTERS
Marvel Comics: Dec, 2011 - No. 4, Mar, 2012 ($3.99, limited series)
1-4-Hopeless-s/Doe-a/c; Morbius, Manphibian, Elsa Bloodstone app. 4.00

LEGION OF NIGHT, THE
Marvel Comics: Oct, 1991 - No. 2, Oct, 1991 ($4.95, 52 pgs.)
1,2-Whilce Portacio-c/a(p) 5.00

LEGION OF SUBSTITUTE HEROES SPECIAL (See Adventure Comics #306)
DC Comics: July, 1985 ($1.25, one-shot, 52 pgs.)
1-Giffen-c/a(p) 4.00

LEGION OF SUPER-HEROES (See Action Comics, Adventure, All New Collectors Edition, Legionnaires, Legends of the Legion, Limited Collectors Edition, Secrets of the..., Superboy & Superman)
National Periodical Publications: Feb, 1973 - No. 4, July-Aug, 1973
1-Legion & Tommy Tomorrow reprints begin 3 6 9 21 33 45
2-4: 2-Forte-r. 3-r/Adv. #340. Action #240. 4-r/Adv. #341, Action #233; Mooney-r 2 4 6 13 18 22

LEGION OF SUPER-HEROES, THE (Formerly Superboy and...; Tales of The Legion #314 on)
DC Comics: No. 259, Jan, 1980 - No. 313, July, 1984
259(#1)-Superboy leaves Legion 2 4 6 8 11 14
260-270: 265-Contains 28 pg. insert "Superman & the TRS-80 computer"; origin Tyroc; Tyroc leaves Legion 6.00
261,263,264,266-(Whitman variants; low print run; no cover #'s) 2 4 6 8 11 14
271-289: 272-Blok joins; origin; 20 pg. insert-Dial 'H' For Hero. 277-Intro. Reflecto. 280-Superboy re-joins Legion. 282-Origin Reflecto. 283-Origin Wildfire 6.00
290-294-Great Darkness saga. 294-Double size (52 pgs.) 1 2 3 5 7 9
295-299,301-313: 297-Origin retold. 298-Free 16 pg. Amethyst preview. 306-Brief origin Star Boy (Swan art). 311-Colan-a 4.00
300-(68 pgs., Mando paper)-Anniversary issue; has c/a by almost everyone at DC 5.00
Annual 1-3(82-84, 52 pgs.)-1-Giffen-c/a; 1st app./origin new Invisible Kid who joins Legion. 2-Karate Kid & Princess Projectra wed & resign 4.00
...The Great Darkness Saga (1989, $17.95, 196 pgs.)-r/LSH #287,290-294 & Annual #3; Giffen-c/a 2 4 6 10 14 18
...The Great Darkness Saga The Deluxe Edition HC (2010, $39.99, dj)-r/LSH #284-296 & Annual #1; new intro. by Levitz, script for #290, Giffen design sketches 40.00
NOTE: ***Aparo** c-282, 283, 300(part). **Austin** c-268i. **Buckler** c-273p, 274p, 276p. **Colan** a-311p. **Ditko** a(p)-267, 268, 272, 274, 276, 281. **Giffen** a-285-313p, Annual 1p; c-287p, 288p, 289, 290p, 291p, 292, 293, 294-299p, 300, 301-313p, Annual 1p, 2p. **Perez** c-268p, 277-280, 281p. **Starlin** a-265. **Staton** a-259p, 260p, 280. **Tuska** a-308p.*

LEGION OF SUPER-HEROES (3rd Series) (Reprinted in Tales of the Legion)
DC Comics: Aug, 1984 - No. 63, Aug, 1989 ($1.25/$1.75, deluxe format)
1-Silver ink logo 1 3 4 6 8 10
2-36,39-44,46-49,51-62: 4-Death of Karate Kid. 5-Death of Nemesis Kid. 12-Cosmic Boy, Lightning Lad, & Saturn Girl resign. 14-Intro new members: Tellus, Sensor Girl, Quislet. 15-17-Crisis tie-ins. 18-Crisis x-over. 25-Sensor Girl i.d. revealed as Princess Projectra. 35-Saturn Girl rejoins. 42,43-Millennium tie-ins. 44-Origin Quislet 3.00
37,38-Death of Superboy 2 4 6 9 13 16
45,50: 45 ($2.95, 68 pgs.)-Anniversary ish. 50-Double size ($2.50-c) 4.00
63-Final issue 4.00
Annual 1-4 (10/85-'88, 52 pgs.)-1-Crisis tie-in 4.00
...: An Eye For An Eye TPB (2007, $17.99)-r/#1-6; intro by Paul Levitz; cover gallery 18.00
...: The More Things Change TPB (2008, $17.99)-r/#7-13; cover gallery 18.00
NOTE: ***Byrne** c-36p. **Giffen** a(p)-1, 2, 50-55, 57-63, Annual 1p, 2; c-1-5p, 54p, Annual 1. **Orlando** a-6p. **Steacy** c-45-50, Annual 3.*

LEGION OF SUPER-HEROES (4th Series)
DC Comics: Nov, 1989 - No. 125, Mar, 2000 ($1.75/$1.95/$2.25)
0-(10/94)-Zero Hour restart of Legion; released between #61 & #62 3.00
1-Giffen-c/a(p)/scripts begin (4 pg.-a only #18) 6.00
2-20,26-49,51-53,55-58: 4-Mon-El (Lar Gand) destroys Time Trapper, changes reality. 5-Alt. reality story where Mordru rules all; Ferro Lad app. 6-1st app. of Laurel Gand (Lar

Legion of Super-Heroes (4th series) #114 © DC

Legion of Super-Heroes (2020 series) #11 © DC

Lenore #8 © Roman Dirge

GD 2.0 | VG 4.0 | FN 6.0 | VF 8.0 | VF/NM 9.0 | NM- 9.2

GD 2.0 | VG 4.0 | FN 6.0 | VF 8.0 | VF/NM 9.0 | NM- 9.2

Gand's cousin). 8-Origin. 13-Free poster by Giffen showing new costumes. 15-(2/91)-1st reference of Lar Gand as Valor. 17-Tornado Twins app. 26-New map of headquarters. 34-Six pg. preview of Timber Wolf mini-series. 40-Minor Legionnaires app. 41-(3/93)-SW6 Legion renamed Legionnaires w/new costumes and some new code-names 4.00
21-25: 21-24-Lobo & Darkseid storyline. 24-Cameo SW6 younger Legion duplicates. 25-SW6 Legion full intro. 5.00
50-($3.50, 68 pgs.) 5.00
54-($2.95)-Die-cut & foil stamped-c 5.00
59-99: 61-(9/94)-Zero Hour. 62-(11/94). 75-XS travels back to the 20th Century (cont'd in Impulse #9). 77-Origin of Brainiac 5. 81-Reintro Sun Boy. 85-Half of the Legion sent to the 20th century, Superman-c/app. 86-Final Night. 87-Deadman-c/app. 88-Impulse-c/app. Adventure Comics #247 cover swipe. 91-Forms one cover image with Legionnaires #47. 96-Wedding of Ultra Boy and Apparition. 99-Robin, Impulse, Superboy app. 3.00
100-($5.95, 96 pgs.)-Legionnaires return to the 30th Century; gatefold-c; 5 stories-art by Simonson, Davis and others 1 2 3 4 5 7
101-121: 101-Armstrong-a(p) begins. 105-Legion past & present vs. Time Trapper. 109-Moder-a. 110-Thunder joins. 114,115-Bizarro Legion. 120,121-Fatal Five. 3.00
122-124: 122,123-Coipel-c/a. 124-Coipel-c 4.00
125-Leads into "Legion Lost" maxi-series; Coipel-c 5.00
#1,000,000 (11/98) Giffen-a 3.00
Annual 1-5 (1990-1994, $3.50, 68 pgs.): 4-Bloodlines. 5-Elseworlds story 4.00
Annual 6 (1995,$3.95)-Year One story 4.00
Annual 7 (1996, $3.50, 48 pgs.)-Legends of the Dead Earth story; intro 75th Century Legion of Super-Heroes; Wildfire app. 4.00
Legion: Secret Files 1 (1/98, $4.95) Retold origin & pin-ups 5.00
Legion: Secret Files 2 (6/99, $4.95) Story and profile pages 5.00
The Beginning of Tomorrow TPB ('99, $17.95) r/post-Zero Hour reboot 18.00
NOTE: ***Giffen** a-1-24; breakdowns-26-32, 34-36; c-1-7, 8(part), 9-24. **Brandon Peterson** a(p)-15(1st for DC), 16, 18, Annual 2(54 pgs.); c-Annual 2p. **Swan/Anderson** c-8(part).*

LEGION OF SUPER-HEROES (5th Series) (Title becomes Supergirl and the Legion of Super-Heroes #16-36) (Intro. in Teen Titans/Legion Special)
DC Comics: Feb, 2005 - No. 15, Apr, 2006; No. 37, Feb, 2008 - No. 50, Mar, 2009 ($2.95/$2.99)
1-15: 1-Waid-s/Kitson-a/c. 4-Kirk & Gibbons-a. 9-Jeanty-a. 15-Dawnstar, Tyroc, Blok-c 3.00
37-50: 37-Shooter-s/Manapul-a begin; two interlocking covers. 50-Wraparound cover 3.00
44-Variant-c by Neal Adams 5.00
... Death of a Dream TPB ('06, $14.99) r/#7-13 15.00
... Enemy Manifest HC ('09, $24.99, dustjacket) r/#45-50 25.00
... Enemy Manifest SC ('10, $14.99) r/#45-50 15.00
... Enemy Rising HC ('08, $19.99, dustjacket) r/#37-44 20.00
... Enemy Rising SC ('09, $14.99) r/#37-44 15.00
...: 1050 Years of the Future TPB ('08, $19.99) r/greatest tales of their 50 year history 20.00
... Teenage Revolution TPB ('05, $14.99) r/#1-6 & Teen Titans/Legion Spec.; sketch pages 15.00

LEGION OF SUPER-HEROES (6th Series)
DC Comics: Jul, 2010 - No. 16, Oct, 2011 ($3.99/$2.99)
1-9: 1-Earth-Man app.; Titan destroyed; Levitz-s/Cinar-a/c. 6-Jimenez back-up-a 4.00
1-6-Variant covers by Jim Lee 8.00
10-16-($2.99) 12-16-Legion of Super-Villains app. 3.00
Annual 1 (2/11, $4.99) New Emerald Empress; Levitz-s/Giffen-a 5.00
...: The Choice HC (2011, $24.99, dustjacket) r/#1-6; variant-c gallery and Cinar art 25.00

LEGION OF SUPER-HEROES (DC New 52)(Also see Legion Lost)
DC Comics: Nov, 2011 - No. 23, Oct, 2013 ($2.99)
1-23: 1-4-Levitz-s/Portela-a. 5-Simonson-c/a. 8-Lightle-a. 17-Giffen-a. 23-Maguire-a 3.00
#0 (11/12, $2.99) Story of Brainiac 5 joining the Legion; Levitz-s/Kolins-a 3.00

LEGION OF SUPER-HEROES (See Superman (2018 series) #14,15)
DC Comics: Jan, 2020 - Present ($3.99)
1-12: 1-Bendis-s/Sook-a; Superboy (Jon Kent) joins the Legion; Mordru app. 3-Robin app. 4,5-Origin retold. 4-Sook & Janin-a. 5-Sook & Godlewski-a. 6-Intro Gold Lantern & Dr. Fate. 8,9-Different artist each page; 8-Mack, Allred, Maleev. 9-Grell, Nowlan, Romita, Jr. 4.00
...: Millennium 1,2 ($4.99, 11/19 - No. 2, 12/19) Bendis-s; Rose & Thorn, Kamandi app. 5.00

LEGION OF SUPER-HEROES/BUGS BUNNY SPECIAL
DC Comics: Aug, 2017 ($4.99, one-shot)
1-Humphries-s/Grummett-a/c; Bugs Bunny in the 31st century; Supergirl & Validus app. 5.00

LEGION OF SUPER-HEROES IN THE 31ST CENTURY (Based on the animated series)
DC Comics: June, 2007 - No. 20, Jan, 2009 ($2.25)
1-20: 1-Chynna Clugston-a; Fatal Five app. 6-Green Lantern Corps app. 15-Impulse app. 3.00
1-(6/07) Free Comic Book Day giveaway 3.00
...: Tomorrow's Heroes (2008, $14.99) r/#1-7; cover gallery 15.00

LEGION OF SUPER-VILLAINS
DC Comics: May, 2011 ($4.99, one-shot)
1-Levitz-s/Portela-a; Saturn Queen, Lightning Lord, Sun-Killer, Micro Lad app. 5.00

LEGION: PROPHETS (Prelude to 2010 movie)
IDW Publishing: Nov, 2009 - No. 4, Dec, 2009 ($3.99, limited series)
1-4: Stewart & Waltz-s. 1-Muriel-a. 2-Holder-a. 3-Paronzini-a. 4-Gaydos-a 4.00

LEGION: SCIENCE POLICE (See Legion of Super-Heroes)
DC Comics: Aug, 1998 - No. 4, Nov, 1998 ($2.25, limited series)
1-4-Ryan-a 3.00

LEGION: SECRET ORIGIN (Legion of Super-Heroes)
DC Comics: Dec, 2011 - No. 6, May, 2012 ($2.99, limited series)
1-6-Levitz-s/Batista-a; formation of the Legion retold 3.00

LEGION WORLDS (Follows Legion Lost series)
DC Comics: Jun, 2001 - No. 6, Nov, 2001 ($3.95, limited series)
1-6-Abnett & Lanning-s; art by various. 5-Dillon-a. 6-Timber Wolf app. 4.00

LEMONADE KID, THE (See Bobby Benson's B-Bar-B Riders)
AC Comics: 1990 ($2.50, 28 pgs.)
1-Powell-c(r); Red Hawk-r by Powell; Lemonade Kid-r/Bobby Benson by Powell (2 stories) 3.00

LENNON SISTERS LIFE STORY, THE
Dell Publishing Co.: No. 951, Nov, 1958 - No. 1014, Aug, 1959
Four Color 951 (#1)-Toth-a, 32pgs, photo-c 11 22 33 73 157 240
Four Color 1014-Toth-a, photo-c 10 20 30 69 147 225

LENORE
Slave Labor Graphics/Titan Comics: Feb, 1998 - Present ($2.95/$3.95, B&W, color #13-on)
1-12: 1-Roman Dirge-s/a, 1,2-2nd printing 4.00
13-($3.95, color) 4.00
Vol. 2 (8/09 - No. 11) 1-11: 1-1st and 2nd printings; Lenore's origin 4.00
Vol. 3 (9/19, $3.99) 1-Two covers 4.00
...: Cooties TPB (3/06, $13.95) r/#9-12; pin-ups by various 14.00
...: Noogies TPB ($11.95) r/#1-4 12.00
...: Pink Bellies HC (Titan, 3/15, $17.99) Vol. 2 #8-11 18.00
...: Purple Nurples HC (8/13, $17.95) Vol. 2 #4-7 18.00
...: Swirlies HC (8/12, $17.95) r/#13 & Vol. 2 #1-3 18.00
...: Wedgies TPB (2000, $13.95) r/#5-8 14.00

LEONARD NIMOY'S PRIMORTALS
Tekno Comix: Mar, 1995 - No. 15, May, 1996 ($1.95)
1-15: Concept by Leonard Nimoy & Isaac Asimov 1-3-w/bound-in game piece & trading card. 4-w/Teknophage Steel Edition coupon. 13,14-Art Adams-c. 15-Simonson-c 4.00

LEONARD NIMOY'S PRIMORTALS
BIG Entertainment: V2#0, June, 1996 - No. 8, Feb, 1997 ($2.25)
V2#0-8: 0-Includes Pt. 9 of "The Big Bang" x-over. 0,1-Simonson-c. 3-Kelley Jones-c 4.00

LEONARD NIMOY'S PRIMORTALS ORIGINS
Tekno Comix: Nov, 1995 - No. 2, Dec, 1995 ($2.95, limited series)
1,2: Nimoy scripts; Art Adams-c; polybagged 4.00

LEONARDO (Also see Teenage Mutant Ninja Turtles)
Mirage Studios: Dec, 1986 ($1.50, B&W, one-shot)
1 3 6 9 21 33 45

LEO THE LION
I. W. Enterprises: No date(1960s) (10¢)
1-Reprint 2 4 6 9 13 16

LEROY (Teen-age)
Standard Comics: Nov, 1949 - No. 6, Nov, 1950
1 21 42 63 122 199 275
2-Frazetta text illo. 14 28 42 82 121 160
3-6: 3-Lubbers-a 12 24 36 69 97 125

LETHAL (Also see Brigade)
Image Comics (Extreme Studios): Feb, 1996 ($2.50, unfinished limited series)
1-Marat Mychaels-c/a. 3.00

LETHAL FOES OF SPIDER-MAN (Sequel to Deadly Foes of Spider-Man)
Marvel Comics: Sept, 1993 - No. 4, Dec, 1993 ($1.75, limited series)
1-4 3.00

LETHARGIC LAD
Crusade Ent.: June, 1996 - No. 3, Sept, 1996 ($2.95, B&W, limited series)
1,2 3.00
3-Alex Ross-c/swipe (Kingdom Come) 4.00
...Jumbo Sized Annual #1 (Summer 2002, $3.99) prints comic stories from internet 4.00

Letter 44 #9 © Charles Soule

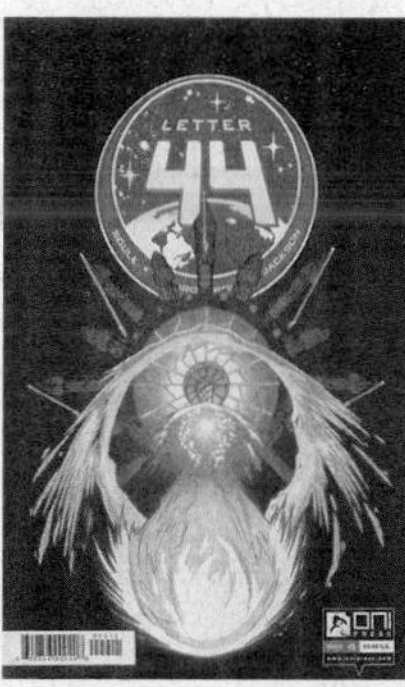

Liberty Annual 2014 © CBLDF

Lidsville #2 © Kroft

	GD 2.0	VG 4.0	FN 6.0	VF 8.0	VF/NM 9.0	NM- 9.2

LETHARGIC LAD ADVENTURES
Crusade Ent./Destination Ent.#3 on: Oct, 1997 - No. 12, Sept./Oct. 1999 ($2.95, B&W)

1-12-Hyland-s/a. 9-Alex Ross sketch page & back-c 3.00

LET ME IN: CROSSROADS (Based on the 2010 movie Let Me In)
Dark Horse Comics: Dec, 2010 - No. 4, Mar, 2011 ($3.99, limited series)

1-4-Prelude to the film; Andreyko-s/Reynolds-a/Phillips-c 4.00
1-4 Variant photo-c 8.00

LET'S PRETEND (CBS radio)
D. S. Publishing Co.: May-June, 1950 - No. 3, Sept-Oct, 1950

1 20 40 60 114 182 250
2,3 15 30 45 86 133 180

LET'S READ THE NEWSPAPER
Charlton Press: 1974

nn-Features Quincy by Ted Sheares 1 3 4 6 8 10

LET'S TAKE A TRIP (TV) (CBS Television Presents)
Pines Comics: Spring, 1958

1-Marv Levy-c/a 5 10 15 24 30 35

LETTER 44
Oni Press: Oct, 2013 - No. 35, Aug, 2017 ($1.00/$3.99)

1-($1.00)-Soule-a/Alberto Alburquerque-a 5.00
2-35-($3.99) 7-Joëlle Jones-a. 14-Drew Moss-a. 28-Gluskova-a 4.00
... #1 Square One Edition (2/17, $1.00) r/#1 3.00

LETTERS TO SANTA (See March of Comics No. 228)

LEVIATHAN DAWN (Also see Event Leviathan)
DC Comics: 2020 ($4.99, one-shot)

1-Follows Event Leviathan series; Bendis-s/Maleev-a 5.00

LEX LUTHOR: MAN OF STEEL
DC Comics: May, 2005 - No. 5, Sept, 2005 ($2.99, limited series)

1-5: 1-Azzarello-s/Bermejo-a/c in all. 3-Batman-c/app. 3.00
TPB (2005, $12.99) r/series 13.00
Luthor HC (2010, $19.99, d.j.) r/#1-5 with 10 new story pages; cover gallery & sketch-a 20.00

LEX LUTHOR/PORKY PIG
DC Comics: Oct, 2018 ($4.99, one-shot)

1-Mark Russell-s/Brad Walker-a/Ben Oliver-c; back-up story in classic cartoon style 5.00

LEX LUTHOR: THE UNAUTHORIZED BIOGRAPHY
DC Comics: 1989 ($3.95, 52 pgs., one-shot, squarebound)

1-Painted-c; Clark Kent app. 6.00

LEX LUTHOR: YEAR OF THE VILLAIN
DC Comics: 2019 ($4.99, one-shot)

1-Latour-s/Hitch-a; multiverse of Luthors app. 5.00

LGBTQ ETC PEOPLE (Reprints from Cerebus in Hell)
Aardvark-Vanaheim: Jun, 2019 ($4.00, B&W)

1-Cerebus figures placed over original Gustave Doré artwork of Hell; X-Men #1-c swipe 4.00

LIBERTY COMICS (Miss Liberty No. 1)
Green Publishing Co.: No. 5, May, 1945 - No. 15, July, 1946 (MLJ & other-r)

5 (5/45)-The Prankster app; Starr-a 33 66 99 194 317 440
10-Hangman & Boy Buddies app.; reprints 3 Hangman stories, incl. Hangman #8
39 78 117 231 378 525
11 (V2#2, 1/46)-Wilbur in women's clothes 19 38 57 111 176 240
12 (V2#4)-Black Hood & Suzie app.; classic Skull-c 90 180 270 576 988 1400
14,15-Patty of Airliner; Starr-a in both 24 48 72 142 234 325

LIBERTY COMICS (The CBLDF Presents...)
Image Comics: July, 2008; Oct, 2009 ($3.99/$4.99, Comic Book Legal Defense Fund benefit)

1-Two covers by Campbell & Mignola; art by Cooke, Aragones, A. Adams & others 4.00
1-(12/08) Second printing with Thor-c by Simonson 4.00
2-(10/09, $4.99) two covers by Romita Jr. & Sale; art by Allred, Templesmith, Jim Lee 5.00
Liberty Annual 2010 (10/10, $4.99) Covers by Gibbons & Robertson 5.00
Liberty Annual 2011 (10/11, $4.99) Covers by Wagner & Cassaday 5.00
Liberty Annual 2012 (10/12, $4.99) Covers by Dodson & Bá; Walking Dead story 5.00
Liberty Annual 2013 (10/13, $4.99) Covers by Corben & Marquez 5.00
Liberty Annual 2014 (10/14, $4.99) Covers by Allred, Simonson, & Charm 5.00
Liberty Annual 2015 (10/15, $4.99) Covers by Fegredo, Fowler & Del Rey 5.00
Liberty Annual 2016 (11/16, $4.99) Stories by Guinan, Pope, Wimberly, Schkade & others 5.00

LIBERTY COMICS
Heroic Publishing: Sept, 2007 ($4.50)

1-Mark Sparacio-c 4.50

LIBERTY GIRL
Heroic Publishing: Aug, 2006 - No. 3, May, 2007 ($3.25/$2.99)

1-3-Mark Sparacio-c/a 3.25

LIBERTY GUARDS
Chicago Mail Order: 1942 (Centaur Publ.)

nn-Reprints Man of War #1 with cover of Liberty Scouts #1; Nazi subs pulling into the harbor in front of the Capitol building & Washington Monument cover by Gustavson
65 130 195 416 708 1000

LIBERTY MEADOWS
Insight Studios Group/Image Comics #27 on: 1999 - No. 37 ($2.95, B&W)

1-Frank Cho-s/a; reprints newspaper strips 3 6 9 17 26 35
1-2nd & 3rd printings 1 2 3 4 5 7
2,3 2 4 6 8 11 14
4-10 1 2 3 4 5 7
11-25,27-37: 20-Adam Hughes-c. 22-Evil Brandy vs. Brandy. 27-1st Image issue, printed sideways 3.00
..., Cover Girl HC (Image, 2006, $24.99, with dustjacket) r/color covers of #1-19,21-37 along with B&W inked versions, sketches and pin-up art 25.00
...: Eden Book 1 SC (Image, 2002, $14.95) r/#1-9; sketch gallery 15.00
...: Eden Book 1 SC 2nd printing (Image, 2004, $19.95) r/#1-9; sketch gallery 20.00
...: Eden Book 1 HC (Image, 2003, $24.95, with dustjacket) r/#1-9; sketch gallery 25.00
...: Creature Comforts Book 2 HC (Image, 2004, $24.95, with d.j.) r/#10-18; sketch gallery 25.00
...: Creature Comforts Book 2 SC (Image, 12/04, $14.95) r/#10-18; sketch gallery 15.00
...Book 3: Summer of Love HC (Image, 12/04, $24.95) r/#19-27; sketch gallery 25.00
...Book 3: Summer of Love SC (Image, 7/05, $14.95) r/#19-27; sketch gallery 15.00
...Book 4: Cold, Cold Heart HC (Image, 9/05, $24.95) r/#28-36; sketch gallery 25.00
...Book 4: Cold, Cold Heart SC (Image, 2006, $14.99) r/#28-36; sketch gallery 15.00
Image Firsts: Liberty Meadows #1 (9/10, $1.00) r/#1 3.00
... Sourcebook (5/04, $4.95) character info and unpublished strips 5.00
... Wedding Album (#26) (2002, $2.95) 3.00

LIBERTY PROJECT, THE
Eclipse Comics: June, 1987 - No. 8, May, 1988 ($1.75, color, Baxter paper)

1-8: 6-Valkyrie app. 3.00

LIBERTY SCOUTS (See Liberty Guards & Man of War)
Centaur Publications: No. 2, June, 1941 - No. 3, Aug, 1941

2(#1)-Origin The Fire-Man, Man of War; Vapo-Man & Liberty Scouts begin; intro Liberty Scouts; Gustavson-c/a in both 174 348 522 1114 1907 2700
3(#2)-Origin & 1st app. The Sentinel 168 336 504 1075 1838 2600

LIBRARIANS, THE (Based on the TV series)
Dynamite Entertainment: 2017 - No. 4, 2018 ($3.99)

1-4-Pfeiffer-s/Buchemi-a; multiple covers 4.00

LICENCE TO KILL (James Bond 007) (Movie)
Eclipse Comics: 1989 ($7.95, slick paper, 52 pgs.)

nn-Movie adaptation; Timothy Dalton photo-c 1 3 4 6 8 10
Limited Hardcover ($24.95) 25.00

LIDSVILLE (TV)
Gold Key: Oct, 1972 - No. 5, Oct, 1973

1-Photo-c on all 5 10 15 31 53 75
2-5 3 6 9 21 33 45

LIEUTENANT, THE (TV)
Dell Publishing Co.: April-June, 1964

1-Photo-c 3 6 9 17 26 35

LIEUTENANT BLUEBERRY (Also see Blueberry)
Marvel Comics (Epic Comics): 1991 - No. 3, 1991 (Graphic novel)

1-($8.95)-Moebius-a in all 4 8 12 23 37 50
2-($8.95) 3 6 9 17 26 35
3-($14.95) 3 6 9 19 30 40

LT. ROBIN CRUSOE, U.S.N. (See Movie Comics & Walt Disney Showcase #26)

LIFE AND DEATH OF TOYO HARADA, THE
Valiant Entertainment: Mar, 2019 - No. 6, Jul, 2019 ($3.99, limited series)

1-6-Dysart-s/Cafu-a. 2-Flashback-a by Guice. 3-Albert Einstein app. 4.00

LIFE EATERS, THE
DC Comics (WildStorm): 2003 ($29.95, hardcover with dust jacket)

HC-David Brin-s; Scott Hampton-painted-a/c; Norse Gods team with the Nazis 30.00
SC-(2004, $19.95) 20.00

The Life of Captain Marvel (2018 series) #5 © MAR

Life Story #45 © FAW

Life With Archie #37 © ACP

LIFE IS STRANGE (Based on the Square Enix video game)
Titan Comics: Dec, 2018 - No. 12, Feb, 2020 ($3.99)

	GD 2.0	VG 4.0	FN 6.0	VF 8.0	VF/NM 9.0	NM- 9.2
1-12-Emma Vieceli-s/Claudia Leonardi-a						4.00

LIFE IS STRANGE (Based on the Square Enix video game)
Titan Comics: Nov, 2020 - Present ($3.99)

	GD 2.0	VG 4.0	FN 6.0	VF 8.0	VF/NM 9.0	NM- 9.2
2.1-2.4-Emma Vieceli-s/Claudia Leonardi-a						4.00

LIFE OF CAPTAIN MARVEL, THE
Marvel Comics Group: Aug, 1985 - No. 5, Dec, 1985 ($2.00, Baxter paper)

	GD 2.0	VG 4.0	FN 6.0	VF 8.0	VF/NM 9.0	NM- 9.2
1-5: 1-All reprint Starlin issues of Iron Man #55, Capt. Marvel #25-34 plus Marvel Feature #12 (all with Thanos). 4-New Thanos back-c by Starlin						6.00

LIFE OF CAPTAIN MARVEL, THE (Carol Danvers)
Marvel Comics: Sept, 2018 - No. 5, Feb, 2019 ($4.99/$3.99, limited series)

	GD 2.0	VG 4.0	FN 6.0	VF 8.0	VF/NM 9.0	NM- 9.2
1-($4.99) Childhood flashbacks; Stohl-s/Pacheco & Sauvage-a						5.00
2-5-($3.99) 4-Origin of Carol's mother						4.00

LIFE OF CHRIST, THE
Catechetical Guild Educational Society: No. 301, 1949 (35¢, 100 pgs.)

	GD 2.0	VG 4.0	FN 6.0	VF 8.0	VF/NM 9.0	NM- 9.2
301-Reprints from Topix(1949)-V5#11,12	10	20	30	54	72	90

LIFE OF CHRIST: THE CHRISTMAS STORY, THE
Marvel Comics/Nelson: Feb, 1993 ($2.99, slick stock)

	GD 2.0	VG 4.0	FN 6.0	VF 8.0	VF/NM 9.0	NM- 9.2
nn						5.00

LIFE OF CHRIST: THE EASTER STORY, THE
Marvel Comics/Nelson: 1993 ($2.99, slick stock)

	GD 2.0	VG 4.0	FN 6.0	VF 8.0	VF/NM 9.0	NM- 9.2
nn						5.00

LIFE OF CHRIST VISUALIZED
Standard Publishers: 1942 - No. 3, 1943

	GD 2.0	VG 4.0	FN 6.0	VF 8.0	VF/NM 9.0	NM- 9.2
1-3: All came in cardboard case, each...	9	18	27	50	65	80
Case only.....	10	20	30	54	72	90

LIFE OF CHRIST VISUALIZED
The Standard Publ. Co.: 1946? (48 pgs. in color)

	GD 2.0	VG 4.0	FN 6.0	VF 8.0	VF/NM 9.0	NM- 9.2
nn	7	14	21	37	46	55

LIFE OF ESTHER VISUALIZED
The Standard Publ. Co.: No. 2062, 1947 (48 pgs. in color)

	GD 2.0	VG 4.0	FN 6.0	VF 8.0	VF/NM 9.0	NM- 9.2
2062	7	14	21	37	46	55

LIFE OF JOSEPH VISUALIZED
The Standard Publ. Co.: No. 1054, 1946 (48 pgs. in color)

	GD 2.0	VG 4.0	FN 6.0	VF 8.0	VF/NM 9.0	NM- 9.2
1054	7	14	21	37	46	55

LIFE OF PAUL (See The Living Bible)

LIFE OF POPE JOHN PAUL II, THE
Marvel Comics Group: Jan, 1983 ($1.50/$1.75)

	GD 2.0	VG 4.0	FN 6.0	VF 8.0	VF/NM 9.0	NM- 9.2
1	2	4	6	8	10	12

LIFE OF RILEY, THE (TV)
Dell Publishing Co.: No. 917, July, 1958

	GD 2.0	VG 4.0	FN 6.0	VF 8.0	VF/NM 9.0	NM- 9.2
Four Color 917-William Bendix photo-c	10	20	30	66	138	210

LIFE ON ANOTHER PLANET
Kitchen Sink Press: 1978 (B&W, graphic novel, magazine size)

	GD 2.0	VG 4.0	FN 6.0	VF 8.0	VF/NM 9.0	NM- 9.2
nn-Will Eisner-s/a						20.00
Reprint (DC Comics, 5/00, $12.95)						13.00

LIFE'S LIKE THAT
Croyden Publ. Co.: 1945 (25¢, B&W, 68 pgs.)

	GD 2.0	VG 4.0	FN 6.0	VF 8.0	VF/NM 9.0	NM- 9.2
nn-Newspaper Sunday strip-r by Neher	7	14	21	35	43	50

LIFE STORIES OF AMERICAN PRESIDENTS (See Dell Giants)

LIFE STORY
Fawcett Publications: Apr, 1949 - V8#46, Jan, 1953; V8#47, Apr, 1953 (All have photo-c?)

	GD 2.0	VG 4.0	FN 6.0	VF 8.0	VF/NM 9.0	NM- 9.2
V1#1	19	38	57	111	176	240
2	12	24	36	67	94	120
3-6, V2#7-12 (3/50)	10	20	30	54	72	90
V3#13-Wood-a (4/50)	15	30	45	90	140	190
V3#14-18, V4#19-24, V5#25-30, V6#31-35	9	18	27	50	65	80
V6#36- "I sold drugs" on-c	14	28	42	82	121	160
V7#37,40-42, V8#44,45	9	18	27	47	61	75
V7#38, V8#43-Evans-a	9	18	27	50	65	80
V7#39-Drug Smuggling & Junkie story	12	24	36	69	97	125
V8#46,47 (Scarce)	10	20	30	56	76	100

NOTE: ***Powell** a-13, 23, 24, 26, 28, 30, 32, 39. **Marcus Swayze** a-1-3, 10-12, 15, 16, 20, 21, 23-25, 31, 35, 37, 40, 44, 46.*

LIFE, THE UNIVERSE AND EVERYTHING (See Hitchhikers Guide to the Galaxy & Restaurant at the End of the Universe)
DC Comics: 1996 - No. 3, 1996 ($6.95, squarebound, limited series)

	GD 2.0	VG 4.0	FN 6.0	VF 8.0	VF/NM 9.0	NM- 9.2
1-3: Adaptation of novel by Douglas Adams.	1	2	3	4	5	7

LIFE WITH ARCHIE
Archie Publications: Sept, 1958 - No. 286, Sept, 1991

	GD 2.0	VG 4.0	FN 6.0	VF 8.0	VF/NM 9.0	NM- 9.2
1	64	128	192	512	1156	1800
2-(9/59)	28	56	84	202	451	700
3-5: 3-(7/60)	17	34	51	117	259	400
6-8,10	12	24	36	79	170	260
9,11-Horror/SciFi-c	15	30	45	105	233	360
12-20	8	16	24	54	102	150
21(7/63)-30	7	14	21	45	89	130
31-34,36-38,40,41	6	12	18	40	73	105
35,39-Horror/Sci-Fi-c	9	18	27	60	120	180
42-Pureheart begins (1st app.-c/s, 10/65)	12	24	36	83	182	280
43,44	7	14	21	44	82	120
45(1/66) 1st Man From R.I.V.E.R.D.A.L.E.	8	16	24	52	99	145
46-Origin Pureheart	7	14	21	46	86	125
47-49	6	12	18	37	66	95
50-United Three begin: Pureheart (Archie), Superteen (Betty), Captain Hero (Jughead)	8	16	24	54	102	150
51-59: 59-Pureheart ends	5	10	15	34	60	85
60-Archie band begins, ends #66	6	12	18	38	69	100
61-66: 61-Man From R.I.V.E.R.D.A.L.E.-c/s	5	10	15	30	50	70
67-80	4	8	12	23	37	50
81-99	3	6	9	19	30	40
100 (8/70), 113-Sabrina & Salem app.	4	8	12	25	40	55
101-112, 114-130(2/73), 139(11/73)-Archie Band c/s	2	4	6	13	18	22
131,134-138,140-146,148-161,164-170(6/76)	2	4	6	10	14	18
132,133,147,163-all horror-c/s	3	6	9	16	23	30
162-UFO c/s	3	6	9	15	22	28
171,173-175,177-184,186,189,191-194,196	2	3	4	6	8	10
172,185,197 : 172-(9/77)-Bi-Cent. spec. ish, 185-2nd 24th cent.-c/s, 197-Time machine/ SF-c/s	2	4	6	8	10	12
176(12/76)-1st app. Capt. Archie of Starship Rivda, in 24th century c/s; 1st app. Stella the Robot	3	6	9	15	22	28
187,188,195,198,199-all horror-c/s	2	4	6	10	14	18
190-1st Dr. Doom-c/s	2	4	6	11	16	20
200 (12/78) Maltese Pigeon-s	2	4	6	8	11	14
201-203,205-237,239,240(1/84): 208-Reintro Veronica	1	2	3	5	6	8
204-Flying saucer-c/s	2	3	4	6	8	10
238-(9/83)-25th anniversary issue; Ol' Betsy (jalopy) replaced	1	2	3	5	7	9
241-278,280-285: 250-Comic book convention-s						5.00
279,286: 279-Intro Mustang Sally ($1.00, 7/90)						6.00

NOTE: ***Gene Colan** a-272-279, 285, 286. Horror/Sci-Fi-c 9, 11, 35, 39, 162.*

LIFE WITH ARCHIE (The Married Life) (Magazine)
Archie Publications: Sept, 2010 - No. 37, Sept, 2014 ($3.99, magazine-size)

	GD 2.0	VG 4.0	FN 6.0	VF 8.0	VF/NM 9.0	NM- 9.2
1-Continuation of Married Life stories from Archie #600-605; articles/interviews	1	3	4	6	8	10
2-10						5.00
11-15,17-34						4.00
16-Kevin Keller gay wedding						10.00
36-($4.99, comic-size) Death of Archie; 5 covers by Allred, Francavilla, Hughes, Ramon Perez & Staples	1	2	3	5	6	8
37-($4.99, comic-size) One Year Later aftermath; 5 covers by Chiang, Edwards, Alex Ross, Simonson & Thompson						5.00
...: The Death of Archie: A Life Celebrated Commemorative Issue (2014, $9.99) reprints #36 & #37 in magazine size; afterword by Jon Goldwater; cover gallery w/artist quotes						10.00

LIFE WITH MILLIE (Formerly A Date With Millie) (Modeling With Millie #21 on)
Atlas/Marvel Comics Group: No. 8, Dec, 1960 - No. 20, Dec, 1962

	GD 2.0	VG 4.0	FN 6.0	VF 8.0	VF/NM 9.0	NM- 9.2
8-Teenage	12	24	36	79	170	260
9-11	9	18	27	59	117	175
12-20	8	16	24	56	108	160

LIFE WITH SNARKY PARKER (TV)
Fox Feature Syndicate: Aug, 1950

	GD 2.0	VG 4.0	FN 6.0	VF 8.0	VF/NM 9.0	NM- 9.2
1-Early TV comic; photo-c from TV puppet show	32	64	96	190	310	430

LIGHT AND DARKNESS WAR, THE
Marvel Comics (Epic Comics): Oct, 1988 - No. 6, Dec, 1989 ($1.95, lim. series)

Lightning Comics #4 © ACE

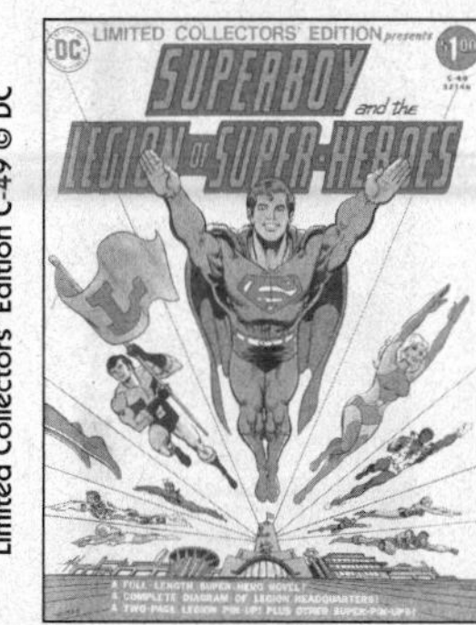

Limited Collectors' Edition C-49 © DC

Lisa Comics #1 © Bongo

GD VG FN VF VF/NM NM-
2.0 4.0 6.0 8.0 9.0 9.2

GD VG FN VF VF/NM NM-
2.0 4.0 6.0 8.0 9.0 9.2

1-6 3.00

LIGHT BRIGADE, THE
DC Comics: 2004 - No. 4, 2004 ($5.95, limited series)
1-4-Archangels in World War II; Tomasi-s/Snejbjerg-a 6.00
TPB (2005, 2009, $19.99) r/series; cover galery 20.00

LIGHT FANTASTIC, THE (Terry Pratchett's)
Innovation Publishing: June, 1992 - No. 4, Sept, 1992 ($2.50, mini-series)
1-4: Adapts 2nd novel in Discworld series 3.00

LIGHT IN THE FOREST (Disney)
Dell Publishing Co.: No. 891, Mar, 1958
Four Color 891-Movie, Fess Parker photo-c 6 12 18 42 79 115

LIGHTNING COMICS (Formerly Sure-Fire No. 1-3)
Ace Magazines: No. 4, Dec, 1940 - No. 13(V3#1), June, 1942
4-Characters continue from Sure-Fire 219 438 657 1402 2401 3400
5,6: 6-Dr. Nemesis begins 155 310 465 992 1696 2400
V2#1-6: 2- "Flash Lightning" becomes "Lash..." 123 246 369 787 1344 1900
V3#1-Intro. Lightning Girl & The Sword 123 246 369 787 1344 1900
NOTE: ***Anderson** a-V2#6. **Mooney** c-V1#5, 6, V2#1-6, V3#1. Bondage c-V2#6. Lightning-c on all.*

LIGHTNING COMICS PRESENTS
Lightning Comics: May, 1994 ($3.50)
1-Red foil-c distr. by Diamond Distr., 1-Black/yellow/blue-c distrib. by Capital Distr., 1-Red/yellow-c distributed by H. World, 1-Platinum 3.50

LIGHTSTEP
Dark Horse Comics (Eipix Comics): Nov, 2018 - No. 5, Apr, 2019 ($3.99, limited series)
1-5-Milos Slavkovic-s/a; Mirko Topalski-s 4.00

LI'L ... (These titles are listed under Little ...)

LILI
Image Comics: No. 0, 1999 ($4.95, B&W)
0-Bendis & Yanover-s 5.00

LILLITH (See Warrior Nun...)
Antarctic Press: Sept, 1996 - No. 3, Feb, 1997 ($2.95, limited series)
1-3: 1-Variant-c 4.00

LIMITED COLLECTORS' EDITION (See Famous First Edition, Marvel Treasury #28, Rudolph The Red-Nosed Reindeer, & Superman Vs. The Amazing Spider-Man; becomes All-New Collectors' Edition)
National Periodical Publications/DC Comics:
(#21-34,51-59: 84 pgs.; #35-41: 68 pgs.; #42-50: 60 pgs.)
C-21, Summer, 1973 - No. C-59, 1978 ($1.00) (10x13-1/2")
(Rudolph...C-20 (implied), 12/72)-See Rudolph The Red-Nosed Reindeer
C-21: Shazam (TV); r/Captain Marvel Jr. #11 by Raboy; C.C. Beck-c, biog. & photo 3 6 9 21 33 45
C-22: Tarzan; complete origin reprinted from #207-210; all Kubert-c/a; Joe Kubert biography & photo inside 3 6 9 17 26 35
C-23: House of Mystery; Wrightson, N. Adams/Orlando, G. Kane/Wood, Toth, Aragones, Sparling reprints 4 8 12 25 40 55
C-24: Rudolph The Red-Nosed Reindeer 6 12 18 40 73 105
C-25: Batman; Neal Adams-c/a(r); G.A. Joker-r; Batman/Enemy Ace-r; Novick-a(r); has photos from TV show 4 8 12 27 44 60
C-26: See Famous First Edition C-26 (same contents)
C-27,C-29,C-31: C-27: Shazam (TV); G.A. Capt. Marvel & Mary Marvel-r; Beck-r. C-29: Tarzan; reprints "Return of Tarzan" from #219-223 by Kubert; Kubert-c. C-31: Superman; origin-r; Giordano-a; photos of George Reeves from 1950s TV show on inside b/c; Burnley, Boring-r 3 6 9 16 23 30
C-32: Ghosts (new-a) 3 6 9 21 33 45
C-33: Rudolph The Red-Nosed Reindeer(new-a) 5 10 15 35 63 90
C-34: Christmas with the Super-Heroes; unpublished Angel & Ape story by Oksner & Wood; Batman & Teen Titans-r 3 6 9 16 23 30
C-35: Shazam (TV); photo cover features TV's Captain Marvel, Jackson Bostwick; Beck-r; TV photos inside b/c 3 6 9 15 22 28
C-36: The Bible; all new adaptation beginning with Genesis by Kubert, Redondo & Mayer; Kubert-c 3 6 9 15 22 28
C-37: Batman; r-1946 Sundays; inside b/c photos of Batman TV show villains (all villain issue; r/G.A. Joker, Catwoman, Penguin, Two-Face, & Scarecrow stories plus 1946 Sundays-r) 3 6 9 18 28 38
C-38: Superman; 1 pg. N. Adams; part photo-c; photos from TV show on inside back-c 3 6 9 16 23 30
C-39: Secret Origins of Super-Villains; N. Adams-i(r); collection reprints 1950's Joker origin, Luthor origin from Adv. Comics #271, Captain Cold origin from Showcase #8 among others; G.A. Batman-r; Beck-r 3 6 9 16 23 30
C-40: Dick Tracy by Gould featuring Flattop; newspaper-r from 12/21/43 - 5/17/44; biog. of Chester Gould 3 6 9 15 22 28
C-41: Super Friends (TV); JLA-r(1965); Toth-c/a 3 6 9 16 24 32
C-42: Rudolph 4 8 12 27 44 60
C-43-C-47: C-43: Christmas with the Super-Heroes; Wrightson, S&K, Neal Adams-a. C-44: Batman; N. Adams-p(r) & G.A.-r; painted-c. C-45: More Secret Origins of Super-Villains; Flash-r/#105; G.A. Wonder Woman & Batman/Catwoman-r. C-46: Justice League of America(1963-r); 3 pgs. Toth-a C-47: Superman Salutes the Bicentennial (Tomahawk interior); 2 pgs. new-a 3 6 9 14 20 26
C-48,C-49: C-48: Superman Vs. The Flash (Superman/Flash race); swipes-c to Superman #199; r/Superman #199 & Flash #175; 6 pgs. Neal Adams-a. C-49: Superboy & the Legion of Super-Heroes 3 6 9 16 23 30
C-50: Rudolph The Red-Nosed Reindeer; contains poster attached at the centerfold with a cardstock flap (1/2 price if poster is missing) 4 8 12 27 44 60
C-51: Batman; Neal Adams-c/a 3 6 9 18 28 38
C-52,C-57: C-52: The Best of DC; Neal Adams-c/a; Toth, Kubert-a. C-57: Welcome Back, Kotter-r(TV)(5/78) includes unpublished #11 3 6 9 16 23 30
C-53 thru C-56, C-58, C-60 thru C-62 (See All-New Collectors' Edition)
C-59: Batman's Strangest Cases; N. Adams-r; Wrightson-r/Swamp Thing #7; N. Adams/Wrightson-c 3 6 9 16 23 30
NOTE: *All-r with exception of some special features and covers. **Aparo** a-52r; c-37. **Grell** c-49. **Infantino** a-25, 39, 44, 45, 52. **Bob Kane** r-25. **Robinson** r-25, 44. **Sprang** r-44. Issues #21-31, 35-39, 45, 48 have back cover cut-outs.*

LINDA (Everybody Loves...) (Phantom Lady No. 5 on)
Ajax-Farrell Publ. Co.: Apr-May, 1954 - No. 4, Oct-Nov, 1954
1-Kamenish-a 20 40 60 115 188 260
2-Lingerie panel 14 28 42 82 121 160
3,4 13 26 39 72 101 130

LINDA CARTER, STUDENT NURSE (Also see Night Nurse)
Atlas Comics (AMI): Sept, 1961 - No. 9, Jan, 1963
1-Al Hartley-c; 1st app. character who becomes Night Nurse in Daredevil V2 #58 (2004) 168 336 504 1075 1838 2600
2-9 25 50 75 150 245 340

LINDA LARK
Dell Publishing Co.: Oct-Dec, 1961 - No. 8, Aug-Oct, 1963
1 3 6 9 19 30 40
2-8 3 6 9 14 19 24

LINE OF DEFENSE 3000AD (Based on the video game)
DC Comics: No. 0, 2012 (no price)
0-Brian Ching-a 3.00

LINUS, THE LIONHEARTED (TV)
Gold Key: Sept, 1965
1 (10155-509) 6 12 18 38 69 100

LION, THE (See Movie Comics)

LIONHEART
Awesome Comics: Sept, 1999 - No. 2, Dec, 1999 ($2.99/$2.50)
1-Ian Churchill-story/a, Jeph Loeb-s; Coven app. 5.00
2-Flip book w/Coven #4 4.00

LION OF SPARTA (See Movie Classics)

LIPPY THE LION AND HARDY HAR HAR (TV)
Gold Key: Mar, 1963 (12¢) (See Hanna-Barbera Band Wagon #1)
1 (10049-303) 7 14 21 46 86 125

LISA COMICS (TV)(See Simpsons Comics)
Bongo Comics: 1995 ($2.25)
1-Lisa in Wonderland 4.00

LITERALS, THE (See Fables and Jack of Fables)
DC Comics (Vertigo): June, 2009 - No. 3, Aug, 2009 ($2.99)
1-3-Crossover with Fables #83-85 and Jack of Fables #33-35; Buckingham-c/a 3.00

LI'L ABNER (See Comics on Parade, Sparkle, Sparkler Comics, Tip Top Comics & Tip Topper)
United Features Syndicate: 1939 - 1940
Single Series 4 ('39) 89 178 267 565 970 1375
Single Series 18 ('40) (#18 on inside, #2 on-c) 65 130 195 416 708 1000

LI'L ABNER (Al Capp's; continued from Comics on Parade #58)
Harvey Publ. No. 61-69 (2/49)/Toby Press No. 70 on: No. 61, Dec, 1947 - No. 97, Jan, 1955
(See Oxydol-Dreft in Promotional Comics section)
61(#1)-Wolverton & Powell-a 25 50 75 150 245 340
62-65: 63-The Wolf Girl app. 65-Powell-a 15 30 45 88 137 185
66,67,69,70 15 30 45 84 127 170

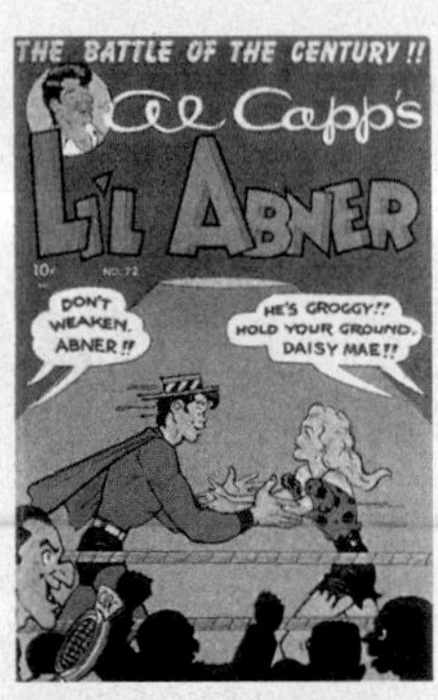

Li'l Abner #72 © TOBY

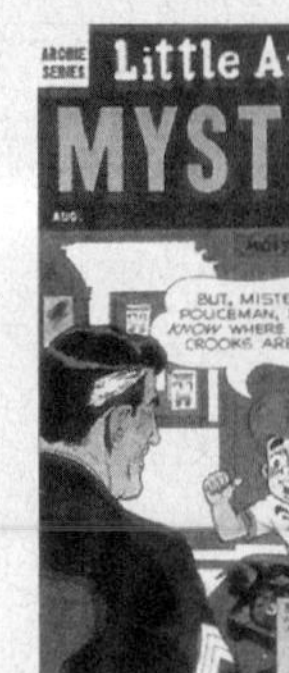

Little Archie Mystery #1 © ACP

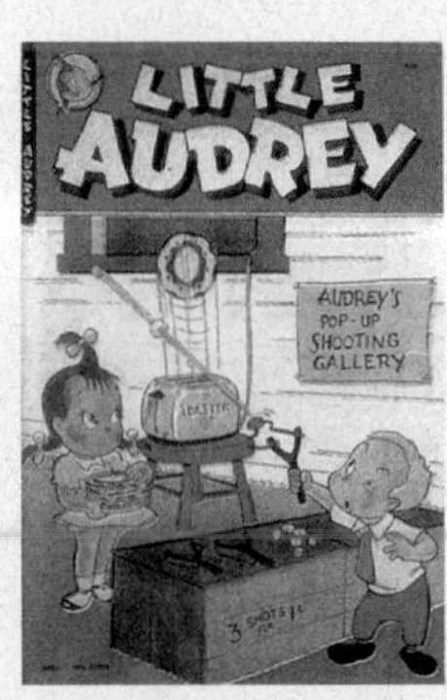

Little Audrey #5 © HARV

	GD 2.0	VG 4.0	FN 6.0	VF 8.0	VF/NM 9.0	NM- 9.2
68-Full length Fearless Fosdick-c/story	16	32	48	92	144	195
71-74,76,80	13	26	39	74	105	135
75,77-79,86,91-All with Kurtzman art; 86-Sadie Hawkins Day. 91-r/#77	15	30	45	83	124	165
81-85,87-90,92-94,96,97: 83-Evil-Eye Fleegle & Double Whammy app. 88-Cousin Weakeyes goes hunting. 94-Six lessons from Adam Lazonga. 96-Football issue	12	24	36	69	97	125
95-Full length Fearless Fosdick story	14	28	42	76	108	140

LI'L ABNER
Toby Press: 1951

	GD 2.0	VG 4.0	FN 6.0	VF 8.0	VF/NM 9.0	NM- 9.2
1	18	36	54	107	169	230

LI'L ABNER'S DOGPATCH (See Al Capp's...)

LITTLE AL OF THE F.B.I.
Ziff-Davis Publications: No. 10, 1950 (no month) - No. 11, Apr-May, 1951 (Saunders painted-c)

	GD 2.0	VG 4.0	FN 6.0	VF 8.0	VF/NM 9.0	NM- 9.2
10(1950)	20	40	60	120	195	270
11(1951)	15	30	45	88	137	185

LITTLE AL OF THE SECRET SERVICE
Ziff-Davis Publications: No. 10, 7-8/51; No, 2, 9-10/51; No. 3, Winter, 1951 (Saunders painted-c)

	GD 2.0	VG 4.0	FN 6.0	VF 8.0	VF/NM 9.0	NM- 9.2
10(#1)	19	38	57	111	176	240
2,3	15	30	45	83	124	165

LITTLE AMBROSE
Archie Publications: September, 1958

	GD 2.0	VG 4.0	FN 6.0	VF 8.0	VF/NM 9.0	NM- 9.2
1-Bob Bolling-c	17	34	51	103	162	220

LITTLE ANGEL
Standard (Visual Editions)/Pines: No. 5, Sept, 1954; No. 6, Sept, 1955 - No. 16, Sept, 1959

	GD 2.0	VG 4.0	FN 6.0	VF 8.0	VF/NM 9.0	NM- 9.2
5-Last pre-code issue	8	16	24	42	54	65
6-16	6	12	18	28	34	40

LITTLE ANNIE ROONEY (Also see Henry)
David McKay Publ.: 1935 (25¢, B&W dailies, 48 pgs.)(10"x10", cardboard-c)

	GD 2.0	VG 4.0	FN 6.0	VF 8.0	VF/NM 9.0	NM- 9.2
Book 1-Daily strip-r by Darrell McClure	39	78	117	231	378	525

LITTLE ANNIE ROONEY (See King Comics & Treasury of Comics)
David McKay/St. John/Standard: 1938; Aug, 1948 - No. 3, Oct, 1948

	GD 2.0	VG 4.0	FN 6.0	VF 8.0	VF/NM 9.0	NM- 9.2
Feature Books 11 (McKay, 1938)	39	78	117	236	388	540
1 (St. John)	16	32	48	92	144	195
2,3	10	20	30	54	72	90

LITTLE ARCHIE (The Adventures of... #13-on) (See Archie Giant Series Mag. #527, 534, 538, 545, 549, 556, 560, 566, 570, 583, 594, 596, 607, 609, 619)
Archie Publications: 1956 - No. 180, Feb, 1983 (Giants No. 3-84)

	GD 2.0	VG 4.0	FN 6.0	VF 8.0	VF/NM 9.0	NM- 9.2
1-(Scarce)	129	258	387	1032	2316	3600
2 (1957)	44	88	132	326	738	1150
3-5: 3-(1958)-Bob Bolling-c & giant issues begin	23	46	69	168	382	560
6-10	16	32	48	111	246	380
11-17,19,21 (84 pgs.)	12	24	36	79	170	260
18,20,22 (84 pgs.)-Horror/Sci-Fi-c	17	34	51	117	259	400
23-39 (68 pgs.)	8	16	24	51	96	140
40 (Fall/66)-Intro. Little Pureheart-c/s (68 pgs.)	8	16	24	55	105	155
41,44-Little Pureheart (68 pgs.)	6	12	18	38	69	100
42-Intro The Little Archies Band, ends #66 (68 pgs.)	6	12	18	41	76	110
43-1st Boy From R.I.V.E.R.D.A.L.E. (68 pgs.)	6	12	18	40	73	105
45-58 (68 pgs.)	5	10	15	33	57	80
59 (68 pgs.)-Little Sabrina begins	8	16	24	51	96	140
60-66 (68 pgs.)	4	8	12	27	44	60
67(9/71)-84: 84-Last 52pg. Giant-Size (2/74)	3	6	9	17	26	35
85-99	2	4	6	10	14	18
100	2	4	6	13	18	22
101-112,114-116,118-129	2	4	6	8	10	12
113,117,130: 113-Halloween Special issue(12/76). 117-Donny Osmond-c cameo 130-UFO cover (5/78)	2	4	6	9	13	16
131-150(1/80), 180(Last issue, 2/83)	1	2	3	5	7	9
151-179						5.00
...In Animal Land 1 (1957)	30	60	90	216	483	750
...In Animal Land 17 (Winter, 1957-58)-19 (Summer,1958)-Formerly Li'l Jinx	12	24	36	79	170	260
Archie Classics - The Adventures of Little Archie Vol. 1 TPB (2004, $10.95) reprints						11.00
Vol. 2 TPB (2008, $9.95) reprints plus new 22 pg. story with Bolling-s/a						10.00

NOTE: *Little Archie Band app. 42-66. Little Sabrina in 59-78,80-180*

LITTLE ARCHIE CHRISTMAS SPECIAL (See Archie Giant Series #581)

LITTLE ARCHIE COMICS DIGEST ANNUAL (...Magazine #5 on)
Archie Publications: 10/77 - No. 48, 5/91 (Digest-size, 128 pgs., later issues $1.35-$1.50)

	GD 2.0	VG 4.0	FN 6.0	VF 8.0	VF/NM 9.0	NM- 9.2
1(10/77)-Reprints	3	6	9	19	30	40
2(4/78,3(11/78)-Neal Adams-a. 3-The Fly-r by S&K	3	6	9	14	20	26
4(4/79) - 10	2	4	6	10	14	18
11-20	2	4	6	8	10	12
21-30: 28-Christmas-c	1	2	3	5	6	8
31-48: 40,46-Christmas-c						5.00

NOTE: *Little Archie, Little Jinx, Little Jughead & Little Sabrina in most issues.*

LITTLE ARCHIE DIGEST MAGAZINE
Archie Comics: July, 1991 - No. 21, Mar, 1998 ($1.50/$1.79/$1.89, digest size, bi-annual)

	GD 2.0	VG 4.0	FN 6.0	VF 8.0	VF/NM 9.0	NM- 9.2
V2#1						6.00
2-10						4.00
11-21						3.00

LITTLE ARCHIE MYSTERY
Archie Publications: Aug, 1963 - No. 2, Oct, 1963 (12¢ issues)

	GD 2.0	VG 4.0	FN 6.0	VF 8.0	VF/NM 9.0	NM- 9.2
1	16	32	48	112	249	385
2	9	18	27	58	114	170

LITTLE ARCHIE, ONE SHOT
Archie Comic Publications: May, 2017 ($4.99, one-shot)

	GD 2.0	VG 4.0	FN 6.0	VF 8.0	VF/NM 9.0	NM- 9.2
nn-Art Baltazar & Franco-s/a; 3 covers; Sabrina app.						5.00

LITTLE ASPIRIN (See Little Lenny & Wisco)
Marvel Comics (CnPC): July, 1949 - No. 3, Dec, 1949 (52 pgs.)

	GD 2.0	VG 4.0	FN 6.0	VF 8.0	VF/NM 9.0	NM- 9.2
1-Oscar app.; Kurtzman-a (4 pgs.)	20	40	60	120	195	270
2-Kurtzman-a (4 pgs.)	14	28	42	76	108	140
3-No Kurtzman-a	10	20	30	58	79	100

LITTLE AUDREY (Also see Playful...)
St. John Publ.: Apr, 1948 - No. 24, May, 1952

	GD 2.0	VG 4.0	FN 6.0	VF 8.0	VF/NM 9.0	NM- 9.2
1-1st app. Little Audrey	148	296	444	947	1624	2300
2	43	86	129	271	461	650
3-5	27	54	81	158	259	360
6-10	20	40	60	114	182	250
11-20: 16-X-Mas-c	15	30	45	63	124	165
21-24	14	28	42	76	108	140

LITTLE AUDREY (See Harvey Hits #11, 19)
Harvey Publications: No. 25, Aug, 1952 - No. 53, April, 1957

	GD 2.0	VG 4.0	FN 6.0	VF 8.0	VF/NM 9.0	NM- 9.2
25-(Paramount Pictures Famous Star... on-c); 1st Harvey Casper and Baby Huey (1 month earlier than Harvey Comic Hits #60(9/52))	27	54	81	194	435	675
26-30: 26-28-Casper app.	9	18	27	58	114	170
31-40: 32-35-Casper app.	6	12	18	41	76	110
41-53	5	10	15	31	53	75
...Clubhouse 1 (9/61, 68 pg. Giant)-New stories & reprints	8	16	24	55	105	155

LITTLE AUDREY
Harvey Comics: Aug, 1992 - No. 8, July, 1994 ($1.25/$1.50)

	GD 2.0	VG 4.0	FN 6.0	VF 8.0	VF/NM 9.0	NM- 9.2
V2#1						5.00
2-8						4.00

LITTLE AUDREY (...Yearbook)
St. John Publishing Co.: 1950 (50¢, 260 pgs.)

	GD 2.0	VG 4.0	FN 6.0	VF 8.0	VF/NM 9.0	NM- 9.2
Contains 8 complete 1949 comics rebound; Casper, Alice in Wonderland, Little Audrey, Abbott & Costello, Pinocchio, Moon Mullins, Three Stooges (from Jubilee), Little Annie Rooney app. (Rare)	190	380	570	1207	2079	2950

(Also see All Good & Treasury of Comics)

NOTE: *This book contains remaindered St. John comics; many variations possible.*

LITTLE AUDREY & MELVIN (Audrey & Melvin No. 62)
Harvey Publications: May, 1962 - No. 61, Dec, 1973

	GD 2.0	VG 4.0	FN 6.0	VF 8.0	VF/NM 9.0	NM- 9.2
1	9	18	27	63	129	195
2-5	4	8	12	25	40	55
6-10	3	6	9	21	33	45
11-20	3	6	9	16	23	30
21-40: 22-Richie Rich app.	2	4	6	13	18	22
41-50,55-61	2	4	6	9	13	16
51-54: All 52 pg. Giants	2	4	6	13	18	22

LITTLE AUDREY TV FUNTIME
Harvey Publ.: Sept, 1962 - No. 33, Oct, 1971 (#1-31: 68 pgs.; #32,33: 52 pgs.)

	GD 2.0	VG 4.0	FN 6.0	VF 8.0	VF/NM 9.0	NM- 9.2
1-Richie Rich app.	9	18	27	63	129	195
2,3: Richie Rich app.	4	8	12	27	44	60
4,5: 5-25¢ & 35¢ issues exist	4	8	12	23	37	50
6-10	3	6	9	17	26	35
11-20	3	6	9	14	19	24
21-33	2	4	6	11	16	20

Little Dot #20 © HARV

The Little Endless Storybook © DC

Li'l Genius #38 © CC

LITTLE BAD WOLF (Disney; see Walt Disney's C&S #52, Walt Disney Showcase #21 & Wheaties)
Dell Publishing Co.: No. 403, June, 1952 - No. 564, June, 1954

	GD 2.0	VG 4.0	FN 6.0	VF 8.0	VF/NM 9.0	NM- 9.2
Four Color 403 (#1)	8	16	24	56	108	160
Four Color 473 (6/53), 564	6	12	18	37	66	95

LI'L BATTLESTAR GALACTICA (Classic 1978 TV series)
Dynamite Entertainment: 2014 ($3.99, one-shot)

	GD 2.0	VG 4.0	FN 6.0	VF 8.0	VF/NM 9.0	NM- 9.2
1-Kid version spoof by Franco & Art Baltazar; covers by Baltazar & Garbowska						4.00

LITTLE BEAVER
Dell Publishing Co.: No. 211, Jan, 1949 - No. 870, Jan, 1958 (All painted-c)

	GD 2.0	VG 4.0	FN 6.0	VF 8.0	VF/NM 9.0	NM- 9.2
Four Color 211('49)-All Harman-a	10	20	30	67	141	215
Four Color 267,294,332(5/51)	7	14	21	44	82	120
3(10-12/51)-8(1-3/53)	5	10	15	31	53	75
Four Color 483(8-10/53),529	5	10	15	35	63	90
Four Color 612,660,695,744,817,870	5	10	15	34	60	85

LI'L BIONIC KIDS (Six Million Dollar Man and Bionic Woman)
Dynamite Entertainment: 2014 ($3.99, one-shot)

	GD 2.0	VG 4.0	FN 6.0	VF 8.0	VF/NM 9.0	NM- 9.2
1-Kid version spoof; Bigfoot app.; Jerwa-s/McGinty-a; covers by Baltazar & Garbowska						4.00

LITTLE BIT
Jubilee/St. John Publishing Co.: Mar, 1949 - No. 2, June, 1949

	GD 2.0	VG 4.0	FN 6.0	VF 8.0	VF/NM 9.0	NM- 9.2
1-Kid humor	14	28	42	78	112	145
2	10	20	30	56	76	95

LI'L DEPRESSED BOY
Image Comics: Feb, 2011 - No. 16, Apr, 2013 ($2.99/$3.99)

	GD 2.0	VG 4.0	FN 6.0	VF 8.0	VF/NM 9.0	NM- 9.2
1-12-S. Steven Struble-s/Sina Grace-a. 5-Guillory-c. 6-Adlard-c. 10-Childish Gambino app.						3.00
13-16-($3.99)						4.00
Vol. 0 (12/11, $9.99) reprints earlier stories from webcomics & anthologies; various-a						10.00

LI'L DEPRESSED BOY: SUPPOSED TO BE THERE TOO
Image Comics: Oct, 2014 - No. 5, Jun, 2015 ($3.99)

	GD 2.0	VG 4.0	FN 6.0	VF 8.0	VF/NM 9.0	NM- 9.2
1-5-S. Steven Struble-s/Sina Grace-a						4.00

LITTLE DOT (See Humphrey, Li'l Max, Sad Sack, and Tastee-Freez Comics)
Harvey Publications: Sept, 1953 - No. 164, Apr, 1976

	GD 2.0	VG 4.0	FN 6.0	VF 8.0	VF/NM 9.0	NM- 9.2
1-Intro./1st app. Richie Rich & Little Lotta	892	1784	2676	6512	11,506	16,500
2-1st app. Freckles & Pee Wee (Richie Rich's poor friends)	174	348	522	1114	1907	2700
3	103	206	309	659	1130	1600
4	90	180	270	576	988	1400
5-Origin dots on Little Dot's dress	100	200	300	640	1095	1550
6-Richie Rich, Little Lotta, & Little Dot all on cover; 1st Richie Rich cover featured	226	452	678	1446	2473	3500
7-10: 9-Last pre-code issue (1/55)	68	136	204	435	743	1050
11-20	39	78	117	231	378	525
21-30	18	36	54	107	169	230
31-40	14	28	42	80	115	150
41-50	11	22	33	62	86	110
51-60	9	18	27	52	69	85
61-80	4	8	12	27	44	60
81-100	3	6	9	19	30	40
101-141: 122-Richie Rich, Little Lotta, & Little Dot birthday-c. 134-Richie Rich, Little Lotta, Little Audrey & Little Dot lemonade-c	3	6	9	16	23	30
142-145: All 52 pg. Giants	3	6	9	17	26	35
146-164	2	4	6	11	16	20

NOTE: *Richie Rich & Little Lotta in all.*

LITTLE DOT
Harvey Comics: Sept, 1992 - No. 7, June, 1994 ($1.25/$1.50)

	GD 2.0	VG 4.0	FN 6.0	VF 8.0	VF/NM 9.0	NM- 9.2
V2#1-Little Dot, Little Lotta, Richie Rich in all						5.00
2-7 ($1.50)						4.00

LITTLE DOT DOTLAND (Dot Dotland No. 62, 63)
Harvey Publications: July, 1962 - No. 61, Dec, 1973

	GD 2.0	VG 4.0	FN 6.0	VF 8.0	VF/NM 9.0	NM- 9.2
1-Richie Rich begins	12	24	36	81	176	270
2,3	7	14	21	44	82	120
4,5	5	10	15	35	63	90
6-10	5	10	15	30	50	70
11-20	4	8	12	23	37	50
21-30	3	6	9	17	26	35
31-50	3	6	9	16	23	30
51-54: All 52 pg. Giants	3	6	9	17	26	35
55-61	2	4	6	11	16	20

LITTLE DOT'S UNCLES & AUNTS (See Harvey Hits No. 4, 13, 24)
Harvey Enterprises: Oct, 1961; No. 2, Aug, 1962 - No. 52, Apr, 1974

	GD 2.0	VG 4.0	FN 6.0	VF 8.0	VF/NM 9.0	NM- 9.2
1-Richie Rich begins; 68 pgs. begin	15	30	45	103	227	350
2,3	8	16	24	51	96	140
4,5	5	10	15	35	63	90
6-10	5	10	15	31	53	75
11-20	4	8	12	23	37	50
21-37: Last 68 pg. issue	3	6	9	18	28	38
38-52: All 52 pg. Giants	3	6	9	16	23	30

LITTLE DRACULA
Harvey Comics: Jan, 1992 - No. 3, May, 1992 ($1.25, quarterly, mini-series)

	GD 2.0	VG 4.0	FN 6.0	VF 8.0	VF/NM 9.0	NM- 9.2
1-3						4.00

LITTLE ENDLESS STORYBOOK, THE (See The Sandman titles and Delirium's Party)
DC Comics: 2001 ($5.95, Prestige format, one-shot)

	GD 2.0	VG 4.0	FN 6.0	VF 8.0	VF/NM 9.0	NM- 9.2
nn-Jill Thompson-s/painted-a/c; puppy Barnabas searches for Delirium						10.00
HC (2011, $14.99) r/story plus original character sketches and merchandise design						15.00

LI'L ERNIE (Evil Ernie)
Dynamite Entertainment: 2014 ($3.99, one-shot)

	GD 2.0	VG 4.0	FN 6.0	VF 8.0	VF/NM 9.0	NM- 9.2
1-Kid version spoof; Roger Langridge-s/a; covers by Baltazar & Garbowska						4.00

LITTLE EVA
St. John Publishing Co.: May, 1952 - No. 31, Nov, 1956

	GD 2.0	VG 4.0	FN 6.0	VF 8.0	VF/NM 9.0	NM- 9.2
1	20	40	60	114	182	250
2	12	24	36	69	97	125
3-5	10	20	30	56	76	95
6-10	9	18	27	47	61	75
11-31	8	16	24	42	54	65
3-D 1,2(10/53, 11/53, 25¢)-Both came w/glasses. 1-Infinity-c	18	36	54	107	169	230
I.W. Reprint #1-3,6-8: 1-r/Little Eva #28. 2-r/Little Eva #29. 3-r/Little Eva #24	2	4	6	8	11	14
Super Reprint #10,12('63),14,16,18('64): 18-r/Little Eva #25.	2	4	6	8	11	14

LI'L GENIUS (Formerly Super Brat; Summer Fun No. 54) (See Blue Bird & Giant Comics #3)
Charlton Comics: No. 6, 1954 - No. 52, 1/65; No. 53, 10/65; No. 54, 10/85 - No. 55, 1/86

	GD 2.0	VG 4.0	FN 6.0	VF 8.0	VF/NM 9.0	NM- 9.2
6 (#1)	11	22	33	62	86	110
7-10	7	14	21	37	46	55
11-1st app. Li'l Tomboy (10/56); same month as 1st issue of Li'l Tomboy (V14#92)	8	16	24	40	50	60
12-15,19,20	6	12	18	29	36	42
16,17-(68 pgs.)	8	16	24	40	50	60
18-(100 pgs., 10/58)	11	22	33	60	83	105
21-35: 34-Atomic bomb explosion	3	6	9	15	22	28
36-53	2	4	6	10	14	18
54,55 (Low print)						6.00

LI'L GHOST
St. John Publ. Co./Fago No. 1 on: 2/58; No. 2,1/59 - No. 3, Mar, 1959

	GD 2.0	VG 4.0	FN 6.0	VF 8.0	VF/NM 9.0	NM- 9.2
1(St. John)	13	26	39	72	101	130
2,3	8	16	24	44	57	70

LITTLE GIANT COMICS
Centaur Publications: 7/38 - No. 3, 10/38; No. 4, 2/39 (132 pgs.) (6-3/4x4-1/2")

	GD 2.0	VG 4.0	FN 6.0	VF 8.0	VF/NM 9.0	NM- 9.2
1-B&W with color-c; stories, puzzles, magic	271	542	813	1734	2967	4200
2,3-B&W with color-c	206	412	618	1318	2259	3200
4 (6-5/8x9-3/8")(68 pgs., B&W inside)	206	412	618	1318	2259	3200

NOTE: ***Filchock** c-2, 4. **Gustavson** a-1. **Pinajian** a-4. **Bob Wood** a-1.*

LITTLE GIANT DETECTIVE FUNNIES
Centaur Publ.: Oct, 1938; No. 4, Jan, 1939 (6-3/4x4-1/2", 132 pgs., B&W)

	GD 2.0	VG 4.0	FN 6.0	VF 8.0	VF/NM 9.0	NM- 9.2
1-B&W with color-c	271	542	813	1734	2967	4200
4(1/39, B&W; color-c; 68 pgs., 6-1/2x9-1/2")-Eisner-r	206	412	618	1318	2259	3200

LITTLE GIANT MOVIE FUNNIES
Centaur Publ.: Aug, 1938 - No. 2, Oct, 1938 (6-3/4x4-1/2", 132 pgs., B&W)

	GD 2.0	VG 4.0	FN 6.0	VF 8.0	VF/NM 9.0	NM- 9.2
1-Ed Wheelan's "Minute Movies" reprints	245	490	735	1568	2684	3800
2-Ed Wheelan's "Minute Movies" reprints	181	362	543	1158	1979	2800

LITTLE GROUCHO (...the Red-Headed Tornado; ...Grouchy No. 2)
Reston Publ. Co.: No. 16; Feb-Mar, 1955 - No. 2, June-July, 1955 (See Tippy Terry)

	GD 2.0	VG 4.0	FN 6.0	VF 8.0	VF/NM 9.0	NM- 9.2
16, 1 (2-3/55)	10	20	30	56	76	95
2(6-7/55)	8	16	24	40	50	60

LITTLE HIAWATHA (Disney; see Walt Disney's C&S #143)

Little Jack Frost #1 © AVON

Little Lulu #221 © Marjorie Buell

Li'l Menace #1 © Fago

Dell Publishing Co.: No. 439, Dec, 1952 - No. 988, May-July, 1959

	GD 2.0	VG 4.0	FN 6.0	VF 8.0	VF/NM 9.0	NM- 9.2
Four Color 439 (#1)	7	14	21	46	86	125
Four Color 787 (4/57), 901 (5/58), 988	5	10	15	34	60	85

LITTLE IKE
St. John Publishing Co.: April, 1953 - No. 4, Oct, 1953

	GD 2.0	VG 4.0	FN 6.0	VF 8.0	VF/NM 9.0	NM- 9.2
1-Kid humor	14	28	42	76	108	140
2	8	16	24	44	57	70
3,4	7	14	21	37	46	55

LITTLE IODINE (See Giant Comic Album)
Dell Publ. Co.: No. 224, 4/49 - No. 257, 1949: 3-5/50 - No. 56, 4-6/62 (1-4-52pgs.)

	GD 2.0	VG 4.0	FN 6.0	VF 8.0	VF/NM 9.0	NM- 9.2
Four Color 224-By Jimmy Hatlo	12	24	36	81	176	270
Four Color 257	8	16	24	55	105	155
1(3-5/50)	10	20	30	64	132	200
2-5	5	10	15	35	63	90
6-10	5	10	15	30	50	70
11-20	4	8	12	27	44	60
21-30: 27-Xmas-c	4	8	12	23	37	50
31-40	3	6	9	21	33	45
41-56	3	6	9	19	30	40

LITTLE JACK FROST
Avon Periodicals: 1951

	GD 2.0	VG 4.0	FN 6.0	VF 8.0	VF/NM 9.0	NM- 9.2
1	15	30	45	84	127	170

LI'L JINX (Little Archie in Animal Land #17) (Also see Pep Comics #62)
Archie Publications: No. 1(#11), Nov, 1956 - No. 16, Sept, 1957

	GD 2.0	VG 4.0	FN 6.0	VF 8.0	VF/NM 9.0	NM- 9.2
1(#11)-By Joe Edwards; "First Issue" on cover	20	40	60	114	182	250
12(1/57)-16	13	26	39	72	101	130

LI'L JINX (See Archie Giant Series Magazine No. 223)

LI'L JINX CHRISTMAS BAG (See Archie Giant Series Mag. No. 195, 206, 219)

LI'L JINX GIANT LAUGH-OUT (See Archie Giant Series Mag. No. 176, 185)
Archie Publications: No. 33, Sept, 1971 - No. 43, Nov, 1973 (52 pgs.)

	GD 2.0	VG 4.0	FN 6.0	VF 8.0	VF/NM 9.0	NM- 9.2
33-43 (52 pgs.)	2	4	6	13	18	22

LITTLE JOE (See Popular Comics & Super Comics)
Dell Publishing Co.: No. 1, 1942

	GD 2.0	VG 4.0	FN 6.0	VF 8.0	VF/NM 9.0	NM- 9.2
Four Color 1	70	140	210	567	1259	1950

LITTLE JOE
St. John Publishing Co.: Apr, 1953

	GD 2.0	VG 4.0	FN 6.0	VF 8.0	VF/NM 9.0	NM- 9.2
1	9	18	27	50	65	80

LI'L KIDS (Also see Li'l Pals)
Marvel Comics Group: 8/70 - No. 2, 10/70; No. 3, 11/71 - No. 12, 6/73

	GD 2.0	VG 4.0	FN 6.0	VF 8.0	VF/NM 9.0	NM- 9.2
1	8	16	24	55	105	155
2-9	4	8	12	28	47	65
10-12-Calvin app.	5	10	15	30	50	70

LITTLE KING
Dell Publishing Co.: No. 494, Aug, 1953 - No. 677, Feb, 1956

	GD 2.0	VG 4.0	FN 6.0	VF 8.0	VF/NM 9.0	NM- 9.2
Four Color 494 (#1)	8	16	24	56	108	160
Four Color 597, 677	5	10	15	34	60	85

LITTLE LANA (Formerly Lana)
Marvel Comics (MjMC): No. 8, Nov, 1949; No. 9, Mar, 1950

	GD 2.0	VG 4.0	FN 6.0	VF 8.0	VF/NM 9.0	NM- 9.2
8,9	20	40	60	114	182	250

LITTLE LENNY
Marvel Comics (CDS): June, 1949 - No. 3, Nov, 1949

	GD 2.0	VG 4.0	FN 6.0	VF 8.0	VF/NM 9.0	NM- 9.2
1-Little Aspirin app.	15	30	45	94	147	200
2,3	11	22	33	62	86	110

LITTLE LIZZIE
Marvel Comics (PrPl)/Atlas (OMC): 6/49 - No. 5, 4/50; 9/53 - No. 3, Jan, 1954

	GD 2.0	VG 4.0	FN 6.0	VF 8.0	VF/NM 9.0	NM- 9.2
1-Kid humor	18	36	54	109	172	235
2-5	12	24	36	67	94	120
1 (9/53, 2nd series by Atlas)-Howie Post-c	13	26	39	74	105	135
2,3	10	20	30	54	72	90

LITTLE LOTTA (See Harvey Hits No. 10)
Harvey Publications: 11/55 - No. 110, 11/73; No. 111, 9/74 - No. 120, 5/76
V2#1, Oct, 1992 - No. 4, July, 1993 ($1.25)

	GD 2.0	VG 4.0	FN 6.0	VF 8.0	VF/NM 9.0	NM- 9.2
1-Richie Rich (r) & Little Dot begin	57	114	171	456	1028	1600
2,3	17	34	51	117	259	400
4,5	10	20	30	69	147	225
6-10	7	14	21	46	86	125
11-20	5	10	15	35	63	90
21-40	4	8	12	23	37	50
41-60	3	6	9	18	28	38
61-80: 62-1st app. Nurse Jenny	3	6	9	15	22	28
81-99	2	4	6	11	16	20
100-103: All 52 pg. Giants	3	6	9	14	19	24
104-120	2	4	6	8	10	12
V2#1-4 (1992-93)						4.00

NOTE: *No. 121 was advertised, but never released.*

LITTLE LOTTA FOODLAND
Harvey Publications: 9/63 - No. 14, 10/67; No. 15, 10/68 - No. 29, Oct, 1972

	GD 2.0	VG 4.0	FN 6.0	VF 8.0	VF/NM 9.0	NM- 9.2
1-Little Lotta, Little Dot, Richie Rich, 68 pgs. begin	11	22	33	73	157	240
2,3	6	12	18	38	69	100
4,5	5	10	15	30	50	70
6-10	4	8	12	23	37	50
11-20	3	6	9	16	23	30
21-26: 26-Last 68 pg. issue	3	6	9	14	20	25
27,28: Both 52 pgs.	2	4	6	11	16	20
29-(36 pgs.)	2	4	6	8	11	14

LITTLE LULU (Formerly Marge's Little Lulu)
Gold Key 207-257/Whitman 258 on: No. 207, Sept, 1972 - No. 268, Mar, 1984

	GD 2.0	VG 4.0	FN 6.0	VF 8.0	VF/NM 9.0	NM- 9.2
207,209,220-Stanley-r. 207-1st app. Henrietta	2	4	6	13	18	22
208,210-219: 208-1st app. Snobbly, Wilbur's butler	2	4	6	9	13	16
221-240,242-249, 250(r/#166), 251-254(r/#206)	2	4	6	8	10	12
241,263-Stanley-r	2	4	6	8	11	14
255-257(Gold Key): 256-r/#212	1	3	4	6	8	10
258,259,262(50¢-c),264(2/82),265(3/82) (Whitman)	2	4	6	11	16	20
260-(9/80)(Whitman pre-pack only - low distribution)	15	30	45	103	227	350
261-(11/80)(Whitman pre-pack only)	7	14	21	44	82	120
262-(1/81) Variant 40¢-c price error (reg. ed. 50¢-c)	3	6	9	15	22	28
266-268 (All #90028 on-c; no date, no date code; 3-pack): 266(7/83). 267(8/83). 268(3/84)-Stanley-r	3	6	9	17	26	35

LITTLE MARY MIXUP (See Comics On Parade)
United Features Syndicate: No. 10, 1939, - No. 26, 1940

	GD 2.0	VG 4.0	FN 6.0	VF 8.0	VF/NM 9.0	NM- 9.2
Single Series 10, 26	36	72	108	211	343	475

LITTLE MAX COMICS (Joe Palooka's Pal; see Joe Palooka)
Harvey Publications: Oct, 1949 - No. 73, Nov, 1961

	GD 2.0	VG 4.0	FN 6.0	VF 8.0	VF/NM 9.0	NM- 9.2
1-Infinity-c; Little Dot begins; Joe Palooka on-c	28	56	84	165	270	375
2-Little Dot app.; Joe Palooka on-c	14	28	42	82	121	160
3-Little Dot app.; Joe Palooka on-c	10	20	30	58	79	100
4-10: 5-Little Dot app., 1pg.	9	18	27	47	61	75
11-20	8	16	24	40	50	60
21-40: 23-Little Dot app. 38-r/#20	6	12	18	31	38	45
41-62,66	3	6	9	17	26	35
63-65,67-73-Include new five pg. Richie Rich stories. 70-73-Little Lotta app.	3	6	9	18	28	38

LI'L MENACE
Fago Magazine Co.: Dec, 1958 - No. 3, May, 1959

	GD 2.0	VG 4.0	FN 6.0	VF 8.0	VF/NM 9.0	NM- 9.2
1-Peter Rabbit app.	9	18	27	52	69	85
2-Peter Rabbit (Vincent Fago's)	7	14	21	35	43	50
3	6	12	18	28	34	40

LITTLE MERMAID, THE (Walt Disney's...; also see Disney's...)
W. D. Publications (Disney): 1990 (no date given)($5.95, no ads, 52 pgs.)

	GD 2.0	VG 4.0	FN 6.0	VF 8.0	VF/NM 9.0	NM- 9.2
nn-Adapts animated movie	1	2	3	5	6	8
nn-Comic version ($2.50)	1	2	3	4	5	7

LITTLE MERMAID, THE (Also see Disney's The Little Mermaid Limited Series)
Disney Comics: 1992 - No. 4, 1992 ($1.50, mini-series)

	GD 2.0	VG 4.0	FN 6.0	VF 8.0	VF/NM 9.0	NM- 9.2
1-Based on movie						6.00
2-4						4.00
1-4: 2nd printings sold at Wal-Mart w/different-c						4.00
Set of #1-4 in unopened 4-issue Collector's Pack						60.00

LITTLE MERMAID, THE
Disney Comics: Oct, 2019 - No. 3, Feb, 2020 ($3.99, limited series)

	GD 2.0	VG 4.0	FN 6.0	VF 8.0	VF/NM 9.0	NM- 9.2
1-3-Adapts the movie; Castellucci-s/Lavina-a/c						4.00

LITTLE MISS MUFFET
Best Books (Standard Comics)/King Features Synd.: No. 11, Dec, 1948 - No. 13, March, 1949

	GD 2.0	VG 4.0	FN 6.0	VF 8.0	VF/NM 9.0	NM- 9.2
11-Strip reprints; Fanny Cory-c/a	12	24	36	69	97	125

Little Nemo: Return to Slumberland #1 © IDW

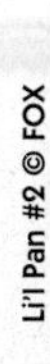

Li'l Pan #2 © FOX

Li'l Sonja #1 © DYN

	GD 2.0	VG 4.0	FN 6.0	VF 8.0	VF/NM 9.0	NM- 9.2
12,13-Strip reprints; Fanny Cory-c/a	9	18	27	47	61	75

LITTLE MISS SUNBEAM COMICS
Magazine Enterprises/Quality Bakers of America: June-July, 1950 - No. 4, Dec-Jan, 1950-51

	GD 2.0	VG 4.0	FN 6.0	VF 8.0	VF/NM 9.0	NM- 9.2
1	20	40	60	115	185	235
2-4	11	22	33	64	90	115
...Advs. In Space ('55)	7	14	21	37	46	55

LITTLE MONSTERS, THE (See March of Comics #423, Three Stooges #17)
Gold Key: Nov, 1964 - No. 44, Feb, 1978

	GD 2.0	VG 4.0	FN 6.0	VF 8.0	VF/NM 9.0	NM- 9.2
1	5	10	15	35	63	90
2	3	6	9	20	31	42
3-10	3	6	9	16	24	32
11-20	3	6	9	15	21	26
21-30: 19-21-Reprints	2	4	6	11	16	20
31-44: 34-39,43-Reprints	2	4	6	8	11	14

LITTLE MONSTERS (Movie)
Now Comics: 1989 - No. 6, June, 1990 ($1.75)

	GD 2.0	VG 4.0	FN 6.0	VF 8.0	VF/NM 9.0	NM- 9.2
1-6: Photo-c from movie						5.00

LITTLE NEMO (See Cocomalt, Future Comics, Help, Jest, Kayo, Punch, Red Seal, & Superworld; most by Winsor McCay Jr., son of famous artist) (Other McCay books: see Little Sammy Sneeze & Dreams of the Rarebit Fiend)

LITTLE NEMO (...in Slumberland)
McCay Features/Nostalgia Press('69): 1945 (11x7-1/4", 28 pgs., B&W)

	GD 2.0	VG 4.0	FN 6.0	VF 8.0	VF/NM 9.0	NM- 9.2
1905 & 1911 reprints by Winsor McCay	11	22	33	62	86	110
1969-70 (Exact reprint)	2	4	6	9	12	15

LITTLE NEMO: RETURN TO SLUMBERLAND
IDW Publishing: Aug, 2014 - No. 4, Feb, 2015 ($3.99)

	GD 2.0	VG 4.0	FN 6.0	VF 8.0	VF/NM 9.0	NM- 9.2
1-4-New stories in McCay style; Shanower-s/Rodriguez-a in all. 1-Multiple covers						4.00

LITTLE ORPHAN ANNIE (See Annie, Famous Feature Stories, Marvel Super Special, Merry Christmas..., Popular Comics, Super Book #7, 11, 23 & Super Comics)

LITTLE ORPHAN ANNIE
David McKay Publ./Dell Publishing Co.: No. 7, 1937 - No. 3, Sept-Nov, 1948; No. 206, Dec, 1948

	GD 2.0	VG 4.0	FN 6.0	VF 8.0	VF/NM 9.0	NM- 9.2
Feature Books(McKay) 7-(1937) (Rare)	126	252	378	806	1378	1950
Four Color 12(1941)	74	148	222	470	810	1150
Four Color 18(1943)-Flag-c	61	122	183	390	670	950
Four Color 52(1944)	25	50	75	175	388	600
Four Color 76(1945)	20	40	60	138	307	475
Four Color 107(1946)	18	36	54	122	271	420
Four Color 152(1947)	12	24	36	79	170	260
1(3-5/48)-r/strips from 5/7/44 to 7/30/44	12	24	36	81	176	270
2-r/strips from 7/21/40 to 9/9/40	9	18	27	57	111	165
3-r/strips from 9/10/40 to 11/9/40	8	16	24	55	105	155
Four Color 206(12/48)	8	16	24	52	99	145

LI'L PALS (Also see Li'l Kids)
Marvel Comics Group: Sept, 1972 - No. 5, May, 1973

	GD 2.0	VG 4.0	FN 6.0	VF 8.0	VF/NM 9.0	NM- 9.2
1	8	16	24	54	102	150
2-5: 5-Super Rabbit story	5	10	15	30	50	70

LI'L PAN (Formerly Rocket Kelly; becomes Junior Comics with #9)(Also see Wotalife Comics)
Fox Feature Syndicate: No. 6, Dec-Jan, 1946-47 - No. 8, Apr-May, 1947

	GD 2.0	VG 4.0	FN 6.0	VF 8.0	VF/NM 9.0	NM- 9.2
6	14	28	42	82	121	160
7,8: 7-Atomic bomb story; robot-c	12	24	36	69	97	125

LITTLE PEOPLE (Also see Darby O'Gill & the...)
Dell Publishing Co.: No. 485, Aug-Oct, 1953 - No. 1062, Dec, 1959 (Walt Scott's)

	GD 2.0	VG 4.0	FN 6.0	VF 8.0	VF/NM 9.0	NM- 9.2
Four Color 485 (#1)	8	16	24	54	102	150
Four Color 573(7/54), 633(6/55)	5	10	15	35	63	90
Four Color 692(3/56),753(11/56),809(7/57),868(12/57),908(5/58),959(12/58),1062	5	10	15	33	57	80

LITTLE RASCALS
Dell Publishing Co.: No. 674, Jan, 1956 - No. 1297, Mar-May, 1962

	GD 2.0	VG 4.0	FN 6.0	VF 8.0	VF/NM 9.0	NM- 9.2
Four Color 674 (#1)	9	18	27	59	117	175
Four Color 778(3/57),825(8/57)	6	12	18	38	69	100
Four Color 883(3/58),936(9/58),974(3/59),1030(9/59),1079(2-4/60),1137(9-11/60)	5	10	15	35	63	90
Four Color 1174(3-5/61),1224(10-12/61),1297	5	10	15	33	57	80

LI'L RASCAL TWINS (Formerly Nature Boy)
Charlton Comics: No. 6, 1957 - No. 18, Jan, 1960

	GD 2.0	VG 4.0	FN 6.0	VF 8.0	VF/NM 9.0	NM- 9.2
6-Li'l Genius & Tomboy in all	6	12	18	31	38	45
7-18: 7-Timmy the Timid Ghost app.	4	8	12	18	22	25

LITTLE RED HOT: (CHANE OF FOOLS)
Image Comics: Feb, 1999 - No. 3, Apr, 1999 ($2.95/$3.50, B&W, limited series)

	GD 2.0	VG 4.0	FN 6.0	VF 8.0	VF/NM 9.0	NM- 9.2
1-3-Dawn Brown-s/a. 2,3-($3.50-c)						4.00
The Foolish Collection TPB ($12.95) r/#1-3						13.00

LITTLE RED HOT: BOUND
Image Comics: July, 2001 - No. 3, Nov, 2001 ($2.95, color, limited series)

	GD 2.0	VG 4.0	FN 6.0	VF 8.0	VF/NM 9.0	NM- 9.2
1-3-Dawn Brown-s/a.						4.00

LITTLE ROQUEFORT COMICS (See Paul Terry's Comics #105)
St. John Publishing Co.(all pre-code)/Pines No. 10: June, 1952 - No. 9, Oct, 1953; No. 10, Summer, 1958

	GD 2.0	VG 4.0	FN 6.0	VF 8.0	VF/NM 9.0	NM- 9.2
1-By Paul Terry; Funny Animal	14	28	42	78	112	145
2	8	16	24	42	54	65
3-10: 10-CBS Television Presents on-c	7	14	21	37	46	55

LITTLE SAD SACK (See Harvey Hits No. 73, 76, 79, 81, 83)
Harvey Publications: Oct, 1964 - No. 19, Nov, 1967

	GD 2.0	VG 4.0	FN 6.0	VF 8.0	VF/NM 9.0	NM- 9.2
1-Richie Rich app. on cover only	5	10	15	34	60	85
2-10	3	6	9	17	26	35
11-19	3	6	9	15	22	28

LITTLE SCOUTS
Dell Publishing Co.: No. 321, Mar, 1951 - No. 587, Oct, 1954

	GD 2.0	VG 4.0	FN 6.0	VF 8.0	VF/NM 9.0	NM- 9.2
Four Color 321 (#1, 3/51)	6	12	18	37	66	95
2(10-12/51) - 6(10-12/52)	4	8	12	25	40	55
Four Color 462,506,550,587	5	10	15	30	50	70

LITTLE SHOP OF HORRORS SPECIAL (Movie)
DC Comics: Feb, 1987 ($2.00, 68 pgs.)

	GD 2.0	VG 4.0	FN 6.0	VF 8.0	VF/NM 9.0	NM- 9.2
1-Colan-c/a	1	3	4	6	8	10

LI'L SONJA (Red Sonja)
Dynamite Entertainment: 2014 ($3.99, one-shot)

	GD 2.0	VG 4.0	FN 6.0	VF 8.0	VF/NM 9.0	NM- 9.2
1-Kid version spoof; Jim Zub-s/Joel Carroll-a; covers by Baltazar & Garbowska						4.00

LITTLE SPUNKY
I. W. Enterprises: No date (1958) (10¢)

	GD 2.0	VG 4.0	FN 6.0	VF 8.0	VF/NM 9.0	NM- 9.2
1-r/Frisky Fables #1	2	4	6	11	16	20

LITTLE STAR
Oni Press: Feb, 2005 - No. 6, Dec, 2005 ($2.99, B&W, limited series)

	GD 2.0	VG 4.0	FN 6.0	VF 8.0	VF/NM 9.0	NM- 9.2
1-6-Andi Watson-s/a						3.00
TPB (4/06, $19.95) r/#1-6						20.00

LITTLE STOOGES, THE (The Three Stooges' Sons)
Gold Key: Sept, 1972 - No. 7, Mar, 1974

	GD 2.0	VG 4.0	FN 6.0	VF 8.0	VF/NM 9.0	NM- 9.2
1-Norman Maurer cover/stories in all	3	6	9	18	28	38
2-7	2	4	6	13	18	22

LITTLEST OUTLAW (Disney)
Dell Publishing Co.: No. 609, Jan, 1955

	GD 2.0	VG 4.0	FN 6.0	VF 8.0	VF/NM 9.0	NM- 9.2
Four Color 609-Movie, photo-c	6	12	18	41	76	110

LITTLEST PET SHOP (Based on the Hasbro toys)
IDW Publishing: May, 2014 - No. 5, Sept, 2014 ($3.99)

	GD 2.0	VG 4.0	FN 6.0	VF 8.0	VF/NM 9.0	NM- 9.2
1-5: 1-Ball-s/Peña-a; multiple covers. 2-5-Two covers on each						4.00
... Spring Cleaning (4/15, $7.99) Four short stories; Ball-s; art by various						8.00

LITTLEST SNOWMAN, THE
Dell Publishing Co.: No. 755, 12/56; No. 864, 12/57; 12-2/1963-64

	GD 2.0	VG 4.0	FN 6.0	VF 8.0	VF/NM 9.0	NM- 9.2
Four Color 755,864, 1(1964)	5	10	15	35	63	90

LI'L TOMBOY (Formerly Fawcett's Funny Animals; see Giant Comics #3)
Charlton Comics: V14#92, Oct, 1956; No. 93, Mar, 1957 - No. 107, Feb, 1960

	GD 2.0	VG 4.0	FN 6.0	VF 8.0	VF/NM 9.0	NM- 9.2
V14#92-Ties as 1st app. with Li'l Genius #11	6	12	18	28	34	40
93-107: 97-Atomic Bunny app.	5	10	15	22	27	30

LI'L VAMPI (Vampirella)
Dynamite Entertainment: 2014 ($3.99, one-shot)

	GD 2.0	VG 4.0	FN 6.0	VF 8.0	VF/NM 9.0	NM- 9.2
1-Kid version spoof; Trautmann-s/Garbowska-a; covers by Baltazar & Garbowska						4.00

LI'L WILLIE COMICS (Formerly & becomes Willie Comics #22 on)
Marvel Comics (MgPC): No. 20, July, 1949 - No. 21, Sept, 1949

	GD 2.0	VG 4.0	FN 6.0	VF 8.0	VF/NM 9.0	NM- 9.2
20,21: 20-Little Aspirin app.	17	34	51	105	165	225

LITTLE WOMEN (See Power Record Comics)

LIVE IT UP
Spire Christian Comics (Fleming H. Revell Co.): 1973, 1974,1976 (39-49 cents)

	GD 2.0	VG 4.0	FN 6.0	VF 8.0	VF/NM 9.0	NM- 9.2
nn-1973 Edition	2	4	6	13	18	22

Livewire #12 © VAL

Lobo #4 © DC

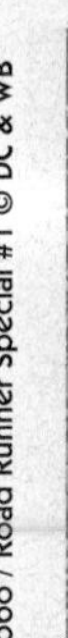

Lobo / Road Runner Special #1 © DC & WB

	GD	VG	FN	VF	VF/NM	NM-
	2.0	4.0	6.0	8.0	9.0	9.2

nn-1974,1976 Editions 2 4 6 8 11 14

LIVEWIRE
Valiant Entertainment: Dec, 2018 - No. 12, Nov, 2019 ($3.99)

1-12: 1-4-Vita Ayala-s/Raúl Allén-a. 5-8-Kano-a. 9-12-Tana Ford-a 4.00

LIVEWIRES
Marvel Comics: Apr, 2005 - No. 6, Sept, 2005 ($2.99, limited series)

1-6-Adam Warren-s/c; Rick Mays-a 3.00
...: Clockwork Thugs, Yo (2005, $7.99, digest) r/#1-6 8.00

LIVING BIBLE, THE
Living Bible Corp.: Fall, 1945 - No. 3, Spring, 1946

1-The Life of Paul; all have L. B. Cole-c 45 90 135 264 480 675
2-Joseph & His Brethren; Jonah & the Whale 33 66 99 194 317 440
3-Chaplains At War (classic-c) 45 90 135 284 480 675

LIVING WITH THE DEAD
Dark Horse Comics: Oct, 2007 - No. 3, Nov, 2007 ($2.99, limited series)

1-3-Zombies; Mike Richardson-s/Ben Stenbeck-a/Richard Corben-c 3.00

LOADED BIBLE
Image Comics: Apr, 2006; May, 2007; Feb, 2008 ($4.99)

...: Jesus vs. Vampires (4/06) Tim Seeley-s/Nate Bellegarde-a 5.00
...2: Blood of Christ (5/07) Seeley-s/Mike Norton-a. ...3: Communion (2/08) 5.00

LOBO
Dell Publishing Co.: Dec, 1965; No. 2, Oct, 1966

1-1st black character to have his own title 38 76 114 285 641 1000
2 17 34 51 117 259 400

LOBO (Also see Action #650, Adventures of Superman, Demon (2nd series), Justice League, L.E.G.I.O.N., Mister Miracle, Omega Men #3 & Superman #41)
DC Comics: Nov, 1990 - No. 4, Feb, 1991 ($1.50, color, limited series)

1-(99¢)-Giffen plots/Breakdowns in all 2 4 6 10 14 18
1-2nd printing 4.00
2-4: 2-Legion '89 spin-off. 1-4 have Bisley painted covers & art 6.00
...: Blazing Chain of Love 1 (9/92, $1.50)-Denys Cowan-c/a; Alan Grant scripts, ...Convention Special 1 (1993, $1.75), ...: Portrait of a Victim 1 (1993, $1.75) 4.00
... Paramilitary Christmas Special 1 (1991, $2.39, 52 pgs.) Bisley-c/a 5.00
...: Portrait of a Bastich TPB (2008, $19.99) r/#1-4 & Lobo's Back #1-4 20.00

LOBO (Also see Showcase '95 #9)
DC Comics: Dec, 1993 - No. 64, Jul, 1999 ($1.75/$1.95/$2.25/$2.50, mature)

1 ($2.95)-Foil enhanced-c; Alan Grant scripts begin 1 3 4 5 6 8
2-9,0,10-64: 2-7-Alan Grant scripts. 9-(9/94). 0-(10/94)-Origin retold. 50-Lobo vs. the DCU. 58-Giffen-a 4.00
#1,000,000 (11/98) 853rd Century x-over 4.00
Annual 1 (1993, $3.50, 68 pgs.)-Bloodlines x-over 5.00
Annual 2 (1994, $3.50)-21 artists (20 listed on-c); Alan Grant script; Elseworlds story 5.00
Annual 3 (1995, $3.95)-Year One story 5.00
.../Authority: Holiday Hell TPB (2006, $17.99) r/Lobo Paramilitary Christmas Special; Authority/Lobo: Jingle Hell and Spring Break Massacre; WildStorm Winter Special 18.00
...Big Babe Spring Break Special (Spr, '95, $1.95)-Balent-a 4.00
...Bounty Hunting for Fun and Profit ('95)-Bisley-c 5.00
... Chained (5/97, $2.50)-Alan Grant story 4.00
.../Deadman: The Brave And The Bald (2/95, $3.50) 4.00
.../Demon: Helloween (12/96, $2.25)-Giarrano-a 4.00
...Fragtastic Voyage 1 ('97, $5.95)-Mejia painted-c/a 6.00
...Gallery (9/95, $3.50)-pin-ups. 4.00
...In the Chair 1 (8/94, $1.95, 36 pgs.), ...I Quit-(12/95, $2.25) 4.00
.../Judge Dredd ('95, $4.95). 5.00
...Lobocop 1 (2/94, $1.95)-Alan Grant scripts; painted-c 4.00

LOBO (Younger version from New 52 Justice League #23.2)
DC Comics: Dec, 2014 - No. 13, Feb, 2016 ($2.99)

1-Bunn-s/Brown-a 6.00
2-13: 2-5-Bunn-s/Brown-a. 4-Superman app. 10,11-Sinestro app. 13-Hal Jordan app. 4.00
Annual 1 (9/15, $4.99) Bunn-s/Rocha-a; the Sinestro Corps app.; leads into Lobo #10 5.00

LOBO: (Title Series), DC Comics

--A CONTRACT ON GAWD, 4/94 - 7/94 (mature) 1-4: Alan Grant scripts. 3-Groo cameo 4.00

--DEATH AND TAXES, 10/96 - No. 4, 1/97, 1-4-Giffen/Grant scripts 4.00

--GOES TO HOLLYWOOD, 8/96 ($2.25), 1-Grant scripts 4.00

--HIGHWAY TO HELL, 1/10 - No. 2, 2/10 ($6.99), 1,2-Scott Ian-s/Sam Kieth-a/c 7.00
TPB (2010, $19.99) r/#1,2; intro. by Scott Ian; Kieth B&W art pages 20.00

--INFANTICIDE, 10/92 - 1/93 ($1.50, mature), 1-4-Giffen-c/a; Grant scripts 4.00

--/ MASK, 2/97 - No. 2, 3/97 ($5.95), 1,2 6.00

--/ ROAD RUNNER, 8/17 ($4.99), 1-Bill Morrison-s/Kelley Jones-a/c; Wile E. Coyote app. 5.00

--'S BACK, 5/92 - No. 4, 11/92 ($1.50, mature), 1-4: 1-Has 3 outer covers. Bisley painted-c 1,2; a-1-3. 3-Sam Kieth-c; all have Giffen plots/breakdown & Grant scripts 4.00
Trade paperback (1993, $9.95)-r/1-4 10.00

--THE DUCK, 6/97 ($1.95), 1-A. Grant-s/V. Semeiks & R. Kryssing-a 4.00

--UNAMERICAN GLADIATORS, 6/93 - No. 4, 9/93 ($1.75, mature), 1-4-Mignola-c; Grant/Wagner scripts 4.00

--UNBOUND, 8/03 - No. 6, 5/04 ($2.95), 1-6-Giffen-s/Horley-c/a. 4-6-Ambush Bug app. 4.00

LOBSTER JOHNSON (One-shots) (See B.P.R.D. and Hellboy titles)
Dark Horse Comics

...: A Chain Forged in Life (7/15, $3.50) Mignola & Arcudi-s; Nixey & Nowlan-a 4.00
...: Caput Mortuum (9/12, $3.50) Mignola & Arcudi-s; Zonjic-c/a 4.00
...: Garden of Bones (1/17, $3.99) Mignola & Arcudi-s; Stephen Green-a/Zonjic-c 4.00
...: Mangekyo (8/17, $3.99) Mignola & Arcudi-s; Stenbeck-a/Zonjic-c 4.00
...: Satan Smells a Rat (5/13, $3.50) Mignola & Arcudi-s; Nowlan-c/a 4.00
...: The Forgotten Man (4/16, $3.50) Mignola & Arcudi-s; Snejbjerg-a/Zonjic-c 4.00
...: The Glass Mantis (12/15, $3.50) Mignola & Arcudi-s; Fejzula-a/Zonjic-c 4.00

LOBSTER JOHNSON: A SCENT OF LOTUS (See B.P.R.D. and Hellboy titles)
Dark Horse Comics: Jul, 2013 - No. 2, Aug, 2013 ($3.50, limited series)

1,2-Mignola & Arcudi-s; Fiumara-a/Zonjic-c 4.00

LOBSTER JOHNSON: GET THE LOBSTER
Dark Horse Comics: Feb, 2014 - No. 5, Aug, 2014 ($3.99, limited series)

1-5-Mignola & Arcudi-s; Zonjic-a/c 4.00

LOBSTER JOHNSON: METAL MONSTERS OF MIDTOWN
Dark Horse Comics: May, 2016 - No. 3, Jul, 2016 ($3.50/$3.99, limited series)

1-3-Mignola & Arcudi-s; Zonjic-a/c. 1-$3.50. 2,3-$3.99 4.00

LOBSTER JOHNSON: THE BURNING HAND
Dark Horse Comics: Jan, 2012 - No. 5, May, 2012 ($3.50, limited series)

1-5-Mignola & Arcudi-s; Zonjic-a. 1-Two covers by Dave Johnson & Mignola 4.00

LOBSTER JOHNSON: THE IRON PROMETHEUS
Dark Horse Comics: Sept, 2007 - No. 5, Jan, 2008 ($2.99, limited series)

1-Mignola-s/c; Armstrong-a 1 3 4 6 8 10
2-5-Mignola-s/c; Armstrong-a 5.00

LOBSTER JOHNSON: THE PIRATE'S GHOST
Dark Horse Comics: Mar, 2017 - No. 3, May, 2017 ($3.99, limited series)

1-3-Mignola & Arcudi-s; Zonjic-a/c 4.00

LOCKE & KEY
IDW Publ.: Feb, 2008 - No. 6, July, 2008 ($3.99, limited series)

1-Joe Hill-s/Gabriel Rodriguez-a 60.00
1-Second printing 8.00
2 14.00
3-6 6.00
...: Free Comic Book Day Edition (5/11) r/story from Crown of Shadows 4.00
...: Grindhouse (8/12, $3.99) EC-style; Hill-s/Rodriguez-a; bonus Guide to the Keyhouse 6.00
...: Guide to the Known Keys (1/12, $3.99) Key to the Moon; bonus Guide to the Keys 15.00
...: Welcome to Lovecraft Legacy Edition #1 (8/10, $1.00) r/#1; synopsis of later issues 4.00
...: Welcome to Lovecraft Special Edition #1 SC (9/09, $5.99) Hill-s/Rodriguez-a; script; back-up story with final art from Seth Fisher 10.00

LOCKE & KEY: ALPHA
IDW Publ.: Aug, 2013 - No. 2, Oct, 2013 ($7.99, limited series)

1,2-Series conclusion; Joe Hill-s/Gabriel Rodriguez-a 8.00

LOCKE & KEY: CLOCKWORKS
IDW Publ.: Jun, 2011 - No. 6, Apr, 2012 ($3.99, limited series)

1-6: 1-Hill-s/Rodriguez-a; set in 1776 4.00

LOCKE & KEY: CROWN OF SHADOWS
IDW Publ.: Nov, 2009 - No. 6, Apr, 2010 ($3.99, limited series)

1-6-Joe Hill-s/Gabriel Rodriguez-a 4.00

LOCKE & KEY: DOG DAYS
IDW Publ.: Oct, 2019 ($4.99, one-shot)

nn - Joe Hill-s/Gabriel Rodriguez-a; bonus preview of Dying is Easy #1 5.00

LOCKE & KEY: HEAD GAMES
IDW Publ.: Jan, 2009 - No. 6, Jun, 2009 ($3.99, limited series)

1-6-Joe Hill-s/Gabriel Rodriguez-a. 3-EC style-c 4.00

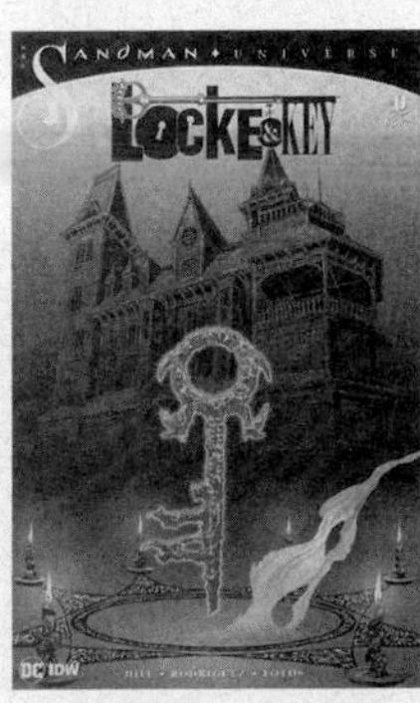

Locke & Key / The Sandman #0 © IDW & DC

Loki (2019 series) #2 © MAR

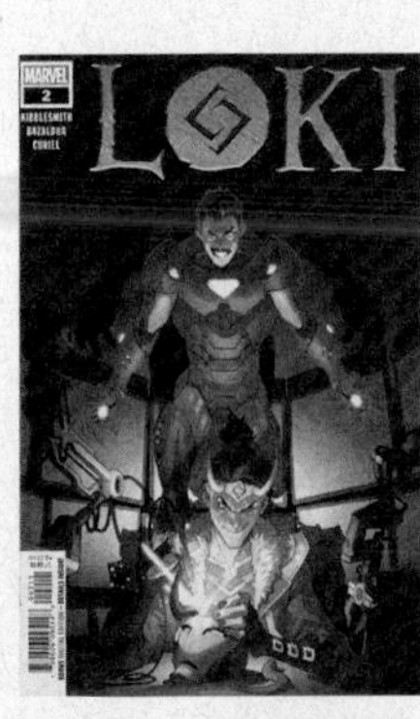

Lonely Receiver #1 © Thompson & Hickman

	GD	VG	FN	VF	VF/NM	NM-
	2.0	4.0	6.0	8.0	9.0	9.2

LOCKE & KEY: ...IN PALE BATTALIONS GO...
IDW Publ.: Aug, 2020 - No. 3, Oct, 2020 ($3.99, limited series)
1-3-Joe Hill-s/Gabriel Rodriguez-a 4.00

LOCKE & KEY: KEYS TO THE KINGDOM
IDW Publ.: Sept, 2010 - No. 6, Mar, 2011 ($3.99, limited series)
1-6-Joe Hill-s/Gabriel Rodriguez-a 4.00

LOCKE & KEY: OMEGA
IDW Publ.: Nov, 2012 - No. 5, May, 2013 ($3.99, limited series)
1-5-Next to Final series; Joe Hill-s/Gabriel Rodriguez-a 4.00

LOCKE & KEY: SMALL WORLD
IDW Publ.: Dec, 2016 ($4.99, one-shot)
1-Set in early 1900s; Joe Hill-s/Gabriel Rodriguez-a; multiple covers 5.00

LOCKE & KEY / THE SANDMAN
IDW Publ.: No. 0, Oct, 2020 ($3.99)
0-"Open the Moon" by Joe Hill-s/Gabriel Rodriguez-a; r/Sandman #1 4.00

LOCKJAW (From the Inhumans)
Marvel Comics: Apr, 2018 - No. 4, Jul, 2018 ($3.99, limited series)
1-4-Kibblesmith-s/Villa-a; D-Man app. 1,2-Ka-Zar app. 3-Spider-Ham app. 4.00

LOCKJAW AND THE PET AVENGERS (Also see Tails of the Pet Avengers)
Marvel Comics: July, 2009 - No. 4, Oct, 2009 ($2.99, limited series)
1-4-Lockheed, Frog Thor, Zabu, Lockjaw and Redwing team up; 2 covers on each 3.00

LOCKJAW AND THE PET AVENGERS UNLEASHED
Marvel Comics: May, 2010 - No. 4, Aug, 2010 ($2.99, limited series)
1-4-Eliopoulos-s/Guara-a; 2 covers on each 3.00

LOCO (Magazine) (Satire)
Satire Publications: Aug, 1958 - V1#3, Jan, 1959

	GD	VG	FN	VF	VF/NM	NM-
V1#1-Chic Stone-a	9	18	27	50	65	80
V1#2,3-Severin-a, 2 pgs. Davis; 3-Heath-a	7	14	21	37	46	55

LODGER
IDW Publishing (Black Crown): Oct, 2018 - No. 5, Feb, 2019 ($3.99, B&W)
1-5-Davis & Maria Lapham-s/David Lapham-a. 1-Covers by Lapham & Sienkiewicz 4.00

LOGAN (Wolverine)
Marvel Comics: May, 2008 - No. 3, Jul, 2008 ($3.99, limited series)
1-3-Vaughan-s/Risso-a/c; regular & B&W editions for each 4.00

LOGAN: PATH OF THE WARLORD
Marvel Comics: Feb, 1996 ($5.95, one-shot)
1-John Paul Leon-a 6.00

LOGAN: SHADOW SOCIETY
Marvel Comics: 1996 ($5.95, one-shot)
1 6.00

LOGAN'S RUN
Marvel Comics Group: Jan, 1977 - No. 7, July, 1977

	GD	VG	FN	VF	VF/NM	NM-
1: 1-5-Based on novel & movie	2	4	6	13	18	22
2-5,7: 6,7-New stories adapted from novel	1	3	4	6	8	10
6-1st Thanos solo story (back-up) by Zeck (6/77)(See Iron Man #55 for debut)	4	8	12	28	47	65
6-(35¢-c variant, limited distribution)	14	28	42	93	204	315
7-(35¢-c variant, limited distribution)	10	20	30	67	141	215

NOTE: **Austin** a-6i. **Gulacy** c-6. **Kane** c-7p. **Perez** a-1-5p; c-1-5p. **Sutton** a-6p, 7p.

LOIS & CLARK, THE NEW ADVENTURES OF SUPERMAN
DC Comics: 1994 ($9.95, one-shot)

	GD	VG	FN	VF	VF/NM	NM-
1-r/Man of Steel #2, Superman Ann. 1, Superman #9 & 11, Action #600 & 655, Adventures of Superman #445, 462 & 466	1	3	4	6	8	10

LOIS LANE (Also see Daring New Adventures of Supergirl, Showcase #9,10 & Superman's Girlfriend...)
DC Comics: Aug, 1986 - No. 2, Sept, 1986 ($1.50, 52 pgs.)
1,2-Morrow-c/a in each 4.00

LOIS LANE
DC Comics: Sept, 2019 - No. 12, Sept, 2020 ($3.99)
1-12: 1-Rucka-s/Perkins-a; The Question (Renee) app. 3-The Question (Charlie) app. 6-Event Leviathan tie-in 4.00

LOKI (Thor)(Also see Vote Loki)
Marvel Comics: Sept, 2004 - No. 4, Nov, 2004 ($3.50)

	GD	VG	FN	VF	VF/NM	NM-
1-Rodi-s/Ribic-a/c in all	2	4	6	8	10	12

2-4 4.00
HC (2005, $17.99, with dustjacket) oversized r/#1-4; original proposal and sketch pages 18.00
SC (2007, $12.99) r/#1-4; original proposal and sketch pages 13.00

LOKI (Thor)
Marvel Comics: Dec, 2010 - No. 4, May, 2011 ($3.99, limited series)
1-4-Aguirre-Sacasa-s/Fiumara-a. 2-Balder dies 4.00

LOKI (Thor)
Marvel Comics: Sept, 2019 - No. 5, Jan, 2020 ($3.99, limited series)
1-5: 1-4-Kibblesmith-s/Bazaldua-a. 2,4-Tony Stark app. 5-Wolverine app. 4.00

LOKI: AGENT OF ASGARD (Thor)
Marvel Comics: Apr, 2014 - No. 17, Oct, 2015 ($2.99/$3.99)
1-5: 1-Ewing-s/Garbett-a/Frison-c; Avengers app. 3.00
6-17-($3.99) 6-9-Axis tie-ins. 6,7-Doctor Doom app. 14-17-Secret Wars tie-ins 4.00

LOKI: RAGNAROK AND ROLL (not the character from Thor)
BOOM! Studios: Feb, 2014 - No. 4, Jun, 2014 ($3.99, limited series)
1,2-Esquivel-s/Gaylord-a/Ziritt-c 4.00

LOLA XOXO
Aspen MLT: Apr, 2014 - No. 6, Mar, 2015 ($3.99)
1-6-Siya Oum-s/a; multiple covers 4.00
The Art of Lolo XOXO 1 (9/16, $5.99) Siya Oum sketch pages and cover gallery 6.00

LOLA XOXO VOLUME 2
Aspen MLT: Jul, 2017 - No. 6, Jan, 2018 ($3.99)
1-6-Siya Oum-s/a; multiple covers 4.00

LOLA XOXO VOLUME 3
Aspen MLT: Jul, 2019 - No. 6, Aug, 2020 ($3.99)
1-6-Siya Oum-s/a; multiple covers 4.00

LOLA XOXO: WASTELAND MADAM
Aspen MLT: Apr, 2015 - No. 4, Feb, 2016 ($3.99)
1-4-Vince Hernandez-s/Siya Oum-a; multiple covers 4.00

LOLLIPOP KIDS, THE
AfterShock Comics: Oct, 2018 - No. 5, Apr, 2019 ($3.99)
1-5-Adam Glass-s/Diego Yapur-a/Robert Hack-c 4.00

LOLLY AND PEPPER
Dell Publishing Co.: No. 832, Sept, 1957 - July, 1962

	GD	VG	FN	VF	VF/NM	NM-
Four Color 832(#1)	6	12	18	40	73	105
Four Color 940,978,1086,1206	4	8	12	28	47	65
01-459-207 (7/62)	3	6	9	17	26	35

LOMAX (See Police Action)

LONE
Dark Horse Comics: Sept, 2003 - No. 6, Mar, 2004 ($2.99)
1-6-Stuart Moore-s/Jerome Opeña-a/Templesmith-c 3.00

LONE EAGLE (The Flame No. 5 on)
Ajax/Farrell Publications: Apr-May, 1954 - No. 4, Oct-Nov, 1954

	GD	VG	FN	VF	VF/NM	NM-
1	14	28	42	82	121	160
2-4: 3-Bondage-c	10	20	30	54	72	90

LONE GUNMEN, THE (From the X-Files)
Dark Horse Comics: June, 2001 ($2.99, one-shot)
1-Paul Lee-a; photo-c 3.00

LONELY HEART (Formerly Dear Lonely Hearts; Dear Heart #15 on)
Ajax/Farrell Publ. (Excellent Publ.): No. 9, Mar, 1955 - No. 14, Feb, 1956

	GD	VG	FN	VF	VF/NM	NM-
9-Kamen-*esque*-a; (Last precode)	15	30	45	85	130	175
10-14	11	22	33	60	83	105

LONELY RECEIVER
AfterShock Comics: Sept, 2020 - No. 5, Jan, 2021 ($4.99/$3.99)
1-($4.99) Zac Thompson-s/Jen Hickman-a/c 5.00
2-5-($3.99) 4.00

LONE RANGER, THE (See Ace Comics, Aurora, Dell Giants, Future Comics, Golden Comics Digest #48, King Comics, Magic Comics & March of Comics #165, 174, 193, 208, 225, 238, 310, 322, 338, 350)

LONE RANGER, THE
Dell Publishing Co.: No. 3, 1939 - No. 167, Feb, 1947

	GD	VG	FN	VF	VF/NM	NM-
Large Feature Comic 3(1939)-Heigh-Yo Silver; text with illus. by Robert Weisman; also exists as a Whitman #710 (scarce)	284	568	852	1818	3109	4400
Large Feature Comic 7(1939)-Illustr. by Henry Vallely; Hi-Yo Silver the Lone Ranger to the Rescue; also exists as Whitman #715 (scarce)	265	530	795	1694	2897	4100

The Lone Ranger #13 © KFS

The Lone Ranger (2006 series) #24 © Classic Media

The Lone Rider #14 © Farrell

	GD 2.0	VG 4.0	FN 6.0	VF 8.0	VF/NM 9.0	NM- 9.2
Feature Book 21(1940), 24(1941)	106	212	318	673	1162	1650
Four Color 82(1945)	38	76	114	285	641	1000
Four Color 98(1945),118(1946)	27	54	81	194	435	675
Four Color 125(1946),136(1947)	19	38	57	131	291	450
Four Color 151,167(1947)	16	32	48	112	249	385

LONE RANGER, THE (Movie, radio & TV; Clayton Moore starred as Lone Ranger in the movies; No. 1-37: strip reprints)(See Dell Giants)
Dell Publishing Co.: Jan-Feb, 1948 - No. 145, May-July, 1962

	GD 2.0	VG 4.0	FN 6.0	VF 8.0	VF/NM 9.0	NM- 9.2
1 (36 pgs.)-The Lone Ranger, his horse Silver, companion Tonto & his horse Scout begin	69	138	207	559	1255	1950
2 (52 pgs. begin, end #41)	27	54	81	194	435	675
3-5	22	44	66	154	340	525
6,7,9,10	16	32	48	112	249	385
8-Origin retold; Indian back-c begin, end #35	19	38	57	131	291	450
11-20: 11- "Young Hawk" Indian boy serial begins, ends #145	12	24	36	80	173	265
21,22,24-31: 51-Reprint. 31-1st Mask logo	10	20	30	64	132	200
23-Origin retold	12	24	36	80	173	265
32-37: 32-Painted-c begin. 36-Animal photo back-c begin, end #49. 37-Last newspaper-r issue; new outfit; red shirt becomes blue; most known copies show the blue shirt on-c & inside	9	18	27	58	114	170
37-Variant issue; Long Ranger wears a red shirt on-c and inside. A few copies of the red shirt outfit were printed before catching the mistake and changing the color to blue (rare)	16	32	48	110	243	375
38-41 (All 52 pgs.) 38-Paul S. Newman-s (wrote most of the stories #38-on)	8	16	24	54	102	150
42-50 (36 pgs.)	7	14	21	46	86	125
51-74 (52 pgs.): 56-One pg. origin story of Lone Ranger & Tonto. 71-Blank inside-c	6	12	18	42	79	115
75,77-99: 79-X-mas-c	6	12	18	40	73	105
76-Classic flag-c	7	14	21	44	82	120
100	7	14	21	46	86	125
101-111: Last painted-c	6	12	18	37	66	95
112-Clayton Moore photo-c begin, end #145	15	30	45	103	227	350
113-117: 117-10¢ &15¢-c exist	9	18	27	60	120	180
118-Origin Lone Ranger, Tonto, & Silver retold; Dan Reid origin; Special Silver anniversary issue	19	38	57	131	291	450
119-140: 139-Fran Striker-s	8	16	24	56	108	160
141-145	9	18	27	58	114	170

NOTE: ***Hank Hartman*** *painted c(signed)-65, 66, 70, 75, 82; unsigned-64?, 67-69?, 71, 72, 73?, 74?, 76-78, 80, 81, 83-91, 92?, 93-111.* ***Ernest Nordli*** *painted c(signed)-42, 50, 52, 53, 56, 59, 60; unsigned-39-41, 44-49, 51, 54, 55, 57, 58, 61-63?*

LONE RANGER, THE
Gold Key (Reprints in #13-20): 9/64 - No. 16, 12/69; No. 17, 11/72; No. 18, 9/74 - No. 28, 3/77

	GD 2.0	VG 4.0	FN 6.0	VF 8.0	VF/NM 9.0	NM- 9.2
1-Retells origin	6	12	18	42	79	115
2	3	6	9	21	33	45
3-10: Small Bear-r in #6-12. 10-Last 12¢ issue	3	6	9	19	30	40
11-17	3	6	9	15	22	28
18-28	2	4	6	11	16	20
Golden West 1(30029-610, 10/66)-Giant; r/most Golden West #3 including Clayton Moore photo front/back-c	6	12	18	40	73	105

LONE RANGER
Dynamite Entertainment: 2006 - No. 25, 2011 ($2.99/$3.50/$3.99)

	NM- 9.2
1-Retells origin; Carriello-a/Matthews-s; badge cover by Cassaday	4.00
1-Variant mask cover by Cassaday	5.00
1-Baltimore Comic-Con 2006 variant cover with masked face and horse silhouette	12.00
1-Directors' Cut ($4.99) r/#1 with comments at page bottoms, script and sketches	5.00
2-23: 2-Origin continues; Tonto app.	3.50
24-($3.99)	4.00
25-($4.99) Carriello-a	5.00
... and Tonto 1-4 (200-2010, $4.99) Cassaday-c	5.00
... Volume 1: Now and Forever TPB (2007, $19.99) r/#1-6; sketch pages	20.00

LONE RANGER: VOLUME 1
Dynamite Entertainment: 2018 - No. 5, 2019 ($3.99, limited series)

	NM- 9.2
1-5-Mark Russell-s/Bob Q-a. 1-Cover by Cassaday, Allred & Francavilla	4.00

LONE RANGER, THE (Volume 2)
Dynamite Entertainment: 2012 - No. 25, 2014 ($3.99)

	NM- 9.2
1-25: 1-Parks-s/Polls-a; two covers by Ross & Francavilla. 2-21-Francavilla-c	4.00
Annual 2013 ($4.99) Denton-s/Triano-a/Worley-c	5.00

LONE RANGER AND TONTO, THE
Topps Comics: Aug, 1994 - No. 4, Nov, 1994 ($2.50, limited series)

	NM- 9.2
1-4: 3-Origin of Lone Ranger; Tonto leaves; Lansdale story, Truman-c/a in all.	3.00
1-4: Silver logo. 1-Signed by Lansdale and Truman	6.00
Trade paperback (1/95, $9.95)	10.00

LONE RANGER AND ZORRO: THE DEATH OF ZORRO, THE
Dynamite Entertainment: 2011 - No. 5, 2011 ($3.99, limited series)

	NM- 9.2
1-5: 1-Four covers by Alex Ross and others; Parks-s/Polls-a	4.00

LONE RANGER GREEN HORNET
Dynamite Entertainment: 2016 - No. 5, 2016 ($3.99, limited series)

	NM- 9.2
1-5-Uslan-s/Timpano-a. 3-Jesse Owens as the new Lone Ranger	4.00

LONE RANGER'S COMPANION TONTO, THE (TV)
Dell Publishing Co.: No. 312, Jan, 1951 - No. 33, Nov-Jan/58-59 (All painted-c)

	GD 2.0	VG 4.0	FN 6.0	VF 8.0	VF/NM 9.0	NM- 9.2
Four Color 312(#1, 1/51)	11	22	33	75	160	245
2(8-10/51),3: (#2 titled "Tonto")	6	12	18	42	79	115
4-10	5	10	15	35	63	90
11-20	5	10	15	31	53	75
21-33	4	8	12	28	47	65

NOTE: ***Ernest Nordli*** *painted c(signed)-2, 7; unsigned-3-6, 8-11, 12?, 13, 14, 18?, 22-24?*
See Aurora Comic Booklets.

LONE RANGER'S FAMOUS HORSE HI-YO SILVER, THE (TV)
Dell Publishing Co.: No. 369, Jan, 1952 - No. 36, Oct-Dec, 1960 (All painted-c, most by Sam Savitt) (Lone Ranger appears in most issues)

	GD 2.0	VG 4.0	FN 6.0	VF 8.0	VF/NM 9.0	NM- 9.2
Four Color 369(#1)-Silver's origin as told by The Lone Ranger	11	22	33	72	154	235
Four Color 392(#2, 4/52)	7	14	21	44	82	120
3(7-9/52)-10(4-6/52)	5	10	15	31	53	75
11-36	4	8	12	27	44	60

LONE RANGER, THE : SNAKE OF IRON
Dynamite Entertainment: 2012 - No. 4, 2013 ($3.99, limited series)

	NM- 9.2
1-4: 1-Dixon-s/Polls-a/Calero-c	4.00

LONE RANGER, THE : VINDICATED
Dynamite Entertainment: 2014 - No. 4, 2015 ($3.99, limited series)

	NM- 9.2
1-4-Justin Gray-s/Rey Villegas-a. 1-Cassaday-c. 2-4-Laming-c	4.00

LONE RIDER (Also see The Rider)
Superior Comics(Farrell Publ.): Apr, 1951 - No. 26, Jul, 1955 (#3-on: 36 pgs.)

	GD 2.0	VG 4.0	FN 6.0	VF 8.0	VF/NM 9.0	NM- 9.2
1 (52 pgs.)-The Lone Rider & his horse Lightnin' begin; Kamen-*ish*-a begins	36	72	108	211	343	475
2 (52 pgs.)-The Golden Arrow begins (origin)	19	38	57	112	179	245
3-6: 6-Last Golden Arrow	17	34	51	103	162	220
7-Golden Arrow becomes Swift Arrow; origin of his shield	18	36	54	107	169	230
8-Origin Swift Arrow	18	36	54	107	169	230
9,10	12	24	36	69	97	125
11-14	10	20	30	54	72	90
15-Golden Arrow origin-r from #2, changing name to Swift Arrow	11	22	33	62	86	110
16-20,22-26: 23-Apache Kid app.	9	18	27	50	65	80
21-3-D effect-c	17	34	51	98	154	210

LONERS, THE
Marvel Comics: June, 2007 - No. 6, Jan, 2008 ($2.99, limited series)

	NM- 9.2
1-6-Cebulski-s/Moline-a/Pearson-c; Lightspeed, Spider-Woman, Ricochet app.	3.00
...: The Secret Lives of Super Heroes TPB (2008, $14.99) r/#1-6; sketch pages	15.00

LONE WOLF AND CUB
First Comics: May, 1987 - No. 45, Apr, 1991 ($1.95-$3.25, B&W, deluxe size)

	GD 2.0	VG 4.0	FN 6.0	VF 8.0	VF/NM 9.0	NM- 9.2
1-Frank Miller-c & intro.; reprints manga series by Koike & Kojima	2	4	6	11	16	20
1-2nd print, 3rd print, 2-2nd print						4.00
2-12: 6-72 pgs. origin issue	1	3	4	6	8	10
13-38,40: 40-Ploog-c						6.00
39-($5.95, 120 pgs.)-Ploog-c	1	2	3	5	6	8
41-44: 41-($3.95, 84 pgs.)-Ploog-c. 42-Ploog-c						6.00
45-Last issue; low print	3	6	9	16	23	30
Deluxe Edition ($19.95, B&W)						20.00

NOTE: ***Sienkiewicz*** *c-13-24.* ***Matt Wagner*** *c-25-30.*

LONE WOLF AND CUB (Trade paperbacks)
Dark Horse Comics: Aug, 2000 - No. 28 ($9.95, B&W, 4" x 6", approx. 300 pgs.)

	NM- 9.2
1-Collects First Comics reprint series; Frank Miller-c	18.00
1-(2nd printing)	12.00
1-(3rd-5th printings)	10.00
2,3-(1st printings)	12.00
2,3-(2nd printings)	10.00

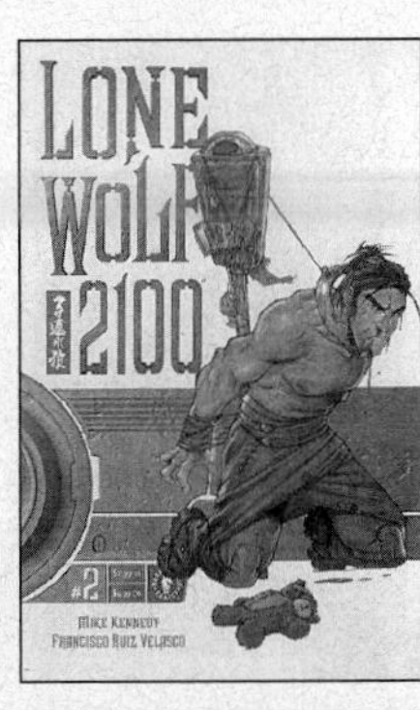

Lone Wolf 2100 #2 © DH & Koike Shoin

Looney Tunes #187 © WB

Lords of Empyre: Swordsman #1 © MAR

GD VG FN VF VF/NM NM-
2.0 4.0 6.0 8.0 9.0 9.2

4-28 10.00

LONE WOLF 2100 (Also see Reveal)
Dark Horse Comics: May, 2002 - No. 11, Dec, 2003 ($2.99, color)

1-New homage to Lone Wolf and Cub; Kennedy-s/Velasco-a 4.00
2-11 3.00
...: The Red File (1/03, $2.99) character and story background files 3.00
... Vol. 1 - Shadows on Saplings TPB (2003, $12.95, 6" x 9") r/#1-4 13.00
... Vol. 2 - The Language of Chaos TPB (2003, $12.95, 6" x 9") r/#5-8, Dirty Tricks short story from Reveal 13.00

LONE WOLF 2100: CHASE THE SETTING SUN
Dark Horse Comics: Jan, 2016 - No. 4, Apr, 2016 ($3.99, color)

1-4-Heisserer-s/Sepulveda-a 4.00

LONG BOW (...Indian Boy)(See Indians & Jumbo Comics #141)
Fiction House Mag. (Real Adventures Publ.): 1951 - No. 8, Fall, 1952; No. 9, Spring, 1953

1-Most covers by Maurice Whitman 20 40 60 114 182 250
2 11 22 33 64 90 115
3-9 10 20 30 56 76 95

LONG HOT SUMMER, THE
DC Comics (Milestone): Jul, 1995 - No. 3, Sept, 1995 ($2.95/$2.50, lim. series)

1-3: 1-($2.95-c). 2,3-($2.50-c) 3.00

LONG JOHN SILVER & THE PIRATES (Formerly Terry & the Pirates)
Charlton Comics: No. 30, Aug, 1956 - No. 32, March, 1957 (TV)

30-32: Whitman-c 11 22 33 60 83 105

LONGSHOT (Also see X-Men, 2nd Series #10)
Marvel Comics: Sept, 1985 - No. 6, Feb, 1986 (60¢, limited series)

1-Art Adams/Whilce Portacio-c/a in all 4 8 12 23 37 50
2-5: 4-Spider-Man app. 2 4 6 10 14 18
6-Double size 3 6 9 14 19 24
Trade Paperback (1989, $16.95)-r/#1-6 17.00

LONGSHOT
Marvel Comics: Feb, 1998 ($3.99, one-shot)

1-DeMatteis-s/Zulli-a 4.00

LONGSHOT SAVES THE MARVEL UNIVERSE
Marvel Comics: Jan, 2014 - No. 4, Feb, 2014 ($2.99, limited series)

1-4-Hastings-s/Camagni-a/Nakayama-c. 3,4-Superior Spider-Man app. 3.00

LOOKING GLASS WARS: HATTER M
Image Comics (Desperado): Dec, 2005 - No. 4, Nov, 2006 ($3.99)

1-4-Templesmith-a/c 4.00

LOONEY TUNES (2nd Series) (TV)
Gold Key/Whitman: April, 1975 - No. 47, June, 1984

1-Reprints 3 6 9 21 33 45
2-10: 2,4-reprints 2 4 6 13 18 22
11-20: 16-reprints 2 4 6 9 12 15
21-30 2 3 4 6 8 10
31,32,36-42(2/82) 1 2 3 5 6 8
33-(8/80)-35 (Whitman pre-pack only, scarce) 3 6 9 21 33 45
43(4/82),44(6/83) (low distribution) 2 4 6 9 13 16
45-47 (All #90296 on-c; nd, nd code, pre-pack) 45(8/83), 46(3/84), 47(6/84) 3 6 9 14 20 26

LOONEY TUNES (3rd Series) (TV)
DC Comics: Apr, 1994 - Present ($1.50/$1.75/$1.95/$1.99/$2.25/$2.50/$2.99)

1-10,120: 1-Marvin Martian-c/sty; Bugs Bunny, Roadrunner, Daffy begin. 120-($2.95-C) 4.00
11-119,121-187: 23-34-($1.75-c). 35-43-($1.95-c). 44-Begin $1.99-c. 93-Begin $2.25-c. 100-Art by various incl. Kyle Baker, Marie Severin, Darwyn Cooke, Jill Thompson 3.00
188-258: 188-Begin $2.99-c; Scooby-Doo spoof. 193-Christmas-c. 237-Duck Dodgers 3.00
...Back In Action Movie Adaptation (12/03, $3.95) photo-c 4.00

LOONEY TUNES AND MERRIE MELODIES COMICS ("Looney Tunes" #166(8/55) on) (Also see Porky's Duck Hunt)
Dell Publishing Co.: 1941 - No. 246, July-Sept, 1962

1-Porky Pig, Bugs Bunny, Daffy Duck, Elmer Fudd, Mary Jane & Sniffles, Pat Patsy and Pete begin (1st comic book app. of each). Bugs Bunny story by Win Smith (early Mickey Mouse artist) 1175 2350 3525 9000 18,900 28,800
2 (11/41) 190 380 570 1568 3534 5500
3-Kandi the Cave Kid begins by Walt Kelly; also in #4-6,8,11,15 125 250 375 1000 2250 3500
4-Kelly-a 122 244 336 988 2219 3450
5-Bugs Bunny The Super-Duper Rabbit story (1st funny animal super hero, 3/42; also see Coo Coo); Kelly-a 93 186 279 744 1672 2600
6,8: 8-Kelly-a 70 140 210 555 1253 1950
7,9,10: 9-Painted-c. 10-Flag-c 50 100 150 390 870 1350
11,15-Kelly-a; 15-Christmas-c 50 100 150 390 870 1350
12-14,16-19 37 74 111 274 612 950
20-25: Pat, Patsy & Pete by Walt Kelly in all. 20-War Bonds-c 30 60 90 219 490 760
26-30 23 46 69 161 356 550
31-40: 33-War Bonds-c. 39-Christmas-c 18 36 54 128 284 440
41-50: 45-War Bonds-c 14 28 42 96 211 325
51-60: 51-Christmas-c 11 22 33 76 163 250
61-80 8 16 24 56 108 160
81-99: 87,99-Christmas-c 7 14 21 49 92 135
100-New Year's-c 8 16 24 55 105 155
101-120 6 12 18 40 73 105
121-150: 124-New Year's-c. 133-Tattoo-c 5 10 15 35 63 90
151-200: 159-Christmas-c 5 10 15 33 57 80
201-240 5 10 15 31 53 75
241-246 5 10 15 33 57 80

LOONY SPORTS (Magazine)
3-Strikes Publishing Co.: Spring, 1975 (68 pgs.)

1-Sports satire 2 4 6 8 11 14

LOOSE CANNON (Also see Action Comics Annual #5 & Showcase '94 #5)
DC Comics: June, 1995 - No. 4, Sept, 1995 ($1.75, limited series)

1-4: Adam Pollina-a. 1-Superman app. 3.00

LOOY DOT DOPE
United Features Syndicate: No. 13, 1939

Single Series 13 34 68 102 199 325 450

LORD JIM (See Movie Comics)

LORD OF THE JUNGLE
Dynamite Entertainment: 2012 - No. 15, 2013 ($1.00/$3.99)

1-($1.00) Retelling of Tarzan's origin; Nelson-s/Castro-a; four covers 3.00
2-15-($3.99) 2-6-Three covers. 7-13-Two covers 4.00
Annual 1 (2012, $4.99) Rahner-s/Davila-a/Parrillo-c 5.00

LORD PUMPKIN
Malibu Comics (Ultraverse): Oct, 1994 ($2.50, one-shot)

0-Two covers 3.00

LORD PUMPKIN/NECROMANTRA
Malibu Comics (Ultraverse): Apr, 1995 - No. 4, July, 1995 ($2.95, limited series, flip book)

1-4 3.00

LORDS OF AVALON: KNIGHT OF DARKNESS
Marvel Comics: Jan, 2008 - No. 6, July, 2009 ($3.99, limited series)

1-6-($3.99)-Kenyon & Furth-s; Ohtsuka-a/c 4.00

LORDS OF AVALON: SWORD OF DARKNESS
Marvel Comics: Apr, 2008 - No. 6, Sept, 2008 ($3.99/$2.99, limited series)

1-($3.99)-Adaptation of Sherrilyn Kenyon's Arthurian fantasy; Ohtsuka-a/c 4.00
2-6-($2.99) 3.00
HC (2008, $19.99) r/#1-6; two covers 20.00

LORDS OF EMPYRE (Tie-in to Empyre series)
Marvel Comics: Sept, 2020 - Oct, 2020 ($4.99, series of one-shots)

...: Celestial Messiah 1 (10/20) Paknadel-s/Lins-a; leads into Empyre #3 5.00
...: Emperor Hulkling 1 (9/20) Zdarsky & Oliveira-s/Garcia-a; prelude to events of Empyre 5.00
...: Swordsman 1 (10/20) Paknadel-s/Nachlik-a 5.00

LORDS OF MARS
Dynamite Entertainment: 2013 - No. 6, 2014 ($3.99, limited series)

1-6-Tarzan and Jane meet John Carter on Mars; Nelson-s/Castro-a; multiple covers 4.00

LORDS OF THE JUNGLE
Dynamite Entertainment: 2016 - No. 6, 2016 ($3.99, limited series)

1-6-Tarzan and Sheena app.; Bechko-s/Castro-a; covers by Castro & Massafera 4.00

LORNA, RELIC WRANGLER
Image Comics: Mar, 2011 ($3.99, one-shot)

1-Micah Harris-s; J. Bone-c 4.00

LORNA THE JUNGLE GIRL (...Jungle Queen #1-5)
Atlas Comics (NPI 1/OMC 2-11/NPI 12-26): July, 1953 - No. 26, Aug, 1957

1-Origin & 1st app. 60 120 180 381 653 925
2-Intro. & 1st app. Greg Knight 32 64 96 190 310 430

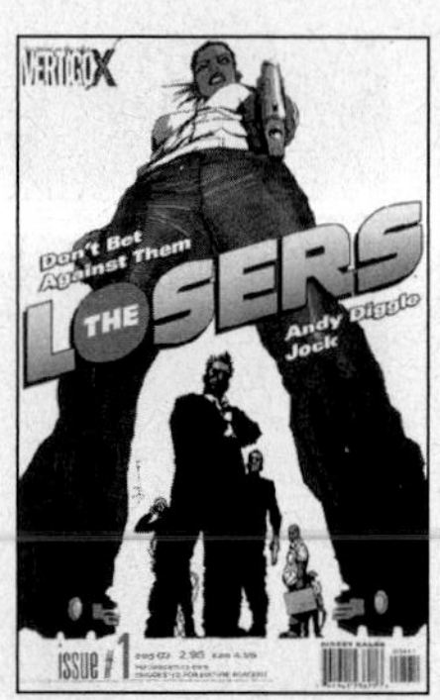

Losers #1 © DC

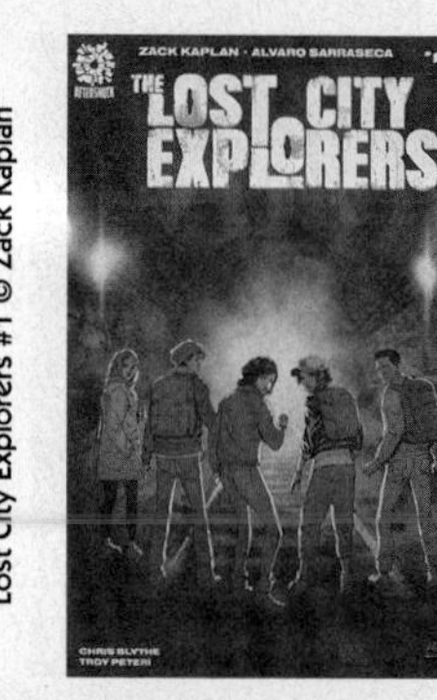

Lost City Explorers #1 © Zack Kaplan

Love and Rockets V2 #5 © Fantagraphics

	GD 2.0	VG 4.0	FN 6.0	VF 8.0	VF/NM 9.0	NM- 9.2
3-5	28	56	84	168	274	380
6-11: 11-Last pre-code (1/55)	24	48	72	144	237	330
12-17,19-26: 14-Colletta & Maneely-c	22	44	66	130	213	295
18-Williamson/Colletta-c	23	46	69	136	223	310

NOTE: ***Brodsky*** *c-1-3, 5, 9.* ***Everett*** *c-21, 23-26.* ***Heath*** *c-6, 7.* ***Maneely*** *c-12, 15.* ***Romita*** *a-18, 20, 22, 24, 26.* ***Shores*** *a-14-16, 18, 24, 26; c-11, 13, 16.* ***Tuska*** *a-6.*

LOSERS (Inspired the 2010 movie)
DC Comics (Vertigo): Aug, 2003 - No. 32, Mar, 2006 ($2.95/$2.99)

1-Andy Diggle-s/Jock-a 4.00
1-Special Edition (6/10, $1.00) r/#1 with "What's Next?" logo on cover 3.00
2-32: 15-Bagged with Sky Captain CD. 20-Oliver-a. 27-Wilson-a 3.00
...: Ante Up TPB (2004, $9.95) r/#1-6 10.00
...: Book Two TPB (2010, $24.99) r/#13-32; Ian Rankin intro.; preliminary art pages 25.00
...: Close Quarters TPB (2005, $14.99) r/#20-25 15.00
...: Double Down TPB (2004, $12.95) r/#7-12 13.00
...: Endgame TPB (2006, $14.99) r/#26-32 15.00
...: Trifecta TPB (2005, $14.99) r/#13-19 15.00
...: Volumes One and Two TPB (2010, $19.99) r/#1-12; new intro. by Diggle 20.00

LOSERS SPECIAL (See Our Fighting Forces #123)(Also see G.I. Combat & Our Fighting Forces)
DC Comics: Sept, 1985 ($1.25, one-shot)

1-Capt. Storm, Gunner & Sarge; Crisis on Infinite Earths x-over 6.00

LOST, THE
Chaos! Comics: Dec, 1997 - No. 3 ($2.95, B&W, unfinished limited series)

1-3-Andreyko-script: 1-Russell back-c 3.00

LOST BOYS, THE (Sequel to the 1987 vampire movie)
DC Comics (Vertigo): Dec, 2016 - No. 6, May, 2017 ($3.99)

1-6-Tim Seeley-s/Scott Godlewski-a/Tony Harris-c; Frog Bros. app. 4.00

LOST BOYS: REIGN OF FROGS (Based on the 1987 vampire movie)
DC Comics (WildStorm): Jul, 2008 - No. 4, Oct, 2008 ($3.50, limited series)

1-4-Rodionoff-s/Gomez-a; Edgar Frog app. 3.50
TPB (2009, $12.99) r/#1-4 13.00

LOST CITY EXPLORERS
AfterShock Comics: Jun, 2018 - No. 5, Oct, 2018 ($3.99, limited series)

1-5-Zack Kaplan-s/Alvaro Sarraseca-a 4.00

LOST CONTINENT
Eclipse Int'l: Sept, 1990 - No. 6, 1991 ($3.50, B&W, squarebound, 60 pgs.)

1-6: Japanese story translated to English 4.00

LOST IN SPACE (Movie)
Dark Horse Comics: Apr, 1998 - No. 3, July, 1998 ($2.95, limited series)

1-3-Continuation of 1998 movie; Erskine-c 3.00

LOST IN SPACE (TV)(Also see Space Family Robinson)
Innovation Publishing: Aug, 1991 - No. 12, Jan, 1993 ($2.50, limited series)

1-12: Bill Mumy (Will Robinson) scripts in #1-9. 9-Perez-c 3.00
1,2-Special Ed.; r/#1,2 plus new art & new-c 3.00
Annual 1,2 (1991, 1992, $2.95, 52 pgs.) 4.00
...: Project Robinson (11/93, $2.50) 1st & only part of intended series 3.00

LOST IN SPACE: COUNTDOWN TO DANGER (Based on the 2018 Netflix series)
Legendary Comics: Oct, 2018 ($17.95, hardcover, one-shot)

HC-Short stories occuring before and during events of the series; Zid-a 18.00

LOST IN SPACE: THE LOST ADVENTURES (IRWIN ALLEN'S...) (TV)
American Gothic Press: Mar, 2016 - No. 6, Nov, 2016 ($3.99, limited series)

1-6-Adaptation of unused scripts. 1-3-The Curious Galactics. 4-6-Malice in Wonderland 4.00

LOST IN SPACE: VOYAGE TO THE BOTTOM OF THE SOUL
Innovation Publishing: No. 13, Aug, 1993 - No. 18, 1994 ($2.50, limited series)

13(V1#1, $2.95)-Embossed silver logo edition; Bill Mumy scripts begin; painted-c 3.00
13(V1#1, $4.95)-Embossed gold logo edition bagged w/poster 5.00
14-18: Painted-c 3.00

NOTE: *Originally intended to be a 12 issue limited series.*

LOST PLANET
Eclipse Comics: 5/87 - No. 5, 2/88; No. 6, 3/89 (Mini-series, Baxter paper)

1-6-Bo Hampton-c/a in all 3.00

LOST SOLDIERS
Image Comics: Jul, 2020 - No. 5, Dec, 2020 ($3.99, limited series)

1-5-Alex Kot-s/Luca Casalanguida-a 4.00

LOST WAGON TRAIN, THE (See Zane Grey Four Color 583)

LOST WORLD, THE
Dell Publishing Co.: No. 1145, Nov-Jan, 1960-61

	GD 2.0	VG 4.0	FN 6.0	VF 8.0	VF/NM 9.0	NM- 9.2
Four Color 1145-Movie, Gil Kane-a, photo-c; 1pg. Conan Doyle biography by Torres	9	18	27	59	117	175

LOST WORLD, THE (See Jurassic Park)
Topps Comics: May, 1997 - No. 4, Aug, 1997 ($2.95, limited series)

1-4-Movie adaptation 3.00

LOST WORLDS (Weird Tales of the Past and Future)
Standard Comics: No. 5, Oct, 1952 - No. 6, Dec, 1952

	GD 2.0	VG 4.0	FN 6.0	VF 8.0	VF/NM 9.0	NM- 9.2
5- "Alice in Terrorland" by Alex Toth; J. Katz-a	55	110	165	352	601	850
6-Toth-a	42	84	126	265	445	625

LOTS 'O' FUN COMICS
Robert Allen Co.: 1940s? (5¢, heavy stock, blue covers)

nn-Contents can vary; Felix, Planet Comics known; contents would determine value. Similar to Up-To-Date Comics. Remainders - re-packaged.

LOT 13
DC Comics: Dec, 2012 - No. 5, Apr, 2013 ($2.99, limited series)

1-5-Niles-s/Fabry-a/c 3.00

LOU GEHRIG (See The Pride of the Yankees)

LOVE ADVENTURES (Actual Confessions #13)
Marvel (IPS)/Atlas Comics (MPI): Oct, 1949; No. 2, Jan, 1950; No. 3, Feb, 1951 - No. 12, Aug, 1952

	GD 2.0	VG 4.0	FN 6.0	VF 8.0	VF/NM 9.0	NM- 9.2
1-Photo-c	29	58	87	170	278	385
2-Powell-a; Tyrone Power, Gene Tierney photo-c	21	42	63	125	206	285
3-8,10-12: 8-Robinson-a	15	30	45	86	133	180
9-Everett-a	15	30	45	88	137	185

LOVE AND AARDVARKS (Reprints from Cerebus in Hell)
Aardvark-Vanaheim: Apr, 2018 ($4.00, B&W)

1-Cerebus figures placed over original Doré artwork; Love and Rockets #1 cover swipe 4.00

LOVE AND MARRIAGE
Superior Comics Ltd. (Canada): Mar, 1952 - No. 16, Sept, 1954

	GD 2.0	VG 4.0	FN 6.0	VF 8.0	VF/NM 9.0	NM- 9.2
1	23	46	69	136	223	310
2	14	28	42	80	115	150
3-10	13	26	39	74	105	135
11-16	11	22	33	62	86	110
I.W. Reprint #1,2,8,11,14: 8-r/Love and Marriage #3. 11-r/Love and Marriage #11	2	4	6	10	14	18
Super Reprint #10('63),15,17('64):15-Love and Marriage #?	2	4	6	10	14	18

NOTE: *All issues have* ***Kamenish*** *art.*

LOVE AND ROCKETS
Fantagraphics Books: 1981 - No. 50, May, 1996 ($2.95/$2.50/$4.95, B&W, mature)

	GD 2.0	VG 4.0	FN 6.0	VF 8.0	VF/NM 9.0	NM- 9.2
1-B&W-c (1981, $1.00; publ. by Hernandez Bros.)(800 printed)	11	22	33	76	163	250
1 (Fall '82; Fantagraphics, color-c)	5	10	15	35	63	90
1-2nd & 3rd printing, 2-11,29-31: 2nd printings						5.00
2	3	6	9	16	24	32
3-10	2	4	6	8	10	12
11-49: 30 ($2.95, 52 pgs.)						5.00
50-($4.95)						6.00

LOVE AND ROCKETS (Volume 2)
Fantagraphics Books: Spring, 2001 - No. 20, Summer, 2007 ($3.95-$7.99, B&W, mature)

	GD 2.0	VG 4.0	FN 6.0	VF 8.0	VF/NM 9.0	NM- 9.2
1-Gilbert, Jaime and Mario Hernandez-s/a	1	3	4	6	8	10
2-9						5.00
10-($5.95)						6.00
11-19-($4.50)						4.50
20-($7.99)						8.00
...: Stories • Free Comic Book Day 2016 Edition (giveaway)						3.00

LOVE AND ROMANCE
Charlton Comics: Sept, 1971 - No. 24, Sept, 1975

	GD 2.0	VG 4.0	FN 6.0	VF 8.0	VF/NM 9.0	NM- 9.2
1	3	6	9	19	30	40
2-5,7-10	2	4	6	10	14	18
6-David Cassidy pin-up; grey-tone cover	3	6	9	14	19	24
11,13-24	2	4	6	8	10	12
12-Susan Dey poster	2	4	6	10	14	18

LOVE AT FIRST SIGHT
Ace Magazines (RAR Publ. Co./Periodical House): Oct, 1949 - No. 43, Nov, 1956 (Photo-c: 18-42)

Love Confessions #47 © QUA

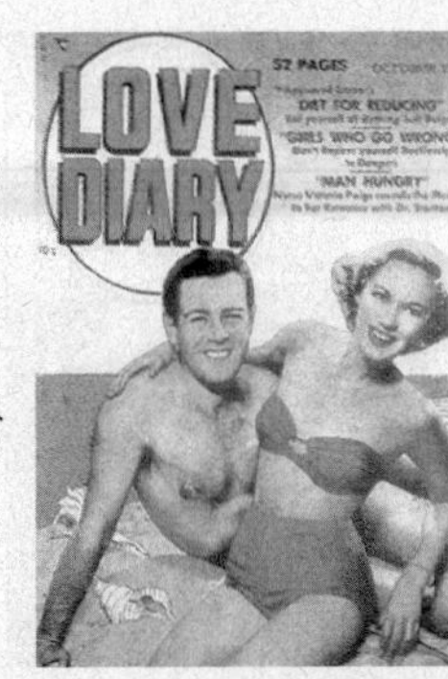

Love Diary #2 © Our Pub. Co.

Love Journal #1 © Our Pub. Co.

	GD 2.0	VG 4.0	FN 6.0	VF 8.0	VF/NM 9.0	NM- 9.2
1-Painted-c	36	72	108	211	343	475
2-Painted-c	17	34	51	105	165	225
3-10: 4,7-Painted-c	15	30	45	88	137	185
11-20	14	28	42	81	118	155
21-33: 33-Last pre-code	14	28	42	78	112	145
34-43	12	24	36	69	97	125

LOVE BUG, THE (See Movie Comics)

LOVEBUNNY AND MR. HELL
Devil's Due Publ./Image Comics: 2002 - 2004 ($2.95, B&W, one-shots)

	GD 2.0	VG 4.0	FN 6.0	VF 8.0	VF/NM 9.0	NM- 9.2
1-Tim Seeley-s						3.00
...: A Day in the Lovelife (Image, 2003) Blaylock-a						3.00
...: Savage Love (Image, 2003) Seeley-s/a; Savage Dragon app.; Seeley & Larsen-c						3.00
TPB (4/04, $9.95, digest-sized) reprints						10.00

LOVE CLASSICS
A Lover's Magazine/Marvel: Nov, 1949 - No. 2, Feb, 1950 (Photo-c, 52 pgs.)

	GD 2.0	VG 4.0	FN 6.0	VF 8.0	VF/NM 9.0	NM- 9.2
1,2: 2-Virginia Mayo photo-c; 30 pg. story "I Turned Into a Small-Town Flirt"	25	50	75	150	245	340

LOVE CONFESSIONS
Quality Comics: Oct, 1949 - No. 54, Dec, 1956 (Photo-c: 3,4,6,7,9,11-18,21,24,25)

	GD 2.0	VG 4.0	FN 6.0	VF 8.0	VF/NM 9.0	NM- 9.2
1-Ward-c/a, 9 pgs; Gustavson-a	45	90	135	284	480	675
2-Gustavson-a; Ward-c	23	46	69	136	223	310
3	16	32	48	98	154	210
4-Crandall-a	17	34	51	105	165	225
5-Ward-a, 7 pgs.	19	38	57	112	179	245
6,7,9,11-13,15,16,18: 7-Van Johnson photo-c. 8-Robert Mitchum & Jane Russell photo-c	15	30	45	83	124	165
8,10-Ward-a (2 stories in #10)	18	36	54	107	169	230
14,17,19,22-Ward-a; 17-Faith Domerque photo-c	17	34	51	103	162	220
20-Ward-a(2)	18	36	54	107	169	230
21,23-28,30-38,40-42: Last precode, 4/55	14	28	42	78	112	145
29-Ward-a	15	30	45	94	147	200
39,53-Matt Baker-a	15	30	45	88	137	185
43,44,46,47,50-52,54: 47-Ward-c?	13	26	39	74	105	135
45,48-Ward-a	14	28	42	82	121	160
49-Baker-c/a	21	42	63	126	206	285

LOVECRAFT
DC Comics: 2003 (graphic novel)

	GD 2.0	VG 4.0	FN 6.0	VF 8.0	VF/NM 9.0	NM- 9.2
Hardcover ($24.95) Rodionoff & Giffen-s/Breccia-a; intro. by John Carpenter						25.00
Softcover ($17.95)						18.00

LOVE DIARY
Our Publishing Co./Toytown/Patches: July, 1949 - No. 48, Oct, 1955 (Photo-c: 1-30) (52 pgs. #1-11?)

	GD 2.0	VG 4.0	FN 6.0	VF 8.0	VF/NM 9.0	NM- 9.2
1-Krigstein-a	34	68	102	204	332	460
2,3-Krigstein & Mort Leav-a in each	20	40	60	115	188	260
4-8	15	30	45	92	144	195
9,10-Everett-a	16	32	48	96	151	205
11-15,17-20	15	30	45	86	133	180
16- Mort Leav-a, 3 pg. Baker-sty. Leav-a	15	30	45	90	140	190
21-30,32-48: 45-Leav-a. 47-Last precode(12/54)	15	30	45	84	127	170
31-John Buscema headlights-c	21	42	63	124	202	280

LOVE DIARY (Diary Loves #2 on; title change due to previously published title)
Quality Comics Group: Sept, 1949

	GD 2.0	VG 4.0	FN 6.0	VF 8.0	VF/NM 9.0	NM- 9.2
1-Ward-c/a, 9 pgs.	45	90	135	284	480	675

LOVE DIARY
Charlton Comics: July, 1958 - No. 102, Dec, 1976

	GD 2.0	VG 4.0	FN 6.0	VF 8.0	VF/NM 9.0	NM- 9.2
1	13	26	39	72	101	130
2	8	16	24	44	57	70
3-5,7-10	7	14	21	35	43	50
6-Torres-a	7	14	21	37	46	55
11-20	3	6	9	17	26	35
21-40	3	6	9	15	22	28
41-60	2	4	6	13	18	22
61-78,80,100-102	2	4	6	9	13	16
79-David Cassidy pin-up	2	4	6	13	18	22
81,83,84,86-99	2	4	6	8	10	12
82,85: 82-Partridge Family poster. 85-Danny poster	2	4	6	10	14	18

LOVE DOCTOR (See Dr. Anthony King...)

LOVE DRAMAS (True Secrets No. 3 on?)
Marvel Comics (IPS): Oct, 1949 - No. 2, Jan, 1950

	GD 2.0	VG 4.0	FN 6.0	VF 8.0	VF/NM 9.0	NM- 9.2
1-Jack Kamen-a; photo-c	28	56	84	165	270	375
2-Photo-c	19	38	57	111	176	240

LOVE EXPERIENCES (Challenge of the Unknown No. 6)
Ace Periodicals (A.A. Wyn/Periodical House): Oct, 1949 - No. 5, June, 1950; No. 6, Apr, 1951 - No. 38, June, 1956

	GD 2.0	VG 4.0	FN 6.0	VF 8.0	VF/NM 9.0	NM- 9.2
1-Painted-c	32	64	96	188	307	425
2	16	32	48	96	151	205
3-5: 5-Painted-c	15	30	45	85	130	175
6-10	14	28	42	82	121	160
11-30: 30-Last pre-code (2/55)	14	28	42	78	112	145
31-38: 38-Indicia date-6/56; c-date-8/56	13	26	39	72	101	130

NOTE: ***Anne Brewster*** *a-15. Photo c-4, 15-35, 38.*

LOVE FIGHTS
Oni Press: June, 2003 - No. 12, Aug, 2004 ($2.99, B&W)

	GD 2.0	VG 4.0	FN 6.0	VF 8.0	VF/NM 9.0	NM- 9.2
1-12-Andi Watson-s/a						3.00
Vol. 1 TPB (4/04, $14.95, digest-size) r/#1-6						15.00

LOVE IS LOVE
IDW Publishing/DC Comics: 2016 ($9.99, TPB)

	GD 2.0	VG 4.0	FN 6.0	VF 8.0	VF/NM 9.0	NM- 9.2
SC-Anthology to benefit the survivors of the Orlando Pulse shooting; Charretier-c	2	4	6	13	18	22

LOVE JOURNAL
Our Publishing Co.: No. 10, Oct, 1951 - No. 25, July, 1954

	GD 2.0	VG 4.0	FN 6.0	VF 8.0	VF/NM 9.0	NM- 9.2
10-Woman on-c "Branded"	103	206	309	659	1130	1600
11-15,17-25: 19-Mort Leav-a	22	44	66	132	216	300
16-Buscema headlight-c	25	50	75	144	237	335

LOVELAND
Mutual Mag./Eye Publ. (Marvel): Nov, 1949 - No. 2, Feb, 1950 (52 pgs.)

	GD 2.0	VG 4.0	FN 6.0	VF 8.0	VF/NM 9.0	NM- 9.2
1,2-Photo-c	20	40	60	115	185	255

LOVELESS
DC Comics: Dec, 2005 - No. 24, Jun, 2008 ($2.99)

	GD 2.0	VG 4.0	FN 6.0	VF 8.0	VF/NM 9.0	NM- 9.2
1-24: 1-Azzarello-s/Frusin-a. 6-8,15,22,23,24-Zezelj-a. 11,12,16-21-Dell'Edera-a						3.00
...: A Kin of Homecoming TPB (2006, $9.99) r/#1-5						10.00
...: Blackwater Falls TPB (2008, $19.99) r/#13-24						20.00
...: Thicker Than Blackwater TPB (2007, $14.99) r/#6-12						15.00

LOVE LESSONS
Harvey Comics/Key Publ. No. 5: Oct, 1949 - No. 5, June, 1950

	GD 2.0	VG 4.0	FN 6.0	VF 8.0	VF/NM 9.0	NM- 9.2
1-Metallic silver-c printed over the cancelled covers of Love Letters #1; indicia title is "Love Letters"	18	36	54	109	172	235
1-Non-metallic version	16	32	48	98	154	210
2-Powell-a; photo-c	11	22	33	62	86	110
3-5: 3,4-Photo-c	9	18	27	52	69	85

LOVE LETTERS (10/49, Harvey; advertised but never published; covers were printed before cancellation and were used as the cover to Love Lessons #1)

LOVE LETTERS (Love Secrets No. 32 on)
Quality Comics: 11/49 - #6, 9/50; #7, 3/51 - #31, 6/53; #32, 2/54 - #51, 12/56

	GD 2.0	VG 4.0	FN 6.0	VF 8.0	VF/NM 9.0	NM- 9.2
1-Ward-c, Gustavson-a	36	72	108	216	351	485
2-Ward-c, Gustavson-a	27	54	81	158	259	360
3-Gustavson-a	18	36	54	107	169	230
4-Ward-a, 9 pgs.; photo-c	22	44	66	128	209	290
5-8,10	14	28	42	82	121	160
9-One pg. Ward "Be Popular with the Opposite Sex"; Robert Mitchum photo-c	15	30	45	85	130	175
11-Ward-r/Broadway Romances #2 & retitled	15	30	45	85	130	175
12-15,18-20	14	28	42	78	112	145
16,17-Ward-a; 16-Anthony Quinn photo-c. 17-Jane Russell photo-c	17	34	51	105	165	225
21-29	14	28	42	76	108	140
30,31(6/53)-Ward-a	14	28	42	82	121	160
32(2/54)-39: 37-Ward-a. 38-Crandall-a. 39-Last precode (4/55)	12	24	36	69	97	125
40-48	11	22	33	64	90	115
49-51: 49,50-Baker-a. 51-Baker-c	16	32	48	98	154	210

NOTE: *Photo-c on most 3-28.*

LOVE LIFE
P. L. Publishing Co.: Nov, 1951

	GD 2.0	VG 4.0	FN 6.0	VF 8.0	VF/NM 9.0	NM- 9.2
1	15	30	45	86	133	180

LOVELORN (Confessions of the Lovelorn #52 on)
American Comics Group (Michel Publ./Regis Publ.): Aug-Sept, 1949 - No. 51, July, 1954 (No. 1-26: 52 pgs.)

Love Romances #62 © MAR

Lovers' Lane #4 © LEV

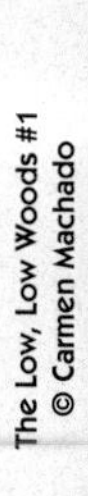
The Low, Low Woods #1 © Carmen Machado

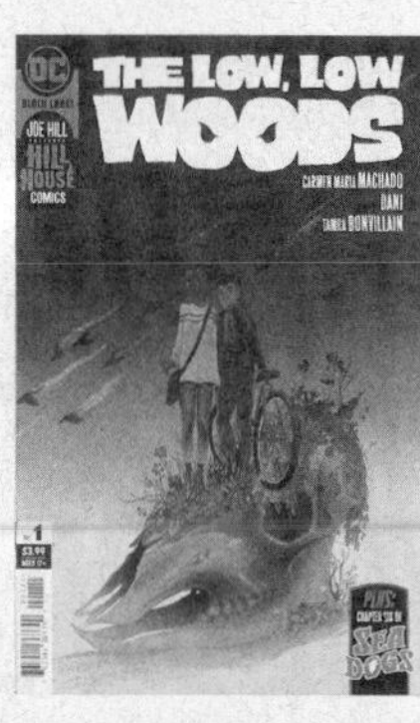

	GD 2.0	VG 4.0	FN 6.0	VF 8.0	VF/NM 9.0	NM- 9.2
1	24	48	72	142	234	325
2	15	30	45	86	133	180
3-10	14	28	42	76	108	140
11-20,22-48: 18-Drucker-a(2 pgs.). 46-Lazarus-a	12	24	36	69	97	125
21-Prostitution story	15	30	45	92	144	195
49-51-Has 3-D effect-c/stories	20	40	60	120	195	270

LOVE MEMORIES
Fawcett Publications: 1949 (no month) - No. 4, July, 1950 (All photo-c)

	GD 2.0	VG 4.0	FN 6.0	VF 8.0	VF/NM 9.0	NM- 9.2
1	18	36	54	109	172	235
2-4: 2-(Win/49-50)	12	24	36	67	94	120

LOVE ME TENDERLOIN: A CAL McDONALD MYSTERY
Dark Horse Comics: Jan, 2004 ($2.99, one-shot)

1-Niles-s/Templesmith-a/c 3.00

LOVE MYSTERY
Fawcett Publications: June, 1950 - No. 3, Oct, 1950 (All photo-c)

	GD 2.0	VG 4.0	FN 6.0	VF 8.0	VF/NM 9.0	NM- 9.2
1-George Evans-a	24	48	72	144	237	330
2,3-Evans-a. 3-Powell-a	17	34	51	98	154	210

LOVE PROBLEMS (See Fox Giants)

LOVE PROBLEMS AND ADVICE ILLUSTRATED (see True Love...)

LOVE ROMANCES (Formerly Ideal #5)
Timely/Marvel/Atlas(TCI No. 7-71/Male No. 72-106): No. 6, May, 1949 - No. 106, July, 1963

	GD 2.0	VG 4.0	FN 6.0	VF 8.0	VF/NM 9.0	NM- 9.2
6-Photo-c	28	56	84	165	270	375
7-Photo-c; Kamen-a	16	32	48	98	154	210
8-Kubert-a; photo-c	16	32	48	98	154	210
9-20: 9-12-Photo-c	15	30	45	88	137	185
21,24-Krigstein-a	15	30	45	92	144	195
22,23,25-35,37,39,40	15	30	45	85	130	175
36,38-Krigstein-a	15	30	45	86	133	180
41-44,46,47: Last precode (2/55)	15	30	45	84	127	170
45,57-Matt Baker-a	16	32	48	98	154	210
48,50-52,54-56,58-74	8	16	24	54	102	150
49,53-Toth-a, 6 & ? pgs.	8	16	24	56	108	160
75,77,82-Matt Baker-a	10	20	30	64	132	200
76,78-81,86,88-90,92-95: 80-Heath-c. 95-Last 10¢-c?	9	18	27	62	126	190
83,84,87,91,106-Kirby-c. 83-Severin-a	11	22	33	77	166	255
85,96,99-105-Kirby-c/a	13	26	39	91	201	310
97-10¢ cover price blacked out, 12¢ printed on cover; Kirby-c/a	22	44	66	154	340	525
98-Kirby-c/a	14	28	42	94	207	320

NOTE: ***Anne Brewster** a-67, 72. **Colletta** a-37, 40, 42, 44, 46, 67(2); c-42, 44, 46, 49, 54, 80. **Everett** c-70. **Hartley** c-20, 21, 30, 31. **Heath** a-87. **Kirby** c-80, 85, 88. **Robinson** a-29.*

LOVE ROMANCES (Marvel 80th Anniversary salute to romance comics)
Marvel Comics: Apr, 2019 ($3.99, one-shot)

1-Short stories by various incl. Simone, Antonio, Hopeless, Martello, Jon Adams 4.00

LOVERS (Formerly Blonde Phantom)
Marvel Comics No. 23,24/Atlas No. 25 on (ANC): No. 23, May, 1949 - No. 86, Aug?, 1957

	GD 2.0	VG 4.0	FN 6.0	VF 8.0	VF/NM 9.0	NM- 9.2
23-Photo-c begin, end #29	27	54	81	162	266	370
24-Toth-*ish* plus Robinson-a	15	30	45	92	144	195
25,30-Kubert-a; 7, 10 pgs.	15	30	45	94	147	200
26-29,31-36,39,40: 35-Maneely-c	15	30	45	84	127	170
37,38-Krigstein-a	15	30	45	88	137	185
41-Everett-a(2)	15	30	45	88	137	185
42,44-65: 65-Last pre-code (1/55)	14	28	42	78	112	145
43-Frazetta 1 pg. ad	14	28	42	78	116	150
66,68-80,82-86	14	28	42	76	108	140
67-Toth-a	14	28	42	80	115	150
81-Baker-a	15	30	45	84	127	170

NOTE: ***Anne Brewster** a-86. **Colletta** a-54, 59, 62, 64, 65, 69, 85; c-61, 64, 65, 75. **Hartley** c-37, 53, 54. **Heath** a-61. **Maneely** a-57. **Powell** a-27, 30. **Robinson** a-42, 54, 56.*

LOVERS' LANE
Lev Gleason Publications: Oct, 1949 - No. 41, June, 1954 (No. 1-18: 52 pgs.)

	GD 2.0	VG 4.0	FN 6.0	VF 8.0	VF/NM 9.0	NM- 9.2
1-Biro-c	21	42	63	126	206	285
2-Biro-c	14	28	42	81	118	155
3-20: 3,4-Painted-c. 20-Frazetta 1 pg. ad	12	24	36	69	97	125
21-38,40,41	11	22	33	60	83	105
39-Story narrated by Frank Sinatra	14	28	42	81	118	155

NOTE: ***Briefer** a-6, 13, 21. **Esposito** a-5. **Fuje** a-4, 16; c-many. **Guardineer** a-1, 3. **Kinstler** c-41. **Sparling** a-3. **Tuska** a-6. Painted c-3-18. Photo c-19-22, 26-28.*

LOVE SCANDALS
Quality Comics: Feb, 1950 - No. 5, Oct, 1950 (Photo-c #2-5) (All 52 pgs.)

	GD 2.0	VG 4.0	FN 6.0	VF 8.0	VF/NM 9.0	NM- 9.2
1-Ward-c/a, 9 pgs.	37	74	111	222	361	500
2,3: 2-Gustavson-a	17	34	51	100	158	215
4-Ward-a, 18 pgs; Gil Fox-a	27	54	81	158	259	360
5-C. Cuidera-a; tomboy story "I Hated Being a Woman"	20	40	60	120	195	270

LOVE SECRETS
Marvel Comics(IPC): Oct, 1949 - No. 2, Jan, 1950 (52 pgs., photo-c)

	GD 2.0	VG 4.0	FN 6.0	VF 8.0	VF/NM 9.0	NM- 9.2
1	23	46	69	136	223	310
2	15	30	45	92	144	195

LOVE SECRETS (Formerly Love Letters #31)
Quality Comics Group: No. 32, Aug, 1953 - No. 56, Dec, 1956

	GD 2.0	VG 4.0	FN 6.0	VF 8.0	VF/NM 9.0	NM- 9.2
32	17	34	51	103	162	220
33,35-39	14	28	42	78	112	145
34-Ward-a	15	30	45	92	144	195
40-Matt Baker-c	17	34	51	103	162	220
41-43: 43-Last precode (3/55)	14	28	42	78	112	145
44,47-50,53,54	13	26	39	72	101	130
45-Ward-a	15	30	45	83	124	165
46-Ward-a; Baker-a	15	30	45	90	140	190
51,52-Ward(r). 52-r/Love Confessions #17	14	28	42	78	112	145
55-Baker-a	15	30	45	86	133	180
56-Baker-c	15	30	45	92	144	195

LOVE STORIES (See Top Love Stories)

LOVE STORIES (Formerly Heart Throbs)
National Periodical Publ.: No. 147, Nov, 1972 - No. 152, Oct-Nov, 1973

	GD 2.0	VG 4.0	FN 6.0	VF 8.0	VF/NM 9.0	NM- 9.2
147-152	3	6	9	14	20	26

LOVE STORIES OF MARY WORTH (See Harvey Comics Hits #55 & Mary Worth)
Harvey Publications: Sept, 1949 - No. 5, May, 1950

	GD 2.0	VG 4.0	FN 6.0	VF 8.0	VF/NM 9.0	NM- 9.2
1-1940's newspaper reprints-#1-4	10	20	30	58	79	100
2-5: 3-Kamen/Baker-a?	8	16	24	42	54	65

LOVE TALES (Formerly The Human Torch #35)
Marvel/Atlas Comics (ZPC No. 36-50/MMC No. 67-75): No. 36, 5/49 - No. 58, 8/52; No. 59, date? - No. 75, Sept, 1957

	GD 2.0	VG 4.0	FN 6.0	VF 8.0	VF/NM 9.0	NM- 9.2
36-Photo-c	26	52	78	154	252	350
37	15	30	45	90	140	190
38-44,46-50: 39-41-Photo-c. 48-Maneely-c	15	30	45	84	127	170
45,51,52,69: 45-Powell-a. 51,69-Everett-a. 52-Krigstein-a	15	30	45	85	130	175
53-60: 60-Last pre-code (2/55)	14	28	42	80	115	150
61-68,70-75: 75-Brewster, Cameron, Colletta-a	14	28	42	76	108	140

LOVE THRILLS (See Fox Giants)

LOVE TRAILS (Western romance)
A Lover's Magazine (CDS)(Marvel): Dec, 1949 - No. 2, Mar, 1950 (52 pgs.)

	GD 2.0	VG 4.0	FN 6.0	VF 8.0	VF/NM 9.0	NM- 9.2
1,2: 1-Photo-c	20	40	60	115	188	260

LOW
Image Comics: Aug, 2014 - No. 26, Feb, 2021 ($3.99/$3.50)

1,11-26-($3.99) Remender-s/Tocchini-a 4.00
2-10-($3.50) Remender-s/Tocchini-a 3.50

LOWELL THOMAS' HIGH ADVENTURE (See High Adventure)

LOWLIFES
IDW Publishing: Jun, 2018 - No. 4, Sept, 2018 ($3.99, limited series)

1-3-Buccellato-s/Sentenac-a 4.00

LOW, LOW WOODS, THE
DC Comics (Hill House Comics): Feb, 2020 - No. 6, Aug, 2020 ($3.99)

1-6-Carmen Machado-s/Dani-a 4.00

LT. (See Lieutenant)

LUCAS STAND
BOOM! Studios: Jun, 2016 - No. 6, Nov, 2016 ($3.99, limited series)

1-6-Kurt Sutter & Caitlin Kittredge-s/Jesús Hervás-a. 1-Multiple covers 4.00

LUCAS STAND: INNER DEMONS
BOOM! Studios: Feb, 2018 - No. 4, May, 2018 ($3.99, limited series)

1-4-Kurt Sutter & Caitlin Kittredge-s/Jesús Hervás-a 4.00

LUCIFER (See The Sandman #4)
DC Comics (Vertigo): Jun, 2000 - No. 75, Aug, 2006 ($2.50/$2.75)

Lucifer #9 © DC

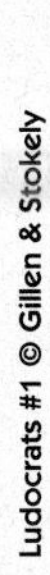
Ludocrats #1 © Gillen & Stokely

Lumberjanes #46 © BOOM

GD VG FN VF VF/NM NM-
2.0 4.0 6.0 8.0 9.0 9.2

1-Carey-s/Weston-a/Fegredo-c 4 8 12 27 44 60
2,3-Carey-s/Weston-a/Fegredo-c 1 2 3 5 6 8
4-10: 4-Pleece-a. 5-Gross-a 4.00
11-49,51-73: 16-Moeller-c begin. 25,26-Death app. 45-Naifeh-a. 53-Kaluta-c begin. 62-Doran-a. 63-Begin $2.75-c 3.00
50-($3.50) P. Craig Russell-a; Mazikeen app. 4.00
74-($2.99) Kaluta-c 3.00
75-($3.99) Last issue; Lucifer's origins retold; Morpheus app.; Gross-a/Moeller-c 4.00
Preview-16 pg. flip book w/Swamp Thing Preview 3.00
Vertigo Essentials: Lucifer #1 Special Edition (3/16, $1.00) Flipbook with GN promos 3.00
...: A Dalliance With the Damned TPB ('02, $14.95) r/#14-20 15.00
...: Children and Monsters TPB ('01, $17.95) r/#5-13 18.00
...: Crux TPB (2006, $14.99) r/#55-61 15.00
...: Devil in the Gateway TPB ('01, $14.95) r/#1-4 & Sandman Presents:..#1-3 15.00
...: Evensong TPB (2007, $14.99) r/#70-75 & Lucifer: Nirvana one-shot 15.00
...: Exodus TPB (2005, $14.95) r/#42-44,46-49 15.00
...: Inferno TPB (2003, $14.95) r/#29-35 15.00
...: Mansions of the Silence TPB (2004, $14.95) r/#36-41 15.00
...: Morningstar TPB (2006, $14.99) r/#62-69 15.00
...: Nirvana (2002, $5.95) Carey-s/Muth-painted-c/a; Daniel app. 6.00
...: The Divine Comedy TPB (2003, $17.95) r/#21-28 18.00
...: The Wolf Beneath the Tree TPB (2005, $14.99) r/#45,50-54 15.00

LUCIFER (See The Sandman #4)
DC Comics (Vertigo): Feb, 2016 - No. 19, Aug, 2017 ($3.99)
1-19: 1-Holly Black-s/Lee Garbett-a/Dave Johnson-c. 6-Stephanie Hans-a 4.00

LUCIFER (The Sandman Universe)
DC Comics (Vertigo): Dec, 2018 - No. 18, May, 2020 ($3.99)
1-18: 1-Dan Watters-s/Max & Sebastian Fiumara-a/Jock-c. 9-Kelley Jones-a 4.00

LUCIFER'S HAMMER (Larry Niven & Jerry Pournelle's...)
Innovation Publishing: Nov, 1993 - No. 6, 1994 ($2.50, painted, limited series)
1-6: Adaptatin of novel, painted-c & art 3.00

LUCKY COMICS
Consolidated Magazines: Jan, 1944; No. 2, Sum, 1945 - No. 5, Sum, 1946
1-Lucky Starr & Bobbie begin 45 90 135 284 480 675
2-4 26 52 78 154 252 350
5-Devil-c by Walter Johnson 34 68 102 204 332 460

LUCKY DUCK
Standard Comics (Literary Ent.): No. 5, Jan, 1953 - No. 8, Sept, 1953
5-Funny animal; Irving Spector-a 13 26 39 74 105 135
6-8-Irving Spector-a 11 22 33 60 83 105
NOTE: *Harvey Kurtzman tried to hire Spector for Mad #1.*

LUCKY "7" COMICS
Howard Publishers Ltd.: 1944 (No date listed)
1-Pioneer, Sir Gallagher, Dick Royce, Congo Raider, Punch Powers; bondage-c
60 120 180 381 653 925

LUCKY STAR (Western)
Nation Wide Publ. Co.: 1950 - No. 7, 1951; No. 8, 1953 - No. 14, 1955 (5x7-1/4"; full color, 5¢)
nn (#1)-(5¢, 52 pgs.)-Davis-a 20 40 60 120 195 270
2,3-(5¢, 52 pgs.)-Davis-a 14 28 42 80 115 150
4-7-(5¢, 52 pgs.)-Davis-a 14 28 42 76 108 140
Given away with Lucky Star Western Wear by the Juvenile Mfg. Co. (SanTone)
7 14 21 35 43 50

LUCY CLAIRE: REDEMPTION
Image Comics: Dec, 2019 - Present ($3.99)
1-4-John Upchurch-s/a 4.00

LUCY SHOW, THE (TV) (Also see I Love Lucy)
Gold Key: June, 1963 - No. 5, June, 1964 (Photo-c: 1,2)
1 11 22 33 77 166 255
2 6 12 18 41 76 110
3-5: Photo back c-1,2,4,5 6 12 18 37 66 95

LUCY, THE REAL GONE GAL (Meet Miss Pepper #5 on)
St. John Publishing Co.: June, 1953 - No. 4, Dec, 1953
1-Negligee panels 37 74 111 222 361 500
2 20 40 60 115 185 255
3,4: 3-Drucker-a 19 38 57 111 176 240

LUDOCRATS, THE
Image Comics: Apr, 2020 - Present ($3.99)
1-5-Kieron Gillen & Jim Rossignol-s/Jeff Stokely-a 4.00

GD VG FN VF VF/NM NM-
2.0 4.0 6.0 8.0 9.0 9.2

LUDWIG BEMELMAN'S MADELEINE & GENEVIEVE
Dell Publishing Co.: No. 796, May, 1957
Four Color 796 5 10 15 31 53 75

LUDWIG VON DRAKE (TV)(Disney)(See Walt Disney's C&S #256)
Dell Publishing Co.: Nov-Dec, 1961 - No. 4, June-Aug, 1962
1 6 12 18 38 69 100
2-4 5 10 15 30 50 70

LUFTWAFFE: 1946 (Volume 1)
Antarctic Press: July, 1996 - No. 4, Jan, 1997 ($2.95, B&W, limited series)
1-4-Ben Dunn & Ted Nomura-s/a, ...Special Ed. 3.00

LUFTWAFFE: 1946 (Volume 2)
Antarctic Press: Mar, 1997 - No. 18 ($2.95/$2.99, B&W, limited series)
1-18: 8-Reviews Tigers of Terra series 3.00
Annual 1 (4/98, $2.95)-Reprints early Nomura pages 4.00
...Color Special (4/98) 3.00
...Technical Manual 1,2 (2/98, 4/99) 4.00

LUGER
Eclipse Comics: Oct, 1986 - No. 3, Feb, 1987 ($1.75, miniseries, Baxter paper)
1-3: Bruce Jones scripts; Yeates-c/a 3.00

LUKE CAGE (Also see Cage & Hero for Hire)
Marvel Comics: Jul, 2017 - No. 5, Nov, 2017; No. 166, Dec, 2017 - No. 170, Apr, 2018 ($3.99)
1-5-Walker-s/Blake-a; Warhawk app. 4.00
[Title switches to legacy numbering after #5 (11/17)]
166-170: 166-Sanna-a; The Ringmaster app.; bonus origin re-cap w/Bagley-a 4.00

LUKE CAGE NOIR
Marvel Comics: Oct, 2009 - No. 4, Jan, 2010 ($3.99, limited series)
1-4-Glass & Benson-a/Martinbrough-a; covers by Bradstreet and Calero 4.00

LUKE SHORT'S WESTERN STORIES
Dell Publishing Co.: No. 580, Aug, 1954 - No. 927, Aug, 1958
Four Color 580(8/54), 651(9/55)-Kinstler-a 5 10 15 33 57 80
Four Color 739,771,807,848,875,927 5 10 15 30 50 70

LUMBERJANES
BOOM! Box: Apr, 2014 - Present ($3.99/$6.99)
1-Noelle Stevenson & Grace Ellis-s/Brooke Allen-a; multiple covers 10.00
2 6.00
3-24,26-49,51-72 4.00
25-($4.99) Two covers by Allen & Wiedle; preview of Lumberjanes/Gotham Academy 5.00
50-($4.99) Four covers by Leyh and Fish 5.00
73-75-($6.99) 7.00
...: A Midsummer Night's Scheme 1 (8/18, $7.99) Andelfinger-s/Gonzalez-a 8.00
...: Beyond Bay Leaf (10/15, $4.99) Faith Erin Hicks-s/Rosemary Valero-O'Connell-a 5.00
...: End of Summer (12/20, $6.99) Watters & Leyh-s/Bosy & Bryant-a 7.00
...: Faire and Square 2017 Special 1 (6/17, $7.99) Black-s/Julia-a; 3 covers 8.00
...: Making the Ghost of It 2016 Special 1 (5/16, $7.99) Wang-s/Norrie-a; Ganucheau-a 8.00
...: Somewhere That's Green 1 (5/19, $7.99) McGuire-s/Bosy-a 8.00
...: The Shape of Friendship GN (11/19, $14.99, SC) Lilah Sturges-s/Polterink-a 15.00
...: The Shape of Friendship Free Comic Book Day Special 2019 (5/19, giveaway) 3.00

LUMBERJANES / GOTHAM ACADEMY
BOOM! Box: Jun, 2016 - No. 6, Nov, 2016 ($3.99)
1-6: 1-Chynna Clugston Flores-s/Rosemary Valero-O'Connell-a; multiple covers 4.00

LUNA
BOOM! Studios: Feb, 2021 - Present ($3.99)
1-Maria Llovet-s/a 4.00

LUNA MOON-HUNTER
WaterWalker Studios: Jul, 2012 - No. 2, Aug, 2012 ($5.95, limited series)
1,2-Rob Hughes-s/Jeff Slemons-a. 1-Posada-c. 2-Buzz-c 6.00
SC-($24.95, 180 pgs.) Painted-c by Buzz & Parrillo; art by Slemons, Buzz & LaRocque 25.00
HC-($49.95, limited edition of 1000) Signed by Hughes & Slemons; 2 bonus articles 50.00

LUNATIC FRINGE, THE
Innovation Publishing: July, 1989 - No. 2, 1989 ($1.75, deluxe format)
1,2 3.00

LUNATICKLE (Magazine) (Satire)
Whitstone Publ.: Feb, 1956 - No. 2, Apr, 1956
1,2-Kubert-a (scarce) 9 18 27 50 65 80

LUNATIK
Marvel Comics: Dec, 1995 - No. 3, Feb, 1996 ($1.95, limited series)

MacGyver: Fugitive Gauntlet #1 © Zlotoff & Lee

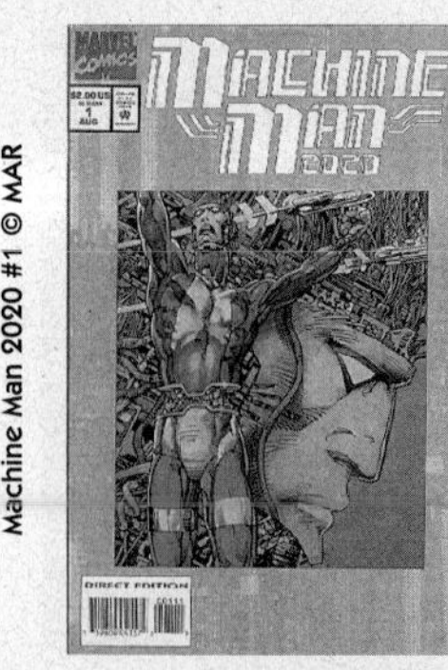

Machine Man 2020 #1 © MAR

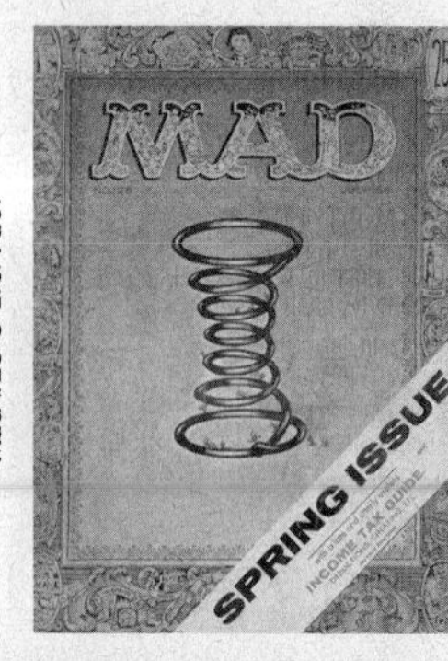

Mad #28 © E.C. Pub.

	GD 2.0	VG 4.0	FN 6.0	VF 8.0	VF/NM 9.0	NM- 9.2

1-3 3.00

LURKERS, THE
IDW Publ.: Oct, 2004 - No. 4, Jan, 2005 ($3.99)
1-4-Niles-s/Casanova-a 4.00

LUST FOR LIFE
Slave Labor Graphics: Feb, 1997 - No. 4, Jan, 1998 ($2.95, B&W)
1-4: 1-Jeff Levin-s/a 3.00

LUTHOR (See Lex Luthor: Man of Steel)

LYCANTHROPE LEO
Viz Communications: 1994 - No. 7($2.95, B&W, limited series, 44 pgs.)
1-7 4.00

LYNCH (See Gen 13)
Image Comics (WildStorm Productions): May, 1997 ($2.50, one-shot)
1-Helmut-c/app. 3.00

LYNCH MOB
Chaos! Comics: June, 1994 - No. 4, Sept, 1994 ($2.50, limited series)
1-4 5.00
1-Special edition full foil-c 1 2 3 5 6 8

LYNDON B. JOHNSON
Dell Publishing Co.: Mar, 1965
12-445-503-Photo-c 3 6 9 19 30 40

M
Eclipse Books: 1990 - No. 4, 1991 ($4.95, painted, 52 pgs.)
1-Adapts movie; contains flexi-disc ($5.95) 6.00
2-4 5.00

MACE GRIFFIN BOUNTY HUNTER (Based on video game)
Image Comics (Top Cow): May, 2003 ($2.99, one-shot)
1-Nocon-a 3.00

MACGYVER: FUGITIVE GAUNTLET (Based on TV series)
Image Comics: Oct, 2012 - No. 5, Feb, 2013 ($3.50, limited series)
1-5-Lee Zlotoff & Tony Lee-s/Will Sliney-a 3.50

MACHETE (Based on the Robert Rodriguez movie)
IDW Publishing: No. 0, Sept, 2010 ($3.99)
0-Origin story; Rodriguez & Kaufman-s/Sayger-a; 3 covers 4.00

MACHINE, THE
Dark Horse Comics: Nov, 1994 - No. 4, Feb, 1995 ($2.50, limited series)
1-4 3.00

MACHINE GUN WIZARDS (See Tommy Gun Wizards)

MACHINE MAN (Also see 2001, A Space Odyssey)
Marvel Comics Group: Apr, 1978 - No. 9, Dec, 1978; No. 10, Aug, 1979 - No. 19, Feb, 1981
1-Jack Kirby-c/a/scripts begin; end #9 3 6 9 20 31 42
2-9-Kirby-c/a/s. 9-(12/78) 2 4 6 9 12 15
10-17: 10-(8/79) Marv Wolfman scripts & Ditko-a begins
1 3 4 6 8 10
18-Wendigo, Alpha Flight-ties into X-Men #140 3 6 9 16 23 30
19-Intro/1st app. Jack O'Lantern (Macendale), later becomes 2nd Hobgoblin
3 6 9 20 31 42
NOTE: ***Austin** c-7i, 19i. **Buckler** c-17p, 18p. **Byrne** c-14p. **Ditko** a-10-19; c-10-13, 14i, 15, 16. **Kirby** a-1-9p; c-1-5, 7-9p. **Layton** c-7i. **Miller** c-19p. **Simonson** c-6.*

MACHINE MAN (Also see X-51)
Marvel Comics Group: Oct, 1984 - No. 4, Jan, 1985 (limited series)
1-4-Barry Smith-c/a(i) & colors in all; Jocasta app. 1-3-Trimpe-a(p). 2-1st app. Arno Stark (Iron Man 2020) 5.00
TPB (1988, $6.95) r/ #1-4; Barry Smith-c 10.00
.../Bastion '98 Annual ($2.99) wraparound-c 4.00

MACHINE MAN 2020 (Also see 2020 Machine Man)
Marvel Comics: Aug, 1994 - No. 2, Sept, 1994 ($2.00, 52 pgs., limited series)
1,2: Reprints Machine Man limited series; Barry Windsor-Smith-c/i(r) 4.00

MACHINE TEEN
Marvel Comics: July, 2005 - No. 5, Nov, 2005 ($2.99, limited series)
1-5-Sumerak-s/Hawthorne-a. 1-James Jean-c 3.00
...: History (2005, $7.99, digest) r/#1-5 8.00

MACK BOLAN: THE EXECUTIONER (Don Pendleton's...)
Innovation Publishing: July, 1993 ($2.50)
1-3-($2.50) 3.00
1-($3.95)-Indestructible Cover Edition 4.00
1-($2.95)-Collector's Gold Edition; foil stamped 4.00
1-($3.50)-Double Cover Edition; red foil outer-c 4.00

MACKENZIE'S RAIDERS (Movie, TV)
Dell Publishing Co.: No. 1093, Apr-June, 1960
Four Color 1093-Richard Carlson photo-c from TV show
6 12 18 37 66 95

MACROSS (Becomes Robotech: The Macross Saga #2 on)
Comico: Dec, 1984 ($1.50)(Low print run)
1-Early manga app. 5 10 15 30 50 70

MACROSS II
Viz Select Comics: 1992 - No. 10, 1993 ($2.75, B&W, limited series)
1-10: Based on video series 4.00

MAD (Tales Calculated to Drive You...)
E. C. Comics (Educational Comics): Oct-Nov, 1952 - No. 550, Apr, 2018
(No. 24-on are magazine format) (Kurtzman editor No. 1-28, Feldstein No. 29 - No. ?)
1-Wood, Davis, Elder start as regulars 457 914 1371 3656 5828 8000
2-Dick Tracy cameo 117 234 351 936 1493 2050
3,4: 3-Stan Lee mentioned. 4-Reefer mention story "Flob Was a Slob" by Davis; Superman parody 83 166 249 664 1057 1450
5-W.M. Gaines biog. 177 354 531 1416 2258 3100
6-11: 6-Popeye cameo. 7,8- "Hey Look" reprints by Kurtzman. 11-Wolverton-a; Davis story was-r/Crime Suspenstories #12 w/new Kurtzman dialogue
60 120 180 480 765 1050
12-15: 12-Archie parody. 15,18-Pot Shot Pete-r by Kurtzman
49 98 147 392 621 850
16-23(5/55): 18-Alice in Wonderland by Jack Davis. 21-1st app. Alfred E. Neuman on-c in fake ad. 22-All by Elder plus photo-montages by Kurtzman.
23-Special cancel announcement 40 80 120 320 510 700
24(7/55)-1st magazine issue (25¢); Kurtzman logo & border on-c; 1st "What? Me Worry?" on-c; 2nd printing exists 94 188 282 752 1201 1650
25-Jaffee starts as regular writer 44 88 132 352 564 775
26,27: 27-Jaffee starts as story artist; new logo 39 78 117 312 499 685
28-Last issue edited by Kurtzman; (three cover variations exist with different wording on contents banner on lower right of cover; value of each the same)
38 76 114 228 372 515
29-Kamen-a; Don Martin starts as regular; Feldstein editing begins
36 72 108 216 351 485
30-1st A. E. Neuman cover by Mingo; last Elder-a; Bob Clarke starts as regular; Disneyland & Elvis Presley spoof 55 110 165 352 601 850
31-Freas starts as regular; last Davis-a until #99 33 66 99 196 321 445
32,33: 32-Orlando, Drucker, Woodbridge start as regulars; Wood back-c. 33-Orlando back-c
27 54 81 162 266 370
34-Berg starts as regular 22 44 66 132 216 300
35-Mingo wraparound-c; Crandall-a 22 44 66 132 216 300
36-40 (7/58): 39-Beall-c 18 36 54 105 165 225
41-50: 42-Danny Kaye-s. 44-Xmas-c. 47-49-Sid Caesar-s. 48-Uncle Sam-c.
50 (10/59)-Peter Gunn-s 15 30 45 90 140 190
51-59: 52-Xmas-c; 77 Sunset Strip. 53-Rifleman-s. 54-Jaffee-a begins. 55-Sid Caesar-s. 59-Strips of Superman, Flash Gordon, Donald Duck & others. 59-Halloween/Headless Horseman-c 14 28 42 80 115 150
60 (1/61)-JFK/Nixon flip-c; 1st Spy vs. Spy by Prohias, who starts as regular
15 30 45 94 147 200
61-70: 64-Rickard starts as regular. 65-JFK-s. 66-JFK-c. 68-Xmas-c by Martin. 70-Route 66-s
6 12 18 41 76 110
71-75,77-80 (7/63): 72-10th Anniv. special; 1/3 pg. strips of Superman, Tarzan & others.
73-Bonanza-s. 74-Dr. Kildare-s 5 10 15 31 53 75
76-Aragonés starts as regular 5 10 15 34 60 85
81-85: 81-Superman strip. 82-Castro-c. 85-Lincoln-c 4 8 12 28 47 65
86-1st Fold-in; commonly creased back covers makes these and later issues scarcer in NM
5 10 15 33 57 80
87,88 5 10 15 31 53 75
89,90: 89-One strip by Walt Kelly; Frankenstein-c; Fugitive-s. 90-Ringo back-c by Frazetta; Beatles app. 5 10 15 33 57 80
91,94,96,100: 94-King Kong-c. 96-Man From U.N.C.L.E. 100-(1/66)-Anniversary issue
4 8 12 28 47 65
92,93,95,97-99: 99-Davis-a resumes 4 8 12 27 44 60
101,104,106,108,114,115,119,121: 101-Infinity-c; Voyage to the Bottom of the Sea-s. 104-Lost in Space-s. 106-Tarzan back-c by Frazetta; 2 pg. Batman by Aragonés. 108-Hogan's Heroes by Davis. 114-Rat Patrol-s. 115-Star Trek. 119-Invaders (TV). 121-Beatles-c; Ringo pin-up; flip-c of Sik-Teen; Flying Nun-s 3 6 9 20 31 42

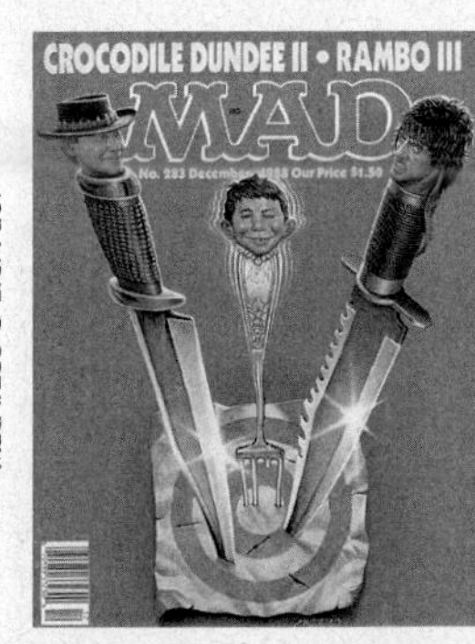

Mad #283 © E.C. Pub.

Madame Xanadu #1 © DC

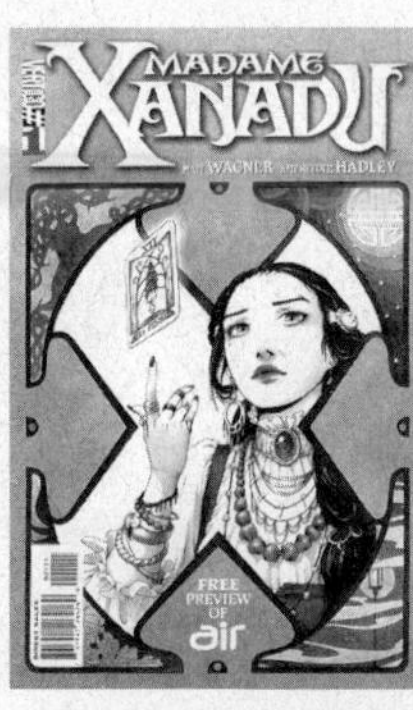

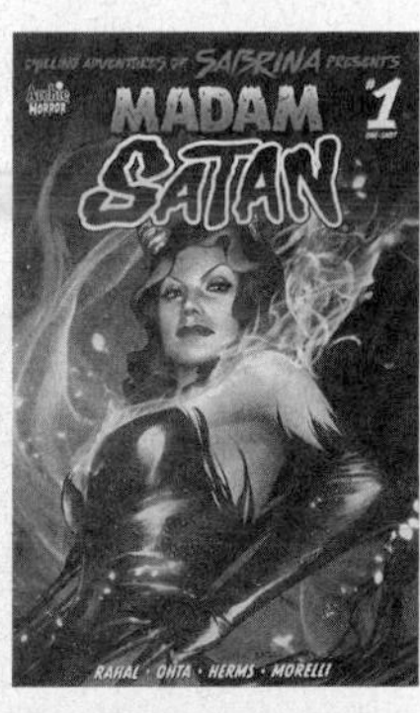

Madam Satan #1 © ACP

GD 2.0 | VG 4.0 | FN 6.0 | VF 8.0 | VF/NM 9.0 | NM- 9.2

102,103,107,109-113,116-118,120(7/68): 118-Beatles cameo 3 6 9 18 28 38
105-Batman-c/s, TV show parody (9/66) 5 10 15 33 57 80
122,124,126,128,129,131-134,136,137,139,140: 122-Ronald Reagan photo inside; Drucker & Mingo-c. 126-Family Affair-s. 128-Last Orlando. 131-Reagan photo back-c. 132-Xmas-c. 133-John Wayne/True Grit. 136-Room 222 3 6 9 15 22 28
123-Four different covers 3 6 9 16 24 32
125,127,130,135,138: 125-2001 Space Odyssey; Hitler back-c. 127-Mod Squad-c/s. 130-Land of the Giants-s; Torres begins as reg. 135-Easy Rider-c by Davis. 138-Snoopy-c; MASH-s 3 6 9 16 24 32
141-149,151-156,158-165,167-170: 141-Hawaii Five-0. 147-All in the Family-s. 153-Dirty Harry-s. 155-Godfather-c/s. 156-Columbo-s. 159-Clockwork Orange-c/s. 161-Tarzan-s. 164-Kung Fu (TV)-s. 165-James Bond-s; Dean Martin-c. 169-Drucker-c; McCloud-s. 170-Exorcist-s 3 6 9 14 19 24
150-(4/72) Partridge Family-s 3 6 9 15 21 26
157-(3/73) Planet of the Apes-c/s 3 6 9 16 23 30
166-(4/74) Classic finger-c 3 6 9 16 23 30
171-185,187,189-192,194,195,198,199: 172-Six Million Dollar Man-s; Hitler back-c. 178-Godfather II-c/s. 180-Jaws-c/s (1/76). 182-Bob Jones starts as regular.185-Starsky & Hutch-s. 187-Fonz/Happy Days-c/s; Harry North starts as regular. 189-Travolta/Kotter-c/s. 190-John Wayne-c/s. 192-King Kong-c/s. 194-Rocky-c/s; Laverne & Shirley-s. 199-James Bond-s 2 4 6 10 14 18
186,188,197,200: 186-Star Trek-c/s. 188-Six Million Dollar Man/ Bionic Woman. 197-Spock-s; Star Wars-s. 200-Close Encounters 2 4 6 13 18 22
193,196: 193-Farrah/Charlie's Angels-c/s. 196-Star Wars-c/s 3 6 9 14 20 26
201,203,205,220: 201-Sat. Night Fever-c/s. 203-Star Wars. 205-Travolta/Grease. 220-Yoda-c, Empire Strikes Back-s 2 4 6 9 13 16
202,204,206,207,209,211-219,221-227,229,230: 204-Hulk TV show. 206-Tarzan. 208-Superman movie. 209-Mork & Mindy. 212-Spider-Man-s; Alien (movie)-s. 213-James Bond, Dracula, Rocky II-s 216-Star Trek. 219-Martin-c. 221-Shining-s. 223-Dallas-c/s. 225-Popeye. 226-Superman II. 229-James Bond. 230-Star Wars 1 3 4 6 8 10
208,228: 208-Superman movie-c/s; Battlestar Galactica-s. 228-Raiders of the Lost Ark-c/s 2 4 6 9 12 15
210-Lord of the Rings 2 4 6 10 14 18
231-235,237-241,243-249,251-260: 233-Pac-Man-c. 234-MASH-c/s. 235-Flip-c with Rocky III & Conan; Boris-a. 239-Mickey Mouse-c. 241-Knight Rider-s. 243-Superman III. 245- Last Rickard-a. 247-Seven Dwarfs-c. 253-Supergirl movie-s; Prince/Purple Rain-s. 254-Rock stars-s. 255-Reagan-c; Cosby-s. 256-Last issue edited by Feldstein; Dynasty, Bev. Hills Cop. 259-Rambo. 260-Back to the Future-c/s; Honeymooners-s 1 2 3 5 6 8
236,242,250: 236-E.T.-c/s;Star Trek II-s. 242-Star Wars/A-Team-c/s. 250-Temple of Doom-c/s; Tarzan-s 1 2 3 5 7 9
261-267,269-276,278-288,290-297: 261-Miami Vice. 262-Rocky IV-c/s, Leave It To Beaver-s. 263-Young Sherlock Holmes-s. 264-Hulk Hogan-c; Rambo-s. 267-Top Gun. 271-Star Trek IV-c/s. 272-ALF-c; Get Smart-s. 273-Pee Wee Herman-c/s. 274-Last Martin-a. 281-California Raisins-c. 282-Star Trek:TNG-s; ALF-s. 283-Rambo III-c/s. 284-Roger Rabbit-c/s. 285-Hulk Hogan-c. 287-3 pgs. Eisner-a. 291-TMNT-c; Indiana Jones-s. 292-Super Mario Bros.-c; Married with Children-s. 295-Back to the Future II. 297-Mike Tyson-c 1 2 3 4 5 7
268,277,289,298-300: 268-Aliens-c/s. 277-Michael Jackson-c/s; Robocop-s. 289-Batman movie parody. 298-Gremlins II-c/s; Robocop II. Batman-s. 299-Simpsons-c/story; Total Recall-s. 300(1/91) Casablanca-s, Dick Tracy-s, Wizard of Oz-s, Gone With The Wind-s 1 2 3 5 6 8
300-303 (1/91-6/91)-Special Hussein Asylum Editions; only distributed to the troops in the Middle East (see Mad Super Spec.) 3 6 9 14 20 25
301-310,312,313,315-320,322,324,326-334,337-349: 303-Home Alone-c/s. 305-Simpsons-s. 306-TMNT II movie. 308-Terminator II. 315-Tribute to William Gaines. 316-Photo-c. 319-Dracula-c/s. 320-Disney's Aladdin-s. 322-Batman Animated series. 327-Seinfeld-s; X-Men-s. 331-Flintstones-c/s. 332-O.J. Simpson-c/s; Simpsons app. in Lion King. 334-Frankenstein-c/s. 338-Judge Dredd-c by Frazetta. 341-Pocahontas-s. 345-Beatles app. (1 pg.) 347-Broken Arrow & Mission Impossible 5.00
311,314,321,323,325,335,336,350,354,358: 311-Addams Family-c/story, Home Improvement-s. 314-Batman Returns-c/story. 321-Star Trek DS9-c/s. 323-Jurassic Park-c/s. 325,336-Beavis & Butthead-c/s. 335-X-Files-s; Pulp Fiction-s; Interview with the Vampire-s. 336-Lois & Clark-s. 350-Polybagged w/CD Rom. 354-Star Wars; Beavis & Butthead-s. 358-X-Files 6.00
351-353,355-357,359-500 5.00
501-550-($5.99) 6.00
Mad About Super Heroes (2002, $9.95) r/super hero app.; Alex Ross-c 10.00

NOTE: ***Aragones** c-210, 293. **Beall** c-39. **Davis** c-2, 27, 135, 139, 173, 178, 212, 213, 219, 246, 260, 296, 308. **Drucker** a-35-62; c-122, 169, 176, 225, 234, 264, 266, 274, 280, 285, 297, 299, 303, 314, 315, 321. **Elder** c-5, 259, 261, 268. **Elder/Kurtzman** a-258-274. **Jules Feiffer** a(r)-42. **Freas** c-40-59, 62-67, 69-70, 72, 74. **Heath** a-14, 27. **Jaffee** c-199, 217, 224, 258. **Kamen** a-29. **Krigstein** a-12, 17, 24, 26. **Kurtzman** c-1, 3, 4, 6-10, 13, 16, 18. **Martin** a-29-62; c-68, 165, 229. **Mingo** c-30-37, 61, 71, 75-80, 82-114, 117-124, 126, 129, 131, 133, 134, 136, 140, 143-148, 150-162, 164, 166-168, 171, 172, 174, 175, 177, 179, 181, 183, 185, 198, 206, 209, 211, 214, 218, 221, 222, 300. **John Severin** a-1-6, 9, 10. **Wolverton** c-11; a-11, 17, 29, 31, 36, 40, 82, 137. **Wood** a-1-21, 23-62; c-26, 28, 29. **Woodbridge** a-35-62. Issues 1-23 are 36 pgs.; 24-28 are 58 pgs.; 29 on are 52 pgs.*

MAD (See Mad Follies, ...Special, More Trash from..., and The Worst from...)

MAD ABOUT MILLIE (Also see Millie the Model)
Marvel Comics Group: April, 1969 - No. 16, Nov, 1970

	GD	VG	FN	VF	VF/NM	NM-
1-Giant issue	10	20	30	68	144	220
2,3 (Giants)	6	12	18	41	76	110
4-10	5	10	15	33	57	80
11-16: 16-r	5	10	15	31	53	75
Annual 1(11/71, 52 pgs.)	5	10	15	34	60	85

MADAME FRANKENSTEIN
Image Comics: May, 2014 - No. 7, Nov, 2014 ($2.99, B&W, limited series)

1-7-Jamie Rich-s/Megan Levens-a/Joëlle Jones-c. 1-Variant-c by Mittens 3.00

MADAME MIRAGE
Image Comics (Top Cow): June, 2007 - No. 6, May, 2008 ($2.99)

1-6: 1-Paul Dini-s/Kenneth Rocafort-a; two covers by Horn and Rocafort 3.00
... First Look (5/07, 99¢) preview of series; Dini interview; cover gallery 3.00
Volume 1 TPB (7/08, $14.99) r/#1-6; cover gallery; cover and design sketches 15.00

MADAME XANADU
DC Comics: July, 1981 ($1.00, no ads, 36 pgs.)

1-Marshall Rogers-a (25 pgs.); Kaluta-c/a (2pgs.); pin-up 1 2 3 5 6 8

MADAME XANADU (Also see Doorway to Nightmare)
DC Comics (Vertigo): Aug, 2008 - No. 29, Jan, 2011 ($2.99)

1-Matt Wagner-s/Amy Reeder Hadley-a/c; Phantom Stranger app. 4.00
1,2-Variant covers. 1-Wagner. 2-Kaluta 5.00
2-29: 2-10-Amy Reeder Hadley-a/c; Phantom Stranger app. 6-Death (from The Sandman) app.; covers by Hadley & Quitely. 9-Zatara app. 10-Jim Corrigan becomes The Spectre. 11-15-Kaluta-a. 14,15-Sandman (Wesley Dodds) app. 16-18-Hadley-a; Det. Jones app. 3.00
...: Broken House of Cards TPB (2011, $17.99) r/#16-23 and story from House of Mystery Halloween Annual #1 18.00
...: Disenchanted TPB (2009, $12.99) r/#1-10; James Robinson intro.; Hadley sketch-a 13.00
...: Exodus TPB (2010, $12.99) r/#11-15; Chris Roberson intro. 13.00
...: Extra-Sensory TPB (2011, $17.99) r/#24-29 18.00

MADAM SATAN (From Chilling Adventures of Sabrina)
Archie Comics: Dec, 2020 ($3.99, one-shot)

1-Eliot Rahal-s/Julius Ohta-a; Madam Satan before becoming Greendale High principal 4.00

MADBALLS
Star Comics/Marvel Comics #9 on: Sept, 1986 - No. 3, Nov, 1986; No. 4, June, 1987 - No. 10, June, 1988

1-10: Based on toys. 9-Post-a 5.00

MAD DISCO
E.C. Comics: 1980 (one-shot, 36 pgs.)

1-Includes 30 minute flexi-disc of Mad disco music 2 4 6 13 18 22

MAD-DOG
Marvel Comics: May, 1993 - No. 6, Oct, 1993 ($1.25)

1-6-Flip book w/2nd story "created" by Bob Newhart's character from his TV show "Bob" set at a comic book company; actual s/a-Ty Templeton 3.00

MAD DOGS
Eclipse Comics: Feb, 1992 - No. 3, July, 1992 ($2.50, B&W, limited series)

1-3 3.00

MAD 84 (Mad Extra)
E.C. Comics: 1984 (84 pgs.)

1 1 3 4 6 8 10

MAD FOLLIES (Special)
E. C. Comics: 1963 - No. 7, 1969

	GD	VG	FN	VF	VF/NM	NM-
nn(1963)-Paperback book covers	19	38	57	133	297	460
2(1964)-Calendar	15	30	45	100	220	340
3(1965)-Mischief Stickers	11	22	33	76	163	250
4(1966)-Mobile; Frazetta-r/back-c Mad #90	9	18	27	57	111	165
5,6: 5(1967)-Stencils. 6(1968)-Mischief Stickers	7	14	21	44	82	120
7(1969)-Nasty Cards	7	14	21	44	82	120

(If bonus is missing, issue is half price)
NOTE: ***Clarke** c-4. **Frazetta** r-4, 6 (1 pg. ea.). **Mingo** c-1-3. **Orlando** a-5.*

MAD HATTER, THE (Costumed Hero)
O. W. Comics Corp.: Jan-Feb, 1946; No. 2, Sept-Oct, 1946

1-Freddy the Firefly begins; Giunta-c/a 81 162 243 518 884 1250

Mad House #122 © ACP

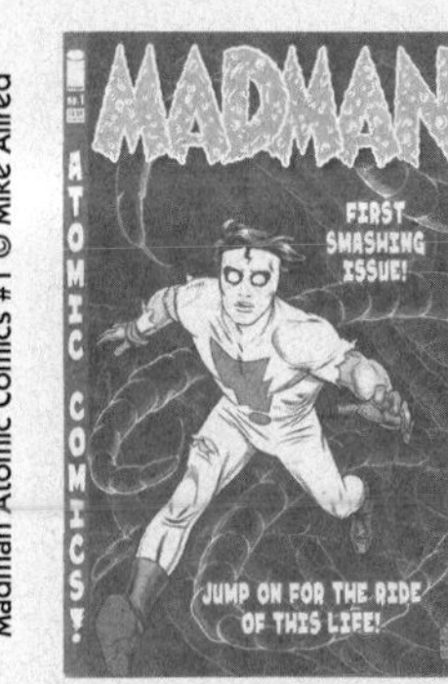

Madman Atomic Comics #1 © Mike Allred

Mae #8 © Gene Ha

	GD 2.0	VG 4.0	FN 6.0	VF 8.0	VF/NM 9.0	NM- 9.2

2-Has ad for E.C.'s Animal Fables #1 43 86 129 271 461 650

MADHOUSE
Ajax/Farrell Publ. (Excellent Publ./4-Star): 3-4/54 - No. 4, 9-10/54; 6/57 - No. 4, Dec?, 1957

1(1954) 40 80 120 246 411 575
2,3 22 44 66 128 209 290
4-Surrealistic-c 31 62 93 182 296 410
1(1957, 2nd series) 16 32 48 98 154 210
2-4 (#4 exist?) 12 24 36 69 97 125

MAD HOUSE (Formerly Madhouse Glads; ...Comics #104? on)
Red Circle Productions/Archie Publications: No. 95, 9/74 - No. 97, 1/75; No. 98, 8/75 - No. 130, 10/82

95,96-Horror stories through #97; Morrow-c 2 4 6 11 16 20
97-Intro. Henry Hobson; Morrow-a/c, Thorne-a 2 4 6 10 14 18
98,99,101-120-Satire/humor stories. 110-Sabrina app.,1pg.
1 3 4 6 8 10
100 2 4 6 8 10 12
121-129 2 4 6 8 10 12
130 2 4 6 9 13 16
Annual 8(1970-71)-Formerly Madhouse Ma-ad Annual; Sabrina app. (6 pgs.)
4 8 12 27 44 60
Annual 9-12(1974-75): 11-Wood-a(r) 3 6 9 14 20 25
...Comics Digest 1('75-76) r/1st & 2nd Sabrina app. 2 4 6 10 14 18
2-8(8/82)(...Mag. #5 on)-Sabrina in many 2 4 6 8 11 14
NOTE: *B. Jones a-96. McWilliams a-97. Wildey a-95, 96. See Archie Comics Digest #1, 13.*

MADHOUSE GLADS (Formerly ...Ma-ad; Madhouse #95 on)
Archie Publ.: No. 73, May, 1970 - No. 94, Aug, 1974 (No. 78-92: 52 pgs.)

73-77,93,94: 74-1 pg. Sabrina 2 4 6 9 13 16
78-92 (52 pgs.) 2 4 6 11 16 20

MADHOUSE MA-AD (...Jokes #67-70; ...Freak-Out #71-74)
(Formerly Archie's Madhouse) (Becomes Madhouse Glads #73 on)
Archie Publications: No. 67, April, 1969 - No. 72, Jan, 1970

67-71: 70-1 pg. Sabrina 3 6 9 15 22 28
72-6 pgs. Sabrina 4 8 12 27 44 60
...Annual 7(1969-70)-Formerly Archie's Madhouse Annual; becomes Madhouse Annual; 6 pgs. Sabrina 4 8 12 28 47 65

MADMAN (See Creatures of the Id #1)
Tundra Publishing: Mar, 1992 - No. 3, 1992 ($3.95, duotone, high quality, lim. series, 52 pgs.)

1-Mike Allred-c/a in all 2 4 6 9 13 16
1-2nd printing 4.00
2,3 6.00

MADMAN ADVENTURES
Tundra Publishing: 1992 - No. 3, 1993 ($2.95, limited series)

1-Mike Allred-c/a in all 1 3 4 6 8 10
2,3 5.00
TPB (Oni Press, 2002, $14.95) r/#1-3 & first app. of Frank Einstein from Creatures of the Id in color; gallery pages 15.00

MADMAN ATOMIC COMICS (Also see The Atomics)
Image Comics: Apr, 2007 - No. 17, Sept, 2009 ($2.99/$3.50)

1-12-Mike Allred-s/c/a. 1-Origin re-told; pin-ups by Rivoche and Powell. 3-Sale back-c 3.50
13-17-($3.50) Wraparound-c. 14-Back up w/Darwyn Cooke-a 3.50
All-New Giant-Size Super Ginchy Special (4/11, $5.99) Allred-s/a; back-ups/pin-ups 6.00
Madman In Your Face 3D Special (11/14, $9.99) Classic stories converted to 3D plus a new short story by Mike Allred and pin-ups by various; glasses included 10.00
... Vol. 1 (2008, $19.99) r/#1-7; bonus art; Jamie Rich intro. 20.00

MADMAN COMICS (Also see The Atomics)
Dark Horse Comics (Legend No. 2 on): Apr, 1994 - No. 20, Dec, 2000 ($2.95/$2.99)

1-Allred-c/a; F. Miller back-c. 1 2 3 5 6 8
2-3: 3-Alex Toth back-c. 5.00
4-11: 4-Dave Stevens back-c. 6,7-Miller/Darrow's Big Guy app. 6-Bruce Timm back-c. 7-Darrow back-c. 8-Origin?; Bagge back-c. 10-Allred/Ross-c; Ross back-c. 11-Frazetta back-c 4.00
12-16: 12-(4/99) 3.50
17-20: 17-The G-Men From Hell #1 on cover; Brereton back-c. 18-(#2). 19,20-($2.99-c). 20-Clowes back-c 3.50
... Boogaloo TPB (6/99, $8.95) r/Nexus Meets Madman & Madman/The Jam 9.00
... Gargantua! (2007, $125.00, HC with dustjacket) r/Madman#1-3, Madman Adventures #1-3, Madman Comics #1-20 and Madman King-Size Super Groovy Special; pin-ups 125.00
Image Firsts: Madman #1 (10/10, $1.00) r/#1 3.00
Ltd. Ed. Slipcover (1997, $99.95, signed and numbered) w/Vol.1 & Vol. 2. Vol.1- reprints #1-5; Vol. 2- reprints #6-10 100.00
The Complete Madman Comics: Vol. 2 (11/96, $17.95, TPB) r/#6-10 plus new material 18.00
Madman King-Size Super Groovy Special (Oni Press, 7/03, $6.95) new short stories by Allred, Derington, Krall and Weissman 7.00
Madman Picture Exhibition No. 1-4 (4-7/02, $3.95) pin-ups by various 4.00
Madman Picture Exhibition Limited Edition (10/02, $29.95) Hardcover collects MPE #1-4 30.00
... Volume 2 SC (2007, $17.99) r/#1-11; Erik Larsen intro. 18.00
... Volume 3 SC (2007, $17.99) r/#12-20 and story from King-Size Groovy; Allred intro. 18.00
Yearbook '95 (1996, $17.95, TPB)-r/#1-5, intro by Teller 18.00

MADMAN / THE JAM
Dark Horse Comics: Jul, 1998 - No. 2, Aug, 1998 ($2.95, mini-series)

1,2-Allred & Mireault-s/a 4.00

MAD MAX: FURY ROAD (Based on the 2015 movie)
DC Comics (Vertigo): Jul, 2015 - Oct, 2015 ($4.99, series of one-shots)

... :Furiosa (8/15, $4.99) Origin of Furiosa; Tristan Jones-a; Edwards-c 5.00
...: Max 1,2 (9/15, 10/15, $4.99) Recap of Max's history & prelude to movie 5.00
...: Nux & Immortan Joe (7/15, $4.99) Origins of Nux & Immortan Joe; Edwards-c 5.00

MAD MONSTER PARTY (See Movie Classics)

MADNESS IN MURDERWORLD
Marvel Comics: 1989 (Came with computer game from Paragon Software)

V1#1-Starring The X-Men 2 4 6 11 16 20

MADRAVEN HALLOWEEN SPECIAL
Hamilton Comics: Oct, 1995 ($2.95, one-shot)

nn-Morrow-a 4.00

MADROX (from X-Factor)
Marvel Comics (Marvel Knights): Nov, 2004 - No. 5, Mar, 2005 ($2.99)

1-5-Peter David-s/Pablo Raimondi-a; Strong Guy app. 3.00
...: Multiple Choice TPB (2005, $13.99) r/#1-5 14.00
X-Factor: Madrox - Multiple Choice HC (2008, $19.99) r/#1-5 20.00

MAD SPECIAL (...Super Special)
E. C. Publications, Inc.: Fall, 1970 - No. 141, Nov, 1999 (84 - 116 pgs.)
(If bonus is missing, issue is one half price)

Fall 1970(#1)-Bonus-Voodoo Doll; contains 17 pgs. new material
9 18 27 63 129 195
Spring 1971(#2)-Wall Nuts; 17 pgs. new material 5 10 15 33 57 80
3-Protest Stickers 5 10 15 33 57 80
4-8: 4-Mini Posters. 5-Mad Flag. 6-Mad Mischief Stickers. 7-Presidential candidate posters, Wild Shocking Message posters. 8-TV Guise 5 10 15 30 50 70
9(1972)-Contains Nostalgic Mad #1 (28 pgs.) 4 8 12 27 44 60
10-13: 10-Nonsense Stickers (Don Martin). 13-Sickie Stickers; 3 pgs. Wolverton-r/Mad #137. 11-Contains 33-1/3 RPM record. 12-Contains Nostalgic Mad #2 (36 pgs.); Davis, Wolverton-a 3 6 9 19 30 40
14,16-21,24: 4-Vital Message posters & Art Depreciation paintings. 16-Mad-hesive Stickers. 17-Don Martin posters. 20-Martin Stickers. 18-Contains Nostalgic Mad #4 (36 pgs.). 21,24-Contains Nostalgic Mad #5 (28 pgs.) & #6 (28 pgs.)
3 6 9 16 23 30
15-Contains Nostalgic Mad #3 (28 pgs.) 3 6 9 16 24 32
22,23,25,27-29,30: 22-Diplomas. 23-Martin Stickers. 25-Martin Posters. 27-Mad Shock-Sticks. 28-Contains Nostalgic Mad #7 (36 pgs.). 29-Mad Collectable-Connectables Posters. 30-The Movies 2 4 6 9 13 16
26-Has 33-1/3 RPM record 2 4 6 13 18 22
31,33-35,37-50 2 4 6 8 11 14
32-Contains Nostalgic Mad #8. 36-Has 96 pgs. of comic book & comic strip spoofs: titles "The Comics" on-c 2 4 6 9 13 16
51-70 1 3 4 6 8 10
71-88,90-100: 71-Batman parodies-r by Wood, Drucker. 72-Wolverton-c r-from 1st panel in Mad #11; Wolverton-s r/new dialogue. 83-All Star Trek spoof issue
1 2 3 5 6 8
76-(Fall, 1991)-Special Hussein Asylum Edition; distributed only to the troops in the Middle East (see Mad #300-303) 2 4 6 13 18 22
89-($3.95)-Polybagged w/1st of 3 Spy vs. Spy hologram trading cards (direct sale only issue) (other cards came w/card set) 1 3 4 6 8 10
101-141: 117-Sci-Fi parodies-r. 4.00
NOTE: *#28-30 have no number on cover.* ***Freas*** *c-76.* ***Mingo*** *c-9, 11, 15, 19, 23.*

MAE
Dark Horse Comics/Lion Forge #7-on: May, 2016 - Present ($3.99)

1-Gene Ha-s/a/c; intro. by Bill Willingham; bonus pin-ups by Graham & Conner 5.00
2-9: 2-5-Ha-s/a/c. 3-Pin-up by Katie Cook. 6-Ha-s/Ganucheau-a. 8-Waid-s. 9-Kremer-s 4.00

MAESTRO
Marvel Comics: Oct, 2020 - No. 5, Feb, 2021 ($4.99/$3.99)

1-($4.99)-Origin of future Hulk; Peter David-s/Germán Peralta; M.O.D.O.K. app.

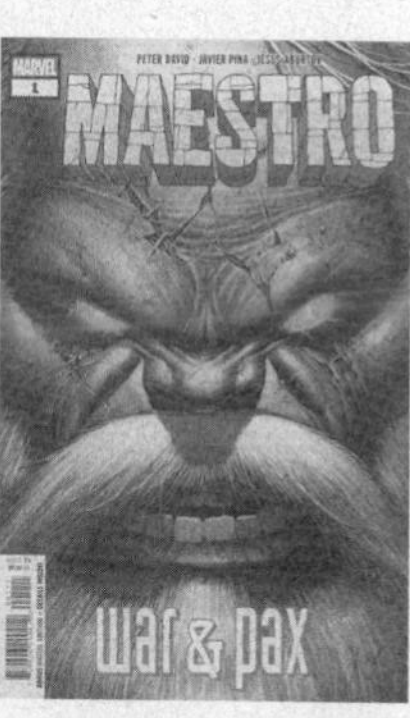

Maestro: War and Pax #1 © MAR

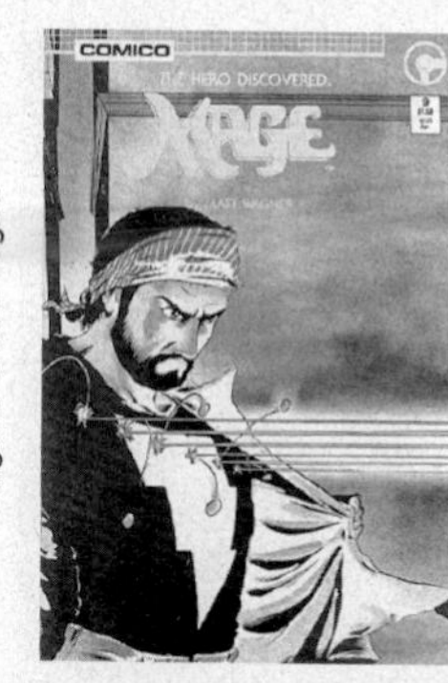

Mage #9 © Matt Wagner

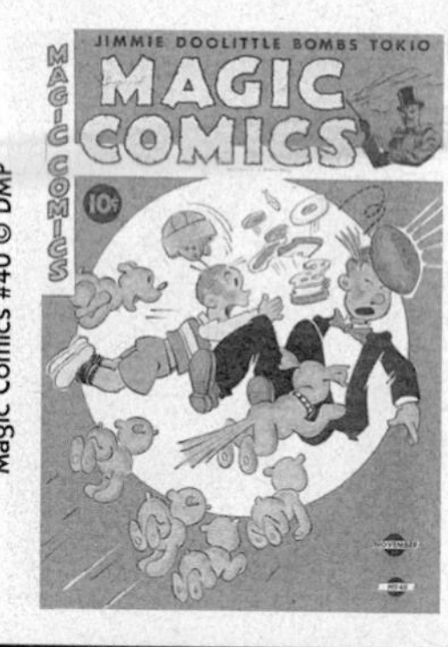

Magic Comics #40 © DMP

GD VG FN VF VF/NM NM-
2.0 4.0 6.0 8.0 9.0 9.2

1 2 3 5 6 8

2-5-($3.99) Hercules app. 4.00

MAESTRO: FUTURE IMPERFECT – MARVEL TALES
Marvel Comics: Oct, 2020 ($7.99, one-shot)

1-Reprints intro. of Maestro in Hulk: Future Imperfect #1,2; Peter David-s/George Pérez-a 8.00

MAESTROS
Image Comics: Oct, 2017 - No. 7, Aug, 2018 ($3.99)

1-7-Steve Skroce-s/a 4.00

MAESTRO: WAR AND PAX (Follows Maestro series)
Marvel Comics: Mar, 2021 - Present ($4.99/$3.99)

1-($4.99)-Future Hulk; Peter David-s/Javier Pina; Machine Man app. 5.00
2-($3.99) Doctor Doom app. 4.00

MAGDALENA, THE (See The Darkness #15-18)
Image Comics (Top Cow): Apr, 2000 - No. 3, Jan, 2001 ($2.50)

Preview Special ('00, $4.95) Flip book w/Blood Legacy preview 5.00
1-Benitez-c/a; variant covers by Silvestri & Turner 3.00
2,3: 2-Two covers 3.00
.../Angelus #1/2 (11/01, $2.95) Benitez-c/Ching-a 3.00
...Blood Divine (2002, $9.95) r/#1-3 & #1/2; cover gallery 10.00
.../Vampirella (7/03, $2.99) Wohl-s/Benitez-a; two covers 3.00

MAGDALENA, THE (Volume 2)
Image Comics (Top Cow): Aug, 2003 - No. 4, Dec, 2003 ($2.99)

Preview (6/03) B&W preview; Wizard World East logo on cover 3.00
1-4-Holguin-s/Basaldua-a 3.00
1-Variant-c by Jim Silke benefitting ACTOR charity 5.00
TPB Volume 1 (12/06, $19.99) r/both series, Darkness #15-18 & Magdalena/Angelus 20.00
.../Daredevil (5/08, $3.99) Phil Hester-s/a; Hester & Sejic-c 4.00
.../Vampirella (12/04, $2.99) Kirkman-s/Manapul-a; two covers by Manapul and Bachalo 3.00
... Vs. Dracula Monster War 2005 (6/05, $2.99) four covers; Joyce Chin-a 3.00

MAGDALENA, THE (Volume 3)
Image Comics (Top Cow): Apr, 2010 - No. 12, May, 2012 ($3.99)

1-12: 1-Marz-s/Blake-a/Sook-c. 7,8-Keu Cha-a 4.00
... Seventh Sacrament 1 (12/14, $3.99) Tini Howard-s/Aileen Oracion-a 4.00

MAGDALENA (Volume 4)
Image Comics (Top Cow): Mar, 2017 - No. 4, Jun, 2017 ($3.99, limited series)

1-4-Howard & Cady-s/DiBari-a 4.00

MAGE (The Hero Discovered...; also see Grendel #16)
Comico: Feb, 1984 (no month) - No. 15, Dec, 1986 ($1.50, Mando paper)

1-Comico's 1st color comic 2 4 6 9 13 16
2-5: 3-Intro Edsel 6.00
6-Grendel begins (1st in color) 3 6 9 14 20 25
7-1st new Grendel story 2 4 6 8 10 12
8-14: 13-Grendel dies. 14-Grendel story ends 6.00
15-($2.95) Double size w/pullout poster 1 2 3 5 6 8
Image Firsts: Mage - The Hero Discovered #1 (10/10, $1.00) r/#1 w/"Image Firsts" logo 3.00
TPB Volume 1-4 (Image, $5.95) 1- r/#1,2. 2- r/#3,4. 3- r/#5,6. 4- r/#7,8 7.00
TPB Volume 5-7 (Image, $6.95) 5- r/#9,10. 6- r/#11,12. 7- r/#13,14 7.00
TPB Volume 8 (Image, 9/99, $7.50) r/#15 7.50
..., Vol. 1 TPB (Image, 2004, $29.99) r/#1-15; cover gallery, promo artwork, bonus art 30.00

MAGE (The Hero Defined) (Volume 2)
Image Comics: July, 1997 - No. 15, Oct, 1999 ($2.50)

0-(7/97, $5.00) American Ent. Ed. 5.00
1-14: Matt Wagner-c/s/a in all. 13-Three covers 3.00
1-"3-D Edition" (2/98, $4.95) w/glasses 5.00
15-($5.95) Acetate cover 6.00
Volume 1,2 TPB ('98,'99, $9.95) 1- r/#1-4. 2-r/#5-8 10.00
Volume 3 TPB ('00, $12.95) r/#9-12 13.00
Volume 4 TPB ('01, $14.95) r/#13-15 15.00
Hardcover Vol. 2 (2005, $49.95) r/#1-15; cover gallery, character design & sketch pages 50.00

MAGE, BOOK THREE: THE HERO DENIED
Image Comics: No. 0 July, 2017 - No. 15, Feb, 2019 ($1.99/$3.99)

0-(7/17, $1.99) Return of Kevin Matchstick 3.00
1-14-Matt Wagner-c/s/a 4.00
15-($7.99) Finale of the trilogy 8.00

MAGE KNIGHT: STOLEN DESTINY (Based on the fantasy game Mage Knight)
Idea + Design Works: Oct, 2002 - No. 5, Feb, 2003 ($3.50, limited series)

1-5: 1-J. Scott Campbell-c; Cabrera-a/Dezago-s, 2-Dave Johnson-c 3.50

GD VG FN VF VF/NM NM-
2.0 4.0 6.0 8.0 9.0 9.2

MAGGIE AND HOPEY COLOR SPECIAL (See Love and Rockets)
Fantagraphics Books: May, 1997 ($3.50, one-shot)

1 4.00

MAGGIE THE CAT (Also see Jon Sable, Freelance #11 & Shaman's Tears #12)
Image Comics (Creative Fire Studio): Jan, 1996 - No. 2, Feb, 1996 ($2.50, unfinished limited series)

1,2: Mike Grell-c/a/scripts 3.00

MAGICA DE SPELL GIANT HALLOWEEN HEX (Also see Walt Disney Showcase #30)
IDW Publisihing: No. 2, Sept, 2018 ($5.99, numbering continues from Disney Giant Halloween Hex)

2-Reprints from Italian & Danish editions; art by Cavazzano & Alfonso 6.00

MAGIC AGENT (See Forbidden Worlds & Unknown Worlds)
American Comics Group: Jan-Feb, 1962 - No. 3, May-June, 1962

1-Origin & 1st app. John Force 5 10 15 30 50 70
2,3 3 6 9 21 33 45

MAGIC COMICS
David McKay Publications: Aug, 1939 - No. 123, Nov-Dec, 1949

1-Mandrake the Magician, Henry, Popeye , Blondie, Barney Baxter, Secret Agent X-9 (not by Raymond), Bunky by Billy DeBeck & Thornton Burgess text stories illustrated by Harrison Cady begin; Henry covers begin 372 744 1116 2195 3798 5400
2 138 276 414 814 1407 2000
3 103 206 309 608 1054 1500
4 76 152 228 448 774 1100
5 64 128 192 378 652 925
6-11: 8-11-Mandrake/Henry funny covers 50 100 150 315 533 750
12-16,18,20: 12-20,22-24-Serious Mandrake mystery covers
68 136 204 435 743 1050
17-The Lone Ranger begins (scarce) 100 200 300 590 1020 1450
19-Classic robot-c (scarce) 161 322 483 1030 1765 2500
21-Mandrake/Henry funny cover 39 78 117 240 395 550
22-24 50 100 150 315 533 750
25-1st Blondie-c 41 82 123 256 428 600
26-30: 26-Dagwood-c begin 30 60 90 177 289 400
31-40: 36-Flag-c 21 42 63 122 199 275
41-50 16 32 48 94 147 200
51-60 14 28 42 80 115 150
61-70 12 24 36 67 94 120
71-99, 107,108-Flash Gordon app; not by Raymond 10 20 30 54 72 90
100 11 22 33 60 83 105
101-106,109-123: 123-Last Dagwood-c 9 18 27 50 65 80

MAGIC FLUTE, THE (See Night Music #9-11)

MAGICIAN: APPRENTICE
Dabel Brothers/Marvel Comics (Dabel Brothers) #3 on: Mar, 2007 - No. 12, Dec, 2007 ($2.95/$2.99)

1-12-Adaptation of the Raymond E. Feist Riftwar Saga series 3.00
1,2-($5.95) 1-Wraparound variant-c by Maitz. 2-Wraparound variant-c by Booth 6.00
Collected Edition (10/06, $3.99) r/#1&2 4.00
Vol. 1 HC (2007, $19.99, dustjacket) r/#1-6; foreword by Feist 20.00
Vol. 1 SC (2007, $15.99) r/#1-6; foreword by Feist 16.00
Vol. 2 HC (2008, $19.99, dustjacket) r/#7-12 20.00

MAGICIANS, THE (Based on the series of novels by Lev Grossman)
Archaia: Nov, 2019 - No. 5, Mar, 2020 ($3.99, limited series)

1-5-Lilah Sturges-s/Pius Bak-a 4.00

MAGIC ORDER, THE
Image Comics: Jun, 2018 - No. 6, Feb, 2019 ($3.99, limited series)

1-6-Mark Millar-s/Olivier Coipel-a/c 4.00

MAGIC PICKLE
Oni Press: Sept, 2001 - No. 4, Dec, 2001 ($2.95, limited series)

1-4-Scott Morse-s/a; Mahfood-a (2 pgs.) 3.00

MAGIC SWORD, THE (See Movie Classics)

MAGIC THE GATHERING (Title Series), **Acclaim Comics (Armada)**

...ANTIQUITIES WAR, 11/95 - 2/96 ($2.50), 1-4-Paul Smith-a(p) 3.00
...ARABIAN NIGHTS, 12/95 - 1/96 ($2.50), 1,2 3.00
...COLLECTION, '95 ($4.95), 1,2-polybagged 5.00
...CONVOCATIONS, '95 ($2.50), 1-nn-pin-ups 3.00
...ELDER DRAGONS, '95 ($2.50), 1,2-Doug Wheatley-a 3.00
...FALLEN ANGEL, '95 ($5.95), nn 6.00

Magilla Gorilla #9 © H-B

Magnificent Ms. Marvel #3 © MAR

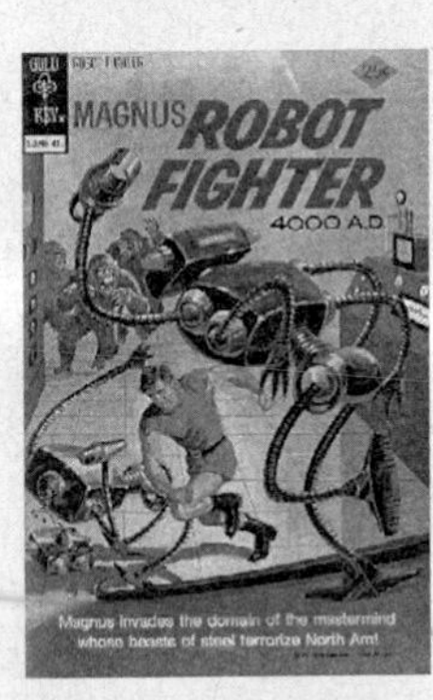

Magnus, Robot Fighter #37 © GK

	GD	VG	FN	VF	VF/NM	NM-
	2.0	4.0	6.0	8.0	9.0	9.2

...FALLEN EMPIRES, 9/95 - 10/95 ($2.75), 1,2 — 3.00
...Collection ($4.95)-polybagged — 5.00
...HOMELANDS, '95 ($5.95), nn-polybagged w/card; Hildebrandts-c — 6.00
... ICE AGE (On The World of...), 7/5 -11/95 ($2.50), 1-4: 1,2-bound-in Magic Card. 3,4-bound-in insert — 3.00
...LEGEND OF JEDIT OJANEN, '96 ($2.50), 1,2 — 3.00
...NIGHTMARE, '95 ($2.50, one shot), 1 — 3.00
...THE SHADOW MAGE, 7/95 - 10/95 ($2.50), 1-4-bagged w/Magic The Gathering card — 3.00
...Collection 1,2 (1995, $4.95)-Trade paperback; polybagged — 5.00
...SHANDALAR, '96 ($2.50), 1,2 — 3.00
...WAYFARER, 11/95 - 2/96 ($2.50), 1-5 — 3.00

MAGIC: THE GATHERING
IDW Publishing: Dec, 2011 - No. 4, Mar, 2012 ($3.99, limited series)
1-4-Forbeck-s/Cóccolo-a — 4.00

MAGIC: THE GATHERING: CHANDRA
IDW Publishing: Nov, 2018 - No. 4, Feb, 2019 ($3.99, limited series)
1-4-Ayala-s/Tolibao-a — 4.00

MAGIC: THE GATHERING: GERRARD'S QUEST
Dark Horse Comics: Mar, 1998 - No. 4, June, 1998 ($2.95, limited series)
1-4: Grell-s/Mhan-a — 3.00

MAGIC: THE GATHERING - PATH OF VENGEANCE
IDW Publishing: Oct, 2012 - No. 4, Feb, 2013 ($4.99, limited series, bagged with card)
1-4-Forbeck-s/Cóccolo-a — 5.00

MAGIC: THE GATHERING - THEROS
IDW Publishing: Oct, 2013 - No. 5 ($4.99, limited series, bagged with card)
1-5-Ciaramella-s/Cóccolo-a — 5.00

MAGIC: THE GATHERING - THE SPELL THIEF
IDW Publishing: May, 2012 - No. 4, Aug, 2012 ($4.99, limited series, bagged with card)
1-4-Forbeck-s/Cóccolo-a — 5.00

MAGIK (Illyana and Storm Limited Series)
Marvel Comics Group: Dec, 1983 - No. 4, Mar, 1984 (60¢, limited series)
1-4: 1-Characters from X-Men; Inferno begins; X-Men cameo (Buscema pencils in #1,2; c-1p. 2-4: 2-Nightcrawler app. & X-Men cameo — 5.00

MAGIK (See Black Sun mini-series)
Marvel Comics: Dec, 2000 - No. 4, Mar, 2001 ($2.99, limited series)
1-4-Liam Sharp-a/Abnett & Lanning-s; Nightcrawler app. — 3.00

MAGILLA GORILLA (TV) (See Kite Fun Book)
Gold Key: May, 1964 - No. 10, Dec, 1968 (Hanna-Barbera)

	GD	VG	FN	VF	VF/NM	NM-
1-1st comic app.	10	20	30	66	138	210
2-4: 3-Vs. Yogi Bear for President. 4-1st Punkin Puss & Mushmouse, Ricochet Rabbit & Droop-a-Long	5	10	15	33	57	80
5-10: 10-Reprints	4	8	12	28	47	65

MAGILLA GORILLA (TV)(See Spotlight #4)
Charlton Comics: Nov, 1970 - No. 5, July, 1971 (Hanna-Barbera)

	GD	VG	FN	VF	VF/NM	NM-
1	6	12	18	41	76	110
2-5	3	6	9	21	33	45

MAGNETIC MEN FEATURING MAGNETO
Marvel Comics (Amalgam): June, 1997 ($1.95, one-shot)
1-Tom Peyer-s/Barry Kitson & Dan Panosian-a — 5.00

MAGNETO (See X-Men #1)
Marvel Comics: nd (Sept, 1993) (Giveaway) (one-shot)
0-Embossed foil-c by Sienkiewicz; r/Classic X-Men #19 & 12 by Bolton — 5.00

MAGNETO
Marvel Comics: Nov, 1996 - No. 4, Feb, 1997 ($1.95, limited series)
1-4: Peter Milligan scripts & Kelley Jones-a(p) — 4.00

MAGNETO
Marvel Comics: Mar, 2011 ($2.99, one-shot)
1-Howard Chaykin-s/a; Roger Cruz-c — 3.00

MAGNETO
Marvel Comics: May, 2014 - No. 21, Oct, 2015 ($3.99)
1-21: 1-Bunn-s/Walta-a/Rivera-c. 9-12-AXIS tie-ins. 18-21-Secret Wars tie-ins — 4.00

MAGNETO AND THE MAGNETIC MEN
Marvel Comics (Amalgam): Apr, 1996 ($1.95, one-shot)
1-Jeff Matsuda-a(p) — 4.00

MAGNETO ASCENDANT
Marvel Comics: May, 1999 ($3.99, squarebound one-shot)
1-Reprints early Magneto appearances — 4.00

MAGNETO: DARK SEDUCTION
Marvel Comics: Jun, 2000 - No. 4, Sept, 2000 ($2.99, limited series)
1-4: Nicieza-s/Cruz-a. 3,4-Avengers-c/app. — 3.00

MAGNETO: NOT A HERO (X-Men Regenesis)
Marvel Comics: Jan, 2012 - No. 4, Apr, 2012 ($2.99, limited series)
1-4-Skottie Young-s/Clay Mann-a; Joseph returns — 3.00

MAGNETO REX
Marvel Comics: Apr, 1999 - No. 3, July, 1999 ($2.50, limited series)
1-3-Rogue, Quicksilver app.; Peterson-a(p) — 4.00

MAGNIFICENT MS. MARVEL
Marvel Comics: May, 2019 - Present ($3.99)
1-17: 1-Saladin Ahmed-s/Minkyu Jung-a. 5-New costume. 10-Intro. Stormranger 13-Intro. Amulet. 15,17-Dum Dum Dugan app. — 4.00
18-($4.99) 75th issue of Ms. Marvel; battles Stormranger — 5.00
Annual 1 (9/19, $4.99) Visaggio-s/Lam-a; The Super-Skrull app. — 5.00

MAGNUS (Robot Fighter)(Volume 1)
Dynamite Entertainment: 2017 - No. 5, 2017 ($3.99)
1-5-Higgins-s/Fornés-a. 1,2-Turok back-up. 3-5-Doctor Spektor back-up — 4.00

MAGNUS, ROBOT FIGHTER (...4000 A.D.)(See Doctor Solar)
Gold Key: Feb, 1963 - No. 46, Jan, 1977 (All painted covers except #5,30,31)

	GD	VG	FN	VF	VF/NM	NM-
1-Origin & 1st app. Magnus; Aliens (1st app.) series begins	75	150	225	600	1350	2100
2,3	12	24	36	83	182	280
4-10: 10-Simonson fan club illo (5/65, 1st-a?)	7	14	21	49	92	135
11-20	5	10	15	33	57	80
21,24-28: 28-Aliens ends	4	8	12	25	40	55
22,23: 22-Origin-r/#1; last 12¢ issue	4	8	12	27	44	60
29-46-Mostly reprints	3	6	9	14	20	25

...: One For One (Dark Horse Comics, 9/10, $1.00) r/#1 — 3.00
Russ Manning's Magnus Robot Fighter - Vol. 1 HC (Dark Horse, 2004, $49.95) r/#1-7 — 70.00
Russ Manning's Magnus Robot Fighter - Vol. 2 HC (DH, 6/05, $49.95) r/#8-14; forward by Steve Rude — 50.00
Russ Manning's Magnus Robot Fighter - Vol. 3 HC (Dark Horse, 10/06, $49.95) r/#15-21 — 50.00
NOTE: *Manning a-1-22, 28-43(r). Spiegle a-23, 44r.*

MAGNUS ROBOT FIGHTER (Also see Vintage Magnus)
Valiant/Acclaim Comics: May, 1991 - No. 64, Feb, 1996 ($1.75/$1.95/$2.25/$2.50)

	GD	VG	FN	VF	VF/NM	NM-
1-Nichols/Layton-c/a; 1-8 have trading cards	3	6	9	14	19	24
2-4,6,8: 4-Rai cameo. 6-1st Solar x-over.	1	3	4	6	8	10
5-Origin & 1st full app. Rai (10/91); #5-8 are in flip book format and back-c & half of book are Rai #1-4 mini-series	3	6	9	16	23	30
7-Magnus vs. Rai-c/story; 1st X-O Armor	2	4	6	11	16	20
0-Origin issue; Layton-a; ordered through mail w/coupons from 1st 8 issues plus 50¢; B. Smith trading card	3	6	9	19	30	40
0-Sold thru comic shops without trading card	3	6	9	14	19	24
9-11						6.00
12-(3.25, 44 pgs.)-Turok-c/story (1st app. in Valiant universe, 5/92); has 8 pg. Magnus story insert	3	6	9	17	26	35
13-24,26-48: 14-1st app. Isak. 15,16-Unity x-overs. 15-Miller-c. 16-Birth of Magnus. 21-New direction & new logo.24-Story cont'd in Rai & the Future Force #9. 33-Timewalker app. 36-Bound-in trading cards. 37-Rai, Starwatchers & Psi-Lords app. 44-Bound-in sneak peek card						4.00
21-Gold ink variant	2	4	6	10	14	18
25-($2.95)-Embossed silver foil-c; new costume						5.00
49-63						4.00
64-($2.50): 64-Magnus dies?	2	4	6	9	12	15
...Invasion (1994, $9.95)-r/Rai #1-4 & Magnus #5-8						12.00
Magnus Steel Nation (1994, $9.95) r/#1-4						12.00
Yearbook (1994, $3.95, 52 pgs.)						5.00

NOTE: ***Ditko/Reese** a-18. **Layton** a(i)-5; c-6-9i, 25; back(i)-5-8. **Reese** a(i)-22, 25, 28; c(i)-22, 24, 28. **Simonson** c-16. Prices for issues 1-8 are for trading cards and coupons intact.*

MAGNUS ROBOT FIGHTER
Acclaim Comics (Valiant Heroes): V2#1, May, 1997 - No. 18, Jun, 1998 ($2.50)
1-18: 1-Reintro Magnus; Donavon Wylie (X-O Manowar) cameo; Tom Peyer scripts & Mike McKone-c/a begin; painted variant-c exists — 4.00

Magog #7 © DC

Man-Bat #1 © DC

Man-eaters #1 © Ministry of Trouble

GD 2.0 VG 4.0 FN 6.0 VF 8.0 VF/NM 9.0 NM- 9.2

MAGNUS ROBOT FIGHTER
Dark Horse Comics: Aug, 2010 - No. 4, May, 2011 ($3.50)
1-4: 1-Shooter-s/Reinhold-a; covers by Swanland & Reinhold; back-up r/#1 (1963) 3.50

MAGNUS ROBOT FIGHTER
Dynamite Entertainment: 2014 - No. 12, 2015 ($3.99)
1-12: 1-8-Fred Van Lente-s/Cory Smith-a; multiple covers on each 4.00
#0 (2014, $3.99) Takes place between #2 & #3; Roberto Castro-a 4.00

MAGNUS ROBOT FIGHTER/NEXUS
Valiant/Dark Horse Comics: Dec, 1993 - No. 2, Apr, 1994 ($2.95, lim. series)
1,2: Steve Rude painted-c & pencils in all 4.00

MAGOG (See Justice Society of America 2007 series)(Continues in Justice Society Special #1)
DC Comics: Nov, 2009 - No.12, Ot. 2010 ($2.99)
1-12: 1-Giffen-s/Porter-a/Fabry-c; variant-c by Porter. 7-Zatanna app. 3.00
...: Lethal Force TPB (2010, $14.99) r/#1-5 15.00

MAID OF THE MIST (See American Graphics)

MAI, THE PSYCHIC GIRL
Eclipse Comics: May, 1987 - No. 28, July, 1989 ($1.50, B&W, bi-weekly, 44pgs.)
1-28, 1,2-2nd print 4.00

MAJESTIC (Mr. Majestic from WildCATS)
DC Comics: Oct, 2004 - No. 4, Jan, 2005 ($2.95, limited series)
1-4-Kerschl-a/Abnett & Lanning-s. 1-Superman app.; Superman #1 cover swipe 3.00
...: Strange New Visitor TPB (2005, $14.99) r/#1-4 & Action #811, Advs. of Superman #624 & Superman #201 15.00

MAJESTIC (Mr. Majestic from WildCATS)
DC Comics (WildStorm): Mar, 2005 - No. 17, July, 2006 ($2.95/$2.99)
1-17: 1-Googe-a/Abnett & Lanning-s; Superman app. 9-Jeanty-a; Zealot app. 3.00
...: Meanwhile, Back on Earth... TPB (2006, $14.99) r/#8-12 15.00
...: The Final Cut TPB (2007, $14.99) r/#13-17 & story fro WildStorm Winter Special 15.00
...: While You Were Out TPB (2006, $12.99) r/#1-7 13.00

MAJOR BUMMER
DC Comics: Aug, 1997 - No. 15, Oct, 1998 ($2.50)
1-15: 1-Origin and 1st app. Major Bummer 3.00

MAJOR HOOPLE COMICS (See Crackajack Funnies)
Nedor Publications: nd (Jan, 1943)

	GD	VG	FN	VF	VF/NM	NM-
1-Mary Worth, Phantom Soldier app. by Moldoff	39	78	117	231	378	525

MAJOR VICTORY COMICS (Also see Dynamic Comics)
H. Clay Glover/Service Publ./Harry 'A' Chesler: 1944 - No. 3, Summer, 1945

	GD	VG	FN	VF	VF/NM	NM-
1-Origin Major Victory (patriotic hero) by C. Sultan (reprint from Dynamic #1); 1st app. Spider Woman; Nazi WWII-c	135	270	405	864	1482	2100
2-Dynamic Boy app.; WWII-c	65	130	195	416	708	1000
3-Rocket Boy app.; WWII-c	61	122	183	390	670	950

MAJOR X
Marvel Comics: Jun, 2019 - No. 6, Aug, 2019 ($4.99/$3.99)
1-($4.99) Rob Liefeld-s/a; Cable, Domino, Deadpool, Wolverine app. 5.00
2-6-($3.99) 2,4,5-Liefeld-s/Peeples-a. 3-Portacio-a. 6-Rob Liefeld-s/a 4.00
No. 0 (10/19, $4.99) r/Wolverine #154,155 with new framing pages; Liefeld-s/a 5.00

MALIBU ASHCAN: RAFFERTY (See Firearm #12)
Malibu Comics (Ultraverse): Nov, 1994 (99¢, B&W w/color-c; one-shot)
1-Previews "The Rafferty Saga" storyline in Firearm; Chaykin-c 3.00

MALTESE FALCON
David McKay Publications: No. 48, 1946

	GD	VG	FN	VF	VF/NM	NM-
Feature Books 48-by Dashiell Hammett	97	194	291	621	1061	1500

MALU IN THE LAND OF ADVENTURE
I. W. Enterprises: 1964 (See White Princess of Jungle #2)

	GD	VG	FN	VF	VF/NM	NM-
1-r/Avon's Slave Girl Comics #1; Severin-c	5	10	15	31	53	75

MAMMOTH COMICS
Whitman Publishing Co.(K. K. Publ.): 1938 (84 pgs.) (B&W, 8-1/2x11-1/2")

	GD	VG	FN	VF	VF/NM	NM-
1-Alley Oop, Terry & the Pirates, Dick Tracy, Little Orphan Annie, Wash Tubbs, Moon Mullins, Smilin' Jack, Tailspin Tommy, Don Winslow, Dan Dunn, Smokey Stover & other reprints (scarce)	252	504	756	1613	2757	3900

MAN AMONG YE, A
Image Comics (Top Cow): Jun, 2020 - Present ($3.99)
1-4-Stephanie Phillips-s/Craig Cermak-a; Caribbean pirates in 1720 4.00

MAN AGAINST TIME
Image Comics (Motown Machineworks): May, 1996 - No. 4, Aug, 1996 ($2.25, lim. series)
1-4: 1-Simonson-c. 2,3-Leon-c. 4-Barreto & Leon-c 3.00

MAN AND SUPERMAN 100-PAGE SUPER SPECTACULAR
DC Comics: Apr, 2019 ($9.99, squarebound, one-shot)
1-Wolfman-s/Castellini-a; Clark Kent's first days in Metropolis re-told 10.00

MAN-BAT (See Batman Family, Brave & the Bold, & Detective #400)
National Periodical Publ./DC Comics: Dec-Jan, 1975-76 - No. 2, Feb-Mar, 1976; Dec, 1984

	GD	VG	FN	VF	VF/NM	NM-
1-Ditko-a(p); Aparo-c; Batman app.; 1st app. She-Bat?; 1st app. Baron Tyme	3	6	9	17	26	35
2-Aparo-c	2	4	6	10	14	18
1 (12/84)-N. Adams-r(3)/Det.(Vs. Batman on-c)	1	2	3	5	6	8

MAN-BAT
DC Comics: Feb, 1996 - No. 3, Apr, 1996 ($2.25, limited series)
1-3: Dixon scripts in all. 2-Killer Croc-c/app. 4.00

MAN-BAT
DC Comics: Jun, 2006 - No. 5, Oct, 2006 ($2.99, limited series)
1-5: Bruce Jones-s/Mike Huddleston-a/c. 1-Hush app. 3.00

MAN-BAT
DC Comics: Apr, 2021 - No. 5, ($3.99, limited series)
1-Dave Wielgosz-s/Sumit Kumar-a; covers by Hotz & Nowlan 4.00

MAN CALLED A-X, THE
Malibu Comics (Bravura): Nov, 1994 - No. 4, Jun, 1995 ($2.95, limited series)
0-4: Marv Wolfman scripts & Shawn McManus-c/a. 0-(2/95). 1-"1A" on cover 3.00

MAN CALLED A-X, THE
DC Comics: Oct, 1997 - No. 8, May, 1998 ($2.50)
1-8: Marv Wolfman scripts & Shawn McManus-c/a. 3.00

MAN CALLED KEV, A (See The Authority)
DC Comics (WildStorm): Sept, 2006 - No. 5, Feb, 2007 ($2.99, limited series)
1-5-Ennis-s/Ezquerra-a/Fabry-c 3.00
TPB (2007, $14.99) r/#1-5; cover gallery 15.00

MAN COMICS
Marvel/Atlas Comics (NPI): Dec, 1949 - No. 28, Sept, 1953 (#1-6: 52 pgs.)

	GD	VG	FN	VF	VF/NM	NM-
1-Tuska-a	39	78	117	231	378	525
2-Tuska-a	20	40	60	118	192	265
3-6	16	32	48	98	154	210
7,8	15	30	45	92	144	195
9-13,15: 9-Format changes to war	15	30	45	92	144	195
14-Henkel (3 pgs.); Pakula-a	15	30	45	94	147	200
16-21,23-28: 28-Crime issue (Bob Brant)	15	30	45	88	137	185
22-Krigstein-a, 5 pgs.	16	32	48	98	154	210

NOTE: ***Berg** a-14, 15, 19. **Colan** a-9, 13, 21, 23. **Everett** a-8, 22; c-22, 25. **Heath** a-11, 13, 16, 17, 21. **Henkel** a-7. Kubertish a-by **Bob Brown**-3. **Maneely** a-5, 11-13; c-5, 10, 11, 16. **Reinman** a-11. **Robinson** a-7, 10, 14. **Robert Sale** a-9, 11. **Sinnott** a-22, 23. **Tuska** a-14, 23.*

MANDRAKE THE MAGICIAN (See Defenders Of The Earth, 123, 46, 52, 55, Giant Comic Album, King Comics, Magic Comics, The Phantom #21, Tiny Tot Funnies & Wow Comics, '36)

MANDRAKE THE MAGICIAN (See Harvey Comics Hits #53)
David McKay Publ./Dell/King Comics (All 12¢): 1938 - 1948; Sept, 1966 - No. 10, Nov, 1967

	GD	VG	FN	VF	VF/NM	NM-
Feature Books 18,19,23 (1938)	110	220	330	704	1202	1700
Feature Books 46	60	120	180	381	653	925
Feature Books 52,55	54	108	162	343	574	825
Four Color 752 (11/56)	10	20	30	70	150	230
1-Begin S.O.S. Phantom, ends #3	7	14	21	46	86	125
2-7,9: 4-Girl Phantom app. 5-Flying Saucer-c/story. 5,6-Brick Bradford app. 7-Origin Lothar. 9-Brick Bradford app.	4	8	12	23	37	50
8-Jeff Jones-a (4 pgs.)	4	8	12	25	40	55
10-Rip Kirby app.; Raymond-a (14 pgs.)	4	8	12	28	47	65

MANDRAKE THE MAGICIAN
Marvel Comics: Apr, 1995 - No. 2, May, 1995 ($2.95, unfinished limited series)
1,2: Mike Barr scripts 3.00

MAN-EATERS
Image Comics: Sept, 2018 - Present ($3.99)
1-12-Chelsea Cain-s/Kate Niemczyk-a 4.00
...: Tomorrow Belongs to You! (3/20, $4.99) 5.00

MAN-EATING COW (See Tick #7,8)
New England Comics: July, 1992 - No. 10, 1994? ($2.75, B&W, limited series)
1-10 3.00

Manhunt! #4 © ME

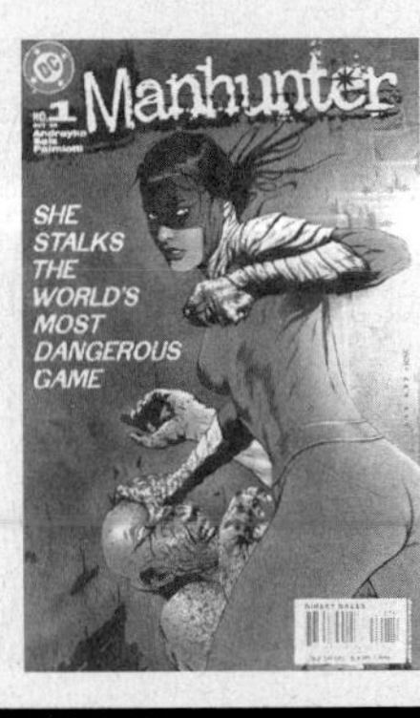

Manhunter (2004 series) #1 © DC

Manifest Destiny #36 © Skybound

	GD	VG	FN	VF	VF/NM	NM-
	2.0	4.0	6.0	8.0	9.0	9.2

Man-Eating Cow Bonanza (6/96, $4.95, 128 pgs.)-r/#1-4. 5.00

MAN FROM ATLANTIS (TV)
Marvel Comics: Feb, 1978 - No. 7, Aug, 1978

1-(84 pgs.)-Sutton-a(p), Buscema-c; origin & cast photos 2 4 6 13 18 22
2-7 6.00

MAN FROM PLANET X, THE
Planet X Productions: 1987 (no price; probably unlicensed)

1-Reprints Fawcett Movie Comic 4.00

MAN FROM U.N.C.L.E., THE (TV) (Also see The Girl From Uncle)
Gold Key: Feb, 1965 - No. 22, Apr, 1969 (All photo-c)

1 13 26 39 91 201 310
2-Photo back c-2-8 7 14 21 44 82 120
3-10: 7-Jet Dream begins (1st app., also see Jet Dream) (all new stories) 5 10 15 33 57 80
11-22: 19-Last 12¢ issue. 21,22-Reprint #10 & 7 5 10 15 30 50 70

MAN FROM U.N.C.L.E., THE (TV)
Entertainment Publishing: 1987 - No. 11 ($1.50/$1.75, B&W)

1-7 ($1.50), 8-11 ($1.75) 4.00

MAN FROM WELLS FARGO (TV)
Dell Publishing Co.: No. 1287, Feb-Apr, 1962 - May-July, 1962 (Photo-c)

Four Color 1287, #01-495-207 6 12 18 40 73 105

MANGA DARKCHYLDE (Also see Darkchylde titles)
Dark Horse Comics: Feb, 2005 - No. 5 ($2.99, limited series)

1,2-Randy Queen-s/a; manga-style pre-teen Ariel Chylde 3.00

MANGA SHI (See Tomoe)
Crusade Entertainment: Aug, 1996 ($2.95)

1-Printed back to front (manga-style) 3.00

MANGA SHI 2000
Crusade Entertainment: Feb, 1997 - No. 3, June, 1997 ($2.95, mini-series)

1-3: 1-Two covers 3.00

MANHATTAN PROJECTS, THE
Image Comics: Mar, 2012 - No. 25, Nov, 2014 ($3.50)

1-Hickman-s/Pitarra-a; intro. Robert and Joseph Oppenheimer 40.00
2 20.00
3 10.00
4-6 8.00
7-25: 10,15,19-Browne-a 4.00

MANHATTAN PROJECTS, THE : THE SUN BEYOND THE STARS
Image Comics: Mar, 2015 - No. 4, Feb, 2016 ($3.50)

1-4-Hickman-s/Pitarra-a 3.50

MANHUNT! (Becomes Red Fox #15 on)
Magazine Enterprises: 10/47 - No. 11, 8/48; No. 12 (no date); No. 13,14, 1953

1-Red Fox by L. B. Cole, Undercover Girl by Whitney, Space Ace begin (1st app.); negligee panels 103 206 309 659 1130 1600
2-Electrocution-c 123 246 369 787 1344 1900
3-5 52 104 156 328 552 775
6-Bondage, torture-c 65 130 195 416 708 1000
7-10: 7-Space Ace ends. 8-Trail Colt begins (intro/1st app., 5/48) by Guardineer; Trail Colt-c. 10-G. Ingels-a 40 80 120 246 411 575
11(8/48)-Frazetta-a, 7 pgs.; The Duke, Scotland Yard begin 55 110 165 352 601 850
12 (no indicia, no date) Same content as Trail Colt nn (A-1 #24); 7 pg. Frazetta-a which were reprinted in Manhunt! #13; Undercover Girl app.; The Red Fox by L.B. Cole; Whitney-c/a; published in Canada 456 912 1368 3329 5765 8200
13(A-1 #63)-Frazetta, r-/Trail Colt #1, 7 pgs. 45 90 135 284 480 675
14(A-1 #77)-Bondage/hypo-c; last L. B. Cole Red Fox; Ingels-a 258 516 774 1651 2826 4000

NOTE: ***Guardineer** a-1-5; c-8. **Paul Parker** c-9, 11. **Whitney** a-2-14; c-1-6, 10, 12. Red Fox by **L. B. Cole**-#1-14. #15 was advertised but came out as Red Fox #15.*

MANHUNTER (See Adventure #58, 73, Brave & the Bold, Detective Comics, 1st Issue Special, House of Mystery #143 and Justice League of America)
DC Comics: 1984 ($2.50, 76 pgs; high quality paper)

1-Simonson-c/a(r)/Detective; Batman app. 5.00

MANHUNTER
DC Comics: July, 1988 - No. 24, Apr, 1990 ($1.00)

1-24: 8,9-Flash app. 9-Invasion. 17-Batman-c/sty 4.00

	GD	VG	FN	VF	VF/NM	NM-
	2.0	4.0	6.0	8.0	9.0	9.2

MANHUNTER
DC Comics: No. 0, Nov, 1994 - No. 12, Nov, 1995 ($1.95/$2.25)

0-12 4.00

MANHUNTER (Also see Batman: Streets of Gotham)
DC Comics: Oct, 2004 - No. 38, Mar, 2009 ($2.50/$2.99)

1-21: 1-Intro. Kate Spencer; Saiz-a/Jae Lee-c/Andreyko-s. 2,3 Shadow Thief app. 13,14-Omac x-over. 20-One Year Later 3.00
22-30: 22-Begin $2.99-c. 23-Sandra Knight app. 27-Chaykin-c. 28-Batman app. 3.00
31-38: 31-(8/08) Gaydos-a. 33,34-Suicide Squad app. 3.00
...: Forgotten (2009, $17.99) r/#31-38 18.00
...: Origins (2007, $17.99) r/#15-23 18.00
...: Street Justice (2005, $12.99) r/#1-5; Andreyko intro. 13.00
...: Trial By Fire (2007, $17.99) r/#6-14 18.00
...: Unleashed (2008, $17.99) r/#24-30 18.00

MANHUNTER: ...
DC Comics: 1979, 1999

The Complete Saga TPB (1979) Reprints stories from Detective Comics #437-443 by Goodwin and Simonson 40.00
The Special Edition TPB (1999, $9.95) r/stories from Detective Comics #437-443 12.00

MANHUNTER SPECIAL (Jack Kirby 100th Birthday tribute)
DC Comics: Oct, 2017 ($4.99, one-shot)

1-Paul Kirk Manhunter & Sandman and Sandy app.; Giffen-s/Buckingham-a; Demon back-up w/Rude-a; bonus Kirby reprint from Tales of the Unexpected #13; Bruce Timm-c 5.00

MANIAC OF NEW YORK
AfterShock Comics: Feb, 2021 - Present ($4.99/$3.99)

1-($4.99) Elliot Kalan-s/Andrea Mutti-a 5.00

MANIFEST DESTINY
Image Comics (Skybound): Nov, 2013 - Present ($2.99/$3.99)

1-Lewis & Clark in 1804 American Frontier encountering zombies & other creatures; Chris Dingess-s/Matthew Roberts-a 3 6 9 16 24 32
2 1 3 4 6 8 10
3-30: 25-Back-up Sacagawea story 3.00
31-42-($3.99) 4.00

MANIFEST ETERNITY
DC Comics: Aug, 2006 - No. 6, Jan, 2007 ($2.99)

1-6-Lobdell-s/Nguyen-a/c 3.00

MAN IN BLACK (See Thrill-O-Rama) (Also see All New Comics, Front Page, Green Hornet #31, Strange Story & Tally-Ho Comics)
Harvey Publications: Sept, 1957 - No. 4, Mar, 1958

1-Bob Powell-c/a 20 40 60 115 188 260
2-4: Powell-c/a 15 30 45 83 124 165

MAN IN BLACK
Lorne-Harvey Publications (Recollections): 1990 - No. 2, July, 1991 (B&W)

1,2 4.00

MAN IN FLIGHT (Disney, TV)
Dell Publishing Co.: No. 836, Sept, 1957

Four Color 836 6 12 18 41 76 110

MAN IN SPACE (Disney, TV, see Dell Giant #27)
Dell Publishing Co.: No. 716, Aug, 1956 - No. 954, Nov, 1958

Four Color 716-A science feat. from Tomorrowland 7 14 21 49 92 135
Four Color 954-Satellites 6 12 18 41 76 110

MANKIND (WWF Wrestling)
Chaos Comics: Sept, 1999 ($2.95, one-shot)

1-Regular and photo-c 5.00
1-Premium Edition ($10.00) Dwayne Turner & Danny Miki-c 10.00

MANN AND SUPERMAN
DC Comics: 2000 ($5.95, prestige format, one-shot)

nn-Michael T. Gilbert-s/a 6.00

MANN'S WORLD
AWA Studios: Jan, 2021 - No. 5 ($3.99, limited series)

1,2-Victor Gischler-s/Niko Walter-a 4.00

MAN OF STEEL, THE (Also see Superman: The Man of Steel)
DC Comics: 1986 (June release) - No. 6, 1986 (75¢, limited series)

1-6: 1-Silver logo; Byrne-c/a/scripts in all; origin, 1-Alternate-c for newsstand sales,1-Distr. to toy stores by So Much Fun, 2-6: 2-Intro. Lois Lane, Jimmy Olsen. 3-Intro/origin Magpie;

Manor Black #1 © Bunn, Hurtt & Crook

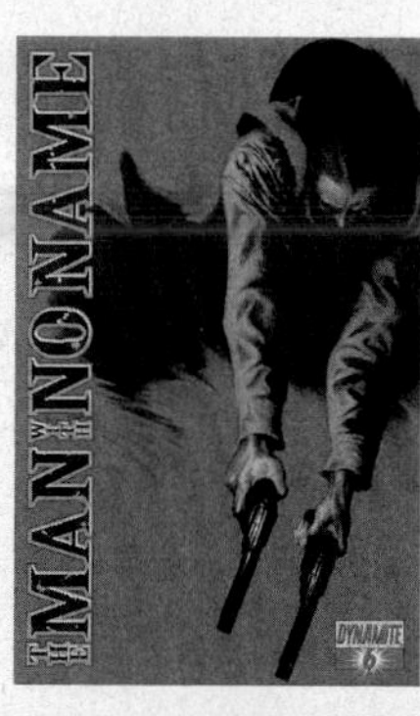

The Man With No Name #6 © MGM

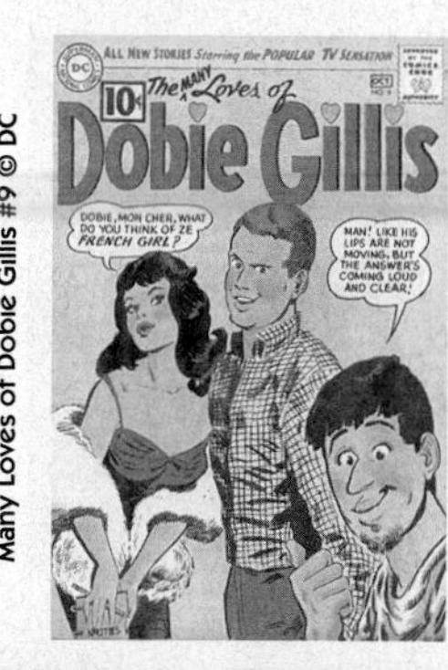

Many Loves of Dobie Gillis #9 © DC

GD VG FN VF VF/NM NM-
2.0 4.0 6.0 8.0 9.0 9.2

Batman-c/story. 4-Intro. new Lex Luthor 1 2 3 5 6 8
1-6-Silver Editions (1993, $1.95)-r/1-6 3.00
...The Complete Saga nn (SC)-Contains #1-6, given away in contest; limited edition 4 8 12 28 47 65
NOTE: *Issues 1-6 were released between Action #583 (9/86) & Action #584 (1/87) plus Superman #423 (9/86) & Advs. of Superman #424 (1/87).*

MAN OF STEEL, THE (Also see Action Comics #1000)(Leads into Superman #1)
DC Comics: Jul, 2018 - No. 6, Sept, 2018 ($3.99, weekly limited series)
1-6-Bendis-s; Rogol Zaar app.; interlocking covers by Reis. 1-Reis-a; intro. Melody Moore. 2-Shaner & Rude-a. 3-Sook-a. 4-Maguire-a. 5-Hughes-a. 6-Fabok-a 4.00

MAN OF THE ATOM (See Solar, Man of the Atom Vol. 2)

MAN OF WAR (See Liberty Guards & Liberty Scouts)
Centaur Publications: Nov, 1941 - No. 2, Jan, 1942
1-The Fire-Man, Man of War, The Sentinel, Liberty Guards, & Vapo-Man begin; Gustavson-c/a; Flag-c 222 444 666 1422 2436 3450
2-Intro The Ferret; Gustavson-c/a 164 328 492 1052 1801 2550

MAN OF WAR
Eclipse Comics: Aug, 1987 - No. 3, Feb, 1988 ($1.75, Baxter paper)
1-3: Bruce Jones scripts 3.00

MAN OF WAR (See The Protectors)
Malibu Comics: 1993 - No. 8, Feb, 1994 ($1.95/$2.50/$2.25)
1-5 ($1.95)-Newsstand Editions w/different-c 3.00
1-8: 1-5-Collector's Edi. w/poster. 6-8 ($2.25): 6-Polybagged w/Skycap. 8-Vs. Rocket Rangers 4.00

MAN O' MARS
Fiction House Magazines: 1953; 1964
1-Space Rangers; Whitman-c 116 232 348 742 1271 1800
I.W. Reprint #1-r/Man O'Mars #1 & Star Pirate; Murphy Anderson-a 7 14 21 46 86 125

MANOR BLACK
Dark Horse Comics: Jul, 2019 - No. 4, Oct, 2019 ($3.99, limited series)
1-4-Cullen Bunn & Brian Hurtt-s/Tyler Crook-a 4.00

MANTECH ROBOT WARRIORS
Archie Enterprises, Inc.: Sept, 1984 - No. 4, Apr, 1985 (75¢)
1-4: Ayers-c/a(p). 1-Buckler-c(i) 4.00

MAN-THING (See Fear, Giant-Size..., Marvel Comics Presents, Marvel Fanfare, Monsters Unleashed, Power Record Comics & Savage Tales)
Marvel Comics Group: Jan, 1974 - No. 22, Oct, 1975; V2#1, Nov, 1979 - V2#11, July, 1981
1-Howard the Duck(2nd app.) cont'd/Fear #19 8 16 24 52 99 145
2 3 6 9 20 31 42
3-1st app. original Foolkiller 3 6 9 16 23 30
4-Origin Foolkiller; last app. 1st Foolkiller 3 6 9 15 22 28
5-11-Ploog-a. 11-Foolkiller cameo (flashback) 3 6 9 14 20 26
12-22: 19-1st app. Scavenger. 20-Spidey cameo. 21-Origin Scavenger, Man-Thing. 22-Howard the Duck cameo 2 4 6 9 13 16
V2#1(1979) 2 4 6 11 16 20
V2#2-11: 4-Dr. Strange-c/app. 11-Mayerik-a 6.00
NOTE: ***Alcala** a-14. **Brunner** c-1. **J. Buscema** a-12p, 13p, 16p. **Gil Kane** c-4p, 10p, 12-20p, 21. **Mooney** a-17, 18, 19p, 20-22, V2#1-3p. **Ploog** Man-Thing-5p, 6p, 7, 8, 9-11p; c-5, 6, 8, 9, 11. **Sutton** a-13i. No. 19 says #10 in indicia.*

MAN-THING (Volume Three, continues in Strange Tales #1 (9/98))
Marvel Comics: Dec, 1997 - No. 8, July, 1998 ($2.99)
1-8-DeMatteis-s/Sharp-a. 2-Two covers. 6-Howard the Duck-c/app. 4.00

MAN-THING (Prequel to 2005 movie)
Marvel Comics: Sept, 2004 - No. 3, Nov, 2004 ($2.99, limited series)
1-3-Hans Rodionoff-s/Kyle Hotz-a 3.00
...: Whatever Knows Fear... (2005, $12.99, TPB) r/#1-3, Savage Tales #1, Adv. Into Fear #16 13.00

MAN-THING
Marvel Comics: May, 2017 - No. 5, Aug, 2017 ($3.99, limited series)
1-5-R.L. Stein-s/German Peralta-a; back-up horror short stories; Stein-s. 1-Origin re-told 4.00

MANTLE
Image Comics: May, 2015 - No. 5, Sept, 2015 ($3.99, limited series)
1-5-Brisson-s/Level-a 4.00

MANTRA
Malibu Comics (Ultraverse): July, 1993 - No. 24, Aug, 1995 ($1.95/$2.50)
1-Polybagged w/trading card & coupon 5.00
1-Newsstand edition w/o trading card or coupon 3.00
1-Full cover holographic edition 2 4 6 8 10 12
1-Ultra-limited silver foil-c 1 2 3 5 6 8
2,3,5-9,11-24: 2-($2.50-Newsstand edition bagged w/card. 3-Intro Warstrike & Kismet. 6-Break-Thru x-over. 7-Prime app.; origin Prototype by Jurgens/Austin (2 pgs.). 11-New costume. 17-Intro NecroMantra & Pinnacle; prelude to Godwheel 3.00
4-($2.50, 48 pgs.)-Rune flip-c/story by B. Smith (3 pgs.) 4.00
10-($3.50, 68 pgs.)-Flip-c w/Ultraverse Premiere #2 4.00
Giant Size 1 (7/94, $2.50, 44 pgs.) 4.00
...Spear of Destiny 1,2 (4/95, $2.50, 36pgs.) 3.00

MANTRA (2nd Series) (Also See Black September)
Malibu Comics (Ultraverse): Infinity, Sept, 1995 - No. 7, Apr, 1996 ($1.50)
Infinity (9/95, $1.50)-Black September x-over, Intro new Mantra 3.00
1-7: 1-(10/95). 5-Return of Eden (original Mantra). 6,7-Rush app. 3.00

MAN WHO F#&%ED UP TIME, THE
AfterShock Comics: Feb, 2020 - No. 5, Aug, 2020 ($3.99, limited series)
1-5-John Layman-s/Karl Mostert-a 4.00

MAN WITH NO NAME, THE (Based on the Clint Eastwood gunslinger character)
Dynamite Entertainment: 2008 - No. 11, 2009 ($3.50)
1-11: 1-Gage-s/Dias-a/Isanove-c. 7-Bernard-a 3.50

MAN WITHOUT FEAR (Follows Daredevil #612)
Marvel Comics: Mar, 2019 - No. 5, Mar, 2019 ($3.99, weekly limited series)
1-5-Jed McKay-s/Kyle Hotz-c. 1,5-Beyruth-a. 3-Defenders app. 4-Kingpin app. 4.00

MAN WITH THE SCREAMING BRAIN (Based on screenplay by Bruce Campbell & David Goodman)
Dark Horse Comics: Apr, 2005 - No. 4, July, 2005 ($2.99, limited series)
1-4-Campbell & Goodman-s; Remender-a/c. 1-Variant-c by Noto. 3-Powell var-c. 4-Mignola var-c 3.00
TPB (11/05, $13.95) r/#1-4; David Goodman intro.; cover gallery 14.00

MAN WITH THE X-RAY EYES, THE (See X,... under Movie Comics)

MANY GHOSTS OF DR. GRAVES, THE (Doctor Graves #73 on)
Charlton Comics: 5/67 - No. 60, 12/76; No. 61, 9/77 - No. 62, 10/77; No. 63, 2/78 - No. 65, 4/78; No. 66, 6/81 - No. 72, 5/82
1-Ditko-a; Palais-a; early issues 12¢-c 8 16 24 54 102 150
2-6,8,10 3 6 9 19 30 40
7,9-Ditko-a 4 8 12 23 37 50
11-13,16-18-Ditko-c/a 3 6 9 19 30 40
14,19,23,25 2 4 6 10 14 18
15,20,21-Ditko-a 3 6 9 14 20 25
22,24,26,27,29-35,38,40-Ditko-c/a 3 6 9 15 22 28
28-Ditko-c 3 6 9 14 20 25
36,46,56,57,59,61,66,67,69,71 2 4 6 8 10 12
37,41,43,51,60-Ditko-a 2 4 6 9 13 16
39,58-Ditko-c. 39-Sutton-a. 58-Ditko-a 2 4 6 9 13 16
42,44,53-Sutton-c; Ditko-a. 42-Sutton-a 2 4 6 9 13 16
45-(5/74) 2nd Newton comic work (8 pgs.); new logo; Sutton-c 2 4 6 11 16 20
47-Newton, Sutton, Ditko-a 2 4 6 10 14 18
48-Ditko, Sutton-a 2 4 6 9 13 16
49-Newton-c/a; Sutton-a. 2 4 6 8 11 14
50-Sutton-a 2 4 6 8 10 12
52-Newton-c; Ditko-a 2 4 6 9 13 16
54-Early Byrne-c; Ditko-a 2 4 6 10 14 18
55-Ditko-c; Sutton-a 2 4 6 9 13 16
62-65,68-Ditko-c/a. 65-Sutton-a 2 4 6 11 16 20
70,72-Ditko-a 2 4 6 10 14 18
Modern Comics Reprint 12,25 (1978) 6.00
NOTE: ***Aparo** a-4, 5, 7, 8, 66r, 69r; c-8, 14, 19, 66r, 67r. **Byrne** c-54. **Ditko** a-1, 7, 9, 11-13, 15-18, 20-22, 24, 26, 27, 29, 30-35, 37, 38, 40-44, 47, 48, 51-54, 58, 60r-65r, 70, 72; c-11-13, 16-18, 22, 24, 26-35, 38, 40, 55, 58, 62-65. **Howard** a-38, 39, 45i, 65; c-48. **Kim** a-36, 46, 52. **Larson** a-58. **Morisi** a-13, 14, 23, 26. **Newton** a-45, 47p, 49p; c-49, 52. **Staton** a-36, 37, 41, 43. **Sutton** a-39, 42, 47-50, 55, 65; c-42, 44, 45; painted c-53. **Zeck** a-56, 59.*

MANY LOVES OF DOBIE GILLIS (TV)
National Periodical Publications: May-June, 1960 - No. 26, Oct, 1964
1-Most covers by Bob Oskner 27 54 81 194 435 675
2-5 15 30 45 105 233 360
6-10: 10-Last 10¢-c 11 22 33 72 154 235
11-26: 20-Drucker-a. 24-(3-4/64). 25-(9/64) 9 18 27 63 129 195

MANY WORLDS OF TESLA STRONG, THE (Also see Tom Strong)
America's Best Comics: July, 2003 ($5.95, one-shot)
1-Two covers by Timm & Art Adams; art by various incl. Campbell, Cho, Noto, Hughes 6.00

MARA

Marauders #3 © MAR

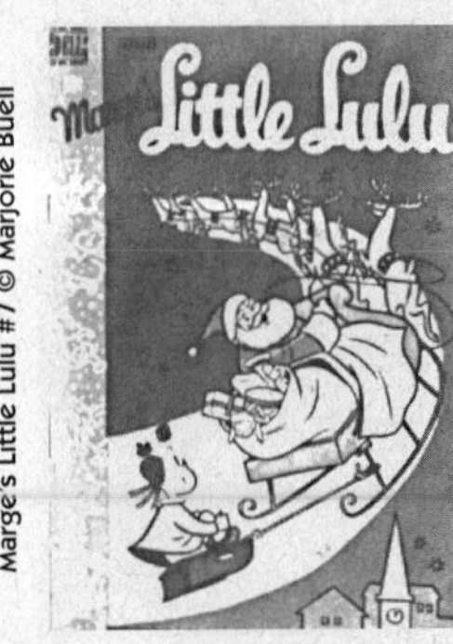

Marge's Little Lulu #7 © Marjorie Buell

Margie Comics #36 © MAR

	GD 2.0	VG 4.0	FN 6.0	VF 8.0	VF/NM 9.0	NM- 9.2

Image Comics: Dec, 2012 - No. 6, Oct, 2013 ($2.99)

1-6-Brian Wood-s/Ming Doyle-a 3.00

MARAUDERS
Marvel Comics: Dec, 2019 - Present ($4.99/$3.99)

1-($4.99) Duggan-s/Lolli-a; Kitty Pryde, Storm, Iceman, Emma Frost, Pyro app. 5.00
2-12-($3.99) 2-Kate becomes the Red Queen. 3-Shinobi Shaw returns 4.00
13-($4.99) "X of Swords" tie-in; Black Panther and Shuri app. 5.00
14-18: 14,15- "X of Swords" tie-ins 4.00

MARAUDER'S MOON (See Luke Short, Four Color #848)

MARCH OF COMICS (See Promotional Comics section)

MARCH OF CRIME (Formerly My Love Affair #1-6) (See Fox Giants)
Fox Feature Synd.: No. 7, July, 1950 - No. 2, Sept, 1950; No. 3, Sept, 1951

7(#1)(7/50)-True crime stories; Wood-a 47 94 141 296 498 700
2(9/50)-Wood-a (exceptional) 43 86 129 271 461 650
3(9/51) 24 48 72 142 234 325

MARCO POLO (Also see Classic Comics #27
Charlton Comics Group: 1962 (Movie classic)

nn (Scarce)-Glanzman-c/a (25 pgs.) 11 22 33 73 157 240

MARC SILVESTRI SKETCHBOOK
Image Comics (Top Cow): Jan, 2004 ($2.99, one-shot)

1-Character sketches, concept artwork, storyboards of Witchblade, Darkness & others 3.00

MARC SPECTOR: MOON KNIGHT (Also see Moon Knight)
Marvel Comics: June, 1989 - No. 60, Mar, 1994 ($1.50/$1.75, direct sales)

1 2 4 6 10 14 18
2-24,26-49,51-54,58,59: 4-Intro new Midnight. 8,9-Punisher app. 15-Silver Sable app. 19-21-Spider-Man & Punisher app. 32,33-Hobgoblin II (Macendale) & Spider-Man (in black costume) app. 35-38-Punisher story. 42-44-Infinity War x-over. 46-Demogoblin app. 51,53-Gambit app. 55-New look. 57-Spider-Man-c/story. 60-Moon Knight dies 4.00
25,50: 25-(52 pgs.)-Ghost Rider app. 50-(56 pgs.)-Special die-cut-c 5.00
55-New look; Platt-c/a 5 10 15 33 57 80
56,60-Platt-c/a 2 4 6 13 18 22
57-Spider-Man-c/app.; Platt-c/a 5 10 15 34 60 85
58,59-Platt-c 2 4 6 8 10 12
...: Divided We Fall ($4.95, 52 pgs.) 5.00
Special 1 (1992, $2.50) 5.00
NOTE: *Cowan c(p) 20-23. Guice c-20. Heath c/a-4. Platt-a 55-57,60; c-55-60.*

MARGARET O'BRIEN (See The Adventures of...)

MARGE'S LITTLE LULU (Continues as Little Lulu from #207 on)
Dell Publishing Co./Gold Key #165-206: No. 74, 6/45 - No. 164, 7-9/62; No. 165, 10/62 - No. 206, 8/72

Marjorie Henderson **Buell**, born in Philadelphia, Pa., in 1904, created Little Lulu, a cartoon character that appeared weekly in the Saturday Evening Post from Feb. 23, 1935 through Dec. 30, 1944. She was not responsible for any of the comic books. **John Stanley** did pencils only on all Little Lulu comics through at least #135 (1959). He did pencils and inks on Four Color #74 & 97. **Irving Tripp** began inking stories from #1 on, and remained the comic's illustrator throughout its entire run. **Stanley** did storyboards (layouts), pencils, and scripts in all cases and inking only on covers. His word balloons were written in cursive. **Tripp** and occasionally other artists at Western Publ. in Poughkeepsie, N.Y. blew up the pencilled pages, inked the blowups, and lettered them. **Arnold Drake** did storyboards, pencils and scripts starting with #197 (1970) on, amidst reprinted issues. **Buell** sold her rights exclusively to Western Publ. in Dec., 1971. The earlier issues had to be approved by **Buell** prior to publication.

Four Color 74('45)-Intro Lulu, Tubby & Alvin 186 372 558 1535 3468 5400
Four Color 97(2/46) 70 140 210 560 1255 1950
(Above two books are all John Stanley - cover, pencils, and inks.)
Four Color 110('46)-1st Alvin Story Telling Time; 1st app. Willy; variant cover exists 44 88 132 326 738 1150
Four Color 115-1st app. Boys' Clubhouse 41 82 123 303 689 1075
Four Color 120, 131: 120-1st app. Eddie 36 72 108 259 580 900
Four Color 139('47),146,158 34 68 102 245 548 850
Four Color 165 (10/47)-Smokes doll hair & has wild hallucinations. 1st Tubby detective story 36 72 108 259 580 900
1(1-2/48)-Lulu's Diary feature begins 76 152 228 616 1333 2050
2-1st app. Gloria; 1st app. Miss Feeny 31 62 93 223 499 775
3-5 27 54 81 194 435 675
6-10: 7-1st app. Annie; Xmas-c 21 42 63 150 330 510
11-20: 18-X-Mas-c. 19-1st app. Wilbur. 20-1st app. Mr. McNabbem 17 34 51 114 252 390
21-30: 26-r/F.C. 110. 30-Xmas-c 15 30 45 100 220 340
31-38,40: 35-1st Mumday story 12 24 36 81 176 270
39-Intro. Witch Hazel in "That Awful Witch Hazel" 12 24 36 82 179 275
41-60: 42-Xmas-c. 45-2nd Witch Hazel app. 49-Gives Stanley & others credit 10 20 30 69 147 225
61-80: 63-1st app. Chubby (Tubby's cousin). 68-1st app. Prof. Cleff. 78-Xmas-c. 80-Intro. Little Itch (2/55) 9 18 27 57 111 165
81-99: 90-Xmas-c 7 14 21 46 86 125
100 7 14 21 49 92 135
101-130: 123-1st app. Fifi 6 12 18 37 66 95
131-164: 135-Last Stanley-p 5 10 15 33 57 80
165-Giant; ...in Paris ('62) 9 18 27 61 123 185
166-Giant; ...Christmas Diary (1962 - '63) 9 18 27 61 123 185
167-169 4 8 12 28 47 65
170,172,175,176,178-196,198-200-Stanley-r. 182-1st app. Little Scarecrow Boy 3 6 9 17 26 35
171,173,174,177,197 3 6 9 16 23 30
201,203,206-Last issue to carry Marge's name 3 6 9 14 20 26
202,204,205-Stanley-r 3 6 9 16 23 30
...Summer Camp 1(8/67-G.K.-Giant) '57-58-r 5 10 15 35 63 90
...Trick 'N' Treat 1(12¢)(12/62-Gold Key) 6 12 18 40 73 105
Marge's Lulu and Tubby in Japan (15¢)(5-7/62) 01476-207 7 14 21 48 89 130
NOTE: *See Dell Giant Comics #23, 29, 36, 42, 50, & Dell Giants for annuals. All Giants not by Stanley from L.L. on Vacation (7/54) on. Irving Tripp a-#1-on. Christmas c-7, 18, 30, 42, 78, 90, 126, 166, 250. Summer Camp issues #173, 177, 181, 189, 197, 201, 206.*

MARGE'S LITTLE LULU (See Golden Comics Digest #19, 23, 27, 29, 33, 36, 40, 43, 46, & March of Comics #251, 267, 275, 293, 307, 323, 335, 349, 355, 369, 385, 406, 417, 427, 439, 456, 468, 475, 488)

MARGE'S TUBBY (Little Lulu)(See Dell Giants)
Dell Publishing Co./Gold Key: No. 381, Aug, 1952 - No. 49, Dec-Feb, 1961-62

Four Color 381(#1)-Stanley script; Irving Tripp-a 19 38 57 129 287 445
Four Color 430,444-Stanley-a 11 22 33 73 157 240
Four Color 461 (4/53)-1st Tubby & Men From Mars story; Stanley-a 10 20 30 68 144 220
5 (7-9/53)-Stanley-a 8 16 24 54 102 150
6-10 7 14 21 44 82 120
11-20 5 10 15 34 60 85
21-30 5 10 15 30 50 70
31-49 4 8 12 27 44 60
...& the Little Men From Mars No. 30020-410(10/64-G.K.)-25¢, 68 pgs. 7 14 21 44 82 120
NOTE: ***John Stanley** did all storyboards & scripts through at least #35 (1959). **Lloyd White** did all art except F.C. 381, 430, 444, 461 & #5.*

MARGIE (See My Little...)

MARGIE (TV)
Dell Publ. Co.: No. 1307, Mar-May, 1962 - No. 2, July-Sept, 1962 (Photo-c)

Four Color 1307(#1) 6 12 18 42 79 115
2 4 8 12 28 47 65

MARGIE COMICS (Formerly Comedy Comics; Reno Browne #50 on)
(Also see Cindy Comics & Teen Comics)
Marvel Comics (ACI): No. 35, Winter, 1946-47 - No. 49, Dec, 1949

35 36 72 108 211 343 475
36-38,42,45,47-49 19 38 57 111 176 240
39,41,43(2),44,46-Kurtzman's "Hey Look" 20 40 60 114 182 250
40-Three "Hey Looks", three "Giggles 'n' Grins" by Kurtzman 20 40 60 120 195 270

MARINEMAN (Ian Churchill's...)
Image Comics: Dec, 2010 - No. 6, Jun, 2011 ($3.99/$4.99)

1-5-Ian Churchill-s/a/c 4.00
6-($4.99) Origin revealed 5.00

MARINES (See Tell It to the...)

MARINES ATTACK
Charlton Comics: Aug, 1964 - No. 9, Feb-Mar, 1966

1-Glanzman-a begins 4 8 12 25 40 55
2-9: 8-1st Vietnam war-c/story 3 6 9 17 25 34

MARINES AT WAR (Formerly Tales of the Marines #4)
Atlas Comics (OPI): No. 5, Apr, 1957 - No. 7, Aug, 1957

5-7 15 30 45 88 137 185
NOTE: ***Colan** a-5. **Drucker** a-5. **Everett** a-5. **Maneely** a-5. **Orlando** a-7. **Severin** c-5.*

MARINES IN ACTION
Atlas News Co.: June, 1955 - No. 14, Sept, 1957

1-Rock Murdock, Boot Camp Brady begin 23 46 69 136 223 310
2-14 15 30 45 88 137 185
NOTE: ***Berg** a-2, 8, 9, 11, 14. **Heath** c-2, 9. **Maneely** c-1, 3. **Severin** a-4; c-7-11, 14.*

MARINES IN BATTLE
Atlas Comics (ACI No. 1-12/WPI No. 13-25): Aug, 1954 - No. 25, Sept, 1958

1-Heath-c; Iron Mike McGraw by Heath; history of U.S. Marine Corps. begins

The Marked #8 © Anomaly Prods.

Married With Children #1 © ELP

Mars Attacks Popeye © Topps

GD 2.0 | VG 4.0 | FN 6.0 | VF 8.0 | VF/NM 9.0 | NM- 9.2

37 74 111 222 361 500
2-Heath-c 20 40 60 114 182 250
3-6,8-10: 4-Last precode (2/55); Romita-a 15 30 45 88 137 185
7-Kubert/Moskowitz-a (6 pgs.) 15 30 45 90 140 190
11-16,18-21,24 15 30 45 85 130 175
17-Williamson-a (3 pgs.) 15 30 45 92 144 195
22,25-Torres-a 15 30 45 85 130 175
23-Crandall-a; Mark Murdock app. 15 30 45 86 133 180
NOTE: ***Berg*** *a-22.* ***G. Colan*** *a-22, 23.* ***Drucker*** *a-6.* ***Everett*** *a-4, 15; c-21.* ***Heath*** *c-1, 2, 4.* ***Maneely*** *c-23, 24.* ***Orlando*** *a-14.* ***Pakula*** *a-6, 23.* ***Powell*** *a-16.* ***Severin*** *a-22; c-12.* ***Sinnott*** *a-23.* ***Tuska*** *a-15.*

MARINE WAR HEROES (Charlton Premiere #19 on)
Charlton Comics: Jan, 1964 - No. 18, Mar, 1967
1-Montes/Bache-c/a 4 8 12 27 44 60
2-16,18: 11-Vietnam sty w/VC tunnels & moles.14,18-Montes/Bache-a
3 6 9 16 23 30
17-Tojo's plan to bomb Pearl Harbor & 1st Atomic bomb blast on Japan
4 8 12 27 44 60

MARK, THE (Also see Mayhem)
Dark Horse Comics: Dec, 1993 - No. 4, Mar, 1994 ($2.50, limited series)
1-4 3.00

MARKED, THE
Image Comics (Shadowline): Oct, 2019 - Present ($3.99, limited series)
1-10: 1-Hine & Haberline-s/Haberline-a 4.00

MARK HAZZARD: MERC
Marvel Comics Group: Nov, 1986 - No. 12, Oct, 1987 (75¢)
1-12: Morrow-a 3.00
Annual 1 (11/87, $1.25) 4.00

MARK OF CHARON (See Negation)
CG Entertainment: Apr, 2003 - No. 5, Aug, 2003 ($2.95, limited series)
1-5-Bedard-s/Bennett-a 3.00

MARK OF ZORRO (See Zorro, Four Color #228)

MARK OF ZORRO, THE
American Mythology Prods.: 2019 ($3.99, one-shot)
1-Reprints Four Color #228 (5/49); Bill Ely-a 4.00

MARK 1 COMICS (Also see Shaloman)
Mark 1 Comics: Apr, 1988 - No. 3, Mar, 1989 ($1.50)
1-3: Early Shaloman app. 2-Origin 3.00

MARKSMAN, THE (Also see Champions)
Hero Comics: Jan, 1988 - No. 5, 1988 ($1.95)
1-5: 1-Rose begins. 1-3-Origin The Marksman 3.00
Annual 1 ('88, $2.75, 52 pgs.)-Champions app. 4.00

MARK TRAIL
Standard Magazines (Hall Syndicate)/Fawcett Publ. No. 5: Oct, 1955; No. 5, Summer, 1959
1(1955)-Sunday strip-r 8 16 24 40 50 60
5(1959) By Ed Dodd 5 10 15 22 26 30
...Adventure Book of Nature 1 (Summer, 1958, 25¢, Pines)-100 pg. Giant; Special Camp Issue; contains 78 Sunday strip-r by Ed Dodd 9 18 27 52 69 85

MARMADUKE MONK
I. W. Enterprises/Super Comics: No date; 1963 (10¢)
I.W. Reprint 1 (nd) 2 4 6 8 11 14
Super Reprint 14 (1963)-r/Monkeyshines Comics #? 2 4 6 8 10 12

MARMADUKE MOUSE
Quality Comics Group (Arnold Publ.): Spring, 1946 - No. 65, Dec, 1956 (Early issues: 52 pgs.)
1-Funny animal 20 40 60 115 188 260
2 12 24 36 69 97 125
3-10 10 20 30 56 76 95
11-30 8 16 24 42 54 65
31-65: Later issues are 36 pgs. 7 14 21 35 43 50
Super Reprint #14(1963) 2 4 6 9 12 15

MARQUIS, THE
Oni Press
...: A Sin of One ($2.99, 5/03) Guy Davis-s/a; Michael Gaydos-c 3.00
...: Intermezzo TPB ($11.95, 12/03) r/A Sin of One and Hell's Courtesan #1,2 12.00

MARQUIS, THE: DANSE MACABRE
Oni Press: May, 2000 - No. 5, Feb, 2001 ($2.95, B&W, limited series)
1-5-Guy Davis-s/a. 1-Wagner-c. 2-Mignola-c. 3-Vess-c. 5-K. Jones-c 3.00
TPB (8/2001, $18.95) r/1-5 & Les Preludes; Seagle intro. 19.00

MARQUIS, THE: DEVIL'S REIGN: HELL'S COURTESAN
Oni Press: Feb, 2002 - No. 2, Apr, 2002 ($2.95, B&W, limited series)
1,2-Guy Davis-s/a 3.00

MARRIAGE OF HERCULES AND XENA, THE
Topps Comics: July, 1998 ($2.95, one-shot)
1-Photo-c; Lopresti-a; Alex Ross pin-up, 1-Alex Ross painted-c 3.00
1-Gold foil logo-c 5.00

MARRIED ... WITH CHILDREN (TV)(Based on Fox TV show)
Now Comics: June, 1990 - No. 7, Feb, 1991(12/90 inside) ($1.75)
V2#1, Sept, 1991 - No. 7, Apr, 1992 ($1.95)
1 2 4 6 8 10 12
2-7: 2-Photo-c, 1,2-2nd printing, V2#2-7: 1,4,6-Photo-c 5.00
V2#1 1 3 4 6 8 10
...Buck's Tale (6/94, $1.95) 4.00
...1994 Annual nn (2/94, $2.50, 52 pgs.)-Flip book format 5.00
Special 1 (7/92, $1.95)-Kelly Bundy photo-c/poster 5.00

MARRIED ... WITH CHILDREN: KELLY BUNDY
Now Comics: Aug, 1992 - No. 3, Oct, 1992 ($1.95, limited series)
1-3: Kelly Bundy photo-c & poster in each 4.00

MARRIED ... WITH CHILDREN: QUANTUM QUARTET
Now Comics: Oct, 1993 - No. 4, 1994, ($1.95, limited series)
1-4: Fantastic Four parody 4.00

MARRIED ... WITH CHILDREN: 2099
Now Comics: June, 1993 - No. 3, Aug, 1993 ($1.95, limited series)
1-3 4.00

MARS
First Comics: Jan, 1984 - No. 12, Jan, 1985 ($1.00, Mando paper)
1-12: Marc Hempel & Mark Wheatley story & art. 2-The Black Flame begins. 10-Dynamo Joe begins 3.00
TPB (IDW Publ., 8/05, $39.99) r/#1-12, creator commentary; bonus art; new Hempel-c 40.00

MARS & BEYOND (Disney, TV)
Dell Publishing Co.: No. 866, Dec, 1957
Four Color 866-A Science feat. from Tomorrowland 8 16 24 52 99 145

MARS ATTACKS
Topps Comics: May, 1994 - No. 5, Sept, 1994 ($2.95, limited series)
1-5-Giffen story; flip books 2 4 6 8 10 12
Special Edition 2 4 6 9 12 15
Trade paperback (12/94, $12.95)-r/limited series plus new 8 pg. story 15.00

MARS ATTACKS
Topps Comics: V2#1, 8/95 - V2#3, 10/95; V2#4, 1/96 - No. 7, 5/96($2.95, bi-monthly #6 on)
V2#1-7: 1-Counterstrike storyline begins. 4-(1/96). 5-(1/96). 5,7-Brereton-c. 6-(3/96)-Simonson-c. 7-Story leads into Baseball Special #1 5.00
Baseball Special 1 (6/96, $2.95)-Bisley-c. 5.00

MARS ATTACKS
IDW Publishing: Jun, 2012 - No. 10, May, 2013 ($3.99, issues #6-10 polybagged with card)
1-10: 1-Layman-s/McCrea-a; 58 covers including all 54 cards from 1962 set 4.00
... #1 IDW's Greatest Hits Edition (3/16, $1.00) reprints #1 3.00
... Art Gallery (9/14, $3.99) Trading card style art by various 4.00
...: Classics Obliterated (6/13, $7.99) Spoofs of Moby Dick, Jekyll & Hyde, Robinson Crusoe 8.00
... KISS (1/13, $3.99) Ryall-s/Robinson-a; 2 variant-c with Judge Dredd & Star Slammers 4.00
... Popeye (1/13, $3.99) Beatty-a; 2 variant-c with Miss Fury & Opus 4.00
... The Holidays (10/12, $7.99) short stories for Halloween-Christmas; 5 covers 8.00
... The Real Ghostbusters (1/13, $3.99) Holder-a; 2 variant-c with Chew & Madman 4.00
... : The Transformers (1/13, $3.99) 2 variant-c with Spike & Strangers in Paradise 4.00
... Zombie vs. Robots (1/13, $3.99) Ryall-s; 2 variant-c with Rog-2000 & Cerebus 4.00

MARS ATTACKS
Dynamite Entertainment: 2018 - No. 5, 2019 ($3.99, limited series)
1-5-Kyle Starks-s/Chris Schweizer-a; multiple covers on each 4.00

MARS ATTACKS FIRST BORN
IDW Publishing: May, 2014 - No. 4, Aug, 2014 ($3.99, limited series)
1-4-Chris Ryall-s/Sam Kieth-a; multiple covers on each 4.00

MARS ATTACKS HIGH SCHOOL
Topps Comics: May, 1997 - No. 2, Sept, 1997 ($2.95, B&W, limited series)
1,2-Stelfreeze-c 4.00

Mars Attacks / Red Sonja #1 © Topps & RS LLC

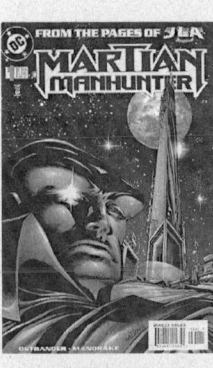

Martian Manhunter #1 © DC

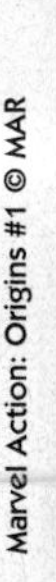

Marvel Action: Origins #1 © MAR

GD 2.0 | VG 4.0 | FN 6.0 | VF 8.0 | VF/NM 9.0 | NM- 9.2

MARS ATTACKS JUDGE DREDD
IDW Publishing: Sept, 2013 - No. 4, Dec, 2013 ($3.99, limited series)

1-4-Al Ewing-s/John McCrea-a/Greg Staples-c — 4.00

MARS ATTACKS IMAGE
Topps Comics: Dec, 1996 - No. 4, Mar, 1997 ($2.50, limited series)

1-4-Giffen-s/Smith & Sienkiewicz-a — 4.00

MARS ATTACKS: OCCUPATION
IDW Publishing: Mar, 2016 - No. 5, Jul, 2016 ($3.99, limited series)

1-5-John Layman-s/Andy Kuhn-a; multiple covers — 4.00

MARS ATTACKS / RED SONJA
Dynamite Entertainment: 2020 - No. 5, 2020 ($3.99, limited series)

1-5-John Layman-s/Fran Strukan-a; multiple covers. 3-Intro. Green Sonja — 4.00

MARS ATTACKS THE SAVAGE DRAGON
Topps Comics: Dec, 1996 - No. 4, Mar, 1997 ($2.95, limited series)

1-4: 1-w/bound-in card — 4.00

MARSHAL BLUEBERRY (See Blueberry)
Marvel Comics (Epic Comics): 1991 ($14.95, graphic novel)

	GD	VG	FN	VF	VF/NM	NM-
1-Moebius-a	3	6	9	21	33	45

MARSHAL LAW (Also see Crime And Punishment: Marshall Law...)
Marvel Comics (Epic Comics): Oct, 1987 - No. 6, May, 1989 ($1.95, mature)

1-6 — 3.00

M.A.R.S. PATROL TOTAL WAR (Formerly Total War #1,2)
Gold Key: No. 3, Sept, 1966 - No. 10, Aug, 1969 (All-Painted-c except #7)

	GD	VG	FN	VF	VF/NM	NM-
3-Wood-a; aliens invade USA	5	10	15	35	63	90
4-10	4	8	12	23	37	50

Wally Wood's M.A.R.S. Patrol Total War TPB (Dark Horse, 9/04, $12.95) r/#3 & Total War #1&2; foreward by Batton Lash; afterword by Dan Adkins — 13.00

MARTHA WASHINGTON (Also see Dark Horse Presents Fifth Anniversary Special, Dark Horse Presents #100-4, Give Me Liberty, Happy Birthday Martha Washington & San Diego Comicon Comics #2)

MARTHA WASHINGTON... (one-shots)
Dark Horse Comics (Legend): ($2.95/$3.50, one-shots)

... Dies (7/07, $3.50) Miller-s/Gibbons-a; r/Miller's original outline for Give Me Liberty — 4.00
... Stranded in Space (11/95, $2.95) Miller-s/Gibbons-a; Big Guy app. — 5.00

MARTHA WASHINGTON GOES TO WAR
Dark Horse Comics (Legend): May, 1994 - No. 5, Sep, 1994 ($2.95, lim. series)

1-5-Miller scripts; Gibbons-c/a — 5.00
TPB ($17.95) r/#1-5 — 18.00

MARTHA WASHINGTON SAVES THE WORLD
Dark Horse Comics: Dec, 1997 - No. 3, Feb, 1998 ($2.95/$3.95, lim. series)

1,2-Miller scripts; Gibbons-c/a in all — 5.00
3-($3.95) — 5.00

MARTHA WAYNE (See The Story of...)

MARTIAN MANHUNTER (See Detective Comics & Showcase '95 #9)
DC Comics: May, 1988 - No. 4, Aug,. 1988 ($1.25, limited series)

1-4: 1,4-Batman app. 2-Batman cameo — 4.00
Special 1-(1996, $3.50) — 4.00

MARTIAN MANHUNTER (See JLA)
DC Comics: No. 0, Oct, 1998 - No. 36, Nov, 2001 ($1.99)

0-(10/98) Origin retold; Ostrander-s/Mandrake-c/a — 3.00
1-36: 1-(12/98). 6-9-JLA app. 18,19-JSA app. 24-Mahnke-a — 3.00
#1,000,000 (11/98) 853rd Century x-over — 3.00
Annual 1,2 (1998,1999; $2.95) 1-Ghosts; Wrightson-c. 2-JLApe — 4.00

MARTIAN MANHUNTER (See DCU Brave New World)
DC Comics: Oct, 2006 - No. 8, May, 2007 ($2.99, limited series)

1-8-Lieberman-s/Barrionuevo-a/c — 3.00
...: The Others Among Us TPB (2007, $19.99) r/#1-8 & story from DCU Brave New World — 20.00

MARTIAN MANHUNTER
DC Comics: Aug, 2015 - No. 12, Jul, 2016 ($2.99)

1-12: 1-Rob Williams-s/Eddy Barrows-a. 1-3-JLA app. 10-Origin — 3.00

MARTIAN MANHUNTER
DC Comics: Feb, 2019 - No. 12, Apr, 2020 ($3.99)

1-12: 1-Orlando-s/Rossmo-a; Earth detective and flashbacks to Mars. 3-Origin retold — 4.00

MARTIAN MANHUNTER: AMERICAN SECRETS
DC Comics: 1992 - Book Three, 1992 ($4.95, limited series, prestige format)

1-3: Barreto-a — 5.00

MARTIAN MANHUNTER/ MARVIN THE MARTIAN SPECIAL
DC Comics: Aug, 2017 ($4.99, one-shot)

1-Orlando & Barbiere-s/Lopresti-a; covers by Lopresti & DeStefano — 5.00

MARTIN KANE (William Gargan as... Private Eye)(Stage/Screen/Radio/TV)
Fox Feature Syndicate (Hero Books): No. 4, June, 1950 - No. 2, Aug, 1950 (Formerly My Secret Affair)

	GD	VG	FN	VF	VF/NM	NM-
4(#1)-True crime stories; Wood-c/a(2); used in **SOTI**, pg. 160; photo back-c	40	80	120	244	402	560
2-Wood/Orlando story, 5 pgs; Wood-a(2)	28	56	84	168	274	380

MARTIN LUTHER KING AND THE MONTGOMERY STORY (See Promotional Comics section)

MARTIN MYSTERY
Dark Horse (Bonelli Comics): Mar, 1999 - No. 6, Aug, 1999 ($4.95, B&W, digest size)

1-6-Reprints Italian series in English; Gibbons-c on #1-3 — 5.00

MARTY MOUSE
I. W. Enterprises: No date (1958?) (10¢)

	GD	VG	FN	VF	VF/NM	NM-
1-Reprint	2	4	6	11	16	20

MARVEL
Marvel Comics: May, 2020 - Present ($4.99)

1-5-Short story anthology; Alex Ross-s/a. 1-Busiek-s/Rude-a. 2-Powell-s/a; Brereton-s/a 3-Weiss-s/a; Sienkiewicz-s/a. 4-Acuña-s/a; Barta-s/a, Dr. Droom app. 5-Hughes-s/a — 5.00

MARVEL ACTION: AVENGERS (All ages)(Title changed from Avengers after #5)
IDW Publishing: No. 6, May, 2019 - No. 9, Sept, 2019 ($3.99)

6-9-Iron Man, Captain America, Thor, Hawkeye, Black Widow, Black Panther & Hulk app. — 4.00

MARVEL ACTION: CAPTAIN MARVEL (All ages)
IDW Publishing: Aug, 2019 - No. 3, Oct, 2019 ($3.99)

1-3-Spider-Woman app.; Sam Maggs-s/Sweeney Boo-a — 4.00

MARVEL ACTION: CHILLERS (All ages)
IDW Publishing: Oct, 2020 - No. 4, Dec, 2020 ($3.99)

1-4-Iron Man, Ironheart & Dr. Strange app. 2-Elsa Bloodstone app. 3-Venom app. — 4.00

MARVEL ACTION CLASSICS (All ages)
IDW Publishing: May, 2019 - Present ($4.99)

... Ant-Man 1 (11/19, $4.99) Ant-Man reprints; Van Lente-s/Lolli-a; Clayton Henry-c — 5.00
... Avengers Featuring Doctor Strange 1 (1/20, $4.99) Reprints; Spider-Man app. — 5.00
... Hulk 1 (7/19, $4.99) Reprints; Doctor Strange, Iron Man and Spider-Man app. — 5.00
... Spider-Man 1 (5/19, $4.99) Reprints; Doctor Strange and Thor app. — 5.00
... Spider-Man Two-In-One 2 (12/19, $4.99) Reprints; Iron Man and Hulk app. — 5.00

MARVEL ACTION HOUR FEATURING IRON MAN (TV cartoon)
Marvel Comics: Nov, 1994 - No. 8, June, 1995 ($1.50/$2.95)

1-8: Based on cartoon series — 4.00
1 ($2.95)-Polybagged w/16 pg Marvel Action Hour Preview & acetate print — 5.00

MARVEL ACTION HOUR FEATURING THE FANTASTIC FOUR (TV cartoon)
Marvel Comics: Nov, 1994 - No. 8, June, 1995 ($1.50/$2.95)

1-8: Based on cartoon series — 4.00
1-($2.95)-Polybagged w/ 16 pg. Marvel Action Hour Preview & acetate print — 5.00

MARVEL ACTION: ORIGINS (All ages stories)
IDW Publishing (Marvel): Dec, 2020 - Present ($3.99)

1-Origins of Spider-Man and Thanos — 4.00

MARVEL ACTION: SPIDER-MAN (All ages stories)
IDW Publishing (Marvel): Nov, 2018 - No. 12, Nov, 2019 ($3.99)

1-12: 1-3-Dawson-s/Ossio-a; teen-age Peter Parker, Miles and Spider-Gwen app. — 4.00
Volume 2 (1/20 - Present) 1-Teen-age Peter Parker, Miles and Spider-Gwen app. — 4.00

MARVEL ACTION UNIVERSE (TV cartoon)
Marvel Comics: Jan, 1989 ($1.00, one-shot)

1-r/Spider-Man And His Amazing Friends — 4.00

MARVEL ADVENTURES
Marvel Comics: Apr, 1997 - No. 18, Sept, 1998 ($1.50)

1-18-"Animated style": 1,4,7-Hulk-c/app. 2,11-Spider-Man. 3,8,15-X-Men. 5-Spider-Man & X-Men. 6-Spider-Man & Human Torch. 9,12-Fantastic Four. 10,16-Silver Surfer. 13-Spider-Man & Silver Surfer. 14-Hulk & Dr. Strange. 18-Capt. America — 4.00

MARVEL ADVENTURES...
Marvel Comics: 2007, 2008 (Free Comic Book Day giveaways)

... Free Comic Book Day 2007 (6/07) 1-Iron Man, Hulk and Franklin Richards app. — 3.00
... Free Comic Book Day 2008 - Iron Man, Hulk, Ant-Man and Spider-Man app. — 3.00

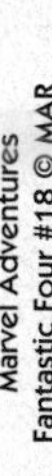

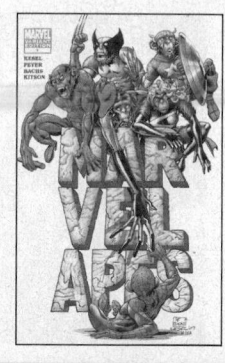

Marvel Adventures Fantastic Four #18 © MAR

Marvel Adventures Super-Heroes #21 © MAR

Marvel Apes #1 © MAR

GD VG FN VF VF/NM NM-
2.0 4.0 6.0 8.0 9.0 9.2

GD VG FN VF VF/NM NM-
2.0 4.0 6.0 8.0 9.0 9.2

MARVEL ADVENTURES FANTASTIC FOUR (All ages title)
Marvel Comics: No. 0, July, 2005 - No. 48, July, 2009 ($1.99/$2.50/$2.99)

0-($1.99) Movie version characters; Dr. Doom app.; Eaton-a 3.00
1-10-($2.50) 1-Skrulls app.; Pagulayan-a. 7-Namor app. 3.00
11-48-($2.99) 12,42-Dr. Doom app. 24-Namor app. 26,28-Silver Surfer app. 3.00
... Vol. 1: Family of Heroes (2005, $6.99, digest) r/#1-4 7.00
... Vol. 2: Fantastic Voyages (2006, $6.99, digest) r/#5-8 7.00
... Vol. 3: World's Greatest (2006, $6.99, digest) r/#9-12 7.00
... Vol. 4: Cosmic Threats (2006, $6.99, digest) r/#13-16 7.00
... Vol. 5: All 4 One, 4 For All (2007, $6.99, digest) r/#17-20 7.00
... Vol. 6: Monsters & Mysteries (2007, $6.99, digest) r/#21-24 7.00
... Vol. 7: The Silver Surfer (2007, $6.99, digest) r/#25-28 7.00
... Vol. 8: Monsters, Moles, Cowboys & Coupons (2008, $7.99, digest) r/#29-32 8.00

MARVEL ADVENTURES FLIP MAGAZINE (All ages title)
Marvel Comics: Aug, 2005 - No. 26, Sept, 2007 ($3.99/$4.99)

1-11: 1-10-Rep. Marvel Advs. Fantastic Four and Marvel Advs. Spider-Man in flip format 4.00
12-14-($4.99) Reprints Marvel Advs. Spider-Man & X-Men/Power Pack in flip format 5.00
15-26-Rep. Marvel Advs. Fantastic Four and Marvel Advs. Spider-Man in flip format 5.00

MARVEL ADVENTURES HULK (All ages title)
Marvel Comics: Sept, 2007 - No. 16, Dec, 2008 ($2.99)

1-16: 1-New version of Hulk's origin; Pagulayan-c. 2-Jamie Madrox app. 13-Mummies 3.00
... Vol. 1: Misunderstood Monster (2007, $6.99, digest) r/#1-4 7.00

MARVEL ADVENTURES IRON MAN (All ages title)
Marvel Comics: July, 2007 - No. 13, Jul, 2008 ($2.99)

1-13: 1-4-Michael Golden-c. 1-New version of Iron Man's origin. 2-Intro. the Mandarin 3.00
... Vol. 1: Heart of Steel (2007, $6.99, digest) r/#1-4 7.00
... Vol. 2: Iron Armory (2008, $7.99, digest) r/#5-8 8.00

MARVEL ADVENTURES SPIDER-MAN (All ages title)
Marvel Comics: May, 2005 - No. 61, May, 2010 ($2.50/$2.99)

1-13-Lee & Ditko stories retold with new art. 13-Conner-c 3.00
14-48: 14-Begin $2.99-c. 14-16-Conner-c. 22,23-Black costume. 35-Venom app. 3.00
50-($3.99) Sinister Six app.; back-up w/Sonny Liew-a 4.00
51-61: 53-Emma Frost becomes a regular; intro. Chat; Skottie Young-c begin 3.00
... Vol. 1 HC (2006, $19.99, with dustjacket) r/#1-8; plot for #7; sketch pages from #6,8 20.00
... Vol. 1: The Sinister Six (2005, $6.99, digest) r/#1-4 7.00
... Vol. 2: Power Struggle (2005, $6.99, digest) r/#5-8 7.00
... Vol. 3: Doom With a View (2006, $6.99, digest) r/#9-12 7.00
... Vol. 4: Concrete Jungle (2006, $6.99, digest) r/#13-16 7.00
... Vol. 5: Monsters on the Prowl (2007, $6.99, digest) r/#17-20 7.00
... Vol. 6: The Black Costume (2007, $6.99, digest) r/#21-24 7.00
... Vol. 7: Secret Identity (2007, $6.99, digest) r/#25-28 7.00
... Vol. 8: Forces of Nature (2008, $7.99, digest) r/#29-32 8.00
... Vol. 9: Fiercest Foes (2008, $7.99, digest) r/#33-36 8.00

MARVEL ADVENTURES SPIDER-MAN (All ages title)
Marvel Comics: June, 2010 - No. 24, May, 2012 ($3.99/$2.99)

1-($3.99) Tobin-s; Franklin Richards back-up 4.00
2-23-($2.99): 3,7-Wolverine app. 3,4-Bullseye app. 6-Doctor Octopus app. 3.00

MARVEL ADVENTURES STARRING DAREDEVIL (...Adventure #3 on)
Marvel Comics Group: Dec, 1975 - No. 6, Oct, 1976

	GD	VG	FN	VF	VF/NM	NM-
1	2	4	6	13	18	22
2-6-r/Daredevil #22-27 by Colan. 3-5-(25¢-c)	1	3	4	6	8	10
3-5-(30¢-c variants, limited distribution)(4,6,8/76)	5	10	15	35	63	90

MARVEL ADVENTURES SUPER HEROES (All ages title)
Marvel Comics: Sept, 2008 - No. 21, May, 2010 ($2.99)

1-21: 1-4: Spider-Man, Hulk and Iron Man team-ups. 1-Hercules app. 5-Dr. Strange app. 6-Ant-Man origin re-told. 7-Thor. 8,12-Capt. America. 17-Avengers begin 3.00

MARVEL ADVENTURES SUPER HEROES (All ages title)
Marvel Comics: June, 2010 - No. 24, May, 2012 ($3.99/$2.99)

1-($3.99) Iron Man and Avengers vs. Magneto 4.00
2-24-($2.99) 4-Deadpool app. 5-Rhino app. 11,12,22-Hulk app. 13,14,19-Thor 3.00

MARVEL ADVENTURES THE AVENGERS (All ages title)
Marvel Comics: July, 2006 - No. 39, Oct, 2009 ($2.99)

1-39-Spider-Man, Wolverine, Hulk, Iron Man, Capt. America, Storm, Giant-Girl app. 3.00
... Vol. 1: Heroes Assembled (2006, $6.99, digest) r/#1-4 7.00
... Vol. 2: Mischief (2007, $6.99, digest) r/#5-8 7.00
... Vol. 3: Bizarre Adventures (2007, $6.99, digest) r/#9-12 7.00
... Vol. 4: The Dream Team (2007, $6.99, digest) r/#13-15 & Giant-Size #1 7.00
... Vol. 5: Some Assembling Required (2008, $7.99, digest) r/#16-19 8.00

MARVEL ADVENTURES TWO-IN-ONE
Marvel Comics: Oct, 2007 - No. 18 ($4.99, bi-weekly)

1-18: 1-9-Reprints Marvel Adventures Spider-Man and Fantastic Four stories. 10-Hulk 5.00

MARVEL AGE (The Official Marvel News Magazine)
(A low priced news Magazine in comic format to promote coming issues)
Marvel Publications: Apr, 1983 - No. 140, Sept, 1994

	GD	VG	FN	VF	VF/NM	NM-
1-Saga of Crystar-c/s	2	4	6	8	10	12
2-7,9,11,14,15						4.00
8-Stan Lee/Jim Shooter-c/interviews	2	4	6	8	10	12
10-Star Wars-c, preview Spider-Man vs. Hobgoblin	1	3	4	6	8	10
12-(3/84) 2 pg. preview/1st app. of Spider-Man in Alien Venom black costume, 2 months before Amazing Spider-Man #252	5	10	15	35	57	80
13,16: 16-New Mutants-c/s						6.00
17-24,26-37,39,40						4.00
25(4/85)-Rocket Raccoon-c/preview art one month before Rocket Raccoon #1						6.00
38-He-Man & Masters of the Universe-c/preview	1	3	4	6	8	10
41(8/86)-Classic Stan Lee-c/sty	4	8	12	27	44	60
42-66: 53-Girls of Marvel swimsuits-c						4.00
67-Jim Lee-c, Wolverine/punisher/Sub-Mariner-c/s						6.00
68-89: 76-She-Hulk swimsuit-c by John Byrne						5.00
90(7/90)-Spider-Man-c by Todd McFarlane; Jim Lee Interview	2	4	6	13	18	22
91-Thanos and Silver Surfer-c	2	4	6	8	10	12
92-94,96,98,100-103,105-137,139						4.00
95-Captain America 50th Anniversary-c/issue						6.00
97(2/91)-Darkhawk-c/preview	4	8	12	23	37	50
99(4/91)-Black Panther Returns-c	1	3	4	6	8	10
104-Wolverine-c by Jim Lee	1	3	4	6	8	10
138(7/94)-Deadpool, Cable-c	2	4	6	10	14	18
140-Last issue	1	2	3	5	6	8
Annual 1(9/85)	1	3	4	6	8	10
Annual 2, 3(9/87)						5.00
Annual 4(6/88)-1st app. Damage Control	2	4	6	8	11	14

MARVEL AGE FANTASTIC FOUR (All ages title)
Marvel Comics: Jun, 2004 - No. 12, Mar, 2005 ($2.25)

1-12-Lee & Kirby stories retold with new art by various. 11-Impossible Man app. 3.00
...Tales (4/05, $2.25) retells first meeting with the Black Panther; O'Hare & Lim-a 3.00
Vol. 1: All For One TPB (2004, $5.99, digest size) r/#1-4 6.00
Vol. 2: Doom TPB (2004, $5.99, digest size) r/#5-8 6.00
Vol. 3: The Return of Doctor Doom TPB (2005, $5.99, digest size) r/#9-12 6.00

MARVEL AGE HULK (All ages title)
Marvel Comics: Nov, 2004 - No. 4, Feb, 2005 ($1.75)

1-3-Lee & Kirby stories retold with new art by various 3.00
Vol. 1: Incredible TPB (2005, $5.99, digest size) r/#1-4 6.00
Vol. 2: Defenders (2008, $7.99, digest) r/#5-8 8.00

MARVEL AGE SPIDER-MAN (All ages title)
Marvel Comics: May, 2004 - No. 20, Mar, 2005 ($2.25)

1-20-Lee & Ditko stories retold with new art. 4-Doctor Doom app. 5-Lizard app. 3.00
1-(Free Comic Book Day giveaway, 8/04) Spider-Man vs. The Vulture; Brooks-a 3.00
Vol. 1 TPB (2004, $5.99, digest) 1-r/#1-4 6.00
Vol. 2: Everyday Hero TPB (2004, $5.99, digest) r/#5-8 6.00
Vol. 3: Swingtime TPB (2004, $5.99, digest) r/#9-12 6.00
Spidey Strikes Back TPB (2005, 5.99, digest) r/#17-20 6.00

MARVEL AGE SPIDER-MAN TEAM-UP (Marvel Adventures on cover)
Marvel Comics: June, 2005 (Free Comic Book Day giveaway)

1-Spider-Man meets the Fantastic Four 3.00

MARVEL AGE TEAM-UP (All ages Spider-Man team-ups) (Also see Free Comic Book Day edition in the Promotional Comics section)
Marvel Comics: Nov, 2004 - No. 5, Apr, 2005 ($1.75)

1-5-Stories retold with new art by various. 1-Fantastic Four app. 3-Kitty Pryde app. 3.00
... Vol. 1: A Little Help From My Friends (2005, $7.99, digest) r/#1-5 8.00

MARVEL AND DC PRESENT FEATURING THE UNCANNY X-MEN AND THE NEW TEEN TITANS
Marvel Comics/DC Comics: 1982 ($2.00, 68 pgs., one-shot, Baxter paper)

	GD	VG	FN	VF	VF/NM	NM-
1-3rd app. Deathstroke the Terminator; Darkseid app.; Simonson/Austin-c/a	3	6	9	18	27	36

MARVEL APES
Marvel Comics: Nov, 2008 - No. 4, Dec, 2008 ($3.99, limited series)

1-4: 1-Kesel-s/Bachs-a; back-up history story with Peyer-s/Kitson-a; two covers 4.00

Marvel Boy (2000 series) #1 © MAR

Marvel Comics #1001 © MAR

Marvel Comics Presents #7 © MAR

GD VG FN VF VF/NM NM-
2.0 4.0 6.0 8.0 9.0 9.2

1-($10.00) Hero Initiative edition with Daredevil gorilla cover by Mike Wieringo 10.00
#0-(2008, $3.99) r/Amazing Spider-Man #110,111; gallery of Marvel Apes variant covers 4.00
...: Amazing Spider-Monkey Special 1 (6/09, $3.99) Sandmonk and the Apevengers app. 4.00
...: Grunt Line 1 (7/09, $3.99) Kesel-s; Charles Darwin app. 4.00
...: Speedball Special 1 (5/09, $3.99) Bachs & Hardin-a 4.00

MARVEL ASSISTANT-SIZED SPECTACULAR
Marvel Comics: Jun, 2009 - No. 2, Jun, 2009 ($3.99, limited series)
1,2-Short stories by various incl. Isanove, Giarrusso, Nauck, Wyatt Cenak, Warren 4.00

MARVEL ATLAS (Styled after the Official Marvel Handbooks)
Marvel Comics: 2007 - No. 2, 2008 ($3.99, limited series)
1,2-Profiles and maps of countries in the Marvel Universe 4.00

MARVEL BOY (Astonishing #3 on; see Marvel Super Action #4)
Marvel Comics (MPC): Dec, 1950 - No. 2, Feb, 1951
1-Origin Marvel Boy by Russ Heath 181 362 543 1158 1979 2800
2-Everett-a; Washington DC under attack 129 258 387 826 1413 2000

MARVEL BOY (Marvel Knights)
Marvel Comics: Aug, 2000 - No. 6, Mar, 2001 ($2.99, limited series)
1-Intro. Marvel Boy; Morrison-s/J.G. Jones-c/a 4.00
1-DF Variant-c 5.00
2-6 3.00
TPB (6/01, $15.95) 16.00

MARVEL BOY: THE URANIAN (Agents of Atlas)
Marvel Comics: Mar, 2010 - No. 3, May, 2010 ($3.99, limited series)
1-3-Origin re-told; back-up reprints from 1950s; Heath & Everett-a 4.00

MARVEL CHILLERS (Also see Giant-Size Chillers)
Marvel Comics Group: Oct, 1975 - No. 7, Oct, 1976 (All 25¢ issues)
1-Intro. Modred the Mystic, ends #2; Kane-c(p) 7 14 21 44 82 120
2,4,5,7: 4-Kraven app. 5,6-Red Wolf app. 7-Kirby-c; Tuska-p
2 4 6 10 14 18
3-Tigra, the Were-Woman begins (origin), ends #7 (see Giant-Size Creatures #1). Chaykin/Wrightson-c. 5 10 15 35 63 90
4-6-(30¢-c variants, limited distribution)(4-8/76) 5 10 15 31 53 75
6-Byrne-a(p); Buckler-c(p) 3 6 9 14 19 24
NOTE: *Bolle a-1.* ***Buckler*** *c-2.* ***Kirby*** *c-7.*

MARVEL CLASSICS COMICS SERIES FEATURING...
(Also see Pendulum Illustrated Classics)
Marvel Comics Group: 1976 - No. 36, Dec, 1978 (52 pgs., no ads)
1-Dr. Jekyll and Mr. Hyde 2 4 6 11 16 20
2-10,28: 28-1st Golden-c/a; Pit and the Pendulum 2 4 6 8 10 12
11-27,29-36 1 2 3 5 7 9
NOTE: ***Adkins*** *c-1i, 4i, 12i.* ***Alcala*** *a-34i; c-34.* ***Bolle*** *a-35.* ***Buscema*** *c-17p, 19p, 26p.* ***Golden*** *c/a-28.* ***Gil Kane*** *c-1-16p, 21p, 22p, 24p, 32p.* ***Nebres*** *a-5; c-24i.* ***Nino*** *a-2, 8, 12.* ***Redondo*** *a-1, 9. No. 1-12 were reprinted from Pendulum Illustrated Classics.*

MARVEL COLLECTIBLE CLASSICS: AVENGERS
Marvel Comics: 1998 ($10.00, reprints with chromium wraparound-c)
1-Reprints Avengers Vol.3, #1; Perez-c 3 6 9 16 24 32

MARVEL COLLECTIBLE CLASSICS: SPIDER-MAN
Marvel Comics: 1998 ($10.00, reprints with chromium wraparound-c)
1-Reprints Amazing Spider-Man #300; McFarlane-c 72 144 216 360 505 650
2-Reprints Spider-Man #1; McFarlane-c 28 56 84 140 195 250

MARVEL COLLECTIBLE CLASSICS: X-MEN
Marvel Comics: 1998 ($10.00, reprints with chromium wraparound-c)
1-Reprints (Uncanny) X-Men #1 & 2; Adam Kubert-c 3 6 9 21 33 45
2-6: 2-Reprints Uncanny X-Men #141 & 142; Byrne-c. 3-Reprints (Uncanny) X-Men #137; Larroca-c. 4-Reprints X-Men #25; Andy Kubert-c. 5-Reprints Giant Size X-Men #1; Gary Frank-c. 6-Reprints X-Men V2#1; Ramos-c 3 6 9 16 24 32

MARVEL COLLECTOR'S EDITION
Marvel Comics: 1992 (Ordered thru mail with Charleston Chew candy wrapper)
1-Flip-book format; Spider-Man, Silver Surfer, Wolverine (by Sam Kieth), & Ghost Rider stories; Wolverine back-c by Kieth 2 4 6 8 10 12

MARVEL COLLECTORS' ITEM CLASSICS (Marvel's Greatest #23 on)
Marvel Comics Group(ATF): Feb, 1965 - No. 22, Aug, 1969 (25¢, 68 pgs.)
1-Fantastic Four, Spider-Man, Thor, Hulk, Iron Man-r begin
13 26 39 90 198 305
2 (4/66) 6 12 18 42 79 115
3,4 5 10 15 35 63 90
5-10 5 10 15 33 57 80
11-22: 22-r/The Man in the Ant Hill/TTA #27 4 8 12 28 47 65
NOTE: *All reprints;* ***Ditko, Kirby*** *art in all.*

MARVEL COMICS (Marvel Mystery Comics #2 on)
Timely Comics (Funnies, Inc.): Oct, Nov, 1939
NOTE: The first issue was originally dated October 1939. Most copies have a black circle stamped over the date (on cover and inside) with "November" printed over it. However, some copies do not have the November overprint and could have a higher value. Most No. 1's have printing defects, i.e., tilted pages which caused trimming into the panels usually on right side and bottom. Covers exist with and without gloss finish.
1-Origin Sub-Mariner by Bill Everett(1st newsstand app.); 1st 8 pgs. were produced for Motion Picture Funnies Weekly #1 which was probably not distributed outside of advance copies; intro Human Torch by Carl Burgos, Kazar the Great (1st Tarzan clone), & Jungle Terror(only app.); intro. The Angel by Gustavson, The Masked Raider & his horse Lightning (ends #12); cover by sci/fi pulp illustrator Frank R. Paul
44,000 88,000 132,000 264,000 415,000 775,000

MARVEL COMICS
Marvel Comics: 1990 ($17.95, hardcover)
1-Reprint of entire Marvel Comics #1 3 6 9 16 23 30

MARVEL COMICS
Marvel Comics
... No. 1 Halloween Comic Fest 2014 (giveaway) Re-colored reprint of Human Torch and Sub-Mariner stories from Marvel Comics #1; cover swipe by Jelena Djurdjevic 3.00
... 70th Anniverary Special (10/09, $4.99) Re-colored reprint of entire Marvel Comics #1; cover swipe by Jelena Djurdjevic 6.00

MARVEL COMICS
Marvel Comics: No. 1000, Oct, 2019 - No. 1001, Dec, 2019 ($9.99/$4.99)
1000-($9.99, square-bound) Single page stories tied in to each year of Marvel from 1939-2020; intro. The Eternity Mask; s/a by various; main cover by Alex Ross 10.00
1001-($4.99) Single page stories; s/a by various 5.00

MARVEL COMICS DIGEST (All-ages Marvel reprint stories printed by Archie Comics)
Archie Comics Publications: Jul, 2017 - No. 8, Oct, 2018 ($6.99, digest-size)
1-8: 1-Spider-Man reprints. 2,6-Avengers. 3-Thor. 4-X-Men. 5-Avengers/Black Panther. 7-Avengers/Ant-Man. 8-Spider-Man & Venom 7.00

MARVEL COMICS PRESENTS
Marvel Comics (Midnight Sons imprint #143 on): Early Sept, 1988 - No. 175, Feb, 1995 ($1.25/$1.50/$1.75, bi-weekly)
1-Wolverine by Buscema in #1-10 3 6 9 14 19 24
2-5 1 2 3 5 6 8
6-10: 6-Sub-Mariner app. 10-Colossus begins 5.00
11-18,20-47,51-71: 17-Cyclops begins. 24-Havok begins. 25-Origin/1st app. Nth Man. 26-Hulk begins by Rogers. 29-Quasar app. 31-Excalibur begins by Austin (i). 32-McFarlane-a(p). 33-Capt. America; Jim Lee-a. 37-Devil-Slayer app. 38-Wolverine begins by Buscema; Hulk app. 39-Spider-Man app. 46-Liefeld Wolverine-c. 51-53-Wolverine by Rob Liefeld. 54-61-Wolverine/Hulk story: 54-Werewolf by Night begins; The Shroud by Ditko. 58-Iron Man by Ditko. 59-Punisher. 62-Deathlok & Wolverine stories 63-Wolverine. 64-71-Wolverine/Ghost Rider 8-part story. 70-Liefeld Ghost Rider/ Wolverine-c 4.00
19-1st app. Damage Control 2 4 6 8 10 12
48-50-Wolverine & Spider-Man team-up by Erik Larsen-c/a. 48-Wasp app. 49,50-Savage Dragon prototype app. by Larsen. 50-Silver Surfer. 50-53-Comet Man; Mumy scripts 6.00
72-Begin 13-part Weapon-X story (Wolverine origin) by B. Windsor-Smith (prologue)
3 6 9 16 23 30
73-Weapon-X part 1; Black Knight, Sub-Mariner 2 4 6 8 10 12
74-84: 74-Weapon-X part 2; Black Knight, Sub-Mariner. 76-Death's Head story. 77-Mr. Fantastic story. 78-Iron Man by Steacy. 80,81-Capt. America by Ditko/Austin. 81-Daredevil by Rogers/Williamson. 82-Power Man. 83-Human Torch by Ditko(a&scripts); $1.00-c direct, $1.25 newsstand. 84-Last Weapon-X (24 pg. conclusion) 4.00
85-Begin 8-part Wolverine story by Sam Kieth (c/a); 1st Kieth-a on Wolverine; begin 8-part Beast story by Jae Lee(p) with Liefeld part pencils #85,86; 1st Jae Lee-a (assisted w/Liefeld, 1991) 5.00
86-90: 86-89-Wolverine, Beast stories continue. 90-Begin 8-part Ghost Rider & Cable story, ends #97; begin flip book format w/two-c 4.00
91-174: 93-Begin 6-part Wolverine story, ends #98. 98-Begin 2-part Ghost Rider story. 99-Spider-Man story. 100-Full-length Ghost Rider/Wolverine story by Sam Kieth w/Tim Vigil assists; anniversary issue, non flip-book. 101-Begin 6-part Ghost Rider/Dr. Strange story & begin 8-part Wolverine/Nightcrawler story by Colan/Williamson; Punisher story. 107-Begin 6-part Ghost Rider/Werewolf by Night story. 109-Begin 8 part Wolverine/Typhoid Mary story. 111-Iron Fist. 113-Begin 6-part Giant-Man & begin 6-part Ghost Rider/Iron Fist stories. 117-Preview of Ravage 2099 (1st app.); begin 6 part Wolverine/Venom story w/Kieth-a. 118-Preview of Doom 2099 (1st app.). 119-Begin Ghost Rider/Cloak & Dagger by Colan. 120,136,138-Spider-Man. 123-Begin 8-part Ghost Rider/Typhoid Mary story; begin 4-part She Hulk story; begin 8-part Wolverine/Lynx story. 125-Begin 6-part Iron Fist story. 130-Begin 6-part Ghost Rider/ Cage story. 136-Daredevil. 137-Begin 6-part

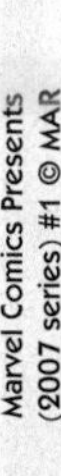
Marvel Comics Presents (2007 series) #1 © MAR

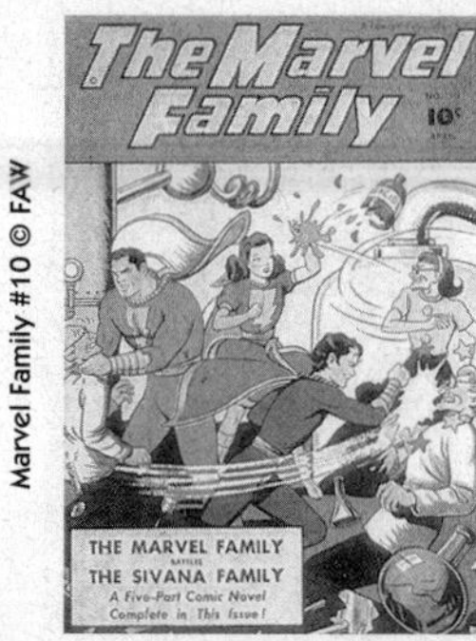

The Marvel Family
10¢
THE MARVEL FAMILY
THE SIVANA FAMILY
A Five-Part Comic Novel
Complete in This Issue!

Marvel Family #10 © FAW

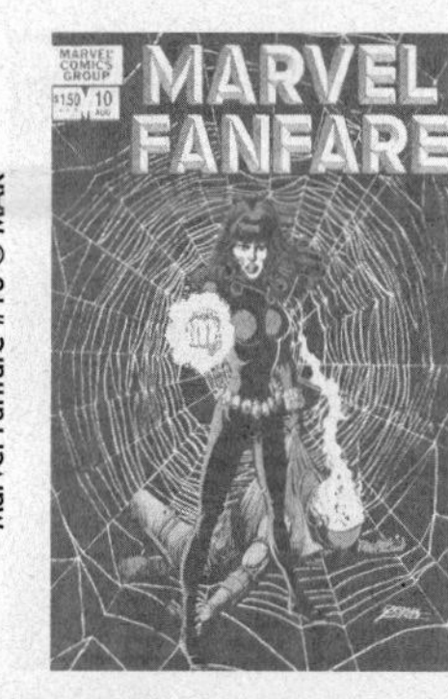

Marvel Fanfare #10 © MAR

GD VG FN VF VF/NM NM-
2.0 4.0 6.0 8.0 9.0 9.2

Wolverine story & 6-part Ghost Rider story. 147-Begin 2-part Vengeance-c/story w/new Ghost Rider. 149-Vengeance-c/story w/new Ghost Rider. 150-Silver ink-c; begin 2-part Bloody Mary story w/Typhoid Mary,Wolverine, Daredevil, new Ghost Rider; intro Steel Raven. 152-Begin 4-part Wolverine, 4-part War Machine, 4-part Vengeance, 3-part Moon Knight stories; same date as War Machine #1. 143-146: Siege of Darkness parts 3,6,11,14; all have spot-varnished-c. 143-Ghost Rider/Scarlet Witch; intro new Werewolf. 144-Begin 2-part Morbius story. 145-Begin 2-part Nightstalkers story. 153-155-Bound-in Spider-Man trading card sheet. 172-Flip-book; intro new Lunatik, Giffen-c/a. 173-Flip-book; Lunatik story; Fabry-c/Giffen-a. 174-Lunatik story, Giffen-a 4.00

175-Flip-book with New Genix-c; Lunatik story, Giffen-a
2 4 6 10 14 18

...Colossus: God's Country (1994, $6.95) r/#10-17 1 2 3 4 5 7

....: Wolverine Vol. 1 TPB (2005, $12.99) r/Wolverine stories from #1-10 13.00

....: Wolverine Vol. 2 TPB (2006, $12.99) r/from #39-50 and Marvel Age Annual #4 13.00

....: Wolverine Vol. 3 TPB (2006, $12.99) r/from #51-61 13.00

....: Wolverine Vol. 4 TPB (2006, $12.99) r/from #62-71 13.00

NOTE: **Austin** *a-31-37i; c(i)-48, 50, 99, 122.* **Buscema** *a-1-10, 38-47; c-6.* **Byrne** *a-79; c-71.* **Colan** *a(p)-36, 37.* **Colan/Williamson** *a-101-108.* **Ditko** *a-7p, 10, 56p, 58, 80, 81, 83.* **Guice** *a-62.* **Sam Kieth** *a-85-92, 117-122; c-85-98, 99p, 100-108, 117, 118, 120-122; back c-109-113, 117.* **Jae Lee** *c-129(back).* **Liefeld** *a-51, 52, 53p(2), 85p; c-46, 70.* **McFarlane** *c-32.* **Mooney** *a-73.* **Rogers** *a-26, 38, 46i, 81p.* **Russell** *a-10-14,16,17i; c-4,19, 30,31i.* **Saltares** *a-8p(early), 38-45p.* **Simonson** *c-1.* **B. Smith** *a-72-84; c-72-84.* **P. Smith** *c-34.* **Sparling** *a-33.* **Starlin** *a-89i.* **Staton** *a-74.* **Steacy** *a-78.* **Sutton** *a-101-105.* **Williamson** *c-62i. Two Gun Kid by* **Gil Kane** *in #116, 122.*

MARVEL COMICS PRESENTS
Marvel Comics: Nov, 2007 - No. 12, Oct, 2008 ($3.99)

1-12-Short stories by various. 1-Wraparound-c by Campbell 4.00

MARVEL COMICS PRESENTS
Marvel Comics: Mar, 2019 - No. 9, Nov, 2019 ($4.99)

1-9: 1-Wolverine serialized story begins; Namor & Capt. America stories. 2-Gorilla Man app. 3-Crusher Hogan app. 4-Moon Knight. 5-Venom app. 6-Intro. Wolverine's daughter Rien 8-White Fox 5.00

MARVEL COMICS SUPER SPECIAL, A (Marvel Super Special #5 on)
Marvel Comics: Sept, 1977 - No. 41(?), Nov, 1986 (nn 7) ($1.50, magazine)

1-Kiss, 40 pgs. comics plus photos & features; John Buscema-a(p); also see Howard the Duck #12; ink contains real KISS blood; Dr. Doom, Spider-Man, Avengers, Fantastic Four, Mephisto app. 13 26 39 91 201 310

2-Conan (1978) 3 6 9 16 23 30

3-Close Encounters of the Third Kind (1978); Simonson-a
3 6 9 14 20 25

4-The Beatles Story (1978)-Perez/Janson-a; has photos & articles
7 14 21 44 82 120

5-Kiss (1978)-Includes poster 12 24 36 82 179 275

6-Jaws II (1978) 3 6 9 15 22 28

7-Sgt. Pepper; Beatles movie adaptation; withdrawn from U.S. distribution (French ed. exists)

8-Battlestar Galactica; tabloid size ($1.50, 1978); adapts TV show
2 4 6 13 18 20

8-Modern-r of tabloid size 2 4 6 10 14 18

8-Battlestar Galactica; publ. in regular magazine format; low distribution ($1.50, 8-1/2x11")
3 6 9 14 20 25

9-Conan 3 6 9 14 20 25

10-Star-Lord (1st color story) 5 10 15 30 50 70

11-13-Weirdworld begins #11; 25 copy special press run of each with gold seal and signed by artists (Proof quality), Spring-June, 1979 8 16 24 55 105 155

11-14: 11-13-Weirdworld (regular issues): 11-Fold-out centerfold. 14-Miller-c(p); adapts movie "Meteor." 1 3 4 6 8 10

15-Star Trek with photos & pin-ups ($1.50-c) 2 4 6 11 16 20

15-With $2.00 price; the price was changed at tail end of a 200,000 press run
3 6 9 14 20 25

16-Empire Strikes Back adaptation; Williamson-a 10 20 30 64 132 200

17-20 (Movie adaptations): 17-Xanadu. 18-Raiders of the Lost Ark. 19-For Your Eyes Only (James Bond). 20-Dragonslayer 6.00

21,23,25,26,28-30 (Movie adaptations): 21-Conan. 23-Annie. 25-Rock and Rule-w/photos; artwork is from movie. 26-Octopussy (James Bond). 28-Krull; photo-c. 29-Tarzan of the Apes (Greystoke movie). 30-Indiana Jones and the Temple of Doom
1 2 3 4 5 7

22-Blade Runner; Williamson-a/Steranko-c 4 8 12 28 47 65

24-The Dark Crystal 2 4 6 11 16 20

27-Return of the Jedi 3 6 9 17 26 35

31-39,41: 31-The Last Star Fighter. 32-The Muppets Take Manhattan. 33-Buckaroo Banzai. 34-Sheena. 35-Conan The Destroyer. 36-Dune. 37-2010. 38-Red Sonja. 39-Santa Claus:The Movie. 41-Howard The Duck
1 3 4 6 8 10

40-Labyrinth 4 8 12 23 37 50

NOTE: **J. Buscema** *a-1, 2, 9, 11-13, 18p, 21, 35, 40; c-11(part), 12.* **Chaykin** *a-9, 19p; c-18, 19.* **Colan** *a(p)-6, 10, 14.* **Morrow** *a-34; c-1i, 34.* **Nebres** *a-11.* **Spiegle** *a-29.* **Stevens** *a-27.* **Williamson** *a-27. #22-28 contain photos from movies.*

GD VG FN VF VF/NM NM-
2.0 4.0 6.0 8.0 9.0 9.2

MARVEL COMICS: 2001
Marvel Comics: 2001 (no cover price, one-shot)

1-Previews new titles for Fall 2001; Wolverine-c 3.00

MARVEL DABEL BROTHERS SAMPLER
Marvel Comics: Dec, 2006 (no cover price, one-shot)

1-Profiles and sample pages of Anita Blake, Magician: Apprentice, Red Prophet, Ptolus 3.00

MARVEL DIVAS
Marvel Comics: Sept, 2009 - No. 4, Dec, 2009 ($3.99, limited series)

1-4-Black Cat, Firestar, Hellcat and Photon app. 1-Campbell-c 4.00

MARVEL DOUBLE FEATURE
Marvel Comics Group: Dec, 1973 - No. 21, Mar, 1977

1-Capt. America, Iron Man-r/T.O.S. begin 4 8 12 25 40 55

2-10: 3-Last 20¢ issue 2 4 6 8 11 14

11-17,20,21:17-Story-r/Iron Man & Sub-Mariner #1; last 25¢ issue
1 3 4 6 8 10

15-17-(30¢-c variants, limited distribution)(4,6,8/76) 4 8 12 27 44 60

18,19-Colan/Craig-r from Iron Man #1 in both 2 4 6 8 10 12

NOTE: **Colan** *r-1-19p.* **Craig** *r-17-19i.* **G. Kane** *r-15p; c-15p.* **Kirby** *r-1-16p, 20, 21; c-17-20.*

MARVEL DOUBLE SHOT
Marvel Comics: Jan, 2003 - No. 4, April, 2003 ($2.99, limited series)

1-4: 1-Hulk by Haynes; Thor w/Asamiya-a; Jusko-c. 2-Dr. Doom by Rivera; Simpsons-style Avengers by Bill Morrison 3.00

MARVEL FAMILY (Also see Captain Marvel Adventures No. 18)
Fawcett Publications: Dec, 1945 - No. 89, Jan, 1954

1-Origin Captain Marvel, Captain Marvel Jr., Mary Marvel, & Uncle Marvel retold; origin/1st app. Black Adam 1225 2450 3675 8200 13,600 19,000

2-The 3 Lt. Marvels & Uncle Marvel app. 77 154 231 493 847 1200

3 54 108 162 346 591 835

4,5 45 90 135 284 480 675

6-10: 6-Classic portrait-c with Uncle Marvel. 7-Shazam app.
39 78 117 231 378 525

11-20 31 62 93 182 296 410

21-30 27 54 81 158 259 360

31-40 23 46 69 136 223 310

41-46,48-50 22 44 66 128 209 290

47-Flying Saucer-c/story (5/50) 29 58 87 170 278 385

51-76 20 40 60 120 195 270

77-Communist Threat-c 40 80 120 244 402 560

78,81-Used in **POP**, pg. 92,93. 23 46 69 136 223 310

79,80,82-88: 79-Horror satire-c 22 44 66 132 216 300

89-Last issue; last Fawcett Captain Marvel app. (low distribution)
40 80 120 244 402 560

MARVEL FANFARE (1st Series)
Marvel Comics Group: Mar, 1982 - No. 60, Jan, 1992 ($1.25/$2.25, slick paper, direct sales)

1-Spider-Man/Angel team-up; 1st Paul Smith-a (1st full story; see King Conan #7); Daredevil app. (many copies were printed missing the centerfold)
2 4 6 9 13 16

2-Spider-Man, Ka-Zar, The Angel. F.F. origin retold 1 3 4 6 8 10

3,4-X-Men & Ka-Zar. 4-Deathlok, Spidey app. 1 2 3 5 6 8

5-14: 5-Dr. Strange, Capt. America. 6-Spider-Man, Scarlet Witch. 7-Incredible Hulk; D.D. back-up(also 15). 8-Dr. Strange; Wolf Boy begins. 9-Man-Thing. 10-13-Black Widow. 14-The Vision 5.00

15,24,33: 15-The Thing by Barry Smith, c/a. 24-Weirdworld; Wolverine back-up. 33-X-Men, Wolverine app.; Punisher pin-up 6.00

16-23,25-32,34-44,46-50: 16,17-Skywolf. 16-Sub-Mariner back-up. 17-Hulk back-up. 18-Capt. America by Miller. 19-Cloak and Dagger. 20-Thing/Dr. Strange. 21-Thing/Dr. Strange /Hulk. 22,23-Iron Man vs. Dr. Octopus. 25,26-Weirdworld. 27-Daredevil/Spider-Man. 28-Alpha Flight. 29-Hulk. 30-Moon Knight. 31,32-Captain America. 34-37-Warriors Three. 38-Moon Knight/Dazzler. 39-Moon Knight/Hawkeye. 40-Angel/Rogue & Storm. 41-Dr. Strange. 42-Spider-Man. 43-Sub-Mariner/Human Torch. 44-Iron Man vs. Dr. Doom by Ken Steacy. 46-Fantastic Four. 47-Hulk. 48-She-Hulk/Vision. 49-Dr. Strange/Nick Fury. 50-X-Factor 4.00

45-All pin-up issue by Steacy, Art Adams & others 5.00

51-($2.95, 52 pgs.)-Silver Surfer; Fantastic Four & Capt. Marvel app.; 51,52-Colan/Williamson back-up (Dr. Strange) 5.00

52,53,56-60: 52,53-Black Knight; 53-Iron Man back up. 56-59-Shanna the She-Devil. 58-Vision & Scarlet Witch back-up. 60-Black Panther/Rogue/Daredevil stories 4.00

54,55-Wolverine back-ups. 54-Black Knight. 55-Power Pack 5.00

... No. 10 Facsimile Edition (12/20, $3.99) Reprints #10 with original ads 4.00

... Vol. 1 TPB (2008, $24.99) r/#1-7 25.00

NOTE: **Art Adams** *c-13.* **Austin** *a-1i, 4i, 33i, 38i; c-8i, 33i.* **Buscema** *a-51p.* **Byrne** *a-1p, 29, 48; c-29.* **Chiodo**

Marvel Feature (2nd series) #7 © MAR

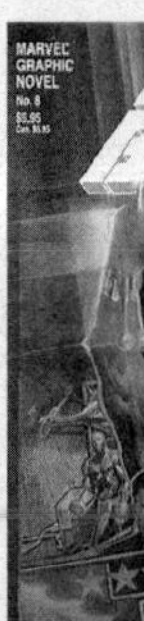
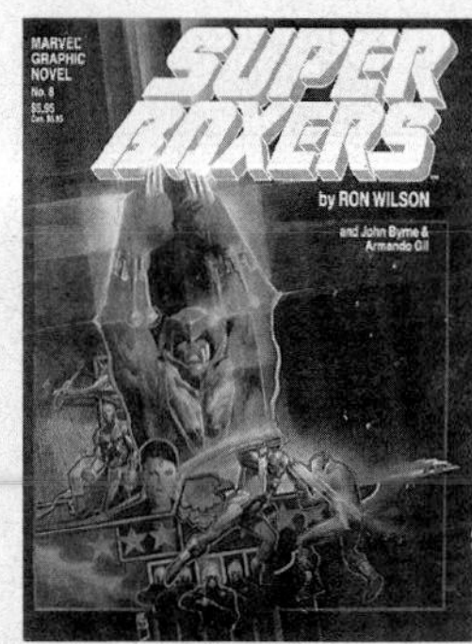

Marvel Graphic Novel #8 © MAR

Marvel Feature #9 © MAR

	GD 2.0	VG 4.0	FN 6.0	VF 8.0	VF/NM 9.0	NM- 9.2

painted c-56-59. ***Colan*** *a-51p.* ***Cowan/Simonson*** *c/a-60.* ***Golden*** *a-1, 2, 4p, 47; c-1, 2, 47.* ***Infantino*** *c/a(p)-8.* ***Gil Kane*** *a-8-11p.* ***Miller*** *a-18; c-1(Back-c), 18.* ***Perez*** *a-10, 11p, 12, 13p; c-10-13p.* ***Rogers*** *a-5p; c-5p.* ***Russell*** *a-5i, 6i, 8-11i, 43i; c-5i, 6.* ***Paul Smith*** *a-1p, 4p, 32, 60;'c-4p.* *Staton c/a-50(p).* ***Williamson*** *a-30i, 51i.*

MARVEL FANFARE (2nd Series)
Marvel Comics: Sept, 1996 - No. 6, Feb, 1997 (99¢)

1-6: 1-Capt. America & The Falcon-c/story; Deathlok app. 2-Wolverine & Hulk-c/app. 3-Ghost Rider & Spider-Man-c/app. 5-Longshot-c/app. 6-Sabretooth, Power Man, & Iron Fist-c/app 4.00

MARVEL FEATURE (See Marvel Two-In-One)
Marvel Comics Group: Dec, 1971 - No. 12, Nov, 1973 (1,2: 25¢, 52 pg. giants) (#1-3: quarterly)

1-Origin/1st app. The Defenders (Sub-Mariner, Hulk & Dr. Strange); see Sub-Mariner #34,35 for prequel; Dr. Strange solo story (predates Dr. Strange #1) plus 1950s Sub-Mariner-r; Neal Adams-c 23 46 69 156 348 540
2-2nd app. Defenders; 1950s Sub-Mariner-r. Rutland, Vermont Halloween x-over 9 18 27 60 120 180
3-Defenders ends 6 12 18 40 73 105
4-Re-intro Antman (1st app. since 1960s), begin series; brief origin; Spider-Man app. 8 16 24 54 102 150
5-7,9,10: 6-Wasp app. & begins team-ups. 9-Iron Man app. 10-Last Antman 3 6 9 21 33 45
8-Origin Antman & Wasp-r/TTA #44; Kirby-a 4 8 12 26 42 55
11-Thing vs. Hulk; 1st Thing solo book (9/73); origin Fantastic Four retold 8 16 24 54 102 150
12-Thing/Iron Man; early Thanos app.; occurs after Capt. Marvel #33; Starlin-a(p) 5 10 15 34 60 85

NOTE: ***Bolle*** *a-9i.* ***Everett*** *a-1i, 3i.* ***Hartley*** *r-10.* ***Kane*** *c-3p, 7p.* ***Russell*** *a-7-10p.* ***Starlin*** *a-8, 11, 12; c-8.*

MARVEL FEATURE (Also see Red Sonja)
Marvel Comics: Nov, 1975 - No. 7, Nov, 1976 (Story cont'd in Conan #68)

1-Red Sonja begins (pre-dates Red Sonja #1); adapts Howard short story; Adams-r/Savage Sword of Conan #1 4 8 12 23 37 50
2-6: Thorne-c/a in #2-7. 4,5-(Regular 25¢ edition)(5,7/76) 1 3 4 6 8 10
4,5-(30¢-c variants, limited distribution) 5 10 15 33 57 80
7-Red Sonja battles Conan 3 6 9 16 23 30

MARVEL FRONTIER COMICS UNLIMITED
Marvel Frontier Comics: Jan, 1994 ($2.95, 68 pgs.)

1-Dances with Demons, Immortalis, Children of the Voyager, Evil Eye, The Fallen stories 4.00

MARVEL FUMETTI BOOK
Marvel Comics Group: Apr, 1984 ($1.00, one-shot)

1-All photos; Stan Lee photo-c; Art Adams touch-ups 5.00

MARVEL FUN & GAMES
Marvel Comics Group: 1979/80 (color comic for kids)

1,11: 1-Games, puzzles, etc. 11-X-Men-c 2 4 6 8 10 12
2-10,12,13: (beware marked pages) 1 2 3 4 5 7

MARVEL GIRL
Marvel Comics: Apr, 2011 ($2.99, one-shot)

1-Early X-Men days of Jean Grey; Fialkov-s/Plati-a/Cruz-c 3.00

MARVEL GRAPHIC NOVEL
Marvel Comics Group (Epic Comics): 1982 - No. 38, 1990? ($5.95/$6.95)

1-Death of Captain Marvel (2nd Marvel graphic novel); Capt. Marvel battles Thanos by Jim Starlin (c/a/scripts) 6 12 18 38 69 100
1 (2nd & 3rd printings) 2 4 6 13 18 22
2-Elric: The Dreaming City 2 4 6 13 18 22
3-Dreadstar; Starlin-c/a, 52 pgs. 3 6 9 14 20 25
4-Origin/1st app. The New Mutants (1982) 9 18 27 57 111 165
4,5-2nd printings 2 4 6 11 16 20
5-X-Men; book-length story (1982) 4 8 12 28 47 65
6-15,20,25,30,31: 6-The Star Slammers. 7-Killraven. 8-Super Boxers; Byrne scripts. 9-The Futurians. 10-Heartburst. 11-Void Indigo. 12-Dazzler. 13-Starstruck. 14-The Swords Of The Swashbucklers. 15-The Raven Banner (a Tale of Asgard). 20-Greenberg the Vampire. 25-Alien Legion. 30-A Sailor's Story. 31-Wolfpack 2 4 6 8 10 12
16,17,21,29: 16-The Aladdin Effect (Storm, Tigra, Wasp, She-Hulk). 17-Revenge Of The Living Monolith (Spider-Man, Avengers, FF app.). 21-Marada the She-Wolf. 29-The Big Chance (Thing vs. Hulk) 2 4 6 9 12 15
18,19,26-28: 18-She Hulk. 19-Witch Queen of Acheron (Conan). 26-Dracula. 27-Avengers (Emperor Doom). 28-Conan the Reaver 2 4 6 10 14 18
22-24: 22-Amaz. Spider-Man in Hooky by Wrightson. 23-Dr. Strange. 24-Love and War (Daredevil); Miller scripts 3 6 9 14 19 24
32-Death of Groo 3 6 9 14 19 24
32-2nd printing ($5.95) 2 4 6 8 10 12
33,34,36,37: 33-Thor. 34-Predator & Prey (Cloak & Dagger). 36-Willow (movie adapt.). 37-Hercules 2 4 6 8 10 12
35-Hitler's Astrologer (The Shadow, $12.95, HC) 2 4 6 11 16 20
35-Soft-c reprint (1990, $10.95) 2 4 6 9 12 15
38-Silver Surfer (Judgement Day)($14.95, HC) 2 4 6 13 18 22
38-Soft-c reprint (1990, $10.95) 2 4 6 9 12 15
nn-Abslom Daak: Dalek Killer (1990, $8.95) Dr. Who 2 4 6 9 12 15
nn-Arena by Bruce Jones (1989, $5.95) Dinosaurs 2 4 6 8 10 12
nn- A-Team Storybook Comics Illustrated (1983) r/ A-Team mini-series #1-3 2 4 6 8 10 12
nn-Ax (1988, $5.95) Ernie Colan-s/a 2 4 6 8 10 12
nn-Black Widow Coldest War (4/90, $9.95) 2 4 6 9 12 15
nn-Chronicles of Genghis Grimtoad (1990, $8.95)-Alan Grant-s 2 4 6 8 10 12
nn-Conan the Barbarian in the Horn of Azoth (1990, $8.95) 2 4 6 8 11 16
nn-Conan of Isles ($8.95) 2 4 6 8 11 16
nn-Conan Ravagers of Time (1992, $9.95) Kull & Red Sonja app. 2 4 6 8 11 16
nn-Conan -The Skull of Set 2 4 6 8 11 16
nn-Doctor Strange and Doctor Doom Triumph and Torment (1989, $17.95, HC) 2 4 6 13 18 22
nn-Dreamwalker (1989, $6.95)-Morrow-a 2 4 6 8 10 12
nn-Excalibur Weird War III (1990, $9.95) 2 4 6 8 10 12
nn-G.I. Joe - The Trojan Gambit (1983, 68 pgs.) 2 4 6 9 12 15
nn-Harvey Kurtzman Strange Adventures (Epic, $19.95, HC) Aragonés, Crumb 3 6 9 14 20 25
nn-Hearts and Minds (1990, $8.95) Heath-a 2 4 6 8 10 12
nn-Inhumans (1988, $7.95)-Williamson-i 3 6 9 14 20 25
nn-Jhereg (Epic, 1990, $8.95) 2 4 6 8 10 12
nn-Kazar-Guns of the Savage Land (7/90, $8.95) 2 4 6 8 10 12
nn-Kull-The Vale of Shadow ('89, $6.95) 2 4 6 8 10 12
nn-Last of the Dragons (1988, $6.95) Austin-a(i) 2 4 6 8 10 12
nn-Nightraven: House of Cards (1991, $14.95) 2 4 6 10 14 18
nn-Nightraven: The Collected Stories (1990, $9.95) Bolton-r/British Hulk mag.; David Lloyd-c/a 2 4 6 8 10 12
nn-Original Adventures of Cholly and Flytrap (Epic, 1991, $9.95) Suydam-s/c/a 2 4 6 10 14 18
nn-Rick Mason Agent (1989, $9.95) 2 4 6 8 10 12
nn-Roger Rabbit In The Resurrection Of Doom (1989, $8.95) 2 4 6 9 12 15
nn-A Sailor's Story Book II: Winds, Dreams and Dragons ('86, $6.95, softcover) Glansman-s/c/a 2 4 6 8 10 12
nn-Squadron Supreme: Death of a Universe (1989, $9.95) Gruenwald-s; Ryan & Williamson-a 3 6 9 14 20 25
nn-Who Framed Roger Rabbit (1989, $6.95) 2 4 6 9 12 15

NOTE: ***Aragones*** *a-27, 32.* ***Buscema*** *a-38.* ***Byrne*** *c/a-18.* ***Heath*** *a-35i.* ***Kaluta*** *a-13, 35p; c-13.* ***Miller*** *a-24p.* ***Simonson*** *a-6; c-6.* ***Starlin*** *c/a-1,3.* ***Williamson*** *a-34.* ***Wrightson*** *c-29i.*

MARVEL HEARTBREAKERS
Marvel Comics: Apr, 2010 ($3.99, one-shot)

1-Romance short stories; Spider-Man, MJ & Gwen app.; Casagrande-a; Beast app. 4.00

MARVEL - HEROES & LEGENDS
Marvel Comics: Oct, 1996; 1997 ($2.95)

nn-Wraparound-c, ...1997 ($2.99) -Original Avengers story 4.00

MARVEL HEROES FLIP MAGAZINE
Marvel Comics: Aug, 2005 - No. 26, Sept, 2007 ($3.99/$4.99)

1-11-Reprints New Avengers and Captain America (2005 series) in flip format thru #13 4.00
12-26: 14-19-Reprints New Avengers and Young Avengers in flip format. 20-Ghost Rider 5.00

MARVEL HOLIDAY SPECIAL
Marvel Comics: No. 1, 1991 - 2011

1-($2.25, 84 pgs.) X-Men, Fantastic Four, Punisher, Thor, Capt. America, Ghost Rider, Capt. Ultra, Spidey stories; Art Adams-c/a 4.00
nn (1992, 1/93 on-c)-Wolverine, Thanos (by Starlin/Lim/Austin) 4.00
nn (1993, 1/94 on-c)-Spider-Man vs. Mephisto; Nick Fury by Chaykin; Hulk app. 4.00
nn (1994)-Capt. America, X-Men, Silver Surfer 4.00
... 1996-Spider-Man by Waid & Olliffe; X-Men, Silver Surfer 4.00
... 2004-Spider-Man by DeFalco & Miyazawa; X-Men, Fantastic Four 4.00
... 2004 TPB ($15.99) r/M.H.S. 2004 & past Christmas-themed stories 16.00
1 (1/06, $3.99) new Christmas-themed stories by various; Immonen-c 4.00
... 2006 (2/07, $3.99) Fin Fang Foom, Hydra, AIM app.; gallery of past covers; Irving-c 4.00
... 2007 (2/08, $3.99) Spider-Man & Wolverine stories; Hembeck-a 4.00
... 2011 (2/12, $3.99) Seeley-c; Spider-Man, Wolverine, Nick Fury, The Thing app. 4.00

Marvel Illustrated: Moby Dick #1 © MAR

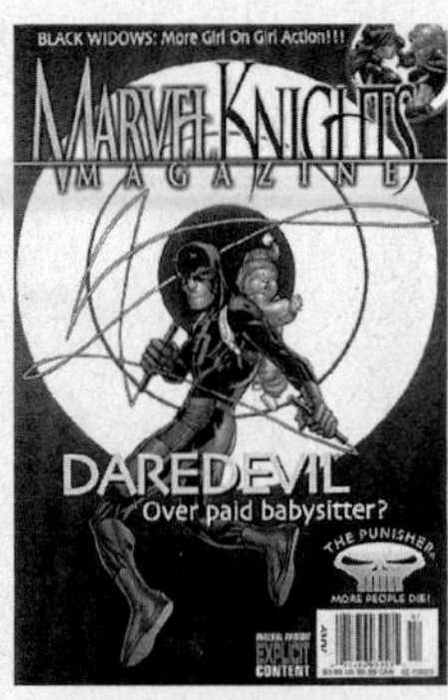

Marvel Knights Magazine #3 © MAR

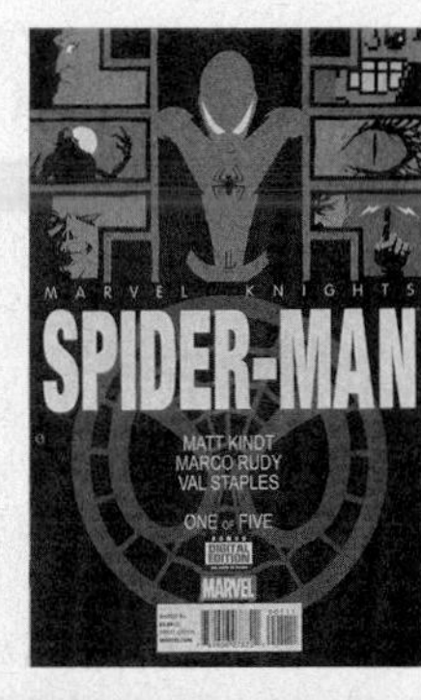

Marvel Knights: Spider-Man #2 © MAR

GD VG FN VF VF/NM NM-
2.0 4.0 6.0 8.0 9.0 9.2

Marvel Holiday (2006, $7.99, digest) reprints from M.H.S. 2004, 2006 & TPB 8.00
Marvel Holiday Spectacular Magazine (2009, $9.99, magazine) reprints from M.H.S. '93, '94, & Amazing Spider-Man #166; and new material w/Doe, Semeiks & Nauck-a 10.00
NOTE: ***Art Adams** a-'92. **Golden** a-'93. **Kaluta** c-'93. **Perez** c-'94.*

MARVEL ILLUSTRATED...
Marvel Comics: 2007 ($2.99)

...Jungle Book - reprints from Marvel Fanfare #8-11; Gil Kane-s/a(p); P. Craig Russell-i 3.00

MARVEL ILLUSTRATED: KIDNAPPED (Title changes to Kidnapped with #5)
Marvel Comics: Jan, 2009 - No. 5, May, 2009 ($3.99, limited series)

1-5-Adaptation of the Stevenson novel; Roy Thomas-s/Mario Gully-a/Parel-c 4.00

MARVEL ILLUSTRATED: LAST OF THE MOHICANS
Marvel Comics: July, 2007 - No. 6, Dec, 2007 ($2.99, limited series)

1-6-Adaptation of the Cooper novel; Roy Thomas-s/Steve Kurth-a. 1-Jo Chen-c 3.00
HC (2008, $19.99) r/#1-6 20.00

MARVEL ILLUSTRATED: MOBY DICK
Marvel Comics: Apr, 2008 - No. 6, Sept, 2008 ($2.99, limited series)

1-6-Adaptation of the Melville novel; Roy Thomas-s/Alixe-a/Watson-c 3.00

MARVEL ILLUSTRATED: PICTURE OF DORIAN GRAY
Marvel Comics: Jan, 2008 - No. 6, July, 2008 ($2.99, limited series)

1-6-Adaptation of the Wilde novel; Roy Thomas-s/Fiumara-a. 1-Parel-c 3.00

MARVEL ILLUSTRATED: SWIMSUIT ISSUE (Also see Marvel Swimsuit Special)
Marvel Comics: 1991 ($3.95, magazine, 52 pgs.)

V1#1-Parody of Sports Illustrated swimsuit issue; Mary Jane Parker centerfold pin-up by Jusko; 2nd print exists 2 4 6 11 16 20

MARVEL ILLUSTRATED: THE ILIAD
Marvel Comics: Feb, 2008 - No. 8, Sept, 2008 ($2.99, limited series)

1-8-Adaptation of Homer's Epic Poem; Roy Thomas-s/Sepulveda-a/Rivera-c 3.00

MARVEL ILLUSTRATED: THE MAN IN THE IRON MASK
Marvel Comics: Sept, 2007 - No. 6, Feb, 2008 ($2.99, limited series)

1-6-Adaptation of the Dumas novel; Roy Thomas-s/Hugo Petrus-a. 1-Djurdjevic-c 3.00
HC (2008, $19.99) r/#1-6 20.00

MARVEL ILLUSTRATED: THE ODYSSEY (Title changes to The Odyssey with #7)
Marvel Comics: Nov, 2008 - No. 8, June, 2009 ($3.99, limited series)

1-8-Adaptation of Homer's Epic Poem; Roy Thomas-s/Greg Tocchini-a/c 4.00

MARVEL ILLUSTRATED: THE THREE MUSKETEERS
Marvel Comics: Aug, 2008 - No. 6, Jan, 2009 ($3.99, limited series)

1-6-Adaptation of the Dumas novel; Roy Thomas-s/Hugo Petrus-a/Parel-c 4.00

MARVEL ILLUSTRATED: TREASURE ISLAND
Marvel Comics: Aug, 2007 - No. 6, Jan, 2008 ($2.99, limited series)

1-6-Adaptation of the Stevenson novel; Roy Thomas-s/Mario Gully-a/Greg Hildebrandt-c 3.00
HC (2008, $19.99) r/#1-6 20.00

MARVEL KNIGHTS (See Black Panther, Daredevil, Inhumans, & Punisher)
Marvel Comics: 1998 (Previews for upcoming series)

Sketchbook-Wizard suppl.; Quesada & Palmiotti-c 4.00
Tourbook-($2.99) Interviews and art previews 4.00

MARVEL KNIGHTS
Marvel Comics: July, 2000 - No. 15, Sept, 2001 ($2.99)

1-Daredevil, Punisher, Black Widow, Shang-Chi, Dagger app. 4.00
2-15: 2-Two covers by Barreto & Quesada 3.00
.../Marvel Boy Genesis Edition (6/00) Sketchbook preview 3.00
...: Millennial Visions (2/02, $3.99) Pin-ups by various; Harris-c 4.00

MARVEL KNIGHTS (Volume 2)
Marvel Comics: May, 2002 - No. 6, Oct, 2002 ($2.99)

1-6-Daredevil, Punisher, Black Widow app.; Ponticelli-a 3.00

MARVEL KNIGHTS: DOUBLE SHOT
Marvel Comics: June, 2002 - No. 4, Sept, 2002 ($2.99, limited series)

1-4: 1-Punisher by Ennis & Quesada; Daredevil by Haynes; Fabry-c 3.00

MARVEL KNIGHTS 4 (Fantastic Four) (Issues #1&2 are titled **Knights 4**) (#28-30 titled **Four**)
Marvel Comics: Apr, 2004 - No. 30, July, 2006 ($2.99)

1-30: 1-7-McNiven-c/a; Aguirre-Sacasa-a. 8,9-Namor app. 13-Cho-c. 14-Land-c. 21-Flashback meeting with Black Panther. 30-Namor app. 3.00
...Vol. 1: The Wolf at the Door (2004, $16.99, TPB) r/#1-7 17.00
...Vol. 2: The Stuff of Nightmares (2005, $13.99, TPB) r/#8-12 14.00
...Vol. 3: Divine Time (2005, $14.99, TPB) r/#13-18 15.00
...Vol. 4: Impossible Things Happen Every Day (2006, $14.99, TPB) r/#19-24 15.00

GD VG FN VF VF/NM NM-
2.0 4.0 6.0 8.0 9.0 9.2

Fantastic Four: The Resurrection of Nicholas Scratch TPB (2006, $14.99) r/#25-30 15.00

MARVEL KNIGHTS: HULK
Marvel Comics: Feb, 2014 - No. 4, May, 2104 ($3.99, limited series)

1-4-Keatinge-s/Kowalski-a; Banner in Paris 4.00

MARVEL KNIGHTS MAGAZINE
Marvel Comics: May, 2001 - No. 6, Oct, 2001 ($3.99, magazine size)

1-6-Reprints of recent Daredevil, Punisher, Black Widow, Inhumans 4.00

MARVEL KNIGHTS SPIDER-MAN (Title continues in Sensational Spider-Man #23)
Marvel Comics: Jun, 2004 - No. 22, Mar, 2006 ($2.99)

1-Wraparound-c by Dodson; Millar-s/Dodson-a; Green Goblin app. 4.00
2-12: 2-Avengers app. 2,3-Vulture & Electro app. 5,8-Cho-c/a. 6-8-Venom app. 3.00
13-18-Reginald Hudlin-s/Billy Tan-a. 13,14,18-New Avengers app. 15-Punisher app. 3.00
19-22-The Other x-over pts. 2,5,8,11; Pat Lee-a 3.00
19-22-var-c: 19-Black costume. 20-Scarlet Spider. 21-Spider-Armor. 22-Peter Parker 5.00
... Vol. 1 HC (2005, $29.99, over-sized with d.j.) r/#1-12; Stan Lee intro.; Dodson & Cho sketch pages 30.00
... Vol. 1: Down Among the Dead Men (2004, $9.99, TPB) r/#1-4 10.00
... Vol. 2: Venomous (2005, $9.99, TPB) r/#5-8 10.00
... Vol. 3: The Last Stand (2005, $9.99, TPB) r/#9-12 10.00
... Vol. 4: Wild Blue Yonder (2005, $14.99, TPB) r/#13-18 15.00

MARVEL KNIGHTS: SPIDER-MAN
Marvel Comics: Dec, 2013 - No. 5, Apr, 2014 ($3.99, limited series)

1-5-Matt Kindt-s/Marco Rudy-a; Arcade app. 4.00

MARVEL KNIGHTS 20TH
Marvel Comics: Jan, 2019 - No. 6, Mar, 2019 ($4.99/$3.99, bi-weekly limited series)

1,6-($4.99) Cates-s/Foreman-a; Daredevil, Frank Castle, Kingpin & Doctor Doom app. 5.00
2-5-($3.99) 2-Henrichon-a. 3-Couceiro-a. 4,5-Black Panther app. 4.00

MARVEL KNIGHTS 2099
Marvel Comics: 2005 ($13.99, TPB)

nn-Reprints one shots: Daredevil 2099, Punisher 2099, Black Panther 2099, Inhumans 2099 and Mutant 2099; Pat Lee-c 14.00

MARVEL KNIGHTS: X-MEN
Marvel Comics: Jan, 2014 - No. 5, May, 2014 ($3.99, limited series)

1-4-Brahm Revel-s/Cris Peter-a; Sabretooth app. 4.00

MARVEL LEGACY
Marvel Comics: Nov, 2017 ($5.99, one-shot)

1-Leads into Marvel's Legacy title re-boot following Secret Empire; Aaron-s/Ribic & McNiven main art, plus art by various; wraparound gatefold front-c by Quesada 6.00

MARVEL LEGACY: ...
Marvel Comics: 2006, 2007 ($4.99, one-shots)

... The 1960s Handbook - Profiles of 1960s iconic and minor characters; info thru 1969 5.00
... The 1970s Handbook - Profiles of 1970s iconic and minor characters; info thru 1979 5.00
... The 1980s Handbook - Profiles of 1980s iconic and minor characters; info thru 1989 5.00
... The 1990s Handbook - Profiles of 1990s iconic and minor characters; Lim-c 5.00
...: The 1960s-1990s Handbook TPB (2007, $19.99) r/one-shots 20.00

MARVELMAN CLASSIC
Marvel Comics: 2010 ($34.99, B&W)

HC-(2010, $34.99) Reprints of 1950s British Marvelman stories; character history 35.00
... Primer (8/10, $3.99) Character history; Mick Anglo interview; Quesada-c 4.00

MARVELMAN FAMILY'S FINEST
Marvel Comics: 2010 - No. 6, Jan, 2011 ($3.99, B&W, limited series)

1-6-Reprints of 1950s Marvelman, Young Marvelman and Marvelman Family stories 4.00

MARVEL MANGAVERSE:... (one-shots)
Marvel Comics: March, 2002 ($2.25, manga-inspired one-shots)

Avengers Assemble! - Udon Studio-s/a 3.00
Eternity Twilight ($3.50) - Ben Dunn-s/a/wrap-around-c 4.00
Fantastic Four - Adam Warren-s/Keron Grant-a 3.00
Ghost Riders - Chuck Austen-s/a 3.00
Punisher - Peter David-s/Lea Hernandez-a 3.00
Spider-Man - Kaare Andrews-s/a 3.00
X-Men - C.B. Cebulski-s/Jeff Matsuda-a 3.00

MARVEL MANGAVERSE (Manga series)
Marvel Comics: June, 2002 - No. 6, Nov., 2002 ($2.25)

1-6: 1-Ben Dunn-s/a; intro. manga Captain Marvel 3.00
Vol. 1 TPB (2002, $24.95) r/one-shots 25.00
Vol. 2 TPB (2002, $12.99) r/#1-6 13.00

Marvel Masterpieces 2 #3 © MAR

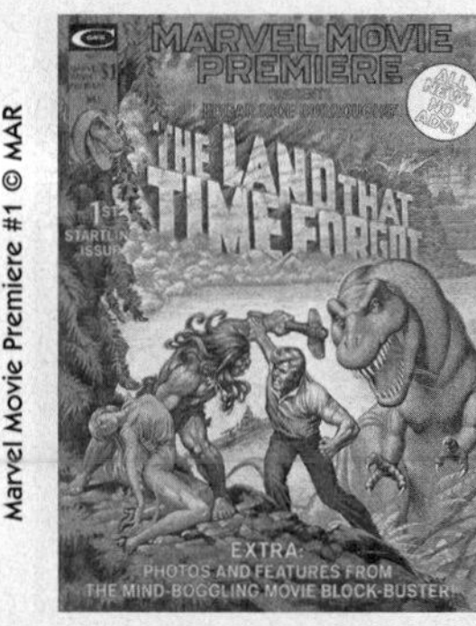

Marvel Movie Premiere #1 © MAR

Marvel Mystery Comics #11 © MAR

	GD 2.0	VG 4.0	FN 6.0	VF 8.0	VF/NM 9.0	NM- 9.2

Vol. 3: Spider-Man-Legend of the Spider-Clan (2003, $11.99, TPB) r/series 12.00

MARVEL MASTERPIECES COLLECTION, THE
Marvel Comics: May, 1993 - No. 4, Aug, 1993 ($2.95, coated paper, lim. series)

1-4-Reprints Marvel Masterpieces trading cards w/ new Jusko paintings in each; Jusko painted-c/a 4.00

MARVEL MASTERPIECES 2 COLLECTION, THE
Marvel Comics: July, 1994 - No. 3, Sept, 1994 ($2.95, limited series)

1-3: 1-Kaluta-c; r/trading cards; new Steranko centerfold 4.00

MARVEL MILESTONE EDITION
Marvel Comics: 1991 - 1999 ($2.95, coated stock)(r/originals with original ads w/silver ink-c)

...: Amazing Fantasy #15 (3/92); ....:Hulk #181 (8/99, $2.99)
3 6 9 17 25 34

...: Amazing Spider-Man #1 (1/93), ...: Amazing Spider-Man #1 (1/93) variation- no price on-c, ...: Amazing Spider-Man #3 (3/95, $2.95), ...: Amazing Spider-Man #129 (11/92), ...: Avengers #1 (9/93), ...:Avengers #4 (3/95, $2.95), ...: Captain America #1 (3/95, $3.95), ...: Fantastic Four #1 (11/91), ...: Fantastic Four #5 (11/92), ...: Giant Size X-Men #1 (1991, $3.95, 68 pgs.), ...: Incredible Hulk #1 (3/92, says 3/91 by error), ...: Iron Man #55 (11/92), ...: Strange Tales-r/Dr. Strange stories from #110, 111, 114, & 115; ...: Tales of Suspense #39 (3/93), ...: X-Men #1-Reprints X-Men #1 (1991)
2 4 6 8 11 14

...: Amazing Spider-Man #149 (11/94, $2.95), ...: Avengers #16 (10/93), ...: X-Men #9 (10/93), ...:X-Men #28 (11/94, $2.95) 1 2 3 5 6 8

...: Iron Fist #14 (11/92) 2 4 6 8 10 12

MARVEL MILESTONES
Marvel Comics: 2005 - 2006 ($3.99, coated stock)(r/originals w/silver ink-c)

...: Beast & Kitty Pryde-r/from Amazing Adventures #11 & Uncanny X-Men #153 5.00
...: Black Panther, Storm & Ka-Zar-r/from Black Panther #26, Marvel Team-Up #100 and Marvel Mystery Comics #7 5.00
...: Blade, Man-Thing & Satana-r/from Tomb of Dracula #10, Adv. Into Fear #16 and Vampire Tales #2 5.00
...: Captain Britain, Psylocke & Sub-Mariner-r/from Spect. Spidey #114, Uncanny X-Men #213 and Human Torch #2 5.00
...: Doom, Sub-Mariner & Red Skull -r/from FF Ann. #2, Sub-Mariner Comics #1, Captain America Comics #1 5.00
...: Dragon Lord, Speedball and The Man in the Sky -r/from Marvel Spotlight #5, Speedball #1 and Amazing Adult Fantasy #14; Ditko-a on all 5.00
...: Dr. Strange, Silver Surfer, Sub-Mariner, & Hulk -r/from Marvel Premiere #3, FF Ann. #5, Marvel Comics #1, Incredible Hulk #3 5.00
...: Ghost Rider, Black Widow & Iceman -r/from Marvel Spotlight #5, Daredevil #81, X-Men #47 5.00
...: Iron Man, Ant-Man & Captain America -r/from TOS #39,40, TTA #27, Capt. America #1 5.00
...: Legion of Monsters, Spider-Man and Brother Voodoo -r/Marvel Premiere #28 & others 5.00
...: Millie the Model & Patsy Walker-r/from Millie the Model #100, Defenders #65 5.00
...: Onslaught -r/Onslaught: Marvel; wraparound-c 5.00
...: Rawhide Kid & Two-Gun Kid-r/Two-Gun Kid #60 and Rawhide Kid #17 5.00
...: Special: Bloodstone, X-51 & Captain Marvel II ($4.99) -r/from Marvel Presents #1, Machine Man #1, Amazing Spider-Man Ann. #19, and Bloodstone #1 6.00
...: Star Brand & Quasar -r/from Star Brand #1 & Quasar #1 5.00
...: Ultimate Spider-Man, Ult. X-Men, Microman & Mantor -r/from Ultimate Spider-Man #1/2, Ultimate X-Men #1/2 and Human Torch #2 5.00
...: Venom & Hercules -r/Marvel S-H Secret Wars #8, Journey Into Mystery Ann. #1 5.00
...: Wolverine, X-Men & Tuk: Caveboy -r/from Marvel Comics Presents #1, Uncanny X-Men #201, Capt. America Comics #1,2 5.00
...: (Jim Lee and Chris Claremont) X-Men and the Starjammers Pt. 1 -r/Unc. X-Men #275 5.00
...: X-Men and the Starjammers Pt. 2 -r/Unc. X-Men #276,277 5.00

MARVEL MINI-BOOKS (See Promotional Comics section)

MARVEL MONSTERS:... (one-shots)
Marvel Comics: Dec, 2005; Oct, 2019 ($3.99/$4.99)

...Devil Dinosaur 1 - Hulk app.; Eric Powell-c/a; Sniegoski-s; r/Journey Into Mystery #62 5.00
...Fin Fang Four 1 - FF app.; Powell-c; Langridge-s/Gray-a; r/Strange Tales #89 5.00
...From the Files of Ulysses Bloodstone 1 - Guide to classic Marvel monsters; Powell-c 5.00
...Monsters on the Prowl 1 - Niles-s/Fegredo-a/Powell-c; Thing, Hulk, Giant-Man & Beast app. 5.00
...Where Monsters Dwell 1 - Giffen-s/a; David-s/Pander-a; Parker-s/Braun-s; Powell-c 5.00
HC (2006, $20.99, dust jacket) r/one-shots 21.00
... No. 1 (10/19, $4.99) Bunn-s/Hepburn-a; monster pin-ups & profiles by various 5.00

MARVEL MOVIE PREMIERE (Magazine)
Marvel Comics Group: Sept, 1975 (B&W, one-shot)

1-Burroughs' "The Land That Time Forgot" adapt. 2 4 6 11 16 20

MARVEL MOVIE SHOWCASE FEATURING STAR WARS
Marvel Comics Group: Nov, 1982 - No. 2, Dec, 1982 ($1.25, 68 pgs.)

1-Star Wars movie adaptation; reprints Star Wars #1-3 by Chaykin; reprints-c to Star Wars #1
5 10 15 34 60 85
2-Reprints Star Wars #4-6; Stevens-r 3 6 9 19 30 40

MARVEL MOVIE SPOTLIGHT FEATURING RAIDERS OF THE LOST ARK
Marvel Comics Group: Nov, 1982 ($1.25, 68 pgs.)

1-Edited-r/Raiders of the Lost Ark #1-3; Buscema-c/a(p); movie adapt. 6.00

MARVEL MUST HAVES (Reprints of recent sold-out issues)
Marvel Comics: Dec, 2001 - 2005 ($2.99/$3.99/$4.99)

1,2,4-6: 1-r/Wolverine: Origin #1, Startling Stories: Banner #1, Tangled Web #4 and Cable #97. 2-Amazing Spider-Man #36 and others. 4-Truth #1, Capt. America V4 #1, and The Ultimates #1. 5-r/Ultimate War #1, Ult. X-Men #26, Ult Spider-Man #33. 6-Ult. Spider-Man #33-36 4.00
3-r/Call of Duty: The Brotherhood #1 & Daredevil #32,33 3.00
Amazing Spider-Man #30-32; Incredible Hulk #34-36; The Ultimates #1-3; Ultimate Spider-Man #1-3; Ultimate X-Men #1-3; (New) X-Men #114-116 each.... 4.00
NYX #1-3 3 6 9 15 22 28
NYX #4-5 with sketch & cover gallery; Ultimates 2 #1-3 each...
2 4 6 9 12 15
Spider-Man and the Black Cat #1-3; preview of #4 5.00

MARVEL MYSTERY COMICS (Formerly Marvel Comics) (Becomes Marvel Tales No. 93 on)
Timely /Marvel Comics (TP #2-17/TCI #18-54/MCI #55-92): No. 2, Dec, 1939 - No. 92, June, 1949 (Some material from #8-10 reprinted in 2004's Marvel 65th Anniversary Special #1)

2-(Rare)-American Ace begins, ends #3; Human Torch (blue costume) by Burgos, Sub-Mariner by Everett continue; 2 pg. origin recap of Human Torch; Angel-c
4000 8000 12,000 30,000 67,500 105,000
3-New logo from Marvel pulp begins; 1st app. of television in comics? in Human Torch story (1/40); Angel-c 2900 5800 8700 21,800 43,400 65,000
4-Intro. Electro, the Marvel of the Age (ends #19), The Ferret, Mystery Detective (ends #9); 1st Sub-Mariner-c by Schomburg; 2nd German swastika on-c of a comic (2/40); one month after Top-Notch Comics #2 3200 6400 9600 24,000 48,000 72,000
5 Classic Schomburg Torch-c, his 1st ever (Scarce)
3900 7800 11,700 28,900 60,450 92,000
6-Angel-c; Gustavson Angel story 1100 2200 3300 8400 15,200 22,000
7-Sub-Mariner attacks N.Y. city & Torch joins police force setting up battle in #8-10. Classic Schomburg Torch-c, his 2nd ever 1300 2600 3900 9900 17,950 26,000
8-1st Human Torch & Sub-Mariner battle(6/40) 1520 3040 4560 11,340 24,420 37,500
9-(Scarce)-Human Torch & Sub-Mariner battle (cover/story); classic-c by Everett
5200 10,400 15,600 38,500 76,250 114,000
10-Human Torch & Sub-Mariner battle, conclusion, 1 pg.; Terry Vance, the Schoolboy Sleuth begins, ends #57 1350 2700 4050 10,000 21,500 33,000
11-Schomburg Torch-c, his 3rd ever 533 1066 1557 3788 6694 9600
12-Classic Angel-c by Kirby 524 1048 1572 3825 6763 9700
13-Intro. of The Vision by S&K (11/40); Sub-Mariner dons new costume, ends #15; Schomburg's 4th Human Torch-c 975 1950 2919 7100 12,550 18,000
14-16: 14-Shows-c to Human Torch #1 on-c (12/40). 15-S&K Vision, Gustavson Angel story
437 874 1311 3190 5645 8100
17-Human Torch/Sub-Mariner team-up by Burgos/Everett; Human Torch pin-up on back-c; shows-c to Human Torch #2 on-c 465 930 1395 3395 5998 8600
18-1st app. villain "The Cat's Paw" 417 834 1251 2918 5159 7400
19,20: 19-Origin Toro in text; shows-c to Sub-Mariner #1 on-c. 20-Origin The Angel in text
423 846 1269 3000 5250 7500
21-The Patriot begins, (intro. in Human Torch #4 (#3)); not in #46-48; Sub-Mariner pin-up on back-c; Gustavson Angel story (7/41) 423 846 1269 3088 5444 7800
22-25: 23-Last Gustavson Angel; origin The Vision in text. 24-Injury-to-eye story
417 834 1251 2918 5159 7400
26-29: 27-Ka-Zar ends; last S&K Vision who battles Satan. 28-Jimmy Jupiter in the Land of Nowhere begins, ends #48; Sub-Mariner vs. The Flying Dutchman
411 822 1233 2877 5039 7200
30-"Remember Pearl Harbor" Japanese war-c 514 1028 1542 3750 6625 9500
31,32-"Remember Pearl Harbor" Japanese war-c. 31-Sub-Mariner by Everett ends, resumes #84. 32-1st app. The Boboes 411 822 1233 2877 5039 7200
33,35,36,38,39: 36-Nazi invasion of NYC cover. 39-WWII Nazi-c
394 788 1182 2758 4829 6900
34-Everett, Burgos, Martin Goodman, Funnies, Inc. office appear in story & battles Hitler; last Burgos Human Torch 405 810 1215 2835 4968 7100
37-Classic Hitler-c 432 864 1296 3154 5577 8000
40-Classic Zeppelin-c 1200 2400 3600 9100 16,550 24,000
41-Hirohito & Tojo-c 423 846 1269 3088 5444 7800
42,43,47 380 760 1140 2660 4680 6700
44-Classic Super Plane-c 1500 3000 4500 11,400 20,700 30,000
45-Red Skull, Nazi hooded Vigilante war-c 463 926 1389 3380 6090 8800
46-Classic Hitler-c 1750 3500 5250 13,300 24,150 35,000
48-Last Vision; flag-c 394 788 1182 2158 4829 6900
49-Origin Miss America 394 788 1182 2158 4829 6900

Marvel Mystery Comics #73 © MAR

Marvel 1985 #1 © MAR

Marvel Premiere #36 © MAR

	GD 2.0	VG 4.0	FN 6.0	VF 8.0	VF/NM 9.0	NM- 9.2
50-Mary becomes Miss Patriot (origin)	365	730	1095	2555	4478	6400
51-60: 54-Bondage-c	300	600	900	2010	3505	5000
61,62,64-Last German war-c	290	580	870	1856	3178	4500
63-Classic Hitler War-c; The Villainess Cat-Woman only app.	463	926	1389	3380	6090	8800
65,66-Last Japanese War-c	290	580	870	1856	3178	4500
67-78: 74-Last Patriot. 75-Young Allies begin. 76-Ten Chapter Miss America serial begins, ends #85	168	336	504	1075	1838	2600
79-New cover format; Super Villains begin on cover; last Angel	187	374	561	1197	2049	2900
80-1st app. Capt. America in Marvel Comics	219	438	657	1402	2401	3400
81-Captain America app.	174	348	522	1114	1907	2700
82-Origin & 1st app. Namora (5/47); 1st Sub-Mariner/Namora team-up; Captain America app.	354	708	1062	2478	4339	6200
83,85: 83-Last Young Allies. 85-Last Miss America; Blonde Phantom app.	168	336	504	1075	1838	2600
84-Blonde Phantom begins (on-c of #84,88,89); Sub-Mariner by Everett begins; Captain America app.; Everett-c	219	438	657	1402	2401	3400
86-Blonde Phantom i.d. revealed; Captain America app.; last Bucky app.	168	336	504	1075	1838	2600
87-1st Capt. America/Golden Girl team-up; last Toro app. (8/48)	174	348	522	1114	1907	2700
88-Golden Girl, Namora, & Sun Girl (1st in Marvel Comics) x-over; Captain America, Blonde Phantom app.	177	354	531	1133	1942	2750
89-1st Human Torch/Sun Girl team-up; 1st Captain America solo; Blonde Phantom app.	174	348	522	1114	1907	2700
90,91: 90-Blonde Phantom un-masked; Captain America app. 91-Capt. America app.; Blonde Phantom & Sub-Mariner end; early Venus app. (4/49) (scarce)	226	452	678	1446	2473	3500
92-Feature story on the birth of the Human Torch and the death of Professor Horton (his creator); 1st app. The Witness in Marvel Comics; Captain America app. (scarce)	415	830	1245	2905	5103	7300
132 Pg. issue, B&W, 25¢ (1943-44)-printed in N. Y.; square binding, blank inside covers); has Marvel No. 33-c in color; contains Capt. America #18 & Marvel Mystery Comics #33; same contents as Captain America Annual	7300	14,600	21,900	45,500	--	--
132 Pg. issue (with variant contents), B&W, 25¢ (1942-'43)- square binding, blank inside covers; has same Marvel No. 33-c in color but contains Capt. America #22 & Marvel Mystery Comics #41 instead	7300	14,600	21,900	45,500	--	--

NOTE: ***Brodsky** c-49, 72, 86, 88-92. **Crandall** a-26i. **Everett** c-9, 27, 84. **Gabrielle** c-30-32. **Schomburg** c-3-11, 13-29, 33-36, 39-48, 50-59, 63-69, 74, 76, 132 pg. issue. **Shores** c-37, 38, 75p, 77, 78p, 79p, 80, 81p, 82-84, 85p, 87p. **Sekowsky** c-73. Bondage covers-3, 4, 7, 12, 28, 29, 49, 50, 52, 56, 57, 58, 59, 65. Angel c-2, 3, 8, 12. Remember Pearl Harbor issues-#30-32.*

MARVEL MYSTERY COMICS
Marvel Comics: Dec, 1999 ($3.95, reprints)

1-Reprints original 1940s stories; Schomburg-c from #74 — 5.00

MARVEL MYSTERY COMICS 70th ANNIVERARY SPECIAL
Marvel Comics: Jul, 2009 ($3.99, one-shot)

1-Rivera-c; new Sub-Mariner/Human Torch team-up set in 1941; reps. from #4 & 5 — 5.00

MARVEL MYSTERY HANDBOOK: 70th ANNIVERARY SPECIAL
Marvel Comics: 2009 ($4.99, one-shot)

1-Official Handbook-style profile pages of characters from Marvel's first year — 5.00

MARVEL NEMESIS: THE IMPERFECTS (EA Games characters)
Marvel Comics: July, 2005 - No. 6, Dec, 2005 ($2.99, limited series)

1-6-Jae Lee-c/Greg Pak-s/Renato Arlem-a; Spider-Man, Thing, Wolverine, Elektra app — 3.00
Digest (2005, $7.99) r/#1-6 — 8.00

MARVEL 1985
Marvel Comics: July, 2008 - No. 6, Dec, 2008 ($3.99, limited series)

1-6: 1-Marvel villains come to the real world; Millar-s/Edwards-a; three covers — 4.00
HC (2009, $24.99) r/#1-6; intro. by Lindelof; Edwards production art — 25.00

MARVEL NO-PRIZE BOOK, THE (The Official... on-c)
Marvel Comics Group: Jan, 1983 (one-shot, direct sales only)

	GD	VG	FN	VF	VF/NM	NM-
1-Stan Lee as Doctor Doom cover by Golden; Kirby-a	1	3	4	6	8	10

MARVEL NOW! POINT ONE
Marvel Comics: Dec, 2012 ($5.99, one-shot)

1-Short story lead-ins to new Marvel Now! series; Nick Fury, Nova, Star-Lord, Ant-Man & others app.; s/a by various; Granov-c and baby variant-c by Skottie Young — 6.00

MARVEL: NOW WHAT?!
Marvel Comics: Dec, 2013 ($3.99, one-shot)

1-Short story spoofs; Doc Octopus, X-Men, Avengers; s/a by various; Skottie Young-c — 4.00

MARVELOUS ADVENTURES OF GUS BEEZER
Marvel Comics: May, 2003; Feb, 2004 ($2.99, one-shots)

...: Gus Beezer & Spider-Man 1 - (5/03) Gurihiru-a — 3.00
...: Hulk 1 - (5/03) Simone-s/Lethcoe-a; She-Hulk app. — 3.00
...: Spider-Man 1 - (5/03) Simone-s/Lethcoe-a; The Lizard & Dr. Doom app. — 3.00
...: X-Men 1 - (5/03) Simone-s/Lethcoe-a — 3.00

MARVELOUS LAND OF OZ (Sequel to Wonderful Wizard of Oz)
Marvel Comics: Jan, 2010 - No. 8, Sept, 2010 ($3.99, limited series)

1-8-Eric Shanower-a/Skottie Young-a/c. 1-Two covers by Young — 4.00
1-Variant Pumpkinhead/Saw-Horse cover by McGuinness — 6.00

MARVEL PETS HANDBOOK (Also see "Lockjaw and the Pet Avengers")
Marvel Comics: 2009 ($3.99, one-shot)

1-Official Handbook-style profile pages of animal characters — 4.00

MARVEL PREMIERE
Marvel Comics Group: April, 1972 - No. 61, Aug, 1981 (A tryout book for new characters)

	GD	VG	FN	VF	VF/NM	NM-
1-Origin Warlock (pre-#1) by Gil Kane/Adkins; origin Counter-Earth; Hulk & Thor cameo (#1-14 are 20¢-c)	19	38	57	133	297	460
2-Warlock ends; Kirby Yellow Claw-r	5	10	15	31	53	75
3-Dr. Strange series begins (pre #1, 7/72), Stan Lee-s/B. Smith-c/a(p)	9	18	27	57	111	165
4-Barry Smith-a; Roy Thomas brings the world of Robert E. Howard into the Marvel Universe (via serpent people)	4	8	12	25	40	55
5-9: 5-1st app. Sligguth; 1st mention of Shuma-Gorath. 6-Brunner-a; 1st N'Gabthoth (Shambler from the sea). 7-1st Dagoth; P. Craig Russell-a. 8-Starlin-(p). 9-Englehart-s; Brunner-a(p) begin	3	6	9	17	26	35
10-Death of the Ancient One; 1st app. Shuma-Gorath	15	30	45	103	227	350
11-14: 11-Three pages of original material; mostly reprint of origin from Strange Tales #115 with Ditko-a. 13-Baron Mordo app; 1st app. Cagliostro & Sise-Neg. 14-Sise-Neg & Shuma-Gorath app.14-Last Dr. Strange (3/74), gets own title 3 months later	3	6	9	14	20	25
15-Origin/1st app. Iron Fist (5/74), ends #25	25	50	75	175	388	600
16,25: 16-2nd app. Iron Fist; origin cont'd from #15; Hama's 1st Marvel-a. 25-1st Byrne Iron Fist (moves to own title next)	5	10	15	34	60	85
17,18,20,22-24: Iron Fist in all	3	6	9	21	33	45
19-1st app. Colleen Wing; Iron Fist app.	7	14	21	49	92	135
21-1st app. Misty Knight; Iron Fist app.	6	12	18	38	69	100
26-Hercules.	2	4	6	8	10	12
27-Satana	3	6	9	16	23	30
28-Legion of Monsters (Ghost Rider, Man-Thing, Morbius, Werewolf)	9	18	27	59	117	175
29-46: 29,30-The Liberty Legion. 29-1st modern app. Patriot. 31-1st app. Woodgod; last 25¢ issue. 32-1st app. Monark Starstalker. 33,34-1st color app. Solomon Kane (Robert E. Howard adaptation "Red Shadows".) 35-Origin/1st app. 3-D Man. 36,37-3-D Man. 38-1st Weirdworld. 39,40-Torpedo. 41-1st Seeker 3000! 42-Tigra. 43-Paladin. 44-Jack of Hearts (1st solo book, 10/78). 45,46-Man-Wolf	1	2	3	5	6	8
29-31-(30¢-c variants, limited distribution)(4,6,8/76)	5	10	15	30	50	70
36-38-(35¢-c variants, limited distribution)(6,8,10/77)	6	12	18	40	73	105
47-Origin/1st app. new Ant-Man (Scott Lang); Byrne-a	9	18	27	58	114	170
48-Ant-Man; Byrne-a	4	8	12	23	37	50
49-The Falcon (1st solo book, 8/79)	3	6	9	16	23	30
50-1st app. Alice Cooper; co-plotted by Alice	4	8	12	23	37	50
51-53-Black Panther vs. KKK	3	6	9	14	20	25
54-56: 54-1st Caleb Hammer. 55-Wonder Man. 56-1st color app. Dominic Fortune						6.00
57-Dr. Who (2nd U.S. app.-see Movie Classics)	3	6	9	21	33	45
58-60-Dr. Who	1	3	4	6	8	10
61-Star Lord	2	4	6	10	14	18

NOTE: ***N. Adams** (Crusty Bunkers) part inks-10, 12, 13. **Austin** a-50i, 56i; c-46i, 50i, 56i, 58. **Brunner** a-4i, 6p, 9-14p; c-9-14. **Byrne** a-47p, 48p. **Chaykin** a-32-34; c-32, 33, 56. **Giffen** a-31p, 44p; c-44. **Gil Kane** a(p)-1, 2, 15; c(p)-1, 2, 15, 16, 22-24, 27, 36, 37. **Kirby** c-26, 29-31, 35. **Layton** a-47i, 48i; c-47. **McWilliams** a-25i. **Miller** c-49p, 53p, 58p. **Nebres** a-44i; c-38i. **Nino** a-38i. **Perez** c/a-38p, 45p, 46p. **Ploog** a-38; c-5-7. **Russell** a-7p. **Simonson** a-60(2pgs.); c-57. **Starlin** a-8p; c-8. **Sutton** a-41, 43, 50p, 61; c-50p, 61. #57-60 publ'd w/two different prices on-c.*

MARVEL PRESENTS
Marvel Comics: October, 1975 - No. 12, Aug, 1977 (#1-6 are 25¢ issues)

	GD	VG	FN	VF	VF/NM	NM-
1-Origin & 1st app. Bloodstone	5	10	15	30	50	70
2-Origin Bloodstone continued; Buckler-c	2	4	6	9	12	15
3-Guardians of the Galaxy (1st solo book, 2/76) begins, ends #12	5	10	15	33	57	80
4-7,9-12: 9,10-Origin Starhawk	2	4	6	8	10	12
4-6-(30¢-c variants, limited distribution)(4-8/76)	4	8	12	27	44	60
8-r/story from Silver Surfer #2 plus 4 pgs. new-a	3	6	9	14	19	24
11,12-(35¢-c variants, limited distribution)(6,8/77)	8	16	24	51	96	140

NOTE: ***Austin** a-6i. **Buscema** r-8p. **Chaykin** a-5p. **Kane** c-1p. **Starlin** layouts-10.*

Marvel Preview #14 © MAR

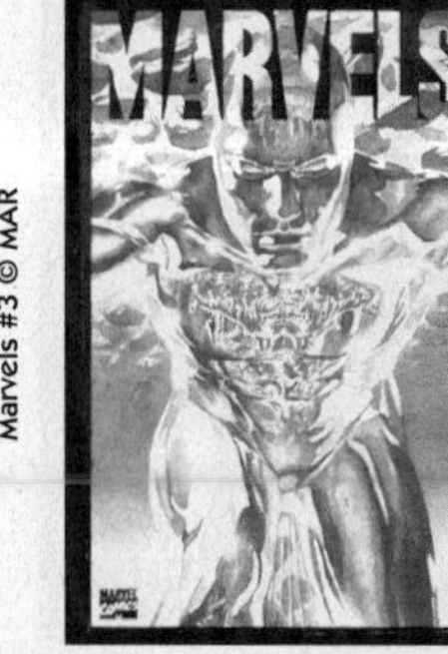

Marvels #3 © MAR

Marvels Comics: X-Men #1 © MAR

GD VG FN VF VF/NM NM-
2.0 4.0 6.0 8.0 9.0 9.2

MARVEL PREVIEW (Magazine) (Bizarre Adventures #25 on)
Marvel Comics: Feb (no month), 1975 - No. 24, Winter, 1980 (B&W) ($1.00)

1-Man-Gods From Beyond the Stars; Crusty Bunkers (Neal Adams)-a(i) & cover; Nino-a 3 6 9 21 33 45
2-1st origin The Punisher (see Amaz. Spider-Man #129 & Classic Punisher); 1st app. Dominic Fortune; Morrow-c 11 22 33 73 157 240
3,8,10: 3-Blade the Vampire Slayer. 8-Legion of Monsters; Morbius app. 10-Thor the Mighty; Starlin frontispiece 4 8 12 23 37 50
4-Star-Lord & Sword in the Star (origins & 1st app.); Morrow-c 17 34 51 119 265 410
5-Sherlock Holmes 3 6 9 14 20 26
6,9: 6-Sherlock Holmes; N. Adams frontispiece. 9-Man-God; origin Star Hawk, ends #20 2 4 6 13 18 22
7-(Summer/76) Debut of Rocket Raccoon (called Rocky Raccoon) in Sword in the Star story (see Incredible Hulk #271 (5/82) for next app.); Satana on cover 31 62 93 223 499 775
11,14,15,18-Star-Lord. 11-Byrne-a; Starlin frontispiece; 2 versions: with and w/o white Heinlein text at lower right corner of front-c; 1st app. Spartax. 14-Starlin painted-c. 18-Sienkiewicz-a; Veitch & Bissette-a 5 10 15 31 53 75
12,16,19,21,23: 12-Haunt of Horror. 16-Masters of Terror. 19-Kull. 21-Moon Knight (Spr/80)-Predates Moon Knight #1; The Shroud by Ditko. 23-Bizarre Advs.; Miller-a 2 4 6 8 10 12
13,17,20,22,24: 17-Blackmark by G. Kane (see Savage Sword of Conan #1-3). 20-Bizarre Advs. 22-King Arthur. 24-Debut Paradox 1 2 3 5 6 8

NOTE: ***N. Adams*** *(C. Bunkers) r-20i.* ***Buscema*** *a-22, 23.* ***Byrne*** *a-11.* ***Chaykin*** *a-20r; c-20 (new).* ***Colan*** *a-8, 16p(3), 18p, 23p; c-16p.* ***Elias*** *a-18.* ***Giffen*** *a-7.* ***Infantino*** *a-14p.* ***Kaluta*** *a-12; c-15.* ***Miller*** *a-23.* ***Morrow*** *a-8i; c-2-4.* ***Perez*** *a-20p.* ***Ploog*** *a-8.* ***Starlin*** *c-13, 14. Nudity in some issues.*

MARVEL RIOT
Marvel Comics: Dec, 1995 ($1.95, one-shot)

1-"Age of Apocalypse" spoof; Lobdell script 4.00

MARVEL RISING
Marvel Comics: Jun, 2018 - Nov, 2018; May, 2019 - No. 5, Sept, 2019 ($5.99/$4.99, lim. series)

0-(6/18, free) Grayson-s/Failla-a; preview of Marvel Super Hero Adventures titles 3.00
1-5: 1-(5/19, $3.99) Capt. Marvel, Ms. Marvel, Squirrel Girl, America & Spider-Gwen app. 4.00
...: Alpha 1 (8/18, $4.99) Part 1; Squirrel Girl & Ms. Marvel team-up; Grayson-s/Duarte-a 5.00
...: Ms. Marvel/Squirrel Girl 1 (10/18, $5.99) Part 3; America Chavez app. 6.00
...: Omega 1 (11/18, $4.99) Part 4 conclusion; Arcade app. 5.00
...: Squirrel Girl/Ms. Marvel 1 (9/18, $5.99) Part 2; battle Emulator 6.00

MARVEL ROMANCE
Marvel Comics: 2006 ($19.99, TPB)

nn-Reprints romance stories from 1960-1972; art by Kirby, Buscema, Colan, Romita 20.00

MARVEL ROMANCE REDUX (Humor stories using art reprinted from Marvel romance comics)
Marvel Comics: Apr, 2006 - Aug, 2006 ($2.99, one-shots)

...: But I Thought He Loved Me Too (4/06) art by Kirby, Colan, Buscema & Romita; Giffen-c 3.00
...: Guys & Dolls (5/06) art by Starlin, Heck, Colan & Buscema; Conner-c 3.00
...: I Should Have Been a Blonde (7/06) art by Brodsky Colletta & Colan; Cho-c 3.00
...: Love is a Four Letter Word (8/06) art by Kirby, Buscema, Colan & Heck; Land-c 3.00
...: Restraining Orders are For Other Girls (6/06) art by Giordano, Kirby; Kyle Baker-c 3.00
...: Another Kind of Love TPB (2007, $13.99) r/one-shots 14.00

MARVELS (Also see Marvels: Eye of the Camera)
Marvel Comics: Jan, 1994 - No. 4, Apr, 1994 ($5.95, painted lim. series)
No. 1 (2nd Printing), Apr, 1996 - No. 4 (2nd Printing), July, 1996 ($2.95)

1-4: Kurt Busiek scripts & Alex Ross painted-c/a in all; double-c w/acetate overlay 1 3 4 6 8 10
Marvel Classic Collectors Pack ($11.90)-Issues #1 & 2 boxed (1st printings). 2 4 6 9 13 16
0-(8/94, $2.95)-no acetate overlay. 5.00
1-4-(2nd printing): r/original limited series w/o acetate overlay 3.00
... Annotated 1-4 (4/19 - No. 4, 8/19, $7.99) reprints with original script, commentary, sketch and unlettered painted art; additional extras 8.00
... Epilogue 1 (9/19, $4.99) Phil Sheldon & family during events of X-Men #98; Busiek-s/Ross-a; new interview with creators; MAD-style spoof (2 pgs.); sketch deign pages 5.00
Hardcover (1994, $59.95)-r/#0-4; w/intros by Stan Lee, John Romita, Sr., Kurt Busiek & Scott McCloud. 60.00
...: 10th Anniversary Edition (2004, $49.99, hardcover w/dustjacket) r/#0-4; scripts and commentaries; Ross sketch pages, cover gallery, behind the scenes art 50.00
Trade paperback ($19.95) 20.00

MARVEL SAGA, THE
Marvel Comics Group: Dec, 1985 - No. 25, Dec, 1987

1-25 4.00

NOTE: ***Williamson*** *a(i)-9, 10; c(i)-7, 10-12, 14, 16.*

MARVEL'S ANT-MAN AND THE WASP PRELUDE (For the 2018 movie)
Marvel Comics: May, 2018 - No. 2, Jun, 2018 ($3.99, limited series)

1,2-Will Corona Pilgrim-s/Chris Allen-a; adaptation of Ant-Man movie 4.00

MARVEL'S ANT-MAN PRELUDE (For the 2015 movie)
Marvel Comics: Apr, 2015 - No. 2, May, 2015 ($2.99, limited series)

1,2-Will Corona Pilgrim-s/Sepulveda-a; photo-c on both; Agent Carter app. 3.00

MARVEL'S AVENGERS (Based on the Marvel's Avengers video game)
Marvel Comics: Feb, 2020 - May, 2020 ($3.99, series of one-shots)

...: Black Widow 1 (5/20) Gage-s/Bandini-a; Taskmaster app. 4.00
...: Captain America 1 (5/20) Allor-s/Jeanty-a; Batroc app. 4.00
...: Hulk 1 (4/20) Jim Zub-s/Ariel Olivetti-a 4.00
...: Iron Man 1 (4/20) Zub-s/Paco Diaz-a; Avengers & Titania app. 4.00
...: Thor 1 (4/20) Zub-s/Robert Gill-a; Loki app. 4.00

MARVEL'S AVENGERS: INFINITY WAR PRELUDE (For the 2018 movie)
Marvel Comics: Mar, 2018 - No. 2, Apr, 2018 ($3.99, limited series)

1,2-Will Corona Pilgrim-s; photo-c on both. 1-Tigh Walker-a. 2-Jorge Fornés-a 4.00

MARVEL'S AVENGERS: UNTITLED PRELUDE (Issue #1 released before final title revealed)
MARVEL'S AVENGERS: ENDGAME PRELUDE (Adaptation of Avengers: Inifinity War)
Marvel Comics: Feb, 2019 - No. 3, Apr, 2019 ($3.99, limited series)

1-3-Will Corona Pilgrim-s/Paco Diaz-a; photo-c on each 4.00

MARVEL'S BLACK PANTHER PRELUDE (For the 2018 movie)
Marvel Comics: Dec, 2017 - No. 2, Jan, 2018 ($3.99, limited series)

1,2-Will Corona Pilgrim-s/Annapaola Martello-a; photo-c on both 4.00

MARVEL'S BLACK WIDOW PRELUDE (For the 2021 movie)
Marvel Comics: Dec, 2017 - No. 2, Jan, 2018 ($3.99, limited series)

1,2-Peter David-s/C.F. Villa-a; photo-c on both; recaps her history with the Avengers 4.00

MARVEL'S CAPTAIN AMERICA: CIVIL WAR PRELUDE (For the 2016 movie)
Marvel Comics: Feb, 2016 - No. 4, Mar, 2016 ($2.99, limited series)

1-4: 1,2-Adaptation of Iron Man 3 movie; Pilgrim-s/Kudranski-a. 3,4-Adapts Captain America: The Winter Soldier movie; Ferguson-a 3.00

MARVEL'S CAPTAIN MARVEL PRELUDE (For the 2019 movie)
Marvel Comics: Jan, 2019 ($3.99, one-shot)

1-Will Corona Pilgrim-s/Andrea Di Vito-a; Fury & Hill's events during Capt. A. Civil War 4.00

MARVELS COMICS: ... (Marvel-type comics read in the Marvel Universe)
Marvel Comics: Jul, 2000 ($2.25, one-shots)

...Captain America #1 -Frenz & Sinnott-a; ...Daredevil #1 -Isabella-s/Newell-a; ...Fantastic Four #1 -Kesel-s/Paul Smith-a; Spider-Man #1 -Oliff-a; ...Thor #1 -Templeton-s/Aucoin-a 3.00
...X-Men #1 -Millar-s/ Sean Phillips & Duncan Fegredo-a 3.00
The History of Marvels Comics (no cover price)-Faux history; previews titles 3.00

MARVEL'S DOCTOR STRANGE PRELUDE (2016 movie)
Marvel Comics: Sept, 2016 - No. 2, Oct, 2016 ($3.99, limited series)

1,2-Corona Pilgrim-s/Fornés-a; photo-c 4.00

MARVEL SELECT FLIP MAGAZINE
Marvel Comics: Aug, 2005 - No. 24 ($3.99/$4.99)

1-11-Reprints Astonishing X-Men and New X-Men: Academy X in flip format 4.00
12-24-($4.99) Reprints recent X-Men mini-series in flip format 5.00

MARVEL SELECTS:
Marvel Comics: Jan, 2000 - No. 6, June, 2000 ($2.75/$2.99, reprints)

...Fantastic Four 1-6: Reprints F.F. #107-112; new Davis-c 3.00
...Spider-Man 1,2,4-6: Reprints AS-M #100,101,103,104,93; Wieringo-c 3.00
...Spider-Man 3 ($2.99): Reprints AS-M #102; new Wieringo-c 3.00

MARVEL 75TH ANNIVERSARY CELEBRATION
Marvel Comics: Dec, 2014 ($5.99, one-shot)

1-Short stories by various incl. Stan Lee, Timm, Bendis, Stan Goldberg; Rivera-c 6.00

MARVELS: EYE OF THE CAMERA (Sequel to Marvels)
Marvel Comics: Feb, 2009 - No. 6, Apr, 2010 ($3.99, limited series)

1-6-Kurt Busiek-s/Jay Anacleto-a; continuing story of photographer Phil Sheldon 4.00
1-6-B&W edition 4.00

MARVEL'S GREATEST COMICS (Marvel Collectors' Item Classics #1-22)
Marvel Comics Group: No. 23, Oct, 1969 - No. 96, Jan, 1981

23-34 (Giants). Begin Fantastic Four-r/#30s?-116 3 6 9 17 26 35
35-37-Silver Surfer-r/Fantastic Four #48-50 2 4 6 11 16 20
38-50: 42-Silver Surfer-r/F.F.(others?) 1 3 4 6 8 10
51-70: 63,64-(25¢ editions) 1 2 3 5 6 8
63,64-(30¢-c variants, limited distribution)(5,7/76) 4 8 12 27 44 60

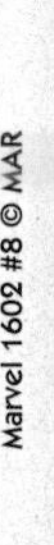
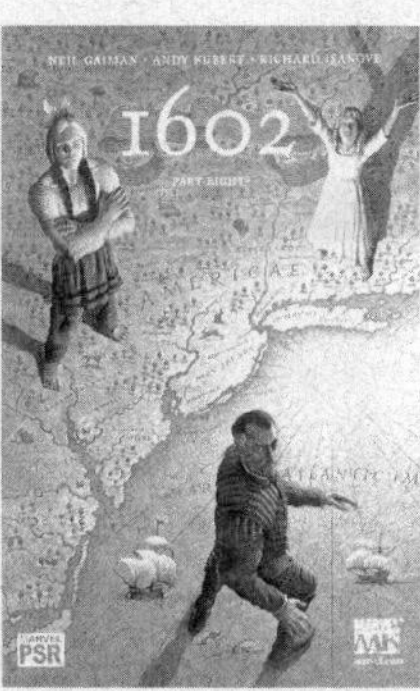

Marvel 1602 #8 © MAR

Marvel Spectacular #2 © MAR

Marvel Spotlight: Halo #1 © MAR & MS

GD 2.0 VG 4.0 FN 6.0 VF 8.0 VF/NM 9.0 NM- 9.2

71-96: 71-73-(30¢ editions) 6.00
71-73-(35¢-c variants, limited distribution)(7,9-10/77) 6 12 18 40 73 105
...: Fantastic Four #52 (2006, $2.99) reprints entire comic with ads and letter column 6.00
NOTE: *Dr. Strange, Fantastic Four, Iron Man, Watcher-#23, 24. Capt. America, Dr. Strange, Iron Man, Fantastic Four-#25-28. Fantastic Four-#38-96. **Buscema** r-85-92; c-87-92r. **Ditko** r-23-28. **Kirby** r-23-82; c-75, 77p, 80p. #81 reprints Fantastic Four #100.*

MARVEL'S GREATEST CREATORS...
Marvel Comics: Jul, 2019 ($1.00, one-shot reprints)
... Avengers – The Origin of Mantis 1 - Reprints Avengers #123; Englehart-s/Brown-a 3.00
... Hulk – The Wedding of Rick Jones 1 - Reprints Inc. Hulk #418; David-s/Frank-a 3.00
... Invaders 1 - Reprints Invaders #1; Roy Thomas-s/Frank Robbins-a 3.00
... Iron Fist – Colleen Wing 1 - Reprints Marvel Premiere #19; Moench-s/Hama-a 3.00
... Iron Fist – Misty Knight 1 - Reprints Marvel Premiere #21; Isabella-s/Arvell Jones-a 3.00
... Luke Cage, Power Man – Piranha 1 - Reprints Power Man #30; McGregor-s 3.00
... Power Pack 1 - Reprints Power Pack #1; Louise Simonson-s/June Brigman-a 3.00
... Silver Surfer – Rude Awakening 1 - Reprints Silver Surfer #51; Marz-s/Lim-a 3.00
... Spider-Man – Kraven's Last Hunt 1 - Reprints Web of Spider-Man #31; Zeck-a 3.00
... What If? – Spider-Girl 1 - Reprints What If? #105; DeFalco-s/Frenz-a 3.00

MARVEL'S GREATEST SUPERHERO BATTLES (See Fireside Book Series)

MARVEL: SHADOWS AND LIGHT
Marvel Comics: Feb, 1997 ($2.95, B&W, one-shot)
1-Tony Daniel-c 4.00

MARVEL 1602
Marvel Comics: Nov, 2003 - No. 8, June, 2004 ($3.50/$3.99, limited series)
1-7-Neil Gaiman-s; Andy Kubert & Richard Isanove-a 3.50
8-($3.99) 4.00
... MGC #1 (7/10, $1.00) r/#1 with "Marvel's Greatest Comics" logo on cover 3.00
HC (2004, $24.99) r/series; script pages for #1, sketch pages and Gaiman afterword 25.00
SC (2005, $19.99) 20.00

MARVEL 1602: FANTASTICK FOUR
Marvel Comics: Nov, 2006 - No. 5, Mar, 2007s ($3.50, limited series)
1-5-Peter David-s/Pascal Alixe-a/Leinil Yu-c 3.50
TPB (2007, $14.99) r/#1-5; sketch page 15.00

MARVEL 1602: NEW WORLD
Marvel Comics: Oct, 2005 - No. 5, Jan, 2006 ($3.50, limited series)
1-5-Greg Pak-s/Greg Tocchini-a; "Hulk" and "Iron Man" app. 3.50
TPB (2006, $14.99) r/#1-5 15.00

MARVEL 65TH ANNIVERSARY SPECIAL
Marvel Comics: 2004 ($4.99, one-shot)
1-Reprints Sub-Mariner & Human Torch battle from Marvel Mystery Comics #8-10 6.00

MARVELS OF SCIENCE
Charlton Comics: March, 1946 - No. 4, June, 1946
1-A-Bomb story 27 54 81 158 259 360
2-4 15 30 45 88 137 185

MARVEL SPECIAL EDITION FEATURING... (Also see Special Collectors' Ed.)
Marvel Comics Group: 1975 - 1978 (84 pgs.) (Oversized)
1-The Spectacular Spider-Man ($1.50); r/Amazing Spider-Man #6,35, Annual 1; Ditko-a(r) 3 6 9 19 30 40
1,2-Star Wars ('77,'78) r/Star Wars #1-3 & #4-6; regular edition 3 6 9 14 20 25
1,2-Star Wars ('77,'78) Whitman variant 3 6 9 19 30 40
3-Star Wars ('78, $2.50, 116 pgs.); r/S. Wars #1-6; regular edition and Whitman variant exist 3 6 9 14 20 26
3-Close Encounters of the Third Kind (1978, $1.50, 56 pgs.)-Movie adaptation; Simonson-a(p) 2 4 6 10 14 18
V2#2(Spring, 1980, $2.00, oversized)- "Star Wars: The Empire Strikes Back"; r/Marvel Comics Super Special #16 3 6 9 17 26 35
NOTE: ***Chaykin** c/a(r)-1(1977), 2, 3. **Stevens** a(r)-2i, 3i. **Williamson** a(r)-V2#2.*

MARVEL SPECTACULAR
Marvel Comics Group: Aug, 1973 - No. 19, Nov, 1975
1-Thor-r from mid-sixties begin by Kirby 3 6 9 15 22 28
2-19 2 4 6 8 10 12

MARVELS: PORTRAITS
Marvel Comics: Mar, 1995 - No. 4, June, 1995 ($2.95, limited series)
1-4: Different artists renditions of Marvel characters 4.00

MARVEL SPOTLIGHT (...& Son of Satan #19, 20, 23, 24)
Marvel Comics Group: Nov, 1971 - No. 33, Apr, 1977; V2#1, July, 1979 - V2#11, Mar, 1981 (A try-out book for new characters)
1-Origin Red Wolf (western hero)(1st solo book, pre-#1); Wood inks, Neal Adams-c; only 15¢ issue 6 12 18 38 69 100
2-(25¢, 52 pgs.)-Venus-r by Everett; origin/1st app. Werewolf By Night (begins) by Ploog; N. Adams-c 38 76 114 285 641 1000
3-Werewolf By Night 6 12 18 42 79 115
4-1st app. of the Darkhold book; Werewolf By Night ends (6/72); gets own title 9/72 8 16 24 56 108 160
5-Origin/1st app. Ghost Rider (8/72) & begins 141 282 423 1142 2571 4000
6-8: 6-Origin G.R. retold. 8-Last Ploog issue 8 16 24 54 102 150
9-11-Last Ghost Rider (gets own title next mo.) 6 12 18 38 69 100
12-Origin & 2nd full app. The Son of Satan (10/73); story cont'd from Ghost Rider #2 & into #3; series begins, ends #24 8 16 24 56 108 160
13-24: 13-Partial origin Son of Satan. 14-Last 20¢ issue. 22-Ghost Rider-c & cameo (5 panels). 24-Last Son of Satan (10/75); gets own title 12/75 2 4 6 10 14 18
25,27,30,31: 27-(Regular 25¢-c), Sub-Mariner app. 30-The Warriors Three. 31-Nick Fury 1 3 4 6 8 10
26-Scarecrow 2 4 6 9 13 16
27-(30¢-c variant, limited distribution) 5 10 15 30 50 70
28-(Regular 25¢-c) 1st solo Moon Knight app. 10 20 30 64 132 200
28-(30¢-c variant, limited distribution) 21 42 63 147 324 500
29-(Regular 25¢-c) (8/76) Moon Knight app.; last 25¢ issue 5 10 15 30 50 70
29-(30¢-c variant, limited distribution) 7 14 21 49 92 135
32-1st app./partial origin Spider-Woman (2/77); Nick Fury app. 10 20 30 68 144 220
33-Deathlok; 1st app. Devil-Slayer (see Demon-Hunter #1) 3 6 9 14 19 24
V2#1-Captain Marvel & Drax app. 2 4 6 9 13 16
1-Variant copy missing issue #1 on cover 4 8 12 23 37 50
2-5,9-11: 2-4-Captain Marvel. 2-Drax app. 4-Ditko-c/a. 5-Dragon Lord. 9-11-Captain Universe (see Micronauts #8) 1 2 3 5 6 8
6-Star-Lord origin 5 10 15 31 53 75
7-Star-Lord; Miller-c 4 8 12 23 37 50
8-Capt. Marvel; Miller-c/a(p) 2 4 6 9 13 16
NOTE: ***Austin** c-V2#2i, 8. **J. Buscema** c/a-30p. **Chaykin** a-31; c-26, 31. **Colan** a-18p, 19p. **Ditko** a-V2#4, 5, 9-11; c-V2#4, 9-11. **Kane** c-21p, 32p. **Kirby** c-29p. **McWilliams** a-20i. **Miller** a-V2#8p; c(p)-V2#2, 5, 7, 8. **Mooney** a-8i, 10i, 14p, 15, 16p, 17p, 24p, 27, 32i. **Nasser** a-33p. **Ploog** a-2-5, 6-8p; c-3-9. **Romita** c-13. **Sutton** a-9-11p, V2#6, 7. #29-25¢ & 30¢ issues exist.*

MARVEL SPOTLIGHT (Most issues spotlight one Marvel artist and one Marvel writer)
Marvel Comics: 2005 - Apr, 2010 ($2.99/$3.99)
...Brian Bendis/Mark Bagley; Daniel Way/Olivier Coipel; David Finch/Roberto Aguirre-Sacasa; Ed Brubaker/Billy Tan; John Cassaday/Sean McKeever; Joss Whedon/Michael Lark; Laurell K. Hamilton/George R.R. Martin; Neil Gaiman/Salvador Larroca; Robert Kirkman/Greg Land; Stan Lee/Jack Kirby; Warren Ellis/Jim Cheung each... 3.00
...Steve McNiven/Mark Millar - Civil War 10.00
...: Captain America (2009) interviews with Brubaker & Hitch; Reborn preview 3.00
...: Captain America Remembered (2007) character features; creator interviews 3.00
...: Civil War Aftermath (2007) Top 10 Moments, casualty list, previews of upcoming series 3.00
...: Dark Reign (2009) features on the Avengers, Fury and others; creator interview 4.00
...: Dark Tower (2007) previews the Stephen King adaptation; creator interviews 5.00
...: Deadpool (2009) character features; interviews with Kelly, Way, Medina & Benson 3.00
...: Fantastic Four and Silver Surfer (2007) character features; creator interviews 3.00
...: Ghost Rider (2007) character and movie features; creator interviews 3.00
...: Halo (2007) a World of Halo feature; Bendis & Maleev interviews 3.00
...: Heroes Reborn/Onslaught Reborn (2006) 3.00
...: Hulk Movie (2008) character and movie features; comic & movie creator interviews 3.00
...: Iron Man Movie (2008) character and movie features; Terrence Howard interview 3.00
...: Iron Man 2 (4/10) movie preview; Granov, Fraction interviews; Whiplash profile 4.00
...: Marvel Knights 10th Anniversary (2008) Quesada interview; series synopsies 3.00
...: Marvel Zombies/Mystic Arcana (2008) character features; creator interviews 3.00
...: Marvel Zombies Return (2009) character features; creator interviews 3.00
...: New Mutants (2009) character features; Claremont & McLeod interviews 3.00
...: Punisher Movie (2008) character and movie features; creator interviews 3.00
...: Secret Invasion (2008) features on the Skrulls; Bendis, Reed & Yu interviews 3.00
...: Secret Invasion Aftermath (2008) Skrull profiles; Bendis, Reed & Diggle interviews 4.00
...: Spider-Man (2007) character features; creator interviews; Ditko art showcase 3.00
...: Spider-Man - Brand New Day (2008) storyline features; Romitas interviews 3.00
...: Spider-Man-One More Day/Brand New Day (2008) storyline features; interviews 3.00
...: Summer Events (2009, $3.99) 2009 title previews; creator interviews 4.00
...: Thor (2007) character features; Straczynski interview; Romita Jr. art showcase 3.00
...: Ultimates 3 (2008) character features; Loeb & Madureira interviews 3.00
...: Ultimatum (2008) previews the limited series; Loeb & Bendis interviews 3.00
...: Uncanny X-Men 500 Issues Celebration (2008) creator interviews; timeline 3.00
...: War of Kings (2009) character features; Abnett, Lanning, Pelletier interviews 3.00

Marvel's The Avengers #1 © MAR

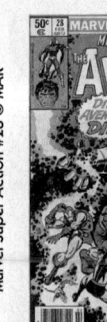

Marvel Super Action #28 © MAR

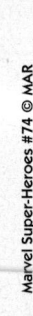

Marvel Super-Heroes #74 © MAR

GD VG FN VF VF/NM NM-
2.0 4.0 6.0 8.0 9.0 9.2

...: Wolverine (2009, $3.99) preview of 2009 Wolverine stories; creator interviews 4.00
...: World War Hulk (2007) character features; creator interviews; early art showcase 3.00
...: X-Men: Messiah Complex (2008) X-Men crossover features; creator interviews 3.00

MARVELS PROJECT, THE
Marvel Comics: Oct, 2009 - No. 8, July, 2010 ($3.99, limited series)

1-8-Emergence of Marvel heroes in 1939-40; Brubaker-s/Epting-a; Epting & McNiven-c 4.00
1-8-Variant covers by Parel 5.00

MARVELS SNAPSHOTS (See Sub-Mariner: ...)

MARVEL'S SPIDER-MAN: CITY AT WAR (Based on the 2018 videogame)
Marvel Comics (Gamerverse): May, 2019 - No. 6, Oct, 2019 ($3.99, limited series)

1-6: 1-Hallum-s/Bandini-a/Crain-c; gets the new costume; Mr. Negative app. 4.00

MARVEL'S SPIDER-MAN: HOMECOMING PRELUDE
Marvel Comics: May, 2017 - No. 2, Jun, 2017 ($3.99, limited series)

1,2-Adaptation from Captain America: Civil War movie; Pilgrim-s/Nauck-a; photo covers 4.00

MARVEL'S SPIDER-MAN: THE BLACK CAT STRIKES (Based on the 2018 videogame)
Marvel Comics (Gamerverse): Mar, 2020 - No. 5, Nov, 2020 ($3.99, limited series)

1-5: 1-Hallum-s/Maresca-a/Takeda-c 4.00

MARVEL'S SPIDER-MAN: VELOCITY (Titled Gamerverse Spider-Man: Velocity for #1)
Marvel Comics (Gamerverse): Oct, 2020 - No. 5, Feb, 2020 ($3.99, limited series)

1-5-Hallum-s/Laiso-a/Skan-c 4.00

MARVEL'S THE AVENGERS
Marvel Comics: Feb, 2015 - No. 2, Mar, 2015 ($2.99, limited series)

1,2-Adaptation of 2012 movie; Pilgrim-s/Bennett-a; photo covers 3.00

MARVEL'S THE AVENGERS: BLACK WIDOW STRIKES
Marvel Comics: Jul, 2012 - No. 3, Aug, 2012 ($2.99, limited series)

1-3-Prelude to 2012 movie; Van Lente-s. 1,3-Photo-c. 2-Granov-c 3.00

MARVEL'S THE AVENGERS PRELUDE
Marvel Comics: May, 2012 - No. 4, Jun, 2012 ($2.99, limited series)

1-4: 1-Prelude to 2012 movie; Luke Ross & Daniel HDR-a 3.00

MARVEL'S THE AVENGERS: THE AVENGERS INITIATIVE
Marvel Comics: Jul, 2012 ($2.99, one-shot)

1-Prelude to 2012 movie; Van Lente-s/Lim-a 3.00

MARVEL'S THOR: RAGNAROK PRELUDE
Marvel Comics: Sept, 2017 - No. 4, Oct, 2017 ($3.99, limited series)

1-4: 1,2-Adapts The Incredible Hulk movie. 3,4-Adapts Thor: The Dark World movie 4.00

MARVEL SUPER ACTION (Magazine)
Marvel Comics Group: Jan, 1976 (B&W, 76 pgs.)

1-2nd app. Dominic Fortune (see Marvel Preview); early Punisher app.; Weird World &
The Huntress; Evans, Ploog-a 9 18 27 58 114 170

MARVEL SUPER ACTION
Marvel Comics Group: May, 1977 - No. 37, Nov, 1981

1-Reprints Capt. America #100 by Kirby 3 6 9 16 24 32
2-13: 2,3,5-13 reprint Capt. America #101,102,103-111. 4-Marvel Boy-r(origin)/M. Boy #1.
11-Origin-r. 12,13-Classic Steranko-c/a(r). 2 4 6 8 11 14
2,3-(35¢-c variants, limited distribution)(6,8/77) 10 20 30 64 132 200
14-20: r/Avengers #55,56, Annual 2, others 1 3 4 6 8 10
21-37: 30-r/Hulk #6 from U.K. 1 2 3 5 6 8

NOTE: ***Buscema*** *a(r)-14p, 15p; c-18-20, 22, 35r-37.* ***Everett*** *a-4.* ***Heath*** *a-4r.* ***Kirby*** *r-1-3, 5-11.* ***B. Smith*** *a-27r, 28r.* ***Steranko*** *a(r)-12p, 13p; c-12r, 13r.*

MARVEL SUPER HERO ADVENTURES (All ages title)
Marvel Comics: Jun, 2018 - Present ($3.99, series of one-shots)

...: Captain Marvel - First Day of School 1 (11/18) Spider-Man and Capt. Marvel team-up 4.00
...: Captain Marvel - Frost Giants Among Us! 1 (2/19) Avengers & Squirrel Girl app. 4.00
...: Captain Marvel - Halloween Spooktacular 1 (12/18) Spider-Man app. 4.00
...: Captain Marvel - Mealtime Mayhem 1 (1/19) Spider-Gwen & Venom app. 4.00
...: Inferno 1 (10/18) Spider-Man and Inferno team-up; Venom & Medusa app. 4.00
...: Ms. Marvel and the Teleporting Dog 1 (9/18) Lockjaw and The Serpent Society app. 4.00
...: Spider-Man - Across the Super-Verse 1 (3/19) Grandmaster and other Spiders app. 4.00
...: Spider-Man and the Stolen Vibranium 1 (6/18) Spider-Man & Black Panther team-up 4.00
...: Spider-Man - Spider-Sense of Adventure 1 (5/19) Ghost-Spider and Arcade app. 4.00
...: Spider-Man - Web Designers 1 (6/19) Mysterio app. 4.00
...: Spider-Man - Web of Intrigue 1 (3/19) Miles, Gwen & Sinister Six app. 4.00
...: The Spider-Doctor 1 (7/18) Spider-Man and Doctor Strange team-up; Hela app. 4.00
...: Webs and Arrows and Ants, Oh My! 1 (8/18) Kate Bishop & Ant-Man app. 4.00

MARVEL SUPER HERO CONTEST OF CHAMPIONS
Marvel Comics Group: June, 1982 - No. 3, Aug, 1982 (Limited series)

GD VG FN VF VF/NM NM-
2.0 4.0 6.0 8.0 9.0 9.2

1-Features nearly all Marvel characters currently appearing in their comics;
1st Marvel limited series 3 6 9 17 26 35
2,3 2 4 6 10 14 18

MARVEL SUPER HEROES
Marvel Comics Group: October, 1966 (25¢, 68 pgs.) (1st Marvel one-shot)

1-r/origin Daredevil from D.D. #1; r/Avengers #2; G.A. Sub-Mariner-r/Marvel Mystery #8
(Human Torch app.). Kirby-a 12 24 36 80 173 265

MARVEL SUPER-HEROES (Formerly Fantasy Masterpieces #1-11)
(Also see Giant-Size Super Heroes) (#12-20: 25¢, 68 pgs.)
Marvel Comics: No. 12, 12/67 - No. 31, 11/71; No. 32, 9/72 - No. 105, 1/82

12-Origin & 1st app. Capt. Marvel of the Kree; G.A. Human Torch, Destroyer, Capt. America,
Black Knight, Sub-Mariner-r (#12-20 all contain new stories and reprints)
27 54 81 194 435 675
13-2nd app. Capt. Marvel; 1st app. of Carol Danvers (later becomes Ms. Marvel);
Golden Age Black Knight, Human Torch, Vision, Capt. America, Sub-Mariner-r
141 282 423 1142 2571 4000
14-Amazing Spider-Man (5/68, new-a by Andru/Everett); G.A. Sub-Mariner, Torch, Mercury
(1st Kirby-a at Marvel), Black Knight, Capt. America reprints
10 20 30 65 135 200
15-Black Bolt cameo in Medusa (new-a); Black Knight, Sub-Mariner, Black Marvel,
Capt. America-r 7 14 21 46 86 125
16-Origin & 1st app. S. A. Phantom Eagle; G.A. Torch, Capt. America, Black Knight,
Patriot, Sub-Mariner-r 5 10 15 34 60 85
17-Origin Black Knight (new-a); G.A. Torch, Sub-Mariner-r; reprint from All-Winners Squad #21
(cover & story) 8 16 24 54 102 150
18-Origin/1st app. Guardians of the Galaxy (1/69); G.A. Sub-Mariner, All-Winners Squad-r
42 84 126 311 706 1100
19-Ka-Zar (new-a); G.A. Torch, Marvel Boy, Black Knight, Sub-Mariner reprints; Smith-c(p);
Tuska-a(r) 4 8 12 28 47 65
20-Doctor Doom (5/69); r/Young Men #24 w/-c 19 38 57 131 291 450
21-31: All-r issues. 21-X-Men, Daredevil, Iron Man-r begin, end #31. 31-Last Giant issue
3 6 9 17 26 35
32-50: 32-Hulk/Sub-Mariner-r begin from TTA. 2 4 6 8 10 12
51-70,100: 56-r/origin Hulk/Inc. Hulk #102; Hulk-r begin
1 3 4 6 8 10
57,58-(30¢-c variants, limited distribution)(5,7/76) 5 10 15 31 53 75
65,66-(35¢-c variants, limited distribution)(7,9/77) 7 14 21 46 86 125
71-99,101-105 1 2 3 5 6 8

NOTE: ***Austin*** *a-104.* ***Colan*** *a(p)-12, 13, 15, 18; c-12, 13, 15, 18.* ***Everett*** *a-14i(new); r-14, 15i, 18, 19, 33; c-85(r). New* ***Kirby*** *c-22, 27, 54.* ***Maneely*** *r-14, 15, 19.* ***Severin*** *r-83-85i, 100-102; c-100-102r.* ***Starlin*** *c-47.* ***Tuska*** *a-19p. Black Knight-r by* ***Maneely*** *in 12-16, 19. Sub-Mariner-r by* ***Everett*** *in 12-20.*

MARVEL SUPER-HEROES
Marvel Comics: May, 1990 - V2#15, Oct, 1993 ($2.95/$2.50, quart., 68-84 pgs.)

1-Moon Knight, Hercules, Black Panther, Magik, Brother Voodoo, Speedball (by Ditko)
& Hellcat; Hembeck-a 1 2 3 5 6 8
2,4,5,V2#3,6,7,9,13-15: 2-Summer Special(7/90); Rogue, Speedball (by Ditko), Iron Man, Falcon, Tigra & Daredevil. 4-Spider-Man/Nick Fury, Daredevil,Speedball, Wonder Man, Spitfire & Black Knight; Byrne-c. 5-Thor, Dr. Strange, Thing & She-Hulk; Speedball by Ditko(p). V2#3-Retells origin Capt. America w/new facts; Blue Shield, Capt. Marvel, Speedball, Wasp; Hulk by Ditko/Rogers V2#6-9: 6,7-($2.25-c) X-Men, Cloak & Dagger, The Shroud (by Ditko) & Marvel Boy in each. 9-West Coast Avengers, Iron Man app.; Kieth-c(p). V2#13-15 ($2.75, 84 pgs.): 13-All Iron Man 30th anniversary.
15-Iron Man/Thor/Volstagg/Dr. Druid 5.00
V2#8-1st app. Squirrel Girl; X-Men, Namor & Iron Man (by Ditko); Larsen-c
5 10 15 34 60 85
V2#10-Ms. Marvel/Sabretooth-c/story (intended for Ms. Marvel #24; shows-c to #24);
Namor, Vision, Scarlet Witch stories; $2.25-c 1 3 4 6 8 10
V2#11-Original Ghost Rider-c/story; Giant-Man, Ms. Marvel stories
2 4 6 8 11 14
V2#12-Dr. Strange, Falcon, Iron Man 4.00

MARVEL SUPER-HEROES MAGAZINE
Marvel Comics: Oct, 1994 - No. 6, Mar, 1995 ($2.95, 100 pgs.)

1-6: 1-r/FF #232, DD #159, Iron Man #115, Incred. Hulk #314 6.00

MARVEL SUPER-HEROES SECRET WARS (See Secret Wars II)
Marvel Comics Group: May, 1984 - No. 12, Apr, 1985 (limited series)

1 4 8 12 25 40 55
1-3-(2nd printings, sold in multi-packs) 4.00
2-6,9-11: 6-The Wasp dies 1 3 4 6 8 10
7,12: 7-Intro. new Spider-Woman. 12-($1.00, 52 pgs.) 2 4 6 10 14 18
8-Spider-Man's new black costume explained as alien costume (1st app. Venom as
alien costume) 6 12 18 42 79 115
Secret Wars Omnibus HC (2008, $99.99, dustjacket) r/#1-12, Thor #383, She-Hulk (2004) #10

Marvel's Voices (2021) #1 © MAR

Marvel Tales #31 © MAR

Marvel Tales: Captain Britain #1 © MAR

GD 2.0 | VG 4.0 | FN 6.0 | VF 8.0 | VF/NM 9.0 | NM- 9.2

and What If? (1989) #4 & #114; photo gallery of related toys; pencil-a from #1 100.00
NOTE: *Zeck a-1-3,6-12; c-1,3,8-12. Additional artists (Romita Sr., Art Adams and others) had uncredited art in #12.*

MARVEL SUPER HERO SPECTACULAR (All ages)
Marvel Comics: Dec, 2015 ($3.99, one-shot)

1-Avengers, Guardians of the Galaxy and Spider-Man app.; bonus puzzle pages 4.00

MARVEL SUPER HERO SQUAD (All ages)
Marvel Comics: Mar, 2009; Nov, 2009 - No. 4, Feb, 2010 ($3.99/$2.99)

1-4-Based on the animated series; back-up humor strips and pin-ups 3.00
...Hero Up! (3/09, $3.99) Collects humor strips from MarvelKids.com; 2 covers 4.00

MARVEL SUPER HERO SQUAD (All ages)
Marvel Comics: Mar, 2010 - No. 12, Feb, 2011 ($2.99)

1-12-Based on the animated series. 1-Wraparound-c 3.00
Super Hero Squad Spectacular 1 (4/11, $3.99) The Beyonder app. 4.00

MARVEL SUPER SPECIAL, A (See Marvel Comics Super...)

MARVEL'S VOICES (Inspired by the Marvel's Voices podcast)
Marvel Comics: Apr, 2020; Jan, 2021 ($4.99)

1-(4/20) Short stories & essays from various creators of color; intro. by Angélique Roché 5.00
1-(1/21) Expanded version of first edition; Miles Morales mask-c 5.00
... Indigenous Voices 1 (1/21, $4.99) Short stories by Native American creators 5.00
...: Legacy 1 (4/21, $4.99) Short stories by African American creators; afterword by Roché 5.00

MARVEL SWIMSUIT SPECIAL (Also see Marvel Illustrated...)
Marvel Comics: 1992 - No. 4, 1995 ($3.95/$4.50, magazine, 52 pgs.)

1-4-Silvestri-c; pin-ups by diff. artists. 2-Jusko-c. 3-Hughes-c
2 4 6 9 12 15

MARVELS X (Prequel to Earth X, Paradise X and Universe X series)
Marvel Comics: Mar, 2020 - No. 6, Dec, 2020 ($4.99)

1-6-Jim Krueger & Alex Ross-s/Well-Bee-a; covers by Ross and others 5.00

MARVEL TAILS STARRING PETER PORKER THE SPECTACULAR SPIDER-HAM
(Also see Peter Porker... and Spider-Ham)(Appears in Spider-Man: Into the Spider-Verse movie)
Marvel Comics Group: Nov, 1983 (one-shot)

1-1st app. Peter Porker, the Spectacular Spider-Ham; Captain Americat, Goose Rider, Hulk Bunny app. 5 10 15 30 50 70

MARVEL TALES (Formerly Marvel Mystery Comics #1-92)
Marvel/Atlas Comics (MCI): No. 93, Aug, 1949 - No. 159, Aug, 1957

93-Horror/weird stories begin 290 580 870 1856 3178 4500
94-Everett-a 165 330 495 1056 1803 2550
95-New logo; classic Sci-Fi cover 206 412 618 1318 2259 3200
96,99,101,103,105 82 164 246 528 902 1275
97-Sun Girl, 2 pgs; Kirbyish-a; one story used in N.Y. State Legislative document
97 194 291 621 1061 1500
98,100: 98-Krigstein-a 74 148 222 470 810 1150
102-Wolverton-a "The End of the World", (6 pgs.) 94 188 282 597 1024 1450
104-Wolverton-a "Gateway to Horror", (6 pgs.) 100 200 300 635 1093 1550
106,107-Krigstein-a. 106-Decapitation story 61 122 183 390 670 950
108-120: 116-(7/53) Werewolf By Night story. 118-Hypo-c/panels in End of World story. 120-Jack Katz-a 54 108 162 343 574 825
121,123-131: 128-Flying Saucer-c. 131-Last precode (2/55)
43 86 129 271 461 650
122-Kubert-a 45 90 135 284 480 675
132,133,135-141,143,145 39 78 117 231 378 525
134-Krigstein, Kubert-a; flying saucer-c 41 82 123 256 428 600
142-Krigstein-a 39 78 117 231 378 525
144-Williamson/Krenkel-a, 3 pgs. 39 78 117 231 378 525
146,148-151,154-156,158: 150-1st S.A. issue. 156-Torres-a
33 66 99 194 317 440
147,152: 147-Ditko-a. 152-Wood, Morrow-a 35 70 105 208 339 470
153-Everett End of World c/story 40 80 120 246 411 575
157,159-Krigstein-a 34 68 102 199 325 450
NOTE: *Andru a-103. **Briefer** a-118. **Check** a-147. **Colan** a-105, 107, 118, 120, 121, 127, 131. **Drucker** a-127, 135, 141, 146, 150. **Everett** a-98, 104, 106(2), 108(2), 131, 148, 151, 153, 155; c-107, 109, 111, 112, 114, 117, 127, 143, 147-151, 153, 155, 156. **Forte** a-119, 125, 130, 158. **Heath** a-110, 113, 118, 119; c-104-106, 110, 130. **Gil Kane** a-117. **Lawrence** a-130. **Maneely** a-111, 126, 129; c-108, 116, 120, 129, 152. **Mooney** a-114. **Morisi** a-153. **Morrow** a-150, 152, 156. **Orlando** a-149, 151, 157. **Pakula** a-119, 121, 133, 135, 144, 150, 152, 156. **Powell** a-136, 137, 150, 154. **Ravielli** a-117, 123. **Rico** a-97, 99. **Romita** a-108. **Sekowsky** a-96-98. **Shores** a-110; c-96. **Sinnott** a-105, 116, 144. **Tuska** a-114. **Whitney** a-107. **Wildey** a-126, 138.*

MARVEL TALES (...Annual #1,2; ...Starring Spider-Man #123 on)
Marvel Comics Group (NPP earlier issues): 1964 - No. 291, Nov, 1994 (No. 1-32: 72 pgs.)
(#1-3 have Canadian variants; back & inside-c are blank, same value)

1-Reprints origins of Spider-Man/Amazing Fantasy #15, Hulk/Inc. Hulk#1, Ant-Man/T.T.A. #35, Giant Man/T.T.A. #49, Iron Man/T.O.S. #39,48, Thor/J.I.M. #83 & r/Sgt. Fury #1
38 76 114 281 628 975
2 ('65)-r/X-Men #1(origin), Avengers #1(origin), origin Dr. Strange-r/Strange Tales #115 & origin Hulk(Hulk #3) 10 20 30 68 144 220
3 (7/66)-Spider-Man, Strange Tales (H. Torch), Journey into Mystery (Thor), Tales to Astonish (Ant-Man)-r begin (r/Strange Tales #101) 6 12 18 40 73 105
4,5 5 10 15 30 50 70
6-8,10: 10-Reprints 1st Kraven/Amaz. S-M #15 3 6 9 21 33 45
9-r/Amazing Spider-Man #14 w/cover 4 8 12 27 44 60
11-33: 11-Spider-Man battles Daredevil-r/Amaz. Spider-Man #16. 13-Origin Marvel Boy-r from M. Boy #1. 22-Green Goblin-c/story-r/Amaz. Spider-Man #27. 30-New Angel story (x-over w/Ka-Zar #2,3). 32-Last 72 pg. iss. 33-(52 pgs.) Kraven-r
3 6 9 16 23 30
34-50: 34-Begin regular size issues 2 3 4 6 8 10
51-65 1 2 3 5 6 8
66-70-(Regular 25¢ editions)(4-8/76) 1 2 3 5 6 8
66-70-(30¢-c variants, limited distribution) 5 10 15 30 50 70
71-105: 75-Origin Spider-Man-r. 77-79-Drug issues-r/Amaz. Spider-Man #96-98. 98-Death of Gwen Stacy-r/Amaz. Spider-Man #121 (Green Goblin). 99-Death Green Goblin-r/Amaz. Spider-Man #122. 100-(52 pgs.)-New Hawkeye/Two Gun Kid story. 101-105-All Spider-Man-r 6.00
80-84-(35¢-c variants, limited distribution)(6-10/77) 6 12 18 38 69 100
106-r/1st Punisher-Amazing Spider-Man #129 5 10 15 33 57 80
107-136: 107-133-All Spider-Man-r. 111,112-r/Spider-Man #134,135 (Punisher). 113,114-r/Spider-Man #136,137(Green Goblin). 126-128-r/clone story from Amazing Spider-Man #149-151. 134-136-Dr. Strange-r begin; SpM stories continue. 134-Dr. Strange-r/Strange Tales #110 5.00
137-Origin-r Dr. Strange; shows original unprinted-c & origin Spider-Man/Amazing Fantasy #15
2 4 6 13 18 22
137-Nabisco giveaway 2 4 6 10 14 18
138-Reprints all Amazing Spider-Man #1; begin reprints of Spider-Man with covers similar to originals 2 4 6 8 11 14
139-144: r/Amazing Spider-Man #2-7 6.00
145-149,151-190,193-199: Spider-Man-r continue w/#8 on. 149-Contains skin "Tattooz" decals. 153-r/1st Kraven/Spider-Man #15. 155-r/2nd Green Goblin/Spider-Man #17. 161,164,165-Gr. Goblin-c/stories-r/Spider-Man #23,26,27. 178,179-Green Goblin-c/story-r/Spider-Man #39,40. 187,189-Kraven-r. 193-Byrne-r/Marvel Team-Up begin w/scripts 5.00
150,191,192,200: 150-($1.00, 52pgs.)-r/Spider-Man Annual #1(Kraven app.). 191-($1.50, 68 pgs.)-r/Spider-Man #96-98. 192-($1.25, 52 pgs.)-r/Spider-Man #121,122. 200-Double size ($1.25)-Miller-c & r/Annual #14 6.00
201-249,251,252,254-257: 208-Last Byrne-r. 210,211-r/Spidey #134,135. 212,213-r/Giant-Size Spidey #4. 213-r/1st solo Silver Surfer story/F.F. Annual #5. 214,215-r/Spidey #161,162. 222-Reprints origin Punisher/Spect. Spider-Man #83; last Punisher reprint. 209-Reprints 1st app. The Punisher/Amazing Spider-Man #129; Punisher reprints begin, end #222. 223-McFarlane-c begins, end #239. 233-Spider-Man/X-Men team-ups begin; r/X-Men #35. 234-r/Marvel Team-Up #4. 235,236-r/M. Team-Up Annual #1. 237,238-r/M. Team-Up #150. 239,240-r/M. Team-Up #38,90(Beast). 242-r/M.Team-Up #89. 243-r/M. Team-Up #117 (Wolverine). 251-r/Spider-Man #100 (Green Goblin-c/story). 252-r/1st app. Morbius/Amaz. Spider-Man #101. 254-r/M. Team-Up #15(Ghost Rider); new painted-c. 255,256-Spider-Man & Ghost Rider-r/Marvel Team-Up #58,91. 257-Hobgoblin-r begin (r/ASM #238) 3.00
250,253: 250-($1.50, 52 pgs.)-r/1st Karma/M. Team-Up #100. 253-($1.50, 52 pgs.) -r/Amaz. S-M #102 4.00
258-291: 258-261-r/A. Spider-Man #239,249-251(Hobgoblin). 262,263-r/Marv. Team-Up #53,54. 262-New X-Men vs. Sunstroke story. 263-New Woodgod origin story. 264,265-r/Amazing Spider-Man Annual 5. 266-273-Reprints alien costume stories/A. S-M 252-259. 277-r/1st Silver Sable/A. S-M 265. 283-r/A. S-M 275 (Hobgoblin). 284-r/A. S-M 276 (Hobgoblin) 4.00
285-variant w/Wonder-Con logo on c-no price-giveaway 4.00
286-($2.95)-p/bagged w/16 page insert & animation print 5.00
NOTE: *All contain reprints; some have new art. #89-97-r/Amazing Spider-Man #110-118; #98-136-r/#121-159; #137-150-r/Amazing Fantasy #15, #1-12 & Annual 1; #151-167-r/#13-28 & Annual 2; #168-186-r/#29-46. **Austin** a-100i; c-272i, 273i. **Byrne** a(r)-193-198p, 201-208p. **Ditko** a-1-30, 83, 100, 137-155. **G. Kane** a-71, 81, 98-101p, 249r; c-125-127p, 130p, 137-155. **Sam Kieth** c-255, 262, 263. **Ron Lim** c-266p-281p, 283p-285p. **McFarlane** c-223-239. **Mooney** a-63, 95-97i, 103(i). **Nasser** a-100p. **Nebres** a-242i. **Perez** c-259-261. **Rogers** c-240, 241, 243-252.*

MARVEL TALES
Marvel Comics: Mar, 2019 - Present ($7.99)

...: Annihilation 1 (2/20) reprints Marvel Two-In-One #53, Daredevil #105 and Darkhawk #6; Inhyuk Lee-c; intro. by Macchio; features Quasar, Moondragon & Darkhawk 8.00
...: Avengers 1 (7/19) reprints Avengers #16,57,264; Bartel-c; intro. by Macchio 8.00
...: Black Panther 1 (11/19) reprints notable appearances; Bartel-c; intro. by Macchio 8.00
...: Black Widow 1 (4/19) reprints notable appearances; Bartel-c; intro. by Macchio 8.00
...: Captain America 1 (9/19) reprints notable appearances; Bartel-c; intro. by Macchio 8.00
...: Captain Britain 1 (11/20) reprints Captain Britain #1-2, Marvel Team-up #65-66, and Excalibur #1; Inhyuk Lee-c; intro. by Macchio 8.00
...: Doctor Strange 1 (1/20) reprints notable appearances; Inhyuk Lee-c; intro. by Macchio 8.00

Marvel Tales Flip Magazine #18 © MAR

Marvel Team-Up #131 © MAR

Marvel Team-Up (2019 series) #5 © MAR

	GD 2.0	VG 4.0	FN 6.0	VF 8.0	VF/NM 9.0	NM- 9.2

...: Fantastic Four 1 (3/19) reprints FF #4, Annual #6, #245; Bartel-c; intro. by Macchio 8.00
...: Ghost Rider 1 (12/19) reprints notable appearances; Inhyuk Lee-c; intro. by Macchio 8.00
...: Hulk 1 (9/19) reprints notable appearances; Bartel-c; intro. by Macchio 8.00
...: Iron Man 1 (7/19) reprints TOS #39,45 & Iron Man #150; Bartel-c; intro. by Macchio 8.00
...: Ravencroft 1 (3/20) reprints notable stories; Inhyuk Lee-c; intro. by Macchio 8.00
...: Silver Surfer 1 (12/19) r/Thor #193 & Sub-Mariner #34,35; Lee-c; intro. by Macchio 8.00
...: Spider-Man 1 (8/19) reprints ASM #66, Marvel Spotlight #32 & Peter Parker #90 8.00
...: Thanos 1 (6/19) reprints Warlock #10, Silver Surfer #45, Warlock & Infinity Watch #8 8.00
...: Thor 1 (5/19) reprints JIM #85 & notable appearances; Bartel-c; intro. by Macchio 8.00
...: Venom 1 (4/19) reprints ASM #316, 361 and Peter Parker Spec. S-M #119; Bartel-c; intro. by Macchio 8.00
...: Wolverine 1 (4/20) reprints notable appearances; Inhyuk Lee-c; intro. by Macchio 8.00
...: X-Men 1 (10/19) reprints notable stories; Bartel-c; intro. by Macchio 8.00

MARVEL TALES FLIP MAGAZINE
Marvel Comics: Sept, 2005 - No. 25, Sept, 2007 ($3.99/$4.99)

1-6-Reprints Amazing Spider-Man #30-up and Amazing Fantasy (2004) in flip format 4.00
7-10-Reprints Amazing Spider-Man #36-up and Runaways Vol. 2 in flip format 4.00
11-25-($4.99) Reprints Amazing Spider-Man #36-up and Runaways Vol. 2 in flip format 5.00

MARVEL TAROT, THE
Marvel Comics: 2007 ($3.99, one-shot)

1-Marvel characters featured in Tarot deck images; Djurdjevic-c 4.00

MARVEL TEAM-UP (See Marvel Treasury Edition #18 & Official Marvel Index To...)
(Replaced by Web of Spider-Man)
Marvel Comics Group: March, 1972 - No. 150, Feb, 1985
NOTE: *Spider-Man team-ups in all but Nos. 18, 23, 26, 29, 32, 35, 97, 104, 105, 137.*

1-Human Torch 15 30 45 103 227 350
2-Human Torch 6 12 18 38 69 100
3-Spider-Man/Human Torch vs. Morbius (part 1); 3rd app. of Morbius (7/72) 7 14 21 46 86 125
4-Spider-Man/X-Men vs. Morbius (part 2 of story); 4th app. of Morbius 7 14 21 48 89 130
5-10: 5-Vision. 6-Thing. 7-Thor. 8-The Cat (4/73, came out between The Cat #3 & 4). 9-Iron Man. 10-Human Torch 3 6 9 20 31 42
11-Inhumans 3 6 9 19 30 40
12-Werewolf (By Night) (8/73) 4 8 12 25 40 55
13,14,16-20: 13-Capt. America. 14-Sub-Mariner. 16-Capt. Marvel. 17-Mr. Fantastic. 18-Human Torch/Hulk. 19-Ka-Zar. 20-Black Panther; last 20¢ issue 2 4 6 13 18 22
15-1st Spider-Man/Ghost Rider team-up (11/73) 5 10 15 31 53 75
21,23-30: 21-Dr. Strange. 23-H-T/Iceman (X-Men cameo). 24-Brother Voodoo. 25-Daredevil. 26-H-T/Thor. 27-Hulk. 28-Hercules. 29-H-T/Iron Man. 30-Falcon 2 4 6 8 10 12
22-Hawkeye 3 6 9 16 23 30
31-45,47-50: 31-Iron Fist. 32-H-T/Son of Satan. 33-Nighthawk. 34-Valkyrie. 35-H-T/Dr. Strange. 36-Frankenstein. 37-Man-Wolf. 38-Beast. 39-H-T. 40-Sons of the Tiger/H-T. 41-Scarlet Witch. 42-The Vision. 43-Dr. Doom; retells origin. 44-Moondragon. 45-Killraven. 47-Thing. 48-Iron Man; last 25¢ issue. 49-Dr. Strange; Iron Man app. 50-Iron Man; Dr. Strange app. 1 3 4 6 8 10
44-48-(30¢-c variants, limited distribution)(4-8/76) 6 12 18 38 69 100
46-Spider-Man/Deathlok team-up 2 4 6 9 12 15
51,52,56,57: 51-Iron Man; Dr. Strange app. 52-Capt. America. 56-Daredevil. 57-Black Widow; 2nd app. Silver Samurai 1 3 4 6 8 10
53-Hulk; Woodgod & X-Men app., 1st Byrne-a on X-Men (1/77) 4 8 12 25 40 55
54,55,58-60: 54,59,60: 54-Hulk; Woodgod app. 59-Yellowjacket/The Wasp. 60-The Wasp (Byrne-a in all). 55-Warlock-c/story; Byrne-a. 58-Ghost Rider 2 4 6 8 10 12
58-62-(35¢-c variants, limited distribution)(6-10/77) 9 18 27 60 120 180
61-64,67-70: All Byrne-a; 61-H-T. 62-Ms. Marvel; last 30¢ issue. 63-Iron Fist. 64-Daughters of the Dragon. 67-Tigra; Kraven the Hunter app. 68-Man-Thing. 69-Havok (from X-Men). 70-Thor 2 4 6 8 10 12
65-Capt. Britain (1st U.S. app.) 5 10 15 35 63 90
66-Capt. Britain; 1st app. Arcade 3 6 9 14 20 26
71-74,76-78,80: 71-Falcon. 72-Iron Man. 73-Daredevil. 74-Not Ready for Prime Time Players (Belushi). 76-Dr. Strange. 77-Ms. Marvel. 78-Wonder Man. 80-Dr. Strange/Clea; last 35¢ issue 1 2 3 5 6 8
75,79,81: Byrne-a(p). 75-Power Man; Cage app. 79-Mary Jane Watson as Red Sonja; Clark Kent cameo (1 panel, 3/79). 81-Death of Satana 1 3 4 6 8 10
82-85,87-94,96-99: 82-Black Widow. 83-Nick Fury. 84-Shang-Chi. 89-Nightcrawler (X-Men). 91-Ghost Rider. 92-Hawkeye. 93-Werewolf by Night. 94-Spider-Man vs. The Shroud. 96-Howard the Duck; last 40¢ issue. 97-Spider-Woman/ Hulk. 98-Black Widow. 99-Machine Man. 85-Shang-Chi/Black Widow/Nick Fury. 87-Black Panther. 88-Invisible Girl. 90-Beast 6.00
86-Guardians of the Galaxy 2 4 6 8 11 14
95-Mockingbird (intro.); Nick Fury app. 4 8 12 28 47 65
100-(Double-size)-Spider-Man & Fantastic Four story with origin/1st app. Karma, one of the New Mutants; X-Men & Professor X cameo; Miller-c/a(p); Storm & Black Panther story; brief origins; Byrne-a(p) 3 6 9 15 22 28
101,102,104-116,118-140,142-149: 101-Nighthawk(Ditko-a). 102-Doc Samson. 104-Hulk/Ka-Zar. 105-Hulk/Power Man/Iron Fist. 106-Capt. America. 107-She-Hulk. 108-Paladin; Dazzler cameo. 109-Dazzler; Paladin app. 110-Iron Man. 111-Devil-Slayer. 112-King Kull; last 50¢ issue. 113-Quasar. 114-Falcon. 115-Thor. 116-Valkyrie. 118-Professor X; Wolverine app. (4 pgs.); X-Men cameo. 119-Gargoyle. 120-Dominic Fortune. 121-Human Torch. 122-Man-Thing. 123-Daredevil. 124-The Beast. 125-Tigra. 126-Hulk & Powerman/Son of Satan. 127-The Watcher. 128-Capt. America; Spider-Man/Capt. America photo-c. 129-Vision. 130-Scarlet Witch. 131-Frogman. 132-Mr. Fantastic. 133-Fantastic Four. 134-Jack of Hearts. 135-Kitty Pryde; X-Men cameo. 136-Wonder Man. 137-Aunt May/Franklin Richards. 138-Sandman. 139-Nick Fury. 140-Black Widow. 142-Capt. Marvel. 143-Starfox. 144-Moon Knight. 145-Iron Man. 146-Nomad. 147-Human Torch; Spider-Man back to old costume. 148-Thor. 149-Cannonball 5.00
103-Ant-Man 2 4 6 11 16 20
117-Wolverine-c/story 3 6 9 14 20 25
141-Daredevil; SpM/Black Widow app. (Spidey in new black costume; ties w/ Amazing Spider-Man #252 for 1st black costume) 5 10 15 34 60 85
150-X-Men ($1.00, double-size); B. Smith-c 2 4 6 8 10 12
Annual 1 (1976)-Spider-Man/X-Men (early app.) 4 8 12 28 47 65
Annual 2 (1979)-Spider-Man/Hulk 2 4 6 8 11 14
Annuals 3,4: 3 (1980)-Hulk/Power Man/Machine Man/Iron Fist; Miller-c(p). 4 (1981)-Spider-Man /Daredevil/Moon Knight/Power Man/Iron Fist; brief origins of each; Miller-c; Miller scripts on Daredevil 1 2 3 4 5 7
Annuals 5-7: 5 (1982)-SpM/The Thing/Scarlet Witch/Dr. Strange/Quasar. 6 (1983)-Spider-Man/ New Mutants (early app.), Cloak & Dagger. 7(1984)-Alpha Flight; Byrne-c(i) 6.00

NOTE: ***Art Adams** c-141p. **Austin** a-79i; c-76i, 79i, 96i, 101i, 112i, 130i. **Bolle** a-9i. **Byrne** a(p)-53-55, 59-70, 75, 79, 100; c-68p, 70p, 72p, 75, 76p, 79p, 129i, 133i. **Colan** a-87p. **Ditko** a-101. **Kane** a(p)-4-6, 13, 14, 16-19, 23; c(p)-4, 13, 14, 17-19, 23, 25, 26, 32-35, 37, 41, 44, 45, 47, 53, 54. **Miller** a-100p; c-95p, 99p, 100p, 102p, 106. **Mooney** a-2i, 7i, 8, 10p, 11p, 16i, 24-31p, 72, 93i, Annual 5i. **Nasser** a-89p; c-101p. **Simonson** c-99i, 148. **Paul Smith** c-131, 132. **Starlin** c-27. **Sutton** a-93p. "H-T" means Human Torch; "SpM" means Spider-Man; "S-M" means Sub-Mariner.*

MARVEL TEAM-UP (2nd Series)
Marvel Comics: Sept, 1997 - No. 11, July, 1998 ($1.99)

1-11: 1-Spider-Man team-ups begin, Generation x-app. 2-Hercules-c/app.; two covers. 3-Sandman. 4-Man-Thing. 7-Blade. 8-Namor team-ups begin, Dr. Strange app. 9-Capt. America. 10-Thing. 11-Iron Man 4.00

MARVEL TEAM-UP
Marvel Comics: Jan, 2005 - No. 25, Dec, 2006 ($2.25/$2.99)

1-7,9: 1,2-Spider-Man & Wolverine; Kirkman-s/Kolins-a. 5,6-X-23 app. 3.00
8,10-25 ($2.99-c) 10-Spider-Man & Daredevil. 12-Origin of Titannus. 14-Invincible app. 15-2nd app. of 2nd Sleepwalker 3.00
... Vol. 1: The Golden Child TPB (2005, $12.99) r/#1-6 13.00
... Vol. 2: Master of the Ring TPB (2005, $17.99) r/#7-13 18.00
... Vol. 3: League of Losers TPB (2006, $13.99) r/#14-18 14.00
... Vol. 4: Freedom Ring TPB (2007, $17.99) r/#19-25 18.00

MARVEL TEAM-UP (Ms. Marvel Team-Up in indicia for #1)
Marvel Comics: Jun, 2019 - No. 6, Nov, 2019 ($3.99, limited series)

1-6: 1-3-Ms. Marvel & Spider-Man team-up. 1-Flip book. 4-6-Ms. Marvel/Captain Marvel 4.00

MARVEL: THE LOST GENERATION
Marvel Comics: No. 12, Mar, 2000 - No. 1, Feb, 2001 ($2.99, issue #s go in reverse)

1-12-Stern-s/Byrne-s/a; untold story of The First Line. 5-Thor app. 3.00

MARVEL/ TOP COW CROSSOVERS
Image Comics (Top Cow): Nov, 2005 ($24.99, TPB)

Vol. 1-Reprints crossovers with Wolverine, Witchblade, Hulk, Darkness; Devil's Reign 25.00

MARVEL TREASURY EDITION
Marvel Comics Group/Whitman #17,18: 1974; #2, Dec, 1974 - #28, 1981 ($1.50/$2.50, 100 pgs., oversized, new-a &-r)(Also see Amazing Spider-Man, The, Marvel Spec. Ed. Feat.--, Savage Fists of Kung Fu, Superman Vs. , & 2001, A Space Odyssey)

1-Spectacular Spider-Man; story-r/Marvel Super-Heroes #14; Romita-c/a(r); G. Kane, Ditko-r; Green Goblin/Hulk-r 5 10 15 35 63 90
1-1,000 numbered copies signed by Stan Lee & John Romita on front-c & sold thru mail for $5.00; these were the 1st 1,000 copies off the press 12 24 36 82 179 275
2-10,12: 2-Fantastic Four-r/F.F. 6,11,48-50(Silver Surfer). 3-The Mighty Thor-r/Thor #125-130. 4-Conan the Barbarian; Barry Smith-c/a(r)/Conan #11. 5-The Hulk (origin-r/Hulk #3). 6-Dr. Strange. 7-Mighty Avengers. 8-Giant Superhero Holiday Grab-Bag; Spider-Man, Hulk, Nick Fury. 9-Giant; Super-hero Team-up. 10-Thor; r/Thor #154-157. 12-Howard the Duck

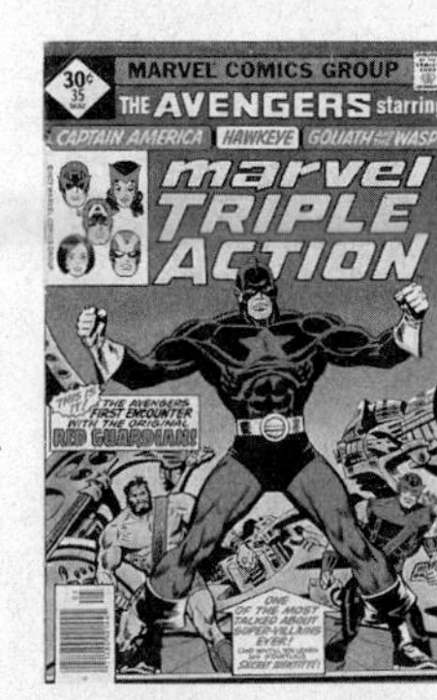

Marvel Triple Action #35 © MAR

Marvel Two-In-One #42 © MAR

Marvel Universe #5 © MAR

	GD 2.0	VG 4.0	FN 6.0	VF 8.0	VF/NM 9.0	NM- 9.2

(r/#H. the Duck #1 & G.S. Man-Thing #4,5) plus new Defenders story. 3 6 9 17 26 35

11,13-20: 11-Fantastic Four. 13-Giant Super-Hero Holiday Grab-Bag. 14-The Sensational Spider-Man; r/1st Morbius from Amazing S-M #101,102 plus #100 & r/Not Brand Echh #6. 15-Conan; B. Smith, Neal Adams-i; r/Conan #24. 16-The Defenders (origin) & Valkyrie; r/Defenders #1,4,13,14. 17-Incredible Hulk; Blob, Havok, Rhino and The Leader app. 18-The Astonishing Spider-Man; r/Spider-Man's 1st team-ups with Iron Fist, The X-Men, Ghost Rider & Werewolf by Night; inside back-c has photos from 1978 Spider-Man TV show. 19-Conan the Barbarian. 20-Hulk 3 6 9 14 20 25

21-24,27: 21-Fantastic Four. 22-Spider-Man. 23-Conan. 24-Rampaging Hulk. 27-Spider-Man 3 6 9 14 20 25

25-Spider-Man vs. The Hulk new story 3 6 9 18 28 38

26-The Hulk; 6 pg. new Wolverine/Hercules-s 3 6 9 17 25 34

28-Spider-Man/Superman; (origin of each) 5 10 15 33 57 80

NOTE: *Reprints-2, 3, 5, 7-9, 13, 14, 16, 17.* ***Neal Adams*** *a(i)-6, 15.* ***Brunner*** *a-6, 12; c-6.* ***Buscema*** *a-15, 19, 28; c-28.* ***Colan*** *a-6r; c-12p.* ***Ditko*** *a-1, 6.* ***Gil Kane*** *c-16p.* ***Kirby*** *a-1-3, 5, 7, 9-11; c-7.* ***Perez*** *a-26.* ***Romita*** *c-1, 5.* ***B. Smith*** *a-4, 15, 19; c-4, 19.*

MARVEL TREASURY OF OZ FEATURING THE MARVELOUS LAND OF OZ
Marvel Comics Group: 1975 ($1.50, oversized) (See MGM's Marvelous...)

1-Roy Thomas-s/Alfredo Alcala-a; Romita-c & bk-c 3 6 9 16 24 32

MARVEL TREASURY SPECIAL (Also see 2001: A Space Odyssey)
Marvel Comics Group: 1974; 1976 ($1.50, oversized, 84 pgs.)

Vol. 1-Spider-Man, Torch, Sub-Mariner, Avengers "Giant Superhero Holiday Grab-Bag"; Wood, Colan/Everett, plus 2 Kirby-r; reprints Hulk vs. Thing from Fantastic Four #25,26 3 6 9 17 25 34

Vol. 1-... Featuring Captain America's Bicentennial Battles (6/76)-Kirby-a; B. Smith inks, 11 pgs. 3 6 9 18 28 38

MARVEL TRIPLE ACTION (See Giant-Size...)
Marvel Comics Group: Feb, 1972 - No. 24, Mar, 1975; No. 25, Aug, 1975 - No. 47, Apr, 1979

1-(25¢ giant, 52 pgs.)-Dr. Doom, Silver Surfer, The Thing begin, end #4 ('66 reprints from Fantastic Four) 4 8 12 28 47 65

2-5 2 4 6 10 14 18

6-10 2 4 6 8 10 12

11-47: 45-r/X-Men #45. 46-r/Avengers #53(X-Men) 1 3 4 6 8 10

29,30-(30¢-c variants, limited distribution)(5,7/76) 5 10 15 30 50 70

36,37-(35¢-c variants, limited distribution)(7,9/77) 8 16 24 54 102 150

NOTE: *#5-44, 46, 47 reprint Avengers #11 thru ?. #40-r/Avengers #48(1st Black Knight).* ***Buscema*** *a(r)-35p, 36p, 38p, 39p, 41, 42, 43p, 44p, 46p, 47p.* ***Ditko*** *a-2r; c-47.* ***Kirby*** *a(r)-1-4p; c-9-19, 22, 24, 29.* ***Starlin*** *c-7.* ***Tuska*** *a(r)-40p, 43i, 46i, 47i. #2 through #17 are 20¢-c.*

MARVEL TRIPLE ACTION
Marvel Comics: May, 2009 - No. 2, Jun, 2009 ($5.99, limited series)

1,2-Reprints stories from Wolverine First Class, Marvel Adventures Avengers & Marvel Super Heroes 6.00

MARVEL TSUM TSUM
Marvel Comics: Oct, 2016 - No. 4, Jan, 2017 ($3.99, limited series)

1-4-Based on Japanese stackable plush toys. 1-Spider-Man and the Avengers app. 4.00

MARVEL TV: GALACTUS - THE REAL STORY
Marvel Comics: Apr, 2009 ($3.99, one-shot)

1-The "hoax" of Galactus, Tieri-s/Santacruz-a; r/Fantastic Four #50 4.00

MARVEL TWO-IN-ONE (...Featuring ... #82 on; also see The Thing)
Marvel Comics Group: January, 1974 - No. 100, June, 1983

1-Thing team-ups begin; Man-Thing 7 14 21 46 86 125

2,3: 2-Sub-Mariner; last 20¢ issue. 3-Daredevil 3 6 9 20 31 42

4,6: 4-Capt. America. 6-Dr. Strange (11/74) 3 6 9 15 22 28

5-Guardians of the Galaxy (9/74, 2nd app.) 4 8 12 25 40 55

7,9,10 2 4 6 10 14 18

8-Early Ghost Rider app. (3/75) 3 6 9 16 24 32

11-14,19,20: 13-Power Man. 14-Son of Satan (early app.) 1 3 4 6 8 10

15-18-(Regular 25¢ editions)(5-7/76) 17-Spider-Man 1 3 4 6 8 10

15-18-(30¢-c variants, limited distribution) 4 8 12 25 40 55

21-29: 27-Deathlok. 29-Master of Kung Fu; Spider-Woman cameo 1 2 3 5 6 8

28,29,31-(35¢-c variants, limited distribution) 5 10 15 33 57 80

30-2nd full app. Spider-Woman (see Marvel Spotlight #32 for 1st app.) 2 4 6 11 16 20

30-(35¢-c variant, limited distribution)(8/77) 9 18 27 57 111 165

31-33-Spider-Woman app. 1 3 4 6 8 10

34-40: 39-Vision 1 2 3 4 5 7

41,42,44,45,47-49: 42-Capt. America. 45-Capt. Marvel 6.00

43,50,53,55-Byrne-a(p). 53-Quasar(7/79, 2nd app.) 1 2 3 5 7 9

46-Thing battles Hulk-c/story 2 4 6 8 11 14

51-The Beast, Nick Fury, Ms. Marvel; Miller-a/c 1 2 3 5 7 9

52-Moon Knight app.; 1st app. Crossfire 2 4 6 10 14 18

54-Death of Deathlok; Byrne-a 3 6 9 14 20 26

56-60,64-68,70-74,76-79,81,82: 60-Intro. Impossible Woman. 68-Angel. 71-1st app. Maelstrom. 76-Iceman 4.00

61-63: 61-Starhawk (from Guardians); "The Coming of Her" storyline begins, ends #63; cover similar to F.F. #67 (Him-c). 62-Moondragon; Thanos & Warlock cameo in flashback; Starhawk app. 63-Warlock revived shortly; Starhawk & Moondragon app. 1 3 4 6 8 10

69-Guardians of the Galaxy 1 3 4 6 8 10

75-Avengers (52 pgs.) 5.00

80,90,100: 80-Ghost Rider. 90-Spider-Man. 100-Double size, Byrne-s 5.00

83-89,91-99: 83-Sasquatch. 84-Alpha Flight app. 93-Jocasta dies. 96-X-Men-c & cameo 4.00

Annual 1 (1976, 52 pgs.)-Thing/Liberty Legion; Kirby-c2 4 6 11 16 20

Annual 2 (1977, 52 pgs.)-Thing/Spider-Man; 2nd death of Thanos; end of Thanos saga; Warlock app.; Starlin-c/a 6 12 18 38 69 100

Annual 3,4 (1978-79, 52 pgs.): 3-Nova. 4-Black Bolt 1 2 3 4 5 7

Annual 5-7 (1980-82, 52 pgs.): 5-Hulk. 6-1st app. American Eagle. 7-The Thing/Champion; Sasquatch, Colossus app.; X-Men cameo (1 pg.) 5.00

NOTE: ***Austin*** *c(i)-42, 54, 56, 58, 61, 63, 66.* ***John Buscema*** *a-30p, 45; c-30p.* ***Byrne*** *(p)-43, 50, 53-55; c-43, 53p, 56p, 98i, 99i.* ***Gil Kane*** *a-1p, 2p; c(p)-1-3, 9-11, 14, 28.* ***Kirby*** *c-12, 19p, 20, 25, 27.* ***Mooney*** *a-18i, 38i, 90i.* ***Nasser*** *a-70p.* ***Perez*** *a(p)-56-58, 60, 64, 65; c(p)-32, 33, 42, 50-52, 54, 55, 57, 58, 61-66, 70.* ***Roussos*** *a-Annual 1i.* ***Simonson*** *c-43i, 97p, Annual 6i.* ***Starlin*** *c-6, Annual 1.* ***Tuska*** *a-6p.*

MARVEL TWO-IN-ONE
Marvel Comics: Sept, 2007 - No. 17, Jan, 2009 ($4.99, 64 pgs.)

1-8,13-16-Reprints Marvel Adventures Avengers and X-Men: First Class stories 5.00

9-12,17-Reprints Marvel Adventures Iron Man and Avengers stories 5.00

MARVEL 2-IN-ONE
Marvel Comics: Feb, 2018 - No. 12, Jan, 2019 ($3.99)

1-12: 1-Human Torch & The Thing team-up; Zdarsky-s/Cheung-a; Doctor Doom app. 4.00

Annual 1 (8/18, $4.99) Spotlight on Infamous Iron Man; Zdarsky-s/Shalvey-a 5.00

MARVEL UNIVERSE (See Official Handbook Of The...)

MARVEL UNIVERSE (Title on variant covers for newsstand editions of some 2001 Marvel titles. See indicia for actual titles and issue numbers)

MARVEL UNIVERSE
Marvel Comics: June, 1998 - No. 7, Dec, 1998 ($2.99/$1.99)

1-($2.99)-Invaders stories from WW2; Stern-s 5.00

2-7-($1.99): 2-Two covers. 4-7-Monster Hunters; Manley-a/Stern-s 4.00

MARVEL UNIVERSE AVENGERS AND ULTIMATE SPIDER-MAN
Marvel Comics: 2012 (no price, Halloween giveaway)

1-Reprints from Marvel Universe Ultimate Spider-Man #1 & Avengers E.M.H #1 4.00

MARVEL UNIVERSE AVENGERS ASSEMBLE (Based on the Disney XD animated series) (Titled Avengers Assemble for #1,2)
Marvel Comics: Dec, 2013 - No. 12, Nov, 2014 ($3.99/$2.99)

1-($3.99) Red Skull app.; bonus Lego-style story 4.00

2-12-($2.99) 5-Dracula app. 7-Hyperion app. 12-Impossible Man app. 3.00

MARVEL UNIVERSE AVENGERS ASSEMBLE: CIVIL WAR
Marvel Comics: May, 2016 - No. 4, Aug, 2016 ($2.99)

1-4: 1,2,4-Ultron app. 3.00

MARVEL UNIVERSE AVENGERS ASSEMBLE SEASON TWO
Marvel Comics: Jan, 2015 - No. 16, Apr, 2016 ($3.99/$2.99)

1-($3.99) Red Skull & Thanos app. 4.00

2-16-($2.99) 2-Thanos & The Watcher app. 4-Winter Soldier app. 9-Ant-Man joins 3.00

MARVEL UNIVERSE AVENGERS: ULTRON REVOLUTION
Marvel Comics: Sept, 2016 - No. 12, Oct, 2017 ($2.99)

1-12-Ultron returns; A.I.M. app. 11-Ms. Marvel joins. 12-Captain Marvel app. 3.00

MARVEL UNIVERSE GUARDIANS OF THE GALAXY (Disney XD animated series)
Marvel Comics: Apr, 2015 - No. 4, Jul, 2015 ($2.99)

1-4: 1-Back-up story with Star-Lord origin 3.00

MARVEL UNIVERSE GUARDIANS OF THE GALAXY (Disney XD animated series)
Marvel Comics: Dec, 2015 - No. 23, Dec, 2017 ($3.99/$2.99)

1-($3.99) Cosmo & Korath app.; bonus Lego story 4.00

2-23-($2.99) 3-Fin Fang Foom app. 4-Grandmaster app. 13-Loki app. 20-Thanos app. 3.00

MARVEL UNIVERSE HULK: AGENTS OF S.M.A.S.H (Disney XD animated series)
Marvel Comics: Dec, 2013 - No. 4, Mar, 2014 ($2.99)

1-4: 1-Hulk, A-Bomb, She-Hulk, Red Hulk and Skaar team-up 3.00

MARVEL UNIVERSE: MILLENNIAL VISIONS

Marvel Versus DC #2 © MAR & DC

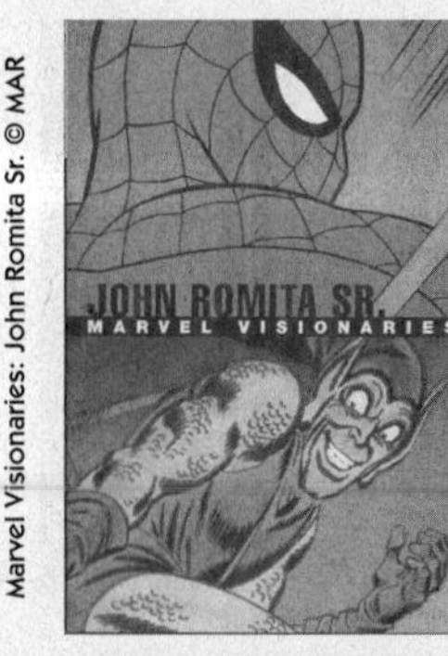

Marvel Visionaries: John Romita Sr. © MAR

Marvel Zombies 2 #1 © MAR

Marvel Comics: Feb, 2002 ($3.99, one-shot)

1-Pin-ups by various; wraparound-c by JH Williams & Gray 4.00

MARVEL UNIVERSE: THE END (Also see Infinity Abyss)
Marvel Comics: May, 2003 - No. 6, Aug, 2003 ($3.50/$2.99, limited series)

1-($3.50)-Thanos, X-Men, FF, Avengers, Spider-Man, Daredevil app.; Starlin-s/a(p) 4.00
2-6-($2.99) Akhenaten, Eternily, Living Tribunal app. 3.00
Thanos Vol. 3: Marvel Universe - The End (2003, $16.99) r/#1-6 17.00

MARVEL UNIVERSE ULTIMATE SPIDER-MAN (Based on the animated series)
Marvel Comics: Jun, 2012 - No. 31, Dec, 2014 ($2.99)

1-31: 1-Agent Coulson app. 13-Iron Man app. 16,19-Venom app. 29-Spider-Ham app. 3.00

MARVEL UNIVERSE ULTIMATE SPIDER-MAN: CONTEST OF CHAMPIONS
Marvel Comics: May, 2016 - No. 4, Aug, 2016 ($2.99, limited series)

1-4-The Collector & Grandmaster app. 1-Iron Man, Hulk & Kraven app. 3.00

MARVEL UNIVERSE ULTIMATE SPIDER-MAN SPIDER-VERSE
Marvel Comics: Jan, 2016 - No. 4, Apr, 2016 ($3.99/$2.99)

1-($3.99) 1-Spider-Man 2099 and Spider-Girl app. 4.00
2-4-($2.99) 3,4-Miles Morales app. 3.00

MARVEL UNIVERSE ULTIMATE SPIDER-MAN VS. THE SINISTER SIX
Marvel Comics: Sept, 2016 - No. 11, Sept, 2017 ($2.99)

1-11: 1,2-Doctor Octopus & Scarlet Spider app. 3-Dr. Strange app. 6-Venom app. 3.00

MARVEL UNIVERSE ULTIMATE SPIDER-MAN: WEB WARRIORS
Marvel Comics: Jan, 2015 - No. 12, Dec, 2015 ($3.99/$2.99)

1-($3.99) Captain America & Doctor Doom app.; back-up with Iron Spider 4.00
2-12-($2.99) 2-Hawkeye app. 3-Iron Man app. 8-Deadpool app. 12-Howling Commandos 3.00
.../Avengers Assemble Halloween ComicFest 2015 #1 (giveaway) reprints 3.00

MARVEL UNIVERSE VS. THE AVENGERS
Marvel Comics: Dec, 2012 - No. 4, Mar, 2013 ($3.99, limited series)

1-4-Avengers vs. Marvel Zombies; Maberry-s/Fernandez-a/Kuder-c 4.00

MARVEL UNIVERSE VS. THE PUNISHER
Marvel Comics: Oct, 2010 - No. 4, Nov, 2010 ($3.99, limited series)

1-4-Punisher vs. Marvel Zombies; Maberry-s/Parlov-a/c 4.00

MARVEL UNIVERSE VS. WOLVERINE
Marvel Comics: Aug, 2011 - No. 4, Nov, 2011 ($3.99, limited series)

1-4-Wolverine vs. Marvel Zombies; Maberry-s/Laurence Campbell-a/c 4.00

MARVEL UNLIMITED (Title on variant covers for newsstand editions of some 2001 Daredevil issues. See indicia for actual titles and issue numbers)

MARVEL VALENTINE SPECIAL
Marvel Comics: Mar, 1997 ($2.99, one-shot)

1-Valentine stories w/Spider-Man, Daredevil, Cyclops, Phoenix 4.00

MARVEL VERSUS DC (See DC Versus Marvel) (Also see Amazon, Assassins, Bruce Wayne: Agent of S.H.I.E.L.D., Bullets & Bracelets, Doctor Strangefate, JLX, Legend of the Dark Claw, Magneto & The Magnetic Men, Speed Demon, Spider-Boy, Super Soldier, & X-Patrol)
Marvel Comics: No. 2, 1996 - No. 3, 1996 ($3.95, limited series)

2,3: 2-Peter David script. 3-Ron Marz script; Dan Jurgens-a(p). 1st app. of Super Soldier, Spider-Boy, Dr. Doomsday, Doctor Strangefate, The Dark Claw, Nightcreeper, Amazon, Wraith & others. Storyline continues in Amalgam books. 5.00

MARVEL VISIONARIES
Marvel Comics: 2002 - 2007 (various prices, HC and TPB)

...: Chris Claremont (2005, $29.99) r/X-Men #137, Uncanny X-Men #153,205,268 & Ann. #12, Iron Fist #14, Wolverine #3, New Mutants #21 and other highlights 30.00
...: Gil Kane (8/02, $24.95) r/Amazing Spider-Man #99, Marvel Premiere #1,#15, TOA #76 & others; plus sketch pages and a cover gallery 25.00
...: Jack Kirby HC (2004, $29.99) r/career highlights- Red Raven Comics #1 (1st work), Captain America Comics #1, Avengers #4, Fantastic Four #48-50 and more 30.00
...: Jack Kirby Vol. 2 HC (2006, $34.99) r/career highlights- Captain America, Two-Gun Kid, Fantastic Four, Thor, Fin Fang Foom, Devil Dinosaur, romance and more 35.00
...: Jim Steranko (9/02, $14.95) r/Captain America #110,111,113; X-Men #50,51 and stories from Tower of Shadows #1 and Our Love Story #5; plus a cover gallery 15.00
...: John Buscema (2007, $34.99) r/career highlights-Avengers, Silver Surfer, Thor, FF, Hulk, Wolverine and others; Roy Thomas intro.; sketch pages and pin-up art 35.00
...: John Romita Jr. (2005, $29.99) r/various stories 1977-2002; debut in AS-M Ann. #11; Iron Man #128, AS-M V2 #36, issues of Hulk, Daredevil: The Man Without Fear, Punisher; sketch pages; intro. by John Romita Sr. 30.00
...: John Romita Sr. (2005, $29.99) r/various stories 1951-1997 including Young Men #24&26, Daredevil #16, ASM #39,42,50; sketch pages; intro. by John Romita Jr. 30.00
...: Roy Thomas (2006, $34.99) r/career highlights; intro. by Stan Lee 35.00
...: Steve Ditko (2005, $29.99) r/various stories 1961-1992; intro. by Blake Bell 30.00
...: Stan Lee HC (2005, $29.99) r/career highlights- Captain America Comics #3 (1st work), and various Spider-Man, FF, Thor, Daredevil stories; 1940-1995; Roy Thomas intro. 30.00

MARVEL WEDDINGS
Marvel Comics: 2005 ($19.99, TPB)

TPB-Reprints weddings of Peter & Mary Jane, Reed & Sue, Scott & Jean, and others 20.00

MARVEL WESTERNS: ...
Marvel Comics: 2006 ($3.99, one-shots)

... Kid Colt and the Arizona Girl 1 (9/06) 2 short stories & 3 Kirby/Ayers reps.; Powell-c 4.00
... Outlaw Files-Profiles and essays about Marvel western characters 4.00
... Strange Westerns Starring The Black Rider 1 (10/06) Englehart-s/Rogers-a & 2 Kirby Rawhide Kid reprints; Rogers-c 4.00
... The Two-Gun Kid 1 (8/06) 2 short stories & a Kirby/Ayers reprint; Powell-c 4.00
... Western Legends 1 (9/06) 2 short stories & r/Rawhide Kid origin by Kirby; Powell-c 4.00
HC (2006, $20.99, dustjacket) r/one-shots 21.00

MARVEL X-MEN COLLECTION, THE
Marvel Comics: Jan, 1994 - No. 3, Mar, 1994 ($2.95, limited series)

1-3-r/X-Men trading cards by Jim Lee 4.00

MARVEL - YEAR IN REVIEW (Magazine)
Marvel Comics: 1989 - No. 3, 1991 (52 pgs.)

1-3: 1-Spider-Man-c by McFarlane. 2-Capt. America-c. 3-X-Men/Wolverine-c 5.00

MARVEL: YOUR UNIVERSE
Marvel Comics: 2008; May, 2009 - No. 3, July, 2009 ($5.99)

1-3-Reprints of 5 recent comics (Ms. Marvel, Nova, Immortal Iron Fist & others) 6.00
...Saga (2008, no cover price) - Re-caps of crossovers (Secret War thru Secret Invasion) 3.00

MARVEL ZOMBIE (Simon Garth)
Marvel Comics: Dec, 2018 ($4.99, one-shot)

1-Prince-s/Raffaele-a; Spider-Man, Moon Girl, Daredevil, others in zombie apocalypse 5.00

MARVEL ZOMBIES (See Ultimate Fantastic Four #21-23, 30-32)
Marvel Comics: Feb, 2006 - No. 5, June, 2006 ($2.99, limited series)

1-Zombies vs. Magneto; Kirkman-s/Phillips-a/Suydam-c swipe of A.F. #15 40.00
1-(2nd-4th printings) Variant Suydam-c swipes of Spider-Man #1, Amazing Spider-Man #50 and Incredible Hulk #1 6.00
2-Avengers #4 cover swipe by Suydam 10.00
3-5: 3-Inc. Hulk #340 c-swipe. 4-X-Men #1 c-swipe. 5-AS-M Ann. #21 c-swipe 6.00
3-5-(2nd printings) 3-Daredevil #179 c-swipe. 4-AS-M #39 c-swipe. 5-Silver Surfer #1 4.00
...: Dead Days (7/07, $3.99) Early days of the plaque; Kirkman-s/Phillips-a/Suydam-c 5.00
...: Dead Days HC (2008, $29.99, oversized) r/Dead Days one-shot, Ultimate Fantastic Four #21-23, 30-32, and Black Panther #28-30 30.00
...: Evil Evolution (1/10, $4.99) Apes vs. Zombies; Marcos Martin-c 5.00
... Halloween (12/12, $3.99) Van Lente-s/Vitti-a/Francavilla-c 4.00
... MGC #1 (7/10, $1.00) r/#1 with "Marvel's Greatest Comics" logo on cover 3.00
...: The Book of Angels, Demons and Various Monstrosities (2007, $3.99) profile pages 5.00
...: The Covers HC (2007, $19.99, d.j.) Suydam's covers with originals and commentary 20.00
HC (2006, $19.99) r/#1-5; Kirkman foreword; cover gallery with variants 20.00

MARVEL ZOMBIES 2
Marvel Comics: Dec, 2007 - No. 5, Apr, 2008 ($2.99, limited series)

1-5-Kirkman-s/Phillips-a/Suydam zombie-fied cover swipes 5.00
HC (2008, $19.99) r/#1-5; cover swipe gallery 20.00

MARVEL ZOMBIES 3
Marvel Comics: Dec, 2008 - No. 4, Mar, 2009 ($3.99, limited series)

1-4-Van Lente-s/Walker-a/Land-c; Machine Man, Jocasta and Morbius app. 5.00

MARVEL ZOMBIES 4
Marvel Comics: Jun, 2009 - No. 4, Sept, 2009 ($3.99, limited series)

1-4-Van Lente-s/Walker-a/Land-c; Zombie Deadpool head app. 4.00

MARVEL ZOMBIES 5
Marvel Comics: Jun, 2010 - No. 5, Sept, 2010 ($3.99, limited series)

1-5-Van Lente-s; Machine Man and Howard the Duck app. 3-Kaluta-a 4.00

MARVEL ZOMBIES (Secret Wars tie-in)
Marvel Comics: Aug, 2015 - No. 4, Dec, 2015 ($3.99, limited series)

1-4-Spurrier-s/Walker-a; Elsa Bloodstone vs. zombies. 2,3-Deadpool app. 4.00

MARVEL ZOMBIES / ARMY OF DARKNESS
Marvel Comics/Dynamite Entertainment: May, 2007 - No. 5, Aug, 2007($2.99, limited series)

1-Zombies vs. Ash during the start of the plaque; Layman-s/Neves-a/Suydam-c 7.00
1-Second printing with Suydam zombie-fied Captain America Comics #1 cover swipe 4.00
2-5-Suydam zombie-fied cover swipes on all 5.00
HC (2007, $19.99) r/#1-5; cover gallery with variants and non-zombied original covers 20.00

Mary Marvel Comics #4 © FAW

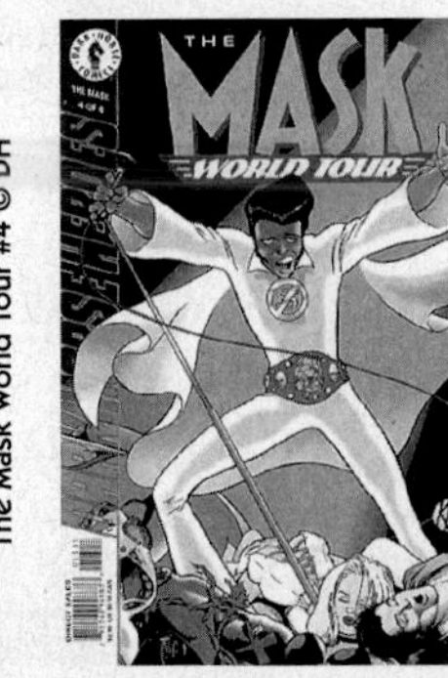

The Mask World Tour #4 © DH

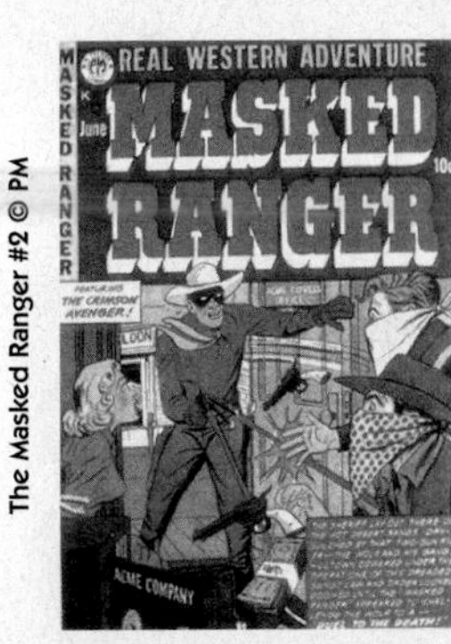

The Masked Ranger #2 © PM

	GD	VG	FN	VF	VF/NM	NM-
	2.0	4.0	6.0	8.0	9.0	9.2

MARVEL ZOMBIES CHRISTMAS CAROL ("Zombies Christmas Carol" on cover)
Marvel Comics: Aug, 2011 - No. 5, Oct, 2011 ($3.99, limited series)
1-5-Adaptation of the Dickens classic with zombies; Kaluta-c/Baldeon-a 4.00

MARVEL ZOMBIES DESTROY!
Marvel Comics: Jul, 2012 - No. 5, Sept, 2012 ($3.99, limited series)
1-5-Howard the Duck, Dum Dum Dugan vs. zombies; Del Mundo-c 4.00

MARVEL ZOMBIES: RESURRECTION
Marvel Comics: Dec, 2019; Nov, 2020 - No. 4, No. 4, Jan, 2021 ($5.99/$3.99)
1-(12/19, $4.99) Phillip Kennedy Johnson-s/Leonard Kirk-a/Inhyuk Lee-c 5.00
1-(11/20, $5.99) Johnson-s/Kirk-a/Inhyuk Lee-c; story continues; Blade app. 6.00
2-4-($3.99) 2-Viv Vision app. 3-Logan & Silver Surfer app. 5.00

MARVEL ZOMBIES RETURN
Marvel Comics: Nov, 2009 - No. 5, Nov, 2009 ($3.99, weekly limited series)
1-5-Suydam-c. 1-Zombie Spider-Man eats the Earth-Z Sinister Six; Dragotta-a 4.00

MARVEL ZOMBIES SUPREME
Marvel Comics: May, 2011 - No. 5, Aug, 2011 ($3.99, limited series)
1-5-Zombies in Squadron Supreme dimension; Blanco-a/Komarck-c; Jack of Hearts app. 4.00

MARVILLE
Marvel Comics: Nov, 2002 - No. 7, Jul, 2003 ($2.25, limited series)
1-6-Satire on DC/AOL-Time-Warner; Jemas-a/Bright-a/Horn-c 3.00
1-($3.95) Variant foil cover by Udon Studios; bonus sketch pages and Jemas afterword 4.00
7-($2.99) Intro. to Epic Comics line with submission guidelines 3.00

MARVIN MOUSE
Atlas Comics (BPC): September, 1957
1-Everett-c/a; Maneely-a 17 34 51 105 165 225

MARY JANE (Spider-Man) (Also see Amazing Mary Jane and Spider-Man Loves Mary Jane)
Marvel Comics: Aug, 2004 - No. 4, Nov, 2004 ($2.25, limited series)
1-4-Marvel Age series with teen-age MJ Watson; Miyazawa-c/a; McKeever-s 3.00
... Vol. 1: Circle of Friends (2004, $5.99, digest-size) r/#1-4 6.00

MARY JANE & SNIFFLES (See Looney Tunes)
Dell Publishing Co.: No. 402, June, 1952 - No. 474, June, 1953
Four Color 402 (#1) 9 18 27 59 117 175
Four Color 474 7 14 21 44 82 120

MARY JANE: HOMECOMING (Spider-Man)
Marvel Comics: May, 2005 - No. 4, Aug, 2005 ($2.99, limited series)
1-4-Teen-age MJ Watson in high school; Miyazawa-c/a; McKeever-s 3.00
... Vol. 2 (2005, $6.99, digest-size) r/#1-4 7.00

MARY MARVEL COMICS (Monte Hale #29 on) (Also see Captain Marvel #18, Marvel Family, Shazam, & Wow Comics)
Fawcett Publications: Dec, 1945 - No. 28, Sept, 1948
1-Captain Marvel introduces Mary on-c; intro/origin Georgia Sivana
174 348 522 1114 1907 2700
2 73 146 219 467 796 1125
3,4: 3-New logo 53 106 159 334 567 800
5-8: 8-Bulletgirl x-over; classic Christmas-c 42 84 126 265 445 625
9,10 39 78 117 231 378 525
11-20 28 56 84 165 270 375
21-28: 28-Western-c 24 48 72 144 237 330

MARY POPPINS (See Movie Comics & Walt Disney Showcase No. 17)

MARY SHELLEY MONSTER HUNTER
AfterShock Comics: Apr, 2019 - No. 5, Aug, 2019 ($3.99, limited series)
1-5-Adam Glass & Olivia Cuartero-Briggs-s/Hayden Sherman-a 4.00

MARY SHELLEY'S FRANKENSTEIN
Topps Comics: Oct, 1994 - Jan, 1995 ($2.95, limited series)
1-4-polybagged w/3 trading cards 5.00
1-4 ($2.50)-Newstand ed. 4.00

MARY WORTH (See Harvey Comics Hits #55 & Love Stories of...)
Argo: March, 1956 (Also see Romantic Picture Novelettes)
1-Senator's mistress makes wife jealous-s 8 16 24 44 57 70

MASK (TV)
DC Comics: Dec, 1985 - No. 4, Mar, 1986; Feb, 1987 - No. 9, Oct, 1987
1-Saturday morning TV show 1 3 4 6 8 10
2-4 6.00
1-9 (2nd series) 4.00

MASK, THE (Also see Mayhem)
Dark Horse Comics: Aug, 1991 - No. 4, Oct, 1991; No. 0, Dec, 1991 ($2.50, 36 pgs., limited series)
1-4: 1-1st app. Lt. Kellaway as The Mask (see Dark Horse Presents #10 for 1st app.) 5.00
0-(12/91, B&W, 56 pgs.)-r/Mayhem #1-4 4.00
...Omnibus Vol. 1 (8/08, $24.95) r/#1-4, Mask Returns and Mask Strikes Back series 25.00
...Omnibus Vol. 2 (4/09, $24.95) r/#1-4, The Hunt For Green October, World Tour, Southern Discomfort, Toys in the Attic series and short stories from DHP 25.00

...: HUNT FOR GREEN OCTOBER July, 1995 - Oct, 1995 ($2.50, lim. series)
1-4-Evan Dorkin scripts 4.00

...: I PLEDGE ALLEGIANCE TO THE MASK Oct, 2019 - No. 4, Jan, 2020 ($3.99, lim. series)
1-4-Christopher Cantwell-s/Patric Reynolds-a 4.00

.../ MARSHAL LAW Feb, 1998 - No. 2, Mar, 1998 ($2.95, lim. series)
1,2-Mills-s/O'Neill-a 4.00

...: OFFICIAL MOVIE ADAPTATION July, 1994 - Aug, 1994 ($2.50, lim. series)
1,2 4.00

... RETURNS Oct, 1992 - No. 4, Mar, 1993 ($2.50, limited series)
1-4 4.00

... SOUTHERN DISCOMFORT Mar, 1996 - No. 4, July, 1996 ($2.50, lim. series)
1-4 4.00

... STRIKES BACK Feb, 1995 - No. 5, Jun, 1995 ($2.50, limited series)
1-5 4.00

... SUMMER VACATION July, 1995 ($10.95, one shot, hard-c)
1-nn-Rick Geary-c/a 11.00

... TOYS IN THE ATTIC Aug, 1998 - No. 4, Nov, 1998 ($2.95, limited series)
1-4-Fingerman-s 4.00

... VIRTUAL SURREALITY July, 1997 ($2.95, one shot)
nn-Mignola, Aragonés, and others-s/a 4.00

... WORLD TOUR Dec, 1995 - No. 4, Mar, 1996 ($2.50, limited series)
1-4: 3-X & Ghost-c/app. 4.00

MASK COMICS
Rural Home Publ.: Feb-Mar, 1945 - No. 2, Apr-May, 1945; No. 2, Fall, 1945
1-Classic L. B. Cole Satan-c/a; Palais-a 1500 3000 4500 11,400 20,700 30,000
2-(Scarce)-Classic L. B. Cole Satan-c; Black Rider, The Boy Magician, & The Collector app.
400 800 1200 2800 4900 7000
2-(Fall, 1945)-No publ.-same as regular #2; L. B. Cole-c
300 600 900 2010 3505 5000

MASKED BANDIT, THE
Avon Periodicals: 1952
nn-Kinstler-a 21 42 63 124 202 280

MASKED MAN, THE
Eclipse Comics: 12/84 - #10, 4/86; #11, 10/87; #12, 4/88 ($1.75/$2.00, color/B&W #9 on, Baxter paper)
1-12: 1-Origin retold. 3-Origin Aphid-Man; begin $2.00-c 3.00

MASKED MARVEL (See Keen Detective Funnies)
Centaur Publications: Sept, 1940 - No. 3, Dec, 1940
1-The Masked Marvel begins 206 412 618 1318 2259 3200
2,3: 2-Gustavson, Tarpe Mills-a 148 296 444 947 1624 2300

MASKED RAIDER, THE (Billy The Kid #9 on; Frontier Scout, Daniel Boone #10-13) (Also see Blue Bird)
Charlton Comics: June, 1955 - No. 8, July, 1957; No. 14, Aug, 1958 - No. 30, June, 1961
1-Masked Raider & Talon the Golden Eagle begin; painted-c
17 34 51 105 165 225
2 10 20 30 54 72 90
3-8,15: 8-Billy The Kid app. 15-Williamson-a, 7 pgs. 8 16 24 42 54 65
14,16-30: 22-Rocky Lane app. 7 14 21 35 43 50

MASKED RANGER
Premier Magazines: Apr, 1954 - No. 9, Aug, 1955
1-The Masked Ranger, his horse Streak, & The Crimson Avenger (origin) begin, end #9; Woodbridge/Frazetta-a 47 94 141 296 498 700
2,3 17 34 51 100 158 215
4-8-All Woodbridge-a. 5-Jesse James by Woodbridge. 6-Billy The Kid by Woodbridge. 7-Wild Bill Hickok by Woodbridge. 8-Jim Bowie's Life Story
17 34 51 105 165 225
9-Torres-a; Wyatt Earp by Woodbridge; Says Death of Masked Ranger on-c
19 38 57 112 179 245

NOTE: *Check a-1. Woodbridge c/a-1, 4-9.*

M.A.S.K.: MOBILE ARMORED STRIKE KOMMAND (Hasbro toy)

The Mask of Dr. Fu Manchu #1 © AVON

Master Comics #1 © FAW

Master of Kung Fu #79 © MAR

	GD	VG	FN	VF	VF/NM	NM-
	2.0	4.0	6.0	8.0	9.0	9.2

IDW Publishing: Nov, 2016 - No. 10, Aug, 2017 ($3.99)

1-10: 1,2-Easton-s/Vargas-a. 3,6,7-Samu-a 4.00
Annual 2017 (2/17, $7.99, squarebound) Griffith-a; bonus character profiles 8.00
M.A.S.K. First Strike 1 (10/17, $3.99) G.I. Joe & Cobra app.; 3 covers; Kyriazis-a 4.00
...: Revolution 1 (9/16, $3.99) Easton-s/Vargas-a 4.00

MASK OF DR. FU MANCHU, THE (See Dr. Fu Manchu)
Avon Periodicals: 1951

1-Sax Rohmer adapt.; Wood-c/a (26 pgs.); Hollingsworth-a
129 258 387 826 1413 2000

MASK OF ZORRO, THE
Image Comics: Aug, 1998 - No. 4, Dec, 1998 ($2.95, limited series)

1-4-Movie adapt. Photo variant-c 3.00

MASKS
Dynamite Entertainment: 2012 - No. 8, 2013 ($3.99)

1-Team-up of the Shadow, Green Hornet, Spider; Alex Ross-a; multiple covers 5.00
2-8: 2-Miss Fury and Green Lama app.; Calero-a. 3-Black Terror app. 4.00

MASKS 2
Dynamite Entertainment: 2015 - No. 8, 2015 ($3.99)

1-8-Pulp hero team-up; Bunn-s/Casallos-a; multiple covers on each 4.00

MASKS: TOO HOT FOR TV!
DC Comics (WildStorm): Feb, 2004 ($4.95)

1-Short stories by various incl. Thompson, Brubaker, Mahnke, Conner; Fabry-c 5.00

MASQUE OF THE RED DEATH (See Movie Classics)

MASQUERADE (See Project Superpowers)
Dynamite Entertainment: 2009 - No. 4, 2009 ($3.50, limited series)

1-4-Alex Ross & Phil Hester-s/Carlos Paul-a; covers by Ross & others 3.50

MASS EFFECT: DISCOVERY (Based on the EA video game)
Dark Horse Comics: May, 2017 - No. 4, Oct, 2017 ($3.99, limited series)

1-4-Barlow-s/Guzmán-a 4.00

MASS EFFECT: EVOLUTION (2nd series based on the EA video game)
Dark Horse Comics: Jan, 2011 - No. 4, Apr, 2011 ($3.50, limited series)

1-4-Walters & Jackson Miller-s/Carnevale-c 3.50

MASS EFFECT: FOUNDATION (Based on the EA video game)
Dark Horse Comics: Jul, 2013 - No. 13, Jul, 2014 ($3.99, limited series)

1-13: 1-Walters-s/Francia-a. 2-4-Parker-a 4.00

MASS EFFECT: HOMEWORLDS (Based on the EA video game)
Dark Horse Comics: Apr, 2012 - No. 4, Aug, 2012 ($3.50, limited series)

1-4: 1-Walters-s/Francisco-a 3.50

MASS EFFECT: INVASION (3rd series based on the EA video game)
Dark Horse Comics: Oct, 2011 - No. 4, Jan, 2012 ($3.50, limited series)

1-4-Walters & Jackson Miller-s/Carnevale-c 3.50

MASS EFFECT: REDEMPTION (Based on the EA video game)
Dark Horse Comics: Jan, 2010 - No. 4, Apr, 2010 ($3.50, limited series)

1-4-Walters & Jackson Miller-s/Francia-a 3.50

MASSIVE, THE
Dark Horse Comics: Jun, 2012 - No. 30, Dec, 2014 ($3.50)

1-30: 1-Brian Wood-s/Kristian Donaldson-a. 4-9,25-30-Brown-a. 10-Erskine-a 3.50
...: Ninth Wave 1-6 ($3.99, 12/15 - No. 6, 5/16) Prequel to series; Wood-s/Brown-a 4.00

MASTER COMICS (Combined with Slam Bang Comics #7 on)
Fawcett Publications: Mar, 1940 - No. 133, Apr, 1953 (No. 1-6: oversized issues) (#1-3: 15¢, 52 pgs.; #4-6: 10¢, 36 pgs.; #7-Begin 68 pg. issues)

1-Origin & 1st app. Master Man; The Devil's Dagger, El Carim, Master of Magic, Rick O'Say, Morton Murch, White Rajah, Shipwreck Roberts, Frontier Marshal, Streak Sloan, Mr. Clue begin (all features end #6) 1000 2000 3000 7400 13,200 19,000
2 (Rare) 300 600 900 2040 3570 5100
3-6: 6-Last Master Man (Rare) 252 504 756 1613 2757 3900
NOTE: *#1-6 rarely found in near mint or very fine condition due to large-size format.*
7-(10/40)-Bulletman, Zoro, the Mystery Man (ends #22), Lee Granger, Jungle King, & Buck Jones begin; only app. The War Bird & Mark Swift & the Time Retarder; Zoro, Lee Granger, Jungle King & Mark Swift all continue from Slam Bang; Bulletman moves from Nickel
313 626 939 1988 3419 4850
8-The Red Gaucho (ends #13), Captain Venture (ends #22) & The Planet Princess begin
168 336 504 1075 1838 2600
9,10: 10-Lee Granger ends 145 290 435 928 1589 2250
11-Origin & 1st app. Minute-Man (2/41) 284 568 852 1818 3109 4400
12 132 264 396 845 1448 2050
13-Origin & 1st app. Bulletgirl; Hitler-c 274 548 822 1754 3002 4250
14-16: 14-Companions Three begins, ends #31 119 238 357 762 1306 1850
17-20: 17-Raboy-a on Bulletman begins. 20-Captain Marvel cameo app. in Bulletman
113 226 339 723 1237 1750
21-(12/41; Scarce)-Captain Marvel & Bulletman team up against Capt. Nazi; origin & 1st app. Capt. Marvel Jr's most famous nemesis Captain Nazi who will cause creation of Capt. Marvel Jr. in Whiz #25. Part I of trilogy origin of Capt. Marvel Jr.; 1st Mac Raboy-c for Fawcett; Capt. Nazi-c 811 1622 2433 5920 10,460 15,000
22-(1/42)-Captain Marvel Jr. moves over from Whiz #25 & teams up with Bulletman against Captain Nazi; part III of trilogy origin of Capt. Marvel Jr. & his 1st cover and adventure
703 1406 2109 5132 9066 13,000
23-Capt. Marvel Jr. c/stories begin (1st solo story); fights Capt. Nazi by himself.
309 618 927 2163 3782 5400
24,25 139 278 417 890 1520 2150
26,28,30-Captain Marvel Jr. vs. Capt. Nazi. 28-Liberty Bell-c. 30-Flag-c
132 264 396 845 1448 2050
27-Captain Marvel Jr. "V For Victory"-c; Capt. Nazi app.
187 374 561 1197 2049 2900
29-Hitler & Hirohito-c 271 542 813 174 2967 4200
31,32,35: 31-Captain Marvel & Spy Smasher Comix Cards on back-c. 32-Last El Carim & Buck Jones; intro Balbo, the Boy Magician in El Carim story; classic Eagle-c by Raboy
113 226 339 723 1237 1750
33-Capt. Marvel Jr. smashing swastika-c; Balbo, the Boy Magician (ends #47), Hopalong Cassidy (ends #49) begins 168 336 504 1075 1858 2600
34-Capt. Marvel Jr. vs. Capt. Nazi-c/story; 1st mention of Capt. Nippon
155 310 465 992 1696 2400
36-Statue of Liberty-c 106 212 318 678 1164 1650
37-39 86 172 258 546 936 1325
40-Classic flag-c 152 304 456 973 1662 2350
41-(8/43)-Bulletman, Capt. Marvel Jr. & Bulletgirl x-over in Minute-Man; only app. Crime Crusaders Club (Capt. Marvel Jr., Minute-Man, Bulletman & Bulletgirl)
94 188 282 597 1025 1450
42-46,49: 46-Hitler story. 49-Last Minute-Man 55 110 165 352 601 850
47-Hitler becomes Corpl. Hitler Jr. 60 120 180 381 653 925
48-Intro. Bulletboy; Capt. Marvel cameo in Minute-Man
58 116 174 371 636 900
50-Intro Radar & Nyoka the Jungle Girl & begin series (5/44); Radar also intro in Captain Marvel #35 (same date); Capt. Marvel x-over in Radar; origin Radar; Capt. Marvel & Capt. Marvel, Jr. introduce Radar on-c 55 110 165 352 601 850
51-58 31 62 93 185 303 420
59-62: Nyoka serial "Terrible Tiara" in all; 61-Capt. Marvel Jr. 1st meets Uncle Marvel
33 66 99 196 321 445
63-80 24 48 72 140 230 320
81,83-87,89-91,95-99: 88-Hopalong Cassidy begins (ends #94). 95-Tom Mix begins (cover only in #123, ends #133) 22 44 66 128 209 290
82,88,92-94-Krigstein-a 22 44 66 132 216 300
100 24 48 72 140 230 320
101-106-Last Bulletman (not in #104) 21 42 63 124 202 280
107-120: 118-Mary Marvel 20 40 60 120 195 270
121-131-(lower print run): 123-Tom Mix-c only 22 44 66 128 209 290
132-B&W and color illos in **POP**; last Nyoka 22 44 66 132 216 300
133-Bill Battle app. 28 56 84 165 270 375
NOTE: ***Mac Raboy** a-15-39, 40(part), 42, 58. c-21-49, 51, 52, 54, 56, 58, 68(part), 69(part). Bulletman c-7-11, 13(half), 15, 18(part), 19, 20, 21(w/Capt. Marvel & Capt. Nazi), 22(w/Capt. Marvel, Jr.). Capt. Marvel, Jr. c-23-133. Master Man c-1-6. Minute Man c-12, 13(half), 14, 16, 17, 18(part).*

MASTER DARQUE
Acclaim Comics (Valiant): Feb, 1998 ($3.95)

1-Manco-a/Christina Z.-s 4.00

MASTER DETECTIVE
Super Comics: 1964 (Reprints)

17-r/Criminals on the Loose V4 #2; r/Young King Cole #?; McWilliams-r
2 4 6 10 14 18

MASTER OF KUNG FU (Formerly Special Marvel Edition; see Deadly Hands of Kung Fu & Giant-Size...)
Marvel Comics Group: No. 17, April, 1974 - No. 125, June, 1983

17-Starlin-a; intro Black Jack Tarr; 3rd Shang-Chi (ties w/Deadly Hands #1)
5 10 15 34 60 85
18,20 3 6 9 16 23 30
19-Man-Thing-c/story 3 6 9 19 30 40
21-23,25-30 2 4 6 10 14 18
24-Starlin, Simonson-a 2 4 6 11 16 20
31-50: 33-1st Leiko Wu. 43-Last 25¢ issue 1 3 4 6 8 10
39-43-(30¢-c variants, limited distribution)(5-7/76) 6 12 18 40 73 105

Masters of the Universe #1 © Mattel

The Matrix Comics TPB © WB

Maverick #13 © DELL

GD VG FN VF VF/NM NM-
2.0 4.0 6.0 8.0 9.0 9.2

51-75 6.00
53-57-(35¢-c variants, limited distribution)(6-10/77) 7 14 21 49 92 135
76-99 5.00
100,118,125-Double size 6.00
101-117,119-124 4.00
Annual 1(4/76)-Iron Fist app. 4 8 12 28 47 65
NOTE: ***Austin*** *c-63i, 74i.* ***Buscema*** *c-44p.* ***Gulacy*** *a(p)-18-20, 22, 25, 29-31, 33-35, 38, 39, 40(p&i), 42-50, 53r(#20); c-51, 55, 64, 67.* ***Gil Kane*** *c(p)-20, 38, 39, 42, 45, 59, 63.* ***Nebres*** *c-73i.* ***Starlin*** *a-17p, 24; c-54.* ***Sutton*** *a-42i. #53 reprints #20.*

MASTER OF KUNG FU (Secret Wars tie-in)
Marvel Comics: Jul, 2015 - No. 4, Oct, 2015 ($3.99, limited series)
1-4-Blackman-s/Talajic-a/Francavilla-c; Shang-Chi & Iron Fist app. 4.00

MASTER OF KUNG FU (Marvel Legacy)
Marvel Comics: No. 126, Jan, 2018 ($3.99, one-shot)
126-CM Punk-s/Talajic-a 4.00

MASTER OF KUNG-FU: BLEEDING BLACK
Marvel Comics: Feb, 1991 ($2.95, 84 pgs., one-shot)
1-The Return of Shang-Chi 4.00

MASTER OF KUNG-FU, SHANG-CHI:... (2002 series, see Shang Chi:...)

MASTER OF THE WORLD
Dell Publishing Co.: No. 1157, July, 1961
Four Color 1157-Movie based on Jules Verne's "Master of the World" and "Robur the Conqueror" novels; with Vincent Price & Charles Bronson 8 16 24 52 99 145

MASTERS OF TERROR (Magazine)
Marvel Comics Group: July, 1975 - No. 2, Sept, 1975 (B&W) (All reprints)
1-Brunner, Barry Smith-a; Morrow/Steranko-c; Starlin-a(p); Gil Kane-a 3 6 9 19 30 40
2-Reese, Kane, Mayerik-a; Adkins/Steranko-c 2 4 6 13 18 22

MASTERS OF THE UNIVERSE (See DC Comics Presents #47 for 1st app.)
DC Comics: Dec, 1982 - No. 3, Feb, 1983 (Mini-series)
1 4 8 12 27 44 60
2,3: 2-Origin He-Man & Ceril 3 6 9 14 19 24
NOTE: ***Alcala*** *a-1i,, 2i.* ***Tuska*** *a-1-3p; c-1-3p. #2 has 75 & 95 cent cover price.*

MASTERS OF THE UNIVERSE (Comic Album)
Western Publishing Co.: 1984 (8-1/2x11", $2.95, 64 pgs.)
11362-Based on Mattel toy & cartoon 3 6 9 17 26 35

MASTERS OF THE UNIVERSE
Star Comics/Marvel #7 on: May 1986 - No. 13, May, 1988 (75¢/$1.00)
1 3 6 9 21 33 45
2-11: 8-Begin $1.00-c 1 3 4 6 8 10
12-Death of He-Man (1st Marvel app.) 5 10 15 31 53 75
13-Return of He-Man & death of Skeletor 4 8 12 27 44 60
The Motion Picture (11/87, $2.00)-Tuska-p 3 6 9 16 23 30

MASTERS OF THE UNIVERSE
Image Comics: Nov, 2002 - No. 4, March, 2003 ($2.95, limited series)
1-($2.95) Two covers by Santalucia and Campbell; Santalucia-a 2 4 6 9 12 15
1-($5.95) Variant-c by Norem w/gold foil logo 1 3 4 6 8 10
2-4($2.95) 2-Two covers by Santalucia and Manapul. 3,4-Two covers 6.00
TPB (CrossGen, 2003, $9.95, 8-1/4" x 5-1/2") digest-sized reprints #1-4 10.00

MASTERS OF THE UNIVERSE (Volume 2)
Image Comics: March, 2003 - No. 6, Aug, 2003 ($2.95)
1-6-($2.95) 1-Santalucia-c. 2-Two covers by Santalucia & JJ Kirby 1 3 4 6 8 10
1-($5.95) Wraparound variant-c by Struzan w/silver foil logo 2 4 6 8 10 12
3,4-($5.95) Wraparound variant holofoil-c. 3-By Edwards 4-By Boris Vallejo & Julie Bell 6.00
Volume 2 Dark Reflections TPB (2004, $18.95) r/#1-6 19.00

MASTERS OF THE UNIVERSE (Volume 3)
MVCreations: Apr, 2004 - No. 8, Dec, 2004 ($2.95)
1-Santalucia-c 1 2 3 5 6 8
2-8 4.00

MASTERS OF THE UNIVERSE...
CrossGen Comics
...Rise of the Snake-Men (Nov, 2003 - No. 3, $2.95) Meyers-a 6.00
...The Power of Fear (12/03, $2.95, one-shot) Santalucia-a 6.00

MASTERS OF THE UNIVERSE, ICONS OF EVIL
Image Comics/CrossGen Comics: 2003 ($4.95, one-shots)
...Beastman -(Image) Origin of Beast Man; Tony Moore-a 5.00
...Mer-Man -(CrossGen) 5.00
...Trapjaw -(CrossGen) 5.00
...Tri-Klops -(CrossGen) Walker-c 5.00
TPB (3/04, $18.95, MVCreations) r/one-shots; sketch pages 19.00

MASTERS OF THE UNIVERSE: ...
DC Comics: Dec, 2012; Mar, 2013; Jul, 2013 ($2.99, one-shots)
... Origin Of He-Man (3/13) Fialkov-s; Ben Oliver-a/c; Prince Adam finds the sword 3.00
... Origin Of Hordak (7/13) Giffen & Keene-s/Giffen-a/c 3.00
... The Origin Of Skeletor (12/12) Fialkov-s; Fraser Irving-a/c; Keldor becomes Skeletor 3.00

MASTERWORKS SERIES OF GREAT COMIC BOOK ARTISTS, THE
Sea Gate Dist./DC Comics: May, 1983 - No. 3, Dec, 1983 (Baxter paper)
1-3: 1,2-Shining Knight by Frazetta r-/Adventure. 2-Tomahawk by Frazetta-r. 3-Wrightson-c/a(r) 6.00

MATADOR
DC Comics (WildStorm): July, 2005 - No. 6, May, 2006 ($2.99, limited series)
1-6-Devin Grayson-s/Brian Stelfreeze-a/c 3.00

MATA HARI
Dark Horse Comics (Berger Books): Feb, 2018 - No. 5, Sept, 2018 ($3.99, limited series)
1-5-Beeby-s/Kristantina-a/c; story of the World War 1 spy 4.00

MATRIX COMICS, THE (Movie)
Burlyman Entertainment: 2003; 2004 ($21.95, trade paperback)
nn-Short stories by various incl. Wachowskis, Darrow, Gaiman, Sienkiewicz, Bagge 22.00
...Volume One Preview (7/03, no cover price) bios of creators; Chadwick-s/a 3.00
Volume 2-(2004) Short stories by various incl. Wachowskis, Sale, McKeever, Dorman 22.00

MATT SLADE GUNFIGHTER (Kid Slade Gunfighter #5 on; See Western Gunfighters)
Atlas Comics (SPI): May, 1956 - No. 4, Nov, 1956
1-Intro Matt & horse Eagle; Williamson/Torres-a 26 52 78 154 252 350
2-Williamson-a 16 32 48 98 154 210
3,4 14 28 42 80 115 150
NOTE: ***Maneely*** *a-1, 3, 4; c-1, 2, 4.* ***Roth*** *a-2-4.* ***Severin*** *a-1, 3, 4.* ***Maneely*** *c/a-1. Issue #s stamped on cover after printing.*

MAUS: A SURVIVOR'S TALE (First graphic novel to win a Pulitzer Prize)
Pantheon Books: 1986, 1991 (B&W)
Vol. 1-(...: My Father Bleeds History)(1986) Art Spiegelman-s/a; recounts stories of Spiegelman's father in 1930s-40s Nazi-occupied Poland; collects first six stories serialized in Raw Magazine from 1980-1985 30.00
Vol. 2-(...: And Here My Troubles Began)(1991) 25.00
Complete Maus Survivor's Tale -HC Vols. 1& 2 w/slipcase 35.00
Hardcover Vol. 1 (1991) 30.00
Hardcover Vol. 2 (1991) 30.00
TPB (1992, $14.00) Vols. 1& 2 18.00

MAVERICK (TV)
Dell Publishing Co.: No. 892, 4/58 - No. 19, 4-6/62 (All have photo-c)
Four Color 892 (#1)-James Garner photo-c begin 19 38 57 131 291 450
Four Color 930,945,962,980,1005 (6-8/59): 945-James Garner/Jack Kelly photo-c begin 10 20 30 65 135 205
7 (10-12/59) - 14: 11-Variant edition has "Time For Change" comic strip on back-c. 14-Last Garner/Kelly-c 8 16 24 54 102 150
15-18: Jack Kelly/Roger Moore photo-c 7 14 21 44 82 120
19-Jack Kelly photo-c (last issue) 7 14 21 46 86 125

MAVERICK (See X-Men)
Marvel Comics: Jan, 1997 ($2.95, one-shot)
1-Hama-s 5.00

MAVERICK (See X-Men)
Marvel Comics: Sept, 1997 - No. 12, Aug, 1998 ($2.99/$1.99)
1,12: 1-($2.99)-Wraparound-c. 12-($2.99) Battles Omega Red 5.00
2-11: 2-Two covers. 4-Wolverine app. 6,7-Sabretooth app. 4.00

MAVERICK MARSHAL
Charlton Comics: Nov, 1958 - No. 7, May, 1960
1 6 12 18 33 41 48
2-7 5 10 15 23 28 32

MAX BRAND (See Silvertip)

MAX HAMM FAIRY TALE DETECTIVE
Nite Owl Comix: 2002 - 2004 ($4.95, B&W, 6 1/2" x 8")
1-(2002) Frank Cammuso-s/a 5.00

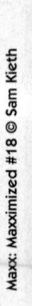

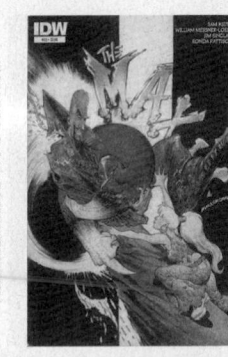

Maximage #7 © Rob Liefeld

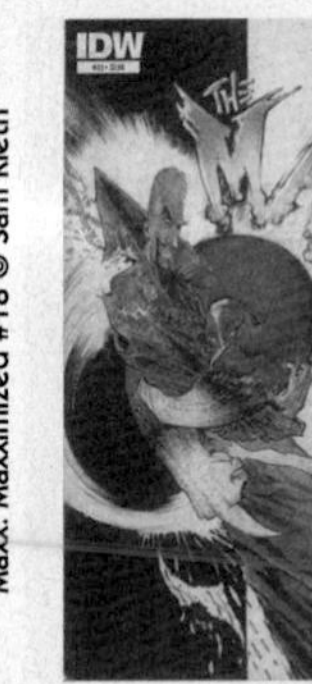

Maxx: Maxximized #18 © Sam Kieth

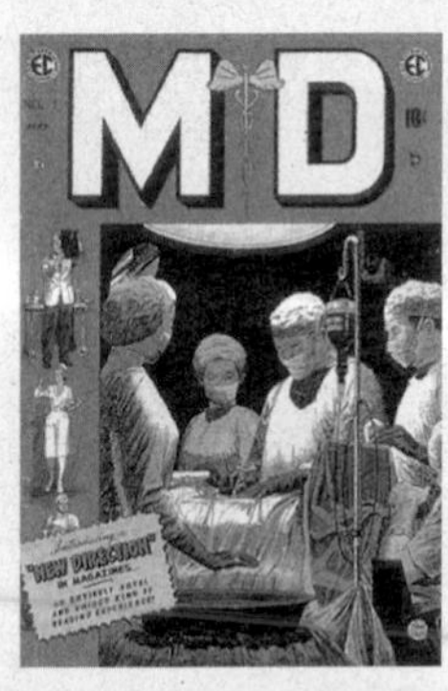

MD #1 © WMG

	GD	VG	FN	VF	VF/NM	NM-
	2.0	4.0	6.0	8.0	9.0	9.2

Vol. 2 #1-3 (2003-2004) Frank Cammuso-s/a 5.00

MAXIMAGE
Image Comics (Extreme Studios): Dec, 1995 - No. 7, June 1996 ($2.50)

1-7: 1-Liefeld-c. 2-Extreme Destroyer Pt. 2; polybagged w/card. 4-Angela & Glory-c/app. 4.00

MAXIMO
Dreamwave Prods.: Jan, 2004 ($3.95, one-shot)

1-Based on the Capcom video game 4.00

MAXIMUM SECURITY (Crossover)
Marvel Comics: Oct, 2000 - No. 3, Jan, 2001 ($2.99)

1-3-Busiek-s/Ordway-a; Ronan the Accuser, Avengers app. 3.00
...Dangerous Planet 1: Busiek-s/Ordway-a; Ego, the Living Planet 3.00
Thor vs. Ego (11/00, $2.99) Reprints Thor #133,160,161; Kirby-a 3.00

MAX RIDE: FINAL FLIGHT (Based on the James Patterson novel Maximum Ride)
Marvel Comics: Nov, 2016 - No. 5, Mar, 2017 ($3.99, limited series)

1-5-Jody Houser-s/Marco Failla-a. 1-Two covers (Nakamura & Oum) 4.00

MAX RIDE: FIRST FLIGHT (Based on the James Patterson novel Maximum Ride)
Marvel Comics: Jun, 2015 - No. 5, Oct, 2015 ($3.99, limited series)

1-5-Marguerite Bennett-s/Alex Sanchez-a. 1-Three covers 4.00

MAX RIDE: ULTIMATE FLIGHT (Based on the James Patterson novel Maximum Ride)
Marvel Comics: Jan, 2016 - No. 5, May, 2016 ($3.99, limited series)

1-5-Jody Houser-s/RB Silva-a. 1-Two covers 4.00

MAXX (Also see Darker Image, Primer #5, & Friends of Maxx)
Image Comics (I Before E): Mar, 1993 - No. 35, Feb, 1998 ($1.95)

	GD	VG	FN	VF	VF/NM	NM-
1/2	1	3	4	6	8	10
1/2 (Gold)						20.00
1-Sam Kieth-c/a/scripts						5.00
1-Glow-in-the-dark variant	2	4	6	8	10	12
1-"3-D Edition" (1/98, $4.95) plus new back-up story						5.00
2-12: 6-Savage Dragon cameo(1 pg.). 7,8-Pitt-c & story						3.00
13-16						3.00
17-35: 21-Alan Moore-s						3.00
Volume 1 TPB (DC/WildStorm, 2003, $17.95) r/#1-6						18.00
Volume 2 TPB (DC/WildStorm, 2004, $17.95) r/#7-13						18.00
Volume 3 TPB (DC/WildStorm, 2004, $17.95) r/#14-20						18.00
Volume 4 TPB (DC/WildStorm, 2005, $17.95) r/#21-27						18.00
Volume 5 TPB (DC/WildStorm, 2005, $19.99) r/#28-35						20.00
Volume 6 TPB (DC/WildStorm, 2006, $19.99) r/Friends of Maxx #1-3 & The Maxx 3-D						20.00

MAXX: MAXXIMIZED
IDW Publishing: Nov, 2013 - No. 35, Sept, 2016 ($3.99)

1-35-Remastered, recolored reprint of the original Maxx issues 4.00

MAYA (See Movie Classics)
Gold Key: Mar, 1968

	GD	VG	FN	VF	VF/NM	NM-
1 (10218-803)(TV) Photo-c	3	6	9	16	24	32

MAYHEM
Dark Horse Comics: May, 1989 - No. 4, Sept, 1989 ($2.50, B&W, 52 pgs.)

	GD	VG	FN	VF	VF/NM	NM-
1-Four part Stanley Ipkiss/Mask story begins; Mask-c	3	6	9	14	19	24
2-4: 2-Mask 1/2 back-c. 4-Mask-c	1	3	4	6	8	10

MAYHEM (Tyrese Gibson's...)
Image Comics: Aug, 2009 - No. 3, Oct, 2009 ($2.99, limited series)

1-3-Tyrese Gibson co-writer; Tone Rodriguez-a/c 3.00

MAZE AGENCY, THE
Comico/Innovation Publ. #8 on: Dec, 1988 - No. 23, Aug, 1991 ($1.95-$2.50, color)

1-23: 1-5,8,9,12-Adam Hughes-c/a. 9-Ellery Queen app. 7 ($2.50)-Last Comico issue 3.00
Annual 1 (1990, $2.75)-Ploog-c; Spirit tribute ish 4.00
Special 1 (1989, $2.75)-Staton-p (Innovation) 4.00
TPB (IDW Publ., 11/05, $24.99) r/#1-5 25.00

MAZE AGENCY, THE (Vol. 2)
Caliber Comics: July, 1997 - No. 3, 1998 ($2.95, B&W)

1-3: 1-Barr-s/Gonzales-a(p). 3-Hughes-c 3.00

MAZE AGENCY, THE
IDW Publishing: Nov, 2005 - No. 3, Jan, 2006 ($3.99, limited series)

1-3-Barr-s/Padilla-a(p)/c 4.00

MAZE RUNNER: THE SCORCH TRIALS (Based on the Maze Runner movies)
BOOM! Studios: Jun, 2015 ($14.99, squarebound SC)

...Official Graphic Novel Prelude - Short stories about the characters; s/a by various 15.00

MAZIE (...& Her Friends) (See Flat-Top, Mortie, Stevie & Tastee-Freez)
Mazie Comics(Magazine Publ.)/Harvey Publ. No. 13-on: 1953 - #12, 1954; #13, 12/54 - #22, 9/56; #23, 9/57 - #28, 8/58

	GD	VG	FN	VF	VF/NM	NM-
1-(Teen-age)-Stevie's girlfriend	15	30	45	84	127	170
2	10	20	30	54	72	90
3-10	8	16	24	42	54	65
11-28	7	14	21	37	46	55

MAZIE
Nation Wide Publishers: 1950 - No. 7, 1951 (5¢) (5x7-1/4"-miniature)(52 pgs.)

	GD	VG	FN	VF	VF/NM	NM-
1-Teen-age	21	42	63	126	206	285
2-7	15	30	45	85	130	175

MAZINGER (See First Comics Graphic Novel #17)

'MAZING MAN
DC Comics: Jan, 1986 - No. 12, Dec, 1986

1-11: 7,8-Hembeck-a 4.00
12-Dark Knight part-c by Miller 5.00
Special 1 ('87), 2 (4/88), 3 ('90)-All $2.00, 52pgs. 5.00

McCANDLESS & COMPANY
Mandalay Books/American Mythology

...: Dead Razor (2001, $7.95) J.C. Vaughn-s/Busch & Sheehan-a; 3 covers 8.00
...: Insecuritues (American Myth., 10/16, $4.99) Vaughn-s/Gonzales-a/Oeming-c 5.00
Crime Scenes: A McCandless & Company Reader TPB (Spring 2006, $17.95) Vaughn-s 18.00

McHALE'S NAVY (TV) (See Movie Classics)
Dell Publ. Co.: May-July, 1963 - No. 3, Nov-Jan, 1963-64 (All have photo-c)

	GD	VG	FN	VF	VF/NM	NM-
1	7	14	21	46	86	125
2,3	5	10	15	31	53	75

McKEEVER & THE COLONEL (TV)
Dell Publishing Co.: Feb-Apr, 1963 - No. 3, Aug-Oct, 1963

	GD	VG	FN	VF	VF/NM	NM-
1-Photo-c	5	10	15	34	60	85
2,3-Photo-c	4	8	12	28	47	65

McLINTOCK (See Movie Comics)

MD
E. C. Comics: Apr-May, 1955 - No. 5, Dec-Jan, 1955-56

	GD	VG	FN	VF	VF/NM	NM-
1-Not approved by code; Craig-c	21	42	63	168	272	375
2-5	13	26	39	104	167	230

NOTE: ***Crandall, Evans, Ingels, Orlando** art in all issues; **Craig** c-1-5.*

MD
Russ Cochran/Gemstone Publishing: Sept, 1999 - No. 5, Jan, 2000 ($2.50)

1-5-Reprints original EC series 4.00
Annual 1 (1999, $13.50) r/#1-5 14.00

MEASLES
Fantagraphics Books: Christmas 1998 - No. 8 ($2.95, B&W, quarterly)

1-8-Anthology: 1-Venus-s by Hernandez 3.00

MECHA (Also see Mayhem)
Dark Horse Comics: June, 1987 - No. 6, 1988 ($1.50/$1.95, color/B&W)

1-6: 1,2 ($1.95, color), 3,4-($1.75, B&W), 5,6-($1.50, B&W) 3.00

MECHANIC, THE
Image Comics: 1998 ($5.95, one-shot, squarebound)

1-Chiodo-painted art; Peterson-s 6.00
1-($10.00) DF Alternate Cover Ed. 10.00

MECHANISM
Image Comics (Top Cow): Jul, 2016 - No. 5, Nov, 2016 ($3.99)

1-5-Raffaele Ienco-s/a 4.00

MECHA SPECIAL
Dark Horse Comics: May, 1995 ($2.95, one-shot)

1 3.00

MECH CADET YU
BOOM! Studios: Aug, 2017 - No. 12, Sept, 2018 ($3.99)

1-12-Greg Pak-s/Takeshi Miyazawa-a 4.00

MECH DESTROYER
Image Comics: Apr, 2001 - No. 4, Sept, 2001 ($2.95, limited series)

1-4-Jae Kim-c/a; Robert Chong-s 3.00

MEDAL FOR BOWZER, A (See Promotional Comics section)

Meet Corliss Archer #2 © FOX

Mega Man: Fully Charged #1 © Capcom

Mega Morphs #1 © MAR

GD 2.0 | VG 4.0 | FN 6.0 | VF 8.0 | VF/NM 9.0 | NM- 9.2

GD 2.0 | VG 4.0 | FN 6.0 | VF 8.0 | VF/NM 9.0 | NM- 9.2

MEDAL OF HONOR COMICS
A. S. Curtis: Spring, 1946
1-War stories 17 34 51 105 165 225

MEDAL OF HONOR SPECIAL
Dark Horse Comics: 1994 ($2.50, one-shot)
1-Kubert-c/a (first story) 3.00

MEDIA STARR
Innovation Publ.: July, 1989 - No. 3, Sept, 1989 ($1.95, mini-series, 28 pgs.)
1-3: Deluxe format 3.00

MEDIEVAL SPAWN/WITCHBLADE
Image Comics (Top Cow Productions): May, 1996 - No. 3, June, 1996 ($2.95, limited series)
1-3-Garth Ennis scripts in all 6.00
1-Platinum foil-c (500 copies from Pittsburgh Con) 35.00
1-Gold 10.00
1-ETM Exclusive Edition; gold foil logo 7.00
TPB ($9.95) r/#1-3 10.00

MEDIEVAL SPAWN & WITCHBLADE
Image Comics: May, 2018 - No. 4, Aug, 2018 ($2.99, limited series)
1-4-Haberlin & Holguin-s/Haberlin-a 3.00

MEET ANGEL (Formerly Angel & the Ape)
National Periodical Publications: No. 7, Nov-Dec, 1969
7-Wood-a(i) 4 8 12 23 37 50

MEET CORLISS ARCHER (Radio/Movie)(My Life #4 on)
Fox Feature Syndicate: Mar, 1948 - No. 3, July, 1948
1-(Teen-age)-Feldstein-c/a; headlight-c 142 284 426 909 1555 2200
2-Feldstein-c/a 65 130 195 416 708 1000
3-Feldstein-c/a 58 116 174 371 636 900
NOTE: *No. 1-3 used in Seduction of the Innocent, pg. 39.*

MEET HERCULES (See Three Stooges)

MEET MERTON
Toby Press: Dec, 1953 - No. 4, June, 1954
1-(Teen-age)-Dave Berg-c/a 22 44 66 128 209 290
2-Dave Berg-c/a 14 28 42 80 115 150
3,4-Dave Berg-c/a 13 26 39 74 105 135
I.W. Reprint #9, Super Reprint #11('63), 18 2 4 6 8 11 14

MEET MISS BLISS (Becomes Stories Of Romance #5 on)
Atlas Comics (LMC): May, 1955 - No. 4, Nov, 1955
1-Al Hartley-c/a 65 130 195 416 708 1000
2-4 30 60 90 177 289 400

MEET MISS PEPPER (Formerly Lucy, The Real Gone Gal)
St. John Publishing Co.: No. 5, April, 1954 - No. 6, June, 1954
5-Kubert/Maurer-a 34 68 102 204 332 460
6-Kubert/Maurer-a; Kubert-c 29 58 87 172 281 390

MEET THE SKRULLS
Marvel Comics: May, 2019 - No. 5, Aug, 2019 ($3.99, limited series)
1-5-Robbie Thompson-s/Niko Henrichon-a 4.00

MEGAGHOST
Albatross Funnybooks: 2018 - No. 5, 2019 ($3.99)
1-5-Gabe Soria-s/Gideon Kendall-a 4.00

MEGALITH (Megalith Deathwatch 2000 #1,2 of second series)
Continuity: 1989 - No. 9, Mar, 1992; No, 0, Apr, 1993 - No. 7, Jan, 1994
1-9-($2.00-c) 1-Neal Adams & Mark Texiera-c/Texiera & Nebres-a 3.00
2nd series: 0-(4/93)-Foil-c; no c-price, giveaway; Adams plot 3.00
1-7: 1-3-Bagged w/card: 1-Gatefold-c by Nebres; Adams plot. 2-Fold-out-c; Adams plot. 3-Indestructible-c. 4-7-Embossed-c: 4-Adams/Nebres-c; Adams part-i. 5-Sienkiewicz-i. 6-Adams part-i. 7-Adams-c(p); Adams plot 3.00

MEGAMAN
Dreamwave Productions: Sept, 2003 - No. 4, Dec, 2003 ($2.95)
1-4-Brian Augustyn-s/Mic Fong-a 3.00
1-($5.95) Chromium wraparound variant-c 6.00

MEGA MAN (Based on the Capcom video game character)
Archie Comics Publications: Jul, 2011 - No. 55, Feb, 2016 ($2.99/$3.99)
1-39 1-Spaziante-a. 20-39-Multiple covers. 24-Worlds Collide x-over begins 3.00
40-49,51-55 ($3.99) Two covers on most. 51,52-Three covers 4.00
50-($4.99) Six covers; "Worlds Unite" Sonic/Mega Man x-over pt. 4 5.00
Free Comic Book Day Edition (2012, giveaway) Origin re-told 3.00
...: Worlds Unite Battles 1 (8/15, $3.99) Sonic/Mega Man x-over; 3 wraparound covers 4.00

MEGA MAN: FULLY CHARGED (Capcom video game character)
BOOM! Studios: Aug, 2020 - No. 6, Jan, 2021 ($4.99)
1-6-Marchisello & Rinehart-s/Simeone-a 5.00

MEGAMIND: BAD. BLUE. BRILLIANT (DreamWorks'...) (Based on the 2010 movie)
Ape Entertainment: 2010 - No. 4, 2011 ($3.95, limited series)
1-4: 1-High school flashback 4.00
nn-($6.95, 9x6") Prequel to the movie; Joe Kelly-s 7.00

MEGA MORPHS
Marvel Comics: Oct, 2005 - No. 4, Dec, 2005 ($2.99, limited series)
1-4-Giant robots based on action figures; McKeever-s; Kang-a 3.00
Digest (2006, $7.99) r/#1-4 plus mini-comics 8.00

MEGATON (A super hero)
Megaton Publ.: Nov, 1983; No. 2, Oct, 1985 - No. 8, Aug, 1987 (B&W)
1-($2.00, 68 pgs.)-Erik Larsen's 1st pro work; Vanguard by Larsen begins (1st app.), ends #4; 1st app. Megaton, Berzerker, & Ethrian; Guice-c/a(p); Gustovich-a(p) in #1,2 3 6 9 15 22 28
2-($2.00, 68 pgs.)-1st brief app. The Dragon (1 pg.) by Larsen (later The Savage Dragon in Image Comics); Guice-c/a(p) 2 4 6 10 14 18
3-(44 pgs.)-1st full app. Savage Dragon-c/story by Larsen; (earlier apps. were in the 1982 fanzine Graphic Fantasy); 1st comic book work by Angel Medina (pin-up) 5 10 15 30 50 70
4-(52 pgs.)-2nd full app. Savage Dragon by Larsen; 4,5-Wildman by Grass Green 2 4 6 8 10 12
5-1st Liefeld published-a (inside f/c, 6/86) 1 2 3 5 7 9
6,7: 6-Larsen-c 1 2 3 4 5 7
8-1st Liefeld story-a (7 pg. super hero story) plus 1 pg. Youngblood ad 3 6 9 14 19 24
...Explosion (6/87, 16 pg. color giveaway)-1st app. Youngblood by Rob Liefeld (2 pg. spread); shows Megaton heroes 5 10 15 33 57 80
...Holiday Special 1 (1994, $2.95, color, 40 pgs., publ. by Entity Comics)-Gold foil logo; bagged w/Kelley Jones card; Vanguard, Megaton plus shows unpublished-c to 1987 Youngblood #1 by Liefeld/Ordway 1 2 3 5 6 8
NOTE: *Copies of Megaton Explosion were also released in early 1992 all signed by Rob Liefeld and were made available to retailers.*

MEGATON MAN (See Don Simpson's Bizarre Heroes)
Kitchen Sink Enterprises: Nov, 1984 - No. 10, 1986
1-10, 1-2nd printing (1989) 4.00
...Meets The Uncategorizable X-Thems 1 (4/89, $2.00) 4.00

MEGATON MAN: BOMB SHELL
Image Comics: Jul, 1999 - No. 2 ($2.95, B&W, mini-series)
1-Reprints stories from Megaton Man internet site 4.00

MEGATON MAN: HARD COPY
Image Comics: Feb, 1999 - No. 2, Apr, 1999 ($2.95, B&W, mini-series)
1,2-Reprints stories from Megaton Man internet site 4.00

MEGATON MAN VS. FORBIDDEN FRANKENSTEIN (Double titled as Don Simpson's Bizarre Heroes #16)
Fiasco Comics: Apr, 1996 ($2.95, B&W, one-shot)
1-Intro The Tomb Team (Forbidden Frankenstein, Drekula, Bride of the Monster, & Moon Wolf). 1 2 3 5 6 8

MEK (See Reload/Mek flipbook for TPB reprint)
DC Comics (Homage): Jan, 2003 - No. 3, Mar, 2003 ($2.95, limited series)
1-3-Warren Ellis-s/Steve Rolston-a 4.00

MEKANIX (See X-Men titles) (See X-Treme X-Men Vol. 4 for TPB)
Marvel Comics: Dec, 2002 - No. 6, May, 2003 ($2.99, limited series)
1-6-Kitty Pryde in college; Claremont-s/Bobillo & Sosa-a 4.00

MEL ALLEN SPORTS COMICS (The Voice of the Yankees)
Standard Comics: No. 5, Nov, 1949; No. 6, June, 1950
5(#1 on inside)-Tuska-a 23 46 69 136 223 310
6(#2)-Lou Gehrig story 16 32 48 94 147 200

MELVIN MONSTER
Dell Publishing Co.: Apr-June, 1965 - No. 10, Oct, 1969
1-By John Stanley 6 12 18 40 73 105
2-10-All by Stanley. #10-r/#1 5 10 15 30 50 70

MELVIN THE MONSTER (See Peter, the Little Pest & Dexter The Demon #7)
Atlas Comics (HPC): July, 1956 - No. 6, July, 1957

Menace #3 © MAR

Men of Wrath #3 © Golgonooza

Mercy #3 © Mirka Andolfo

	GD 2.0	VG 4.0	FN 6.0	VF 8.0	VF/NM 9.0	NM- 9.2
1-Maneely-c/a	17	34	51	98	154	210
2-6: 4-Maneely-c/a	12	24	36	67	94	120

MENACE
Atlas Comics (HPC): Mar, 1953 - No. 11, May, 1954

	GD 2.0	VG 4.0	FN 6.0	VF 8.0	VF/NM 9.0	NM- 9.2
1-Horror & sci/fi stories begin; Everett-c/a	226	452	678	1446	2473	3500
2-Post-atom bomb disaster by Everett; anti-Communist propaganda/torture scenes; Sinnott sci/fi story "Rocket to the Moon"	155	310	465	992	1696	2400
3,4,6-Everett-a. 4-Sci/fi story "Escape to the Moon". 6-Romita sci/fi story "Science Fiction"	110	220	330	704	1202	1700
5-Origin & 1st app. The Zombie by Everett (reprinted in Tales of the Zombie #1)(7/53); 5-Sci/fi story "Rocket Ship"	300	600	900	2010	3505	5000
7,8,10,11: 7-Frankenstein story. 8-End of world story; Heath 3-D art(3 pgs.). 10-H-Bomb panels	84	168	252	538	919	1300
9-Everett-a r-in Vampire Tales #1	129	258	387	826	1413	2000

NOTE: ***Brodsky** c-7, 8, 11. **Colan** a-6; c-9. **Everett** a-1-6, 9; c-1-6. **Heath** a-1-8; c-10. **Katz** a-11. **Maneely** a-3-5, 7-9. **Powell** a-11. **Romita** a-3, 6, 8, 11. **Shelly** a-10. **Shores** a-7. **Sinnott** a-2, 7. **Tuska** a-1, 2, 5.*

MENACE
Awesome-Hyperwerks: Nov, 1998 ($2.50)

	GD 2.0	VG 4.0	FN 6.0	VF 8.0	VF/NM 9.0	NM- 9.2
1-Jada Pinkett Smith-s/Fraga-a						3.00

MEN AGAINST CRIME (Formerly Mr. Risk; Hand of Fate #8 on)
Ace Magazines: No. 3, Feb, 1951 - No. 7, Oct, 1951

	GD 2.0	VG 4.0	FN 6.0	VF 8.0	VF/NM 9.0	NM- 9.2
3-Mr. Risk app.	15	30	45	85	130	175
4-7: 4-Colan-a; entire book-r as Trapped! #4. 5-Meskin-a	11	22	33	62	85	110

MEN, GUNS, & CATTLE (See Classics Illustrated Special Issue)

MEN IN ACTION (Battle Brady #10 on)
Atlas Comics (IPS): April, 1952 - No. 9, Dec, 1952 (War stories)

	GD 2.0	VG 4.0	FN 6.0	VF 8.0	VF/NM 9.0	NM- 9.2
1-Berg, Reinman-a	34	68	102	204	332	460
2,3: 3-Heath-c/a	17	34	51	105	165	225
4-6,8,9	15	30	45	94	147	200
7-Krigstein-a; Heath-c	17	34	51	105	165	225

NOTE: ***Brodsky** a-3; c-1, 4-6. **Maneely** a-4; c-5. **Pakula** a-1, 6. **Robinson** c-8. **Shores** c-9. **Sinnott** a-6.*

MEN IN ACTION
Ajax/Farrell Publications: Apr, 1957 - No. 6, Jun, 1958

	GD 2.0	VG 4.0	FN 6.0	VF 8.0	VF/NM 9.0	NM- 9.2
1	14	28	42	76	108	140
2	8	16	24	44	57	70
3-6	8	16	24	40	50	60

MEN IN BLACK, THE (1st series)
Aircel Comics (Malibu): Jan, 1990 - No. 3 Mar, 1990 ($2.25, B&W, lim. series)

	GD 2.0	VG 4.0	FN 6.0	VF 8.0	VF/NM 9.0	NM- 9.2
1-Cunningham-s/a in all	7	14	21	44	82	120
2,3	3	6	9	19	30	40
Graphic Novel (Jan, 1991) r/#1-3	3	6	9	16	23	30

MEN IN BLACK (2nd series)
Aircel Comics (Malibu): May, 1991 - No. 3, Jul, 1991 ($2.50, B&W, lim. series)

	GD 2.0	VG 4.0	FN 6.0	VF 8.0	VF/NM 9.0	NM- 9.2
1-Cunningham-s/a in all	3	6	9	19	30	40
2,3	2	4	6	11	16	20

MEN IN BLACK: FAR CRY
Marvel Comics: Aug, 1997 ($3.99, color, one-shot)

	GD 2.0	VG 4.0	FN 6.0	VF 8.0	VF/NM 9.0	NM- 9.2
1-Cunningham-s	1	3	4	6	8	10

MEN IN BLACK: RETRIBUTION
Marvel Comics: Dec, 1997 ($3.99, color, one-shot)

	GD 2.0	VG 4.0	FN 6.0	VF 8.0	VF/NM 9.0	NM- 9.2
1-Cunningham-s; continuation of the movie	1	3	4	6	8	10

MEN IN BLACK: THE MOVIE
Marvel Comics: Oct, 1997 ($3.99, one-shot, movie adaptation)

	GD 2.0	VG 4.0	FN 6.0	VF 8.0	VF/NM 9.0	NM- 9.2
1-Cunningham-s	1	3	4	6	8	10

MEN INTO SPACE
Dell Publishing Co.: No. 1083, Feb-Apr, 1960

	GD 2.0	VG 4.0	FN 6.0	VF 8.0	VF/NM 9.0	NM- 9.2
Four Color 1083-Anderson-a, photo-c	6	12	18	38	69	100

MEN OF BATTLE (Also see New Men of Battle)
Catechetical Guild: V1#5, March, 1943 (Hardcover)

	GD 2.0	VG 4.0	FN 6.0	VF 8.0	VF/NM 9.0	NM- 9.2
V1#5-Topix reprints	8	16	24	40	50	60

MEN OF WAR
DC Comics, Inc.: August, 1977 - No. 26, March, 1980 (#9,10: 44 pgs.)

	GD 2.0	VG 4.0	FN 6.0	VF 8.0	VF/NM 9.0	NM- 9.2
1-Enemy Ace, Gravedigger (origin #1,2) begin	3	6	9	19	30	40
2-4,8-10,12-14,19,20: All Enemy Ace stories. 4-1st Dateline Frontline. 9-Unknown Soldier app.	2	4	6	11	16	20
5-7,11,15-18,21-25: 17-1st app. Rosa	2	4	6	9	13	16
26-Sgt. Rock & Easy Co.-c/s	3	6	9	14	20	26

NOTE: ***Chaykin** a-9, 10, 12-14, 19, 20. **Evans** c-25. **Kubert** c-2-23, 24p, 26.*

MEN OF WAR (DC New 52)
DC Comics: Nov, 2011 - No. 8, Jun, 2012 ($3.99)

	GD 2.0	VG 4.0	FN 6.0	VF 8.0	VF/NM 9.0	NM- 9.2
1-8: 1-Sgt. Rock's grandson in modern times; Derenick-a; Navy Seals back-up; Winslade-a 6-Back-up w/Corben-a. 8-Frankenstein & G.I. Robot app.						4.00

MEN OF WRATH
Marvel Comics (ICON): Oct, 2014 - No. 5, Feb, 2015 ($3.50, limited series)

	GD 2.0	VG 4.0	FN 6.0	VF 8.0	VF/NM 9.0	NM- 9.2
1-5-Jason Aaron-s/Ron Garney-a; two covers on each. 5-Alex Ross var-c						3.50

MEN'S ADVENTURES (Formerly True Adventures)
Marvel/Atlas Comics (CCC): No. 4, Aug, 1950 - No. 28, July, 1954

	GD 2.0	VG 4.0	FN 6.0	VF 8.0	VF/NM 9.0	NM- 9.2
4(#1)(52 pgs.)	40	80	120	246	411	575
5-Flying Saucer story	27	54	81	158	259	360
6-8: 7-Buried alive story. 8-Sci/fic story	24	48	72	144	237	330
9-20: All war format	18	36	54	109	172	235
21,22,24,26: All horror format	42	84	126	265	445	625
23-Crandall-a; Fox-a(i); horror format	43	86	129	271	461	650
25-Shrunken head-c	84	168	252	538	919	1300
27,28-Human Torch & Toro-c/stories; Captain America & Sub-Mariner stories in each (also see Young Men #24-28)	171	342	513	1094	1872	2650

NOTE: ***Ayers** a-20, 27(H. Torch). **Berg** a-15, 16. **Brodsky** c-4-9, 11, 12, 16-18, 24. **Burgos** c-27, 28 (Human Torch). **Colan** a-13, 14, 19. **Everett** a-10, 14, 22, 25, 28; c-14, 21-23. **Hartley** a-12. **Heath** a-8, 11, 24; c-13, 20, 26. **Lawrence** a-23; 27(Captain America). **Maneely** a-24; c-10, 15. **Mac Pakula** a-15, 25. **Post** a-23. **Powell** a-27(Sub-Mariner). **Reinman** a-10-12, 16. **Robinson** c-19. **Romita** a-22. **Sale** a-12-14. **Shores** c-25. **Sinnott** a-13, 21. **Tuska** a-24. Adventure-#4-8; War-#9-20; Weird/Horror-#21-26.*

MENZ INSANA
DC Comics (Vertigo): 1997 ($7.95, one-shot)

	GD 2.0	VG 4.0	FN 6.0	VF 8.0	VF/NM 9.0	NM- 9.2
nn-Fowler-s/Bolton painted art	1	2	3	5	6	8

MEPHISTO VS... (See Silver Surfer #3)
Marvel Comics Group: Apr, 1987 - No. 4, July, 1987 ($1.50, mini-series)

	GD 2.0	VG 4.0	FN 6.0	VF 8.0	VF/NM 9.0	NM- 9.2
1-4: 1-Fantastic Four; Austin-i. 2-X-Factor. 3-X-Men. 4-Avengers						4.00

MERA: QUEEN OF ATLANTIS (Leads into Aquaman #38)
DC Comics: Apr, 2018 - No. 6, Sept, 2018 ($3.99, limited series)

	GD 2.0	VG 4.0	FN 6.0	VF 8.0	VF/NM 9.0	NM- 9.2
1-6: 1-Abnett-s/Medina-a; origin retold; Ocean Master app.						4.00

MERC (See Mark Hazzard: Merc)

MERCENARIES (Based on the Pandemic video game)
Dynamite Entertainment: 2007 - No. 3, 2008 ($3.99, limited series)

	GD 2.0	VG 4.0	FN 6.0	VF 8.0	VF/NM 9.0	NM- 9.2
1-3-Michael Turner-c; Brian Reed-s/Edgar Salazar-a						4.00

MERCHANTS OF DEATH
Acme Press (Eclipse): Jul, 1988 - No. 4, Nov, 1988 ($3.50, B&W/16 pgs. color, 44 pg. mag.)

	GD 2.0	VG 4.0	FN 6.0	VF 8.0	VF/NM 9.0	NM- 9.2
1-4: 4-Toth-c						4.00

MERCILESS: THE RISE OF MING (Also see Flash Gordon: Zeitgeist)
Dynamite Entertainment: 2012 - No. 4, 2012 ($3.99, limited series)

	GD 2.0	VG 4.0	FN 6.0	VF 8.0	VF/NM 9.0	NM- 9.2
1-4 Ming the Merciless' rise to power; Alex Ross-c; Beatty-c/Adrian-a						4.00

MERCY (Mirka Andolfo's...)
Image Comics: Mar, 2020 - No. 6, Sept, 2020 ($3.99, limited series)

	GD 2.0	VG 4.0	FN 6.0	VF 8.0	VF/NM 9.0	NM- 9.2
1-6-Mirka Andolfo-s/a. 1-Five covers						4.00

MERCY THOMPSON (Patricia Briggs'...)
Dynamite Entertainment: 2014 - No. 6, 2015 ($3.99, limited series)

	GD 2.0	VG 4.0	FN 6.0	VF 8.0	VF/NM 9.0	NM- 9.2
1-6-Patricia Briggs & Rik Hoskin-s/Tom Garcia-a						4.00

MERIDIAN
CrossGeneration Comics: Jul, 2000 - No. 44, Apr, 2004 ($2.95)

	GD 2.0	VG 4.0	FN 6.0	VF 8.0	VF/NM 9.0	NM- 9.2
1-44: Barbara Kesel-s						3.00
Flying Solo Vol. 1 TPB (2001, $19.95) r/#1-7; cover by Steve Rude						20.00
Going to Ground Vol. 2 TPB (2002, $19.95) r/#8-14						20.00
Taking the Skies Vol. 3 TPB (2002, $15.95) r/#15-20						16.00
Vol. 4: Coming Home (12/02, $15.95) r/#21-26						16.00
Vol. 5: Minister of Cadador (7/03, $15.95) r/#27-32						16.00
Vol. 6: Changing Course (1/04, $15.95) r/#33-38						16.00
Traveler Vol. 1-4 ($9.95): Digest-size reprints of TPBs						10.00

MERLIN JONES AS THE MONKEY'S UNCLE (See Movie Comics and The Misadventures of... under Movie Comics)

MERRILL'S MARAUDERS (See Movie Classics)

MERRY CHRISTMAS (See A Christmas Adventure, Donald Duck..., Dell Giant #39, & March of Comics #153 in the Promotional Comics section)

MERRY COMICS
Carlton Publishing Co.: Dec, 1945 (10¢)

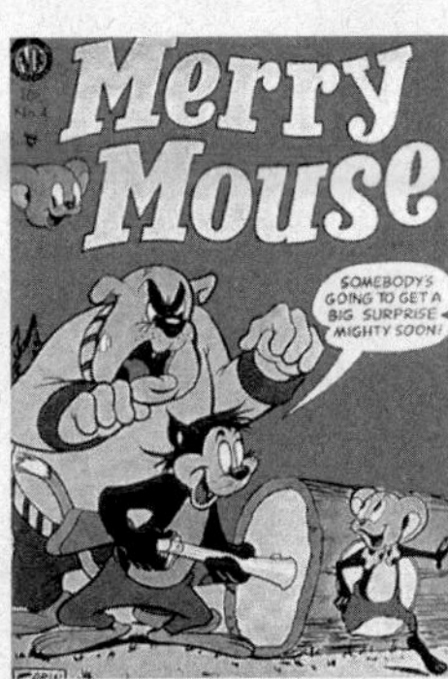

Metal Men #41 © DC

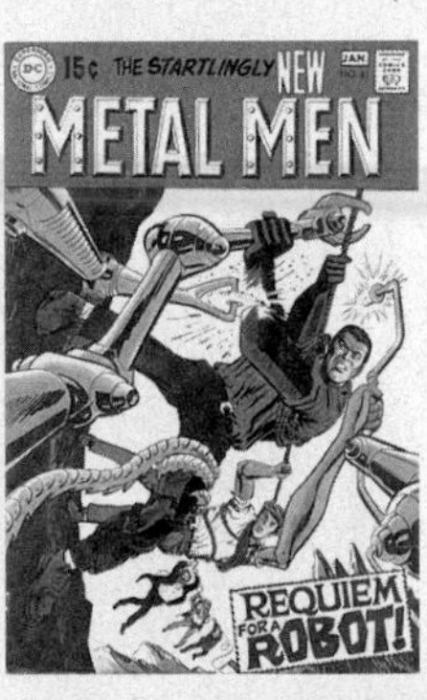

Metamorpho #9 © DC

	GD 2.0	VG 4.0	FN 6.0	VF 8.0	VF/NM 9.0	NM- 9.2
nn-Boogeyman app.	26	52	78	154	252	350

MERRY COMICS: Four Star Publications: 1947 (Advertised, not published)

MERRY-GO-ROUND COMICS
LaSalle Publ. Co./Croyden Publ./Rotary Litho.: 1944 (25¢, 132 pgs.); 1946; 9-10/47 - No. 2, 1948

	GD	VG	FN	VF	VF/NM	NM-
nn(1944)(LaSalle)-Funny animal; 29 new features	22	44	66	132	216	300
21 (Publisher?)	11	22	33	60	83	105
1(1946)(Croyden)-Al Fago-c; funny animal	14	28	42	80	115	150
V1#1,2(1947-48; 52 pgs.)(Rotary Litho. Co. Ltd., Canada); Ken Hultgren-a	11	22	33	60	83	105

MERRY MAILMAN (See Fawcett's Funny Animals #87-89)

MERRY MOUSE (Also see Funny Tunes & Space Comics)
Avon Periodicals: June, 1953 - No. 4, Jan-Feb, 1954

	GD	VG	FN	VF	VF/NM	NM-
1-1st app.; funny animal; Frank Carin-c/a	13	26	39	74	105	135
2-4	8	16	24	44	57	70

MERRY X-MEN HOLIDAY SPECIAL
Marvel Comics: Feb, 2019 ($4.99, one-shot)

	GD	VG	FN	VF	VF/NM	NM-
1-Holiday short stories by various; Nakayama-c						4.00

MERV PUMPKINHEAD, AGENT OF D.R.E.A.M. (See The Sandman)
DC Comics (Vertigo): 2000 ($5.95, one-shot)

	GD	VG	FN	VF	VF/NM	NM-
1-Buckingham-a(p); Nowlan painted-c						6.00

META-4
First Comics: Feb, 1991 - No. 4, 1991 ($2.25)

	GD	VG	FN	VF	VF/NM	NM-
1-($3.95, 52pgs.)						4.00
2-4						3.00

METAL GEAR SOLID (Based on the video game)
IDW Publ.: Sept, 2004 - No. 12, Aug, 2005 ($3.99)

	GD	VG	FN	VF	VF/NM	NM-
1-12: 1-Two covers; Ashley Wood-a/Kris Oprisko-s						4.00
1-Retailer edition with foil cover						15.00

METAL GEAR SOLID: SONS OF LIBERTY
IDW Publ.: Sept, 2005 - No. 12, Sept, 2007 ($3.99)

	GD	VG	FN	VF	VF/NM	NM-
#0 (9/05) profile pages on characters; Ashley Wood-a						4.00
1-12: 1-Two covers; Ashley Wood-a/Alex Garner-s						4.00

METALLIX
Future Comics: Dec, 2002 - No. 6, June, 2003 ($3.50)

	GD	VG	FN	VF	VF/NM	NM-
0-6-Ron Lim-a. 0-(6/03) Origin. 1-Layton-c						3.50
1-Collector's Edition with variant cover by Lim						3.50
1-Free Comic Book Day Edition (4/03) Layton-c						3.00

METAL MEN (See Brave & the Bold, DC Comics Presents, and Showcase #37-40)
National Periodical Publications/DC Comics: 4-5/63 - No. 41, 12-1/69-70; No. 42, 2-3/73 - No. 44, 7-8/73; No. 45, 4-5/76 - No. 56, 2-3/78

	GD	VG	FN	VF	VF/NM	NM-
1-(4-5/63)-5th app. Metal Men	56	112	168	448	999	1550
2	20	40	60	135	300	465
3-5	13	26	39	89	195	300
6-10	9	18	27	59	117	175
11-20: 12-Beatles cameo (2-3/65)	7	14	21	46	86	125
21-Batman, Robin & Flash x-over	6	12	18	41	76	110
22-26,28-30	5	10	15	34	60	85
27-Origin Metal Men retold	6	12	18	42	79	115
31-41(1968-70): 38-Last 12¢ issue. 41-Last 15¢	5	10	15	31	53	75
42-44(1973)-Reprints	2	4	6	10	14	18
45('76)-49-Simonson-a in all: 48,49-Re-intro Eclipso	2	4	6	10	14	18
50-56: 50-Part-r. 54,55-Green Lantern x-over	2	4	6	9	12	15

NOTE: ***Andru/Esposito** c-1-30. **Aparo** c-53-56. **Giordano** c-45, 46. **Kane/Esposito** a-30, 31; c-31. **Simonson** a-45-49; c-47-52. **Staton** a-50-56.*

METAL MEN (Also see Tangent Comics/ Metal Men)
DC Comics: Oct, 1993 - No. 4, Jan, 1994 ($1.25, mini-series)

	GD	VG	FN	VF	VF/NM	NM-
1-($2.50)-Multi-colored foil-c						5.00
2-4: 2-Origin						4.00

METAL MEN (Also see 52)
DC Comics: Oct, 2007 - No. 8, Jul, 2008 ($2.99, limited series)

	GD	VG	FN	VF	VF/NM	NM-
1-8-Duncan Rouleau-s/a; origin re-told. 3-Chemo returns						3.00
HC (2008, $24.99, dustjacket) r/#1-8; cover gallery and sketch pages						25.00
SC (2009, $14.99) r/#1-8; cover gallery and sketch pages						15.00

METAL MEN
DC Comics: Dec, 2019 - No. 12, Feb, 2021 ($3.99, limited series)

	GD	VG	FN	VF	VF/NM	NM-
1-12-Dan DiDio-s/Shane Davis-a. 1-Intro. Nth Metal Man. 3-Devil Ray monster returns. 7-Intro. Animal Gas Gang. 7-9-Chemo app. 10-Origin of Nth Metal Man						4.00

METAMORPHO (See Action Comics #413, Brave & the Bold #57,58, 1st Issue Special, & World's Finest #217)
National Periodical Publications: July-Aug, 1965 - No. 17, Mar-Apr, 1968 (All 12¢ issues)

	GD	VG	FN	VF	VF/NM	NM-
1-(7-8/65)-3rd app. Metamorpho	14	28	42	97	214	330
2,3	7	14	21	46	86	125
4-6,10: 10-Origin & 1st app. Element Girl (1-2/67)	6	12	18	37	66	95
7-9	5	10	15	33	57	80
11-17: 17-Sparling-c/a	5	10	15	30	50	70

NOTE: ***Ramona Fradon** a-B&B 57, 58, 1-4. **Orlando** a-5, 6; c-5-9, 11. **Trapani** a(p)-7-16; i-16.*

METAMORPHO
DC Comics: Aug, 1993 - No. 4, Nov, 1993 ($1.50, mini-series)

	GD	VG	FN	VF	VF/NM	NM-
1-4						4.00

METAMORPHO: YEAR ONE
DC Comics: Early Dec, 2007 - No. 6, Late Feb, 2008 ($2.99, limited series)

	GD	VG	FN	VF	VF/NM	NM-
1-6-Origin re-told; Jurgens-s/Jurgens & Delperdang-a/Nowlan-c. 6-Justice League app.						3.00
TPB ('08, $14.99) r/#1-6						15.00

METAPHYSIQUE
Malibu Comics (Bravura): Apr, 1995 - No. 6, Oct, 1995 ($2.95, limited series)

	GD	VG	FN	VF	VF/NM	NM-
1-6: Norm Breyfogle-c/a/scripts						3.00

METEOR COMICS
L. L. Baird (Croyden): Nov, 1945

	GD	VG	FN	VF	VF/NM	NM-
1-Captain Wizard, Impossible Man, Race Wilkins app.; origin Baldy Bean, Capt. Wizard's sidekick; bare-breasted mermaids story	57	114	171	362	619	875

METEOR MAN
Marvel Comics: Aug, 1993 - No. 6, Jan, 1994 ($1.25, limited series)

	GD	VG	FN	VF	VF/NM	NM-
1-6: 1-Regular unbagged. 4-Night Thrasher-c/story. 6-Terry Austin-c(i)						3.00
1-Polybagged w/button & rap newspaper						4.00
...: The Movie (4/93 [7/93 on cover], $2.25) movie adaptation						3.00

METROPOL (See Ted McKeever's...)

METROPOL A.D. (See Ted McKeever's...)

METROPOLIS S.C.U. (Also see Showcase '96 #1)
DC Comics: Nov, 1995 - No. 4, Feb, 1996 ($1.50, limited series)

	GD	VG	FN	VF	VF/NM	NM-
1-4:1-Superman-c & app.						4.00

MEZZ: GALACTIC TOUR 2494 (Also See Nexus)
Dark Horse Comics: May, 1994 ($2.50, one-shot)

	GD	VG	FN	VF	VF/NM	NM-
1						3.00

MGM'S MARVELOUS WIZARD OF OZ (See Marvel Treasury of Oz)
Marvel Comics Group/National Periodical Publications: 1975 ($1.50, 84 pgs.; oversize)

	GD	VG	FN	VF	VF/NM	NM-
1-Adaptation of MGM's movie; J. Buscema-a	4	8	12	23	37	50

M.G.M'S MOUSE MUSKETEERS (Formerly M.G.M.'s The Two Mouseketeers)
Dell Publishing Co.: No. 670, Jan, 1956 - No. 1290, Mar-May, 1962

	GD	VG	FN	VF	VF/NM	NM-
Four Color 670 (#4)	6	12	18	38	69	100
Four Color 711,728,764	5	10	15	31	53	75
8 (4-6/57) - 21 (3-5/60)	4	8	12	27	44	60
Four Color 1135,1175,1290	4	8	12	28	47	65

M.G.M.'S SPIKE AND TYKE (also see Tom & Jerry #79)
Dell Publishing Co.: No. 499, Sept, 1953 - No. 1266, Dec-Feb, 1961-62

	GD	VG	FN	VF	VF/NM	NM-
Four Color 499 (#1)	7	14	21	49	92	135
Four Color 577,638	5	10	15	35	63	90
4(12-2/55-56)-10	4	8	12	27	44	60
11-24(12-2/60-61)	4	8	12	23	37	50
Four Color 1266	4	8	12	28	47	65

M.G.M.'S THE TWO MOUSKETEERS
Dell Publishing Co.: No. 475, June, 1953 - No. 642, July, 1955

	GD	VG	FN	VF	VF/NM	NM-
Four Color 475 (#1)	9	18	27	57	111	165
Four Color 603 (11/54), 642	6	12	18	41	76	110

MIAMI VICE REMIX
IDW Publishing (Lion Forge): Mar, 2015 - No. 5, Jul, 2015 ($3.99, limited series)

	GD	VG	FN	VF	VF/NM	NM-
1-5-Joe Casey-s/Jim Mahfood-a; re-imagined Crockett & Tubbs						4.00

MICE TEMPLAR, THE
Image Comics: Sept, 2007 - No. 6, Oct, 2008 ($3.99/$2.99)

	GD	VG	FN	VF	VF/NM	NM-
1-($3.99)-Bryan Glass-s/Michael Avon Oeming-a/c						4.00
2-6-($2.99)						3.00

MICE TEMPLAR, THE , VOLUME 2: DESTINY

Mice Templar V4 #7 © Oeming & Glass

Mickey Malone nn © Hale Nass Corp

Mickey Mouse #34 © DIS

GD 2.0 | VG 4.0 | FN 6.0 | VF 8.0 | VF/NM 9.0 | NM- 9.2

Image Comics: July, 2009 - No. 9, May, 2010 ($3.99/$2.99/$4.99)
1,2-($3.99) 1-Bryan Glass-s/Oeming & Santos-a; 2 covers. 2-Santos-a 4.00
3-8-($2.99)-Santos-a; 2 covers by Oeming & Santos 3.00
9-($4.99) 5.00

MICE TEMPLAR, THE , VOLUME 3: A MIDWINTER NIGHT'S DREAM
Image Comics: Dec, 2010 - No. 8, Mar, 2012 ($3.99/$2.99)
1,8-($3.99) 1-Bryan Glass-s/Oeming & Santos-a; 2 covers 4.00
2-7-($2.99)-Santos-a; 2 covers by Oeming & Santos 3.00

MICE TEMPLAR, THE , VOLUME 4: LEGEND
Image Comics: Mar, 2013 - No. 14, Oct, 2014 ($3.99/$2.99/$4.99)
1-($3.99)-Bryan Glass-s/Victor Santos-a; 2 covers 4.00
2-7-($2.99)-Santos-a; 2 covers by Oeming & Santos 3.00
8-($4.99) 5.00
9-13-($3.99) 4.00
14-($5.99) Bonus back-up Hammer of the Gods by Oeming & Wheatley 6.00

MICE TEMPLAR, THE , VOLUME 5: NIGHT'S END
Image Comics: Mar, 2015 - No. 5, Sept, 2015 ($3.99/$5.99)
1,3,5-($3.99)-Bryan Glass-s/Victor Santos-a; 2 covers by Oeming & Santos 4.00
2,4-($5.99)-Bonus back-up Hammer of the Gods 6.00

MICHAELANGELO CHRISTMAS SPECIAL (See Teenage Mutant Ninja Turtles Christmas Special)

MICHAELANGELO, TEENAGE MUTANT NINJA TURTLE
Mirage Studios: 1986 (One shot) ($1.50, B&W)
1-Christmas-c/story 4 8 12 23 37 50
1-2nd printing ('89, $1.75)-Reprint plus new-a 6.00

MICHAEL CHABON PRESENTS THE AMAZING ADVENTURES OF THE ESCAPIST
Dark Horse Comics: Feb, 2004 - No. 8, Nov, 2005 ($8.95, squarebound)
1-5,7,8-Short stories by Chabon and various incl. Chaykin, Starlin, Brereton, Baker 9.00
6-Includes 6 pg. Spirit & Escapist story (Will Eisner's last work); Spirit on cover 9.00
... Vol. 1 (5/04, $17.95, digest-size) r/#1&2; wraparound-c by Chris Ware 18.00
... Vol. 2 (11/04, $17.95, digest-size) r/#3&4; wraparound-c by Matt Kindt 18.00
... Vol. 3 (4/06, $14.95, digest-size) r/#5&6; Tim Sale-c 15.00

MICHAEL MOORCOCK'S ELRIC: THE MAKING OF A SORCEROR
DC Comics: 2004 - No. 4, 2006 ($5.95, prestige format, limited series)
1-4-Moorcock-s/Simonson-a 6.00
TPB (2007, $19.99) r/#1-4 20.00

MICHAEL MOORCOCK'S MULTIVERSE
DC Comics (Helix): Nov, 1997 - No. 12, Oct, 1998 ($2.50, limited series)
1-12: Simonson, Reeve & Ridgway-a 3.00
TPB (1999, $19.95) r/#1-12 20.00

MICHAEL TURNER, A TRIBUTE TO...
Aspen MLT: 2008 ($8.99, squarebound)
nn-Pin-ups and tributes from Turner's colleagues and friends; Turner & Ross-c 9.00
Michael Turner Legacy Vol. 1 #1 (6/18, $5.99) Pin-ups and tributes 6.00

MICHAEL TURNER PRESENTS: ASPEN (See Aspen)

MICKEY AND DONALD (See Walt Disney's...)

MICKEY AND DONALD CHRISTMAS PARADE
IDW Publishing: Dec, 2015 - Present ($5.99/$6.99, squarebound, annual)
1,2-($5.99) English translations of Dutch, Italian and Swedish Disney Christmas stories 6.00
3-5-($6.99) English translations of Dutch & Italian Christmas stories. 3-r/Four Color #62 7.00

MICKEY AND DONALD IN VACATIONLAND (See Dell Giant No. 47)

MICKEY & THE BEANSTALK (See Story Hour Series)

MICKEY & THE SLEUTH (See Walt Disney Showcase #38, 39, 42)

MICKEY FINN (Also see Big Shot Comics #74 & Feature Funnies)
Eastern Color 1-4/McNaught Synd. #5 on (Columbia)/Headline V3#2:
Nov?, 1942 - V3#2, May, 1952

	GD	VG	FN	VF	VF/NM	NM-
1	32	64	96	188	307	425
2	16	32	48	96	151	205
3-Charlie Chan story	13	26	39	72	101	130
4	10	20	30	58	79	100
5-10	9	18	27	50	65	80
11-15(1949): 12-Sparky Watts app.	8	16	24	42	54	65
V3#1,2(1952)	7	14	21	35	43	50

MICKEY MALONE
Hale Nass Corp.: 1936 (Color, punchout-c) (B&W-a on back)
nn - 1pg. of comics 315 630 1260 -- -- --

MICKEY MANTLE (See Baseball's Greatest Heroes #1)

MICKEY MOUSE (See Adventures of Mickey Mouse, The Best of Walt Disney Comics, Cheerios giveaways, Donald and ..., Dynabrite Comics, 40 Big Pages..., Gladstone Comic Album, Merry Christmas From..., Walt Disney's Mickey and Donald, Walt Disney's Comics & Stories, Walt Disney's..., & Wheaties)

MICKEY MOUSE (...Secret Agent #107-109; Walt Disney's... #148-205?)
(See Dell Giants for annuals) (#204 exists from both G.K. & Whitman)
Dell Publ. Co./Gold Key #85-204/Whitman #204-218/Gladstone #219 on:
#16, 1941 - #84, 7-9/62; #85, 11/62 - #218, 6/84; #219, 10/86 - #256, 4/90

	GD	VG	FN	VF	VF/NM	NM-
Four Color 16(1941)-1st Mickey Mouse comic book; "...vs. the Phantom Blot" by Gottfredson	1350	2700	4050	17,500	--	--
Four Color 27(1943)- "7 Colored Terror"	73	146	219	584	1317	2050
Four Color 79(1945)-By Carl Barks (1 story)	94	188	282	752	1651	2550
Four Color 116(1946)	27	54	81	184	410	635
Four Color 141,157(1947)	22	44	66	155	345	535
Four Color 170,181,194('48)	19	38	57	133	297	460
Four Color 214('49),231,248,261	15	30	45	105	233	360
Four Color 268-Reprints/WDC&S #22-24 by Gottfredson ("Surprise Visitor")	14	28	42	98	217	335
Four Color 279,286,296	12	24	36	79	170	260
Four Color 304,313(#1),325(#2),334	11	22	33	72	154	235
Four Color 343,352,362,371,387	9	18	27	62	126	190
Four Color 401,411,427(10-11/52)	8	16	24	56	108	160
Four Color 819-Mickey Mouse in Magicland	6	12	18	41	76	110
Four Color 1057,1151,1246(1959-61)-Album; #1057 has 10¢ & 12¢ editions; back covers are different	6	12	18	37	66	95
28(12-1/52-53)-32,34	6	12	18	40	73	105
33-(Exists with 2 dates, 10-11/53 & 12-1/54)	6	12	18	40	73	105
35-50	5	10	15	35	63	90
51-73,75-80	5	10	15	31	53	75
74-Story swipe "The Rare Stamp Search" from 4-Color #422- "The Gilded Man"	5	10	15	35	63	90
81-105: 93,95-titled "Mickey Mouse Club Album". 100-105: Reprint 4-Color #427,194,279, 170,343,214 in that order	4	8	12	25	40	55
106-120	3	6	9	19	30	40
121-130	3	6	9	16	23	30
131-146	3	6	9	14	20	25
147,148: 147-Reprints "The Phantom Fires" from WDC&S #200-202.148-Reprints "The Mystery of Lonely Valley" from WDC&S #208-210	3	6	9	14	20	25
149-158	2	4	6	10	14	18
159-Reprints "The Sunken City" from WDC&S #205-207	2	4	6	10	14	18
160-178: 162-165,167-170-r	2	4	6	10	14	18
167-Whitman edition	2	4	6	10	14	18
179-(52 pgs.)	2	4	6	11	16	20
180-203: 200-r/Four Color #371	2	4	6	8	10	12
204-(Whitman or G.K.), 205,206	2	4	6	9	13	16
207(8/80), 209(pre-pack?)	6	12	18	38	69	100
208-(8-12/80)-Only distr. in Whitman 3-pack	10	20	30	69	147	225
210(2/81),211-214	2	4	6	9	13	16
215-218: 215(2/82), 216(4/82), 217(3/84), 218(misdated 8/82; actual date 7/84)	2	4	6	10	14	18
219-1st Gladstone issue; The Seven Ghosts serial-r begins by Gottfredson	2	4	6	11	16	20
220,221	2	3	4	6	8	10
222-225: 222-Editor-in Grief strip-r						5.00
226-230						5.00
231-243,246-254: 240-r/March of Comics #27. 245-r/F.C. #279. 250-r/F.C. #248						4.00
244 (1/89, $2.95, 100 pgs.)-Squarebound 60th anniversary issue; gives history of Mickey						5.00
245,255,256: 245-r/F.C. #279. 255,256-($1.95, 68 pgs.)						5.00

NOTE: *Reprints #195-197, 198(2/3), 199(1/3), 200-208, 211(1/2), 212, 213, 215(1/3), 216-on.* ***Gottfredson*** *Mickey Mouse serials in #219-239, 241-244, 246-249, 251-253, 255.*

	GD	VG	FN	VF	VF/NM	NM-
Album 01-518-210(Dell), 1(10082-309)(9/63-Gold Key)	3	6	9	21	33	45
...Club 1(1/64-Gold Key)(TV)	4	8	12	22	35	48
Mini Comic 1(1976)(3-1/4x6-1/2")-Reprints 158	1	2	3	5	6	8
Surprise Party 1(30037-901, G.K.)(1/69)-40th Anniversary (see Walt Disney Showcase #47)	3	6	9	20	31	42
Surprise Party 1(1979)-r/1969 issue	1	2	3	5	6	8

MICKEY MOUSE (Continued from Mickey Mouse and Friends)
BOOM! Studios: No. 304, Jan, 2011 - No. 309, Jun, 2011 ($3.99)
304-309: 304-Peg-Leg Pete app. 309-Continues in Walt Disney's C&S #720 4.00

MICKEY MOUSE
IDW Publishing: Jun, 2015 - No. 21, Jun, 2017 ($3.99)

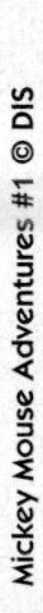
Mickey Mouse Adventures #1 © DIS

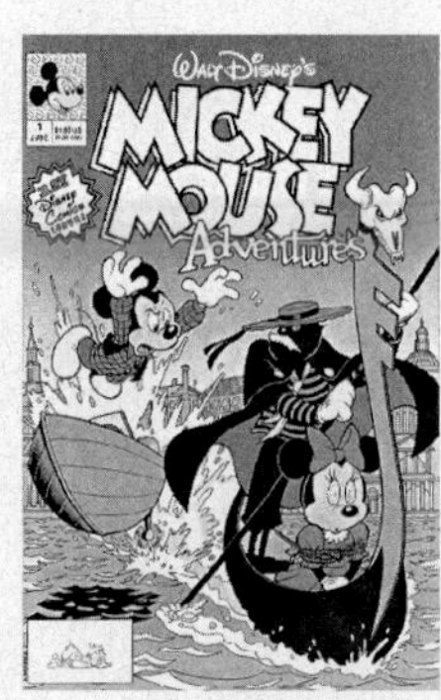

Mickey Mouse Magazine V2 #3 © DIS

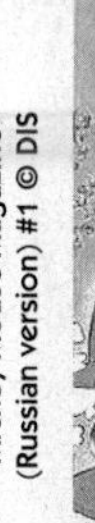
Mickey Mouse Magazine (Russian version) #1 © DIS

GD VG FN VF VF/NM NM-
2.0 4.0 6.0 8.0 9.0 9.2

1-Legacy numbered #310; art by Cavazzano and others; multiple covers 4.00
2-21-Classic Disney and foreign reprints; multiple covers on each. 21-(Legacy #330) 4.00

MICKEY MOUSE ADVENTURES
Disney Comics: June, 1990 - No. 18, Nov, 1991 ($1.50)

1,8,9: 1-Bradbury, Murry-r/M.M. #45,73 plus new-a. 8-Byrne-c. 9-Fantasia 50th ann. issue w/new adapt. of movie 4.00
2-7,10-18: 2-Begin all new stories. 10-r/F.C. #214 3.00

MICKEY MOUSE AND FRIENDS (Continued from Walt Disney's Mickey Mouse and Friends) (Title continues as Mickey Mouse #304-on)
BOOM! Studios: No. 296, Sept, 2009 - No. 303, Dec, 2010 ($2.99/$3.99)

296-299,301-303: 296-299-Wizards of Mickey stories. 301-Conclusion to story in #300 3.00
300-($3.99, 9/10) Petrucha-s/Pelaez-a; back-up Tanglefoot story w/Gottfredson-a 4.00
300 Deluxe Edition ($6.99) Variant cover by Daan Jippes 7.00

MICKEY MOUSE CLUB FUN BOOK
Golden Press: 1977 (1.95, 228 pgs.)(square bound)

11190-1950s-r; 20,000 Leagues, M. Mouse Silly Symphonys, The Reluctant Dragon, etc.
4 8 12 28 47 65

MICKEY MOUSE CLUB MAGAZINE (See Walt Disney...)

MICKEY MOUSE COMICS DIGEST
Gladstone: 1986 - No. 5, 1987 (96 pgs.)

1 ($1.25-c) 1 2 3 5 6 8
2-5: 3-5 ($1.50-c) 5.00

MICKEY MOUSE IN COLOR
Another Rainbow/Pantheon: 1988 (Deluxe, 13"x17", hard-c, $250.00) (Trade, 9-7/8"x11-1/2", hard-c, $39.95)

Deluxe limited edition of 3,000 copies signed by Floyd Gottfredson and Carl Barks, designated as the "Official Mickey Mouse 60th Anniversary" book. Mickey Sunday and daily reprints, plus Barks "Riddle of the Red Hat" from Four Color #79. Comes with 45 r.p.m. record interview with Gottfredson and Barks. 240 pgs. 12 24 36 82 179 275
Deluxe, limited to 100 copies, as above, but with a unique colored pencil original drawing of Mickey Mouse by Carl Barks. 800.00
Pantheon trade edition, edited down & without Barks, 192 pgs.
3 6 9 19 30 40

MICKEY MOUSE MAGAZINE (Becomes Walt Disney's Comics & Stories)(Also see 40 Big Pages of Mickey Mouse)
K. K. Publ./Western Publishing Co.: Summer, 1935 (June-Aug, indicia) - V5#12, Sept, 1940; V1#1-5, V3#11,12, V4#1-3 are 44 pgs; V2#3-100 pgs; V5#12-68 pgs; rest are 36 pgs.(No V3#1, V4#6)

V1#1 (Large size, 13-1/4x10-1/4"; 25¢)-Contains puzzles, games, cels, stories & comics of Disney characters. Promotional magazine for Disney cartoon movies and paraphernalia
1425 2850 4275 9200 19,000 --

Note: *Some copies were autographed by the editors & given away with all early one year subscriptions.*

2 (Size change, 11-1/2x8-1/2"; 10/35; 10¢)-High quality paper begins; Messmer-a
329 658 987 2800 -- --
3,4: 3-Messmer-a 194 388 582 1650 -- --
5-1st Donald Duck solo-c; 2nd cover app. ever; last 44 pg. & high quality paper issue
394 788 1182 3350 -- --
6-9: 6-36 pg. issues begin; Donald becomes editor. 8-2nd Donald solo-c. 9-1st Mickey/Minnie-c 165 330 495 1400 -- --
10-12, V2#1,2: 11-1st Pluto/Mickey-c; Donald fires himself and appoints Mickey as editor
153 306 459 1300 -- --
V2#3-Special 100 pg. Christmas issue (25¢); Messmer-a; Donald becomes editor of Wise Quacks 476 952 1428 4050 -- --
4-Mickey Mouse Comics & Roy Ranger (adventure strip) begin; both end V2#9; Messmer-a 135 270 405 1150 -- --
5-9: 5-Ted True (adventure strip, ends V2#9) & Silly Symphony Comics (ends V3#3) begin. 6-1st solo Minnie-c. 6-9-Mickey Mouse Movies cut-out in each
61 122 183 390 670 950
10-1st full color issue; Mickey Mouse (by Gottfredson; ends V3#12) & Silly Symphony (ends V3#3) full color Sunday-r, Peter The Farm Detective (ends V5#8) & Ole Of The North (ends V3#3) begins 105 210 315 672 1149 1625
11-13: 12-Hiawatha-c & feature story 58 116 174 371 636 900
V3#2-Big Bad Wolf Halloween-c 68 136 204 435 743 1050
3 (12/37)-1st app. Snow White & The Seven Dwarfs (before release of movie) (possibly 1st in print); Mickey X-Mas-c 129 258 387 826 1413 2000
4 (1/38)-Snow White & The Seven Dwarfs serial begins (on stands before release of movie); Ducky Symphony (ends V3#11) begins
98 196 294 627 1076 1525
5-1st Snow White & Seven Dwarfs-c (St. Valentine's Day)
121 242 363 774 1325 1875
6-Snow White serial ends; Lonesome Ghosts app. (2 pp.)
69 138 207 442 759 1075
7-Seven Dwarfs Easter-c 63 126 189 403 689 975
8-10: 9-Dopey-c. 10-1st solo Goofy-c 52 104 156 328 552 775
11,12 (44 pgs; 8 more pgs. color added). 11-Mickey the Sheriff serial (ends V4#3) & Donald Duck strip-r (ends V3#12) begin. Color feature on Snow White's Forest Friends 57 114 171 362 619 875
V4#1 (10/38; 44 pgs.)-Brave Little Tailor-c/feature story, nominated for Academy Award; Bobby & Chip by Otto Messmer (ends V4#2) & The Practical Pig (ends V4#2) begin
57 114 171 362 619 875
2 (44 pgs.)-1st Huey, Dewey & Louie-c 63 126 189 403 689 975
3 (12/38, 44 pgs.)-Ferdinand The Bull-c/feature story, Academy Award winner; Mickey Mouse & The Whalers serial begins, ends V4#12
55 110 165 352 601 850
4-Spotty, Mother Pluto strip-r begin, end V4#8 52 104 156 328 552 775
5-St. Valentine's day-c. 1st Pluto solo-c 58 116 174 371 636 900
7 (3/39)-The Ugly Duckling-c/feature story, Academy Award winner
54 108 162 343 574 825
7 (4/39)-Goofy & Wilbur The Grasshopper classic-c/feature story from 1st Goofy solo cartoon movie; Timid Elmer begins, ends V5#5
57 114 171 362 619 875
8-Big Bad Wolf-c from Practical Pig movie poster; Practical Pig feature story
54 108 162 343 574 825
9-Donald Duck & Mickey Mouse Sunday-r begin; The Pointer feature story, nominated for Academy Award 54 108 162 343 574 825
10-Classic July 4th drum & fife-c; last Donald Sunday-r
84 168 252 538 919 1300
11-1st slick-c; last over-sized issue 54 108 162 343 574 825
12 (9/39; format change, 10-1/4x8-1/4")-1st full color, cover to cover issue; Donald's Penguin-c/feature story 58 116 174 371 636 900
V5#1-Black Pete-c; Officer Duck-c/feature story; Autograph Hound feature story; Robinson Crusoe serial begins 73 146 219 467 796 1125
2-Goofy-c; 1st brief app. Pinocchio 79 158 237 502 864 1225
3 (12/39)-Pinocchio Christmas-c (Before movie release). 1st app. Jiminy Cricket; Pinocchio serial begins 97 194 291 621 1061 1500
4,5: 5-Jiminy Cricket-c; Pinocchio serial ends; Donald's Dog Laundry feature story
58 116 174 371 636 900
6,7: 6-Tugboat Mickey feature story; Rip Van Winkle feature begins, ends V5#8. 7-2nd Huey, Dewey & Louie-c 57 114 171 362 619 875
8-Last magazine size issue; 2nd solo Pluto-c; Figaro & Cleo feature story
60 120 180 381 653 925
9-11: 9 (6/40; change to comic book size)-Jiminy Cricket feature story; Donald-c & Sunday-r begin. 10-Special Independence Day issue. 11-Hawaiian Holiday & Mickey's Trailer feature stories; last 36 pg. issue 65 130 195 416 708 1000
12 (Format change)-The transition issue (68 pgs.) becoming a comic book. With only a title change to follow, becomes Walt Disney's Comics & Stories #1 with the next issue 481 962 1443 3511 6206 8900

NOTE: ***Otto Messmer**-a is in many issues of the first two-three years. The following story titles and issues have gags created by **Carl Barks**: V4#3(12/38)-'Donald's Better Self' & 'Donald's Golf Game;' V4#4(1/39)-'Donald's Lucky Day;' V4#7(3/39)-'Hockey Champ;' V4#7(4/39)-'Donald's Cousin Gus;' V4#9(6/39)-'Sea Scouts;' V4#12(9/39)-'Donald's Penguin;' V5#9 (6/40)-'Donald's Vacation;' V5#10(7/40)-'Bone Trouble;' V5#12(9/40)-'Window Cleaners.'*

MICKEY MOUSE MAGAZINE (Russian Version)
May 16, 1991 (1st Russian printing of a modern comic book)

1-Bagged w/gold label commemoration in English 2 4 6 10 14 18

MICKEY MOUSE MARCH OF COMICS (See March of Comics #8,27,45,60,74)

MICKEY MOUSE SHORTS: SEASON ONE
IDW Publishing: Jul, 2016 - No. 4, Oct, 2016 ($3.99, limited series)

1-4-Adaptations of new Disney cartoon shorts 4.00

MICKEY MOUSE'S SUMMER VACATION (See Story Hour Series)

MICKEY MOUSE SUMMER FUN (See Dell Giants)

MICKEY SPILLANE'S MIKE DANGER
Tekno Comix: Sept, 1995 - No. 11, May, 1996 ($1.95)

1-11: 1-Frank Miller-c. 7-polybagged; Simonson-c. 8,9-Simonson-c 3.00

MICKEY SPILLANE'S MIKE DANGER
Big Entertainment: V2#1, June, 1996 - No. 10, Apr, 1997 ($2.25)

V2#1-10: Max Allan Collins scripts 3.00

MICKEY SPILLANE'S MIKE HAMMER
Titan Comics: Jul, 2018 - No. 4, Oct, 2018 ($3.99, limited series)

1-4-Max Allan Collins-s/Marcelo Salaza & Marcio Freire-a 4.00

MICKEY'S TWICE UPON A CHRISTMAS (Disney)

Micronauts #26 © MAR

Middlewest #4 © Young & Corona

Midnight of the Soul #1 © Howard Chaykin

	GD	VG	FN	VF	VF/NM	NM-
	2.0	4.0	6.0	8.0	9.0	9.2

Gemstone Publishing: 2004 ($3.95, square-bound, one-shot)

nn-Christmas short stories with Mickey, Minnie, Donald, Uncle Scrooge, Goofy and others 4.00

MICROBOTS, THE
Gold Key: Dec, 1971 (one-shot)

1 (10271-112) Painted-c 3 6 9 15 22 28

MICRONAUTS (Toys)
Marvel Comics Group: Jan, 1979 - No. 59, Aug, 1984 (Mando paper #53 on)

1-Intro/1st app. Baron Karza 3 6 9 17 26 35
2-7,9,10,35,37,57: 7-Man-Thing app.9-1st app. Cilicia. 35-Double size; origin Microverse; intro Death Squad; Dr. Strange app. 37-Nightcrawler app.; X-Men cameo (2 pgs.). 57-(52 pgs.) 6.00
8-1st app. Capt. Universe (8/79) 4 8 12 23 37 50
11-34,36,38-56,58,59: 13-1st app. Jasmine. 15-Death of Microtron. 15-17-Fantastic Four app. 17-Death of Jasmine. 20-Ant-Man app. 21-Microverse series begins. 25-Origin Baron Karza. 25-29-Nick Fury app. 27-Death of Biotron. 34-Dr. Strange app. 38-First direct sale. 40-Fantastic Four app. 48-Early Guice-a begins. 59-Golden painted-c 4.00
Annual 1,2 (12/79,10/80)-Ditko-c/a 5.00
NOTE: *#38-on distributed only through comic shops.* ***N. Adams*** *c-7i.* ***Chaykin*** *a-13-18p.* ***Ditko*** *a-39p.* ***Giffen*** *a-36p, 37p(part).* ***Golden*** *a-1-12p; c-2-7p, 8-23, 24p, 38, 39, 59.* ***Guice*** *a-48-58p; c-49-58.* ***Gil Kane*** *a-38, 40-45p; c-40-45.* ***Layton*** *c-33-37.* ***Miller*** *c-31.*

MICRONAUTS (Micronauts: The New Voyages on cover)
Marvel Comics Group: Oct, 1984 - No. 20, May, 1986

V2#1-20 4.00
NOTE: ***Kelley Jones*** *a-1; c-1, 6.* ***Guice*** *a-4p; c-2p.*

MICRONAUTS
Image Comics: 2002 - No. 11, Sept, 2003 ($2.95)

2002 Convention Special (no cover price, B&W) previews series 3.00
1-11: 1-3-Hanson-a; Dave Johnson-c. 4-Su-a; 2 covers by Linsner & Hanson 3.00
...Vol. 1: Revolution (2003, $12.95, digest size) r/#1-5 13.00

MICRONAUTS (Volume 2)
Devil's Due Publishing: Mar, 2004 - No. 3, May, 2004 ($2.95)

1-3-Jolley-s/Broderick-a 3.00

MICRONAUTS
IDW Publishing: Apr, 2016 - No. 11, Mar, 2017 ($4.99/$3.99)

1-($4.99) Cullen Bunn-s/David Baldeón-a; multiple covers; Baron Karza app. 5.00
2-11-($3.99) Max Dunbar-a. 5-Revolution tie-in 4.00
Annual #1 (1/17, $7.99) Bunn-s/Ferreira-a; future Micronauts app. 8.00
... First Strike 1 (9/17, $3.99) Rom app.; leads into Rom First Strike; Gage-s/Panda-a 4.00
...: Revolution 1 (9/16, $3.99) Tie-in w/Transformers, G.I. Joe, M.A.S.K.,Action Man, Rom 4.00

MICRONAUTS: KARZA
Image Comics: Feb, 2003 - No. 4, May, 2003 ($2.95)

1-4-Krueger-s/Kurth-a 3.00

MICRONAUTS SPECIAL EDITION
Marvel Comics Group: Dec, 1983 - No. 5, Apr, 1984 ($2.00, limited series, Baxter paper)

1-5: r-/original series 1-12; Guice-c(p)-all 4.00

MICRONAUTS: WRATH OF KARZA (Leads into First Strike #1)
IDW Publishing: Apr, 2017 - No. 5, Aug, 2017 ($3.99)

1-5-Cullen Bunn & Jimmy Johnston-s/Andrew Griffith-a; multiple covers 4.00

MIDDLEWEST
Image Comics: Nov, 2018 - No. 18 ($3.99)

1-18-Skottie Young-s/Jorge Corona-a. 1-Three covers 4.00

MIDGET COMICS (Fighting Indian Stories)
St. John Publishng Co.: Feb, 1950 - No. 2, Apr, 1950 (5-3/8x7-3/8", 68 pgs.)

1-Fighting Indian Stories; Matt Baker-c 37 74 111 222 361 500
2-Tex West, Cowboy Marshal (also in #1) 15 30 45 94 147 200

MIDNIGHT (See Smash Comics #18)

MIDNIGHT
Ajax/Farrell Publ. (Four Star Comic Corp.): Apr, 1957 - No. 6, June, 1958

1-Reprints from Voodoo & Strange Fantasy with some changes 19 38 57 112 179 245
2-6 14 28 42 76 108 140

MIDNIGHTER (See The Authority)
DC Comics (WildStorm): Jan, 2007 - No. 20, Aug, 2008 ($2.99)

1-20: 1-Ennis-s/Sprouse-a/c. 6-Fabry-a. 7-Vaughan-s. 8-Gage-s. 9-Stelfreeze-a 3.00
1-4-Variant covers. 1-Michael Golden. 2-Art Adams 3-Jason Pearson. 4-Glenn Fabry 4.00
...: Anthem TPB (2008, $14.99) r/#7,10-15 15.00
...: Armageddon (12/07, $2.99) Gage-s/Coleby-a/McKone-c 3.00
...: Assassin8 TPB (2009, $14.99) r/#16-20 15.00
...: Killing Machine TPB (2008, $14.99) r/#1-6 15.00

MIDNIGHTER (See The Authority)
DC Comics: Aug, 2015 - No. 12, Jul, 2016 ($2.99)

1-12: 1-Orlando-s/Aco-a. 3-5-Grayson app. 9-12-Harley Quinn & Suicide Squad app. 3.00

MIDNIGHTER AND APOLLO (The Authority)
DC Comics: Dec, 2016 - No. 6, May, 2017 ($3.99, limited series)

1-6-Orlando-s/Blanco-a. 1,2-Henry Bendix app. 2-6-Neron app. 4.00

MIDNIGHT MASS
DC Comics (Vertigo): Jun, 2002 - No. 8, Jan, 2003 ($2.50)

1-8-Rozum-s/Saiz & Palmiotti-a 3.00

MIDNIGHT MASS: HERE THERE BE MONSTERS
DC Comics (Vertigo): March, 2004 - No. 6, Aug, 2004 ($2.95, limited series)

1-6-Rozum-s/Paul Lee-a 3.00

MIDNIGHT MEN
Marvel Comics (Epic Comics/Heavy Hitters): June, 1993 - No. 4, Sept, 1993 ($2.50/$1.95, limited series)

1-($2.50)-Embossed-c; Chaykin-c/a & scripts in all 4.00
2-4 3.00

MIDNIGHT MYSTERY
American Comics Group: Jan-Feb, 1961 - No. 7, Oct, 1961

1-Sci/Fi story 9 18 27 60 120 180
2-7: 7-Gustavson-a 5 10 15 33 57 80
NOTE: ***Reinman*** *a-1, 3.* ***Whitney*** *a-1, 4-6; c-1-3, 5, 7.*

MIDNIGHT NATION
Image Comics (Top Cow): Oct, 2000 - No. 12, July, 2002 ($2.50/$2.95)

1-Straczynski-s/Frank-a; 2 covers 3.50
2-11: 9-Twin Towers cover 3.00
12-($2.95) Last issue 3.00
Wizard #1/2 (2001) Michael Zulli-a; two covers by Frank 3.00
Vol. 1 ('03, $29.99, TPB) r/#1-12 & Wizard #1/2; cover gallery; afterword by Straczynski 30.00

MIDNIGHT OF THE SOUL
Image Comics: Jun, 2016 - No. 5, Oct, 2016 ($3.50, limited series)

1-5-Howard Chaykin-s/a/c; set in 1950s New York City 3.50

MIDNIGHT SOCIETY: THE BLACK LAKE
Dark Horse Comics: Jun, 2015 - No. 4, Oct, 2015 ($3.99)

1-4-Drew Johnson-s/a/c 4.00

MIDNIGHT SONS UNLIMITED
Marvel Comics (Midnight Sons imprint #4 on): Apr, 1993 - No. 9, May, 1995 ($3.95, 68 pgs.)

1-9: Blaze, Darkhold (by Quesada #1), Ghost Rider, Morbius & Nightstalkers in all. 1-Painted-c. 3-Spider-Man app. 4-Siege of Darkness part 17; new Dr. Strange & new Ghost Rider app.; spot varnish-c 4.00
NOTE: ***Sears*** *a-2.*

MIDNIGHT TALES
Charlton Press: Dec, 1972 - No. 18, May, 1976

V1#1 3 6 9 17 26 35
2-10 2 4 6 10 14 18
11-18: 11-14-Newton-a(p) 2 4 6 8 11 14
12,17(Modern Comics reprint, 1977) 6.00
NOTE: ***Adkins*** *a-12i, 13i.* ***Ditko*** *a-12.* ***Howard*** *(Wood imitator) a-1-15, 17, 18; c-1-18.* ***Don Newton*** *a-11-14p.* ***Staton*** *a-1, 3-11, 13.* ***Sutton*** *a-3-10.*

MIDNIGHT VISTA
AfterShock Comics: Sept, 2019 - No. 5, Jan, 2020 ($3.99, limited series)

1-5-Eliot Rahal-s/Clara Meath-a/Juan Doe-c 4.00

MIGHTY, THE
DC Comics: Apr, 2009 - No. 12, Mar, 2010 ($2.99)

1-12: Tomasi & Champagne-s/Dave Johnson-c. 1-4-Snejbjerg-a. 5-12-Samnee-a 3.00
...: Volume 1 TPB (2009, $17.99) r/#1-6 18.00
...: Volume 2 TPB (2010, $17.99) r/#7-12 18.00

MIGHTY ATOM, THE (...& the Pixies #6) (Formerly The Pixies #1-5)
Magazine Enterprises: No. 6, 1949; Nov, 1957 - No. 6, Aug-Sept, 1958

6(1949-M.E.)-no month (1st Series) 8 16 24 40 50 60
1-6(2nd Series)-Pixies-r 5 10 15 20 24 28
I.W. Reprint #1(nd) 2 4 6 8 11 14

MIGHTY AVENGERS

The Mighty Captain Marvel #0 © MAR

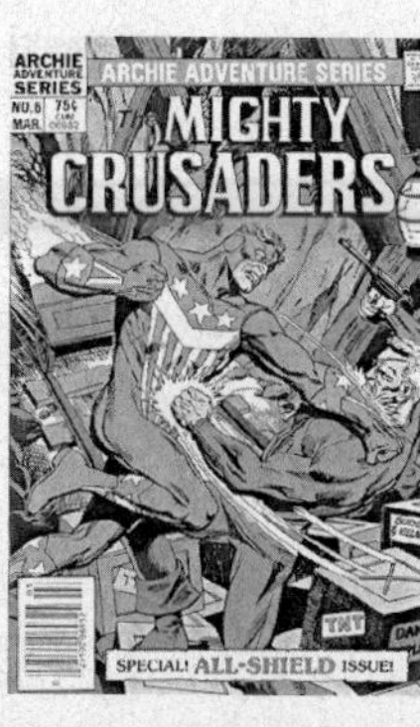

The Mighty Crusaders #6 © ACP

Mighty Midget Comics Golden Arrow #11 © DC

GD VG FN VF VF/NM NM-
2.0 4.0 6.0 8.0 9.0 9.2

Marvel Comics: May, 2007 - No. 36, Jun, 2010 ($3.99/$2.99)

1-($3.99) Iron Man, Ms. Marvel select new team; Bendis-s/Cho-a/c; Mole Man app. 5.00
2-20: 2-6-($2.99) Ultron returns. 7-15: 7-Bagley-a begins; Venom on-c. 9-11-Dr. Doom app. 12-20-Secret Invasion. 12,13-Maleev-a. 15-Romita Jr.-a. 16-Elektra. 20-Wasp funeral 3.00
21-($3.99) Dark Reign; Scarlet Witch returns; new team assembled; Pham-a 4.00
22-36: 25,26-Fantastic Four app. 35,36-Siege; Ultron returns 3.00
...: Most Wanted Files (2007, $3.99) profiles of members, accomplices & adversaries 4.00
... Vol. 1: The Ultron Initiative HC (2008, $19.99) r/#1-6; variant covers and sketch art 20.00
... Vol. 2: Venom Bomb HC (2008, $19.99) r/#7-11; B&W cover art 20.00

MIGHTY AVENGERS (Continues in Captain America and the Mighty Avengers)
Marvel Comics: Nov, 2013 - No. 14, Nov, 2014 ($3.99)

1-14: 1-Luke Cage, White Tiger, Power Man, Spectrum & Superior Spider-Man team; Land-a. 4-Falcon app. 5-She-Hulk app. 6-8-Schiti-a. 9-Ronin unmasked. 10-12-Original Sin 4.00

MIGHTY BEAR (Formerly Fun Comics; becomes Unsane #15)
Star Publ. No. 13,14/Ajax-Farrell (Four Star): No. 13, Jan, 1954 - No. 14, Mar, 1954; 9/57 - No. 3, 2/58

13,14-L. B. Cole-c 18 36 54 109 172 235
1-3('57-58)Four Star; becomes Mighty Ghost #4 8 16 24 40 50 60

MIGHTY CAPTAIN MARVEL, THE (Follows Civil War II)(Continues in Captain Marvel #125)
Marvel Comics: No. 0, Feb, 2017 - No. 9, Nov, 2017 ($3.99)

0-Stohl-s/Laiso-a; Alpha Flight app. 4.00
1-9: 1-(3/17) Stohl-s/Rosanas-a. 5-8-Secret Empire tie-ins 4.00

MIGHTY COMICS (...Presents) (Formerly Flyman)
Radio Comics (Archie): No. 40, Nov, 1966 - No. 50, Oct, 1967 (All 12¢ issues)

40-Web 5 10 15 30 50 70
41-50: 41-Shield, Black Hood. 42-Black Hood. 43-Shield, Web & Black Hood. 44-Black Hood, Steel Sterling & The Shield. 45-Shield & Hangman; origin Web retold. 46-Steel Sterling, Web & Black Hood. 47-Black Hood & Mr. Justice. 48-Shield & Hangman; Wizard x-over in Shield. 49-Steel Sterling & Fox; Black Hood x-over in Steel Sterling. 50-Black Hood & Web; Inferno x-over in Web 4 8 12 28 47 65
NOTE: *Paul Reinman a-40-50.*

MIGHTY CRUSADERS, THE (Also see Adventures of the Fly, The Crusaders & Fly Man)
Mighty Comics Group (Radio Comics): Nov, 1965 - No. 7, Oct, 1966 (All 12¢)

1-Origin The Shield 7 14 21 49 92 135
2-Origin Comet 4 8 12 28 47 65
3,5-7: 3-Origin Fly-Man. 5-Intro. Ultra-Men (Fox, Web, Capt. Flag) & Terrific Three (Jaguar, Mr. Justice, Steel Sterling). 7-Steel Sterling feature; origin Fly-Girl 4 8 12 27 44 60
4-1st S.A. app. Fireball, Inferno & Fox; Firefly, Web, Bob Phantom, Blackjack, Hangman, Zambini, Kardak, Steel Sterling, Mr. Justice, Wizard, Capt. Flag, Jaguar x-over 4 8 12 28 47 65
Volume 1: Origin of a Super Team TPB (2003, $12.95) r/#1 & Fly Man #31-33 13.00
NOTE: *Reinman a-6.*

MIGHTY CRUSADERS, THE (All New Advs. of...#2)
Red Circle Prod./Archie Ent. No. 6 on: Mar, 1983 - No. 13, Sept, 1985 ($1.00, 36 pgs, Mando paper)

1-Origin Black Hood, The Fly, Fly Girl, The Shield, The Wizard, The Jaguar, Pvt. Strong & The Web; return of MLJ heroes 1 2 3 4 5 7
2-10: 2-Mister Midnight begins. 4-Darkling replaces Shield. 5-Origin Jaguar, Shield begins. 7-Untold origin Jaguar. 10-Veitch-a 5.00
11-13-Lower print run 6.00
NOTE: *Buckler a-1-3, 4i, 5p, 7p, 8i, 9i; c-1-10p.*

MIGHTY CRUSADERS, THE (Also see The Shield, The Web and The Red Circle)
DC Comics: Sept, 2010 - No. 6, Feb, 2011 ($3.99, limited series)

1-6-The Shield, The Web, Fly-Girl, Inferno, War Eagle & The Comet team-up 4.00
... Special 1 (7/10, $4.99) Prequel to series; Pina-a/Lau-c 5.00

MIGHTY CRUSADERS, THE (Volume 3)
Archie Comic Publications (Dark Circle): Jan, 2018 - No. 4, May, 2018 ($3.99)

1-4-The Shield, Jaguar, Firefly, Darkling, Steel Sterling, The Comet & The Web team-up 4.00

MIGHTY GHOST (Formerly Mighty Bear #1-3)
Ajax/Farrell Publ.: No. 4, June, 1958

4 7 14 21 37 46 55

MIGHTY HERCULES, THE (TV)
Gold Key: July, 1963 - No. 2, Nov, 1963

1 (10072-307) 11 22 33 77 166 265
2 (10072-311) 12 24 36 80 173 240

MIGHTY HEROES, THE (TV) (Funny)
Dell Publishing Co.: Mar, 1967 - No. 4, July, 1967

1-Also has a 1957 Heckle & Jeckle-r 10 20 30 66 138 210
2-4: 4-Has two 1958 Mighty Mouse-r 7 14 21 44 82 120

MIGHTY HEROES
Spotlight Comics: 1987 (B&W, one-shot)

1-Heckle & Jeckle backup 5.00

MIGHTY HEROES
Marvel Comics: Jan, 1998 ($2.99, one-shot)

1-Origin of the Mighty Heroes 3.00

MIGHTY LOVE
DC Comics: 2003 ($24.99/$17.95, graphic novel)

HC-($24.95) Howard Chaykin-s/a; intro. Skylark and the Iron Angel 25.00
SC-($17.95) 18.00

MIGHTY MAN (From Savage Dragon titles)
Image Comics: Dec, 2004 ($7.95, one-shot)

1-Reprints the serialized back-ups from Savage Dragon #109-118 8.00

MIGHTY MAN (From Savage Dragon)
Image Comics: Apr, 2017 ($3.99, one-shot)

1-Larsen-s/Koutsis-a; Superpatriot, Malcolm Dragon, Horridus, Barbaric, Ricochet app. 4.00

MIGHTY MARVEL TEAM-UP THRILLERS
Marvel Comics: 1983 ($5.95, trade paperback)

1-Reprints team-up stories 3 6 9 18 28 38

MIGHTY MARVEL WESTERN, THE
Marvel Comics Group (LMC earlier issues): Oct, 1968 - No. 46, Sept, 1976 (#1-14: 68 pgs.; #15,16: 52 pgs.)

1-Begin Kid Colt, Rawhide Kid, Two-Gun Kid-r 7 14 21 48 89 130
2-5: (2-14 are 68 pgs.) 4 8 12 27 44 60
6-16: (15,16 are 52 pgs.) 3 6 9 21 33 45
17-20 2 4 6 13 18 22
21-30,32,37: 24-Kid Colt-r end. 25-Matt Slade-r begin. 32-Origin-r/Rawhide Kid #23; Williamson-r/Kid Slade #7. 37-Williamson, Kirby-r/Two-Gun Kid 51 2 4 6 9 13 16
31,33-36,38-46: 31-Baker-r. 2 4 6 8 11 14
45-(30¢-c variant, limited distribution)(6/76) 9 18 27 61 123 185
NOTE: *Jack Davis a(r)-21-24. **Keller** r-1-13, 22. **Kirby** a(r)-1-3, 6, 9, 12-14, 16, 25-29, 32-38, 40, 41, 43-46; c-29. **Maneely** a(r)-22. **Severin** c-3i, 9. No Matt Slade-#43.*

MIGHTY MIDGET COMICS, THE (Miniature)
Samuel E. Lowe & Co.: No date; circa 1942-1943 (Sold 2 for 5¢, B&W and red, 36 pgs, approx. 5x4")

Bulletman #11(1943)-r/cover/Bulletman #3 16 32 48 94 147 200
Captain Marvel Adventures #11 16 32 48 94 147 200
Captain Marvel #11 (Same as above except for full color ad on back cover; this issue was glued to cover of Captain Marvel #20 and is not found in fine-mint condition) 345 690 1035 -- -- --
Captain Marvel Jr. #11 (Same-c as Master #27 16 32 48 94 147 200
Captain Marvel Jr. #11 (Same as above except for full color ad on back-c; this issue was glued to cover of Captain Marvel #21 and is not found in fine-mint condition) 345 690 1035 -- -- --
Golden Arrow #11 15 30 45 90 140 190
Golden Arrow #11 (Same as above except for full color ad on back-c; this issue was glued to cover of Captain Marvel #21 and is not found in fine-mint condition) 285 570 855 -- -- --
Ibis the Invincible #11(1942)-Origin; reprints cover to Ibis #1 (Predates Fawcett's Ibis the Invincible #1). 18 36 54 105 165 225
Spy Smasher #11(1942) 16 32 48 94 147 200
NOTE: *The above books came in a box called "box full of books" and was distributed with other Samuel Lowe puzzles, paper dolls, coloring books, etc. They are not titled Mighty Midget Comics. All have a war bond seal on back cover which is otherwise blank. These books came in a "Mighty Midget" flat cardboard counter display rack.*
Balbo, the Boy Magician #12 (1943)-1st book devoted entirely to character. 10 20 30 54 72 90
Bulletman #12 12 24 36 69 97 125
Commando Yank #12 (1943)-Only comic devoted entirely to character. 10 20 30 56 76 95
Dr. Voltz the Human Generator (1943)-Only comic devoted entirely to character. 10 20 30 54 72 90
Lance O'Casey #12 (1943)-1st comic devoted entirely to character (Predates Fawcett's Lance O'Casey #1). 10 20 30 54 72 90
Leatherneck the Marine (1943)-Only comic devoted entirely to character. 10 20 30 54 72 90
Minute Man #12 12 24 36 67 94 120
Mister "Q" (1943)-Only comic devoted entirely to character.

Mighty Morphin #1 © SCG PR & Hasbro

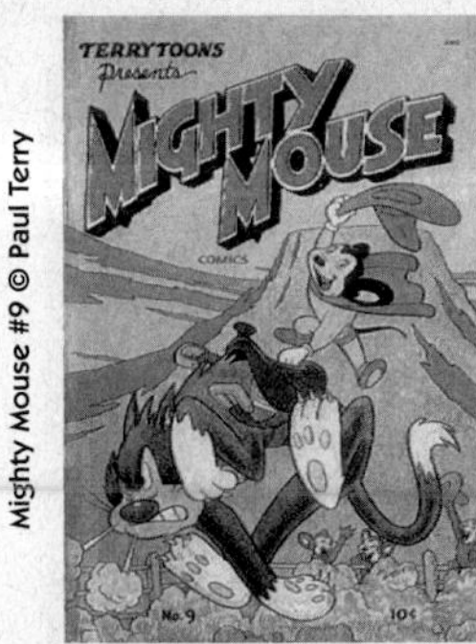

Mighty Mouse #9 © Paul Terry

The Mighty Thor #2 © MAR

	GD 2.0	VG 4.0	FN 6.0	VF 8.0	VF/NM 9.0	NM- 9.2
	10	20	30	54	72	90
Mr. Scarlet and Pinky #12 (1943)-Only comic devoted entirely to character.	10	20	30	58	79	100
Pat Wilton and His Flying Fortress (1943)-1st comic devoted entirely to character.	10	20	30	54	72	90
The Phantom Eagle #12 (1943)-Only comic devoted entirely to character.	10	20	30	54	72	90
State Trooper Stops Crime (1943)-Only comic devoted entirely to character.	10	20	30	54	72	90
Tornado Tom (1943)-Origin, r/from Cyclone #1-3; only comic devoted entirely to character.	10	20	30	54	72	90

MIGHTY MORPHIN (Mighty Morphin' Power Rangers)
BOOM! Studios: Nov, 2020 - Present ($4.99)

1-($4.99) Parrott-s/Renna-a; multiple covers 5.00
2-4-($3.99) 4-Green Ranger unmasks 4.00

MIGHTY MORPHIN POWER RANGERS (Also see Saban's Mighty Morphin' Power Rangers)
BOOM! Studios: No. 0, Jan, 2016; Mar, 2016 - Present ($3.99)

0-Higgins-s/Prasetya-a; Rita Repulsa & Scorpina app.; multiple covers 4.00
1-24,26-49,51-55: 1-4,6-9,11-Higgins-s/Prasetya-a. 5-Silas-a. 10-Lam-a 4.00
25,50-($4.99) 25-Sold in black polybag; Tommy dies 5.00
2016 Annual 1 (8/16, $7.99) Short stories; art by Guillory, Terry Moore, Kochalka 8.00
2017 Annual 1 (5/17, $7.99) Short stories; art by Mora, Irving, Montes; 3 covers 8.00
2018 Annual 1 (4/18, $7.99) Shattered Grid; short stories; 3 covers 8.00
... FCBD 2018 Special (5/18, giveaway) Shattered Grid; Galindo-a 3.00
... Shattered Grid 1 (8/18, $7.99) Di Nicuolo & Galindo-a 8.00
... 25th Anniversary Special 1 (6/18, $7.99) Short stories; art by Quinones & others 8.00

MIGHTY MORPHIN POWER RANGERS: PINK
BOOM! Studios: Jun, 2016 - No. 6, Jan, 2017 ($3.99, limited series)

1-6-Fletcher & Thompson-s/DiNicuolo-a; multiple covers 4.00

MIGHTY MORPHIN POWER RANGERS / TEENAGE MUTANT NINJA TURTLES
BOOM! Studios: Dec, 2019 - No. 5, Jun, 2020 ($4.99/$3.99, limited series)

1-($4.99) Ryan Parrott-s/Simone di Meo-a; Shredder app.; multiple covers 5.00
2-5-($3.99) Rita Repulsa, BeBop & Rocksteady app. 4.00

MIGHTY MORPHIN' POWER RANGERS: THE MOVIE (Also see Saban's Mighty Morphin' Power Rangers)
Marvel Comics: Sept, 1995 ($3.95, one-shot)

	GD	VG	FN	VF	VF/NM	NM-
nn-Adaptation of movie	1	2	3	5	6	8

MIGHTY MOUSE (See Adventures of..., Dell Giant #43, Giant Comics Edition, March of Comics #205, 237, 247, 257, 447, 459, 471, 483, Oxydol-Dreft, Paul Terry's, & Terry-Toons Comics)

MIGHTY MOUSE (1st Series)
Timely/Marvel Comics (20th Century Fox): Fall, 1946 - No. 4, Summer, 1947

	GD	VG	FN	VF	VF/NM	NM-
1	200	400	600	1280	2190	3100
2	76	152	228	486	831	1175
3,4	48	96	144	302	514	725

MIGHTY MOUSE (2nd Series) (Paul Terry's... #62-71)
St. John Publishing Co./Pines No. 68 (3/56) on (TV issues #72 on): Aug, 1947 - No. 67, 11/55; No. 68, 3/56 - No. 83, 6/59

	GD	VG	FN	VF	VF/NM	NM-
5(#1)	68	136	204	435	743	1050
6-10: 10-Over-sized issue	25	50	75	150	245	340
11-19	15	30	45	90	140	190
20 (11/50) - 25-(52 pg. editions)	14	28	42	76	108	140
20-25-(36 pg. editions)	12	24	36	67	94	120
26-37: 35-Flying saucer-c	11	22	33	62	86	110
38-45-(100 pgs.)	20	40	60	120	195	270
46-83: 62-64,67-Painted-c. 82-Infinity-c	10	20	30	58	79	100
Album nn (nd, 1952/53?, St. John)(100 pgs.)(Rebound issues w/new cover)	28	56	84	165	270	375
Album 1(10/52, 25¢, 100 pgs., St. John)-Gandy Goose app.	36	72	108	216	351	485
Album 2,3(11/52 & 12/52, St. John) (100 pgs.)	27	54	81	158	259	360
Fun Club Magazine 1(Fall, 1957-Pines, 25¢, 100 pgs.) (CBS TV)-Tom Terrific, Heckle & Jeckle, Dinky Duck, Gandy Goose	20	40	60	120	195	270
Fun Club Magazine 2-6(Winter, 1958-Pines)	12	24	36	67	94	120
3-D 1-(1st printing-9/53, 25¢)(St. John)-Came w/glasses; stiff covers; says World's First! on-c; 1st 3-D comic	29	58	87	170	278	385
3-D 1-(2nd printing-10/53, 25¢)-Came w/glasses; slick, glossy covers, slightly smaller	20	40	60	114	182	250
3-D 2,3(11/53, 12/53, 25¢)-(St. John)-With glasses	20	40	60	114	182	250

MIGHTY MOUSE (TV)(3rd Series)(Formerly Adventures of Mighty Mouse)
Gold Key/Dell Publ. Co. No. 166-on: No. 161, Oct, 1964 - No. 172, Oct, 1968

	GD	VG	FN	VF	VF/NM	NM-
161(10/64)-165(9/65)-(Becomes Adventures of... No. 166 on)	4	8	12	28	47	65
166(3/66), 167(6/66)-172	3	6	9	20	31	42

MIGHTY MOUSE (TV)
Spotlight Comics: 1987 - No. 2, 1987 ($1.50, color)

1,2-New stories 4.00
...And Friends Holiday Special (11/87, $1.75) 4.00

MIGHTY MOUSE (TV)
Marvel Comics: Oct, 1990 - No. 10, July, 1991 ($1.00)(Based on Sat. cartoon)

1-10: 1-Dark Knight-c parody. 2-10: 3-Intro Bat-Bat; Byrne-c. 4,5-Crisis-c/story parodies w/Perez-c. 6-Spider-Man-c parody. 7-Origin Bat-Bat 3.00

MIGHTY MOUSE (TV)
Dynamite Entertainment: 2017 - No. 5, 2017 ($3.99)

1-5: 1-Multiple covers incl. Alex Ross & Neal Adams; Mighty Mouse in the real world 4.00

MIGHTY MOUSE ADVENTURE MAGAZINE
Spotlight Comics: 1987 ($2.00, B&W, 52 pgs., magazine size, one-shot)

1-Deputy Dawg, Heckle & Jeckle backup stories 5.00

MIGHTY MOUSE ADVENTURES (Adventures of... #2 on)
St. John Publishing Co.: November, 1951

	GD	VG	FN	VF	VF/NM	NM-
1	41	82	123	256	428	600

MIGHTY MOUSE ADVENTURE STORIES (Paul Terry's... on-c only)
St. John Publishing Co.: 1953 (50¢, 384 pgs.)

	GD	VG	FN	VF	VF/NM	NM-
nn-Rebound issues	60	120	180	381	653	925

MIGHTY MUTANIMALS (See Teenage Mutant Ninja Turtles Adventures #19)
May, 1991 - No. 3, July, 1991 ($1.00, limited series)
Archie Comics: Apr, 1992 - No. 9, June, 1993 ($1.25)

	GD	VG	FN	VF	VF/NM	NM-
1-3: 1-Story cont'd from TMNT Advs. #19.	1	2	3	5	6	8
1-4 (1992)	1	2	3	5	6	8
5-9: 7-1st app. Merdude	2	4	6	8	10	12

MIGHTY SAMSON (Also see Gold Key Champion)
Gold Key/Whitman #32: July, 1964 - No. 20, Nov, 1969; No. 21, Aug, 1972; No. 22, Dec, 1973 - No. 31, Mar, 1976; No. 32, Aug, 1982 (Painted-c #1-31)

	GD	VG	FN	VF	VF/NM	NM-
1-Origin/1st app.; Thorne-a begins	8	16	24	55	105	155
2-5	4	8	12	28	47	65
6-10: 7-Tom Morrow begins, ends #20	3	6	9	20	30	40
11-20	3	6	9	16	23	30
21-31: 21,22-r	2	4	6	11	16	20
32(Whitman, 8/82)-r	2	4	6	8	10	12

MIGHTY SAMSON
Dark Horse Comics: Dec, 2010 - No. 4, Oct, 2011 ($3.50)

1-4: 1-Origin retold; Shooter & Vaughn-s/Olliffe-a/Swanland-c; r/1st app. from 1964 3.50
1-Variant-c by Olliffe 4.00

MIGHTY THOR, THE (Continues in Thor; God of Thunder)
Marvel Comics: Jun, 2011 - No. 22, Dec, 2012 ($3.99)

1-Fraction-s/Coipel-a; Silver Surfer app.; bonus concept art from the movie 4.00
1-Variant-c by Charest 6.00
1-Variant-c by Simonson 10.00
2-22: 3-6-Galactus app. 7-Fear Itself tie-in; Odin's 1st battle vs. the Serpent. 8-Tanarus. 13-17-Simonson-c. 18-21-Alan Davis-a 4.00
12.1 (6/12, $2.99) Kitson-a/Coipel-c; flashbacks from Volstagg & Sif 3.00
Annual 1 (8/12, $4.99) Silver Surfer & Galactus app.; DeMatteis-s/Elson-a 5.00

MIGHTY THOR (Jane Foster as Thor)
Marvel Comics: Jan, 2016 - No. 23, Nov, 2017; No. 700, Dec, 2017 - No. 706, Jun, 2018 ($4.99/$3.99)

1-($4.99) Tri-fold cover; Aaron-s/Dauterman-a; Loki app. 5.00
2-23-($3.99) 3-Multiple Lokis app. 12-Origin of Mjolnir; Frazer Irving-a. 14-Epting-a. 20-Volstagg becomes the War Thor 4.00
[Title switches to legacy numbering after #23 (11/17)]
700-(12/17, $5.99) Aaron-s; art by various incl. Dauterman, Simonson, Acuna, Coipel 6.00
701-706: 701-Mangog vs. War Thor; Harren-a. 703-706-Dauterman-a 4.00
...: At the Gates of Valhalla 1 (7/18, $4.99) Intro Goddesses of Thunder; Bartel-a 5.00
... 3D #1 (6/19, $7.99, polybagged with 3D glasses) r/#1 in 3D; wraparound-c 8.00

MIKE BARNETT, MAN AGAINST CRIME (TV)
Fawcett Publications: Dec, 1951 - No. 6, Oct, 1952

	GD	VG	FN	VF	VF/NM	NM-
1	23	46	69	136	223	310
2	14	28	42	82	121	160
3,4,6	13	26	39	72	101	130

Miles Morales: Spider-Man #17 © MAR

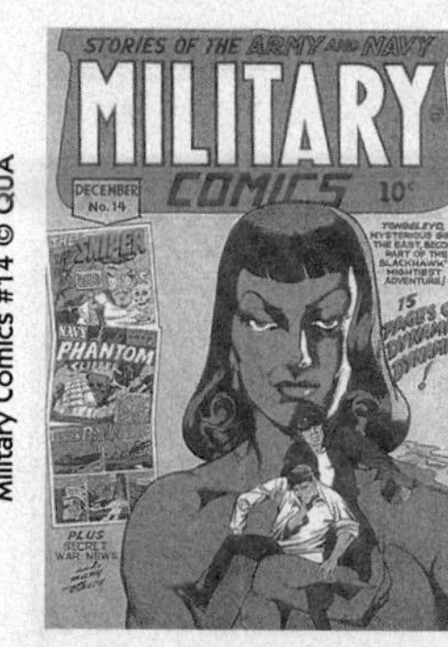

Military Comics #14 © QUA

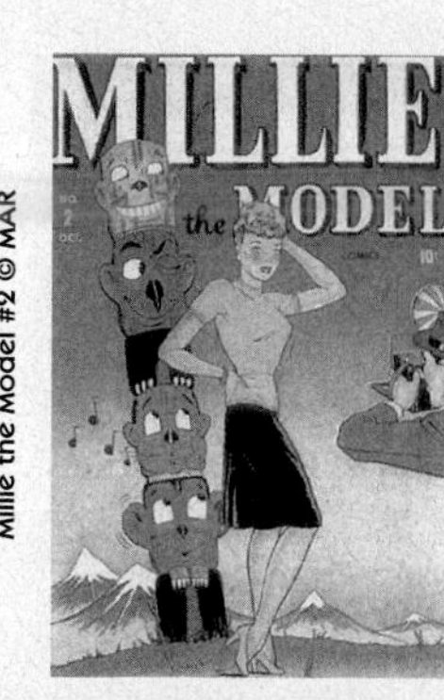

Millie the Model #2 © MAR

	GD 2.0	VG 4.0	FN 6.0	VF 8.0	VF/NM 9.0	NM- 9.2
5- "Market for Morphine" cover/story	16	32	48	96	151	205

MIKE DANGER (See Mickey Spillane's...)

MIKE DEODATO'S...
Caliber Comics: 1996, ($2.95, B&W)

...FALLOUT 3000 #1, **...JONAS** (mag. size) #1,**...PRIME CUTS** (mag. size) #1, **...PROTHEUS** #1,2, **...RAMTHAR** #1,**...RAZOR NIGHTS** #1 — 3.00

MIKE GRELL'S SABLE (Also see Jon Sable & Sable)
First Comics: Mar, 1990 - No. 10, Dec, 1990 ($1.75)

1-10: r/Jon Sable Freelance #1-10 by Grell — 3.00

MIKE MIST MINUTE MIST-ERIES (See Ms. Tree/Mike Mist in 3-D)
Eclipse Comics: April, 1981 ($1.25, B&W, one-shot)

1 — 3.00

MIKE SHAYNE PRIVATE EYE
Dell Publishing Co.: Nov-Jan, 1962 - No. 3, Sept-Nov, 1962

	GD 2.0	VG 4.0	FN 6.0	VF 8.0	VF/NM 9.0	NM- 9.2
1	4	8	12	23	37	50
2,3	3	6	9	16	24	32

MILES MORALES: SPIDER-MAN
Marvel Comics: Feb, 2019 - Present ($3.99)

1-23: 1-Ahmed-s/Garrón-a; Rhino app. 3,20,21-Captain America app. 5,6-Intro. Starling. 10-Ultimatum app. 13-Rhino app.; Billie born. 23-"King in Black" tie-in — 4.00
Miles Morales: The End 1 (3/20, $4.99) Damion Scott-a; future Miles' last adventure — 5.00

MILES MORALES: ULTIMATE SPIDER-MAN
Marvel Comics: Jul, 2014 - No. 12, Jun, 2015 ($3.99)

1-11: 1-Bendis-s/Marquez-a; Peter Parker & Norman Osborn return. 11-Dr. Doom app. — 4.00
12-Doctor Doom and the Ultimates app.; leads into Secret Wars #1 — 4.00

MILES TO GO
AfterShock Comics: Sept, 2020 - Present ($3.99)

1-3-B. Clay Moore-s/Stephen Molnar-a — 4.00

MILESTONE FOREVER
DC Comics: Apr, 2010 - No. 2, May, 2010 ($5.99, squarebound, limited series)

1,2-McDuffie-s/Leon & Bright-a; Icon, Blood Syndicate, Hardware and Static app. — 6.00

MILITARY COMICS (Becomes Modern Comics #44 on)
Quality Comics Group: Aug, 1941 - No. 43, Oct, 1945

	GD 2.0	VG 4.0	FN 6.0	VF 8.0	VF/NM 9.0	NM- 9.2
1-Origin/1st app. Blackhawk by C. Cuidera (Eisner scripts); Miss America, The Death Patrol by Jack Cole (also #2-7,27-30), & The Blue Tracer by Guardineer; X of the Underground, The Yankee Eagle, Q-Boat & Shot & Shell, Archie Atkins, Loops & Banks by Bud Ernest (Bob Powell)(ends #13) begin	476	952	1428	3475	6188	8900
2-Secret War News begins (by McWilliams #2-16); Cole-a; new uniform with yellow circle & hawk's head for Blackhawk	155	310	465	992	1696	2400
3-Origin/1st app. Chop Chop (9/41)	123	246	369	787	1344	1900
4	105	210	315	667	1146	1625
5-The Sniper begins; Miss America in costume #4-7	94	188	282	397	1025	1450
6-9: 8-X of the Underground begins (ends #13). 9-The Phantom Clipper begins (ends #16)	73	146	219	467	796	1125
10-Classic Eisner-c	98	196	294	627	1076	1525
11-Flag-c	71	142	213	454	777	1100
12-Blackhawk by Crandall begins, ends #22	73	146	219	467	796	1125
13-15: 14-Private Dogtag begins (ends #83)	58	116	174	371	636	900
16-20: 16-Blue Tracer ends. 17-P.T. Boat begins	53	106	159	334	567	800
21-31: 22-Last Crandall Blackhawk. 23-Shrunken head-c. 27-Death Patrol revived. 28-True story of Mussolini	47	94	141	296	498	700
32-43	41	82	123	256	428	600

NOTE: **Berg** *a-6.* **Al Bryant** *c-31-34, 38, 40-43.* **J. Cole** *a-1-3, 27-32.* **Crandall** *a-12-22; c-13-20.* **Cuidera** *c-2-9.* **Eisner** *c-1, 2(part), 9, 10.* **Kotsky** *c-21-29, 35, 37, 39.* **McWilliams** *a-2-16.* **Powell** *a-1-13.* **Ward** *Blackhawk-30, 31(15 pgs. each); c-30.*

MILK AND CHEESE (Also see Cerebus Bi-Weekly #20)
Slave Labor: 1991 - No. 7, Jan, 1997 ($2.50, B&W)

	GD 2.0	VG 4.0	FN 6.0	VF 8.0	VF/NM 9.0	NM- 9.2
1-Evan Dorkin story & art in all	5	10	15	33	57	80
1-2nd-6th printings						4.00
2-"Other #1"	3	6	9	16	24	32
2-reprint						3.00
3-"Third #1"	2	4	6	11	16	20
4-"Fourth #1", 5-"First Second Issue"	1	3	4	6	8	10
6,7: 6-"#666"						5.00

NOTE: *Multiple printings of all issues exist and are worth cover price unless listed here.*

MILKMAN MURDERS, THE
Dark Horse Comics: Jun, 2004 - No. 4, Aug, 2004 ($2.99, limited series)

1-4-Casey-s/Parkhouse-a — 3.00

MILLARWORLD (Mark Millar characters)
Image Comics: Jul, 2016; Sept, 2017 ($2.99)

...Annual 2016 1 (7/16) Short stories of Kick-Ass, Hit-Girl, Chrononauts and others — 3.00
...Annual 2017 1 (9/17) Short stories of Kick-Ass, Superior, Huck, Nemesis and others — 3.00

MILLENNIUM
DC Comics: Jan, 1988 - No. 8, Feb, 1988 (Weekly limited series)

1-Englehart-s/Staton c/a(p) — 4.00
2-8 — 3.00
TPB (2008, $19.99) r/#1-8 — 20.00

MILLENNIUM (TV, spin-off from The X-Files)
IDW Publishing: Jan, 2015 - No. 5, May, 2015 ($3.99, limited series)

1-5: 1-Frank Black & Agent Mulder app.; Joe Harris-s/Colin Lorimer-a; three covers — 4.00

MILLENNIUM EDITION:... (Reprints of classic DC issues, plus some WildStorm and non-DC issues with characters now published by DC)
DC Comics: Feb, 2000 - Feb, 2001 (gold foil cover stamps)

Action Comics #1, Adventure Comics #61, All Star Comics #3, All Star Comics #8, Batman #1, Detective Comics #1, Detective Comics #27, Detective Comics #38, Flash Comics #1, Military Comics #1, More Fun Comics #73, Police Comics #1, Sensation Comics #1, Superman #1, Whiz Comics #2, Wonder Woman #1 -($3.95-c) — 5.00
Action Comics #252, Adventure Comics #247, Brave and the Bold #28, Brave and the Bold #85, Crisis on Infinte Earths #1, Detective #225, Detective #327, Detective #359, Detective #395, Flash #123, Gen13 #1, Green Lantern #76, House of Mystery #1, House of Secrets #92, JLA #1, Justice League #1, Mad #1, Man of Steel #1, Mysterious Suspense #1, New Gods, #1, New Teen Titans #1, Our Army at War #81, Plop! #1, Saga of the Swamp Thing #21, Shadow #1, Showcase #4, Showcase #9, Showcase #22, Superman #233, Superman (2nd) #75, Superman's Pal Jimmy Olsen #1, Watchmen #1, WildC.A.T.s #1, Wonder Woman (2nd) #1, World's Finest #71 -($2.50-c) — 4.00
All-Star Western #10, Hellblazer #1, More Fun Comics #101, Preacher #1, Sandman #1, Spirit #1, Superboy #1, Superman #76, Young Romance #1-($2.95-c) — 4.00
Batman: The Dark Knight Returns #1, Kingdom Come #1 -($5.95-c) — 6.00
All Star Comics #3, Batman #1, Justice League #1: Chromium cover — 12.00
Crisis on Infinite Earths #1 Chromium cover — 20.00

MILLENNIUM FEVER
DC Comics (Vertigo): Oct, 1995 - No.4, Jan, 1996 ($2.50, limited series)

1-4: Duncan Fegredo-c/a — 3.00

MILLENNIUM: THE GIRL WHO DANCED WITH DEATH
Titan Comics: Sept, 2018 - No. 3, Nov, 2018 ($5.99, limited series)

1-3-Adaptation of the Stieg Larsson novel; Runberg-s/Ortega-a — 6.00

MILLENNIUM: THE GIRL WHO KICKED THE HORNET'S NEST
Titan Comics: Jan, 2018 - No. 2, Feb, 2018 ($5.99, limited series)

1,2-Adaptation of the Stieg Larsson novel; Runberg-s. 1-Homs-a. 2-Carot-a — 6.00

MILLENNIUM: THE GIRL WHO PLAYED WITH FIRE
Titan Comics: Oct, 2017 - No. 2, Nov, 2017 ($5.99, limited series)

1,2-Adaptation of the Stieg Larsson novel; Runberg-s. 1-Gonzalez-a. 2-Carot-a — 6.00

MILLENNIUM: THE GIRL WITH THE DRAGON TATTOO
Titan Comics: Jul, 2017 - No. 2, Aug, 2017 ($5.99, limited series)

1,2-Adaptation of the Stieg Larsson novel; Runberg-s/Homs-a — 6.00

MILLENNIUM 2.5 A.D.
ACG Comics: No. 1, 2000 ($2.95)

1-Reprints 1934 Buck Rogers daily strips #1-48 — 3.00

MILLIE, THE LOVABLE MONSTER
Dell Publishing Co.: Sept-Nov, 1962 - No. 6, Jan, 1973

	GD 2.0	VG 4.0	FN 6.0	VF 8.0	VF/NM 9.0	NM- 9.2
12-523-211-Bill Woggon c/a in all	5	10	15	31	53	75
2(8-10/63)	4	8	12	28	47	65
3(8-10/64)	4	8	12	25	40	55
4(7/72), 5(10/72), 6(1/73)	3	6	9	14	19	24

NOTE: **Woggon** *a-3-6; c-3-6. 4 reprints 1; 5 reprints 2; 6 reprints 3.*

MILLIE THE MODEL (See Comedy Comics, A Date With..., Joker Comics #28, Life With..., Mad About..., Marvel Mini-Books, Misty & Modeling With...)
Marvel/Atlas/Marvel Comics(CnPC #1)(SPI/Male/VPI):1945 - No. 207, Dec, 1973

	GD 2.0	VG 4.0	FN 6.0	VF 8.0	VF/NM 9.0	NM- 9.2
1-Origin	354	708	1062	2478	4339	6200
2 (10/46)-Millie becomes The Blonde Phantom to sell Blonde Phantom perfume; a pre-Blonde Phantom app. (see All-Select #11, Fall, 1946)	97	194	291	621	1061	1500
3-8,10: 4-7-Willie app. 7-Willie smokes extra strong tobacco. 8,10-Kurtzman's "Hey Look". 8-Willie & Rusty app.	57	114	171	362	619	875

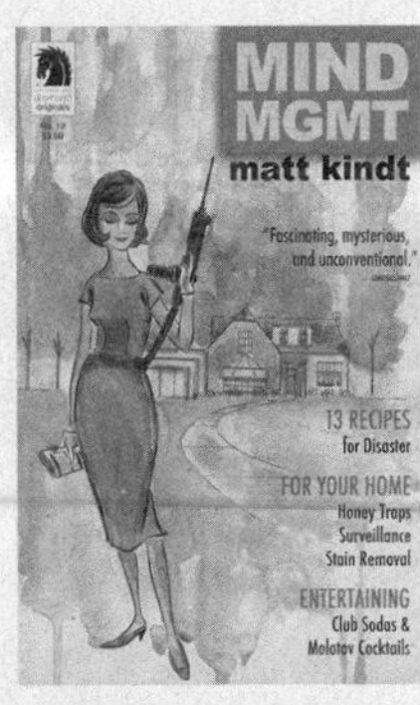

Mind MGMT #13 © Matt Kindt

Ministry of Space #1 © Ellis & Weston

Miracleman #1 © ECL

	GD 2.0	VG 4.0	FN 6.0	VF 8.0	VF/NM 9.0	NM- 9.2
9-Powerhouse Pepper by Wolverton, 4 pgs.	71	142	213	454	777	1100
11-Kurtzman-a, "Giggles 'n' Grins"	40	80	120	245	411	575
12,15,17,19,20: 12-Rusty & Hedy Devine app.	39	78	117	240	395	550
13,14,16,18: 13,14,16-Kurtzman's "Hey Look". 13-Hedy Devine app. 18-Dan DeCarlo-a begins	32	64	96	192	314	435
21-30	31	62	93	182	296	410
31-40	17	34	51	115	255	395
41-60: 47-Millie's 3-D poses	16	32	48	111	246	380
61-80	14	28	42	96	211	325
81-99: 93-Last DeCarlo issue?	11	22	33	72	154	235
100	11	22	33	77	166	255
101-106,108-130	7	14	21	44	82	120
107-Jack Kirby app. in story	7	14	21	48	89	130
131-134,136,138-153: 141-Groovy Gears-c/s	5	10	15	33	57	80
135-(2/66) 1st app. Groovy Gears	6	12	18	38	69	100
137-2nd app. Groovy Gears	5	10	15	35	63	90
154-New Millie begins (10/67)	6	12	18	42	79	115
155-190	5	10	15	33	57	80
191,193-199,201-206	5	10	15	30	50	70
192-(52 pgs.)	5	10	15	33	57	80
200,207(Last issue)	5	10	15	33	57	80
(Beware: cut-up pages are common in all Annuals)						
Annual 1(1962)-Early Marvel annual (2nd?)	35	70	105	252	564	875
Annual 2(1963)	18	36	54	128	284	440
Annual 3-5 (1964-1966)	9	18	27	60	120	180
Annual 6-10(1967-11/71)	7	14	21	48	89	130
Queen-Size 11(9/74), 12(1975)	6	12	18	41	76	110

NOTE: *Dan DeCarlo a-18-93.*

MILLION DOLLAR DIGEST (Richie Rich... #23 on; also see Richie Rich...)
Harvey Publications: 11/86 - No. 7, 11/87; No. 8, 4/88 - No. 34, Nov, 1994 ($1.25/$1.75, digest size)

	GD	VG	FN	VF	VF/NM	NM-
1	1	2	3	5	6	8
2-8: 8-(68 pgs.)						6.00
9-20: 9-Begin $1.75-c. 14-May not exist	1	2	3	4	5	7
21-34	1	3	4	6	8	10

MILT GROSS FUNNIES (Also see Picture News #1)
Milt Gross, Inc. (ACG?): Aug, 1947 - No. 2, Sept, 1947

	GD	VG	FN	VF	VF/NM	NM-
1	29	58	87	170	278	385
2	20	40	60	114	182	250

MILTON THE MONSTER & FEARLESS FLY (TV)
Gold Key: May, 1966

	GD	VG	FN	VF	VF/NM	NM-
1 (10175-605)	8	16	24	54	102	150

MINDFIELD
Aspen MLT: No. 0, May, 2010 - No. 6, Sept, 2011 ($2.50/$2.99)

	NM-
0-($2.50) Krul-s/Konat-a; 3 covers	3.00
1-6-($2.99) Multiples covers on each	3.00

MIND MGMT
Dark Horse Comics: May, 2012 - No. 35, Jul, 2015 ($3.99)

	NM-
1-Matt Kindt-s/a/c	30.00
2-6	10.00
7-35	4.00
#0 (11/12, $2.99) Prints background stories from Mind MGMT Secret Files digital site	3.00
New MGMT#1/Mind Mgmt #36 (8/15, $3.99) Series conclusion	4.00

MIND THE GAP
Image Comics: May, 2012 - No. 17, May, 2014 ($2.99)

	NM-
1-17: 1-8,10-McCann-s/Esquejo-a/c. 9-McDaid-a. 11,12-Basri-a	3.00

MINIMUM CARNAGE
Marvel Comics: Dec, 2012 - Jan, 2013 ($3.99, limited series)

	NM-
...: Alpha (12/12) Venom, Carnage and Scarlet Spider app.; Medina-a/Crain-c	4.00
...: Omega (1/13) The Enigma Force in the Microverse app.	4.00

MINIMUM WAGE
Fantagraphics Books: V1#1, July, 1995 ($9.95, B&W, graphic novel, mature)
V2#1, 1995 - 1997 ($2.95, B&W, mature)

	GD	VG	FN	VF	VF/NM	NM-
V1#1-Bob Fingerman story & art	1	3	4	6	8	10
V2#1-9($2.95): Bob Fingerman story & art. 2-Kevin Nowlan back-c. 4-w/pin-ups. 5-Mignola back-c						3.00
Book Two TPB ('97, $12.95) r/V2#1-5						13.00

MINIMUM WAGE
Image Comics: Jan, 2014 - No. 6, Jun, 2014 ($3.50, B&W&Green, mature)

	NM-
1-6-Bob Fingerman story & art; story resumes in May 2000	3.50

MINIMUM WAGE: SO MANY BAD DECISIONS
Image Comics: May, 2015 - No. 6, Oct, 2015 ($3.99, B&W&Green/color pages, mature)

	NM-
1-6-Bob Fingerman story & art. 3-Marc Maron app.	4.00

MINIONS (From Despicable Me movies)
Titan Comics: Jul, 2015 - No. 2, Aug, 2015 ($3.99, limited series)

	NM-
1,2-Short stories and one-page gags; Ah-Koon-s/Collin-a	4.00

MINIONS PAELLA! (From Despicable Me movies)
Titan Comics: Nov, 2019 - No. 2, Dec, 2019 ($3.99, limited series)

	NM-
1,2-Short stories and one-page gags; Lapuss-s/Collin-a	4.00

MINIONS VIVA LE BOSS! (From Despicable Me movies)
Titan Comics: Nov, 2018 - No. 2, Jan, 2018 ($3.99, limited series)

	NM-
1,2-Short stories and one-page gags; Lapuss-s/Collin-a	4.00

MINISTRY OF SPACE
Image Comics: Apr, 2001 - No. 3, Apr, 2004 ($2.95, limited series)

	NM-
1-3-Warren Ellis-s/Chris Weston-a	3.00
...Vol. 1 Omnibus (3/04, $4.95) r/1&2	5.00
TPB (12/04, $12.95) r/series; sketch & design pages; intro by Mark Millar	13.00

MINKY WOODCOCK: THE GIRL WHO HANDCUFFED HOUDINI
Titan Comics: Nov, 2017 - No. 4, May, 2018 ($3.99, limited series)

	NM-
1-4-Cynthia Von Buhler-s/a. 1-Covers by Mack, McGinnis, Von Buhler & photo	4.00

MINOR MIRACLES
DC Comics: 2000 ($12.95, B&W, squarebound)

	NM-
nn-Will Eisner-s/a	13.00

MINUTE MAN (See Master Comics & Mighty Midget Comics)
Fawcett Publications: Summer, 1941 - No. 3, Spring, 1942 (68 pgs.)

	GD	VG	FN	VF	VF/NM	NM-
1	219	438	657	1402	2401	3400
2-Japanese invade NYC Statue of Liberty WWII-c	161	322	483	1030	1765	2500
3	126	252	378	806	1378	1950

MINX, THE
DC Comics (Vertigo): Oct, 1998 - No. 8, May, 1999 ($2.50, limited series)

	NM-
1-8-Milligan-s/Phillips-c/a	3.00

MIRACLE COMICS
Hillman Periodicals: Feb, 1940 - No. 4, Mar, 1941

	GD	VG	FN	VF	VF/NM	NM-
1-Sky Wizard Master of Space, Dash Dixon, Man of Might, Pinkie Parker, Dusty Doyle, The Kid Cop, K-7, Secret Agent, The Scorpion, & Blandu, Jungle Queen begin; Masked Angel only app. (all 1st app.)	311	622	933	2225	3913	5600
2-Classic Sky Wizard-c	194	388	582	1242	2121	3000
3,4: 3-Devil-c; Bill Colt, the Ghost Rider begins. 4-The Veiled Prophet & Bullet Bob (by Burnley) app.	148	296	444	947	1624	2300

MIRACLEMAN
Eclipse Comics: Aug, 1985 - No. 15, Nov, 1988; No. 16, Dec, 1989 - No. 24, Aug, 1993

	GD	VG	FN	VF	VF/NM	NM-
1-r/British Marvelman series; Alan Moore scripts in #1-16	2	4	6	11	16	20
1-Gold variant (edition of 400, same as regular comic, but signed by Alan Moore, came with signed & #'d gold certificate of authenticity)	54	108	162	432	966	1500
1-Blue variant (edition of 600, comic came with signed blue certificate of authenticity)	34	68	102	245	548	850
2-8,10: 8-Airboy preview. 6,9,10-Origin Miracleman. 10-Snyder-c	1	2	3	5	6	8
9-Shows graphic scenes of childbirth	2	4	6	8	10	12
11-14(5/87-4/88) Totleben-a	2	4	6	11	16	20
15-($1.75-c, low print) death of Kid Miracleman	6	12	18	41	76	110
16-Last Alan Moore-s; 1st $1.95-c (low print)	3	6	9	16	24	32
17-22: 17-"The Golden Age" begins, ends #22. Dave McKean-c begins, end #22; Neil Gaiman scripts in #17-24	2	4	6	11	16	20
23-"The Silver Age" begins; Barry W. Smith-c	3	6	9	16	23	30
24-Last issue; Smith-c	3	6	9	19	30	40
3-D #1 (12/85)	2	4	6	8	10	12
3-D #1 Blue variant (edition of 99)	3	6	9	21	33	45
3-D #1 Gold variant (edition of 199)	3	6	9	16	23	30

NOTE: *Miracleman 3-D #1 (12/85) (2D edition) Interior is the same as the 3-D version except in non 3-D format. Indicia are the same for both versions of the book with only the non 3-D art distinguishing this book from the standard 3-D version. Standard 3-D edition has house ad mentioning the non 3-D edition. Two known copies exist, one in the Michigan State University Special Collection Department. (No known sales)*

	NM-
Book One: A Dream of Flying (1988, $9.95, TPB) r/#1-5; Leach-c	25.00
Book One: A Dream of Flying-Hardcover (1988, $29.95) r/#1-5	70.00
Book Two: The Red King Syndrome (1990, $12.95, TPB) r/#6-10; Bolton-c	30.00
Book Two: The Red King Syndrome-Hardcover (1990, $30.95) r/#6-10	85.00

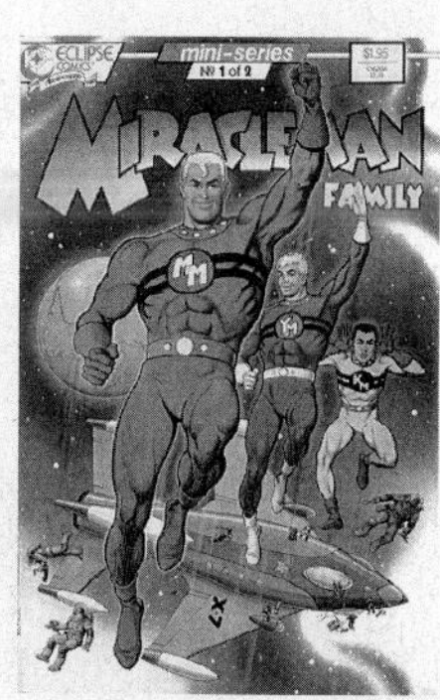

Miracleman Family #1 © ECL

Miss America Magazine V7 #24 © MAR

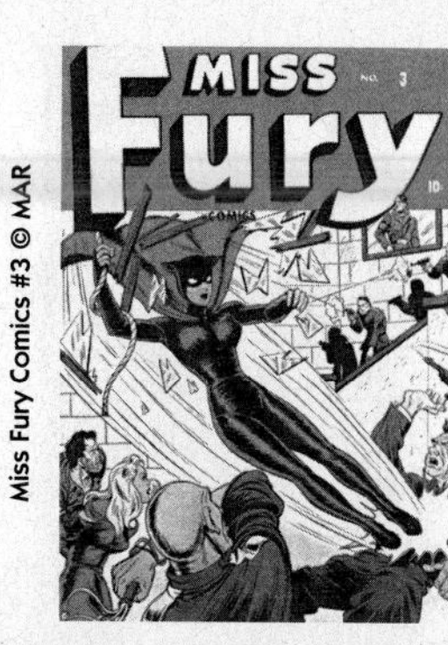

Miss Fury Comics #3 © MAR

	GD 2.0	VG 4.0	FN 6.0	VF 8.0	VF/NM 9.0	NM- 9.2

Book Three: Olympus (1990, $12.95, TPB) r/#11-16 130.00
Book Three: Olympus-Hardcover (1990, $30.95) r/#11-16 250.00
Book Four: The Golden Age (1992, $15.95, TPB) r/#17-22 30.00
Book Four: The Golden Age Hardcover (1992, $33.95) r/#17-22 50.00
Book Four: The Golden Age (1993, $12.99, TPB) new McKean-c 15.00
NOTE: *Eclipse archive copies exist for #4,5,8,17,23. Each has a small Miracleman image foil-stamped on the cover.* ***Chaykin*** *c-3.* ***Gulacy*** *c-7.* ***McKean*** *c-17-22.* ***B. Smith*** *c-23, 24.* ***Starlin*** *c-4.* ***Totleben*** *a-11-13; c-9, 11-13.* ***Truman*** *c-6.*

MIRACLEMAN
Marvel Comics: Mar, 2014 - No. 16, May, 2015 ($5.99/$4.99)

1-($5.99) Remastered reprints of Miracleman #1 and stories from Warrior #1&2; interview with Mick Anglo; reprints of 1950s Marvelman stories; Quesada-c 6.00
2-15: 2-($4.99) R/Warrior #3-5 and Kid Marvelman debut (1955) 5.00
16-($5.99) End of Book Three; bonus pencil art and design sketches 6.00
All-New Miracleman Annual 1 (2/15, $4.99) New stories; Morrison-s/Quesada-a and Milligan-s/Allred-a; bonus script and art pages 5.00

MIRACLEMAN: APOCRYPHA
Eclipse Comics: Nov, 1991 - No. 3, Feb, 1992 ($2.50, limited series)

1-3: 1-Stories by Neil Gaiman, Mark Buckingham, Alex Ross & others. 3-Stories by James Robinson, Kelley Jones, Matt Wagner, Neil Gaiman, Mark Buckingham & others 1 2 3 4 5 7
TPB (12/92, $15.95) r/#1-3; Buckingham-c 20.00

MIRACLEMAN BY GAIMAN & BUCKINGHAM (The Golden Age)
Marvel Comics: Nov, 2015 - No. 6, Mar, 2016 ($4.99)

1-6-Remastered reprints of Miracleman #17-22 with bonus script and art pages 5.00

MIRACLEMAN FAMILY
Eclipse Comics: May, 1988 - No. 2, Sept, 1988 ($1.95, lim. series, Baxter paper)

1,2: 2-Gulacy-c 5.00

MIRACLE OF THE WHITE STALLIONS, THE (See Movie Comics)

MIRROR'S EDGE (Based on the EA video game)
DC Comics (WildStorm): Dec, 2008 - No. 6, Jun, 2009 ($3.99, limited series)

1-6: 1-Origin of Faith; Rhianna Pratchett-s/Matthew Dow Smith-a 4.00
TPB (2009, $19.99) r/#1-6 20.00

MIRROR'S EDGE: EXORDIUM (Based on the EA video game)
Dark Horse Comics: Sept, 2015 - No. 6, Feb, 2016 ($3.99, limited series)

1-6: 1-Emgård-s/Häggström & Sammelin-a 4.00

MISADVENTURES OF ADAM WEST, THE
Bluewater Comics: Jul, 2011 - Feb, 2012 ($3.99)

1-4: 1-Two covers; co-created by Adam West 4.00
Second series 1-3 (1/12 - No. 3, 2/12) 4.00

MISADVENTURES OF MERLIN JONES, THE (See Movie Comics & Merlin Jones as the Monkey's Uncle under Movie Comics)

MISFIT CITY
BOOM! Studios (BOOM! Box): May, 2017 - No. 8, Dec, 2017 ($3.99)

1-8-Kirsten Smith & Kurt Lustgarten-s/Naomi Franquiz-a 4.00

MISPLACED
Image Comics: May, 2003 - No. 4, Dec, 2004 ($2.95)

1-4: 1-Three covers by Blaylock, Green and Clugston-Major; Blaylock-s/a 3.00
... @17 (12/04, $4.95) Nara from "Dead @17 " app.; Blaylock-s/a 5.00

MISS AMERICA COMICS (Miss America Magazine #2 on; also see Blonde Phantom & Marvel Mystery Comics)
Marvel Comics (20CC): 1944 (one-shot)

1-2 pgs. pin-ups 343 686 1029 2400 4200 6000

MISS AMERICA COMICS 70th ANNIVERARY SPECIAL
Marvel Comics: Aug, 2009 ($3.99, one-shot)

1-Eaglesham-c; new Miss America & Whizzer story; reps. from All Winners #9-11 5.00

MISS AMERICA MAGAZINE (Formerly Miss America; Miss America #51 on)
Miss America Publ. Corp./Marvel/Atlas (MAP): V1#2, Nov, 1944 - No. 93, Nov, 1958

V1#2-Photo-c of teenage girl in Miss America costume; Miss America, Patsy Walker (intro.) comic stories plus movie reviews & stories; intro. Buzz Baxter & Hedy Wolfe;
1 pg. origin Miss America 303 606 909 2121 3711 5300
3-5-Miss America & Patsy Walker stories 106 212 318 678 1164 1650
6-Patsy Walker only 65 130 195 416 708 1000
V2#1(4/45)-6(9/45)-Patsy Walker continues 26 52 78 154 252 350
V3#1(10/45)-6(4/46) 21 42 63 124 202 280
V4#1(5/46),2,5(9/46) 18 36 54 107 169 230
V4#3(7/46)-Liz Taylor photo-c 43 86 129 271 461 650
V4#4 (8/46; 68 pgs.), V4#6 (10/46; 92 pgs.) 16 32 48 96 151 205
V5#1(11/46)-6(4/47), V6#1(5/47)-3(7/47) 15 30 45 94 147 200
V7#1(8/47)-23(#56, 6/49) 15 30 45 90 140 190
V7#24(#57, 7/49)-Kamen-a (becomes Best Western #58 on?)
15 30 45 92 144 195
V7#25(8/49), 27-44(3/52), VII,nn(5/52) 15 30 45 88 137 185
V7#26(9/49)-All comics 15 30 45 94 147 200
V1,nn(7/52)-V1,nn(1/53)(#46-49), V7#50(Spring '53), V1#51-V7?#54(7/53),
55-93 15 30 45 85 130 175
NOTE: *Photo-c #1, 4, V2#1, 4, 5, V3#5, V4#3, 4, 6, V7#15, 16, 24, 26, 34, 37, 38. Painted c-3.* ***Powell*** *a-V7#31.*

MISS BEVERLY HILLS OF HOLLYWOOD (See Adventures of Bob Hope)
National Periodical Publ.: Mar-Apr, 1949 - No. 9, July-Aug, 1950 (52 pgs.)

1 (Meets Alan Ladd) 65 130 195 416 708 1000
2-William Holden photo on-c 48 96 144 302 514 725
3-5: 2-9-Part photo-c. 5-Bob Hope photo on-c 41 82 123 256 428 600
6,7,9: 6-Lucille Ball photo on-c 39 78 117 231 378 525
8-Reagan photo on-c 42 84 126 265 445 625
NOTE: *Beverly meets Alan Ladd in #1, Eve Arden #2, Betty Hutton #4, Bob Hope #5.*

MISS CAIRO JONES
Croyden Publishers: 1945

1-Bob Oksner daily newspaper-r (1st strip story); lingerie panels
26 52 78 154 252 350

MISS FURY
Adventure Comics: 1991 - No. 4, 1991 ($2.50, limited series)

1-4: 1-Origin; granddaughter of original Miss Fury 4.00
1-Limited ed. ($4.95) 5.00

MISS FURY
Dynamite Entertainment: 2013 - No. 11, 2014 ($3.99)

1-11: 1-Multiple covers on all; Herbert-a; origin 4.00

MISS FURY (VOLUME 2)
Dynamite Entertainment: 2016 - No. 5, 2016 ($3.99, limited series)

1-5-Corinna Bechko-s/Jonathan Lau-a; covers by Lotay & Lau 4.00

MISS FURY COMICS (Newspaper strip reprints)
Timely Comics (NPI 1/CmPI 2/MPC 3-8): Winter, 1942-43 - No. 8, Winter, 1946 (Published twice a year)

1-Origin Miss Fury by Tarpe' Mills (68 pgs.) in costume w/paper dolls with cut-out costumes
459 918 1377 3350 5925 8500
2-(60 pgs.)-In costume w/paper dolls; hooded Nazi-c
271 542 813 1734 2967 4200
3-(60 pgs.)-In costume w/paper dolls; Hitler-c 226 452 678 1446 2473 3500
4-(52 pgs.)-Classic Nazi WWII-c with giant swastika, Tojo & Hitler photo on wall; in costume, 2 pgs. w/paper dolls 194 388 582 1242 2121 3000
5-(52 pgs.)-In costume w/paper dolls; Japanese WWII-c
148 296 444 947 1624 2300
6-(52 pgs.)-Not in costume in inside stories, w/paper dolls
123 246 369 787 1344 1900
7,8-(36 pgs.)-In costume 1 pg. each; no paper dolls 100 200 300 640 1095 1550
NOTE: ***Schomburg*** *c-1, 5, 6.*

MISS FURY DIGITAL FIRST
Dynamite Entertainment: 2013 - No. 2, 2013 ($3.99, limited series)

1,2-Prints online stories. 1-Reis, Desjardins, Casas-a. 2-Casas-a 4.00

MISSION IMPOSSIBLE (TV) (Also see Wild!)
Dell Publ. Co.: May, 1967 - No. 4, Oct, 1968; No. 5, Oct, 1969 (All have photo-c)

1 9 18 27 59 117 175
2-5: 5-Reprints #1 5 10 15 35 63 90

MISSION IMPOSSIBLE (Movie) (1st Paramount Comics book)
Marvel Comics (Paramount Comics): May, 1996 ($2.95, one-shot)

1-Liefeld-c & back-up story 4.00

MISS LIBERTY (Becomes Liberty Comics)
Burten Publishing Co.: 1945 (MLJ reprints)

1-The Shield & Dusty, The Wizard, & Roy, the Super Boy app.; r/Shield-Wizard #13
40 80 120 246 411 575

MISS MELODY LANE OF BROADWAY (See The Adventures of Bob Hope)
National Periodical Publ.: Feb-Mar, 1950 - No. 3, June-July, 1950 (52 pgs.)

1-Movie stars photos app. on all-c. 77 154 231 493 847 1200
2,3: 3-Ed Sullivan photo on-c. 41 82 123 256 428 600

MISS PEACH
Dell Publishing Co.: Oct-Dec, 1963; 1969

Mr. & Mrs. X #3 © MAR

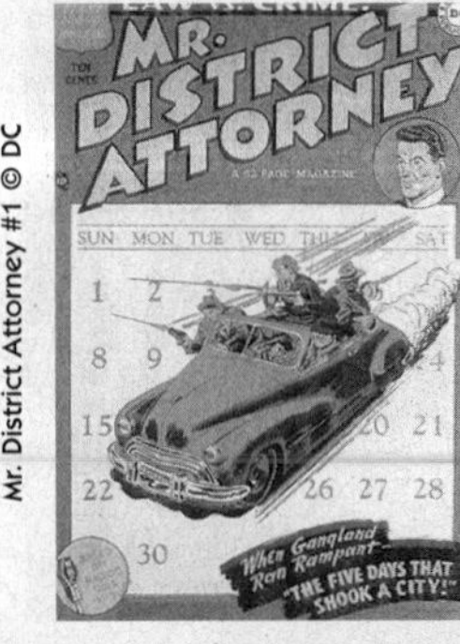

Mr. District Attorney #1 © DC

Mister Miracle (2017 series) #12 © DC

	GD	VG	FN	VF	VF/NM	NM-
	2.0	4.0	6.0	8.0	9.0	9.2

1-Jack Mendelsohn-a/script 7 14 21 44 82 120
...Tells You How to Grow (1969; 25¢)-Mel Lazarus-a; also given away (36 pgs.)
5 10 15 30 50 70

MISS PEPPER (See Meet Miss Pepper)

MISS SUNBEAM (See Little Miss...)

MISS VICTORY (See Captain Fearless #1,2, Holyoke One-Shot #3, Veri Best Sure Fire & Veri Best Sure Shot Comics)

MISTER AMERICA
Endeavor Comics: Apr, 1994 - No. 2, May, 1994 ($2.95, limited series)
1,2 4.00

MR. & MRS. BEANS
United Features Syndicate: No. 11, 1939
Single Series 11 37 74 111 222 361 500

MR. & MRS. J. EVIL SCIENTIST (TV)(See The Flintstones & Hanna-Barbera Band Wagon #3)
Gold Key: Nov, 1963 - No. 4, Sept, 1966 (Hanna-Barbera, all 12¢)
1 6 12 18 41 76 110
2-4 4 8 12 23 37 50

MR. AND MRS. X (Gambit and Rogue)
Marvel Comics: Sept, 2018 - No. 12, Aug, 2019 ($3.99)
1-12: 1-Thompson-s/Bazaldua-a; the wedding. 2,3-Deadpool app. 4-Starjammers app. 4.00

MR. ANTHONY'S LOVE CLINIC (Based on radio show)
Hillman Periodicals: Nov, 1949 - No. 5, Apr-May, 1950 (52 pgs.)
1-Photo-c on all 22 44 66 132 216 300
2 15 30 45 85 130 175
3-5 14 28 42 78 112 145

MISTER BLANK
Amaze Ink: No. 0, Jan, 1996 - No. 14, May, 2000 ($1.75/$2.95, B&W)
0-($1.75, 16 pgs.) Origin of Mr. Blank 3.00
1-14-($2.95) Chris Hicks-s/a 3.00

MR. DISTRICT ATTORNEY (Radio/TV)
National Per. Publ.: Jan-Feb, 1948 - No. 67, Jan-Feb, 1959 (1-23: 52 pgs.)
1-Howard Purcell c-5-23 (most) 103 206 309 659 1130 1600
2 45 90 135 284 480 675
3-5 31 62 93 182 296 410
6-10: 8-Rise & fall of Lucky Lynn 24 48 72 140 230 320
11-20 17 34 51 105 165 225
21-43: 43-Last pre-code (1-2/55) 14 28 42 81 118 155
44-67: 55-UFO story 12 24 36 69 97 125

MR. DISTRICT ATTORNEY (SeeThe Funnies #35)
Dell Publishing Co.: No. 13, 1942
Four Color 13-See The Funnies #35 for 1st app. 29 58 87 209 467 725

MISTER E (Also see Books of Magic limited series)
DC Comics: Jun, 1991- No. 4, Sept, 1991($1.75, limited series)
1-4-Snyder III-c/a; follow-up to Books of Magic limited series 3.00

MISTER ED, THE TALKING HORSE (TV)
Dell Publishing Co./Gold Key: Mar-May, 1962 - No. 6, Feb, 1964 (All photo-c; photo back-c: 1-6)
Four Color 1295 12 24 36 80 173 265
1(11/62) (Gold Key)-Photo-c 9 18 27 58 114 170
2-6: Photo-c 5 10 15 34 60 85
(See March of Comics #244, 260, 282, 290)

MR. GUM (From The Atomics)
Oni Press: April, 2003 ($2.99, one-shot)
1-Mike Allred-s/J. Bone-a; Madman & The Atomics app. 3.00

MR. HERO, THE NEWMATIC MAN (See Neil Gaiman's...)

MR. MAGOO (TV) (The Nearsighted..., ...& Gerald McBoing Boing 1954 issues; formerly Gerald McBoing-Boing And ...)
Dell Publishing Co.: No. 6, Nov-Jan, 1953-54; 5/54 - 3-5/62; 9-11/63 - 3-5/65
6 9 18 27 58 114 170
Four Color 561(5/54),602(11/54) 9 18 27 58 114 170
Four Color 1235(#1, 12-2/62),1305(#2, 3-5/62) 7 14 21 48 89 130
3(9-11/63) - 5 6 12 18 42 79 115
Four Color 1235(12-536-505)(3-5/65)-2nd Printing 5 10 15 35 63 90

MR. MAJESTIC (See WildC.A.T.S.)
DC Comics (WildStorm): Sept, 1999 - No. 9, May, 2000 ($2.50)
1-9: 1-McGuinness-a/Casey & Holguin-s. 2-Two covers 3.00
TPB (2002, $14.95) r/#1-6 & Wildstorm Spotlight #1 15.00

MISTER MIRACLE (1st series) (See Cancelled Comic Cavalcade)
National Periodical Publications/DC Comics: 3-4/71 - V4#18, 2-3/74; V5#19, 9/77 - V6#25, 8-9/78; 1987 (Fourth World)
1-1st app. Mr. Miracle (#1-3 are 15¢) 15 30 45 105 233 360
2,3: 2-Intro. Granny Goodness. 3-Last 15¢ issue 5 10 15 35 63 90
4-Intro. Barda; Boy Commandos-r begin; (52 pgs.) 16 32 48 112 249 385
5-8: All 52 pgs. 5 10 15 31 53 75
9-18: 9-Origin Mr. Miracle; Darkseid cameo. 15-Intro/1st app. Shilo Norman. 18-Barda & Scott Free wed; New Gods app. & Darkseid cameo; Last Kirby issue.
3 6 9 16 23 30
19-25 (1977-78) 2 4 6 8 10 12
Special 1(1987, $1.25, 52 pgs.) 1 2 3 5 6 8
Jack Kirby's Fourth World TPB ('01, $12.95) B&W&Grey-toned reprint of #11-18; Mark Evanier intro. 13.00
Jack Kirby's Mister Miracle TPB ('98, $12.95) B&W&Grey-toned reprint of #1-10; David Copperfield intro. 13.00
NOTE: ***Austin** a-19i. **Ditko** a-6r. **Golden** a-23-25p; c-25p. **Heath** a-24i, 25i; c-25i. **Kirby** a(p)/c-1-18. **Nasser** a-19i. **Rogers** a-19-22p; c-19, 20p, 21p, 22-24. 4-8 contain **Simon & Kirby** Boy Commandos reprints from Detective 82,76, Boy Commandos 1, 3 & Detective 64 in that order.*

MISTER MIRACLE (2nd Series) (See Justice League)
DC Comics: Jan, 1989 - No. 28, June, 1991 ($1.00/$1.25)
1-28: 13,14-Lobo app. 22-1st new Mr. Miracle w/new costume 4.00

MISTER MIRACLE (3rd Series)
DC Comics: Apr, 1996 - No. 7, Oct, 1996 ($1.95)
1-7: 2-Vs. JLA. 6-Simonson-c 4.00

MISTER MIRACLE (4th Series)
DC Comics: Oct, 2017 - No. 12, Jan, 2019 ($3.99, limited series)
1-Tom King-s/Mitch Gerads-a; covers by Derington & Gerads 22.00
1-Director's Cut (4/18, $5.99) r/#1 B&W art; bonus script 6.00
2-12-King-s/Gerads-a. 7-Jacob born 5.00

MR. MIRACLE (See Capt. Fearless #1 & Holyoke One-Shot #4)

MR. MONSTER (1st Series)(Doc Stearn... #7 on; See Airboy-Mr. Monster Special, Dark Horse Presents, Super Duper Comics & Vanguard Illustrated #7)
Eclipse Comics: Jan, 1985 - No. 10, June, 1987 ($1.75, Baxter paper)
1,3: 1-1st story-r from Vanguard Ill. #7(1st app.). 3-Alan Moore scripts; Wolverton-r/Weird Mysteries #5. 5.00
2-Dave Stevens-c 2 4 6 8 10 12
4-10: 6-Ditko-r/Fantastic Fears #5 plus new Giffen-a. 10- "6-D" issue 4.00

MR. MONSTER
Dark Horse Comics: Feb, 1988 - No. 8, July, 1991 ($1.75, B&W)
1-7 3.00
8-($4.95, 60 pgs.)-Origins conclusion 5.00

MR. MONSTER ATTACKS! (Doc Stearn...)
Tundra Publ.: Aug, 1992 - No. 3, Oct, 1992 ($3.95, limited series, 32 pgs.)
1-3: Michael T. Gilbert-a/scripts; Gilbert/Dorman painted-c 4.00

MR. MONSTER PRESENTS (CRACK-A-BOOM!)
Caliber Comics: 1997 - No. 3, 1997 ($2.95, B&W&Red, limited series)
1-3: Michael T. Gilbert-a/scripts: 1-Wraparound-c 3.00

MR. MONSTER'S GAL FRIDAY...KELLY!
Image Comics: Jan, 2000 - No. 3, May, 2004 ($3.50, B&W)
1-3-Michael T. Gilbert-c; story & art by various. 3-Alan Moore-s 3.50

MR. MONSTER'S SUPER-DUPER SPECIAL
Eclipse Comics: May, 1986 - No. 8, July, 1987
1-(5/86)...3-D High Octane Horror #1 5.00
1-(5/86)...2-D version, 100 copies 2 4 6 11 16 20
2-(8/86)...High Octane Horror #1, 3-(9/86)...True Crime #1, 4-(11/86)...True Crime #2, 5-(1/87)...Hi-Voltage Super Science #1, 6-(3/87)...High Shock Schlock #1, 7-(5/87)...High Shock Schlock #2, 8-(7/87)...Weird Tales Of The Future #1 4.00
NOTE: ***Jack Cole** r-3, 4. **Evans** a-2r. **Kubert** a-1r. **Powell** a-5r. **Wolverton** a-2r, 7r, 8r.*

MR. MONSTER VS. GORZILLA
Image Comics: July, 1998 ($2.95, one-shot)
1-Michael T. Gilbert-a 3.00

MR. MONSTER: WORLDS WAR TWO
Atomeka Press: 2004 ($6.99, one-shot)
nn-Michael T. Gilbert-s/George Freeman-a; two covers by Horley & Dorman 7.00

Mister Mystery #5 © Media Pub.

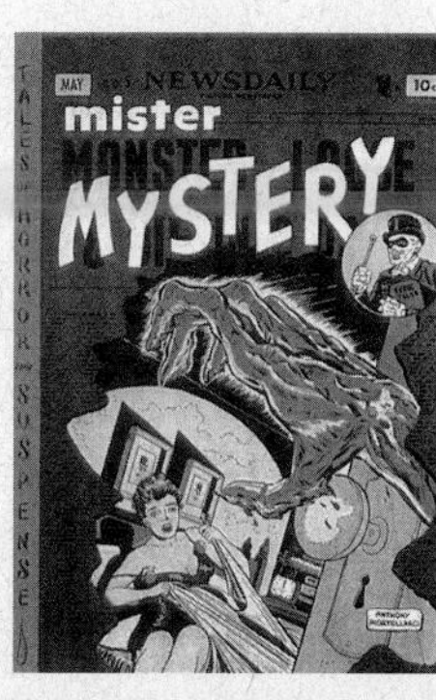

Mister X V2 #10 © Dean Motter

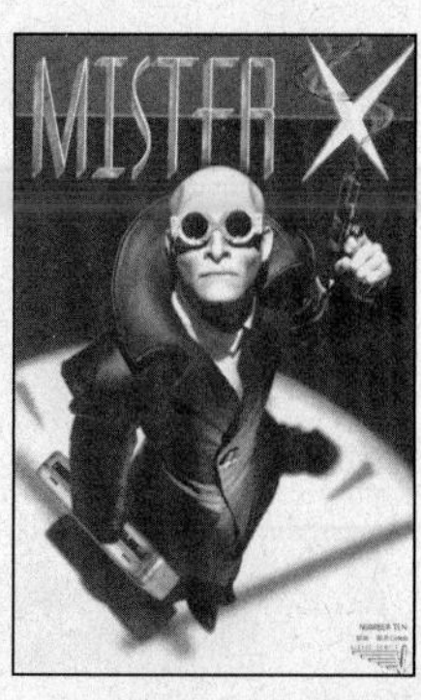

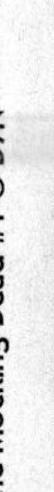
The Mocking Dead #1 © DYN

GD VG FN VF VF/NM NM-
2.0 4.0 6.0 8.0 9.0 9.2

MR. MUSCLES (Formerly Blue Beetle #18-21)
Charlton Comics: No. 22, Mar, 1956; No. 23, Aug, 1956
22,23 10 20 30 58 79 100

MR. MXYZPTLK (VILLAINS)
DC Comics: Feb, 1998 ($1.95, one-shot)
1-Grant-s/Morgan-a/Pearson-c 3.00

MISTER MYSTERY (Tales of Horror and Suspense)
Mr. Publ. (Media Publ.) No. 1-3/SPM Publ./Stanmore (Aragon): Sept, 1951 - No. 19, Oct, 1954
1-Kurtzman-*esque* horror story 148 296 444 947 1624 2300
2,3-Kurtzman-*esque* story. 3-Anti-Wertham edit. 81 162 243 518 884 1250
4-Bondage-c 123 246 369 787 1344 1900
5,8,10 81 162 243 518 884 1250
6-Classic torture-c 306 612 918 2198 3849 5500
7- "The Brain Bats of Venus" by Wolverton; partially re-used in Weird Tales of the Future #7
306 612 918 2198 3849 5500
9-Nostrand-a 90 180 270 576 988 1400
11-(5-6/53) Wolverton "Robot Woman" story/Weird Mysteries #2, cut up, rewritten, retitled "Beauty & the Beast"" & partially redrawn; girl in "Beauty & the Beast", splash pg. redrawn from cover of Weird Tales of the Future #4 (11/52); woman on pg. 6 taken from cover of Weird Tales of the Future #2 (6/52) 306 612 918 2198 3849 5500
12-Classic injury to eye-c 423 846 1269 3000 5250 7500
13-16,19: 15- "Living Dead" junkie story. 16-Bondage-c. 19-Reprints
63 126 189 403 689 975
17-Severed heads-c 116 232 346 742 1271 1800
18- "Robot Woman" by Wolverton reprinted from Weird Mysteries #2; decapitation, bondage-c
135 270 405 864 1482 2100

NOTE: ***Andru** a-1, 2p, 3p. **Andru/Esposito** c-1-3. **Baily** c-10-18(most). **Mortellaro** c-5-7. Bondage c-7, 16. Some issues have graphic dismemberment scenes.*

MR. PEABODY AND SHERMAN (Based on the 2014 Dreamworks movie)
IDW Publishing: Nov, 2013 - No. 4, Jan, 2014 ($3.99)
1-4: 1-Fisch-s/Monlongo-a; 3 covers. 2-Three covers. 3,4-Two covers 4.00

MR. PUNCH
DC Comics (Vertigo): 1994 ($24.95, one-shot)
nn (Hard-c)-Gaiman scripts; McKean-c/a 40.00
nn (Soft-c) 18.00

MISTER Q (See Mighty Midget Comics & Our Flag Comics #5)

MR. RISK (Formerly All Romances; Men Against Crime #3 on)(Also see Our Flag Comics & Super-Mystery Comics)
Ace Magazines: No. 7, Oct, 1950; No. 2, Dec, 1950
7,2 15 30 45 84 127 170

MR. SCARLET & PINKY (See Mighty Midget Comics)

MR. T
APComics: May, 2005 ($3.50)
1-Chris Bunting-s/Neil Edwards-a 3.50

MR. T AND THE T-FORCE
Now Comics: June, 1993 - No. 10, May, 1994 ($1.95, color)
1-10-Newsstand editions: 1-7-polybagged with photo trading card in each. 1,2-Neal Adams-c/a(p). 3-Dave Dorman painted-c 4.00
1-10-Direct Sale editions polybagged w/line drawn trading cards. 1-Contains gold foil trading card by Neal Adams 4.00

MISTER TERRIFIC (DC New 52)(Leads into Earth 2 series)
DC Comics: Nov, 2011 - No. 8, Jun, 2012 ($2.99)
1-8: 1-Wallace-s/Gugliotta-a/JG Jones-c; origin re-told. 2-Intro. Brainstorm 3.00

MISTER UNIVERSE (Professional wrestler)
Mr. Publications Media Publ. (Stanmor, Aragon): July, 1951; No. 2, Oct, 1951 - No. 5, April, 1952
1 26 52 78 154 252 350
2- "Jungle That Time Forgot", (24 pg. story); Andru/Esposito-c
15 30 45 90 140 190
3-Marijuana story 15 30 45 90 140 190
4,5-"Goes to War" cover/stories (Korean War) 14 28 43 78 112 145

MISTER X (See Vortex)
Mr. Publications/Vortex Comics/Caliber V3#1 on: 6/84 - No. 14, 8/88 ($1.50/$2.25, direct sales, coated paper);V2#1, Apr, 1989 - V2#12, Mar, 1990 ($2.00/$2.50, B&W, newsprint) V3#1, 1996 - No. 4, 1996 ($2.95, B&W)
1-14: 11-Dave McKean story & art (6 pgs.) 4.00
V2 #1-12: 1-11 (Second Coming, B&W): 1-Four diff.-c. 10-Photo-c 3.00
V3 #1-4 3.00
Return of... ($11.95, graphic novel)-r/V1#1-4 12.00
Return of... ($34.95, hardcover limited edition)-r/1-4 35.00
Special (no date, 1990?) 3.00

MISTER X
Dark Horse Comics: Mar, 2013 ($2.99, one-shot)
...: Hard Candy (3/13) Dean Motter-s/a 3.00

MISTER X: CONDEMNED
Dark Horse Comics: Dec, 2008 - No. 4, Mar, 2009 ($3.50, limited series)
1-4-Dean Motter-s/a 3.50

MISTER X: EVICTION
Dark Horse Comics: May, 2013 - No. 3, Jul, 2013 ($3.99, limited series)
1-3-Dean Motter-s/a 4.00

MISTER X: RAZED
Dark Horse Comics: Feb, 2015 - No. 4, May, 2015 ($3.99, limited series)
1-4-Dean Motter-s/a 4.00

MISTY
Marvel Comics (Star Comics): Dec, 1985 - No. 6, May, 1986 (Limited series)
1-6: Millie The Model's niece 4.00

MITZI COMICS (Becomes Mitzi's Boy Friend #2-7)(See All Teen)
Timely Comics: Spring, 1948 (one-shot)
1-Kurtzman's "Hey Look" plus 3 pgs. "Giggles 'n' Grins"
61 122 183 390 670 950

MITZI'S BOY FRIEND (Formerly Mitzi Comics; becomes Mitzi's Romances)
Marvel Comics (TCI): No. 2, June, 1948 - No. 7, April, 1949
2 29 58 87 172 281 390
3-7 21 42 63 122 199 275

MITZI'S ROMANCES (Formerly Mitzi's Boy Friend)
Timely/Marvel Comics (TCI): No. 8, June, 1949 - No. 10, Dec, 1949
8-Becomes True Life Tales #8 (10/49) on? 21 42 63 124 202 280
9,10: 10-Painted-c 18 36 54 107 169 230

MNEMOVORE
DC Comics (Vertigo): Jun, 2005 - No. 6, Nov, 2005 ($2.99, limited series)
1-6-Rodionoff & Fawkes-s/Huddleston-a/c 3.00

MOBY DICK (See Feature Presentations #6, King Classics, and Classic Comics #5)
Dell Publishing Co.: No. 717, Aug, 1956
Four Color 717-Movie, Gregory Peck photo-c 8 16 24 52 99 145

MOBY DUCK (See Donald Duck #112 & Walt Disney Showcase #2,11)
Gold Key (Disney): Oct, 1967 - No. 11, Oct, 1970; No. 12, Jan, 1974 - No. 30, Feb, 1978
1-Three Little Pigs app. 3 6 9 20 31 42
2-5: 2-Beagle Boys app. 5-Captain Hook app. 2 4 6 11 16 20
6-11: 6-Huey, Dewey & Louie app. 2 4 6 9 13 16
12-30: 21,30-r 1 3 4 6 8 10

MOCKINGBIRD (From S.H.I.E.L.D.)
Marvel Comics: May, 2016 - No. 8, Dec, 2016 ($3.99)
1-8: 1-4-Chelsea Cain-s/Kate Niemczyk-a/Joëlle Jones-c. 5-Moustafa-a. 6-Civil War II tie-in 4.00
... S.H.I.E.L.D. 50th Anniversary (11/15, $3.99) Joëlle Jones-a; back-up with Red Widow 4.00

MOCKING DEAD, THE
Dynamite Entertainment: 2013 - No. 5, 2014 ($3.99, B&W, limited series)
1-5: 1-Fred Van Lente-s/Max Dunbar-a 4.00

MODEL FUN (With Bobby Benson)
Harle Publications: No. 2, Fall, 1954 - No. 5, July, 1955
2-Bobby Benson 7 14 21 37 46 55
3-5-Bobby Benson 5 10 15 24 29 34

MODELING WITH MILLIE (Formerly Life With Millie)
Atlas/Marvel Comics (Male Publ.): No. 21, Feb, 1963 - No. 54, June, 1967
21 9 18 27 61 123 185
22-30 6 12 18 38 69 100
31-53 5 10 15 34 60 85
54-Last issue; Gears-c & 6 pg. story; Beatles swipe imitators; FF #63 comic appears in story; "Millie the Marvel" 6 pg. story as super-hero 5 10 15 35 63 90

MODELS, INC.
Marvel Comics: Oct, 2009 - No. 4, Jan, 2010 ($3.99, limited series)
1-4-Millie the Model, Patsy Walker, Mary Jane Watson app.; Land-c. 1-Tim Gunn app. 4.00

Modern Comics #51 © QUA

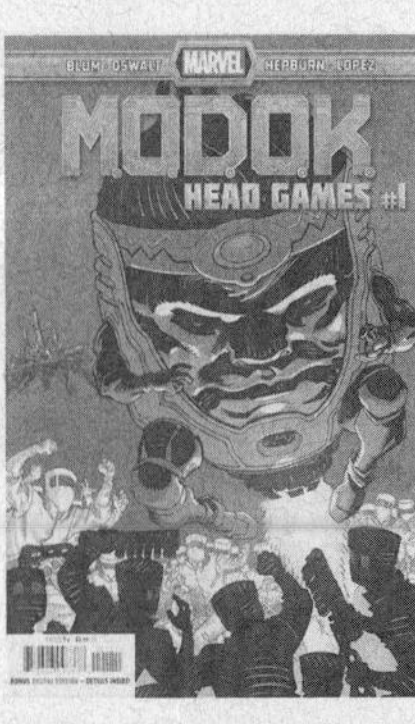

M.O.D.O.K.: Head Games #1 © MAR

The Monolith #1 © Palmiotti, Gray & DC

MODERN COMICS (Formerly Military Comics #1-43)
Quality Comics Group: No. 44, Nov, 1945 - No. 102, Oct, 1950

	GD 2.0	VG 4.0	FN 6.0	VF 8.0	VF/NM 9.0	NM- 9.2
44-Blackhawk continues	54	108	162	343	574	825
45-52: 49-1st app. Fear, Lady Adventuress	38	76	114	228	369	510
53-Torchy by Ward begins (9/46)	43	86	129	271	461	650
54-60: 55-J. Cole-a	32	64	96	192	314	435
61-Classic-c	39	78	117	240	395	550
62-64,66-77,79,80: 73-J. Cole-a	31	62	93	182	296	410
65-Classic Grim Reaper Skull-c	63	126	189	403	689	975
78-1st app. Madame Butterfly	36	72	108	211	343	475
81-99,101: 82,83-One pg. J. Cole-a. 83-Last 52 pg. issue 99-Blackhawks on the moon-c/story	31	62	93	182	296	410
100	32	64	96	192	314	435
102-(Scarce)-J. Cole-a; Spirit by Eisner app.	39	78	117	240	395	550

NOTE: ***Al Bryant** c-44-51, 54, 55, 66, 69. **Jack Cole** a-55, 73. **Crandall** Blackhawk-#46, 47, 50, 51, 54, 56, 58-60, 64, 67-70, 73, 74, 76-78, 80-83; c-60-65, 67, 68, 70-95. **Crandall/Cuidera** c-56-59, 96-102. **Gustavson** a-47, 49. **Ward** Blackhawk-#52, 53, 55 (15 pgs. each). Torchy in #53-102; by **Ward** only in #53-89(9/49); by **Gil Fox** #92, 93, 102.*

MODERN FANTASY
Dark Horse Comics: Jun, 2018 - No. 4, Sept, 2018 ($3.99, limited series)

	GD 2.0	VG 4.0	FN 6.0	VF 8.0	VF/NM 9.0	NM- 9.2
1-4-Rafer Roberts-s/Kristen Gudsnuk-a						4.00

MODERN LOVE
E. C. Comics: June-July, 1949 - No. 8, Aug-Sept, 1950

	GD 2.0	VG 4.0	FN 6.0	VF 8.0	VF/NM 9.0	NM- 9.2
1-Feldstein, Ingels-a	116	232	348	742	1271	1800
2-Craig/Feldstein-c/s	84	168	252	538	919	1300
3	68	136	204	435	743	1050
4-6 (Scarce): 4-Bra/panties panels	92	184	276	593	1009	1425
7	68	136	204	435	743	1050
8-Bill Gaines/Al Feldstein app. in comic industry parody sty.	81	162	243	518	884	1250

NOTE: ***Craig** a-3. **Feldstein** a-in most issues; c-1, 2i, 3-8. **Harrison** a-4. **Iger** a-6-8. **Ingels** a-1, 2, 4-7. **Palais** a-5. **Wood** a-7. **Wood/Harrison** a-5-7. (Canadian reprints known; see Table of Contents.)*

MODERN WARFARE 2: GHOST (Based on the videogame)
DC Comics (WildStorm): Jan, 2010 - No. 6, Sept, 2010 ($3.99, limited series)

	GD 2.0	VG 4.0	FN 6.0	VF 8.0	VF/NM 9.0	NM- 9.2
1-6: 1-Two covers; Lapham-s/West-a						4.00
TPB (2010, $17.99) r/#1-6; cover sketches and sketch art						18.00

MOD LOVE
Western Publishing Co.: 1967 (50¢, 36 pgs.)

	GD 2.0	VG 4.0	FN 6.0	VF 8.0	VF/NM 9.0	NM- 9.2
1-(Low print)	8	16	24	56	108	160

MODNIKS, THE
Gold Key: Aug, 1967 - No. 2, Aug, 1970

	GD 2.0	VG 4.0	FN 6.0	VF 8.0	VF/NM 9.0	NM- 9.2
10206-708(#1)	3	6	9	21	33	45
2	3	6	9	15	22	28

M.O.D.O.K. ASSASSIN (Secret Wars tie-in)
Marvel Comics: Jul, 2015 - No. 5, Nov, 2015 ($3.99, limited series)

	GD 2.0	VG 4.0	FN 6.0	VF 8.0	VF/NM 9.0	NM- 9.2
1-5-Yost-s/Pinna-a; Angela app. 1-Bullseye, Baron Mordo & Clea app.						4.00

M.O.D.O.K.: HEAD GAMES
Marvel Comics: Feb, 2021 - No. 4 ($3.99, limited series)

	GD 2.0	VG 4.0	FN 6.0	VF 8.0	VF/NM 9.0	NM- 9.2
1-3-Blum & Oswalt-s/Hepburn-a; Monica Rappaccini app. 2-Tony Stark app. 3-Gwenpool app.						4.00

M.O.D.O.K.: REIGN DELAY
Marvel Comics: Nov, 2009 ($3.99, one-shot)

	GD 2.0	VG 4.0	FN 6.0	VF 8.0	VF/NM 9.0	NM- 9.2
1-M.O.D.O.K. cartoony humor stories from Marvel Digital Comics; Ryan Dunlavey-s/a						4.00

MOD SQUAD (TV)
Dell Publishing Co.: Jan, 1969 - No. 3, Oct, 1969 - No. 8, April, 1971

	GD 2.0	VG 4.0	FN 6.0	VF 8.0	VF/NM 9.0	NM- 9.2
1-Photo-c	7	14	21	44	82	120
2-4: 2-4-Photo-c	4	8	12	27	44	60
5-8: 8-Photo-c; Reprints #2	4	8	12	23	37	50

MOD WHEELS
Gold Key: Mar, 1971 - No. 19, Jan, 1976

	GD 2.0	VG 4.0	FN 6.0	VF 8.0	VF/NM 9.0	NM- 9.2
1	4	8	12	25	40	55
2-9	3	6	9	16	23	30
10-19: 11,15-Extra 16 pgs. ads	3	6	9	14	19	24

MOE & SHMOE COMICS
O. S. Publ. Co.: Spring, 1948 - No. 2, Summer, 1948

	GD 2.0	VG 4.0	FN 6.0	VF 8.0	VF/NM 9.0	NM- 9.2
1	11	22	33	62	86	110
2	8	16	24	40	50	60

MOEBIUS (Graphic novel)
Marvel Comics (Epic Comics): Oct, 1987 - No. 6, 1988; No. 7, 1990; No. 8, 1991; No. 9, 1994 ($9.95, 8x11", mature)

	GD 2.0	VG 4.0	FN 6.0	VF 8.0	VF/NM 9.0	NM- 9.2
1	4	8	12	27	44	60
2	5	10	15	33	57	80
3-(1st & 2nd printings, $12.95)	6	12	18	41	76	110
4-6,8	3	6	9	21	33	45
7,0: 0 (1990, $12.95)	4	8	12	23	37	50
9-(1994) Printed 3 years after #8	7	14	21	46	86	125
Moebius I-Signed & #'d hard-c ($45.95, Graphitti Designs, 1,500 copies printed)-r/#1-3	8	16	24	51	96	140

MOEBIUS COMICS
Caliber: May, 1996 - No. 6 ($2.95, B&W)

	GD 2.0	VG 4.0	FN 6.0	VF 8.0	VF/NM 9.0	NM- 9.2
1,5,6-Moebius-c/a on all; William Stout-a	3	6	9	14	20	25
2-4-Moebius-c/a	2	4	6	9	12	15

MOEBIUS: THE MAN FROM CIGURI
Dark Horse Comics: 1996 ($7.95, digest-size)

	GD 2.0	VG 4.0	FN 6.0	VF 8.0	VF/NM 9.0	NM- 9.2
nn-Moebius-c/a	4	8	12	23	37	50

MOLLY MANTON'S ROMANCES (Romantic Affairs #3)
Marvel Comics (SePI): Sept, 1949 - No. 2, Dec, 1949 (52 pgs.)

	GD 2.0	VG 4.0	FN 6.0	VF 8.0	VF/NM 9.0	NM- 9.2
1-Photo-c (becomes Blaze the Wonder Collie #2 (10/49) on? & Molly Manton's Romances #2	25	50	75	150	245	340
2-Titled "Romances of…"; photo-c	16	32	48	98	154	210

MOLLY O'DAY (Super Sleuth)
Avon Periodicals: February, 1945 (1st Avon comic)

	GD 2.0	VG 4.0	FN 6.0	VF 8.0	VF/NM 9.0	NM- 9.2
1-Molly O'Day, The Enchanted Dagger by Tuska (r/Yankee #1), Capt'n Courage, Corporal Grant app.	81	162	243	518	884	1250

MOMENT OF SILENCE
Marvel Comics: Feb, 2002 ($3.50, one-shot)

	GD 2.0	VG 4.0	FN 6.0	VF 8.0	VF/NM 9.0	NM- 9.2
1-Tributes to the heroes and victims of Sept. 11; s/a by various						3.50

MONARCHY, THE (Also see The Authority and StormWatch)
DC Comics (WildStorm): Apr, 2001 - No. 12, May, 2002 ($2.50)

	GD 2.0	VG 4.0	FN 6.0	VF 8.0	VF/NM 9.0	NM- 9.2
1-12: 1-McCrea & Leach-a/Young-s						3.00
Bullets Over Babylon TPB (2001, $12.95) r/#1-4, Authority #21						13.00

MONKEES, THE (TV)(Also see Circus Boy, Groovy, Not Brand Echh #3, Teen-Age Talk, Teen Beam & Teen Beat)
Dell Publishing Co.: March, 1967 - No. 17, Oct, 1969

	GD 2.0	VG 4.0	FN 6.0	VF 8.0	VF/NM 9.0	NM- 9.2
1-Photo-c	10	20	30	69	147	225
2-17: All photo-c. 17-Reprints #1	6	12	18	38	69	100

MONKEY AND THE BEAR, THE
Atlas Comics (ZPC): Sept, 1953 - No. 3, Jan, 1954

	GD 2.0	VG 4.0	FN 6.0	VF 8.0	VF/NM 9.0	NM- 9.2
1-Howie Post-c/a in all; funny animal	14	28	42	81	118	155
2,3	10	20	30	56	76	95

MONKEYMAN AND O'BRIEN (Also see Dark Horse Presents #80, 100-5, Gen[13]/..., Hellboy: Seed of Destruction, & San Diego Comic Con #2)
Dark Horse Comics (Legend): Jul, 1996 - No. 3, Sept, 1996 ($2.95, lim. series)

	GD 2.0	VG 4.0	FN 6.0	VF 8.0	VF/NM 9.0	NM- 9.2
1-3: New stories; Art Adams-c/a/scripts						4.00
nn-(2/96, $2.95)-r/back-up stories from Hellboy: Seed of Destruction; Adams-c/a/scripts						4.00

MONKEYSHINES COMICS
Ace Periodicals/Publishers Specialists/Current Books/Unity Publ.: Summer, 1944 - No. 27, July, 1949

	GD 2.0	VG 4.0	FN 6.0	VF 8.0	VF/NM 9.0	NM- 9.2
1-Funny animal	19	38	57	109	172	235
2-(Aut/44)	12	24	36	69	97	125
3-10: 3-(Win/44)	11	22	33	60	83	105
11-18,20-27: 23,24-Fago-c/a	9	18	27	52	69	85
19-Frazetta-a	11	22	33	60	83	105

MONKEY'S UNCLE, THE (See Merlin Jones As... under Movie Comics)

MONOLITH, THE
DC Comics: Apr, 2004 - No. 12, Mar, 2005 ($3.50/$2.95)

	GD 2.0	VG 4.0	FN 6.0	VF 8.0	VF/NM 9.0	NM- 9.2
1-($3.50) Palmiotti & Gray-s/Winslade-a						3.50
2-12-($2.95): 6-8-Batman app.; Coker-a						3.00
...: Volume One HC (Image Comics, 2012, $17.99) r/#1-4; intro. by Jim Steranko						18.00

MONROES, THE (TV)
Dell Publishing Co.: Apr, 1967

	GD 2.0	VG 4.0	FN 6.0	VF 8.0	VF/NM 9.0	NM- 9.2
1-Photo-c	3	6	9	17	26	35

Monster Hunters #11 © CC

Monstress #5 © Liu & Takeda

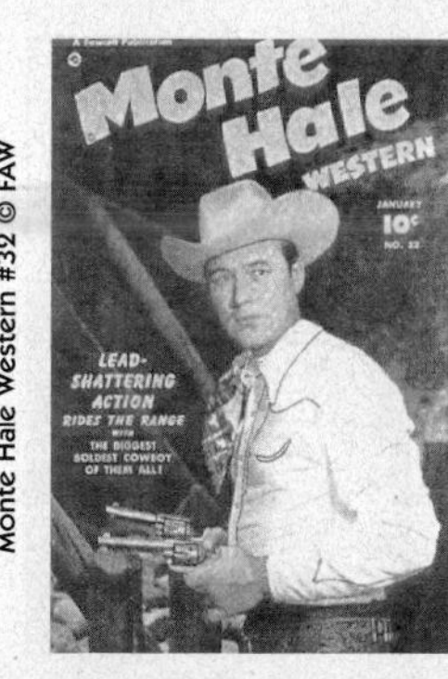

Monte Hale Western #32 © FAW

MONSTER
Fiction House Magazines: 1953 - No. 2, 1953

	GD 2.0	VG 4.0	FN 6.0	VF 8.0	VF/NM 9.0	NM- 9.2
1-Dr. Drew by Grandenetti; reprint from Rangers Comics #48; Whitman-c	82	164	246	528	902	1275
2-Whitman-c	54	108	162	343	574	825

MONSTER CRIME COMICS (Also see Crime Must Stop)
Hillman Periodicals: Oct, 1952 (15¢, 52 pgs.)

	GD 2.0	VG 4.0	FN 6.0	VF 8.0	VF/NM 9.0	NM- 9.2
1 (Scarce)	232	464	696	1485	2543	3600

MONSTER HOUSE (Companion to the 2006 movie)
IDW Publishing: June, 2006 ($7.99, one-shot)

nn-Two stories about Bones and Skull by Joshua Dysart and Simeon Wilkins 8.00

MONSTER HOWLS (Magazine)
Humor-Vision: December, 1966 (Satire) (35¢, 68 pgs.)

	GD 2.0	VG 4.0	FN 6.0	VF 8.0	VF/NM 9.0	NM- 9.2
1-John Severin-a	5	10	15	34	60	85

MONSTER HUNTERS
Charlton Comics: Aug, 1975 - No. 9, Jan, 1977; No. 10, Oct, 1977 - No. 18, Feb, 1979

	GD 2.0	VG 4.0	FN 6.0	VF 8.0	VF/NM 9.0	NM- 9.2
1-Howard-a; Newton-c; 1st Countess Von Bludd and Colonel Whiteshroud	3	6	9	17	26	35
2-Sutton-c/a; Ditko-a	3	6	9	14	19	24
3,4,5,7: 4-Sutton-c/a	2	4	6	9	12	15
6,8,10: 6,8,10-Ditko-a	2	4	6	10	14	18
9,11,12	1	3	4	6	8	10
13,15,18-Ditko-c/a. 18-Sutton-a	2	4	6	10	14	18
14-Special all-Ditko issue	3	6	9	16	24	32
16,17-Sutton-a	2	3	4	6	8	10
1,2 (Modern Comics reprints, 1977)						6.00

NOTE: *Ditko a-2, 6, 8, 10, 13-15r, 18r; c-13-15, 18.* ***Howard*** *a-1, 3, 17; r-13.* ***Morisi*** *a-1.* ***Staton*** *a-1, 13.* ***Sutton*** *a-2, 4; c-2, 4; r-16-18.* ***Zeck*** *a-4-9. Reprints in #12-18.*

MONSTER MADNESS (Magazine)
Marvel Comics: 1972 - No. 3, 1973 (60¢, B&W)

	GD 2.0	VG 4.0	FN 6.0	VF 8.0	VF/NM 9.0	NM- 9.2
1-3: Stories by "Sinister" Stan Lee. 1-Frankenstein photo-c. 2-Son of Frankenstein photo-c. 3-Bride of Frankenstein photo-c	4	8	12	27	44	60

MONSTER MAN
Image Comics (Action Planet): Sept, 1997 ($2.95, B&W)

1-Mike Manley-c/s/a 3.00

MONSTER MASTERWORKS
Marvel Comics: 1989 ($12.95, TPB)

nn-Reprints 1960's monster stories; art by Kirby, Ditko, Ayers, Everett 20.00

MONSTER MATINEE
Chaos! Comics: Oct, 1997 - No. 3, Oct, 1997 ($2.50, limited series)

1-3: pin-ups 3.00

MONSTER MENACE
Marvel Comics: Dec, 1993 - No. 4, Mar, 1994 ($1.25, limited series)

1-4: Pre-code Atlas horror reprints. 6.00

NOTE: ***Ditko****-r &* ***Kirby****-r in all.*

MONSTER OF FRANKENSTEIN (See Frankenstein and Essential Monster of Frankenstein)

MONSTER PILE-UP
Image Comics: Aug, 2008 ($1.99)

1-New short stories of Astounding Wolf-Man, Firebreather, Perhapanauts, Proof 3.00

MONSTERS ATTACK (Magazine)
Globe Communications Corpse: Sept, 1989 - No. 5, Dec, 1990 (B&W)

	GD 2.0	VG 4.0	FN 6.0	VF 8.0	VF/NM 9.0	NM- 9.2
1-5-Ditko, Morrow, J. Severin-a. 5-Toth, Morrow-a	1	2	3	4	5	7

MONSTERS, INC. (Based on the Disney/Pixar movie)
BOOM! Studios: Jun, 2009 - No. 4, Nov, 2009 ($2.99, limited series)

...: Laugh Factory 1-4: 1,3-Three covers. 2,4-Two covers 3.00

MONSTERS, INC. (Based on the Disney/Pixar movie)
Marvel Worldwide Inc.: Feb, 2013 - No. 2 ($2.99, limited series)

1,2-Movie adaptation 3.00
...: A Perfect Date (2013, $2.99) 3.00
...: The Humanween Party (4/13, $2.99) 3.00

MONSTERS ON THE PROWL (Chamber of Darkness #1-8)
Marvel Comics Group (No. 13,14: 52 pgs.): No. 9, 2/71 - No. 27, 11/73; No. 28, 6/74 - No. 30, 10/74

	GD 2.0	VG 4.0	FN 6.0	VF 8.0	VF/NM 9.0	NM- 9.2
9-Barry Smith inks	5	10	15	31	53	75
10-12,15: 12-Last 15¢ issue	3	6	9	19	30	40
13,14-(52 pgs.)	4	8	12	22	35	48
16-(4/72)-King Kull 4th app.; Severin-c	4	8	12	22	35	48
17-30	3	6	9	16	24	32

NOTE: ***Ditko*** *r-9, 14, 16.* ***Kirby*** *r-10-17, 21, 23, 25, 27, 28, 30; c-9, 25.* ***Kirby/Ditko*** *r-14, 17-20, 22, 24, 26, 29.* ***Marie/John Severin*** *a-16(Kull). 9-13, 15 contain one new story. Woodish art by* ***Reese****-11. King Kull created by Robert E. Howard.*

MONSTERS TO LAUGH WITH (Magazine) (Becomes Monsters Unlimited #4)
Marvel Comics Group: 1964 - No. 3, 1965 (B&W)

	GD 2.0	VG 4.0	FN 6.0	VF 8.0	VF/NM 9.0	NM- 9.2
1-Humor by Stan Lee	7	14	21	49	92	135
2,3: 3-Frankenstein photo-c	5	10	15	31	53	75

MONSTERS UNLEASHED (Magazine)
Marvel Comics Group: July, 1973 - No. 11, Apr, 1975; Summer, 1975 (B&W)

	GD 2.0	VG 4.0	FN 6.0	VF 8.0	VF/NM 9.0	NM- 9.2
1-Soloman Kane sty; Werewolf app.	6	12	18	40	73	105
2-4: 2-The Frankenstein Monster begins, ends #10. 3-Neal Adams-c/a; The Man-Thing begins (origin-r); Son of Satan preview. 4-Werewolf app.	4	8	12	25	40	55
5-7: Werewolf in all. 5-Man-Thing. 7-Williamson-a(r)	3	6	9	19	30	40
8-11: 8-Man-Thing; N. Adams-r. 9-Man-Thing; Wendigo app. 10-Origin Tigra	3	6	9	19	30	40
Annual 1 (Summer,1975, 92 pgs.)-Kane-a	3	6	9	21	33	45

NOTE: ***Boris*** *c-2, 6.* ***Brunner*** *a-2; c-11.* ***J. Buscema*** *a-2p, 4p, 5p.* ***Colan*** *a-1, 4r.* ***Davis*** *a-3r.* ***Everett*** *a-2r.* ***G. Kane*** *a-3.* ***Krigstein*** *r-4.* ***Morrow*** *a-3; c-1.* ***Perez*** *a-8.* ***Ploog*** *a-6.* ***Reese*** *a-1, 2.* ***Tuska*** *a-3p.* ***Wildey*** *a-1r.*

MONSTERS UNLEASHED
Marvel Comics: Mar, 2017 - No. 5, May, 2017 ($4.99, limited series with tie-ins)

1-5: 1-Cullen Bunn-s/Steve McNiven-a; Avengers, X-Men, Guardians of the Galaxy, Inhumans & Champions app. 2-Land-a. 3-Leinil Yu-a. 4-Larroca-a. 5-Adam Kubert-a 5.00

MONSTERS UNLEASHED (Ongoing series)
Marvel Comics: Jun, 2017 - No. 12, May, 2018 ($3.99)

1-12: 1-Bunn-s/Baldeón-a; Elsa Bloodstone & Mole Man app. 7,8-Fin Fang Foom app. 4.00

MONSTERS UNLIMITED (Magazine) (Formerly Monsters To Laugh With)
Marvel Comics Group: No. 4, 1965 - No. 7, 1966 (B&W)

	GD 2.0	VG 4.0	FN 6.0	VF 8.0	VF/NM 9.0	NM- 9.2
4-7: 4,7-Frankenstein photo-c	5	10	15	34	60	85

MONSTER WORLD
DC Comics (WildStorm): Jul, 2001 - No. 4, Oct, 2001 ($2.50, limited series)

1-4-Lobdell-s/Meglia-c/a 3.00

MONSTER WORLD
American Gothic Press: Dec, 2015 - No. 4, May, 2016 ($3.99)

1-4-Philip Kim & Steve Niles-s/Piotr Kowalski-a 4.00

MONSTRESS
Image Comics: Nov, 2015 - Present ($4.99/$3.99)

1-($4.99) Marjorie Liu-s/Sana Takeda-a 22.00
2 12.00
3,4 6.00
5-32-($3.99) 4.00

MONSTRESS: TALK-STORIES
Image Comics: Nov, 2020 - No. 2, Dec, 2020 ($3.99)

1,2-Marjorie Liu-s/Sana Takeda-a; spotlight on Kippa 4.00

MONSTRO MECHANICA
AfterShock Comics: Dec, 2017 - No. 5, Apr, 2018 ($3.99)

1-5-Paul Allor-s/Chris Evenhuis-a; Leonardo Da Vinci and his robot in 1472 4.00

MONTANA KID, THE (See Kid Montana)

MONTE HALE WESTERN (Movie star; Formerly Mary Marvel #1-28; also see Fawcett Movie Comic, Motion Picture Comics, Picture News #8, Real Western Hero, Six-Gun Heroes, Western Hero & XMas Comics)
Fawcett Publ./Charlton No. 83 on: No. 29, Oct, 1948 - No. 88, Jan, 1956

	GD 2.0	VG 4.0	FN 6.0	VF 8.0	VF/NM 9.0	NM- 9.2
29-(#1, 52 pgs.)-Photo-c begin, end #82; Monte Hale & his horse Pardner begin	26	52	78	154	252	350
30-(52 pgs.)-Big Bow and Little Arrow begin, end #34; Captain Tootsie by Beck	14	28	42	80	115	150
31-36,38-40-(52 pgs.): 34-Gabby Hayes begins, ends #80. 39-Captain Tootsie by Beck	12	24	36	67	94	120
37,41,45,49-(36 pgs.)	10	20	30	54	72	90
42-44,46-48,50-(52 pgs.): 47-Big Bow & Little Arrow app.	10	20	30	58	79	100
51,52,54-56,58,59-(52 pgs.)	9	18	27	52	69	85
53,57-(36 pgs.): 53-Slim Pickens app.	8	16	24	44	57	70
60-81: 36 pgs. #60-on. 80-Gabby Hayes ends	8	16	24	42	54	65
82-Last Fawcett issue (6/53)	9	18	27	52	69	85

83-1st Charlton issue (2/55); B&W photo back-c begin. Gabby Hayes returns, ends #86

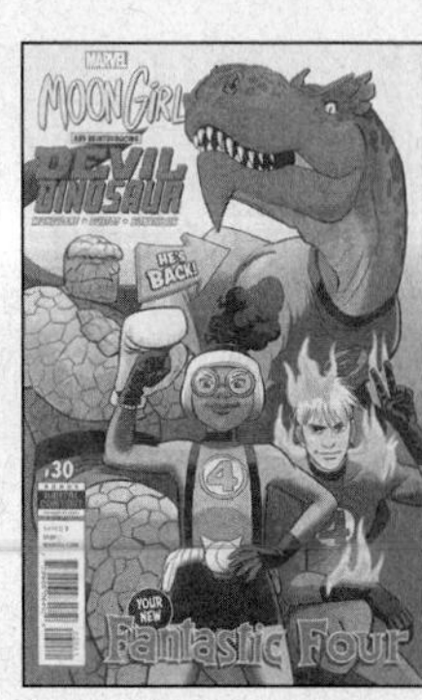

Moon Girl and Devil Dinosaur #30 © MAR

Moon Knight #189 © MAR

Moonshine #16 © Azzarello & Risso

	GD 2.0	VG 4.0	FN 6.0	VF 8.0	VF/NM 9.0	NM- 9.2
	10	20	30	58	79	100
84 (4/55)	8	16	24	44	57	70
85-86	8	16	24	42	54	65
87,88: 87-Wolverton-r, 1/2 pg. 88-Last issue	8	16	24	44	57	70

NOTE: ***Gil Kane** a-33?, 34? Rocky Lane -1 pg. (Carnation ad)-38, 40, 41, 43, 44, 46, 55.*

MONTY HALL OF THE U.S. MARINES (See With the Marines...)
Toby Press: Aug, 1951 - No. 11, Apr, 1953

	GD	VG	FN	VF	VF/NM	NM-
1	15	30	45	92	144	195
2	10	20	30	56	76	95
3-5	9	18	27	47	61	75
6-11	8	16	24	42	54	65

NOTE: *Full page pin-ups (Pin-Up Pete) by **Jack Sparling** in #1-9.*

MOON, A GIRL...ROMANCE, A (Becomes Weird Fantasy #13 on; formerly Moon Girl #1-8)
E. C. Comics: No. 9, Sept-Oct, 1949 - No. 12, Mar-Apr, 1950

	GD	VG	FN	VF	VF/NM	NM-
9-Moon Girl cameo	123	246	369	787	1344	1900
10,11	106	212	318	678	1164	1650
12-(Scarce)	129	258	387	826	1413	2000

NOTE: ***Feldstein, Ingels** art in all. **Feldstein** c-9-12. **Wood/Harrison** a-10-12. Canadian reprints known; see Table of Contents.*

MOON GIRL AND DEVIL DINOSAUR
Marvel Comics: Jan, 2016 - No. 47, Nov, 2019 ($3.99)

	GD	VG	FN	VF	VF/NM	NM-
1-47: 1-Reeder & Montclare-s/Bustos-a; intro. Lunella Lafayette. 4-Hulk app. 9-11-Ms. Marvel app. 14-Thing & Hulk (Cho) app. 15-Ironheart app. 19-Intro. Girl-Moon. 22,23-Ego the Living Planet app. 25-30-The Thing and Human Torch app.						4.00

MOON GIRL AND THE PRINCE (#1) (Moon Girl #2-6; Moon Girl Fights Crime #7, 8; becomes A Moon, A Girl, Romance #9 on)(Also see Animal Fables #7, Int. Crime Patrol #6, Happy Houlihans & Tales From The Crypt #22)
E. C. Comics: Fall, 1947 - No. 8, Summer, 1949

	GD	VG	FN	VF	VF/NM	NM-
1-Origin Moon Girl (see Happy Houlihans #1). Intro Santana, Queen of the Underworld	161	322	483	1030	1765	2500
2-Moon Girl battles Futureman	97	194	291	621	1061	1500
3,4: 3-Santana, Queen of the Underworld returns. 4-Moon Girl vs. a vampire	90	180	270	576	988	1400
5-E.C.'s 1st horror story, "Zombie Terror"	232	464	696	1485	2543	3600
6-8 (Scarce): 7-Origin Star (Moongirl's sidekick)	103	206	309	659	1130	1600

NOTE: ***Craig** a-2, 5; c-1, 2. **Moldoff** a-1-8; c-3-8 (Shelly). **Wheelan's** Fat and Slat app. in #3, 4, 6. #2 & #3 are 52 pgs., #4 on, 36 pgs. Canadian reprints known; (see Table of Contents.)*

MOON KNIGHT (Also see The Hulk, Marc Spector..., Marvel Preview #21, Marvel Spotlight & Werewolf by Night #32)
Marvel Comics Group: Nov, 1980 - No. 38, Jul, 1984 (Mando paper #33 on)

	GD	VG	FN	VF	VF/NM	NM-
1-Origin resumed in #4	5	10	15	33	57	80
2	2	4	6	11	16	20
3,4: 4-Intro Midnight Man	2	4	6	9	12	15
5-15,25,35: 25-Double size. 35-($1.00, 52 pgs.)-X-Men app.; F.F. cameo						6.00
16-24,26-28,31-34,36-38: 16-The Thing app.						5.00
29,30-Werewolf By Night app.	2	4	6	11	16	20

NOTE: ***Austin** c-27i, 31i. **Cowan** a-16; c-16, 17. **Kaluta** c-36-38; back c-35. **Miller** c-9, 12p, 13p, 15p, 27p. **Ploog** back c-35. **Sienkiewicz** a-1-15, 17-20, 22-26, 28-30, 33i, 36(4), 37; c-1-5, 7, 8, 10, 11, 14-16, 18-26, 28-30, 31p, 33, 34.*

MOON KNIGHT
Marvel Comics Group: June, 1985 - V2#6, Dec, 1985

	GD	VG	FN	VF	VF/NM	NM-
V2#1-Double size; new costume	1	2	3	5	6	8
V2#2-6: 6-Sienkiewicz painted-c						4.00

MOON KNIGHT
Marvel Comics: Jan, 1998 - No. 4, Apr, 1998 ($2.50, limited series)

	NM-
1-4-Moench-s/Edwards-c/a	4.00

MOON KNIGHT (Volume 3)
Marvel Comics: Jan, 1999 - No. 4, Feb, 1999 ($2.99, limited series)

	NM-
1-4-Moench-s/Texeira-a(p)	4.00

MOON KNIGHT (Fourth series) (Leads into Vengeance of the Moon Knight)
Marvel Comics: June, 2006 - No. 30, Jul, 2009 ($2.99)

	NM-
1-Finch-a/c; Huston-s	4.00
1-B&W sketch variant-c	6.00
2-19,21-26: 7-Spider-Man app. 9,10-Punisher app. 13-Suydam-c begin. 23-25-Bullseye	3.00
20-($3.99) Deodato-a; back-up r/1st app. in Werewolf By Night #32,33	4.00
Annual 1 (1/08, $3.99) Swierczynski-s/Palo-a	4.00
... Saga (2009, free) synopsis of origin and major storylines	3.00
...: Silent Knight 1 (1/09, $3.99) Milligan-s/Laurence Campbell-a/Crain-c	4.00

MOON KNIGHT (Fifth series)
Marvel Comics: Jul, 2011 - No. 12, Jun, 2012 ($3.99, limited series)

	NM-
1-Bendis-s/Maleev-a/c; Wolverine, Spider-Man and Capt. America "app."	4.00
2-12: 2-Echo returns. 3-Bullseye-c	4.00

MOON KNIGHT (Sixth series)
Marvel Comics: May, 2014 - No. 17, Sept, 2015 ($3.99)

	NM-
1-17: 1-6-Ellis-s/Shalvey-a. 7-12-Wood-s/Smallwood-a. 13-17-Bunn	4.00

MOON KNIGHT (Seventh series)
Marvel Comics: Jun, 2016 - No. 14, Jul, 2017 ($4.99/$3.99)

	NM-
1-($4.99)-Lemire-s/Smallwood-a	5.00
2-14-($3.99) 5-9-Art by Smallwood, Stokoe, Torres, and Francavilla	4.00

MOON KNIGHT (Marvel Legacy)
Marvel Comics: No. 188, Jan, 2018 - No. 200, Dec, 2018 ($3.99)

	NM-
188-199: 188-Bemis-s/Burrows-a	4.00
200-($4.99) Davidson-a	5.00
Annual 1 (11/19, $4.99) Acts of Evil; Moustafa & Horak-a; Kang the Conqueror app.	5.00

MOON KNIGHT: DIVIDED WE FALL
Marvel Comics: 1992 ($4.95, 52 pgs.)

	NM-
nn-Denys Cowan-c/a(p)	5.00

MOON KNIGHT SPECIAL
Marvel Comics: Oct, 1992 ($2.50, 52 pgs.)

	NM-
1-Shang Chi, Master of Kung Fu-c/story	4.00

MOON KNIGHT SPECIAL EDITION
Marvel Comics Group: Nov, 1983 - No. 3, Jan, 1984 ($2.00, limited series, Baxter paper)

	NM-
1-3: Reprints from Hulk mag. by Sienkiewicz	4.00

MOON MULLINS (See Popular Comics, Super Book #3 & Super Comics)
Dell Publishing Co.: 1941 - 1945

	GD	VG	FN	VF	VF/NM	NM-
Four Color 14(1941)	50	100	150	315	533	750
Large Feature Comic 29(1941)	37	74	111	222	361	500
Four Color 31(1943)	16	32	48	110	243	375
Four Color 81(1945)	10	20	30	68	144	220

MOON MULLINS
Michel Publ. (American Comics Group)#1-6/St. John #7,8: Dec-Jan, 1947-48 - No. 8, Mar-May, 1949 (52 pgs)

	GD	VG	FN	VF	VF/NM	NM-
1-Alternating Sunday & daily strip-r	27	54	81	158	259	360
2	15	30	45	88	137	185
3-8: 7,8-St. John Publ. 7,8-...Featuring Kayo on-c	15	30	45	85	130	175

NOTE: ***Milt Gross** a-2-6, 8. **Frank Willard** r-all.*

MOON PILOT
Dell Publishing Co.: No. 1313, Mar-May, 1962

	GD	VG	FN	VF	VF/NM	NM-
Four Color 1313-Movie, photo-c	6	12	18	41	76	110

MOONSHADOW (Also see Farewell, Moonshadow)
Marvel Comics (Epic Comics): 5/85 - #12, 2/87 ($1.50/$1.75, mature)
(1st fully painted comic book)

	GD	VG	FN	VF	VF/NM	NM-
1-Origin; J. M. DeMatteis scripts & Jon J. Muth painted-c/a.						6.00
2-12: 11-Origin						4.00
Trade paperback (1987?)-r/#1-12						14.00
Signed & #ed HC ($39.95, 1,200 copies)-r/#1-12	4	8	12	27	44	60

MOONSHADOW
DC Comics (Vertigo): Oct, 1994 - No. 12, Aug, 1995 ($2.25/$2.95)

	NM-
1-11: Reprints Epic series.	3.00
12 ($2.95)-w/expanded ending	4.00
The Complete Moonshadow TPB ('98, $39.95) r/#1-12 and Farewell Moonshadow; new Muth painted-c	40.00

MOONSHINE
Image Comics: Oct, 2016 - Present ($2.99/$3.99)

	NM-
1-6-Brian Azzarello-s/Eduardo Risso-a. 1-Covers by Risso & Frank Miller	3.00
7-22-($3.99) Azzarello-s/Risso-a	4.00

MOON-SPINNERS, THE (See Movie Comics)

MOONSTONE MONSTERS
Moonstone: 2003 - 2005 ($2.95, B&W)

	NM-
...: Demons ($2.95) - Short stories by various; Frenz-c	3.00
...: Ghosts ($2.95) - Short stories by various; Frenz-c	3.00
...: Sea Creatures ($2.95) - Short stories by various; Frenz-c	3.00
...: Witches ($2.95) - Short stories by various; Frenz-c	3.00
...: Zombies ($2.95) - Short stories by various; Frenz-c	3.00
Volume 1 (2004, $16.95, TPB) r/short stories from series; Wolak-c	17.00

MOONSTONE NOIR

Morbius: Bond of Blood #1 © MAR

More Fun Comics #117 © DC

More Fund Comics TPB © CBLDF

	GD 2.0	VG 4.0	FN 6.0	VF 8.0	VF/NM 9.0	NM- 9.2

Moonstone: 2003 - 2004 ($2.95/$4.95/$5.50, B&W)
...: Bulldog Drummond (2004, $4.95) - Messner-Loebs-s/Barkley-a 5.00
...: Johnny Dollar ($4.95) - Gallaher-s/Theriault-a 5.00
...: Mr. Keen, Tracer of Lost Persons 1,2 ($2.95, limited series) - Ferguson-a 3.00
...: Mysterious Traveler (2003, $5.50) - Trevor Von Eeden-a/Joe Gentile-s 5.50
...: Mysterious Traveler Returns (2004, $4.95) - Trevor Von Eeden-a/Joe Gentile-s 5.00
...: The Lone Wolf ($4.95) - Jolley-s/Croall-a 5.00

MOPSY (See Pageant of Comics & TV Teens)
St. John Publ. Co.: Feb, 1948 - No. 19, Sept, 1953

	GD	VG	FN	VF	VF/NM	NM-
1-Part-r; reprints "Some Punkins" by Neher	42	84	126	265	445	625
2	16	32	48	98	154	210
3-10(1953): 8-Lingerie panels	15	30	45	92	144	195
11-19: 19-Lingerie-c	15	30	45	85	130	175

NOTE: *#1-7, 13, 18, 19 have paper dolls.*

MORBIUS
Marvel Comics: Jan, 2020 - No. 5, May, 2020 ($3.99)
1-5-Ayala-s/Ferreira-a. 1-Intro. Elizabeth; the Melter app. 2-5-Spider-Man app. 4.00

MORBIUS: BOND OF BLOOD
Marvel Comics: Apr, 2021 ($3.99, one-shot)
1-Ralph Macchio-s/Tom Reilly-a; origin told in flashback; Mister Hyde app. 4.00

MORBIUS REVISITED
Marvel Comics: Aug, 1993 - No. 5, Dec, 1993 ($1.95, mini-series)
1-5-Reprints Fear #27-31 4.00

MORBIUS: THE LIVING VAMPIRE (Also see Amazing Spider-Man #101,102, Fear #20, Marvel Team-Up #3, 4, Midnight Sons Unl. & Vampire Tales)
Marvel Comics (Midnight Sons imprint #16 on): Sep, 1992 - No. 32, Apr, 1995 ($1.75/$1.95)
1-($2.75, 52 pgs.)-Polybagged w/poster; Ghost Rider & Johnny Blaze x-over (part 3 of Rise of the Midnight Sons) 5.00
2-11,13-24,26-32: 3,4-Vs. Spider-Man-c/s.15-Ghost Rider app. 16-Spot varnish-c. 16,17-Siege of Darkness, parts 5 &13. 18-Deathlok app. 21-Bound-in Spider-Man trading card sheet; Spider-Man app. 4.00
12-($2.25)-Outer-c is a Darkhold envelope made of black parchment w/gold ink; Midnight Massacre x-over 5.00
25-($2.50, 52 pgs.)-Gold foil logo 5.00

MORBIUS: THE LIVING VAMPIRE (Marvel NOW!)
Marvel Comics: Mar, 2013 - No. 9, Nov, 2013 ($2.99)
1-9: 1-Keatinge-s/Elson-a/Dell'Otto-c. 6,7-Superior Spider-Man app. 3.00

MORE FUN COMICS (Formerly New Fun Comics #1-6)
National Periodical Publs: No. 7, Jan, 1936 - No. 127, Nov-Dec, 1947 (No. 7,9-11: paper-c)

	GD	VG	FN	VF	VF/NM	NM-
7(1/36)-Oversized, paper-c; 1 pg. Kelly-a	1063	2126	3189	8500	--	--
8(2/36)-Oversized (10x12"), paper-c; 1 pg. Kelly-a; Sullivan-c	1063	2026	3189	8500	--	--
9(3-4/36)(Very rare, 1st standard-sized comic book with original material)-Last multiple panel-c	1475	2950	4425	11,800	--	--
10,11(7/36): 10-Last Henri Duval by Siegel & Shuster. 11-1st "Calling All Cars" by Siegel & Shuster; new classic logo begins	763	1526	2289	6100	--	--
12(8/36)-Slick-c begin	563	1126	1689	4500	--	--
V2#1(9/36, #13) 1 pg. Fred Astaire photo/bio	513	1026	1539	4100	--	--
2(10/36, #14)-Dr. Occult in costume (1st in color)(Superman prototype; 1st DC appearance) continues from The Comics Magazine, ends #17	2025	4050	6075	16,200	--	--
V2#3(11/36, #15), 17(V2#5)	825	1650	2475	6600	--	--
16(V2#4)-Cover numbering begins; ties with New Comics #11 as 1st DC Christmas-c; last Superman tryout issue	925	1850	2775	7400	--	--
18-20(V2#8, 5/37)	381	762	1143	3050	--	--
21(V2#9)-24(V2#12, 9/37)	252	504	756	1613	2757	3900
25(V3#1, 10/37)-27(V3#3, 12/37): 27-Xmas-c	252	504	756	1613	2757	3900
28-30: 30-1st non-funny cover	245	490	735	1568	2684	3800
31-Has ad for Action Comics #1	300	600	900	2070	3535	5000
32-35: 32-Last Dr. Occult	223	446	669	1427	2438	3450
36-40: 36-(10/38)-The Masked Ranger & sidekick Pedro begins; Ginger Snap by Bob Kane (2 pgs.; 1st-a?). 39-Xmas-c	206	412	618	1318	2259	3200
41-50: 41-Last Masked Ranger. 43-Beany (1 pg.) and Ginger Snap centerfold by Bob Kane	194	388	582	1242	2121	3000
51-The Spectre app. (in costume) in one panel ad at end of Buccaneer story	503	1006	1509	5405	7352	9300
52-(2/40)-Origin/1st app. The Spectre (in costume splash panel only), part 1 by Bernard Baily (parts 1 & 2 written by Jerry Siegel; Spectre's costume changes color from purple & blue to green & grey; last Wing Brady; Spectre-c	12,200	24,400	36,600	85,000	152,500	220,000
53-Origin The Spectre (in costume at end of story), part 2; Capt. Desmo begins; Spectre-c	3380	6760	10,140	23,700	55,850	88,000
54-The Spectre in costume; last King Carter; classic-Spectre-c	2150	4300	6450	15,000	29,500	44,000
55-(Scarce, 5/40)-Dr. Fate begins (1st app.); last Bulldog Martin; Spectre-c	2150	4300	6450	15,000	29,500	44,000
56-1st Dr. Fate-c (classic), origin continues. Congo Bill begins (6/40), 1st app.;	1000	2000	3000	7500	13,800	20,000
57-60-All Spectre-c	503	1006	1509	3672	6486	9300
61,65: 61-Classic Dr. Fate-c. 65-Classic Spectre-c	481	962	1443	3511	6206	8900
62-64,66: 63-Last Lt. Bob Neal. 64-Lance Larkin begins; all Spectre-c	360	720	1080	2520	4410	6300
67-(5/41)-Origin (1st) Dr. Fate; last Congo Bill & Biff Bronson (Congo Bill continues in Action Comics #37, 6/41)-Spectre-c	865	1730	2595	6315	11,158	16,000
68-70: 68-Clip Carson begins. 70-Last Lance Larkin; all Dr. Fate-c	300	600	900	1980	3440	4900
71-Origin & 1st app. Johnny Quick by Mort Weisinger (9/41); classic sci/fi Dr. Fate-c	459	918	1377	3350	5925	8500
72-Dr. Fate's new helmet; last Sgt. Carey, Sgt. O'Malley & Captain Desmo; German submarine-c (Nazi war-c)	300	600	900	1970	3410	4850
73-Origin & 1st app. Aquaman (11/41) by Paul Norris; intro. Green Arrow & Speedy; Dr. Fate-c	12,600	25,200	37,800	82,000	113,500	145,000
74-2nd Aquaman; 1st Percival Popp, Supercop; Dr. Fate-c	730	1460	2190	5329	9415	13,500
75,76: 75-New origin Spectre; Nazi spy ring cover w/Hitler's photo. 76-Last Dr. Fate-c; Johnny Quick (by Meskin #76-97) begins, ends #107; last Clip Carson	300	600	900	2040	3570	5100
77-Green Arrow-c begin	248	496	744	1587	2719	3850
78-80	177	354	531	1133	1942	2750
81-83,85,88,90: 81-Last large logo. 82-1st small logo.	119	238	357	762	1306	1850
84-Green Arrow Japanese war-c	139	278	417	890	1520	2150
86,87-Johnny Quick-c. 87-Last Radio Squad	119	238	357	762	1306	1850
89-Origin Green Arrow & Speedy Team-up	145	290	435	928	1589	2250
91-97,99: 91-1st bi-monthly issue. 93-Dover & Clover begin (1st app., 9-10/43). 97-Kubert-a	87	174	261	553	952	1350
98-Last Dr. Fate (scarce)	110	220	330	704	1202	1700
100 (11-12/44)-Johnny Quick-c	100	200	300	640	1095	1550
101-Origin & 1st app. Superboy (1-2/45)(not by Siegel & Shuster); last Spectre issue; Green Arrow-c	1000	2000	3000	7300	12,900	18,500
102-2nd Superboy app; 1st Dover & Clover-c	161	322	483	1030	1765	2500
103-3rd Superboy app; last Green Arrow-c	119	238	357	762	1306	1850
104-1st Superboy-c w/Dover & Clover	113	226	339	723	1237	1750
105,106-Superboy-c	90	180	270	576	988	1400
107-Last Johnny Quick & Superboy	84	168	252	538	919	1300
108-120: 108-Genius Jones begins; 1st c-app. (3-4/46; cont'd from Adventure Comics #102)	28	56	84	165	270	375
121-124,126: 121-123,126-Post funny animal (Jimminy & the Magic Book)-c	26	52	78	154	252	350
125-Superman c-app.w/Jimminy	100	200	300	640	1095	1550
127-(Scarce)-Post-c/a	47	94	141	296	498	725

NOTE: *All issues are scarce to rare. Cover features: The Spectre-#52-55, 57-60, 62-67. Dr. Fate-#56, 61, 68-76. The Green Arrow & Speedy-#77-85, 88-97, 99, 101 (w/Dover & Clover-#98, 103). Johnny Quick-#86, 87, 100. Dover & Clover-#102, (104, 106 w/Superboy), 107, 108(w/Genius Jones), 110, 112, 114, 117, 119. Genius Jones-#109, 111, 113, 115, 116, 118, 120.* ***Baily*** *a-45, 52-on; c-52-55, 57-60, 62-67.* ***Al Capp*** *a-45(signed Koppy).* ***Ellsworth*** *c-7.* ***Creig Flessel*** *c-30, 31, 35-48(most).* ***Guardineer*** *c-47, 49, 50.* ***Kiefer*** *a-20.* ***Meskin*** *c-86, 87, 100?* ***Moldoff*** *c-51.* ***George Papp*** *c-77-85.* ***Post*** *c-121-127.* ***Vincent Sullivan*** *c-8-28, 32-34.*

MORE FUND COMICS (Benefit book for the Comic Book Legal Defense Fund)
(Also see Even More Fund Comics)
Sky Dog Press: Sept, 2003 ($10.00, B&W, trade paperback)
nn-Anthology of short stories and pin-ups by various; Hulk-c by Pérez 10.00

MORE SEYMOUR (See Seymour My Son)
Archie Publications: Oct, 1963

	GD	VG	FN	VF	VF/NM	NM-
1-DeCarlo-a?	3	6	9	21	33	45

MORE THAN MORTAL (Also see Lady Pendragon/...)
Liar Comics: June, 1997 - No. 4, Apr, 1998 ($2.95, limited series)
Image Comics: No. 5, Dec, 1999 - No. 6, Mar, 2000 ($2.95)
1-Blue forest background-c, 1-Variant-c 4.00
1-White-c 6.00
1-2nd printing; purple sky cover 3.00
2-4: 3-Silvestri-c, 4-Two-c, one by Randy Queen 3.00
5,6: 5-1st Image Comics issue 3.00

MORE THAN MORTAL: OTHERWORLDS
Image Comics: July, 1999 - No. 4, Dec, 1999 ($2.95, limited series)

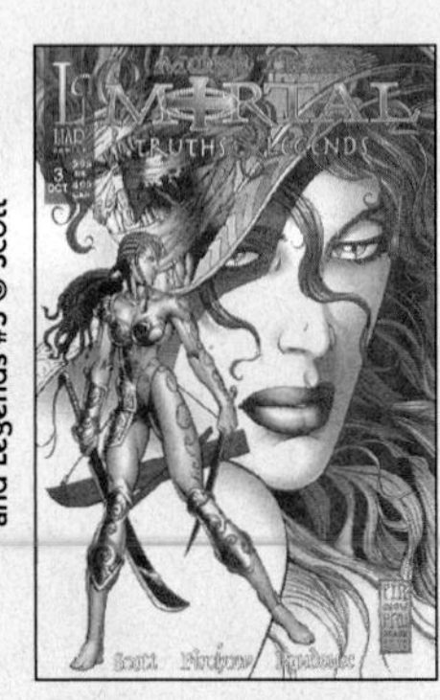

More Than Mortal Truths and Legends #3 © Scott

Mosaic #8 © MAR

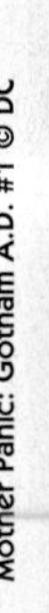

Mother Panic: Gotham A.D. #1 © DC

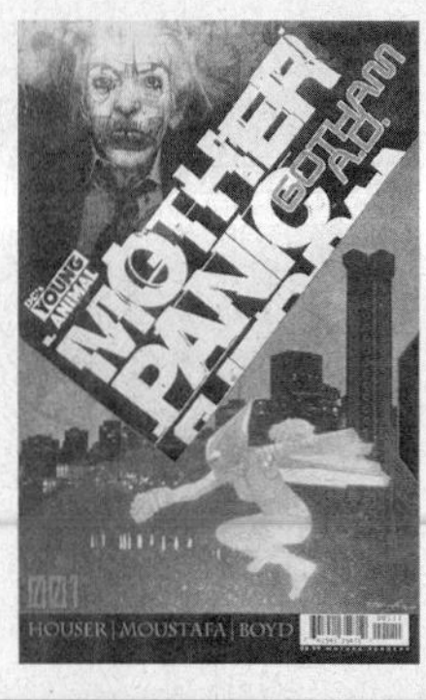

	GD	VG	FN	VF	VF/NM	NM-
	2.0	4.0	6.0	8.0	9.0	9.2

1-4-Firchow-a. 1-Two covers 3.00

MORE THAN MORTAL SAGAS
Liar Comics: Jun, 1998 - No. 3, Dec, 1998 ($2.95, limited series)

1,2-Painted art by Romano. 2-Two-c, one by Firchow 3.00
1-Variant-c by Linsner 5.00

MORE THAN MORTAL TRUTHS AND LEGENDS
Liar Comics: Aug, 1998 - No. 6, Apr, 1999 ($2.95)

1-6-Firchow-a(p) 3.00
1-Variant-c by Dan Norton 4.50

MORE TRASH FROM MAD (Annual)
E. C. Comics: 1958 - No. 12, 1969
(Note: Bonus missing = half price)

nn(1958)-8 pgs. color Mad reprint from #20 18 36 54 122 271 420
2(1959)-Market Product Labels 11 22 33 76 163 250
3(1960)-Text book covers 10 20 30 69 147 225
4(1961)-Sing Along with Mad booklet 10 20 30 69 147 225
5(1962)-Window Stickers; r/from Mad #39 8 16 24 54 102 150
6(1963)-TV Guise booklet 8 16 24 54 102 150
7(1964)-Alfred E. Neuman commemorative stamps 7 14 21 44 82 120
8(1965)-Life size poster-Alfred E. Neuman 5 10 15 35 63 90
9-12: 9,10(1966-67)-Mischief Sticker. 11(1968)-Campaign poster & bumper sticker. 12(1969)-Pocket medals 5 10 15 35 63 90

NOTE: *Kelly Freas c-1, 2, 4. Mingo c-3, 5-9, 12.*

MORGAN THE PIRATE (Movie)
Dell Publishing Co.: No. 1227, Sept-Nov, 1961

Four Color 1227-Photo-c 7 14 21 46 86 125

MORLOCKS
Marvel Comics: June, 2002 - No. 4, Sept, 2002 ($2.50, limited series)

1-4-Johns-s/Martinbrough-c/a. 1-1st app. Angel Dust 3.00

MORLOCK 2001
Atlas/Seaboard Publ.: Feb, 1975 - No. 3, July, 1975

1,2: 1-(Super-hero)-Origin & 1st app.; Milgrom-c 2 4 6 11 16 20
3-Ditko/Wrightson-a; origin The Midnight Man & The Mystery Men 3 6 9 15 22 28

MORNING GLORIES
Image Comics: Aug, 2010 - Present ($3.99/$3.50/$2.99)

1-($3.99) Nick Spencer-s/Joe Eisma-a/Rodin Esquejo-c; group cover 10.00
1-Second-Fourth printings 4.00
2-($3.50) Regular cover and white background 2nd printing 5.00
3-6-Regular covers and white background 2nd printings 4.00
7-23-($2.99) 3.00
24,25,27,28-($3.99) 4.00
26-($1.00) Start of Season Two 3.00
29-48-($3.50) 3.50
49-($4.99) Spencer-s/Eisma-a 5.00
50-(7/16, $5.99) 6.00
...Vol. 1 TPB (2/11, $9.99) r/#1-6 10.00

MORNINGSTAR SPECIAL
Comico: Apr, 1990 ($2.50)

1-From the Elementals; Willingham-c/a/scripts 3.00

MORTAL KOMBAT
Malibu Comics: July, 1994 - No. 6, Dec, 1994 ($2.95)

1-Two diff. covers exist 2 4 6 9 12 15
1-Limited edition gold foil embossed-c 3 6 9 14 20 25
2-6 5.00
0 (12/94), Special Edition 1 (11/94) 3 6 9 14 20 25
Tournament Edition I12/94, $3.95), II('95)($3.95) 2 4 6 11 16 20
...: **BARAKA** ,June, 1995 ($2.95, one-shot) #1; ...**BATTLEWAVE** ,2/95 - No. 6, 7/95 , #1-6; ...**GORO, PRINCE OF PAIN** ,9/94 - No. 3, 11/94, #1-3; ...**KITANA AND MILEENA** ,8/95 , ...**KUNG LAO** ,7/95 , #1; ... **RAYDON & KANO** ,3/95 - No. 3, 5/95, #1-3: ...(all $2.95-c) 2 4 6 9 12 15
...: **U.S. SPECIAL FORCES** (1/95 - No. 2, $3.50), 1,2 2 4 6 9 12 15

MORTAL KOMBAT X
DC Comics: Mar, 2015 - No. 12, Jan, 2016 ($3.99, printings of digital-first stories)

1-Kittelsen-s/Soy-a/Reis-c 2 4 6 9 12 15
2-6 1 2 3 5 6 8
7-12: 9-12-Jae Lee-c 5.00

MORTIE (Mazie's Friend; also see Flat-Top)
Magazine Publishers: Dec, 1952 - No. 4, June, 1953?

1 12 24 36 69 97 125
2-4 8 16 24 42 54 65

MORTIGAN GOTH: IMMORTALIS (See Marvel Frontier Comics Unlimited)
Marvel Comics: Sept, 1993 - No. 4, Mar, 1994 ($1.95, mini-series)

1-($2.95)-Foil-c 4.00
2-4 3.00

MORT THE DEAD TEENAGER
Marvel Comics: Nov, 1993 - No. 4, Mar, 1994 ($1.75, mini-series)

1-4 3.00

MORTY MEEKLE
Dell Publishing Co.: No. 793, May, 1957

Four Color 793 5 10 15 30 50 70

MOSAIC
Marvel Comics: Dec, 2016 - No. 8, Jul, 2017 ($4.99/$3.99)

1-($4.99) Geoffrey Thorne-s/Khary Randolph-a; intro. Morris Sackett 5.00
2-8-($3.99) 3,4-Spider-Man app. 6-Inhumans app. 8-Diablo app. 4.00

MOSES & THE TEN COMMANDMENTS (See Dell Giants)

MOSTLY WANTED
DC Comics (WildStorm): Jul, 2000 - No. 4, Nov, 2000 ($2.50, limited series)

1-4-Lobdell-s/Flores-a 3.00

MOTEL HELL (Based on the 1980 movie)
IDW Publishing: Oct, 2010 - No. 3, Dec, 2010 ($3.99, limited series)

1-3-Matt Nixon-s/Chris Moreno-a. 1,2-Bradstreet-c. 3-Moreno-c 4.00

MOTH, THE
Dark Horse Comics: Apr, 2004 - No. 4, Aug, 2004 ($2.99)

1-4-Steve Rude-c/a; Gary Martin-s 3.00
... Special (3/04, $4.95) 5.00
TPB (5/05, $12.95) r/#1-4 and Special; gallery of extras 13.00

MOTH, THE
Rude Dude Productions: May 2008 (Free Comic Book Day giveaway)

... Special Edition - Steve Rude-s/a; sketch pages 3.00

MOTH & WHISPER
AfterShock Comics: Sept, 2018 - No. 5, Jan, 2019 ($3.99, limited series)

1-5-Ted Anderson-s/Jen Hickman-a 4.00

MOTHER GOOSE AND NURSERY RHYME COMICS (See Christmas With Mother Goose)
Dell Publishing Co.: No. 41, 1944 - No. 862, Nov, 1957

Four Color 41-Walt Kelly-c/a 23 46 69 161 356 550
Four Color 59, 68-Kelly c/a 18 36 54 125 276 430
Four Color 862-The Truth About..., Movie (Disney) 7 14 21 44 82 120

MOTHERLANDS
DC Comics (Vertigo): Mar, 2018 - No. 6, Aug, 2018 ($3.99, limited series)

1-6-Spurrier-s/Stott-a/Canete-c 4.00

MOTHER PANIC
DC Comics (Young Animal): Jan, 2017 - No. 12, Dec, 2017 ($3.99)

1-12: 1-Houser-s/Edwards-a; Batman cameo. 3-Batman & Batwoman app. 7-9-Leon-a 4.00
.../ Batman Special 1 (4/18, $4.99) Part 2 of Milk Wars crossover; Templeton-a/Quitely-c 5.00

MOTHER PANIC: GOTHAM A.D.
DC Comics (Young Animal): May, 2018 - No. 6, Oct, 2018 ($3.99)

1-6: 1-Houser-s/Moustafa-a/Edwards-c. 1-Joker cameo. 2-Catwoman app. 4.00

MOTHER TERESA OF CALCUTTA
Marvel Comics Group: 1984

1-(52 pgs.) No ads 2 4 6 9 12 15

MOTION PICTURE COMICS (See Fawcett Movie Comics)
Fawcett Publications: No. 101, 1950 - No. 114, Jan, 1953 (All-photo-c)

101- "Vanishing Westerner"; Monte Hale (1950) 16 32 48 98 154 210
102- "Code of the Silver Sage"; Rocky Lane (1/51) 15 30 45 83 124 165
103- "Covered Wagon Raid"; Rocky Lane (3/51) 15 30 45 83 124 165
104- "Vigilante Hideout"; Rocky Lane (5/51)-Book length Powell-a 15 30 45 83 124 165
105- "Red Badge of Courage"; Audie Murphy; Bob Powell-a (7/51) 20 40 60 114 182 250
106- "The Texas Rangers"; George Montgomery (9/51) 15 30 45 83 124 165

Motor Crush #8 © Fletcher, Stewart & Tarr

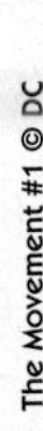
The Movement #1 © DC

Movie Classics - Tomb of Ligeia © DELL

	GD 2.0	VG 4.0	FN 6.0	VF 8.0	VF/NM 9.0	NM- 9.2
107- "Frisco Tornado"; Rocky Lane (11/51)	14	28	42	80	115	150
108- "Mask of the Avenger"; John Derek	12	24	36	69	97	125
109- "Rough Rider of Durango"; Rocky Lane	14	28	42	80	115	150
110- "When Worlds Collide"; George Evans-a (5/52); Williamson & Evans drew themselves in story; (also see Famous Funnies No. 72-88)	77	154	231	493	847	1200
111- "The Vanishing Outpost"; Lash LaRue	15	30	45	90	140	190
112- "Brave Warrior"; Jon Hall & Jay Silverheels	12	24	36	67	94	120
113- "Walk East on Beacon"; George Murphy; Schaffenberger-a	10	20	30	54	72	90
114- "Cripple Creek"; George Montgomery (1/53)	10	20	30	58	79	100

MOTION PICTURE FUNNIES WEEKLY (See Promotional Comics section)

MOTOR CRUSH
Image Comics: Dec, 2016 - No. 11, Apr, 2018 ($3.99)

1-11-Fletcher & Stewart-s/Tarr-a; covers by Tarr & Stewart. 6-Stewart-a 4.00

MOTOR GIRL
Abstract Studio: 2016 - No. 10, 2017 ($3.99, B&W)

1-10-Terry Moore-s/a/c 4.00

MOTORHEAD (See Comic's Greatest World)
Dark Horse Comics: Aug, 1995 - No. 6, Jan, 1996 ($2.50)

1-6: Bisley-c on all. 1-Predator app. 3.00
Special 1 (3/94, $3.95, 52pgs.)-Jae Lee-c; Barb Wire, The Machine & Wolf Gang app. 4.00

MOTORMOUTH (... & Killpower #7? on)
Marvel Comics UK: June, 1992 - No. 12, May, 1993 ($1.75)

1-13: 1,2-Nick Fury app. 3-Punisher-c/story. 5,6-Nick Fury & Punisher app. 6-Cable cameo. 7-9-Cable app. 3.00

MOUNTAIN MEN (See Ben Bowie)

MOUSE MUSKETEERS (See M.G.M.'s...)

MOUSE ON THE MOON, THE (See Movie Classics)

MOVEMENT, THE
DC Comics: Jul, 2013 - No. 12, Jul. 2014 ($2.99)

1-12: 1-Gail Simone-s/Freddie Williams-a/Amanda Conner-c. 2-4-Rainmaker app. 9,10-Batgirl app. 3.00

MOVIE CARTOONS
DC Comics: Dec, 1944 (cover only ashcan)

nn-Ashcan comic, not distributed to newsstands, only for in house use. Covers were produced, but not the rest of the book. A copy sold in 2006 for $500.

MOVIE CLASSICS
Dell Publishing Co.: Apr, 1956; May-Jul, 1962 - Dec, 1969

(Before 1963, most movie adaptations were part of the 4-Color series)
(Disney movie adaptations after 1970 are in Walt Disney Showcase)

	GD 2.0	VG 4.0	FN 6.0	VF 8.0	VF/NM 9.0	NM- 9.2
Around the World Under the Sea 12-030-612 (12/66)	3	6	9	21	33	45
Bambi 3(4/56)-Disney; r/4-Color #186	4	8	12	28	47	65
Battle of the Bulge 12-056-606 (6/66)	3	6	9	20	31	42
Beach Blanket Bingo 12-058-509	6	12	18	42	79	115
Bon Voyage 01-068-212 (12/62)-Disney; photo-c	3	6	9	21	33	45
Castilian, The 12-110-401	3	6	9	19	30	40
Cat, The 12-109-612 (12/66)	3	6	9	18	28	38
Cheyenne Autumn 12-112-506 (4-6/65)	5	10	15	31	53	75
Circus World, Samuel Bronston's 12-115-411; John Wayne app.; John Wayne photo-c	9	18	27	58	114	170
Countdown 12-150-710 (10/67)-James Caan photo-c	3	6	9	20	31	42
Creature, The 1 (12-142-302) (12-2/62-63)	25	50	75	175	388	600
Creature, The 12-142-410 (10/64)	6	12	18	38	69	100
David Ladd's Life Story 12-173-212 (10-12/62)-Photo-c	6	12	18	40	73	105
Die, Monster, Die 12-175-603 (3/66)-Photo-c	5	10	15	35	63	90
Dirty Dozen 12-180-710 (10/67)	4	8	12	28	47	65
Dr. Who & the Daleks 12-190-612 (12/66)-Peter Cushing photo-c; 1st U.S. app. of Dr. Who	23	46	69	168	382	560
Dracula 12-231-212 (10-12/62)	10	20	30	64	132	200
El Dorado 12-240-710 (10/67)-John Wayne; photo-c	11	22	33	73	157	240
Ensign Pulver 12-257-410 (8-10/64)	3	6	9	18	28	38
Frankenstein 12-283-305 (3-5/63)(see Frankenstein 8-10/64 for 2nd printing)	10	20	30	64	132	200
Great Race, The 12-299-603 (3/66)-Natallie Wood, Tony Curtis photo-c	4	8	12	28	47	65
Hallelujah Trail, The 12-307-602 (2/66) (Shows 1/66 inside); Burt Lancaster, Lee Remick photo-c	5	10	15	30	50	70
Hatari 12-340-301 (1/63)-John Wayne	7	14	21	48	89	130
Horizontal Lieutenant, The 01-348-210 (10/62)	3	6	9	18	28	38
Incredible Mr. Limpet, The 12-370-408; Don Knotts photo-c	5	10	15	30	50	70
Jack the Giant Killer 12-374-301 (1/63)	7	14	21	44	82	120
Jason & the Argonauts 12-376-310 (8-10/63)-Photo-c	9	18	27	60	120	180
Lancelot & Guinevere 12-416-310 (10/63)	5	10	15	30	50	70
Lawrence 12-426-308 (8/63)-Story of Lawrence of Arabia; movie ad on back-c; not exactly like movie	5	10	15	30	50	70
Lion of Sparta 12-439-301 (1/63)	3	6	9	21	33	45
Mad Monster Party 12-460-801 (9/67)-Based on Kurtzman's screenplay	9	18	27	59	117	175
Magic Sword, The 01-496-209 (9/62)	5	10	15	31	53	75
Masque of the Red Death 12-490-410 (8-10/64)-Vincent Price photo-c	6	12	18	38	69	100
Maya 12-495-612 (12/66)-Clint Walker & Jay North part photo-c	4	8	12	23	37	50
McHale's Navy 12-500-412 (10-12/64)	4	8	12	27	44	60
Merrill's Marauders 12-510-301 (1/63)-Photo-c	3	6	9	18	28	38
Mouse on the Moon, The 12-530-312 (10/12/63)-Photo-c	3	6	9	21	33	45
Mummy, The 12-537-211 (9-11/62) 2 versions with different back-c	13	26	39	89	195	300
Music Man, The 12-538-301 (1/63)	3	6	9	19	30	40
Naked Prey, The 12-545-612 (12/66)-Photo-c	5	10	15	31	53	75
Night of the Grizzly, The 12-558-612 (12/66)-Photo-c	3	6	9	21	33	45
None But the Brave 12-565-506 (4-6/65)	5	10	15	31	53	75
Operation Bikini 12-597-310 (10/63)-Photo-c	3	6	9	21	33	45
Operation Crossbow 12-590-512 (10-12/65)	3	6	9	19	30	40
Prince & the Pauper, The 01-654-207 (5-7/62)-Disney	3	6	9	21	33	45
Raven, The 12-680-309 (9/63)-Vincent Price photo-c	6	12	18	37	66	95
Ring of Bright Water 01-701-910 (10/69) (inside shows #12-701-909)	3	6	9	21	33	45
Runaway, The 12-707-412 (10-12/64)	3	6	9	18	28	38
Santa Claus Conquers the Martians #? (1964)-Photo-c	11	22	33	75	160	245
Santa Claus Conquers the Martians 12-725-603 (3/66, 12¢)-Reprints 1964 issue; photo-c	7	14	21	44	82	120
Another version given away with a Golden Record, SLP 170, nn, no price (3/66)-Complete with record	11	22	33	75	160	245
Six Black Horses 12-750-301 (1/63)-Photo-c	3	6	9	19	30	40
Ski Party 12-743-511 (9-11/65)-Frankie Avalon photo-c; photo inside-c; Adkins-a	4	8	12	28	47	65
Smoky 12-746-702 (2/67)	3	6	9	18	28	38
Sons of Katie Elder 12-748-511 (9-11/65); John Wayne app.; photo-c	10	20	30	66	138	210
Tales of Terror 12-793-302 (2/63)-Evans-a	5	10	15	33	57	80
Three Stooges Meet Hercules 01-828-208 (8/62)-Photo-c	9	18	27	59	117	175
Tomb of Ligeia 12-830-506 (4-6/65)	5	10	15	31	53	75
Treasure Island 01-845-211 (7-9/62)-Disney; r/4-Color #624	3	6	9	19	30	40
Twice Told Tales (Nathaniel Hawthorne) 12-840-401 (11-1/63-64); Vincent Price photo-c	5	10	15	33	57	80
Two on a Guillotine 12-850-506 (4-6/65)	3	6	9	21	33	45
Valley of Gwangi 01-880-912 (12/69)	8	16	24	55	105	155
War Gods of the Deep 12-900-509 (7-9/65)	3	6	9	19	30	40
War Wagon, The 12-533-709 (9/67); John Wayne app.	7	14	21	48	89	130
Who's Minding the Mint? 12-924-708 (8/67)	3	6	9	18	28	38
Wolfman, The 12-922-308 (6-8/63)	9	18	27	62	126	190
Wolfman, The 1(12-922-410)(8-10/64)-2nd printing; r/#12-922-308	4	8	12	25	40	55
Zulu 12-950-410 (8-10/64)-Photo-c	7	14	21	44	82	120

MOVIE COMICS (See Cinema Comics Herald & Fawcett Movie Comics)

MOVIE COMICS
National Periodical Publications/Picture Comics: April, 1939 - No. 6, Sept-Oct, 1939 (Most all photo-c)

	GD 2.0	VG 4.0	FN 6.0	VF 8.0	VF/NM 9.0	NM- 9.2
1- "Gunga Din", "Son of Frankenstein", "The Great Man Votes", "Fisherman's Wharf", & "Scouts to the Rescue" part 1; Wheelan "Minute Movies" begin	366	732	1098	2562	4481	6400
2- "Stagecoach", "The Saint Strikes Back", "King of the Turf", "Scouts to the Rescue" part 2, "Arizona Legion", Andy Devine photo-c	274	548	822	1740	2995	4250

Movie Comics #4 © DC

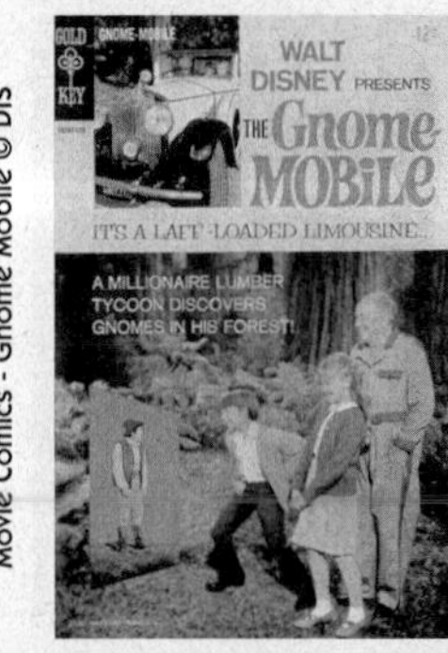
Movie Comics - Gnome Mobile © DIS

Movie Comics - Lord Jim © DIS

GD VG FN VF VF/NM NM-
2.0 4.0 6.0 8.0 9.0 9.2

3- "East Side of Heaven", "Mystery in the White Room", "Four Feathers", "Mexican Rose" with Gene Autry, "Spirit of Culver", "Many Secrets", "The Mikado"
(1st Gene Autry photo cover) 203 406 609 1289 2220 3150
4- "Captain Fury", Gene Autry in "Blue Montana Skies", "Streets of N.Y." with Jackie Cooper, "Oregon Trail" part 1 with Johnny Mack Brown, "Big Town Czar" with Barton MacLane, & "Star Reporter" with Warren Hull 152 304 456 965 1658 2350
5- "The Man in the Iron Mask", "Five Came Back", "Wolf Call", "The Girl & the Gambler", "The House of Fear", "The Family Next Door", "Oregon Trail" part 2 165 330 495 1056 1803 2550
6- "The Phantom Creeps", "Chumps at Oxford", & "The Oregon Trail" part 3; 2nd Robot-c 245 490 735 1568 2684 3800

NOTE: *Above books contain many original movie stills with dialogue from movie scripts. All issues are scarce.*

MOVIE COMICS
Fiction House Magazines: Dec, 1946 - No. 4, 1947

1-Big Town (by Lubbers), Johnny Danger begin; Celardo-a; Mitzi of the Movies by Fran Hopper 42 84 126 265 445 625
2-(2/47)- "White Tie & Tails" with William Bendix; Mitzi of the Movies begins; Matt Baker-a 32 64 96 190 310 430
3-(6/47)-Andy Hardy starring Mickey Rooney 32 64 96 190 310 430
4-Mitzi In Hollywood by Matt Baker; Merton of the Movies with Red Skelton; Yvonne DeCarlo & George Brent in "Slave Girl" 39 78 117 240 395 550

MOVIE COMICS
Gold Key/Whitman: Oct, 1962 - 1984

Alice in Wonderland 10144-503 (3/65)-Disney; partial reprint of 4-Color #331 4 8 12 23 37 50
Alice In Wonderland #1 (Whitman pre-pack, 3/84) 2 4 6 11 16 20
Aristocats, The 1 (30045-103)(3/71)-Disney; with pull-out poster (25¢) (No poster = half price) 6 12 18 40 73 105
Bambi 1 (10087-309)(9/63)-Disney; r/4-C #186 4 8 12 25 40 55
Bambi 2 (10087-607)(7/66)-Disney; r/4-C #186 3 6 9 19 30 40
Beneath the Planet of the Apes 30044-012 (12/70)-with pull-out poster; photo-c (No poster = half price) 8 16 24 56 108 160
Big Red 10026-211 (11/62)-Disney; photo-c 3 6 9 19 30 40
Big Red 10026-503 (3/65)-Disney; reprints 10026-211; photo-c 3 6 9 16 23 30
Blackbeard's Ghost 10222-806 (6/68)-Disney 3 6 9 18 28 38
Bullwhip Griffin 10181-706 (6/67)-Disney; Spiegle-a; photo-c 3 6 9 21 33 45
Captain Sindbad 10077-309 (9/63)-Manning-a; photo-c 5 10 15 35 63 90
Chitty Chitty Bang Bang 1 (30038-902)(2/69)-with pull-out poster; Disney; photo-c (No poster = half price) 6 12 18 40 73 105
Cinderella 10152-508 (8/65)-Disney; r/4-C #786 4 8 12 27 44 60
Darby O'Gill & the Little People 10251-001(1/70)-Disney; reprints 4-Color #1024 (Toth-a); photo-c 4 8 12 28 47 65
Dumbo 1 (10090-310)(10/63)-Disney; r/4-C #668 3 6 9 21 33 45
Emil & the Detectives 10120-502 (11/64)-Disney; photo-c & back-c photo pin-up 3 6 9 19 30 40
Escapade in Florence 1 (10043-301)(1/63)-Disney; starring Annette Funicello 7 14 21 48 89 130
Fall of the Roman Empire 10118-407 (7/64); Sophia Loren photo-c 4 8 12 23 37 50
Fantastic Voyage 10178-702 (2/67)-Wood/Adkins-a; photo-c 5 10 15 34 60 85
55 Days at Peking 10081-309 (9/63)-Photo-c 3 6 9 19 30 40
Fighting Prince of Donegal, The 10193-701 (1/67)-Disney 3 6 9 18 28 38
First Men in the Moon 10132-503 (3/65)-Fred Fredericks-a; photo-c 4 8 12 25 40 55
Gay Purr-ee 30017-301(1/63, 84 pgs.) 5 10 15 31 53 75
Gnome Mobile, The 10207-710 (10/67)-Disney; Walter Brennan photo-c & back-c photo pin-up 4 8 12 21 33 45
Goodbye, Mr. Chips 10246-006 (6/70)-Peter O'Toole photo-c 3 6 9 19 30 40
Happiest Millionaire, The 10221-804 (4/68)-Disney 3 6 9 21 33 45
Hey There, It's Yogi Bear 10122-409 (9/64)-Hanna-Barbera 6 12 18 37 66 95
Horse Without a Head, The 10109-401 (1/64)-Disney 3 6 9 18 28 38
How the West Was Won 10074-307 (7/63)-Based on the L'Amour novel; Tufts-a 4 8 12 27 44 60
In Search of the Castaways 10048-303 (3/63)-Disney; Hayley Mills photo-c 6 12 18 37 66 95
Jungle Book, The 1 (6022-801)(1/68-Whitman)-Disney; large size (10x13-1/2"); 59¢ 6 12 18 38 69 100

GD VG FN VF VF/NM NM-
2.0 4.0 6.0 8.0 9.0 9.2

Jungle Book, The 1 (30033-803)(3/68, 68 pgs.)-Disney; same contents as Whitman #1 4 8 12 23 37 50
Jungle Book, The 1 (6/78, $1.00 tabloid) 3 6 9 16 23 30
Jungle Book (7/84)-r/Giant; Whitman pre-pack 2 4 6 10 14 18
Kidnapped 10080-306 (6/63)-Disney; reprints 4-Color #1101; photo-c 3 6 9 21 33 45
King Kong 30036-809(9/68-68 pgs.)-painted-c 5 10 15 33 57 80
King Kong nn-Whitman Treasury($1.00, 68 pgs.,1968), same cover as Gold Key issue 6 12 18 38 69 100
King Kong 11299(#1-786, 10x13-1/4", 68 pgs., $1.00, 1978) 3 6 9 19 30 40
Lady and the Tramp 10042-301 (1/63)-Disney; r/4-Color #629 3 6 9 21 33 45
Lady and the Tramp 1 (1967-Giant; 25¢)-Disney; reprints part of Dell #1 5 10 15 33 57 80
Lady and the Tramp 2 (10042-203)(3/72)-Disney; r/4-Color #629 3 6 9 17 26 35
Legend of Lobo, The 1 (10059-303)(3/63)-Disney; photo-c 3 6 9 16 23 30
Lt. Robin Crusoe, U.S.N. 10191-610 (10/66)-Disney; Dick Van Dyke photo-c & back-c photo pin-up 3 6 9 17 26 35
Lion, The 10035-301 (1/63)-Photo-c 3 6 9 16 24 32
Lord Jim 10156-509 (9/65)-Photo-c 3 6 9 16 24 32
Love Bug, The 10237-906 (6/69)-Disney; Buddy Hackett photo-c 4 8 12 21 33 45
Mary Poppins 10136-501 (1/65)-Disney; photo-c 5 10 15 30 50 70
Mary Poppins 30023-501 (1/65-68 pgs.)-Disney; photo-c 6 12 18 41 76 110
McLintock 10110-403 (3/64); John Wayne app.; John Wayne & Maureen O'Hara photo-c 10 20 30 66 138 210
Merlin Jones as the Monkey's Uncle 10115-510 (10/65)-Disney; Annette Funicello front/back photo-c 5 10 15 34 60 85
Miracle of the White Stallions, The 10065-306 (6/63)-Disney 3 6 9 18 28 38
Misadventures of Merlin Jones, The 10115-405 (5/64)-Disney; Annette Funicello photo front/back-c 5 10 15 34 60 85
Moon-Spinners, The 10124-410 (10/64)-Disney; Hayley Mills photo-c 6 12 18 37 66 95
Mutiny on the Bounty 1 (10040-302)(2/63)-Marlon Brando photo-c 3 6 9 21 33 45
Nikki, Wild Dog of the North 10141-412 (12/64)-Disney; reprints 4-Color #1226 3 6 9 16 23 30
Old Yeller 10168-601 (1/66)-Disney; reprints 4-Color #869; photo-c 3 6 9 16 23 30
One Hundred & One Dalmations 1 (10247-002) (2/70)-Disney; reprints Four Color #1183 3 6 9 19 30 40
Peter Pan 1 (10086-309)(9/63)-Disney; reprints Four Color #442 3 6 9 21 33 45
Peter Pan 2 (10086-909)(9/69)-Disney; reprints Four Color #442 3 6 9 17 25 34
Peter Pan 1 (3/84)-r/4-Color #442; Whitman pre-pack 2 4 6 11 16 20
P.T. 109 10123-409 (9/64)-John F. Kennedy 4 8 12 28 47 65
Rio Conchos 10143-503(3/65) 3 6 9 21 33 45
Robin Hood 10163-506 (6/65)-Disney; reprints Four Color #413 3 6 9 16 24 32
Shaggy Dog & the Absent-Minded Professor 30032-708 (8/67-Giant, 68 pgs.) Disney; reprints 4-Color #985,1199 5 10 15 30 50 70
Sleeping Beauty 1 (30042-009)(9/70)-Disney; reprints Four Color #973; with pull-out poster (No poster = half price) 6 12 18 40 73 105
Snow White & the Seven Dwarfs 1 (10091-310)(10/63)-Disney; reprints Four Color #382 3 6 9 21 33 45
Snow White & the Seven Dwarfs 10091-709 (9/67)-Disney; reprints Four Color #382 3 6 9 17 26 35
Snow White & the Seven Dwarfs 90091-204 (2/84)-Reprints Four Color #382; Whitman pre-pack 2 4 6 11 16 20
Son of Flubber 1 (10057-304)(4/63)-Disney; sequel to "The Absent-Minded Professor" 3 6 9 21 33 45
Summer Magic 10076-309 (9/63)-Disney; Hayley Mills photo-c; Manning-a 6 12 18 38 69 100
Swiss Family Robinson 10236-904 (4/69)-Disney; reprints Four Color #1156; photo-c 3 6 9 19 30 40
Sword in the Stone, The 30019-402 (2/64-Giant, 68 pgs.)-Disney (see March of Comics #258 & Wart and the Wizard 6 12 18 37 66 95
That Darn Cat 10171-602 (2/66)-Disney; Hayley Mills photo-c 6 12 18 37 66 95

Movie Comics - Yellow Submarine © GK

Movie Love #12 © FF

Ms. Marvel (2016 series) #9 © MAR

GD 2.0 | VG 4.0 | FN 6.0 | VF 8.0 | VF/NM 9.0 | NM- 9.2

Those Magnificent Men in Their Flying Machines 10162-510 (10/65); photo-c
3 6 9 19 30 40
Three Stooges in Orbit 30016-211 (11/62-Giant, 32 pgs.)-All photos from movie; stiff-photo-c
9 18 27 58 114 170
Tiger Walks, A 10117-406 (6/64)-Disney; Torres?, Tufts-a; photo-c
4 8 12 23 37 50
Toby Tyler 10142-502 (2/65)-Disney; reprints Four Color #1092; photo-c
3 6 9 17 26 35
Treasure Island 1 (10200-703)(3/67)-Disney; reprints Four Color #624; photo-c
3 6 9 16 23 30
20,000 Leagues Under the Sea 1 (10095-312)(12/63)-Disney; reprints Four Color #614
3 6 9 19 30 40
Wonderful Adventures of Pinocchio, The 1 (10089-310)(10/63)-Disney; reprints Four Color #545
(see Wonderful Advs. of...) 3 6 9 20 31 42
Wonderful Adventures of Pinocchio, The 10089-109 (9/71)-Disney; reprints Four Color #545
3 6 9 16 23 30
Wonderful World of the Brothers Grimm 1 (10008-210)(10/62)
4 8 12 27 44 60
X, the Man with the X-Ray Eyes 10083-309 (9/63)-Ray Milland photo on-c
7 14 21 44 82 120
Yellow Submarine 35000-902 (2/69-Giant, 68 pgs.)-With pull-out poster;
The Beatles cartoon movie; Paul S. Newman-s 26 52 78 182 404 625
Without poster 10 20 30 64 132 200

MOVIE FABLES
DC Comics: Dec, 1944 (cover only ashcan)

nn-Ashcan comic, not distributed to newsstands, only for in house use. Covers were produced, but not the rest of the book. A copy sold in 2006 for $500.

MOVIE GEMS
DC Comics: Dec, 1944 (cover only ashcan)

nn-Ashcan comic, not distributed to newsstands, only for in house use. Covers were produced, but not the rest of the book. A copy sold in 2006 for $500.

MOVIE LOVE (Also see Personal Love)
Famous Funnies: Feb, 1950 - No. 22, Aug, 1953 (All photo-c)

1-Dick Powell, Evelyn Keyes, & Mickey Rooney photo-c
24 48 72 142 234 325
2-Myrna Loy photo-c 15 30 45 84 127 170
3-7,9: 6-Ricardo Montalban photo-c. 9-Gene Tierney, John Lund, Glenn Ford, & Rhonda Fleming photo-c. 14 28 42 78 112 145
8-Williamson/Frazetta-a, 6 pgs. 55 110 165 352 601 850
10-Frazetta-a, 6 pgs. 55 110 165 352 601 850
11,14-16: 14-Janet Leigh photo-c 14 28 42 76 108 140
12-Dean Martin & Jerry Lewis photo-c (12/51, pre-dates Advs. of Dean Martin & Jerry Lewis comic) 27 54 81 158 259 360
13-Ronald Reagan photo-c with 1 pg. biog. 34 68 102 199 325 450
17-Leslie Caron & Ralph Meeker photo-c; 1 pg. Frazetta ad
14 28 42 78 112 145
18-22: 19-John Derek photo-c. 20-Donald O'Connor & Debbie Reynolds photo-c. 21-Paul Henreid & Patricia Medina photo-c. 22-John Payne & Coleen Gray photo-c
13 26 39 74 105 135

NOTE: *Each issue has a full-length movie adaptation with photo covers.*

MOVIE MONSTERS (Magazine)
Atlas/Seaboard: Dec, 1974 - No. 4, Aug, 1975 (B&W; Film, photo & article magazine)

1-(84 pages) Planet of the Apes, King Kong, Sindbad & Harryhausen, Christopher Lee Dracula, Star Trek, Werewolf, Creature from the Black Lagoon, Hammer's Mummy, Gorgo, & Exorcist 4 8 12 27 44 60
2-(2/1975) 2001: Planet of the Apes-c; 2001: A Space Odyssey; Doc Savage; Frankenstein; Rodan; One Million Years BC; (lower print run) 4 8 12 27 44 60
3-(4/1975) Phantom of the Opera-c; Wolfman, Godzilla, Boris Karloff, Batman, Forbidden Planet, Jack the Giant Killer 4 8 12 25 40 55
4-(8/1975) Thing, Flash Gordon, Lon Chaney Jr., Lost Worlds, Loch Ness Monster, Day the Earth Stood Still, Star Trek 4 8 12 25 40 55

MOVIE THRILLERS (Movie)
Magazine Enterprises: 1949

1-Adaptation of "Rope of Sand" w/Burt Lancaster; Burt Lancaster photo-c
30 60 90 177 289 400

MOVIE TOWN ANIMAL ANTICS (Formerly Animal Antics; becomes Raccoon Kids #52 on)
National Periodical Publ.: No. 24, Jan-Feb, 1950 - No. 51, July-Aug, 1954

24-Raccoon Kids continue 12 24 36 67 94 120
25-51 10 20 30 54 72 90
NOTE: ***Sheldon Mayer** a-28-33, 35, 37-41, 43, 44, 47, 49-51.*

MOVIE TUNES COMICS (Formerly Animated...; Frankie No. 4 on)

Marvel Comics (MgPC): No. 3, Fall, 1946

3-Super Rabbit, Krazy Krow, Silly Seal & Ziggy Pig 20 40 60 115 188 260

MOWGLI JUNGLE BOOK (Rudyard Kipling's...)
Dell Publ. Co.: No. 487, Aug-Oct, 1953 - No. 620, Apr, 1955

Four Color 487 (#1) 7 14 21 46 86 125
Four Color 582 (8/54), 620 5 10 15 33 57 80

MPH
Image Comics: May, 2014 - No. 5, Feb, 2015 ($2.99/$4.99)

1-4-($2.99) Mark Millar-s/Duncan Fegredo-a; multiple covers on each 3.00
5-($4.99) Two covers 5.00

MR. (See Mister)

MRS. DEADPOOL AND THE HOWLING COMMANDOS (Secret Wars tie-in)
Marvel Comics: Aug, 2015 - No. 4, Nov, 2015 ($3.99, limited series)

1-4-Duggan-s/Espin-a; Dracula and Ghost Deadpool app. 4.00

M. REX
Image Comics: July, 1999 - No. 2, Dec, 1999 ($2.95)

Preview ($5.00) B&W pages and sketchbook; Rouleau-a 5.00
1,2-($2.95) 1-Joe Kelly-s/Rouleau-a/Anacleto-c. 2-Rouleau-c 3.00

MS. MARVEL (Also see The Avengers #183)
Marvel Comics Group: Jan, 1977 - No. 23, Apr, 1979

1-1st app. Ms. Marvel; Scorpion app. in #1,2 9 18 27 63 129 195
2-Origin 3 6 9 21 33 45
3-10: 5-Vision app. 6-10-(Reg. 30¢-c). 9-1st Deathbird. 10-Last 30¢ issue
2 4 6 13 18 22
6-10-(35¢-c variants, limited dist.)(6/77) 14 28 42 94 207 320
11-15,19-22: 19-Capt. Marvel app. 20-New costume 2 4 6 10 14 18
16-1st brief app. Mystique (Raven Darkholme) 6 12 18 37 66 95
17-Brief app. Mystique, disguised as Nick Fury 5 10 15 30 50 70
18-1st full app. Mystique; Avengers x-over 8 16 24 56 108 160
23-Vance Astro (leader of the Guardians) app. 3 6 9 16 23 30
NOTE: ***Austin** c-14i, 16i, 17i, 22i. **Buscema** a-1-3p; c(p)-2, 4, 6, 7, 15. **Infantino** a-14p, 19p. **Gil Kane** c-8. **Mooney** a-4-8p, 13p, 15-18p. **Starlin** c-12.*

MS. MARVEL (Also see New Avengers)
Marvel Comics: May, 2006 - No. 50, Apr, 2010 ($2.99)

1-Cho-c/Reed-s/De La Torre-a; Stilt-Man app. 3 6 9 15 22 28
1-Variant cover by Michael Turner 3 6 9 19 30 40
2-24: 4,5-Dr. Strange app. 6,7-Araña app. 4.00
25-($3.99) Two covers by Horn and Dodson; Secret Invasion 5.00
26-49: 26-31-Secret Invasion. 34-Spider-Man app. 35-Dark Reign. 37-Carol explodes. 39,40,46,48,49-Takeda-a. 40-Deadpool app. 41-Carol returns. 47-Spider-Man app. 3.00
50-($3.99) Mystique and Captain Marvel app.; Takeda & Oliver-a 5.00
... Annual 1 (11/08, $3.99) Spider-Man app.; Horn-c 4.00
... Special (3/07, $2.99) Reed-s/Camuncoli-a/c 3.00
... Storyteller (1/09, $2.99) Reed-s/Camuncoli-a/c 3.00
... Vol. 1: Best of the Best HC (2006, $19.99) r/#1-5 & Giant-Size Ms. Marvel #1 20.00
... Vol. 1: Best of the Best SC (2007, $14.99) r/#1-5 & Giant-Size Ms. Marvel #1 15.00
... Vol. 2: Civil War HC (2007, $19.99) r/#6-10 & Ms. Marvel Special #1 20.00
... Vol. 2: Civil War SC (2007, $14.99) r/#6-10 & Ms. Marvel Special #1 15.00
... Vol. 3: Operation Lightning Storm HC (2007, $19.99) r/#11-17 20.00
... Vol. 4: Monster Smash HC (2008, $19.99) r/#18-24 20.00

MS. MARVEL (Kamala Khan)(See Captain Marvel [2012-2014] #14&17 for cameo 1st apps.)
Marvel Comics: Apr, 2014 - No. 19, Dec, 2015 ($2.99)

1-Intro. Kamala Khan; G. Willow Wilson-s/Adrian Alphona-a; Pichelli-c
4 8 12 28 47 65
2-McKelvie-c 2 4 6 9 12 15
3-7: 3-5-Alphona-a. 3-McKelvie-c. 6,7-Wolverine app.; Wyatt-a 5.00
8-15: 8-11-Alphona-a. 9-Medusa app. 12-Loki app.; Bondoc-a. 13-15-Miyazawa-a 3.00
16-19-Secret Wars tie-ins; Captain Marvel app.; Alphona-a 3.00

MS. MARVEL (Kamala Khan)(Follows events of Secret Wars)
Marvel Comics: Jan, 2016 - No. 38, Apr, 2019 ($4.99/$3.99)

1-($4.99) Wilson-s/Miyazawa & Alphona-a; Chiang-c 5.00
2-11,13-30,32-38-($3.99) 2,3-Dr. Faustus app. 4-6-Nico Leon-a. 8-11-Civil War II tie-in. 4.00
12-($4.99) Andolfo-a; back-up Red Widow story 5.00
31-($4.99) 50th issue special; Wilson, Ahmed, Minhaj & Rowell-s; art by Leon & various 5.00

MS. MYSTIC
Pacific Comics: Oct, 1982 - No. 2, Feb, 1984 ($1.00/$1.50)

1,2: Neal Adams-c/a/script. 1-Origin; intro Erth, Ayre, Fyre & Watr 5.00

MS. MYSTIC

Ms. Tree #33 © Collins & Beatty

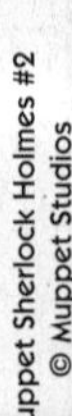
Multiple Man #3 © MAR

Muppet Sherlock Holmes #2 © Muppet Studios

	GD	VG	FN	VF	VF/NM	NM-
	2.0	4.0	6.0	8.0	9.0	9.2

Continuity Comics: 1988 - No. 9, May, 1992 ($2.00)

1-9: 1,2-Reprint Pacific Comics issues 3.00

MS. MYSTIC
Continunity Comics: V2#1, Oct, 1993 - V2#4, Jan, 1994 ($2.50)

V2#1-4: 1-Adams-c(i)/part-i. 2-4-Embossed-c. 2-Nebres part-i. 3-Adams-c(i)/plot. 4-Adams-c(p)/plot 3.00

MS. MYSTIC DEATHWATCH 2000 (Ms. Mystic #3)
Continuity: May, 1993 - No. 3, Aug, 1993 ($2.50)

1-3-Bagged w/card; Adams plots 3.00

MS. TREE QUARTERLY / SPECIAL
DC Comics: Summer, 1990 -No. 10, 1992 ($3.95/$3.50, 84 pgs, mature)

1-10: 1-Midnight story; Batman text story, Grell-a. 2,3-Midnight stories; The Butcher text stories 4.00

NOTE: *Cowan c-2. Grell c-1, 6. Infantino a-8.*

MS. TREE'S THRILLING DETECTIVE ADVENTURES (Ms. Tree #4 on; also see The Best of Ms. Tree)(Baxter paper #4-9) (See Eclipse Magazine #1 for 1st app.)
Eclipse Comics/Aardvark-Vanaheim 10-18/Renegade Press 19 on: 2/83 - #9, 7/84; #10, 8/84 - #18, 5/85; #19, 6/85 - #50, 6/89

1 4.00
2-49: 2-Schythe begins. 9-Last Eclipse & last color issue. 10,11-two-tone 3.00
50-Contains flexi-disc ($3.95, 52 pgs.) 4.00
Ms. Tree 3-D 1 (Renegade, 8/85)-With glasses; Mike Mist app. 3.00
Summer Special 1 (8/86) 3.00
1950s Three-Dimensional Crime (7/87, no glasses)-Johnny Dynamite in 3-D 3.00

NOTE; *Miller pin-up 1-4. Johnny Dynamite-r begin #36 by Morisi.*

MS. VICTORY SPECIAL(Also see Capt. Paragon & Femforce)
Americomics: Jan, 1985 (nd)

1 4.00

MUCHA LUCHA (Based on Kids WB animated TV show)
DC Comics: Jun, 2003 - No. 3, Aug, 2003 ($2.25, limited series)

1-3-Rikochet, Buena Girl and The Flea app. 4.00

MUDMAN
Image Comics: Nov, 2011 - No. 6 ($3.50)

1-6-Paul Grist-s/a 3.50

MUGGSY MOUSE (Also see Tick Tock Tales)
Magazine Enterprises: 1951 - No. 3, 1951; No. 4, 1954 - No. 5, 1954; 1963

	GD	VG	FN	VF	VF/NM	NM-
1(A-1 #33)	14	28	42	82	121	160
2(A-1 #36)-Racist-c	21	42	63	122	199	275
3(A-1 #39), 4(A-1 #95), 5(A-1 #99)	9	18	27	52	69	85
Super Reprint #14(1963), I.W. Reprint #1,2 (nd)	2	4	6	9	13	16

MUGGY-DOO, BOY CAT
Stanhall Publ.: July, 1953 - No. 4, Jan, 1954

	GD	VG	FN	VF	VF/NM	NM-
1-Funny animal; Irving Spector-a	12	24	36	67	94	120
2-4	7	14	21	35	43	50
Super Reprint #12('63), 16('64)	2	4	6	8	11	14

MULAN: REVELATIONS
Dark Horse Comics: Jun, 2015 - No. 4, Nov, 2015 ($3.99)

1-4-Andreyko-s/Kaneshiro-a; Mulan in 2125 Shanghai 4.00

MULTIPLE MAN (Jamie Madrox from X-Factor)
Marvel Comics: Aug, 2018 - No. 5, Dec, 2018 ($3.99, limited series)

1-5: 1-Rosenberg-s/MacDonald-a; New Mutants & Beast app. 4.00

MULTIVERSITY, THE
DC Comics: Oct, 2014 - No. 2, Jun, 2015 ($4.99/$5.99)

1-($4.99) Morrison-s/Reis-a; Earth-23 Superman, Capt. Carrot, alternate Earth heroes gather 5.00
2-($5.99) Morrison-s/Reis-a/c 6.00
... 1&2 Director's Cut (2/16, $7.99, squarebound) reprints #1&2 with original B&W pencil art plus Morrison's original story proposals 8.00
...: Guidebook (3/15, $7.99) Legion of Sivanas, Kamandi app.; Multiverse map 8.00
...: Mastermen (4/15, $4.99) Earth-10 Overman & The Freedom Fighters; Jim Lee-a 5.00
...: Pax Americana 1 (1/15, $4.99) Earth-4 Charlton heroes; Quitely-a 5.00
...: Pax Americana Director's Cut 1 (7/15, $9.99) Quitely pencil art and Morrison's script excerpts; polybagged with large folded Multiverse map 10.00
...: The Just 1 (12/14, $4.99) Earth-16 Super-Sons and Justice League offspring; Oliver-a 5.00
...: The Society of Super-Heroes: Conquerors of the Counter-World 1 (11/14, $4.99) Earth-40 Dr. Fate, Green Lantern, Blackhawks, The Atom vs. Vandal Savage; Sprouse-a 5.00
...: Thunderworld Adventures 1 (2/15, $4.99) Earth-5 Shazam Family; Cam Stewart-c 5.00

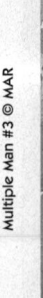

	GD	VG	FN	VF	VF/NM	NM-
	2.0	4.0	6.0	8.0	9.0	9.2

...: Ultra Comics 1 (5/15, $4.99) Earth-33 Ultra; Mahnke-a 5.00

MUMMY, THE (See Universal Presents... under Dell Giants & Movie Classics)

MUMMY, THE: PALIMPSEST
Titan Comics (Hammer Comics): Dec, 2016 - No. 5, May, 2017 ($3.99)

1-5-Peter Milligan-s/Ronilson Freire-a 4.00

MUMMY, THE: THE RISE AND FALL OF XANGO'S AX (Based on the Brendan Fraser movies)
IDW Publishing: Apr, 2008 - No. 4, July, 2008 ($3.99, limited series)

1-4-Prequel to '08 movie The Mummy: Tomb of the Dragon Emperor; Stephen Mooney-a 4.00

MUNCHKIN
BOOM! Studios (BOOM! Box): Jan, 2015 - No. 25, Jan, 2017 ($3.99)

1-24-Short stories of characters from the card game; each issue contains a card 4.00
25-($4.99) Covers by McGinty & Fridolfs 5.00
...: Deck the Dungeons (12/15, $4.99) Katie Cook-s/Mike Luckas-a; 2 covers 5.00

MUNDEN'S BAR ANNUAL
First Comics: Apr, 1988; 1989 ($2.95/$5.95)

	GD	VG	FN	VF	VF/NM	NM-
1-($2.95)-r/from Grimjack; Fish Police story; Ordway-c						4.00
2-($5.95)-Teenage Mutant Ninja Turtles app.	2	4	6	9	12	15

MUNSTERS, THE (TV)
Gold Key: Jan, 1965 - No. 16, Jan, 1968 (All photo-c)

	GD	VG	FN	VF	VF/NM	NM-
1 (10134-501)	24	48	72	168	372	575
2	11	22	33	76	163	250
3-5	9	18	27	61	123	185
6-16	9	18	27	57	111	165

MUNSTERS, THE (TV)
TV Comics!: Aug, 1997 - No. 4 ($2.95, B&W)

	GD	VG	FN	VF	VF/NM	NM-
1-4-All have photo-c						5.00
1,4-($7.95)-Variant-c	1	3	4	6	8	10
2-Variant-c w/Beverly Owens as Marilyn						6.00
Special Comic Con Ed. (7/97, $9.95)						10.00

MUPPET... (TV)
BOOM! Studios

... King Arthur 1-4 (12/09 - No. 4, 3/10, $2.99) Benjamin & Storck-s/Alvarez-a; 2 covers 3.00
... Peter Pan 1-4 (8/09 - No. 4, 11/09, $2.99) Randolph-s/Mebberson-a; multiple covers 3.00
... Robin Hood 1-4 (4/09 - No. 4, 7/09, $2.99) Beedle-s/Villavert Jr.-a; multiple covers 3.00
... Sherlock Holmes 1-4 (8/10 - No. 4, 11/10, $2.99) Storck-s/Mebberson-a/c 3.00
... Snow White 1-4 (4/10 - No. 4, 7/10, $2.99) Snider & Storck-s/Paroline-a; 2 covers 3.00

MUPPET BABIES, THE (TV)(See Star Comics Magazine)
Marvel Comics (Star Comics)/Marvel #18 on: Aug, 1985 - No. 26, July, 1989 (Children's book)

1-26 5.00

MUPPETS (The Four Seasons)
Marvel Worldwide: Sept, 2012 - No. 4, Dec, 2012 ($2.99, limited series)

1-4-Roger Landridge-s/a 3.00

MUPPET SHOW, THE (TV)
BOOM! Studios: Mar, 2009 - No. 4, Jun, 2009 ($2.99, limited series)

1-4-Roger Landridge-s/a; multiple covers 3.00
...: The Treasure of Peg Leg Wilson (7/09 - No. 4, 10/09) 1-4-Landridge-s/a; multiple-c 3.00

MUPPET SHOW COMIC BOOK, THE (TV)
BOOM! Studios: No. 0, Nov, 2009 - No. 11, Oct, 2010 ($2.99)

0-11: 0-3-Roger Landridge-s/a; multiple covers. 0-Paroline-a; Pigs in Space 3.00

MUPPETS TAKE MANHATTAN, THE
Marvel Comics (Star Comics): Nov, 1984 - No. 3, Jan, 1985

1-3-Movie adapt. r-/Marvel Super Special 4.00

MURCIELAGA, SHE-BAT
Heroic Publishing: Jan, 1993 - No. 2, 1993 (B&W)

1-($1.50, 28 pgs.) 3.00
2-($2.95, 36 pgs.)-Coated-c 3.00

MURDER CAN BE FUN
Slave Labor Graphics: Feb, 1996 - No. 12 ($2.95, B&W)

1-12: 1-Dorkin-c. 2-Vasquez-c. 3.00

MURDER INCORPORATED (My Private Life #16 on)
Fox Feature Syndicate: 1/48 - No. 15, 12/49; (2 No.9's); 6/50 - No. 3, 8/51

	GD	VG	FN	VF	VF/NM	NM-
1 (1st Series); 1,2 have 'For Adults Only' on-c	73	146	219	467	796	1125
2-Electrocution story	52	104	156	328	552	775
3,5-7,9(4/49),10(5/49),11-15	35	70	105	208	339	470

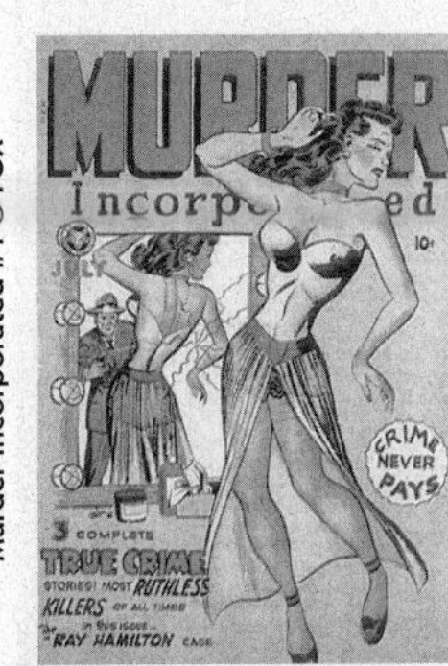

Murder Incorporated #4 © FOX

Muties #1 © MAR

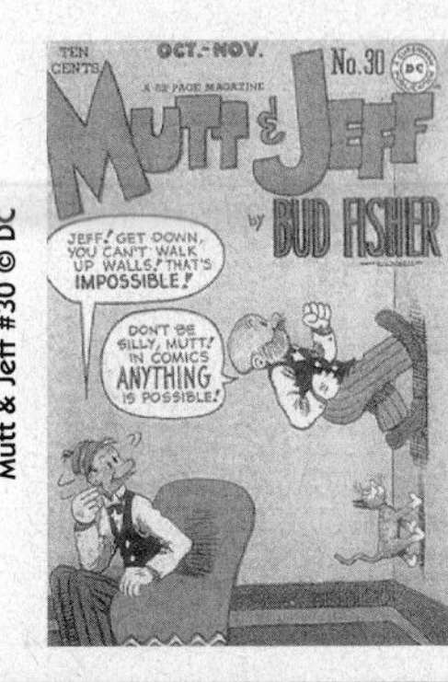

Mutt & Jeff #30 © DC

GD VG FN VF VF/NM NM-
2.0 4.0 6.0 8.0 9.0 9.2

4-Classic lingerie-c 103 206 309 659 1130 1600
8-Used in **SOTI**, pg. 160 39 78 117 231 378 525
9(3/49)-Possible use in **SOTI**, pg. 145; r/Blue Beetle #56('48)
34 68 102 204 332 460
5(#1, 6/50)(2nd Series)-Formerly My Desire #4; bondage-c.
27 54 81 162 266 370
2(8/50)-Morisi-a 25 50 75 150 245 340
3(8/51)-Used in **POP**, pg. 81; Rico-a; lingerie-c/panels
33 66 99 194 317 440

MURDERLAND
Image Comics: Aug, 2010 - No. 3, Nov, 2010 ($2.99)
1-3-Stephen Scott-s/David Haun-a 3.00

MURDER ME DEAD
El Capitán Books: July, 2000 - No. 9, Oct, 2001 ($2.95/$4.95, B&W)
1-8-David Lapham-s/a 3.00
9-($4.95) 5.00

MURDEROUS GANGSTERS
Avon Per./Realistic No. 3 on: Jul, 1951; No. 2, Dec, 1951 - No. 4, Jun, 1952
1-Pretty Boy Floyd, Leggs Diamond; 1 pg. Wood-a 87 174 261 553 952 1350
2-Baby-Face Nelson; 1 pg. Wood-a; classic painted-c
81 162 243 518 884 1250
3-Painted-c 43 86 129 271 461 650
4- "Murder by Needle" drug story; Mort Lawrence-a; Kinstler-c
47 94 141 296 498 700

MURDER MYSTERIES (Neil Gaiman's...)
Dark Horse Comics: 2002 ($13.95, HC, one-shot)
HC-Adapts Gaiman story; P. Craig Russell-script/art 14.00

MURDER TALES (Magazine)
World Famous Publications: V1#10, Nov, 1970 - V1#11, Jan, 1971 (52 pgs.)
V1#10-One pg. Frazetta ad 6 12 18 40 73 105
11-Guardineer-r; bondage-c 5 10 15 31 53 75

MUSHMOUSE AND PUNKIN PUSS (TV)
Gold Key: September, 1965 (Hanna-Barbera)
1 (10153-509) 8 16 24 55 105 155

MUSIC BOX (Jennifer Love Hewitt's...)
IDW Publishing: Nov, 2009 - No. 5, Apr, 2010 ($3.99, lim. series)
1-5-Anthology; Scott Lobdell-s/art by various. 1-Gaydos-a. 3-Archer-a 4.00

MUSIC MAN, THE (See Movie Classics)

MUTANT CHRONICLES (Video game)
Acclaim Comics (Armada): May, 1996 - No. 4, Aug, 1996 ($2.95, lim. series)
1-4: Simon Bisley-c on all, Sourcebook (#5) 4.00

MUTANT EARTH (Stan Winston's...)
Image Comics: April, 2002 - No. 4, Jan, 2003 ($2.95)
1-4-Flip book w/Realm of the Claw 3.00
Trakk...His Adventures in Mutant Earth TPB (2003, $16.95) r/#1-4; Winston interview 17.00

MUTANT MISADVENTURES OF CLOAK AND DAGGER, THE
(Becomes Cloak and Dagger #14 on)
Marvel Comics: Oct, 1988 - No. 19, Aug, 1991 ($1.25/$1.50)
1-8,10-15: 1-X-Factor app. 10-Painted-c. 12-Dr. Doom app. 14-Begin new direction 4.00
9,16-19: 9-(52 pgs.) The Avengers x-over; painted-c. 16-18-Spider-Man x-over. 18-Infinity Gauntlet x-over; Thanos cameo; Ghost Rider app. 19-(52 pgs.) Origin Cloak & Dagger 5.00
NOTE: *Austin a-12i; c(i)-4, 12, 13; scripts-all.* ***Russell*** *a-2i.* ***Williamson*** *a-14i-16i; c-15i.*

MUTANTS & MISFITS
Silverline Comics (Solson): 1987 - No. 3, 1987 ($1.95)
1-3 3.00

MUTANTS VS. ULTRAS
Malibu Comics (Ultraverse): Nov, 1995 ($6.95, one-shot)
1-r/Exiles vs. X-Men, Night Man vs. Wolverine, Prime vs. Hulk 7.00

MUTANT, TEXAS: TALES OF SHERIFF IDA RED (Also see Jingle Belle)
Oni Press: May, 2002 - No. 4, Nov, 2002 ($2.95, B&W, limited series)
1-4-Paul Dini-s/J. Bone-c/a 3.00
TPB (2003, $11.95) r/#1-4; intro. by Joe Lansdale 12.00

MUTANT 2099
Marvel Comics (Marvel Knights): Nov, 2004 ($2.99, one-shot)
1-Kirkman-s/Pat Lee-c 3.00

MUTANT X (See X-Factor)
Marvel Comics: Nov, 1998 - No. 32, June, 2001 ($2.99/$1.99/$2.25)
1-($2.99) Alex Summers with alternate world's X-Men 4.00
2-11,13-19-($1.99): 2-Two covers. 5-Man-Spider-c/app. 3.00
12,25-($2.99): 12-Pin-up gallery by Kaluta, Romita, Byrne 4.00
20-24,26-32: 20-Begin $2.25-c. 28-31-Logan-c/app. 32-Last issue 3.00
Annual '99, '00 (5/99,'00, $3.50) '00-Doran-a(p) 4.00
Annual 2001 ($2.99) Story occurs between #31 & #32; Dracula app. 4.00

MUTANT X (Based on TV show)
Marvel Comics: May, 2002; June, 2002 ($3.50)
...: Dangerous Decisions (6/02) -Kuder-s/Immonen-a 3.50
...: Origin (5/02) -Tischman & Chaykin-s/Ferguson-a 3.50

MUTATIS
Marvel Comics (Epic Comics): 1992 - No. 3, 1992 ($2.25, mini-series)
1-3: Painted-c 3.00

MUTIES
Marvel Comics: Apr, 2002 - No. 6, Sept, 2002 ($2.50)
1-6: 1-Bollars-s/Ferguson-a. 2-Spaziante-a. 3-Haspiel-a. 4-Kanuiga-a 3.00

MUTINY (Stormy Tales of the Seven Seas)
Aragon Magazines: Oct, 1954 - No. 3, Feb, 1955
1 19 38 57 112 179 245
2,3: 2-Capt. Mutiny. 3-Lashing torture bondage-c 15 30 45 84 127 170

MUTINY ON THE BOUNTY (See Classics Illustrated #100 & Movie Comics)

MUTOPIA X (Also see House of M and related titles)
Marvel Comics: Sept, 2005 - No. 5, Jan, 2006 ($2.99, limited series)
1-5-Medina-a/Hine-s 3.00
House of M: Mutopia X (2006, $13.99, TPB) r/series 14.00

MUTT AND JEFF (See All-American, All-Flash #18, Cicero's Cat, Comic Cavalcade, Famous Feature Stories, The Funnies, Popular & Xmas Comics)
All American/National 1-103(6/58)/Dell 104(10/58)-115 (10-12/59)/Harvey 116(2/60)-148: Summer, 1939 (nd) - No. 148, Nov, 1965
1(nn)-Lost Wheels 203 406 609 1289 2220 3150
2(nn)-Charging Bull (Summer, 1940, nd; on sale 6/20/40)
90 180 270 576 988 1400
3(nn)-Bucking Broncos (Summer, 1941, nd) 60 120 180 381 653 925
4(Winter, '41), 5(Summer, '42) 54 108 162 343 574 825
6-10: 6-Includes Minute Man Answers the Call 32 64 96 188 307 425
11-20: 20-X-Mas-c 21 42 63 126 206 285
21-30 16 32 48 94 147 200
31-50: 32-X-Mas-c 14 28 42 82 121 160
51-75-Last Fisher issue. 53-Last 52 pgs. 12 24 36 67 94 120
76-99,101-103: 76-Last pre-code issue(1/55) 5 10 15 35 63 90
100 6 12 18 37 66 95
104-115,132-148 5 10 15 30 48 65
116-131-Richie Rich app. 5 10 15 32 51 70
...Jokes 1-3(8/60-61, Harvey)-84 pgs.; Richie Rich in all; Little Dot in #2,3; Lotta in #2
5 10 15 30 48 65
...New Jokes 1-4(10/63-11/65, Harvey)-68 pgs.; Richie Rich in #1-3; Stumbo in #1
4 8 12 24 37 50
NOTE: *Most all issues by* ***Al Smith****. Issues from 1963 on have* ***Fisher*** *reprints. Clarification: early issues signed by Fisher are mostly drawn by Smith.*

MY BROTHERS' KEEPER
Spire Christian Comics (Fleming H. Revell Co.): 1973 (35/49¢, 36 pgs.)
nn 2 4 6 13 18 22

MY CONFESSIONS (My Confession #7&8; formerly Western True Crime; A Spectacular Feature Magazine #11)
Fox Feature Syndicate: No. 7, Aug, 1949 - No. 10, Jan-Feb, 1950
7-Wood-a (10 pgs.) 77 154 231 493 847 1200
8,9: 8-Harrison/Wood-a (19 pgs.). 9-Wood-a 39 78 117 240 395 550
10 23 46 69 138 227 315

MYCROFT HOLMES AND THE APOCALYPSE HANDBOOK
Titan Comics: Sept, 2016 - No. 5, Mar, 2017 ($3.99)
1-5-Sherlock Holmes' older brother; Kareem Abdul-Jabbar & Raymond Obstfeld-s 4.00

MY DATE COMICS (Teen-age)
Hillman Periodicals: July, 1947 - V1#4, Jan, 1948 (2nd Romance comic; see Young Romance)
1-S&K-c/a 53 106 159 334 567 800
2-4-S&K-c/a; Dan Barry-a 34 68 102 199 325 450

MY DESIRE (Formerly Jo-Jo Comics; becomes Murder, Inc. #5 on)

My Faith in Frankie #1 © Carey & Liew

My Greatest Adventure #17 © DC

My Little Pony: Friendship Is Magic #21 © Hasbro

Fox Feature Syndicate: No. 30, Aug, 1949 - No. 4, April, 1950

	GD 2.0	VG 4.0	FN 6.0	VF 8.0	VF/NM 9.0	NM- 9.2
30 (#1)	31	62	93	182	296	410
31 (#2, 10/49),3(2/50),4	21	42	63	124	202	280
31 (Canadian edition)	14	28	42	80	115	150
32(12/49)-Wood-a	34	68	102	199	325	450

MY DIARY (Becomes My Friend Irma #3 on?)
Marvel Comics (A Lovers Mag.): Dec, 1949 - No. 2, Mar, 1950

	GD 2.0	VG 4.0	FN 6.0	VF 8.0	VF/NM 9.0	NM- 9.2
1,2-Photo-c	23	46	69	136	223	310

MY EXPERIENCE (Formerly All Top; becomes Judy Canova #23 on)
Fox Feature Syndicate: No. 19, Sept, 1949 - No. 22, Mar, 1950

	GD 2.0	VG 4.0	FN 6.0	VF 8.0	VF/NM 9.0	NM- 9.2
19,21: 19-Wood-a. 21-Wood-a(2)	37	74	111	218	354	490
20	20	40	60	115	188	260
22-Wood-a (9 pgs.)	33	66	99	194	317	440

MY FAITH IN FRANKIE
DC Comics (Vertigo): March, 2004 - No. 4, June, 2004 ($2.95, limited series)

	GD 2.0	VG 4.0	FN 6.0	VF 8.0	VF/NM 9.0	NM- 9.2
1-4-Mike Carey-s/Sonny Liew & Marc Hempel-a						3.00
TPB (2004, $6.95, digest-size) r/series in B&W; Dead Boy Detectives preview						7.00

MY FAVORITE MARTIAN (TV)
Gold Key: 1/64; No.2, 7/64 - No. 9, 10/66 (No. 1,3-9 have photo-c)

	GD 2.0	VG 4.0	FN 6.0	VF 8.0	VF/NM 9.0	NM- 9.2
1-Russ Manning-a	11	22	33	72	154	235
2	6	12	18	42	79	115
3-9	5	10	15	35	63	90

MY FRIEND IRMA (Radio/TV) (Formerly My Diary? and/or Western Life Romances?)
Marvel/Atlas Comics (BFP): No. 3, June, 1950 - No. 47, Dec, 1954; No. 48, Feb, 1955

	GD 2.0	VG 4.0	FN 6.0	VF 8.0	VF/NM 9.0	NM- 9.2
3-Dan DeCarlo-a in all; 52 pgs. begin, end ?	77	154	231	493	847	1200
4-Kurtzman-a (10 pgs.)	37	74	111	222	361	500
5- "Egghead Doodle" by Kurtzman (4 pgs.)	24	48	72	142	234	325
6,8-10: 9-Paper dolls, 1 pg; Millie app. (5 pgs.)	19	38	57	111	176	240
7-One pg. Kurtzman-a	19	38	57	112	179	245
11-23: 23-One pg. Frazetta-a	15	30	45	88	137	185
24-48: 41,48-Stan Lee & Dan DeCarlo app.	15	30	45	84	127	170

MY GIRL PEARL
Atlas Comics: 4/55 - #4, 10/55; #5, 7/57 - #6, 9/57; #7, 8/60 - #11, ?/61

	GD 2.0	VG 4.0	FN 6.0	VF 8.0	VF/NM 9.0	NM- 9.2
1-Dan DeCarlo-c/a in #1-6	82	164	246	528	902	1275
2	39	78	117	240	395	550
3-6	31	62	93	186	303	420
7-11	14	28	42	94	207	320

MY GREATEST ADVENTURE (Doom Patrol #86 on)
National Periodical Publications: Jan-Feb, 1955 - No. 85, Feb, 1964

	GD 2.0	VG 4.0	FN 6.0	VF 8.0	VF/NM 9.0	NM- 9.2
1-Before CCA	148	296	444	1221	2761	4300
2	56	112	168	454	990	1525
3-5	38	76	114	285	641	1000
6-10: 6-Science fiction format begins	32	64	96	230	515	800
11-14: 12-1st S.A. issue	24	48	72	168	372	575
15-17: Kirby-a in all	27	54	81	189	420	650
18-Kirby-c/a	28	56	84	202	451	700
19,23-25	20	40	60	140	310	480
20,21,28-Kirby-a	24	48	72	168	372	575
22-Space Ranger prototype (7-8/58)(see Showcase #15 for Space Ranger debut)	23	46	69	168	382	560
26,27,29,30	17	34	51	114	252	390
31-40	14	28	42	94	207	320
41,42,44-57,59	12	24	36	83	182	280
43-Kirby-a	13	26	39	87	191	295
58,60,61-Toth-a; Last 10¢ issue	12	24	36	84	185	285
62-76,78,79: 79-Promotes "Legion of the Strange" for next issue; renamed Doom Patrol for #80	10	20	30	68	144	220
77-Toth-a; Robotman prototype	11	22	33	78	163	250
80-(6/63)-Intro/origin Doom Patrol and begin series; origin & 1st app. Negative Man, Elasti-Girl & S.A. Robotman	136	272	408	1088	2444	3800
81,85-Toth-a	23	46	69	161	356	550
82-84	21	42	63	142	316	490

NOTE: ***Anderson*** *a-42.* ***Cameron*** *a-24.* ***Colan*** *a-77.* ***Meskin*** *a-25, 26, 32, 39, 45, 50, 56, 57, 61, 64, 70, 73, 74, 76, 79; c-76.* ***Moreira*** *a-11, 12, 15, 17, 20, 23, 25, 27, 37, 40-43, 46, 48, 55-57, 59, 60, 62-65, 67, 69, 70; c-1-4, 7-10.* ***Roussos*** *c/a-71-73.* ***Wildey*** *a-32.*

MY GREATEST ADVENTURE (Also see 2011 Weird Worlds series)
DC Comics: Dec, 2011 - No. 6, May, 2012 ($3.99, limited series)

	GD 2.0	VG 4.0	FN 6.0	VF 8.0	VF/NM 9.0	NM- 9.2
1-6-Short stories of Tanga, Robotman, and Garbage Man; Lopresti-s/a, Maguire-s/a						4.00

MY GREAT LOVE (Becomes Will Rogers Western #5)
Fox Feature Syndicate: Oct, 1949 - No. 4, Apr, 1950

	GD 2.0	VG 4.0	FN 6.0	VF 8.0	VF/NM 9.0	NM- 9.2
1	28	56	84	168	274	380
2-4	15	30	45	94	147	200

MY INTIMATE AFFAIR (Inside Crime #3)
Fox Feature Syndicate: Mar, 1950 - No. 2, May, 1950

	GD 2.0	VG 4.0	FN 6.0	VF 8.0	VF/NM 9.0	NM- 9.2
1	34	68	102	204	332	460
2	16	32	48	98	154	210

MY LIFE (Formerly Meet Corliss Archer)
Fox Feature Syndicate: No. 4, Sept, 1948 - No. 15, July, 1950

	GD 2.0	VG 4.0	FN 6.0	VF 8.0	VF/NM 9.0	NM- 9.2
4-Used in **SOTI**, pg. 39; Kamen/Feldstein-a	57	114	171	362	619	875
5-Kamen-a	37	74	111	222	361	500
6-Kamen/Feldstein-a	39	78	117	240	395	550
7-Wood-a; wash cover	40	80	120	246	411	575
8,9,11-15	20	40	60	120	195	270
10-Wood-a	31	62	93	186	303	420

MY LITTLE MARGIE (TV)
Charlton Comics: July, 1954 - No. 54, Nov, 1964

	GD 2.0	VG 4.0	FN 6.0	VF 8.0	VF/NM 9.0	NM- 9.2
1-Photo front/back-c	39	78	117	240	395	550
2-Photo front/back-c	20	40	60	118	192	265
3-7,10	14	28	42	76	108	140
8,9-Infinity-c	14	28	42	76	108	140
11-14: Part-photo-c (#13, 8/56). 14-UFO cover	11	22	33	62	86	110
15-19	10	20	30	58	79	100
20-(25¢, 100 pg. issue)	16	32	48	92	144	195
21-40: 40-Last 10¢ issue	5	10	15	33	57	80
41-53	5	10	15	30	50	70
54-(11/64) Beatles on cover; lead story spoofs the Beatle haircut craze of the 1960's; Beatles app. (scarce)	18	36	54	128	284	440

NOTE: Doll cut-outs in 32, 33, 40, 45, 50.

MY LITTLE MARGIE'S BOY FRIENDS (TV) (Freddy V2#12 on)
Charlton Comics: Aug, 1955 - No. 11, Apr?, 1958

	GD 2.0	VG 4.0	FN 6.0	VF 8.0	VF/NM 9.0	NM- 9.2
1-Has several Archie swipes	17	34	51	100	158	215
2	10	20	30	58	79	100
3-11	9	18	27	50	65	80

MY LITTLE MARGIE'S FASHIONS (TV)
Charlton Comics: Feb, 1959 - No. 5, Nov, 1959

	GD 2.0	VG 4.0	FN 6.0	VF 8.0	VF/NM 9.0	NM- 9.2
1	21	42	63	122	199	275
2-5	10	20	30	56	76	95

MY LITTLE PHONY: A BRONY ADVENTURE
Dynamite Entertainment: 2014 ($5.99, one-shot)

	NM- 9.2
1-My Little Pony fandom parody; Moreci & Seeley-a/Haeser & Baal-a; 2 covers	6.00

MY LITTLE PONY
IDW Publishing

	NM- 9.2
... Annual #1: Equestria Girls (10/13, $7.99) Price & Fleecs-a; multiple covers	8.00
... Annual 2014 (9/14, $7.99) Anderson-s/Bates-a; two covers	8.00
... Annual 2017 (2/17, $7.99) Short stories by Whitley, Rice, Price & others; two covers	8.00
... Art Gallery (11/13, $3.99) Pin-ups by Sara Richard & others	4.00
... Cover Gallery (8/13, $3.99) Gallery of regular and variant covers	4.00
... Halloween Comicfest 2016 (10/16, giveaway) reprints Friends Forever #4	3.00
... Holiday Special (12/15, $3.99) Cook-s/Hickey, Garbowska, Price, Cook-a; 3 covers	4.00
... Holiday Special 2017 (12/17, $4.99) Asmus-s/Hickey-a; 3 covers	5.00
... Holiday Special (11/19, $4.99) Asmus-s/Price & Forstner-a; 3 covers	5.00

MY LITTLE PONY: FEATS OF FRIENDSHIP
IDW Publishing: Aug, 2019 - No. 3, Oct, 2019 ($3.99, limited series)

	NM- 9.2
1-3-Ian Flynn-s/Tony Fleecs-a	4.00

MY LITTLE PONY: FIENDS FOREVER
IDW Publishing: Apr, 2015 - No. 5, May, 2015 ($3.99, weekly mini-series)

	NM- 9.2
1-5-Spotlight on Equestria's villains. 1-Whitley-s/Hickey-a. 3-Garbowska-a	4.00

MY LITTLE PONY: FRIENDS FOREVER
IDW Publishing: Jan, 2014 - No. 38, Mar, 2017 ($3.99)

	NM- 9.2
1-38: 1-de Campi-s/McNeil-a; multiple covers. 3,6,10,13,14,21,27,30,34,37-Garbowska-a. 8-Katie Cook-s	4.00
... - Halloween Fest 2014 (10/14, giveaway) reprints #2	3.00

MY LITTLE PONY: FRIENDSHIP IS MAGIC
IDW Publishing: Nov, 2012 - Present ($3.99)

	NM- 9.2
1-Katie Cook-s/Andy Price-a; 7 covers	5.00
1-Subscription variant cover by Jill Thompson	5.00
2-49,51-74,76-94-Multiple covers on each. 18,19-Interlocking covers	4.00
50-($5.99) Anderson-s/Price-a; Whitley-s/Fosgitt-a	6.00

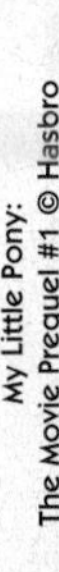

My Little Pony: The Movie Prequel #1 © Hasbro

My Love Memoirs #11 © FOX

My Own Romance #74 © MAR

	GD 2.0	VG 4.0	FN 6.0	VF 8.0	VF/NM 9.0	NM- 9.2
75-($7.99) Katie Cook-s/Andy Price-s/a; four covers						8.00
... #1 Greatest Hits (8/16, $1.00) reprints #1						3.00
... #1 Hundred Penny Press (2/14, $1.00) reprints #1						3.00
... Deviations 1 (3/17, $4.99) Cook-s/Garbowska-a; 3 covers; Prince Blueblood app.						5.00
... 20/20 (1/19, $4.99) Ponies meet their future selves; Anderson-s/Kuusisto-a						5.00

MY LITTLE PONY: LEGENDS OF MAGIC
IDW Publishing: Apr, 2017 - No. 12, Mar, 2018 ($3.99)

	GD 2.0	VG 4.0	FN 6.0	VF 8.0	VF/NM 9.0	NM- 9.2
1-12: 1-6-Whitley-s/Hickey-a. 7-12-Fleecs-a						4.00
Annual 2018 (4/18, $7.99) Whitley-s/Hickey-a						8.00

MY LITTLE PONY MICRO-SERIES
IDW Publishing: Feb, 2013 - No. 10, Dec, 2013 ($3.99)

	GD 2.0	VG 4.0	FN 6.0	VF 8.0	VF/NM 9.0	NM- 9.2
1-Twilight Sparkle - Zahler-s/a						5.00
2-10: 2-Rainbow Dash. 3-Rarity. 4-Fluttershy						4.00

MY LITTLE PONY: NIGHTMARE KNIGHTS
IDW Publishing: Oct, 2018 - No. 5, Feb, 2019 ($3.99, limited series)

	GD 2.0	VG 4.0	FN 6.0	VF 8.0	VF/NM 9.0	NM- 9.2
1-5-Whitley-s/Fleecs-a						4.00

MY LITTLE PONY: PONYVILLE MYSTERIES
IDW Publishing: May, 2018 - Aug, 2018 ($3.99, limited series)

	GD 2.0	VG 4.0	FN 6.0	VF 8.0	VF/NM 9.0	NM- 9.2
1-4-Christina Rice-s/Agnes Garbowska-a						4.00

MY LITTLE PONY: SPIRIT OF THE FOREST
IDW Publishing: May, 2019 - No. 3, Jul, 2019 ($3.99, limited series)

	GD 2.0	VG 4.0	FN 6.0	VF 8.0	VF/NM 9.0	NM- 9.2
1-3-Whitley-s/Hickey-a						4.00

MY LITTLE PONY: THE MOVIE PREQUEL
IDW Publishing: Jun, 2017 - No. 4, Sept, 2017 ($3.99, limited series)

	GD 2.0	VG 4.0	FN 6.0	VF 8.0	VF/NM 9.0	NM- 9.2
1-4-Ted Anderson-s/Andy Price-a; The Storm King app.						4.00

MY LOVE (Becomes Two Gun Western #5 (11/50) on?)
Marvel Comics (CLDS): July, 1949 - No. 4, Apr, 1950 (All photo-c)

	GD 2.0	VG 4.0	FN 6.0	VF 8.0	VF/NM 9.0	NM- 9.2
1	25	50	75	150	245	340
2,3	16	32	48	98	154	210
4-Bettie Page photo-c (see Cupid #2)	54	108	162	343	574	825

MY LOVE
Marvel Comics Group: Sept, 1969 - No. 39, Mar, 1976

	GD 2.0	VG 4.0	FN 6.0	VF 8.0	VF/NM 9.0	NM- 9.2
1	9	18	27	59	117	175
2-9: 4-6-Colan-a	5	10	15	33	57	80
10-Williamson-r/My Own Romance #71; Kirby-a	5	10	15	34	60	85
11-13,15-19	4	8	12	27	44	60
14-(52 pgs.)-Woodstock-c/sty; Morrow-c/a; Kirby/Colletta-r	9	18	27	58	114	170
20-Starlin-a	4	8	12	28	47	65
21,22,24-27,29-38: 38-Reprints	4	8	12	23	37	50
23-Steranko-r/Our Love Story #5	4	8	12	27	44	60
28-Kirby-a	4	8	12	25	40	55
39-Last issue; reprints	4	8	12	27	44	60
Special 1 (12/71)(52 pgs.)	5	10	15	34	60	85

NOTE: ***John Buscema** a-1-7, 10, 18-21, 22r(2), 24r, 25r, 29r, 34r, 36r, 37r, Spec. (r)(4); c-13, 15, 25, 27, Spec. **Colan** a-4, 5, 6, 8, 9, 16, 17, 20, 21, 22, 24r, 27r, 30r, 35r, 39r. **Colan/Everett** a-13, 15, 16, 27(r/#13). **Kirby** a-(r)-10, 14, 26, 28. **Romita** a-1-3, 19, 20, 25, 34, 38; c-1-3, 15.*

MY LOVE AFFAIR (March of Crime #7 on)
Fox Feature Syndicate: July, 1949 - No. 6, May, 1950

	GD 2.0	VG 4.0	FN 6.0	VF 8.0	VF/NM 9.0	NM- 9.2
1	36	72	108	211	343	475
2	17	34	51	103	162	220
3-6-Wood-a. 5-(3/50)-Becomes Love Stories #6	31	62	93	182	296	410

MY LOVE LIFE (Formerly Zegra)
Fox Feature Synd.: No. 6, June, 1949 - No. 13, Aug, 1950; No. 13, Sept, 1951

	GD 2.0	VG 4.0	FN 6.0	VF 8.0	VF/NM 9.0	NM- 9.2
6-Kamenish-a	29	58	87	172	281	390
7-13	17	34	51	100	158	215
13 (9/51)(Formerly My Story #12)	15	30	45	92	144	195

MY LOVE MEMOIRS (Formerly Women Outlaws; Hunted #13 on)
Fox Feature Syndicate: No. 9, Nov, 1949 - No. 12, May, 1950

	GD 2.0	VG 4.0	FN 6.0	VF 8.0	VF/NM 9.0	NM- 9.2
9,11,12-Wood-a	31	62	93	184	300	415
10	16	32	48	98	154	210

MY LOVE SECRET (Formerly Phantom Lady; Animal Crackers #31)
Fox Feature Syndicate/M. S. Distr.: No. 24, June, 1949 - No. 30, June, 1950; No. 53, 1954

	GD 2.0	VG 4.0	FN 6.0	VF 8.0	VF/NM 9.0	NM- 9.2
24-Kamen/Feldstein-a	31	62	93	186	303	420
25-Possible caricature of Wood on-c?	20	40	60	115	185	255
26,28-Wood-a	30	60	90	177	289	400
27,29,30: 30-Photo-c	18	36	54	107	169	230
53-(Reprint, M.S. Distr.) 1954? nd given; formerly Western Thrillers; becomes Crimes by Women #54; photo-c	12	24	36	67	94	120

MY LOVE STORY (Hoot Gibson Western #5 on)
Fox Feature Syndicate: Sept, 1949 - No. 4, Mar, 1950

	GD 2.0	VG 4.0	FN 6.0	VF 8.0	VF/NM 9.0	NM- 9.2
1	27	54	81	162	266	370
2	16	32	48	98	154	210
3,4-Wood-a	30	60	90	177	289	400

MY LOVE STORY
Atlas Comics (GPS): April, 1956 - No. 9, Aug, 1957

	GD 2.0	VG 4.0	FN 6.0	VF 8.0	VF/NM 9.0	NM- 9.2
1	20	40	60	115	188	260
2	14	28	42	78	112	145
3,7: Matt Baker-a. 7-Toth-a	15	30	45	92	144	195
4-6,8,9	13	26	39	72	101	130

NOTE: ***Brewster** a-3. **Colletta** a-1(2), 3, 4(2), 5; c-3.*

MYLO XYLOTO COMICS
Bongo Comics: 2013 - No. 6, 2013 ($3.99, limited series)

	GD 2.0	VG 4.0	FN 6.0	VF 8.0	VF/NM 9.0	NM- 9.2
1-6-Mark Osborne & Coldplay-s/Fuentes-a						4.00

MY NAME IS BRUCE
Dark Horse Comics: Sept, 2008 ($3.50, one-shot)

	GD 2.0	VG 4.0	FN 6.0	VF 8.0	VF/NM 9.0	NM- 9.2
nn-Adaptation of the Bruce Campbell movie; Cliff Richards-a/Bart Sears-c						3.50

MY NAME IS HOLOCAUST
DC Comics: May, 1995 - No. 5, Sept, 1995 ($2.50, limited series)

	GD 2.0	VG 4.0	FN 6.0	VF 8.0	VF/NM 9.0	NM- 9.2
1-5						5.00

MY ONLY LOVE
Charlton Comics: July, 1975 - No. 9, Nov, 1976

	GD 2.0	VG 4.0	FN 6.0	VF 8.0	VF/NM 9.0	NM- 9.2
1	3	6	9	15	22	28
2,4-9	2	4	6	9	13	16
3-Toth-a	2	4	6	11	16	20

MY OWN ROMANCE (Formerly My Romance; Teen-Age Romance #77 on)
Marvel/Atlas (MjPC/RCM No. 4-59/ZPC No. 60-76): No. 4, Mar, 1949 - No. 76, July, 1960

	GD 2.0	VG 4.0	FN 6.0	VF 8.0	VF/NM 9.0	NM- 9.2
4-Photo-c	25	50	75	150	245	340
5-10: 5,6,8-10-Photo-c	15	30	45	90	140	190
11-20: 14-Powell-a	15	30	45	83	124	165
21-42,55: 42-Last precode (2/55). 55-Toth-a	14	28	42	81	118	155
43-54,56-60	8	16	24	51	96	140
61-70,72,73,75,76	7	14	21	48	89	130
71-Williamson-a	8	16	24	52	99	145
74-Kirby-a	8	16	24	52	99	145

NOTE: ***Brewster** a-59. **Colletta** a-45(2), 48, 50, 55, 57(2), 59; c-58i, 59, 61. **Everett** a-25; c-58p. **Kirby** c-71, 75, 76. **Maneely** c-18. **Morisi** a-18. **Orlando** a-61. **Romita** a-36. **Tuska** a-10.*

MY PAL DIZZY (See Comic Books, Series I)

MY PAST (...Confessions) (Formerly Western Thrillers)
Fox Feature Syndicate: No. 7, Aug, 1949 - No. 11, Apr, 1950 (Crimes Inc. #12)

	GD 2.0	VG 4.0	FN 6.0	VF 8.0	VF/NM 9.0	NM- 9.2
7	30	60	90	177	289	400
8-10	16	32	48	98	154	210
11-Wood-a	30	60	90	177	289	400

MY PERSONAL PROBLEM
Ajax/Farrell/Steinway Comic: 11/55; No. 2, 2/56; No. 3, 9/56 - No. 4, 11/56; 10/57 - No. 3, 5/58

	GD 2.0	VG 4.0	FN 6.0	VF 8.0	VF/NM 9.0	NM- 9.2
1	13	26	39	74	105	135
2-4	8	16	24	44	57	70
1-3('57-'58)-Steinway	7	14	21	37	46	55

MY PRIVATE LIFE (Formerly Murder, Inc.; becomes Pedro #18)
Fox Feature Syndicate: No. 16, Feb, 1950 - No. 17, April, 1950

	GD 2.0	VG 4.0	FN 6.0	VF 8.0	VF/NM 9.0	NM- 9.2
16,17	20	40	60	115	185	255

MYRA NORTH (See The Comics, Crackajack Funnies & Red Ryder)
Dell Publishing Co.: No. 3, Jan, 1940

	GD 2.0	VG 4.0	FN 6.0	VF 8.0	VF/NM 9.0	NM- 9.2
Four Color 3	116	232	348	742	1271	1800

MY REAL LOVE
Standard Comics: No. 5, June, 1952 (Photo-c)

	GD 2.0	VG 4.0	FN 6.0	VF 8.0	VF/NM 9.0	NM- 9.2
5-Toth-a, 3 pgs.; Tuska, Cardy, Vern Greene-a	17	34	51	100	158	215

MY ROMANCE (Becomes My Own Romance #4 on)
Marvel Comics (RCM): Sept, 1948 - No. 3, Jan, 1949

	GD 2.0	VG 4.0	FN 6.0	VF 8.0	VF/NM 9.0	NM- 9.2
1	28	56	84	165	270	375
2,3: 2-Anti-Wertham editorial (11/48)	17	34	51	103	162	220

MY ROMANTIC ADVENTURES (Formerly Romantic Adventures)
American Comics Group: No. 72, 12/56 - No. 115, 12/60; No. 116, 7/61 - No. 138, 3/64

My Secret Life #22 © FOX

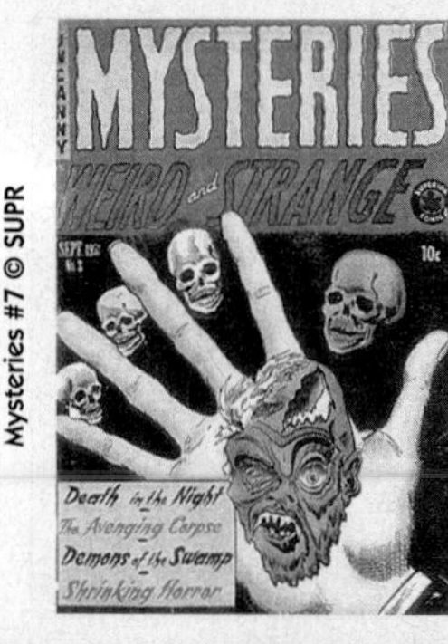

Mysteries #7 © SUPR

Mysterious Suspense #1 © CC

	GD 2.0	VG 4.0	FN 6.0	VF 8.0	VF/NM 9.0	NM- 9.2
72	10	20	30	56	76	95
73-85	7	14	21	37	46	55
86-Three pg. Williamson-a (2/58)	9	18	27	47	61	75
87-100	3	6	9	21	33	45
101-138	3	6	9	17	26	35

NOTE: ***Whitney** art in most issues.*

MY SECRET (Becomes Our Secret #4 on)
Superior Comics, Ltd.: Aug, 1949 - No. 3, Oct, 1949

	GD 2.0	VG 4.0	FN 6.0	VF 8.0	VF/NM 9.0	NM- 9.2
1	22	44	66	132	216	300
2,3	15	30	45	94	147	200

MY SECRET AFFAIR (Becomes Martin Kane #4)
Hero Book (Fox Feature Syndicate): Dec, 1949 - No. 3, April, 1950

	GD 2.0	VG 4.0	FN 6.0	VF 8.0	VF/NM 9.0	NM- 9.2
1-Harrison/Wood-a (10 pgs.)	39	78	117	231	378	525
2,3-Wood-a	31	62	93	186	303	420

MY SECRET CONFESSION
Sterling Comics: September, 1955

	GD 2.0	VG 4.0	FN 6.0	VF 8.0	VF/NM 9.0	NM- 9.2
1-Sekowsky-a	13	26	39	74	105	135

MY SECRET LIFE (Formerly Western Outlaws; Romeo Tubbs #26 on)
Fox Feature Syndicate: No. 22, July, 1949 - No. 27, July, 1950; No. 27, 9/51

	GD 2.0	VG 4.0	FN 6.0	VF 8.0	VF/NM 9.0	NM- 9.2
22	23	46	69	136	223	310
23,26-Wood-a, 6 pgs.	31	62	93	186	303	420
24,25,27	17	34	51	103	162	220
27 (9/51)	15	30	45	90	140	190

NOTE: *The title was changed to Romeo Tubbs after #25 even though #26 & 27 did come out.*

MY SECRET LIFE (Formerly Young Lovers; Sue & Sally Smith #48)
Charlton Comics: No. 19, Aug, 1957 - No. 47, Sept, 1962

	GD 2.0	VG 4.0	FN 6.0	VF 8.0	VF/NM 9.0	NM- 9.2
19	4	8	12	28	47	65
20-35	3	6	9	17	26	35
36-47: 44-Last 10¢ issue. 47-1st app. Sue & Sally Smith	3	6	9	16	23	30

MY SECRET MARRIAGE
Superior Comics, Ltd.: May, 1953 - No. 24, July, 1956 (Canadian)

	GD 2.0	VG 4.0	FN 6.0	VF 8.0	VF/NM 9.0	NM- 9.2
1	21	42	63	126	206	285
2	13	26	39	74	105	135
3-24	11	22	33	64	90	115
I.W. Reprint #9	2	4	6	9	13	16

NOTE: *Many issues contain **Kamen-ish** art.*

MY SECRET ROMANCE (Becomes A Star Presentation #3)
Hero Book (Fox Feature Syndicate): Jan, 1950 - No. 2, March, 1950

	GD 2.0	VG 4.0	FN 6.0	VF 8.0	VF/NM 9.0	NM- 9.2
1	27	54	81	158	259	360
2-Wood-a	31	62	93	182	296	410

MY SECRETS (Magazine) (Also see Gothic Romances)
Atlas/Seaboard: Feb, 1975 (B&W, 68 pgs.)

	GD 2.0	VG 4.0	FN 6.0	VF 8.0	VF/NM 9.0	NM- 9.2
Vol. 1 #1	16	32	48	112	249	385

MY SECRET STORY (Formerly Captain Kidd #25; Sabu #30 on)
Fox Feature Syndicate: No. 26, Oct, 1949 - No. 29, April, 1950

	GD 2.0	VG 4.0	FN 6.0	VF 8.0	VF/NM 9.0	NM- 9.2
26	22	44	66	132	216	300
27-29	15	30	45	92	144	195

MYSPACE DARK HORSE PRESENTS
Dark Horse Books: Sept, 2008 - Feb, 2011 ($19.95/$19.99, TPB)

Vol. 1 - Short stories previously appearing on Dark Horse's MySpace.com webpage; s/a by various incl. Whedon, Bá, Bagge, Mignola, Moon, Nord, Trimpe, Warren, Way 20.00
Vol. 2 - Collects stories from online #7-12; s/a by Way, Niles, Dorkin, Hotz & others 20.00
Vol. 3 - Collects stories from online #13-19; s/a by Mignola, Cloonan & others 20.00
Vol. 4 - Collects stories from online #20-24; s/a by Whedon, Chen & others 20.00
Vol. 5 - Collects stories from online #25-30; s/a by Thompson, Aragonés & others 20.00
Vol. 6 - Collects stories from online #31-36; s/a by Sakai, Dorkin & others 20.00

MYSTERIES (...Weird & Strange)
Superior/Dynamic Publ. (Randall Publ. Ltd.): May, 1953 - No. 11, Jan, 1955

	GD 2.0	VG 4.0	FN 6.0	VF 8.0	VF/NM 9.0	NM- 9.2
1-All horror stories	58	116	174	371	636	900
2-A-Bomb blast story	37	74	111	222	361	500
3-11: 10-Kamenish-c/a reprinted from Strange Mysteries #2; cover is from a panel in Strange Mysteries #2	34	68	102	199	325	450

MYSTERIES IN SPACE (See Fireside Book Series)

MYSTERIES OF LOVE IN SPACE
DC Comics: Mar, 2019 ($9.99, square-bound, one shot)

1-Anthology by various; Superman, Lois, Darkseid, Bizarro, Space Cabbie, Crush app. 10.00

MYSTERIES OF SCOTLAND YARD (Also see A-1 Comics)
Magazine Enterprises: No. 121, 1954 (one shot)

	GD 2.0	VG 4.0	FN 6.0	VF 8.0	VF/NM 9.0	NM- 9.2
A-1 121-Reprinted from Manhunt (5 stories)	18	36	54	107	169	230

MYSTERIES OF UNEXPLORED WORLDS (See Blue Bird)(Becomes Son of Vulcan V2#49 on)
Charlton Comics: Aug, 1956; No. 2, Jan, 1957 - No. 48, Sept, 1965

	GD 2.0	VG 4.0	FN 6.0	VF 8.0	VF/NM 9.0	NM- 9.2
1	40	80	120	244	402	560
2-No Ditko	19	38	57	112	179	245
3,4,8,9 Ditko-a. 3-Diko c/a (4). 4-Ditko c/a (2).	32	64	96	190	310	430
5,6,10,11: 5,6-Ditko-c/a (all). 10-Ditko-c/a(4). 11-Ditko-c/a(3); signed J. Kotdi	34	68	102	199	325	450
7-(2/58, 68 pgs.) 4 stories w/Ditko-a	37	74	111	222	361	500
12-Ditko sty (3); Baker story "The Charm Bracelet"	32	64	96	190	310	430
13-18,20	11	22	33	62	86	110
19,21-24,26-Ditko-a	24	48	72	144	237	330
25,27-30: 28-Communist A-bomb story w/Khrushchev	5	10	15	34	60	85
31-45: 43-Atomic bomb panel	4	8	12	28	47	65
46(5/65)-Son of Vulcan begins (origin/1st app.)	5	10	15	30	50	70
47,48	4	8	12	25	40	55

NOTE: ***Ditko** c-3-6, 10, 11, 19, 21-24. Covers to #19, 21-24 reprint story panels.*

MYSTERIOUS ADVENTURES
Story Comics: Mar, 1951 - No. 24, Mar, 1955; No. 25, Aug, 1955

	GD 2.0	VG 4.0	FN 6.0	VF 8.0	VF/NM 9.0	NM- 9.2
1-All horror stories	106	212	318	678	1164	1650
2-(6/51)	55	110	165	352	601	850
3,4,6,10	53	106	159	334	567	800
5-Severed heads/bondage-c	60	120	180	381	653	925
7-Dagger in eye panel; dismemberment stories	68	136	204	435	743	1050
8-Eyeball story	65	130	195	416	708	1000
9-Extreme violence (8/52)	58	116	174	371	636	900
11-(12/52)-Used in **SOTI**, pg. 84	55	110	165	352	601	850
12,14: 14-E.C. Old Witch swipe	53	106	159	334	567	800
13-Classic skull-c	116	232	348	742	1271	1800
15-21: 18-Used in Senate Investigative report, pgs. 5,6; E.C. swipe/TFTC #35; The Coffin-Keeper & Corpse (hosts). 20-Electric chair-c; used by Wertham in the Senate hearings. 21-Bondage/beheading-c; extreme violence	84	168	252	538	919	1300
22- "Cinderella" parody	55	110	165	352	601	850
23-Disbrow-a (6 pgs.); E.C. swipe "The Mystery Keeper's Tale" (host) and "Mother Ghoul's Nursery Tale"	52	104	156	328	552	775
24,25	42	84	126	265	445	625

NOTE: ***Tothish** art by **Ross Andru**-#22, 23. **Bache** a-8. **Cameron** a-5-7. **Harrison** a-12. **Hollingsworth** a-3-8, 12. **Schaffenberger** a-24, 25. **Wildey** a-15, 17.*

MYSTERIOUS ISLAND (Also see Classic Comics #34)
Dell Publishing Co.: No. 1213, July-Sept, 1961

	GD 2.0	VG 4.0	FN 6.0	VF 8.0	VF/NM 9.0	NM- 9.2
Four Color 1213-Movie, photo-c	8	16	24	52	99	145

MYSTERIOUS ISLE
Dell Publishing Co.: Nov-Jan, 1963/64 (Jules Verne)

	GD 2.0	VG 4.0	FN 6.0	VF 8.0	VF/NM 9.0	NM- 9.2
1-Painted-c	3	6	9	21	33	45

MYSTERIOUS RIDER, THE (See Zane Grey, 4-Color 301)

MYSTERIOUS STORIES (Formerly Horror From the Tomb #1)
Premier Magazines: No. 2, Dec-Jan, 1954-1955 - No. 7, Dec, 1955

	GD 2.0	VG 4.0	FN 6.0	VF 8.0	VF/NM 9.0	NM- 9.2
2-Woodbridge-c; last pre-code issue	57	114	171	362	619	875
3-Woodbridge-c/a	40	80	120	246	411	575
4-7: 5-Cinderella parody. 6-Woodbridge-c	39	78	117	231	378	525

NOTE: ***Hollingsworth** a-2, 4.*

MYSTERIOUS STRANGER
DC Comics: Aug/Sept. 1952

nn-Ashcan comic, not distributed to newsstands, only for in-house use. Cover art is All Star Western #60 with interior being Sensation Comics #100. A FN/VF copy sold for $2,357.50 in 2002.

MYSTERIOUS SUSPENSE (Also see Blue Beetle #1 (1967))
Charlton Comics: Oct, 1968 (12¢)

	GD 2.0	VG 4.0	FN 6.0	VF 8.0	VF/NM 9.0	NM- 9.2
1-Return of the Question by Ditko (c/a)	8	16	24	52	99	145

MYSTERIOUS TRAVELER (See Tales of the...)

MYSTERIOUS TRAVELER COMICS (Radio)
Trans-World Publications: Nov, 1948

	GD 2.0	VG 4.0	FN 6.0	VF 8.0	VF/NM 9.0	NM- 9.2
1-Powell-c/a(2); Poe adaptation, "Tell Tale Heart"	77	154	231	493	847	1200

MYSTERIUS
DC Comics (WildStorm): Mar, 2009 - No. 6, Aug, 2009 ($2.99, limited series)

Mystery Comics #3 © WHW

Mystery in Space #117 © DC

Mystery Tales #4 © MAR

GD VG FN VF VF/NM NM-
2.0 4.0 6.0 8.0 9.0 9.2

1-6-Jeff Parker-a/Tom Fowler-a 3.00
TPB (2010, $17.99) r/#1-6 18.00

MYSTERY COMICS
William H. Wise & Co.: 1944 - No. 4, 1944 (No months given)

1-The Magnet, The Silver Knight, Brad Spencer, Wonderman, Dick Devins, King of Futuria, & Zudo the Jungle Boy begin (all 1st app.); Schomburg-c on all 187 374 561 1197 2049 2900
2-Bondage-c 123 246 369 787 1344 1900
3,4: 3-Lance Lewis, Space Detective begins (1st app.); Robot-c. 4-(V2#1 inside); KKK-c 116 232 348 742 1271 1800

MYSTERY COMICS DIGEST
Gold Key/Whitman?: Mar, 1972 - No. 26, Oct, 1975

1-Ripley's Believe It or Not; reprint of Ripley's #1 origin Ra-Ka-Tep the Mummy; Wood-a 4 8 12 26 41 55
2-9: 2-Boris Karloff Tales of Mystery; Wood-a; 1st app. Werewolf Count Wulfstein. 3-Twilight Zone (TV); Crandall, Toth & George Evans-a; 1st app. Tragg & Simbar the Lion Lord; (2) Crandall/Frazetta-r/Twilight Zone #1 4-Ripley's Believe It or Not; 1st app. Baron Tibor, the Vampire. 5-Boris Karloff Tales of Mystery; 1st app. Dr. Spektor. 6-Twilight Zone (TV); 1st app. U.S. Marshal Reid & Sir Duane; Evans-r. 7-Ripley's Believe It or Not; origin The Lurker in the Swamp; 1st app. Duroc. 8-Boris Karloff Tales of Mystery; McWilliams-r; Orlando-r. 9-Twilight Zone (TV); Williamson, Crandall, McWilliams-a; 2nd Tragg app.;Torres, Evans, Heck/Tuska-r 3 6 9 20 30 40
10-26: 10,13-Ripley's Believe It or Not: 13-Orlando-r. 11,14-Boris Karloff Tales of Mystery. 14-1st app. Xorkon. 12,15-Twilight Zone (TV). 16,19,22,25-Ripley's Believe It or Not. 17-Boris Karloff Tales of Mystery; Williamson-r; Orlando-r. 18,21,24-Twilight Zone (TV). 20,23,26-Boris Karloff Tales of Mystery 3 6 9 16 23 30

NOTE: *Dr. Spektor app.-#5, 10-12, 21. Durak app.-#15. Duroc app.-#14 (later called Durak). King George 1st app.-#8.*

MYSTERY GIRL
Dark Horse Comics: Dec, 2015 - No. 4, Mar, 2016 ($3.99)

1-4-Tobin-s/Albuquerque-a 4.00

MYSTERY IN SPACE (Also see Fireside Book Series and Pulp Fiction Library: ...)
National Periodical Pub.: 4-5/51 - No. 110, 9/66; No. 111, 9/80 - No. 117, 3/81 (#1-3: 52 pgs.)

1-Frazetta-a, 8 pgs.; Knights of the Galaxy begins, ends #8 269 538 807 2219 5010 7800
2 94 188 282 761 1706 2650
3 64 128 192 512 1156 1800
4,5 52 104 156 420 935 1450
6-10: 7-Toth-a 42 84 126 311 706 1100
11-15 34 68 102 245 548 850
16-18,20-25: Interplanetary Insurance feature by Infantino in all. 21-1st app. Space Cabbie. 24-Last pre-code issue 30 60 90 216 483 750
19-Virgil Finlay-a 33 66 99 238 532 825
26-40: 26-Space Cabbie feature begins. 34-1st S.A. issue. 36,40-Grey-tone-c 23 46 69 164 362 560
41-52: 45,46-Grey-tone-c. 47-Space Cabbie ends 17 34 51 119 265 410
53-Adam Strange begins (8/59, 10pg. sty); robot-c 157 314 471 1295 2923 4550
54 44 88 132 326 738 1150
55-Grey tone-c 44 88 132 326 738 1150
56-60: 59-Kane/Anderson-a 23 46 69 164 362 560
61-71: 61-1st app. Adam Strange foe Ulthoon. 62-1st app. A.S. foe Mortan. 63-Origin Vandor. 66-Star Rovers begin (1st app.). 68-1st app. Dust Devils (6/61). 69-1st Mailbag. 70-2nd app. Dust Devils. 71-Last 10¢ issue 18 36 54 128 284 440
72-74,76-80 13 26 39 86 188 290
75-JLA x-over in Adam Strange (5/62)(sequel to J.L.A. #3, 2nd app. of Kanjar Ro) 22 44 66 152 336 520
75 (Facsimile Edition) (2020, $3.99) Reprints #75 with original 1962 ads & letter column 4.00
81-86 10 20 30 64 132 200
87-(11/63)-Adam Strange/Hawkman double feat begins; 3rd Hawkman tryout series 15 30 45 105 233 360
88-Adam Strange & Hawkman stories 14 28 42 96 211 325
89-Adam Strange & Hawkman stories 13 26 39 89 195 300
90-Book-length Adam Strange & Hawkman story; 1st team-up (3/64); Hawkman moves to own title next month; classic-c 15 30 45 103 227 350
91-102: 91-End Infantino art on Adam Strange; double-length Adam Strange story. 92-Space Ranger begins (6/64), ends #103. 92-94,96,98-Space Ranger-c. 94,98-Adam Strange/Space Ranger team-up. 102-Adam Strange ends (no Space Ranger) 7 14 21 44 82 120
103-Origin Ultra, the Multi-Alien; last Space Ranger 6 12 18 38 69 100
104-110: 110-(9/66)-Last 12¢ issue 5 10 15 30 50 70
V17#111(9/80)-117: 117-Newton-a(3 pgs.) 2 4 6 8 11 14

NOTE: ***Anderson** a-2, 4, 8-10, 12-17, 19, 45-48, 51, 57, 59i, 61-64, 70, 76, 87-91; c-9, 10, 15-25, 87, 89, 105-108, 110. **Aparo** a-111. **Austin** a-112i. **Bolland** a-115. **Craig** a-114, 116. **Ditko** a-111, 114-116. **Drucker** a-13, 14. **Elias** a-98, 102, 103. **Golden** a-113p. **Sid Greene** a-78, 91. **Infantino** a-1-8, 11, 14-25, 27-46, 48, 49, 51, 53-91, 103, 117; c-60-86, 88, 90, 91, 105, 107. **Gil Kane** a-14p, 15p, 18p, 19p, 26p, 29-59p(most), 100-102; c-52, 101. **Kubert** a-113; c-111-115. **Moreira** c-27, 28. **Rogers** a-111. **Sekowsky** a-52. **Simon & Kirby** a-4(2 pgs.). **Spiegle** a-111, 114. **Starlin** c-116. **Sutton** a-112. **Tuska** a-115p, 117p.*

MYSTERY IN SPACE
DC Comics: Nov, 2006 - No. 8, Jul, 2007 ($3.99, limited series)

1-8: 1-Captain Comet's rebirth; Starlin-s/Shane Davis-a; The Weird by Starlin 4.00
1-Variant cover by Neal Adams 10.00
Volume One TPB (2007, $17.99) r/#1-5 18.00
Volume Two TPB (2007, $17.99) r/#6-8 and The Weird from #1-4 18.00

MYSTERY IN SPACE
DC Comics (Vertigo): Jul, 2012 ($7.99, one-shot)

1-Short sci-fi stories by various incl. Kaluta, Allred, Baker, Diggle, Gianfelice; Sook-c 8.00

MYSTERY MEN
Marvel Comics: Aug, 2011 - No. 5, Nov, 2011 ($2.99, limited series)

1-5-Zircher-a/c; Liss-s; Pulp-era characters in 1932 3.00

MYSTERY MEN COMICS
Fox Feature Syndicate: Aug, 1939 - No. 31, Feb, 1942

1-Intro. & 1st app. The Blue Beetle, The Green Mask, Rex Dexter of Mars by Briefer, Zanzibar by Tuska, Lt. Drake, D-13-Secret Agent by Powell, Chen Chang, Wing Turner, & Captain Denny Scott 1800 3600 5400 13,500 23,750 34,000
2-Robot & sci/fi-c (2nd Robot-c w/Movie #6) 432 864 1296 3154 5577 8000
3 (10/39)-Classic Lou Fine-c 811 1622 2433 5920 10,460 15,000
4,5: 4-Capt. Savage begins (11/39) 360 720 1080 2520 4410 6300
6-Tuska-c 303 606 909 2121 3711 5300
7-1st Blue Beetle-c app. 389 778 1187 2723 4762 6800
8-Lou Fine bondage-c 343 686 1029 2400 4200 6000
9-The Moth begins; Lou Fine-c 252 504 756 1613 2757 3900
10-Wing Turner by Kirby; Simon bondage-c 276 552 828 1764 3032 4300
11,12: Both Joe Simon-c. 11-Intro. Domino 245 490 735 1568 2684 3800
13-Intro. Lynx & sidekick Blackie (8/40) 174 348 522 1114 1907 2700
14-18: 16-Bondage/Hypo needle-c 161 322 463 1030 1765 2500
19-Intro. & 1st app. Miss X (ends #21) 174 348 522 1114 1907 2700
20-31: 26-The Wraith begins 152 304 456 973 1662 2350

NOTE: ***Briefer** a-1-15, 20, 24; c-9. **Cuidera** a-22. **Lou Fine** c-1-5,8,9. **Powell** a-1-15, 24. **Simon** c-10-12. **Tuska** a-1-16, 22, 24, 27; c-6. Bondage-c 1, 3, 7, 8, 10, 16, 25, 27-29, 31. Blue Beetle c-7, 8, 10-31. D-13 Secret Agent c-6. Green Mask c-1, 3-5. Rex Dexter of Mars c-2, 9.*

MYSTERY MEN MOVIE ADAPTION
Dark Horse Comics: July, 1999 - No. 2, Aug, 1999 ($2.95, mini-series)

1,2-Fingerman-s; photo-c 3.00

MYSTERY PLAY, THE
DC Comics (Vertigo): 1994 ($19.95, one-shot)

nn-Hardcover-Morrison-s/Muth-painted art 25.00
Softcover ($9.95)-New Muth cover 10.00

MYSTERY SCIENCE THEATER 3000: THE COMIC
Dark Horse Comics: Sept, 2018 - No. 6, May, 2019 ($3.99)

1-6-Hodgson and others-s. 1-Nauck & Manley-a. 5,6-Black Cat app. 4.00

MYSTERY SOCIETY
IDW Publishing: May, 2010 - No. 5, Oct, 2010 ($3.99, limited series)

1-5-Niles-s/Staples-a 4.00
... Special (3/13, $3.99) Niles-s/Ritchie-a/c 4.00

MYSTERY TALES
Atlas Comics (20CC): Mar, 1952 - No. 54, Aug, 1957

1-Horror/weird stories in all 203 406 609 1299 2225 3150
2-Krigstein-a 119 238 357 762 1306 1850
3-10: 6-A-Bomb panel. 10-Story similar to "The Assassin" from Shock SuspenStories 100 200 300 635 1093 1550
11,13-21: 14-Maneely s/f story. 20-Electric chair issue. 21-Matt Fox-a; decapitation story 63 126 189 403 689 975
12,22: 12-Matt Fox-a. 22-Forte/Matt Fox-c; a(i) 66 132 198 419 722 1025
23-26 (2/55)-Last precode issue 57 114 171 362 619 875
27,29-35,37,38,41-43,48,49: 43-Morisi story contains Frazetta art swipes from Untamed Love 47 94 141 296 498 700
28,36,39,40,45: 28-Jack Katz-a. 36,39-Krigstein-a. 40,45-Ditko-a. (#45 is 3 pgs. only) 45 90 135 284 480 675
44-Labyrinth-c/s; Williamson/Krenkel-a 54 108 162 343 574 825
46,51-Williamson/Krenkel-a. 46-Crandall text illos 48 96 144 302 514 725
47-Crandall, Ditko, Powell-a 48 96 144 302 514 725
50,52,53: 50-Torres, Morrow-a 47 94 141 296 498 700
54-Crandall, Check-a 45 90 135 284 480 675

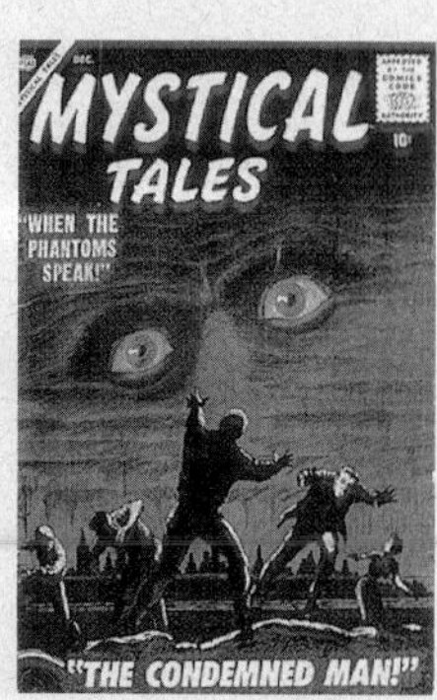

Mystical Tales #4 © MAR

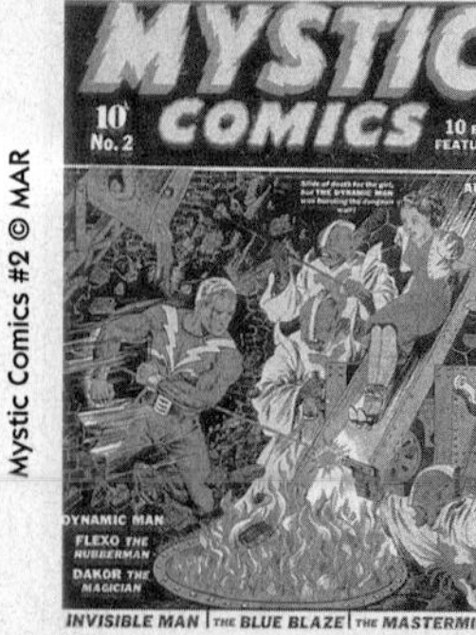

Mystic Comics #2 © MAR

Mystique #1 © MAR

GD 2.0 | VG 4.0 | FN 6.0 | VF 8.0 | VF/NM 9.0 | NM- 9.2

NOTE: ***Ayers*** *a-18, 49, 52.* ***Berg*** *a-17, 51.* ***Colan*** *a-1, 3, 18, 35, 43.* ***Colletta*** *a-18.* ***Drucker*** *a-41.* ***Everett*** *a-2, 29, 33, 35, 41; c-8-11, 14, 38, 39, 41, 43, 44, 46, 48-51, 53.* ***Fass*** *a-16.* ***Forte*** *a-21, 22, 45, 46.* ***Matt Fox*** *a-12?, 21, 22; c-22.* ***Heath*** *a-3; c-3, 15, 17, 26.* ***Heck*** *a-25.* ***Kinstler*** *a-15.* ***Mort Lawrence*** *a-26, 32, 34.* ***Maneely*** *a-1, 9, 14, 22; c-12, 23, 24, 27.* ***Mooney*** *a-3, 40.* ***Morisi*** *a-43, 49, 52.* ***Morrow*** *a-50.* ***Orlando*** *a-51.* ***Pakula*** *a-16.* ***Powell*** *a-21, 29, 37, 38, 47.* ***Reinman*** *a-1, 14, 17.* ***Robinson*** *a-7p, 42.* ***Romita*** *a-37.* ***Roussos*** *a-4, 44.* ***R.Q. Sale*** *a-45, 46, 49.* ***Severin*** *c-52.* ***Shores*** *a-17, 45.* ***Tuska*** *a-10, 12, 14.* ***Whitney*** *a-2.* ***Wildey*** *a-37.*

MYSTERY TALES
Super Comics: 1964

Super Reprint #16,17('64): 16-r/Tales of Horror #2. 17-r/Eerie #14(Avon), 18-Kubert-r/Strange Terrors #4 3 6 9 15 22 28

MYSTERY TRAIL
DC Comics: Feb/Mar 1950

nn - Ashcan comic, not distributed to newsstands, only for in-house use. Cover art is Danger Trail #3 with interior being Star Spangled Comics #109. A FN/VF copy sold for $2,357.50 in 2002.

MYSTIC (3rd Series)
Marvel/Atlas Comics (CLDS 1/CSI 2-21/OMC 22-35/CSI 35-61): March, 1951 - No. 61, Aug, 1957

1-Atom bomb panels; horror/weird stories in all 148 296 444 947 1624 2300
2 74 148 222 470 810 1150
3-Eyes torn out 65 130 195 416 708 1000
4- "The Devil Birds" by Wolverton (6 pgs.) 110 220 330 704 1202 1700
5,7-10 53 106 159 334 567 800
6- "The Eye of Doom" by Wolverton (7 pgs.) 106 212 318 678 1164 1650
11-17,19,20: 16-Bondage/torture c/story 47 94 141 296 498 700
18-Classic Everett skeleton-c 110 220 330 704 1202 1700
21-25,27-36-Last precode (3/55). 25-E.C. swipe 40 80 120 246 411 575
26-Atomic War story; severed head story/cover 50 100 150 315 533 750
37-51,53-56,61 36 72 108 211 343 475
52-Wood-a; Crandall-a? 37 74 111 222 361 500
57-Story "Trapped in the Ant-Hill" (1957) is very similar to "The Man in the Ant Hill" in TTA #27 50 100 150 315 533 750
58,59-Krigstein-a 36 72 108 211 343 475
60-Williamson/Mayo-a (4 pgs.) 36 72 108 214 347 480

NOTE: ***Andru*** *a-23, 25.* ***Ayers*** *a-35, 53; c-8.* ***Berg*** *a-49.* ***Cameron*** *a-49, 51.* ***Check*** *a-31, 60.* ***Colan*** *a-3, 7, 12, 21, 37, 60.* ***Colletta*** *a-29.* ***Drucker*** *a-46, 52, 56.* ***Everett*** *a-8, 9, 17, 40, 44, 57; c-13; 18, 21, 42, 47, 49, 51-55, 57-59, 61.* ***Forte*** *a-35, 52, 58.* ***Fox*** *a-24i.* ***Al Hartley*** *a-35.* ***Heath*** *a-10; c-10, 20, 22, 23, 25, 30.* ***Infantino*** *a-12.* ***Kane*** *a-8, 24p.* ***Jack Katz*** *a-31, 33.* ***Mort Law.rence*** *a-19, 37.* ***Maneely*** *a-22, 24, 58; c-7, 15, 28, 29, 31.* ***Moldoff*** *a-29.* ***Morisi*** *a-48, 49, 52.* ***Morrow*** *a-51.* ***Orlando*** *a-57, 61.* ***Pakula*** *a-52, 57, 59.* ***Powell*** *a-52, 54-56.* ***Robinson*** *a-5.* ***Romita*** *a-11, 15.* ***R.Q. Sale*** *a-35, 53, 58.* ***Sekowsky*** *a-1, 2, 4, 5.* ***Severin*** *c-56, 60.* ***Tuska*** *a-15.* ***Whitney*** *a-33.* ***Wildey*** *a-28, 30.* ***Ed Win*** *a-17, 20. Canadian reprints known-title 'Startling.'*

MYSTIC (Also see CrossGen Chronicles)
CrossGeneration Comics: Jul, 2000 - No. 43, Jan, 2004 ($2.95)

1-43: 1-Marz-s/Peterson & Dell-a. 15-Cameos by DC & Marvel characters 3.00

MYSTIC (CrossGen characters)
Marvel Comics: Oct, 2011 - No. 4, Jan, 2012 ($2.99, limited series)

1-4-G. Willow Wilson-s/David López-a/Amanda Conner-c 3.00

MYSTICAL TALES
Atlas Comics (CCC 1/EPI 2-8): June, 1956 - No. 8, Aug, 1957

1-Everett-c/a 65 130 195 416 708 1000
2-4: 2-Berg-a. 3,4-Crandall-a. 37 74 111 222 361 500
5-Williamson-a (4 pgs.) 39 78 117 240 395 550
6-Torres, Krigstein-a 36 72 108 214 347 480
7-Bolle, Forte, Torres, Orlando-a 35 70 105 208 339 470
8-Krigstein, Check-a 36 72 108 214 347 480

NOTE: ***Ayers*** *a-6.* ***Everett*** *a-1; c-1-4, 6, 7.* ***Orlando*** *a-1, 2, 7.* ***Pakula*** *a-3.* ***Powell*** *a-1, 4.* ***Sale*** *a-5.* ***Sinnott*** *a-6.*

MYSTIC ARCANA
Marvel Comics: Aug, 2007 - Jan, 2008 ($2.99)

1-Magik on-c; art by Scott and Nguyen; Ian McNee and Dani Moonstar app. 3.00
(#2)...: Black Knight 1 (9/07, $2.99) Djurdjevic-c/Grummett & Hanna-a; origin retold 3.00
3-("Scarlet Witch" on cover)(10/07, $2.99) Djurdjevic-c/Santacruz-a; childhood 3.00
(#4)...: Sister Grimm 1 (1/08, $2.99) Nico Minoru from Runaways; Djurdjevic-c/Noto-a 3.00
...: The Book of Marvel Magic ('07, $3.99) Official Handbook profiles of the magic-related 4.00
HC (2007, $24.99, d.j.) r/series and ...: The Book of Marvel Magic 25.00

MYSTIC COMICS (1st Series)
Timely Comics (TPI 1-5/TCI 8-10): March, 1940 - No. 10, Aug, 1942

1-Origin The Blue Blaze, The Dynamic Man, & Flexo the Rubber Robot; Zephyr Jones, 3X's & Deep Sea Demon app.; The Magician begins (all 1st app.); c-from Spider pulp V18#1, 6/39 1600 3200 4800 12,800 27,400 42,000
2-The Invisible Man & Master Mind Excello begin; Space Rangers, Zara of the Jungle, Taxi Taylor app. (scarce) 811 1622 2433 5920 10,460 15,000
3-Origin Hercules, who last appears in #4 497 994 1491 3628 6414 9200
4-Origin The Thin Man & The Black Widow; Merzak the Mystic app.; last Flexo, Dynamic Man, Invisible Man & Blue Blaze (some issues have date sticker on cover; others have July w/August overprint in silver color); Roosevelt assassination-c 865 1730 2595 6315 11,158 16,000
5-(3/41)-Origin The Black Marvel, The Blazing Skull, The Sub-Earth Man, Super Slave & The Terror; The Moon Man & Black Widow app.; 5-German war-c begin, end #10 443 886 1329 3234 5717 8200
6-(10/41)-Origin The Challenger & The Destroyer (1st app.?; also see All-Winners #2, Fall, 1941) 1000 2000 3000 7600 13,800 20,000
7-The Witness begins (12/41, origin & 1st app.); origin Davey & the Demon; last Black Widow; Hitler opens his trunk of terror-c by Simon & Kirby (classic-c) 865 1730 2595 6315 11,158 16,000
8,10: 8-Classic Destroyer WWII Nazi bondage/torture-c. 10-Father Time, World of Wonder, & Red Skeleton app.; last Challenger & Terror 649 1298 1947 4738 8369 12,000
9-Gary Gaunt app.; last Black Marvel, Mystic & Blazing Skull; Hitler-c 838 1676 2514 6117 10,809 15,500

NOTE: ***Gabrielle*** *c-8-10.* ***Rico*** *a-9(2).* ***Schomburg*** *a-1-4; c-1-6.* ***Sekowsky*** *a-9.* ***Sekowsky/Klein*** *a-8 (Challenger). Bondage c-1, 2, 9.*

MYSTIC COMICS (2nd Series)
Timely Comics (ANC): Oct, 1944 - No. 3, Win, 1944-45; No. 4, Mar, 1945

1-The Angel, The Destroyer, The Human Torch, Terry Vance the Schoolboy Sleuth, & Tommy Tyme begin 300 600 900 2010 3505 5000
2-(Fall/44)-Last Human Torch & Terry Vance; bondage/hypo-c 200 400 600 1280 2190 3100
3-Last Angel (two stories) & Tommy Tyme 158 316 474 1011 1731 2450
4-The Young Allies-c & app.; Schomburg-c 152 304 456 973 1662 2350

MYSTIC COMICS 70th ANNIVERARY SPECIAL
Marvel Comics: Oct, 2009 ($3.99, one-shot)

1-New story of The Vision; r/G.A. Vision app. from Marvel Myst. Comics #13 & 16 5.00

MYSTIC HANDS OF DR. STRANGE
Marvel Comics: May, 2010 ($3.99, B&W, one-shot)

1-Short stories; art by Irving, Brunner, McKeever & Marcos Martin; Parrillo-c 4.00

MYSTIK U
DC Comics: Jan, 2018 - No. 3, Mar, 2018 ($5.99, limited series)

1-3: 1-Teenage Zatanna, Enchantress at magic college; intro. Plop; Kwitney-s/Norton-a 6.00

MYSTIQUE (See X-Men titles)
Marvel Comics: June, 2003 - No. 24, Apr, 2005 ($2.99)

1-24: 1-6-Linsner-c/Vaughan-s/Lucas-a. 7-Ryan-a begins. 8-Horn-c. 9-24-Mayhew-c 23-Wolverine & Rogue app. 3.00
... Vol. 1: Drop Dead Gorgeous TPB (2004, $14.99) r/#1-6 15.00
... Vol. 2: Tinker, Tailor, Mutant, Spy TPB (2004, $17.99) r/#7-13 18.00
... Vol. 3: Unnatural TPB (2004, $13.99) r/#14-18 14.00

MYSTIQUE & SABRETOOTH (Sabretooth and Mystique on-c)
Marvel Comics: Dec, 1996 - No. 4, Mar, 1997 ($1.95, limited series)

1-4: Characters from X-Men 4.00

MY STORY (...True Romances in Pictures #5,6; becomes My Love Life #13) (Formerly Zago)
Hero Books (Fox Feature Syndicate): No. 5, May, 1949 - No. 12, Aug, 1950

5-Kamen/Feldstein-a 37 74 111 222 361 500
6-8,11,12: 12-Photo-c 20 40 60 114 182 250
9,10-Wood-a 30 60 90 177 289 400

MYTHIC
Image Comics: May, 2015 - No. 8, 2016 ($1.99/$2.99/$3.99)

1-3: 1-($1.99) Phil Hester-s/John McCrea-a. 2,3-($2.99) 3.00
4-8-($3.99) 4.00

MYTHOS
Marvel Comics: Mar, 2006 - Dec, 2007 ($3.99)

1-Retelling of X-Men #1 with painted-a by Paolo Rivera; Paul Jenkins-s 4.00
...: Captain America 1 (8/08) Retelling of origin; painted-a by Rivera; Jenkins-s 4.00
...: Fantastic Four 1 (12/07) Retelling of Fantastic Four #1; painted-a by Rivera; Jenkins-s 4.00
...: Ghost Rider 1 (3/07) Retelling of Marvel Spotlight #5; painted-a by Rivera; Jenkins-s 4.00
...: Hulk 1 (10/06) Retelling of Incredible Hulk #1; painted-a by Rivera; Jenkins-s 4.00
...: Spider-Man 1 (8/07) Retelling of Amazing Fantasy #15; painted-a by Rivera; Jenkins-s 4.00

MYTHOS: THE FINAL TOUR
DC Comics/Vertigo: Dec, 1996 - No. 3, Feb, 1997 ($5.95, limited series)

1-3: 1-Ney Rieber-s/Amaro-a. 2-Snejbjerg-a; Constantine-app. 3-Kristiansen-a; Black Orchid-app. 6.00

MYTHSTALKERS
Image Comics: Mar, 2003 - No. 8, Mar, 2004 ($2.95)

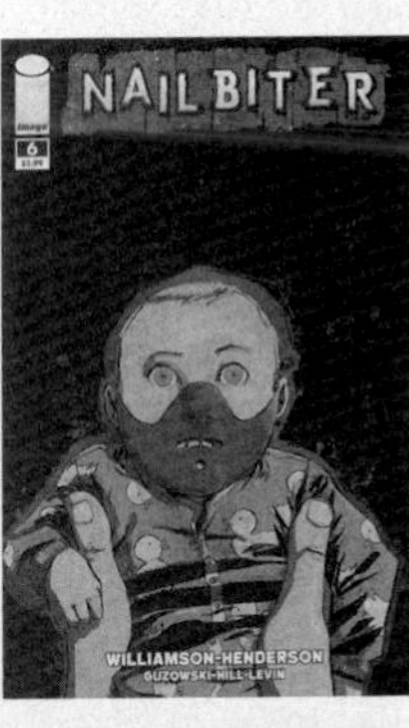

Nailbiter #6 © Williamson & Henderson

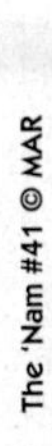
The 'Nam #41 © MAR

Namor, The Best Defense #1 © MAR

	GD 2.0	VG 4.0	FN 6.0	VF 8.0	VF/NM 9.0	NM- 9.2

1-8-Jiro-a 3.00

MY TRUE LOVE (Formerly Western Killers #64; Frank Buck #70 on)
Fox Feature Syndicate: No. 65, July, 1949 - No. 69, March, 1950

	GD	VG	FN	VF	VF/NM	NM-
65	31	62	93	182	296	410
66,68,69: 69-Morisi-a	20	40	60	116	188	260
67-Wood-a	31	62	93	182	296	410

NAIL, THE
Dark Horse Comics: June, 2004 - No. 4, Oct, 2004 ($2.99, limited series)

1-4-Rob Zombie & Steve Niles-s/Nat Jones-a/Simon Bisley-c 3.00
TPB (2005, $12.95) r/series 13.00

NAILBITER
Image Comics: May, 2014 - No. 30, Mar, 2017 ($2.99)

1-29: 1-Williamson-s/Henderson-a. 7-Brian Bendis appears as a character. 13-Archie style cover 3.00
30-($3.99) Final issue 4.00
.../ Hack/Slash 1 (3/15, $4.99) Flip book with Hack/Slash / Nailbiter 1 5.00

NAILBITER RETURNS
Image Comics: Apr, 2020 - No. 10, Feb, 2021 ($3.99)

1-10-Williamson-s/Henderson-a 4.00

NAKED BRAIN (Marc Hempel's...)
Insight Studios Group: 2002 - No. 3, 2002 ($2.95, B&W, limited series)

1-3-Marc Hempel cartoons and sketches; Tug & Buster app. 3.00

NAKED PREY, THE (See Movie Classics)

'NAM, THE (See Savage Tales #1, 2nd series & Punisher Invades...)
Marvel Comics Group: Dec, 1986 - No. 84, Sept, 1993

	GD	VG	FN	VF	VF/NM	NM-
1-Golden a(p)/c begins, ends #13	2	4	6	8	11	14
1 (2nd printing)						3.00
2-7,9-25,27-66,70-74: 7-Golden-a (2 pgs.). 32-Death R. Kennedy. 52,53-Frank Castle (The Punisher) app. 52,53-Gold 2nd printings. 58-Silver logo. 65-Heath-c/a. 70-Lomax scripts begin						3.00
8-1st app. Fudd Verzyl, Tunnel Rat	1	3	4	6	8	10
26-2nd app. Fudd Verzyl, Tunnel Rat						4.00
67-69-Punisher 3 part story						4.00
75-($2.25, 52 pgs.)						6.00
76-84						3.00
Trade Paperback 1,2: 1-r/#1-4. 2-r/#5-8	1	2	3	5	6	8
TPB ('99, $14.95) r/#1-4; recolored						15.00

'NAM MAGAZINE, THE
Marvel Comics: Aug, 1988 - No. 10, May, 1989 ($2.00, B&W, 52pgs.)

1-10: Each issue reprints 2 issues of the comic 4.00

NAMELESS
Image Comics: Feb, 2015 - No. 6, Dec, 2015 ($2.99)

1-6-Morrison-s/Burnham-a 3.00

NAMELESS, THE
Image Comics: May, 1997 - No. 5, Sept, 1997 ($2.95, B&W)

1-5: Pruett/Hester-s/a 3.00
...: The Director's Cut TPB (2006, $15.99) r/#1-5; original proposal by Pruett 16.00

NAMES, THE
DC Comics (Vertigo): Nov, 2014 - No. 9, Jul, 2015 ($2.99, limited series)

1-9-Peter Milligan-s/Leandro Fernandez-a 3.00

NAMESAKE
BOOM! Studios: Nov, 2016 - No. 4, Feb, 2017 ($3.99, limited series)

1-4-Orlando-s/Rebelka-a 4.00

NAMES OF MAGIC, THE (Also see Books of Magic)
DC Comics (Vertigo): Feb, 2001 - No. 5, June, 2001 ($2.50, limited series)

1-5: Bolton painted-c on all; Case-a; leads into Hunter: The Age of Magic 3.00
TPB (2002, $14.95) r/#1-5 15.00

NAME OF THE GAME, THE
DC Comics: 2001 ($29.95, graphic novel)

Hardcover ($29.95) Will Eisner-s/a 30.00

NAMOR (Volume 2)
Marvel Comics: June, 2003 - No. 12, May, 2004 (25¢/$2.25/$2.99)

1-(25¢-c)Young Namor in the 1920s; Larroca-c/a 3.00
2-6-($2.25) Larroca-a 3.00
7-12-($2.99): 7-Olliffe-a begins 3.00

NAMORA (See Marvel Mystery Comics #82 & Sub-Mariner Comics)
Marvel Comics (PrPI): Fall, 1948 - No. 3, Dec, 1948

	GD	VG	FN	VF	VF/NM	NM-
1-Sub-Mariner x-over in Namora; Namora by Everett(2), Sub-Mariner by Rico (10 pgs.)	306	612	918	2198	3849	5500
2-The Blonde Phantom & Sub-Mariner story; Everett-a	239	478	717	1530	2615	3700
3-(Scarce)-Sub-Mariner app.; Everett-a	265	530	795	1694	2897	4100

NAMORA (See Agents of Atlas)
Marvel Comics: Aug, 2010 ($3.99, one-shot)

1-Parker-s/Pichelli-a 4.00

NAMOR: THE BEST DEFENSE (Also see Immortal Hulk, Doctor Strange, Silver Surfer)
Marvel Comics: Feb, 2019 ($4.99, one-shot)

1-Chip Zdarsky-s/Carlos Magno-a; Ron Garney-c 5.00

NAMOR: THE FIRST MUTANT (Curse of the Mutants x-over with X-Men titles)
Marvel Comics: Oct, 2010 - No. 11, Aug, 2011 ($3.99/$2.99)

1-($3.99) Olivetti-a/Stuart Moore-s/Jae Lee-c; back-up retelling of origin and history 4.00
2-11-($2.99) 2-Emma Frost app. 5-Mayhew-c. 6-10-Noto-c 3.00
... Annual 1 (7/11, $3.99) Part 3 of "Escape From the Negative Zone" x-over; Fiumara-a 4.00

NAMOR, THE SUB-MARINER (See Prince Namor & Sub-Mariner)
Marvel Comics: Apr, 1990 - No. 62, May, 1995 ($1.00/$1.25/$1.50)

	GD	VG	FN	VF	VF/NM	NM-
1-Byrne-c/a/scripts in 1-25 (scripts only #26-32)	2	4	6	8	10	12
2-5: 5-Iron Man app.						5.00
6-11,13-23,25,27-36,38-49,51-62: 16-Re-intro Iron Fist (8-cameo only). 18-Punisher cameo (1 panel); 21-23,25-Wolverine cameos. 22,23-Iron Fist app. 28-Iron Fist-c/story. 31-Dr. Doom-c/story. 33,34-Iron Fist cameo. 35-New Tiger Shark-c/story. 48-The Thing app.						4.00
12,24: 12-(52pgs.)-Re-intro. The Invaders. 24-Namor vs. Wolverine						5.00
26-Namor w/new costume; 1st Jae Lee-c/a this title (5/92) & begins	1	3	4	6	8	10
37-Aqua holografx foil-c						5.00
50-($1.75, 52 pgs.)-Newsstand ed.; w/bound-in S-M trading card sheet (both versions)						5.00
50-($2.95, 52 pgs.)-Collector edition w/foil-c						5.00
Annual 1-4 ('91-94, 68 pgs.): 1-3 pg. origin recap. 2-Return/Defenders. 3-Bagged w/card. 4-Painted-c						5.00

NOTE: *Jae Lee a-26-30p, 31-37, 38p, 39, 40; c-26-40.*

'NAMWOLF
Albatross Funnybooks: 2017 - No. 4, 2017 ($3.99, limited series)

1-4-Fabian Rangel Jr.-s/Logan Faerber-a; werewolf in 1970 Viet Nam 4.00

NANCY AND SLUGGO (See Comics On Parade & Sparkle Comics)
United Features Syndicate: No. 16, 1949 - No. 23, 1954

	GD	VG	FN	VF	VF/NM	NM-
16(#1)	11	22	33	62	86	110
17-23	8	16	24	40	50	60

NANCY & SLUGGO (Nancy #146-173; formerly Sparkler Comics)
St. John/Dell #146-187/Gold Key #188 on: No. 121, Apr, 1955-No. 192, Oct, 1963

	GD	VG	FN	VF	VF/NM	NM-
121(4/55)(St. John)	10	20	30	54	72	90
122-145(7/57)(St. John)	8	16	24	44	57	70
146(9/57)-Peanuts begins, ends #192 (Dell)	8	16	24	56	108	160
147-161 (Dell) Peanuts in all	8	16	24	51	86	120
162-165,177-180-John Stanley-a	7	14	21	44	82	120
166-176-Oona & Her Haunted House series; Stanley-a	7	14	21	49	92	135
181-187(3-5/62)(Dell)	5	10	15	35	63	90
188(10/62)-192 (Gold Key)	5	10	15	35	63	90
Four Color 1034(9-11/59)-Summer Camp	5	10	15	30	50	70

(See Dell Giant #34, 45 & Dell Giants)

NANCY DREW
Dynamite Entertainment: 2018 - No. 5, 2018 ($3.99, limited series)

1-5-Kelly Thompson-s/Jenn St-Onge-a; Hardy Boys app. 4.00

NANCY DREW AND THE HARDY BOYS: THE BIG LIE
Dynamite Entertainment: 2017 - No. 6, 2017 ($3.99, limited series)

1-6-Anthony Del Col-s/Werther Dell'Edera-a; multiple-c on each; Bobbsey twins app. 4.00

NANCY DREW: THE DEATH OF NANCY DREW
Dynamite Entertainment: 2020 - No. 6, 2020 ($3.99, limited series)

1-6-Anthony Del Col-s/Joe Eisma-a; Hardy Boys app. 4.00

NANNY AND THE PROFESSOR (TV)
Dell Publishing Co.: Aug, 1970 - No. 2, Oct, 1970 (Photo-c)

	GD	VG	FN	VF	VF/NM	NM-
1-(01-546-008)	5	10	15	30	50	70

Naomi #6 © DC

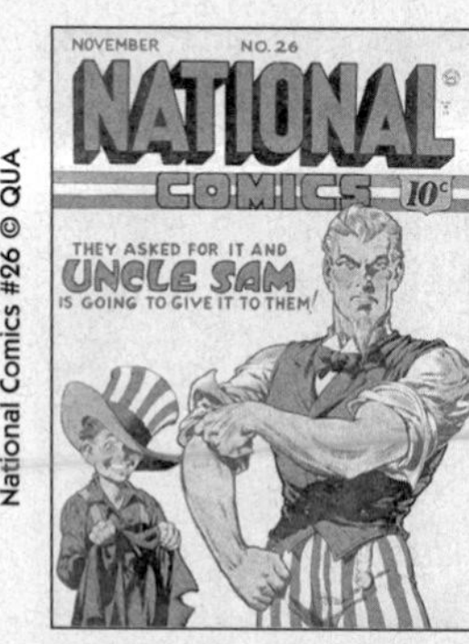

National Comics #26 © QUA

National Comics: Madame X #1 © DC

GD VG FN VF VF/NM NM-
2.0 4.0 6.0 8.0 9.0 9.2

2 4 8 12 25 40 55

NAOMI
DC Comics (Wonder Comics): Mar, 2019 - No. 6, Sept, 2019 ($3.99)
1-6-Brian Bendis & David F. Walker-s/Jamal Campbell-a. 1-Superman app. 3-6-Origin 4.00

NAPOLEON
Dell Publishing Co.: No. 526, Dec, 1953
Four Color 526 5 10 15 30 50 70

NAPOLEON & SAMANTHA (See Walt Disney Showcase No. 10)

NAPOLEON & UNCLE ELBY (See Clifford McBride's...)
Eastern Color Printing Co.: July, 1942 (68 pgs.) (One Shot)
1 48 96 194 302 514 725
1945-American Book-Strafford Press (128 pgs.) (8x10-1/2"; B&W reprints; hardcover)
15 30 45 86 133 190

NAPOLEON DYNAMITE (Based on the 2004 movie)
IDW Publishing: Sept, 2019 - No. 4, Dec, 2019 ($3.99, limited series)
1-4-Sequel to movie; Monlongo-a; multiple covers on each 4.00
... Valentine's Day Special (2/20, $3.99) Megan Brown-s/Christine Larsen-a; 3 covers 4.00

NARCOS (Based on the 2015-2017 TV series)
IDW Publishing: Dec, 2019 - Present ($3.99)
1,2-Ferrier-s/Malhotra-a. 1-Three covers. 2-Two covers 4.00

NARRATIVE ILLUSTRATION, THE STORY OF THE COMICS (Also see Good Triumphs Over Evil!)
M.C. Gaines: Summer, 1942 (32 pgs., 7-1/4"x10", B&W w/color inserts)
nn-16 pgs. text with illustrations of ancient art, strips and comic covers; 4 pg. WWII War Bond promo, "The Minute Man Answers the Call" color comic drawn by Shelly and a special 8-page color comic insert of "The Story of Saul" (from Picture Stories from the Bible #10 or soon to appear in PS #10) or "Noah and His Ark" or "The Story of Ruth". Insert has special title page indicating it was part of a Sunday newspaper supplement insert series that had already run in a New England "Sunday Herald." Another version exists with insert from Picture Stories from the Bible #7.
(very rare) Estimated value... 1700.00
NOTE: ***Print, A Quarterly Journal of the Graphic Arts*** *Vol. 3 No. 2 (88 pg., square bound) features the 1st printing of Narrative Illustration, The Story of The Comics. A VG+ copy sold for $750 in 2005.*

NASCAR HEROES
Starbridge Media: 2007 - No. 3 ($3.95)
1-3: 1-Origin of fictional racer Jimmy Dash. 3-Origin of the Daytona 500; DeStefano-s 4.00
nn-(2008, Free Comic Book Day giveaway) The Mystery of Driver Z 3.00

NASH (WCW Wrestling)
Image Comics: July, 1999 - No. 2, July, 1999 ($2.95)
1,2-Regular and photo-c 3.00
1-($6.95) Photo-split-cover Edition 7.00

NATHANIEL DUSK
DC Comics: Feb, 1984 - No. 4, May, 1984 ($1.25, mini-series, direct sales, Baxter paper)
1-4: 1-Intro/origin; Gene Colan-c/a in all 3.00

NATHANIEL DUSK II
DC Comics: Oct, 1985 - No. 4, Jan, 1986 ($2.00, mini-series, Baxter paper)
1-4: Gene Colan-c/a in all 3.00

NATIONAL COMICS
Quality Comics Group: July, 1940 - No. 75, Nov, 1949
1-Uncle Sam begins (1st app.); origin sidekick Buddy by Eisner; origin Wonder Boy & Kid Dixon; Merlin the Magician (ends #45); Cyclone, Kid Patrol, Sally O'Neil Policewoman, Pen Miller (by Klaus Nordling; ends #22), Prop Powers (ends #26), & Paul Bunyan (ends #22) begin 730 1460 2190 5329 9415 13,500
2 290 580 870 1856 3178 4500
3-Last Eisner Uncle Sam 219 438 657 1402 2401 3400
4-Last Cyclone 165 330 495 1056 1803 2550
5-(11/40)-Quicksilver begins (1st app.; 3rd w/lightning speed?; re-intro'd by DC in 1993 as Max Mercury in Flash #76, 2nd series); origin Uncle Sam; bondage-c
194 388 582 1242 2121 3000
6,8-11: 8-Jack & Jill begins (ends #22). 9-Flag-c 158 316 474 1011 1731 2450
7-Classic Lou Fine-c 459 918 1377 3350 5925 8500
12-15-Lou Fine-a 123 246 369 787 1344 1900
16-Classic skeleton-c; Lou Fine-a 232 464 696 1485 2543 3600
17,19-22: 21-Classic Nazi swastika cover. 22-Last Pen Miller (moves to Crack #23)
97 194 291 621 1061 1500
18-(12/41)-Shows Asians attacking Pearl Harbor; on stands one month before actual event
213 426 639 1363 2332 3300
23-The Unknown & Destroyer 171 begin 97 194 291 621 1061 1500
24-Japanese War-c 100 200 300 635 1093 1550
25-30: 25-Nazi drug usage/hypodermic needle in story. 26-Wonder Boy ends. 27- G-2 the Unknown begins (ends #46). 29-Origin The Unknown
68 136 204 435 743 1050
31-33: 33-Chic Carter begins (ends #47) 63 126 189 403 689 975
34-37,40: 35-Last Kid Patrol 57 114 171 362 619 875
38-Hitler, Tojo, Mussolini-c 103 206 309 659 1130 1600
39-Hitler-c 110 220 330 704 1202 1700
41-Classic Uncle Sam American Eagle WWII-c 55 110 165 352 601 850
42-The Barker begins (1st app?, 5/44); The Barker covers begin
42 84 126 265 445 625
43-50: 48-Origin The Whistler 29 58 87 170 278 385
51-Sally O'Neil by Ward, 8 pgs. (12/45) 31 62 93 182 296 410
52-60 21 42 63 122 199 275
61-67: 67-Format change; Quicksilver app. 16 32 48 92 144 195
68-75: The Barker ends 15 30 45 84 127 170
NOTE: ***Cole*** *Quicksilver-13; Barker-43; c-43, 46, 47, 49-51.* ***Crandall*** *Uncle Sam-11-13 (with* ***Fine****), 25, 26; c-24-26, 30-33, 43.* ***Crandall*** *Paul Bunyan-10-13.* ***Fine*** *Uncle Sam-13 (w/****Crandall****), 17, 18; c-1-14, 16, 18, 21.* ***Gill Fox*** *c-69-74.* ***Guardineer*** *Quicksilver-27, 35.* ***Gustavson*** *Quicksilver-14-26.* ***McWilliams*** *a-23-28, 55, 57. Uncle Sam c-1-41. Barker c-42-75.*

NATIONAL COMICS (Also see All Star Comics 1999 crossover titles)
DC Comics: May, 1999 ($1.99, one-shot)
1-Golden Age Flash and Mr. Terrific; Waid-s/Lopresti-a 4.00

NATIONAL COMICS
DC Comics: Sept, 2012 ($3.99, one-shots)
... Eternity 1 (9/12) Re-intro of Kid Eternity; Lemire-s/Hamner-a/c 4.00
... Looker 1 (10/12) Vampire supermodel; Edginton-s/Mike S. Miller-a/March-c 4.00
... Madame X 1 (12/12) Rob Williams-s/Trevor Hairsine-a/Fiona Staples-c 4.00
... Rose & Thorn 1 (11/12) Taylor-s/Googe-a/Sook-c 4.00

NATIONAL CRUMB, THE (Magazine-Size)
Mayfair Publications: August, 1975 (52 pgs., B&W) (Satire)
1-Grandenetti-c/a, Ayers-a 2 4 6 11 16 20

NATIONAL VELVET (TV)
Dell Publishing Co./Gold Key: May-July, 1961 - No. 2, Mar, 1963 (All photo-c)
Four Color 1195 (#1) 6 12 18 41 76 110
Four Color 1312, 01-556-207, 12-556-210 (Dell) 4 8 12 27 44 60
1,2: 1(12/62) (Gold Key). 2(3/63) 4 8 12 27 44 60

NATION OF SNITCHES
Piranha Press (DC): 1990 ($4.95, color, 52 pgs.)
nn 5.00

NATION X (X-Men on the Utopia island)
Marvel Comics: Feb, 2010 - No. 4, May, 2010 ($3.99, limited series)
1-4-Short stories by various. 1,4-Allred-a. 2-Choi, Cloonan-a. 4-Doop app. 4.00
...: X-Factor (3/10, $3.99) David-s/DeLandro-a 4.00

NATURE BOY (Formerly Danny Blaze; Li'l Rascal Twins #6 on)
Charlton Comics: No. 3, March, 1956 - No. 5, Feb, 1957
3-1st app./origin; Blue Beetle story (last Golden Age app.); Buscema-c/a
24 48 72 142 234 325
4,5 17 34 51 103 162 220
NOTE: ***John Buscema*** *a-3, 4p, 5; c-3.* ***Powell*** *a-4.*

NATURE OF THINGS (Disney, TV/Movie)
Dell Publishing Co.: No. 727, Sept, 1956 - No. 842, Sept, 1957
Four Color 727 (#1), 842-Jesse Marsh-a 5 10 15 33 57 80

NAUSICAA OF THE VALLEY OF WIND
Viz Comics: 1988 - No. 7, 1989; 1989 - No. 4, 1990 ($2.50, B&W, 68pgs.)
Book 1-7: 1-Contains Moebius poster 5.00
Part II, Book 1-4 ($2.95) 5.00

NAVY ACTION (Sailor Sweeney #12-14)
Atlas Comics (CDS): Aug, 1954 - No. 11, Apr, 1956; No. 15, 1/57 - No. 18, 8/57
1-Powell-a 45 90 135 284 480 675
2-Lawrence-a; RQ Sale-a 25 50 75 150 245 340
3-11: 4-Last precode (2/55) 21 42 63 124 202 280
15-18 20 40 60 114 182 250
NOTE: ***Berg*** *a-7, 9.* ***Colan*** *a-8.* ***Drucker*** *a-7, 17.* ***Everett*** *a-3, 7, 16; c-16, 17.* ***Heath*** *c-1, 2, 5, 6.* ***Maneely*** *a-5, 7, 8, 18; c-9, 11.* ***Pakula*** *a-2, 3, 9.* ***Reinman*** *a-17.*

NAVY COMBAT
Atlas Comics (MPI): June, 1955 - No. 20, Oct, 1958
1-Torpedo Taylor begins by Don Heck; Heath-c 41 82 123 256 428 600
2 22 44 66 132 216 300

Navy Heroes #1 © APC

Negan Lives! #1 © Robert Kirkman

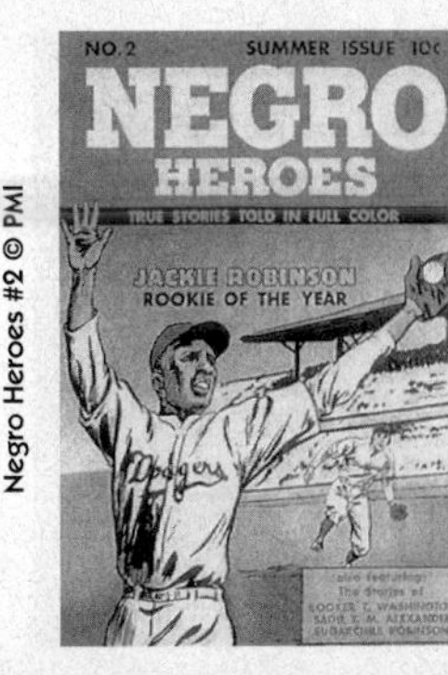

Negro Heroes #2 © PMI

	GD 2.0	VG 4.0	FN 6.0	VF 8.0	VF/NM 9.0	NM- 9.2
3-10	20	40	60	115	188	260
11,13-16,18-20: 14-Torres-a	18	36	54	107	169	230
12-Crandall-a	19	38	57	112	179	245
17-Williamson-a, 4 pgs.; Torres-a	19	38	57	112	179	245

NOTE: ***Ayers** a-15. **Berg** a-10, 11. **Colan** a-11. **Drucker** a-7. **Everett** a-3, 20; c-8 & 9 w/**Tuska**, 10, 13-16. **Forte** a-15, 18. **Heck** a-11(2), 15, 19. **Maneely** c-1, 5, 6, 11, 17. **Morisi** a-8. **Pakula** a-7, 18. **Powell** a-20. **Reinman** a-18.*

NAVY HEROES
Almanac Publishing Co.: 1945

	GD	VG	FN	VF	VF/NM	NM-
1-Heavy in propaganda	17	34	51	105	165	225

NAVY PATROL
Key Publications: May, 1955 - No. 4, Nov, 1955

	GD	VG	FN	VF	VF/NM	NM-
1	10	20	30	58	79	100
2-4	8	16	24	42	54	65

NAVY TALES
Atlas Comics (CDS): Jan, 1957 - No. 4, July, 1957

	GD	VG	FN	VF	VF/NM	NM-
1-Everett-c; Berg, Powell-a	39	78	117	231	378	525
2-Williamson/Mayo-a(5 pgs); Crandall-a	22	44	66	132	216	300
3,4-Reinman-a; Severin-c. 4-Crandall-a	19	38	57	111	176	240

NOTE: ***Colan** a-4. **Maneely** c-2. **Reinman** a-2-4. **Sinnott** a-4.*

NAVY TASK FORCE
Stanmor Publications/Aragon Mag. No. 4-8: Feb, 1954 - No. 8, April, 1956

	GD	VG	FN	VF	VF/NM	NM-
1	14	28	42	76	108	140
2	9	18	27	47	61	75
3-8: 8-r/Navy Patrol #1; defeat of the Japanese Navy	8	16	24	40	50	60

NAVY WAR HEROES
Charlton Comics: Jan, 1964 - No. 7, Mar-Apr, 1965

	GD	VG	FN	VF	VF/NM	NM-
1	4	8	12	23	37	50
2-7	3	6	9	15	22	28

NAZA (Stone Age Warrior)
Dell Publishing Co.: Nov-Jan, 1963-64 - No. 9, March, 1966

	GD	VG	FN	VF	VF/NM	NM-
12-555-401 (#1)-Painted-c	5	10	15	34	60	85
2-9: 2-4-Painted-c	4	8	12	25	40	55

NEBBS, THE (Also see Crackajack Funnies)
Dell Publishing Co./Croydon Publishing Co.: 1941; 1945

	GD	VG	FN	VF	VF/NM	NM-
Large Feature Comic 23(1941)	24	48	72	144	237	330
1(1945, 36 pgs.)-Reprints	14	28	42	78	112	145

NEBULA (Guardians of the Galaxy)
Marvel Comics: Apr, 2020 - Present ($3.99)

1,2-Vita Ayala-s/Claire Roe-a 4.00

NECESSARY EVIL
Desperado Publishing: Oct, 2007 - No. 9, Nov, 2008 ($3.99)

1-9: 1-Joshua Williamson-s/Marcus Harris-a/Dustin Nguyen-c 4.00

NECROMANCER
Image Comics (Top Cow): Sept, 2005 - No. 6, July 2006 ($2.99)

1-6: 1-Manapul-a/Ortega-s; three covers by Manapul, Horn & Bachalo 3.00
... Pilot Season Vol. 1 #1 (11/07, $2.99) Ortega-s/Meyers-a/Manapul-c 3.00

NECROMANCER: THE GRAPHIC NOVEL
Marvel Comics (Epic Comics): 1989 ($8.95)

nn 9.00

NECROWAR
Dreamwave Productions: July, 2003 - No. 3, Sept, 2003 ($2.95)

1-3-Furman-s/Granov-digital art 3.00

NEGAN LIVES! (The Walking Dead)
Image Comics: Jul, 2020 ($4.99, one-shot)

1-Kirkman-s/Adlard-a; takes place between Walking Dead #174-193 8.00
1-2nd printing with blue title logo 5.00
1-Variant with Gold foil title logo 55.00
1-Variant with Silver foil title logo 30.00
1-2nd printing with Bronze foil title logo 8.00

NEGATION
CrossGeneration Comics: Dec, 2001 - No. 27, Mar, 2004 ($2.95)

Prequel (12/01) 3.00
1-27: 1-(1/02) Pelletier-a/Bedard & Waid-s 3.00
... Lawbringer (11/02, $2.95) Nebres-a 3.00
Vol. 1: Bohica! (10/02, $19.95, TPB) r/ Prequel & #1-6 20.00
Vol. 2: Baptism of Fire (5/03, $15.95, TPB) r/#7-12 16.00
Vol. 3: Hounded (12/03, $15.95, TPB) r/#13-18 16.00

NEGATION WAR
CrossGeneration Comics: Apr, 2004 - No. 6 ($2.95)

1-4-Bedard-s/Pelletier-a 3.00

NEGATIVE BURN
Caliber: 1993 - No. 50, 1997 ($2.95, B&W, anthology)

1,2,4-12,14-47: Anthology by various including Bolland, Burden, Doran, Gaiman, Moebius, Moore, & Pope 4.00

	GD	VG	FN	VF	VF/NM	NM-
3,13: 3-Bone story. 13-Strangers in Paradise story	2	4	6	8	10	12

48,49-($4.95) 5.00
50-($6.95, 96 pgs.)-Gaiman, Robinson, Bolland 7.00
...Summer Special 2005 (Image, 2005, $9.99) new short stories by various 10.00
...: The Best From 1993-1998 (Image, 1/05, $19.95) r/short stories by various 20.00
...Winter Special 2005 (Image, 2005, $9.99) new short stories by various 10.00

NEGATIVE BURN
Image Comics (Desperado): May, 2006 - No. 21 ($5.99, B&W, anthology)

1-21: 1-Art by Bolland, Powell, Luna, Smith, Hester. 2-Milk & Cheese by Dorkin 6.00

NEGRO (See All-Negro)

NEGRO HEROES (Calling All Girls, Real Heroes, & True Comics reprints)
Parents' Magazine Institute: Spring, 1947 - No. 2, Summer, 1948

	GD	VG	FN	VF	VF/NM	NM-
1	181	362	543	1158	1979	2800
2-Jackie Robinson-c/story	165	330	495	1056	1803	2550

NEGRO ROMANCE (Negro Romances #4)
Fawcett Publications: June, 1950 - No. 3, Oct, 1950 (All photo-c)

	GD	VG	FN	VF	VF/NM	NM-
1-Evans-a (scarce)	245	490	735	1568	2684	3800
2,3 (scarce)	206	412	618	1318	2259	3200

NEGRO ROMANCES (Formerly Negro Romance; Romantic Secrets #5 on)
Charlton Comics: No. 4, May, 1955

	GD	VG	FN	VF	VF/NM	NM-
4-Reprints Fawcett #2 (scarce)	206	412	618	1318	2259	3200

NEIL GAIMAN AND CHARLES VESS' STARDUST
DC Comics (Vertigo): 1997 - No. 4, 1998 ($5.95/$6.95, square-bound, lim. series)

1-4: Gaiman text with Vess paintings in all 7.00
Hardcover (1998, $29.95) r/series with new sketches 35.00
Softcover (1999, $19.95) oversized; new Vess-c 20.00

NEIL GAIMAN'S LADY JUSTICE
Tekno Comix: Sept, 1995 - No. 11, May, 1996 ($1.95/$2.25)

1-11: 1-Sienkiewicz-c; pin-ups. 1-5-Brereton-c. 7-Polybagged. 11-The Big Bang Pt. 7 3.00
Free Comic Book Day (Super Genius, 2015, giveaway) r/#1 3.00

NEIL GAIMAN'S LADY JUSTICE
BIG Entertainment: V2#1, June, 1996 - No. 9, Feb, 1997 ($2.25)

V2#1-9: Dan Brereton-c on all. 6-8-Dan Brereton script 3.00

NEIL GAIMAN'S MIDNIGHT DAYS
DC Comics (Vertigo): 1999 ($17.95, trade paperback)

nn-Reprints Gaiman's short stories; new Swamp Thing w/ Bissette-a 18.00

NEIL GAIMAN'S MR. HERO-THE NEWMATIC MAN
Tekno Comix: Mar, 1995 - No. 17, May, 1996 ($1.95/$2.25)

1-17: 1-Intro Mr. Hero & Teknophage; bound-in game piece and trading card. 4-w/Steel edition Neil Gaiman's Teknophage #1 coupon. 13-Polybagged 3.00

NEIL GAIMAN'S MR. HERO-THE NEWMATIC MAN
BIG Entertainment: V2#1, June, 1996 ($2.25)

V2#1-Teknophage destroys Mr. Hero; includes The Big Bang Pt. 10 3.00

NEIL GAIMAN'S NEVERWHERE
DC Comics (Vertigo): Aug, 2005 - No. 9, Sept, 2006 ($2.99, limited series)

1-9-Adaptation of Gaiman novel; Carey-s/Fabry-a/c 3.00
TPB (2007, $19.99) r/series; intro. by Carey 20.00

NEIL GAIMAN'S PHAGE-SHADOWDEATH
BIG Entertainment: June, 1996 - No. 6, Nov, 1996 ($2.25, limited series)

1-6: Bryan Talbot-c & scripts in all. 1-1st app. Orlando Holmes 3.00

NEIL GAIMAN'S TEKNOPHAGE
Tekno Comix: Aug, 1995 - No. 10, Mar, 1996 ($1.95/$2.25)

1-6-Rick Veitch scripts & Bryan Talbot-c/a. 3.00
1-Steel Edition 4.00
7-10: Paul Jenkins scripts in all. 8-polybagged 3.00

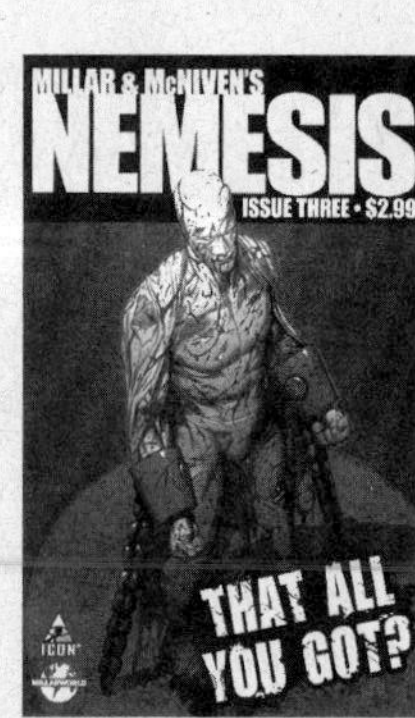

Nemesis #3 © Millar & McNiven

Nemo: Heart of Ice HC © Moore & O'Neill

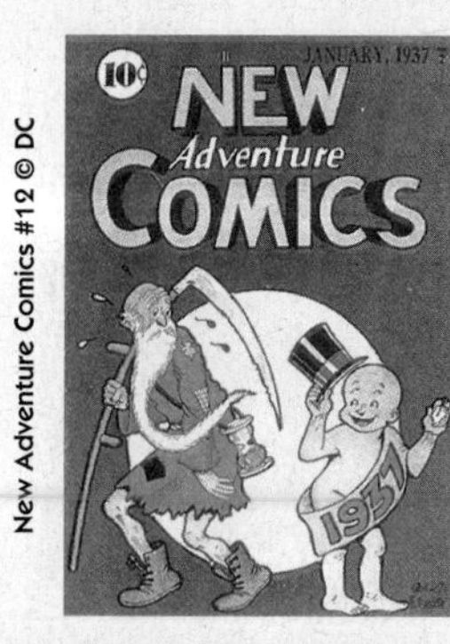

New Adventure Comics #12 © DC

	GD 2.0	VG 4.0	FN 6.0	VF 8.0	VF/NM 9.0	NM- 9.2

NEIL GAIMAN'S WHEEL OF WORLDS
Tekno Comix: Apr, 1995 - No. 1, May, 1996 ($2.95/$3.25)

0-1st app. Lady Justice; 48 pgs.; bound-in poster 5.00
0-Regular edition 4.00
1 ($3.25, 5/96)-Bruce Jones scripts; Lady Justice & Teknophage app.; CGI photo-c 4.00

NEIL THE HORSE (See Charlton Bullseye #2)
Aardvark-Vanaheim #1-10/Renegade Press #11 on: 2/83 - No. 10, 12/84; No. 11, 4/85 - #15, 1985 (B&W)

1($1.40) 4.00
1-2nd print 3.00
2-12: 11-w/paperdolls 3.00
13-15: Double size ($3.00). 13-w/paperdolls. 15 is a flip book(2-c) 4.00

NEIL YOUNG'S GREENDALE
DC Comics (Vertigo): 2010 ($19.99, hardcover graphic novel)

HC-Story based on the Neil Young album; Dysart-s/Chiang-a; intro. by Neil Young 20.00

NELLIE THE NURSE (Also see Gay Comics & Joker Comics)
Marvel/Atlas Comics (SPI/LMC): 1945 - No. 36, Oct, 1952; 1957

1-(1945) 142 284 426 909 1555 2200
2-(Spring/46) 42 84 126 265 445 625
3,4: 3-New logo (9/46) 34 68 102 199 325 450
5-Kurtzman's "Hey Look" (3); Georgie app. 33 66 99 194 317 440
6-8,10: 7,8-Georgie app. 10-Millie app. 27 54 81 162 266 370
9-Wolverton-a (1 pg.); Mille the Model app. 28 56 84 168 274 380
11,14-16,18-Kurtzman's "Hey Look" 29 58 87 172 281 390
12- "Giggles 'n' Grins" by Kurtzman 27 54 81 162 266 370
13,17,19,20: 17-Annie Oakley app. 23 46 69 136 223 310
21-30: 28-Mr. Nexdoor-r (3 pgs.) by Kurtzman/Rusty #22
20 40 60 118 192 265
31-36: 36-Post-c 19 38 57 111 176 240
1('57)-Leading Mag. (Atlas)-Everett-a, 20 pgs 32 64 96 192 314 435

NELLIE THE NURSE
Dell Publishing Co.: No. 1304, Mar-May, 1962

Four Color 1304-Stanley-a 9 18 27 57 111 165

NEMESIS (Millar & McNiven's...)
Marvel Comics (Icon): May, 2010 - No. 4, Feb, 2011 ($2.99)

1-4-Millar-s/McNiven-a 3.00
1,2-Variant covers: 1-Yu. 2-Cassaday 8.00

NEMESIS ARCHIVES (Listed with Adventures Into the Unknown)

NEMESIS: THE IMPOSTERS
DC Comics: May, 2010 - No. 4, Aug, 2010 ($2.99, limited series)

1-4-Richards-a/Luvisi-c. 1-Joker app. 2-4-Batman app. 3.00

NEMESIS THE WARLOCK (Also see Spellbinders)
Eagle Comics: Sept, 1984 - No. 7, Mar, 1985 (limited series, Baxter paper)

1-7: 2000 A.D. reprints 3.00

NEMESIS THE WARLOCK
Quality Comics/Fleetway Quality #2 on: 1989 - No. 19, 1991 ($1.95, B&W)

1-19 3.00

NEMO (The League of Extraordinary Gentlemen)
Top Shelf Productions: ($14.95, hardcover, one-shots)

...: Heart of Ice HC (2/13) Alan Moore-s/Kevin O'Neill-a 15.00
...: River of Ghosts HC (2015) Alan Moore-s/Kevin O'Neill-a 15.00
...: Roses of Berlin HC (3/14) Alan Moore-s/Kevin O'Neill-a 15.00

NEON FUTURE (Steve Aoki Presents...)
Impact Theory, LLC: Oct, 2018 - No. 6, Aug, 2019 ($3.99)

1-6: 1-Neil Edwards & Jheremy Raapack-a 4.00

NEON JOE, WEREWOLF HUNTER (Based on Adult Swim TV series)
DC Comics: 2015 (no price, one-shot)

nn - Origin of Neon Joe; Glaser-s/Mandrake & Duursema-a/Panosian-c 3.00

NEUTRO
Dell Publishing Co.: Jan, 1967

1-Jack Sparling-c/a (super hero); UFO-s 4 8 12 27 44 60

NEVADA (See Zane Grey's Four Color 412, 996 & Zane Grey's Stories of the West #1)

NEVADA (Also see Vertigo Winter's Edge #1)
DC Comics (Vertigo): May, 1998 - No. 6, Oct, 1998 ($2.50, limited series)

1-6-Gerber-s/Winslade-c/a 3.00
TPB-(1999, $14.95) r/#1-6 & Vertigo Winter's Edge preview 15.00

NEVER AGAIN (War stories; becomes Soldier & Marine V2#9)
Charlton Comics: Aug, 1955; No. 8, July, 1956 (No #2-7)

1-WWII 13 26 39 72 101 130
8-(Formerly Foxhole?) 8 16 24 44 57 70

NEVERBOY
Dark Horse Comics: Mar, 2015 - No. 6, Aug, 2015 ($3.99)

1-6-Shaun Simon-s/Tyler Jenkins-a 4.00

NEVERMEN, THE (See Dark Horse Presents #148-150)
Dark Horse Comics: May, 2000 - No. 4, Aug, 2000 ($2.95, limited series)

1-4-Phil Amara-s/Guy Davis-a 3.00

NEVERMEN, THE: STREETS OF BLOOD
Dark Horse Comics: Jan, 2003 - No. 3, Apr, 2003 ($2.99, limited series)

1-3-Phil Amara-s/Guy Davis-a 3.00
TPB (7/03, $9.95) r/#1-3; Paul Jenkins intro.; Davis sketch pages 10.00

NEW ADVENTURE COMICS (Formerly New Comics; becomes Adventure Comics #32 on; V1#12 indicia says NEW COMICS #12)
National Periodical Publications: V1#12, Jan, 1937 - No. 31, Oct, 1938

V1#12-Federal Men by Siegel & Shuster continues; Jor-L mentioned;
Whitney Ellsworth-c begin, end #14 700 1400 2100 5600 – –
V2#1(2/37, #13)-(Rare) 700 1400 2100 5600 – –
V2#2 (#14) 588 1176 1764 4700 – –
15(V2#3)-20(V2#8): 15-1st Adventure logo; Creig Flessel-c begin, end #31.
16-1st non-funny cover. 17-Nadir, Master of Magic begins, ends #30
454 908 1362 2497 4199 5900
21(V2#9),22(V2#10, 2/37): 22-X-Mas-c 392 784 1176 2156 3628 5100
23-25,28-31 358 716 1074 1969 3310 4650
26(5/38) (rare) has house ad for Action Comics #1 showing B&W image of cover
(early published image of Superman)(prices vary widely on this book)
4940 9880 14,820 35,800 – –
27(6/38) has house ad for Action Comics #1 showing B&W image of cover (rare)
(early published image of Superman) 1850 3700 5550 10,500 15,750 21,000

NEW ADVENTURES OF ABRAHAM LINCOLN, THE
Image Comics (Homage): 1998 ($19.95, one-shot)

1-Scott McCloud-s/computer art 20.00

NEW ADVENTURES OF CHARLIE CHAN, THE (TV)
National Periodical Publications: May-June, 1958 - No. 6, Mar-Apr, 1959

1 (Scarce)-John Broome-s/Sid Greene-a in all 97 194 291 621 1061 1500
2 (Scarce) 60 120 180 381 653 925
3-6 (Scarce)-Greene/Giella-a 53 106 159 334 567 800

NEW ADVENTURES OF CHOLLY AND FLYTRAP, THE
Epic Comics: Dec, 1990 - No. 3, Feb, 1991 ($4.95, limited series)

1-3-Arthur Suydam-s/a/c; painted covers 5.00

NEW ADVENTURES OF HUCK FINN, THE (TV)
Gold Key: December, 1968 (Hanna-Barbera)

1- "The Curse of Thut"; part photo-c 3 6 9 21 33 45

NEW ADVENTURES OF PINOCCHIO (TV)
Dell Publishing Co.: Oct-Dec, 1962 - No. 3, Sept-Nov, 1963

12-562-212(#1) 7 14 21 48 89 130
2,3 6 12 18 38 69 100

NEW ADVENTURES OF ROBIN HOOD (See Robin Hood)

NEW ADVENTURES OF SHERLOCK HOLMES (Also see Sherlock Holmes)
Dell Publishing Co.: No. 1169, Mar-May, 1961 - No. 1245, Nov-Jan, 1961/62

Four Color 1169(#1) 12 24 36 79 170 260
Four Color 1245 10 20 30 70 150 230

NEW ADVENTURES OF SPEED RACER
Now Comics: Dec, 1993 - No. 7, 1994? ($1.95)

1-7 3.00
0-(Premiere)-3-D cover 3.00

NEW ADVENTURES OF SUPERBOY, THE (Also see Superboy)
DC Comics: Jan, 1980 - No. 54, June, 1984

1 2 4 6 9 13 16
2-6,8-10 5.00
11-49,51-54: 11-Superboy gets new power. 14-Lex Luthor app. 15-Superboy gets new parents. 28-Dial "H" For Hero begins, ends #49. 45-47-1st app. Sunburst. 48-Begin 75¢-c.
4.00

New Avengers (2014 series) #22 © MAR

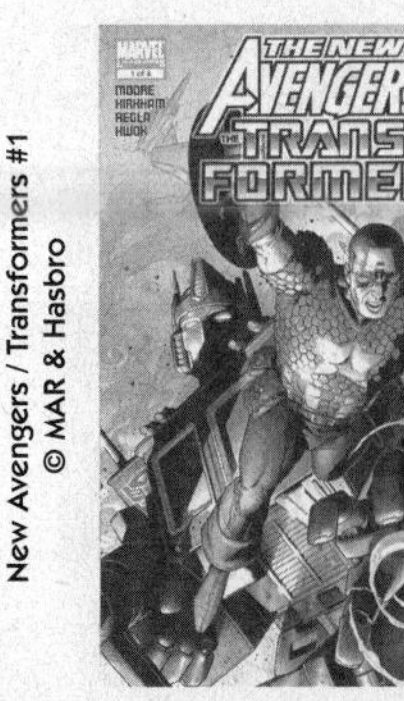

New Avengers / Transformers #1 © MAR & Hasbro

New Crusaders #1 © ACP

GD VG FN VF VF/NM NM-
2.0 4.0 6.0 8.0 9.0 9.2

1,2,5,6,8 (Whitman variants; low print run; no issue # shown on cover)
3 6 9 16 23 30
7,50: 7-Has extra story "The Computers That Saved Metropolis" by Starlin (Radio Shack giveaway w/indicia). 50-Legion app. 5.00
NOTE: *Buckler a-9p; c-36p. Giffen a-50; c-50. 40i. Gil Kane c-32p, 33p, 35, 39, 41-49. Miller c-51. Starlin a-7. Krypto back-ups in 17, 22. Superbaby in 11, 14, 19, 24.*

NEW ADVENTURES OF THE PHANTOM BLOT, THE (See The Phantom Blot)

NEW AMERICA
Eclipse Comics: Nov, 1987 - No. 4, Feb, 1988 ($1.75, Baxter paper)
1-4: Scout limited series 3.00

NEW ARCHIES, THE (TV)
Archie Comic Publications: Oct, 1987 - No. 22, May, 1990 (75¢)
1 5.00
2-10: 3-Xmas issue 4.00
11-22: 17-22 (95¢-$1.00): 21-Xmas issue 3.00

NEW ARCHIES DIGEST (TV)(...Comics Digest Magazine #4?-10; ...Digest Magazine #11 on)
Archie Comics: May, 1988 - No. 14, July, 1991 ($1.35/$1.50, quarterly)
1 6.00
2-14: 6-Begin $1.50-c 3.50

NEW AVENGERS, THE (Also see Promotional section for military giveaway)
Marvel Comics: Jan, 2005 - No. 64, Jun, 2010 ($2.25/$2.50/$2.99/$3.99)
1-Bendis-s/Finch-a; Spider-Man app.; re-intro The Sentry; 4 covers by McNiven, Quesada & Finch; variants from #1-6 combine for one team image 5.00
1-Director's Cut ($3.99) includes alternate covers, script, villain gallery 4.00
1-MGC (6/10 $1.00) r/#1 with "Marvel's Greatest Comics" cover logo 3.00
2-20: 2-6-Finch-a. 4-1st app. Maria Hill. 5-Wolverine app. 7-10-Origin of the Sentry; McNiven-a. 11-Debut of Ronin. 14,15-Cho-c/a. 17-20-Deodato-a 3.00
21-48: 21-26-Civil War. 21-Chaykin-a/c. 26-Maleev-a. 27-31-Yu-a; Echo & "Elektra" app. 33-37-The Hood app. 38-Gaydos-a. 39-Mack-a. 40-47-Secret Invasion 3.00
49-($3.99) Dark Reign 4.00
50-($4.99) Dark Reign; Tan, Hitch, McNiven, Yu, Horn & others-a; Tan wraparound-c 5.00
50-($4.99) Adam Kubert variant-c 6.00
51-64-($3.99) Dark Reign. 51,52-Tan & Bachalo-a. 54-Brother Voodoo becomes Sorceror Supreme. 56-Wrecking Crew app. 61-64-Siege; Steve Rogers app. 4.00
51-54-Variant covers by Bachalo 7.00
56,57-Variant covers. 56-70th Anniversary frame. 57-Super Hero Squad 6.00
Annual 1 (6/06, $3.99) Wedding of Luke Cage and Jessica Jones; Bendis-s/Coipel-a 4.00
Annual 2 (2/08, $3.99) Avengers vs. The Hood's gang; Bendis-s/Pagulayan-a 4.00
Annual 3 (2/10, $4.99) Mayhew-c/a; Dark Avengers app.; Siege preview 5.00
... Finale (6/10, $4.99) Follows Siege #4; Bendis-s/Hitch-a/c; Count Nefaria app. 5.00
...: Illuminati (5/06, $3.99) Bendis-s/Maleev-a; leads into Planet Hulk; Civil War preview 4.00
... Most Wanted Files (2006, $3.99) profile pages of Avenger villains 4.00
... Volume 1 HC (2007, $29.99) oversized r/#1-10, ... Most Wanted Files, and ... Guest Starring the Fantastic Four (military giveaway); new intro. by Bendis; script & sketch pages 30.00
... Volume 2 HC (2008, $29.99) oversized r/#11-20, ... Annual #1, and story from Giant-Size Spider-Woman; variant covers & sketch pages 30.00

NEW AVENGERS (The Heroic Age)
Marvel Comics: Aug, 2010 - No. 34, Jan, 2013 ($3.99)
1-Bendis-s/Immonen-a/c; Luke Cage forms new team; back-up text Avengers history 4.00
1-Variant-c by Djurdjevic 6.00
2-16: Hellstrom & Doctor Voodoo app.; back-up text Avengers history. 6-Doctor Voodoo killed. 9-13-Nick Fury flashback w/Chaykin-a. 10-Intro. Avengers 1959. 14-16-Fear Itself. 16-Daredevil joins 4.00
16.1 (11/11, $2.99) Neal Adams-a/c; Bendis-s; Norman Osborn app. 3.00
17-23-($3.99) 17-Norman Osborn attacks; Iron Man app.; Deodato-a 4.00
24-33: 24-30-Avengers vs. X-Men tie-in. 26,27-DaVinci app. 31-Gaydos-a. 32-Pacheco-a 4.00
34-($4.99) Dr. Strange become Sorcerer Supreme again; Deodato-a; gallery of Bendis-era Avengers covers 5.00
Annual 1 (11/11, $4.99) Dell'Otto-a; Wonder Man app.; continues in Avengers Annual #1 5.00

NEW AVENGERS (Marvel NOW!)
Marvel Comics: Mar, 2013 - No. 33, Jun, 2015 ($3.99)
1-7: 1-Hickman-s/Epting-a; Black Panther and the Illuminati. 4-Galactus app. 4.00
8-23: 8-12-Infinity tie-ins; Deodato-a. 13-Inhumanity; Bianchi-a. 17-21-Great Society app. 4.00
24-($4.99) Doctor Doom, Thanos and the Cabal app. 5.00
25-32: 27-Kudranski-a. 28,32-Deodato-a 4.00
33-($4.99) Doctor Doom & Molecule Man app.; leads into Secret Wars x-over; Deodato-a 5.00
Annual 1 (8/14, $4.99) Spotlight on Doctor Strange; Marco Rudy-a 5.00

NEW AVENGERS (Follows events of Secret Wars)(See U.S.Avengers)
Marvel Comics: Dec, 2015 - No. 18, Jan, 2017 ($3.99)
1-18: 1-Ewing-s/Sandoval-a; Squirrel Girl app. 5,6-Avengers of 20XX app. 8-10-Standoff tie-in; Marcus To-a. 12-17-Civil War II tie-in. 12-16-Interlocking covers 4.00

NEW AVENGERS: ILLUMINATI (Also see Civil War and Secret Invasion)
Marvel Comics: Feb, 2007 - No. 5, Jan, 2008 ($2.99, limited series)
1-5-Bendis & Reed-s/Cheung-a. 3-Origin of The Beyonder. 5-Secret Invasion 3.00
HC (2008, $19.99, dustjacket) r/#1-5; cover sketch art 20.00
SC (2008, $14.99) r/#1-5; cover sketch art 15.00

NEW AVENGERS: LUKE CAGE
Marvel Comics: Jun, 2010 - No. 3, Aug, 2010 ($3.99, limited series)
1-3-Arcudi-s/Canete-a; Spider-Man & Ronin app. 4.00

NEW AVENGERS: THE REUNION
Marvel Comics: May, 2009 - No. 4, Aug, 2009 ($3.99, limited series)
1-4-Mockingbird and Ronin (Hawkeye); McCann-s/López-a/Jo Chen-c 4.00

NEW AVENGERS/TRANSFORMERS
Marvel Comics: Sept, 2007 - No. 4, Dec, 2007 ($2.99, limited series)
1-4-Kirkham-a; Capt. America app. 1-Cheung-c. 2-Pearson-c 3.00
TPB (2008, $10.99) r/#1-4 11.00

NEW AVENGERS: ULTRON FOREVER
Marvel Comics: Jun, 2015 ($4.99)(Continues in Uncanny Avengers: Ultron Forever)
1-Part 2 of 3-part crossover with Avengers and Uncanny Avengers; Ewing-s/Alan Davis-a; team-up of past, present and future Avengers vs. Ultron 5.00

NEW BOOK OF COMICS (Also see Big Book Of Fun)
National Periodical Publ.: 1937; No. 2, Spring, 1938 (100 pgs. each) (Reprints)
1(Rare)-1st regular size comic annual; 2nd DC annual; contains r/New Comics #1-4 & More Fun #9; r/Federal Men (8 pgs.), Henri Duval (1 pg.), & Dr. Occult in costume (1 pg.) by Siegel & Shuster; Moldoff, Sheldon Mayer (15 pgs.)-a
1850 3700 5550 12,000 21,000 30,000
2-Contains-r/More Fun #15 & 16; r/Dr. Occult in costume (a Superman prototype), & Calling All Cars (4 pgs.) by Siegel & Shuster 892 1784 2576 6512 11,506 16,500

NEW CHALLENGERS (Challengers of the Unknown)(Follows events of Dark Nights: Metal)
DC Comics: Jul, 2018 - No. 6, Dec, 2018 ($2.99)
1-5: 1-New team recruited; Snyder & Gillespie-s/Andy Kubert-a/c. 2-Original team returns. 4-6-Marion-a 3.00

NEW COMICS (New Adventure #12 on)
National Periodical Publ.: 12/35 - No. 11, 12/36 (No. 1-6: paper cover) (No. 1-5: 84 pgs.)
V1#1-Billy the Kid, Sagebrush 'n' Cactus, Jibby Jones, Needles, The Vikings, Sir Loin of Beef, Now-When I Was a Boy, & other 1-2 pg. strips; 2 pgs. Kelly art(1st)-(Gulliver's Travels); Sheldon Mayer-a(1st)(2 2pg. strips); Vincent Sullivan-c(1st)
2365 4730 7095 14,900 – –
2-1st app. Federal Men by Siegel & Shuster & begins (also see The Comics Magazine #2); Mayer, Kelly-a (Rare)(1/36) 1365 2730 4095 8600 – –
3-6: 3,4-Sheldon Mayer-a which continues in The Comics Magazine #1. 3-Vincent Sullivan-c. 4-Dickens' "A Tale of Two Cities" adaptation begins. 5-Junior Federal Men Club; Kiefer-a. 6- "She" adaptation begins 937 1874 2811 5900 – –
7-10 603 1206 1809 3800 – –
11-Ties with More Fun #16 as DC's 1st Christmas-c 683 1366 2049 4300 – –
NOTE: *#1-6 rarely occur in mint condition. Whitney Ellsworth c-4-11.*

NEW CRUSADERS (Rise of the Heroes)
Archie Comics (Red Circle Comics): Oct, 2012 - No. 6, Mar, 2013 ($2.99)
1-6-The Shield and the offspring of the Mighty Crusaders 3.00

NEW DEADWARDIANS, THE
DC Comics (Vertigo): May, 2012 - No. 8, Dec, 2012 ($2.99, limited series)
1-8-Abnett-s/Culbard-a 3.00

NEW DEFENDERS (See Defenders)

NEW DNAGENTS, THE (Formerly DNAgents)
Eclipse Comics: V2#1, Oct, 1985 - V2#17, Mar, 1987 (Whole #s 25-40; Mando paper)
V2#1-17: 1-Origin recap. 7-Begin 95 cent-c. 9,10-Airboy preview 3.00
3-D 1 (1/86, $2.25) 3.00
2-D 1 (1/86)-Limited ed. (100 copies) 10.00

NEW DYNAMIX
DC Comics (WildStorm): May, 2008 - No. 5, Sept, 2008 ($2.99, limited series)
1-5-Warner-s/J.J. Kirby-a/c. 1-Variant-c by Jim Lee. 1-Convention Ed. with Lee-c 3.00

NEW ETERNALS: APOCALYPSE NOW (Also see Eternals, The)
Marvel Comics: Feb, 2000 ($3.99, one-shot)
1-Bennett & Hanna-a; Ladronn-c 4.00

NEW EXCALIBUR
Marvel Comics: Jan, 2006 - No. 24, Dec, 2007 ($2.99)

New 52: Future's End #1 © DC

New Gods #9 © DC

Newmen #4 © Rob Liefeld

	GD	VG	FN	VF	VF/NM	NM-
	2.0	4.0	6.0	8.0	9.0	9.2

1-24: 1-Claremont-s/Ryan-a; Dazzler app. 3-Juggernaut app. 4-Lionheart app. 3.00
... Vol. 1: Defenders of the Realm TPB (2006, $17.99) r/#1-7 18.00
... Vol. 2: Last Days of Camelot TPB (2007, $19.99) r/#8-15 20.00
... Vol. 3: Battle for Eternity TPB (2007, $24.99) r/#16-24; sketch pages 25.00

NEW EXILES (Continued from Exiles #100 and Exiles - Days of Then and Now)
Marvel Comics: Mar, 2008 - No. 18, Apr, 2009 ($2.99)
1-18: 1-Claremont-s/Grummett-a; 2 covers by Land & Golden; new team 3.00
1-2nd printing with Grummett-c 3.00
Annual 1 (2/09, $3.99) Claremont-s/Grummett-a 4.00

NEW 52: FUTURE'S END
DC Comics: No 0, Jun, 2014 - No. 48, Jun, 2015 ($2.99, weekly limited series)
... FCBD Special Edition #0 (6/14, giveaway) Part 1; 35 years in the future 3.00
1-36: 1-Set 5 years in the future; Azzarello, Lemire, Jurgens & Giffen-s. 29-New Firestorm. 33-Kid Deathstroke-c. 44-Brainiac steals New York (Convergence) 3.00

NEWFORCE (Also see Newmen)
Image Comics (Extreme Studios): Jan, 1996-No. 4, Apr, 1996 ($2.50, lim. series)
1-4: 1-"Extreme Destroyer" Pt. 8; polybagged w/gaming card. 4-Newforce disbands 3.00

NEW FUN COMICS (More Fun #7 on; see Big Book of Fun Comics)
National Periodical Publications: Feb, 1935 - No. 6, Oct, 1935 (10x15", No. 1-4,: slick-c) (No. 1-5: 36 pgs; 40 pgs. No. 6)
V1#1 (1st DC comic); 1st app. Oswald The Rabbit; Jack Woods (cowboy) begins
8571 17,142 25,713 60,000 – –
2(3/35)-(Very Rare) 4129 8258 12,387 28,900 – –
3-5(8/35): 3-Don Drake on the Planet Soro-c/story (sci/fi, 4/35); early (maybe 1st) DC letter column. 5-Soft-c 2743 5486 8229 19,200 – –
6(10/35)-1st Dr. Occult by Siegel & Shuster (Leger & Reuths); last "New Fun" title. "New Comics" #1 begins in Dec. which is reason for title change to More Fun; Henri Duval (ends #10) by Siegel & Shuster begins; paper-c
4429 8858 13,287 31,000 – –

NEW FUNNIES (The Funnies #1-64; Walter Lantz...#109 on; New TV... #259, 260, 272, 273; TV Funnies #261-271)
Dell Publishing Co.: No. 65, July, 1942 - No. 288, Mar-Apr, 1962
65(#1)-Andy Panda in a world of real people, Raggedy Ann & Andy, Oswald the Rabbit (with Woody Woodpecker x-overs), Li'l Eight Ball & Peter Rabbit begin; Bugs Bunny and Elmer app. 96 192 288 768 1734 2700
66-70: 66-Felix the Cat begins. 67-Billy & Bonny Bee by Frank Thomas begins. 69-Kelly-a (2 pgs.); The Brownies begin (not by Kelly); Halloween-c
31 62 93 223 499 775
71-75: 71-Christmas-c. 72-Kelly illos. 75-Brownies by Kelly?
21 42 63 146 311 475
76-Andy Panda (Carl Barks & Pabian-a); Woody Woodpecker x-over in Oswald ends
50 100 150 400 900 1400
77,78: 77-Kelly-c. 78-Andy Panda in a world with real people ends
15 30 45 103 227 350
79-81 10 20 30 69 147 225
82-Brownies by Kelly begins 11 22 33 73 157 240
83-85-Brownies by Kelly in ea. 83-X-mas-c; Homer Pigeon begins. 85-Woody Woodpecker, 1 pg. strip begins 11 22 33 72 154 235
86-90: 87-Woody Woodpecker stories begin 9 18 27 57 111 165
91-99 8 16 24 51 96 140
100 (6/45) 8 16 24 54 102 150
101-120: 119-X-Mas-c 7 14 21 46 86 125
121-150: 131,143-X-Mas-c 6 12 18 40 73 105
151-200: 155-X-Mas-c. 167-X-Mas-c. 182-Origin & 1st app. Knothead & Splinter. 191-X-Mas-c 5 10 15 35 63 90
201-240 5 10 15 35 57 80
241-288: 270,271-Walter Lantz c-app. 281-1st story swipes/WDC&S #100
5 10 15 30 50 70
NOTE: *Early issues written by* ***John Stanley.***

NEW GODS, THE (1st Series)(New Gods #12 on)(See Adventure #459, DC Graphic Novel #4, 1st Issue Special #13 & Super-Team Family)
National Periodical Publications/DC Comics: 2-3/71 - V2#11, 10-11/72; V3#12, 7/77 - V3#19, 7-8/78 (Fourth World)
1-Intro/1st app. Orion; 4th app. Darkseid (cameo; 3 weeks after Forever People #1) (#1-3 are 15¢ issues) 12 24 36 83 182 280
2-Darkseid-c/story (2nd full app., 4-5/71) 7 14 21 44 82 120
3-1st app. Black Racer; last 15¢ issue 6 12 18 38 69 100
4-6,8,9: (25¢, 52 pg. giants): 4-Darkseid cameo; origin Manhunter-r. 5,8-Young Gods feature. 9-1st app. Forager 4 8 12 25 40 55
7-1st app. Steppenwolf (2-3/72); Darkseid app.; origin Orion; 1st origin of all New Gods as a group; Young Gods feature 12 24 36 80 173 265
10,11: 11-Last Kirby issue. 3 6 9 21 33 45
12-19: Darkseid storyline w/minor apps. 12-New costume Orion (see 1st Issue Special #13 for 1st new costume). 19-Story continued in Adventure Comics #459,460
2 4 6 8 11 14
Jack Kirby's New Gods TPB ('98, $11.95, B&W&Grey) r/#1-11 plus cover gallery of original series and "84 reprints 12.00
NOTE: *#4-9(25¢, 52 pgs.) contain Manhunter-r by* ***Simon*** *&* ***Kirby*** *from Adventure #73, 74, 75, 76, 77, 78 with covers in that order.* ***Adkins*** *i-12-14, 17-19.* ***Buckler*** *a(p)-15.* ***Kirby*** *c/a-1-11p.* ***Newton*** *a(p)-12-14, 16-19.* ***Starlin*** *c-17.* ***Staton*** *c-19p.*

NEW GODS (Also see DC Graphic Novel #4)
DC Comics: June, 1984 - No. 6, Nov, 1984 ($2.00, Baxter paper)
1-5: New Kirby-c; r/New Gods #1-10. 5.00
6-Reprints New Gods #11 w/48 pgs of new Kirby story & art; leads into DC Graphic Novel #4
2 4 6 8 10 12

NEW GODS (2nd Series)
DC Comics: Feb, 1989 - No. 28, Aug, 1991 ($1.50)
1-28: 1,5-28-Evanier-s. 2-4-Starlin-s. 13-History of New Gods 20th anniv. 4.00

NEW GODS (3rd Series) (Becomes Jack Kirby's Fourth World) (Also see Showcase '94 #1 & Showcase '95 #7)
DC Comics: Oct, 1995 - No. 15, Feb, 1997 ($1.95)
1-11,13-15: 9-Giffen-a(p). 10,11-Superman app. 13-Takion, Mr. Miracle & Big Barda app. 13-15-Byrne-a(p)/scripts & Simonson-c. 15-Apokolips merged w/ New Genesis; story cont'd in Jack Kirby's Fourth World 4.00
12-(11/96, 99¢)-Byrne-a(p)/scripts & Simonson-c begin; Takion cameo; indicia reads October 1996 4.00
...Secret Files 1 (9/98, $4.95) Origin-s 5.00

NEW GODS SPECIAL, THE (Jack Kirby's 100th Birthday tribute)
DC Comics: Oct, 2017 ($4.99, one-shot)
1-Spotlight on Orion; Shane Davis-s/a; back-up by Walt Simonson-s/a; short reprints 5.00

NEW GUARDIANS, THE
DC Comics: Sept, 1988 - No. 12, Sept, 1989 ($1.25)
1-($2.00, 52 pgs)-Staton-c/a in #1-9 5.00
2-12 4.00

NEW HEROIC (See Heroic)

NEW INVADERS (Titled Invaders for #0 & #1) (See Avengers V3#83,84)
Marvel Comics: No. 0, Aug, 2004 - No. 9, June, 2005 ($2.99)
0-9-Roster of U.S. Agent, Sub-Mariner, Blazing Skull and others. 0-Avengers app. 3.00

NEW JUSTICE MACHINE, THE (Also see The Justice Machine)
Innovation Publishing: 1989 - No. 3, 1989 ($1.95, limited series)
1-3 4.00

NEW KIDS ON THE BLOCK, THE (Also see Richie Rich and...)
Harvey Comics: Dec, 1990 - No. 8, Dec, 1991 ($1.25)
1-8 4.00
...**Back Stage Pass** 1(12/90) - 7(11/91) **Chillin'** 1(12/90) - 7(12/91): 1-Photo-c ...**Comic Tour** '90/91 1 (12/90) - 7(12/91) **Digest** 1(1/91) - 5(1/92) **Hanging Tough** 1 (2/91) **Magic Summer Tour** 1 (Fall/90) **Magic Summer Tour** nn (Fall/90, sold at concerts) **Step By Step** 1 (Fall/90, one-shot) **Valentine Girl** 1 (Fall/90, one-shot)-Photo-c 4.00

NEW LINE CINEMA'S TALES OF HORROR (Anthology)
DC Comics (WildStorm): Nov, 2007 ($2.99, one-shot)
1-Freddy Krueger and Leatherface app.; Darick Robertson-c 3.00

NEW LOVE (See Love & Rockets)
Fantagraphics Books: Aug, 1996 - No. 6, Dec, 1997 ($2.95, B&W, lim. series)
1-6: Gilbert Hernandez-s/a 3.00

NEWMAN
Image Comics (Extreme Studios): Jan, 1996 - No. 4, Apr, 1996 ($2.50, lim. series)
1-4: 1-Extreme Destroyer Pt. 3; polybagged w/card. 4-Shadowhunt tie-in; Eddie Collins becomes new Shadowhawk 3.00

NEW MANGVERSE (Also see Marvel Mangaverse)
Marvel Comics: Mar, 2006 - No. 5, July, 2006 ($2.99, lim. series)
1-5: Cebulski-s/Ohtsuka-a; The Hand and Elektra app. 3.00
...: The Rings of Fate (2006, $7.99, digest) r/#1-5 8.00

NEWMEN (becomes The Adventures Of The...#22)
Image Comics (Extreme Studios): Apr, 1994 - No. 20, Nov, 1995; No. 21, Nov, 1996 ($1.95/$2.50)
1-21: 1-5: Matsuda-c/a. 10-Polybagged w/trading card. 11-Polybagged. 20-Has a variant-c; Babewatch! x-over. 21-(11/96)-Series relaunch; Chris Sprouse-a begins; pin-up. 16-Has a variant-c by Quesada & Palmiotti 3.00

New Mutants #10 © MAR

New Mutants (2009 series) #14 © MAR

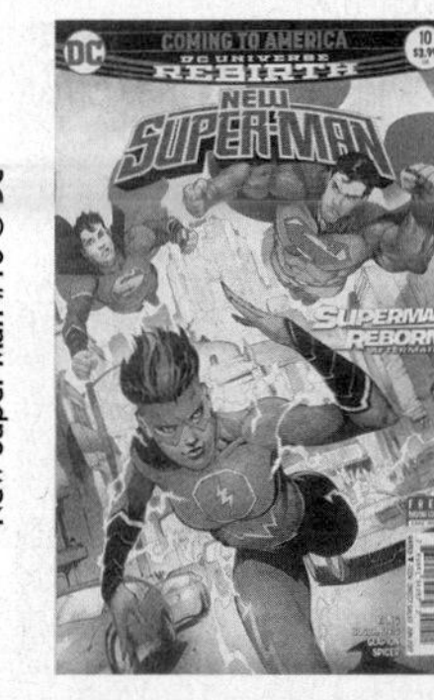
New Super-Man #10 © DC

	GD 2.0	VG 4.0	FN 6.0	VF 8.0	VF/NM 9.0	NM- 9.2

TPB-(1996, $12.95) r/#1-4 w/pin-ups 13.00

NEW MEN OF BATTLE, THE
Catechetical Guild: 1949 (nn) (Carboard-c)
nn(V8#1-3,5,6)-192 pgs.; contains 6 issues of Topix rebound 11 22 33 60 83 105
nn(V8#7-V8#11)-160 pgs.; contains 5 iss. of Topix 10 20 30 54 72 90

NEW MGMT (See Mind MGMT)

NEW MUTANTS, THE (See Marvel Graphic Novel #4 for 1st app.)(Also see X-Force & Uncanny X-Men #167)
Marvel Comics Group: Mar, 1983 - No. 100, Apr, 1991
1-Claremont-s/McLeod-a 3 6 9 17 26 35
2-,8,10: 3,4-Ties into X-Men #167. 10-1st app. Magma 1 2 3 5 6 8
9-1st app. Selene, the Black Queen 2 4 6 9 12 15
11-15,17,19,20: 13-Kitty Pryde app. 5.00
16-1st app. Warpath (w/out costume); see Uncanny X-Men #193 3 6 9 14 20 26
18-Intro. new Warlock 2 4 6 11 16 20
21-Double size; origin new Warlock; newsstand version has cover price written in by Sienkiewicz 2 4 6 8 10 12
22-24,27-30: 23-25-Cloak & Dagger app. 5.00
25-1st brief app. Legion (David Haller) 3 6 9 17 25 34
26-1st full Legion app. 3 6 9 19 30 40
31-49,51-58: 35-Magneto intro'd as new headmaster. 43-Portacio-i. 58-Contains pull-out mutant registration form 5.00
50,73: 50-Double size. 73-(52 pgs.). 6.00
59-61: Fall of The Mutants series. 60-(52 pgs.) 6.00
62-72,74-85: 68-Intro Spyder. 63-X-Men & Wolverine clones app. 76-X-Factor & X-Terminator app. 85-Liefeld-c begin 5.00
86-Rob Liefeld-a begins; McFarlane-c(i) swiped from Ditko splash pg.; 1st brief app. Cable (last page teaser) 3 6 9 17 26 35
87-1st full app. Cable (3/90) 9 18 27 59 117 175
87-2nd printing; gold metallic ink-c ($1.00) 3 6 9 15 22 28
88-2nd app. Cable 2 4 6 9 13 16
92-No Liefeld-a; Liefeld-c 5.00
89,90,91,93-97,99: 89-3rd app. Cable. 90-New costumes. 90,91-Sabretooth app. 93,94-Cable vs. Wolverine. 95-97-X-Tinction Agenda x-over. 95-Death of new Warlock. 97-Wolverine & Cable-c, but no app. 99-1st app. of Feral (of X-Force); 2nd app. Shatterstar (cameo); Byrne-c/swipe (X-Men, 1st Series #138) 6.00
95,100-Gold 2nd printing. 100-Silver ink 3rd printing 6.00
98-1st app. Deadpool, Gideon & Domino (2/91); Liefeld-c/a 14 28 42 96 211 325
100-(52 pgs.)-1st brief app. X-Force; 1st full app. of Shatterstar 3 6 9 15 22 28
Annual 1 (1984) 2 4 6 8 11 14
Annual 2 (1986, $1.25)-1st Psylocke 5 10 15 31 53 75
Annual 3,4,6,7 ('87, '88,'90,'91, 68 pgs.): 4-Evolutionary War x-over. 6-1st new costumes by Liefeld (3 pgs.); 1st brief app. Shatterstar (of X-Force). 7-Liefeld pin-up only; X-Terminators back-up story; 2nd app. X-Force (cont'd in New Warriors Annual #1) 5.00
Annual 5 (1989, $2.00, 68 pgs.)-Atlantis Attacks; 1st Liefeld-a on New Mutants 6.00
... Classic Vol. 1 TPB (2006, $24.99) r/#1-7, Marvel Graphic Novel #4, Uncanny X-Men #167 25.00
... Classic Vol. 2 TPB (2007, $24.99) r/#8-17 25.00
... Classic Vol. 3 TPB (2008, $24.99) r/#18-25 & Annual #1 25.00
... No. 98 Facimile Edition (9/19, $3.99) Reprints #98 with original 1991 ads and letters 4.00
Special 1-Special Edition ('85, 68 pgs.)-Ties in w/X-Men Alpha Flight limited series; cont'd in X-Men Annual #9; Art Adams/Austin-a 2 4 6 8 11 14
Summer Special 1(Sum/90, $2.95, 84 pgs.) 5.00
NOTE: ***Art Adams** c-38, 39. **Austin** c-57i. **Byrne** c/a-75p. **Liefeld** a-86-91p, 93-96p, 98-100, Annual 5p, 6(3 pgs.); c-85-91p, 92, 93p, 94, 95, 96p, 97-100, Annual 5, 6p. **McFarlane** c-85-89i, 93i. **Portacio** a(i)-43. **Russell** a-48i. **Sienkiewicz** a-18-31, 35-38i; c-17-31, 35i, 37i, Annual 1. **Simonson** c-11p. **B. Smith** c-36, 40-48. **Williamson** a(i)-69, 71-73, 78-80, 82, 83; c(i)-69, 72, 73, 78.*

NEW MUTANTS (Continues as New X-Men (Academy X))
Marvel Comics: July, 2003 - No. 13, June, 2004 ($2.50/$2.99)
1-13: 1-6-Josh Middleton-c. 7-11-Bachalo-c. 8-Begin $2.99 3.00
... Vol. 1: Back To School TPB (2005, $16.99) r/#1-6; new Middleton-c 17.00

NEW MUTANTS
Marvel Comics: July, 2009 - No. 50, Dec, 2012 ($3.99/$2.99)
1-($3.99) Neves-a; Legion app.; covers by Ross, Adam Kubert, McLeod, Benjamin 4.00
2-24-($2.99) 2-10-Adam Kubert-c. 11-Siege; Dodson-c. 12-14-Second Coming 3.00
25-($3.99) Fernandez-a; wraparound-c by Djurdjevic; Nate Grey returns 4.00
26-50: 29-32-Fear Itself tie-in. 33-Regenesis. 34-Blink returns. 42,43-Exiled x-over with Exiled #1 & Journey Into Mystery #637,638 3.00
... Saga (2009, giveaway) New Mutants character profiles and story synopsies; Neves-c 3.00

NEW MUTANTS
Marvel Comics: Jan, 2020 - Present ($4.99/$3.99)
1-($4.99) Brisson & Hickman-s/Rod Reis-a; Starjammers app. 5.00
2-16-($3.99) 13- "X of Swords" tie-in 4.00
...: War Children 1 (11/19, $4.99) Claremont-s/Sienkiewicz-a/c 5.00

NEW MUTANTS: DEAD SOULS
Marvel Comics: May, 2018 - No. 6, Oct, 2018 ($3.99, limited series)
1-6-Rosenberg-s/Gorham-a; Rictor, Boom Boom, Magik, Strong Guy & Wolfsbane app. 4.00

NEW MUTANTS FOREVER
Marvel Comics: Oct, 2010 - No. 5, Feb, 2011 ($3.99, limited series)
1-5-Claremont-s/Rio & McLeod-a; Red Skull app. 1-Back-up history of New Mutants 4.00

NEW MUTANTS, THE: TRUTH OR DEATH
Marvel Comics: Nov, 1997 - No. 3, Jan, 1998 ($2.50, limited series)
1-3-Raab-s/Chang-a(p) 3.00

NEW PEOPLE, THE (TV)
Dell Publishing Co.: Jan, 1970 - No. 2, May, 1970
1 3 6 9 16 24 32
2-Photo-c 3 6 9 15 21 26

NEW ROMANCER
DC Comics (Vertigo): Feb, 2016 - No. 6, Jul, 2016 ($3.99, limited series)
1-6-Milligan-s/Parson-a; Lord Byron & Casanova in present day 4.00

NEW ROMANCES
Standard Comics: No. 5, May, 1951 - No. 21, May, 1954
5-Photo-c 21 42 63 124 202 280
6-9: 6-Barbara Bel Geddes, Richard Basehart "Fourteen Hours" photo-c. 7-Ray Milland & Joan Fontaine photo-c. 9-Photo-c from '50s movie 15 30 45 84 127 170
10,14,16,17-Toth-a 15 30 45 86 133 180
11-Toth-a; Liz Taylor, Montgomery Clift photo-c 39 78 117 240 395 550
12,13,15,18-21 14 28 42 78 112 145
NOTE: ***Celardo** a-9. **Moreira** a-6. **Tuska** a-7, 20. Photo c-5-16.*

NEWSBOY LEGION AND THE BOY COMMANDOS SPECIAL, THE (Jack Kirby's 100th Birthday tribute)
DC Comics: Oct, 2017 ($4.99, one-shot)
1-Howard Chaykin-s/a/c; reprint from Star Spangled Comics #29; Simon-s/Kirby-a 5.00

NEWSBOY LEGION BY JOE SIMON AND JACK KIRBY, THE
DC Comics: 2010 ($49.99, hardcover with dustjacket)
Vol. 1 - Reprints apps. in Star Spangled Comics #7-32; new intro. by Joe Simon 50.00

NEW SHADOWHAWK, THE (Also see Shadowhawk & Shadowhunt)
Image Comics (Shadowline Ink): June, 1995 - No. 7, Mar, 1996 ($2.50)
1-7: Kurt Busiek scripts in all 3.00

NEWSTRALIA
Innovation Publ.: July, 1989 - No. 5, 1989 ($1.75, color)(#2 on, $2.25, B&W)
1-5: 1,2: Timothy Truman-c/a; Gustovich-i 3.00

NEW SUICIDE SQUAD (DC New 52)
DC Comics: Sept, 2014 - No. 22, Sept, 2016 ($2.99)
1-New team of Harley Quinn, Joker's Daughter, Black Manta, Deathstroke, Deadshot 3 6 9 17 26 35
2,3 1 2 3 5 6 8
4-10 4.00
11-22: 22-Cliquet-a 3.00
Annual 1 (11/15, $4.99) Continues story from #12; Briones-a 5.00
...: Futures End 1 (11/14, $2.99, regular-c) Five years later; Coelho-a 3.00
...: Futures End 1 (11/14, $3.99, 3-D cover) 4.00

NEW SUPER-MAN (DC Rebirth)(See Batman/Superman #32 for 1st app.)
DC Comics: Sept, 2016 - No. 19, Mar, 2018 ($2.99/$3.99)
1-9: 1-Kong Kenan as China's Superman; origin; Gene Luen Yang-s/Bogdanovic-a. 7-9-Master I-Ching app. 8-Ching Lung (from Detective Comics #1) app. 9-Luthor app. 3.00
10-19-($3.99) 10-Superman app. 15-Suicide Squad app. 17,18-Justice League app. 4.00

NEW SUPER-MAN & THE JUSTICE LEAGUE OF CHINA
DC Comics: No. 20, Apr, 2018 - No. 24, Aug, 2018 ($3.99)
20-24-Yang-s/Peeples-a 4.00

NEW TALENT SHOWCASE (Talent Showcase #16 on)
DC Comics: Jan, 1984 - No. 19, Oct, 1985 (Direct sales only)
1-19: Features new strips & artists. 18-Williamson-c(i) 3.00

New Talent Showcase 2018 #1 © DC

New Teen Titans #9 © DC

New Warriors #9 © MAR

GD VG FN VF VF/NM NM-
2.0 4.0 6.0 8.0 9.0 9.2

GD VG FN VF VF/NM NM-
2.0 4.0 6.0 8.0 9.0 9.2

NEW TALENT SHOWCASE
DC Comics: Jan, 2017 ($7.99, one-shot)

1-Janson-c; short stories by various; Wonder Woman, Harley Quinn, Deadman app. 8.00
... 2017 #1 (1/18, $7.99) Short stories by various; Wonder Woman, Red Hood, Duke, Katana, Deadshot, Poison Ivy and Dr. Fate app. 8.00
... 2018 #1 (2/19, $7.99) Short stories by various; Batman, Catwoman, Wonder Woman, Constantine, John Stewart and Zatanna app. 8.00

NEW TEEN TITANS, THE (See DC Comics Presents #26, Marvel and DC Present & Teen Titans; Tales of the Teen Titans #41 on)
DC Comics: Nov, 1980 - No. 40, Mar, 1984

1-Robin, Kid Flash, Wonder Girl, The Changeling (1st app.), Starfire, The Raven, Cyborg begin; partial origin 5 10 15 31 53 75
2-1st app. Deathstroke the Terminator 10 20 30 64 132 200
3-9: 3-Origin Starfire; Intro The Fearsome Five. 4-Origin continues; J.L.A. app. 6-Origin Raven. 7-Cyborg origin. 8-Origin Kid Flash retold. 9-Minor app. Deathstroke on last pg. 2 4 6 9 12 15
10-2nd app. Deathstroke the Terminator (see Marvel & DC Present for 3rd app.); origin Changeling retold 2 4 6 13 18 22
11-20: 13-Return of Madame Rouge & Capt. Zahl; Robotman revived. 14-Return of Mento; origin Doom Patrol. 15-Death of Madame Rouge & Capt. Zahl; intro. new Brotherhood of Evil. 16-1st app. Captain Carrot (free 16 pg. preview). 18-Return of Starfire. 19-Hawkman teams-up 1 2 3 5 6 8
21-Intro Night Force in free 16 pg. insert; intro Brother Blood 2 4 6 9 13 16
22-25,27-33,35-40: 22-1st app. Bethany Snow. 23-1st app. Vigilante (not in costume), & Blackfire; bondage-c. 24-Omega Men app. 25-Omega Men cameo; free 16 pg. preview Masters of the Universe. 27-Free 16 pg. preview Atari Force. 29-The New Brotherhood of Evil & Speedy app. 30-Terra joins the Titans. 37-Batman & The Outsiders x-over. 38-Origin Wonder Girl. 39-Last Dick Grayson as Robin; Kid Flash quits 6.00
26-1st app. Terra 2 4 6 9 13 16
34-4th app. Deathstroke the Terminator 2 4 6 8 10 12
Annual 1(11/82)-Omega Men app. 2 4 6 8 10 12
Annual V2#2(9/83)-1st app. Vigilante in costume; 1st app. Lyla 3 6 9 19 30 40
Annual 3 (See Tales of the Teen Titans Annual #3)
...: Games GN (2011, $24.99, HC) Wolfman-s/Pérez-a/c; original GN started in 1988, finished in 2011; '80s NTT roster; afterword by Pérez; Wolfman's original plot 25.00
...: Games GN (2013, $16.99, SC) same contents as HC 17.00
...: Terra Incognito TPB (2006, $19.99) r/#26,28-34 & Annual #2 20.00
...: The Judas Contract TPB (2003, $19.95) r/#39,40 plus Tales of the Teen Titans #41-44 & Annual #3 20.00
...: Who is Donna Troy? TPB (2005, $19.99) r/#38,Tales of the Teen Titans #50, New Titans #50-55 and Teen Titans/Outsiders Secret Files 2003 20.00
NOTE: *Pérez a-1-4p, 6-34p, 37-40p, Annual 1p, 2p; c-1-12, 13-17p, 18-21, 22p, 23p, 24-37, 38, 39(painted), 40, Annual 1, 2.*

NEW TEEN TITANS, THE (Becomes The New Titans #50 on)
DC Comics: Aug, 1984 - No. 49, Nov, 1988 ($1.25/$1.75; deluxe format)

1-New storyline; Pérez-c/a begins 2 4 6 8 11 14
2,3: 2-Re-intro Lilith 6.00
4-10: 5-Death of Trigon. 7-9-Origin Lilith. 8-Intro Kole. 10-Kole joins 5.00
11-49: 13,14-Crisis x-over. 20-Robin (Jason Todd) joins; original Teen Titans return. 38-Infinity, Inc. x-over. 47-Origin of all Titans; Titans (East & West) pin-up by Pérez 4.00
Annual 1-4 (9/85-'88): 1-Intro. Vanguard. 2-Byrne c/a(p); origin Brother Blood; intro new Dr. Light. 3-Intro. Danny Chase. 4-Pérez-c 4.00
...: The Terror of Trigon TPB (2003, $17.95) r/#1-5; new cover by Phil Jimenez 18.00
NOTE: ***Buckler** c-10. **Kelley Jones** a-47, Annual 4. **Erik Larsen** a-33. **Orlando** c-33p. **Perez** a-1-5; c-1-7, 19-23, 43. **Steacy** c-47.*

NEW TERRYTOONS (TV)
Dell Publishing Co./Gold Key: 6-8/60 - No. 8, 3-5/62; 10/62 - No. 54, 1/79

1(1960-Dell)-Deputy Dawg, Dinky Duck & Hashimoto-San begin (1st app. of each) 10 20 30 64 132 200
2-8(1962) 6 12 18 41 76 110
1(30010-210)(10/62-Gold Key, 84 pgs.)-Heckle & Jeckle begins 9 18 27 58 114 170
2(30010-301)-84 pgs. 7 14 21 49 92 135
3-5 4 8 12 27 44 60
6-10 4 8 12 21 33 45
11-20 3 6 9 15 22 28
21-30 2 4 6 9 13 16
31-43 1 3 4 6 8 10
44-54: Mighty Mouse-c/s in all 2 4 6 8 11 14
NOTE: *Reprints: #4-12, 38, 40, 47. (See March of Comics #379, 393, 412, 435)*

NEW TESTAMENT STORIES VISUALIZED
Standard Publishing Co.: 1946 - 1947

"New Testament Heroes–Acts of Apostles Visualized, Book I"
"New Testament Heroes–Acts of Apostles Visualized, Book II"
"Parables Jesus Told" Set.... 17 34 51 100 158 215
NOTE: *All three are contained in a cardboard case, illustrated on front and info about the set.*

NEW THUNDERBOLTS (Continues in Thunderbolts #100)
Marvel Comics: Jan, 2005 - No. 18, Apr, 2006 ($2.99)

1-18: 1-Grummett-a/Nicieza-s. 1-Captain Marvel app. 2-Namor app. 4-Wolverine app. 3.00
... Vol. 1: One Step Forward (2005, $14.99) r/#1-6 15.00
... Vol. 2: Modern Marvels (2005, $14.99) r/#7-12 15.00
... Vol. 3: Right of Power (2006, $17.99) r/#13-18 & Thunderbolts #100 18.00

NEW TITANS, THE (Formerly The New Teen Titans)
DC Comics: No. 50, Dec, 1988 - No. 130, Feb, 1996 ($1.75/$2.25)

50-Perez-c/a begins; new origin Wonder Girl 6.00
51-59: 50-55-Painted-c. 55-Nightwing (Dick Grayson) forces Danny Chase to resign; Batman app. in flashback, Wonder Girl becomes Troia 4.00
60,61: 60-A Lonely Place of Dying Part 2 continues from Batman #440; new Robin tie-in; Timothy Drake app. 61-A Lonely Place of Dying Part 4 4.00
62-70,72-99,101-124,126-130: 62-65: Deathstroke the Terminator app. 65-Tim Drake (Robin) app. 70-1st Deathstroke solo cover/sty. 72-79-Deathstroke in all: 74-Intro. Pantha. 79-Terra brought back to life; 1 panel cameo Team Titans (1st app.). Deathstroke in #80-84,86. 80-2nd full app. Team Titans. 83,84-Deathstroke kills his son, Jericho. 85-Team Titans app. 86-Deathstroke vs. Nightwing-c/story; last Deathstroke app. 87-New costume Nightwing. 90-92-Parts 2,5,8 Total Chaos (Team Titans). 99-1st app. Arsenal. 115-(11/94) 3.00
71-(44 pgs.)-10th anniversary issue; Deathstroke cameo 4.00
100-($3.50, 52 pgs.)-Holo-grafx foil-c 4.00
125 (3.50)-wraparound-c 4.00
#0-(10/94) Zero Hour, released between #114 & 115 3.00
Annual 5-10 ('89-'94, 68 pgs.. 7-Armaggedon 2001 x-over; 1st full app. Teen (Team) Titans (new group). 8-Deathstroke app.; Eclipso app. (minor). 10-Elseworlds story 4.00
Annual 11 (1995, $3.95)-Year One story 4.00
NOTE: ***Perez** a-50-55p, 57,60p, 58,59,61(layouts); c-50-61, 62-67i, Annual 5i; co-plots-66.*

NEW TV FUNNIES (See New Funnies)

NEW TWO-FISTED TALES, THE
Dark Horse Comics/Byron Preiss:1993 ($4.95, limited series, 52 pgs.)

1-Kurtzman-r & new-a 5.00
NOTE: ***Eisner** c-1i. **Kurtzman** c-1p, 2.*

NEWUNIVERSAL
Marvel Comics: Feb, 2007 - No. 6, July, 2007 ($2.99)

1-6-Warren Ellis-s/Salvador Larroca-a. 1,2-Variant covers by Ribic 3.00
...: 1959 (9/08, $3.99) Aftermath of the White Event of 1953; Tony Stark app. 4.00
...: Conqueror (10/08, $3.99) The White Event of 2689 B.C.; Eric Nguyen-a 4.00
... : Everything Went White HC (2007, $19.99) r/#1-6; sketch pages 20.00
... : Everything Went White SC (2008, $14.99) r/#1-6; sketch pages 15.00

NEWUNIVERSAL: SHOCKFRONT
Marvel Comics: Jul, 2008 - No. 2 ($2.99)

1,2-Warren Ellis-s/Steve Kurth-a 3.00

NEW WARRIORS, THE (See Thor #411,412)
Marvel Comics: July, 1990 - No. 75, 1996 ($1.00/$1.25/$1.50)

1-Williamson-i; Bagley-c/a(p) in #1-13, (1st printing has red cover) 3 6 9 15 22 28
1-Gold 2nd printing (7/91) 1 2 3 5 6 8
2-5: 1,3-Guice-c(i). 2-Williamson-c/a(i). 5.00
6-24,26-49,51-75: 7-Punisher cameo (last pg.). 8,9-Punisher app. 14-Darkhawk & Namor x-over. 17-Fantastic Four & Silver Surfer x-over. 19-Gideon (of X-Force) app. 28-Intro Turbo & Cardinal. 31-Cannonball & Warpath app. 42-Nova vs. Firelord. 46-Photo-c. 47-Bound-in S-M trading card sheet. 52-12 pg. ad insert. 62-Scarlet Spider-c/app. 70-Spider-Man-c/app. 72-Avengers-c/app. 4.00
25-($2.50, 52 pgs.)-Die-cut cover 5.00
40,60: 40-($2.25)-Gold foil collector's edition 5.00
50-($2.95, 52 pgs.)-Glow in the dark-c 5.00
Annual 1-4('91-'94,68 pgs.)-1-Origins all members; 3rd app. X-Force (cont'd from New Mutants Ann. #7 & cont'd in X-Men Ann. #15); x-over before X-Force #1; Bagley-c/a(p); Williamson-i. 3-Bagged w/card 5.00

NEW WARRIORS, THE
Marvel Comics: Oct, 1999 - No. 10, July, 2000 ($2.99/$2.50)

0-Wizard supplement; short story and preview sketchbook 3.00
1-($2.99) 4.00
2-10: 2-Two covers. 5-Generation X app. 9-Iron Man-c 3.00

The New Wave #13 © ECL

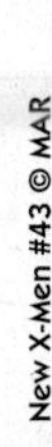

New X-Men #43 © MAR

Nexus #19 © FC

GD 2.0 | VG 4.0 | FN 6.0 | VF 8.0 | VF/NM 9.0 | NM- 9.2

NEW WARRIORS (See Civil War #1)
Marvel Comics: Aug, 2005 - No. 6, Feb, 2006 ($2.99, limited series)

1-6-Scottie Young-a 3.00
...: Reality Check TPB (2006, $14.99) r/#1-6 15.00

NEW WARRIORS (The Initiative)
Marvel Comics: Aug, 2007 - No. 20, Mar, 2009 ($2.99)

1-19: 1-Medina-a; new team is formed. 2-Jubilee app. 14-16-Secret Invasion 3.00
20-($3.99) 4.00
...: Defiant TPB (2008, $14.99) r/#1-6 15.00

NEW WARRIORS (All-New Marvel Now)
Marvel Comics: Apr, 2014 - No. 12, Jan, 2015 ($3.99)

1-12: 1-Nova, Speedball, Justice, Sun Girl, Scarlet Spider team; Yost-s/To-a 4.00

NEW WAVE, THE
Eclipse Comics: 6/10/86 - No. 13, 3/87 (#1-8: bi-weekly, 20pgs; #9-13: monthly)

1-13:1-Origin, concludes #5. 6-Origin Megabyte. 8,9-The Heap returns. 13-Snyder-c 3.00
...Versus the Volunteers 3-D #1,2(4/87): 1-Snyder-c 3.00

NEW WEST, THE
Black Bull Comics: Mar, 2005 - No. 2, Jun, 2005 ($4.99, limited series)

1,2-Phil Noto-a/c; Jimmy Palmiotti-s 5.00

NEW WORLD (See Comic Books, series I)

NEW WORLD, THE
Image Comics: Jul, 2018 - No. 5, Nov, 2018 ($4.99/$3.99, limited series)

1-($4.99) Ales Kot-s/Tradd Moore-a 5.00
2-5-($3.99) 4.00

NEW WORLDS
Caliber: 1996 - No. 6 ($2.95/$3.95, 80 pgs., B&W, anthology)

1-6: 1-Mister X & other stories 4.00

NEW X-MEN (See X-Men *2nd series* #114-156)

NEW X-MEN (Academy X) (Continued from New Mutants)
Marvel Comics: July, 2004 - No. 46, Mar, 2008 ($2.99)

1-46: 1,2-Green-c/a. 16-19-House of M. 20,21-Decimation. 40-Endangered Species back-ups begin. 44-46-Messiah Complex x-over; Ramos-a 3.00
Yearbook 1 (12/05, $3.99) new story and profile pages 4.00
...: Childhood's End Vol. 1 TPB (2006, $10.99) r/#20-23 11.00
...: Childhood's End Vol. 2 TPB (2006, $10.99) r/#24-27 11.00
...: Childhood's End Vol. 3 TPB (2006, $10.99) r/#28-32 11.00
...: Childhood's End Vol. 4 TPB (2007, $10.99) r/#33-36 11.00
...: Childhood's End Vol. 5 TPB (2007, $17.99) r/#37-43 18.00
House of M: New X-Men TPB (2006, $13.99) r/#16-19 and selections from Secrets Of The House of M one-shot 14.00
... Vol. 1: Choosing Sides TPB (2004, $14.99) r/#1-6 15.00
... Vol. 2: Haunted TPB (2005, $14.99) r/#7-12 15.00
... Vol. 3: X-Posed TPB (2006, $14.99) r/#12-15 & Yearbook Special 15.00

NEW X-MEN: HELLIONS
Marvel Comics: July, 2005 - No. 4, Oct, 2005 ($2.99, limited series)

1-4-Henry-a/Weir & DeFilippis-s 3.00
TPB (2006, $9.99) r/#1-4 10.00

NEW YEAR'S EVIL
DC Comics: Feb, 2020 ($9.99, squarebound one-shot)

1-Short Holiday stories featuring DC villains; Harley Quinn app.; Cheung-c 10.00

NEW YORK FIVE, THE
DC Comics (Vertigo): Mar, 2011 - No. 4, Jun, 2011 ($2.99, B&W, limited series)

1-4-Brian Wood-s/Ryan Kelly-a 3.00

NEW YORK GIANTS (See Thrilling True Story of the Baseball Giants)

NEW YORK STATE JOINT LEGISLATIVE COMMITTEE TO STUDY THE PUBLICATION OF COMICS, THE
N.Y. State Legislative Document: 1951, 1955

This document was referenced by Wertham for **Seduction of the Innocent.** Contains numerous repros from comics showing violence, sadism, torture, and sex. 1955 version (196p, No. 37, 2/23/55) - Sold for $180 in 1986.

NEW YORK, THE BIG CITY
Kitchen Sink Press: 1986 ($10.95, B&W); **DC Comics:** July, 2000 ($12.95, B&W)

nn-(1986, $10.95) Will Eisner-s/a 25.00
nn-(2000, $12.95) new printing 13.00

NEW YORK WORLD'S FAIR (Also see Big Book of Fun & New Book of Fun)
National Periodical Publ.: 1939, 1940 (100 pgs.; cardboard covers)
(DC's 4th & 5th annuals)

1939-Scoop Scanlon, Superman (blond haired Superman on-c), Sandman, Zatara, Slam Bradley, Ginger Snap by Bob Kane begin; 1st published app. The Sandman (see Adventure #40 for his 1st drawn story); Vincent Sullivan-c; cover background by Guardineer
1800 3600 5400 13,000 31,200 –
1940-Batman, Hourman, Johnny Thunderbolt, Red, White & Blue & Hanko (by Creig Flessel) app.; Superman, Batman & Robin-c (1st time they all appear together); early Robin app.; 1st Burnley-c/a (per Burnley) 975 1950 2925 7200 17,000 –

NOTE: *The 1939 edition was published 4/29/39 and released 4/30/39, the day the fair opened, at 25¢, and was first sold only at the fair. Since all other comics were 10¢, it didn't sell. Remaining copies were advertised beginning in the August issues of most DC comics for 25¢, but soon the price was dropped to 15¢. Everyone that sent a quarter through the mail for it received a free Superman #1 or a #2 to make up the dime difference. 15¢ stickers were placed over the 25¢ price. Four variations on the 15¢ stickers are known. The 1940 edition was published 5/11/40 and was priced at 15¢. It was a precursor to World's Best #1.*

NEW YORK: YEAR ZERO
Eclipse Comics: July, 1988 - No. 4, Oct, 1988 ($2.00, B&W, limited series)

1-4 3.00

NEXT, THE
DC Comics: Sept, 2006 - No. 6, Feb, 2007 ($2.99, limited series)

1-6-Tad Williams-s/Dietrich Smith-a; Superman app. 3.00

NEXT MEN (See John Byrne's...)

NEXT MEN: AFTERMATH (Continued from John Byrne's Next Men 2010-2011 series)
IDW Publishing: No. 40, Feb, 2012 - No. 44, Jun, 2012 ($3.99)

40-44-John Byrne-s/a/c 4.00

NEXT NEXUS, THE
First Comics: Jan, 1989 - No. 4, April, 1989 ($1.95, limited series, Baxter paper)

1-4: Mike Baron scripts & Steve Rude-c/a. 3.00
TPB (10/89, $9.95) r/series 10.00

NEXTWAVE: AGENTS OF H.A.T.E
Marvel Comics: Mar, 2006 - No. 12, Mar, 2007 ($2.99)

1-12-Warren Ellis-s/Stuart Immonen-a. 2-Fin Fang Foom app. 12-Devil Dinosaur app. 3.00
Vol. 1 - This Is What They Want HC (2006, $19.99) r/#1-6; Ellis original pitch 20.00
Vol. 1 - This Is What They Want SC (2007, $14.99) r/#1-6; Ellis original pitch 15.00
Vol. 2 - I Kick Your Face HC (2007, $19.99) r/#7-12 20.00
Vol. 2 - I Kick Your Face SC (2008, $14.99) r/#7-12 15.00

NEXUS (See First Comics Graphic Novel #4, 19 & The Next Nexus)
Capital Comics/First Comics No. 7 on: June, 1981 - No. 6, Mar, 1984; No. 7, Apr, 1985 - No. 80?, May, 1991 (Direct sales only, 36 pgs.; V2#1('83)-printed on Baxter paper)

1-B&W version; mag. size; w/double size poster 3 6 9 19 30 40
1-B&W 1981 limited edition; 500 copies printed and signed; same as above except this version has a 2-pg. poster & a pencil sketch on paperboard by Steve Rude
6 12 18 41 76 110
2-B&W, magazine size 2 4 6 13 18 22
3-B&W, magazine size; Brunner back-c; contains 33-1/3 rpm record ($2.95 price)
2 4 6 9 13 16
V2#1-Color version 5.00
2-49,51-80: 2-Nexus' origin begins. 67-Snyder-c/a 3.00
50-($3.50, 52 pgs.) 4.00
Hardcover Volume One (Dark Horse Books, 11/05, $49.95) r/#1-3 & V2 #1-4; creator bios 50.00
HC Volume Two (Dark Horse Books, 3/06, $49.95) r/V2 #5-11; creator bios 50.00
HC Volume Three (Dark Horse Books, 5/06, $49.95) r/V2 #12-18; Marz forward 50.00
HC Volume Four (Dark Horse Books, 8/06, $49.95) r/V2 #19-25; Powell forward 50.00
HC Volume Five (Dark Horse Books, 2/07, $49.95) r/V2 #26-32; Brubaker forward 50.00
HC Volume Six (Dark Horse Books, 2/07, $49.95) r/V2 #33-39; Evanier forward 50.00
HC Volume Seven (Dark Horse Books, 2/08, $49.95) r/V2 #40-46; Brunning forward 50.00
HC Volume Eight (Dark Horse Books, 1/09, $49.95) r/V2 #47-52 and The Next Nexus #1; interview with original publishers John Davis and Milton Griepp 50.00
HC Volume Nine (Dark Horse Books, 8/09, $49.95) r/V2 #53-57 & The Next Nexus #2-4 50.00

NOTE: ***Bissette** c-V2#29. **Giffen** c/a-V2#23. **Gulacy** c-1 (B&W), 2(B&W). **Mignola** c/a-V2#28. **Rude** c-3(B&W), V2#1-22, 24-27, 33-36, 39-42, 45-48, 50, 58-60, 75; a-1-3, V2#1-7, 8-16p, 18-22p, 24-27p, 33-36p, 39-42p, 45-48p, 50, 58, 59p, 60. **Paul Smith** a-V2#37, 38, 43, 44, 51-55p; c-V2#37, 38, 43, 44, 51-55.*

NEXUS
Rude Dude Productions: No. 99, July, 2007 - No. 102, Jun, 2009 ($2.99)

99-Mike Baron scripts & Steve Rude-c/a 3.00
100-($4.99) Part 2 of Space Opera; back-up feature: History of Nexus 5.00
101/102-(6/09, $4.95) Combined issue 5.00
..., Free Comic Book Day 2007 - Excerpts from previous issues and preview of #99 3.00
... Greatest Hits (8/07, $1.99) same content as Free Comic Book Day 2007 3.00
...: The Origin (11/07, $3.99) reprints the 7/96 one-shot 4.00

NEXUS: ALIEN JUSTICE
Dark Horse Comics: Dec, 1992 - No. 3, Feb, 1993 ($3.95, limited series)

NFL Rush Zone #1 © NFL

Nickel Comics #413 © DC

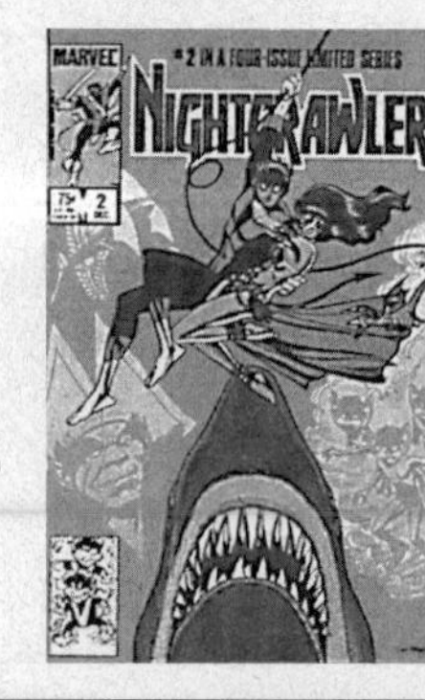

Nightcrawler #2 © MAR

	GD 2.0	VG 4.0	FN 6.0	VF 8.0	VF/NM 9.0	NM- 9.2

1-3: Mike Baron scripts & Steve Rude-c/a 4.00

NEXUS: EXECUTIONER'S SONG
Dark Horse Comics: June, 1996 - No. 4, Sept, 1996 ($2.95, limited series)
1-4: Mike Baron scripts & Steve Rude-c/a 3.00

NEXUS FILES
First Comics: 1989 ($4.50, color/16pgs. B&W, one-shot, squarebound, 52 pgs.)
1-New Rude-a; info on Nexus 4.50

NEXUS: GOD CON
Dark Horse Comics: Apr, 1997 - No. 2, May, 1997 ($2.95, limited series)
1,2-Baron-s/Rude-c/a 3.00

NEXUS LEGENDS
First Comics: May, 1989 - No. 23, Mar, 1991 ($1.50, Baxter paper)
1-23: R/1-3(Capital) & early First Comics issues w/new Rude covers #1-6,9,10 3.00

NEXUS MEETS MADMAN (...Special)
Dark Horse Comics: May, 1996 ($2.95, one-shot)
nn-Mike Baron & Mike Allred scripts, Steve Rude-c/a. 3.00

NEXUS: NIGHTMARE IN BLUE
Dark Horse Comics: July, 1997 - No. 4, Oct, 1997 ($2.95, limited series)
1-4: 1,2,4-Adam Hughes-c 3.00

NEXUS: THE LIBERATOR
Dark Horse Comics: Aug, 1992 - No. 4, Nov, 1992 ($2.95, limited series)
1-4 3.00

NEXUS: THE ORIGIN
Dark Horse Comics: July, 1996 ($3.95, one-shot)
nn-Mike Baron- scripts, Steve Rude-c/a. 4.00

NEXUS: THE WAGES OF SIN
Dark Horse Comics: Mar, 1995 - No. 4, June, 1995 ($2.95, limited series)
1-4 3.00

NFL RUSH ZONE: SEASON OF THE GUARDIANS
Action Lab Comics: Feb, 2013 - No. 4 ($3.99)
1-4: 1-Matt Ryan & Roddy White app. 4.00
Free Comic Book Day edition (2013, giveaway) 3.00

NFL SUPERPRO
Marvel Comics: Oct, 1991 - No. 12, Sept, 1992 ($1.00)
1-12: 1-Spider-Man-c/app. 3.00
Special Edition (9/91, $2.00) Jusko painted-c 4.00
Super Bowl Edition (3/91, squarebound) Jusko painted-c 4.00

NICK CALM, AGENT OF C.O.D.P.I.E.C.E. (Reprints from Cerebus in Hell)
Aardvark-Vanaheim: Aug, 2018 ($4.00, B&W)
1-Cerebus figures placed over original Gustave Doré artwork; Nick Fury #4-c swipe 4.00

NICKEL COMICS
Dell Publishing Co.: 1938 (Pocket size - 7-1/2x5-1/2")(68 pgs.)
1- "Bobby & Chip" by Otto Messmer, Felix the Cat artist. Contains some English reprints
90 180 270 576 988 1400

NICKEL COMICS
Fawcett Publications: Feb 1940
nn - Ashcan comic, not distributed to newsstands, only for in-house use. A CGC certified 9.6 copy sold for $7,200 in 2003. In 2008, a CGC certified 8.5 sold for $2,390 and an uncertified Near Mint copy sold for $3,100.

NICKEL COMICS
Fawcett Publications: May, 1940 - No. 8, Aug, 1940 (36 pgs.; Bi-Weekly; 5¢)

	GD	VG	FN	VF	VF/NM	NM-
1-Origin/1st app. Bulletman	397	794	1191	2779	4865	6950
2	129	258	387	826	1413	2000
3	94	188	282	597	1025	1450
4-The Red Gaucho begins	77	154	231	493	847	1200
5-7	77	154	231	493	847	1200
8-World's Fair-c; Bulletman moved to Master Comics #7 in October (scarce)	97	194	291	621	1061	1500

NOTE: ***Beck** c-5-8. **Jack Binder** c-1-4. Bondage c-5. Bulletman c-1-8.*

NICK FURY
Marvel Comics: Jun, 2017 - No. 6, Nov, 2017 ($3.99, limited series)
1-6-James Robinson-s/Aco-a; Nick Fury Jr. vs. Hydra; Frankie Noble app. 4.00

NICK FURY, AGENT OF SHIELD (See Fury, Marvel Spotlight #31 & Shield)
Marvel Comics Group: 6/68 - No. 15, 11/69; No. 16, 11/70 - No. 18, 3/71

	GD	VG	FN	VF	VF/NM	NM-
1	15	30	45	103	227	350
2-4: 4-Origin retold	8	16	24	51	96	140
5-Classic-c	8	16	24	56	108	160
6,7: 7-Salvador Dali painting swipe	7	14	21	46	86	125
8-11,13: 9-Hate Monger begins, ends #11. 10-Smith layouts/pencil. 11-Smith-c. 13-1st app. Super-Patriot; last 12¢ issue	4	8	12	28	47	65
12-Smith-c/a	5	10	15	30	50	70
14-Begin 15¢ issues	4	8	12	25	40	55
15-1st app. & death of Bullseye-c/story(11/69); Nick Fury shot & killed; last 15¢ issue	7	14	21	49	92	135
16-18-(25¢, 52 pgs.)-r/Str. Tales #135-143	3	6	9	20	31	42

TPB (May 2000, $19.95) r/ Strange Tales #150-168 20.00
...: Who is Scorpio? TPB (11/00, $12.95) r/#1-3,5; Steranko-c 13.00
NOTE: ***Adkins** a-3i. **Craig** a-10i. **Sid Greene** a-12i. **Kirby** a-16-18r. **Springer** a-4, 6, 7, 8p, 9, 10p, 11; c-8, 9. **Steranko** a(p)-1-3, 5; c-1-7.*

NICK FURY AGENT OF SHIELD (Also see Strange Tales #135)
Marvel Comics: Dec, 1983 - No. 2, Jan, 1984 (2.00, 52 pgs., Baxter paper)
1,2-r/Nick Fury #1-4; new Steranko-c 1 3 4 6 8 10

NICK FURY, AGENT OF S.H.I.E.L.D.
Marvel Comics: Sept, 1989 - No. 47, May, 1993 ($1.50/$1.75)
V2#1 5.00
2-26,30-47: 10-Capt. America app. 13-Return of The Yellow Claw. 15-Fantastic Four app. 30,31-Deathlok app. 36-Cage app. 37-Woodgod c/story. 38-41-Flashes back to pre-Shield days after WWII. 44-Capt. America-c/s. 45-Viper-c/s. 46-Gideon x-over 3.00
27-29-Wolverine-c/stories 4.00
NOTE: ***Alan Grant** scripts-11. **Guice** a(p)-20-23, 25, 26; c-20-28.*

NICK FURY'S HOWLING COMMANDOS
Marvel Comics: Dec, 2005 - No. 6, May, 2006 ($2.99)
1-6: 1-Giffen-s/Francisco-a 3.00
1-Director's Cut ($3.99) r/#1 with original script and sketch design pages 4.00

NICK FURY VS. S.H.I.E.L.D.
Marvel Comics: June, 1988 - No. 6, Nov, 1988 ($3.50, 52 pgs, deluxe format)
1,2: 1-Steranko-c. 2-(Low print run) Sienkiewicz-c 6.00
3-6 5.00

NICK HALIDAY (Thrill of the Sea)
Argo: May, 1956
1-Daily & Sunday strip-r by Petree 10 20 30 58 79 100

NIGHT AND THE ENEMY (Graphic Novel)
Comico: 1988 (8-1/2x11") ($11.95, color, 80 pgs.)
1-Harlan Ellison scripts/Ken Steacy-c/a; r/Epic Illustrated & new-a (1st & 2nd printings) 12.00
1-Limited edition ($39.95) 40.00

NIGHT BEFORE CHRISTMAS, THE (See March of Comics No. 152 in the Promotional Comics section)

NIGHT BEFORE CHRISTMASK, THE
Dark Horse Comics: Nov, 1994 ($9.95, one-shot)
nn-Hardcover book; The Mask; Rick Geary-c/a 10.00

NIGHTBREED (See Clive Barker's Nightbreed)

NIGHT CLUB
Image Comics: Apr, 2005 - No. 4, Dec, 2006 ($2.95/$2.99, limited series)
1-4: 1-Mike Baron-s/Mike Norton-a 3.00

NIGHTCRAWLER (X-Men)
Marvel Comics Group: Nov, 1985 - No. 4, Feb, 1986 (Mini-series from X-Men)
1-4: 1-Cockrum-c/a 6.00

NIGHTCRAWLER (Volume 2)
Marvel Comics: Feb, 2002 - No. 4, May, 2002 ($2.50, limited series)
1-4-Matt Smith-a 3.00

NIGHTCRAWLER
Marvel Comics: Nov, 2004 - No. 12, Jan, 2006 ($2.99)
1-12: 1-6-Robertson-a/Land-c. 2-Magik app. 8-Wolverine app. 10-Man-Thing app. 3.00
...: The Devil Inside TPB (2005, $14.99) r/#1-6 15.00
...: The Winding Way TPB (2006, $14.99) r/#7-12 15.00

NIGHTCRAWLER
Marvel Comics: Jun, 2014 - No. 12, May, 2015 ($3.99)
1-12: 1-Claremont-s/Nauck-a. 7-Death of Wolverine tie-in 4.00

NIGHTFALL: THE BLACK CHRONICLES
DC Comics (Homage): Dec, 1999 - No. 3, Feb, 2000 ($2.95, limited series)
1-3-Coker-a/Gilmore-s 3.00

Nighthawk #1 © MAR

Nightmare #3 © STJ

Nightmare Theater #1 © Chaos!

GD VG FN VF VF/NM NM-
2.0 4.0 6.0 8.0 9.0 9.2

NIGHT FORCE, THE (See New Teen Titans #21)
DC Comics: Aug, 1982 - No. 14, Sept, 1983 (60¢)

1 4.00
2-14: 13-Origin Baron Winter. 14-Nudity panels 3.00
NOTE: *Colan* c/a-1-14p. *Giordano* c-1i, 2i, 4i, 5i, 7i, 12i.

NIGHT FORCE
DC Comics: Dec, 1996 - No. 12, Nov, 1997 ($2.25)

1-12: 1-3-Wolfman-s/Anderson-a(p). 8-"Convergence" part 2 3.00

NIGHT FORCE
DC Comics: May, 2012 - No. 7, Nov, 2012 ($2.99, limited series)

1-7-Wolfman-s/Mandrake-a/Manco-c 3.00

NIGHT GLIDER
Topps Comics (Kirbyverse): April, 1993 ($2.95, one-shot)

1-Kirby c-1, Heck-a; polybagged w/Kirbychrome trading card 4.00

NIGHTHAWK
Marvel Comics: Sept, 1998 - No. 3, Nov, 1998 ($2.99, mini-series)

1-3-Krueger-s; Daredevil app. 3.00

NIGHTHAWK (From Squadron Supreme)
Marvel Comics: Jul, 2016 - No. 6, Dec, 2016 ($3.99)

1-6: 1-Walker-s/Villalobos-a/Cowan-c. 3-Morazzo-a 4.00

NIGHTINGALE, THE
Henry H. Stansbury Once-Upon-A-Time Press, Inc.: 1948 (10¢, 7-1/4x10-1/4", 14 pgs., 1/2 B&W)

(Very Rare)-Low distribution; distributed to Westchester County & Bronx, N.Y. only; used in **Seduction of the Innocent**, pg. 312,313 as the 1st and only "good" comic book ever published. Ill. by Dong Kingman; 1,500 words of text, printed on high quality paper & no word balloons. Copyright registered 10/22/48, distributed week of 12/5/48. Only 5000 copies printed, 6 currently known to still exist. (By Hans Christian Andersen)
Estimated value........ 350.00

NIGHT MAN, THE (See Sludge #1)
Malibu Comics (Ultraverse): Oct, 1993 - No. 23, Aug, 1995 ($1.95/$2.50)

1-($2.50, 48 pgs.)-Rune flip-c/story by B. Smith (3 pgs.) 5.00
1-Ultra-Limited silver foil-c 1 3 4 6 8 10
2-15, 17: 3-Break-Thru x-over; Freex app. 4-Origin Firearm (2 pgs.) by Chaykin. 6-TNTNT app. 8-1st app. Teknight 4.00
16 ($3.50)-flip book (Ultraverse Premiere #11) 5.00
...:The Pilgrim Conundrum Saga (1/95, $3.95, 68 pgs.)-Strangers app. 5.00
18-23: 22-Loki-c/app. 4.00
Infinity ($1.50) 4.00
...Vs. Wolverine #0-Kelley Jones-c; mail in offer 1 3 4 6 8 10
NOTE: *Zeck* a-16.

NIGHT MAN, THE
Malibu Comics (Ultraverse): Sept, 1995 - No.4, Dec, 1995 ($1.50, lim. series)

1-4: Post Black September storyline 3.00

NIGHT MAN, THE /GAMBIT
Malibu Comics (Ultraverse): Mar, 1996 - No. 3, May, 1996 ($1.95, lim. series)

0-Limited Premium Edition 4.00
1-3: David Quinn scripts in all. 3-Rhiannon discovered to be The Night Man's mother 3.00

NIGHTMARE
Ziff-Davis (Approved Comics)/St. John No. 3: Summer, 1952 - No. 3, Winter, 1952, 53 (Painted-c)

1-1 pg. Kinstler-a; Tuska-a(2) 74 148 222 470 810 1150
2-Kinstler-a-Poe's "Pit & the Pendulum" 52 104 156 328 552 775
3-Kinstler-a 47 94 141 296 498 700

NIGHTMARE (Weird Horrors #1-9) (Amazing Ghost Stories #14 on)
St. John Publishing Co.: No. 10, Dec, 1953 - No. 13, Aug, 1954

10-Reprints Ziff-Davis Weird Thrillers #2 w/new Kubert-c plus 2 pgs. Kinstler-a; Anderson, Colan & Toth-a 68 136 204 435 743 1050
11-Krigstein-a; painted-c; Poe adapt., "Hop Frog" 52 104 156 328 552 775
12-Kubert bondage-c; adaptation of Poe's "The Black Cat"; Cannibalism story 50 100 150 315 533 750
13-Reprints Z-D Weird Thrillers #3 with new cover; Powell-a(2), Tuska-a; Baker-c 165 330 495 1056 1803 2550

NIGHTMARE (Magazine) (Also see Psycho)
Skywald Publishing Corp.: Dec, 1970 - No. 23, Feb, 1975 (B&W, 68 pgs.)

1-Everett-a; Heck-a; Shores-a 10 20 30 68 144 220
2-5,8,9: 2,4-Decapitation story. 5-Nazi-s; Boris Karloff 4 pg. photo/text-s. 8-Features E.C. movie "Tales From the Crypt"; reprints some E.C. comics panels. 9-Wrightson-a; bondage-c; 1st Lovecraft Saggoth Chronicles/Cthulhu 6 12 18 38 69 100
6-Kaluta-a; Jeff Jones-c, photo & interview; 1st Living Gargoyle; Love Witch-s w/nudity; Boris Karloff-s 6 12 18 41 76 110
7 5 10 15 33 57 80
10-Wrightson-a (1 pg.); Princess of Earth-c/s; Edward & Mina Sartyros, the Human Gargoyles series continues from Psycho #8 6 12 18 38 69 100
11-19: 12-Excessive gore, severed heads. 13-Lovecraft-s. 15-Dracula-c/s. 17-Vampires issue; Autobiography of a Vampire series begins 4 8 12 28 47 65
20-John Byrne's 1st artwork (2 pgs.)(8/74); severed head-c; Hitler app. 8 16 24 54 102 150
21-23: 21-(1974 Summer Special)-Kaluta-a. 22-Tomb of Horror issue. 23-(1975 Winter Special) 5 10 15 31 53 75
Annual 1(1972)-Squarebound; B. Jones-a 5 10 15 31 53 75
Winter Special 1(1973)-All new material 4 8 12 28 47 65
Yearbook nn(1974)-B. Jones, Reese, Wildey-a 4 8 12 28 47 65
NOTE: *Adkins* a-5. *Boris* c-2, 3, 5 (#4 is not by Boris). *Buckler* a-3, 15. *Byrne* a-20p. *Everett* a-1, 2, 4, 5, 12. *Jeff Jones* a-6, 21r(Psycho #6); c-6. *Katz* a-3, 5, 21. *Reese* a-4, 5. *Wildey* a-4, 5, 6, 21, '74 Yearbook. *Wrightson* a-9, 10.

NIGHTMARE (Alex Nino's)
Innovation Publishing: 1989 ($1.95)

1-Alex Nino-a 3.00

NIGHTMARE
Marvel Comics: Dec, 1994 - No. 4, Mar, 1995 ($1.95, limited series)

1-4 3.00

NIGHTMARE & CASPER (See Harvey Hits #71) (Casper & Nightmare #6 on) (See Casper The Friendly Ghost #19)
Harvey Publications: Aug, 1963 - No. 5, Aug, 1964 (25¢)

1-All reprints? 7 14 21 49 92 135
2-5: All reprints? 5 10 15 30 50 70

NIGHTMARE ON ELM STREET, A (Also see Freddy Krueger's...)
DC Comics (WildStorm): Dec, 2006 - No. 8, Aug, 2007 ($2.99)

1-8: 1-Two covers by Harris & Bradstreet; Dixon-s/West-a 5.00

NIGHTMARES (See Do You Believe in Nightmares)

NIGHTMARES
Eclipse Comics: May, 1985 - No. 2, May, 1985 ($1.75, Baxter paper)

1,2 3.00

NIGHTMARE THEATER
Chaos! Comics: Nov, 1997 - No. 4, Nov, 1997 ($2.50, mini-series)

1-4-Horror stories by various; Wrightson-a 3.00

NIGHTMASK
Marvel Comics Group: Nov, 1986 - No. 12, Oct, 1987

1-12 3.00

NIGHT MASTER
Silverwolf: Feb, 1987 ($1.50, B&W)

1-Tim Vigil-c/a 3.00

NIGHTMASTER (See Shadowpact)
DC Comics: Jan, 2011 ($2.99, one-shot)

1-Wrightson-c/Beechen-s/Dwyer-a; Shadowpact app. 3.00

NIGHT MUSIC (See Eclipse Graphic Album Series, The Magic Flute)
Eclipse Comics: Dec, 1984 - No. 11, 1990 ($1.75/$3.95/$4.95, Baxter paper)

1-7: 3-Russell's Jungle Book adapt. 4,5-Pelleas And Melisande (double titled) 6-Salomé (double titled). 7-Red Dog #1 3.00
8-($3.95) Ariane and Bluebeard 4.00
9-11-($4.95) The Magic Flute; Russell adapt. 5.00

NIGHT NURSE (Also see Linda Carter, Student Nurse)
Marvel Comics Group: Nov, 1972 - No. 4, May, 1973

1 30 60 90 216 483 750
2-4 10 20 30 70 150 230

NIGHT NURSE
Marvel Comics: Jul, 2015 ($7.99, one-shot)

1-Reprints 1972 series #1-4 and Daredevil V2 #80; Siya Oum-c 8.00

NIGHT OF MYSTERY
Avon Periodicals: 1953 (no month) (one-shot)

nn-1 pg. Kinstler-a, Hollingsworth-c 77 154 231 493 847 1200

NIGHT OF THE GRIZZLY, THE (See Movie Classics)

NIGHT OF THE LIVING DEADPOOL
Marvel Comics: Mar, 2014 - No. 4, May, 2014 ($3.99, limited series)

Nights into Dreams #6 © Sega

Nightwing (2016 series) #24 © DC

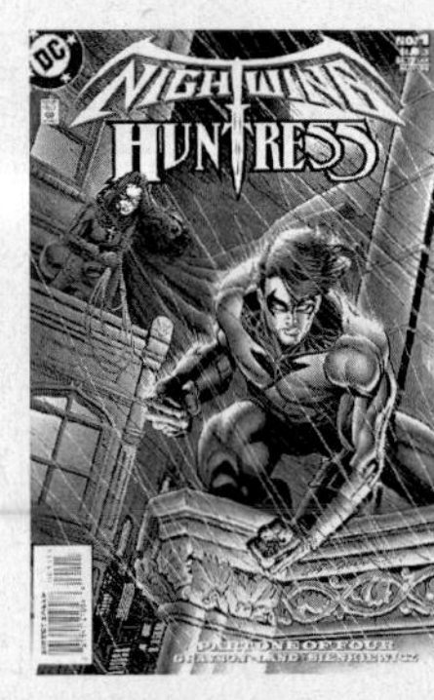

Nightwing & Huntress #1 © DC

	GD	VG	FN	VF	VF/NM	NM-
	2.0	4.0	6.0	8.0	9.0	9.2

1-4-Bunn-s/Rosanas-a; Deadpool in a zombie apocalypse 4.00

NIGHTRAVEN (See Marvel Graphic Novel)

NIGHT RIDER (Western)
Marvel Comics Group: Oct, 1974 - No. 6, Aug, 1975

1: 1-6 reprint Ghost Rider #1-6 (#1-origin)	5	10	15	31	53	75
2-6	3	6	9	14	19	24

NIGHT'S CHILDREN: THE VAMPIRE
Millenium: July, 1995 - No. 2, Aug, 1995 ($2.95, B&W)

1,2: Wendy Snow-Lang story & art 3.00

NIGHTSIDE
Marvel Comics: Dec, 2001 - No. 4, Mar, 2002 ($2.99)

1-4: 1-Weinberg-s/Derenick-a; intro Sydney Taine 3.00

NIGHTS INTO DREAMS (Based on video game)
Archie Comics: Feb, 1998 -No. 6, Oct, 1998 ($1.75, limited series)

1-6 3.00

NIGHTSTALKERS (Also see Midnight Sons Unlimited)
Marvel Comics (Midnight Sons #14 on): Nov, 1992 - No. 18, Apr, 1994 ($1.75)

1-($2.75, 52 pgs.)-Polybagged w/poster; part 5 of Rise of the Midnight Sons storyline; Garney/Palmer-c/a begins; Hannibal King, Blade & Frank Drake begin 4.00
2-9,11-18: 5-Punisher app. 7-Ghost Rider app. 8,9-Morbius app. 14-Spot varnish-c. 14,15-Siege of Darkness Pts 1 & 9 3.00
10-($2.25)-Outer-c is a Darkhold envelope made of black parchment w/gold ink; Midnight Massacre part 1 4.00

NIGHT TERRORS,THE
Chanting Monks Studios: 2000 ($2.75, B&W)

1-Bernie Wrightson-c; short stories, one by Wrightson-s/a 3.00

NIGHT THRASHER (Also see The New Warriors)
Marvel Comics: Aug, 1993 - No. 21, Apr, 1995 ($1.75/$1.95)

1-($2.95, 52 pgs.)-Red holo-grafx foil-c; origin 4.00
2-21: 2-Intro Tantrum. 3-Gideon (of X-Force) app. 10-Bound-in trading card sheet; Iron Man app. 15-Hulk app. 3.00

NIGHT THRASHER: FOUR CONTROL
Marvel Comics: Oct, 1992 - No. 4, Jan, 1993 ($2.00, limited series)

1-4: 2-Intro Tantrum. 3-Gideon (of X-Force) app. 3.00

NIGHT TRIBES
DC Comics (WildStorm): July, 1999 ($4.95, one-shot)

1-Golden & Sniegoski-s/Chin-a 5.00

NIGHTVEIL (Also see Femforce)
Americomics/AC Comics: Nov, 1984 - No. 7, 1987 ($1.75)

1-7 3.00
...'s Cauldron Of Horror 1 (1989, B&W)-Kubert, Powell, Wood-r plus new Nightveil story 3.00
...'s Cauldron Of Horror 2 (1990, $2.95, B&W)-Pre-code horror-r by Kubert & Powell 3.00
...'s Cauldron Of Horror 3 (1991) 3.00
Special 1 ('88, $1.95)-Kaluta-c 3.00
One Shot ('96, $5.95)-Flip book w/ Colt 6.00

NIGHTWATCH
Marvel Comics: Apr, 1994 - No. 12, Mar, 1995 ($1.50)

1-($2.95)-Collectors edition; foil-c; Ron Lim-c/a begins; Spider-Man app. 4.00
1-12-Regular edition. 2-Bound-in S-M trading card sheet; 5,6-Venom-c & app. 7,11-Cardiac app. 3.00

NIGHTWING (Also see New Teen Titans, New Titans, Showcase '93 #11,12, Tales of the New Teen Titans & Teen Titans Spotlight)
DC Comics: Sept, 1995 - No. 4, Dec, 1995 ($2.25, limited series)

1-Dennis O'Neil story/Greg Land-a in all	2	4	6	9	13	16

2-4 4.00
...: Alfred's Return (7/95, $3.50) Giordano-a 4.00
...Ties That Bind (1997, $12.95, TPB) r/mini-series & Alfred's Return 13.00

NIGHTWING
DC Comics: Oct, 1996 - No. 153, Apr, 2009 ($1.95/$1.99/$2.25/$2.50/$2.99)

1-Chuck Dixon scripts & Scott McDaniel-c/a	3	6	9	21	33	45
2,3	1	2	3	5	6	8

4-10: 6-Robin-c/app. 5.00
11-20: 13-15-Batman app. 19,20-Cataclysm pts. 2,11 4.00
21-49,51-64: 23-Green Arrow app. 26-29-Huntress-c/app. 30-Superman-c/app. 35-39-No Man's Land. 41-Land/Geraci-a begins. 46-Begin $2.25-c. 47-Texiera-c. 52-Catwoman-c/app. 54-Shrike app. 3.00
50-($3.50) Nightwing battles Torque 4.00
65-74,76-99: 65,66-Bruce Wayne: Murderer x-over pt. 3,9. 68,69: B.W.: Fugitive pt. 6,9. 70-Last Dixon-s. 71-Devin Grayson-s begin. 81-Batgirl vs. Deathstroke. 93-Blockbuster killed. 94-Copperhead app. 96-Bagged w/CD. 96-98-War Games 3.00
75-(1/03, $2.95) Intro. Tarantula 4.00
100-(2/05, $2.95) Tarantula app. 4.00
101-117: 101-Year One begins. 103-Jason Todd & Deadman app. 107-110-Hester-a. 109-Begin $2.50-c. 109,110-Villains United tie-ins. 112-Deathstroke app. 3.00
118-149,151-153: 118-One Year Later; Jason Todd as 2nd Nightwing. 120-Begin $2.99-c. 138,139-Resurrection of Ra's al Ghul x-over. 138-2nd printing. 147-Two-Face app. 3.00
150-($3.99) Batman R.I.P. x-over; Nightwing vs. Two-Face; Tan-c 4.00
#1,000,000 (11/98) teams with future Batman 3.00
Annual 1(1997, $3.95) Pulp Heroes 4.00
Annual 2 (6/07, $3.99) Dick Grayson and Barbara Gordon's shared history 4.00
...Eighty Page Giant 1 (12/00, $5.95) Intro. of Hella; Dixon-s/Haley-c 6.00
...: Big Guns (2004, $14.95, TPB) r/#47-50; Secret Files 1, Eighty Page Giant 1 15.00
...: Brothers in Blood (2007, $14.99, TPB) r/#118-124 15.00
...: A Darker Shade of Justice (2001, $19.95, TPB) r/#30-39, Secret Files #1 20.00
...: Freefall (2008, $17.99, TPB) r/#140-146 18.00
...: A Knight in Blüdhaven (1998, $14.95, TPB) r/#1-8 15.00
...: Love and Bullets (2000, $17.95, TPB) r/#1/2, 19,21,22,24-29 18.00
...: Love and War (2007, $14.99, TPB) r/#125-132 15.00
...: On the Razor's Edge (2005, $14.99, TPB) r/#52,54-60 15.00
...: Our Worlds at War (9/01, $2.95) Jae Lee-c 3.00
...: Renegade TPB (2006, $17.95) r/#112-117 18.00
...: Rough Justice (1999, $17.95, TPB) r/#9-18 18.00
Secret Files 1 (10/99, $4.95) Origin-s and pin-ups 5.00
...: The Great Leap (2009, $19.99) r/#147-153 20.00
...: The Hunt for Oracle (2003, $14.95, TPB) r/#41-46 & Birds of Prey #20,21 15.00
...: The Lost Year (2008, $14.99) r/#133-137 & Annual #2 15.00
...: The Target (2001, $5.95) McDaniel-c/a 6.00
Wizard 1/2 (Mail offer) 5.00
...: Year One (2005, $14.99) r/#101-106 15.00

NIGHTWING (DC New 52)(Leads into Grayson series)
DC Comics: Nov, 2011 - No. 30, Jul, 2014 ($2.99)

1-Dick Grayson in black/red costume; Higgins-s/Barrows-a/c 20.00
1-2nd printing with red background-c 10.00
2-7,10-14: 2-4-Batgirl app. 13,14-Lady Shiva app. 14-Joker cameo 4.00
8,9: 8-Night of the Owls prelude. 9-Night of the Owls x-over 5.00
15-Die-cut cover with Joker mask; Death of the Family tie-in 5.00
16-18: 16-Death of the Family tie-in. 18-Requiem; Tony Zucco returns 4.00
19-24,26-29: 19-24-Prankster app. 26,27-Mad Hatter app. 28,29-Mr. Zsasz app. 3.00
25-($3.99) Zero Year flashback to Haly's Circus days; Higgins-s/Conrad & Richards-a 4.00
30-($3.99) Aftermath of Forever Evil series; Grayson joins Spyral 4.00
#0-(11/12, $2.99) Origin re-told/updated; Lady Shiva app.; DeFalco-s/Barrows-a 4.00
Annual #1 (12/13, $4.99) Batgirl Wanted! tie-in; Firefly app. 5.00

NIGHTWING (DC Rebirth)
DC Comics: Sept, 2016 - Present ($2.99/$3.99)

1-24: 1-Seeley-s/Fernandez-a. 1-Intro. Raptor. 5,6-Night of the Monster Men x-over. 17-20-Deathwing & Prof. Pyg app. 21-Flash (Wally) app. 22-24-Blockbuster app. 3.00
25-($3.99) Blockbuster & Tiger Shark app. 4.00
26-43: 26-28-Huntress app. 29-Dark Nights: Metal tie-in 3.00
44-49: 44-($3.99) Mooneyham-a. 49-Silencer app. 4.00
50-($4.99) Follows Grayson's shooting in Batman #55; flashback art by Janson 5.00
51-74,76,77: 51-Foil-c. 53-56-Scarecrow app. 57,58-Joker's Daughter app. 62-69-Talon app. 70,71-Joker app. 72-74-Punchline app. 73,74-Joker War tie-in 4.00
75-($5.99) Joker War tie-in; Nightwing regains real memory; KGBeast app. 6.00
Annual 1 (10/18, $4.99) Percy-s/Schmidt-a; Vicki Vale app. 5.00
Annual 2 (12/19, $4.99) Jurgens-s/Moore-a; follows shooting in Batman #55 5.00
Annual 3 (8/20, $4.99) Jurgens-s/Miranda-a; Condor Red app. 5.00
.../Magilla Gorilla Special 1 (12/18, $4.99) Grape Ape app.; Secret Squirrel back-up 5.00
...: Rebirth (9/16, $2.99) Seeley-s/Paquette-a; Damian app.; back in Nightwing costume 3.00

NIGHTWING (See Tangent Comics/ Nightwing)

NIGHTWING AND HUNTRESS
DC Comics: May, 1998 - No. 4, Aug, 1998 ($1.95, limited series)

1-4-Grayson-s/Land & Sienkiewicz-a 3.00
TPB (2003, $9.95) r/#1/4; cover gallery 10.00

NIGHTWINGS (See DC Science Fiction Graphic Novel)

NIGHTWING: THE NEW ORDER
DC Comics: Oct, 2017 - No. 6, Mar, 2018 ($3.99, limited series)

1-6-Higgins-s/McCarthy-a; future Nightwing in 2040. 4,5-Titans app. 5-Superman app. 4.00

1963 Book 6 © Image

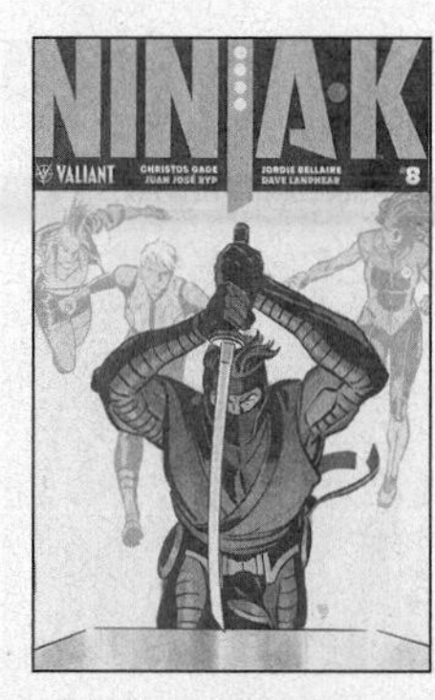

Ninjak (2018 series) #8 © VAL

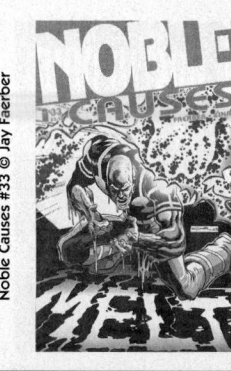

Noble Causes #33 © Jay Faerber

	GD 2.0	VG 4.0	FN 6.0	VF 8.0	VF/NM 9.0	NM- 9.2

NIGHTWORLD
Image Comics: Aug, 2014 - No. 4, Nov, 2014 ($3.99, limited series)

1-4-McGovern-s/Leandri-a/c 4.00

NIKKI, WILD DOG OF THE NORTH (Disney, see Movie Comics)
Dell Publishing Co.: No. 1226, Sept, 1961

Four Color 1226-Movie, photo-c 5 10 15 33 57 80

9-11 - ARTISTS RESPOND
Dark Horse Comics: 2002 ($9.95, TPB, proceeds donated to charities)

Volume 1-Short stories about the September 11 tragedies by various Dark Horse, Chaos! and Image writers and artists; Eric Drooker-c 10.00

9-11: EMERGENCY RELIEF
Alternative Comics: 2002 ($14.95, TPB, proceeds donated to the Red Cross)

nn-Short stories by various inc. Pekar, Eisner, Hester, Oeming, Noto; Cho-c 15.00

9-11 - THE WORLD'S FINEST COMIC BOOK WRITERS AND ARTISTS TELL STORIES TO REMEMBER
DC Comics: 2002 ($9.95, TPB, proceeds donated to charities)

Volume 2-Short stories about the September 11 tragedies by various DC, MAD, and WildStorm writers and artists ; Alex Ross-c 10.00

NINE RINGS OF WU-TANG
Image Comics: July, 1999 - No. 5, July, 2000 ($2.95)

Preview (7/99, $5.00, B&W) 5.00
1-5: 1-(11/99, $2.95) Clayton Henry-a 3.00
Tower Records Variant-c 5.00
Wizard #0 Prelude 3.00
TPB (1/01, $19.95) r/#1-5, Preview & Prelude; sketchbook & cover gallery 20.00

1963
Image Comics (Shadowline Ink): Apr, 1993 - No. 6, Oct, 1993 ($1.95, lim. series)

1-6: Alan Moore scripts; Veitch, Bissette & Gibbons-a(p) 3.00
1-Gold 4.00
*NOTE: **Bissette** a-2-4; **Gibbons** a-1i, 2i, 6i; c-2.*

1984 (Magazine) (1994 #11 on)
Warren Publishing Co.: June, 1978 - No. 10, Jan, 1980 ($1.50, B&W with color inserts, mature content with nudity; 84 pgs. except #4 has 92 pgs.)

1-Nino-a in all; Mutant World begins by Corben 3 6 9 15 22 28
2-10: 4-Rex Havoc begins. 7-1st Ghita of Alizarr by Thorne. 9-1st Starfire 2 4 6 10 14 18
NOTE: ***Alcala** a-1-3,5,7i. **Corben** a-1-8; c-1,2. **Nebres** a-1-8,10. **Thorne** a-7,8,10. **Wood** a-1,2,5i.*

1994 (Formerly 1984) (Magazine)
Warren Publishing Co.: No. 11, Feb, 1980 - No. 29, Feb, 1983 (B&W with color; mature; #11-(84 pgs.); #12-16,18-21,24-(76 pgs.); #17,22,23,25-29-(68 pgs.)

11,17,18,20,22,23,29: 11,17-8 pgs. color insert. 18-Giger-c. 20-1st Diana Jacklighter Manhuntress by Maroto. 22-1st Sigmund Pavlov by Nino; 1st Ariel Hart by Hsu. 23-All Nino issue 2 4 6 8 11 14
12-16,19,21,24-28: 21-1st app. Angel by Nebres. 27-The Warhawks return 1 3 4 6 8 10
NOTE: ***Corben** c-26. **Maroto** a-20, 21, 24-28. **Nebres** a-11-13, 15, 16, 18, 21, 22, 25, 28. **Nino** a-11-19, 20(2), 21, 25, 26, 28; c-21. **Redondo** c-20. **Thorne** a-11-14, 17-21, 24-26, 28, 29.*

NINJA BOY
DC Comics (WildStorm): Oct, 2001 - No. 6, Mar, 2002 ($3.50/$2.95)

1-($3.50) Ale Garza-a/c 3.50
2-6-($2.95) 3.00
...: Faded Dreams TPB (2003, $14.95) r/#1-6; sketch pages 15.00

NINJA HIGH SCHOOL (1st series)
Antarctic Press: 1986 - No. 3, Aug, 1987 (B&W)

1-Ben Dunn-s/c/a; early Manga series 2 4 6 10 14 18
2,3 2 4 6 8 10 12

NINJAK (See Bloodshot #6, 7 & Deathmate)
Valiant/Acclaim Comics (Valiant) No. 16 on: Feb, 1994 - No. 26, Nov. 1995 ($2.25/$2.50)

1 ($3.50)-Chromium-c; Quesada-c/a(p) in #1-3 6.00
1-Gold 2 4 6 13 18 22
2-13: 3-Batman, Spawn & Random (from X-Factor) app. as costumes at party (cameo). 4-w/bound-in trading card. 5,6-X-O app. 4.00
0,00,14-26: 14-(4/95)-Begin $2.50-c. 0-(6/95, $2.50). 00-(6/95, $2.50) 3.00
... Black Water HC (2013, $24.99) r/#1-6, #0, #00; bonus Quesada sketch-a 25.00
Yearbook 1 (1994, $3.95) 4.00

NINJAK
Acclaim Comics (Valiant Heroes): V2#1, Mar, 1997 -No. 12, Feb, 1998 ($2.50)

V2#1-12: 1-Intro new Ninjak; 1st app. Brutakon; Kurt Busiek scripts begin; painted variant-c exists. 2-1st app. Karnivor & Zeer. 3-1st app. Gigantik, Shurikai, & Nixie. 4-Origin; 1st app. Yasuiti Motomiya; intro The Dark Dozen; Colin King cameo. 9-Copycat-c 3.00

NINJAK (See Rapture)
Valiant Entertainment: Mar, 2015 - No. 27, May, 2017 ($3.99)

1-27-Multiple covers on each: 1-Kindt-s/Guice and Mann-a. 4-Origin of Roku; Ryp-a 4.00

NINJA·K
Valiant Entertainment: No. 0, Sept, 2017; No. 1, Nov, 2017 - No. 14, Dec, 2018 ($3.99)

0-Kindt-s/Portela-a; recaps origin 4.00
1-14: 1-5-Gage-s/Giorello-a. 1-History of Ninja-A in 1917. 6-9-Ryp-a 4.00
... One Dollar Debut (5/19, $1.00) r/#1 3.00

NINJAK VS. THE VALIANT UNIVERSE
Valiant Entertainment: Jan, 2018 - No. 4, Apr, 2018 ($3.99, limited series)

1-4-Rahal-s/Bennett-a 4.00

NINJA SCROLL
DC Comics (WildStorm): Nov, 2006 - No. 12, Oct, 2007 ($2.99)

1-12: 1-J. Torres-s/Michael Chang Ting Yu-a/c. 11-Puckett-s/Meyers-a 3.00
1-3-Variant covers by Jim Lee 5.00
TPB (2007, $19.99) r/#1-3,5-7 20.00

NINJETTES (See Jennifer Blood #4)
Dynamite Entertainment: 2012 - No. 6, 2012 ($3.99, limited series)

1-6-Origin of the team; Ewing-s/Casallos-a. 6-Jennifer Blood app. 4.00

NINTENDO COMICS SYSTEM (Also see Adv. of Super Mario Brothers)
Valiant Comics: Feb, 1990 - No. 9, Oct, 1991 ($4.95, card stock-c, 68 pgs.)

1-9: 1-Featuring Game Boy, Super Mario, Clappwall. 3-Layton-c. 5-8-Super Mario Bros. 9-Dr. Mario 1st app. 2 4 6 8 11 14

(Ninth) **IXTH GENERATION** (See Aphrodite IX & Poseidon IX)
Image Comics (Top Cow): Jan, 2015 - No. 8, Mar, 2016 ($3.99)

1-8: 1-4-Hawkins-s/Sejic-a; Aphrodite IX app. 5-7-Atilio Rojo-a 4.00
... Hidden Files 1 (4/15, $3.99) Short story and guide to the cities; Hawkins-s/Rojo-a 4.00

NOAH (Adaptation of the 2014 movie)
Image Comics: Mar, 2014 (HC, $29.99, 8-3/4" x 11-1/2")

HC-Darren Aronofsky & Ari Handel-s/Niko Henrichon-a 30.00

NOAH'S ARK
Spire Christian Comics/Fleming H. Revell Co.: 1973,1975 (35/49¢)

nn-By Al Hartley 2 4 6 11 16 20

NOBLE CAUSES
Image Comics: July, 2001; Jan, 2002 - No. 4, May, 2002 ($2.95)

...First Impressions (7/01) Intro. the Noble family; Faerber-s 3.00
1-4: 1-(1/02) Back-up-s with Conner-a. 2-Igle back-up-a. 2-4-Two covers 3.00
...: Extended Family (5/03, $6.95) short stories by various 7.00
...: Extended Family 2 (6/04, $7.95) short stories by various 8.00
Vol. 1: In Sickness and in Health (2003, $12.95) r/#1-4 & ...First Impresssions 13.00

NOBLE CAUSES (Volume 3)
Image Comics: July, 2004 - No. 40, Mar, 2009 ($3.50)

1-24,26-40-Faerber-s. 1-Two covers. 2-Venture app. 5-Invincible app. 3.50
25-($4.99) Art by various; Randolph-c 5.00
Vol. 4: Blood and Water (2005, $14.95) r/#1-6 15.00
Vol. 5: Betrayals (2006, $14.99) r/#7-12 & The Pact V2 #2 15.00
Vol. 6: Hidden Agendas (2006, $15.99) r/#13-18 and Image Holiday Spec. 2005 story 16.00
Vol. 7: Powerless (2007, $15.99) r/#19-25; Wieringo sketch page 16.00

NOBLE CAUSES: DISTANT RELATIVES
Image Comics: Jul, 2003 - No. 4, Oct, 2003 ($2.95, B&W, limited series)

1-4-Faerber-s/Richardson & Ponce-a 3.00
Vol. 3: Distant Relatives (1/05, $12.95) r/#1-4; intro. by Joe Casey 13.00

NOBLE CAUSES: FAMILY SECRETS
Image Comics: Oct, 2002 - No. 4, Jan, 2003 ($2.95, limited series)

1,2,4-Faerber-s/Oeming-c. 1-Variant cover by Walker. 2-Valentino var-c. 4-Hester var-c 3.00
3-1st app. of Invincible (cameo & Valentino var-c) 3 6 9 18 28 38
3-1st app. of Invincible (cameo); regular Oeming-c 2 4 6 11 16 20
Vol. 2: Family Secrets (2004, $12.95) r/#1-4; sketch pages 13.00

NOBODY (Amado, Cho & Adlard's...)
Oni Press: Nov, 1998 - No. 4, Feb, 1999 ($2.95, B&W, mini-series)

1-4 3.00

NOCTURNALS, THE

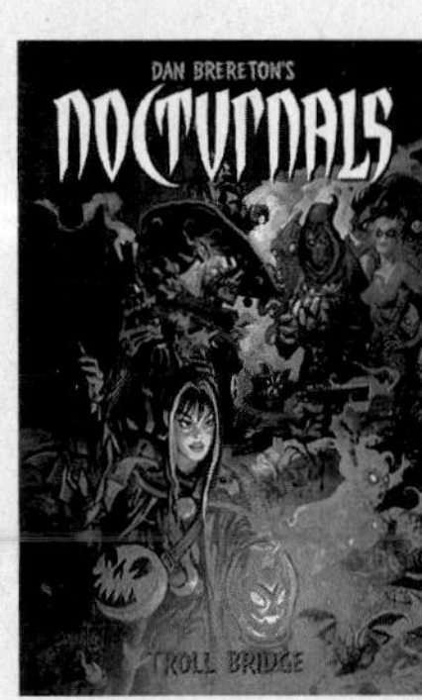

Nocturnals: Troll Bridge © Dan Brereton

Nomen Omen #11 © Bucci & Camagni

Northwest Mounties #4 © STJ

	GD	VG	FN	VF	VF/NM	NM-
	2.0	4.0	6.0	8.0	9.0	9.2

GD VG FN VF VF/NM NM-
2.0 4.0 6.0 8.0 9.0 9.2

Malibu Comics (Bravura): Jan, 1995 - No. 6, Aug, 1995 ($2.95, limited series)

1-6: Dan Brereton painted-c/a & scripts 3.00
1-Glow-in-the-Dark premium edition 5.00

NOCTURNALS, THE
Dark Horse Comics/Image Comics/Oni Press: one-shots and trade paperbacks

Black Planet TPB (Oni Press, 1998, $19.95) r/#1-6 (Malibu Comics series) 20.00
Black Planet and Other Stories HC (Olympian Publ.; 7/07, $39.95) r/Black Planet & Witching Hour contents; cover & sketch gallery with Brereton interviews 40.00
Carnival of Beasts (Image, 7/08, $6.99) short stories; Brereton-s/Brereton & others-a 7.00
Sinister Path (Big Wow! Art, 2017) original GN; Brereton-s/a 16.00
Troll Bridge (Oni Press, 2000, $4.95, B&W & orange) Brereton-s/painted-c; art by Brereton, Chin, Art Adams, Sakai, Timm, Warren, Thompson, Purcell, Stephens and others 5.00
Unhallowed Eve TPB (Oni Press, 10/02, $9.95) r/Witching Hour & Troll Bridge one-shots 10.00
Witching Hour (Dark Horse, 5/98, $4.95) Brereton-s/a; reprints DHP stories + 8 new pgs. 5.00

NOCTURNALS: THE DARK FOREVER
Oni Press: Jul, 2001 -No. 3, Feb, 2002 ($2.95, limited series)

1-3-Brereton-s/painted-a/c 3.00
TPB (5/02, $9.95) r/#1-3; afterword & pin-ups by Alex Ross 10.00

NOCTURNE
Marvel Comics: June, 1995 - No. 4, Sept. 1995 ($1.50, limited series)

1-4 3.00

NO ESCAPE (Movie)
Marvel Comics: June, 1994 - No. 3, Aug, 1994 ($1.50)

1-3: Based on movie 3.00

NO HONOR
Image Comics (Top Cow): Feb, 2001 - No. 4, July, 2001 ($2.50)

Preview (12/00, B&W) Silvestri-c 3.00
1-4-Avery-s/Crain-a 3.00
TPB (8/03, $12.99) r/#1-4; intro. by Straczynski 13.00

NOIR
Dynamite Entertainment: 2013 - No. 5, 2014 ($3.99, limited series)

1-5: 1-Miss Fury, Black Sparrow & The Shadow app.; Gischler-s/Mutti-a 4.00

NOMAD (See Captain America #180)
Marvel Comics: Nov, 1990 - No. 4, Feb, 1991 ($1.50, limited series)

1-4: 1,4-Captain America app. 3.00

NOMAD
Marvel Comics: V2#1, May, 1992 - No. 25, May, 1994 ($1.75)

V2#1-25: 1-Has gatefold-c w/map/wanted poster. 4-Deadpool x-over. 5-Punisher vs. Nomad-c/story. 6-Punisher & Daredevil-c/story cont'd in Punisher War Journal #48. 7-Gambit-c/story. 10-Red Wolf app. 21-Man-Thing-c/story. 25-Bound-in trading card sheet 3.00

NOMAD: GIRL WITHOUT A WORLD (Rikki Barnes from Captain America V2 Heroes Reborn)
Marvel Comics: Nov, 2009 - No. 4, Feb, 2010 ($3.99, limited series)

1-4-McKeever-s. 2-Falcon app. 4-Young Avengers app. 4.00

NOMAN (See Thunder Agents)
Tower Comics: Nov, 1966 - No. 2, March, 1967 (25¢, 68 pgs.)

	GD	VG	FN	VF	VF/NM	NM-
1-Wood/Williamson-c; Lightning begins; Dynamo cameo; Kane-a(p) & Whitney-a	8	16	24	55	105	155
2-Wood-c only; Dynamo x-over; Whitney-a	5	10	15	34	60	85

NOMEN OMEN
Image Comics: Oct, 2019 - Present ($3.99)

1-12-Bucci-s/Camagni-a; 3 covers 4.00

NO MERCY
Image Comics: Apr, 2015 - No. 14, Mar, 2017 ($2.99/$3.99)

1-4-Alex de Campi-s/Carla Speed McNeil-a 3.00
5-14-($3.99) 6-EC-style cover 4.00

NONE BUT THE BRAVE (See Movie Classics)

NON-HUMANS
Image Comics: Oct, 2012 - No. 4, Jul, 2013 ($2.99)

1-4-Brunswick-s/Portacio-a/c 3.00

NOODNIK COMICS (See Pinky the Egghead)
Comic Media/Mystery/Biltmore: Dec, 1953; No. 2, Feb, 1954 - No. 5, Aug, 1954

	GD	VG	FN	VF	VF/NM	NM-
3-D(1953, 25¢; Comic Media)(#1)-Came w/glasses	32	64	96	190	310	430
2-5	11	22	33	64	90	115

NO ONE LEFT TO FIGHT
Dark Horse Comics: Jul, 2019 - No. 5, Nov, 2019 ($3.99)

1-5-Aubrey Sitterson-s/Fico Ossio-a 4.00

NORMALMAN (See Cerebus the Aardvark #55, 56)
Aardvark-Vanaheim/Renegade Press #6 on: Jan, 1984 - No. 12, Dec, 1985 ($1.70/$2.00)

1-12: 1-Jim Valentino-c/a in all. 6-12 ($2.00, B&W): 10-Cerebus cameo; Sim-a (2 pgs.) 3.00
...- Megaton Man Special 1 (Image Comics, 8/94, $2.50) 3.00
...3-D 1 (Annual, 1986, $2.25) 3.00
...Twentieth Anniversary Special (7/04, $2.95) 3.00

NORMALS
AfterShock Comics: May, 2017 - No. 6, Oct, 2017 ($3.99, limited series)

1-6-Adam Glass-s/Dennis Calero-a 4.00

NORSE MYTHOLOGY
Dark Horse Comics: Oct, 2020 - Present ($3.99, limited series)

1-4-Neil Gaiman & P. Craig Russell-s. 1-Art by Russell, Mignola, & Ordway. 2-Ordway-a 4.00

NORTHANGER ABBEY (Adaptation of the Jane Austen novel)
Marvel Comics: Jan, 2012 - No. 5, May, 2012 ($3.99, mini-series)

1-5-Nancy Butler-s/Janet K. Lee-a/Julian Tedesco-c 4.00

NORTH AVENUE IRREGULARS (See Walt Disney Showcase #49)

NORTH 40
DC Comics (WildStorm): Sept, 2009 - No. 6, Feb, 2010 ($2.99)

1-6-Aaron Williams-s/Fiona Staples-a 3.00
TPB (2010, $17.99) r/#1-6 18.00

NORTHLANDERS
DC Comics (Vertigo): Feb, 2008 - No. 50, Jun, 2012 ($2.99)

1-50: 1-Vikings in 980 A.D.; Wood-s/Gianfelice-a; covers by Carnivale. 35-Cloonan-a 3.00
1-3-Variant covers. 1-Adam Kubert. 2-Andy Kubert. 3-Dave Gibbons 5.00
...: Blood in the Snow TPB (2010, $14.99) r/#9,10,17-20 15.00
...: Metal and Other Stories TPB (2011, $17.99) r/#29-36 18.00
...: Sven the Returned TPB (2008, $9.99) r/#1-8; cover gallery 10.00
...: The Cross + The Hammer TPB (2009, $14.99) r/#11-16 15.00
...: The Plague Widow TPB (2010, $16.99) r/#21-28 17.00

NORTHSTAR
Marvel Comics: Apr, 1994 - No. 4, July, 1994 ($1.75, mini-series)

1-4: Character from Alpha Flight 3.00

NORTH TO ALASKA
Dell Publishing Co.: No. 1155, Dec, 1960

	GD	VG	FN	VF	VF/NM	NM-
Four Color 1155-Movie, John Wayne photo-c	15	30	45	100	220	340

NORTHWEST MOUNTIES (Also see Approved Comics #12)
Jubilee Publications/St. John: Oct, 1948 - No. 4, July, 1949

	GD	VG	FN	VF	VF/NM	NM-
1-Rose of the Yukon by Matt Baker; Walter Johnson-a; Lubbers-c	55	110	165	352	601	850
2-Baker-a; Lubbers-c. Ventrilo app.	41	82	123	255	428	600
3-Bondage-c, Baker-a; Sky Chief, K-9 app.	45	90	135	284	480	675
4-Baker-c/a(2 pgs.); Blue Monk & The Desperado app.	54	108	162	343	574	825

NOSFERATU WARS
Dark Horse Comics: Mar, 2014 ($3.99, one-shot)

1-Reprints serial story from Dark Horse Presents #26-29; Niles-s/Menton3-a 4.00

NO SLEEP 'TIL DAWN
Dell Publishing Co.: No. 831, Aug, 1957

	GD	VG	FN	VF	VF/NM	NM-
Four Color 831-Movie, Karl Malden photo-c	6	12	18	42	79	115

NOSTALGIA ILLUSTRATED
Marvel Comics: Nov, 1974 - V2#8, Aug, 1975 (B&W, 76 pgs.)

	GD	VG	FN	VF	VF/NM	NM-
V1#1	3	6	9	21	33	45
V1#2, V2#1-8	3	6	9	15	22	28

NOT BRAND ECHH (Brand Echh #1-4; See Crazy, 1973)
Marvel Comics Group (LMC): Aug, 1967 - No. 13, May, 1969; No. 14, Jan, 2018
(1st Marvel parody book)

	GD	VG	FN	VF	VF/NM	NM-
1: 1-8 are 12¢ issues	7	14	21	48	89	130
2-8: 3-Origin Thor, Hulk & Capt. America; Monkees, Alfred E. Neuman cameo. 4-X-Men app. 5-Origin/intro. Forbush Man. 7-Origin Fantastical-4 & Stuporman. 8-Beatles cameo; X-Men satire; last 12¢-c	4	8	12	25	40	55
9-13 (25¢, 68 pgs., all Giants) 9-Beatles cameo. 10-All-r; The Old Witch, Crypt Keeper & Vault Keeper cameos. 12,13-Beatles cameo	5	10	15	30	50	70
14-(1/18, $3.99) Forbush Man app.; s/a by Zdarsky, Spencer & others; Nakamura-c						4.00

NOTE: ***Colan** a(p)-4, 5, 8, 9, 13. **Everett** a-1i. **Kirby** a(p)-1, 3, 5-7, 10r; c-1p. **J. Severin** a-1; c-3, 6-8, 11. **M. Severin** a-1-13; c-2, 9, 10, 12, 13. **Sutton** a-3, 4, 5i, 6i, 8, 9, 10r, 11-13; c-5. Archie satire in #9. Avengers satire in #8, 12.*

Nova #25 © MAR

Nova (2007 series) #7 © MAR

Nova (2013 series) #27 © MAR

GD 2.0 | VG 4.0 | FN 6.0 | VF 8.0 | VF/NM 9.0 | NM- 9.2

NOTHING CAN STOP THE JUGGERNAUT
Marvel Comics: 1989 ($3.95)

1-r/Amazing Spider-Man #229 & 230 5.00

NO TIME FOR SERGEANTS (TV)
Dell Publ. Co.: No. 914, July, 1958; Feb-Apr, 1965 - No. 3, Aug-Oct, 1965

Four Color 914 (Movie)-Toth-a; Andy Griffith photo-c 9 18 27 60 120 180
1(2-4/65) (TV): Photo-c 5 10 15 34 60 85
2,3 (TV): Photo-c 4 8 12 28 47 65

NOVA (The Man Called... No. 22-25)(See New Warriors)
Marvel Comics Group: Sept, 1976 - No. 25, May, 1979

1-Origin/1st app. Nova (Richard Rider) Marv Wolfman-s; John Buscema-a 9 18 27 58 114 170
2,3: 2-1st app. Condor & Powerhouse. 3-1st app. Diamondhead; Sal Buscema-p begin 2 4 6 13 18 22
4,12: 4-Thor x-over; 1st app. The Corrupter; Kirby-c. 12-Spider-Man x-over w/Amazing Spider-Man #171 3 6 9 14 20 25
5-11: 5-Nova vs. Tyrannus; Kirby-c; Marvel Bullpen app (incl. Stan Lee) 6-1st app. The Sphinx & Megaman. 7-Sphinx, Condor, Powerhouse & Diamondhead app. 8-Origin Megaman. 9-Megaman app. 10-Sphinx, Condor, Powerhouse & Diamondhead app. 11-vs. Sphinx 2 4 6 8 10 12
10,11-(35¢-c variants, limited distribution)(6,7/77) 9 18 27 62 126 190
12-(35¢-c variant, limited distribution)(8/77) 10 20 30 68 144 220
13,14-(Regular 30¢ editions)(9/77) 13-Intro Crime-Buster; Sandman app. 14-vs. Sandman 1 3 4 6 8 10
13,14-(35¢-c variants, limited distribution) 9 18 27 62 126 190
15-24: 15-Infantino-a begins. 16-18-vs. Yellow Claw; Nick Fury and SHIELD app. 19-Wally West (Kid Flash) cameo; 1st app Blackout. 20-1st Project X (Sherlock Holmes robot). 21-Richard reveals his Nova I.D to parents; vs Corrupter. 22-1st app the Comet (in costume). 23-Dr. Sun app. (origin) from Tomb of Dracula; Sphinx cameo. 24-Origin Powerhouse, Diamondhead, Crime-Buster, Comet Man, Sphinx & Dr. Sun app. 1 2 3 5 6 8
25-Last issue; Powerhouse, Diamondhead, Crime-Buster, Comet Man, Sphinx & Dr. Sun app. story continues in Fantastic Four #204-214 3 6 9 14 19 24

NOTE: ***Austin** c-21i, 23i. **John Buscema** a(p)-1-3, 8, 21; c-1p, 2, 15. **Infantino** a(p)-15-20, 22-25; c-17-20, 21p, 23p, 24p. **Kirby** c-4p, 5, 7. **Nebres** c-25i. **Simonson** a-23i.*

NOVA
Marvel Comics: Jan, 1994 - June, 1995 ($1.75/$1.95) (Started as 4-part mini-series)

1-($2.95, 52 pgs.)-Collector's Edition w/gold foil-c; new Nova costume; Nicieza-s/Marrinan-a; continued from New Warriors #42; re-intro Richard Rider's supporting cast – Ginger Jaye, Bernie Dillon & Roger 'Caps' Cooper; origin & history recap; vs. Gladiator of the Shi'ar Imperial Guard; Queen Adora app. 1 3 4 6 8 10
1-($2.25, 52 pgs.)-Newsstand Edition w/o foil-c 5.00
2-5: 2-1st app. Tailhook; Speedball app. 3-vs. Spider-Man; Corrupter app; 1st app Nova 00. 4-Vs. Nova 00; contains Rock Video Monthly insert (centerfold). 5-Re-intro Condor; Sphinx cameo; leads into New Warriors #47; contains centerfold insert for Marvel 'Masterprints' 3.00
6,7: 6-'Time and Time Again', pt.3; story continued from Night Thrasher #11; Rage & Firestar solo stories; continues in New Warriors #48. 7- 'Time and Time Again' pt.6; continued from Night Thrasher #12; Rage & Firestar solo stories; Cloak and Dagger app; continues in New Warriors #49; last Nicieza-s 4.00
8-12: 8-1st app. Shatterforce. 9-Vs. Shatterforce. 10-Vs. Diamondhead & Rhino; New Warriors and Corrupter app. 11-She-Hulk, the Thing & Ant-Man guest star; Nick Fury cameo; contains two inserts – a Marvel Subscription offer and a centerfold insert for a personalized X-Men/Captain Universe comic. 12-Vs. Nova 00; Nick Fury, Black Bolt & the Inhumans app. 13-'Deathstorm' T-Minus 3; Firestar, Night Thrasher & Nick Fury app. 14-'Deathstorm' T-Minus 2; Nova 00, Darkhawk & the New Warriors app. 15-'Deathstorm' T-Minus 1; 1st app. Kraa (brother of Zorr from Nova #1, 1976) 3.00
16-18: 16-'Deathstorm' conclusion; vs. Kraa; Nova-Corps app; death of Nova 00. 17-vs. Supernova (Garthan Saal); Richard is stripped of his rank; Queen Adora app. 18-Last issue; Richard Rider de-powered; Supernova becomes Nova-Prime; Dire Wraith Queen app; story continues in New Warriors #60 6.00

NOVA
Marvel Comics: May, 1999 - No. 7, Nov, 1999 ($2.99/$1.99)

1-($2.99, 38 pgs.) –Larsen-s/Bennett-a; wraparound-c by Larsen; origin retold; Nebula app; reveals her father to be Zorr (from issue #1, 1976); She-Hulk, Spider-Man, Speedball, Namorita app. 5.00
2-6: 2-Two covers; vs. Diamondhead; Captain America app.; Namorita's skin returns to normal. 3-Savage Dragon app.; (as a Skrull); New Warriors, Thor, Fantastic Four & the Condor app.; return of the Sphinx. 4-vs. Condor; Fantastic Four app; Red Raven cameo. 5-Spider-Man app. 6-vs. the Sphinx; Venom cameo 3.00
7-Last issue; Red Raven & Bi-Beast app. vs. Venom 4.00

NOVA (See Secret Avengers and The Thanos Imperative)

Marvel Comics: June, 2007 - No. 36, Jun, 2010 ($2.99)

1-Abnett/Lanning-s; Chen-a; Granov-c; continued from Annihilation #6; brief Iron Man app. 3 6 9 16 24 32
2-The Initiative x-over; Nova returns to Earth; vs. Diamondhead; Iron Man & the Thunderbolts (Penance, Radioactive Man, Venom & Moonstone) app. 1 3 4 6 8 10
3-The Initiative x-over; vs. the Thunderbolts; Iron Man app.; Nova leaves Earth 1 2 3 5 6 8
4-7,9: Annihilation Conquest x-overs. 4-Phalanx and Gamora app. 5-Nova infected with the Phalanx virus; Gamora app. 6-Gamora-c by Granov; Drax app. 7-Gamora and Drax app; last Chen-a. 9-Cosmo, Gamora and Drax app. 7.00
8-1st app. Cosmo - the Russian telepathic dog; 1st app. Knowhere – a space station formed out of the severed head of a Celestial (as seen in the GOTG movie); 1st app. of the Luminals; 1st Wellington Alves-a; brief Peter Quill (Star-Lord) app. 3 6 9 20 31 42
10-14: 10-Nova and Gamora solo story; Drax app.; leads into Nova Annual #1. 11-Gamora, Drax & Warlock of the New Mutants app; Pelletier-a begins. 12-Warlock of the New Mutants app. Nova, Gamora & Drax cured of the Phalanx virus; leads into Annihilation Conquest #6. 13-Galactus & Silver Surfer app.; contains 5-pg preview of the new Eternals series; Alves-a. 14-Galactus app.; Nova vs. Silver Surfer. 15-Galactus & Silver Surfer app. 6.00
16-18: Secret Invasion x-over. 16-Super-Skrull app.; Nova returns to Earth. 17-Team up w/Darkhawk at Project Pegasus vs. the Skrulls; Quasar (Wendell Vaughn) returns. 18-Quasar & Darkhawk app; vs. the Skrulls; return of the Nova Corps 5.00
18-Zombie 1:10 variant-c by Wellington Alves 6.00
19-Darkhawk app.; Robbie Rider joins the Nova-Corps; Serpent Society app. 20-New Warriors flashback; Justice & Firestar app; Ego the Living Planet app. 21-Fantastic Four app; Ego the Living Planet becomes new base for the Nova Corps; Nova's powers are taken away. 22-Quasar app.; Andrea Divito-a begins 4.00
20-Villain 'Sphinx' variant-c by Mike Deodato Jr. 1 2 3 5 6 8
23-28: War of Kings x-over. 23-Richard Rider dons the Quantum Bands – becomes the new Quasar. 24-Gladiator & the Shi'ar Imperial Guard app. 25-Richard regains his Nova powers; Wendell Vaughn (Quasar) regains the Quantum Bands; Emperor Vulcan app. 26-Lord Ravenous app. 27-Blastaar & Lord Ravenous app. 28-War of Kings ends; Robbie Rider officially joins the Nova Corps. Quasar app. 6.00
25-'Dirty Dancing' 1980s decade 1:10 variant by Alina Urusov 5.00
28-Marvel Comics 70th Anniversary frame variant 6.00
29,30: 'Starstalker' parts 1-2. 29-1st Marvel Universe app. of Monark Starstalker (previously from Marvel Premiere #32). 30-vs. Ego the Living Planet 3.00
31-Darkhawk app. 5.00
32-34: Realm of Kings x-over; 32,33-Reed Richards, Black Bolt, Darkhawk, Namorita & the Sphinx app. 33-Moonstone, Man-Wolf, Bloodstone, Basilisk app. 34-'Death' of Black Bolt; Nova vs. Moonstone, Reed Richards vs. Bloodstone, Namorita vs. Man-Wolf, Darkhawk vs. Gyre the Raptor; contains 6 pg. preview of the New Ultimates series 1 2 3 5 6 8
34-Deadpool variant-c 2 4 6 8 12 15
35-Realm of Kings x-over; Reed Richards, Darkhawk, Namorita vs. Sphinx; Namorita brought back to current continuity 1 3 4 6 8 10
36-Last issue; Darkhawk & Quasar app.; leads into Thanos Imperative Ignition 2 4 6 8 12 15
Annual #1 (4/08, $3.99); Slightly altered origin retold; Annihilation Conquest tie-in; Quasar app.; takes place between Nova issues #10-11 1 2 3 5 6 8
...: Origin of Richard Rider (2009, $4.99) origin retold from Nova #1 & 4 ('76) 5.00
... Vol. 1: Annihilation - Conquest TPB (2007, $17.99) r/#1-7; cover sketches 18.00

NOVA (Marvel NOW!)
Marvel Comics: Apr, 2013 - No. 31, Jul, 2015 ($3.99)

1-Loeb-s/McGuinness-a/c; Rocket Raccoon & Gamora app.; multiple variant covers 6.00
2-9: 2,3-Rocket Raccoon & Gamora app. 7-Superior Spider-Man app. 8,9-Infinity tie-in 4.00
10-($4.99) "Issue #100"; Speedball & Justice app.; cover gallery 5.00
11-24,26-31: 12-16-Beta Ray Bill app. 18-20-Original Sin tie-in. 19,20-Rocket Raccoon app. 23,24-Axis tie-in. 28-Black Vortex crossover 4.00
25-($4.99) Axis tie-in; Sam joins the Avengers 5.00
Annual 1 (5/15, $4.99) The Hulk app.; Duggan-s/Baldeon-a 5.00
... Special 1 (10/14, $4.99) Part 3 of x-over with Iron Man & Uncanny X-Men 5.00

NOVA
Marvel Comics: Jan, 2016 - No. 11, Nov, 2016 ($3.99)

1-11: 1-Sean Ryan-s/Cory Smith-a. 3,4-Ms. Marvel & Spider-Man (Miles) app. 8,9-Civil War II tie-in. 10,11-Richard Rider returns 4.00

NOVA
Marvel Comics: Feb, 2017 - No. 7, Aug, 2017 ($3.99)

1-7: 1-Ramón Pérez-a; Richard Rider & Ego app. 4-Gamora app. 4.00

NOW AGE ILLUSTRATED (See Pendulum Illustrated Classics)

Nuclear Family #1 © Bromberg & AS

Nutty Comics #7 © FAW

NYX #5 © MAR

	GD	VG	FN	VF	VF/NM	NM-
	2.0	4.0	6.0	8.0	9.0	9.2

NOW AGE BOOKS ILLUSTRATED (See Pendulum Illustrated Classics)

NOWHERE MAN
Dynamite Entertainment: 2011 - No. 4, 2011 ($3.99)

1-4-Marc Guggenheim-s/Jeevan J. Kang-a 4.00

NOWHERE MEN
Image Comics: Nov, 2012 - No. 11, Sept, 2016 ($2.99)

1-Stephenson-s/Bellegarde-a 15.00
1-2nd thru 5th printings 4.00
2 6.00
3-11 4.00

NO WORLD
Aspen MLT: Apr, 2017 - No. 6, Oct, 2017 ($3.99, limited series)

1-6-Lobdell-s/Gunderson-a; multiple covers on each 4.00

NTH MAN THE ULTIMATE NINJA (See Marvel Comics Presents #25)
Marvel Comics: Aug, 1989 - No. 16, Sept, 1990 ($1.00)

1-16-Ninja mercenary. 8-Dale Keown's 1st Marvel work (1/90, pencils) 3.00

NUCLEAR FAMILY (Based on the short story Breakfast at Twilight by Philip K. Dick)
AfterShock Comics: Feb, 2021 - Present ($4.99)

1-Stephanie Phillips-s/Tony Shasteen-a 5.00

NUCLEUS (Also see Cerebus)
Heiro-Graphic Publications: May, 1979 ($1.50, B&W, adult fanzine)

1-Contains "Demonhorn" by Dave Sim; early app. of Cerebus The Aardvark (4 pg. story)
5 10 15 34 60 85

NUKLA
Dell Publishing Co.: Oct-Dec, 1965 - No. 4, Sept, 1966

1-Origin & 1st app. Nukla (super hero) 5 10 15 30 50 70
2,3 3 6 9 19 30 40
4-Ditko-a, c(p) 4 8 12 23 37 50

NUMBER OF THE BEAST
DC Comics (WildStorm): June, 2008 - No. 8, Sept, 2008 ($2.99, limited series)

1-8-Beatty-s/Sprouse-a/c. 1-Variant-c by Mahnke. 6-The Authority app. 3.00
TPB (2008, $19.99) r/#1-8; character dossiers 20.00

NURSE BETSY CRANE (Formerly Teen Secret Diary) (Also see Registered Nurse for reprints)
Charlton Comics: V2#12, Aug, 1961 - V2#27, Mar, 1964 (See Soap Opera Romances)

V2#12-27 4 8 12 28 47 65

NURSE HELEN GRANT (See The Romances of...)

NURSE LINDA LARK (See Linda Lark)

NURSERY RHYMES
Ziff-Davis Publ. Co. (Approved Comics): No. 10, July-Aug, 1951 - No. 2, Winter, 1951 (Painted-c)

10 (#1), 2: 10-Howie Post-a 20 40 60 115 188 260

NURSES, THE (TV)
Gold Key: April, 1963 - No. 3, Oct, 1963 (Photo-c: #1,2)

1 5 10 15 30 50 70
2,3 3 6 9 18 28 38

NUTS! (Satire)
Premiere Comics Group: March, 1954 - No. 5, Nov, 1954

1-Hollingsworth-a 37 74 111 222 361 500
2,4,5: 5-Capt. Marvel parody 24 48 72 140 230 320
3-Drug "reefers" mentioned; Marilyn Monroe & Joe DiMaggio parody-c
26 52 78 152 248 345

NUTS (Magazine) (Satire)
Health Knowledge: Feb, 1958 - No. 2, April, 1958

1 10 20 30 54 72 90
2 7 14 21 37 46 55

NUTS & JOLTS
Dell Publishing Co.: No. 22, 1941

Large Feature Comic 22 21 42 63 122 199 275

NUTSY SQUIRREL (Formerly Hollywood Funny Folks)(See Comic Cavalcade)
National Periodical Publications: #61, 9-10/54 - #69, 1-2/56; #70, 8-9/56 - #71, 10-11/56; #72, 11/57

61-Mayer-a; Grossman-a in all 14 28 42 80 115 150
62-72: Mayer a-62,65,67-72 10 20 30 56 76 95

NUTTY COMICS
Fawcett Publications: Winter, 1946

1-Capt. Kidd story; 1 pg. Wolverton-a 15 30 45 84 127 170

NUTTY COMICS
Home Comics (Harvey Publications): 1945; No. 4, May-June, 1946 - No. 8, June-July, 1947 (No #2,3)

nn-Helpful Hank, Bozo Bear & others (funny animal) 9 18 27 52 69 85
4 8 16 24 40 50 60
5-Rags Rabbit begins(1st app.); infinity-c 9 18 27 47 61 75
6-8 7 14 21 35 43 50

NUTTY LIFE (Formerly Krazy Life #1; becomes Wotalife Comics #3 on)
Fox Feature Syndicate: No. 2, Summer, 1946

2 23 46 69 136 223 310

NU WAY
Aspen MLT: Jul, 2018 - No. 5, Jan, 2019 ($3.99, limited series)

1-5-Krul-s/Konat-a; multiple covers on each 4.00

NYOKA, THE JUNGLE GIRL (Formerly Jungle Girl; see The Further Adventures of..., Master Comics #50 & XMas Comics)
Fawcett Publications: No. 2, Winter, 1945 - No. 77, June, 1953 (Movie serial)

2 68 136 204 435 743 1050
3 39 78 117 231 378 525
4,5-Bondage covers 32 64 96 190 310 430
6-11,13,14,16-18-Krigstein-a: 17-Sam Spade ad by Lou Fine
20 40 60 118 192 265
12,15,19,20 19 38 57 111 176 240
21-30: 25-Clayton Moore photo-c? 14 28 42 78 112 145
31-40 11 22 33 64 90 115
41-50 10 20 30 58 79 100
51-60 9 18 27 52 69 85
61-77 9 18 27 47 61 75

NOTE: *Photo-c from movies 25, 30-70, 72, 75-77. Bondage c-4, 5, 7, 8, 14, 24.*

NYOKA, THE JUNGLE GIRL (Formerly Zoo Funnies; Space Adventures #23 on)
Charlton Comics: No. 14, Nov, 1955 - No. 22, Nov, 1957

14 12 24 36 67 94 120
15-22 10 20 30 54 72 90

NYX (Also see X-23 title)
Marvel Comics: Nov, 2003 - No. 7, Oct, 2005 ($2.99)

1-Quesada-s/Middleton-a/c; intro. Kiden Nixon 3 6 9 14 20 25
2 2 4 6 10 14 18
3-1st app. X-23 16 32 48 110 243 375
4-2nd app X-23 4 8 12 27 44 60
5,6-Teranishi-a 2 4 6 8 11 14
7-($3.99) Teranishi-a 1 3 4 6 8 10
NYX X-23 (2005, $34.99, oversized with d.j.) r/X-23 #1-6 & NYX #1-7; intro by Craig Kyle; sketch pages, development art and unused covers 45.00
...: Wannabe TPB (2006, $19.99) r/#1-7; development art and unused covers 20.00

NYX: NO WAY HOME
Marvel Comics: Oct, 2008 - No. 6, Apr, 2009 ($3.99)

1-6: 1-Andrasofszky-a/Liu-s/Urusov-c; sketch pages, character and cover design art 5.00

OAKLAND PRESS FUNNYBOOK, THE
The Oakland Press: 9/17/78 - 4/13/80 (16 pgs.) (Weekly)
Full color in comic book form; changes to tabloid size 4/20/80-on

Contains Tarzan by Manning, Marmaduke, Bugs Bunny, etc. (low distribution); 9/23/79 - 4/13/80 contain Buck Rogers by Gray Morrow & Jim Lawrence 5.00

OAKY DOAKS (See Famous Funnies #190)
Eastern Color Printing Co.: July, 1942 (One Shot)

1 37 74 111 222 361 500

OBERGEIST: RAGNAROK HIGHWAY
Image Comics (Top Cow/Minotaur): May, 2001 - No. 6, Nov, 2001 ($2.95, limited series)

Preview ('01, B&W, 16 pgs.) Harris painted-c 3.00
1-6-Harris-c/a/Jolley-s. 1-Three covers 3.00
...:The Directors' Cut (2002, $19.95, TPB) r/#1-6; Bruce Campbell intro. 20.00
... :The Empty Locket (3/02, $2.95, B&W) Harris & Snyder-a 3.00

OBERON
AfterShock Comics: Feb, 2019 - No. 5, Jul, 2019 ($3.99)

1-5-Ryan Parrott-s/Milos Slavkovic-a 4.00

OBIE
Store Comics: 1953 (6¢)

Oblivion Song #1 © Kirkman & De Felici

Occupy Avengers #8 © MAR

Official Handbook of the Marvel Universe #3 © MAR

	GD 2.0	VG 4.0	FN 6.0	VF 8.0	VF/NM 9.0	NM- 9.2
1	9	18	27	47	61	75

OBI-WAN AND ANAKIN (Star Wars)
Marvel Comics: Mar, 2016 - No. 5, Jul, 2016 ($3.99)
1-5-Takes place a few years after Episode One; Soule-s/Checchetto-a/c 4.00

OBJECTIVE FIVE
Image Comics: July, 2000 - No. 6, Jan, 2001 ($2.95)
1-6-Lizalde-a 3.00

OBLIVION
Comico: Aug, 1995 - No. 3, May, 1996 ($2.50)
1-3: 1-Art Adams-c. 2-(1/96)-Bagged w/gaming card. 3-(5/96)-Darrow-c 3.00

OBLIVION SONG
Image Comics: Mar, 2018 - Present ($3.99)
1-24,26-30-Kirkman-s/De Felici-a 4.00
25-($4.99) Flip book with Science Dog #25 - Kirkman-s/Cory Walker-a 5.00

OBNOXIO THE CLOWN (Character from Crazy Magazine)
Marvel Comics Group: April, 1983 (one-shot)
1-Vs. the X-Men 5.00

OCCULT CRIMES TASKFORCE
Image Comics: July, 2006 - No. 4, May, 2007 ($2.99, limited series)
1-4-Rosario Dawson & David Atchison-s/Tony Shasteen-a 3.00
... Vol. 1 TPB (2007, $14.99) r/#1-4; sketch and cover development art 15.00

OCCULTIST, THE
Dark Horse Comics: Dec, 2010 ($3.50, one-shot)
1-Richardson & Seeley-s/Drujiniu-a/Morris-c 3.50

OCCULTIST, THE
Dark Horse Comics: Nov, 2011 - No. 3, Jan, 2012 ($3.50, limited series)
1-3-Seeley-s/Drujiniu-a/Morris-c. 1-Variant-c by Frison 3.50

OCCULTIST, THE
Dark Horse Comics: Oct, 2013 - No. 5, Feb, 2014 ($3.50, limited series)
1-5-Seeley-s/Norton-a/Morris-c. 1-Variant-c by Rivera 3.50

OCCULT FILES OF DR. SPEKTOR, THE
Gold Key/Whitman No. 25: Apr, 1973 - No. 24, Feb, 1977; No. 25, May, 1982 (Painted-c #1-24)

	GD	VG	FN	VF	VF/NM	NM-
1-1st app. Lakota; Baron Tibor begins	5	10	15	34	60	85
2-5: 3-Mummy-c/s. 5-Jekyll & Hyde-c/s	3	6	9	19	30	40
6-10: 6,9-Frankenstein. 8,9-Dracula c/s. 9.-Jekyll & Hyde c/s. 9,10-Mummy-c/s	3	6	9	15	22	28
11-13,15-17,19-22,24: 11-1st app. Spektor as Werewolf. 11-13-Werewolf-c/s. 12,16-Frankenstein c/s. 17-Zombie/Voodoo-c. 19-Sea monster-c/s. 20-Mummy-s. 21-Swamp monster-c/s. 24-Dragon-c/s	2	4	6	11	16	20
14-Dr. Solar app.	3	6	9	16	24	32
18,23-Dr. Solar cameo	2	4	6	13	18	22
22-Return of the Owl-c/s	2	4	6	13	18	22
25(Whitman, 5/82)-r/#1 with line drawn-c	2	4	6	9	13	16

NOTE: *Also see Dan Curtis, Golden Comics Digest 33, Gold Key Spotlight, Mystery Comics Digest 5, & Spine Tingling Tales.*

OCCUPY AVENGERS (Follows Civil War II)
Marvel Comics: Jan, 2017 - No. 9, Sept, 2017 ($3.99)
1-4-Hawkeye and Red Wolf team; Pacheco-a. 3,4-Nighthawk & Nick Fury LMD app. 8,9-Secret Empire tie-ins. 9-Leads into Secret Empire #7 4.00

OCCUPY COMICS
Black Mask Studios: 2013 - No. 3, 2013 ($3.50)
1-3-Short stories and essays about the Occupy movement; s/a by various. 1-Allred-c 3.50

OCEAN
DC Comics (WildStorm): Dec, 2005 - No. 6, Sept, 2006 ($2.95/$2.99/$3.99, limited series)
1-5-Warren Ellis-s/Chris Sprouse-a 3.00
6-($3.99) Conclusion 4.00

OCEAN MASTER: YEAR OF THE VILLAIN
DC Comics: 2019 ($4.99, one-shot)
1-Watters-s/Mendonca-a; Apex Lex and Marine Marauder app. 5.00

OCTOBER FACTION, THE
IDW Publishing: Oct, 2014 - No. 18, Jul, 2016 ($3.99)
1-18-Steve Niles-s/Damien Worm-a/c 4.00
... #1 Special Edition (9/19, $3.99) r/#1 with added Netflix logo on cover 4.00

OCTOBER FACTION, THE: DEADLY SEASON
IDW Publishing: Oct, 2016 - No. 5, Feb, 2017 ($3.99, limited series)
1-5-Steve Niles-s/Damien Worm-a/c 4.00

OCTOBER FACTION: SUPERNATURAL DREAMS
IDW Publishing: Mar, 2018 - No. 5, Jul, 2018 ($3.99, limited series)
1-5-Steve Niles-s/Damien Worm-a/c 4.00

ODDLY NORMAL
Image Comics: Sept, 2014 - No. 10, Sept, 2015 ($2.99)
1-10-Otis Frampton-s/a 3.00

ODELL'S ADVENTURES IN 3-D (See Adventures in 3-D)

ODY-C
Image Comics: Nov, 2014 - No. 12, Oct, 2016 ($3.99)
1-12: 1-Matt Fraction-s/Christian Ward-a; 8-page gatefold 4.00

ODYSSEY, THE (See Marvel Illustrated: The Odyssey)

ODYSSEY OF THE AMAZONS
DC Comics: Mar, 2017 - No. 6, Aug, 2017 ($3.99, limited series)
1-6-Early history of the Amazons; Kevin Grevioux-s/Ryan Benjamin-a 4.00

OFFCASTES
Marvel Comics (Epic Comics/Heavy Hitters): July, 1993 - No. 3, Sept, 1993 ($1.95, limited series)
1-3: Mike Vosburg-c/a/scripts in all 3.00

OFFICIAL CRISIS ON INFINITE EARTHS INDEX, THE
Independent Comics Group (Eclipse): Mar, 1986 ($1.75)
1 5.00

OFFICIAL CRISIS ON INFINITE EARTHS CROSSOVER INDEX, THE
Independent Comics Group (Eclipse): July, 1986 ($1.75)
1-Pérez-c. 5.00

OFFICIAL DOOM PATROL INDEX, THE
Independent Comics Group (Eclipse): Feb, 1986 - No. 2, Mar, 1986 ($1.50, limited series)
1,2: Byrne-c. 4.00

OFFICIAL HANDBOOK OF THE CONAN UNIVERSE ANNIVERSARY EDITION
Marvel Comics: Dec, 2020 ($5.99, one-shot)
1-Reprints The Handbook of the Conan Universe ('85,'86); Kaluta wraparound-c 6.00

OFFICIAL HANDBOOK OF THE MARVEL UNIVERSE, THE
Marvel Comics Group: Jan, 1983 - No. 15, May, 1984 (Limited series)
1-Lists Marvel heroes & villains (letter A) 6.00
2-15: 2 (B-C, 3-(C-D). 4-(D-G). 5-(H-J), 6-(K-L). 7-(M). 8-(N-P); Punisher-c. 9-(Q-S), 10-(S). 11-(S-U). 12-(V-Z); Wolverine-c. 13,14-Book of the Dead. 15-Weaponry catalogue 5.00
NOTE: ***Bolland** a-8. **Byrne** c/a(p)-1-14; c-15p. **Grell** a-6, 9. **Kirby** a-1, 3. **Layton** a-2, 5, 7. **Mignola** a-3, 4, 5, 6, 8, 12. **Miller** a-4-6, 8, 10. **Nebres** a-3, 4, 8. **Redondo** a-3, 4, 8, 13, 14. **Simonson** a-1, 4, 6-13. **Paul Smith** a-1-12. **Starlin** a-5, 7, 8, 10, 13, 14. **Steranko** a-8p. **Zeck**-2-14.*

OFFICIAL HANDBOOK OF THE MARVEL UNIVERSE, THE
Marvel Comics Group: Dec, 1985 - No. 20, Feb, 1988 ($1.50, maxi-series)
V2#1-Byrne-c 5.00
2-20: 2,3-Byrne-c 4.00

	GD	VG	FN	VF	VF/NM	NM-
Trade paperback Vol. 1-10 ($6.95)	1	3	4	6	8	10

NOTE: ***Art Adams** a-7, 8, 11, 12, 14. **Bolland** a-8, 10, 13. **Buckler** a-1, 3, 5, 10. **Buscema** a-1, 5, 8, 9, 10, 13, 14. **Byrne** a-1-14; c-1-11. **Ditko** a-1, 2, 4, 6, 7, 11, 13. a-7, 11. **Mignola** a-2, 4, 9, 11, 13. **Miller** a-2, 4, 12. **Simonson** a-1, 2, 4-13, 15. **Paul Smith** a-1-5, 7-12, 14. **Starlin** a-6, 8, 9, 12, 16. **Zeck** a-1-4, 6, 7, 9-14, 16.*

OFFICIAL HANDBOOK OF THE MARVEL UNIVERSE, THE
Marvel Comics: July, 1989 - No. 8, Mid-Dec, 1990 ($1.50, lim. series, 52 pgs.)
V3#1-8: 1-McFarlane-a (2 pgs.) 4.00

OFFICIAL HANDBOOK OF THE MARVEL UNIVERSE, THE (Also see Spider-Man)
Marvel Comics: 2004 - Present ($3.99, one-shots)
...: Alternate Universes 2005 - Profile pages of 1602, MC2, 2099, Earth X, Mangaverse, Days of Future Past, Squadron Supreme, Spider-Ham's Larval Earth and others 4.00
...: Avengers 2004 - Profile pages; art by various; lists of character origins and 1st apps. 4.00
...: Avengers 2005 - Profile pages and info for New Avengers, Young Avengers & others 4.00
...: Book of the Dead 2004 - Profile pages of deceased Marvel characters; art by various; 4.00
...: Daredevil 2004 - Profile pages; art by various; lists of character origins and 1st apps. 4.00
...: Fantastic Four 2005 - Profile pages of members, friends & enemies 4.00
...: Golden Age 2005 - Profile pages; art by various; lists of character origins and 1st apps. 4.00
...: Horror 2005 - Profile pages; art by various; lists of character origins and 1st apps. 4.00
...: Hulk 2004 - Profile pages; art by various; lists of character origins and 1st apps. 4.00
...: Marvel Knights 2005 - Profile pages of characters from Marvel Knights line 4.00
...: Spider-Man 2004 - Profile pages; art by various; lists of character origins and 1st apps. 4.00
...: Spider-Man 2005 - Profile pages of Spidey's friends and foes, emphasizing the recent 4.00
...: Wolverine 2004 - Profile pages; art by various; lists of character origins and 1st apps. 4.00
...: Teams 2005 - Profile pages of Avengers, X-Men and other teams 4.00

Official Marvel Index to The Amazing Spider-Man #1 © MAR

Oh My Goddess! Pt. 4 #2 © Kosuke

O.K. Comics #2 © UFS

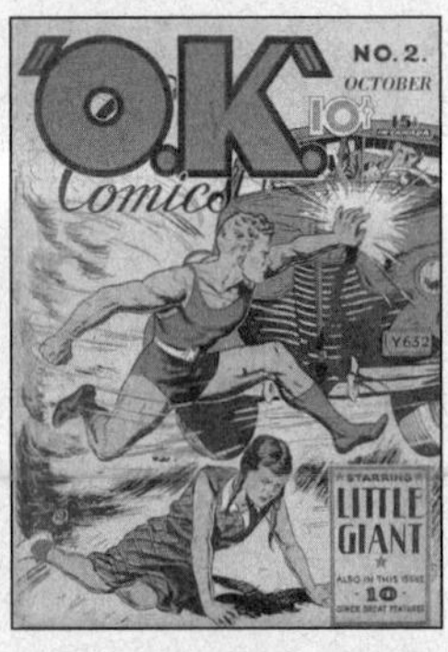

	GD 2.0	VG 4.0	FN 6.0	VF 8.0	VF/NM 9.0	NM- 9.2
...: Women of Marvel 2005 - Profile pages; art by various; Greg Land-c						4.00
...: X-Men 2004 - Profile pages; art by various; lists of character origins and 1st apps.						4.00
...: X-Men 2005 - Profile pages; art by various; lists of character origins and 1st apps.						4.00
...: X-Men - The Age of Apocalypse 2005 - Profile pages of characters plus Exiles						4.00

OFFICIAL HANDBOOK OF THE MARVEL UNIVERSE A-Z UPDATE
Marvel Comics: Apr, 2010 - No. 5, 2010 ($3.99, limited series)

	GD 2.0	VG 4.0	FN 6.0	VF 8.0	VF/NM 9.0	NM- 9.2
1-5-Profile pages; Andrasofszky-c						4.00

OFFICIAL HANDBOOK OF THE ULTIMATE MARVEL UNIVERSE, THE
Marvel Comics: 2005 ($3.99, one-shots)

	GD 2.0	VG 4.0	FN 6.0	VF 8.0	VF/NM 9.0	NM- 9.2
... 2005: The Fantastic Four and Spider-Man - Profile pages; art by various						4.00
... The Ultimates and X-Men 2005 - Profile pages; art by various; Bagley-c						4.00

OFFICIAL HAWKMAN INDEX, THE
Independent Comics Group: Nov, 1986 - No. 2, Dec, 1986 ($2.00)

	GD 2.0	VG 4.0	FN 6.0	VF 8.0	VF/NM 9.0	NM- 9.2
1,2						4.00

OFFICIAL INDEX TO THE MARVEL UNIVERSE (Also see "Avengers, Thor...")
Marvel Comics: 2009 - No. 14, April, 2010 ($3.99)

	GD 2.0	VG 4.0	FN 6.0	VF 8.0	VF/NM 9.0	NM- 9.2
1-14-Each issue has chronological synopsies, creator credits, character lists for 40-50 issues of apps. for Iron Man, Spider-Man and the X-Men starting with 1st apps. in issue #1						4.00

OFFICIAL JUSTICE LEAGUE OF AMERICA INDEX, THE
Independent Comics Group (Eclipse): April, 1986 - No. 8, Mar, 1987 ($2.00, Baxter paper)

	GD 2.0	VG 4.0	FN 6.0	VF 8.0	VF/NM 9.0	NM- 9.2
1-8: 1,2-Perez-c.						6.00

OFFICIAL LEGION OF SUPER-HEROES INDEX, THE
Independent Comics Group (Eclipse): Dec, 1986 - No. 5, 1987 ($2.00, limited series)
(No Official in Title #2 on)

	GD 2.0	VG 4.0	FN 6.0	VF 8.0	VF/NM 9.0	NM- 9.2
1-5: 4-Mooney-c						6.00

OFFICIAL MARVEL INDEX TO MARVEL TEAM-UP
Marvel Comics Group: Jan, 1986 - No. 6, 1987 ($1.25, limited series)

	GD 2.0	VG 4.0	FN 6.0	VF 8.0	VF/NM 9.0	NM- 9.2
1-6						4.00

OFFICIAL MARVEL INDEX TO THE AMAZING SPIDER-MAN
Marvel Comics Group: Apr, 1985 - No. 9, Dec, 1985 ($1.25, limited series)

	GD 2.0	VG 4.0	FN 6.0	VF 8.0	VF/NM 9.0	NM- 9.2
1 ($1.00)-Byrne-c.						5.00
2-9: 5,6,8,9-Punisher-c.						4.00

OFFICIAL MARVEL INDEX TO THE AVENGERS, THE
Marvel Comics: Jun, 1987 - No. 7, Aug, 1988 ($2.95, limited series)

	GD 2.0	VG 4.0	FN 6.0	VF 8.0	VF/NM 9.0	NM- 9.2
1-7						5.00

OFFICIAL MARVEL INDEX TO THE AVENGERS, THE
Marvel Comics: V2#1, Oct, 1994 - V2#6, 1995 ($1.95, limited series)

	GD 2.0	VG 4.0	FN 6.0	VF 8.0	VF/NM 9.0	NM- 9.2
V2#1-#6						4.00

OFFICIAL MARVEL INDEX TO THE FANTASTIC FOUR
Marvel Comics Group: Dec, 1985 - No. 12, Jan, 1987 ($1.25, limited series)

	GD 2.0	VG 4.0	FN 6.0	VF 8.0	VF/NM 9.0	NM- 9.2
1-12: 1-Byrne-c. 1,2-Kirby back-c (unpub. art)						4.00

OFFICIAL MARVEL INDEX TO THE X-MEN, THE
Marvel Comics: May, 1987 - No. 7, July, 1988 ($2.95, limited series)

	GD 2.0	VG 4.0	FN 6.0	VF 8.0	VF/NM 9.0	NM- 9.2
1-7						5.00

OFFICIAL MARVEL INDEX TO THE X-MEN, THE
Marvel Comics: V2#1, Apr, 1994 - V2#5, 1994 ($1.95, limited series)

	GD 2.0	VG 4.0	FN 6.0	VF 8.0	VF/NM 9.0	NM- 9.2
V2#1-5: 1-Covers X-Men #1-51. 2-Covers #52-122,Special #1,2,Giant-Size #1,2. 3-Byrne-c; covers #123-177, Annuals 3-7, Spec. Ed. #1. 4-Covers Uncanny X-Men #178-234, Annuals 8-12. 5-Covers #235-287, Annuals 13-15						4.00

OFFICIAL SOUPY SALES COMIC (See Soupy Sales)

OFFICIAL TEEN TITANS INDEX, THE
Indep. Comics Group (Eclipse): Aug, 1985 - No. 5, 1986 ($1.50, lim. series)

	GD 2.0	VG 4.0	FN 6.0	VF 8.0	VF/NM 9.0	NM- 9.2
1-5						4.00

OFFICIAL TRUE CRIME CASES (Formerly Sub-Mariner #23; All-True Crime Cases #26 on)
Marvel Comics (OCI): No. 24, Fall, 1947 - No. 25, Winter, 1947-48

	GD 2.0	VG 4.0	FN 6.0	VF 8.0	VF/NM 9.0	NM- 9.2
24(#1)-Burgos-a; Syd Shores-c	29	58	87	170	278	385
25-Syd Shores-c; Kurtzman's "Hey Look"	21	42	63	124	202	280

OF SUCH IS THE KINGDOM
George A. Pflaum: 1955 (15¢, 36 pgs.)

	GD 2.0	VG 4.0	FN 6.0	VF 8.0	VF/NM 9.0	NM- 9.2
nn-Reprints from 1951 Treasure Chest	4	8	12	16	22	25

O.G. WHIZ (See Gold Key Spotlight #10)
Gold Key: 2/71 - No. 6, 5/72; No. 7, 5/78 - No. 11, 1/79 (No. 7: 52 pgs.)

	GD 2.0	VG 4.0	FN 6.0	VF 8.0	VF/NM 9.0	NM- 9.2
1-John Stanley script	5	10	15	31	53	75
2-John Stanley script	4	8	12	23	37	50
3-6(1972)	3	6	9	17	26	35
7-11(1978-79)-Part-r: 9-Tubby issue	2	4	6	9	12	15

OH, BROTHER! (Teen Comedy)
Stanhall Publ.: Jan, 1953 - No. 5, Oct, 1953

	GD 2.0	VG 4.0	FN 6.0	VF 8.0	VF/NM 9.0	NM- 9.2
1-By Bill Williams	17	34	51	105	165	225
2-5	13	26	39	72	101	130

OH MY GODDESS! (Manga)
Dark Horse Comics: Aug, 1994 - No. 112 ($2.50-$3.99, B&W)

	GD 2.0	VG 4.0	FN 6.0	VF 8.0	VF/NM 9.0	NM- 9.2
1-6-Kosuke Fujishima-s/a in all						3.00
... PART II 2/95 - No. 9, 9/95 ($2.50, B&W, lim.series) #1-9						3.00
... PART III 11/95 - No. 11, 9/96 ($2.95, B&W, lim. series) #1-11						3.00
... PART IV 12/96 - No. 8, 7/97 ($2.95, B&W, lim. series) #1-8						3.00
... PART V 9/97 - No. 12, 8/98 ($2.95, B&W, lim. series)						
1,2,5,8: 5-Ninja Master pt. 1						3.00
3,4,6,7,10-12-($3.95, 48 pgs.) 10-Fallen Angel. 11-Play The Game						4.00
9-($3.50) "It's Lonely At The Top"						3.50
... PART VI 10/98 - No. 5, 3/99 ($3.50/$2.95, B&W, lim. series)						
1-($3.50)						3.50
2-6-($2.95)-6-Super Urd one-shot						3.00
... PART VII 5/99 - No. 8, 12/99 ($2.95, B&W, lim. series) #1-3						3.00
4-8-($3.50)						3.50
... PART VIII 1/00 - No. 6, 6/00 ($3.50, B&W, lim. series) #1-3,5,7						3.50
4-($2.95) "Hail To The Chief" begins						3.00
... PART IX 7/00 - No. 7, 1/01 ($3.50/$2.99) #1-4: 3-Queen Sayoko						3.50
5-7-($2.99)						3.00
... PART X 2/01 - No. 5, 6/01 ($3.50) #1-5						3.50
... PART XI 10/01 - No. 10, 3/02 ($3.50) #1,2,7,8						3.50
3-6,9-($2.99) Mystery Child						3.00
10-($3.99)						4.00
(Series adapts new numbering) 88-90-($3.50) Learning to Love						3.50
91-94,96-103,105,107-110: 91-94 ($2.99) Traveler. 96-98-The Phantom Racer						3.00
95,104,106-($3.50) 95-Traveler pt. 5						3.50
111,112-($3.99)						4.00

OH SUSANNA (TV)
Dell Publishing Co.: No. 1105, June-Aug, 1960 (Gale Storm)

	GD 2.0	VG 4.0	FN 6.0	VF 8.0	VF/NM 9.0	NM- 9.2
Four Color 1105-Toth-a, photo-c	10	20	30	66	138	210

OKAY COMICS
United Features Syndicate: July, 1940

	GD 2.0	VG 4.0	FN 6.0	VF 8.0	VF/NM 9.0	NM- 9.2
1-Captain & the Kids & Hawkshaw the Detective reprints	52	104	156	328	552	775

O.K. COMICS
Hit Publications: May, 1940 (ashcan)

nn-Ashcan comic, not distributed to newsstands, only for in house use. A CGC certified 8.0 copy sold in 2003 for $1,000.

O.K. COMICS
United Features Syndicate/Hit Publications: July, 1940 - No. 2, Oct, 1940

	GD 2.0	VG 4.0	FN 6.0	VF 8.0	VF/NM 9.0	NM- 9.2
1-Little Giant (w/super powers), Phantom Knight, Sunset Smith, & The Teller Twins begin	84	168	252	538	919	1300
2 (Rare)-Origin Mister Mist by Chas. Quinlan	87	174	261	553	952	1350

OKLAHOMA KID
Ajax/Farrell Publ.: June, 1957 - No. 4, 1958

	GD 2.0	VG 4.0	FN 6.0	VF 8.0	VF/NM 9.0	NM- 9.2
1	11	22	33	62	86	110
2-4	7	14	21	37	46	55

OKLAHOMAN, THE
Dell Publishing Co.: No. 820, July, 1957

	GD 2.0	VG 4.0	FN 6.0	VF 8.0	VF/NM 9.0	NM- 9.2
Four Color 820-Movie, photo-c	8	16	24	54	102	150

OKTANE
Dark Horse Comics: Aug, 1995 - Nov, 1995 ($2.50, color, limited series)

	GD 2.0	VG 4.0	FN 6.0	VF 8.0	VF/NM 9.0	NM- 9.2
1-4-Gene Ha-a						3.00

OKTOBERFEST COMICS
Now & Then Publ.: Fall 1976 (75¢, Canadian, B&W, one-shot)

	GD 2.0	VG 4.0	FN 6.0	VF 8.0	VF/NM 9.0	NM- 9.2
1-Dave Sim-s/a; Gene Day-a; 1st app. Uncle Hans & Natter P. Bombast; The Beavers sty; 1st Cap'n Riverrat, Sim-s/Day-a	3	6	9	16	23	30

OLD GLORY COMICS
DC Comics: 1941

nn - Ashcan comic, not distributed to newsstands, only for in-house use. Cover art is Flash Comics #12 with interior being Action Comics #37 (no known sales)

Old Haunts #1 © AWA Studios

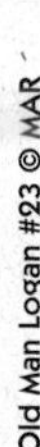
Old Man Logan #23 © MAR

Once & Future #11 © Kieron Gillen

	GD 2.0	VG 4.0	FN 6.0	VF 8.0	VF/NM 9.0	NM- 9.2

OLD GUARD, THE (Inspired the 2020 Netflix movie)
Image Comics: Feb, 2017 - No. 5, Jun, 2017 ($3.99)

1-5-Greg Rucka-s/Leandro Fernández-a 4.00

OLD GUARD, THE: FORCE MULTIPLIED
Image Comics: Dec, 2019 - No. 5, Jul, 2020 ($3.99)

1-5-Greg Rucka-s/Leandro Fernández-a 4.00

OLD HAUNTS
AWA Studios: Jun, 2020 - No. 5 ($3.99)

1-5-Ollie Masters & Rob Williams-s/Laurence Campbell-a 4.00

OLD IRONSIDES (Disney)
Dell Publishing Co.: No. 874, Jan, 1958

Four Color 874-Movie w/Johnny Tremain 6 12 18 42 79 115

OLD LADY HARLEY (See Harley Quinn #42)
DC Comics: Dec, 2018 - No. 5, Apr, 2019 ($3.99, limited series)

1-5-Tieri-s/Miranda-a/Conner-c; future Harley, Joker, Red Tool and Catwoman app. 4.00

OLD MAN HAWKEYE
Marvel Comics: Mar, 2018 - No. 12, Feb, 2019 ($3.99)

1-12-Sacks-s/Checchetto-a; takes place 5 years before the original Old Man Logan 4.00

OLD MAN LOGAN (Secret Wars tie-in)
Marvel Comics: Jul, 2015 - No. 5, Dec, 2015 ($4.99/$3.99, limited series)

1-($4.99) Bendis-s/Sorrentino-a; future Logan from Wolverine V3 #66; Emma Frost app. 5.00
2-5-($3.99) 2-Sabretooth app. 3-Apocalypse app. 5-X-Men app. 4.00

OLD MAN LOGAN (Follows Secret Wars)(Continues in Dead Man Logan)
Marvel Comics: Mar, 2016 - No. 50, Dec, 2018 ($4.99/$3.99)

1-($4.99) Lemire-s/Sorrentino-a; future Logan in current Marvel Universe 5.00
2-49-($3.99) 2-Amadeus Cho Hulk app. 4-Steve Rogers app. 7-Lady Deathstrike app. 14,15-Dracula app.; Andrade-a. 21-24-Past Lives. 25-30-Maestro app. 25-32-Deodato-a 31-35-Scarlet Samurai. 36-38,43-45-Bullseye app. 41,42-Kraven app. 4.00
50-($4.99) Brisson-s/Roberson & Edwards-a; Maestro app. 5.00
Annual 1 (11/18, $4.99) Frank Castle app.; Brisson-s/Di Meo-a/Shane Davis-c 5.00

OLD MAN QUILL
Marvel Comics: Apr, 2019 - No. 12, Feb, 2020 ($3.99)

1-12: 1-Sacks-s/Gill-a; Star-Lord with Guardians of the Galaxy 45+ years in the future. 6,11,12-Galactus app. 4.00

OLD YELLER (Disney, see Movie Comics, and Walt Disney Showcase #25)
Dell Publishing Co.: No. 869, Jan, 1958

Four Color 869-Movie, photo-c 6 12 18 38 69 100

OLIVER
Image Comics: Jan, 2019 - Present ($3.99)

1-4-Gary Whitta-s/Darick Robertson-a. 1-Covers by Robertson & Fabry 4.00

OLIVIA TWIST
Dark Horse Comics (Berger Books): Sept, 2018 - No. 4, Jan, 2019 ($4.99, limited series)

1-4-Darin Strauss & Adam Dalva-s/Emma Vieceli-a. 3-Tula Lotay-c. 4-Sana Takeda-c 5.00

OMAC (One Man Army; ...Corps. #4 on; also see Kamandi #59 & Warlord)
(See Cancelled Comic Cavalcade)
National Periodical Publications: Sept-Oct, 1974 - No. 8, Nov-Dec, 1975

1-Origin 5 10 15 34 60 85
2-8: 8-2 pg. Neal Adams ad 3 6 9 17 26 35
Jack Kirby's Omac: One Man Army Corps HC (2008, $24.99, d.j.) r/#1-8; Evanier intro. 25.00
NOTE: *Kirby a-1-8p; c-1-7p. Kubert c-8.*

OMAC (See DCU Brave New World)
DC Comics: Sept, 2006 - No. 8, Apr, 2007 ($2.99, limited series)

1-8: 1-Bruce Jones-s/Renato Guedes-a. 1-3-Firestorm & Cyborg app. 8-Superman app. 3.00

O.M.A.C. (DC New 52)
DC Comics: Nov, 2011 - No. 8, Jun, 2012 ($2.99)

1-8: 1-DiDio-s/Giffen-a/c; Dubbilex and Brother Eye app. 2-Max Lord & Sarge Steel app. 5-Crossover with Frankenstein, Agent of SHADE #5. 6-Kolins-a 3.00

OMAC: ONE MAN ARMY CORPS
DC Comics: 1991 - No. 4, 1991 ($3.95, B&W, mini-series, mature, 52 pgs.)

Book One - Four: John Byrne-c/a & scripts 5.00

OMAC PROJECT, THE
DC Comics: June, 2005 - No. 6, Nov, 2005 ($2.50, limited series)

1-6-Prelude to Infinite Crisis x-over; Rucka-s/Saiz-a 3.00
...: Infinite Crisis Special 1 (5/06, $4.99) Rucka-s/Saiz-a; follows destruction of satellite 5.00
TPB (2005, $14.99) r/#1-6, Countdown to Infinite Crisis, Wonder Woman #219 15.00

O'MALLEY AND THE ALLEY CATS
Gold Key: April, 1971 - No. 9, Jan, 1974 (Disney)

1 3 6 9 16 23 30
2-9 2 4 6 9 13 16

OMEGA ELITE
Blackthorne Publishing: 1987 ($1.25)

1-Starlin-c 4.00

OMEGA FLIGHT
Marvel Comics: Jun, 2007 - No. 5, Oct, 2007 ($2.99, limited series)

1-Oeming-s/Kolins-a; Wrecking Crew app. 4.00
1-Second printing with Sasquatch variant-c 3.00
2-5: 5-Beta Ray Bill app. 3.00
...: Alpha to Omega TPB ('07, $13.99) r/#1-5, USAgent story/Civil War: Choosing Sides 14.00

OMEGA MEN, THE (See Green Lantern #141)
DC Comics: Dec, 1982 - No. 38, May, 1986 ($1.00/$1.25/$1.50; Baxter paper)

1-Giffen-c/a 1 3 4 6 8 10
2,4-9,11-19,21-25,28-30,32,33,36,38: 2-Origin Broot. 5,9-2nd & 3rd app. Lobo (cameo, 2 pgs. each). 7-Origin The Citadel. 19-Lobo cameo. 30-Intro new Primus 3.00
3-1st app. Lobo (5 pgs.)(6/83); Lobo-c 5 10 15 31 53 75
10-1st full Lobo story 2 4 6 9 12 15
20: 20-2nd full Lobo story 5.00
26,27,31,34,35: 26,27-Alan Moore scripts. 31-Crisis x-over. 34,35-Teen Titans x-over 4.00
37-1st solo Lobo story (8 pg. back-up by Giffen) 6.00
Annual 1(11/84, 52 pgs.), 2(11/85) 4.00
NOTE: *Giffen c/a-1-6p. Morrow a-24r. Nino c/a-16, 21; a-Annual 1i.*

OMEGA MEN, THE
DC Comics: Dec, 2006 - No. 6, May, 2007 ($2.99, limited series)

1-6: 1-Superman, Wonder Girl, Green Lantern app.; Flint-a/Gabrych-s 3.00

OMEGA MEN, THE
DC Comics: Aug, 2015 - No. 12, Jul, 2016 ($2.99)

1-12: 1-Tom King-s/Barnaby Bagenda-a; Kyle Rayner app. 4-Cypress-a 3.00

OMEGA THE UNKNOWN
Marvel Comics Group: March, 1976 - No. 10, Oct, 1977

1-1st app. Omega 3 6 9 17 26 35
2,3-(Regular 25¢ editions). 2-Hulk-c/story. 3-Electro-c/story. 2 3 4 6 8 10
2,3-(30¢-c variants, limited distribution) 3 6 9 19 30 40
4-10: 8-1st brief app. 2nd Foolkiller (Greg Salinger), 1 panel only. 9,10-(Reg. 30¢ editions). 9-1st full app. 2nd Foolkiller 1 2 3 5 6 8
9,10-(35¢-c variants, limited distribution) 6 12 18 41 76 110
... Classic TPB (2005, $29.99) r/#1-10 30.00
NOTE: *Kane c(p)-3, 5, 8, 9. Mooney a-1-3, 4p, 5, 6p, 7, 8i, 9, 10.*

OMEGA: THE UNKNOWN
Marvel Comics: Dec, 2007 - No. 10, Sept, 2008 ($2.99, limited series)

1-10-Jonathan Lethem-s/Farel Dalrymple-a 3.00

OMEN
Northstar Publishing: 1989 - No. 3, 1989 ($2.00, B&W, mature)

1-Tim Vigil-c/a in all 1 2 3 5 7 9
1, (2nd printing) 3.00
2,3 6.00

OMEN, THE
Chaos! Comics: May, 1998 - No. 5, Sept, 1998 ($2.95, limited series)

1-5: 1-Six covers, ...: Vexed (10/98, $2.95) Chaos! characters appear 3.00

OMNI MEN
Blackthorne Publishing: 1987 - No. 3, 1987 ($1.25)

1-3 3.00
Graphic Novel (1989, $3.50) 4.00

ONCE & FUTURE
BOOM! Studios: Aug, 2019 - Present ($3.99)

1-Kieron Gillen-s/Dan Mora-a in all 2 4 6 8 11 14
2 1 3 4 6 8 10
3-8 5.00
9-16: 9-12-Beowulf and Grendel app. 4.00

ONCE UPON A TIME: OUT OF THE PAST (TV)
Marvel Comics: 2015 ($24.99, hardcover with dustjacket)

HC-Sequel to Shadow of the Queen HC; Bechko & Vazquez-s; Stacy Lee-c 25.00

100 Bullets #94 © Azzarello, Risso & DC

Oni Double Feature #12 © Oni Press

Onslaught Reborn #5 © MAR

	GD	VG	FN	VF	VF/NM	NM-
	2.0	4.0	6.0	8.0	9.0	9.2

ONCE UPON A TIME: SHADOW OF THE QUEEN (TV)
Marvel Comics: 2013 ($19.99, hardcover with dustjacket)
HC-Regina and the Huntsman; Bechko-s; art by Del Mundo, Lolos, Henderson, & Kaluta 20.00

ONE, THE
Marvel Comics (Epic Comics): July, 1985 - No. 6, Feb, 1986 (Limited series, mature)
1-6: Post nuclear holocaust super-hero. 2-Intro The Other 3.00

ONE-ARM SWORDSMAN, THE
Victory Prod./Lueng's Publ. #4 on: 1987 - No. 12, 1990 ($2.75/$1.80, 52 pgs.)
1-3 ($2.75) 4.00
4-12: 4-6-$1.80-c. 7-12-$2.00-c 4.00

ONE-HIT WONDER
Image Comics: Feb, 2014 - No. 5, Apr, 2015 ($3.50)
1-5: 1-4-Sapolsky-s/Olivetti-a/c. 5-Thompson & Fiorelli-a/Roux-a 3.50

ONE HUNDRED AND ONE DALMATIANS (Disney, see Cartoon Tales, Movie Comics, and Walt Disney Showcase #9, 51)
Dell Publishing Co.: No. 1183, Mar, 1961
Four Color 1183-Movie 10 20 30 66 138 210

101 DALMATIONS (Movie)
Disney Comics: 1991 (52 pgs., graphic novel)
nn-($4.95, direct sales)-r/movie adaptation & more 5.00
1-($2.95, newsstand edition) 3.00

101 WAYS TO END THE CLONE SAGA (See Spider-Man)
Marvel Comics: Jan, 1997 ($2.50, one-shot)
1 4.00

100 BULLETS
DC Comics (Vertigo): Aug, 1999 - No. 100, Jun, 2009 ($2.50/$2.75/$2.99)
1-Azzarello-s/Risso-a/Dave Johnson-c 4 8 12 23 37 50
2-5 6.00
6-49,51-61: 26-Series summary; art by various. 45-Preview of Losers 4.00
50-($3.50) History of the Trust 5.00
62-71: 62-Begin $2.75-c. 64-Preview of Loveless 3.00
72-99: 72-Begin $2.99-c 3.00
100-($4.99) Final issue 6.00
...#1/Crime Line Sampler Flip-Book (9/09, $1.00) r/#1 with previews of upcoming GNs 3.00
....: A Foregone Tomorrow TPB (2002, $17.95) r/#20-30 18.00
....: Decayed TPB (2006, $14.99) r/#68-75; Darwyn Cooke intro. 15.00
....: First Shot, Last Call TPB (2000, $9.95) r/#1-5, Vertigo Winter's Edge #3 10.00
....: Hang Up on the Hang Low TPB (2001, $9.95) r/#15-19; Jim Lee intro. 10.00
....: Once Upon a Crime TPB (2007, $12.99) r/#76-83 13.00
....: Samurai TPB (2003, $12.95) r/#43-49 13.00
....: Six Feet Under the Gun TPB (2003, $12.95) r/#37-42 13.00
....: Split Second Chance TPB (2001, $14.95) r/#6-14 15.00
....: Strychnine Lives TPB (2006, $14.99) r/#59-67; Manuel Ramos intro. 15.00
....: The Counterfifth Detective TPB (2003, $12.95) r/#31-36 13.00
....: The Hard Way TPB (2005, $14.99) r/#50-58 15.00
....: Wilt TPB (2009, $19.99) r/#89-100; Azzarello intro. 20.00

100 BULLETS: BROTHER LONO
DC Comics (Vertigo): Aug, 2013 - No. 8, Apr, 2014 ($3.99/$2.99, limited series)
1-($3.99) Azzarello-s/Risso-a/Dave Johnson-c 4.00
2-8-($2.99) Azzarello-s/Risso-a/Dave Johnson-c on all 3.00

100 GREATEST MARVELS OF ALL TIME
Marvel Comics: Dec, 2001 ($7.50/$3.50, limited series)
1-5-Reprints top #6-#25 stories voted by poll for Marvel's 40th ann. 7.50
6-($3.50) (#5 on-c) Reprints X-Men (2nd series) #1 4.00
7-($3.50) (#4 on-c) Reprints Giant-Size X-Men #1 4.00
8-($3.50) (#3 on-c) Reprints (Uncanny) X-Men #137 (Death of Jean Grey) 4.00
9-($3.50) (#2 on-c) Reprints Fantastic Four #1 4.00
10-($3.50) (#1 on-c) Reprints Amazing Fantasy #15 (1st app. Spider-Man) 4.00

100 PAGES OF COMICS
Dell Publishing Co.: 1937 (Stiff covers, square binding)
101(Found on back cover)-Alley Oop, Wash Tubbs, Capt. Easy, Og Son of Fire, Apple Mary, Tom Mix, Dan Dunn, Tailspin Tommy, Doctor Doom 165 330 495 1056 1803 2550

100 PAGE SUPER SPECTACULAR (See DC 100 Page Super Spectacular)

100%
DC Comics (Vertigo): Aug, 2002 - No. 5, July, 2003 ($5.95, B&W, limited series)
1-5-Paul Pope-s/a 6.00
HC (2009, $39.99, dustjacket) r/#1-5; sketch pages and background info 40.00
TPB (2005, $24.99) r/#1-5; sketch pages and background info 25.00
TPB (2009, $29.99) r/#1-5; sketch pages and background info 30.00

100% TRUE?
DC Comics (Paradox Press): Summer 1996 - No. 2 ($4.95, B&W)
1,2-Reprints stories from various Paradox Press books. 5.00

$1,000,000 DUCK (See Walt Disney Showcase #5)

ONE MILLION YEARS AGO (Tor #2 on)
St. John Publishing Co.: Sept, 1953
1-Origin & 1st app. Tor; Kubert-c/a; Kubert photo inside front cover 23 46 69 136 223 310

ONE MONTH TO LIVE ("Heroic Age: ..." in indicia)
Marvel Comics: Nov, 2010 - No. 5, Nov, 2010 ($2.99, weekly limited series)
1-5-Remender-s; Spider-Man and the Fantastic Four app. 3.00

ONE SHOT (See Four Color...)

1001 HOURS OF FUN
Dell Publishing Co.: No. 13, 1943
Large Feature Comic 13 (nn)-Puzzles & games; by A.W. Nugent. This book was bound as #13 w/Large Feature Comics in publisher's files 36 72 108 211 343 475

ONE TRICK RIP OFF, THE (See Dark Horse Presents)

ONI (Adaption of video game)
Dark Horse Comics: Feb, 2001 - No. 3, Apr, 2001 ($2.99, limited series)
1-3-Sunny Lee-a(p) 3.00

ONIBA: SWORDS OF THE DEMON
Aspen MLT: No. 0, Oct, 2015 ($2.50)
0-Hernandez-s/Pantalena-a; two covers 3.00

ONI DOUBLE FEATURE (See Clerks: The Comic Book and Jay & Silent Bob)
Oni Press: Jan, 1998 - No. 13, Sept, 1999 ($2.95, B&W)
1-Jay & Silent Bob; Kevin Smith-s/Matt Wagner-a 1 3 4 6 8 10
1-2nd printing 3.00
2-11,13: 2,3-Paul Pope-s/a. 3,4-Nixey-s/a. 4,5-Sienkewicz-s/a. 6,7-Gaiman-s. 9-Bagge-c. 13-All Paul Dini-s; Jingle Belle 3.00
12-Jay & Silent Bob as Bluntman & Chronic; Smith-s/Allred-a 5.00

ONI PRESS COLOR SPECIAL
Oni Press: Jun, 2001; Jul, 2002 ($5.95, annual)
...2001-Oeming "Who Killed Madman?" cover; stories & art by various 6.00
...2002-Allred wraparound-c; stories & art by various 6.00

ONSLAUGHT: EPILOGUE
Marvel Comics: Feb, 1997 ($2.95, one-shot)
1-Hama-s/Green-a; Xavier-c; Bastion-app. 4.00

ONSLAUGHT: MARVEL
Marvel Comics: Oct, 1996 ($3.95, one-shot)
1-Conclusion to Onslaught x-over; wraparound-c 1 2 3 4 5 7

ONSLAUGHT REBORN
Marvel Comics: Jan, 2007 - No. 5, Feb, 2008 ($2.99, limited series)
1-5-Loeb-s/Liefeld-a; female Bucky app. 2-Variant-c by Joe Madureira. 3-McGuiness var-c. 4-Campbell var-c. 5-Bianchi var-c; female Bucky goes to regular Marvel Universe 3.00
1-Variant-c by Michael Turner 4.00
HC (2008, $19.99) r/#1-5; sketch pages; foreword by Liefeld 20.00

ONSLAUGHT UNLEASHED
Marvel Comics: Apr, 2011 - No. 4, Jul, 2011 ($3.99, limited series)
1-4-McKeever-s/Andrade-a/Ramos-c; Secret Avengers & Young Allies app. 4.00

ONSLAUGHT: X-MEN
Marvel Comics: Aug, 1996 ($3.95, one-shot)
1-Waid & Lobdell script; Fantastic Four & Avengers app.; Xavier as Onslaught 1 2 3 5 6 8
1-Variant-c 2 4 6 11 16 20

ON STAGE
Dell Publishing Co.: No. 1336, Apr-June, 1962
Four Color 1336-Not by Leonard Starr 5 10 15 34 60 85

ON THE DOUBLE (Movie)
Dell Publishing Co.: No. 1232, Sept-Nov, 1961
Four Color 1232 5 10 15 34 60 85

ON THE ROAD TO PERDITION (Movie)

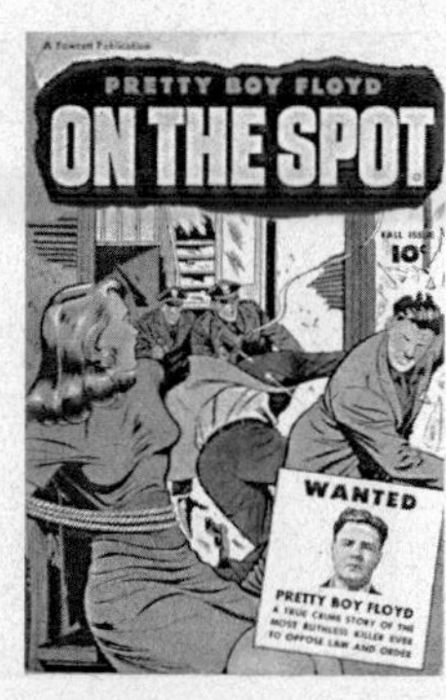

On the Spot nn © FAW

Optimus Prime #25 © Hasbro

The Order #1 © MAR

	GD	VG	FN	VF	VF/NM	NM-
	2.0	4.0	6.0	8.0	9.0	9.2

DC Comics (Paradox Press): 2003 - Book 3, 2004 ($7.95, 8"x5 1/2", B&W, limited series)
...: Oasis, Book 1-Max Allan Collins-s/José Luis García-López-a/David Beck-c 8.00
...: Sanctuary, Book 2-Max Allan Collins-s/Steve Lieber-a/José Luis García-López-c 8.00
...: Detour, Book 3-Max Allan Collins-s/José Luis García-López-a/Steve Lieber-c/a(i) 8.00
Road to Perdition 2: On the Road (2004, $14.95) r/series; Collins intro. 15.00

ON THE ROAD WITH ANDRAE CROUCH
Spire Christian Comics (Fleming H. Revell): 1973, 1974 (39¢)
nn-1973 Edition 2 4 6 13 18 22
nn-1974 Edition 2 4 6 9 13 16

ON THE SCENE PRESENTS:...
Warren Publishing Co.: Oct, 1966 - No. 2, 1967 (B&W magazine, two #1 issues)
#1 "Super Heroes" (68 pgs.) Batman 1966 movie photo-c/s; has articles/photos/comic art from serials on Superman, Flash Gordon, Capt. America, Capt. Marvel and The Phantom 5 10 15 31 53 75
#1 "Freak Out, USA" (Fall/1966, 60 pgs.) (lower print run) articles on musicians like Zappa, Jefferson Airplane, Supremes 5 10 15 33 57 80
#2 "Freak Out, USA" (2/67, 52 pgs.) Beatles, Country Joe, Doors/Jim Morrison, Bee Gees 5 10 15 33 57 80

ON THE SPOT (Pretty Boy Floyd...)
Fawcett Publications: Fall, 1948
nn-Pretty Boy Floyd photo on-c; bondage-c 40 80 120 244 402 550

ONYX
IDW Publishing: Jul, 2015 - No. 4, Oct, 2015 ($3.99)
1-4-Gabriel Rodriguez & Chris Ryall-s&a. 1-Three covers 4.00

ONYX OVERLORD
Marvel Comics (Epic): Oct, 1992 - No. 4, Jan, 1993 ($2.75, mini-series)
1-4: Moebius scripts 3.00

OPEN SPACE
Marvel Comics: Mid-Dec, 1989 - No. 4, Aug, 1990 ($4.95, bi-monthly, 68 pgs.)
1-4: 1-Bill Wray-a; Freas-c 5.00
0-(1999) Wizard supplement; unpubl. early Alex Ross-a; new Ross-c 3.00

OPERATION BIKINI (See Movie Classics)

OPERATION: BROKEN WINGS, 1936
BOOM! Studios: Nov, 2011 - No. 3, Jan, 2012 ($3.99, limited series)
1-3-Hanna-s/Hairsine-a; English translation of French comic 4.00

OPERATION BUCHAREST (See The Crusaders)

OPERATION CROSSBOW (See Movie Classics)

OPERATION: KNIGHTSTRIKE (See Knightstrike)
Image Comics (Extreme Studios): May, 1995 - No.3, July, 1995 ($2.50)
1-3 3.00

OPERATION PERIL
American Comics Group (Michel Publ.): Oct-Nov, 1950 - No. 16, Apr-May, 1953 (#1-5: 52 pgs.)
1-Time Travelers, Danny Danger (by Leonard Starr) & Typhoon Tyler (by Ogden Whitney) begin 42 84 126 265 445 625
2-War-c 25 50 75 150 245 340
3-War-c; horror story 23 46 69 136 223 310
4,5-Sci/fi-c/story 37 74 111 222 361 500
6-10: 6,8,9,10-Sci/fi-c. 6-Tank vs. T-Rex-c. 7-Sabretooth-c 22 44 66 128 209 290
11,12-War-c; last Time Travelers 15 30 45 83 124 165
13-16: All war format 10 20 30 56 76 105
NOTE: *Starr a-2, 5. Whitney a-1, 2, 5-10, 12; c-1, 3, 5, 8, 9.*

OPERATION: S.I.N.
Marvel Comics: Mar, 2015 - No. 5, Jul, 2015 ($3.99, limited series)
1-5-Peggy Carter & Howard Stark in 1952; Kathryn Immonen-s/Rich Ellis-a 4.00

OPERATION: STORMBREAKER
Acclaim Comics (Valiant Heroes): Aug, 1997 ($3.95, one-shot)
1-Waid/Augustyn-s, Braithwaite-a 4.00

OPTIC NERVE
Drawn and Quarterly: Apr, 1995 - Present ($2.95-$3.95, bi-annual)
1-7: Adrian Tomine-c/a/scripts in all 3.00
8-11: 8-($3.50). 9-11-($3.95) 4.00
12,13-($5.95) Half front-c. 12-Amber Sweet story 6.00
14-($6.95) Half front-c 7.00
32 Stories-($9.95, trade paperback)-r/Optic Nerve mini-comics 10.00
32 Stories-($29.95, hardcover)-r/Optic Nerve mini-comics; signed & numbered 30.00

OPTIMUS PRIME (Transformers)
IDW Publishing: Nov, 2016 - No. 18, Oct, 2018 ($3.99)
1-25-Follows Revolution x-over. 1-3-Barber-s/Zama-a; multiple covers on each. 4-Milne-a 4.00
Annual 2018 (2/18, $7.99) Barber-s/Tramontano & Griffith-a 8.00
... First Strike 1 (9/17, $3.99) Barber-s/Guidi & Wycough-a; part of Hasbro x-over 4.00

ORACLE: THE CURE
DC Comics: May, 2009 - No. 3, Jul, 2009 ($2.99, limited series)
1-3-Guillem March-c; Calculator app. 3.00
TPB (2010, $17.99) r/#1-3 and Birds of Prey #126,127 18.00

ORAL ROBERTS' TRUE STORIES (Junior Partners #120 on)
TelePix Publ. (Oral Roberts' Evangelistic Assoc./Healing Waters): 1956 (no month) - No. 119, 7/59 (15¢)(No. 102: 25¢)
V1#1(1956)-(Not code approved)- "The Miracle Touch" 19 38 57 109 172 235
102-(Only issue approved by code, 10/56) "Now I See" 13 26 39 74 105 135
103-119: 115-(114 on inside) 10 20 30 54 72 90
NOTE: *Also see Happiness & Healing For You.*

ORANGE BIRD, THE
Walt Disney Educational Media Co.: No date (1980) (36 pgs.; in color; slick cover)
nn-Included with educational kit on foods, ...in Nutrition Adventures nn (1980) ...and the Nutrition Know-How Revue nn (1983) 3.00

ORB (Magazine)
Orb Publishing: 1974 - No. 6, Mar/Apr 1976 (B&W/color)
1-1st app. Northern Light & Kadaver, both series begin 5 10 15 30 50 70
2,3 (72 pgs.) 3 6 9 16 23 30
4-6 (60 pgs.): 4,5-origin Northern Light 2 4 6 10 14 18
NOTE: ***Allison** a-1-3. **Gene Day** a-1-6. **P. Hsu** a-4-6. **Steacy** s/a-3,4.*

ORBIT
Eclipse Books: 1990 - No. 3, 1990 ($4.95, 52 pgs., squarebound)
1-3: Reprints from Isaac Asimov's Science Fiction Magazine; 1-Dave Stevens-c, Bolton-a. 3-Bolton-c/a, Yeates-a 5.00

ORBITER
DC Comics (Vertigo): 2003 ($24.95, hardcover with dust jacket)
HC-Warren Ellis-s/Colleen Doran-a 25.00
SC-(2004, $17.95) Warren Ellis-s/Colleen Doran-a 18.00

ORCHID
Dark Horse Comics: Oct, 2011 - No. 12, Jan, 2013 ($1.00/$3.50)
1-Tom Morello-s/Scott Hepburn-a; covers by Carnevale & Fairey 3.00
2-12-($3.50) Carnevale-c 3.50

ORCS!
BOOM! Studios (kaboom!): Feb, 2021 - Present ($4.99)
1-Christine Larsen-s/a 5.00

ORDER, THE (cont'd from Defenders V2#12)
Marvel Comics: Apr, 2002 - No. 6, Sept, 2002 ($2.25, limited series)
1-6: 1-Haley-a/Duffy & Busiek-s. 3-Avengers-c/app. 4-Jurgens-a 3.00

ORDER, THE (The Initiative following Civil War)
Marvel Comics: Sept, 2007 - No. 10, Jun, 2008 ($2.99)
1-10-California's Initiative team; Fraction-s/Kitson-a/c 3.00
... Vol. 1: The Next Right Thing TPB (2008, $14.99) r/#1-7 15.00

ORIENTAL HEROES
Jademan Comics: Aug, 1988 - No. 55, Feb, 1993 ($1.50/$1.95, 68 pgs.)
1,55 5.00
2-54 4.00

ORIGINAL ADVENTURES OF CHOLLY & FLYTRAP, THE
Image Comics: Feb, 2006 - No. 2, June, 2006 ($5.99, limited series)
1,2-Arthur Suydam-s/a; interview with Suydam and art pages 6.00

ORIGINAL ASTRO BOY, THE
Now Comics: Sept, 1987 - No. 20, Jun, 1989 ($1.50/$1.75)
1-20-All have Ken Steacy painted-c/a 5.00

ORIGINAL BLACK CAT, THE
Recollections: Oct. 6, 1988 - No. 9, 1992 ($2.00, limited series)
1-9: Elias-r; 1-Bondage-c. 2-Murphy Anderson-c 4.00

ORIGINAL DICK TRACY, THE

Original Sin #3.4 © MAR

Orion #1 © DC

The Orville: Launch Day #1 © 20Fx

	GD	VG	FN	VF	VF/NM	NM-
	2.0	4.0	6.0	8.0	9.0	9.2

Gladstone Publishing: Sept, 1990 - No. 5, 1991 ($1.95, bi-monthly, 68pgs.)

1-5: 1-Vs. Pruneface. 2-& the Evil influence; begin $2.00-c 4.00

NOTE: *#1 reprints strips 7/16/43 - 9/30/43. #2 reprints strips 12/1/46 - 2/2/47. #3 reprints 8/31/46 - 11/14/46. #4 reprints 9/17/45 - 12/23/45. #5 reprints 6/10/46 - 8/28/46.*

ORIGINAL DOCTOR SOLAR, MAN OF THE ATOM, THE
Valiant: Apr, 1995 ($2.95, one-shot)

1-Reprints Doctor Solar, Man of the Atom #1,5; Bob Fugitani-r; Paul Smith-c; afterword by Seaborn Adamson 4.00

ORIGINAL E-MAN AND MICHAEL MAUSER, THE
First Comics: Oct, 1985 - No. 7, April, 1986 ($1.75/$2.00, Baxter paper)

1-6: 1-Has r-/Charlton's E-Man, Vengeance Squad. 2-Shows #4 in indicia by mistake 3.00
7-($2.00, 44 pgs.)-Staton-a 4.00

ORIGINAL GHOST RIDER, THE
Marvel Comics: July, 1992 - No. 20, Feb, 1994 ($1.75)

1-20: 1-7-r/Marvel Spotlight #5-11 by Ploog w/new-c. 3-New Phantom Rider (former Night Rider) back-ups begin by Ayers. 4-Quesada-c(p). 8-Ploog-c. 8,9-r/Ghost Rider #1,2. 10-r/Marvel Spotlight #12. 11-18,20-r/Ghost Rider #3-12. 19-r/Marvel Two-in-One #8 3.00

ORIGINAL GHOST RIDER RIDES AGAIN, THE
Marvel Comics: July, 1991 - No. 7, Jan, 1992 ($1.50, limited series, 52 pgs.)

1-7: 1-r/Ghost Rider #68(origin),69 w/covers. 2-7: R/ G.R. #70-81 w/covers 4.00

ORIGINAL MAGNUS ROBOT FIGHTER, THE
Valiant: Apr, 1995 ($2.95, one-shot)

1-Reprints Magnus, Robot Fighter 4000 #2; Russ Manning-r; Rick Leonardi-c; afterword by Seaborn Adamson 5.00

ORIGINAL MARVEL ZOMBIES, THE: MARVEL TALES
Marvel Comics: Dec, 2020 ($7.99, one-shot)

1-Reprints Ultimate Fantastic Four #21-23 and Marvel Zombies #1; Macchio foreword 8.00

ORIGINAL NEXUS GRAPHIC NOVEL (See First Comics Graphic Novel #19)

ORIGINALS, THE
DC Comics (Vertigo): 2004 ($24.95/$17.99, B&W graphic novel)

HC (2004, $24.95) Dave Gibbons-s/a 25.00
SC (2005, $17.99) 18.00

ORIGINAL SHIELD, THE
Archie Enterprises, Inc.: Apr, 1984 - No. 4, Oct, 1984

1-4: 1,2-Origin Shield; Ayers p-1-4, Nebres c-1,2 5.00

ORIGINAL SIN
Marvel Comics: No. 0, Jun, 2014 - No. 8, Nov, 2014 ($4.99/$3.99, limited series)

0-($4.99) Origin of the Watcher re-told; Nova (Sam Alexander) app.; Waid-s/Cheung-a 5.00
1-($4.99) The Watcher is murdered; Aaron-s/Deodato-a 5.00
2-7-($3.99) 5-Nick Fury's origin. 7-Thor loses use of his hammer 4.00
8-($4.99) Murderer revealed; new Watcher begins 5.00
Annual 1 (12/14, $4.99) Fury and Howard Stark in 1958; Cisic-a/Tedesco-c 5.00
#3.1 - #3.4 (Hulk vs. Iron Man) ($3.99, 8/14 - 10/14) Flashback to the Gamma bomb 4.00
#5.1 - #5.5 (Thor & Loki: The Tenth Realm) ($3.99, 9/14 - 11/14) Angela revealed as Thor's sister; Aaron & Ewing-s 4.00

ORIGINAL SINS (Secrets from the Watcher's Eyes unleashed in Original Sin #3)
Marvel Comics: Aug, 2014 - No. 5, Oct, 2014 ($3.99, limited series)

1-5-Short stories; Young Avengers in all issue; The Hood apps. 1-Deathlok prelude. 5-Secret of Dum Dum Dugan 4.00

ORIGINAL SWAMP THING SAGA, THE (See DC Special Series #2, 14, 17, 20)

ORIGINAL TUROK, SON OF STONE, THE
Valiant: Apr, 1995 - No. 2, May, 1995 ($2.95, limited series)

1,2: 1-Reprints Turok, Son of Stone #24,25,42; Alberto Gioletti-r; Rags Morales-c; afterword by Seaborn Adamson. 2-Reprints Turok, Son of Stone #24,33; Gioletti-r; McKone-c 4.00

ORIGIN OF GALACTUS (See Fantastic Four #48-50)
Marvel Comics: Feb, 1996 ($2.50, one-shot)

1-Lee & Kirby reprints w/pin-ups 4.00

ORIGIN OF THE DEFIANT UNIVERSE, THE
Defiant Comics: Feb, 1994 ($1.50, 20 pgs., one-shot)

1-David Lapham, Adam Pollina & Alan Weiss-a; Weiss-c 5.00

NOTE: *The comic was originally published as Defiant Genesis and was distributed at the 1994 Philadelphia ComicCon.*

ORIGINS
BOOM! Studios: Nov, 2020 - No. 6 ($3.99, limited series)

1-4-Clay McLeod Chapman-s/Jakub Rebelka-a 4.00

ORIGINS OF MARVEL COMICS (Also see Fireside Book Series)
Marvel Comics: July, 2010 ($3.99, one-shot)

1-Single page origins of prominent Marvel characters; text and art by various 4.00
...: X-Men (11/10, $3.99) single page origins of X-Men and other mutants; s/a-various 4.00

ORIGIN II (Sequel to Wolverine: The Origin)
Marvel Comics: Feb, 2014 - No. 5, Jun, 2014 ($4.99/$3.99, limited series)

1-($4.99) Gillen-s/Adam Kubert-a/c; acetate overlay on cover; set in 1907 5.00
2-5-($3.99) Sabretooth app. 4.00

ORION (Manga)
Dark Horse Comics: Sept, 1992 - No. 6, July, 1993 ($2.95/$3.95, B&W, bimonthly, lim. series)

1-6: 1,2,6-Squarebound: 1-Masamune Shirow-c/a/s in all 4.00

ORION (See New Gods)
DC Comics: June, 2000 - No. 25, June, 2002 ($2.50)

1-14-Simonson-s/a. 3-Back-up story w/Miller-a. 4-Gibbons-a back-up. 7-Chaykin back-up. 8-Loeb/Liefeld back-up. 10-A. Adams back-up-a 12-Jim Lee back-up-a. 13-JLA-c/app.; Byrne-a 3.00
15-($3.95) Black Racer app.; back-up story w/J.P. Leon-a 4.00
16-24-Simonson-s/a: 19-Joker: Last Laugh x-over 3.00
25-($3.95) Last issue; Mister Miracle-c/app. 4.00
The Gates of Apocalypse (2001, $12.95, TPB) r/#1-5 & various short-s 13.00

ORORO: BEFORE THE STORM (Storm from X-Men)
Marvel Comics: Aug, 2005 - No. 4, Nov, 2005 ($2.99, limited series)

1-4-Barberi-a/Sumerak-s; young Storm in Egypt 3.00
... Digest (2006, $6.99) r/#1-4 7.00

ORPHAN AGE
AfterShock Comics.: Apr, 2019 - No. 5, Aug, 2019 ($3.99)

1-5-Ted Anderson-s/Nuno Plati-a 4.00

ORPHAN BLACK (Based on the BBC TV show)
IDW Publishing: Feb, 2015 - No. 5, Jun, 2015 ($3.99)

1-6: Multiple covers on all. 1-Kudranski-a; spotlight on Sarah. 2-Spotlight on Helena. 3-Alison. 4-Cosima. 5-Rachel 4.00
... #1: IDW's Greatest Hits (6/18, $1.00) r/#1 3.00

ORPHAN BLACK: CRAZY SCIENCE
IDW Publishing: Jun, 2018 ($3.99, unfinished limited series)

1-Heli Kennedy-s/Fico Ossio-a; 3 covers 4.00

ORPHAN BLACK: DEVIATIONS
IDW Publishing: Mar, 2017 - No. 6, Aug, 2017 ($4.99/$3.99)

1-($4.99) Kennedy-s/Nichols-a; what if Beth wasn't hit by the train; multiple covers 5.00
2-6-($3.99) Kennedy-s/Nichols-a 4.00

ORPHAN BLACK: HELSINKI
IDW Publishing: Nov, 2015 - No. 5, Mar, 2016 ($3.99)

1-5: Multiple covers on all. 1-Alan Quah-a 4.00

ORVILLE, THE (Based on the 2017 sci-fi TV show)
Dark Horse Comics: Jul, 2019 - No. 4, Oct, 2019 ($3.99, limited series)

1-4: 1,2-New Beginnings; Goodman-s/Cabeza-a. 3,4-The Word of Avis; the Krill app. 4.00

ORVILLE, THE (Based on the 2017 sci-fi TV show)
Dark Horse Comics: Sept, 2020 - No. 4, Dec, 2020 ($3.99, limited series)

1-4: 1,2-Launch Day; Goodman-s/Cabeza-a; the Krill app. 3,4-Heroes 4.00

OSBORN (Green Goblin)
Marvel Comics: Jan, 2011 - No. 5, Jun, 2011 ($3.99, limited series)

1-5-Deconnick-s/Rios-a/Oliver-c 4.00

OSBORN JOURNALS (See Spider-Man titles)
Marvel Comics: Feb, 1997 ($2.95, one-shot)

1-Hotz-c/a 3.00

OSCAR COMICS (Formerly Funny Tunes; Awful...#11 & 12) (Also see Cindy Comics)
Marvel Comics: No. 24, Spring, 1947 - No. 10, Apr, 1949; No. 13, Oct, 1949

	GD	VG	FN	VF	VF/NM	NM-
24(#1, Spring, 1947)	30	60	90	177	289	400
25(#2, Sum, 1947)-Wolverton-a plus Kurtzman's "Hey Look"	31	62	93	182	296	410
26(#3)-Same as regular #3 except #26 was printed over in black ink with #3 appearing on-c below the over print	20	40	60	120	165	270
3-9,13: 8-Margie app.	20	40	60	120	165	270
10-Kurtzman's "Hey Look"	23	46	69	134	220	305

OSWALD THE RABBIT (Also see New Fun Comics #1)
Dell Publishing Co.: No. 21, 1943 - No. 1268, 12-2/61-62 (Walter Lantz)

Oswald the Rabbit FC #183 © W. Lantz

Our Army at War #159 © DC

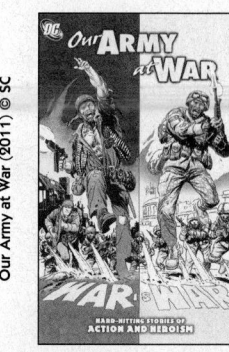

Our Army at War (2011) © SC

	GD 2.0	VG 4.0	FN 6.0	VF 8.0	VF/NM 9.0	NM- 9.2
Four Color 21(1943)	40	80	120	296	673	1050
Four Color 39(1943)	27	54	81	194	435	675
Four Color 67(1944)	16	32	48	112	249	385
Four Color 102(1946)-Kelly-a, 1 pg.	14	28	42	94	207	320
Four Color 143,183	9	18	27	59	117	175
Four Color 225,273	7	14	21	46	86	125
Four Color 315,388	6	12	18	40	73	105
Four Color 458,507,549,593	5	10	15	35	63	90
Four Color 623,697,792,894,979,1268	5	10	15	33	57	80

OSWALD THE RABBIT (See The Funnies, March of Comics #7, 38, 53, 67, 81, 95, 111, 126, 141, 156, 171, 186, New Funnies & Super Book #8, 20)

OTHER DEAD, THE
IDW Publishing: Sept, 2013 - No. 6, Feb, 2014 ($3.99)

1-6-Zombie animals; Ortega-s/Mui-a. 1-Variant-c by Dorman. 2-6-Pres. Obama app. 4.00

OTHER HISTORY OF THE DC UNIVERSE, THE
DC Comics (Black Label): Jan, 2021 - No. 5 ($6.99, 10-3/4" x 8-1/2", lim. series)

1,2-Ridley-s/Camuncoli & Cucchi-a; two covers by Camuncoli & Jamal Campbell. 1-Black Lightning origin and history. 2-History of Mal Duncan & Bumblebee 7.00

OTHER SIDE, THE
DC Comics (Vertigo): Dec, 2006 - No. 5, Apr, 2007 ($2.99, limited series)

1-5-Soldiers from both sides of the Vietnam War; Aaron-s/Stewart-a/c 3.00
TPB (2007, $12.99) r/#1-5; sketch pages, Stewart's travelogue to Saigon 13.00

OTHERWORLD
DC Comics (Vertigo): May, 2005 - No. 7, Nov, 2005 ($2.99)

1-7-Phil Jimenez-s/a(p) 3.00
...: Book One TPB (2006, $19.99) r/#1-7; cover gallery 20.00

OUR ARMY AT WAR (Becomes Sgt. Rock #302 on; also see Army At War)
National Periodical Publications: Aug, 1952 - No. 301, Feb, 1977

	GD 2.0	VG 4.0	FN 6.0	VF 8.0	VF/NM 9.0	NM- 9.2
1	241	482	723	1988	4494	7000
2	104	208	312	832	1866	2900
3,4: 4-Krigstein-a	77	154	231	616	1383	2150
5-7	56	112	168	448	999	1550
8-11,14-Krigstein-a	53	106	159	416	933	1450
12,15-20	46	92	138	350	788	1225
13-Krigstein-c/a; flag-c	56	112	168	448	999	1550
21-31: Last precode (2/55)	33	66	99	238	532	825
32-40	29	58	87	209	467	725
41-60: 51-1st S.A. issue. 57,60-Grey tone-c	26	52	78	182	404	625
61-70: 61-(8/57) Pre-Sgt. Rock Easy Co.-c/s. 67-Minor Sgt. Rock prototype	24	48	72	168	372	575
71-80	22	44	66	154	340	525
81-(4/59) "The Rock of Easy" - Sgt. Rock prototype. Part of lead-up trio to 1st definitive Sgt. Rock. Story features a character named "Sgt. Rocky" as a "4th grade rate" sergeant (three stripes/chevrons) who is referred to as "The Rock of Easy". Editor also promises more stories of "...Rock-like Sergeant". Andru & Esposito-a/Haney-s	350	700	1050	2975	6738	10,500
82-(5/59) "Hold up Easy"- 1st app. of a Sgt. Rock. Part of lead-up trio to 1st definitive Sgt. Rock. Character named Sgt. Rock appears in a supporting "motivator" role as a "4th grade rate" sergeant (three stripes/chevrons) in six panels in six page story; Haney-s/Drucker-a	136	272	408	1088	2444	3800
83-(6/59) "The Rock and Wall" - 1st true appearance of Sgt. Rock. Sgt. Rock finally introduced as a Master Sergeant (three chevrons and three rockers) and is main character of story. 1st specific narration that defines the "Rock of Easy" as Sgt. Rock. 1st actual "Sgt. Rock" collaboration between creators Robert Kanigher and Joe Kubert	900	1800	2700	7600	17,800	28,000
84-(7/59) "Laughter on Snakehead Hill" - 2nd appearance of Sgt. Rock. Story advances true Sgt. Rock continuity in 13-page title story featuring Sgt. Rock and Easy Co.; Kanigher-s/Novick-a/Kubert-c	93	186	279	744	1672	2600
85-Origin & 1st app. Ice Cream Soldier	71	142	213	568	1284	2000
86,87-Early Sgt. Rock; Kubert-a	54	108	162	432	966	1500
88-1st Sgt. Rock-c; Kubert-c/a	72	144	216	583	1267	1950
89-"No Shot From Easy!" story; Heath-c	45	90	135	333	754	1175
90-Kubert-c/a; How Rock got his stripes	80	160	240	648	1399	2150
91-All-Sgt. Rock issue; Grandenetti-c/Kubert-a	123	246	369	984	2217	3450
92,94,96-99: 97-Regular Kubert-c begin	33	66	99	238	532	825
93-1st Zack Nolan	37	74	111	274	612	950
95-1st app. Bulldozer	42	84	126	311	706	1100
100	46	92	138	357	805	1250
101,108,113: 101-1st app. Buster. 113-1st app. Wildman & Jackie Johnson	27	54	81	189	420	650
102-104,106,107,109,110,114,116-120: 104-Nurse Jane-c/s. 109-Pre Easy Co. Sgt. Rock-s. 118-Sunny injured	24	48	72	168	372	575
105-1st app. Junior	31	62	93	223	499	775
111-1st app. Wee Willie & Sunny	34	68	102	245	548	850
112-Classic Easy Co. roster-c	70	140	210	560	1255	1950
115-Rock revealed as orphan; 1st x-over Mlle. Marie. 1st Sgt. Rock's battle family	31	62	93	223	499	775
121-125	16	32	48	112	249	385
126-1st app. Canary; grey tone-c	26	52	78	182	404	625
127-2nd all-Sgt. Rock issue; 1st app. Little Sure Shot	27	54	81	194	435	675
128-Training & origin Sgt. Rock; 1st Sgt. Krupp	38	76	114	285	641	1000
129-139: 138-1st Sparrow. 141-1st Shaker	15	30	45	103	227	350
140-3rd all-Sgt. Rock issue	17	34	51	119	265	410
141-150: 147,148-Rock becomes a General	11	22	33	76	163	250
151-Intro. Enemy Ace by Kubert (2/65), black-c	46	92	138	340	770	1200
152-4th all-Sgt. Rock issue	14	28	42	96	211	325
153-2nd app. Enemy Ace (4/65)	20	40	60	138	307	475
154,156,157,159-161,165-167: 157-2 pg. centerfold spread pin-up as part of story. 159-1st Nurse Wendy Winston-c/s. 165-2nd Iron Major	10	20	30	64	132	200
155-3rd app. Enemy Ace (6/65)(see Showcase)	14	28	42	96	211	325
158-Book-length Sgt. Rock story; origin & 1st app. Iron Major(9/65), formerly Iron Captain; flashback to death of Rock's brother Josh	11	22	33	72	154	235
162,163-Viking Prince x-over in Sgt. Rock	10	20	30	69	147	225
164-Giant G-19	15	30	45	103	227	350
168-1st Unknown Soldier app.; referenced in Star-Spangled War Stories #157; (Sgt. Rock x-over) (6/66)	30	60	90	216	483	750
169,170	8	16	24	56	108	160
171-176,178-181: 171-1st Mad Emperor	8	16	24	51	96	140
177-(80 pg. Giant G-32)	10	20	30	64	132	200
182,183,186-Neal Adams-a. 186-Origin retold	9	18	27	57	111	165
184-Wee Willie dies	9	18	27	61	123	185
185,187,188,193-195,197-199	6	12	18	41	76	110
189,191,192,196: 189-Intro. The Teen-age Underground Fighters of Unit 3. 196-Hitler cameo	6	12	18	42	79	115
190-(80 pg. Giant G-44)	8	16	24	54	102	150
200-12 pg. Rock story told in verse; Evans-a	7	14	21	44	82	120
201,202,204-207: 201-Krigstein-r/#14. 204,205-All reprints; no Sgt. Rock. 207-Last 12¢ cover	5	10	15	34	60	85
203-(80 pg. Giant G-56)-All-r, Sgt. Rock story	7	14	21	48	89	130
208-215	4	8	12	27	44	60
216,229-(80 pg. Giants G-68, G-80): 216-Has G-58 on-c by mistake	6	12	18	40	73	105
217-219: 218-1st U.S.S. Stevens	4	8	12	25	40	55
220-Classic dinosaur/Sgt. Rock-c/s	5	10	15	30	50	70
221-228,230-234: 231-Intro/death Rock's brother. 234-Last 15¢ issue	3	6	9	21	33	45
235-239,241: 52 pg. Giants	4	8	12	27	44	60
240-Neal Adams-a; 52 pg. Giant	5	10	15	31	53	75
242-Also listed as DC 100 Page Super Spectacular #9	9	18	27	58	114	170
243-246: (All 52 pgs.) 244-No Adams-a	4	8	12	25	40	55
247-250,254-268,270: 247-Joan of Arc	3	6	9	15	22	28
251-253-Return of Iron Major	3	6	9	16	24	32
269,275-(100 pgs.)	5	10	15	31	53	75
271,272,274,276-279	3	6	9	14	19	24
273-Crucifixion-c	3	6	9	16	24	32
280-(68 pgs.)-200th app. Sgt. Rock; reprints Our Army at War #81,83	4	8	12	22	35	48
281-299,301: 295-Bicentennial cover	2	4	6	13	18	22
300-Sgt. Rock-s by Kubert (2/77)	3	6	9	15	22	28

NOTE ***Alcala*** *a-251.* ***Drucker*** *a-27, 67, 68, 79, 82, 83, 96, 164, 177, 203, 212, 243r, 244, 269r, 275r, 280r.* ***Evans*** *a-165-175, 200, 266, 269, 270, 274, 276, 278, 280.* ***Glanzman*** *a-218, 220, 222, 223, 225, 227, 230-232, 238-241, 244, 247, 248, 256-259, 261, 265-267, 271, 282, 283, 298.* ***Grandenetti*** *c-91,120.* ***Grell*** *a-287.* ***Heath*** *a-44, 50, 164, & most 176-281.* ***Kubert*** *a-38, 59, 67, 68 & most issues from 83-165, 171, 233, 236, 267, 275, 300; c-84, 280.* ***Maurer*** *a-233, 237, 239, 240, 45, 280, 284, 288, 290, 291, 295.* ***Severin*** *a-236, 252, 265, 267, 269r, 272.* ***Toth*** *a-235, 241, 254.* ***Wildey*** *a-283-285, 287p.* ***Wood*** *a-249.*

OUR ARMY AT WAR
DC Comics: Nov, 2010 ($3.99, one-shot)

1-Joe Kubert-c; Mike Marts-s/Victor Ibáñez-a 4.00
TPB (2011, $14.99) r/#1 and other 2010 war one-shots Weird War Tales #1, Our Fighting Forces #1, G.I. Combat #1 and Star-Spangled War Stories #1 15.00

OUR FIGHTING FORCES
National Per. Publ./DC Comics: Oct-Nov, 1954 - No. 181, Sept-Oct, 1978

	GD 2.0	VG 4.0	FN 6.0	VF 8.0	VF/NM 9.0	NM- 9.2
1-Grandenetti-c/a	145	290	435	1196	2698	4200
2	54	108	162	432	966	1500
3-Kubert-c; last precode issue (3/55)	44	88	132	326	738	1150

Our Fighting Forces #11 © DC

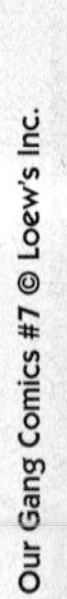

Our Gang Comics #7 © Loew's Inc.

Outcast #32 © Robert Kirkman

	GD 2.0	VG 4.0	FN 6.0	VF 8.0	VF/NM 9.0	NM- 9.2
4,5	37	74	111	274	612	950
6-9: 7-1st S.A. issue	31	62	93	223	479	735
10-Wood-a	32	64	96	230	515	800
11-19	25	50	75	175	388	600
20-Grey tone-c (4/57)	35	70	105	252	564	875
21-30	20	40	60	141	313	485
31-40	18	36	54	122	271	420
41-Unknown Soldier tryout	24	48	72	168	372	575
42-44	17	34	51	117	259	400
45-1st app. of Gunner & Sarge, app. thru #94	59	118	177	472	1061	1650
46	27	54	81	189	420	650
47	19	38	57	129	287	445
48,50	15	30	45	103	227	350
49-1st Pooch	28	56	84	202	451	700
51-Grey tone-c	26	52	78	182	404	625
52-64: 64-Last 10¢ issue	12	24	36	82	179	275
65-70: 66-Panel inspired a famous Roy Lichtenstein painting	10	20	30	64	132	200
71-Classic grey tone-c; Pooch fires machine gun; panel inspired a famous Roy Lichtenstein painting	25	50	75	175	388	600
72-80	8	16	24	56	108	160
81-90	7	14	21	44	82	120
91-98: 95-Devil-Dog begins, ends #98.	6	12	18	37	66	95
99-Capt. Hunter begins, ends #106	7	14	21	46	86	125
100	6	12	18	38	69	100
101-105,107-120: 116-Mlle. Marie app. 120-Last 12¢ issue	5	10	15	30	50	70
106-Hunters Hellcats begin	5	10	15	31	53	75
121,122: 121-Intro. Heller	4	8	12	27	44	60
123-The Losers (Capt. Storm, Gunner & Sarge, Johnny Cloud) begin	9	18	27	60	120	180
124-132: 132-Last 15¢ issue	4	8	12	23	37	50
133-137 (Giants). 134-Toth-a	4	8	12	27	44	60
138-145,147-150: 149-Frank Thorne-c	3	6	9	16	23	30
146-Classic "Burma Sky" story; Toth-a/Goodwin-s	3	6	9	17	26	35
151-162-Kirby a(p)	3	6	9	18	28	38
163-180	3	6	9	14	19	24
181-Last issue	3	6	9	16	23	30
... (War One-Shot) 1 (11/10, $3.99) The Losers app.; B. Clay Moore-s/Chad Hardin-a						4.00

NOTE: ***N. Adams*** *c-147.* ***Drucker*** *a-28, 37, 39, 42-44, 49, 53, 133r.* ***Evans*** *a-149, 164-174, 177-181.* ***Glanzman*** *a-125-128, 132, 134, 138-141, 143, 144.* ***Heath*** *a-2, 16, 18, 28, 41, 44, 49, 50, 59, 64, 114, 135-138r; c-51.* ***Kirby*** *a-151-162p; c-152-159.* ***Kubert*** *c/a in many issues.* ***Maurer*** *a-135.* ***Redondo*** *a-166.* ***Severin*** *a-123-130, 131i, 132-150.*

OUR FIGHTING FORCES GIANT
DC Comics: 2020 ($4.99, one-shot, 100 pgs., squarebound, Mass Market & Direct Market editions exist with different covers)

	GD	VG	FN	VF	VF/NM	NM-
1-New stories of The Unknown Soldier, Batwoman, and Batman w/Jim Lee-a and reprints from Men of War #4-7; art by Corben, Winslade, Kolins and others						5.00

OUR FIGHTING MEN IN ACTION (See Men In Action)

OUR FLAG COMICS
Ace Magazines: Aug, 1941 - No. 5, April, 1942

	GD	VG	FN	VF	VF/NM	NM-
1-Captain Victory, The Unknown Soldier (intro.) & The Three Cheers begin	295	590	885	1918	3259	4600
2-Origin The Flag (patriotic hero); 1st app?	174	348	522	1114	1907	2700
3-5: 5-Intro & 1st app. Mr. Risk	161	322	483	1030	1765	2500

NOTE: ***Anderson*** *a-1, 4.* ***Mooney*** *a-1, 2; c-2.*

OUR GANG COMICS (With Tom & Jerry #39-59; becomes Tom & Jerry #60 on; based on film characters)
Dell Publishing Co.: Sept-Oct, 1942 - No. 59, June, 1949

	GD	VG	FN	VF	VF/NM	NM-
1-Our Gang & Barney Bear by Kelly, Tom & Jerry, Pete Smith, Flip & Dip, The Milky Way begin (all 1st app.)	106	212	318	859	1855	2850
2-Benny Burro begins (#2 by Kelly)	38	76	114	285	641	1000
3-5	23	46	69	161	356	550
6-Bumbazine & Albert only app. by Kelly	29	58	87	209	467	725
7-No Kelly story	16	32	48	110	243	375
8-Benny Burro begins by Barks	38	76	114	285	641	1000
9-Barks-a(2): Benny Burro & Happy Hound; no Kelly story	34	68	102	245	548	850
10-Benny Burro by Barks	25	50	75	175	388	600
11-1st Barney Bear & Benny Burro by Barks (5-6/44); Happy Hound by Barks	34	68	102	242	541	840
12-20	16	32	48	107	236	365
21-30: 30-X-Mas-c	11	22	33	77	166	255
31-36-Last Barks issue	9	18	27	63	129	195
37-40	7	14	21	44	82	120
41-50	6	12	18	38	69	100
51-57	5	10	15	35	63	90
58,59-No Kelly art or Our Gang stories	5	10	15	33	57	80
Our Gang Volume 1 (Fantagraphics Books, 2006, $12.95, TPB) r/Our Gang stories written and by Walt Kelly from #1-8; Leonard Maltin intro.; Jeff Smith-c						13.00
Our Gang Volume 2 (Fantagraphics Books, 2007, $12.95, TPB) r/Our Gang stories written and by Walt Kelly from #9-15; Steve Thompson intro.; Jeff Smith-c						13.00
Our Gang Volume 3 (Fantagraphics Books, 2008, $14.99, TPB) r/Our Gang stories written and by Walt Kelly from #16-23; Steve Thompson intro.; Jeff Smith-c						15.00

NOTE: ***Barks*** *art in part only.* ***Barks*** *did not write Barney Bear stories #30-34. (See March of Comics #3, 26). Early issues have photo back-c.*

OUR LADY OF FATIMA (Also see Fatima...)
Catechetical Guild Educational Society: 3/11/55 (15¢) (36 pgs.)

	GD	VG	FN	VF	VF/NM	NM-
395	6	12	18	28	34	40

OUR LOVE (True Secrets #3 on? or Romantic Affairs #3 on?)
Marvel Comics (SPC): Sept, 1949 - No. 2, Jan, 1950

	GD	VG	FN	VF	VF/NM	NM-
1-Photo-c	28	56	84	168	274	380
2-Photo-c	16	32	48	98	154	210

OUR LOVE STORY
Marvel Comics Group: Oct, 1969 - No. 38, Feb, 1976

	GD	VG	FN	VF	VF/NM	NM-
1	12	24	36	79	170	260
2-4,6-8,10,11	5	10	15	34	60	85
5-Steranko-a	11	22	33	75	160	245
9,12-Kirby-a	5	10	15	35	63	90
13-(10/71, 52 pgs.)	6	12	18	38	69	100
14-New story by Gary Fredrich & Tarpe' Mills	5	10	15	34	60	85
15-20,27:27-Colan/Everett-a(r?); Kirby/Colletta-r	4	8	12	27	44	60
21-26,28-37	4	8	12	25	40	55
38-Last issue	4	8	12	28	47	65

NOTE: ***J. Buscema*** *a-1-3, 5-7, 9, 13r, 16r, 19r(2), 21r, 22r(2), 23r, 34r, 35r; c-11, 13, 16, 22, 23, 24, 27, 35.* ***Colan*** *a-3-6, 21r(#6), 22r, 23r(#3), 24r(#4), 27; c-19.* ***Katz*** *a-17.* ***Maneely*** *a-13r.* ***Romita*** *a-13r; c-1, 2, 4-6.* ***Weiss*** *a-16, 17, 29r(#17).*

OUR MEN AT WAR
DC Comics: Aug/Sept 1952

nn - Ashcan comic, not distributed to newsstands, only for in-house use. Cover art is All Star Western #60, interior being Detective Comics #181 (a FN/VF copy sold for $1195 in 2012)

OUR MISS BROOKS
Dell Publishing Co.: No. 751, Nov, 1956

	GD	VG	FN	VF	VF/NM	NM-
Four Color 751-Photo-c	8	16	24	52	99	145

OUR SECRET (Exciting Love Stories)(Formerly My Secret)
Superior Comics Ltd.: No. 4, Nov, 1949 - No. 8, Jun, 1950

	GD	VG	FN	VF	VF/NM	NM-
4-Kamen-a; spanking scene	32	64	96	188	307	425
5,6,8	15	30	45	88	137	185
7-Contains 9 pg. story intended for unpublished Ellery Queen #5; lingerie panels	15	30	45	92	144	195

OUTCAST, THE
Valiant: Dec, 1995 ($2.50, one-shot)

	GD	VG	FN	VF	VF/NM	NM-
1-Breyfogle-a.						3.00

OUTCAST BY KIRKMAN & AZACETA
Image Comics: Jun, 2014 - No. 48 ($2.99/$3.99)

	GD	VG	FN	VF	VF/NM	NM-
1-Kirkman-s/Azaceta-a/c						10.00
2						5.00
3-47: 25-(25¢-c)						4.00

OUTCASTS
DC Comics: Oct, 1987 - No. 12, Sept, 1988 ($1.75, limited series)

	GD	VG	FN	VF	VF/NM	NM-
1-12: John Wagner & Alan Grant scripts in all						3.00

OUTER DARKNESS
Image Comics (Skybound): Nov, 2018 - Present ($3.99)

	GD	VG	FN	VF	VF/NM	NM-
1-12-John Layman-s/Afu Chan-a						4.00
.../ Chew (3/20 - Present, $3.99) 1-3-Tony Chu brought to the future						4.00

OUTER LIMITS, THE (TV)
Dell Publishing Co.: Jan-Mar, 1964 - No. 18, Oct, 1969 (Most painted-c)

	GD	VG	FN	VF	VF/NM	NM-
1	12	24	36	81	176	270
2-5	6	12	18	42	79	115
6-10	6	12	18	37	66	95
11-18: 17-Reprints #1. 18-r/#2	5	10	15	33	57	80

OUTER SPACE (Formerly This Magazine Is Haunted, 2nd Series)

Outlanders #22 © DH

Outlaw Nation #1 © Delano & Sudzuka

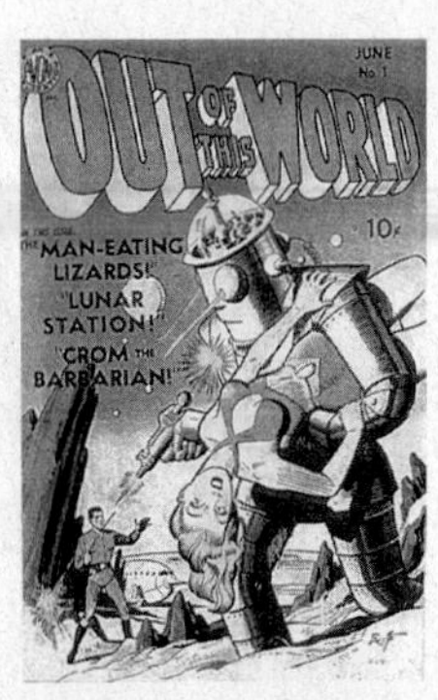

Out of This World #1 © AVON

	GD 2.0	VG 4.0	FN 6.0	VF 8.0	VF/NM 9.0	NM- 9.2

Charlton Comics: No. 17, May, 1958 - No. 25, Dec, 1959; Nov, 1968

	GD	VG	FN	VF	VF/NM	NM-
17-Williamson/Wood-a	15	30	45	84	127	170
18-20-Ditko-a	25	50	75	150	245	340
21-Ditko-c	20	40	60	120	195	270
22-25	15	30	45	83	124	165
V2#1(11/68)-Ditko-a, Boyette-c	5	10	15	33	57	80

OUT FOR BLOOD
Dark Horse: Sept, 1999 - No. 4, Dec, 1999 ($2.95, B&W, limited series)

	GD	VG	FN	VF	VF/NM	NM-
1-4-Kelley Jones-c; Erskine-a						3.00

OUTLANDERS (Manga)
Dark Horse Comics: Dec, 1988 - No. 33, Sept,1991 ($2.00-$2.50, B&W, 44 pgs.)

	GD	VG	FN	VF	VF/NM	NM-
1-33: Japanese Sci-fi manga						4.00

OUTLAW (See Return of the...)

OUTLAWED
Marvel Comics: May, 2020 ($4.99, one-shot)

	GD	VG	FN	VF	VF/NM	NM-
1-Eve L. Ewing-s/Kim Jacinto-a; teen heroes banned; leads into Champions #1 (2020)	1	3	4	6	8	10

OUTLAW FIGHTERS
Atlas Comics (IPC): Aug, 1954 - No. 5, Apr, 1955

	GD	VG	FN	VF	VF/NM	NM-
1-Tuska-a	17	34	51	100	158	215
2-5: 5-Heath-c/a, 7 pgs.	13	26	39	72	101	130

NOTE: ***Colan** a-4. **Hartley** a-3. **Heath** c/a-5. **Maneely** c-2, 4. **Pakula** a-2. **Reinman** a-2, 4. **Tuska** a-1-3.*

OUTLAW KID, THE (1st Series; see Wild Western)
Atlas Comics (CCC No. 1-11/EPI No. 12-29): Sept, 1954 - No. 19, Sept, 1957

	GD	VG	FN	VF	VF/NM	NM-
1-Origin; The Outlaw Kid & his horse Thunder begin; Black Rider app.	39	78	117	231	378	525
2-Black Rider app.	17	34	51	100	158	215
3-7,9: 3-Wildey-a(3)	14	28	42	80	115	150
8-Williamson/Woodbridge-a, 4 pgs.	14	28	42	82	121	160
10-Williamson-a	14	28	42	82	121	160
11-17,19: 13-Baker text illo. 15-Williamson text illo (unsigned)	11	22	33	62	86	110
18-Williamson/Mayo-a	12	24	36	67	94	120

NOTE: ***Berg** a-4, 7, 13. **Maneely** c-1-3, 5-8, 11-13, 15, 16, 18. **Pakula** a-3. **Severin** c-10, 17, 19. **Shores** a-1. **Wildey** a-1(3), 2-8, 10, 11, 12(4), 13(4), 15-19(4 each); c-4.*

OUTLAW KID, THE (2nd Series)
Marvel Comics Group: Aug, 1970 - No. 30, Oct, 1975

	GD	VG	FN	VF	VF/NM	NM-
1-Reprints; 1-Orlando-r, Wildey-r(3)	4	8	12	23	37	50
2,3,9: 2-Reprints. 3,9-Williamson-a(r)	2	4	6	13	18	22
4-7: 7-Last 15¢ issue	2	4	6	11	16	20
8-Double size (52 pgs.); Crandall-r	3	6	9	16	24	32
10-Origin	3	6	9	19	30	40
11-20: new-a in #10-16	2	4	6	13	18	22
21-30: 27-Origin-r/#10	2	4	6	9	13	16

NOTE: ***Ayers** a-10, 27r. **Berg** a-7, 25r. **Everett** a-2(2 pgs.). **Gil Kane** c-10, 11, 15, 27r, 28. **Roussos** a-10i, 27i(r). **Severin** c-1, 9, 20, 25. **Wildey** r-1-4, 6-9, 19-22, 25, 26. **Williamson** a-28r. **Woodbridge/Williamson** a-9r.*

OUTLAW NATION
DC Comics (Vertigo): Nov, 2000 - No. 19, May, 2002 ($2.50)

	GD	VG	FN	VF	VF/NM	NM-
1-19-Fabry painted-c/Delano-s/Sudzuka-a						3.00
TPB (Image Comics, 11/06, $15.99) B&W reprint of #1-19; Delano intro.						16.00

OUTLAW PRINCE, THE
Dark Horse Books: 2011 ($12.99, SC, 80 pgs.)

	GD	VG	FN	VF	VF/NM	NM-
SC-Adaptation of ERB's The Outlaw of Torn; Rob Hughes-s/Thomas Yeates painted-a; origin/1st app. Norman of Torn; intro. & death of Lady Maud						13.00
Deluxe HC Limited Edition ($49.99, 112 pgs.) Bonus 2 articles (approx. 200 signed)						50.00

OUTLAWS
D. S. Publishing Co.: Feb-Mar, 1948 - No. 9, June-July, 1949

	GD	VG	FN	VF	VF/NM	NM-
1-Violent & suggestive stories	39	78	117	231	378	525
2-Ingels-a; Baker-a	39	78	117	231	378	525
3,5,6: 3-Not Frazetta. 5-Sky Sheriff by Good app. 6-McWilliams-a	18	36	54	109	172	235
4-Orlando-a	19	38	57	112	179	245
7,8-Ingels-a in each	26	52	78	156	256	355
9-(Scarce)-Frazetta-a (7 pgs.)	52	104	156	328	552	800

NOTE: *Another #3 was printed in Canada with **Frazetta** art "Prairie Jinx," 7 pgs.*

OUTLAWS, THE (Formerly Western Crime Cases)
Star Publishing Co.: No. 10, May, 1952 - No. 13, Sep, 1953; No. 14, Apr, 1954

	GD	VG	FN	VF	VF/NM	NM-
10-L.B. Cole-c	24	48	72	140	230	330
11-14-L.B. Cole-c. 14-Reprints Western Thrillers #4 (Fox) w/new L.B. Cole-c; Kamen, Feldstein-r	19	38	57	109	172	245

OUTLAWS
DC Comics: Sept, 1991 - No. 8, Apr, 1992 ($1.95, limited series)

	GD	VG	FN	VF	VF/NM	NM-
1-8: Post-apocalyptic Robin Hood.						3.00

OUTLAWS OF THE WEST (Formerly Cody of the Pony Express #10)
Charlton Comics: No. 11, 7/57 - No. 81, 5/70; No. 82, 7/79 - No. 88, 4/80

	GD	VG	FN	VF	VF/NM	NM-
11	8	16	24	44	57	70
12,13,15-17,19,20	6	12	18	27	33	38
14-(68 pgs., 2/58)	9	18	27	50	65	80
18-Ditko-a	10	20	30	56	76	95
21-30	3	6	9	16	23	30
31-50: 34-Gunmaster app.	2	4	6	13	18	22
51-63,65,67-70: 54-Kid Montana app.	2	4	6	10	14	18
64,66: 64-Captain Doom begins (1st app.). 68-Kid Montana series begins	2	4	6	13	18	22
71-79: 73-Origin & 1st app. The Sharp Shooter, last app. #74. 75-Last Capt. Doom	2	4	6	9	12	15
80,81-Ditko-a	2	4	6	13	18	22
82-88						6.00
64,79(Modern Comics-r, 1977, '78)						6.00

OUTLAWS OF THE WILD WEST
Avon Periodicals: 1952 (25¢, 132 pgs.) (4 rebound comics)

	GD	VG	FN	VF	VF/NM	NM-
1-Wood back-c; Kubert-a (3 Jesse James-r)	41	82	123	256	428	600

OUTLAW TRAIL (See Zane Grey 4-Color 511)

OUT OF SANTA'S BAG (See March of Comics #10 in the Promotional Comics section)

OUT OF THE NIGHT (The Hooded Horseman #18 on)
Amer. Comics Group (Creston/Scope): Feb-Mar, 1952 - No. 17, Oct-Nov, 1954

	GD	VG	FN	VF	VF/NM	NM-
1-Williamson/LeDoux-a (9 pgs.); ACG's 1st editor's page	97	194	291	521	1061	1500
2-Williamson-a (5 pgs.)	60	120	180	381	653	925
3,5-10: 9-Sci/Fic story	39	78	117	240	395	550
4-Williamson-a (7 pgs.)	50	100	150	315	533	750
11-17: 13-Nostrand-a? 17-E.C. Wood swipe	31	62	93	186	303	420

NOTE: ***Landau** a-14, 16, 17. **Shelly** a-12.*

OUT OF THE SHADOWS
Standard Comics/Visual Editions: No. 5, July, 1952 - No. 14, Aug, 1954

	GD	VG	FN	VF	VF/NM	NM-
5-Toth-p; Moreira, Tuska-a; Roussos-c	77	154	231	493	847	1200
6-Toth/Celardo-a; Katz-a(2)	48	96	144	302	514	725
7,9: 7-Jack Katz-c/a(2). 9-Crandall-a(2)	42	84	126	265	445	625
8-Katz shrunken head-c	129	258	387	826	1413	2000
10-Spider-c; Sekowsky-a	48	96	144	302	514	725
11-Toth-a, 2 pgs.; Katz-a; Andru-c	42	84	126	265	445	625
12-Toth/Peppe-a(2); Katz-a	50	100	150	315	533	750
13-Cannabalism story; Sekowsky-a; Roussos-c	52	104	156	328	552	775
14-Toth-a	42	84	126	265	445	625

OUT OF THE VORTEX (Comics' Greatest World:... #1-4)
Dark Horse Comics: Oct., 1993 - No. 12, Oct, 1994 ($2.00, limited series)

	GD	VG	FN	VF	VF/NM	NM-
1-12: 1-Foil logo. 4-Dorman-c(p). 6-Hero Zero x-over. 12-$2.50-c						3.00

NOTE: ***Art Adams** c-7. **Golden** c-8. **Mignola** c-2. **Simonson** c-3. **Zeck** c-10.*

OUT OF THIS WORLD
Charlton Comics: Aug, 1956 - No. 16, Dec, 1959

	GD	VG	FN	VF	VF/NM	NM-
1	37	74	111	222	361	500
2	18	36	54	107	169	230
3-6-Ditko-c/a (3) each	36	72	108	211	343	475
7-(2/58, 15¢, 68 pgs.)-Ditko-c/a(4)	39	78	117	236	388	540
8-(5/58, 15¢, 68 pgs.)-Ditko-a(2)	38	76	117	231	378	525
9,10,12,16-Ditko-a	26	52	78	154	252	350
11-Ditko c/a (3)	34	68	102	204	332	460
13,15	14	28	42	81	118	155
14-Matt Baker-a, 7 pg. story	15	30	45	88	137	185

NOTE: ***Ditko** c-3-12, 16. **Reinman** a-10.*

OUT OF THIS WORLD
Avon Periodicals: June, 1950; Aug, 1950

	GD	VG	FN	VF	VF/NM	NM-
1-Kubert-a(2) (one reprinted/Eerie #1, 1947) plus Crom the Barbarian by Gardner Fox & John Giunta (origin); Fawcette-c	148	296	444	947	1624	2300
1-(8/50) Reprint; no month on cover	82	164	246	528	902	1275

OUT OF THIS WORLD ADVENTURES
Avon Periodicals: July, 1950 - No. 2, Apr, 1951 (25¢ sci-fi pulp magazine with 32-page color comic insert)

Outsiders #9 © DC

Over the Garden Wall: Hollow Town #1 © CN

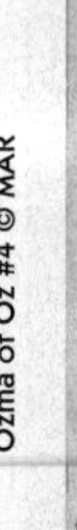

Ozma of Oz #4 © MAR

GD VG FN VF VF/NM NM-
2.0 4.0 6.0 8.0 9.0 9.2

1-Kubert-a(2); Crom the Barbarian by Fox & Giunta; text stories by Cummings, Van Vogt, del Rey, Chandler 95 190 285 603 1039 1475
2-Kubert-a plus The Spider God of Akka by Gardner Fox & John Giunta pulp magazine w/comic insert; Wood-a (21 pgs.); mentioned in **SOTI,** page 120 61 122 183 390 670 950

OUT OUR WAY WITH WORRY WART
Dell Publishing Co.: No. 680, Feb, 1956
Four Color 680 5 10 15 31 53 75

OUTPOSTS
Blackthorne Publishing: June, 1987 - No. 4, 1987 ($1.25)
1-4: 1-Kaluta-c(p) 3.00

OUTSIDERS, THE
DC Comics: Nov, 1985 - No. 28, Feb, 1988
1 4.00
2-28: 18-26-Batman returns. 21-Intro. Strike Force Kobra; 1st app. Clayface IV. 22-E.C. parody; Orlando-a. 21- 25-Atomic Knight app. 27,28-Millennium tie-ins 3.00
Annual 1 (12/86, $2.50), Special 1 (7/87, $1.50) 4.00
NOTE: ***Aparo** a-1-7, 9-14, 17-22, 25, 26; c-1-7, 9-14, 17, 19-26.* ***Byrne** a-11.* ***Bolland** a-6, 18; c-16.* ***Ditko** a-13p.* ***Erik Larsen** a-24, 27 28; c-27, 28.* ***Morrow** a-12.*

OUTSIDERS
DC Comics: Nov, 1993 - No. 24, Nov, 1995 ($1.75/$1.95/$2.25)
1-11,0,12-24: 1-Alpha; Travis Charest-c. 1-Omega; Travis Charest-c. 5-Atomic Knight app. 8-New Batman-c/story. 11-(9/94)-Zero Hour. 0-(10/94).12-(11/94). 21-Darkseid cameo. 22-New Gods app. 3.00

OUTSIDERS (See Titans/Young Justice: Graduation Day)(Leads into Batman and the Outsiders)
DC Comics: Aug, 2003 - No. 50, Nov, 2007 ($2.50/$2.99)
1-Nightwing, Arsenal, Metamorpho app.; Winick-s/Raney-a 5.00
2-Joker and Grodd app. 4.00
3-33: 3-Joker-c. 5,6-ChrisCross-a. 8-Huntress app. 9,10-Capt. Marvel Jr. app. 24,25-X-over with Teen Titans. 26,27-Batman & old Outsiders 3.00
34-50: 34-One Year Later. 36-Begin $2.99-c. 37-Superman app. 44-Red Hood app. 3.00
Annual 1 (6/07, $3.99) McDaniel-a; Black Lightning app. 4.00
.../Checkmate: Checkout TPB (2008, $14.99) r/#47-49 & Checkmate #13-15 15.00
... Double Feature (10/03, $4.95) r/#1,2 5.00
...: Crisis Intervention TPB (2006, $12.99) r/#29-33 13.00
...: Looking For Trouble TPB (2004, $12.95) r/#1-7 & Teen Titans/Outsiders Secret Files & Origins 2003; intro. by Winick 13.00
...: Pay As You Go TPB (2007, $14.99) r/#42-46 & Annual #1 15.00
...: Sum of All Evil TPB (2004, $14.95) r/#8-15 15.00
...: The Good Fight TPB (2006, $14.99) r/#34-41 15.00
...: Wanted TPB (2005, $14.99) r/#16-23 15.00

OUTSIDERS, THE (See Batman and the Outsiders for #1-14 and #40)
DC Comics: No. 15, Apr, 2009 - No. 39, Jun, 2011 ($2.99)
15-23,26-39: 15-Alfred assembles a new team; Garbett-a. 17-19-Deathstroke app. 3.00
24,25-($3.99) Blackest Night; Terra rises as a Black Lantern 4.00
...: The Deep TPB (2009, $14.99) r/#15-20 & Batman and the Outsiders Special #1 15.00
...: The Great Divide TPB (2011, $17.99) r/#32-40; cover gallery 18.00
...: The Hunt TPB (2010, $14.99) r/#21-25 15.00
...: The Road to Hell TPB (2010, $14.99) r/#26-31 15.00

OUTSIDERS: FIVE OF A KIND (Bridges Outsiders #49 & 50)
DC Comics: Oct, 2007 ($2.99, weekly limited series)
...Katana/Shazam! (part 2 of 5) - Barr-s/Sharpe-a 3.00
...Metamorpho/Aquaman (part 4 of 5) - Wilson-s/Middleton-a 3.00
...Nightwing/Captain Boomerang (part 1 of 5) - DeFilippis & Weir-s/Willams-a 3.00
...Thunder/Martian Manhunter (part 3 of 5) - Bedard-s/Turnbull-a; Grayven app. 3.00
...Wonder Woman/Grace (part 5 of 5) - Andreyko-s/Richards-a 3.00
TPB (2008, $14.99) r/series & Outsiders #50 15.00

OUT THERE
DC Comics(Cliffhanger): July, 2001 - No. 18, Aug, 2003 ($2.50/$2.95)
1-Humberto Ramos-c/a; Brian Augustyn-s 3.00
1-Variant-c by Carlos Meglia 4.00
2-18: 3-Variant-c by Bruce Timm. 9-Begin $2.95-c 3.00
...: The Evil Within TPB (2002, $12.95) r/#1-6; Ramos sketch pages 13.00

OVERKILL: WITCHBLADE/ ALIENS/ DARKNESS/ PREDATOR
Image Comics/Dark Horse Comics: Dec, 2000 - No. 2, 2001 ($5.95)
1,2-Jenkins-s/Lansing, Ching & Benitez-a 6.00

OVERTAKEN
Aspen/MLT: Aug, 2013 - No. 5, Jan, 2018 ($1.00/$3.99)

GD VG FN VF VF/NM NM-
2.0 4.0 6.0 8.0 9.0 9.2

1-5-Mastromauro-s/Lorenzana-a; multiple covers on each. 1-($1.00-c). 2-(3/16) 4.00

OVER THE EDGE
Marvel Comics: Nov, 1995 - No. 10, Aug, 1996 (99¢)
1-10: 1,6,10-Daredevil-c/story. 2,7-Dr. Strange-c/story. 3-Hulk-c/story. 4,9-Ghost Rider-c/story. 5-Punisher-c/story. 8-Elektra-c/story 3.00

OVER THE GARDEN WALL (Based on the Cartoon Network mini-series)
Boom Entertainment (KaBOOM!): Aug, 2015 - No. 4, Nov, 2015 ($3.99, limited series)
1-4-Pat McHale-s/Jim Campbell-a; multiple covers on each 4.00
Special 1 (11/14, $4.99)-Prequel to the Cartoon Network mini-series; McHale-s/Campbell-a 5.00

OVER THE GARDEN WALL: HOLLOW TOWN (Cartoon Network)
Boom Entertainment (KaBOOM!): Sept, 2018 - No. 5, Jan, 2019 ($3.99, limited series)
1-5-Celia Lowenthal-s/Jorge Monlongo-a; multiple covers on each 4.00

OVER THE GARDEN WALL ONGOING (Cartoon Network)
Boom Entertainment (KaBOOM!): Apr, 2016 - No. 20, Nov, 2018 ($3.99, limited series)
1-20: 1-4-Two stories in each; Campbell-s/Burgos-a & Levari-s/McGee-a; multiple covers 4.00
... 2017 Special 1 (9/17, $7.99) Three stories; covers by Mercado & Derek Kim 8.00

OVER THE GARDEN WALL: SOULFUL SYMPHONIES (Cartoon Network)
Boom Entertainment (KaBOOM!): Aug, 2019 - No. 5, Dec, 2019 ($3.99, limited series)
1-5-Birdie Willis-s/Rowan MacColl-a; multiple covers on each 4.00

OVERWATCH: TRACER – LONDON CALLING (Based on the video game)
Dark Horse Comics: Dec, 2020 - No. 5, ($3.99, limited series)
1-3-Mariko Tamaki-s/Babs Tarr-a 4.00

OWL, THE (See Crackajack Funnies #25, Popular Comics #72 and Occult Files of Dr. Spektor #22)
Gold Key: April, 1967; No. 2, April, 1968
1-Written by Jerry Siegel; '40s super hero 5 10 15 34 60 85
2 4 8 12 28 47 65

OWL, THE (See Project Superpowers)
Dynamite Entertainment: 2013 - No. 4, 2013 ($3.99, limited series)
1-4-Golden Age hero in modern times; Krul-s/H.K. Michael-a; covers by Ross & Syaf 4.00

OZ (See First Comics Graphic Novel, Marvel Treaury Of Oz & MGM's Marvelous...)

OZ
Caliber Press: 1994 - 1997 ($2.95, B&W)
0-20: 0-Released between #10 & #11 3.00
1 ($5.95)-Limited Edition; double-c 6.00
...Specials: Freedom Fighters. Lion. Scarecrow. Tin Man 3.00

OZARK IKE
Dell Publishing Co./Standard Comics B11 on: Feb, 1948; Nov, 1948 - No. 24, Dec, 1951; No. 25, Sept, 1952
Four Color 180(1948-Dell) 11 22 33 73 157 240
B11, B12, 13-15 14 28 42 76 108 140
16-25 12 24 36 67 94 120

OZ: DAEMONSTORM
Caliber Press: 1997 ($3.95, B&W, one-shot)
1 4.00

OZMA OF OZ (Dorothy Gale from Wonderful Wizard of Oz)
Marvel Comics: Jan, 2011 - No. 8, Sept, 2011 ($3.99, limited series)
1-6-Eric Shanower-s/Skottie Young-a/c 4.00
Oz Primer (5/11, $3.99) creator interviews and character profiles 4.00

OZ: ROMANCE IN RAGS
Caliber Press: 1996 ($2.95, B&W, limited series)
1-3, ..Special 3.00

OZ SQUAD
Brave New Worlds/Patchwork Press: 1992 - No. 4, 1994 ($2.50/$2.75, B&W)
1-4-Patchwork Press 3.00

OZ SQUAD
Patchwork Press: Dec, 1995 - No. 10, 1996 ($3.95/$2.95, B&W)
1-($3.95) 4.00
2-10 3.00

OZ: STRAW AND SORCERY
Caliber Press: 1997 ($2.95, B&W, limited series)
1-3 3.00

OZ-WONDERLAND WARS, THE
DC Comics: Jan, 1986 - No. 3, March, 1986 (Mini-series)(Giants)

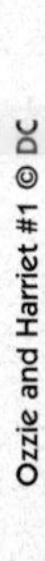

Ozzie and Harriet #1 © DC

Panic #5 © WMG

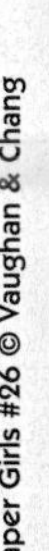
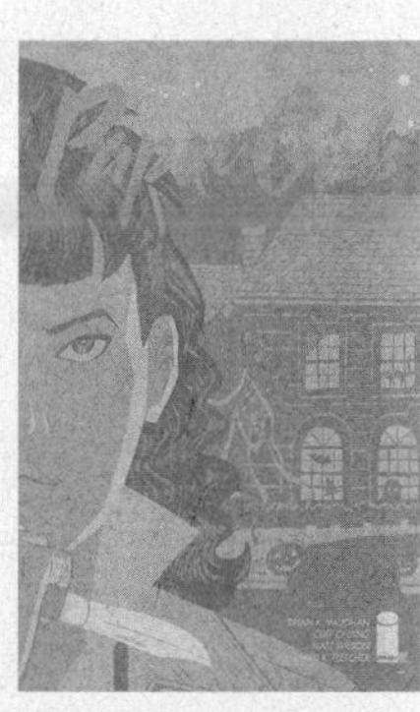
Paper Girls #26 © Vaughan & Chang

GD 2.0 | VG 4.0 | FN 6.0 | VF 8.0 | VF/NM 9.0 | NM- 9.2

1-3-Capt. Carrot app.; funny animals 4.00

OZZIE & BABS (TV Teens #14 on)
Fawcett Publications: Dec, 1947 - No. 13, Fall, 1949

1-Teen-age 15 30 45 88 137 185
2 10 20 30 56 76 95
3-13 9 18 27 50 65 80

OZZIE AND HARRIET (The Adventures of... on cover) (Radio)
National Periodical Publications: Oct-Nov, 1949 - No. 5, June-July, 1950

1-Photo-c 106 212 318 678 1164 1650
2 52 104 156 328 552 775
3-5 42 84 126 265 445 625

OZZY OSBOURNE (Todd McFarlane Presents)
Image Comics (Todd McFarlane Prod.): June, 1999 ($4.95, magazine-sized)

1-Bio, interview and comic story; Ormston painted-a; Ashley Wood-c
1 2 3 5 6 8

PACIFIC COMICS GRAPHIC NOVEL (See Image Graphic Novel)

PACIFIC PRESENTS (Also see Starslayer #2, 3)
Pacific Comics: Oct, 1982 - No. 2, Apr, 1983; No. 3, Mar, 1984 - No. 4, Jun, 1984

1-Chapter 3 of The Rocketeer; Stevens-c/a; Bettie Page model
3 6 9 14 19 24
2-Chapter 4 of The Rocketeer (4th app.); nudity; Stevens-c/a
2 4 6 11 16 20
3,4: 3-1st app. Vanity 3.00
NOTE: ***Conrad** a-3, 4; c-3. **Ditko** a-1-3; c-1(1/2). **Dave Stevens** a-1, 2; c-1(1/2), 2.*

PACIFIC RIM: AFTERMATH
Legendary Comics: Jan, 2018 - No. 5, May, 2018 ($3.99)

1-5-Cavan Scott-s 4.00

PACIFIC RIM: TALES FROM THE DRIFT
Legendary Comics: Nov, 2015 - No. 4, Apr, 2016 ($3.99)

1-4-Beachum & Fialkov-s/Marz-a 4.00

PACIFIC RIM: TALES FROM YEAR ZERO
Legendary Comics: Jun, 2013 ($24.99, HC graphic novel)

HC - Prequel to the 2013 movie; Beacham-s/Alex Ross-c; art by various 25.00

PACT, THE
Image Comics: Feb, 1994 - No. 3, June, 1994 ($1.95, limited series)

1-3: Valentino co-scripts & layouts 3.00

PACT, THE
Image Comics: Apr, 2005 - No. 4, Jan, 2006 ($2.99/$2.95)

1-4: Invincible, Shadowhawk, Firebreather & Zephyr team-up. 1-Valentino-s/a 3.00

PAGEANT OF COMICS (See Jane Arden & Mopsy)
Archer St. John: Sept, 1947 - No. 2, Oct, 1947

1-Mopsy strip-r 22 44 66 130 213 295
2-Jane Arden strip-r 14 28 42 82 121 160

PAINKILLER JANE
Event Comics: June, 1997 - No. 5, Nov, 1997 ($3.95/$2.95)

1-Augustyn/Waid-s/Leonardi/Palmiotti-a, variant-c 4.00
2-5: Two covers (Quesada, Leonardi) 3.00
0-(1/99, $3.95) Retells origin; two covers 4.00
Essential Painkiller Jane TPB (2007, $19.99) r/#0-5; cover gallery and pin-ups 20.00

PAINKILLER JANE
Dynamite Entertainment: 2006 - No. 3, 2006 ($2.99)

1-3-Quesada & Palmiotti-s/Moder-a. 1-Four covers by Q&P, Moder, Tan and Conner 3.00
Volume #1 TPB (2007, $9.99) r/#1-3; cover gallery and Palmiotti interview 10.00

PAINKILLER JANE
Dynamite Entertainment: No. 0, 2007 - No. 5, 2007 ($3.50)

0-(25¢) Quesada & Palmiotti-s/Moder-a 3.00
1-5-($3.50) 1-Continued from #0; 5 covers. 4,5-Crossover with Terminator 2 #6,7 3.50
Volume #2 TPB (2007, $11.99) r/#0-3; cover gallery 12.00

PAINKILLER JANE / DARKCHYLDE
Event Comics: Oct, 1998 ($2.95, one-shot)

Preview-($6.95) DF Edition, 1-($6.95) DF Edition 7.00
1-Three covers; J.G. Jones-a 3.00

PAINKILLER JANE / HELLBOY
Event Comics: Aug, 1998 ($2.95, one-shot)

1-Leonardi & Palmiotti-a 5.00

GD 2.0 | VG 4.0 | FN 6.0 | VF 8.0 | VF/NM 9.0 | NM- 9.2

PAINKILLER JANE: THE PRICE OF FREEDOM
Marvel Comics (ICON): Nov, 2013 - No. 4, Jan, 2014 ($3.99/$2.99, limited series)

1-($3.99) Palmiotti-s/Santacruz & Lotfi-a; covers by Amanda Conner & Dave Johnson 4.00
2-4-($2.99) Santacruz-a/Conner-c 3.00

PAINKILLER JANE: THE 22 BRIDES
Marvel Comics (ICON): May, 2014 - No. 3, Oct, 2014 ($4.99/$3.99, limited series)

1-($4.99) Palmiotti-s/Santacruz & Fernandez-a; covers by Christian & Conner 5.00
2,3-($3.99) Santacruz-a2-Photo-c. 3-Conner-c 4.00

PAINKILLER JANE VS. THE DARKNESS
Event Comics: Apr, 1997 ($2.95, one-shot)

1-Ennis-s; four variant-c (Conner, Hildebrandts, Quesada, Silvestri) 3.50

PAKLIS
Image Comics: May, 2017 - No. 5 ($5.99/$3.99/$4.99)

1,2,5-($5.99) Serialized anthology by Dustin Weaver-s/a/c 6.00
3-($3.99) Dustin Weaver-s/a/c 4.00
4-($4.99) Dustin Weaver-s/a/c 5.00

PANCHO VILLA
Avon Periodicals: 1950

nn-Kinstler-c 30 60 90 177 289 400

PANDEMICA
IDW Publishing: Sept, 2019 - No. 5, Jan, 2020 ($3.99)

1-5-Jonathan Maberry-s/Alex Sanchez-a 4.00

PANHANDLE PETE AND JENNIFER (TV) (See Gene Autry #20)
J. Charles Laue Publishing Co.: July, 1951 - No. 3, Nov, 1951

1 13 26 39 74 105 135
2,3: 2-Interior photo-cvrs 9 18 27 50 65 80

PANIC (Companion to Mad)
E. C. Comics (Tiny Tot Comics): Feb-Mar, 1954 - No. 12, Dec-Jan, 1955-56

1-Used in Senate Investigation hearings; Elder draws entire E. C. staff; Santa Claus & Mickey Spillane parody 47 94 141 376 601 825
2-Atomic bomb-c 22 44 66 176 281 385
3,4: 3-Senate Subcommittee parody; Davis draws Gaines, Feldstein & Kelly, 1 pg.; Old King Cole smokes marijuana. 4-Infinity-c; John Wayne parody
18 36 54 144 227 310
5-11: 8-Last pre-code issue (5/55). 9-Superman, Smilin' Jack & Dick Tracy app. on-c; has photo of Walter Winchell on-c. 11-Wheedies cereal box-c
16 32 48 128 207 285
12 (Low distribution; thousands were destroyed) 24 48 72 192 309 425
NOTE: ***Davis** a-1-12; c-12. **Elder** a-1-12. **Feldstein** c-1-3, 5. **Kamen** a-1. **Orlando** a-1-9. **Wolverton** c-4, panel-3. **Wood** a-2-9, 11, 12.*

PANIC (Magazine) (Satire)
Panic Publ.: July, 1958 - No. 6, July, 1959; V2#10, Dec, 1965 - V2#12, 1966

1 14 28 42 80 115 150
2-6 9 18 27 50 65 80
V2#10-12: Reprints earlier issues 3 6 9 17 26 35
NOTE: ***Davis** a-3(2 pgs.), 4, 5, 10; c-10. **Elder** a-5. **Powell** a-V2#10, 11. **Torres** a-1-5. **Tuska** a-V2#11.*

PANIC
Gemstone Publishing: March, 1997 - No. 12, Dec, 1999 ($2.50, quarterly)

1-12: E.C. reprints 4.00

PANTHA (See Vampirella-The New Monthly #16,17)

PANTHA (Also see Prophecy)
Dynamite Entertainment: 2012 - No. 6, 2013 ($3.99)

1-6: 1-Jerwa-s/Rodrix-a; covers by Sean Chen & Texiera. 2-6-Texiera-c 4.00

PANTHA: HAUNTED PASSION (Also see Vampirella Monthly #0)
Harris Comics: May, 1997 ($2.95, B&W, one-shot)

1-r/Vampirella #30,31 3.00

PANTHEON
IDW Publishing: Apr, 2010 - No. 5, Aug, 2010 ($3.99)

1-5-Andreyko-s/Molnar-a; co-created by Michael Chiklis 4.00

PAPA MIDNITE (See John Constantine - Hellblazer Special:...)

PAPER GIRLS
Image Comics: Oct, 2015 - No. 30, Jul, 2019 ($2.99/$3.99)

1-20-Brian K. Vaughn-s/Cliff Chiang-a 3.00
21-29-($3.99) 4.00
30-($4.99) Last issue 5.00

Paradise X #4 © MAR

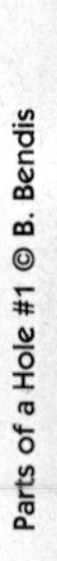

Parts of a Hole #1 © B. Bendis

Pathfinder: Origins #3 © Paizo

GD VG FN VF VF/NM NM-
2.0 4.0 6.0 8.0 9.0 9.2

GD VG FN VF VF/NM NM-
2.0 4.0 6.0 8.0 9.0 9.2

PARADE (See Hanna-Barbera...)

PARADE COMICS (See Frisky Animals on Parade)

PARADE OF PLEASURE
Derric Verschoyle Ltd., London, England: 1954 (192 pgs.) (Hardback book)

By Geoffrey Wagner. Contains section devoted to the censorship of American comic books with illustrations in color and black and white. (Also see **Seduction of the Innocent**).
Distributed in USA by Library Publishers, N. Y. 150 300 450 600 750 900
with dust jacket.... 283 566 849 1132 1416 1700

PARADISE TOO!
Abstract Studios: 2000 - No. 14, 2003 ($2.95, B&W)

1-14-Terry Moore's unpublished newspaper strips and sketches 3.00
Complete Paradise Too TPB (2010, $29.95) r/#1-14 with bonus material 30.00
...: Checking For Weirdos TPB (4/03, $14.95) r/#8-12 15.00
...: Drunk Ducks! TPB (7/02, $15.95) r/#1-7 16.00

PARADISE X (Also see Earth X and Universe X)
Marvel Comics: Apr, 2002 - No. 12, Aug, 2003 ($4.50/$2.99)

0-Ross-c; Braithwaite-a 4.50
1-12-($2.99) Ross-c; Braithwaite-a. 7-Punisher on-c. 10-Kingpin on-c 3.00
...:A (10/03, $2.99) Braithwaite-a; Ross-c 3.00
...:Devils (11/02, $4.50) Sadowski-a; Ross-c 4.50
...:Ragnarok 1,2 (3/02, 4/03; $2.99) Yeates-a; Ross-c 3.00
...:X (11/03, $2.99) Braithwaite-a; Ross-c; conclusion of story 3.00
...:Xen (7/02, $4.50) Yeowell & Sienkiewicz-a; Ross-c 4.50
Earth X Vol. 4: Paradise X Book 1 (2003, $29.99, TPB) r/#0,1-5, ...: Xen; Heralds #1-3 30.00
Vol. 5: Paradise X Book 2 (2004, $29.99, TPB) r/#6-12, Ragnarok #1&2; Devils, A & X 30.00

PARADISE X: HERALDS (Also see Earth X and Universe X)
Marvel Comics: Dec, 2001 - No. 3, Feb, 2002 ($3.50)

1-3-Prelude to Paradise X series; Ross-c; Pugh-a 3.50
Special Edition (Wizard preview) Ross-c 3.00

PARADOX
Dark Visions Publ: June, 1994 - No. 2, Aug, 1994 ($2.95, B&W, mature)

1,2: 1-Linsner-c. 2-Boris-c. 3.00

PARALLAX: EMERALD NIGHT (See Final Night)
DC Comics: Nov, 1996 ($2.95, one-shot, 48 pgs.)

1-Final Night tie-in; Green Lantern (Kyle Rayner) app. 4.00

PARAMOUNT ANIMATED COMICS (See Harvey Comics Hits #60, 62)
Harvey Publications: No. 3, Jun, 1953 - No. 22, Jul, 1956

3-Baby Huey, Herman & Katnip, Buzzy the Crow begin
32 64 96 192 314 435
4-6 15 30 45 85 130 175
7-Baby Huey becomes permanent cover feature; cover title becomes Baby Huey with #9
26 52 78 156 256 355
8-10: 9-Infinity-c 14 28 42 76 108 140
11-22 10 20 30 58 79 100

PARENT TRAP, THE (Disney)
Dell Publishing Co.: No. 1210, Oct-Dec, 1961

Four Color 1210-Movie, Hayley Mills photo-c 9 18 27 58 114 170

PARIAH (Aron Warner's...)
Dark Horse Comics: Feb, 2014 - No. 8, Sept, 2014 ($3.99)

1-8-Aron Warner & Philip Gelatt-s/Brett Weldele-a 4.00

PARLIAMENT OF JUSTICE
Image Comics: Mar, 2003 ($5.95, B&W, one-shot, square-bound)

1-Michael Avon Oeming-c/s; Neil Vokes-a 6.00

PARODY
Armour Publishing: Mar, 1977 - No. 3, Aug, 1977 (B&W humor magazine)

1 3 6 9 15 22 28
2,3: 2-King Kong, Happy Days. 3-Charlie's Angels, Rocky
2 4 6 10 14 18

PAROLE BREAKERS
Avon Periodicals/Realistic #2 on: Dec, 1951 - No. 3, July, 1952

1(#2 on inside)-r-c/Avon paperback #283 (painted-c)
61 122 183 390 670 950
2-Kubert-a; r-c/Avon paperback #114 (photo-c) 47 94 141 296 498 700
3-Kinstler-c 40 80 120 246 411 575

PARTRIDGE FAMILY, THE (TV)(Also see David Cassidy)
Charlton Comics: Mar, 1971 - No. 21, Dec, 1973

1-(2 versions: B&W photo-c & tinted color photo-c) 7 14 21 48 89 130
2-4,6-10 4 8 12 27 44 60
5-Partridge Family Summer Special (52 pgs.); The Shadow, Lone Ranger, Charlie McCarthy, Flash Gordon, Hopalong Cassidy, Gene Autry & others app.
8 16 24 51 96 140
11-21 3 6 9 21 33 45

PARTS OF A HOLE
Caliber Press: 1991 ($2.50, B&W)

1-Short stories & cartoons by Brian Michael Bendis 3.00

PARTS UNKNOWN
Eclipse Comics/FX: July, 1992 - No. 4, Oct, 1992 ($2.50, B&W, mature)

1-4: All contain FX gaming cards 3.00

PARTS UNKNOWN
Image Comics: May, 2000 - Sept, 2000 ($2.95, B&W)

...: Killing Attractions 1 (5/00) Beau Smith-s/Brad Gorby-a 3.00
...: Hostile Takeover 1-4 (6-9/00) 3.00

PASSION, THE
Catechetical Guild: No. 394, 1955

394 8 16 24 44 57 70

PASSOVER (See Avengelyne)
Maximum Press: Dec, 1996 ($2.99, one-shot)

1 3.00

PAST AWAYS
Dark Horse Comics: Mar, 2015 - No. 9, Mar, 2016 ($3.99)

1-9: 1-Matt Kindt-s/Scott Kolins-a; two covers by Kolins & Kindt 4.00

PAT BOONE (TV)(Also see Superman's Girlfriend Lois Lane #9)
National Per. Publ.: Sept-Oct, 1959 - No. 5, May-Jun, 1960 (All have photo-c)

1 42 84 126 265 445 625
2-5: 3-Fabian, Connie Francis & Paul Anka photos on-c. 4-Previews "Journey To The Center Of The Earth". 4-Johnny Mathis & Bobby Darin photos on-c. 5-Dick Clark & Frankie Avalon photos on-c 34 68 102 199 325 450

PATCHES
Rural Home/Patches Publ. (Orbit): Mar-Apr, 1945 - No. 11, Nov, 1947

1-L. B. Cole-c 48 96 144 302 514 725
2 20 40 60 114 182 250
3,4,6,8-11: 6-Henry Aldrich story. 8-Smiley Burnette-c/s (6/47); pre-dates Smiley Burnette #1. 9-Mr. District Attorney story (radio). Leav/Keigstein-a (16 pgs.). 9-11-Leav-c. 10-Jack Carson (radio) c/story; Leav-c. 11-Red Skelton story 17 34 51 103 162 220
5-Danny Kaye-c/story; L.B. Cole-c. 22 44 66 132 216 300
7-Hopalong Cassidy-c/story 20 40 60 118 192 265

PATH, THE (Also see Negation War)
CrossGeneration Comics: Apr, 2002 - No. 23, Apr, 2004 ($2.95)

1-23: 1-Ron Marz-s/Bart Sears-a. 13-Matthew Smith-a begins 3.00

PATHFINDER (Based on the Pathfinder roleplaying game)
Dynamite Entertainment: 2012 - No. 12, 2013 ($3.99)

1-12: 1-Jim Zub-s/Andrew Huerta-a; four covers. 2-12-Multiple covers on each 4.00
... Special 2013 ($4.99, 40 pgs.) Jim Zub-s/Kevin Stokes-a 5.00

PATHFINDER: CITY OF SECRETS (Based on the Pathfinder roleplaying game)
Dynamite Entertainment: 2014 - No. 6, 2014 ($4.99)

1-6-Zub-s/Oliveira-a; Bound-in poster; multiple covers on each 5.00

PATHFINDER: GOBLINS! (Based on the Pathfinder roleplaying game)
Dynamite Entertainment: 2013 - No. 5, 2013 ($3.99)

1-5: Short stories by various; multiple covers on each 4.00

PATHFINDER: HOLLOW MOUNTAIN (Based on the Pathfinder roleplaying game)
Dynamite Entertainment: 2015 - No. 6, 2016 ($4.99)

1-6: 1-Sutter-s/Garcia-a; multiple covers 5.00

PATHFINDER: ORIGINS (Based on the Pathfinder roleplaying game)
Dynamite Entertainment: 2015 - No. 6, 2015 ($4.99)

1-6: 1-Spotlight on Valeros; multiple-c. 2-Kyra. 3-Seoni. 4-Merisiel. 5-Harsk. 6-Ezren 5.00

PATHFINDER: RUNESCARS (Based on the Pathfinder roleplaying game)
Dynamite Entertainment: 2017 - No. 5, 2017 ($3.99/$4.99)

1-($3.99) Schneider-s/Silva-a; multiple covers 4.00
2-5-($4.99) 2,4,5-Sutter-s. 3,5-Schneider-s 5.00

PATHFINDER: SPIRAL OF BONES (Based on the Pathfinder roleplaying game)
Dynamite Entertainment: 2018 - No. 5, 2018 ($4.99)

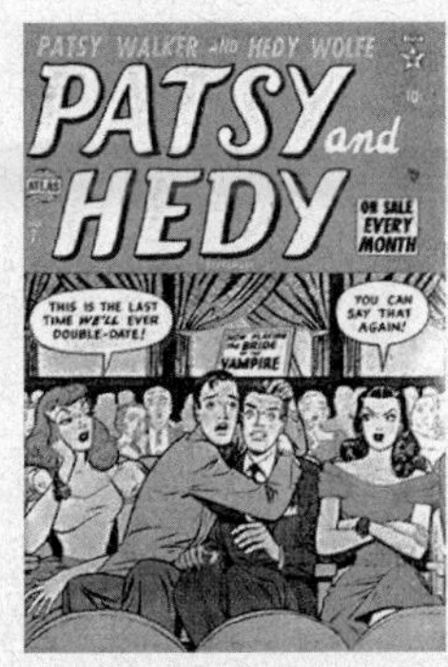

Patsy and Hedy #7 © MAR

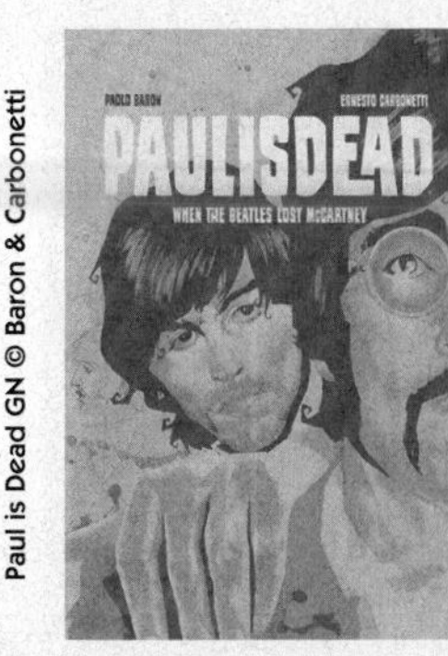

Paul is Dead GN © Baron & Carbonetti

Peacemaker #1 © CC

	GD 2.0	VG 4.0	FN 6.0	VF 8.0	VF/NM 9.0	NM- 9.2
1-5: 1-Frasier-s/Garcia-a; multiple covers; encounter map included in each						5.00

PATHFINDER: WORLDSCAPE (Based on the Pathfinder roleplaying game)
Dynamite Entertainment: 2016 - No. 6, 2017 ($4.99)

	GD	VG	FN	VF	VF/NM	NM-
1-6-Red Sonja, John Carter and Tarzan app.; Jonathan Lau-a						5.00

PATHWAYS TO FANTASY
Pacific Comics: July, 1984

	GD	VG	FN	VF	VF/NM	NM-
1-Barry Smith-c/a; Jeff Jones-a (4 pgs.)						4.00

PATORUZU (See Adventures of...)

PATRIOTS, THE
DC Comics (WildStorm): Jan, 2000 - No. 10, Oct, 2000 ($2.50)

	GD	VG	FN	VF	VF/NM	NM-
1-10-Choi and Peterson-s/Ryan-a						3.00

PATSY & HEDY (Teenage)(Also see Hedy Wolfe)
Atlas Comics/Marvel (GPI/Male): Feb, 1952 - No. 110, Feb, 1967

	GD	VG	FN	VF	VF/NM	NM-
1-Patsy Walker & Hedy Wolfe; Al Jaffee-c	65	130	195	416	708	1000
2	24	48	72	144	237	330
3-10: 3,7,8,9-Al Jaffee-c	21	42	63	124	202	280
11-20: 17,19,20-Al Jaffee-c	18	36	54	103	162	220
21-40	15	30	45	88	137	185
41-50	8	16	24	54	102	150
51-60	8	16	24	51	96	140
61-80,100: 88-Lingerie panel	7	14	21	44	82	120
81-87,89-99,101-110	6	12	18	41	76	110
Annual 1(1963)-Early Marvel annual	12	24	36	79	170	260

PATSY & HER PALS (Teenage)
Atlas Comics (PPI): May, 1953 - No. 29, Aug, 1957

	GD	VG	FN	VF	VF/NM	NM-
1-Patsy Walker	41	82	123	256	428	600
2	20	40	60	118	192	265
3-10	17	34	51	103	162	220
11-29: 24-Everett-c	15	30	45	85	130	175

PATSY WALKER (See All Teen, A Date With Patsy, Girls' Life, Miss America Magazine, Patsy & Hedy, Patsy & Her Pals & Teen Comics)
Marvel/Atlas Comics (BPC): 1945 (no month) - No. 124, Dec, 1965

	GD	VG	FN	VF	VF/NM	NM-
1-Teenage	417	834	1257	2919	5110	7300
2	52	104	156	328	552	775
3,4,6-10	39	78	117	236	388	540
5-Injury-to-eye-c	41	82	123	256	428	600
11,12,15,16,18	25	50	75	147	241	335
13,14,17,19-22-Kurtzman's "Hey Look"	26	52	78	154	252	350
23,24	21	42	63	124	202	280
25-Rusty by Kurtzman; painted-c	27	54	81	158	259	360
26-29,31: 26-31: 52 pgs.	19	38	57	111	176	240
30(52 pgs.)-Egghead Doodle by Kurtzman (1 pg.)	20	40	60	114	182	250
32-57: Last precode (3/55)	17	34	51	100	158	215
58-80,100	9	18	27	59	117	175
81-98: 92,98-Millie x-over	8	16	24	55	105	155
99-Linda Carter x-over	12	24	36	81	176	270
101-124	7	14	21	44	82	120
Fashion Parade 1(1966, 68 pgs.) (Beware cut-out & marked pages)	11	22	33	73	157	240

NOTE: *Painted c-25-28. Anti-Wertham editorial in #21. Georgie app. in #8, 11, 17. Millie app. in #10, 92, 98. Mitzi app. in #11. Rusty app. in #12, 25. Willie app. in #12.* ***Al Jaffee*** *c-44, 47, 49, 51, 57, 58.*

PATSY WALKER, A.K.A. HELLCAT
Marvel Comics: Feb, 2016 - No. 17, Jun, 2017 ($3.99)

	GD	VG	FN	VF	VF/NM	NM-
1-17: 1-Kate Leth-s/Brittney Williams-a; She-Hulk and Tom Hale app. 2-Hedy Wolfe app. 6-Natasha Allegri-a. 6,7-Jessica Jones app. 8-Civil War II tie-in						4.00

PATSY WALKER: HELLCAT
Marvel Comics: Sept, 2008 - No. 5, Feb, 2009 ($2.99, limited series)

	GD	VG	FN	VF	VF/NM	NM-
1-5-Lafuente-a/Kathryn Immonen-s/Stuart Immonen-c; Hellcat joins The Initiative						3.00

PAT THE BRAT (Adventures of Pipsqueak #34 on)
Archie Publications (Radio): June, 1953; Summer, 1955 - No. 4, 5/56; No. 15, 7/56 - No. 33, 7/59

	GD	VG	FN	VF	VF/NM	NM-
nn(6/53)	19	38	57	111	176	240
1(Summer, 1955)	17	34	51	100	158	215
2-4-(5/56) (#5-14 not published). 3-Early Bolling-a	10	20	30	54	72	90
15-(7/56)-33: 18-Early Bolling-a	5	10	15	31	53	75

PAT THE BRAT COMICS DIGEST MAGAZINE
Archie Publications: October, 1980 (95¢)

	GD	VG	FN	VF	VF/NM	NM-
1-Li'l Jinx & Super Duck app.	2	4	6	9	13	16

PATTY CAKE
Permanent Press: Mar, 1995 - No. 9, Jul, 1996 ($2.95, B&W)

	GD	VG	FN	VF	VF/NM	NM-
1-9: Scott Roberts-s/a						3.00

PATTY CAKE
Caliber Press (Tapestry): Oct, 1996 - No. 3, Apr, 1997 ($2.95, B&W)

	GD	VG	FN	VF	VF/NM	NM-
1-3: Scott Roberts-s/a, ...Christmas (12/96)						3.00

PATTY CAKE & FRIENDS
Slave Labor Graphics: Nov, 1997 - Nov, 2000 ($2.95, B&W)

	GD	VG	FN	VF	VF/NM	NM-
Here There Be Monsters (10/97), 1-14: Scott Roberts-s/a						3.00
Volume 2 #1 (11/00, $4.95)						5.00

PATTY POWERS (Formerly Della Vision #3)
Atlas Comics: No. 4, Oct, 1955 - No. 7, Oct, 1956

	GD	VG	FN	VF	VF/NM	NM-
4	19	38	57	112	179	245
5-7	15	30	45	86	133	180

PAT WILTON (See Mighty Midget Comics)

PAUL
Spire Christian Comics (Fleming H. Revell Co.): 1978 (49¢)

	GD	VG	FN	VF	VF/NM	NM-
nn	2	4	6	10	14	18

PAULINE PERIL (See The Close Shaves of...)

PAUL IS DEAD (The Beatles)
Image Comics: Apr, 2020 ($16.99, graphic novel)

	GD	VG	FN	VF	VF/NM	NM-
nn-Speculative fiction about the legend of Paul McCartney's 1966 death						17.00

PAUL REVERE'S RIDE (TV, Disney, see Walt Disney Showcase #34)
Dell Publishing Co.: No. 822, July, 1957

	GD	VG	FN	VF	VF/NM	NM-
Four Color 822-w/Johnny Tremain, Toth-a	7	14	21	49	92	135

PAUL TERRY (See Heckle and Jeckle)

PAUL TERRY'S ADVENTURES OF MIGHTY MOUSE (See Adventures of...)

PAUL TERRY'S COMICS (Formerly Terry-Toons Comics; becomes Adventures of Mighty Mouse No. 126 on)
St. John Publishing Co.: No. 85, Mar, 1951 - No. 125, May, 1955

	GD	VG	FN	VF	VF/NM	NM-
85,86-Same as Terry-Toons #85, & 86 with only a title change; published at same time?; Mighty Mouse, Heckle & Jeckle & Gandy Goose continue from Terry-Toons	13	26	39	72	101	130
87-99	10	20	30	54	72	90
100	10	20	30	58	79	100
101-104,107-125: 121,122,125-Painted-c	9	18	27	52	69	85
105,106-Giant Comics Edition (25¢, 100 pgs.) (9/53 & ?). 105-Little Roquefort-c/story	19	38	57	111	176	240

PAUL TERRY'S MIGHTY MOUSE (See Mighty Mouse)

PAUL TERRY'S MIGHTY MOUSE ADVENTURE STORIES (See Mighty Mouse Adventure Stories)

PAUL THE SAMURAI (See The Tick #4)
New England Comics: July, 1992 - No. 6, July, 1993 ($2.75, B&W)

	GD	VG	FN	VF	VF/NM	NM-
1-6						3.00

PAWNEE BILL
Story Comics (Youthful Magazines?): Feb, 1951 - No. 3, July, 1951

	GD	VG	FN	VF	VF/NM	NM-
1-Bat Masterson, Wyatt Earp app.	15	30	45	86	133	180
2,3: 3-Origin Golden Warrior; Cameron-a	10	20	30	56	76	90

PAYBACKS, THE
Dark Horse Comics: Sept, 2015 - No. 4, Dec, 2015 ($3.99)

	GD	VG	FN	VF	VF/NM	NM-
1-4: 1-Cates & Rahal-s/Shaw-a						4.00

PAY-OFF (This Is the..., ...Crime, ...Detective Stories)
D. S. Publishing Co.: July-Aug, 1948 - No. 5, Mar-Apr, 1949 (52 pgs.)

	GD	VG	FN	VF	VF/NM	NM-
1-True Crime Cases #1,2	34	68	102	206	336	465
2	19	38	57	111	176	240
3-5-Thrilling Detective Stories	15	30	45	90	140	190

PEACEMAKER, THE (Also see Fightin' Five)
Charlton Comics: V3#1, Mar, 1967 - No. 5, Nov, 1967 (All 12¢ cover price)

	GD	VG	FN	VF	VF/NM	NM-
1-Fightin' Five begins	10	20	30	64	132	200
2,3,5	4	8	12	23	37	50
4-Origin The Peacemaker	4	8	12	27	44	60
1,2(Modern Comics reprint, 1978)						6.00

PEACEMAKER (Also see Crisis On Infinite Earths & Showcase '93 #7,9,10)
DC Comics: Jan, 1988 - No. 4, Apr, 1988 ($1.25, limited series)

	GD	VG	FN	VF	VF/NM	NM-
1-Paul Kupperberg-s/Tod Smith-a	2	4	6	8	10	12

Peanuts #1 © UFS

Pearl #12 © Jinxworld

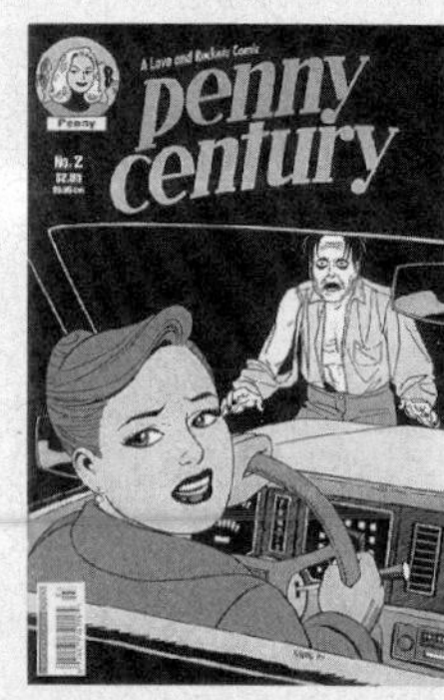

Penny Century #2 © Jaime Hernandez

GD VG FN VF VF/NM NM-
2.0 4.0 6.0 8.0 9.0 9.2

2-4 5.00

PEANUTS (Charlie Brown) (See Tip Top #173 and United Comics #21 for Peanuts 1st comic book app.)(Also see Fritzi Ritz, Nancy & Sluggo, Sparkle & Sparkler, Tip Top, Tip Topper & United Comics)
United Features Syndicate/Dell Publishing Co./Gold Key: 1953-54; No. 878, 2/58 - No. 13, 5-7/62; 5/63 - No. 4, 2/64

	GD 2.0	VG 4.0	FN 6.0	VF 8.0	VF/NM 9.0	NM- 9.2
1(U.F.S.)(1953-54)-Reprints United Features' Strange As It Seems, Willie, Ferdnand (scarce)	1000	2000	3000	7300	12,900	18,500
Four Color 878(#1) (Dell) Schulz-s/a, with assistance from Dale Hale and Jim Sasseville thru #4	148	296	444	1243	2697	4150
Four Color 969,1015('59)	34	68	102	245	548	850
4(2-4/60) Schulz-s/a; one story by Anthony Pocrnich, Schulz's assistant cartoonist	17	34	51	117	259	400
5-13-Schulz-c only; s/a by Pocrnich	15	30	45	101	223	345
1(Gold Key, 5/63)	32	64	96	230	515	800
2-4	13	26	39	86	188	290

PEANUTS (Charlie Brown)
BOOM! Entertainment: No. 0, Nov, 2011 - No. 4, Apr, 2012; V2 No. 1, Aug, 2012 - No. 32, Apr, 2016 ($1.00/$3.99)

0-(11/11, $1.00) New short stories and Sunday page reprints 3.00
1-4: 1-(1/12, $3.99) New short stories and Sunday page reprints; Snoopy sled cover 4.00
1-4-Variant-c with first appearance image. 1-Charlie Brown. 2-Lucy. 3-Linus. 4-Snoopy 6.00
(Volume 2)
1-32: 1-(8/12, "#1 of 4" on-c) 4.00
1-12-Variant-c with first appearance image. 1-Schroeder. 2-Pig-Pen. 4-Woodstock 10.00
... Free Comic Book Day Edition (5/12) Giveaway flip book with Adventure Time 3.00
...: Friends Forever 2016 Special (7/16, $7.99) New and classic short stories 8.00
Happiness is a Warm Blanket, Charlie Brown HC (Boom Entertainment, 3/2011, $19.99) adaptation of new animated special 20.00
It's Tokyo, Charlie Brown (10/12, $13.99, squarebound GN) Vicki Scott-s/a; bonus art 14.00
...: The Snoopy Special 1 (11/15, $4.99) New and classic Snoopy short stories 5.00
...: Where Beagles Dare! GN (9/15, $9.99, SC) Jason Cooper-s/Vicki Scott-a 10.00

PEANUTS HALLOWEEN
Fantagraphics Books: Sept, 2008 (8-1/2" x 5-3/8" ashcan giveaway)

nn-Halloween themed reprints in color and B&W 2.00

PEARL
DC Comics (Jinxworld): Oct, 2018 - No. 12, Oct, 2019 ($3.99)

1-12-Bendis-s/Gaydos-a. 1-Bonus reprint of 1st Bendis Batman-s (Batman Chrons. #21) 4.00

PEBBLES & BAMM BAMM (TV) (See Cave Kids #7, 12)
Charlton Comics: Jan, 1972 - No. 36, Dec, 1976 (Hanna-Barbera)

	GD 2.0	VG 4.0	FN 6.0	VF 8.0	VF/NM 9.0	NM- 9.2
1-From the Flintstones; "Teen Age..." on cover	5	10	15	31	53	75
2-10	3	6	9	16	24	32
11-20	2	4	6	13	18	22
21-36	2	4	6	9	13	16
nn (1973, digest, 100 pgs.) B&W one page gags	3	6	9	17	26	35

PEBBLES & BAMM BAMM (TV)
Harvey Comics: Nov, 1993 - No. 3, Mar, 1994 ($1.50) (Hanna-Barbera)

V2#1-3 3.00
...Giant Size 1 (10/93, $2.25, 68 pgs.)("Summer Special" on-c) 4.00

PEBBLES FLINTSTONE (TV) (See The Flintstones #11)
Gold Key: Sept, 1963 (Hanna-Barbera)

	GD 2.0	VG 4.0	FN 6.0	VF 8.0	VF/NM 9.0	NM- 9.2
1 (10088-309)-Early Pebbles app.	9	18	27	58	114	170

PEDRO (Formerly My Private Life #17; also see Romeo Tubbs)
Fox Feature Syndicate: No. 18, June, 1950 - No. 2, Aug, 1950?

	GD 2.0	VG 4.0	FN 6.0	VF 8.0	VF/NM 9.0	NM- 9.2
18(#1)-Wood-c/a(p)	27	54	81	158	259	360
2-Wood-a?	17	34	51	105	165	225

PEE-WEE PIXIES (See The Pixies)

PELLEAS AND MELISANDE (See Night Music #4, 5)

PENALTY (See Crime Must Pay the...)

PENANCE: RELENTLESS (See Civil War, Thunderbolts and related titles)
Marvel Comics: Nov, 2007 - No. 5 ($2.99)

1-5-Speedball/Penance; Jenkins-s/Gulacy-a. 3-Wolverine app. 3.00
TPB (2008, $13.99) r/#1-5 14.00

PENDRAGON (Knights of... #5 on; also see Knights of...)
Marvel Comics UK, Ltd.: July, 1992 - No. 15, Sept, 1993 ($1.75)

1-15: 1-4-Iron Man app. 6-8-Spider-Man app. 3.00

PENDULUM ILLUSTRATED BIOGRAPHIES
Pendulum Press: 1979 (B&W)

19-355x-George Washington/Thomas Jefferson, 19-3495-Charles Lindbergh/Amelia Earhart, 19-3509-Harry Houdini/Walt Disney, 19-3517-Davy Crockett/Daniel Boone-Redondo-a, 19-3525-Elvis Presley/Beatles, 19-3533-Benjamin Franklin/Martin Luther King Jr, 19-3541-Abraham Lincoln/Franklin D. Roosevelt, 19-3568-Marie Curie/Albert Einstein-Redondo-a, 19-3576-Thomas Edison/Alexander Graham Bell-Redondo-a, 19-3584-Vince Lombardi/Pele, 19-3592-Babe Ruth/Jackie Robinson, 19-3606-Jim Thorpe/Althea Gibson

	GD 2.0	VG 4.0	FN 6.0	VF 8.0	VF/NM 9.0	NM- 9.2
Softback						5.00
Hardback	1	2	3	4	5	7

PENDULUM ILLUSTRATED CLASSICS (Now Age Illustrated)
Pendulum Press: 1973 - 1978 (75¢, 62pp, B&W, 5-3/8x8")
(Also see Marvel Classics)

64-100x(1973)-Dracula-Redondo art, 64-131x-The Invisible Man-Nino art, 64-0968-Dr. Jekyll and Mr. Hyde-Redondo art, 64-1005-Black Beauty, 64-1010-Call of the Wild, 64-1020-Frankenstein, 64-1025-Hucklebury Finn, 64-1030-Moby Dick-Nino-a, 64-1040-Red Badge of Courage, 64-1045-The Time Machine-Nino-a, 64-1050-Tom Sawyer, 64-1055-Twenty Thousand Leagues Under the Sea, 64-1069-Treasure Island, 64-1328(1974)-Kidnapped, 64-1336-Three Musketeers-Nino art, 64-1344-A Tale of Two Cities, 64-1352-Journey to the Center of the Earth, 64-1360-The War of the Worlds-Nino-a, 64-1379-The Greatest Advs. of Sherlock Holmes-Redondo art, 64-1387-Mysterious Island, 64-1395-Hunchback of Notre Dame, 64-1409-Helen Keller-story of my life, 64-1417-Scarlet Letter, 64-1425-Gulliver's Travels, 64-2618(1977)-Around the World in Eighty Days, 64-2626-Captains Courageous, 64-2634-Connecticut Yankee, 64-2642-The Hound of the Baskervilles, 64-2650-The House of Seven Gables, 64-2669-Jane Eyre, 64-2677-The Last of the Mohicans, 64-2685-The Best of O'Henry, 64-2693-The Best of Poe-Redondo-a, 64-2707-Two Years Before the Mast, 64-2715-White Fang, 64-2723-Wuthering Heights, 64-3126(1978)-Ben Hur-Redondo art, 64-3134-A Christmas Carol, 64-3142-The Food of the Gods, 64-3150-Ivanhoe, 64-3169-The Man in the Iron Mask, 64-3177-The Prince and the Pauper, 64-3185-The Prisoner of Zenda, 64-3193-The Return of the Native, 64-3207-Robinson Crusoe, 64-3215-The Scarlet Pimpernel, 64-3223-The Sea Wolf, 64-3231-The Swiss Family Robinson, 64-3851-Billy Budd, 64-386x-Crime and Punishment, 64-3878-Don Quixote, 64-3886-Great Expectations, 64-3894-Heidi, 64-3908-The Iliad, 64-3916-Lord Jim, 64-3924-The Mutiny on Board H.M.S. Bounty, 64-3932-The Odyssey, 64-3940-Oliver Twist, 64-3959-Pride and Prejudice, 64-3967-The Turn of the Screw

	GD 2.0	VG 4.0	FN 6.0	VF 8.0	VF/NM 9.0	NM- 9.2
Softback						6.00
Hardback	1	2	3	5	6	8

NOTE: *All of the above books can be ordered from the publisher; some were reprinted as Marvel Classic Comics #1-12. In 1972 there was another brief series of 12 titles which contained Classics Ill. artwork. They were entitled* ***Now Age Books*** *Illustrated, but can be easily distinguished from later series by the small Classics Illustrated logo at the top of the front cover. The format is the same as the later series. The 48 pg. C.I. art was stretched out to make 62 pgs. After Twin Circle Publ. terminated the Classics Ill. series in 1971, they made a one year contract with Pendulum Press to print these twelve titles of C.I. art. Pendulum was unhappy with the contract, and at the end of 1972 began their own art series, utilizing the talents of the Filipino artist group. One detail which makes this rather confusing is that when they redid the art in 1973, they gave it the same identifying no. as the 1972 series. All 12 of the 1972 C.I. editions have new covers, taken from internal art panels. In spite of their recent age, all of the 1972 C.I. series are very rare. Mint copies would fetch at least $50. Here is a list of the 1972 series, with C.I. title no. counterpart:*

64-1005 (CI#60-A2) 64-1010 (CI#91) 64-1015 (CI-Jr #503) 64-1020 (CI#26)
64-1025 (CI#19-A2) 64-1030 (CI#5-A2) 64-1035 (CI#169) 64-1040 (CI#98)
64-1045 (CI#133) 64-1050 (CI#50-A2) 64-1055 (CI#47) 64-1060 (CI-Jr#535)

PENDULUM ILLUSTRATED ORIGINALS
Pendulum Press: 1979 (In color)

94-4254-Solarman: The Beginning (See Solarman) 6.00

PENDULUM'S ILLUSTRATED STORIES
Pendulum Press: 1990 - No. 72, 1990? (No cover price ($4.95), squarebound, 68 pgs.)

1-72: Reprints Pendulum Ill. Classics series 5.00

PENGUIN: PAIN & PREJUDICE (Batman)
DC Comics: Dec, 2011 - No. 5, Apr, 2012 ($2.99, limited series)

1-5-Hurwitz-s/Kudranski-a/c; Penguin's childhood and rise to power 3.00

PENGUINS OF MADAGASCAR (Based on the DreamWorks movie and TV series)
Ape Entertainment: 2010 - No. 4, 2011 ($3.95, limited series)

1-4-Skipper, Kowalski, Private and Rico app. 4.00

PENGUINS OF MADAGASCAR (Based on the DreamWorks movie and TV series)
Titan Comics: Dec, 2014 - No. 4, Mar, 2015 ($3.99, limited series)

1-4-Skipper, Kowalski, Private and Rico app. 4.00

PENNY
Avon Comics: 1947 - No. 6, Sept-Oct, 1949 (Newspaper reprints)

	GD 2.0	VG 4.0	FN 6.0	VF 8.0	VF/NM 9.0	NM- 9.2
1-Photo & biography of creator	36	72	108	211	343	475
2-5	17	34	51	98	154	210
6-Perry Como photo on-c	17	34	51	103	162	220

PENNY CENTURY (See Love and Rockets)
Fantagraphics Books: Dec, 1997 - No. 7, Jul, 2000 ($2.95, B&W, mini-series)

1-7-Jaime Hernandez-s/a 3.00

PENNY DORA AND THE WISHING BOX
Image Comics: Nov, 2014 - No. 5, Jun, 2015 ($2.99)

1-5-Michael Stock-s/Sina Grace-a 3.00

PENNY DREADFUL (Based on the Showtime TV series)
Titan Comics: Jun, 2016 - No. 5, Nov, 2016 ($3.99)

Penultiman #1 © AHOY Comics

Pep Comics #85 © ACP

Perfect Love #10 (#1) © Z-D

	GD 2.0	VG 4.0	FN 6.0	VF 8.0	VF/NM 9.0	NM- 9.2

1-5: 1-Wilson-Cairns-s/De Martinis-a; multiple covers 4.00

PENNY DREADFUL (Volume 2) (Based on the Showtime TV series)
Titan Comics: May, 2017 - No. 12, Dec, 2018 ($3.99)

1-($4.99)-Chris King-s/Jesús Hervás-a; multiple covers 5.00
2-12-($3.99) 4.00

PENULTIMAN (See Steel Cage #1 for debut)
AHOY Comics: 2020 - No. 5, 2021 ($3.99)

1-5-Tom Peyer-s/Alan Robinson-a 4.00

PEP COMICS (See Archie Giant Series #576, 589, 601, 614, 624)
MLJ Magazines/Archie Publications No. 56 (3/46) on: Jan, 1940 - No. 411, Mar, 1987

Issue	GD	VG	FN	VF	VF/NM	NM-
1-Intro. The Shield (1st patriotic hero) by Irving Novick; origin & 1st app. The Comet by Jack Cole, The Queen of Diamonds & Kayo Ward; The Rocket, The Press Guardian (The Falcon #1 only), Sergeant Boyle, Fu Chang, & Bentley of of Scotland Yard; Robot-c; Shield-c begin	1000	2000	3000	7500	13,500	19,500
2-Origin The Rocket	322	644	966	2254	4027	5800
3-Nazi WWII-c	271	542	813	1734	2967	4200
4-WWII brought to U.S. Capitol building; Wizard cameo; early robot-s	245	490	735	1568	2884	3800
5-Wizard cameo in Shield story	245	490	735	1568	2884	3800
6,7,9,10	200	400	600	1280	2190	3100
8-Last Jack Cole Comet; no Cole-a in #6,7; torture by branding-c	258	516	774	1651	2826	4000
11-Dusty, Shield's sidekick begins (1st app.); last Press Guardian, Fu Chang	219	438	657	1402	2401	3400
12-Origin & 1st app. Fireball (2/41); last Rocket & Queen of Diamonds; Danny in Wonderland begins; bondage-c	232	464	696	1465	2543	3600
13-15: All bondage/torture covers	181	362	543	1158	1979	2800
16-Origin Madam Satan; blood drainage-c	343	686	1029	2400	4200	6000
17-Origin/1st app. The Hangman (7/41); death of The Comet; Comet is revealed as Hangman's brother	649	1298	1947	4738	8369	12,000
18,19,21: 19-WWII Nazi-c. 21-Last Madam Satan	181	362	543	1158	1979	2800
20-Classic Nazi swastika-c; last Fireball	541	1082	1623	3950	6975	10,000
22-Intro. & 1st app. Archie, Betty, & Jughead (12/41); (on sale 10/41)(also see Jackpot)	31,500	63,200	94,500	210,000	310,000	410,000
23-Statue of Liberty-c (1/42; on sale 11/41)	2500	5000	7500	15,000	21,250	27,500
24-Coach Kleats app. (unnamed until Archie #94); bondage/torture-c	811	1622	2433	5920	10,460	15,000
25-1st app. Archie's jalopy; 1st skinny Mr. Weatherbee prototype	524	1048	1572	3825	6763	9700
26-1st app. Veronica Lodge (4/42); "Remember Pearl Harbor!" cover caption	1100	2200	3300	8400	15,200	22,000
27-Bill of Rights-c	418	836	1254	2926	5163	7400
28-Classic swastika/Hangman-c	400	800	1200	2800	4900	7000
29,30: 29-Origin Shield retold; 30-Capt. Commando begins; bondage/torture-c; 1st Miss Grundy (definitive version); see Jackpot #4	371	742	1113	2600	4550	6500
31-MLJ offices & artists are visited in Sgt. Boyle story; 1st app. Mr. Lodge; cover has woman steam-broiled alive, Nazi bondage-c	432	864	1296	3154	5577	8000
32,33,35: 32-Shield dons new costume. 33-Pre-Moose tryout (see Jughead #1)	314	628	951	2251	3976	5700
34-Classic Bondage/Hypo-c	2500	5000	7500	15,600	24,300	33,000
36-1st full Archie-c in Pep (2/43) w/Shield & Hangman (see Jackpot #4 where Archie's face appears in a small circle)	1900	3800	5700	13,300	22,150	31,000
37-40	274	548	822	1754	3002	4250
41-Archie-c begin	331	662	993	2317	4059	5800
42-45	213	426	639	1363	2332	3300
46,47,49,50: 47-Last Hangman issue; infinity-c	184	368	552	1178	2014	2850
48-Black Hood begins (5/44); ends #51,59,60; Archie fish-c	239	478	717	1530	2615	3700
51-60: 52-Suzie begins; 1st Mr Weatherbee-c. 56-Last Capt. Commando. 59-Black Hood not in costume; lingerie panels; Archie dresses as his aunt; Suzie ends. 60-Katy Keene begins(3/47), ends #154	90	180	270	576	988	1400
61-65-Last Shield. 62-1st app. Li'l Jinx (7/47)	73	146	219	467	796	1125
66-80: 66-G-Man Club becomes Archie Club (2/48); Nevada Jones by Bill Woggon. 76-Katy Keene story. 78-1st app. Dilton	41	82	123	256	428	600
81-99	26	52	78	154	252	350
100	32	64	96	190	310	430
101-130	17	34	51	103	162	220
131(2/59)-137	8	16	24	51	96	140
138-140-Neal Adams-a (1 pg.) in each	8	16	24	52	99	145
141-149(9/61)	6	12	18	41	76	110
150-160-Super-heroes app. in each (see note). 150 (10/61?)-2nd or 3rd app. The Jaguar? 151-154,156-158-Horror/Sci/Fi-c. 157-Li'l Jinx. 159-Both 12¢ and 15¢ covers exist	8	16	24	56	108	160
161(3/63) 3rd Josie app.; early Josie stories w/DeCarlo-a begin (see Note for others)	7	14	21	46	86	125
162-167,169-180	5	10	15	30	50	70
168,200: 168-(1/64)-Jaguar app. 200-(12/66)	5	10	15	31	53	75
181(5/65)-199: 187-Pureheart try-out story. 192-UFO-c. 198-Giantman-c(only)	4	8	12	23	37	50
201-217,219-226,228-240(4/70): 224-(12/68) 1st app. Archie's pet, Hot Dog (later becomes Jughead's pet)	3	6	9	16	23	30
218,227-Archies Band-c only	3	6	9	17	26	35
241-270(10/72)	2	4	6	13	18	22
271-297,299	2	4	6	9	12	15
298, 300: 298-Josie and the Pussycats-c. 300(4/75)	2	4	6	13	18	22
301-340(8/78)	1	3	4	6	8	10
341-382	1	2	3	4	5	7
383(4/82),393(3/84): 383-Marvelous Maureen begins (Sci/fi). 393-Thunderbunny begins	1	2	3	5	6	8
384-392,394,395,397-399,401-410						5.00
396-Early Cheryl Blossom-c	2	4	6	9	12	15
400(5/85),411: 400-Story featuring Archie staff (DeCarlo-a)	1	2	3	4	5	7

NOTE: ***Biro*** *a-2, 4, 5.* ***Jack Cole*** *a-1-5, 8.* ***Al Fagaly*** *c-55-72.* ***Fuje*** *a-39, 45, 47; c-34.* ***Meskin*** *a-2, 4, 5, 11(2).* ***Montana*** *c-30, 32, 33, 36, 73-87(most).* ***Novick*** *c-1-28, 29(w/****Schomburg****), 31i.* ***Harry Sahle*** *c-35, 39-50.* ***Schomburg*** *c-38.* ***Bob Wood*** *a-2, 4-6, 11. The Fly app. in 151, 154, 160. Flygirl app. in 153, 155, 156, 158. Jaguar app. in 150, 152, 157, 159, 168. Josie by* ***DeCarlo*** *in 161-166, 168-171, 173, 175-177, 179, 181. Katy Keene by* ***Bill Woggon*** *in 73-126. Bondage c-7, 12, 13, 15, 18, 21, 31, 32. Cover features: Shield #1-16; Shield/Hangman #17-27, 29-41; Hangman #28. Archie #36, 41-on.*

PEP COMICS FEATURING BETTY AND VERONICA
Archie Comic Publications: May, 2011 (Giveaway)

Free Comic Book Day Edition - Little Archie flashback 3.00

PEPE
Dell Publishing Co.: No. 1194, Apr, 1961

Issue	GD	VG	FN	VF	VF/NM	NM-
Four Color 1194-Movie, photo-c	5	10	15	30	50	70

PERFECT CRIME, THE
Cross Publications: Oct, 1949 - No. 33, May, 1953 (#2-14, 52 pgs.)

Issue	GD	VG	FN	VF	VF/NM	NM-
1-Powell-a(2)	50	100	150	315	533	750
2 (4/50)	28	56	84	165	270	375
3-10: 7-Steve Duncan begins, ends #30. 10-Flag-c	24	48	72	140	230	320
11-Used in **SOTI**, pg. 159	26	52	78	154	252	350
12-14	22	44	66	132	216	300
15- "The Most Terrible Menace" 2 pg. drug editorial (8/51)	24	48	72	144	237	330
16,17,19-25,27-29,31-33	20	40	60	114	182	250
18-Drug cover, heroin drug propaganda story, plus 2 pg. anti-drug editorial (11/51)	41	82	123	252	424	595
26-Drug-c with hypodermic needle; drug propaganda story (7/52)	41	82	123	252	424	595
30-Strangulation cover (11/52)	43	86	129	271	461	650

NOTE: ***Powell*** *a-No. 1, 2, 4.* ***Wildey*** *a-1, 5. Bondage c-11.*

PERFECT LOVE
Ziff-Davis(Approved Comics)/St. John No. 9 on: #10, 8-9/51 (cover date; 5-6/51 indicia date); #2, 10-11/51 - #10, 12/53

Issue	GD	VG	FN	VF	VF/NM	NM-
10(#1)(8-9/51)-Painted-c	30	60	90	177	289	400
2(10-11/51)	20	40	60	115	185	255
3,5-7: 3-Painted-c. 5-Photo-c	16	32	48	98	154	210
4,8 (Fall, 1952)-Kinstler-a; last Z-D issue	16	32	48	98	154	210
9,10 (10/53, 12/53, St. John): 9-Painted-c. 10-Photo-c	15	30	45	94	147	200

PERHAPANAUTS, THE
Dark Horse Comics: Nov, 2005 - No. 4, Feb, 2006 ($2.99, limited series)

1-4-Todd Dezago-s/Craig Rousseau-a/c 3.00
... Annual #1 (2/08, $3.50) Two covers by Rousseau and Allred 3.50
...: Danger Down Under! 1-5 (11/12 - No. 5, 6/13, $3.50) Two covers on each 3.50
... Halloween Spooktacular 1 (10/09, $3.50) Hembeck, Rousseau and others-a 3.50
,,, - Molly's Story (2/10, $3.50) Copland-a 3.50
(2nd series) (4/08 - No. 6, $3.50) 1-6: 1-Two covers by Art Adams and Rousseau 3.50

PERHAPANAUTS: SECOND CHANCES, THE
Dark Horse Comics: Oct, 2006 - No. 4, Jan, 2007 ($2.99, limited series)

1-4-Todd Dezago-s/Craig Rousseau-a/c 3.00

PERRI (Disney)
Dell Publishing Co.: No. 847, Jan, 1958

Issue	GD	VG	FN	VF	VF/NM	NM-
Four Color 847-Movie, w/2 diff-c publ.	6	12	18	37	66	95

Personal Love #13 © FF

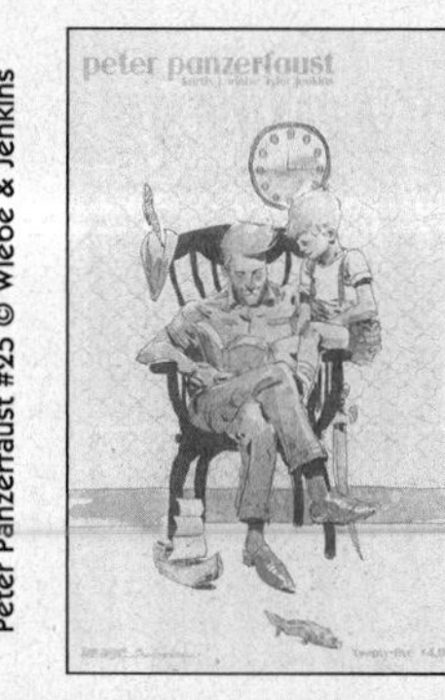

Peter Panzerfaust #25 © Wiebe & Jenkins

Peter Parker: Spider-Man #5 © MAR

	GD 2.0	VG 4.0	FN 6.0	VF 8.0	VF/NM 9.0	NM- 9.2

PERRY MASON
David McKay Publications: No. 49, 1946 - No. 50, 1946

Feature Books 49, 50-Based on Gardner novels	40	80	120	244	402	560

PERRY MASON MYSTERY MAGAZINE (TV)
Dell Publishing Co.: June-Aug, 1964 - No. 2, Oct-Dec, 1964

1-Raymond Burr painted-c	8	16	24	55	105	155
2-Raymond Burr photo-c	6	12	18	37	66	95

PERSONAL LOVE (Also see Movie Love)
Famous Funnies: Jan, 1950 - No. 33, June, 1955

1-Photo-c	26	52	78	154	252	350
2-Kathryn Grayson & Mario Lanza photo-c	15	30	45	88	137	185
3-7,10: 7-Robert Walker & Joanne Dru photo-c. 10-Loretta Young & Joseph Cotton photo-c	15	30	45	84	127	170
8,9: 8-Esther Williams & Howard Keel photo-c. 9-Debra Paget & Louis Jourdan photo-c	15	30	45	85	130	175
11-Toth-a; Glenn Ford & Gene Tierney photo-c	15	30	45	94	147	200
12,16,17-One pg. Frazetta each. 17-Rock Hudson & Yvonne DeCarlo photo-c	15	30	45	85	130	175
13-15,18-23: 12-Jane Greer & William Lundigan photo-c. 14-Kirk Douglas photo-c. 15-Dale Robertson & Joanne Dru photo-c. 18-Gregory Peck & Susan Hayworth photo-c. 19-Anthony Quinn & Suzan Ball photo-c. 20-Robert Wagner & Kathleen Crowley photo-c. 21-Roberta Peters & Byron Palmer photo-c. 22-Dale Robertson photo-c. 23-Rhonda Fleming-c	14	28	42	82	121	160
24,27,28-Frazetta-a in each (8,8&6 pgs.). 27-Rhonda Fleming & Fernando Lamas photo-c. 28-Mitzi Gaynor photo-c	55	110	165	352	601	850
25-Frazetta-a (tribute to Bettie Page, 7 pg. story); Tyrone Power/Terry Moore photo-c from "King of the Khyber Rifles"	86	172	258	546	936	1325
26,29,30,33: 26-Constance Smith & Byron Palmer photo-c. 29-Charlton Heston & Nicol Morey photo-c. 30-Johnny Ray & Mitzi Gaynor photo-c. 33-Dana Andrews & Piper Laurie photo-c	14	28	42	82	121	160
31-Marlon Brando & Jean Simmons photo-c; last pre-code (2/55)	17	34	51	103	162	220
32-Classic Frazetta-a (8 pgs.); Kirk Douglas & Bella Darvi photo-c	82	164	246	528	902	1275

NOTE: *All have photo-c. Many feature movie stars.* ***Everett*** *a-5, 9, 10, 24.*

PERSONAL LOVE (Going Steady V3#3 on)
Prize Publ. (Headline): V1#1, Sept, 1957 - V3#2, Nov-Dec, 1959

V1#1	14	28	42	82	121	160
2	10	20	30	54	72	90
3-6(7-8/58)	9	18	27	47	61	75
V2#1(9-10/58)-V2#6(7-8/59)	8	16	24	40	50	60
V3#1-Wood?/Orlando-a	8	16	24	42	54	65
2	7	14	21	37	46	55

PESTILENCE
AfterShock Comics: May, 2017 - No. 6, Jan, 2018 ($3.99)

1-6-Tieri-s/Okunev-a/Bradstreet-c; Crusaders and zombies in the year 1347						4.00

PESTILENCE: A STORY OF SATAN
AfterShock Comics: May, 2018 - No. 5, Nov, 2018 ($3.99)

1-5-Tieri-s/Okunev-a/Bradstreet-c						4.00

PETER CANNON - THUNDERBOLT (See Crisis on Infinite Earths)(Also see Thunderbolt)
DC Comics: Sept, 1992 - No. 12, Aug, 1993 ($1.25)

1-12						3.00

PETER CANNON: THUNDERBOLT
Dynamite Entertainment: 2012 - No. 13, 2013 ($3.99)

1-10: 1-Darnell & Ross-s/Lau-a; back-up unpublished '80s Thunderbolt story; Pete Morisi-s/a. 1-3-Four covers on each. 4-7-Covers by Ross & Segovia						4.00

PETER CANNON: THUNDERBOLT, VOLUME 1
Dynamite Entertainment: 2019 - No. 5, 2019 ($3.99)

1-5-Gillen-s/Wijngaard-a						4.00

PETER COTTONTAIL
Key Publications: Jan, 1954; Feb, 1954 - No. 2, Mar, 1954 (Says 3/53 in error)

1(1/54)-Not 3-D	10	20	30	58	79	100
1(2/54)-(3-D, 25¢)-Came w/glasses; written by Bruce Hamilton	22	44	66	130	213	295
2-Reprints 3-D #1 but not in 3-D	7	14	21	35	43	50

PETER GUNN (TV)
Dell Publishing Co.: No. 1087, Apr-June, 1960

Four Color 1087-Photo-c	8	16	24	52	99	145

PETE ROSE: HIS INCREDIBLE BASEBALL CAREER
Masstar Creations Inc.: 1995

1-John Tartaglione-a						4.00

PETER PAN (Disney) (See Hook, Movie Classics & Comics, New Adventures of... & Walt Disney Showcase #36)
Dell Publishing Co.: No. 442, Dec, 1952 - No. 926, Aug, 1958

Four Color 442 (#1)-Movie	10	20	30	70	150	230
Four Color 926-Reprint of 442	5	10	15	35	63	90

PETER PAN
Disney Comics: 1991 ($5.95, graphic novel, 68 pgs.)(Celebrates video release)

nn-r/Peter Pan Treasure Chest from 1953						7.00

PETER PANDA
National Periodical Publications: Aug-Sept, 1953 - No. 31, Aug-Sept, 1958

1-Grossman-c/a in all	65	130	195	416	708	1000
2	33	66	99	196	321	445
3,4,6-8,10	26	52	78	154	252	350
5-Classic-c (scarce)	113	226	339	723	1237	1750
9-Robot-c	39	78	117	240	395	550
11-31	20	40	60	115	188	260

PETER PAN RECORDS (See Power Records)

PETER PAN TREASURE CHEST (See Dell Giants)

PETER PANZERFAUST
Image Comics (Shadowline): Feb, 2012 - No. 25, Dec, 2016 ($3.50/$3.99)

1-Kurtis Wiebe-s/Tyler Jenkins-a/c; Peter Pan-type character in WWII Europe	5	10	15	31	53	75
1-Second printing	2	4	6	11	16	20
2	2	4	6	9	12	15
3	2	4	6	8	10	12
4-8						5.00
9-1st full app. Kapitan Haken						6.00
10-24						4.00
25-Last issue; bonus preview of Rat Queens v2						5.00

PETER PARKER (See The Spectacular Spider-Man)

PETER PARKER
Marvel Comics: May, 2010 - No. 5, Sept, 2010 ($3.99/$2.99)

1-($3.99) Prints material from Marvel Digital Comics; Olliffe-a; back-up w/Hembeck-s/a						4.00
2-5-($2.99): 2-4-Olliffe-a. 3-Braithwaite-c. 5-Nauck-a; Thing app.						3.00

PETER PARKER: SPIDER-MAN
Marvel Comics: Jan, 1999 - No. 57, Aug, 2003 ($2.99/$1.99/$2.25)

1-Mackie-s/Romita Jr.-a; wraparound-c	1	3	4	6	8	10
1-($6.95) DF Edition w/variant-c by the Romitas	2	4	6	8	11	14
2-11,13-17-($1.99): 2-Two covers; Thor app. 3-Iceman-c/app. 4-Marrow-c/app. 5-Spider-Woman app. 7,8-Blade app. 9,10-Venom app. 11-Iron Man & Thor-c/app.						4.00
12-($2.99) Sinister Six and Venom app.						5.00
18-24,26-43: 18-Begin $2.25-c. 20-Jenkins-s/Buckingham-a start. 23-Intro Typeface. 24-Maximum Security x-over. 29-Rescue of MJ. 30-Ramos-c. 42,43-Mahfood-a						4.00
25-($2.99) Two covers; Spider-Man & Green Goblin						5.00
44-47-Humberto Ramos-c/a; Green Goblin-c/app.						4.00
48,49,51-57: 48,49-Buckingham-c/a. 51,52-Herrera-a. 56,57-Kieth-a; Sandman returns						4.00
50-($3.50) Buckingham-c/a						5.00
#156.1 (10/12, $2.99, 50th Anniversary one-shot) Stern-s/De La Torre-a/Romita Jr.-c						4.00
...'99 Annual (8/99, $3.50) Man-Thing app.						5.00
...'00 Annual ($3.50) Bounty app.; Joe Bennett-a; Black Cat back-up story						5.00
...'01 Annual ($2.99) Avery-s						5.00
...: A Day in the Life TPB (5/01, $14.95) r/#20-22,26; Webspinners #10-12						15.00
...: One Small Break TPB (2002, $16.95) r/#27,28,30-34; Andrews-c						17.00
Spider-Man: Return of the Goblin TPB (2002, $8.99) r/#44-47; Ramos-c						9.00
...Vol. 4: Trials & Tribulations TPB (2003, $11.99) r/#35,37,48-50; Cho-c						12.00

PETER PARKER: THE SPECTACULAR SPIDER-MAN
Marvel Comics: Aug, 2017 - No. 6, Jan, 2018; No. 297, Feb, 2018 - No. 313, Feb, 2019 ($4.99/$3.99)

1-($4.99) Zdarsky-s/Adam Kubert-a; Johnny Storm app.; back-up w/Black Widow app.						5.00
2-6-($3.99) 3,4-Kingpin app. 6-Walsh-a						4.00

[Title switches to legacy numbering after #6 (1/18)]

297-299-Kubert-a. 298,299-Black Panther app.						4.00
300-($5.99) Black Panther, Human Torch, Ironheart app.; bonus cover gallery						6.00
301-313: 301-303-Spider-Man teams with younger version; Quinones-a. 310-Zdarsky-a. 311-313-Spider-Geddon tie-in; Morlun app.						4.00
Annual 1 (8/18, $4.99) Zdarsky-s/Allred-a/c; spotlight on J. Jonah Jameson; Bachalo-a						5.00

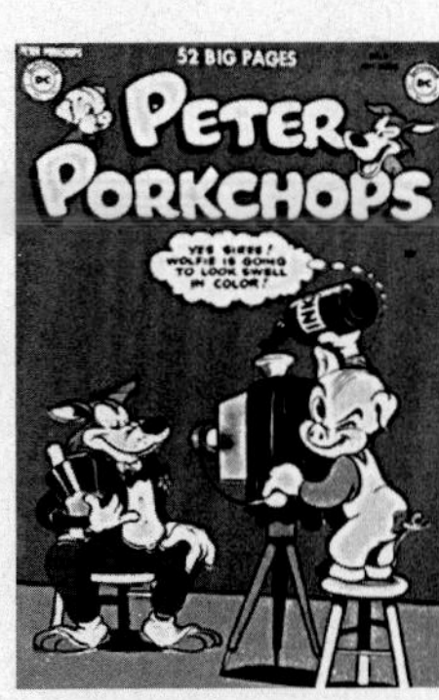

Peter Porkchops #4 © DC

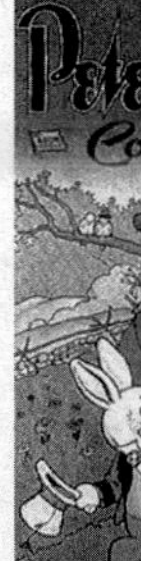

Peter Rabbit #1 © AVON

The Phantom #3 © KFS

	GD 2.0	VG 4.0	FN 6.0	VF 8.0	VF/NM 9.0	NM- 9.2

PETER PAT
United Features Syndicate: No. 8, 1939

Single Series 8	39	78	117	231	378	525

PETER PAUL'S 4 IN 1 JUMBO COMIC BOOK
Capitol Stories (Charlton): No date (1953)

1-Contains 4 comics bound; Space Adventures, Space Western, Crime & Justice, Racket Squad in Action	43	86	129	271	461	650

PETER PIG
Standard Comics: No. 5, May, 1953 - No. 6, Aug, 1953

5,6	8	16	24	40	50	60

PETER PORKCHOPS (See Leading Comics #23) (Also see Capt. Carrot)
National Periodical Publications: 11-12/49 - No. 61, 9-11/59; No. 62, 10-12/60 (1-11: 52 pgs.)

1	37	74	111	222	361	500
2	17	34	51	103	162	220
3-10: 6- "Peter Rockets to Mars!" c/story	13	26	39	74	105	135
11-30	10	20	30	56	76	95
31-62	9	18	27	47	61	75

NOTE: ***Otto Feuer** a-all. **Rube Grossman**-a most issues. **Sheldon Mayer** a-30-38, 40-44, 46-52, 61.*

PETER PORKER, THE SPECTACULAR SPIDER-HAM
Star Comics (Marvel): May, 1985 - No. 17, Sept, 1987 (Also see Marvel Tails)

1-Michael Golden-c	1	3	4	6	8	10
2-17: 12-Origin/1st app. Bizarro Phil. 13-Halloween issue						5.00

NOTE: *Back-up features: 2-X-Bugs. 3-Iron Mouse. 4-Croctor Strange. 5-Thrr, Dog of Thunder.*

PETER POTAMUS (TV)
Gold Key: Jan, 1965 (Hanna-Barbera)

1-1st app. Peter Potamus & So-So, Breezly & Sneezly	9	18	27	61	123	185

PETER RABBIT (See New Funnies #65 & Space Comics)
Dell Publishing Co.: No. 1, 1942

Large Feature Comic 1	81	162	243	518	884	1250

PETER RABBIT (Adventures of...; New Advs. of... #9 on)(Also see Funny Tunes & Space Comics)
Avon Periodicals: 1947 - No. 34, Aug-Sept, 1956

1(1947)-Reprints 1943-44 Sunday strips; contains a biography & drawing of Cady	39	78	117	240	395	550
2 (4/48)	25	50	75	150	245	340
3 ('48) - 6(7/49)-Last Cady issue	22	44	66	130	213	295
7-10(1950-8/51): 9-New logo	12	24	36	67	94	120
11(11/51)-34('56)-Avon's character	10	20	30	56	76	95
...Easter Parade (1952, 25¢, 132 pgs.)	22	44	66	128	209	290
...Jumbo Book (1954-Giant Size, 25¢)-Jesse James by Kinstler (6 pgs.); space ship-c	26	52	78	154	252	350

PETER RABBIT 3-D
Eternity Comics: April, 1990 ($2.95, with glasses; sealed in plastic bag)

1-By Harrison Cady (reprints)						4.00

PETER, THE LITTLE PEST (#4 titled Petey)
Marvel Comics Group: Nov, 1969 - No. 4, May, 1970

1	8	16	24	51	96	140
2-4-r-Dexter the Demon & Melvin the Monster	5	10	15	31	53	75

PETE'S DRAGON (See Walt Disney Showcase #43)

PETE THE PANIC
Stanmor Publications: November, 1955

nn-Code approved	8	16	24	44	57	70

PETEY (See Peter, the Little Pest)

PETTICOAT JUNCTION (TV, inspired Green Acres)
Dell Publ. Co.: Oct-Dec, 1964 - No. 5, Oct-Dec, 1965 (#1-3, 5 have photo-c)

1	6	12	18	41	76	110
2-5	5	10	15	31	53	75

PETUNIA (Also see Looney Tunes and Porky Pig)
Dell Publishing Co.: No. 463, Apr, 1953

Four Color 463	5	10	15	33	57	80

PHAGE (See Neil Gaiman's Teknophage & Neil Gaiman's Phage-Shadowdeath)

PHANTACEA
McPherson Publishing Co.: Sept, 1977 - No. 6, Summer, 1980 (B&W)

1-Early Dave Sim-a (32 pgs.)	4	8	12	28	47	65
2-Dave Sim-a(10 pgs.)	3	6	9	14	19	24
3-6: 3-Flip-c w/Damnation Bridge. 4-Gene Day-a	2	4	6	10	14	18

PHANTASMO (See The Funnies #45)
Dell Publishing Co.: No. 18, 1941

Large Feature Comic 18	45	90	135	284	480	675

PHANTOM, THE
David McKay Publishing Co.: 1939 - 1949

Feature Books 20	174	348	522	1114	1907	2700
Feature Books 22	94	188	282	597	1025	1450
Feature Books 39	71	142	213	454	777	1100
Feature Books 53,56,57	55	110	165	352	601	850

PHANTOM, THE (See Ace Comics, Defenders Of The Earth, Eat Right to Work and Win, Future Comics, Harvey Comics Hits #51,56, Harvey Hits #1, 6, 12, 15, 26, 36, 44, 48, & King Comics)

PHANTOM, THE (nn (#29)-Published overseas only) (Also see Comics Reading Libraries in the Promotional Comics section)
Gold Key(#1-17)/King(#18-28)/Charlton(#30 on): Nov, 1962 - No. 17, Jul, 1966; No. 18, Sept, 1966 - No. 28, Dec, 1967; No. 30, Feb, 1969 - No. 74, Jan, 1977

1-Origin revealed on inside-c & back-c	25	50	75	175	388	600
2-King, Queen & Jack begins, ends #11	11	22	33	72	154	235
3-5	9	18	27	58	114	170
6-10	7	14	21	46	86	125
11-17: 12-Track Hunter begins	6	12	18	38	69	100
18-Flash Gordon begins; Wood-a	5	10	15	31	53	75
19-24: 20-Flash Gordon ends (both by Gil Kane). 21-Mandrake begins. 20,24-Girl Phantom app.	4	8	12	28	47	65
25-28: 25-Jeff Jones-a(4 pgs.); 1 pg. Williamson ad. 26-Brick Bradford app. 28-Brick Bradford app.	4	8	12	23	37	50
30-33: 33-Last 12¢ issue	3	6	9	17	25	
34						
34-40: 36,39-Ditko-a	3	6	9	16	24	32
41-66,72: 46-Intro. The Piranha. 51-Grey tone-c. 62-Bolle-c	3	6	9	14	20	26
67-Origin retold; Newton-c/a; Humphrey Bogart, Lauren Bacall & Peter Lorre app.	3	6	9	17	25	34
68,70,71,73-Newton-c/a	3	6	9	14	19	24
69-Newton-c only	3	6	9	14	19	24
74-Classic flag-c by Newton; Newton-a;	3	6	9	18	28	38

NOTE: ***Aparo** a-31-34, 36-38; c-31-38, 60, 61. Painted c-1-17.*

PHANTOM, THE
DC Comics: May, 1988 - No. 4, Aug, 1988 ($1.25, mini-series)

1-4: Orlando-c/a in all						4.00

PHANTOM, THE
DC Comics: Mar, 1989 - No. 13, Mar, 1990 ($1.50)

1-13: 1-Brief origin						4.00

PHANTOM, THE
Wolf Publishing: 1992 - No. 8, 1993 ($2.25)

1-8						4.00

PHANTOM, THE
Moonstone: 2003 - No. 26, Dec, 2008 ($3.50/$3.99)

1-26: 1-Cassaday-c/Raab-s/Quinn-a						4.00
... Annual #1 (2007, $6.50) Blevins-c; stroy and art by various incl. Nolan						6.50
... - Captain Action 1 (2010, $3.99) covers by Thibert, Sparacio, and Gilbert						4.00

PHANTOM, THE
Hermes Press: 2014 - No. 6, 2016 ($3.99)

1-6: 1-Peter David-s/Sal Velluto-a; four covers						4.00

PHANTOM BLOT, THE (#1 titled New Adventures of...)
Gold Key: Oct, 1964 - No. 7, Nov, 1966 (Disney)

1 (Meets The Mysterious Mr. X)	7	14	21	46	86	125
2-1st Super Goof	5	10	15	34	60	85
3-7	3	6	9	21	33	45

PHANTOM EAGLE (See Mighty Midget, Marvel Super Heroes #16 & Wow #6)

PHANTOM FORCE
Image Comics/Genesis West #0, 3-7: 12/93 - #2, 1994; #0, 3/94; #3, 5/94 - #8, 10/94 ($2.50/$3.50, limited series)

0 (3/94, $2.50)-Kirby/Jim Lee-c; Kirby-p pgs. 1,5,24-29.						4.00
1 (12/93, $2.50)-Polybagged w/trading card; Kirby/Liefeld-c; Kirby plots/pencils w/inks by Liefeld, McFarlane, Jim Lee, Silvestri, Larsen, Williams, Ordway & Miki						4.00
2 ($3.50)-Kirby-a(p); Kirby/Larson-c						5.00

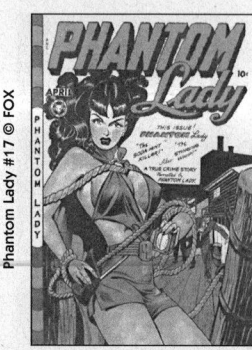

Phantom Lady #17 © FOX

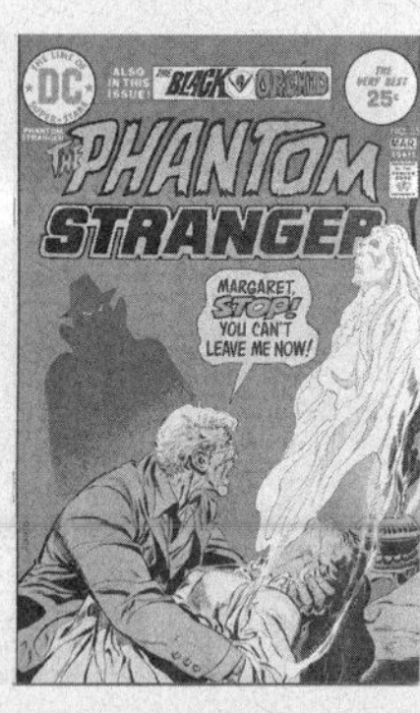

Phantom Stranger #35 © DC

Phoenix (2010) #0 © Nemesis

GD VG FN VF VF/NM NM-
2.0 4.0 6.0 8.0 9.0 9.2

3-8: 3-(5/94, $2.50)-Kirby/McFarlane-c 4-(5/94)-Kirby-c(p). 5-(6/94) 4.00

PHANTOM GUARD
Image Comics (WildStorm Productions): Oct, 1997 - No. 6, Mar, 1998 ($2.50)

1-6: 1-Two covers 3.00
1-($3.50)-Voyager Pack w/Wildcore preview 4.00

PHANTOM JACK
Image Comics: Mar, 2004 - No. 5, July, 2004 ($2.95)

1-5-Mike San Giacomo-s/Mitchell Breitweiser-a. 4-Initial printings with errors exist 3.00
The Collected Edition (Speakeasy Comics, 2005, $17.99) r/series; Bendis intro 18.00

PHANTOM LADY (1st Series) (My Love Secret #24 on) (Also see All Top, Daring Adventures, Freedom Fighters, Jungle Thrills, & Wonder Boy)
Fox Feature Syndicate: No. 13, Aug, 1947 - No. 23, Apr, 1949

13(#1)-Phantom Lady by Matt Baker begins (see Police Comics #1 for 1st app.); Blue Beetle story 524 1048 1572 3825 6763 9700
14-16: 14(#2)-Not Baker-c. 15-P.L. injected with experimental drug. 16-Negligee-c, panels; true crime stories begin 303 606 909 2121 3711 5300
17-Classic bondage cover; used in **SOTI**, illo "Sexual stimulation by combining 'headlights' with the sadist's dream of tying up a woman" 2000 4000 6000 15,300 28,650 42,000
18,19 295 590 885 1918 3259 4600
20-22 252 504 758 1613 2757 3900
23-Classic bondage-c 811 1622 2433 5920 10,460 15,000
NOTE: ***Matt Baker** a-in all; c-13, 15-21. **Kamen** a-22, 23.*

PHANTOM LADY (2nd Series) (See Terrific Comics) (Formerly Linda)
Ajax/Farrell Publ.: V1#5, Dec-Jan, 1954/1955 - No. 4, June, 1955

V1#5(#1)-By Matt Baker 174 348 522 1114 1907 2700
V1#2-Last pre-code 119 238 357 762 1306 1850
3,4-Red Rocket. 3-Heroin story 97 194 291 621 1061 1500

PHANTOM LADY
Verotik Publications: 1994 ($9.95)

1-Reprints G. A. stories from Phantom Lady and All Top Comics; Adam Hughes-c 2 4 6 10 14 18

PHANTOM LADY
DC Comics: Oct, 2012 - No. 4, Jan, 2013 ($2.99, limited series)

1-4-Gray and Palmiotti-s/Staggs-a. 1-Re-intro with Doll Man; Conner-c 3.00

PHANTOM PLANET, THE
Dell Publishing Co.: No. 1234, 1961

Four Color 1234-Movie 7 14 21 49 92 135

PHANTOM STRANGER, THE (1st Series)(See Saga of Swamp Thing)
National Periodical Publications: Aug-Sept, 1952 - No. 6, June-July, 1953

1(Scarce)-1st app. 415 830 1245 2905 5153 7400
2 (Scarce) 265 530 795 1694 2897 4100
3-6 (Scarce) 258 516 774 1651 2826 4000
Ashcan (8,9/52) Not distributed to newsstands, only for in house use (no known sales)

PHANTOM STRANGER, THE (2nd Series) (See Showcase #80) (See Showcase Presents for B&W reprints)
National Periodical Publs.: May-June, 1969 - No. 41, Feb-Mar, 1976; No. 42, Mar, 2010

1-2nd S.A. app. P. Stranger; only 12¢ issue 11 22 33 76 163 250
2,3 6 12 18 38 69 100
4-1st new look Phantom Stranger; N. Adams-a 6 12 18 41 76 110
5-7 5 10 15 31 53 75
8-14: 14-Last 15¢ issue 4 8 12 23 37 50
15-19: All 25¢ giants (52 pgs.) 4 8 12 25 40 55
20-Dark Circle begins, ends #24. 3 6 9 16 24 32
21,22 3 6 9 14 20 25
23-Spawn of Frankenstein begins by Kaluta 4 8 12 25 40 55
24,25,27-30-Last Spawn of Frankenstein 3 6 9 19 30 40
26- Book-length story featuring Phantom Stranger, Dr. 13 & Spawn of Frankenstein 3 6 9 21 33 45
31-The Black Orchid begins (6-7/74). 3 6 9 18 28 38
32,34-38: 34-Last 20¢ issue (#35 on are 25¢) 2 4 6 13 18 22
33,39-41: 33-Deadman-c/story. 39-41-Deadman app. 3 6 9 14 20 25
42-(3/10, $2.99) Blackest Night one-shot; Syaf-a; Spectre, Deadman and Blue Devil app. 3.00
NOTE: ***N. Adams** a-4; c-3-19. **Anderson** a-4, 5i. **Aparo** a-7-17, 19-26; c-20-24, 33-41. **B. Bailey** a-27-30. **DeZuniga** a-12-16, 18, 19, 21, 22, 31, 34. **Grell** a-33. **Kaluta** a-23-25; c-26. **Meskin** r-15, 16, 18, 19. **Redondo** a-32, 35, 36. **Sparling** a-20. **Starr** a-17r. **Toth** a-15r. Black Orchid by **Carrilo**-38-41. Dr. 13 solo in-13, 18, 19, 20, 21, 34. Frankenstein by **Kaluta**-23-25; by **Baily**-27-30. No Black Orchid-33, 34, 37.*

PHANTOM STRANGER (See Justice League of America #103)
DC Comics: Oct, 1987 - No. 4, Jan, 1988 (75¢, limited series)

1-4-Mignola/Russell-c/a & Eclipso app. in all. 3,4-Eclipso-c 5.00

PHANTOM STRANGER (See intro. in DC Comics - The New 52 FCBD Special Edition) (Title changes to Trinity of Sin: The Phantom Stranger with #9 (Aug, 2013))
DC Comics: No. 0, Nov, 2012 - No. 22, Oct, 2015 ($2.99)

0-22: 0-Origin retold; Spectre app.; DiDio-s/Anderson-a. 2-Pandora app. 4,5-Jae Lee-c; Justice League Dark app. 6,7-Gene Ha-a/c; The Question app. 11-Trinity War. 12-17-Forever Evil tie-in. 18-Superman app. 20-The Spectre app. 3.00
...: Future's End (11/14, $3.99) 3-D lenticular cover; five years later; Winslade-a 4.00
...: Future's End (11/14, $2.99) regular cover; five years later 3.00

PHANTOM STRANGER (See Vertigo Visions-The Phantom Stranger)

PHANTOM: THE GHOST WHO WALKS
Marvel Comics: Feb, 1995 - No. 3, Apr, 1995 ($2.95, limited series)

1-3 4.00

PHANTOM: THE GHOST WHO WALKS
Moonstone: 2003 ($16.95, TPB)

nn-Three new stories by Raab, Goulart, Collins, Blanco and others; Klauba painted-c 17.00

PHANTOM 2040 (TV cartoon)
Marvel Comics: May, 1995 - No. 4, Aug, 1995 ($1.50)

1-4-Based on animated series; Ditko-a(p) in all 4.00

PHANTOM WITCH DOCTOR (Also see Durango Kid #8 & Eerie #8)
Avon Periodicals: 1952

1-Kinstler-c/a (7 pgs.) 100 200 300 635 1093 1550

PHANTOM ZONE, THE (See Adventure #283 & Superboy #100, 104)
DC Comics: January, 1982 - No. 4, April, 1982

1-4-Superman app. in all. 2-4: Batman, Green Lantern, Supergirl, Wonder Woman app. 4.00
NOTE: ***Colan** a-1-4p; c-1-4p. **Giordano** c-1-4i.*

PHAZE
Eclipse Comics: Apr, 1988 - No. 2, Oct, 1988 ($2.25)

1,2: 1-Sienkiewicz-c. 2-Gulacy painted-c 3.00

PHIL RIZZUTO (Baseball Hero)(See Sport Thrills, Accepted reprint)
Fawcett Publications: 1951 (New York Yankees)

nn-Photo-c 74 148 222 470 810 1150

PHOENIX
Atlas/Seaboard Publ.: Jan, 1975 - No. 4, Oct, 1975

1-Origin; Rovin-s/Amendola-a 2 4 6 13 18 22
2-4: 3-Origin & only app. The Dark Avenger. 4-New origin/costume The Protector (formerly Phoenix) 2 4 6 9 13 16
NOTE: ***Infantino** appears in #1, 2. **Austin** a-3i. **Thorne** c-3.*

PHOENIX
Ardden Entertainment (Atlas Comics): Mar, 2011 - No. 6, May, 2012 ($2.99)

1-6-Krueger & Deneen-s/Zachary-a; origin re-told 3.00
... Issue Zero - NY Comicon Edtion (10/10, $2.99) Dorien-a; origin prequel to #1 3.00

PHOENIX (...The Untold Story)
Marvel Comics Group: April, 1984 ($2.00, one-shot)

1-Byrne/Austin-r/X-Men #137 with original unpublished ending 2 4 6 10 14 18

PHOENIX RESURRECTION, THE
Malibu Comics (Ultraverse): 1995 - 1996 ($3.95)

Genesis #1 (12/95)-X-Men app; wraparound-c, Revelations #1 (12/95)-X-Men app; wraparound-c, Aftermath #1 (1/96)-X-Men app. 5.00
0-($1.95)-r/series 4.00
0-American Entertainment Ed. 5.00

PHOENIX RESURRECTION: THE RETURN OF JEAN GREY
Marvel Comics: Feb, 2018 - No. 5 ($4.99/$3.99, limited series)

1,5-($4.99) Yu-a. 5-Leads into Jean Grey #11 and X-Men Red #1 5.00
2-4-($3.99) 2-Pacheco-a. 3-Bennett-a. 4-Rosanas-a 4.00

PHOENIX WITHOUT ASHES
IDW Publishing: Aug, 2010 - No. 4, Nov, 2010 ($3.99, limited series)

1-4-Harlan Ellison-s/Alan Robinson-a 4.00

PHONOGRAM
Image Comics: Aug, 2006 - No. 6, May, 2007 ($3.50, limited series)

1-Gillen-s/McKelvie-a 15.00
2-6 5.00

PHONOGRAM: THE SINGLES CLUB (Volume 2)
Image Comics: Dec, 2008 - No. 7, Feb, 2010 ($3.50, limited series)

Pictorial Romances #21 © STJ

Picture News #5 © 299 Lafayette

Pinhead & Foodini #3 © FAW

GD 2.0 | VG 4.0 | FN 6.0 | VF 8.0 | VF/NM 9.0 | NM- 9.2

1-7-Gillen-s/McKelvie-a. 5-Recalled for bar-code error 4.00

PHONOGRAM (Volume 3)(The Immaterial Girl)
Image Comics: Aug, 2015 - No. 6, Jan, 2016 ($3.99, limited series)

1-6-Gillen-s/McKelvie-a 4.00

PICNIC PARTY (See Dell Giants)

PICTORIAL CONFESSIONS (Pictorial Romances #4 on)
St. John Publishing Co.: Sept, 1949 - No. 3, Dec, 1949

1-Baker-c/a(3) 100 200 300 635 1093 1550
2-Baker-a; photo-c 41 82 123 256 428 600
3-Kubert, Baker-a; part Kubert-c 43 86 129 271 461 650

PICTORIAL LOVE STORIES (Formerly Tim McCoy)
Charlton Comics: No. 22, Oct, 1949 - No. 26, July, 1950 (all photo-c)

22-26: All have "Me-Dan Cupid". 25-Fred Astaire-c 22 44 66 130 213 295

PICTORIAL LOVE STORIES
St. John Publishing Co.: October, 1952

1-Baker-c 50 100 150 315 533 750

PICTORIAL ROMANCES (Formerly Pictorial Confessions)
St. John Publ. Co.: No. 4, Jan, 1950; No. 5, Jan, 1951 - No. 24, Mar, 1954

4-Baker-a; photo-c 53 106 159 334 567 800
5,10-All Matt Baker issues. 5-Reprints all stories from #4 w/new Baker-c
60 120 180 380 653 925
6-9,12,13,15,16-Baker-c, 2-3 stories 58 116 174 371 636 900
11-Baker-c/a(3); Kubert-r/Hollywood Confessions #1
60 120 180 380 653 925
14,21-24: Baker-c/a each. 21,24-Each has signed story by Estrada
61 122 183 390 670 950
17-20(7/53, 25¢, 100 pgs.): Baker-c/a; each has two signed stories by Estrada
113 226 339 723 1237 1750

NOTE: *Matt Baker art in most issues.* ***Estrada*** *a-17-20(2), 21, 24.*

PICTURE CRIMES
David McKay Publ.: June, 1937

1-Story in photo panels (a GD+ copy sold in 2012 for $478 and a certified 5.5 copy sold for $2051 in 2017)

PICTURE NEWS
Lafayette Street Corp.: Jan, 1946 - No. 10, Jan-Feb, 1947

1-Milt Gross begins, ends No. 6; 4 pg. Kirby-a; A-Bomb-c/story
52 104 156 328 552 775
2-Atomic explosion panels; Frank Sinatra/Perry Como story
27 54 81 158 259 360
3-Atomic explosion panels; Frank Sinatra, June Allyson, Benny Goodman stories 23 46 69 136 223 310
4-Atomic explosion panels; "Caesar and Cleopatra" movie adapt. w/Claude Raines & Vivian Leigh; Jackie Robinson story 27 54 81 158 259 360
5-7: 5-Hank Greenberg story; Atomic explosion panel. 6-Joe Louis-c/story
20 40 60 117 189 260
8,10: 8-Monte Hale story (9-10/46; 1st?). 10-Dick Quick; A-Bomb story; Krigstein, Gross-a
20 40 60 120 195 270
9-A-Bomb story; "Crooked Mile" movie adaptation; Joe DiMaggio story.
23 46 69 136 223 310

PICTURE PARADE (Picture Progress #5 on)
Gilberton Company (Also see A Christmas Adventure): Sept, 1953 - V1#4, Dec, 1953 (28 pgs.)

V1#1-Andy's Atomic Adventures; A-bomb blast-c; (Teachers version distributed to schools exists) 22 44 66 130 213 295
2-Around the World with the United Nations 14 28 42 76 108 140
3-Adventures of the Lost One(The American Indian), 4-A Christmas Adventure (r-under same title in 1969) 14 28 42 76 108 140

PICTURE PROGRESS (Formerly Picture Parade)
Gilberton Corp.: V1#5, Jan, 1954 - V3#2, Oct, 1955 (28-36 pgs.)

V1#5-9,V2#1-9: 5-News in Review 1953. 6-The Birth of America. 7-The Four Seasons. 8-Paul Revere's Ride. 9-The Hawaiian Islands(5/54). V2#1-The Story of Flight(9/54). 2-Vote for Crazy River (The Meaning of Elections). 3-Louis Pasteur. 4-The Star Spangled Banner. 5-News in Review 1954. 6-Alaska: The Great Land. 7-Life in the Circus. 8-The Time of the Cave Man. 9-Summer Fun(5/55)
9 18 27 50 65 80
V3#1,2: 1-The Man Who Discovered America. 2-The Lewis & Clark Expedition
9 18 27 47 61 75

PICTURE SCOPE JUNGLE ADVENTURES (See Jungle Thrills)

PICTURE STORIES FROM AMERICAN HISTORY
National/All-American/E. C. Comics: 1945 - No. 4, Sum, 1947 (#1,2: 10¢, 56 pgs.; #3,4: 15¢, 52 pgs.)

1 30 60 90 177 289 400
2-4 24 48 72 140 230 320

PICTURE STORIES FROM SCIENCE
E.C. Comics: Spring, 1947 - No. 2, Fall, 1947

1-(15¢) 31 62 93 182 296 410
2-(10¢) 24 48 72 144 237 330

PICTURE STORIES FROM THE BIBLE (See Narrative Illustration, the Story of the Comics by M.C. Gaines)
National/All-American/E.C. Comics: 1942 - No. 4, Fall, 1943; 1944-46

1-4('42-Fall, '43)-Old Testament (DC) 25 50 75 150 245 340
Complete Old Testament Edition, (12/43-DC, 50¢, 232 pgs.);-1st printing; contains #1-4; 2nd - 8th (1/47) printings exist; later printings by E.C. some with 65¢-c
34 68 102 199 325 450
Complete Old Testament Edition (1945-publ. by Bible Pictures Ltd.)-232 pgs., hardbound, in color with dust jacket 34 68 102 199 325 450

NOTE: *Both Old and New Testaments published in England by Bible Pictures Ltd. in hardback, 1943, in color, 376 pgs. (2 vols.: O.T. 232 pgs. & N.T. 144 pgs.), and were also published by Scarf Press in 1979 (Old Test., $9.95) and in 1980 (New Test., $7.95)*

1-3(New Test.; 1944-46, DC)-52 pgs. ea. 20 40 60 115 188 260
The Complete Life of Christ Edition (1945, 25¢, 96 pgs.)-Contains #1&2 of the New Testament Edition 34 68 102 199 325 450
1,2(Old Testament-r in comic book form)(E.C., 1946; 52 pgs.)
20 40 60 115 188 260
1(DC),2(AA),3(EC)(New Testament-r in comic book form)(E.C., 1946; 52 pgs.)
20 40 60 115 188 260
Complete New Testament Edition (1945-E.C., 40¢, 144 pgs.)-Contains #1-3 1946 printing has 50¢-c 34 68 102 199 325 450

NOTE: *Another British series entitled* ***The Bible Illustrated*** *from 1947 has recently been discovered, with the same internal artwork. This eight edition series (5-OT, 3-NT) is of particular interest to Classics Ill. collectors because it exactly copied the C.I. logo format. The British publisher was Thorpe & Porter, who in 1951 began publishing the British Classics Ill. series. All editions of The Bible Ill. have new British painted covers. While this market is still new, and not all editions have as yet been found, current market value is about the same as the first U.S. editions of Picture Stories From The Bible.*

PICTURE STORIES FROM WORLD HISTORY
E.C. Comics: Spring, 1947 - No. 2, Summer, 1947 (52, 48 pgs.)

1-(15¢) 31 62 93 186 303 420
2-(10¢) 24 48 72 140 230 320

PIGS
Image Comics: Sept, 2011 - No. 8, Aug, 2012 ($2.99)

1-8: 1-Cosby & McCool-s/Tamura-a/Jock-c. 3-Conner-c. 5-Gibbons-c. 7-Ramos-c 3.00

PILGRIM, THE
IDW Publishing: Apr, 2010 - No. 2, Jun, 2010 ($3.99, limited series)

1,2-Mike Grell-a/c; Mark Ryan-s 4.00

PILOT SEASON...
Image Comics (Top Cow): 2008 - 2011 ($1.00/$2.99/$3.99, one-shots)

...: Asset (9/10, $3.99) Sablik-s/Marquez-a/Frison-c 4.00
...: City of Refuge (10/11, $3.99) Foehl-s/Calero-a/c 4.00
...: Crosshair (10/10, $3.99) Katz-s/Jefferson-a/Silvestri-c 4.00
...: Declassified (10/09, $1.00) Preview of one-shots with covers, script and sketch pgs. 3.00
...: Demonic (1/10, $2.99) Kirkman-s/Benitez-a; two covers by Silvestri 3.00
...: Fleshdigger (10/11, $3.99) Denton & Keene-s; Sanchez-a; Francavilla-c 4.00
...: Forever (10/10, $3.99) Inglesby-s/Nachlik-a/Hutomo-c 4.00
...: Murdered (11/09, $2.99) Kirkman-s/Blake-a; two covers by Silvestri 3.00
...: 7 Days From Hell (10/10, $3.99) Noto-a/Hill & Levin-s/Stelfreeze-c 4.00
...: Stellar (7/10, $2.99) Kirkman-s/Chang-a/Silvestri-c 3.00
...: The Beauty (10/11, $3.99) Haun & Hurley-s/Haun-a/c (becomes a 2015 series) 10.00
...: The Test (10/10, $3.99) Fialkov-s/Ekedal-a/Hutomo-c 4.00
...: 39 Minutes (9/10, $3.99) Harms-s/Lando-a/Albuquerque-c 4.00
...: Twilight Guardian (5/08, $3.99) Hickman-s 4.00

PINHEAD
Marvel Comics (Epic Comics): Dec, 1993 - No. 6, May, 1994 ($2.50)

1-($2.95)-Embossed foil-c by Kelley Jones; Intro Pinhead & Disciples (Snakeoil, Hangman, Fan Dancer & Dixie) 4.00
2-6 3.00

PINHEAD & FOODINI (TV)(Also see Foodini & Jingle Dingle Christmas...)
Fawcett Publications: July, 1951 - No. 4, Jan, 1952 (Early TV comic)

1-(52 pgs.)-Photo-c; based on TV puppet show 32 64 96 192 314 435

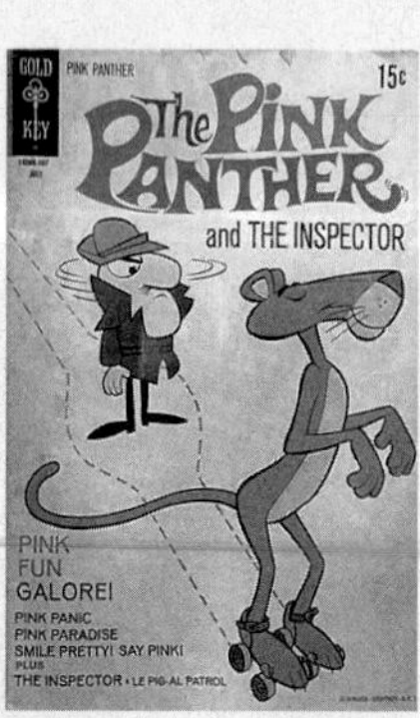

The Pink Panther #2 © GK

Pinky and the Brain #25 © WB

Pitt #14 © Dale Keown

	GD 2.0	VG 4.0	FN 6.0	VF 8.0	VF/NM 9.0	NM- 9.2
2,3-Photo-c	16	32	48	98	154	210
4	14	28	42	82	121	160

PINHEAD VS. MARSHALL LAW (Law in Hell)
Marvel Comics (Epic): Nov, 1993 - No. 2, Dec, 1993 ($2.95, lim. series)

	GD	VG	FN	VF	VF/NM	NM-
1,2: 1-Embossed red foil-c. 2-Embossed silver foil-c						4.00

PINK DUST
Kitchen Sink Press: 1998 ($3.50, B&W, mature)

	GD	VG	FN	VF	VF/NM	NM-
1-J. O'Barr-s/a						3.50

PINK PANTHER, THE (TV)(See The Inspector & Kite Fun Book)
Gold Key #1-70/Whitman #71-87: April, 1971 - No. 87, Mar, 1984

	GD	VG	FN	VF	VF/NM	NM-
1-The Inspector begins	6	12	18	41	76	110
2-5	3	6	9	17	26	35
6-10	3	6	9	14	19	24
11-30: Warren Tufts-a #16-on	2	4	6	9	13	16
31-60	2	4	6	8	11	14
61-70	1	2	3	5	7	9
71-74,81-83: 81(2/82), 82(3/82), 83(4/82)	2	4	6	8	10	12
75(8/80)-77 (Whitman pre-pack) (scarce)	4	8	12	27	44	60
78(1/81)-80 (Whitman pre-pack) (not as scarce)	2	4	6	11	16	20
78 (1/81, 40¢-c) Cover price error variant	3	6	9	15	22	28
84-87(All #90266 on-c, no date or date code): 84(6/83), 85(8/83), 87(3/84)	3	6	9	14	20	26
Mini-comic No. 1(1976)(3-1/4x6-1/2")	1	3	4	6	8	10

NOTE: *Pink Panther began as a movie cartoon. (See Golden Comics Digest #38, 45 and March of Comics #376, 384, 390, 409, 418, 429, 441, 449, 461, 473, 486); #37, 72, 80-85 contain reprints.*

PINK PANTHER SUPER SPECIAL (TV)
Harvey Comics: Oct, 1993 ($2.25, 68 pgs.)

	GD	VG	FN	VF	VF/NM	NM-
V2#1-The Inspector & Wendy Witch stories also						5.00

PINK PANTHER, THE
Harvey Comics: Nov, 1993 - No. 9, July, 1994 ($1.50)

	GD	VG	FN	VF	VF/NM	NM-
V2#1-9						4.00

PINK PANTHER, THE (Volume 3)
American Mythology Productions: 2016 - Present ($3.99)

	GD	VG	FN	VF	VF/NM	NM-
1-4-New and classic short stories by various; multiple covers on each. 4-Trick or Pink						4.00
... Anniversary Special 1 (2017, $3.99) New short stories and reprints; 3 covers						4.00
...: Cartoon Hour Special 1,2 (2017, $4.99) Short stories by various; 3 covers						5.00
...: Classic Christmas 1 (2018, $3.99) Reprint from Pink Panther #60 (1979)						4.00
... 55th Anniversary Special 1 (2019, $3.99) New short stories and reprints; 3 covers						4.00
... Presents the Ant & the Aardvark 1 (2018, $3.99) New short stories and reprints						4.00
...: Snow Day (2017, $3.99) New short stories by S.A. Check and reprint; 3 covers						4.00
... Super-Pink Special 1 (2017, $3.99) New short stories and reprint; 3 covers						4.00
... Surfside Special 1 (2018, $3.99) New short stories and reprints; 2 covers						4.00
... Vs. The Inspector 1 (2018, $3.99) New short stories and reprints; 2 covers						4.00
... Winter Special 1 (2018, $3.99) New short stories and reprints; 2 covers						4.00

PINKY & THE BRAIN (See Animaniacs)
DC Comics: July, 1996 - No. 27, Nov, 1998 ($1.75/$1.95/$1.99)

	GD	VG	FN	VF	VF/NM	NM-
1-27, ...Christmas Special (1/96, $1.50)						4.00

PINKY LEE (See Adventures of...)

PINKY THE EGGHEAD
I.W./Super Comics: 1963 (Reprints from Noodnik)

	GD	VG	FN	VF	VF/NM	NM-
I.W. Reprint #1,2(nd)	2	4	6	8	11	14
Super Reprint #14-r/Noodnik Comics #4	2	4	6	8	11	14

PINOCCHIO (See 4-Color #92, 252, 545, 1203, Mickey Mouse Mag. V5#3, Movie Comics under Wonderful Advs. of..., New Advs. of..., Thrilling Comics #2, Walt Disney Showcase, Walt Disney's..., Wonderful Advs. of..., & World's Greatest Stories #2)
Dell Publishing Co.: No. 92, 1945 - No. 1203, Mar, 1962 (Disney)

	GD	VG	FN	VF	VF/NM	NM-
Four Color 92-The Wonderful Adventures of...; 16 pg. Donald Duck story ; entire book by Kelly	49	98	147	382	866	1350
Four Color 252 (10/49)-Origin, not by Kelly	12	24	36	79	170	260
Four Color 545 (3/54)-The Wonderful Advs. of...; part-r of 4-Color #92; Disney-movie	8	16	24	56	108	160
Four Color 1203 (3/62)	6	12	18	42	79	115

PINOCCHIO AND THE EMPEROR OF THE NIGHT
Marvel Comics: Mar, 1988 ($1.25, 52 pgs.)

	GD	VG	FN	VF	VF/NM	NM-
1-Adapts film						4.00

PINOCCHIO LEARNS ABOUT KITES (See Kite Fun Book)

PIN-UP PETE (Also see Great Lover Romances & Monty Hall...)
Toby Press: 1952

	GD	VG	FN	VF	VF/NM	NM-
1-Jack Sparling pin-ups	26	52	78	154	252	350

PIONEER MARSHAL (See Fawcett Movie Comics)

PIONEER PICTURE STORIES
Street & Smith Publications: Dec, 1941 - No. 9, Dec, 1943

	GD	VG	FN	VF	VF/NM	NM-
1-The Legless Air Ace begins; WWII-c	52	104	156	328	552	775
2 -True life story of Errol Flynn	24	48	72	142	234	325
3-5,7-9	21	42	63	122	199	275
6-Classic Japanese WWII "Remember Pearl Harbor"-c	142	284	426	909	1555	2200

PIONEER WEST ROMANCES (Firehair #1,2,7-11)
Fiction House Magazines: No. 3, Spring, 1950 - No. 6, Winter, 1950-51

	GD	VG	FN	VF	VF/NM	NM-
3-(52 pgs.)-Firehair continues	20	40	60	115	188	260
4-6	20	40	60	115	188	260

PIPSQUEAK (See The Adventures of...)

PIRACY
E. C. Comics: Oct-Nov, 1954 - No. 7, Oct-Nov, 1955

	GD	VG	FN	VF	VF/NM	NM-
1-Williamson/Torres-a; has full page subscription ad for unpublished Crypt of Terror #1	36	72	108	288	457	625
2-Williamson/Torres-a	22	44	66	176	278	380
3-7: 5-7-Comics Code symbol on cover	17	34	51	136	216	295

NOTE: ***Crandall*** *a-in all; c-2-4.* ***Davis*** *a-1, 2, 6.* ***Evans*** *a-3-7; c-7.* ***Ingels*** *a-3-7.* ***Krigstein*** *a-3-5, 7; c-5, 6.* ***Wood*** *a-1, 2; c-1.*

PIRACY
Gemstone Publishing: March, 1998 - No. 7, Sept, 1998 ($2.50)

	GD	VG	FN	VF	VF/NM	NM-
1-7: E.C. reprints						4.00
Annual 1 ($10.95) Collects #1-4						11.00
Annual 2 ($7.95) Collects #5-7						8.00

PIRANA (See The Phantom #46 & Thrill-O-Rama #2, 3)

PIRATE CORP$, THE (See Hectic Planet)
Eternity Comics/Slave Labor Graphics: 1987 - No. 4, 1988 ($1.95)

	GD	VG	FN	VF	VF/NM	NM-
1-4: 1,2-Color. 3,4-B&W						3.00
Special 1 ('89, B&W)-Slave Labor Publ.						3.00

PIRATE CORP$, THE (Volume 2)
Slave Labor Graphics: 1989 - No. 6, 1992 ($1.95)

	GD	VG	FN	VF	VF/NM	NM-
1-6-Dorkin-s/a						3.00

PIRATE OF THE GULF, THE (See Superior Stories #2)

PIRATES COMICS
Hillman Periodicals: Feb-Mar, 1950 - No. 4, Aug-Sept, 1950 (All 52 pgs.)

	GD	VG	FN	VF	VF/NM	NM-
1	30	60	90	177	289	400
2-Dave Berg-a	18	36	54	107	169	230
3,4-Berg-a	16	32	48	96	151	205

PIRATES OF CONEY ISLAND, THE
Image Comics: Oct, 2006 - No. 8 ($2.99)

	GD	VG	FN	VF	VF/NM	NM-
1-6-Rick Spears-s/Vasilis Lolos-a; two covers. 2-Cloonan var-c						3.00

PIRATES OF DARK WATER, THE (Hanna Barbera)
Marvel Comics: Nov, 1991 - No. 9, Aug, 1992 ($1.95)

	GD	VG	FN	VF	VF/NM	NM-
1-9: 9-Vess-c						3.00

PISCES
Image Comics: Apr, 2015 - No. 3, Jul, 2015 ($3.50/$3.99, unfinished series)

	GD	VG	FN	VF	VF/NM	NM-
1-3-Kurtis Wiebe-s/Johnnie Christmas-a						4.00

P.I.'S: MICHAEL MAUSER AND MS. TREE, THE
First Comics: Jan, 1985 - No. 3, May, 1985 ($1.25, limited series)

	GD	VG	FN	VF	VF/NM	NM-
1-3: Staton-c/a(p)						3.00

PITT, THE (Also see The Draft & The War)
Marvel Comics: Mar, 1988 ($3.25, 52 pgs., one-shot)

	GD	VG	FN	VF	VF/NM	NM-
1-Ties into Starbrand, D.P.7						4.00

PITT (See Youngblood #4 & Gen 13 #3,#4)
Image Comics #1-9/Full Bleed #1/2,10-on: Jan, 1993 - No. 20 ($1.95, intended as a four part limited series)

	GD	VG	FN	VF	VF/NM	NM-
1/2-(12/95)-1st Full Bleed issue						4.00
1-Dale Keown-c/a. 1-1st app. The Pitt						5.00
2-13: All Dale Keown-c/a. 3 (Low distribution). 10 (1/96)-Indicia reads "January 1995"						3.00
14-20: 14-Begin $2.50-c, pullout poster						3.00
TPB-(1997, $9.95) r/#1/2, 1-4						12.00
TPB 2-(1999, $11.95) r/#5-9						12.00

Planetary #14 © WSP

Planet Comics #7 © FH

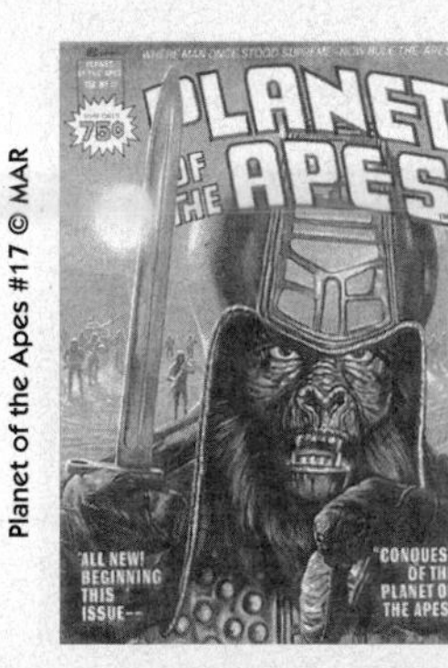
Planet of the Apes #17 © MAR

PITT CREW
Full Bleed Studios: Aug, 1998 - No. 5, Dec, 1999 ($2.50)

	GD 2.0	VG 4.0	FN 6.0	VF 8.0	VF/NM 9.0	NM- 9.2
1-5: 1-Richard Pace-s/Ken Lashley-a. 2-4-Scott Lee-a						3.00

PITT IN THE BLOOD
Full Bleed Studios: Aug, 1996 ($2.50, one-shot)

	GD 2.0	VG 4.0	FN 6.0	VF 8.0	VF/NM 9.0	NM- 9.2
nn-Richard Pace-a/script						3.00

PIXIE & DIXIE & MR. JINKS (TV)(See Jinks, Pixie, and Dixie & Whitman Comic Books)
Dell Publishing Co./Gold Key: July-Sept, 1960 - Feb, 1963 (Hanna-Barbera)

	GD 2.0	VG 4.0	FN 6.0	VF 8.0	VF/NM 9.0	NM- 9.2
Four Color 1112	7	14	21	49	92	135
Four Color 1196,1264, 01-631-207 (Dell, 7/62)	5	10	15	35	63	90
1(2/63-Gold Key)	6	12	18	37	66	95

PIXIE PUZZLE ROCKET TO ADVENTURELAND
Avon Periodicals: Nov, 1952

	GD 2.0	VG 4.0	FN 6.0	VF 8.0	VF/NM 9.0	NM- 9.2
1	23	46	69	136	223	310

PIXIES, THE (Advs. of...)(The Mighty Atom and ...#6 on)(See A-1 Comics #16)
Magazine Enterprises: Winter, 1946 - No. 4, Fall?, 1947; No. 5, 1948

	GD 2.0	VG 4.0	FN 6.0	VF 8.0	VF/NM 9.0	NM- 9.2
1-Mighty Atom	14	28	42	78	112	145
2-5-Mighty Atom	8	16	24	44	57	70
I.W. Reprint #1(1958), 8-(Pee-Wee Pixies), 10-I.W. on cover, Super on inside	2	4	6	10	14	18

PIZZAZZ
Marvel Comics: Oct, 1977 - No. 16, Jan, 1979 (slick-color kids mag. w/puzzles, games, comics)

	GD 2.0	VG 4.0	FN 6.0	VF 8.0	VF/NM 9.0	NM- 9.2
1-Star Wars photo-c/article; origin Tarzan; KISS photos/article; Iron-On bonus; 2 pg. pin-up calendars thru #8	4	8	12	25	40	55
2-Spider-Man-c; Beatles pin-up calendar	2	4	6	13	18	22
3-8: 3-Close Encounters-s; Bradbury-s. 4-Alice Cooper, Travolta; Charlie's Angels/Fonz/Hulk/Spider-Man-c. 5-Star Trek quiz. 6-Asimov-s. 7-James Bond; Spock/Darth Vader-c. 8-TV Spider-Man photo-c/article	2	4	6	11	16	20
9-14: 9-Shaun Cassidy-c. 10-Sgt. Pepper-c/s. 12-Battlestar Galactica-s; Spider-Man app. 13-TV Hulk-c/s. 14-Meatloaf-c/s	2	4	6	10	14	18
15,16: 15-Battlestar Galactica-s. 16-Movie Superman photo-c/s, Hulk.	2	4	6	11	16	20

NOTE: ***Star Wars*** *comics in all (1-6:Chaykin-a, 7-9: DeZuniga-a, 10-13:Simonson/Janson-a. 14-16:Cockrum-a).* ***Tarzan*** *comics, 1pg.-#1-8. 1pg. "Hey Look" by Kurtzman #12-16.*

PLANETARY (See Preview in flip book Gen13 #33)
DC Comics (WildStorm Prod.): Apr, 1999 - No. 27, Dec, 2009 ($2.50/$2.95/$2.99)

	GD 2.0	VG 4.0	FN 6.0	VF 8.0	VF/NM 9.0	NM- 9.2
1-Ellis-s/Cassaday-a/c	2	4	6	10	14	18
1-Special Edition (6/09, $1.00) r/#1 with "After Watchmen" cover frame						3.00
2-5						6.00
6-10						5.00
11-15: 12-Fourth Man revealed						4.00
16-26: 16-Begin $2.95-c. 23-Origin of The Drummer						3.00
27-($3.99) Wraparound gatefold-c						4.00
...: All Over the World and Other Stories (2000, $14.95) r/#1-6 & Preview						15.00
...: All Over the World and Other Stories-Hardcover (2000, $24.95) r/#1-6 & Preview; with dustjacket						25.00
.../Batman: Night on Earth 1 (8/03, $5.95) Ellis-s/Cassaday-a						6.00
...: Crossing Worlds (2004, $14.95) r/Batman, JLA, and The Authority x-overs						15.00
.../JLA: Terra Occulta (11/02, $5.95) Elseworlds; Ellis-s/Ordway-a						6.00
...: Leaving the 20th Century -HC (2004, $24.95) r/#13-18						25.00
...: Leaving the 20th Century -SC (2004, $14.99) r/#13-18						15.00
...: Spacetime Archaeology -HC (2010, $24.99) r/#19-27						25.00
...: Spacetime Archaeology -SC (2010, $17.99) r/#19-27						18.00
.../The Authority: Ruling the World (8/00, $5.95) Ellis-s/Phil Jimenez-a						6.00
...: The Fourth Man -Hardcover (2001, $24.95) r/#7-12						25.00
...: The Planetary Reader (8/03, $5.95) r/#13-15						6.00

PLANETARY BRIGADE (Also see Hero Squared)
BOOM! Studios: Feb, 2006 - No. 2, Mar, 2006 ($2.99)

	GD 2.0	VG 4.0	FN 6.0	VF 8.0	VF/NM 9.0	NM- 9.2
1-3-Giffen & DeMatteis-s/art by various; Haley-c						3.00
... Origins 1-3 (10/06-4/07, $3.99) Giffen & DeMatteis-s/Julia Bax-a						4.00

PLANET COMICS
Fiction House Magazines: 1/40 - No. 62, 9/49; No. 63, Wint, 1949-50; No. 64, Spring, 1950; No. 65, 1951(nd); No. 66-68, 1952(nd); No. 69, Wint, 1952-53; No. 70-72, 1953(nd); No. 73, Winter, 1953-54

	GD 2.0	VG 4.0	FN 6.0	VF 8.0	VF/NM 9.0	NM- 9.2
1-Origin Auro, Lord of Jupiter by Briefer (ends #61); Flint Baker & The Red Comet begin; Eisner/Fine-c	1500	300	4500	11,200	21,600	32,000
2-Lou Fine-c (Scarce)	703	1406	2109	5132	9066	13,000
3-Eisner-c	411	822	1233	2877	5039	7200
4-Gale Allen and the Girl Squadron begins	354	708	1062	2478	4339	6200
5,6-(Scarce): 5-Eisner/Fine-c	383	766	1149	2681	4691	6700
7-12: 8-Robot-c. 12-The Star Pirate begins	300	600	900	1950	3375	4800
13,14: 13-Reff Ryan begins	271	542	813	1734	2967	4200
15-(Scarce)-Mars, God of War begins (11/41); see Jumbo Comics #31 for 1st app.	1000	2000	3000	7600	13,800	20,000
16-20,22	200	400	600	1280	2190	3100
21-The Lost World & Hunt Bowman begin	206	412	618	1318	2259	3200
23-26: 26-Space Rangers begin (9/43), end #71	174	348	522	1114	1907	2700
27-30	139	278	417	890	1520	2150
31-35: 33-Origin Star Pirates Wonder Boots, reprinted in #52. 35-Mysta of the Moon begins, ends #62	123	246	369	787	1344	1900
36-45: 38-1st Mysta of the Moon-c. 41-New origin of "Auro, Lord of Jupiter". 42-Last Gale Allen. 43-Futura begins	110	220	330	704	1202	1700
46-60: 48-Robot-c. 53-Used in **SOTI**, pg. 32	90	180	270	576	988	1400
61-68,70: 64,70-Robot-c. 65-70-All partial-r of earlier issues. 70-r/stories from #41	73	146	219	467	796	1125
69-Used in **POP**, pgs. 101,102	74	148	222	470	810	1150
71-73-No series stories. 71-Space Rangers strip	65	130	195	416	708	1000
I.W. Reprint 1,8,9: 1(nd)-r/#70; cover-r from Attack on Planet Mars. 8 (r/#72), 9-r/#73	9	18	27	59	117	175

NOTE: ***Anderson*** *a-33-38, 40-51 (Star Pirate), 58.* ***Matt Baker*** *a-53-59 (Mysta of the Moon).* ***Celardo*** *c-12.* ***Bill Discount*** *a-71 (Space Rangers).* ***Elias*** *c-70.* ***Evans*** *a-46-49 (Auro, Lord of Jupiter), 50-64 (Lost World).* ***Fine*** *c-2, 5.* ***Hopper*** *a-31, 35 (Gale Allen), 41, 42, 48, 49 (Mysta of the Moon).* ***Ingels*** *a-24-31 (Lost World), 56-61 (Auro, Lord of Jupiter).* ***Lubbers*** *a-44-47 (Space Rangers); c-40, 41.* ***Moreira*** *a-43, 44 (Mysta of the Moon).* ***Renee*** *a-40-49 (Lost World); c-33, 35, 39.* ***Tuska*** *a-30 (Star Pirate).* ***M. Whitman*** *a-50-52 (Mysta of the Moon), 53-58 (Star Pirate); c-71-73.* ***Starr*** *a-59.* ***Zolnerwich*** *c-10. 13-25. Bondage c-53.*

PLANET COMICS
Pacific Comics: 1984 ($5.95)

	GD 2.0	VG 4.0	FN 6.0	VF 8.0	VF/NM 9.0	NM- 9.2
1-Reprints Planet Comics #1(1940)	1	2	3	5	6	8

PLANET COMICS
Blackthorne Publishing: Apr, 1988 - No. 3 ($2.00, color/B&W #3)

	GD 2.0	VG 4.0	FN 6.0	VF 8.0	VF/NM 9.0	NM- 9.2
1-New stories; Dave Stevens-c	4	8	12	25	40	55
2,3: New stories	1	2	3	5	6	8

PLANET HULK (See Incredible Hulk and Giant-Size Hulk #1 (2006))

PLANET HULK (Secret Wars tie-in)
Marvel Comics: Jul, 2015 - No. 5, Nov, 2015 ($4.99/$3.99, limited series)

	GD 2.0	VG 4.0	FN 6.0	VF 8.0	VF/NM 9.0	NM- 9.2
1-($4.99) Humphries-s/Laming-a; Steve Rogers app.; back-up Pak-s//Miyazawa-a						5.00
2-5-($3.99) Doc Green & Devil Dinosaur app.						4.00

PLANET OF THE APES (Magazine) (Also see Adventures on the... & Power Record Comics)
Marvel Comics Group: Aug, 1974 - No. 29, Feb, 1977 (B&W) (Based on movies)

	GD 2.0	VG 4.0	FN 6.0	VF 8.0	VF/NM 9.0	NM- 9.2
1-Ploog-a	5	10	15	33	57	80
2-Ploog-a	3	6	9	16	24	32
3-10	3	6	9	14	20	26
11-20	3	6	9	15	22	28
21-28 (low distribution)	3	6	9	21	33	45
29 (low distribution)	5	10	15	35	63	90

NOTE: ***Alcala*** *a-7-11, 17-22, 24.* ***Ploog*** *a-1-4, 6, 8, 11, 13, 14, 19.* ***Sutton*** *a-11, 12, 15, 17, 19, 20, 23, 24, 29.* ***Tuska*** *a-1-6.*

PLANET OF THE APES
Adventure Comics: Apr, 1990 - No. 24, 1992 ($2.50, B&W)

	GD 2.0	VG 4.0	FN 6.0	VF 8.0	VF/NM 9.0	NM- 9.2
1-New movie tie-in; comes w/outer-c (3 colors)						4.00
1-Limited serial numbered edition ($5.00)	1	2	3	5	6	8
1-2nd printing (no outer-c, $2.50)						3.00
2-24						3.00
Annual 1 ($3.50)						4.00
...Urchak's Folly 1-4 ($2.50, mini-series)						3.00

PLANET OF THE APES (The Human War)
Dark Horse Comics: Jun, 2001 - No. 3, Aug, 2001 ($2.99, limited series)

	GD 2.0	VG 4.0	FN 6.0	VF 8.0	VF/NM 9.0	NM- 9.2
1-3-Follows the 2001 movie; Edginton-s						3.00

PLANET OF THE APES
Dark Horse Comics: Sept, 2001 - No. 6, Feb, 2002 ($2.99, ongoing series)

	GD 2.0	VG 4.0	FN 6.0	VF 8.0	VF/NM 9.0	NM- 9.2
1-6: 1-3-Edginton-s. 1-Photo & Wagner covers. 2-Plunkett & photo-c						3.00

PLANET OF THE APES
BOOM! Studios: Apr, 2011 - No. 15, Jun, 2012 ($3.99)

	GD 2.0	VG 4.0	FN 6.0	VF 8.0	VF/NM 9.0	NM- 9.2
1-4,6-15-Takes place 1200 years before Taylor's arrival; Magno-a; three covers						4.00
5-($1.00) Three covers						3.00
Annual 1 (8/12, $4.99) Short stories by various; six covers						5.00
Giant 1 (9/13, $4.99) Gregory-s/Barreto-a						5.00
Special 1 (2/13, $4.99) Continued from #15; Diego Barreto-a						5.00
Spectacular 1 (7/13, $4.99) Gregory-s/Barreto-a						5.00
...: The Simian Age 1 (12/18, $7.99) Short stories by various; 2 covers						8.00
...: The Time of Man 1 (10/18, $7.99) Short stories by various incl. Magno; 2 covers						8.00

Planet of the Nerds #1 © Constant & Robinson

Plastic Man (2018 series) #2 © DC

Plunge #6 © Joe Hill

	GD 2.0	VG 4.0	FN 6.0	VF 8.0	VF/NM 9.0	NM- 9.2

PLANET OF THE APES: CATACLYSM
BOOM! Studios: Sept, 2012 - No. 12, Aug, 2013 ($3.99)

1-12-Takes place 8 years before Taylor's arrival; Couceiro-a. 1-Multiple covers 4.00

PLANET OF THE APES/ GREEN LANTERN
BOOM! Studios: Feb, 2017 - No. 6, Jul, 2017 ($3.99, limited series)

1-6-Bagenda-a; Hal Jordan & Sinestro on the POTA; Cornelius app.; multiple covers 4.00

PLANET OF THE APES: URSUS
BOOM! Studios: Jan, 2018 - No. 6, Jun, 2018 ($3.99, limited series)

1-6-Spotlight on General Ursus; Walker-s/Mooneyham-a 4.00

PLANET OF THE APES VISIONARIES
BOOM! Studios: Aug, 2018 ($19.99, hardcover graphic novel)

HC-Alternate version in an adaptation of Rod Serling's original screenplay; Dana Gould-s/ Chad Lewis-a/Paolo Rivera-c; bonus character design art 20.00

PLANET OF THE NERDS
AHOY Comics: 2019 - No. 5, 2019 ($3.99, limited series)

1-5-Paul Constant-s/Alan Robinson-a. 1,2-Nakayama-c 4.00

PLANET OF VAMPIRES
Seaboard Publications (Atlas): Feb, 1975 - No. 3, July, 1975

Issue	GD	VG	FN	VF	VF/NM	NM-
1-Neal Adams-c(i); 1st Broderick-c/a(p); Hama-s	3	6	9	16	24	32
2,3: 2-Neal Adams-c. 3-Heath-c/a	2	4	6	13	18	22

PLANET TERRY
Marvel Comics (Star Comics)/Marvel: April, 1985 - No. 12, March, 1986 (Children's comic)

1-12 5.00
1-Variant with "Star Chase" game on last page & inside back-c 15.00

PLANTS VS. ZOMBIES (Based on the Electronic Arts game)
Dark Horse Comics: Jun, 2015 - No. 12, Jun, 2016 ($2.99)

1-12: 1-3-Bully For You; Tobin-s/Chan-a. 4-6-Grown Sweet Home. 7-9-Petal to the Metal 3.00
...: Garden Warfare 1-3 (10/15 - No. 3, 12/15, $2.99) Tobin-s/Chabot-a 3.00

PLASM (See Warriors of Plasm)
Defiant: June, 1993

0-Came bound into Diamond Previews V3#6 (6/93); price is for complete Previews with comic still attached 5.00
0-Comic only removed from Previews 3.00

PLASMER
Marvel Comics UK: Nov, 1993 - No. 4, Feb, 1994 ($1.95, limited series)

1-($2.50)-Polybagged w/4 trading cards 4.00
2-4: Capt. America & Silver Surfer app. 3.00

PLASTIC FORKS
Marvel Comis (Epic Comics): 1990 - No. 5, 1990 ($4.95, 68 pgs., limited series, mature)

Book 1-5: Squarebound 5.00

PLASTIC MAN (Also see Police Comics & Smash Comics #17)
Vital Publ. No. 1,2/Quality Comics No. 3 on: Sum, 1943 - No. 64, Nov, 1956

Issue	GD	VG	FN	VF	VF/NM	NM-
nn(#1)- "In The Game of Death"; Skull-c; Jack Cole-c/a begins; ends-#64?	470	940	1410	3431	6066	8700
nn(#2, 2/44)- "The Gay Nineties Nightmare"	181	362	543	1158	1979	2800
3 (Spr, '46)	118	236	354	749	1287	1825
4 (Sum, '46)	89	178	267	565	970	1375
5 (Aut, '46)	73	146	219	467	796	1125
6-10	60	120	180	381	653	925
11-15,17-20	53	106	159	334	567	800
16-Classic-c	61	122	183	390	670	950
21-30: 26-Last non-r issue?	41	82	123	256	428	600
31-40: 40-Used in POP, pg. 91	34	68	102	199	325	450
41-64: 53-Last precode issue. 54-Robot-c. 64-Sci-fi-c	28	56	84	165	270	375
Super Reprint 11,16,18: 11('63)-r/#16. 16-r/#18 & #21; Cole-a. 18('64)-Spirit-r by Eisner from Police #95	4	8	12	24	37	50

NOTE: ***Cole** r-44, 49, 56, 58, 59 at least. **Cuidera** c-32-64i.*

PLASTIC MAN (See DC Special #15 & House of Mystery #160)
National Periodical Publications/DC Comics: 11-12/66 - No. 10, 5-6/68; V4#11, 2-3/76 - No. 20, 10-11/77

Issue	GD	VG	FN	VF	VF/NM	NM-
1-Real 1st app. Silver Age Plastic Man (House of Mystery #160 is actually tryout); Gil Kane-c/a; 12¢ issues begin	11	22	33	77	166	255
2-5: 4-Infantino-c; Mortimer-a	5	10	15	31	53	75
6-10('68): 7-G.A. Plastic Man & Woozy Winks (1st S.A. app.) app.; origin retold. 10-Sparling-a; last 12¢ issue	4	8	12	27	44	60
V4#11('76)-20: 11-20-Fradon-p. 17-Origin retold	2	4	6	8	11	14

...80-Page Giant (2003, $6.95) reprints origin and other stories in 80-Pg. Giant format 7.00
...Special 1 (8/99, $3.95) 4.00

PLASTIC MAN
DC Comics: Nov, 1988 - No. 4, Feb, 1989 ($1.00, mini-series)

1-4: 1-Origin; Woozy Winks app. 4.00

PLASTIC MAN
DC Comics: Feb, 2004 - No. 20, Mar, 2006 ($2.95/$2.99)

1-20-Kyle Baker-s/a in most. 1-Retells origin. 7,12-Scott Morse-s/a. 8-JLA cameo 3.00
...: On the Lam TPB (2004, $14.95) r/#1-6 15.00
...: Rubber Bandits TPB (2005, $14.99) r/#8-11,13,14 15.00

PLASTIC MAN
DC Comics: Aug, 2018 - No. 6, Jan, 2019 ($3.99, limited series)

1-6-Gail Simone-s/Adriana Melo-a. 1-Origin re-told. 2,3-Man-Bat app. 3-Ross-c 4.00

PLASTRON CAFE
Mirage Studios: Dec, 1992 - No. 4, July, 1993 ($2.25, B&W)

1-4: 1-Teenage Mutant Ninja Turtles app.; Kelly Freas-c. 2-Hildebrandt painted-c. 4-Spaced & Alien Fire stories 3.00

PLAYFUL LITTLE AUDREY (TV)(Also see Little Audrey #25)
Harvey Publications: 6/57 - No. 110, 11/73; No. 111, 8/74 - No. 121, 4/76

Issue	GD	VG	FN	VF	VF/NM	NM-
1	32	64	96	230	515	800
2	12	24	36	82	179	275
3-5	8	16	24	54	102	150
6-10	6	12	18	40	73	105
11-20	5	10	15	31	53	75
21-40	4	8	12	25	40	55
41-60	3	6	9	19	30	40
61-84: 84-Last 12¢ issue	3	6	9	15	22	28
85-99	2	4	6	11	16	20
100-52 pg. Giant	3	6	9	16	23	30
101-103: 52 pg. Giants	3	6	9	14	20	25
104-121	1	3	4	6	8	10

...In 3-D (Spring, 1988, $2.25, Blackthorne #66) 4.00

PLOP! (Also see The Best of DC #60,63 digests)
National Periodical Publications: Sept-Oct, 1973 - No. 24, Nov-Dec, 1976

Issue	GD	VG	FN	VF	VF/NM	NM-
1-Sergio Aragonés-a begins; Wrightson-a	4	8	12	23	37	50
2-4,6-20	3	6	9	14	20	26
5-Wrightson-a	3	6	9	15	22	28
21-24 (52 pgs.). 23-No Aragonés-a; Lord of the Rings parody with Wally Wood-s/a	3	6	9	16	23	30

NOTE: ***Alcala** a-1-3. **Anderson** a-5. **Aragonés** a-1-22, 24. **Ditko** a-16p. **Evans** a-1. **Mayer** a-1. **Orlando** a-21, 22; c-21. **Sekowsky** a-5, 6p. **Toth** a-11. **Wolverton** r-4, 22-24(1 pg.ea.); c-1-12, 14, 17, 18. **Wood** a-14, 16i, 18-24; c-13, 15, 16, 19.*

PLUNGE
DC Comics (Black Label/Hill House Comics): Apr, 2020 - No. 6, Oct, 2020 ($3.99)

1-6-Joe Hill-s/Stuart Immonen-a; back-up Sea Dogs serial in #1-5 4.00

PLUTO (See Cheerios Premiums, Four Color #537, Mickey Mouse Magazine, Walt Disney Showcase #4, 7, 13, 20, 23, 33 & Wheaties)
Dell Publ. Co.: No. 7, 1942; No. 429, 10/52 - No. 1248, 11-1/61-62 (Disney)

Issue	GD	VG	FN	VF	VF/NM	NM-
Large Feature Comic 7(1942)-Written by Carl Barks, Jack Hannah, & Nick George (Barks' 1st comic book work)	232	464	696	1485	2543	3600
Four Color 429 (#1)	11	22	33	73	157	240
Four Color 509	7	14	21	46	86	125
Four Color 595,654,736,853	6	12	18	40	73	105
Four Color 941,1039,1143,1248	5	10	15	33	57	80

PLUTONA
Image Comics: Sept, 2015 - No. 5, Jun, 2016 ($2.99)

1-5-Lemire-s/Lenox-a 3.00

POCKET CLASSICS
Academic Inc. Publications: 1984 (B&W, 4 1/4" x 6 3/4", 68 pages)

C1(Black Beauty. C2(The Call of the Wild). C3(Dr. Jekyll and Mr. Hyde). C4(Dracula). C5(Frankenstein). C6(Huckleberry Finn). C7(Moby Dick). C8(The Red Badge of Courage). C9(The Time Machine). C10(Tom Sawyer). C11(Treasure Island). C12(20,000 Leagues Under the Sea). C13(The Great Adventures of Sherlock Holmes). C14(Gulliver's Travels). C15(The Hunchback of Notre Dame). C16(The Invisible Man). C17(Journey to the Center of the Earth). C18(Kidnapped). C19(The Mysterious Island). C20(The Scarlet Letter). C21(The Story of My Life). C22(A Tale of Two Cities). C23(The Three Musketeers). C24(The War of the Worlds). C25(Around the World in Eighty Days). C26(Captains Courageous). C27 (A Connecticut Yankee in King Arthur's Court). C28(Sherlock Holmes - The Hound of the Baskervilles). C29(The House of the Seven Gables). C30(Jane Eyre). C31(The Last of the

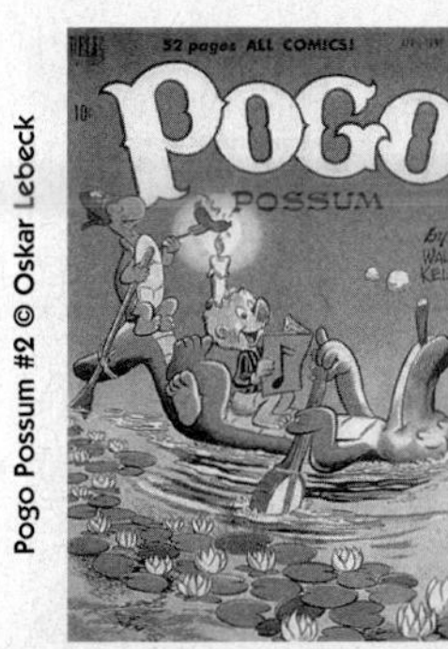

Pogo Possum #2 © Oskar Lebeck

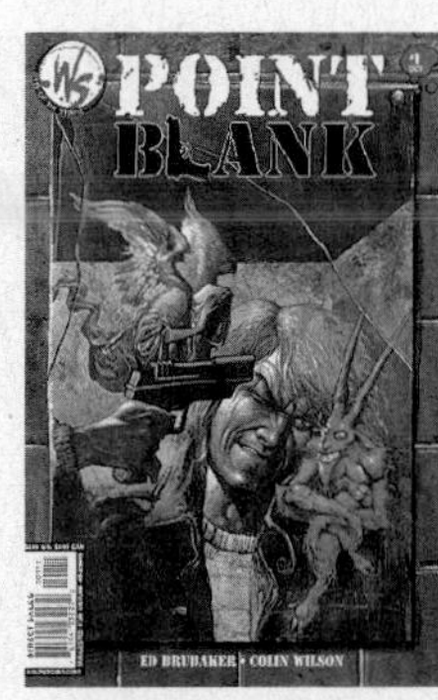

Point Blank #1 © WSP

Poison Elves #33 © Drew Hayes

GD VG FN VF VF/NM NM-
2.0 4.0 6.0 8.0 9.0 9.2

GD VG FN VF VF/NM NM-
2.0 4.0 6.0 8.0 9.0 9.2

Mohicans). C32(The Best of O. Henry). C33(The Best of Poe). C34(Two Years Before the Mast). C35(White Fang). C36(Wuthering Heights). C37(Ben Hur). C38(A Christmas Carol). C39(The Food of the Gods). C40(Ivanhoe). C41(The Man in the Iron Mask). C42(The Prince and the Pauper). C43(The Prisoner of Zenda). C44(The Return of the Native). C45(Robinson Crusoe). C46(The Scarlet Pimpernel). C47(The Sea Wolf). C48(The Swiss Family Robinson). C49(Billy Budd). C50(Crime and Punishment). C51(Don Quixote). C52(Great Expectations). C53(Heidi). C54(The Illiad). C55(Lord Jim). C56(The Mutiny on Board H.M.S. Bounty). C57(The Odyssey). C58(Oliver Twist). C59(Pride and Prejudice). C60(The Turn of the Screw) each... 8.00

Shakespeare Series:
S1(As You Like It). S2(Hamlet). S3(Julius Caesar). S4(King Lear). S5(Macbeth). S6(The Merchant of Venice). S7(A Midsummer Night's Dream). S8(Othello). S9(Romeo and Juliet). S10(The Taming of the Shrew). S11(The Tempest). S12(Twelfth Night) each... 9.00

POCKET COMICS (Also see Double Up)
Harvey Publications: Aug, 1941 - No. 4, Jan, 1942 (Pocket size; 100 pgs.)
(Tied with Spitfire Comics #1 for earliest Harvey comic)

1-Origin & 1st app. The Black Cat, Cadet Blakey the Spirit of '76, The Red Blazer, The Phantom, Sphinx, & The Zebra; Phantom Ranger, British Agent #99, Spin Hawkins, Satan, Lord of Evil begin (1st app. of each); classic Simon horror cover showing an army battling a gigantic monster with the Statue of Liberty in its claws; Simon-c/a in #1-3 300 600 900 2010 3505 5000
2 (9/41)-Black Cat & Nazi WWII-c by Simon 200 400 600 1280 2190 3100
3,4-Black Cat & Nazi WWII-c. 3-Simon-c 187 374 561 1197 2049 2900

POE DAMERON (Star Wars) (Title changes to Star Wars: Poe Dameron with #13)
Marvel Comics: Jun, 2016 - No. 12, May, 2017 ($4.99/$3.99)

1-($4.99) Soule-s/Noto-a/c; prelude to The Force Awakens; back-up w/Eliopoulos-a 5.00
2-6,8-12-($3.99) Black Squadron app. 4.00
7-($4.99) Anzueta-a; Leia cameo 5.00

POGO PARADE (See Dell Giants)

POGO POSSUM (Also see Animal Comics & Special Delivery)
Dell Publishing Co.: No. 105, 4/46 - No. 148, 5/47; 10-12/49 - No. 16, 4-6/54

Four Color 105(1946)-Kelly-c/a 57 114 171 456 1028 1600
Four Color 148-Kelly-c/a 40 80 120 296 673 1050
1-(10-12/49)-Kelly-c/a in all 36 72 108 266 596 925
2 23 46 69 161 356 550
3-5 15 30 45 105 233 360
6-10: 10-Infinity-c 13 26 39 91 201 310
11-16: 11-X-Mas-c 10 20 30 69 147 225
NOTE: *#1-4, 9-13: 52 pgs.; #5-8, 14-16: 36 pgs.*

POINT BLANK (See Wildcats)
DC Comics (WildStorm): Oct, 2002 - No. 5, Feb, 2003 ($2.95, limited series)

1-5-Brubaker-s/Wilson-a/Bisley-c. 1-Variant-c by Wilson; Grifter and John Lynch app. 3.00
TPB (2003, $14.95), (2009, $14.99) r/#1-5; afterword by Brubaker 15.00

POINT ONE
Marvel Comics: Jan, 2012 ($5.99, one-shot)

1-Short story preludes to Marvel's event storylines for 2012; s/a by various 6.00

POISON ELVES (Formerly I, Lusiphur)
Mulehide Graphics: No. 8, 1993- No. 20, 1995 (B&W, magazine/comic size, mature readers)

8-Drew Hayes-c/a/scripts. 2 4 6 8 10 12
9-11: 11-1st comic size issue 2 4 6 8 10 12
12,14,16 1 2 3 5 6 8
13,15-(low print) 2 4 6 8 11 14
15-2nd print 4.00
17-20 1 2 3 5 6 8
...Desert of the Third Sin-(1997, $14.95, TPB)-r/#13-18 15.00
...Patrons-($4.95, TPB)-r/#19,20 5.00
...Traumatic Dogs-(1996, $14.95,TPB)-Reprints I, Lusiphur #7, Poison Elves #8-12 15.00

POISON ELVES (See I, Lusiphur)
Sirius Entertainment: June, 1995 - No. 79, Sept, 2004 ; No. 80, Nov, 2007 ($2.50/$2.95, B&W, mature readers)

1-Linsner-c; Drew Hayes-a/scripts in all. 6.00
1-2nd print 3.00
2-25: 12-Purple Marauder-c/app. 3.00
26-45, 47-49 3.00
46,50-79: 61-Fillbäch Brothers-s/a. 74-Art by Crilley (3 pgs.) 3.00
80-($3.50) Tribute issue to Drew Hayes; sketchbook and notebook art with commentary 3.50
... Baptism By Fire-(2003, $19.95, TPB)-r/#48-59 20.00
... Color Special #1 (12/98, $2.95) 5.00
... Companion (12/02, $3.50) Back-story and character bios 3.50
... : Dark Wars TPB Vol. 1 (2005, $15.95) r/#60,62-68 16.00
... FAN Edition #1 mail-in offer; Drew Hayes-c/s/a 1 2 3 5 6 8
... Rogues-(2002, $15.95, TPB)-r/#40-47 16.00
...Salvation-(2001, $19.95, TPB)-r/#26-39 20.00
...Sanctuary-(1999, $14.95, TPB)-r/#1-12 15.00

POISON ELVES
Ape Entertainment: 2013 - No. 3 ($2.99, B&W)

1-3: 1-Horan-s/Montos-a; Davidsen-s/Ritchie-a; 3 covers by Robertson, Montos & Moore 3.00

POISON ELVES: DOMINION
Sirius Entertainment: Sept, 2005 - No. 6, Sept, 2006 ($3.50, B&W, limited series)

1-6-Keith Davidsen-s/Scott Lewis-a 3.50

POISON ELVES: HYENA
Sirius Entertainment: Sept, 2004 - No. 4, Feb, 2005 ($2.95, B&W, limited series)

1-4-Keith Davidsen-s/Scott Lewis-a 3.00
Ventures TPB Vol. 1: The Hyena Collection (2006, $14.95) r/#1-4 & 2 short stories 15.00

POISON ELVES: LOST TALES
Sirius Entertainment: Jan, 2006 - No. 11 ($2.95, B&W, limited series)

1-11-Aaron Bordner-a; Bordner & Davidsen-s 3.00

POISON ELVES: LUSIPHUR & LIRILITH
Sirius Entertainment: 2001 - No. 4, 2001 ($2.95, B&W, limited series)

1-4-Drew Hayes-s/Jason Alexander-a 3.00
TPB (2002, $11.95) r/#1-4 12.00

POISON ELVES: PARINTACHIN
Sirius Entertainment: 2001 - No. 3, 2002 ($2.95, B&W, limited series)

1-3-Drew Hayes-c/Fillbäch Brothers-s/a 3.00
TPB (2003, $8.95) r/#1-3 9.00

POISON ELVES VENTURES
Sirius Entertainment: May, 2005 - No. 4, Apr, 2006 ($3.50, B&W, limited series)

... #1: Cassanova; ...#2: Lynn; ...#3: The Purple Marauder; #4: Jace - Bordner-a 3.50

POISON IVY: CYCLE OF LIFE AND DEATH
DC Comics: Mar, 2016 - No. 6 ($2.99, limited series)

1-6: 1-Amy Chu-s/Clay Mann-a; covers by Mann & Dodson; Harley Quinn app. 3.00

POKÉMON (TV) (Also see Magical Pokémon Journey)
Viz Comics: Nov, 1998 - 2000 ($3.25/$3.50, B&W)

...Part 1: The Electric Tale of Pikachu
1-Toshiro Ono-s/a 2 4 6 8 10 12
1-4 (2nd through current printings) 4.00
2 6.00
3,4 5.00
TPB ($12.95) 13.00

...Part 2: Pikachu Strikes Back
1 6.00
2-4 5.00
TPB 13.00

...Part 3: Electric Pikachu Boogaloo
1 6.00
2-4 ($2.95-c) 5.00
TPB 13.00

...Part 4: Surf's Up Pikachu
1,3,4 5.00
2 ($2.95-c) 5.00
TPB 13.00
NOTE: Multiple printings exist for most issues

POKÉMON ADVENTURES
Viz Comics: Sept, 1999 - No. 4 ($5.95, B&W, magazine-size)

1-4-Includes stickers bound in 6.00

POKÉMON ADVENTURES
Viz Comics: 2000 - 2002 ($2.95/$4.95, B&W)

Part 2 (2/00-7/00) 1-6-Includes stickers bound in 5.00
Part 3 (8/00-2/01) 1-7 5.00
Part 4 (3/00-6/01) 1-4 5.00
Part 5 (7/01-10/01) 1-4 5.00
Part 6: 1-4, Part 7 1-5 5.00

POKÉMON: THE FIRST MOVIE
Viz Comics: 1999 ($3.95)

Mewtwo Strikes Back 1-4 5.00
Pikachu's Vacation 5.00

POKÉMON: THE MOVIE 2000

Polarity #3 © BOOM!

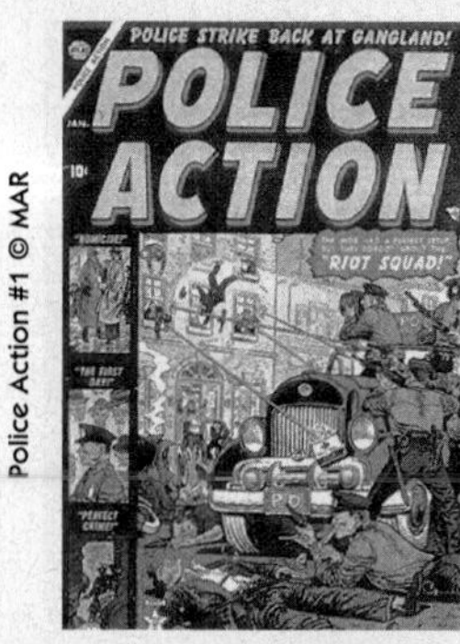

Police Action #1 © MAR

Police Comics #100 © QUA

	GD	VG	FN	VF	VF/NM	NM-
	2.0	4.0	6.0	8.0	9.0	9.2

Viz Comics: 2000 ($3.95)
1-Official movie adaption 5.00
Pikachu's Rescue Adventure 5.00
...:The Power of One (mini-series) 1-3 5.00

POLARITY
BOOM! Studios: Apr, 2013 - No. 4 ($3.99, limited series)
1-4: 1-Bemis-s/Coelho-a; 3 covers 4.00

POLICE ACADEMY (TV)
Marvel Comics: Nov, 1989 - No. 6, Feb, 1990 ($1.00)
1-6: Based on TV cartoon; Post-c/a(p) in all 4.00

POLICE ACTION
Atlas News Co.: Jan, 1954 - No. 7, Nov, 1954
1-Violent-a by Robert Q. Sale 34 68 102 204 332 460
2 17 34 51 100 158 215
3-7: 7-Powell-a 15 30 45 90 140 190
NOTE: *Ayers a-4, 5. Colan a-1. Forte a-1, 2. Mort Lawrence a-5. Maneely a-3; c-1, 5. Reinman a-6, 7.*

POLICE ACTION
Atlas/Seaboard Publ.: Feb, 1975 - No. 3, June, 1975
1-3: 1-Lomax, N.Y.P.D., Luke Malone begin; McWilliams-a. 2-Origin Luke Malone, Manhunter; Ploog-a 2 4 6 10 14 18
NOTE: *Ploog art in all. Sekowsky/McWilliams a-1-3. Thorne c-3.*

POLICE AGAINST CRIME
Premiere Magazines: April, 1954 - No. 9, Aug, 1955
1-Disbrow-a; extreme violence (man's face slashed with knife); Hollingsworth-a
48 96 144 302 514 725
2-Hollingsworth-a 27 54 81 158 259 360
3-9 22 44 66 130 213 295

POLICE BADGE #479 (Formerly Spy Thrillers #1-4)
Atlas Comics (PrPl): No. 5, Sept, 1955
5-Maneely-c/a (6 pgs.); Heck-a 15 30 45 84 127 170

POLICE CASE BOOK (See Giant Comics Editions)

POLICE CASES (See Authentic... & Record Book of...)

POLICE COMICS
Quality Comics Group (Comic Magazines): Aug, 1941 - No. 127, Oct, 1953
1-Origin/1st app. Plastic Man by Jack Cole (r-in DC Special #15), The Human Bomb by Gustavson, & No. 711; intro. The Firebrand by Reed Crandall, The Mouthpiece by Guardineer, Phantom Lady, & The Sword; Chic Carter by Eisner app.; Firebrand-c 1-4
1200 2400 3600 9100 16,550 24,000
2-Plastic Man smuggles opium 320 640 960 2240 3920 5600
3 245 490 735 1568 2684 3800
4 210 420 630 1334 2292 3250
5-Plastic Man covers begin, end #102; Plastic Man forced to smoke marijuana
366 732 1098 2562 4481 6400
6,7 177 354 531 1124 1937 2750
8-Manhunter begins (origin/1st app.) (3/42) 200 400 600 1280 2190 3100
9,10 139 278 417 883 1517 2150
11-The Spirit strip reprints begin by Eisner (origin-strip #1); 1st comic book app. The Spirit & 1st cover app. (9/42) 406 812 1218 2842 4971 7100
12-Intro. Ebony 184 368 552 1168 2009 2850
13-Intro. Woozy Winks; last Firebrand 194 388 582 1242 2121 3000
14-19: 15-Last No. 711; Destiny begins 77 154 231 493 847 1200
20-The Raven x-over in Phantom Lady; features Jack Cole himself
81 162 243 518 884 1250
21,22: 21-Raven & Spider Widow x-over in Phantom Lady (cameo in #22)
65 130 195 416 708 1000
23-30: 23-Last Phantom Lady. 24-26-Flatfoot Burns by Kurtzman in all
58 116 174 371 636 900
31-41: 37-1st app. Candy by Sahle & begins (12/44). 41-Last Spirit-r by Eisner
50 100 150 315 533 750
42,43-Spirit-r by Eisner/Fine 42 84 126 265 445 625
44-Fine Spirit-r begin, end #88,90,92 42 84 126 265 445 625
45-50: 50-(#50 on-c, #49 on inside, 1/46) 36 72 108 214 347 480
51-60: 58-Last Human Bomb 30 60 90 177 289 400
61-88,90,92: 63-(Some issues have #65 printed on cover, but #63 on inside) Kurtzman-a, 6 pgs. 90,92-Spirit by Fine 25 50 75 150 245 340
89,91,93-No Spirit stories 23 46 69 136 223 310
94-99,101,102: Spirit by Eisner in all; 101-Last Manhunter. 102-Last Spirit & Plastic Man by Jack Cole 32 64 96 192 314 435
100 39 78 117 231 378 525
103-Content change to crime; Ken Shannon & T-Man begin (1st app. of each, 12/50) 37 74 111 222 361 500
104-112,114-127: Crandall-a most issues (not in 104,105,122,125-127). 109-Atomic bomb story. 112-Crandall-a 22 44 66 132 216 300
113-Crandall-c/a(2), 9 pgs. each 25 50 75 147 241 335
NOTE: *Most Spirit stories signed by Eisner are not by him; all are reprints. Crandall Firebrand-1-8. Spirit by Eisner 1-41, 94-102; by Eisner/Fine-42, 43; by Fine-44-88, 90, 92. 103, 109. Al Bryant c-33, 34. Cole c-17-32, 35-102(most). Crandall c-13, 14. Crandall/Cuidera c-105-127. Eisner c-4i. Gill Fox c-1-3, 4p, 5-12, 15. Bondage c-103, 109, 125.*

POLICE LINE-UP
Avon Periodicals/Realistic Comics #3,4: Aug, 1951 - No. 4, July, 1952 (Painted-c #1-3)
1-Wood-a, 1 pg. plus part-c; spanking panel-r/Saint #5
52 104 156 328 552 775
2-Classic story "The Religious Murder Cult", drugs, perversion; r/Saint #5; c-r/Avon paperback #329 39 78 117 240 395 550
3,4: 3-Kubert-a(r?)/part-c; Kinstler-a (inside-c only) 28 56 84 168 274 380

POLICE TRAP (Public Defender In Action #7 on)
Mainline #1-4/Charlton #5,6: 8-9/54 - No. 4, 2-3/55; No. 5, 7/55 - No. 6, 9/55
1-S&K covers-all issues; Meskin-a; Kirby scripts 40 80 120 246 411 575
2-4 24 48 72 140 230 320
5,6-S&K-c/a 30 60 90 177 289 400

POLICE TRAP
Super Comics: No. 11, 1963; No. 16-18, 1964
Reprint #11,16-18: 11-r/Police Trap #3. 16-r/Justice Traps the Guilty #? 17-r/Inside Crime #3 & r/Justice Traps The Guilty #83; 18-r/Inside Crime #3
2 4 6 9 13 16

POLLY & HER PALS (See Comic Monthly #1)

POLLY & THE PIRATES
Oni Press: Sept, 2005 - No. 6, June, 2006 ($2.99, B&W, limited series)
1-6-Ted Naifeh-s/a; Polly is shanghaied by the pirate ship Titania 3.00
TPB (7/06, $11.95, digest) r/#1-6 12.00

POLLYANNA (Disney)
Dell Publishing Co.: No. 1129, Aug-Oct, 1960
Four Color 1129-Movie, Hayley Mills photo-c 7 14 21 49 92 135

POLLY PIGTAILS (Girls' Fun & Fashion Magazine #44 on)
Parents' Magazine Institute/Polly Pigtails: Jan, 1946 - V4#43, Oct-Nov, 1949
1-Infinity-c; photo-c 23 46 69 136 223 310
2-Photo-c 14 28 42 82 121 160
3-5: 3,4-Photo-c 11 22 33 64 90 115
6-10: 7-Photo-c 10 20 30 56 76 95
11-30: 22-Photo-c 9 18 27 50 65 80
31-43: 38-Natalie Wood photo-c 8 16 24 42 54 65

PONY EXPRESS (See Tales of the...)

PONYTAIL (Teen-age)
Dell Publishing Co./Charlton No. 13 on: 7-9/62 - No. 12, 10-12/65; No. 13, 11/69 - No. 20, 1/71
12-641-209(#1) 4 8 12 23 37 50
2-12 3 6 9 17 26 35
13-20 3 6 9 14 19 24

POP
Dark Horse Comics: Aug, 2014 - No. 4, Nov, 2014 ($3.99, limited series)
1-4-Curt Pires-s/Jason Copland-a 4.00

POP COMICS
Modern Store Publ.: 1955 (36 pgs.; 5x7"; in color) (7¢)
1-Funny animal 9 18 27 47 61 75

POPEYE (See Comic Album #7, 11, 15, Comics Reading Libraries *in the Promotional Comics section,* Eat Right to Work and Win, Giant Comic Album, King Comics, Kite Fun Book, Magic Comics, March of Comics #37,52, 66, 80, 96, 117, 134, 148, 157, 169, 194, 246, 264, 274, 294, 453, 465, 477 & Wow Comics, 1st series)

POPEYE
David McKay Publications: 1937 - 1939 (All by Segar)
Feature Books nn (100 pgs.) (Very Rare) 1050 2100 3150 8000 14,500 21,000
Feature Books 2 (52 pgs.) 148 296 444 947 1624 2300
Feature Books 3 (100 pgs.)-r/nn issue with new-c 110 220 330 704 1202 1700
Feature Books 5,10 (76 pgs.) 100 200 300 635 1093 1550
Feature Books 14 (76 pgs.) (Scarce) 116 232 348 742 1271 1800

POPEYE (Strip reprints through 4-Color #70)
Dell #1-65/Gold Key #66-80/King #81-92/Charlton #94-138/Gold Key #139-155/Whitman #156 on: 1941 - 1947; #1, 2-4/48 - #65, 7-9/62; #66, 10/62 - #80, 5/66; #81, 8/66 - #92, 12/67;

Popeye FC #70 © KFS

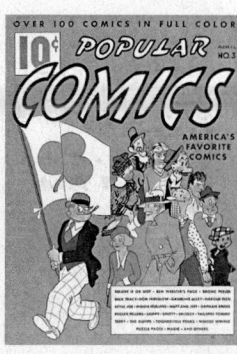

Popular Comics #3 © DELL

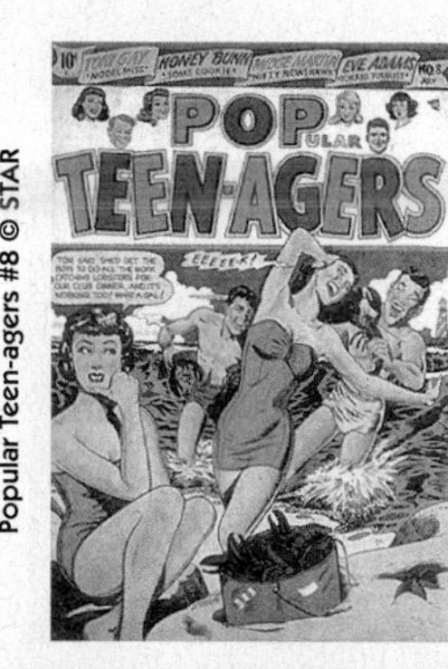

Popular Teen-agers #8 © STAR

	GD 2.0	VG 4.0	FN 6.0	VF 8.0	VF/NM 9.0	NM- 9.2
#94, 2/69 - #138, 1/77; #139, 5/78 - #171, 6/84 (no #93,160,161)						
Large Feature Comic 24('41)-Half by Segar	100	200	300	635	1093	1550
Four Color 25('41)-by Segar	113	226	339	718	1234	1750
Large Feature Comic 10('43)	73	146	219	467	796	1125
Four Color 17('43),26('43)-by Segar	49	98	147	382	866	1350
Four Color 43('44)	30	60	90	216	483	750
Four Color 70('45)-Title: ...& Wimpy	23	46	69	156	348	540
Four Color 113('46-original strips begin),127,145('47),168	14	28	42	94	207	320
1(2-4/48)(Dell)-All new stories continue	34	68	102	245	548	850
2	15	30	45	105	233	360
3-10: 5-Popeye on moon w/rocket-c	12	24	36	79	170	260
11-20	9	18	27	60	120	180
21-40,46: 46-Origin Swee' Pee	8	16	24	51	96	140
41-45,47-50	6	12	18	40	73	105
51-60	5	10	15	35	63	90
61-65 (Last Dell issue)	5	10	15	31	53	75
66(10/62),67-Both 84 pgs. (Gold Key)	6	12	18	40	73	105
68-80	4	8	12	25	40	55
81-92,94-97 (no #93): 97-Last 12¢ issue	3	6	9	20	31	42
98,99,101-107,109-138: 123-Wimpy beats Neil Armstrong to the moon. 130-1st app. Superstuff	3	6	9	14	19	24
100	3	6	9	17	26	35
108-Traces Popeye's origin from 1929	3	6	9	15	22	28
139-155: 144-50th Anniversary issue	2	4	6	8	10	12
156,157,162-167(Whitman)(no #160,161).167(3/82)	2	4	6	10	14	18
158(9/80),159(11/80)-pre-pack only	5	10	15	34	60	85
168-171:(All #90069 on-c; pre-pack) 168(6/83). 169(#168 on-c)(8/83). 170(3/84). 171(6/84)	3	6	9	17	26	35

NOTE: *Reprints-#145, 147, 149, 151, 153, 155, 157, 163-168(1/3), 170.*

POPEYE
Harvey Comics: Nov, 1993 - No. 7, Aug, 1994 ($1.50)

V2#1-7						3.00
...Summer Special V2#1-(10/93, $2.25, 68 pgs.)-Sagendorf-r & others						4.00

POPEYE
IDW Publishing: Apr, 2012 - No. 12, Apr, 2013 ($3.99)

1-12-New stories in classic style; Langridge-s. 1-Action #1 cover swipe. 12-Barney Google and Spark Plug app.						4.00

POPEYE (CLASSIC...)
IDW Publishing: Aug, 2012 - No. 65, Dec, 2017 ($3.99/$4.99)

1-43-Reprints of Bud Sagendorf's classic stories						4.00
44-65-($4.99)						5.00

POPEYE SPECIAL
Ocean Comics: Summer, 1987 - No. 2, Sept, 1988 ($1.75/$2.00)

1,2: 1-Origin						4.00

POPPLES (TV, movie)
Star Comics (Marvel): Dec, 1986 - No. 4, Jun, 1987

1-4-Based on toys						5.00

POPPO OF THE POPCORN THEATRE
Fuller Publishing Co. (Publishers Weekly): 10/29/55 - No. 13, 1956 (weekly)

1	10	20	30	56	76	95
2-5	7	14	21	37	46	55
6-13	6	12	18	31	38	45

NOTE: *By **Charles Biro**. 10¢ cover, given away by supermarkets such as IGA.*

POP-POP COMICS
R. B. Leffingwell Co.: No date (Circa 1945) (52 pgs.)

1-Funny animal	17	34	51	100	158	215

POPULAR COMICS
Dell Publishing Co.: Feb, 1936 - No. 145, July-Sept, 1948

1-Dick Tracy (1st comic book app.), Little Orphan Annie, Terry & the Pirates, Gasoline Alley, Don Winslow (1st app.), Harold Teen, Little Joe, Skippy, Moon Mullins, Mutt & Jeff, Tailspin Tommy, Smitty, Smokey Stover, Winnie Winkle & The Gumps begin (all strip-r)	986	1972	2958	6900	--	--
2	300	600	900	2100	--	--
3	229	458	687	1600	--	--
4-6(7/36): 5-Tom Mix begins. 6-1st app. Scribbly	179	358	537	1250	--	--
7-10: 8,9-Scribbly & Reglar Fellers app.	143	286	429	1000	--	--
11-20: 12-X-Mas-c	86	172	301	495	785	1075
21-27: 27-Last Terry & the Pirates, Little Orphan Annie, & Dick Tracy	62	124	217	357	566	775
28-37: 28-Gene Autry app. 31,32-Tim McCoy app. 35-Christmas-c; Tex Ritter app.	48	96	168	276	438	600
38-43: Tarzan in text only. 38-(4/39)-Gang Busters (Radio, 2nd app.) & Zane Grey's Tex Thorne begins? 43-The Masked Pilot app.; 1st non-funny-c?	46	92	161	265	423	580
44,45: 45-Hurricane Kid-c	42	84	149	242	384	525
46-Origin/1st app. Martan, the Marvel Man(12/39)	56	112	196	322	511	700
47-49-Martan, the Marvel Man-c	46	92	161	265	420	575
50-Gang Busters-c	39	78	137	224	355	485
51-Origin The Voice (The Invisible Detective) strip begins (5/40)	42	84	147	242	384	525
52-Classic Martan blasting robots-c/sty	68	136	238	391	621	850
53-56: 55-End of World story	37	74	130	213	337	460
57-59-Martan, the Marvel Man-c	46	92	161	265	420	575
60-Origin/1st app. Professor Supermind and Son (2/41)	43	86	151	247	394	540
61-64,66-Professor Supermind-c. 63-Smilin' Jack begins	35	70	123	201	318	435
65-Classic Professor Supermind WWII-c	46	92	161	265	420	575
67-71	23	46	69	136	223	310
72-The Owl & Terry & the Pirates begin (2/42); Smokey Stover reprints begin	42	84	126	242	371	500
73-75	29	58	87	167	259	350
76-78-Capt. Midnight in all (see The Funnies #57)	40	80	120	230	358	485
79-85-Last Owl	27	54	81	155	238	320
86-99: 86-Japanese WWII-c. 98-Felix the Cat, Smokey Stover-r begin	18	36	54	104	157	210
100	20	40	60	115	175	235
101-130	10	20	30	58	89	120
131-145: 142-Last Terry & the Pirates	9	18	27	52	79	105

NOTE: *Martan, the Marvel Man c-47-49, 52, 57-59. Professor Supermind c-60-63, 64(1/2), 65, 66. The Voice c-53.*

POPULAR FAIRY TALES (See March of Comics #6, 18)

POPULAR ROMANCE
Better-Standard Publications: No. 5, Dec, 1949 - No. 29, July, 1954

5	20	40	60	115	185	255
6-9: 7-Palais-a; lingerie panels	15	30	45	83	124	165
10-Wood-a (2 pgs.)	15	30	45	90	140	190
11,12,14-16,18-21,28,29	14	28	42	76	108	140
13,17-Severin/Elder-a (3&8 pgs.)	14	28	42	80	115	150
22-27-Toth-a	15	30	45	83	124	165

NOTE: *All have photo-c. **Tuska** art in most issues.*

POPULAR TEEN-AGERS (Secrets of Love) (School Day Romances #1-4)
Star Publications: No. 5, Sept, 1950 - No. 23, Nov, 1954

5-Toni Gay, Midge Martin & Eve Adams continue from School Day Romances; Ginger Bunn (formerly Ginger Snapp & becomes Honey Bunn #6 on) begins; all features end #8	47	94	141	296	498	700
6-8 (7/51)-Honey Bunn begins; all have L. B. Cole-c; 6-Negligee panels	40	80	120	246	411	575
9-(...Romances; 1st romance issue, 10/51)	36	72	108	216	351	485
10-(...Secrets of Love thru #23)	34	68	102	204	332	460
11,16,18,19,22,23	31	62	93	182	296	410
12,13,17,20,21-Disbrow-a	32	64	96	190	310	430
14-Harrison/Wood-a	39	78	117	240	395	550
15-Wood?, Disbrow-a	34	68	102	204	332	460
Accepted Reprint 5,6 (nd); L.B. Cole-c	10	20	30	53	76	95

NOTE: *All have **L. B. Cole** covers.*

PORKY PIG (See Bugs Bunny &..., Kite Fun Book, Looney Tunes, March of Comics #42, 57, 71, 89, 99, 113, 130, 143, 164, 175, 192, 209, 218, 367, and Super Book #6, 18, 30)

PORKY PIG (...& Bugs Bunny #40-69)
Dell Publishing Co./Gold Key No. 1-93/Whitman No. 94 on: No. 16, 1942 - No. 81, Mar-Apr, 1962; Jan, 1965 - No. 109, June, 1984

Four Color 16(#1, 1942)	100	200	300	800	1800	2800
Four Color 48(1944)-Carl Barks-a	98	196	294	794	1772	2750
Four Color 78(1945)	28	56	84	202	451	700
Four Color 112(7/46)	16	32	48	111	246	380
Four Color 156,182,191('49)	11	22	33	75	160	245
Four Color 226,241('49),260,271,277,284,295	9	18	27	61	123	185
Four Color 303,311,322,330: 322-Sci/fi-c/story	8	16	24	51	96	140
Four Color 342,351,360,370,385,399,410,426	6	12	18	40	73	105
25 (11-12/52)-30	5	10	15	33	57	80
31-40	5	10	15	30	50	70
41-60	4	8	12	25	40	55
61-81(3-4/62)	3	6	9	21	33	45

Post Americana #1 © Steve Skroce

The Power Company #1 © DC

Powerhouse Pepper #1 © MAR

	GD	VG	FN	VF	VF/NM	NM-
	2.0	4.0	6.0	8.0	9.0	9.2
1(1/65-Gold Key)(2nd Series)	5	10	15	31	53	75
2,4,5-r/4-Color 226,284 & 271 in that order	3	6	9	19	30	40
3,6-10: 3-r/Four Color #342	3	6	9	16	24	32
11-30	3	6	9	14	19	24
31-54	2	4	6	10	14	18
55-70	2	4	6	8	11	14
71-93(Gold Key)	2	3	4	6	8	10
94-96	2	4	6	8	10	12
97(9/80),98-pre-pack only (99 known not to exist)	4	8	12	27	44	60
100	2	4	6	10	14	18
101-105: 104(2/82). 105(4/82)	2	4	6	8	11	14
106-109 (All #90140 on-c, no date or date code): 106(7/83), 107(8/83), 108(2/84), 109(6/84) low print run	3	6	9	14	20	26

NOTE: *Reprints-#1-8, 9-35(2/3); 36-46(1/4-1/2), 58, 67, 69-74, 76, 78, 102-109(1/3-1/2).*

PORKY PIG'S DUCK HUNT
Saalfield Publishing Co.: 1938 (12pgs.)(large size)(heavy linen-like paper)

2178-1st app. Porky Pig & Daffy Duck by Leon Schlesinger. Illustrated text story book written in verse. 1st book ever devoted to these characters. (see Looney Tunes #1 for their 1st comic book app.) 77 154 231 493 847 1200

PORTAL BOUND
Aspen MLT: No. 0, Feb, 2018 - No. 5, Aug, 2018 ($1.50/$3.99)

0-($1.50) Roslan & Carrasco-s/Arizmendi-a; 2 covers; bonus character sketches 3.00
1-5-($3.99) Roslan & Carrasco-s/Arizmendi-a 4.00

PORTENT, THE
Image Comics: Feb, 2006 - No. 4, Aug, 2006 ($2.99)

1-4-Peter Bergting-s/a 3.00
Vol. 1: Duende TPB (2006, 12.99) r/#1-4; pin-up art; intro. by Kaluta 13.00

PORTIA PRINZ OF THE GLAMAZONS
Eclipse Comics: Dec, 1986 - No. 6, Oct, 1987 ($2.00, B&W, Baxter paper)

1-6 3.00

POSEIDON IX (Also see Aphrodite IX and (Ninth) IX Generation)
Image Comics (Top Cow): Sept, 2015 ($3.99, one-shot)

1-Howard-s/Sevy-a; story continues in IX Generation #5 4.00

POSSESSED, THE
DC Comics (Cliffhanger): Sept, 2003 - No. 6, March, 2004 ($2.95, limited series)

1-6-Johns & Grimminger-s/Sharp-a 3.00
TPB (2004, $14.95) r/#1-6; promo art and sketch pages 15.00

POSTAL (Also see Eden's Fall)
Image Comics (Top Cow): Feb, 2015 - Present ($3.99)

1-24: 1-Matt Hawkins & Bryan Hill-s/Issac Goodheart-a 4.00
25-($5.99) Matt Hawkins & Bryan Hill-s/Issac Goodheart-a 6.00
...: Dossier 1 (11/15, $3.99) Ryan Cady-a; background on Eden and character profiles 4.00
...: Mark 1 (2/18, $3.99) Spotlight on Mark; Ienco-a 4.00
...: Night Shift 1 (12/20, $3.99) Spotlights on Roy Magnus & Molly; Goodheart-c 4.00

POSTAL: DELIVERANCE
Image Comics (Top Cow): Jul, 2019 - Present ($3.99)

1-8-Bryan Hill-s/Raffaele Ienco-a 4.00

POST AMERICANA
Image Comics: Dec, 2020 - Present ($3.99)

1-3-Steve Skroce-s/a 4.00

POST GAZETTE (See Meet the New... in the Promotional Comics section)

POWDER RIVER RUSTLERS (See Fawcett Movie Comics)

POWER & GLORY (See American Flagg! & Howard Chaykin's American Flagg!
Malibu Comics (Bravura): Feb, 1994 - No. 4, May, 1994 ($2.50, limited series, mature)

1A, 1B-By Howard Chaykin; w/Bravura stamp 3.00
1-Newsstand ed. (polybagged w/children's warning on bag), Gold ed., Silver-foil ed., Blue-foil ed.(print run of 10,000), Serigraph ed. (print run of 3,000)($2.95)-Howard Chaykin-c/a begin 4.00
2-4-Contains Bravura stamp 3.00
Holiday Special (Win '94, $2.95) 3.00

POWER COMICS
Holyoke Publ. Co./Narrative Publ.: 1944 - No. 4, 1945

	GD	VG	FN	VF	VF/NM	NM-
1-L. B. Cole-c	219	438	657	1402	2401	3400
2-Hitler, Hirohito-c (scarce)	432	864	1296	3154	5577	8000
3-Classic L.B. Cole-c; Dr. Mephisto begins?	432	864	1296	3154	5577	8000
4-L.B. Cole-c; Miss Espionage app. #3,4; Leav-a	258	516	774	1651	2826	4000

POWER COMICS
Power Comics Co.: 1977 - No. 5, Dec, 1977 (B&W)

	GD	VG	FN	VF	VF/NM	NM-
1- "A Boy And His Aardvark" by Dave Sim; first Dave Sim aardvark (not Cerebus)	3	6	9	17	26	35
1-Reprint (3/77, black-c)	1	2	3	5	6	8
2-Cobalt Blue by Gustovich	1	3	4	6	8	10
3-5: 3-Nightwitch. 4-Northern Light. 5-Bluebird	1	3	4	6	8	10

POWER COMICS
Eclipse Comics (Acme Press): Mar, 1988 - No. 4, Sept, 1988 ($2.00, B&W, mini-series)

1-4: Bolland, Gibbons-r in all 3.00

POWER COMPANY, THE
DC Comics: Apr, 2002 - No. 18, Sep, 2003 ($2.50/$2.75)

1-6-Busiek-s/Grummett-a. 6-Green Arrow & Black Canary-c/app. 3.00
7-18: 7:Begin $2.75-c. 8,9-Green Arrow app. 11-Firestorm joins. 15-Batman app. 3.00
...Bork (3/02) Busiek-s/Dwyer-a; Batman & Flash (Barry Allen) app. 3.00
...Josiah Power (3/02) Busiek-s/Giffen-a; Superman app. 3.00
...Manhunter (3/02) Busiek-s/Jurgens-a; Nightwing app. 3.00
...Sapphire (3/02) Busiek-s/Bagley-a; JLA & Kobra app. 3.00
...Skyrocket (3/02) Busiek-s/Staton-a; Green Lantern (Hal Jordan) app. 3.00
...Striker Z (3/02) Busiek-s/Bachs-a; Superboy app. 3.00
...Witchfire (3/02) Busiek-s/Haley-a; Wonder Woman app. 3.00

POWER CUBED
Dark Horse Comics: Sept, 2015 - No. 4, Jan, 2016 ($3.99, limited series)

1-4-Aaron Lopresti-s/a 4.00

POWER FACTOR
Wonder Color Comics #1/Pied Piper #2: May, 1987 - No. 2, 1987 ($1.95)

1,2: Super team. 2-Infantino-c 3.00

POWER FACTOR
Innovation Publishing: Oct, 1990 - No. 3, 1991 ($1.95/$2.25)

1-3: 1-R-/1st story + new-a, 2-r/2nd story + new-a. 3-Infantino-a 3.00

POWER GIRL (See All-Star #58, Infinity, Inc., JSA Classified, Showcase #97-99)
DC Comics: June, 1988 - No. 4, Sept, 1988 ($1.00, color, limited series)

	GD	VG	FN	VF	VF/NM	NM-
1	3	6	9	14	20	26
2-4	1	2	3	5	6	8

TPB (2006, $14.99) r/Showcase #97-99; Secret Origins #11; JSA Classified #1-4 and pages from JSA #32,39; cover gallery 15.00

POWER GIRL
DC Comics: Jul, 2009 - No. 27, Oct, 2011 ($2.99)

	GD	VG	FN	VF	VF/NM	NM-
1-Amanda Conner-a; covers by Conner and Hughes; Ultra-Humanite app.	3	6	9	17	25	34
2-Conner-a; covers by Conner and Hughes	2	4	6	13	18	22

3-10: 3-6-Covers by Conner and March 5.00
11-26: 13-23-Winick-s/Basri-a. 20,21-Crossover with Justice League: Generation Lost #18-22 23-Zatanna app. 24,25-Batman app.; Prasetya-a 4.00
27-Ample cleavage cover; Cyclone app. 5 10 15 33 57 80
...: Aliens and Apes SC (2010, $17.99) r/#7-12 18.00
...: A New Beginning SC (2010, $17.99) r/#1-6; gallery of variant covers 18.00
...: Bomb Squad SC (2011, $14.99) r/#13-18 15.00

POWERHOUSE PEPPER COMICS (See Gay Comics, Joker Comics & Tessie the Typist)
Marvel Comics (20CC): No. 1, 1943; No. 2, May, 1948 - No. 5, Nov, 1948

	GD	VG	FN	VF	VF/NM	NM-
1-(60 pgs.)-Wolverton-a in all; c-2,3	235	470	705	1492	2571	3650
2	103	206	309	659	1130	1600
3,4	97	194	291	621	1061	1500
5-(Scarce)	113	226	339	723	1237	1750

POWERLESS
Marvel Comics: Aug, 2004 - No. 6, Jan, 2005 ($2.99, limited series)

1-6-Peter Parker, Matt Murdock and Logan without powers; Gaydos-a 3.00
TPB (2005, $14.99) r/series; sketch page by Gaydos 15.00

POWER LINE
Marvel Comics (Epic Comics): May, 1988 - No. 8, Sept, 1989 ($1.25/$1.50)

1-8: 2-Williamson-i. 3-Dr. Zero app. 4-7-Morrow-a. 8-Williamson-i 3.00

POWER LINES
Image Comics: Mar, 2016 - No. 3 ($3.50/$3.99)

1-3-Jimmie Robinson-s/a. 1-($3.50-c). 2-Begin $3.99-c 4.00

POWER LORDS
DC Comics: Dec, 1983 - No. 3, Feb, 1984 (Limited series, Mando paper)

1-3: Based on Revell toys 4.00

Power Man #49 © MAR

The Power of Shazam! #42 © DC

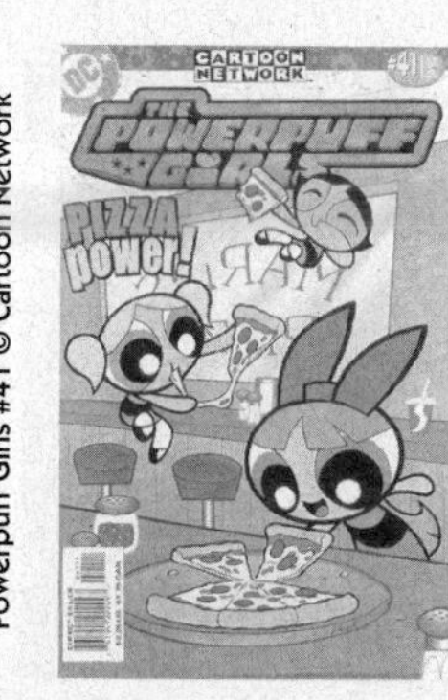

Powerpuff Girls #41 © Cartoon Network

	GD 2.0	VG 4.0	FN 6.0	VF 8.0	VF/NM 9.0	NM- 9.2
POWER MAN (Formerly Hero for Hire; ...& Iron Fist #50 on; see Cage & Giant-Size...)						
Marvel Comics Group: No. 17, Feb, 1974 - No. 125, Sept, 1986						
17-Luke Cage continues; Iron Man app.	4	8	12	28	47	65
18,20: 18-Last 20¢ issue; intro. Wrecking Crew	3	6	9	16	23	30
19-1st app. Cottonmouth	4	8	12	28	47	65
21-23,25-30	2	4	6	9	12	15
24-Intro. Black Goliath	7	14	21	46	86	125
30-(30¢-c variant, limited distribution)(4/76)	4	8	12	28	47	65
31-46: 31-Part Neal Adams-i. 34-Last 25¢ issue. 36-r/Hero For Hire #12. 41-1st app. Thunderbolt. 45-Starlin-c.	1	3	4	6	8	10
31-34-(30¢-c variants, limited distribution)(5-8/76)	5	10	15	30	50	70
44-46-(35¢-c variants, limited distribution)(6-8/77)	9	18	27	62	126	190
47-Barry Smith-a	2	4	6	8	10	12
47-(35¢-c variant, limited distribution)(10/77)	9	18	27	58	114	170
48-Power Man/Iron Fist 1st meet; Byrne-a(p)	5	10	15	35	63	90
49-Byrne-a(p)	3	6	9	15	22	28
50-Iron Fist joins Cage; Byrne-a(p)	5	10	15	33	57	80
51-56,58-65,67-77: 58-Intro El Aguila. 75-Double size. 77-Daredevil app.	1	2	3	5	6	8
57-New X-Men app. (6/79)	4	8	12	25	40	55
66-2nd app. Sabretooth (see Iron Fist #14)	5	10	15	35	63	90
78,84: 78-3rd app. Sabretooth (cameo under cloak). 84-4th app. Sabretooth	4	8	12	25	40	55
79-83,85-99,101-124: 87-Moon Knight app. 109-The Reaper app.						4.00
100-Double size; Origin K'un L'un	1	2	3	5	6	8
125-Double size; Death of Iron Fist	2	4	6	9	12	15
Annual 1(1976)-Punisher cameo in flashback	3	6	9	15	23	30
NOTE: *Austin c-102i. **Byrne** a-48-50; c-102, 104, 106, 107, 112-116. **Kane** c(p)-24, 25, 28, 48. **Miller** a-68, 76(2 pgs.); c-66-68, 70-74, 80i. **Mooney** a-38i, 53i, 55i. **Nebres** a-76p. **Nino** a-42i, 43i. **Perez** a-27. **B. Smith** a-47i. **Tuska** a(p)-17, 20, 24, 26, 28, 29, 36, 47. Painted c-75, 100.*						
POWER MAN AND IRON FIST						
Marvel Comics: Apr, 2011 - No. 5, Jul, 2011 ($2.99, limited series)						
1-5-Van Lente-s/Alves-a; Victor Alvarez as Power Man						3.00
POWER MAN AND IRON FIST						
Marvel Comics: Apr, 2016 - No. 15, Jun, 2017 ($3.99)						
1-15: 1-Luke Cage and Danny Rand; David Walker-s/Sanford Greene-a; Tombstone app. 6-9-Civil War II tie-in						4.00
...: Sweet Christmas Annual 1 (2/17, $4.99) Walker-s/Hepburn-a; Daimon Hellstrom app.						5.00
POWER OF PRIME						
Malibu Comics (Ultraverse): July, 1995 - No. 4, Nov, 1995 ($2.50, lim. series)						
1-4						3.00
POWER OF SHAZAM!, THE (See SHAZAM!)						
DC Comics: 1994 (Painted graphic novel) (Prequel to new series)						
Hardcover-($19.95)-New origin of Shazam!; Ordway painted-c/a & script	3	6	9	14	20	25
Softcover-($7.50), Softcover-($9.95)-New-c.	2	4	6	8	10	12
POWER OF SHAZAM!, THE						
DC Comics: Mar, 1995 - No. 47, Mar, 1999; No. 48, Mar, 2010 ($1.50/$1.75/$1.95/$2.50)						
1-Jerry Ordway scripts begin	2	4	6	8	11	14
2-20: 4-Begin $1.75-c. 6:Re-intro of Capt. Nazi. 8-Re-intro of Spy Smasher, Bulletman & Minuteman; Swan-a (7 pgs.). 11-Re-intro of Ibis, Swan-a(2 pgs.). 14-Gil Kane-a(p). 20-Superman-c/app.; "Final Night"						3.00
21-47: 21-Plastic Man-c/app. 22-Batman-c/app. 24-Spy Smasher WWII story. 35,36-X-over w/Starman #39,40. 38-41-Mr. Mind. 43-Bulletman app. 45-JLA-c/app.						3.00
48-(3/10, $2.99) Blackest Night one-shot; Osiris rises as a Black Lantern; Kramer-a						3.00
#1,000,000 (11/98) 853rd Century x-over; Ordway-c/s/a						3.00
Annual 1 (1996, $2.95)-Legends of the Dead Earth story; Jerry Ordway-c; Mike Manley-a						4.00
POWER OF STRONGMAN, THE (Also see Strongman)						
AC Comics: 1989 ($2.95)						
1-Powell G.A.-r						3.00
POWER OF THE ATOM (See Secret Origins #29)						
DC Comics: Aug, 1988 - No. 18, Nov, 1989 ($1.00)						
1-18: 6-Chronos returns; Byrne-p. 9-JLI app.						3.00
POWER OF THE DARK CRYSTAL (Jim Henson)						
BOOM! Studios (Archaia): Feb, 2017 - No. 12, Mar, 2018 ($3.99)						
1-12-Simon Spurrier-s/Kelly & Nichole Matthews-a; multiple covers						4.00
POWER PACHYDERMS						
Marvel Comics: Sept, 1989 ($1.25, one-shot)						
1-Elephant super-heroes; parody of X-Men, Elektra, & 3 Stooges						3.00

	GD 2.0	VG 4.0	FN 6.0	VF 8.0	VF/NM 9.0	NM- 9.2
POWER PACK						
Marvel Comics Group: Aug, 1984 - No. 62, Feb, 1991						
1-($1.00, 52 pgs.)-Origin & 1st app. Power Pack						5.00
2-18,20-26,28,30-45,47-62						3.00
19-(52 pgs.)-Cloak & Dagger, Wolverine app.						4.00
27-Mutant massacre; Wolverine & Sabretooth app.						5.00
29,46: 29-Spider-Man & Hobgoblin app. 46-Punisher app.						4.00
Graphic Novel: Power Pack & Cloak & Dagger: Shelter From the Storm ('89, SC, $7.95) Velluto/Farmer-a						10.00
...Holiday Special 1 (2/92, $2.25, 68 pgs.)						4.00
NOTE: ***Austin** scripts-53. **Mignola** c-20. **Morrow** a-51. **Spiegle** a-55i. **Williamson** a(i)-43, 50, 52.*						
POWER PACK (Volume 2)						
Marvel Comics: Aug, 2000 - No. 4, Nov, 2000 ($2.99, limited series)						
1-4-Doran & Austin-c/a						3.00
POWER PACK						
Marvel Comics: June, 2005 - No. 4, Aug, 2005 ($2.99, limited series)						
1-4-Sumerak-s/Gurihiru-a; back-up Franklin Richards story. 3-Fantastic Four app.						3.00
... Digest (2006, $6.99) r/#1-4						7.00
POWER PACK (Marvel Legacy)						
Marvel Comics: No. 63, Jan, 2018 ($3.99, one-shot)						
63-Devin Grayson-s/Marika Cresta-a						4.00
POWER PACK (Also see Outlawed #1 and Champions)						
Marvel Comics: Jun, 2020 - Present ($3.99)						
1-3-Ryan North-s/Nico Leon-a. 1-Origin retold. 2-The Wizard app. 3-Taskmaster app.						4.00
POWER PACK: DAY ONE						
Marvel Comics: May, 2008 - No. 4, Aug, 2008($2.99, limited series)						
1-4-Van Lente-s/Gurihiru-a; origin retold; Coover-a back-ups. 1-Fantastic Four cameo						3.00
POWER PACK: GROW-UP						
Marvel Comics: Oct, 2019 ($4.99, one-shot)						
1-Louise Simonson-s/June Brigman-a; back-up w/art by Gurihiru; Kofi & Wolverine app.						5.00
POWERPUFF GIRLS, THE (Also see Cartoon Network Starring... #1)						
DC Comics: May, 2000 - No. 70, Mar, 2006 ($1.99/$2.25)						
1	2	4	6	8	10	12
2-10						5.00
11-55,57-70: 25-Pin-ups by Allred, Byrne, Baker, Mignola, Hernandez, Warren						4.00
56-($2.95) Bonus pages; Mojo Jojo-c						5.00
...Double Whammy (12/00, $3.95) r/#1,2 & a Dexter's Lab story						5.00
...Movie: The Comic (9/02, $2.95) Movie adaptation; Phil Moy & Chris Cook-a						4.00
POWERPUFF GIRLS						
IDW Publishing: Sept, 2013 - No. 10, Jun, 2014 ($3.99)						
1-10: 1-Five covers; Troy Little-s/a; Mojo Jojo app. 2-10-Multiple covers on each						4.00
POWERPUFF GIRLS (Based on the 2016 TV reboot)						
IDW Publishing: Jul, 2016 - No. 6, Dec, 2016 ($3.99)						
1-6: 1-4-Derek Charm-a; multiple covers on each. 1-Mojo Jojo app.						4.00
POWERPUFF GIRLS: BUREAU OF BAD						
IDW Publishing: Nov, 2017 - No. 3, Jan, 2018 ($3.99, limited series)						
1-3-Mancini & Goldman-s/Murphy-a; multiple covers on each						4.00
POWERPUFF GIRLS: SUPER SMASH-UP!						
IDW Publishing: Jan, 2015 - No. 5, May, 2015 ($3.99, limited series)						
1-5-Dexter's Laboratory's Dexter & Dee-Dee app.; multiple covers on each						4.00
POWERPUFF GIRLS: THE TIME TIE						
IDW Publishing: May, 2017 - No. 3, Jul, 2017 ($3.99, limited series)						
1-3-Mancini & Goldman-s/Murphy-a; multiple covers on each						4.00
POWER RANGERS (Mighty Morphin Power Rangers)						
BOOM! Studios: Nov, 2020 - Present ($4.99/$3.99)						
1-($4.99) Parrott-s/Mortarino-a; multiple covers; Omega Rangers app.						5.00
2-4-($3.99)						4.00
POWER RANGERS: DRAKKON NEW DAWN (Mighty Morphin Power Rangers)						
BOOM! Studios: Aug, 2020 - No. 3, Oct, 2020 ($4.99, limited series)						
1-3-Burch-s/Ragazzoni-a; multiple covers						5.00
POWER RANGERS: RANGER SLAYER (Mighty Morphin Power Rangers)						
BOOM! Studios: Jul, 2020 ($7.99, one-shot)						
1-Parrott-s/Mora-a; multiple covers						8.00
POWER RANGERS ZEO (TV)(Saban's...)(Also see Saban's Mighty Morphin Power Rangers)						

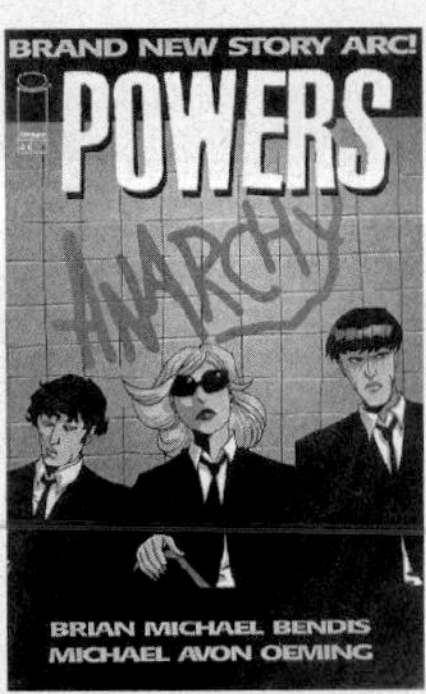

Powers #21 © Jinxworld

Power Up #6 © Leth & Cummings

Preacher #50 © Ennis & Dillon

	GD	VG	FN	VF	VF/NM	NM-
	2.0	4.0	6.0	8.0	9.0	9.2

GD VG FN VF VF/NM NM-
2.0 4.0 6.0 8.0 9.0 9.2

Image Comics (Extreme Studios): Aug, 1996 ($2.50)

1-Based on TV show 4.00

POWER RECORD COMICS (Named Peter Pan Record Comics for #33-47)
Marvel Comics/Power Records: 1974 - 1978 ($1.49, 7x10" comics, 20 pgs. with 45 R.P.M. record) (Clipped corners - reduce value 20%) (Comic alone - 50%; record alone - 50%) (Some copies significantly warped by shrinkwrapping - reduce value 20%) (PR22, PR23, PR38, PR43, PR44 do not exist)

PR10-Spider-Man-r/from #124,125; Man-Wolf app. PR18-Planet of the Apes-r. PR19-Escape From the Planet of the Apes-r. PR20-Beneath the Planet of the Apes-r. PR21-Battle for the Planet of the Apes-r. PR24-Spider-Man II-New-a begins. PR27-Batman "Stacked Cards"; N. Adams-a(p). PR30-Batman "Robin Meets Man-Bat"; N. Adams-r/Det.(7 pgs.).
With record; each... 5 10 15 35 63 90

PR11-Incredible Hulk-r/#171. PR12-Captain America-r/#168. PR13-Fantastic Four-r/#126. PR14-Frankenstein-Ploog-r/#1. PR15-Tomb of Dracula-Colan-r/#2. PR16-Man-Thing-Ploog-r/#5. PR17-Werewolf By Night-Ploog-r/Marvel Spotlight #2. PR28-Superman "Alien Creatures". PR29-Space: 1999 "Breakaway". PR31-Conan-N. Adams-a; reprinted in Conan #116. PR32-Space: 1999 "Return to the Beginning". PR33-Superman-G.A. origin, Buckler-a(p). PR34-Superman. PR35-Wonder Woman-Buckler-a(p)
With record; each... 5 10 15 31 53 75

PR11, PR24-(1981 Peter Pan records re-issues) PR11-New Abomination & Rhino-c
With record; each... 5 10 15 33 57 80

PR25-Star Trek "Passage to Moauv". PR26-Star Trek "Crier in Emptiness." PR36-Holo-Man. PR37-Robin Hood. PR39-Huckleberry Finn. PR40-Davy Crockett. PR41-Robinson Crusoe. PR42-20,000 Leagues Under the Sea. PR47-Little Women
With record; each... 4 8 12 28 47 65

PR25, PR26 (Peter Pan records re-issues with photo covers). PR45-Star Trek "Dinosaur Planet". PR46-Star Trek "The Robot Masters" 4 8 12 28 47 65

NOTE: *Peter Pan re-issues exist for #25-32 and are valued the same.*

POWERS
Image Comics: 2000 - No. 37, Feb, 2004 ($2.95)

1-Bendis-s/Oeming-a; murder of Retro Girl 3 6 9 16 23 30
2-6: 6-End of Retro Girl arc. 1 3 4 6 8 10
7-14: 7-Warren Ellis app. 12-14-Death of Olympia 4.00
15-37: 31-36-Origin of the Powers 3.00
Annual 1 (2001, $3.95) 4.00
...: Anarchy TPB (11/03, $14.95) r/#21-24; interviews, sketchbook, cover gallery 15.00
...Coloring/Activity Book (2001, $1.50, B&W, 8 x 10.5") Oeming-a 3.00
... Firsts 1 (6/15, $1.00) r/#1 3.00
...: Forever TPB (2005, $19.95) r/#31-37; script for #31, sketchbook, cover gallery 20.00
...: Little Deaths TPB (2002, $19.95) r/#7,12-14, Ann. #1, Coloring/Activity Book; sketch pages, cover gallery 20.00
...: Roleplay TPB (2001, $13.95) r/#8-11; sketchbook, cover gallery 14.00
... Scriptbook (2001, $19.95) scripts for #1-11; Oeming sketches 20.00
...: Supergroup TPB (2003, $19.95) r/#15-20; sketchbook, cover gallery 20.00
...: The Definitive Collection Vol. 1 HC (2006, $29.99, dust jacket) r/#1-11 & Coloring/Activity Book, script for #1, sketch pages and covers, interviews, letter column highlights 30.00
...: The Definitive Collection Vol. 2 HC (2009, $29.99, dust jacket) r/#12-24 & Annual #1; cover gallery; 1st Bendis/Oeming Jinx story; interviews, letter column highlights 30.00
...: Who Killed Retro Girl TPB (2000, $21.95) r/#1-6; sketchbook, cover gallery, and promotional strips from Comic Shop News 22.00

POWERS
Marvel Comics (Icon): Jul, 2004 - No. 30, Sept, 2008 ($2.95/$3.95)

1-11,13-24-Bendis-s/Oeming-a. 14-Cover price error 3.00
12-($3.95, 64 pages) 2 covers; Bendis & Oeming interview 4.00
25-30-($3.95, 40 pages) 25-Two covers; Bendis interview 4.00
Annual 2008 (5/08, $4.95) Bendis-s/Oeming-a; interview with Brubaker, Simone, others 5.00
...: Legends TPB (2005, $17.95) r/#1-6; sketchbook, cover gallery 18.00
...: Psychotic TPB (1/06, $19.95) r/#7-12; Bendis & Oeming interview, cover gallery 20.00
...: Cosmic TPB (10/07, $19.95) r/#13-18; script and sketch pages 20.00
...: Secret Identity TPB (12/07, $19.95) r/#19-24; script pages 20.00

POWERS (Volume 3)
Marvel Comics (Icon): Nov, 2009 - No. 11, Jul, 2012 ($3.95)

1-11-Bendis-s/Oeming-a 4.00

POWERS (Volume 5)
Marvel Comics (Icon): Jan, 2015 - No. 8, Apr, 2017 ($3.99)

1-8-Bendis-s/Oeming-a. 1-Bonus photo spread of TV show cast 4.00

POWERS: BUREAU (Follows Volume 3)
Marvel Comics (Icon): Feb, 2013 - No. 12, Nov, 2014 ($3.95)

1-12-Bendis-s/Oeming-a 4.00

POWERS OF X (Weekly series alternating with House of X #1-6)
Marvel Comics: Sept, 2019 - No. 6, Dec, 2019 ($5.99/$4.99)

1-($5.99) Hickman-s/Silva-a 6.00
2-6-($4.99) 4-Mr. Sinister app. 5.00

POWERS THAT BE (Becomes Star Seed No.7 on)
Broadway Comics: Nov, 1995 - No. 6, June, 1996 ($2.50)

1-6: 1-Intro of Fatale & Star Seed. 6-Begin $2.95-c. 3.00
Preview Editions 1-3 (9/95 - 11/95, B&W) 3.00

POWER UP
BOOM! Studios: Jul, 2015 - No. 6, Dec, 2015 ($3.99)

1-6-Katie Leth-s/Matt Cummings-a. 1-Multiple covers 4.00

POW MAGAZINE (Bob Sproul's) (Satire Magazine)
Humor-Vision: Aug, 1966 - No. 3, Feb, 1967 (30¢)

1,2: 2-Jones-a 4 8 12 28 47 65
3-Wrightson-a 5 10 15 34 60 85

PREACHER
DC Comics (Vertigo): Apr, 1995 - No. 66, Oct, 2000 ($2.50, mature)

nn-Preview 10 20 30 69 147 225
1 ($2.95)-Ennis scripts, Dillon-a & Fabry-c in all; 1st app. Jesse, Tulip, & Cassidy
10 20 30 69 147 225
1-Retailer Incentive Edition (5/16, $3.99) r/#1 with new cover by Steve Dillon 4.00
1-Special Edition (6/09, $1.00) r/#1 with "After Watchmen" cover frame 4.00
2-1st app. Saint of Killers. 4 8 12 28 47 65
3 3 6 9 20 31 42
4,5 3 6 9 16 23 30
6-10 2 4 6 10 14 18
11,12,14,15: 12-Polybagged w/videogame w/Ennis text
1 3 4 6 8 10
13-Hunters storyline begins; ends #17; 1st app. Herr Starr
3 6 9 21 33 45
16-20: 19-Saint of Killers app.; begin "Crusaders", ends #24 6.00
21-25: 21-24-Saint of Killers app. 25-Origin of Cassidy. 4.00
26-49,52-64: 52-Tulip origin 3.00
50-($3.75) Pin-ups by Jim Lee, Bradstreet, Quesada and Palmiotti 4.00
51-Includes preview of 100 Bullets; Tulip origin 1 3 4 6 8 10
65,66-($3.75) 65-Almost everyone dies. 66-Final issue
1 3 4 6 8 10
Alamo (2001, $17.95, TPB) r/#59-66; Fabry-c 18.00
All Hell's a-Coming (2000, $17.95, TPB)-r/#51-58, ...:Tall in the Saddle 18.00
... Book One HC (2009, $39.99, d.j.) r/#1-12; new Ennis intro.; pin-ups from #50,66 40.00
... Book Two HC (2010, $39.99, d.j.) r/#13-26; new Stuart Moore intro. 40.00
... Book Three HC (2010, $39.99, d.j.) r/#27-33, ...Special: Saint of Killers #1-4 & ...Special: Cassidy: Blood & Whiskey #1; new Ennis intro. 40.00
... Book Four HC (2011, $39.99, d.j.) r/#34-40, ...Special: One Man's War, ...Special: The Story of You-Know-Who, & ...Special: The Good Old Boys; new Dillon intro. 40.00
...: Dead or Alive HC (2000, $29.95) Gallery of Glenn Fabry's cover paintings for every Preacher issue; commentary by Fabry & Ennis 30.00
...: Dead or Alive SC (2003, $19.95) 20.00
Dixie Fried (1998, $14.95, TPB)-r/#27-33, Special: Cassidy 15.00
Gone To Texas (1996, $14.95, TPB)-r/#1-7; Fabry-c 15.00
Proud Americans (1997, $14.95, TPB)-r/#18-26; Fabry-c 15.00
Salvation (1999, $14.95, TPB)-r/#41-50; Fabry-c 15.00
Until the End of the World (1996, $14.95, TPB)-r/#8-17; Fabry-c 15.00
War in the Sun (1999, $14.95, TPB)-r/#34-40 15.00

PREACHER SPECIAL: CASSIDY: BLOOD & WHISKEY
DC Comics (Vertigo): 1998 ($5.95, one-shot)

1-Ennis-scripts/Fabry-c/Dillon-a 6.00

PREACHER SPECIAL: ONE MAN'S WAR
DC Comics (Vertigo): Mar, 1998 ($4.95, one-shot)

1-Ennis-scripts/Fabry-c /Snejbjerg-a 5.00

PREACHER SPECIAL: SAINT OF KILLERS
DC Comics (Vertigo): Aug, 1996 - No. 4, Nov, 1996 ($2.50, lim. series, mature)

1-4: Ennis-scripts/Fabry-c. 1,2-Pugh-a. 3,4-Ezquerra-a 4.00
1-Signed & numbered 20.00

PREACHER SPECIAL: THE GOOD OLD BOYS
DC Comics (Vertigo): Aug, 1997 ($4.95, one-shot, mature)

1-Ennis-scripts/Fabry-c /Esquerra-a 5.00

PREACHER SPECIAL: THE STORY OF YOU-KNOW-WHO
DC Comics (Vertigo): Dec, 1996 ($4.95, one-shot, mature)

Predator Big Game #4 © 20th Fox

Prelude to Infinite Crisis TPB © DC

Pretty Deadly #1 © MCM & Rios

	GD 2.0	VG 4.0	FN 6.0	VF 8.0	VF/NM 9.0	NM- 9.2

1-Ennis-scripts/Fabry-c/Case-a 5.00

PREACHER: TALL IN THE SADDLE
DC Comics (Vertigo): 2000 ($5.95, one-shot)

1-Ennis-scripts/Fabry-c/Dillon-a; early romance of Tulip and Jesse 6.00

PRECINCT, THE
Dynamite Entertainment: 2015 - No. 5, 2016 ($3.99)

1-5-Barbarie-s/Zamora-a. 1-Covers by Benitez & Robertson 4.00

PREDATOR (Also see Aliens Vs. ..., Batman vs. ..., Dark Horse Comics, & Dark Horse Presents)
Dark Horse Comics: June, 1989 - No. 4, Mar, 1990 ($2.25, limited series)

	GD	VG	FN	VF	VF/NM	NM-
1-Based on movie; 1st app. Predator	5	10	15	30	50	70
1-2nd printing	2	4	6	8	11	14
2	2	4	6	9	13	16
3,4	2	4	6	8	10	12

Trade paperback (1990, $12.95)-r/#1-4 15.00

... Omnibus Volume 1 (8/07, $24.95, 6" x 9") r/#1-4, ... Cold War, ... Dark River, ...Bloody Sands of Time mini-series and stories from Dark Horse Comics #1,2,4-7,10-12 25.00

... Omnibus Volume 2 (2/08, $24.95, 6" x 9") r/ ... Big Game, ... Race War, ...Invaders From The, Fourth Dimension mini-series and stories from Dark Horse Comics #16-18,20,21; Dark Horse Presents #46 and A Decade of Dark Horse 25.00

... Omnibus Volume 3 (6/08, $24.95, 6" x 9") r/ ... Bad Blood, ... Kindred, ...Hell and Hot Water, ... Strange Roux mini-series and stories from Dark Horse Comics #12-14 and Dark Horse Presents #119 & 124 25.00

PREDATOR
Dark Horse Comics: June, 2009 - No. 4, Jan, 2010 ($3.50, limited series)

1-4-Arcudi-s/Saltares-a/Swanland-c; variant-c by Warner 3.50

PREDATOR: (title series) **Dark Horse Comics**

--BAD BLOOD, 12/93 - No. 4, 1994 ($2.50) 1-4 5.00

--BIG GAME, 3/91 - No. 4, 6/91 ($2.50) 1-4: 1-3-Contain 2 Dark Horse trading cards 5.00

--BLOODY SANDS OF TIME, 2/92 - No. 2, 2/92 ($2.50) 1,2-Dan Barry-c/a(p)/scripts 5.00

--CAPTIVE, 4/98 ($2.95, one-shot) 1 5.00

--COLD WAR, 9/91 - No. 4, 12/91 ($2.50) 1-4: All have painted-c 5.00

--DARK RIVER, 7/96 - No.4, 10/96 ($2.95)1-4: Miran Kim-c 5.00

--HELL & HOT WATER, 4/97 - No. 3, 6/97 ($2.95) 1-3 5.00

--HELL COME A WALKIN', 2/98 - No. 2, 3/98 ($2.95) 1,2-In the Civil War 5.00

--HOMEWORLD, 3/99 - No. 4, 6/99 ($2.95) 1-4 5.00

--HUNTERS, 5/17 - No. 5, 8/17 ($3.99) 1-5-Warner-s/Velasco-a/Doug Wheatley-c 4.00

--HUNTERS II, 8/18 - No. 4, 1/19 ($3.99) 1-4-Warner-s/Padilla-a 4.00

--HUNTERS III, 2/20 - No. 4, ($3.99) 1,2-Warner-s/Thies-a 4.00

--INVADERS FROM THE FOURTH DIMENSION, 7/94 ($3.95, one-shot, 52 pgs.) 1 5.00

--JUNGLE TALES. 3/95 ($2.95) 1-r/Dark Horse Comics 5.00

--KINDRED, 12/96 - No. 4, 3/97 ($2.50) 1-4 5.00

--NEMESIS, 12/97 - No. 2, 1/98 ($2.95) 1,2-Predator in Victorian England; Taggart-c 5.00

--PRIMAL, 7/97 - No. 2, 8/97 ($2.95) 1,2 5.00

--RACE WAR (See Dark Horse Presents #67), 2/93 - No. 4,10/93 ($2.50, color)
1-4,0: 1-4-Dorman painted-c #1-4, 0(4/93) 5.00

--STRANGE ROUX, 11/96 ($2.95, one-shot) 1 5.00

--XENOGENESIS (Also see Aliens Xenogenesis), 8/99 - No. 4, 11/99 ($2.95)
1,2-Edginton-s 5.00

PREDATOR: FIRE AND STONE (Crossover with Aliens, AvP, and Prometheus)
Dark Horse Comics: Oct, 2014 - No. 4, Jan, 2015 ($3.50, limited series)

1-4-Williamson-s/Mooneyham-a 3.50

PREDATOR: LIFE AND DEATH (Continues in Prometheus: Life and Death)
Dark Horse Comics: Mar, 2016 - No. 4, Jun, 2016 ($3.99, limited series)

1-4-Abnett-s/Thies-a 4.00

PREDATORS (Based on the 2010 movie)
Dark Horse Comics: Jun, 2010 - No. 4, Jun, 2010 ($2.99, weekly limited series)

1-4-Prequel to the 2010 movie; stories by Andreyko and Lapham; Paul Lee-c 3.00
... Film Adaptation (7/10, $6.99) Tobin-s/Drujiniu-s/photo-c 7.00
...: Preserve the Game (7/10, $3.50) Sequel to the movie; Lapham-s/Jefferson-a 3.50

PREDATOR 2
Dark Horse Comics: Feb, 1991 - No. 2, June, 1991 ($2.50, limited series)

1,2: 1-Adapts movie; both w/trading cards & photo-c 5.00

PREDATOR VS. JUDGE DREDD
Dark Horse Comics: Oct, 1997 - No. 3 ($2.50, limited series)

1-3-Wagner-s/Alcatena-a/Bolland-c 5.00

PREDATOR VS. JUDGE DREDD VS. ALIENS
Dark Horse Comics/IDW: Jul, 2016 - No. 4, Jun, 2017 ($3.99, limited series)

1-4-Layman-s/Mooneyham-a/Fabry-c 4.00

PREDATOR VS. MAGNUS ROBOT FIGHTER
Dark Horse/Valiant: Oct, 1992 - No. 2, 1993 ($2.95, limited series)
(1st Dark Horse/Valiant x-over)

1,2: (Reg.)-Barry Smith-c; Lee Weeks-a. 2-w/trading cards 5.00
1 (Platinum edition, 11/92)-Barry Smith-c 10.00

PREHISTORIC WORLD (See Classics Illustrated Special Issue)

PRELUDE TO DEADPOOL CORPS (Leads into Deadpool Corps #1)
Marvel Comics: May, 2010 - No. 5, May, 2010 ($3.99/$2.99, weekly limited series)

1-($3.99) Deadpool & Lady Deadpool vs. alternate dimension Capt. America; Liefeld-a 4.00
2-5-($2.99) Alternate reality Deadpools team-up; Dave Johnson interlocking covers 3.00

PRELUDE TO INFINITE CRISIS
DC Comics: 2005 ($5.99, squarebound)

nn-Reprints stories and panels with commentary leading into Infinite Crisis series 6.00

PREMIERE (See Charlton Premiere)

PRESIDENTIAL MATERIAL
IDW Publishing: Oct, 2008 ($3.99/$7.99)

...: Barack Obama - Biography of the candidate; Mariotte-s/Morgan-a/Campbell-c 4.00
...: John McCain - Biography of the candidate; Helfer-s/Thompson-a/Campbell-c 4.00
Flipbook ($7.99) Both issues in flipbook format 8.00

PRESTO KID, THE (See Red Mask)

PRETTY BOY FLOYD (See On the Spot)

PRETTY DEADLY
Image Comics: Oct, 2013 - No. 10, Jun, 2016 ($3.50)

1-10-DeConnick-s/Rios-a/c 3.50

PRETTY DEADLY: THE RAT
Image Comics: Sept, 2019 - No. 5, Jan, 2020 ($3.99, limited series)

1-5-DeConnick-s/Rios-a/c 4.00

PRETTY VIOLENT
Image Comics: Aug, 2019 - No. 11, Nov, 2020 ($3.99)

1-11-Derek Hunter-a; Hunter & Jason Young-s 4.00

PREZ (See Cancelled Comic Cavalcade, Sandman #54 & Supergirl #10)
National Periodical Publications: Aug-Sept, 1973 - No. 4, Feb-Mar, 1974

	GD	VG	FN	VF	VF/NM	NM-
1-Origin; Joe Simon scripts	3	6	9	17	26	35
2-4	2	4	6	13	18	22

PREZ
DC Comics: Aug, 2015 - No. 6, Feb, 2016 ($2.99)

1-6: 1-Intro. Beth Ross; Mark Russell-s/Ben Caldwell-a 3.00

PRICE, THE (See Eclipse Graphic Album Series)

PRIDE & JOY
DC Comics (Vertigo): July, 1997 - No. 4, Oct, 1997 ($2.50, limited series)

1-4-Ennis-s 3.00
TPB (2004, $14.95) r/#1-4 15.00

PRIDE & PREJUDICE
Marvel Comics: June, 2009 - No. 5, Oct, 2009 ($3.99, limited series)

1-5-Adaptation of the Jane Austen novel; Nancy Butler-s/Hugo Petrus-a 4.00

PRIDE AND THE PASSION, THE
Dell Publishing Co.: No. 824, Aug, 1957

	GD	VG	FN	VF	VF/NM	NM-
Four Color 824-Movie, Frank Sinatra & Cary Grant photo-c	9	18	27	61	123	185

PRIDE OF BAGHDAD
DC Comics (Vertigo): 2006 ($19.99, hardcover with dustjacket)

HC-A pride of lions escaping from the Baghdad zoo in 2003; Vaughan-s/Henrichon-a 20.00
SC-(2007, $12.99) 13.00

PRIDE OF THE YANKEES, THE (See Real Heroes & Sport Comics)
Magazine Enterprises: 1949 (The Life of Lou Gehrig)

	GD	VG	FN	VF	VF/NM	NM-
nn-Photo-c; Ogden Whitney-a	87	174	261	553	952	1350

PRIEST (Also see Asylum)

Prime #8 © MAL

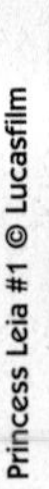
Princess Leia #1 © Lucasfilm

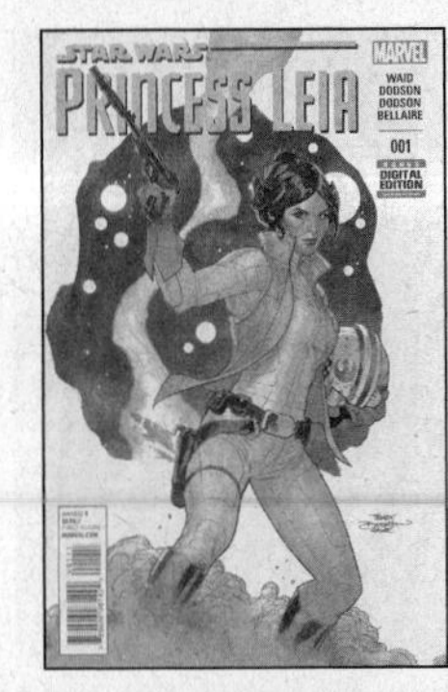

Prison Break! #2 © AVON

	GD 2.0	VG 4.0	FN 6.0	VF 8.0	VF/NM 9.0	NM- 9.2

Maximum Press: Aug, 1996 - No. 2, Oct, 1996 ($2.99)

1,2 — 3.00

PRIMAL FORCE
DC Comics: No. 0, Oct, 1994 - No. 14, Dec, 1995 ($1.95/$2.25)

0-14: 0- Teams Red Tornado, Golem, Jack O'Lantern, Meridian & Silver Dragon. 9-begin $2.25-c — 3.00

PRIMAL MAN (See The Crusaders)

PRIMAL RAGE
Sirius Entertainment: 1996 ($2.95)

1-Dark One-c; based of video game — 3.00

PRIME (See Break-Thru, Flood Relief & Ultraforce)
Malibu Comics (Ultraverse): June, 1993 - No. 26, Aug, 1995 ($1.95/$2.50)

1-1st app. Prime; has coupon for Ultraverse Premiere #0 — 4.00
1-With coupon missing — 2.00
1-Full cover holographic edition; 1st of kind w/Hardcase #1 & Strangers #1 — 10.00
1-Ultra 5,000 edition w/silver ink-c — 6.00
2-4,6-11,14-26: 2-Polybagged w/card & coupon for U. Premiere #0. 3,4-Prototype app. 4-Direct sale w/o card.4-($2.50)-Newsstand ed. polybagged w/card. 6-Bill & Chelsea Clinton app.115-Intro Papa Verite; Pérez-c/a. 16-Intro Turbo Charge — 3.00
5-($2.50, 48 pgs.)-Rune flip-c/story part B by Barry Smith; see Sludge #1 for 1st app. Rune; 3-pg. Night Man preview — 4.00
12-($3.50, 68 pgs.)-Flip book w/Ultraverse Premiere #3; silver foil logo — 4.00
13-($2.95, 52 pgs.)-Variant covers — 4.00
...: Gross and Disgusting 1 (10/94, $3.95)-Boris-c; "Annual" on cover, published monthly in indicia — 4.00
...Month "Ashcan" (8/94, 75¢)-Boris-c — 3.00
... Time: A Prime Collection (1994, $9.95)-r/1-4 — 10.00
...Vs. The Incredible Hulk (1995)-mail away limited edition — 10.00
...Vs. The Incredible Hulk Premium edition — 10.00
...Vs. The Incredible Hulk Super Premium edition — 15.00

NOTE: *Perez a-15; c-15, 16.*

PRIME (Also see Black September)
Malibu Comics (Ultraverse): Infinity, Sept, 1995 - V2#15, Dec, 1996 ($1.50)

Infinity, V2#1-15: Post Black September storyline. 6-8-Solitaire app. 9-Breyfogle-c/a. 10-12-Ramos-c. 15-Lord Pumpkin app. — 3.00
Infinity Signed Edition (2,000 printed) — 1 2 3 5 6 8

PRIME/CAPTAIN AMERICA
Malibu Comics: Mar, 1996 ($3.95, one-shot)

1-Norm Breyfogle-a — 5.00

PRIME8: CREATION
Two Morrows Publishing: July, 2001 ($3.95, B&W)

1-Neal Adams-c — 4.00

PRIMER (Comico...)
Comico: Oct (no month), 1982 - No. 6, Feb, 1984 (B&W)

	GD	VG	FN	VF	VF/NM	NM-
1 (52 pgs.)	3	6	9	15	22	28
2-1st app. Grendel & Argent by Wagner	15	30	45	105	233	360
3,4	2	4	6	10	14	18
5-1st Sam Kieth art in comics ('83) & 1st The Maxx	6	12	18	41	76	110
6-Intro & 1st app. Evangeline	3	6	9	14	19	24

PRIMORTALS (Leonard Nimoy's...)

PRIMUS (TV)
Charlton Comics: Feb, 1972 - No. 7, Oct, 1972

	GD	VG	FN	VF	VF/NM	NM-
1-Staton-a in all	2	4	6	11	16	20
2-7: 6-Drug propaganda story	2	4	6	8	11	14

PRINCE NAMOR, THE SUB-MARINER (Also see Namor ...)
Marvel Comics Group: Sept, 1984 - No. 4, Dec, 1984 (Limited-series)

1-4 — 5.00

PRINCE OF PERSIA: BEFORE THE SANDSTORM (Based on the 2010 movie)
Dynamite Entertainment: 2010 - No. 4, 2010 ($3.99, limited series)

1-4-Art by Fowler and various. 1-Chang-a. 2-Lopez-a. 3-Edwards-a — 5.00

PRINCESS LEIA (Star Wars)
Marvel Comics: May, 2015 - No. 5, Sept, 2015 ($3.99)

1-5-Mark Waid-s/Terry Dodson-a; story follows the ending of Episode IV — 4.00

PRINCESS SALLY (Video game)
Archie Publications: Apr, 1995 - No. 3, June, 1995 ($1.50, limited series)

1-3: Spin-off from Sonic the Hedgehog — 4.00

PRINCESS UGG
Oni Press: Jun, 2014 - No. 8, Mar, 2015 ($3.99)

1-8-Ted Naifeh-s/a — 4.00

PRINCE VALIANT (See Ace Comics, Comics Reading Libraries *in the Promotional Comics section*, & King Comics #146, 147)
David McKay Publ./Dell: No. 26, 1941; No. 67, June, 1954 - No. 900, May, 1958

	GD	VG	FN	VF	VF/NM	NM-
Feature Books 26 ('41)-Harold Foster-c/a; newspaper strips reprinted, pgs. 1-28,30-63; color & 68 pgs; Foster cover is only original comic book artwork by him	168	336	504	1075	1838	2600
Four Color 567 (6/54)(#1)-By Bob Fuje-Movie, photo-c	10	20	30	66	138	210
Four Color 650 (9/55), 699 (4/56), 719 (8/56),-Fuje-a	8	16	24	51	96	140
Four Color 788 (4/57), 849 (1/58), 900-Fuje-a	7	14	21	44	82	120

PRINCE VALIANT
Marvel Comics: Dec, 1994 - No. 4, Mar, 1995 ($3.95, limited series)

1-4: Kaluta-c in all — 4.00

PRINCE VANDAL
Triumphant Comics: Nov, 1993 - Apr?, 1994 ($2.50)

1-6: 1,2-Triumphant Unleashed x-over — 3.00

PRIORITY: WHITE HEAT
AC Comics: 1986 - No. 2, 1986 ($1.75, mini-series)

1,2-Bill Black-a — 3.00

PRISCILLA'S POP
Dell Publishing Co.: No. 569, June, 1954 - No. 799, May, 1957

	GD	VG	FN	VF	VF/NM	NM-
Four Color 569 (#1), 630 (5/55), 704 (5/56),799	6	12	18	37	66	95

PRISON BARS (See Behind...)

PRISON BREAK!
Avon Per./Realistic No. 3 on: Sept, 1951 - No. 5, Sept, 1952 (Painted c-3)

	GD	VG	FN	VF	VF/NM	NM-
1-Wood-c & 1 pg.; has-r/Saint #7 retitled Michael Strong Private Eye	129	258	387	826	1413	2000
2-Wood-c; Kubert-a; Kinstler inside front-c	53	106	159	334	567	800
3-Orlando, Check-a; c-/Avon paperback #179	39	78	117	240	395	550
4,5: 4-Kinstler-c & inside f/c; Lawrence, Lazarus-a. 5-Kinstler-c; Infantino-a	36	72	108	211	343	475

PRISONER, THE (TV)
DC Comics: 1988 - No. 4, 1989 ($3.50, squarebound, mini-series)

1-4 (Books a-d) — 5.00

PRISONER, THE: THE UNCERTAINTY MACHINE (TV)
Titan Comics: Jun, 2018 - No. 4, Sept, 2018 ($3.99, limited series)

1-4-Milligan-s/Lorimer-a — 4.00

PRISON RIOT
Avon Periodicals: 1952

	GD	VG	FN	VF	VF/NM	NM-
1-Marijuana Murders-1 pg. text; Kinstler-c; 2 Kubert illos on text pages	45	90	135	284	480	675

PRISON TO PRAISE
Logos International: 1974 (35¢) (Religious, Christian)

	GD	VG	FN	VF	VF/NM	NM-
nn-True Story of Merlin R. Carothers	3	6	9	14	20	25

PRIVATE BUCK
Dell Publishing Co./Rand McNally: No. 21, 1941 - No. 12, 1942 (4-1/2" x 5-1/2", 1942)

	GD	VG	FN	VF	VF/NM	NM-
Large Feature Comic 21 (#1)(1941)(Series I), 22 (1941)(Series I), 12 (1942)(Series II)	21	42	63	122	199	275
382-Rand McNally, one panel per page; small size	12	24	36	67	94	120

PRIVATE EYE (Cover title: Rocky Jorden...#6-8)
Atlas Comics (MCI): Jan, 1951 - No. 8, March, 1952

	GD	VG	FN	VF	VF/NM	NM-
1-Cover title: Crime Cases... #1-5	28	56	84	165	270	375
2,3-Tuska c/a(3)	15	30	45	90	140	190
4-8	14	28	42	81	118	155

NOTE: *Henkel a-6(3), 7; c-7. Sinnott a-6.*

PRIVATE EYE (See Mike Shayne...)

PRIVATE SECRETARY
Dell Publishing Co.: Dec-Feb, 1962-63 - No. 2, Mar-May, 1963

	GD	VG	FN	VF	VF/NM	NM-
1	4	8	12	28	47	65
2	3	6	9	21	33	45

PRIVATE STRONG (See The Double Life of...)

PRIZE COMICS (...Western #69 on) (Also see Treasure Comics)

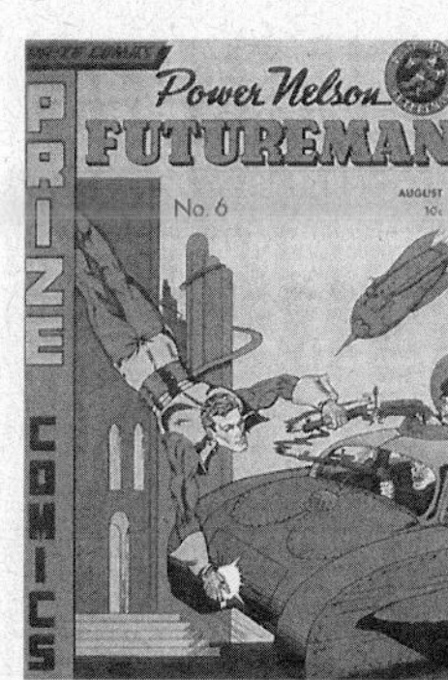
Prize Comics #6 © PRIZE

The Programme #7 © Milligan & Smith

Project Superpowers: Ch. 2 #5 © DYN

Prize Publications: March, 1940 - No. 68, Feb-Mar, 1948

	GD 2.0	VG 4.0	FN 6.0	VF 8.0	VF/NM 9.0	NM- 9.2
1-Origin Power Nelson, The Futureman & Jupiter, Master Magician; Ted O'Neil, Secret Agent M-11, Jaxon of the Jungle, Bucky Brady & Storm Curtis begin (1st app. of each)	356	712	1068	2492	4346	6200
2-The Black Owl begins (1st app.)	239	478	717	1530	2615	3700
3-Classic sci-fi-c	226	452	678	1446	2473	3500
4-Classic robot-c	276	552	828	1766	3033	4300
5-Dr. Dekkar, Master of Monsters app.	181	362	543	1158	1979	2800
6-Classic sci-fi-c; Dr. Dekkar app.	206	412	618	1318	2259	3200
7-(Scarce)-1st app. The Green Lama (12/40); Black Owl by S&K; origin/1st app. Dr. Frost & Frankenstein; Capt. Gallant, The Great Voodini & Twist Turner begin;	975	1950	2919	7100	12,550	18,000
8,9-Black Owl & Ted O'Neil by S&K	194	388	582	1242	2121	3000
10-12,14,15: 11-Origin Bulldog Denny. 14-War-c	145	290	435	928	1589	2250
13-Yank & Doodle begin (8/41, origin/1st app.)	184	368	552	1178	2014	2850
16-19: 16-Spike Mason begins	132	264	396	845	1448	2050
20-(Rare) Frankenstein, Black Owl, Green Lama, Yank and Doodle WWII parade-c	423	846	1269	3000	5250	7500
21,25,27,28,31-All WWII covers	113	226	339	723	1237	1750
22-24,26: 22-Statue of Liberty Japanese attack war-c. 23-Uncle Sam patriotic war-c. 24-Lincoln statue patriotic-c. 26-Liberty Bell-c	145	290	435	928	1589	2250
29,30,32	97	194	291	621	1061	1500
33-Classic bondage/torture-c	194	388	582	1242	2121	3000
34-Origin Airmale, Yank & Doodle; The Black Owl joins army, Yank & Doodle's father assumes Black Owl's role	77	154	231	493	847	1200
35-36,38-39: 35-Flying Fist & Bingo begin	61	122	183	390	670	950
37-Intro. Stampy, Airmale's sidekick; Hitler-c	300	600	900	2010	3505	5000
40-Nazi WWII-c	71	142	213	454	777	1100
41-45,47-50: 45-Yank & Doodle learn Black Owl's I.D. (their father). 48-Prince Ra begins	64	128	162	343	574	825
46-Classic Zombie Horror-c/story	123	246	369	787	1344	1900
51-62,64,67,68: 53-Transvestism story. 55-No Frankenstein. 57-X-Mas-c. 64-Black Owl retires	39	78	117	231	378	525
63-Simon & Kirby c/a	42	84	126	265	445	625
65,66-Frankenstein-c by Briefer	45	90	135	284	480	675

NOTE: ***Briefer** a 7-on; c-65, 66. **J. Binder** a-16; c-21-29. **Guardineer** a-62. **Kiefer** c-62. **Palais** c-68. **Simon & Kirby** c-63, 75, 83.*

PRIZE COMICS WESTERN (Formerly Prize Comics #1-68)
Prize Publications (Feature): No. 69(V7#2), Apr-May, 1948 - No. 119, Nov-Dec, 1956 (No. 69-84: 52 pgs.)

	GD 2.0	VG 4.0	FN 6.0	VF 8.0	VF/NM 9.0	NM- 9.2
69(V7#2)	17	34	51	103	162	220
70-75: 74-Kurtzman-a (8 pgs.)	15	30	45	85	130	175
76-Randolph Scott photo-c; "Canadian Pacific" movie adaptation	15	30	45	88	137	185
77-Photo-c; Severin/Elder, Mart Bailey-a; "Streets of Laredo" movie adaptation	15	30	45	84	127	170
78-Photo-c; S&K-a, 10 pgs.; Severin, Mart Bailey-a; "Bullet Code", & "Roughshod" movie adaptations	18	36	54	107	169	230
79-Photo-c; Kurtzman-a, 8 pgs.; Severin/Elder, Severin, Mart Bailey-a; "Stage To Chino" movie adaptation w/George O'Brien	18	36	54	103	169	230
80-82-Photo-c; 80,81-Severin/Elder-a(2). 82-1st app. The Preacher by Mart Bailey; Severin/Elder-a(3)	15	30	45	84	127	170
83,84	13	26	39	74	105	135
85-1st app. American Eagle by John Severin & begins (V9#6, 1-2/51)	21	42	63	124	202	280
86,101-105, 109-Severin/Williamson-a	14	28	42	78	112	145
87-99,110,111-Severin/Elder-a(2-3) each	14	28	42	81	110	155
100	15	30	45	85	124	165
106-108,112	10	20	30	56	76	95
113-Williamson/Severin-a(2)/Frazetta?	14	28	42	81	118	155
114-119: Drifter series in all; by Mort Meskin #114-118	9	18	27	52	69	85

NOTE: ***Fass** a-81. **Severin & Elder** c-84-99. **Severin** a-72, 75, 77-79, 83-86, 96, 97, 100-105; c-92,100-109(most), 110-119. **Simon & Kirby** c-75, 83.*

PRIZE MYSTERY
Key Publications: May, 1955 - No. 3, Sept, 1955

	GD 2.0	VG 4.0	FN 6.0	VF 8.0	VF/NM 9.0	NM- 9.2
1	14	28	42	78	112	175
2,3	10	20	30	54	72	95

PRO, THE
Image Comics: July, 2002 ($5.95, squarebound, one-shot)

	NM- 9.2
1-Ennis-s/Conner & Palmiotti-a; prostitute gets super-powers	8.00
1-Second printing with different cover	6.00
Hardcover Edition (10/04, $14.95) oversized reprint plus new 8 pg. story; sketch pages	15.00

PRODIGY
Image Comics: Dec, 2018 - No. 6, Jun, 2019 ($3.99)

1-6-Mark Millar-s/Rafael Albuquerque-a 4.00

PROFESSIONAL FOOTBALL (See Charlton Sport Library)

PROFESSOR COFFIN
Charlton Comics: No. 19, Oct, 1985 - No. 21, Feb, 1986

	GD 2.0	VG 4.0	FN 6.0	VF 8.0	VF/NM 9.0	NM- 9.2
19-21: Wayne Howard-a(r); low print run	1	2	3	5	6	8

PROFESSOR OM
Innovation Publishing: May, 1990 - No. 2, 1990 ($2.50, limited series)

1,2-East Meets West spin-off 3.00

PROFESSOR XAVIER AND THE X-MEN (Also see X-Men, 1st series)
Marvel Comics: Nov, 1995 - No. 18 (99¢)

1-18: Stories featuring the Original X-Men. 2-vs. The Blob. 5-Vs. the Original Brotherhood of Evil Mutants. 10-Vs. The Avengers 4.00

PROGRAMME, THE
DC Comics (WildStorm): Sept, 2007 - No. 12, Aug, 2008 ($2.99, limited series)

1-12: 1-Milligan-s/C.P. Smith-a; covers by Smith & Van Sciver 3.00
Book One TPB (2008, $17.99) r/#1-6; cover sketches 18.00
Book Two TPB (2008, $17.99) r/#7-12; cover sketches 18.00

PROJECT A-KO (Manga)
Malibu Comics: Mar, 1994 - No. 4, June, 1994 ($2.95)

1-4-Based on anime film 3.00

PROJECT A-KO 2 (Manga)
CPM Comics: May, 1995 - No. 3, Aug, 1995 ($2.95, limited series)

1-3 3.00

PROJECT A-KO VERSUS THE UNIVERSE (Manga)
CPM Comics: Oct, 1995 - No. 5, June, 1996 ($2.95, limited series, bi-monthly)

1-5 3.00

PROJECT BLACK SKY
Dark Horse Comics

... Sampler (10/14, $4.99) 1-Reprints The Occultist (2013) #1, Brain Boy (2013) #0, Ghost (2013) #1, Blackout #1 5.00
Free Comic Book Day: Project Black Sky (5/14, giveaway) Capt. Midnight & Brain Boy app. 3.00

PROJECT SUPERPOWERS
Dynamite Entertainment: 2008 - No. 7, 2008 ($1.00/$3.50/$2.99)

0-($1.00) Two connecting covers by Alex Ross; re-intro of Golden Age heroes 3.00
0-($1.00) Variant cover by Michael Turner 5.00
1-($3.50) Covers by Ross and Turner; Jim Krueger-s/Carlos Paul-a 3.50
2-7-($2.99) 3.00
... Chapter One HC (2008, $29.99, dustjacket) r/#0-7; Ross sketch pages; layout art 30.00

PROJECT SUPERPOWERS: BLACKCROSS
Dynamite Entertainment: 2015 - No. 6, 2015 ($3.99)

1-6-Warren Ellis-s/Colton Worley-a; multiple covers on each 4.00

PROJECT SUPERPOWERS: CHAPTER TWO
Dynamite Entertainment: 2009 - No. 12, 2010 ($1.00/$2.99)

... Chapter Two Prelude (2008, $1.00) Ross sketch pages and mini-series previews 3.00
0-($1.00) Three connecting covers by Alex Ross; The Inheritors assemble 3.00
1-12-($2.99) 1-Krueger & Ross-s/Salazar-a; Ross sketch pages; 2 Ross covers 3.00
... X-Mas Carol (2010, $5.99) Berkenkotter-a/Ross-c 6.00

PROJECT SUPERPOWERS: CHAPTER THREE
Dynamite Entertainment: 2018 - No. 6, 2018 ($1.00/$2.99)

0-(10¢) Six covers; Rob Williams-s/Sergio Davila-a 3.00
1-6-($3.99)-Rob Williams-s/Sergio Davila-a; multiple covers on each 4.00

PROJECT SUPERPOWERS: HERO KILLERS
Dynamite Entertainment: 2017 - No. 5, 2017 ($3.99)

1-5-Browne-s/Woods-a. 1-Black Terror killed 4.00

PROJECT SUPERPOWERS: MEET THE BAD GUYS
Dynamite Entertainment: 2009 - No. 4, 2009 ($2.99)

1-4: Ross & Casey-s. 1-Bloodlust. 2-The Revolutionary. 3-Dagon. 4-Supremacy 3.00

PROMETHEA
America's Best Comics: Aug, 1999 - No. 32, Apr, 2005 ($3.50/$2.95)

1-Alan Moore-s/Williams III & Gray-a; Alex Ross painted-c 4.00
1-Variant-c by Williams III & Gray 4.00
2-31-($2.95): 7-Villarrubia photo-a. 10-"Sex, Stars & Serpents". 26-28-Tom Strong app.

Propeller Man #5 © DH

Proposition Player #3 © Bill Willingham

Psi-Lords #5 © VAL

GD 2.0 VG 4.0 FN 6.0 VF 8.0 VF/NM 9.0 NM- 9.2

27-Cover swipe of Superman vs. Spider-Man treasury ed. 3.00
32-($3.95) Final issue; pages can be cut & assembled into a 2-sided poster 2 4 6 9 12 15
32-Limited edition of 1000; variant issue printed as 2-sided poster, signed by Moore and Williams; each came with a 48 page book of Promethea covers 120.00
Book 1 Hardcover ($24.95, dust jacket) r/#1-6 25.00
Book 1 TPB ($14.95) r/#1-6 15.00
Book 2 Hardcover ($24.95, dust jacket) r/#7-12 25.00
Book 2 TPB ($14.95) r/#7-12 15.00
Book 3 Hardcover ($24.95, dust jacket) r/#13-18 25.00
Book 3 TPB ($14.95) r/#13-18 15.00
Book 4 Hardcover ($24.95, dust jacket) r/#19-25 25.00
Book 4 TPB ($14.99) r/#19-25 15.00
Book 5 Hardcover ($24.95, d.j.) r/#26-32; includes 2-sided poster image from #32 25.00
Book 5 TPB ($14.99) r/#26-32; includes 2-sided poster image from #32 15.00

PROMETHEUS: FIRE AND STONE (Crossover with Aliens, AvP, and Predator)
Dark Horse Comics: Sept, 2014 - No. 4, Dec, 2014 ($3.50, limited series)
1-4-Tobin-s/Ferreyra-a 3.50
... – Omega (2/15, $4.99) DeConnick-s/Alessio-a; finale to the crossover 4.00

PROMETHEUS: LIFE AND DEATH (Continues in Aliens: Life and Death)
Dark Horse Comics: Jun, 2016 - No. 4, Sept, 2016 ($3.99, limited series)
1-4-Abnett-s/Mutti-a 4.00
... – Final Conflict (4/17, $5.99) Abnett-s/Thies-a; finale of Life and Death x-over 6.00

PROMETHEUS (VILLAINS) (Leads into JLA #16,17)
DC Comics: Feb, 1998 ($1.95, one-shot)
1-Origin & 1st app.; Morrison-s/Pearson-c 3.00

PROPELLERMAN
Dark Horse Comics: Jan, 1993 - No. 8, Mar, 1994 ($2.95, limited series)
1-8: 2,4,8-Contain 2 trading cards 3.00

PROPHECY
Dynamite Entertainment: 2012 - No. 7, 2013 ($3.99, limited series)
1-7: 1-Marz-s/Geovani-a; Vampirella,Red Sonja, Dracula & Pantha app. 4-Ash app. 4.00

PROPHET (See Youngblood #2)
Image Comics (Extreme Studios): Oct, 1993 - No. 10, 1995 ($1.95)
1-($2.50)-Liefeld/Panosian-c/a; 1st app. Mary McCormick; Liefeld scripts in 1-4; #1-3 contain coupons for Prophet #0 4.00
1-Gold foil embossed-c edition rationed to dealers 6.00
2-10: 2-Liefeld-c(p). 3-1st app. Judas. 4-1st app. Omen; Black and White Pt. 3 by Thibert. 4-Alternate-c by Stephen Platt. 5,6-Platt-c/a. 7-(9/94, $2.50)-Platt-c/a. 8-Bloodstrike app. 10-Polybagged w/trading card; Platt-c. 3.00
0-(7/94, $2.50)-San Diego Comic Con ed. (2200 copies) 4.00

PROPHET
Image Comics (Extreme Studios): V2#1, Aug, 1995 - No. 8 ($3.50)
V2#1-8: Dixon scripts in all. 1-4-Platt-a. 1-Boris-c; F. Miller variant-c. 4-Newmen app. 5,6-Wraparound-c 3.50
Annual 1 (9/95, $2.50)-Bagged w/Youngblood gaming card; Quesada-c 3.00
Babewatch Special 1 (12/95, $2.50)-Babewatch tie-in 3.00
1995 San Diego Edition-B&W preview of V2#1. 3.00
TPB-(1996, $12.95) r/#1-7 13.00

PROPHET (Volume 3)
Awesome Comics: Mar, 2000 ($2.99)
1-Flip-c by Jim Lee and Liefeld 3.00

PROPHET
Image Comics: No. 21, Jan, 2012 - No. 45, Jul, 2014 ($2.99/$3.99)
21-27-($2.99): 21-Two covers; Graham-s 3.00
28-45-($3.99): 29-Dalrymple-a 4.00

PROPHET/CABLE
Image Comics (Extreme): Jan, 1997 - No. 2, Mar, 1997 ($3.50, limited series)
1,2-Liefeld-c/a: 2-#1 listed on cover 4.00

PROPHET/CHAPEL: SUPER SOLDIERS
Image Comics (Extreme): May, 1996 - No. 2, June, 1996 ($2.50, limited series)
1,2: 1-Two covers exist 3.00
1-San Diego Edition; B&W-c 3.00

PROPHET EARTHWAR
Image Comics: Jan, 2016 - No. 6, Nov, 2016 ($3.99)
1-6: 1-Graham & Roy-s/Milonogiannis & Roy-a 4.00

PROPHET: STRIKEFILE
Image Comics: Sept, 2014 - No. 2, Nov, 2015 ($3.99)
1,2-Short stories and profile pages by various 4.00

PROPOSITION PLAYER
DC Comics (Vertigo): Dec, 1999 - No. 6, May, 2000 ($2.50, limited series)
1-6-Willingham-s/Guinan-a/Bolton-c 3.00
TPB (2003, $14.95) r/#1-6; intro. by James McManus 15.00

PROTECTORS (Also see The Ferret)
Malibu Comics: Sept, 1992 - No. 20, May, 1994 ($1.95-$2.95)
1-20 ($2.50, direct sale)-With poster & diff-c: 1-Origin; has 3/4 outer-c. 3-Polybagged w/Skycap 3.50
1-12 ($1.95, newsstand)-Without poster 3.00

PROTECTORS, INC.
Image Comics: Nov, 2013 - No. 10, Nov, 2014 ($2.99)
1-10-Straczynski-s/Purcell-a; multiple covers on #1-7 3.00

PROTOTYPE (Also see Flood Relief & Ultraforce)
Malibu Comics (Ultraverse): Aug, 1993 - No. 18, Feb, 1995 ($1.95/$2.50)
1-Holo-c 1 2 3 5 6 8
1-Ultra Limited silver foil-c 6.00
1,3: 3-($2.50, 48 pgs.)-Rune flip-c/story by B. Smith (3 pgs.) 4.00
2,4-12,14-18: 4-Intro Wrath. 5-Break-Thru & Strangers x-over. 6-Arena cameo. 7,8-Arena-c/story. 12-(7/94). 14 (10/94) 3.00
13 (8/94, $3.50)-Flip book (Ultraverse Premiere #6) 4.00
#0-(8/94, $2.50, 44 pgs.) 4.00
Giant Size 1 (10/94, $2.50, 44 pgs.) 4.00

PROTOTYPE (Based on the Activision video game)
DC Comics (WildStorm): Jun, 2009 - No. 6, Nov, 2009 ($3.99, limited series)
1-6-Darick Robertson-c/a 4.00
TPB (2010, $19.99) r/#1-6 20.00

PROWLER (Also see Clone Conspiracy and Amazing Spider-Man)
Marvel Comics: Dec, 2016 - May, 2017 ($3.99)
1-6-Sean Ryan-s/Javier Saltares-a. 6-Spider-Man app. 4.00

PRUDENCE & CAUTION (Also see Dogs of War & Warriors of Plasm)
Defiant: May, 1994 - No. 2, June, 1994 ($3.50/$2.50)(Spanish versions exist)
1-($3.50, 52 pgs.)-Chris Claremont scripts in all 4.00
2-($2.50) 3.00

PRYDE AND WISDOM (Also see Excalibur)
Marvel Comics: Sept, 1996 - No. 3, Nov, 1996 ($1.95, limited series)
1-3: Warren Ellis scripts; Terry Dodson & Karl Story-c/a 3.00

PSI-FORCE
Marvel Comics Group: Nov, 1986 - No. 32, June, 1989 (75¢/$1.50)
1-25: 11-13-Williamson-i 3.00
26-32 3.00
Annual 1 (10/87) 4.00
... Classic Vol. 1 TPB (2008, $24.99) r/#1-9 25.00

PSI-JUDGE ANDERSON
Fleetway Publications (Quality): 1989 - No. 15, 1990 ($1.95, B&W)
1-15 4.00

PSI-LORDS
Valiant: Sept, 1994 - No. 10, June, 1995 ($2.25)
1-($3.50)-Chromium wraparound-c 5.00
1-Gold 8.00
2-10: 3-Chaos Effect Epsilon Pt. 2 3.00

PSI-LORDS
Valiant Entertainment: Jun, 2019 - No. 8, Jan, 2020 ($3.99)
1-8-Fred Van Lente-s/Renato Guedes-a. 7-X-O Manowar app. 4.00

PSYBA-RATS (Also see Showcase '94 #3,4)
DC Comics: Apr, 1995-No. 3, June, 1995 ($2.50, limited series)
1-3 3.00

PSYCHO (Magazine) (Also see Nightmare)
Skywald Publ. Corp.: Jan, 1971 - No. 24, Mar, 1975 (68 pgs.; B&W)
1-All reprints 8 16 24 55 105 155
2-Origin & 1st app. The Heap, series begins 6 12 18 38 69 100
3-Frankenstein series by Adkins begins 6 12 18 37 66 95
4-7,9,10: 4-7-Squarebound. 4-1st Out of Chaos/Satan-c/s 5 10 15 34 60 85

Psychoanalysis #3 © WMG

Pulp HC © Basement Gang

Punchline #1 © DC

GD VG FN VF VF/NM NM-
2.0 4.0 6.0 8.0 9.0 9.2

8-(Squarebound)1st app. Edward & Mina Sartyros, the Human Gargoyles
6 12 18 37 66 95
11-17: 13-Cannabalism; 3 pgs of Christopher Lee as Dracula photos
4 8 12 27 44 60
18-Injury to eye-c 5 10 15 31 53 75
19-Origin Dracula. 4 8 12 28 47 65
20-Severed Head-c 5 10 15 33 57 80
21-24: 22-1974 Fall Special; Reese, Wildey-a(r). 24-1975 Winter Special; Dave Sim scripts (1st pro work) 5 10 15 30 50 70
Annual 1 (1972)(68 pgs.) Dracula & the Heap app. 5 10 15 30 50 70
Yearbook (1974-nn)-Everett, Reese-a 4 8 12 27 44 60
NOTE: *Boris c-3, 5. Buckler a-2, 4, 5. Gene Day a-21, 23, 24. Everett a-3-6. B. Jones a-4. Jeff Jones a-6, 7, 9; c-12. Kaluta a-13. Katz/Buckler a-3. Kim a-24. Morrow a-1. Reese a-5. Dave Sim s-24. Sutton a-3. Wildey a-5.*

PSYCHO, THE
DC Comics: 1991 - No. 3, 1991 ($4.95, squarebound, limited series)
1-3-Hudnall-s/Brereton painted-a/c 5.00
TPB (Image Comics, 2006, $17.99) r/series; Brereton sketch pages; Hudnall afterword 18.00

PSYCHOANALYSIS
E. C. Comics: Mar-Apr, 1955 - No. 4, Sept-Oct, 1955
1-All Kamen-c/a; not approved by code 26 52 78 208 334 460
2-4-Kamen-c/a in all 17 34 51 136 213 290

PSYCHOANALYSIS
Gemstone Publishing: Oct, 1999 - No. 4, Jan, 2000 ($2.50)
1-4-Reprints E.C. series 4.00
Annual 1 (2000, $10.95) r/#1-4 11.00

PSYCHO BONKERS
Aspen MLT: May, 2015 - No. 4, Sept, 2015 ($3.99)
1-4-Vince Hernandez-s/Adam Archer-a 4.00

PSYCHONAUTS
Marvel Comics (Epic Comics): Oct, 1993 - No. 4, Jan, 1994 ($4.95, lim. series)
1-4: American/Japanese co-produced comic 5.00

PSYLOCKE
Marvel Comics: Jan, 2010 - No. 4, Apr, 2010 ($3.99, limited series)
1-Finch-c/Yost-s/Tolibao-a in all 4 8 12 27 44 60
2 2 4 6 13 18 22
3,4-Wolverine app. 2 4 6 8 11 14

PSYLOCKE & ARCHANGEL CRIMSON DAWN
Marvel Comics: Aug, 1997 - No. 4, Nov, 1997 ($2.50, limited series)
1-4-Raab-s/Larroca-a(p) 4.00

PTOLUS: CITY BY THE SPIRE
Dabel Brothers Productions/Marvel Comics (Dabel Brothers) #2 on: June, 2006 - No. 6, Mar, 2007 ($2.99)
1-(1st printing, Dabel) Adaptation of the Monte Cook novel; Cook-s 4.00
1-(2nd printing, Marvel), 2-6 3.00
Monte Cooke's Ptolus: City By the Spire TPB (2007, $14.99) r/#1-6 15.00

P.T. 109 (See Movie Comics)

PUBLIC DEFENDER IN ACTION (Formerly Police Trap)
Charlton Comics: No. 7, Mar, 1956 - No. 12, Oct, 1957
7 14 28 42 81 118 155
8-12 10 20 30 54 72 90

PUBLIC ENEMIES
D. S. Publishing Co.: 1948 - No. 9, June-July, 1949
1-True Crime Stories 40 80 120 246 411 575
2-Used in **SOTI**, pg. 95 31 62 93 182 296 410
3-5: 5-Arrival date of 10/1/48 20 40 60 118 192 265
6,8,9 20 40 60 114 182 250
7-McWilliams-a; injury to eye panel 20 40 60 115 188 260

PUBLIC RELATIONS
Devil's Due/1First Comics: 2015 - No. 13, Nov, 2016 ($3.99)
1-13: 1-3-Sturges & Justus-s/Hahn-a; Annie Wu-c 4.00

PUBO
Dark Horse Comics: Dec, 2002 - No. 3, Mar, 2003 ($3.50, B&W, limited series)
1-3-Leland Purvis-s/a 3.50

PUDGY PIG
Charlton Comics: Sept, 1958 - No. 2, Nov, 1958
1,2 3 6 9 19 30 40

GD VG FN VF VF/NM NM-
2.0 4.0 6.0 8.0 9.0 9.2

PUFFED
Image Comics: Jul, 2003 - No. 3, Sept, 2003 ($2.95, B&W)
1-3-Layman-s/Crosland-a. 1-Two covers by Crosland & Quitely 3.00

PULP
Image Comics: Jul, 2020 ($16.95, HC graphic novel)
HC - Ed Brubaker-s/Sean Phillips-a/c 17.00

PULP FANTASTIC (Vertigo V2K)
DC Comics (Vertigo): Feb, 2000 - No. 3, Apr, 2000 ($2.50, limited series)
1-3-Chaykin & Tischman-s/Burchett-a 3.00

PULP FICTION LIBRARY: MYSTERY IN SPACE
DC Comics: 1999 ($19.95, TPB)
nn-Reprints classic sci-fi stories from Mystery in Space, Strange Adventures, Real Fact Comics and My Greatest Adventure 20.00

PULSE, THE (Also see Alias and Deadline)
Marvel Comics: Apr, 2004 - No. 14, May, 2006 ($2.99)
1-Jessica Jones, Ben Urich, Kat Farrell app.; Bendis-s/Bagley-a 5.00
2-14: 2-5-Bendis-s/Bagley-a. 3-5-Green Goblin app. 6,7-Brent Anderson-a 9-Wolverine app. 10-House of M. 11-14-Gaydos-a 3.00
...: House of M Special (9/05, 50¢) tabloid newspaper format; Mayhew- "photos" 3.00
Vol. 1: Thin Air (2004, $13.99) r/#1-5, gallery of cover layouts and sketches 14.00
Vol. 2: Secret War (2005, $11.99) r/#6-9 12.00
Vol. 3: Fear (2006, $14.99) r/#11-14 and New Avengers Annual #1 15.00

PUMA BLUES
Aardvark One International/Mirage Studios #21 on: 1986 - No. 26, 1990 ($1.70-$1.75, B&W)
1-19, 21-26: 1-1st & 2nd printings. 25,26-$1.75-c 3.00
20 ($2.25)-By Alan Moore, Miller, Grell, others 5.00
Trade Paperback (12/88, $14.95) 15.00

PUMPKINHEAD (Movie)
Dynamite Entertainment: 2018 - No. 5, 2018 ($3.99, limited series)
1-5-Cullen Bunn-s/Blacky Shepherd-a. 1-Three covers. 2-5-Two covers 4.00

PUMPKINHEAD: THE RITES OF EXORCISM (Movie)
Dark Horse Comics: 1993 - No. 2, 1993 ($2.50, limited series)
1,2: Based on movie; painted-c by McManus 4.00

PUNCH & JUDY COMICS
Hillman Per.: 1944; No. 2, Fall, 1944 - V3#2, 12/47; V3#3, 6/51 - V3#9, 12/51
V1#1-(60 pgs.) 31 62 93 182 296 410
2 15 30 45 92 144 195
3-12(7/46) 14 28 42 82 121 160
V2#1(8/49),3-9 12 24 36 67 94 120
V2#2,10-12, V3#1-Kirby-a(2) each 23 46 69 138 227 315
V3#2-Kirby-a 21 42 63 124 202 280
3-9 10 20 30 56 76 95

PUNCH COMICS
Harry 'A' Chesler: 12/41; #2, 2/42; #9, 7/44 - #19, 10/46; #20, 7/47 - #23, 1/48
1-Mr. E, The Sky Chief, Hale the Magician, Kitty Kelly begin
258 516 774 1651 2826 4000
2-Captain Glory app. 129 258 387 826 1413 2000
9-Rocketman & Rocket Girl & The Master Key begin; classic-c
432 864 1296 3154 5577 8000
10-Sky Chief app.; J. Cole-a; Master Key-r/Scoop #3
90 180 270 576 988 1400
11-Origin Master Key-r/Scoop #1; Sky Chief, Little Nemo app.; Jack Cole-a; Fine-*ish* art by Sultan 103 206 309 659 1130 1600
12-Rocket Boy & Capt. Glory app; classic Skull-c 3400 6800 10,200 18,700 28,350 38,000
13-Cover has list of 4 Chesler artists' names on tombstone
123 246 369 787 1344 1900
14,15,21: 21-Hypo needle story 84 168 252 538 919 1300
16,17-Gag-c 42 84 126 265 445 625
18-Bondage-c; hypodermic panels 87 174 261 553 952 1350
19-Giant bloody hands-c 168 336 504 1075 1838 2600
20-Unique cover with bare-breasted women. Rocket Girl-c
187 374 561 1197 2049 2900
22,23-Little Nemo-not by McCay. 22-Intro Baxter (teenage)(68 pgs.)
30 60 90 177 289 400

PUNCHLINE
DC Comics: Jan, 2021 ($4.99, one-shot)
1-Origin revealed; Tynion IV & Sam Johns-s/Mirka Andolfo-a 5.00

PUNCHY AND THE BLACK CROW

Punisher #92 © MAR

Punisher V2 #3 © MAR

Punisher (2004 series) #1 © MAR

GD VG FN VF VF/NM NM-
2.0 4.0 6.0 8.0 9.0 9.2

Charlton Comics: No. 10, Oct, 1985 - No. 12, Feb, 1986

10-12: Al Fago funny animal-r; low print run 6.00

PUNISHER (See Amazing Spider-Man #129, Blood and Glory, Born, Captain America #241, Classic Punisher, Daredevil #182-184, 257, Daredevil and the..., Ghost Rider V2#5, 6, Marc Spector #8 & 9, Marvel Preview #2, Marvel Super Action, Marvel Tales, Power Pack #46, Spectacular Spider-Man #81-83, 140, 141, 143 & new Strange Tales #13 & 14)

PUNISHER (The...)
Marvel Comics Group: Jan, 1986 - No. 5, May, 1986 (Limited series)

1-Double size; Grant-s/Zeck-a; Jigsaw app. 5 10 15 35 63 90
2 3 6 9 17 26 35
3-5 2 4 6 13 18 22
Trade Paperback (1988)-r/#1-5 16.00
Circle of Blood TPB (8/01, $15.95) Zeck-c 16.00
Circle of Blood HC (2008, $19.99) two covers 20.00
NOTE: *Zeck a-1-4; c-1-5.*

PUNISHER (The...) (Volume 2)
Marvel Comics: July, 1987 - No. 104, July, 1995

1 3 6 9 21 33 45
2-9: 8-Portacio/Williams-c/a begins, ends #18. 9-Scarcer, low dist. 6.00
10-Daredevil app; ties in w/Daredevil #257 3 6 9 14 20 26
11-25,50: 13-18-Kingpin app. 19-Stroman-c/a. 20-Portacio-c(p). 24-1st app. Shadowmasters. 25,50:($1.50,52 pgs.). 25-Shadowmasters app. 4.00
26-49,51-74,76-85,87-89: 57-Photo-c; came w/outer-c (newsstand ed. w/o outer-c). 59-Punisher is severely cut & has skin grafts (has black skin). 60-62-Luke Cage app. 62-Punisher back to white skin. 68-Tarantula-c/story. 85-Prequel to Suicide Run Pt. 0. 87,88-Suicide Run Pt. 6 & 9 3.00
75-($2.75, 52 pgs.)-Embossed silver foil-c 4.00
86-($2.95, 52 pgs.)-Embossed & foil stamped-c; Suicide Run part 3 4.00
90-99: 90-bound-in cards. 99-Cringe app. 3.00
100,104: 100-($2.95, 68 pgs.). 104-Last issue 4.00
100-($3.95, 68 pgs.)-Foil cover 5.00
101-103: 102-Bullseye 3.50
"Ashcan" edition (75¢)-Joe Kubert-c 3.00
Annual 1-7 ('88-'94, 68 pgs.) 1-Evolutionary War x-over. 2-Atlantis Attacks x-over; Jim Lee-a(p) (back-up story, 6 pgs.); Moon Knight app. 4-Golden-c(p). 6-Bagged w/card. 4.00
...: A Man Named Frank (1994, $6.95, TPB) 7.00
...and Wolverine in African Saga nn (1989, $5.95, 52 pgs.)-Reprints Punisher War Journal #6 & 7; Jim Lee-c/a(r) 6.00
... Assassin Guild ('88, $6.95, graphic novel) 10.00
Back to School Special 1-3 (11/92-10/94, $2.95, 68 pgs.) 4.00
.../Batman: Deadly Knights (10/94, $4.95) 6.00
.../Black Widow: Spinning Doomsday's Web (1992, $9.95, graphic novel) 12.00
...Bloodlines nn (1991, $5.95, 68 pgs.) 6.00
...: Die Hard in the Big Easy nn ('92, $4.95, 52 pgs.) 6.00
...: Empty Quarter nn ('94, $6.95) 7.00
...G-Force nn (1992, $4.95, 52 pgs.)-Painted-c 6.00
...Holiday Special 1-3 (1/93-1/95,, 52 pgs.,68pgs.)-1-Foil-c 4.00
...Intruder Graphic Novel (1989, $14.95, hardcover) 20.00
...Intruder Graphic Novel (1991, $9.95, softcover) 12.00
...Invades the 'Nam: Final Invasion nn (2/94, $6.95)-J. Kubert-c & chapter break art; reprints The 'Nam #84 & unpublished #85,86 10.00
...Kingdom Gone Graphic Novel (1990, $16.95, hardcover) 20.00
...Meets Archie (8/94, $3.95, 52 pgs.)-Die cut-c; no ads; same contents as Archie Meets The Punisher 6.00
...Movie Special 1 (6/90, $5.95, squarebound, 68 pgs.) painted-c; Brent Anderson-a; contents intended for a 3 issue series which was advertised but not published 6.00
...: No Escape nn (1990, $4.95, 52 pgs.)-New-a 6.00
...Return to Big Nothing Graphic Novel (Epic, 1989, $16.95, hardcover) 25.00
...Return to Big Nothing Graphic Novel (Marvel, 1989, $12.95, softcover) 15.00
...The Prize nn (1990, $4.95, 68 pgs.)-New-a 6.00
Summer Special 1-4(8/91-7/94, 52 pgs.):1-No ads. 2-Bisley-c; Austin-a(i). 3-No ads 4.00
NOTE: ***Austin** c(i)-47, 48. **Cowan** c-39. **Golden** c-50, 85, 86, 100. **Heath** a-26, 27, 89, 90, 91; c-26, 27. **Quesada** c-56p, 62p. **Sienkiewicz** c-Back to School 1.**Stroman** a-76p(9 pgs.). **Williamson** a(i)-25, 60-62i, 64-70, 74, Annual 5; c(i)-62, 65-68.*

PUNISHER (Also see Double Edge)
Marvel Comics: Nov, 1995 - No. 18, Apr, 1997 ($2.95/$1.95/$1.50)

1 ($2.95)-Ostrander scripts begin; foil-c. 5.00
2-18: 7-Vs. S.H.I.E.L.D. 11-"Onslaught." 12-17-X-Cutioner-c/app. 17-Daredevil, Spider-Man-c/app. 4.00

PUNISHER (Marvel Knights)
Marvel Comics: Nov, 1998 - No. 4, Feb, 1999 ($2.99, limited series)

1-4: 1-Wrightson-a; Wrightson & Jusko-c 4.00
1-($6.95) DF Edition; Jae Lee variant-c 7.00

GD VG FN VF VF/NM NM-
2.0 4.0 6.0 8.0 9.0 9.2

PUNISHER (Marvel Knights) (Volume 3)
Marvel Comics: Apr, 2000 - No. 12, Mar, 2001 ($2.99, limited series)

1-Ennis-s/Dillon & Palmiotti-a/Bradstreet-c 1 3 4 6 8 10
1-Bradstreet white variant-c 2 4 6 8 10 12
1-($6.95) DF Edition; Jurgens & Ordway variant-c 2 4 6 9 12 15
2-Two covers by Bradstreet & Dillon 3.00
3-($3.99) Bagged with Marvel Knights Genesis Edition; Daredevil app. 4.00
4-12: 9-11-The Russian app. 3.00
HC (6/02, $34.95) r/#1-12, Punisher Kills the Marvel Universe, and Marvel Knights Double Shot #1 35.00
... By Garth Ennis Omnibus (2008, $99.99) oversized r/#1-12, #1-7 & #13-37 of 2001 series, Punisher Kills the Marvel Universe, and Marvel Knights Double Shot #1; extras 100.00
.../Painkiller Jane (1/01, $3.50) Jusko-c; Ennis-s/Jusko and Dave Ross-a(p) 3.50
...: Welcome Back Frank TPB (4/01, $19.95) r/#1-12 20.00

PUNISHER (Marvel Knights) (Volume 4)
Marvel Comics: Aug, 2001 - No. 37, Feb, 2004 ($2.99)

1-Ennis-s/Dillon & Palmiotti-a/Bradstreet-c; The Russian app. 4.00
2-Two covers (Dillon & Bradstreet) Spider-Man-c/app. 3.00
3-37: 3-7-Ennis-s/Dillon-a. 9-12-Peyer-s/Gutierrez-a. 13,14-Ennis-s/Dilllon-a. 16,17-Wolverine app.; Robertson-a. 18-23,32-Dillon-a. 24-27-Mandrake-a. 27-Elektra app. 33-37-Spider-Man, Daredevil, & Wolverine app. 36,37-Hulk app. 3.00
...Army of One TPB (2/02, $15.95) r/#1-7; Bradstreet-c 16.00
Vol. 2 HC (2003, $29.95) r/#1-7,13-18; intro. by Mike Millar 30.00
Vol. 3 HC (2004, $29.95) r/#19-27; script pages for #19 30.00
Vol. 3: Business as Usual TPB (2003, $14.99) r/#13-18; Bradstreet-c 15.00
Vol. 4: Full Auto TPB (2003, $17.99) r/#20-26; Bradstreet-c 18.00
Vol. 5: Streets of Laredo TPB (2003, $17.99) r/#19,27-32 18.00
Vol. 6: Confederacy of Dunces TPB (2004, $13.99) r/#33-37 14.00

PUNISHER (Marvel MAX)(Title becomes "Punisher: Frank Castle MAX" with #66)
Marvel Comics: Mar, 2004 - No. 75, Dec, 2009 ($2.99/$3.99)

1-49,51-60: 1-Ennis-s/LaRosa-a/Bradstreet-c; flashback to his family's murder; Micro app. 6-Micro killed. 7-12,19-25-Fernandez-a. 13-18-Braithwaite-a. 31-36-Barracuda. 43-49-Medina-a. 51-54-Barracuda app. 60-Last Ennis-s/Bradstreet-c 3.00
50-($3.99) Barracuda returns; Chaykin-a 4.00
61-65-Gregg Hurwitz-s/Dave Johnson-c/Laurence Campbell-a 3.00
66-73-($3.99) 66-70-Six Hours to Kill; Swierczynski-s. 71-73-Parlov-a 4.00
74,75-($4.99) 74-Parlov-a. 75-Short stories; art by Lashley, Coker, Parlov & others 5.00
Annual (11/07, $3.99) Mike Benson-s/Laurence Campbell-a 4.00
...: Bloody Valentine (4/06, $3.99) Palmiotti & Gray-s/Gulacy & Palmiotti-a; Gulacy-c 4.00
...: Force of Nature (4/08, $4.99) Swierczynski-s/Lacombe-a/Deodato-c 5.00
...: MAX MGC #1 (5/10, $1.00) reprints #1 with "Marvel's Greatest Comics" cover logo 3.00
...: MAX: Naked Kill (8/09, $3.99) Campbell-a/Bradstreet-c 4.00
...: MAX Special: Little Black Book (8/08, $3.99) Gischler-s/Palo-a/Johnson-c 4.00
...: MAX X-Mas Special (2/09, $3.99) Aaron-s/Boschi-a/Bachalo-c 4.00
...: Red X-Mas (2/05, $3.99) Palmiotti & Gray-s/Texeira & Palmiotti-a; Texeira-c 4.00
...: Silent Night (2/06, $3.99) Diggle-s/Hotz-a/Deodato-c 4.00
...: The Cell (7/05, $4.99) Ennis-s/LaRosa-a/Bradstreet-c 5.00
...: The Tyger (2/06, $4.99) Ennis-s/Severin-a/Bradstreet-c; Castle's childhood 5.00
...: Very Special Holidays TPB ('06, $12.99) r/Red X-Mas, Bloody Valentine and Silent Night 13.00
...: X-Mas Special (1/07, $3.99) Stuart Moore-s/CP Smith-a 4.00
... MAX: From First to Last HC (2006, $19.99) r/The Tyger, The Cell and The End 1-shots 20.00
... MAX Vol. 1 (2005, $29.99) oversized r/#1-12; gallery of Fernandez art from #7 shown from layout to colored pages 30.00
... MAX Vol. 2 (2006, $29.99) oversized r/#13-24; gallery of Fernandez pencil art 30.00
... MAX Vol. 3 (2007, $29.99) oversized r/#25-36; gallery of Fernandez & Parlov art 30.00
... MAX Vol. 4 (2008, $29.99) oversized r/#37-49; gallery of Fernandez & Medina art 30.00
Vol. 1: In the Beginning TPB (2004, $14.99) r/#1-6 15.00
Vol. 2: Kitchen Irish TPB (2004, $14.99) r/#7-12 15.00
Vol. 3: Mother Russia TPB (2005, $14.99) r/#13-18 15.00
Vol. 4: Up is Down and Black is White TPB (2005, $14.99) r/#19-24 15.00
Vol. 5: The Slavers TPB (2006, $15.99) r/#25-30; Fernandez pencil pages 16.00
Vol. 6: Barracuda TPB (2006, $15.99) r/#31-36; Parlov sketch page 16.00
Vol. 7: Man of Stone TPB (2007, $15.99) r/#37-42 16.00
Vol. 8: Widowmaker TPB (2007, $17.99) r/#43-49 18.00
Vol. 9: Long Cold Dark TPB (2008, $15.99) r/#50-54 16.00

PUNISHER (Frank Castle in the Marvel Universe after Secret Invasion)
(Title changes to Franken-Castle for #17-21)
Marvel Comics: Mar, 2009 - No. 21, Nov, 2010 ($3.99/$2.99)

1-($3.99) Dark Reign; Sentry app.; Remender-s/Opena-a; character history; 2 covers 4.00
2-5,710($2.99) 2-7-The Hood app. 4-Microchip returns. 5-Daredevil #183 cover swipe 3.00
6-($3.99) Huat-a/McKone-c; profile pages of resurrected villains 4.00
11-Follows Dark Reign: The List - Punisher; Franken-Castle begins; Tony Moore-a 4.00
12-16-Franken-Castle continues; Legion of Monsters app. 14-Brereton & Moore-a 3.00

Punisher #218 © MAR

PunisherMax #18 © MAR

Punisher War Journal #31 © MAR

GD VG FN VF VF/NM NM-
2.0 4.0 6.0 8.0 9.0 9.2

GD VG FN VF VF/NM NM-
2.0 4.0 6.0 8.0 9.0 9.2

Franken-Castle 17-20: 19, 20-Wolverine & Daken app. 3.00
Franken-Castle 21-($3.99) Brereton-a/c; Legion of Monsters app.; Frank gets body back 4.00
Annual 1 (11/09, $3.99) Pearson-a/c; Spider-Man app. 4.00
...: Franken-Castle - The Birth of the Monster 1 (7/10, $4.99) r/#11 & Dark Reign: The List 5.00

PUNISHER (Frank Castle in the Marvel Universe)(Continues in Punisher: War Zone [2012])
Marvel Comics: Oct, 2011 - No. 16, Nov, 2012 ($3.99/$2.99)

1-($3.99) Rucka-s/Checchetto-a/Hitch-c 4.00
1-Variant-c by Sal Buscema 6.00
1-Variant-c by Neal Adams 10.00
2-16-($2.99): 2,3-Vulture app. 10-Spider-Man & Daredevil app. 3.00
..., Moon Knight & Daredevil: The Big Shots (10/11, $3.99) Previews new series for Punisher, Moon Knight & Daredevil; creator interviews and production art 4.00

PUNISHER, THE
Marvel Comics: Apr, 2014 - No. 20, Sept, 2015 ($3.99)

1-20: 1-Edmonson-s/Gerads-a; Howling Commandos app. 2-6-Electro app. 16,17-Captain America (Falcon) app. 19,20-Secret Wars tie-ins 4.00

PUNISHER, THE
Marvel Comics: Jul, 2016 - No. 17, Dec, 2017; No. 218, Jan, 2018 - No. 228, Sept, 2018 ($3.99)

1-17: 1-Becky Cloonan-s/Steve Dillon-a. 7-Steve Dillon's last work. 8-12-Horak-a. 13-Anka-a 14-17-Horak-a 4.00

[Title switches to legacy numbering after #11 (11/17)]

218-228-Castle gets the War Machine armor. 218-223-Vilanova-a 4.00
Annual 1 (12/16, $4.99) Gerry Conway-s/Felix Ruiz-a 5.00

PUNISHER, THE
Marvel Comics: Oct, 2018 - No. 16, Dec, 2019 ($4.99/$3.99)

1-($4.99) Rosenberg-s/Kudranski-a; Baron Zemo & The Mandarin app. 5.00
2-16-($3.99) 2-Luke Cage, Iron Fist & Daredevil app. 3-Daredevil app. 13-Thunderbolts 4.00
Annual 1 (9/19, $4.99) Acts of Evil; Karla Pacheco-s/Gorham-a; J. Jonah Jameson app. 5.00

PUNISHER AND WOLVERINE: DAMAGING EVIDENCE (See Wolverine and...)

PUNISHER ARMORY, THE
Marvel Comics: 7/90 ($1.50); No. 2, 6/91; No. 3, 4/92 - 10/94($1.75/$2.00)

1-10: 1-r/weapons pgs. from War Journal. 1,2-Jim Lee-c. 3-10-All new material. 3-Jusko painted-c 4.00

PUNISHER: IN THE BLOOD (Marvel Universe Frank Castle)
Marvel Comics: Jan, 2011 - No. 5, May, 2011 ($3.99, limited series)

1-5-Remender-s/Boschi-a; Jigsaw & Microchip app. 4.00

PUNISHER KILL KREW (Follows War of the Realms series)
Marvel Comics: Oct, 2019 - No. 5, Jan, 2020 ($3.99, limited series)

1-5-Duggan-s/Ferreyra-a; Juggernaut & The Black Knight app. 4.00

PUNISHER KILLS THE MARVEL UNIVERSE
Marvel Comics: Nov, 1995 ($5.95, one-shot)

1-Garth Ennis script/Doug Braithwaite-a 4 8 12 27 44 60
1-2nd printing (3/00) Steve Dillon-c 6.00
1-3rd printing (2008, $4.99) original 1995 cover 5.00

PUNISHER MAGAZINE, THE
Marvel Comics: Oct, 1989 - No. 16, Nov, 1990 ($2.25, B&W, Magazine, 52 pgs.)

1-16: 1-r/Punisher #1('86). 2,3-r/Punisher 2-5. 4-16: 4-7-r/Punisher V2#1-8. 4-Chiodo-c. 8-r/Punisher #10 & Daredevil #257; Portacio & Lee-r. 14-r/Punisher War Journal #1,2 w/new Lee-c. 16-r/Punisher W. J. #3,8 4.00
NOTE: ***Chiodo*** *painted c-4, 7, 16.* ***Jusko*** *painted c-6, 8.* ***Jim Lee*** *r-8, 14-16; c-14.* ***Portacio/Williams*** *r-7-12.*

PUNISHERMAX
Marvel Comics (MAX): Jan, 2010 - No. 22, Apr, 2012 ($3.99)

1-22-Aaron-s/Dillon-a/Johnson-c. 1-5-Rise of the Kingpin. 6-11-Bullseye. 17-20-Elektra app. 21-Castle dies. 22-Afterword by Aaron 4.00
...: Butterfly (5/10, $4.99) Valerie D'Orazio-s/Laurence Campbell-a/c 5.00
...: Get Castle (3/10, $4.99) Rob Williams-s/Laurence Campbell-a/Bradstreet-c 5.00
...: Happy Ending (10/10, $3.99) Milligan-s/Ryp-a/c 4.00
...: Hot Rods of Death (11/10, $4.99) Huston-s/Martinbrough-a/Bradstreet-c 5.00
...: Tiny Ugly World (12/10, $4.99) Lapham-s/Talajic-a/Bradstreet-c 5.00

PUNISHER MAX: THE PLATOON (Titled Punisher: The Platoon for #3-6)
Marvel Comics: Dec, 2017 - No. 6, Apr, 2018 ($3.99, limited series)

1-6-Ennis-s/Parlov-a; Castle's first tour of Vietnam 4.00

PUNISHER: NIGHTMARE
Marvel Comics: Mar, 2013 - No. 5, Mar, 2013 ($3.99, weekly limited series)

1-5-Texeira-a/c; Gimple-s 4.00

PUNISHER NOIR
Marvel Comics: Oct, 2009 - No. 4, Jan, 2010 ($3.99, limited series)

1-4-Pulp-style set in 1935; Tieri-s/Azaceta-a 4.00

PUNISHER: OFFICIAL MOVIE ADAPTATION
Marvel Comics: May, 2004 - No. 3, May, 2004 ($2.99, limited series)

1-3-Photo-c of Thomas Jane; Milligan-s/Olliffe-a 3.00

PUNISHER: ORIGIN OF MICRO CHIP, THE
Marvel Comics: July, 1993 - No. 2, Aug, 1993 ($1.75, limited series)

1,2 4.00

PUNISHER: P.O.V.
Marvel Comics: 1991 - No. 4, 1991 ($4.95, painted, limited series, 52 pgs.)

1-4: Starlin scripts & Wrightson painted-c/a in all. 2-Nick Fury app. 6.00

PUNISHER PRESENTS: BARRACUDA MAX
Marvel Comics (MAX): Apr, 2007 - No. 5, Aug, 2007 ($3.99, limited series)

1-5-Ennis-s/Parlov-a/c 4.00
SC (2007, $17.99) r/series; sketch pages 18.00

PUNISHER: SOVIET
Marvel Comics (MAX): Jan, 2020 - No. 6, May, 2020 ($3.99, limited series)

1-6-Ennis-s/Burrows-a 4.00

PUNISHER: THE END
Marvel Comics: June, 2004 ($4.50, one-shot)

1-Ennis-s/Corben-a/c 4.50

PUNISHER: THE GHOSTS OF INNOCENTS
Marvel Comics: Jan, 1993 - No. 2, Jan, 1993 ($5.95, 52 pgs.)

1,2-Starlin scripts 6.00

PUNISHER: THE MOVIE
Marvel Comics: 2004 ($12.99,TPB)

nn-Reprints Amazing Spider-Man #129; Official Movie Adaptation and Punisher V3 #1 13.00

PUNISHER: THE PLATOON (See Punisher MAX: The Platoon)

PUNISHER: THE TRIAL OF THE PUNISHER
Marvel Comics: Nov, 2013 - No. 2, Dec, 2013 ($3.99, limited series)

1-Guggenheim-s/Yu-a/c. 2-Suayan-a; Matt Murdock app. 4.00

PUNISHER 2099 (See Punisher War Journal #50)
Marvel Comics: Feb, 1993 - No. 34, Nov, 1995 ($1.25/$1.50/$1.95)

1-Foil stamped-c 4.00
1-(Second printing) 3.00
2-24,26-34: 13-Spider-Man 2099 x-over; Ron Lim-c(p). 16-bound-in card sheet 3.00
25-($2.95, 52 pgs.)-Deluxe edition; embossed foil-cover 5.00
25-($2.25, 52 pgs.) 4.00
(Marvel Knights) #1 (11/04, $2.99) Kirkman-s/Mhan-a/Pat Lee-c 3.00
... No. 1 (1/20, $4.99) Matt Horak-a 5.00

PUNISHER VS. BULLSEYE
Marvel Comics: Jan, 2006 - No. 5, May, 2006 ($2.99, limited series)

1-5-Daniel Way-s/Steve Dillon-a 3.00
TPB (2006, $13.99) r/#1-5; cover sketch pages 14.00

PUNISHER VS. DAREDEVIL
Marvel Comics: Jun, 2000 ($3.50, one-shot)

1-Reprints Daredevil #183,#184 & #257 4.00

PUNISHER WAR JOURNAL, THE
Marvel Comics: Nov, 1988 - No. 80, July, 1995 ($1.50/$1.75/$1.95)

1-Origin The Punisher; Matt Murdock cameo; Jim Lee inks begin 3 6 9 15 22 28
2-7: 2,3-Daredevil x-over; Jim Lee-c(i). 4-Jim Lee c/a begins. 6-Two part Wolverine story begins. 7-Wolverine-c, story ends 5.00
8-49,51-60,62,63,65: 13-16,20-22: No Jim Lee-a. 13-Lee-c only. 13-15-Heath-i. 14,15-Spider-Man x-over. 19-Last Jim Lee-c/a.29,30-Ghost Rider app. 31-Andy & Joe Kubert art. 36-Photo-c. 47,48-Nomad/Daredevil-c/stories; see Nomad. 57,58-Daredevil & Ghost Rider-c/stories. 62,63-Suicide Run Pt. 4 & 7 4.00
50,61,64($2.95, 52 pgs.): 50-Preview of Punisher 2099 (1st app.); embossed-c. 61-Embossed foil cover; Suicide Run Pt. 1. 64-Die-cut-c; Suicide Run Pt. 10 5.00
64-($2.25, 52 pgs.)-Regular cover edition 5.00
66-74,76-80: 66-Bound-in card sheet 4.00
75 ($2.50, 52 pgs.) 5.00
NOTE: ***Golden*** *c-25-30, 40, 61, 62.* ***Jusko*** *painted c-31, 32.* ***Jim Lee*** *a-1i-3i, 4p-13p, 17p-19p; c-2i, 3i, 4p-15p, 17p, 18p, 19p. Painted c-40.*

PUNISHER WAR JOURNAL (Frank Castle back in the regular Marvel Universe)
Marvel Comics: Jan, 2007 - No. 26, Feb, 2009 ($2.99)

Punisher War Zone #10 © MAR

Punk Mambo #3 © VAL

Purgatori #5 © Chaos!

	GD	VG	FN	VF	VF/NM	NM-
	2.0	4.0	6.0	8.0	9.0	9.2

1-Civil War tie-in; Spider-Man app; Fraction-s/Olivetti-a 5.00
1-B&W edition (11/06) 5.00
2-5: 2,3-Civil War tie-in. 4-Deodato-a 4.00
6-11,13-24,26: 6-10-Punisher dons Captain America-*esque* outfit. 7-Two covers. 11-Winter Soldier app. 16-23-Chaykin-a. 18-23-Jigsaw app. 24-Secret Invasion 3.00
12,25-($3.99) 12-World War Hulk x-over; Fraction-s/Olivetti-a. 25-Secret Invasion 4.00
... Annual 1 (1/09, $3.99) Spurrier-s/Dell'edera-a 4.00
... Vol. 1: Civil War HC (2007, $19.99) r/#1-4 and #1 B&W edition; Olivetti sketch pages 20.00
... Vol. 1: Civil War SC (2007, $14.99) r/#1-4 and #1 B&W edition; Olivetti sketch pages 15.00
... Vol. 2: Goin' Out West HC (2007, $24.99) r/#5-11; Olivetti sketch page 25.00
... Vol. 2: Goin' Out West SC (2008, $17.99) r/#5-11; Olivetti sketch page 18.00
... Vol. 3: Hunter Hunted HC (2008, $19.99) r/#12-17 20.00

PUNISHER: WAR ZONE, THE
Marvel Comics: Mar, 1992 - No. 41, July, 1995 ($1.75/$1.95)

1-($2.25, 40 pgs.)-Die cut-c; Romita, Jr.-c/a begins 6.00
2-22,24,26,27-41: 8-Last Romita, Jr.-c/a. 19-Wolverine app. 24-Suicide Run Pt. 5. 27-Bound-in card sheet. 31-36-Joe Kubert-a 4.00
23-($2.95, 52 pgs.)-Embossed foil-c; Suicide Run part 2; Buscema-a(part) 5.00
25-($2.25, 52 pgs.)-Suicide Run part 8; painted-c 5.00
Annual 1,2 ('93, 94, $2.95, 68 pgs.)-1-Bagged w/card; John Buscema-a 5.00
...: River Of Blood TPB (2006, $15.99) r/#31-36; Joe Kubert-a 16.00
NOTE: *Golden c-23. Romita, Jr. c/a-1-8.*

PUNISHER: WAR ZONE
Marvel Comics: Feb, 2009 - No. 6, Mar, 2009 ($3.99, weekly limited series)

1-6-Ennis-s/Dillon-a/c; return of Ma Gnucci 4.00
1-Variant cover by John Romita, Jr. 6.00

PUNISHER: WAR ZONE (Follows Punisher 2011-2012 series)
Marvel Comics: Dec, 2012 - No. 5, Apr, 2013 ($3.99, limited series)

1-5: Rucka-s; Spider-Man and The Avengers app. 4.00

PUNISHER: YEAR ONE
Marvel Comics: Dec, 1994 - No. 4, Apr, 1995 ($2.50, limited series)

1-4 4.00

PUNK MAMBO
Valiant Entertainment: No. 0, Nov, 2014; Apr, 2019 - No. 5, Aug, 2019 ($3.99, limited series)

0-(11/14) Milligan-s/Gill-a; bonus preview of The Valiant #1 4.00
1-5-Cullen Bunn-s/Adam Gorham-a/ Dan Brereton-c 4.00

PUNK ROCK JESUS
DC Comics (Vertigo): Sept, 2012 - No. 6, Feb, 2013 ($2.99, B&W, limited series)

1-6-Sean Murphy-s/a/c; cloning of Jesus 3.00

PUNKS NOT DEAD
IDW Publishing (Black Crown): Feb, 2018 - No. 6, Jul, 2018 ($3.99)

1-6-Barnett-s/Simmonds-a; 3 covers 4.00

PUNKS NOT DEAD: LONDON CALLING
IDW Publishing (Black Crown): Feb, 2019 - No. 5, Jun, 2019 ($3.99)

1-5-Barnett-s/Simmonds-a 4.00

PUNX
Acclaim (Valiant): Nov, 1995 - No. 3, Jan, 1996 ($2.50, unfinished lim. series)

1-3: Giffen story & art in all. 2-Satirizes Scott McCloud's Understanding Comics 3.00
(Manga) Special 1 (3/96, $2.50)-Giffen scripts 3.00

PUPPET COMICS
George W. Dougherty Co.: Spring, 1946 - No. 2, Summer, 1946

	GD	VG	FN	VF	VF/NM	NM-
1-Funny animal in both	25	50	75	150	245	350
2	15	30	45	90	140	190

PUPPETOONS (See George Pal's...)

PUREHEART (See Archie as...)

PURGATORI
Chaos! Comics: Prelude #-1, 5/96 ($1.50, 16 pgs.); 1996 - No. 3 Dec, 1996 (limited series)

Prelude #-1-Pulido story; Balent-c/a; contains sketches & interviews 3.00
0-(2/01, $2.99) Prelude to "Love Bites"; Rio-c/a 3.00
1/2 (12/00, $2.95) Al Rio-c/a 3.00
1-($3.50)-Wraparound cover; red foil embossed-c; Jim Balent-a 5.00
1-($19.95)-Premium Edition (1000 print run) 20.00
2-($3.00)-Wraparound-c 3.00
2-Variant-c 5.00
..: Heartbreaker 1 (3/02, $2.99) Jolley-s 3.00
..: Love Bites 1 (3/01, $2.99) Turnbull-a/Kaminski-s 3.00
..: Mischief Night 1 (11/01, $2.99) 3.00
..: Re-Imagined 1 (7/02, $2.99) Jolley-s/Neves-a 3.00
...The Dracula Gambit-($2.95) 3.00
...The Dracula Gambit Sketchbook-($2.95) 3.00
...The Vampire's Myth 1-($19.95) Premium Ed. (10,000) 20.00
...Vs. Chastity (7/00, $2.95) Two versions (Alpha and Omega) with different endings; Rio-a 3.00
...Vs. Lady Death (1/01, $2.95) Kaminski-s 3.00
...Vs. Vampirella (4/00, $2.95) Zanier-a; Chastity app. 3.00

PURGATORI
Chaos! Comics: Oct, 1998 - No. 7, Apr, 1999 ($2.95)

1-7-Quinn-s/Rio-c/a. 2-Lady Death-c 3.00

PURGATORI
Dynamite Entertainment: 2014 - No. 5, 2015 ($3.99)

1-5: 1-Gillespie-s; multiple covers. 2-4-Jade app. 4.00

PURGATORI: DARKEST HOUR
Chaos! Comics: Sept, 2001 - No. 2, Oct, 2001 ($2.99, limited series)

1,2 3.00

PURGATORI: EMPIRE
Chaos! Comics: May, 2000 - No. 3, July, 2000 ($2.95, limited series)

1-3-Cleavenger-c 3.00

PURGATORI: GODDESS RISING
Chaos! Comics: July, 1999 - No. 4, Oct, 1999 ($2.95, limited series)

1-4-Deodato-c/a 3.00

PURGATORI: GOD HUNTER
Chaos! Comics: Apr, 2002 - No. 2, May, 2002 ($2.99, limited series)

1,2-Molenaar-a/Jolley-s 3.00

PURGATORI: GOD KILLER
Chaos! Comics: Jun, 2002 - No. 2, July, 2002 ($2.99, limited series)

1,2-Molenaar-a/Jolley-s 3.00

PURGATORI: THE HUNTED
Chaos! Comics: Jun, 2001 - No. 2, Aug, 2001 ($2.99, limited series)

1,2 3.00

PURPLE CLAW, THE (Also see Tales of Horror)
Minoan Publishing Co./Toby Press: Jan, 1953 - No. 3, May, 1953

	GD	VG	FN	VF	VF/NM	NM-
1-Origin; horror/weird stories in all	47	94	141	296	498	700
2,3: 1-3 r-in Tales of Horror #9-11	32	64	96	188	307	425
I.W. Reprint #8-Reprints #1	3	6	9	19	30	40

PUSH (Based on the 2009 movie)
DC Comics (WildStorm): Early Jan, 2009 - No. 6, Apr, 2009 ($3.50, limited series)

1-6-Movie prequel; Bruno Redondo-a. 1-Jock-c 3.50
TPB (2009, $19.99) r/#1-6 20.00

PUSSYCAT (Magazine)
Marvel Comics Group: Oct, 1968 (B&W reprints from Men's magazines)

	GD	VG	FN	VF	VF/NM	NM-
1-(Scarce)-Ward, Everett, Wood-a; Everett-c	61	122	183	390	670	950

PUZZLE FUN COMICS (Also see Jingle Jangle)
George W. Dougherty Co.: Spring, 1946 - No. 2, Summer, 1946 (52 pgs.)

	GD	VG	FN	VF	VF/NM	NM-
1-Gustavson-a	28	56	84	168	274	380
2	18	36	54	107	169	230

NOTE: *#1 & 2('46) each contain a **George Carlson** cover plus a 6 pg. story "Alec in Fumbleland"; also many puzzles in each.*

PvP (Player vs. Player)
Image Comics: Mar, 2003 - No. 45, Mar, 2010 ($2.95/$2.99/$3.50, B&W, reads sideways)

1-34,36-Scott Kurtz-s/a in all. 1,16-Frank Cho-c. 11-Savage Dragon-c/app. 14-Invincible app. 19-Jonathan Luna-c. 25-Cho-a (2 pgs.) 3.00
35,37-45 ($3.50): 45-Brandy from Liberty Meadows app. 3.50
#0 (7/05, 50¢) Secret Origin of Skull 3.00
...: At Large TPB (7/04, $11.95) r/#1-6 12.00
... Vol. 2: Reloaded TPB (12/04, $11.95) r/#7-12 12.00
... Vol. 3: Rides Again TPB (2005, $11.99) r/#13-18 12.00
... Vol. 4: PVP Goes Bananas TPB (2007, $12.99) r/#19-24 13.00
... Vol. 5: PVP Treks On TPB (2008, $14.99) r/#25-31 15.00
...: The Dork Ages TPB (2/04, $11.95) r/#1-6 from Dork Storm Press 12.00

Q2: THE RETURN OF QUANTUM & WOODY
Valiant Entertainment: Oct, 2014 - No. 5, Feb, 2015 ($3.99, limited series)

1-5: 1-Priest-s/Bright-a; multiple covers 4.00

QUACK!
Star Reach Productions: July, 1976 - No. 6, 1977? ($1.25, B&W)

Quantum and Woody Must Die #4 © VAL

Quarantine Zone HC © DC & Aloy Ent.

Queen & Country #29 © Greg Rucka

	GD 2.0	VG 4.0	FN 6.0	VF 8.0	VF/NM 9.0	NM- 9.2

1-Brunner-c/a on Duckaneer (Howard the Duck clone); Dave Stevens, Gilbert, Shaw-a 2 4 6 10 14 18
1-2nd printing (10/76) 5.00
2-6: 2-Newton the Rabbit Wonder by Aragonés/Leialoha; Gilbert, Shaw-a; Leialoha-c. 3-The Beavers by Dave Sim begin, end #5; Gilbert, Shaw-a; Sim/Leialoha-c. 6-Brunner-a (Duckeneer); Gilbert-a 2 4 6 8 10 12

QUADRANT
Quadrant Publications: 1983 - No. 8, 1986 (B&W, nudity, adults)

1-Peter Hsu-c/a in all 2 4 6 13 18 22
2-8 2 4 6 8 10 12

QUAKE: S.H.I.E.L.D. 50TH ANNIVERSARY
Marvel Comics: Nov, 2015 ($3.99, one-shot)

1-Spotlight on Daisy Johnson; Daniel Johnson-a/Nakayama-c; Avengers app. 4.00

QUANTUM AGE, THE (Also see Black Hammer)
Dark Horse Comics: Jul, 2018 - No. 6, Jan, 2019 ($3.99, limited series)

1-6-Lemire-s/Torres-a. 4-6-Colonel Weird app. 4.00

QUANTUM & WOODY
Acclaim Comics: June, 1997 - No. 17, No. 32 (9/99), No. 18 - No. 21, Feb, 2000 ($2.50)

1-17: 1-1st app.; two covers. 6-Copycat-c. 9-Troublemakers app. 3.00
32-(9/99); 18-(10/99),19-21 3.00
The Director's Cut TPB ('97, $7.95) r/#1-4 plus extra pages 8.00

QUANTUM & WOODY
Valiant Entertainment: Jul, 2013 - No. 12, Jul, 2014 ($3.99)

1-12: 1-Asmus-s/Fowler-a; covers by Ryan Sook & Marcos Martin; origin re-told 4.00
#0 -(3/14, $3.99) Story of the goat; Asmus-s/Fowler-a/c 4.00
... Valiant-Sized #1 (12/14, $4.99) Thomas Edison app. 5.00

QUANTUM AND WOODY!
Valiant Entertainment: Dec, 2017 - No. 12, Nov, 2018 ($3.99)

1-3: 1-Daniel Kibblesmith-s/Kano-a. 3,6,7,12-Portela-a. 8-11-Eisma-a 4.00

QUANTUM AND WOODY
Valiant Entertainment: Jan, 2020 - Present ($3.99)

1-4-Hastings-s/Browne-a 4.00

QUANTUM & WOODY MUST DIE
Valiant Entertainment: Jan, 2015 - No. 4, Apr, 2015 ($3.99, limited series)

1-4: 1-James Asmus-s/Steve Lieber-a; multiple covers on each 4.00

QUANTUM LEAP (TV) (See A Nightmare on Elm Street)
Innovation Publishing: Sept, 1991 - No. 12, Jun, 1993 ($2.50, painted-c)

1-12: Based on TV show; all have painted-c. 8-Has photo gallery 4.00
Special Edition 1 (10/92)-r/#1 w/8 extra pgs. of photos & articles 4.00
Time and Space Special 1 (#13) ($2.95)-Foil logo 4.00

QUANTUM TUNNELER, THE
Revolution Studio: Oct, 2001 (no cover price, one-shot)

1-Prequel to "The One" movie; Clayton Henry-a 3.00

QUARANTINE ZONE
DC Comics: Apr, 2016 ($22.99, HC graphic novel)

HC - Daniel Wilson-s/Fernando Pasarin-a 23.00

QUASAR (See Avengers #302, Captain America #217, Incredible Hulk #234, Marvel Team-Up #113 & Marvel Two-in-One #53)
Marvel Comics: Oct, 1989 - No. 60, Jul, 1994 ($1.00/$1.25, Direct sales #17 on)

1-Gruenwald-s/Paul Ryan-c/a begin; Origin of Wendell Vaughn from Marvel Man to Quasar; Marvel Boy & Fantastic Four app. 6.00
2-6: 2-Origin of the Quantum-Bands; Deathurge & Eon app; Quasar becomes 'Protector of the Universe'. 3-Human Torch app. 4-Aquarian app. 5,6-Acts of Vengeance tie-in. 5-Absorbing Man & Loki app. 6-Red Ghost, Living Laser, Uatu the Watcher app; Venom cameo (2pgs); last Ryan-a(p) 3.00
7-Spider-Man & Quasar vs. Terminus 4.00
8-14,18: 8-Secret Wars x-over; Mike Manley-a begins. 9-Modam (female Modok) app. 10-Dr. Minerva app. 11-Excalibur & Mordred app; first Moondragon as 'H.D Steckley'. 12-Eternals app.; death of Quasar's father (Gilbert). 13-Squadron Supreme & Overmind app. 14-McFarlane-c; Squadron Supreme, Overmind app. 18-1st app. Origin & Unbeing; new Quasar costume; 1st Greg Capullo-a 3.00
15,16: 15-Mignola-c; Squadron Supreme, Overmind, the Stranger & the Watchers app. 16-($1.50, 52 pgs.) Squadron Supreme, Overmind, Stranger & the Watchers app. 4.00
17-Features Marvel's speedsters: Quicksilver, Makkari, Captain Marvel (Monica Rambeau), Speed Demon, Black Racer, Super Sabre & the Runner; Flash parody 'Buried Alien' 5.00
19-(2/91)-Re-intro Jack of Hearts & Maelstrom (neither one seen since 1984); Dr. Strange app. 6.00
20,21: 20-Fantastic Four & the Presence app. 21-Maelstrom revealed as the 'Cosmic Assassin' 5.00
22,23,27,29: 22-Quasar dies; Deathurge app. 'H.D Steckley' revealed to be Moondragon. 23-Ghost Rider app. 27-Original Marvel Boy app. 29-Kismet (Her) app; Vanity Fair Demi Moore pregnancy parody-c 3.00
24-Brief Infinity Gauntlet reference; Thanos & Mephisto app.; vs. Maelstrom; 1st app. Infinity (the female aspect of Eternity) 1 2 3 5 6 8
25-($1.50)-New costume Quasar (returns to life); Eternity, Infinity, Oblivion, Death, Celestials, Galactus, Watchers app.; 'death' of Maelstrom 4.00
26-Infinity Gauntlet tie-in; Thanos & Moondragon app. 5.00
28,30-33: 28-Kismet (Her) app.; Avengers; Warlock, Moondragon, Jack of Hearts app. 30-What If..? issue; Watcher, Thanos, Maelstrom app. 31-Quasar in the New Universe; gains the power of the Starbrand. 32-Operation Galactic Storm Pt. 3; continued from Avengers West Coast #80; Shi'ar Imperial Guard app.; 1st app. Korath the Pursuer. 33-Operation Galactic Storm Pt.10; continued from Avengers West Coast #81; story continues in Wonder Man #8 (#32-34 same as Special #1-3) 4.00
34-39,41-49,51-53: 34-Opertation Galactic Storm Pt. 17; continued from Captain America #400; continued in Avengers West Coast #82. 35-Operation Galactic Storm aftermath; Quasar quits the Avengers. 38-Infinity War x-over; Quasar & the Avengers vs. Warlock, Thanos & the Infinity Watch; last Capullo-a. 39-Infinity War x-over; Thanos & Deathurge app. 41-Avengers app. 42-Punisher app. 43-Quasar returns to life. 47,48-Thunderstrike app. 49-Kismet app. 51,52: 52-Squadron Supreme app. 53-Warlock & the Infinity Watch app. 3.00
40,50: 40-Infinity War x-over; Quasar uses the Ultimate Nullifier and dies; Thanos app. 50-($2.95, 52 pgs.)-Holo-grafix foil-c Silver Surfer, Man-Thing, Ren & Stimpy app. 4.00
54,55: 53-Warlock & the Infinity Watch app. 54-Starblast tie-in; continued from Starblast #1; Hyperion vs. Gladiator. 55-Starblast tie-in; continued from Starblast #2; Black Bolt app; continued in Starblast #3 4.00
56-57: 56-Starblast tie-in; continued from Starblast #4; New Universe app.; continued in Starblast #4. 57-Living Tribunal & the New Universe app. 5.00
58,59: 58-w/bound-in card sheet; Makkari wins the Galactic Race; DC Comics Flash (as Fastforward) app. 59-Thanos & Starfox app. 6.00
60-Last issue; Avengers, New Warriors & Fantastic Four app; Quasar leaves Earth 1 2 3 5 6 8
Special #1-3 ($1.25, newsstand)-Same as #32-34 3.00

QUEEN & COUNTRY (See Whiteout)
Oni Press: Mar, 2001 - No. 32, Aug, 2007 ($2.95/$2.99, B&W)

1-Rucka-s in all. Rolston-a/Sale-c 1 2 3 4 5 7
2-5: 2-4-Rolston-a/Sale-c. 5-Snyder-c/Hurtt-a 4.00
6-24,26-32: 6,7-Snyder-c/Hurtt-a. 13-15-Alexander-a. 16-20-McNeil-a. 21-24-Hawthorne-a 26-28-Norton-a 3.00
25-($5.99) Rolston-a 6.00
Free Comic Book Day giveaway (5/02) r/#1 with "Free Comic Book Day" banner on-c 3.00
Operation: Blackwall (10/03, $8.95, TPB) r/#13-15; John Rogers intro. 9.00
Operation: Broken Ground (2002, $11.95, TPB) r/#1-4; Ellis intro. 12.00
Operation: Crystal Ball (1/03, $14.95, TPB) r/#8-12; Judd Winick intro. 15.00
Operation: Dandelion HC (8/04, $25.00) r/#21-24; Jamie S. Rich intro. 25.00
Operation: Dandelion (8/04, $11.95, TPB) r/#21-24; Jamie S. Rich intro. 12.00
Operation: Morningstar (9/02, $8.95, TPB) r/#5-7; Stuart Moore intro. 9.00
Operation: Storm Front (3/04, $14.95, TPB) r/#16-20; Geoff Johns intro. 15.00

QUEEN & COUNTRY: DECLASSIFIED
Oni Press: Nov, 2002 - No. 3, Jan, 2003 ($2.95, B&W, limited series)

1-3-Rucka-s/Hurtt-a/Morse-c 3.00
TPB (7/03, $8.95) r/#1-3; intro. by Micah Wright 9.00

QUEEN & COUNTRY: DECLASSIFIED (Volume 2)
Oni Press: Jan, 2005 - No. 3, Feb, 2006 ($2.95/$2.99, B&W, limited series)

1-3-Rucka-s/Burchett-a/c 3.00
TPB (3/06, $8.95) r/#1-3 9.00

QUEEN & COUNTRY: DECLASSIFIED (Volume 3)
Oni Press: Jun, 2005 - No. 3, Aug, 2005 ($2.95, B&W, limited series)

1-3- "Sons & Daughters;" Johnston-s/Mitten-a/c 3.00
TPB (3/06, $8.95) r/#1-3 9.00

QUEEN OF THE WEST, DALE EVANS (TV)(See Dale Evans Comics, Roy Rogers & Western Roundup under Dell Giants)
Dell Publ. Co.: No. 479, 7/53 - No. 22, 1-3/59 (All photo-c; photo back c-4-8,15)

	GD 2.0	VG 4.0	FN 6.0	VF 8.0	VF/NM 9.0	NM- 9.2
Four Color 479(#1, '53)	16	32	48	110	243	375
Four Color 528(#2, '54)	9	18	27	60	120	180
3,4: 3(4-6/54)-Toth-a. 4-Toth, Manning-a	7	14	21	46	86	125
5-10-Manning-a. 5-Marsh-a	6	12	18	40	73	105
11,19,21-No Manning 21-Tufts-a	5	10	15	31	53	75
12-18,20,22-Manning-a	5	10	15	34	60	85

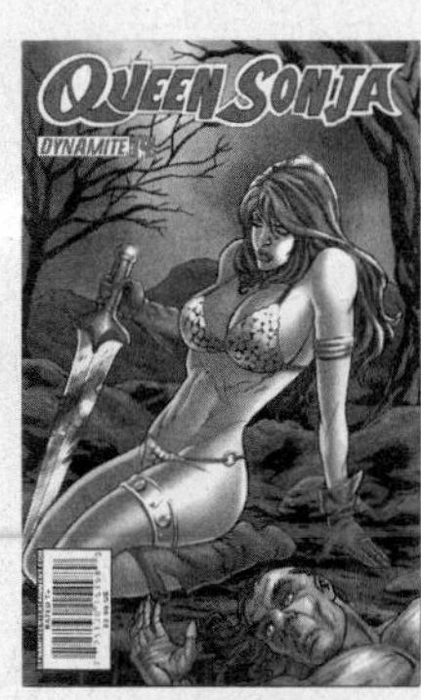

Queen Sonja #14 © RS LLC

Quicksilver: No Surrender #4 © MAR

Rachel Rising #7 © Terry Moore

	GD	VG	FN	VF	VF/NM	NM-
	2.0	4.0	6.0	8.0	9.0	9.2

GD VG FN VF VF/NM NM-
2.0 4.0 6.0 8.0 9.0 9.2

QUEEN SONJA (See Red Sonja)
Dynamite Entertainment: 2009 - No. 35, 2013 ($2.99/$3.99)

1-10: 1-Rubi-a/Ortega-s; 3 covers; back-up r/Marvel Feature #1 — 4.00
11-35-($3.99) 16-Thulsa Doom returns — 4.00

QUENTIN DURWARD
Dell Publishing Co.: No. 672, Jan, 1956

	GD	VG	FN	VF	VF/NM	NM-
Four Color 672-Movie, photo-c	6	12	18	42	79	115

QUESTAR ILLUSTRATED SCIENCE FICTION CLASSICS
Golden Press: 1977 (224 pgs.) ($1.95)

	GD	VG	FN	VF	VF/NM	NM-
11197-Stories by Asimov, Sturgeon, Silverberg & Niven; Starstream-r	3	6	9	20	30	40

QUEST FOR CAMELOT
DC Comics: July, 1998 ($4.95)

1-Movie adaption — 5.00

QUEST FOR DREAMS LOST (Also see Word Warriors)
Literacy Volunteers of Chicago: July 4, 1987 ($2.00, B&W, 52 pgs.)(Proceeds donated to help fight illiteracy)

1-Teenage Mutant Ninja Turtles by Eastman/Laird, Trollords, Silent Invasion, The Realm, Wordsmith, Reacto Man, Eb'nn, Aniverse — 4.00

QUESTION, THE (See Americomics, Blue Beetle (1967), Charlton Bullseye & Mysterious Suspense)

QUESTION, THE (Also see Showcase '95 #3)
DC Comics: Feb, 1987 - No. 36, Mar, 1990; No. 37, Mar, 2010 ($1.50)

1-36: Denny O'Neil scripts in all. 17-Rorshach app. — 3.00
37-(3/10, $2.99) Blackest Night one-shot; Victor Sage rises; Shiva app.; Cowan-a — 3.00
Annual 1 (1988, $2.50) — 4.00
Annual 2 (1989, $3.50) — 4.00
...: Epitaph For a Hero TPB (2008, $19.99) r/#13-18 — 20.00
...: Peacemaker TPB (2010, $19.99) r/#31-36 — 20.00
...: Pipeline TPB (2011, $14.99) r/stories from Detective Comics #854-865; sketch-a — 15.00
...: Poisoned Ground TPB (2008, $19.99) r/#7-12 — 20.00
...: Riddles TPB (2009, $19.99) r/#25-30 — 20.00
...: Welcome to Oz TPB (2009, $19.99) r/#19-24 — 20.00
...: Zen and Violence TPB (2007, $19.99) r/#1-6 — 20.00

QUESTION, THE (Also see Crime Bible and 52)
DC Comics: Jan, 2005 - No. 6, Jun, 2005 ($2.95, limited series)

1-6-Rick Veitch-s/Tommy Lee Edwards-a. 4,6-Superman app. — 3.00

QUESTION QUARTERLY, THE
DC Comics: Summer, 1990 - No. 5, Spring, 1992 ($2.50/$2.95, 52pgs.)

1-5 — 4.00

NOTE: ***Cowan** a-1, 2, 4, 5; c-1-3, 5. **Mignola** a-5i. **Quesada** a-3-5.*

QUESTION RETURNS, THE
DC Comics: Feb, 1997 ($3.50, one-shot)

1-Brereton-c — 4.00

QUESTION, THE : THE DEATHS OF VIC SAGE
DC Comics (Black Label): Jan, 2020 - No. 4, Oct, 2020 ($6.99, over-sized 10-7/8" x 8-1/2", limited series)

1-4-Jeff Lemire-s/Denys Cowan & Bill Sienkiewicz-a; two covers on each — 7.00

QUESTPROBE
Marvel Comics: 8/84; No. 2, 1/85; No. 3, 11/85 (lim. series)

1-3: 1-The Hulk app. by Romita. 2-Spider-Man; Mooney-a(i). 3-Human Torch & Thing — 4.00

QUICK DRAW McGRAW (TV) (Hanna-Barbera)(See Whitman Comic Books)
Dell Publishing Co./Gold Key No. 12 on: No. 1040, 12-2/59-60 - No. 11, 7-9/62; No. 12, 11/62; No. 13, 2/63; No. 14, 4/63; No. 15, 6/69 (1st show aired 9/29/59)

	GD	VG	FN	VF	VF/NM	NM-
Four Color 1040(#1) 1st app. Quick Draw & Baba Looey, Augie Doggie & Doggie Daddy and Snooper & Blabber	12	24	36	83	182	280
2(4-6/60)-4,6: 2-Augie Doggie & Snooper & Blabber stories (8 pgs. each); pre-dates both of their #1 issues. 4-Augie Doggie & Snooper & Blabber stories.	5	10	15	35	63	90
5-1st Snagglepuss app.; last 10¢ issue	6	12	18	38	69	100
7-11	5	10	15	30	50	70
12,13-Title change to ...Fun-Type Roundup (84pgs.)	6	12	18	38	69	100
14,15: 15-Reprints	4	8	12	27	44	60

QUICK DRAW McGRAW (TV)(See Spotlight #2)
Charlton Comics: Nov, 1970 - No. 8, Jan, 1972 (Hanna-Barbera)

	GD	VG	FN	VF	VF/NM	NM-
1	5	10	15	30	50	70
2-8	3	6	9	18	28	38

QUICKSILVER (See Avengers)
Marvel Comics: Nov, 1997 - No. 13, Nov, 1998 ($2.99/$1.99)

1-($2.99)-Peyer-s/Casey Jones-a; wraparound-c — 4.00
2-11: 2-Two covers-variant by Golden. 4-6-Inhumans app. — 3.00
12-($2.99) Siege of Wundagore pt. 4 — 4.00
13-Magneto-c/app.; last issue — 3.00

QUICKSILVER: NO SURRENDER (Avengers)
Marvel Comics: Jul, 2018 - No. 5, Nov, 2018 ($3.99, limited series)

1-5-Saladin Ahmed-s/Eric Nguyen-a; Scarlet Witch app. — 4.00

QUICK-TRIGGER WESTERN (...Action #12; Cowboy Action #5-11)
Atlas Comics (ACI #12/WPI #13-19): No. 12, May, 1956 - No. 19, Sept, 1957

	GD	VG	FN	VF	VF/NM	NM-
12-Baker-a	22	44	66	128	209	290
13-Williamson-a, 5 pgs.	18	36	54	107	169	230
14-Everett, Crandall, Torres-a; Heath-c	16	32	48	94	147	200
15,16: 15-Torres, Crandall-a. 16-Orlando, Kirby-a	15	30	45	84	127	170
17,18: 18-Baker-a	15	30	45	83	124	165
19	13	26	39	74	105	135

NOTE: ***Ayers** a-17. **Colan** a-16. **Maneely** a-15, 17; c-15, 18. **Morrow** a-18. **Powell** a-14. **Severin** a-19; c-12, 13, 16, 17, 19. **Shores** a-16. **Tuska** a-17.*

QUINCY (See Comics Reading Libraries in the Promotional Comics section)

QUITTER, THE
DC Comics (Vertigo): 2005 ($19.99, B&W graphic novel)

HC ($19.99) Autobiography of Harvey Pekar; Pekar-s/Daen Haspiel-a — 20.00
SC (2006, $12.99) — 13.00

RACCOON KIDS, THE (Formerly Movietown Animal Antics)
National Periodical Publications (Arleigh No. 63,64): No. 52, Sept-Oct, 1954 - No. 62, Oct-Nov, 1956; No. 63, Sept, 1957; No. 64, Nov, 1957

	GD	VG	FN	VF	VF/NM	NM-
52-Doodles Duck by Mayer	15	30	45	83	124	165
53-64: 53-62-Doodles Duck by Mayer	11	22	33	62	86	110

NOTE: ***Otto Feuer**-a most issues. **Rube Grossman**-a most issues.*

RACE FOR THE MOON
Harvey Publications: Mar, 1958 - No. 3, Nov, 1958

	GD	VG	FN	VF	VF/NM	NM-
1-Powell-a(5); 1/2-pg. S&K-a; cover redrawn from Galaxy Science Fiction pulp (5/53)	20	40	60	115	188	260
2-Kirby/Williamson-c(r)/a(3); Kirby-p 7 more stys	29	58	87	172	281	390
3-Kirby/Williamson-c/a(4); Kirby-p 6 more stys	32	64	96	190	310	430

RACER-X
Now Comics: 8/88 - No. 11, 8/89; V2#1, 9/89 - V2#10, 1990 ($1.75)

0-Deluxe ($3.50) — 5.00
1 (9/88) - 11, V2#1-10 — 4.00

RACER X (See Speed Racer)
DC Comics (WildStorm): Oct, 2000 - No. 3, Dec, 2000 ($2.95, limited series)

1-3: 1-Tommy Yune-s/Jo Chen-a; 2 covers by Yune. 2,3-Kabala app. — 4.00

RACHEL RISING
Abstract Studio: 2011 - No. 42, 2016 ($3.99, B&W)

1-Terry Moore-s/a/c; back cover by Fabio Moon; green background on cover — 85.00
1-(2nd printing) Red background on cover — 35.00
1-(3rd printing) Red background on cover — 35.00
2 — 35.00
3-6 — 10.00
7-42: 42-Final issue — 4.00
Halloween ComicFest Edition (2014, giveaway) Reprints #1 with orange bkgd on cover — 5.00

RACING PETTYS
STP Corp.: 1980 ($2.50, 68 pgs., 10 1/8" x 13 1/4")

	GD	VG	FN	VF	VF/NM	NM-
1-Bob Kane-a. Kane bio on inside back-c.	2	4	6	8	11	14

RACK & PAIN
Dark Horse Comics: Mar, 1994 - No. 4, June, 1994 ($2.50, limited series)

1-4: Brian Pulido scripts in all. 1-Greg Capullo-c — 3.00

RACK & PAIN: KILLERS
Chaos! Comics: Sept, 1996 - No. 4, Jan, 1997 ($2.95, limited series)

1-4: Reprints Dark Horse series; Jae Lee-c — 3.00

RACKET SQUAD IN ACTION
Capitol Stories/Charlton Comics: May-June, 1952 - No. 29, Mar, 1958

	GD	VG	FN	VF	VF/NM	NM-
1	36	72	109	216	351	485
2-4,6: 3,4,6-Dr. Neff, Ghost Breaker app.	19	38	57	111	176	240
5-Dr. Neff, Ghost Breaker app; headlights-c	53	106	159	334	567	800
7-10: 10-Explosion-c	16	32	48	98	154	210

Radiant Black #1 © Higgins & Costa

Radioactive Man #4 © Bongo

Ragnarok #5 © Walt Simonson

	GD 2.0	VG 4.0	FN 6.0	VF 8.0	VF/NM 9.0	NM- 9.2
11-Ditko-c/a	40	80	120	244	402	560
12-Ditko explosion-c (classic); Shuster-a(2)	68	136	204	435	743	1050
13-Shuster-c(p)/a.	15	30	45	85	130	175
14-Marijuana story "Shakedown"; Giordano-c	20	40	60	118	192	265
15-28: 15,20,22,23-Giordano-c	14	28	42	81	118	155
29-(15¢, 68 pgs.)	15	30	45	92	144	195

RADIANT BLACK
Image Comics: Feb, 2021 - Present ($3.99)
1-Kyle Higgins-s/Marcelo Costa-a 4.00

RADIANT LOVE (Formerly Daring Love #1)
Gilmor Magazines: No. 2, Dec, 1953 - No. 6, Aug, 1954
2 24 48 72 140 230 320
3-6 17 34 51 100 158 215

RADICAL DREAMER
Blackball Comics: No. 0, May, 1994 - No. 4, Nov, 1994 ($1.99, bi-monthly) (1st poster format comic)
0-4: 0-2-($1.99, poster format): 0-1st app. Max Wrighter. 3,4-($2.50-c) 3.00

RADICAL DREAMER
Mark's Giant Economy Size Comics: V2#1, June, 1995 - V2#6, Feb, 1996 ($2.95, B&W, limited series)
V2#1-6 3.00
Prime (5/96, $2.95) 3.00
Dreams Cannot Die!-(1996, $20.00, softcover)-Collects V1#0-4 & V2#1-6; intro by Kurt Busiek; afterward by Mark Waid 20.00
Dreams Cannot Die!-(1996, $60.00, hardcover)-Signed & limited edition; collects V1#0-4 & V2#1-6; intro by Kurt Busiek; afterward by Mark Waid 60.00

RADICALLY REARRANGED RONIN RAGDOLLS
Kevin Eastman Studios, Inc.: 2019 ($3.99)
1-TMNT pastiche with cats; Kevin Eastman & Troy Little-a; David Avallone-s 4.00

RADIOACTIVE MAN (Simpsons TV show)
Bongo Comics: 1993 - No. 6, 1994 ($1.95/$2.25, limited series)
1-($2.95)-Glow-in-the-dark-c; bound-in jumbo poster; origin Radioactive Man; (cover dated Nov. 1952) 2 4 6 8 11 14
2-6: 2-Says #88 on-c & inside & dated May 1962; cover parody of Atlas Kirby monster-c; Superior Squad app.; origin Fallout Boy. 3-($1.95)-Cover "dated" Aug 1972 #216. 4-($2.25)-Cover "dated" Oct 1980 #412; w/trading card. 5-Cover "dated" Jan 1986 #679; w/trading card. 6-(Jan 1995 #1000) 4.00
Colossal #1-($4.95) 1 2 3 5 6 8
#4 (2001, $2.50) Faux 1953 issue; Murphy Anderson-i (6 pgs.) 3.00
#100 (2000, $2.50) Comic Book Guy-c/app.; faux 1963 issue inside 3.00
#136 (2001, $2.50) Dan DeCarlo-c/a 3.00
#222 (2001, $2.50) Batton Lash-s; Radioactive Man in 1972-style 3.00
#575 (2002, $2.50) Chaykin-c; Radioactive Man in 1984-style 3.00
1963-106 (2002, $2.50) Radioactive Man in 1960s Gold Key-style; Groening-c 3.00
#7 Bongo Super Heroes Starring... (2003, $2.50) Marvel Silver Age-style Superior Squad 3.00
#8 Official Movie Adaptation (2004, $2.99) starring Rainier Wolfcastle and Milhouse 3.00
#9 (#197 on-c) (2004, $2.50) Kirby-esque New Gods spoof; Golden Age Radio Man app. 3.00

RADIO FUNNIES
DC Comics: Mar. 1939; undated variant
nn-(3/39) Ashcan comic, not distributed to newsstands, only for in-house use. Cover art is Adventure Comics #39 with interior being Detective Comics #19 (no known sales)
nn - Ashcan comic. No date. Cover art is Detective #26 with interior from Detective #17; one copy, graded at GD/VG, sold at auction for $4481.25 in Nov, 2009. Another copy graded at GD/VG sold at auction for $3346 in Feb, 2010.

RAGAMUFFINS
Eclipse Comics: Jan, 1985 ($1.75, one shot)
1-Eclipse Magazine-r, w/color; Colan-a 3.00

RAGE (Based on the id video game)
Dark Horse Comics: Jun, 2011 - No. 3, Aug, 2011 ($3.50, limited series)
1-3-Nelson-s/Mutti-a/Fabry-c. 1-Variant-c by Martiniere 3.50

RAGEMOOR
Dark Horse Comics: Mar, 2012 - No. 4, Jun, 2012 ($3.50, B&W, limited series)
1-4-Richard Corben-a/c; Jan Strnad-s 3.50

RAGGEDY ANN AND ANDY (See Dell Giants, March of Comics #23 & New Funnies)
Dell Publishing Co.: No. 5, 1942 - No. 533, 2/54; 10-12/64 - No. 4, 3/66
Four Color 5(1942) 48 96 144 362 831 1300
Four Color 23(1943) 34 68 102 245 548 850
Four Color 45(1943) 26 52 78 182 404 625
Four Color 72(1945) 20 40 60 141 313 485
1(6/46)-Billy & Bonnie Bee by Frank Thomas 29 58 87 209 467 725
2,3: 3-Egbert Elephant by Dan Noonan begins 15 30 45 100 220 340
4-Kelly-a, 16 pgs. 15 30 45 105 233 360
5,6,8-10 12 24 36 80 173 265
7-Little Black Sambo, Black Mumbo & Black Jumbo only app; Christmas-c 14 28 42 97 214 330
11-20 10 20 30 64 132 200
21-Alice In Wonderland cover/story 12 24 36 80 173 265
22-27,29-39(8/49), Four Color 262 (1/50): 34-"...In Candyland" 9 18 27 57 111 165
28-Kelly-c 9 18 27 59 117 175
Four Color 306,354,380,452,533 7 14 21 46 86 125
1(10-12/64-Dell) 4 8 12 23 37 50
2,3(10-12/65), 4(3/66) 3 6 9 16 23 30
NOTE: *Kelly art ("Animal Mother Goose")-#1-34, 36, 37; c-28. Peterkin Pottle by* ***John Stanley*** *in 32-38.*

RAGGEDY ANN AND ANDY
Gold Key: Dec, 1971 - No. 6, Sept, 1973
1 3 6 9 18 28 38
2-6 3 6 9 15 21 26

RAGGEDY ANN & THE CAMEL WITH THE WRINKLED KNEES (See Dell Jr. Treasury #8)

RAGMAN (See Batman Family #20, The Brave & The Bold #196 & Cancelled Comic Cavalcade)
National Per. Publ./DC Comics No. 5: Aug-Sept, 1976 - No. 5, Jun-Jul, 1977
1-Origin & 1st app. 3 6 9 19 30 40
2-5: 2-Origin ends; Kubert-c. 4-Drug use story 2 4 6 8 10 12
NOTE: ***Kubert*** *a-4, 5; c-1-5.* ***Redondo*** *studios a-1-4.*

RAGMAN (2nd Series)
DC Comics: Oct, 1991 - No. 8, May, 1992 ($1.50, limited series)
1-8: 1-Giffen plots/breakdowns. 3-Origin. 8-Batman-c/story 3.00

RAGMAN (3rd Series)
DC Comics: Dec, 2017 - No. 6, May, 2018 ($2.99, limited series)
1-6-Ray Fawkes-s/Inaki Miranda-a/Guillem March-c; new origin. 3-6-Etrigan app. 3.00

RAGMAN: CRY OF THE DEAD
DC Comics: Aug, 1993 - No. 6, Jan, 1994 ($1.75, limited series)
1-6: Joe Kubert-c 3.00

RAGMAN: SUIT OF SOULS
DC Comics: Dec, 2010 ($3.99, one-shot)
1-Gage-s/Segovia-a/Saiz-c; origin retold 4.00

RAGNAROK
IDW Publishing: Jul, 2014 - No. 12, Feb, 2017 ($3.99/$4.99)
1-7-Walt Simonson-s/a; two covers on each 4.00
8-12-($4.99) 5.00

RAGNAROK: THE BREAKING OF HELHEIM
IDW Publishing: Jul, 2019 - Present ($4.99)
1-4-Walt Simonson-s/a; multiple covers on each 4.00

RAGS RABBIT (Formerly Babe Ruth Sports #10 or Little Max #10?; also see Harvey Hits #2, Harvey Wiseguys & Tastee Freez)
Harvey Publications: No. 11, June, 1951 - No. 18, March, 1954 (Written & drawn for little folks)
11-(See Nutty Comics #5 for 1st app.) 8 16 24 40 50 60
12-18 6 12 18 28 34 40

RAI (Rai and the Future Force #9-23) (See Magnus #5-8)
Valiant: Mar, 1992 - No. 0, Oct, 1992; No. 9, May, 1993 - No. 33, Jun, 1995 ($1.95/$2.25)
1-Valiant's 1st original character 2 4 6 13 18 22
2-5: 4-Low print run 2 4 6 9 12 15
6-10: 6,7-Unity x-overs. 7-Death of Rai. 9-($2.50)-Gatefold-c; story cont'd from Magnus #24; Magnus, Eternal Warrior & X-O app. 6.00
11-33: 15-Manowar Armor app. 17-19-Magnus x-over. 21-1st app. The Starwatchers (cameo); trading card. 22-Death of Rai. 26-Chaos Effect Epsilon Pt. 3 4.00
#0-(11/92)-Origin/1st app. new Rai (Rising Spirit) & 1st full app. & partial origin Bloodshot; also see Eternal Warrior #4; tells future of all characters 4 8 12 23 37 50
NOTE: ***Layton*** *c-2i, 9i.* ***Miller*** *c-6.* ***Simonson*** *c-7.*

RAI
Valiant Entertainment: May, 2014 - No. 16, Aug, 2016 ($3.99)
1-16: 1-Kindt-s/Crain-a; Rai in Japan in the year 4001. 15,16-4001 AD tie-ins 4.00
...: The History of the Valiant Universe 1 (6/17, $3.99) Roberts-s/Portela-a; 2 covers 4.00

RAI

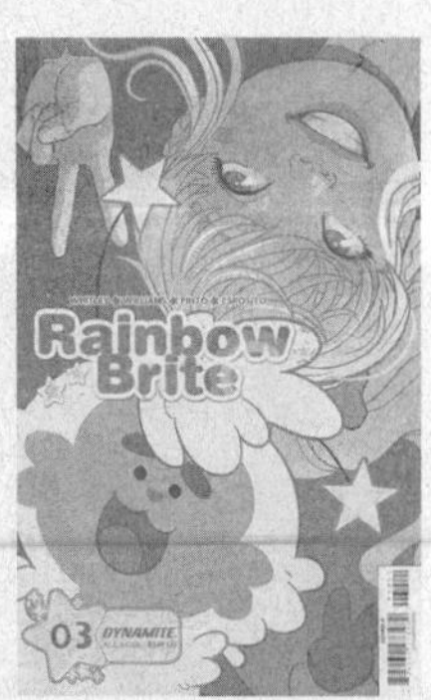

Rainbow Brite #3 © Hallmark

Range Romances #1 © QUA

Rann-Thanagar War #5 © DC

	GD	VG	FN	VF	VF/NM	NM-
	2.0	4.0	6.0	8.0	9.0	9.2

Valiant Entertainment: Nov, 2019 - Present ($3.99)
1-10: 1-Abnett-s/Ryp-a 4.00

RAIDERS OF THE LOST ARK (Movie)
Marvel Comics Group: Sept, 1981 - No. 3, Nov, 1981 (Movie adaptation)
1-r/Marvel Comics Super Special #18 3 6 9 14 20 25
2,3 2 4 6 8 10 12
NOTE: ***Buscema** a(p)-1-3; c(p)-1. **Simonson** a-3i; scripts-1-3.*

RAINBOW BRITE
Dynamite Entertainment: 2018 - No. 5, 2019 ($3.99, limited series)
1-5-Origin story; Jeremy Whitley-s/Brittney Williams-a; multiple covers on each 4.00

RAINBOW BRITE AND THE STAR STEALER
DC Comics: 1985
nn-Movie adaptation 2 4 6 10 14 18

RAISE THE DEAD
Dynamite Entertainment: 2007 - No. 4, Aug, 2007 ($3.50)
1-4-Arthur Suydam-c/Leah Moore & John Reppion-s/Petrus-a; Phillips var-c on all 4.00
... Vol. 1 HC (2007, $19.99) r/#1-4; script, interview & sketch pages; cover gallery 20.00

RAISE THE DEAD 2
Dynamite Entertainment: 2010 - No. 4, 2011 ($3.99)
1-4-Leah Moore & John Reppion-s/Vilanova-a 4.00

RALPH KINER, HOME RUN KING
Fawcett Publications: 1950 (Pittsburgh Pirates)
nn-Photo-c; life story 60 120 180 381 658 935

RALPH SNART ADVENTURES
Now Comics: June, 1986 - V2#9, 1987; V3#1 - #26, Feb, 1991; V4#1, 1992 - #4, 1992
1-3, V2#1-7,V3#1-23,25,26:1-($1.00, B&W)-1(B&W),V2#1(11/86), B&W), 8,9-color. V3#1(9/88)-Color begins 3.00
V3#24-($2.50)-3-D issue, V4#1-3-Direct sale versions w/cards 3.00
V4#1-3-Newsstand versions w/random cards 3.00
Book 1 1 2 3 5 6 8
3-D Special (11/92, $3.50)-Complete 12-card set w/3-D glasses 4.00

RAMAR OF THE JUNGLE (TV)
Toby Press No. 1/Charlton No. 2 on: 1954 (no month); No. 2, Sept, 1955 - No. 5, Sept, 1956
1-Jon Hall photo-c; last pre-code issue 25 50 75 150 246 340
2-5: 2-Jon Hall photo-c 17 34 51 103 162 220

RAMAYAN 3392 A.D.
Virgin Comics: Sept, 2006 - No. 8, Aug, 2008 ($2.99)
1-8: 1-Alex Ross-c; re-imagining of the Indian myth of Ramayana; poster of cover inside 3.00
... Reloaded (8/07 - No. 7, 7/08, $2.99) 1-7: 1-Two covers by Kang and Oeming 3.00
... Reloaded Guidebook (4/08, $2.99) Profiles of characters and weapons 3.00

RAMM
Megaton Comics: May, 1987 - No. 2, Sept, 1987 ($1.50, B&W)
1,2-Both have 1 pg. Youngblood ad by Liefeld 3.00

RAMPAGING HULK (The Hulk #10 on; also see Marvel Treasury Edition)
Marvel Comics Group: Jan, 1977 - No. 9, June, 1978 ($1.00, B&W magazine)
1-Bloodstone story w/Buscema & Nebres-a. Origin re-cap w/Simonson-a; Gargoyle, UFO story; Ken Barr-c 4 8 12 25 40 55
2-Old X-Men app; origin old w/Simonson-a & new X-Men in text w/Cockrum illos; Bloodstone story w/Brown & Nebres-a 3 6 9 17 26 35
3-9: 3-Iron Man app.; Norem-c. 4-Gallery of villains w/Giffen-a. 5,6-Hulk vs. Sub-Mariner. 7-Man-Thing story. 8-Original Avengers app. 9-Thor vs. Hulk battle; Shanna the She-Devil story w/DeZuniga-a 3 6 9 14 19 24
NOTE: ***Alcala** a-1-3i, 5i, 8i. **Buscema** a-1. **Giffen** a-4. **Nino** a-4i. **Simonson** a-1-3p. **Starlin** a-4(w/**Nino**), 7; c-4, 5, 7.*

RAMPAGING HULK
Marvel Comics: Aug, 1998 - No. 6, Jan, 1999 ($2.99/$1.99)
1-($2.99) Flashback stories of Savage Hulk; Leonardi-a 5.00
2-6-($1.99): 2-Two covers 4.00

RAMPAGING WOLVERINE
Marvel Comics: June, 2009 ($3.99, B&W, one-shot)
1-Short stories by Fialkov, Luque, Ted McKeever, Yost, Santolouco, Firth, Nelson 4.00

RANDOLPH SCOTT (Movie star)(See Crack Western #67, Prize Comics Western #76, Western Hearts #8, Western Love #1 & Western Winners #7)

RANGE BUSTERS
Fox Feature Syndicate: Sept, 1950 (10¢, one shot)
1-Saga of John Wesley Hardin 21 42 63 124 202 280

RANGE BUSTERS (Formerly Cowboy Love?; Wyatt Earp, Frontier Marshall #11 on)
Charlton Comics: No. 8, May, 1955 - No. 10, Sept, 1955
8 8 16 24 42 54 65
9,10 6 12 18 28 34 40

RANGELAND LOVE
Atlas Comics (CDS): Dec, 1949 - No. 2, Mar, 1950 (52 pgs.)
1-Robert Taylor & Arlene Dahl photo-c 21 42 63 122 199 275
2-Photo-c 15 30 45 90 140 190

RANGER, THE (See Zane Grey, Four Color #255)

RANGE RIDER, THE (TV)(See Flying A's...)

RANGE ROMANCES
Comic Magazines (Quality Comics): Dec, 1949 - No. 5, Aug, 1950 (#5: 52 pg)
1-Gustavson-c/a 28 56 84 168 274 380
2-Crandall-c/a 28 56 84 165 270 375
3-Crandall, Gustavson-a; photo-c 23 46 69 136 223 310
4-Crandall-a; photo-c 20 40 60 120 195 270
5-Gustavson-a; Crandall-a(p); photo-c 20 40 60 120 195 270

RANGERS COMICS (...of Freedom #1-7)
Fiction House Magazines: 10/41 - No. 67, 10/52; No. 68, Fall, 1952; No. 69, Winter, 1952-53 (Flying stories)
1-Intro. Ranger Girl & The Rangers of Freedom; ends #7, cover app. only #5 568 1136 1704 4146 7323 10,500
2 219 438 657 1402 2401 3400
3 161 322 483 1030 1765 2500
4,5 110 220 330 704 1202 1700
6-10-All Japanese war covers. 8-U.S. Rangers begin 87 174 261 553 952 1350
11,12-Commando Rangers app. 81 162 243 518 884 1250
13-Commando Ranger begins-not same as Commando Rangers; Nazi war-c 90 180 270 576 988 1400
14-Classic Japanese bondage/torture WWII-c 113 226 339 723 1237 1750
15-20: 15,17,19-Japanese war-c. 18-Nazi war-c 68 136 204 435 743 1050
21-Intro/origin Firehair (begins, 2/45) 161 322 483 1030 1765 2500
22-25,27,29-Japanese war-c. 23-Kazanda begins, ends #28 54 108 162 343 574 825
26-Classic Japanese WWII good girl-c 90 180 270 576 988 1400
28,30: 28-Tiger Man begins (origin/1st app., 4/46), ends #46. 30-Crusoe Island begins, ends #40 42 84 126 265 445 625
31-40: 33-Hypodermic panels 37 74 111 222 361 500
41-46: 41-Last Werewolf Hunter 27 54 81 162 266 370
47-56- "Eisnerish" Dr. Drew by Grandenetti. 48-Last Glory Forbes. 53-Last 52 pg. issue. 55-Last Sky Rangers 26 52 78 152 249 345
57-60-Straight run of Dr. Drew by Grandenetti 19 38 57 112 179 245
61-69: 64-Suicide Smith begins. 63-Used in **POP**, pgs. 85, 99. 67-Space Rangers begin, end #69 16 32 48 98 154 210
NOTE: *Bondage, discipline covers, lingerie panels are common. Crusoe Island by **Larsen**-#30-36. Firehair by **Lubbers**-#30-49. Glory Forbes by **Baker**-#36-45, 47; by **Whitman**-#34, 35. I Confess in #41-53. Jan of the Jungle in #42-58. King of the Congo in #49-53. Tiger Man by **Celardo**-#30-39. **M. Anderson** a-30? **Baker** a-36-38, 42, 44. **John Celardo** a-34, 36-39. **Lee Elias** a-21-28. **Evans** a-19, 38-46, 48-52. **Hopper** a-25, 26. **Ingels** a-13-16. **Larsen** a-34. **Bob Lubbers** a-30-38, 40-44; c-40-45. **Moreira** a-41-47. **Tuska** a-16, 17, 19, 22. **M. Whitman** c-61-66. **Zolnerwich** c-1-17.*

RANGO (TV)
Dell Publishing Co.: Aug, 1967
1-Photo-c of comedian Tim Conway 4 8 12 28 47 65

RANN-THANAGAR HOLY WAR (Also see Hawkman Special #1)
DC Comics: July, 2008 - No. 8, Feb, 2009 ($3.50, limited series)
1-8-Adam Strange & Hawkman app.; Starlin-s/Lim-a. 1-Two covers by Starlin & Lim 3.50
Volume One TPB (2009, $19.99) r/#1-4 & Hawkman Special #1 20.00
Volume Two TPB (2009, $19.99) r/#5-8 & Adam Strange Special #1 20.00

RANN-THANAGAR WAR (See Adam Strange 2004 mini-series)(Prelude to Infinite Crisis)
DC Comics: July, 2005 - No. 6, Dec, 2005 ($2.50, limited series)
1-6-Adam Strange, Hawkman and Green Lantern (Kyle Rayner) app.; Gibbons-s/Reis-a 3.00
...: Infinite Crisis Special (4/06, $4.99) Kyle Rayner becomes Ion again; Jade dies 5.00
TPB (2005, $12.99) r/#1-6; cover gallery; new Bolland-c 13.00

RAPHAEL (See Teenage Mutant Ninja Turtles)
Mirage Studios: 1985 ($1.50, 7-1/2x11", B&W w/2 color cover, one-shot)
1-1st Turtles one-shot spin-off; contains 1st drawing of the Turtles as a group from 1983; 1st app. Casey Jones 25 50 75 175 388 600
1-2nd printing (11/87); new-c & 8 pgs. art 4 8 12 23 37 50

RAPHAEL BAD MOON RISING (See Teenage Mutant Ninja Turtles)

Rat God #1 © Richard Corben

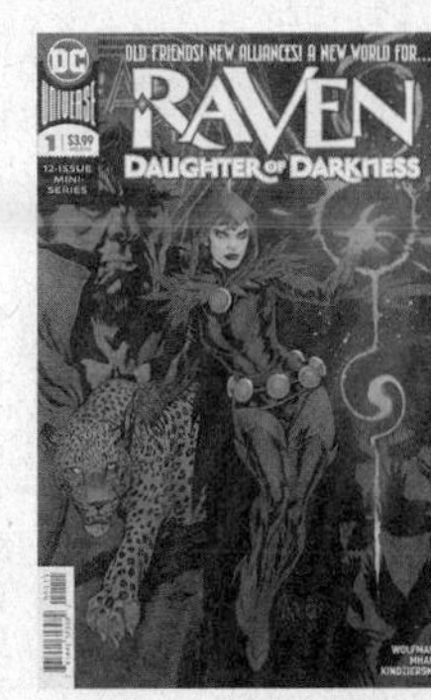

Raven: Daughter of Darkness #1 © DC

Rawhide Kid #17 © MAR

	GD 2.0	VG 4.0	FN 6.0	VF 8.0	VF/NM 9.0	NM- 9.2

Mirage Publishing: July, 2007 - No. 4, Oct, 2007 ($3.25, B&W, limited series)

1-4-Continued from Tales of the TMNT #7; Lawson-a	1	3	4	6	8	10

RAPTURE
Dark Horse Comics: May, 2009 - No. 6, Jan, 2010 ($2.99, limited series)

1-6-Taki Soma & Michael Avon Oeming-s/a/c. 1-Maleev var-c. 2-Mack var-c 3.00

RAPTURE
Valiant Entertainment: May, 2017 - No. 4, Aug, 2017 ($3.99)

1-4-Kindt-s/Cafu-a; Ninjak, Shadowman & Punk Mambo app. 4-Ryp-a; preview of Eternity 4.00

RASCALS IN PARADISE
Dark Horse Comics: Aug, 1994 - No. 3, Dec, 1994 ($3.95, magazine size)

1-3-Jim Silke-a/story 4.00
Trade paperback-($16.95)-r/#1-3 17.00

RASL
Cartoon Books: Mar, 2008 - No. 15, Jul, 2012 ($3.50/$4.99, B&W)

1-14-Jeff Smith-s/a/c 3.50
15-($4.99) Conclusion 5.00

RASPUTIN: VOICE OF THE DRAGON
Dark Horse Comics: Nov, 2017 - No. 5, Mar, 2018 ($3.99, limited series)

1-5-Mignola & Roberson-s/Mittens-a; Rasputin in 1941 Nazi Germany 4.00

RATCHET & CLANK (Based on the Sony videogame)
DC Comics (WildStorm thru #4): Nov, 2010 - No. 6, Apr, 2011 ($3.99/$2.99, limited series)

1-4-Fixman-s/Archer-a 4.00
5,6-($2.99) 3.00
TPB (2011, $17.99) r/#1-6 18.00

RATFINK (See Frantic and Zany)
Canrom, Inc.: Oct, 1964

1-Woodbridge-a	9	18	27	61	123	185

RAT GOD
Dark Horse Comics: Feb, 2015 - No. 5, Jun, 2015 ($3.99, limited series)

1-5-Richard Corben-s/a/c 4.00

RAT PATROL, THE (TV) (Also see Wild!)
Dell Publishing Co.: Mar, 1967 - No. 5, Nov, 1967; No. 6, Oct, 1969

1-Christopher George photo-c	6	12	18	41	76	110
2-6: 3-6-Photo-c	4	8	12	28	47	65

RAT QUEENS
Image Comics (Shadowline): Sept, 2013 - No. 16, May, 2016 ($3.50/$3.99)

1-Kurtis Wiebe-s/Roc Upchurch-a/c	1	3	4	6	8	10

1-Variant-c by Fiona Staples 40.00
2-10: 2-8-Two covers on each. 9,10-Sejic-a. 9-Frison-c 3.50
11-16-($3.99) Fowler-a 4.00
... Special: Braga #1 (1/15, $3.50) Wiebe-s/Tess Fowler-a; origin of Braga the Orc 3.50

RAT QUEENS (Volume 2)
Image Comics (Shadowline): Mar, 2017 - Present ($3.99)

1-24: 1-15-Kurtis Wiebe-s/Owen Gieni-a/c. 16-19-Ferrier-s/Petraites-a. 22-24-Moritat-a 4.00
... Special: Neon Static 1 (7/18, $3.99) Wiebe-s/Kirkby-a/c; set in future city 4.00
... Special: Orc Dave 1 (9/17, $3.99) Staples-c; Dave's 1st meeting with the Queens 4.00
... Special: Swamp Romp 1 (4/19, $3.99) Ferrier-s/Petraites-a 4.00

RAVAGERS, THE (See Teen Titans and Superboy New 52 series)
DC Comics: Jul, 2012 - No. 12, Jul, 2013 ($2.99)

1-12: 1-Fairchild, Beast Boy, Terra, Thunder, Lightning, Ridge team; Churchill-a 3.00
#0 (11/12, $2.99) Churchill-a; origin of Beast Boy & Terra 3.00

RAVAGE 2099 (See Marvel Comics Presents #117)
Marvel Comics: Dec, 1992 - No. 33, Aug, 1995 ($1.25/$1.50)

1-($1.75)-Gold foil stamped-c; Stan Lee scripts 4.00
1-($1.75)-2nd printing 3.00
2-24,26-33: 5-Last Ryan-c. 6-Last Ryan-a. 14-Punisher 2099 x-over. 15-Ron Lim-c(p). 18-Bound-in card sheet 3.00
25 ($2.25, 52 pgs.) 4.00
25 ($2.95, 52 pgs.)-Silver foil embossed-c 5.00

RAVEN (See DC Special: Raven and Teen Titans titles)

RAVEN (From Teen Titans)
DC Comics: Nov, 2016 - No. 6, Apr, 2017 ($2.99, limited series)

1-6: 1-3-Wolfman-s/Borges-a. 4-6-Neves-a 3.00

RAVEN, THE (See Movie Classics)

RAVEN CHRONICLES
Caliber (New Worlds): 1995 - No. 16 ($2.95, B&W)

1-16: 10-Flip book w/Wordsmith #6. 15-Flip book w/High Caliber #4 3.00

RAVENCROFT (Also see Ruins of Ravencroft)(Leads into King in Black series)
Marvel Comics: Mar, 2020 - No. 5, Nov, 2020 ($3.99, limited series)

1-5-Tieri-s/Unzueta-a; Misty Knight app. 4.00

RAVEN: DAUGHTER OF DARKNESS (From Teen Titans)
DC Comics: Mar, 2018 - No. 12, Mar, 2019 ($3.99, limited series)

1-12-Wolfman-s/Mhan-a; Baron Winters app. 4.00

RAVENS AND RAINBOWS
Pacific Comics: Dec, 1983 (Baxter paper)(Reprints fanzine work in color)

1-Jeff Jones-c/a(r); nudity scenes 3.00

RAWHIDE (TV)
Dell Publishing Co./Gold Key: Sept-Nov, 1959 - June-Aug, 1962; July, 1963 - No. 2, Jan, 1964

Four Color 1028 (#1)	23	46	69	161	356	550
Four Color 1097,1160,1202,1261,1269	13	26	39	91	201	310
01-684-208 (8/62, Dell)	11	22	33	73	157	240
1(10071-307) (7/63, Gold Key)	11	22	33	73	157	240
2-(12¢)	10	20	30	66	138	210

NOTE: *All have Clint Eastwood photo-c.* **Tufts** *a-1028.*

RAWHIDE KID
Atlas/Marvel Comics (CnPC No. 1-16/AMI No. 17-30): Mar, 1955 - No. 16, Sept, 1957; No. 17, Aug, 1960 - No. 151, May, 1979

1-Rawhide Kid, his horse Apache & sidekick Randy begin; Wyatt Earp app.; #1 was not code approved; Maneely splash pg.	213	426	639	1363	2332	3300
2	57	114	171	362	619	875
3-5	42	84	126	265	445	625
6-10: 7-Williamson-a (4 pgs.)	36	72	108	214	347	480
11-16: 16-Torres-a	31	62	93	182	296	410
17-Origin by Jack Kirby; Kirby-a begins	355	710	1065	2485	4343	6200
18-21,24-30	27	54	81	189	420	650
22-Monster-c/story by Kirby/Ayers	35	70	105	252	564	875
23-Origin retold by Jack Kirby	48	96	138	368	834	1300
31-35,40: 31,32-Kirby-a. 33-35-Davis-a. 34-Kirby-a. 35-Intro & death of The Raven. 40-Two-Gun Kid x-over.	14	28	42	98	217	335
36,37,39,41,42-No Kirby. 42-1st Larry Lieber issue	11	22	33	76	163	250
38-Red Raven-c/story; Kirby-c (2/64); Colan-a	17	34	51	115	255	395
43-Kirby-a (beware: pin-up often missing)	14	28	42	94	207	320
44,46: 46-Toth-a. 46-Doc Holliday-c/s	10	20	30	66	138	210
45-Origin retold, 17 pgs.	13	26	39	86	188	290
47-49,51-60	7	14	21	46	86	125
50-Kid Colt x-over; vs. Rawhide Kid	7	14	21	49	92	135
61-70: 64-Kid Colt story. 66-Two-Gun Kid story. 67-Kid Colt story. 70-Last 12¢ issue	5	10	15	34	60	85
71-78,80-83,85	3	6	9	20	31	42
79,84,86,95: 79-Williamson-a(r). 84,86: Kirby-a. 86-Origin-r; Williamson-r/Ringo Kid #13 (4 pgs.)	3	6	9	21	33	45
87-91: 90-Kid Colt app. 91-Last 15¢ issue	3	6	9	18	28	38
92,93 (52 pg.Giants). 92-Kirby-a	4	8	12	25	40	55
94,96-99	3	6	9	16	24	32
100 (6/72)-Origin retold & expanded	3	6	9	21	33	45
101-120: 115-Last new story	3	6	9	14	19	24
121-151	2	4	6	10	14	18
133,134-(30¢-c variants, limited distribution)(5,7/76)	7	14	21	48	89	130
140,141-(35¢-c variants, limited distribution)(7,9/77)	15	30	45	101	223	345
Special 1(9/71, 25¢, 68 pgs.)-All Kirby/Ayers-r	5	10	15	33	57	80

NOTE: **Ayers** *a-13, 14, 16, 29, 37-39, 61.* **Colan** *a-5, 35, 37, 38; c-145p, 148p, 149p.* **Davis** *a-125r.* **Everett** *a-54i, 65, 66, 88, 96i, 148i(r).* **Gulacy** *c-147.* **Heath** *c-4.* **G. Kane** *c-101, 144.* **Keller** *a-5, 39, 41, 144r.* **Kirby** *a-17-32, 34, 42, 43, 84, 86, 92, 109r, 112r, 116r, 117r, 137r, Spec. 1; c-17-35, 37, 38, 40, 41, 43-47, 137r.* **Maneely** *c-1-3, 5, 6, 14.* **Morisi** *a-13.* **Morrow/Williamson** *r-111.* **Roussos** *r-146i, 147i, 149-151i.* **Severin** *a-16; c-8, 13.* **Sutton** *a-61, 93.* **Torres** *a-99r.* **Tuska** *a-14.* **Wildey** *r-146-151(Outlaw Kid).* **Williamson** *r-79, 86, 95.*

RAWHIDE KID
Marvel Comics Group: Aug, 1985 - No. 4, Nov, 1985 (Mini-series)

1-4 5.00

RAWHIDE KID
Marvel Comics (MAX): Apr, 2003 - No. 5, June, 2003 ($2.99, limited series)

1-John Severin-a/Ron Zimmerman-s; Dave Johnson-c 3.00
2-5: 3-Dodson-c. 4-Darwyn Cooke-c. 5-J. Scott Campbell-c 3.00
Vol. 1: Slap Leather TPB (2003, $12.99) r/#1-5 13.00

RAWHIDE KID (The Sensational Seven)
Marvel Comics: Aug, 2010 - No. 4, Nov, 2010 ($3.99, limited series)

The Ray #10 © DC

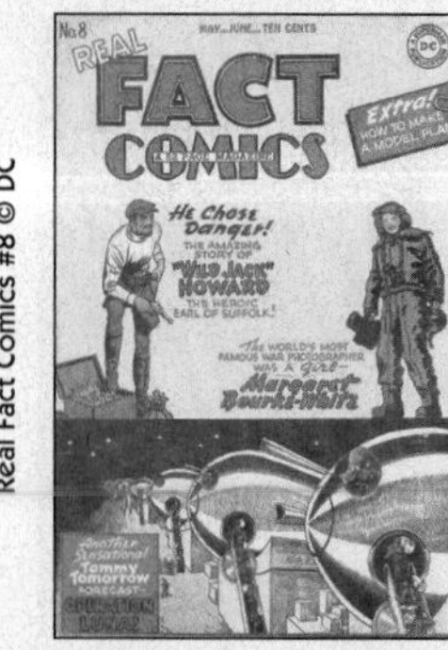

Real Fact Comics #8 © DC

Real Heroes #2 © PMI

GD VG FN VF VF/NM NM-
2.0 4.0 6.0 8.0 9.0 9.2

1-4-Chaykin-a/Zimmerman-s. 1-Cassaday-c. 2-Dave Johnson-c. 4-Suydam-c 4.00

RAY, THE (See Freedom Fighters & Smash Comics #14)
DC Comics: Feb, 1992 - No. 6, July, 1992 ($1.00, mini-series)

1-Sienkiewicz-c; Joe Quesada-a(p) in 1-5 5.00
2-6: 3-6-Quesada-c(p). 6-Quesada layouts only 3.00
...In a Blaze of Power (1994, $12.95)-r/#1-6 w/new Quesada-c 13.00

RAY, THE
DC Comics: May, 1994 - No. 28, Oct, 1996 ($1.75/$1.95/$2.25)

1-Quesada-c(p); Superboy app. 3.00
1-($2.95)-Collectors Edition w/diff. Quesada-c; embossed foil-c 4.00
2-5,0,6-24,26-28: 2-Quesada-c(p); Superboy app. 5-(9/94). 0-(10/94) 3.00
25-($3.50)-Future Flash (Bart Allen)-c/app; double size 4.00
Annual 1 ($3.95, 68 pgs.)-Superman app. 4.00

RAY, THE
DC Comics: Feb, 2012 - No. 4, May, 2012 ($2.99, limited series)

1-4: 1-Igle-a/Palmiotti & Gray-s; origin of the new Ray; intro. Lucien Gates 3.00

RAY BRADBURY COMICS
Topps Comics: Feb, 1993 - V4#1, June, 1994 ($2.95)

1-5-Polybagged w/3 trading cards each. 1-All dinosaur issue; Corben-a; Williamson/Torres/Krenkel-r/Weird Science-Fantasy #25. 3-All dinosaur issue; Steacy painted-c; Stout-a 3.00
Special Edition 1 (1994, $2.95)-The Illustrated Man 3.00
...Special: Tales of Horror #1 ($2.50), ...Trilogy of Terror V3#1 (5/94, $2.50), ...Martian Chronicles V4#1 (6/94, $2.50)-Steranko-c 3.00
NOTE: ***Kelley Jones** a-Trilogy of Terror V3#1. **Kaluta** a-Martian Chronicles V4#1. **Kurtzman/Matt Wagner** c-2. **McKean** c-4. **Mignola** a-4. **Wood** a-Trilogy of Terror V3#1r.*

RAZORLINE
Marvel Comics: Sept, 1993 (75¢, one-shot)

1-Clive Barker super-heroes: Ectokid, Hokum & Hex, Hyperkind & Saint Sinner 3.00

RAZOR'S EDGE, THE
DC Comics (WildStorm): Dec, 2004 - No. 5, Apr, 2005 ($2.95)

1-5-Warblade; Bisley-c/a; Ridley-s 3.00

REAL ADVENTURE COMICS (Action Adventure #2 on)
Gillmor Magazines: Apr, 1955

1 12 24 36 69 97 125

REAL ADVENTURES OF JONNY QUEST, THE
Dark Horse Comics: Sept, 1996 - No. 12, Sept, 1997 ($2.95)

1-12 3.00

REAL CLUE CRIME STORIES (Formerly Clue Comics)
Hillman Periodicals: V2#4, June, 1947 - V8#3, May, 1953

V2#4(#1)-S&K c/a(3); Dan Barry-a 50 100 150 315 533 750
5-7-S&K c/a(3-4). 7-Iron Lady app. 40 80 120 244 402 560
8-12 15 30 45 83 124 165
V3#1-8,10-12, V4#1-3,5-8,11,12 14 28 42 76 108 140
V3#9-Used in **SOTI**, pg. 102 15 30 45 85 130 175
V4#4-S&K-a 15 30 45 86 138 180
V4#9,10-Krigstein-a 14 28 42 78 112 145
V5#1-5,7,8,10,12 10 20 30 58 79 100
6,9,11(1/54)-Krigstein-a 11 22 33 62 86 110
V6#1-5,8,9,11 10 20 30 54 72 90
6,7,10,12-Krigstein-a. 10-Bondage-c 11 22 33 62 86 110
V7#1-3,5-11, V8#1-3: V7#6-1 pg. Frazetta ad "Prayer" - 1st app.? 10 20 30 58 79 100
4,12-Krigstein-a 11 22 33 62 86 110
NOTE: ***Barry** a-9, 10; c-V2#8. **Briefer** a-V6#6. **Fuje** a- V2#7(2), 8, 11. **Infantino** a-V2#8; c-V2#11. **Lawrence** a-V3#8, V5#7. **Powell** a-V4#11, 12. V5#4, 5, 7 are 68 pgs.*

REAL EXPERIENCES (Formerly Tiny Tessie)
Atlas Comics (20CC): No. 25, Jan, 1950

25-Virginia Mayo photo-c from movie "Red Light" 15 30 45 88 137 185

REAL FACT COMICS
National Periodical Publications: Mar-Apr, 1946 - No. 21, July-Aug, 1949

1-S&K-c/a; Harry Houdini story; Just Imagine begins (not by Finlay); Fred Ray-a 48 96 144 302 514 725
2-S&K-a; Rin-Tin-Tin & P. T. Barnum stories 28 56 84 165 270 375
3-H.G. Wells, Lon Chaney stories; early DC letter column (New Fun Comics #3 from 1935 may be the 1st) 26 52 78 154 252 350
4-Virgil Finlay-a on 'Just Imagine' begins, ends #12 (2 pgs. each); Jimmy Stewart & Jack London stories; Joe DiMaggio 1 pg. biography 29 58 87 172 281 390
5-Batman/Robin-c taken from cover of Batman #9; 5 pg. story about creation of Batman & Robin; Tom Mix story 155 310 465 992 1696 2400
6-Origin & 1st app. Tommy Tomorrow by Weisinger and Sherman (1-2/47); Flag-c; 1st writing by Harlan Ellison (letter column, non-professional); "First Man to Reach Mars" epic-c/story 84 168 252 538 919 1300
7-(No. 6 on inside)-Roussos-a; D. Fairbanks sty. 15 30 45 94 147 200
8-2nd app. Tommy Tomorrow by Finlay (5-6/47) 48 96 144 302 514 725
9-S&K-a; Glenn Miller, Indianapolis 500 stories 21 42 63 122 199 275
10-Vigilante by Meskin (based on movie serial); 4 pg. Finlay s/f story 20 40 60 118 192 265
11,12: 11-Annie Oakley, G-Men stories; Kinstler-a 14 28 42 82 121 160
13-Dale Evans and Tommy Tomorrow-c/stories 37 74 111 222 361 500
14,17,18: 14-Will Rogers story 14 28 42 80 115 150
15-Nuclear explosion part-c ("Last War on Earth" story); Clyde Beatty story 15 30 45 94 147 200
16-Tommy Tomorrow app.; 1st Planeteers? 36 72 108 211 343 475
19-Sir Arthur Conan Doyle story 15 30 45 83 124 165
20-Kubert-a, 4 pgs; Daniel Boone story 15 30 45 88 137 185
21-Kubert-a, 2 pgs; Kit Carson story 14 28 42 80 115 150
Ashcan (2/46) nn-Not distributed to newsstands, only for in house use. Covers were produced, but not the rest of the book. A copy sold in 2008 for $500.
NOTE: ***Barry** c-16. **Virgil Finlay** c-6, 8. **Meskin** c-10. **Roussos** a-1-4, 6.*

REAL FUNNIES
Nedor Publishing Co.: Jan, 1943 - No. 3, June, 1943

1-Funny animal, humor; Black Terrier app. (clone of The Black Terror) 36 72 108 211 343 475
2,3 18 36 54 107 169 230

REAL GHOSTBUSTERS, THE (Also see Slimer)
Now Comics: Aug, 1988 - No. 28, Feb, 1991 ($1.75/$1.95)

1-Based on Ghostbusters movie 3 6 9 16 23 30
2 1 3 4 6 8 10
3-28 5.00

REAL HEROES
Image Comics: Mar, 2014 - No. 4, Nov, 2014 ($3.99)

1-3-Bryan Hitch-s/a 4.00
4-($4.99) 5.00

REAL HEROES COMICS
Parents' Magazine Institute: Sept, 1941 - No. 16, Oct, 1946

1-Roosevelt-c/story 32 64 96 192 314 435
2-J. Edgar Hoover-c/story 15 30 45 85 130 175
3-5,7-10: 4-Churchill, Roosevelt stories 14 28 42 78 112 145
6-Lou Gehrig-c/story 20 40 60 114 182 250
11-16: 13-Kiefer-a 10 20 30 54 72 90

REALISTIC ROMANCES
Realistic Comics/Avon Periodicals: July-Aug, 1951 - No. 17, Aug-Sept, 1954 (No #9-14)

1-Kinstler-a; c-/Avon paperback #211 42 84 126 265 445 625
2 23 46 69 136 223 310
3,4 22 44 66 128 209 290
5,8-Kinstler-a 22 44 66 130 213 295
6-c-/Diversey Prize Novels #6; Kinstler-a 22 44 66 132 216 300
7-Evans-a?; c-/Avon paperback #360 22 44 66 132 216 300
15,17: 17-Kinstler-c 21 42 63 124 202 280
16-Kinstler marijuana story-r/Romantic Love #6 22 44 66 130 213 295
I.W. Reprint #1,8,9: #1-r/Realistic Romances #4; Astarita-a. 9-r/Women To Love #1 3 6 9 15 22 28
NOTE: ***Astarita** a-2-4, 7, 8, 17. Photo c-1, 2. Painted c-3, 4.*

REALITY CHECK
Image Comics: Sept, 2013 - No. 4, Dec, 2013 ($2.99)

1-4-Brunswick-s/Bogdanovic-a 3.00

REAL LIFE COMICS
Nedor/Better/Standard Publ./Pictorial Magazine No. 13: Sept, 1941 - No. 59, Sept, 1952

1-Uncle Sam-c/story; Daniel Boone story 79 158 237 502 864 1225
2-Woodrow Wilson-c/story 39 78 117 240 395 550
3-Classic Schomburg Hitler-c with "Emperor of Hate" emblazoned in blood behind him. Cover shows world at war, concentration camps and Nazis killing civilians; Hitler 10 pg. bio 1000 2000 3000 7400 13,200 19,000
4,5: 4-Story of American flag "Old Glory" 33 66 99 196 321 445
6-10: 6-Wild Bill Hickok story 29 58 87 170 278 385
11-14,16-20: 17-Albert Einstein story 23 46 69 136 223 310
15-Japanese WWII-c by Schomburg 30 60 90 177 289 400
21-23,25,26,29,30: 29-A-Bomb story. 28-Japanese WWII-c 20 40 60 120 195 270
24-Story of Baseball (Babe Ruth); Japanese WWII-c

The Realm #10 © Peck & Haun

Real Western Hero #74 © FAW

Reaver #6 © Skybound

	GD 2.0	VG 4.0	FN 6.0	VF 8.0	VF/NM 9.0	NM- 9.2
	29	58	87	170	278	385
27,28: 27-Schomburg A-Bomb-c; story of A-Bomb	27	54	81	158	259	360
31-33,35,36,42-44,48,49: 32-Frank Sinatra story. 49-Baseball issue	17	34	51	100	158	215
34,37-41,45-47: 34-Jimmy Stewart story. 37-Story of motion pictures; Bing Crosby story. 38-Jane Froman story. 39- "1,000,000 A.D." story. 40-Bob Feller. 41-Jimmie Foxx story ("Jimmy" on-c); "Home Run" Baker story. 45-Story of Olympic games; Burl Ives & Kit Carson story. 46-Douglas Fairbanks Jr. & Sr. story. 47-George Gershwin story	18	36	54	105	165	225
50-Frazetta-a (5 pgs.)	31	62	93	186	303	420
51-Jules Verne "Journey to the Moon" by Evans; Severin/Elder-a	22	44	66	130	213	295
52-Frazetta-a (4 pgs.); Severin/Elder-a(2); Evans-a	34	68	102	204	332	460
53-57-Severin/Elder-a. 54-Bat Masterson-c/story	18	36	54	105	165	225
58-Severin/Elder-a(2)	18	36	54	107	169	230
59-1 pg. Frazetta; Severin/Elder-a	18	36	54	107	169	230

NOTE: ***Guardineer** a-40(2), 44. **Meskin** a-52. **Roussos** a-50. **Schomburg** c-1-5, 7, 11, 13-21, 23, 24, 26-28, 30-32-40, 42, 44-50, 54, 55. **Tuska** a-53. Photo-c 5, 6.*

REAL LIFE SECRETS (Real Secrets #2 on)
Ace Periodicals: Sept, 1949 (one-shot)

	GD	VG	FN	VF	VF/NM	NM-
1-Painted-c	19	38	57	112	179	245

REAL LIFE STORY OF FESS PARKER (Magazine)
Dell Publishing Co.: 1955

	GD	VG	FN	VF	VF/NM	NM-
1	8	16	24	56	108	160

REAL LIFE TALES OF SUSPENSE (See Suspense)

REAL LOVE (Formerly Hap Hazard)
Ace Periodicals (A. A. Wyn): No. 25, April, 1949 - No. 76, Nov, 1956

	GD	VG	FN	VF	VF/NM	NM-
25	20	40	60	115	188	260
26	15	30	45	86	133	180
27-L. B. Cole-a	15	30	45	92	144	195
28-35	14	28	42	82	121	160
36-66: 66-Last pre-code (2/55)	14	28	42	80	115	150
67-76	13	26	39	72	101	130

NOTE: *Photo c-50-76. Painted c-46.*

REALM, THE
Arrow Comics/WeeBee Comics #13/Caliber Press #14 on: Feb, 1986 - No. 21, 1991 (B&W)

1-3,5-21 — 3.00
4-1st app. Deadworld (9/86) — 4.00
Book 1 ($4.95, B&W) — 5.00

REALM, THE
Image Comics: Sept, 2017 - Present ($3.99)

1-15-Seth Peck & Jeremy Haun-s/a. 1-Covers by Haun & Tony Moore — 4.00

REAL McCOYS, THE (TV)
Dell Publ. Co.: No. 1071, 1-3/60 - 5-7/1962 (All have Walter Brennan photo-c)

	GD	VG	FN	VF	VF/NM	NM-
Four Color 1071,1134-Toth-a in both	8	16	24	54	102	150
Four Color 1193,1265	7	14	21	48	89	130
01-689-207 (5-7/62)	6	12	18	42	79	115

REALM OF KINGS (Also see Guardians of the Galaxy and Nova)
Marvel Comics: Jan, 2010 ($3.99, one-shot)

1-Abnett & Lanning-s/Manco & Asrar-a; Guardians of the Galaxy app. — 4.00

REALM OF KINGS: IMPERIAL GUARD
Marvel Comics: Jan, 2010 - No. 5, May, 2010 ($3.99, limited series)

1-5-Abnett & Lanning-s/Walker-a; Starjammers app. — 4.00

REALM OF KINGS: INHUMANS
Marvel Comics: Jan, 2010 - No. 5, May, 2010 ($3.99, limited series)

1-5-Abnett & Lanning-s/Raimondi-a; Mighty Avengers app. — 4.00

REALM OF KINGS: SON OF HULK
Marvel Comics: Apr, 2010 - No. 4, July, 2010 ($3.99, limited series)

1-4-Reed-s/Munera-a; leads into Incredible Hulk #609 — 4.00

REALM OF THE CLAW (Also see Mutant Earth as part of a flipbook)
Image Comics: Oct, 2003 - No. 2 ($2.95)

0-(7/03, $5.95) Convention Special; cover has gold-foil title logo — 6.00
1,2-Two covers by Yardin — 3.00
Vol. 1 TPB (2006, $16.99) r/series; concept art & sketch pages — 17.00

REAL SCREEN COMICS (#1 titled Real Screen Funnies; TV Screen Cartoons #129-138)
National Periodical Publications: Spring, 1945 - No. 128, May-June, 1959 (#1-40: 52 pgs.)

	GD	VG	FN	VF	VF/NM	NM-
1-The Fox & the Crow, Flippity & Flop, Tito & His Burrito begin	123	246	369	787	1344	1900
2	50	100	150	315	533	750
3-5	32	64	96	188	307	425
6-10 (2-3/47)	21	42	63	122	199	275
11-20 (10-11/48): 13-The Crow x-over in Flippity & Flop	16	32	48	94	147	200
21-30 (6-7/50)	14	28	42	76	108	140
31-50	11	22	33	60	83	105
51-99	10	20	30	54	72	90
100	10	20	30	56	76	95
101-128	8	16	24	44	57	70

REAL SCREEN FUNNIES
DC Comics: Spring 1945

1-Ashcan comic, not distributed to newsstands, only for in-house use. Cover art is Real Screen Funnies #1 with interior being Detective Comics #92. Only ashcan cover to be produced using the regular production first issue art and only using the color yellow. A copy sold in 2008 for $3,000. A FN/VF copy sold for $1314.50 in 2012. A CGC 6.5 copy sold for $1050 in 2018.

REAL SECRETS (Formerly Real Life Secrets)
Ace Periodicals: No. 2, Nov, 1950 - No. 5, May, 1950

	GD	VG	FN	VF	VF/NM	NM-
2-Painted-c	15	30	45	88	137	185
3-5: 3-Photo-c	13	26	39	74	105	135

REAL SPORTS COMICS (All Sports Comics #2 on)
Hillman Periodicals: Oct-Nov, 1948 (52 pgs.)

	GD	VG	FN	VF	VF/NM	NM-
1-Powell-a (12 pgs.)	42	84	126	265	445	625

REAL WAR STORIES
Eclipse Comics: July, 1987; No. 2, Jan, 1991 ($2.00, 52 pgs.)

1-Bolland-a(p), Bissette-a, Totleben-a(i); Alan Moore scripts (2nd printing exists, 2/88) — 5.00
2-($4.95) — 5.00

REAL WESTERN HERO (Formerly Wow #1-69; Western Hero #76 on)
Fawcett Publications: No. 70, Sept, 1948 - No. 75, Feb, 1949 (All 52 pgs.)

	GD	VG	FN	VF	VF/NM	NM-
70(#1)-Tom Mix, Monte Hale, Hopalong Cassidy, Young Falcon begin	22	44	66	132	216	300
71-75: 71-Gabby Hayes begins. 71,72-Captain Tootsie by Beck. 75-Big Bow and Little Arrow app.	15	30	45	85	130	175

NOTE: *Painted/photo c-70-73; painted c-74, 75.*

REAL WEST ROMANCES
Crestwood Publishing Co./Prize Publ.: 4-5/49 - V1#6, 3/50; V2#1, Apr-May, 1950 (All 52 pgs. & photo-c)

	GD	VG	FN	VF	VF/NM	NM-
V1#1-S&K-a(p)	29	58	87	172	281	390
2-Gail Davis and Rocky Shahan photo-c	15	30	45	85	130	175
3-Kirby-a(p) only	15	30	45	88	137	185
4-S&K-a; Whip Wilson, Reno Browne photo-c	20	40	60	118	192	265
5-Audie Murphy, Gale Storm photo-c; S&K-a	18	36	54	109	172	235
6-Produced by S&K, no S&K-a; Robert Preston & Cathy Downs photo-c	14	28	42	81	118	155
V2#1-Kirby-a(p)	14	28	42	81	118	155

NOTE: ***Meskin** a-V1#5, 6. **Severin/Elder** a-V1#3-6, V2#1. **Meskin** a-V1#6. **Leonard Starr** a-1-3. Photo-c V1#1-6, V2#1.*

REALWORLDS :...
DC Comics: 2000 ($5.95, one-shots, prestige format)

Batman - Marshall Rogers-a/Golden & Sniegoski-s; Justice League of America -Dematteis-s/Barr-painted art; Superman - Vance-s/García-López & Rubenstein-a; Wonder Woman - Hanson & Neuwirth-s/Sam-a — 6.00

REANIMATOR (Based on the 1985 horror movie)
Dynamite Entertainment: 2015 - No. 4, 2015 ($3.99, mini-series)

1-4-Further exploits of Herbert West; Davidsen-s/Valiente-a; four covers on each — 4.00

RE-ANIMATOR IN FULL COLOR
Adventure Comics: Oct, 1991 - No. 3, 1992 ($2.95, mini-series)

1-3: Adapts horror movie. 1-Dorman painted-c — 3.00

REAP THE WILD WIND (See Cinema Comics Herald)

REAVER
Image Comics (Skybound): Jul, 2019 - No. 11, Sept, 2020 ($3.99)

1-11: 1-Justin Jordan-s/Rebekah Isaacs-a. 7-11-Henrichon-a — 4.00

REBEL, THE (TV)(Nick Adams as Johnny Yuma)
Dell Publishing Co.: No. 1076, Feb-Apr, 1960 - No. 1262, Dec-Feb, 1961-62

	GD	VG	FN	VF	VF/NM	NM-
Four Color 1076 (#1)-Sekowsky-a, photo-c	10	20	30	66	138	210

Four Color 1138 (9-11/60), 1207 (9-11/61), 1262-Photo-c

Reborn #3 © Millarworld & Cappulo

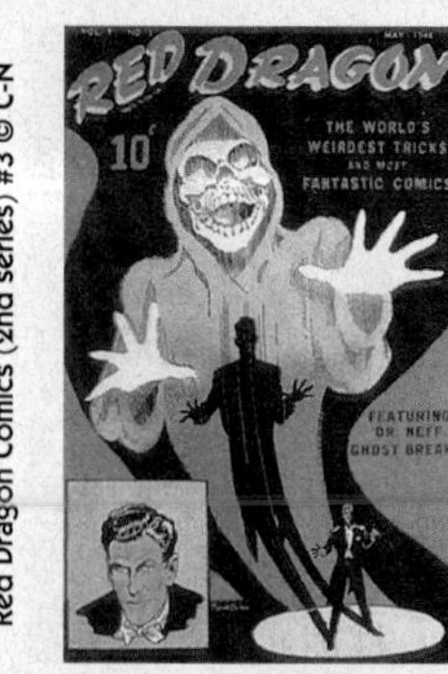

Red Dragon Comics (2nd series) #3 © C-N

Redemption #1 © AWA Inc.

	GD	VG	FN	VF	VF/NM	NM-
	2.0	4.0	6.0	8.0	9.0	9.2

8 16 24 55 105 155

REBELS (Also see Rebels: These Free And Independent States)
Dark Horse Comics: Apr, 2015 - No. 10, Jan, 2016 ($3.99)

1-Set in Revolutionary War 1775 Vermont; Brian Wood-s/Andrea Mutti-a/Tula Lotay-c 5.00
2-10: 4-General Washington app. 4.00

R.E.B.E.L.S.
DC Comics: Apr, 2009 - No. 28, Jul, 2011 ($2.99)

1-9,12-28: 1-Bedard-s/Clarke-a; Vril Dox returns; Supergirl app.; 2 covers. 15-Starfire app. 19-28-Lobo app. 3.00
10,11-($3.99) Blackest Night x-over; Vril Dox joins the Sinestro Corps 4.00
Annual 1 (12/09, $4.99) Origin of Starro the Conqueror; Despero app. 5.00
...: Sons of Brainiac TPB (2011, $14.99) r/#15-20 15.00
...: Strange Companions TPB (2010, $14.99) r/#7-9 & Annual #1 15.00
...: The Coming of Starro TPB (2010, $17.99) r/#1-6 18.00
...: The Son and the Stars TPB (2010, $17.99) r/#10-14 18.00

R.E.B.E.L.S. '94 (Becomes R.E.B.E.L.S. '95 & R.E.B.E.L.S. '96)
DC Comics: No. 0, Oct, 1994 - No. 17, Mar, 1996 ($1.95/$2.25)

0-17: 8-$2.25-c begins. 15-R.E.B.E.L.S '96 begins. 3.00

REBELS: THESE FREE AND INDEPENDENT STATES
Dark Horse Comics: Mar, 2017 - No. 8, Oct, 2017 ($3.99)

1-8: 1-5-Birth of the U.S. Navy in 1794; Brian Wood-s/Andrea Mutti-a 4.00

REBORN
Image Comics: Oct, 2016 - No. 6, Jun, 2017 ($3.99)

1-Mark Millar-s/Greg Capullo-a 5.00
2-5 4.00
6-($5.99) Bonus sketch pages and creator interview 6.00

RECORD BOOK OF FAMOUS POLICE CASES
St. John Publishing Co.: 1949 (25¢, 132 pgs.)

nn-Kubert-a(3); r/Son of Sinbad; Baker-c 60 120 180 381 653 925

RED (Inspired the 2010 Bruce Willis movie)
DC Comics (Homage): Sept, 2003 - No. 3, Feb, 2004 ($2.95, limited series)

1-3-Warren Ellis-s/Cully Hamner-a/c 5.00
Red/Tokyo Storm Warning TPB (2004, $14.95) Flip book r/both series 15.00
Red: Eyes Only (2/11, $4.99) comic prequel; Hamner-s/a/c 5.00
Red: Frank (11/10, $3.99) movie prequel; Noveck-s/Masters-a/Hamner & photo-c 4.00
Red: Joe (11/10, $3.99) movie prequel; Wagner-s/Redondo-a/Hamner & photo-c 4.00
Red: Marvin (11/10, $3.99) movie prequel; Hoeber-s/Olmos-a/Hamner & photo-c 4.00
Red: Victoria (11/10, $3.99) movie prequel; Hoeber-s/Hahn-a/Hamner & photo-c 4.00
...: Better R.E.D. Than Dead TPB (2011, $14.99) r/movie prequel issues; sketch-a 15.00

RED ARROW
P. L. Publishing Co.: May-June, 1951 - No. 3, Oct, 1951

1-Bondage-c 16 32 48 98 154 210
2,3 12 24 36 67 94 120

RED ATLANTIS
AfterShock Comics: Nov, 2020 - Present ($4.99, limited series)

1-4-Stephanie Phillips-s/Robert Carey-a 5.00

RED BAND COMICS
Enwil Associates: Nov, 1944, No. 2, Jan, 1945 - No. 4, May, 1945

1-Bogeyman-c/intro. (The Spirit swipe) 52 104 156 328 552 775
2-Origin Bogeyman & Santanas; c-reprint/#1 36 72 108 214 347 480
3,4-Captain Wizard app. in both (1st app.); each has identical contents/cover
34 68 102 199 325 450

REDBLADE
Dark Horse Comics: Apr, 1993 - No. 3, July, 1993 ($2.50, mini-series)

1-3: 1-Double gatefold-c 3.00

RED BORDER
AWA Studios: Mar, 2020 - No. 4, Aug, 2020 ($3.99, limited series)

1-4-Jason Starr-s/Will Conrad-a 4.00

RED CIRCLE, THE (Re-introduction of characters from MLJ/Archie publications)
DC Comics: Oct, 2009 ($2.99, series of one-shots)

...Inferno 1 - Hangman app.; Straczynski-s/Greg Scott-a 5.00
...The Hangman 1 - Origin retold; Straczynski-s/Derenick & Sienkiewicz-a 5.00
...The Shield 1 - Origin retold; Straczynski-s/McDaniel-a 5.00
...The Web 1 - Straczynski-s/Robinson-a 5.00

RED CIRCLE COMICS (Also see Blazing Comics & Blue Circle Comics)
Rural Home Publications (Enwil): Jan, 1945 - No. 4, April, 1945

1-The Prankster & Red Riot begin 77 154 231 493 847 1200
2-Starr-a; The Judge (costumed hero) app. 39 78 117 236 388 540
3,4-Starr-c/a. 3-The Prankster not in costume 32 64 96 188 307 425
4-(Dated 4/45)-Leftover covers to #4 were later restapled over early 1950s coverless comics; variations in the coverless comics used are endless; Woman Outlaws, Dorothy Lamour, Crime Does Not Pay, Sabu, Diary Loves, Love Confessions & Young Love V3#3 known
22 44 66 130 213 295

RED CIRCLE SORCERY (Chilling Adventures in Sorcery #1-5)
Red Circle Prod. (Archie): No. 6, Apr, 1974 - No. 11, Feb, 1975 (All 25¢ iss.)

6,8,9,11: 6-Early Chaykin-a. 7-Pino-a. 8-Only app. The Cobra
2 4 6 9 13 16
7-Bruce Jones-a with Wrightson, Kaluta, Jeff Jones 3 6 9 14 19 24
10-Wood-a(i) 2 4 6 10 14 18

NOTE: ***Chaykin*** *a-6, 10.* ***McWilliams*** *a-10(2 & 3 pgs.).* ***Mooney*** *a-11p.* ***Morrow*** *a-6-8, 9(text illos), 10, 11i; c-6-11.* ***Thorne*** *a-8, 10.* ***Toth*** *a-8, 9.*

RED DOG (See Night Music #7)

RED DRAGON
Comico: June, 1996 ($2.95)

1-Bisley-c 3.00

RED DRAGON COMICS (1st Series) (Formerly Trail Blazers; see Super Magician V5#7, 8)
Street & Smith Publications: No. 5, Jan, 1943 - No. 9, Jan, 1944

5-Origin Red Rover, the Crimson Crimebuster; Rex King, Man of Adventure, Captain Jack Commando, & The Minute Man begin; text origin Red Dragon; Binder-c
110 220 330 704 1202 1700
6-Origin The Black Crusader & Red Dragon (3/43); 1st story app. Red Dragon & 1st cover (classic-c) 258 516 774 1651 2826 4000
7-Classic Japanese exploding soldier WWII-c 377 754 1131 2639 4620 6600
8-The Red Knight app. 71 142 213 454 777 1100
9-Origin Chuck Magnon, Immortal Man 71 142 213 454 777 1100

RED DRAGON COMICS (2nd Series)(See Super Magician V2#8)
Street & Smith Publications: Nov, 1947 - No. 6, Jan, 1949; No. 7, July, 1949

1-Red Dragon begins; Elliman, Nigel app.; Edd Cartier-c/a
126 252 378 806 1378 1950
2-Cartier-c 63 126 189 403 689 975
3-1st app. Dr. Neff Ghost Breaker by Powell; Elliman, Nigel app.
52 104 156 328 552 775
4-Cartier c/a 65 130 195 416 708 1000
5-7 39 78 117 240 395 550

NOTE: ***Maneely*** *a-5, 7.* ***Powell*** *a-2-7; c-3, 5, 7.*

RED EAGLE
David McKay Publications: No. 16, Aug, 1938

Feature Books 16 37 74 111 222 361 500

REDEMPTION
AWA Studios: Feb, 2021 - No. 5 ($3.99, limited series)

1-Christa Faust-s/Mike Deodato Jr.-a; afterwords from the creators 4.00

REDEYE (See Comics Reading Libraries in the Promotional Comics section)

RED FOX (Formerly Manhunt! #1-14; also see Extra Comics)
Magazine Enterprises: No. 15, 1954

15(A-1 #108)-Undercover Girl story; L.B. Cole-c/a (Red Fox); r-from Manhunt; Powell-a
20 40 60 115 185 255

RED GOBLIN: RED DEATH (See Absolute Carnage series)
Marvel Comics: Dec, 2019 ($4.99)

1-Norman Osborn and the Carnage symbiote 5.00

RED GOOSE COMIC SELECTIONS (See Comic Selections)

RED HAWK (See A-1 Comics, Bobby Benson's ..#14-16 & Straight Arrow #2)
Magazine Enterprises: No. 90, 1953

11-(A-1 Comics #90)-Powell-c/a 14 28 42 76 108 140

RED HERRING
DC Comics (WildStorm): Oct, 2009 - No. 6, Mar, 2010 ($2.99, limited series)

1-6-Tischman-s/Bond-a 3.00

RED HOOD (Title changed from Red Hood: Outlaw #50)
DC Comics: No. 51, Jan, 2021 - Present ($3.99)

51,52-Shawn Martinbrough-s/Tony Akins-a 4.00

RED HOOD AND THE OUTLAWS (DC New 52)
DC Comics: Nov, 2011 - No. 40, May, 2015 ($2.99)

1-Jason Todd, Starfire, Roy Harper team; Lobdell-s/Rocafort-a/c
2 4 6 8 11 14

Red Hood and the Outlaws #14 © DC

Red Mother #1 © Jeremy Haun

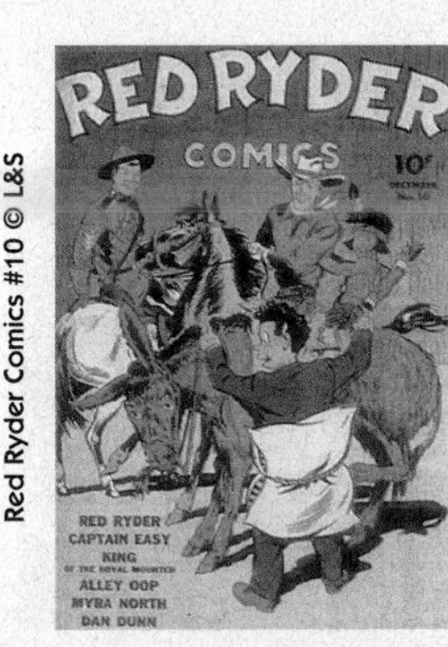

Red Ryder Comics #10 © L&S

2-4 6.00
5-8 4.00
9-Night of the Owls tie-in; Mr. Freeze vs. Talon 5.00
10-14 3.00
15-(2/13) Death of the Family tie-in; die-cut cover; Joker app. 5.00
16-18: 16,17-Death of the Family tie-in 4.00
19-24,26-40: 24,26,27-Ra's al Ghul app. 30,31-Lobo app. 37-Arsenal's origin 3.00
25-($3.99) Zero Year tie-in; Talia and the Red Hood Gang app.; Haun-a 4.00
#0-(11/12, $2.99) Jason Todd's origin re-told; Joker app. 6.00
Annual 1 (7/13, $4.99) Takes place between #20 & 21; Green Arrow app.; Barrionuevo-a 5.00
Annual 2 (2/15, $4.99) Christmas-themed; Derenick-a 5.00
...: Futures End 1 (11/14, $2.99, regular-c) Five years later; Lobdell-s/Kolins-a 3.00
...: Futures End 1 (11/14, $3.99, 3-D cover) 4.00

RED HOOD AND THE OUTLAWS (DC Rebirth)(Title changes to Red Hood: Outlaw with #27)
DC Comics: Oct, 2016 - No. 26, Nov, 2018 ($2.99/$3.99)

1-8: 1-Jason Todd, Artemis & Bizarro team; Lobdell-s/Soy-a; Blask Mask app. 3.00
9-24,26-($3.99) 12-Solomon Grundy app. 13-Lex Luthor app. 16,17-Harley Quinn app. 18-The Creeper app. 4.00
25-($4.99) Art by Soy & Hairsine; back-up with Hester-a; leads into Annual 2 5.00
Annual 1 (10/17, $4.99) Nightwing & KGBeast app.; Kirkham-a/c 5.00
Annual 2 (10/18, $4.99) Arsenal app.; Lobdell-s/Henry-a/Rocafort-c 5.00
Annual 3 (9/19, $4.99) Lobdell-s/Pollina-a/Soy-c; leads into Red Hood: Outlaw #37 5.00
...: Rebirth (9/16, $2.99) Jason Todd origin re-told; Batman app. 3.00

RED HOOD / ARSENAL
DC Comics: Aug, 2015 - No. 13, Aug, 2016 ($2.99)

1-13: 1-Jason Todd & Roy Harper team; Lobdell-s/Medri. 3-5-Batman (Gordon) app. 6-13-Joker's Daughter app. 7-"Robin War" tie-in. 13-Bonus flashback 1st meeting 3.00

RED HOOD: OUTLAW (Title changed from Red Hood and the Outlaws)(Becomes Red Hood #51)
DC Comics: No. 27, Dec, 2018 - No. 50, Dec, 2020 ($3.99)

27-49: 27-31,33,34-Lobdell-s/Woods-a. 28,29-Batwoman app. 32-Segovia-a. 48-Joker War tie-in; Punchline app. 4.00
50-($5.99) Duela Dent (Joker's Daughter) app.; Pantalena-a 6.00

RED HOOD: THE LOST DAYS
DC Comics: Aug, 2010 - No. 6, Jan, 2011 ($2.99, limited series)

1-6-The Return of Jason Todd; Winick-s/Raimondi-a/Tucci-c. 6-Joker & Hush app. 4.00
TPB (2011, $14.99) r/#1-6 15.00

RED LANTERNS (DC New 52)
DC Comics: Nov, 2011 - No. 40, May, 2015 ($2.99)

1-34: 1-Milligan-s/Benes-a/c; Atrocitus, Dex-Starr & Bleez app. 6-8,11-Guy Gardner app. 10-Stormwatch app. 13-15-Rise of the Third Army. 17-First Lantern app. 24-Lights Out pt. 4. 28-Flipbook with Green Lantern #28; Supergirl app. 29-Superman app. 3.00
35-40: 35-37-Godhead x-over; Simon Baz app. 3.00
#0-(11/12, $2.99) Origin of Atrocitus, the 1st Red Lantern; Syaf-a 3.00
Annual 1 (9/14, $4.99) Story occurs between #33 & 34; Batman cameo 5.00
...: Futures End 1 (11/14, $2.99, regular-c) Five years later; Soule-s/Calafiore-a 3.00
...: Futures End 1 (11/14, $3.99, 3-D cover) 4.00

RED MASK (Formerly Tim Holt; see Best Comics, Blazing Six-Guns)
Magazine Enterprises No. 42-53/Sussex No. 54 (M.E. on-c): No. 42, June-July, 1954 - No. 53, May, 1956; No. 54, Sept, 1957

	GD	VG	FN	VF	VF/NM	NM-
42-Ghost Rider by Ayers continues, ends #50; Black Phantom continues; 3-D effect c/stories begin	21	42	63	122	199	275
43- 3-D effect-c/stories	19	38	57	109	172	235
44-52: 3-D effect stories only. 47-Last pre-code issue. 50-Last Ghost Rider. 51-The Presto Kid begins by Ayers (1st app.); Presto Kid-c begins; last 3-D effect story.						
52-Origin The Presto Kid	17	34	51	98	154	210
53,54-Last Black Phantom; last Presto Kid-c	15	30	45	83	124	165
I.W. Reprint #1 (r-/#52). 2 (nd, r/#51 w/diff.-c). 3, 8 (nd; Kinstler-c); 8-r/Red Mask #52	3	6	9	16	22	28

NOTE: ***Ayers** art on Ghost Rider & Presto Kid. **Bolle** art in all (Red Mask); c-43, 44, 49. **Guardineer** a-52. Black Phantom in #42-44, 47-50, 53, 54.*

REDMASK OF THE RIO GRANDE
AC Comics: 1990 ($2.50, 28 pgs.)(Has photos of movie posters)

1-Bolle-c/a(r); photo inside-c 3.00

RED MENACE
DC Comics (WildStorm): Jan, 2007 - No. 6, Jun, 2007 ($2.99, limited series)

1-6-Ordway-a/c; Bilson, DeMeo & Brody-s 3.00
TPB (2007, $17.99) r/series, sketch pages & variant covers 18.00

RED MOTHER, THE
BOOM! Studios: Dec, 2019 - No. 12, Jan, 2021 ($3.99)

1-12-Jeremy Haun-s/Danny Luckert-a 4.00

RED MOUNTAIN FEATURING QUANTRELL'S RAIDERS (Movie)(Also see Jesse James #28)
Avon Periodicals: 1952

	GD	VG	FN	VF	VF/NM	NM-
nn-Alan Ladd; Kinstler-c	34	68	102	204	332	460

REDNECK
Image Comics (Skybound): Apr, 2017 - Present ($3.99)

1-Donny Cates-s/Lisandro Estherren-a 5.00
2-29 4.00

RED ONE
Image Comics: Mar, 2015 - No. 4, Oct, 2016 ($2.99)

1-4-Xavier Dorison-s/Terry Dodson-a/c 3.00

RED PROPHET: THE TALES OF ALVIN MAKER
Dabel Brothers Prods./Marvel Comics (Dabel Brothers): Mar, 2006 - No. 12, Mar, 2008 ($2.99)

1-12-Adaptation of Orson Scott Card novel. 1-Miguel Montenegro-a 3.00
... Vol. 1 HC (2007, $19.99, dustjacket) r/#1-6 20.00
... Vol. 1 SC (2007, $15.99) r/#1-6 16.00
... Vol. 2 HC (2008, $19.99, dustjacket) r/#7-12 20.00

"RED" RABBIT COMICS
Dearfield Comic/J. Charles Laue Publ. Co.: Jan, 1947 - No. 22, Aug-Sep, 1951

	GD	VG	FN	VF	VF/NM	NM-
1	16	32	48	94	147	200
2	11	22	33	62	86	110
3-10	10	20	30	54	72	90
11-17,19-22	8	16	24	47	61	75
18-Flying Saucer-c (1/51)	10	20	30	58	79	100

RED RAVEN COMICS (Human Torch #2 on)(See X-Men #44 & Sub-Mariner #26, 2nd series)
Timely Comics: August, 1940

	GD	VG	FN	VF	VF/NM	NM-
1-Jack Kirby-c (his 1st signed work); origin & 1st app. Red Raven; Comet Pierce & Mercury by Kirby, The Human Top & The Eternal Brain; intro. Magar, the Mystic & only app.	2250	4500	6750	17,000	31,000	45,000

RED ROBIN (Batman: Reborn)
DC Comics: Aug, 2009 - No. 26, Oct, 2011 ($2.99)

1-26-Tim (Drake) Wayne in the Kingdom Come costume; Bachs-a. 1-Two covers 3.00

RED ROCKET 7
Dark Horse Comics: Aug, 1997 - No. 7, June, 1998 ($3.95, square format, limited series)

1-7-Mike Allred-c/s/a 4.00

RED RYDER COMICS (Hi Spot #2)(Movies, radio)(See Crackajack Funnies & Super Book of Comics)
Hawley Publ. No. 1/Dell Publishing Co.(K.K.) No. 3 on: 9/40; No. 3, 8/41 - No. 5, 12/41; No. 6, 4/42 - No. 151, 4-6/57 (Beware of almost identical reprints of #1 made in the late 1980s)

	GD	VG	FN	VF	VF/NM	NM-
1-Red Ryder, his horse Thunder, Little Beaver & his horse Papoose strip reprints begin by Fred Harman; 1st meeting of Red & Little Beaver; Harman line-drawn-c #1-85	265	530	795	1694	2897	4100
3-(Scarce)-Alley Oop, Capt. Easy, Dan Dunn, Freckles & His Friends, King of the Royal Mtd., Myra North strip-r begin	54	108	162	432	966	1500
4-6: 6-1st Dell issue (4/42)	27	54	81	189	420	650
7-10	23	46	69	161	356	550
11-20	16	32	48	108	239	370
21-32-Last Alley Oop, Dan Dunn, Capt. Easy, Freckles	10	20	30	69	147	225
33-40 (52 pgs.): 40-Photo back-c begin, end #57	9	18	27	58	114	170
41 (52 pgs.)-Rocky Lane photo back-c	9	18	27	60	120	180
42-46 (52 pgs.): 46-Last Red Ryder strip-r	7	14	21	49	92	135
47-53 (52 pgs.): 47-New stories on Red Ryder begin. 49,52-Harmon photo back-c	6	12	18	41	76	110
54-92: 54-73 (36 pgs.). 59-Harmon photo back-c. 73-Last King of the Royal Mtd; strip-r by Jim Gary. 74-85 (52 pgs.)-Harman line-drawn-c. 86-92 (52 pgs.)-Harman painted-c	6	12	18	37	66	95
93-99,101-106: 94-96 (36 pgs.)-Harman painted-c. 97,98,(36 pgs.)-Harman line-drawn-c. 99,101-106 (36 pgs.)-Jim Bannon Photo-c	5	10	15	33	57	80
100 (36 pgs.)-Bannon photo-c	5	10	15	34	60	85
107-118 (52 pgs.)-Harman line-drawn-c	5	10	15	31	53	75
119-129 (52 pgs.): 119-Painted-c begin, not by Harman, end #151	5	10	15	30	50	70
130-151 (36 pgs.): 145-Title change to Red Ryder Ranch Magazine. 149-Title change to Red Ryder Ranch Comics	4	8	12	28	47	65
Four Color 916 (7/58)	4	8	12	28	47	65

NOTE: ***Fred Harman** a-1-99; c-1-98, 107-118. Don Red Barry, Allan Rocky Lane, Wild Bill Elliott & Jim Bannon starred as Red Ryder in the movies. Robert Blake starred as Little Beaver.*

Red Seal Comics #20 © SUPR

Red Skull #2 © MAR

Red Sonja #35 © RS LLC

	GD	VG	FN	VF	VF/NM	NM-
	2.0	4.0	6.0	8.0	9.0	9.2

RED RYDER PAINT BOOK
Whitman Publishing Co.: 1941 (8-1/2x11-1/2", 148 pgs.)

	GD	VG	FN	VF	VF/NM	NM-
nn-Reprints 1940 daily strips	76	152	228	479	810	1140

RED SEAL COMICS (Formerly Carnival Comics, and/or Spotlight Comics?)
Harry 'A' Chesler/Superior Publ. No. 19 on: No. 14, 10/45 - No. 18, 10/46; No. 19, 6/47 - No. 22, 12/47

	GD	VG	FN	VF	VF/NM	NM-
14-The Black Dwarf begins (continued from Spotlight?); Little Nemo app; bondage/hypo-c; Tuska-a	116	232	348	742	1271	1800
15-Torture story; funny-c	45	90	135	284	480	675
16-Used in **SOTI**, pg. 181, illo "Outside the forbidden pages of de Sade, you find draining a girl's blood only in children's comics;" drug club story r-later in Crime Reporter #1; Veiled Avenger & Barry Kuda app; Tuska-a; funny-c	68	136	204	435	743	1050
17,18,20: Lady Satan, Yankee Girl & Sky Chief app; 17-Tuska-a	65	130	195	416	708	1000
19-No Black Dwarf (on-c only); Zor, El Tigre app.	63	126	189	403	689	975
21-Lady Satan & Black Dwarf app.	39	78	117	240	395	550
22-Zor, Rocketman app. (68 pgs.)	39	78	117	240	395	550

RED SHE-HULK (Title continues from Hulk (2008 series) #57)
Marvel Comics: No. 58, Dec, 2012 - No. 67, Sept, 2013 ($2.99)

58-67-Betty Ross character; Pagulayan-a/c. 59,60-Avengers app. 66-Man-Thing app. 3.00

REDSKIN (Thrilling Indian Stories)(Famous Western Badmen #13 on)
Youthful Magazines: Sept, 1950 - No. 12, Oct, 1952

	GD	VG	FN	VF	VF/NM	NM-
1-Walter Johnson-a (7 pgs.)	22	44	66	130	213	295
2	15	30	45	84	127	170
3-12: 3-Daniel Boone story. 6-Geronimo story	13	26	39	74	105	135

NOTE: ***Walter Johnson** c-3, 4. **Palais** a-11. **Wildey** a-5, 11. Bondage c-6, 12.*

RED SKULL
Marvel Comics: Sept, 2011 - No. 5, Jan, 2012 ($2.99, limited series)

1-5-Pak-s/Colak-a/Aja-c; Red Skull's childhood and origin 3.00

RED SKULL (Secret Wars Battleworld tie-in)
Marvel Comics: Sept, 2015 - No. 3, Nov, 2015 ($3.99, limited series)

1-3-Joshua Williamson-s/Luca Pizzari-a; Crossbones, Magneto & Bucky app. 4.00

RED SONJA (Also see Conan #23, Kull & The Barbarians, Marvel Feature & Savage Sword Of Conan #1)
Marvel Comics Group: 1/77 - No. 15, 5/79; V1#1, 2/83 - V2#2, 3/83; V3#1, 8/83 - V3#4, 2/84; V3#5, 1/85 - V3#13, 5/86

	GD	VG	FN	VF	VF/NM	NM-
1-Created by Robert E. Howard	4	8	12	27	44	60
2-10: 5-Last 30¢ issue	2	4	6	8	10	12
4,5-(35¢-c variants, limited distribution)(7,9/77)	9	18	27	62	126	190
11-15, V2#1,V2#2: 14-Last 35¢ issue	1	3	4	6	8	10
V3#1 ($1.00, 52 pgs.)	1	3	4	6	8	10
V3#2-13: #2-4 ($1.00, 52 pgs.)						5.00

NOTE: ***Brunner** c-12-14. **J. Buscema** a(p)-12, 13, 15; c-V#1. **Nebres** a-V3#3i(part). **N. Redondo** a-8i, V3#2i, 3i. **Simonson** a-V3#1. **Thorne** c/a-1-11.*

RED SONJA (Continues in Queen Sonja) (Also see Classic Red Sonja)
Dynamite Entertainment: No. 0, Apr, 2005 - No. 80, 2013 (25¢/$2.99/$3.99)

0-(4/05, 25¢) Greg Land-c/Mel Rubi-a/Oeming & Carey-s 4.00
1-(6/05, $2.99) Five covers by Ross, Linsner, Cassaday, Turner, Rivera; Rubi-a 10.00
2-46-Multiple covers on all. 29-Sonja dies. 34-Sonja reborn 3.00
5-RRP Edition with Red Foil logo and Isanove-a 15.00
50-('10, $4.99) new stories and reprints; Marcos, Chin, Desjardins-a; 4 covers 5.00
51-79-($3.99): 51-56-Geovani-a; multiple covers on each 4.00
80-($4.99) Red Sonja vs. Dracula; bonus interview with Gail Simone 5.00
Annual #1 (2007, $3.50) Oeming-s/Sadowski-a; Red Sonja Comics Chronology 4.00
Annual #2 (2009, $3.99) Gage-s/Marcos-a; wraparound Prado-c & Marcos-c 4.00
Annual #3 (2010, $5.99) Brereton-s/c/a; Batista-a 6.00
Annual #4 (2013, $4.99) Beatty-s/Mena-a 5.00
... Blue (2011, $4.99) Brett-s/Geovani-a; covers by Geovani & Rubi 5.00
... Break the Skin (2011, $4.99) Winslade-c/Van Meter-s/Salazar-a 5.00
... Cover Showcase Vol. 1 (2007, $5.99) gallery of variant covers; Cho sketches 6.00
... Deluge (2011, $4.99) Brereton-s/c; Bolson-a/var-c; reprint from Conan #48 ('74) 5.00
Giant Size Red Sonja #1 (2007, $4.99) Chaykin-c; new story and reprints and pin-ups 5.00
Giant Size Red Sonja #2 (2008, $4.99) Segovia-c; new story and reprints and pin-ups 5.00
... Goes East ($4.99) three covers; Joe Ng-a 5.00
...: Monster Isle ($4.99) two covers; Pablo Marcos-a/Roy Thomas-s 5.00
... One More Day ($4.99) two covers; Liam Sharp-a 5.00
... Raven ('12, $4.99) Antonio-a/Martin-c; bonus pin-up gallery 5.00
...: Revenge of the Gods 1-5 (2011 - No. 5, 2011, $3.99) Sampare-a/Lieberman-s 4.00
... Vacant Shell ($4.99) two covers; Remender-s/Renaud-a 5.00
...: Wrath of the Gods 1-5 (2010 - No. 5, 2010, $3.99) Geovani-a 4.00
The Adventures of Red Sonja TPB (2005, $19.99) r/Marvel Feature #1-7 20.00
The Adventures of Red Sonja Vol. 2 TPB (2007, $19.99) r/#1-7 of '77 Marvel series 20.00
... Vol. 1 TPB (2006, $19.99) r/#0-6; gallery of covers and variants; creators interview 20.00
... Vol. 2 Arrowsmith TPB (2007, $19.99) r/#7-12; gallery of covers and variants 20.00
... Vol. 3 The Rise of Gath TPB (2007, $19.99) r/#13-18; gallery of covers and variants 20.00
... Vol. 4 Animals & More TPB (2007, $24.99) r/#19-24; gallery of covers and variants 25.00

RED SONJA (Volume 2)
Dynamite Entertainment: 2013 - No. 18, 2015 ($3.99)

1-18: 1-Gail Simone-s/Walter Geovani-a; six covers. 2-18-Multiple covers 4.00
#0 (2014, $3.99) Simone-s/Salonga-a/Hardman-c 4.00
#100 (2015, $7.99) Five short stories by various incl. Simone, Oeming, Marcos; 5 covers 8.00
#1973 (2015, $7.99) Five short stories by various incl. Simone, Bunn, Thomas & others 8.00
...: and Cub (2014, $4.99) Nancy Collins-s/Fritz Casas-a/J.M. Linsner-c 5.00
...: Berserker (2014, $4.99) Jim Zub-s/Jonathan Lau-a/Jeffrey Cruz-c 5.00
...: Sanctuary (2014, $4.99) Mason-s/Salonga-a/Davila-c; includes full script 5.00

RED SONJA (Volume 3)
Dynamite Entertainment: 2016 - No. 6, 2016 ($3.99)

1-6: 1-Marguerite Bennett-s/Aneke-a; multiple covers 4.00

RED SONJA (Volume 4)
Dynamite Entertainment: No. 0, 2016 - No. 25, 2019 ($3.99)

0-(25¢) Sonja transported to present day New York City; Amy Chu-s/Carlos Gomez-a 3.00
1-25-($3.99) Chu-s/Gomez-a in most; multiple covers. 17-HDR-a. 23-Castro-a 4.00
... Halloween Special One-Shot (2018, $4.99) Burnham-s/Garcia-a; Reilly Brown-c 5.00
... Holiday Special One-Shot (2018, $4.99) Chu & Burnham-s/Jamie-a; Romero-c 5.00

RED SONJA (Volume 5) (Also see Killing Red Sonja)
Dynamite Entertainment: 2019 - No. 24, 2021 ($3.99)

1-24: 1-6-Mark Russell-s/Mirko Colak-a; multiple covers. 7-9,13-Bob Q-a. 10-12-Colak-a 4.00
..., Lord of Fools One-Shot (2019, $4.99) Russell-s/Bob Q-a; takes place around #6 5.00
... Valentine's Special (2021, $4.99) Willingham-s/Cafaro-a 5.00

RED SONJA: AGE OF CHAOS
Dynamite Entertainment: 2020 - No. 6, 2020 ($3.99, limited series)

1-6-Erik Burnham-s/Jonathan Lau-a; Evil Ernie, Purgatori app.; multiple covers 4.00

RED SONJA AND VAMPIRELLA MEET BETTY AND VERONICA
Dynamite Entertainment: 2019 - No. 12, 2020 ($3.99)

1-12: 1-8,10,11-Amy Chu-s/Maria Sanapo-a; multiple covers. 6-11-Draculina app. 9-Parent-a 4.00

RED SONJA: ATLANTIS RISES
Dynamite Entertainment: 2012 - No. 4, 2012 ($3.99, limited series)

1-4-Lieberman-s/Dunbar-a/Parrillo-c 4.00

RED SONJA: BIRTH OF THE SHE-DEVIL
Dynamite Entertainment: 2019 - No. 4, 2019 ($3.99, limited series)

1-4-Luke Lieberman-s/Sergio Davila-a 4.00

RED SONJA/CLAW: THE DEVIL'S HANDS (See Claw the Unconquered)
DC Comics (WildStorm)/Dynamite Ent.: May, 2006 - No. 4, Aug, 2006 ($2.99, limited series)

1-4-Covers by Jim Lee & Dell'Otto; Andy Smith-a 1-Alex Ross var-c. 2-Dell'Otto var-c. 3-Bermejo var-c. 4-Andy Smith var-c 3.00
TPB (2007, $12.99) r/#1-4; cover gallery 13.00

RED SONJA/ CONAN
Dynamite Entertainment: 2015 - No. 4, 2015 ($3.99, limited series)

1-4-Gischler-s/Castro-a; multiple covers 4.00

RED SONJA: SCAVENGER HUNT
Marvel Comics: Dec, 1995 ($2.95, one-shot)

1 4.00

RED SONJA/ TARZAN
Dynamite Entertainment: 2018 - No. 6, 2018 ($3.99, limited series)

1-6-Simone-s/Geovani-a; multiple covers 4.00

RED SONJA: THE BLACK TOWER
Dynamite Entertainment: 2014 - No. 4, 2015 ($3.99, limited series)

1-4-Tieri-s/Razek-a/Conner-c 4.00

RED SONJA: THE MOVIE
Marvel Comics Group: Nov, 1985 - No. 2, Dec, 1985 (Limited series)

1,2-Movie adapt-r/Marvel Super Spec. #38 4.00

RED SONJA: THE PRICE OF BLOOD
Dynamite Entertainment: 2020 - No. 3, 2021 ($3.99, limited series)

1-3-Lieberman-s/Geovani-a; multiple covers 4.00

Red Sonja: The Superpowers #1 © RS LLC

Reform School Girl! nn © AVON

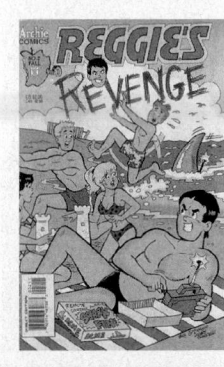

Reggie's Revenge #2 © ACP

	GD 2.0	VG 4.0	FN 6.0	VF 8.0	VF/NM 9.0	NM- 9.2

RED SONJA: THE SUPERPOWERS
Dynamite Entertainment: 2020 - Present ($3.99, limited series)
1,2-Abnett-s/Lau-a; multiple covers; Captain Future, Vana, Mr. Raven & The Sword app. 4.00

RED SONJA: UNCHAINED
Dynamite Entertainment: 2013 - No. 4, 2013 ($3.99, limited series)
1-4-Follows the Red Sonja: Blue one-shot; Jadsen-a 4.00

RED SONJA: VULTURE'S CIRCLE
Dynamite Entertainment: 2015 - No. 5, 2015 ($3.99, limited series)
1-5-Collins & Lieberman-s/Casas-a; three covers on each 4.00

RED SONJA VS. THULSA DOOM
Dynamite Entertainment: 2005 - No. 4, 2006 ($3.50)
1-4-Conrad-a; Conrad & Dell'Otto covers 3.50
..., Volume 1 TPB (2006, $14.99) r/series; cover gallery 15.00

RED STAR, THE
Image Comics/Archangel Studios: June, 2000 - No. 9, June, 2002 ($2.95)
1-Christian Gossett-s/a(p) 4.00
2-9: 9-Beck-c 3.00
#(7.5) Reprints Wizard #1/2 story with new pages 3.00
Annual 1 (Archangel Studios, 11/02, $3.50) "Run Makita Run" 4.00
TPB (4/01, $24.95, 9x12") oversized r/#1-4; intro. by Bendis 25.00
Nokgorka TPB (8/02, $24.95, 9x12") oversized r/#6-9; w/sketch pages 25.00
Wizard 1/2 (mail order) 10.00

RED STAR, THE (Volume 2)
CrossGen #1,2/Archangel Studios #3 on: Feb, 2003 - No. 5, July, 2004 ($2.95/$2.99)
1-5-Christian Gossett-s/a(p) 3.00
Prison of Souls TPB (8/04, $24.95, 9x12") oversized r/#1-5; w/sketch pages 25.00

RED STAR, THE: SWORD OF LIES
Archangel Studios: Aug, 2006 ($4.50)
1-Christian Gossett-s/a(p); origin of the Red Star team 4.50

RED TEAM
Dynamite Entertainment: 2013 - No. 7, 2014 ($3.99)
1-7: 1-Ennis-s/Cermak-a; covers by Chaykin & Sook 4.00

RED TEAM, VOLUME 2: DOUBLE TAP, CENTER MASS
Dynamite Entertainment: 2016 - No. 9, 2017 ($3.99)
1-8: 1-Ennis-s/Cermak-a/Panosian-c 4.00
9-($4.99) 5.00

RED THORN
DC Comics (Vertigo): Jan, 2016 - No. 13, Feb, 2017 ($3.99)
1-13: 1-6-David Baillie-s/Meghan Hetrick-a. 7-Steve Pugh-a 4.00

RED TORNADO (See All-American #20 & Justice League of America #64)
DC Comics: July, 1985 - No. 4, Oct, 1985 (Limited series)
1-4: Kurt Busiek scripts in all. 1-3-Superman & Batman cameos 4.00

RED TORNADO
DC Comics: Nov, 2009 - No. 6, Apr, 2010 ($2.99, limited series)
1-6: 1-3-Benes-c. 5,6-Vixen app. 3.00
...: Family Reunion TPB (2010, $17.99) r/#1-6 18.00

RED WARRIOR
Marvel/Atlas Comics (TCI): Jan, 1951 - No. 6, Dec, 1951

	GD	VG	FN	VF	VF/NM	NM-
1-Red Warrior & his horse White Wing; Tuska-a	21	42	63	122	199	275
2-Tuska-c	12	24	36	69	97	125
3-6: 4-Origin White Wing. 6-Maneely-c	10	20	30	58	79	100

RED, WHITE & BLUE COMICS
DC Comics: 1941
nn - Ashcan comic, not distributed to newsstands, only for in-house use. Cover art is All-American Comics #20 with interior being Flash Comics #17 (no known sales)

RED WING
Image Comics: Jul, 2011 - No. 4, Oct, 2011 ($3.50, limited series)
1-4-Hickman-s/Pitarra-a 3.50

RED WOLF (See Avengers #80 & Marvel Spotlight #1)
Marvel Comics Group: May, 1972 - No. 9, Sept, 1973

	GD	VG	FN	VF	VF/NM	NM-
1-(Western hero); Gil Kane/Severin-c; Shores-a	4	8	12	28	47	65
2-9: 2-Kane-c; Shores-a. 6-Tuska-r in back-up. 7-Red Wolf as super hero begins. 9-Origin sidekick, Lobo (wolf)	3	6	9	16	23	30

RED WOLF (From the Secret Wars tie-in series 1872)
Marvel Comics: Feb, 2016 - No. 6, Jul, 2016 ($3.99)
1-6: 1-Edmondson-s/Talajic-a. 2-Red Wolf in the present 4.00

REESE'S PIECES
Eclipse Comics: Oct, 1985 - No.2, Oct, 1985 ($1.75, Baxter paper)
1,2-B&W-r in color 3.00

REFORM SCHOOL GIRL!
Realistic Comics: 1951

	GD	VG	FN	VF	VF/NM	NM-
nn-Used in **SOTI**, pg. 358, & cover ill. with caption "Comic books are supposed to be like fairy tales"; classic photo-c	1300	2600	3900	9900	17,950	26,000

(Prices vary widely on this book)

NOTE: *The cover and title originated from a digest-sized book published by Diversey Publishing Co. of Chicago in 1948. The original book "House of Fury", Doubleday, came out in 1941. The girl's real name which appears on the cover of the digest and comic is Marty Collins, Canadian model and ice skating star who posed for this special color photograph for the Diversey novel.*

REGENTS ILLUSTRATED CLASSICS
Prentice Hall Regents, Englewood Cliffs, NJ 07632: 1981 (Plus more recent reprintings) (48 pgs., B&W-a with 14 pgs. of teaching helps)

NOTE: *This series contains Classics Ill. art, and was produced from the same illegal source as* **Cassette Books.** *But when Twin Circle sued to stop the sale of the Cassette Books, they decided to permit this series to continue. This series was produced as a teaching aid. The 20 title series is divided into four levels based upon number of basic words used therein. There is also a teacher's manual for each level. All of the titles are still available from the publisher for about $5 each retail. The number to call for mail order purchases is (201)767-5937. Almost all of the issues have new covers taken from some interior art panel. Here is a list of the series by Regents ident. no. and the Classics Ill. counterpart.*

16770(Cl#24-A2)18333(Cl#3-A2)21668(Cl#13-A2)32224(Cl#21)33051(Cl#26)35788(Cl#84)37153(Cl#16)44460(Cl#19-A2)44808(Cl#18-A2)52395(Cl#4-A2)58627(Cl#5-A2)60067(Cl#30)68405(Cl#23A1)70302(Cl#29)78192(Cl#7-A2)78193(Cl#10-A2)79679(Cl#85)92046(Cl#1-A2)93062(Cl#64)93512(Cl#25)

RE: GEX
Awesome-Hyperwerks: Jul, 1998 - No. 0, Dec, 1998; ($2.50)
Preview (7/98) Wizard Con Edition 3.00
0-(12/98) Loeb-s/Liefeld-a/Pat Lee-c, 1-(9/98) Loeb-s/Liefeld-a/c 3.00

REGGIE (Formerly Archie's Rival...; Reggie & Me #19 on)
Archie Publications: No. 15, Sept, 1963 - No. 18, Nov, 1965

	GD	VG	FN	VF	VF/NM	NM-
15(9/63), 16(10/64), 17(8/65), 18(11/65)	5	10	15	33	57	80

NOTE: *Cover title No. 15 & 16 is Archie's Rival Reggie.*

REGGIE AND ME (Formerly Reggie)
Archie Publ.: No. 19, Aug, 1966 - No. 126, Sept, 1980 (No. 50-68: 52 pgs.)

	GD	VG	FN	VF	VF/NM	NM-
19-Evilheart app.	4	8	12	27	44	60
20-23-Evilheart app.; with Pureheart #22	3	6	9	21	33	45
24-40(3/70)	3	6	9	16	23	30
41-49(7/71)	2	4	6	13	18	22
50(9/71)-68 (1/74, 52 pgs.)	3	6	9	14	20	26
69-99	2	4	6	8	10	12
100(10/77)	2	4	6	9	12	15
101-126	1	2	3	5	7	9

REGGIE AND ME (Volume 2)
Archie Comic Publications: Jan, 2017 - No. 5, ($3.99)
1-5-Multiple covers and classic back-up reprints in#1,2. Tom DeFalco-s/Sandy Jarrell-a 4.00

REGGIE'S JOKES (See Reggie's Wise Guy Jokes)

REGGIE'S REVENGE!
Archie Comic Publications, Inc.: Spring, 1994 - No. 3 ($2.00, 52 pgs.) (Published semi-annually)

	GD	VG	FN	VF	VF/NM	NM-
1-Bound-in pull-out poster	1	2	3	5	6	8
2,3						5.00

REGGIE'S WISE GUY JOKES
Archie Publications: Aug, 1968 - No. 55, 1980 (#5-28 are Giants)

	GD	VG	FN	VF	VF/NM	NM-
1	5	10	15	31	53	75
2-4	3	6	9	15	22	28
5-16 (1/71)(68 pg. Giants)	3	6	9	16	24	32
17-28 (52 pg. Giants)	2	4	6	13	18	22
29-40(1/77)	1	3	4	6	8	10
41-55	1	2	3	5	6	8

REGISTERED NURSE
Charlton Comics: Summer, 1963

	GD	VG	FN	VF	VF/NM	NM-
1-r/Nurse Betsy Crane & Cynthia Doyle	4	8	12	27	44	60

REG'LAR FELLERS
Visual Editions (Standard): No. 5, Nov, 1947 - No. 6, Mar, 1948

	GD	VG	FN	VF	VF/NM	NM-
5,6	10	20	30	54	72	90

REG'LAR FELLERS HEROIC (See Heroic Comics)

Regression #11 © Bunn, Luckert & Enger

The Ren & Stimpy Show #38 © Nickelodeon

Resident Alien #2 © Hogan & Parkhouse

GD VG FN VF VF/NM NM-
2.0 4.0 6.0 8.0 9.0 9.2

GD VG FN VF VF/NM NM-
2.0 4.0 6.0 8.0 9.0 9.2

REGRESSION
Image Comics: May, 2017 - No. 15, Jan, 2019 ($3.99)
1-15-Bunn-s/Luckert-a 4.00

REGULAR SHOW (Based on Cartoon Network series)
Boom Entertainment (kaBOOM!): Apr, 2013 - No. 40, Oct, 2016 ($3.99)
1-40-Multiple covers on all 4.00
2014 Annual 1 (6/14, $4.99) Four short stories by various; three covers 5.00
2015 Special 1 (3/15, $4.99) Four short stories by various; two covers 5.00
2017 Special 1 (4/17, $7.99) Six short stories by various; two covers 8.00
2018 Special 1 (2/18, $7.99) Four short stories; McCreery-s; art by various 8.00

REGULAR SHOW: SKIPS (Based on Cartoon Network series)
Boom Entertainment (kaBOOM!): Nov, 2013 - No. 6, Apr, 2014 ($3.99)
1-6-Mad Rupert-s/a; multiple covers on all 4.00

REGULAR SHOW: 25 YEARS LATER (Based on Cartoon Network series)
Boom Entertainment (kaBOOM!): Jun, 2018 - No. 6, Nov, 2018 ($3.99)
1-6-Christopher Hastings-s/Anna Johnstone-a; multiple covers on all 4.00

REID FLEMING, WORLD'S TOUGHEST MILKMAN
Eclipse Comics/ Deep Sea Comics: 1980; 8/86; V2#1, 12/86 - V2#3, 12/88; V2#4, 11/89; V2#5, 11/90 - V2#9, 4/98 (B&W)
1-(1980, self-published) David Boswell-s/a 5.00
1-2nd, 4th & 5th printings ($2.50); (3rd print, large size, 8/86, $2.50) 3.00
V2#1 (10/86, regular size, $2.00), 1-2nd print, 3rd print ($2.00, 2/89) 3.00
2-9 , V2#2-2nd & 3rd printings, V2#4-2nd printing, V2#5 ($2.00), V2#6 (Deep Sea, r/V2#5) 7-9-New stories 3.00

REIGN IN HELL
DC Comics: Sept, 2008 - No. 8, Apr, 2009 ($3.50, limited series)
1-8-Neron, Shadowpact app.; Giffen-s; Dr. Occult back-up w/Segovia-a. 1-Two covers 3.50
TPB (2009, $19.99) r/#1-8 20.00

REIGN OF THE ZODIAC
DC Comics: Oct, 2003 - No. 8, May, 2004 ($2.75)
1-8: 1-6,8-Giffen-s/Doran-a/Harris-c. 7-Byrd-a 3.00

RELATIVE HEROES
DC Comics: Mar, 2000 - No. 6, Aug, 2000 ($2.50, limited series)
1-6-Grayson-s/Guichet & Sowd-a. 6-Superman-c/app. 3.00

RELAY
AfterShock Comics: Jul, 2018 - No. 5, Apr, 2019 ($3.99, limited series)
1-5-Zac Thompson-s/Andy Clarke-a 4.00
#0 (Free Comic Book Day, 5/18, giveaway) Thompson-s/Clarke-a 3.00

RELOAD
DC Comics (Homage): May, 2003 - No. 3, Sept, 2003 ($2.95, limited series)
1-3-Warren Ellis-s/Paul Gulacy & Jimmy Palmiotti-a 3.00
.../Mek TPB (2004, $14.95, flip book) r/Reload #1-3 & Mek #1-3 15.00

RELUCTANT DRAGON, THE (Walt Disney's...)
Dell Publishing Co.: No. 13, 1940
Four Color 13-Contains 2 pgs. of photos from film; 2 pg. foreword to Fantasia by Leopold Stokowski; Donald Duck, Goofy, Baby Weems & Mickey Mouse (as the Sorcerer's Apprentice) app. 226 452 678 1446 2473 3500

REMAINS
IDW Publishing: May, 2004 - No. 5, Sept, 2004 ($3.99)
1-5-Steve Niles-s/Kieron Dwyer-a 4.00

REMARKABLE WORLDS OF PROFESSOR PHINEAS B. FUDDLE, THE
DC Comics (Paradox Press): 2000 - No. 4, 2000 ($5.95, limited series)
1-4-Boaz Yakin-s/Erez Yakin-a 6.00
TPB (2001, $19.95) r/series 20.00

REMEMBER PEARL HARBOR
Street & Smith Publications: 1942 (68 pgs.) (Illustrated story of the battle)
nn-Uncle Sam-c; Jack Binder-a 97 194 291 621 1061 1500

REN & STIMPY SHOW, THE (TV) (Nickelodeon cartoon characters)
Marvel Comics: Dec, 1992 - No. 44, July, 1996 ($1.75/$1.95)
1-($2.25)-Polybagged w/scratch & sniff Ren or Stimpy air fowler (equal numbers of each were made) 2 4 6 8 13 16
1-2nd & 3rd printing; different dialogue on-c 4.00
2-6: 4-Muddy Mudskipper back-up. 5-Bill Wray painted-c. 6-Spider-Man vs. Powdered Toast Man 5.00
7-17: 12-1st solo back-up story w/Tank & Brenner 4.00
18-44: 18-Powered Toast Man app. 4.00
25 ($2.95) Deluxe edition w/die cut cover 5.00
...Don't Try This at Home (3/94, $12.95, TPB)-r/#9-12 13.00
...Eenteractive Special ('95, $2.95) 6.00
...Holiday Special 1994 (2/95, $2.95, 52 pgs.) 6.00
...Mini Comic (1995) 1 2 3 5 6 8
...Pick of the Litter nn (1993, $12.95, TPB)-r/#1-4 13.00
...Radio Daze (11/95, $1.95) 6.00
...Running Joke nn (1993, $12.95, TPB)-r/#1-4 plus new-a 13.00
...Seeck Little Monkeys (1/95, $12.95)-r/#17-20 13.00
...Special 2 (7/94, $2.95, 52 pgs.), ...Special 3 (10/94, $2.95, 52 pgs.)-Choose adventure, ...Special: Around the World in a Daze ($2.95), ...Special: Four Swerks (1/95, $2.95, 52 pgs.)-FF #1 cover swipe; cover reads "Four Swerks w/5 pg. coloring book.", ...Special: Powdered Toast Man 1 (4/94, $2.95, 52 pgs.), ...Special: Powdered Toast Man's Cereal Serial (4/95, $2.95), ...Special: Sports (10/95, $2.95) 6.00
...Tastes Like Chicken nn (11/93,$12.95,TPB)-r/#5-8 13.00
...Your Pals (1994, $12.95, TPB)-r/#13-16 13.00

RENATO JONES: THE ONE %
Image Comics: May, 2016 - No. 5, Oct, 2016 ($3.99)
1-5-Kaare Andrews-s/a/c 4.00
Renato Jones, Season 2: Freelancer (5/17 - No. 5, 11/17, $3.99) 1-5-Andrews-s/a/c 4.00

RENFIELD
Caliber Press: 1994 - No. 3, 1995 ($2.95, B&W, limited series)
1-3 3.00

RENO BROWNE, HOLLYWOOD'S GREATEST COWGIRL (Formerly Margie Comics; Apache Kid #53 on; also see Western Hearts, Western Life Romances & Western Love)
Marvel Comics (MPC): No. 50, April, 1950 - No. 52, Sept, 1950 (52 pgs.)
50-Reno Browne photo-c on all 32 64 96 188 307 425
51,52 27 54 81 162 266 370

REPLACER, THE
AfterShock Comics: Apr, 2019 ($7.99, one-shot)
1-Zac Thompson-s/Arjuna Susini-a 8.00

REPLICA
AfterShock Comics: Dec, 2015 - No. 5, Apr, 2016 ($3.99)
1-5-Paul Jenkins-s/Andy Clarke-a 4.00

REPTILICUS (Becomes Reptisaurus #3 on)
Charlton Comics: Aug, 1961 - No. 2, Oct, 1961
1 (Movie) 22 44 66 154 340 525
2 11 22 33 73 157 240

REPTISAURUS (Reptilicus #1,2)
Charlton Comics: V2#3, Jan, 1962 - No. 8, Dec, 1962; Summer, 1963
V2#3-8: 3-Flying saucer-c/s. 8-Montes/Bache-c/a 5 10 15 35 63 90
Special Edition 1 (Summer, 1963) 5 10 15 34 60 85

REQUIEM FOR DRACULA
Marvel Comics: Feb, 1993 ($2.00, 52 pgs.)
nn-r/Tomb of Dracula #69,70 by Gene Colan 4.00

RESCUE (Pepper Potts in Iron Man armor)
Marvel Comics: July, 2010 ($3.99, one-shot)
1-DeConnick-s/Mutti-a/Foreman-c 4.00

RESCUERS, THE (See Walt Disney Showcase #40)

RESIDENT ALIEN
Dark Horse Comics: No. 0, Apr, 2012 - No. 3, Jul, 2012 ($3.50, limited series)
0-3-Hogan-s/Parkhouse-a: 0-Reprints chapters from Dark Horse Presents #4-6 3.50

RESIDENT ALIEN: AN ALIEN IN NEW YORK
Dark Horse Comics: Apr, 2018 - No. 4, Jul, 2018 ($3.99, limited series)
1-4-Hogan-s/Parkhouse-a 4.00

RESIDENT ALIEN: THE MAN WITH NO NAME
Dark Horse Comics: Sept, 2016 - No. 4, Dec, 2016 ($3.99, limited series)
1-4-Hogan-s/Parkhouse-a 4.00

RESIDENT ALIEN: THE SAM HAIN MYSTERY
Dark Horse Comics: No. 0, Apr, 2015 - No. 3, Jul, 2015 ($3.99, limited series)
0-3-Hogan-s/Parkhouse-a: 0-Reprints chapters from Dark Horse Presents V3 #1-3 4.00

RESIDENT ALIEN: THE SUICIDE BLONDE
Dark Horse Comics: No. 0, Aug, 2013 - No. 3, Nov, 2013 ($3.99, limited series)
0-3-Hogan-s/Parkhouse-a: 0-Reprints chapters from Dark Horse Presents #18-20 4.00

The Resistance #1 © AWA

Resurrection Man (2011 series) #1 © DC

Revenge #1 © Ross & Churchill

	GD 2.0	VG 4.0	FN 6.0	VF 8.0	VF/NM 9.0	NM- 9.2

RESIDENT ALIEN: YOUR RIDE'S HERE
Dark Horse Comics: Nov, 2020 - No. 6 ($3.99, limited series)
1-3-Hogan-s/Parkhouse-a 4.00

RESIDENT EVIL (Based on video game)
Image Comics (WildStorm): Mar, 1998 - No. 5 ($4.95, quarterly magazine)
1 5 10 15 35 63 90
2-5 3 6 9 21 33 45
...Code: Veronica 1-4 (2002, $14.95) English reprint of Japanese comics 15.00
...Collection One ('99, $14.95, TPB) r/#1-4 15.00

RESIDENT EVIL (Volume 2)
DC Comics (WildStorm): May, 2009 - No. 6, Feb, 2011 ($3.99)
1-6: 1,2-Liam Sharpe-a. 1-Two covers 4.00
...: Volume 2 TPB (2011, $19.99) r/#1-6 20.00

RESIDENT EVIL: FIRE AND ICE
DC Comics (WildStorm): Dec, 2000 - No. 4, May, 2001 ($2.50, limited series)
1-4-Bermejo-c 5.00
TPB (2009, $24.99) r/#1-4 plus short stories from Resident Evil magazine 25.00

RESISTANCE (Based on the video game)
DC Comics (WildStorm): Early Mar, 2009 - No. 6, Jul, 2009 ($3.99, limited series)
1-6-Ramón Pérez-a/C.P. Smith-c 4.00
TPB (2010, $19.99) r/#1-6 20.00

RESISTANCE, THE
DC Comics (WildStorm): Nov, 2002 - No. 8, June, 2003 ($2.95)
1-8-Palmiotti & Gray-s/Santacruz-a 3.00

RESISTANCE, THE
AWA Studios: Mar, 2020 - No. 6, Sept, 2020 ($3.99, limited series)
1-6-Straczynski-s/Deodato Jr.-a 4.00
...: Reborns (1/21, $3.99) Straczynski-s/C.P. Smith-a 4.00

REST (Milo Ventimiglia Presents...)
Devil's Due Publ.: No. 0, Aug, 2008 - No. 2 (99¢/$3.50)
0-(99¢) Prelude to series; Powers-s/McManus-a 3.00
1,2-($3.50) 1-Two covers (Tim Sale art & Milo Ventimiglia photo) 3.50

RESTAURANT AT THE END OF THE UNIVERSE, THE (See Hitchhiker's Guide to the Galaxy & Life, the Universe & Everything)
DC Comics: 1994 - No. 3, 1994 ($6.95, limited series)
1-3 7.00

RESTLESS GUN (TV)
Dell Publishing Co.: No. 934, Sept, 1958 - No. 1146, Nov-Jan, 1960-61
Four Color 934 (#1)-Photo-c 9 18 27 61 123 185
Four Color 986 (5/59), 1045 (11-1/60), 1089 (3/60), 1146-Wildey-a; all photo-c 7 14 21 46 86 125

RESURRECTIONISTS
Dark Horse Comics: Nov, 2014 - No. 4, Feb, 2015 ($3.50)
1-4-Van Lente-s/Rosenzweig-a 3.50

RESURRECTION MAN
DC Comics: May, 1997 - No. 27, Aug, 1999 ($2.50)
1-Lenticular disc on cover 5.00
2-5: 2-JLA app. 4.00
6-27: 6-Genesis-x-over. 7-Batman app. 10-Hitman-c/app. 16,17-Supergirl x-over. 18-Deadman & Phantom Stranger-c/app. 21-JLA-c/app. 3.00
#1,000,000 (11/98) 853rd Century x-over 3.00

RESURRECTION MAN (DC New 52)
DC Comics: Nov, 2011 - No. 12, Oct, 2012; No. 0, Nov, 2012 ($2.99)
1-12: 1-Abnett & Lanning-s/Dagnino-a/Reis-c; Body Doubles app. 9-Suicide Squad app. 3.00
#0 (11/12) Origin of Mitch Shelley and the Body Doubles; Bachs-a/Francavilla-c 3.00

RETIEF (Keith Laumer's)
Adventure Comics (Malibu): Dec, 1989 - Vol. 2, No.6, ($2.25, B&W)
1-6,Vol. 2, #1-6,Vol. 3 (...of The CDT) #1-6 3.00
...and The Warlords #1-6, ...: Diplomatic Immunity #1 (4/91), ...: Giant Killer #1 (9/91), ...: Crime & Punishment #1 (11/91) 3.00

RETROVIRUS
Image Comics: Nov, 2012 ($12.99, hardcover GN)
HC-Gray & Palmiotti-s/Fernandez-a/Conner-c 13.00

RETURN FROM WITCH MOUNTAIN (See Walt Disney Showcase #44)

RETURNING, THE
BOOM! Studios: Mar, 2014 - No. 4, Jun, 2014 ($3.99, limited series)
1-4-Jason Starr-s/Andrea Mutti-a/Frazer Irving-c 4.00

RETURN OF ALISON DARE: LITTLE MISS ADVENTURES, THE (Also see Alison Dare: Little Miss Adventures)
Oni Press: Apr, 2001 - No. 3, Sept, 2001 ($2.95, B&W, limited series)
1-3-J. Torres-s/J.Bone-c/a 3.00

RETURN OF GORGO, THE (Formerly Gorgo's Revenge)
Charlton Comics: No. 2, Aug, 1963; No. 3, Fall, 1964 (12¢)
2,3-Ditko-c/a; based on M.G.M. movie 7 14 21 49 92 135

RETURN OF KONGA, THE (Konga's Revenge #2 on)
Charlton Comics: 1962
nn 8 16 24 51 96 140

RETURN OF MEGATON MAN
Kitchen Sink Press: July, 1988 - No. 3, 1988 ($2.00, limited series)
1-3: Simpson-c/a 4.00

RETURN OF THE GREMLINS (The Roald Dahl characters)
Dark Horse Comics: Mar, 2008 - No. 3, May, 2008 ($2.99, limited series)
1-3-Richardson-s/Yeagle-a. 1-Back-up reprint of intro. from 1943. 2-Back-up reprints of three Gremlin Gus 2-pagers from 1943. 3-Back-up reprints 3.00

RETURN OF THE LIVING DEADPOOL
Marvel Comics: Apr, 2015 - No. 4, Jul, 2015 ($3.99, limited series)
1-4-Cullen Bunn-s/Nik Virella-a 6.00

RETURN OF THE OUTLAW
Toby Press (Minoan): Feb, 1953 - No. 11, 1955
1-Billy the Kid 12 24 36 67 94 120
2 8 16 24 40 50 60
3-11 7 14 21 37 46 55

RETURN OF WOLVERINE (Continued in Wolverine: Infinity Watch)
Marvel Comics: Nov, 2018 - No. 5, Apr, 2019 ($4.99/$3.99, limited series)
1,5-($4.99) Soule-s/McNiven-a 5.00
2-4-($3.99) Shalvey-a 4.00

RETURN TO JURASSIC PARK
Topps Comics: Apr, 1995 - No. 9, Feb, 1996 ($2.50/$2.95)
1-9: 3-Begin $2.95-c. 9-Artists' Jam issue 4.00

RETURN TO THE AMALGAM AGE OF COMICS: THE MARVEL COMICS COLLECTION
Marvel Comics: 1997 ($12.95, TPB)
nn-Reprints Amalgam one-shots: Challengers of the Fantastic #1, The Exciting X-Patrol #1, Iron Lantern #1, The Magnetic Men Featuring Magneto #1, Spider-Boy Team-Up #1 & Thorion of the New Asgods #1 13.00

REVEAL
Dark Horse Comics: Nov, 2002 ($6.95, squarebound)
1-Short stories of Dark Horse characters by various; Lone Wolf 2100, Buffy, Spyboy app. 7.00

REVEALING LOVE STORIES (See Fox Giants)

REVEALING ROMANCES
Ace Magazines: Sept, 1949 - No. 6, Aug, 1950
1 20 40 60 115 188 260
2 14 28 42 78 112 145
3-6 12 24 36 69 97 125

REVELATIONS
Dark Horse Comics: Aug, 2005 - No. 6, Jan, 2006 ($2.99, limited series)
1-6-Paul Jenkins-s/Humberto Ramos-a/c 3.00
1-6-(BOOM! Studios, 1/14 - No. 6, 6/14, $3.99) reprints original series 4.00

REVENGE
Image Comics: Feb, 2014 - No. 4, Jun, 2014 ($2.99)
1-4-Jonathan Ross-s/Ian Churchill-a 3.00

REVENGE OF THE COSMIC GHOST RIDER (Also see Cosmic Ghost Rider)
Marvel Comics: Feb, 2020 - No. 5, Oct, 2020 ($4.99/$3.99, limited series)
1-($4.99) Hallum-s/Hepburn-a; back-up w/Gates-s/Shaw-a; present-day Frank Castle app. 5.00
2-5-($3.99) 3-5-Mephisto app. 4.00

REVENGE OF THE PROWLER (Also see The Prowler)
Eclipse Comics: Feb, 1988 - No. 4, June, 1988 ($1.75/$1.95)
1,3,4: 1-$1.75. 3,4-$1.95-c; Snyder III-a(p) 3.00
2 ($2.50)-Contains flexi-disc 4.00

The Revisionist #1 © Frank Barbiere

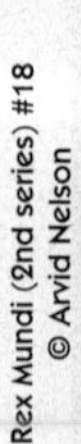

Rex Mundi (2nd series) #18 © Arvid Nelson

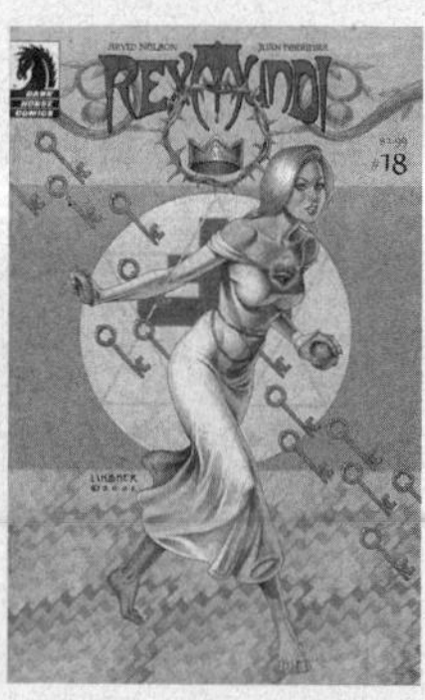

Richard Dragon, Kung-Fu Fighter #1 © DC

	GD 2.0	VG 4.0	FN 6.0	VF 8.0	VF/NM 9.0	NM- 9.2

REVISIONIST, THE
AfterShock Comics: Jun, 2016 - No. 6, Nov, 2016 ($3.99)

1-6: 1-Frank Barbiere-s/Garry Brown-a 4.00

REVIVAL
Image Comics: Jul, 2012 - No. 47, Feb, 2017 ($2.99/$3.99)

1-Tim Seeley-s/Mike Norton-a/Jenny Frison-c 12.00
1-Variant-c by Craig Thompson 18.00
1-Second-fourth printings 4.00
2-26 3.00
27-47-($3.99) 4.00

REVOLUTION
IDW Publishing: Sept, 2016 - No. 5, Nov, 2016 ($3.99, limited series)

1-5-Barber & Bunn-s/Ossio-a; multiple covers on each; G.I. Joe, Transformers, Rom, Micronauts, and M.A.S.K. app. 2-5-Bonus character profile pages 4.00

REVOLUTIONARIES (Follows the Revolution x-over)
IDW Publishing: Dec, 2016 - No. 8, Jul, 2017 ($3.99)

1-7: 1,2-Barber-s/Ossio-a; multiple covers on each; G.I. Joe, Transformers, Rom app. 4.00
8-($4.99) Barber-s/Ossio & Joseph-a 5.00

REVOLUTIONARY WAR
Marvel Comics: Mar, 2014 - May, 2014 ($3.99)

...: Alpha 1 (3/14) Part 1; Lanning & Cowsill-s/Elson-a; Capt. Britain & Pete Wisdom app. 4.00
...: Dark Angel 1 (3/14) Part 2; Gillen-s/Dietrich Smith-a; Mephisto app. 4.00
...: Death's Head II 1 (4/14) Part 4; Lanning & Cowsill-s/Roche-a 4.00
...: Knights of Pendragon 1 (3/14) Part 3; Williams-s/Sliney-a; Union Jack app. 4.00
...: Motormouth 1 (5/14) Part 6; Dakin-s/Cliquet-a; Killpower app. 4.00
...: Omega 1 (5/14) Part 8; conclusion; Lanning & Cowsill-s/Elson-a 4.00
...: Supersoldiers 1 (4/14) Part 5; Williams-s/Brent Anderson-a 4.00
...: Warheads 1 (5/14) Part 7; Lanning & Cowsill-s/Erskine-a 4.00

REVOLUTION: AW YEAH!
IDW Publishing: Feb, 2017 - No. 3, Jul, 2017 ($3.99, limited series)

1-3-All ages x-over of Rom, Transformers, G.I. Joe, Micronauts; Art Baltazar-s/a 4.00

REVOLUTION ON THE PLANET OF THE APES
Mr. Comics: Dec, 2005 - No. 6, Aug, 2006 ($3.95)

1-6: 1,2-Salgood Sam-a 4.00

REX ALLEN COMICS (Movie star)(Also see Four Color #877 & Western Roundup under Dell Giants)
Dell Publ. Co.: No. 316, Feb, 1951 - No. 31, Dec-Feb, 1958-59 (All-photo-c)

	GD	VG	FN	VF	VF/NM	NM-
Four Color 316(#1)(52 pgs.)-Rex Allen & his horse Koko begin; Marsh-a	13	26	39	86	188	290
2 (9-11/51, 36 pgs.)	8	16	24	55	105	150
3-10	6	12	18	38	69	100
11-20	5	10	15	34	60	85
21-23,25-31	5	10	15	31	53	75
24-Toth-a	5	10	15	34	60	85

NOTE: *Manning a-20, 27-30. Photo back-c F.C. #316, 2-12, 20, 21.*

REX DEXTER OF MARS (See Mystery Men Comics)
Fox Feature Syndicate: Fall, 1940 (68 pgs.)

	GD	VG	FN	VF	VF/NM	NM-
1-Rex Dexter, Patty O'Day, & Zanzibar (Tuska-a) app.; Briefer-c/a	271	542	813	1734	2967	4200

REX HART (Formerly Blaze Carson; Whip Wilson #9 on)
Timely/Marvel Comics (USA): No. 6, Aug, 1949 - No. 8, Feb, 1950 (All photo-c)

	GD	VG	FN	VF	VF/NM	NM-
6-Rex Hart & his horse Warrior begin; Black Rider app; Captain Tootsie by Beck; Heath-a	27	54	81	158	259	360
7,8: 18 pg. Thriller in each. 7-Heath-a. 8-Blaze the Wonder Collie app. in text	19	38	57	109	172	235

REX MORGAN, M.D. (Also see Harvey Comics Library)
Argo Publ.: Dec, 1955 - No. 3, Apr?, 1956

	GD	VG	FN	VF	VF/NM	NM-
1-r/Rex Morgan daily newspaper strips & daily panel-r of "These Women" by D'Alessio & "Timeout" by Jeff Keate	15	30	45	88	137	185
2,3	13	26	39	72	101	120

REX MUNDI (Latin for "King of the World")
Image Comics: No. 0, Aug, 2002 - No. 18, Apr, 2006 ($2.95/$2.99)

0-18-Arvid Nelson-s. 0-13-Eric Johnson-a. 14,15-Jim DiBartolo-a. 18-Ramos-c 3.00
Vol. 1: The Guardian of the Temple TPB (1/04, $14.95) r/#0-5 15.00
Book 1: The Guardian of the Temple TPB (Dark Horse, 11/06, $16.95) r/#0-5 & Brother Matthew web comic; Dysart intro. 17.00
Vol. 2: The River Underground TPB (4/05, $14.95) r/#6-11 15.00
Book 2: The River Underground (Dark Horse, 2006, $16.95) r/#6-11 17.00
Vol. 3: The Lost Kings TPB (Dark Horse, 9/06, $16.95) r/#12-17 17.00
Book Four: Crowd and Sword TPB (Dark Horse, 12/07, $16.95) r/#18 plus V2 #1-5 and story from Dark Horse Book of Monsters 17.00

REX MUNDI (Volume 2)
Dark Horse Comics: July, 2006 - No. 19, Aug, 2009 ($2.99)

1-19-Arvid Nelson-s. 1-JH Williams-c. 16-Chen-c. 18-Linsner-c 3.00
Book Five: The Valley at the End of the World TPB (11/08, $17.95) r/#6-12 18.00

REX THE WONDER DOG (See The Adventures of...)

REYN
Image Comics: Jan, 2015 - No. 10, Nov, 2015 ($2.99)

1-10-Symons-s/Stockman-a 3.00

RHUBARB, THE MILLIONAIRE CAT
Dell Publishing Co.: No. 423, Sept-Oct, 1952 - No. 563, June, 1954

	GD	VG	FN	VF	VF/NM	NM-
Four Color 423 (#1)	7	14	21	44	82	120
Four Color 466(5/53),563	6	12	18	37	66	95

RIB
Dilemma Productions: Oct, 1995 - April, 1996 ($1.95, B&W)

Ashcan, 1 3.00

RIB
Bookmark Productions: 1996 ($2.95, B&W)

1-Sakai-c; Andrew Ford-s/a 3.00

RIB
Caliber Comics: May, 1997 - No. 5, 1998 ($2.95, B&W)

1-5: 1-"Beginnings" pts. 1 & 2 3.00

RIBIT! (Red Sonja imitation)
Comico: Jan, 1989 - No. 4, April?, 1989 ($1.95, limited series)

1-4: Frank Thorne-c/a/scripts 3.00

RIBTICKLER (Also see Fox Giants)
Fox Feature Synd./Green Publ. (1957)/Norlen (1959): 1945, No. 2, 1946, No. 3, Jul-Aug, 1946 - No. 9, Jul-Aug, 1947; 1957; 1959

	GD	VG	FN	VF	VF/NM	NM-
1-Funny animal	23	46	69	136	223	310
2-(1946)	14	28	42	78	112	145
3-9: 3,5,7-Cosmo Cat app.	11	22	33	62	86	110
3,7,8 (Green Publ.-1957), 3,7,8 (Norlen Mag.-1959)	3	6	9	16	23	30

RICHARD DRAGON
DC Comics: July, 2004 - No. 12, Jun, 2005 ($2.50)

1-12: 1-Dixon-s/McDaniel-a/c; Ben Turner app. 2,3-Nightwing app. 4-6,11,12-Lady Shiva 3.00

RICHARD DRAGON, KUNG-FU FIGHTER (See The Batman Chronicles #5, Brave & the Bold, & The Question)
National Periodical Publ./DC Comics: Apr-May, 1975 - No. 18, Nov-Dec, 1977

	GD	VG	FN	VF	VF/NM	NM-
1-Intro Richard Dragon, Ben Stanley (later Ben Turner) & O-Sensei; 1st app. Barney Ling; adaptation of Jim Dennis (Denny O'Neil) novel "Dragon's Fists" begins, ends #4	5	10	15	31	53	75
2,3: 2-Intro Carolyn Woosan; Starlin/Weiss-c/a; bondage-c. 3-Kirby-a(p); Giordano bondage-c	2	4	6	9	12	15
4,6-8-Wood inks. 4-Carolyn Woosan dies	2	4	6	8	10	12
5-1st app. Lady Shiva; Wood inks	7	14	21	46	86	125
9-13,15-17: 9-Ben Stanley becomes Ben Turner; intro Preying Mantis. 16-1st app. Prof Ojo.	1	3	4	6	8	10
14-"Spirit of Bruce Lee"	3	6	9	14	20	26
18-1st app. Ben Turner as The Bronze Tiger	2	4	6	10	14	18

NOTE: ***Buckler** a-14. c-15, 18. **Chua** c-13. **Estrada** a-9, 13-18. **Estrada/Abel** a-10-12. **Estrada/Wood** a-4-8. **Giordano** c-1, 3-11. **Weiss** a-2(partial) c-2i.*

RICHARD THE LION-HEARTED (See Ideal a Classical Comic)

RICHIE RICH (See Harvey Collectors Comics, Harvey Hits, Little Dot, Little Lotta, Little Sad Sack, Million Dollar Digest, Mutt & Jeff, Super Richie & 3-D Dolly; also Tastee-Freez Comics in the Promotional Comics section)

RICHIE RICH (...the Poor Little Rich Boy) (See Harvey Hits #3, 9)
Harvey Publ.: Nov, 1960 - #218, Oct, 1982; #219, Oct, 1986 - #254, Jan, 1991

	GD	VG	FN	VF	VF/NM	NM-
1-(See Little Dot #1 for 1st app.)	362	724	1086	3149	6825	10,500
2	89	178	267	712	1606	2500
3-5	46	92	138	340	770	1200
6-10: 8-Christmas-c	27	54	81	189	420	650
11-20	16	32	48	112	249	385
21-30	11	22	33	76	163	250
31-40	9	18	27	61	123	185
41-50: 42(2/66)-X-mas-c	7	14	21	49	92	135

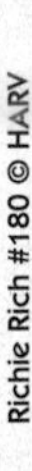
Richie Rich #180 © HARV

Richie Rich Bank Book #10 © HARV

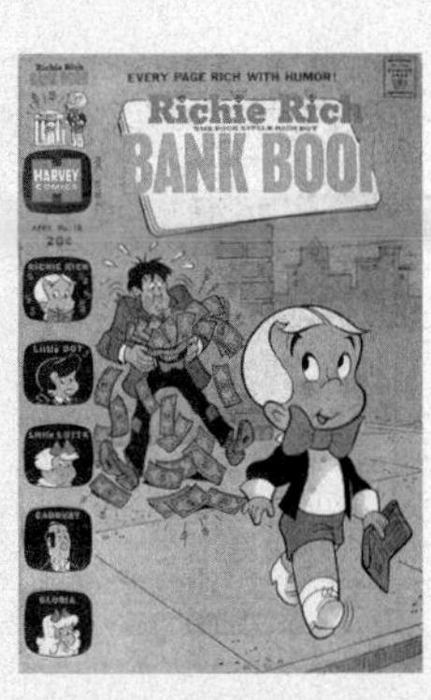

Richie Rich Cash #15 © HARV

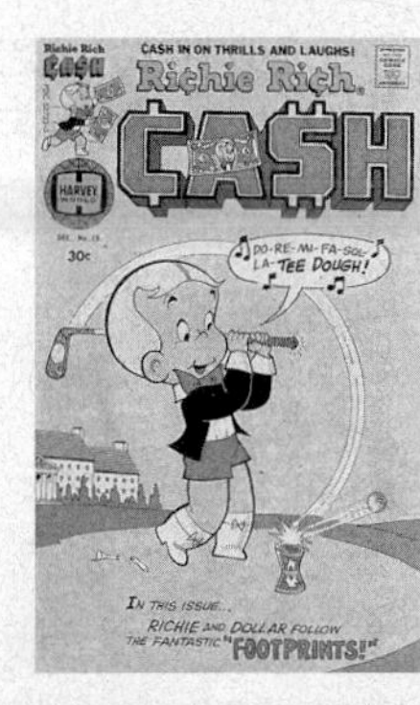

	GD 2.0	VG 4.0	FN 6.0	VF 8.0	VF/NM 9.0	NM- 9.2
51-55,57-60: 59-Buck, prototype of Dollar the Dog	5	10	15	35	63	90
56-1st app. Super Richie	6	12	18	41	76	110
61-64,66-80: 71-Nixon & Robert Kennedy caricatures; outer space-c	4	8	12	28	47	65
65-Buck the Dog (Dollar prototype) on cover	6	12	18	37	66	95
81-99	3	6	9	21	33	45
100(12/70)-1st app. Irona the robot maid	4	8	12	25	40	55
101-111,117-120	3	6	9	14	20	26
112-116: All 52 pg. Giants	3	6	9	16	24	32
121-140: 137-1st app. Mr. Cheepers and Professor Keenbean	2	4	6	9	13	16
141-160: 145-Infinity-c. 155-3rd app. The Money Monster	2	4	6	8	10	12
161-180	1	3	4	6	8	10
181-199	1	2	3	5	6	8
200	1	3	4	6	8	10
201-218: 210-Stone-Age Riches app	1	2	3	4	5	7
219-254: 237-Last original material						6.00
Harvey Comics Classics Vol. 2 TPB (Dark Horse Books, 10/07, $19.95) Reprints Richie Rich's early appearances in this title, Little Dot and Richie Rich Success Stories, mostly B&W with some color stories; history and interview with Ernie Colón						20.00

RICHIE RICH
Harvey Comics: Mar, 1991 - No. 28, Nov, 1994 ($1.00, bi-monthly)

	GD	VG	FN	VF	VF/NM	NM-
1-28: Reprints best of Richie Rich						3.00
Giant Size 1-4 (10/91-10/93, $2.25, 68 pgs.)						4.00

RICHIE RICH ADVENTURE DIGEST MAGAZINE
Harvey Comics: 1992 - No. 7, Sept, 1994 ($1.25, quarterly, digest-size)

	GD	VG	FN	VF	VF/NM	NM-
1-7						4.00

RICHIE RICH AND...
Harvey Comics: Oct, 1987 - No. 11, May, 1990 ($1.00)

	GD	VG	FN	VF	VF/NM	NM-
1-Professor Keenbean						4.00
2-11: 2-Casper. 3-Dollar the Dog. 4-Cadbury. 5 Mayda Munny. 6-Irona. 7-Little Dot. 8-Professor Keenbean. 9-Little Audrey. 10-Mayda Munny. 11-Cadbury						3.00

RICHIE RICH AND BILLY BELLHOPS
Harvey Publications: Oct, 1977 (52 pgs., one-shot)

	GD	VG	FN	VF	VF/NM	NM-
1	2	4	6	11	16	20

RICHIE RICH AND CADBURY
Harvey Publ.: 10/77; #2, 9/78 - #23, 7/82; #24, 7/90 - #29, 1/91 (1-10: 52pgs.)

	GD	VG	FN	VF	VF/NM	NM-
1-(52 pg. Giant)	2	4	6	11	16	20
2-10-(52 pg. Giant)	2	4	6	8	10	12
11-23						6.00
24-29: 24-Begin $1.00-c						4.00

RICHIE RICH AND CASPER
Harvey Publications: Aug, 1974 - No. 45, Sept, 1982

	GD	VG	FN	VF	VF/NM	NM-
1	3	6	9	19	30	40
2-5	2	4	6	13	18	22
6-10: 10-Xmas-c	2	4	6	9	13	16
11-20	1	3	4	6	8	10
21-45: 22-Xmas-c						6.00

RICHIE RICH AND DOLLAR THE DOG (See Richie Rich #65)
Harvey Publications: Sept, 1977 - No. 24, Aug, 1982 (#1-10: 52 pgs.)

	GD	VG	FN	VF	VF/NM	NM-
1-(52 pg. Giant)	2	4	6	11	16	20
2-10-(52 pg. Giant)	2	4	6	8	10	12
11-24						6.00

RICHIE RICH AND DOT
Harvey Publications: Oct, 1974 (one-shot)

	GD	VG	FN	VF	VF/NM	NM-
1	3	6	9	15	22	28

RICHIE RICH AND GLORIA
Harvey Publications: Sept, 1977 - No. 25, Sept, 1982 (#1-11: 52 pgs.)

	GD	VG	FN	VF	VF/NM	NM-
1-(52 pg. Giant)	2	4	6	11	16	20
2-11-(52 pg. Giant)	2	4	6	8	10	12
12-25						6.00

RICHIE RICH AND HIS GIRLFRIENDS
Harvey Publications: April, 1979 - No. 16, Dec, 1982

	GD	VG	FN	VF	VF/NM	NM-
1-(52 pg. Giant)	2	4	6	9	13	16
2-(52 pg. Giant)	1	3	4	6	8	10
3-10	1	2	3	5	6	8
11-16						6.00

RICHIE RICH AND HIS MEAN COUSIN REGGIE
Harvey Publications: April, 1979 - No. 3, 1980 (50¢) (#1,2: 52 pgs.)

	GD	VG	FN	VF	VF/NM	NM-
1	2	4	6	9	13	16
2-3:	1	3	4	6	8	10

NOTE: *No. 4 was advertised, but never released.*

RICHIE RICH AND JACKIE JOKERS (Also see Jackie Jokers)
Harvey Publications: Nov, 1973 - No. 48, Dec, 1982

	GD	VG	FN	VF	VF/NM	NM-
1: 52 pg. Giant; contains material from unpublished Jackie Jokers #5	4	8	12	23	37	50
2,3-(52 pg. Giants). 2-R.R. & Jackie 1st meet	3	6	9	15	22	28
4,5	2	4	6	13	18	22
6-10	2	4	6	9	13	16
11-20,26: 11-1st app. Kool Katz. 26-Star Wars parody	1	3	4	6	8	10
21-25,27-40	1	2	3	4	5	7
41-48						6.00

RICHIE RICH AND PROFESSOR KEENBEAN
Harvey Comics: Sept, 1990 - No. 2, Nov, 1990 ($1.00)

	GD	VG	FN	VF	VF/NM	NM-
1,2						3.00

RICHIE RICH AND THE NEW KIDS ON THE BLOCK
Harvey Publications: Feb, 1991 - No. 3, June, 1991 ($1.25, bi-monthly)

	GD	VG	FN	VF	VF/NM	NM-
1-3: 1,2-New Richie Rich stories						4.00

RICHIE RICH AND TIMMY TIME
Harvey Publications: Sept, 1977 (50¢, 52 pgs, one-shot)

	GD	VG	FN	VF	VF/NM	NM-
1	2	4	6	11	16	20

RICHIE RICH BANK BOOK
Harvey Publications: Oct, 1972 - No. 59, Sept, 1982

	GD	VG	FN	VF	VF/NM	NM-
1	5	10	15	30	50	70
2-5: 2-2nd app. The Money Monster	3	6	9	16	23	30
6-10	2	4	6	11	16	20
11-20: 18-Super Richie app.	2	4	6	8	10	12
21-30	1	2	3	5	7	9
31-40	1	2	3	4	5	7
41-59						6.00

RICHIE RICH BEST OF THE YEARS
Harvey Publications: Oct, 1977 - No. 6, June, 1980 (128 pgs., digest-size)

	GD	VG	FN	VF	VF/NM	NM-
1(10/77)-Reprints	2	4	6	9	12	15
2-6(11/79-6/80, 95¢). #2(10/78)-Rep.. #3(6/79, 75¢)	1	2	3	5	7	9

RICHIE RICH BIG BOOK
Harvey Publications: Nov, 1992 - No. 2, May, 1993 ($1.50, 52 pgs.)

	GD	VG	FN	VF	VF/NM	NM-
1,2						4.00

RICHIE RICH BIG BUCKS
Harvey Publications: Apr, 1991 - No. 8, July, 1992 ($1.00, bi-monthly)

	GD	VG	FN	VF	VF/NM	NM-
1-8						3.00

RICHIE RICH BILLIONS
Harvey Publications: Oct, 1974 - No. 48, Oct, 1982 (#1-33: 52 pgs.)

	GD	VG	FN	VF	VF/NM	NM-
1	3	6	9	21	33	45
2-5: 2-Christmas issue	3	6	9	14	20	25
6-10	2	4	6	10	14	18
11-20	2	4	6	8	10	12
21-33	1	2	3	5	6	8
34-48: 35-Onion app.						6.00

RICHIE RICH CASH
Harvey Publications: Sept, 1974 - No. 47, Aug, 1982

	GD	VG	FN	VF	VF/NM	NM-
1-1st app. Dr. N-R-Gee	3	6	9	19	30	40
2-5	2	4	6	13	18	22
6-10	2	4	6	9	13	16
11-20	1	3	4	6	8	10
21-30	1	2	3	4	5	7
31-47: 33-Dr. Blemish app.						6.00

RICHIE RICH CASH MONEY
Harvey Comics: May, 1992 - No. 2, Aug, 1992 ($1.25)

	GD	VG	FN	VF	VF/NM	NM-
1,2						3.00

RICHIE RICH, CASPER AND WENDY - NATIONAL LEAGUE
Harvey Comics: June, 1976 (50¢)

	GD	VG	FN	VF	VF/NM	NM-
1-Newsstand version of the baseball giveaway	2	4	6	13	18	22

RICHIE RICH COLLECTORS COMICS (See Harvey Collectors Comics)

Richie Rich Dollars & Cents #69 © HARV

Richie Rich Gems #2 © HARV

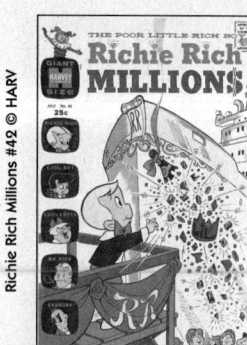

Richie Rich Millions #42 © HARV

RICHIE RICH DIAMONDS
Harvey Publications: Aug, 1972 - No. 59, Aug, 1982 (#1, 23-45: 52 pgs.)

	GD 2.0	VG 4.0	FN 6.0	VF 8.0	VF/NM 9.0	NM- 9.2
1-(52 pg. Giant)	5	10	15	30	50	70
2-5	3	6	9	16	23	30
6-10	2	4	6	11	16	20
11-22	2	4	6	8	10	12
23-30-(52 pg. Giants)	2	4	6	8	11	14
31-45: 39-r/Origin Little Dot	1	2	3	5	7	9
46-50	1	2	3	4	5	7
51-59						6.00

RICHIE RICH DIGEST MAGAZINE
Harvey Publications: Oct, 1986 - No. 42, Oct, 1994 ($1.25/$1.75, digest-size)

	GD 2.0	VG 4.0	FN 6.0	VF 8.0	VF/NM 9.0	NM- 9.2
1	1	2	3	5	6	8
2-10						5.00
11-20						4.00
21-42						4.00

RICHIE RICH DIGEST STORIES (...Magazine #?-on)
Harvey Publications: Oct, 1977 - No., 17, Oct, 1982 (75¢/95¢, digest-size)

	GD 2.0	VG 4.0	FN 6.0	VF 8.0	VF/NM 9.0	NM- 9.2
1-Reprints	2	4	6	9	12	15
2-10: Reprints	1	2	3	5	7	9
11-17: Reprints						6.00

RICHIE RICH DIGEST WINNERS
Harvey Publications: Dec, 1977 - No. 16, Sept, 1982 (75¢/95¢, 132 pgs., digest-size)

	GD 2.0	VG 4.0	FN 6.0	VF 8.0	VF/NM 9.0	NM- 9.2
1	2	4	6	9	12	15
2-5	1	2	3	5	7	9
6-16						6.00

RICHIE RICH DOLLARS & CENTS
Harvey Publications: Aug, 1963 - No. 109, Aug, 1982 (#1-43: 68 pgs.; 44-60, 71-94: 52 pgs.)

	GD 2.0	VG 4.0	FN 6.0	VF 8.0	VF/NM 9.0	NM- 9.2
1: (#1-64 are all reprint issues)	19	38	57	133	297	460
2	10	20	30	66	138	210
3-5: 5-r/1st app. of R.R. from Little Dot #1	8	16	24	54	102	150
6-10	6	12	18	40	73	105
11-20	4	8	12	28	47	65
21-30: 25-r/1st app. Nurse Jenny (Little Lotta #62)	3	6	9	21	33	45
31-43: 43-Last 68 pg. issue	3	6	9	17	26	35
44-60: All 52 pgs.	3	6	9	14	19	25
61-71	1	3	4	6	8	10
72-94: All 52 pgs.	2	4	6	8	10	12
95-99,101-109						6.00
100-Anniversary issue	1	2	3	5	7	9

RICHIE RICH FORTUNES
Harvey Publications: Sept, 1971 - No. 63, July, 1982 (#1-15: 52 pgs.)

	GD 2.0	VG 4.0	FN 6.0	VF 8.0	VF/NM 9.0	NM- 9.2
1	5	10	15	34	60	85
2-5	3	6	9	19	30	40
6-10	2	4	6	13	18	22
11-15: 11-r/1st app. The Onion	2	4	6	9	12	15
16-30	1	2	3	5	7	9
31-40	1	2	3	4	5	7
41-63: 62-Onion app.						6.00

RICHIE RICH GEMS
Harvey Publications: Sept, 1974 - No. 43, Sept, 1982

	GD 2.0	VG 4.0	FN 6.0	VF 8.0	VF/NM 9.0	NM- 9.2
1	3	6	9	19	30	40
2-5	2	4	6	13	18	22
6-10	2	4	6	9	13	16
11-20	1	3	4	6	8	10
21-30	1	2	3	4	5	7
31-43: 36-Dr. Blemish, Onion app. 38-1st app. Stone-Age Riches						6.00
44-48 (Ape Entertainment, 2011-2012, $3.99) new stories w/Colon-a & reprints						4.00
... Special Collection (Ape Entertainment, 2012, $6.99) r/Valentine & Winter Specials						7.00
... Valentines Special (Ape Entertainment, 2012, $3.99) new story w/Colon-a & reprints						4.00
... Winter Special (Ape Entertainment, 2011, $3.99) new story w/Colon-a & reprints						4.00

RICHIE RICH GOLD AND SILVER
Harvey Publications: Sept, 1975 - No. 42, Oct, 1982 (#1-27: 52 pgs.)

	GD 2.0	VG 4.0	FN 6.0	VF 8.0	VF/NM 9.0	NM- 9.2
1	3	6	9	17	26	35
2-5	2	4	6	11	16	20
6-10	2	4	6	8	11	14
11-27	1	2	3	5	7	9
28-42: 34-Stone-Age Riches app.						6.00

RICHIE RICH GOLD NUGGETS DIGEST
Harvey Publications: Dec., 1990 - No. 4, June, 1991 ($1.75, digest-size)

	GD 2.0	VG 4.0	FN 6.0	VF 8.0	VF/NM 9.0	NM- 9.2
1-4						4.00

RICHIE RICH HOLIDAY DIGEST MAGAZINE (...Digest #4)
Harvey Publications: Jan, 1980 - #3, Jan, 1982; #4, 3/88; #5, 2/89 (annual)

	GD 2.0	VG 4.0	FN 6.0	VF 8.0	VF/NM 9.0	NM- 9.2
1-X-Mas-c	1	3	4	6	8	10
2-5: 2,3: All X-Mas-c. 4-(3/88, $1.25), 5-(2/89, $1.75)	1	2	3	4	5	7

RICHIE RICH INVENTIONS
Harvey Publications: Oct, 1977 - No. 26, Oct, 1982 (#1-11: 52 pgs.)

	GD 2.0	VG 4.0	FN 6.0	VF 8.0	VF/NM 9.0	NM- 9.2
1	2	4	6	11	16	20
2-5	2	4	6	8	10	12
6-11	1	2	3	5	6	8
12-26						6.00

RICHIE RICH JACKPOTS
Harvey Publications: Oct, 1972 - No. 58, Aug, 1982 (#41-43: 52 pgs.)

	GD 2.0	VG 4.0	FN 6.0	VF 8.0	VF/NM 9.0	NM- 9.2
1-Debut of Cousin Jackpots	4	8	12	28	47	65
2-5	3	6	9	16	23	30
6-10	2	4	6	11	16	20
11-15,17-20	2	4	6	8	10	12
16-Super Richie app.	2	4	6	9	12	15
21-30	1	2	3	5	7	9
31-40,44-50: 37-Caricatures of Frank Sinatra, Dean Martin, Sammy Davis, Jr. 45-Dr. Blemish app.	1	2	3	4	5	7
41-43 (52 pgs.)	1	3	4	6	8	10
51-58						6.00

RICHIE RICH MILLION DOLLAR DIGEST (...Magazine #?-on)(See Million Dollar Digest)
Harvey Publications: Oct, 1980 - No. 10, Oct, 1982 ($1.50)

	GD 2.0	VG 4.0	FN 6.0	VF 8.0	VF/NM 9.0	NM- 9.2
1	1	3	4	6	8	10
2-10						7.00

RICHIE RICH MILLIONS
Harvey Publ.: 9/61; #2, 9/62 - #113, 10/82 (#1-48: 68 pgs.; 49-64, 85-97: 52 pgs.)

	GD 2.0	VG 4.0	FN 6.0	VF 8.0	VF/NM 9.0	NM- 9.2
1: (#1-3 are all reprint issues)	23	46	69	168	382	560
2	11	22	33	73	157	240
3-5: All other giants are new & reprints. 5-1st 15 pg. Richie Rich story	8	16	24	56	108	160
6-10	7	14	21	49	92	135
11-20	5	10	15	35	63	90
21-30	4	8	12	27	44	60
31-48: 31-1st app. The Onion. 48-Last 68 pg. Giant	3	6	9	19	30	40
49-64: 52 pg. Giants	3	6	9	14	20	25
65-67,69-73,75-84	2	4	6	8	10	12
68-1st Super Richie-c (11/74)	2	4	6	13	18	22
74-1st app. Mr. Woody; Super Richie app.	2	4	6	8	11	14
85-97: 52 pg. Giants	2	4	6	8	11	14
98,99	1	2	3	4	5	7
100	1	2	3	5	7	9
101-113						6.00

RICHIE RICH MONEY WORLD
Harvey Publications: Sept, 1972 - No. 59, Sept, 1982

	GD 2.0	VG 4.0	FN 6.0	VF 8.0	VF/NM 9.0	NM- 9.2
1-(52 pg. Giant)-1st app. Mayda Munny	5	10	15	33	57	80
2-Super Richie app.	3	6	9	17	26	35
3-5	3	6	9	16	23	30
6-10: 9,10-Richie Rich mistakenly named Little Lotta on covers	2	4	6	11	16	20
11-20: 16,20-Dr. N-R-Gee	2	4	6	8	10	12
21-30	1	2	3	5	7	9
31-50	1	2	3	4	5	7
51-59						6.00
Digest 1 (2/91, $1.75)						5.00
2-8 (12/93, $1.75)						3.00

RICHIE RICH PROFITS
Harvey Publications: Oct, 1974 - No. 47, Sept, 1982

	GD 2.0	VG 4.0	FN 6.0	VF 8.0	VF/NM 9.0	NM- 9.2
1	3	6	9	19	30	40
2-5	2	4	6	13	18	22
6-10: 10-Origin of Dr. N-R-Gee	2	4	6	9	13	16
11-20: 15-Christmas-c	1	3	4	6	8	10
21-30	1	2	3	4	5	7
31-47						6.00

RICHIE RICH RELICS
Harvey Comics: Jan, 1988 - No.4, Feb, 1989 (75¢/$1.00, reprints)

	GD 2.0	VG 4.0	FN 6.0	VF 8.0	VF/NM 9.0	NM- 9.2
1-4						3.00

Richie Rich Success Stories #6 © HARV

Rick and Morty #60 © Cartoon Network

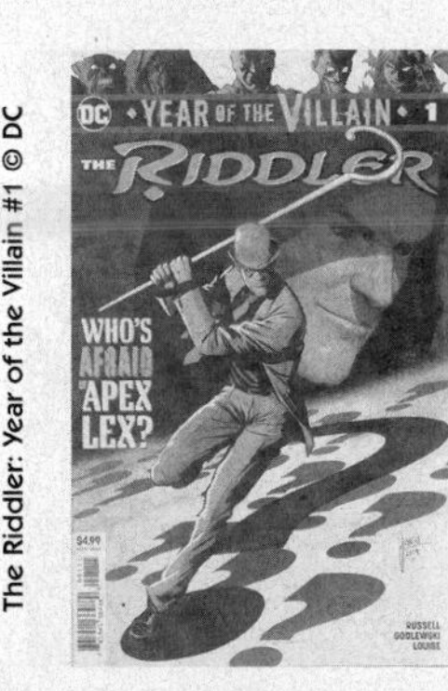

The Riddler: Year of the Villain #1 © DC

RICHIE RICH RICHES
Harvey Publications: July, 1972 - No. 59, Aug, 1982 (#1, 2, 41-45: 52 pgs.)

	GD 2.0	VG 4.0	FN 6.0	VF 8.0	VF/NM 9.0	NM- 9.2
1-(52 pg. Giant)-1st app. The Money Monster	5	10	15	33	57	80
2-(52 pg. Giant)	3	6	9	19	30	40
3-5	3	6	9	16	23	30
6-10: 7-1st app. Aunt Novo	2	4	6	11	16	20
11-20: 17-Super Richie app. (3/75)	2	4	6	8	10	12
21-40	1	2	3	5	6	8
41-45: 52 pg. Giants	1	3	4	6	8	10
46-59: 56-Dr. Blemish app.						6.00

RICHIE RICH: RICH RESCUE
Ape Entertainment: 2011 - No. 4, 2011 ($3.95, limited series)

	GD 2.0	VG 4.0	FN 6.0	VF 8.0	VF/NM 9.0	NM- 9.2
1-6-New short stories by various incl. Ernie Colon; Jack Lawrence-c						4.00
FCBD Edition (2011, giveaway) Flip book with Kung Fu Panda						3.00

RICHIE RICH SUCCESS STORIES
Harvey Publications: Nov, 1964 - No. 105, Sept, 1982 (#1-38: 68 pgs., 39-55, 67-90: 52 pgs.)

	GD 2.0	VG 4.0	FN 6.0	VF 8.0	VF/NM 9.0	NM- 9.2
1	18	36	54	128	284	440
2	9	18	27	58	114	170
3-5	8	16	24	51	96	140
6-10	5	10	15	35	63	90
11-20	5	10	15	31	53	75
21-30: 27-1st Penny Van Dough (8/69)	4	8	12	23	37	50
31-38: 38-Last 68 pg. Giant	3	6	9	19	30	40
39-55-(52 pgs.): 44-Super Richie app.	3	6	9	14	20	25
56-66	2	4	6	8	10	12
67-90: 52 pgs.	2	4	6	8	11	14
91-99,101-105: 91-Onion app. 101-Dr. Blemish app.						6.00
100	1	2	3	5	7	9

RICHIE RICH SUMMER BONANZA
Harvey Comics: Oct, 1991 ($1.95, one-shot, 68 pgs.)

	GD 2.0	VG 4.0	FN 6.0	VF 8.0	VF/NM 9.0	NM- 9.2
1-Richie Rich, Little Dot, Little Lotta						4.00

RICHIE RICH TREASURE CHEST DIGEST (...Magazine #3)
Harvey Publications: Apr, 1982 - No. 3, Aug, 1982 (95¢, Digest Mag.)
(#4 advertised but not publ.)

	GD 2.0	VG 4.0	FN 6.0	VF 8.0	VF/NM 9.0	NM- 9.2
1	1	3	4	6	8	10
2,3	1	2	3	4	5	7

RICHIE RICH VACATION DIGEST
Harvey Comics: Oct, 1991; Oct, 1992; Oct, 1993 ($1.75, digest-size)

	GD 2.0	VG 4.0	FN 6.0	VF 8.0	VF/NM 9.0	NM- 9.2
1-(10/91), 1-(10/92), 1-(10/93)						4.00

RICHIE RICH VACATIONS DIGEST
Harvey Publ.: 11/77; No. 2, 10/78 - No. 7, 10/81; No. 8, 8/82; No. 9, 10/82 (Digest, 132 pgs.)

	GD 2.0	VG 4.0	FN 6.0	VF 8.0	VF/NM 9.0	NM- 9.2
1-Reprints	2	4	6	9	12	15
2-6	1	2	3	5	7	9
7-9						6.00

RICHIE RICH VAULT OF MYSTERY
Harvey Publications: Nov, 1974 - No. 47, Sept, 1982

	GD 2.0	VG 4.0	FN 6.0	VF 8.0	VF/NM 9.0	NM- 9.2
1	4	8	12	23	37	50
2-5: 5-The Condor app.	2	4	6	13	18	22
6-10	2	4	6	9	13	16
11-20	1	3	4	6	8	10
21-30	1	2	3	4	5	7
31-47						6.00

RICHIE RICH ZILLIONZ
Harvey Publ.: Oct, 1976 - No. 33, Sept, 1982 (#1-4: 68 pgs.; #5-18: 52 pgs.)

	GD 2.0	VG 4.0	FN 6.0	VF 8.0	VF/NM 9.0	NM- 9.2
1	3	6	9	17	26	35
2-4: 4-Last 68 pg. Giant	2	4	6	11	16	20
5-10	2	4	6	8	10	12
11-18: 18-Last 52 pg. Giant	1	2	3	5	6	8
19-33						6.00

RICH JOHNSTON'S... (Parody of the Avengers movie characters)
BOOM! Studios: Apr, 2012 ($3.99, series of one-shots)

	GD 2.0	VG 4.0	FN 6.0	VF 8.0	VF/NM 9.0	NM- 9.2
... Captain American Idol 1 - Rich Johnston-s/Chris Haley-a						4.00
... Iron Muslim 1 - Rich Johnston-s/Bryan Turner-a; Demon in a Bottle cover swipe						4.00
... Scienthorlogy 1 - Rich Johnston-s/Michael Netzer-a						4.00
... The Avengefuls 1 - Rich Johnston-s/Joshua Covey; two printings						4.00

RICK AND MORTY (Based on the Adult Swim animated series)
Oni Press: Apr, 2015 - No. 60, Mar, 2020 ($3.99)

	GD 2.0	VG 4.0	FN 6.0	VF 8.0	VF/NM 9.0	NM- 9.2
1-Zac Gorman-s/CJ Cannon-a; multiple covers	10	20	30	66	138	210
2,3	3	6	9	17	26	35
4-49,51-60: 44-The Vindicators app.						4.00
50-($6.99) Morty's Mind Blowers						7.00
...#1 50th Issue Celebration Reprint (5/19, $3.99) r/#1						4.00
... Free Comic Book Day 2017 (5/17, giveaway) r/#1; preview of Pocket Like You Stole It						3.00
... Presents: Birdperson 1 (7/20, $4.99) Origin & 1st meeting with Rick						5.00
... Presents: Council of Ricks 1 (6/20, $4.99) Goldman-s/Ellerby & Murphy-a						5.00
... Presents: Death Stalkers 1 (1/21, $4.99) Phillips-s/Ryan Lee-a; Hemorrhage app.						5.00
... Presents: Jaguar 1 (11/20, $4.99) Ellerby-s/a						5.00
... Presents: Jerry 1 (3/19, $4.99) Ferrier-s/Cannon-a						5.00
... Presents: Krombopulos Michael 1 (6/18, $4.99) Ortberg-s/Cannon-a						5.00
... Presents: Mr. Meeseeks 1 (6/19, $4.99) Asmus & Festante-s/Cannon-a						5.00
... Presents: Pickle Rick 1 (11/18, $4.99) Delilah S. Dawson-s/CJ Cannon-a; Jaguar app.						5.00
... Presents: Sleepy Gary 1 (9/18, $4.99) Visaggio-s/Cannon-a						5.00
... Presents: The Flesh Curtains 1 (9/19, $4.99) Sturges-s/Cannon-a; Birdman app.						5.00
... Presents: The Vindicators 1 (3/18, $4.99) Cannon-a; Pickle Rick app.						5.00
... Presents: Unity 1 (11/19, $4.99) Tini Howard-s/Marco Mazzarello-a						5.00

RICK AND MORTY EVER AFTER (Adult Swim)
Oni Press: Oct, 2020 - No. 4, Jan, 2021 ($3.99, limited series)

	GD 2.0	VG 4.0	FN 6.0	VF 8.0	VF/NM 9.0	NM- 9.2
1-4-Sam Maggs-s/Sarah Stern-a; multiple covers						4.00

RICK AND MORTY GO TO HELL (Adult Swim)
Oni Press: Jun, 2020 - No. 5, Oct, 2020 ($3.99, limited series)

	GD 2.0	VG 4.0	FN 6.0	VF 8.0	VF/NM 9.0	NM- 9.2
1-5-Ferrier-s/Oroza-a; multiple covers						4.00

RICK AND MORTY: LIL' POOPY SUPERSTAR (Adult Swim)
Oni Press: Jul, 2016 - No. 5, Nov, 2016 ($3.99, limited series)

	GD 2.0	VG 4.0	FN 6.0	VF 8.0	VF/NM 9.0	NM- 9.2
1-5-Sarah Graley-s/a; multiple covers						4.00

RICK AND MORTY: POCKET LIKE YOU STOLE IT (Adult Swim)
Oni Press: Jul, 2017 - No. 5, Nov, 2017 ($3.99, limited series)

	GD 2.0	VG 4.0	FN 6.0	VF 8.0	VF/NM 9.0	NM- 9.2
1-5-Tim Howard-s/Marc Ellerby-a; multiple covers						4.00

RICK AND MORTY VS. DUNGEONS & DRAGONS (Adult Swim)
Oni Press/IDW Publishing: Aug, 2018 - No. 4, Dec, 2018 ($3.99, limited series)

	GD 2.0	VG 4.0	FN 6.0	VF 8.0	VF/NM 9.0	NM- 9.2
1-4-Patrick Rothfuss & Jim Zub-s/Troy Little-a						4.00
1: Director's Cut Edition (2/19, $4.99) r/#1 with some script pages and B&W art						5.00

RICK AND MORTY VS. DUNGEONS & DRAGONS II: PAINSCAPE (Adult Swim)
Oni Press/IDW Publishing: Aug, 2019 - No. 4, Dec, 2019 ($3.99, limited series)

	GD 2.0	VG 4.0	FN 6.0	VF 8.0	VF/NM 9.0	NM- 9.2
1-4-Jim Zub-s/Troy Little-a						4.00

RICK AND MORTY WORLDS APART (Adult Swim)
Oni Press: Feb, 2021 - Present ($3.99, limited series)

	GD 2.0	VG 4.0	FN 6.0	VF 8.0	VF/NM 9.0	NM- 9.2
1-Trujillo-s/Fleecs-a; the dragon Balthrowmaw app.						4.00

RICKY
Standard Comics (Visual Editions): No. 5, Sept, 1953

	GD 2.0	VG 4.0	FN 6.0	VF 8.0	VF/NM 9.0	NM- 9.2
5-Teenage humor	10	20	30	54	72	90

RICKY NELSON (TV)(See Sweethearts V2#42)
Dell Publishing Co.: No. 956, Dec, 1958 - No. 1192, June, 1961 (All photo-c)

	GD 2.0	VG 4.0	FN 6.0	VF 8.0	VF/NM 9.0	NM- 9.2
Four Color 956,998	15	30	45	103	227	350
Four Color 1115,1192: 1192-Manning-a	12	24	36	80	173	265

RIDDLER, THE : YEAR OF THE VILLAIN
DC Comics: 2019 ($4.99, one-shot)

	GD 2.0	VG 4.0	FN 6.0	VF 8.0	VF/NM 9.0	NM- 9.2
1-King Tut and Apex Lex app.; origin re-told; Russell-s/Godlewski-a/Janin-c						4.00

RIDE, THE (Also see Gun Candy flip-book)
Image Comics: June, 2004 - No. 2, July, 2004 ($2.95, B&W, anthology)

	GD 2.0	VG 4.0	FN 6.0	VF 8.0	VF/NM 9.0	NM- 9.2
1,2: Hughes-c/Wagner-s. 1-Hamner & Stelfreeze-a. 2-Jeanty & Pearson-a						3.00
... Burning Desire 1-5 (6/19 - No. 5, 10/19, $3.99) 1-Hughes-c/a(6 pgs.) 4-Coker-a						4.00
... Die Valkyrie 1-3 (6/07 - No. 3, 2/08, $2.99) Stelfreeze-a/Wagner-s/Pearson-c						3.00
... Foreign Parts 1 (1/05, $2.95) Dixon-s/Haynes-a; Marz-s/Brunner-a; Pearson-c						3.00
... Halloween Special: The Key to Survival (10/07, $3.50) Tomm Coker-s/a						3.50
... Savannah 1 (4/07, $4.99) s/a by students of Savannah College of Art						5.00
... 2 For the Road 1 (10/04, $2.95) Dixon-s/Hamner & Gregory-a/Johnson-c						3.00
Vol. 1 TPB (2005, $9.99) r/#1,2, Foreign Parts, 2 For the Road; Chaykin intro.						10.00
Vol. 2 TPB (2005, $15.99) r/Gun Candy #1,2 & Die Valkyrie #1-3; sketch pages						16.00

RIDER, THE (Frontier Trail #6; also see Blazing Sixguns I.W. Reprint #10, 11)
Ajax/Farrell Publ. (Four Star Comic Corp.): Mar, 1957 - No. 5, 1958

	GD 2.0	VG 4.0	FN 6.0	VF 8.0	VF/NM 9.0	NM- 9.2
1-Swift Arrow, Lone Rider begin	14	28	42	76	108	140
2-5	8	16	24	42	54	65

RIDERS OF THE PURPLE SAGE (See Zane Grey & Four Color #372)

RIFLEMAN, THE (TV)

Rima, The Jungle Girl #1 © DC

The Rinse #1 © BOOM & Phillips

Rip Hunter Time Master #16 © DC

	GD 2.0	VG 4.0	FN 6.0	VF 8.0	VF/NM 9.0	NM- 9.2
Dell Publ. Co./Gold Key No. 13 on: No. 1009, 7-9/59 - No. 12, 7-9/62; No. 13, 11/62 - No. 20, 10/64						
Four Color 1009 (#1)	23	46	69	156	348	540
2 (1-3/60)	10	20	30	67	141	215
3-Toth-a (4 pgs.); variant edition has back-c with "Something Special" comic strip	10	20	30	65	135	205
4-9: 6-Toth-a (4 pgs.)	9	18	27	59	117	175
10-Classic-c	38	76	114	281	628	975
11-20	7	14	21	46	86	125

NOTE: *Warren Tufts a-2-9. All have Chuck Connors & Johnny Crawford photo-c. Photo back c-13-15.*

RIFTWAR
Marvel Comics: July, 2009 - No. 5, Dec, 2009 ($3.99, limited series)

	GD	VG	FN	VF	VF/NM	NM-
1-5-Adaptation of Raymond E. Feist novel; Glass-s/Stegman-a						4.00

RIMA, THE JUNGLE GIRL
National Periodical Publications: Apr-May, 1974 - No. 7, Apr-May, 1975

	GD	VG	FN	VF	VF/NM	NM-
1-Origin, part 1 (#1-5: 20¢; 6,7: 25¢)	3	6	9	14	20	26
2-7: 2-4-Origin, parts 2-4. 7-Origin & only app. Space Marshal	2	3	4	6	8	10

NOTE: *Kubert c-1-7. Nino a-1-7. Redondo a-1-7.*

RING OF BRIGHT WATER (See Movie Classics)

RING OF THE NIBELUNG, THE
DC Comics: 1989 - No. 4, 1990 ($4.95, squarebound, 52 pgs., mature readers)

	GD	VG	FN	VF	VF/NM	NM-
1-4: Adapts Wagner cycle of operas, Gil Kane-c/a						5.00

RING OF THE NIBELUNG, THE
Dark Horse Comics: Feb, 2000 - Sept, 2001 ($2.95/$2.99/$5.99, limited series)

	GD	VG	FN	VF	VF/NM	NM-
Vol. 1 (The Rhinegold) 1-4: Adapts Wagner; P. Craig Russell-s/a						3.00
Vol. 2,3: Vol. 2 (The Valkyrie) 1-3: 1-(8/00). Vol. 3 (Siegfried) 1-3: 1-(12/00)						3.00
Vol. 4 (The Twilight of the Gods) 1-3: 1-(6/01)						3.00
4-(9/01, $5.99, 64 pgs.) Conclusion with sketch pages						6.00

RINGO KID, THE (2nd Series)
Marvel Comics Group: Jan, 1970 - No. 23, Nov, 1973; No. 24, Nov, 1975 - No. 30, Nov, 1976

	GD	VG	FN	VF	VF/NM	NM-
1-Williamson-a r-from #10, 1956.	4	8	12	28	47	65
2-11: 2-Severin-c. 11-Last 15¢ issue	2	4	6	11	16	20
12 (52 pg. Giant)	3	6	9	16	24	32
13-20: 13-Wildey-r. 20-Williamson-r/#1	2	4	6	9	13	16
21-30	2	4	6	8	10	12
27,28-(30¢-c variant, limited distribution)(5,7/76)	13	26	39	86	188	290

RINGO KID WESTERN, THE (1st Series) (See Wild Western & Western Trails)
Atlas Comics (HPC)/Marvel Comics: Aug, 1954 - No. 21, Sept, 1957

	GD	VG	FN	VF	VF/NM	NM-
1-Origin; The Ringo Kid begins	39	78	117	240	395	550
2-Black Rider app.; origin/1st app. Ringo's Horse Arab	20	40	60	120	195	270
3-5	15	30	45	86	133	180
6-8-Severin-a(3) each	15	30	45	90	140	190
9,11,12,14-21: 12-Orlando-a (4 pgs.)	14	28	42	78	112	145
10,13-Williamson-a (4 pgs.)	14	28	42	81	118	155

NOTE: *Berg a-8. Maneely a-1-5, 15, 16(text illos only), 17(4), 18, 20, 21; c-1-6, 8, 13, 15-18, 20. J. Severin c-10, 11. Sinnott a-1. Wildey a-16-18.*

RINGSIDE
Image Comics: Nov, 2015 - No. 15, Apr, 2018 ($3.99)

	GD	VG	FN	VF	VF/NM	NM-
1-15-Keatinge-s/Barber-a						4.00

RINSE, THE
BOOM! Studios: Sept, 2011 - No. 4, Dec, 2011 ($1.00/$3.99)

	GD	VG	FN	VF	VF/NM	NM-
1-($1.00)-Phillips-s/Laming-a						3.00
2-4-($3.99)						4.00

RIN TIN TIN (See March of Comics #163,180,195)

RIN TIN TIN (TV) (...& Rusty #21 on; see Western Roundup under Dell Giants)
Dell Publishing Co./Gold Key: Nov, 1952 - No. 38, May-July, 1961; Nov, 1963 (All Photo-c)

	GD	VG	FN	VF	VF/NM	NM-
Four Color 434 (#1)	15	30	45	103	227	350
Four Color 476,523	9	18	27	59	117	175
4(3-5/54)-10	6	12	18	40	73	105
11-17,19,20	6	12	18	37	66	95
18-(4-5/57) 1st app. of Rusty and the Cavalry of Fort Apache; photo-c	7	14	21	46	86	125
21-38: 36-Toth-a (4 pgs.)	5	10	15	31	53	75
... & Rusty 1 (11/63-Gold Key)	5	10	15	33	57	80

RIO (Also see Eclipse Monthly)
Comico: June, 1987 ($8.95, 64 pgs.)

	GD	VG	FN	VF	VF/NM	NM-
1-Wildey-c/a						9.00

RIO AT BAY
Dark Horse Comics: July, 1992 - No. 2, Aug, 1992 ($2.95, limited series)

	GD	VG	FN	VF	VF/NM	NM-
1,2-Wildey-c/a						3.00

RIO BRAVO (Movie) (See 4-Color #1018)
Dell Publishing Co.: June, 1959

	GD	VG	FN	VF	VF/NM	NM-
Four Color 1018-Toth-a; John Wayne, Dean Martin, & Ricky Nelson photo-c.	27	54	81	189	420	650

RIO CONCHOS (See Movie Comics)

RIOT (Satire)
Atlas Comics (ACI No. 1-5/WPI No. 6): Apr, 1954 - No. 3, Aug, 1954; No. 4, Feb, 1956 - No. 6, June, 1956

	GD	VG	FN	VF	VF/NM	NM-
1-Russ Heath-a	48	96	144	302	514	725
2-Li'l Abner satire by Post	31	62	93	182	296	410
3-Last precode (8/54)	27	54	81	158	259	360
4-Infinity-c; Marilyn Monroe "7 Year Itch" movie satire; Mad Rip-off ads	34	68	102	199	325	450
5-Marilyn Monroe, John Wayne parody; part photo-c	34	68	102	204	332	460
6-Lorna of the Jungle satire by Everett; Dennis the Menace satire-c/story; part photo-c	27	54	81	158	259	360

NOTE: *Berg a-3. Burgos c-1, 2. Colan a-1. Everett a-4, 6. Heath a-1. Maneely a-1, 2, 4-6; c-3, 4, 6. Post a-1-4. Reinman a-2. Severin a-4-6.*

RIOT GEAR
Triumphant Comics: Sept, 1993 - No. 11, July, 1994 ($2.50, serially numbered)

	GD	VG	FN	VF	VF/NM	NM-
1-11: 1-2nd app. Riot Gear. 2-1st app. Rabin. 3,4-Triumphant Unleashed x-over. 3-1st app. Surzar. 4-Death of Captain Tich						3.00
Violent Past 1,2: 1-(2/94, $2.50)						3.00

R.I.P.
TSR, Inc.:1990 - No. 8, 1991 ($2.95, 44 pgs.)

	GD	VG	FN	VF	VF/NM	NM-
1-8-Based on TSR game						4.00

RIPCLAW (See Cyberforce)
Image Comics (Top Cow Prod.): Apr, 1995 - No. 3, June, 1995 (Limited series)

	GD	VG	FN	VF	VF/NM	NM-
1/2-Gold, 1/2-San Diego ed., 1/2-Chicago ed.	1	3	4	6	8	10
1-3: Brandon Peterson-a(p)						3.00
Special 1 (10/95, $2.50)						3.00

RIPCLAW
Image Comics (Top Cow Prod.): V2#1, Dec, 1995 - No. 6, June, 1996 ($2.50)

	GD	VG	FN	VF	VF/NM	NM-
V2#1-6: 5-Medieval Spawn/Witchblade Preview						3.00
...: Pilot Season 1 (2007, $2.99) Jason Aaron-s/Jorge Lucas-a/Tony Moore-c						3.00

RIPCORD (TV)
Dell Publishing Co.: Mar-May, 1962

	GD	VG	FN	VF	VF/NM	NM-
Four Color 1294	6	12	18	40	73	105

R.I.P.D.
Dark Horse Comics: Oct, 1999 - No. 4, Jan, 2000 ($2.95, limited series)

	GD	VG	FN	VF	VF/NM	NM-
1-4						3.00
TPB (2003, $12.95) r/#1-4						13.00

R.I.P.D.: CITY OF THE DAMNED
Dark Horse Comics: Nov, 2012 - No. 4, Mar, 2013 ($3.50, limited series)

	GD	VG	FN	VF	VF/NM	NM-
1-4-Barlow-s/Parker-a/Wilkins-c						3.50

RIP HUNTER TIME MASTER (See Showcase #20, 21, 25, 26 & Time Masters)
National Periodical Publications: Mar-Apr, 1961 - No. 29, Nov-Dec, 1965

	GD	VG	FN	VF	VF/NM	NM-
1-(3-4/61)	66	132	198	335	1193	1850
2	25	50	75	175	388	600
3-5: 5-Last 10¢ issue	15	30	45	105	232	360
6,7-Toth-a in each	11	22	33	73	157	240
8-15	8	16	24	54	102	150
16-19	6	12	18	41	76	110
20-Hitler-c/s	9	18	27	58	114	170
21-28	6	12	18	37	66	95
29-Gil Kane-c	7	14	21	46	86	125

RIP IN TIME (Also see Teenage Mutant Ninja Turtles #5-7)
Fantagor Press: Aug, 1986 - No.5, 1987 ($1.50, B&W)

	GD	VG	FN	VF	VF/NM	NM-
1-5: Corben-c/a in all						4.00

RIP KIRBY (Also see Harvey Comics Hits #57, & Street Comix)
David McKay Publications: 1948

Ripley's Believe It or Not! #26 © GK

The Rise of Ultraman #1 © Tsuburaya Prods.

Riverdale Digest #1 © ACP

GD 2.0 | VG 4.0 | FN 6.0 | VF 8.0 | VF/NM 9.0 | NM- 9.2

Feature Books 51,54: Raymond-c; 51-Origin 39 78 117 236 388 540

RIPLEY'S BELIEVE IT OR NOT! (See Ace Comics, All-American Comics, Mystery Comics Digest #1, 4, 7, 10, 13, 16, 19, 22, 25)

RIPLEY'S BELIEVE IT OR NOT!
Harvey Publications: Sept, 1953 - No. 4, March, 1954
1-Powell-a 19 38 57 112 179 245
2-4 10 20 30 56 76 95

RIPLEY'S BELIEVE IT OR NOT! (Continuation of Ripleys'...True Ghost Stories & Ripley's...True War Stories)
Gold Key: No. 4, April, 1967 - No. 94, Feb, 1980
4-Shrunken head photo-c; McWilliams-a 4 8 12 25 40 55
5-Subtitled "True War Stories"; Evans-a; 1st Jeff Jones-a in comics? (2 pgs.) 4 8 12 23 37 50
6-10: 6-McWilliams-a. 10-Evans-a(2) 3 6 9 19 30 40
11-20: 15-Evans-a 3 6 9 16 23 30
21-30 2 4 6 13 18 22
31-38,40-60 2 4 6 9 13 16
39-Crandall-a 2 4 6 10 14 18
61-73 1 3 4 6 8 10
74,77-83-(52 pgs.) 2 4 6 9 13 16
75,76,84-94 1 2 3 5 6 8
Story Digest Mag. 1(6/70)-4-3/4x6-1/2", 148pp. 5 10 15 31 53 75
NOTE: *Evanish art by* ***Luiz Dominguez*** *#22-25, 27, 30, 31, 40.* ***Jeff Jones*** *a-5(2 pgs.).* ***McWilliams*** *a-65, 66, 70, 89.* ***Orlando*** *a-8.* ***Sparling*** *c-68. Reprints-74, 77-84, 87 (part); 91, 93 (all).* ***Williamson, Wood*** *a-80r/#1.*

RIPLEY'S BELIEVE IT OR NOT!
Dark Horse Comics: May, 2002 - No. 3, Oct, 2002 ($2.99, B&W, unfinished limited series)
1-3-Nord-c/a. 1-Stories of Amelia Earhart & D.B. Cooper 3.00

RIPLEY'S BELIEVE IT OR NOT! TRUE GHOST STORIES (Along with Ripley's...True War Stories, the three issues together precede the 1967 series that starts its numbering with #4) (Also see Dan Curtis)
Gold Key: June, 1965 - No. 2, Oct, 1966
1-Williamson, Wood & Evans-a; photo-c 8 16 24 51 96 140
2-Orlando, McWilliams-a; photo-c 5 10 15 30 50 70
Mini-Comic 1(1976-3-1/4x6-1/2") 2 4 6 8 11 14
11186(1977)-Golden Press; ($1.95, 224 pgs.)-All-r 4 8 12 25 40 55
11401(3/79)-Golden Press; ($1.00, 96 pgs.)-All-r 3 6 9 15 22 28

RIPLEY'S BELIEVE IT OR NOT! TRUE WAR STORIES (Along with Ripley's...True Ghost Stories, the three issues together precede the 1967 series that starts its numbering with #4)
Gold Key: Nov, 1965 (Aug, 1965 in indicia)
1-No Williamson-a 5 10 15 30 50 70

RIPLEY'S BELIEVE IT OR NOT! TRUE WEIRD
Ripley Enterprises: June, 1966 - No. 2, Aug, 1966 (B&W Magazine)
1,2-Comic stories & text 3 6 9 21 33 45

RISE OF APOCALYPSE
Marvel Comics: Oct, 1996 - No. 4, Jan, 1997 ($1.95, limited series)
1-Adam Pollina-c/a in all 1 3 4 6 8 10
2-4 5.00

RISE OF THE BLACK FLAME
Dark Horse Comics: Sept, 2016 - No. 5, Jan, 2017 ($3.99, limited series)
1-5-Mignola & Roberson-s/Mitten-a/Laurence Campbell-c 4.00

RISE OF THE BLACK PANTHER
Marvel Comics: Mar, 2018 - No. 6, Aug, 2018 ($3.99, limited series)
1-6: 1-Origin of T'Challa; Narcisse-s/Renaud-a/Stelfreeze-c; Klaw app. 2-Namor app. 4.00

RISE OF THE MAGI
Image Comics (Top Cow): No. 0, May, 2014 - No. 5 ($3.50)
0 (5/14, Free Comic Book Day giveaway) Silvestri-s/c; bonus character & concept art 3.00
1-5: 1-(6/14) Silvestri-s/Kesgin-a; four covers 3.50

RISE OF THE TEENAGE MUTANT NINJA TURTLES
Image Comics (Top Cow): No. 0, Jul, 2018 - No. 5, Jan, 2019 ($3.99)
0-5-Based on the Nickelodeon animated series; Matthew K. Manning-s/Chad Thomas-a 4.00

RISE OF THE TEENAGE MUTANT NINJA TURTLES: SOUND OFF!
Image Comics (Top Cow): Jul, 2019 - No. 3, Sept, 2019 ($3.99)
1-3-Matthew K. Manning-s/Chad Thomas-a 4.00

RISE OF ULTRAMAN, THE
Marvel Comics: Nov, 2020 - No. 5, Mar, 2021 ($5.99/$3.99, limited series)
1-($5.99) Intro. Shin Hayata; Higgins & Groom-s/Manna-a; main cover by Alex Ross 6.00
2-5-($3.99) Origin of Ultraman 4.00

RISING STARS
Image Comics (Top Cow): Mar, 1999 - No. 24, Mar, 2005 ($2.50/$2.99)
Preview-(3/99, $5.00) Straczynski-s 6.00
0-(6/00, $2.50) Gary Frank-a/c 3.00
1/2-(8/01, $2.95) Anderson-c; art & sketch pages by Zanier 3.00
1-Four covers; Keu Cha-c/a 5.00
1-($10.00) Gold Editions-four covers 10.00
1-($50.00) Holofoil-c 50.00
2-7: 5-7-Zanier & Lashley-a(p) 4.00
8-23: 8-13-Zanier & Lashley-a(p). 14-Immonen-a. 15-Flip book B&W preview of Universe. 15-23-Brent Anderson-a 3.00
24-($3.99) Series finale; Anderson-a/c 4.00
Born In Fire TPB (11/00, $19.95) r/#1-8; foreword by Neil Gaiman 20.00
Power TPB (2002, $19.95) r/#9-16 20.00
Prelude-(10/00, $2.95) Cha-a/Lashley-c 3.00
...: Visitations (2002, $8.99) r/#0, 1/2, Preview; new Anderson-c; cover gallery 9.00
Vol. 3: Fire and Ash TPB (2005, $19.99) r/#17-24; design pages & cover gallery 20.00
Vol. 4 TPB (2006, $19.99) r/Rising Stars Bright #1-3 and Voices of the Dead #1-6 20.00
Vol. 5 TPB (2007, $16.99) r/Rising Stars: Untouchable #1-5 and ...: Visitations 17.00
Wizard #0-(3/99) Wizard supplement; Straczynski-s 3.00
Wizard #1/2 5.00

RISING STARS BRIGHT
Image Comics (Top Cow): Mar, 2003 - No. 3, May, 2003 ($2.99, limited series)
1-3-Avery-s/Jurgens & Gorder-a/Beck-c 3.00

RISING STARS: UNTOUCHABLE
Image Comics (Top Cow): Mar, 2006 - No. 5, July, 2006 ($2.99, limited series)
1-5-Avery-s/Anderson-a 3.00

RISING STARS: VOICES OF THE DEAD
Image Comics (Top Cow): June, 2005 - No. 6, Dec, 2005 ($2.99, limited series)
1-6-Avery-s/Staz Johnson-a 3.00

RISING SUN (Based on the CMON board game)
IDW Publishing: Nov, 2019 - Present ($4.99)
1,2-Ron Marz & David Rodriguez-s/Martin Coccolo-a 5.00

RIVERDALE (Based on the 2017 TV series)
Archie Comic Publications: Apr, 2017; May, 2017 - No. 12, Jul, 2018 ($3.99)
1-12: 1-4-Eisma-a. 5-12-Pitilli-a. 6-History of Pop's 4.00
... FCBD Edition (5/18, giveaway) r/#6 3.00
... One-Shot (4/17, $4.99) Short story prologues to the TV series; multiple covers 4.00

RIVERDALE (Volume 2)(Season 3 on cover)
Archie Comic Publications: May, 2019 - No. 5, Sept, 2019 ($3.99)
1-5-Short stories; Ostow-s; art by Pitilli & Eisma 4.00
... FCBD Edition (5/19, giveaway) new story; Ostow-s/Pitilli-a 3.00

RIVERDALE DIGEST (Tie-in to 2017 TV series)
Archie Comic Publications: Jun, 2017 - No. 7, May, 2018 ($5.99/$6.99)
1,2-($5.99): 1-Reprints of first issues of recent 2015-2017 Archie series; Francavilla TV cast-c. 2-Reprints of early 2015-2017 issues and classic reprints 6.00
3-7-($6.99)-Reprints of early 2015-2017 issues and classic reprints 7.00

RIVERDALE HIGH (Archie's... #7,8)
Archie Comics: Aug, 1990 - No. 8, Oct, 1991 ($1.00, bi-monthly)
1 4.00
2-8 3.00

RIVER FEUD (See Zane Grey & Four Color #484)

RIVETS
Dell Publishing Co.: No. 518, Nov, 1953
Four Color 518 5 10 15 31 53 75

RIVETS (A dog)
Argo Publ.: Jan, 1956 - No. 3, May, 1956
1-Reprints Sunday & daily newspaper strips 7 14 21 35 43 50
2,3 5 10 15 22 26 30

ROACHMILL
Blackthorne Publ.: Dec, 1986 - No. 6, Oct, 1987 ($1.75, B&W)
1-6 3.00

ROACHMILL
Dark Horse Comics: May, 1988 - No. 10, Dec, 1990 ($1.75, B&W)
1-10: 10-Contains trading cards 3.00

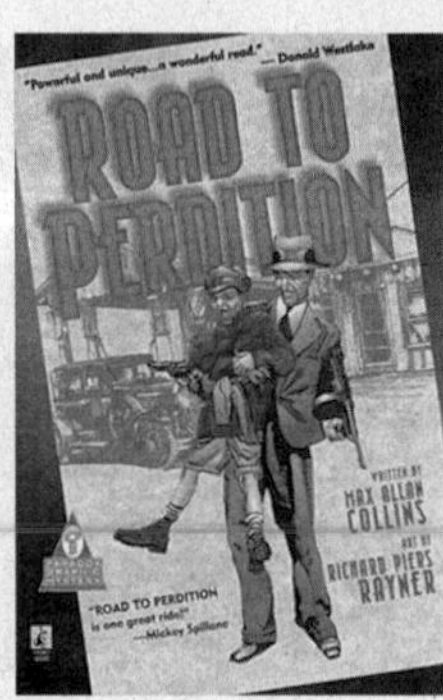

Road to Perdition GN © DC

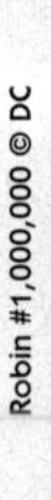
Robin #1,000,000 © DC

Robin Hood Tales #7 © DC

GD VG FN VF VF/NM NM-
2.0 4.0 6.0 8.0 9.0 9.2

ROAD OF THE DEAD: HIGHWAY TO HELL
IDW Publishing: Oct, 2018 - No. 3, Dec, 2018 ($4.99, limited series)
1-3-Jonathan Maberry-s/Drew Moss-a 5.00

ROAD RUNNER (See Beep Beep, the...)

ROAD TO EMPYRE: THE KREE/SKRULL WAR (Leads into Empyre series)
Marvel Comics: May, 2020 ($4.99, one-shot)
1-Thompson-s/De Iulis & Rodriguez-a; origin of Hulkling & Kree/Skrull history re-told 4.00

ROAD TO OZ (Adaptation of the L. Frank Baum book)
Marvel Comics: Nov, 2012 - No. 6, May, 2013 ($3.99, limited series)
1-6-Eric Shanower-s/Skottie Young-a/c 4.00

ROAD TO PERDITION (Inspired the 2002 Tom Hanks/Paul Newman movie)
(Also see On the Road to Perdition)
DC Comics/Paradox Press: 1998, 2002 ($13.95, B&W paperback graphic novel)
nn-(1st printing) Max Allan Collins-s/Richard Piers Rayner-a 30.00
2nd & 3rd printings (2002, $13.95) 14.00
Movie photo cover edition (2002) 14.00

ROADTRIP
Oni Press: Aug, 2000 ($2.95, B&W, one-shot)
1-Reprints Judd Winick's back-up stories from Oni Double Feature #9,10 3.00

ROADWAYS
Cult Press: May, 1994 ($2.75, B&W, limited series)
1 3.00

ROARIN' RICK'S RARE BIT FIENDS
King Hell Press: July, 1994 - No. 21, Aug, 1996 ($2.95, B&W, mature)
1-21: Rick Veitch-c/a/scripts in all. 20-(5/96). 21-(8/96)-Reads Subtleman #1 on cover 3.00
Rabid Eye: The Dream Art of Rick Veitch ($14.95, B&W, TPB)-r/#1-8 & the appendix from #12 15.00
Pocket Universe (6/96, $14.95, B&W, TPB)-Reprints 15.00

ROBERT E. HOWARD'S CONAN THE BARBARIAN
Marvel Comics: 1983 ($2.50, 68 pgs., Baxter paper)
1-r/Savage Tales #2,3 by Smith, c-r/Conan #21 by Smith. 5.00

ROBERT LOUIS STEVENSON'S KIDNAPPED (See Kidnapped)

ROBIN (See Aurora, Birds of Prey, Detective Comics #38, New Teen Titans, Robin II, Robin III, Robin 3000, Star Spangled Comics #65, Teen Titans & Young Justice)

ROBIN (See Batman #457)
DC Comics: Jan, 1991 - No. 5, May, 1991 ($1.00, limited series)
1-Free poster by N. Adams; Bolland-c on all 6.00
1-2nd & 3rd printings (without poster) 3.00
2-5 4.00
2-2nd printing 3.00
Annual 1,2 (1992-93, $2.50, 68 pgs.): 1-Grant/Wagner scripts; Sam Kieth-c. 2-Intro Razorsharp; Jim Balent-c(p) 4.00

ROBIN (See Detective #668) (Also see Red Robin)
DC Comics: Nov, 1993 - No. 183, Apr, 2009 ($1.50/$1.95/$1.99/$2.25/$2.50/$2.99)
1-($2.95)-Collector's edition w/foil embossed-c; 1st app. Robin's car, The Redbird; Azrael as Batman app. 6.00
1-Newsstand ed. 3.00
0,2-49,51-66-Regular editions: 3-5-The Spoiler app. 6-The Huntress-c/story cont'd from Showcase '94 #5. 7-Knightquest: The Conclusion w/new Batman (Azrael) vs. Bruce Wayne. 8-KnightsEnd Pt. 5. 9-KnightsEnd Aftermath; Batman-c & app. 10-(9/94)-Zero Hour. 0-(10/94). 11-(11/94). 25-Green Arrow-c/app. 26-Batman app. 27-Contagion Pt. 3; Catwoman-c/app; Penguin & Azrael app. 28-Contagion Pt. 11. 29-Penguin app. 31-Wildcat-c/app. 32-Legacy Pt. 3. 33-Legacy Pt. 7. 35-Final Night. 46-Genesis. 52,53-Cataclysm pt. 7, conclusion. 55-Green Arrow app. 62-64-Flash-c/app. 3.50
14 ($2.50)-Embossed-c; Troika Pt. 4 4.00
50-($2.95)-Lady Shiva & King Snake app. 4.00
67-74,76-97: 67-72-No Man's Land. 79-Green Arrow app. 86-Pander Bros.-a 3.00
75-($2.95) 4.00
98,99-Bruce Wayne: Murderer x-over pt. 6, 11 3.00
100-($3.50) Last Dixon-s 4.00
101-174: 101-Young Justice x-over. 106-Kevin Lau-c. 121,122-Willingham-s/Mays-a. 125-Tim Drake quits. 126-Spoiler becomes the new Robin. 129-131-War Games. 132-Robin moves to Bludhaven, Batgirl app. 138-Begin $2.50-c. 139-McDaniel-a begins. 146-147-Teen Titans app. 148-One Year Later; new costume. 150-Begin $2.99-c. 152,153-Boomerang app. 168,169-Resurrection of Ra's al Ghul x-over. 174 Spoiler unmasked 3.00
175-183: 175,176-Batman R.I.P. x-over. 180-Robin vs. Red Robin 3.00
#1,000,000 (11/98) 853rd Century x-over 3.00
Annual 3-5: 3-(1994, $2.95)-Elseworlds story. 4-(1995, $2.95)-Year One story.
5-(1996, $2.95)-Legends of the Dead Earth story 4.00
Annual 6 (1997, $3.95)-Pulp Heroes story 4.00
Annual 7 (12/07, $3.99)-Pearson-c/a; prelude to Resurrection of Ra's al Ghul x-over 4.00
.../Argent 1 (2/98, $1.95) Argent (Teen Titans) app. 3.00
.../Batgirl: Fresh Blood TPB (2005, $12.99) r/#132,133 & Batgirl #58,59 13.00
...: Days of Fire and Madness (2006, $12.99, TPB) r/#140-145 13.00
...Eighty-Page Giant 1 (9/00, $5.95) Chuck Dixon-s/Diego Barreto-a 6.00
...: Flying Solo (2000, $12.95, TPB) r/#1-6, Showcase '94 #5,6 13.00
...Plus 1 (12/96, $2.95) Impulse-c/app.; Waid-s 4.00
...Plus 2 (12/97, $2.95) Fang (Scare Tactics) app. 4.00
...: Search For a Hero (2009, $19.99, TPB) r/#175-183; cover gallery 20.00
.../Spoiler Special 1 (8/08, $3.99) Follows Spoiler's return in Robin #174; Dixon-s 4.00
...: Teenage Wasteland (2007, $17.99, TPB) r/#154-162 18.00
...: The Big Leagues (2008, $12.99, TPB) r/#163-167 13.00
...: Unmasked (2004, $12.95, TPB) r/#121-125; Pearson-c 13.00
...: Violent Tendencies (2008, $17.99, TPB) r/#170-174 & Robin/Spoiler Special 1 18.00
....: Wanted (2007, $12.99, TPB) r/#148-153 13.00

ROBIN: A HERO REBORN
DC Comics: 1991 ($4.95, squarebound, trade paperback)
nn-r/Batman #455-457 & Robin #1-5; Bolland-c 2 4 6 8 10 12

ROBIN 80TH ANNIVERSARY 100-PAGE SUPER SPECTACULAR
DC Comics: May, 2020 ($9.99, squarebound, one-shot)
1-Short stories and pin-ups of the various Robins; s/a by various; multiple covers 10.00

ROBIN HOOD (See The Advs. of..., Brave and the Bold, Classic Comics #7, Classics Giveaways (12/44), Four Color #413, 669, King Classics, Movie Comics & Power Record Comics) (...& His Merry Men, The Illustrated Story of...)

ROBIN HOOD (Disney)
Dell Publishing Co.: No. 413, Aug, 1952; No. 669, Dec, 1955
Four Color 413-(1st Disney movie Four Color book)(8/52)-Photo-c 9 18 27 60 120 180
Four Color 669 (12/55)-Reprints #413 plus photo-c 5 10 15 35 63 90

ROBIN HOOD (Adventures of... #6-8)
Magazine Enterprises (Sussex Pub. Co.): No. 52, Nov, 1955 - No. 5, Mar, 1957
52 (#1)-Origin Robin Hood & Sir Gallant of the Round Table 16 32 48 92 144 195
53 (#2), 3-5 12 24 36 69 97 125
I.W. Reprint #1,2,9: 1-r/#3. 2-r/#4. 9-r/#52 (1963) 2 4 6 9 13 16
Super Reprint #10,15: 10-r/#53. 15-r/#5 2 4 6 9 13 16
NOTE: *Bolle a-in all; c-52.*

ROBIN HOOD (Not Disney)
Dell Publishing Co.: May-July, 1963 (one-shot)
1 3 6 9 16 23 30

ROBIN HOOD (Disney) (Also see Best of Walt Disney)
Western Publishing Co.: 1973 ($1.50, 8-1/2x11", 52 pgs., cardboard-c)
96151- "Robin Hood", based on movie, 96152- "The Mystery of Sherwood Forest", 96153- "In King Richard's Service", 96154- "The Wizard's Ring" each.... 3 6 9 15 22 28

ROBIN HOOD
Eclipse Comics: July, 1991 - No. 3, Dec, 1991 ($2.50, limited series)
1-3: Timothy Truman layouts 3.00

ROBIN HOOD AND HIS MERRY MEN (Formerly Danger & Adventure)
Charlton Comics: No. 28, Apr, 1956 - No. 38, Aug, 1958
28 10 20 30 54 72 90
29-37 8 16 24 42 54 65
38-Ditko-a (5 pgs.); Rocke-c 14 28 42 76 108 140

ROBIN HOOD TALES (Published by National Periodical #7 on)
Quality Comics Group (Comic Magazines): Feb, 1956 - No. 6, Nov-Dec, 1956
1-All have Baker/Cuidera-c 34 68 102 199 325 450
2-6-Matt Baker-a 32 64 96 192 314 435

ROBIN HOOD TALES (Cont'd from Quality series)(See Brave & the Bold #5)
National Periodical Publ.: No. 7, Jan-Feb, 1957 - No. 14, Mar-Apr, 1958
7-All have Andru/Esposito-c 36 72 108 211 343 475
8-14 30 60 90 177 289 400

ROBIN RISES: OMEGA (See Batman & Robin #33-37)
DC Comics: Sept, 2014; Feb, 2015 ($4.99, one-shots)
Alpha 1 (2/15)-Tomasi-s/Andy Kubert-a/c; Damien returns; Talia app. 5.00
Omega 1 (9/14)-Tomasi-s/Andy Kubert-a/c; Ra's al Ghul and Justice League app. 5.00

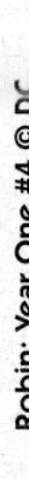
Robin: Year One #4 © DC

Robocop: Last Stand #1 © Orion

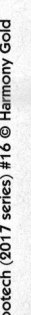

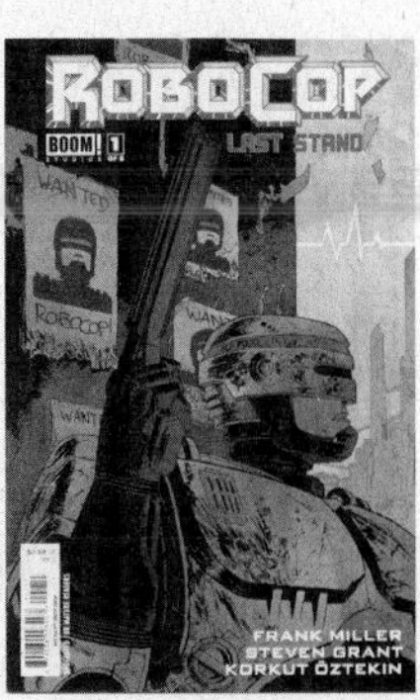

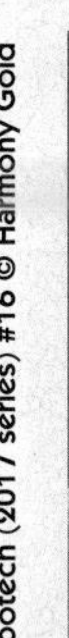
Robotech (2017 series) #16 © Harmony Gold

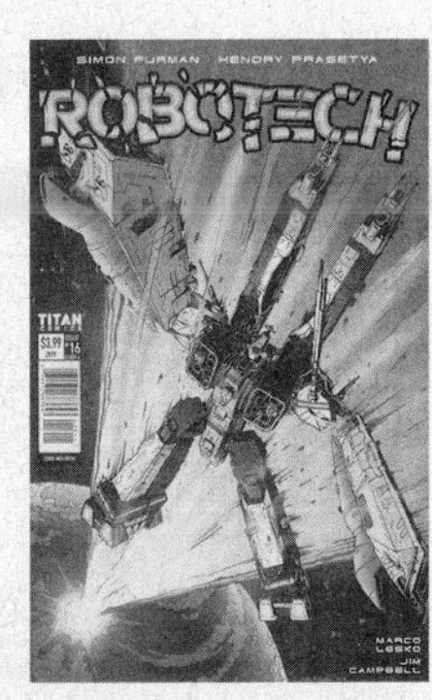

	GD 2.0	VG 4.0	FN 6.0	VF 8.0	VF/NM 9.0	NM- 9.2

ROBINSON CRUSOE (See King Classics & Power Record Comics)
Dell Publishing Co.: Nov-Jan, 1963-64

1	3	6	9	15	21	26

ROBIN: SON OF BATMAN (Damian Wayne)
DC Comics: Aug, 2015 - No. 13, Aug, 2016 ($3.99)

1-13: 1-Gleason-s/a. 4-Deathstroke app. 5-Damian vs. Talia. 7-"Robin War" tie-in 4.00

ROBIN II (The Joker's Wild)
DC Comics: Oct, 1991 - No. 4, Dec, 1991 ($1.50, mini-series)

1-(Direct sales, $1.50)-With 4 diff.-c; same hologram on each 6.00
1-(Newsstand, $1.00)-No hologram; 1 version 4.00
1-Collector's set ($10.00)-Contains all 5 versions bagged with hologram trading card inside 18.00
2-(Direct sales, $1.50)-With 3 different-c 5.00
2-4-(Newsstand, $1.00)-1 version of each 4.00
2-Collector's set ($8.00)-Contains all 4 versions bagged with hologram trading card inside 12.00
3-(Direct sale, $1.50)-With 2 different-c 4.00
3-Collector's set ($6.00)-Contains all 3 versions bagged with hologram trading card inside 10.00
4-(Direct sales, $1.50)-Only one version 4.00
4-Collector's set ($4.00)-Contains both versions bagged with Bat-Signal hologram trading card 6.00
Multi-pack (All four issues w/hologram sticker) 14.00
Deluxe Complete Set ($30.00)-Contains all 14 versions of #1-4 plus a new hologram trading card; numbered & limited to 25,000; comes with slipcase & 2 acid free backing boards 45.00

ROBIN III: CRY OF THE HUNTRESS
DC Comics: Dec, 1992 - No. 6, Mar, 1993 (Limited series)

1-6 ($2.50, collector's ed.)-Polybagged w/movement enhanced-c plus mini-poster of newsstand-c by Zeck 5.00
1-6 ($1.25, newsstand ed.): All have Zeck-c 4.00

ROBIN 3000
DC Comics (Elseworlds): 1992 - No. 2, 1992 ($4.95, mini-series, 52 pgs.)

1,2-Foil logo; Russell-c/a 6.00

ROBIN WAR (Crossover with Grayson, Robin: Son of Batman, and We Are Robin)
DC Comics: Feb, 2016 - No. 2, Mar, 2016 ($4.99)

1,2-Tom King-s; art by various; The Court of Owls app. 5.00

ROBIN: YEAR ONE
DC Comics: 2000 - No. 4, 2001 ($4.95, square-bound, limited series)

1-4: Earliest days of Robin's career; Javier Pulido-c/a. 2,4-Two-Face app. 6.00
TPB (2002, 2008, $14.95/$14.99, 2 printings) r/#1-4 15.00

ROBOCOP
Marvel Comics: Oct, 1987 ($2.00, B&W, magazine, one-shot)

1-Movie adaptation	2	4	6	8	10	12

ROBOCOP (Also see Dark Horse Comics)
Marvel Comics: Mar, 1990 - No. 23, Jan, 1992 ($1.50)

1-Based on movie	1	3	4	6	8	10
2-23						3.00
nn (7/90, $4.95, 52 pgs.)-r/B&W magazine in color; adapts 1st movie						5.00

ROBOCOP
Dynamite Entertainment: 2010 - No. 6, 2010 ($3.50, limited series)

1-6-Follows the events of the first film; Neves-a 3.50

ROBOCOP
BOOM! Studios: Jul, 2014 - No. 12, Jun, 2015 ($3.99)

1-12: 1-8-Williamson-s/Magno-a. 1-Multiple covers. 9,10-Aragon-a 4.00

ROBOCOP (FRANK MILLER'S...)
Avatar Press: July, 2003 - No. 9, Jan, 2006 ($3.50/$3.99, limited series)

1-9-Frank Miller-s/Juan Ryp-a. 1-Three covers by Miller, Ryp, and Barrows. 2-Two covers 4.00
Free Comic Book Day Edition (4/03) Previews Robocop & Stargate SG•1; Busch-c 3.00

ROBOCOP (Tie-ins to the 2014 movie)
BOOM! Studios: Feb, 2014 ($3.99)

...: Beta (2/14) Brisson-s/Laiso-a 4.00
...: Hominem Ex Machina (2/14) Moreci-s/Copland-a 4.00
...: Memento Mori (2/14) Barbiere-s/Vieira-a 4.00
...: To Live and Die in Detroit (2/14) Joe Harris-s/Piotr Kowalski-a 4.00

ROBOCOP: CITIZENS ARREST
BOOM! Studios: Apr, 2018 - No. 5, Aug, 2018 ($3.99, limited series)

1-5-Brian Wood-s/Jorge Coelho-a 4.00

ROBOCOP: LAST STAND
BOOM! Studios: Aug, 2013 - No. 8, Mar, 2014 ($3.99, limited series)

1-8: 1-Miller & Grant-s/Oztekin-a 4.00

ROBOCOP: MORTAL COILS
Dark Horse Comics: Sept, 1993 - No. 4, Dec, 1993 ($2.50, limited series)

1-4: 1,2-Cago painted-c 4.00

ROBOCOP: PRIME SUSPECT
Dark Horse Comics: Oct, 1992 - No. 4, Jan, 1993 ($2.50, limited series)

1-4: 1,3-Nelson painted-c. 2,4-Bolton painted-c 4.00

ROBOCOP: ROAD TRIP
Dynamite Entertainment: 2012 - No. 4, 2012 ($3.99, limited series)

1-4-De Zarate-a 4.00

ROBOCOP: ROULETTE
Dark Horse Comics: Dec, 1993 - No. 4, 1994 ($2.50, limited series)

1-4: 1,3-Nelson painted-c. 2,4-Bolton painted-c 4.00

ROBOCOP 2
Marvel Comics: Aug, 1990 ($2.25, B&W, magazine, 68 pgs.)

1-Adapts movie sequel scripted by Frank Miller; Bagley-a 5.00

ROBOCOP 2
Marvel Comics: Aug, 1990; Late Aug, 1990 - #3, Late Sept, 1990 ($1.00, limited series)

nn-(8/90, $4.95, 68 pgs., color)-Same contents as B&W magazine 5.00
1: #1-3 reprint no number issue 3.00
2,3: 2-Guice-c(i) 3.00

ROBOCOP 3
Dark Horse Comics: July, 1993 - No. 3, Nov, 1993 ($2.50, limited series)

1-3: Nelson painted-c; Nguyen-a(p) 4.00

ROBOCOP VERSUS THE TERMINATOR
Dark Horse Comics: Sept, 1992 - No. 4, 1992 (Dec.) ($2.50, limited series)

1-4: Miller scripts & Simonson-c/a in all 4.00
1-Platinum Edition 10.00
NOTE: *All contain a different Robocop cardboard cut-out stand-up.*

ROBO DOJO
DC Comics (WildStorm): Apr, 2002 - No. 6, Sept, 2002 ($2.95, limited series)

1-6-Wolfman-s 3.00

ROBO-HUNTER (Also see Sam Slade...)
Eagle Comics: Apr, 1984 - No. 5, 1984 ($1.00)

1-5-2000 A.D. 4.00

R.O.B.O.T. BATTALION 2050
Eclipse Comics: Mar, 1988 ($2.00, B&W, one-shot)

1 3.00

ROBOT COMICS
Renegade Press: No. 0, June, 1987 ($2.00, B&W, one-shot)

0-Bob Burden story & art 3.00

ROBOTECH
Antarctic Press: Mar, 1997 - No. 11, Nov, 1998 ($2.95)

1-11, Annual 1 (4/98, $2.95) 4.00
...Class Reunion (12/98, $3.95, B&W) 4.00
...Escape (5/98, $2.95, B&W), ...Final Fire (12/98, $2.95, B&W) 4.00

ROBOTECH
DC Comics (WildStorm): No. 0, Feb, 2003 - No. 6, Jul, 2003 ($2.50/$2.95, limited series)

0-Tommy Yune-s; art by Jim Lee, Garza, Bermejo and others; pin-up pages by various 3.00
1-6 ($2.95)-Long Vo-a 3.00
...: From the Stars (2003, $9.95, digest-size) r/#0-6 & Sourcebook 10.00
... Sourcebook (3/03, $2.95) pin-ups and info on characters and mecha; art by various 3.00

ROBOTECH
Titan Comics: Aug, 2017 - No. 24, Oct, 2019 ($3.99)

1-24: 1-11-Brian Wood-s/Marco Turini-a; multiple covers on each. 12-14-Prasetya-a 4.00
... Free Comic Book Day 2019 - Furman-s/Prasetya-a 3.00

ROBOTECH: COVERT-OPS
Antarctic Press: Aug, 1998 - No. 2, Sept, 1998 ($2.95, B&W, limited series)

1,2-Gregory Lane-s/a 4.00

Robotech: Vermilion #1 © Harmony Gold

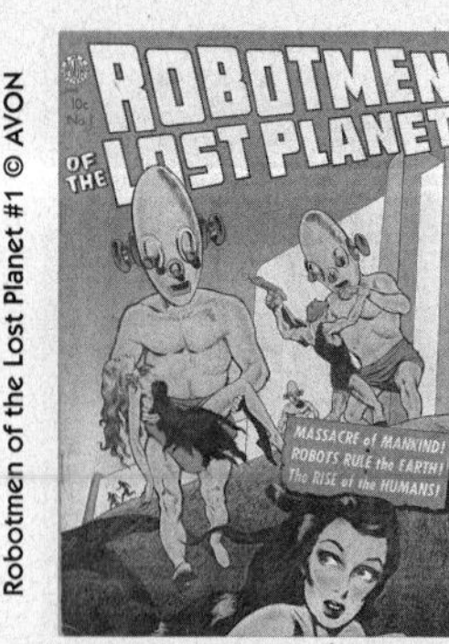

Robotmen of the Lost Planet #1 © AVON

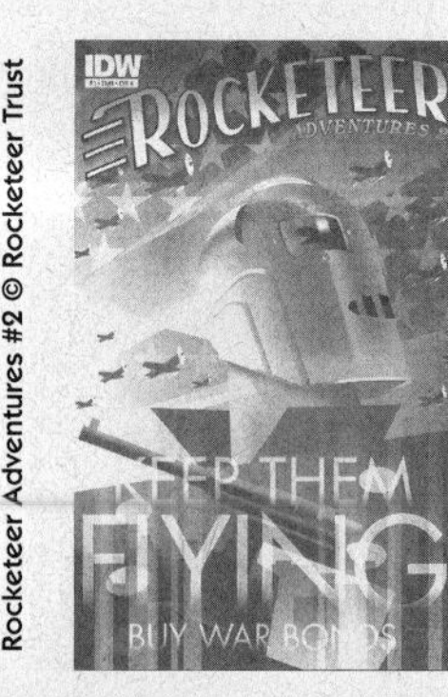

Rocketeer Adventures #2 © Rocketeer Trust

	GD	VG	FN	VF	VF/NM	NM-
	2.0	4.0	6.0	8.0	9.0	9.2

ROBOTECH DEFENDERS
DC Comics: Mar, 1985 - No. 2, Apr, 1985 (Mini-series)
1,2 4.00

ROBOTECH IN 3-D (TV)
Comico: Aug, 1987 ($2.50)
1-Steacy painted-c 5.00

ROBOTECH: INVASION
DC Comics (WildStorm): Feb, 2004 - No. 5, July, 2004 ($2.95, limited series)
1-5-Faerber & Yune-s/Miyazawa & Dogan-a 3.00

ROBOTECH: LOVE AND WAR
DC Comics (WildStorm): Aug, 2003 - No. 6, Jan, 2004 ($2.95, limited series)
1-6-Long Vo & Charles Park-a/Faerber & Yune-s. 2-Variant-c by Warren 3.00

ROBOTECH MASTERS (TV)
Comico: July, 1985 - No. 23, Apr, 1988 ($1.50)
1 6.00
2-23 4.00

ROBOTECH: PRELUDE TO THE SHADOW CHRONICLES
DC Comics (WildStorm): Dec, 2005 - No. 5, Mar, 2006 ($3.50, limited series)
1-5-Yune-s/Dogan & Udon Studios-a 3.50
TPB (2010, $17.99) r/#1-5; production art 18.00

ROBOTECH: REMIX
Titan Comics: Nov, 2019 - Present ($3.99)
1-4-Continues from Robotech 2017-19 series; Fletcher-s/Damaso-a 4.00

ROBOTECH: SENTINELS - RUBICON
Antarctic Press: July, 1998 ($2.95, B&W)
1 4.00

ROBOTECH SPECIAL
Comico: May, 1988 ($2.50, one-shot, 44 pgs.)
1-Steacy wraparound-c; partial photo-c 5.00

ROBOTECH THE GRAPHIC NOVEL
Comico: Aug, 1986 ($5.95, 8-1/2x11", 52 pgs.)
1-Origin SDF-1; intro T.R. Edwards, Steacy-c/a 15.00
1-Second printing (12/86) 10.00

ROBOTECH: THE MACROSS SAGA (TV)(Formerly Macross)
Comico: No. 2, Feb, 1985 - No. 36, Feb, 1989 ($1.50)
2 1 2 3 5 6 8
3-10 5.00
11-36: 12,17-Ken Steacy painted-c. 26-Begin $1.75-c. 35,36-($1.95) 4.00
Volume 1-4 TPB (WildStorm, 2003, $14.95, 5-3/4" x 8-1/4")1-Reprints #2-6 & Macross #1. 2- r/#7-12. 3-r/#13-18. 4-r/#19-24 15.00

ROBOTECH: THE NEW GENERATION
Comico: July, 1985 - No. 25, July, 1988
1 6.00
2-25 4.00

ROBOTECH: VERMILION
Antarctic Press: Mar, 1997 - No. 4, ($2.95, B&W, limited series)
1-4 4.00

ROBOTECH / VOLTRON
Dynamite Entertainment: 2013 - No. 5, 2014 ($3.99, limited series)
1-5-Tommy Yune-s 4.00

ROBOTECH: WINGS OF GIBRALTAR
Antarctic Press: Aug, 1998 - No. 2, Sept, 1998 ($2.95, B&W, limited series)
1,2-Lee Duhig-s/a 4.00

ROBOTIX
Marvel Comics: Feb, 1986 (75¢, one-shot)
1-Based on toy 4.00

ROBOTMEN OF THE LOST PLANET (Also see Space Thrillers)
Avon Periodicals: 1952 (Also see Strange Worlds #19)
1-McCann-a (3 pgs.); Fawcette-a 181 362 543 1158 1979 2800

ROB ROY
Dell Publishing Co.: 1954 (Disney-Movie)
Four Color 544-Manning-a, photo-c 8 16 24 52 99 145

ROCK, THE (WWF Wrestling)

	GD	VG	FN	VF	VF/NM	NM-
	2.0	4.0	6.0	8.0	9.0	9.2

Chaos! Comics: June, 2001 ($2.99, one-shot)
1-Photo-c; Grant-s/Neves-a 4.00

ROCK & ROLL HIGH SCHOOL
Roger Corman's Cosmic Comics: Oct, 1995 ($2.50)
1-Bob Fingerman scripts 3.00

ROCK AND ROLLO (Formerly TV Teens)
Charlton Comics: V2#14, Oct, 1957 - No. 19, Sept, 1958
V2#14-19 6 12 18 31 38 45

ROCK COMICS
Landgraphic Publ.: Jul/Aug, 1979 ($1.25, tabloid size, 28 pgs.)
1-N. Adams-c; Thor (not Marvel's) story by Adams 3 6 9 14 20 25

ROCKET (Rocket Raccoon from Guardians of the Galaxy)
Marvel Comics: Jul, 2017 - No. 6, Dec, 2017 ($3.99, limited series)
1-6: 1-Ewing-s/Gorham-a/Mayhew-c. 4-Deadpool app. 4.00

ROCKET COMICS
Hillman Periodicals: Mar, 1940 - No. 3, May, 1940
1-Rocket Riley, Red Roberts the Electro Man (origin), The Phantom Ranger, The Steel Shark, The Defender, Buzzard Barnes and his Sky Devils, Lefty Larson, & The Defender, the Man with a Thousand Faces begin (1st app. of each); all have Rocket Riley-c 300 600 900 2070 3635 5200
2,3: 2-Jack Cole-a 213 426 639 1363 2332 3300

ROCKET COMICS: IGNITE
Dark Horse Comics: Apr, 2003 (Free Comic Book Day giveaway)
1-Previews Dark Horse series Syn, Lone, and Go Boy 7 3.00

ROCKETEER, THE (See Eclipse Graphic Album Series, Pacific Presents & Starslayer)

ROCKETEER ADVENTURE MAGAZINE, THE
Comico/Dark Horse Comics No. 3: July, 1988 ($2.00); No. 2, July, 1989 ($2.75); No. 3, Jan, 1995 ($2.95)
1-(7/88, $2.00)-Dave Stevens-c/a in all; Kaluta back-up-a; 1st app. Jonas (character based on The Shadow) 2 4 6 9 13 16
2-(7/89, $2.75)-Stevens/Dorman painted-c 1 3 4 6 8 10
3-(1/95, $2.95)-Includes pinups by Stevens, Gulacy, Plunkett, & Mignola 5.00
Volume 2-(9/96, $9.95, magazine size TPB)-Reprints #1-3 10.00

ROCKETEER ADVENTURES
IDW Publishing: May, 2011 - No. 4, Aug, 2011 ($3.99, limited series)
1-4-Anthology of new stories by various; covers by Alex Ross and Dave Stevens 4.00
The Rocketeer: The Best of Rocketeer Adventures: Funko Edition 1 (1/18, $4.99) r/stories from series; art by Cassaday, Ha, Kaluta, Sakai, & Weston; Funko fig cover 5.00

ROCKETEER ADVENTURES VOLUME 2
IDW Publishing: Mar, 2012 - No. 4, Jun, 2012 ($3.99, limited series)
1-4-Anthology by various; covers by Darwyn Cooke and Stevens. 1-Sakai-a. 4-Simonson & Byrne-a 4.00

ROCKETEER AT WAR, THE
IDW Publishing: Dec, 2015 - No. 4, Apr, 2016 ($4.99, limited series)
1-4-Guggenheim-s; covers by Bullock & Bradshaw. 1,2-Bullock-a. 3,4-J. Bone-a 5.00

ROCKETEER: CARGO OF DOOM
IDW Publishing: Aug, 2012 - No. 4, Nov, 2012 ($3.99, limited series)
1-4-Waid-s/Samnee-a/c; variant-c by Stevens on all 4.00

ROCKETEER: HOLLYWOOD HORROR
IDW Publishing: Feb, 2013 - No. 4, May, 2013 ($3.99, limited series)
1-4-Langridge-s/Bone-a/Simonson-c; variant-c on all 4.00

ROCKETEER JETPACK TREASURY EDITION
IDW Publishing: Nov, 2011 ($9.99, oversized 13" x 9-3/4" format)
1-Recolored r/Starslayer #1-3, Pacific Presents #1,2 & Rocketeer Special Edition 10.00

ROCKETEER SPECIAL EDITION, THE
Eclipse Comics: Nov, 1984 ($1.50, Baxter paper)(Chapter 5 of Rocketeer serial)
1-Stevens-c/a; Kaluta back-c; pin-ups inside 3 6 9 14 20 25
NOTE: *Originally intended to be published in Pacific Presents.*

ROCKETEER, THE: THE COMPLETE ADVENTURES
IDW Publishing: Oct, 2009 ($29.99/$75.00, hardcover)
HC-Reprints of Dave Stevens' Rocketeer stories in Starslayer #1-3, Pacific Presents #1,2, Rocketeer Special Edition and Rocketeer Adventure Magazine #1-3; all re-colored 30.00
... Deluxe Edition ($75.00, 8"x12" slipcased HC) larger size reprints of HC content plus 100 bonus pages of sketch art, layouts, design work; intro. by Thomas Jane 110.00

Rocket Girl #1 © Montclare & Reeder

Rock Fantasy Comics #9 © RFC

Rocky Lane Western #5 © FAW

	GD 2.0	VG 4.0	FN 6.0	VF 8.0	VF/NM 9.0	NM- 9.2

... Deluxe Edition 2nd printing ($75.00, oversized slipcased HC) 75.00

ROCKETEER, THE: THE OFFICIAL MOVIE ADAPTATION
W. D. Publications (Disney): 1991
nn-($5.95, 68 pgs.)-Squarebound deluxe edition 6.00
nn-($2.95, 68 pgs.)-Stapled regular edition 4.00
3-D Comic Book (1991, $7.98, 52 pgs.) 8.00

ROCKETEER/THE SPIRIT: PULP FRICTION
IDW Publishing: Jul, 2013 - No. 4, Dec, 2013 ($3.99, limited series)
1-4: 1-Waid-s/Paul Smith-a; covers by Smith & Darwyn Cooke. 2-Wallace-a. 3,4-Bone-a 4.00

ROCKET GIRL
Image Comics: Oct, 2013 - No. 10, Oct, 2017 ($3.50/$3.99)
1-10-Brandon Montclare-a/Amy Reeder-a/c. 6-Begin $3.99-c 4.00

ROCKET KELLY (See The Bouncer, Green Mask #10); becomes Li'l Pan #6)
Fox Feature Syndicate: 1944; Fall, 1945 - No. 5, Oct-Nov, 1946
nn (1944), 1 (Fall, 1945) 45 90 135 284 480 675
2-The Puppeteer app. (costumed hero) 34 68 102 199 325 450
3-5: 5-(#5 on cover, #4 inside) 29 58 87 172 281 390

ROCKETMAN (Strange Fantasy #2 on) (See Hello Pal & Scoop Comics)
Ajax/Farrell Publications: June, 1952 (Strange Stories of the Future)
1-Rocketman & Cosmo 57 114 171 362 619 875

ROCKET RACCOON (Also see Marvel Preview #7 and Incredible Hulk #271)
Marvel Comics: May, 1985 - No. 4, Aug, 1985 (color, limited series)
1-Mignola-a/Mantlo-s in all 4 8 12 28 47 65
2-4 2 4 6 11 16 20
...: Tales From Half-World 1 (10/13, $7.99) r/#1-4; new cover by McNiven 8.00

ROCKET RACCOON (Guardians of the Galaxy)
Marvel Comics: Sept, 2014 - No. 11, Jul, 2015 ($3.99)
1-Skottie Young-s/a; Groot app. 5.00
2-11-Skottie Young-s. 7,8-Andrade-a 4.00
Free Comic Book Day 2014 (5/14, giveaway) Archer-a; Groot and Wal-rus app. 3.00

ROCKET RACCOON (Guardians of the Galaxy)
Marvel Comics: Feb, 2017 - No. 5, Jun, 2017 ($3.99)
1-5-Rosenberg-s/Coelho-a. 1-Johnny Storm app. 2-5-Kraven app. 4.00

ROCKET RACCOON & GROOT (Guardians of the Galaxy)
Marvel Comics: Mar, 2016 - No. 10, Nov, 2016 ($3.99)
1-10: 1-6-Skottie Young-s. 1-3-Filipe Andrade-a. 8-10-Gwenpool app. 4.00

ROCKET SHIP X
Fox Feature Syndicate: September, 1951; 1952
1 71 142 213 454 777 1100
1952 (nn, nd, no publ.)-Edited 1951-c (exist?) 41 82 123 256 428 600

ROCKET TO ADVENTURE LAND (See Pixie Puzzle...)

ROCKET TO THE MOON
Avon Periodicals: 1951
nn-Orlando-c/a; adapts Otis Adelbert Kline's "Maza of the Moon"
184 368 552 1178 2014 2850

ROCK FANTASY COMICS
Rock Fantasy Comics: Dec, 1989 - No. 16?, 1991 ($2.25/$3.00, B&W)(No cover price)
1-Pink Floyd part 1 5.00
1-2nd printing ($3.00-c) 3.00
2,3: 2-Rolling Stones #1. 3-Led Zeppelin #1 4.00
2,3: 2nd printings ($3.00-c, 1/90 & 2/90) 3.00
4-Stevie Nicks Not published
5-Monstrosities of Rock #1; photo back-c 4.00
5-2nd printing ($3.00, 3/90 indicia, 2/90-c) 3.00
6-9,11-15,17,18: 6-Guns n' Roses #1 (1st & 2nd printings, 3/90)-Begin $3.00-c. 7-Sex Pistols #1. 8-Alice Cooper; not published. 9-Van Halen #1; photo back-c. 11-Jimi Hendrix #1; wraparound-c 3.00
10-Kiss #1; photo back-c 2 4 6 8 10 12
16-($5.00, 68 pgs.)-The Great Gig in the Sky(Floyd) 5.00

ROCK HAPPENING (See Bunny and Harvey Pop Comics:...)

ROCK N' ROLL COMICS
DC Comics: Dec./Jan 1956 (ashcan)
nn-Ashcan comic, not distributed to newsstands, only for in house use (no known sales)

ROCK N' ROLL COMICS
Revolutionary Comics: Jun, 1989 - No. 65 ($1.50/$1.95/$2.50, B&W/col. #15 on)
1-Guns N' Roses 1 3 4 6 8 10
1-2nd thru 7th printings. 7th printing (full color w/new-c/a) 3.00
2-Metallica 1 3 4 6 8 10
2-2nd thru 6th printings (6th in color) 3.00
3-Bon Jovi (no reprints) 1 2 3 5 6 8
4-8,10-65: 4-Motley Crue(2nd printing only, 1st destroyed). 5-Def Leppard (2 printings). 6-Rolling Stones(4 printings). 7-The Who (3 printings). 8-Skid Row; not published. 10-Warrant/Whitesnake(2 printings; 1st has 2 diff.-c). 11-Aerosmith (2 printings?). 12-New Kids on the Block(2 printings). 12-3rd printing; rewritten & titled NKOTB Hate Book. 13-Led Zeppelin. 14-Sex Pistols. 15-Poison; 1st color issue. 16-Van Halen. 17-Madonna. 18-Alice Cooper. 19-Public Enemy/2 Live Crew. 20-Queensryche/Tesla. 21-Prince? 22-AC/DC; begin $2.50-c. 23-Living Colour. 26-Michael Jackson. 29-Ozzy. 45,46-Grateful Dead. 49-Rush. 50,51-Bob Dylan. 56-David Bowie 5.00
9-Kiss 2 4 6 8 10 12
9-2nd & 3rd printings 3.00
NOTE: *Most issues were reprinted except #3. Later reprints are in color. #8 was not released.*

ROCKO'S MODERN AFTERLIFE (TV)
BOOM! Studios (kaboom!): Apr, 2019 - No. 4, Jul, 2019 ($3.99, limited series)
1-4-Burch-s/Di Meo-a; multiple covers; the undead attach O-Town 4.00

ROCKO'S MODERN LIFE (TV) (Nickelodeon cartoon)
Marvel Comics: June, 1994 - No. 7, Dec, 1994 ($1.95)
1-7 3.00

ROCKO'S MODERN LIFE (TV) (Nickelodeon cartoon)
BOOM! Studios (kaboom!): Dec, 2017 - No. 8, Sept, 2018 ($3.99)
1-8-Ferrier-s/McGinty-a; multiple covers 4.00

ROCKSTARS
Image Comics: Dec, 2016 - No. 8 ($3.99)
1-8-Joe Harris-s/Megan Hutchison-a 4.00

ROCKY AND BULLWINKLE (TV)
IDW Publishing: Mar, 2014 - No. 4, Jun, 2014 ($3.99)
1-4-Evanier-s/Langridge-a; bonus Dudley Do-Right short story in each; two covers 4.00

ROCKY AND BULLWINKLE SHOW, THE (TV)
American Mythology: 2017 - No. 3, 2018 ($3.99, limited series)
1-3: 1-New short stories and reprints from Bullwinkle #1&2; three covers 4.00

ROCKY AND BULLWINKLE (TV)
American Mythology: 2019 - 2020 ($3.99, one-shots)
... As Seen on TV 1-3 (2019-2020, $3.99) new story & reprints; Peabody & Sherman app. 4.00
... Present: The Best of Boris & Natasha 1 (2019, $3.99) reprints from 1973-1976 4.00
... Present: The Best of Dudley Do-Right of the Mounties 1 (2019, $3.99) reps. from 1973 4.00
... Present: The Best of Mr. Peaboy & Sherman 1 (2019, $3.99) reprints from 1963-1974 4.00

ROCKY AND HIS FIENDISH FRIENDS (TV)(Bullwinkle)
Gold Key: Oct, 1962 - No. 5, Sept, 1963 (Jay Ward)
1 (25¢, 80 pgs.) 13 26 39 89 195 300
2,3 (25¢, 80 pgs.) 9 18 27 62 126 190
4,5 (Regular size, 12¢) 7 14 21 46 86 125

ROCKY AND HIS FRIENDS (See Kite Fun Book & March of Comics #216 in the Promotional Comics section)

ROCKY AND HIS FRIENDS (TV)
Dell Publishing Co.: No. 1128, 8-10/60 - No.1311,1962 (Jay Ward)
Four Color 1128 (#1) (8-10/60) 26 52 78 182 404 625
Four Color 1152 (12-2/61), 1166, 1208, 1275, 1311('62)
16 32 48 107 236 365

ROCKY HORROR PICTURE SHOW THE COMIC BOOK, THE
Caliber Press: Jul, 1990 - No. 3, Jan, 1991 ($2.95, mini-series, 52 pgs.)
1-3: 1-Adapts cult film plus photos, etc., 1-2nd printing
2 4 6 8 11 14
...Collection ($4.95) 2 4 6 9 13 16

ROCKY JONES SPACE RANGER (See Space Adventures #15-18)

ROCKY JORDEN PRIVATE EYE (See Private Eye)

ROCKY LANE WESTERN (Allan Rocky Lane starred in Republic movies & TV for a short time as Allan Lane, Red Ryder & Rocky Lane) (See Black Jack Fawcett Movie Comics, Motion Picture Comics & Six-Gun Heroes)
Fawcett Publications/Charlton No. 56 on: May, 1949 - No. 87, Nov, 1959
1 (36 pgs.)-Rocky, his stallion Black Jack, & Slim Pickens begin; photo-c begin, end #57; photo back-c 55 110 165 352 601 850
2 (36 pgs.)-Last photo back-c 22 44 66 132 216 300
3-5 (52 pgs.): 4-Captain Tootsie by Beck 17 34 51 98 154 210
6,10 (36 pgs.): 10-Complete western novelette "Badman's Reward"

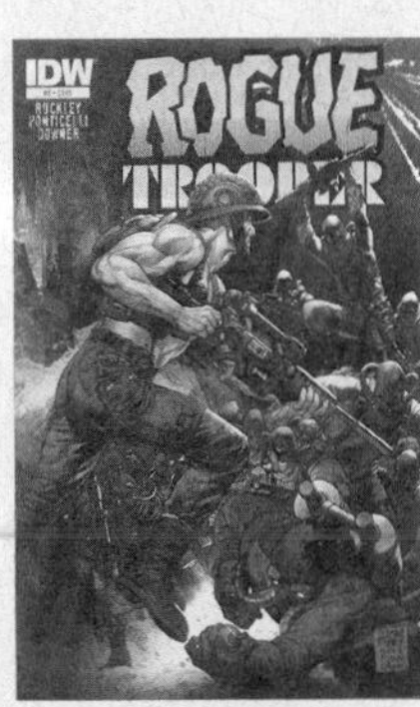

Rogue Trooper #2 © Rebellion

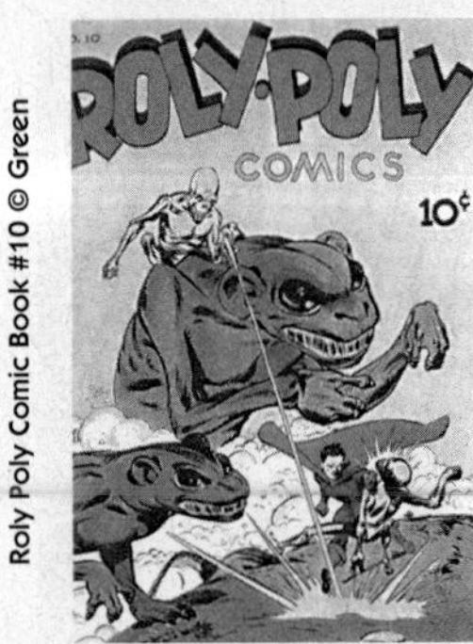

Roly Poly Comic Book #10 © Green

Rom (2016 series) #4 © Hasbro

	GD 2.0	VG 4.0	FN 6.0	VF 8.0	VF/NM 9.0	NM- 9.2
	14	28	42	76	108	140
7-9 (52 pgs.)	14	28	42	82	121	160
11-13,15-17,19,20 (52 pgs.): 15-Black Jack's Hitching Post begins, ends #25. 20-Last Slim Pickens	12	24	36	67	94	120
14,18 (36 pgs.)	10	20	30	58	79	100
21,23,24 (52 pgs.): 21-Dee Dickens begins, ends #55,57,65-68	10	20	30	58	79	100
22,25-28,30 (36 pgs. begin)	10	20	30	54	72	90
29-Classic complete novel "The Land of Missing Men" with hidden land of ancient temple ruins (r-in #65)	14	28	42	76	108	140
31-40	9	18	27	52	69	85
41-54	9	18	27	47	61	75
55-Last Fawcett issue (1/54)	9	18	27	52	69	85
56-1st Charlton issue (2/54)-Photo-c	14	28	42	82	121	160
57,60-Photo-c	10	20	30	54	72	90
58,59,61-64,66-78,80-86: 59-61-Young Falcon app. 64-Slim Pickens app. 66-68: Reprints #30,31,32	8	16	24	44	57	70
65-r/#29, "The Land of Missing Men"	9	18	27	50	65	80
79-Giant Edition (68 pgs.)	10	20	30	58	79	100
87-Last issue	9	18	27	52	69	85

NOTE: *Complete novels in #10, 14, 18, 22, 25, 30-32, 36, 38, 39, 49. Captain Tootsie in #4, 12, 20. Big Bow and Little Arrow in #11, 28, 63. Black Jack's Hitching Post in #15-25, 64, 73.*

ROCKY LANE WESTERN
AC Comics: 1989 ($2.50, B&W, one-shot?)

1-Photo-c; Giordano reprints — 4.00
Annual 1 (1991, $2.95, B&W, 44 pgs.)-photo front/back & inside-c; reprints — 4.00

ROD CAMERON WESTERN (Movie star)
Fawcett Publications: Feb, 1950 - No. 20, Apr, 1953

	GD	VG	FN	VF	VF/NM	NM-
1-Rod Cameron, his horse War Paint, & Sam The Sheriff begin; photo front/back-c begin	31	62	93	182	296	410
2	15	30	45	90	140	190
3-Novel length story "The Mystery of the Seven Cities of Cibola"	14	28	42	82	121	160
4-10: 9-Last photo back-c	12	24	36	69	97	125
11-19	10	20	30	58	79	100
20-Last issue & photo-c	11	22	33	62	86	110

NOTE: *Novel length stories in No. 1-8, 12-14.*

RODEO RYAN (See A-1 Comics #8)

ROGAN GOSH
DC Comics (Vertigo): 1994 ($6.95, one-shot)

nn-Peter Milligan scripts — 7.00

ROGER DODGER (Also in Exciting Comics #57 on)
Standard Comics: No. 5, Aug, 1952

	GD	VG	FN	VF	VF/NM	NM-
5-Teen-age	17	34	51	103	162	220

ROGER RABBIT (Also see Marvel Graphic Novel)
Disney Comics: June, 1990 - No. 18, Nov, 1991 ($1.50)

	GD	VG	FN	VF	VF/NM	NM-
1-All new stories	1	3	4	6	8	10
2-18-All new stories						4.00
In 3-D 1 (1992, $2.50)-Sold at Wal-Mart?; w/glasses	1	2	3	5	6	8

ROGER RABBIT'S TOONTOWN
Disney Comics: Aug, 1991 - No. 5, Dec, 1991 ($1.50)

1-5 — 4.00

ROGER ZELAZNY'S AMBER: THE GUNS OF AVALON
DC Comics: 1996 - No. 3, 1996 ($6.95, limited series)

1-3: Based on novel — 7.00

ROG 2000
Pacific Comics: June, 1982 ($2.95, 44 pgs., B&W, one-shot, magazine)

	GD	VG	FN	VF	VF/NM	NM-
nn-Byrne-c/a (r)	2	4	6	8	11	14
2nd printing (7/82)	1	2	3	4	5	7

ROGUE (From X-Men)
Marvel Comics: Jan, 1995 - No. 4, Apr, 1995 ($2.95, limited series)

1-4: 1-Gold foil logo — 4.00
TPB-($12.95) r/#1-4 — 13.00

ROGUE (Volume 2)
Marvel Comics: Sept, 2001 - No. 4, Dec, 2001 ($2.50, limited series)

1-4-Julie Bell painted-c/Lopresti-a; Rogue's early days with X-Men — 3.00

ROGUE (From X-Men)
Marvel Comics: Sept, 2004 - No. 12, Aug, 2005 ($2.99)

1-12: 1-Richards-a. 4-Gambit app. 11-Sunfire dies, Rogue absorbs his powers — 3.00
...: Going Rogue TPB (2005, $14.99) r/#1-6 — 15.00
...: Forget-Me-Not TPB (2006, $14.99) r/#7-12 — 15.00

ROGUE & GAMBIT
Marvel Comics: Mar, 2018 - No. 5, Jul, 2018 ($3.99, limited series)

1-5-Kelly Thompson-s/Pere Pérez-a — 4.00

ROGUE ANGEL: TELLER OF TALL TALES (Based on the Alex Archer novels)
IDW Publishing: Feb, 2008 - No. 5, Jun, 2008 ($3.99)

1-5-Annja Creed adventures; Barbara-Kesel-s/Renae De Liz-a — 4.00

ROGUES GALLERY
DC Comics: 1996 ($3.50, one-shot)

1-Pinups of DC villains by various artists — 4.00

ROGUE TROOPER
IDW Publishing: Feb, 2014 - No. 4, May, 2014 ($3.99)

1-4-Ruckley-s/Ponticelli-a/Fabry-c — 4.00

ROGUE TROOPER CLASSICS
IDW Publishing: May, 2014 - No. 8, Dec, 2014 ($3.99)

1-8-Newly colored reprints of strips from 2000 AD magazine. 1-4-Gibbons-a — 4.00

ROGUES, THE (VILLAINS) (See The Flash)
DC Comics: Feb, 1998 ($1.95, one-shot)

1-Augustyn-s/Pearson-c — 3.00

ROKKIN
DC Comics (WildStorm): Sept, 2006 - No. 6, Feb, 2007 ($2.99, limited series)

1-6-Hartnell-s/Bradshaw-a — 3.00

ROKU
Valiant Entertainment: Oct, 2019 - No. 4, Jan, 2020 ($3.99, limited series)

1-4-Cullen Bunn-s/Ramón Bachs-a; multiple covers on each — 4.00

ROLLING STONES: VOODOO LOUNGE
Marvel Comics: 1995 ($6.95, Prestige format, one-shot)

nn-Dave McKean-script/design/art — 7.00

ROLY POLY COMIC BOOK
Green Publishing Co.: 1945 - No. 15, 1946 (MLJ reprints)

	GD	VG	FN	VF	VF/NM	NM-
1-(No number on cover or indicia, "1945 issue" on cover) Red Rube & Steel Sterling begin; Sahle-c	39	78	117	240	395	550
6-The Blue Circle & The Steel Fist app.	27	54	81	158	259	360
10-Origin Red Rube retold; Steel Sterling story (Zip #41)	29	58	87	174	285	395
11,12: The Black Hood app. in both	31	62	93	186	303	420
14-Classic decapitation-c; the Black Hood app.	304	608	912	2128	3764	5400
15-The Blue Circle & The Steel Fist app.; cover exact swipe from Fox Blue Beetle #1	39	78	117	236	388	540

ROM (Based on the Parker Brothers toy)
Marvel Comics Group: Dec, 1979 - No. 75, Feb, 1986

	GD	VG	FN	VF	VF/NM	NM-
1-Origin/1st app.	5	10	15	33	57	80
2-16,19-23,28-30: 5-Dr. Strange. 13-Saga of the Space Knights begins. 19-X-Men cameo. 23-Powerman & Iron Fist app.	1	2	3	5	6	8
17,18-X-Men app.	2	4	6	9	12	15
24-27: 24-F.F. cameo; Skrulls, Nova & The New Champions app. 25-Double size. 26,27-Galactus app.	1	2	3	5	7	9
31-49,51-60: 31,32-Brotherhood of Evil Mutants app. 32-X-Men cameo. 34,35-Sub-Mariner app. 41,42-Dr. Strange app. 56,57-Alpha Flight app. 58,59-Ant-Man app.						6.00
50-Skrulls app. (52 pgs.) Pin-ups by Konkle, Austin	1	2	3	4	5	7
61-74: 65-West Coast Avengers & Beta Ray Bill app. 65,66-X-Men app.						6.00
75-Last issue	2	4	6	9	12	15
Annual 1-4: (1982-85, 52 pgs.)						6.00

NOTE: ***Austin** c-3i, 18i, 61i. **Byrne** a-74i; c-56, 57, 74. **Ditko** a-59-75p, Annual 4. **Golden** c-7-12, 19. **Guice** a-61i; c-55, 58, 60p, 70p. **Layton** a-59i, 72i; c-15, 59i, 69. **Miller** c-2p?, 3p, 17p, 18p. **Russell** a(i)-64, 65, 67, 69, 71, 75; c-64, 65i, 66, 71i, 75. **Severin** c-41p. **Sienkiewicz** a-53i; c-46, 47, 52-54, 68, 71p, Annual 2. **Simonson** c-18. **P. Smith** c-59p. **Starlin** c-67. **Zeck** c-50.*

ROM (Based on the Parker Brothers toy) (Also see Rom & The Micronauts)
IDW Publishing: Jul, 2016 - No. 14, Aug, 2017 ($4.99/$3.99)

1-($4.99) Ryall & Gage-s/Messina-a — 5.00
2-14-($3.99) 2-4-Revolution tie-in. 2-G.I. Joe app. 5-Transformers app. — 4.00
Annual 2017 (1/17, $7.99) Origin of Rom; Ryall & Gage-s/Messina-a — 8.00
... First Strike 1 (10/17, $3.99) Part of the Hasbro character x-over; Gage-s/Panda-a — 4.00
FCBD 2016 Edition #0 - (5/16, giveaway) Prelude to series; Action Man flip book — 3.00
...: Revolution (9/16, $3.99) Revolution x-over; Ryall-s/Gage-a; multiple covers — 4.00
...: Tales of the Solstar Order (3/18, $4.99) Ryall & Gage-s/Dorian-a — 5.00

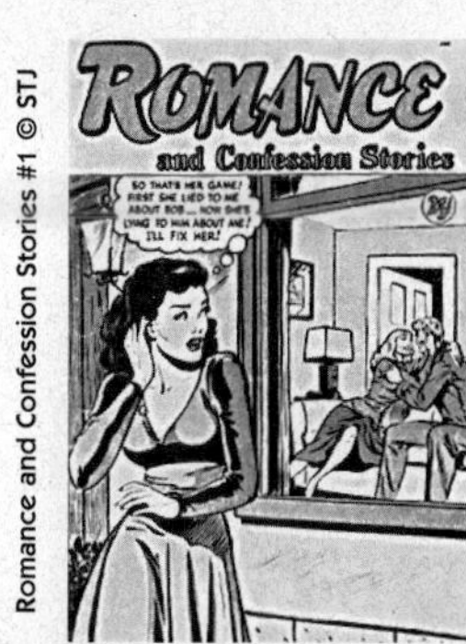

Romance and Confession Stories #1 © STJ

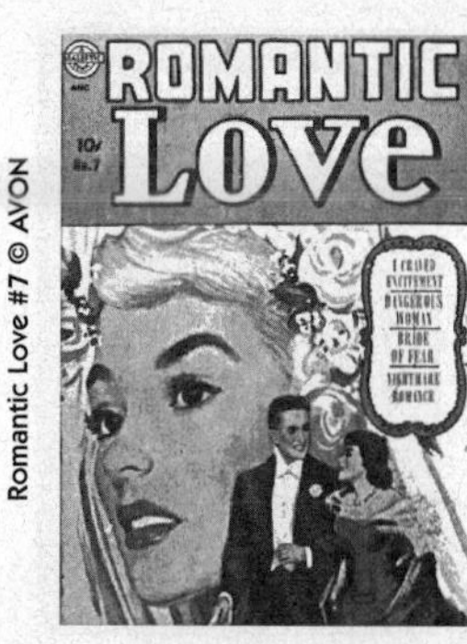

Romantic Love #7 © AVON

Romantic Story #1 © FAW

ROMANCE (See True Stories of...)

ROMANCE AND CONFESSION STORIES (See Giant Comics Edition)
St. John Publishing Co.: No date (1949) (25¢, 100 pgs.)

	GD 2.0	VG 4.0	FN 6.0	VF 8.0	VF/NM 9.0	NM- 9.2
1-Baker-c/a; remaindered St. John love comics	110	220	330	704	1202	1700

ROMANCE DIARY
Marvel Comics (CDS)(CLDS): Dec, 1949 - No. 2, Mar, 1950

	GD 2.0	VG 4.0	FN 6.0	VF 8.0	VF/NM 9.0	NM- 9.2
1,2-Photo-c	21	42	63	122	199	275

ROMANCE OF FLYING, THE
David McKay Publications: 1942

	GD 2.0	VG 4.0	FN 6.0	VF 8.0	VF/NM 9.0	NM- 9.2
Feature Books 33 (nn)-WW II photos	19	38	57	112	179	245

ROMANCES OF MOLLY MANTON (See Molly Manton)

ROMANCES OF NURSE HELEN GRANT, THE
Atlas Comics (VPI): Aug, 1957

	GD 2.0	VG 4.0	FN 6.0	VF 8.0	VF/NM 9.0	NM- 9.2
1	21	42	63	122	199	275

ROMANCES OF THE WEST (Becomes Romantic Affairs #3?)
Marvel Comics (SPC): Nov, 1949 - No. 2, Mar, 1950 (52 pgs.)

	GD 2.0	VG 4.0	FN 6.0	VF 8.0	VF/NM 9.0	NM- 9.2
1-Movie photo-c of Yvonne DeCarlo & Howard Duff (Calamity Jane & Sam Bass)	30	60	90	177	289	400
2-Photo-c	18	36	54	103	162	220

ROMANCE STORIES OF TRUE LOVE (Formerly True Love Problems & Advice Illustrated)
Harvey Publications: No. 45, 5/57 - No. 50, 3/58; No. 51, 9/58 - No. 52, 11/58

	GD 2.0	VG 4.0	FN 6.0	VF 8.0	VF/NM 9.0	NM- 9.2
45-51: 45,46,48-50-Powell-a	7	14	21	37	46	55
52-Matt Baker-a	9	18	27	52	69	85

ROMANCE TALES (Formerly Western Winners #6?)
Marvel Comics (CDS): No. 7, Oct, 1949 - No. 9, April, 1950 (7-9: photo-c)

	GD 2.0	VG 4.0	FN 6.0	VF 8.0	VF/NM 9.0	NM- 9.2
7	19	38	57	112	179	245
8,9: 8-Everett-a	14	28	42	80	115	150

ROMANCE TRAIL
National Periodical Publications: July-Aug, 1949 - No. 6, May-June, 1950 (All photo-c & 52 pgs.)

	GD 2.0	VG 4.0	FN 6.0	VF 8.0	VF/NM 9.0	NM- 9.2
1-Kinstler, Toth-a; Jimmy Wakely photo-c	60	120	180	381	653	925
2-Kinstler-a; Jim Bannon photo-c	33	66	100	196	321	445
3-Tex Williams photo-c; Kinstler, Toth-a	35	70	105	208	339	470
4-Jim Bannon as Red Ryder photo-c; Toth-a	26	52	78	154	252	350
5,6: Photo-c on both. 5-Kinstler-a	24	48	72	140	230	320

ROM & THE MICRONAUTS (Based on the Parker Brothers toys)
IDW Publishing: Dec, 2017 - No. 5, Apr, 2018 ($3.99, limited series)

	GD 2.0	VG 4.0	FN 6.0	VF 8.0	VF/NM 9.0	NM- 9.2
1-5-Gage-s/Villanelli-a; multiple covers; Baron Karza app.						4.00

ROMAN HOLIDAYS, THE (TV)
Gold Key: Feb, 1973 - No. 4, Nov, 1973 (Hanna-Barbera)

	GD 2.0	VG 4.0	FN 6.0	VF 8.0	VF/NM 9.0	NM- 9.2
1	4	8	12	27	44	60
2-4	3	6	9	17	26	35

ROMANTIC ADVENTURES (My... #49-67, covers only)
American Comics Group (B&I Publ. Co.): Mar-Apr, 1949 - No. 71, Nov, 1956 (Becomes My... #72 on)

	GD 2.0	VG 4.0	FN 6.0	VF 8.0	VF/NM 9.0	NM- 9.2
1	25	50	75	150	245	340
2	15	30	45	86	133	180
3-10	12	24	36	69	97	125
11-20 (4/52)	11	22	33	60	83	105
21-45,51,52: 52-Last Pre-code (2/55)	10	20	30	56	76	95
46-49-3-D effect-c/stories (TrueVision)	15	30	45	86	135	180
50-Classic cover/story "Love of A Lunatic"	103	206	309	659	1130	1600
53-71	9	18	27	52	69	85

NOTE: *#1-23, 52 pgs.* ***Shelly*** *a-40. Whitney c/art in many issues.*

ROMANTIC AFFAIRS (Formerly Molly Manton's Romances #2 and/or Romances of the West #2 and/or Our Love #2?)
Marvel Comics (SPC): No. 3, Mar, 1950

	GD 2.0	VG 4.0	FN 6.0	VF 8.0	VF/NM 9.0	NM- 9.2
3-Photo-c from Molly Manton's Romances #2	15	30	45	92	144	195

ROMANTIC CONFESSIONS
Hillman Periodicals: Oct, 1949 - V3#1, Apr-May, 1953

	GD 2.0	VG 4.0	FN 6.0	VF 8.0	VF/NM 9.0	NM- 9.2
V1#1-McWilliams-a	24	48	72	142	234	325
2-Briefer-a; negligee panels	15	30	45	86	133	180
3-12	14	28	42	78	112	145
V2#1,2,4-8,10-12: 2-McWilliams-a	13	26	39	72	101	130
3-Krigstein-a	14	28	42	78	112	145
9-One pg. Frazetta ad	13	26	39	72	101	130
V3#1	12	24	36	69	97	125

ROMANTIC HEARTS
Story Comics/Master/Merit Pubs.: Mar, 1951 - No. 10, Oct, 1952; July, 1953 - No. 12, July, 1955

	GD 2.0	VG 4.0	FN 6.0	VF 8.0	VF/NM 9.0	NM- 9.2
1(3/51) (1st Series)	20	40	60	120	195	270
2	14	28	42	78	112	145
3-10: Cameron-a	13	26	39	74	105	135
1(7/53) (2nd Series)-Some say #11 on-c	15	30	45	86	133	180
2	13	26	39	72	101	130
3-12	11	22	33	64	90	115

ROMANTIC LOVE
Avon Periodicals/Realistic (No #14-19): 9-10/49 - #3, 1-2/50; #4, 2-3/51 - #13, 10/52; #20, 3-4/54 - #23, 9-10/54

	GD 2.0	VG 4.0	FN 6.0	VF 8.0	VF/NM 9.0	NM- 9.2
1-c-/Avon paperback #252	45	90	135	284	480	675
2-5: 3-c-/paperback Novel Library #12. 4-c-/paperback Diversey Prize Novel #5. 5-c-/paperback Novel Library #34	28	56	84	168	274	380
6- "Thrill Crazy" marijuana story; c-/Avon paperback #207; Kinstler-a	40	80	120	244	402	560
7,8: 8-Astarita-a(2)	27	54	81	162	266	370
9-c-/paperback Novel Library #41; Kinstler-a; headlights-c	40	80	120	244	402	560
10-12: 10-c-/Avon paperback #212. 11-c-/paperback Novel Library #17; Kinstler-a. 12-c-/paperback Novel Library #13	30	60	90	177	289	400
13,21-23: 22,23-Kinstler-c	27	54	81	162	266	370
20-Kinstler-c/a	28	56	84	168	274	380
nn(1-3/53)(Realistic-r)	18	36	54	107	169	230

NOTE: ***Astarita*** *a-7, 10, 11, 21. Painted c-1-3, 5, 7-11, 13. Photo c-4, 6.*

ROMANTIC LOVE
Quality Comics Group: 1963-1964

	GD 2.0	VG 4.0	FN 6.0	VF 8.0	VF/NM 9.0	NM- 9.2
I.W. Reprint #2,3,8,11: 2-r/Romantic Love #2	3	6	9	14	19	24

ROMANTIC MARRIAGE (Cinderella Love #25 on)
Ziff-Davis/St. John No. 18 on (#1-8: 52 pgs.): #1-3 (1950, no months); #4, 5-6/51 - #17, 9/52; #18, 9/53 - #24, 9/54

	GD 2.0	VG 4.0	FN 6.0	VF 8.0	VF/NM 9.0	NM- 9.2
1-Photo-c; Cary Grant/Betsy Drake photo back-c.	31	62	93	182	296	410
2-Painted-c; Anderson-a (also #15)	20	40	60	118	192	265
3-9: 3,4,8,9-Painted-c; 5-7-Photo-c	18	36	54	109	172	235
10-Unusual format; front-c is a painted-c; back-c is a photo-c complete with logo, price, etc.	31	62	93	182	295	410
11-17 13-Photo-c. 15-Signed story by Anderson. 17-(9/52)-Last Z-D issue	16	32	48	98	154	210
18-22: 20-Photo-c	16	32	48	98	154	210
23-Baker-c; all stories are reprinted from #15	50	100	150	315	633	750
24-Baker-c	90	180	270	576	988	1400

ROMANTIC PICTURE NOVELETTES
Magazine Enterprises: 1946

	GD 2.0	VG 4.0	FN 6.0	VF 8.0	VF/NM 9.0	NM- 9.2
1-Mary Worth-r; Creig Flessel-c	21	42	63	122	199	275

ROMANTIC SECRETS (Becomes Time For Love)
Fawcett/Charlton Comics No. 5 (10/55) on: Sept, 1949 - No. 39, 4/53; No. 5, 10/55 - No. 52, 11/64 (#1-39: photo-c)

	GD 2.0	VG 4.0	FN 6.0	VF 8.0	VF/NM 9.0	NM- 9.2
1-(52 pg. issues begin, end #?)	19	38	57	112	179	245
2,3	12	24	36	69	97	125
4,9-Evans-a	13	26	39	74	105	135
5-8,10(9/50)	10	20	30	54	72	90
11-23	9	18	27	47	61	75
24-Evans-a	9	18	27	52	69	85
25-39('53)	8	16	24	44	57	70
5 (Charlton, 2nd Series)(10/55, formerly Negro Romances #4)	10	20	30	58	79	100
6-10	8	16	24	44	57	70
11-20	4	8	12	22	35	48
21-35	3	6	9	19	30	40
36-52('64)	3	6	9	16	23	30

NOTE: ***Bailey*** *a-20.* ***Powell*** *a(1st series)-5, 7, 10, 12, 16, 17, 20, 26, 29, 33, 34, 36, 37.* ***Sekowsky*** *a-26.* ***Swayze*** *a(1st series)-16, 18, 19, 23, 26-28, 31, 32, 39.*

ROMANTIC STORY (Cowboy Love #28 on)
Fawcett/Charlton Comics No. 23 on: 11/49 - #22, Sum, 1953; #23, 5/54 - #27, 12/54; #28, 8/55 - #130, 11/73

	GD 2.0	VG 4.0	FN 6.0	VF 8.0	VF/NM 9.0	NM- 9.2
1-Photo-c begin, end #24; 52 pgs. begins	19	38	57	112	179	245
2	13	26	39	72	101	130
3-5	10	20	30	56	76	95
6-14	9	18	27	52	69	85
15-Evans-a	10	20	30	56	76	95

Rom: Dire Wraiths #1 © Hasbro

Room 222 #1 © 20th Fox

Rorschach #1 © DC

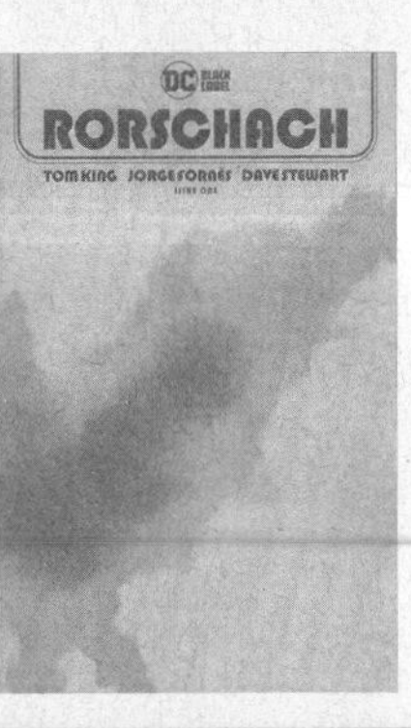

	GD 2.0	VG 4.0	FN 6.0	VF 8.0	VF/NM 9.0	NM- 9.2
16-22(Sum, '53; last Fawcett issue). 21-Toth-a?	8	16	24	42	54	65
23-39: 26,29-Wood swipes	7	14	21	37	46	55
40-(100 pgs.)	11	22	33	64	90	115
41-50	3	6	9	20	31	42
51-80: 57-Hypo needle story	3	6	9	16	23	30
81-99	2	4	6	10	14	18
100	2	4	6	13	28	22
101-130: 120-Bobby Sherman pin-up	2	4	6	9	12	15

NOTE: ***Jim Aparo** a-94.* ***Powell** a-7, 8, 16, 20, 30.* ***Marcus Swayze** a-2, 12, 20, 32.*

ROMANTIC THRILLS (See Fox Giants)

ROMANTIC WESTERN
Fawcett Publications: Winter, 1949 - No. 3, June, 1950 (All Photo-c)

	GD	VG	FN	VF	VF/NM	NM-
1	24	48	72	140	230	320
2-(Spr/50)-Williamson, McWilliams-a	20	40	60	120	195	270
3	15	30	45	92	144	195

ROMEO TUBBS (...That Lovable Teenager; formerly My Secret Life)
Fox Features Syndicate/Green Publ. Co. No. 27: No. 26, 5/50 - No. 28, 7/50; No. 1, 1950; No. 27, 12/52

	GD	VG	FN	VF	VF/NM	NM-
26-Teen-age	14	28	42	81	118	155
28 (7/50)	13	26	39	72	101	130
27 (12/52)-Contains Pedro on inside; Wood-a	16	32	48	98	154	210

ROM: DIRE WRAITHS
IDW Publishing: Oct, 2019 - Present ($4.99, limited series)

1-Ryall-s/Pizzari & Dorian Sr.-a 5.00

ROMULUS
Image Comics: Oct, 2016 - No. 4, May, 2017 ($3.99)

1-4-Bryan Hill-s/Nelson Blake II-a 4.00

ROM VS. TRANSFORMERS: SHINING ARMOR
IDW Publishing: Jul, 2017 - No. 5, Nov, 2017 ($3.99, limited series)

1-5-Barber & Gage-s/Milne-a 4.00

RONALD McDONALD (TV)
Charlton Press: Sept, 1970 - No. 4, March, 1971

	GD	VG	FN	VF	VF/NM	NM-
1-Bill Yates-a in all	8	16	24	52	99	145
2-4: 2 & 3 both dated Jan, 1971	5	10	15	33	57	80
V2#1-4-Special reprint for McDonald systems; new cover art on each; "Not for resale" on cover	6	12	18	38	69	100

RONIN
DC Comics: July, 1983 - No. 6, Aug, 1984 ($2.50, limited series, 52 pgs.)

	GD	VG	FN	VF	VF/NM	NM-
1-Frank Miller-c/a/scripts in all	2	4	6	11	16	20
2-5	2	4	6	8	11	14
6-Scarcer; has fold-out poster.	2	4	6	11	16	20

Trade paperback (1987, $12.95)-Reprints #1-6 18.00

RONIN ISLAND
BOOM! Studios: Mar, 2019 - No. 12, Jul, 2020 ($3.99, limited series)

1-12-Greg Pak-s/Giannis Milonogiannis-a 4.00

RONNA
Knight Press: Apr, 1997 ($2.95, B&W, one-shot)

1-Beau Smith-s 3.00

ROOK (See Eerie Magazine & Warren Presents: The Rook)
Warren Publications: Oct, 1979 - No. 14, April, 1982 (B&W magazine)

	GD	VG	FN	VF	VF/NM	NM-
1-Nino-a/Corben-c; with 8 pg. color insert	3	6	9	16	23	30
2-4,6,7: 2-Voltar by Alcala begins. 3,4-Toth-a	2	4	6	9	13	16
5,8-14: 11-Zorro-s. 12-14-Eagle by Severin	2	4	6	9	13	16

ROOK
Harris Comics: No. 0, Jun, 1995 - No. 4, 1995 ($2.95)

0-4: 0-short stories (3) w/preview. 4-Brereton-c. 3.00

ROOK, THE
Dark Horse Comics: Oct, 2015 - No. 4, Jan, 2016 ($3.99)

1-4-Steven Grant-s/Paul Gulacy-a/c 4.00

ROOKIE COP (Formerly Crime and Justice?)
Charlton Comics: No. 27, Nov, 1955 - No. 33, Aug, 1957

	GD	VG	FN	VF	VF/NM	NM-
27	11	22	33	62	86	110
28-33	8	16	24	42	54	65

ROOM 222 (TV)
Dell Publishing Co.: Jan, 1970; No. 2, May, 1970 - No. 4, Jan, 1971

	GD 2.0	VG 4.0	FN 6.0	VF 8.0	VF/NM 9.0	NM- 9.2
1	6	12	18	37	66	95
2-4-Photo-c. 3-Marijuana story. 4 r/#1	4	8	12	25	40	55

ROOTIE KAZOOTIE (TV)(See 3-D-ell)
Dell Publishing Co.: No. 415, Aug, 1952 - No. 6, Oct-Dec, 1954

	GD	VG	FN	VF	VF/NM	NM-
Four Color 415 (#1)	9	18	27	61	123	185
Four Color 459,502(#2,3), 4(4-6/54)-6	6	12	18	41	76	110

ROOTS OF THE SWAMP THING
DC Comics: July, 1986 - No.5, Nov, 1986 ($2.00, Baxter paper, 52 pgs.)

1-5: r/Swamp Thing #1-10 by Wrightson & House of Mystery-r. 1-new Wrightson-c (2-5 reprinted covers). 5.00

RORSCHACH
DC Comics (Black Label): Dec, 2020 - No. 12 ($4.99)

1-5-Tom King-s/Jorge Fornés-a 5.00

ROSE (See Bone)
Cartoon Books: Nov, 2000 - No. 3, Feb, 2002 ($5.95, lim. series, square-bound)

1-3-Prequel to Bone; Jeff Smith-s/Charles Vess painted-a/c 6.00
HC (2001, $29.95) r/#1-3; new Vess cover painting 30.00
SC (2002, $19.95) r/#1-3; new Vess cover painting 20.00
1-($6.00)-Blood & Glory Edition 6.00

ROSE
Image Comics: Apr, 2017 - No. 17, Feb, 2019 ($3.99)

1-17-Meredith Finch-s/Ig Guara-a 4.00

ROSE AND THORN
DC Comics: Feb, 2004 - No. 6, July, 2004 ($2.95, limited series)

1-6-Simone-s/Melo-a/Hughes-c 3.00

ROSWELL: LITTLE GREEN MAN (See Simpsons Comics #19-22)
Bongo Comics: 1996 - No. 6 ($2.95, quarterly)

1-6 4.00
...Walks Among Us ('97, $12.95, TPB) r/ #1-3 & Simpsons flip books 13.00

ROUGH RIDERS
AfterShock Comics: Apr, 2016 - No. 7, Nov, 2016 ($3.99)

1-7: 1-Teddy Roosevelt, Annie Oakley, Houdini, Jack Johnson, Thomas Edison team 4.00
... Nation 1 (11/16, $3.99) Dossier of other Rough Rider teams; art by various 4.00

ROUGH RIDERS: RIDE OR DIE
AfterShock Comics: Feb, 2018 - No. 4, May, 2018 ($3.99)

1-4-Glass-s/Olliffe-a; H.P. Lovecraft app. 4.00

ROUGH RIDERS: RIDERS ON THE STORM
AfterShock Comics: Feb, 2017 - No. 6, Sept, 2017 ($3.99)

1-6-Glass-s/Olliffe-a; Monk Eastman joins team 4.00

ROUND TABLE OF AMERICA: PERSONALITY CRISIS (See Big Bang Comics)
Image Comics: Aug, 2005 ($3.50, one-shot)

1-Carlos Rodriguez-a/Pedro Angosto-s 3.50

ROUNDUP (...Western Crime Stories)
D. S. Publishing Co.: July-Aug, 1948 - No. 5, Mar-Apr, 1949 (All 52 pgs.)

	GD	VG	FN	VF	VF/NM	NM-
1-Kiefer-a	20	40	60	120	195	270
2-5: 2-Marijuana drug mention story	15	30	45	86	133	180

ROUTE 666
CrossGeneration Comics: July, 2002 - No. 22, Jun, 2004 ($2.95)

1-22-Bedard-s/Moline-a in most. 5-Richards-a. 15-McCrea-a 3.00

ROWANS RUIN
BOOM! Studios: Oct, 2015 - No. 4, Jan, 2016 ($3.99, limited series)

1-4-Mike Carey-s/Mike Perkins-a. 1-Multiple covers 4.00

ROYAL CITY
Image Comics: Mar, 2017 - No. 14, Aug, 2018 ($4.99/$3.99)

1-($4.99) Jeff Lemire-s/a 5.00
2-14-($3.99) 4.00

ROYAL ROY
Marvel Comics (Star Comics): May, 1985 - No. 6, Mar, 1986 (Children's book)

1-6 4.00

ROYALS (The Inhumans) (Leads into Inhumans: Judgment Day)
Marvel Comics: Jun, 2017 - No. 12, Feb, 2018 ($3.99)

1-12: 1-Ewing-s/Meyers-a; Marvel Boy app. 2-Maximus returns. 4,5-Ronan app. 4.00

ROYALS, THE: MASTERS OF WAR

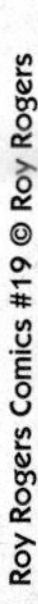
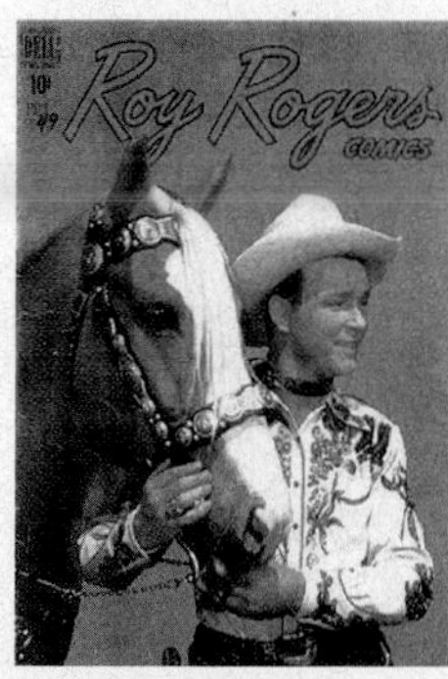
Roy Rogers Comics #19 © Roy Rogers

Ruby Falls #1 © Nocenti & Biondi

Rulah Jungle Goddess #19 © FOX

	GD 2.0	VG 4.0	FN 6.0	VF 8.0	VF/NM 9.0	NM- 9.2

GD VG FN VF VF/NM NM-
2.0 4.0 6.0 8.0 9.0 9.2

DC Comics (Vertigo): Apr, 2014 - No. 6, Sept, 2014 ($2.99, limited series)
1-6-Rob Williams-s/Simon Coleby-a/c; super-powered Royal families during WWII 3.00

ROY CAMPANELLA, BASEBALL HERO
Fawcett Publications: 1950 (Brooklyn Dodgers)
nn-Photo-c; life story 62 124 186 394 677 960

ROY ROGERS (See March of Comics #17, 35, 47, 62, 68, 73, 77, 86, 91, 100, 105, 116, 121, 131, 136, 146, 151, 161, 167, 176, 191, 206, 221, 236, 250)

ROY ROGERS AND TRIGGER
Gold Key: Apr, 1967
1-Photo-c; reprints 4 8 12 27 44 60

ROY ROGERS ANNUAL
Wilson Publ. Co., Toronto/Dell: 1947 ("Giant Edition" on-c)(132 pgs., 50¢)
nn-Seven known copies. Front and back cover art are from Roy Rogers #2. Stories reprinted from Roy Rogers #2, Four Color #137 and Four Color #153. (A copy in VG/FN was sold in 1986 for $400, in 1996 for $1200 & in 2000 for $1500; a FN+ sold for $1,650; a GD sold for $448 in 2008, a FN sold for $717 in 2009 and a FR sold for $156 in 2015.)

ROY ROGERS COMICS (See Western Roundup under Dell Giants)
Dell Publishing Co.: No. 38, 4/44 - No. 177, 12/47 (#38-166: 52 pgs.)
Four Color 38 (1944)-49 pg. story; photo front/back-c on all 4-Color issues (1st western comic with photo-c) 155 310 465 1279 2890 4500
Four Color 63 (1945)-Color photos on all four-c 40 80 120 296 673 1050
Four Color 86,95 (1945) 29 58 87 209 467 725
Four Color 109 (1946) 22 44 66 154 340 525
Four Color 117,124,137,144 17 34 51 119 265 410
Four Color 153,160,166: 166-48 pg. story 15 30 45 105 233 360
Four Color 177 (36 pgs.)-32 pg. story 15 30 45 100 220 340
HC (Dark Horse Books, 8/08, $49.95) r/Four Color #38,63,86,95,109; Roy Rogers Jr intro. 50.00

ROY ROGERS COMICS (...& Trigger #92(8/55)-on)(Roy starred in Republic movies, radio & TV) (Singing cowboy) (Also see Dale Evans, It Really Happened #8, Queen of the West Dale Evans, & Roy Rogers' Trigger)
Dell Publishing Co.: Jan, 1948 - No. 145, Sept-Oct, 1961 (#1-19: 36 pgs.)
1-Roy, his horse Trigger, & Chuck Wagon Charley's Tales begin; photo-c begin, end #145 60 122 183 488 1094 1700
2 20 40 60 138 307 475
3-5 14 28 42 96 211 325
6-10 12 24 36 80 173 265
11-19: 19-Chuckwagon Charley's Tales ends 10 20 30 68 144 220
20 (52 pgs.)-Trigger feature begins, ends #46 10 20 30 69 147 225
21-30 (52 pgs.) 9 18 27 60 120 180
31-46 (52 pgs.): 37-X-Mas-c 8 16 24 51 96 140
47-56 (36 pgs.): 47-Chuck Wagon Charley's Tales returns, ends #133. 49-X-mas-c. 55-Last photo back-c 6 12 18 40 73 105
57 (52 pgs.)-Heroin drug propaganda story 6 12 18 41 76 110
58-70 (52 pgs.): 58-Heroin drug use/dealing story. 61-X-Mas-c 6 12 18 40 73 105
71-80 (52 pgs.): 73-X-Mas-c 5 10 15 35 63 90
81-91 (36 pgs. #81-on): 85-X-Mas-c 5 10 15 34 60 85
92-99,101-110,112-118: 92-Title changed to Roy Rogers and Trigger (8/55) 5 10 15 33 57 80
100-Trigger feature returns, ends #131 6 12 18 37 66 95
111,119-124-Toth-a 6 12 18 38 69 100
125-131: 125-Toth-a (1 pg.) 5 10 15 31 53 75
132-144-Manning-a. 132-1st Dale Evans-sty by Russ Manning. 138,144-Dale Evans featured 5 10 15 34 60 85
145-Last issue 6 12 18 40 73 105
NOTE: ***Buscema*** *a-74-108(2 stories each).* ***Manning*** *a-123, 124, 132-144.* ***Marsh*** *a-110. Photo back-c No. 1-9, 11-35, 38-55.*

ROY ROGERS' TRIGGER
Dell Publishing Co.: No. 329, May, 1951 - No. 17, June-Aug, 1955
Four Color 329 (#1)-Painted-c 14 28 42 97 214 330
2 (9-11/51)-Photo-c 10 20 30 64 132 200
3-5: 3-Painted-c begin, end #17, most by S. Savitt 6 12 18 38 69 100
6-17: Title merges with Roy Rogers after #17 5 10 15 31 53 75

ROY ROGERS WESTERN CLASSICS
AC Comics: 1989 -No. 4 ($2.95/$3.95, 44pgs.) (24 pgs. color, 16 pgs. B&W)
1-4: 1-Dale Evans-r by Manning, Trigger-r by Buscema; photo covers & interior photos by Roy & Dale. 2-Buscema-r (3); photo-c & B&W photos inside. 3-Dale Evans-r by Manning; Trigger-r by Buscema plus other Buscema-r; photo-c 4.00

RUBY FALLS
Dark Horse Comics (Berger Books): Oct, 2019 - No. 4, Jan, 2020 ($3.99, limited series)
1-4-Ann Nocenti-s/Flavia Biondi-a 4.00

RUDOLPH, THE RED-NOSED REINDEER
National Per. Publ.: 1950 - No. 13, Winter, 1962-63 (Issues are not numbered)
1950 issue (#1); Grossman-c/a in all 42 84 126 265 445 625
1951-53 issues (3 total) 24 48 72 142 234 325
1954/55, 55/56, 56/57 20 40 60 115 188 260
1957/58, 58/59, 59/60, 60/61, 61/62 10 20 30 68 144 220
1962/63 (rare)(84 pgs.)(shows "Annual" in indicia) 20 40 60 136 303 470
NOTE: *13 total issues published. Has games & puzzles also.*

RUDOLPH, THE RED-NOSED REINDEER (Also see Limited Collectors' Edition C-20, C-24, C-33, C-42, C-50; and All-New Collectors' Edition C-53 & C-60)
National Per. Publ.: Christmas 1972 (Treasury-size)
nn-Precursor to Limited Collectors' Edition title (scarce) (implied to be Lim. Coll .Ed. C-20) 19 38 57 133 297 460

RUFF AND REDDY (TV)
Dell Publ. Co.: No. 937, 9/58 - No. 12, 1-3/62 (Hanna-Barbera)(#9 on: 15¢)
Four Color 937(#1)(1st Hanna-Barbera comic book) 10 20 30 69 147 225
Four Color 981,1038 7 14 21 44 82 120
4(1-3/60)-12: 8-Last 10¢ issue 6 12 18 38 69 100

RUFF & REDDY SHOW, THE
DC Comics: Dec, 2017 - No. 6, May, 2018 ($3.99, limited series)
1-6-Ruff & Ready in the real world; Chaykin-s/Mac Rey-a; 2 covers (Chaykin & Rey) 4.00

RUGGED ACTION (Strange Stories of Suspense #5 on)
Atlas Comics (CSI): Dec, 1954 - No. 4, June, 1955
1-Brodsky-c 18 36 54 109 172 235
2-4: 2-Last precode (2/55) 14 28 42 78 112 145
NOTE: ***Ayers*** *a-2, 3.* ***Maneely*** *c-2, 3.* ***Severin*** *a-2.*

RUGRATS (TV) (Nickelodeon cartoon)
BOOM! Studios (kaboom!): Oct, 2017 - No. 8, May, 2018 ($3.99)
1-8: 1-3,5-Box Brown-s/Lisa DuBois-a; multiple covers 4.00
...: C Is For Chanukah 2018 Special 1 (11/18, $7.99) Kibblesmith & Crawford-s/Sherron-a 8.00
...: R Is For Reptar 2018 Special 1 (4/18, $7.99) Short stories by various 8.00

RUINS
Marvel Comics (Alterniverse): July, 1995 - No. 2, Sept, 1995 ($5.00, painted, limited series)
1,2: Phil Sheldon from Marvels; Warren Ellis scripts; acetate-c 6.00
Reprint (2009, $4.99) r/#1,2; cover gallery 5.00

RUINS OF RAVENCROFT
Marvel Comics: Mar, 2020 ($4.99, series of one-shots)
...: Carnage - Tieri-s/Unzueta-a; Set in the early 1400s New York 5.00
...: Dracula - Tieri-s/Unzueta-a; Dracula vs. Golden Age Captain America 5.00
...: Sabretooth - Tieri-s/Unzueta-a; Wolverine vs. Sabretooth in 1909 5.00

RULAH JUNGLE GODDESS (Formerly Zoot; I Loved #28 on) (Also see All Top Comics & Terrors of the Jungle)
Fox Feature Syndicate: No. 17, Aug, 1948 - No. 27, June, 1949
17 148 296 444 947 1624 2300
18-Classic girl-fight interior splash 97 194 291 621 1061 1500
19,20 94 188 282 397 1025 1450
21-Used in **SOTI**, pg. 388,389 132 264 396 845 1448 2050
22-Used in **SOTI**, pg. 22,23 94 188 282 597 1025 1450
23-27 71 142 213 454 777 1100
NOTE: ***Kamen*** *c-17-19, 21, 22.*

RUNAWAY, THE (See Movie Classics)

RUNAWAYS
Marvel Comics: July, 2003 - No. 18, Nov, 2004 ($2.95/$2.25/$2.99)
1-($2.95) Vaughan-s/Alphona-a/Jo Chen-c 4.00
2-9-($2.50) 3.00
10-18-($2.99) 11,12-Miyazawa-a; Cloak and Dagger app. 16-The mole revealed 3.00
Hardcover (2005, $34.99) oversized r/#1-18; proposal & sketch pages; Vaughan intro. 35.00
Marvel Age Runaways Vol. 1: Pride and Joy (2004, $7.99, digest size) r/#1-6 8.00
...Vol. 2: Teenage Wasteland (2004, $7.99, digest size) r/#7-12 8.00
...Vol. 3: The Good Die Young (2004, $7.99, digest size) r/#13-18 8.00

RUNAWAYS (Also see X-Men/Runaways 2006 FCBD Edition)
Marvel Comics: Apr, 2005 - No. 30, Aug, 2008 ($2.99)
1-24: 1-6-Vaughan-s/Alphona-a/Jo Chen-c. 7,8-Miyazawa-a/Bachalo-c. 11-Spider-Man app. 12-New Avengers app. 18-Gert killed 3.00
25-30-Joss Whedon-s/Michael Ryan-a. 25-Punisher app. 3.00
...: Dead End Kids HC (2008, $19.99) r/#25-30 20.00
... Saga (2007, $3.99) re-caps the 2 series thru #24; 4 new pages w/Ramos-a; Ramos-c 4.00

Runaways (2017 series) #24 © MAR

RWBY #3 © Rooster Teeth Prods.

Saban's Go Go Power Rangers #16 © Saban

GD VG FN VF VF/NM NM-
2.0 4.0 6.0 8.0 9.0 9.2

Hardcover (2006, $24.99) oversized r/#1-12 & X-Men/Runaways; script & sketch pages 25.00
Hardcover Vol. 3 (2007, $24.99) oversized r/#13-24; sketch pages 25.00
...Vol. 4: True Believers (2006, $7.99, digest size) r/#1-6 8.00
...Vol. 5: Escape To New York (2006, $7.99, digest size) r/#7-12 8.00
...Vol. 6: Parental Guidance (2006, $7.99, digest size) r/#13-18 8.00

RUNAWAYS (3rd series)
Marvel Comics: Oct, 2008 - No. 14, Nov, 2009 ($2.99/$3.99)
1-9,11-14: 1-6-Terry Moore-s/Humberto Ramos-a/c. 7-9-Miyazawa-a 3.00
10-($3.99) Wolverine & the X-Men app.; Yost & Asmus-s; Pichelli & Rios-a; Lafuente-c 4.00

RUNAWAYS (Secret Wars Battleworld tie-in)
Marvel Comics: Aug, 2015 - No. 4, Nov, 2015 ($3.99, limited series)
1-4-Noelle Stevenson-s/Sanford Greene-a 4.00

RUNAWAYS
Marvel Comics: Nov, 2017 - Present ($3.99)
1-33: 1-Gert revived; Rowell-s/Anka-a. 8-Julie Power app. 33-Wolverine app. 4.00
... Halloween Comic Fest 2017 1 (12/17, giveaway) r/#1 (2003) first app. 3.00

RUN BABY RUN
Logos International: 1974 (39¢, Christian religious)
nn-By Tony Tallarico from Nicky Cruz's book 2 4 6 11 16 20

RUN, BUDDY, RUN (TV)
Gold Key: June, 1967 (Photo-c)
1 (10204-706) 3 6 9 17 26 35

RUNE (See Curse of Rune, Sludge & all other Ultraverse titles for previews)
Malibu Comics (Ultraverse): 1994 - No. 9, Apr, 1995 ($1.95)
0-Obtained by sending coupons from 11 comics; came w/Solution #0, poster, temporary tattoo, card 1 2 3 5 6 8
1,2,4-9: 1-Barry Windsor-Smith-c/a/stories begin, ends #6. 5-1st app. of Gemini. 6-Prime & Mantra app. 3.00
1-(1/94)-"Ashcan" edition flip book w/Wrath #1 3.00
1-Ultra 5000 Limited silver foil edition 6.00
3-(3/94, $3.50, 68 pgs.)-Flip book w/Ultraverse Premiere #1 4.00
Giant Size 1 ($2.50, 44 pgs.)-B.Smith story & art. 4.00

RUNE (2nd Series)(Formerly Curse of Rune)(See Ultraverse Unlimited #1)
Malibu Comics (Ultraverse): Infinity, Sept, 1995 - V2#7, Apr, 1996 ($1.50)
Infinity, V2#1-7: Infinity-Black September tie-in; black-c & painted-c exist. 1,3-7-Marvel's Adam Warlock app; regular & painted-c exist. 2-Flip book w/ "Phoenix Resurrection" Pt. 6 3.00
...Vs. Venom 1 (12/95, $3.95) 4.00

RUNE: HEARTS OF DARKNESS
Malibu Comics (Ultraverse): Sept, 1996 - No. 3, Nov, 1996 ($1.50, lim. series)
1-3: Moench scripts & Kyle Hotz-c/a; flip books w/6 pg. Rune story by the Pander Bros. 3.00

RUNE/SILVER SURFER
Marvel Comics/Malibu Comics (Ultraverse): Apr, 1995 ($5.95/$2.95, one-shot)
1 ($5.95, direct market)-BWS-c 6.00
1 ($2.95, newstand)-BWS-c 3.00
1-Collector's limited edition 6.00

RUNLOVEKILL
Image Comics: Apr, 2015 - No. 8 ($2.99, limited series)
1-4: 1-Tsuei-s/Canete-a 3.00

RUSE (Also see Archard's Agents)
CrossGeneration Comics: Nov, 2001 - No. 26, Jan, 2004 ($2.95)
1-Waid-s/Guice & Perkins-a 5.00
2-26: 6-Jeff Johnson-a. 11,15-Paul Ryan-a. 12-Last Waid-s 3.00
Enter the Detective Vol. 1 TPB (2002, $15.95) r/#1-6; Guice-c 16.00
...: The Silent Partner Vol. 2 (3/03, $15.95, TPB) r/#7-12 16.00
...: Criminal Intent Vol. 3 ('03, $15.95, TPB) r/#13-18 16.00
Traveler 1,2 ($9.95): Digest-size editions of the TPBs 10.00

RUSE
Marvel Comics: May, 2011 - No. 4 ($2.99, limited series)
1-4-Waid-s/Guice-c. 1,3,4-Pierfederici-a 3.00

RUSH CITY
DC Comics: Sept, 2006 - No. 6, May, 2007 ($2.99, limited series)
1-6: 1-Dixon-s/Green-a/Jock-c. 2,3-Black Canary app. 3.00

RUSTLERS, THE (See Zane Grey Four Color 532)

RUSTY, BOY DETECTIVE
Good Comics/Lev Gleason: Mar-April, 1955 - No. 5, Nov, 1955
1-Bob Wood, Carl Hubbell-a begins 11 22 33 62 80 110
2-5 9 18 27 47 61 75

RUSTY COMICS (Formerly Kid Movie Comics; Rusty and Her Family #21, 22; The Kelleys #23 on; see Millie The Model)
Marvel Comics (HPC): No. 12, Apr, 1947 - No. 22, Sept, 1949
12-Mitzi app. 32 64 96 192 314 435
13 20 40 60 114 182 250
14-Wolverton's Powerhouse Pepper (4 pgs.) plus Kurtzman's "Hey Look" 30 60 90 177 289 400
15-17-Kurtzman's "Hey Look" 22 44 66 128 209 290
18,19 18 36 54 107 169 230
20-Kurtzman-a (5 pgs.) 22 44 66 132 216 300
21,22-Kurtzman-a (17 & 22 pgs.) 28 56 84 168 274 380

RUSTY DUGAN (See Holyoke One-Shot #2)

RUSTY RILEY
Dell Publishing Co.: No. 418, Aug, 1952 - No. 554, April, 1954 (Frank Godwin strip reprints)
Four Color 418 (...a Boy, a Horse, and a Dog #1) 7 14 21 44 82 120
Four Color 451(2/53), 486 ('53), 554 5 10 15 30 50 70

RUULE
Beckett Comics: Dec, 2003 - No. 5, Apr, 2004 ($2.99)
1-5-David Mack-c/Mike Hawthorne-a 3.00

RUULE: KISS & TELL
Beckett Comics: Jun, 2004 - No. 8 ($1.99)
1-8: 1-Amano-s/c; Rousseau-a. 4-Maleev-c 3.00
TPB (2005, $19.99) r/#1-8 20.00

RWBY (Based on the online series from Rooster Teeth)(Issue #7 printing cancelled, digital only)
DC Comics: Dec, 2019 - No. 6, May, 2020 ($3.99)
1-6-Marguerite Bennett-s; two covers on each. 1-3,6-Mirka Andolfo-a. 4,5-Hetrick-a 4.00

RYDER OF THE STORM
Radical Comics: Oct, 2010 - No. 3, Apr, 2011 ($4.99, limited series)
1-3-David Hine-s/Wayne Nichols-a 5.00

SAARI ("The Jungle Goddess")
P. L. Publishing Co.: November, 1951
1 57 114 171 362 619 875

SABAN POWERHOUSE (TV)
Acclaim Books: 1997 ($4.50, digest size)
1,2-Power Rangers, BeetleBorgs, and others 1 3 4 6 8 10

SABAN PRESENTS POWER RANGERS TURBO VS. BEETLEBORGS METALLIX (TV)
Acclaim Books: 1997 ($4.50, digest size, one-shot)
nn 1 3 4 6 8 10

SABAN'S GO GO POWER RANGERS
BOOM! Studios: Jul, 2017 - No. 32, Jun, 2020 ($3.99)
1-32: 1-Parrott-s/Mora-a; multiple covers; retells 1st meeting with Rita Repulsa 4.00
...: Back To School 1 (9/18, $7.99) Rangers separately on Spring Break; art by various 8.00
...: Forever Rangers 1 (6/19, $7.99) Parrott-s/Carlini & Mortarino-a; origin of Zordon 8.00

SABAN'S MIGHTY MORPHIN POWER RANGERS
Hamilton Comics: Dec, 1994 - No. 6, May, 1995 ($1.95, limited series)
1-w/bound-in Power Ranger Barcode Card 3 6 9 16 23 30
2-6 5.00

SABAN'S MIGHTY MORPHIN POWER RANGERS (TV)
Marvel Comics: 1995 - No. 8, 1996 ($1.75)
1 1 3 4 6 8 10
2-8 4.00

SABAN'S POWER RANGERS: AFTERSHOCK
BOOM! Studios: Mar, 2017 ($14.99, SC)
SC - Sequel to the 2017 movie; Parrott-s/Werneck-a; movie photo-c 15.00

SABLE (Formerly Jon Sable, Freelance; also see Mike Grell's...)
First Comics: Mar, 1988 - No. 27, May, 1990 ($1.75/$1.95)
1-27: 10-Begin $1.95-c 3.00

SABLE & FORTUNE (Also see Silver Sable and the Wild Pack)
Marvel Comics: Mar, 2006 - No. 4, June, 2006 ($2.99, limited series)
1-4-John Burns-a/Brendan Cahill-s 3.00

SABRE (See Eclipse Graphic Album Series)
Eclipse Comics: Aug, 1982 - No. 14, Aug, 1985 (Baxter paper #4 on)

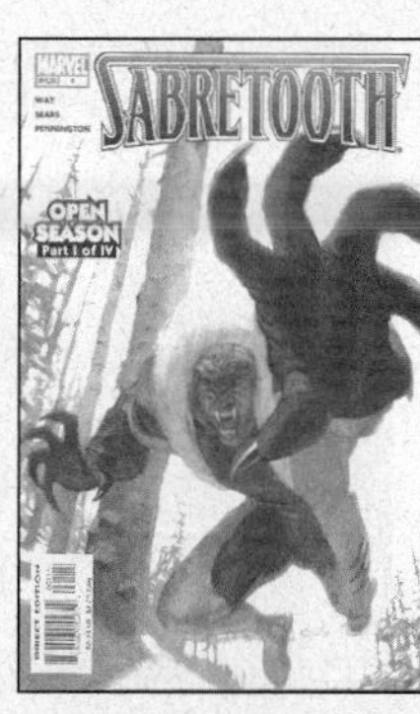

Sabretooth (2004 series) #1 © MAR

Sabrina the Teenage Witch V4 #1 © ACP

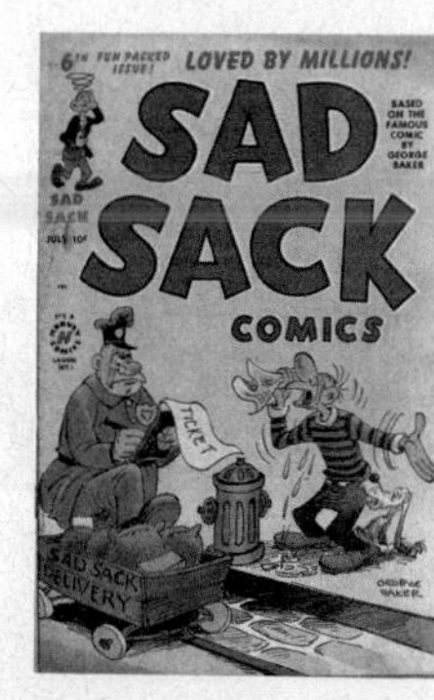

Sad Sack Comics #6 © HARV

GD 2.0 | VG 4.0 | FN 6.0 | VF 8.0 | VF/NM 9.0 | NM- 9.2

1-14: 1-Sabre & Morrigan Tales begin. 4-6-Incredible Seven origin 3.00

SABRETOOTH (See Iron Fist, Power Man, X-Factor #10 & X-Men)
Marvel Comics: Aug, 1993 - No. 4, Nov, 1993 ($2.95, lim. series, coated paper)
1-4: 1-Die-cut-c. 3-Wolverine app. 5.00
...Special 1 "In the Red Zone" (1995, $4.95) Chromium wraparound-c 6.00
V2 #1 (1/98, $5.95, one-shot) Wildchild app. 6.00
Trade paperback (12/94, $12.95) r/#1-4 13.00

SABRETOOTH
Marvel Comics: Dec, 2004 - No. 4, Feb, 2005 ($2.99, limited series)
1-4-Sears-a. 3,4-Wendigo app. 3.00
...: Open Season TPB (2005, $9.99) r/#1-4 10.00

SABRETOOTH AND MYSTIQUE (See Mystique and Sabretooth)

SABRETOOTH CLASSIC
Marvel Comics: May, 1994 - No. 15, July, 1995 ($1.50)
1-15: 1-3-r/Power Man & Iron Fist #66,78,84. 4-r/Spec. S-M #116. 9-Uncanny X-Men #212, 10-r/Uncanny X-Men #213. 11-r/ Daredevil #238. 12-r/Classic X-Men #10 3.00

SABRETOOTH: MARY SHELLEY OVERDRIVE
Marvel Comics: Aug, 2002 - No. 4, Nov, 2002 ($2.99, limited series)
1-4-Jolley-s; Harris-c 3.00

SABRINA (Volume 2) (Based on animated series)
Archie Publications: Jan, 2000 - No. 104, Sept, 2009 ($1.79/$1.99/$2.19/$2.25/$2.50)
1-Teen-age Witch magically reverted to 12 years old 2 4 6 8 10 12
2-10: 4-Begin $1.99-c 4.00
11-104: 38-Sabrina aged back to 16 years old. 39-Begin $2.19-c. 58-Manga-style begins; Tania Del Rio-a. 67-Josie and the Pussycats app. 101-Young Salem; begin $2.50-c 3.00
... And The Archies (2004, 8 1/2"x 5 1/2", Diamond Comic Dist. Halloween giveaway) - Tania Del Rio-s/a; manga-style; Josie and the Pussycats app. 3.00

SABRINA'S CHRISTMAS MAGIC (See Archie Giant Series Magazine #196, 207, 220, 231, 243, 455, 467, 479, 491, 503, 515)

SABRINA'S HALLOWEEN SPOOOKTACULAR
Archie Publications: 1993 - 1995 ($2.00, 52 pgs.)
1-Neon orange ink-c; bound-in poster 2 4 6 8 10 12
2,3-Titled "Sabrina's Holiday Spectacular" 6.00

SABRINA, THE TEEN-AGE WITCH (TV)(See Archie Giant Series, Archie's Madhouse 22, Archie's TV…, Chilling Advs. In Sorcery, Little Archie #59)
Archie Publications: April, 1971 - No. 77, Jan, 1983 (52 pg.Giants No. 1-17)

Issue	GD	VG	FN	VF	VF/NM	NM-
1-52 pgs. begin, end #17	23	46	69	161	356	550
2-Archie's group x-over	9	18	27	59	117	175
3-5: 3,4-Archie's Group x-over	6	12	18	40	73	105
6-10	5	10	15	33	57	80
11-17(2/74)	4	8	12	27	44	60
18-30	3	6	9	19	30	40
31-40(8/77)	3	6	9	14	20	26
41-60(6/80)	2	4	6	10	14	18
61-70	2	4	6	8	11	14
71-76-low print run	2	4	6	11	16	20
77-Last issue; low print run	3	6	9	15	22	28

SABRINA, THE TEEN-AGE WITCH
Archie Publications: 1996 ($1.50, 32 pgs., one-shot)
1-Updated origin 2 4 6 8 10 12

SABRINA, THE TEEN-AGE WITCH (Continues in Sabrina, Vol. 2)
Archie Publications: May, 1997 - No. 32, Dec, 1999 ($1.50/$1.75/$1.79)
1-Photo-c with Melissa Joan Hart 2 4 6 8 10 12
2-10: 9-Begin $1.75-c 6.00
11-20 5.00
21-32: 24-Begin $1.79-c. 28-Sonic the Hedgehog-c/app. 4.00

SABRINA THE TEEN-AGE WITCH (Volume 3)
Archie Comic Publications: May, 2019 - No. 5, Nov, 2019 ($3.99)
1-5-Kelly Thompson-s/Veronica & Andy Fish-a; multiple covers 4.00

SABRINA THE TEEN-AGE WITCH (Volume 4)
Archie Comic Publications: May, 2020 - No. 5, Apr, 2021 ($3.99)
1-5-Kelly Thompson-s/Veronica & Andy Fish-a; multiple covers 4.00

SABU, "ELEPHANT BOY" (Movie; formerly My Secret Story)
Fox Feature Syndicate: No. 30, June, 1950 - No. 2, Aug, 1950
30(#1)-Wood-a; photo-c from movie 27 54 81 158 259 360
2-Photo-c from movie; Kamen-a 20 40 60 114 182 250

SACHS & VIOLENS
Marvel Comics (Epic Comics): Nov, 1993 - No. 4, July, 1994 ($2.25, limited series, mature)
1-($2.75)-Embossed-c w/bound-in trading card 3.00
1-($3.50)-Platinum edition (1 for each 10 ordered) 4.00
2-4: Perez-c/a; bound-in trading card: 2-(5/94) 3.00
TPB (DC, 2006, $14.99) r/series; intro. by Peter David; creator bios. 15.00

SACRAMENTS, THE
Catechetical Guild Educational Society: Oct, 1955 (35¢)
30304 8 16 24 42 54 65

SACRED AND THE PROFANE, THE (See Eclipse Graphic Album Series #9 & Epic Illustrated #20)

SACRED CREATURES
Image Comics: Jul, 2017 - No. 6, May, 2018 ($4.99/$3.99)
1,4-6-($4.99) Pablo Raimondi & Klaus Janson-s/Raimondi-a. 4-6-Janson partial-a 5.00
2,3-($3.99) 4.00

SACRED SIX
Dynamite Entertainment: 2020 - Present ($3.99)
1-7-Vampirella, Draculina, Pantha, Nyx, Chastity & Lilith app. 1-Jae Lee & Gabriel Ibarra-a 5.00

SADDLE JUSTICE (Happy Houlihans #1,2) (Saddle Romances #9 on)
E. C. Comics: No. 3, Spring, 1948 - No. 8, Sept-Oct, 1949
3-The 1st E.C. by Bill Gaines to break away from M. C. Gaines' old Educational Comics format. Craig, Feldstein, H. C. Kiefer, & Stan Asch-a; mentioned in Love and Death 71 142 213 454 777 1100
4-1st Graham Ingels-a for E.C. 58 116 174 371 636 900
5-8-Ingels-a in all 54 108 162 343 574 825
NOTE: *Craig and Feldstein art in most issues. Canadian reprints known; see Table of Contents.* ***Craig*** *c-3, 4.* ***Ingels*** *c-5-8. #4 contains a biography of* ***Craig****.*

SADDLE ROMANCES (Saddle Justice #3-8; Weird Science #12 on)
E. C. Comics: No. 9, Nov-Dec, 1949 - No. 11, Mar-Apr, 1950
9,11: 9-Ingels-c/a. 11-Ingels-a; Feldstein-c 57 114 171 362 619 875
10-Wally Wood's 1st work at E. C.; Ingels-a; Feldstein-c 77 154 231 493 847 1200
NOTE: *Canadian reprints known; see Table of Contents.* ***Wood/Harrison*** *a-10, 11.*

SADIE SACK (See Harvey Hits #93)

SAD SACK AND THE SARGE
Harvey Publications: Sept, 1957 - No. 155, June, 1982

Issue	GD	VG	FN	VF	VF/NM	NM-
1	12	24	36	82	179	275
2	7	14	21	46	86	125
3-10	5	10	15	35	63	90
11-20	5	10	15	30	50	70
21-30	3	6	9	19	30	40
31-50	3	6	9	14	20	25
51-70	2	4	6	9	13	16
71-90,97-99	1	3	4	6	8	10
91-96: All 52 pg. Giants	2	4	6	9	13	16
100	2	4	6	8	10	12
101-120	1	2	3	4	5	7
121-155						5.00

NOTE: ***George Baker*** *covers on numerous issues.*

SAD SACK COMICS (See Harvey Collector's Comics #16, Little Sad Sack, Tastee Freez Comics #4 & True Comics #55 for 1st app.)
Harvey Publications/Lorne-Harvey Publications (Recollections) #288 On: Sept, 1949 - No. 287, Oct, 1982; No. 288, 1992 - No. 291, 1993
1-Infinity-c; Little Dot begins (1st app.); civilian issues begin, end #21; based on comic strip (first app. in True Comics #55) 139 278 417 1112 2506 3900

Issue	GD	VG	FN	VF	VF/NM	NM-
2-Flying Fool by Powell	31	62	93	223	499	775
3	17	34	51	117	259	400
4-10	12	24	36	79	170	260
11-21	8	16	24	54	102	150
22-("Back In The Army Again" on covers #22-36); "The Specialist" story about Sad Sack's return to Army	9	18	27	59	117	175
23-30	5	10	15	34	60	85
31-50	4	8	12	28	47	65
51-80,100: 62-"The Specialist" reprinted	3	6	9	21	33	45
81-99	3	6	9	16	23	30
101-140	3	6	9	14	19	24
141-170,200	2	4	6	11	16	20
171-199	2	4	6	9	13	16
201-207: 207-Last 12¢ issue	2	4	6	8	11	14
208-222	1	3	4	6	8	10

Sad Sack Laugh Special #6 © HARV

Saga #1 © Vaughan & Staples

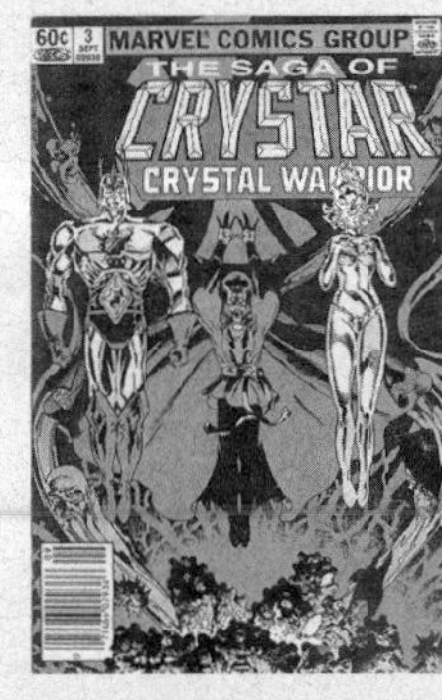

Saga of Crystar, Crystal Warrior #3 © MAR

	GD 2.0	VG 4.0	FN 6.0	VF 8.0	VF/NM 9.0	NM- 9.2
223-228 (25¢ Giants, 52 pgs.)	2	4	6	8	11	14
229-250	1	3	4	6	8	10
251-285						6.00
286,287-Limited distribution	1	2	3	5	7	9
288,289 ($2.75, 1992): 289-50th anniversary issue						6.00
290,291 ($1.00, 1993, B&W)						3.00
3-D 1 (1/54, 25¢)-Came with 2 pairs of glasses; titled "Harvey 3-D Hits"	14	28	42	93	204	315
...At Home for the Holidays 1 (1993, no-c price)-Publ. by Lorne-Harvey' X-Mas issue						4.00

NOTE: *The Sad Sack Comics comic book was a spin-off from a Sunday Newspaper strip launched through John Wheeler's Bell Syndicate. The previous Sunday page and the first 21 comics depicted the Sad Sack in civvies. Unpopularity caused the Sunday page to be discontinued in the early '50s. Meanwhile Sad Sack returned to the Army, by popular demand, in issue No. 22, remaining there ever since. Incidentally, relatively few of the first 21 issues were ever collected and remain scarce due to this.* ***George Baker*** *covers on numerous issues.*

SAD SACK FUN AROUND THE WORLD
Harvey Publications: 1974 (no month)

	GD	VG	FN	VF	VF/NM	NM-
1-About Great Britain	2	4	6	11	16	20

SAD SACK GOES HOME
Harvey Publications: 1951 (16 pgs. in color, no cover price)

	GD	VG	FN	VF	VF/NM	NM-
nn-By George Baker	5	10	15	31	53	75

SAD SACK LAUGH SPECIAL
Harvey Publications: Winter, 1958-59 - No. 93, Feb, 1977 (#1-9: 84 pgs.; #10-60: 68 pgs.; #61-76: 52 pgs.)

	GD	VG	FN	VF	VF/NM	NM-
1-Giant 25¢ issues begin	9	18	27	60	120	180
2	5	10	15	35	63	90
3-10	5	10	15	30	50	70
11-30	4	8	12	25	40	55
31-60: 31-Hi-Fi Tweeter app. 60-Last 68 pg. Giant	3	6	9	16	23	30
61-76-(All 52 pg. issues)	2	4	6	10	14	18
77-93	1	2	3	5	6	8

SAD SACK NAVY, GOBS 'N' GALS
Harvey Publications: Aug, 1972 - No. 8, Oct, 1973

	GD	VG	FN	VF	VF/NM	NM-
1: 52 pg. Giant	3	6	9	16	23	30
2-8	2	4	6	9	12	15

SAD SACK'S ARMY LIFE (See Harvey Hits #8, 17, 22, 28, 32, 39, 43, 47, 51, 55, 58, 61, 64, 67, 70)

SAD SACK'S ARMY LIFE (...Parade #1-57, ...Today #58 on)
Harvey Publications: Oct, 1963 - No. 60, Nov, 1975; No. 61, May, 1976

	GD	VG	FN	VF	VF/NM	NM-
1-(68 pg. issues begin)	7	14	21	44	82	120
2-10	4	8	12	27	44	60
11-20	3	6	9	19	30	40
21-34: Last 68 pg. issue	3	6	9	16	23	30
35-51: All 52 pgs.	2	4	6	10	14	18
52-61	1	3	4	6	8	10

SAD SACK'S FUNNY FRIENDS (See Harvey Hits #75)
Harvey Publications: Dec, 1955 - No. 75, Oct, 1969

	GD	VG	FN	VF	VF/NM	NM-
1	9	18	27	60	120	180
2-10	5	10	15	35	63	90
11-20	4	8	12	23	37	50
21-30	3	6	9	17	26	35
31-50	3	6	9	14	20	25
51-75	2	4	6	9	13	16

SAD SACK'S MUTTSY (See Harvey Hits #74, 77, 80, 82, 84, 87, 89, 92, 96, 99, 102, 105, 108, 111, 113, 115, 117, 119, 121)

SAD SACK USA (...Vacation #8)
Harvey Publications: Nov, 1972 - No. 7, Nov, 1973; No. 8, Oct, 1974

	GD	VG	FN	VF	VF/NM	NM-
1	3	6	9	14	20	25
2-8	2	4	6	8	10	12

SAD SACK WITH SARGE & SADIE
Harvey Publications: Sept, 1972 - No. 8, Nov, 1973

	GD	VG	FN	VF	VF/NM	NM-
1-(52 pg. Giant)	3	6	9	14	20	25
2-8	2	4	6	8	10	12

SAD SAD SACK WORLD
Harvey Publ.: Oct, 1964 - No. 46, Dec, 1973 (#1-31: 68 pgs.; #32-38: 52 pgs.)

	GD	VG	FN	VF	VF/NM	NM-
1	6	12	18	41	76	110
2-10	4	8	12	25	40	55
11-20	3	6	9	19	30	40
21-31: 31-Last 68 pg. issue	3	6	9	16	23	30
32-39-(All 52 pgs)	2	4	6	10	14	18
40-46	1	3	4	6	8	10

SAFEST PLACE IN THE WORLD, THE
Dark Horse Comics: 1993 ($2.50, one-shot)

	GD	VG	FN	VF	VF/NM	NM-
1-Steve Ditko-c/a/scripts						4.00

SAFETY-BELT MAN
Sirius Entertainment: June, 1994 - No. 6, 1995 ($2.50, B&W)

	GD	VG	FN	VF	VF/NM	NM-
1-6: 1-Horan-s/Dark One-a/Sprouse-c. 2,3-Warren-c. 4-Linsner back-up story. 5,6-Crilley-a						3.00

SAFETY-BELT MAN ALL HELL
Sirius Entertainment: June, 1996 - No. 6, Mar, 1997 ($2.95, color)

	GD	VG	FN	VF	VF/NM	NM-
1-6-Horan-s/Fillbach Bros.-a						3.00

SAGA
Image Comics: Mar, 2012 - Present ($2.99)

	GD	VG	FN	VF	VF/NM	NM-
1-Brian K. Vaughan-s/Fiona Staples-a/c; 1st app. Alana, Marko, Hazel, The Will, and Lying Cat	9	18	27	60	120	180
1-Second printing	3	6	9	15	22	28
2-1st app. The Stalk	3	6	9	17	26	35
3-5: 3-1st app. Izabel	3	6	9	14	20	25
6,7,9-12						6.00
8-1st app. Gwendolyn	3	6	9	14	19	24
13-53: 19-Intro. Ginny. 24-Lying Cat returns. 25,37-Wraparound-c. 43-(25¢-c). 51-Doff killed. 53-Prince Robot killed						4.00
54-(7/18) Marko dies						4.00

SAGA OF BIG RED, THE
Omaha World-Herald: Sept, 1976 ($1.25) (In color)

	GD	VG	FN	VF	VF/NM	NM-
nn-by Win Mumma; story of the Nebraska Cornhuskers (sports)						6.00

SAGA OF CRYSTAR, CRYSTAL WARRIOR, THE
Marvel Comics: May, 1983 - No. 11, Feb, 1985 (Remco toy tie-in)

	GD	VG	FN	VF	VF/NM	NM-
1,6: 1-(Baxter paper). 6-Nightcrawler app; Golden-c						5.00
2-5,7-11: 3-Dr. Strange app. 3-11-Golden-c (painted-4,5). 11-Alpha Flight app.						4.00

SAGA OF RA'S AL GHUL, THE
DC Comics: Jan, 1988 - No. 4, Apr, 1988 ($2.50, limited series)

	GD	VG	FN	VF	VF/NM	NM-
1-4-r/N. Adams Batman						6.00

SAGA OF SABAN'S MIGHTY MORPHIN POWER RANGERS (Also see Saban's Mighty Morphin Power Rangers)
Hamilton Comics: 1995 - No. 4, 1995 ($1.95, limited series)

	GD	VG	FN	VF	VF/NM	NM-
1-4						4.00

SAGA OF SEVEN SUNS, THE : VEILED ALLIANCES
DC Comics (WildStorm): 2004 ($24.95, hardcover graphic novel with dustjacket)

	GD	VG	FN	VF	VF/NM	NM-
HC-Kevin J. Anderson-s/Robert Teranishi-a						25.00
SC-(2004, $17.95)						18.00

SAGA OF THE ORIGINAL HUMAN TORCH
Marvel Comics: Apr, 1990 - No. 4, July, 1990 ($1.50, limited series)

	GD	VG	FN	VF	VF/NM	NM-
1-4: 1-Origin; Buckler-c/a(p). 3-Hitler-c						4.00

SAGA OF THE SUB-MARINER, THE
Marvel Comics: Nov, 1988 - No. 12, Oct, 1989 ($1.25/$1.50 #5 on, maxi-series)

	GD	VG	FN	VF	VF/NM	NM-
1-12: 9-Original X-Men app.						4.00

SAGA OF THE SWAMP THING, THE (See Swamp Thing)

SAILOR MOON (Manga)
Mixx Entertainment Inc.: 1998 - No. 25 ($2.95)

	GD	VG	FN	VF	VF/NM	NM-
1	3	6	9	14	20	25
1-(San Diego edition)	3	6	9	17	26	35
2-5	2	4	6	9	12	15
6-10	1	3	4	6	8	10
11-25	1	2	3	4	5	7
26-35						5.00
... Rini's Moon Stick 1						15.00

SAILOR ON THE SEA OF FATE (See First Comics Graphic Novel #11)

SAILOR SWEENEY (Navy Action #1-11, 15 on)
Atlas Comics (CDS): No. 12, July, 1956 - No. 14, Nov, 1956

	GD	VG	FN	VF	VF/NM	NM-
12-14: 12-Shores-a. 13,14-Severin-c	27	54	81	158	259	360

SAINT, THE (Also see Movie Comics(DC) #2 & Silver Streak #18)
Avon Periodicals: Aug, 1947 - No. 12, Mar, 1952

	GD	VG	FN	VF	VF/NM	NM-
1-Kamen bondage-c/a	155	310	465	992	1696	2400
2	57	114	171	362	619	875
3,5	52	104	156	328	552	775

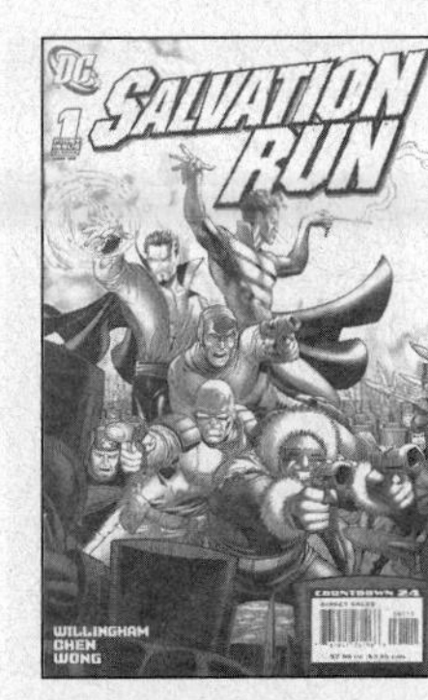

Salvation Run #1 © DC

Sam and Twitch #6 © TMP

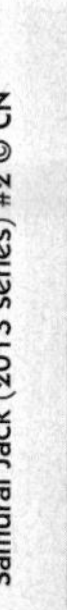
Samurai Jack (2013 series) #2 © CN

	GD 2.0	VG 4.0	FN 6.0	VF 8.0	VF/NM 9.0	NM- 9.2
4-Lingerie panels, black background, Good Girl art-c	61	122	183	390	670	950
6-Miss Fury app. by Tarpe Mills (14 pgs.)	77	154	231	493	847	1200
7-c-/Avon paperback #118	42	84	126	265	445	625
8,9(12/50): Saint strip-r in #8-12; 9-Kinstler-c	40	80	120	246	411	575
10-Wood-a, 1 pg; c-/Avon paperback #289	40	80	120	246	411	575
11	36	72	108	214	347	480
12-c-/Avon paperback #123	38	76	114	228	369	510

NOTE: *Lucky Dale, Girl Detective in #1,2,4,6.* ***Hollingsworth** a-4, 6. Painted-c 7, 8, 10-12.*

SAINT ANGEL
Image Comics: Mar, 2000 - No. 4, Mar, 2001 ($2.95/$3.95)

0-Altstaetter & Napton-s/Altstaetter-a 3.00
1-4-($3.95) Flip book w/Deity. 1-(6/00). 2-(10/00) 4.00

ST. GEORGE
Marvel Comics (Epic Comics): June, 1988 - No.8, Oct, 1989 ($1.25,/$1.50)

1-8: Sienkiewicz-c. 3-begin $1.50-c 3.00

SAINT GERMAINE
Caliber Comics: 1997 - No. 8, 1998 ($2.95)

1-8: 1,5-Alternate covers 3.00

ST. SWITHIN'S DAY
Trident Comics: Apr, 1990 ($2.50, one-shot)

1-Grant Morrison scripts 3.00

ST. SWITHIN'S DAY
Oni Press: Mar, 1998 ($2.95, B&W, one-shot)

1-Grant Morrison-s/Paul Grist-a 3.00

SALOMÉ (See Night Music #6)

SALVATION RUN
DC Comics: Jan, 2008 - No. 7, Jul, 2008 ($2.99/$3.50, limited series)

1-6-DC villains banished to an alien planet; Willingham-s/Chen-a/c. 1-Var-c by Corroney 3.00
7-($3.50) Luthor cover by Chen 3.50

	GD	VG	FN	VF	VF/NM	NM-
7-($3.50) Variant Joker cover by Neal Adams	4	8	12	25	40	55

SAM AND MAX, FREELANCE POLICE SPECIAL
Fishwrap Prod./Comico: 1987 ($1.75, B&W); Jan, 1989 ($2.75, 44 pgs.)

1 ($1.75, B&W, Fishwrap) 4.00
2 ($2.75, color, Comico) 4.00

SAM AND TWITCH (See Spawn and Case Files:...)
Image Comics (Todd McFarlane Prod.): Aug, 1999 - No. 26, Feb, 2004 ($2.50)

1-26: 1-19-Bendis-s. 1-14-Medina-a. 15-19-Maleev-a. 20-24-McFarlane-s/Maleev-a 3.00
Book One: Udaku (2000, $21.95, TPB) B&W reprint of #1-8 22.00
...: The Brian Michael Bendis Collection Vol. 1 (2/06, $24.95) r/#1-9 in color; sketch pages 25.00
...: The Brian Michael Bendis Collection Vol. 2 (6/07, $24.95) r/#10-19; cover gallery 25.00

SAM AND TWITCH: THE WRITER
Image Comics (Todd McFarlane Prod.): May, 2010 - No. 4, Jun, 2010 ($2.99)

1-4-Blengino-s/Erbetta-a/c 3.00

SAMARITAN VERITAS
Image Comics: May, 2017 - No. 3, Jul, 2017 ($3.99)

1-3-Hawkins-s/Rojo-a 4.00

SAM HILL PRIVATE EYE
Close-Up (Archie): 1950 - No. 7, 1951

	GD	VG	FN	VF	VF/NM	NM-
1	23	46	69	136	223	310
2	14	28	42	78	112	145
3-7	10	20	30	58	79	100

SAMSON (1st Series) (Captain Aero #7 on; see Big 3 Comics)
Fox Feature Syndicate: Fall, 1940 - No. 6, Sept, 1941 (See Fantastic Comics)

	GD	VG	FN	VF	VF/NM	NM-
1-Samson begins, ends #6; Powell-a, signed 'Rensie;' Wing Turner by Tuska app; Fine-c?	213	426	639	1363	2332	3300
2-Dr. Fung by Powell; Fine-c?	97	194	291	621	1061	1500
3-Navy Jones app.; Joe Simon-c	73	146	219	467	796	1125
4-Yarko the Great, Master Magician begins	68	136	204	435	743	1050
5,6: 5-WWII Nazi-c. 6-Origin The Topper	58	116	174	371	636	900

SAMSON (2nd Series) (Formerly Fantastic Comics #10, 11)
Ajax/Farrell Publications (Four Star): No. 12, April, 1955 - No. 14, Aug, 1955

	GD	VG	FN	VF	VF/NM	NM-
12-Wonder Boy	36	72	108	211	343	475
13,14: 13-Wonder Boy, Rocket Man	31	62	93	186	303	420

SAMSON (See Mighty Samson)

SAMSON & DELILAH (See A Spectacular Feature Magazine)

SAMUEL BRONSTON'S CIRCUS WORLD (See Circus World under Movie Classics)

SAMURAI (Also see Eclipse Graphic Album Series #14)
Aircel Publications: 1985 - No. 23, 1987 ($1.70, B&W)

1, 14-16-Dale Keown-a 4.00
1-(reprinted),2-12,17-23: 2 (reprinted issue exists) 3.00
13-Dale Keown's 1st published artwork (1987) 6.00

SAMURAI
Warp Graphics: May, 1997 ($2.95, B&W)

1 3.00

SAMURAI: BROTHERS IN ARMS
Titan Comics: Oct, 2016 - No. 6 ($3.99)

1-6-Genet-a/DiGiorgio-s; English version of French comic 4.00

SAMURAI CAT
Marvel Comics (Epic Comics): June, 1991 - No. 3, Sept, 1991 ($2.25, limited series)

1-3: 3-Darth Vader-c/story parody 3.00

SAMURAI: HEAVEN & EARTH
Dark Horse Comics: Dec, 2004 - No. 5, Dec, 2005 ($2.99)

1-5-Luke Ross-a/Ron Marz-s 3.00
TPB (4/06, $14.95) r/#1-5; sketch pages and cover and pin-up gallery 15.00

SAMURAI: HEAVEN & EARTH (Volume 2)
Dark Horse Comics: Nov, 2006 - No. 5, June, 2007 ($2.99)

1-5-Luke Ross-a/Ron Marz-s 3.00
TPB (10/07, $14.95) r/#1-5; sketch pages and cover and pin-up gallery 15.00

SAMURAI JACK (TV)
IDW Publishing: Oct, 2013 - No. 20, May, 2015 ($3.99)

1-20: 1-5-Jim Zub-s/Andy Suriano-a; multiple covers on each 4.00
... Special - Director's Cut (2/14, $7.99) Reprints '02 DC issue; commentary by Bill Wray 8.00

SAMURAI JACK: LOST WORLDS (TV)
IDW Publishing: Apr, 2019 - No. 4, Jul, 2019 ($3.99, limited series)

1-4-Paul Allor-s/Adam Bryce Thomas-a; multiple covers on each 4.00

SAMURAI JACK: QUANTUM JACK (TV)
IDW Publishing: Sept, 2017 - No. 5, Jan, 2018 ($3.99, limited series)

1-5-Rangel, Jr.-s/Johnson-Cadwell-a; multiple covers 4.00

SAMURAI JACK SPECIAL (TV)
DC Comics: Sept, 2002 ($3.95, one-shot)

1-Adaptation of pilot episode with origin story; Tartakovsky-s/Naylor & Wray-a 4.00

SAMURAI: LEGEND
Marvel Comics (Soleil): 2008 - No. 4, 2009 ($5.99)

1-4-Genet-a/DiGiorgio-s; English version of French comic; preview of other titles 6.00

SAMUREE
Continuity Comics: May, 1987 - No. 9, Jan, 1991

1-9 3.00

SAMUREE
Continuity Comics: V2#1, May, 1993 - V2#4, Jan,1994 ($2.50)

V2#1-4-Embossed-c: 2,4-Adams plot, Nebres-i. 3-Nino-c(i) 3.00

SAMUREE
Acclaim Comics (Windjammer): Oct, 1995 - No. 2, Nov,1995 ($2.50, lim. series)

1,2 3.00

SAN DIEGO COMIC CON COMICS
Dark Horse Comics: 1992 - No.4, 1995 (B&W, promo comic for the San Diego Comic Con)

	GD	VG	FN	VF	VF/NM	NM-
1-(1992)-Includes various characters published from Dark Horse including Concrete, The Mask, RoboCop and others; 1st app. of Sprint from John Byrne's Next Men; art by Quesada, Byrne, Rude, Burden, Moebius & others; pin-ups by Rude, Dorkin, Allred & others; Chadwick-c	2	4	6	8	11	14
2-(1993)-Intro of Legend imprint; 1st app. of John Byrne's Danger Unlimited, Mike Mignola's Hellboy (also see John Byrne's Next Men #21), Art Adams' Monkeyman & O'Brien; contains stories featuring Concrete, Sin City, Martha Washington & others; Grendel, Madman, & Big Guy pin-ups; Don Martin-c	9	18	27	59	117	175
3-(1994)-Contains stories featuring Barb Wire, The Mask, The Dirty Pair, & Grendel by Matt Wagner; contains pin-ups of Ghost, Predator & Rascals In Paradise; The Mask-c	1	2	3	5	6	8
4-(1995)-Contains Sin City story by Miller (3pg.), Star Wars, The Mask, Tarzan, Foot Soldiers; Sin City & Star Wars flip-c	1	2	3	5	6	8

Sandman #62 © DC

Sandman Mystery Theatre #50 © DC

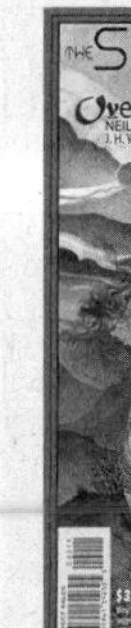

Sandman: Overture #2 © DC

GD	VG	FN	VF	VF/NM	NM-
2.0	4.0	6.0	8.0	9.0	9.2

SANDMAN, THE (1st Series) (Also see Adventure Comics #40, New York World's Fair, Sandman Special (2017) and World's Finest #3)
National Periodical Publ.: Winter, 1974; No. 2, Apr-May, 1975 - No. 6, Dec-Jan, 1975-76

1-1st app. Bronze Age Sandman by Simon & Kirby (last S&K collaboration) 6 12 18 41 76 110
2-6: 6-Kirby/Wood-c/a 3 6 9 21 33 45
The Sandman By Joe Simon & Jack Kirby HC (2009, $39.99, d.j.) r/Sandman app. from World's Finest #6,7, Adventure Comics #72-102 and Sandman #1; Morrow intro. 40.00
NOTE: *Kirby a-1p, 4-6p; c-1-5, 6p.*

SANDMAN (2nd Series) (See Books of Magic, Vertigo Jam & Vertigo Preview)
DC Comics (Vertigo imprint #47 on): Jan, 1989 - No. 75, Mar, 1996 ($1.50-$2.50, mature)

1 ($2.00, 52 pgs.)-1st app. Modern Age Sandman (Morpheus); Neil Gaiman scripts begin; Sam Kieth-a(p) in #1-5; Wesley Dodds (G.A. Sandman) cameo. 8 16 24 51 96 140
2-Cain & Abel app. (from HOM & HOS) 3 6 9 17 26 35
3,5: 3-John Constantine app. 2 4 6 13 18 22
4-1st app. Lucifer Morningstar; The Demon app. 5 10 15 31 53 75
6,7 2 4 6 9 12 15
8-Death-c/story (1st app.)-Regular ed. has Jeanette Kahn publishorial & American Cancer Society ad w/no indicia on inside front-c 7 14 21 46 86 125
8-Limited ed. (600+ copies?); has Karen Berger editorial and next issue teaser on inside covers (has indicia) 23 46 69 161 356 550
9-14: 10-Has explaination about #8 mixup; has bound-in Shocker movie poster. 14-(52 pgs.)-Bound-in Nightbreed fold-out 2 4 6 8 10 12
15-20: 16-Photo-c. 17,18-Kelley Jones-a. 19-Vess-a 1 2 3 5 6 8
18-Error version w/1st 3 panels on pg. 1 in blue ink 17 34 51 117 259 400
19-Error version w/pages 18 & 20 facing each other 2 4 6 11 16 20
21,23-27: Seasons of Mist storyline. 22-World Without End preview. 24-Kelley Jones/Russell-a 6.00
22-1st Daniel (Later becomes new Sandman) 3 6 9 15 22 28
28-30 5.00
31-49,51-74: 36-(52 pgs.). 41,44-48-Metallic ink on-c. 48-Cerebus appears as a doll. 54-Re-intro Prez; Death app.; Belushi, Nixon & Wildcat cameos. 57-Metallic ink on c. 65-w/bound-in trading card. 69-Death of Sandman. 70-73-Zulli-a. 74-Jon J. Muth-a. 4.00
50-($2.95, 52 pgs.)-Black-c w/metallic ink by McKean; Russell-a; McFarlane pin-up 1 2 3 5 6 8
50-($2.95)-Signed & limited (5,000) Treasury Edition with sketch of Neil Gaiman 3 6 9 14 19 24
50-Platinum 28.00
75-($3.95)-Vess-a. 5.00
Special 1 (1991, $3.50, 68 pgs.)-Glow-in-the-dark-c 5.00
Absolute Sandman Special Edition #1 (2006, 50¢) sampling from HC; recolored r/#1 3.00
Absolute Sandman Volume One (2006, $99.00, slipcased hardcover) recolored r/#1-20; Gaiman's original proposal; script and pencils from #19; character sketch gallery 100.00
Absolute Sandman Volume Two (2007, $99.00, slipcased hardcover) recolored r/#21-39; r/A Gallery of Dreams one-shot; bonus stories, scripts and pencil art 100.00
Absolute Sandman Volume Three (2008, $99.00, slipcased hardcover) recolored r/#40-56; & Special #1; bonus galleries, scripts and pencil art; Jill Thompson intro. 100.00
Absolute Sandman Volume Four (2008, $99.00, slipcased hardcover) recolored r/#57-75; scripts & sketch pages for #57 & 75; gallery of Dreaming memorabilia; Berger intro. 100.00
...: A Gallery of Dreams ($2.95)-Intro by N. Gaiman 4.00
...: Preludes & Nocturnes ($29.95, HC)-r/#1-8. 30.00
...: The Doll's House (1990, $29.95, HC)-r/#8-16. 30.00
...: Dream Country ($29.95, HC)-r/#17-20. 30.00
...: Season of Mists ($29.95, Leatherbound HC)-r/#21-28. 50.00
...: A Game of You ($29.95, HC)-r/32-37, ...: Fables and Reflections ($29.95, HC)-r/Vertigo Preview #1, Sandman Special #1, #29-31, #38-40 & #50. ...: Brief Lives ($29.95, HC)-r/#41-49. ...: World's End ($29.95, HC)-r/#51-56 30.00
...: The Kindly Ones (1996, $34.95, HC)-r/#57-69 & Vertigo Jam #1 35.00
...: The Wake ($29.95, HC)-r/#70-75. 30.00
NOTE: *A new set of hardcover printings with new covers was introduced in 1998-99. Multiple printings exist of softcover collections. Recolored (from the Absolute HC) softcover editions were released in 2010.* ***Bachalo*** *a-12;* ***Kelley Jones*** *a-17, 18, 22, 23, 26, 27.* ***Vess*** *a-19, 75.*

SANDMAN: ENDLESS NIGHTS
DC Comics (Vertigo): 2003 ($24.95, hardcover, with dust jacket)

HC-Neil Gaiman stories of Morpheus and the Endless illustrated by Fabry, Manara, Prado, Quitely, Russell, Sienkiewicz, and Storey; McKean-c 25.00
...Special (11/03, $2.95) Previews hardcover; Dream story w/Prado-a; McKean-c 4.00
SC (2004, $17.95) 18.00

SANDMAN MIDNIGHT THEATRE
DC Comics (Vertigo): Sept, 1995 ($6.95, squarebound, one-shot)

nn-Modern Age Sandman (Morpheus) meets G.A. Sandman; Gaiman & Wagner story; McKean-c; Kristiansen-a 7.00

GD	VG	FN	VF	VF/NM	NM-
2.0	4.0	6.0	8.0	9.0	9.2

SANDMAN MYSTERY THEATRE (Also see Sandman (2nd Series) #1)
DC Comics (Vertigo): Apr, 1993 - No. 70, Feb, 1999 ($1.95/$2.25/$2.50)

1-G.A. Sandman advs. begin; Matt Wagner scripts begin 5.00
2-49,51-70: 5-Neon ink logo. 29-32-Hourman app. 38-Ted Knight (G.A. Starman) app. 42-Jim Corrigan (Spectre) app. 45-48-Blackhawk app. 3.00
50-($3.50, 48 pgs.) w/bonus story of S.A. Sandman, Torres-a 4.00
Annual 1 (10/94, $3.95, 68 pgs.)-Alex Ross, Bolton & others-a 5.00
...: Dr. Death and the Night of the Butcher (2007, $19.99) r/#21-28 20.00
...: The Blackhawk and The Return of the Scarlet Ghost (2010, $19.99) r/#45-52 20.00
...: The Face and the Brute (2004, $19.95) r/#5-12 20.00
...: The Hourman and The Python (2008, $19.99) r/#29-36 20.00
...: The Mist and The Phantom of the Fair (2009, $19.99) r/#37-44 20.00
...: The Scorpion (2006, $12.99) r/#17-20 13.00
...: The Tarantula (1995, $14.95) r/#1-4 15.00
...: The Vamp (2005, $12.99) r/#13-16 13.00

SANDMAN MYSTERY THEATRE (2nd Series)
DC Comics (Vertigo): Feb, 2007 - No. 5, Jun, 2007 ($2.99, limited series)

1-5-Wesley Dodds and Dian in 1997; Rieber-s/Nguyen-a 3.00

SANDMAN: OVERTURE
DC Comics (Vertigo): Dec, 2013 - No. 6, Nov, 2015 ($4.99/$3.99, limited series)

1-($4.99) Prelude to Sandman #1 ('89); Gaiman-s/JH Williams III-a/c; var-c by McKean 5.00
2-6-($3.99) Gaiman-s/JH Williams III-a/c 4.00
... Special Edition 1 (1/14, $5.99) B&W version of #1 with creator interviews; bonus info 6.00
... Special Edition 2-6 ($4.99) B&W versions with creator interviews; bonus info. 6-(12/15) 5.00

SANDMAN PRESENTS...
DC Comics (Vertigo)

Taller Tales TPB (2003, $19.95) r/S.P: The Thessaliad #1-4; Merv Pumpkinhead, Agent...; The Dreaming #55; S.P. Everything You Always...; new McKean-c; intro by Willingham 20.00

SANDMAN PRESENTS: BAST
DC Comics (Vertigo): Mar, 2003 - No. 3, May, 2003 ($2.95, limited series)

1-3-Kiernan-s/Bennett-a/McKean-c 3.00

SANDMAN PRESENTS: DEADBOY DETECTIVES (See Sandman #21-28)
DC Comics (Vertigo): Aug, 2001 - No. 4, Nov, 2001 ($2.50, limited series)

1-4:Talbot-a/McKean-c/Brubaker-s 3.00
TPB (2008, $12.99) r/#1-4 13.00

SANDMAN PRESENTS: EVERYTHING YOU ALWAYS WANTED TO KNOW ABOUT DREAMS...BUT WERE AFRAID TO ASK
DC Comics (Vertigo): Jul, 2001 ($3.95, one-shot)

1-Short stories by Willingham; art by various; McKean-c 4.00

SANDMAN PRESENTS: LOVE STREET
DC Comics (Vertigo): Jul, 1999 - No. 3, Sept, 1999 ($2.95, limited series)

1-3: Teenage Hellblazer in 1968 London; Zulli-a 3.00

SANDMAN PRESENTS: LUCIFER
DC Comics (Vertigo): Mar, 1999 - No. 3, May, 1999 ($2.95, limited series)

1-Scott Hampton painted-c/a in all 1 2 3 5 6 8
2,3 4.00

SANDMAN PRESENTS: PETREFAX
DC Comics (Vertigo): Mar, 2000 - No. 4, Jun, 2000 ($2.95, limited series)

1-4-Carey-s/Leialoha-a 3.00

SANDMAN PRESENTS: THE CORINTHIAN
DC Comics (Vertigo): Dec, 2001 - No. 3, Feb, 2002 ($2.95, limited series)

1-3-Macan-s/Zezelj-a/McKean-c 3.00

SANDMAN PRESENTS, THE: THE FURIES
DC Comics (Vertigo): 2002 ($24.95, one-shot)

Hardcover-Mike Carey-s/John Bolton-painted art; Lyta Hall's reunion with Daniel 30.00
Softcover-(2003, $17.95) 18.00

SANDMAN PRESENTS, THE: THESSALY: WITCH FOR HIRE
DC Comics (Vertigo): Apr, 2004 - No. 4, July, 2004 ($2.95, limited series)

1-4-Willingham-s/McManus-a/McPherson-c 3.00
TPB-(2005, $12.99) r/#1-4 13.00

SANDMAN PRESENTS, THE: THE THESSALIAD
DC Comics (Vertigo): Mar, 2002 - No. 4, Jun, 2002 ($2.95, limited series)

1-4-Willingham-s/McManus-a/McKean-c 3.00

SANDMAN SPECIAL, THE (Jack Kirby 100th Birthday tribute)
DC Comics: Oct, 2017 ($4.99, one-shot)

The Sandman: The Dream Hunters #1 © DC

Satan's Six #1 © Jack Kirby

Savage (2021 series) #1 © VAL

	GD 2.0	VG 4.0	FN 6.0	VF 8.0	VF/NM 9.0	NM- 9.2

1-Jurgens-s/Bogdanove-a and Orlando-s/Leonardi-a; Brute & Glob app.; Paul Pope-c 5.00

SANDMAN, THE: THE DREAM HUNTERS
DC Comics (Vertigo): Oct, 1999 ($29.95/$19.95, one-shot graphic novel)

Hardcover-Neil Gaiman-s/Yoshitaka Amano-painted art 30.00
Softcover-(2000, $19.95) new Amano-c 20.00

SANDMAN, THE: THE DREAM HUNTERS
DC Comics (Vertigo): Jan, 2009 - No. 4, Apr, 2009 ($2.99, limited series)

1-4-Adaptation of the Gaiman/Amano GN by P. Craig Russell-s/a; 2 covers on each 3.00
HC (2009, $24.99) afterwords by Gaiman, Russell, Berger; cover gallery & sketch art 25.00
SC (2010, $19.99) afterwords by Gaiman, Russell, Berger; cover gallery & sketch art 20.00

SANDMAN UNIVERSE, THE
DC Comics: Oct, 2018 ($4.99, one-shot)

1-Intro to 4 new related series (The Dreaming, Books of Magic, House of Whispers & Lucifer); stories by Gaiman & others; Jae Lee-c; Cain, Abel & Lucien app. 5.00

SANDMAN UNIVERSE PRESENTS HELLBLAZER, THE
DC Comics (Black Label): 2019 ($4.99)

1-Spurrier-s/Takara-a; two covers 5.00

SANDS OF THE SOUTH PACIFIC
Toby Press: Jan, 1953

	GD	VG	FN	VF	VF/NM	NM-
1-Good Girl Art-c	53	106	159	334	567	800

SANTA AND HIS REINDEER (See March of Comics #166)

SANTA AND THE ANGEL (See Dell Junior Treasury #7)
Dell Publishing Co.: Dec, 1949 (Combined w/Santa at the Zoo) (Gollub-a condensed from FC#128)

	GD	VG	FN	VF	VF/NM	NM-
Four Color 259	7	14	21	49	92	135

SANTA AT THE ZOO (See Santa And The Angel)

SANTA CLAUS AROUND THE WORLD (See March of Comics #241 in Promotional Comics section)

SANTA CLAUS CONQUERS THE MARTIANS (See Movie Classics)

SANTA CLAUS FUNNIES (Also see Dell Giants)
Dell Publishing Co.: Dec?, 1942 - No. 1274, Dec, 1961

	GD	VG	FN	VF	VF/NM	NM-
nn(#1)(1942)-Kelly-a	36	72	108	259	580	900
2(12/43)-Kelly-a	24	48	72	168	372	575
Four Color 61(1944)-Kelly-a	23	46	69	161	356	550
Four Color 91(1945)-Kelly-a	17	34	51	117	259	400
Four Color 128('46),175('47)-Kelly-a	14	28	42	94	207	320
Four Color 205,254-Kelly-a	12	24	36	84	185	285
Four Color 302,361,525,607,666,756,867	8	16	24	51	96	140
Four Color 958,1063,1154,1274	6	12	18	41	76	110

NOTE: *Most issues contain only one Kelly story.*

SANTA CLAUS PARADE
Ziff-Davis (Approved Comics)/St. John Publishing Co.: 1951; No. 2, Dec, 1952; No. 3, Jan, 1955 (25¢)

	GD	VG	FN	VF	VF/NM	NM-
nn(1951-Ziff-Davis)-116 pgs. (Xmas Special 1,2)	37	74	111	218	354	490
2(12/52-Ziff-Davis)-100 pgs.; Dave Berg-a	29	58	87	172	281	390
V1#3(1/55-St. John)-100 pgs.; reprints-c/#1	22	44	66	132	216	300

SANTA CLAUS' WORKSHOP (See March of Comics #50,168 in Promotional Comics section)

SANTA IS COMING (See March of Comics #197 in Promotional Comics section)

SANTA IS HERE (See March of Comics #49 in Promotional Comics section)

SANTA'S BUSY CORNER (See March of Comics #31 in Promotional Comics section)

SANTA'S CANDY KITCHEN (See March of Comics #14 in Promotional Comics section)

SANTA'S CHRISTMAS BOOK (See March of Comics #123 in Promotional Comics section)

SANTA'S CHRISTMAS COMICS
Standard Comics (Best Books): Dec, 1952 (100 pgs.)

	GD	VG	FN	VF	VF/NM	NM-
nn-Supermouse, Dizzy Duck, Happy Rabbit, etc.	24	48	72	142	234	325

SANTA'S CHRISTMAS LIST (See March of Comics #255 in Promotional Comics section)

SANTA'S HELPERS (See March of Comics #64, 106, 198 in Promotional Comics section)

SANTA'S LITTLE HELPERS (See March of Comics #270 in Promotional Comics section)

SANTA'S SHOW (See March of Comics #311 in Promotional Comics section)

SANTA'S SLEIGH (See March of Comics #298 in Promotional Comics section)

SANTA'S SURPRISE (See March of Comics #13 in Promotional Comics section)

SANTA'S TINKER TOTS
Charlton Comics: 1958

	GD	VG	FN	VF	VF/NM	NM-
1-Based on "The Tinker Tots Keep Christmas"	6	12	18	40	73	105

SANTA'S TOYLAND (See March of Comics #242 in Promotional Comics section)

SANTA'S TOYS (See March of Comics #12 in Promotional Comics section)

SANTA'S VISIT (See March of Comics #283 in Promotional Comics section)

SANTA THE BARBARIAN
Maximum Press: Dec, 1996 ($2.99, one-shot)

1-Fraga/Mhan-s/a 3.00

SANTERIA: THE GODDESS KISS
Aspen MLT: Mar, 2016 - No. 5, Nov, 2017 ($3.99, limited series)

1-5-Wohl-s/Cafaro-a 4.00

SANTIAGO (Movie)
Dell Publishing Co.: Sept, 1956 (Alan Ladd photo-c)

	GD	VG	FN	VF	VF/NM	NM-
Four Color 723-Kinstler-a	9	18	27	60	120	180

SARGE SNORKEL (Beetle Bailey)
Charlton Comics: Oct, 1973 - No. 17, Dec, 1976

	GD	VG	FN	VF	VF/NM	NM-
1	2	4	6	11	16	20
2-10	2	4	6	8	10	12
11-17	1	2	3	5	7	9

SARGE STEEL (Becomes Secret Agent #9 on; also see Judomaster)
Charlton Comics: Dec, 1964 - No. 8, Mar-Apr, 1966 (All 12¢ issues)

	GD	VG	FN	VF	VF/NM	NM-
1-Origin & 1st app.	4	8	12	25	40	55
2-5,7,8	3	6	9	16	23	30
6-2nd app. Judomaster	3	6	9	19	30	40

SASQUATCH DETECTIVE SPECIAL
DC Comics: Feb, 2019 ($7.99, one-shot)

1-New origin story; Stilwell-s/Randall-a; also reprints back-ups from Exit Stage Left: The Snagglepus Chronicles; bonus sketch art 8.00

SATAN'S SIX
Topps Comics (Kirbyverse): Apr, 1993 - No. 4, July, 1993 ($2.95, lim. series)

1-4: 1-Polybagged w/Kirbychrome trading card; Kirby/McFarlane-c plus 8 pgs. Kirby-a(p); has coupon for Kirbychrome ed. of Secret City Saga #0. 2-4-Polybagged w/3 cards. 4-Teenagents preview 4.00
NOTE: *Ditko a-1. Miller a-1.*

SATAN'S SIX: HELLSPAWN
Topps Comics (Kirbyverse): June, 1994 - No. 3, July, 1994 ($2.50, limited series)

1-3: 1-(6/94)-Indicia incorrectly shows "Vol 1 #2". 2-(6/94) 3.00

SATELLITE FALLING
IDW Publishing: May, 2016 - No. 5, May, 2017 ($3.99)

1-5-Steve Horton-s/Stephen Thompson-a 4.00

SATELLITE SAM
Image Comics: Jul, 2013 - No. 15, Jul, 2015 ($3.50, B&W, mature)

1-15-Matt Fraction-s/Howard Chaykin-a/c 3.50

SAUCER COUNTRY
DC Comics (Vertigo): May, 2012 - No. 14, Jun, 2013 ($2.99)

1-14: 1-Cornell-s/Kelly-a. 6-Broxton-a. 11-Colak-a 3.00

SAUCER STATE (Sequel to Saucer Country)
IDW Publishing: May, 2017 - No. 6, Oct, 2017 ($3.99)

1-6-Cornell-s/Kelly-a 4.00

SAURIANS: UNNATURAL SELECTION (See Sigil)
CrossGeneration Comics: Feb, 2002 - No. 2, Mar, 2002 ($2.95, limited series)

1,2-Waid-s/DiVito-a 3.00

SAVAGE
Image Comics (Shadowline): Oct, 2008 - No. 4, Jan, 2009 ($3.50, limited series)

1-4-Mayhew-c/a; Niles and Frank-s 3.50

SAVAGE
Valiant Entertainment: Nov, 2016 - No. 4, Feb, 2017 ($3.99, limited series)

1-4-B. Clay Moore-s/Larosa & Henry-a 4.00

SAVAGE
Valiant Entertainment: Feb, 2021 - Present ($3.99)

1-Max Bemis-s/Nathan Stockman-a 4.00

SAVAGE AVENGERS
Marvel Comics: Jul, 2019 - Present ($4.99/$3.99)

1-($4.99) Team of Conan, Wolverine, Punisher, Doctor Voodoo; Duggan-s/Deodato-a 5.00
2-17-($3.99) 2-5-Kulan Gath & Venom app. 6-Jacinto-a. 13-16-Zircher-a. 14,16-Juggernaut

Savage Combat Tales #2 © Seaboard

The Savage Dragon #97 © Erik Larsen

The Savage Hawkman #11 © DC

	GD	VG	FN	VF	VF/NM	NM-
	2.0	4.0	6.0	8.0	9.0	9.2

& Black Knight app. 17-King In Black tie-in; Deadpool app. 4.00
#0 (4/20, $4.99) Reprints Uncanny X-Men #190 & 191 with Kulan Gath, new framing story 5.00
Annual 1 (12/19, $4.99) Garney-a; Conan, Black Widow & Hellstrom app. 5.00

SAVAGE AXE OF ARES
Marvel Comics: June, 2010 ($3.99, B&W, one-shot)

1-B&W short stories by Hurwitz, Palo, McKeever, Swierczynski, Manco and others 4.00

SAVAGE COMBAT TALES
Atlas/Seaboard Publ.: Feb, 1975 - No. 3, July, 1975

1,3: 1-Sgt. Stryker's Death Squad begins (origin); Goodwin-s
2 4 6 11 16 20
2-Toth-a; only app. War Hawk; Goodwin-s 2 4 6 13 18 22
NOTE: *Buckler c-3. McWilliams a-1-3; c-1. Sparling a-1, 3.*

SAVAGE DRAGON, THE (See Megaton #3 & 4)
Image Comics (Highbrow Entertainment): July, 1992 - No. 3, Dec, 1992 ($1.95, lim. series)

1-Erik Larsen-c/a/scripts & bound-in poster in all; 4 cover color variations w/4 different posters; 1st Highbrow Entertainment title 1 3 4 6 8 10
2-Intro SuperPatriot-c/story (10/92) 5.00
3-Contains coupon for Image Comics #0 4.00
3-With coupon missing 2.00
...Vs. Savage Megaton Man 1 (3/93, $1.95)-Larsen & Simpson-c/a. 4.00
TPB-('93, $9.95) r/#1-3 10.00

SAVAGE DRAGON, THE
Image Comics (Highbrow Entertainment): June, 1993 - Present ($1.95/$2.50/$2.99/$3.50)

1-Erik Larsen-c/a/scripts 1 2 3 5 6 8
2-($2.95, 52 pgs.)-Teenage Mutant Ninja Turtles-c/story; flip book features Vanguard #0 (See Megaton for 1st app.); 1st app. Supreme 5.00
3-30: 3-7: Erik Larsen-c/a/scripts. 3-Mighty Man back-up story w/Austin-a(i). 4-Flip book w/Ricochet. 5-Mighty Man flip-c & back-up plus poster. 6-Jae Lee poster. 7-Vanguard poster. 8-Deadly Duo poster by Larsen. 13A (10/94)-Jim Lee-c/a; 1st app. Max Cash (Condition Red). 13B (6/95)-Larsen story. 15-Dragon poster by Larsen. 22-TMNT-c/a; Bisley pin-up. 27-"Wondercon Exclusive" new-c. 28-Maxx-c/app. 29-Wildstar-c/app. 30-Spawn app. 4.00
25 ($3.95)-variant-c exists. 5.00
31-49,51-71: 31-God vs. The Devil; alternate version exists w/o expletives (has "God Is Good" inside Image logo) 33-Birth of Dragon/Rapture's baby. 34,35-Hellboy-c/app. 51-Origin of She-Dragon. 70-Ann Stevens killed 4.00
50-($5.95, 100 pgs.) Kaboom and Mighty Man app.; Matsuda back-c; pin-ups by McFarlane, Simonson, Capullo and others 6.00
72-74: 72-Begin $2.95-c 4.00
75-($5.95) 6.00
76-99,101-106,108-114,116-124,126-127,129-131,133-136,138: 76-New direction starts. 83,84-Madman-c/app. 84-Atomics app. 97-Dragon returns home; Mighty Man app. 134-Bomb Queen app. 3.50
100-($8.95) Larsen-s/a; inked by various incl. Sienkiewicz, Timm, Austin, Simonson, Royer; plus pin-ups by Timm, Silvestri, Miller, Cho, Art Adams, Pacheco 9.00
107-($3.95) Firebreather, Invincible, Major Damage-c/app.; flip book w/Major Damage 4.00
115-($7.95, 100 pgs.) Wraparound-c; Freak Force app.; Larsen & Englert-a 8.00
125-($4.99, 64 pgs.) new story, The Fly, & various Mr. Glum reprints 5.00
128-Wesley and the villains from Wanted app.; J.G. Jones-c 4.00
132-($6.99, 80 pgs.) new story with Larsen-a; back-up story with Fosco-a 7.00
137-(8/08) Madman & Amazing Joy Buzzards-c/app. 1 2 3 5 6 8
137-(8/08) Variant cover with Barack Obama endorsed by Savage Dragon; yellow bkgrd
7 14 21 48 89 130
137-(8/08) 2nd printing of variant cover with Barack Obama and red background
1 3 4 6 8 10
137-3rd & 4th printings: 3rd-Blue background. 4th-Purple background 6.00
139-144,146-149,151-174,176-183: 139-Start $3.50-c; Invincible app. 140,141-Witchblade, Spawn app. 148-Also a FCBD edition.155-160-Dragon War. 160-163-Flip book 3.50
145-Obama-c/app. 1 2 3 5 6 8
150-($5.99, 100 pgs.) back up r/Daredevil's origin from Daredevil #18 (1943) 6.00
175-($3.99, 48 pgs.) Darklord app.; Vanguard back-c and back-up story 4.00
184-199,201-224 ($3.99) 184,186-188-The Claw app. 190-Regular & digest-size versions. 209-Malcolm's wedding. 217-Spawn app. 4.00
200-(12/14, $8.99, 100 pgs., squarebound) Back-up story w/Trimpe-a; Burnhum-a 9.00
225-(7/17, $9.99, 100 pgs., squarebound) Death of Savage Dragon; back-up by various 10.00
226-249,251-257: 226-Donald Trump on cover. 227-Malcolm & family move to Toronto. 252-Salutes the Funnies; newspaper comics homages 4.00
250-(7/20, $9.99, 100 pgs., squarebound) Savage Dragon returns; back-up by various 10.00
#0-(7/06, $1.95) reprints origin story from 2005 Image Comics Hardcover 3.50
...Archives Vol. 1 (12/06, $19.99) B&W rep. 1st mini-series #1-3 & #1-21 20.00
...Archives Vol. 2 (2007, $19.99) B&W rep. #22-50; roster pages of Dragon's fellow cops 20.00
...Companion (7/02, $2.95) guide to issues #1-100, character backgrounds 3.50
...Endgame (2/04, $15.95, TPB) r/#47-52 16.00
The Fallen (11/97, $12.95, TPB) r/#7-11, ...Possessed (9/98, $12.95, TPB) r/#12-16, ...Revenge (1998, $12.95, TPB) r/#17-21 13.00
...Gang War (4/00, $16.95, TPB) r/#22-26 17.00
.../Hellboy (10/02, $5.95) r/#34 & #35; Mignola-c 6.00
Image Firsts: Savage Dragon #1 (4/10, $1.00) reprints #1 3.00
... Legacy FCBD 1 (5/15, giveaway) Story later re-worked for issue #211 3.00
...Team-Ups (10/98, $19.95, TPB) r/team-ups 20.00
...: Terminated HC (2/03, $28.95) r/#34-40 & #1/2 29.00
...: This Savage World HC (2002, $24.95) r/#76-81; intro. by Larsen 25.00
...: This Savage World SC (2003, $15.95) r/#76-81; intro. by Larsen 16.00
...: Worlds at War SC (2004, $16.95) r/#41-46; intro. by Larsen; sketch pages 17.00

SAVAGE DRAGON ARCHIVES (Also see Dragon Archives, The)

SAVAGE DRAGONBERT: FULL FRONTAL NERDITY
Image Comics: Oct, 2002 ($5.95, B&W, one-shot)

1-Reprints of the Savage Dragon/Dilbert spoof strips 6.00

SAVAGE DRAGON/DESTROYER DUCK, THE
Image Comics/ Highbrow Entertainment: Nov, 1996 ($3.95, one-shot)

1 4.00

SAVAGE DRAGON: GOD WAR
Image Comics: July, 2004 - No. 4, Oct, 2005 ($2.95, limited series)

1-4-Kirkman-s/Englert-a 3.50

SAVAGE DRAGON/MARSHALL LAW
Image Comics: July, 1997 - No. 2, Aug, 1997 ($2.95, B&W, limited series)

1,2-Pat Mills-s, Kevin O'Neill-a 4.00

SAVAGE DRAGON: SEX & VIOLENCE
Image Comics: Aug, 1997 - No. 2, Sept, 1997 ($2.50, limited series)

1,2-T&M Bierbaum-s, Mays, Lupka, Adam Hughes-a 4.00

SAVAGE DRAGON/TEENAGE MUTANT NINJA TURTLES CROSSOVER
Mirage Studios: Sept, 1993 ($2.75, one-shot)

1-Erik Larsen-c(i) only 5.00

SAVAGE DRAGON: THE RED HORIZON
Image Comics/ Highbrow Entertainment: Feb, 1997 - No. 3 ($2.50, lim. series)

1-3 4.00

SAVAGE FISTS OF KUNG FU
Marvel Comics Group: 1975 (Marvel Treasury)

1-Iron Fist, Shang Chi, Sons of Tiger; Adams, Starlin-a
3 6 9 17 26 40

SAVAGE HAWKMAN, THE (DC New 52)
DC Comics: Nov, 2011 - No. 20, Jun, 2013 ($2.99)

1-20: 1-Tony Daniel-s/Philip Tan-a/c; Carter Hall bonds with the Nth metal 3.00
#0-(11/12, $2.99) Origin story of Katar Hol on Thanagar; Bennett-a/c 3.00

SAVAGE HULK, THE (Also see Incredible Hulk)
Marvel Comics: Jan, 1996 ($6.95, one-shot)

1-Bisley-c; David, Lobdell, Wagner, Loeb, Gibbons, Messner-Loebs scripts; McKone, Kieth, Ramos & Sale-a 7.00

SAVAGE HULK
Marvel Comics: Aug, 2014 - No. 6, Jan, 2015 ($3.99, limited series)

1-6: 1-4-Alan Davis-s/a; follows story from X-Men #66 ('70) Silver Age X-Men & The Leader app. 2-Abomination app. 5,6-Bechko-s/Hardman-a; Dr. Strange app. 4.00

SAVAGE RAIDS OF GERONIMO (See Geronimo #4)

SAVAGE RANGE (See Luke Short, Four Color 807)

SAVAGE RED SONJA: QUEEN OF THE FROZEN WASTES
Dynamite Entertainment: 2006 - No. 4, 2006 ($3.50, limited series)

1-4: 1-Three covers by Cho, Texeira & Homs; Cho & Murray-s/Homs-a 3.50
TPB (2007, $14.99) r/series; cover gallery and sketch pages 15.00

SAVAGE RETURN OF DRACULA
Marvel Comics: 1992 ($2.00, 52 pgs.)

1-r/Tomb of Dracula #1,2 by Gene Colan 4.00

SAVAGE SHE-HULK, THE (See The Avengers, Marvel Graphic Novel #18 & The Sensational She-Hulk)
Marvel Comics Group: Feb, 1980 - No. 25, Feb, 1982

1-Origin & 1st app. She-Hulk 9 18 27 59 117 175
2-5,25: 25-(52 pgs.) 2 4 6 8 11 14

The Savage She-Hulk #23 © MAR

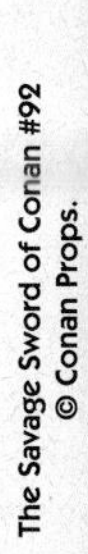
The Savage Sword of Conan #92 © Conan Props.

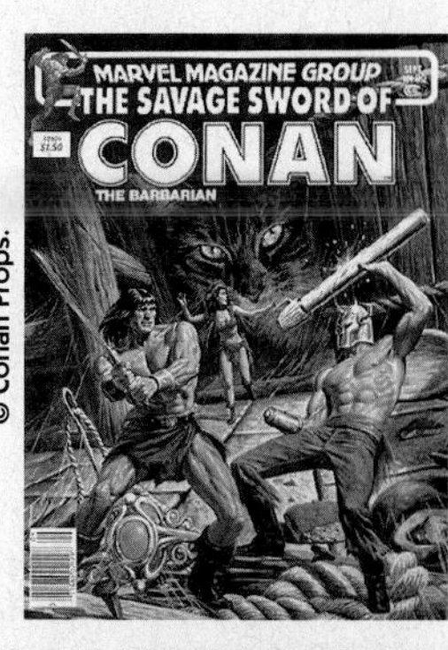

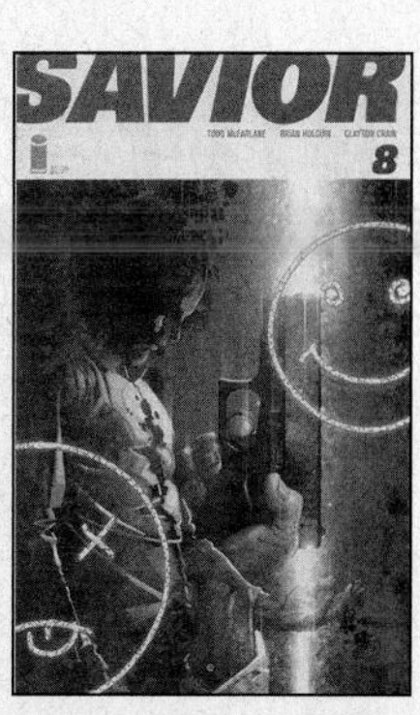

Savior #8 © TMP

	GD	VG	FN	VF	VF/NM	NM-
	2.0	4.0	6.0	8.0	9.0	9.2

6,7,10-24: 6-She-Hulk vs. Iron Man. 1 3 4 6 8 10
8-Vs. Man-Thing 2 4 6 9 12 15
9-1st Ultiman 2 4 6 11 16 20
NOTE: *Austin a-25i; c-23i-25i. J. Buscema a-1p; c-1, 2p. Golden c-8-11.*

SAVAGE SHE-HULK (Titled All New Savage She Hulk for #3,4)
Marvel Comics: Jun, 2009 - No. 4, Sept, 2009 ($3.99, limited series)
1-4-Lyra, daughter of the Hulk; She-Hulk & Dark Avengers app. 2-Campbell-c 4.00

SAVAGE SKULLKICKERS (See Skullkickers #20)

SAVAGE SWORD (ROBERT E. HOWARD'S...)
Dark Horse Comics: Dec, 2010 - No. 9 ($7.99, squarebound)
1-9-Short stories by various incl. Roy Thomas, Barry-Windsor-Smith; Conan app. 8.00

SAVAGE SWORD OF CONAN (The... #41 on; ...The Barbarian #175 on)
Marvel Comics Group: Aug, 1974 - No. 235, July, 1995 ($1.00/$1.25/$2.25, B&W magazine, mature)
1-Smith-r; J. Buscema/N. Adams/Krenkel-a; origin Blackmark by Gil Kane (part 1, ends #3); Blackmark's 1st app. in magazine form-r/from paperback) & Red Sonja (3rd app.) 9 18 27 63 129 195
2-Neal Adams-c; Chaykin/N. Adams-a 5 10 15 34 60 85
3-Severin/B. Smith-a; N. Adams-a 4 8 12 28 47 65
4-Neal Adams/Kane-a(r) 3 6 9 21 33 45
5-10: 5-Jeff Jones frontispiece (r) 3 6 9 17 26 35
11-20 2 4 6 13 18 22
21-30 2 4 6 10 14 18
31-50: 34-3 pg. preview of Conan newspaper strip. 35-Cover similar to Savage Tales #1. 45-Red Sonja returns; begin $1.25-c 2 4 6 8 11 14
51-99: 63-Toth frontispiece. 65-Kane-a w/Chaykin/Miller/Simonson/Sherman finishes. 70-Article on movie. 83-Red Sonja-r by Neal Adams from #1 1 2 3 5 7 9
100 1 3 4 6 8 10
101-176: 163-Begin $2.25-c. 169-King Kull story. 171-Soloman Kane by Williamson (i): 172-Red Sonja story 6.00
177-199: 179,187,192-Red Sonja app. 190-193-4 part King Kull story. 196-King Kull story 5.00
200-220: 200-New Buscema-a; Robert E. Howard app. with Conan in story. 202-King Kull story. 204-60th anniversary (1932-92). 211-Rafael Kayanan's 1st Conan-a. 214-Sequel to Red Nails by Howard 6.00
221-230 2 4 6 8 10 12
231-234 2 4 6 11 16 20
235-Last issue 4 8 12 27 44 60
Special 1(1975, B&W)-B. Smith-r/Conan #10,13 3 6 9 18 27 36
Volume 1 TPB (Dark Horse Books, 12/07, $17.95, B&W) r/#1-10 and selected stories from Savage Tales #1-5 with covers 18.00
Volume 2 TPB (Dark Horse Books, 3/08, $17.95, B&W) r/#11-24 18.00
Volume 3 TPB (Dark Horse Books, 5/08, $19.95, B&W) r/#25-36 and selected pin-ups 20.00
Volume 4 TPB (Dark Horse Books, 9/08, $19.95, B&W) r/#37-48 and selected pin-ups 20.00
Volume 5 TPB (Dark Horse Books, 2/09, $19.95, B&W) r/#49-60 and selected pin-ups 20.00
NOTE: *N. Adams a-14p, 60, 83p(r). Alcala a-2 ,4, 7, 12, 15-20, 23, 24, 28, 59, 67, 69, 75, 76i, 80i, 82i, 83i, 89, 180i, 184i, 187i, 189i, 216p. Austin a-78i. Boris painted c-1, 4, 5, 7, 9, 10, 12, 15. Brunner a-30; c-8, 30. Buscema a-1-5, 7, 10-12, 15-24, 26-28, 31, 32, 36-43, 45, 47-58p, 60-67p, 70, 71-74p, 76-81p, 87-96p, 98, 99-101p, 190-204p; painted c-40. Chaykin c-31. Chiodo painted c-71, 76, 79, 81, 84, 85, 178. Conrad c-215, 217. Corben a-4, 16, 29. Finlay a-16. Golden a-98, 101; c-98, 101, 105, 106, 117, 124, 150. Kaluta a-11, 18; c-3, 91, 93. Gil Kane a-2, 3, 8, 13r, 29, 47, 64, 65, 67, 85p, 86p. Rafael Kayanan a-211-213, 215, 217. Krenkel a-9, 11, 14, 16, 24. Morrow a-7. Nebres a-93i, 101i, 107, 114. Newton a-6. Nino c/a-6. Redondo painted c-48-50, 52, 56, 57, 85i, 90, 96i. Marie & John Severin a-Special 1. Simonson a-7, 8, 12, 15-17. Barry Smith a-7, 16, 24, 82r, Special 1r. Starlin c-26. Toth a-64. Williamson a(i)-162, 171, 186. No. 8 , 10 & 16 contain a Robert E. Howard Conan adaptation.*

SAVAGE SWORD OF CONAN
Marvel Comics: Apr, 2019 - No. 12, Feb, 2020 ($4.99/$3.99)
1-($4.99) Duggan-s/Garney-a; main cover by Alex Ross; bonus text story 5.00
2-5-($3.99) Duggan-s/Garney-a; main cover by Alex Ross; bonus text story 4.00
6-12: 6-Meredith Finch-s/Luke Ross-a; main cover by David Finch. 10,11-Alan Davis-a 4.00

SAVAGE TALES (...Featuring Conan #4 on)(Magazine)
Marvel Comics Group: May, 1971; No. 2, 10/73; No. 3, 2/74 - No. 12, Summer, 1975 (B&W)
1-Origin/1st app. The Man-Thing by Morrow; Conan the Barbarian by Barry Smith (1st Conan x-over outside his own title); Femizons by Romita-r/in #3; Ka-Zar story by Buscema 32 64 96 230 515 800
2-B. Smith, Brunner, Morrow, Williamson-a; Wrightson King Kull reprint/ Creatures on the Loose #10 5 10 15 35 63 90
3-B. Smith, Brunner, Steranko, Williamson-a 5 10 15 30 50 70
4,5-N. Adams-c; last Conan (Smith-r/#4) plus Kane/N. Adams-a. 5-Brak the Barbarian begins, ends #8 4 8 12 27 44 60
6-Ka-Zar begins; Williamson-r; N. Adams-c 3 6 9 19 30 40
7-N. Adams-i 3 6 9 15 22 28
8,9,11: 8-Shanna, the She-Devil app. thru #10; Williamson-r

	GD	VG	FN	VF	VF/NM	NM-
	2.0	4.0	6.0	8.0	9.0	9.2

3 6 9 14 20 26
10-Neal Adams-a(i), Williamson-r 3 6 9 15 22 28
...Featuring Ka-Zar Annual 1 (Summer, '75, B&W)(#12 on inside)-Ka-Zar origin by Gil Kane; B. Smith-r/Astonishing Tales 3 6 9 17 26 35
NOTE: *Boris c-7, 10. Buscema a-5r, 6p, 8p; c-2. Colan a-1p. Fabian c-8. Golden a-1, 4; c-1. Heath a-10p, 11p. Kaluta c-9. Maneely r-2, 4(The Crusader in both). Morrow a-1, 2, Annual 1. Reese a-2. Severin a-1-7. Starlin a-5. Robert E. Howard adaptations-1-4.*

SAVAGE TALES (Volume 2)
Marvel Comics Group: Oct, 1985 - No. 8, Dec, 1986 ($1.50, B&W, magazine, mature)
1-1st app. The Nam; Golden, Morrow-a (indicia incorrectly lists this as Volume 1) 6.00
2-8: 2,7-Morrow-a. 4-2nd Nam story; Golden-a 4.00

SAVAGE TALES
Dynamite Entertainment: 2007 - No. 10, 2008 ($4.99)
1-10: 1-Anthology; Red Sonja app.; three covers 5.00
... Red Sonja One-Shot (2019, $4.99) Russell-s; Sorcerers of Wigur-Nomadene app. 5.00
... Vampirella One-Shot (2018, $4.99) Burnham-s; back-up Valaka story; Robert Hack-c 5.00

SAVAGE THINGS
DC Comics (Vertigo): May, 2017 - No. 8, Dec, 2018 ($3.99)
1-8-Justin Jordan-s/Ibrahim Moustafa-a/J.P. Leon-c 4.00

SAVAGE WOLVERINE
Marvel Comics: Mar, 2013 - No. 23, Nov, 2014 ($3.99)
1-5-Frank Cho-s/a/c; Shanna & Amadeus Cho app. 4.00
1-Variant-c by Skottie Young 8.00
6-23: 6-8-Wells-s/Madureira-a/c; Elektra, Kingpin & Spider-Man app. 9-11-Jock-s/a. 14-17-Isanove-s/a. 19-Simone-s. 21,22-WWI; Quinones-a/Nowlan-c 4.00

SAVANT GARDE (Also see WildC.A.T.S...)
Image Comics/WildStorm Productions: Mar, 1997 - No. 7, Sept, 1997 ($2.50)
1-7 3.00

SAVED BY THE BELL (TV)
Harvey Comics: Mar, 1992 - No. 5, May, 1993 ($1.25, limited series)
1 2 4 6 8 10 12
2-5, Holiday Special (3/92), Special 1 (9/92, $1.50)-photo-c, Summer Break 1 (10/92) 6.00

SAVIOR
Image Comics/Todd McFarlane Productions: Apr, 2015 - No. 8, Nov, 2015 ($2.99)
1-8-Todd McFarlane & Brian Holguin-s/Clayton Crain-a/c 3.00

SAW: REBIRTH (Based on 2004 movie Saw)
IDW Publ.: Oct, 2005 ($3.99, one-shot)
1-Guedes-a 4.00

SCALPED
DC Comics (Vertigo): Mar, 2007 - No. 60, Oct, 2012 ($2.99, limited series)
1-Aaron-s/Guera-a/Jock-c 4 8 12 28 47 65
1-Special Edition (7/10, $1.00) r/#1 with "What's Next?" cover frame 3.00
2-5 1 2 3 5 6 8
6-20: 12-Leon-a 4.00
21-60: 50-Bonus pin-ups by various 3.00
...: Casino Blood TPB (2008, $14.99) r/#6-11; intro. by Garth Ennis 15.00
...: Dead Mothers TPB (2008, $17.99) r/#12-18 18.00
...: High Lonesome TPB (2009, $14.99) r/#25-29; intro. by Jason Starr 15.00
...: Indian Country TPB (2007, $9.99) r/#1-5; intro. by Brian K. Vaughan 10.00
...: Rez Blues (2011, $17.99) r/#35-42 18.00
...: The Gnawing (2010, $14.99) r/#30-34; intro. by Matt Fraction 15.00
...: The Gravel in Your Guts (2009, $14.99) r/#19-24; intro. by Ed Brubaker 15.00

SCAMP (Walt Disney)(See Walt Disney's Comics & Stories #204)
Dell Publ. Co./Gold Key: No. 703, 5/56 - No. 1204, 8-10/61; 11/67 - No. 45, 1/79
Four Color 703(#1) 9 18 27 59 117 175
Four Color 777,806('57),833 6 12 18 40 73 105
5(3-5/58)-10(6-8/59) 5 10 15 31 53 75
11-16(12-2/60-61), Four Color 1204(1961) 4 8 12 27 44 60
1(12/67-Gold Key)-Reprints begin 4 8 12 25 40 55
2(3/69)-10 2 4 6 13 18 22
11-20 2 4 6 8 11 14
21-45 1 2 3 4 5 7
NOTE: *New stories-#20(in part), 22-25, 27, 29-31, 34, 36-40, 42-45. New covers-#11, 12, 14, 15, 17-25, 27, 29-31, 34, 36-38.*

SCARAB
DC Comics (Vertigo): Nov, 1993 - No. 8, June, 1994 ($1.95, limited series)
1-8-Glenn Fabry painted-c: 1-Silver ink-c. 2-Phantom Stranger app. 3.00

SCARECROW OF ROMNEY MARSH, THE (See W. Disney Showcase #53)

Scarlet #5 © Jinxworld

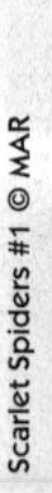
Scarlet Spiders #1 © MAR

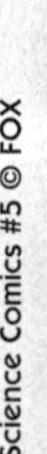
Science Comics #5 © FOX

GD 2.0 | VG 4.0 | FN 6.0 | VF 8.0 | VF/NM 9.0 | NM- 9.2

Gold Key: April, 1964 - No. 3, Oct, 1965 (Disney TV Show)

10112-404 (#1) 6 12 18 40 73 105
2,3 4 8 12 28 47 65

SCARECROW (VILLAINS) (See Batman)
DC Comics: Feb, 1998 ($1.95, one-shot)

1-Fegredo-a/Milligan-s/Pearson-c 3.00

SCARE TACTICS
DC Comics: Dec, 1996 - No. 12, Mar, 1998 ($2.25)

1-12: 1-1st app. 3.00

SCAR FACE (See The Crusaders)

SCARFACE: SCARRED FOR LIFE (Based on the 1983 movie)
IDW Publishing: Dec, 2006 - No. 5, Apr, 2007 ($3.99, limited series)

1-5-Tony Montana survives his shooting; Layman-s/Crosland-a 4.00
Scarface: Devil in Disguise (7/07 - No. 4, 10/07, $3.99) Alberto Dose-a 4.00

SCARLET
Marvel Comics (ICON): July, 2010 - No. 10, Aug, 2016 ($3.95)

1-10-Bendis-s/Maleev-a. 1-Second printing exists. 8-(5/16) 4.00
1-5-Variant covers. 1-Deodato & Lafuente. 2-Oeming & Mack. 3,4-Oeming. 5-Bendis 6.00

SCARLET
DC Comics (Jinxworld): Oct, 2018 - No. 5, Mar, 2019 ($3.99)

1-5-Bendis-s/Maleev-a 4.00

SCARLET O'NEIL (See Harvey Comics Hits #59 & Invisible...)

SCARLET SPIDER
Marvel Comics: Nov, 1995 - No. 2, Jan, 1996 ($1.95, limited series)

1,2: Replaces Spider-Man title 4.00

SCARLET SPIDER
Marvel Comics: Mar, 2012 - No. 25, Feb, 2014 ($3.99/$2.99)

1-Kaine following "Spider Island"; Yost-s/Stegman-a; 2 covers by Stegman 4.00
2-12, 12.1, 13-24-($2.99) 10,11-Carnage & Venom app. 17-19-Wolverine app. 3.00
25-($3.99) Last issue; Yost-s/Baldeon-a 4.00

SCARLET SPIDERS (Tie-in for Spider-Verse in Amazing Spider-Man [2014] #9-15)
Marvel Comics: Jan, 2015 - No. 3, Mar, 2015 ($3.99, limited series)

1-3-Kaine, Ben Reilly and Jessica Drew app.; Costa-s/Diaz-a 4.00

SCARLET SPIDER UNLIMITED
Marvel Comics: Nov, 1995 ($3.95, one-shot)

1-Replaces Spider-Man Unlimited title 4.00

SCARLETT COUTURE
Titan Comics: May, 2015 - No. 4, Aug, 2015 ($3.99)

1-4-Des Taylor-s/a 4.00

SCARLETT'S STRIKE FORCE (G.I. Joe)
IDW Publishing: Dec, 2017 - No. 3, Feb, 2018 ($3.99, limited series)

1-3-Sitterson-s/Daniel-a; Cobra Commander app. 4.00

SCARLET WITCH (See Avengers #16, Vision &... & X-Men #4)
Marvel Comics: Jan, 1994 - No. 4, Apr, 1994 ($1.75, limited series)

1-Abnett & Lanning-s; Agatha Harkness app. 1 3 4 6 8 10
2-1st Lore 2 4 6 11 16 20
3,4 5.00

SCARLET WITCH
Marvel Comics: Feb, 2016 - No. 15, Apr, 2017 ($3.99)

1-15: 1-3: 1-Robinson-s/Del Rey-a; Agatha Harkness app. 3-Dillon-a. 7-Wu-a.
9-Civil War II tie-in; Quicksilver app.; Joelle Jones-a 4.00

SCARY GODMOTHER (Hardcover story books)
Sirius: 1997 - 2002 ($19.95, HC with dust jackets, one-shots)

Volume 1 (9/97) Jill Thompson-s/a; first app. of Scary Godmother 20.00
Vol. 2 - The Revenge of Jimmy (9/98, $19.95) 20.00
Vol. 3 - The Mystery Date (10/99, $19.95) 20.00
Vol. 4 - The Boo Flu (9/02, $19.95) 20.00

SCARY GODMOTHER
Sirius: 2001 - No. 6, 2002 ($2.95, B&W, limited series)

1-6-Jill Thompson-s/a 3.00
...: Activity Book (12/00, $2.95, B&W) Jill Thompson-s/a 3.00
...: Bloody Valentine Special (2/98, $3.95, B&W) Jill Thompson-s/a; pin-ups by Ross, Mignola, Russell 4.00
...: Ghoul's Out For Summer (2002,$14.95, B&W) r/#1-6 15.00
...: Holiday Spooktakular (11/98, $2.95, B&W) Jill Thompson-s/a; pin-ups by Brereton, LaBan, Dorkin, Fingerman 3.00

SCARY GODMOTHER: WILD ABOUT HARRY
Sirius: 2000 - No. 3 ($2.95, B&W, limited series)

1-3-Jill Thompson-s/a 3.00
TPB (2001, $9.95) r/series 10.00

SCARY TALES
Charlton Comics: 8/75 - #9, 1/77; #10, 9/77 - #20, 6/79; #21, 8/80 - #46, 10/84

1-Origin/1st app. Countess Von Bludd, not in #2 4 8 12 25 40 55
2,4,6,9,10: 4,9-Sutton-c/a. 4-Man-Thing copy 2 4 6 11 16 20
3-Sutton painted-c; Ditko-a 3 6 9 14 20 25
5,11-Ditko-c/a. 3 6 9 16 23 30
7,8-Ditko-a 2 4 6 13 18 22
12,15,16,19,21,39-Ditko-a 2 4 6 11 16 20
13,17,20 2 4 6 9 12 15
14,18,30,32-Ditko-c/a 3 6 9 14 20 25
22-29,33-37,39,40: 37,38,40-New-a. 39-All Ditko reprints and cover 2 4 6 8 10 12
31,38: 31-Newton-c/a. 38-Mr. Jigsaw app. 2 4 6 8 10 12
41-45-New-a. 41-Ditko-a(3). 42-45-(Low print) 2 4 6 9 12 15
46-Reprints (Low print) 2 4 6 11 16 20
1(Modern Comics reprint, 1977) 1 3 4 6 8 10

NOTE: ***Adkins** a-31i; c-31i. **Ditko** a-3, 5, 7, 8(2), 11, 12, 14-16r, 18(3)r, 19r, 21r, 30r, 32, 39r, 41(3); c-5, 11, 14, 18, 30, 32. **Newton** a-31p; c-31p. **Powell** a-18r. **Staton** a-1(2 pgs.), 4, 20r; c-1, 20. **Sutton** a-4, 9; c-4, 9. **Zeck** a-9.*

SCATTERBRAIN
Dark Horse Comics: Jun, 1998 - No. 4, Sept, 1998 ($2.95, limited series)

1-4-Humor anthology by Aragonés, Dorkin, Stevens and others 3.00

SCAVENGERS
Triumphant Comics: 1993(nd, July) - No. 11, May, 1994 ($2.50, serially numbered)

1-9,0,10,11: 5,6-Triumphant Unleashed x-over. 9-(3/94). 0-Retail ed. (3/94, $2.50, 36 pgs.). 0-Giveaway edition (3/94, 20 pgs.). 0-Coupon redemption edition. 10-(4/94) 3.00

SCENE OF THE CRIME (Also see Vertigo: Winter's Edge #2)
DC Comics (Vertigo): May, 1999 - No. 4, Aug, 1999 ($2.50, limited series)

1-4-Brubaker-s/Lark-a 3.00
...: A Little Piece of Goodnight TPB ('00, $12.95) r/#1-4; Winter's Edge #2 13.00

SCHOOL DAY ROMANCES (...of Teen-Agers #4; Popular Teen-Agers #5 on)
Star Publications: Nov-Dec, 1949 - No. 4, May-June, 1950 (Teenage)

1-Toni Gayle (later Toni Gay), Ginger Snapp, Midge Martin & Eve Adams begin 40 80 120 246 411 575
2,3: 3-Jane Powell photo on-c & true life story 31 62 93 186 303 420
4-Ronald Reagan photo on-c; L.B. Cole-c 43 86 129 271 461 650

NOTE: *All have **L. B. Cole** covers.*

SCHWINN BICYCLE BOOK (...Bike Thrills, 1959)
Schwinn Bicycle Co.: 1949; 1952; 1959 (10¢)

1949 7 14 21 37 46 55
1952-Believe It or Not facts; comic format; 36 pgs. 5 10 15 23 28 32
1959 4 8 11 16 19 22

SCIENCE COMICS (1st Series)
Fox Feature Syndicate: Feb, 1940 - No. 8, Sept, 1940

1-Origin Dynamo (1st app., called Electro in #1), The Eagle (1st app.), & Navy Jones; Marga, The Panther Woman (1st app.), Cosmic Carson & Perisphere Payne, Dr. Doom begin; bondage/hypo-c; Electro-c 865 1730 2595 6315 11,158 16,000
2-Classic Lou Fine Dynamo-c 459 918 1377 3350 5925 8500
3-Classic Lou Fine Dynamo-c 389 778 1167 2723 4762 6800
4-Kirby-a; Cosmic Carson-c by Joe Simon 389 778 1167 2723 4762 6800
5-8: 5,8-Eagle-c. 6,7-Dynamo-c 232 464 696 1485 2543 3600

NOTE: *Cosmic Carson by **Tuska**-#1-3; by **Kirby**-#4. **Lou Fine** c-1-3 only.*

SCIENCE COMICS (2nd Series)
Humor Publications (Ace Magazines?): Jan, 1946 - No. 5, 1946

1-Palais-c/a in #1-3; A-Bomb-c 28 59 84 168 274 380
2 15 30 45 90 140 190
3-Feldstein-a (6 pgs.); Palais-c 20 40 60 120 195 270
4,5: 4-Palais-c 14 28 42 78 112 145

SCIENCE COMICS
Ziff-Davis Publ. Co.: May, 1947 (8 pgs. in color)

nn-Could be ordered by mail for 10¢; like the nn Amazing Adventures (1950) & Boy Cowboy (1950); used to test the market 63 126 159 334 567 800

SCIENCE COMICS (True Science Illustrated)
Export Publication Ent., Toronto, Canada: Mar, 1951 (Distr. in U.S. by Kable News Co.)

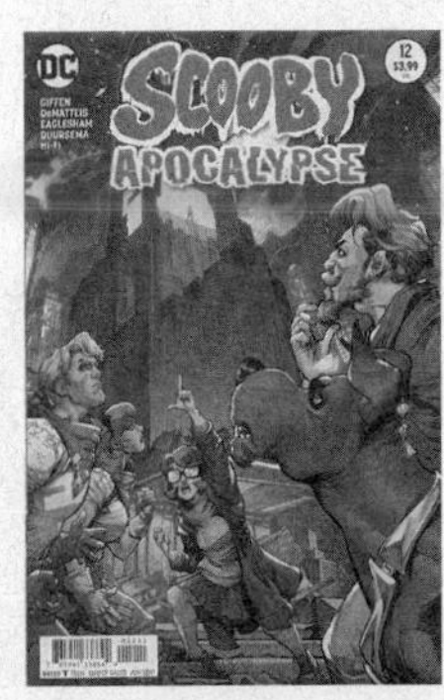

Scooby Apocalypse #12 © H-B

Scooby-Doo: Where are You? #25 © H-B

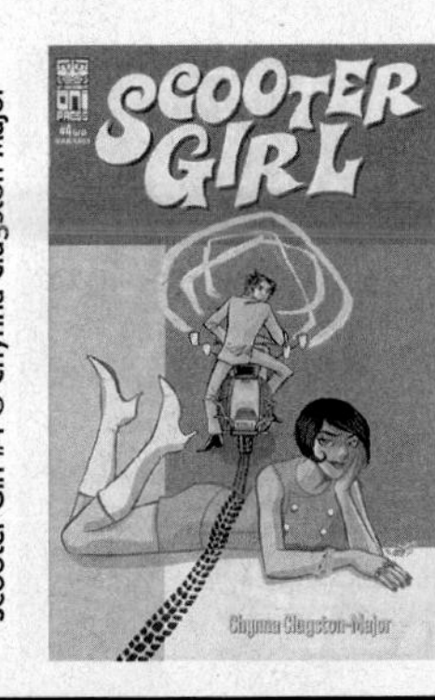

Scooter Girl #4 © Chynna Clugston-Major

GD 2.0 | VG 4.0 | FN 6.0 | VF 8.0 | VF/NM 9.0 | NM- 9.2

1-Science Adventure stories plus some true science features; man on moon story 21 42 63 122 199 275

SCIENCE DOG SPECIAL (Also see Invincible)
Image Comics: Aug, 2010; No. 2, May, 2011 ($3.50)
1,2: 1-Kirkman-s/Walker-a/c; leads into Invincible #75 3.50

SCIENCE FICTION SPACE ADVENTURES (See Space Adventures)

SCION (Also see CrossGen Chronicles)
CrossGeneration Comics: July, 2000 - No. 43, Apr, 2004 ($2.95)
1-43: 1-Marz-s/Cheung-a 3.00

SCI-SPY
DC Comics (Vertigo): Apr, 2002 - No. 6, Sept, 2002 ($2.50, limited series)
1-6-Moench-s/Gulacy-c/a 3.00

SCI-TECH
DC Comics (WildStorm): Sept, 1999 - No. 4, Dec, 1999 ($2.50, limited series)
1-4-Benes-a/Choi & Peterson-s 3.00

SCOOBY APOCALYPSE (Scooby Doo)
DC Comics: Jul, 2016 - No. 36, Jun, 2019 ($3.99)
1-36: 1-Giffen & DeMatteis-s/Porter-a; covers by Jim Lee and various; team's 1st meeting 4-Intro. Scrappy-Doo. 6-Velma's origin. 7-Eaglesham-a. 9-18-Scrappy-Doo app. 16-29-Secret Squirrel back-up. 25-Fred killed. 30-36-Atom Ant back-up; JLA app. 4.00
.../Hanna-Barbera Halloween Comics Fest Special Edition 1 (12/16, giveaway) previews Scooby Apocalypse, Future Quest, The Flintstones, and Wacky Races 3.00

SCOOBY DOO (TV)(...Where are you? #1-16,26; ...Mystery Comics #17-25, 27 on)
(See March Of Comics #356, 368, 382, 391 in the Promotional Comics section)
Gold Key: Mar, 1970 - No. 30, Feb, 1975 (Hanna-Barbera)

	GD	VG	FN	VF	VF/NM	NM-
1-First comic book app.	175	350	525	1400	2450	3500
2	19	38	57	133	297	460
3-5	17	34	51	117	259	400
6-10	12	24	36	80	173	265
11-20: 11-Tufts-a	9	18	27	59	117	175
21-30: 28-Whitman edition	8	16	24	52	99	145

SCOOBY DOO (TV)
Charlton Comics: Apr, 1975 - No. 11, Dec, 1976 (Hanna-Barbera)

	GD	VG	FN	VF	VF/NM	NM-
1	11	22	33	72	154	235
2-5	7	14	21	48	89	130
6-11	6	12	18	37	66	95
nn-(1976, digest, 68 pgs., B&W)	5	10	15	31	53	75

SCOOBY-DOO (TV) (Newsstand sales only) (See Dynamutt & Laff-A-Lympics)
Marvel Comics Group: Oct, 1977 - No. 9, Feb, 1979 (Hanna-Barbera)

	GD	VG	FN	VF	VF/NM	NM-
1-Dyno-Mutt begins	5	10	15	35	63	90
1-(35¢-c variant, limited distribution)(10/77)	11	22	33	73	163	250
2-5	3	6	9	19	30	40
6-9	3	6	9	21	33	45

SCOOBY-DOO (TV)
Harvey Comics: Sept, 1992 - No. 3, May, 1993 ($1.25)

	GD	VG	FN	VF	VF/NM	NM-
V2#1-3: 3-(Low print and scarce)	2	4	6	10	14	18
Big Book 1,2 (11/92, 4/93, $1.95, 52 pgs.)	2	4	6	8	10	12
Giant Size 1,2 (10/92, 3/93, $2.25, 68 pgs.)	2	4	6	8	10	12

SCOOBY DOO (TV)
Archie Comics: Oct, 1995 -No. 21, June, 1997 ($1.50)

	GD	VG	FN	VF	VF/NM	NM-
1	3	6	9	14	20	25
2-21: 12-Cover by Scooby Doo creative designer Iwao Takamoto						6.00

SCOOBY DOO (TV)
DC Comics: Aug, 1997 - No. 159, Oct, 2010 ($1.75/$1.95/$1.99/$2.25/$2.50/$2.99)

	GD	VG	FN	VF	VF/NM	NM-
1	2	4	6	9	12	15
2-10: 5-Begin-$1.95-c						5.00
11-45: 14-Begin $1.99-c						4.00
46-89,91-157: 63-Begin $2.25-c. 75-With 2 Garbage Pail Kids stickers. 100-Wray-c						3.00
90,158,159: 90-($2.95) Bonus stories. 158,159-($2.99-c)						4.00
...Spooky Spectacular 1 (10/99, $3.95) Comic Convention story						4.00
...Spooky Spectacular 2000 (10/00, $3.95)						4.00
...Spooky Summer Special 2001 (8/01, $3.95) Staton-a						4.00
...Super Scarefest (8/02, $3.95) r/#20,25,30-32						4.00

SCOOBY-DOO 50TH ANNIVERSARY GIANT (TV)
DC Comics: 2019 ($4.99, squarebound one-shot)
1-Three new stories plus reprints from Scooby-Doo: Where Are You?; Brizuela-a 5.00

SCOOBY-DOO TEAM-UP (TV)
DC Comics: Jan, 2014 - No. 50, Nov, 2019 ($2.99)

	GD	VG	FN	VF	VF/NM	NM-
1-11,13-20,22-50: 1-Batman & Robin app.; Man-Bat app. 2-Ace the Bat-Hound app. 3-Bat-Mite app. 4-Teen Titans Go! 6-Super Friends & Legion of Doom app. 7-Flintstones. 8-Jetsons. 10-Jonny Quest. 13-Spectre, Deadman & Phantom Stranger. 27-Plastic Man. 28-Jonah Hex app. 31-The Atom. 33-Legion of Super-Heroes. 34-Birds of Prey. 43-Doom Patrol. 45-Mr. Miracle & Big Barda. 46-Black Lightning. 50-Bat-Mite, Scooby-Mite, cartoon & movie versions and Scooby Apocalypse versions app.						3.00
12-Harley Quinn, Poison Ivy, Catwoman & Batgirl app.	2	4	6	8	10	12
21-Harley Quinn, Joker, Batman, Robin & Batgirl app.						6.00
... FCBD Special Edition 1 (6/15, giveaway) flipbook with Teen Titans Go!						4.00
... Halloween Special Edition (12/14, giveaway) r/#1						4.00

SCOOBY-DOO: WHERE ARE YOU? (TV)
DC Comics: Nov, 2010 - Present ($2.99)

	GD	VG	FN	VF	VF/NM	NM-
1	3	6	9	14	20	25
2-5	1	3	4	6	8	10
6-20						6.00
21-31,33-50						4.00
32-KISS spoof	3	6	9	14	20	25
51-108						3.00

SCOOP COMICS (Becomes Yankee Comics #4-7, a digest sized cartoon book; then after #8 it becomes Snap #9)
Harry 'A' Chesler (Holyoke): November, 1941 - No. 3, Mar, 1943; No. 8, 1944

	GD	VG	FN	VF	VF/NM	NM-
1-Intro. Rocketman & Rocketgirl & begins; origin The Master Key & begins; Dan Hastings begins; Charles Sultan-c/a	155	310	465	992	1696	2400
2-Rocket Boy begins; injury to eye story (reprinted in Spotlight #3); classic-c	400	800	1200	2800	4900	7000
3-Injury to eye story-r from #2; Rocket Boy	110	220	330	704	1202	1700
8-Formerly Yankee Comics; becomes Snap	68	136	204	435	743	1050

SCOOTER (See Swing With...)

SCOOTER COMICS
Rucker Publ. Ltd. (Canadian): Apr, 1946
1-Teen-age/funny animal 22 44 66 128 209 290

SCOOTER GIRL
Oni Press: May, 2003 - No. 6, Feb, 2004 ($2.99, B&W, limited series)
1-6-Chynna Clugston-Major-s/a 3.00
TPB (5/04, $14.95, digest size) r/series; sketch pages 15.00

SCORPION
Atlas/Seaboard Publ.: Feb, 1975 - No. 3, July, 1975

	GD	VG	FN	VF	VF/NM	NM-
1-Intro.; bondage-c by Chaykin	3	6	9	15	22	28
2-Chaykin-a w/Wrightson, Kaluta, Simonson assists(p)	3	6	9	15	22	28
3-Jim Craig-c/a	2	4	6	11	16	20

NOTE: *Chaykin a-1, 2; c-1. Colon c-2. Craig c/a-3.*

SCORPION KING, THE (Movie)
Dark Horse Comics: March, 2002 - No. 2, Apr, 2002 ($2.99, limited series)
1,2-Photo-c of the Rock; Richards-a 3.00

SCORPIO ROSE
Eclipse Comics: Jan, 1983 - No. 2, Oct, 1983 ($1.25, Baxter paper)
1,2: Dr. Orient back-up story begins. 2-origin. 4.00

SCOTLAND YARD (Inspector Farnsworth of)(Texas Rangers in Action #5 on?)
Charlton Comics Group: June, 1955 - No. 4, Mar, 1956

	GD	VG	FN	VF	VF/NM	NM-
1-Tothish-a	15	30	45	86	133	180
2-4: 2-Tothish-a	10	20	30	56	76	95

SCOTT PILGRIM, ... (Inspired the 2010 movie)
Oni Press: Jul, 2004 - Vol. 6, Jul, 2010 ($11.99, B&W, 7-1/2" x 5", multiple printings exist)
Scott Pilgrim's Precious Little Life (Vol. 1) Bryan Lee O'Malley-s/a in all 12.00
Scott Pilgrim Vs. The World (Vol. 2), S.P. & The Infinite Sadness (Vol. 3), S.P. Gets it Together (Vol. 4), S.P. Vs. The Universe (Vol. 5), Scott Pilgrim's Finest Hour (Vol. 6) each 12.00
Free Scott Pilgrim #1 (Free Comic Book Day Edition, 2006) 15.00
Full-Colour Odds & Ends 2008 12.00

SCOURGE, THE
Aspen MLT: No. 0, Aug, 2010 - No. 6, Dec, 2011 ($2.50/$2.99)
0-($2.50) Lobdell-s/Battle-a; multiple covers 3.00
1-6-($2.99) Lobdell-s/Battle-a; multiple covers 3.00

SCOURGE OF THE GODS
Marvel Comics (Soleil): 2009 - No. 3, 2009 ($5.99, limited series)
1-3-Mangin-s/Gajic-a; English version of French comic 6.00

Scratch #1 © I Before E Inc.

The Scumbag #1 © Rick Remender

Sea Devils #7 © DC

	GD 2.0	VG 4.0	FN 6.0	VF 8.0	VF/NM 9.0	NM- 9.2
...: The Fall 1-3 (2009 - No. 3, 2009)						6.00

SCOUT (See Eclipse Graphic Album #16, New America & Swords of Texas)
(Becomes Scout: War Shaman)
Eclipse Comics: Dec, 1985 - No. 24, Oct, 1987($1.75/$1.25, Baxter paper)

1-15,17,18,20-24: 19-Airboy preview. 10-Bissette-a. 11-Monday, the Eliminator begins. 15-Swords of Texas						3.00
16,19: 16-Scout 3-D Special ($2.50), 16-Scout 2-D Limited Edition, 19-contains flexidisk ($2.50)						4.00
...Handbook 1 (8/87, $1.75, B&W)						3.00
Mount Fire (1989, $14.95, TPB) r/#8-14						15.00

SCOUT'S HONOR
AfterShock Comics: Jan, 2021 - Present ($4.99/$3.99)

1-($4.99) David Pepose-s/Luca Casalanguida-a						5.00
2-($3.99)						4.00

SCOUT: WAR SHAMAN (Formerly Scout)
Eclipse Comics: Mar, 1988 - No. 16, Dec, 1989 ($1.95)

1-16						3.00

SCRATCH
DC Comics: Aug, 2004 - No. 5, Dec, 2004 ($2.50, limited series)

1-5-Sam Kieth-s/a/c; Batman app.						3.00

SCREAM (...Comics) (Andy Comics #20 on)
Humor Publications/Current Books(Ace Magazines): Autumn, 1944 - No. 19, Apr, 1948

1-Teenage humor	21	42	63	124	202	280
2	14	28	42	80	115	150
3-16: 11-Racist humor (Indians). 16-Intro. Lily-Belle	11	22	33	64	90	115
17,19	10	20	30	58	79	100
18-Hypo needle story	11	22	33	64	90	115

SCREAM (Magazine)
Skywald Publ. Corp.: Aug, 1973 - No. 11, Feb, 1975 (68 pgs., B&W) (Painted-c on all)

1-Nosferatu-c/1st app. (series thru #11); Morrow-a. Cthulhu/Necronomicon-s	9	18	27	58	114	170
2,3: 2-(10/73) Lady Satan 1st app. & series begins; Edgar Allan Poe adaptations begin (thru #11); Phantom of the Opera-s. 3-(12/73) Origin Lady Satan	5	10	15	33	57	80
4-1st Cannibal Werewolf and 1st Lunatic Mummy	4	8	12	28	50	70
5,7,8: 5,7-Frankenstein app. 8-Buckler-a; Werewolf-s; Slither-Slime Man-s	4	8	12	28	50	70
6, 9,10: 6-(6/74) Saga of The Victims/ I Am Horror, classic GGA Hewetson series begins (thru #11); Frankenstein 2073-s. 9-Severed head-c; Marcos-a. 9,10-Werewolf-s. 10-Dracula-c/s	5	10	15	31	53	75
11- (1975 Winter Special) "Mr. Poe and the Raven" story	5	10	15	33	57	80

NOTE: ***Buckler** a-8. **Hewetson** s-1-11. **Marcos** a-9. **Miralles** c-2. **Morrow** a-1. **Poe** s-2-11. **Segrelles** a-7; c-1.*

SCREAM: CURSE OF CARNAGE (Follows the Absolute Carnage series)
Marvel Comics: Jan, 2020 - Present ($4.99/$3.99, limited series)

1-($4.99) Andi Benton with the Scream symbiote; Chapman-s/Mooneyham-a						5.00
2-5-($3.99) Brown & Mooneyham-a. 4,5-Thor app.						4.00

SCREEN CARTOONS
DC Comics: Dec, 1944 (cover only ashcan)
nn-Ashcan comic, not distributed to newsstands, only for in house use. Covers were produced, but not the rest of the book. A copy sold in 2006 for $400 and in 2008 for $500.

SCREEN COMICS
DC Comics: Dec, 1944 (cover only ashcan)
nn-Ashcan comic, not distributed to newsstands, only for in house use. Covers were produced, but not the rest of the book. A copy sold in 2006 for $400, in 2008 for $500 and in 2013 for $500.

SCREEN FABLES
DC Comics: Dec, 1944 (cover only ashcan)
nn-Ashcan comic, not distributed to newsstands, only for in house use. Covers were produced, but not the rest of the book. A copy sold in 2006 for $400 and in 2008 for $500.

SCREEN FUNNIES
DC Comics: Dec, 1944 (cover only ashcan)
nn-Ashcan comic, not distributed to newsstands, only for in house use. Covers were produced, but not the rest of the book. A copy sold in 2006 for $400 and in 2008 for $500.

SCREEN GEMS
DC Comics: Dec, 1944 (cover only ashcan)
nn-Ashcan comic, not distributed to newsstands, only for in house use. Covers were produced, but not the rest of the book. A copy sold in 2010 for $891 and a VF copy sold for $775.

SCREWBALL SQUIRREL
Dark Horse Comics: July, 1995 - No. 3, Sept, 1995 ($2.50, limited series)

1-3: Characters created by Tex Avery						3.00

SCRIBBLENAUTS UNMASKED: A CRISIS OF IMAGINATION (Based on the video game)
DC Comics: Mar, 2014 - No. 7, Sept, 2014 ($2.99)

1-7: 1-The Bat Family, the Joker and Phantom Stranger app. 3-The Anti-Monitor app.						3.00

SCRIBBLY (See All-American Comics, Buzzy, The Funnies, Leave It To Binky & Popular Comics)
National Periodical Publ.: 8-9/48 - No. 13, 8-9/50; No. 14, 10-11/51 - No. 15, 12-1/51-52

	GD 2.0	VG 4.0	FN 6.0	VF 8.0	VF/NM 9.0	NM- 9.2
1-Sheldon Mayer-c/a in all; 52 pgs. begin	100	200	300	640	1095	1550
2	61	122	183	390	670	950
3-5	52	104	156	328	552	775
6-10	39	78	117	240	395	550
11-15: 13-Last 52 pgs.	33	66	99	196	321	445

SCUD: TALES FROM THE VENDING MACHINE
Fireman Press: 1998 - No. 5 ($2.50, B&W)

1-5: 1-Kaniuga-a. 2-Ruben Martinez-a						3.00

SCUD: THE DISPOSABLE ASSASSIN
Fireman Press: Feb, 1994 - No. 20, 1997 ($2.95, B&W)
Image Comics: No. 21, Feb, 2008 - No. 24, May, 2008 ($3.50, B&W)

1	6	12	18	37	66	95
1-2nd printing in color						5.00
2	2	4	6	9	12	15
3						6.00
4-20						3.00
21-24: 21-(2/08, $3.50) Ashley Wood-c. 22-Mahfood-c						3.50
Heavy 3PO ($12.95, TPB) r/#1-4						13.00
Programmed For Damage ($14.95, TPB) r/#5-9						15.00
Solid Gold Bomb ($17.95, TPB) r/#10-15						18.00

SCUMBAG, THE
Image Comics: Oct, 2020 - Present ($3.99)

1-5: 1-Remender-s/Larosa-a; intro. Ernie Ray Clementine. 2-Robinson-a. 3-Eric Powell-a						4.00

SEA DEVILS (See Showcase #27-29)
National Periodical Publications: Sept-Oct, 1961 - No. 35, May-June, 1967

1-(9-10/61)	59	118	177	472	1061	1650
2-Last 10¢ issue; grey-tone-c	27	54	81	194	435	675
3-Begin 12¢ issues thru #35; grey-tone-c	18	36	54	124	275	425
4,5-Grey-tone-c	15	30	45	105	233	360
6-10	10	20	30	69	147	225
11,12,14-20: 12-Grey-tone-c	8	16	24	54	102	150
13-Kubert, Colan-a; Joe Kubert app. in story	8	16	24	55	105	155
21-35: 22-Intro. International Sea Devils; origin & 1st app. Capt. X & Man Fish. 33,35-Grey-tone-c	6	12	18	40	73	105

NOTE: ***Heath** a-Showcase 27-29, 1-10; c-Showcase 27-29, 1-10, 14-16. **Moldoff** a-16i.*

SEA DEVILS (See Tangent Comics/ Sea Devils)

SEADRAGON (Also see the Epsilion Wave)
Elite Comics: May, 1986 - No. 8, 1987 ($1.75)

1-8: 1-1st & 2nd printings exist						3.00

SEAGUY
DC Comics (Vertigo): July, 2004 - No. 3, Sept, 2004 ($2.95, limited series)

1-3-Grant Morrison-s/Cameron Stewart-a/c						3.00
TPB (2005, $9.95) r/#1-3						10.00

SEAGUY: THE SLAVES OF MICKEY EYE
DC Comics (Vertigo): Jun, 2009 - No. 3, Aug, 2009 ($3.99, limited series)

1-3-Grant Morrison-s/Cameron Stewart-a/c						4.00

SEA HOUND, THE (Captain Silver's Log Of The...)
Avon Periodicals: 1945 (no month) - No. 2, Sept-Oct, 1945

nn (#1)-29 pg. novel length sty-"The Esmeralda's Treasure"	18	36	54	105	165	225
2	13	26	39	74	105	135

SEA HOUND, THE (Radio)
Capt. Silver Syndicate: No. 3, July, 1949 - No. 4, Sept, 1949

3,4	10	20	30	54	72	90

SEA HUNT (TV)
Dell Publishing Co.: No. 928, 8/58 - No. 1041, 10-12/59; No. 4, 1-3/60 - No. 13, 4-6/62 (All

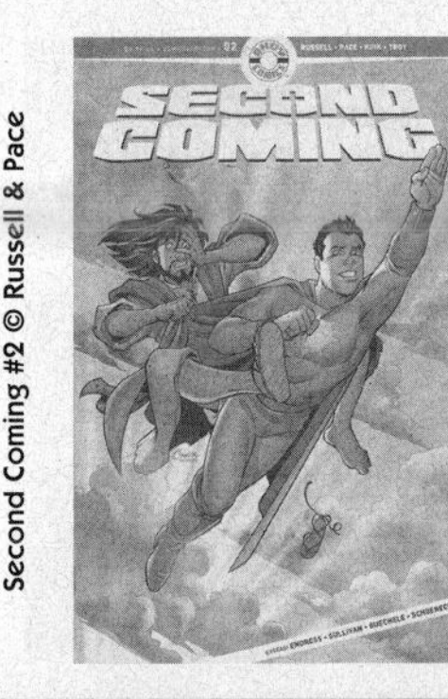

Second Coming #2 © Russell & Pace

Secret Avengers (2013 series) #1 © MAR

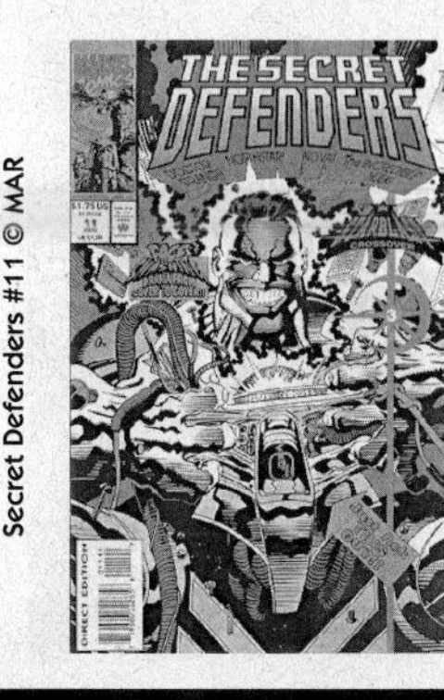

Secret Defenders #11 © MAR

GD 2.0 | VG 4.0 | FN 6.0 | VF 8.0 | VF/NM 9.0 | NM- 9.2

have Lloyd Bridges photo-c)
Four Color 928(#1) 10 20 30 68 144 220
Four Color 994(#2), 4-13: Manning-a #4-6,8-11,13 8 16 24 51 96 140
Four Color 1041(#3)-Toth-a 8 16 24 51 96 140

SEA OF RED
Image Comics: Mar, 2005 - No. 13, Nov, 2006 ($2.95/$2.99/$3.50)
1-12-Vampirates at sea; Remender & Dwyer-s/Dwyer & Sam-a 3.00
13-($3.50) 3.50
Vol. 1: No Grave But The Sea (9/05, $8.95) r/#1-4 9.00
Vol. 2: No Quarter (2006, $11.99) r/#5-8 12.00
Vol. 3: The Deadlights (2006, $14.99) r/#9-13 15.00

SEA OF STARS
Image Comics: Jul, 2019 - Present ($3.99, limited series)
1-8-Jason Aaron & Dennis Hallum-s/Stephen Green-a 4.00

SEA OF THIEVES (Based on the Microsoft computer game)
Titan Comics: Apr, 2018 - No. 4, Jul, 2018 ($3.99)
1-4-Jeremy Whitley-s/Rhoald Marcellius-a; multiple covers; bonus character profiles 4.00

SEAQUEST (TV)
Nemesis Comics: Mar, 1994 ($2.25)
1-Has 2 diff-c stocks (slick & cardboard); Alcala-i 3.00

SEARCHERS, THE (Movie)
Dell Publishing Co.: No. 709, 1956
Four Color 709-John Wayne photo-c 26 52 78 182 404 625

SEARCHERS, THE
Caliber Comics: 1996 - No. 4, 1996 ($2.95, B&W)
1-4 3.00

SEARCHERS, THE : APOSTLE OF MERCY
Caliber Comics: 1997 - No. 2, 1997 ($2.95/$3.95, B&W)
1-($2.95) 3.00
2-($3.95) 4.00

SEARCH FOR LOVE
American Comics Group: Feb-Mar, 1950 - No. 2, Apr-May, 1950 (52 pgs.)
1-Ken Bald-c 15 30 45 94 147 200
2 12 24 36 67 94 120

SEARS (See Merry Christmas From...)

SEASON'S BEATINGS
Marvel Comics: Feb, 2019 ($4.99, one-shot)
1-Christmas-themed short stories; Deadpool, X-Force, Spider-Man, Squirrel Girl app. 5.00

SEASON'S GREETINGS
Hallmark (King Features): 1935 (6-1/4x5-1/4", 24 pgs. in color)
nn-Cover features Mickey Mouse, Popeye, Jiggs & Skippy. "The Night Before Christmas" told one panel per page, each panel by a famous artist featuring their character. Art by Alex Raymond, Gottfredson, Swinnerton, Segar, Chic Young, Milt Gross, Sullivan (Messmer), Herriman, McManus, Percy Crosby & others (22 artists in all)
Estimated value... 1000.00

SEBASTIAN O
DC Comics (Vertigo): May, 1993 - No. 3, July, 1993 ($1.95, limited series)
1-3-Grant Morrison scripts; Steve Yeowell-a 3.00
TPB (2004, $9.95) r/#1-3; intro. chronology by Morrison 10.00

SECOND COMING
AHOY Comics: 2019 - No. 6, 2020 ($3.99, limited series)
1-6-Russell-s/Pace & Kirk-a/Conner-c; Jesus meets Sunstar. 1-3-Variant-c by Pace 4.00

SECOND COMING: ONLY BEGOTTEN SON
AHOY Comics: 2020 - Present ($3.99, limited series)
1,2-Russell-s/Pace & Kirk-a/Pace-c. 1-Origin of Sunstar 4.00

SECOND LIFE OF DOCTOR MIRAGE, THE (See Shadowman #16)
Valiant: Nov, 1993 - No. 18, May, 1995 ($2.50)
1-18: 1-With bound-in poster. 5-Shadowman x-over. 7-Bound-in trading card 3.00
1-Gold ink logo edition; no price on-c 1 3 4 6 8 10

SECOND SIGHT
AfterShock Comics: Feb, 2016 - No. 6, Jul, 2016 ($3.99)
1-6-David Hine-s/Alberto Ponticelli-a 4.00

SECRET AGENT (Formerly Sarge Steel)
Charlton Comics: V2#9, Oct, 1966; V2#10, Oct, 1967
V2#9-Sarge Steel part-r begins 3 6 9 17 26 35
10-Tiffany Sinn, CIA app. (from Career Girl Romances #39); Aparo-a
3 6 9 14 20 26

SECRET AGENT (TV) (See Four Color #1231)
Gold Key: Nov, 1966; No. 2, Jan, 1968
1-John Drake photo-c 8 16 24 52 99 145
2-Photo-c 6 12 18 37 66 95

SECRET AGENT X-9 (See Flash Gordon #4 by King)
David McKay Publ.: 1934 (Book 1: 84 pgs.; Book 2: 124 pgs.) (8x7-1/2")
Book 1-Contains reprints of the first 13 weeks of the strip by Alex Raymond; complete except for 2 dailies 52 104 156 328 552 775
Book 2-Contains reprints immediately following contents of Book 1, for 20 weeks by Alex Raymond; complete except for two dailies. Note: Raymond mis-dated the last five strips from 6/34, and while the dating sequence is confusing, the continuity is correct
42 84 126 265 445 625

SECRET AGENT X-9 (See Magic Comics)
Dell Publishing Co.: Dec, 1937 (Not by Raymond)
Feature Books 8 55 110 165 352 601 850

SECRET AGENT Z-2 (See Holyoke One-Shot No. 7)

SECRET AVENGERS (The Heroic Age)
Marvel Comics: Jul, 2010 - No. 37, Mar, 2013 ($3.99)
1-Bendis-s/Deodato-a/Djurdjevic-c; Steve Rogers assembles covert squad 4.00
1-Variant-c by Yardin 6.00
2-12: 2-Two covers. 2-4-Deodato-a. 5-Nick Fury app.; Aja-a 4.00
12.1 ($2.99) Spencer-s/Eaton-a/Deodato-c 3.00
13-21: 13-15-Fear Itself tie-in; Granov-c. 15-Aftermath of Bucky's demise. 16-21-Ellis-s 4.00
21.2-($2.99) Remender-s/Zircher-a; intro. new Masters of Evil 3.00
22-37: 22-25-Remender-s/Hardman-a/Art Adams-c. 23-Venom joins. 26-28-A vs. X 4.00

SECRET AVENGERS (Marvel NOW!)
Marvel Comics: Apr, 2013 - No. 16, Apr, 2014 ($3.99)
1-16: 1-5-Spencer-s/Luke Ross-a/Coker-c; Agent Coulson app. 5,7-Hulk app. 7,9-Guice-a 9,16-Winter Soldier app. 4.00

SECRET AVENGERS (All-New Marvel NOW!)
Marvel Comics: May, 2014 - No. 15, Jun, 2015 ($3.99)
1-15: 1-Ales Kot-s/Michael Walsh-a; M.O.D.O.K. app. 7-Deadpool app. 4.00

SECRET CITY SAGA (See Jack Kirby's Secret City Saga)

SECRET DEFENDERS (Also see The Defenders & Fantastic Four #374)
Marvel Comics: Mar, 1993 - No. 25, Mar, 1995 ($1.75/$1.95)
1-($2.50)-Red foil stamped-c; Dr. Strange, Nomad, Wolverine, Spider Woman & Darkhawk begin 4.00
2-11,13-24: 9-New team w/Silver Surfer, Thunderstrike, Dr. Strange & War Machine. 13-Thanos replaces Dr. Strange as leader; leads into Cosmic Powers limited series; 14-Dr. Druid. 15-Bound in card sheet. 15-17-Deadpool app. 18-Giant Man & Iron Fist app. 3.00
12,25: 12-($2.50)-Prismatic foil-c. 25 ($2.50, 52 pgs.) 4.00

SECRET DIARY OF EERIE ADVENTURES
Avon Periodicals: 1953 (25¢ giant, 100 pgs., one-shot)
nn-(Rare)-Kubert-a; Hollingsworth-c; Sid Check back-c
415 830 1245 2905 5103 7300

SECRET EMPIRE (Also see Free Comic Book Day 2017 Secret Empire)
Marvel Comics: No. 0, Jun, 2017 - No. 10, Oct, 2017 ($4.99/$3.99, limited series)
0-2-($4.99): 0-Spencer-s/Acuña-a; Steve Rogers and Hydra take over. 1-McNiven-a 5.00
3-5,7-($3.99) 3,5-Sorrentino-a. 4-Yu-a. 5-Bruce Banner returns 4.00
6,8-10-($4.99): 6,9-Yu-a. 7-Black Widow killed. 8-Acuña-a. 10-McNiven-a 5.00
... Omega 1 (11/17, $4.99) Epilogue to series; Sorrentino & Bennett-a 5.00
...: Underground 1 (8/17, $4.99) Whitley-s/Koda-a; takes place after #4; Sauron app. 5.00
...: United 1 (8/17, $4.99) X-Men & Deadpool app.; Anindito-a 5.00
...: Uprising 1 (7/17, $4.99) The Champions & Black Widow app.; Landy-s/Cassara-a 5.00

SECRET EMPIRE: BRAVE NEW WORLD
Marvel Comics: Aug, 2017 - No. 5, Oct, 2017 ($3.99, limited series)
1-5: Namor/Invaders and back-up short stories of various heroes under Hydra rule 5.00

SECRET FILES & ORIGINS GUIDE TO THE DC UNIVERSE
DC Comics: Mar, 2000; Feb, 2002 ($6.95/$4.95)
2000 (3/00, $6.95)-Overview of DC characters; profile pages by various 7.00
2001-2002 (2/02, $4.95) Olivetti-c 5.00

SECRET FILES PRESIDENT LUTHOR
DC Comics: Mar, 2001 ($4.95, one-shot)

Secret Hearts #26 © DC

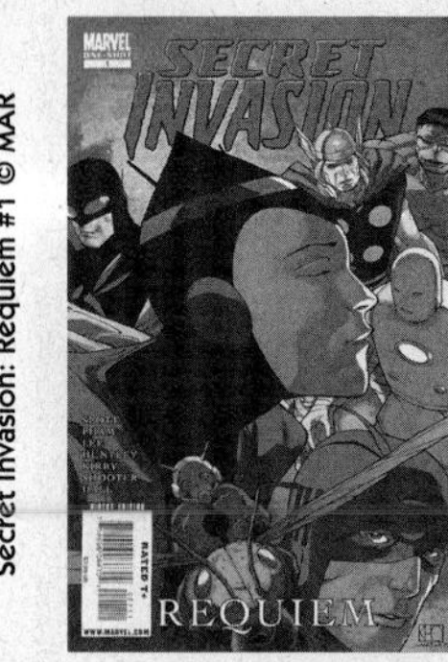

Secret Invasion: Requiem #1 © MAR

Secret Mysteries #16 © Ribage

	GD 2.0	VG 4.0	FN 6.0	VF 8.0	VF/NM 9.0	NM- 9.2
1-Short stories & profile pages by various; Harris-c						5.00

SECRET HEARTS
National Periodical Publications (Beverly)(Arleigh No. 50-113):
9-10/49 - No. 6, 7-8/50; No. 7, 12-1/51-52 - No. 153, 7/71

	GD	VG	FN	VF	VF/NM	NM-
1-Kinstler-a; photo-c begin, end #6	71	142	213	454	777	1100
2-Toth-a (1 pg.); Kinstler-a	37	74	111	222	361	500
3,6 (1950)	33	66	99	194	317	440
4,5-Toth-a	34	68	102	199	325	450
7(12-1/51-52) (Rare)	47	94	141	296	498	700
8-10 (1952)	25	50	75	150	245	340
11-20	19	38	57	111	176	240
21-26: 26-Last precode (2-3/55)	16	32	48	92	144	195
27-40	8	16	24	51	96	140
41-50	6	12	18	40	73	105
51-60	5	10	15	35	63	90
61-75,100: 75-Last 10¢ issue	5	10	15	31	53	75
76-99,101-109: 83,88-Each has panel which inspired a famous Roy Lichtenstein painting	4	8	12	23	37	50
110- "Reach for Happiness" serial begins, ends #138	4	8	12	25	40	55
111-119,121-126: 114-Colan-a/c	3	6	9	17	26	35
120,134-Neal Adams-c	4	8	12	25	40	55
127 (4/68)-Beatles cameo	4	8	12	27	44	60
128-133,135-142: 141,142- "20 Miles to Heartbreak", Chapter 2 & 3 (see Young Love for Chapters 1 & 4); Toth, Colletta-a	3	6	9	16	24	32
143-148,150-152: 144-Morrow-a	3	6	9	14	20	26
149,153: 149-Toth-a. 153-Kirby-i	3	6	9	15	22	28

SECRET HISTORY OF THE AUTHORITY: HAWKSMOOR
DC Comics (WildStorm): May, 2008 - No. 6, Oct, 2008 ($2.99, limited series)

	NM-
1-6-Costa-s/Staples-a/Hamner-c	3.00
TPB (2009, $19.99) r/#1-6	20.00

SECRET IDENTITIES
Image Comics: Feb, 2015 - No. 7, Sept, 2015 ($3.50/$3.99)

	NM-
1-6-Faerber & Joines-s/Kyriazis-a	3.50
7-($3.99)	4.00

SECRET INVASION (Also see Mighty Avengers, New Avengers, and Skrulls!)
Marvel Comics: June, 2008 - No. 8, Jan, 2009 ($3.99, limited series)

	NM-
1-Skrull invasion; Bendis-s/Yu-a/Dell'Otto-c	5.00
1-Variant cover with blank area for sketches	5.00
1-McNiven variant-c	12.00
1-Yu variant-c	30.00
1-2nd printing with old Avengers variant-c by Yu	4.00
1 Director's Cut (2008, $4.99) r/#1 with script; concept and promo art; cover gallery	5.00
2-8-Dell'Otto-c. 8-Wasp killed	4.00
2-4-McNiven variant-c. 2-Avengers. 3-Nick Fury. 4-Tony Stark, Spider-Woman, Black Widow	6.00
2-8-Yu variant-c. 2-Hawkeye & Mockingbird. 3-Spider-Woman. 4-Nick Fury	10.00
5-Rubi variant-c	5.00
6-Cho Spider-Woman variant-c	8.00
...:Aftermath: Beta Ray Bill - The Green of Eden (6/09, $3.99) Brereton-a	4.00
...: Chronicles 1,2 (4/09,6/09, $5.99) reprints from New Avengers & Illuminati issues	6.00
... Dark Reign (2/09, $3.99) villain meeting after #8; previews new series; Maleev-a/c	4.00
... Dark Reign (2/09, $3.99) Variant Green Goblin cover by Bryan Hitch	8.00
... Requiem (2009, $3.99) Hank Pym becomes The Wasp; r/TTA #44 & Avengers #215	4.00
... Saga (2008, giveaway) history of the Skrulls told through reprint panels and text	3.00
...: The Infiltration TPB (2008, $19.99) r/FF #2; New Avengers #31,32,38,39; New Avengers: Illuminati #1,5; Mighty Avengers #7; and Avengers: The Initiative Annual #1	20.00
...: War of Kings (2/09, $3.99) Black Bolt and the Inhumans; Pelletier & Dazo-a	4.00
...: Who Do You Trust? (8/08, $3.99) short tie-in stories by various; Jimenez-c	4.00

SECRET INVASION: AMAZING SPIDER-MAN
Marvel Comics: Oct, 2008 - No. 3, Dec, 2008 ($2.99, limited series)

	NM-
1-3-Jackpot battles a Super-Skrull; Santucci-a. 2-Menace app.	3.00

SECRET INVASION: FANTASTIC FOUR
Marvel Comics: July, 2008 - No. 3, Sept, 2008 ($2.99, limited series)

	NM-
1-3-Skrulls and Lyja invade; Kitson-a/Davis-c	3.00
1-Variant Skrull cover by McKone	5.00

SECRET INVASION: FRONT LINE
Marvel Comics: Sept, 2008 - No. 5, Jan, 2009 ($2.99, limited series)

	NM-
1-5-Ben Urich covering the Skrull invasion; Reed-s/Castiello-a	3.00

SECRET INVASION: INHUMANS
Marvel Comics: Oct, 2008 - No. 4, Jan, 2009 ($2.99, limited series)

	NM-
1-4-Raney-a/Sejic-c/Pokasky-s; search for Black Bolt	3.00

SECRET INVASION: RUNAWAYS/YOUNG AVENGERS (Follows Runaways #30)
Marvel Comics: Aug, 2008 - No. 3, Nov, 2008 ($2.99, limited series)

	NM-
1-3-Miyazawa-a/Ryan-c	3.00

SECRET INVASION: THOR
Marvel Comics: Oct, 2008 - No. 3, Dec, 2008 ($2.99, limited series)

	NM-
1-3-Fraction-s/Braithwaite-a; Skrulls invade Asgard; Beta Ray Bill app.	3.00
1-2nd printing with Beta Ray Bill cover	3.00

SECRET INVASION: X-MEN
Marvel Comics: Oct, 2008 - No. 4, Jan, 2009 ($2.99, limited series)

	NM-
1-4-Carey-s/Nord-a/Dodson-c; Skrulls invade San Francisco	3.00
1-2nd printing with variant Nord-c	3.00

SECRET ISLAND OF OZ, THE (See First Comics Graphic Novel)

SECRET LIFE OF PETS, THE (Based on the 2016 animated movie)
Titan Comics: Jun, 2019 - Dec, 2019 ($3.99)

	NM-
1,2-Lapuss-s/Goum-a	4.00
...Volume 2 (11/19 - No. 2, 12/19) 1,2-Lapuss-s/Goum-a	

SECRET LOVE (See Fox Giants & Sinister House of...)

SECRET LOVE
Ajax-Farrell/Four Star Comic Corp. No. 2 on: 12/55 - No. 3, 8/56; 4/57 - No. 5, 2/58; No. 6, 6/58

	GD	VG	FN	VF	VF/NM	NM-
1(12/55-Ajax, 1st series)	15	30	45	84	127	170
2,3	11	22	33	60	83	105
1(4/57-Ajax, 2nd series)	13	26	39	72	101	130
2-6: 5-Bakerish-a	10	20	30	54	72	90

SECRET LOVES
Comic Magazines/Quality Comics Group: Nov, 1949 - No. 6, Sept, 1950

	GD	VG	FN	VF	VF/NM	NM-
1-Ward-c	35	70	105	208	339	470
2-Ward-c	27	54	81	162	266	370
3-Crandall-a	19	38	57	111	176	240
4,6	15	30	45	90	140	190
5-Suggestive art "Boom Town Babe"; photo-c	22	44	66	128	209	290

SECRET LOVE STORIES (See Fox Giants)

SECRET MISSIONS (Admiral Zacharia's...)
St. John Publishing Co.: February, 1950

	GD	VG	FN	VF	VF/NM	NM-
1-Joe Kubert-c; stories of U.S. foreign agents	24	48	72	140	230	320

SECRET MYSTERIES (Formerly Crime Mysteries & Crime Smashers)
Ribage/Merit Publications No. 17 on: No. 16, Nov, 1954 - No. 19, July, 1955

	GD	VG	FN	VF	VF/NM	NM-
16-Horror, Palais-a; Myron Fass-c	41	82	123	256	428	600
17-19-Horror. 17-Fass-c; mis-dated 3/54?	32	64	96	190	310	430

SECRET ORIGINS (1st Series) (See 80 Page Giant #8)
National Periodical Publications: Aug-Oct, 1961 (Annual) (Reprints)

	GD	VG	FN	VF	VF/NM	NM-
1-Origin Adam Strange (Showcase #17), Green Lantern (Green Lantern #1), Challengers (partial-r/Showcase #6, 6 pgs. Kirby-a), J'onn J'onzz (Det. #225), The Flash (Showcase #4), Green Arrow (1 pg. text), Superman-Batman team (World's Finest #94), Wonder Woman (Wonder Woman #105)	46	92	138	350	788	1225
Replica Edition (1998, $4.95) r/entire book and house ads						5.00
Even More Secret Origins (2003, $6.95) reprints origins of Hawkman, Eclipso, Kid Flash, Blackhawks, Green Lantern's oath, and Jimmy Olsen-Robin team in 80 pg. Giant style						7.00

SECRET ORIGINS (2nd Series)
National Periodical Publications: Feb-Mar, 1973 - No. 6, Jan-Feb, 1974; No. 7, Oct-Nov, 1974 (All 20¢ issues) (All origin reprints)

	GD	VG	FN	VF	VF/NM	NM-
1-Superman(r/1 pg. origin/Action #1, 1st time since G.A.), Batman(Detective #33), Ghost(Flash #88), The Flash(Showcase #4)	5	10	15	34	60	85
2-7: 2-Green Lantern & The Atom(Showcase #22 & 34), Supergirl(Action #252). 3-Wonder Woman (W.W. #1), Wildcat (Sensation #1). 4-Vigilante (Action #42) by Meskin, Kid Eternity(Hit #25). 5-The Spectre by Baily (More Fun #52,53). 6-Blackhawk(Military #1) & Legion of Super-Heroes(Superboy #147). 7-Robin (Detective #38), Aquaman (More Fun #73)	3	6	9	19	30	40

NOTE: *Infantino a-1. Kane a-2. Kubert a-1.*

SECRET ORIGINS (3rd Series)
DC Comics: Apr, 1986 - No. 50, Aug, 1990 (All origins)(52 pgs. #6 on)(#27 on: $1.50)

	GD	VG	FN	VF	VF/NM	NM-
1,3: 1-Origin Superman. 3-Shazam	1	2	3	5	6	8
2,4-6: 2-Blue Beetle. 4-Firestorm. 5-Crimson Avenger. 6-Halo/G.A. Batman						5.00
7-9,11,12,15-20,22-26: 7-Green Lantern (Guy Gardner)/G.A. Sandman. 8-Shadow Lass/Doll Man. 9-G.A. Flash/Skyman.11-G.A. Hawkman/Power Girl. 12-Challengers of Unknown/ G.A. Fury (2nd modern app.). 15-Spectre/Deadman. 16-G.A. Hourman/Warlord. 17-Adam Strange story by Carmine Infantino; Dr. Occult. 18-G.A. Gr. Lantern/The Creeper.						

Secret Origins (2014 series) #10 © DC

Secret Six (2015 series) #5 © DC

Secrets of Haunted House #31 © DC

GD VG FN VF VF/NM NM-
2.0 4.0 6.0 8.0 9.0 9.2

19-Uncle Sam/The Guardian. 20-Batgirl/G.A. Dr. Mid-Nite. 22-Manhunters. 23-Floronic Man/Guardians of the Universe. 24-Blue Devil/Dr. Fate. 25-LSH/Atom. 26-Black Lightning/Miss America 5.00
10-Phantom Stranger w/Alan Moore scripts; Legends spin-off 5.00
13-Origin Nightwing; Johnny Thunder app. 5.00
14-Suicide Squad; Legends spin-off 1 2 3 5 6 8
21-Jonah Hex/Black Condor 5.00
27-30,36-38,40-49: 27-Zatara/Zatanna. 28-Midnight/Nightshade. 29-Power of the Atom/Mr. America; new 3 pg. Red Tornado story by Mayer (last app. of Scribbly, 8/88). 30-Plastic Man/Elongated Man. 36-Poison Ivy by Neil Gaiman & Mark Buckingham/Green Lantern. 37-Legion Of Substitute Heroes/Doctor Light. 38-Green Arrow/Speedy; Grell scripts. 40-All Ape issue. 41-Rogues Gallery of Flash. 42-Phantom Girl/GrimGhost. 43-Original Hawk & Dove/Cave Carson/Chris KL-99. 44-Batman app.; story based on Det. #40. 45-Blackhawk/El Diablo. 46-JLA/LSH/New Titans. 47-LSH. 48-Ambush Bug/Stanley & His Monster/Rex the Wonder Dog/Trigger Twins. 49-Newsboy Legion/Silent Knight/Bouncing Boy 4.00
31-35,39: 31-JSA. 32-JLA. 33-35-JLI. 39-Animal Man-c/story continued in Animal Man #10; Grant Morrison scripts; Batman app. 4.00
50-($3.95, 100 pgs.)-Batman & Robin in text, Flash of Two Worlds, Johnny Thunder, Dolphin, Black Canary & Space Museum 5.00
Annual 1 (8/87)-Capt. Comet/Doom Patrol 5.00
Annual 2 ('88, $2.00)-Origin Flash II & Flash III 5.00
Annual 3 ('89, $2.95, 84 pgs.)-Teen Titans; 1st app. new Flamebird who replaces original Bat-Girl 5.00
Special 1 (10/89, $2.00)-Batman villains: Penguin, Riddler, & Two-Face; Bolland-c; Sam Kieth-a; Neil Gaiman scripts(2) 5.00

NOTE: ***Art Adams** a-33i(part). **M. Anderson** 8, 19, 21, 25i; c-19(part). **Aparo** c/a-10. **Bissette** c-23. **Bolland** c-7. **Byrne** c/a-Annual 1. **Colan** c/a-5p. **Forte** a-37. **Giffen** a-18p, 44p, 48. **Infantino** a-17, 50p. **Kaluta** c-39. **Gil Kane** a-2, 28; c-2p. **Kirby** c-19(part). **Erik Larsen** a-13. **Mayer** a-29. **Morrow** a-21. **Orlando** a-10. **Perez** a-50i, Annual 3i; c- Annual 3. **Rogers** a-6p. **Russell** a-27i. **Simonson** c-22. **Staton** a-36, 50p. **Steacy** a-35. **Tuska** a-4p, 9p.*

SECRET ORIGINS (4th Series)(DC New 52)
DC Comics: Jun, 2014 - No. 11, May, 2015 ($4.99)

1-3,5-9,11: 1-Origin Superman, Robin. 2-Batman. 6-Wonder Woman 5.00
4-Harley Quinn 2 4 6 8 10 12
10-Batgirl; Stewart & Fletcher-s/Koh-a; Firestorm & Poison Ivy 6.00

SECRET ORIGINS 80 PAGE GIANT (Young Justice)
DC Comics: Dec, 1998 ($4.95, one-shot)

1-Origin-s of Young Justice members; Ramos-a (Impulse) 5.00

SECRET ORIGINS FEATURING THE JLA
DC Comics: 1999 ($14.95, TPB)

1-Reprints recent origin-s of JLA members; Cassaday-c 15.00

SECRET ORIGINS OF SUPER-HEROES (See DC Special Series #10, 19)

SECRET ORIGINS OF SUPER-VILLAINS 80 PAGE GIANT
DC Comics: Dec, 1999 ($4.95, one-shot)

1-Origin-s of Sinestro, Amazo and others; Gibbons-c 5.00

SECRET ORIGINS OF THE WORLD'S GREATEST SUPER-HEROES
DC Comics: 1989 ($4.95, 148 pgs.)

nn-Reprints Superman, JLA origins; new Batman origin-s; Bolland-c 1 3 4 6 8 10

SECRET ROMANCE
Charlton Comics: Oct, 1968 - No. 41, Nov, 1976; No. 42, Mar, 1979 - No. 48, Feb, 1980

1-Begin 12¢ issues, ends #? 3 6 9 18 28 38
2-10: 9-Reese-a 2 4 6 11 16 20
11-16,18,19,21-30 2 4 6 9 13 16
17,20: 17-Susan Dey poster. 20-David Cassidy pin-up2 4 6 11 16 20
31-48 2 4 6 8 10 12

NOTE: *Beyond the Stars apps.-No. 9, 11, 12, 14.*

SECRET ROMANCES (Exciting Love Stories)
Superior Publications Ltd.: Apr, 1951 - No. 27, July, 1955

1 23 46 69 136 223 310
2 15 30 45 94 147 200
3-10 14 28 42 82 121 160
11-13,15-18,20-27 13 26 39 74 105 135
14,19-Lingerie panels 14 28 42 78 108 140

SECRET SERVICE (See Kent Blake of the...)

SECRET SERVICE (Inspired the 2015 movie Kingsmen: The Secret Service)(Also see Kingsmen: The Red Diamond)
Marvel Comics (Icon): Jun, 2012 - No. 6, Jun, 2013 ($2.99/$4.99, limited series)

1-5-Mark Millar-s/Dave Gibbons-a/c 3.00
6-($4.99) 5.00

SECRET SIX (See Action Comics Weekly)
National Periodical Publications: Apr-May, 1968 - No. 7, Apr-May, 1969 (12¢)

1-Origin/1st app. 7 14 21 49 92 135
2-7 4 8 12 25 40 55

SECRET SIX (See Tangent Comics/ Secret Six)

SECRET SIX (See Villains United)
DC Comics: Jul, 2006 - No. 6, Jan, 2007 ($2.99, limited series)

1-6-Gail Simone-s/Brad Walker-a. 4-Doom Patrol app. 3.00
...: Six Degrees of Devastation TPB (2007, $14.99) r/#1-6 15.00

SECRET SIX
DC Comics: Nov, 2008 - No. 36, Oct, 2011 ($2.99)

1-36: 1-Gail Simone-s/Nicola Scott-a. 2-Batman app. 8-Rodriguez-a. 11-13-Wonder Woman & Artemis app. 16-Black Alice app. 17,18-Blackest Night 3.00
...: Cats in the Cradle TPB (2011, $14.99) r/#19-24 15.00
...: Danse Macabre TPB (2010, $14.99) r/#15-18 & Suicide Squad #67 (Blackest Night) 15.00
...: Depths TPB (2010, $14.99) r/#8-14 15.00
...: The Reptile Brain TPB (2011, $14.99) r/#25-29 15.00
...: Unhinged TPB (2009, $14.99) r/#1-7; intro. by Paul Cornell 15.00

SECRET SIX
DC Comics: Feb, 2015 - No. 14, Jul, 2016 ($2.99)

1-14: 1,2-Simone-s/Lashley-a; Catman & Black Alice app. 10-Superman app. 12-14-Shiva app.; Elongated Man returns 3.00

SECRET SOCIETY OF SUPER-VILLAINS
National Per. Publ./DC Comics: May-June, 1976 - No. 15, June-July, 1978

1-Origin; JLA cameo & Capt. Cold app. 3 6 9 16 23 30
2-5,15: 2-Re-intro/origin Capt. Comet; Green Lantern x-over. 5-Green Lantern, Hawkman x-over; Darkseid app. 15-G.A. Atom, Dr. Midnite, & JSA app. 2 4 6 8 11 14
6-14: 9,10-Creeper x-over. 11-Capt. Comet; Orlando-i2 3 4 6 8 10

SECRET SOCIETY OF SUPER-VILLAINS SPECIAL (See DC Special Series #6)

SECRETS OF HAUNTED HOUSE
National Periodical Publications/DC Comics: 4-5/75 - #5, 12-1/75-76; #6, 6-7/77 - #14, 10-11/78; #15, 8/79 - #46, 3/82

1 5 10 15 34 60 85
2-4 3 6 9 19 30 40
5-Wrightson-c 4 8 12 23 37 50
6-14 2 4 6 11 16 20
15-30 2 4 6 8 11 14
31,44: 31-(12/80) Mr. E series begins (1st app.), ends #41. 44-Wrightson-c 2 4 6 9 13 16
32-(1/81) Origin of Mr. E 2 4 6 8 11 14
33-43,45,46: 34,35-Frankenstein Monster app. 1 3 4 6 8 10

NOTE: ***Aparo** c-7. **Aragones** a-1. **B. Bailey** a-8. **Bissette** a-46. **Buckler** c-32-40p. **Ditko** a-9, 12, 41, 45. **Golden** a-10. **Howard** a-13i. **Kaluta** c-8, 10, 11, 14, 16, 29. **Kubert** c-41, 42. **Sheldon Mayer** a-43p. **McWilliams** a-35. **Nasser** a-24. **Newton** a-30p. **Nino** a-1, 13, 19. **Orlando** c-13, 30, 43, 45i. **N. Redondo** a-4, 5, 29. **Rogers** c-26. **Spiegle** a-31-41. **Wrightson** c-5, 44.*

SECRETS OF HAUNTED HOUSE SPECIAL (See DC Special Series #12)

SECRETS OF LIFE (Movie)
Dell Publishing Co.: 1956 (Disney)

Four Color 749-Photo-c 5 10 15 31 53 75

SECRETS OF LOVE (See Popular Teen-Agers...)

SECRETS OF LOVE AND MARRIAGE
Charlton Comics: V2#1, Aug, 1956 - V2#25, June, 1961

V2#1-Matt Baker-c? 8 16 24 51 96 140
V2#2-6 4 8 12 28 47 65
V2#7-9-(All 68 pgs.) 6 12 18 40 73 105
10-25 4 8 12 25 40 55

SECRETS OF MAGIC (See Wisco)

SECRETS OF SINISTER HOUSE (Sinister House of Secret Love #1-4)
National Periodical Publ.: No. 5, June-July, 1972 - No. 18, June-July, 1974

5-(52 pgs.). 7 14 21 46 86 125
6-9: 7-Redondo-a 4 8 12 23 37 50
10-Neal Adams-a(i) 4 8 12 25 40 55
11-18: 15-Redondo-a. 17-Barry-a; early Chaykin 1 pg. strip 3 6 9 16 23 30

NOTE: ***Alcala** a-6, 13, 14. **Glanzman** a-7. **Kaluta** c-6, 7. **Nino** a-8, 11-13. Ambrose Bierce adapt.-#14.*

SECRETS OF SINISTER HOUSE
DC Comics: Dec, 2019 ($9.99, square-bound oneshot, 80 pgs.)

Secrets of Young Brides #2 © CC

Secret Wars: Battleworld #4 © MAR

Secret Weapons #10 © VAL

GD VG FN VF VF/NM NM-
2.0 4.0 6.0 8.0 9.0 9.2

1-Short stories of horror by various incl. Dini, Hester, Layman, Raney; Romita Jr.-c 10.00

SECRETS OF THE LEGION OF SUPER-HEROES
DC Comics: Jan, 1981 - No. 3, Mar, 1981 (Limited series)

1-3: 1-Origin of the Legion. 2-Retells origins of Brainiac 5, Shrinking Violet, Sun-Boy, Bouncing Boy, Ultra-Boy, Matter-Eater Lad, Mon-El, Karate Kid & Dream Girl 5.00

SECRETS OF TRUE LOVE
St. John Publishing Co.: Feb, 1958

1-Matt Baker-c 30 60 90 177 289 400

SECRETS OF YOUNG BRIDES
Charlton Comics: No. 5, Sept, 1957 - No. 44, Oct, 1964; July, 1975 - No. 9, Nov, 1976

5 5 10 15 34 60 85
6-10: 8-Negligee panel 4 8 12 25 40 55
11-20 4 8 12 23 37 50
21-30: Last 10¢ issue? 3 6 9 21 33 45
31-44(10/64) 3 6 9 16 23 30
1-(2nd series) (7/75) 3 6 9 16 24 32
2-9 2 4 6 9 12 15

SECRET SQUIRREL (TV)(See Kite Fun Book)
Gold Key: Oct, 1966 (12¢) (Hanna-Barbera)

1-1st Secret Squirrel and Morocco Mole, Squiddly Diddly, Winsome Witch
10 20 30 66 138 210

SECRET STORY ROMANCES (Becomes True Tales of Love)
Atlas Comics (TCI): Nov, 1953 - No. 21, Mar, 1956

1-Everett-a; Jay Scott Pike-c 26 52 78 154 252 350
2 15 30 45 88 137 185
3-11: 11-Last pre-code (2/55) 14 28 42 82 121 160
12-21 13 26 39 72 101 130

NOTE: ***Colletta** a-10, 14, 15, 17, 21; c-10, 14, 17.*

SECRET VOICE, THE (See Great American Comics Presents...)

SECRET WAR
Marvel Comics: Apr, 2004 - No. 5, Dec, 2005 ($3.99, limited series)

1-Bendis-s/Dell'Otto painted-a/c; 6.00
1-2nd printing with gold logo on white cover and full-color Spider-Man 4.00
1-3rd printing with white cover and B&W sketched Spider-Man 4.00
2-Wolverine-c; intro. Daisy Johnson (Quake) 14.00
2-2nd printing with white cover and B&W sketched Wolverine 12.00
3-5: 3-Capt. America-c. 4-Black Widow-c. 5-Daredevil-c 4.00
... : From the Files of Nick Fury (2005, $3.99) Fury's journal entries; profiles of characters 4.00
HC (2005, $29.99, dust jacket) r/#1-5 & ...From the Files of Nick Fury; additional art 30.00
SC (2006, $24.99) r/#1-5 & ...From the Files of Nick Fury; additional art 25.00

SECRET WARPS (Characters merging within the Soul Stone)
Marvel Comics: Sept, 2019 ($4.99, weekly series of one-shots)

...: Arachknight Annual 1 - Part 4; Spider-Man/Moon Knight vs Supreme Seven 5.00
...: Ghost Panther Annual 1 - Part 3; Ghost Rider/Black Panther 5.00
...: Iron Hammer Annual 1 - Part 5; Iron Man/Thor 5.00
...: Soldier Supreme Annual 1 - Part 1; Captain America/Doctor Strange vs. Madame Hel 5.00
...: Weapon Hex Annual 1 - Part 2; X-23/Scarlet Witch 5.00

SECRET WARRIORS (Also see 2009 Dark Reign titles)
Marvel Comics: Apr, 2009 - No. 28, Sept, 2011 ($3.99/$2.99)

1-Bendis & Hickman-s/Caselli-a/Cheung-c; Nick Fury app.; Hydra dossier; sketch pages 4.00
2-24,26-28-($2.99) 8-Dark Avengers app. 17-19-Howling Commandos return 3.00
25-($3.99) Baron Strucker app.; Vitti-a 4.00

SECRET WARRIORS (Tie-in to Secret Empire)
Marvel Comics: Jul, 2017 - No. 12, Mar, 2018 ($3.99)

1-12: 1-Rosenberg-s/Garrón-a; Ms. Marvel, Moon Girl, Karnak app. 7-Deadpool app. 4.00

SECRET WARS
Marvel Comics: 2014 (Giveaway)

... No. 1 Halloween Comic Fest 2014 - Reprints Marvel Super Heroes Secret Wars #1 3.00

SECRET WARS (See Free Comic Book Day 2015 for prelude)
Marvel Comics: Jul, 2015 - No. 9, Mar, 2016 ($4.99/$3.99, limited series, originally planned as 8 issues)

1,2-($4.99) Hickman-s/Ribic-a; end of the Marvel 616 and Ultimate universes 5.00
3-8-($3.99): 3-Miles Morales app. 4.00
9-($4.99) End of Battleworld, beginning of the Prime Earth 5.00
...: Agents of Atlas (12/15, $4.99) Taylor-s/Pugh-a/Kirk-c; Baron Zemo app. 5.00
...: Official Guide to the Marvel Multiverse 1 (12/15, $4.99) Handbook-style info on characters, events and realities tied-in with the Secret Wars series 5.00
...: Secret Love 1 (10/15, $4.99) Romance stories by various; Ms. Marvel, Squirrel Girl, Daredevil, Ghost Rider, Iron Fist & Misty Knight app.; 2 covers 5.00
..., Too 1 (1/16, $4.99) Humor short stories by various incl. Powell, Guillory, Leth 5.00

SECRET WARS: BATTLEWORLD
Marvel Comics: Jul, 2015 - No. 4, Oct, 2015 ($3.99, limited series)

1-4-Short stories by various. 2-Howard the Duck app. 4-Silver Surfer app.; Francavilla-c 4.00

SECRET WARS: JOURNAL
Marvel Comics: Jul, 2015 - No. 5, Nov, 2015 ($3.99, limited series)

1-5-Short stories by various. 1-Leads into Siege #1. 3-Isanove-a. 4-Lashley-a 4.00

SECRET WARS 2099
Marvel Comics: Jul, 2015 - No. 5, Nov, 2015 ($3.99, limited series)

1-5-Peter David-s/Will Sliney-a; Avengers vs. Defenders; Baron Mordo app. 4.00

SECRET WARS II (Also see Marvel Super Heroes...)
Marvel Comics Group: July, 1985 - No. 9, Mar, 1986 (Maxi-series)

1,9: 9-(52 pgs.) X-Men app., Spider-Man app. 6.00
2-8: 2,8-X-Men app. 5-1st app. Boom Boom. 5,8-Spider-Man app. 4.00

SECRET WEAPONS
Valiant: Sept, 1993 - No. 21, May, 1995 ($2.25)

1-10,12-21: 3-Reese-a(i). 5-Ninjak app. 9-Bound-in trading card. 12-Bloodshot app. 4.00
11-(Sept. on envelope, Aug on-c, $2.50)-Enclosed in manilla envelope; Bloodshot app; intro new team. 5.00

SECRET WEAPONS
Valiant Entertainment: Jun, 2017 - No. 4, Sept, 2017 ($3.99)

1-4-Heisserer-s/Allén-a 4.00
#0-(1/18, $3.99) Heisserer-s/Pollina-a; origin of Nikki Finch 4.00
...: Owen's Story #0 (3/18, $3.99) Heisserer-s/Allén-a 4.00

SECTAURS
Marvel Comics: June, 1985 - No. 8, Sept, 1986 (75¢) (Based on Coleco Toys)

1-8, 1-Giveaway; same-c with "Coleco 1985 Toy Fair Collectors' Edition" 4.00

SECTION ZERO
Image Comics (Gorilla): June, 2000 - No. 3, Sept, 2000 ($2.50)

1-3-Kesel-s/Grummett-a 3.00

SECTION ZERO
Image Comics (Gorilla): Apr, 2019 - No. 6, Sept, 2019 ($3.99)

1-6-Kesel-s/Grummett-a; 3 covers on each 4.00

SEDUCTION OF THE INNOCENT (Also see New York State Joint Legislative Committee to Study...)
Rinehart & Co., Inc., N. Y.: 1953, 1954 (400 pgs.) (Hardback, $4.00)(Written by Fredric Wertham, M.D.)(Also printed in Canada by Clarke, Irwin & Co. Ltd.)

(1st Version)-with bibliographical note intact (pages 399 & 400)(several copies got out before the comic publishers forced the removal of this page)
258 516 774 1109 1330 1550
Dust jacket only 45 90 135 284 467 675
(1st Version)-without bibliographical note 117 234 351 503 602 725
Dust jacket only 26 52 78 151 251 350
(2nd Version)-Published in England by Rinehart, 1954, 399 pgs. has bibliographical page; "Second print" listed on inside flap of the dust jacket; publication page has no "R" colophon; unlike 1st version 20 40 60 117 189 260
1972 r-/of 2nd version; 400 pgs. w/bibliography page; Kennikat Press
7 14 21 48 89 130
2004 r/with new intro. by Wertham scholar James E. Reibman, 424 pgs; 6" x 9"; limited to 220 copies 7 14 21 46 86 125

NOTE: *Material from this book appeared in the November, 1953 (Vol.70, pp50-53,214) issue of the **Ladies' Home Journal** under the title "What Parents Don't Know About Comic Books". With the release of this book, Dr. Wertham reveals seven years of research attempting to link juvenile delinquency to comic books. Many illustrations showing excessive violence, sex, sadism, and torture are shown. This book was used at the Kefauver Senate hearings which led to the Comics Code Authority. Because of the influence this book had on the comic industry and the collector's interest in it, we feel this listing is justified. Modern printings exist in limited editions. Also see **Parade of Pleasure**.*

SEDUCTION OF THE INNOCENT! (Also see Halloween Horror)
Eclipse Comics: Nov, 1985 - 3-D#2, Apr, 1986 ($1.75)

1-6: Double listed under cover title from #7 on 6.00
3-D 1 (10/85, $2.25, 36 pgs.)-contains unpublished Advs. Into Darkness #15 (pre-code); Dave Stevens-c 2 4 6 10 14 18
2-D 1 (100 copy limited signed & #ed edition)(B&W) 4 8 12 25 40 55
3-D 2 (4/86)-Baker, Toth, Wrightson-c 1 2 3 5 6 8
2-D 2 (100 copy limited signed & #ed edition)(B&W) 3 6 9 17 26 35

NOTE: ***Anderson** r-2, 3. **Crandall** c/a(r)-1. **Meskin** c/a(r)-3, 3-D 1. **Moreira** r-2. **Toth** a-1-6r; c-4r. **Tuska** r-6.*

SEDUCTION OF THE INNOCENT

Self / Made #1 © Groom & Ferigato

The Sensational Spider-Man #6 © MAR

Sensation Comics #3 © DC

	GD 2.0	VG 4.0	FN 6.0	VF 8.0	VF/NM 9.0	NM- 9.2

Dynamite Entertainment: 2015 - No. 4, 2016 ($3.99, limited series)
1-4-Ande Parks-s/Esteve Polls-a/Francesco Francavilla-c 4.00

SEEDS, THE
Dark Horse Comics (Berger Books): Aug, 2018 - No. 4 ($3.99, limited series)
1,2-Ann Nocenti-s/David Aja-a 4.00

SEEKERS INTO THE MYSTERY
DC Comics (Vertigo): Jan, 1996 - No. 15, Apr, 1997 ($2.50)
1-14: J.M. DeMatteis scripts in all. 1-4-Glenn Barr-a. 5,10-Muth-c/a. 6-9-Zulli-c/a. 11-14-Bolton-c; Jill Thompson-a 3.00
15-($2.95)-Muth-c/a 3.00

SEEKER 3000 (See Marvel Premiere #41)
Marvel Comics: Jun, 1998 - No. 4, Sept, 1998 ($2.99/$2.50, limited series)
1-($2.99)-Set 25 years after 1st app.; wraparound-c 4.00
2-4-($2.50) 3.00
...Premiere 1 (6/98, $1.50) Reprints 1st app. from Marvel Premiere #41; wraparound-c 3.00

SELECT DETECTIVE (Exciting New Mystery Cases)
D. S. Publishing Co.: Aug-Sept, 1948 - No. 3, Dec-Jan, 1948-49
1-Matt Baker-a 39 78 117 240 395 550
2-Baker, McWilliams-a 26 52 78 154 252 350
3 20 40 60 114 182 250

SELF / MADE
Image Comics: Dec, 2018 - No. 6, May, 2019 ($3.99)
1-6-Mat Groom-s/Eduardo Ferigato-a 4.00

SEMPER FI (Tales of the Marine Corp)
Marvel Comics: Dec, 1988- No. 9, Aug, 1989 (75¢)
1-9: Severin-c/a 4.00

SENSATIONAL POLICE CASES (Becomes Captain Steve Savage, 2nd Series)
Avon Periodicals: 1952; No. 2, 1954 - No. 4, July-Aug, 1954
nn-(1952, 25¢, 100 pgs.)-Kubert-a?; Check, Larsen, Lawrence & McCann-a; Kinstler-c 55 110 165 352 601 850
2-4: 2-Kirbyish-a (3-4/54). 4-Reprint/Saint #5 22 44 66 128 209 290
I.W. Reprint #5-(1963?, nd)-Reprints Prison Break #5(1952-Realistic); Infantino-a 3 6 9 17 26 35

SENSATIONAL SHE-HULK, THE (She-Hulk #21-23) (See Savage She-Hulk)
Marvel Comics: V2#1, 5/89 - No. 60, Feb, 1994 ($1.50/$1.75, deluxe format)
V2#1-Byrne-c/a(p)/scripts begin, end #8 3 6 9 17 26 35
2,3,5-8: 3-Spider-Man app. 5.00
4,14-17,21-23: 4-Reintro G.A. Blonde Phantom. 14-17-Howard the Duck app. 21-23-Return of the Blonde Phantom. 22-All Winners Squad app. 5.00
9-13,18-20,24-49,51-60: 25-Thor app. 26-Excalibur app.; Guice-c. 29-Wolverine app. (3 pgs.). 30-Hobgoblin-c & cameo. 31-Byrne-c/a/scripts begin again. 35-Last $1.50-c. 37-Wolverine/Punisher/Spidey-c, but no app. 39-Thing app. 56-War Zone app.; Hulk cameo. 57-Vs. Hulk-c/story. 58-Electro-c/story. 59-Jack O'Lantern app. 4.00
50-($2.95, 52 pgs.)-Embossed green foil-c; Byrne app.; last Byrne-c/a; Austin, Chaykin, Simonson-a; Miller-a(2 pgs.) 2 4 6 8 10 12
NOTE: *Dale Keown a(p)-13, 15-22.*

SENSATIONAL SHE-HULK IN CEREMONY, THE
Marvel Comics: 1989 - No. 2, 1989 ($3.95, squarebound, 52 pgs.)
nn-Part 1, nn-Part 2 6.00

SENSATIONAL SPIDER-MAN
Marvel Comics: Apr, 1989 ($5.95, squarebound, 80 pgs.)
1-r/Amazing Spider-Man Annual #14,15 by Miller & Annual #8 by Kirby & Ditko 6.00

SENSATIONAL SPIDER-MAN, THE
Marvel Comics: Jan, 1996 - No. 33, Nov, 1998 ($1.95/$1.99)
0 ($4.95)-Lenticular-c; Jurgens-a/scripts 2 4 6 8 10 12
1 1 2 3 5 6 8
1-($2.95) variant-c; polybagged w/cassette 4 8 12 25 40 55
2-5: 2-Kaine & Rhino app. 3-Giant-Man app. 5.00
6-18: 9-Onslaught tie-in; revealed that Peter & Mary Jane's unborn baby is a girl. 11-Revelations. 13-15-Ka-Zar app. 14,15-Hulk app. 4.00
19-24: Living Pharoah app. 22,23-Dr. Strange app. 4.00
25-($2.99) Spiderhunt pt. 1; Normie Osborne kidnapped 5.00
25-Variant-c 1 2 3 5 6 8
26-33: 26-Nauck-a. 27-Double-c with "The Sensational Hornet #1"; Vulture app. 28-Hornet vs. Vulture. 29,30-Black Cat-c/app. 33-Last issue; Gathering of Five concludes 4.00
33.1, 33.2 (10/12, $2.99) DeFalco-s/Barberi-a/Bianchi-c 4.00
#(-1) Flashback(7/97) Dezago-s/Wieringo-a 4.00
'96 Annual ($2.95) 5.00

SENSATIONAL SPIDER-MAN, THE (Previously Marvel Knights Spider-Man #1-22)
Marvel Comics: No. 23, Apr, 2006 - No. 41, Dec, 2007 ($2.99)
23-40: 23-25-Aguirre-Sacasa-s/Medina-a. 23-Wraparound-c. 24,34,37-Black Cat app. 26-New costume. 28-Unmasked; Dr. Octopus app.; Crain-a. 35-Black costume resumes 3.00
41-($3.99) One More Day pt. 3; Straczynski-s/Quesada-a/c 4.00
... Annual 1 (2007, $3.99) Flashbacks of Peter & MJ's relationship; Larroca-a/Fraction-s 4.00
... Feral HC (2006, $19.99, dustjacket) r/#23-27; sketch pages 20.00
Civil War: Peter Parker, Spider-Man TPB (2007, $17.99) r/#28-34; Crain cover concepts 18.00
...: Self Improvement 1(10/19, $4.99) Unpublished story of Spidey's 1st black costume 5.00

SENSATION COMICS (Sensation Mystery #110 on)
National Per. Publ./All-American: Jan, 1942 - No. 109, May-June, 1952
1-Origin Mr. Terrific (1st app.), Wildcat (1st app.), The Gay Ghost, & Little Boy Blue; Wonder Woman (cont'd from All Star #8), The Black Pirate begin; intro. Justice & Fair Play Club 10,500 21,000 31,500 70,000 122,500 175,000
1-Reprint, Oversize 13-1/2x10". WARNING: This comic is an exact duplicate reprint of the original except for its size. DC published it in 1974 with a second cover titling it as a Famous First Edition. There have been many reported cases of the outer cover being removed and the interior sold as the original edition. The reprint with the new outer cover removed is practically worthless. See Famous First Edition for value.
2-Etta Candy begins 784 1568 2352 5723 10,112 14,500
3-W. Woman gets secretary's job 459 918 1377 3350 5925 8500
4-1st app. Stretch Skinner in Wildcat 303 606 909 2121 3711 5300
5-Intro. Justin, Black Pirate's son 284 568 852 1818 3109 4400
6-Origin/1st app. Wonder Woman's magic lasso 443 886 1329 3234 5717 8200
7-10 232 464 696 1485 2543 3600
11,12,14-20 158 316 474 1011 1731 2450
13-Hitler, Tojo, Mussolini-c (as bowling pins) 423 846 1269 3000 5250 7500
21-30: 22-Cheetah app. (2nd cover) 123 246 369 787 1344 1900
31-33 100 200 300 640 1095 1550
34-Sargon, the Sorcerer begins (10/44), ends #36; begins again #52 103 206 309 654 1130 1600
35-40: 36-2nd app. Giganta/1st cover; Cheetah app. 38-Christmas-c 97 194 291 621 1061 1500
41-50: 43-The Whip app. 87 174 261 553 952 1350
51-60: 51-Last Black Pirate. 56,57-Sargon by Kubert 84 168 252 538 919 1300
61-67,70-80: 63-Last Mr. Terrific. 66-Wildcat by Kubert 74 148 222 470 810 1150
68-Origin & 1st app. Huntress (8/47) 271 542 813 1734 2967 4200
69-2nd app. Huntress 87 174 261 553 952 1350
81-Used in **SOTI**, pg. 33,34; Krigstein-a 86 172 258 546 936 1325
82-93: 83-Last Sargon. 86-The Atom app. 90-Last Wildcat. 91-Streak begins by Alex Toth. 92-Toth-a (2 pgs.) 79 158 237 502 864 1225
94-1st all girl issue 132 264 396 845 1448 2050
95-99,101-106: 95-Unmasking of Wonder Woman-c/story. 99-1st app. Astra, Girl of the Future, ends #106. 103-Robot-c. 105-Last 52 pgs. 106-Wonder Woman ends 110 220 330 704 1202 1700
100-(11-12/50) 145 290 435 928 1589 2250
107-(Scarce, 1-2/52)-1st mystery issue; Johnny Peril by Toth(p), 8 pgs. & begins; continues from Danger Trail #5 (3-4/51)(see Comic Cavalcade #15 for 1st app.) 110 220 330 704 1202 1700
108-(Scarce)-Johnny Peril by Toth(p) 100 200 300 640 1095 1550
109-(Scarce)-Johnny Peril by Toth(p) 106 212 318 678 1164 1650
NOTE: ***Krigstein** a-(Wildcat)-81, 83, 84. **Moldoff** Black Pirate-1-25; Black Pirate not in 34-36, 43-48. **Oskner** c(i)-89-91, 94-106. Wonder Woman by **H. G. Peter**, all issues except #8, 17-19, 21; c-4-7, 9-18, 20-88, 92, 93. **Toth** a-91, 98; c-107. Wonder Woman c-1-106.*

SENSATION COMICS (Also see All Star Comics 1999 crossover titles)
DC Comics: May, 1999 ($1.99, one-shot)
1-Golden Age Wonder Woman and Hawkgirl; Robinson-s 4.00

SENSATION COMICS FEATURING WONDER WOMAN
DC Comics: Oct, 2014 - No. 17, Feb, 2016 ($3.99, printing of digital-first comics)
1-17-Short story anthology. 1-Simone-s/Van Sciver-a. 2-Gene Ha-c. 5-Darkseid app. 8-Noelle Stevenson-a; Jae Lee-c. 10-Francavilla-c. 12-Poison Ivy app. 13-Superwoman app. 15-Garcia-López-a; Cheetah app.; McNeil-s/a. 16-Scott Hampton-a; Harley Quinn app. 4.00

SENSATION MYSTERY (Formerly Sensation Comics #1-109)
National Periodical Publ.: No. 110, July-Aug, 1952 - No. 116, July-Aug, 1953
110-Johnny Peril continues 65 130 195 419 710 1000
111-116-Johnny Peril in all. 116-M. Anderson-a 65 130 195 419 710 1000
NOTE: ***M. Anderson** c-110. **Colan** a-114p. **Giunta** a-112. **G. Kane** c(p)-108, 109, 111-115.*

SENSE & SENSABILITY
Marvel Comics: July, 2010 - No. 5, Nov, 2010 ($3.99, limited series)

The Sentry (2018 series) #1 © MAR

Serenity: Float Out #1 © Universal

Sgt. Fury #147 © MAR

GD 2.0 | VG 4.0 | FN 6.0 | VF 8.0 | VF/NM 9.0 | NM- 9.2

1-5-Adaptation of the Jane Austen novel; Nancy Butler-s/Sonny Liew-a/c 4.00

SENTENCES: THE LIFE OF M.F. GRIMM
DC Comics (Vertigo): 2007 ($19.99, B&W graphic novel)

HC-Autobiography of Percy Carey (M.F. Grimm); Ronald Wimberly-a 20.00
SC (2008, $14.99) 15.00

SENTINEL
Marvel Comics: June, 2003 - No. 12, April, 2004 ($2.99/$2.50)

1-Sean McKeever-s/Udon Studios-a 3.00
2-12 3.00
Marvel Age Sentinel Vol. 1: Salvage (2004, $7.99, digest size) r/#1-6 8.00
Vol. 2: No Hero (2004, $7.99, digest size) r/#7-12; sketch pages 8.00

SENTINEL (2nd series)
Marvel Comics: Jan, 2006 - No. 5, May, 2006 ($2.99, limited series)

1-5-Sean McKeever-s/Joe Vriens-a 3.00
Vol. 3: Past Imperfect (2006, $7.99, digest size) r/#1-5 8.00

SENTINELS OF JUSTICE, THE (See Americomics & Captain Paragon &...)

SENTINEL SQUAD O*N*E
Marvel Comics: Mar, 2006 - No. 5, July, 2006 ($2.99, limited series)

1-5-Lopresti-a/Layman-s 3.00
Decimation: Sentinel Squad O*N*E (2006, $13.99, TPB) r/series; sketch pg. by Caliafore 14.00

SENTRY (Also see New Avengers and Siege)
Marvel Comics: Sept, 2000 - No. 5, Jan, 2001 ($2.99, limited series)

1-5-Paul Jenkins-s/Jae Lee-a. 3-Spider-Man-c/app. 4-X-Men, FF app. 3.00
.../Fantastic Four (2/01, $2.99) Continues story from #5; Winslade-a 3.00
.../Hulk (2/01, $2.99) Sienkiewicz-c/a 3.00
.../Spider-Man (2/01, $2.99) back story of the Sentry; Leonardi-a 3.00
.../The Void (2/01, $2.99) Conclusion of story; Jae Lee-a 3.00
.../X-Men (2/01, $2.99) Sentry and Archangel; Texeira-a 3.00
TPB (10/01, $24.95) r/#1-5 & all one-shots; Stan Lee interview 25.00
TPB (2nd edition, 2005, $24.99) 25.00

SENTRY (Follows return in New Avengers #10)
Marvel Comics: Nov, 2005 - No. 8, Jun, 2006 ($2.99, limited series)

1-8-Paul Jenkins-s/John Romita Jr.-a. 1-New Avengers app. 3-Hulk app. 3.00
1-(Rough Cut) (12/05, $3.99) Romita sketch art and Jenkins script; cover sketches 4.00
...: Fallen Sun (7/10, $3.99) Siege epilogue; Jenkins-s/Raney-a/Yu-c 4.00
...: Reborn TPB (2006, $21.99) r/#1-8 22.00

SENTRY
Marvel Comics: Aug, 2018 - No. 5, Dec, 2018 ($3.99, limited series)

1-5: 1-Lemire-s/Jacinto-a/Hitch-c; Misty Knight app. 4.00

SEPTEMBER MOURNING
Image Comics (Top Cow): Feb, 2017 ($4.99)

1-Marc Silvestri-c; Lazar & McCourt-s 5.00

SERENITY (Based on 2005 movie Serenity and 2003 TV series Firefly)
Dark Horse Comics: July, 2005 - No. 3, Sept, 2005 ($2.99, limited series)

1-3: Whedon & Matthews-s/Conrad-a. Three covers for each issue by various 4.00
...: Float Out (6/10, $3.50) Story of Wash; Patton Oswalt-s; covers by Jo Chen & Stockton 3.50
...: One For One (9/10, $1.00) reprints #1, Cassaday-c with red cover frame 3.00
...: Those Left Behind HC (11/07, $19.95, dustjacket) r/series; intro. by Nathan Fillion; pre-production art for the movie; Hughes-c 20.00
...: Those Left Behind TPB (1/06, $9.95) r/series; intro. by Nathan Fillion; Hughes-c 10.00

SERENITY BETTER DAYS (Firefly)
Dark Horse Comics: Mar, 2008 - No. 3, May, 2008 ($2.99, limited series)

1-3: Whedon & Matthews-s/Conrad-a; Adam Hughes-c 3.00

SERENITY: FIREFLY CLASS 03-K64 - LEAVES ON THE WIND (Follows movie)
Dark Horse Comics: Jan, 2014 - No. 6, Jun, 2014 ($3.50, limited series)

1-6: Zack Whedon-s/Georges Jeanty-a; covers by Dos Santos & Jeanty 3.50

SERENITY: FIREFLY CLASS 03-K64 - NO POWER IN THE 'VERSE (Follows movie)
Dark Horse Comics: Oct, 2016 - No. 6, Mar, 2017 ($3.99, limited series)

1-6: Chris Roberson-s/Georges Jeanty-a; covers by Dos Santos & Jeanty 4.00

SERGEANT BARNEY BARKER (Becomes G. I. Tales #4 on)
Atlas Comics (MCI): Aug, 1956 - No. 3, Dec, 1956

1-Severin-c/a(4) 26 52 78 154 252 350
2,3: 2-Severin-c/a(4). 3-Severin-c/a(5) 17 34 51 100 158 215

SERGEANT BILKO (Phil Silvers Starring as...) (TV)
National Periodical Publications: May-June, 1957 - No. 18, Mar-Apr, 1960

1-All have Bob Oskner-c 63 126 189 403 689 975
2 34 68 102 199 325 450
3-5 27 54 81 162 266 370
6-18: 11,12,15-17-Photo-c 22 44 66 128 209 290

SGT. BILKO'S PVT. DOBERMAN (TV)
National Periodical Publications: June-July, 1958 - No. 11, Feb-Mar, 1960

1-Bob Oskner c-1-4,7,11 26 52 78 182 404 625
2 12 24 36 82 179 275
3-5: 5-Photo-c 19 18 27 60 120 180
6-11: 6,9-Photo-c 7 14 21 44 82 120

SGT. DICK CARTER OF THE U.S. BORDER PATROL (See Holyoke One-Shot)

SGT. FURY (& His Howling Commandos)(See Fury & Special Marvel Edition)
Marvel Comics Group (BPC earlier issues): May, 1963 - No. 167, Dec, 1981

1-1st app. Sgt. Nick Fury (becomes agent of Shield in Strange Tales #135); Kirby/Ayers-c/a; 1st Dum-Dum Dugan & the Howlers 480 960 1440 4100 9300 14,500
2-Kirby-a 61 122 183 488 1094 1700
3-5: 3-Reed Richards x-over. 4-Death of Junior Juniper. 5-1st Baron Strucker app.; Kirby-a 31 62 93 223 499 775
6-10: 8-Baron Zemo, 1st Percival Pinkerton app. 9-Hitler-c & app. 10-1st app. Capt. Savage (the Skipper)(9/64) 16 32 48 112 249 385
11,12,14-20: 14-1st Blitz Squad. 18-Death of Pamela Hawley 9 18 27 61 123 185
13-Captain America & Bucky app.(12/64); 2nd solo Capt. America x-over outside The Avengers; Kirby-a 48 96 144 370 835 1300
13-2nd printing (1994) 2 4 6 9 12 15
21-24,26,28-30 6 12 18 40 73 105
25,27: 25-Red Skull app. 27-1st app. Eric Koenig; origin Fury's eye patch 6 12 18 41 76 110
31-33,35-50: 35-Eric Koenig joins Howlers. 43-Bob Hope, Glen Miller app. 44-Flashback on Howlers' 1st mission 4 8 12 27 44 60
34-Origin Howling Commandos 5 10 15 34 60 85
51-60 4 8 12 23 37 50
61-67: 64-Capt. Savage & Raiders x-over; peace symbol-c. 67-Last 12¢ issue; flag-c 3 6 9 19 30 40
68-80: 76-Fury's Father app. in WWI story 3 6 9 16 24 32
81-91: 91-Last 15¢ issue 3 6 9 14 20 26
92-(52 pgs.) 3 6 9 16 24 32
93-99: 98-Deadly Dozen x-over 3 6 9 14 19 24
100-Capt. America, Fantastic 4 cameos; Stan Lee, Martin Goodman & others app. 3 6 9 18 27 36
101-120: 101-Origin retold 2 4 6 10 14 18
121-130: 121-123-r/#19-21 2 4 6 8 11 14
131-167: 167-Reprints (from 1963) 2 4 6 8 10 12
133,134-(30¢-c variants, limited dist.)(5,7/76) 9 18 27 58 114 170
141,142-(35¢-c variants, limited dist.)(7,9/77) 22 44 66 154 340 525
Annual 1(1965, 25¢, 72 pgs.)-r/#4,5 & new-a 13 26 39 89 195 300
Special 2(1966) 6 12 18 42 79 115
Special 3(1967) All new material 5 10 15 30 50 70
Special 4(1968) 3 6 9 21 33 45
Special 5-7(1969-11/71) 3 6 9 17 26 35

NOTE: ***Ayers** a-8, Annual 1. **Ditko** a-15i. **Gil Kane** c-37, 96. **Kirby** a-1-7, 13p, 167p(r). Special 5; c-1-8, 10-20, 25, 167p. **Severin** a-44-46, 48, 162, 164; inks-49-79, Special 4, 6; c-4i, 5, 6, 44, 46, 110, 149i, 155i, 162-166. **Sutton** a-57p. Reprints in #80, 82, 85, 87, 89, 91, 93, 95, 99, 101, 103, 105, 107, 109, 111, 121-123, 145-155, 167.*

SGT. FURY AND HIS HOWLING COMMANDOS
Marvel Comics: July, 2009 ($3.99, one-shot)

1-John Paul Leon-a/c; WWII tale set in 1942; Baron Strucker app. 4.00

SGT. FURY AND HIS HOWLING DEFENDERS (See The Defenders #147)

SERGEANT PRESTON OF THE YUKON (TV)
Dell Publishing Co.: No. 344, Aug, 1951 - No. 29, Nov-Jan, 1958-59

Four Color 344(#1)-Sergeant Preston & his dog Yukon King begin; painted-c begin, end #18 12 24 36 83 182 280
Four Color 373,397,419('52) 8 16 24 56 108 160
5(11-1/52-53)-10(2-4/54): 6-Bondage-c. 5 10 15 35 63 90
11,12,14-17 5 10 15 33 57 80
13-Origin Sgt. Preston 5 10 15 35 63 90
18-Origin Yukon King; last painted-c 5 10 15 35 63 90
19-29: All photo-c 6 12 18 41 76 110

SGT. ROCK (Formerly Our Army at War; see Brave & the Bold #52 & Showcase #45)
National Periodical Publications/DC Comics: No. 302, Mar, 1977 - No. 422, July, 1988

302 5 10 15 30 50 70
303-310 3 6 9 16 23 30

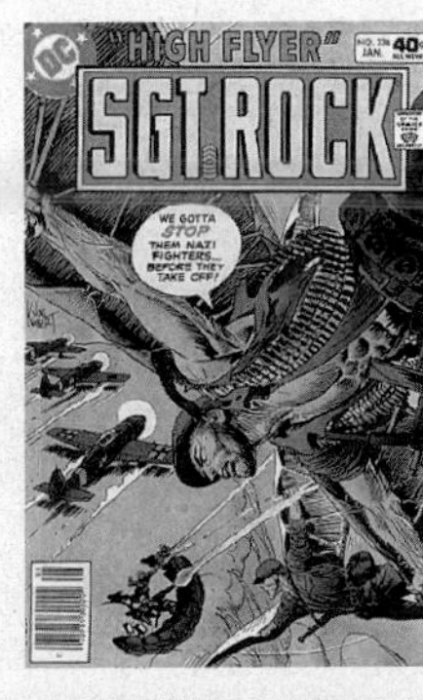

Sgt. Rock #336 © DC

Serial #1 © Terry Moore

7 Brothers #1 © Virgin

GD 2.0 VG 4.0 FN 6.0 VF 8.0 VF/NM 9.0 NM- 9.2

311-320: 318-Reprints 2 4 6 10 16 20
321-350 2 4 6 8 11 14
329-Whitman variant 3 6 9 14 19 24
351-399,401-421: 412-Mlle Marie & Haunted Tank 1 2 3 5 7 9
400-(6/85) Anniversary issue 2 4 6 8 11 14
422-1st Joe, Adam, Andy Kubert-a team; last issue 2 4 6 10 14 18
Annual 2-4: 2(1982)-Formerly Sgt. Rock's Prize Battle Tales #1. 3(1983). 4(1984) 2 4 6 8 10 12

NOTE: ***Estrada*** *a-322, 327, 331, 336, 337, 341, 342i.* ***Glanzman*** *a-384, 421.* ***Kubert*** *a-302, 303, 305r, 306, 328, 351, 356, 368, 373, 422; c-317, 318r, 319-323, 325-333-on, Annual 2, 3.* ***Severin*** *a-347.* ***Spiegle*** *a-382, Annual 2, 3.* ***Thorne*** *a-384.* ***Toth*** *a-385r.* ***Wildey*** *a-307, 311, 313, 314.*

SGT. ROCK: BETWEEN HELL AND A HARD PLACE
DC Comics (Vertigo): 2003 ($24.95, hardcover one-shot)

HC-Joe Kubert-a/c; Brian Azzarello-s 25.00
SC (2004, $17.95) 18.00

SGT. ROCK'S COMBAT TALES
DC Comics: 2005 ($9.99, digest)

Vol. 1-Reprints early app. in Our Army at War, G.I. Combat, Star Spangled War Stories 10.00

SGT. ROCK SPECIAL (Sgt. Rock #14 on; see DC Special Series #3)
DC Comics: Oct, 1988 - No. 21, Feb, 1992; No. 1, 1992; No. 2, 1994 ($2.00, quarterly/monthly, 52 pgs)

1-Reprint begin 2 4 6 8 11 14
2-21: All-r; 5-r/early Sgt. Rock/Our Army at War #81. 7-Tomahawk-r by Thorne. 9-Enemy Ace-r by Kubert. 10-All Rock issue. 11-r/1st Haunted Tank story. 12-All Kubert issue; begins monthly. 13-Dinosaur story by Heath(r). 14-Enemy Ace-r (22 pgs.) by Adams/Kubert. 15-Enemy Ace (22 pgs.) by Kubert. 16-Iron Major-c/story. 16,17-Enemy Ace-r. 19-r/Batman/Sgt. Rock team-up/B&B #108 by Aparo 1 2 3 5 6 8
1 (1992, $2.95, 68 pgs.)-Simonson-c; unpubbed Kubert-a; Glanzman, Russell, Pratt, & Wagner-a 6.00
2 (1994, $2.95) Brereton painted-c 4.00

NOTE: ***Neal Adams*** *r-1, 8, 14p.* ***Chaykin*** *a-2; r-3, 9(2pgs.); c-3.* ***Drucker*** *r-6.* ***Glanzman*** *r-20.* ***Golden*** *a-1.* ***Heath*** *a-2; r-5, 9-13, 16, 19; 21.* ***Krigstein*** *r-4, 8.* ***Kubert*** *r-1-17, 20, 21; c-1p, 2, 8, 14-21.* ***Miller*** *r-6p.* ***Severin*** *r-3, 6, 10.* ***Simonson*** *r-2, 4; c-4.* ***Thorne*** *r-7.* ***Toth*** *r-2, 8, 11.* ***Wood*** *r-4.*

SGT. ROCK SPECTACULAR (See DC Special Series #13)

SGT. ROCK'S PRIZE BATTLE TALES (Becomes Sgt. Rock Annual #2 on; see DC Special Series #18 & 80 Page Giant #7)
National Periodical Publications: Winter, 1964 (Giant - 80 pgs., one-shot)

1-Kubert, Heath-r; new Kubert-c 36 72 108 259 580 900
... Replica Edition (2000, $5.95) Reprints entire issue 6.00

SGT. ROCK: THE LOST BATTALION
DC Comics: Jan, 2009 - No. 6, Jun, 2009 ($2.99, limited series)

1-6-Billy Tucci-s/a. 1-Tucci & Sparacio-c 3.00
HC (2009, $24.99, d.j.) r/#1-6; production art; cover art gallery 25.00
SC (2010, $17.99) r/#1-6; production art; cover art gallery 18.00

SGT. ROCK: THE PROPHECY
DC Comics: Mar, 2006 - No. 6, Aug, 2006 ($2.99, limited series)

1-6-Joe Kubert-s/a/c. 1-Variant covers by Andy and Adam Kubert 3.00
TPB (2007, $17.99) r/#1-6 18.00

SGT. STRYKER'S DEATH SQUAD (See Savage Combat Tales)

SERGIO ARAGONÉS' ACTIONS SPEAK
Dark Horse Comics: Jan, 2001 - No. 6, Jun, 2001 ($2.99, B&W, limited series)

1-6-Aragonés-c/a; wordless one-page cartoons 3.00

SERGIO ARAGONÉS' BLAIR WHICH?
Dark Horse Comics: Dec, 1999 ($2.95, B&W, one-shot)

nn-Aragonés-c/a; Evanier-s. Parody of "Blair Witch Project" movie 4.00

SERGIO ARAGONÉS' BOOGEYMAN
Dark Horse Comics: June, 1998 - No. 4, Sept, 1998 ($2.95, B&W, lim. series)

1-4-Aragonés-c/a 4.00

SERGIO ARAGONÉS DESTROYS DC
DC Comics: June, 1996 ($3.50, one-shot)

1-DC Superhero parody book; Aragonés-c/a; Evanier scripts 4.00

SERGIO ARAGONÉS' DIA DE LOS MUERTOS
Dark Horse Comics: Oct, 1998 ($2.95, one-shot)

1-Aragonés-c/a; Evanier scripts 4.00

SERGIO ARAGONÉS FUNNIES
Bongo Comics: 2011 - No. 12, 2014 ($3.50)

1-12-Color and B&W humor strips by Aragonés 3.50

SERGIO ARAGONÉS' GROO & RUFFERTO
Dark Horse Comics: Dec, 1998 - No. 4, Mar, 1999 ($2.95, lim. series)

1-3-Aragonés-c/a 4.00

SERGIO ARAGONÉS' GROO: DEATH AND TAXES
Dark Horse Comics: Dec, 2001 - No. 4, Apr, 2002 ($2.99, lim. series)

1-4-Aragonés-c/a; Evanier-s 3.00

SERGIO ARAGONÉS' GROO: HELL ON EARTH
Dark Horse Comics: Nov, 2007 - No. 4, Apr, 2008 ($2.99, lim. series)

1-4-Aragonés-c/a; Evanier-s 3.00

SERGIO ARAGONÉS' GROO: MIGHTIER THAN THE SWORD
Dark Horse Comics: Jan, 2000 - No. 4, Apr, 2000 ($2.95, lim. series)

1-4-Aragonés-c/a; Evanier-s 3.00

SERGIO ARAGONÉS' GROO: THE HOGS OF HORDER
Dark Horse Comics: Oct, 2009 - No. 4, Mar, 2010 ($3.99, lim. series)

1-4-Aragonés-c/a; Evanier-s 4.00

SERGIO ARAGONÉS' GROO THE WANDERER (See Groo...)

SERGIO ARAGONÉS' GROO: 25TH ANNIVERSARY SPECIAL
Dark Horse Comics: Aug, 2007 ($5.99, one-shot)

nn-Aragonés-c/a; Evanier scripts; wraparound cover 6.00

SERGIO ARAGONÉS' LOUDER THAN WORDS
Dark Horse Comics: July, 1997 - No. 6, Dec, 1997 ($2.95, B&W, limited series)

1-6-Aragonés-c/a 3.00

SERGIO ARAGONÉS MASSACRES MARVEL
Marvel Comics: June, 1996 ($3.50, one-shot)

1-Marvel Superhero parody book; Aragonés-c/a; Evanier scripts 4.00

SERGIO ARAGONÉS STOMPS STAR WARS
Marvel Comics: Jan, 2000 ($2.95, one-shot)

1-Star Wars parody; Aragonés-c/a; Evanier scripts 4.00

SERIAL (See Rachel Rising and Five Years)
Abstract Studios: 2021 - No. 10 ($3.99)

1-Zoe from Rachel Rising app.; Terry Moore-s/a/c 4.00

SESAME STREET
Ape Entertainment: 2013 ($3.99)

1-Short stories by various; multiple covers 4.00
Free Comic Book Day edition (2013) Flip book with Strawberry Shortcake 3.00

SEVEN
Intrinsic Comics: July, 2007 ($3.00)

1-Jim Shooter-s/Paul Creddick-a 3.00

SEVEN BLOCK
Marvel Comics (Epic Comics): 1990 ($4.50, one-shot, 52 pgs.)

1-Dixon-s/Zaffino-a 6.00
nn-(IDW Publ., 2004, $5.99) reprints #1 6.00

SEVEN BROTHERS (John Woo's...)
Virgin Comics: Oct, 2006 - No. 5, Feb, 2007 ($2.99)

1-5-Garth Ennis-s/Jeevan Kang-a. 1-Two covers by Amano & Horn. 2-Kang var-c 3.00
TPB (6/07, $14.99) r/#1-5; cover gallery, deleted scenes and concept art 15.00
Volume 2 (9/07 - No. 5, 2/08) 1-Edison George-a. 4,5-David Mack-c 3.00

SEVEN DEAD MEN (See Complete Mystery #1)

SEVEN DWARFS (Also see Snow White)
Dell Publishing Co.: No. 227, 1949 (Disney-Movie)

Four Color 227 10 20 30 69 147 225

SEVEN MILES A SECOND
DC Comics (Vertigo Verité): 1996 ($7.95, one-shot)

nn-Wojnarowicz-s/Romberg-a 8.00

SEVEN-PER-CENT SOLUTION
IDW Publishing: Aug, 2015 - No. 5 ($3.99)

1-4-Sherlock Holmes/Sigmund Freud team-up; David & Scott Tipton-s/Joseph-a/Jones-c 4.00

SEVEN SAMUROID, THE (See Image Graphic Novel)

SEVEN SEAS COMICS
Universal Phoenix Features/Leader No. 6: Apr, 1946 - No. 6, 1947(no month)

1-South Sea Girl by Matt Baker, Capt. Cutlass begin; Tugboat Tessie by Baker app.

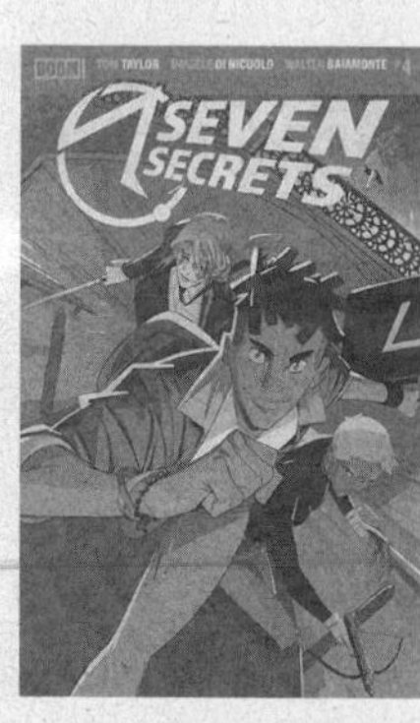

Seven Secrets #4 © Tom Taylor

Sex Criminals #30 © Milkfed & Zdarsco

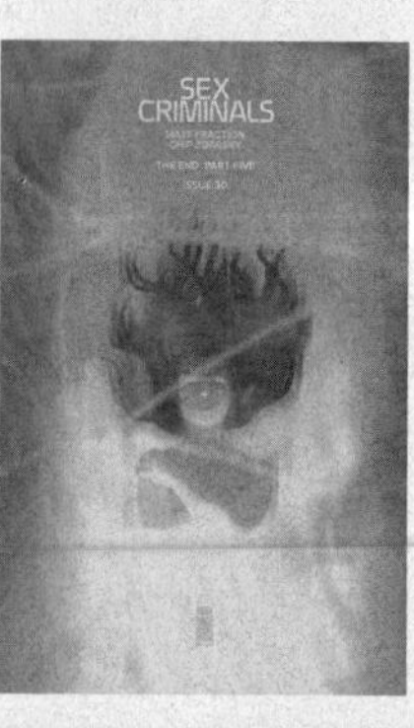

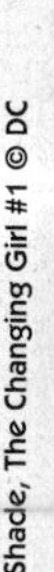

Shade, The Changing Girl #1 © DC

	GD 2.0	VG 4.0	FN 6.0	VF 8.0	VF/NM 9.0	NM- 9.2
	94	188	282	602	1026	1450
2-Swashbuckler-c	71	142	213	454	777	1100
3-Six pg. Feldstein-a	155	310	465	992	1696	2400
4-Classic Baker-c	649	1298	1947	4738	8369	12,000
5-Baker Headlights Good Girl-c	187	374	561	1197	2049	2900
6-Baker Good Girl-c	371	742	1113	2600	4550	6500
NOTE: *Baker a-1-6; c-3-6.*						
SEVEN SECRETS						
BOOM! Studios: Aug, 2020 - Present ($3.99)						
1-6-Tom Taylor-s/Danielle Di Nicuolo-a						4.00
SEVEN SOLDIERS OF VICTORY (Book-ends for seven related mini-series)						
DC Comics: No. 0, Apr, 2005; No. 1; Dec, 2006 ($2.95/$3.99)						
0-Grant Morrison-s/J.H. Williams-a						3.00
1-($3.99) Series conclusion; Grant Morrison-s/J.H. Williams-a						4.00
... Volume One (2006, $14.99) r/#0, Shining Knight #1,2; Zatanna #1,2; Guardian #1,2; and Klarion the Witch Boy #1; intro. by Morrison; character design sketches						15.00
... Volume Two (2006, $14.99) r/Shining Knight #3,4; Zatanna #3; Guardian #3,4; and Klarion the Witch Boy #2,3						15.00
... Volume Three ('06, $14.99) r/Zatanna #4; Mister Miracle #1,2; Bulleteer #1,2; Frankenstein #1 and Klarion the Witch Boy #4;						15.00
... Volume Four ('07, $14.99) r/Mister Miracle #3,4; Bulleteer #3,4; Frankenstein #2-4 and Seven Soldiers of Victory #1; script pages						15.00
SEVEN SOLDIERS: BULLETEER						
DC Comics: Jan, 2006 - No. 4, May, 2006 ($2.99, limited series)						
1-4-Grant Morrison-s/Yanick Paquette-a/c						3.00
SEVEN SOLDIERS: FRANKENSTEIN						
DC Comics: Jan, 2006 - No. 4, May, 2006 ($2.99, limited series)						
1-4-Grant Morrison-s/Doug Mahnke-a/c						3.00
SEVEN SOLDIERS: GUARDIAN						
DC Comics: May, 2005 - No. 4, Nov, 2005 ($2.99, limited series)						
1-4-Grant Morrison-s/Cameron Stewart-a; Newsboy Army app.						3.00
SEVEN SOLDIERS: KLARION THE WITCH BOY						
DC Comics: June, 2005 - No. 4, Dec, 2005 ($2.99, limited series)						
1-4-Grant Morrison-s/Frazer Irving-a						3.00
SEVEN SOLDIERS: MISTER MIRACLE						
DC Comics: Nov, 2005 - No. 4, May, 2006 ($2.99, limited series)						
1-4: 1-Grant Morrison-s/Pasqual Ferry-a/c. 3,4-Freddie Williams II-a/c						3.00
SEVEN SOLDIERS: SHINING KNIGHT						
DC Comics: May, 2005 - No. 4, Oct, 2005 ($2.99, limited series)						
1-4-Grant Morrison-s/Simone Bianchi-a						3.00
SEVEN SOLDIERS: ZATANNA						
DC Comics: June, 2005 - No. 4, Dec, 2005 ($2.99, limited series)						
1-4-Grant Morrison-s/Ryan Sook-a						3.00
1776 (See Charlton Classic Library)						
7TH SWORD, THE						
IDW Publishing (Darby Pop): Apr, 2014 - No. 6 ($3.99)						
1-6: 1-John Raffo-s/Nelson Blake II-a. 3-6-Nur Iman-a						4.00
7TH VOYAGE OF SINBAD, THE (Movie)						
Dell Publishing Co.: Sept, 1958 (photo-c)						
Four Color 944-Buscema-a	11	22	33	77	166	255
SEVEN TO ETERNITY						
Image Comics: Sept, 2016 - No. 17 ($3.99)						
1-Rick Remender-s/Jerome Opeña-a						45.00
2						10.00
3-16: 7,8-James Harren-a						4.00
77 SUNSET STRIP (TV)						
Dell Publ. Co./Gold Key: No. 1066, Jan-Mar, 1960 - No. 2, Feb, 1963 (All photo-c)						
Four Color 1066-Toth-a	9	18	27	61	123	185
Four Color 1106,1159-Toth-a	7	14	21	49	92	135
Four Color 1211,1263,1291, 01-742-209(7-9/62)-Manning-a in all	7	14	21	46	86	125
1,2: Manning-a. 1(11/62-G.K.)	7	14	21	46	86	125
77TH BENGAL LANCERS, THE (TV)						
Dell Publishing Co.: May, 1957						

	GD 2.0	VG 4.0	FN 6.0	VF 8.0	VF/NM 9.0	NM- 9.2
Four Color 791-Photo-c	7	14	21	44	82	120
SEVERED						
Image Comics: Aug, 2011 - No. 7, Feb, 2012 ($2.99)						
1-7-Scott Snyder & Scott Tuft-s/Attila Futaki-a/c						3.00
SEX						
Image Comics: Mar, 2013 - No. 34, Dec, 2016 ($2.99/$3.99)						
1-26-Joe Casey-s/Piotr Kowalski-a/c						3.00
27-34-($3.99)						4.00
SEX CRIMINALS						
Image Comics: Sept, 2013 - No. 30, Aug, 2020; No. 69, Oct, 2020 ($3.50/$3.99)						
1-Matt Fraction-s/Chip Zdarsky-a/c	3	6	9	16	24	32
1-Variant-c by Shimizu	3	6	9	14	20	25
2	1	3	4	6	8	10
3-10						5.00
11-24,26-30						4.00
11-24,26-30,69-($4.69) Variant cover in pink polybag						5.00
25-($4.99)						5.00
25-($5.69) Variant cover by Skottie Young, in pink polybag						6.00
69-($3.99) Final issue; numbering skips from 30 to 69						4.00
...: Sexual Gary Special (9/20, $4.99) Matt Fraction-s/Rachael Stott-a						5.00
SEYMOUR, MY SON (See More Seymour)						
Archie Publications (Radio Comics): Sept, 1963						
1-DeCarlo-c/a	5	10	15	33	57	80
SFSX						
Image Comics: Sept, 2019 - Present ($3.99)						
1-7-Tina Horn-s. 1,2,4-Michael Dowling-a. 6,7-Jen Hickman-a						4.00
SHADE, THE (See Starman)						
DC Comics: Apr, 1997 - No. 4, July, 1997 ($2.25, limited series)						
1-4-Robinson-s/Harris-c: 1-Gene Ha-a. 2-Williams/Gray-a 3-Blevins-a. 4-Zulli-a						3.00
SHADE, THE (From Starman)						
DC Comics: Dec, 2011 - No. 12, Nov, 2012 ($2.99, limited series)						
1-12: 1-Robinson-s/Hamner-a/Harris-c; Deathstroke app. 4-Cooke-a. 8-Thompson-a 12-Origin of the Shade; Gene Ha-a						3.00
1-12-Variant covers. 1-3-Hamner. 4-Darwyn Cooke. 5-7-Pulido. 11-Irving						4.00
SHADE, THE CHANGING GIRL (Continues as Shade, The Changing Woman)						
DC Comics (Young Animal): Dec, 2016 - No. 12, Nov, 2017 ($3.99)						
1-12: 1-Castellucci-s/Zarcone-a; intro. Megan Boyer/Loma Shade. 4-Element Girl back-up. 7-Sauvage-a						4.00
.../ Wonder Woman Special 1 (4/18, $4.99) Part 3 of Milk Wars crossover; Quitely-c						5.00
SHADE, THE CHANGING MAN (See Cancelled Comic Cavalcade)						
National Per. Publ./DC Comics: June-July, 1977 - No. 8, Aug-Sept, 1978						
1-1st app. Shade; Ditko-c/a in all	3	6	9	16	23	30
2-8	2	3	4	6	8	10
SHADE, THE CHANGING MAN (2nd series) (Also see Suicide Squad #16)						
DC Comics (Vertigo imprint #33 on): July, 1990 - No. 70, Apr, 1996 ($1.50-$2.25, mature)						
1-($2.50, 52 pgs.)-Peter Milligan scripts in all						4.00
2-41,45-49,51-59: 6-Preview of World Without End. 17-Begin $1.75-c. 33-Metallic ink on-c. 41-Begin $1.95-c						3.00
42-44-John Constantine app.						3.50
50-($2.95, 52 pgs.)						4.00
60-70: 60-begin $2.25-c						3.00
...: Edge of Vision TPB (2009, $19.99) r/#7-13						20.00
...: Scream Time TPB (2010, $19.99) r/#14-19						20.00
...: The American Scream TPB (2003, 2009, $17.95/$17.99) r/#1-6						18.00
NOTE: *Bachalo a-1-9, 11-13, 15-21, 23-26, 33-39, 42-45, 47, 49, 50; c-30, 33-41.*						
SHADE, THE CHANGING WOMAN (Continues from Shade, The Changing Girl)						
DC Comics (Young Animal): May, 2018 - No. 6, Oct, 2018 ($3.99)						
1-6-Castellucci-s/Zarcone-a						4.00
SHADO: SONG OF THE DRAGON (See Green Arrow #63-66)						
DC Comics: 1992 - No. 4, 1992 ($4.95, limited series, 52 pgs.)						
Book One - Four: Grell scripts; Morrow-a(i)						6.00
SHADOW, THE (See Batman #253, 259 & Marvel Graphic Novel #35)						
SHADOW, THE (Pulp, radio)						
Archie Comics (Radio Comics): Aug, 1964 - No. 8, Sept, 1965 (All 12¢)						
1-Jerry Siegel scripts in all; Shadow-c.	9	18	27	57	111	165
2-8: 2-App. in super-hero costume on-c only; Reinman-a(backup). 3-Superhero begins;						

The Shadow V2 #5 © Advance Mag.

Shadow Comics #10 © Condé Nast

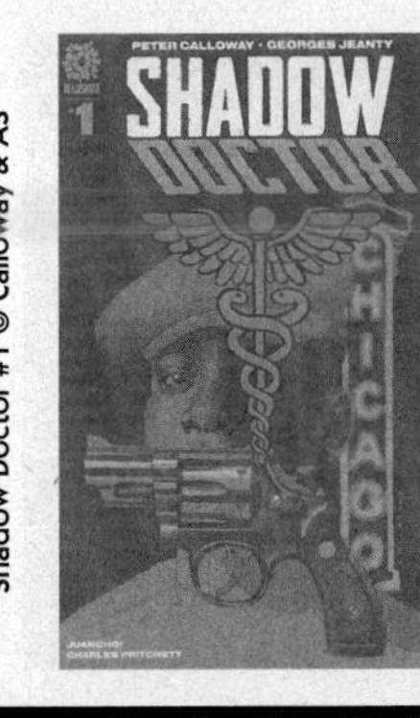

Shadow Doctor #1 © Calloway & AS

	GD 2.0	VG 4.0	FN 6.0	VF 8.0	VF/NM 9.0	NM- 9.2

Reinman-a (book-length novel). 3,4,6,7-The Fly 1 pg. strips. 4-8-Reinman-a. 5-8-Siegel scripts. 7-Shield app. 5 10 15 33 57 80

SHADOW, THE
National Periodical Publications: Oct-Nov, 1973 - No. 12, Aug-Sept, 1975

1-Kaluta-a begins 6 12 18 38 69 100
2 3 6 9 21 33 45
3-Kaluta/Wrightson-a 4 8 12 23 37 50
4,6-Kaluta-a ends. 4-Chaykin, Wrightson part-i 3 6 9 18 28 38
5,7-12: 11-The Avenger (pulp character) x-over 2 4 6 13 18 22
NOTE: ***Craig** a-10. **Cruz** a-10-12. **Kaluta** a-1, 2, 3p, 4, 6; c-1-4, 6, 10-12. **Kubert** c-9. **Robbins** a-5, 7-9; c-5, 7, 8.*

SHADOW, THE
DC Comics: May, 1986 - No. 4, Aug, 1986 (limited series)

1-4: Howard Chaykin art in all 4.00
Blood & Judgement ($12.95)-r/1-4 13.00

SHADOW, THE
DC Comics: Aug, 1987 - No. 19, Jan, 1989 ($1.50)

1-19: Andrew Helfer scripts in all. 4.00
Annual 1,2 (12/87, '88,)-2-The Shadow dies; origin retold (story inspired by the movie "Citizen Kane"). 5.00
NOTE: ***Kyle Baker** a-7i, 8-19, Annual 2. **Chaykin** c-Annual 1. **Helfer** scripts in all. **Orlando** a-Annual 1. **Rogers** c/a-7. **Sienkiewicz** c/a-1-6.*

SHADOW, THE (Movie)
Dark Horse Comics: June, 1994 - No. 2, July, 1994 ($2.50, limited series)

1,2-Adaptation from Universal Pictures film 4.00
NOTE: ***Kaluta** c/a-1, 2.*

SHADOW, THE
Dynamite Entertainment: 2012 - No. 25, 2014 ($3.99)

1-25: 1-Ennis-s/Campbell-a; multiple covers on all. 7-10-Gischler-s 4.00
#0-(2014, $3.99) Cullen Bunn-s/Colton Worley-a/Gabriel Hardman-c 4.00
#100-(2014, $7.99, squarebound) Short stories by various incl. Francavilla, Chaykin, Wagner, Uslan; 2 covers by Wagner & Hack 8.00
Annual 1 (2012, $4.99) Sniegoski-s/Calero-a/Alex Ross-c 5.00
Annual 2013 ($4.99) Parks-s/Evely-a/Worley-c 5.00
One Shot 2014: Agents of the Shadow ($7.99, squarebound) Robert Hack-c 8.00
... Over Innsmouth (2014, $4.99) Ron Marz-s/Ivan Rodriguez-a 5.00
Special 1 (2012, $4.99) Beatty-s/Cliquet-a/Alex Ross-c 5.00
Special 2014: Death Factory ($7.99, squarebound) Phil Hester-s/c; Ivan Rodriguez-a 8.00

SHADOW, THE (Volume 2)
Dynamite Entertainment: 2014 - No. 5, 2015 ($1.00/$3.99, limited series)

1-($1.00) Bunn-s/Timpano-a/Guice-c 3.00
2-5-($3.99) Bunn-s/Timpano-a/Guice-c 4.00

SHADOW, THE (Volume 3)
Dynamite Entertainment: 2017 - No. 6, 2018 ($3.99, limited series)

1-6: 1-Spurrier & Watters-s/Daniel HDR-a; multiple covers on all. 4-Jaime-a 4.00

SHADOW AND DOC SAVAGE, THE
Dark Horse Comics: July, 1995 - No. 2, Aug, 1995 ($2.95, limited series)

1,2 4.00

SHADOW AND THE MYSTERIOUS 3, THE
Dark Horse Comics: Sept, 1994 ($2.95, one-shot)

1-Kaluta co-scripts. 4.00
NOTE: ***Stevens** c-1.*

SHADOW, THE / BATMAN
Dynamite Entertainment: 2017 - No. 6, 2018 ($3.99, limited series)

1-6-Orlando-s/Timpano-a; multiple covers on each; Ra's al Ghul & Shiwan Khan app. 4.00

SHADOW CABINET (See Heroes)
DC Comics (Milestone): No. 0, Jan, 1994 - No. 17, Oct, 1995 ($1.75/$2.50)

0-(1/94, $2.50, 52 pgs.)-Silver ink-c; Simonson-c 4.00
1-17: 1-(6/94) Byrne-c 3.00

SHADOW COMICS (Pulp, radio)
Street & Smith Publications: Mar, 1940 - V9#5, Aug-Sept, 1949
NOTE: *The Shadow first appeared on radio in 1929 and was featured in pulps beginning in April, 1931, written by Walter Gibson. The early covers of this series were reprinted from the pulp covers.*

V1#1-Shadow, Doc Savage, Bill Barnes, Nick Carter (radio), Frank Merriwell, Iron Munro, the Astonishing Man begin 784 1568 2352 5723 10,112 14,500
2-The Avenger begins, ends #6; Capt. Fury only app. 248 496 744 1587 2719 3850
3(nn-5/40)-Norgil the Magician app.; cover is exact swipe of Shadow pulp from 1/33 184 368 552 1178 2014 2850
4-The Three Musketeers begins, ends #8; classic painted decapitation-c 184 368 552 1178 2014 2850
5-Doc Savage ends 129 258 387 826 1413 2000
6,8,9: 9-Norgil the Magician app. 106 212 318 678 1164 1650
7-Origin/1st app. The Hooded Wasp & Wasplet (11/40); series ends V3#8; Hooded Wasp/Wasplet app. on-c thru #9 110 220 330 704 1202 1700
10-Origin The Iron Ghost, ends #11; The Dead End Kids begins, ends #14 103 206 309 659 1130 1600
11-Origin Hooded Wasp & Wasplet retold 103 206 309 659 1130 1600
12-Dead End Kids app. 94 188 282 597 1025 1450
V2#1(11/41, Vol. II#2 in indicia) Dead End Kids -s 94 188 282 597 1025 1450
2-(Rare, 1/42, Vol. II#3 in indicia) Giant ant-c 194 388 582 1242 2121 3000
3-Origin & 1st app. Supersnipe (3/42); series begins; Little Nemo story (Vol.II#4 in indicia) 148 296 444 947 1624 2300
4,5: 4,8-Little Nemo story 84 168 252 538 919 1300
6-9: 6-Blackstone the Magician story 81 162 243 518 884 1250
10,12: 10-Supersnipe app.' Skull-c 77 154 231 493 847 1200
11-Classic Devil Kyoti World War 2 sunburst-c 100 200 300 640 1095 1550
V3#1,2,5,7-12: 10-Doc Savage begins, not in V5#5, V6#10-12, V8#4 77 154 231 493 847 1200
3-1st Monstrodamus-c/sty 106 212 318 678 1164 1650
4-2nd Monstrodamus; classic-c of giant salamander getting shot in the head 113 226 339 723 1237 1750
6-Classic underwater-c 116 232 348 742 1271 1800
V4#1,3-12 53 106 159 334 567 800
2-Classic severed head-c 158 316 474 1011 1731 2450
V5#1-12: 1-(4/45). 12-(3/46) 50 100 150 315 533 750
V6#1-11: 9-Intro. Shadow, Jr. (12/46) 47 94 141 296 498 700
12-Powell-c/a; atom bomb panels 50 100 150 315 533 750
V7#1,2,5,7-9,12: 2,5-Shadow, Jr. app.; Powell-a 43 86 129 271 461 650
3,6,11-Powell-c/a 50 100 150 315 535 750
4-Powell-c/a; Atom bomb panels 52 104 156 328 552 775
10(1/48)-Flying Saucer-c/story (2nd of this theme; see The Spirit 9/28/47); Powell-c/a 77 154 231 493 847 1200
V8#1,2,4-12-Powell-a. 50 100 150 315 533 750
3-Powell Spider-c/a 53 106 159 334 567 800
V9#1,5-Powell-a 48 96 144 302 514 725
2-4-Powell-c/a 50 100 150 315 533 750
NOTE: ***Binder** c-V3#1. **Powell** art in most issues beginning V6#12. Painted c-1-6.*

SHADOW DOCTOR
AfterShock Comics: Feb, 2021 - Present ($3.99)

1-Peter Calloway-s/Georges Jeanty-a; covers by Chiarello & Jeanty 4.00

SHADOWDRAGON
DC Comics: 1995 ($3.50, annual)

Annual 1-Year One story 4.00

SHADOW EMPIRES: FAITH CONQUERS
Dark Horse Comics: Aug, 1994 - No. 4, Nov, 1994 ($2.95, limited series)

1-4 3.00

SHADOW/GREEN HORNET: DARK NIGHTS (Pulp characters)
Dynamite Entertainment: 2013 - No. 5, 2013 ($3.99)

1-5-Lamont Cranston & Britt Reid team-up in 1939; Uslan-s; multiple covers on each 4.00

SHADOWHAWK (See Images of Shadowhawk, New Shadowhawk, Shadowhawk II, Shadowhawk III & Youngblood #2)
Image Comics (Shadowline Ink): Aug, 1992 - No. 4, Mar, 1993; No. 12, Aug, 1994 - No. 18, May, 1995 ($1.95/$2.50)

1-($2.50)-Embossed silver foil stamped-c; Valentino/Liefeld-c; Valentino-c/a/ scripts in all; has coupon for Image #0; 1st Shadowline Ink title 5.00
1-With coupon missing 2.00
1-($1.95)-Newsstand version w/o foil stamp 3.00
2-13,0,1418: 2-Shadowhawk poster w/McFarlane-i; brief Spawn app.; wraparound-c w/silver ink highlights. 3-($2.50)-Glow-in-the-dark-c. 4-Savage Dragon-c/story; Valentino/Larsen-c. 5-11-(See Shadowhawk II and III). 12-Cont'd from Shadowhawk III; pull-out poster by Texeira.13-w/ShadowBone poster; WildC.A.T.s app. 0 (10/94)-Liefeld c/a/story; ShadowBart poster. 14-(10/94, $2.50)-The Others app. 16-Supreme app. 17-Spawn app.; story cont'd from Badrock & Co. #6. 18-Shadowhawk dies; Savage Dragon & Brigade app. 3.00
Special 1(12/94, $3.50, 52 pgs.)-Silver Age Shadowhawk flip book 4.00
Gallery (4/94, $1.95) 3.00
Out of the Shadows ($19.95)-r/Youngblood #2, Shadowhawk #1-4, Image Zero #0, Operation: Urban Storm (Never published) 20.00
.../Vampirella (2/95, $4.95)-Pt.2 of x-over (See Vampirella/Shadowhawk for Pt. 1) 5.00
NOTE: *Shadowhawk was originally a four issue limited series. The story continued in Shadowhawk II, Shadowhawk III & then became Shadowhawk again with issue #12.*

Shadow Hunter #2 © Virgin

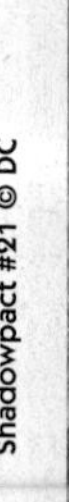
Shadowman (2018 series) #1 © VAL

Shadowpact #21 © DC

	GD	VG	FN	VF	VF/NM	NM-
	2.0	4.0	6.0	8.0	9.0	9.2

GD VG FN VF VF/NM NM-
2.0 4.0 6.0 8.0 9.0 9.2

SHADOWHAWK II (Follows Shadowhawk #4)
Image Comics (Shadowline Ink): V2#1, May, 1993 - V2#3, Aug, 1993 ($3.50/$1.95/$2.95, limited series)

V2#1 ($3.50)-Cont'd from Shadowhawk #4; die-cut mirricard-c 4.00
2 ($1.95)-Foil embossed logo; reveals identity; gold-c variant exists 4.00
3 ($2.95)-Pop-up-c w/Pact ashcan insert 4.00

SHADOWHAWK III (Follows Shadowhawk II #3)
Image Comics (Shadowline Ink): V3#1, Nov, 1993 - V3#4, Mar, 1994 ($1.95, limited series);

V3#1-4: 1-Cont'd from Shadowhawk II; intro Valentine; gold foil & red foil stamped-c variations. 2-(52 pgs.)-Shadowhawk contracts HIV virus; U.S. Male by M. Anderson (p) in free 16 pg.insert. 4-Continues in Shadowhawk #12 4.00

SHADOWHAWK (Volume 2) (Also see New Man #4)
Image Comics: May, 2005 - No. 15, Sept, 2006 ($2.99/$3.50)

1-4-Eddie Collins as Shadowhawk; Rodríguez-a; Valentino-co-plotter 3.50
5-15-($3.50) 5-Cover swipe of Superman Vs. Spider-Man treasury edition 3.50
...One Shot #1 (7/06, $1.99) r/Return of Shadowhawk 3.00
Return of Shadowhawk (12/04, $2.99) Valentino-s/a/c; Eddie Collins origin retold 3.00

SHADOWHAWK (Volume 3)
Image Comics: May, 2010 - No. 5, Dec, 2010 ($3.50)

1-5-Rodríguez-a. 1-Back-up with Valentino-a/Niles-s 3.50

SHADOWHAWKS OF LEGEND
Image Comics (Shadowline Ink): Nov, 1995 ($4.95, one-shot)

nn-Stories of past Shadowhawks by Kurt Busiek, Beau Smith & Alan Moore 5.00

SHADOW, THE: HELL'S HEAT WAVE (Movie, pulp, radio)
Dark Horse Comics: Apr, 1995 - No. 3, June, 1995 ($2.95, limited series)

1-3: Kaluta story 4.00

SHADOW HUNTER (Jenna Jameson's...)
Virgin Comics: No. 0, Dec, 2007 - No. 3 ($2.99)

0-Preview issue; creator interviews; gallery of covers for upcoming issues; Greg Horn-c 3.00
1-3: 1-Two covers by Horn & Land; Jameson & Christina Z-s/Singh-a. 2-Three covers 3.00

SHADOWHUNT SPECIAL
Image Comics (Extreme Studios): Apr, 1996 ($2.50)

1-Retells origin of past Shadowhawks; Valentino script; Chapel app. 3.00

SHADOW, THE: IN THE COILS OF THE LEVIATHAN (Movie, pulp, radio)
Dark Horse Comics: Oct, 1993 - No. 4, Apr, 1994 ($2.95, limited series)

1-4-Kaluta-c & co-scripter 4.00
Trade paperback (10/94, $13.95)-r/1-4 14.00

SHADOWLAND (Also see Daredevil #508-512 & Black Panther: The Man Without Fear #513)
Marvel Comics: Sept, 2010 - No. 5, Jan, 2011 ($3.99, limited series)

1-5: 1-Diggle-s/Tan-a; Bullseye killed; Cassaday-c. 2-Ghost Rider app. 4.00
1-Variant-c by Tan 6.00
...: After the Fall 1 (2/11, $3.99) Finch-c; Black Panther app. 4.00
...: Bullseye 1 (10/10, $3.99) Chen-a; Bullseye's funeral 4.00
...: Elektra 1 (11/10, $3.99) Wells-s/Rios-a/Takeda-c 4.00
...: Ghost Rider 1 (11/10, $3.99) Williams-s/Crain-a/c 4.00
...: Spider-Man 1 (12/10, $3.99) Shang-Chi & Mr. Negative app.; Siqueira-a 4.00

SHADOWLAND: BLOOD IN THE STREETS (Leads into Heroes For Hire)
Marvel Comics: Oct, 2010 - No. 4, Jan, 2011 ($3.99, limited series)

1-4-Johnston-s/Alves-a; Misty Knight, Silver Sable, Paladin, Shroud app. 4.00

SHADOWLAND: DAUGHTERS OF THE SHADOW
Marvel Comics: Oct, 2010 - No. 3, Dec, 2010 ($3.99, limited series)

1-3-Henderson-s/Rodriguez-a; Colleen Wing app. 3-Preview of Black Panther #513 4.00

SHADOWLAND: MOON KNIGHT
Marvel Comics: Oct, 2010 - No. 3, Dec, 2010 ($3.99, limited series)

1-3-Hurwitz-s/Dazo-a 4.00

SHADOWLAND: POWER MAN
Marvel Comics: Oct, 2010 - No. 4, Jan, 2011 ($3.99, limited series)

1-4-Van Lente-s/Asrar-a. 1-New Power Man debut; Iron Fist app. 4.00

SHADOWLINE SAGA: CRITICAL MASS, A
Marvel Comics (Epic): Jan, 1990 - No. 7, July, 1990 ($4.95, lim. series, 68 pgs)

1-6: Dr. Zero, Powerline, St. George 5.00
7 ($5.95, 84 pgs.)-Morrow-a, Williamson-c(i) 6.00

SHADOWMAN (See X-O Manowar #4)
Valiant/Acclaim Comics (Valiant): May, 1992 - No. 43, Dec, 1995 ($2.50)

1-Partial origin 3 6 9 16 23 30
2-5: 3-1st app. Sousa the Soul Eater 5.00
6,7,9-42: 15-Minor Turok app. 16-1st app. Dr. Mirage (8/93). 17,18-Archer & Armstrong x-over. 19-Aerosmith-c/story. 23-Dr. Mirage x-over. 24-(4/94). 25-Bound-in trading card. 29-Chaos Effect. 4.00
8-1st app. Master Darque 2 4 6 8 10 12
43-Shadowman jumps to his death 1 2 3 5 6 8
0-($2.50, 4/94)-Regular edition 6.00
0-($3.50)-Wraparound chromium-c edition 1 2 3 5 6 8
0-Gold 20.00
Yearbook 1 (12/94, $3.95) 5.00

SHADOWMAN (Volume 2)
Acclaim Comics (Valiant Heroes): Mar, 1997 - No. 20, Jun, 1998 ($2.50, mature)

1-1st app. Zero; Garth Ennis scripts begin, end #4 1 2 3 5 6 8
2-20: 2-Zero becomes new Shadowman. 4-Origin; Jack Boniface (original Shadowman) rises from the grave. 5-Jamie Delano scripts begin. 9-Copycat-c 3.00
1-Variant painted cover 1 2 3 5 6 8
#0 Gold 5.00

SHADOWMAN (Volume 3)
Acclaim Comics: July, 1999 - No. 5, Nov, 1999 ($3.95/$2.50)

1-($3.95)-Abnett & Lanning-s/Broome & Benjamin-a 1 2 3 5 6 8
2-5-($2.50): 3,4-Flip book with Unity 2000 3.00

SHADOWMAN
Valiant Entertainment: Nov, 2012 - No. 16, Mar, 2014 ($3.99)

1-Jordan-s/Zircher-a; two covers by Zircher (regular & pullbox) 5.00
1-Variant-c by Dave Johnson 8.00
1-Variant-c by Bill Sienkiewicz 20.00
2-16: 2-6-Jordan-s/Zircher-a 4.00
2-4-Pullbox variants 6.00
5-16-Pullbox variants 4.00
11-Variant-c with detachable Halloween mask 4.00
13X-(10/13, bagged with Bleeding Cool Magazine #7) prelude to #13; Milligan-s 3.00
#0-(5/13, $3.99) Origin of Master Darque 4.00

SHADOWMAN
Valiant Entertainment: Mar, 2018 - No. 11, Jan, 2019 ($3.99)

1-11: 1-Diggle-s/Segovia-a. 4-Martinbrough & Segovia-a. 6-11-Guedes-a 4.00

SHADOWMAN END TIMES
Valiant Entertainment: Apr, 2014 - No. 3, Jun, 2014 ($3.99, limited series)

1-3-Milligan-s/De Landro-a 4.00

SHADOWMAN / RAE SREMMURD
Valiant Entertainment: Oct, 2017 ($3.99, one-shot)

1-Rahal-s/Guedes-a; bonus preview of Ninja•K #1 4.00

SHADOWMASTERS
Marvel Comics: Oct, 1989 - No.4, Jan, 1990 ($3.95, squarebound, 52 pgs.)

1-4: Heath-a(i). 1-Jim Lee-c; story cont'd from Punisher 4.00

SHADOW, THE: MIDNIGHT IN MOSCOW (Pulp character)
Dynamite Entertainment: 2014 - No. 6, 2014 ($3.99, limited series)

1-6:-Howard Chaykin-s/a/c 4.00

SHADOW NOW, THE (Pulp character)
Dynamite Entertainment: 2013 - No. 6, 2014 ($3.99, limited series)

1-6: 1-David Liss-s/ColtonWorley-a; The Shadow in present day New York 4.00

SHADOW OF THE BATMAN
DC Comics: Dec, 1985 - No. 5, Apr, 1986 ($1.75, limited series)

1-Detective-r (all have wraparound-c) 1 3 4 6 8 10
2,3,5: 3-Penguin-c & cameo. 5-Clayface app. 6.00
4-Joker-c/story 1 2 3 4 6 8
NOTE: ***Austin** a(new)-2i, 3i; r-2-4i.* ***Rogers** a(new)-1, 2p, 3p, 4, 5; r-1-5p; c-1-5.* ***Simonson** a-1r.*

SHADOW ON THE TRAIL (See Zane Grey & Four Color #604)

SHADOWPACT (See Day of Vengeance)
DC Comics: Jul, 2006 - No. 25, Jul, 2008 ($2.99)

1-25: 1-Bill Willingham-s; Detective Chimp, Ragman, Blue Devil, Nightshade, Enchantress and Nightmaster app. 1-Superman app. 13-Zauriel app.; S. Hampton-a 3.00
...: Cursed TPB (2007, $14.99) r/#4,9-13 15.00
...: Darkness and Light TPB (2008, $14.99) r/#14-19 15.00
...: The Burning Age TPB (2008, $17.99) r/#20-25 18.00
...: The Pentacle Plot TPB (2007, $14.99) r/#1-3,5-8 15.00

SHADOW PLAY (Tales of the Supernatural)
Whitman Publications: June, 1982

Shadows on the Grave #8 © Richard Corben

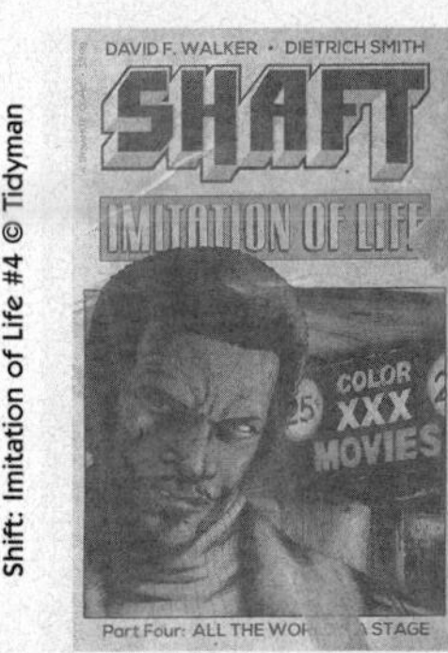

Shift: Imitation of Life #4 © Tidyman

Shang-Chi (2020 series) #1 © MAR

	GD 2.0	VG 4.0	FN 6.0	VF 8.0	VF/NM 9.0	NM- 9.2

1-Painted-c 1 2 3 5 6 8

SHADOWPLAY
IDW Publ.: Sept, 2005 - No. 4, Dec, 2005 ($3.99)
1-4-Benson-s/Templesmith-a; Christina Z-s/Wood-a; 2 covers by Templesmith & Wood 4.00
TPB (3/06, $17.99) r/series; flip book format 18.00

SHADOW REAVERS
Black Bull Ent.: Oct, 2001 - No. 5, Mar, 2002 ($2.99)
1-5-Nelson-a; two covers for each issue 3.00
Limited Preview Edition (5/01, no cover price) 3.00

SHADOW RIDERS
Marvel Comics UK, Ltd.: June, 1993 - No. 4, Sept, 1993 ($1.75, limited series)
1-($2.50)-Embossed-c; Cable-c/story 4.00
2-4-Cable app. 2-Ghost Rider app. 3.00

SHADOWS
Image Comics: Feb, 2003 - No. 4, Nov, 2003 ($2.95)
1-4-Jade Dodge-s/Matt Camp-a/c 3.00

SHADOWS & LIGHT
Marvel Comics: Feb, 1998 - No. 3, July, 1998 ($2.99, B&W, quarterly)
1-3: 1-B&W anthology of Marvel characters; Black Widow art by Gene Ha, Hulk by Wrightson, Iron Man by Ditko & Daredevil by Stelfreeze; Stelfreeze painted-c. 2-Weeks, Sharp, Starlin, Thompson-a. 3-Buscema, Grindberg, Giffen, Layton-a 3.00

SHADOW'S FALL
DC Comics (Vertigo): Nov, 1994 - No. 6, Apr, 1995 ($2.95, limited series)
1-6: Van Fleet-c/a in all. 3.00

SHADOWS FROM BEYOND (Formerly Unusual Tales)
Charlton Comics: V2#50, October, 1966
V2#50-Ditko-c 4 8 12 28 47 65

SHADOWS ON THE GRAVE
Dark Horse Comics: Dec, 2016 - No. 8, Sept, 2017 ($3.99, B&W, limited series)
1-8-Horror story anthology; Richard Corben-s/a/c 4.00

SHADOW STATE
Broadway Comics: Dec, 1995 - No. 5, Apr, 1996 ($2.50)
1-5: 1,2-Fatale back-up story; Cockrum-a(p) 3.00
Preview Edition 1,2 (10-11/95, $2.50, B&W) 3.00

SHADOW STRIKES!, THE (Pulp, radio)
DC Comics: Sept, 1989 - No.31, May, 1992 ($1.75)
1-4,7-31: 31-Mignola-c 4.00
5,6-Doc Savage x-over 5.00
Annual 1 (1989, $3.50, 68 pgs.)-Spiegle a; Kaluta-c 5.00

SHADOW, THE : THE DEATH OF MARGO LANE (Pulp characters)
Dynamite Entertainment: 2016 - No. 5, 2016 ($3.99, limited series)
1-5-Matt Wagner-s/a/c. 4-The Red Empress app. 4.00

SHADOW WALK
Legendary Comics: Nov, 2013 ($24.99, graphic novel)
HC - Mark Waid-s/Shane Davis-a 25.00

SHADOW WAR OF HAWKMAN
DC Comics: May, 1985 - No. 4, Aug, 1985 (limited series)
1-4 4.00

SHADOW, THE: YEAR ONE
Dynamite Entertainment: 2012 - No. 10, 2014 ($3.99)
1-9: 1-Matt Wagner-s/Wilfredo Torres-a; multiple covers 4.00
10-($4.99) 5.00

SHAFT (Based on the movie character)
Dynamite Entertainment: 2014 - No. 6, 2015 ($3.99, limited series)
1-6-David F. Walker-s/Bilquis Evely-a; multiple covers on each 4.00

SHAFT: IMITATION OF LIFE (Based on the movie character)
Dynamite Entertainment: 2016 - No. 4, 2016 ($3.99, limited series)
1-4-David F. Walker-s/Dietrich Smith-a/Matthew Clark-c 4.00

SHAGGY DOG & THE ABSENT-MINDED PROFESSOR (See Movie Comics & Walt Disney Showcase #46)(Disney-Movie)
Dell Publ. Co.: No. 985, Apr-Jun, 1959; No. 1199, Apr, 1961; Aug, 1967
Four Color 985 7 14 21 49 92 135
Four Color 1199 (4/61) Movie, photo-c; variant "Double Feature" edition; has a "Fabulous Formula" strip on back-c 7 14 21 49 92 135
Four Color 1199-(8/67) Movie, photo-c 7 14 21 49 92 135

SHAHRAZAD
Big Dog Ink: No. 0, Apr, 2013 - No. 5, Apr, 2014 ($1.99/$3.99)
0-($1.99) Hutchison-s/Krome-a; multiple covers 3.00
1-3 ($3.99) Hutchison & Castor-s/Krome-a; multiple covers on each 4.00

SHAHRAZAD
Aspen MLT: Apr, 2015 - No. 5, Aug, 2015 ($2.99/$3.99)
1,2-($2.99) Remastered reprints of 2013 series; multiple covers on each 3.00
3-5-($3.99) Hutchison & Castor-s/Krome-a; multiple covers on each 4.00

SHALOMAN (Jewish-themed stories and history)
Al Wiesner/ Mark 1 Comics: 1988 - 2012 (B&W)
V1#1-Al Wiesner-s/a in all 5.00
2-9 3.00
V2 #1(The New Adventures)-4,6-10, V3 (The Legend of...) #1-12 3.00
V2 #5 (Color)-Shows Vol 2, No. 4 in indicia 3.00
V4 (The Saga of ...) #1(2004), 2-8: 8-Chanukah & The Holocaust 3.00
...: The Sequel (2010) "11-9", ...: The Sequel 2 (2011) Genesis #2 Jews in Space 3.00
...: The Sequel 3 (2012) Purim and the X-Suit 3.00
The Saga of Shaloman (20th Anniversary Edition) TPB (10/08, $15.99) r/V4 #1-8 16.00

SHAMAN'S TEARS (Also see Maggie the Cat)
Image Comics (Creative Fire Studio): 5/93 - No. 2, 8/93; No. 3, 11/94 - No. 0, 1/96 ($2.50/$1.95)
0-2: 0-(DEC-c, 1/96)-Last Issue. 1-(5/93)-Embossed red foil-c; Grell-c/a & scripts in all. 2-Cover unfolds into poster (8/93-c, 7/93 inside) 4.00
3-12: 3-Begin $1.95-c. 5-Re-intro Jon Sable. 12-Re-intro Maggie the Cat (1 pg.) 3.00

SHAME ITSELF
Marvel Comics: Jan, 2012 ($3.99, one-shot)
1-Spoof of "Fear Itself" x-over event; short stories by various incl. Cenac & Kupperman 4.00

SHANG-CHI
Marvel Comics: Nov, 2020 - No. 5, Mar, 2021 ($3.99)
1-5-Gene Luen Yang-s/Dike Ruan & Philip Tan-a. 1-Fin Fang Foom cameo 4.00

SHANG-CHI: MASTER OF KUNG-FU ("Master of Kung Fu" on cover for #1&2)
Marvel Comics: Nov, 2002 - No. 6, Apr, 2003 ($2.99, limited series)
1-6-Moench-s/Gulacy-c/a 3.00
...One-Shot 1 (11/09, $3.99, B&W) Deadpool app. 4.00
... Vol. 1: The Hellfire Apocalypse TPB (2003, $14.99) r/#1-6 15.00

SHANNA, THE SHE-DEVIL (See Savage Tales #8)
Marvel Comics Group: Dec, 1972 - No. 5, Aug, 1973 (All are 20¢ issues)
1-1st app. Shanna; Steranko-c; Tuska-a(p) 8 16 24 54 102 150
2-Steranko-c; heroin drug story 4 8 12 23 37 50
3-5 3 6 9 14 20 25

SHANNA, THE SHE-DEVIL
Marvel Comics: Apr, 2005 - No. 7, Oct, 2005 ($3.50, limited series)
1-7-Reintro of Shanna; Frank Cho-s/a/c in all 3.50
HC (2005, $24.99, dust jacket) r/#1-7 25.00
SC (2006, $16.99) r/#1-7 17.00

SHANNA, THE SHE-DEVIL: SURVIVAL OF THE FITTEST
Marvel Comics: Oct, 2007 - No. 4, Jan, 2008 ($2.99, limited series)
1-4-Khari Evans-a/c; Gray & Palmiotti-s 3.00
SC (2008, $10.99) r/#1-4 11.00

SHAOLIN COWBOY
Burlyman Entertainment: Dec, 2004 - No. 7, May, 2007 ($3.50)
1-7-Geof Darrow-s/a. 3-Moebius-c 3.50

SHAOLIN COWBOY
Dark Horse Comics: Oct, 2013 - No. 4, Feb, 2014 ($3.99)
1-4-Geof Darrow-s/a. 1-Variant-c by Simonson 4.00

SHAOLIN COWBOY: WHO'LL STOP THE REIGN?
Dark Horse Comics: Apr, 2017 - No. 4, Jul, 2017 ($3.99)
1-4-Geof Darrow-s/a. 1-Variant-c by Frank Miller 4.00

SHAPER
Dark Horse Comics: Mar, 2015 - No. 5, Jul, 2015 ($3.99)
1-5: 1-Heisserer-s/Massafera-a. 2-5-Continuado-a 4.00

SHARKEY THE BOUNTY HUNTER
Image Comics: Feb, 2019 - No. 6, Oct, 2019 ($3.99, limited series)
1-6-Mark Millar-s/Simone Bianchi-a/c 4.00

Shatter #1 © FC

Shazam! (2019 serie) #15 © DC

Sheena, Queen of the Jungle #5 © FH

	GD	VG	FN	VF	VF/NM	NM-
	2.0	4.0	6.0	8.0	9.0	9.2

SHARK FIGHTERS, THE (Movie)
Dell Publishing Co.: Jan, 1957

Four Color 762 - Buscema-a; photo-c 8 16 24 52 99 145

SHARK-MAN
Thrill House/Image Comics: Jul, 2006; Jul, 2007; Jan, 2008 - No. 3, Jun, 2008 ($3.99/$3.50)

1,2: 1-(Thrill House, 7/06, $3.99)-Steve Pugh-s/a. 2-(Image Comics, 7/07) 4.00
1-3: 1-(Image, 1/08, $3.50) reprints Thrill House #1 3.50

SHARKY
Image Comics: Feb, 1998 - No. 4, 1998 ($2.50, bi-monthly)

1-4: 1-Mask app.; Elliot-s/a. Horley painted-c. 3-Three covers by Horley, Bisley, & Horley/Elliot. 4-Two covers (swipe of Avengers #4 and wraparound) 3.00
1-($2.95) "$1,000,000" variant 3.00
2-($2.50) Savage Dragon variant-c 3.00

SHARP COMICS (Slightly large size)
H. C. Blackerby: Winter, 1945-46 - V1#2, Spring, 1946 (52 pgs.)

V1#1-Origin Dick Royce Planetarian 55 110 165 352 601 850
2-Origin The Pioneer; Michael Morgan, Dick Royce, Sir Gallagher, Planetarian, Steve Hagen, Weeny and Pop app. 55 110 165 352 601 850

SHARPY FOX (See Comic Capers & Funny Frolics)
I. W. Enterprises/Super Comics: 1958; 1963

1,2-I.W. Reprint (1958): 2-r/Kiddie Kapers #1 2 4 6 9 13 16
14-Super Reprint (1963) 2 4 6 8 11 14

SHATTER (See Jon Sable #25-30)
First Comics: June, 1985; Dec, 1985 - No. 14, Apr, 1988 ($1.75, Baxter paper/deluxe paper)

1 (6/85)-1st computer generated-a in a comic book (1st printing) 4.00
1-(2nd print.); 1(12/85)-14: computer generated-a & lettering in all 3.00
Special 1 (1988) 3.00

SHATTERED IMAGE
Image Comics (WildStorm Productions): Aug, 1996 - No. 4, Dec, 1996 ($2.50, lim. series)

1-4: 1st Image company-wide x-over; Kurt Busiek scripts in all. 1-Tony Daniel-c/a(p). 2-Alex Ross-c/swipe (Kingdom Come) by Ryan Benjamin & Travis Charest 3.00

SHATTERSTAR (From X-Force)
Marvel Comics: Dec, 2018 - No. 5, Apr, 2019 ($3.99, limited series)

1-Tim Seeley-s/Carlos Villa-a; Grandmaster app. 4.00

SHAUN OF THE DEAD (Movie)
IDW Publishing: June, 2005 - No. 4, Sept, 2005 ($3.99, limited series)

1-4-Adaptation of 2004 movie; Zach Howard-a 4.00
TPB (12/05, $17.99) r/series; sketch pages and cover gallery 18.00

SHAZAM (See Billy Batson and the Magic of Shazam!, Giant Comics to Color, Limited Collectors' Edition, Power Of Shazam! and Trials of Shazam!)

SHAZAM! (TV)(See World's Finest #253 for story from unpublished #36)
National Periodical Publ./DC Comics: Feb, 1973 - No. 35, May-June, 1978

1-1st revival of original Captain Marvel since G.A. (origin retold), by C.C. Beck; Mary Marvel & Captain Marvel Jr. app.; Superman-c 7 14 21 49 92 135
2-5: 2-Infinity photo-c.; re-intro Mr. Mind & Tawny. 3-Capt. Marvel-r. (10/46). 4-Origin retold; Capt. Marvel-r. (1949). 5-Capt. Marvel Jr. origin retold; Capt. Marvel-r. (1948, 7 pgs.) 3 6 9 18 28 38
6,7,9-11: 6-photo-c; Capt. Marvel-r (1950, 6 pgs.). 9-Mr. Mind app. 10-Last C.C. Beck issue. 11-Schaffenberger-a begins. 3 6 9 15 22 28
8-(100 pgs.) 8-r/1st Black Adam app. from Marvel Family #1; r/Capt. Marvel Jr. by Raboy; origin/C.M. #80; origin Mary Marvel/C.M.A. #18; origin Mr. Tawny/C.M.A. #79 6 12 18 41 76 120
12-17-(All 100 pgs.). 15-vs. Lex Luthor & Mr. Mind 5 10 15 30 50 70
18-24,26,27,29,30: 21-24-All reprints. 26-Sivana app. (10/76). 27-Kid Eternity teams up w/Capt. Marvel. 30-1st DC app. 3 Lt. Marvels 3 6 9 14 20 25
25-1st app. Isis 7 14 21 46 86 135
28-(3-4/77) 1st Bronze Age app. of Black Adam 15 30 45 105 233 375
31-35: 31-1st DC app. Minuteman. 34-Origin Capt. Nazi & Capt. Marvel Jr. retold 3 6 9 16 23 30
...: The Greatest Stories Ever Told TPB (2008, $24.99) reprints; Alex Ross-c 25.00

NOTE: *Reprints in #1-8, 10, 12-17, 21-24.* **Beck** *a-1-10, 12-17r, 21-24r; c-1, 3-9.* **Nasser** *c-35p.* **Newton** *a-35p.* **Raboy** *a-5r, 8r, 17r.* **Schaffenberger** *a-11, 14-20, 25, 26, 27p, 28, 29-31p, 33i, 35i; c-20, 22, 23, 25, 26i, 27i, 28-33.*

SHAZAM!
DC Comics: March, 2011 ($2.99, one-shot)

1-Richards-a/Chiang-c; Blaze app.; story continues in Titans #32 3.00

SHAZAM! (See back-up stories in Justice League [2011 series] #0,7-11,14-16,18-21)
DC Comics: Feb, 2019 - No. 15, Nov, 2020 ($4.99/$3.99)

1-($4.99) Johns-s/Eaglesham-a; back-up origin of Hoppy w/Naito-a 5.00
2-13,15-($3.99): 2-Johns-s/Santucci-a; Sivana & Mr. Mind app.; intro. King Kid. 4-6,8-11-Black Adam app. 8-Billy's father gains the power. 11,13-Monster Society app. 12-Batman & Scarecrow app.; Loveness-s/Peterson-a. 13-Eaglesham-a. 15-Peterson-a 4.00
14-($4.99) Superboy Prime app.; Eaglesham-a 5.00

SHAZAM! AND THE SHAZAM FAMILY! ANNUAL
DC Comics: 2002 ($5.95, squarebound, one-shot)

1-Reprints Golden Age stories including 1st Mary Marvel and 1st Black Adam 1 3 4 6 8 10

SHAZAM!: POWER OF HOPE
DC Comics: Nov, 2000 ($9.95, treasury size, one-shot)

nn-Painted art by Alex Ross; story by Alex Ross and Paul Dini 10.00

SHAZAM!: THE MONSTER SOCIETY OF EVIL
DC Comics: 2007 - No. 4, 2007 ($5.99, square-bound, limited series)

1-4: Jeff Smith-s/a/c in all. 1-Retelling of origin. 2-Mary Marvel & Dr. Sivana app. 6.00
HC (2007, $29.99, over-sized with dust jacket that unfolds to a poster) r/#1-4; Alex Ross intro.; Smith afterword; sketch pages, script pages and production notes 30.00
SC (2009, $19.99) r/#1-4; Alex Ross intro. 20.00

SHAZAM: THE NEW BEGINNING
DC Comics: Apr, 1987 - No. 4, July, 1987 (Legends spin-off) (Limited series)

1-4: 1-New origin & 1st modern app. Captain Marvel; Marvel Family cameo. 2-4-Sivana & Black Adam app. 4.00

SHEA THEATRE COMICS
Shea Theatre: No date (1940's) (32 pgs.)

nn-Contains Rocket Comics; MLJ cover in one color 17 34 51 98 154 220

SHE-BAT (See Murcielaga, She-Bat & Valeria the She-Bat)

SHE COULD FLY
Dark Horse Comics (Berger Books): Jul, 2018 - No. 4, Oct, 2018 ($4.99, limited series)

1-4-Christopher Cantwell-s/Martín Morazzo-a 5.00

SHE COULD FLY: THE LOST PILOT
Dark Horse Comics (Berger Books): Apr, 2019 - No. 5, Aug, 2019 ($3.99, limited series)

1-5-Christopher Cantwell-s/Martín Morazzo-a 4.00

SHE-DRAGON (See Savage Dragon #117)
Image Comics: July, 2006 ($5.99, one-shot)

nn- She-Dragon in Dimension-X; origin retold; Franchesco-a/Larsen-s; sketch pages 6.00

SHEENA (Movie)
Marvel Comics: Dec, 1984 - No. 2, Feb, 1985 (limited series)

1,2-r/Marvel Comics Super Special #34; Tanya Roberts movie 5.00

SHEENA, QUEEN OF THE JUNGLE (See Jerry Iger's Classic..., Jumbo Comics, & 3-D Sheena)
Fiction House Magazines: Spr, 1942; No. 2, Wint, 1942-43; No. 3, Spr, 1943; No. 4, Fall, 1948; No. 5, Sum, 1949; No. 6, Spr, 1950; No. 7-10, 1950(nd); No. 11, Spr, 1951 - No. 18, Wint, 1952-53 (#1-3: 68 pgs.; #4-7: 52 pgs.)

1-Sheena begins 300 600 900 1980 3440 4900
2 (Winter, 1942-43) 168 336 504 1075 1838 2600
3 (Spring, 1943) Classic Giant Ape-c 168 336 504 1075 1838 2600
4,5 (Fall, 1948, Sum, 1949): 4-New logo; cover swipe from Jumbo #20 61 122 183 390 670 950
6,7 (Spring, 1950, 1950) 50 100 150 315 533 750
8-10(1950 - Win/50, 36 pgs.) 43 86 129 271 461 650
11-17: 15-Cover swipe from Jumbo #43 40 80 120 246 411 575
18-Used in **POP**, pg. 98 42 84 126 265 445 625
I.W. Reprint #9-r/#18; c-r/White Princess #3 4 8 12 28 44 60

NOTE: **Baker** *c-5-10?* **Whitman** *c-11-18(most).* **Zolnerowich** *c-1-3.*

SHEENA, QUEEN OF THE JUNGLE
Devil's Due Publishing: Mar, 2007; Jun, 2007 - No. 5, Jan, 2008 (99¢/$3.50)

1-5: 1-Rodi-s/Merhoff-a; 5 covers 3.50
... 99¢ Special (3/07) Revival of the character; Rodi-s/Cummings-a; sketch pages; history 3.00
...: Dark Rising (10/08 - No. 3, 12/08) 1-3 3.50
... Trail of the Mapinguari (4/08, $5.50) Two covers 5.50

SHEENA, QUEEN OF THE JUNGLE
Dynamite Entertainment: No. 0, 2017 - No. 10, 2018 (25¢/$3.99)

0-(25¢) Marguerite Bennett & Christina Trujillo-s/Moritat-a; multiple covers 3.00
1-10-($3.99) 1-Bennett & Trujillo-s/Moritat-a. 4-10-Sanapo-a 4.00

SHEENA 3-D SPECIAL (Also see Blackthorne 3-D Series #1)
Eclipse Comics: Jan, 1985 ($2.00)

She-Hulk (2005 series) #22 © MAR

Sherlock: The Blind Banker #1 © Hartswood

Sheva's War #5 © Christopher Moeller

	GD	VG	FN	VF	VF/NM	NM-
	2.0	4.0	6.0	8.0	9.0	9.2

1-Dave Stevens-c 2 4 6 10 14 18

SHE-HULK (Also see The Savage She-Hulk & The Sensational She-Hulk)
Marvel Comics: May, 2004 - No. 12, Apr, 2005 ($2.99)

1-Bobillo-a/Slott-s/Granov-c; Avengers app. 1 2 3 5 6 8
2-4-Bobillo-a/Slott-s/Granov-c. 4-Spider-Man-c/app. 3.00
5-12: Mayhew-c. 9-12-Pelletier-a. 10-Origin of Titania 3.00
Vol. 1: Single Green Female TPB (2004, $14.99) r/#1-6 15.00
Vol. 2: Superhuman Law TPB (2005, $14.99) r/#7-12 15.00

SHE-HULK (2nd series)
Marvel Comics: Dec, 2005 - No. 38, Apr, 2009 ($2.99)

1-Bobillo-a/Slott-s/Horn-c; New Avengers app. 5.00
2,4-7,9-24: 2-Hawkeye-c/app. 9-Jen marries John Jameson. 12-Thanos app. 16-Wolverine app. 3.00
3-($3.99) 100th She-Hulk issue; new story w/art by various incl. Bobillo, Conner, Mayhew & Powell; r/Savage She-Hulk #1 and r/Sensational She-Hulk #1 4.00
8-Civil War 15.00
8-2nd printing with variant Bobillo-c 3.00
25-($3.99) Intro. the Behemoth; Juggernaut cameo; Handbook bio pages of She-Hulk 4.00
26-37: 27-Iron Man app. 30-Hercules app. 31-X-Factor app. 32,33-Secret Invasion 3.00
38-($3.99) Thundra, Valkyrie and Invisible Woman app. 4.00
...: Cosmic Collision 1 (2/09, $3.99) Lady Liberators app.; David-s/Asrar-a/Sejic-c 4.00
... Sensational 1 (5/10, $4.99) 30th Anniversary celebration; Stan Lee app.; Frank-c 5.00
Vol. 3: Time Trials (2006, $14.99) r/#1-5; Bobillo sketch page 15.00
Vol. 4: Laws of Attraction (2007, $19.99) r/#6-12; Paul Smith sketch page 20.00
Vol. 5: Planet Without a Hulk (2007, $19.99) r/#14-21; Slott's original series pitch 20.00
...: Jaded HC (2008, $19.99) r/#22-27; cover gallery 20.00

SHE-HULK (3rd series)
Marvel Comics: Apr, 2014 - No. 12, Apr, 2015 ($2.99)

1-12: 1-4-Soule-s/Pulido-a/Wada-c. 1-Tony Stark app. 2-Hellcat app. 3.00

SHE-HULK (Marvel Legacy)
Marvel Comics: No. 159, Jan, 2018 - No. 163, May, 2018 ($3.99)

159-163: 159-Tamaki-s/Lindsay-a. 159-161-The Leader app. 4.00
Annual 1(10/19, $4.99) Acts of Evil; Bullseye-c/app.; Andolfo-c 5.00

SHE-HULKS
Marvel Comics: Jan, 2011 - No. 4, Apr, 2011 ($3.99/$2.99, limited series)

1-($3.99) She-Hulk & Lyra team-up; Stegman-a/McGuinness-c; character profile pages 4.00
2-4-($2.99) McGuinness-c 3.00

SHELTERED
Image Comics: Jul, 2013 - No. 15, Mar, 2015 ($2.99)

1-15-Brisson-s/Christmas-a 3.00

SHERIFF BOB DIXON'S CHUCK WAGON (TV) (See Wild Bill Hickok #22)
Avon Periodicals: Nov, 1950

1-Kinstler-c/a(3) 16 32 48 98 154 210

SHERIFF OF BABYLON, THE
DC Comics (Vertigo): Feb, 2016 - No. 12, Jan, 2017 ($3.99)

1-12-Tom King-s/Mitch Gerads-a/John Paul Leon-c 4.00

SHERIFF OF TOMBSTONE
Charlton Comics: Nov, 1958 - No. 17, Sept, 1961

V1#1-Giordano-c; Severin-a 6 12 18 37 66 95
2 4 8 12 22 35 48
3-10 3 6 9 17 25 32
11-17 3 6 9 14 20 25

SHERLOCK: A SCANDAL IN BELGRAVIA (Adaptation of episode from the BBC TV series)
Titan Comics: Jan, 2020 - No. 5, May, 2020 ($4.99/$3.99, B&W, reads back to front, right to left)

1-5-($4.99) English version of original Japanese manga; art by Jay.; multiple covers 5.00

SHERLOCK: A STUDY IN PINK (Adaptation of episode from the BBC TV series)
Titan Comics: Jul, 2016 - No. 6, Dec, 2016 ($4.99/$3.99, B&W, reads back to front, right to left)

1-($4.99) English version of original Japanese manga; art by Jay.; multiple covers 5.00
2-6-($3.99) 4.00

SHERLOCK FRANKENSTEIN AND THE LEGION OF EVIL (Also see Black Hammer)
Dark Horse Comics: Oct, 2017 - No. 4, Jan, 2018 ($3.99, limited series)

1-4-Lemire-s/Rubín-a 4.00

SHERLOCK HOLMES (See Classic Comics #33, Marvel Preview, New Adventures of..., & Spectacular Stories)

SHERLOCK HOLMES (All New Baffling Adventures of...)(Young Eagle #3 on?)
Charlton Comics: Oct, 1955 - No. 2, Mar, 1956

1-Dr. Neff, Ghost Breaker app. 43 86 129 271 461 650
2 39 78 117 231 378 525

SHERLOCK HOLMES (Also see The Joker)
National Periodical Publications: Sept-Oct, 1975

1-Cruz-a; Simonson-c 3 6 9 17 26 35

SHERLOCK HOLMES
Dynamite Entertainment: 2009 - No. 5, 2009 ($3.50, limited series)

1-5-Cassaday-c/Moore & Reppion-s/Aaron Campbell-a 3.50

SHERLOCK HOLMES: MORIARTY LIVES
Dynamite Entertainment: 2014 - No. 5, 2014 ($3.99, limited series)

1-5-Liss-s/Indro-a/Francavilla-c 4.00

SHERLOCK HOLMES: THE LIVERPOOL DEMON
Dynamite Entertainment: 2012 - No. 5, 2013 ($3.99, limited series)

1-5-Moore & Reppion-s/Triano-a/Francavilla-c 4.00

SHERLOCK HOLMES: THE VANISHING MAN
Dynamite Entertainment: 2018 - No. 4, 2018 ($3.99, limited series)

1-4-Moore & Reppion-s/Ohta-a/Cassaday-c 4.00

SHERLOCK HOLMES VS. HARRY HOUDINI
Dynamite Entertainment: 2014 - No. 5, 2015 ($3.99, limited series)

1-5-Del Col & McCreery-s/Furuzono-a; multiple covers on each 4.00

SHERLOCK HOLMES: YEAR ONE
Dynamite Entertainment: 2011 - No. 6, 2011 ($3.99, limited series)

1-6-Beatty-s; multiple covers on each 4.00

SHERLOCK: THE BLIND BANKER (Adaptation of episode from the BBC TV series)
Titan Comics: Feb, 2017 - No. 6, Jul, 2017 ($4.99/$3.99, B&W, reads back to front, right to left)

1-6-English version of original Japanese manga; art by Jay.; multiple covers 5.00

SHERLOCK: THE GREAT GAME (Adaptation of episode from the BBC TV series)
Titan Comics: Sept, 2017 - No. 6, Feb, 2018 ($4.99, B&W, reads back to front, right to left)

1-6-English version of original Japanese manga; art by Jay.; multiple covers 5.00

SHERRY THE SHOWGIRL (Showgirls #4)
Atlas Comics: July, 1956 - No. 3, Dec, 1956; No. 5, Apr, 1957 - No. 7, Aug, 1957

1-Dan DeCarlo-c/a in all 258 516 774 1651 2826 4000
2 97 194 291 621 1061 1500
3,5-7 65 130 195 416 708 1000

SHE'S JOSIE (See Josie)

SHEVA'S WAR
DC Comics (Helix): Oct, 1998 - No. 5, Feb, 1999 ($2.95, mini-series)

1-5-Christopher Moeller-s/painted-a/c 3.00

SHI (one-shots and TPBs)
Crusade Comics

...: Akai (2001, $2.99)-Intro. Victoria Cross; Tucci-a/c; J.C. Vaughn-s 3.00
...: Akai Victoria Cross Ed. ($5.95, edition of 2000) variant Tucci-c 6.00
...: C.G.I. (2001, $4.99) preview of unpublished series 5.00
.../ Cyblade: The Battle for the Independents (9/95, $2.95) Tucci-c; Hellboy, Bone app. 3.00
.../ Cyblade: The Battle for the Independents (9/95, $2.95) Silvestri variant-c 3.00
.../ Daredevil: Honor Thy Mother (1/97, $2.95) Flip book 3.00
...: Judgment Night (200, $3.99) Wolverine app.; Battlebook card and pages; Tucci-a 4.00
...: Kaidan (10/96, $2.95) Two covers; Tucci-c; Jae Lee wraparound-c 3.00
...: Masquerade (3/98, $3.50) Painted art by Lago, Texeira, and others 3.50
...: Nightstalkers (9/97, $3.50) Painted art by Val Mayerik 3.50
...: Rekishi (1/97, $2.95) Character bios and story summaries of Shi: The Way of the Warrior told in Detective Joe Labianca's point of view; Christopher Golden script; Tucci-c; J.G. Jones-a; flip book w/Shi: East Wind Rain preview 3.00
...: The Art of War Tourbook (1998, $4.95) Blank cover for sketches; early Tucci-a inside 5.00
.../ Vampirella (10/97, $2.95) Ellis-s/Lau-a 3.00
... Vs. Tomoe (8/96, $3.95) Tucci-a/scripts; wraparound foil-c 4.00
... Vs. Tomoe (6/96, $5.00. B&W)-Preview Ed.; sold at San Diego Comic Con 5.00
The Definitive Shi Vol. 1 (2006-2007, $24.99, TPB) B&W r/Way of the Warrior, Tomoe, Rekishi, and Senryaku series; cover gallery with sketches; Tucci & Sparacio-c 25.00

SHI: BLACK, WHITE AND RED
Crusade Comics: Mar, 1998 - No. 2, May, 1998 ($2.95, B&W&Red, mini-series)

1,2-J.G. Jones-painted art 3.00
...- Year of the Dragon Collected Edition (2000, $5.95) r/#1&2 6.00

S.H.I.E.L.D. (2015 series) #1 © MAR

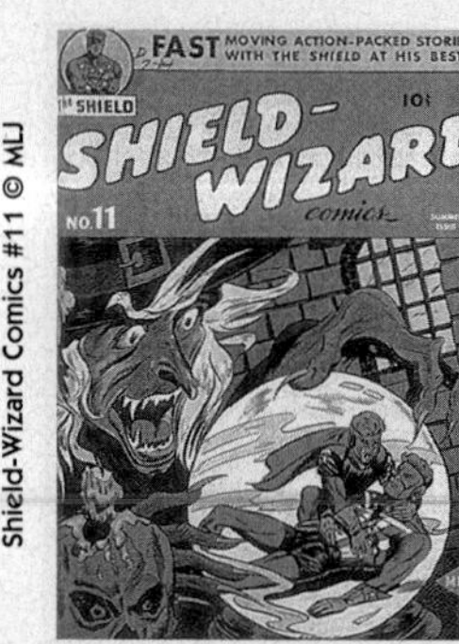

Shield-Wizard Comics #11 © MLJ

Shi: The Series #8 © William Tucci

	GD 2.0	VG 4.0	FN 6.0	VF 8.0	VF/NM 9.0	NM- 9.2

SHIDIMA
Image Comics: Jan, 2001 - No. 7, Nov, 2002 ($2.95, limited series)

1-7-Prequel to Warlands 3.00
#0-(10/01, $2.25) Short story and sketch pages 3.00

SHI: EAST WIND RAIN
Crusade Comics: Nov, 1997 - No. 2, Feb, 1998 ($3.50, limited series)

1,2-Shi at WW2 Pearl Harbor 3.50

S.H.I.E.L.D. (Nick Fury & His Agents of...) (Also see Nick Fury)
Marvel Comics Group: Feb, 1973 - No. 5, Oct, 1973 (All 20¢ issues)

	GD	VG	FN	VF	VF/NM	NM-
1-All contain reprint stories from Strange Tales #146-155; new Steranko-c	4	8	12	23	37	50
2-New Steranko flag-c	3	6	9	15	22	28
3-5: 3-Kirby/Steranko-c(r). 4-Steranko-c(r)	2	4	6	9	12	15

NOTE: *Buscema a-3p(r). Kirby layouts 1-5; c-3 (w/Steranko). Steranko a-3r, 4r(2).*

S.H.I.E.L.D.
Marvel Comics: Jun, 2010 - No. 6, Apr, 2011 ($3.99/$2.99)

1-($3.99) Leonardo DaVinci app.; Weaver-a/Hickman-s/Parel-c; 4 printings 4.00
1-Variant-c by Weaver 6.00
1-Director's Cut (9/10, $4.99) r/#1 with character sketch-a and bios; design-a 5.00
2-6-($2.99) 2-Three printings. 3-Galactus app. 3.00
Infinity (6/11, $4.99) DaVinci, Nostradamus, Newton & Tesla app.; Parel-c 5.00
... Origins (1/14, $7.99) r/Battle Scars #6, Secret Avengers #1; Strange Tales #135 8.00

S.H.I.E.L.D. (2nd series; title becomes S.H.I.E.L.D. by Hickman & Weaver with #5)
Marvel Comics: Aug, 2011 - No. 4, Feb, 2012; No. 5, Jul, 2018 - No. 6, Aug, 2018 ($3.99/$2.99)

1-($3.99) Weaver-a/Hickman-s/Parel-c; profile pgs of main characters 4.00
2-4-($2.99) 3.00
5,6: 5-(7/18, $3.99) Continuation after 6-year hiatus 4.00
... By Hickman & Weaver: The Rebirth 1 (7/18, $5.99) r/#1-4; Parel-c 6.00

S.H.I.E.L.D. (Based on the TV series)
Marvel Comics: Feb, 2015 - No. 12, Jan, 2016 ($4.99/$3.99)

1-($4.99) Waid-s/Pacheco-a/Tedesco-c; Avengers app. 5.00
2-8-($3.99) 2-Ms. Marvel (Kamala Khan) app.; Ramos-a. 3-Spider-Man app.; Davis-a 4.00
9-($5.99) 50th Anniversary issue; Howling Commandos app.; r/Strange Tales #135 6.00
10-12: 10-Howard the Duck app. 11-Dominic Fortune app.; Chaykin-a 4.00

SHIELD, THE (Becomes Shield-Steel Sterling #3; #1 titled Lancelot Strong; also see Advs. of the Fly, Double Life of Private Strong, Fly Man, Mighty Comics, The Mighty Crusaders, The Original... & Pep Comics #1)
Archie Enterprises, Inc.: June, 1983 - No. 2, Aug, 1983

1,2: Steel Sterling app. 1-Weiss-c/a. 2-Kanigher-s/Buckler-c/Nebres-a 5.00
America's 1st Patriotic Comic Book Hero, The Shield (2002, $12.95, TPB) r/Pep Comics #1-5, Shield-Wizard Comics #1; foreward by Robert M. Overstreet 13.00

SHIELD, THE (Archie Ent. character) (Continued from The Red Circle)
DC Comics: Nov, 2009 - No. 10, Aug, 2010 ($3.99)

1-10: 1-Magog app.; Inferno back-up feature thru #6; Green Arrow app. 2,3-Grodd app. 4,5-The Great Ten app. 7-10-The Fox back-up feature; Oeming-a 4.00
...: Kicking Down the Door TPB ('10, $19.99) r/#1-6, Red Circle: The Web & RC: The Shield 20.00

SHIELD, THE
Archie Comic Publications: Dec, 2015 - No. 4, Jan, 2017 ($3.99)

1-4-Christopher & Wendig-s/Drew Johnson-a; a new Shield recruited; multiple covers 4.00

SHIELD, THE: SPOTLIGHT (TV)
IDW Publishing: Jan, 2004 - No. 5, May, 2004 ($3.99)

1-5-Jeff Marriote-s/Jean Diaz-a/Tommy Lee Edwards-c 4.00
TPB (7/04, $19.99) r/#1-5; Michael Chiklis photo-c 20.00

SHIELD-STEEL STERLING (Formerly The Shield)
Archie Enterprises, Inc.: No. 3, Dec, 1983 (Becomes Steel Sterling No. 4)

3-Nino-a; Steel Sterling by Kanigher & Barreto 5.00

SHIELD WIZARD COMICS (Also see Pep Comics & Top-Notch Comics)
MLJ Magazines: Summer, 1940 - No. 13, Spring, 1944

	GD	VG	FN	VF	VF/NM	NM-
1-(V1#5 on inside)-Origin The Shield by Irving Novick & The Wizard by Ed Ashe, Jr; Flag-c	450	900	1350	3300	6650	10,000
2-(Winter/40)-Origin The Shield retold; Wizard's sidekick, Roy the Super Boy begins (see Top-Notch #8 for 1st app.)	290	580	870	1856	3178	4500
3,4	200	400	600	1280	2190	3100
5-Dusty, the Boy Detective begins; Nazi bondage-c	174	348	522	1114	1907	2700
6,7: 6-Roy the Super Boy app. 7-Shield dons new costume (Summer, 1942); S & K-c?	165	330	495	1048	1799	2550
8-Nazi bondage-c; HItler photo on-c	284	568	852	1818	3109	4400
9-Japanese WWII bondage-c	181	362	543	1158	1979	2800
10-Nazi swastica-c	194	388	582	1242	2121	3000
11,12	129	258	387	826	1413	2000
13-Japanese WWII bondage/torture-c (scarce)	213	426	639	1363	2332	3300

NOTE: ***Bob Montana** c-13. **Novick** c-1,3-6,8-11. **Harry Sahle** c-12.*

SHI: FAN EDITIONS
Crusade Comics: 1997

1-3-Two covers polybagged in FAN #19-21 3.00
1-3-Gold editions 4.00

SHI: HEAVEN AND EARTH
Crusade Comics: June, 1997 - No. 4, Apr, 1998 ($2.95)

1-4 3.00
4-($4.95) Pencil-c variant 5.00
Rising Sun Edition-signed by Tucci in FanClub Starter Pack 4.00
"Tora No Shi" variant-c 3.00

SHI: JU-NEN
Dark Horse Comics: July, 2004 - No. 4, May, 2005 ($2.99, mini-series)

1-4-Tucci-a/Tucci & Vaughn-s; origin retold 3.00
TPB (2/06, $12.95) r/#1-4; Tucci and Sparacio-c 13.00

SHINING KNIGHT (See Adventure Comics #66)

SHINKU
Image Comics: Jun, 2011 - No. 5, Oct, 2012 ($2.99)

1-5-Marz-s/Moder-a 3.00

SHINOBI (Based on Sega video game)
Dark Horse Comics: Aug, 2002 ($2.99, one-shot)

1-Medina-a/c 3.00

SHIP AHOY
Spotlight Publishers: Nov, 1944 (52 pgs.)

	GD	VG	FN	VF	VF/NM	NM-
1-L. B. Cole-c	27	54	81	158	259	360

SHIP OF FOOLS
Image Comics: Aug, 1997 - No. 3 ($2.95, B&W)

0-3-Glass-s/Oeming-a 3.00

SHI: POISONED PARADISE
Avatar Press: July, 2002 - No. 2, Aug, 2002 ($3.50, limited series)

1,2-Vaughn and Tucci-s/Waller-a; 1-Four covers 3.50

SHIPWRECK
AfterShock Comics: Oct, 2016 - No. 6, Jun, 2018 ($3.99)

1-6-Warren Ellis-s/Phil Hester-a 3.00

SHIPWRECKED! (Disney-Movie)
Disney Comics: 1990 ($5.95, graphic novel, 68 pgs.)

nn-adaptation; Spiegle-a 6.00

SHIRTLESS BEAR FIGHTER
Image Comics: Jun, 2017 - No. 5, Oct, 2017 ($3.99, limited series)

1-5-Leheup & Girner-s/Vendrell-a; multiple covers on each 4.00

SHI: SEMPO
Avatar Press: Aug, 2003 - No. 2, ($3.50, B&W, limited series)

1,2-Vaughn and Tucci-s/Alves-a; 1-Four covers 3.50

SHI: SENRYAKU
Crusade Comics: Aug, 1995 - No. 3, Nov, 1995 ($2.95, limited series)

1-3: 1-Tucci-c; Quesada, Darrow, Sim, Lee, Smith-a. 2-Tucci-c; Silvestri, Balent, Perez, Mack-a. 3-Jusko-c; Hughes, Ramos, Bell, Moore-a 3.00
1-variant-c (no logo) 4.00
Hardcover ($24.95)-r/#1-3; Frazetta-c. 25.00
Trade Paperback ($13.95)-r/#1-3; Frazetta-c. 14.00

SHI: THE ILLUSTRATED WARRIOR
Crusade Comics: 2002 - No. 7, 2003 ($2.99, B&W)

1-7-Story text with Tucci full page art 3.00

SHI: THE SERIES
Crusade Comics: Aug, 1997 - No. 13 ($2.95, color #1-10, B&W #11)

1-10 3.00
11-13: 11-B&W. 12-Color; Lau-a 3.00
#0 Convention Edition 5.00

SHI: THE WAY OF THE WARRIOR
Crusade Comics: Mar, 1994 - No. 12, Apr, 1997 ($2.50/$2.95)

Shocking Mystery Cases #60 © Star

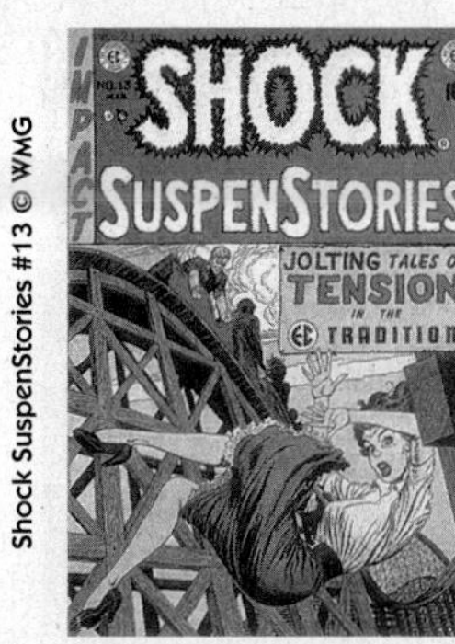

Shock SuspenStories #13 © WMG

Showcase #9 © DC

GD 2.0 | VG 4.0 | FN 6.0 | VF 8.0 | VF/NM 9.0 | NM- 9.2

1/2 4.00
1 2 4 6 8 10 12
1-Commemorative ed., B&W, new-c; given out at 1994 San Diego Comic Con
2 4 6 10 14 18
1-Fan appreciation edition -r/#1 3.00
1-Fan appreciation edition (variant) 6.00
1- 10th Anniversary Edition (2004, $2.99) 3.00
2 5.00
2-Commemorative edition (3,000) 2 4 6 9 13 16
2-Fan appreciation edition -r/#2 3.00
3 4.00
4-7: 4-Silvestri poster. 7-Tomoe app. 3.00
5,6: 5-Silvestri variant-c. 6-Tomoe #1 variant-c 3.50
5-Gold edition 12.00
6,8-12: 6-Fan appreciation edition 3.00
8-Combo Gold edition 6.00
8-Signed Edition-(5000) 4.00
Trade paperback (1995, $12.95)-r/#1-4 15.00
Trade paperback (1995, $14.95)-r/#1-4 revised; Julie Bell-c 15.00

SHI: YEAR OF THE DRAGON
Crusade Comics: 2000 - No. 3, 2000 ($2.99, limited series)
1-3: 1-Two covers; Tucci-a/c; flashback to teen-aged Ana 3.00

SHMOO (See Al Capp's... & Washable Jones &...)

SHOCK (Magazine)
Stanley Publ.: May, 1969 - V3#4, Sept, 1971 (B&W reprints from horror comics, including some pre-code) (No V2#1,3)
V1#1-Cover-r/Weird Tales of the Future #7 by Bernard Baily; r/Weird Chills #1
7 14 21 48 89 130
2-Wolverton-r/Weird Mysteries 5; r-Weird Mysteries #7 used in **SOTI**; cover reprints cover to Weird Chills #1 5 10 15 35 63 90
3,5,6 4 8 12 28 47 65
4-Harrison/Williamson-r/Forbid. Worlds #6 5 10 15 30 50 70
V2#2(5/70), V1#8(7/70), V2#4(9/70)-6(1/71), V3#1-4: V2#4-Cover swipe from Weird Mysteries #6 4 8 12 27 44 60
NOTE: ***Disbrow** r-V2#4; Bondage c-V1#4, V2#6, V3#1.*

SHOCK DETECTIVE CASES (Formerly Crime Fighting Detective) (Becomes Spook Detective Cases No. 22)
Star Publications: No. 20, Sept, 1952 - No. 21, Nov, 1952
20,21-L.B. Cole-c; based on true crime cases 60 120 180 381 653 925
NOTE: ***Palais** a-20. No. 21-Fox-r.*

SHOCK ILLUSTRATED (...Adult Crime Stories; Magazine format)
E. C. Comics: Sept-Oct, 1955 - No. 3, Spring, 1956 (Adult Entertainment on-c #1,2)(All 25¢)
1-All by Kamen; drugs, prostitution, wife swapping 27 54 81 158 259 360
2-Williamson-a redrawn from Crime SuspenStories #13 plus Ingels, Crandall, Evans & part Torres-i; painted-c 24 48 72 140 230 320
3-Only 100 known copies bound & given away at E.C. office; Crandall, Evans-a; painted-c; shows May, 1956 on-c 194 388 582 1242 2121 3000

SHOCKING MYSTERY CASES (Formerly Thrilling Crime Cases)
Star Publications: No. 50, Sept, 1952 - No. 60, Oct, 1954 (All crime reprints?)
50-Disbrow "Frankenstein" story 71 142 213 454 777 1100
51-Disbrow-a 42 84 126 265 445 625
52-60: 56-Drug use story 39 78 117 240 395 550
NOTE: ***L. B. Cole** covers on all; a-60(2 pgs.). **Hollingsworth** a-52. **Morisi** a-55.*

SHOCKING TALES DIGEST MAGAZINE
Harvey Publications: Oct, 1981 (95¢)
1-1957-58-r; Powell, Kirby, Nostrand-a 2 4 6 9 13 16

SHOCK ROCKETS
Image Comics (Gorilla): Apr, 2000 - No. 6, Oct, 2000 ($2.50)
1-6-Busiek-s/Immonen & Grawbadger-a. 6-Flip book w/Superstar preview 3.00
...: We Have Ignition TPB (Dark Horse, 8/04, $14.95, 6" x 9") r/#1-6 15.00

SHOCK SUSPENSTORIES (Also see EC Archives • Shock SuspenStories)
E. C. Comics: Feb-Mar, 1952 - No. 18, Dec-Jan, 1954-55
1-Classic Feldstein electrocution-c 131 262 393 1048 1674 2300
2 57 114 171 456 728 1000
3,4: 3-Classic decapitation splash. 4-Used in **SOTI**, pg. 387,388
50 100 150 400 638 875
5-Hanging-c 63 126 189 504 802 1100
6-Classic hooded vigilante bondage-c 183 366 549 1464 2332 3200
7-Classic face melting-c 80 160 240 640 1020 1400
8-Williamson-a 49 98 147 392 621 850
9-11: 9-Injury to eye panel. 10-Junkie story 40 80 120 320 510 700
12- "The Monkey" classic junkie cover/story; anti-drug propaganda issue
69 138 207 552 876 1200
13-Frazetta's only solo story for E.C., 7 pgs, draws himself as main male character
60 120 180 480 765 1050
14-Used in Senate Investigation hearings 40 80 120 320 510 700
15-Used in 1954 Reader's Digest article, "For the Kiddies to Read"
37 74 111 296 473 650
16-18: 16- "Red Dupe" editorial; rape story 36 72 108 288 457 625
NOTE: ***Ray Bradbury** adaptations-1, 7, 9. **Craig** a-11; c-11. **Crandall** a-9-13, 15-18. **Davis** a-1-5. **Evans** a-7, 8, 14-18; c-16-18. **Feldstein** c-1, 7-9, 12. **Ingels** a-1, 2, 6. **Kamen** a-in all; c-10, 13, 15. **Krigstein** a-14, 18. **Orlando** a-1, 3-7, 9, 10, 12, 16, 17. **Wood** a-2-15; c-2-6, 14.*

SHOCK SUSPENSTORIES (Also see EC Archives • Shock SuspenStories)
Russ Cochran/Gemstone Publishing: Sept, 1992 - No. 18, Dec, 1996 ($1.50/$2.00/$2.50, quarterly)
1-18: 1-3: Reprints with original-c. 17-r/HOF #17 4.00

SHOGUN WARRIORS
Marvel Comics Group: Feb, 1979 - No. 20, Sept, 1980 (Based on Mattel toys of the classic Japanese animation characters) (1-3: 35¢; 4-19: 40¢; 20: 50¢)
1-Raydeen, Combatra, & Dangard Ace begin; Trimpe-a
3 6 9 17 26 35
2-20: 2-Lord Maurkon & Elementals of Evil app.; Rok-Korr app. 6-Shogun vs. Shogun. 7,8-Cerberus. 9-Starchild. 11-Austin-c. 12-Simonson-c. 14-16-Doctor Demonicus. 17-Juggernaut. 19,20-FF x-over 2 3 4 6 8 10

SHOOK UP (Magazine) (Satire)
Dodsworth Publ. Co.: Nov, 1958
V1#1 4 8 12 28 47 65

SHOPLIFTERS WILL BE LIQUIDATED
AfterShock Comics: Oct, 2019 - No. 5, Mar, 2020 ($3.99, limited series)
1-5-Patrick Kindlon-s/Stefano Simeone-a 4.00

SHORT RIBS
Dell Publishing Co.: No. 1333, Apr - June, 1962
Four Color 1333 5 10 15 35 63 90

SHORTSTOP SQUAD (Baseball)
Ultimate Sports Ent. Inc.: 1999 ($3.95, one-shot)
1-Ripken Jr., Larkin, Jeter, Rodriguez app.; Edwards-c/a 4.00

SHORT STORY COMICS (See Hello Pal,...)

SHORTY SHINER (The Five-Foot Fighter in the Ten Gallon Hat)
Dandy Magazine (Charles Biro): June, 1956 - No. 3, Oct, 1956
1 9 18 27 47 61 75
2,3 7 14 21 37 46 55

SHOTGUN SLADE (TV)
Dell Publishing Co.: No. 1111, July-Sept, 1960
Four Color 1111-Photo-c 6 12 18 37 66 95

SHOWCASE (See Cancelled Comic Cavalcade & New Talent...)
National Per. Publ./DC Comics: 3-4/56 - No. 93, 9/70; No. 94, 8-9/77 - No. 104, 9/78
1-Fire Fighters; w/Fireman Farrell 331 662 993 2880 6240 9600
2-Kings of the Wild; Kubert-a (animal stories) 136 272 408 1088 2444 3800
3-The Frogmen by Russ Heath; Heath greytone-c (early DC example, 7-8/56)
118 236 354 944 2122 3300
4-Origin/1st app. The Flash (1st DC Silver Age hero, Sept-Oct, 1956); Kanigher-s; Infantino & Kubert-c/a; 1st app. Iris West and The Turtle; r/in Secret Origins #1 ('61 & '73); Flash shown reading G.A. Flash Comics #13; back-up story w/Broome-s/Infantino & Kubert-a
7600 15,200 30,400 68,400 121,700 175,000
5-Manhunters; Meskin-a 104 208 312 832 1866 2900
6-Origin/1st app. Challengers of the Unknown by Kirby, partly r/in Secret Origins #1 & Challengers #64,65 (1st S.A. hero team & 1st original concept S.A. series)(1-2/57)
383 766 1149 3256 7378 11,500
7-Challengers of the Unknown by Kirby (2nd app.) reprinted in Challengers of the Unknown #75 162 324 486 1337 3019 4700
8-The Flash (5-6/57, 2nd app.); origin & 1st app. Captain Cold
940 1880 2820 8500 16,000 23,500
9-Lois Lane (Pre-#1, 7-8/57) (1st Showcase character to win own series)
Superman app. on-c 700 1400 2100 5600 10,050 14,500
10-Lois Lane; Jor-El cameo; Superman app. on-c 220 440 660 1815 4108 6400
11-Challengers of the Unknown by Kirby (3rd) 141 284 423 1142 2571 4000
12-Challengers of the Unknown by Kirby (4th) 141 284 423 1142 2571 4000
13-The Flash (3rd app.); origin Mr. Element 383 766 1149 3256 7378 11,500
14-The Flash (4th app.); origin Dr. Alchemy, former Mr. Element (rare in NM)

Showcase #19 © DC

Showcase #75 © DC

Showcase '96 #12 © DC

	GD 2.0	VG 4.0	FN 6.0	VF 8.0	VF/NM 9.0	NM- 9.2
	367	734	1101	3120	7060	11,000
15-Space Ranger (7-8/58, 1st app., also see My Greatest Aventure #22)	172	344	516	1419	3210	5000
16-Space Ranger (9-10/58, 2nd app.)	94	188	282	761	1706	2650
17-(11-12/58)-Adventures on Other Worlds; origin/1st app. Adam Strange by Gardner Fox & Mike Sekowsky	500	1000	1500	4250	9625	15,000
18-Adventures on Other Worlds (2nd A. Strange)	100	200	300	800	1800	2800
19-Adam Strange; 1st Adam Strange logo	102	204	306	816	1833	2850
20-Rip Hunter; origin & 1st app. (5-6/59); Moreira-a	145	290	435	1196	2698	4200
21-Rip Hunter (7-8/59, 2nd app.); Sekowsky-c/a	59	118	177	472	1061	1650
22-Origin & 1st app. Silver Age Green Lantern by Gil Kane and John Broome (9-10/59); reprinted in Secret Origins #2	1400	2800	5600	17,000	37,500	58,000
23-Green Lantern (11-12/59, 2nd app.); nuclear explosion-c	207	414	621	178	3854	6000
24-Green Lantern (1-2/60, 3rd app.)	169	338	507	1394	3147	4900
25,26-Rip Hunter by Kubert. 25-Grey tone-c	48	96	144	370	835	1300
27-Sea Devils (7-8/60, 1st app.); Heath-c/a; Grey tone-c	80	160	240	640	1445	2250
28-Sea Devils (9-10/60, 2nd app.); Heath-c/a; Grey tone-c	39	78	117	289	657	1025
29-Sea Devils; Heath-c/a; grey tone c-27-29	42	84	126	311	706	1100
30-Origin Silver Age Aquaman (1-2/61) (see Adventure #260 for 1st S.A. origin)	276	552	828	2277	5139	8000
31-Aquaman	56	112	168	444	997	1550
32,33-Aquaman	41	82	123	303	689	1075
34-Origin & 1st app. Silver Age Atom by Gil Kane & Murphy Anderson (9-10/61); reprinted in Secret Origins #2	169	338	507	1394	3147	4900
35-The Atom by Gil Kane (2nd); last 10¢ issue	50	100	150	400	900	1400
36-The Atom by Gil Kane (1-2/62, 3rd app.)	40	80	120	296	673	1050
37-Metal Men (3-4/62, 1st app.)	111	222	333	888	1994	3100
38-Metal Men (5-6/62, 2nd app.)	30	60	90	219	490	760
39-Metal Men (7-8/62, 3rd app.)	23	46	69	164	362	560
40-Metal Men (9-10/62, 4th app.)	21	42	63	147	324	500
41,42-Tommy Tomorrow (parts 1 & 2). 42-Origin	13	26	39	91	201	310
43-Dr. No (James Bond); Nodel-a; originally published as British Classics Illustrated #158A & as #6 in a European Detective series, all with diff. painted-c. This Showcase #43 version is actually censored, deleting all racial skin color and dialogue thought to be racially demeaning (1st DC S.A. movie adaptation)(based on Ian Fleming novel & movie)	57	114	171	456	1028	1600
44-Tommy Tomorrow	10	20	30	66	138	210
45-Sgt. Rock (7-8/63); pre-dates B&B #52; origin retold; Heath-c	34	68	102	245	548	850
46,47-Tommy Tomorrow	9	18	27	61	123	185
48,49-Cave Carson (3rd tryout series; see B&B)	8	16	24	54	102	150
50,51-I Spy (Danger Trail-r by Infantino), King Farady story (#50 has new 4 pg. story)	7	14	21	48	89	130
52-Cave Carson	7	14	21	49	92	135
53,54-G.I. Joe (11-12/64, 1-2/65); Heath-a	11	22	33	75	160	245
55-Dr. Fate & Hourman (3-4/65); origin of each in text; 1st solo app. G.A. Green Lantern in Silver Age (pre-dates Gr. Lantern #40); 1st S.A. app. Solomon Grundy	42	84	126	311	706	1100
56-Dr. Fate & Hourman	13	26	39	87	191	295
57-Enemy Ace by Kubert (7-8/65, 4th app. after Our Army at War #155)	19	38	57	131	291	450
58-Enemy Ace by Kubert (5th app.)	16	32	48	107	236	365
59-Teen Titans (11-12/65, 3rd app.)	18	36	54	124	275	425
60-1st S. A. app. The Spectre; Anderson-a (1-2/66); origin in text	26	52	78	182	404	625
61-The Spectre by Anderson (2nd app.)	12	24	36	82	179	275
62-Origin & 1st app. Inferior Five (5-6/66)	9	18	27	61	123	185
63,65-Inferior Five. 63-Hulk parody. 65-X-Men parody (11-12/66)	6	12	18	37	66	95
64-The Spectre by Anderson (5th app.)	12	24	36	82	179	275
66,67-B'wana Beast	5	10	15	35	63	90
68-Maniaks (1st app., spoof of The Monkees)	5	10	15	35	63	90
69,71-Maniaks. 71-Woody Allen-c/app.	5	10	15	34	60	85
70-Binky (9-10/67)-Tryout issue; 1950's Leave It To Binky reprints with art changes	6	12	18	37	66	95
72-Top Gun (Johnny Thunder-r)-Toth-a	5	10	15	31	53	75
73-Origin/1st app. Creeper; Ditko-c/a (3-4/68)	11	22	33	76	163	250
74-Intro/1st app. Anthro; Post-c/a (5/68)	7	14	21	49	92	135
75-Origin/1st app. Hawk & the Dove; Ditko-c/a	11	22	33	76	163	250
76-1st app. Bat Lash (8/68)	8	16	24	52	99	145
77-1st app. Angel & The Ape (9/68)	6	12	18	41	76	110
78-1st app. Jonny Double (11/68)	5	10	15	30	50	70
79-1st app. Dolphin (12/68); Aqualad origin-r	13	26	39	89	195	300
80-1st S.A. app. Phantom Stranger (1/69); Neal Adams-c	15	30	45	100	220	340
81-Windy & Willy; r/Many Loves of Dobie Gillis #26 with art changes	5	10	15	34	60	85
82-1st app. Nightmaster (5/69) by Grandenetti & Giordano; Kubert-c	7	14	21	44	82	120
83,84-Nightmaster by Wrightson w/Jones/Kaluta ink assist in each; Kubert-c. 83-Last 12¢ issue 84-Origin retold; begin 15¢	6	12	18	41	76	110
85-87-Firehair; Kubert-a	3	6	9	16	23	30
88-90-Jason's Quest: 90-Manhunter 2070 app.	3	6	9	14	20	25
91-93-Manhunter 2070: 92-Origin. 93-(9/70) Last 15¢ issue	3	6	9	14	20	25
94-Intro/origin new Doom Patrol & Robotman(8-9/77)	3	6	9	14	20	25
95,96-The Doom Patrol. 95-Origin Celsius	2	3	4	6	8	10
97-Power Girl; origin; JSA cameos	4	8	12	25	40	55
98,99-Power Girl; origin in #98; JSA cameos	2	4	6	11	16	20
100-(52 pgs.)-Most Showcase characters featured	2	4	6	11	16	20
101-103-Hawkman; Adam Strange x-over	2	4	6	8	10	12
104-(52 pgs.)-O.S.S. Spies at War	2	4	6	8	10	12

NOTE: ***Anderson*** *a-22-24i, 34-36i, 55, 56, 60, 61, 64, 101-103i; c-50i, 51i, 55, 56, 60, 61, 64.* ***Aparo*** *c-94-96.* ***Boring*** *c-10.* ***Estrada*** *a-104.* ***Fraden*** *c(p)-30, 31, 33.* ***Heath*** *c-3, 27-29.* ***Infantino*** *c/a(p)-4, 8, 13, 14; c-50p, 51p.* ***Gil Kane*** *a-22-24p, 34-36p; c-17-19, 22-24p(w/****Giella****), 31.* ***Kane/Anderson*** *c-34-36.* ***Kirby*** *c-11, 12.* ***Kirby/Stein*** *c-6, 7.* ***Kubert*** *a-2, 4i, 25, 26, 45, 53, 54, 72; c-25, 26, 53, 54, 57, 58, 82-87, 101-104; c-2, 4i.* ***Moreira*** *c-5.* ***Orlando*** *a-62p, 63p, 97i; c-62, 63, 97i.* ***Sekowsky*** *a-65p.* ***Sparling*** *a-78.* ***Staton*** *a-94, 95-99p, 100; c-97-100p.*

SHOWCASE '93

DC Comics: Jan, 1993 - No. 12, Dec, 1993 ($1.95, limited series, 52 pgs.)

1-12: 1-Begin 4 part Catwoman story & 6 part Blue Devil story; begin Cyborg story; Art Adams/Austin-c. 3-Flash by Charest (p). 6-Azrael in Bat-costume (2 pgs.). 7,8-Knightfall parts 13 & 14. 6-10-Deathstroke app. (6,10-cameo). 9,10-Austin-i. 10-Azrael as Batman in new costume app.; Gulacy-c. 11-Perez-c. 12-Creeper app.; Alan Grant scripts 4.00

NOTE: ***Chaykin*** *c-9.* ***Fabry*** *c-8.* ***Giffen*** *a-12.* ***Golden*** *c-3.* ***Zeck*** *c-6.*

SHOWCASE '94

DC Comics: Jan, 1994 - No. 12, Dec, 1994 ($1.95, limited series, 52 pgs.)

1-12: 1,2-Joker & Gunfire stories. 1-New Gods. 4-Riddler story. 5-Huntress-c/story w/app. new Batman. 6-Huntress-c/story w/app. Robin; Atom story. 7-Penguin story by Peter David, P. Craig Russell, & Michael T. Gilbert; Penguin-c by Jae Lee. 8,9-Scarface origin story by Alan Grant, John Wagner,& Teddy Kristiansen; Prelude to Zero Hour. 10-Zero Hour tie-in story. 11-Man-Bat. 4.00

NOTE: ***Alan Grant*** *scripts-3, 4.* ***Kelley Jones*** *c-12.* ***Mignola*** *c-3.* ***Nebres*** *a(i)-2.* ***Quesada*** *c-10.* ***Russell*** *a-7p.* ***Simonson*** *c-5.*

SHOWCASE '95

DC Comics: Jan, 1995 - No. 12, Dec, 1995 ($2.50/$2.95, limited series)

1-4-Supergirl story. 3-Eradicator-c.; The Question story. 4-Thorn c/story 4.00

5-12: 5-Thorn-c/story; begin $2.95-c. 8-Spectre story. 12-The Shade story by James Robinson & Wade Von Grawbadger; Maitresse story by Claremont & Alan Davis 4.00

SHOWCASE '96

DC Comics: Jan, 1996 - No. 12, Dec, 1996 ($2.95, limited series)

1-12: 1-Steve Geppi cameo. 3-Black Canary & Lois Lane-c/story; Deadman story by Jamie Delano & Wade Von Grawbadger, Gary Frank-c. 4-Firebrand & Guardian-c/story; The Shade & Dr. Fate "Times Past" story by James Robinson & Matt Smith begins, ends #5. 6-Superboy-c/app.; Atom app.; Capt. Marvel (Mary Marvel)-c/app. 8-Supergirl by David & Dodson. 11-Scare Tactics app. 11,12-Legion of Super-Heroes vs. Brainiac. 12-Jesse Quick app. 4.00

SHOWCASE PRESENTS...

(B&W archive reprints of DC Silver Age stories)

DC Comics: 2005 - 2011 ($9.99/$16.99/$17.99/$19.99, B&W, over 500 pgs., squarebound)

Adam Strange Vol. 1 (2007, $16.99) r/Showcase #17-19 & Mystery in Space #53-84 17.00
Ambush Bug (2009, $16.99) r/first app. in DC Comics Presents #52 other early app. 17.00
Aquaman Vol. 1 (2007, $16.99) r/Aquaman #1-6 & other early app. 17.00
Aquaman Vol. 2 (2008, $16.99) r/Aquaman #7-23 & other early app. 17.00
Aquaman Vol. 3 (2009, $16.99) r/Aquaman #24-39 & other early app. 17.00
The Atom Vol. 1 (2007, $16.99) r/Showcase #34-36 & The Atom #1-17 17.00
The Atom Vol. 2 (2008, $16.99) r/The Atom #18-38 17.00
Batgirl Vol. 1 (2007, $16.99) r/early apps. from Detective #359 (1967) thru 1975 17.00
Bat Lash Vol. 1 (2009, $9.99) r/#1-7, Showcase #76, DC Special Series #16, and Jonah Hex #49,51,52 10.00
Batman Vol. 1 (2006, $16.99) r/"new look" from Detective #327-342, Batman #164-174 17.00
Batman Vol. 2 (2007, $16.99) r/"new look" from Detective #343-358, Batman #175-188 17.00
Batman Vol. 3 (2008, $16.99) r/"new look" from Detective #359-375, Batman #189, 190-192,194-197,199-202 17.00
Batman and the Outsiders Vol. 1 (2007, $16.99) r/#1-19, Annual #1; Brave and the Bold #200; and New Teen Titans #37 17.00
Blackhawk Vol. 1 (2008, $16.99) r/#108-127 17.00

Showcase Presents Metamorpho Vol. 1 © DC

Shrek #2 © Dreamworks

Shuri #8 © MAR

	GD 2.0	VG 4.0	FN 6.0	VF 8.0	VF/NM 9.0	NM- 9.2

Booster Gold Vol. 1 (2008, $16.99) r/#1-25 & Action Comics #594 17.00
The Brave and the Bold Batman Team-ups Vol. 1 (2007, $16.99) r/#59,64,67-71,74-87 17.00
The Brave and the Bold Batman Team-ups Vol. 2 (2007, $16.99) r/#88-108 17.00
The Brave and the Bold Batman Team-ups Vol. 3 (2008, $16.99) r/#109-134 17.00
Challengers of the Unknown Vol. 1 (2006, $16.99) r/#1-17 & Showcase #6,7,11,12 17.00
Challengers of the Unknown Vol. 2 (2008, $16.99) r/#18-37 17.00
DC Comics Presents: The Superman Team-ups Vol. 1 (2009, $17.99) r/#1-26 18.00
Dial H For Hero ('10, $9.99) r/early apps. in House of Mystery #156-173 10.00
Doc Savage ('11, $19.99) r/Doc Savage #1-8 (1975-77 Marvel B&W magazine) 20.00
The Doom Patrol Vol. 1 (2009, $16.99) r/#86-101 and My Greatest Adventure #80-85 17.00
The Doom Patrol Vol. 2 (2010, $19.99) r/#102-121 20.00
The Elongated Man Vol. 1 ('06, $16.99) r/early apps. in Flash & Detective ('60-'68) 17.00
Eclipso Vol. 1 (2009, $9.99) r/stories from House of Secrets #61-80 10.00
Enemy Ace Vol. 1 (2008, $16.99) r/Our Army at War #151 & other early app. 17.00
The Flash Vol. 1 (2007, $16.99) r/Flash Comics #104 (last G.A. issue), Showcase #4,8,13,14 & The Flash #105-119 17.00
The Flash Vol. 2 (2008, $16.99) r/The Flash #120-140 17.00
The Flash Vol. 3 (2009, $16.99) r/The Flash #141-161 17.00
The Flash, The Trial of ... (2011, $19.99) r/The Flash #323-327,329-336,340-350 20.00
The Great Disaster Featuring The Atomic Knights and Hercules Vol. 1 (2007, $16.99) 17.00
Green Arrow Vol. 1 (2006, $16.99) r/Adventure #250-269, Brave and the Bold #50,71,85; Justice League of America #4; World's Finest #95-134,136,138,140 17.00
Green Lantern Vol. 1 (2005, $9.99) r/Showcase #22-24 & Green Lantern #1-17 20.00
Green Lantern Vol. 1 (2010, $19.99) r/Showcase #22-24 & Green Lantern #1-17 20.00
Green Lantern Vol. 2 (2007, $16.99) r/Green Lantern #18-38 17.00
Green Lantern Vol. 3 (2008, $16.99) r/Green Lantern #39-59 17.00
Green Lantern Vol. 4 (2009, $16.99) r/Green Lantern #60-75 17.00
Green Lantern Vol. 5 (2011, $19.99) r/Green Lantern #76-87,89 and back up stories from Flash #217-246 20.00
Haunted Tank Vol. 1 ('06, $16.99) r/G.I. Combat #87-119, Brave & The Bold #52 and Our Army at War #155; Russ Heath-c 17.00
Haunted Tank Vol. 2 ('08, $16.99) r/G.I. Combat #120-156 17.00
Hawkman Vol. 1 ('07, $16.99) r/Brave & The Bold #34-36,42-44, Mystery in Space #87-90, Hawkman #1-11, and The Atom #7 17.00
Hawkman Vol. 2 ('08, $16.99) r/Brave & The Bold #70, Hawkman #12-27, The Atom #31, & The Atom and Hawkman #39-45 17.00
The House of Mystery Vol. 1 ('06, $16.99) r/House of Mystery #174-194 ('68-'71) 17.00
The House of Mystery Vol. 2 ('07, $16.99) r/House of Mystery #195-211 ('71-'73) 17.00
The House of Mystery Vol. 3 ('09, $16.99) r/House of Mystery #212-226 ('73-'74) 17.00
The House of Secrets Vol. 1 ('08, $16.99) r/House of Secrets #81-98 ('69-'72) 17.00
The House of Secrets Vol. 2 ('09, $17.99) r/House of Secrets #99-119 ('72-'74) 18.00
Jonah Hex Vol. 1 (2005, $16.99) r/All Star Western #10-12, Weird Western Tales #13,14, 16-33; plus the complete adventures of Outlaw from All Star Western #2-8 17.00
Justice League of America Vol. 1 ('05, $16.99) r/Brave & the Bold #28-30, J.L. of A. #1-16 and Mystery in Space #75 17.00
Justice League of America Vol. 2 ('07, $16.99) r/Justice League of America #17-36 17.00
Justice League of America Vol. 3 ('07, $16.99) r/Justice League of America #37-60 17.00
Justice League of America Vol. 4 ('09, $16.99) r/Justice League of America #61-83 17.00
Justice League of America Vol. 5 ('11, $19.99) r/Justice League of America #84-106 20.00
Legion of Super-Heroes Vol. 1 ('07, $16.99) r/Adventure #247 & early app. thru 1964 17.00
Legion of Super-Heroes Vol. 2 ('08, $16.99) r/app. in Adventure & Superboy 1964-66 17.00
Legion of Super-Heroes Vol. 3 ('09, $16.99) r/Adventure #349-368 & S.P. Jimmy Olsen #106 17.00
Legion of Super-Heroes Vol. 4 ('10, $19.99) r/app. in Adv., Action & Superboy 1968-72 20.00
Martian Manhunter Vol. 1 (2007, $16.99) r/Detective #225-304 & Batman #78 (prototype) 17.00
Martian Manhunter Vol. 2 ('09, $16.99) r/Detective #305-326 & House of Myst. #143-173 17.00
Metal Men Vol. 1 (2007, $16.99) r/#1-16; Brave & Bold #55, Showcase #37-40 17.00
Metamorpho Vol. 1 ('05, $16.99) r/Brave&Bold #57,58,66,68; Metamorpho #1-17;JLA #42 17.00
Our Army at War Vol. 1 ('10, $19.99) r/#1-20 20.00
Phantom Stranger Vol. 1 (2006, $16.99) r/#1-21 (2nd series) & Showcase #80 17.00
Phantom Stranger Vol. 2 (2008, $16.99) r/#22-41 and various 1970-1978 appearances 17.00
Robin The Boy Wonder Vol. 1 (2007, $16.99) r/back-ups from Batman, Detective, WF 17.00
Secrets of Sinister House ('10, $17.99) r/#5-18 and Sinister House of Secret Love #1-4 18.00
Sgt. Rock Vol. 1 ('07, $16.99) r/G.I. Combat #68, Our Army at War #81-117 17.00
Sgt. Rock Vol. 2 ('08, $16.99) r/Our Army at War #118-148 17.00
Sgt. Rock Vol. 3 ('10, $19.99) r/Our Army at War #149-163,165-172,174-176,178-180 20.00
Shazam! Vol. 1 ('06, $16.99) r/#1-33 17.00
Strange Adventures Vol. 1 ('08, $16.99) r/#54-73 17.00
Supergirl Vol. 1 ('07, $16.99) r/prototype from Superman #123 (8/58); 1st app. Action #252 (5/59) and early appearances thru Nov. 1961 17.00
Supergirl Vol. 2 ('08, $16.99) r/appearances in Action Comics #283-321 (1961-1965) 17.00
Superman Vol. 1 ('05, $9.99) r/Action #241-257 & Superman #122-134 (1958-59) 20.00
Superman Vol. 1 ('10, $19.99) r/Action #241-257 & Superman #122-134 (1958-59) 20.00
Superman Vol. 2 ('06, $16.99) r/Action #258-275 & Superman #134-145 (1959-61) 17.00
Superman Vol. 3 ('07, $16.99) r/Action #279-292 & Superman #146-156 & Annual #3,4 17.00
Superman Vol. 4 ('08, $16.99) r/Action #293-309 & Superman #157-166 (1962-64) 17.00
Superman Family Vol. 1 ('06, $16.99) Superman's Pal, Jimmy Olsen #1-22; Showcase #9 and Superman #22 17.00
Superman Family Vol. 2 ('08, $16.99) Superman's Pal, Jimmy Olsen #23-34; Showcase #10 and Superman's Girl Friend, Lois Lane #1-7 17.00
Superman Family Vol. 3 ('09, $16.99) Superman's Pal, Jimmy Olsen #35-44 and Superman's Girl Friend, Lois Lane #8-16 17.00
Teen Titans Vol. 1 ('06, $16.99) r/#1-18; Brave & the Bold #54,60; Showcase #59 17.00
Teen Titans Vol. 2 ('07, $16.99) r/#19-37, World's Finest #205 and Brave & Bold #83,94 17.00
The Unknown Soldier Vol. 1 ('06, $16.99) r/Star Spangled War Stories #158-188 17.00
The War That Time Forgot Vol. 1 ('07, $16.99) r/S.S.W.S. #90,92,94-125,127,128 17.00
Warlord Vol. 1 ('09, $16.99) r/#1-28 and debut in 1st Issue Special #1 17.00
The Witching Hour Vol. 1 ('11, $19.99) r/#1-19 20.00
Wonder Woman Vol. 1 ('07, $16.99) r/#98-117 17.00
Wonder Woman Vol. 2 ('08, $16.99) r/#118-137 17.00
World's Finest Vol. 1 ('07, $16.99) r/#71-111 & Superman #76 17.00
World's Finest Vol. 2 ('08, $16.99) r/#112-145 17.00
World's Finest Vol. 3 ('10, $17.99) r/#146-160,162-169,171-173 ('64-'68) 18.00

SHOWGIRLS (Formerly Sherry the Showgirl #3)
Atlas Comics (MPC No. 2): No. 4, 2/57; June, 1957 - No. 2, Aug, 1957

	GD 2.0	VG 4.0	FN 6.0	VF 8.0	VF/NM 9.0	NM- 9.2
4-(2/57) Dan DeCarlo-c/a begins	81	162	243	518	884	1250
1-(6/57) Millie, Sherry, Chili, Pearl & Hazel begin	87	174	261	553	952	1350
2	48	96	144	302	514	725

SHREK (Movie)
Dark Horse Comics: Sept, 2003 - No. 3, Dec, 2003 ($2.99, limited series)

1-3-Takes place after 1st movie; Evanier-s/Bachs-a; CGI cover 4.00

SHREK (Movie)
Ape Entertainment: 2010 - No. 4, 2011 ($3.95, limited series)

1-3-Short stories by various 4.00

SHROUD, THE (See Super-Villain Team-Up #5)
Marvel Comics: Mar, 1994 - No. 4, June, 1994 ($1.75, mini-series)

1-4: 1,2,4-Spider-Man & Scorpion app. 4.00

SHROUD OF MYSTERY
Whitman Publications: June, 1982

	GD 2.0	VG 4.0	FN 6.0	VF 8.0	VF/NM 9.0	NM- 9.2
1	1	2	3	4	5	7

SHRUGGED
Aspen MLT, Inc.: No. 0, June, 2006 - No. 8, Feb, 2009 ($2.50/$2.99)

0-($2.50) Turner & Mastromauro-s/Gunnell-a; intro. story and character profiles 3.00
1-8-($2.99) 1-Six covers. 2-Three covers 3.00
... : Beginnings (5/06, $1.99) Prequel intro. to Ange and Dev; Gunnell-a; development art 3.00
Volume 2 (3/13, $1.00) 1-Marks & Gunnell-a; multiple covers 3.00
V2 #2-6-($3.99) Mastromauro-s/Marks-a. 6-(2/18) 4.00
Volume 3 (2/18, $3.99) 1-4-Mastromauro-s/André Risso-a; multiple covers 4.00

SHURI (From Black Panther)
Marvel Comics: Dec, 2018 - No. 10, Sept, 2019 ($3.99)

	GD 2.0	VG 4.0	FN 6.0	VF 8.0	VF/NM 9.0	NM- 9.2
1-Nnedi Okorafor-s/Leonardo Romero-a	2	4	6	11	16	20
2-Rocket & Groot app.; Okorafor-s/Romero-a	2	4	6	9	12	15

3-10: 3-5-Okorafor-s/Romero-a. 3-Rocket & Groot app. 6,7-Miles Morales app.; Ayala-s/Davidson-a. 8-10-Shuri in the Black Panther costume 6.00

SHUTTER
Image Comics: Apr, 2014 - No. 30, Jul, 2017 ($3.50/$3.99)

1-11-Keatinge-s/Del Duca-a 3.50
12-30-($3.99) 4.00

SHUT UP AND DIE
Image Comics/Halloween: 1998 - No. 3, 1998 ($2.95,B&W, bi-monthly)

1-3: Hudnall-s 3.00

SICK (Sick Special #131) (Magazine) (Satire)
Feature Publ./Headline Publ./Crestwood Publ. Co./Hewfred Publ./ Pyramid Comm./ Charlton Publ. No. 109 (4/76) on: Aug, 1960 - No. 134, Fall, 1980

	GD 2.0	VG 4.0	FN 6.0	VF 8.0	VF/NM 9.0	NM- 9.2
V1#1-Jack Paar photo on-c; Torres-a; Untouchables-s; Ben Hur movie photo-s	14	28	42	98	217	335
2-Torres-a; Elvis app.; Lenny Bruce app.	9	18	27	62	126	190
3-5-Torres-a in all. 3-Khruschev-c; Hitler-s. 4-Newhart-s; Castro-s; John Wayne. 5-JFK/Castro-c; Elvis pin-up; Hitler.	8	16	24	55	105	155
6-Photo-s of Ricky Nelson & Marilyn Monroe; JFK	9	18	27	57	111	165

V2#1,2,4-8 (#7,8,10-14): 1-(#7) Hitler-s; Brando photo-s. 2-(#8) Dick Clark-s. 4-(#10) Untouchables-c; Candid Camera-s. 5-(#11) Nixon-c; Lone Ranger-s; JFK-s. 6-(#12) Beatnik-c/s. 8-(#14) Liz Taylor pin-up, JFK-s; Dobie Gillis-s; Sinatra & Dean Martin photo-s

Sick #43 © Prize

Sidekick #9 © Studio JMS

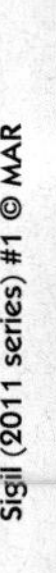
Sigil (2011 series) #1 © MAR

	GD 2.0	VG 4.0	FN 6.0	VF 8.0	VF/NM 9.0	NM- 9.2
	8	16	24	51	96	140
3-(#9) Marilyn Monroe/JFK-c; Kingston Trio-s	8	16	24	55	105	155
V3#1-7(#15-21): 1-(#15) JFK app.; Liz Tayor/Richard Burton-s. 2-(#16) Ben Casey/ Frankenstein-c/s; Hitler photo-s. 5-(#19) Nixon back-c/s; Sinatra photo-s. 6-(#20) 1st Huckleberry Fink-c	5	10	15	33	57	80
8-(#22) Cassius Clay vs. Liston-s; 1st Civil War Blackouts-/Pvt. Bo Reargard w/ Jack Davis-a	5	10	15	35	63	90
V4#1-5 (#23-27): Civil War Blackouts-/Pvt. Bo Reargard w/ Jack Davis-a in all. 1-(#23) Smokey Bear-c; Tarzan-s. 2-(#24) Goldwater & Paar-s; Castro-s. 3-(#25) Frankenstein-c; Cleopatra/Liz Taylor-s; Steve Reeves photo-s. 4-(#26) James Bond-s; Hitler-s. 5-(#27) Taylor/Burton pin-up; Sinatra, Martin, Andress, Ekberg photo-s	4	8	12	27	44	60
28,31,36,39: 31-Pink Panther movie photo-s; Burke's Law-s. 39-Westerns; Elizabeth Montgomery photo-s; Beat mag-s	4	8	12	23	37	50
29,34,37,38: 29-Beatles-c by Jack Davis. 34-Two pg. Beatles-s & photo pin-up. 37-Playboy parody issue. 38-Addams Family-s	4	8	12	27	44	60
30,32,35,40: 30-Beatles photo pin-up; James Bond photo-s. 32-Ian Fleming-s; LBJ-s; Tarzan-s. 35-Beatles cameo; Three Stooges parody. 40-Tarzan-s; Crosby/Hope-s; Beatles parody	4	8	12	28	47	65
33-Ringo Starr photo-c & spoof on "A Hard Day's Night"; inside-c has Beatles photos	5	10	15	35	63	90
41,50,51,53,54,60: 41-Sports Illustrated parody-c/s. 50-Mod issue; flip-c w/1967 calendar w/Bob Taylor-a. 51-Get Smart-s. 53-Beatles cameo; nudity panels. 54-Monkees-c. 60-TV Daniel Boone-s	3	6	9	19	30	40
42-Fighting American-c revised from Simon/Kirby-c; "Good girl" art by Sparling; profile on Bob Powell; superhero parodies	5	10	15	33	57	80
43-49,52,55-59: 43-Sneaker set begins by Sparling. 45-Has #44 on-c & #45 on inside; TV Westerns-s; Beatles cameo. 46-Hell's Angels-s; NY Mets-s. 47-UFO/Space-c. 49-Men's Adventure mag. parody issue; nudity. 52-LBJ-s. 55-Underground culture special. 56-Alfred E. Neuman-c; inventors issue. 58-Hippie issue-c/s. 59-Hippie-s	3	6	9	16	24	32
61-64,66-69,71,73,75-80: 63-Tiny Tim-c & poster; Monkees-s. 64-Flip-c. 66-Flip-c; Mod Squad-s. 69-Beatles cameo; Peter Sellers photo-s. 71-Flip-c; Clint Eastwood-s. 76-Nixon-s; Marcus Welby-s. 78-Ma Barker-s; Courtship of Eddie's Father-s; Abbie Hoffman-s	3	6	9	15	22	28
65,70,74: 65-Cassius Clay/Brando/J. Wayne-c; Johnny Carson-s. 70-(9/69) John & Yoko-c, 1/2 pg. story. 74-Clay, Agnew, Namath & others as superheroes-c/s; Easy Rider-s; Ghost and Mrs. Muir-s	3	6	9	16	24	32
72-(84 pgs.) Xmas issue w/2 pg. slick color poster; Tarzan-s; 2 pg. Superman & superheroes-s	3	6	9	21	33	45
81-85,87-95,98,99: 81-(2/71) Woody Allen photo-s. 85 Monster Mag. parody-s; Nixon-s w/Ringo & John cameo. 88-Klute photo-s; Nixon paper dolls page. 92-Lily Tomlin; Archie Bunker pin-up. 93-Woody Allen	2	4	6	13	18	22
86,96,97,100: 86-John & Yoko, Tiny Tim-c; Love Story movie photo-s. 96-Kung Fu-c; Mummy-s, Dracula & Frankenstein app. 97-Superman-s; 1974 Calendar; Charlie Brown & Snoopy pin-up. 100-Serpico-s; Cosell-s; Jacques Cousteau-s	3	6	9	14	19	24
101-103,105-114,116,119,120: 101-Three Musketeers-s; Dick Tracy-s. 102-Young Frankenstein-s. 103-Kojak-s; Evel Knievel-s. 105-Towering Inferno-s; Peanuts/Snoopy-s. 106-Cher-c/s. 10 7-Jaws-c/s. 108-Pink Panther-c/s; Archie-s. 109-Adam & Eve-s(nudity). 110-Welcome Back Kotter-s. 111-Sonny & Cher-s. 112-King Kong-c/s. 120-Star Trek-s	2	4	6	9	13	16
104,115,117,118: 104-Muhammad Ali-c/s. 115-Charlie's Angels-s. 117-Bionic Woman & Six Million $ Man-c/s; Cher D'Flower begins by Sparling (nudity). 118-Star Wars-s; Popeye-s	2	4	6	11	16	20
121-125,128-130: 122-Darth Vader-s. 123-Jaws II-s. 128-Superman-c/movie parody. 130-Alien movie-s	2	4	6	10	14	18
126,127: 126-(68 pgs.) Battlestar Galactica-c/s; Star Wars-s; Wonder Woman-s. 127-Mork & Mindy-s; Lord of the Rings-s	2	4	6	13	18	22
131-(1980 Special) Star Wars/Star Trek/Flash Gordon wraparound-c/s; Superman parody; Battlestar Galactica-s	3	6	9	14	19	24
132,133: 132-1980 Election-c/s; Apocalypse Now-s. 133-Star Trek-s; Chips-s; Superheroes page	2	4	6	13	18	22
134 (scarce)(68 pg. Giant)-Star Wars-c; Alien-s; WKRP-s; Mork & Mindy-s; Taxi-s; MASH-s	4	8	12	19	30	40
Annual 1- Birthday Annual (1966)-3 pg. Huckleberry Fink fold out	4	8	12	23	37	50
Annual 2- 7th Annual Yearbook (1967)-Davis-c, 2 pg. glossy poster insert	4	8	12	23	37	50
Annual 3 (1968) "Big Sick Laff-in" on-c (84 pgs.)-w/psychedelic posters; Frankenstein poster	3	6	9	17	26	35
Annual 1969 "Great Big Fat Annual Sick", 1969 "9th Year Annual Sick", 1970, 1971	3	6	9	16	24	32
Annual 12,13-(1972,1973, 84 pgs.) 13-Monster-c	3	6	9	16	24	32
Annual 14,15-(1974,1975, 84 pgs.) 14-Hitler photo-s	3	6	9	16	24	32
Annual 2-4 (1980)	2	4	6	9	13	16
Special 1 (1980) Buck Rogers-c/s; MASH-s	3	6	9	14	19	24
Special 2 (1980) Wraparound Star Wars: Empire Strikes Back-c; Charlie's Angels/Farrah-s; Rocky-s; plus reprints	3	6	9	14	19	24
Yearbook 15(1975, 84 pgs.) Paul Revere-c	3	6	9	16	23	30

NOTE: ***Davis*** *a-42, 87; c-22, 23, 25, 29, 31, 32.* ***Powell*** *a-7, 31, 57.* ***Simon*** *a-1-3, 10, 41, 42, 87, 99; c-1, 47, 57, 59, 69, 91, 95-97, 99, 100, 102, 107, 112.* ***Torres*** *a-1-3, 29, 31, 47, 49.* ***Tuska*** *a-14, 41-43. Civil War Blackouts-23, 24. #42 has biography of Bob Powell.*

SIDEKICK (Paul Jenkins'...)
Image Comics (Desperado): June, 2006 - No. 5, May, 2007 ($3.50, limited series)

1-5-Paul Jenkins-s/Chris Moreno-a 3.50
... Super Summer Sidekick Spectacular 1 (7/07, $2.99) 3.50
... Super Summer Sidekick Spectacular 2 (9/07, $3.50) 3.50

SIDEKICK
Image Comics (Joe's Comics): Aug, 2013 - No. 12, Dec, 2015 ($2.99)

1-7,9-12: 1-Straczynski-a/Mandrake-a; intro. The Cowl and Flyboy; 6 covers. 4-6-Two covers 3.00
8-($3.99) Chrome-c 4.00

SIDEKICKS
Fanboy Ent., Inc.: Jun, 2000 - No. 3, Apr, 2001 ($2.75, B&W, lim. series)

1-3-J.Torres-s/Takesi Miyazawa-a. 3-Variant-c by Wieringo 3.00
...: Super Fun Summer Special (Oni Press, 7/03, $2.99) art by various incl. Wieringo 3.00
...: The Substitute (Oni Press, 7/02, $2.95) 3.00
...: The Transfer Student TPB (Oni Press, 6/02, $8.95, 9" x 6") r/#1-3 9.00
...: The Transfer Student TPB 2nd Ed. (10/03, $11.95, 9" x 6") r/#1-3; The Substitute 12.00

SIDESHOW
Avon Periodicals: 1949 (one-shot)

	GD 2.0	VG 4.0	FN 6.0	VF 8.0	VF/NM 9.0	NM- 9.2
1-(Rare)-Similar to Bachelor's Diary	142	284	426	909	1555	2200

SIDEWAYS (Follows events from Dark Nights: Metal)
DC Comics: Apr, 2018 - No. 13, Apr, 2019 ($2.99)

1-13: 1-Didio-s/Rocafort-a; intro Derek James 4.00
Annual 1 (1/19, $4.99) Takes place after #9; New 52 Superman & Seven Soldiers app. 5.00

SIEGE
Marvel Comics: Mar, 2010 - No. 4, Jun, 2010 ($3.99, limited series)

1-4-Asgard is invaded; Bendis-s/Coipel-a. 4-End of The Sentry 4.00
1-4-Variant covers by Dell'Otto 8.00
...: Captain America (6/10, $2.99) Gage-s/Dallocchio-a/Djurdjevic-c; both Caps app. 4.00
...: Loki (6/10, $2.99) Gillen-s/McKelvie-a/Djurdjevic-c; Hela & Mephisto app. 4.00
...: Secret Warriors (6/10, $2.99) Hickman-s/Vitti-a/Djurdjevic-c; Phobos attacks 4.00
...: Spider-Man (6/10, $2.99) Reed-s/Santucci-a/Djurdjevic-c; Venom & Ms. Marvel app. 4.00
...: Storming Asgard - Heroes & Villains (3/10, $3.99) Dossiers on participants; Land-c 4.00
...: The Cabal (2/10, $3.99) series prelude; Bendis-s/Lark-a; covers by Finch & Davis 4.00
...: Young Avengers (6/10, $2.99) McKeever-s/Asrar-a/Djurdjevic-c; Wrecking Crew app. 4.00

SIEGE (Secret Wars tie-in) (Continued from Secret Wars: Journal #1)
Marvel Comics: Sept, 2015 - No. 4, Dec, 2015 ($3.99, limited series)

1-4-Gillen-s/Andrade-a; Abigail Brand, Kate Bishop & Ms. America app. 4.00

SIEGE: EMBEDDED
Marvel Comics: Mar, 2010 - No. 4, Jul, 2010 ($3.99, limited series)

1-4-Reed-s/Samnee-a/Granov-c; Ben Urich & Volstagg cover the invasion 4.00

SIEGEL AND SHUSTER: DATELINE 1930s
Eclipse Comics: Nov, 1984 - No. 2, Sept, 1985 ($1.50/$1.75, Baxter paper #1)

1,2: 1-Unpublished samples of strips from the '30s; includes 'Interplanetary Police'; Shuster-c. 2 ($1.75, B&W)-unpublished strips; Shuster-c 4.00

SIF (See Thor titles)
Marvel Comics: Jun, 2010 ($3.99, one shot)

1-Deconnick-s/Stegman-a/Foreman-c; Beta Ray Bill app. 4.00

SIGIL (Also see CrossGen Chronicles)
CrossGeneration Comics: Jul, 2000 - No. 43, Jan, 2004 ($2.95)

1-43: 1-Barbara Kesel-s/Ben & Ray Lai-a. 12-Waid-s begin. 21-Chuck Dixon-s begin 3.00

SIGIL
Marvel Comics: May, 2011 - No. 4, Aug, 2011 ($2.99)

1-4-Carey-s/Kirk-a 3.00
1-Variant-c by McGuinness 5.00

SIGMA
Image Comics (WildStorm): March, 1996 - No. 3, June, 1996 ($2.50, limited series)

1-3: 1-"Fire From Heaven" prelude #2; Coker-a. 2-"Fire From Heaven" pt. 6.

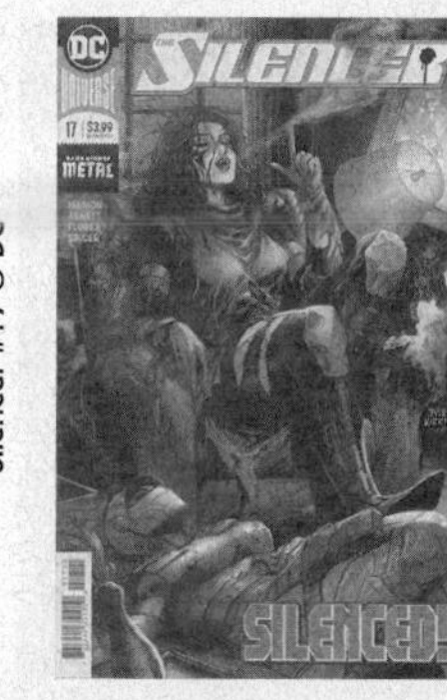

Silencer #17 © DC

Silly Tunes #4 © MAR

Silver Sable and the Wild Pack #36 © MAR

GD VG FN VF VF/NM NM-
2.0 4.0 6.0 8.0 9.0 9.2

3-"Fire From Heaven" pt. 14. 3.00

SILENCER, THE
DC Comics: Mar, 2018 - No. 18, Aug, 2019 ($2.99/$3.99)
1-12: 1-Abnett-s/Romita Jr.-a; intro. Honor Guest; Talia al Ghul app. 3-6-Deathstroke app. 4-8-Bogdanovic-a 3.00
13-18-($3.99): 13-Origin of Silencer; Talia al Ghul app.; Marion-a/Kirkham-c 4.00

SILENT DRAGON
DC Comics (WildStorm): Sept, 2005 - No. 6, Feb, 2006 ($2.99, limited series)
1-6-Tokyo 2066 A.D.; Leinil Yu-a/c; Andy Diggle-s 3.00
TPB (2006, $19.99) r/series; sketch page 20.00

SILENT HILL: DEAD/ALIVE
IDW Publishing: Dec, 2005 - No. 5, Apr, 2006 ($3.99, limited series)
1-5-Stakal-a/Ciencin-s. 1-Four covers. 2-5-Two covers 4.00

SILENT HILL DOWNPOUR: ANNE'S STORY
IDW Publishing: Aug, 2014 - No. 4, Nov, 2014 ($3.99, limited series)
1-4-Tom Waltz-s/Tristan Jones-a; two covers on each 4.00

SILENT HILL: DYING INSIDE
IDW Publishing: Feb, 2004 - No. 5, June, 2004 ($3.99, limited series)
1-5-Based on the Konami computer game. 1-Templesmith-a; Ashley Wood-c 4.00
...: Paint It Black (2/05, $7.49) Ciencin-s/Thomas-a 7.50
...: The Grinning Man 5/05, $7.49) Ciencin-s/Stakal-a 7.50
TPB (8/04, $19.99) r/#1-5; Ashley Wood-c 20.00

SILENT HILL: PAST LIFE
IDW Publishing: Oct, 2010 - No. 4, Jan, 2011 ($3.99, limited series)
1-4-Waltz-s; two covers on each 4.00

SILENT HILL: SINNER'S REWARD
IDW Publishing: Feb, 2008 - No. 4, Apr, 2008 ($3.99, limited series)
1-4-Waltz-s/Stamb-a 4.00

SILENT INVASION, THE
Rengade Press: Apr, 1986 - No.12, Mar, 1988 ($1.70/$2.00, B&W)
1-12-UFO sightings of the '50's 3.00
Book 1- reprints ($7.95) 8.00

SILENT MOBIUS
Viz Select Comics: 1991 - No. 5, 1992 ($4.95, color, squarebound, 44 pgs.)
1-5: Japanese stories translated to English 5.00

SILENT SCREAMERS (Based on the Aztech Toys figures)
Image Comics: Oct, 2000 ($4.95)
Nosferatu Issue - Alex Ross front & back-c 5.00

SILENT WAR
Marvel Comics: Mar, 2007 - No. 6, Aug, 2007 ($2.99, limited series)
1-6-Inhumans, Black Bolt and Fantastic Four app.; Hine-s/Irving-a/Watson-c 3.00
TPB (2007, $14.99) r/series 15.00

SILK (See Amazing Spider-Man 2014 series #1 & #4 for debut)
Marvel Comics: Apr, 2015 - No. 7, Nov, 2015 ($3.99)
1-Robbie Thompson-s/Stacey Lee-a/Dave Johnson-c; Spider-Man app. 2 4 6 10 14 18
2-7: 3-6-Black Cat app. 4-Fantastic Four app. 7-Secret Wars tie-in 4.00

SILK (Spider-Man)
Marvel Comics: Jan, 2016 - No. 19, Jun, 2017 ($3.99)
1-19: 1-Robbie Thompson-s/Stacey Lee-a; Black Cat & Mockingbird app. 4,5-Fish-a. 7,8-"Spider-Women" tie-in; Spider-Woman & Spider-Gwen app. 14-17-Clone Conspiracy 4.00

SILKE
Dark Horse Comics: Jan, 2001 - No. 4, Sept, 2001 ($2.95)
1-4-Tony Daniel-s/a 3.00

SILKEN GHOST
CrossGen Comics: June, 2003 - No. 5, Oct, 2003 ($2.95, limited series)
1-5-Dixon-s/Rosado-a 3.00
Traveler Vol. 1 (2003, $9.95) digest-sized reprint #1-5 10.00

SILLY PILLY (See Frank Luther's...)

SILLY SYMPHONIES (See Dell Giants)

SILLY TUNES
Timely Comics: Fall, 1945 - No. 7, June, 1947
1-Silly Seal, Ziggy Pig begin 32 64 96 190 310 430
2-(2/46) 18 36 54 107 169 230
3-7: 6-New logo 15 30 45 92 144 195

SILVER (See Lone Ranger's Famous Horse...)

SILVER AGE
DC Comics: July, 2000 ($3.95, limited series)
1-Waid-s/Dodson-a; "Silver Age" style x-over; JLA & villains switch bodies 4.00
...: Challengers of the Unknown ($2.50) Joe Kubert-c; vs. Chronos 3.00
...: Dial H For Hero ($2.50) Jim Mooney-c; Waid-s/Kitson-a; vs. Martian Manhunter 3.00
...: Doom Patrol ($2.50) Ramona Fradon-c/Peyer-s 3.00
...: Flash ($2.50) Carmine Infantino-c; Kid Flash and Elongated Man app. 3.00
...: Green Lantern ($2.50) Gil Kane-c/Busiek-s/Anderson-a; vs. Sinestro 3.00
...: Justice League of America ($2.50) Ty Templeton-c; Millar-s/Kolins-a 3.00
...: Showcase ($2.50) Dick Giordano-c/a; Johns-s; Batgirl, Adam Strange app. 3.00
... Secret Files ($4.95) Intro. Agamemno; short stories & profile pages 5.00
...: Teen Titans ($2.50) Nick Cardy-c; vs. Penguin, Mr. Element, Black Manta 3.00
...: The Brave and the Bold ($2.50) Jim Aparo-c; Batman & Metal Men 3.00
... 80-Page Giant ($5.95) Conclusion of x-over; "lost" Silver Age stories 6.00

SILVERBACK
Comico: 1989 - No. 3, 1990 ($2.50, color, limited series, mature readers)
1-3: Character from Grendel: Matt Wagner-a 3.00

SILVERBLADE
DC Comics: Sept, 1987 - No. 12, Sept, 1988
1-12: Colan-c/a in all 4.00

SILVER CEREBUS
Aardvark-Vanaheim: Feb, 2020 ($4.00, B&W, one-shot)
1-Cerebus figures placed over outer space backgrounds; Silver Surfer #1-c swipe 4.00

SILVERHAWKS
Star Comics/Marvel Comics #6: Aug, 1987 - No. 6, June, 1988 ($1.00)
1-6 4.00

SILVERHEELS
Pacific Comics: Dec, 1983 - No. 3, May, 1984 ($1.50)
1-3-Bruce Jones-s, Scott Hampton-c/a; Steacy-a in back-up stories 4.00

SILVER KID WESTERN
Key/Stanmor Publications: Oct, 1954 - No. 5, July, 1955
1 11 22 33 62 86 110
2 7 14 21 35 43 50
3-5 6 12 18 29 36 42
I.W. Reprint #1,2-Severin-c: 1-r/#? 2-r/#1 2 4 6 8 11 14

SILVER SABLE AND THE WILD PACK (See Amazing Spider-Man #265 and Sable & Fortune)
Marvel Comics: June, 1992 - No. 35, Apr, 1995; No. 36, Jan, 2018 ($1.25/$1.50)
1-($2.00)-Embossed & foil stamped-c; Spider-Man app. 4.00
2-24,26-35: 4,5-Dr. Doom-c/story. 6,7-Deathlok-c/story. 9-Origin Silver Sable. 10-Punisher-c/s. 15-Capt. America-c/s. 16,17-Intruders app. 18,19-Venom-c/s. 19-Siege of Darkness x-over. 23-Daredevil (in new costume) & Deadpool app. 24-Bound-in card sheet. Li'l Sylvie backup story 3.00
25-($2.00, 52 pgs.)-Li'l Sylvie backup story 4.00
36-(1/18, $3.99) Marvel Legacy one-shot; Faust-s/Siqueira-a 4.00

SILVER STAR (Also see Jack Kirby's...)
Pacific Comics: Feb, 1983 - No. 6, Jan, 1984 ($1.00)
1-6: 1-1st app. Last of the Viking Heroes. 1-5-Kirby-c/a. 2-Ditko-a 5.00
...: Graphite Edition TPB (TwoMorrows Publ., 3/06, $19.95) r/series in B&W including Kirby's original pencils; sketch pages; original screenplay 20.00
Jack Kirby's Silver Star, Volume 1 HC (Image Comics, 2007, $34.99) r/series in color; sketch pages; original screenplay 35.00

SILVER STREAK COMICS (Crime Does Not Pay #22 on)
Your Guide Publs. No. 1-7/New Friday Publs. No. 8-17/Comic House Publ./ Newsbook Publ.: Dec, 1939 - No. 21, May, 1942; No. 23, 1946; nn, Feb, 1946 (Silver logo-#1-5)
1-(Scarce)-Intro the Claw by Cole (r-in Daredevil #21), Red Reeves Boy Magician (ends #2), Captain Fearless (ends #2), The Wasp (ends #2), Mister Midnight (ends #2) begin; Spirit Man only app. Calling The Duke begins (ends #2). Barry Lane only app. Silver Metallic-c begin, end #5; Claw-c 1,2,6-8 1100 2200 3300 8400 16,200 24,000
2-The Claw ends (by Cole); makes pact w/Hitler; Simon-c/a (The Claw); ad for Marvel Mystery Comics #2 (12/39). Lance Hale begins (receives super powers). Solar Patrol app. 454 908 1362 3314 5857 8400
3-1st app. & origin Silver Streak (2nd with Lightning speed); Dickie Dean the Boy Inventor, Lance Hale, Ace Powers (ends #6), Bill Wayne The Texas Terror (ends #6) & The Planet Patrol (ends #6) begin. Detective Snoop, Sergeant Drake only app. 420 840 1260 2940 5170 7400

Silver Streak Comics #10 © LEV

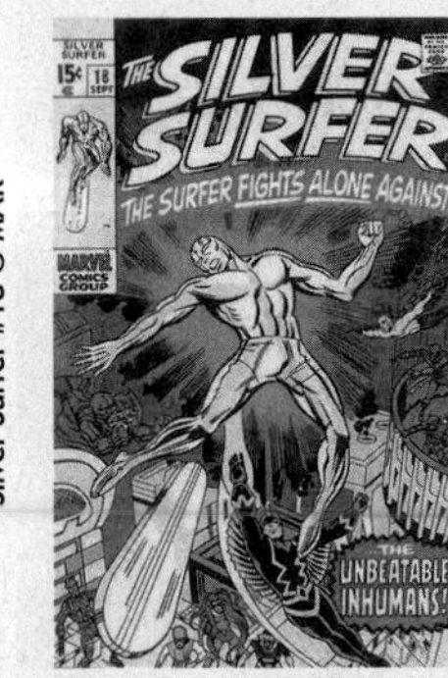

Silver Surfer #18 © MAR

Silver Surfer (2nd series) #96 © MAR

GD VG FN VF VF/NM NM-
2.0 4.0 6.0 8.0 9.0 9.2

4-Sky Wolf begins (ends #6); Silver Streak by Jack Cole (new costume); 1st app. Jackie, Lance Hale's sidekick. Lance Hale gains immortality 190 380 570 1207 2079 2950
5-Cole c/a(2); back-c ad for Claw app. in #6 225 450 675 1440 2470 3500
6-(Scarce, 9/40)-Origin & 1st app. Daredevil (blue & yellow costume) by Jack Binder; The Claw returns as the Green Claw; classic Cole Claw-c 2700 5400 8100 18,900 33,450 48,000
7-Claw vs. Daredevil serial begins c/sty, ends #11. Daredevil new costume-blue & red by Jack Cole & 3 other Cole stories (38 pgs.). Origin Whiz, S. S.'s Falcon 2nd app. Daredevil & 1st Daredevil-c (by Cole). Cloud Curtis, Presto Martin begins. Dynamo Hill & Zongar The Miracleman only app. 865 1730 2595 6315 11,158 16,000
8-Classic Claw vs. Daredevil by Cole c/sty; last Cole Silver streak. Dan Dearborn begins (ends #12). Secret Agent X-101 begins, (ends #9) 811 1622 2433 5920 10,460 15,000
9-Claw vs. Daredevil by Cole. Silver Streak-c by Bob Wood 265 530 795 1694 2897 4100
10-Origin & 1st app. Captain Battle (5/41) by Binder; Claw vs. Daredevil by Cole; Silver Streak/robot-c by Bob Wood 226 452 675 1446 2473 3500
11-Intro./origin Mercury by Bob Wood, Silver Streak's sidekick; conclusion Claw vs. Daredevil by Rico; in 'Presto Martin,' 2nd pg., newspaper says 'Roussos does it again' 181 362 543 1158 1979 2800
12-Daredevil-c by Rico; Lance Hale finds lost valley w/cave men, battles dinosaurs, sabre-toothed cats; his last app. 161 322 483 1030 1765 2500
13-Origin Thun-Dohr; Scarlet Skull (a Red Skull swipe) vs. Daredevil; Bingham Boys app. 155 310 465 992 1696 2400
14-Classic Nazi skull men-c/sty 245 490 735 1568 2684 3800
15-Classic Mummy horror-c 226 452 675 1446 2473 3500
16-(11/41) Hitler-c; Silver Streak battles Hitler sty w/classic splash page. Capt. Battle fights walking corpses 454 908 1362 3314 5857 8400
17-Last Daredevil issue. 161 322 483 1030 1765 2500
18-The Saint begins (2/42, 1st app.) by Leslie Charteris (see Movie Comics #2 by DC); The Saint-c 148 296 444 947 1624 2300
19,20 (1942)-Ned of the Navy app. 19-Silver Streak ends. 20-Japanese WWII-c/sty; last Captain Battle, Dickie Dean, Cloud Curtis; Red Reed, Alonzo Appleseed only app.; Wolverton's Scoop Scuttle app. 71 142 213 454 777 1100
21-(5/42)-Hitler app. in strip on cover; Wolverton's Scoop Scuttle app. 100 200 300 640 1095 1550
nn(#22, 2/46, 60 pgs.)(Newsbook Publ.)-R-/S.S. story from #4-7 by Jack Cole plus 2 Captain Fearless stories-r from #1&2, all in color; bondage/torture-c by Dick Briefer w/torture meter 343 686 1029 2400 4200 6000
23 (nd, 11/1946?, 52 pgs.)(An Atomic Comic) bondage-c, Silver Streak c/sty 106 212 318 618 1164 1650

NOTE: **Jack Binder** *a-8-12, 15; c-3, 4, 13-15, 17.* **Dick Briefer** *a-9-20; c-nn(#22).* **Jack Cole** *a-(Claw)-#2, 3, 6-10, nn(#22). (Daredevil)-#6-10, (Dickie Dean)-#3-10, (Pirate Prince)-#7, (Silver Streak)-#4-8, nn; c-5 (Silver Streak), 6 (Claw), 7, 8 (Daredevil).* **Bill Everett** *Red Reed begins #20.* **Fred Guardineer** *a-#8-12.* **Don Rico** *a-11-17 (Daredevil), 15, 19 (Silver Streak); c-11, 12, 16.* **Joe Simon** *a-2 (Solar Patrol), 3 (Silver Streak); c-2.* **Basil Wolverton** *a-20, 21.* **Bob Wood** *a-8-15 (Presto Martin), 9 (Silver Streak); c-9, 10. Captain Battle c-11, 13-15, 17. Claw c-#1, 2, 6-8. Daredevil c-7, 8, 12. Dickie Dean c-19. Ned of the Navy c-20 (war). The Saint c-18. Silver Streak c-5, 10, 16, nn(#22), 23.*

SILVER STREAK COMICS (Homage with Golden Age size and Golden Age art styles)
Image Comics: No. 24, Dec, 2009 ($3.99, one-shot)

24-New Daredevil, Claw, Silver Streak & Captain Battle stories; Larsen, Grist, Gilbert-a 5.00

SILVER SURFER (See Fantastic Four, Fantasy Masterpieces V2#1, Fireside Book Series, Marvel Graphic Novel, Marvel Presents #8, Marvel's Greatest Comics & Tales To Astonish #92)

SILVER SURFER, THE (Also see Essential Silver Surfer)
Marvel Comics Group: Aug, 1968 - No. 18, Sept, 1970; June, 1982

1-More detailed origin by John Buscema (p); The Watcher back-up stories begin (origin), end #7; (No. 1-7: 25¢, 68 pgs.) 155 310 465 1279 2890 4500
2-1st app. Badoon 20 40 60 136 303 470
3-1st app. Mephisto 64 128 192 512 1156 1800
4-Lower distribution; Thor & Loki app. 68 136 204 544 1222 1900
5-7-Last giant size. 5-The Stranger app.; Fantastic Four app. 6-Brunner inks. 7-(8/69)-Early cameo Frankenstein's monster (see X-Men #40) 13 26 39 91 201 310
8-10: 8-18-(15¢ issues) 11 22 33 75 160 245
11-13,15-18: 15-Silver Surfer vs. Human Torch; Fantastic Four app. 17-Nick Fury app. 18-Vs. The Inhumans; Kirby-a; Trimpe-c 10 20 30 68 144 220
14-Spider-Man x-over 16 32 48 111 246 380
14 Facsimile Edition (3/2019, $3.99) reprints #14 with original ads and letter column 4.00
... Omnibus Vol. 1 Hardcover (2007, $74.99, dustjacket) r/#1-18 re-colored with original letter pages, Fantastic Four Annual #5 & Not Brand Echh #13; Lee and Buscema bios 75.00
V2#1 (6/82, 52 pgs.)-Byrne-c/a 2 4 6 9 12 15

NOTE: **Adkins** *a-8-15i.* **Brunner** *a-6i.* **J. Buscema** *a-1-17p.* **Colan** *a-1-3p.* **Reinman** *a-1-4i. #1-14 were reprinted in Fantasy Masterpieces V2#1-14.*

SILVER SURFER (Volume 3) (See Marvel Graphic Novel #38)
Marvel Comics Group: V3#1, July, 1987 - No. 146, Nov, 1998

GD VG FN VF VF/NM NM-
2.0 4.0 6.0 8.0 9.0 9.2

1-Double-size ($1.25)-Englehart & Rogers-s/a begins; vs. the Champion; Fantastic Four app. w/She-Hulk; Nova (Frankie Raye) & Galactus app; Surfers exile on Earth ends 2 4 6 10 14 18
2-9: 2-Surfer returns to Zenn-La; Shalla-Bal app. as Empress of Zenn-La; Skrulls app.; Surfer story next in West Coat Avengers Annual #2 and Avengers Annual #16. 3-Collector & Champion app.; Surfer vs. the Runner; re-intro Mantis (not seen since 1975). 4-Elders of the Universe app.; Collector, Champion, Runner, Gardener, Contemplator, Grandmaster & Possessor; 1st app. of Astronomer, Obliterator & Trader; Ego revealed as an Elder; origin Mantis. 5-vs. the Obliterator. 6-Origin of the Obliterator. 7-Supreme Intelligence & the Elders app. 8-Supreme Intelligence app.; Surfer gains the Soul Gem. 9-Elders vs. Galactus; six Soul Gems app. 6.00
10-Galactus absorbs the Elders; Eternity app. 2 4 6 8 10 12
11-14: 11-1st app. Reptyl, Clumsy Foulup & the fake Surfer; Nova (Frankie Raye) app. 12-Death of fake Contemplator; Reptyl & Nova (Frankie Raye) app. 13-Ronan the Accuser vs. Surfer and Nova (Frankie Raye); fake Surfer app.; last Rogers-a. 14-Origin & death of the fake Surfer; Ronan app.; Nova (Frankie Raye) app.; story continues in Surfer Ann. #1 5.00
15,16: 15-Ron Lim-c/a begin (9/88); Soul Gems app.; Reed, Sue and Franklin of the Fantastic Four app.; Galactus & Nova (Frankie Raye), Elders of the Universe app.: Astronomer, Possessor & Trader. 16-Astromoner, Trader & In-Betweener app.; brief x-over w/Fantastic Four #319 6.00
17,18: 17-Elders of the Universe, In-Betweener, Death & Galactus app. 18-Galactus vs. the In-Betweener; Elders of the Universe, the Soul Gems & Lord Order & Master Chaos app. 1 2 3 5 6 7
19,20-Firelord & Starfox app. 5.00
21-24,26-30,32,33,39-43: 21-vs. the Obliterator. 22-Ego the Living Planet app. 26-Super-Skrull app. 27-Stranger & Super-Skrull app. 28-Death of Super-Skrull; Reptyl app. 29-Midnight Sun app; death of Reptyl. 30-Midnight Sun & the Stranger app. 32,33-Jim Valentino-s; 33-Impossible Man app. 39-Alan Grant scripts. 40-43-Surfer in Dynamo City 4.00
25,31-($1.50, 52 pgs.) 25-New Kree/Skrull war; Badoon app; Skrulls regain their shape-shifting ability. 31-Conclusion of Kree/Skrull war; Stranger & the Living Tribunal app. 5.00
34-Thanos returns (cameo); Starlin scripts begin; Death app. 3 6 9 18 27 36
35-38: 35-1st full Thanos in Silver Surfer (3/90); reintro Drax the Destroyer on last pg. (cameo). 36-Recaps history of Thanos, Captain Marvel & Warlock app. in recap. 37-Full reintro Drax the Destroyer; Drax-c. 38-Silver Surfer battles Thanos; Nebula app; Thanos story continues in Thanos Quest #1-2 1 3 4 6 8 10
44-Classic Thanos-c; 1st app. of the Infinity Gauntlet; Thanos defeats the Surfer & Drax; Mephisto cameo 5 10 15 34 60 85
45-Thanos-c; Mephisto app.; origin of the Infinity Gems 3 6 9 15 23 30
46-Return of Adam Warlock (2/91); reintro Gamora & Pip the Troll (within Soul World) 2 4 6 11 16 20
47-49: 47-Warlock vs. Drax. 48-Galactus app; last Starlin scripts (also #50). 49-Thanos & Mephisto app.; Ron Marz scripts begin 1 3 4 6 8 10
50-($1.50, 52 pgs.)-Embossed & silver foil-c; Silver Surfer has brief battle w/Thanos; story cont'd in Infinity Gauntlet #1; extended origin flashback to the Silver Surfer's life on Zenn-La 3 6 9 14 20 25
50-2nd & 3rd printings 5.00
51-59-Infinity Gauntlet x-overs; 51-Galactus and Nova (Frankie Raye) app. 52-Firelord vs. Drax; continued in Infinity Gauntlet #2. 53-Death of Clumsy Foulup. 54-vs the Rhino; Hulk cameo. 55,56-Thanos kills everyone (Surfer dream sequence); Warlock app; continued in Infinity Gauntlet #4. 57-x-over w/Infinity Gauntlet #4. 58-Defenders app. (dream sequence); Warlock app. 59-Warlock, Dr. Strange, Dr. Doom, Thor, Firelord, Drax & Thanos app; concluded in Infinity Gauntlet #6 6.00
60-69,71-73: 60-vs. Midnight Sun; Warlock & Dr. Strange cameo; Black Bolt, Gorgon & Karnak of the Inhumans app. 61-Collector app. 63-Captain Marvel app. 64-Collector app. 65-Reptyl returns. 66-Mistress Love & Master Hate app. 67-69-Infinity War x-overs. 67-Continued from Infinity War #1; x-over w/Dr. Strange #42; Nebula, Galactus, Nova (Frankie Raye) & Dr. Strange app; Magus cameo; continued in Infinity War #2. 68,69-Galactus, Nova & Dr. Strange app. 69-Magus cameo; continues in Infinity War #3. 71-Herald Ordeal Pt. 2; Nebula, Firelord & Galactus app; Surfer vs. Morg. 72-Herald Ordeal Pt. 3; 1st app. Cyborg Nebula (as seen in the GOTG movie); Firelord, Nova, Galactus & Morg app. 73-Herald Ordeal Pt. 4; reintro Gabriel the Airwalker; Firelord, Galactus, Nova, Morg app; Terrax cameo 4.00
70,74: Herald Ordeal Pts.1,5. 70-1st app. Morg (becomes the new Herald of Galactus), Nova released of her duties; Nebula app. 74-Terrax, Firelord, Airwalker, Nova, Nebula app. 5.00
75-($2.50, 52 pgs.)-Embossed foil-c; Lim-c/a; Herald Ordeal Pt. 6; Surfer, Firelord, Airwalker, Terrax & Nova vs. Morg; death of Nova; Morg stripped of the power cosmic; Firelord & Airwalker resume Herald duties 5.00
76-81,83-87,90-97: 76-Origin Jack of Hearts retold; Galactus, Airwalker, Firelord & Nebula app.; Morg cameo. 77-Jack of Hearts & Nebula app; return of Morg. 78-New Jack of Hearts costume; Nebula, Morg & Galactus app. 79-Captain Atlas & Dr. Minerva app.; Morg vs. Terrax; Gladiator & Beta Ray Bill cameo. 80-1st app. Ganymede (named in issue #81);

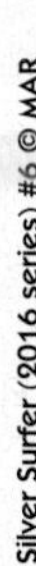
Silver Surfer (2016 series) #6 © MAR

Silver Surfer: Black #5 © MAR

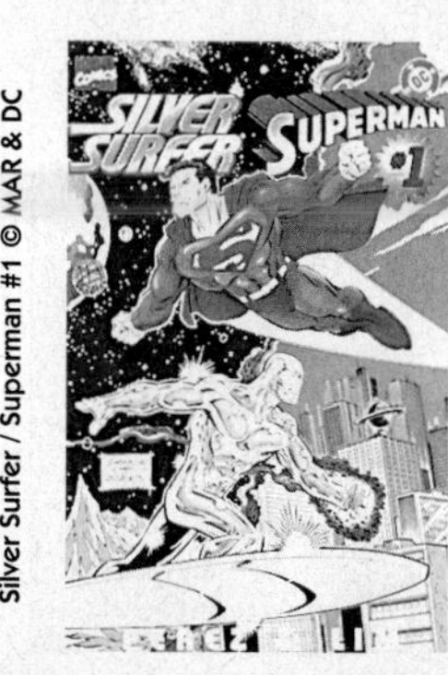

Silver Surfer / Superman #1 © MAR & DC

	GD 2.0	VG 4.0	FN 6.0	VF 8.0	VF/NM 9.0	NM- 9.2

Morg vs. Terrax. 81-1st cameo app. Tyrant; Morg, Terrax, Gladiator, Beta Ray Bill cameos. 83-85-Infinity Crusade x-overs. 83-Surfer vs. Firelord; x-over w/Infinity Crusade #3; Thanos cameo; cont'd in Infinity Crusade #4. 84-Thanos app. 85-Wonder Man & Storm vs. Surfer; concluded in Infinity Crusade #6. 86-Blood & Thunder Pt. 2; cont'd from Thor #468; Surfer & Beta Ray Bill vs. insane Thor; Pip the Troll & Warlock cameo; cont'd in Warlock Chronicles #6. 87-Blood & Thunder Pt. 6; cont'd from Thor #469; Dr. Strange, Warlock & the Infinity Watch app; cont'd in Warlock Chronicles #7. 89-Colleen Doran-a(p). 90-Legacy (son of Capt. Marvel) app. 92-Marvel Masterprints card insert; last Lim-a. 93-Fantastic Four app; Thing, Human Torch & Ant-Man (Scott Lang); Spider-Man cameo. 94-Fantastic Four & Warlock and the Infinity Watch app. 95-Fantastic Four app.; Hulk cameo. 97-Terrax app; Champion cameo 4.00

82-($1.75, 52 pgs.)-Surfer, Morg, Terrax, Gladiator, Beta Ray Bill, Jack of Hearts & Ganymede vs. Tyrant; Galactus app. 5.00

88,99: 88-Blood & Thunder Pt. 10-cont'd from Thor #470; Thanos vs. insane Thor; Dr. Strange, Warlock & the Infinity Watch app; cont'd in Warlock Chronicles #8; 'Kay-bee Toys' coupon insert for Ghost Rider 'Hot Pursuit' comic; 7-pg. Punisher 'Suicide Run' advertisement; 7-pg. 'Juice' magazine insert featuring interviews with the New Warriors. 99-Mephisto cameo 5.00

98-vs. Champion; Drax & Thanos app. 5.00

100-($2.25, 52 pgs.)-Wraparound-c; vs. Mephisto 6.00

100-($3.95, 52 pgs.)-Enhanced-silver holofoil-c 5.00

101-108,110: 101-Tyrant cameo; Surfer returns to Zenn-La; Shalla-Bal app. 102-Galactus & Morg app; Tyrant cameo; last Marz script. 104-Morg app. Galactus, Morg & Legacy app; Surfer vs. Super-Skrull; 4-pg Rune/Silver Surfer preview. 106-Galactus, Morg & Tyrant app. 108-Tyrant vs. Galactus; Morg & Legacy app. 110-Legacy & Nebula app; John Buscema-a. 4.00

109-Tyrant vs. Galactus; Legacy app.; Morg no longer Herald. 5.00

111-121: 111-New direction; Pérez scripts begin. 112-1st app. Uni-Lord. 114-Watcher app. 120-vs. Uni-Lord. 121-End of the Uni-Lord saga; Beta Ray Bill & Quasar cameo 4.00

122-Legacy & Beta Ray Bill app. 5.00

123-124,126-127,129-130: 123-1st Dematteis script; Surfer returns to Earth; Alicia Masters app. 124-Kymaera (Namorita) app. 126-Dr. Strange app. 127-Alicia Masters & the Puppet Master app. 130-Surfer learns that Zenn-La has been destroyed; Galactus app. 4.00

125 ($2.95)-Wraparound-c; vs. Hulk-c/app. 5.00

128-Spider-Man & Daredevil-c/app. 1 3 4 6 8 10

131-134: 131-Galactus app. 133-Puppet Master app. 134-Scrier & The Other app. 4.00

135-140: 135-Agatha Harkness, Scrier & the Thing app. 136,137-Scrier & Mephisto app. 138-Thing app. 140-Jon J. Muth-a begins 6.00

141-144: 143,144-Psycho-Man app. 1 2 3 4 6 7

145-Alicia Masters; Surfer returns to Earth 1 2 3 4 6 8

146-Firelord app; last issue. 2 4 6 9 12 15

#(-1) Flashback (7/97)-Stan Lee app; 1st app. The Other; Galactus app. 4.00

Annual 1 (1988, $1.75)-Evolutionary War Pt. 3; continued from Punisher Annual #1; 1st Ron Lim-a on Silver Surfer (20 pg. back-up story & pin-ups); Eternals app. Surfer & Super-Skrull team-up; Mantis app.; story continues in West Coast Avengers #37; Evolutionary War continues in New Mutants Annual #4 6.00

Annual 2 (1989, $2.00)-Atlantis Attacks Pt. 1; Ghaur the Deviant app; Dr. Strange cameo; story continues in Iron Man Annual #10 5.00

Annual 3-6: 3-(1990, $2.00)-Lifeform Pt. 4; continued from Punisher Annual #3. 4-(1991, $2.00)-The Korvac Quest Pt. 3; continued from Thor Annual #16; 3-pg. origin story; Silver Surfer battles the Guardians of the Galaxy (30th Century version); continued in Guardians of the Galaxy Annual #1. 5-(1992, $2.25)- Return of the Defenders Pt. 3; continued from Namor the Sub-Mariner Annual #2; Hulk & Dr. Strange app.; continued in Dr. Strange Annual #2; Nebula app. in Firelord & Starfox back-up story. 6-(1993, $2.95)-Polybagged w/trading card; 1st app. Legacy; card is by Lim/Austin; Surfer & Legacy vs. Ronan the Accuser; Terrax, Jack of Hearts & Ganymede back up features 5.00

Annual 7-(1994, $2.95)-Morg resumes being Herald to Galactus; Firelord leaves; Legacy app. in back-up 5.00

Annual '97-($2.99)-Scrier app. Annual '98-($2.99)..& Thor; vs. Millennius; Avengers app. 5.00

...Dangerous Artifacts-(1996, 48 pgs.)-Marz scripts w/Claudio Castellini-a; Galactus & Thanos app; 1st app. White Raven 1 3 4 6 8 10

Graphic Novel (1988, HC, $14.95)-Judgment Day; Lee-s/Buscema-a; Galactus vs. Mephisto 30.00

Graphic Novel (1988, SC, $10.95)-Judgment Day; Jusko-c 20.00

Graphic Novel (1990, HC, $16.95)-The Enslavers; Stan Lee-s & Pollard-a; non-canon Marvel universe story 25.00

Graphic Novel (1991, SC, $12.95)-Homecoming; Starlin-a; death of Shalla-Bal 15.00

Inner Demons TPB (4/98, $3.50)r/#123,125,126 5.00

...: Rebirth of Thanos TPB (2006, $24.99) r/#34-38, Thanos Quest #1,2; Logan's Run #6 25.00

...: The First Coming of Galactus nn (11/92, $5.95, 68 pgs.)-Reprints Fantastic Four #48-50 with new Lim-c 6.00

Wizard 1/2 2 4 6 9 12 15

NOTE: ***Austin*** *c(i)-7, 8, 71, 73, 74, 76, 79.* ***Cowan*** *a-143,146.* ***Cully Hamner*** *a-83p.* ***Ron Lim*** *a(p)-15-31, 33-38, 40-55, (56, 57-part-p), 60-65, 73-82, Annual 2, 4; c(p)-15-31, 32-38, 40-84, 86-92, Annual 2, 4-6.* ***Muth*** *c/a-140-142,144,145.* ***M. Rogers*** *a-1-10, 12, 19, 21; c-1-9, 11, 12, 21.*

SILVER SURFER (Volume 4)
Marvel Comics: Sept, 2003 - No. 14, Dec, 2004 ($2.25/$2.99)

1-6: 1-Milx-a; Jusko-c. 2-Jae Lee-c 3.00
7-14-($2.99) 3.00
...Vol. 1: Communion (2004, $14.99) r/#1-6 15.00

SILVER SURFER (Volume 5)
Marvel Comics: Apr, 2011 - No. 5, Aug, 2011 ($2.99, limited series)

1-5-Pagulayan-c. 1-Segovia-a. 4,5-Fantastic Four app. 3.00

SILVER SURFER (6th series)
Marvel Comics: May, 2014 - No. 15, Jan, 2016 ($3.99)

1-10: 1-Dan Slott-s/Michael Allred-a/c. 3-Guardians of the Galaxy app. 8-10-Galactus app. 4.00
11-($4.99) Story runs upside down on top or bottom halves of the pages 5.00
12-15: 13-15-Secret Wars tie-in 4.00

SILVER SURFER (7th series)
Marvel Comics: Mar, 2016 - No. 14, Dec, 2017 ($3.99)

1-5,7-14-Slott-s/Allred-a. 1-4-The Thing app. 3-50th Anniversary issue; Shalla Bal app. 4.00
6-(10/16, $4.99) 200th issue; Spider-Man app.; cover gallery 5.00
Annual 1 (11/18, $4.99) Ethan Sacks-s/André Lima Araujo-a; Galactus app. 5.00
...: The Prodigal Sun 1 (10/19, $4.99) Peter David-s/Francesco Manna-a; Prah'd'gul app. 5.00

SILVER SURFER, THE
Marvel Comics (Epic): Dec, 1988 - No. 2, Jan, 1989 ($1.00, lim. series)

1-By Stan Lee scripts & Moebius-c/a 2 4 6 9 13 16
2 1 2 3 5 6 8
HC (1988, $19.95, dust jacket) r/#1,2; "Making Of" text section and sketch pages 30.00
... By Stan Lee & Moebius (3/13, $7.99) r/#1&2; bonus production diary from Moebius 8.00
...: Parable ('98, $5.99) r/#1&2 6.00

SILVER SURFER: BLACK
Marvel Comics: Aug, 2019 - No. 5, Dec, 2019 ($3.99, limited series)

1-5-Donny Cates-s/Tradd Moore-a; Ego & Knull app. 4.00

SILVER SURFER: IN THY NAME
Marvel Comics: Jan, 2008 - No. 4, Apr, 2008 ($2.99, limited series)

1-4-Spurrier-s/Huat-a. 1-Turner-c. 2-Dell'Otto-c. 3-Paul Pope-c. 4-Galactus app. 3.00

SILVER SURFER: LOFTIER THAN MORTALS
Marvel Comics: Oct, 1999 - No. 2, Oct, 1999 ($2.50, limited series)

1,2-Remix of Fantastic Four #57-60; Velluto-a 3.00

SILVER SURFER: REQUIEM
Marvel Comics: July, 2007 - No. 4, Oct, 2007 ($3.99, limited series)

1-4-Straczynski-s/Ribic-a. 1-Origin retold; Fantastic Four app. 4.00
HC (2007, $19.99) r/#1-4, Ribic cover sketches 20.00

SILVER SURFER/SUPERMAN
Marvel Comics: 1996 ($5.95,one-shot)

1-Perez-s/Lim-c/a(p) 2 4 6 8 10 12

SILVER SURFER: THE BEST DEFENSE (Also see Immortal Hulk, Doctor Strange, Namor)
Marvel Comics: Feb, 2019 ($4.99, one-shot)

1-Jason Latour-s/a; Ron Garney-c; Galactus app. 5.00

SILVER SURFER VS. DRACULA
Marvel Comics: Feb, 1994 ($1.75, one-shot)

1-r/Tomb of Dracula #50; Everett Vampire-r/Venus #19; Howard the Duck back-up by Brunner; Lim-c(p) 1 3 4 6 8 10

SILVER SURFER/WARLOCK: RESURRECTION
Marvel Comics: Mar, 1993 - No. 4, June, 1993 ($2.50, limited series)

1-4-Starlin-c/a & scripts. 1-Surfer joins Warlock & the Infinity Watch to rescue Shalla-Bal; story continued from the 'Homecoming' GN. 2-Death app.; Mephisto cameo. 3-Surfer vs. Mephisto. 4-Warlock vs. Mephisto; Shalla-Bal revived. 4.00

SILVER SURFER/WEAPON ZERO
Marvel Comics: Apr, 1997 ($2.95, one-shot)

1-"Devil's Reign" pt. 8 3.00

SILVERTIP (Max Brand)
Dell Publishing Co.: No. 491, Aug, 1953 - No. 898, May, 1958

Four Color 491 (#1); all painted-c 8 16 24 52 99 145
Four Color 572,608,637,667,731,789,898-Kinstler-a 5 10 15 34 60 85
Four Color 835 5 10 15 34 60 85

SIM CITY
Aardvark-Vanaheim: ($4.00, B&W, with cover swipes from Sin City)

Simpsons Comics #150 © Bongo

Simpsons Comics Presents Bart Simpson #100 © Bongo

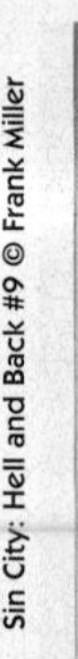

Sin City: Hell and Back #9 © Frank Miller

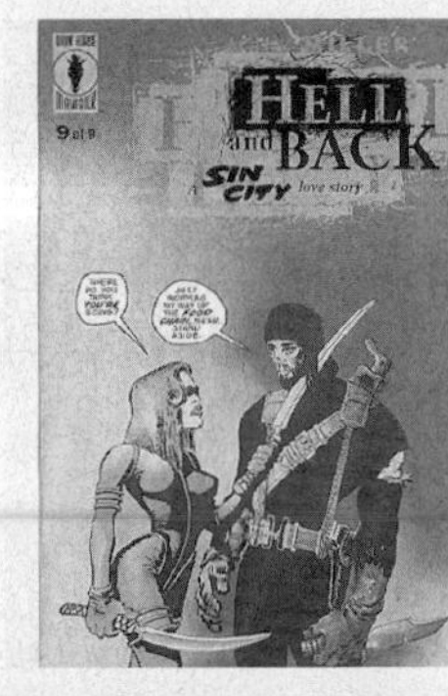

	GD	VG	FN	VF	VF/NM	NM-
	2.0	4.0	6.0	8.0	9.0	9.2

...: A Dave To Kill For 1 (2/19) Cerebus figures in Frank Miller style backgrounds 4.00
... - That Issue After 1 (3/19) Cerebus figures with Gustave Doré artwork of Hell 4.00

SIMON DARK
DC Comics: Dec, 2007 - No. 18, May, 2009 ($2.99)

1-Intro. Simon Dark; Steve Niles-s/Scott Hampton-a/c 4.00
1-Second printing with full face variant cover 3.00
2-18 3.00
...: Ashes TPB (2009, $17.99) r/#7-12 18.00
...: The Game of Life TPB (2009, $17.99) r/#13-18 18.00
...: What Simon Does TPB (2008, $14.99) r/#1-6 18.00

SIMPSONS COMICS (See Bartman, Futurama, Itchy & Scratchy & Radioactive Man)
Bongo Comics Group: 1993 - No. 245, 2018 ($1.95/$2.50/$2.99/$3.99)

1-($2.25)-FF#1-c swipe; pull-out poster; flip book 3 6 9 17 26 35
2-5: 2-Patty & Selma flip-c/sty. 3-Krusty, Agent of K.L.O.W.N. flip-c/story. 4-Infinity-c; flip-c of Busman #1; w/trading card. 5-Wraparound-c w/trading card 1 3 4 6 8 10
6-40: All Flip books. 6-w/Chief Wiggum's "Crime Comics". 7-w/"McBain Comics". 8-w/"Edna, Queen of the Congo". 9-w/"Barney Gumble". 10-w/"Apu". 11-w/"Homer". 12-w/"White Knuckled War Stories". 13-w/"Jimbo Jones' Wedgie Comics". 14-w/"Grampa". 15-w/"Itchy & Scratchy". 16-w/"Bongo Grab Bag". 17-w/"Headlight Comics". 18-w/"Milhouse". 19,20-w/"Roswell." 21,22-w/"Roswell". 23-w/"Hellfire Comics". 24-w/"Lil' Homey". 36-39-Flip book w/Radioactive Man 6.00
41-49,51-99: 43-Flip book w/Poochie. 52-Dini-s. 77-Dixon-s. 85-Begin $2.99-c 5.00
50-($5.95) Wraparound-c; 80 pgs.; square-bound 1 2 3 5 6 8
100-($6.99) 100 pgs.; square-bound; clip issue of past highlights 1 2 3 5 6 8
101-182,184-199,201-224: 102-Barks Ducks homage. 117-Hank Scorpio app. 122-Archie spoof. 132-Movie poster enclosed. 132-133-Two-parter. 144-Flying Hellfish flashback. 150-w/Poster. 163-Aragonés-s/a. 218-Guardians of the Galaxy spoof 3.00
183-Archie Comics #1 cover swipe; Archie homage with Stan Goldberg-a 3.00
200-(2013, $4.99) Wraparound-c; short stories incl. Dorkin-s/a; Matt Groening cameo 5.00
225-244-($3.99) 225-Bonus back-up 1970s Eddie & Lou story. 237-Bartman app. 4.00
245-($3.99) Last issue; Bongo the rabbit app.; bonus cover gallery of #1-245 4.00
... A Go-Go (1999, $11.95)-r/#32-35; ...Big Bonanza (1998, $11.95)-r/#28-31, ...Extravaganza (1994, $10.00)-r/#1-4; infinity-c, ...On Parade (1998, $11.95)-r/#24-27, ...Simpsorama (1996, $10.95)-r/#11-14 12.00
Simpsons Classics 1-30 (2004 - 2011, $3.99, magazine-size, quarterly) reprints 4.00
Simpsons Comics Barn Burner ('04, $14.95) r/#57-61,63 15.00
Simpsons Comics Beach Blanket Bongo ('07, $14.95) r/#71-75,77 15.00
Simpsons Comics Belly Buster ('04, $14.95) r/#49,51,53-56 15.00
Simpsons Comics Hit the Road! ('08, $15.95) r/#85,86,88,89,90 16.00
Simpsons Comics Jam-Packed Jamboree ('06, $14.95) r/#64-69 15.00
Simpsons Comics Madness ('03, $14.95) r/#43-48 15.00
Simpsons Comics Royale ('01, $14.95) r/various Bongo issues 15.00
Simpsons Comics Treasure Trove 1-4 ('08-'09, $3.99, 6" x 8") r/various Bongo issues 4.00
Simpsons Summer Shindig ('07-'15, $4.99) 1-9-Anthology. 1-Batman/Ripken insert 5.00
Simpsons Winter Wing Ding ('06-'14, $4.99) 1-10-Holiday anthology. 1-Dini-s 5.00

SIMPSONS COMICS AND STORIES
Welsh Publishing Group: 1993 ($2.95, one-shot)

1-(Direct Sale)-Polybagged w/Bartman poster 3 6 9 16 23 30
1-(Newsstand Edition)-Without poster 6.00

SIMPSONS COMICS PRESENTS BART SIMPSON
Bongo Comics Group: 2000 - No. 100, 2016 ($2.50/$2.99)

1-Bill Morrison-c 1 3 4 6 8 10
2-40: 7-9-Dan DeCarlo-layouts. 13-Begin $2.99-c. 17,37-Bartman app. 5.00
41-99: 50-Aragonés-s/a 3.00
100-($4.99) 100-year old Bart, Mrs. Krabappel, Fruit Bat Man app. 5.00
The Big Book of Bart Simpson TPB (2002, $12.95) r/#1-4 15.00
The Big Bad Book of Bart Simpson TPB (2003, $12.95) r/#5-8 15.00
The Big Bratty Book of Bart Simpson TPB (2004, $12.95) r/#9-12 15.00
The Big Beefy Book of Bart Simpson TPB (2005, $13.95) r/#13-16 15.00
The Big Bouncy Book of Bart Simpson TPB (2006, $13.95) r/#17-20 15.00
The Big Beastly Book of Bart Simpson TPB (2007, $14.95) r/#21-24 15.00
The Big Brilliant Book of Bart Simpson TPB (2008, $14.95) r/#25-28 15.00

SIMPSONS FUTURAMA CROSSOVER CRISIS II (TV) (Also see Futurama/Simpsons Infinitely Secret Crossover Crisis)
Bongo Comics: 2005 - No. 2, 2005 ($3.00, limited series)

1,2-The Professor brings the Simpsons' Springfield crew to the 31st century 5.00

SIMPSONS ILLUSTRATED (TV)
Bongo Comics: 2012 - No. 27, 2017 ($3.99, quarterly)

1-20-Reprints 4.00
21-27-($4.99) 25-All-monster issue 5.00

SIMPSONS ONE-SHOT WONDERS (TV)
Bongo Comics: 2012 - 2018 ($2.99/$3.99)

...: Bart Simpson's Pal Milhouse 1 - Short stories; centerfold with decal 3.00
...: Chief Wiggum's Felonius Funnies 1 ($3.99) - Future Cop app. 4.00
...: Duffman 1 ($3.99) - Green Lantern spoof; centerfold with die-cut Duffman mask 4.00
...: Grampa 1 ($3.99) - "Choose Your Adventure" format; wraparound-c 4.00
...: Jimbo 1 ($3.99) - Short stories; centerfold with die-cut skull sticker 4.00
...: Kang & Kodos 1 ($3.99) - Short stories; centerfold with bumper stickers 4.00
...: Krusty 1 ($3.99) - Krusty's backstory; back-c swipe of Uncanny X-Men #141 4.00
...: Li'l Homer 1 - Short stories of Homer's childhood; centerfold with cut-outs 3.00
...: Lisa 1 ($3.99) - Short stories by Matsumoto and others; sticker page centerfold 4.00
...: Maggie 1 - Short stories by Aragonés and others; paperdoll centerfold; Aragonés-c 3.00
...: McBain 1 ($3.99) - Entire issue unfolds for a poster on the back 4.00
...: Mr. Burns 1 ($3.99) - Short stories incl. Richie Rich spoof; Fruit Bat Man mask 4.00
...: Professor Frink 1 ($3.99) - Short stories; 3-D glasses insert; 3-D story and back-c 4.00
...: Ralph Wiggums Comics 1 - Short stories by Aragonés and others 3.00
...: The Mighty Moe Szyslak 1 - Short stories by various; Flintstones homage back-c 3.00

SIMPSONS SUPER SPECTACULAR (TV)
Bongo Comics: 2006 - No. 16, 2013 ($2.99)

1-16: 2-Bartman, Stretch Dude and The Cupcake Kid team up; back-up story Brereton-a. 5-Fradon-a on Metamorpho spoof. 8-Spirit spoof. 9,10,14-16-Radioactive Man app. 3.00

SINBAD, JR (TV Cartoon)
Dell Publishing Co.: Sept-Nov, 1965 - No. 3, May, 1966

1 4 8 12 23 37 50
2,3 3 6 9 17 26 35

SIN BOLDLY
Image Comics: Dec, 2013 ($3.50, B&W, one-shot)

1-J.M. Linsner-s/a/c; short stories with Sinful Suzi and Obsidian Stone 3.50

SIN CITY (See Dark Horse Presents, A Decade of Dark Horse, & San Diego Comic Con Comics #2,4)
Dark Horse Comics (Legend)

TPB ($15.00) Reprints early DHP stories 15.00
Booze, Broads & Bullets TPB ($15.00) 15.00
Frank Miller's Sin City: One For One (8/10, $1.00) reprints debut story from DHP #51 3.00

SIN CITY (FRANK MILLER'S...) (Reissued TPBs to coincide with the April 2005 movie)
Dark Horse Books: Feb, 2005 ($17.00/$19.00, 6" x 9" format with new Miller covers)

Volume 1: The Hard Goodbye ($17.00) reprints stories from Dark Horse Presents #51-62 and DHP Fifth Anniv. Special; covers and publicity pieces 17.00
Volume 2: A Dame to Kill For ($17.00) r/Sin City: A Dame to Kill For #1-6 17.00
Volume 3: The Big Fat Kill ($17.00) r/Sin City: The Big Fat Kill #1-5; pin-up gallery 17.00
Volume 4: That Yellow Bastard ($19.00) r/Sin City: That Yellow Bastard #1-6; pin-up gallery by Mike Allred, Kyle Baker, Jeff Smith and Bruce Timm; cover gallery 19.00
Volume 5: Family Values ($12.00) r/Sin City: Family Values GN 12.00
Volume 6: Booze, Broads & Bullets ($15.00) r/Sin City: The Babe Wore Red and Other Stories; Silent Night; story from A Decade of Dark Horse; Lost Lonely & Lethal; Sex & Violence; and Just Another Saturday Night 15.00
Volume 7: Hell and Back ($28.00) r/Sin City: Hell and Back #1-9; pin-up gallery 28.00

SIN CITY: A DAME TO KILL FOR
Dark Horse Comics (Legend): Nov, 1993 - No. 6, May, 1994 ($2.95, B&W, limited series)

1-6: Frank Miller-c/a & story in all. 1-1st app. Dwight. 6.00
1-3-Second printing 3.00
Limited Edition Hardcover 85.00
Hardcover 25.00
TPB ($15.00) 15.00

SIN CITY: FAMILY VALUES
Dark Horse Comics (Legend): Oct, 1997 ($10.00, B&W, squarebound, one-shot)

nn-Miller-c/a & story 10.00
Limited Edition Hardcover 75.00

SIN CITY: HELL AND BACK
Dark Horse (Maverick): Jul, 1999 - No. 9 ($2.95/$4.95, B&W, limited series)

1-8-Miller-c/a & story. 7-Color 5.00
9-($4.95) 6.00

SIN CITY: JUST ANOTHER SATURDAY NIGHT
Dark Horse Comics (Legend): Aug, 1997 (Wizard 1/2 offer, B&W, one-shot)

1/2-Miller-c/a & story 1 2 3 5 6 8
nn (10/98, $2.50) r/#1/2 4.00

SIN CITY: LOST, LONELY & LETHAL

Sinestro #8 © DC

SIP Kids #1 © Terry Moore

Sisterhood of Steel #4 © MAR

	GD	VG	FN	VF	VF/NM	NM-
	2.0	4.0	6.0	8.0	9.0	9.2

Dark Horse Comics (Legend): Dec, 1996 ($2.95, B&W and blue, one-shot)

nn-Miller-c/s/a; w/pin-ups 5.00

SIN CITY: SEX AND VIOLENCE
Dark Horse Comics (Legend): Mar, 1997 ($2.95, B&W and blue, one-shot)

nn-Miller-c/a & story 5.00

SIN CITY: SILENT NIGHT
Dark Horse Comics (Legend): Dec, 1995 ($2.95, B&W, one-shot)

1-Miller-c/a & story; Marv app. 6.00

SIN CITY: THAT YELLOW BASTARD (Second Ed. TPB listed under Sin City (Frank Miller's...)
Dark Horse Comics (Legend): Feb, 1996 - No. 6, July, 1996 ($2.95/$3.50, B&W and yellow, limited series)

1-5: Miller-c/a & story in all. 1-1st app. Hartigan. 6.00
6-($3.50) Error & corrected 6.00
Limited Edition Hardcover 25.00
TPB ($15.00) 15.00

SIN CITY: THE BABE WORE RED AND OTHER STORIES
Dark Horse Comics (Legend): Nov, 1994 ($2.95, B&W and red, one-shot)

1-r/serial run in Previews as well as other stories; Miller-c/a & scripts; Dwight app. 6.00

SIN CITY: THE BIG FAT KILL (Second Edition TPB listed under Sin City (Frank Miller's...)
Dark Horse Comics (Legend): Nov, 1994 - No. 5, Mar, 1995 ($2.95, B&W, limited series)

1-5-Miller story & art in all; Dwight app. 6.00
Hardcover 25.00
TPB ($15.00) 15.00

SIN CITY: THE FRANK MILLER LIBRARY
Dark Horse Books: Set 1, Nov, 2005; Set 2, Mar, 2006 ($150, slipcased hardcover, 8" x 12")

Set 1 - Individual hardcovers for Volume 1: The Hard Goodbye, Volume 2: A Dame to Kill For, Volume 3: The Big Fat Kill, Volume 4: That Yellow Bastard; new red foil stamped covers; slipcase box is black with red foil graphics 150.00
Set 2 - Individual hardcovers for Volume 5: Family Values, Volume 6: Booze, Broads & Bullets, Volume 7: Hell and Back, new red foil stamped covers; The Art of Sin City red hardcover; slipcase box is black with red foil graphics 150.00

SINDBAD (See Capt. Sindbad under Movie Comics, and Fantastic Voyages of Sindbad)

SINERGY
Image Comics (Shadowline): Nov, 2014 - No. 5, Mar, 2015 ($3.50)

1-5: 1-Oeming & Soma-s/Oeming-a/c 3.50

SINESTRO
DC Comics: Jun, 2014 - No. 23, Jul, 2016 ($2.99)

1-23: 1-Bunn-s/Eaglesham-a; Lyssa Drak & Arkillo app. 6-8-Godhead x-over; New Gods app. 7-Van Sciver-a. 9-11-Mongul app. 15-Lobo app. 16-20-Black Adam app. 17-20-Wonder Woman app. 19,20-Harley Quinn & Superman app. 3.00
Annual 1 (6/15, $4.99) Bunn-s/Eaglesham-c; art by various 5.00
...: Futures End 1 (11/14, $2.99, regular-c) Five years later; Bunn-s/Lima-a/Nowlan-c 3.00
...: Futures End 1 (11/14, $3.99, 3-D cover) 4.00
...: Year of the Villain 1 (10/19, $4.99) Russell-s/Cinar-a; Apex Lex Luthor app. 5.00

SINGING GUNS (See Fawcett Movie Comics)

SINGLE SERIES (Comics on Parade #30 on)(Also see John Hix...)
United Features Syndicate: 1938 - No. 28, 1942 (All 68 pgs.)

Note: See Individual Alphabetical Listings for prices

1-Captain and the Kids (#1)	2-Broncho Bill (1939) (#1)
3-Ella Cinders (1939)	4-Li'l Abner (1939) (#1)
5-Fritzi Ritz (#1)	6-Jim Hardy by Dick Moores (#1)
7-Frankie Doodle	8-Peter Pat (On sale 7/14/39)
9-Strange As It Seems	10-Little Mary Mixup
11-Mr. and Mrs. Beans	12-Joe Jinks
13-Looy Dot Dope	14-Billy Make Believe
15-How It Began (1939)	16-Illustrated Gags (1940)-Has ad for Captain and the Kids #1 reprint listed below
17-Danny Dingle	
18-Li'l Abner (#2 on-c)	
19-Broncho Bill (#2 on-c)	20-Tarzan by Hal Foster
21-Ella Cinders (#2 on-c; on sale 3/19/40)	22-Iron Vic
23-Tailspin Tommy by Hal Forrest (#1)	24-Alice in Wonderland (#1)
25-Abbie and Slats	26-Little Mary Mixup (#2 on-c, 1940)
27-Jim Hardy by Dick Moores (1942)	28-Ella Cinders & Abbie and Slats (1942)
1-Captain and the Kids (1939 reprint)-2nd Edition	1-Fritzi Ritz (1939 reprint)-2nd ed.

NOTE: *Some issues given away at the 1939-40 New York World's Fair (#6).*

SINISTER DEXTER
IDW Publishing: Dec, 2013 - No. 7, Jun, 2014 ($3.99)

1-7: 1-Dan Abnett-s/Andy Clarke-a; two covers by Clarke and Fuso 4.00

SINISTER HOUSE OF SECRET LOVE, THE (Becomes Secrets of Sinister House No. 5 on)
National Periodical Publ.: Oct-Nov, 1971 - No. 4, Apr-May, 1972

	GD 2.0	VG 4.0	FN 6.0	VF 8.0	VF/NM 9.0	NM- 9.2
1 (All 52 pgs.) -Grey-tone-c	13	26	39	91	201	310
2,4	7	14	21	48	89	130
3-Toth-a; Grey-tone-c	8	16	24	51	96	140

SINS OF YOUTH... (Also see Young Justice: Sins of Youth)
DC Comics: May 2000 ($4.95/$2.50, limited crossover series)

Secret Files 1 ($4.95) Short stories and profile pages; Nauck-c 5.00
...Aquaboy/Lagoon Man; Batboy and Robin; JLA Jr.; Kid Flash/Impulse; Starwoman and the JSA, Superman, Jr./Superboy, Sr.; The Secret/ Deadboy, Wonder Girls ($2.50-c) Old and young heroes switch ages 3.00

SIP KIDS (Strangers in Paradise)
Abstract Studio: 2014 - No. 4, 2015 ($4.99, color)

1-4-Strangers in Paradise characters as young kids; Terry Moore-s/a/c 5.00

SIR CHARLES BARKLEY AND THE REFEREE MURDERS
Hamilton Comics: 1993 ($9.95, 8-1/2" x 11", 52 pgs.)

	GD 2.0	VG 4.0	FN 6.0	VF 8.0	VF/NM 9.0	NM- 9.2
nn-Photo-c; Sports fantasy comic book fiction (uses real names of NBA superstars). Script by Alan Dean Foster, art by Joe Staton. Comes with bound-in sheet of 35 gummed "Moods of Charles Barkley" stamps. Photo/story on Barkley	2	4	6	9	12	15
Special Edition of 100 copies for charity signed on an affixed book plate by Barkley, Foster & Staton						175.00
Ashcan edition given away to dealers, distributors & promoters (low distribution). Four pages in color, balance of story in b&w	2	4	6	9	12	15

SIR EDWARD GREY, WITCHFINDER: IN THE SERVICE OF ANGELS (From Hellboy)
Dark Horse Comics: July, 2009 - No. 5, Nov, 2009 ($2.99, limited series)

1-5-Mignola-s/c; Stenbeck-a 3.00

SIR EDWARD GREY, WITCHFINDER: THE MYSTERIES OF UNLAND (From Hellboy)
Dark Horse Comics: Jun, 2014 - No. 5, Oct, 2014 ($3.50, limited series)

1-5-Newman & McHugh-s/Crook-a/Tedesco-c 3.50

SIREN (Also see Eliminator & Ultraforce)
Malibu Comics (Ultraverse): Sept, 1995 - No. 3, Dec, 1995 ($1.50)

Infinity, 1-3: Infinity-Black-c & painted-c exists. 1-Regular-c & painted-c; War Machine app. 2-Flip book w/Phoenix Resurrection Pt. 3 3.00
Special 1-(2/96, $1.95, 28 pgs.)-Origin Siren; Marvel Comic's Juggernaut-c/app. 3.00

SIRENS (See George Pérez's Sirens)

SIR LANCELOT (TV)
Dell Publishing Co.: No. 606, Dec, 1954 - No. 775, Mar, 1957

	GD 2.0	VG 4.0	FN 6.0	VF 8.0	VF/NM 9.0	NM- 9.2
Four Color 606 (not TV)	6	12	18	42	79	115
Four Color 775(...and Brian)-Buscema-a; photo-c	9	18	27	59	117	175

SIR WALTER RALEIGH (Movie)
Dell Publishing Co.: May, 1955 (Based on movie "The Virgin Queen")

	GD 2.0	VG 4.0	FN 6.0	VF 8.0	VF/NM 9.0	NM- 9.2
Four Color 644-Photo-c	6	12	18	42	79	115

SISTERHOOD OF STEEL (See Eclipse Graphic Adventure Novel #13)
Marvel Comics (Epic Comics): Dec, 1984 - No. 8, Feb, 1986 ($1.50, Baxter paper, mature)

1-8 4.00

SISTERS OF SORROW
BOOM! Studios: Jul, 2017 - No. 4, Oct, 2017 ($3.99, limited series)

1-4-Kurt Sutter & Courtney Alameda-s/Hyeonjin Kim-a. 1-Jae Lee-c 4.00

SITUATION, THE (TV's Jersey Shore)
Wizard World: July, 2012 (no cover price)

1-Jenkins-s/Caldwell-a; two covers by Horn & Caldwell 3.00

6 BLACK HORSES (See Movie Classics)

SIX FROM SIRIUS
Marvel Comics (Epic Comics): July, 1984 - No. 4, Oct, 1984 ($1.50, limited series, mature)

1-4: Moench scripts; Gulacy-c/a in all 4.00

SIX FROM SIRIUS II
Marvel Comics (Epic Comics): Feb, 1986 - No. 4, May, 1986 ($1.50, limited series, mature)

1-4: Moench scripts; Gulacy-c/a in all 4.00

SIX-GUN GORILLA
BOOM! Studios: Jun, 2013 - No. 6, Nov, 2013 ($3.99, limited series)

1-6: 1-Spurrier-s/Stokely-a 4.00

SIX-GUN HEROES

Six-Gun Heroes #4 © FAW

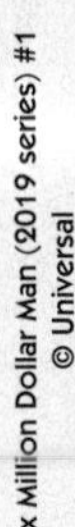
Six Million Dollar Man (2019 series) #1 © Universal

Skrulls! #1 © MAR

GD VG FN VF VF/NM NM-
2.0 4.0 6.0 8.0 9.0 9.2

GD VG FN VF VF/NM NM-
2.0 4.0 6.0 8.0 9.0 9.2

Fawcett Publications: March, 1950 - No. 23, Nov, 1953 (Photo-c #1-23)

1-Rocky Lane, Hopalong Cassidy, Smiley Burnette begin (same date as Smiley Burnette #1)
31 62 93 186 303 420
2 16 32 48 94 147 200
3-5: 5-Lash LaRue begins 14 28 42 76 108 140
6-15 11 22 33 62 86 110
16-22: 17-Last Smiley Burnette. 18-Monte Hale begins
10 20 30 54 72 90
23-Last Fawcett issue 10 20 30 58 79 100

NOTE: *Hopalong Cassidy photo c-1-3. Monte Hale photo c-18. Rocky Lane photo c-4, 5, 7, 9, 11, 13, 15, 17, 20, 21, 23. Lash LaRue photo c-6, 8, 10, 12, 14, 16, 19, 22.*

SIX-GUN HEROES (Cont'd from Fawcett; Gunmasters #84 on) (See Blue Bird)
Charlton Comics: No. 24, Jan, 1954 - No. 83, Mar-Apr, 1965 (All Vol. 4)

24-Lash LaRue, Hopalong Cassidy, Rocky Lane & Tex Ritter begin; photo-c
14 28 42 80 115 150
25 10 20 30 54 72 90
26-30: 26-Rod Cameron story. 28-Tom Mix begins? 9 18 27 47 61 75
31-40: 38-40-Jingles & Wild Bill Hickok (TV) 8 16 24 42 54 65
41-46,48,50: 41-43-Wild Bill Hickok (TV) 8 16 24 40 50 60
47-Williamson-a, 2 pgs; Torres-a 8 16 24 42 54 65
49-Williamson-a (5 pgs.) 9 18 27 50 65 80
51-56,58-60: 58-Gunmaster app. 3 6 9 19 30 40
57-Origin & 1st app. Gunmaster 4 8 12 25 40 55
61-70 3 6 9 16 23 30
71-75,77,78,80-83 2 4 6 13 18 22
76,79: 76-Gunmaster begins. 79-1st app. & origin of Bullet, the Gun-Boy
3 6 9 14 19 24

SIXGUN RANCH (See Luke Short & Four Color #580)

SIX GUNS
Marvel Comics: Jan, 2012 - No. 5, Apr, 2012 ($2.99, limited series)

1-5-Diggle-s/Gianfelice-a; Tarantula and Tex Dawson app. 3.00

SIX-GUN WESTERN
Atlas Comics (CDS): Jan, 1957 - No. 4, July, 1957

1-Crandall-a; two Williamson text illos 23 46 69 136 223 310
2,3-Williamson-a in both 16 32 48 94 147 200
4-Woodbridge-a 14 28 42 80 115 150

NOTE: ***Ayers** a-2, 3. **Maneely** a-1; c-2, 3. **Orlando** a-2. **Pakula** a-2. **Powell** a-3. **Romita** a-1, 4. **Severin** c-1, 4. **Shores** a-2.*

SIX MILLION DOLLAR MAN, THE (TV) (Also see The Bionic Man)
Charlton Comics: 6/76 - No. 4, 12/76; No. 5, 10/77; No. 6, 2/78 - No. 9, 6/78

1-Staton-c/a; Lee Majors photo on-c 5 10 15 35 63 90
2-Neal Adams-c; Staton-a 4 8 12 25 40 55
3-9 3 6 9 14 19 24

SIX MILLION DOLLAR MAN, THE (TV)(Magazine)
Charlton Comics: July, 1976 - No. 7, Nov, 1977 (B&W)

1-Neal Adams-c/a 4 8 12 27 44 60
2-Neal Adams-c 3 6 9 16 24 32
3-N. Adams part inks; Chaykin-a 3 6 9 14 19 24
4-7 2 4 6 11 16 20

SIX MILLION DOLLAR MAN, THE: FALL OF MAN (TV)
Dynamite Entertainment: 2016 - No. 5, 2016 ($3.99)

1-5: 1-Van Jensen-s/Ron Salas-a; three covers 4.00

SIX MILLION DOLLAR MAN, THE: SEASON 6 (TV)
Dynamite Entertainment: 2014 - No. 6, 2014 ($3.99)

1-Jim Kuhoric-s/Juan Antonio Ramirez-a; covers by Alex Ross & Ken Haeser & photo-c 4.00
2-6-Two covers by Ross & Haeser on each. 2-Maskatron returns 4.00

SIX MILLION DOLLAR MAN, THE: VOLUME 1 (TV)
Dynamite Entertainment: 2019 - No. 5, 2019 ($3.99, limited series)

1-5-Christopher Hastings-s/David Hahn-a; set in 1974 4.00

SIXPACK AND DOGWELDER: HARD TRAVELIN' HEROZ (See All-Star Section Eight)
DC Comics: Oct, 2016 - No. 6, Mar, 2017 ($3.99, limited series)

1-6-Ennis-s/Braun-a/Dillon-c. 1-Power Girl, Catwoman, & Starfire app. 2-6-Constantine app. 2-The Spectre app. 4.00

SIX STRING SAMURAI
Awesome-Hyperwerks: Sept, 1998 ($2.95)

1-Stinsman & Fraga-a; Liefeld-c 3.00

1602 WITCH HUNTER ANGELA (Secret Wars tie-in)
Marvel Comics: Aug, 2015 - No. 4, Dec, 2015 ($3.99, limited series)

1-4-Marguerite Bennett-s; Hans & Sauvage-a; The Enchantress app. 4.00

67 SECONDS
Marvel Comics (Epic Comics): 1992 ($15.95, 54 pgs., graphic novel)

nn-James Robinson scripts; Steve Yeowell-c/a 2 4 6 11 14 18

SKAAR: KING OF THE SAVAGE LAND
Marvel Comics: Jun, 2011 - No. 5 ($2.99, limited series)

1-5-Shanna & Ka-Zar app.; Ching-a. 1-Komarck-c. 2-McGuinness-c 3.00

SKAAR: SON OF HULK (Title continues in Son of Hulk #13)(Also see World War Hulk x-over)
Marvel Comics: Aug, 2008 - No. 12, Aug, 2009 ($2.99)

1-Garney-a/Pak-s; 2 covers by Pagulayan and Julie Bell; origin 4.00
1-Second printing - 2 covers by Garney and Hulk movie image 3.00
1-Third printing - Garney sketch variant-c 3.00
2-12: 2-6-Back-up story with Guice-a. 7-12-Silver Surfer app. 3.00
Planet Skaar Prologue 1 (7/09, $3.99) Panosian-a; Fantastic Four & She-Hulk app. 4.00
... Presents - Savage World of Sakaar (11/08, $3.99) Pak-s/art by various; Garney-c 4.00

SKATEMAN
Pacific Comics: Nov, 1983 (Baxter paper, one-shot)

1-Adams-c/a 4.00

SKELETON HAND (...In Secrets of the Supernatural)
American Comics Gr. (B&M Dist. Co.): Sept-Oct, 1952 - No. 6, Jul-Aug, 1953

1 81 162 243 518 884 1250
2 42 84 126 265 445 625
3-6 39 78 117 231 378 525

SKELETON KEY
Amaze Ink: July, 1995 - No. 30, Jan, 1998 ($1.25/$1.50/$1.75, B&W)

1-30 3.00
Special #1 (2/98, $4.95) Unpublished short stories 5.00
Sugar Kat Special (10/98, $2.95) Halloween stories 3.00
Beyond The Threshold TPB (6/96. $11.95)-r/#1-6 12.00
Cats and Dogs TPB ($12.95)-r/#25-30 13.00
The Celestial Calendar TPB ($19.95)-r/#7-18 20.00
Telling Tales TPB ($12.95)-r/#19-24 13.00

SKELETON KEY (Volume 2)
Amaze Ink: 1999 - No. 4, 1999 ($2.95, B&W)

1-4-Andrew Watson-s/a 3.00

SKELETON WARRIORS
Marvel Comics: Apr, 1995 - No. 4, July, 1995 ($1.50)

1-4: Based on animated series. 3.00

SKIN GRAFT: THE ADVENTURES OF A TATTOOED MAN
DC Comics (Vertigo): July, 1993 - No. 4, Oct, 1993 ($2.50, lim. series, mature)

1-4 3.00

SKINWALKER
Oni Press: May, 2002 - No. 4, Sept, 2002 ($2.95, limited series)

1-4-Hurtt & Dela Cruz-a; Talon-c 3.00
1-(5/05) Free Comic Book Day Edition 3.00

SKI PARTY (See Movie Classics)

SKREEMER
DC Comics: May, 1989 - No. 6, Oct, 1989 ($2.00, limited series, mature)

1-6: Contains graphic violence; Milligan-s 3.00
TPB (2002, $19.95) r/#1-6 20.00

SKRULL KILL KREW
Marvel Comics: Sept, 1995 - No. 5, Dec, 1995 ($2.95, limited series)

1-5: Grant Morrison & Mark Millar scripts; Steve Yeowell-a. 2,3-Cap America app. 5.00
TPB (2006, $16.99) r/#1-5 17.00

SKRULL KILL KREW
Marvel Comics: Jun, 2009 - No. 5, Dec, 2009 ($3.99, limited series)

1-5-Felber-s/Robinson-a 4.00

SKRULLS! (Tie-in to Secret Invasion crossover)
Marvel Comics: 2008 ($4.99, one-shot)

1-Skrull history, profiles of Skrulls, their allies & foes; checklist of appearances; Horn-c 5.00

SKRULLS VS. POWER PACK (Tie-in to Secret Invasion crossover)
Marvel Comics: Sept, 2008 - No. 4 ($2.99, limited series)

1-4-Van Lente-s/Hamscher-a; Franklin Richards app. 3.00

SKUL, THE

Skullkickers #23 © Jim Zub

Skylanders #7 © Activision

Slam! #3 © Ribon & Fish

	GD 2.0	VG 4.0	FN 6.0	VF 8.0	VF/NM 9.0	NM- 9.2

Virtual Comics (Byron Preiss Multimedia): Oct, 1996 - No. 3, Dec, 1996 ($2.50, lim. series)
1-3: Ron Lim & Jimmy Palmiotti-a 3.00

SKULL & BONES
DC Comics: 1992 - No. 3, 1992 ($4.95, limited series, 52 pgs.)
Book 1-3: 1-1st app. 5.00

SKULLDIGGER AND SKELETON BOY (From Black Hammer)
Dark Horse Comics: Dec, 2019 - No. 6, Feb, 2021 ($3.99)
1-6-Lemire-s/Zonjic-a; origin of Skeleton Boy 5.00

SKULLKICKERS
Image Comics: Sept, 2010 - No. 33, Jul, 2015; No. 100, Aug, 2015 ($2.99/$3.50)
1-Jim Zubkavich-s/Edwin Huang-a; two covers 4.00
1-(2nd & 3rd printings), 2-18 3.00
24-29,31-33: 24-($3.50) "Before Watchmen" cover swipe (no issues #34-99) 3.50
30-($3.99) Multi-dimensional variant Skullkickers 4.00
#100 ($3.99, 8/15) Last issue; conclusion of Infinite Icons of the Endless Epic 4.00
All-New Secret Skullkickers 1 (6/13, $3.50) issue #22; cover swipe of X-Men #125 ('79) 3.50
Dark Skullkickers Dark 1 (7/13, $3.50) issue #23; cover swipe of Green Lantern #85 ('71) 3.50
Savage Skullkickers 1 (3/13, $3.50) issue #20; cover swipe of Savage Wolverine #1 3.50
The Mighty Skullkickers 1 (4/13, $3.50) issue #21; cover swipe of Thor #337 3.50
Uncanny Skullkickers 1 (2/13, $3.50) issue #19 3.50

SKULL, THE SLAYER
Marvel Comics Group: Aug, 1975 - No. 8, Nov, 1976 (20¢/25¢)
1-Origin & 1st app.; Gil Kane-c 3 6 9 17 25 34
2-8: 2-Gil Kane-c. 5,6-(Regular 25¢-c). 8-Kirby-c 2 4 6 8 10 12
5,6-(30¢-c variants, limited distribution)(5,7/76) 4 8 12 23 37 50

SKY BLAZERS (CBS Radio)
Hawley Publications: Sept, 1940 - No. 2, Nov, 1940
1-Sky Pirates, Ace Archer, Flying Aces begin 82 164 246 528 902 1275
2-WWII air battle grey-tone-c 42 84 126 265 445 625

SKYBOURNE
BOOM! Studios: Sept, 2016 - No. 5, Feb, 2018 ($3.99)
1-5-Frank Cho-s/a 4.00

SKY DOLL
Marvel Comics (Soleil): 2008 - No. 3, 2008 ($5.99, mature)
1-3-Barbucci & Canepa-s/a; English version of French comic; preview of other titles 6.00
...: Doll's Factory 1,2 (2009 - No. 2, 2009, $5.99) Barbucci & Canepa-s/a 6.00
...: Lacrima Christi 1,2 (9/10 - No. 2, 10/10, $5.99) Barbucci & Canepa and others-s/a 6.00
...: Space Ship 1,2 (7/10 - No. 2, 8/10, $5.99) Barbucci & Canepa and others-s/a 6.00

SKY DOLL: SUDRA
Titan Comics: Apr, 2017 - No. 2, May, 2017 ($3.99, mature)
1,2-Barbucci & Canepa-s/a; English version of French comic 4.00

SKYE RUNNER
DC Comics (WildStorm): June, 2006 - No. 6, Mar, 2007 ($2.99)
1-6: 1-Three covers; Warner-s/Garza-a. 2-Three covers, incl. Campbell 3.00

SKYLANDERS (Based on the Activision video game)
IDW Publishing: No. 0, Jul, 2014 - No. 12, Aug, 2015 ($3.99)
0-(no cover price) Lord Kaos app.; Bowden-a; character bios 3.00
1-12: 1-Marz & Rodriguez-s/Baldeón-a 4.00
... Quarterly - Spyro & Friends: Biting Back (3/18, $4.99) Marz & Rodriguez-s 5.00
... Quarterly - Spyro & Friends: Full Blast (7/17, $4.99) Marz & Rodriguez-s 5.00
... Quarterly - Spyro & Friends: Goldslinger (11/17, $4.99) Marz & Rodriguez-s 5.00
... Superchargers 1-6 (10/15 - No. 6, 3/16, $3.99) Marz & Rodriguez-s 4.00

SKYMAN (See Big Shot Comics & Sparky Watts)
Columbia Comics Gr.: Fall?, 1941 - No. 2, Fall?, 1942; No. 3, 1948 - No. 4, 1948
1-Origin Skyman, The Face, Sparky Watts app.; Whitney-c/a; 3rd story-r from Big Shot #1;
Whitney c-1-4 132 264 396 845 1448 2050
2 (1942)-Yankee Doodle 71 142 213 454 777 1100
3,4 (1948) 42 84 126 265 445 625

SKYMAN (Also see Captain Midnight 2013 series #4)
Dark Horse Comics: Jan, 2014 - No. 4, Apr, 2014 ($2.99)
1-4: 1-Fialkov-s/Garcia-a; origin of a new Skyman. 3,4-Captain Midnight app. 3.00
... One-Shot (11/14, $2.99) Garcia-a 3.00

SKYPILOT
Ziff-Davis Publ. Co.: No. 10, 1950(nd) - No. 11, Apr-May, 1951
10,11-Frank Borth-a; Saunders painted-c 19 38 57 111 176 240

SKY RANGER (See Johnny Law...)

SKYROCKET
Harry 'A' Chesler: 1944
nn-Alias the Dragon, Dr. Vampire, Skyrocket & The Desperado app.; WWII Japan zero-c
58 116 174 371 636 900

SKY SHERIFF (Breeze Lawson...) (Also see Exposed & Outlaws)
D. S. Publishing Co.: Summer, 1948
1-Edmond Good-c/a 19 38 57 111 176 240

SKYWARD
Image Comics: Apr, 2018 - No. 15, Jul, 2019 ($3.99)
1-15: 1-Joe Henderson-s/Lee Garbett-a 4.00

SKY WOLF (Also see Airboy)
Eclipse Comics: Mar, 1988 - No. 3, Oct, 1988 ($1.25/$1.50/$1.95, lim. series)
1-3 3.00

SLAINE, THE BERSERKER (Slaine the King #21 on)
Quality: July, 1987 - No. 28, 1989 ($1.25/$1.50)
1-28 3.00

SLAINE, THE HORNED GOD
Fleetway: 1998 - No. 3 ($6.99)
1-3-Reprints series from 2000 A.D.; Bisley-a 7.00

SLAM!
BOOM! Studios (Boom! Box): Nov, 2016 - No. 4, Feb, 2017 ($3.99)
1-4-Roller derby; Pamela Ribon-s/Veronica Fish-a 4.00

SLAM BANG COMICS (Western Desperado #8)
Fawcett Publications: Mar, 1940 - No. 7, Sept, 1940 (Combined with Master Comics #7)
1-Diamond Jack, Mark Swift & The Time Retarder, Lee Granger, Jungle King begin &
continue in Master 275 550 825 1760 3030 4300
2 119 238 357 762 1306 1850
3-Classic monster-c (scarce) 320 640 960 2240 3970 5700
4,6,7: 6-Intro Zoro, the Mystery Man (also in #7) 100 200 300 640 1095 1550
5-Classic Dragon-c 113 226 339 723 1237 1750
Ashcan (1940) Not distributed to newsstands, only for in house use. A copy sold in 2006 for $4,500.

SLAM! THE NEXT JAM
BOOM! Studios (Boom! Box): Sept, 2017 - No. 4, Dec, 2017 ($3.99)
1-4-Roller derby; Pamela Ribon-s/Marina Julia-a 4.00

SLAPSTICK
Marvel Comics: Nov, 1992 - No. 4, Feb, 1993 ($1.25, limited series)
1-4: Fry/Austin-c/a. 4-Ghost Rider, D.D., F.F. app. 3.00

SLAPSTICK
Marvel Comics: Feb, 2017 - No. 6, Jul, 2017 ($3.99, limited series)
1-6-Brown & Van Lente-s/Olortegui-a 4.00

SLAPSTICK COMICS
Comic Magazines Distributors: nd (1946?) (36 pgs.)
nn-Firetop feature; Post-a(2); Munson Paddock-c 40 80 120 244 402 560

SLASH & BURN
DC Comics (Vertigo): Jan, 2016 - No. 6, Jun, 2016 ($3.99/$4.99)
1-5-Si Spencer-s/Max Dunbar-a 4.00
6-($4.99) 5.00

SLASH-D DOUBLECROSS
St. John Publishing Co.: 1950 (Pocket-size, 132 pgs.)
nn-Western comics 24 48 72 144 237 330

SLASH MARAUD
DC Comics: Nov, 1987 - No. 6, Apr, 1988 ($1.75, limited series)
1-6-Moench-s/Gulacy-a/c 3.00

SLAVE GIRL COMICS (See Malu... & White Princess of the Jungle #2)
Avon Periodicals/Eternity Comics (1989): Feb, 1949 - No. 2, 1949 (52 pgs.); Mar, 1989 (B&W, 44 pgs)
1-Larsen-c/a 158 316 474 1011 1731 2450
2-Larsen-a (no month listed) 129 258 387 826 1413 2000
1-(3/89, $2.25, B&W, 44 pgs.)-r/#1 5.00

SLAVE LABOR STORIES
SLG Publishing: May, 2003 (Giveaway, B&W)
1-Free Comic Book Day Edition; short stories by various; Dorkin Milk & Cheese-c 3.00

SLAYER: REPENTLESS (Based on the band Slayer)

Sleepy Hollow #2 © 20th Fox

Sludge #7 © MAL

Smallville Season 11 #6 © DC

	GD 2.0	VG 4.0	FN 6.0	VF 8.0	VF/NM 9.0	NM- 9.2

Dark Horse Comics: Jan, 2017 - No. 3, Jun, 2017 ($4.99, limited series)
1-3-Jon Schnepp-s/Guiu Villanova-a/Glenn Fabry-c; Slayer app. 5.00

SLEDGE HAMMER (TV)
Marvel Comics: Feb, 1988 - No. 2, Mar,1988 ($1.00, limited series)
1,2 3.00

SLEDGEHAMMER 44
Dark Horse Comics: Mar, 2013 - No. 2, Apr, 2013 ($3.50, limited series)
1,2-Mignola & Arcudi-s/Latour-a; Mignola-c 3.50

SLEDGEHAMMER 44: THE LIGHTNING WAR
Dark Horse Comics: Nov, 2013 - No. 3, Jan, 2014 ($3.50, limited series)
1-3-Mignola & Arcudi-s/Laurence Campbell-a. 1-Mignola-c. 2,3-Campbell-c 3.50

SLEEPER
DC Comics (WildStorm): Mar, 2003 - No. 12, Mar, 2004 ($2.95)
1-12-Brubaker-s/Phillips-c/a. 3-Back-up preview of The Authority: High Stakes pt. 2 3.00
...: All False Moves TPB (2004, $17.95) r/#7-12 18.00
...: Out in the Cold TPB (2004, $17.95) r/#1-6 18.00

SLEEPER: SEASON TWO
DC Comics (WildStorm): Aug, 2004 - No. 12, July, 2005 ($2.95/$2.99)
1-12-Brubaker-s/Phillips-c/a. 3.00
TPB (2009, $24.99) r/#1-12 25.00
...: A Crooked Line TPB (2005, $17.99) r/#1-6 18.00
...: The Long Way Home TPB (2005, $14.99) r/#7-12 15.00

SLEEPING BEAUTY (See Dell Giants & Movie Comics)
Dell Publishing Co.: No. 973, May, 1959 - No. 984, June, 1959 (Disney)
Four Color 973 (...and the Prince) 11 22 33 76 163 250
Four Color 984 (...Fairy Godmother's) 9 18 27 62 126 190

SLEEPLESS
Image Comics: Dec, 2017 - No. 11, Jan, 2019 ($3.99)
1-11-Sarah Vaughn-s/Leila Del Duca-a 4.00

SLEEPWALKER (Also see Infinity Wars: Sleepwalker)
Marvel Comics: June, 1991 - No. 33, Feb, 1994 ($1.00/$1.25)
1-1st app. Sleepwalker 4.00
2-33: 4-Williamson-i. 5-Spider-Man-c/story. 7-Infinity Gauntlet x-over. 8-Vs. Deathlok-c/story. 11-Ghost Rider-c/story. 12-Quesada-c/a(p) 14-Intro Spectra. 15-F.F.-c/story. 17-Darkhawk & Spider-Man x-over. 18-Infinity War x-over; Quesada/Williamson-c. 21,22-Hobgoblin app. 19-($2.00)-Die-cut Sleepwalker mask-c 3.00
25-($2.95, 52 pgs.)-Holo-grafx foil-c; origin 4.00
Holiday Special 1 (1/93, $2.00, 52 pgs.)-Quesada-c(p) 4.00

SLEEPWALKING
Hall of Heroes: Jan, 1996 ($2.50, B&W)
1-Kelley Jones-c 3.00

SLEEPY HOLLOW (Movie Adaption)
DC Comics (Vertigo): 2000 ($7.95, one-shot)
1-Kelley Jones-a/Seagle-s 8.00

SLEEPY HOLLOW (Based on the Fox TV show)
BOOM! Studios: Oct, 2014 - No. 4, Jan, 2015 ($3.99, limited series)
1-4-Marguerite Bennett-s/Jorge Coelho-a/Phil Noto-c 4.00
...: Origins 1 (4/15, $4.99) Mike Johnson-s/Matias Bergara-a; Quinones-c 5.00
...: Providence 1-4 (8/15 - No. 4 11/15, $3.99) Carrasco-s/Santos-a 4.00

SLEEZE BROTHERS, THE
Marvel Comics (Epic Comics): Aug, 1989 - No. 6, Jan, 1990 ($1.75, mature)
1-6: 4-6 (9/89 - 11/89 indicia dates) 3.00
nn-(1991, $3.95, 52 pgs.) 4.00

SLICK CHICK COMICS
Leader Enterprises: 1947(nd) - No. 3, 1947(nd)
1-Teenage humor 40 80 120 246 411 575
2,3 27 54 81 158 259 360

SLIDERS (TV)
Acclaim Comics (Armada): June, 1996 - No. 2, July, 1996 ($2.50, lim. series)
1,2: D.G. Chichester scripts; Dick Giordano-a. 3.00

SLIDERS: DARKEST HOUR (TV)
Acclaim Comics (Armada): Oct, 1996 - No. 3, Dec, 1996 ($2.50, limited series)
1-3 3.00

SLIDERS SPECIAL
Acclaim Comics (Armada): Nov, 1996 - No 3, Mar, 1997 ($3.95, limited series)
1-3: 1-Narcotica-Jerry O'Connell-s. 2-Blood and Splendor. 3-Deadly Secrets 4.00

SLIDERS: ULTIMATUM (TV)
Acclaim Comics (Armada): Sept, 1996 - No. 2, Sept, 1996 ($2.50, lim. series)
1,2 3.00

SLIMER! (TV cartoon) (Also see the Real Ghostbusters)
Now Comics: 1989 - No. 19, Nov, 1990 ($1.75)
1-19: Based on animated cartoon 4.00

SLIM MORGAN (See Wisco)

SLINGERS (See Spider-Man: Identity Crisis issues)
Marvel Comics: Dec, 1998 - No. 12, Nov, 1999 ($2.99/$1.99)
0-(Wizard #88 supplement) Prelude story 3.00
1-($2.99) Four editions w/different covers for each hero, 16 pages common to all, the other pages from each hero's perspective 4.00
2-12: 2-Two-c. 12-Saltares-a 3.00

SLITHISS ATTACKS! (Also see Very Weird Tales)
Oceanspray Comics Group: Dec, 2001 – No. 4, Aug, 2004 ($3.00/$4.00)
1-($3.00) Origin and 1st app. of the monster Slithiss; 1st app. Overconfident Man 15.00
2-($4.00) 2nd app. Overconfident Man; "Chris Lamo" Newport, OR murder parody 12.00
3-($3.00) Rutland Vermont Halloween x-over; 3rd app. Overconfident Man 12.00
4-($3.00) 4th app. Overconfident Man 10.00
Special Edition 1($20.00) reprints #1-2 without letter column 20.00
Special Edition 1($20.00) second printing 20.00
NOTE: *Created in prevention classes taught by Jon McClure at the Oceanspray Family Center in Newport, OR and paid for by the Housing Authority of Lincoln County, all books are b&w with color covers. Bob Overstreet and other comics' professionals wrote letters of encouragement that were published in issues #2-4. Issues #1-2 penciled and inked by various artists; #3-4 penciled by James Gilmer. All comics feature characters created by students, signed and numbered by Jon McClure. Issue #1 had a 200 issue print run, while issues #2-4 have print runs of 100 each. Special Edition #1 had a print run of 26 issues, while the second printing had a 10 issue print run. Ties in with live action movie Face Eater released in 2007 and card game FaceEater released in 2010.*

SLOTS
Image Comics: Oct, 2017 - No. 6, Mar, 2018 ($3.99)
1-6-Dan Panosian-s/a/c 4.00

SLUDGE
Malibu Comics (Ultraverse): Oct, 1993 - No. 12, Dec, 1994 ($2.50/$1.95)
1-($2.50, 48 pgs.)-Intro/1st app. Sludge; Rune flip-c/story Pt. 1 (1st app., 3 pgs.) by Barry Smith; The Night Man app. (3 pg. preview); The Mighty Magnor 1 pg strip begins by Aragonés (cont. in other titles) 4.00
1-Ultra 5000 Limited silver foil 8.00
2-11: 3-Break-Thru x-over. 4-2 pg. Mantra origin. 8-Bloodstorm app. 3.00
12 ($3.50)-Ultraverse Premiere #8 flip book; Alex Ross poster 4.00
...:Red Xmas (12/94, $2.50, 44 pgs.) 4.00

SLUGGER (Little Wise Guys Starring...)(Also see Daredevil Comics)
Lev Gleason Publications: April, 1956
1-Biro-c 9 18 27 52 69 85

SMALLVILLE (Based on TV series)
DC Comics: May, 2003 - No. 11, Jan, 2005 ($3.50/$3.95, bi-monthly)
1-6-Photo-c. 1-Plunkett-a; interviews with cast; season 1 episode guide begins 4.00
7-11-($3.95) 7-Chloe Chronicles begin; season 2 episode guide begins 4.00
Vol. 1 TPB (2004, $9.95) r/#1-4 & Smallville: The Comic; photo-c 10.00

SMALLVILLE: ALIEN (Based on TV series)
DC Comics: Feb, 2014 - No. 4, May, 2014 ($3.99, printings of previously released digital comics)
1-4: 1-The Monitor lands on Earth; Staggs-a. 2-4-Batman app. 4.00

SMALLVILLE: CHAOS (Based on TV series)(Season 11)
DC Comics: Oct, 2014 - No. 4, Jan, 2015 ($3.99, printings of previously released digital comics)
1-4: 1-Eclipso app.; Padilla-a. 3-Darkseid app. 3,4-Supergirl & Superboy app. 4.00

SMALLVILLE: LANTERN (Based on TV series)
DC Comics: Jun, 2014 - No. 4, Sept, 2014 ($3.99, printings of previously released digital comics)
1-4: 1-Kal-El joins the Green Lantern Corps; Takara-a. 2-4-Parallax app. 4.00

SMALLVILLE SEASON 11 (Based on TV series)
DC Comics: Jul, 2012 - No. 19, Jan, 2014 ($3.99, printings of previously released digital comics)
1-19: 1-Two covers by Gary Frank & Cat Staggs; Pere Perez-a. 5-8-Batman app. 13-15-Legion app. 15-Doomsday app. 16-19-Diana of Themyscira app. 4.00
... Special 1 (7/13, $4.99) Batman, Nightwing and Martian Manhunter app. 5.00
... Special 2 (9/13, $4.99) Lana Lang and John Corben app. 5.00
... Special 3 (12/13, $4.99) Spotlight on Luthor and Tess; Lobel-a 5.00
... Special 4 (3/14, $4.99) Superboy, Jay Garrick, Blue Beetle, Wonder Twins app. 5.00

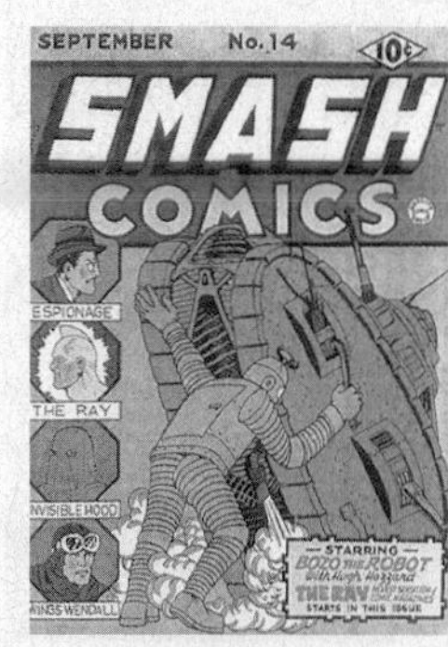

Smash Comics #14 © QUA

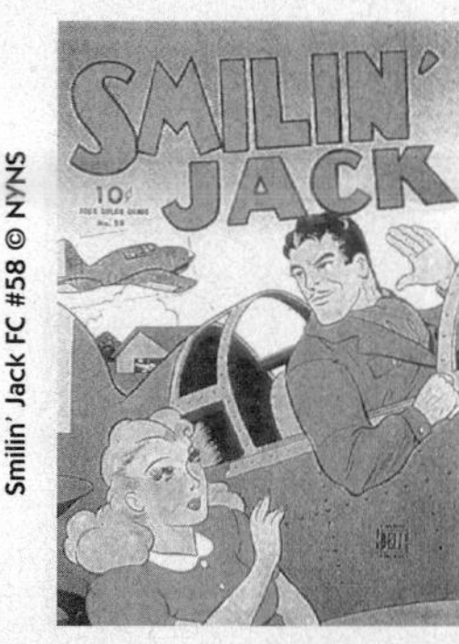

Smilin' Jack FC #58 © NYNS

Smokey the Bear FC #703 © DELL

	GD	VG	FN	VF	VF/NM	NM-
	2.0	4.0	6.0	8.0	9.0	9.2
... Special 5 (9/14, $4.99) Zatanna and John Constantine app.						5.00

SMALLVILLE SEASON 11: CONTINUITY (Based on TV series)
DC Comics: Feb, 2015 - No. 4, May, 2015 ($3.99, printings of previously released digital comics)

1-4-The Crisis vs. the Monitors; Legion of Super-Heroes app.; Guara-a						4.00

SMALLVILLE: THE COMIC (Based on TV series)
DC Comics: Nov, 2002 ($3.95, 64 pages, one-shot)

1-Photo-c; art by Martinez and Leon; interviews with cast; season 2 preview						5.00

SMASH COMICS (Becomes Lady Luck #86 on)
Quality Comics Group: Aug, 1939 - No. 85, Oct, 1949

1-Origin Hugh Hazard & His Iron Man, Bozo the Robot, Espionage, Starring Black X by Eisner, & Hooded Justice (Invisible Justice #2 on); Chic Carter & Wings Wendall begin; 1st Robot on the cover of a comic book (Bozo)	354	708	1062	2478	4339	6200
2-The Lone Star Rider app; Invisible Hood gains power of invisibility; bondage/torture-c	155	310	465	992	1696	2400
3-Captain Cook & Eisner's John Law begin	94	188	282	597	1025	1450
4,5: 4-Flash Fulton begins	90	180	270	576	988	1400
6-12: 12-One pg. Fine-a	87	174	261	553	952	1350
13-Magno begins (8/40); last Eisner issue; The Ray app. in full page ad; The Purple Trio begins	87	174	261	553	952	1350
14-Intro. The Ray (9/40) by Lou Fine & others	331	662	993	2317	4059	5800
15-1st Ray-c, 2nd app.	168	336	504	1075	1838	2600
16-The Scarlet Seal begins	135	270	405	864	1482	2100
17-Wun Cloo becomes plastic super-hero by Jack Cole (9-months before Plastic Man); Ray-c	145	290	435	928	1589	2250
18-Midnight by Jack Cole begins (origin & 1st app., 1/41)	181	362	543	1158	1979	2800
19-22: Last Ray by Fine; The Jester begins-#22. 19,21-Ray-c	94	188	282	597	1024	1450
23,24: 23-Ray-c. 24-The Sword app.; last Chic Carter; Wings Wendall dons new costume #24,25	79	158	237	502	864	1225
25-Origin/1st app. Wildfire; Rookie Rankin begins; Ray-c	81	162	243	518	884	1250
26-30: 28-Midnight-c begin, end #85	66	132	198	419	722	1025
31,32,34: The Ray by Rudy Palais; also #33	61	122	183	390	670	950
33-Origin The Marksman	63	126	189	403	689	975
35-37	50	100	150	315	533	750
38-The Yankee Eagle begins; last Midnight by Jack Cole; classic-c by Cole	102	204	306	653	1114	1575
39,40-Last Ray issue	50	100	150	315	533	750
41,44-50	41	82	123	256	428	600
42-Lady Luck begins by Klaus Nordling	135	270	405	864	1482	2100
43-Lady Luck-c (1st & only in Smash)	90	180	270	576	988	1400
51-60	32	64	96	188	307	425
61-70	24	48	72	142	234	325
71-85: 79-Midnight battles the Men from Mars-c/s	21	42	63	122	199	275

NOTE: ***Al Bryant** c-54, 63-68. **Cole** a-17-38, 68, 69, 72, 73, 78, 80, 83, 85; c-38, 60-62, 69-84. **Crandall** a-(Ray)-23-29, 35-38; c-36, 39, 40, 42-44, 46. **Fine** a(Ray)-14, 15, 16(w/**Tuska**), 17-22. **Fox** c-24-35. **Fuje** Ray-30. **Gil Fox** a-6-7, 9, 11-13. **Guardineer** a-(The Marksman)-39-?, 49, 52. **Gustavson** a-4-7, 9, 11-13 (The Jester)-22-46; (Magno)-13-21; (Midnight)-39(Cole inks), 49, 52, 63-65. **Kotzky** a-(Espionage)-33-38; c-45, 47-53. **Nordling** a-49, 52, 63-65. **Powell** a-11, 12, (Abdul the Arab)-13-24.Black X c-2, 6, 9, 11, 13, 16. Bozo the Robot c-1, 3, 5, 8, 10, 12, 14, 18, 20, 22, 24, 26. Midnight c-28-85. The Ray c-15, 17, 19, 21, 23, 25, 27. Wings Wendall c-4, 7.*

SMASH COMICS (Also see All Star Comics 1999 crossover titles)
DC Comics: May, 1999 ($1.99, one-shot)

1-Golden Age Doctor Mid-nite and Hourman						4.00

SMASH HIT SPORTS COMICS
Essankay Publications: V2#1, Jan, 1949

V2#1-L.B. Cole-c/a	29	58	87	170	278	385

SMAX (Also see Top Ten)
America's Best Comics: Oct, 2003 - No. 5, May, 2004 ($2.95, limited series)

1-5-Alan Moore-s/Zander Cannon-a						3.00
... Collected Edition (2004, $19.95, HC with dustjacket) r/#1-5						20.00
... Collected Edition SC (2005, $12.99) r/#1-5						13.00

SMILE COMICS (Also see Gay Comics, Tickle, & Whee)
Modern Store Publ.: 1955 (52 pgs.; 5x7-1/4") (7¢)

1	9	18	27	52	69	85

SMILEY BURNETTE WESTERN (Also see Patches #8 & Six-Gun Heroes)
Fawcett Publ.: March, 1950 - No. 4, Oct, 1950 (All photo front & back-c)

1-Red Eagle begins	26	52	78	154	252	350
2-4	17	34	51	98	154	210

SMILEY (THE PSYCHOTIC BUTTON) (See Evil Ernie)
Chaos! Comics: July, 1998 - May, 1999 ($2.95, one-shots)

1-Ivan Reis-a						3.00
... Holiday Special (1/99), ...'s Spring Break (4/99), ...Wrestling Special (5/99)						3.00

SMILIN' JACK (See Famous Feature Stories and Popular Comics) (Also see Super Book of Comics #1&2 and Super-Book of Comics #7&19 in the Promotional Comics section)
Dell Publishing Co.: No. 5, 1940 - No. 8, Oct-Dec, 1949

Four Color 5 (1940)	94	188	282	597	1025	1450
Four Color 10 (1940)	77	154	231	493	847	1200
Large Feature Comic 12,14,25 (1941)	71	142	213	454	777	1100
Four Color 4 (1942)	71	142	213	454	777	1100
Four Color 14 (1943)	32	64	96	230	515	800
Four Color 36,58 (1943-44)	22	44	66	154	340	525
Four Color 80 (1945)	13	26	39	89	195	300
Four Color 149 (1947)	9	18	27	62	126	190
1 (1-3/48)	11	22	33	72	154	235
2	6	12	18	38	69	100
3-8 (10-12/49)	5	10	15	33	57	80

SMILING SPOOK SPUNKY (See Spunky)

SMITTY (See Popular Comics, Super Book #2, 4 & Super Comics)
Dell Publishing Co.: No. 11, 1940 - No. 7, Aug-Oct, 1949; No. 909, Apr, 1958

Four Color 11 (1940)	57	114	171	362	619	875
Large Feature Comic 26 (1941)	43	86	129	271	461	650
Four Color 6 (1942)	25	50	75	175	388	600
Four Color 32 (1943)	16	32	48	112	249	385
Four Color 65 (1945)	13	26	39	87	191	295
Four Color 99 (1946)	10	20	30	66	138	210
Four Color 138 (1947)	9	18	27	59	117	175
1 (2-4/48)	9	18	27	57	111	165
2-(5-7/48)	5	10	15	31	53	75
3,4: 3-(8-10/48), 4-(11-1/48-49)	4	8	12	27	44	60
5-7, Four Color 909 (4/58)	4	8	12	23	37	50

SMOKEY BEAR (TV) (See March Of Comics #234, 362, 372, 383, 407)
Gold Key: Feb, 1970 - No. 13, Mar, 1973

1	3	6	9	18	28	38
2-5	2	4	6	10	14	18
6-13	2	4	6	8	10	12

SMOKEY STOVER (See Popular Comics, Super Book #5,17,29 & Super Comics)
Dell Publishing Co.: No. 7, 1942 - No. 827, Aug, 1957

Four Color 7 (1942)-Reprints	25	50	75	175	388	600
Four Color 35 (1943)	15	30	45	105	233	360
Four Color 64 (1944)	12	24	36	84	185	285
Four Color 229 (1949)	6	12	18	42	79	115
Four Color 730,827	5	10	15	34	60	85

SMOKEY THE BEAR (See Forest Fire for 1st app.)
Dell Publ. Co.: No. 653, 10/55 - No. 1214, 8/61 (See March of Comics #234)

Four Color 653 (#1)	10	20	30	67	141	215
Four Color 708,754,818,932	6	12	18	40	73	105
Four Color 1016,1119,1214	5	10	15	31	53	75

SMOKY (See Movie Classics)

SMOOTH CRIMINALS
BOOM! Studios (BOOM! Box): Nov, 2018 - No. 8, Aug, 2019 ($3.99)

1-8-Kurt Lustgarten & Kirsten Smith-s/Leisha Riddel-a						4.00

SMOSH
Dynamite Entertainment: 2016 - No. 6, 2016 ($3.99)

1-6: 1-3-McDermott-s/Viglino-a; back-up with Yale Stewart-s/a. 4-Boxman origin						4.00

SMURFS (TV)
Marvel Comics: 1982 (Dec) - No. 3, 1983

1-3	3	6	9	14	20	26
...Treasury Edition 1 (64 pgs.)-r/#1-3	3	6	9	18	28	38

SNAFU (Magazine)
Atlas Comics (RCM): Nov, 1955 - V2#2, Mar, 1956 (B&W)

V1#1-Heath/Severin-a; Everett, Maneely-a	17	34	51	98	154	210
V2#1,2-Severin-a	14	28	42	78	112	145

SNAGGLEPUSS (TV)(See Hanna-Barbera Band Wagon, Quick Draw McGraw #5 & Spotlight #4)
Gold Key: Oct, 1962 - No. 4, Sept, 1963 (Hanna-Barbera)

Snake Eyes: Deadgame #1 © Hasbro

Snotgirl #11 © O'Malley & Hung

Sojourn #4 © CRO

	GD 2.0	VG 4.0	FN 6.0	VF 8.0	VF/NM 9.0	NM- 9.2

1 8 16 24 56 108 160
2-4 6 12 18 37 66 95

SNAGGLEPUSS CHRONICLES (See Exit Stage Left: The Snagglepuss Chronicles)

SNAKE EYES (G.I. Joe)
Devil's Due Publ.: Aug, 2005 - No. 6, Jan, 2006 ($2.95)
1-6-Santalucia-a 3.00
...: Declassified TPB (4/06, $18.95) r/series; source guide 19.00

SNAKE EYES (... and Storm Shadow #13-on)(Cont. from G.I. Joe: Snake Eyes, Volume 2 #7)
IDW Publishing: No. 8, Dec, 2011 - No. 21, Nov, 2011 ($3.99)
8-21: 13-Title change to Snake Eyes and Storm Shadow 4.00

SNAKE EYES: DEADGAME
IDW Publishing: Jul, 2020 - Present ($4.99)
1-4-Rob Liefeld-s/a; multiple covers; Joseph Colton app. 5.00

SNAKE PLISSKEN CHRONICLES, (John Carpenter's...)
Hurricane Entertainment: June, 2003 - No. 4 ($2.99)
Preview Issue (8/02, no cover price) B&W preview; John Carpenter interview 3.00
1-4: 1-Three covers; Rodriguez-a 3.00

SNAKES AND LADDERS
Eddie Campbell Comics: 2001 ($5.95, B&W, one-shot)
nn-Alan Moore-s/Eddie Campbell-a 6.00

SNAKES ON A PLANE (Adaptation of the 2006 movie)
Virgin Comics: Oct, 2006 - No. 2, Nov, 2006 ($2.99, limited series)
1,2: 1-Dixon-s/Purcell-a. JG Jones and photo-c. 2-Klebs, Jr.-a; Moore & photo-c 3.00

SNAKE WOMAN (Shekhar Kapur's...)
Virgin Comics: July, 2006 - No. 10, Apr, 2007 ($2.99)
1-10: 1-6-Michael Gaydos-a/Zeb Wells-s. 1-Two covers by Gaydos & Singh 3.00
#0 (5/07, 99¢) origin of the Snake Goddess; background info; Gaydos-a/c 3.00
... Curse of the 68 (3/08 - No. 4, 5/08, $2.99) 1-4: 1-Ingale-a. 2-Manu-a 3.00
... Tale of the Snake Charmer 1-6 (6/07-12/07, $2.99) Vivek Shinde-a 3.00
... Vol. 1 TPB (6/07, $14.99) r/#1-5; Gaydos sketch pages; creator commentary 15.00
... Vol. 2 TPB (9/07, $14.99) r/#6-10; Cebulski intro. 15.00

SNAP (Formerly Scoop #8; becomes Jest #10,11 & Komik Pages #10)
Harry 'A' Chesler: No. 9, 1944
9-Manhunter, The Voice; WWII gag-c 36 72 108 211 343 475

SNAPPY COMICS
Cima Publ. Co. (Prize Publ.): 1945
1-Airmale app.; 9 pg. Sorcerer's Apprentice adapt; Kiefer-a
39 78 117 240 395 550

SNAPSHOT
Image Comics: Feb, 2013 - No. 4, May, 2013 ($2.99, B&W, limited series)
1-4-Andy Diggle-s/Jock-a/c 3.00

SNARKED
Boom Entertainment (Kaboom!): No. 0, Aug, 2011 - No. 12, Sept, 2012 ($1.00/$3.99)
0-($1.00) Roger Langridge-s/a; sketch gallery, bonus content and games 3.00
1-12: 1-($3.99) Covers by Langridge & Samnee 4.00

SNARKY PARKER (See Life With...)

SNIFFY THE PUP
Standard Publ. (Animated Cartoons): No. 5, Nov, 1949 - No. 18, Sept, 1953
5-Two Frazetta text illos 14 28 42 82 121 160
6-10 9 18 27 50 65 80
11-18 8 16 24 42 54 65

SNOOPER AND BLABBER DETECTIVES (TV) (See Whitman Comic Books)
Gold Key: Nov, 1962 - No. 3, May, 1963 (Hanna-Barbera)
1 6 12 18 42 79 115
2,3 5 10 15 33 57 80

SNOTGIRL
Image Comics: Jul, 2016 - Present ($2.99/$3.99)
1-10-Bryan O'Malley-s/Leslie Hung-a; two covers by O'Malley & Hung on each 3.00
11-15-($3.99) 4.00

SNOW BLIND
BOOM! Studios: Dec, 2015 - No. 4, Mar, 2016 ($3.99)
1-4-Ollie Masters-s/Tyler Jenkins-a 4.00

SNOWFALL
Image Comics: Feb, 2016 - No. 9, Jun, 2017 ($3.99)
1-9-Joe Harris-s/Martín Morazzo-a 4.00

SNOW WHITE (See Christmas With... (in Promotional Comics section), Mickey Mouse Magazine, Movie Comics & Seven Dwarfs)
Dell Publishing Co.: No. 49, July, 1944 - No. 382, Mar, 1952 (Disney-Movie)
Four Color 49 (...& the Seven Dwarfs) 50 100 150 400 900 1400
Four Color 382 (1952)-origin; partial reprint of Four Color 49
11 22 33 73 157 240

SNOW WHITE
Marvel Comics: Jan, 1995 ($1.95, one-shot)
1-r/1937 Sunday newspaper pages 4.00

SNOW WHITE AND THE SEVEN DWARFS
Whitman Publications: April, 1982 (60¢)
nn-r/Four Color 49 1 3 4 6 8 10

SNOW WHITE AND THE SEVEN DWARFS
Dark Horse Comics: Jun, 2019 - No. 3, Aug, 2019 ($3.99, limited series)
1-3-Cecil Castellucci-s/Gabriele Bagnoli-a 4.00

SNOW WHITE AND THE SEVEN DWARFS GOLDEN ANNIVERSARY
Gladstone: Fall, 1987 ($2.95, magazine size, 52 pgs.)
1-Contains poster 2 4 6 9 13 16

SOAP OPERA LOVE
Charlton Comics: Feb, 1983 - No. 3, June, 1983
1-3-Low print run 3 6 9 19 30 40

SOAP OPERA ROMANCES
Charlton Comics: July, 1982 - No. 5, March, 1983
1-5-Nurse Betsy Crane-r; low print run 3 6 9 19 30 40

SOCK MONKEY
Dark Horse Comics: Sept, 1998 - No. 2, Oct, 1998 ($2.95/$2.99, B&W)
1,2-Tony Millionaire-s/a 1 2 3 5 6 8
Vol. 2 -(Tony Millionaire's Sock Monkey) July, 1999 - No. 2, Aug, 1999
1,2 3.00
Vol. 3 -(Tony Millionaire's Sock Monkey) Nov, 2000 - No. 2, Dec, 2000
1,2 3.00
Vol. 4 -(Tony Millionaire's Sock Monkey) May, 2003 - No. 2, Aug, 2003
1,2 3.00
...The Inches Incident (Sept, 2006 - No. 4, Apr, 2007) 1-4-Tony Millionaire-s/a 3.00

SOJOURN
White Cliffs Publ. Co.: Sept, 1977 - No. 2, 1978 ($1.50, B&W & color, tabloid size)
1,2: 1-Tor by Kubert, Eagle by Severin, E. V. Race, Private Investigator by Doug Wildey, T. C. Mars by Aragonés begin plus other strips 2 4 6 8 10 12
NOTE: Most copies came folded. Unfolded copies are worth 50% more.

SOJOURN
CrossGeneration Comics: July, 2001 - No. 34, May, 2004 ($2.95)
Prequel -Ron Marz-s/Greg Land-c/a; preview pages 3.00
1-Ron Marz-s/Greg Land-c/a in most 6.00
2,3 5.00
4-24: 7-Immonen-a. 12-Brigman-a. 17-Lopresti-a. 21-Luke Ross-a 3.00
25-34: 25-$1.00-c. 34-Cariello-a 3.00
...: From the Ashes TPB (2001, $19.95) r/#1-6; Land painted-c 20.00
...: The Dragon's Tale TPB (2002, $15.95) r/#7-12; Jusko painted-c 16.00
...: The Warrior's Tale TPB (2003, $15.95) r/#13-18 16.00
Vol. 4: The Thief's Tale (2003, $15.95) r/#19-24 16.00
Vol. 5: The Sorcerer's Tale (Checker Book Publ.,2007, $17.95) r/#25-30 18.00
Vol. 6: The Berzerker's Tale (Checker Book Publ.,2007, $17.95) r/#31-34, Prequel 18.00
Traveler Vol.1,2 ($9.95) digest-sized reprints of TPBs 10.00

SOLAR (...Man of the Atom) (Also see Doctor Solar)
Valiant/Acclaim Comics (Valiant): Sept, 1991 - No. 60, Apr, 1996 ($1.75-$2.50, 44 pgs.)
1-Layton-a(i) on Solar; Barry Windsor-Smith-c/a 2 4 6 11 16 20
2,4-9: 2-Layton-a(i) on Solar, B. Smith-a. 7-vs. X-O Armor
1 2 3 5 6 8
3-1st app. Harada (11/91); intro. Harbinger 4 8 12 22 35 48
10-(6/92, $3.95)-1st app. Eternal Warrior (6 pgs.); black embossed-c; origin & 1st app. Geoff McHenry (Geomancer) 4 8 12 23 37 50
10-($3.95)-2nd printing 6.00
11-15: 11-1st full app. Eternal Warrior. 12,13-Unity x-overs. 14-1st app. Fred Bender (becomes Dr. Eclipse). 15-2nd Dr. Eclipse 5.00
16-60: 17-X-O Manowar app. 23-Solar splits. 29-1st Valiant Vision book. 33-Valiant Vision; bound-in trading card. 38-Chaos Effect Epsilon Pt.1. 46-52-Dan Jurgens-a(p)/scripts w/Giordano-i. 53,54-Jurgens scripts only. 60-Giffen scripts; Jeff Johnson-a(p) 4.00

Solar, Man of the Atom (2014 series) #1 © RH

Solid Blood #17 © Kirkman & Ottley

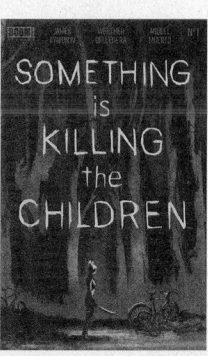

Something is Killing the Children #1 © James Tynion IV

	GD 2.0	VG 4.0	FN 6.0	VF 8.0	VF/NM 9.0	NM- 9.2
0-($9.95, trade paperback)-r/Alpha and Omega origin story; polybagged w/poster						12.00
...: Second Death (1994, $9.95)-r/issues #1-4.						10.00

NOTE: *#1-10 all have free 8 pg. insert "Alpha and Omega" which is a 10 chapter Solar origin story. All 10 centerfolds can pieced together to show climax of story.* ***Ditko*** *a-11p, 14p.* ***Giordano*** *a-46, 47, 48, 49, 50, 51, 52i.* ***Johnson*** *a-60p.* ***Jurgens*** *a-46, 47, 48, 49, 50 , 51, 52p.* ***Layton*** *a-1-3i; c-2i, 11i, 17i, 25i.* ***Miller*** *c-12.* ***Quesada*** *c-17p, 20-23p, 29p.* ***Simonson*** *c-13.* ***B. Smith*** *a-1-10; c-1, 3, 5, 7, 19i.* ***Thibert*** *c-22i, 23i.*

SOLARMAN (See Pendulum Ill. Originals)
Marvel Comics: Jan, 1989 - No. 2, May, 1990 ($1.00, limited series)

1,2 — 3.00

SOLAR, MAN OF THE ATOM (Man of the Atom on cover)
Acclaim Comics (Valiant Heroes): Vol. 2, May, 1997 ($3.95, one-shot, 46 pgs) (1st Valiant Heroes Special Event)

Vol. 2-Reintro Solar; Ninjak cameo; Warren Ellis scripts; Darick Robertson-a — 4.00

SOLAR: MAN OF THE ATOM
Dynamite Entertainment: 2014 - No. 12, 2015 ($3.99)

1-12: 1-Barbiere-s/Bennett-a; 5 covers. 3-Female Solar in costume. 5-White costume — 4.00

SOLAR, MAN OF THE ATOM: HELL ON EARTH
Acclaim Comics (Valiant Heroes): Jan, 1998 - No. 4 ($2.50, limited series)

1-4-Priest-s/ Zircher-a(p) — 3.00

SOLAR, MAN OF THE ATOM: REVELATIONS
Acclaim Comics (Valiant Heroes): Nov, 1997 ($3.95, one-shot, 46 pgs.)

1-Krueger-s/ Zircher-a(p) — 4.00

SOLDIER & MARINE COMICS (Fightin' Army #16 on)
Charlton Comics (Toby Press of Conn. V1#11): No. 11, Dec, 1954 - No. 15, Aug, 1955; V2#9, Dec, 1956

	GD 2.0	VG 4.0	FN 6.0	VF 8.0	VF/NM 9.0	NM- 9.2
V1#11 (12/54)-Bob Powell-a	13	26	39	72	101	130
V1#12(2/55)-15: 12-Photo-c. 14-Photo-c; Colan-a	9	18	27	52	69	85
V2#9(Formerly Never Again; Jerry Drummer V2#10 on)	9	18	27	47	61	75

SOLDIER COMICS
Fawcett Publications: Jan, 1952 - No. 11, Sept, 1953

	GD 2.0	VG 4.0	FN 6.0	VF 8.0	VF/NM 9.0	NM- 9.2
1	15	30	45	90	140	190
2	10	20	30	54	72	90
3-5: 4-What Happened in Taewah	9	18	27	52	69	85
6-11: 8-Illo. in **POP**	9	18	27	47	61	75

SOLDIERS OF FORTUNE
American Comics Group (Creston Publ. Corp.): Mar-Apr, 1951 - No. 13, Feb-Mar, 1953

	GD 2.0	VG 4.0	FN 6.0	VF 8.0	VF/NM 9.0	NM- 9.2
1-Capt. Crossbones by Shelly, Ace Carter, Lance Larson begin	28	56	84	165	270	375
2-(52 pgs.)	15	30	45	90	140	190
3-10: 6-Bondage-c	14	28	42	81	118	155
11-13 (War format)	10	20	30	56	76	95

NOTE: ***Shelly*** *a-1-3, 5.* ***Whitney*** *a-6, 8-11, 13; c-1-3, 5, 6.*

SOLDIERS OF FREEDOM
Americomics: 1987 - No. 2, 1987 ($1.75)

1,2 — 3.00

SOLDIER X (Continued from Cable)
Marvel Comics: Sept, 2002 - No. 12, Aug, 2003 ($2.99/$2.25)

1,10,11,12-($2.99) 1-Kordey-a/Macan-s. 10-Bollers-s/Ranson-a — 3.00
2-9-($2.25) — 3.00

SOLDIER ZERO (From Stan Lee)
BOOM! Studios: Oct, 2010 - No. 12, Sept, 2011 ($3.99)

1-12: 1-4-Cornell-s/Pina-a — 4.00

SOLID BLOOD
Image Comics: No. 17, Dec, 2020 ($3.99, one-shot, newsprint paper)

17-Robert Kirkman-s/Ryan Ottley-a; homage to 1990s Image comics; Michonne cameo — 4.00

SOLITAIRE (Also See Prime V2#6-8)
Malibu Comics (Ultraverse): Nov, 1993 - No. 12, Dec, 1994 ($1.95)

1-($2.50)-Collector's edition bagged w/playing card — 4.00
1-12: 1-Regular edition w/o playing card. 2,4-Break-Thru x-over. 3-2 pg. origin The Night Man. 4-Gatefold-c. 5-Two pg. origin the Strangers — 3.00

SOLO
Marvel Comics: Sept, 1994 - No. 4, Dec, 1994 ($1.75, limited series)

1-4: Spider-Man app. — 3.00

SOLO (Movie)
Dark Horse Comics: July, 1996 - No. 2, Aug, 1996 ($2.50, limited series)

1,2: Adaptation of film; photo-c — 3.00

SOLO (Anthology showcasing individual artists)
DC Comics: Dec, 2004 - No. 12, Oct, 2006 ($4.95/$4.99)

1-12: 1-Tim Sale-a; stories by Sale and various. 2-Richard Corben-a; stories by Corben and Arcudi. 3-Paul Pope. 4-Howard Chaykin. 5-Darwyn Cooke. 6-Jordi Bernet. 7-Michael Allred; Teen Titans & Doom Patrol app. 8-Teddy Kristiansen. 9-Scott Hampton. 10-Damion Scott. 11-Sergio Aragonés. 12-Brendan McCarthy — 5.00

SOLO
Marvel Comics: Dec, 2016 - No. 5, Apr, 2017 ($3.99)

1-5: 1-Thorne & Duggan-s/Diaz-a; Dum Dum Dugan app. — 4.00

SOLO: A STAR WARS STORY ADAPTATION (Titled Star Wars: Solo Adaptation for #1)
Marvel Comics: Dec, 2018 - No. 7, Jun, 2019 ($4.99/$3.99, limited series)

	GD 2.0	VG 4.0	FN 6.0	VF 8.0	VF/NM 9.0	NM- 9.2
1-($4.99) Thompson-s/Sliney-a						5.00
2-5,7-($3.99) Noto-c						4.00
6-1st Darth Maul Crime Syndicate	2	4	6	9	12	15

SOLO AVENGERS (Becomes Avenger Spotlight #21 on)
Marvel Comics: Dec, 1987 - No. 20, July, 1989 (75¢/$1.00)

	GD 2.0	VG 4.0	FN 6.0	VF 8.0	VF/NM 9.0	NM- 9.2
1-Jim Lee-a on back-up story	1	3	4	6	8	10
2-20: 11-Intro Bobcat						4.00

SOLOMON AND SHEBA (Movie)
Dell Publishing Co.: No. 1070, Jan-Mar, 1960

	GD 2.0	VG 4.0	FN 6.0	VF 8.0	VF/NM 9.0	NM- 9.2
Four Color 1070-Sekowsky-a; photo-c	9	18	27	60	120	180

SOLOMON GRUNDY
DC Comics: May, 2009 - No. 7, Nov, 2009 ($2.99)

1-7-Scott Kolins-s/a. 2-Bizarro app. 7-Blackest Night prelude — 3.00
TPB (2010, $19.99) r/#1-7 — 20.00

SOLOMON KANE (Based on the Robert E. Howard character. Also see Blackthorne 3-D Series #60 & Marvel Premiere)
Marvel Comics: Sept, 1985 - No. 6, July, 1986 (Limited series)

1-Double size — 5.00
2-6: 3-6-Williamson-a(i) — 4.00

SOLOMON KANE
Dark Horse Comics: Sept, 2008 - No. 5, Feb, 2009 ($2.99)

1-5: 1-Two covers by Cassaday and Joe Kubert; Guevara-a — 3.00
...: Death's Black Riders 1-4 (1/10 - No. 4, 6/10, $3.50) Robertson-c — 3.50
...: Red Shadows 1-4 (4/11 - No. 4, 7/11, $3.50) Bruce Jones-s/Rahsan Ekedal-a; two covers by Davis & Manchess on each — 3.50

SOLUS
CG Entertainment, Inc.: Apr, 2003 - No. 8, Jan, 2004 ($2.95)

1-8: 1-4,6,7-George Pérez-a/c; Barbara Kesel-s. 5-Ryan-a. 8-Kirk-a — 3.00

SOLUTION, THE
Malibu Comics (Ultraverse): Sept, 1993 - No. 17, Feb, 1995 ($1.95)

1,3-15: 1-Intro Meathook, Deathdance, Black Tiger, Tech. 4-Break-Thru x-over; gatefold-c. 5-2 pg. origin The Strangers. 11-Brereton-c — 3.00
1-($2.50)-Newsstand ed. polybagged w/trading card — 4.00
1-Ultra 5000 Limited silver foil — 8.00
0-Obtained w/Rune #0 by sending coupons from 11 comics — 5.00
2-($2.50, 48 pgs.)-Rune flip-c/story by B. Smith; The Mighty Magnor 1 pg. strip by Aragonés — 4.00
16 ($3.50)-Flip-c Ultraverse Premiere #10 — 4.00
17 ($2.50) — 3.00

SOMERSET HOLMES (See Eclipse Graphic Novel Series)
Pacific Comics/ Eclipse Comics No. 5, 6: Sept, 1983 - No. 6, Dec, 1984 ($1.50, Baxter paper)

1-6: 1-Brent Anderson-c/a. Cliff Hanger by Williamson in all — 4.00

SOMETHING IS KILLING THE CHILDREN
BOOM! Studios: Sept, 2019 - Present ($3.99)

	GD 2.0	VG 4.0	FN 6.0	VF 8.0	VF/NM 9.0	NM- 9.2
1-Tynion IV-s/Dell'edera-a	11	22	33	76	163	250
2	3	6	9	19	30	40
3	3	6	9	16	23	30
4-9	2	4	6	9	12	15
10-15						4.00

SONATA
Image Comics: Jun, 2019 - Present ($3.99)

1-12-David Hine-s/Brian Haberlin-s/a. 12-Flashback to the 1st meeting of Sonata and Treen — 4.00
12-(3D Edition, $7.99) Polybagged with 3D glasses; bonus cover gallery in 3D — 8.00

SONG OF THE SOUTH (See Brer Rabbit)

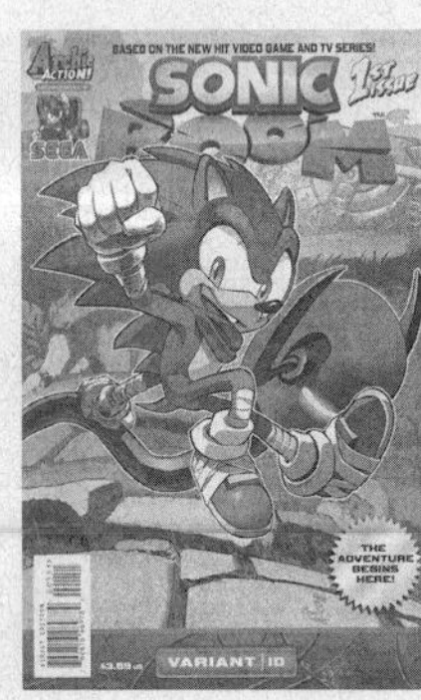

Sonic Boom #1 © Sega

Sonjaversal #1 © RS LLC

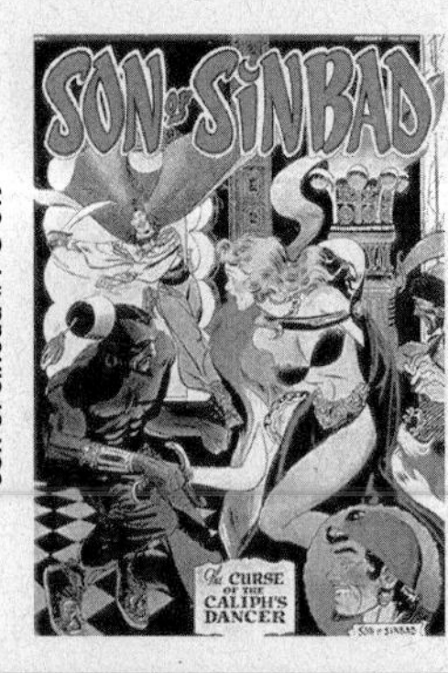

Son of Sinbad #1 © STJ

	GD	VG	FN	VF	VF/NM	NM-
	2.0	4.0	6.0	8.0	9.0	9.2

SONIC & KNUCKLES
Archie Comics: Aug, 1995 ($2.00)
1 2 4 6 8 11 14

SONIC BOOM
Archie Comic Publications: Dec, 2014 - No. 11, Oct, 2015 ($3.99)
1-11: 1-Regular-c and 4 interlocking variant covers. 2-7,11-Two covers on each. 8-10-"Worlds Unite" Sonic/Mega Man x-over; 3 covers 4.00

SONIC COMIC ORIGINS AND MEGA MAN X
Archie Comic Publications: Jun/Jul 2014 (giveaway)
... Free Comic Book Day Edition - Flipbook; Freedom Fighters app. 3.00

SONIC DISRUPTORS
DC Comics: Dec, 1987 - No. 7, July, 1988 ($1.75, unfinished limited series)
1-7 3.00

SONIC MEGA DRIVE
Archie Comic Publications: Aug, 2016 ($3.99, limited series)
1-25th Anniversary celebration; Flynn-s/Hesse-a 4.00
... - The Next Level (12/16, $4.99) Flynn-s/Hesse-a; Metal Sonic app. 5.00

SONIC'S FRIENDLY NEMESIS KNUCKLES
Archie Publications: July, 1996 - No. 3, Sept, 1996 ($1.50, limited series)
1-3 1 2 3 5 6 8

SONIC SUPER DIGEST
Archie Publications: Dec, 2012 - No. 17 ($3.99/$4.99)
1-7-($3.99) 4.00
8-17-($4.99) 5.00

SONIC SUPER SPECIAL
Archie Publications: 1997 - No. 15, Feb, 2001 ($2.00/$2.25/$2.29, 48 pgs)
1 2 4 6 11 16 20
2,3 5.00
4-6,8-15: 10-Sabrina-c/app. 15-Sin City spoof 4.00
7-(w/Image) Spawn, Maxx, Savage Dragon-c/app.; Valentino-a 2 4 6 9 12 15

SONIC THE HEDGEHOG (TV, video game)
Archie Comics: No. 0, Feb, 1993 - No. 3, May, 1993 ($1.25, mini-series)
0(2/93),1: Shaw-a(p) & covers on all 4 8 12 25 40 55
2,3 3 6 9 16 23 30
Beginnings TPB (2003, $10.95) r/#0-3 11.00
...: The Beginning TPB (2006, $10.95) r/#0-3 11.00

SONIC THE HEDGEHOG (TV, video game)
Archie Comics: July, 1993 - No. 290, Feb, 2017 ($1.25-$2.99)
1 5 10 15 35 63 90
2 3 6 9 21 33 45
3 3 6 9 16 23 30
4-10: 8-Neon ink-c. 2 4 6 11 16 20
11-20 2 4 6 9 13 16
21-30 ($1.50): 25-Silver ink-c 2 4 6 8 10 12
31-50 1 2 3 5 6 8
51-93 4.00
94-212: 117-Begin $2.19-c. 152-Begin $2.25-c. 157-Shadow app. 198-Begin $2.50 3.00
213-249,251-263: 213-Begin $2.99-c. 248-263-Two covers 3.00
250-($3.99) Wraparound-c; part 9 of Worlds Collide x-over with Mega Man 4.00
264-274,276-290-($3.99) Two covers on most. 273,274-"Worlds Unite" Sonic/Mega Man x-over; 3 covers on each. 288-290-Genesis of a Hero 4.00
275-($4.99) "Worlds Unite" Sonic/Mega Man x-over; six covers 5.00
Free Comic Book Day Edition 1 (2007)- Leads into Sonic the Hedgehog #175 3.00
Free Comic Book Day Edition 2009 - Reprints Sonic the Hedgehog #1 from July 1993 3.00
Free Comic Book Day Edition 2010 - 2012: 2010-New story 3.00
Sonic and Mega Man: World's Collide Prelude, FCBD Edition (6-7/13) 3.00
Sonic and Mega Man: Worlds Unite FCBD Edition (6-7/15) Prelude to crossover 3.00
Sonic Sampler: Free Comic Book Day Edition (5/16) Sonic & Sonic Universe stories 3.00
Sonic: Worlds Unite Battles (9/15, $3.99) Sonic/Mega Man x-over; 3 wraparound covers 4.00
Triple Trouble Special (10/95, $2.00, 48 pgs.) 1 3 4 6 8 10

SONIC THE HEDGEHOG (TV, video game)
IDW Publishing: Apr, 2018 - Present ($3.99, #1-4 weekly, #5-on monthly)
1-12,14-24,26-37: 1-Flynn-s/Yardley-a. 3-Knuckles app. 4-Intro. Tangle the Lemur 4.00
13,25-($4.99) 13-Tails, Rough & Tumble app.; four covers. 25-The Deadly Six app. 5.00
... Halloween Comicfest 1 (10/19, free giveaway) r/#1 3.00

SONIC THE HEDGEHOG: BAD GUYS
IDW Publishing: Sept, 2020 - No. 4, Dec, 2020 ($3.99)
1-4-Ian Flynn-s/Jack Lawrence-a. 1-Five covers. 2-4-Three covers 4.00

SONIC THE HEDGEHOG: TANGLE & WHISPER
IDW Publishing: No. 0, Apr, 2019 - No. 4, Oct, 2019 ($3.99, limited series)
0-(4/19, no price) Ian Flynn-s/Evan Stanley-a; previews series and Sonic storyline 3.00
1-4-($3.99) Ian Flynn-s/Evan Stanley-a; Mimic app.; multiple covers on each 4.00

SONIC UNIVERSE (Sonic the Hedgehog)
Archie Publications: Apr, 2009 - No. 94, Mar, 2017 ($2.50/$2.99/$3.99)
1-15 3.00
16-66: 16-Begin $2.99-c. 51-66-Two covers. 51-54-Worlds Collide 3.00
67-94-($3.99) Two covers on most. 75-"Worlds Unite" Sonic/Mega Man x-over prelude with nine covers. 76-78-"Worlds Unite" x-over; 3 covers on each. 87-90-Shattered 4.00

SONIC VS. KNUCKLES "BATTLE ROYAL" SPECIAL
Archie Publications: 1997 ($2.00, one-shot)
1 2 4 6 9 12 15

SONIC X (Sonic the Hedgehog)
Archie Publications: Nov, 2005 - No. 40, Feb, 2009 ($2.25)
1-Sam Speed app. 4.00
2-40 3.00

SONJAVERSAL (Red Sonja)
Dynamite Entertainment: 2021 - Present ($3.99)
1-Hastings-s/Qualano & Perez-a; alternate Sonjas meet 4.00

SON OF AMBUSH BUG (See Ambush Bug)
DC Comics: July, 1986 - No. 6, Dec, 1986 (75¢)
1-6: Giffen-c/a in all. 5-Bissette-a. 4.00

SON OF BLACK BEAUTY (Also see Black Beauty)
Dell Publishing Co.: No. 510, Oct, 1953 - No. 566, June, 1954
Four Color 510,566 5 10 15 31 53 75

SON OF FLUBBER (See Movie Comics)

SON OF HULK (Continues from Skaar: Son of Hulk #12) (See Realm of Kings)
Marvel Comics: No. 13, Sept, 2009 - No. 17, Jan, 2010 ($2.99)
13-17: 13,15-17-Galactus app. 3.00

SON OF M (Also see House of M series)
Marvel Comics: Feb, 2006 - No. 6, July, 2006 ($2.99, limited series)
1-6: 1-Powerless Quicksilver; Martinez-a. 2-Quicksilver regains powers; Inhumans app. 3.00
Decimation: Son of M (2006, $13.99, TPB) r/series; Martinez sketch pages 14.00

SON OF MERLIN
Image Comics (Top Cow): Feb, 2013 - No. 5, Jun, 2013 ($1.00/$2.99, limited series)
1-5: 1-($1.00-c); Napton-s/Zid-a; covers by Zid & Sejic. 2-($2.99) 3.00

SON OF MUTANT WORLD
Fantagor Press: 1990 - No. 5, 1990? ($2.00, bi-monthly)
1-5: 1-3: Corben-c/a. 4,5 ($1.75, B&W) 3.00

SON OF ORIGINS OF MARVEL COMICS (See Fireside Book Series)

SON OF SATAN (Also see Ghost Rider #1 & Marvel Spotlight #12)
Marvel Comics Group: Dec, 1975 - No. 8, Feb, 1977 (25¢)
1-Mooney-a; Kane-c(p), Starlin splash(p) 4 8 12 28 47 65
2,6-8: 2-Origin The Possessor. 8-Heath-a 2 4 6 11 16 20
3-5-(Regular 25¢ editions)(4-8/76): 5-Russell-p 2 4 6 11 16 20
3-5-(30¢-c variants, limited distribution) 4 8 12 27 44 60
...: Marvel Spotlight #12 Facsimile Edition (11/19, $3.99) r/issue with original 1973 ads 4.00

SON OF SINBAD (Also see Abbott & Costello & Daring Adventures)
St. John Publishing Co.: Feb, 1950
1-Kubert-c/a 57 114 171 362 619 875

SON OF SUPERMAN (Elseworlds)
DC Comics: 1999 ($14.95, prestige format, one-shot)
nn-Chaykin & Tischman-s/Williams III & Gray-a 15.00

SON OF TOMAHAWK (See Tomahawk)

SON OF VULCAN (Formerly Mysteries of Unexplored Worlds #1-48; Thunderbolt V3#51 on)
Charlton Comics: V2#49, Nov, 1965 - V2#50, Jan, 1966
V2#49,50: 50-Roy Thomas scripts (1st pro work) 3 6 9 17 26 35

SONS OF ANARCHY (Based on the TV series)
BOOM! Studios: Sept, 2013 - No. 25, Sept, 2015 ($3.99, originally a 6-issue limited series)
1-24: 1-6-Christopher Golden-s/Damian Couceiro-a; multiple covers on each 4.00

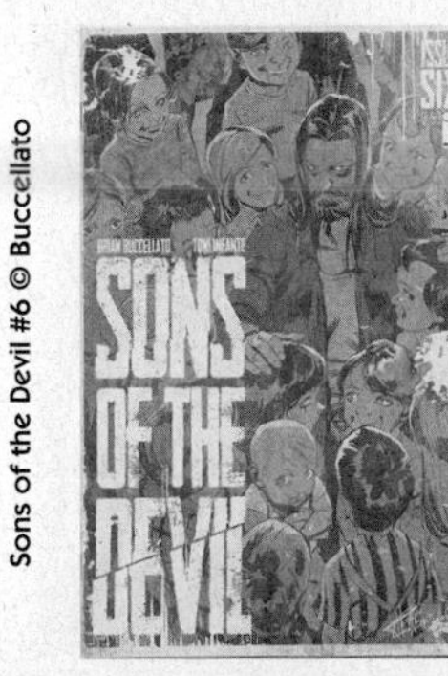
Sons of the Devil #6 © Buccellato

Soulfire V8 #1 © AspenMLT

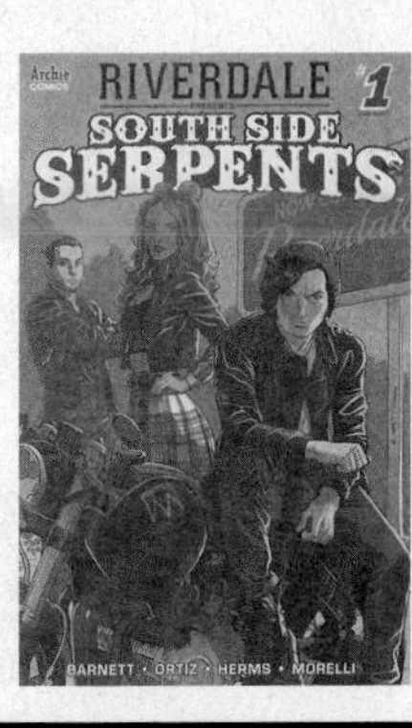
South Side Serpents #1 © ACP

	GD 2.0	VG 4.0	FN 6.0	VF 8.0	VF/NM 9.0	NM- 9.2

25-($4.99) Last issue; Ferrier-s/Bergara-a; three covers 5.00

SONS OF ANARCHY REDWOOD ORIGINAL (TV series)
BOOM! Studios: Aug, 2016 - No. 12, Jul, 2017 ($3.99)

1-12: 1-Prequel with 18-year-old Jax Teller. 1-4-Masters-s/Pizzari-a; multiple covers 4.00

SONS OF KATIE ELDER (See Movie Classics)

SONS OF THE DEVIL
Image Comics: May, 2015 - No. 14, Jul, 2017 ($2.99/$3.99)

1-5: 1-Brian Buccellato-s/Toni Infante-a 3.00
6-14-($3.99) 4.00

SORCERY (See Chilling Adventures in... & Red Circle...)

SORORITY SECRETS
Toby Press: July, 1954

	GD	VG	FN	VF	VF/NM	NM-
1	23	46	69	136	223	310

SOULFIRE (MICHAEL TURNER PRESENTS:...) (Also see Eternal Soulfire)
Aspen MLT, Inc.: No. 0, 2004 - No. 10, Jul, 2009 ($2.50/$2.99)

0-($2.50) Turner-a/c; Loeb-s; intro. to characters & development sketches 3.00
1-($2.99) Two covers 3.00
1-Diamond Previews Exclusive 5.00
2-9: 2,3-Two covers. 4-Four covers 3.00
10-($3.99) Benitez-a 4.00
... Sourcebook 1 (3/15, $4.99) Character profiles; two covers by Turner 5.00
...: The Collected Edition Vol. 1 (5/05, $6.99) r/#1,2; cover gallery 7.00
Hardcover Volume 1 (12/05, $24.99) r/#0-5 & preview from Wizard Mag.; Johns intro. 25.00

SOULFIRE (MICHAEL TURNER PRESENTS:...) (Volume 2)
Aspen MLT, Inc.: No. 0, Oct, 2009 - No. 9, Jan, 2011 ($2.50/$2.99)

0-($2.50) Marcus To-a 3.00
1-9-($2.99) 1-Five covers. 9-Covers by To and Linsner 3.00

SOULFIRE (MICHAEL TURNER'S...) (Volume 3)
Aspen MLT, Inc.: No. 0, Apr, 2011 - No. 8, May, 2012 ($1.99/$2.99)

0-($1.99) Krul-s/Fabok-a; 4 covers 3.00
1-8-($2.99) 1-Four covers 3.00
... Despair (7/12, $3.99) Schwartz-s/Marks-a; 3 covers 4.00
... Faith (7/12, $3.99) McMurray-s/Oum-a; 3 covers 4.00
... Hope (7/12, $3.99) Krul-s/Varese-a; 3 covers 4.00
... Power (7/12, $3.99) Wohl-s/Randolph-a; 3 covers 4.00
... Primer (6/12, $1.00) Reprints and story summaries 3.00

SOULFIRE (MICHAEL TURNER'S...) (Volume 4)
Aspen MLT, Inc.: Aug, 2012 - No. 8, Oct, 2013 ($3.99)

1-8-Krul-s/DeBalfo-a; multiple covers on each 4.00

SOULFIRE (MICHAEL TURNER'S...) (Volume 5)
Aspen MLT, Inc.: Nov, 2013 - No. 8, Oct, 2014 ($1.00/$3.99)

1-($1.00) Krul-s/Marion-a; multiple covers 3.00
2-8-($3.99) Multiple covers on each 4.00
Annual 1 2014 (7/14, $5.99) Art by Garbowska, Hanson, Turner, Cafaro 6.00

SOULFIRE (ALL NEW MICHAEL TURNER'S...) (Volume 6)
Aspen MLT, Inc.: Mar, 2017 - No. 8, Oct, 2017 ($3.99)

1-8-($3.99) Multiple covers on each. 1-Krul-s/Cafaro-a 4.00

SOULFIRE (MICHAEL TURNER'S...) (Volume 7)
Aspen MLT, Inc.: Jul, 2018 - No. 8, Feb, 2019 ($3.99)

1-8: 1-Krul-s/Ladjouze-a; multiple covers 4.00
... Primer 1 (7/18, 25¢) Series intro. and bonus text recaps of previous volumes 3.00

SOULFIRE (MICHAEL TURNER'S...) (Volume 8)
Aspen MLT, Inc.: Jun, 2019 - No. 6, Nov, 2019 ($3.99)

1-6: 1-Krul-s/Forté-a; multiple covers 4.00

SOULFIRE: CHAOS REIGN
Aspen MLT, Inc.: No. 0, June, 2006 - No. 3, Jan, 2007 ($2.50/$2.99)

0-($2.50) Three covers; Marcus To-a; J.T. Krul-s 3.00
1-3-($2.99) 1-Three covers 3.00
...: Beginnings (7/06, $1.99) Marcus To-a; J.T. Krul-s 3.00
...: Beginnings 1 (7/07, $1.99) Francisco Herrera-a; J.T. Krul-s 3.00

SOULFIRE: DYING OF THE LIGHT
Aspen MLT, Inc.: No. 0, 2004 - No. 5, Feb, 2006 ($2.50/$2.99)

0-($2.50) Three covers; Gunnell-a; Krul-s; back-story to the Soulfire universe 3.00
1-5-($2.99) 1-Five covers 3.00
... Vol. 1 TPB (2007, $14.99) r/#0-5; Gunnell sketch pages, cover gallery 15.00

SOULFIRE: NEW WORLD ORDER
Aspen MLT, Inc.: No. 0, Jul, 2007; May, 2009 - No. 5, Dec, 2009 ($2.50/$2.99)

0 (7/07, $2.50) Two covers; Herrera-a/Krul-s 3.00
1-5-($2.99) 1-Four covers 3.00

SOULFIRE: SHADOW MAGIC
Aspen MLT, Inc.: No. 0, Nov, 2008 - No. 5, May, 2009 ($2.50/$2.99)

0-($2.50) Two covers; Sana Takeda-a 3.00
1-5-($2.99) 1-Two covers 3.00

SOUL SAGA
Image Comics (Top Cow): Feb, 2000 - No. 5, Apr, 2001 ($2.50)

1-5: 1-Madureira-c; Platt & Batt-a 3.00

SOULSEARCHERS AND COMPANY
Claypool Comics: June, 1995 - No. 82, Jan, 2007 ($2.50, B&W)

1-10: Peter David scripts 5.00
11-82 3.00

SOULWIND
Image Comics: Mar, 1997 - No. 8 ($2.95, B&W, limited series)

1-8: 5-"The Day I Tried To Live" pt. 1 3.00
Book Five; The August Ones (Oni Press, 3/01, $8.50) 8.50
...The Kid From Planet Earth (1997, $9.95, TPB) 10.00
...The Kid From Planet Earth (Oni Press, 1/00, $8.50, TPB) 8.50
...The Day I Tried to Live (Oni Press, 4/00, $8.50, TPB) 8.50
The Complete Soulwind TPB ($29.95, 11/03, 8" x 5 1/2") r/Oni Books #1-5 30.00

SOUPY SALES COMIC BOOK (TV)(The Official...)
Archie Publications: 1965

	GD	VG	FN	VF	VF/NM	NM-
1-(Teen-age)	8	16	24	56	108	160

SOUTHERN BASTARDS
Image Comics: Apr, 2014 - No. 20, May, 2018 ($3.50/$3.99)

1-Jason Aaron-s/Jason Latour-a 8.00
2-20: 18-Chris Brunner-a 4.00

SOUTHERN CROSS
Image Comics: Mar, 2014 - No. 14, Mar, 2018 ($2.99/$3.99)

1-6-Becky Cloonan-s/c; Andy Belanger-a 3.00
7-14-($3.99) Cloonan-s/c; Belanger-a 4.00

SOUTHERN KNIGHTS, THE (See Crusaders #1)
Guild Publ/Fictioneer Books: No. 2, 1983 - No. 41, 1993 (B&W)

	GD	VG	FN	VF	VF/NM	NM-
2-Magazine size	1	2	3	5	6	8
3-35, 37-41						3.00
36-($3.50-c)						4.00
Dread Halloween Special 1, Primer Special 1 (Spring, 1989, $2.25)						3.00
Graphic Novels #1-4						4.00

SOUTH SIDE SERPENTS (Based on the Riverdale TV series)
Archie Comic Publications: Mar, 2021 ($3.99, one-shot)

1-Jughead, FP Jones & Toni Topaz app.; David Barnett-s/Richard Ortiz-a 4.00

SOVEREIGNS
Dynamite Entertainment: No. 0, 2017 - No. 5, 2017 ($1.00/$3.99)

0-($1.00) Short stories of Magnus, Turok, Solar and Doctor Spektor 3.00
1-5-($3.99) Fawkes-s/Desjardins-a; back-up stories on each 4.00

SOVEREIGN SEVEN (Also see Showcase '95 #12)
DC Comics: July, 1995 - No. 36, July, 1998 ($1.95) (1st creator-owned mainstream DC comic)

1-1st app. Sovereign Seven (Reflex, Indigo, Cascade, Finale, Cruiser, Network & Rampart); 1st app. Maitresse; Darkseid app.; Chris Claremont-s & Dwayne Turner-c/a begins 4.00
1-Gold 8.00
1-Platinum 40.00
2-36: 2-Wolverine cameo. 4-Neil Gaiman cameo. 5,8-Batman app. 7-Ramirez cameo (from the movie Highlander). 9-Humphrey Bogart cameo from Casablanca. 10-Impulse app; Manoli Wetherell & Neal Conan cameo from Uncanny X-Men #226. 11-Robin app. 16-Final Night. 24-Superman app. 25-Power Girl app. 28-Impulse-c/app. 3.00
Annual 1 (1995, $3.95)-Year One story; Big Barda & Lobo app.; Jeff Johnson-c/a 4.00
Annual 2 (1996, $2.95)-Legends of the Dead Earth; Leonardi-c/a 4.00
...Plus 1(2/97, $2.95)-Legion-c/app. 4.00
TPB-($12.95) r/#1-5, Annual #1 & Showcase '95 #12 13.00

SPACE: ABOVE AND BEYOND (TV)
Topps Comics: Jan, 1996 - No. 3, Mar, 1996 ($2.95, limited series)

1-3: Adaptation of pilot episode; Steacy-c. 3.00

SPACE: ABOVE AND BEYOND--THE GAUNTLET (TV)

Space Adventures #3 © CC

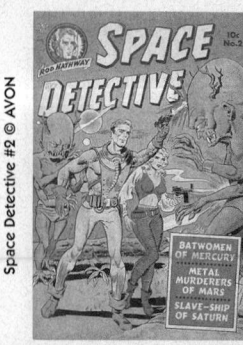

Space Detective #2 © AVON

Spaceman #5 © MAR

	GD	VG	FN	VF	VF/NM	NM-
	2.0	4.0	6.0	8.0	9.0	9.2

Topps Comics: May, 1996 -No. 2, June, 1996 ($2.95, limited series)

1,2 3.00

SPACE ACE (Also see Manhunt!)
Magazine Enterprises: No. 5, 1952

5(A-1 #61)-Guardineer-a 74 148 222 470 810 1150

SPACE ACE: DEFENDER OF THE UNIVERSE (Based on the Don Bluth video game)
CrossGen Comics: Oct, 2003 - No. 6 ($2.95, limited series)

1,2-Kirkman-s/Borges-a 3.00

SPACE ACTION
Ace Magazines (Junior Books): June, 1952 - No. 3, Oct, 1952

1-Cameron-a in all (1 story) 100 200 300 635 1093 1550
2,3 63 126 189 403 689 975

SPACE ADVENTURES (War At Sea #22 on)
Capitol Stories/Charlton Comics: 7/52 - No. 21, 8/56; No. 23, 5/58 - No. 59, 11/64; V3#60, 10/67; V1#2, 7/68 - V1#8, 7/69; No. 9, 5/78 - No. 13, 3/79

1-Fago/Morales world on fire-c 77 134 231 493 847 1200
2 34 68 102 204 332 460
3-5: 4,6-Flying saucer-c/stories 28 56 84 168 274 380
6,8,9: 8-Robot-c. 9-A-Bomb panel 25 50 75 150 245 340
7-Sex change story "Transformation" 97 194 291 621 1061 1500
10,11-Ditko-c/a. 10-Robot-c. 11-Two Ditko stories 74 148 222 470 810 1150
12-Ditko-c (classic) 290 580 870 1856 3178 4500
13-(Fox-r, 10-11/54); Blue Beetle-c/story 17 34 51 105 165 235
14,15,17,18: 14-Blue Beetle-c/story; Fox-r (12-1/54-55, last pre-code).
15,17,18-Rocky Jones-c/s.(TV); 15-Part photo-c 22 44 66 128 209 290
16-Krigstein-a; Rocky Jones-c/story (TV) 24 48 72 140 230 320
19-Robot-c by Giordano 16 32 48 98 154 210
20-Reprints Fawcett's "Destination Moon" 24 48 72 142 234 325
21-(8/56) (no #22)(Becomes War At Sea) 16 32 48 98 154 210
23-(5/58; formerly Nyoka, The Jungle Girl)-Reprints Fawcett's "Destination Moon"
22 44 66 128 209 290
24,25,31,32-Ditko-a. 24-Severin-a(signed "LePoer") 22 44 66 128 209 290
26,27-Ditko-a(4) each. 26,28-Flying saucer-c 23 46 69 136 223 310
28-30 13 26 39 72 101 130
33-Origin/1st app. Capt. Atom by Ditko (3/60) 161 322 483 1030 1765 2500
34-40,42-All Captain Atom by Ditko 28 56 84 168 274 380
41,43,45-59: 43-Alan Shephard strory, 2nd man in space. 45-Mercury Man app.
5 10 15 33 57 80
44-1st app. Mercury Man 6 12 18 40 73 105
V3#60(#1, 10/67)-Presents UFO origin & 1st app. Paul Mann & The Saucers From the Future
5 10 15 33 57 80
2,5,6,8 (1968-69)-Ditko-a: 2-Aparo-c/a 3 6 9 21 33 45
3,4,7: 4-Aparo-c/a 3 6 9 17 26 35
9-13(1978-79)-Capt. Atom-r/Space Adventures by Ditko; 9-Reprints origin/1st app. Capt. Atom from #33 6.00

NOTE: *Aparo a-V3#60. c-V3#8.* ***Ditko*** *c-12, 31-42.* ***Giordano*** *c-3, 4, 7-9, 18p, 19* ***Krigstein*** *c-15.* ***Shuster*** *a-11. Issues 13 & 14 have Blue Beetle logos; #15-18 have Rocky Jones logos.*

SPACE BANDITS
Image Comics: Jul, 2019 - No. 5, Nov, 2019 ($3.99/$5.99, limited series)

1-4-($3.99) Mark Millar-s/Matteo Scalera-a 4.00
5-($5.99) 6.00

SPACE BASTARDS
Humanoids Inc.: Jul, 2019 - No. 5, Nov, 2019 ($5.99)

1-Darick Robertson-a/Eric Peterson & Joe Aubrey-s 6.00

SPACE BUSTERS
Ziff-Davis Publ. Co.: Spring, 1952 - No. 2, Fall, 1952

1-Krigstein-a(3); Painted-c by Norman Saunders 94 188 282 597 1025 1450
2-Kinstler-a(2 pgs.); Saunders painted-c 77 154 231 493 847 1200

NOTE: ***Anderson*** *a-2. Bondage c-2.*

SPACE CADET (See Tom Corbett,...)

SPACE CIRCUS
Dark Horse Comics: July, 2000 - No. 4, Oct, 2000 ($2.95, limited series)

1-4-Aragonés-a/Evanier-s 3.00

SPACE COMICS (Formerly Funny Tunes)
Avon Periodicals: No. 4, Mar-Apr, 1954 - No. 5, May-June, 1954

4,5-Space Mouse, Peter Rabbit, Super Pup (formerly Spotty the Pup), & Merry Mouse continue from Funny Tunes 10 20 30 54 72 90
I.W. Reprint #8 (nd)-Space Mouse-r 2 4 6 9 13 16

	GD	VG	FN	VF	VF/NM	NM-
	2.0	4.0	6.0	8.0	9.0	9.2

SPACE DETECTIVE
Avon Periodicals: July, 1951 - No. 4, July, 1952

1-Rod Hathway, Space Detective begins, ends #4; Wood-c/a(3)-23 pgs.; "Opium Smugglers of Venus" drug story; Lucky Dale-r/Saint #4 171 342 513 1094 1872 2650
2-Tales from the Shadow Squad story; Wood/Orlando-c; Wood inside layouts; "Slave Ship of Saturn" story 123 246 369 787 1344 1900
3,4: 3-Kinstler-c. 4-Kinstlerish-a by McCann 58 116 174 371 636 900
I.W. Reprint #1(Reprints #2), 8(Reprints cover #1 & part Famous Funnies #191)
4 8 12 25 40 55

SPACE EXPLORER (See March of Comics #202)

SPACE FAMILY ROBINSON (TV)(...Lost in Space #15-37, ...Lost in Space On Space Station One #38 on)(See Gold Key Champion)
Gold Key: Dec, 1962 - No. 36, Oct, 1969; No. 37, 10/73 - No. 54, 11/78; No. 55, 3/81 - No. 59, 5/82 (All painted covers)

1-(Low distribution); Spiegle-a in all 33 66 99 238 532 825
2(3/63)-Family becomes lost in space 12 24 36 81 176 270
3-5 8 16 24 51 96 140
6-10: 6-Captain Venture back-up stories begin 6 12 18 38 69 100
11-20: 14-(10/65). 15-Title change (1/66) 5 10 15 30 50 70
21-36: 28-Last 12¢ issue. 36-Captain Venture ends 4 8 12 23 37 50
37-48: 37-Origin retold 2 4 6 11 16 20
49-59: Reprints #49,50,55-59 2 4 6 8 10 12

NOTE: *The TV show first aired on 9/15/65. Title changed after TV show debuted.*

SPACE FAMILY ROBINSON (See March of Comics #320, 328, 352, 404, 414)

SPACE GHOST (TV) (Also see Golden Comics Digest #2 & Hanna-Barbera Super TV Heroes #3-7)
Gold Key: March, 1967 (Hanna-Barbera) (TV debut was 9/10/66)

1 (10199-703)-Spiegle-a 31 62 93 223 499 775

SPACE GHOST (TV cartoon)
Comico: Mar, 1987 ($3.50, deluxe format, one-shot) (Hanna-Barbera)

1-Steve Rude-c/a; Evanier-s; Steacy painted-a 3 6 9 14 19 24

SPACE GHOST (TV cartoon)
DC Comics: Jan, 2005 - No. 6, June, 2005 ($2.95/$2.99, limited series)

1-6-Alex Ross-c/Ariel Olivetti-a/Joe Kelly-s; origin of Space Ghost 3.00
TPB (2005, $14.99) r/series; cover gallery 15.00

SPACE GIANTS, THE (TV cartoon)
FBN Publications: 1979 ($1.00, B&W, one-shots)

1-Based on Japanese TV series 3 6 9 14 20 25

SPACEHAWK
Dark Horse Comics: 1989 - No. 3, 1990 ($2.00, B&W)

1-3-Wolverton-c/a(r) plus new stories by others. 5.00

SPACE JAM
DC Comics: 1996 ($5.95, one-shot, movie adaption)

1-Wraparound photo cover of Michael Jordan 2 4 6 8 10 12

SPACE KAT-ETS (...in 3-D)
Power Publishing Co.: Dec, 1953 (25¢, came w/glasses)

1 32 64 96 192 314 435

SPACEKNIGHTS
Marvel Comics: Oct, 2000 - No. 5, Feb, 2001 ($2.99, limited series)

1-5-Starlin-s/Batista-a 3.00

SPACEKNIGHTS
Marvel Comics: Dec, 2012 - No. 3, Feb, 2013 ($3.99, limited series)

1-3-Reprints the 2000-2001 series & Annihilation: Conquest Prologue 4.00

SPACEMAN (Speed Carter...)
Atlas Comics (CnPC): Sept, 1953 - No. 6, July, 1954

1-Grey tone-c 113 226 339 723 1237 1750
2 58 116 174 371 636 900
3-6: 4-A-Bomb explosion-c 54 108 162 343 574 825

NOTE: ***Everett*** *c-1, 3.* ***Heath*** *a-1.* ***Maneely*** *a-1(3), 2(4), 3(3), 4-6; c-5, 6.* ***Romita*** *a-1.* ***Sekowsky*** *c-4.* ***Sekowsky/Abel*** *a-4(3).* ***Tuska*** *a-5(3).*

SPACE MAN
Dell Publ. Co.: No. 1253, 1-3/62 - No. 8, 3-5/64; No. 9, 7/72 - No. 10, 10/72

Four Color 1253 (#1)(1-3/62)(15¢-c) 8 16 24 51 96 140
2,3: 2-(15¢-c). 3-(12¢-c) 4 8 12 27 44 60
4-8-(12¢-c) 3 6 9 21 33 45
9,10-(15¢-c): 9-Reprints #1253. 10-Reprints #2 2 4 6 9 12 15

SPACEMAN (From the Atomics)

Spaceman #9 © Azzarello & Risso

Space Worlds #6 © MAR

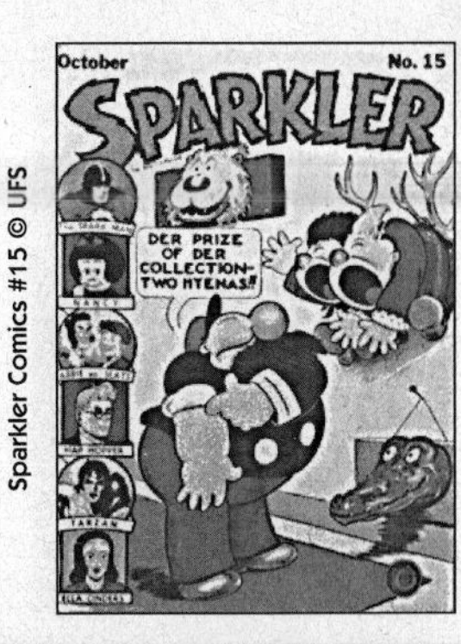

Sparkler Comics #15 © UFS

Oni Press: July, 2002 ($2.95, one-shot)

	GD 2.0	VG 4.0	FN 6.0	VF 8.0	VF/NM 9.0	NM- 9.2
1-Mike Allred-s/a; Lawrence Marvit additional art						3.00

SPACEMAN
DC Comics (Vertigo): Dec, 2011 - No. 9, Oct, 2012 ($1.00/$2.99, limited series)

	GD 2.0	VG 4.0	FN 6.0	VF 8.0	VF/NM 9.0	NM- 9.2
1-($1.00) Azzarello-s/Risso-a/Johnson-c						4.00
2-9-($2.99)						3.00

SPACE MOUSE (Also see Funny Tunes & Space Comics)
Avon Periodicals: April, 1953 - No. 5, Apr-May, 1954

	GD 2.0	VG 4.0	FN 6.0	VF 8.0	VF/NM 9.0	NM- 9.2
1	14	28	42	82	121	160
2	9	18	27	50	65	80
3-5	8	16	24	40	50	60

SPACE MOUSE (Walter Lantz...#1; see Comic Album #17)
Dell Publishing Co./Gold Key: No. 1132, Aug-Oct, 1960 - No. 5, Nov, 1963 (Walter Lantz)

	GD 2.0	VG 4.0	FN 6.0	VF 8.0	VF/NM 9.0	NM- 9.2
Four Color 1132,1244, 1(11/62)(G.K.)	5	10	15	33	57	80
2-5	4	8	12	23	37	50

SPACE MYSTERIES
I.W. Enterprises: 1964 (Reprints)

	GD 2.0	VG 4.0	FN 6.0	VF 8.0	VF/NM 9.0	NM- 9.2
1-r/Journey Into Unknown Worlds #4 w/new-c	3	6	9	15	22	28
8,9: 9-r/Planet Comics #73	3	6	9	15	22	28

SPACE: 1999 (TV) (Also see Power Record Comics)
Charlton Comics: Nov, 1975 - No. 7, Nov, 1976

	GD 2.0	VG 4.0	FN 6.0	VF 8.0	VF/NM 9.0	NM- 9.2
1-Origin Moonbase Alpha; Staton-c/a	3	6	9	21	33	45
2,7: 2-Staton-a	2	4	6	13	18	22
3-6: All Byrne-a; c-3,5,6	3	6	9	16	23	30
nn (Charlton Press, digest, 100 pgs., B&W, no cover price) new stories & art	4	8	12	27	44	60

SPACE: 1999 (TV)(Magazine)
Charlton Comics: Nov, 1975 - No. 8, Nov, 1976 (B&W) (#7 shows #6 inside)

	GD 2.0	VG 4.0	FN 6.0	VF 8.0	VF/NM 9.0	NM- 9.2
1-Origin Moonbase Alpha; Morrow-c/a	3	6	9	16	24	32
2-8: 2,3-Morrow-c/a. 4-6-Morrow-c. 5,8-Morrow-a	2	4	6	11	16	20

SPACE PATROL (TV)
Ziff-Davis Publishing Co. (Approved Comics): Summer, 1952 - No. 2, Oct-Nov, 1952 (Painted-c by Norman Saunders)

	GD 2.0	VG 4.0	FN 6.0	VF 8.0	VF/NM 9.0	NM- 9.2
1-Krigstein-a	97	194	291	621	1061	1500
2-Krigstein-a(3)	69	138	207	442	759	1075

SPACE PIRATES (See Archie Giant Series #533)

SPACE: PUNISHER
Marvel Comics: Sept, 2012 - No. 4, Dec, 2012 ($3.99, limited series)

	GD 2.0	VG 4.0	FN 6.0	VF 8.0	VF/NM 9.0	NM- 9.2
1-4-Outer space sci-fi pulp version of the Punisher; Tieri-s/Texeira-a/c						4.00

SPACE RANGER (See Mystery in Space #92, Showcase #15 & Tales of the Unexpected)

SPACE SQUADRON (In the Days of the Rockets)(Becomes Space Worlds #6)
Marvel/Atlas Comics (ACI): June, 1951 - No. 5, Feb, 1952

	GD 2.0	VG 4.0	FN 6.0	VF 8.0	VF/NM 9.0	NM- 9.2
1-Space team; Brodsky c-1,5	100	200	300	645	1098	1550
2: Tuska c-2-4	74	148	222	470	810	1150
3-5: 3-Capt. Jet Dixon by Tuska(3); Maneely-a. 4-Weird advs. begin	65	130	195	416	708	1000

SPACE THRILLERS
Avon Periodicals: 1954 (25¢ Giant)

	GD 2.0	VG 4.0	FN 6.0	VF 8.0	VF/NM 9.0	NM- 9.2
nn-(Scarce)-Robotmen of the Lost Planet; contains 3 rebound comics of The Saint & Strange Worlds. Contents could vary	161	322	483	1030	1765	2500

SPACE TRIP TO THE MOON (See Space Adventures #23)

SPACE USAGI
Mirage Studios: June, 1992 - No. 3, 1992 ($2.00, B&W, mini-series)
V2#1, Nov, 1993 - V2#3, Jan, 1994 ($2.75)

	GD 2.0	VG 4.0	FN 6.0	VF 8.0	VF/NM 9.0	NM- 9.2
1-3: Stan Sakai-c/a/scripts, V2#1-3						3.00

SPACE USAGI
Dark Horse Comics: Jan, 1996 - No. 3, Mar, 1996 ($2.95, B&W, limited series)

	GD 2.0	VG 4.0	FN 6.0	VF 8.0	VF/NM 9.0	NM- 9.2
1-3: Stan Sakai-c/a/scripts						3.00

SPACE WAR (Fightin' Five #28 on)
Charlton Comics: Oct, 1959 - No. 27, Mar, 1964; No. 28, Mar, 1978 - No. 34, 3/79

	GD 2.0	VG 4.0	FN 6.0	VF 8.0	VF/NM 9.0	NM- 9.2
V1#1-Giordano-c begin, end #3	13	26	39	89	195	300
2,3	8	16	24	54	102	150
4-6,8,10-Ditko-c/a	12	24	36	83	182	280
7,9,11-15 (3/62): Last 10¢ issue	6	12	18	38	69	100
16 (6/62)-27 (3/64): 18,19-Robot-c	5	10	15	33	57	80
28 (3/78),29-31,33,34-Ditko-c/a(r): 30-Staton, Sutton/Wood-a. 31-Ditko-c/a(3); same-c as Strange Suspense Stories #2 (1968); atom blast-c	1	3	4	6	8	10
32-r/Charlton Premiere V2#2; Sutton-a						6.00

SPACE WARPED
Boom Entertainment (Kaboom!): Jun, 2011 - No. 6, Dec, 2011 ($3.99, limited series)

	GD 2.0	VG 4.0	FN 6.0	VF 8.0	VF/NM 9.0	NM- 9.2
1-6-Star Wars spoof; Bourhis-s/Spiessert-a						4.00

SPACE WESTERN (Formerly Cowboy Western Comics; becomes Cowboy Western Comics #46 on)
Charlton Comics (Capitol Stories): No. 40, Oct, 1952 - No. 45, Aug, 1953

	GD 2.0	VG 4.0	FN 6.0	VF 8.0	VF/NM 9.0	NM- 9.2
40-Intro Spurs Jackson & His Space Vigilantes; flying saucer story	135	270	405	864	1482	2100
41,43: 41-Flying saucer-c	61	122	183	390	670	950
42-Atom bomb explosion-c	65	130	195	416	708	1000
44-Cowboys battle Nazis on Mars	110	220	330	704	1202	1700
45-"The Valley That Time Forgot", a pre-Turok story with dinosaurs & a bow-hunting Indian; Hitler app.	68	136	204	435	743	1050

SPACE WORLDS (Formerly Space Squadron #1-5)
Atlas Comics (Male): No. 6, April, 1952

	GD 2.0	VG 4.0	FN 6.0	VF 8.0	VF/NM 9.0	NM- 9.2
6-Sol Brodsky-c	57	114	171	362	619	875

SPANKY & ALFALFA & THE LITTLE RASCALS (See The Little Rascals)

SPARKIE, RADIO PIXIE (Radio)(Becomes Big Jon & Sparkie #4)
Ziff-Davis Publ. Co.: Winter, 1951 - No. 3, July-Aug, 1952 (Painted-c)(Sparkie #2,3; #1?)

	GD 2.0	VG 4.0	FN 6.0	VF 8.0	VF/NM 9.0	NM- 9.2
1-Based on children's radio program	29	58	87	170	278	385
2,3: 3-Big Jon and Sparkie on-c only	19	38	57	112	179	245

SPARKLE COMICS
United Features Synd.: Oct-Nov, 1948 - No. 33, Dec-Jan, 1953-54

	GD 2.0	VG 4.0	FN 6.0	VF 8.0	VF/NM 9.0	NM- 9.2
1-Li'l Abner, Nancy, Captain & the Kids, Ella Cinders (#1-3: 52 pgs.)	16	32	48	98	154	210
2	10	20	30	58	79	100
3-10	8	16	24	44	57	70
11-20	8	16	24	40	50	60
21-32	7	14	21	35	43	50
33-(2-3/54) 2 pgs. early Peanuts by Schulz	15	30	45	83	124	165

SPARKLE PLENTY (See Harvey Comics Library #2 & Dick Tracy)
Dell Publishing Co.: 1949

	GD 2.0	VG 4.0	FN 6.0	VF 8.0	VF/NM 9.0	NM- 9.2
Four Color 215 - Dick Tracy reprint by Gould	11	22	33	75	160	245

SPARKLER COMICS (1st series)
United Feature Comic Group: July, 1940 - No. 2, 1940

	GD 2.0	VG 4.0	FN 6.0	VF 8.0	VF/NM 9.0	NM- 9.2
1-Jim Hardy	42	84	126	265	445	625
2-Frankie Doodle	34	68	102	201	328	455

SPARKLER COMICS (2nd series)(Nancy & Sluggo #121 on)(Cover title becomes Nancy and Sluggo #101? on)
United Features Syndicate: July, 1941 - No. 120, Jan, 1955

	GD 2.0	VG 4.0	FN 6.0	VF 8.0	VF/NM 9.0	NM- 9.2
1-Origin 1st app. Sparkman; Tarzan (by Hogarth in all issues), Captain & the Kids, Ella Cinders, Danny Dingle, Dynamite Dunn, Nancy, Abbie & Slats, Broncho Bill, Frankie Doodle, begin; Spark Man c-1-9,11,12; Hap Hopper c-10,13	194	388	582	1242	2121	3000
2	65	130	195	416	708	1000
3,4	50	100	150	315	533	750
5-9: 9-Spark Man's new costume	42	84	126	265	445	625
10-Spark Man's secret ID revealed	45	90	135	284	480	675
11,12-Spark Man war-c. 12-Spark Man's new costume (color change)	40	80	120	246	411	575
13-Hap Hopper war-c	32	64	96	190	310	430
14-Tarzan-c by Hogarth	66	132	198	419	722	1025
15,17: 15-Capt & Kids-c. 17-Nancy & Sluggo-c	24	48	72	144	237	330
16,18-Spark Man-c. 16-Japanese WWII-c. 18-Nazi WWII-c	41	82	123	256	428	600
19-1st Race Riley and the Commandos-c/s	39	78	117	236	388	540
20-Nancy war-c	29	58	87	172	281	390
21,25,28,31,34,37-Tarzan-c by Hogarth	50	100	150	315	533	750
22-24,26,27,29,30: 22-Race Riley & the Commandos strips begin, ends #44	22	44	66	132	216	300
32,33,35,36,38,40	14	28	42	80	115	150
39-Classic Tarzan shooting an arrow into a dinosaur's eye on cover by Hogarth	82	164	246	528	902	1275
41,43,45,46,48,49	11	22	33	60	83	105
42,44,47,50-Tarzan-c (42,47,50 by Hogarth)	27	54	81	158	259	360

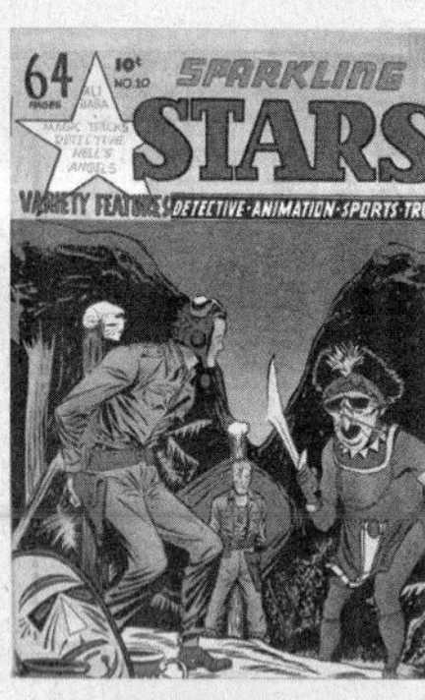

Sparkling Stars #10 © HOKE

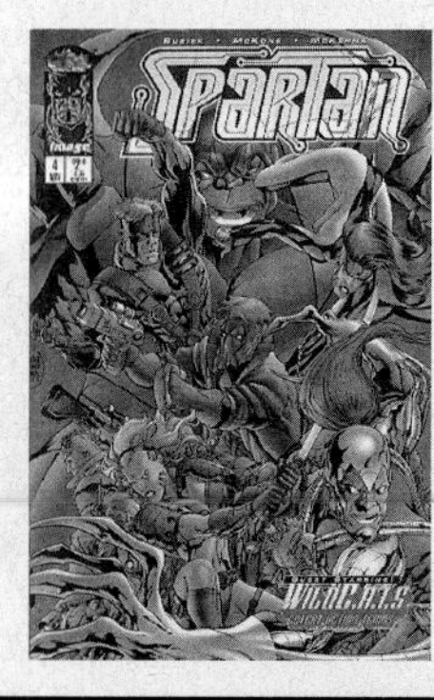

Spartan: Warrior Spirit #4 © WSP

Spawn #179 © TMP

GD VG FN VF VF/NM NM-
2.0 4.0 6.0 8.0 9.0 9.2

51,52,54-68,70: 57-Li'l Abner begins (not in #58); Fearless Fosdick app. in #58
10 20 30 58 79 100
53-Tarzan-c by Hogarth 26 52 78 154 252 350
69-Wolverton-*esque* Horror-c 12 24 36 67 94 120
71-80 9 18 27 47 61 75
81,82,84-86: 86 Last Tarzan; lingerie panels 8 16 24 40 50 60
83-Tarzan-c; Li'l Abner ends 13 26 39 72 101 130
87-96,98-99 7 14 21 37 46 55
97-Origin Casey Ruggles by Warren Tufts 8 16 24 42 54 65
100 8 16 24 42 54 65
101-107,109-112,114-119 6 12 18 31 38 45
108,113-Toth-a 7 14 21 37 46 55
120-(10-11/54) 2 pgs. early Peanuts by Schulz 13 26 39 72 101 130

SPARKLING LOVE
Avon Periodicals/Realistic (1953): June, 1950; 1953

1(Avon)-Kubert-a; photo-c 36 72 109 216 351 485
nn(1953)-Reprint; Kubert-a 15 30 45 84 127 170

SPARKLING STARS
Holyoke Publishing Co.: June, 1944 - No. 33, March, 1948

1-Hell's Angels, FBI, Boxie Weaver, Petey & Pop, & Ali Baba begin
25 50 75 150 245 340
2-Speed Spaulding story 15 30 45 86 133 180
3-Actual FBI case photos & war photos 12 24 36 67 94 120
4-10: 7-X-Mas-c 10 20 30 58 79 100
11-19: 13-Origin/1st app. Jungo the Man-Beast-c/s 10 20 30 54 72 90
20-Intro Fangs the Wolf Boy 10 20 30 58 79 100
21-33: 29-Bondage-c. 31-Sid Greene-a 9 18 27 52 69 85

SPARK MAN (See Sparkler Comics)
Frances M. McQueeny: 1945 (36 pgs., one-shot)

1-Origin Spark Man r/Sparkler #1-3; female torture story; cover redrawn from Sparkler #1
39 78 117 231 378 525

SPARKY WATTS (Also see Big Shot Comics & Columbia Comics)
Columbia Comic Corp.: Nov?, 1942 - No. 10, 1949

1(1942)-Skyman & The Face app; Hitler/Goering story/c
129 258 387 826 1413 2000
2(1943) 39 78 117 240 395 550
3(1944) "6000 Lbs. Block Buster to Bust Adolf"-c 26 52 78 156 256 355
4(1944)-Origin 20 40 60 120 195 270
5(1947)-Skyman app.; Boody Rogers-c/a 17 34 51 103 162 220
6,7,9,10: 6(1947). 9-Haunted House-c. 10(1949) 13 26 39 74 105 135
8(1948)-Surrealistic-c 15 30 45 83 124 165
NOTE: *Boody Rogers c-1-8.*

SPARROWHAWK
BOOM! Studios: Oct, 2018 - No. 5, Mar, 2019 ($3.99, limited series)

1-5-Delilah S. Dawson-s/Matias Basla-a 4.00

SPARTACUS (Movie)
Dell Publishing Co.: No. 1139, Nov, 1960 (Kirk Douglas photo-c)

Four Color 1139-Buscema-a 11 22 33 75 160 245

SPARTACUS (Television series)
Devil's Due Publishing: Oct, 2009 - No. 2 ($3.99)

1,2: 1-DeKnight-s. 2-Palmiotti-s 4.00

SPARTAN: WARRIOR SPIRIT (Also see WildC.A.T.S: Covert Action Teams)
Image Comics (WildStorm Productions): July, 1995 - No. 4, Nov, 1995 ($2.50, lim. series)

1-4: Kurt Busiek scripts; Mike McKone-c/a 3.00

SPARTA: USA
DC Comics (WildStorm): May, 2010 - No. 6, Oct, 2010 ($2.99, limited series)

1-6: 1-Lapham-s/Timmons-a; covers by Timmons and Lapham 3.00

SPAWN (Also see Curse of the Spawn and Sam & Twitch)
Image Comics (Todd McFarlane Prods.): May, 1992 - Present ($1.95/$2.50/$2.99)

1-1st app. Spawn; McFarlane-c/a begins; McFarlane/Steacy-c; 1st Todd McFarlane Productions title. 4 8 12 23 37 50
1-Black & white edition 16 32 48 110 243 375
2,3: 2-1st app. Violator; McFarlane/Steacy-c 3 6 9 14 19 24
4-Contains coupon for Image Comics #0 2 4 6 11 16 20
4-With coupon missing 3.00
4-Newsstand edition w/o poster or coupon 6.00
5-Cerebus cameo (1 pg.) as stuffed animal; Spawn mobile poster #1
2 4 6 9 13 16
6-8,10: 7-Spawn Mobile poster #2. 8-Alan Moore scripts; Miller poster. 10-Cerebus app.; Dave Sim scripts; 1 pg. cameo app. by Superman 2 4 6 8 10 12
9-Neil Gaiman scripts; Jim Lee poster; 1st Angela. 3 6 9 17 25 34
11-17,19,20,22-30: 11-Miller script; Darrow poster. 12-Bloodwulf poster by Liefeld. 14,15-Violator app. 16,17-Grant Morrison scripts; Capullo-c/a(p). 23,24-McFarlane-a/stories. 25-(10/94). 19-(10/94). 20-(11/94) 1 2 3 5 6 8
18-Grant Morrison script, Capullo-c/a(p); low distr. 2 4 6 8 10 12
21-low distribution 2 4 6 8 10 12
31-49: 31-1st app. The Redeemer; new costume (brief). 32-1st full app. new costume. 38-40,42,44,46,48-Tony Daniel-c/a(p). 38-1st app. Cy-Gor. 40,41-Cy-Gor & Curse app. 6.00
50-($3.95, 48 pgs.) 1 2 3 5 6 8
51-96: 52-Savage Dragon app. 56-w/ Darkchylde preview. 57-Cy-Gor-c/app. 64-Polybagged w/McFarlane Toys catalog. 65-Photo-c of movie Spawn and McFarlane. 81-Billy Kincaid returns 6.00
97-Angela-c/app. 2 4 6 8 11 14
98,99-Angela app. 1 2 3 5 6 8
100-($4.95) Angela dies; 6 total covers; the 3 variants by McFarlane, Miller, and Mignola
2 4 6 9 13 16
100-($4.95) 3 variant covers by Ross, Capullo, and Wood
1 3 4 6 8 10
101-149,151-173,176-199,201-219: 101-149-($2.50). 119-Gunslinger Spawn cameo. 151-($2.95) Wraparound-c by Tan. 167-Clown app. 179-Mayhew-a. 185-McFarlane & Holguin-s; Portacio-a begins. 193-Sam & Twitch app. 210-215-Michael Golden-c 5.00
150-($4.95) 4 covers by McFarlane, Capullo, Tan, Jim Lee
1 2 3 5 6 8
174-Origin/1st full app. of Gunslinger Spawn 21 42 63 147 324 500
175-Origin of Gunslinger Spawn continues 13 26 39 89 195 300
200-(1/11, $3.99) 7 covers by McFarlane, Capullo, Finch, Jim Lee, Liefeld, Silvestri, Wood 5.00
220-(6/12, $3.99) 20th Anniversary issue; McFarlane-s/Kudranski-a; bonus interview, timeline and cover gallery 1 3 4 6 8 10
220: 20th Anniversary Collector's Special-(6/12, $4.99) B&W version of #220 w/bonuses
2 4 6 9 12 15
221-249,251-299: 221-231-Cover swipes of classic covers. 221-Amazing Fantasy #15. 225-Election special with 2 covers (Obama & Romney). 228-Action #1 c-swipe. 231-Spider-Man #1 ('90) c-swipe. 234-Haunt app. 251-Follows Spawn Resurrection #1. 258-Erik Larsen & McFarlane-a begin. 265-Ant app. 266-Savage Dragon app. 267-275,291,292-Kudranski-a. 276-282-Darragh Savage-s/Alexander-a 5.00
250-($5.99) McFarlane-s/Kudranski-a; Al Simmons returns; multiple covers
1 2 3 5 6 8
300-(9/19, $7.99) McFarlane-s; art by Capullo, McFarlane, JS Campbell, Alexander & Opeña; intro. She-Spawn, bonus cover gallery; multiple covers
1 2 3 5 6 8
301-($4.99) McFarlane-s; art by Capullo, McFarlane, Crain, Alexander & Opeña 5.00
302-315: 302-305-Alexander-a; She-Spawn app. 306-Tan-a; intro. Raptor. 309,311-313-Gunslinger Spawn returns 3.00
309-Gunslinger Spawn variant-c by McFarlane 10.00
Annual 1-Blood & Shadows ('99, $4.95) Ashley Wood-c/a; Jenkins-s 6.00
... #1 Director's Cut (5/17, $4.99) 25th Anniversary edition; r/#1 B&W inked art with McFarlane commentary; bonus promotional art; 3 covers (McFarlane, Crain, Ashley Wood) 5.00
... #1 Free Comic Book Day 2019 (giveaway) r/#1; new cover by Francesco Mattina 3.00
...: Architects of Fear (2/11, $6.99, squarebound GN) Briclot-a 7.00
...: Armegeddon Complete Collection TPB ('07, $29.95) r/#150-163 30.00
...: Armegeddon, Part 1 TPB (10/06, $14.99) r/#150-155 15.00
...: Armegeddon, Part 2 TPB (2/07, $15.95) r/#156-164 16.00
...Bible-(8/96, $1.95)-Character bios 4.00
Book 1 TPB($9.95) r/#1-5; Book 2-r/#6-9,11; Book 3 -r/#12-15, Book 4- r/#16-20; Book 5-r/#21-25; Book 6- r/#26-30; Book 7-r/#31-34; Book 8-r/#35-38; Book 9-r/#39-42; Book 10-r/#43-47 11.00
Book 11 TPB ($10.95) r/#48-50; Book 12-r/#51-54 11.00
... Collection Vol. 1 (10/05, $19.95) r/#1-8,11,12; intro. by Frank Miller 20.00
... Collection Vol. 2 HC (7/07, $49.95) r/#13-33 50.00
... Collection Vol. 2 SC (9/06, $29.95) r/#13-33 30.00
... Collection Vol. 3 (3/07, $29.95) r/#34-54 30.00
... Collection Vol. 4 (9/07, $29.95) r/#55-75 30.00
... Collection Vol. 5 ('08, $29.95) r/#76-95 30.00
... Collection Vol. 6 (8/08, $29.95) r/#96-116; cover gallery 30.00
Image Firsts: Spawn #1 (4/10, $1.00) reprints #1 3.00
... Godslayer Vol. 1 (9/06, $6.99) Anacleto-c/a; Holguin-s; sketch pages 7.00
... Kills Everyone! 1 (8/16, $2.99) McFarlane-s/JJ Kirby-a; mini Spawn vs. cosplayers 3.00
...: Neonoir TPB (11/08, $14.95) r/#170-175 15.00
...: New Flesh TPB ('07, $14.95) r/#166-169 15.00
... Resurrection 1 (3/15, $2.99) Follows issue #250; Jenkins-s/Jonboy-a 3.00
...Simony (5/04, $7.95) English translation of French Spawn story; Briclot-a 8.00
NOTE: *Capullo a-16p-18p; c-16p-18p. Daniel a-38-40, 42, 44, 46. McFarlane a-1-15; c-1-15p. Thibert a-16i(part). Posters come with issues 1, 4, 7-9, 11, 12. #25 was released before #19 & 20.*

Part 3 of 4 'Introducing the superbad CLOWNOS!'
SPAWN KILLS 2

Spawn Kills Everyone Too #3 © TMP

Special Forces #1 © Kyle Baker

The Spectacular Spider-Man #15 © MAR

	GD 2.0	VG 4.0	FN 6.0	VF 8.0	VF/NM 9.0	NM- 9.2

SPAWN-BATMAN (Also see Batman/Spawn: War Devil under Batman: One-Shots)
Image Comics (Todd McFarlane Productions): 1994 ($3.95, one-shot)
1-Miller scripts; McFarlane-c/a 3 6 9 14 20 26

SPAWN: BLOOD FEUD
Image Comics (Todd McFarlane Prods.): June, 1995 - No. 4, Sept, 1995 ($2.25, lim. series)
1-4-Alan Moore scripts, Tony Daniel-a 6.00

SPAWN FAN EDITION
Image Comics (Todd McFarlane Productions): Aug, 1996 - No. 3, Oct, 1996 (Giveaway, 12 pgs.) (Polybagged w/Overstreet's FAN)
1-3: Beau Smith scripts; Brad Gorby-a(p). 1-1st app. Nordik, the Norse Hellspawn. 2-1st app. McFallon. 3-1st app. Mercy 1 2 3 5 6 8
1-3-(Gold): All retailer incentives 16.00
1-3-Variant-c 1 2 3 5 6 8
2-(Platinum)-Retailer incentive 25.00

SPAWN GODSLAYER
Image Comics (Todd McFarlane Prods.): May, 2007 - No. 8, Apr, 2008 ($2.99)
1-8: 1-Holguin-s/Tan-a/Anacleto-c 3.00

SPAWN KILLS EVERYONE TOO (Also titled Spawn Kills Everyone 2)
Image Comics (Todd McFarlane Prod.): Dec, 2018 - No. 4, Mar, 2019 ($3.99, limited series)
1-4-McFarlane-s/Robson-a; Baby Spawn having babies. 3,4-Infinity Gauntlet spoof 4.00

SPAWN: THE DARK AGES
Image Comics (Todd McFarlane Productions): Mar, 1999 - No. 28, Oct, 2001 ($2.50)
1-Fabry-c; Holguin-s/Sharp-a; variant-c by McFarlane 6.00
2-28 4.00

SPAWN THE IMPALER
Image Comics (Todd McFarlane Prods.): Oct, 1996 - No. 3, Dec, 1996 ($2.95, limited series)
1-3-Mike Grell scripts, painted-a 5.00

SPAWN: THE UNDEAD
Image Comics (Todd McFarlane Prod.): Jun, 1999 - No. 9, Feb, 2000 ($1.95/$2.25)
1-9-Dwayne Turner-c/a; Jenkins-s. 7-9-($2.25-c) 5.00
TPB (6/08, $24.99) r/#1-9 25.00

SPAWN/WILDC.A.T.S
Image Comics (WildStorm): Jan, 1996 - No. 4, Apr, 1996 ($2.50, lim. series)
1-4: Alan Moore scripts in all. 4.00

SPEAKER FOR THE DEAD (ORSON SCOTT CARD'S...) (Ender's Game)
Marvel Comics: Mar, 2011 - No. 5, Jul, 2011 ($3.99, limited series)
1-3-Johnston-s/Mhan-a/Camuncoli-c 4.00

SPECIAL AGENT (Steve Saunders...)(Also see True Comics #68)
Parents' Magazine Institute (Commended Comics No. 2): Dec, 1947 - No. 8, Sept, 1949 (Based on true FBI cases)
1-J. Edgar Hoover photo on-c 15 30 45 92 144 195
2 10 20 30 58 79 100
3-8 9 18 27 52 69 85

SPECIAL COLLECTORS' EDITION (See Savage Fists of Kung-Fu)

SPECIAL COMICS (Becomes Hangman #2 on)
MLJ Magazines: Winter, 1941-42
1-Origin The Boy Buddies (Shield & Wizard x-over); death of The Comet retold (see Pep #17); origin The Hangman retold; Hangman-c 420 840 1260 2940 5170 7400

SPECIAL EDITION (See Gorgo and Reptisaurus)

SPECIAL EDITION COMICS (See Promotional Section)

SPECIAL EDITION COMICS
Fawcett Publications: 1940 (August) (68 pgs., one-shot)
1-1st book devoted entirely to Captain Marvel; C.C. Beck-c/a; only app. of Captain Marvel with belt buckle; Capt. Marvel appears with button-down flap; 1st story (came out before Captain Marvel #1) 946 1892 2838 6906 12,203 17,500
NOTE: *Prices vary widely on this book. Since this book is all Captain Marvel stories, it is actually a pre-Captain Marvel #1. There is speculation that this book almost became* ***Captain Marvel #1****. After* ***Special Edition*** *was published, there was an editor change at Fawcett. The new editor commissioned Kirby to do a nn* ***Captain Marvel*** *book early in 1941. This book was followed by a 2nd book several months later. This 2nd book was advertised as a #3 (making Special Edition the #1, & the nn issue the #2). However, the 2nd book did come out as a #2.*

SPECIAL EDITION: SPIDER-MAN VS. THE HULK (See listing under The Amazing Spider-Man)

SPECIAL EDITION X-MEN
Marvel Comics Group: Feb, 1983 ($2.00, one-shot, Baxter paper)
1-r/Giant-Size X-Men #1 plus one new story 3 6 9 14 20 26

SPECIAL FORCES
Image Comics: Oct, 2007 - No. 4, Mar, 2009 ($2.99)
1-4-Iraq war combat; Kyle Baker-s/a/c 3.00

SPECIAL MARVEL EDITION (Master of Kung Fu #17 on)
Marvel Comics Group: Jan, 1971 - No. 16, Feb, 1974 (#1-3: 25¢, 68 pgs.; #4: 52 pgs.; #5-16: 20¢, regular ed.)
1-Thor-r by Kirby; 68 pgs. 4 8 12 28 47 65
2-4: Thor-r by Kirby; 2,3-68 pg. Giant. 4-(52 pgs.) 3 6 9 16 24 32
5-14: Sgt. Fury-r; 11-r/Sgt. Fury #13 (Capt. America) 2 4 6 9 12 15
15-Master of Kung Fu (Shang-Chi) begins (1st app., 12/73); Starlin-a; origin/1st app. Nayland Smith & Dr. Petrie 35 70 105 252 564 875
16-1st app. Midnight; Starlin-a (2nd Shang-Chi) 6 12 18 42 79 115
NOTE: *Kirby c-10-14.*

SPECIAL MISSIONS (See G.I. Joe...)

SPECIAL WAR SERIES (Attack V4#3 on?)
Charlton Comics: Aug, 1965 - No. 4, Nov, 1965
V4#1-D-Day (also see D-Day listing) 4 8 12 28 47 65
2-Attack! 3 6 9 16 23 30
3-War & Attack (also see War & Attack) 3 6 9 14 20 25
4-Judomaster (intro/1st app.; see Sarge Steel) 9 18 27 60 120 180

SPECIES (Movie)
Dark Horse Comics: June, 1995 - No. 4, Sept, 1995 ($2.50, limited series)
1-4: Adaptation of film 3.00

SPECIES: HUMAN RACE (Movie)
Dark Horse Comics: Nov, 1996 - No. 4, Feb, 1997 ($2.95, limited series)
1-4 3.00

SPECTACULAR ADVENTURES (See Adventures)

SPECTACULAR FEATURE MAGAZINE, A (Formerly My Confession) (Spectacular Features Magazine #12)
Fox Feature Syndicate: No. 11, April, 1950
11 (#1)-Samson and Delilah 30 60 90 177 289 400

SPECTACULAR FEATURES MAGAZINE (Formerly A Spectacular Feature Magazine)
Fox Feature Syndicate: No. 12, June, 1950 - No. 3, Aug, 1950
12 (#2)-Iwo Jima; photo flag-c 27 54 81 162 266 370
3-True Crime Cases From Police Files 22 44 66 132 216 300

SPECTACULAR SCARLET SPIDER
Marvel Comics: Nov, 1995 - No. 2, Dec, 1995 ($1.95, limited series)
1,2: Replaces Spectacular Spider-Man 3.00

SPECTACULAR SPIDER-GIRL
Marvel Comics: Jul, 2010 - No. 4, Oct, 2010 ($3.99, limited series)
1-4-Frenz-a; Frank Castle and the Hobgoblin app. 4.00

SPECTACULAR SPIDER-MAN, THE (See Marvel Special Edition and Marvel Treasury Edition)

SPECTACULAR SPIDER-MAN, THE (Magazine)
Marvel Comics Group: July, 1968 - No. 2, Nov, 1968 (35¢)
1-(B&W)-Romita/Mooney 52 pg. story plus updated origin story with Everett-a(i) 11 22 33 76 163 250
1-Variation w/single c-price of 40¢ 11 22 33 73 157 240
2-(Color)-Green Goblin-c & 58 pg. story; Romita painted-c (story reprinted in King Size Spider-Man #9); Romita/Mooney-a 9 18 27 62 126 190

SPECTACULAR SPIDER-MAN, THE (Peter Parker...#54-132, 134)
Marvel Comics Group: Dec, 1976 - No. 263, Nov, 1998
1-Origin recap in text; return of Tarantula 6 12 18 37 66 95
2-Kraven the Hunter app. 3 6 9 19 30 40
3-5: 3-Intro Lightmaster. 4-Vulture app. 3 6 9 14 20 25
6-8-Morbius app.; 6-r/Marvel Team-Up #3 w/Morbius 3 6 9 15 22 28
7,8-(35¢-c variants, limited distribution)(6,7/77) 9 18 27 57 111 165
9-20: 9,10-White Tiger app. 11-Last 30¢-c. 17,18-Angel & Iceman app. (from Champions); Ghost Rider cameo. 18-Gil Kane-c 2 4 6 8 11 14
9-11-(35¢-c variants, limited distribution)(8-10/77) 8 16 24 54 102 150
21,24-26: 21-Scorpion app. 26-Daredevil app. 2 3 4 6 8 10
22,23-Moon Knight app. 2 4 6 8 10 12
27-Miller's 1st art on Daredevil (2/79); also see Captain America #235 5 10 15 34 60 85
28-Miller Daredevil (p) 4 8 12 25 40 55
29-55,57,59: 33-Origin Iguana. 38-Morbius app. 1 2 3 4 5 7
56-2nd app. Jack O'Lantern (Macendale) & 1st Spidey/Jack O'Lantern battle (7/81) 1 2 3 5 6 8

The Spectacular Spider-Man #263 © MAR

The Spectre (3rd series) #62 © DC

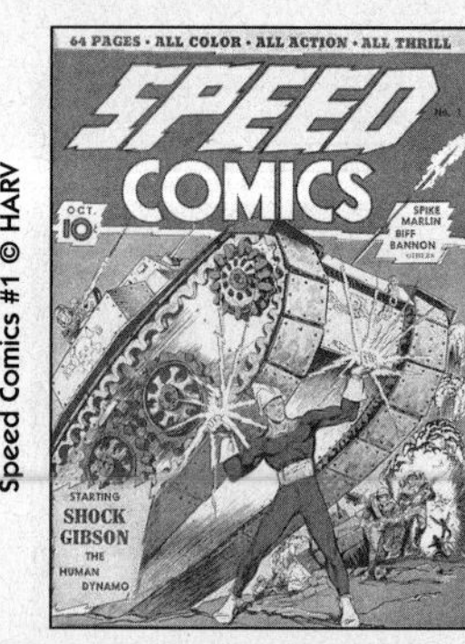

Speed Comics #1 © HARV

GD VG FN VF VF/NM NM-
2.0 4.0 6.0 8.0 9.0 9.2

58-Byrne-a(p) 1 2 3 5 6 8
60-Double size; origin retold with new facts revealed 1 2 3 5 6 8
61-63,65-68,71-74: 65-Kraven the Hunter app. 6.00
64-1st app. Cloak & Dagger (3/82) 6 12 18 42 79 115
69,70-Cloak & Dagger app. (origin retold in #69). 70-1st app. of Silvermane in cyborg form 2 4 6 8 10 12
75-Double size 1 2 3 5 6 8
76-80: 78,79-Punisher cameo 6.00
81,82-Punisher, Cloak & Dagger app. 1 3 4 6 8 10
83-Origin Punisher retold (10/83) 2 4 6 9 12 15
84,86-89,91-99: 94-96-Cloak & Dagger app. 98-Intro The Spot 6.00
85-Hobgoblin (Ned Leeds) app. (12/83); gains powers of original Green Goblin (see Amazing Spider-Man #238) 2 4 6 8 10 12
90-Spider-Man's new black costume, last panel (ties w/Amazing Spider-Man #252 & Marvel Team-Up #141 for 1st app.) 4 8 12 25 40 55
100-(3/85)-Double size 1 2 3 4 5 7
101-115,117,118,120-129: 107-110-Death of Jean DeWolff. 111-Secret Wars II tie-in. 128-Black Cat new costume 5.00
116,119-Sabretooth-c/story 2 4 6 9 12 15
130-132: 130-Hobgoblin app. 131-Six part Kraven tie-in. 132-Kraven tie-in 2 3 4 6 8 10
133-137,139,140: 140-Punisher cameo 5.00
138-1st full app. Tombstone (origin #139) 1 3 4 6 8 10
141-143-Punisher app. 1 2 3 4 5 7
144-146,148-157: 151-Tombstone returns 4.00
147-1st brief app. new Hobgoblin (Macendale), 1 page; continued in Web of Spider-Man #48 2 4 6 9 13 16
158-Spider-Man gets new powers (1st Cosmic Spidey, cont'd in Web of Spider-Man #59) 2 4 6 9 12 15
159-Cosmic Spider-Man app. 1 2 3 4 5 7
160-188,190-199: 161-163-Hobgoblin app. 168-170-Avengers x-over. 169-1st app. The Outlaws. 180-184-Green Goblin app. 197-199-Original X-Men-c/story 4.00
189-($2.95, 52 pgs.)-Silver hologram on-c; battles Green Goblin; origin Spidey retold; Vess poster w/Spidey & Hobgoblin 6.00
189-(2nd printing)-Gold hologram on-c 4.00
195-(Deluxe ed.)-Polybagged w/"Dirt" magazine #2 & Beastie Boys/Smithereens music cassette 1 3 4 6 8 10
200-($2.95)-Holo-grafx foil-c; Green Goblin-c/story 6.00
201-219,221,222,224,226-228,230-247: 212-w/card sheet. 203-Maximum Carnage x-over. 204-Begin 4 part death of Tombstone story. 207,208-The Shroud-c/story. 208-Siege of Darkness x-over (#207 is a tie-in). 209-Black Cat back-up. 215,216-Scorpion app. 217-Power & Responsibility Pt. 4. 231-Return of Kaine; Spider-Man corpse discovered. 232-New Doc Octopus app. 233-Carnage-c/app. 235-Dragon Man cameo. 236-Dragon Man-c/app; Lizard app.; Peter Parker regains powers. 238,239-Lizard app. 239-w/card insert. 240-Revelations storyline begins. 241-Flashback 5.00
213-Collectors ed. polybagged w/16 pg. preview & animation cel; foil-c; 1st meeting Spidey & Typhoid Mary 5.00
213-Version polybagged w/Gamepro #7; no-c date, price 4.00
217,219 ($2.95)-Deluxe edition foil-c: flip book 5.00
220 ($2.25, 52 pgs.)-Flip book, Mary Jane reveals pregnancy 5.00
223,229: ($2.50) 229-Spidey quits 5.00
223,225: ($2.95)-223-Die Cut-c. 225-Newsstand ed. 5.00
225,229: ($3.95) 225-Direct Market Holodisk-c (Green Goblin). 229-Acetate-c, Spidey quits 5.00
240-Variant-c 5.00
248,249,251-254,256: 249-Return of Norman Osborn 256-1st app. Prodigy 4.00
250-($3.25) Double gatefold-c 5.00
255-($2.99) Spiderhunt pt. 4 5.00
257-262: 257-Double cover with "Spectacular Prodigy #1"; battles Jack O'Lantern. 258-Spidey is cleared. 259,260-Green Goblin & Hobgoblin app. 262-Byrne-s 4.00
263-Final issue; Byrne-c; Aunt May returns 5.00
#(-1) Flashback (7/97) 4.00
1000 (6/11, $4.99) Punisher app.; Nauck & Ryan-a/Rivera-c; r/ASM #129 5.00
Annual 1 (1979)-Doc Octopus-c & 46 pg. story 2 4 6 10 14 18
Annual 2 (1980)-Origin/1st app. Rapier 1 2 3 5 6 8
Annual 3-5: ('81-'83) 3-Last Man-Wolf 5.00
Annual 6-14: 8 ('88,$ 1.75)-Evolutionary War x-over; Daydreamer returns Gwen Stacy "clone" back to real self (not Gwen Stacy). 9 ('89, $2.00, 68 pgs.)-Atlantis Attacks. 10 ('90, $2.00, 68 pgs.)-McFarlane-a. 11 ('91, $2.00, 68 pgs.)-Iron Man app. 12 ('92, $2.25, 68 pgs.)-Venom solo story cont'd from Amazing Spider-Man Annual #26. 13 ('93, $2.95, 68 pgs.)-Polybagged w/trading card; John Romita, Sr. back-up-a 5.00
Special 1 (1995, $3.95)-Flip book 5.00

NOTE: ***Austin*** *c-21i, Annual 11i.* ***Buckler*** *a-103, 107-111, 116, 117, 119, 122, Annual 1, Annual 10; c-103, 107-111, 113, 116-119, 122, Annual 1.* ***Buscema*** *a-121.* ***Byrne*** *c(p)-17, 43, 58, 101, 102.* ***Giffen*** *a-120p.* ***Hembeck*** *c/a-86p.* ***Larsen*** *c-Annual 11p.* ***Miller*** *c-46p, 48p, 50, 51p, 52p, 54p, 55, 56p, 57, 60.* ***Mooney*** *a-7i, 11i, 21p, 23p, 25p, 26p, 29-34p, 36p, 37p, 39i, 41, 42i, 49p, 50i, 51i, 53p, 54-57i, 59-66i, 68i, 71i, 73-79i, 81-83i, 85i, 87-99i, 102i, 125p, Annual 1i, 2p.* ***Nasser*** *c-37p.* ***Perez*** *c-10.* ***Simonson*** *c-54i.* ***Zeck*** *a-22, 118, 131, 132; c-131, 132.*

SPECTACULAR SPIDER-MAN (2nd series)
Marvel Comics: Sept, 2003 - No. 27, June, 2005 ($2.25/$2.99)

1-Jenkins-s/Ramos-a/c; Venom-c/app. 4.00
2-26: 2-5-Venom app. 6-9-Dr. Octopus app. 11-13-The Lizard app. 14-Rivera painted-a. 15,16-Capt. America app. 17,18-Ramos-a. 20-Spider-Man gets organic webshooters 21,22-Caldwell-a. 23-26-Sarah & Gabriel app.; Land-c 3.00
27-($2.99) Last issue; Uncle Ben app. in flashback; Buckingham-a 4.00
... Vol. 1: The Hunger TPB (2003, $11.99) r/#1-5 12.00
... Vol. 2: Countdown TPB (2004, $11.99) r/#6-10 12.00
... Vol. 3: Here There Be Monsters TPB (2004, $9.99) r/#11-14 10.00
... Vol. 4: Disassembled TPB (2004, $14.99) r/#15-20 15.00
... Vol. 5: Sins Remembered (2005, $9.99) r/#23-26 10.00
... Vol. 6: The Final Curtain (2005, $14.99) r/#21,22,27 & Peter Parker: Spider-Man #39-41 15.00

SPECTACULAR STORIES MAGAZINE (Formerly A Star Presentation)
Fox Feature Syndicate (Hero Books): No. 4, July, 1950; No. 3, Sept, 1950

4-Sherlock Holmes (true crime stories) 39 78 117 240 395 550
3-The St. Valentine's Day Massacre (true crime) 26 52 78 154 252 350

SPECTER INSPECTORS
BOOM! Studios (BOOM! Box): Feb, 2021 - Present ($4.99)

1-Bowen McCurdy & Kaityn Musto-s/Musto-a 5.00

SPECTRE, THE (1st Series) (See Adventure Comics #431-440, More Fun & Showcase)
National Periodical Publ.: Nov-Dec, 1967 - No. 10, May-June, 1969 (All 12¢)

1-(11-12/67)-Anderson-c/a 15 30 45 105 233 360
2-5-Neal Adams-c/a; 3-Wildcat x-over 9 18 27 57 111 165
6-8,10: 6-8-Anderson inks. 7-Hourman app. 6 12 18 41 76 110
9-Wrightson-a 7 14 21 46 86 125

SPECTRE, THE (2nd Series) (See Saga of the Swamp Thing #58, Showcase '95 #8 & Wrath of the...)
DC Comics: Apr, 1987 - No. 31, Oct, 1989 ($1.00, new format)

1-Colan-a begins 1 2 3 5 6 8
2-32: 9-Nudity panels. 10-Batman cameo. 10,11-Millennium tie-ins 4.00
Annual 1 (1988, $2.00)-Deadman app. 5.00

NOTE: ***Art Adams*** *c-Annual 1.* ***Colan*** *a-1-6.* ***Kaluta*** *c-1-3.* ***Mignola*** *c-7-9.* ***Morrow*** *a-9-15.* ***Sears*** *c/a-22.* ***Vess*** *c-13-15.*

SPECTRE, THE (3rd Series) (Also see Brave and the Bold #72, 75, 116, 180, 199 & Showcase '95 #8)
DC Comics: Dec, 1992 - No. 62, Feb, 1998 ($1.75/$1.95/$2.25/$2.50)

1-($1.95)-Glow-in-the-dark-c; Mandrake-a begins 1 2 3 5 6 8
2,3 5.00
4-7,9-12,14-20: 10-Kaluta-c. 11-Hildebrandt painted-c. 16-Aparo/K. Jones-a. 19-Snyder III-c. 20-Sienkiewicz-c 4.00
8,13-($2.50)-Glow-in-the-dark-c 6.00
21-62: 22-(9/94)-Superman-c & app. 23-(11/94). 43-Kent Williams-c. 44-Kaluta-c. 47-Final Night x-over. 49-Begin Bolton-c. 51-Batman-c/app. 52-Gianni-c. 54-1st app. Michael Holt (Mr. Terrific); Corben-c. 60-Harris-c 3.00
#0 (10/94) Released between #22 & #23 3.00
Annual 1 (1995, $3.95)-Year One story 5.00

NOTE: ***Bisley*** *c-27.* ***Fabry*** *c-2.* ***Kelley Jones*** *c-31.* ***Vess*** *c-5.*

SPECTRE, THE (4th Series) (Hal Jordan; also see Day of Judgment #5 and Legends of the DC Universe #33-36)
DC Comics: Mar, 2001 - No. 27, May, 2003 ($2.50/$2.75)

1-DeMatteis-s/Ryan Sook-c/a 4.00
2-27: 3,4-Superman & Batman-c/app. 5-Two-Face-c/app. 20-Begin $2.75-c. 21-Sinestro returns. 24-JLA app. 3.00

SPECTRE, THE (See Crisis Aftermath: The Spectre)

SPEEDBALL (See Amazing Spider-Man Annual #12, Marvel Super-Heroes & The New Warriors)
Marvel Comics: Sept, 1988(10/88-inside) - No. 10, Jun, 1989 (75¢)

1-Ditko/Guice-a/c 1 3 4 6 8 10
2-10: Ditko/Guice-a-2-4; Ditko a-2-10; c-2-10p 4.00

SPEED BUGGY (TV)(Also see Fun-In #12, 15)
Charlton Comics: July, 1975 - No. 9, Nov, 1976 (Hanna-Barbera)

1 3 6 9 16 23 30
2-9 2 4 6 11 16 20

SPEED CARTER SPACEMAN (See Spaceman)

SPEED COMICS (New Speed)(Also see Double Up)
Brookwood Publ./Speed Publ./Harvey Publications No. 14 on:
10/39 - #11, 8/40; #12, 3/41 - #44, 1-2/47 (#14-16: pocket size, 100 pgs.)

Speed Force #1 © DC

Spellbound #17 © MAR

The Spider #12 © Argosy

	GD 2.0	VG 4.0	FN 6.0	VF 8.0	VF/NM 9.0	NM- 9.2
1-Origin & 1st app. Shock Gibson; Ted Parrish, the Man with 1000 Faces begins; Powell-a; becomes Champion #2 on?; has earliest? full page panel in comics; classic war-c	443	886	1329	3234	5717	8200
2-Powell-a	213	426	639	1363	2332	3300
3-War-c	158	316	474	1011	1731	2450
4,5: 4-Powell-a. 5-Dinosaur-c	145	290	435	928	1589	2250
6-9,11: 7-Mars Mason begins, ends #11. 9,11-War-c	135	270	405	864	1482	2100
10-Classsic Giant Moth Monster-c	181	362	543	1158	1979	2800
12 (3/41; shows #11 in indicia)-The Wasp begins; Major Colt app. (Capt. Colt #12)	151	302	453	966	1658	2350
13-Intro. Captain Freedom & Young Defenders; Girl Commandos, Pat Parker (costumed heroine), War Nurse begins; Major Colt app.	168	336	504	1075	1838	2600
14,15-(100 pg. pocket size, 1941): 14-2nd Harvey comic (See Pocket); Shock Gibson dons new costume; Nazi war-c. 15-Pat Parker dons costume, last in costume #23; no Girl Commandos; Nazi monsters war-c.	300	600	900	2040	3570	5100
16-(100 pg. pocket size, 1941) Cover with Hitler leading an army of Nazi ghouls to the White House	314	628	942	2224	3912	5600
17-Classic Simon & Kirby WWII Nazi bondage/torture-c; Black Cat begins (4/42, early app.; see Pocket #1); origin Black Cat-r/Pocket #1; not in #40,41	300	600	900	2070	3635	5200
18-20-S&K-c. 18-Bondage/torture-c. 19,20-Japanese war-c	252	504	756	1613	2757	3900
21-Hitler, Tojo-c; Kirby-c	320	640	960	2251	3976	5700
22-Nazi WWII-c by Kirby	219	438	657	1402	2401	3400
23-Origin Girl Commandos; war-c by Kirby	219	438	657	1402	2401	3400
24-Pat Parker team-up with Girl Commandos; Hitler, Tojo, & Mussolini-c	284	568	852	1818	3109	4400
25,27,29: 25-War-c. 27 Nazi WWII-c. 29-Nazi WWII bondage-c	190	380	570	1216	2083	2950
26-Flag-c	252	504	756	1613	2757	3900
28-Classic Nazi monster WWII-c	371	742	1113	2600	4550	6500
30-Nazi WWII Death Chamber bondage-c	232	464	696	1485	2543	3600
31-Classic Schomburg Hitler & Tojo-c	371	742	1113	2600	4550	6800
32-35-Schomburg-c. 32,34-Nazi war-c. 33,35-Japanese war-c	194	388	582	1242	2121	3000
36-Schomburg Japanese war-c	123	246	369	787	1344	1900
37,39-42,44: 37-Japanese war-c. 41-War-c	48	96	144	302	514	725
38-Iwo-Jima Flag-c	55	110	165	352	601	850
43-Robot-c	57	114	171	362	619	875

NOTE: ***Al Avison*** *c-14-16, 30, 43.* ***Briefer*** *a-6, 7.* ***Jon Henri*** *(Kirbyesque) c-17-20.* ***Kubert*** *a-37, 38, 42-44.* ***Kirby/Caseneuve*** *c-21-23.* ***Cecelia Munson*** *a-7-11(Mars Mason).* ***Palais*** *c-37, 39-42.* ***Powell*** *a-1, 2, 4-7, 28, 31, 44.* ***Schomburg*** *c-31-36.* ***Tuska*** *a-3, 6, 7. Bondage c-18, 35. Captain Freedom c-16-24, 25(part), 26-44(w/Black Cat #27, 29, 31, 32-40). Shock Gibson c-1-15.*

SPEED DEMON (Also see Marvel Versus DC #3 & DC Versus Marvel #4)
Marvel Comics (Amalgam): Apr, 1996 ($1.95, one-shot)

	GD	VG	FN	VF	VF/NM	NM-
1						3.00

SPEED DEMONS (Formerly Frank Merriwell at Yale #1-4?; Submarine Attack #11 on)
Charlton Comics: No. 5, Feb, 1957 - No. 10, 1958

	GD	VG	FN	VF	VF/NM	NM-
5-10	7	14	21	35	43	50

SPEED FORCE (See The Flash 2nd Series #143-Cobalt Blue)
DC Comics: Nov, 1997 ($3.95, one-shot)

	GD	VG	FN	VF	VF/NM	NM-
1-Flash & Kid Flash vs. Cobalt Blue; Waid-s/Aparo & Sienkiewicz-a; Flash family stories and pin-ups by various						4.00

SPEED RACER (Also see The New Adventures of...)
Now Comics: July, 1987 - No. 38, Nov, 1990 ($1.75)

	GD	VG	FN	VF	VF/NM	NM-
1						4.00
2-38, 1-2nd printing						3.00
Special 1 (1988, $2.00), Special 2 (1988, $3.50)						4.00

SPEED RACER (Also see Racer X)
DC Comics (WildStorm): Oct, 1999 - No. 3, Dec, 1999 ($2.50, limited series)

	GD	VG	FN	VF	VF/NM	NM-
1-3-Tommy Yune-s/a; origin of Racer X; debut of the Mach 5						3.00
...: Born To Race (2000, $9.95, TPB) r/series & conceptual art						10.00
...: The Original Manga Vol. 1 ('00, $9.95, TPB) r/1950s B&W manga						10.00

SPEED RACER: CHRONICLES OF THE RACER
IDW Publishing: 2007 - No. 4, Apr, 2008 ($3.99)

	GD	VG	FN	VF	VF/NM	NM-
1-4-Multiple covers for each						4.00

SPEED RACER FEATURING NINJA HIGH SCHOOL
Now Comics: Aug, 1993 - No. 2, 1993 ($2.50, mini-series)

	GD	VG	FN	VF	VF/NM	NM-
1,2: 1-Polybagged w/card. 2-Exists?						3.00

SPEED RACER: RETURN OF THE GRX
Now Comics: Mar, 1994 - No. 2, Apr, 1994 ($1.95, limited series)

	GD	VG	FN	VF	VF/NM	NM-
1,2						3.00

SPEED SMITH-THE HOT ROD KING (Also see Hot Rod King)
Ziff-Davis Publishing Co.: Spring, 1952

	GD	VG	FN	VF	VF/NM	NM-
1-Saunders painted-c	26	52	78	154	252	350

SPEEDY GONZALES
Dell Publishing Co.: No. 1084, Mar, 1960

	GD	VG	FN	VF	VF/NM	NM-
Four Color 1084	6	12	18	41	76	110

SPEEDY RABBIT (See Television Puppet Show)
Realistic/I. W. Enterprises/Super Comics: nd (1953); 1963

	GD	VG	FN	VF	VF/NM	NM-
nn (1953)-Realistic Reprint?	3	6	9	14	20	26
I.W. Reprint #1 (2 versions w/diff. c/stories exist)-Peter Cottontail #?						
Super Reprint #14(1963)	2	4	6	8	11	14

SPELLBINDERS
Quality: Dec, 1986 - No. 12, Jan, 1988 ($1.25)

	GD	VG	FN	VF	VF/NM	NM-
1-12: Nemesis the Warlock, Amadeus Wolf						3.00

SPELLBINDERS
Marvel Comics: May, 2005 - No. 6, Oct, 2005 ($2.99, limited series)

	GD	VG	FN	VF	VF/NM	NM-
1-6-Carey-s/Perkins-a						3.00
...: Signs and Wonders TPB (2006, $7.99, digest) r/#1-6						8.00

SPELLBOUND (See The Crusaders)

SPELLBOUND (Tales to Hold You... #1, Stories to Hold You...)
Atlas Comics (ACI 1-15/Male 16-23/BPC 24-34): Mar, 1952 - #23, June, 1954; #24, Oct, 1955 - #34, June, 1957

	GD	VG	FN	VF	VF/NM	NM-
1-Horror/weird stories in all	132	264	396	845	1448	2050
2-Edgar A. Poe app.	71	142	213	454	777	1100
3-Whitney-a; cannibalism story; classic Heath-c	110	220	330	704	1202	1700
4,5	61	122	183	390	670	950
6-Krigstein-a	63	126	189	403	689	975
7-10: 7,8-Ayers-a	54	108	162	343	574	825
11-13,15,16,18-20	50	100	150	315	533	750
14-Ed Win-a; classic Everett-c	151	302	453	966	1658	2350
17-Krigstein-a; classic Everett skeleton-c	132	264	396	845	1448	2050
21-23: 23-Last precode (6/54)	42	84	126	265	445	625
24-28,30,31,34: 25-Orlando-a	34	68	102	201	328	455
29-Ditko-a (4 pgs.)	36	72	108	216	351	485
32,33-Torres-a	34	68	102	201	328	455

NOTE: ***Brodsky*** *a-5; c-1, 5-7, 10, 11, 13, 15, 25-27, 32.* ***Colan*** *a-17.* ***Everett*** *a-2, 5, 7, 10, 16, 28, 31; c-2, 8, 9, 14, 17-19, 28, 30.* ***Forgione/Abel*** *a-29.* ***Forte/Fox*** *a-16.* ***Al Hartley*** *a-2.* ***Heath*** *a-2, 4, 8, 9, 12, 14, 16; c-3, 4, 12, 16, 20, 21.* ***Infantino*** *a-15.* ***Keller*** *a-5.* ***Kida*** *a-2, 14.* ***Maneely*** *a-7, 14, 27; c-24, 29, 31.* ***Mooney*** *a-5, 13, 18.* ***Mac Pakula*** *a-22, 32.* ***Post*** *a-8.* ***Powell*** *a-19, 20, 32.* ***Robinson*** *a-1.* ***Romita*** *a-24, 26, 27.* ***R.Q. Sale*** *a-29.* ***Sekowsky*** *a-5.* ***Severin*** *c-29.* ***Sinnott*** *a-8, 16, 17.*

SPELLBOUND
Marvel Comics: Jan, 1988 - Apr, 1988 ($1.50, bi-weekly, Baxter paper)

	GD	VG	FN	VF	VF/NM	NM-
1-5						4.00
6 ($2.25, 52 pgs.)						5.00

SPELLJAMMER (Also see TSR Worlds Comics Annual)
DC Comics: Sept, 1990 - No. 15, Nov, 1991 ($1.75)

	GD	VG	FN	VF	VF/NM	NM-
1-15: Based on TSR game. 11-Heck-a.						3.00

SPELL ON WHEELS
Dark Horse Comics: Oct, 2016 - No. 5, Feb, 2017 ($3.99)

	GD	VG	FN	VF	VF/NM	NM-
1-5-Kate Leth-s/Megan Levens-a. 1-Ming Doyle-c						4.00

SPENCER SPOOK (Formerly Giggle Comics)
American Comics Group: No. 100, Mar-Apr, 1955 - No. 101, May-June, 1955

	GD	VG	FN	VF	VF/NM	NM-
100,101	8	16	24	44	57	70

SPIDER, THE
Eclipse Books: 1991 - Book 3, 1991 ($4.95, 52 pgs., limited series)

	GD	VG	FN	VF	VF/NM	NM-
Book 1-3-Truman-c/a						5.00

SPIDER, THE
Dynamite Entertainment: 2012 - No. 18, 2014 ($3.99)

	GD	VG	FN	VF	VF/NM	NM-
1-18: 1-Revival of the pulp character; Liss-s/Worley-a; 4 covers. 2-18-Multiple covers						4.00
Annual 1 (2013, $4.99) Denton-s/Vitorino-a/c						5.00

SPIDER-BOY (Also see Marvel Versus DC #3)
Marvel Comics (Amalgam): Apr, 1996 ($1.95)

	GD	VG	FN	VF	VF/NM	NM-
1-Mike Wieringo-c/a; Karl Kesel story; 1st app. of Bizarnage, Insect Queen, Challengers of the Fantastic, Sue Storm: Agent of S.H.I.E.L.D., & King Lizard						3.00

Spider-Girl (2011 series) #5 © MAR

Spider-Ham #1 © MAR

Spider-Man #48 © MAR

GD VG FN VF VF/NM NM-
2.0 4.0 6.0 8.0 9.0 9.2

SPIDER-BOY TEAM-UP
Marvel Comics (Amalgam): June, 1997 ($1.95, one-shot)
1-Karl Kesel & Roger Stern-s/Jo Ladronn-a(p) 3.00

SPIDER-FORCE (Tie-in to Spider-Geddon)
Marvel Comics: Dec, 2018 - No. 3, Feb, 2019 ($3.99, limited series)
1-3: 1-Priest-s/Siqueira-a; Spider-Woman, Spider-Kid, Scarlet Spider app. 4.00

SPIDER-GEDDON (Also see Edge of Spider-Geddon, Spider-Girls and Superior Octopus)
Marvel Comics: No. 0, Nov, 2018 - No. 5, Feb, 2019 ($4.99/$3.99)
0,5-($4.99) 0-Clayton Crain-a; 1st app. Spider-Man from PS4 videogame 5.00
1-4-($3.99) 1-Gage-s/Molina-a; multiverse of Spider-Mans app.; Morlun returns 4.00
... Handbook 1 (2/19, $4.99) Profiles of various Spider-Men of the Multiverse 5.00

SPIDER-GIRL (See What If... #105)
Marvel Comics: Oct, 1998 - No. 100, Sept, 2006 ($1.99/$2.25/$2.99)
0-($2.99)-r/1st app. Peter Parker's daughter from What If #105; previews regular series, Avengers-Next and J2 2 4 6 8 10 12
1-DeFalco-s/Olliffe & Williamson-s 1 3 4 6 8 10
2-Two covers 4.00
3-16,18-20: 3-Fantastic Five-c/app. 10,11-Spider-Girl time-travels to meet teenaged Spider-Man 3.00
17-($2.99) Peter Parker suits up 4.00
21-24,26-49,51-59: 21-Begin $2.25-c. 31-Avengers app. 3.00
25-($2.99) Spider-Girl vs. the Savage Six 4.00
50-($3.50) 4.00
59-99-($2.99) 59-Avengers app.; Ben Parker born. 75-May in Black costume. 82-84-Venom bonds with Normie Osborn. 93-Venom-c. 95-Tony Stark app. 3.00
100-($3.99) Last issue; story plus Rogues Gallery, profile pages; r/#27,53 4.00
1999 Annual ($3.99) 4.00
...: The End! (10/10, $3.99) Frenz & Buscema-a; Mayhem app. 4.00
Wizard #1/2 (1999) 3.00
... A Fresh Start (1/99,$5.99, TPB) r/#1&2 6.00
... Presents The Buzz and Darkdevil (2007, $7.99, digest) r/mini-series 8.00

SPIDER-GIRL (Araña Corazon from Arana Heart of the Spider)
Marvel Comics: Jan, 2011 - No. 8, Sept, 2011 ($3.99/$2.99)
1-($3.99) Tobin-s/Henry-a/Kitson-c; back-up w/Haspiel-a; Fantastic Four app. 4.00
1-Variant-c by Del Mundo 5.00
2-8-($2.99) 2,3-Red Hulk app. 4,5-Ana Kravenoff app. 6-Hobgoblin app. 8-Powers return 3.00

SPIDER-GIRLS (Spider-Geddon tie-in)
Marvel Comics: Dec, 2018 - No. 3, Feb, 2019 ($3.99, limited series)
1-3-Houser-s/Genolet-a; Mayday Parker, Anya Corazon & Annie Parker app. 4.00

SPIDER-GWEN (See debut in Edge of Spider-Verse #2)
Marvel Comics: Apr, 2015 - No. 5, Aug, 2015 ($3.99)
1-Latour-s/Robbi Rodriguez-a/c; The Vulture app. 1 3 4 6 8 10
2-5: 2-Spider-Ham app. 3-The Vulture & The Punisher app. 4.00

SPIDER-GWEN
Marvel Comics: Dec, 2015 - No. 34, Sept, 2018 ($3.99)
1-Latour-s/Robbi Rodriguez-a; The Lizard & female Capt. America app. 1 2 3 5 6 8
2-23,25-34: 7,8-"Spider-Women" tie-in; Silk & Spider-Woman app. 10-Kraven app. 16-18-Miles app.; x-over with Spider-Man #12-14. 25-32-Gwenom app. 4.00
24-1st app. Gwenom 3 6 9 19 30 40
#0 (1/16, $4.99) Reprints #1 (4/15) plus script of Edge of Spider-Verse #2 5.00
Annual 1 (8/16, $4.99) Short stories; Latour-s; art by various 5.00

SPIDER-GWEN: GHOST-SPIDER (Spider-Geddon tie-in)(Also see Ghost-Spider series)
Marvel Comics: Dec, 2018 - No. 10, Sept, 2019 ($3.99)
1-10: 1-Spider-Ham app. 4-10-Miyazawa-a. 10-Adapts Ghost-Spider name 4.00

SPIDER-HAM (Peter Porker, The Spectacular...)(See Marvel Tails & Spider-Geddon)
Marvel Comics: Feb, 2020 - No. 5, Jun, 2020 ($3.99)
1-5: 1-Origin re-told; Sca-vengers and the Unhumanati app. 2-5-Spider-Man app. 4.00

SPIDER-HAM 25TH ANNIVERSARY SPECIAL
Marvel Comics: Aug, 2010 ($3.99, one-shot)
1-Jusko-c/DeFalco-s/Chabot-a; Peter Porker vs. the Swinester Six 4.00

SPIDER ISLAND... (one-shots) (See Amazing Spider-Man #666-673)
Marvel Comics
...: Deadly Foes 1 (10/11, $4.99) Hobgoblin & Jackal stories; Caselli-c 5.00
...: Emergence of Evil - Jackal & Hobgoblin 1 (10/11, $4.99) Hobgoblin & Jackal reprints 5.00
...: Heroes For Hire 1 (12/11, $2.99) Misty Knight & Paladin; Hotz-a/Yardin-c 3.00
...: I Love New York City 1 (11/11, $3.99) Short stories by various; Punisher app. 4.00
...: Spider-Woman 1 (11/11, $2.99) Van Lente-s/Camuncoli-a; Alicia Masters app. 3.00
... Spotlight 1 ('11, $3.99) Creator interviews and story previews 4.00
...: The Avengers 1 (11/11, $2.99) McKone-a/Yu-c; Frog-Man app. 3.00

SPIDER-ISLAND (Secret Wars tie-in)(Back-up MC2 Spider-Girl story in each issue)
Marvel Comics: Sept, 2015 - No. 5, Dec, 2015 ($4.99/$3.99, limited series)
1-($4.99) Gage-s/Diaz-a/Ramos-c; Venom and Werewolf By Night app. 5.00
2-5-($3.99) Tony Stark as the Green Goblin. 3-5-Peter Parker returns 4.00

SPIDER ISLAND: CLOAK & DAGGER (See Amazing Spider-Man #666-673)
Marvel Comics: Oct, 2011 - No. 3, Dec, 2011 ($2.99, limited series)
1-3-Spencer-s/Rios-a/Choi-c; Mr. Negative app. 3.00

SPIDER ISLAND: DEADLY HANDS OF KUNG FU (See Amazing Spider-Man #666-673)
Marvel Comics: Oct, 2011 - No. 3, Dec, 2011 ($2.99, limited series)
1-3-Johnston-s/Fiumara-a; Madame Web & Iron Fist app. 3.00

SPIDER ISLAND: THE AMAZING SPIDER-GIRL (Continued from Spider-Girl #8)
Marvel Comics: Oct, 2011 - No. 3, Dec, 2011 ($2.99, limited series)
1-3-Hobgoblin & Kingpin app.; Tobin-s/Larraz-a 3.00

SPIDER-MAN (See Amazing..., Friendly Neighborhood..., Giant-Size..., Marvel Age..., Marvel Knights..., Marvel Tales, Marvel Team-Up, Spectacular..., Spidey Super Stories, Ultimate Marvel Team-Up, Ultimate..., Venom, & Web Of...)

SPIDER-MAN (Peter Parker Spider-Man on cover but not indicia #75-on)
Marvel Comics: Aug, 1990 - No. 98, Nov, 1998 ($1.75/$1.95/ $1.99)
1-Silver edition, direct sale only (unbagged) 2 4 6 10 14 18
1-Silver bagged edition; direct sale, no price on comic, but $2.00 on plastic bag (125,000 print run) 3 6 9 16 24 32
1-Regular edition w/Spidey face in UPC area (unbagged); green-c 2 4 6 8 11 14
1-Regular bagged edition w/Spidey face in UPC area; green cover (125,000) 12.00
1-Newsstand bagged w/UPC code 2 4 6 8 10 12
1-Gold edition, 2nd printing (unbagged) with Spider-Man in box (400,000-450,000) 3 6 9 17 26 35
1-Gold 2nd printing w/UPC code; (less than 10,000 print run) intended for Wal-Mart; much scarcer than originally believed 12 24 36 81 176 270
1-Platinum ed. mailed to retailers only (10,000 print run); has new McFarlane-a & editorial material instead of ads; stiff-c, no cover price 13 26 39 89 195 300
1-Facsimile Edition (10/20, $3.99) reprints #1 with original ads and letter page 4.00
2-10: 2-McFarlane-c/a/scripts cont.; Lizard origin retold in brief. 3-Spider-Man origin retold in brief. 6,7-Ghost Rider & Hobgoblin app. 8-Wolverine cameo; Wolverine storyline begins 6.00
11-25: 12-Wolverine storyline ends. 13-Spidey's black costume returns; Morbius app. 14-Morbius app. 15-Erik Larsen-c/a; Beast c/s. 16-X-Force-c/story w/Liefeld assists; continues in X-Force #4; reads sideways; last McFarlane issue. 17-Thanos-c/story; Leonardi/Williamson-c/a. 18-Ghost Rider-c/story. 18-23-Sinister Six storyline w/Erik Larsen-c/a/scripts. 19-Hulk & Hobgoblin-c & app. 20-22-Deathlok app. 22,23-Ghost Rider, Hulk, Hobgoblin app. 23-Wrap-around gatefold-c. 24-Infinity War x-over w/Demogoblin & Hobgoblin-c/story. 24-Demogoblin dons new costume & battles Hobgoblin-c/story 4.00
26-($3.50, 52 pgs.)-Silver hologram on-c w/gatefold poster by Ron Lim; origin retold 6.00
26-2nd printing; gold hologram on-c 4.00
27-45: 32-34-Punisher-c/story. 37-Maximum Carnage x-over. 39,40-Electro-c/s (cameo #38). 41-43-Iron Fist-c/stories w/Jae Lee-c/a. 42-Intro Platoon. 44-Hobgoblin app. 3.50
46-49,51-53, 55, 56,58-74,76-81: 46-Begin $1.95-c; bound-in card sheet. 51-Power & Responsibility Pt. 3. 52,53-Venom app. 60-Kaine revealed. 61-Origin Kaine. 65-Mysterio app. 66-Kaine-c/app.; Peter Parker app. 67-Carnage-c/app. 68,69-Hobgoblin-c/app. 72-Onslaught x-over; Spidey vs. Sentinels. 74-Daredevil-c/app. 77-80-Morbius-c/app. 3.00
46-($2.95)-Polybagged; silver ink-c w/16 pg. preview of cartoon series & animation style print; bound-in trading card sheet 4.00
50-($2.50)-Newsstand edition 4.00
50-($3.95)-Collectors edition w/holographic-c 5.00
51-($2.95)-Deluxe edition foil-c; flip book 4.00
54-($2.75, 52 pgs.)-Flip book 4.00
57-($2.50) 4.00
57-($2.95)-Die cut-c 5.00
65-($2.95)-Variant-c; polybagged w/cassette 4.00
75-($2.95)-Wraparound-c; Green Goblin returns; death of Ben Reilly (who was the clone) 4.00
82-97: 84-Juggernaut app. 91-Double cover with "Dusk #1"; battles the Shocker. 93-Ghost Rider app. 3.00
98-Double cover; final issue 4.00
#(-1) Flashback (7/97) 3.00
Annual '97 ($2.99), '98 ($2.99)-Devil Dinosaur-c/app. 5.00
NOTE: *Erik Larsen c/a-15, 18-23. M. Rogers/Keith Williams c/a-27, 28.*

SPIDER-MAN (Miles Morales in regular Marvel Universe)
Marvel Comics: Apr, 2016 - No. 21, Dec, 2017; No. 234, Jan, 2018 - No. 240, Jul, 2018 ($3.99)
1-19,21: 1,2-Bendis-s/Pichelli-a; Avengers & Peter Parker app. 3-Ms. Marvel app.

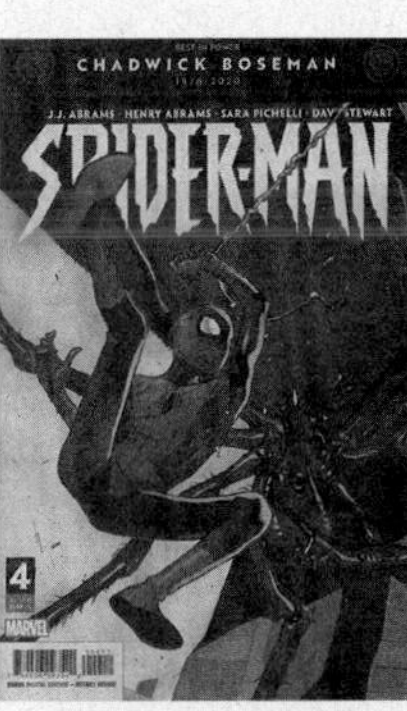

Spider-Man (2019 series) #4 © MAR

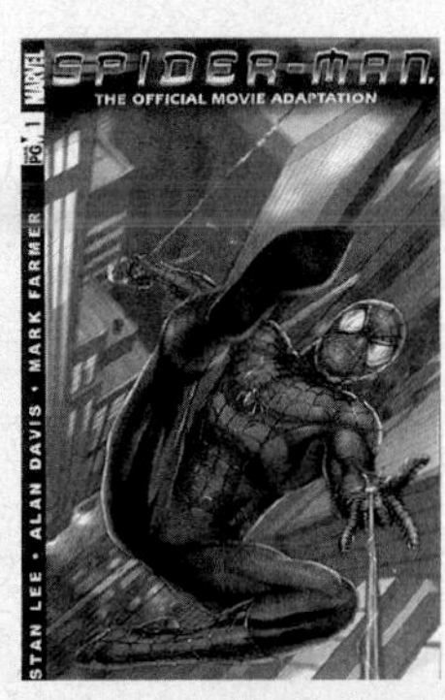

Spider-Man: The Official Movie Adaptation © MAR

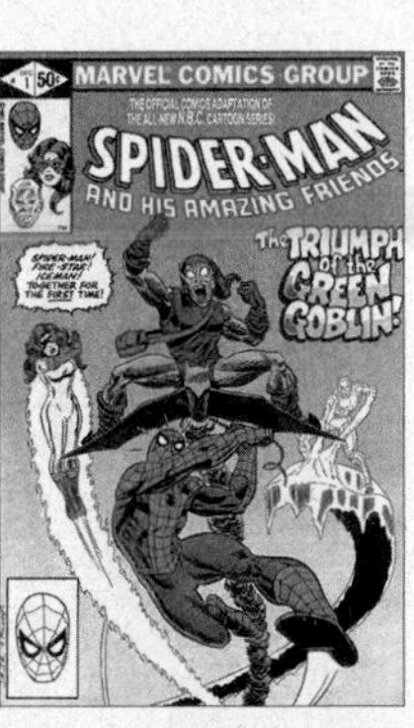

Spider-Man and His Amazing Friends #1 © MAR

GD	VG	FN	VF	VF/NM	NM-
2.0	4.0	6.0	8.0	9.0	9.2

6-10-Civil War II tie-ins. 12,13-Crossover with Spider-Gwen #16-18. 16,18-Black Cat app. 21-Nico Leon-a 4.00
20-Miles Morales pinned down by police officer-c; Nico Leon-a 2 4 6 9 12 15
[Title switches to legacy numbering after #21 (12/17)]
234-240: 234-239-Hobgoblin, Sandman, Electro, The Spot, Bombshell, Iron Spider app. 4.00
Annual 1 (10/18, $4.99) Morbius app. 5.00

SPIDER-MAN
Marvel Comics: Nov, 2019 - No. 5, Feb, 2021 ($3.99)

1-($4.99) J.J. & Henry Abrams-s/Pichelli-a; intro Cadaverous and future Ben Parker 5.00
2-5-($3.99) Ben becomes the new Spider-Man. 3-5-Tony Stark and Riri Williams app. 4.00

SPIDER-MAN (one-shots, hardcovers and TPBs)
...& Arana Special: The Hunter Revealed (5/06, $3.99) Del Rio-s; art by Del Rio & various 4.00
...and Batman ('95, $5.95) DeMatteis-s; Joker, Carnage app. 3 6 9 14 19 24
...and Daredevil ('84, $2.00) 1-r/Spectacular Spider-Man #26-28 by Miller 6.00
...and The Human Torch in...Bahia de Los Muertos! 1 (5/09, $3.99) Beland-s/Juan Doe-a; Diablo app.; printed in two versions (English and Spanish language) 4.00
... Annual 1 (8/19, $4.99) Spider-Ham spotlight; back-up by Phil Lord & Christopher Miller 5.00
...: Back in Black HC (2007, $34.99, dustjacket) oversized r/Amaz. S-M #539-543, Friendly Neighborhood S-M #17-23 & Annual #1; cover pencils and sketch pages 35.00
...: Back in Black SC (2008, $24.99) same contents as HC 25.00
...: Back in Black Handbook (2007, $3.99) Official Handbook format; Lopresti-c 10.00
...: Back in Quack (11/10, $3.99) Howard the Duck, Beverly and Man-Thing app. 4.00
...: Birth of Venom TPB (2007, $29.99) r/Secret Wars #8, AS-M #252-259,298-300,315-317, AS-M Annual #25, Fantastic Four #274 and Web of Spider-Man #1 30.00
...: Brand New Day HC (2008, $24.99, dustjacket) r/Amaz. S-M #546-551, Spider-Man: Swing Shift and story from Venom Super-Special 25.00
...: Carnage nn (6/93, $6.95, TPB)-r/Amazing S-M #344,345,359-363; spot varnish-c 10.00
.../Daredevil (10/02, $2.99) Vatche Mavlian-c/a; Brett Matthews-s 3.00
...: Dead Man's Hand 1 (4/97, $2.99) 3.00
...: Death of the Stacys HC (2007, $19.99, dustjacket) r/Amazing Spider-Man #88-92 and #121,122; intro. by Gerry Conway; afterword by Romita; cover gallery incl. reprints 20.00
.../Dr. Strange: "The Way to Dusty Death" nn (1992, $6.95, 68 pgs.) 8.00
...: Election Day HC (2009, $29.99) r/#584-588; includes Barack Obama app from #583 30.00
.../Elektra '98-($2.99) vs. The Silencer 3.00
... Family (2005, $4.99, 100 pgs.) new story and reprints; Spider-Ham app. 5.00
... Fear Itself (3/09, $3.99) Spider-Man and Man-Thing; Stuart Moore-s/Joe Suitor-a 4.00
... Fear Itself Graphic Novel (2/92, $12.95) 18.00
Free Comic Book Day 2012 (Spider-Man: Season One) #1 (Giveaway) Previews the GN 3.00
Giant-Sized Spider-Man (12/98, $3.99) r/team-ups 4.00
...: Grim Hunt - The Kraven Saga (5/10, free) prelude to Grim Hunt arc; Kraven history 3.00
Holiday Special 1995 ($2.95) 6.00
...: Hot Shots nn (1/96, $2.95) fold out posters by various, inc. Vess and Ross 4.00
Identity Crisis (9/98, $19.95, TPB) 20.00
...: Kraven's Last Hunt HC (2006, $19.99) r/Amaz. S-M #293,294; Web of S-M #31,32 and Spect. S-M #131-132; intro. by DeMatteis; Zeck-a; cover pencils and interior pencils 20.00
...: Legacy of Evil 1 (6/96, $3.95) Kurt Busiek script & Mark Texeira-c/a 4.00
...Legends Vol. 1: Todd McFarlane ('03, $19.95, TPB)-r/Amaz. S-M #298-305 20.00
...Legends Vol. 2: Todd McFarlane ('03, $19.99, TPB)-r/Amaz. S-M #306-314, & Spec. Spider-Man Annual #10 20.00
...Legends Vol. 3: Todd McFarlane ('04, $24.99, TPB)-r/Amaz. S-M #315-323,325,328 25.00
...Legends Vol. 4: Spider-Man & Wolverine ('03, $13.95, TPB) r/Spider-Man & Wolverine #1-4 and Spider-Man/Daredevil #1 14.00
.../Marrow (2/01, $2.99) Garza-a 5.00
...: Marvels Snapshots 1 (12/20, $4.99) Howard Chaykin-s/a; Alex Ross-c 5.00
.../Mary Jane: ... You Just Hit the Jackpot TPB (2009, $24.99) early apps. & key stories 25.00
...: Master Plan 1 (9/17, $3.99) Thompson-s/Stockman-a; bonus r/ASM #2 4.00
100th Anniversary Special: Spider-Man 1 (9/14, $3.99) In-Hyk Lee-a/c; Venom app. 4.00
...: One More Day HC (2008. $24.99, dustjacket) r/Amaz. S-M #544-545, Friendly N.S-M #24, Sensational S-M #41 and Marvel Spotlight: Spider-Man-One More Day 25.00
...: Origin of the Hunter (6/10, $3.99) r/Kraven apps. in ASM #15 & 34; new Mayhew-a 4.00
..., Peter Parker: Back in Black HC (2007, $34.99) oversized r/Sensational Spider-Man #35-40 & Annual #1, Spider-Man Family #1,2; Marvel Spotlight: Spider-Man and Spider-Man Back in Black Handbook; cover sketches 35.00
..., Punisher, Sabretooth: Designer Genes (1993, $8.95) 10.00
...: Reptilian Rage 1 (8/19, $3.99) Macchio-s/Chris Allen-a; The Lizard app. 4.00
...Return of the Goblin TPB (See Peter Parker: Spider-Man)
...Revelations ('97, $14.99, TPB) r/end of Clone Saga plus 14 new pages by Romita Jr. 15.00
...: Saga of the Sandman TPB (2007, $19.99) r/1st app. Amazing S-M #4 and other app. 20.00
...: Season One HC (2012, $24.99) Origin and early days; Bunn-s/Neil Edwards-a 25.00
...: Son of the Goblin (2004, $15.99, TPB) r/AS-M#136-137,312 & Spec. S-M #189,200 16.00
... Special: Black and Blue and Read All Over 1 (11/06, $3.99) new story and r/ASM #12 4.00
Special Edition 1 (12/92-c, 11/92 inside)-The Trial of Venom; ordered thru mail with $5.00 donation or more to UNICEF; embossed metallic ink; came bagged w/bound-in poster; Daredevil app. 3 6 9 14 20 25
... Spectacular 1 (8/14, $4.99) Reprints all-ages tales; Green Goblin, Kraven app. 5.00
Super Special (7/95, $3.95)-Planet of the Symbiotes 4.00
The Best of Spider-Man Vol. 2 (2003, $29.99, HC with dust jacket) r/AS-M V2 #37-45, Peter Parker: S-M #44-47, and S-M's Tangled Web #10,11; Pearson-c 30.00
The Best of Spider-Man Vol. 3 (2004, $29.99, HC with d.j.) r/AS-M V2 #46-58, 500 30.00
The Best of Spider-Man Vol. 4 (2005, $29.99, HC with d.j.) r/#501-514; sketch pages 30.00
The Best of Spider-Man Vol. 5 (2006, $29.99, HC with d.j.) r/#515-524; sketch pages 30.00
The Complete Frank Miller Spider-Man (2002, $29.95, HC) r/Miller-s/a 30.00
The Death of Captain Stacy (2000, $3.50) r/AS-M#88-90 5.00
The Death of Gwen Stacy ($14.95) r/AS-M#96-98,121,122 15.00
...: The Movie ($12.95) adaptation by Stan Lee-s/Alan Davis-a; plus r/Ultimate Spider-Man #8, Peter Parker #35, Tangled Web #10; photo-c 13.00
...: The Official Movie Adaptation (2002, $5.95) Stan Lee-s/Alan Davis-a 6.00
...: The Other HC (2006, $29.99, dust jacket) r/Amazing S-M #525-528, Friendly Neighborhood S-M #1-4 and Marvel Knights S-M #19-22; gallery of variant covers 30.00
...: The Other SC (2006, $24.99) r/crossover; gallery of variant covers 25.00
...: The Other Sketchbook (2005, $2.99) sketch page preview of 2005-6 x-over 3.00
Torment TPB (5/01$15.95) r/#1-5, Spec. S-M #10 16.00
... Vs. Doctor Octopus ($17.95) reprints early battles; Sean Chen-c 18.00
... Vs. Punisher (7/00, $2.99) Michael Lopez-c/a 5.00
...Vs. Silver Sable (2006, $15.99, TPB)-r/Amazing Spider-Man #265,279-281 & Peter Parker, The Spectacular Spider-Man #128,129 16.00
...Vs. The Black Cat (2005, $14.99, TPB)-r/Amaz. S-M #194,195,204,205,226,227 15.00
...Vs. Vampires (12/10, $3.99) Blade app.; Castro-a/Grevioux-s 4.00
...Vs. Venom (1990, $8.95, TPB)-r/Amaz. S-M #300,315-317 w/new McFarlane-c 15.00
...Visionaries (10/01, $19.95, TPB)-r/Amaz. S-M #298-305; McFarlane-a 20.00
...Visionaries: John Romita (8/01, $19.95, TPB)-r/Amaz. S-M #39-42, 50,68,69,108,109; new Romita-c 20.00
...Visionaries: Kurt Busiek (2006, $19.99, TPB)-r/Untold Tales of Spider-Man #1-8 20.00
...Visionaries: Roger Stern (2007, $24.99, TPB)-r/Amazing Spider-Man #206 & Spectacular Spider-Man #43-52,54; Stern interview 25.00
Wizard 1/2 ($10.00) Leonardi-a; Green Goblin app. 10.00

SPIDER-MAN ADVENTURES
Marvel Comics: Dec, 1994 - No. 15, Mar, 1996 ($1.50)

1-15 ($1.50)-Based on animated series 4.00
1-($2.95)-Foil embossed-c 5.00

SPIDER-MAN AND HIS AMAZING FRIENDS (See Marvel Action Universe)
Marvel Comics Group: Dec, 1981 (one-shot)

1-Adapted from NBC TV cartoon show; Green Goblin-c/story; 1st Spidey, Firestar, Iceman team-up; Spiegle-p 5 10 15 31 53 75

SPIDER-MAN AND POWER PACK
Marvel Comics: Jan, 2007 - No. 4, Apr, 2007 ($2.99, limited series)

1-4-Sumerak-s/Gurihiru-a; Sandman app. 3,4-Venom app. 3.00
...: Big City Heroes (2007, $6.99, digest) r/#1-4 7.00

SPIDER-MAN AND THE FANTASTIC FOUR
Marvel Comics: Jun, 2007 - No. 4, Sept, 2007 ($2.99, limited series)

1-4-Mike Wieringo-a/c; Jeff Parker-s. 1,4-Impossible Man app. 3.00
...: Silver Rage TPB (2007, $10.99) r/#1-4; series outline and cover sketches 11.00

SPIDER-MAN AND THE LEAGUE OF REALMS (War of the Realms tie-in)
Marvel Comics: Jul, 2019 - No. 3, Aug, 2019 ($3.99, limited series)

1-3-Sean Ryan-s/Nico Leon-a 4.00

SPIDER-MAN AND THE SECRET WARS
Marvel Comics: Feb, 2010 - No. 4, May, 2010 ($2.99, limited series)

1-4-Tobin-s/Scherberger-a. 3-Black costume app. 3.00

SPIDER-MAN AND THE INCREDIBLE HULK (See listing under Amazing...)

SPIDER-MAN AND THE UNCANNY X-MEN
Marvel Comics: Mar, 1996 ($16.95, trade paperback)

nn-r/Uncanny X-Men #27, Uncanny X-men #35, Amazing Spider-Man #92, Marvel Team-Up Annual #1, Marvel Team-Up #150, & Spectacular Spider-Man #197-199 17.00

SPIDER-MAN & THE X-MEN
Marvel Comics: Feb, 2015 - No. 6, Jub, 2015 ($3.99)

1-3: Spider-Man teaching at the Jean Grey School; Kalan-s/Failla-a. 2,3-Mojo app. 4.00

SPIDER-MAN & VENOM: DOUBLE TROUBLE (All-ages)
Marvel Comics: Jan, 2020 - No. 4, Apr, 2020 ($3.99, limited series)

1-4-Spider-Man & Venom as roommates; Tamaki-s/Gurihiru-a; Ghost-Spider app. 4.00

SPIDER-MAN & WOLVERINE (See Spider-Man Legends Vol. 4 for TPB reprint)

Spider-Man: Blue #4 © MAR

Spider-Man / Deadpool #20 © MAR

Spider-Man: Lifeline #1 © MAR

	GD	VG	FN	VF	VF/NM	NM-
	2.0	4.0	6.0	8.0	9.0	9.2

Marvel Comics: Aug, 2003 - No. 4, Nov, 2003 ($2.99, limited series)

1-4-Matthews-s/Mavlian-a 3.00

SPIDER-MAN AND X-FACTOR
Marvel Comics: May, 1994 - No. 3, July, 1994 ($1.95, limited series)

1-3 4.00

SPIDER-MAN /BADROCK
Maximum Press: Mar, 1997 ($2.99, mini-series)

1A, 1B(#2)-Jurgens-s 4.00

SPIDER-MAN/BLACK CAT: THE EVIL THAT MEN DO (Also see Marvel Must Haves)
Marvel Comics: Aug, 2002 - No. 6, Mar, 2006 ($2.99, limited series)

1-6-Kevin Smith-s/Terry Dodson-c/a 3.00
HC (2006, $19.99, dust jacket) r/#1-6; script to #6 with sketches 20.00

SPIDER-MAN: BLUE
Marvel Comics: July, 2002 - No. 6, Apr, 2003 ($3.50, limited series)

1-6: Jeph Loeb-s/Tim Sale-a/c; flashback to early MJ and Gwen Stacy 3.50
HC (2003, $21.99, with dust jacket) over-sized r/#1-6; intro. by John Romita 22.00
SC (2004, $14.99) r/#1-6; cover gallery 15.00

SPIDER-MAN: BRAND NEW DAY (See Amazing Spider-Man Vol. 2)

SPIDER-MAN: BREAKOUT (See New Avengers #1)
Marvel Comics: June, 2005 - No. 5, Oct, 2005 ($2.99, limited series)

1-5-Bedard-s/Garcia-a. 1-U-Foes app. 5-New Avengers app. 3.00
TPB (2006, $13.99) r/#1-5 14.00

SPIDER-MAN: CHAPTER ONE
Marvel Comics: Dec, 1998 - No. 12, Oct, 1999 ($2.50, limited series)

1-Retelling/updating of origin; John Byrne-s/c/a 4.00
1-($6.95) DF Edition w/variant-c by Jae Lee 7.00
2-11: 2-Two covers (one is swipe of ASM #1); Fantastic Four app. 9-Daredevil. 11-Giant-Man-c/app. 4.00
12-($3.50) Battles the Sandman 5.00
0-(5/99) Origins of Vulture, Lizard and Sandman 4.00

SPIDER-MAN CLASSICS
Marvel Comics: Apr, 1993 - No. 16, July, 1994 ($1.25)

1-14,16: 1-r/Amaz. Fantasy #15 & Strange Tales #115. 2-16-r/Amaz. Spider-Man #1-15. 6-Austin-c(i) 4.00
15-($2.95)-Polybagged w/16 pg. insert & animation style print; r/Amazing Spider-Man #14 (1st Green Goblin) 5.00

SPIDER-MAN COLLECTOR'S PREVIEW
Marvel Comics: Dec, 1994 ($1.50, 100 pgs., one-shot)

1-wraparound-c; no comics 4.00

SPIDER-MAN COMICS MAGAZINE
Marvel Comics Group: Jan, 1987 - No. 13, 1988 ($1.50, digest-size)

1-13-Reprints 6.00

SPIDER-MAN/DEADPOOL
Marvel Comics: Mar, 2016 - No. 50, Jul, 2019 ($3.99)

1-49: 1-Joe Kelly-s/Ed McGuinness-a; back-up reprint of Vision #1. 6-Aukerman-s. 7-Art in 1968 Ditko-style by Koblish. 8-New black Spidey suit. 11-Penn Jillette-s. 16-Dracula app. 17,18-McGuinness-a. 19,20-Slapstick app. 23-25,27,28-Bachalo-a. 48,49-Gwenpool app. 4.00
50-($4.99) Last issue; Gwenpool app. 5.00
#1.MU (3/17, $4.99) Corin-s/Walker-a/Dave Johnson-c 5.00

SPIDER-MAN: DEATH AND DESTINY
Marvel Comics: Aug, 2000 - No. 3, Oct, 2000 ($2.99, limited series)

1-3-Aftermath of the death of Capt. Stacy 3.00

SPIDER-MAN/ DOCTOR OCTOPUS: OUT OF REACH
Marvel Comics: Jan, 2004 - No. 5, May, 2004 ($2.99, limited series)

1-5: 1-Keron Grant-a/Colin Mitchell-s 3.00
Marvel Age... TPB (2004, $5.99, digest size) r/#1-5 6.00

SPIDER-MAN/ DOCTOR OCTOPUS: YEAR ONE
Marvel Comics: Aug, 2004 - No. 5, Dec, 2004 ($2.99, limited series)

1-5-Kaare Andrews-a/Zeb Wells-s 3.00

SPIDER-MAN: ENTER THE SPIDER-VERSE
Marvel Comics: Jan, 2019 ($4.99, one-shot)

1-Web-Warriors and Sinister Six app.; Macchio-s/Flaviano-a; r/Spider-Man #1 (2016) 5.00

SPIDER-MAN FAIRY TALES
Marvel Comics: July, 2007 - No. 4, Oct, 2007 ($2.99, limited series)

1-4: 1-Cebulski-s/Tercio-a. 2-Henrichon-a. 3-Kobayashi-a. 4-Dragotta-p/Allred-i 3.00
TPB (2007, $10.99) r/#1-4 11.00

SPIDER-MAN FAMILY (Also see Amazing Spider-Man Family)
Marvel Comics: Apr, 2007 - No. 9, Aug, 2008 ($4.99, anthology)

1-9-New tales and reprints. 1-Black costume, Sandman, Black Cat app. 4-Agents of Atlas app., Kirk-a; Puppet Master by Eliopoulos. 8-Iron Man app. 9-Hulk app. 5.00
... Featuring Spider-Clan 1 (1/07, $4.99) new Spider-Clan story; reprints w/Spider-Man 2099 and Amazing Spider-Man #252 (black costume) 5.00
... Featuring Spider-Man's Amazing Friends 1 (10/06, $4.99) new story with Iceman and Firestar; Mini Marvels w/Giarrusso-a; reprints w/Spider-Man 2099 5.00
...: Back In Black (2007, $7.99, digest) r/new content from #1-3 8.00
...: Untold Team-Ups (2008, $9.99, digest) r/new content from #4-6 10.00

SPIDER-MAN/FANTASTIC FOUR (Spider-Man and the Fantastic Four on cover)
Marvel Comics: Sept, 2010 - No. 4, Dec, 2010 ($3.99, limited series)

1-4-Gage-s/Alberti-a; Dr. Doom app. 4.00

SPIDER-MAN: FAR FROM HOME PRELUDE
Marvel Comics: May, 2019 - No. 2, Jun, 2019 ($3.99, limited series)

1,2-Adaptation of Spider-Man: Homecoming movie; Pilgrim-s/Maresca-a; photo-c 4.00

SPIDER-MAN: FEVER
Marvel Comics: Jun, 2010 - No. 3, Aug, 2010 ($3.99, limited series)

1-3-Brendan McCarthy-s/a; Dr. Strange app. 4.00

SPIDER-MAN: FRIENDS AND ENEMIES
Marvel Comics: Jan, 1995 - No. 4, Apr, 1995 ($1.95, limited series)

1-4-Darkhawk, Nova & Speedball app. 4.00

SPIDER-MAN: FUNERAL FOR AN OCTOPUS
Marvel Comics: Mar, 1995 - No. 3, May, 1995 ($1.50, limited series)

1-3 4.00

SPIDER-MAN/ GEN 13
Marvel Comics: Nov, 1996 ($4.95, one-shot)

nn-Peter David-s/Stuart Immonen-a 5.00

SPIDER-MAN: GET KRAVEN
Marvel Comics: Aug, 2002 - No. 6, Jan, 2003 ($2.99/$2.25, limited series)

1-($2.99) McCrea-a/Quesada-c; back-up story w/Rio-a 4.00
2-6-($2.25) 2-Sub-Mariner app. 3.00

SPIDER-MAN: HOBGOBLIN LIVES
Marvel Comics: Jan, 1997 - No. 3, Mar, 1997 ($2.50, limited series)

1-3-Wraparound-c 4.00
TPB (1/98, $14.99) r/#1-3 plus timeline 15.00

SPIDER-MAN: HOUSE OF M (Also see House of M and related x-overs)
Marvel Comics: Aug, 2005 - No. 5, Dec, 2005 ($2.99, limited series)

1-5-Waid & Peyer-s/Larroca-a; rich and famous Peter Parker in mutant-ruled world 3.00
House of M: Spider-Man TPB (2006, $13.99) r/series 14.00

SPIDER-MAN/ HUMAN TORCH
Marvel Comics: Mar, 2005 - No. 5, July, 2005 ($2.99, limited series)

1-5-Ty Templeton-a/Dan Slott-s; team-ups from early days to the present 3.00
...: I'm With Stupid (2006, $7.99, digest) r/#1-5 8.00

SPIDER-MAN: INDIA
Marvel Comics: Jan, 2005 - No. 4, Apr, 2005 ($2.99, limited series)

1-4-Pavitr Prabhakar gains spider powers; Kang-a/Seetharaman-s 3.00

SPIDER-MAN: LEGEND OF THE SPIDER-CLAN (See Marvel Mangaverse for TPB)
Marvel Comics: Dec, 2002 - No. 5, Apr, 2003 ($2.25, limited series)

1-5-Marvel Mangaverse Spider-Man; Kaare Andrews-s/Skottie Young-c/a 3.00

SPIDER-MAN: LIFELINE
Marvel Comics: Apr, 2001 - No. 3, June, 2001 ($2.99, limited series)

1-3-Nicieza-s/Rude-c/a; The Lizard app. 3.00

SPIDER-MAN: LIFE STORY
Marvel Comics: May, 2019 - No. 6, Oct, 2019 ($4.99, limited series)

1-5-The 1962 Spider-Man ages in real time; Zdarsky-s/Bagley-a. 2-The '70s. 3-The'80s; Venom app. 5-Morlun app.; Civil War. 6-The 2010s; Venom/Kraven & Miles app. 5.00

SPIDER-MAN LOVES MARY JANE (Also see Mary Jane limited series)
Marvel Comics: Feb, 2006 - No. 20, Sept, 2007 ($2.99)

1-20-Mary Jane & Peter in high school; McKeever-s/Miyazawa-a/c. 5-Gwen Stacy app. 16-18,20-Firestar app. 17-Felicia Hardy app. 3.00
... Vol. 1: Super Crush (2006, $7.99, digest) r/#1-5; cover concepts page 8.00

Spider-Man Noir (2020 series) #4 © MAR

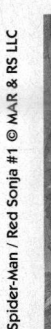

Spider-Man / Red Sonja #1 © MAR & RS LLC

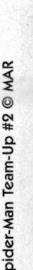

Spider-Man Team-Up #2 © MAR

GD 2.0 | VG 4.0 | FN 6.0 | VF 8.0 | VF/NM 9.0 | NM- 9.2

... Vol. 2: The New Girl (2006, $7.99, digest) r/#6-10; sketch pages 8.00
... Vol. 3: My Secret Life (2007, $7.99, digest) r/#11-15; sketch pages 8.00
... Vol. 4: Still Friends (2007, $7.99, digest) r/#16-20 8.00
Hardcover Vol. 1 (2007, $24.99) oversized reprints of #1-5, Mary Jane #1-4 and Mary Jane: Homecoming #1-4; series proposals, sketch pages and covers; coloring process 25.00
Hardcover Vol. 2 (2008, $39.99) oversized reprints of #6-20, sketch & layout pages 40.00

SPIDER-MAN LOVES MARY JANE SEASON 2
Marvel Comics: Oct, 2008 - No. 5, Feb, 2009 ($2.99, limited series)

1-5-Terry Moore-s/c; Craig Rousseau-a 3.00
1-Variant-c by Alphona 8.00

SPIDER-MAN: MADE MEN
Marvel Comics: Aug, 1998 ($5.99, one-shot)

1-Spider-Man & Daredevil vs. Kingpin 6.00

SPIDER-MAN MAGAZINE
Marvel Comics: 1994 - No. 3, 1994 ($1.95, magazine)

1-3: 1-Contains 4 S-M promo cards & 4 X-Men Ultra Fleer cards; Spider-Man story by Romita, Sr.; X-Men story; puzzles & games. 2-Doc Octopus & X-Men stories 4.00

SPIDER-MAN: MAXIMUM CLONAGE
Marvel Comics: 1995 ($4.95)

Alpha #1-Acetate-c, Omega #1-Chromium-c. 6.00

SPIDER-MAN MEGAZINE
Marvel Comics: Oct, 1994 - No. 6, Mar, 1995 ($2.95, 100 pgs.)

1-6: 1-r/ASM #16,224,225, Marvel Team-Up #1 5.00

SPIDER-MAN NOIR
Marvel Comics: Dec, 2008 - No. 4, May, 2009 ($3.99, limited series)

1-4-Pulp-style Spider-Man in 1933; DiGiandomenico-a; covers by Zircher & Calero 4.00
...: Eyes Without a Face 1-4 (2/10 - No. 4, 5/10) DiGiandomenico-a; Zircher & Calero-c 4.00

SPIDER-MAN NOIR
Marvel Comics: May, 2020 - No. 5, Dec, 2020 ($3.99, limited series)

1-5-Pulp-style Spider-Man in 1939; Stohl-s/Ferreyra-a 4.00

SPIDER-MAN: POWER OF TERROR
Marvel Comics: Jan, 1995 - No. 4, Apr, 1995 ($1.95, limited series)

1-4-Silvermane & Deathlok app. 4.00

SPIDER-MAN/PUNISHER: FAMILY PLOT
Marvel Comics: Feb, 1996 - No. 2, Mar, 1996 ($2.95, limited series)

1,2 4.00

SPIDER-MAN: QUALITY OF LIFE
Marvel Comics: Jul, 2002 - No. 4, Oct, 2002 ($2.99, limited series)

1-4-All CGI art by Scott Sava; Rucka-s; Lizard app. 3.00
TPB (2002, $12.99) r/#1-4; a "Making of..." section detailing the CGI process 13.00

SPIDER-MAN: REDEMPTION
Marvel Comics: Sept, 1996 - No. 4, Dec, 1996 ($1.50, limited series)

1-4: DeMatteis scripts; Zeck-a 4.00

SPIDER-MAN/ RED SONJA
Marvel Comics: Oct, 2007 - No. 5, Feb, 2008 ($2.99, limited series)

1-5-Rubi-a/Oeming-s/Turner-c; Venom & Kulan Gath app. 3.00
HC (2008, $19.99, dustjacket) r/#1-5 and Marvel Team-Up #79; sketch pages 20.00

SPIDER-MAN: REIGN
Marvel Comics: Feb, 2007 - No. 4, May, 2007 ($3.99, limited series)

1-Kaare Andrews-s/a; red costume on cover 4.00
1-Variant cover with black costume 10.00
2-4 4.00
HC (2007, $19.99, dustjacket) r/#1-4; sketch pages and cover variant gallery 20.00
HC 2nd printing (2007, $19.99, dustjacket) with variant black cover 20.00
SC (2008, $14.99) r/#1-4; sketch pages and cover variant gallery 15.00

SPIDER-MAN: REVENGE OF THE GREEN GOBLIN
Marvel Comics: Oct, 2000 - No. 3, Dec, 2000 ($2.99, limited series)

1-3-Frenz & Olliffe-a; continues in AS-M #25 & PP:S-M #25 3.00

SPIDER-MAN SAGA
Marvel Comics: Nov, 1991 - No. 4, Feb, 1992 ($2.95, limited series)

1-4: Gives history of Spider-Man: text & illustrations 4.00

SPIDER-MAN 1602
Marvel Comics: Dec, 2009 - No. 5, Apr, 2010 ($3.99, limited series)

1-5- Peter Parquagh from Marvel 1602; Parker-s/Rosanas-a 4.00

SPIDER-MAN: SWEET CHARITY
Marvel Comics: Aug, 2002 ($4.95, one-shot)

1-The Scorpion-c/app.; Campbell-c/Zimmerman-s/Robertson-a 5.00

SPIDER-MAN'S TANGLED WEB (Titled **"Tangled Web"** in indicia for #1-4)
Marvel Comics: Jun, 2001 - No. 22, Mar, 2003 ($2.99)

1-3: "The Thousand" on-c; Ennis-s/McCrea-a/Fabry-c 4.00
4-"Severance Package" on-c; Rucka-s/Risso-a; Kingpin-c/app. 5.00
5,6-Flowers for Rhino; Milligan-s/Fegredo-a 3.00
7-10,12,15-20,22: 7-9-Gentlemen's Agreement; Bruce Jones-s/Lee Weeks-a. 10-Andrews-s/a. 12-Fegredo-a. 15-Paul Pope-s/a. 18-Ted McKeever-s/a. 19-Mahfood-a. 20-Haspiel-a 3.00
11,13,21-($3.50) 11-Darwyn Cooke-s/a. 13-Phillips-a. 21-Christmas-s by Cooke & Bone 4.00
14-Azzarello & Scott Levy (WWE's Raven)-s about Crusher Hogan 4.00
TPB (10/01, $15.95) r/#1-6 16.00
Volume 2 TPB (4/02, $14.95) r/#7-11 15.00
Volume 3 TPB (2002, $15.99) r/#12-17; Jason Pearson-c 16.00
Volume 4 TPB (2003, $15.99) r/#18-22; Frank Cho-c 16.00

SPIDER-MAN TEAM-UP
Marvel Comics: Dec, 1995 - No. 7, June, 1996 ($2.95)

1-7: 1-w/ X-Men. 2-w/Silver Surfer. 3-w/Fantastic Four. 4-w/Avengers. 5-Gambit & Howard the Duck-c/app. 7-Thunderbolts-c/app. 4.00
... Special 1 (5/05, $2.99) Fantastic Four app.; Todd Dezago-s/Shane Davis-a 4.00

SPIDER-MAN: THE ARACHNIS PROJECT
Marvel Comics: Aug, 1994 - No. 6, Jan, 1995 ($1.75, limited series)

1-6-Venom, Styx, Stone & Jury app. 4.00

SPIDER-MAN: THE CLONE JOURNAL
Marvel Comics: Mar, 1995 ($2.95, one-shot)

1 4.00

SPIDER-MAN: THE CLONE SAGA
Marvel Comics: Nov, 2009 - No. 6, Apr, 2010 ($3.99, limited series)

1-6-Retelling of the saga with different ending; DeFalco & Mackie-s/Nauck-a 4.00

SPIDER-MAN: THE FINAL ADVENTURE
Marvel Comics: Nov, 1995 - No. 4, Feb, 1996 ($2.95, limited series)

1-4: 1-Nicieza scripts; foil-c 4.00

SPIDER-MAN: THE JACKAL FILES
Marvel Comics: Aug, 1995 ($1.95, one-shot)

1 4.00

SPIDER-MAN: THE LOST YEARS
Marvel Comics: Aug, 1995-No. 3, Oct, 1995; No. 0, 1996 ($2.95/$3.95,lim. series)

0-(1/96, $3.95)-Reprints. 5.00
1-3-DeMatteis scripts, Romita, Jr.-c/a 4.00
NOTE: *Romita c-0i. Romita, Jr. a-0r, 1-3p. c-0-3p. Sharp a-0r.*

SPIDER-MAN: THE MANGA
Marvel Comics: Dec, 1997 - No. 31, June, 1999 ($3.99/$2.99, B&W, bi-weekly)

1-($3.99)-English translation of Japanese Spider-Man 5.00
2-31-($2.99) 4.00

SPIDER-MAN: THE MUTANT AGENDA
Marvel Comics: No. 0, Feb, 1994; No. 1, Mar, 1994 - No. 3, May, 1994 ($1.75, limited series)

0-(2/94, $1.25, 52 pgs.)-Crosses over w/newspaper strip; has empty pages to paste in newspaper strips; gives origin of Spidey 5.00
1-3: Beast & Hobgoblin app. 1-X-Men app. 4.00

SPIDER-MAN: THE MYSTERIO MANIFESTO (Listed as "Spider-Man and Mysterio" in indicia)
Marvel Comics: Jan, 2001 - No. 3, Mar, 2001 ($2.99, limited series)

1-3-Daredevil-c/app.; Weeks & McLeod-a 3.00

SPIDER-MAN: THE PARKER YEARS
Marvel Comics: Nov, 1995 ($2.50, one-shot)

1 4.00

SPIDER-MAN 2: THE MOVIE
Marvel Comics: Aug, 2004 ($3.50/$12.99, one-shot)

1-($3.50) Movie adaptation; Johnson, Lim & Olliffe-a 4.00
TPB-($12.99) Movie adaptation; r/Amazing Spider-Man #50, Ultimate Spider-Man #14,15 13.00

SPIDER-MAN 2099 (See Amazing Spider-Man #365)
Marvel Comics: Nov, 1992 - No. 46, Aug, 1996 ($1.25/$1.50/$1.95)

1-(stiff-c)-Red foil stamped-c; begins origin of Miguel O'Hara (Spider-Man 2099); Leonardi/Williamson-c/a begins 1 3 4 6 8 10

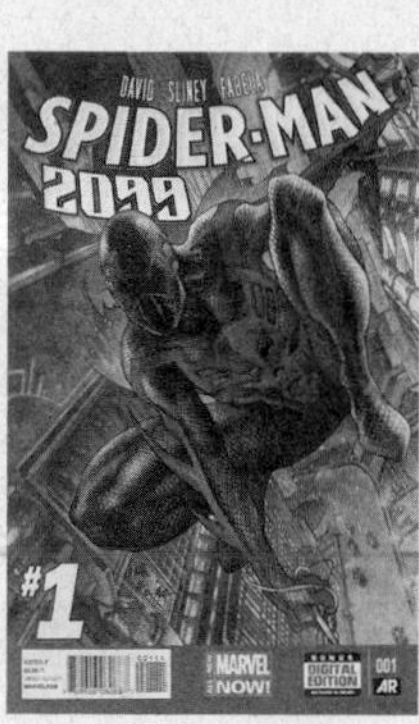

Spider-Man 2099 (2014 series) #1 © MAR

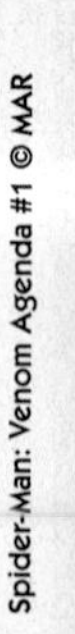

Spider-Man: Venom Agenda #1 © MAR

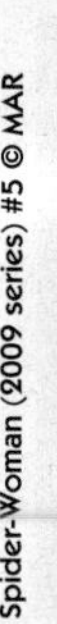
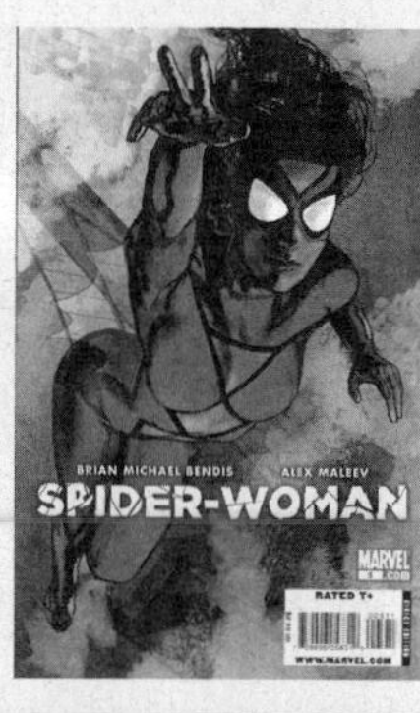

Spider-Woman (2009 series) #5 © MAR

GD VG FN VF VF/NM NM-
2.0 4.0 6.0 8.0 9.0 9.2

1-2nd printing, 2-12,14-24,26-34,39,40: 2-Origin continued, ends #3. 4-Doom 2099 app. 19-Bound-in trading cards. 3.00
13-Extra 16 pg. insert on Midnight Sons 4.00
25-($2.25, 52 pgs.)-Newsstand edition 4.00
25-($2.95, 52 pgs.)-Deluxe edition w/embossed foil-c 5.00
35-38-Venom app. 35-Variant-c. 36-Two-c; Jae Lee-a. 37,38-Two-c 5.00
41-46: 46-The Vulture app; Mike McKone-a(p) 3.00
Annual 1 (1994, $2.95, 68 pgs.) 5.00
Special 1 (1995, $3.95) 5.00
NOTE: *Chaykin c-37. Ron Lim a(p)-18; c(p)-13, 16, 18. Kelley Jones c/a-9. Leonardi/Williamson a-1-8, 10-13, 15-17, 19, 20, 22-25; c-1-13, 15, 17-19, 20, 22-25, 35.*

SPIDER-MAN 2099
Marvel Comics: Sept, 2014 - No. 12, Jul, 2015 ($3.99)
1-12: 1-Miguel O'Hara in 2014; Peter David-s/Will Sliney-a. 5-8-Spider-Verse tie-in 4.00

SPIDER-MAN 2099
Marvel Comics: Dec, 2015 - No. 25, Sept, 2017 ($3.99)
1-24: 1-Miguel O'Hara still in the present; David-s/Sliney-a. 2-New costume. 13-16-Civil War II tie-ins. 14-16-Power Pack app. 17-19-Elektra app. 4.00
25-($4.99) David-s/Sliney-a 5.00

SPIDER-MAN 2099 (Tie-in to 2099 Alpha & 2099 Omega crossover)
Marvel Comics: Feb, 2020 ($4.99)
1-Spencer-s/Carlos-a 5.00

SPIDER-MAN 2099 MEETS SPIDER-MAN
Marvel Comics: 1995 ($5.95, one-shot)
nn-Peter David script; Leonardi/Williamson-c/a. 6.00

SPIDER-MAN UNIVERSE
Marvel Comics: Mar, 2000 - No. 7, Oct, 2000 ($4.95/$3.99, reprints)
1-5-Reprints recent issues from the various Spider-Man titles 5.00
6,7-($3.99) 4.00

SPIDER-MAN UNLIMITED
Marvel Comics: May, 1993 - No. 22, Nov, 1998 ($3.95, #1-12 were quarterly, 68 pgs.)
1-Begin Maximum Carnage storyline, ends; Carnage-c/story 2 4 6 8 10 12
2-12: 2-Venom & Carnage-c/story; Lim-c/a(p) in #2-6. 10-Vulture app. 4.00
13-22: 13-Begin $2.99-c; Scorpion-c/app. 15-Daniel-c; Puma-c/app. 19-Lizard-c/app. 20-Hannibal King and Lilith app. 21,22-Deodato-a 4.00

SPIDER-MAN UNLIMITED (Based on the TV animated series)
Marvel Comics: Dec, 1999 - No. 5, Apr, 2000 ($2.99/$1.99)
1-($2.99) Venom and Carnage app. 5.00
2-5: 2-($1.99) Green Goblin app. 4.00

SPIDER-MAN UNLIMITED (3rd series)
Marvel Comics: Mar, 2004 - No. 15, July, 2006 ($2.99)
1-16: 1-Short stories by various incl. Miyazawa & Chen-a. 2-Mays-a. 6-Allred-c. 14-Finch-c/a; Black Cat app. 3.00

SPIDER-MAN UNMASKED
Marvel Comics: Nov, 1996 ($5.95, one-shot)
nn-Art w/text 6.00

SPIDER-MAN: VENOM AGENDA
Marvel Comics: Jan, 1998 ($2.99, one-shot)
1-Hama-s/Lyle-c/a 5.00

SPIDER-MAN VS. DRACULA
Marvel Comics: Jan, 1994 ($1.75, 52 pgs., one-shot)
1-r/Giant-Size Spider-Man #1 plus new Matt Fox-a 4.00

SPIDER-MAN VS. WOLVERINE
Marvel Comics Group: Feb, 1987; V2#1, 1990 (68 pgs.)
1-Williamson-c/a(i); intro Charlemagne; death of Ned Leeds (old Hobgoblin) 3 6 9 21 33 45
V2#1 (1990, $4.95)-Reprints #1 (2/87) 6.00

SPIDER-MAN: WEB OF DOOM
Marvel Comics: Aug, 1994 - No. 3, Oct, 1994 ($1.75, limited series)
1-3 4.00

SPIDER-MAN: WITH GREAT POWER...
Marvel Comics: Mar, 2008 - No. 5, Sept, 2008 ($3.99, limited series)
1-5-Origin and early days re-told; Lapham-s/Harris-a/c 4.00

SPIDER-MAN: WITH GREAT POWER COMES GREAT RESPONSIBILITY
Marvel Comics: Jun, 2011 - No. 7, Dec, 2011 ($3.99, limited series)
1-7: Reprints of noteworthy Spider-Man stories. 1-R/Ultimate Spider-Man #33,97, and Ultimate Comics Spider-Man #1. 4-R/ Amazing Spider-Man #1,11,20 4.00

SPIDER-MAN: YEAR IN REVIEW
Marvel Comics: Feb, 2000 ($2.99)
1-Text recaps of 1999 issues 3.00

SPIDER-MEN
Marvel Comics: Aug, 2012 - No. 5, Nov, 2012 ($3.99, limited series)
1-5-Peter Parker goes to Ultimate Universe; teams with Miles Morales; Pichelli-a 4.00

SPIDER-MEN II
Marvel Comics: Sept, 2017 - No. 5, Feb, 2018 ($3.99, limited series)
1-5-Peter Parker teams with Miles Morales; Bendis-s/Pichelli-a 4.00

SPIDER REIGN OF THE VAMPIRE KING, THE (Also see The Spider)
Eclipse Books: 1992 - No. 3, 1992 ($4.95, limited series, coated stock, 52 pgs.)
Book One - Three: Truman scripts & painted-c 5.00

SPIDER'S WEB, THE (See G-8 and His Battle Aces)

SPIDER-VARK
Aardvark-Vanaheim: Aug, 2020 ($8.00, B&W, one-shot)
1-Cerebus figures w/Doré artwork of Hell; cover swipe of Amazing Spider-Man Annual #21 8.00

SPIDER-VERSE (See Amazing Spider-Man 2014 series #7-14)
Marvel Comics: Jan, 2015 - No. 2, Mar, 2015 ($4.99, limited series)
1,2-Short stories of alternate Spider-Men; s/a by various. 2-Anarchic Spider-Man 5.00

SPIDER-VERSE (Secret Wars tie-in)
Marvel Comics: Jul, 2015 - No. 5, Nov, 2015 ($4.99/$3.99, limited series)
1-($4.99) Costa-s/Araujo-a; Spider-Gwen, Spider-Ham & Norman Osborn app. 5.00
2-5-($3.99) Alternate Spider-Men vs. Sinister Six 4.00

SPIDER-VERSE (Secret Wars tie-in)
Marvel Comics: Dec, 2019 - No. 6, May, 2020 ($3.99, limited series)
1-6: Miles teams up with Spider-heroes. 4-Killam-s/Gedeon-a. 5-Spider-Man Noir app. 4.00

SPIDER-VERSE TEAM-UP (See Amazing Spider-Man 2014 series #7-14)
Marvel Comics: Jan, 2015 - No. 3, Mar, 2015 ($3.99, limited series)
1-3-Short stories of alternate Spider-Men team-ups; s/a by various. 2-Spider-Gwen, Miles Morales and '67 animated Spider-Man app. 4.00

SPIDER-WHORE
Aardvark-Vanaheim: Nov, 2020 ($4.00, B&W, one-shot)
1-Cerebus figures with Gustave Doré artwork of Hell; cover swipe of What If #105 4.00

SPIDER-WOMAN (Also see The Avengers #240, Marvel Spotlight #32, Marvel Super Heroes Secret Wars #7, Marvel Two-In-One #29 and New Avengers)
Marvel Comics Group: April, 1978 - No. 50, June, 1983 (New logo #47 on)
1-New complete origin & mask added 4 8 12 27 44 60
2-5,7-18: 2-Excalibur app. 3,11,12-Brother Grimm app. 13,15-The Shroud-c/s. 16-Sienkiewicz-c 1 2 3 4 5 7
6,19,20,28,29,32: 6-Morgan LeFay app. 6,19,32-Werewolf by Night-c/s. 20,28,29-Spider-Man app. 32-Universal Monsters photo/Miller-c 1 2 3 5 6 8
21-27,30,31,33-36 6.00
37-1st app. Siryn of X-Force; X-Men x-over; origin retold 3 6 9 17 26 35
38-X-Men x-over 2 4 6 8 11 14
39-49: 46-Kingpin app. 49-Tigra-c/story 5.00
50-(52 pgs.)-Death of Spider-Woman; photo-c 2 4 6 11 16 20
... No. 1 Facsimile Edition (11/19, $3.99) Reprints #1 with original 1978 ads
NOTE: *Austin a-37i. Byrne c-26p. Infantino a-1-19. Layton c-19. Miller c-32p.*

SPIDER-WOMAN
Marvel Comics: Nov, 1993 - No. 4, Feb, 1994 ($1.75, mini-series)
V2#1-4: 1,2-Origin; U.S. Agent app. 4.00

SPIDER-WOMAN
Marvel Comics: July, 1999 - No. 18, Dec, 2000 ($2.99/$1.99/$2.25)
1-($2.99) Byrne-s/Sears-a 5.00
2-18: 2-11-($1.99). 2-Two covers. 12-Begin $2.25-c. 15-Capt. America-c/app. 4.00

SPIDER-WOMAN (Printed version of the motion comic for computers)
Marvel Comics: Nov, 2009 - No. 7, May, 2010 ($3.99/$2.99)
1-($3.99) Bendis-s/Maleev-a; covers by Maleev & Alex Ross; Jessica joins S.W.O.R.D. 4.00
2-6-($2.99) 2-4-Madame Hydra app. 6-Thunderbolts app. 3.00
7-($3.99) New Avengers app. 4.00

SPIDER-WOMAN (Also see Spider-Verse event in Amazing Spider-Man 2014 series #7-14)
Marvel Comics: Jan, 2015 - No. 10, Oct, 2015 ($3.99)

Spider-Woman (2020 series) #2 © MAR

Spike vs. Dracula #2 © 20th Fox

The Spirit #22 © Will Eisner

	GD 2.0	VG 4.0	FN 6.0	VF 8.0	VF/NM 9.0	NM- 9.2
1-4-Spider-Verse tie-ins; Silk app.; Hopeless-s/Land-a/c. 4-Avengers app.						4.00
5-10: 5-New costume; Javier Rodriguez-a/c. 10-Black Widow app.						4.00

SPIDER-WOMAN
Marvel Comics: Jan, 2016 - No. 17, May, 2017 ($3.99)

1-17: 1-5-Hopeless-s/Javier Rodriguez-a. 4-Jessica's baby is born. 6,7-"Spider-Women x-over; Spider-Gwen & Silk app.; Joelle Jones-a. 9-11-Civil War II tie-in. 13-16-Hobgoblin app. 4.00

SPIDER-WOMAN
Marvel Comics: May, 2020 - Present ($4.99/$3.99)

1-($4.99) Karla Pacheco-s/Pere Pérez-a; new costume debuts; Siqueira-a 5.00
2-4,6-9-($3.99) 2-Night Nurse & Rhino app. 6-Capt. Marvel app. 7,8-King in Black tie-in 4.00
5-($4.99) Legacy issue #100; back-up story with Captain Marvel app. 5.00

SPIDER-WOMAN: ORIGIN (Also see New Avengers)
Marvel Comics: Feb, 2006 - No. 5, June, 2006 ($2.99, limited series)

1-5-Bendis & Reed-s/Jonathan & Joshua Luna-a/c 3.00
1-Variant cover by Olivier Coipel 3.00
HC (2006, $19.99) r/series 20.00
SC (2007, $13.99) r/series 14.00

SPIDER-WOMEN (Crossover with Silk, Spider-Gwen and Spider-Woman)
Marvel Comics: Alpha, Jun, 2016 - Omega, Aug, 2016 ($4.99, limited series)

... Alpha 1 - Thompson-s/Del Rey-a/Putri-c; part 1 of x-over; intro. Earth-65 Cindy Moon 5.00
... Omega 1 - Hopeless-s/Leon-a/Putri-c; part 8 conclusion of x-over 5.00

SPIDEY (Spider-Man)
Marvel Comics: Feb, 2016 - No. 12, Jan, 2017 ($3.99)

1-12-High school-era Spider-Man. 1-3-Bradshaw-a. 1-Doc Ock app. 7-Black Panther app. 4.00
... No. 1 Halloween Comic Fest 2016 (12/16, giveaway) r/#1 3.00

SPIDEY SUPER STORIES (Spider-Man) (Also see Fireside Books)
Marvel/Children's TV Workshop: Oct, 1974 - No. 57, Mar, 1982 (35¢, no ads)

	GD	VG	FN	VF	VF/NM	NM-
1-Origin (stories simplified for younger readers)	6	12	18	38	69	100
2-Kraven	3	6	9	19	30	40
3-10,15: 6-Iceman. 15-Storm-c/sty	3	6	9	14	20	26
11-14,16-20: 19,20-Kirby-c	3	6	9	14	19	24
21-30: 22-Early Ms. Marvel app.	2	4	6	13	18	22
31-53: 31-Moondragon-c/app.; Dr. Doom app. 33-Hulk. 34-Sub-Mariner. 38-F.F. 39-Thanos-c/story. 44-Vision. 45-Silver Surfer & Dr. Doom app.	2	4	6	11	16	20
54-57: 56-Battles Jack O'Lantern-c/sty (exactly one year after 1st app. in Machine Man #19)	3	6	9	14	20	26

SPIKE AND TYKE (See M.G.M.'s...)

SPIKE... (Also see Buffy the Vampire Slayer and related titles)
IDW Publ.: Aug, 2005; Jan, 2006; Apr, 2006 ($7.49, squarebound, one-shots)

...: Lost & Found (4/06, $7.49) Scott Tipton-s/Fernando Goni-a 8.00
...: Old Times (8/05, $7.49) Peter David-s/Fernando Goni-a; Cecily/Halfrek app. 8.00
...: Old Wounds (1/06, $7.49) Tipton-s/Goni-a; flashback to Black Dahlia murder case 8.00
TPB (7/06, $19.99) r/one-shots 20.00

SPIKE (Buffy the Vampire Slayer)
IDW Publ.: Oct, 2010 - No. 8, May, 2011 ($3.99, limited series)

1-8-Lynch-s; multiple covers on each. 1,2-Urru-a. 5-7-Willow app. 4.00
... 100 Page Spectacular (6/11, $7.99) reprints of four IDW Spike stories; Frison-c 8.00

SPIKE (A Dark Place) (From Buffy the Vampire Slayer)
Dark Horse Comics: Aug, 2012 - No. 5, Dec, 2012 ($2.99, limited series)

1-5-Paul Lee-a; 2 covers by Frison & Morris on each 3.00

SPIKE: AFTER THE FALL (Also see Angel: After the Fall) (Follows the last Angel TV episode)
IDW Publ.: July, 2008 - No. 4, Oct, 2008 ($3.99, limited series)

1-4-Lynch-s/Urru-a; multiple covers on each 4.00

SPIKE: ASYLUM (Buffy the Vampire Slayer)
IDW Publ.: Sept, 2006 - No. 5, Jan, 2007 ($3.99, limited series)

1-5-Lynch-s/Urru-a; multiple covers on each 4.00

SPIKE: SHADOW PUPPETS (Buffy the Vampire Slayer)
IDW Publ.: June, 2007 - No. 4, Sept, 2007 ($3.99, limited series)

1-4-Lynch-s/Urru-a; multiple covers on each 4.00

SPIKE: THE DEVIL YOU KNOW (Buffy the Vampire Slayer)
IDW Publ.: Jun, 2010 - No. 4, Sept, 2010 ($3.99, limited series)

1-4-Bill Williams-s/Chris Cross-a/Urru-c 4.00

SPIKE VS. DRACULA (Buffy the Vampire Slayer)
IDW Publ.: Feb, 2006 - No. 5, Mar, 2006 ($3.99, limited series)

1-5: 1-Peter David-s/Joe Corroney-a; Dru and Bela Lugosi app. 4.00

SPIN & MARTY (TV) (Walt Disney's)(See Walt Disney Showcase #32)
Dell Publishing Co. (Mickey Mouse Club): No. 714, June, 1956 - No. 1082, Mar-May, 1960 (All photo-c)

	GD	VG	FN	VF	VF/NM	NM-
Four Color 714 (#1)	11	22	33	75	160	245
Four Color 767,808 (#2,3)	9	18	27	58	114	170
Four Color 826 (#4)-Annette Funicello photo-c	18	36	54	126	281	435
5(3-5/58) - 9(6-8/59)	7	14	21	44	82	120
Four Color 1026,1082	7	14	21	44	82	120

SPIN ANGELS
Marvel Comics (Soleil): 2009 - No. 4, 2009 ($5.99)

1-4-English version of French comics; Jean-Luc Sala-s/Pierre-Mony Chan-a 6.00

SPINE-TINGLING TALES (Doctor Spektor Presents...)
Gold Key: May, 1975 - No. 4, Jan, 1976 (All 25¢ issues)

	GD	VG	FN	VF	VF/NM	NM-
1-1st Tragg-r/Mystery Comics Digest #3	2	4	6	10	14	18
2-4: 2-Origin Ra-Ka-Tep-r/Mystery Comics Digest #1; Dr. Spektor #12. 3-All Durak-r issue; 4-Baron Tibor's 1st app.-r/Mystery Comics Digest #4; painted-c	1	2	3	5	7	9

SPINWORLD
Amaze Ink (Slave Labor Graphics): July, 1997 - No. 4, Jan, 1998 ($2.95/$3.95, B&W, mini-series)

1-3-Brent Anderson-a(p) 3.00
4-($3.95) 4.00

SPIRAL ZONE
DC Comics: Feb, 1988 - No. 4, May, 1988 ($1.00, mini-series)

1-4-Based on Tonka toys 3.00

SPIRIT, THE (Newspaper comics - see Promotional Comics section)

SPIRIT, THE (1st Series)(Also see Police Comics #11 and The Best of the Spirit TPB)
Quality Comics Group (Vital): 1944 - No. 22, Aug, 1950

	GD	VG	FN	VF	VF/NM	NM-
nn(#1)- "Wanted Dead or Alive"	148	296	444	947	1624	2300
nn(#2)- "Crime Doesn't Pay"	55	110	165	352	601	850
nn(#3)- "Murder Runs Wild"	50	100	150	315	533	750
4,5: 4-Flatfoot Burns begins, ends #22. 5-Wertham app.	42	84	126	265	445	625
6-10	36	72	108	216	351	485
11-Crandall-c	35	70	105	208	339	470
12-17-Eisner-c. 19-Honeybun app.	48	96	144	302	514	725
18,19-Strip-r by Eisner; Eisner-c	65	130	195	416	708	1000
20,21-Eisner good girl covers; strip-r by Eisner	116	232	348	742	1271	1800
22-Used by N.Y. Legis. Comm; classic Eisner-c	541	1082	1623	3950	6975	10,000
Super Reprint #11-r/Quality Spirit #19 by Eisner	3	6	9	18	27	35
Super Reprint #12-r/Spirit #17 by Fine; Sol Brodsky-c	3	6	9	18	27	35

SPIRIT, THE (2nd Series)
Fiction House Magazines: Spring, 1952 - No. 5, 1954

	GD	VG	FN	VF	VF/NM	NM-
1-Not Eisner	58	116	174	371	636	900
2-Eisner-c/a(2)	55	110	165	352	601	850
3-Eisner/Grandenetti-c	52	104	156	328	552	775
4-Eisner/Grandenetti-c; Eisner-a	53	106	159	334	567	800
5-Eisner-c/a(4)	55	110	165	352	601	850

SPIRIT, THE
Harvey Publications: Oct, 1966 - No. 2, Mar, 1967 (Giant Size, 25¢, 68 pgs.)

	GD	VG	FN	VF	VF/NM	NM-
1-Eisner-r plus 9 new pgs.(origin Denny Colt, Take 3, plus 2 filler pgs.) (#3 was advertised, but never published)	8	16	24	54	102	150
2-Eisner-r plus 9 new pgs.(origin of the Octopus)	7	14	21	44	82	120

SPIRIT, THE (Underground)
Kitchen Sink Enterprises (Krupp Comics): Jan, 1973 - No. 2, Sept, 1973 (Black & White)

	GD	VG	FN	VF	VF/NM	NM-
1-New Eisner-c & 4 pgs. new Eisner-a plus-r (titled Crime Convention)	4	8	12	23	37	50
2-New Eisner-c & 4 pgs. new Eisner-a plus-r (titled Meets P'Gell)	4	8	12	25	40	55

SPIRIT, THE (Magazine)
Warren Publ. Co./Krupp Comic Works No. 17 on: 4/74 - No. 16, 10/76; No. 17, Winter, 1977 - No. 41, 6/83 (B&W w/color) (#6-14,16 are squarebound)

	GD	VG	FN	VF	VF/NM	NM-
1-Eisner-r begin; 8 pg. color insert	6	12	18	41	76	110
2-5: 2-Powder Pouf-s; UFO-s. 4-Silk Satin-s	4	8	12	27	44	60
6-9,11-15: 7-All Ebony issue. 8-Female Foes issue. 8,12-Sand Seref-s. 9-P'Gell & Octopus-s. 12-X-Mas issue	4	8	12	25	40	55
10-Giant Summer Special ($1.50)-Origin	4	8	12	27	44	60
16-Giant Summer Special ($1.50)-Olga Bustle-c/s	4	8	12	25	40	55
17,18(8/78): 17-Lady Luck-r	3	6	9	17	26	35

19-21-New Eisner-a. 20,21-Wood-r (#21-r/A DP on the Moon by Wood). 20-Outer Space-r

The Spirit (2015 series) #9 © Will Eisner

Spitfire Comics #133 © Malverne Herald

Spongebob Comics #29 © UPP

	GD	VG	FN	VF	VF/NM	NM-
	2.0	4.0	6.0	8.0	9.0	9.2

3 6 9 17 26 35

22-41: 22,23-Wood-r (#22-r/Mission the Moon by Wood). 28-r/last story (10/5/52). 30-(7/81)-Special Spirit Jam issue w/Caniff, Corben, Bolland, Byrne, Miller, Kurtzman, Rogers, Sienkiewicz-a & 40 others. 36-Begin Spirit Section-r; r/1st story (6/2/40) in color; new Eisner-c/a(18 pgs.)($2.95). 37-r/2nd story in color plus 18 pgs. new Eisner-a. 38-41: r/3rd - 6th stories in color. 41-Lady Luck Mr. Mystic in color
3 6 9 15 22 28

Special 1(1975)-All Eisner-a (mail only, 1500 printed, full color)
13 26 39 89 195 300

NOTE: *Covers pencilled/inked by **Eisner** only #1-9,12-16; painted by Eisner & Ken Kelly #10 & 11; painted by Eisner #17-up; one color story reprinted in #1-10. **Austin** a-30i. **Byrne** a-30p. **Miller** a-30p.*

SPIRIT, THE
Kitchen Sink Enterprises: Oct, 1983 - No. 87, Jan, 1992 ($2.00, Baxter paper)

1-60: 1-Origin-r/12/23/45 Spirit Section. 2-r/ 1/20/46-2/10/46. 3-r/2/17/46-3/10/46. 4-r/3/17/46-4/7/46. 11-Last color issue. 54-r/section 2/19/50 4.00
61-87: 85-87-Reprint the Outer Space Spirit stories by Wood. 86-r/A DP on the Moon by Wood from 1952 4.00

SPIRIT, THE (Also see Batman/The Spirit in Batman one-shots)
DC Comics: Feb, 2007 - No. 32, Oct, 2009 ($2.99)

1-32: 1-6,8-12-Darwyn Cooke-s/a/c. 2-P'Gell app. 3-Origin re-told. 7-Short stories by Baker, Bernet, Palmiotti, Simonson & Sprouse; Cooke-c. 13-Short stories by various 3.00
... Femme Fatales TPB (2008, $19.99) r/1940s stories focusing on the Spirit's female adversaries like Silk Satin, P'gell, Powder Pouf and Silken Floss; Michael Uslan intro. 20.00
... Special 1 (2008, $2.99) r/stories from '47, '49, '50 newspaper strips; the Octopus app. 3.00

SPIRIT, THE (First Wave)
DC Comics: Jun, 2010 - No. 17, Oct, 2011 ($3.99/$2.99)(B&W back-up stories by various)

1-10: 1-Schultz-s/Moritat-a; covers by Ladronn and Schultz; back-up by O'Neil & Sienkiewicz. 2-Back-up by Ellison & Baker. 7-Corben-a back-up. 8-Ploog-a back-up 4.00
11-17-($2.99) 11-16-Hine-s/Moritat-a; no back-up story. 17-B&W; Bolland, Russell-a 3.00
...: Angel Smerti TPB (2011, $17.99) r/#1-7 18.00

SPIRIT, (WILL EISNER'S THE...)
Dynamite Entertainment: 2015 - No. 12, 2016 ($3.99)

1-12: 1-Wagner-s/Schkade-a; multiple covers. 2-12-Powell-c 4.00

SPIRIT, (WILL EISNER'S THE...): CORPSE MAKERS (Volume 2)
Dynamite Entertainment: 2017 - No. 5, 2018 ($3.99)

1-5-Francesco Francavilla-s/a/c 4.00

SPIRIT JAM
Kitchen Sink Press: Aug, 1998 ($5.95, B&W, oversized, square-bound)

nn-Reprints Spirit (Magazine) #30 by Eisner & 50 others; and "Cerebus Vs. The Spirit" from Cerebus Jam #1 6.00

SPIRIT, THE: THE NEW ADVENTURES
Kitchen Sink Press: 1997 - No. 8, Nov, 1998 ($3.50, anthology)

1-Moore-s/Gibbons-c/a 4.00
2-8: 2-Gaiman-s/Eisner-c. 3-Moore-s/Bolland-c/Moebius back-c. 4-Allred-s/a; Busiek-s/Anderson-a. 5-Chadwick-s/c/a(p); Nyberg-i. 6-S.Hampton & Mandrake-a 3.50
Will Eisner's The Spirit Archives Volume 27 (Dark Horse, 2009, $49.95) r/#1-8 50.00

SPIRIT: THE ORIGIN YEARS
Kitchen Sink Press: May, 1992 - No. 10, Dec, 1993 ($2.95, B&W)

1-10: 1-r/sections 6/2/40(origin)-6/23/40 (all 1940s) 3.00

SPIRITMAN (Also see Three Comics)
No publisher listed: No date (1944) (10¢)(Triangle Sales Co. ad on back cover)

1-Three 16pg. Spirit sections bound together, (1944, 10¢, 52 pgs.)
34 68 102 204 332 460
2-Two Spirit sections (3/26/44, 4/2/44) bound together; by Lou Fine
29 58 87 170 278 385

SPIRIT OF THE BORDER (See Zane Grey & Four Color #197)

SPIRIT OF THE TAO
Image Comics (Top Cow): Jun, 1998 - No. 15, May, 2000 ($2.50)

Preview 5.00
1-14: 1-D-Tron-s/Tan & D-Tron-a 3.00
15-($4.95) 5.00

SPIRITS OF GHOST RIDER: MOTHER OF DEMONS (Story continues in Ghost Rider #5)
Marvel Comics: Apr, 2020 ($3.99, one-shot)

1-Story of Lilith; Jack O'Lantern app.; Brisson-s/Boschi-a 4.00

SPIRITS OF VENGEANCE (Marvel Legacy)
Marvel Comics: Dec, 2017 - No. 5, Apr, 2018 ($3.99)

1-5-Gischler-s/Baldeón-a; Blade, Ghost Rider, Daimon Hellstrom, Satana app. 4.00

SPIRIT WORLD (Magazine)
Hampshire Distributors Ltd.: Fall, 1971 (B&W)

1-New Kirby-a; Neal Adams-c; poster inside 6 12 18 40 73 105
(1/2 price without poster)

SPITFIRE (Female undercover agent)
Malverne Herald (Elliot)(J. R. Mahon): No. 132, 1944 (Aug) - No. 133, 1945
Both have Classics Gift Box ads on back-c with checklist to #20

132-British spitfire WWII-c. 40 80 120 244 402 560
133-Female agent/Nazi WWII-c 194 388 582 1242 2121 3000

SPITFIRE (WW2 speedster from MI:13)
Marvel Comics: Oct, 2010 ($3.99, one-shot)

1-Cornell-s/Casagrande-a; Blade app. 4.00

SPITFIRE AND THE TROUBLESHOOTERS
Marvel Comics: Oct, 1986 - No. 9, June, 1987 (Codename: Spitfire #10 on)

1-3,5-9 3.00
4-McFarlane-a 4.00

SPITFIRE COMICS (Also see Double Up) (Tied with Pocket Comics #1 for earliest Harvey)
Harvey Publications: Aug, 1941 - No. 2, Oct, 1941 (Pocket size; 100 pgs.)

1-Origin The Clown, The Fly-Man, The Spitfire & The Magician From Bagdad; British spitfire, Nazi bomber WWII-c 106 212 318 678 1164 1650
2-(Rare) Fly-Man-c 97 194 291 621 1061 1500

SPLITTING IMAGE
Image Comics: Mar, 1993 - No. 2, 1993 ($1.95)

1,2-Simpson-c/a; parody comic 3.00
...80-Page Giant 1 (4/17, $7.99) r/#1,2 plus Normalman - Megaton Man Special 8.00

SPONGEBOB COMICS (TV's Spongebob Squarepants)
United Plankton Pictures: 2011 - No. 85, 2018 ($2.99/$3.99)

1-51-Short stories by various. 1-Kochalka back-c. 3-Aquaman homage w/Fradon-a. 32-36-Showdown at the Shady Shoals; Mermaid Man app; Ordway-a 3.00
52-85-($3.99) 53,59,60,68-Chuck Dixon-s. 63,64-Mermaid Girl spotlight. 66-70-Ordway-a 4.00
Annual-Size Super-Giant Swimtacular 1 (2013, $4.99) art by Fradon, Ordway, Kochalka 5.00
Annual-Size Super-Giant Swimtacular 2 (2014, $4.99) Mermaid Man app. 5.00
Annual-Size Super-Giant Swimtacular 3 (2015, $4.99) art by Barta, Kochalka, Chabot 5.00
Annual-Size Super-Giant Swimtacular 4 (2016, $4.99) Neal Adams & others-a; Ordway-c 5.00
Annual-Size Super-Giant Swimtacular 2017 (2017, $4.99) Mayerik & others-a; Chabot-c 5.00
Annual-Size Super-Giant Swimtacular 2018 (2018, $4.99) Ordway & others-a; Gianni-c 5.00
SpongeBob Freestyle Funnies 1 (2013, Free Comic Book Day giveaway) Short stories 3.00
SpongeBob Freestyle Funnies 2014 (Free Comic Book Day giveaway) Short stories 3.00
SpongeBob Freestyle Funnies 2015 (Free Comic Book Day giveaway) Short stories 3.00
SpongeBob Freestyle Funnies 2016 (FCBD giveaway) Short stories; Fradon-a 3.00
SpongeBob Freestyle Funnies 2017 (FCBD giveaway) Short stories; Kochalka-a 3.00
SpongeBob Freestyle Funnies 2018 (FCBD giveaway) Short stories; Mermaid Man app. 3.00

SPOOF
Marvel Comics Group: Oct, 1970; No. 2, Nov, 1972 - No. 5, May, 1973

1-Infinity-c; Dark Shadows-c & parody 4 8 12 25 40 55
2-5: 2-All in the Family. 3-Beatles, Osmonds, Jackson 5, David Cassidy, Nixon & Agnew-c. 5-Rod Serling, Woody Allen, Ted Kennedy-c 3 6 9 16 24 32

SPOOK (Formerly Shock Detective Cases)
Star Publications: No. 22, Jan, 1953 - No. 30, Oct, 1954

22-Sgt. Spook-r; acid in face story; hanging-c 226 452 678 1446 2473 3500
23,25,27: 25-Jungle Lil-r. 27-Two Sgt. Spook-r 55 110 165 352 601 850
24-Used in **SOTI**, pgs. 182,183-r/Inside Crime #2; Transvestism story
58 116 174 371 636 900
26,28-30: 26-Disbrow-a. 28,29-Rulah app. 29-Jo-Jo app. 30-Disbrow-c/a(2); only Star-c 53 106 159 334 567 800

NOTE: ***L. B. Cole** covers-all issues except #30; a-28(1 pg.). **Disbrow** a-26(2), 28, 29(2), 30(2); No. 30 r/Blue Bolt Weird Tales #114.*

SPOOK COMICS
Baily Publications/Star: 1946

1-Mr. Lucifer story 55 110 165 352 601 850

SPOOK HOUSE
Albatross Funnybooks: 2016 - No. 5, 2017 ($3.99)

1-5-Horror anthology by Eric Powell and others; Powell-c 4.00
... 2019 Halloween Special (2019, $3.99) Short stories by Eric Powell & others; Powell-c 4.00

SPOOK HOUSE 2
Albatross Funnybooks: 2018 - No. 4, 2018 ($3.99)

1-4-Horror anthology by Eric Powell and others; Powell-c. 2-Lula app. 4.00

Spooky #35 © HARV

Sports Action #8 © MAR

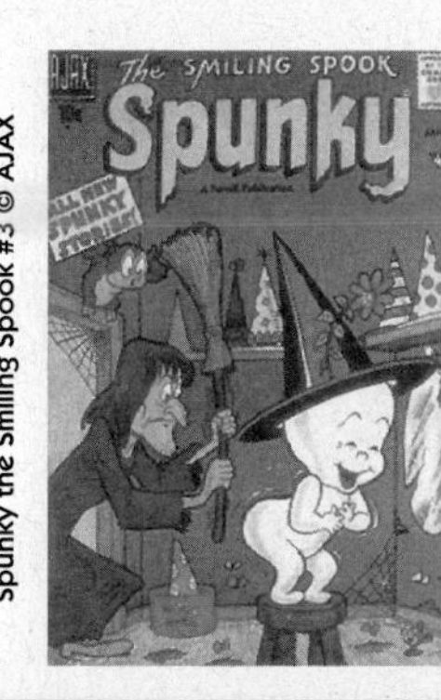

Spunky the Smiling Spook #3 © AJAX

SPOOKY (The Tuff Little Ghost; see Casper The Friendly Ghost)
Harvey Publications: 11/55 - 139, 11/73; No. 140, 7/74 - No. 155, 3/77; No. 156, 12/77 - No. 158, 4/78; No. 159, 9/78; No. 160, 10/79; No. 161, 9/80

	GD 2.0	VG 4.0	FN 6.0	VF 8.0	VF/NM 9.0	NM- 9.2
1-Nightmare begins (see Casper #19)	71	142	213	568	1284	2000
2	22	44	66	154	340	525
3-10(1956-57)	12	24	36	79	170	260
11-20(1957-58)	7	14	21	44	82	120
21-40(1958-59)	5	10	15	33	57	80
41-60	4	8	12	27	44	60
61-80,100	3	6	9	19	30	40
81-99	3	6	9	16	24	32
101-120	2	4	6	11	16	20
121-126,133-140	2	4	6	8	11	14
127-132: All 52 pg. Giants	2	4	6	11	16	20
141-161	1	2	3	5	7	9

SPOOKY
Harvey Comics: Nov, 1991 - No. 4, Sept, 1992 ($1.00/$1.25)

	GD 2.0	VG 4.0	FN 6.0	VF 8.0	VF/NM 9.0	NM- 9.2
1						4.00
2-4: 3-Begin $1.25-c						3.00
...Digest 1-3 (10/92, 6/93, 10/93, $1.75, 100 pgs.)-Casper, Wendy, etc.						4.00

SPOOKY HAUNTED HOUSE
Harvey Publications: Oct, 1972 - No. 15, Feb, 1975

	GD 2.0	VG 4.0	FN 6.0	VF 8.0	VF/NM 9.0	NM- 9.2
1	3	6	9	17	26	35
2-5	2	4	6	10	14	18
6-10	2	4	6	8	10	12
11-15	1	2	3	5	7	9

SPOOKY MYSTERIES
Your Guide Publ. Co.: No date (1946) (10¢)

	GD 2.0	VG 4.0	FN 6.0	VF 8.0	VF/NM 9.0	NM- 9.2
1-Mr. Spooky, Super Snooper, Pinky, Girl Detective app.	30	60	90	177	289	400

SPOOKY SPOOKTOWN
Harvey Publ.: 9/61; No. 2, 9/62 - No. 52, 12/73; No. 53, 10/74 - No. 66, 12/76

	GD 2.0	VG 4.0	FN 6.0	VF 8.0	VF/NM 9.0	NM- 9.2
1-Casper, Spooky; 68 pgs. begin	14	28	42	94	207	320
2	8	16	24	54	102	150
3-5	6	12	18	38	69	100
6-10	5	10	15	31	53	75
11-20	4	8	12	23	37	50
21-39: 39-Last 68 pg. issue	3	6	9	19	30	40
40-45: All 52 pgs.	2	4	6	11	16	20
46-66: 61-Hot Stuff/Spooky team-up story	1	2	3	5	7	9

SPORT COMICS (Becomes True Sport Picture Stories #5 on)
Street & Smith Publications: Oct, 1940 (No mo.) - No. 4, Nov, 1941

	GD 2.0	VG 4.0	FN 6.0	VF 8.0	VF/NM 9.0	NM- 9.2
1-Life story of Lou Gehrig	60	120	180	381	653	925
2	32	64	96	190	310	430
3,4: 4-Story of Notre Dame coach Frank Leahy	27	54	81	162	266	370

SPORT LIBRARY (See Charlton Sport Library)

SPORTS ACTION (Formerly Sport Stars)
Marvel/Atlas Comics (ACI No. 2,3/SAI No. 4-14): No. 2, Feb, 1950 - No. 14, Sept, 1952

	GD 2.0	VG 4.0	FN 6.0	VF 8.0	VF/NM 9.0	NM- 9.2
2-Powell-a; George Gipp life story	43	86	129	269	455	640
1-(nd,no price, no publ., 52pgs, #1 on-c; has same-c as #2; blank inside-c (giveaway?)	22	44	66	132	216	300
3-Everett-a	24	48	72	142	234	325
4-11,14: Weiss-a	22	44	66	128	209	290
12,13: 12-Everett-c. 13-Krigstein-a	23	46	69	136	223	310

NOTE: *Title may have changed after No. 3, to Crime Must Lose No. 4 on, due to publisher change.* ***Sol Brodsky*** *c-4-7, 13, 14.* ***Maneely*** *c-3, 8-11.*

SPORT STARS
Parents' Magazine Institute (Sport Stars): Feb-Mar, 1946 - No. 4, Aug-Sept, 1946 (Half comic, half photo magazine)

	GD 2.0	VG 4.0	FN 6.0	VF 8.0	VF/NM 9.0	NM- 9.2
1- "How Tarzan Got That Way" story of Johnny Weissmuller	40	80	120	243	402	560
2-Baseball greats	26	52	78	154	252	350
3,4	23	46	69	136	223	310

SPORT STARS (Becomes Sports Action #2 on)
Marvel Comics (ACI): Nov, 1949 (52 pgs.)

	GD 2.0	VG 4.0	FN 6.0	VF 8.0	VF/NM 9.0	NM- 9.2
1-Knute Rockne; painted-c	45	90	135	284	480	675

SPORT THRILLS (Formerly Dick Cole; becomes Jungle Thrills #16)
Star Publications: No. 11, Nov, 1950 - No. 15, Nov, 1951

	GD 2.0	VG 4.0	FN 6.0	VF 8.0	VF/NM 9.0	NM- 9.2
11-Dick Cole begins; Ted Williams & Ty Cobb life stories	31	62	93	182	296	410
12-Joe DiMaggio, Phil Rizzuto stories & photos on-c; L.B. Cole-c/a	25	50	75	147	241	335
13-15-All L. B. Cole-c. 13-Jackie Robinson, Pee Wee Reese stories & photo on-c. 14-Johnny Weissmuler life story	25	50	75	147	241	335
Accepted Reprint #11 (#15 on-c, nd); L.B. Cole-c	10	20	30	54	72	90
Accepted Reprint #12 (nd); L.B. Cole-c; Joe DiMaggio & Phil Rizzuto life stories-r/#12	10	20	30	54	72	90

SPOTLIGHT (TV) (newsstand sales only)
Marvel Comics Group: Sept, 1978 - No. 4, Mar, 1979 (Hanna-Barbera)

	GD 2.0	VG 4.0	FN 6.0	VF 8.0	VF/NM 9.0	NM- 9.2
1-Huckleberry Hound, Yogi Bear; Shaw-a	3	6	9	19	30	40
2,4: 2-Quick Draw McGraw, Augie Doggie, Snooper & Blabber. 4-Magilla Gorilla, Snagglepuss	3	6	9	16	23	30
3-The Jetsons; Yakky Doodle	3	6	9	19	30	40

SPOTLIGHT COMICS
Country Press Inc.: Sept, 1940

nn-Ashcan, not distributed to newsstands, only for in house use. A NM copy sold in 2009 for $1015.

SPOTLIGHT COMICS (Becomes Red Seal Comics #14 on?)
Harry 'A' Chesler (Our Army, Inc.): Nov, 1944, No. 2, Jan, 1945 - No. 3, 1945

	GD 2.0	VG 4.0	FN 6.0	VF 8.0	VF/NM 9.0	NM- 9.2
1-The Black Dwarf (cont'd in Red Seal?), The Veiled Avenger, & Barry Kuda begin; Tuska-c	142	284	426	909	1555	2200
2	77	154	231	493	847	1200
3-Injury to eye story (reprinted from Scoop #3)	81	162	243	518	884	1250

SPOTTY THE PUP (Becomes Super Pup #4, see Television Puppet Show)
Avon Periodicals/Realistic Comics: No. 2, Oct-Nov, 1953 - No. 3, Dec-Jan, 1953-54 (Also see Funny Tunes)

	GD 2.0	VG 4.0	FN 6.0	VF 8.0	VF/NM 9.0	NM- 9.2
2,3	9	18	27	47	61	75
nn (1953, Realistic-r)	6	12	18	28	34	40

SPUNKY (...Junior Cowboy)(...Comics #2 on)
Standard Comics: April, 1949 - No. 7, Nov, 1951

	GD 2.0	VG 4.0	FN 6.0	VF 8.0	VF/NM 9.0	NM- 9.2
1-Text illos by Frazetta	15	30	45	92	144	195
2-Text illos by Frazetta	12	24	36	69	97	125
3-7	9	18	27	52	69	85

SPUNKY THE SMILING SPOOK
Ajax/Farrell (World Famous Comics/Four Star Comic Corp.): Aug, 1957 - No. 4, May, 1958

	GD 2.0	VG 4.0	FN 6.0	VF 8.0	VF/NM 9.0	NM- 9.2
1-Reprints from Frisky Fables	12	24	36	67	94	120
2-4	7	14	21	37	46	55

SPY AND COUNTERSPY (Becomes Spy Hunters #3 on)
American Comics Group: Aug-Sept, 1949 - No. 2, Oct-Nov, 1949 (52 pgs.)

	GD 2.0	VG 4.0	FN 6.0	VF 8.0	VF/NM 9.0	NM- 9.2
1-Origin, 1st app. Jonathan Kent, Counterspy	33	66	99	194	317	440
2	20	40	60	115	185	255

SPYBOY
Dark Horse Comics: Oct, 1999 - No. 17, May, 2001 ($2.50/$2.95/$2.99)

	GD 2.0	VG 4.0	FN 6.0	VF 8.0	VF/NM 9.0	NM- 9.2
1-17: 1-6-Peter David-s/Pop Mhan-a. 7,8-Meglia-a. 9-17-Mhan-a						3.00
13.1-13.3 (4/03-8/03, $2.99), 13.2,13.3-Mhan-a						3.00
... Special (5/02, $4.99) David-s/Mhan-a						5.00

SPYBOY: FINAL EXAM
Dark Horse Comics: May, 2004 - No. 4, Aug, 2004 ($2.99, limited series)

	GD 2.0	VG 4.0	FN 6.0	VF 8.0	VF/NM 9.0	NM- 9.2
1-4-Peter David-s/Pop Mhan-a/c						3.00
TPB (2005, $12.95) r/series						13.00

SPYBOY/ YOUNG JUSTICE
Dark Horse Comics: Feb, 2002 - No. 3, Apr, 2002 ($2.99, limited series)

	GD 2.0	VG 4.0	FN 6.0	VF 8.0	VF/NM 9.0	NM- 9.2
1-3: 1-Peter David-s/Todd Nauck-a/Pop Mhan-c. 2-Mhan-a						3.00

SPY CASES (Formerly The Kellys)
Marvel/Atlas Comics (Hercules Publ.): No. 26, Sept, 1950 - No. 19, Oct, 1953

	GD 2.0	VG 4.0	FN 6.0	VF 8.0	VF/NM 9.0	NM- 9.2
26 (#1)	34	68	102	204	332	460
27(#2),28(#3, 2/51): 27-Everett-a; bondage-c	19	38	57	112	179	245
4(4/51) - 7,9,10: 4-Heath-a	17	34	51	103	162	220
8-A-Bomb-c/story	19	38	57	111	176	240
11-19: 10-14-War format	15	30	45	92	144	195

NOTE: ***Sol Brodsky*** *c-1-5, 8, 9, 11-14, 17, 18.* ***Maneely*** *a-8; c-7, 10.* ***Tuska*** *a-7.*

SPY FIGHTERS
Marvel/Atlas Comics (CSI): March, 1951 - No. 15, July, 1953 (Cases from official records)

	GD 2.0	VG 4.0	FN 6.0	VF 8.0	VF/NM 9.0	NM- 9.2
1-Clark Mason begins; Tuska-a; Brodsky-c	34	68	102	204	332	460
2-Tuska-a	19	38	57	112	179	245

Spy Smasher #9 © FAW

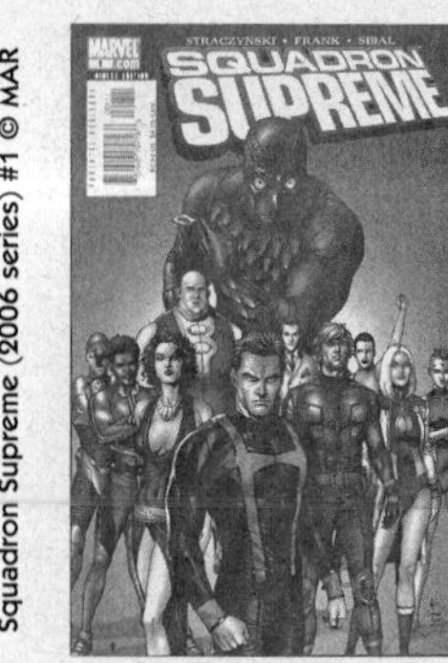

Squadron Supreme (2006 series) #1 © MAR

Stamps Comics #7 © YM

	GD 2.0	VG 4.0	FN 6.0	VF 8.0	VF/NM 9.0	NM- 9.2
3-13: 3-5-Brodsky-c. 7-Heath-c	16	32	48	98	154	210
14,15-Pakula-a(3), Ed Win-a. 15-Brodsky-c	17	34	51	103	162	220

SPY-HUNTERS (Formerly Spy & Counterspy)
American Comics Group: No. 3, Dec-Jan, 1949-50 - No. 24, June-July, 1953 (#3-14: 52 pgs.)

	GD 2.0	VG 4.0	FN 6.0	VF 8.0	VF/NM 9.0	NM- 9.2
3-Jonathan Kent continues, ends #10	24	48	72	144	237	330
4-10: 4,8,10-Starr-a	15	30	45	84	127	170
11-15,17-22,24: 18-War-c begin. 21-War-c/stories begin	11	22	33	62	86	110
16-Williamson-a (9 pgs.)	16	32	48	96	151	205
23-Graphic torture, injury to eye panel	20	40	60	120	195	270

NOTE: ***Drucker** a-12. **Whitney** a-many issues; c-7, 8, 10-12, 15, 16.*

SPY ISLAND
Dark Horse Comics: Apr, 2020 - No. 4, Dec, 2020 ($3.99, limited series)

1-4-Chelsea Cain-s/Elise McCall-a 4.00

SPYMAN (Top Secret Adventures on cover)
Harvey Publications (Illustrated Humor): Sept, 1966 - No. 3, Feb, 1967 (12¢)

	GD 2.0	VG 4.0	FN 6.0	VF 8.0	VF/NM 9.0	NM- 9.2
1-Origin and 1st app. of Spyman. Steranko-a(p)-1st pro work; 1 pg. Neal Adams ad; Tuska-c/a, Crandall-a(i)	9	18	27	59	117	175
2-Simon-c; Steranko-a(p)	5	10	15	33	57	80
3-Simon-c	4	8	12	28	47	65

SPY SMASHER (See Mighty Midget, Whiz & Xmas Comics) (Also see Crime Smasher)
Fawcett Publications: Fall, 1941 - No. 11, Feb, 1943

	GD 2.0	VG 4.0	FN 6.0	VF 8.0	VF/NM 9.0	NM- 9.2
1-Spy Smasher begins; silver metallic-c	343	686	1029	2400	4200	6000
2-Raboy-c	158	316	474	1011	1731	2450
3,4: 3-Bondage-c. 4-Irvin Steinberg-c	113	226	339	723	1237	1750
5-7: Raboy-a; 6-Raboy-c/a. 7-Part photo-c (movie) Japanese dragon-c	94	188	282	597	1025	1450
8,11: War-c	81	162	243	518	884	1250
9-Hitler, Tojo, Mussolini-c.	158	316	474	1011	1731	2450
10-Hitler-c	145	290	435	928	1589	2250

SPY THRILLERS (Police Badge No. 479 #5)
Atlas Comics (PrPI): Nov, 1954 - No. 4, May, 1955

	GD 2.0	VG 4.0	FN 6.0	VF 8.0	VF/NM 9.0	NM- 9.2
1-Brodsky c-1,2	29	58	87	172	281	390
2-Last precode (1/55)	17	34	51	100	158	215
3,4	15	30	45	85	130	175

SQUADRON SINISTER (Secret Wars tie-in)
Marvel Comics: Aug, 2015 - No. 4, Jan, 2016 ($3.99, limited series)

1-4-Guggenheim-s/Pacheco-a/c. 1-Squadron Supreme app. 2-Frightful Four app. 4.00

SQUADRON SUPREME (Also see Marvel Graphic Novel - ...: Death of a Universe)
Marvel Comics Group: Aug, 1985 - No. 12, Aug, 1986 (Maxi-series)

1-Double size 5.00
2-12 4.00
TPB ($24.99) r/#1-12; Alex Ross painted-c; printing inks contain some of the cremated remains of late writer Mark Gruenwald 50.00
TPB-2nd printing ($24.99): Inks contain no ashes 25.00
...Death of a Universe TPB (2006, $24.99) r/Marvel Graphic Novel, Thor #280, Avengers #5,6; Avengers/Squadron Supreme Annual and Squadron Supreme: New World Order 25.00

SQUADRON SUPREME (Also see Supreme Power)
Marvel Comics: May, 2006 - No. 7, Nov, 2006 ($2.99)

1-7-Straczynski-s/Frank-a/c 3.00
Saga of Squadron Supreme (2006, $3.99) summary of Supreme Power #1-18; plus Hyperion and Nighthawk limited series; wraparound-c; preview of Squadron Supreme #1 4.00
... Vol. 1: The Pre-War Years (2006, $20.99, dustjacket) r/#1-5 & Saga of S.S. 21.00

SQUADRON SUPREME
Marvel Comics: Sept, 2008 - No. 12, Aug, 2009 ($2.99)

1-12: 1-Set 5 years after Ultimate Power; Nick Fury app.; Chaykin-s/Turini-a/Land-c 3.00

SQUADRON SUPREME
Marvel Comics: Feb, 2016 - No. 15, Mar, 2017 ($3.99)

1-15-Robinson-s; main covers by Alex Ross thru #4. 1-Kirk-a; Namor killed. 3-Avengers app. 9-12-Civil War II tie-in. 10-Thundra & Blue Marvel app. 11,12-Spider-Man app. 4.00

SQUADRON SUPREME: HYPERION VS. NIGHTHAWK
Marvel Comics: Mar, 2007 - No. 4, June, 2007 ($2.99, limited series)

1-4-Hyperion and Nighthawk in Darfur; Gulacy-a/c; Guggenheim-s 3.00
TPB (2007, $10.99) r/#1-4 11.00

SQUADRON SUPREME: NEW WORLD ORDER
Marvel Comics: Sept, 1998 ($5.99, one-shot)

1-Wraparound-c; Kaminski-s 6.00

SQUALOR
First Comics: Dec, 1989 - Aug, 1990 ($2.75, limited series)

1-4: Sutton-a 3.00

SQUEE (Also see Johnny The Homicidal Maniac)
Slave Labor Graphics: Apr, 1997 - No. 4, May, 1998 ($2.95, B&W)

1-4: Jhonen Vasquez-s/a in all 3.00

SQUEEKS (Also see Boy Comics)
Lev Gleason Publications: Oct, 1953 - No. 5, June, 1954

	GD 2.0	VG 4.0	FN 6.0	VF 8.0	VF/NM 9.0	NM- 9.2
1-Funny animal; Biro-c; Crimebuster's pet monkey "Squeeks" begins	12	24	36	67	94	120
2-Biro-c	8	16	24	42	54	65
3-5: 3-Biro-c	7	14	21	37	46	55

S.R. BISSETTE'S SPIDERBABY COMIX
SpiderBaby Grafix: Aug, 1996 - No. 2 ($3.95, B&W, magazine size)

Preview-(8/96, $3.95)-Graphic violence & nudity; Laurel & Hardy app. 4.00
1,2 4.00

S.R. BISSETTE'S TYRANT
SpiderBaby Grafix: Sept, 1994 - No. 4 ($2.95, B&W)

1-4 4.00

STALKER (Also see All Star Comics 1999 and crossover issues)
National Periodical Publications: June-July, 1975 - No. 4, Dec-Jan, 1975-76

	GD 2.0	VG 4.0	FN 6.0	VF 8.0	VF/NM 9.0	NM- 9.2
1-Origin & 1st app; Ditko/Wood-c/a	2	4	6	10	14	18
2-4-Ditko/Wood-c/a	2	3	4	6	8	10

STALKERS
Marvel Comics (Epic Comics): Apr, 1990 - No. 12, Mar, 1991 ($1.50)

1-12: 1-Chadwick-c 3.00

STAMP COMICS (Stamps... on-c; Thrilling Adventures In...#8)
Youthful Magazines/Stamp Comics, Inc.: Oct, 1951 - No. 7, Oct, 1952

	GD 2.0	VG 4.0	FN 6.0	VF 8.0	VF/NM 9.0	NM- 9.2
1-(15¢) ('Stamps' on indicia No. 1-3,5,7)	26	52	78	156	256	355
2	15	30	45	90	140	190
3-6: 3,4-Kiefer, Wildey-a	15	30	45	83	124	165
7-Roy Krenkel (4 pgs.)	18	36	54	103	162	220

NOTE: *Promotes stamp collecting; gives stories behind various commemorative stamps. No. 2, 10¢ printed over 15¢ c-price. **Kiefer** a-1-7. **Kirkel** a-1-6. **Napoli** a-2-7. **Palais** a-2-4, 7.*

STAND, THE ... (Based on the Stephen King novel)
Marvel Comics: 2008 - 2012 ($3.99, limited series)

...: American Nightmares 1-5 (5/09 - No. 5, 10/09, $3.99) Aguirre-Sacasa-s/Perkins-a 4.00
...: Captain Trips 1-5 (12/08 - No. 5, 3/09, $3.99) Aguirre-Sacasa-s/Perkins-a 4.00
...: Hardcases 1-5 (8/10 - No. 5, 1/11, $3.99) Aguirre-Sacasa-s/Perkins-a 4.00
...: No Man's Land 1-5 (4/11 - No. 5, 8/11, $3.99) Aguirre-Sacasa-s/Perkins-a 4.00
...: Soul Survivors 1-5 (12/09 - No. 5, 5/10, $3.99) Aguirre-Sacasa-s/Perkins-a 4.00
...: The Night Has Come 1-6 (10/11 - No. 6, 3/12, $3.99) Aguirre-Sacasa-s/Perkins-a 4.00

STAN LEE MEETS...
Marvel Comics: Nov, 2006 - Jan, 2007 ($3.99, series of one-shots)

Doctor Doom 1 (12/06) Lee-s/Larroca-a/c; Loeb-s/McGuinness-a; r/Fantastic Four #87 4.00
Doctor Strange 1 (11/06) Lee-s/Davis-a/c; Bendis-s/Bagley-a; r/Marvel Premiere #3 4.00
Silver Surfer 1 (1/07) Lee-s/Wieringo-a/c; Jenkins-s/Buckingham-a; r/S.S. #14 4.00
Spider-Man 1 (11/06) Lee-s/Coipel-a/c; Whedon-s/Gaydos-a; Hembeck-s/a; r/AS-M #87 4.00
The Thing 1 (12/06) Lee-s/Weeks-a/c; Thomas-s/Kolins-a; r/FF #79; FF #51 cover swipe 4.00
HC (2007, $24.99, dustjacket) r/one-shots; interviews and features 25.00

STAN LEE'S MIGHTY 7
Archie Comics (Stan Lee Comics): May, 2012 - No. 3, Sept, 2012 ($2.99, limited series)

1-3-Co-written by Stan Lee; Alex Saviuk-a; multiple covers on each 3.00

STANLEY & HIS MONSTER (Formerly The Fox & the Crow)
National Periodical Publ.: No. 109, Apr-May, 1968 - No. 112, Oct-Nov, 1968

	GD 2.0	VG 4.0	FN 6.0	VF 8.0	VF/NM 9.0	NM- 9.2
109-112	3	6	9	21	33	45

STANLEY & HIS MONSTER
DC Comics: Feb, 1993 - No. 4, May, 1993 ($1.50, limited series)

1-4 3.00

STAN SHAW'S BEAUTY & THE BEAST
Dark Horse Comics: Nov, 1993 ($4.95, one-shot)

1 5.00

STAR (See Captain Marvel 2019 series #8)
Marvel Comics: Mar, 2020 - No. 5, Nov, 2020 ($3.99)

1-5: 1-Loki, Jessica Jones and Scarlet Witch app. 2-5-The Black Order app. 3-5-Captain Marvel. 3,5-Scarlet Witch app. 4.00

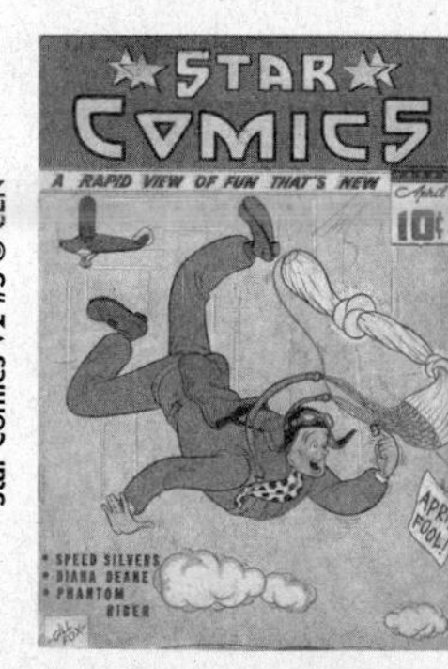

Star Comics V2 #3 © CEN

Starfire (2015 series) #11 © DC

Stargate Universe #4 © MGM

	GD	VG	FN	VF	VF/NM	NM-
	2.0	4.0	6.0	8.0	9.0	9.2

STARBLAST
Marvel Comics: Jan, 1994 - No. 4, Apr, 1994 ($1.75, limited series)

1-($2.00, 52 pgs.)-Nova, Quasar, Black Bolt; painted-c 4.00
2-4 3.00

STAR BLAZERS
Comico: Apr, 1987 - No. 4, July, 1987 ($1.75, limited series)

1-4 3.00

STAR BLAZERS
Comico: 1989 ($1.95/$2.50, limited series)

1-5- Steacy wraparound painted-c on all 3.00

STAR BLAZERS (The Magazine of Space Battleship Yamato)
Argo Press: No. 0, Aug, 1995 - No. 3, Dec, 1995 ($2.95)

0-3 3.00

STARBORN (From Stan Lee)
BOOM! Studios: Dec, 2010 - No. 12, Nov, 2011 ($3.99)

1-12: 1-9,11-Roberson-s/Randolph-a. 1-7-Three covers on each. 10-Scalera-a 4.00

STAR BRAND
Marvel Comics (New Universe): Oct, 1986 - No. 19, May, 1989 (75¢/$1.25)

1-15: 14-begin $1.25-c 3.00
16-19-Byrne story & art; low print run 5.00
Annual 1 (10/87) 4.00
... Classic Vol. 1 TPB (2006, $19.99) r/#1-7 20.00

STARBRAND & NIGHTMASK
Marvel Comics: Feb, 2016 - No. 6, Jul, 2016 ($3.99)

1-6: 1-Weisman-s/Stanton-a; Kevin and Adam go to college; Nitro & Graviton app. 4.00

STARCADIA QUEST (Based on the tabletop game)
IDW Publishing: Aug, 2019 - No. 3, Oct, 2019 ($4.99, limited series)

1-3-James Roberts-s/Aurelio Mazzara-a 5.00

STARCHILD
Tailspin Press: 1992 - No. 12 ($2.25/$2.50, B&W)

1,2-('92),0(4/93),3-12: 0-Illos by Chadwick, Eisner, Sim, M. Wagner. 3-(7/93). 4-(11/93). 6-(2/94) 3.00

STARCHILD: MYTHOPOLIS
Image Comics: No. 0, July, 1997 - No. 4, Apr, 1998 ($2.95, B&W, limited series)

0-4-James Owen-s/a 3.00

STAR COMICS
Ultem Publ. (Harry `A' Chesler)/Centaur Publications: Feb, 1937 - V2#7 (No. 23), Aug, 1939 (#1-6: large size)

V1#1-Dan Hastings (s/f) begins 423 846 1269 3088 5444 7800
2-(4/37) 252 504 756 1613 2757 3900
3-Classic Black Americana cover (rare) 432 864 1296 3154 5577 8000
4,5-Classic Winsor McCay Little Nemo-c/stories (rare) 290 580 870 1856 3178 4500
6-(9/37) 239 478 717 1530 2615 3700
7-9: 8-Severed head centerspread; Impy & Little Nemo by Winsor McCay Jr, Popeye app. by Bob Wood; Mickey Mouse & Popeye app. as toys in Santa's bag on-c; X-Mas-c 168 336 504 1075 1838 2600
10 (1st Centaur; 3/38)-Impy by Winsor McCay Jr; Don Marlow by Guardineer begins 200 400 600 1280 2190 3100
11-1st Jack Cole comic-a, 1 pg. (4/38) 245 490 735 1568 2684 3800
12-15: 12-Riders of the Golden West begins; Little Nemo app. 15-Speed Silvers by Gustavson & The Last Pirate by Burgos begins 119 238 357 762 1306 1850
16 (12/38)-The Phantom Rider & his horse Thunder begins, ends V2#6 135 270 405 864 1482 2100
V2#1(#17, 2/39)-Phantom Rider-c (only non-funny-c) 168 336 504 1075 1838 2600
2-7(#18-23): 2-Diana Deane by Tarpe Mills app. 3-Drama of Hollywood by Mills begins. 7-Jungle Queen app. 97 194 291 621 1061 1500

NOTE: ***Biro** c-6, 9, 10. **Burgos** a-15, 16, V2#1-7. **Ken Ernst** a-10, 12, 14. **Filchock** c-15, 18, 22. **Gill Fox** c-14, 19. **Guardineer** a-6, 8-14. **Gustavson** a-13-16, V2#1-7. **Winsor McCay** c-4, 5. **Tarpe Mills** a-15, V2#1-7. **Schwab** c-20, 23. **Bob Wood** a-10, 12, 13; c-7, 8.*

STAR COMICS MAGAZINE
Marvel Comics (Star Comics): Dec, 1986 - No. 13, 1988 ($1.50, digest-size)

1,9-Spider-Man-c/s 2 4 6 8 11 14
2-8-Heathcliff, Ewoks, Top Dog, Madballs-r in #1-13 1 2 3 5 7 9
10-13 2 4 6 8 10 12

S.T.A.R. CORPS
DC Comics: Nov, 1993 - No. 6, Apr, 1994 ($1.50, limited series)

1-6: 1,2-Austin-c(i). 1-Superman app. 3.00

STARCRAFT (Based on the video game)
DC Comics (WildStorm): Jul, 2009 - No. 7, Jan, 2010 ($2.99)

1-7-Furman-s; two covers on each 3.00
HC (2010, $19.99, dustjacket) r/#1-7 20.00
SC (2011, $14.99) r/#1-7 15.00

STARCRAFT: SCAVENGERS (Based on the Blizzard Ent. video game)
Dark Horse Comics: Jul, 2018 - No. 4, Oct, 2018 ($3.99, limited series)

1-4-Jody Houser-s/Gabriel Guzmán-a 4.00

STARCRAFT: SOLDIERS (Based on the Blizzard Ent. video game)
Dark Horse Comics: Jan, 2019 - No. 4, Apr, 2019 ($3.99, limited series)

1-4-Jody Houser & Andrew Robinson-s/Miguel Sepulveda-a 4.00

STARCRAFT: SURVIVORS (Based on the Blizzard Ent. video game)
Dark Horse Comics: Jul, 2019 - No. 4, Apr, 2019 ($3.99, limited series)

1-4-Jody Houser-s/Gabriel Guzmán-a 4.00

STAR CROSSED
DC Comics (Helix): June, 1997 - No. 3, Aug, 1997 ($2.50, limited series)

1-3-Matt Howarth-s/a 3.00

STARDUST (See Neil Gaiman and Charles Vess' Stardust)

STARDUST KID, THE
Image Comics/Boom! Studios #4-on: May, 2005 - No. 4 ($3.50)

1-4-J.M. DeMatteis-s/Mike Ploog-a 3.50

STAR FEATURE COMICS
I. W. Enterprises: 1963

Reprint #9-Stunt-Man Stetson-r/Feat. Comics #141 2 4 6 10 13 16

STARFIRE (Not the Teen Titans character)
National Periodical Publ./DC Comics: Aug-Sept, 1976 - No. 8, Oct-Nov, 1977

1-Origin (CCA stamp fell off cover art; so it was approved by code) 2 4 6 13 18 22
2-8 1 2 3 5 6 8

STARFIRE (Teen Titans character)(Also see Red Hood and the Outlaws)
DC Comics: Aug, 2015 - No. 12, Jul, 2016 ($2.99)

1-12: 1-Conner & Palmiotti-s/Lupacchino-a; Conner-c. 3-Intro. Atlee. 7,8-Grayson app. 9-Charretier-a begins; intro. Syl'khee 3.00

STARGATE
Dynamite Entertainment

...: Daniel Jackson 1-4 (2010 - No. 4, 2010, $3.99) Watson-a/Murray-s 4.00
...: Vala Mal Doran 1-5 (2010 - No. 5, 2010, $3.99) Razek-a/Jerwa-s 4.00

STARGATE ATLANTIS (Based on the TV series)
American Mythology Prods.: 2016 - No. 6 ($3.99)

1-6: 1-Haynes & Vaughn-s/LaRocque-a; covers by Wheatley & LaRocque. 4-6-Gateways #1-3 on cover; Watson-a 4.00

STARGATE ATLANTIS HEARTS & MINDS
American Mythology Prods.: 2017 - No. 3, 2017 ($3.99)

1-3-Haynes & Vaughn-s/LaRocque-a 4.00

STARGATE ATLANTIS SINGULARITY
American Mythology Prods.: 2018 - No. 3, 2018 ($3.99)

1-3: 1-Haynes & Vaughn-s/Purcell & LaRocque-a. 2,3-Purcell-a 4.00

STARGATE ATLANTIS / STARGATE UNIVERSE ANTHOLOGY
American Mythology Prods.: 2018 ($3.99)

1-Haynes & Vaughn-s/LaRocque & Purcell-a; 3 covers 4.00

STARGATE ATLANTIS / STARGATE UNIVERSE ANTHOLOGY ONGOING
American Mythology Prods.: 2018 - No. 3, 2018 ($3.99)

1-3: 1-Haynes & Vaughn-s/Hilinski-a; Check-s/Gouveia-a; 3 covers. 3-Purcell-a 4.00

STARGATE UNIVERSE (Based on the TV series)
American Mythology Prods.: 2017 - No. 6, 2018 ($3.99)

1-6: 1-Haynes & Vaughn-s/Caracuzzo-a. 2,3-Gouveia-a. 4-6-Hilinski-a 4.00

STAR HUNTERS (See DC Super Stars #16)
National Periodical Publ./DC Comics: Oct-Nov, 1977 - No. 7, Oct-Nov, 1978

1,7: 1-Newton-a(p). 7-44 pgs. 2 4 6 8 10 12
2-6 1 2 3 4 5 7

NOTE: ***Buckler** a-4-7p; c-1-7p. **Layton** a-1-5i; c-1-6i. **Nasser** a-3p. **Sutton** a-6i.*

STARJAMMERS (See X-Men Spotlight on Starjammers)

Starlight #6 © Millarworld & Parlov

Starman (2nd series) #42 © DC

Star Ranger #1 © CHES

	GD	VG	FN	VF	VF/NM	NM-
	2.0	4.0	6.0	8.0	9.0	9.2

STARJAMMERS (Also see Uncanny X-Men)
Marvel Comics: Oct, 1995 - No. 4, Jan, 1996 ($2.95, limited series)
1-4: Foil-c; Ellis scripts 4.00

STARJAMMERS
Marvel Comics: Sept, 2004 - No. 6, Jan, 2005 ($2.99, limited series)
1-6-Kevin J. Anderson-s. 1-Garza-a. 2-6-Lucas-a 3.00

STARK TERROR
Stanley Publications: Dec, 1970 - No. 5, Aug, 1971 (B&W, magazine, 52 pgs.)
(1950s Horror reprints, including pre-code)

	GD	VG	FN	VF	VF/NM	NM-
1-Bondage, torture-c	8	16	24	51	96	140
2-4 (Gillmor/Aragon-r)	5	10	15	31	53	75
5 (ACG-r)	4	8	12	28	47	65

STARLET O'HARA IN HOLLYWOOD (Teen-age) (Also see Cookie)
Standard Comics: Dec, 1948 - No. 4, Sept, 1949

	GD	VG	FN	VF	VF/NM	NM-
1-Owen Fitzgerald-a in all	52	104	156	328	552	775
2	40	80	120	246	411	575
3,4	34	68	102	204	332	460

STARLIGHT
Image Comics: Mar, 2014 - No. 6, Oct, 2014 ($2.99)
1-5-Mark Millar-s/Goran Parlov-a. 1-Covers by Cassaday & Parlov. 2-Sienkiewicz var-c 3.00
6-($4.99) Two covers by Cassaday and Chiang 5.00

STARLORD
Marvel Comics: Dec, 1996 - No. 3, Feb, 1997 ($2.50, limited series)
1-3-Timothy Zahn-s 4.00

STAR-LORD (Guardians of the Galaxy)
Marvel Comics: Aug, 2013; 2014 ($7.99, series of reprints)
...: Annihilation - Conquest 1 (2014) r/Annihilation: Conquest - Starlord #1-4; design art 8.00
...: Tears For Heaven 1 (2014) r/Marvel Preview #18, Marvel Spotlight #6,7, and Marvel Premiere #61; bonus art; new cover by Pichelli 8.00
...: The Hollow Crown 1 (8/13) r/Marvel Preview #4,11 and Star-Lord Special Edition 8.00

STAR-LORD
Marvel Comics: Jan, 2016 - No. 8, Aug, 2016 ($3.99)
1-8: 1-Humphries-s/Garron-a; 18-year-old Peter Quill's 1st meeting with Yondu 4.00

STAR-LORD
Marvel Comics: Feb, 2017 - No. 6, Jun, 2017 ($3.99)
1-6-Zdarsky-s/Anka-a. 1,5,6-Old Man Logan app. 3-5-Daredevil app. 4.00
Annual 1 (7/17, $4.99) Zdarsky-s/Morissette-a/Anka-c 5.00

STAR-LORD & KITTY PRYDE (Secret Wars tie-in)
Marvel Comics: Sept, 2015 - No. 3, Nov, 2015 ($3.99, limited series)
1-3-Humphries-s/Firmansyah-a; Gambit app. 4.00

STARLORD MEGAZINE
Marvel Comics: Nov, 1996 ($2.95, one-shot)
1-Reprints w/preview of new series 4.00

STAR-LORD THE SPECIAL EDITION (Also see Marvel Comics Super Special #10, Marvel Premiere & Preview & Marvel Spotlight V2#6,7)
Marvel Comics Group: Feb, 1982 (one-shot, direct sales) (1st Baxter paper comic)

	GD	VG	FN	VF	VF/NM	NM-
1-Byrne/Austin-a; Austin-c; 8 pgs. of new-a by Golden (p); Dr. Who story by Dave Gibbons; 1st deluxe format comic	3	6	9	14	20	26

STAR MAGE
IDW Publishing: Apr, 2014 - No. 6, Sept, 2014 ($3.99, limited series)
1-6: 1-JC De La Torre-s/Ray Dillon-a. 2-6-Franco Cespedes-a 4.00

STARMAN (1st Series) (Also see Justice League & War of the Gods)
DC Comics: Oct, 1988 - No. 45, Apr, 1992 ($1.00)

	GD	VG	FN	VF	VF/NM	NM-
1-Origin	1	2	3	5	6	8

2-25,29-45: 4-Intro The Power Elite. 9,10,34-Batman app. 14-Superman app. 17-Power Girl app. 38-War of the Gods x-over. 42-45-Eclipso-c/stories 3.00
26-1st app. David Knight (G.A.Starman's son). 5.00
27,28: 27-Starman (David Knight) app. 28-Starman disguised as Superman; leads into Superman #50 4.00

STARMAN (2nd Series) (Also see The Golden Age, Showcase 95 #12, Showcase 96 #4,5)
DC Comics: No. 0, Oct, 1994 - No. 80, Aug, 2001; No. 81, Mar, 2010 ($1.95/$2.25/$2.50)

	GD	VG	FN	VF	VF/NM	NM-
0,1: 0-James Robinson scripts, Tony Harris-c/a(p) & Wade Von Grawbadger-a(i) begins; Sins of the Father storyline begins, ends #3; 1st app. new Starman (Jack Knight); reintro of the G.A. Mist & G.A. Shade; 1st app. Nash; David Knight dies	1	3	4	6	8	10

	GD	VG	FN	VF	VF/NM	NM-
	2.0	4.0	6.0	8.0	9.0	9.2

2-7: 2-Reintro Charity from Forbidden Tales of Dark Mansion. 3-Reintro/2nd app. "Blue" Starman (1st app. in 1st Issue Special #12); Will Payton app. (both cameos). 5-David Knight app. 6-The Shade "Times Past" story; Kristiansen-a. 7-The Black Pirate cameo 5.00
8-17: 8-Begin $2.25-c. 10-1st app. new Mist (Nash). 11-JSA "Times Past" story; Matt Smith-a. 12-16-Sins of the Child. 17-The Black Pirate app. 4.00
18-37: 18-G.A. Starman "Times Past" story; Watkiss-a. 19-David Knight app. 20-23-G.A. Sandman app. 24-26-Demon Quest; all 3 covers make-up triptych. 33-36-Batman-c/app. 37-David Knight and deceased JSA members app. 3.00
38-49,51-56: 38-Nash vs. Justice League Europe. 39,40-Crossover w/ Power of Shazam! #35,36; Bulletman app. 42-Demon-c/app. 43-JLA-c/app. 44-Phantom Lady-c/app. 46-Gene Ha-a. 51-Jor-El app. 52,53-Adam Strange-c/app. 3.00
50-($3.95) Gold foil logo on-c; Star Boy (LSH) app. 4.00
57-79: 57-62-Painted covers by Harris and Alex Ross. 72-Death of Ted Knight 3.00
80-($3.95) Final issue; cover by Harris & Robinson 4.00
81-(3/10, $2.99) Blackest Night one-shot; The Shade vs. David Knight; Harris-c 3.00
#1,000,000 (11/98) 853rd Century x-over; Snejbjerg-a 3.00
Annual 1 (1996, $3.50)-Legends of the Dead Earth story; Prince Gavyn & G.A. Starman stories; J.H. Williams III, Bret Blevins, Craig Hamilton-c/a(p) 4.00
Annual 2 (1997, $3.95)-Pulp Heroes story; 4.00
...80 Page Giant (1/99, $4.95) Harris-c 5.00
...Secret Files 1 (4/98, $4.95)-Origin stories and profile pages 5.00
...The Mist (6/98, $1.95) Girlfrenzy; Mary Marvel app. 3.00
A Starry Knight-($17.95, TPB) r/#47-53 18.00
Grand Guignol-(2004, $19.95, TPB)-r/#61-73 20.00
Infernal Devices-($17.95, TPB) r/#29-35,37,38 18.00
Night and Day-($14.95, TPB)-r/#7-10,12-16 15.00
Sins of the Father-($12.95, TPB)-r/#0-5 13.00
Sons of the Father-($14.99, TPB)-r/#75-80 15.00
Stars My Destination-(2003, $14.95, TPB)-r/#55-60 15.00
Times Past-($17.95, TPB)-r/stories of other Starmen 18.00
The Starman Omnibus Vol. One (2008, $49.99, HC with dj) r/#0,1-16; James Robinson intro. 50.00
The Starman Omnibus Vol. Two (2009, $49.99, HC with dj) r/#17-29, Annual #1, Showcase '95 #12, Showcase '96 #4,5; Harris intro.; merchandise gallery 50.00
The Starman Omnibus Vol. Three (2009, $49.99, HC with dj) r/#30-38, Annual #2, Starman Secret Files #1 and The Shade #1-4 50.00
The Starman Omnibus Vol. Four (2010, $49.99, HC with dj) r/#39-46, 80 Page Giant #1, Power of Shazam! #35,36; Starman: The Mist #1 and Batman/Hellboy/Starman #1,2 50.00
The Starman Omnibus Vol. Five (2010, $49.99, HC with dj) r/#47-60, #1,000,000; Stars and S.T.R.I.P.E. #0; All Star Comics 80 Page Giant #1; JSA: All Stars #4 50.00
The Starman Omnibus Vol. Six (2011, $49.99, HC with dj) r/#61-81, Johns intro. 50.00

STARMAN/CONGORILLA (See Justice League: Cry For Justice)
DC Comics: Mar, 2011 ($2.99, one-shot)
1-Animal Man and Rex the Wonder Dog app.; Robinson-s/Booth-a/Ha-c 3.00

STARMASTERS
Marvel Comics: Dec, 1995 - No. 3, Feb, 1996 ($1.95, limited series)
1-3-Continues in Cosmic Powers Unlimited #4 3.00

STAR PIG
IDW Publishing: Jul, 2019 - No. 4, Oct, 2019 ($3.99, limited series)
1-4-Delilah S. Dawson-s/Francesco Gaston-a; two covers on each 4.00

STAR PRESENTATION, A (Formerly My Secret Romance #1,2; Spectacular Stories #4 on) (Also see This Is Suspense)
Fox Feature Syndicate (Hero Books): No. 3, May, 1950

	GD	VG	FN	VF	VF/NM	NM-
3-Dr. Jekyll & Mr. Hyde by Wood & Harrison (reprinted in Startling Terror Tales #10); "The Repulsing Dwarf" by Wood; Wood-c	77	154	231	493	847	1200

STAR QUEST COMIX (Warren Presents... on cover)
Warren Publications: Oct, 1978 ($1.50, B&W magazine, 84 pgs., square-bound)

	GD	VG	FN	VF	VF/NM	NM-
1-Corben, Maroto, Neary-a; Ken Kelly-c; Star Wars	2	4	6	9	12	15

STAR RAIDERS (See DC Graphic Novel #1)

STAR RANGER (Cowboy Comics #13 on)
Chesler Publ./Centaur Publ.: Feb, 1937 - No. 12, May, 1938 (Large size: No. 1-6)

	GD	VG	FN	VF	VF/NM	NM-
1-(1st Western comic)-Ace & Deuce, Air Plunder; Creig Flessel-a	304	608	912	2128	3764	5400
2	171	342	513	1094	1872	2650
3-6	161	322	483	1030	1765	2500
7-9: 8(12/37)-Christmas-c; Air Patrol, Gold coast app.; Guardineer centerfold	126	252	378	806	1378	1950
V2#10 (1st Centaur; 3/38)	142	284	426	909	1555	2200
11,12	119	238	357	762	1306	1850

NOTE: ***J. Cole** a-10, 12; c-12. **Ken Ernst** a-11. **Gill Fox** a-8(illo), 9, 10. **Guardineer** a-1-3, 5-7, 8(illos), 9, 10, 12. **Gustavson** a-8-10, 12. **Fred Schwab** c-2-11. **Bob Wood** a-8-10.*

Star Reach #1 © SRP

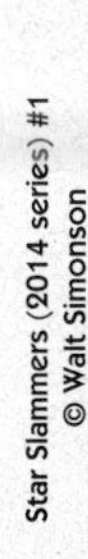

Star Slammers (2014 series) #1 © Walt Simonson

Star Spangled Comics #8 © DC

GD VG FN VF VF/NM NM-
2.0 4.0 6.0 8.0 9.0 9.2

STAR RANGER FUNNIES (Formerly Cowboy Comics)
Centaur Publications: V1#15, Oct, 1938 - V2#5, Oct, 1939

V1#15-Lyin Lou, Ermine, Wild West Junior, The Law of Caribou County by Eisner, Cowboy Jake, The Plugged Dummy, Spurs by Gustavson, Red Coat, Two Buckaroos & Trouble Hunters begin 132 264 396 845 1448 2050

V2#1 (1/39) 110 220 330 704 1202 1700

2-5: 2-Night Hawk by Gustavson. 4-Kit Carson app. 90 180 270 576 988 1400

NOTE: **Jack Cole** *a-V2#1, 3; c-V2#1.* **Filchock** *c-V2#2, 3.* **Guardineer** *a-V2#3.* **Gustavson** *a-V2#2.* **Pinajian** *c/a-V2#5.*

STAR REACH (Mature content)
Star Reach Publ.: Apr, 1974 - No. 18, Oct, 1979 (B&W, #12-15 w/color)

1-(75¢, 52 pgs.) Art by Starlin, Simonson. Chaykin-c/a; origin Death. Cody Starbuck-sty 3 6 9 17 26 35

1-2nd, 3th, and 4th printings ($1.00-$1.50-c) 6.00

2-11: 2-Adams, Giordano-a; 1st Stephanie Starr-c/s. 3-1st Linda Lovecraft. 4-1st Sherlock Duck. 5-1st Gideon Faust by Chaykin. 6-Elric-c. 7-BWS-c. 9-14-Sacred & Profane-c/s by Steacy. 11-Samurai 2 4 6 8 11 14

2-2nd printing 4.00

12-15 (44 pgs.): 12-Zelazny-s. Nasser-a, Brunner-c 2 4 6 9 13 16

16-18-Magazine size: 17-Poe's Raven-c/s 2 4 6 9 13 16

NOTE: **Adams** *c-2.* **Bonivert** *a-17.* **Brunner** *a-3,5; c-3,10,12.* **Chaykin** *a-1,4,5; c-1(1st ed),4,5; back-c-1(2nd,3rd,4th ed).* **Gene Day** *a-6,8,9,11,15.* **Friedrich** *s-2,3,8,10.* **Gasbarri** *a-7.* **Gilbert** *a-9,12.* **Giordano** *a-2.* **Gould** *a-6.* **Hirota/Mukaide** *s/a-7.* **Jones** *c-6.* **Konz** *a-17.* **Leialoha** *a-3,4,6-i, 13,15; c-13,15.* **Lyda** *a-6,12-15.* **Marrs** *a-2-5,7,10,14,15,16,18; c-18; back-c-2.* **Mukaide** *a-18.* **Nasser** *a-12.* **Nino** *a-6;* **Russell** *a-8,10; c-8.* **Dave Sim** *s-7; lettering-9.* **Simonson** *a-1.* **Skeates** *a-1,2.* **Starlin** *a-1(x2), 2(x2); back-c-1(1st ed); c-1(2nd,3rd,4th ed).* **Barry Smith** *c-7.* **Staton** *a-5,6,7.* **Steacy** *a-8-14; c-9,11,14,16.* **Vosburg** *a-2-5,7,10.* **Workman** *a-2-5,8.* *Nudity panels in most. Wraparound-c: 3-5,7-11,13-16,18.*

STAR REACH CLASSICS
Eclipse Comics: Mar, 1984 - No. 6, Aug, 1984 ($1.50, Baxter paper)

1-6: 1-Neal Adams-r/Star Reach #1; Sim & Starlin-a 3.00

STARR FLAGG, UNDERCOVER GIRL (See Undercover...)

STARRIORS
Marvel Comics: Aug, 1984 - Feb, 1985 (Limited series) (Based on Tomy toys)

1-4 4.00

STARR THE SLAYER
Marvel Comics (MAX): Nov, 2009 - No. 4, Feb, 2010 ($3.99, limited series)

1-4- Richard Corben-c/a; Daniel Way-s 4.00

STARS AND S.T.R.I.P.E. (Also see JSA)
DC Comics: July, 1999 - No. 14, Sept, 2000 ($2.95/$2.50)

0-($2.95) 1st app. Courtney Whitmore; Moder and Weston-a; Starman app. 3.00

1-Johns and Robinson-s/Moder-a; origin new Star Spangled Kid 3.00

2-14: 4-Marvel Family app. 9-Seven Soldiers of Victory-c/app. 3.00

JSA Presents: Stars and S.T.R.I.P.E. Vol. 1 TPB (2007, $17.99) r/#1-8; Johns intro. 18.00

JSA Presents: Stars and S.T.R.I.P.E. Vol. 2 TPB (2008, $17.99) r/#0,9-14 18.00

STARS AND STRIPES COMICS
Centaur Publications: No. 2, May, 1941 - No. 6, Dec, 1941

2(#1)-The Shark, The Iron Skull, A-Man, The Amazing Man, Mighty Man, Minimidget begin; The Voice & Dash Dartwell, the Human Meteor, Reef Kinkaid app.; Gustavson Flag-c 271 542 813 1734 2967 4200

3-Origin Dr. Synthe; The Black Panther app. 181 362 543 1158 1979 2800

4-Origin/1st app. The Stars and Stripes; injury to eye-c 155 310 465 992 1696 2400

5(#5 on cover & inside) 123 246 369 787 1344 1900

5(#6)-(#5 on cover, #6 on inside) 123 246 369 787 1344 1900

NOTE: **Gustavson** *c/a-3.* **Myron Strauss** *c-4, 5(#5), 5(#6).*

STAR SEED (Formerly Powers That Be)
Broadway Comics: No. 7, 1996 - No. 9 ($2.95)

7-9 3.00

STARSHIP DOWN
Dark Horse Comics: Mar, 2020 - Present ($3.99)

1-Justin Giampaoli-s/Andrea Mutti-a 4.00

STARSHIP TROOPERS
Dark Horse Comics: 1997 - No. 2, 1997 ($2.95, limited series)

1,2-Movie adaptation 3.00

STARSHIP TROOPERS: BRUTE CREATIONS
Dark Horse Comics: 1997 ($2.95, one-shot)

1 3.00

STARSHIP TROOPERS: DOMINANT SPECIES
Dark Horse Comics: Aug, 1998 - No. 4, Nov, 1998 ($2.95, limited series)

1-4-Strnad-s/Bolton-c 3.00

STARSHIP TROOPERS: INSECT TOUCH
Dark Horse Comics: 1997 - No. 3, 1997 ($2.95, limited series)

1-3 3.00

STAR SLAMMERS (See Marvel Graphic Novel #6)
Malibu Comics (Bravura): May, 1994 - No. 4, Aug, 1994 ($2.50, unfinished limited series)

1-4: W. Simonson-a/stories; contain Bravura stamps 3.00

STAR SLAMMERS
IDW Publishing: Mar, 2014 - No. 8, Oct, 2014 ($3.99)

1-8-Recolored reprint of 1994 series; Walt Simonson-s/a. 1-4-Two covers by Simonson 4.00

STAR SLAMMERS SPECIAL
Dark Horse Comics (Legend): June, 1996 ($2.95, one-shot)

nn-Simonson-c/a/scripts; concludes Bravura limited series. 3.00

STARSLAYER
Pacific Comics/First Comics No. 7 on: Feb, 1982 - No. 6, Apr, 1983; No. 7, Aug, 1983 - No. 34, Nov, 1985

1-Origin & 1st app.; 1 pg. Rocketeer brief app. which continues in #2 2 4 6 11 16 20

2-Origin/1st full app. the Rocketeer (4/82) by Dave Stevens (Chapter 1 of Rocketeer saga; see Pacific Presents #1,2) 3 6 9 17 26 35

3-Chapter 2 of Rocketeer saga by Stevens 2 4 6 11 16 20

4,6,7: 7-Grell-a ends 4.00

5-2nd app. Groo the Wanderer by Aragonés 2 4 6 8 10 12

8,9,11-34: 18-Starslayer meets Grimjack. 20-The Black Flame begins (9/84, 1st app.), ends #33. 27-Book length Black Flame story 4.00

10-1st app. Grimjack (11/83, ends #17) 5.00

NOTE: **Grell** *a-1-7; c-1-8.* **Stevens** *back c-2, 3.* **Sutton** *a-17p, 20-22p, 24-27p, 29-33p.*

STARSLAYER (The Director's Cut)
Acclaim Comics (Windjammer): June, 1994 - No. 8, Dec, 1995 ($2.50)

1-8: Mike Grell-c/a/scripts 4.00

STAR SPANGLED COMICS (Star Spangled War Stories #131 on)
National Periodical Publications: Oct, 1941 - No. 130, July, 1952

GD VG FN VF VF/NM NM-
2.0 4.0 6.0 8.0 9.0 9.2

1-Origin/1st app. Tarantula; Captain X of the R.A.F., Star Spangled Kid (see Action #40), Armstrong of the Army begin; Robot-c 530 1060 1590 3869 6835 9800

2 194 388 582 1242 2121 3000

3-5 116 232 348 742 1271 1800

6-Last Armstrong/Army; Penniless Palmer begins 73 146 219 467 796 1125

7-(4/42)-Origin/1st app. The Guardian by S&K, & Robotman (by Paul Cassidy & created by Siegel);The Newsboy Legion (1st app.), Robotman & TNT begin; last Captain X 811 1622 2433 5920 10,460 15,000

8-Origin TNT & Dan the Dyna-Mite 252 504 756 1613 2757 3900

9,10 168 336 504 1075 1838 2600

11-17 123 246 369 787 1344 1900

18-Origin Star Spangled Kid 155 310 465 992 1696 2400

19-Last Tarantula 123 246 369 787 1344 1900

20-Liberty Belle begins (5/43) 155 310 465 992 1696 2400

21-29-Last S&K issue; 23-Last TNT. 25-Robotman by Jimmy Thompson begins. 29-Intro Robbie the Robotdog 103 206 309 659 1130 1600

30-40: 31-S&K-c 63 126 189 403 689 975

41-51: 41,49-Kirby-c. 51-Robot-c by Kirby 57 114 171 362 619 875

52-64: 53 by S&K. 64-Last Newsboy Legion & The Guardian 52 104 156 328 552 775

65-Robin begins with c/app. (2/47); Batman cameo in 1 panel; Robin-c begins, end #95 219 438 657 1402 2401 3400

66-Batman cameo in Robin story 94 188 282 597 1024 1450

67,68,70-80: 68-Last Liberty Belle? 72-Burnley Robin-c 74 148 222 470 810 1150

69-Origin/1st app. Tomahawk by F. Ray; atom bomb story & splash (6/47); black-c (rare in high grade) 245 490 735 1568 2684 3800

81-Origin Merry, Girl of 1000 Gimmicks in Star Spangled Kid story 61 122 183 390 670 950

82,85: 82-Last Robotman? 85-Last Star Spangled Kid? 55 110 165 352 601 850

83-Tomahawk enters the lost valley, a land of dinosaurs; Capt. Compass begins, ends #130 58 116 174 371 636 900

84,87 (Rare): 87-Batman cameo in Robin 87 174 261 553 952 1350

86-Batman cameo in Robin story 62 124 186 395 678 960

88(1/49)-94: Batman-c/stories in all. 91-Federal Men begin, end #93. 94-Manhunters Around the World begin, end #121 69 138 207 442 759 1075

Star Spangled War Stories #151 © DC

Star Spangled War Stories (2014 series) #1 © DC

Startling Comics #7 © Nedor

	GD 2.0	VG 4.0	FN 6.0	VF 8.0	VF/NM 9.0	NM- 9.2
95-Batman story; last Robin-c	58	116	174	371	636	900
96,98-Batman cameo in Robin stories. 96-1st Tomahawk-c (also #97-121)	41	82	123	256	428	600
97,99	37	74	111	222	361	500
100 (1/50)-Pre-Bat-Hound tryout in Robin story (pre-dates Batman #92).	43	86	129	271	461	650
101-109,118,119,121: 121-Last Tomahawk-c	34	68	102	199	325	450
110,111,120-Batman cameo in Robin stories. 120-Last 52 pg. issue	34	68	102	206	336	465
112-Batman & Robin story	37	74	111	222	361	500
113-Frazetta-a (10 pgs.)	41	82	123	260	435	610
114-Retells Robin's origin (3/51); Batman & Robin story	45	90	135	284	480	675
115,117-Batman app. in Robin stories	37	74	111	222	361	500
116-Flag-c	39	78	117	231	378	525
122-(11/51)-Ghost Breaker-c/stories begin (origin/1st app.), ends #130 (Ghost Breaker covers #122-130)	60	120	180	381	653	925
123-126,128,129	39	78	117	240	395	550
127-Batman app.	41	82	123	256	428	600
130-Batman cameo in Robin story	43	86	129	271	461	650

NOTE: *Most all issues after #29 signed by Simon & Kirby are not by them.* ***Bill Ely*** *c-122-130.* ***Mortimer*** *c-65-74(most), 76-95(most).* ***Fred Ray*** *c-96-106, 109, 110, 112, 113, 115-120.* ***S&K*** *c-7-31, 33, 34, 36, 37, 39, 40, 48, 49, 50-54, 56-58.* ***Hal Sherman*** *c-1-6.* ***Dick Sprang*** *c-75.*

STAR SPANGLED COMICS (Also see All Star Comics 1999 crossover titles)
DC Comics: May, 1999 ($1.99, one-shot)

1-Golden Age Sandman and the Star Spangled Kid — 3.00

STAR SPANGLED KID (See Action #40, Leading Comics & Star Spangled Comics)

STAR SPANGLED WAR STORIES
DC Comics: Aug/Sept 1952

nn - Ashcan comic, not distributed to newsstands, only for in-house use. Cover art is Western Comics #28 with interior being Western Comics #13 (a VG- copy sold for $2151 in 2012)

STAR SPANGLED WAR STORIES (Formerly Star Spangled Comics #1-130; Becomes The Unknown Soldier #205 on) (See Showcase)
National Periodical Publ.: No. 131, 8/52 - No. 133, 10/52; No. 3, 11/52 - No. 204, 2-3/77

	GD	VG	FN	VF	VF/NM	NM-
131(#1)	209	418	627	1338	2294	3250
132	119	238	357	762	1306	1850
133-Used in **POP**, pg. 94	103	206	309	659	1130	1600
3,5,6: 6-Evans-a	68	136	204	435	743	1050
4-Devil Dog Dugan app.	69	138	207	442	759	1075
7-10	32	64	96	230	515	800
11-20	27	54	81	194	435	675
21-30: 30-Last precode (2/55)	24	48	72	168	372	575
31-33,35-40	20	40	60	138	307	475
34-Krigstein-a	20	40	60	144	317	490
41-44,46-50: 50-1st S.A. issue	18	36	54	125	276	430
45-1st DC grey tone war-c (5/56)	46	92	138	368	834	1300
51,52,54-63,65,66, 68-83	16	32	48	108	239	370
53-"Rock Sergeant," 3rd Sgt. Rock prototype; inspired "P.I. & The Sand Fleas" in G.I. Combat #56 (1/57)	27	54	81	194	435	675
64-Pre-Sgt. Rock Easy Co. story (12/57)	20	40	60	140	310	480
67-Two Easy Co. stories without Sgt. Rock	20	40	60	142	314	490
84-Origin Mlle. Marie	125	250	375	1000	2250	3500
85-89-Mlle. Marie in all	32	64	96	230	515	800
90-1st app. "War That Time Forgot" series; dinosaur issue-c/story (4-5/60) (also see Weird War Tales #94 & #99)	100	200	300	800	1800	2800
91,93-No dinosaur stories	17	34	51	119	265	410
92-2nd dinosaur-c/s	31	62	93	223	499	775
94 (12/60)- "Ghost Ace" story; Baron Von Richter as The Enemy Ace (predates Our Army at War #151)	35	70	105	252	564	875
95-99: Dinosaur-c/s	23	46	69	156	348	540
100-Dinosaur-c/story.	23	46	69	168	382	560
101-115: All dinosaur issues. 102-Panel inspired a famous Roy Lichtenstein painting	17	34	51	115	255	395
116-125,127-133,135-137: 120-1st app. Caveboy and Dino. 137-Last dinosaur story; Heath Birdman-#129,131	14	28	42	94	207	320
126-No dinosaur story	11	22	33	73	157	240
134-Dinosaur story; Neal Adams-a	15	30	45	105	233	360
138-New Enemy Ace-c/stories begin by Joe Kubert (4-5/68), end #150 (also see Our Army at War #151 and Showcase #57)	16	32	48	112	249	385
139-Origin Enemy Ace (7/68)	10	20	30	69	147	225
140-143,145: 145-Last 12¢ issue (6-7/69)	8	16	24	54	102	150
144-Neal Adams/Kubert-a	9	18	27	58	114	170
146-Enemy Ace-c/app.	6	12	18	41	76	110
147,148-New Enemy Ace stories	7	14	21	48	89	130
149,150-Last new Enemy Ace by Kubert. Viking Prince by Kubert	7	14	21	44	82	120
151-1st solo app. Unknown Soldier (6-7/70); Enemy Ace-r begin (from Our Army at War, Showcase & SSWS); end #161	18	36	54	125	276	430
152-Reprints 2nd Enemy Ace app.	6	12	18	38	69	100
153,155-Enemy Ace reprints; early Unknown Soldier stories	5	10	15	34	60	85
154-Origin Unknown Soldier	13	26	39	87	191	295
156-1st Battle Album; Unknown Soldier story; Kubert-c/a	5	10	15	31	53	75
157-Sgt. Rock x-over in Unknown Soldier story.	4	8	12	28	47	65
158-163-(52 pgs.): New Unknown Soldier stories; Kubert-c/a. 161-Last Enemy Ace-r	4	8	12	25	40	55
164-183,200: 181-183-Enemy Ace vs. Balloon Buster serial app; Frank Thorne-a. 200-Enemy Ace back-up	3	6	9	15	22	28
184-199,201-204	2	4	6	13	18	22

NOTE: ***Anderson*** *a-28.* ***Chaykin*** *a-167.* ***Drucker*** *a-59, 61, 64, 66, 67, 73-84.* ***Estrada*** *a-149.* ***John Giunta*** *a-72.* ***Glanzman*** *a-167, 171, 172, 174.* ***Heath*** *a-42,122, 132, 133; c-67, 122, 132-134.* ***Kaluta*** *a-197i; c-167.* ***G. Kane*** *a-169.* ***Kubert*** *a-6-163(most later issues), 200.* ***Maurer*** *a-160, 165.* ***Severin*** *a-65, 162.* ***S&K*** *c-7-31, 33, 34, 37, 40.* ***Simonson*** *a-170, 172, 174, 180.* ***Sutton*** *a-168.* ***Thorne*** *a-183.* ***Toth*** *a-164.* ***Wildey*** *a-161. Suicide Squad in 110, 116-118, 120, 121, 127.*

STAR SPANGLED WAR STORIES (Featuring Mademoiselle Marie)
DC Comics: Nov, 2010 ($3.99, one-shot)

1-Mademoiselle Marie in 1944 France; Tucci-s/Justiniano-a/Bolland-c — 4.00

STAR SPANGLED WAR STORIES (Featuring G.I. Zombie)
DC Comics: Sept, 2014 - No. 8, May, 2015 ($2.99)

1-8-Palmiotti & Gray-s/Scott Hampton-a. 1-6-Darwyn Cooke-c. 7-Dave Johnson-c — 3.00
...: Futures End 1 (11/14, $2.99, regular-c) Five years later; Dave Johnson-c — 3.00
...: Futures End 1 (11/14, $3.99, 3-D cover) — 4.00

STARSTREAM (Adventures in Science Fiction)(See Questar illustrated)
Whitman/Western Publishing Co.: 1976 (79¢, 68 pgs, cardboard-c)

	GD	VG	FN	VF	VF/NM	NM-
1-4: 1-Bolle-a. 2-4-McWilliams & Bolle-a	2	4	6	10	14	18

STARSTRUCK
Marvel Comics (Epic Comics): Feb, 1985 - No. 6, Feb, 1986 ($1.50, mature)

1-6: Kaluta-a — 6.00

STARSTRUCK
Dark Horse Comics: Aug, 1990 - No. 4, Nov?, 1990 ($2.95, B&W, 52pgs.)

1-3: Kaluta-r/Epic series plus new-c/a in all — 4.00
4 (68 pgs.)-contains 2 trading cards — 5.00
Reprint 1-13 (IDW, 8/09 - No. 13, Sept, 2010, $3.99) newly colored; Galactic Girl Guides — 4.00

STARSTRUCK: OLD PROLDIERS NEVER DIE
IDW Publishing: Feb, 2017 - No. 6, Jul, 2017 ($4.99)

1-Expanded version of old stories with new art; Elaine Lee-s/Michael Kaluta-a — 5.00

STAR STUDDED
Cambridge House/Superior Publishers: 1945 (25¢, 132 pgs.); 1945 (196 pgs.)

	GD	VG	FN	VF	VF/NM	NM-
nn-Captain Combat by Giunta, Ghost Woman, Commandette, & Red Rogue app.; Infantino-a	47	94	141	296	498	700
nn-The Cadet, Edison Bell, Hoot Gibson, Jungle Lil (196 pgs.); copies vary; Blue Beetle in some	50	100	150	315	533	750

STARTLING COMICS
Better Publications (Nedor): June, 1940 - No. 53, Sept, 1948

	GD	VG	FN	VF	VF/NM	NM-
1-Origin Captain Future-Man Of Tomorrow, Mystico (By Sansone), The Wonder Man; The Masked Rider & his horse Pinto begins; Masked Rider formerly in pulps; drug use story	360	720	1080	2520	4410	6300
2 -Don Davis, Espionage Ace begins	187	374	561	1197	2049	2900
3	151	302	453	966	1658	2350
4	126	252	378	806	1378	1950
5,6,9	106	212	318	678	1164	1650
7,8-Nazi WWII-c	135	270	405	864	1482	2100
10-The Fighting Yank begins (9/41, origin/1st app.); Nazi WWII-c	919	1838	2757	6709	11,855	17,000
11-2nd app. Fighting Yank; Nazi WWII-c	265	530	795	1694	2897	4100
12-Hitler, Tojo, Mussolini-c	300	600	900	2010	3505	5000
13-15	126	252	378	806	1378	1950
16-Origin The Four Comrades; not in #32,35	145	290	435	928	1589	2250
17-Last Masked Rider & Mystico	129	258	387	826	1413	2000
18-Pyroman begins (12/42, origin)(also see America's Best Comics #3 for 1st app., 11/42)	187	374	561	1197	2049	2900
19-Nazi WWII-c	219	438	657	1402	2401	3400

20-Classic hooded Nazi giant snake bondage/torture-c (scarce); The Oracle begins (3/43);

Startling Stories: The Thing #1 © MAR

Star Trek #49 © Paramount

Star Trek (2011 series) #27 © CBS Studios

	GD 2.0	VG 4.0	FN 6.0	VF 8.0	VF/NM 9.0	NM- 9.2
not in issues 26,28,33,34	304	608	912	2128	3764	5400
21-Origin The Ape, Oracle's enemy; Schomburg hypo-c	181	362	543	1158	1979	2800
22-34: All have Schomburg WWII-c. 34-Origin The Scarab & only app.	151	302	453	966	1658	2350
35-Hypodermic syringe attacks Fighting Yank in drug story; Schomburg WWII-c	155	310	465	992	1696	2400
36-43: 36-Last Four Comrades. 38-Bondage/torture-c. 40-Last Capt. Future & Oracle. 41-Front Page Peggy begins; A-Bomb-c. 43-Last Pyroman	68	136	204	435	743	1050
44,45: 44-Lance Lewis, Space Detective begins; Ingels-c; sci/fi-c begin. 45-Tygra begins (intro/origin, 5/47); Ingels-c/a (splash pg. & inside f/c B&W ad)	116	232	348	742	1271	1800
46-Classic Ingels-c; Ingels-a	174	348	522	1114	1907	2700
47,48,50-53: 50,51-Sea-Eagle app.	132	264	396	845	1448	2050
49-Classic Schomburg Robot-c; last Fighting Yank	1200	2400	3600	8900	15,950	23,000

NOTE: ***Ingels** a-44, 45; c-44, 45, 46(wash). **Schomburg** (**Xela**) c-21-43; 47-53 (airbrush). **Tuska** c-45? Bondage c-16, 21, 37, 46-49. Captain Future c-1-9, 13, 14. Fighting Yank c-10-12, 15-17, 21, 22, 24, 26, 28, 30, 32, 34, 36, 38, 40, 42. Pyroman c-18-20, 23, 25, 27, 29, 31, 33, 35, 37, 39, 41, 43.*

STARTLING STORIES: BANNER
Marvel Comics: July, 2001 - No. 4, Oct, 2001 ($2.99, limited series)

1-4-Hulk story by Azzarello; Corben-c/a 3.00
TPB (11/01, $12.95) r/1-4 13.00

STARTLING STORIES: FANTASTIC FOUR - UNSTABLE MOLECULES (See Fantastic Four - ...)

STARTLING STORIES: THE MEGALOMANIACAL SPIDER-MAN
Marvel Comics: Jun, 2002 ($2.99, one-shot)

1-Spider-Man spoof; Peter Bagge-s/a 3.00

STARTLING STORIES: THE THING
Marvel Comics: 2003 ($3.50, one-shot)

1-Zimmerman-s/Kramer-a; Inhumans and the Hulk app. 3.50

STARTLING STORIES: THE THING - NIGHT FALLS ON YANCY STREET
Marvel Comics: Jun, 2003 - No. 4, Sept, 2003 ($3.50, limited series)

1-4-Dorkin-s/Haspiel-a. 2,3-Frightful Four app. 3.50

STARTLING TERROR TALES
Star Publications: No. 10, May, 1952 - No. 14, Feb, 1953; No. 4, Apr, 1953 - No. 11, 1954

	GD 2.0	VG 4.0	FN 6.0	VF 8.0	VF/NM 9.0	NM- 9.2
10-(1st Series)-Wood/Harrison-a (r/A Star Presentation #3) Disbrow/Cole-c; becomes 4 different titles after #10; becomes Confessions of Love #11 on, The Horrors #11 on, Terrifying Tales #11 on, Terrors of the Jungle #11 on & continues w/Startling Terror #11	119	238	357	762	1306	1850
11-(8/52)-L. B. Cole Spider-c; r-Fox's "A Feature Presentation" #5 (blue-c)	314	628	942	2224	3912	5600
11-Black-c (variant; believed to be a pressrun change) (Unique)	331	662	993	2317	4059	5800
12,14	47	94	141	296	498	700
13-Jo-Jo-r; Disbrow-a	50	100	150	315	533	750
4-9,11(1953-54) (2nd Series): 11-New logo	42	84	126	265	445	625
10-Disbrow-a	47	94	141	296	498	700

NOTE: ***L. B. Cole** covers-all issues. **Palais** a-V2#8r, V2#11r.*

STAR TREK (TV) (See Dan Curtis Giveaways, Dynabrite Comics & Power Record Comics)
Gold Key: 7/67; No. 2, 6/68; No. 3, 12/68; No. 4, 6/69 - No. 61, 3/79

	GD 2.0	VG 4.0	FN 6.0	VF 8.0	VF/NM 9.0	NM- 9.2
1-Photo-c begin, end #9; photo back-c is on all copies, no variant exists with an ad on the back-c	82	164	246	656	1478	2300
2-Regular version has an ad on back-c	25	50	75	175	388	600
2 (rare variation w/photo back-c)	49	98	147	382	866	1350
3-5-All have back-c ads	17	34	51	117	259	400
3 (rare variation w/photo back-c)	32	64	96	230	515	800
6-9	11	22	33	76	163	250
10-20	6	12	18	37	66	95
21-30	5	10	15	31	53	80
31-40	4	8	12	27	44	60
41-61: 52-Drug propaganda story	3	6	9	21	33	45
... Gold Key 100-Page Spectacular (IDW, 2/17, $7.99) r/#1,8,14; cover & pin-up gallery						8.00
...the Enterprise Logs nn (8/76)-Golden Press, ($1.95, 224 pgs.)-r/#1-8 plus 7 pgs. by McWilliams (#11185)-Photo-c	6	12	18	41	76	110
...the Enterprise Logs Vol. 2 ('76)-r/#9-17 (#11187)-Photo-c	5	10	15	34	60	85
...the Enterprise Logs Vol. 3 ('77)-r/#18-26 (#11188); McWilliams-a (4 pgs.)-Photo-c	5	10	15	33	57	80
Star Trek Vol. 4 (Winter '77)-Reprints #27,28,30-34,36,38 (#11189) plus 3 pgs. new art	5	10	15	31	53	75
... : The Key Collection (Checker Book Publ. Group, 2004, $22.95) r/#1-8						23.00
... : The Key Collection Volume 2 (Checker, 2004, $22.95) r/#9-16						23.00
... : The Key Collection Volume 3 (Checker, 2005, $22.95) r/#17-24						23.00
... : The Key Collection Volume 4 (Checker, 2005, $22.95) r/#25-33						23.00
... : The Key Collection Volume 5 (Checker, 2006, $22.95) r/#34,36,38,39,40-43						23.00

NOTE: ***McWilliams** a-38, 40-44, 46-61. #29 reprints #1; #35 reprints #4; #37 reprints #5; #45 reprints #7. The tabloids all have photo covers and blank inside covers. Painted covers #10-44, 46-59.*

STAR TREK
Marvel Comics Group: April, 1980 - No. 18, Feb, 1982

	GD 2.0	VG 4.0	FN 6.0	VF 8.0	VF/NM 9.0	NM- 9.2
1: 1-3-r/Marvel Super Special; movie adapt.	3	6	9	14	20	25
2-16: 5-Miller-c	1	3	4	6	8	10
17-Low print run	2	4	6	9	13	16
18-Last issue; low print run	2	4	6	11	16	20

NOTE: ***Austin** c-18i. **Buscema** a-13. **Gil Kane** a-15. **Nasser** c/a-7. **Simonson** c-17.*

STAR TREK (Also see Who's Who In Star Trek)
DC Comics: Feb, 1984 - No. 56, Nov, 1988 (75¢, Mando paper)

	GD 2.0	VG 4.0	FN 6.0	VF 8.0	VF/NM 9.0	NM- 9.2
1-Sutton-a(p) begins	2	4	6	11	16	20
2-5						6.00
6-10: 7-Origin Saavik						5.00
11-32,34-49,51-56: 19-Walter Koenig story. 37-Painted-c						4.00
33-($1.25, 52 pgs.)-20th anniversary issue						5.00
50-($1.50, 52 pgs.)						5.00
Annual 1-3: 1(1985). 2(1986). 3(1988, $1.50)						5.00
...: To Boldly Go TPB (Titan Books, 7/05, $19.95) r/#1-6; Koenig foreward; cast interviews						20.00
...: The Trial of James T. Kirk TPB (Titan Books, 6/06, $19.95) r/#7-12; cast interviews						20.00
...: The Return of the Worthy TPB (Titan Books, 12/06, $19.95) r/#13-18; cast interviews						20.00

NOTE: ***Morrow** a-28, 35, 36, 56. **Orlando** c-8i. **Perez** c-1-3. **Spiegle** a-19. **Starlin** c-24, 25. **Sutton** a-1-6p, 8-18p, 20-27p, 29p, 31-34p, 39-52p, 55p; c-4-6p, 8-22p, 46p.*

STAR TREK
DC Comics: Oct, 1989 - No. 80, Jan, 1996 ($1.50/$1.75/$1.95/$2.50)

	GD 2.0	VG 4.0	FN 6.0	VF 8.0	VF/NM 9.0	NM- 9.2
1-Capt. Kirk and crew	1	3	4	6	8	10
2,3						5.00
4-23,25-30: 10-12-The Trial of James T. Kirk. 21-Begin $1.75-c						3.00
24-($2.95, 68 pgs.)-40 pg. epic w/pin-ups						4.00
31-49,51-74,76-80						3.00
50-($3.50, 68 pgs.)-Painted-c						4.00
75 ($3.95)						4.00
Annual 1-6('90-'95, 68 pgs.): 1-Morrow-a. 3-Painted-c						4.00
Special 1-3 ('9-'95, 68 pgs.)-1-Sutton-a.						4.00
...: The Ashes of Eden (1995, $14.95, 100 pgs.)-Shatner story						18.00
...Generations (1994, $3.95, 68 pgs.)-Movie adaptation						4.00
...Generations (1994, $5.95, 68 pgs.)-Squarebound						6.00

STAR TREK...(TV)
DC Comics (WildStorm): one-shots

All of Me (4/00, $5.95, prestige format) Lopresti-a 6.00
Enemy Unseen TPB (2001, $17.95) r/Perchance to Dream, Embrace the Wolf, The Killing Shadows; Struzan-c 18.00
Enter the Wolves (2001, $5.95) Crispin & Weinstein-s; Mota-a/c 6.00
New Frontier - Double Time (11/00, $5.95)-Captain Calhoun's USS Excalibur; Peter David-s; Stelfreeze-c 6.00
Other Realities TPB (2001, $14.95) r/All of Me, New Frontier - Double Time, and DS9-N-Vector; Van Fleet-c 15.00
Special (2001, $6.95) Stories from all 4 series by various; Van Fleet-c 7.00

STAR TREK (Further adventures of the crew from the 2009 movie)
IDW Publishing: Sept, 2011 - No. 60, Aug, 2016 ($3.99)

1-49: 1,2-Gary Mitchell app.; Molnar-a. 11,12-Tribbles. 15,16-Mirror Universe. 21-Follows the 2013 movie; Klingons & Section 31 app. 35-40-The Q Gambit; DS9 crew app. 4.00
50-($4.99) Mirror Universe; Khan app.; bonus history of Star Trek comics, aliens 5.00
51-60: 51,52-Mirror Universe. 52-Variant Archie Comics cover. 55-58-Legacy of Spock 4.00
Annual (12/13, $7.99) "Strange New Worlds" on cover; photonovel by John Byrne 8.00
... #1: Greatest Hits (3/16, $1.00) reprints #1 3.00
... #1: Hundred Penny Press (8/13, $1.00) reprints #1 3.00
...: Deviations 1 (3/17, $4.99) Timeline where Romulans, not Vulcans made 1st Contact 5.00
...: Flesh and Stone (7/14, $3.99) Doctors Bashir, Crusher, Pulaski, McCoy app. 4.00
...: 50th Anniversary Cover Celebration (8/16, $7.99) Gallery of IDW Star Trek covers 8.00
...: IDW 20/20 (1/19, $4.99) Picard on the Stargazer 20 years before TNG; Woodward-a 5.00
... Space Spanning Treasury Edition (4/13, $9.99, 13" x 8.5") Reprints #9,10,13 10.00

STAR TREK: ALIEN SPOTLIGHT
IDW Publishing: Sept, 2007 - Feb, 2008 ($3.99, series of one-shots)

... Andorians (11/07) Storrie-s/O'Grady-a; Counselor Troi app.; two art & one photo-c 4.00
... Borg (1/08) Harris-s/Murphy-a; Janeway & Next Gen crew app.; two art & one photo-c 4.00
... Cardassians (12/09) Padilla-a; Garak & Kira app. 4.00
... The Gorn (9/07) Messina-a; Chekov app.; two art & one photo-c 4.00

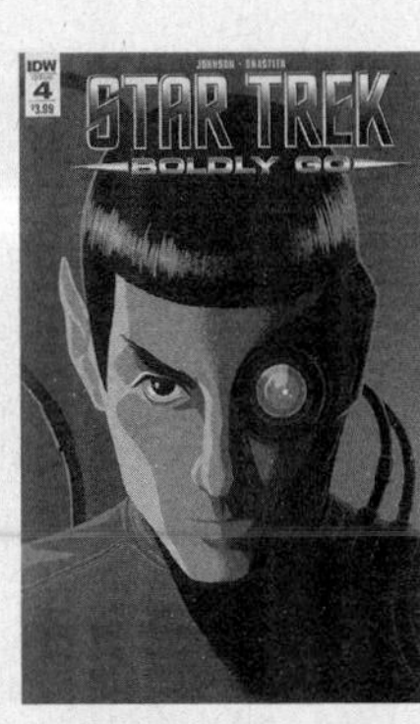

Star Trek: Boldly Go #4 © CBS Studios

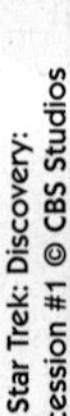

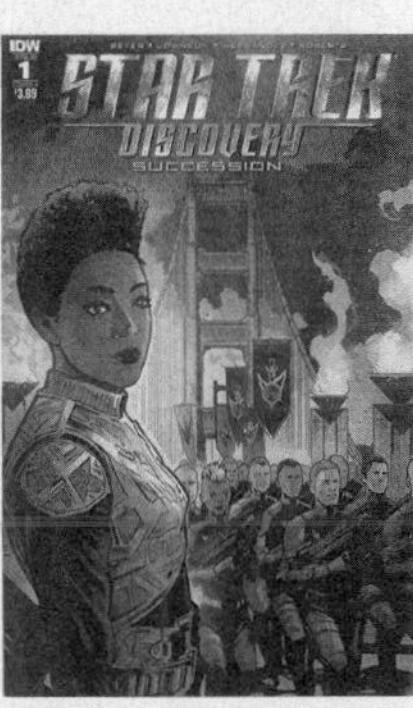

Star Trek: Discovery: Succession #1 © CBS Studios

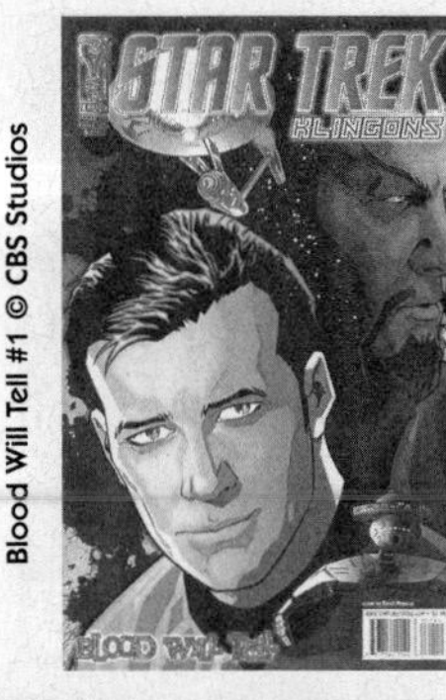

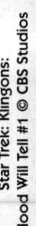

Star Trek: Klingons: Blood Will Tell #1 © CBS Studios

GD 2.0 VG 4.0 FN 6.0 VF 8.0 VF/NM 9.0 NM- 9.2

... Orions (12/07) Casagrande-a; Capt. Pike app.; two art & one photo-c 4.00
... Q (8/09) Casagrande-a; takes place after Star Trek 8 movie; two art & one photo-c 4.00
... Romulans (2/08) John Byrne-s/a; Kirk era; two art & one photo-c 4.00
... Romulans (5/09) Wagner Reis-a; David Williams-c 4.00
... Tribbles (3/09) Hawthorne-a; first encounter with Klingons; one art & one photo-c 4.00
... Vulcans (10/07) Spock's early Enterprise days with Capt. Pike; two art & one photo-c 4.00

STAR TREK: ASSIGNMENT EARTH
IDW Publishing: May, 2008 - No. 5, Sept, 2008 ($3.99, limited series)
1-5-Further adventures of Gary Seven and Roberta; John Byrne-s/a/c. 5-Nixon app. 4.00

STAR TREK: BOLDLY GO (Takes place after the 2016 movie Star Trek Beyond)
IDW Publishing: Oct, 2016 - No. 18, Mar, 2018 ($3.99)
1-18-The 2009 movie crew; Mike Johnson-s/Shasteen-a; The Borg app.; multiple covers 4.00

STAR TREK: BURDEN OF KNOWLEDGE
IDW Publishing: Jun, 2010 - No. 4, Sept, 2010 ($3.99, limited series)
1-4-Original series Kirk and crew; Manfredi-a 4.00

STAR TREK: CAPTAIN'S LOG
IDW Publishing: one-shots
...: Harriman (4/10, $3.99) Captain of the Enterprise-B following Kirk's "demise"; Currie-a 4.00
...: Jellico (10/10, $3.99) Woodward-a 4.00
...: Pike (9/10, $3.99) Events that put Pike in the chair; Woodward-a 4.00
...: Sulu (1/10, $3.99) Manfredi-a 4.00

STAR TREK: COUNTDOWN (Prequel to the 2009 movie)
IDW Publishing: Jan, 2009 - No. 4, Apr, 2009 ($3.99, limited series)
1-4: 1-Ambassador Spock on Romulus; intro. Nero; Messina-a 4.00
Hundred Penny Press: Star Trek: Countdown #1 (4/11, $1.00) r/#1 w/new cover frame 3.00

STAR TREK: COUNTDOWN TO DARKNESS (Prequel to the 2013 movie)
IDW Publishing: Jan, 2013 - No. 4, Apr, 2013 ($3.99, limited series)
1-4-Captain April app.; Messina-a; regular & photo covers on each 4.00

STAR TREK: CREW
IDW Publishing: Mar, 2009 - No. 5, Jul, 2009 ($3.99, limited series)
1-5: John Byrne-s/a; Captain Pike era 4.00

STAR TREK: DEBT OF HONOR
DC Comics: 1992 ($24.95/$14.95, graphic novel)
Hardcover ($24.95) Claremont-s/Hughes-a(p) 25.00
Softcover ($14.95) 15.00

STAR TREK: DEEP SPACE NINE (TV)
Malibu Comics: Aug, 1993 - No. 32, Jan, 1996 ($2.50)
1-Direct Sale Edition w/line drawn-c 1 2 3 5 6 8
1-Newsstand Edition with photo-c 6.00
0-(1/95, $2.95)-Terok Nor 4.00
2-30: 2-Polybagged w/trading card. 9-4 pg. prelude to Hearts & Minds 4.00
31-($3.95) 5.00
32-($3.50) 5.00
Annual 1 (1/95, $3.95, 68 pgs.) 5.00
Special 1 (1995, $3.50) 5.00
Ultimate Annual 1 (12/95, $5.95) 6.00
...:Lightstorm (12/94, $3.50) 5.00

STAR TREK: DEEP SPACE NINE (TV)
Marvel Comics (Paramount Comics): Nov, 1996 - No. 15, Mar, 1998 ($1.95/$1.99)
1-15: 12,13-"Telepathy War" pt. 2,3 4.00

STAR TREK: DEEP SPACE NINE: FOOL'S GOLD
IDW Publishing: Dec, 2009 - No. 4, Mar, 2010 ($3.99)
1-4-Mantovani-a 4.00

STAR TREK: DEEP SPACE NINE -- N-VECTOR (TV)
DC Comics (WildStorm): Aug, 2000 - No. 4, Nov, 2000 ($2.50, limited series)
1-4-Cypress-a 3.00

STAR TREK DEEP SPACE NINE-THE CELEBRITY SERIES
Malibu Comics: May, 1995 ($2.95)
1-Blood and Honor; Mark Lenard script 4.00
1-Rules of Diplomacy; Aron Eisenberg script 4.00

STAR TREK: DEEP SPACE NINE HEARTS AND MINDS
Malibu Comics: June, 1994 - No. 4, Sept, 1994 ($2.50, limited series)
1-4 4.00
1-Holographic-c 5.00

STAR TREK: DEEP SPACE NINE, THE MAQUIS
Malibu Comics: Feb, 1995 - No. 3, Apr, 1995 ($2.50, limited series)
1-3-Newsstand-c, 1-Photo-c 4.00

STAR TREK: DEEP SPACE NINE/THE NEXT GENERATION
Malibu Comics: Oct, 1994 - No. 2, Nov, 1994 ($2.50, limited series)
1,2: Parts 2 & 4 of x-over with Star Trek: TNG/DS9 from DC Comics 4.00

STAR TREK: DEEP SPACE NINE – TOO LONG A SACRIFICE
IDW Publishing: Apr, 2020 - No. 4, Oct, 2020 ($3.99, limited series)
1-4-Steve & David Tipton-s/Greg Scott-a 4.00

STAR TREK: DEEP SPACE NINE WORF SPECIAL
Malibu Comics: Dec, 1995 ($3.95, one-shot)
1-Includes pinups 6.00

STAR TREK: DISCOVERY (Based on the 2017 TV series)
IDW Publishing: Mar, 2018 ($7.99)
Annual 2018 (3/18, $7.99)-Beyer & Johnson-s/Hernandez-a; spotlight on Lt. Stamets 8.00
...: Captain Saru (2/19, $7.99) Beyer & Johnson-s/Hernandez-a; two covers 8.00

STAR TREK: DISCOVERY – AFTERMATH (Based on the 2017 TV series)
IDW Publishing: Aug, 2019 - No. 3, Oct, 2019 ($3.99, limited series)
1-3-Beyer & Johnson-s/Shasteen-a; takes place before Spock joins the Enterprise 4.00

STAR TREK: DISCOVERY: SUCCESSION (Based on the 2017 TV series)
IDW Publishing: Apr, 2018 - No. 4, Jul, 2018 ($3.99, limited series)
1-4-Beyer & Johnson-s/Hernandez-a; takes place in the Mirror Universe 4.00

STAR TREK: DISCOVERY: THE LIGHT OF KAHLESS (Based on the 2017 TV series)
IDW Publishing: Oct, 2017 - No. 4, Jan, 2018 ($3.99, limited series)
1-4-Beyer & Johnson-s/Shasteen-a 4.00

STAR TREK: DIVIDED WE FALL
DC Comics (WildStorm): July, 2001 - No. 4, Oct, 2001 ($2.95, limited series)
1-4: Ordover & Mack-s; Lenara Kahn, Verad and Odan app. 3.00

STAR TREK EARLY VOYAGES (TV)
Marvel Comics (Paramount Comics): Feb, 1997 - No. 17, Jun, 1998 ($2.95/$1.95/$1.99)
1-($2.95) 6.00
2-17 4.00

STAR TREK: ENTERPRISE EXPERIMENT
IDW Publishing: Apr, 2008 - No. 5, Aug, 2008 ($3.99, limited series)
1-5-Year Four story; D.C. Fontana & Derek Chester-s; Purcell-a 4.00

STAR TREK: FIRST CONTACT (Movie)
Marvel Comics (Paramount Comics): Nov, 1996 ($5.95, one-shot)
nn-Movie adaption 6.00

STAR TREK/ GREEN LANTERN (The Spectrum War)
IDW Publishing: Jul, 2015 - No. 6, Dec, 2015 ($3.99, limited series)
1-6-Crew from 2009 movie and Hal Jordan; Sinestro & Nekron app.; multiple covers 4.00

STAR TREK/ GREEN LANTERN (Stranger Worlds)
IDW Publishing: Dec, 2016 - No. 6, May, 2017 ($3.99, limited series)
1-6-Sinestro & The Manhunters app.; multiple covers. 2-6-Khan app. 4.00

STAR TREK: HARLAN ELLISON'S ORIGINAL CITY ON THE EDGE OF FOREVER TELEPLAY
IDW Publishing: Jun, 2014 - No. 5, Oct, 2014 ($3.99, limited series)
1-5-Adaptation of Ellison's teleplay; J.K. Woodward-a; two covers on each 4.00

STAR TREK: INFESTATION (Crossover with G.I. Joe, Transformers & Ghostbusters)
IDW Publishing: Feb, 2011 - No. 2, Feb, 2011 ($3.99, limited series)
1,2-Zombies in the Kirk era; Maloney & Erskine-a; two covers on each 4.00

STAR TREK: KHAN
IDW Publishing: Oct, 2013 - No. 5, Feb, 2014 ($3.99, limited series)
1-5-Follows the 2013 movie; Khan's origin; Messina & Balboni-a 4.00

STAR TREK: KHAN RULING IN HELL
IDW Publishing: Oct, 2010 - No. 4, Jan, 2011 ($3.99, limited series)
1-4-Khan and the Botany Bay crew after banishment on Ceti Alpha V; Mantovani-a 4.00

STAR TREK: KLINGONS: BLOOD WILL TELL
IDW Publishing: Apr, 2007 - No. 5 ($3.99, limited series)
1-5-Star Trek TOS episodes from the Klingon viewpoint; Messina-a. 2-Tribbles 4.00
1-($4.99) Klingon Language Variant; comic with Kliingon text; English script 5.00

STAR TREK/ LEGION OF SUPER-HEROES
IDW Publishing: Oct, 2011 - No. 6, Mar, 2012 ($3.99, limited series)

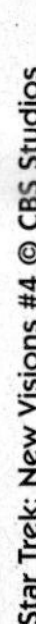
Star Trek: New Visions #4 © CBS Studios

Star Trek: Starfleet Academy #2 © CBS Studios

Star Trek: The Next Generation #24 © Paramount

	GD 2.0	VG 4.0	FN 6.0	VF 8.0	VF/NM 9.0	NM- 9.2

1-6-Jeff Moy-a/Jimenez-c 1-Giffen var-c. 2-Lightle var-c. 3-Grell var-c. 5-Allred var-c 4.00

STAR TREK: LEONARD McCOY, FRONTIER DOCTOR
IDW Publishing: Apr, 2010 - No. 4, Jul, 2010 ($3.99, limited series)

1-4-Dr. McCoy right before Star Trek: TMP; John Byrne-s/a 4.00

STAR TREK: MANIFEST DESTINY
IDW Publishing: Apr, 2016 - No. 4, May, 2016 ($4.99/$3.99, limited series)

1-The 2009 movie crew vs. Klingons; Angel Hernandez-a 5.00
2-4-($3.99) 4.00

STAR TREK: MIRROR BROKEN (Series previewed in Star Trek: The Next Generation: Mirror Broken #0 FCBD giveaway)
IDW Publishing: May, 2017 - No. 5, Oct, 2017 ($3.99, limited series)

1-5-The Mirror Universe Next Generation crew; David & Scott Tipton-s/Woodward-a 4.00

STAR TREK: MIRROR IMAGES
IDW Publishing: June, 2008 - No. 5, Nov, 2008 ($3.99, limited series)

1-5-Further adventures in the Mirror Universe. 3-Mirror-Picard app. 4.00

STAR TREK: MIRROR MIRROR
Marvel Comics (Paramount Comics): Feb, 1997 ($3.95, one-shot)

1-DeFalco-s 4.00

STAR TREK: MISSION'S END
IDW Publishing: Mar, 2009 - No. 5, July, 2009 ($3.99, limited series)

1-5-Kirk, Spock, Bones crew, their last mission on the pre-movie Enterprise 4.00

STAR TREK MOVIE ADAPTATION
IDW Publishing: Feb, 2010 - No. 6, Aug, 2010 ($3.99, limited series)

1-6-Adaptation of 2009 movie; Messina-a; regular & photo-c on each 4.00

STAR TREK MOVIE SPECIAL
DC Comics: 1984 (June) - No. 2, 1987 ($1.50); No. 1, 1989 ($2.00, 52 pgs)

nn-(#1)-Adapts Star Trek III; Sutton-p (68 pgs.) 5.00
2-Adapts Star Trek IV; Sutton-a; Chaykin-c. (68 pgs.) 5.00
1 (1989)-Adapts Star Trek V; painted-c 5.00

STAR TREK: NERO
IDW Publishing: Aug, 2009 - No. 4, Nov, 2009 ($3.99, limited series)

1-4-Nero's ship after the attack on the Kelvin to the arrival of Spock 4.00

STAR TREK: NEW FRONTIER
IDW Publishing: Mar, 2008 - No. 5, July, 2008 ($3.99, limited series)

1-5-Capt. Calhoun & Adm. Shelby app.; Peter David-s 4.00

STAR TREK: NEW VISIONS
IDW Publishing: May, 2014 - No. 22, Jun, 2018 ($7.99, squarebound)

1-22-Photonovels of original crew by John Byrne. 1-Mirror Universe 8.00
... Special: More Of The Serpent Than The Dove (9/16, Humble Bundle) Gorn app. 20.00
... Special: The Cage (7/16, $7.99) 8.00

STAR TREK 100 PAGE...
IDW Publishing: Nov, 2011 - 2012 ($7.99)

...Spectacular #1 (11/11) Reprints stories of the original crew; s/a by Byrne and others 8.00
...Spectacular 2012 (2/12) Reprints; Khan, Q, Capt. Pike, the Gorn app. 8.00
...Spectacular Summer 2012 (8/12) Reprints of TNG and Voyager stories 8.00
...Spectacular Winter 2012 - Reprints; Capt. Harriman, Mirror Universe 8.00

STAR TREK: OPERATION ASSIMILATION
Marvel Comics (Paramount Comics): Dec, 1996 ($2.95, one-shot)

1 4.00

STAR TREK: PICARD COUNTDOWN (Prelude to the 2020 TV series)
IDW Publishing: Nov, 2019 - No. 3, Jan, 2020 ($3.99, limited series)

1-3-Beyer & Johnson-s/Hernandez-a; intro. Raffi Musiker, Laris & Zhaban 4.00

STAR TREK/PLANET OF THE APES: THE PRIMATE DIRECTIVE
IDW Publishing: Dec, 2014 - No. 5, Apr, 2015 ($3.99, limited series)

1-5-Classic crew on the Planet of the Apes; Klingons app. 2-Kirk meets Taylor 8.00

STAR TREK: ROMULANS SCHISMS
IDW Publishing: Sept, 2009 - No. 3, Nov, 2009 ($3.99, limited series)

1-3-John Byrne-s/a/c 4.00

STAR TREK: ROMULANS THE HOLLOW CROWN
IDW Publishing: Sept, 2008 - No. 2, Oct, 2008 ($3.99, limited series)

1,2-John Byrne-s/a/c 4.00

STAR TREK VI: THE UNDISCOVERED COUNTRY (Movie)
DC Comics: 1992

1-($2.95, regular edition, 68 pgs.)-Adaptation of film 5.00
nn-($5.95, prestige edition)-Has photos of movie not included in regular edition; painted-c by Palmer; photo back-c 1 2 3 5 6 8

STAR TREK: SPOCK: REFLECTIONS
IDW Publishing: July, 2009 - No. 4, Oct, 2009 ($3.99, limited series)

1-4-Flashbacks of Spock's childhood and career; Messina & Manfredi-a 4.00

STAR TREK: STARFLEET ACADEMY
Marvel Comics (Paramount Comics): Dec, 1996 - No. 19, Jun, 1998 ($1.95/$1.99)

1-19: Begin new series. 12-"Telepathy War" pt. 1. 18-English & Klingon editions 4.00

STAR TREK: STARFLEET ACADEMY
IDW Publishing: Dec, 2015 - No. 5, Apr, 2016 ($3.99, limited series)

1-5-Crew of the 2009 movie at the academy; Charm-a 4.00

STAR TREK: TELEPATHY WAR
Marvel Comics (Paramount Comics): Nov, 1997 ($2.99, 48 pgs., one-shot)

1-"Telepathy War" x-over pt. 6 4.00

STAR TREK - THE MODALA IMPERATIVE
DC Comics: Late July, 1991 - No. 4, Late Sept, 1991 ($1.75, limited series)

1-4 4.00
TPB ($19.95) r/series and ST:TNG - The Modala Imperative 20.00

STAR TREK: THE NEXT GENERATION (TV)
DC Comics: Feb, 1988 - No. 6, July, 1988 (limited series)

1 ($1.50, 52 pgs.)-Sienkiewicz painted-c 2 4 6 8 11 14
2-6 ($1.00) 5.00

STAR TREK: THE NEXT GENERATION (TV)
DC Comics: Oct, 1989 -No. 80, 1995 ($1.50/$1.75/$1.95)

1-Capt. Picard and crew from TV show 2 4 6 8 11 14
2,3 6.00
4-10 5.00
11-23,25-49,51-60 4.00
24,50: 24-($2.50, 52 pgs.). 50-($3.50, 68 pgs.)-Painted-c 6.00
61-74,76-80 4.00
75-($3.95, 50 pgs.) 5.00
Annual 1-6 ('90-'95, 68 pgs.) 5.00
Special 1 -3('93-'95, 68 pgs.)-1-Contains 3 stories 5.00
...-The Series Finale (1994, $3.95, 68 pgs.) 5.00

STAR TREK: THE NEXT GENERATION (TV)
DC Comics (WildStorm): one-shots

Embrace the Wolf (6/00, $5.95, prestige format) Golden & Sniegoski-s 6.00
Forgiveness (2001, $24.95, HC) David Brin-s/Scott Hampton painted-a; dust jacket-c 30.00
Forgiveness (2002, $17.95, SC) 18.00
The Gorn Crisis (1/01, $29.95, HC) Kordey painted-a/dust jacket-c 30.00
The Gorn Crisis (1/01, $17.95, SC) Kordey painted-a 18.00

STAR TREK: THE NEXT GENERATION/DEEP SPACE NINE (TV)
DC Comics: Dec, 1994 - No. 2, Jan, 1995 ($2.50, limited series)

1,2-Parts 1 & 3 of x-over with Star Trek: DS9/TNG from Malibu Comics 4.00

STAR TREK: THE NEXT GENERATION / DOCTOR WHO: ASSIMILATION²
IDW Publishing: May, 2012 - No. 8, Dec, 2012 ($3.99, limited series)

1-8-The Borg and Cybermen team-up; Tipton-s/Woodward-a; multiple covers on each 4.00

STAR TREK: THE NEXT GENERATION: GHOSTS
IDW Publishing: Nov, 2009 - No. 5, Mar, 2010 ($3.99)

1-5-Cannon-s/Aranda-a 4.00

STAR TREK: THE NEXT GENERATION - ILL WIND
DC Comics: Nov, 1995 - No. 4, Feb, 1996 ($2.50, limited series)

1-4: Hugh Fleming painted-c on all 4.00

STAR TREK: THE NEXT GENERATION: INTELLIGENCE GATHERING
IDW Publishing: Jan, 2008 - No. 5, May, 2008 ($3.99)

1-5-Messina-a/Scott & David Tipton-s; two covers on each 4.00

STAR TREK: THE NEXT GENERATION: MIRROR BROKEN (See Star Trek: Mirror Broken)
IDW Publishing: May, 2017 (free giveaway)

0-(5/17, FCBD giveaway) Mirror Universe crew, prelude to series; J.K. Woodward-a/c; bonus design art 3.00

STAR TREK: THE NEXT GENERATION - PERCHANCE TO DREAM
DC Comics/WildStorm: Feb, 2000 - No. 4, May, 2000 ($2.50, limited series)

1-4-Bradstreet-c 3.00

STAR TREK: THE NEXT GENERATION - RIKER

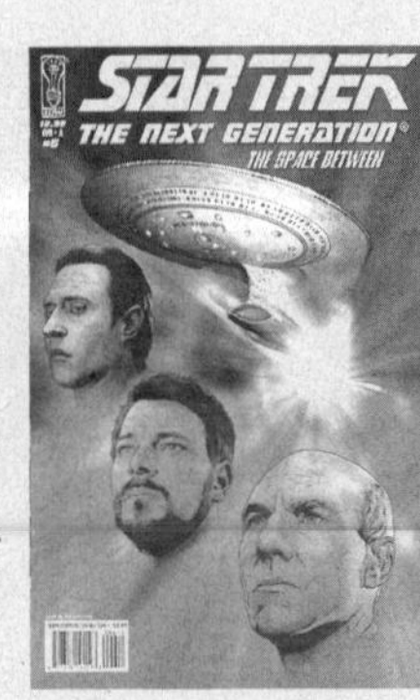

Star Trek: The Next Generation: The Space Between #6 © Paramount

Star Trek: Year Five #1 © CBS Studios

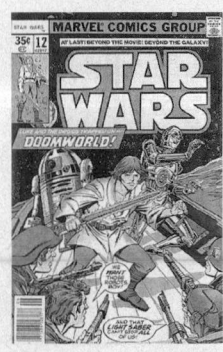

Star Wars #12 © Lucasfilm

	GD 2.0	VG 4.0	FN 6.0	VF 8.0	VF/NM 9.0	NM- 9.2

Marvel Comics (Paramount Comics): July, 1998 ($3.50, one-shot)
1-Riker joins the Maquis 4.00

STAR TREK: THE NEXT GENERATION - SHADOWHEART
DC Comics: Dec, 1994 - No. 4, Mar, 1995 ($1.95, limited series)
1-4 4.00

STAR TREK: THE NEXT GENERATION: TERRA INCOGNITA
IDW Publishing: Jul, 2018 - No. 6, Dec, 2018 ($3.99)
1-6: 1-Shasteen-a; Mirror Universe Barclay app. 4.00

STAR TREK: THE NEXT GENERATION - THE KILLING SHADOWS
DC Comics/WildStorm: Nov, 2000 - No. 4, Feb, 2001 ($2.50, limited series)
1-4-Scott Ciencin-s; Sela app. 3.00

STAR TREK: THE NEXT GENERATION: THE LAST GENERATION
IDW Publishing: Nov, 2008 - No. 5, Mar, 2009 ($3.99, limited series)
1-5-Purcell-a; alternate timeline with Klingon war; Sulu app. 4.00

STAR TREK: THE NEXT GENERATION - THE MODALA IMPERATIVE
DC Comics: Early Sept, 1991 - No. 4, Late Oct, 1991 ($1.75, limited series)
1-4 4.00

STAR TREK: THE NEXT GENERATION: THE SPACE BETWEEN
IDW Publishing: Jan, 2007 - No. 6, June, 2007 ($3.99)
1-6-Single issue stories from various seasons; photo & art covers 4.00

STAR TREK: THE NEXT GENERATION: THROUGH THE MIRROR
IDW Publishing: May, 2018 - No. 5, May, 2018 ($3.99, weekly limited series)
1-5-David & Scott Tipton-s; Mirror Universe crew crosses over 4.00

STAR TREK: THE Q CONFLICT
IDW Publishing: Jan, 2019 - No. 6, Jun, 2019 ($3.99, limited series)
1-6-Crews of Kirk, Picard, Sisko, Janeway vs. Q, Metron, Ayelborne & Trelane; Messina-a 4.00

STAR TREK: THE WRATH OF KHAN
IDW Publishing: Jun, 2009 - No. 3, Jul, 2009 ($3.99, limited series)
1-3-Movie adaptation; Chee Yang Ong-a 4.00

STAR TREK: TNG: HIVE
IDW Publishing: Sept, 2012 - No. 4, Feb, 2013 ($3.99, limited series)
1-4-Brannon Braga-s/Joe Corroney-a; Next Generation crew vs. the Borg 4.00

STAR TREK UNLIMITED
Marvel Comics (Paramount Comics): Nov, 1996 - No. 10, July, 1998 ($2.95/$2.99)
1,2-Stories from original series and Next Generation 5.00
3-10: 3-Begin $2.99-c. 6-"Telepathy War" pt. 4. 7-Q & Trelane swap Kirk & Picard 4.00

STAR TREK UNTOLD VOYAGES
Marvel Comics (Paramount Comics): May, 1998 - No. 5, July, 1998 ($2.50)
1-5-Kirk's crew after the 1st movie 4.00

STAR TREK: VOYAGER
Marvel Comics (Paramount Comics): Nov, 1996 - No. 15, Mar, 1998 ($1.95/$1.99)
1-15: 13-"Telepathy War" pt. 5. 14-Seven of Nine joins crew 4.00

STAR TREK: VOYAGER
DC Comics/WildStorm/IDW: one-shots and trade paperbacks
- Elite Force (7/00, $5.95) The Borg app.; Abnett & Lanning-s 6.00
... Encounters With the Unknown TPB (2001, $19.95) reprints 20.00
- False Colors (1/00, $5.95) Photo-c and Jim Lee-c; Jeff Moy-a 6.00
...: Mirrors and Smoke (IDW, 10/19, $4.99) Mirror Universe Janeway's crew; Woodward-a 5.00

STAR TREK: VOYAGER – SEVEN'S RECKONING
IDW Publishing: Nov, 2020 - No. 4, Feb, 2021 ($3.99, limited series)
1-4-Dave Baker-s/Angel Hernandez-a 4.00

STAR TREK: VOYAGER-- THE PLANET KILLER
DC Comics/WildStorm: Mar, 2001 - No. 3, May, 2001 ($2.95, limited series)
1-3-Voyager vs. the Planet Killer from the ST:TOS episode; Teranishi-a 3.00

STAR TREK: VOYAGER SPLASHDOWN
Marvel Comics (Paramount Comics): Apr, 1998 - No. 4, July, 1998 ($2.50, limited series)
1-4-Voyager crashes on a water planet 4.00

STAR TREK VS. TRANSFORMERS
IDW Publishing: Sept, 2018 - No. 5, Jan, 2019 ($3.99, limited series)
1-5-Crew from Star Trek animated series meets Transformers; multiple covers 4.00

STAR TREK: WAYPOINT
IDW Publishing: Sept, 2016 - No. 6, Jul, 2017 ($4.99/$3.99)
1-($4.99) Short story anthology; future Next Gen Data & Geordi; multiple covers 5.00
2-6-($3.99) 2-Gold Key style story. 3-Voyager & DS9 crews 4.00
... Special 1 (11/18, $7.99) Ezri Dax, Q, Will Decker & Ilia app.; Sonny Liew-a 8.00
... Special 2019 (3/19, $7.99) Short stories by various; Mooney-c 8.00

STAR TREK/ X-MEN
Marvel Comics (Paramount Comics): Dec, 1996 ($4.99, one-shot)
1-Kirk's crew & X-Men; art by Silvestri, Tan, Winn & Finch; Lobdell-s 6.00

STAR TREK/ X-MEN: 2ND CONTACT
Marvel Comics (Paramount Comics): May, 1998 ($4.99, 64 pgs., one-shot)
1-Next Gen. crew & X-Men battle Kang, Sentinels & Borg following First Contact movie 6.00
1-Painted wraparound variant cover 6.00

STAR TREK: YEAR FIVE
IDW Publishing: Apr, 2019 - Present ($3.99)
1-18-Original series crew; multiple covers on each. 7-Intro. Ayal. 10-Lt. Arex app. 17-Origin of Gary Seven & Isis; Woodward painted-a 4.00
...: Valentine's Day Special (2/20, $3.99) Paul Cornell-s/Christopher Jones-a; 3 covers 4.00

STAR TREK: YEAR FOUR (Also see Star Trek: Enterprise Experiment)
IDW Publishing: July, 2007 - No. 5, Nov, 2007 ($3.99, limited series)
1-5: 1-Original series crew; Tischman-s/Conley-a; three covers on each 4.00

STARVE
Image Comics: Jun, 2015 - No. 10, Jun, 2016 ($3.99)
1-10-Brian Wood-s/Danijel Zezelj-a 4.00

STAR WARS (Movie) (See Classic..., Contemporary Motivators, Dark Horse Comics, The Droids, The Ewoks, Marvel Movie Showcase, Marvel Special Ed.)
Marvel Comics Group: July, 1977 - No. 107, Sept, 1986

	GD 2.0	VG 4.0	FN 6.0	VF 8.0	VF/NM 9.0	NM- 9.2
1-(Regular 30¢ edition)-Price in square w/UPC code; #1-6 adapt first movie; first issue on sale before movie debuted	13	26	39	89	195	300
1-(35¢-c; limited distribution - 1500 copies?)- Price in square w/UPC code (Prices vary widely on this book. In 2005 a CGC certified 9.4 sold for $6,500, a CGC certified 9.2 sold for $3,403, and a CGC certified 6.0 sold for $610)	400	800	1200	3400	7950	12,500

NOTE: *The rare 35¢ edition has the cover price in a square box, and the UPC box in the lower left hand corner has the UPC code lines running through it.*

	GD 2.0	VG 4.0	FN 6.0	VF 8.0	VF/NM 9.0	NM- 9.2
1-Reprint; has "reprint" in upper lefthand corner of cover or on inside or price and number inside a diamond with no date or UPC on cover; 30¢ and 35¢ issues published	5	10	15	33	57	80
2-9: Reprints; has "reprint" in upper lefthand corner of cover or on inside or price and number inside a diamond with no date or UPC on cover; 30¢ and 35¢ issues published	1	3	4	6	8	10
2-4-(30¢ issues). 4-Battle with Darth Vader	5	10	15	31	53	75
2-4-(35¢ with UPC code; not reprints)	66	132	198	535	1193	1850
5,6: 5-Begin 35¢-c on all editions. 6-Stevens-a(i)	3	6	9	21	33	45
7-20	2	4	6	11	16	20
21-38,45-67,69,70: 50-Giant	2	4	6	8	10	12
39-41,43,44-The Empire Strikes Back-r by Al Williamson in all	2	4	6	9	12	15
42-Reprints 1st Boba Fett app. in comics	13	26	39	89	195	300
68-Reintro Boba Fett	10	20	30	64	132	200
71-80	2	4	6	8	11	14
81-Boba Fett app.	6	12	18	41	76	110
82-90	2	4	6	9	13	16
91,93-99: 98-Williamson-a	2	4	6	11	16	20
92,100-106: 92,100-($1.00, 52 pgs.)	3	6	9	14	20	26
107 (low dist.); Portacio-a(i)	6	12	18	37	66	95
Annual 1 (12/79, 52 pgs.)-Simonson-c	3	6	9	15	22	28
Annual 2 (11/82, 52 pgs.), 3(12/83, 52 pgs.)	2	4	6	10	14	18

... A Long Time Ago...Vol. 1 TPB (Dark Horse Comics, 6/02, $29.95) r/#1-14 30.00
... A Long Time Ago...Vol. 2 TPB (Dark Horse Comics, 7/02, $29.95) r/#15-28 30.00
... A Long Time Ago...Vol. 3 TPB (Dark Horse Comics, 11/02, $29.95) r/#39-53 30.00
... A Long Time Ago...Vol. 4 TPB (Dark Horse Comics, 1/03, $29.95) r/#54-67 & Ann. 2 30.00
... A Long Time Ago...Vol. 5 TPB (Dark Horse Comics, 3/03, $29.95) r/#68-81 & Ann. 3 30.00
... A Long Time Ago...Vol. 6 TPB (Dark Horse Comics, 5/03, $29.95) r/#82-93 30.00
... A Long Time Ago...Vol. 7 TPB (Dark Horse Comics, 6/03, $29.95) r/#96-107 30.00
... No. 1 Facsimile Edition (2/20, $3.99) Reprints #1 with original 1977 ads 4.00

__Austin__ a-11-15i, 21i, 38; c-12-15i, 21i. __Byrne__ c-13p. __Chaykin__ a-1-10p; c-1. __Golden__ c/a-38. __Miller__ c-47p; pin-up-43. __Nebres__ c/a-Annual 2i. __Portacio__ a-107i. __Sienkiewicz__ c-92i, 98. __Simonson__ a-16p, 49p, 51-63p, 65p, 66p; c-16, 49-51, 52p, 53-62, Annual 1. __Steacy__ painted a-105i, 106i; c-105. __Williamson__ a-39-44p, 50p, 98; c-39, 40, 41-44p. Painted c-81, 87, 92, 95, 98, 100, 105.

STAR WARS (Modern continuation from 1986's Star Wars #107)
Marvel Comics: No. 108, Jul, 2019 ($5.99, one-shot)
108-Valence the Hunter, Jaxon & Amaiza app.; Rosenberg-s; art by various; Simonson-c 6.00

Star Wars (2015 series) #75 © Lucasfilm

Star Wars Adventures #26 © Lucasfilm

Star Wars: Age of Republic Special #1 © Lucasfilm

	GD	VG	FN	VF	VF/NM	NM-
	2.0	4.0	6.0	8.0	9.0	9.2

STAR WARS (Monthly series) (Becomes Star Wars Republic #46-on)
Dark Horse Comics: Dec, 1998 - No. 45, Aug, 2005 ($2.50/$2.95/$2.99)

1-Prelude To Rebellion; Strnad-s 1 2 3 5 6 8
2-6,8,9,11-45: 2-6-Prelude To Rebellion; Strnad-s. 4-Brereton-c. 8-12-Outlander. 13,17-18-($2.95). 13-18-Emissaries to Malastare; Truman-s. 14-16-($2.50) Schultz-c. 19-22-Twilight; Duursema-a. 23-26-Infinity's End. 42-45-Rite of Passage 3.00
5,6 (Holochrome-c variants) 6.00
7-1st app. Aurra Sing; Outlander story arc begins 4 8 12 25 40 55
10-1st A'shared Hett (later becomes Darth Krayt) 5 10 15 30 50 70
#0 Another Universe.com Ed.($10.00) r/serialized pages from Pizzazz Magazine; new Dorman painted-c 12.00
... A Valentine Story (2/03, $3.50) Leia & Han Solo on Hoth; Winick-s/Chadwick-a/c 3.50
...: Rite of Passage (2004, $12.95) r/#42-45 13.00
...: The Stark Hyperspace War (903, $12.95) r/#36-39 13.00

STAR WARS (Monthly series)
Dark Horse Comics: Jan, 2013 - No. 20, Aug, 2014 ($2.99)

1-Takes place after Episode IV; Brian Wood-s/Carlos D'Anda-a/Alex Ross-c 8.00
2-Ross-c 5.00
3-20: 3,4-Ross-c. 5-7-Migliari-c 3.00

STAR WARS
Dark Horse Comics (Free Comic Book Day giveaways)

...: and Captain Midnight (5/13) flip book with new Captain Midnight story & Avatar 3.00
...: Clone Wars #0 (5/09) flip book with short stories of Usagi Yojimbo, Emily the Strange 3.00
...: Clone Wars Adventures (7/04) based on Cartoon Network series; Fillbach Bros. -a 3.00
...: FCBD 2005 Special (5/05) Anakin & Obi-Wan during Clone Wars 3.00
...: FCBD 2006 Special (5/06) Clone Wars story; flip book with Conan FCBD Special 3.00
...: Tales - A Jedi's Weapon (5/02, 16 pgs.) Anakin Skywalker Episode 2 photo-c 3.00
Free Comic Book Day and Star Wars: The Clone Wars (5/11) flip book with Avatar: The Last Airbender 3.00

STAR WARS (Also see Darth Vader and Star Wars: Vader Down)
Marvel Comics: Mar, 2015 - No. 75, Jan, 2020 ($4.99/$3.99)

1-($4.99) Takes place after Episode IV; Aaron-s/Cassaday-a; multiple covers 5.00
2-6-($3.99) Darth Vader app.; Cassaday-a. 4-6-Boba Fett app. 6-Intro Sana Solo 4.00
7-24,26-36: 7-Bianchi-a; Obi-Wan flashback. 8-12-Immonen-a. 13,14-Vader Down pts. 3,5; Deodato-a. 15,20-Obi-Wan flashback; Mayhew-a. 16-19-Yu-a. 26-30-Yoda app. 31,32-Doctor Aphra app. 4.00
25-($4.99) Darth Vader app.; Molina-a; back-up Droids story by Eliopoulos 5.00
37-($4.99) SCAR Squadron app.; back-up Tusken Raiders story; Sorrentino-a 5.00
38-49,51-55-Larroca-a. 45-Wedge app. 55-Leia promoted to General 4.00
50-(9/18, $5.99) Larroca-a; back-up with Camuncoli-a; bonus cover gallery 6.00
56-74: 56,61,62-Broccardo-a. 57-60,63-67-Unzueta-a. 57-Intro Thane Markona & Tula 4.00
75-($4.99) Luke & Chewbacca vs. Vader; Noto-a 5.00
Annual 1 (2/16, $4.99) Gillen-s/Unzueta-a/Cassaday-c; Emperor Palpatine app. 5.00
Annual 2 (1/17, $4.99) Kelly Thompson-s/Emilio Laiso-a; intro. Pash Davane 5.00
Annual 3 (11/17, $4.99) Latour-s/Walsh-a 5.00
Annual 4 (7/18, $4.99) Bunn-s/Anindito, Boschi & Laming-a; Sana Starros app. 5.00
...: Empire Ascendant 1 (2/20, $5.99) Short stories following #75; the Rebels reach Hoth; Beilert Valance app.; leads into events of Empire Strikes Back 6.00
... Saga 1 (2/20, $3.99) Synopsis of the 2015-2020 series; panels and summaries 4.00
... Special: C-3PO 1 (6/16, $4.99) Robinson-s/Harris-a/c; story of C-3PO's red arm 5.00

STAR WARS (Also see Star Wars: Darth Vader 2020 series)
Marvel Comics: Mar, 2020 - Present ($4.99/$3.99)

1-($4.99) Takes place after Empire Strikes Back; Soule-s/Saiz-a; multiple covers 5.00
2-10-($3.99): 2-Jabba the Hutt app. 3,4-Return to Cloud City; Lobot app. 4.00

STAR WARS, THE
Dark Horse Comics: Sept, 2013 - No. 8, May, 2014 ($3.99)

1-8-Adaptation of George Lucas' original rough-draft screenplay; Mayhew-a/Runge-c 4.00
#0-(1/14, $3.99) Design work of characters, settings, vehicles 4.00

STAR WARS ADVENTURES (Anthology of All-ages stories)
IDW Publishing: Sept, 2017 - No. 32, Mar, 2020 ($3.99)

1-32: 2-Charretier-a. 3-Tudyk-s. 5-Porgs app. 10,11-Lando app. 30-Kylo Ren-c 4.00
Annual 2018 (4/18, $7.99) John Jackson Miller-s; Jaxxon app.; Sommariva-c 8.00
Annual 2019 (5/19, $7.99) Lando & Jaxxon app.; Stan Sakai-c 8.00
...: Flight of the Falcon (1/19, $4.99) Moreci-s/Florean-a; Chewbacca app. 5.00
... Free Comic Book Day 2018 (5/18, giveaway) Derek Charm-a/c; Han & Chewie app. 3.00
... Free Comic Book Day 2019 (5/19, giveaway) Derek Charm-a/c; Han & Chewie app. 3.00
... Greatest Hits (12/19, $1.00) Reprints #1; Scott-s/Charm-a; Rey on Jakku 3.00

STAR WARS ADVENTURES (Anthology of All-ages stories)
IDW Publishing: Sept, 2020 - Present ($3.99)

1-3-Francavilla-c. 3-Darth Maul app. 4.00
Annual 2020 (8/20, $5.99) Jaxxon app.; Scott-s/Gaston-a; IG-88 app.;Brokenshire-s/a 6.00

STAR WARS ADVENTURES: DESTROYER DOWN (All-ages stories)
IDW Publishing: Nov, 2018 - No. 3, Jan, 2019 ($3.99, limited series)

1-3: Rey app.; Beatty-s/Charm-a; back-up with Beatty-s/Sommariva-a 4.00

STAR WARS ADVENTURES: RETURN TO VADER'S CASTLE (All-ages stories)
IDW Publishing: Oct, 2019 - No. 5, Oct, 2019 ($3.99, weekly limited series)

1-5-Francavilla-c on all. 1-Darth Maul app. 2-Kelley Jones-a. 5-Darth Vader spotlight 4.00

STAR WARS ADVENTURES: SMUGGLER'S RUN (All-ages stories)
IDW Publishing: Dec, 2020 - No. 2, Jan, 2021 ($5.99, limited series)

1,2-Adaptation of the Greg Rucka novel; Han Solo & Chewbacca app.; Römling-a 6.00

STAR WARS ADVENTURES: TALES FROM VADER'S CASTLE (All-ages stories)
IDW Publishing: Oct, 2018 - No. 5, Oct, 2018 ($3.99, weekly limited series)

1-5-Francavilla-c on all. 2-Count Dooku app.; Kelley Jones-a. 4-Hack-a 4.00

STAR WARS: AGENT OF THE EMPIRE - HARD TARGETS
Dark Horse Comics: Oct, 2012 - No. 5, Feb, 2013 ($2.99, limited series)

1-5: 1-Ostrander-s/Fabbri-a; Boba Fett app. 3.00

STAR WARS: AGENT OF THE EMPIRE - IRON ECLIPSE
Dark Horse Comics: Dec, 2011 - No. 5, Apr, 2012 ($3.50, limited series)

1-5: 1-Ostrander-s/Roux-a; Han Solo & Chewbacca app. 3.50

STAR WARS: AGE OF REBELLION ...
Marvel Comics: Jun, 2019 - Aug, 2019 ($3.99, series of one-shots)

... - Boba Fett 1 (7/19) Pak-s/Laming-a/Dodson-c 4.00
... - Grand Moff Tarkin 1 (6/19) Pak-s/Laming-a/Dodson-c; Princess Leia app. 4.00
... - Han Solo 1 (7/19) Pak-s/Sprouse-a/Dodson-c; Luke and Chewbacca app. 4.00
... - Jabba The Hutt 1 (7/19) Pak-s/Laiso, Boschi & Turini-a/Dodson-c 4.00
... - Lando Calrissian 1 (7/19) Pak-s/Buffagni-a/Dodson-c; Lobot app. 4.00
... - Luke Skywalker 1 (8/19) Pak-s/Sprouse-a/Dodson-c; Vader & The Emperor app. 4.00
... - Princess Leia 1 (6/19) Pak-s/Sprouse-a/Dodson-c; Lando & Chewbacca app. 4.00
... Special 1 (6/19, $4.99) Short stories of Yoda, IG-88, Biggs and Porkins 5.00

STAR WARS: AGE OF REPUBLIC ...
Marvel Comics: Feb, 2019 - Aug, 2019 ($3.99, series of one-shots)

... - Anakin Skywalker 1 (4/19) Houser-s/Smith & Santos-a; Obi-Wan Kenobi app. 4.00
... - Count Dooku 1 (4/19) Houser-s/Luke Ross-a 4.00
... - Darth Maul 1 (2/19) Houser-s/Smith & Santos-a; Darth Sidious app. 4.00
... - Darth Vader 1 (8/19) Greg Pak-s/Ramon Bachs-a 4.00
... - General Grievous 1 (5/19) Houser-s/Luke Ross-a 4.00
... - Jango Fett 1 (3/19) Houser-s/Luke Ross-a; young Boba Fett app. 4.00
... - Obi-Wan Kenobi 1 (3/19) Houser-s/Smith & Santos-a; early days of Anakin's training 4.00
... - Padmé Amidala 1 (5/19) Houser-s/Smith & Santos-a; takes place during Clone Wars 4.00
... - Qui-Gon Jinn 1 (2/19) Houser-s/Cory Smith-a; Yoda app. 4.00
... Special 1 (3/19, $4.99) Short stories of Mace Windu, Asajj Ventress, Jar Jar Binks 5.00

STAR WARS: AGE OF RESISTANCE ... (Each has a bonus character essay)
Marvel Comics: Sept, 2019 - Nov, 2019 ($3.99, series of one-shots)

... - Captain Phasma 1 (9/19) Taylor-s/Kirk-a/Noto-c 4.00
... - Finn 1 (9/19) Taylor-s/Rosanas/Noto-c; FN-2187's custodian days 4.00
... - General Hux 1 (109/19) Taylor-s/Kirk-a/Noto-c; Kylo Ren app. 4.00
... - Kylo Ren 1 (11/19) Taylor-s/Kirk-a/Noto-c 4.00
... - Poe Dameron 1 (10/19) Taylor-s/Rosanas/Noto-c 4.00
... - Rey 1 (9/19) Taylor-s/Rosanas/Noto-c; takes place after Han Solo's death; Leia app. 4.00
... - Rose Tico 1 (11/19) Taylor-s/Rosanas/Noto-c; Paige and Leia app. 4.00
... Special 1 (9/19, $4.99) Short stories of Maz Kanata, Adm. Holdo, BB-8 by various 5.00
... - Supreme Leader Snoke 1 (11/19) Taylor-s/Rosanas/Noto-c; training Kylo Ren 4.00

STAR WARS: A NEW HOPE - THE SPECIAL EDITION
Dark Horse Comics: Jan, 1997 - No. 4, Apr, 1997 ($2.95, limited series)

1-4-Dorman-c 4.00

STAR WARS BECKETT (From Solo: A Star Wars Story movie)
Marvel Comics: Oct, 2018 ($4.99, one-shot)

1-Prelude to Star Wars: Solo Adaptation; Duggan-s; art by Salazar, Laming, Sliney 5.00

STAR WARS: BLOOD TIES - BOBA FETT IS DEAD
Dark Horse Comics: Apr, 2012 - No. 4, Jul, 2012 ($3.50, limited series)

1-4-Scalf painted-a/c 3.50

STAR WARS: BLOOD TIES: JANGO AND BOBA FETT
Dark Horse Comics: Aug, 2010 - No. 4, Nov, 2010 ($3.50, limited series)

1-4-Scalf painted-a/c 3.50

STAR WARS: BOBA FETT
Dark Horse Comics: Dec, 1995 - No. 3, Aug, 1997 ($3.95) (Originally intended as a one-shot)

Star Wars: Bounty Hunters #4 © Lucasfilm

Star Wars: Darth Maul #4 © Lucasfilm

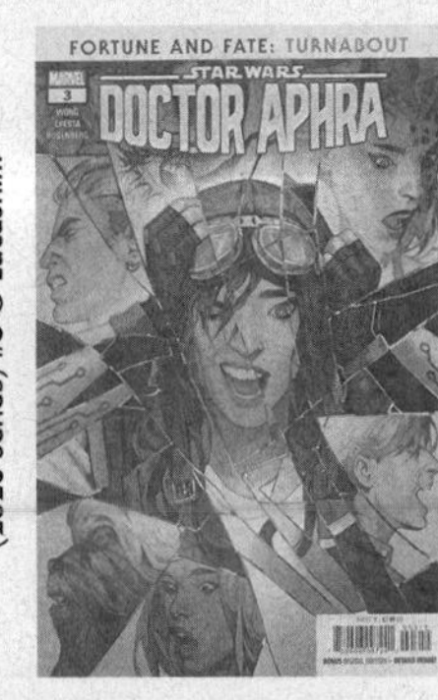

Star Wars: Doctor Aphra (2020 series) #3 © Lucasfilm

	GD 2.0	VG 4.0	FN 6.0	VF 8.0	VF/NM 9.0	NM- 9.2
1-Kennedy-c/a	2	4	6	9	12	15
2,3						5.00
Death, Lies, & Treachery TPB (1/98, $12.95) r/#1-3						13.00
... - Agent of Doom (11/00, $2.99) Ostrander-s/Cam Kennedy-a						3.00
... - Overkill (3/06, $2.99) Hughes-c/Andrews-s/Velasco-a						3.00
Twin Engines of Destruction (1/97, $2.95)						6.00

STAR WARS: BOBA FETT: ENEMY OF THE EMPIRE
Dark Horse Comics: Jan, 1999 - No. 4, Apr, 1999 ($2.95, limited series)

1-4-Recalls 1st meeting of Fett and Vader 4.00

STAR WARS: BOUNTY HUNTERS
Marvel Comics: May, 2020 - Present ($3.99)

1-9-Valance, Bossk, Boba Fett, Doctor Aphra app.; Sacks-s/Villanelli-a 4.00

STAR WARS: CHEWBACCA
Dark Horse Comics: Jan, 2000 - No. 4, Apr, 2000 ($2.95, limited series)

1-4-Macan-s/art by various incl. Anderson, Kordey, Gibbons; Phillips-c 3.00

STAR WARS: CLONE WARS ADVENTURES
Dark Horse Comics: 2004 - No. 10, 2007 ($6.95, digest-sized)

1-10-Short stories inspired by Clone Wars animated series 7.00

STAR WARS: CRIMSON EMPIRE
Dark Horse Comics: Dec, 1997 - No. 6, May, 1998 ($2.95, limited series)

	GD	VG	FN	VF	VF/NM	NM-
1-Richardson-s/Gulacy-a	2	4	6	11	18	20
2-6						5.00

STAR WARS: CRIMSON EMPIRE II: COUNCIL OF BLOOD
Dark Horse Comics: Nov, 1998 - No. 6, Apr, 1999 ($2.95, limited series)

1-Richardson & Stradley-s/Gulacy-a in all 6.00
2-6 4.00

STAR WARS: CRIMSON EMPIRE III: EMPIRE LOST
Dark Horse Comics: Oct, 2011 - No. 6, Apr, 2012 ($3.50, limited series)

1-6: 1-Richardson-s/Gulacy-a/Dorman-c 3.50

STAR WARS: DARK EMPIRE
Dark Horse Comics: Dec, 1991 - No. 6, Oct, 1992 ($2.95, limited series)

	GD	VG	FN	VF	VF/NM	NM-
Preview-(99¢)						4.00
1-All have Dorman painted-c	2	4	6	9	12	15
1-3-2nd printing						4.00
2-Low print run	2	4	6	9	12	15
3						6.00
4-6						4.00
Gold Embossed Set (#1-6)-With gold embossed foil logo (price is for set)						60.00
Platinum Embossed Set (#1-6)						90.00
Trade paperback (4/93, $16.95)						24.00
Dark Empire 1 - TPB 3rd printing (2003, $16.95)						17.00
Ltd. Ed. Hardcover ($99.95) Signed & numbered						100.00

STAR WARS: DARK EMPIRE II
Dark Horse Comics: Dec, 1994 - No. 6, May, 1995 ($2.95, limited series)

	GD	VG	FN	VF	VF/NM	NM-
1-Dave Dorman painted-c	2	4	6	9	12	15
2-6: Dorman-c in all.						4.00
Platinum Embossed Set (#1-6)						35.00
Trade paperback ($17.95)						18.00
TPB Second Edition (9/06, $19.95) r/#1-6 and Star Wars: Empire's End #1,2						20.00

STAR WARS: DARK FORCE RISING
Dark Horse Comics: May, 1997 - No. 6, Oct, 1997 ($2.95, limited series)

1-6 4.00
TPB (2/98, $17.95) r/#1-6 18.00

STAR WARS: DARK TIMES (Continued from Star Wars Republic #83)(Storyline continues in Star Wars: Rebellion #15)
Dark Horse Comics: Oct, 2006 - No. 17, Jun, 2010 ($2.99)

1-17-Nineteen years before Episode IV; Doug Wheatley-a. 11-Celeste Morne awakens 13-17-Blue Harvest 3.00
#0-(7/09, $2.99) Prologue to Blue Harvest 3.00

STAR WARS: DARK TIMES - A SPARK REMAINS
Dark Horse Comics: Jul, 2013 - No. 5, Dec, 2013 ($3.50, limited series)

1-5-Stradley-s/Wheatley-a; Darth Vader app. 3.50

STAR WARS: DARK TIMES - FIRE CARRIER
Dark Horse Comics: Feb, 2013 - No. 5, Jun, 2013 ($2.99, limited series)

1-5-Stradley-s/Guzman-a; Darth Vader app. 3.00

STAR WARS: DARK TIMES - OUT OF THE WILDERNESS
Dark Horse Comics: Aug, 2011 - No. 5, Apr, 2012 ($2.99, limited series)

1-5-Doug Wheatley-a 3.00

STAR WARS: DARTH MAUL
Dark Horse Comics: Sept, 2000 - No. 4, Dec, 2000 ($2.95, limited series)

1-4-Photo-c and Struzan painted-c; takes place 6 months before Ep. 1 3.00

STAR WARS: DARTH MAUL (Issue #1 titled Darth Maul)
Marvel Comics: Apr, 2017 - No. 5, Sept, 2017 ($4.99/$3.99)

1-($4.99) Cullen Bunn-s/Luke Ross-a; back-up by Eliopoulos-s/a 5.00
2-5-($3.99) Aurra Sing & Cad Bane app. 4.00
... Halloween Comic Fest 2017 1 (12/17, giveaway) r/#1 without Eliopoulos back-up 3.00

STAR WARS: DARTH MAUL - DEATH SENTENCE
Dark Horse Comics: Jul, 2012 - No. 4, Oct, 2012 ($2.99, limited series)

1-4-Tom Taylor-s/Bruno Redondo-a/Dave Dorman-c 3.00

STAR WARS: DARTH MAUL - SON OF DATHOMIR
Dark Horse Comics: May, 2014 - No. 4, Aug, 2014 ($3.50, limited series)

1-4-Barlow-s/Frigeri-a/Scalf-c 3.50

STAR WARS: DARTH VADER (Also see Star Wars 2020 series)
Marvel Comics: Apr, 2020 - Present ($4.99/$3.99)

1-($4.99) Takes place after Empire Strikes Back; Pak-s/Ienco-a; multiple covers 5.00
2-10-($3.99) 2-Intro. Sabé 4.00

STAR WARS: DARTH VADER AND THE CRY OF SHADOWS
Dark Horse Comics: Dec, 2013 - No. 5, Apr, 2014 ($3.50, limited series)

1-5-Siedell-s/Guzman-a/Massaferra-c 3.50

STAR WARS: DARTH VADER AND THE GHOST PRISON
Dark Horse Comics: May, 2012 - No. 5, Sept, 2012 ($3.50, limited series)

1-5-Blackman-s/Alessio-a/Wilkins-c. 1-Variant-c by Sanda 3.50

STAR WARS: DARTH VADER AND THE LOST COMMAND
Dark Horse Comics: Jan, 2011 - No. 5, May, 2011 ($3.50, limited series)

1-5-Blackman-s/Leonardi-a/Sanda-c. 1-Variant-c by Wheatley 3.50

STAR WARS: DARTH VADER AND THE NINTH ASSASSIN
Dark Horse Comics: Apr, 2013 - No. 5, Aug, 2013 ($3.50, limited series)

1-5-Siedell-s. 1,2,4-Thompson-a. 3,5-Fernandez-a 3.50

STAR WARS: DAWN OF THE JEDI
Dark Horse Comics: No. 0, Feb, 2012 - Mar, 2014 ($3.50)

0-Guide to the worlds, characters, sites, vehicles; Migliari-c 3.50
... - Force Storm (2/12 - No. 5, 6/12, $3.50) 1-5-Ostrander-s/Duursema-a/c 3.50
... - Force War (11/13 - No. 5, 3/14, $3.50) 1-5-Ostrander-s/Duursema-a/c 3.50
... - Prisoner of Bogan (11/12 - No. 5, 5/13, $2.99) 1-5-Ostrander-s/Duursema-a/c 3.00

STAR WARS: DOCTOR APHRA (See Doctor Aphra for #1-6)(See Darth Vader #3 for debut)
Marvel Comics: No. 7, Jul, 2017 - No. 40, Feb, 2020 ($3.99)

7-24: 7,8-Luke, Han, Leia & Sana app. 12,13-Darth Vader app. 20-24-Sana Starros app. 4.00
25-($4.99) Darth Vader & Sana Starros app. 5.00
26-40: 26-31-Laiso-a. 40-Darth Vader app. 4.00
Annual 1 (10/17, $4.99) Gillen-s/Laming & Sliney-a 5.00
Annual 2 (11/18, $4.99) Spurrier-s/Wijngaard-a 5.00
Annual 3 (12/19, $4.99) Spurrier-s/Charretier-a 5.00

STAR WARS: DOCTOR APHRA (Star Wars)(2nd series)(First issue titled Doctor Aphra)
Marvel Comics: Jun, 2020 - Present ($3.99)

1-7: 1-5-Alyssa Wong-s/Marika Cresta-a. 5-Lady Domina app. 7-Sana Starros app. 4.00

STAR WARS: DROIDS (See Dark Horse Comics #17-19)
Dark Horse Comics: Apr, 1994 - #6, Sept, 1994; V2#1, Apr, 1995 - V2#8, Dec, 1995 ($2.50, limited series)

1-($2.95)-Embossed-c 5.00
2-6, Special 1 (1/95, $2.50), V2#1-8 4.00
Star Wars Omnibus: Droids One TPB (6/08, $24.95) r/#1-6, Special 1, V2#1-8, Star Wars: The Protocol Offensive and "Artoo's Day Out" story from Star Wars Galaxy Magazine #1 25.00

STAR WARS: DROIDS UNPLUGGED
Marvel Comics: Aug, 2017 ($4.99, one-shot)

1-Chris Eliopoulos-s/a; short stories with R2-D2, BB-8 and a probe droid 5.00

STAR WARS: EMPIRE
Dark Horse Comics: Sept, 2002 - No. 40, Feb, 2006 ($2.99)

1-40: 1-Benjamin-a; takes place weeks before SW: A New Hope. 7,28-Boba Fett-c. 14-Vader after the destruction of the Death Star. 15-Death of Biggs; Wheatley-a 3.00
... Volume 1 (2003, $12.95, TPB) r/#1-4 13.00
... Volume 2 (2004, $17.95, TPB) r/#8-12,15 18.00

Star Wars: Empire #35 © Lucasfilm

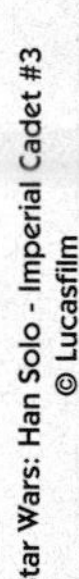

Star Wars: Han Solo - Imperial Cadet #3 © Lucasfilm

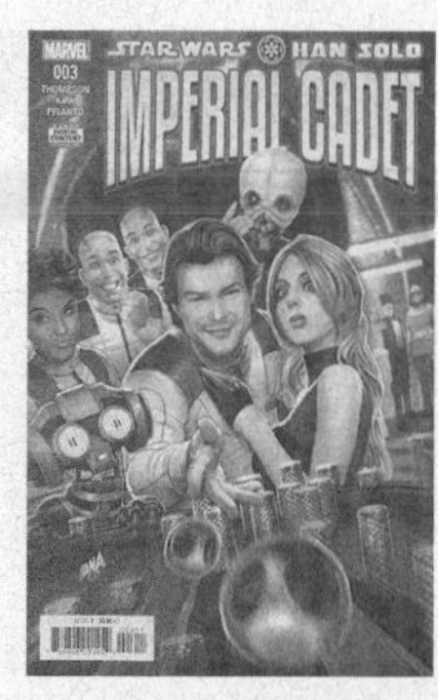

Star Wars: Legacy #16 © Lucasfilm

	GD 2.0	VG 4.0	FN 6.0	VF 8.0	VF/NM 9.0	NM- 9.2

... Volume 3: The Imperial Perspective (2004, $17.95, TPB) r/#13,14,16-19 18.00
... Volume 4: The Heart of the Rebellion (2005, $17.95, TPB) r/#5,6,20-22 & Star Wars: A Valentine Story 18.00
... Volume 5 (2006, $14.95, TPB) r/#23-27 15.00
... Volume 6: In the Shadows of Their Fathers (10/06, $17.95, TPB) r/#29-34 18.00
... Volume 7: The Wrong Side of the War (1/07, $17.95, TPB) r/#34-40 18.00

STAR WARS: EMPIRE'S END
Dark Horse Comics: Oct, 1995 - No. 2, Nov, 1995 ($2.95, limited series)

1,2-Dorman-c 1 3 4 6 8 10

STAR WARS: EPISODE 1 THE PHANTOM MENACE
Dark Horse Comics: May, 1999 - No. 4 ($2.95, movie adaptation)

1-4-Regular and photo-c; Damaggio & Williamson-a 5.00
TPB ($12.95) r/#1-4 13.00
...Anakin Skywalker-Photo-c & Bradstreet-c, ...Obi-Wan Kenobi-Photo-c & Egeland-c, ...Queen Amidala-Photo-c & Bradstreet-c, ...Qui-Gon Jinn-Photo-c & Bradstreet-c 5.00
Gold foil covers; Wizard 1/2 10.00

STAR WARS: EPISODE II - ATTACK OF THE CLONES
Dark Horse Comics: Apr, 2002 - No. 4, May, 2002 ($3.99, movie adaptation)

1-4-Regular and photo-c; Duursema-a 4.00
TPB ($17.95) r/#1-4; Struzan-c 18.00

STAR WARS: EPISODE III - REVENGE OF THE SITH
Dark Horse Comics: May, 2005 - No. 4, May, 2005 ($2.99, movie adaptation)

1-4-Wheatley-a/Dorman-c 3.00
TPB ($12.95) r/#1-4; Dorman-c 13.00

STAR WARS FORCES OF DESTINY (All-ages anthology spotlighting female characters)
IDW Publishing: Jan, 2018 ($3.99, series of one-shots)

... – Ahsoka & Padme - Revis-s/Pinto-a 4.00
... – Hera - Grayson-s/Widermann-a 4.00
... – Leia - Charretier-a; Leia on planet Hoth before the events of Empire 4.00
... – Rey - Houser-s/Florean-a; Rey meets BB-8 on Jakku 4.00
... – Rose & Paige - Dawson-s/Baldari-a; the sisters before the events of The Last Jedi 4.00

STAR WARS: GALAXY'S EDGE
Marvel Comics: Jun, 2019 - No. 5, Oct, 2019 ($3.99, limited series)

1-5: 1-Han Solo & Chewbacca app.; Sacks-s/Sliney-a. 2-Greedo app. 4-Dr. Aphra app. 4.00

STAR WARS: GENERAL GRIEVOUS
Dark Horse Comics: Mar, 2005 - No. 4, June, 2005 ($2.99, limited series)

1-4-Leonardi-a/Dixon-s 3.00
TPB (2005, $12.95) r/#1-4 13.00

STAR WARS HANDBOOK
Dark Horse Comics: July, 1998 - Mar, 2000 ($2.95, one-shots)

... X-Wing Rogue Squadron (7/98)-Guidebook to characters and spacecraft 1 3 4 6 8 10
... Crimson Empire (7/99) Dorman-c 1 3 4 6 8 10
... Dark Empire (3/00) Dorman-c 1 3 4 6 8 10

STAR WARS: HAN SOLO - IMPERIAL CADET
Marvel Comics: Jan, 2019 - No. 5, May, 2019 ($3.99)

1-5-Robbie Thompson-s/Leonard Kirk-a; Han's early days in Imperial Navy; Qi'Ra app. 4.00

STAR WARS: HEIR TO THE EMPIRE (Adaptation of Timothy Zahn novel)
Dark Horse Comics: Oct, 1995 - No. 6, Apr, 1996 ($2.95, limited series)

1-1st app. Grand Admiral Thrawn & Mara Jade 8 16 24 56 108 160
2-2nd app. of Admiral Thrawn 3 6 9 16 23 30
3,5,6 5.00
4-1st cover app. of Mara Jade 3 6 9 16 23 30

STAR WARS: INFINITIES - A NEW HOPE
Dark Horse Comics: May, 2001 - No. 4, Oct, 2001 ($2.99, limited series)

1-4: "What If..." the Death Star wasn't destroyed in Episode 4 3.00
TPB (2002, $12.95) r/ #1-4 13.00

STAR WARS: INFINITIES - THE EMPIRE STRIKES BACK
Dark Horse Comics: July, 2002 - No. 4, Oct, 2002 ($2.99, limited series)

1-4: "What If..." Luke died on the ice planet Hoth; Bachalo-c 3.00
TPB (2/03, $12.95) r/ #1-4 13.00

STAR WARS: INFINITIES - RETURN OF THE JEDI
Dark Horse Comics: Nov, 2003 - No. 4, Mar, 2004 ($2.99, limited series)

1-4:"What If..." ; Benjamin-a 3.00

STAR WARS: INVASION
Dark Horse Comics: July, 2009 - No. 5, Nov, 2009 ($2.99)

1-5-Jo Chen-c 3.00
#0-(10/09, $3.50) Dorman-c; Han Solo and Chewbacca app. 3.50
... - Rescues 1-6 (5/10 - No. 6, 12/10) Chen-c 3.00
... - Revelations 1-5 (7/11 - No. 5, 11/11, $3.50) Luke Skywalker app.; Scalf-c 3.50

STAR WARS: JABBA THE HUTT
Dark Horse Comics: Apr, 1995 ($2.50, one-shots)

nn, ...The Betrayal, ...The Dynasty Trap, ...The Hunger of Princess Nampi 1 3 4 6 8 10

STAR WARS: JANGO FETT - OPEN SEASONS
Dark Horse Comics: Apr, 2002 - No. 4, July, 2002 ($2.99, limited series)

1-4: 1-Bachs & Fernandez-a 3.00

STAR WARS: JEDI
Dark Horse Comics: Feb, 2003 - Jun, 2004 ($4.99, one-shots)

... - Aayla Secura (8/03) Ostrander-s/Duursema-a 2 4 6 11 16 20
... - Count Dooku (11/03) Duursema-a 2 4 6 8 10 12
... - Mace Windu (2/03) Duursema-a; 1st app. Asajj Ventress 10 20 30 64 132 200
... - Shaak Ti (5/03) Ostrander-s/Duursema-a 2 4 6 11 16 20
... - Yoda (6/04) Barlow-s/Hoon-a 3 6 9 21 33 45

STAR WARS: JEDI ACADEMY - LEVIATHAN
Dark Horse Comics: Oct, 1998 - No. 4, Jan, 1999 ($2.95, limited series)

1-1st app. Kyp Durron; Lago-c 3 6 9 16 23 30
2-4-Chadwick-c 5.00

STAR WARS: JEDI COUNCIL: ACTS OF WAR
Dark Horse Comics: Jun, 2000 - No. 4, Sept, 2000 ($2.95, limited series)

1-4-Stradley-s; set one year before Episode 1 3.00

STAR WARS: JEDI FALLEN ORDER – DARK TEMPLE (Based on video game)
Marvel Comics: Nov, 2019 - No. 5, Feb, 2020 ($3.99, limited series)

1-5-Rosenburg-s/Villanelli-a/Checchetto-c 4.00

STAR WARS: JEDI QUEST
Dark Horse Comics: Sept, 2001 - No. 4, Dec, 2001 ($2.99, limited series)

1-4-Anakin's Jedi training; Windham-s/Mhan-a 3.00

STAR WARS: JEDI - THE DARK SIDE
Dark Horse Comics: May, 2011 - No. 5, Sept, 2011 ($2.99, limited series)

1-5: 1-Qui-Gon Jinn 21 years befor Episode 1; Asrar-a 3.00

STAR WARS: JEDI VS. SITH
Dark Horse Comics: Apr, 2001 - No. 6, Sept, 2001 ($2.99, limited series)

1-6: Macan-s/Bachs-a/Robinson-c 3.00

STAR WARS: KNIGHT ERRANT
Dark Horse Comics: Oct, 2010 - No. 5, Feb, 2011 ($2.99)

1-5: 1-John Jackson Miller-s/Federico Dallocchio-a 3.00
... - Deluge 1-5 (8/11 - No. 5 12/11, $3.50) 1-Miller-s/Rodriguez-a/Quinones-c 3.50
... - Escape 1-5 (6/12 - No. 5 10/12, $3.50) 1-Miller-s/Castiello-a/Carré-c 3.50

STAR WARS: KNIGHTS OF THE OLD REPUBLIC
Dark Horse Comics: Jan, 2006 - No. 50, Feb, 2010 ($2.99)

1-8,10-50-Takes place 3,964 years before Episode IV. 1-6-Brian Ching-a/Charest-c 3.00
9-1st full app. of Revan 15 30 45 103 227 350
... Handbook (11/07, $2.99) profiles of characters, ships, locales 3.00
.../Rebellion #0 (3/06, 25¢) flip book preview of both series 3.00
... - War 1-5 (1/12 - No. 5, 5/12, $3.50) J.J. Miller-s/Mutti-a 3.50
... Vol. 1 Commencement TPB (11/06, $18.95) r/#0-6 19.00
... Vol. 2 Flashpoint TPB (5/07, $18.95) r/#17-12 19.00
... Vol. 3 Days of Fear, Nights of Anger TPB (1/08, $18.95) r/#13-18 19.00

STAR WARS: LANDO - DOUBLE OR NOTHING
Marvel Comics: Jul, 2018 - No. 5, Nov, 2018 ($3.99, limited series)

1-5: 1-Barnes-s/Villanelli-a; young Lando & L3-37 before Solo movie 4.00

STAR WARS: LEGACY
Dark Horse Comics: No. 0, June, 2006 - No. 50, Aug, 2010 ($2.99)
Volume 2, Mar, 2013 - No. 18, Aug, 2014 ($2.99)

0-(25¢) Dossier of characters, settings, ships and weapons; Duursema-c 3.00
0 1/2-(1/08, $2.99) Updated dossier of characters, settings, ships, and history 3.00
1-50: 1-Takes place 130 years after Episode IV; Hughes-c/Duursema-a. 4-Duursema-c 7,39-Luke Skywalker on-c. 16-Obi-Wan Kenobi app. 50-Wraparound-c 3.00
...: Broken Vol. 1 TPB (4/07, $17.95) r/#1-3,5,6 18.00
...: One for One (9/10, $1.00) reprints #1 with red cover frame 3.00
... Volume Two 1 (3/13 - No. 18, 8/14, $2.99) 1-18: 1-Bechko-s/Hardman-a/Wilkins-c 3.00

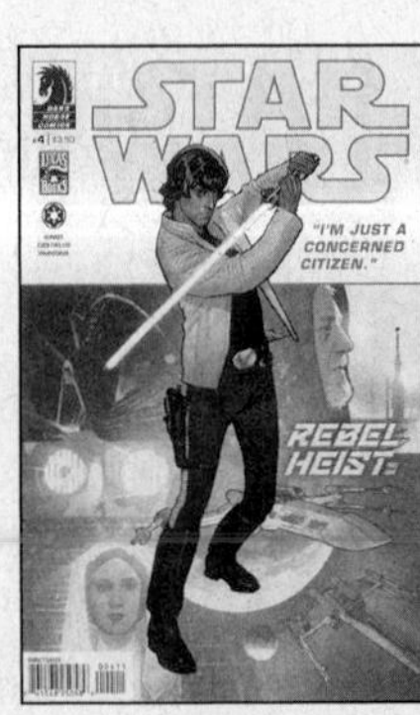

Star Wars: Rebel Heist #4 © Lucasfilm

Star Wars: Shadows of the Empire #4 © Lucasfilm

Star Wars: Tales of the Jedi - Dark Lords of the Sith #6 © Lucasfilm

GD 2.0 | VG 4.0 | FN 6.0 | VF 8.0 | VF/NM 9.0 | NM- 9.2

... War 1-6 (12/10 - No. 6, 5/11, $3.50) 1-Ostrander-s/Duursema-a; Darth Krayt app. 3.50

STAR WARS: LOST TRIBE OF THE SITH - SPIRAL
Dark Horse Comics: Aug, 2012 - No. 5, Dec, 2012 ($2.99, limited series)
1-5-J.J. Miller-s/Mutti-a/Renaud-c 3.00

STAR WARS: MACE WINDU
Marvel Comics: Oct, 2017 - No. 5, Feb, 2018 ($3.99, limited series)
1-5-Matt Owens-s/Denys Cowan-a; follows after the Battle of Geonosis 4.00

STAR WARS: MARA JADE
Dark Horse Comics: Aug, 1998 - No. 6, Jan, 1999 ($2.95, limited series)
1-Ezquerra-a in all 4 6 12 23 37 50
2-6 6.00

STAR WARS: OBSESSION (Clone Wars)
Dark Horse Comics: Nov, 2004 - No. 5, Apr, 2005 ($2.99, limited series)
1-5-Blackman-s/Ching-a/c; Anakin & Obi-Wan 5 months before Episode III 3.00
...: Clone Wars Vol. 7 (2005, $17.95) r/#1-5 and 2005 Free Comic Book Day edition 18.00

STAR WARS: POE DAMERON (Titled Poe Dameron for #1-12)
Marvel Comics: No. 13, Jun, 2017 - No. 31, Nov, 2018 ($3.99)
13-31: 13-Soule-s/Noto-a. 14-22-Unzueta-a. 20-25-Lor San Tekka app. 26-28-Recounts events from Episode VII & VIII 4.00
Annual 1 (8/17, $4.99) Thompson-s/Virella-a; General Organa app. 5.00
Annual 2 (10/18, $4.99) Houser-s/Broccardo-a; Leia, Han Solo & Chewbacca app. 5.00

STAR WARS: PURGE
Dark Horse Comics: Dec, 2005 ($2.99, one-shot)
nn-Vader vs. remaining Jedi one month after Episode III; Hughes-c/Wheatley-a 5.00
... - Seconds To Die (11/09, $3.50) Vader app.; Charest-c/Ostrander-s 3.50
... - The Hidden Blade (4/10, $3.50) Vader app.; Scalf-c/a; Blackman-s 3.50
... - The Tyrant's Fist 1,2 (12/12 - No, 2, 1/13, $3.50) Vader app.; Freed-s/Dan Scott-c 3.50

STAR WARS: QUI-GON & OBI-WAN - LAST STAND ON ORD MANTELL
Dark Horse Comics: Dec, 2000 - No. 3, Mar, 2001 ($2.99, limited series)
1-3: 1-Three covers (photo, Tony Daniel, Bachs) Windham-s 3.00

STAR WARS: QUI-GON & OBI-WAN - THE AURORIENT EXPRESS
Dark Horse Comics: Feb, 2002 - No. 2, Mar, 2002 ($2.99, limited series)
1,2-Six years prior to Phantom Menace; Marangon-a 3.00

STAR WARS: REBEL HEIST
Dark Horse Comics: Apr, 2014 - No. 4, Jul, 2014 ($3.50)
1-4-Kindt-s/Castiello-a; two covers by Kindt and Adam Hughes on each 3.50

STAR WARS: REBELLION (Also see Star Wars: Knights of the Old Republic flip book)
Dark Horse Comics: Apr, 2006 - No. 16, Aug, 2008 ($2.99)
1-16-Takes place 9 months after Episode IV; Luke Skywalker app. 1-Badeaux-a/c 3.00
Vol. 1 TPB (2/07, $14.95) r/#0 (flip book) & #1-5 15.00

STAR WARS: REPUBLIC (Formerly Star Wars monthly series)
Dark Horse Comics: No. 46, Sept, 2002 - No. 83, Feb, 2006 ($2.99)
46-83-Events of the Clone Wars 3.00
...: Clone Wars Vol. 1 (2003, $14.95) r/#46-50 15.00
...: Clone Wars Vol. 2 (2003, $14.95) r/#51-53 & Star Wars: Jedi - Shaak Ti 15.00
...: Clone Wars Vol. 3 (2004, $14.95) r/#55-59 15.00
...: Clone Wars Vol. 4 (2004, $16.95) r/#54, 63 & Star Wars: Jedi - Aayla Secura & Dooku 17.00
...: Clone Wars Vol. 5 (2004, $17.95) r/#60-62, 64 & Star Wars: Jedi - Yoda 18.00
...: Clone Wars Vol. 6 (2005, $17.95) r/#65-71 18.00
(Clone Wars Vol. 7 - see Star Wars: Obsession)
...: Clone Wars Vol. 8 (2006, $17.95) r/#72-78 18.00
...: Clone Wars Vol. 9 (2006, $17.95) r/#79-83 & Star Wars: Purge 18.00
...: Honor and Duty TPB (5/06, $12.95) r/#46-48,78 13.00

STAR WARS: RETURN OF THE JEDI (Movie)
Marvel Comics Group: Oct, 1983 - No. 4, Jan, 1984 (limited series)
1-Williamson-p in all; r/Marvel Super Special #27 2 4 6 11 16 20
2-4-Continues r/Marvel Super Special #27 2 4 6 9 12 15
Oversized issue (1983, $2.95, 10-3/4x8-1/4", 68 pgs., cardboard-c)-r/#1-4 2 4 6 10 13 16

STAR WARS: RIVER OF CHAOS
Dark Horse Comics: June, 1995 - No. 4, Sept, 1995 ($2.95, limited series)
1-4: Louise Simonson scripts 4.00

STAR WARS: ROGUE ONE ADAPTATION
Marvel Comics: Jun, 2017 - No. 6, Nov, 2017 ($4.99/$3.99, limited series)
1-($4.99) Houser-s/Laiso & Bazaldua-a; Noto-c; afterword by director Gareth Edwards 5.00
2-6-($3.99) 3-Villanelli-a. 4-6-Laiso-a 4.00

Star Wars: Rogue One - Cassian & K2-SO Special 1 (10/17, $4.99) Swierczynski-s 5.00

STAR WARS: SHADOWS OF THE EMPIRE
Dark Horse Comics: May, 1996 - No. 6, Oct, 1996 ($2.95, limited series)
1-6: Story details events between The Empire Strikes Back & Return of the Jedi; Russell-a(i). 5.00

STAR WARS: SHADOWS OF THE EMPIRE - EVOLUTION
Dark Horse Comics: Feb, 1998 - No. 5, June, 1998 ($2.95, limited series)
1-5: Perry-s/Fegredo-c. 4.00

STAR WARS: SHADOW STALKER
Dark Horse Comics: Sept, 1997 ($2.95, one-shot)
nn-Windham-a. 4.00

STAR WARS: SOLO ADAPTATION (See Solo: A Star Wars Story Adaptation)

STAR WARS: SPLINTER OF THE MIND'S EYE
Dark Horse Comics: Dec, 1995 - No. 4, June, 1996 ($2.50, limited series)
1-4: Adaption of Alan Dean Foster novel 4.00

STAR WARS: STARFIGHTER
Dark Horse Comics: Jan, 2002 - No. 3, March, 2002 ($2.99, limited series)
1-3-Williams & Gray-c 3.00

STAR WARS: TAG & BINK ARE DEAD
Dark Horse Comics: Oct, 2001 - No. 2, Nov, 2001($2.99, limited series)
1,2-Rubio-s 3.00
Star Wars: Tag & Bink Were Here TPB (11/06, $14.95) r/both SW: Tag & Bink series 15.00
Star Wars: Tag & Bink Were Here (Marvel, 7/18, $7.99) r/both SW: Tag & Bink series 8.00

STAR WARS: TAG & BINK II
Dark Horse Comics: Mar, 2006 - No. 2, Apr, 2006($2.99, limited series)
1-Tag & Bink invade Return of the Jedi; Rubio-s. 2-Tag & Bink as Jedi younglings during Ep II 3.00

STAR WARS TALES
Dark Horse Comics: Sept, 1999 - No. 24, Jun, 2005 ($4.95/$5.95/$5.99, anthology)
1-4-Short stories by various 6.00
5-24 ($5.95/$5.99-c) Art and photo-c on each 6.00
Volume 1-6 ($19.95) 1-(1/02) r/#1-4. 2-('02) r/#5-8. 3-(1/03) r/#9-12. 4-(1/04) r/#13-16 5-(1/05) r/#17-20; introduction pages from #1-20. 6-(1/06) r/#21-24 20.00

STAR WARS: TALES FROM MOS EISLEY
Dark Horse Comics: Mar, 1996 ($2.95, one-shot)
nn-Bret Blevins-a. 4.00

STAR WARS: TALES OF THE JEDI (See Dark Horse Comics #7)
Dark Horse Comics: Oct, 1993 - No. 5, Feb, 1994 ($2.50, limited series)
1-5: All have Dave Dorman painted-c. 3-r/Dark Horse Comics #7-9 w/new coloring & some panels redrawn 5.00
1-5-Gold foil embossed logo; limited # printed-7500 (set) 50.00
Star Wars Omnibus: Tales of the Jedi Volume One TPB (11/07, $24.95) r/#1-5, ... - The Golden Age of the Sith #0-5 and ... - The Fall of the Sith Empire #1-5 25.00

STAR WARS: TALES OF THE JEDI-DARK LORDS OF THE SITH
Dark Horse Comics: Oct, 1994 - No. 6, Mar, 1995 ($2.50, limited series)
1-6: 1-Polybagged w/trading card 1 2 3 5 6 8

STAR WARS: TALES OF THE JEDI-REDEMPTION
Dark Horse Comics: July, 1998 - No. 5, Nov, 1998 ($2.95, limited series)
1-5: 1-Kevin J. Anderson-s/Kordey-c 1 3 4 6 8 10

STAR WARS: TALES OF THE JEDI-THE FALL OF THE SITH EMPIRE
Dark Horse Comics: June, 1997 - No. 5, Oct, 1997 ($2.95, limited series)
1-5 5.00

STAR WARS: TALES OF THE JEDI-THE FREEDON NADD UPRISING
Dark Horse Comics: Aug, 1994 - No. 2, Nov, 1994 ($2.50, limited series)
1,2 1 3 4 6 8 10

STAR WARS: TALES OF THE JEDI-THE GOLDEN AGE OF THE SITH
Dark Horse Comics: July, 1996 - No. 5, Feb, 1997 (99¢/$2.95, limited series)
0-(99¢)-Anderson-s 5.00
1-5-Anderson-s 1 2 3 5 6 8

STAR WARS: TALES OF THE JEDI-THE SITH WAR
Dark Horse Comics: Aug, 1995 - No. 6, Jan, 1996 ($2.50, limited series)
1-6: Anderson scripts 4.00

STAR WARS: TARGET VADER
Marvel Comics: Sept, 2019 - No. 6, Feb, 2020 ($3.99, limited series)

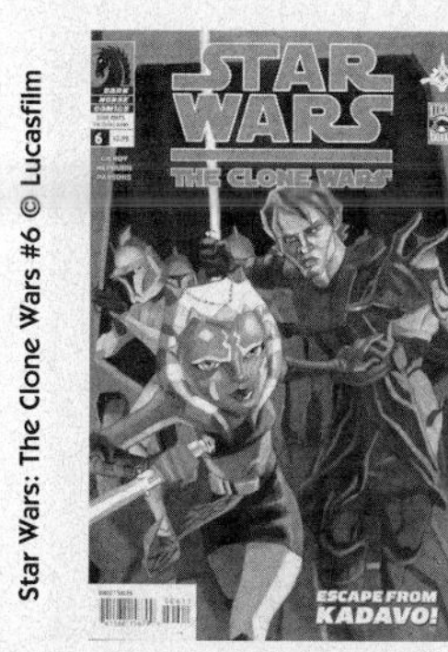

Star Wars: The Clone Wars #6 © Lucasfilm

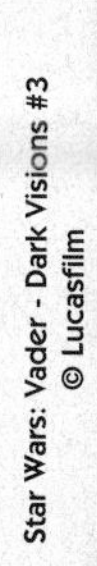
Star Wars: Vader - Dark Visions #3 © Lucasfilm

Static Shock: Rebirth of the Cool #1 © Milestone Media

	GD 2.0	VG 4.0	FN 6.0	VF 8.0	VF/NM 9.0	NM- 9.2

1-6-Robbie Thompson-s; Valance app. 4.00

STAR WARS: THE BOUNTY HUNTERS
Dark Horse Comics: July, 1999 - Oct, 1999 ($2.95, one-shots)

...Aurra Sing (7/99), ...Kenix Kil (10/99), ...Scoundrel's Wages (8/99) Lando Calrissian app. 4.00

STAR WARS: THE CLONE WARS (Based on the Cartoon Network series)
Dark Horse Comics: Sept, 2008 - No. 12, Jan, 2010 ($2.99)

	GD	VG	FN	VF	VF/NM	NM-
1-1st comic app. of Ahsoka Tano	28	56	84	202	451	700
2-Gilroy-s/Hepburn-a/Filoni-c	4	8	12	23	37	50
3,4-Gilroy-s/Hepburn-a/Filoni-c	3	6	9	14	20	25
5-12: 5,6-Gilroy-s/Hepburn-a/Filoni-c	2	4	6	9	12	15

STAR WARS: THE FORCE AWAKENS ADAPTATION (Episode VII movie)
Marvel Comics: Aug, 2016 - No. 6, Jan, 2017 ($4.99, limited series)

1-6: 1-Chuck Wendig-s/Luke Ross-a/Esad Ribic-c. 3-Marc Laming-a 5.00

STAR WARS: THE FORCE UNLEASHED (Based on the LucasArts video game)
Dark Horse Comics: Aug, 2008 ($15.95, one-shot graphic novel)

GN-Intro. Starkiller, Vader's apprentice; takes place 2 years before Battle of Yavin 16.00

STAR WARS: THE HIGH REPUBLIC (Takes place before Phantom Menace)
Marvel Comics: Mar, 2021 - Present ($3.99)

1,2: 1-Cavan Scott-s/Ario Anindito-a; intro Keeve Trennis; Yoda app. 4.00

STAR WARS: THE HIGH REPUBLIC ADVENTURES (Takes place before Phantom Menace)
IDW Publishing: Feb, 2021 - Present ($3.99)

1-Older-s/Talibao-a 4.00

STAR WARS: THE JABBA TAPE
Dark Horse Comics: Dec, 1998 ($2.95, one-shot)

nn-Wagner-s/Plunkett-a 4.00

STAR WARS: THE LAST COMMAND
Dark Horse Comics: Nov, 1997 - No. 6, July, 1998 ($2.95, limited series)

1-6: Based on the Timothy Zaun novel 4.00

STAR WARS: THE LAST JEDI ADAPTATION
Marvel Comics: Jul, 2018 - No. 6, Nov, 2018 ($4.99/$3.99, limited series)

1,6-($4.99) Whitta-s/Walsh-a. 1-Del Mundo-c 5.00
2-5-($3.99) 2-Shirahama-c. 3-Noto-c. 4-Rahzzah-c. 5-Rivera-c 4.00

STAR WARS: THE LAST JEDI - DJ - MOST WANTED
Marvel Comics: Mar, 2018 ($4.99, one-shot)

1-Acker & Blacker-s/Walker-a 5.00

STAR WARS: THE OLD REPUBLIC (Based on the video game)
Dark Horse Comics: July, 2010 - No. 6, Dec, 2010 ($2.99, limited series)

1-3 (Threat of Peace)-Chestny-s/Sanchez-a. 1-Two covers 3.00
4-6 (Blood of the Empire)-Freed-s/Dave Ross-a 3.00

STAR WARS: THE OLD REPUBLIC - THE LOST SUNS (Based on the video game)
Dark Horse Comics: Jun, 2011 - No. 5, Oct, 2011 ($3.50, limited series)

1-5-Freed-s/Carré-c/Freeman-a 3.50

STAR WARS: THE PROTOCOL OFFENSIVE
Dark Horse Comics: Sept, 1997 ($4.95, one-shot)

nn-Anthony Daniels & Ryder Windham-s 5.00

STAR WARS: THE RISE OF KYLO REN
Marvel Comics: Feb, 2020 - No. 4, May, 2020 ($4.99/$3.99, limited series)

1-($4.99)-Soule-s/Sliney-a; Ben Solo after the burning of the temple 5.00
2-4-($3.99) 2-Young Ben meets the Knights of Ren; Snoke app. 4.00

STAR WARS: THRAWN
Marvel Comics: Apr, 2018 - No. 6, Sept, 2018 ($3.99, limited series)

1-6-Houser-s/Luke Ross-a; Thrawn's intro to the Empire; Palpatine app. 4.00

STAR WARS: TIE FIGHTER (Tie-in to Alphabet Squadron novel)
Marvel Comics: Jun, 2019 - No. 5, Oct, 2019 ($3.99, limited series)

1-5-Houser-s/Antonio-a; spotlight on Shadow Wing squad 4.00

STAR WARS: UNDERWORLD - THE YAVIN VASSILIKA
Dark Horse Comics: Dec, 2000 - No. 5, June, 2001 ($2.99, limited series)

1-5-(Photo and Robinson covers) 3.00

STAR WARS: UNION
Dark Horse Comics: Nov, 1999 - No. 4, Feb, 2000 ($2.95, limited series)

1-4-Wedding of Luke and Mara Jade; Teranishi-a/Stackpole-s 4.00

STAR WARS: VADER – DARK VISIONS
Marvel Comics: May, 2019 - No. 5, Aug, 2019 ($4.99/$3.99, limited series)

1-($4.99)-Hallum-s/Villanelli-a/Smallwood-c 5.00
2-5-($3.99)-Hallum-s/Smallwood-c. 2-Level-a. 3-David Lopez-a. 4-Mooney-a. 5-Borges-a 4.00

STAR WARS: VADER DOWN
Marvel Comics: Jan, 2016 ($4.99, one-shot)

1-Part 1 of x-over with Star Wars (2015) #13,14 and Darth Vader #13-15; Deodato-a 5.00

STAR WARS: VADER'S QUEST
Dark Horse Comics: Feb, 1999 - No. 4, May, 1999 ($2.95, limited series)

1-4-Follows destruction of 1st Death Star; Gibbons-a 4.00

STAR WARS: VISIONARIES
Dark Horse Comics: Apr, 2005 ($17.95, TPB)

nn-Short stories from the concept artists for Revenge of the Sith movie 18.00

STAR WARS: X-WING ROGUE SQUADRON (Star Wars: X-Wing Rogue Squadron-The Phantom Affair #5-8 appears on cover only)
Dark Horse Comics: July, 1995 - No. 35, Nov, 1998 ($2.95)

1/2 8.00
1-24,26-35: 1-4-Baron scripts. 5-20-Stackpole scripts 4.00
25-($3.95) 5.00
The Phantom Affair TPB ($12.95) r/#5-8 13.00

STAR WARS: X-WING ROGUE SQUADRON: ROGUE LEADER
Dark Horse Comics: Sept, 2005 - No. 3, Nov, 2005 ($2.99)

1-3-Takes place one week after the Batttle of Endor 3.00

STATIC (See Charlton Action: Featuring "Static")

STATIC (See Heroes)
DC Comics (Milestone): June, 1993 - No. 45, Mar, 1997 ($1.50/$1.75/$2.50)

1-($2.95)-Collector's Edition; polybagged w/poster & trading card & backing board (direct sales only) 6.00
1-Platinum Edition with red background cover 12.00
1-Intro. Virgil Hawkins 6.00
2-13,15-24,26-45: 2-Origin. 8-Shadow War; Simonson silver ink-c. 27-Kent Williams-c 3.00
14-($2.50, 52 pgs.)-Worlds Collide Pt. 14 4.00
25 ($3.95) 4.00
...: Trial by Fire (2000, $9.95) r/#1-4; Leon-c 10.00

STATIC SHOCK (DC New 52)
DC Comics: Nov, 2011 - No. 8, Jun, 2012 ($2.99)

1-8: 1-McDaniel & Rozum-s/McDaniel-a/c. 6-Hardware & Technique app. 8-Origin retold 3.00

STATIC SHOCK!: REBIRTH OF THE COOL (TV)
DC Comics: Jan, 2001 - No. 4, Sept, 2001 ($2.50, limited series)

1-4: McDuffie-s/Leon-c/a 3.00

STATIC SHOCK SPECIAL
DC Comics: Aug, 2011 ($2.99, one-shot)

1-Cowan-a/Williams III-c; pin-ups by various; tribute to Dwayne McDuffie 3.00

STATIC-X
Chaos! Comics: Aug, 2002 ($5.99)

1-Polybagged with music CD; metal band as super-heroes; Pulido-s 6.00

STEALTH (Pilot Season: ...)
Image Comics (Top Cow): May, 2010; Mar, 2020 - No. 6, Oct, 2020 ($2.99/$3.99)

1-(5/10) Kirkman-s/Mitchell-a/Silvestri-c 3.00
1-6: 1-(3/20, $3.99) Costa-s/Bellegarde-a 4.00

STEAM MAN, THE
Dark Horse Comics: Oct, 2015 - No. 5, Feb, 2016 ($3.99)

1-5-Kowalski-a; Steam robot and crew in 1899 4.00

STEAMPUNK
DC/WildStorm (Cliffhanger): Apr, 2000 - No. 12, Aug, 2002 ($2.50/$3.50)

Catechism (1/00) Prologue -Kelly-s/Bachalo-a 3.00
1-4,6-11: 4-Four covers by Bachalo, Madureira, Ramos, Campbell 3.00
5,12-($3.50) 4.00
...: Drama Obscura ('03, $14.95) r/#6-12 15.00
...: Manimatron ('01, $14.95) r/#1-5, Catechism, Idiosincratica 15.00

STEAMPUNK BATTLESTAR GALACTICA 1880 (See Battlestar Galactica 1880)

STEED AND MRS. PEEL (TV)(Also see The Avengers)
Eclipse Books/ ACME Press: 1990 - No. 3, 1991 ($4.95, limited series)

Books One - Three: Grant Morrison scripts/Ian Gibson-a 5.00
1-6: 1-(BOOM! Studios, 1/12 - No. 6, 6/12, $3.99) r/Books One - Three 4.00

STEED AND MRS. PEEL (TV)(The Avengers)
BOOM! Studios: No. 0, Aug, 2012 - No. 11, Jul, 2013 ($3.99)

Steel #48 © DC

Steve Rogers: Super-Soldier #4 © MAR

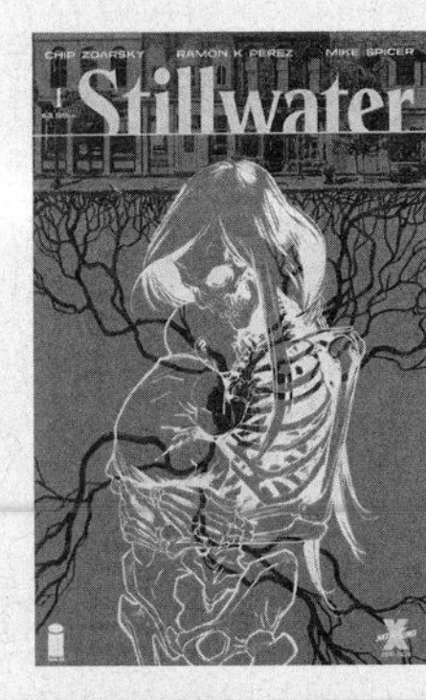

Stillwater #1 © Skybound

	GD	VG	FN	VF	VF/NM	NM-
	2.0	4.0	6.0	8.0	9.0	9.2

GD VG FN VF VF/NM NM-
2.0 4.0 6.0 8.0 9.0 9.2

0-11: 0-Mark Waid-s/Steve Bryant-a; eight covers. 1-3-Sliney-a; five covers 4.00

STEED AND MRS. PEEL: WE'RE NEEDED (TV)(The Avengers)
BOOM! Studios: Jul, 2014 - No. 3, Sept, 2014 ($3.99)(Issue #1 says "1 of 6")

1-3-Edginton-s/Cosentino-a. 1-Two covers 4.00

STEEL (Also see JLA)
DC Comics: Feb, 1994 - No. 52, July, 1998 ($1.50/$1.95/$2.50)

1-8,0,9-52: 1-From Reign of the Supermen storyline. 6,7-Worlds Collide Pt. 5 &12. 8-(9/94). 0-(10/94). 9-(11/94). 46-Superboy-c/app. 50-Millennium Giants x-over 3.00
1-(3/11, $2.99, one-shot) Benes-a/Garner-c; Reign of Doomsday x-over 4.00
Annual 1 (1994, $2.95)-Elseworlds story 4.00
Annual 2 (1995, $3.95)-Year One story 4.00
...Forging of a Hero TPB (1997, $19.95) reprints early app. 20.00

STEEL: THE OFFICIAL COMIC ADAPTATION OF THE WARNER BROS. MOTION PICTURE
DC Comics: 1997 ($4.95, Prestige format, one-shot)

nn-Adaptation of the Shaquille O'Neal movie; Bogdanove & Giordano-a 5.00

STEEL CAGE (Also see Penultiman)
AHOY Comics: 2019 ($3.99)

1-Series try-outs for Bright Boy, Noah Zark and Penultiman; Elsa Charretier-c 4.00

STEELGRIP STARKEY
Marvel Comics (Epic): June, 1986 - No. 6, July, 1987 ($1.50, lim. series, Baxter paper)

1-6 3.00

STEEL STERLING (Formerly Shield-Steel Sterling; see Blue Ribbon, Jackpot, Mighty Comics, Mighty Crusaders, Roly Poly & Zip Comics)
Archie Enterprises, Inc.: No. 4, Jan, 1984 - No. 7, July, 1984

4-7: 4-6-Kanigher-s; Barreto-a. 5,6-Infantino-a. 6-McWilliams-a 5.00

STEEL, THE INDESTRUCTIBLE MAN (See All-Star Squadron #8 and J.L. of A. Annual #2)
DC Comics: Mar, 1978 - No. 5, Oct-Nov, 1978

	GD	VG	FN	VF	VF/NM	NM-
1	3	6	9	15	22	28
2-5: 5-44 pgs.	1	2	3	4	6	8

STEELTOWN ROCKERS
Marvel Comics: Apr, 1990 - No. 6, Sept, 1990 ($1.00, limited series)

1-6: Small town teens form rock band 3.00

STEEPLE
Dark Horse Comics: Sept, 2019 - No. 5, Jan, 2020 ($3.99, limited series)

1-5-John Allison-s/a/c; variant-c for each by various 4.00

STELLAR
Image Comics (Skybound): Jun, 2018 - No. 6, Nov, 2018 ($3.99, limited series)

1-6-Joseph Keatinge-s/Bret Blevins-a 4.00

STEPHEN COLBERT'S TEK JANSEN (From the animated shorts on The Colbert Report)
Oni Press: July, 2007 - No. 5, Jan, 2009 ($3.99, limited series)

1-Chantier-a/Layman & Peyer-s; back-up story by Massey-s/Rodriguez-a; Chantier-c 4.00
1-Variant-c by John Cassaday 6.00
1-Second printing with flip book of Cassaday & Chantier covers 4.00
2-5: 2-(6/08) Flip book with covers by Rodriguez & Wagner. 3-Flip-c by Darwyn Cooke 4.00

STEPHEN KING'S N. THE COMIC SERIES
Marvel Comics: May, 2010 - No. 4, Aug, 2010 ($3.99, limited series)

1-4-Guggenheim-s/Maleev-a/c 4.00

STEVE AUSTIN (See Stone Cold Steve Austin)

STEVE CANYON (See Harvey Comics Hits #52)
Dell Publishing Co.: No. 519, 11/53 - No. No. 1033, 9/59 (All Milton Caniff-a except #519, 939, 1033)

	GD	VG	FN	VF	VF/NM	NM-
Four Color 519 (1, 1953)	8	16	24	56	108	160
Four Color 578 (8/54), 641 (7/55), 737 (10/56), 804 (5/57), 939 (10/58), 1033 (9/59) (photo-c)	5	10	15	35	63	90

STEVE CANYON
Grosset & Dunlap: 1959 (6-3/4x9", 96 pgs., B&W, no text, hardcover)

	GD	VG	FN	VF	VF/NM	NM-
100100-Reprints 2 stories from strip (1953, 1957)	6	12	18	31	38	45
100100 (softcover edition)	5	10	15	24	30	35

STEVE CANYON COMICS
Harvey Publ.: Feb, 1948 - No. 6, Dec, 1948 (Strip reprints, No. 4,5: 52pgs.)

	GD	VG	FN	VF	VF/NM	NM-
1-Origin; has biography of Milton Caniff; Powell-a, 2 pgs.; Caniff-a	20	40	60	120	195	270
2-Caniff, Powell-a in #2-6	14	28	42	80	115	150
3-6: 6-Intro Madame Lynx-c/story	14	28	42	76	108	140

STEVE CANYON IN 3-D
Kitchen Sink Press: June, 1986 ($2.25, one-shot)

1-Contains unpublished story from 1954 5.00

STEVE DITKO'S STRANGE AVENGING TALES
Fantagraphics Books: Feb, 1997 ($2.95, B&W)

1-Ditko-c/s/a 5.00

STEVE DONOVAN, WESTERN MARSHAL (TV)
Dell Publishing Co.: No. 675, Feb, 1956 - No. 880, Feb, 1958 (All photo-c)

	GD	VG	FN	VF	VF/NM	NM-
Four Color 675-Kinstler-a	7	14	21	48	89	130
Four Color 768-Kinstler-a	6	12	18	38	69	100
Four Color 880	5	10	15	31	53	75

STEVEN UNIVERSE (TV)
BOOM! Studios (kaBOOM): Aug, 2014 - No. 8, Mar, 2015 ($3.99)

1-8: 1-Four covers; Uncle Grandpa preview. 2-8-Three covers 4.00
...: Anti-Gravity OGN (11/17, $14.99, 9" x 6") Perper-s/Chan & Ayoub-a 15.00
...: Greg Universe Special 1 (4/15, $4.99) Short stories by various; two covers 5.00
...: 2016 Special 1 (12/16, $7.99) Short donut-themed stories by various; two covers 8.00

STEVEN UNIVERSE (Ongoing)(TV)
BOOM! Studios (kaBOOM): Feb, 2017 - No. 36, Jan, 2020 ($3.99)

1-24,26-36: 1-Four covers; Lapis & Peridot app. 19-Sugilite app. 4.00
25-($4.99) Captain Lars and his crew vs. Emerald 5.00
...: Fusion Frenzy 1 (3/19, $7.99) Short stories by various; 3 covers 8.00

STEVEN UNIVERSE AND THE CRYSTAL GEMS (TV)
BOOM! Studios (kaBOOM): Mar, 2016 - No. 4, Jun, 2016 ($3.99)

1-4-Fenton-s/Garland-a; multiple covers on each. 1-Preview of Over the Garden Wall 4.00

STEVEN UNIVERSE: HARMONY (TV)
BOOM! Studios (kaBOOM): Aug, 2018 - No. 5, Dec, 2018 ($3.99, 8" x 8" square size)

1-5-S.M. Vidaurri-s/Mollie Rose-a; Aquamarine, Topaz & Sugilite app. 4.00

STEVE ROGERS: SUPER-SOLDIER (Captain America - The Heroic Age)
Marvel Comics: Sept, 2010 - No. 4, Dec, 2010 ($3.99, limited series)

1-4-Brubaker-s/Eaglesham-a/Pacheco-c. 1-Back-up rep. of origin from CA #1 ('41) 4.00
Annual 1 (6/11, $3.99) Continued from Uncanny X-Men Annual #3; Roberson-a 4.00

STEVE ROPER
Famous Funnies: Apr, 1948 - No. 5, Dec, 1948

	GD	VG	FN	VF	VF/NM	NM-
1-Contains 1944 daily newspaper-r	14	28	42	78	112	145
2	9	18	27	52	69	85
3-5	8	16	24	42	54	65

STEVE SAUNDERS SPECIAL AGENT (See Special Agent)

STEVE SAVAGE (See Captain...)

STEVE ZODIAC & THE FIRE BALL XL-5 (TV)
Gold Key: Jan, 1964

	GD	VG	FN	VF	VF/NM	NM-
10108-401 (#1)	8	16	24	56	108	160

STEVIE (Mazie's boy friend)(Also see Flat-Top, Mazie & Mortie)
Mazie (Magazine Publ.): Nov, 1952 - No. 6, Apr, 1954

	GD	VG	FN	VF	VF/NM	NM-
1-Teenage humor; Stevie, Mortie & Mazie begin	14	28	42	80	115	150
2-6	9	18	27	47	61	75

STEVIE MAZIE'S BOY FRIEND (See Harvey Hits #5)

STEWART THE RAT (See Eclipse Graphic Album Series)

ST. GEORGE (See listing under Saint...)

STIG'S INFERNO
Vortex/Eclipse: 1985 - No. 7, Mar, 1987 ($1.95, B&W)

1-7 ($1.95) 3.00
Graphic Album (1988, $6.95, B&W, 100 pgs.) 7.00

STILLWATER
Image Comics (Skybound): Sept, 2020 - Present ($3.99)

1-6-Chip Zdarsky-s/Ramón Perez-a 4.00

STING OF THE GREEN HORNET (See The Green Hornet)
Now Comics: June, 1992 - No. 4, 1992 ($2.50, limited series)

1-4: Butler-c/a 3.00
1-4 ($2.75)-Collectors Ed.; polybagged w/poster 4.00

STOKER'S DRACULA (Reprints unfinished Dracula story from 1974-75 with new ending)
Marvel Comics: 2004 - No. 4, May, 2005 ($3.99, B&W)

1-4: 1-Reprints from Dracula Lives! #5-8; Roy Thomas-s/Dick Giordano-a. 2-R/#10,11 & Legion of Monsters #1. 3,4-New story/artwork to finish story. 4-Giordano afterword 4.00

Stone #1 © Haberlin & Portacio

Storm (2014 series) #1 © MAR

StormWatch #20 © WSP

	GD 2.0	VG 4.0	FN 6.0	VF 8.0	VF/NM 9.0	NM- 9.2

HC (2005, $24.99) r/#1-4; foreward by Thomas; Giordano afterword; bonus art & covers 25.00

STONE
Avalon Studios: Aug, 1998 - No. 4, Apr, 1999 ($2.50, limited series)

1-4-Portacio-a/Haberlin-s 3.00
1-Alternate-c 5.00
2-($14.95) DF Stonechrome Edition 15.00

STONE (Volume 2)
Avalon Studios: Aug, 1999 - No. 4, May, 2000 ($2.50)

1-4-Portacio-a/Haberlin-s 3.00
1-Chrome-c 5.00

STONE COLD STEVE AUSTIN (WWF Wrestling)
Chaos! Comics: Oct, 1999 - No. 4, Feb, 2000 ($2.95)

1-4-Reg. & photo-c; Steven Grant-s 4.00
1-Premium Ed. ($10.00) 10.00
Preview ($5.00) 5.00

STONE PROTECTORS
Harvey Pubications: May, 1994 - No. 3, Sept, 1994

nn (1993, giveaway)(limited distribution, scarce) 6.00
1-3-Ace Novelty action figures 4.00

STONEY BURKE (TV Western)
Dell Publishing Co.: June-Aug, 1963 - No. 2, Sept-Nov, 1963

1,2-Jack Lord photo-c on both 3 6 9 16 24 32

STONY CRAIG
Pentagon Publishing Co.: 1946 (No #)

nn-Reprints Bell Syndicate's "Sgt. Stony Craig" newspaper strips; story of the Japanese soldier who wouldn't surrender 12 24 36 67 94 120

STORIES BY FAMOUS AUTHORS ILLUSTRATED (Fast Fiction #1-5)
Seaboard Publ./Famous Authors Ill.: No. 6, Aug, 1950 - No. 13, Mar, 1951

1-Scarlet Pimpernel-Baroness Orczy 27 54 81 160 263 365
2-Capt. Blood-Raphael Sabatini 26 52 78 154 252 350
3-She, by Haggard 30 60 90 177 289 400
4-The 39 Steps-John Buchan 18 36 54 107 169 230
5-Beau Geste-P. C. Wren 18 36 54 107 169 230
NOTE: *The above five issues are exact reprints of Fast Fiction #1-5 except for the title change and new Kiefer covers on #1 and 2. Kiefer c(r)-3-5. The above 5 issues were released before Famous Authors #6.*
6-Macbeth, by Shakespeare; Kiefer art (8/50); used in **SOTI**, pg. 22,143; Kiefer-c; 36 pgs. 24 48 72 142 234 325
7-The Window; Kiefer-c/a; 52 pgs. 18 36 54 107 169 230
8-Hamlet, by Shakespeare; Kiefer-c/a; 36 pgs. 21 42 63 126 206 285
9,10: 9-Nicholas Nickleby, by Dickens; G. Schrotter-a; 52 pgs. 10-Romeo & Juliet, by Shakespeare; Kiefer-c/a; 36 pgs. 18 36 54 107 169 230
11-13: 11-Ben-Hur; Schrotter-a; 52 pgs. 12-La Svengali; Schrotter-a; 36 pgs. 13-Scaramouche; Kiefer-c/a; 36 pgs. 18 36 54 103 162 220
NOTE: *Artwork was prepared/advertised for #14, The Red Badge Of Courage. Gilberton bought out Famous Authors, Ltd. and used that story as C.I. #98. Famous Authors, Ltd. then published the Classics Junior series. The Famous Authors titles were published as part of the regular Classics Ill. Series in Brazil starting in 1952.*

STORIES FROM THE TWILIGHT ZONE
Skylark Pub: Mar, 1979, 68 pgs. (B&W comic digest, 5-1/4x7-5/8")

15405-2: Pfevfer-a, 56 pgs, new comics 3 6 9 17 26 35

STORIES OF ROMANCE (Formerly Meet Miss Bliss)
Atlas Comics (LMC): No. 5, Mar, 1956 - No. 13, Aug, 1957

5-Baker-a? 20 40 60 114 182 250
6-10,12,13 14 28 42 80 115 150
11-Baker, Romita-a; Colletta-c/a 20 40 60 114 182 250
NOTE: ***Ann Brewster** a-13. **Colletta** a-9(2), 11; c-5, 11.*

STORM (X-Men)
Marvel Comics: Feb, 1996 - No. 4, May, 1996 ($2.95, limited series)

1-4-Foil-c; Dodson-a(p); Ellis-s: 2-4-Callisto app. 4.00

STORM (X-Men)
Marvel Comics: Apr, 2006 - No. 6, Sept, 2006 ($2.99, limited series)

1-6: Ororo and T'Challa meet as teens; Eric Jerome Dickey-s 3.00
HC (2007, $19.99, dustjacket) r/#1-6 20.00
SC (2008, $14.99) r/#1-6 15.00

STORM (X-Men)
Marvel Comics: Sept, 2014 - No. 11, Jul, 2015 ($3.99)

1-11: 1-Greg Pak-s/Victor Ibañez-a. 9-Gambit app. 4.00

STORMBREAKER: THE SAGA OF BETA RAY BILL (Also see Thor)
Marvel Comics: Mar, 2005 - No. 6, Aug, 2005 ($2.99, limited series)

1-6-Oeming & Berman-s/DiVito-a; Galactus app. 6-Spider-Man app. 3.00
TPB (2006, $16.99) r/#1-6 17.00

STORMING PARADISE
DC Comics (WildStorm): Sept, 2008 - No. 6, Aug, 2009 ($2.99, limited series)

1-6-WWII invasion of Japan; Dixon-s/Guice-a/c 3.00
TPB (2009, $19.99) r/#1-6 20.00

STORM SHADOW (G.I. Joe character)
Devil's Due Publishing: May, 2007 - No. 7, Nov, 2007 ($3.50)

1-7-Larry Hama-s 3.50

STORMWATCH (Also see The Authority)
Image Comics (WildStorm Prod.): May, 1993 - No. 50, Jul, 1997 ($1.95/$2.50)

1-8,0,9-36: 1-Intro StormWatch (Battalion, Diva, Winter, Fuji, & Hellstrike); 1st app. Weatherman; Jim Lee-c & part scripts; Lee plots in all. 1-Gold edition.1-3-Includes coupon for limited edition StormWatch trading card #00 by Lee. 3-1st brief app. Backlash. 0-($2.50)-Polybagged w/card; 1st full app. Backlash. 9-(4/94, $2.50)-Intro Defile. 10-(6/94),11,12-Both (8/94). 13,14-(9/94). 15-(10/94). 21-Reads #1 on-c. 22-Direct Market; Wildstorm Rising Pt. 9, bound-in card. 23-Spartan joins team. 25-(6/94, June 1995 on-c, $2.50). 35-Fire From Heaven Pt. 5. 36-Fire From Heaven Pt. 12 3.00
10-Alternate Portacio-c, see Deathblow #5 3.00
22-($1.95)-Newsstand, Wildstorm Rising Pt. 9 3.00
37-(7/96, $3.50, 38 pgs.)-Weatherman forms new team; 1st app. Jenny Sparks, Jack Hawksmoor & Rose Tattoo; Warren Ellis scripts begin; Justice League #1-c/swipe 4.00
38-49: 44-Three covers. 3.00
50-($4.50) 4.50
Special 1 ,2(1/94, 5/95, $3.50, 52 pgs.) 4.00
Sourcebook 1 (1/94, $2.50) 3.00

STORMWATCH (Also see The Authority)
Image Comics (WildStorm): Oct, 1997 - No. 11, Sept, 1998 ($2.50)

1-Ellis-s/Jimenez-a(p); two covers by Bennett 3.00
1-($3.50)-Voyager Pack bagged w/Gen 13 preview 4.00
2-11: 4-1st app. Midnighter and Apollo. 7,8-Freefall app. 9-Gen13 & DV8 app. 3.00
A Finer World ('99, $14.95, TPB) r/V2 #4-9 15.00
Change or Die ('99, $14.95, TPB) r/V1 #48-50 & V2 #1-3 15.00
Final Orbit ('01, $9.95, TPB) r/V2 #10,11 & WildC.A.T.S./Aliens; Hitch-c 10.00

STORMWATCH (DC New 52)
DC Comics: Nov, 2011 - No. 30, Jun, 2014 ($2.99)

1-Cornell-s/Sepulveda-a; Martian Manhunter app.; blue bkgrd cover 4.00
1-(2nd printing, cover has red bkgrd), 2-8: 7,8-Jenkins-s. 12-Martian Manhunter leaves 3.00
13-30: 13,14-Etrigan returns. 18-Team re-booted; Starlin-s/c. 20-Lobo origin 3.00
#0-(11/12, $2.99) Flashback to Demon Knights; Milligan-s/Conrad-a 3.00

STORMWATCH: P.H.D. (Post Human Division)
DC Comics (WildStorm): Jan, 2007 - No. 24, Jan, 2010 ($2.99)

1-24: 1-Two covers by Mahnke & Hairsine; Gage-s/Mahnke-a. 2-Var-c by Dell'Otto 3.00
...: Armageddon 1 (2/08, $2.99) Gage-s/Fernández-a/McKone-c 3.00
TPB (2007, $17.99) r/#1-4,6,7 & story from Worldstorm #1 18.00
... Book Two TPB (2008, $17.99) r/#5,8-12; sketch pages and concept art 18.00
... Book Three TPB (2009, $17.99) r/#13-19 18.00

STORMWATCH: TEAM ACHILLES
DC Comics (WildStorm): Sept, 2002 - No. 23, Aug, 2004 ($2.95)

1-8: 1-Two covers by Portacio; Portacio-a/Wright-s. 5,6-The Authority app. 3.00
9-23: 9-Back-up preview of The Authority: High Stakes pt. 1 3.00
TPB (2003, $14.95) r/Wizard Preview and #1-6; Portacio art pages 15.00
Book 2 (2004, $14.95) r/#7-11 & short story from Eye of the Storm Annual 15.00

STORMY (Disney) (Movie)
Dell Publishing Co.: No. 537, Feb, 1954

Four Color 537 (...the Thoroughbred)-on top 2/3 of each page; Pluto story on bottom 1/3 5 10 15 34 60 85

STORY OF JESUS (See Classics Illustrated Special Issue)

STORY OF MANKIND, THE (Movie)
Dell Publishing Co.: No. 851, Jan, 1958

Four Color 851-Vincent Price/Hedy Lamarr photo-c 7 14 21 48 89 130

STORY OF MARTHA WAYNE, THE
Argo Publ.: April, 1956

1-Newspaper strip-r 7 14 21 35 43 50

STORY OF RUTH, THE
Dell Publishing Co.: No. 1144, Nov-Jan, 1961 (Movie)

Four Color 1144-Photo-c 9 18 27 57 111 165

Straight Arrow #9 © ME

Strange Academy #1 © MAR

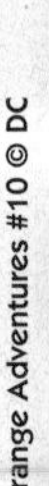
Strange Adventures #10 © DC

GD VG FN VF VF/NM NM-
2.0 4.0 6.0 8.0 9.0 9.2

STORY OF THE COMMANDOS, THE (Combined Operations)
Long Island Independent: 1943 (15¢, B&W, 68 pgs.) (Distr. by Gilberton)
nn-All text (no comics); photos & illustrations; ad for Classic Comics on back cover (Rare) 47 94 141 296 498 700

STORY OF THE GLOOMY BUNNY, THE (See March of Comics #9)

STORYTELLER, THE: FAIRIES (Jim Henson's)
BOOM! Studios (Archaia): Dec, 2017 - No. 4, Mar, 2018 ($3.99, limited series)
1-4: 1-Matt Smith-s/a. 2-Benjamin Schipper-s/a. 3-Tyler Jenkins-s/a. 4-Celia Lowenthal-s/a 4.00

STORYTELLER, THE: GIANTS (Also see Jim Henson's The Storyteller)
BOOM! Studios (Archaia): Dec, 2016 - No. 4, Mar, 2017 ($3.99, limited series)
1-4: 1-Conor Nolan-s/a. 2-Brandon Dayton-s/a. 3-Jared Cullum-s/a. 4-Feifei Ruan-s/a 4.00

STORYTELLER, THE: SIRENS (Jim Henson's)
BOOM! Studios (Archaia): Apr, 2019 - No. 4 ($3.99, limited series)
1-4: 1-Rebelka-a. 2-Chan Chau-s/a. 3-Sarah Webb-s/a. 4-Aud Koch-s/a 4.00

STRAIGHT ARROW (Radio)(See Best of the West & Great Western)
Magazine Enterprises: Feb-Mar, 1950 - No. 55, Mar, 1956 (All 36 pgs.)
1-Straight Arrow (alias Steve Adams) & his palomino Fury begin; 1st mention of Sundown Valley & the Secret Cave 47 94 141 296 498 700
2-Red Hawk begins (1st app?) by Powell (origin), ends #55 24 48 72 140 230 320
3-Frazetta-c 41 82 123 256 428 600
4,5: 4-Secret Cave-c 21 42 63 126 206 285
6-10 17 34 51 100 158 215
11-Classic story "The Valley of Time", with an ancient civilization made of gold 23 46 69 136 223 310
12-19 14 28 42 82 121 160
20-Origin Straight Arrow's Shield 16 32 48 92 144 195
21-Origin Fury 19 38 57 109 172 235
22-Frazetta-c 34 68 102 204 332 460
23,25-30: 25-Secret Cave-c. 28-Red Hawk meets The Vikings 11 22 33 62 86 110
24-Classic story "The Dragons of Doom!" with prehistoric pteradactyls 15 30 45 84 127 170
31-38: 36-Red Hawk drug story by Powell 10 20 30 54 72 90
39-Classic story "The Canyon Beast", with a dinosaur egg hatching a Tyranosaurus Rex 14 28 42 76 108 140
40-Classic story "Secret of The Spanish Specters", with Conquistadors' lost treasure 11 22 33 64 90 115
41,42,44-54: 45-Secret Cave-c 9 18 27 50 65 80
43-Intro & 1st app. Blaze, S. Arrow's Warrior dog 10 20 30 58 79 100
55-Last issue 11 22 33 62 86 110
NOTE: ***Fred Meagher** a 1-55; c-1, 2, 4-21, 23-55. **Powell** a 2-55. **Whitney** a-1. Many issues advertise the radio premiums associated with Straight Arrow.*

STRAIGHT ARROW'S FURY (Also see A-1 Comics)
Magazine Enterprises: No. 119, 1954 (one-shot)
A-1 119-Origin; Fred Meagher-c/a 16 32 48 98 154 210

STRAIN, THE (Adaptation of novels by Guillermo del Toro and Chuck Hogan)
Dark Horse Comics: Dec, 2011 - No. 11, Feb, 2013 ($1.00/$3.50)
1-($1.00) Lapham, Hogan & del Toro-s/Huddleston-a/c; variant-c by Morris 3.50
2-11-($3.50) Lapham-s/Huddleston-a/c 3.50

STRAIN, THE: MISTER QUINLAN - VAMPIRE HUNTER
Dark Horse Comics: Sept, 2016 - No. 5 ($3.99)
1-5: 1-Lapham, Hogan & del Toro-s/Salazar-a; origin of Mister Quinlan in ancient Rome 4.00

STRAIN, THE: THE FALL (Guillermo del Toro and Chuck Hogan)
Dark Horse Comics: Jul, 2013 - No. 9, Mar, 2014 ($3.99)
1-9-Lapham, Hogan & del Toro-s/Huddleston-a/Gist-c 4.00

STRAIN, THE: THE NIGHT ETERNAL (Guillermo del Toro and Chuck Hogan)
Dark Horse Comics: Aug, 2014 - No. 12, Aug, 2015 ($3.99)
1-12-Lapham, Hogan & del Toro-s/Huddleston-a/Gist-c 4.00

STRANGE (Tales You'll Never Forget)
Ajax-Farrell Publ. (Four Star Comic Corp.): March, 1957 - No. 6, May, 1958
1 29 58 87 172 281 390
2-Censored r/Haunted Thrills 16 32 48 96 151 205
3-6 14 28 42 82 121 160

STRANGE (Dr. Strange)
Marvel Comics (Marvel Knghts): Nov, 2004 - No. 6, July, 2005 ($3.50)
1-6-Straczynski & Barnes-s/Peterson-a; Dr. Strange's origin retold 3.50
...: Beginnings and Endings TPB (2006, $17.99) r/#1-6 18.00

STRANGE (Dr. Strange)
Marvel Comics: Jan, 2010 - No. 4, Apr, 2010 ($3.99, limited series)
1-4-Waid-s/Rios-a/Coker-c 4.00

STRANGE ACADEMY
Marvel Comics: May, 2020 - Present ($4.99/$3.99)
1-($4.99) Skottie Young-s/Humberto Ramos-a; Dr. Strange, Doctor Voodoo, Loki app. 6 12 18 38 69 100
2-($3.99) Ancient One, Man-Thing app. 4 8 12 23 37 50
3-7 4.00

STRANGE ADVENTURE MAGAZINE
CJH Publications: Dec, 1936 (10¢)
1-Flash Gordon, The Master of Mars, text stories w/some full pg. panels of art by Fred Meagher (a FN+ copy sold for $1075 in 2012)

STRANGE ADVENTURES
DC Comics: July/Aug 1950
nn - Ashcan comic, not distributed to newsstands, only for in-house use. Cover art is All Star Comics #47 with interior being Detective Comics #140. A second example has the interior of Detective Comics #146. A third example has an unidentified issue of Detective Comics as the interior. This is the only ashcan with multiple interiors. A FN+ copy sold for $1,000 in 2007.

STRANGE ADVENTURES
National Periodical Publ.: Aug-Sept, 1950 - No. 244, Oct-Nov, 1973 (No. 1-12: 52 pgs.)
1-Adaptation of "Destination Moon"; preview of movie w/photo-c from movie (also see Fawcett Movie Comic #2); adapt. of Edmond Hamilton's "Chris KL-99" in #1-3; Darwin Jones begins 181 362 543 1493 3372 5250
2 80 160 240 644 1447 2250
3,4 57 114 171 456 1028 1600
5-8,10: 7-Origin Kris KL-99 46 92 138 359 805 1250
9-(6/51)-Origin/1st app. Captain Comet (c/story) 111 222 333 888 1994 3100
11-20: 12,13,17,18-Toth-a. 14-Robot-c 32 64 96 230 515 800
21-30: 28-Atomic explosion panel. 30-Robot-c 30 60 90 216 483 750
31,34-38 27 54 81 196 441 685
32,33-Krigstein-a 29 58 87 202 451 700
39-Ill. in **SOTI** "Treating police contemptuously" (top right) 35 70 105 252 564 875
40-49-Last Capt. Comet; not in 45,47,48 27 54 81 191 426 660
50-53-Last precode issue (2/55) 23 46 69 161 356 550
54-70 19 38 57 131 291 450
71-79,81-99 15 30 45 103 227 350
80-Grey-tone-c 26 52 78 182 404 625
100 17 34 51 119 265 410
101-110: 104-Space Museum begins by Sekowsky 12 24 36 81 176 270
111-116,118,119: 114-Star Hawkins begins, ends #185; Heath-a in Wood E.C. style 12 24 36 79 170 260
117-(6/60)-Origin/1st app. Atomic Knights. 46 92 138 364 820 1275
120-2nd app. Atomic Knights 21 42 63 147 324 500
121,122,125,127,128,130,131,133,134: 134-Last 10¢ issue 10 20 30 69 147 225
123,126-3rd & 4th app. Atomic Knights 13 26 39 89 195 300
124-Intro/origin Faceless Creature 15 30 45 105 233 360
129,132,135,138,141,147-Atomic Knights app. 11 22 33 76 163 250
136,137,139,140,143,145,146,148,149,151,152,154,155,157-159: 136-Robot cover. 159-Star Rovers app.; Gil Kane/Anderson-a. 9 18 27 59 117 175
142-2nd app. Faceless Creature 10 20 30 68 144 220
144-Only Atomic Knights-c (by M. Anderson) 13 26 39 91 201 310
150,153,156,160: Atomic Knights in each. 150-Greytone-c. 153-(6/63)-3rd app. Faceless Creature; atomic explosion-c. 160-Last Atomic Knights 10 20 30 66 138 210
161-179: 161-Last Space Museum. 163-Star Rovers app. 170-Infinity-c. 177-Intro/origin Immortal Man 7 14 21 46 86 125
180-Origin/1st app. Animal Man 57 114 171 456 1028 1600
181-183,185,186,188,189 6 12 18 37 66 95
184-2nd app. Animal Man by Gil Kane 11 22 33 72 154 235
187-Intro/origin The Enchantress 35 70 105 252 564 875
190-1st app. Animal Man in costume 14 28 42 94 207 320
191-194,196-200,202-204 5 10 15 34 60 85
195-1st full app. Animal Man 8 16 24 55 105 155
201-Last Animal Man; 2nd full app. 6 12 18 41 76 110
205-(10/67)-Intro/origin Deadman by Infantino & begin series, ends #216 57 114 171 456 1028 1600
206-Neal Adams-a begins 13 26 39 91 201 310
207-210 10 20 30 64 132 200

Strange Adventures (2020 series) #6 © DC

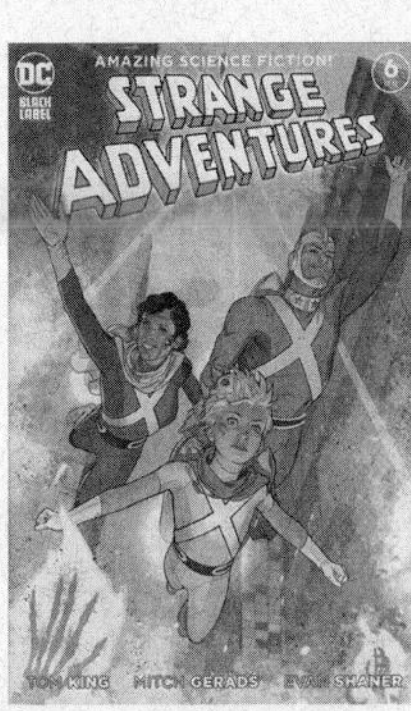

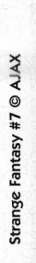

Strange Fantasy #7 © AJAX

Strange Mysteries #5 © SUPR

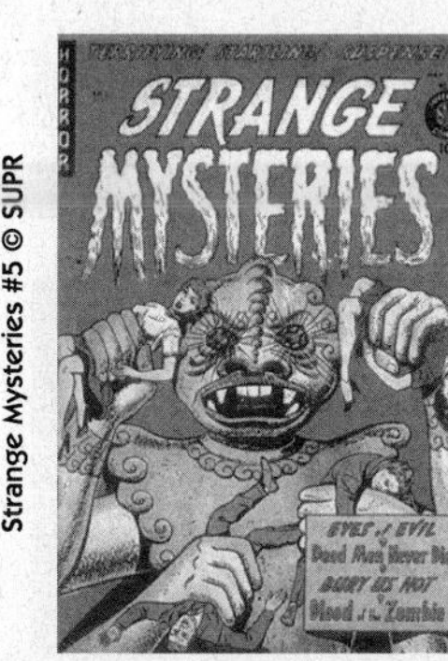

	GD	VG	FN	VF	VF/NM	NM-
	2.0	4.0	6.0	8.0	9.0	9.2

211-216: 211-Space Museum-r. 215-1st app. League of Assassins. 216-(1-2/69)-Deadman story finally concludes in Brave & the Bold #86 (10-11/69); secret message panel by Neal Adams (pg. 13); tribute to Steranko 9 18 27 58 114 170
217-r/origin & 1st app. Adam Strange from Showcase #17, begin-r; Atomic Knights-r begin 3 6 9 18 28 38
218-221,223-225: 218-Last 12¢ issue. 225-Last 15¢ issue 3 6 9 14 20 26
222-New Adam Strange story; Kane/Anderson-a 3 6 9 21 33 45
226,227,230-236-(68-52 pgs.): 226, 227-New Adam Strange text story w/illos by Anderson (8,6 pgs.) 231-Last Atomic Knights-r. 235-JLA-c/s 3 6 9 14 20 26
228,229 (68 pgs.) 3 6 9 16 24 32
237-243 2 4 6 10 14 18
244-Last issue 2 4 6 11 16 20

NOTE: ***Neal Adams*** *a-206-216; c-207-218, 228, 235.* ***Anderson*** *a-8-52, 94, 96, 99, 115, 117, 119-163, 217r, 218r, 222, 223-225r, 226, 229r, 242i(r); c-18, 19, 21, 23, 24, 27, 30, 32-44(most); c/r-157i, 190i, 217-224, 228-231, 233, 235-239, 241-243.* ***Ditko*** *a-188, 189.* ***Drucker*** *a-42, 43, 45.* ***Elias*** *a-212.* ***Finlay*** *a-2, 3, 6, 7, 210r, 229r.* ***Giunta*** *a-237r.* ***Heath*** *a-116.* ***Infantino*** *a-10-101, 106-151, 154, 157-163, 180, 190, 218-221r, 223-244p(r); c-50; c(r)-190p, 197, 199-211, 218-221, 223-244.* ***Kaluta*** *c-238, 240.* ***Gil Kane*** *a-8-116, 124, 125, 130, 138, 146-157, 173-186, 204r, 222r, 227-231r; c(p)-11-17, 25, 154, 157.* ***Kubert*** *a-55(2 pgs.), 226; c-219, 220, 225-227, 232, 234.* ***Moreira*** *c-26, 28, 29, 71.* ***Morrow*** *c-230.* ***Mortimer*** *c-8.* ***Powell*** *a-4.* ***Sekowsky*** *a-71p, 97-162p, 217p(r), 218p(r); c-206, 217-219r.* ***Simon & Kirby*** *a-2r (2 pgs)* ***Sparling*** *a-201.* ***Toth*** *a-8, 12, 13, 17-19.* ***Wood*** *a-154i. Atomic Knights in #117, 120, 123, 126, 129, 132, 135, 138, 141, 144, 147, 150, 153, 156, 160. Atomic Knights reprints by* ***Anderson*** *in 217-221, 223-231. Chris KL99 in 1-3, 5, 7, 9, 11, 15. Capt. Comet covers-9-14, 17-19, 24, 26, 27, 32-44.*

STRANGE ADVENTURES
DC Comics (Vertigo): Nov, 1999 - No. 4, Feb, 2000 ($2.50, limited series)

1-4: 1-Bolland-c; art by Bolland, Gibbons, Quitely 3.00

STRANGE ADVENTURES
DC Comics: May, 2009 - No. 8, Dec, 2009 ($3.99, limited series)

1-8: 1-Starlin-s in all; Adam Strange, Capt. Comet, Bizarro & Prince Gavyn app. 4.00
TPB (2010, $19.99) r/#1-8; cover gallery 20.00

STRANGE ADVENTURES
DC Comics (Vertigo): Jul, 2011 ($7.99, one-shot)

1-Short story anthology; s/a by Azzarello, Risso, Milligan and others; Paul Pope-c 8.00

STRANGE ADVENTURES
DC Comics (Black Label): May, 2020 - No. 12 ($4.99, limited series)

1-8-Adam Strange's book tour; Tom King-s/Mitch Gerads & Evan Shaner-a; 2 covers on each. 2-8-Mister Terrific & Batman app. in most 5.00
1-Director's Cut (1/21, $5.99) Original script with black & white art 6.00

STRANGE AS IT SEEMS (See Famous Funnies-A Carnival of Comics, Feature Funnies #1, The John Hix Scrap Book & Peanuts)

STRANGE AS IT SEEMS
United Features Syndicate: 1939

Single Series 9, 1, 2 39 78 117 240 395 550

STRANGE CEREBUS (Reprints from Cerebus in Hell)
Aardvark-Vanaheim: Oct, 2017 ($4.00, B&W)

1-Cerebus figures placed over original Doré artwork of Hell; Dr. Strange #180-c swipe 4.00

STRANGE COMBAT TALES
Marvel Comics (Epic Comics): Oct, 1993 - No. 4, Jan, 1994 ($2.50, limited series)

1-4 3.00

STRANGE CONFESSIONS
Ziff-Davis Publ. Co.: Jan-Mar (Spring on-c), 1952 - No. 4, Fall, 1952 (All have photo-c)

1(Scarce)-Kinstler-a 84 168 252 538 919 1300
2(Scarce, 7-8/52) 54 108 162 343 574 825
3(Scarce, 9-10/52)-#3 on-c, #2 on inside; Reformatory girl story; photo-c 53 106 159 334 567 800
4(Scarce) 52 104 156 328 552 775

STRANGE DAYS
Eclipse Comics: Oct, 1984 - No. 3, Apr, 1985 ($1.75, Baxter paper)

1-3: Freakwave, Johnny Nemo, & Paradax from Vanguard Illustrated; nudity, violence & strong language 4.00

STRANGE DAYS (Movie)
Marvel Comics: Dec, 1995 ($5.95, squarebound, one-shot)

1-Adaptation of film 6.00

STRANGE FANTASY (Eerie Tales of Suspense!)(Formerly Rocketman #1)
Ajax-Farrell: Aug, 1952 - No. 14, Oct-Nov, 1954

2(#1, 8/52)-Jungle Princess story; Kamenish-a; reprinted from Ellery Queen #1 84 168 252 538 919 1300
2(10/52)-No Black Cat or Rulah; Bakerish, Kamenish-a; hypo/meathook-c 71 142 213 454 777 1100
3-Rulah story, called Pulah 54 108 162 343 574 825
4-Rocket Man app. (2/53) 50 100 150 315 533 750
5,6,8,10,12,14 43 86 129 271 461 650
7-Madam Satan/Slave story 53 106 159 334 567 800
9(w/Black Cat), 9(w/Boy's Ranch; S&K-a), 9(w/War)(A rebinding of Harvey interiors; not publ. by Ajax) 47 94 141 296 498 700
9-Regular issue; Steve Ditko's 3rd published work (tied with Captain 3D) 87 174 261 553 952 1350
11-Jungle story 50 100 150 315 533 750
13-Bondage-c; Rulah (Kolah) story 54 108 162 343 574 825

STRANGE FRUIT
BOOM! Studios: Jul, 2015 - No. 4, Nov, 2016 ($3.99, limited series)

1-4-J.G. Jones-a; Jones & Mark Waid-s 4.00

STRANGE GALAXY
Eerie Publications: V1#8, Feb, 1971 - No. 11, Aug, 1971 (B&W, magazine)

V1#8-Reprints-c/Fantastic V19#3 (2/70) (a pulp) 3 6 9 21 33 45
9-11 3 6 9 17 26 35

STRANGE GIRL
Image Comics: June, 2005 - No. 18, Sept, 2007 ($2.95/$2.99/$3.50)

1-18: 1-Rick Remender-s/Eric Nguyen-a. 13-18-($3.50) 3.50
... Vol. 1: Girl Afraid TPB (2005, $12.99) r/#1-4; sketch pages and pin-ups 13.00

STRANGE JOURNEY
America's Best (Steinway Publ.) (Ajax/Farrell): Sept, 1957 - No. 4, Jun, 1958 (Farrell reprints)

1-The Phantom Express 24 48 72 140 230 320
2-4: 2-Flying saucer-c. 3-Titanic-c 17 34 51 103 162 220

STRANGE LOVE (See Fox Giants)

STRANGE MYSTERIES
Superior/Dynamic Publications: Sept, 1951 - No. 21, Jan, 1955

1-Kamenish-a & horror stories begin 90 180 270 576 988 1400
2 52 104 156 328 552 775
3-5 48 96 144 302 514 725
6-8 43 86 129 271 461 650
9-Bondage 3-D effect-c 54 108 162 343 574 825
10-Used in **SOTI**, pg. 181 48 96 144 302 514 725
11-18: 13-Eyeball-c 37 74 111 218 354 490
19-r/Journey Into Fear #1; cover is a splash from one story; Baker-r(2) 39 78 117 231 378 525
20,21-Reprints; 20-r/#1 with new-c (The Devil) 30 60 90 177 289 400

STRANGE MYSTERIES
I. W. Enterprises/Super Comics: 1963 - 1964

I.W. Reprint #9; Rulah-r/Spook #28; Disbrow-a 3 6 9 19 30 40
Super Reprint #10-12,15-17(1963-64): 10,11-r/Strange #2,1. 12-r/Tales of Horror #5 (3/53) less-c. 15-r/Dark Mysteries #23. 16-r/The Dead Who Walk. 17-r/Dark Mysteries #22 3 6 9 19 30 40
Super Reprint #18-r/Witchcraft #1; Kubert-a 3 6 9 19 30 40

STRANGE PLANETS
I. W. Enterprises/Super Comics: 1958; 1963-64

I.W. Reprint #1(nd)-Reprints E. C. Incredible S/F #30 plus-c/Strange Worlds #3 6 12 18 38 69 100
I.W. Reprint #9-Orlando/Wood-r/Strange Worlds #4; cover-r from Flying Saucers #1 7 14 21 48 89 130
Super Reprint #10-Wood-r (22 pg.) from Space Detective #1; cover-r/Attack on Planet Mars 7 14 21 48 89 130
Super Reprint #11-Wood-r (25 pg.) from An Earthman on Venus 8 16 24 52 99 145
Super Reprint #12-Orlando-r/Rocket to the Moon 8 16 24 54 102 150
Super Reprint #15-Reprints Journey Into Unknown Worlds #8; Heath, Colan-r 5 10 15 31 53 75
Super Reprint #16-Reprints Avon's Strange Worlds #6; Kinstler, Check-a 5 10 15 33 57 80
Super Reprint #18-r/Great Exploits #1 (Daring Adventures #6); Space Busters, Explorer Joe, The Son of Robin Hood; Krigstein-a 4 8 12 28 47 65

STRANGERS
Image Comics: Mar, 2003 - No. 6, Sept, 2003 ($2.95)

1-6-Randy & Jean-Marc Lofficier-s; two covers. 2-Nexus back-up story 3.00

STRANGERS, THE
Malibu Comics (Ultraverse): June, 1993 - No. 24, May, 1995 ($1.95/$2.50)

1-4,6-12,14-20: 1-1st app. The Strangers; has coupon for Ultraverse Premiere #0; 1st app.

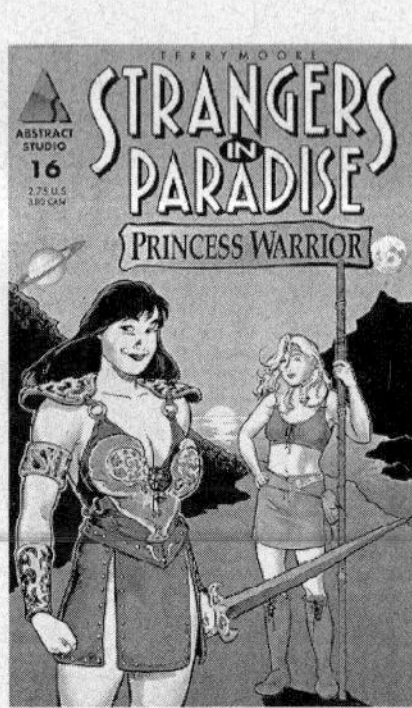

Strangers in Paradise V3 #16 © Terry Moore

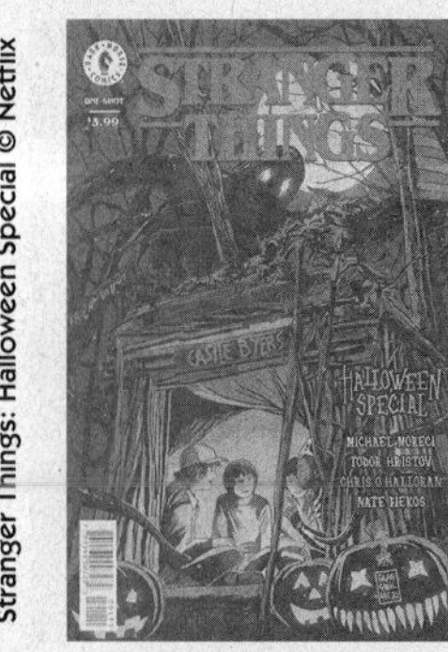

Stranger Things: Halloween Special © Netflix

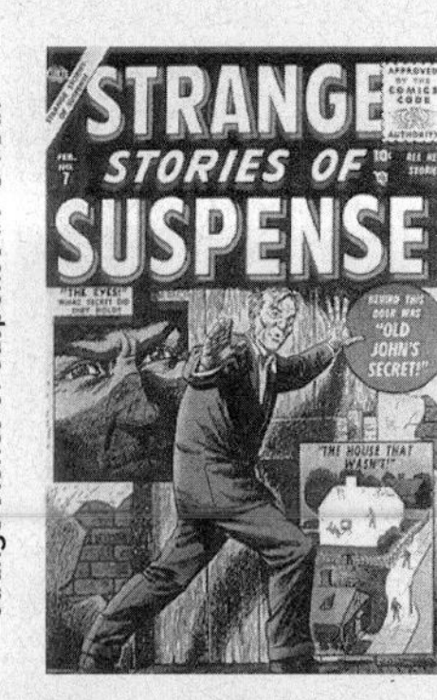

Strange Stories of Suspense #7 © MAR

GD VG FN VF VF/NM NM-
2.0 4.0 6.0 8.0 9.0 9.2

the Night Man (not in costume). 2-Polybagged w/trading card. 7-Break-Thru x-over. 8-2 pg. origin Solution. 12-Silver foil logo; wraparound-c. 17-Rafferty app. 3.00
1-With coupon missing 2.00
1-Full cover holographic edition, 1st of kind w/Hardcase #1 & Prime #1 1 2 3 5 6 8
1-Ultra 5000 limited silver foil 6.00
4-($2.50)-Variant Newsstand edition bagged w/card 4.00
5-($2.50, 52 pgs.)-Rune flip-c/story by B. Smith (3 pgs.); The Mighty Magnor 1 pg. strip by Aragones; 3-pg. Night Man preview 4.00
13-($3.50, 68 pgs.)-Mantra app.; flip book w/Ultraverse Premiere #4 4.00
21-24 ($2.50) 3.00
...:The Pilgrim Conundrum Saga (1/95, $3.95, 68pgs.) 4.00

STRANGERS IN PARADISE (Also see SIP Kids)
Antarctic Press: Nov, 1993 - No. 3, Feb, 1994 ($2.75, B&W, limited series)

1 10 20 30 69 147 225
1-2nd/3rd prints 2 4 6 9 12 15
2 (2300 printed) 5 10 15 30 50 70
3 3 6 9 17 26 35
Trade paperback (Antarctic Press, $6.95)-Red -c (5000 print run) 10.00
Trade paperback (Abstract Studios, $6.95)-Red-c (2000 print run) 15.00
Trade paperback (Abstract Studios, $6.95, 1st-4th printing)-Blue- 7.00
Hardcover ('98, $29.95) includes first draft pages 30.00
Gold Reprint Series ($2.75) 1-3-r/#1-3 3.00

STRANGERS IN PARADISE
Abstract Studios: Sept, 1994 - No. 14, July, 1996 ($2.75, B&W)

1 2 4 6 9 13 16
1,3- 2nd printings 4.00
2,3: 2-Color dream sequence 1 2 3 5 6 8
4-10 5.00
4-6-2nd printings 4.00
11-14: 14-The Letters of Molly & Poo 4.00
Gold Reprint Series ($2.75) 1-13-r/#1-13 4.00
I Dream Of You ($16.95, TPB) r/#1-9 17.00
It's a Good Life ($8.95, TPB) r/#10-13 9.00

STRANGERS IN PARADISE (Volume Three)
Homage Comics #1-8/Abstract Studios #9-on: Oct, 1996 - No. 90, May, 2007 ($2.75-$2.99, color #1-5, B&W #6-on)

1-Terry Moore-c/s/a in all; dream seq. by Jim Lee-a 1 2 3 5 6 8
1-Jim Lee variant-c 2 4 6 8 10 12
2-5 5.00
6-16: 6-Return to B&W. 13-15-High school flashback. 16-Xena Warrior Princess parody; two covers 4.00
17-89: 33-Color issue. 46-Molly Lane. 49-Molly & Poo. 86-David dies 4.00
90-Last issue; 3 covers of Katchoo, Francine and David forming a triptych 5.00
...Lyrics and Poems (2/99) 4.00
...Source Book (2003, $2.95) Background on characters & story arcs, checklists 4.00
Brave New World ('02, $8.95, TPB) r/#44,45,47,48 9.00
Child of Rage ($15.95, TPB) r/#31-38 16.00
David's Story (6/04, $8.95, TPB) r/#61-63 9.00
Ever After ('07, $15.95, TPB) r/#83-90 16.00
Flower to Flame ('03, $15.95, TPB) r/#55-60 16.00
Heart in Hand ('03, $12.95, TPB) r/#50-54 13.00
High School ('98, $8.95, TPB) r/#13-16 9.00
Immortal Enemies ('98, $14.95, TPB) r/#6-12 15.00
Love & Lies (2006, $14.95, TPB)r/#77-82 15.00
Love Me Tender ($12.95, TPB) r/#1-5 in B&W w/ color Lee seq. 13.00
Molly & Poo (2005, $8.95, TPB)r/#46,49,73 9.00
My Other Life ($14.95, TPB) r/#25-30 15.00
Pocket Book 1-5 ($17.95, 5 1/2" x 8", TPB) 1-r/Vol.1 & 2. 2-r/#1-17 in B&W. 3-r/#18-24,26-32,34-38. 4-r/#41-45,47,48,50-60. 5-r/#46,49,61-76 18.00
Sanctuary ($15.95, TPB) r/#17-24 16.00
Tattoo ($14.95, TPB) r/#70-76; sketch pages and fan tattoo photos 15.00
Tomorrow Now (11/04, $14.95, TPB) r/#64-69 15.00
Tropic of Desire ($12.95, TPB) r/#39-43 13.00
The Complete... : Volume 3 Part 1 HC ($49.95) r/#1-12 50.00
The Complete... : Volume 3 Part 2 HC ($49.95) r/#13-15,17-25 50.00
The Complete... : Volume 3 Part 3 HC ('01, $49.95) r/#26-38 50.00
The Complete... : Volume 3 Part 4 HC ('02, $39.95) r/#39-46,49 40.00
The Complete... : Volume 3 Part 5 HC ('03, $49.95) r/#47,48,50-57 50.00
The Complete... : Volume 3 Part 6 HC ('04, $49.95) r/#58-69 50.00
The Complete... : Volume 3 Part 7 HC ('06, $49.95) r/#70-80 50.00

STRANGERS IN PARADISE XXV
Abstract Studio: 2018 - No. 10, 2019 ($3.99, B&W)

GD VG FN VF VF/NM NM-
2.0 4.0 6.0 8.0 9.0 9.2

1-10-Terry Moore-c/s/a; Rachel, Zoe & Lilith app. 4.00
1-Free Comic Book Day edition (2018, giveaway) r/#1 3.00

STRANGER THINGS (Based on the Netflix TV series)
Dark Horse Comics: Sept, 2018 - No. 4, Jan 2019 ($3.99, limited series)

1-4-Will Byers time in the Upside Down; Houser-s/Martino-a; multiple covers 4.00
...: Halloween Special One Shot (10/20, $3.99) Moreci-s/Hristov-a/Francavilla-c 4.00

STRANGER THINGS / D&D CROSSOVER (Based on the Netflix TV series)
Dark Horse Comics: Nov, 2020 - No. 4 Feb, 2021 ($3.99, limited series)

1-4-Houser & Zub-s/Galindo-a/multiple covers 4.00

STRANGER THINGS: INTO THE FIRE (Based on the Netflix TV series)
Dark Horse Comics: Jan, 2020 - No. 4, Jul, 2020 ($3.99, limited series)

1-4-The search for subject Eight; Houser-s/Kelly-a/Kalvachev-c 4.00

STRANGER THINGS: SCIENCE CAMP (Based on the Netflix TV series)
Dark Horse Comics: Sept, 2020 - No. 4, Dec, 2020 ($3.99, limited series)

1-4-Houser-s/Salazar-a/Kalvachev-c 4.00

STRANGER THINGS SIX (Based on the Netflix TV series)
Dark Horse Comics: May, 2019 - No. 4, Aug, 2019 ($3.99, limited series)

1-4-Prequel focusing on subject Six, Francine; Houser-s/Salazar-a 4.00

STRANGE SKIES OVER EAST BERLIN
BOOM! Studios: Oct, 2019 - No. 4, Jan, 2020 ($3.99, limited series)

1-4-Jeff Loveness-s/Lisandro Estherren-a 4.00

STRANGE SPORTS STORIES (See Brave & the Bold #45-49, DC Special, and DC Super Stars #10)
National Periodical Publications: Sept-Oct, 1973 - No. 6, July-Aug, 1974

1-Devil-c 3 6 9 17 25 34
2-6: 2-Swan/Anderson-a 2 4 6 9 13 16

STRANGE SPORTS STORIES
DC Comics (Vertigo): May, 2015 - No. 4, Aug, 2015 ($4.99, limited series)

1-4-Anthology of short stories by various. 1-Paul Pope-c. 4-Pope-s/a 5.00

STRANGE STORIES FROM ANOTHER WORLD (Unknown World #1)
Fawcett Publications: No. 2, Aug, 1952 - No. 5, Feb, 1953

2-Saunders painted-c 55 110 165 352 601 850
3-5-Saunders painted-c 43 86 129 271 461 650

STRANGE STORIES OF SUSPENSE (Rugged Action #1-4)
Atlas Comics (CSI): No. 5, Oct, 1955 - No. 16, Aug, 1957

5(#1) 55 110 165 352 601 850
6,7,9 39 78 117 240 395 550
8-Morrow/Williamson-a; Pakula-a 40 80 120 246 411 575
10-Crandall, Torres, Meskin-a 37 74 111 222 361 500
11-13: 12-Torres, Pakula-a. 13-E.C. art swipes 33 66 99 194 317 440
14-16: 14-Williamson/Mayo-a. 15-Krigstein-a. 16-Fox, Powell-a 34 68 102 204 332 460

NOTE: ***Everett** a-6, 7, 13; c-8, 9, 11-14. **Forte** a-12, 16. **Heath** a-5. **Maneely** c-5. **Morisi** a-11. **Morrow** a-13. **Powell** a-8. **Sale** a-11. **Severin** c-7. **Wildey** a-14.*

STRANGE STORY (Also see Front Page)
Harvey Publications: June-July, 1946 (52 pgs.)

1-The Man in Black Called Fate by Powell 42 84 126 265 445 625

STRANGE SUSPENSE STORIES (Lawbreakers Suspense Stories #10-15; This Is Suspense #23-26; Captain Atom V1#78 on)
Fawcett Publications/Charlton Comics No. 16 on: 6/52 - No. 5, 2/53; No. 16, 1/54 - No. 22, 11/54; No. 27, 10/55 - No. 77, 10/65; V3#1, 10/67 - V1#9, 9/69

1-(Fawcett)-Powell, Sekowsky-a 94 188 282 597 1024 1450
2-George Evans horror story 53 106 159 334 567 800
3-5 (2/53)-George Evans horror stories 43 86 129 271 461 650
16(1-2/54)-Formerly Lawbreakers S.S. 36 72 108 214 347 480
17 27 54 81 162 266 370
18-E.C. swipe/HOF 7; Ditko-c/a(2) 54 108 162 343 574 825
19-Ditko electric chair-c; Ditko-a 541 1082 1623 3950 6975 10,000
20-Ditko-c/a(2) 47 94 141 296 498 700
21-Shuster-a; a woman dangling over an alligator pit while a madman smashes her fingers with a hammer 48 96 144 302 514 725
22(11/54)-Ditko-c, Shuster-a; last pre-code issue; becomes This Is Suspense 45 90 135 284 480 675
27(10/55)-(Formerly This Is Suspense #26) 17 34 51 103 162 220
28-30,38 14 28 42 80 115 150
31-33,35,37,40-Ditko-c/a(2-3 each) 22 44 66 130 213 295
34-Story of ruthless business man, Wm. B. Gaines; Ditko-c/a

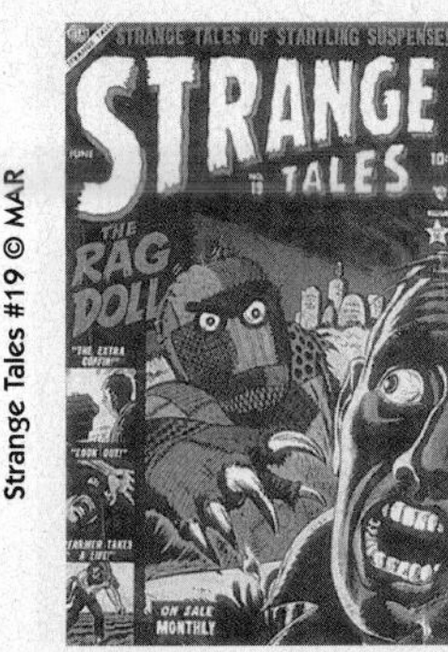

Strange Tales #19 © MAR

Strange Tales #108 © MAR

Strange Tales #160 © MAR

	GD 2.0	VG 4.0	FN 6.0	VF 8.0	VF/NM 9.0	NM- 9.2
	55	110	165	352	601	850
36-(15¢, 68 pgs.); Ditko-a(4)	27	54	81	158	259	360
39,41,52,53-Ditko-a	20	40	60	114	182	250
42-44,46,49,54-60	5	10	15	34	60	85
45,47,48,50,51-Ditko-c/a	12	24	36	82	179	275
61-74: 72-Has panel which inspired a famous Roy Lichtenstein painting	5	10	15	30	50	70
75(6/65)-Reprints origin/1st app. Captain Atom by Ditko from Space Advs. #33; r/Severin-a/Space Advs. #24 (75-77: 12¢ issues)	10	20	30	66	138	210
76,77-Captain Atom-r by Ditko/Space Advs.	6	12	18	40	73	105
V3#1(10/67): 12¢ issues begin	3	6	9	19	30	40
V1#2-Ditko-c/a; atom bomb-c	3	6	9	19	30	40
V1#3-9: 3-8-All 12¢ issues. 9-15¢ issue	2	4	6	13	18	22

NOTE: ***Alascia** a-19. **Aparo** a-60, V3#1, 2, 4; c-V1#4, 8, 9. **Baily** a-1-3; c-2, 5. **Evans** c-3, 4. **Giordano** c-16, 17p, 24p, 25p. **Montes/Bache** c-66. **Powell** a-4. **Shuster** a-19, 21. **Marcus Swayze** a-27.*

STRANGE TALENT OF LUTHER STRODE, THE (Also see The Legend of Luther Strode)
Image Comics: Oct, 2011 - No. 6, Mar, 2012 ($2.99, limited series)

	GD 2.0	VG 4.0	FN 6.0	VF 8.0	VF/NM 9.0	NM- 9.2
1-6: Justin Jordan-s/Tradd Moore-a						3.00

STRANGE TALES (...Featuring Warlock #178-181; Doctor Strange #169 on)
Atlas (CCPC #1-67/ZPC #68-79/VPI #80-85)/Marvel #86(7/61) on:
June, 1951 - No. 168, May, 1968; No. 169, Sept, 1973 - No. 188, Nov, 1976

	GD 2.0	VG 4.0	FN 6.0	VF 8.0	VF/NM 9.0	NM- 9.2
1-Horror/weird stories begin	757	1514	2271	5526	9763	14,000
2	209	418	627	1338	2294	3250
3,5: 3-Atom bomb panels	161	322	483	1030	1705	2500
4-Cosmic eyeball story "The Evil Eye"	168	336	504	1075	1838	2600
6-9: 6-Heath-c/a. 7-Colan-a	131	262	393	838	1442	2025
10-Krigstein-a	132	264	396	845	1448	2050
11-14,16-20	105	210	315	672	1149	1625
15-Krigstein-a; detached head-c	110	220	330	704	1202	1700
21,23-27,29-34: 27-Atom bomb panels. 33-Davis-a. 34-Last pre-code issue (2/55)	90	180	270	576	988	1400
22-Krigstein, Forte/Fox-a	97	194	291	621	1061	1500
28-Jack Katz story used in Senate Investigation report, pgs. 7 & 169; classic skull-c	514	1028	1542	3750	6625	9500
35-41,43,44: 37-Vampire story by Colan	47	94	141	364	820	1275
42,45,59,61-Krigstein-a; #61 (2/58)	48	96	144	370	835	1300
46-57,60: 51-(10/56) 1st S.A. issue. 53,56-Crandall-a. 60-(8/57)	44	88	132	326	738	1150
58,64-Williamson-a in each, with Mayo-#58	45	90	135	333	754	1175
62,63,65,66: 62-Torres-a. 66-Crandall-a	44	88	132	326	738	1150
67-Prototype ish. (Quicksilver)	49	96	147	382	866	1350
68,71,72,74,77,80: Ditko/Kirby-a in #67-80	44	88	132	326	738	1150
69,70,73,75,76,78,79: 69-Prototype ish. (Prof. X). 70-Prototype ish. (Giant Man). 73-Prototype ish. (Ant-Man). 75-Prototype ish. (Iron Man). 76-Prototype ish. (Human Torch). 78-Prototype ish. (Ant-Man). 79-Prototype ish. (Dr. Strange) (12/60)	48	96	144	370	835	1300
81-83,85-88,90,91-Ditko/Kirby-a in all: 86-Robot-c. 90-(11/61)-Atom bomb blast panel	42	84	126	311	706	1100
84-Prototype ish. (Magneto)(5/61); has powers like Magneto of X-Men, but two years earlier; Ditko/Kirby-a	51	102	153	400	900	1400
89-1st app. Fin Fang Foom (10/61) by Kirby	290	580	870	2440	5520	8600
92-Prototype ish. (Ancient One & Ant-Man); last 10¢ issue	43	86	129	318	722	1125
93,95,96,98-100: Kirby-a	36	72	108	266	596	925
94-Creature similar to The Thing; Kirby-a	43	86	129	318	722	1125
97-1st app. of an Aunt May & Uncle Ben by Ditko (6/62), before Amazing Fantasy #15; (see Tales Of Suspense #7); Kirby-a	129	258	387	1032	2316	3600
101-Human Torch begins by Kirby (10/62); origin recap Fantastic Four & Human Torch; Human Torch-c begin	173	346	519	1394	3147	4900
102-1st app. Wizard; robot-c	46	92	138	359	805	1250
103-105: 104-1st app. Trapster (as Paste-Pot Pete). 105-2nd Wizard	41	82	123	303	689	1075
106,108,109: 106-Fantastic Four guests (3/63)	34	68	102	245	548	850
107-(4/63)-Human Torch/Sub-Mariner battle; 4th S.A. Sub-Mariner app. & 1st x-over outside of Fantastic Four	61	122	183	488	1094	1700
110-(7/63)-Intro Doctor Strange, Ancient One & Wong by Ditko	660	1320	2640	6200	13,600	21,000
111-2nd Dr. Strange; intro. Baron Mordo	66	132	198	535	1193	1850
112-1st Eel	28	56	84	202	451	700
113-Origin/1st app. Plantman	27	54	81	194	435	675
114-Acrobat disguised as Captain America, 1st app. since the G.A.; intro. & 1st app. Victoria Bentley; 3rd Dr. Strange app. & begin series (11/63)	52	104	156	421	936	1450
115-Origin Dr. Strange; Human Torch vs. Sandman (Spidey villain; 2nd app. & brief origin); early Spider-Man x-over, 12/63	94	188	282	761	1706	2650
116-(1/64)-Human Torch battles The Thing; 1st Thing x-over	24	48	72	168	372	575
117,118,120: 118-1st cover app. of Dr. Strange. 120-1st Iceman x-over (from X-Men)	16	32	48	111	246	380
119-Spider-Man x-over (2 panel cameo)	18	36	54	125	276	430
121,122,124,127-134: Thing/Torch team-up in 121-134. 128-Quicksilver & Scarlet Witch app. (1/65). 130-The Beatles cameo. 134-Last Human Torch; The Watcher-c/story; Wood-a(i)	13	26	39	87	191	295
123-1st app. The Beetle (see Amazing Spider-Man #21 for next app.); 1st Thor x-over (8/64); Loki app.	16	32	48	110	243	375
125-Torch & Thing battle Sub-Mariner (10/64)	17	34	51	117	259	400
126-Intro Clea and Dormammu (cont'd in #127)	45	90	135	333	754	1175
135-Col. (formerly Sgt.) Nick Fury becomes Nick Fury Agent of Shield (origin/1st app.) by Kirby (8/65); series begins	42	84	126	311	706	1100
136,137,139,140	8	16	24	54	102	150
138-Intro Eternity	21	42	63	147	324	500
141-147,149: 145-Begins alternating-c features w/Nick Fury (odd #'s) & Dr. Strange (even #'s). 146-Last Ditko Dr. Strange who is in consecutive stories since #113; only full Ditko Dr. Strange-c this title. 147-Dr. Strange (by Everett #147-152) continues thru #168, then Dr. Strange #169	6	12	18	41	76	110
148-Origin Ancient One	8	16	24	54	102	150
150(11/66)-John Buscema's 1st work at Marvel	8	16	24	51	96	140
151-Kirby/Steranko-c/a; 1st Marvel work by Steranko	9	18	27	61	123	185
152,153-Kirby/Steranko-a	7	14	21	44	82	120
154-158-Steranko-a/script. 157,158-Debut of The Living Tribunal	7	14	21	44	82	120
159-Origin Nick Fury retold; Intro Val; Captain America-c/story; Steranko-a	10	20	30	64	132	200
160-162-Steranko-a/scripts; Capt. America app.	7	14	21	44	82	120
163-166,168-Steranko-a(p). 168-Last Nick Fury (gets own book next month) & last Dr. Strange who also gets own book	6	12	18	42	79	115
167-Steranko pen/script; classic flag-c	9	18	27	63	129	195
169-1st app. Brother Voodoo(origin in #169,170) & begin series, ends #173	25	50	75	175	388	600
170-174: 174-Origin Golem	3	6	9	16	23	30
175-177: 177-Brunner-c	3	6	9	14	20	25
178-(2/75)-Warlock by Starlin begins; origin Warlock & Him retold; 1st app. Magus; Starlin-c/a/scripts in #178-181 (all before Warlock #9)	9	18	27	62	126	190
179-Intro/1st app. Pip the Troll; Warlock app.	5	10	15	35	63	90
180-(6/75) Intro. Gamora (Guardians of the Galaxy) (5 panels); Warlock by Starlin	11	22	33	72	154	235
181-(8/75)-Warlock story continued in Warlock #9; 1st full app. of Gamora	5	10	15	33	57	80
182-188: 185,186-(Regular 25¢ editions)	2	4	6	8	10	12
185,186-(30¢-c variants, limited distribution)(5,7/76)	5	10	15	30	50	70
Annual 1(1962)-Reprints from Strange Tales #73,76,78, Tales of Suspense #7,9, Tales to Astonish #1,6,7, & Journey Into Mystery #53,55,59; (1st Marvel annual)	71	142	213	568	1284	2000
Annual 2(7/63)-New Human Torch vs. Spider-Man story by Kirby/Ditko (1st Spidey x-over; 4th app.); reprints from Strange Tales #67, Strange Worlds (Atlas) #1-3, World of Fantasy #16; Kirby-c	114	228	342	923	2062	3200

NOTE: ***Briefer** a-17. **Burgos** a-123p. **J. Buscema** a-174p. **Colan** a-7, 11, 20, 37, 53, 169-173p, 188p. **Davis** c-71. **Ditko** a-46, 50, 67-122, 123-125p, 126-146, 175r, 182-188r; c-51, 93, 115, 121, 146. **Everett** a-4, 21, 40-42, 73, 147-152, 164i; c-8, 10, 11, 13, 15, 24, 45, 49-54, 56, 58, 60, 61, 63, 148, 150, 152, 158i. **Forte** a-27, 43, 50, 53, 54, 60. **Heath** a-2, 6; c-6, 18-20. **Kamen** a-45. **G. Kane** c-170-173, 182p. **Kirby** Human Torch-101-105, 108, 109, 114, 120; Nick Fury-135p, 141-143p; (Layouts)-135-153; other **Kirby** a-67-100p; c-68-70, 72-74, 76-92, 94, 95, 101-114, 116-123, 125-130, 132-135, 136p, 138-145, 147, 149, 151p. **Kirby/Ayers** c-101-106, 108-110. **Kirby/ Ditko** a-80, 88, 121; c-75, 93, 97, 100, 139. **Lawrence** a-29. **Leiber/ Fox** a-110-113. **Maneely** a-3, 7, 37, 42; c-33, 40. **Moldoff** a-20. **Mooney** a-174i. **Morisi** a-53, 56. **Morrow** a-54. **Orlando** a-41, 44, 46, 49, 52. **Powell** a-42, 44, 49, 54, 130-134p; c-131p. **Reinman** a-11, 50, 74, 80, 88, 91, 95, 104, 106, 112i, 124-127i. **Robinson** a-17. **Romita** c-169. **Roussos** c-201i. **R.Q. Sale** a-56; c-16. **Sekowski** a-3, 11. **Severin** a(i)-136-138; c-137. **Starlin** a-178, 179, 180p, 181p; c-178-180, 181p. **Steranko** a-151-161, 162-168p; c-151i, 153, 155, 157, 159, 161, 163, 165, 167. **Torres** a-53, 62. **Tuska** a-14, 166p. **Whitney** a-149. **Wildey** a-42, 56. **Woodbridge** a-59. Fantastic Four cameos #101-134. Jack Katz app.-26.*

STRANGE TALES
Marvel Comics Group: Apr, 1987 - No. 19, Oct, 1988

	GD 2.0	VG 4.0	FN 6.0	VF 8.0	VF/NM 9.0	NM- 9.2
V2#1-19						5.00

STRANGE TALES
Marvel Comics: Nov, 1994 ($6.95, one-shot)

	GD 2.0	VG 4.0	FN 6.0	VF 8.0	VF/NM 9.0	NM- 9.2
V3#1-acetate-c	1	2	3	5	6	8

STRANGE TALES (Anthology; continues stories from Man-Thing #8 and Werewolf By Night #6)
Marvel Comics: Sept, 1998 - No. 2, Oct, 1998 ($4.99)

	GD 2.0	VG 4.0	FN 6.0	VF 8.0	VF/NM 9.0	NM- 9.2
1,2: 1-Silver Surfer app. 2-Two covers						5.00

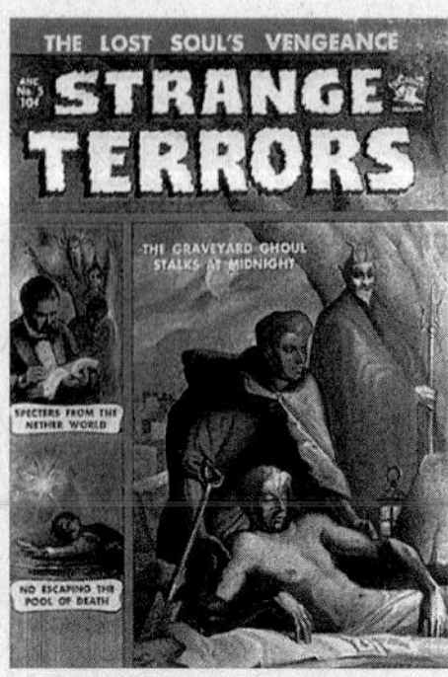

Strange Terrors #5 © STJ

Strange Worlds #2 © AVON

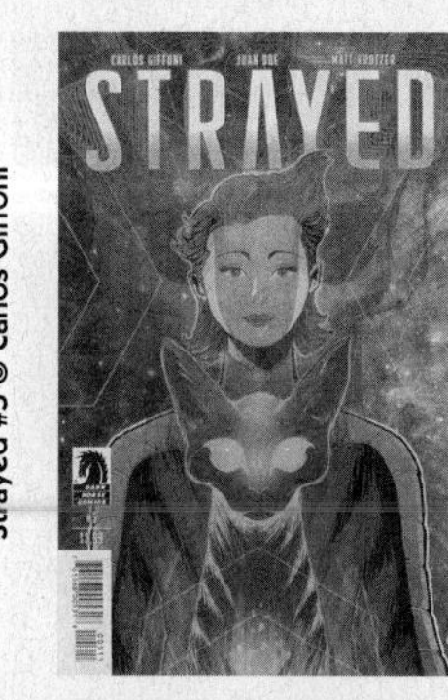

Strayed #5 © Carlos Giffoni

STRANGE TALES (Humor anthology)
Marvel Comics: Nov, 2009 - No. 3, Jan, 2010 ($4.99, limited series)

	GD 2.0	VG 4.0	FN 6.0	VF 8.0	VF/NM 9.0	NM- 9.2
1-3: 1-Paul Pope, Kochalka, Bagge and others-s/a. 2-Bagge-c/a. 3-Sakai-c/a						5.00

STRANGE TALES II (Humor anthology)
Marvel Comics: Dec, 2010 - No. 3, Feb, 2011 ($4.99, limited series)

	GD 2.0	VG 4.0	FN 6.0	VF 8.0	VF/NM 9.0	NM- 9.2
1-3: 2-Jaime Hernandez-c. 3-Terry Moore-s/a; Pekar-s/Templeton-a						5.00

STRANGE TALES: DARK CORNERS
Marvel Comics: May, 1998 ($3.99, one-shot)

	GD 2.0	VG 4.0	FN 6.0	VF 8.0	VF/NM 9.0	NM- 9.2
1-Anthology; stories by Baron & Maleev, McGregor & Dringenberg, DeMatteis & Badger; Estes painted-c						4.00

STRANGE TALES OF THE UNUSUAL
Atlas Comics (ACI No. 1-4/WPI No. 5-11): Dec, 1955 - No. 11, Aug, 1957

	GD 2.0	VG 4.0	FN 6.0	VF 8.0	VF/NM 9.0	NM- 9.2
1-Powell-a	60	120	180	381	653	925
2	39	78	117	231	378	525
3-Williamson-a (4 pgs.)	39	78	117	240	395	550
4,6,8,11: 4-UFO-c	31	62	93	182	296	410
5-Crandall, Ditko-a	35	70	105	208	339	470
7,9: 7-Kirby, Orlando-a. 9-Krigstein-a	33	66	99	194	217	440
10-Torres, Morrow-a	31	62	93	182	296	410

NOTE: *Baily a-6. **Brodsky** c-2-4. **Everett** a-2, 6; c-6, 9, 11. **Heck** a-1. **Maneely** c-1. **Orlando** a-7. **Pakula** a-10. **Romita** a-1. **R.Q. Sale** a-3. **Wildey** a-3.*

STRANGE TERRORS
St. John Publishing Co.: June, 1952 - No. 7, Mar, 1953

	GD 2.0	VG 4.0	FN 6.0	VF 8.0	VF/NM 9.0	NM- 9.2
1-Bondage-c; Zombies spelled Zoombies on-c; Fine-*esque* -a	87	174	261	553	952	1350
2	43	86	129	271	461	650
3-Kubert-a; painted-c	53	106	159	334	567	800
4-Kubert-a (reprinted in Mystery Tales #18); Ekgren painted-c; Fine-*esque* -a; Jerry Iger caricature	94	188	282	597	1025	1450
5-Kubert-a; painted-c	53	106	159	334	567	800
6-Giant (25¢, 100 pgs.)(1/53); Tyler classic bondage/skull-c	81	162	243	518	884	1250
7-Giant (25¢, 100 pgs.); Kubert-c/a	71	142	213	454	777	1100

NOTE: ***Cameron** a-6, 7. **Morisi** a-6.*

STRANGE WORLD OF YOUR DREAMS
Prize Publications: Aug, 1952 - No. 4, Jan-Feb, 1953

	GD 2.0	VG 4.0	FN 6.0	VF 8.0	VF/NM 9.0	NM- 9.2
1-Simon & Kirby-a	81	162	243	518	884	1250
2,3-Simon & Kirby-c/a. 2-Meskin-a	57	114	171	362	619	875
4-S&K-c; Meskin-a	48	96	144	302	514	725

STRANGE WORLDS (#18 continued from Avon's Eerie #1-17)
Avon Periodicals: 11/50 - No. 9, 11/52; No. 18, 10-11/54 - No. 22, 9-10/55 (No #11-17)

	GD 2.0	VG 4.0	FN 6.0	VF 8.0	VF/NM 9.0	NM- 9.2
1-Kenton of the Star Patrol by Kubert (r/Eerie #1 from 1947); Crom the Barbarian by John Giunta	171	342	513	1094	1872	2650
2-Wood-a; Crom the Barbarian by Giunta; Dara of the Vikings app.; used in **SOTI**, pg. 112; injury to eye panel	155	310	465	992	1696	2400
3-Wood/Orlando-a (Kenton), Wood/Williamson/Frazetta/Krenkel/Orlando-a (7 pgs.); Malu Slave Girl Princess app.; Kinstler-c	258	516	774	1651	2826	4000
4-Wood-c/a (Kenton); Orlando-a; origin The Enchanted Daggar; Sultan-a; classic cover	219	438	657	1402	2401	3400
5-Orlando/Wood-a (Kenton); Wood-c	129	258	387	826	1413	2000
6-Kinstler-a(2); Orlando/Wood-c; Check-a	68	136	204	435	743	1050
7-Fawcette & Becker/Alascia-a	63	126	189	403	689	975
8-Kubert, Kinstler, Hollingsworth & Lazarus-a; Lazarus Robot-c	60	120	180	381	653	925
9-Kinstler, Fawcette, Alascia, Kubert-a	55	100	165	352	601	850
18-(Formerly Eerie #17)-Reprints "Attack on Planet Mars" by Kubert	41	82	123	256	428	600
19-r/Avon's "Robotmen of the Lost Planet"; last pre-code issue; Robot-c	41	82	123	256	428	600
20-War-c/story; Wood-c(r)/U.S. Paratroops #1	14	28	42	81	118	155
21,22-War-c/stories. 22-New logo	13	26	39	72	101	130
I.W. Reprint #5-Kinstler-a(r)/Avon's #9	5	10	15	30	50	70

STRANGE WORLDS
Marvel Comics (MPI No. 1,2/Male No. 3,5): Dec, 1958 - No. 5, Aug, 1959

	GD 2.0	VG 4.0	FN 6.0	VF 8.0	VF/NM 9.0	NM- 9.2
1-Kirby & Ditko-a; flying saucer issue	123	246	369	787	1344	1900
2-Ditko-c/a	68	136	204	435	743	1050
3-Kirby-a(2)	61	122	183	390	670	950
4-Williamson-a	55	110	165	352	601	850
5-Ditko-a	53	106	159	334	567	800

NOTE: ***Buscema** a-3, 4. **Ditko** a-1-5; c-2.. **Heck** a-2. **Kirby** a-1, 3. **Kirby/Brodsky** c-1, 3-5.*

STRAWBERRY SHORTCAKE
Marvel Comics (Star Comics): Jun, 1985 - No. 6, Feb, 1986 (Children's comic)

	GD 2.0	VG 4.0	FN 6.0	VF 8.0	VF/NM 9.0	NM- 9.2
1-6: Howie Post-a	2	4	6	8	10	12

STRAWBERRY SHORTCAKE
Ape Entertainment: 2011 - No. 4, 2011 ($3.95, limited series)

	GD 2.0	VG 4.0	FN 6.0	VF 8.0	VF/NM 9.0	NM- 9.2
1-4: 1-Scratch 'n' sniff cover						4.00
Volume 2 (2012, $3.99) 1,2						4.00

STRAWBERRY SHORTCAKE
IDW Publishing: Apr, 2016 - No. 8, Nov, 2016 ($3.99)

	GD 2.0	VG 4.0	FN 6.0	VF 8.0	VF/NM 9.0	NM- 9.2
1-8: Multiple covers on each. 1-Georgia Ball-s/Amy Mebberson-a						4.00
... Funko Universe One-Shot (5/17, $4.99) Ball-s; art in Funko Pop! style						5.00

STRAY
DC Comics (Homage Comics): 2001 ($5.95, prestige format, one-shot)

	GD 2.0	VG 4.0	FN 6.0	VF 8.0	VF/NM 9.0	NM- 9.2
1-Pollina-c/a; Lobdell & Palmiotti-s						6.00

STRAY
Dark Horse Comics: 2004 (8 1/2"x 5 1/2", Diamond Comic Dist. Halloween giveaway)

	GD 2.0	VG 4.0	FN 6.0	VF 8.0	VF/NM 9.0	NM- 9.2
nn-Reprint from The Dark Horse Book of Hauntings; Evan Dorkin-s/Jill Thompson-a						3.00

STRAY BULLETS
El Capitan Books/Image Comics: 1995 - No. 41, Mar, 2014 ($2.95/$3.50, B&W, mature)

	GD 2.0	VG 4.0	FN 6.0	VF 8.0	VF/NM 9.0	NM- 9.2
1-David Lapham-c/a/scripts	2	4	6	11	16	20
2,3						6.00
4-8						4.00
9-21,31,32-($2.95)						3.50
22-30,33-41-($3.50) 22-Includes preview to Murder Me Dead. 40-(10/05). 41-(3/14)						3.50
Free Comic Book Day giveaway (5/02) Reprints #2 with "Free Comic Book Day" banner on-c; flip book with The Matrix (printing of internet comic)						3.00
Innocence of Nihilism Volume 1 HC ($29.95, hardcover) r/#1-7						30.00
Somewhere Out West Volume 2 HC ($34.95, hardcover) r/#8-14						35.00
Other People Volume 3 HC ($34.95, hardcover) r/#15-22						35.00
Volume 1-3 TPB ($11.95, softcover) 1-r/#1-4. 2-r/#5-8. 3-r/ #9-12						12.00
Volume 4-7 TPB ($14.95) 4- r/#13-16. 5- r/#17-20. 6- r/#21-24. 7-r/#25-28						15.00

NOTE: *Multiple printings of most issues exist & are worth cover price.*

STRAY BULLETS: KILLERS
Image Comics (El Capitan Books): Mar, 2014 - No. 8, Oct, 2014 ($3.50, B&W)

	GD 2.0	VG 4.0	FN 6.0	VF 8.0	VF/NM 9.0	NM- 9.2
1-8-David Lapham-c/a/scripts; set in 1978						3.50

STRAY BULLETS: SUNSHINE AND ROSES
Image Comics (El Capitan Books): Feb, 2015 - No. 41, Jun, 2019 ($3.50/$3.99, B&W)

	GD 2.0	VG 4.0	FN 6.0	VF 8.0	VF/NM 9.0	NM- 9.2
1-10-David Lapham-c/a/scripts; set in 1979 Baltimore						3.50
11-36,41-($3.99) 20-Amy Racecar app.						4.00
37-40-($4.99)						5.00

STRAYED
Dark Horse Comics: Aug, 2019 - No. 5, Dec, 2019 ($3.99, limited series)

	GD 2.0	VG 4.0	FN 6.0	VF 8.0	VF/NM 9.0	NM- 9.2
1-5-Carlos Giffoni-s/Juan Doe-a						4.00

STRAYER
AfterShock Comics: Jan, 2016 - No. 5 ($3.99)

	GD 2.0	VG 4.0	FN 6.0	VF 8.0	VF/NM 9.0	NM- 9.2
1-5-Justin Jordan-s/Juan Gedeon-a						4.00

STRAY TOASTERS
Marvel Comics (Epic Comics): Jan, 1988 - No. 4, April, 1989 ($3.50, squarebound, limited series)

	GD 2.0	VG 4.0	FN 6.0	VF 8.0	VF/NM 9.0	NM- 9.2
1-4: Sienkiewicz-c/a/scripts						4.00

STREET COMIX
Street Enterprises/King Features: 1973 (50¢, B&W, 36 pgs.)(20,000 print run)

	GD 2.0	VG 4.0	FN 6.0	VF 8.0	VF/NM 9.0	NM- 9.2
1-Rip Kirby	2	4	6	8	11	14
2-Flash Gordon	2	4	6	10	14	18

STREETFIGHTER
Ocean Comics: Aug, 1986 - No. 4, Spr, 1987 ($1.75, limited series)

	GD 2.0	VG 4.0	FN 6.0	VF 8.0	VF/NM 9.0	NM- 9.2
1-4: 2-Origin begins						3.00

STREET FIGHTER
Malibu Comics: Sept, 1993 - No. 3, Nov, 1993 ($2.95)

	GD 2.0	VG 4.0	FN 6.0	VF 8.0	VF/NM 9.0	NM- 9.2
1-3: 3-Includes poster; Ferret x-over						4.00

STREET FIGHTER
Image Comics: Sept, 2003 - No. 14, Feb, 2005 ($2.95)

	GD 2.0	VG 4.0	FN 6.0	VF 8.0	VF/NM 9.0	NM- 9.2
1-Back-up story w/Madureira-a; covers by Madureira and Tsang						4.00
2-6,8-14: 2-Two covers by Campbell and Warren; back-up story w/Warren-a						3.00
7-($4.50) Larocca-c						4.50
... Vol. 1 (3/04, $9.99, digest-size) r/main stories from #1-6						10.00

Strike! #3 © ECL

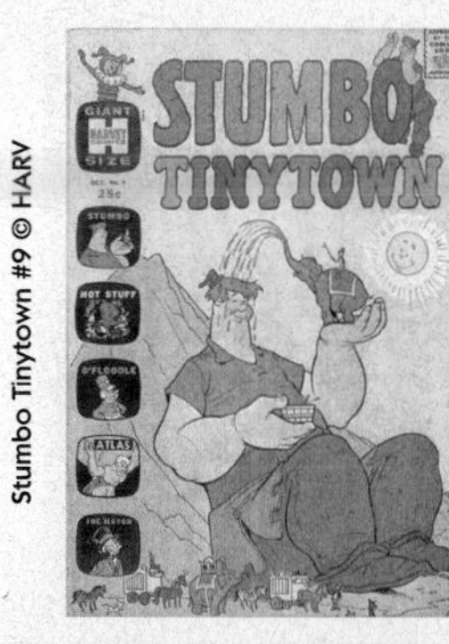

Stumbo Tinytown #9 © HARV

Sub-Mariner #4 © MAR

GD VG FN VF VF/NM NM-
2.0 4.0 6.0 8.0 9.0 9.2

GD VG FN VF VF/NM NM-
2.0 4.0 6.0 8.0 9.0 9.2

STREET FIGHTER: THE BATTLE FOR SHADALOO
DC Comics/CAP Co. Ltd.: 1995 ($3.95, one-shot)

1-Polybagged w/trading card & Tattoo 4.00

STREET FIGHTER II
Tokuma Comics (Viz): Apr, 1994 - No. 8, Nov, 1994 ($2.95, limited series)

1-8 3.00

STREET FIGHTER II
UDON Comics: No. 0, Oct, 2005 - No. 6, Nov, 2006 ($1.99/$3.95/$2.95)

0-(10/05, $1.99) prelude to series; Alvin Lee-a 3.00
1-($3.95) Two covers by Alvin Lee & Ed McGuinness 4.00
2-6-($2.95) 3.00
... Legends 1 (8/06, $3.95) Spotlight on Sakura; two covers 4.00

STREET FIGHTER X G.I. JOE
IDW Publishing: Feb, 2016 - No. 6, Jul, 2016 ($4.99)

1-Sitterson-s/Laiso-a; multiple covers; Destro, Snake Eyes, Baroness, Ryu app. 5.00
2-6-($3.99) Multiple covers on each 4.00

STREET SHARKS
Archie Publications: Jan, 1996 - No. 3, Mar, 1996 ($1.50, limited series)

1-3 3.00

STREET SHARKS
Archie Publications: May, 1996 - No. 6 ($1.50)

1-6 3.00

STRETCH ARMSTRONG AND THE FLEX FIGHTERS (Based on the Netfix animated series)
IDW Publishing: Jan, 2018 - No. 3, Mar, 2018 ($3.99, limited series)

1-3-Burke & Wyatt-s/Koutsis-a; 3 covers 4.00

STRICTLY PRIVATE (You're in the Army Now)
Eastern Color Printing Co.: July, 1942 (#1 on sale 6/15/42)

1,2: Private Peter Plink. 2-Says 128 pgs. on-c 36 72 108 211 343 475

STRIKE!
Eclipse Comics: Aug, 1987 - No. 6, Jan, 1988 ($1.75)

1-6, ...Vs. Sgt. Strike Special 1 (5/88, $1.95) 3.00

STRIKEBACK! (The Hunt For Nikita)
Malibu Comics (Bravura): Oct, 1994 - No. 3, Jan, 1995 ($2.95, unfinished limited series)

1-3: Jonathon Peterson script, Kevin Maguire-c/a 3.00
1-Gold foil embossed-c 5.00

STRIKEBACK!
Image Comics (WildStorm Productions): Jan, 1996 - No. 5, May, 1996 ($2.50, lim. series)

1-5: Reprints original Bravura series w/additional story & art by Kevin Maguire & Jonathon Peterson; new Maguire-c in all. 4,5-New story & art 3.00

STRIKEFORCE
Marvel Comics: Nov, 2019 - No. 9, Oct, 2020 ($3.99)

1-9: 1-Team of Blade, Angela, Spectrum, Winter Soldier, Spider-Woman, Wiccan and Hellstrom; Howard-s/Peralta-a. 7-9-Deadpool app. 4.00

STRIKEFORCE: AMERICA
Comico: Dec, 1995 ($2.95)

V2#1-Polybagged w/gaming card; S. Clark-a(p) 5.00

STRIKEFORCE: MORITURI
Marvel Comics Group: Dec, 1986 - No. 31, July, 1989

1,13: 13-Double size 4.00
2-12,14-31: 14-Williamson-i. 25-Heath-c 3.00
... – We Who Are About To Die 1 (3/12, $0.99) r/#1 with profile pages and cover gallery 3.00

STRIKEFORCE MORITURI: ELECTRIC UNDERTOW
Marvel Comics: Dec, 1989 - No. 5, Mar, 1990 ($3.95, 52 pgs., limited series)

1-5 Squarebound 4.00

STRONG GUY REBORN (See X-Factor)
Marvel Comics: Sept, 1997 ($2.99, one-shot)

1-Dezago-s/Andy Smith, Art Thibert-a 3.00

STRONGHOLD
AfterShock Comics: Feb, 2019 - No. 5, Aug, 2019 ($3.99)

1-5-Phil Hester-s/Ryan Kelly-a 4.00

STRONG MAN (Also see Complimentary Comics & Power of...)
Magazine Enterprises: Mar-Apr, 1955 - No. 4, Sept-Oct, 1955

1(A-1 #130)-Powell-c/a 24 48 72 140 230 320
2-4: (A-1 #132,134,139)-Powell-a. 2-Powell-c 18 36 54 109 172 235

STRONTIUM DOG
Eagle Comics: Dec, 1985 - No. 4, Mar, 1986 ($1.25, limited series)

1-4, Special 1: 4-Moore script. Special 1 (1986)-Moore script 4.00

STRYFE'S STRIKE FILE
Marvel Comics: Jan, 1993 ($1.75, one-shot, no ads)

1-Stroman, Capullo, Andy Kubert, Brandon Peterson-a; silver metallic ink-c; X-Men tie-in to X-Cutioner's Song 4.00
1-Gold metallic ink 2nd printing 3.00

STRYKEFORCE
Image Comics (Top Cow): May, 2004 - No. 5, Oct, 2004 ($2.99)

1-5-Faerber-s/Kirkham-a. 4,5-Preview of HumanKind 3.00
Vol. 1 TPB (2005, $16.99) r/#1-5 & Codename: Strykeforce #0-3; sketch pages 17.00

STUMBO THE GIANT (See Harvey Hits #49,54,57,60,63,66,69,72,78,88 & Hot Stuff #2)

STUMBO TINYTOWN
Harvey Publications: Oct, 1963 - No. 13, Nov, 1966 (All 25¢ giants)

1-Stumbo, Hot Stuff & others begin 14 28 42 98 217 335
2 8 16 24 54 102 150
3-5 6 12 18 38 69 100
6-13 5 10 15 33 57 80

STUNTMAN COMICS (Also see Thrills Of Tomorrow)
Harvey Publ.: Apr-May, 1946 - No. 2, June-July, 1946; No. 3, Oct-Nov, 1946

1-Origin Stuntman by S&K reprinted in Black Cat #9; S&K-c
123 246 369 787 1344 1900
2-S&K-c/a; The Duke of Broadway story 68 136 204 435 743 1050
3-Small size (5-1/2x8-1/2"; B&W; 32 pgs.); distributed to mail subscribers only; S&K-a; Kid Adonis by S&K reprinted in Green Hornet #37
123 246 369 787 1344 1900
(Also see All-New #15, Boy Explorers #2, Flash Gordon #5 & Thrills of Tomorrow)

STUPID COMICS (Also see 40 oz. Collected)
Oni Press/Image Comics: July, 2000; Sept, 2002 - No. 3, Aug, 2005 ($2.95, B&W)

1-(Oni Press, 7/00) Jim Mahfood 1 page satire strips reprinted from JAVA magazine 3.00
1-3-(Image Comics, 9/02; 10/03) Jim Mahfood 1 page and 2 page satire strips 3.00
TPB (4/06, $12.99) r/#1(Oni) and #1-3(Image); Phoenix New Times strips 13.00

STUPID HEROES
Mirage Studios: Sept, 1993 - No. 3, Dec, 1994 ($2.75, unfinished limited series)

1-3-Laird-c/a & scripts; 2 trading cards bound in 3.00

STUPID, STUPID RAT TAILS (See Bone)
Cartoon Books: Dec, 1999 - No. 3, Feb, 2000 ($2.95, limited series)

1-3-Jeff Smith-a/Tom Sniegoski-s 4.00

SUBMARINE ATTACK (Formerly Speed Demons)
Charlton Comics: No. 11, May, 1958 - No. 54, Feb-Mar, 1966

11 4 8 12 27 44 60
12-20: 16-Atomic bomb panels 3 6 9 19 30 40
21-30 3 6 9 17 26 35
31-54: 43-Cuban missile crisis story. 47-Atomic bomb panels
3 6 9 15 22 28

NOTE: *Glanzman c/a-25. Montes/Bache a-38, 40, 41.*

SUB-MARINER (See All-Select, All-Winners, Blonde Phantom, Daring, The Defenders, Fantastic Four #4, Human Torch, The Invaders, Iron Man &..., Marvel Mystery, Marvel Spotlight #27, Men's Adventures, Motion Picture Funnies Weekly, Namora, Namor, The..., Prince Namor, The Sub-Mariner, Saga Of The..., Tales to Astonish #70 & 2nd series, USA & Young Men)

SUB-MARINER, THE (2nd Series)(Sub-Mariner #31 on)
Marvel Comics Group: May, 1968 - No. 72, Sept, 1974 (No. 43: 52 pgs.)

1-Origin Sub-Mariner; story continued from Iron Man & Sub-Mariner #1
37 74 111 274 612 950
2-Triton app. 10 20 30 64 132 200
3,4 7 14 21 49 92 135
5-1st Tiger Shark (9/68) 22 44 66 154 340 525
6,7,9,10: 6-Tiger Shark-c & 2nd app., cont'd from #5. 7-Photo-c. (1968). 9-1st app. Serpent Crown (origin in #10 & 12) 5 10 15 35 63 90
8-Sub-Mariner vs. Thing 11 22 33 73 157 240
8-2nd printing (1994) 2 4 6 9 12 15
11-13,15: 15-Last 12¢ issue 5 10 15 30 50 70
14-Sub-Mariner vs. G. A. Toro, who assumes identity of G. A. Human Torch; death of Toro (1st modern app. & only app. Toro, 6/69) 6 12 18 42 79 115
16-20: 19-1st Sting Ray (11/69); Stan Lee, Romita, Heck, Thomas, Everett & Kirby cameos. 20-Dr. Doom app. 3 6 9 21 33 45
21,23-33,37-42: 25-Origin Atlantis. 30-Capt. Marvel x-over. 37-Death of Lady Dorma.

Sub-Mariner Comics #7 © MAR

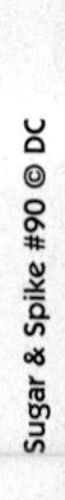

Sugar & Spike #90 © DC

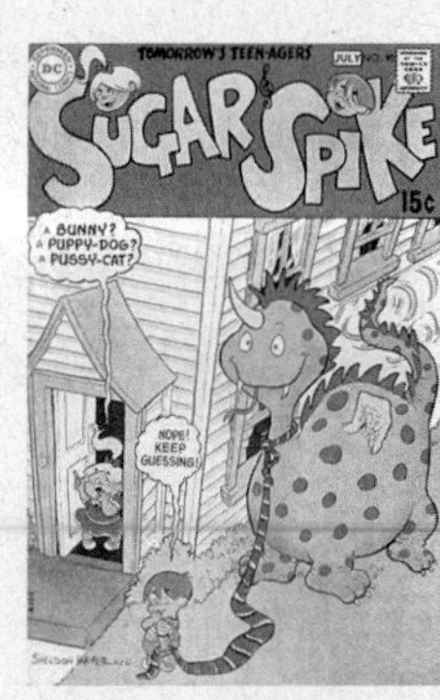

Suicide Risk #24 © BOOM & Carey

	GD 2.0	VG 4.0	FN 6.0	VF 8.0	VF/NM 9.0	NM- 9.2
38-Origin retold. 40-Spider-Man x-over. 42-Last 15¢ issue	3	6	9	16	24	32
22-Dr. Strange x-over	5	10	15	35	63	90
34-Prelude (w/#35) to 1st Defenders story; Hulk & Silver Surfer x-over	10	20	30	66	138	210
35-Namor/Hulk/Silver Surfer team-up to battle The Avengers-c/story (3/71); hints at teaming up again	8	16	24	54	102	150
36-Wrightson-a(i)	3	6	9	19	30	40
43-King Size Special (52 pgs.)	3	6	9	20	31	42
44,45-Sub-Mariner vs. Human Torch	3	6	9	18	30	40
46-49,56,62,64-72: 47,48-Dr. Doom app. 49-Cosmic Cube story. 52-1st app. Dragon-Lord. 52,53-Sunfire app. 62-1st Tales of Atlantis, Chaykin-s/a; ends #66. 64-Hitler cameo. 67-New costume; F.F. x-over. 69-Spider-Man x-over (6 panels)	2	4	6	9	13	16
50-1st app. Nita, Namor's niece (later Namorita in New Warriors)	9	18	27	57	111	165
51-55,57,58,60,61,63-Everett issues: 57-Venus app. (1st since 4/52); anti-Vietnam War panels. 61-Last artwork by Everett; 1st 4 pgs. completed by Mortimer; pgs. 5-20 by Mooney	2	4	6	10	14	18
59-1st battle with Thor; Everett-a	5	10	15	33	57	80
Special 1 (1/71)-r/Tales to Astonish #70-73	4	8	12	28	47	65
Special 2 (1/72)-(52 pgs.)-r/T.T.A. #74-76; Everett-a	3	6	9	19	30	40

NOTE: ***Bolle*** *a-67i.* ***Buscema*** *a(p)-1-8, 20, 24.* ***Colan*** *a(p)-10, 11, 40, 43, 46-49, Special 1, 2; c(p)-10, 11, 40.* ***Craig*** *a-17i, 19-23i.* ***Everett*** *a-45r, 50-55, 57, 58, 59-61(plot), 63(plot); c-47, 48i, 55, 57, 58-59i, 61, Spec. 2.* ***G. Kane*** *c(p)-42-52, 58, 66, 70, 71.* ***Mooney*** *a-24i, 25i, 32-35i, 39i, 42i, 44i, 45i, 60i, 61i, 65p, 66p, 68i.* ***John Severin*** *c/a-38i.* ***Marie Severin*** *c-a 14p.* ***Starlin*** *c-59p.* ***Tuska*** *a-41p, 42p, 69-71p.* ***Wrightson*** *a-36i. #53, 54-r/stories Sub-Mariner Comics #41 & 39.*

SUB-MARINER (The Initiative, follows Civil War series)
Marvel Comics: Aug, 2007 - No. 6, Jan, 2008 ($2.99, limited series)

1-6: 1-Turner-c/Briones-a/Cherniss & Johnson-s; Iron Man app. 3-Yu-c; Venom app.						4.00
...: Revolution TPB (2008, $14.99) r/#1-6						15.00

SUB-MARINER: MARVELS SNAPSHOTS
Marvel Comics: May, 2020 ($4.99, one-shot)

1-Alan Brennert-s/Jerry Ordway-a; set in Spring 1946; All-Winners Squad app.						5.00

SUB-MARINER COMICS (1st Series) (The Sub-Mariner #1, 2, 33-42)(Official True Crime Cases #24 on; Amazing Mysteries #32 on; Best Love #33 on)
Timely/Marvel Comics (TCI 1-7/SePI 8/MPI 9-32/Atlas Comics (CCC 33-42)): Spring, 1941 - No. 23, Sum, 1947; No. 24, Wint, 1947 - No. 31, 4/49; No. 32, 7/49; No. 33, 4/54 - No. 42, 10/55

	GD 2.0	VG 4.0	FN 6.0	VF 8.0	VF/NM 9.0	NM- 9.2
1-The Sub-Mariner by Everett & The Angel begin: Nazi WWII-c	3800	7600	11,400	28,500	69,250	110,000
2-Everett-a; Nazi WWII-c	838	1676	2514	6117	10,809	15,500
3-Churchill assassination-c; 40 pg. S-M story	703	1406	2109	5132	9066	13,000
4-Everett-a, 40 pgs.; 1 pg. Wolverton-a; Nazi WWII-c	481	962	1467	3511	6206	8900
5-Gabrielle/Klein-c; Japanese WWII-c	423	846	1269	3067	5384	7700
6-8,10-Japanese WWII-c	405	810	1215	2835	4968	7100
9-Classic Japanese WWII flag-c (Spr. 1943); Wolverton-a, 3 pgs.	423	846	1269	3000	5250	7500
11-Classic Schomburg-c	514	1028	1542	3750	6625	9500
12,14-Nazi WWII-c	337	674	1011	2359	4130	5900
13-Classic Schomburg hooded Japanese WWII bondage-c	432	864	1296	3154	5577	8000
15-Schomburg Japanese WWII-c	320	640	960	2251	3976	5700
16,17-Japanese WWII-c	300	600	900	2010	3505	5000
18-20	258	516	774	1651	2826	4000
21-Last Angel; Everett-a	168	336	504	1075	1838	2600
22-Young Allies app.	168	336	504	1075	1838	2600
23-The Human Torch, Namora x-over (Sum/47); 2nd app. Namora after Marvel Mystery #82	200	400	600	1280	2190	3100
24-Namora x-over (3rd app.)	203	406	609	1299	2225	3150
25-The Blonde Phantom begins (Spr/48), ends No. 31; Kurtzman-a; Namora x-over; last quarterly issue	190	380	570	1216	2083	2950
26,27: 26-Namora c/app.	177	354	531	1133	1942	2750
28-Namora cover; Everett-a	213	426	639	1363	2332	3300
29-31 (4/49): 29-The Human Torch app. 31-Capt. America app.	194	388	582	1242	2121	3000
32 (7/49, Scarce)-Origin Sub-Mariner	423	846	1269	3046	5323	7600
33 (4/54)-Origin Sub-Mariner; The Human Torch app.; Namora x-over in Sub-Mariner #33-42	161	322	483	1030	1765	2500
34,35-Human Torch in ea. 34-Namora bondage-c	119	238	357	762	1306	1850
36,37,39-41: 36,39-41-Namora app.	116	232	346	742	1271	1800
38-Origin Sub-Mariner's wings; Namora app.; last pre-code (2/55)	132	264	396	845	1448	2050
42-Last issue	138	276	414	883	1517	2150

NOTE: *Angel by* ***Gustavson****-#1, 8.* ***Brodsky*** *c-34-36, 42.* ***Everett*** *a-1-4, 22-24, 26-42; c-32, 33, 40.* ***Maneely*** *a-38; c-37, 39-41.* ***Rico*** *c-27-31.* ***Schomburg*** *c-1-4, 6, 8-18, 20.* ***Sekowsky*** *c-24. 25, 26(w/****Rico****).* ***Shores*** *c-21-23, 38. Bondage c-13, 22, 24, 25, 34.*

SUB-MARINER COMICS 70th ANNIVERARY SPECIAL
Marvel Comics: June, 2009 ($3.99, one-shot)

1-New WWII story, Breitweiser-a; Williamson-a; r/debut app. from Marvel Comics #1						5.00

SUB-MARINER: THE DEPTHS
Marvel Comics: Nov, 2008 - No. 5, May, 2009 ($3.99, limited series)

1-5-Peter Milligan-s/Esad Ribic-a/c						4.00

SUBSPECIES
Eternity Comics: May, 1991 - No. 4, Aug, 1991 ($2.50, limited series)

1-4: New stories based on horror movie						4.00

SUBTLE VIOLENTS
CFD Productions: 1991 ($2.50, B&W, mature)

	GD 2.0	VG 4.0	FN 6.0	VF 8.0	VF/NM 9.0	NM- 9.2
1-Linsner-c & story	1	3	4	8	10	12
San Diego Limited Edition	4	8	12	27	44	60

SUE & SALLY SMITH (Formerly My Secret Life)
Charlton Comics: V2#48, Nov, 1962 - No. 54, Nov, 1963 (Flying Nurses)

	GD 2.0	VG 4.0	FN 6.0	VF 8.0	VF/NM 9.0	NM- 9.2
V2#48-2nd app.	3	6	9	18	27	36
49-54	3	6	9	14	20	26

SUGAR & SPIKE (Also see The Best of DC, DC Silver Age Classics and Legends of Tomorrow)
National Periodical Publications: Apr-May, 1956 - No. 98, Oct-Nov, 1971

	GD 2.0	VG 4.0	FN 6.0	VF 8.0	VF/NM 9.0	NM- 9.2
1 (Scarce)	481	962	1443	3511	6206	8900
2	161	322	483	1030	1765	2500
3-5: 3-Letter column begins	90	180	270	576	988	1400
6-10	53	106	159	334	567	800
11-20	39	78	117	240	395	550
21-29: 26-Christmas-c	27	54	81	162	266	370
30-Scribbly & Scribbly, Jr. x-over	28	56	84	168	274	380
31-40	21	42	63	124	202	280
41-60	9	18	27	58	114	170
61-80: 69-1st app. Tornado-Tot-c/story. 72-Origin & 1st app. Bernie the Brain	7	14	21	48	89	130
81-84,86-93,95: 84-Bernie the Brain apps. as Superman in 1 panel (9/69)	6	12	18	37	66	95
85 (68 pgs.)-r/#72	6	12	18	41	76	110
94-1st app. Raymond, African-American child	6	12	18	41	76	110
96 (68 pgs.)	7	14	21	44	82	120
97,98 (52 pgs.)	6	12	18	41	76	110
No. 1 Replica Edition (2002, $2.95) reprint of #1						4.00

NOTE: *All written and drawn by* ***Sheldon Mayer.*** *Issues with Paper Doll pages cut or missing are common.*

SUGAR BOWL COMICS (Teen-age)
Famous Funnies: May, 1948 - No. 5, Jan, 1949

	GD 2.0	VG 4.0	FN 6.0	VF 8.0	VF/NM 9.0	NM- 9.2
1-Toth-c/a	16	32	48	98	154	210
2,4,5	10	20	30	58	79	100
3-Toth-a	11	22	33	64	90	115

SUGARFOOT (TV)
Dell Publishing Co.: No. 907, May, 1958 - No. 1209, Oct-Dec, 1961

	GD 2.0	VG 4.0	FN 6.0	VF 8.0	VF/NM 9.0	NM- 9.2
Four Color 907 (#1)-Toth-a, photo-c	10	20	30	67	141	215
Four Color 992 (5-7/59), Toth-a, photo-c	9	18	27	63	129	195
Four Color 1059 (11-1/60), 1098 (5-7/60), 1147 (11-1/61), 1209-all photo-c. 1059,1098,1147-all have variant edition, back-c comic strip	7	14	21	49	92	135

SUGARSHOCK (Also see MySpace Dark Horse Presents)
Dark Horse Comics: Oct, 2009 ($3.50, one-shot)

1-Joss Whedon-s/Fabio Moon-a/c; story from online comic; Moon sketch pgs.						3.50

SUICIDE RISK
BOOM! Studios: May, 2013 - No. 25, May, 2015 ($3.99)

1-25: 1-Carey-s/Casagrande-a. 5-Joëlle Jones-a. 10-Coelho-a						4.00

SUICIDERS
DC Comics (Vertigo): Apr, 2015 - No. 6, Nov, 2015 ($3.99)

1-6-Lee Bermejo-s/a/c						4.00

SUICIDERS: KINGS OF HELL.A.
DC Comics (Vertigo): May, 2016 - No. 6 ($3.99)

1-6-Lee Bermejo-s/c. 1-5-Alessandro Vitti-a. 6-Gerardo Zaffino-a; Bermejo-a (2 pgs.)						4.00

SUICIDE SQUAD (See Brave & the Bold, Doom Patrol & Suicide Squad Spec., Legends #3 & note under Star Spangled War stories)

Suicide Squad (2011 series) #11 © DC

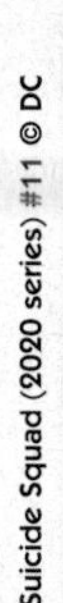
Suicide Squad (2020 series) #11 © DC

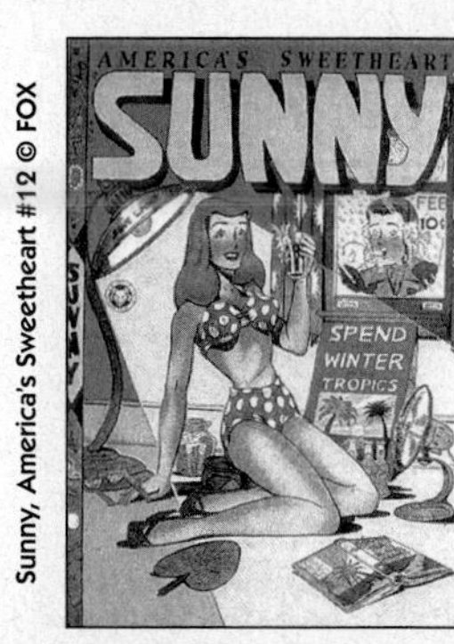
Sunny, America's Sweetheart #12 © FOX

	GD	VG	FN	VF	VF/NM	NM-
	2.0	4.0	6.0	8.0	9.0	9.2

DC Comics: May, 1987 - No. 66, June, 1992; No. 67, Mar, 2010 (Direct sales only #32 on)

1-Chaykin-c 5 10 15 33 57 80
2-10: 9-Millennium x-over. 10-Batman-c/story 6.00
11-22,24-47,50-66: 13-JLI app. (Batman). 16-Re-intro Shade The Changing Man. 27-34,36,37-Snyder-a. 38-Origin Bronze Tiger. 40-43-"The Phoenix Gambit" Batman storyline. 40-Free Batman/Suicide Squad poster 4.00
23-1st Oracle 3 6 9 21 33 45
48-Joker/Batgirl-c/s 3 6 9 20 31 42
49-Joker/Batgirl-c/s 2 4 6 11 16 20
67-(3/10, $2.99) Blackest Night one-shot; Fiddler rises as a Black Lantern; Califiore-a 4.00
Annual 1 (1988, $1.50)-Manhunter x-over 5.00
...: Trial By Fire TPB (2011, $19.99) r/#1-8 & Secret Origins #14 20.00

SUICIDE SQUAD (2nd series)
DC Comics: Nov, 2001 - No. 12, Oct, 2002 ($2.50)

1-Giffen-s/Medina-a; Sgt. Rock app. 5.00
2-9: 4-Heath-a 4.00
10-12-Suicide Squad vs. Antiphon: 10-J. Severin-a. 12-JSA app.
1 3 4 6 8 10

SUICIDE SQUAD (3rd series)
DC Comics: Nov, 2007 - No. 8, Jun, 2008 ($2.99, limited series)

1-8-Ostrander-s/Pina-a/Snyder III-c 4.00
...: From the Ashes TPB (2008, $19.99) r/#1-8 20.00

SUICIDE SQUAD (DC New 52)(Also see New Suicide Squad)
DC Comics: Nov, 2011 - No. 30, Jul, 2014 ($2.99)

1-Harley Quinn, Deadshot, King Shark, El Diablo, Voltaic, Black Spider team up
5 10 15 30 50 70
1-(2nd printing) 2 4 6 13 28 22
1 Special Edition (5/16, FCBD giveaway) 3.00
2-5 1 2 3 5 6 8
6-Origin Harley Quinn part 1 3 6 9 17 26 35
6,7-(2nd printing) 1 2 3 5 6 8
7-Origin Harley Quinn part 2 3 6 9 14 20 25
8-13,16-20,22-30: 19-Unknown Soldier joins. 24-29-Forever Evil tie-in. 24-Omac returns 4.00
14,15-Death of the Family tie-in; Joker app. 5.00
14-Variant die-cut Joker mask-c; Death of the Family tie-in 6.00
21-Harley Quinn-c/s 1 3 4 6 8 10
30-($3.99) Forever Evil tie-in; Coelho-a/Mahnke-c 4.00
#0 (11/12, $2.99) Amanda Waller pre-Suicide Squad; Dagnino-a 5.00
...: Amanda Waller (5/14, $4.99) Jim Zub-s/Coelho-a 5.00

SUICIDE SQUAD (DC Rebirth)
DC Comics: Oct, 2016 - No. 50, Mar, 2019 ($2.99)

1-Harley Quinn, Deadshot, Killer Croc, Katana, Boomerang team up; Jim Lee-a; back-up origin of Deadshot retold; Fabok-a 3.00
1-Director's Cut (5/17, $5.99) r/#1,2 with pencil-a; bonus original script for #1 6.00
2-7: 2,3-Zod app. 2-Back-up Boomerang origin w/Reis-a. 3-Back-up Katana origin 3.00
8-24: 8-Killer Frost joins; Justice League vs. Suicide Squad prelude; Lee-a. 9,10-JL vs. SS tie-ins. 11-15-Romita Jr.-a. 16-18-Daniel-a. 20-Sejic-a. 23,24-Batman app. 3.00
25-($3.99) Batman app.; Cafaro-a; cameo app. Rick Flag & Karin Grace 4.00
26-49: 26-Dark Nights: Metal tie-in. 27-32-Secret History of Task Force X. 41-44-Batman app. 3.00
50-($4.99) Williams-s/Peralta, Schoonover & Conrad-a 5.00
Annual 1 (10/18, $4.99) New team with Merlyn vs. Swamp Thing; Cliquet-a 5.00
.../Banana Splits Special 1 (5/17, $4.99) Caldwell-a; Snagglepuss back-up; Porter-a 5.00
...: Rebirth (10/16, $2.99) Rick Flag joins; Harley Quinn, Deadshot, Boomerang app. 3.00
... Special: War Crimes 1 (10/16, $4.99) Ostrander-s/Gus Vazquez-a; Shado app. 5.00

SUICIDE SQUAD
DC Comics: Feb, 2020 - No. 11, Jan, 2021 ($4.99/$3.99)

1-($4.99) Harley Quinn, Deadshot, The Shark, Zebra-Man; intro The Revolutionaries 5.00
2-11-($3.99) 6-Batman app. 4.00

SUICIDE SQUAD BLACK FILES
DC Comics: Jan, 2019 - No. 6, Jun, 2019 ($4.99, limited series)

1-6-New squad incl. Gentleman Ghost, El Diablo, Klarion, Enchantress; Eaton-a 5.00

SUICIDE SQUAD MOST WANTED: DEADSHOT & KATANA
DC Comics: Mar, 2016 - No. 6, Aug, 2016 ($4.99, limited series)

1-6-Deadshot by Buccellato-s/Bogdanovic-a; Katana by Barr-s/Neves-a; Nord-c 5.00

SUICIDE SQUAD MOST WANTED: EL DIABLO & BOOMERANG (Title changes to Suicide Squad Most Wanted: El Diablo & Amanda Waller for #5,6)
DC Comics: Oct, 2016 - No. 6, Mar, 2017 ($4.99, limited series)

1-4-El Diablo by Nitz-s/Richards-a; Boomerang by Moreci-s/Bazaldua-a; Huddleston-c 5.00
5,6-Amanda Waller by Ayala-s/Merhoff-a; El Diablo by Nitz-s/Richards-a 5.00

SUMMER FUN (See Dell Giants)

SUMMER FUN (Formerly Li'l Genius; Holiday Surprise #55)
Charlton Comics: No. 54, Oct, 1966 (Giant)

54 3 6 9 21 33 45

SUMMER FUN (Walt Disney's...)
Disney Comics: Summer, 1991 ($2.95, annual, 68 pgs.)

1-D. Duck, M. Mouse, Brer Rabbit, Chip 'n' Dale & Pluto, Li'l Bad Wolf, Super Goof, Scamp stories 4.00

SUMMER LOVE (Formerly Brides in Love?)
Charlton Comics: V2#46, Oct, 1965; V2#47, Oct, 1966; V2#48, Nov, 1968

V2#46-Beatles-c & 8 pg. story 12 24 36 83 182 280
47-(68 pgs.) Beatles-c & 12 pg. story 10 20 30 66 138 210
48 3 6 9 17 26 35

SUMMER MAGIC (See Movie Comics)

SUNDANCE (See Hotel Deparee...)

SUNDANCE KID (Also see Blazing Six-Guns)
Skywald Publications: June, 1971 - No. 3, Sept, 1971 (52 pgs.)(Pre-code reprints & new-s)

1-Durango Kid; Two Kirby Bullseye-r 3 6 9 16 23 30
2,3: 2-Swift Arrow, Durango Kid, Bullseye by S&K; Meskin plus 1 pg. origin. 3-Durango Kid, Billy the Kid, Red Hawk-r 2 4 6 11 16 20

SUNDAY PIX (Christian religious)
David C. Cook Pub/USA Weekly Newsprint Color Comics: V1#1, Mar,1949 - V16#26, July 19, 1964 (7x10", 12 pgs., mail subscription only)

V1#1 8 16 24 44 57 70
V1#2-35 6 12 18 27 33 38
V2#1-52 (1950) 5 10 15 23 28 32
V3-V6 (1951-1953) 4 9 13 18 22 26
V7-V11#1-7,23-52 (1954-1959) 2 4 6 13 18 22
V11#8-22 (2/22-5/31/59) H.G. Wells First Men in the Moon serial
3 6 9 14 19 24
V12#1-19,21-52; V13-V15#1,2,9-52; V16#1-26(7/19/64)
2 4 6 10 14 18
V12#20 (5/15/60) 2 page interview with Peanuts' Charles Schulz
4 8 12 23 37 50
V15#3-8 (2/24/63) John Glenn, Christian astronaut 3 6 9 16 23 30

SUN DEVILS
DC Comics: July, 1984 - No. 12, June, 1985 ($1.25, maxi series)

1-12: 6-Death of Sun Devil 4.00

SUNDIATA: A LEGEND OF AFRICA
NBM Publishing Inc.: 2002 ($15.95, hardcover with dustjacket)

nn-Will Eisner-s/a; adaptation of an African folk tale 16.00

SUNDOWNERS
Dark Horse Comics: Aug, 2014 - No. 6, Jan, 2015 ($3.50)

1-6: 1-Tim Seeley-s/Jim Terry-a 3.50

SUN FUN KOMIKS
Sun Publications: 1939 (15¢, B&W & red)

1-Satire on comics (rare); 1st Hitler app. in comics?
703 1406 2109 5132 9066 13,000

NOTE: *Hitler, Stalin and Mussolini featured gag in 1-page story written in Hebrew and English. Nazi swastika and Nazi flag app. in a different 1-page "Gussie the Gob" story.*

SUNFIRE & BIG HERO SIX (See Alpha Flight)
Marvel Comics: Sept, 1998 - No. 3, Nov, 1998 ($2.50, limited series)

1-Lobdell-s 5 10 15 30 50 70
2,3 2 4 6 11 16 20

SUN GIRL (See The Human Torch & Marvel Mystery Comics #88)
Marvel Comics (CCC): Aug, 1948 - No. 3, Dec, 1948

1-1st app. Sun Girl; Miss America app. 290 580 870 1856 3178 4500
2,3: 2-The Blonde Phantom begins 200 400 600 1280 2190 3100

SUNNY, AMERICA'S SWEETHEART (Formerly Cosmo Cat #1-10)
Fox Feature Syndicate: No. 11, Dec, 1947 - No. 14, June, 1948

11-Feldstein-c/a 161 322 483 1030 1765 2500
12-14: 12,13-Feldstein-a; 13,14-Lingerie panels. 13-L.B. Cole-a
106 212 318 678 1164 1650
I.W. Reprint #8-Feldstein-a; r/Fox issue 10 20 30 64 132 210

SUN-RUNNERS (Also see Tales of the...)

Superboy #44 © DC

Superboy #228 © DC

Superboy (3rd series) #32 © DC

GD VG FN VF VF/NM NM-
2.0 4.0 6.0 8.0 9.0 9.2

Pacific Comics/Eclipse Comics/Amazing Comics: 2/84 - No. 3, 5/84; No. 4, 11/84 - No. 7, 1986 (Baxter paper)

1-7: P. Smith-a in #2-4 4.00
Christmas Special 1 (1987, $1.95)-By Amazing 4.00

SUNSET CARSON (Also see Cowboy Western)
Charlton Comics: Feb, 1951 - No. 4, 1951 (No month) (Photo-c on each)

1-Photo/retouched-c (Scarce, all issues) 60 120 180 381 653 925
2-Kit Carson story; adapts "Kansas Raiders" w/Brian Donlevy, Audie Murphy & Margaret Chapman 42 84 126 265 445 625
3,4 34 68 102 204 332 460

SUNSET PASS (See Zane Grey & 4-Color #230)

SUPER ANGRY BIRDS (Based on Rovio videogame Angry Birds)
IDW Publishing: Sept, 2015 - No. 4, Dec, 2015 ($3.99, limited series)

1-4: 1-The Eagle's Eye - Jeff Parker-s/Ron Randall-a; two covers 4.00

SUPER ANIMALS PRESENTS PIDGY & THE MAGIC GLASSES
Star Publications: Dec, 1953 (25¢, came w/glasses)

1-(3-D Comics)-L. B. Cole-c 42 84 126 265 445 625

SUPER BAD JAMES DYNOMITE
5-D Comics: Dec, 2005 - No. 5, Feb, 2007 ($3.99)

1-5-Created by the Wayans brothers 4.00

SUPERBOY
DC Comics: Jan, 1942

nn-Ashcan comic, not distributed to newsstands, only for in house use. Covers were produced, but not the rest of the book. A CGC certified 9.2 copy sold in 2003 for $6,600.

SUPERBOY (See Adventure, Aurora, DC Comics Presents, DC 100 Page Super Spectacular #15, DC Super Stars, 80 Page Giant #10, More Fun Comics, The New Advs. of... & Superman Family #191, Young Justice)

SUPERBOY (1st Series)(...& the Legion of Super-Heroes with #231)
(Becomes The Legion of Super-Heroes No. 259 on)
National Periodical Publ./DC Comics: Mar-Apr, 1949 - No. 258, Dec, 1979 (#1-16: 52 pgs.)

1-Superman cover; intro in More Fun #101 (1-2/45) 1050 2100 3150 8000 14,500 21,000
2-Used in **SOTI**, pg. 35-36,226 274 548 822 1754 3027 4300
3 197 394 591 1261 2156 3050
4 145 290 435 928 1589 2250
5-1st pre-Supergirl tryout (c/story, 11-12/49) 164 328 492 1050 1800 2550
6-9: 8-1st Superbaby 124 248 372 794 1360 1925
10-1st app. Lana Lang 158 316 474 1011 1731 2450
11-15: 11-2nd Lana Lang app.; 1st Lana cover 92 184 276 593 1009 1425
16-20: 20-2nd Jor-El cover 63 126 189 403 689 975
21-26,28-30: 21-Lana Lang app. 54 108 162 343 574 825
27-Low distribution 63 126 189 403 689 975
31-38: 38-Last pre-code issue (1/55) 47 94 141 296 498 700
39-48,50 (7/56) 42 84 126 265 445 625
49 (6/56)-1st app. Metallo (this one's Jor-El's robot) 84 168 252 538 919 1300
51-60: 51-Krypto app. 52-1st S.A. issue. 56-Krypto-c 34 68 102 199 325 450
61-67 28 56 84 165 270 375
68-Origin/1st app. original Bizarro (10-11/58) 375 750 1125 2850 5425 8000
69-77,79: 76-1st Supermonkey 24 48 72 142 234 325
78-Origin Mr. Mxyzptlk & Superboy's costume 36 72 108 211 343 475
80-1st meeting Superboy/Supergirl (4/60) 40 80 120 246 411 575
81,83-85,87,88: 83-Origin/1st app. Kryptonite Kid 13 26 39 86 188 290
82-1st Bizarro Krypto 17 34 51 115 255 395
86-(1/61)-4th Legion app; Intro Pete Ross 27 54 81 194 435 675
89-(6/61)-1st app. Mon -El; 2nd Phantom Zone 38 76 114 285 641 1000
90-92: 90-Pete Ross learns Superboy's I.D. 92-Last 10¢ issue 11 22 33 76 163 250
93-10th Legion app.(12/61); Chameleon Boy app. 12 24 36 84 185 285
94-97,99: 94-1st app. Superboy Revenge Squad 10 20 30 68 144 220
98-(7/62) Legion app; origin & 1st app. Ultra Boy; Pete Ross joins Legion 16 32 48 107 236 365
100-(10/62)-Ultra Boy app; 1st app. Phantom Zone villains, Dr. Xadu & Erndine. 2 pg. map of Krypton; origin Superboy retold; r-cover of Superman #1 18 36 54 121 268 415
101-120: 104-Origin Phantom Zone. 115-Atomic bomb-c. 117-Legion app. 9 18 27 57 111 165
121-128: 124-(10/65)-1st app. Insect Queen (Lana Lang). 125-Legion cameo. 126-Origin Krypto the Super Dog retold with new facts 7 14 21 49 92 135
129-(80-pg. Giant G-22)-Reprints origin Mon-El 9 18 27 57 111 165
130-137,139,140: 131-Legion statues cameo in Dog Legionnaires story. 132-1st app. Supremo. 133-Superboy meets Robin 6 12 18 41 76 110

GD VG FN VF VF/NM NM-
2.0 4.0 6.0 8.0 9.0 9.2

138 (80-pg. Giant G-35) 7 14 21 46 86 125
141-146,148-155,157: 145-Superboy's parents regain their youth. 148-Legion app. 157-Last 12¢ issue 5 10 15 35 63 90
147(6/68)-Giant G-47; 1st origin of L.S.H. (Saturn Girl, Lightning Lad, Cosmic Boy); origin Legion of Super-Pets-r/Adv. #293 8 16 24 51 96 140
147 Replica Edition (2003, $6.95) reprints entire issue; cover recreation by Ordway 7.00
156-(Giant G-59) 6 12 18 38 69 100
158-164,166-171,175: 171-1st app. Aquaboy 3 6 9 18 28 38
165,174 (Giant G-71,G-83): 165-r/1st app. Krypto the Superdog from Adventure Comics #210 5 10 15 34 60 85
172,173,176-Legion app.: 172-1st app. & origin Yango (The Super Ape). 176-Partial photo-c; last 15¢ issue 3 6 9 19 30 40
177-184,186,187 (All 52 pgs.): 182-All new origin of the classic World's Finest team (Superman & Batman) as teenagers (2/72, 22pgs). 184-Origin Dial H for Hero-r 3 6 9 20 31 42
185-Also listed as DC 100 Pg. Super Spectacular #12; Legion-c/story; Teen Titans, Kid Eternity(r/Hit #46), Star Spangled Kid-r(S.S. #55) 8 16 24 51 96 140
188-190,192,194,196: 188-Origin Karkan. 196-Last Superboy solo story 3 6 9 14 19 24
191,193,195: 191-Origin Sunboy retold; Legion app. 193-Chameleon Boy & Shrinking Violet get new costumes. 195-1st app. Erg-1/Wildfire; Phantom Girl gets new costume 3 6 9 14 20 26
197-Legion series begins; Lightning Lad's new costume 4 8 12 28 47 65
198,199: 198-Element Lad & Princess Projectra get new costumes 3 6 9 14 20 26
200-Bouncing Boy & Duo Damsel marry; J'onn J'onzz cameo 3 6 9 16 23 30
201,204,206,207,209: 201-Re-intro Erg-1 as Wildfire. 204-Supergirl resigns from Legion. 206-Ferro Lad & Invisible Kid app. 209-Karate Kid gets new costume 2 4 6 11 16 20
202,205-(100 pgs.): 202-Light Lass gets new costume; Mike Grell's 1st comic work-i (5-6/74) 5 10 15 30 50 70
203-Invisible Kid killed by Validus 3 6 9 16 24 32
208,210: 208-(68 pgs.). 208-Legion of Super-Villains app. 210-Origin Karate Kid 3 6 9 14 20 26
211-220: 212-Matter-Eater Lad resigns. 216-1st app. Tyroc, who joins the Legion in #218 2 4 6 9 13 16
221-230,246-249: 226-Intro. Dawnstar. 228-Death of Chemical King 2 4 6 8 10 12
231-245: (Giants). 240-Origin Dawnstar; Chaykin-a. 242-(52 pgs.). 243-Legion of Substitute Heroes app. 243-245-(44 pgs.). 2 4 6 9 13 16
244,245-(Whitman variants; low print run, no issue# shown on cover) 3 6 9 14 20 26
246-248-(Whitman variants; low ...) 2 4 6 11 16 20
250-258: 253-Intro Blok. 257-Return of Bouncing Boy & Duo Damsel by Ditko 2 3 4 6 8 10
251-258-(Whitman variants; low print run) 2 4 6 10 14 18
Annual 1 (Sum/64, 84 pgs.)-Origin Krypto-r 16 32 48 111 246 380
Spectacular 1 (1980, Giant)-1st comic distributed only through comic stores; mostly-r 2 4 6 8 11 14
...: The Greatest Team-Up Stories Ever Told TPB (2010, $19.99) r/team-ups with Robin, Supergirl, young versions of Aquaman, Green Arrow, Bruce Wayne; Davis-c 20.00

NOTE: ***Neal Adams** c-143, 145, 146, 148-155, 157-161, 163, 164, 166-168, 172, 173, 175, 176, 178. **M. Anderson** a-178,179, 245i. **Ditko** a-257p. **Grell** a-202i, 203-219, 220-224p, 235p; c-207-232, 235, 236p, 237, 239p, 240p, 243p, 246, 258. **Nasser** a(p)-222, 225, 226, 230, 231, 233, 236. **Simonson** a-237p. **Starlin** a(p)-239, 250, 251; c-238. **Staton** a-227p, 243-249p, 252-258p; c-247-251p. **Swan/Moldoff** c-109. **Tuska** a-172, 173, 176, 183, 235p. **Wood** inks-153-155, 157-161. Legion app.-172, 173, 176, 177, 183, 184, 188, 190, 191, 193, 195, 197-258.*

SUPERBOY (TV)(2nd Series)(The Adventures of...#19 on)
DC Comics: Feb, 1990 - No. 22, Dec, 1991 ($1.00/$1.25)

1-Photo-c from TV show; Mooney-a(p) 5.00
2-22: Mooney-a in 2-8,18-20; 8-Bizarro-c/story; Arthur Adams-a(i). 9-12,14-17-Swan-a 4.00
...Special 1 (1992, $1.75) Swan-a 5.00

SUPERBOY (3rd Series)
DC Comics: Feb, 1994 - No. 100, Jul, 2002 ($1.50/$1.95/$1.99/$2.25)

1-Metropolis Kid from Reign of the Supermen 1 3 4 6 8 10
2-8,0,9-24,26-76: 6,7-Worlds Collide Pts. 3 & 8. 8-(9/94)-Zero Hour x-over. 0-(10/94). 9-(11/94)-King Shark app. 21-Legion app. 28-Supergirl-c/app. 33-Final Night. 38-41-"Meltdown". 45-Legion-c/app. 47-Green Lantern-c/app. 50-Last Boy on Earth begins. 60-Crosses Hypertime. 68-Demon-c/app. 4.00
25-($2.95)-New Gods & Female Furies app.; w/pin-ups 5.00
77-99: 77-Begin $2.25-c. 79-Superboy's powers return. 80,81-Titans app. 83-New costume. 85-Batgirl app. 90,91-Our Worlds at War x-over 4.00
100-($3.50) Sienkiewicz-c; Grummett & McCrea-a; Superman cameo 5.00

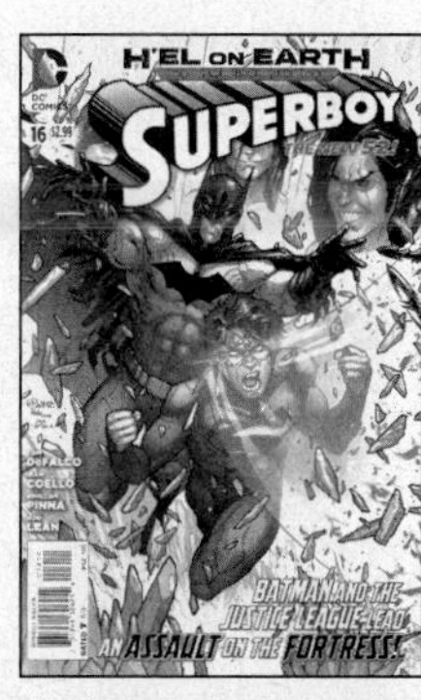

Superboy (2011 series) #16 © DC

Supercar #3 © GK

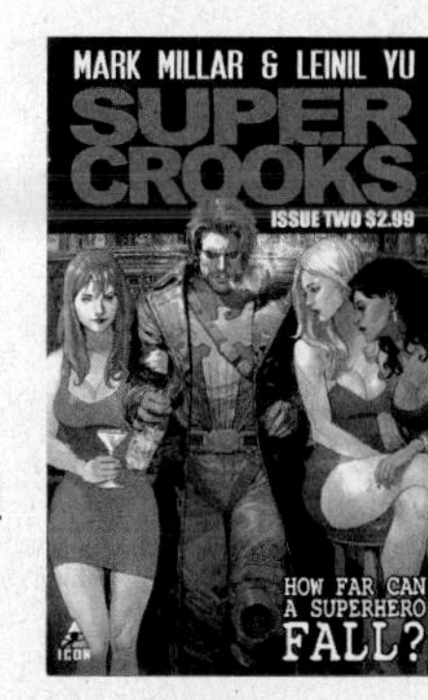

Supercrooks #2 © Millar & Yu

GD 2.0 | VG 4.0 | FN 6.0 | VF 8.0 | VF/NM 9.0 | NM- 9.2

#1,000,000 (11/98) 853rd Century x-over 4.00
Annual 1 (1994, $2.95, 68 pgs.)-Elseworlds story, Pt. 2 of The Super Seven (see Adventures Of Superman Annual #6) 5.00
Annual 2 (1995, $3.95)-Year One story 5.00
Annual 3 (1996, $2.95)-Legends of the Dead Earth 5.00
Annual 4 (1997, $3.95)-Pulp Heroes story 5.00
...Plus 1 (Jan, 1997, $2.95) w/Capt. Marvel Jr. 4.00
...Plus 2 (Fall, 1997, $2.95) w/Slither (Scare Tactics) 4.00
.../Risk Double-Shot 1 (Feb, 1998, $1.95) w/Risk (Teen Titans) 4.00

SUPERBOY (4th Series)
DC Comics: Jan, 2011 - No. 11, Early Oct, 2011 ($2.99)

1-11: 1-Lemire-s/Gallo-a/Albuquerque-c; Parasite & Poison Ivy app. 2,3-Noto-c 3.00
1-5: 1-Variant-c by Cassaday. 2-March-var-c. 3-Nguyen var-c. 4-Lau var-c. 5-Manapul 4.00

SUPERBOY (DC New 52)
DC Comics: Nov, 2011 - No. 34, Oct, 2014 ($2.99)

1-34: 1-New origin; Lobdell-s/Silva-a/Canete-c; Caitlin Fairchild app. 6-Supergirl app. 8-Grunge, Beast Boy & Terra app. 9-"The Culling" x-over cont. from Teen Titans Annual #1; Teen Titans and the Legion app. 14-17-H'El on Earth tie-in; Batman app. 3.00
#0-(11/12, $2.99) Origin of Kryptonian clones; Silva-a 3.00
Annual 1 (3/13, $4.99) H'El on Earth tie-in between Superboy #16 & Superman #16 5.00
...: Futures End 1 (11/14, $2.99, regular-c) Five years later, Freefall app.; Caldwell-a 3.00
...: Futures End 1 (11/14, $3.99, 3-D cover) 4.00

SUPERBOY AND THE LEGION OF SUPER-HEROES
DC Comics: 2011 ($14.99, TPB)

SC-Reprints stories from Adventure Comics #515-520 15.00

SUPERBOY & THE RAVERS
DC Comics: Sept, 1996 - No. 19, March, 1998 ($1.95)

1-19: 4-Adam Strange app. 7-Impulse-c/app. 9-Superman-c/app. 3.00

SUPERBOY COMICS
DC Comics: Jan. 1942

nn - Ashcan comic, not distributed to newsstands, only for in-house use. Cover art is Detective Comics #57 with interior being Action Comics #38. A CGC certified 9.2 copy sold for $6,600 in 2003 and for $15,750 in 2008.

SUPERBOY/ROBIN: WORLD'S FINEST THREE
DC Comics: 1996 - No. 2, 1996 ($4.95, squarebound, limited series)

1,2: Superboy & Robin vs. Metallo & Poison Ivy; Karl Kesel & Chuck Dixon scripts; Tom Grummett-c(p)/a(p) 5.00

SUPERBOY'S LEGION (Elseworlds)
DC Comics: 2001 - No. 2, 2001 ($5.95, squarebound, limited series)

1,2- 31st century Superboy forms Legion; Farmer-s/i; Davis-a(p)/c 6.00

SUPERBOY: THE BOY OF STEEL
DC Comics: 2010 ($19.99, hardcover with dustjacket)

HC-Reprints stories from Adventure Comics #0-3,5,6 & Superman Secret Files 2009 20.00
SC-(2011, $14,99) Same contents as HC 15.00

SUPER BRAT (Li'l Genius #6 on)
Toby Press: Jan, 1954 - No. 4, July, 1954

	GD	VG	FN	VF	VF/NM	NM-
1	12	24	36	69	97	125
2-4: 4-Li'l Teevy by Mel Lazarus	7	14	21	35	43	50
I.W. Reprint #1,2,3,7,8('58): 1-r/#1	2	4	6	8	11	14
I.W. (Super) Reprint #10('63)	2	4	6	8	10	12

SUPERCAR (TV)
Gold Key: Nov, 1962 - No. 4, Aug, 1963 (All painted-c)

	GD	VG	FN	VF	VF/NM	NM-
1	11	22	33	72	154	235
2,3	7	14	21	44	82	120
4-Last issue	7	14	21	49	92	135

SUPER CAT (Formerly Frisky Animals; also see Animal Crackers)
Star Publications #56-58/Ajax/Farrell Publ. (Four Star Comic Corp.):
No. 56, Nov, 1953 - No. 58, May, 1954; Aug, 1957 - No. 4, May, 1958

	GD	VG	FN	VF	VF/NM	NM-
56-58-L.B. Cole-c on all	21	42	63	122	199	275
1(1957-Ajax)- "The Adventures of..." c-only	11	22	33	60	83	105
2-4	8	16	24	40	50	60

SUPER CEREBUS ANNUAL
Aardvark-Vanaheim: Apr, 2019 ($8.00, B&W)

1-Cerebus figures with original Gustave Doré artwork; Superman Annual #1-c swipe 8.00

SUPER CIRCUS (TV)
Cross Publishing Co.: Jan, 1951 - No. 5, Sept, 1951 (Mary Hartline)

	GD	VG	FN	VF	VF/NM	NM-
1-(52 pgs.)-Cast photos on-c	20	40	60	114	182	250
2-Cast photos on-c	13	26	39	72	101	130
3-5	10	20	30	58	79	100

SUPER CIRCUS (TV)
Dell Publ. Co.: No. 542, Mar, 1954 - No. 694, Mar, 1956 (Mary Hartline)

	GD	VG	FN	VF	VF/NM	NM-
Four Color 542: Mary Hartline photo-c	7	14	21	49	92	135
Four Color 592,694: Mary Hartline photo-c	6	12	18	38	69	100

SUPER COMICS
Dell Publishing Co.: May, 1938 - No. 121, Feb-Mar, 1949

	GD	VG	FN	VF	VF/NM	NM-
1-Terry & The Pirates, The Gumps, Dick Tracy, Little Orphan Annie, Little Joe, Gasoline Alley, Smilin' Jack, Smokey Stover, Smitty, Tiny Tim, Moon Mullins, Harold Teen, Winnie Winkle begin	248	496	744	1587	2719	3850
2	90	180	270	576	988	1400
3	81	162	243	518	884	1250
4,5: 4-Dick Tracy-c; also #8-10,17,26(part),31	60	120	180	381	653	925
6-10	48	96	144	302	514	725
11-20: 20-Smilin' Jack-c (also #29,32)	40	80	120	244	402	560
21-29: 21-Magic Morro begins (origin & 1st app., 2/40). 22,27-Ken Ernst-c (also #25?); Magic Morro c-22,25,27,34	34	68	102	204	332	460
30- "Sea Hawk" movie adaptation-c/story with Errol Flynn	36	72	108	214	347	480
31-40: 34-Ken Ernst-c	29	58	87	170	278	385
41-50: 41-Intro Lightning Jim. 43-Terry & The Pirates ends	24	48	72	142	234	325
51-60	19	38	57	112	179	245
61-70: 62-Flag-c. 65-Brenda Starr-r begin? 67-X-Mas-c	17	34	51	103	162	220
71-80	14	28	42	82	121	160
81-99	14	28	42	78	112	145
100	14	28	42	81	118	155
101-115-Last Dick Tracy (moves to own title)	10	20	30	58	79	100
116-121: 116,118-All Smokey Stover. 117-All Gasoline Alley. 119-121-Terry & The Pirates app. in all	9	18	27	52	69	85

SUPER COPS, THE
Red Circle Productions (Archie): July, 1974 (one-shot)

	GD	VG	FN	VF	VF/NM	NM-
1-Morrow-c/a; art by Pino, Hack, Thorne	2	4	6	8	11	14

SUPER COPS
Now Comics: Sept, 1990 - No. 4, Dec?, 1990 ($1.75)

1-($2.75, 52 pgs.)-Dave Dorman painted-c (both printings) 4.00
2-4 3.00

SUPER CRACKED (See Cracked)

SUPERCROOKS
Marvel Comics (Icon): May, 2012 - No. 4, Aug, 2012 ($2.99/$4.99)

1-3-($2.99) Millar-s/Yu-a. 1-Covers by Yu & Gibbons. 2-Covers by Yu & Hitch 3.00
4-($4.99) Bonus preview of Jupiter's Children (later re-titled Jupiter's Legacy) 5.00

SUPER DC GIANT (25-50¢, all 68-52 pg. Giants)
National Per. Publ.: No. 13, 9-10/70 - No. 26, 7-8/71; V3#27, Summer, 1976 (No #1-12)

	GD	VG	FN	VF	VF/NM	NM-
S-13-Binky	10	20	30	64	132	200
S-14-Top Guns of the West; Kubert-c; Trigger Twins, Johnny Thunder, Wyoming Kid-r; Moreira-r (9-10/70)	5	10	15	33	57	80
S-15-Western Comics; Kubert-c; Pow Wow Smith, Vigilante, Buffalo Bill-r; new Gil Kane-a (9-10/70)	5	10	15	33	57	80
S-16-Best of the Brave & the Bold; Batman-r & Metamorpho origin-r from Brave & the Bold; Spectre pin-up.	4	8	12	27	44	60
S-17-Love 1970 (scarce)	24	48	72	168	372	575
S-18-Three Mouseketeers; Dizzy Dog, Doodles Duck, Bo Bunny-r; Sheldon Mayer-a	9	18	27	57	111	165
S-19-Jerry Lewis; Neal Adams pin-up	9	18	27	59	117	175
S-20-House of Mystery; N. Adams-c; Kirby-r(3)	7	14	21	44	82	120
S-21-Love 1971 (scarce)	28	56	84	202	451	700
S-22-Top Guns of the West; Kubert-c	4	8	12	25	40	55
S-23-The Unexpected	4	8	12	28	47	65
S-24-Supergirl	4	8	12	25	40	55
S-25-Challengers of the Unknown; all Kirby/Wood-r	4	8	12	22	35	48
S-26-Aquaman (1971)-r/S.A. Aquaman origin story from Showcase #30	4	8	12	27	44	60
27-Strange Flying Saucers Adventures (Sum, 1976)	3	6	9	18	28	38

NOTE: ***Sid Greene** r-27p(2), **Heath** r-27. **G. Kane** a-14r(2), 15, 27r(p). **Kubert** r-16.*

SUPER DINOSAUR
Image Comics: Apr, 2011 - No. 23, Dec, 2014 ($2.99)

Super Duck Comics #20 © MAR

Super Friends #31 © DC

Supergirl (2005 series) #50 © DC

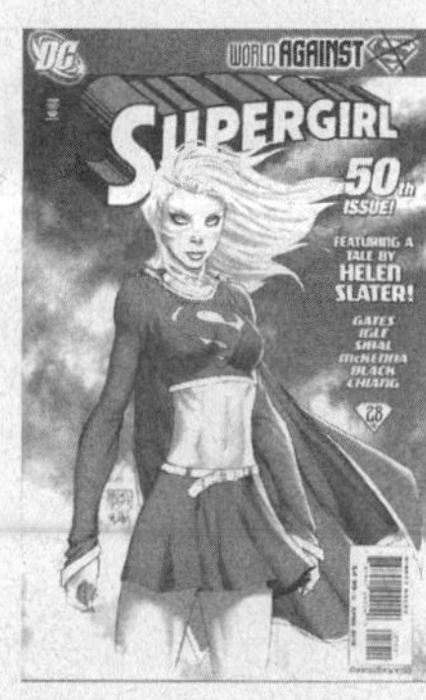

	GD	VG	FN	VF	VF/NM	NM-
	2.0	4.0	6.0	8.0	9.0	9.2

1-23: 1-Robert Kirkman-s/Jason Howard-a; origin story and character profiles 3.00
... Origin Special #1 FCBD Edition (5/11, giveaway) r/#1 3.00

SUPER-DOOPER COMICS
Able Mfg. Co./Harvey: 1946 - No. 7, May, 1946; No. 8, 1946 (10¢, 32 pgs., paper-c)

1-The Clock, Gangbuster app. (scarce) 100 200 300 645 1098 1550
2 20 40 60 120 195 270
3-6 18 36 54 111 176 240
7,8-Shock Gibson. 7-Where's Theres A Will by Ed Wheelan, Steve Case Crime Rover, Penny & Ullysses Jr. 8-Sam Hill app. 24 48 72 140 230 320

SUPER DUCK
Archie Comics Publications: May, 2020 - No. 4 ($3.99, limited series)

1-Frank Tieri & Ian Flynn-s/Ryan Jampole-a; revival of Golden Age character 4.00

SUPER DUCK COMICS (The Cockeyed Wonder) (See Jolly Jingles)
MLJ Mag. No. 1-4(9/45)/Close-Up No. 5 on (Archie): Fall, 1944 - No. 94, Dec, 1960 (Also see Laugh #24)(#1-5 are quarterly)

1-Origin; Hitler & Hirohito-c 171 342 513 1094 1872 2650
2-Bill Vigoda-c 37 74 111 222 361 500
3-5: 4-20-Al Fagaly-c (most) 26 52 78 154 252 350
6-10 15 30 45 90 140 190
11-20(6/48) 13 26 39 72 101 130
21,23-40 (10/51) 11 22 33 62 86 110
22-Used in **SOTI**, pg. 35,307,308 14 28 42 78 112 145
41-60 (2/55) 10 20 30 54 72 90
61-94 8 16 24 44 57 70

SUPER DUPER (Formerly Pocket Comics #1-4?)
Harvey Publications: No. 5, 1941 - No. 11, 1941

5-Captain Freedom & Shock Gibson app. 74 148 222 470 810 1150
8,11 53 106 159 334 567 800

SUPER DUPER COMICS (Formerly Latest Comics?)
F. E. Howard Publ.: No. 3, May-June, 1947

3-1st app. Mr. Monster 81 162 243 518 884 1250

SUPER FRIENDS (TV) (Also see Best of DC & Limited Collectors' Edition)
National Periodical Publications/DC Comics: Nov, 1976 - No. 47, Aug, 1981 (#14 is 44 pgs.)

1-Superman, Batman, Robin, Wonder Woman, Aquaman, Atom, Wendy, Marvin & Wonder Dog begin (1st Super Friends) 6 12 18 38 69 100
2-Penguin-c/sty 3 6 9 16 23 30
3-5 3 6 9 14 20 26
6,8-10,14: 8-1st app. Jack O'Lantern. 9-1st app. Icemaiden. 14-Origin Wonder Twins 2 4 6 13 18 22
7-1st app. Wonder Twins & The Seraph 8 16 24 54 102 150
11-13,15-30: 13-1st app. Dr. Mist. 25-1st app. Fire as Green Fury. 28-Bizarro app. 2 4 6 9 13 16
13-16,20-23,25,32-(Whitman variants; low print run, no issue# on cover) 2 4 6 11 16 20
31,47: 31-Black Orchid app. 47-Origin Fire & Green Fury 2 4 6 10 14 18
32-46: 36,43-Plastic Man app. 2 4 6 8 11 14
TBP (2001, $14.95) r/#1,6-9,14,21,27 & Limited Collectors' Edition C-41; Alex Ross-c 15.00
...: Truth, Justice and Peace TPB (2003, $14.95) r/#10,12,13,25,28,29,31,36,37 15.00
NOTE: *Estrada a-1p, 2p. Orlando a-1p. Staton a-43, 45.*

SUPER FRIENDS (All ages stories with puzzles and games)(Based on Mattel toy line)
DC Comics: May, 2008 - No. 29, Sept, 2010 ($2.25/$2.99)

1-29-Superman, Batman, Wonder Woman, Aquaman, Flash & Green Lantern. 29-Begin $2.99-c; Bat-Mite & Mr. Mxyzptlk app. 3.00
...: Calling All Super Friends TPB (2009, $12.99) r/#8-14; puzzles and games 13.00
...: For Justice TPB (2009, $12.99) r/#1-7; puzzles and games 13.00
...: Head of the Class TPB (2010, $12.99) r/#15-21; puzzles and games 13.00
...: Mystery in Space TPB (2011, $12.99) r/#22-28; puzzles and games 13.00

SUPER FUN
Gillmor Magazines: Jan, 1956 (By A.W. Nugent)

1-Comics, puzzles, cut-outs by A.W. Nugent 10 20 30 54 72 90

SUPER FUNNIES (...Western Funnies #3,4)
Superior Comics Publishers Ltd. (Canada): Dec, 1953 - No. 4, Sept, 1954

1-(3-D, 10¢)-...Presents Dopey Duck; make your own 3-D glasses cut-out inside front-c; did not come w/glasses 39 78 117 240 395 550
2-Horror & crime satire 15 30 45 94 147 200
3-Phantom Ranger-c/s; Geronimo, Billy the Kid app. 10 20 30 58 79 100
4-Phantom Ranger-c/story 10 20 30 58 79 100

SUPERGIRL
DC Comics: Feb. 1944

nn - Ashcan comic, not distributed to newsstands, only for in-house use. Cover art is Boy Commandos #1 with interior being Action Comics #80. A copy sold for $15,750 in 2008.

SUPERGIRL (See Action, Adventure #281, Brave & the Bold, Crisis on Infinite Earths #7, Daring New Advs. of..., Super DC Giant, Superman Family, & Super-Team Family)

SUPERGIRL
National Periodical Publ.: Nov, 1972 - No. 9, Dec-Jan, 1973-74; No. 10, Sept-Oct, 1974 (1st solo title)(20¢)

1-Zatanna back-up stories begin, end #5 12 24 36 81 176 270
2-4,6,7,9: 7-Zatanna battles Supergirl 4 8 12 27 44 60
5,8,10: 5-Zatanna origin-r. 8-JLA x-over; Batman cameo. 10-Prez app. 4 8 12 28 47 65
NOTE: *Zatanna in #1-5, 7(Guest); Prez app. in #10. #1-10 are 20¢ issues.*

SUPERGIRL (Formerly Daring New Adventures of...)
DC Comics: No. 14, Dec, 1983 - No. 23, Sept, 1984

14-23: 16-Ambush Bug app. 20-JLA & New Teen Titans app. 5.00
...Movie Special (1985)-Adapts movie; Morrow-a; photo back-c 5.00

SUPERGIRL
DC Comics: Feb, 1994 - No. 4, May, 1994 ($1.50, limited series)

1-Matrix clone Supergirl; Stern-s/Brigman-a 1 3 4 6 8 10
2-4: Guice-a(i) 5.00

SUPERGIRL (See Showcase '96 #8)
DC Comics: Sept, 1996 - No. 80, May, 2003 ($1.95/$1.99/$2.25/$2.50)

1-Peter David scripts & Gary Frank-c/a 2 4 6 11 16 24
1-2nd printing 4.00
2,4-9: 4-Gorilla Grodd-c/app. 6-Superman-c/app. 9-Last Frank-a 5.00
3-Final Night, Gorilla Grodd app. 6.00
10-19: 14-Genesis x-over. 16-Power Girl app. 4.00
20-35: 20-Millennium Giants x-over; Superman app. 23-Steel-c/app. 24-Resurrection Man x-over. 25-Comet ID revealed; begin $1.99-c 4.00
36-46: 36,37-Young Justice x-over 4.00
47-49,51-74: 47-Begin $2.25-c. 51-Adopts costume from animated series. 54-Green Lantern app. 59-61-Our Worlds at War x-over. 62-Two-Face-c/app. 66,67-Demon-c/app. 68-74-Mary Marvel app. 70-Nauck-a. 73-Begin $2.50-c 4.00
50-($3.95) Supergirl's final battle with the Carnivore 5.00
75-80: 75-Re-intro. Kara Zor-El; cover swipe of Action Comics #252 by Haynes; Benes-a. 78-Spectre app. 80-Last issue; Romita-c 4.00
#1,000,000 (11/98) 853rd Century x-over 4.00
Annual 1 (1996, $2.95)-Legends of the Dead Earth 5.00
Annual 2 (1997, $3.95)-Pulp Heroes; LSH app.; Chiodo-c 5.00
...: Many Happy Returns TPB (2003, $14.95) r/#75-80; intro. by Peter David 15.00
...Plus (2/97, $2.95) Capt.(Mary) Marvel-c/app.; David-s/Frank-a 4.00
.../Prysm Double-Shot 1 (Feb, 1998, $1.95) w/Prysm (Teen Titans) 3.00
...: Wings (2001, $5.95) Elseworlds; DeMatteis-s/Tolagson-a 6.00
TPB-('98, $14.95) r/Showcase '96 #8 & Supergirl #1-9 15.00

SUPERGIRL (See Superman/Batman #8 & #19)
DC Comics: No. 0, Oct, 2005 - No. 67, Oct, 2011 ($2.99)

0-Reprints Superman/Batman #19 with white variant of that cover 3.00
1-Loeb-s/Churchill-a; two covers by Churchill & Turner; Power Girl app. 5.00
1-2nd printing with B&W sketch variant of Turner-c 3.00
1-3rd printing with variant-c homage to Action Comics #252 by Churchill 3.00
2-4: 2-Teen Titans app. 3-Outsiders app.; covers by Turner & Churchill 3.00
5-($3.99) Supergirl vs. Supergirl; Churchill & Turner-c 4.00
6-49: 6-9-One Year Later; Power Girl app. 11-Intro. Powerboy. 12-Terra debut; Conner-a 20-Amazons Attack x-over. 21,22-Karate Kid app. 28-31-Resurrection Man app. 35,36-New Krypton x-over; Argo City story re-told; Superwoman app. 35-Ross-c. 36-Zor-El dies 3.00
50-($4.99) Lana Lang Insect Queen app.; Superwoman returns; back-up story co-written by Helen Slater with Chiang-a; Turner-c 5.00
50-Variant cover by Middleton 6.00
51-67: 51-52-New Krypton. 52-Brainiac 5 app. 53-57-Bizarro-Girl app. 55-63-Reeder-c 3.00
58-DC 75th Anniversary variant cover by Conner 6.00
Annual 1 (11/09, $3.99) Origin of Superwoman 4.00
Annual 2 (12/10, $4.99) Silver Age Legion of Super-Heroes app.; Reeder-c 5.00
...: Beyond Good and Evil TPB (2008, $17.99) r/#23-27 and Action Comics #850 18.00
...: Bizarrogirl TPB (2011, $19.99) r/#53-59 & Annual #2 20.00
...: Candor TPB (2007, $14.99) r/#6-9; and pages from JSA Classified #2, Superman #223, Superman/Batman #27 and JLA #122,123 15.00
...: Death & The Family TPB (2010, $17.99) r/#48-50 & Annual #1 18.00
...: Friends & Fugitives TPB (2010, $17.99) r/#43,45-47; Action Comics #881,882 18.00
...: Identity TPB (2007, $19.99) r/#10-16 and story from DCU Infinite Holiday Special 20.00
...: Power TPB (2006, $14.99) r/#1-5 and Superman/Batman #19; variant-c gallery 15.00

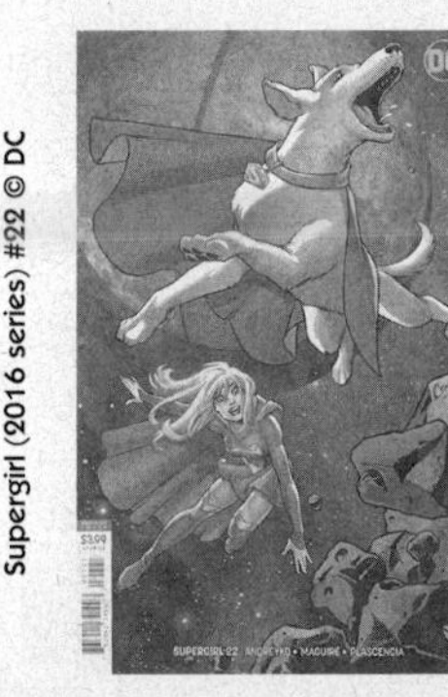
Supergirl (2016 series) #22 © DC

Super Goof #60 © DIS

Superior Spider-Man (2019 series) #6 © MAR

	GD 2.0	VG 4.0	FN 6.0	VF 8.0	VF/NM 9.0	NM- 9.2
...: Way of the World TPB (2009, $17.99) r/#28-33						18.00
...: Who is Superwoman TPB (2009, $17.99) r/#34,37-42						18.00

SUPERGIRL (DC New 52)
DC Comics: Nov, 2011 - No. 40, May, 2015 ($2.99)

	GD	VG	FN	VF	VF/NM	NM-
1-New origin; Green & Johnson-s/Asrar-a/c; Superman app.						4.00
2-40: 2,3-Superman app. 8-Pérez-a. 14-17-H'El on Earth tie-in. 17-Wonder Woman app. 19,20-Power Girl app. 19-Power Girl gets classic costume. 23,24-Cyborg Superman app. 26-28-Lobo app. 28-33-Kara joins Red Lanterns. 33-Gen13 app. 36-40-Maxima app.						3.00
#0-(11/12, $2.99) Kara's escape from Krypton						3.00
...: Futures End 1 (11/14, $2.99, regular-c) Five years later; Cyborg Superman app.						3.00
...: Futures End 1 (11/14, $3.99, 3-D cover)						4.00
... Special Edition 1 (12/15, $1.00) reprints #1 with Supergirl TV banner at top of cover						3.00

SUPERGIRL (DC Rebirth)(Issues #41 & #42 were only released digitally)
DC Comics: Nov, 2016 - No. 40, May, 2020 ($2.99/$3.99)

	GD	VG	FN	VF	VF/NM	NM-
1-7: 1-Orlando-s/Ching-a; Cyborg Superman app.						3.00
8-24,26-40-($3.99) 8-Superman & Emerald Empress app. 9-11-Batgirl app. 12-Fatal Five. 12-20-Variant covers by Stanley "Artgerm" Lau. 20-The Unexpected app. 26-Omega Men app. 31-33-Maguire-a. 33-Legion of Super-Heroes app. 36-40-The Infected						4.00
25-($4.99) Lupacchino-a						5.00
Annual 1 (10/17, $4.99) The new Fatal Five app.; takes place between #11,12						5.00
Annual 2 (1/20, $4.99) Venditti-s/Braga-a; follows #36; The Batman Who Laughs app.						5.00
...: Rebirth 1 (10/16, $2.99) Orlando-s/Lupacchino-a; gets the Kara Danvers identity						3.00

SUPERGIRL AND THE LEGION OF SUPER-HEROES (Continues from Legion of Super-Heroes #15, Apr, 2006)(Continues as Legion of Super-Heroes #37)
DC Comics: No. 16, May, 2006 - No. 36, Jan, 2008 ($2.99)

	GD	VG	FN	VF	VF/NM	NM-
16-Supergirl appears in the 31st century						4.00
16-2nd printing						3.00
17-36: 23-Mon-El cameo. 24,25-Mon-El returns						3.00
...: Adult Education TPB (2007, $14.99) r/#20-25 & LSH #6,9,13-15						15.00
...: Dominator War TPB (2007, $14.99) r/#26-30						15.00
...: Strange Visitor From Another Century TPB (2006, $14.99) r/#16-19 & LSH #11,12,15						15.00
...: The Quest For Cosmic Boy TPB (2008, $14.99) r/#31-36						15.00

SUPERGIRL: BEING SUPER
DC Comics: Feb, 2017 - No. 4, Aug, 2017 ($5.99, limited series)

	GD	VG	FN	VF	VF/NM	NM-
1-4-Mariko Tamaki-s/Joëlle Jones-a						6.00

SUPERGIRL: COSMIC ADVENTURES IN THE 8TH GRADE (Cartoony all-ages title)
DC Comics: Feb, 2008 - No. 6, Jul, 2009 ($2.50, limited series)

	GD	VG	FN	VF	VF/NM	NM-
1-6: 1-Supergirl lands on Earth; Eric Jones-a. 5,6-Comet & Streaky app.						3.00

SUPERGIRL/LEX LUTHOR SPECIAL (Supergirl and Team Luthor on-c)
DC Comics: 1993 ($2.50, 68 pgs., one-shot)

	GD	VG	FN	VF	VF/NM	NM-
1-Pin-ups by Byrne & Thibert						4.00

SUPERGOD (Warren Ellis'...)
Avatar Press: Oct, 2009 - No. 5, Nov, 2010 ($3.99, limited series)

	GD	VG	FN	VF	VF/NM	NM-
1-5-Warren Ellis-s/Garrie Gastony-a; multiple covers on each						4.00

SUPER GOOF (Walt Disney) (See Dynabrite & The Phantom Blot)
Gold Key No. 1-57/Whitman No. 58 on: Oct, 1965 - No. 74, July, 1984

	GD	VG	FN	VF	VF/NM	NM-
1	5	10	15	33	57	80
2-5	3	6	9	17	26	35
6-10	3	6	9	14	19	24
11-20	2	4	6	8	11	14
21-30	1	3	4	6	8	10
31-50	1	2	3	4	5	7
51-57						6.00
58,59 (Whitman)	1	2	3	5	6	8
60(8/80), 62(11/80) 3-pack only (scarce)	6	12	18	41	76	110
61(9-10/80) 3-pack only (rare)	9	18	27	63	129	195
63-66('81)	1	2	3	5	6	8
63 (1/81, 40¢-c) Cover price error variant (scarce)	3	6	9	14	19	24
67-69: 67(2/82), 68(2-3/82), 69(3/82)						6.00
70-74 (#90180 on-c; pre-pack, nd, nd code): 70(5/83), 71(8/83), 72(5/84), 73(6/84), 74(7/84)	3	6	9	15	22	28

NOTE: *Reprints in #16, 24, 28, 29, 37, 38, 43, 45, 46, 54(1/2), 56-58, 65(1/2), 72(r-#2).*

SUPER GREEN BERET (Tod Holton...)
Lightning Comics (Milson Publ. Co.): Apr, 1967 - No. 2, Jun, 1967

	GD	VG	FN	VF	VF/NM	NM-
1-(25¢, 68 pgs)	5	10	15	30	50	70
2-(25¢, 68 pgs)	3	6	9	21	33	45

SUPER HEROES (See Giant-Size... & Marvel...)

SUPER HEROES
Dell Publishing Co.: Jan, 1967 - No. 4, June, 1967

	GD	VG	FN	VF	VF/NM	NM-
1-Origin & 1st app. Fab 4	5	10	15	33	57	80
2-4	3	6	9	16	24	32

SUPER-HEROES BATTLE SUPER-GORILLAS (See DC Special #16)
National Periodical Publications: Winter, 1976 (52 pgs., all reprints, one-shot)

	GD	VG	FN	VF	VF/NM	NM-
1-Superman, Batman, Flash stories; Infantino-a(p)	2	4	6	11	16	20

SUPER HEROES VERSUS SUPER VILLAINS
Archie Publications (Radio Comics): July, 1966 (no month given)(68 pgs.)

	GD	VG	FN	VF	VF/NM	NM-
1-Flyman, Black Hood, Web, Shield-r; Reinman-a	6	12	18	37	66	95

SUPER HERO SQUAD (See Marvel Super Hero Squad)

SUPERHERO WOMEN, THE - FEATURING THE FABULOUS FEMALES OF MARVEL COMICS (See Fireside Book Series)

SUPERICHIE (Formerly Super Richie)
Harvey Publications: No. 5, Oct, 1976 - No. 18, Jan, 1979 (52 pgs. giants)

	GD	VG	FN	VF	VF/NM	NM-
5-Origin/1st app. new costumes for Rippy & Crashman	2	4	6	9	13	16
6-18	2	4	6	8	10	12

SUPERIOR
Marvel Comics (ICON): Dec, 2010 - No. 7, Mar, 2012 ($2.99/$4.99)

	GD	VG	FN	VF	VF/NM	NM-
1-6-Mark Millar-s/Leinil Yu-a. 1-1st & 2nd printings						3.00
7-($4.99) Bonus preview of Supercrooks #1						5.00
... World Record Special 1 (12/11, $2.99, B&W) Comic created in less than 12 hours						3.00

SUPERIOR CARNAGE
Marvel Comics: Sept, 2013 - No. 5, Jan, 2014 ($3.99)

	GD	VG	FN	VF	VF/NM	NM-
1-5: 1-Shinick-s/Segovia-a; covers by Crain & Checchetto. 2-5-Superior Spider-Man app.						4.00
Annual 1 (4/14, $4.99) Bunn-s/Jacinto & Henderson-a; follows #5; Kasady in prison						5.00

SUPERIOR FOES OF SPIDER-MAN (Superior Spider-Man)
Marvel Comics: Sept, 2013 - No. 17, Jan, 2015 ($3.99)

	GD	VG	FN	VF	VF/NM	NM-
1-17: 1-Boomerang, Shocker, Overdrive, Speed Demon & Beetle team; Spencer-s						4.00

SUPERIOR IRON MAN (Follows events of the Avengers & X-Men: Axis series)
Marvel Comics: Jan, 2015 - No. 9, Aug, 2015 ($3.99)

	GD	VG	FN	VF	VF/NM	NM-
1-9: 1-Tom Taylor-s/Yildiray Cinar-a. 1-4-Daredevil app.						4.00

SUPERIOR OCTOPUS (Tie-in to Spider-Geddon event)
Marvel Comics: Dec, 2018 ($3.99)

	GD	VG	FN	VF	VF/NM	NM-
1-Cloned Otto Octavius; Arnim Zola & The Gorgon app.; Gage-s/Hawthorne-a						4.00

SUPERIOR SPIDER-MAN (Follows Amazing Spider-Man #700)
Marvel Comics: Mar, 2013 - No. 31, Jun, 2014; No. 32, Oct, 2014 - No. 33, Nov, 2014 ($3.99)

	GD	VG	FN	VF	VF/NM	NM-
1-Doc Ock as Spider-Man; new Sinister Six app.; Slott-s/Stegman-a						8.00
1-Variant baby-c by Skottie Young						10.00
2-6: 4,5-Camuncoli-a. 4-Green Goblin cameo. 6-Ramos-a						5.00
6AU (5/13, $3.99) Alternate timeline Age of Ultron tie-in; Gage-s/Soy-a						4.00
7-24: 7,8-Ramos-a; Avengers app. 9-Peter's memories removed. 14-New costume. 17-19-Spider-Man 2099 app. 20-Black Cat app. 22-24-Venom app.						4.00
25-($4.99) Superior Venom vs. the Avengers; Ramos-a						5.00
26-30: 27-Goblin Nation begins. 29-Spider-Man 2099 app.						4.00
31-($5.99) Goblin Nation finale; covers by Camuncoli & Campbell; Silver Surfer bonus						6.00
32,33-($4.99) Edge of Spider-Verse tie-ins; takes place during issue #19						5.00
Annual 1 (1/14, $4.99) Blackout app.; Gage-s/Rodriguez-a						5.00
Annual 2 (5/14, $4.99) Leads into Superior Spider-Man #30; Gage-s/Rodriguez-a						5.00

SUPERIOR SPIDER-MAN (Otto Octavius)(See Spider-Geddon)
Marvel Comics: Feb, 2019 - No. 12, Dec, 2019 ($3.99)

	GD	VG	FN	VF	VF/NM	NM-
1-6-Gage-s/Hawthorne-a. 1-Stilt-Man app. 1-3-Terrax app. 5,6-Doctor Strange app.						4.00
7-12: 7,8-War of the Realms tie-ins. 11-Doctor Octopus returns; Mephisto app.						4.00

SUPERIOR SPIDER-MAN TEAM UP
Marvel Comics: Sept, 2013 - No. 12, Jun, 2014 ($3.99)

	GD	VG	FN	VF	VF/NM	NM-
1-10: 1-Avengers app. 8-Namor app. 9,10-Daredevil & The Punisher app.						4.00
... Special 1 (12/13, $4.99) Hulk & the original X-Men app.; Dialynas-a/Lozano-c						5.00

SUPERIOR STORIES
Nesbit Publishers, Inc.: May-June, 1955 - No. 4, Nov-Dec, 1955

	GD	VG	FN	VF	VF/NM	NM-
1-The Invisible Man by H.G. Wells	25	50	75	154	252	350
2-4: 2-The Pirate of the Gulf by J.H. Ingrahams. 3-Wreck of the Grosvenor by William Clark Russell. 4-The Texas Rangers by O'Henry	13	26	39	72	101	130

NOTE: ***Morisi** c/a in all. Kiwanis stories in #3 & 4. #4 has photo of Gene Autry on-c.*

SUPER MAGIC (Super Magician Comics #2 on)
Street & Smith Publications: May, 1941

	GD	VG	FN	VF	VF/NM	NM-
V1#1-Blackstone the Magician-c/story; origin/1st app. Rex King (Black Fury); Charles Sultan-c; Blackstone-c begin	206	412	618	1318	2259	3200

SUPER MAGICIAN COMICS (Super Magic #1)

Superman #2 © DC

Superman #96 © DC

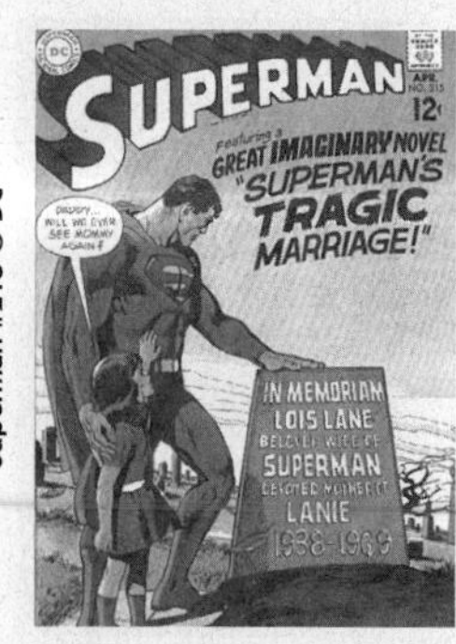

Superman #215 © DC

Street & Smith Publications: No. 2, Sept, 1941 - V5#8, Feb-Mar, 1947

	GD 2.0	VG 4.0	FN 6.0	VF 8.0	VF/NM 9.0	NM- 9.2
V1#2-Blackstone the Magician continues; Rex King, Man of Adventure app.	87	174	261	553	952	1350
3-Tao-Anwar, Boy Magician begins	54	108	162	343	574	825
4-7,9-12: 4-Origin Transo. 11-Supersnipe app.	50	100	150	315	533	750
8-Abbott & Costello story (1st app?, 11/42)	53	106	159	334	567	800
V2#1-The Shadow app.	48	96	144	302	514	725
2-12: 5-Origin Tigerman. 8-Red Dragon begins	29	58	87	174	285	395
V3#1-12: 5-Origin Mr. Twilight	27	54	81	162	266	370
V4#1-4,6-12: 11-Nigel Elliman Ace of Magic begins (3/46)	23	46	69	136	223	310
5-KKK-c/sty	47	94	141	296	498	700
V5#1-6	22	44	66	130	213	295
7,8-Red Dragon by Edd Cartier-c/a	42	84	126	265	445	625

NOTE: ***Jack Binder** c-1-14(most). Red Dragon c-V5#7, 8.*

SUPERMAN (See Action Comics, Advs. of..., All-New Coll. Ed., All-Star Comics, Best of DC, Brave & the Bold, Cosmic Odyssey, DC Comics Presents, Heroes Against Hunger, JLA, The Kents, Krypton Chronicles, Limited Coll. Ed., Man of Steel, Phantom Zone, Power Record Comics, Special Edition, Steel, Super Friends, Superman: The Man of Steel, Superman: The Man of Tomorrow, Taylor's Christmas Tabloid, Three-Dimension Advs., World Of Krypton, World Of Metropolis, World Of Smallville & World's Finest)

SUPERMAN (Becomes Adventures of...#424 on)
National Periodical Publ./DC Comics: Summer, 1939 - No. 423, Sept, 1986
(#1-5 are quarterly)

	GD 2.0	VG 4.0	FN 6.0	VF 8.0	VF/NM 9.0	NM- 9.2
1(nn)-1st four Action stories reprinted; origin Superman by Siegel & Shuster; has a new 2 pg. origin plus 4 pgs. omitted in Action story; see The Comics Magazine #1 & More Fun #14-17 for Superman prototype app.; cover r/splash page from Action #10; 1st pin-up Superman on back-c - 1st pin-up in comics	126,500	253,000	506,000	950,000	1,425,000	1,900,000

1-Reprint, Oversize 13-1/2x10". **WARNING:** This comic is an exact duplicate reprint of the original except for its size. DC published it in 1978 with a second cover titling it as a Famous First Edition. There have been many reported cases of the outer cover being removed and the interior sold as the original edition. The reprint with the new outer cover removed is practically worthless. See Famous First Edition for value.

	GD 2.0	VG 4.0	FN 6.0	VF 8.0	VF/NM 9.0	NM- 9.2
2-All daily strip-r; full pg. ad for N.Y. World's Fair	3500	7000	10,500	26,200	55,600	85,000
3-2nd story-r from Action #5; 3rd story-r from Action #6	1675	3350	5025	12,200	25,000	40,000
4-2nd mention of Daily Planet (Spr/40); also see Action #23; 2nd & 3rd app. Luthor (red-headed; also see Action #23); first issue of title to feature original stories	1000	2000	3000	7400	13,200	19,000
5-4th Luthor app. (grey hair)	784	1568	2352	5723	10,112	14,500
6,7: 6-1st splash pg. in a Superman comic. 7-1st Perry White? (11-12/40)	514	1028	1542	3750	6625	9500
8-10: 10-5th app. Luthor (1st bald Luthor, 5-6/41)	454	908	1362	3314	5857	8400
11-13,15: 13-Jimmy Olsen & Luthor app.	366	732	1098	2562	4481	6400
14-Patriotic Shield-c classic by Fred Ray	1100	2200	3300	8350	15,175	22,000
16,19,20: 16-1st Lois Lane-c this title (5-6/42); 2nd Lois-c after Action #29	304	608	912	2128	3764	5400
17-Hitler, Hirohito-c	1075	2150	3225	8200	14,850	21,500
18-Classic WWII-c	371	742	1113	2600	4550	6500
21,22,25: 25-Clark Kent's only military service; Fred Ray's only super-hero story	239	478	717	1530	2615	3700
23-Classic periscope-c	343	686	1029	2400	4200	6000
24-Classic Jack Burnley flag-c	432	864	1296	3154	5577	8000
26-Classic war-c	415	830	1245	2905	5103	7300
27-29: 27,29-Lois Lane-c. 28-Lois Lane Girl Reporter series begins, ends #40,42	194	388	582	1242	2121	3000
28-Overseas edition for Armed Forces; same as reg. #28	194	388	582	1242	2121	3000
30-Origin & 1st app. Mr. Mxyztplk (9-10/44)(pronounced "Mix-it-plk") in comic books; name later became Mxyzptlk ("Mix-yez-pit-l-ick"); the character was inspired by a combination of the name of Al Capp's Joe Blyfstyk (the little man with the black cloud over his head) & the devilish antics of Bugs Bunny; he first app. in newspapers 3/7/44; Superman flies for the first time	309	618	927	2198	3849	5500
31-40: 33-(3-4/45)-3rd app. Mxyztplk. 35,36-Lois Lane-c. 38-Atomic bomb story (1-2/46); delayed because of gov't censorship; Superman shown reading Batman #32 on cover. 40-Mxyztplk-c	152	304	456	973	1662	2350
41-50: 42-Lois Lane-c. 45-Lois Lane as Superwoman (see Action #60 for 1st app.). 46-(5-6/47)-1st app. Superboy this title? 48-1st time Superman travels thru time	129	258	387	826	1413	2000
51,52: 51-Lois Lane-c	123	246	369	787	1344	1900
53-Third telling of Superman origin; 10th anniversary issue ('48); classic origin-c by Boring	394	788	1182	2758	4829	6900
54,56-60: 57-Lois Lane as Superwoman-c. 58-Intro Tiny Trix. 59-Early use of heat vision (possibly first time)	119	238	357	762	1306	1850
55-Used in **SOTI**, pg. 33	123	246	369	787	1344	1900
61-Origin Superman retold; origin Green Kryptonite (1st Kryptonite story); Superman returns to Krypton for 1st time & sees his parents for 1st time since infancy, discovers he's not an Earth man	219	438	657	1402	2401	3400
62-70: 62-Orson Welles-c/story. 65-1st Krypton Foes: Mala, Kizo, & U-Ban. 66-2nd Superbaby story. 67-Perry Como-c/story. 68-1st Luthor-c this title (see Action Comics)	116	232	348	742	1271	1800
71-75: 74-2nd Luthor-c this title. 75-Some have #74 on-c	113	226	339	723	1237	1750
76-Batman x-over; Superman & Batman learn each other's I.D. for the 1st time (5-6/52) (also see World's Finest #71)	377	754	1131	2639	4620	6600
77-81: 78-Last 52 pg. issue; 1st meeting of Lois Lane & Lana Lang. 81-Used in **POP**, pg. 88. 81-"Superwoman From Space" story	100	200	300	640	1095	1550
82-87,89,90: 89-1st Curt Swan-c in title	92	184	276	593	1009	1425
88-Prankster, Toyman & Luthor team-up	97	194	291	621	1061	1500
91-95: 95-Last precode issue (2/55)	84	168	252	538	919	1300
96-99: 96-Mr. Mxyztplk-c/story	77	154	231	493	847	1200
100 (9-10/55)-Shows cover to #1 on-c	274	548	822	1740	2995	4250
101-105,107-110: 109-1st S.A. issue	56	112	168	353	752	1150
106 (7/56)-Retells origin	59	118	177	372	786	1200
111-120	50	100	150	315	670	1025
121,122,124-127,129: 127-Origin/1st app. Titano. 129-Intro/origin Lori Lemaris, The Mermaid	44	88	132	277	589	900
123-Pre-Supergirl tryout-c/story (8/58).	175	350	700	1630	3715	5800
128-(4/59)-Red Kryptonite used. Bruce Wayne x-over who protects Superman's i.d. (3rd story)	50	100	150	300	625	950
130-(7/59)-2nd app, Krypto, the Superdog with Superman (see Sup.'s Pal Jimmy Olsen #29) (all other previous app. w/Superboy)	52	104	156	312	644	975
131-139: 135-2nd Lori Lemaris app. 139-Lori Lemaris app.;	37	74	111	222	461	700
140-1st Blue Kryptonite & Bizarro Supergirl; origin Bizarro Jr. #1	37	74	111	222	461	700
141-145,148: 142-2nd Batman x-over	32	64	96	192	396	600
146-(7/61)-Superman's life story; back-up hints at Earth II. Classic-c	49	98	147	294	610	925
147(8/61)-7th Legion app; 1st app. Legion of Super-Villains; 1st app. Adult Legion; swipes-c to Adv. #247	41	82	123	246	511	775
149(11/61)-8th Legion app. (cameo); "The Death of Superman" imaginary story; last 10¢ issue	39	78	117	234	492	750
150,151,153,154,157,159,160: 157-Gold Kryptonite used (see Adv. #299); Mon -El app.; Lightning Lad cameo (11/62)	14	28	42	94	207	320
152,155,156,158,162: 152(4/62)-15th Legion app. 155-(8/62)-Legion app; Lightning Man & Cosmic Man, & Adult Legion app. 156,162-Legion app. 158-1st app. Superman as Nightwing & Jimmy Olsen as Flamebird & Nor-Kann of Kandor (12/62)	14	28	42	97	214	330
161-1st told death of Ma and Pa Kent	15	30	45	100	220	340
161-2nd printing (1987, $1.25)-New DC logo; sold thru So Much Fun Toy Stores (cover title: Superman Classic)						5.00
163-166,168-180: 166-XMas-c. 168-All Luthor issue; JFK tribute/memorial. 169-Bizarro Invasion of Earth-c/story; last Sally Selwyn. 170-Pres. Kennedy story is finally published after delay from #168 due to assassination. 172,173-Legion cameos. 174-Super-Mxyzptlk; Bizarro app. 176-Legion of Super-Pets	11	22	33	75	160	245
167-New origin Brainiac, text reference of Brainiac 5 descending from adopted human son Brainiac II; intro Tharla (later Luthor's wife)	14	28	42	98	217	335
181,182,184-186,188-192,194-196,198,200: 181-1st 2965 story/series. 182-1st S.A. app. of The Toyman (1/66). 189-Origin/destruction of Krypton II.	9	18	27	60	120	180
183 (Giant G-18)	12	24	36	79	170	260
187,193,197 (Giants G-23,G-31,G-36)	9	18	27	63	129	195
199-1st Superman/Flash race (8/67): also see Flash #175 & World's Finest #198,199 (r-in Limited Coll. Ed. C-48)	42	84	126	311	706	1100
201,203-206,208-211,213-216: 213-Brainiac-5 app. 216-Last 12¢ issue	6	12	18	38	69	100
202 (80-pg. Giant G-42)-All Bizarro issue	7	14	21	44	82	120
207,212,217 (Giants G-48,G-54,G-60): 207-30th anniversary Superman (6/68)	6	12	18	42	79	115
218-221,223-226,228-231	5	10	15	33	57	85
222,239(Giants, G-66,G-84)	6	12	18	41	76	110
227,232(Giants, G-72,G-78): 232-All Krypton issue	6	12	18	41	76	110
233-2nd app. Morgan Edge; Clark Kent switches from newspaper reporter to TV newscaster; all Kryptonite on Earth destroyed; classic Neal Adams-c; 1st Fabulous World of Krypton story; Superman pin-up by Swan	18	36	54	124	275	425
234-238	5	10	15	33	57	80
240-Kaluta-a; last 15¢ issue	5	10	15	31	53	75
241-244 (All 52 pgs.): 241-New Wonder Woman app. 243-G.A.-r/#38	5	10	15	30	50	70
245-Also listed as DC 100 Pg. Super Spectacular #7; Air Wave, Kid Eternity, Hawkman-r; Atom-r/Atom #3	9	18	27	62	126	190

Superman #330 © DC

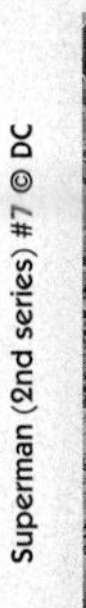

Superman (2nd series) #7 © DC

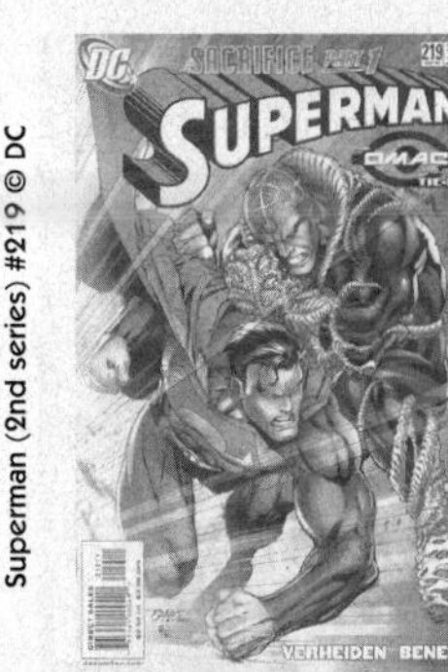

Superman (2nd series) #219 © DC

GD 2.0 VG 4.0 FN 6.0 VF 8.0 VF/NM 9.0 NM- 9.2

246-248,250,251,253 (All 52 pgs.): 246-G.A.-r/#40. 248-World of Krypton story. 251-G.A.-r/#45. 253-Finlay-a, 2 pgs., G.A.-r/#1 5 10 15 30 50 70

249,254-Neal Adams-a. 249-(52 pgs.); 1st app. Terra-Man (Swan-a) & origin-s by Dick Dillin (p) & Neal Adams (inks) 5 10 15 35 63 90

252-Also listed as DC 100 Pg. Super Spectacular #13; Ray(r/Smash #17), Black Condor, (r/Crack #18), Hawkman(r/Flash #24); Starman-r/Adv. #67; Dr. Fate & Spectre-r/More Fun #57; N. Adams-c 10 20 30 66 138 210

255-271,273-277,279-283: 263-Photo-c. 264-1st app. Steve Lombard. 276-Intro Capt. Thunder. 279-Batman, Batgirl app. 282-Luthor battlesuit 3 6 9 14 20 26

272,278,284-All 100 pgs. G.A.-r in all. 272-r/2nd app. Mr. Mxyztplk from Action #80 5 10 15 30 50 70

285-299: 289-Partial photo-c. 292-Origin Lex Luthor retold 2 4 6 10 14 18

300-(6/76) Superman in the year 2001 4 8 12 25 40 55

301-316,318-350: 301,320-Solomon Grundy app. 323-Intro. Atomic Skull. 327-329-(44 pgs.). 327-Kobra app. 330-More facts revealed about I.D. 331,332-1st/2nd app. Master Jailer. 335-Mxyzptlk marries Ms. Bgbznz. 336-Rose & Thorn app. 338-(8/79) 40th Anniv. issue; the bottled city of Kandor enlarged. 344-Frankenstein & Dracula app. 2 4 6 8 10 12

317-Classic Neal Adams kryptonite cover 3 6 9 21 33 45

321-323,325-327,329-332,335-345,348,350 (Whitman variants; low print run; no issue # on cover) 2 4 6 10 14 18

351-399: 353-Brief origin. 354,355,357-Superman 2020 stories (354-Debut of Superman III). 356-World of Krypton story (also #360,367,375). 366-Fan letter by Todd McFarlane. 369-Christmas-c. 372-Superman 2021 story. 376-Free 6 pg. preview Daring New Advs. of Supergirl. 377-Terra-Man-c/app.; free 16 pg. preview Masters of the Universe. 378-Origin & 1st app. Colonel Future. 379-Bizarro World app. 1 3 4 6 8 10

400 (10/84, $1.50, 68 pgs.)-Many top artists featured; Chaykin painted cover, Miller back-c; Steranko-s/a (10 pages) 2 4 6 8 10 12

401-422: 405-Super-Batman story. 408-Nuclear Holocaust-c/story. 411-Special Julius Schwartz tribute issue. 414,415-Crisis x-over. 422-Horror-c by Bolland 1 2 3 5 6 8

409-(7/85) Var-c with Superman/Superhombre logo 16 32 48 107 236 365

423-Alan Moore scripts; Curt Swan-a/George Pérez-a(i); "Whatever Happened to the Man of Tomorrow?" story, cont'd in Action #583 2 4 6 11 16 20

Annual 1 (10/60, 84 pgs.)-Reprints 1st Supergirl story/Action #252; r/Lois Lane #1; Krypto-r (1st Silver Age DC annual) 87 174 261 705 1578 2450

Annual 2 (Win, 1960-61)-Super-villain issue; Brainiac, Titano, Metallo, Bizarro origin-r 36 72 108 259 580 900

Annual 3 (Sum, 1961)-Strange Lives of Superman 25 50 75 175 388 600

Annual 4(Win, 1961-62)-11th Legion app; 1st Legion origins (text & pictures); advs. in time, space & on alien worlds 20 40 60 138 307 475

Annual 5 (Sum, 1962)-All Krypton issue 16 32 48 112 249 385

Annual 6 (Win, 1962-63)-Legion-r/Adv. #247; Superman Family portrait on back-c 15 30 45 100 220 340

Annual 7 (Sum, 1963)-Silver Anniversary Issue; origin-r/Superman-Batman team/Adv. #275; cover gallery of famous issues 11 22 33 76 163 250

Annual 8 (Win, 1963-64)-All origins issue 11 22 33 73 157 240

Annual 9 (8/64)-Was advertised but came out as 80 Page Giant #1 instead

Annual 9 (1983)-Toth/Austin-a 1 3 4 6 8 10

Annuals 10,12: 10(1984, $1.25)-M. Anderson-i. 12(1986)-Bolland-c 1 2 3 5 6 8

Annual 11 (1985) "For the Man Who Has Everything" story; Alan Moore-s/Dave Gibbons-a; Mongul and the Black Mercy app.; Wonder Woman, Batman & Robin app. (adapted for a Justice League Unlimited animated episode 4 8 12 27 44 60

Special 1-3 ('83-'85): 1-G. Kane-c/a; contains German-r 6.00

The Amazing World of Superman "Official Metropolis Edition" (1973, $2.00, treasury-size)-Origin retold; Wood-r(i) from Superboy #153,161; poster incl. (half price if poster missing) 4 8 12 27 44 60

11195 (2/79, $1.95, 224 pgs.)-Golden Press 4 8 12 23 37 50

NOTE: ***N. Adams*** *a-249i, 254p; c-204-206, 210, 212-215, 219, 231i, 233-237, 240-243, 249-252, 254, 263, 307, 308, 313, 314, 317.* ***Adkins*** *a-323i.* ***Austin*** *c-368i.* ***Wayne Boring*** *art-late 1940's to early 1960's.* ***Buckler*** *a(p)-352, 363, 364, 369; c(p)-324-327, 356, 363, 368, 369, 373, 376, 378.* ***Burnley*** *a-252r; c-19-25, 30, 33, 34, 35p, 38p, 39p, 45p.* ***Fine*** *a-252r.* ***Kaluta*** *a-400.* ***Gil Kane*** *a-272r, 367, 372, 375, Special 2; c-374p, 375p, 377, 381, 382, 384-390, 392, Annual 9, Special 2.* ***Joe Kubert*** *c-216.* ***Morrow*** *a-238.* ***Mortimer*** *a-250r.* ***Perez*** *c-364p.* ***Fred Ray*** *a-25; c-6, 8-18.* ***Starlin*** *c-355.* ***Staton*** *a-354i, 355i.* ***Swan/Moldoff*** *c-149.* ***Williamson*** *a(i)-408-410, 412-416; c-408i, 409i.* ***Wrightson*** *a-400, 416.*

SUPERMAN (2nd Series) (Title continues numbering from Adventures of Superman #649)
DC Comics: Jan, 1987 - No. 226, Apr, 2006; No. 650, May, 2006 - No. 714, Oct, 2011

0-(10/94) Zero Hour; released between #93 & #94 5.00

1-Byrne-c/a begins; intro new Metallo 2 4 6 10 14 18

2-8,10: 3-Legends x-over; Darkseid-c & app. 7-Origin/1st app. Rampage. 8-Legion app. 5.00

9-Joker-c 6.00

11-15,17-20,22-49,51,52,54-56,58-67: 11-1st new Mr. Mxyzptlk. 12-Lori Lemaris revived. 13-1st app. new Toyman. 13,14-Millennium x-over. 20-Doom Patrol app.; Supergirl cameo. 31-Mr. Mxyzptlk app. 37-Newsboy Legion app. 41-Lobo app. 44-Batman storyline, part 1. 45-Free extra 8 pgs. 54-Newsboy Legion story. 63-Aquaman x-over. 67-Last $1.00-c 4.00

16,21: 16-1st app. new Supergirl (4/88). 21-Supergirl-c/story; 1st app. Matrix who becomes new Supergirl 5.00

50-($1.50, 52 pgs.)-Clark Kent proposes to Lois 5.00

50-2nd printing 4.00

53-Clark reveals i.d. to Lois (Cont'd from Action #662) 5.00

53-2nd printing 4.00

57-($1.75, 52 pgs.) 5.00

68-72: 65,66,68-Deathstroke-c/stories. 70-Superman & Robin team-up 4.00

73-Doomsday cameo 6.00

74-Doomsday Pt. 2 (Cont'd from Justice League #69); Superman battles Doomsday 2 4 6 9 12 15

73,74-2nd printings 4.00

75-(1/93, $2.50)-Collector's Ed.; Doomsday Pt. 6; Superman dies; polybagged w/poster of funeral, obituary from Daily Planet, postage stamp & armband premiums (direct sales only) 3 6 9 18 27 36

75-Direct sales copy (no upc code, 1st print) 2 4 6 9 12 15

75-Direct sales copy (no upc code, 2nd-4th prints) 4.00

75-Newsstand copy w/upc code 1 3 4 6 8 10

75-Platinum Edition; given away to retailers 8 16 24 54 102 150

76,77-Funeral For a Friend parts 4 & 8 5.00

78-($1.95)-Collector's Edition with die-cut outer-c & mini poster; Doomsday cameo 5.00

78-($1.50)-Newsstand Edition w/poster and different-c; Doomsday-c & cameo 4.00

79-81,83-89: 83-Funeral for a Friend epilogue; new Batman (Azrael) cameo. 87,88-Bizarro-c/story 4.00

82-($3.50)-Collector's Edition w/all chromium-c; real Superman revealed; Green Lantern x-over from G.L. #46; no ads 6.00

82-($2.00, 44 pgs.)-Regular Edition w/different-c 5.00

90-99: 93-(9/94)-Zero Hour. 94-(11/94). 95-Atom app. 96-Brainiac returns 4.00

100-Death of Clark Kent foil-c 5.00

100-Newsstand 4.00

101-122: 101-Begin $1.95-c; Black Adam app. 105-Green Lantern app. 110-Plastic Man-c/app. 114-Brainiac app; Dwyer-c. 115-Lois leaves Metropolis. 116-(10/96)-1st app. Teen Titans by Jurgens & Perez in 8 pg. preview. 117-Final Night. 118-Wonder Woman app. 119-Legion app. 122-New powers 4.00

123-Collector's Edition w/glow in the dark-c, new costume 1 3 4 6 8 10

123-Standard ed., new costume 5.00

124-149: 128-Cyborg-c/app. 131-Birth of Lena Luthor. 132-Superman Red/Superman Blue. 134-Millennium Giants. 136,137-Superman 2999. 139-Starlin-a. 140-Grindberg-a 4.00

150-($2.95) Standard Ed.; Brainiac 2.0 app.; Jurgens-s 5.00

150-($3.95) Collector's Ed. w/holo-foil enhanced variant-c 5.00

151-158: 151-Loeb-s begins; Daily Planet reopens 4.00

159-174: 159-$2.25-c begin. 161-Joker-c/app. 162-Aquaman-c/app. 163-Young Justice app. 165-JLA app.; Ramos; Madureira, Liefeld, A. Adams, Wieringo, Churchill-a. 166-Collector's and reg. editions. 167-Return to Krypton. 168-Batman-c/app.(cont'd in Detective #756). 171-173-Our Worlds at War. 173-Sienkiewicz-a (2 pgs.). 174-Adopts black & red "S" logo 3.00

175-($3.50) Joker: Last Laugh x-over; Doomsday-c/app. 4.00

176-189,191-199: 176,180-Churchill-a. 180-Dracula app. 181-Bizarro-c/app. 184-Return to Krypton II. 189-Van Fleet-c. 192,193,195,197-199-New Supergirl app. 3.00

190-($2.25) Regular edition 3.00

190-($3.95) Double-Feature Issue; included reprint of Superman: The 10¢ Adventure 4.00

200-($3.50) Gene Ha-c/art by various; preview art by Yu & Bermejo 4.00

201-Mr Majestic-c/app.; cover swipe of Action #1 3.00

202,203-Godfall parts 3,6; Turner-c; Caldwell-a(p). 203-Jim Lee sketch pages 3.00

204-Jim Lee-c/a begins; Azzarello-s 3.00

204-Diamond Retailer Summit edition with sketch-c 5 10 15 35 63 90

205-214: 205-Two covers by Jim Lee and Michael Turner. 208-JLA app. 211-Battles Wonder Woman 3.00

215-($2.99) Conclusion to Azzarello/Lee arc 4.00

216-218,220-226: 216-Captain Marvel app. 221-Bizarro & Zoom app. 226-Earth-2 Superman story; Chaykin,Sale, Benes, Ordway-a 3.00

219-Omac/Sacrifice pt. 1; JLA app. 4.00

219-2nd printing with red background variant-c 3.00

(Title continues numbering from Adventures of Superman #649)

650-(5/06) One Year Later; Clark powerless after Infinite Crisis 4.00

651-665,667-669,671-674,676-680: 652-Begin $2.99-c. 654-658,662-664,667-Pacheco-a. 665-Origin of Jimmy Olsen. 671-673-Insect Queen. 676-680-Ross-c 3.00

666, 670,675-($3.99) 666-Simonson-a. 670-The Third Kryptonian. 675-Ross-c 4.00

681-699: 681-683-New Krypton x-over; Ross-c. 685-Mon-El freed from Phantom Zone. 694-Mon-El new costume. 698,699-Last Stand of New Krypton x-over 3.00

700-(8/10, $4.99) Cover by Gary Frank; Robinson-s; Straczynski-s begin 5.00

700-Variant-c by Risso 8.00

701-714: 701-"Grounded" begins; Straczynski-s/Cassaday-c. 704,706-Wilson-s 3.00

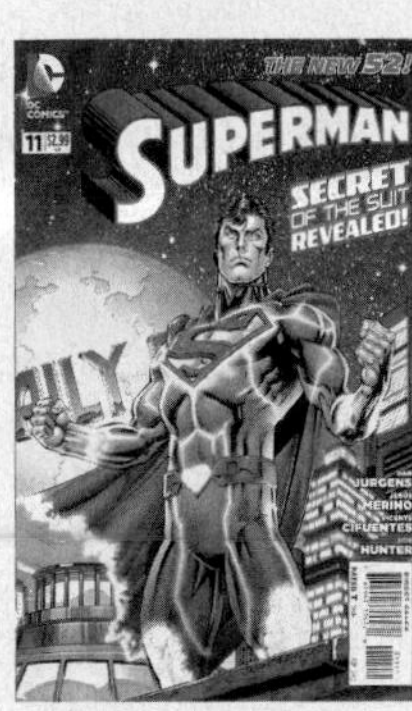

Superman (2011 series) #11 © DC

Superman (2018 series) #15 © DC

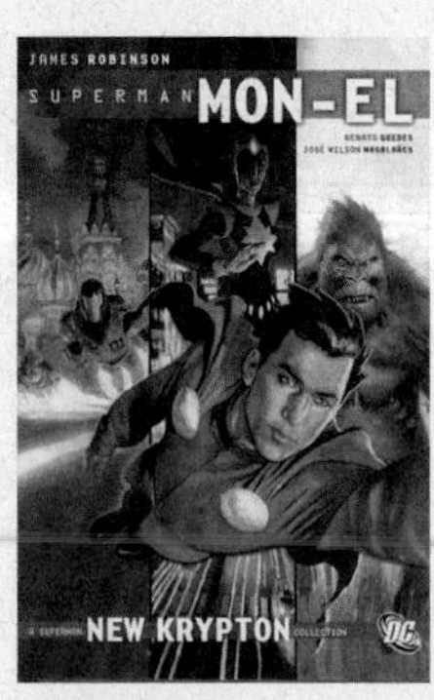

Superman Mon-El SC © DC

GD VG FN VF VF/NM NM-
2.0 4.0 6.0 8.0 9.0 9.2

701-DC 75th Variant-c by Cassaday (Superman #1 swipe) 8.00
#1,000,000 (11/98) 853rd Century x-over; Gene Ha-c 4.00
Annual 1,2: 1 (1987)-No Byrne-a. 2 (1988)-Byrne-a; Newsboy Legion; Guardian returns 5.00
Annual 3-6 ('91-'94 68 pgs.): 1-Armageddon 2001 x-over; Batman app.; Austin-c(i) & part inks. 4-Eclipso app. 6-Elseworlds sty 5.00
Annual 3-2nd & 3rd printings; 3rd has silver ink 5.00
Annual 7 (1995, $3.95, 69 pgs.)-Year One story 5.00
Annual 8 (1996, $2.95)-Legends of the Dead Earth story 5.00
Annual 9 (1997, $3.95)-Pulp Heroes story 5.00
Annual 10 (1998, $2.95)-Ghosts; Wrightson-c 5.00
Annual 11 (1999, $2.95)-JLApe; Art Adams-c 5.00
Annual 12 (2000, $3.50)-Planet DC 4.00
Annual 13 (1/08, $3.99) Finale of Camelot Falls 4.00
Annual 14 (10/09, $3.99) Origin of Mon-El re-told; Pina-a/Guedes-c 4.00
...: 80 Page Giant (2/99, $4.95) Jurgens-c 6.00
...: 80 Page Giant 1 (5/10, $5.99) Lopresti-c; short stories by various 6.00
...: 80 Page Giant 2 (6/99, $4.95) Harris-c 6.00
...: 80 Page Giant 3 (11/00, $5.95) Nowlan-c; art by various 6.00
...: 80 Page Giant 2011 (4/11, $5.99) Nguyen-c; art by various; Bizarros app. 6.00
Special 1 (1992, $3.50, 68 pgs.)-Simonson-c/a 6.00

SUPERMAN (DC New 52)
DC Comics: Nov, 2011 - No. 52, Jul, 2016 ($2.99/$3.99)

1-Pérez-s/c; Merino-a 2 4 6 10 14 18
1-Variant-c by Jim Lee 18.00
2-23: 3-6-Nicola Scott-a. 6-Supergirl app. 13-Clark quits job. 14-17-H'El on Earth x-over with Superboy & Supergirl. 17-H'El on Earth conclusion. 19,20-Orion app. 3.00
23.1, 23.2, 23.3, 23.4 (11/13, $2.99, regular covers) 3.00
23.1 (11/13, $3.99, 3-D cover) "Bizarro #1" on cover; Fisch-s/Kuder-c/Jeff Johnson-a 5.00
23.2 (11/13, $3.99, 3-D cover) "Brainiac #1" on cover; origin; Bedard-s/Alixe-a 5.00
23.3 (11/13, $3.99, 3-D cover) "H'El #1" on cover; Jor-El app.; Lobdell-s/Jurgens-a 5.00
23.4 (11/13, $3.99, 3-D cover) "Parasite #1" on cover; origin; Kuder-s/a 5.00
24-31: 25-Krypton Returns pt. 4. 26,27-Parasite app. 28,29-Starfire app. 3.00
32-($3.99) Romita Jr.-a/Johns-s begin; intro. Ulysses; wraparound-c by Romita Jr. 4.00
33-49: 33-39-Romita Jr.-a/Johns-s. 41-Yang-s begin. 45-48-Porter-a. 49-Vandal Savage 4.00
50-($4.99) Conclusion vs. Vandal Savage; Romita Jr. -c 5.00
51,52-Final Days of Superman x-over. 52-Superman dies; pre-Flashpoint Superman app. 4.00
#0-(11/12, $2.99) Jor-El & Lara flashback on Krypton; Rocafort-a/c 3.00
Annual 1 (10/12, $4.99) Alixe-a/Rocafort-c; Helspont app. 5.00
Annual 2 (9/13, $4.99) Jurgens-a/Andy Kubert-c; Brainiac app. 5.00
Annual 3 (2/16, $4.99) Origin/history of Vandal Savage; art by Sienkiewicz & others 5.00
... By Geoff Johns and John Romita Jr. Director's Cut 1 (11/14, $4.99) r/#32 B&W pencil art and full script 5.00
...: Futures End 1 (11/14, $2.99, regular-c) Five years later; Jurgens-s/Weeks-a 3.00
...: Futures End 1 (11/14, $3.99, 3-D cover) 4.00

SUPERMAN (DC Rebirth)
DC Comics: Aug, 2016 - No. 45, Jun, 2018 ($2.99)

1-24-Tomasi & Gleason-s. 2-The Eradicator returns. 8,9-Dinosaur Island. 10,11-Batman & Robin (Damian) app. 14-16-Multiplicity; alternate Earth Supermans & Capt. Carrot app. 18,19-Superman Reborn. 23,24-Manchester Black app. 3.00
25-($3.99) Manchester Black & Batman app.; Mahnke & Gleason-a 4.00
26-45: 29,30-Parallax & Sinestro app. 31,32-Deathstroke app. 38-Teen Titans app. 3.00
Annual 1 (1/17, $4.99) Swamp Thing app.; Tomasi & Gleason-s/Jimenez-a 5.00
...: Rebirth (8/16, $2.99) Pre-52 Superman and Lana Lang app.; Tomasi-s/Mahnke-a 3.00
... Special 1 (7/18, $4.99) Dinosaur Island; Capt. Storm app.; bonus short stories 5.00

SUPERMAN
DC Comics: Sept, 2018 - Present ($3.99)

1-17: 1-Bendis-s/Reis-a; Martian Manhunter app. 2-6,12-Rogol Zaar app. 7-Lobo app. 8-10-Crime Syndicate app. 14,15-Legion of Super-Heroes app. 4.00
13-($4.99) Variant "Year of the Villain" Lois Lane-c by Adam Hughes 5.00
18-24,26-28: 18-Superman reveals his Clark Kent ID to the world. 19-22-Mongul app. 22-24-Maguire-a. 23,24-Dr. Fate app. 4.00
25-($5.99) Intro. Synmar 6.00

SUPERMAN (Hardcovers and Trade Paperbacks)

... and the Legion of Super-Heroes HC (2008, $24.99) r/Action Comics #858-863, covers and variants; intro. by Giffen; Gary Frank design sketch pages 25.00
... and the Legion of Super-Heroes SC (2009, $14.99) same contents as HC 15.00
...: Back in Action TPB (2007, $14.99) r/Action Comics #841-843 and DC Comics Presents #4,17,24; commentary by Busiek 15.00
.../Batman: Saga of the Super Sons TPB (2007, $19.99) r/Super Sons stories from '70s World's Finest #215,216,221,222,224,228,230,231,233,242,263 & Elseworlds 80-Page Giant 20.00
...: Brainiac HC (2009, $19.99, dustjacket) r/Action Comics #866-870 & Superman: New Krypton Special #1 20.00
...: Brainiac SC (2010, $12.99) r/Action #866-870 & Superman: New Krypton Spec. #1 13.00

GD VG FN VF VF/NM NM-
2.0 4.0 6.0 8.0 9.0 9.2

...: Camelot Falls HC (2007, $19.99, dustjacket) r/Superman #654-658 20.00
...: Camelot Falls SC (2008, $12.99) r/Superman #654-658 13.00
...: Camelot Falls Vol. 2 HC (2008, $19.99, dj) r/Superman #662-664,667 & Ann. #13 20.00
...: Camelot Falls Vol. 2 The Weight of the World SC (2008, $12.99) r/Superman #662-664,667 & Ann. #13 13.00
...: Chronicles Vol. 1 ('06, $14.99, TPB) r/early Superman app. in Action Comics #1-13, New York World's Fair 1939 and Superman #1 15.00
...: Chronicles Vol. 2 ('07, $14.99, TPB) r/early Superman app. in Action Comics #14-20 and Superman #2,3 15.00
...: Chronicles Vol. 3 ('07, $14.99, TPB) r/early Superman app. in Action Comics #21-25, Superman #3,4 and New York World's Fair 1940 15.00
...: Chronicles Vol. 4 ('08, $14.99, TPB) r/early Superman app. in Action Comics #26-31, Superman #6,7 15.00
...: Chronicles Vol. 5 ('08, $14.99, TPB) r/early Superman app. in Action Comics #32-36, Superman #8,9 and World's Best Comics #1 15.00
...: Chronicles Vol. 6 ('09, $14.99, TPB) r/early Superman app. in Action Comics #37-40, Superman #10,11 and World's Finest Comics #2,3 15.00
...: Chronicles Vol. 7 ('09, $14.99, TPB) r/early Superman app. in Action Comics #41-43, Superman #12,13 and World's Finest Comics #4 15.00
...: Chronicles Vol. 8 ('10, $14.99, TPB) r/early Superman app. in Action Comics #44-47, and Superman #14,15 15.00
...: Chronicles Vol. 9 ('11, $17.99, TPB) r/early Superman app. in Action Comics #48-52, and Superman #16,17 and World's Finest Comics #6 18.00
...: Codename: Patriot HC ('10, $24.99, d.j.) r/partial New Krypton storyline 25.00
...: Codename: Patriot SC ('11, $14.99) r/partial New Krypton storyline 15.00
...: Critical Condition ('03, $14.95, TPB) r/2000 Kryptonite poisoning storyline 15.00
.../ Doomsday: The Collection Edition (2006, $19.99) r/Superman/Doomsday: Hunter/Prey #1-3, Doomsday Ann. #1, Superman: The Doomsday Wars #1-3, Advs. of Superman #594 and Superman #175; intro. by Dan Jurgens 20.00
...: Daily Planet (2006, $19.99, TPB)-Reprints stories of Daily Planet staff 20.00
... Earth One HC (2010, $19.99)-Updated re-imagining of Superman's debut in Metropolis; Straczynski-s/Shane Davis-a; sketch pages by Davis 20.00
... Earth One Volume Two HC (2012, $22.99)-Straczynski-s/Davis-a; sketch pages 23.00
... Earth One Volume Three HC (2014, $22.99)-Straczynski-s/Syaf-a; sketch pages 23.00
...: Emperor Joker TPB (2007, $14.99) reprints 2000 x-over from Superman titles 15.00
...: Endgame (2000, $14.95, TPB)-Reprints Y2K and Brainiac story line 15.00
...: Ending Battle (2009, $14.99, TPB) r/crossover of Superman titles from 2002 15.00
...: Eradication! The Origin of the Eradicator (1996, $12.95, TPB) 13.00
...: Escape From Bizarro World HC (2008, $24.99, dustjacket) r/Action #855-857; early apps. in Superman #140, DC Comics Presents #71 and Man of Steel #5; Vaughan intro. 25.00
...: Escape From Bizarro World SC (2009, $14.99) same contents as hardcover 15.00
...: Exile (1998, $14.95, TPB)-Reprints space exile following execution of Kryptonian criminals; 1st Eradicator 15.00
...: For Tomorrow Volume 1 HC (2005, $24.99, dustjacket) r/#204-209; intro by Azzarello; new cover and sketch section by Lee 25.00
...: For Tomorrow Volume 1 SC (2005, $14.99) r/#204-209; foil-stamped S emblem-c 15.00
...: For Tomorrow Volume 2 HC (2005, $24.99, dustjacket) r/#210-215; afterword and sketch section by Lee; new Lee-c with foil-stamped S emblem 25.00
...: For Tomorrow Volume 2 SC (2005, $14.99) r/#210-215; foil-stamped S emblem-c 15.00
...: Godfall HC (2004, $19.95, dustjacket) r/Action #812-813, Advs. of Superman #625-626, Superman #202-203; Caldwell sketch pages; Turner cover gallery; new Turner-c 20.00
...: Godfall SC (2004, $9.99) r/Action #812-813, Advs. of Superman #625-626, Superman #202-203; Caldwell sketch pages; Turner cover gallery; new Turner-c 10.00
...: Infinite Crisis TPB (2006, $12.99) r/Infinite Crisis #5, I.C. Secret Files and Origins 2006, Action Comics #836, Superman #226 and Advs. of Superman #649 13.00
... In the Forties ('05, $19.99, TPB) Intro. by Bob Hughes 20.00
... In the Fifties ('02, $19.95, TPB) Intro. by Mark Waid 20.00
... In the Sixties ('01, $19.95, TPB) Intro. by Mark Waid 20.00
... In the Seventies ('00, $19.95, TPB) Intro. by Christopher Reeve 20.00
... In the Eighties ('06, $19.99, TPB) Intro. by Jerry Ordway 20.00
... In the Name of Gog ('05, $17.99, TPB) r/Action Comics #820-825 18.00
... Kryptonite HC ('08, $24.99) r/Superman Confidential #1-5,11; Darwyn Cooke intro. 25.00
...: Last Son HC (2008, $19.99) r/Action Comics #844-846,851 and Annual #11; sketch pages and variant covers; Marc McClure intro. 20.00
... Mon-El HC ('10, $24.99) r/Superman #684-690, Action #874 & Annual #1, Superman: Secret Files 2009 #1 25.00
... Mon-El SC ('11, $17.99) r/Superman #684-690, Action #874 & Annual #1, Superman: Secret Files 2009 #1 18.00
... Mon-El - Man of Valor HC ('10, $24.99) r/Superman #692-697 & Annual #14, Adventure #11, Superman: Secret Files 2009 #1 25.00
... : New Krypton Vol. 1 HC ('09, $24.99, d.j.) r/Superman #681, Action #871 & one-shots 25.00
... : New Krypton Vol. 1 SC ('10, $17.99) r/Superman #681, Action #871 & one-shots 18.00
... : New Krypton Vol. 2 HC ('09, $24.99, d.j.) r/Superman #682,683, Action #872,873 & Supergirl #35,36; gallery of covers and variants 25.00
... : New Krypton Vol. 2 SC ('10, $17.99) same contents as HC 18.00

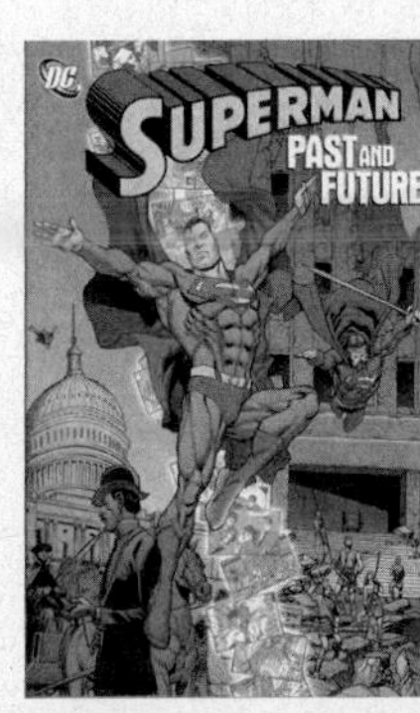

Superman: Past and Future SC © DC

Superman: Tales From the Phantom Zone © DC

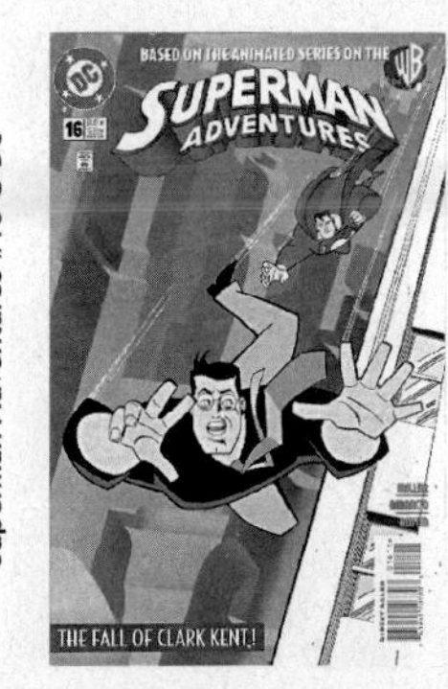

Superman Adventures #16 © DC

GD VG FN VF VF/NM NM-
2.0 4.0 6.0 8.0 9.0 9.2

GD VG FN VF VF/NM NM-
2.0 4.0 6.0 8.0 9.0 9.2

... : New Krypton Vol. 3 HC ('10, $24.99, d.j.) r/Superman: World of New Krypton #1-5 & Action Comics Annual #10; gallery of covers and variants 25.00
... : New Krypton Vol. 3 SC ('11, $17.99) same contents as HC 18.00
... : New Krypton Vol. 4 HC ('10, $24.99, d.j.) r/Superman: World of New Krypton #6-12; gallery of covers and variants; sketch and design art 25.00
... : New Krypton Vol. 4 SC ('11, $17.99) same contents as HC 18.00
... : Nightwing and Flamebird HC ('10, $24.99, d.j.) r/Action #875-879 & Annual #12 25.00
... : Nightwing and Flamebird SC ('10, $17.99) r/Action #875-879 & Annual #12 18.00
... : Nightwing and Flamebird Vol. 2 HC ('10, $24.99, d.j.) r/Action #883-889, Superman #696 & Adventure Comics #8-10 25.00
... No Limits ('00, $14.95, TPB) Reprints early 2000 stories 15.00
...: Our Worlds at War Book 1 ('02, $19.95, TPB) r/1st half of x-over 20.00
...: Our Worlds at War Book 2 ('02, $19.95, TPB) r/2nd half of x-over 20.00
...: Our Worlds at War - The Complete Collection ('06, $24.99, TPB) r/entire x-over 25.00
...: Past and Future (2008, $19.99, TPB) r/time travel stories 1947-1983 20.00
...: President Lex TPB (2003, $17.95) r/Luthor's run for the White House; Harris-c 18.00
...: Redemption TPB (2007, $12.99) r/Superman #659,666 & Action Comics #848,849 13.00
...: Return to Krypton (2004, $17.95, TPB) r/2001-2002 x-over 18.00
...: Sacrifice (2005, $14.99, TPB) prelude x-over to Infinite Crisis; r/Superman #218-220, Advs. of Superman #642,643; Action #829, Wonder Woman #219,220 15.00
...: Shadows Linger (2008, $14.99, TPB) r/Superman #671-675 15.00
... : Strange Attractors (2006, $14.99, TPB) r/Action Comics #827,828,830-835 15.00
... : Tales From the Phantom Zone ('09, $19.99, TPB) r/Phantom Zone stories 1961-68 20.00
...: That Healing Touch TPB (2005, $14.99) r/Advs. of Superman #633-638 & Superman Secret Files 2004 15.00
...: The Adventures of Nightwing and Flamebird TPB (2009, $19.99)-reprints appearances in Superman Family #173,183-194 20.00
...: The Black Ring Volume One HC (2011, $19.99, d.j.) r/Action Comics #890-895 20.00
The Bottle City of Kandor TPB (2007, $14.99)-Reprints 1st app. in Action #242 and other stories; Nightwing and Flamebird app. 15.00
The Coming of Atlas HC (2009, $19.99, dustjacket)-r/Superman #677-680 & Atlas' debut from First Issue Special #1 (1975); intro by James Robinson 20.00
The Coming of Atlas SC (2010, $14.99) same contents as HC 15.00
The Death of Clark Kent (1997, $19.95, TPB)-Reprints Man of Steel #43 (1 page), Superman #99 (1 page),#100-102, Action #709 (1 page), #710,711, Advs. of Superman #523-525, Superman:The Man of Tomorrow #1 20.00
The Death of Superman (1993, $4.95, TPB)-Reprints Man of Steel #17-19, Superman #73-75, Advs. of Superman #496,497, Action #683,684, & Justice League #69 2 4 6 9 12 15
The Death of Superman, 2nd & 3rd printings 1 3 4 6 8 10
The Death of Superman Platinum Edition 25.00
...: The Greatest Stories Ever Told ('04, $19.95, TPB) Ross-c, Uslan intro. 20.00
...: The Greatest Stories Ever Told Vol. 2 ('06, $19.99, TPB) Ross-c, Greenberger intro. 20.00
...: The Journey ('06, $14.99, TPB) r/Action Comics #831 & Superman #217,221-225 15.00
...: The Man of Steel Vol. 2 ('03, $19.95, TPB) r/Superman #1-3, Action #584-586, Advs. of Superman #424-426 & Who's Who Update '87 20.00
...: The Man of Steel Vol. 3 ('04, $19.95, TPB) r/Superman #4-6, Action #587-589, Advs. of Superman #427-429; intro. by Ordway; new Ordway-c 20.00
...: The Man of Steel Vol. 4 ('05, $19.99, TPB) r/Superman #7,8; Action #590,591; Advs. of Superman #430,431; Legion of Super-Heroes #37,38; new Ordway-c 20.00
...: The Man of Steel Vol. 5 ('06, $19.99, TPB) r/Superman #9-11, Action #592-593, Advs. of Superman #432-435; intro. by Mike Carlin; new Ordway-c 20.00
...: The Man of Steel Vol. 6 ('08, $19.99, TPB) r/Superman #12 & Ann. #1, Action #594-595 & Ann. #1, Advs. of Superman Ann.#1; Booster Gold #23; new Ordway-c 20.00
The Third Kryptonian ('08, $14.99, TPB) r/Action #847, Superman #668-670 & Ann. #13 15.00
The Trial of Superman ('97, $14.95, TPB) reprints story arc 15.00
The World of Krypton ('08, $14.99, TPB) r/World of Krypton Vol. 2 #1-4 and various tales of Krypton and its history; Kupperberg intro. 15.00
The Wrath of Gog ('05, $14.99, TPB) reprints Action Comics #812-819 15.00
...: They Saved Luthor's Brain ('00, $14.95) r/ "death" and return of Luthor 15.00
...: 3-2-1 Action! ('08, $14.99) Jimmy Olsen super-powered stories; Steve Rude-c 15.00
...: 'Til Death Do Us Part ('01, $17.95) reprints; Mahnke-c 18.00
...: Time and Time Again (1994, $7.50, TPB)-Reprints 10.00
...: Transformed ('98, $12.95, TPB) r/post Final Night powerless Superman to Electric Superman 13.00
...: Unconventional Warfare (2005, $14.95, TPB) r/Adventures of Superman #625-632 and pages from Superman Secret Files 2004 15.00
...: Up, Up and Away! (2006, $14.99, TPB) r/Superman #650-653 and Action #837-840 15.00
... Vs. Brainiac (2008, $19.99, TPB) reprints 1st meeting in Action #242 and other duels 20.00
... Vs. Lex Luthor (2006, $19.99, TPB) reprints 1st meeting in Action #23 and 11 other classic duels 1940-2001 20.00
... Vs. The Flash (2005, $19.99, TPB) reprints their races from Superman #199, Flash #175, World's Finest #198, DC Comics Presents #1&2, Advs. of Superman #463 & DC First: Flash/Superman; new Alex Ross-c 20.00
... Vs. The Revenge Squad (1999, $12.95, TPB) 13.00
...: Whatever Happened to the Man of Tomorrow? TPB (1/97, $5.99) r/Superman #423 & Action Comics #583, intro. by Paul Kupperberg 8.00
...: Whatever Happened to the Man of Tomorrow? Deluxe Edition HC (2009, $24.99, d.j.) r/Superman #423, Action #583, DC Comics Presents #85, Superman Ann #11 25.00
...: Whatever Happened to the Man of Tomorrow? SC (2010, $14.99) r/same as HC 15.00

NOTE: ***Austin*** *a(i)-1-3.* ***Byrne*** *a-1-16p, 17, 19-21p, 22; c-1-17, 20-22; scripts-1-22.* ***Guice*** *c/a-64.* ***Kirby*** *c-37p.* ***Joe Quesada*** *c-Annual 4.* ***Russell*** *c/a-23i.* ***Simonson*** *c-69i. #19-21 2nd printings sold in multi-packs.*

SUPERMAN (one-shots)

Daily News Magazine Presents DC Comics' Superman nn-(1987, 8 pgs.)-Supplement to New York Daily News; Perez-c/a 5.00
...: A Nation Divided (1999, $4.95)-Elseworlds Civil War story 5.00
... & Savage Dragon: Chicago (2002, $5.95) Larsen-a; Ross-c 6.00
... & Savage Dragon: Metropolis (11/99, $4.95) Bogdanove-a 5.00
...: At Earth's End (1995, $4.95)-Elseworlds story 5.00
...Beyond #0 (10/11, $3.99) The Batman Beyond future; Frenz-a/Nguyen-c 4.00
...: Blood of My Ancestors (2003, $6.95)-Gil Kane & John Buscema-a 7.00
...: Distant Fires (1998, $5.95)-Elseworlds; Chaykin-s 6.00
...: Emperor Joker (10/00, $3.50)-Follows Action #769 4.00
... : Endless Winter Special 1 (2/21, $3.99) Part 3 of crossover event; Hester-a 5.00
...: End of the Century (2/00, $24.95, HC)-Immonen-s/a 25.00
...: End of the Century (2003, $17.95, SC)-Immonen-s/a 18.00
... For Earth (1991, $4.95, 52 pgs, printed on recycled paper)-Ordway wraparound-c 6.00
...IV Movie Special (1987, $2.00)-Movie adaptation; Heck-a 4.00
...Gallery, The 1 (1993, $2.95)-Poster-a 3.00
...: Heroes 1 (4/20, $5.99) Aftermath of revealing Clark Kent ID to world; art by various 6.00
..., Inc. (1999, $6.95)-Elseworlds Clark as a sports hero; Garcia-Lopez-a 7.00
...: Infinite City HC (2005, $24.99, dustjacket) Mike Kennedy-s/Carlos Meglia-a 25.00
...: Infinite City SC (2006, $17.99) Mike Kennedy-s/Carlos Meglia-a 18.00
...: Kal (1995, $5.95)-Elseworlds story 6.00
...: Leviathan Rising Special 1 (7/19, $9.99) Leads into Event Leviathan series 10.00
...: Lex 2000 (1/01, $3.50) Election night for the Luthor Presidency 4.00
...: Lois Lane 1 (4/14, $4.99) Marguerite Bennett-s; Rocafort-c 5.00
...: Monster (1999, $5.95)-Elseworlds story; Anthony Williams-a 6.00
... Movie Special-(9/83)-Adaptation of Superman III; other versions exist with store logos on bottom 1/3 of-c 4.00
...: New Krypton Special 1 (12/08, $3.99) Funeral of Pa Kent; newly enlarged Kandor 4.00
...: Our Worlds at War Secret Files 1-(8/01, $5.95)-Stories & profile pages 6.00
... Plus 1(2/97, $2.95)-Legion of Super-Heroes-c/app. 4.00
...'s Metropolis-(1996, $5.95, prestige format)-Elseworlds; McKeever-c/a 6.00
...: Speeding Bullets-(1993, $4.95, 52 pgs.)-Elseworlds 6.00
.../Spider-Man-(1995, $3.95)-r/DC and Marvel Presents... 4.00
... 10-Cent Adventure 1 (3/02, 10¢) McDaniel-a; intro. Cir-El Supergirl 3.00
...: The Earth Stealers 1-(1988, $2.95, 52 pgs, prestige format) Byrne script; painted-c 6.00
...: The Earth Stealers 1-2nd printing 4.00
...: The Legacy of Superman #1 (3/93, $2.50, 68 pgs.)-Art Adams-c; Simonson-a 6.00
...: The Last God of Krypton ('99,$4.95) Hildebrandt Bros.-a/Simonson-s 5.00
...: The Last Son of Krypton FCBD Special Edition (7/13) r/Action #844; Jim Lee-c 3.00
...: The Odyssey ('99, $4.95) Clark Kent's post-Smallville journey 5.00
...: 3-D (12/98, $3.95)-with glasses 4.00
.../Thundercats (1/04, $5.95) Winick-s/Garza-a; two covers by Garza & McGuinness 6.00
.../Through the Ages (2006, $3.99) r/Action #1, Superman ('87) #7; origins and pin-ups 4.00
.../Top Cat Special 1 (12/18, $4.99) Amazo app.; Shane Davis-a; Secret Squirrel back-up 5.00
.../Toyman-(1996, $1.95) 3.00
...: True Brit (2004, $24.95, HC w/dust jacket) Elseworlds; Kal-El's rocket lands in England; co-written by John Cleese and Kim Howard Johnson; John Byrne-a 25.00
...: True Brit (2005, $17.99, TPB) Elseworlds; Kal-El's rocket lands in England 18.00
...: Under A Yellow Sun (1994, $5.95, 68 pgs.)-A Novel by Clark Kent; embossed-c 6.00
... Vs. Darkseid: Apokolips Now! 1 (3/03, $2.95) McKone-a; Kara (Supergirl #75) app. 4.00
...: Villains 1 (5/20, $5.99) Aftermath of revealing Clark Kent ID to world; art by various 6.00
...: War of the Worlds (1999, $5.95)-Battles Martians 6.00
...: Where is thy Sting? (2001, $6.95)-McCormack-Sharp-c/a 7.00
...: Y2K (2/00, $4.95)-1st Brainiac 13 app.; Guice-c/a 5.00

SUPERMAN ADVENTURES, THE (Based on animated series)
DC Comics: Oct, 1996 - No. 66, Apr, 2002 ($1.75/$1.95/$1.99)

1-Rick Burchett-c/a begins; Paul Dini script; Lex Luthor app.; 1st app. Mercy Graves in comics; silver ink, wraparound-c 5.00
2-20,22: 2-McCloud scripts begin; Metallo-c/app. 3-Brainiac-c/app. 5-1st app. Livewire in comics. 6-Mxyzptlk-c/app. 3.00
21-($3.95) 1st animated Supergirl 5.00
23-66: 23-Begin $1.99-c; Livewire app. 25-Batgirl-c/app. 28-Manley-a. 54-Retells Superman #233 "Kryptonite Nevermore" 58-Ross-c 3.00
Annual 1 (1997, $3.95)-Zatanna and Bruce Wayne app. 4.00
Special 1 (2/98, $2.95) Superman vs. Lobo 4.00
TPB (1998, $7.95) r/#1-6 8.00

Superman & Batman: World's Funnest © DC

Superman / Batman #9 © DC

Superman Family #195 © DC

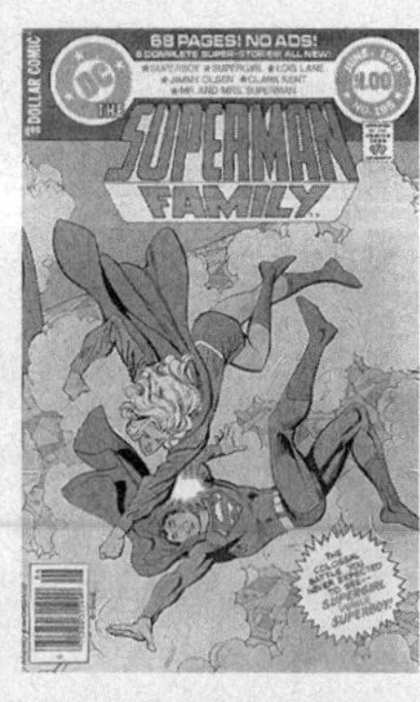

	GD	VG	FN	VF	VF/NM	NM-
	2.0	4.0	6.0	8.0	9.0	9.2

... Vol 1: Up, Up and Away (2004, $6.95, digest) r/#16,19,22-24; Amancio-a 7.00
... Vol 2: The Never-Ending Battle (2004, $6.95) r/#25-29 7.00
... Vol 3: Last Son of Krypton (2006, $6.99) r/#30-34 7.00
... Vol 4: The Man of Steel (2006, $6.99) r/#35-39 7.00

SUPERMAN ALIENS 2: GOD WAR (Also see Superman Vs. Aliens)
DC Comics/Dark Horse Comics: May, 2002 - No. 4, Nov, 2002 ($2.99, limited series)

1-4-Bogdanove & Nowlan-a; Darkseid & New Gods app. 3.00
TPB (6/03, $12.95) r/#1-4 13.00

SUPERMAN: AMERICAN ALIEN
DC Comics: Jan, 2016 - No. 7, Jul, 2016 ($3.99, limited series)

1-7-Flashbacks to Clark Kent's upbringing; Max Landis-s in all. 1-Dragotta-a. 4-Jae Lee-a; Batman app. 7-Lobo app.; Jock-a 4.00

SUPERMAN & BATMAN: GENERATIONS (Elseworlds)
DC Comics: 1999 - No. 4, 1999 ($4.95, limited series)

1-4-Superman & Batman team-up from 1939 to the future; Byrne-c/s/a 5.00
TPB (2000, $14.95) r/series 15.00

SUPERMAN & BATMAN: GENERATIONS II (Elseworlds)
DC Comics: 2001 - No. 4, 2001 ($5.95, limited series)

1-4-Superman, Batman & others team-up from 1942-future; Byrne-c/s/a 6.00
TPB (2003, $19.95) r/series 20.00

SUPERMAN & BATMAN: GENERATIONS III (Elseworlds)
DC Comics: Mar, 2003 - No. 12, Feb, 2004 ($2.95, limited series)

1-12-Superman & Batman through the centuries; Byrne-c/s/a 3.00

SUPERMAN & BATMAN VS. ALIENS AND PREDATOR
DC Comics: 2007 - No. 2, 2007 ($5.99, squarebound, limited series)

1,2-Schultz-s/Olivetti-a 6.00
TPB (2007, $12.99) r/#1,2; pencil breakdown pages 13.00

SUPERMAN AND BATMAN VS. VAMPIRES AND WEREWOLVES
DC Comics: Early Dec, 2008 - No. 6, Late Feb, 2009 ($2.99, limited series)

1-6-Van Hook-s/Mandrake-a/c. 1-Wonder Woman app. 5-Demon-c/app. 3.00
TPB (2009, $14.99) r/#1-6; intro. by John Landis 15.00

SUPERMAN & BATMAN: WORLD'S FUNNEST (Elseworlds)
DC Comics: 2000 ($6.95, square-bound, one-shot)

nn-Mr. Mxyzptlk and Bat-Mite destroy each DC Universe; Dorkin-s; art by various incl. Ross, Timm, Miller, Allred, Moldoff, Gibbons, Cho, Jimenez 7.00

SUPERMAN & BUGS BUNNY
DC Comics: Jul, 2000 - No. 4, Oct, 2000 ($2.50, limited series)

1-4-JLA & Looney Tunes characters meet 3.00

SUPERMAN/BATMAN
DC Comics: Oct, 2003 - No. 87, Oct, 2011 ($2.95/$2.99)

1-Two covers (Superman or Batman in foreground) Loeb-s/McGuinness-a; Metallo app.
1 2 3 6 8 10
1-2nd printing (Batman cover) 3.00
1-3rd printing; new McGuinness cover 3.00
1-Diamond/Alliance Retailer Summit Edition-variant 7 14 21 46 86 125
1-(6/06, Free Comic Book Day giveaway) reprints #1 3.00
2-6: 2,5-Future Superman app. 6-Luthor in battlesuit 3.00
7-Pat Lee-c/a; Superboy & Robin app. 3.00
8-Michael Turner-c/a; intro. new Kara Zor-El 5.00
8-Second printing with sketch cover 3.00
8-Third printing with new Turner cover 3.00
9-13-Michael Turner-c/a; Wonder Woman app. 10,13-Variant-c by Jim Lee 3.00
14-25: 14-18-Pacheco-a; Lightning Lord, Saturn Queen & Cosmic King app. 19-Supergirl app.; leads into Supergirl #1. 21-25-Bizarro app. 25-Superman & Batman covers; 2nd printing with white bkgrd cover 3.00
26-($3.99) Sam Loeb tribute issue; 2 covers by Turner; story & art by 26 various; back-up by Loeb & Sale 5.00
27-49: 27-Flashback to Earth-2 Power Girl & Huntress; Maguire-a. 34-36-Metal Men app. 3.00
50-($3.99) Thomas Wayne meets Jor-El; Justice League app. 4.00
51-74: 51,52-Mr. Mxyzptlk app. 66,67-Blackest Night; Man-Bat and Bizarro app. 3.00
75-($4.99) Quitely-c; Legion of Super-Heroes app.; Ordway-a; 2-pg. features by various 5.00
76-87: 76-Aftermath of Batman's "death". 77-Supergirl/Damian team-up 3.00
Annual #1 (12/06, $3.99) Re-imaging of 1st meeting from World's Finest #71 4.00
Annual #2 (5/08, $3.99) Kolins-a; re-imaging of Superman as Supernova story 4.00
Annual #3 (3/09, $3.99) Composite Superman-c by Wrightson; Batista-a 4.00
Annual #4 (8/10, $4.99) Batman Beyond; Levitz-s/Guedes-a/Lau-c 8.00
Annual #5 (6/11, $4.99) Reign of Doomsday x-over, Cyborg Superman app.; Sepulveda-a 5.00
...Absolute Power HC (2005, $19.99) r/#14-18 20.00
...Absolute Power SC (2006, $12.99) r/#14-18 13.00
..."Batman V Superman: Dawn of Justice Day" Special Edition 1 (4/16, free) r/#1 3.00
...Big Noise SC (2010, $14.99) r/#64,68-71 15.00
...Enemies Among Us SC (2009, $12.99) r/#28-33 13.00
...Finest Worlds SC (2010, $14.99) r/#50-56 15.00
...Night and Day HC (2010, $19.99) r/#60-63,65-67 20.00
...Public Enemies HC (2004, $19.95) r/#1-6 & Secret Files 2003; sketch art pages 20.00
...Public Enemies SC (2005, $12.99) r/#1-6 & Secret Files 2003; sketch art pages 15.00
...Public Enemies SC (2009, $14.99) r/#1-6 & Secret Files 2003; sketch art pages 15.00
...Secret Files 2003 (11/03, $4.95) Reis-a; pin-ups by various; Loeb/Sale short-s 5.00
... : Supergirl HC (2004, $19.95) r/#8-13; intro by Loeb, cover gallery, sketch pages 20.00
... : Supergirl SC (2005, $12.99) r/#8-13; intro by Loeb, cover gallery, sketch pages 13.00
... : The Search For Kryptonite HC (2008, $19.99) r/#44-49; Davis sketch pages 20.00
... : The Search For Kryptonite SC (2009, $12.99) r/#44-49; Davis sketch pages 13.00
... : Torment HC (2008, $19.99) r/#37-42; cover gallery, Nguyen sketch pages 20.00
... : Vengeance HC (2006, $19.99) r/#20-25; sketch pages 20.00
... : Vengeance SC (2008, $12.99) r/#20-25; sketch pages 13.00
... : Worship SC (2011, $17.99) r/#72-75 & Annual #4 18.00

SUPERMAN/BATMAN: ALTERNATE HISTORIES
DC Comics: 1996 ($14.95, trade paperback)

nn-Reprints Detective Comics Annual #7, Action Comics Annual #6, Steel Annual #1, Legends of the Dark Knight Annual #4 15.00

SUPERMAN: BIRTHRIGHT
DC Comics: Sept, 2003 - No. 12, Sept, 2004 ($2.95, limited series)

1-12-Waid-s/Leinil Yu-a; retelling of origin and early Superman years 3.00
HC (2004, $29.95, dustjacket) r/series; cover gallery; Waid proposal with Yu concept art 30.00
SC (2005, $19.99) r/series; cover gallery; Waid proposal with Yu concept art 20.00

SUPERMAN COMICS
DC Comics: 1939

nn - Ashcan comic, not distributed to newsstands, only for in-house use. Cover art is Action Comics #7 with interior being Action Comics #8. A CGC certified 9.0 copy sold for $37,375 in 2005, for $90,000 in 2007 and for $83,000 in Sept. 2018.

SUPERMAN CONFIDENTIAL (See Superman Hardcovers and TPBs listings for reprint)
DC Comics: Jan, 2007 - No. 14, Jun, 2008 ($2.99)

1-14: 1-5,9-Darwyn Cooke-s/Tim Sale-a/c; origin of Kryptonite re-told. 8-10-New Gods and Darkside app. 3.00
...: Kryptonite TPB (2009, $14.99) r/#1-5,11; intro. by Darwyn Cooke; Tim Sale sketch-a 15.00

SUPERMAN: DAY OF DOOM
DC Comics: Jan, 2003 - No. 4, Feb, 2003 ($2.95, weekly limited series)

1-4-Jurgens-s/Jurgens & Sienkiewicz-a 3.00
TPB (2003, $9.95) r/#1-4 10.00

SUPERMAN DOOMED (DC New 52) (See Action Comics #31-34 and Superman/Wonder Woman)
DC Comics: Jul, 2014 - No. 2, Nov, 2014 ($4.99, bookends for crossover)

1,2: 1-Lashley-a; Wonder Woman & Steel app. 2-Superman vs. Brainiac 6.00

SUPERMAN/DOOMSDAY: HUNTER/PREY
DC Comics: 1994 - No. 3, 1994 ($4.95, limited series, 52 pgs.)

1-3 6.00

SUPERMAN FAMILY, THE (Formerly Superman's Pal Jimmy Olsen)
National Per. Publ./DC Comics: No. 164, Apr-May, 1974 - No. 222, Sept, 1982

164-(100 pgs.) Jimmy Olsen, Supergirl, Lois Lane begin
4 8 12 28 47 65
165-169 (100 pgs.) 3 6 9 18 28 38
170-176 (68 pgs.) 3 6 9 14 19 24
177-190 (52 pgs.): 177-181-52 pgs. 182-Marshall Rogers-a; $1.00 issues begin; Krypto begins, ends #192. 183-Nightwing-Flamebird begins, ends #194. 189-Brainiac 5, Mon -El app. 2 4 6 9 13 16
191-193,195-199: 191-Superboy begins, ends #198 2 3 4 6 8 10
194,200: 194-Rogers-a. 200-Book length sty 2 4 6 8 10 12
201-210,212-222 1 2 3 5 6 8
211-Earth II Batman & Catwoman marry 2 4 6 8 11 14

NOTE: ***N. Adams*** *c-182-185.* ***Anderson*** *a-186i.* ***Buckler*** *c(p)-190, 191, 209, 210, 215, 217, 220.* ***Jones*** *a-191-193.* ***Gil Kane*** *c(p)-221, 222.* ***Mortimer*** *a(p)-191-193, 199, 201-222.* ***Orlando*** *a(i)-186, 187.* ***Rogers*** *a-182, 194.* ***Staton*** *a-191-194, 196p.* ***Tuska*** *a(p)-203, 207-209.*

SUPERMAN FAMILY ADVENTURES
DC Comics: Jul, 2012 - No. 12, Jun, 2013 ($2.99)

1-12-Young-reader stories, games and DC Nation character profiles; Baltazar-a 3.00

SUPERMAN/FANTASTIC FOUR
DC Comics/Marvel Comics: 1999 ($9.95, tabloid size, one-shot)

1-Battle Galactus and the Cyborg; wraparound-c by Alex Ross and Dan Jurgens;

Superman Forever #1 © DC

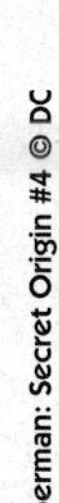
Superman: Secret Origin #4 © DC

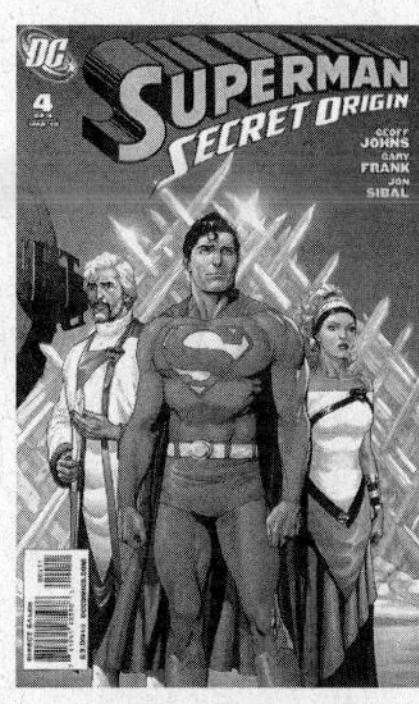

Superman's Girlfriend Lois Lane #15 © DC

	GD	VG	FN	VF	VF/NM	NM-
	2.0	4.0	6.0	8.0	9.0	9.2

Jurgens-s/a; Thibert-a 10.00

SUPERMAN FOR ALL SEASONS
DC Comics: 1998 - No, 4, 1998 ($4.95, limited series, prestige format)

1-Loeb-s/Sale-a/c; Superman's first year in Metropolis 6.00
2-4 5.00
Hardcover (1999, $24.95) r/#1-4 25.00

SUPERMAN FOR EARTH (See Superman one-shots)

SUPERMAN FOREVER
DC Comics: Jun, 1998 ($5.95, one-shot)

1-($5.95)-Collector's Edition with a 7-image lenticular-c by Alex Ross; Superman returns to normal; s/a by various 7.00
1-($4.95) Standard Edition with single image Ross-c 5.00

SUPERMAN/GEN13
DC Comics (WildStorm): Jun, 2000 - No. 3, Aug, 2000 ($2.50, limited series)

1-3-Hughes-s/ Bermejo-a; Campbell variant-c for each 3.00
TPB (2001, $9.95) new Bermejo-c; cover gallery 10.00

SUPERMAN GIANT (See reprint of new stories in Superman: Up In The Sky)
DC Comics: 2018 - No. 16, 2019 ($4.99, 100 pgs., squarebound, Walmart exclusive)

1-New story Palmiotti-s/Derenick-a; reprints from Superman/Batman, Green Lantern ('05), and The Terrifics in all 8.00
2-6,8-16: 2-Palmiotti-s/Derenick-a. 3-Tom King-s/Andy Kubert-a begins plus reprints 5.00
7-Many deaths of Lois Lane 10.00

SUPERMAN GIANT
DC Comics: Dec, 2019 - No. 3, 2020 ($4.99, 100 pgs., squarebound, Mass Market & Direct Market editions exist for each issue, with different covers)

1-3: 1-New story w/Parasite; plus reprints. 2,3-New story w/Pelletier-a 5.00

SUPERMAN: KING OF THE WORLD
DC Comics: June, 1999 ($3.95/$4.95, one-shot)

1-($3.95) Regular Ed. 4.00
1-($4.95) Collectors' Ed. with gold foil enhanced-c 5.00

SUPERMAN: LAST SON OF EARTH
DC Comics: 2000 - No. 2, 2000 ($5.95, limited series, prestige format)

1,2-Elseworlds; baby Clark rockets to Krypton; Gerber-s/Wheatley-a 6.00

SUPERMAN: LAST STAND OF NEW KRYPTON
DC Comics: May, 2010 - No. 3, Late June, 2010 ($3.99, limited series)

1-3-Robinson & Gates-s/Woods-a. 2-Pérez-c. 3-Sook-c 4.00
HC (2010, $24.99, DJ) r/#1,2, Adventure Comics #8,9, Supergirl #51 & Superman #698 25.00
Vol. 2 HC (2010, $19.99, DJ) r/#3, Adventure #10,11, Supergirl #52 & Superman #699 20.00

SUPERMAN: LAST STAND ON KRYPTON
DC Comics: 2003 ($6.95, one-shot, prestige format)

1-Sequel to Superman: Last Son of Earth; Gerber-s/Wheatley-a 7.00

SUPERMAN: LOIS & CLARK (See Convergence Superman #1 & 2)
DC Comics: Dec, 2015 - No. 8, Jul, 2016 ($3.99)

1-8: 1-Pre-Flashpoint Superman & Lois on New 52 Earth; Jurgens-s/Weeks-a 4.00

SUPERMAN: LOIS LANE (Girlfrenzy)
DC Comics: Jun, 1998 ($1.95, one shot)

1-Connor & Palmiotti-a 4.00

SUPERMAN/MADMAN HULLABALOO!
Dark Horse Comics: June, 1997 - No. 3, Aug, 1997 ($2.95, limited series)

1-3-Mike Allred-c/s/a 4.00
TPB (1997, $8.95) 9.00

SUPERMAN: METROPOLIS
DC Comics: Apr, 2003 - No. 12, Mar, 2004 ($2.95, limited series)

1-12-Focus on Jimmy Olsen; Austen-s. 1-6-Zezelj-a. 7-12-Kristiansen-a. 8,9-Creeper app. 3.00

SUPERMAN METROPOLIS SECRET FILES
DC Comics: Jun, 2000 ($4.95, one shot)

1-Short stories, pin-ups and profile pages; Hitch and Neary-c 5.00

SUPERMAN: PEACE ON EARTH
DC Comics: Jan, 1999 ($9.95, Treasury-sized, one-shot)

1-Alex Ross painted-c/a; Paul Dini-s 12.00

SUPERMAN: RED SON
DC Comics: 2003 - No. 3, 2003 ($5.95, limited series, prestige format)

1-Elseworlds; Superman's rocket lands in Russia; Mark Millar-s/Dave Johnson-c/a 25.00
2,3 15.00

TPB (2004, $17.95) r/#1-3; intro. by Tom DeSanto; sketch pages 18.00
... - The Deluxe Edition HC (2009, $24.99, d.j.) r/#1-3; sketch art by various 35.00

SUPERMAN RED/ SUPERMAN BLUE
DC Comics: Feb, 1998 ($4.95, one shot)

1-Polybagged w/3-D glasses and reprint of Superman 3-D (1955); Jurgens-plot/3-D cover; script and art by various 5.00
1-($3.95)-Standard Ed.; comic only, non 3-D cover 4.00

SUPERMAN RETURNS... (2006 movie)
DC Comics: Aug, 2006 ($3.99, movie tie-in stories by Singer, Dougherty and Harris)

Prequel 1 - Krypton to Earth; Olivetti-a/Hughes-c; retells Jor-El's story 6.00
Prequel 2 - Ma Kent; Kerschl-a/Hughes-c; Ma Kent during Clark childhood and absence 4.00
Prequel 3 - Lex Luthor; Leonardi-a/Hughes-c; Luthor's 5 years in prison 4.00
Prequel 4 - Lois Lane; Dias-a/Hughes-c; Lois during Superman's absence 4.00
The Movie and Other Tales of the Man of Steel (2006, $12.99, TPB) adaptation; origin from Amazing World of Superman; Action #810, Superman #185; Advs. of Superman #575 13.00
The Official Movie Adaptation (2006, $6.99) Pasko-s/Haley-a; photo-c 7.00
...: The Prequels TPB (2006, $12.99) r/the 4 prequels 13.00

SUPERMAN: SAVE THE PLANET
DC Comics: Oct, 1998 ($2.95, one-shot)

1-($2.95) Regular Ed.; Luthor buys the Daily Planet 4.00
1-($3.95) Collector's Ed. with acetate cover 5.00

SUPERMAN SCRAPBOOK (Has blank pages; contains no comics)

SUPERMAN: SECRET FILES
DC Comics: Jan, 1998; May 1999 ($4.95)

1,2: 1-Retold origin story, "lost" pages & pin-ups 5.00
... & Origins 2004 (8/04) pin-ups by Lee, Turner and others 5.00
... & Origins 2005 (1/06) short stories and pin-ups by various 5.00
... 2009 (10/09, $4.99) short stories and pin-ups about New Krypton x-over 5.00

SUPERMAN: SECRET IDENTITY
DC Comics: 2004 - No. 4, 2004 ($5.95, squarebound, limited series)

1-4-Busiek-s/Immonen-a/c 6.00

SUPERMAN: SECRET ORIGIN
DC Comics: Nov, 2009 - No. 6, Oct, 2010 ($3.99, limited series)

1-6-Geoff Johns-s/Gary Frank-a/c; origin mythos re-told. 2-Legion app. 5-Metallo app. 4.00
1-6-Variant covers by Frank 6.00
HC (2011, $29.99) r/#1-6; intro. by David Goyer; variant covers 30.00

SUPERMAN'S GIRLFRIEND LOIS LANE (See Action Comics #1, 80 Page Giant #3, 14, Lois Lane, Showcase #9, 10, Superman #28 & Superman Family)

SUPERMAN'S GIRLFRIEND LOIS LANE (See Showcase #9,10)
National Periodical Publ.: Mar-Apr, 1958 - No. 136, Jan-Feb, 1974; No. 137, Sept-Oct, 1974

	GD 2.0	VG 4.0	FN 6.0	VF 8.0	VF/NM 9.0	NM- 9.2
1-(3-4/58)	360	720	1440	3950	9225	14,500
2	104	208	312	832	1866	2900
3	70	140	210	560	1255	1950
4,5	46	92	138	368	834	1300
6,7	38	76	114	281	628	975
8-10: 9-Pat Boone-c/story	32	64	96	230	515	800
11-13,15-19: 12-(10/59)-Aquaman app. 17-(5/60) 2nd app. Brainiac.	19	38	57	131	291	450
14-Supergirl x-over; Batman app. on-c only	23	46	69	161	356	550
20-Supergirl-c/sty	22	44	66	154	340	525
21-28: 23-1st app. Lena Thorul, Lex Luthor's sister; 1st Lois as Elastic Lass. 27-Bizarro-c/story	14	28	42	96	211	325
29-Aquaman, Batman, Green Arrow cover app. and cameo; last 10¢ issue	17	34	51	115	255	395
30-32,34-46,48,49	9	18	27	59	117	175
33(5/62)-Mon -El app.	9	18	27	63	129	195
47-Legion app.	9	18	27	63	129	195
50(7/64)-Triplicate Girl, Phantom Girl & Shrinking Violet app.	9	18	27	63	129	195
51-55,57-67,69: 59-Jor -El app.; Batman back-up sty	7	14	21	44	82	120
56-Saturn Girl app.	7	14	21	49	92	135
68-(Giant G-26)	8	16	24	54	102	150
70-Penguin & Catwoman app. (1st S.A. Catwoman, 11/66; also see Detective #369 for 3rd app.); Batman & Robin cameo	32	64	96	230	515	800
71-Batman & Robin cameo (3 panels); Catwoman story cont'd from #70 (2nd app.); see Detective #369 for 3rd app	10	20	30	69	147	225
72,73,75,76,78	5	10	15	34	60	85
74-1st Bizarro Flash (5/67); JLA cameo	6	12	18	41	76	110
77-(Giant G-39)	6	12	18	42	79	115
79-Neal Adams-c or c(i) begin, end #95,108	6	12	18	37	66	95

Supermansion #1 © Colton Prods.

Superman's Pal Jimmy Olsen #138 © DC

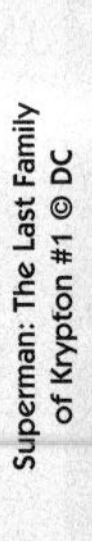
Superman: The Last Family of Krypton #1 © DC

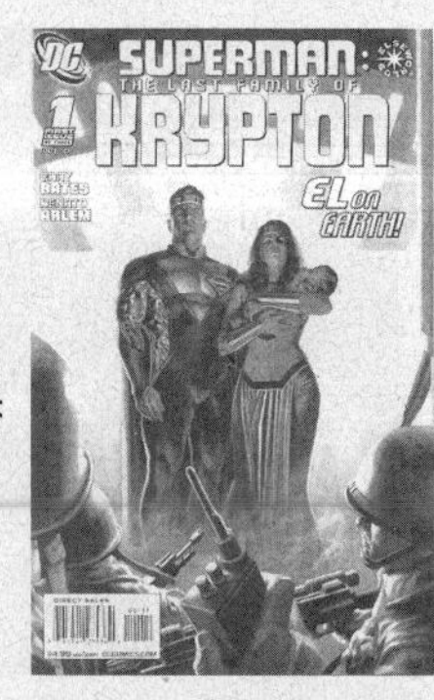

	GD	VG	FN	VF	VF/NM	NM-
	2.0	4.0	6.0	8.0	9.0	9.2

80-85,87,88,90-92: 92-Last 12¢ issue 4 8 12 28 47 65
86,95 (Giants G-51,G-63)-Both have Neal Adams-c 6 12 18 37 66 95
89,93: 89-Batman x-over; all N. Adams-c. 93-Wonder Woman-c/story
5 10 15 30 50 70
94,96-99,101-103,107-110 4 8 12 23 37 50
100 4 8 12 25 40 55
104-(Giant G-75) 5 10 15 34 60 85
105-Origin/1st app. The Rose & the Thorn. 6 12 18 41 76 110
106-"I Am Curious (Black)" story; Lois changes her skin color to black (11/70)
21 42 63 147 324 500
111-Justice League-c/s; Morrow-a; last 15¢ issue 5 10 15 31 53 75
112,114-123 (52 pgs.): 115-Black Racer app. 116,119-Darkseid app. 122-G.A. Lois Lane-r/ Superman #30. 123-G.A.Batman-r/Batman #35 (w/Catwoman)
4 8 12 23 37 50
113-(Giant G-87) Kubert-a (previously unpublished G.A. story)(scarce in NM)
6 12 18 38 69 100
124-135: 130-Last Rose & the Thorn. 132-New Zatanna story
3 6 9 16 23 30
136,137: 136-Wonder Woman x-over 3 6 9 19 30 40
Annual 1(Sum, 1962)-r/L. Lane #12; Aquaman app. 19 38 57 131 291 450
Annual 2(Sum, 1963) 13 26 39 91 201 310
NOTE: *Buckler a-117-121p. Curt Swan or Kurt Schaffenberger a-1-81(most); c(p)-1-15.*

SUPERMAN/SHAZAM: FIRST THUNDER
DC Comics: Nov, 2005 - No. 4, Feb, 2006 ($3.50, limited series)

1-4-Retells first meeting; Winick-s/Middleton-a. Dr. Sivana app. 6.00

SUPERMAN: SILVER BANSHEE
DC Comics: Dec, 1998 - No. 2, Jan, 1999 ($2.25, mini-series)

1,2-Brereton-s/c; Chin-a 4.00

SUPERMANSION (Based on the animated series)
Titan Comics: May, 2018 - No. 2, Jun, 2018 ($5.99, limited series)

1,2-Hutchinson-s/Elphick-a; multiple covers 6.00

SUPERMAN SMASHES THE KLAN (Inspired by the 1940s Superman radio show)
DC Comics: Oct, 2019 - No. 3, Feb, 2020 ($7.99, 6" x 9" squarebound, limited series)

1-3-Gene Luen Yang-s/Gurihiru-a/c; set in 1946. 1-Variant-c by Kyle Baker 8.00

SUPERMAN'S NEMESIS: LEX LUTHOR
DC Comics: Mar, 1999 - No. 4, Jun, 1999 ($2.50, mini-series)

1-4-Semeiks-a 4.00

SUPERMAN'S PAL JIMMY OLSEN (Superman Family #164 on)
(See Action Comics #6 for 1st app. & 80 Page Giant)
National Periodical Publ.: Sept-Oct, 1954 - No. 163, Feb-Mar, 1974 (Fourth World #133-148)

1 510 1025 1785 5100 11,700 18,300
2 179 358 537 1477 3339 5200
3-Last pre-code issue 114 228 342 923 2062 3200
4,5 70 140 210 560 1268 1975
6-10 46 92 138 350 788 1225
11-20: 15-1st S.A. issue 33 66 99 238 532 825
21-28,30 22 44 66 154 340 525
29-(6/58) 1st app. Krypto with Superman 26 52 78 182 404 625
31-Origin & 1st app. Elastic Lad (Jimmy Olsen) 23 46 69 161 356 550
32-40: 33-One pg. biography of Jack Larson (TV Jimmy Olsen). 36-Intro Lucy Lane. 37-2nd app. Elastic Lad & 1st cover app. 13 26 39 91 201 310
41-50: 41-1st J.O. Robot. 48-Intro/origin Superman Emergency Squad
10 20 30 68 144 220
51-56: 56-Last 10¢ issue 8 16 24 54 102 150
57-62,64-70: 57-Olsen marries Supergirl. 62-Mon-El & Elastic Lad app. but not as Legionnaires. 70-Element Boy (Lad) app. 6 12 18 40 73 105
63 (9/62)-Legion of Super-Villains app. 7 14 21 48 89 130
71,74,75,78,80-84,86,89,90: 86-Jimmy Olsen Robot becomes Congorilla
5 10 15 33 57 80
72,73,76,77,79,85,87,88: 72(10/63)-Legion app; Elastic Lad (Olsen) joins. 73-Ultra Boy app. 76,85-Legion app. 76-Legion app. 77-Olsen with Colossal Boy's powers & costume; origin Titano retold. 79-(9/64)-Titled The Red-headed Beatle of 1000 B.C. 85-Legion app. 87-Legion of Super-Villains app. 88-Star Boy app. 5 10 15 34 60 85
91-94,96-98 4 8 12 28 47 65
95 (Giant G-25) 7 14 21 44 82 120
99-Olsen w/powers & costumes of Lightning Lad, Sun Boy & Element Lad
5 10 15 31 53 75
100-Legion cameo 5 10 15 31 53 75
101-103,105-112,114-120: 106-Legion app. 110-Infinity-c. 117-Batman & Legion cameo. 120-Last 12¢ issue 4 8 12 23 37 50
104 (Giant G-38) 5 10 15 34 60 85
113,122,131,140 (Giants G-50,G-62,G-74,G-86) 5 10 15 31 53 75
121,123-130,132 3 6 9 21 33 45
133-(10/70)-Jack Kirby story & art begins; re-intro Newsboy Legion; 1st app. Morgan Edge
7 14 21 49 92 135
134-1st app. Darkseid (1 panel, 12/70) 54 108 162 378 652 925
135-2nd app. Darkseid (1 pg. cameo; see New Gods & Forever People); G.A. Guardian app. 9 18 27 60 120 180
136-139: 136-Origin new Guardian. 138-Partial photo-c. 139-Last 15¢ issue
4 8 12 23 37 50
141-150: (25¢,52 pgs.). 141-Photo-c with Don Rickles; Newsboy Legion-r by S&K begin; full pg. self-portrait of Jack Kirby; Don Rickles cameo. 149,150-G.A. Plastic Man-r in both; 150-Newsboy Legion app. 3 6 9 21 33 45
151-163 3 6 9 16 23 30
... Special 1 (12/08, $4.99) New Krypton tie-in; The Guardian and Dubbilex app. 5.00
... Special 2 (10/09, $4.99) New Krypton tie-in; Mon-El app.; Chang-a 5.00
Superman: The Amazing Transformations of Jimmy Olsen TPB (2007, $14.99) reprints Olsen's transformations into Wolf-Man, Elastic Lad, Turtle Boy and others; new Bolland-c 15.00
NOTE: *Issues #141-148 contain **Simon & Kirby** Newsboy Legion reprints from Star Spangled #7, 8, 9, 10, 11, 12, 13, 14 in that order. **N. Adams** c-109-112, 115, 117, 118, 120, 121, 132, 134-136, 147, 148. **Kirby** a-133-139p, 141-148p; c-133, 137, 139, 142, 145p. **Kirby/N. Adams** c-137, 138, 141-144, 146. **Curt Swan** c-1-14(most)., 140.*

SUPERMAN'S PAL JIMMY OLSEN
DC Comics: Sept, 2019 - No. 12, Sept, 2020 ($3.99)

1-12-Matt Fraction-s/Steve Lieber-a. 5,6-Batman app. 4.00

SUPERMAN SPECTACULAR (Also see DC Special Series #5)
DC Comics: 1982 (Magazine size, 52 pgs., square binding)

1-Saga of Superman Red/ Superman Blue; Luthor and Terra-Man app.; Gonzales & Colletta-a 2 4 6 9 13 16

SUPERMAN: STRENGTH
DC Comics: 2005 - No. 3, 2005 ($5.95, limited series)

1-3: Alex Ross-c/Scott McCloud-s/Aluir Amancio-a 6.00

SUPERMAN / SUPERGIRL: MAELSTROM
DC Comics: Early Jan, 2009 - No. 5, Mar, 2009 ($2.99, limited series)

1-5: Palmiotti & Gray-s/Noto-c/a; Darkseid app. 3.00
TPB (2009, $12.99) r/#1-5 13.00

SUPERMAN / SUPERHOMBRE
DC Comics: Apr, 1945

nn - Ashcan comic, not distributed to newsstands, only for in-house use (no known sales)

SUPERMAN / TARZAN: SONS OF THE JUNGLE
Dark Horse Comics: Oct, 2001 - No. 3, May, 2002 ($2.99, limited series)

1-3-Elseworlds; Kal-El lands in the jungle; Dixon-s/Meglia-a/Ramos-c 3.00

SUPERMAN: THE COMING OF THE SUPERMEN
DC Comics: Apr, 2016 - No. 6, Sept, 2016 ($3.99, limited series)

1-6: 1-Neal Adams-s/a/c in all; Kalibak app. 3,4-Orion app. 3-6-Darkseid app. 4.00

SUPERMAN: THE DARK SIDE
DC Comics: 1998 - No. 3, 1998 ($4.95, squarebound, mini-series)

1-3: Elseworlds; Kal-El lands on Apokolips 5.00

SUPERMAN: THE DOOMSDAY WARS
DC Comics: 1998 - No. 3, 1999 ($4.95, squarebound, mini-series)

1-3: Superman & JLA vs. Doomsday; Jurgens-s/a(p) 5.00

SUPERMAN: THE KANSAS SIGHTING
DC Comics: 2003 - No. 2, 2003 ($6.95, squarebound, mini-series)

1,2-DeMatteis-s/Tolagson-a 7.00

SUPERMAN: THE LAST FAMILY OF KRYPTON
DC Comics: Oct, 2010 - No. 3, Dec, 2010 ($4.99, limited series)

1-3-Elseworlds; the El family lands on Earth; Bates-s/Arlem-a/Massafera-c 5.00

SUPERMAN: THE MAN OF STEEL (Also see Man of Steel, The)
DC Comics: July, 1991 - No. 134, Mar, 2003 ($1.00/$1.25/$1.50/$1.95/$2.25)

0-(10/94) Zero Hour; released between #37 & #38 5.00
1-($1.75, 52 pgs.)-Painted-c 1 2 3 5 6 8
2-16: 3-War of the Gods x-over. 5-Reads sideways. 10-Last $1.00-c. 14-Superman & Robin team-up 4.00
17-1st brief app. Doomsday 4 8 12 25 40 55
17-(2nd printing) 3 6 9 17 26 35
18-1st full app. Doomsday 3 6 9 19 30 40
18-(2nd-4th printings) 2 4 6 11 16 20
18-(5th printing) 4 8 12 27 44 60
19-Doomsday battle issue (c/story) 2 4 6 8 11 14
19-(2nd & 3rd printings) 3 6 9 16 23 30

Superman: The Man of Steel #37 © DC

Superman / Wonder Woman #12 © DC

Supermouse #1 © STD

	GD 2.0	VG 4.0	FN 6.0	VF 8.0	VF/NM 9.0	NM- 9.2

20-22: 20,21-Funeral for a Friend. 22-($1.95)-Collector's Edition w/die-cut outer-c & bound-in poster; Steel-c/story 5.00
22-($1.50)-Newsstand Ed. w/poster & different-c 5.00
23-49,51-99: 30-Regular edition. 32-Bizarro-c/story. 35,36-Worlds Collide Pt. 1 & 10. 37-(9/94)-Zero Hour x-over. 38-(11/94). 48-Aquaman app. 54-Spectre-c/app; Lex Luthor app. 56-Mxyzptlk-c/app. 57-G.A. Flash app. 58-Supergirl app. 59-Parasite-c/app.; Steel app. 60-Reintro Bottled City of Kandor. 62-Final Night. 64-New Gods app. 67-New powers. 75-"Death" of Mxyzptlk. 78,79-Millennium Giants. 80-Golden Age style. 92-JLA app. 98-Metal Men app. 4.00
30-($2.50)-Collector's Edition; polybagged with Superman & Lobo vinyl clings that stick to wraparound-c; Lobo-c/story 5.00
50 ($2.95)-The Trial of Superman 4.00
100-($2.99) New Fortress of Solitude revealed 3.00
100-($3.99) Special edition with fold out cardboard-c 4.00
101,102-101-Batman app. 3.00
103-133: 103-Begin $2.25. 105-Batman-c/app. 111-Return to Krypton. 115-117-Our Worlds at War. 117-Maxima killed. 121-Royal Flush Gang app. 128-Return to Krypton II. 3.00
134-($2.75) Last issue; Steel app.; Bogdanove-c 3.00
#1,000,000 (11/98) 853rd Century x-over; Gene Ha-c 4.00
Annual 1-5 ('92-'96,68 pgs.): 1-Eclipso app.; Joe Quesada-c(p). 2-Intro Edge. 3 -Elseworlds; Mignola-c; Batman app. 4-Year One story. 5-Legends of the Dead Earth story 5.00
Annual 6 (1997, $3.95)-Pulp Heroes story 5.00
...Gallery (1995, $3.50) Pin-ups by various 4.00

SUPERMAN: THE MAN OF TOMORROW
DC Comics: 1995 - No. 15, Fall, 1999 ($1.95-$2.95, quarterly)
1-15: 1-Lex Luthor app. 3-Lex Luthor-c/app; Joker app. 4-Shazam! app. 5-Wedding of Lex Luthor. 10-Maxima-c/app. 13-JLA-c/app. 4.00
#1,000,000 (11/98) 853rd Century x-over; Gene Ha-c 4.00

SUPERMAN: THE SECRET YEARS
DC Comics: Feb, 1985 - No. 4, May, 1985 (limited series)
1-4-Miller-c on all 5.00

SUPERMAN: THE WEDDING ALBUM
DC Comics: Dec, 1996 ($4.95, 96 pgs, one-shot)
1-Standard Edition-Story & art by past and present Superman creators; gatefold back-c. Byrne-c 5.00
1-Collector's Edition-Embossed cardstock variant-c w/ metallic silver ink and matte and gloss varnishes 8.00
Retailer Rep. Program Edition (#'d to 250, signed by Bob Rozakis on back-c) 55.00
TPB ('97, $14.95) r/Wedding and honeymoon stories 15.00

SUPERMAN 3-D (See Three-Dimension Adventures)

SUPERMAN-TIM (See Promotional Comics section)

SUPERMAN UNCHAINED (DC New 52)
DC Comics: Aug, 2013 - No. 9, Jan, 2015 ($4.99/$3.99)
1-($4.99) Snyder-s/Jim Lee-a/c; back-up with Nguyen-a; bonus creator interviews 5.00
1-Director's Cut (9/13, $5.99) Lee's pencil art and Scott Snyder's scripts; cover gallery 6.00
2-8-($3.99) 2,6,7-Batman app. 4.00
9-($4.99) Wraparound-c by Jim Lee 5.00

SUPERMAN: UP IN THE SKY (Reprints serialized story in Walmart exclusive Superman Giant)
DC Comics: Sept, 2019 - No. 6, Feb, 2020 ($4.99, limited series)
1-6:1-Reprints Superman Giant #3,4; Andy Kubert-a. 2-R/#5,6. 3-R/#7,8; Sgt. Rock app. 4-R/#9,10; Flash app. 5-R/#12,13; Darkseid app. 6-R/#15,16 5.00

SUPERMAN VILLAINS SECRET FILES
DC Comics: Jun, 1998 ($4.95, one shot)
1-Origin stories, "lost" pages & pin-ups 5.00

SUPERMAN VS. ALIENS (Also see Superman Aliens 2: God War)
DC Comics/Dark Horse Comics: July, 1995 - No. 3, Sept, 1995 ($4.95, limited series)
1-3: Jurgens/Nowlan-a 5.00

SUPERMAN VS. MUHAMMAD ALI (See All-New Collectors' Edition C-56 for original 1978 printing)
DC Comics: 2010
... Deluxe Edition (2010, $19.99, HC w/dustjacket) recolored reprint in comic size; new intro. by Neal Adams; afterword by Jenette Kahn; sketch pages, key to cover celebs 20.00
... Facsimile Edition (2010, $39.99, HC no dustjacket) recolored reprint in original Treasury size; new intro. by Neal Adams; key to cover celebs 40.00

SUPERMAN VS. PREDATOR
DC Comics/Dark Horse Comics: 2000 - No. 3, 2000 ($4.95, limited series)
1-3-Micheline-s/Maleev-a 5.00
TPB (2001, $14.95) r/series 15.00

SUPERMAN VS. THE AMAZING SPIDER-MAN (Also see Marvel Treasury Edition No. 28)
National Periodical Publications/Marvel Comics Group: 1976
($2.00, Treasury sized, 100 pgs.)

	GD 2.0	VG 4.0	FN 6.0	VF 8.0	VF/NM 9.0	NM- 9.2
1-Superman and Spider-Man battle Lex Luthor and Dr. Octopus; Andru/Giordano-a; 1st Marvel/DC x-over.	9	18	27	62	126	190
1-2nd printing; 2000 numbered copies signed by Stan Lee on front cover & sold through mail	17	34	51	117	259	400
nn-(1995, $5.95)-r/#1	2	4	6	11	16	20

SUPERMAN VS. THE TERMINATOR: DEATH TO THE FUTURE
Dark Horse/DC Comics: Dec, 1999 - No. 4, Mar, 2000 ($2.95, limited series)
1-4-Grant-s/Pugh-a/c: Steel and Supergirl app. 4.00

SUPERMAN: WAR OF THE SUPERMEN
DC Comics: No. 0, Jun, 2010 - No. 4, Jul, 2010 ($2.99, limited series)
0-Free Comic Book Day issue; Barrows-c 3.00
1-4: 1-New Krypton destroyed 3.00
HC (2011, $19.99) r/#0-4 & Superman #700 20.00

SUPERMAN/WONDER WOMAN (DC New 52)
DC Comics: Dec, 2013 - No. 29, Jul, 2016 ($3.99)
1-Soule-s/Daniel-a; wraparound gatefold-c; Doomsday app. 5.00
2-29: 2-6-Zod app. 4-6-Faora app. 7-Doomsday app. 8-12-Doomed x-over. 14-17-Magog app. 18,19-Suicide Squad app. 26,27-Vandal Savage app. 28,29-Supergirl app. 4.00
Annual 1 (9/14, $4.99) Doomsday Superman vs. Cyborg Superman 5.00
Annual 2 (2/16, $4.99) Short stories by various; Paquette-c 5.00
...: Futures End 1 (11/14, $2.99, regular-c) Cont'd from Wonder Woman: FE #1 3.00
...: Futures End 1 (11/14, $3.99, 3-D cover) 4.00

SUPERMAN/WONDER WOMAN: WHOM GODS DESTROY
DC Comics: 1997 ($4.95, prestige format, limited series)
1-4-Elseworlds; Claremont-s 5.00

SUPERMAN WORKBOOK
National Periodical Publ./Juvenile Group Foundation: 1945 (B&W, reprints, 68 pgs)

	GD 2.0	VG 4.0	FN 6.0	VF 8.0	VF/NM 9.0	NM- 9.2
nn-Cover-r/Superman #14	295	590	885	1888	3244	4600

SUPERMAN: WORLD OF NEW KRYPTON
DC Comics: May, 2009 - No. 12,Apr, 2010 ($2.99, limited series)
1-12: Robinson & Rucka-s/Woods-a; Frank-c and variant for each. 4-Green Lantern app. 3.00

SUPERMAN YEAR ONE
DC Comics (Black Label): Aug, 2019 - No. 3, Dec, 2019 ($7.99, 10-7/8" x 8-1/2", lim. series)
1-3-Frank Miller-s/John Romita Jr.-a; two covers on each; origin re-told 8.00

SUPER MARIO BROS. (Also see Adventures of the..., Blip, Gameboy, and Nintendo Comics System)
Valiant Comics: 1990 - No. 6, 1991 ($1.95, slick-c) V2#1, 1991 - No. 5, 1991

	GD 2.0	VG 4.0	FN 6.0	VF 8.0	VF/NM 9.0	NM- 9.2
1-Wildman-a	6	12	18	38	69	100
2	3	6	9	16	23	30
3-6, V2#1-5-($1.50)	2	4	6	9	12	15
Special Edition 1 (1990, $1.95)-Wildman-a; 1st Valiant comic	3	6	9	19	30	40

SUPER MARKET COMICS
Fawcett Publications: No date (1950s)
nn - Ashcan comic, not distributed to newsstands, only for in-house use (no known sales)

SUPER MARKET VARIETIES
Fawcett Publications: No date (1950s)
nn - Ashcan comic, not distributed to newsstands, only for in-house use (no known sales)

SUPERMEN OF AMERICA
DC Comics: Mar, 1999 ($3.95/$4.95, one-shot)
1-($3.95) Regular Ed.; Immonen-s/art by various 4.00
1-($4.95) Collectors' Ed. with membership kit 5.00

SUPERMEN OF AMERICA (Mini-series)
DC Comics: Mar, 2000 - No. 6, Aug, 2000 ($2.50)
1-6-Nicieza-s/Braithwaite-a 3.00

SUPERMOUSE (...the Big Cheese; see Coo Coo Comics)
Standard Comics/Pines No. 35 on (Literary Ent.): Dec, 1948 - No. 34, Sept, 1955; No. 35, Apr, 1956 - No. 45, Fall, 1958

	GD 2.0	VG 4.0	FN 6.0	VF 8.0	VF/NM 9.0	NM- 9.2
1-Frazetta text illos (3)	40	80	120	246	411	575
2-Frazetta text illos	19	38	57	111	176	240
3,5,6-Text illos by Frazetta in all	15	30	45	83	124	165
4-Two pg. text illos by Frazetta	15	30	45	85	130	175
7-10	10	20	30	54	72	90
11-20: 13-Racist humor (Indians)	8	16	24	44	57	70

Super-Mystery Comics V7 #2 © ACE

Supernatural: Origins #6 © WB

Super Rabbit #13 © MAR

	GD 2.0	VG 4.0	FN 6.0	VF 8.0	VF/NM 9.0	NM- 9.2
21-45	7	14	21	37	46	55
1-Summer Holiday issue (Summer, 1957, 25¢, 100 pgs.)-Pines	15	30	45	84	127	170
2-Giant Summer issue (Summer, 1958, 25¢, 100 pgs.)-Pines; has games, puzzles & stories	11	22	33	60	83	105

SUPER-MYSTERY COMICS
Ace Magazines (Periodical House): July, 1940 - V8#6, July, 1949

	GD	VG	FN	VF	VF/NM	NM-
V1#1-Magno, the Magnetic Man & Vulcan begins (1st app.); Q-13, Corp. Flint, & Sky Smith begin	423	846	1269	3000	5250	7500
2	226	452	678	1446	2473	3500
3-The Black Spider begins (1st app.)	187	374	561	1197	2049	2900
4-Origin Davy	126	252	378	806	1378	1950
5-Intro. The Clown & begin series (12/40)	132	264	396	845	1448	2050
6(2/41)	110	220	330	704	1202	1700
V2#1(4/41)-Origin Buckskin	105	210	315	672	1149	1625
2-6(2/42): 3-Hitler & Mussolini app. 4-WWII Nazi-c. 6-Vulcan begins again; bondage/torture-c	98	196	294	627	1076	1525
V3#1(4/42),2: 1-Black Ace begins	105	210	315	672	1149	1625
3-Classic Kurtzman Japanese WWII giant robot bondage-c; intro. The Lancer; Dr. Nemesis & The Sword begin; Kurtzman-a(2)(Mr. Risk & Paul Revere Jr.)	158	316	474	1011	1731	2450
4-Kurtzman-c/a; classic-c	232	464	696	1485	2543	3600
5-Kurtzman-a(2); L.B. Cole-a; Mr. Risk app.	118	236	354	755	1290	1825
6(10/43)-Mr. Risk app.; Kurtzman's Paul Revere Jr.; L.B. Cole-a	98	196	294	627	1076	1525
V4#1(1/44)-L.B. Cole-a; Hitler app.	69	138	207	442	759	1075
2-6(4/45): 2,5,6-Mr. Risk app.	60	120	180	381	653	925
V5#1(7/45)-6	57	114	171	362	619	875
V6#1,2,4,5,6: 4-Last Magno. Mr. Risk app. in #2,4-6. 6-New logo	54	108	162	343	574	825
3-Classic torture c/story	206	412	618	1318	2259	3200
V7#1-6, V8#1-4,6	52	104	156	328	552	775
V8#5-Meskin, Tuska, Sid Greene-a	53	106	159	334	567	800

NOTE: ***Sid Greene** a-V7#4. **Mooney** c-V1#5, 6, V2#1-6. **Palais** a-V5#3, 4; c-V4#6-V5#4, V6#2, V8#4. Bondage c-V2#5, 6, V3#2, 5. Magno c-V1#1-V3#6, V4#2-V5#5, V6#2. The Sword c-V4#1, 6(w/Magno).*

SUPERNATURAL (Volume 4) (Based on the CW television series)
DC Comics: Dec, 2011 - No. 6, May, 2012 ($2.99, limited series)

1-6: 1-Sam in Scotland; Brian Wood-s/Grant Bond-a 3.00

SUPERNATURAL: BEGINNING'S END (Based on the CW television series)
DC Comics (WildStorm): Mar, 2010 - No. 6, Aug, 2010 ($2.99, limited series)

1-6-Prequel to the series; Dabb & Loflin-s/Olmos-a. 1-Olmos and photo-c 3.00
TPB (2010, $14.99) r/#1-6; character sketch pages 15.00

SUPERNATURAL FREAK MACHINE: A CAL MCDONALD MYSTERY
IDW Publishing: Mar, 2005 - No. 3 ($3.99)

1-3-Steve Niles-s/Kelley Jones-a 4.00

SUPERNATURAL LAW (Formerly Wolff & Byrd, Counselors of the Macabre)
Exhibit A Press: No. 24, Oct, 1999 - No. 45, 2008 ($2.50/$2.95/$3.50, B&W)

24-35-Batton Lash-s/a. 29-Marie Severin-c. 33-Cerebus spoof 3.00
36-40-($2.95). 37-Frank Cho pin-up and story panels 3.00
(#41) ...First Amendment Issue (2005, $3.50) anti-censorship story; CBLDF info 3.50
(#42) With a Silver Bullet (2006, $3.50) new stories and pin-ups 3.50
(#43) At the Box Office (2006, $3.50) new stories and pin-ups 3.50
(#44) Wolff & Byrd: The Movie (2007, $3.50) new stories and pin-ups 3.50
45-($3.50) Toxic Avenger and Lloyd Kaufman app. 3.50
#1 (2005, $2.95) r/Wolff & Byrd with redrawn and re-toned art; relettered 3.00

SUPERNATURAL LAW SECRETARY MAVIS
Exhibit A Press: 2001 - No. 5, 2008 ($2.95/$3.50, B&W)

1-3: 3-DeCarlo-c 3.00
4,5-($3.50) Jaime Hernandez-c 3.50

SUPERNATURAL: ORIGINS (Based on the CW television series)
DC Comics (WildStorm): July, 2007 - No. 6, Dec, 2007 ($2.99, limited series)

1-6: 1-Bradstreet-c; Johnson-s/Smith-a; back-up w/Johns-s/Hester-a 3.00
TPB (2008, $14.99) r/#1-6; sketch pages 15.00

SUPERNATURAL: RISING SON (Based on the CW television series)
DC Comics (WildStorm): Jun, 2008 - No. 6, Nov, 2008 ($2.99, limited series)

1-6-Johnson & Dessertine-s/Olmos-a. 1-Oliver-c 3.00
1-Variant-c by Nguyen 6.00
TPB (2009, $14.99) r/#1-6 15.00

SUPERNATURALS
Marvel Comics: Dec, 1998 - No. 4, Dec, 1998 ($3.99, weekly limited series)

1-4-Pulido-s/Balent-c; bound-in Halloween masks 4.00
1-4-With bound-in Ghost Rider mask (1 in 10) 4.00
... Preview Tour Book (10/98, $2.99) Reis-c 4.00

SUPERNATURAL THRILLERS
Marvel Comics Group: Dec, 1972 - No. 6, Nov, 1973; No. 7, Jun, 1974 - No. 15, Oct, 1975

	GD	VG	FN	VF	VF/NM	NM-
1-It!; Sturgeon adap. (see Astonishing Tales #21)	5	10	15	30	50	70
2-4,6: 2-The Invisible Man; H.G. Wells adapt. 3-The Valley of the Worm; R.E. Howard adapt. 4-Dr. Jekyll & Mr. Hyde; R.L. Stevenson adapt.. 6-The Headless Horseman; last 20¢ issue	3	6	9	14	20	25
5-1st app. The Living Mummy	6	12	18	42	79	115
7-15: 7-The Living Mummy begins. 8-1st app. The Elementals	3	6	9	17	26	35

NOTE: ***Brunner** c-11. **Buckler** a-5p. **Ditko** a-8r, 9r. **G. Kane** a-3p; c-3, 9p, 15p. **Mayerik** a-2p, 7, 8, 9p, 10p, 11. **McWilliams** a-14i. **Mortimer** a-4. **Steranko** c-1, 2. **Sutton** a-15. **Tuska** a-6p.*

SUPERPATRIOT (Also see Freak Force & Savage Dragon #2)
Image Comics (Highbrow Entertainment): July, 1993 - No. 4, Dec, 1993 ($1.95, lim. series)

1-4: Dave Johnson-c/a; Larsen scripts; Giffen plots 3.00

SUPERPATRIOT: AMERICA'S FIGHTING FORCE
Image Comics: July, 2002 - No. 4, Oct, 2002 ($2.95, limited series)

1-4-Cory Walker-a/c; Savage Dragon app. 3.00

SUPERPATRIOT: LIBERTY & JUSTICE
Image Comics (Highbrow Entertainment): July, 1995 - No. 4, Oct, 1995 ($2.50, lim. series)

1-4: Dave Johnson-c/a. 1-1st app. Liberty & Justice 3.00
TPB (2002, $12.95) r/#1-4; new cover by Dave Johnson; sketch pages 13.00

SUPERPATRIOT: WAR ON TERROR
Image Comics: July, 2004 - No. 4, May, 2007 ($2.95/$2.99, limited series)

1-4-Kirkman-s/Su-a 3.00

SUPER POWERS (1st Series)
DC Comics: July, 1984 - No. 5, Nov, 1984

1-5: 1-Joker/Penguin-c/story; Batman app.; all Kirby-c. 5-Kirby c/a 6.00

SUPER POWERS (2nd Series)
DC Comics: Sept, 1985 - No. 6, Feb, 1986

1-6: Kirby-c/a; Capt. Marvel & Firestorm join; Batman cameo; Darkseid storyline in all. 4-Batman cameo. 5,6-Batman app. 5.00

SUPER POWERS (3rd Series)
DC Comics: Sept, 1986 - No. 4, Dec, 1986

1-4: 1-Cyborg joins; 1st app. Samurai from Super Friends TV show. 1-4-Batman cameos; Darkseid storyline in #1-4 4.00

SUPER POWERS (All ages series)
DC Comics: Jan, 2017 - No. 6, Jun, 2017 ($2.99, limited series)

1-6-Franco & Baltazar-s/Baltazar-a/c; Superman, Batman & Wonder Woman vs. Brainiac 3.00

SUPER PUP (Formerly Spotty The Pup) (See Space Comics)
Avon Periodicals: No. 4, Mar-Apr, 1954 - No. 5, 1954

	GD	VG	FN	VF	VF/NM	NM-
4,5: 4-Atom bomb-c. 5-Robot-c	9	18	27	52	69	85

SUPER RABBIT (See All Surprise, Animated Movie Tunes, Comedy Comics, Comic Capers, Ideal Comics, It's A Duck's Life, Li'l Pals, Movie Tunes & Wisco)
Timely Comics (CmPl): Fall, 1944 - No. 14, Nov, 1948

	GD	VG	FN	VF	VF/NM	NM-
1-Hitler & Hirohito-c; war effort paper recycling PSA by S&K; Ziggy Pig & Silly Seal begin	271	542	613	1734	2967	4200
2	53	106	159	334	567	800
3-5	34	68	102	201	328	455
6-Origin	35	70	105	208	339	470
7-10: 9-Infinity-c	22	44	66	132	216	300
11-Kurtzman's "Hey Look"	25	50	75	150	245	340
12-14	22	44	66	132	216	300
I.W. Reprint #1,2('58),7,10('63): 1-r/#13. 2-r/#10.	3	6	9	15	22	28

SUPER RICHIE (Superichie #5 on) (See Richie Rich Millions #68)
Harvey Publications: Sept, 1975 - No. 4, Mar, 1976 (All 52 pg. Giants)

	GD	VG	FN	VF	VF/NM	NM-
1	3	6	9	16	23	30
2-4	2	4	6	11	16	20

SUPER SECRET CRISIS WAR! (Crossover of Cartoon Network characters)
IDW Publishing: Jun, 2014 - No. 6, Nov, 2014 ($3.99, limited series)

1-6-Powerpuff Girls, Samurai Jack, Dexter, Ben 10 vs. Aku, Mojo Jojo, Mandark 4.00
... Codename: Kids Next Door One-Shot (11/14 $3.99) 3 covers; Jampole-a 4.00
... Cow and Chicken One-Shot (10/14 $3.99) 3 covers; Jim Zub-s 4.00
... Foster's Home For Imaginary Friends One-Shot (9/14 $3.99) 3 covers; Ganucheau-a 4.00
... Johnny Bravo One-Shot (7/14 $3.99) 3 covers; Erica Henderson-a 4.00

Super Spy #2 © CEN

Super-Villain Team-Up #6 © MAR

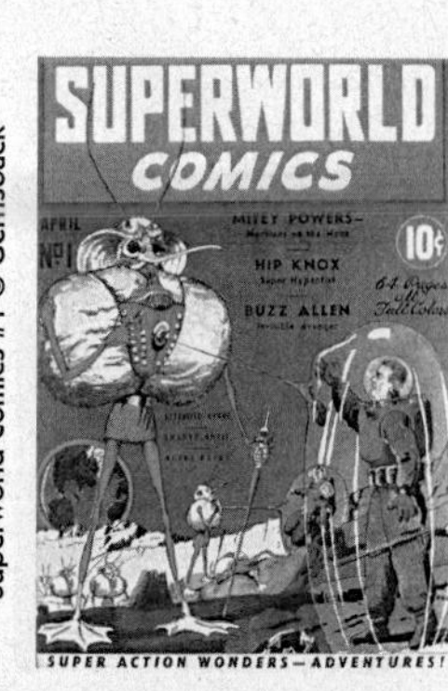

Superworld Comics #1 © Gernsback

GD VG FN VF VF/NM NM-
2.0 4.0 6.0 8.0 9.0 9.2

... The Grimm Adventures of Billy and Mandy One-Shot (7/14 $3.99) 3 covers; Leth-s 4.00

SUPER SLUGGERS (Baseball)
Ultimate Sports Ent. Inc.: 1999 ($3.95, one-shot)

1-Bonds, Piazza, Caminiti, Griffey Jr. app.; Martinbrough-c/a 4.00

SUPERSNIPE COMICS (Formerly Army & Navy #1-5)
Street & Smith Publications: V1#6, Oct, 1942 - V5#1, Aug-Sept, 1949
(See Shadow Comics V2#3)

V1#6-Rex King - Man of Adventure (costumed hero, see Super Magic/Magician) by Jack Binder begins; Supersnipe by George Marcoux continues from Army & Navy #5; Bill Ward-a 84 168 252 538 919 1300
7,10-12: 10,11-Little Nemo app. 52 104 156 328 552 775
8-Hitler, Tojo, Mussolini in Hell with Devil-c 343 686 1029 2400 4200 6000
9-Doc Savage x-over in Supersnipe; Hitler-c 258 516 774 1651 2826 4000
V2 #1: Both V2#1(2/44) & V2#2(4/44) have V2#1 on outside-c; Huck Finn by Clare Dwiggins begins, ends V3#5 (rare) 58 116 174 371 636 900
V2#2 (4/44) has V2#1 on outside-c; classic shark-c 45 90 135 264 480 675
3-12: 12-Statue of Liberty-c 23 46 69 136 223 310
V3#1-12: 8-Bobby Crusoe by Dwiggins begins, ends V3#12. 9-X-Mas-c 20 40 60 117 189 260
V4#1-12, V5#1: V4#10-X-Mas-c 17 34 51 98 154 210
NOTE: ***George Marcoux** c-V1#6-V3#4. Doc Savage app. in some issues.*

SUPER SOLDIER (See Marvel Versus DC #3)
DC Comics (Amalgam): Apr, 1996 ($1.95, one-shot)

1-Mark Waid script & Dave Gibbons-c/a. 4.00

SUPER SOLDIER: MAN OF WAR
DC Comics (Amalgam): June, 1997 ($1.95, one-shot)

1-Waid & Gibbons-s/Gibbons & Palmiotti-c/a. 4.00

SUPER SOLDIERS
Marvel Comics UK: Apr, 1993 - No. 8, Nov, 1993 ($1.75)

1-($2.50)-Embossed silver foil logo 5.00
2-8: 5-Capt. America app. 6-Origin; Nick Fury app.; neon ink-c 4.00

SUPER SONS
DC Comics: Apr, 2017 - No. 16, Jul, 2018 ($2.99/$3.99)

1,2: 1-Damian Wayne (Robin) & Jon Kent (Superboy) team-up; Tomasi-s/Jimenez-a 3.00
3-16-($3.99) 3,4-Battle Kid Amazo. 6,7-Teen Titans app. 11,12-Future adult Superboy (Conner), Wonder Girl (Cassie) and Kid Flash (Bart) app. 13,14-Talia app. 4.00
Annual 1 (1/18, $4.99) Tomasi-s/Pelletier-a; Krypto, Titus & the Super-Pets app. 5.00
... / Dynomutt Special 1 (7/18, $4.99) Blue Falcon and Red Vulture app.; Pasarin-a 5.00

SUPERSPOOK (Formerly Frisky Animals on Parade)
Ajax/Farrell Publications: No. 4, June, 1958

4 9 18 27 50 65 80

SUPER SPY (See Wham Comics)
Centaur Publications: Oct, 1940 - No. 2, Nov, 1940 (Reprints)

1-Origin The Sparkler 103 206 309 659 1130 1600
2-The Inner Circle, Dean Denton, Tim Blain, The Drew Ghost, The Night Hawk by Gustavson, & S.S. Swanson by Glanz app. 71 142 213 454 777 1100

SUPERSTAR: AS SEEN ON TV
Image Comics (Gorilla): 2001 ($5.95)

1-Busiek-s/Immonen-a 6.00

SUPER STAR HOLIDAY SPECIAL (See DC Special Series #21)

SUPER-TEAM FAMILY
National Periodical Publ./DC Comics: Oct-Nov, 1975 - No. 15, Mar-Apr, 1978

1-Reprints by Neal Adams & Kane/Wood; 68 pgs. begin, ends #4. New Gods app. 3 6 9 17 25 34
2,3: New stories 3 6 9 14 20 25
4-7: Reprints. 4-G.A. JSA-r & Superman/Batman/Robin-r from World's Finest. 5-52 pgs. begin 2 4 6 10 14 18
8-14: 8-10-New Challengers of the Unknown stories. 9-Kirby-a. 11-14: New stories 3 6 9 14 19 24
15-New Gods app. New stories 3 6 9 14 20 26
NOTE: ***Neal Adams** r-1-3. **Brunner** c-3. **Buckler** c-8p. **Tuska** a-7r. **Wood** a-1i(r), 3.*

SUPER TV HEROES (See Hanna-Barbera...)

SUPER-VILLAIN CLASSICS
Marvel Comics Group: May, 1983

1-Galactus -The Origin; Kirby-a 3 6 9 15 22 28

SUPER-VILLAIN TEAM-UP (See Fantastic Four #6 & Giant-Size...)
Marvel Comics Group: 8/75 - No. 14, 10/77; No. 15, 11/78; No. 16, 5/79; No. 17, 6/80

GD VG FN VF VF/NM NM-
2.0 4.0 6.0 8.0 9.0 9.2

1-Continued from Giant-Size Super-Villain Team-Up #2; Sub-Mariner & Dr. Doom begin, end #10 5 10 15 30 50 70
2-5: 5-1st app. The Shroud 3 6 9 14 19 24
5-(30¢-c variant, limited distribution)(4/76) 5 10 15 31 53 75
6,7-(25¢ editions) 6-(6/76)-F.F., Shroud app. 7-Origin Shroud 2 4 6 8 11 14
6,7-(30¢-c, limited distribution)(6,8/76) 5 10 15 31 53 75
8,9,11-17: 9-Avengers app. 11-15-Dr. Doom & Red Skull app. 2 4 6 8 11 14
10-Classic Dr. Doom, Red Skull, Captain America battle-c 2 4 6 11 16 20
12-14-(35¢-c variants, limited distribution)(6,8,10/77) 11 22 33 73 157 240
NOTE: ***Buckler** c-4p, 5p, 7p. **Buscema** c-1. **Byrne/Austin** c-14. **Evans** a-1p, 3p. **Everett** a-1p. **Giffen** a-8p, 13p; c-13p. **Kane** c-2p, 9p. **Mooney** a-4i. **Starlin** c-6. **Tuska** r-1p, 15p. **Wood** r-15p.*

SUPER-VILLAIN TEAM-UP/ MODOK'S 11
Marvel Comics: Sept, 2007 - No. 5, Jan, 2008 ($2.99, limited series)

1-5: 1-MODOK's origin re-told; Portela-a/Powell-c; Purple Man & Mentallo app. 3.00
... TPB (2008, $13.99) r/#1-5 14.00

SUPER WESTERN COMICS (Also see Buffalo Bill)
Youthful Magazines: Aug, 1950 (One shot)

1-Buffalo Bill begins; Wyatt Earp, Calamity Jane & Sam Slade app; Powell-c/a 18 36 54 107 169 230

SUPER WESTERN FUNNIES (See Super Funnies)

SUPERWOMAN
DC Comics: Jan 1942

nn - Ashcan comic, not distributed to newsstands, only for in-house use. Cover art is More Fun Comics #73 with interior being Action Comics #38 (no known sales)

SUPERWOMAN (DC Rebirth)
DC Comics: Oct, 2016 - No. 18, Mar, 2018 ($2.99/$3.99)

1-8: 1-Phil Jimenez-s/a; Lois and Lana with powers. 2-8-Lena Luthor app. 3.00
9-18-($3.99): 9,10-Segovia-a. 13-15-Supergirl app. 14-18-Maxima app. 4.00

SUPERWORLD COMICS
Hugo Gernsback (Komos Publ.): Apr, 1940 - No. 3, Aug, 1940 (68 pgs.)

1-Origin & 1st app. Hip Knox, Super Hypnotist; Mitey Powers & Buzz Allen, the Invisible Avenger, Little Nemo begin; cover by Frank R. Paul (all have sci/fi-c) (Scarce) 890 1780 2670 6500 13,750 21,000
2-Marvo 1-2 Go+, the Super Boy of the Year 2680 (1st app.); Paul-c (Scarce) 649 1298 1947 4738 8369 12,000
3 (Scarce) 486 972 1458 3550 6275 9000

SUPERZERO
AfterShock Comics: Dec, 2015 - No. 6, Jun, 2016 ($3.99)

1-6-Conner & Palmiotti-s/De Latorre-a. 1-Covers by Conner, Cooke & Hester 4.00

SUPER ZOMBIES
Dynamite Entertainment: 2009 - No. 5, 2009 ($3.50)

1-5-Mel Rubi-a; Guggenheim & Gonzales-s; two covers for each by Rubi & Neves 3.50

SUPREME (Becomes ...The New Adventures #43-48)(See Youngblood #3)
(Also see Bloodwulf Special, Legend of Supreme, & Trencher #3)
Image Comics (Extreme Studios)/ Awesome Entertainment #49 on:
V2#1, Nov, 1992 - V2#42, Sept, 1996; V3#49 - No. 56, Feb, 1998

V2#1-Liefeld-a(i) & scripts; embossed foil logo 4.00
1-Gold Edition 1 2 3 5 6 8
2-(3/93)-Liefeld co-plots & inks; 1st app. Grizlock 3.00
3-42: 3-Intro Bloodstrike; 1st app. Khrome. 5-1st app. Thor. 6-1st brief app. The Starguard. 7-1st full app. The Starguard. 10-Black and White Pt 1 (1st app.) by Art Thibert (2 pgs. ea. installment). 25-(5/94)-Platt-c. 11-Coupon #4 for Extreme Prejudice #0; Black and White Pt. 7 by Thibert. 12-(4/94)-Platt-c. 13,14-(6/94). 15 (7/94). 16 (7/94)-Stormwatch app. 18-Kid Supreme Sneak Preview; Pitt app.19,20-Polybagged w/trading card. 20-1st app. Woden & Loki (as a dog); Overtkill app. 21-1st app. Loki (in true form). 21-23-Poly-bagged trading card. 32-Lady Supreme cameo. 33-Origin & 1st full app. of Lady Supreme (Probe from the Starguard); Babewatch! tie-in. 37-Intro Loki; Fraga-c. 40-Retells Supreme's past advs. 41-Alan Moore scripts begin; Supreme revised; intro The Supremacy; Jerry Ordway-c (Joe Bennett variant-c exists). 42-New origin w/Rick Veitch-a; intro Radar, The Hound Supreme & The League of Infinity 3.00
28-Variant-c by Quesada & Palmiotti 3.00
(#43-48-**See Supreme: The New Adventures**)
V3#49,51: 49-Begin $2.99-c 3.00
50-($3.95)-Double sized, 2 covers, pin-up gallery 4.00
52a,52b-($3.50) 4.00
53-56: 53-Sprouse-a begins. 56-McGuinness-c 3.00

Supreme Blue Rose #1 © Rob Liefeld

Surf N' Wheels #1 © CC

Suspense Comics #10 © Continental

	GD	VG	FN	VF	VF/NM	NM-
	2.0	4.0	6.0	8.0	9.0	9.2

Annual 1-(1995, $2.95) 4.00
...: Supreme Sacrifice (3/06, $3.99) Flip book with Suprema; Kirkman-s/Malin-a 4.00
...: The Return TPB (Checker Book Publ., 2003, $24.95) r/#53-56 & Supreme; The Return #1-6; Ross-c; additional sketch pages by Ross 25.00
...: The Story of the Year TPB (Checker Book Publ., 2002, $26.95) r/#41-52; Ross-c 27.00
NOTE: ***Rob Liefeld** a(i)-1, 2; co-plots-2-4; scripts-1, 5, 6. **Ordway** c-41. **Platt** c-12, 25. **Thibert** c(i)-7-9.*

SUPREME
Image Comics: No. 63, Apr, 2012 - No. 68, Jan, 2013 ($2.99)

63-66: 63-Moore-s; two covers by Larsen & Hamscher; Larsen-a in all 3.00
67,68-($3.99) 67-Omni-Man (from Invincible) app.; Larsen-a 4.00

SUPREME BLUE ROSE
Image Comics: Jul, 2014 - No. 7, Mar, 2015 ($2.99)

1-7-Warren Ellis-s/Tula Lotay-a 3.00

SUPREME: GLORY DAYS
Image Comics (Extreme Studios): Oct, 1994 - No. 2, Dec, 1994 ($2.95/$2.50, limited series)

1,2: 2-Diehard, Roman, Superpatriot, & Glory app. 3.00

SUPREME POWER (Also see Squadron Supreme 2006 series)
Marvel Comics (MAX): Oct, 2003 - No. 18, Oct, 2005 ($2.99)

1-($2.99) Straczynski-s/Frank-a; Frank-c 3.00
1-($4.99) Special Edition with variant Quesada-c; includes r/early Squadron Supreme apps. 5.00
2-18: 4-Intro. Nighthawk. 6-The Blur debuts. 10-Princess Zarda returns. 17-Hyperion revealed as alien. 18-Continues in mini-series 3.00
... MGC #1 (7/11, $1.00) r/#1 with "Marvel's Greatest Comics" banner on cover 3.00
Vol. 1: Contact TPB (2004, $14.99) r/#1-6 15.00
Vol. 2: Powers & Principalities TPB (2004, $14.99) r/#7-12 15.00
Vol. 3: High Command TPB (2005, $14.99) r/#13-18 15.00
Vol. 1 HC (2005, $29.99, 7 1/2" x 11" with dustjacket) r/#1-12; Avengers #85 & 86, Straczynski intro., Frank cover sketches and character design pages 30.00
Vol. 2 HC (2006, $29.99, 7 1/2" x 11" with dustjacket) r/#13-18; ...: Hyperion #1-5; character design pages 30.00

SUPREME POWER
Marvel Comics (MAX): Aug, 2011 - No. 4, Nov, 2011 ($3.99, limited series)

1-4-Higgins-s/Garcia-a/Fiumara-c; Doctor Spectrum app. 4.00

SUPREME POWER: HYPERION
Marvel Comics (MAX): Nov, 2005 - No. 5, Mar, 2006 ($2.99, limited series)

1-5: 1-Straczynski-s/Jurgens-a/Dodson-c 3.00
TPB (2006, $14.99) r/#1-5 15.00

SUPREME POWER: NIGHTHAWK
Marvel Comics (MAX): Nov, 2005 - No. 6, Apr, 2006 ($2.99, limited series)

1-6-Daniel Way-s/Steve Dillon-a; origin of Whiteface 3.00
TPB (2006, $16.99) r/#1-6; cover concept art 17.00

SUPREME: THE NEW ADVENTURES (Formerly Supreme)
Maximum Press: V3#43, Oct, 1996 - V3#48, May, 1997 ($2.50)

V3#43-48: 43-Alan Moore scripts in all; Joe Bennett-a; Rick Veitch-a (8 pgs.); Dan Jurgens-a (1 pg.); intro Citadel Supreme & Suprematons; 1st Allied Supermen of America 4.00

SUPREME: THE RETURN
Awesome Entertainment: May, 1999 - No. 6, June, 2000 ($2.99)

1-6: Alan Moore-s. 1,2-Sprouse & Gordon-a/c. 2,4-Liefeld-c. 6-Kirby app. 4.00

SUPURBIA (GRACE RANDOLPH'S...)
BOOM! Studios: Mar, 2012 - No. 4, Jun, 2012 ($3.99, limited series)

1-4-Grace Randolph-s/Dauterman-a. 1-Garza-c 4.00

SUPURBIA (GRACE RANDOLPH'S...)(Volume 2)
BOOM! Studios: Nov, 2012 - No. 12, Oct, 2013 ($3.99, limited series)

1-12-Grace Randolph-s/Dauterman-a; multiple covers on #1-5 4.00

SURE-FIRE COMICS (Lightning Comics #4 on)
Ace Magazines: June, 1940 - No. 4, Oct, 1940 (Two No. 3's)

V1#1-Origin Flash Lightning & begins; X-The Phantom Fed, Ace McCoy, Buck Steele, Marvo the Magician, The Raven, Whiz Wilson (Time Traveler) begin (all 1st app.); Flash Lightning c-1-4 284 568 852 1818 3109 4400
2 155 310 465 992 1696 2400
3(9/40), 3(#4)(10/40)-nn on-c, #3 on inside 123 246 369 787 1344 1900

SURFACE TENSION
Titan Comics: Jun, 2015 - No. 5, Oct, 2015 ($3.99, limited series)

1-5-Jay Gunn-s/a. 1,2-Two covers 4.00

SURF 'N' WHEELS
Charlton Comics: Nov, 1969 - No. 6, Sept, 1970

1 3 6 9 19 30 40
2-6 3 6 9 14 19 24

SURGE
Eclipse Comics: July, 1984 - No. 4, Jan, 1985 ($1.50, lim. series, Baxter paper)

1-4-Ties into DNAgents series 3.00

SURGEON X
Image Comics: Sept, 2016 - No. 6, Feb, 2017 ($3.99)

1-6: 1-Sara Kenney-s/John Watkiss-a/c. 6-Watkiss & Pleece-a 4.00

SURPRISE ADVENTURES (Formerly Tormented)
Sterling Comic Group: No. 3, Mar, 1955 - No. 5, July, 1955

3-5: 3,5-Sekowsky-a 12 24 36 69 97 125

SURVIVE (Follows Cataclysm: The Ultimates Last Stand)
Marvel Comics: May, 2014 ($3.99, one-shot)

1-Bendis-s/Quinones-a; the new Ultimates team is formed 4.00

SURVIVORS' CLUB
DC Comics (Vertigo): Dec, 2015 - No. 9, Aug, 2016 ($3.99)

1-9-Beukes & Halvorsen-s/Ryan Kelly-a/Sienkiewicz-c 4.00

SUSIE Q. SMITH
Dell Publishing Co.: No. 323, Mar, 1951 - No. 553, Apr, 1954

Four Color 323 (#1) 6 12 18 38 69 100
Four Color 377, 453 (2/53), 553 5 10 15 31 53 75

SUSPENSE (Radio/TV issues #1-11; Real Life Tales of... #1-4) (Amazing Detective Cases #3 on?)
Marvel/Atlas Comics (CnPC No. 1-10/BFP No. 11-29): Dec, 1949 - No. 29, Apr, 1953 (#1-8, 17-23: 52 pgs.)

1-Powell-a; Peter Lorre, Sidney Greenstreet photo-c from Hammett's "The Verdict" 110 220 330 704 1202 1700
2-Crime stories; Dennis O'Keefe & Gale Storm photo-c from Universal movie "Abandoned" 48 96 144 302 514 725
3-Change to horror 58 116 174 371 636 900
4,7-10: 7-Dracula-sty 48 96 144 302 514 725
5-Krigstein, Tuska, Everett-a 50 100 150 315 533 750
6-Tuska, Everett, Morisi-a 47 94 141 296 498 700
11-13,15-17,19,20 42 84 126 265 445 625
14-Classic Heath Hypo-c; A-Bomb panels 55 110 165 352 601 850
18,22-Krigstein-a 42 84 126 265 445 625
21,23,24,26-29: 24-Tuska-a 39 78 117 240 395 550
25-Electric chair-c/story 48 96 144 302 514 725
NOTE: ***Ayers** a-20. **Briefer** a-5, 7, 27. **Brodsky** c-4, 6-9, 11, 16, 17, 25. **Colan** a-8(2), 9. **Everett** a-5, 6(2), 19, 23, 28; c-21-23, 26. **Fuje** a-29. **Heath** a-5, 6, 8, 10, 12, 14; c-14, 19, 24. **Maneely** a-11, 12, 23, 24, 28, 29; c-5, 6p, 10, 13, 15, 18. **Mooney** a-24, 28. **Morisi** a-6, 12. **Palais** a-10. **Rico** a-7-9. **Robinson** a-29. **Romita** a-20(2), 25. **Sekowsky** a-11, 13, 14. **Sinnott** a-23, 25. **Tuska** a-5, 6(2), 12; c-12. **Whitney** a-15, 16, 22. **Ed Win** a-27.*

SUSPENSE COMICS
Continental Magazines: Dec, 1943 - No. 12, Sept, 1946

1-The Grey Mask begins; bondage/torture-c; L. B. Cole-a (7 pgs.) 703 1406 2109 5132 9066 13,000
2-Intro. The Mask; Rico, Giunta, L. B. Cole-a (7 pgs.) 300 600 900 2040 3570 5100
3-L.B. Cole-a; classic Schomburg-c (Scarce) 9500 19,000 28,500 57,000 98,500 140,000
4-L. B. Cole-c begin 300 600 900 1980 3440 4900
5,6 265 530 795 1694 2897 4100
7,9,10,12: 9-L.B. Cole eyeball-c 206 412 618 1318 2259 3200
8-Classic L. B. Cole spider-c 481 962 1443 3511 6206 8900
11-Classic Devil-c 400 800 1200 2800 4900 7000
NOTE: ***L. B. Cole** c-4-12. **Fuje** a-8. **Larsen** a-11. **Palais** a-10, 11. Bondage c-1, 3, 4.*

SUSPENSE DETECTIVE
Fawcett Publications: June, 1952 - No. 5, Mar, 1953

1-Evans-a (11 pgs); Baily-c/a 53 106 159 334 567 800
2-Evans-a (10 pgs.) 31 62 93 182 296 410
3-5 26 52 78 154 252 350
NOTE: ***Baily** a-4, 5; c-1-3. **Sekowsky** a-2, 4, 5; c-5.*

SUSPENSE STORIES (See Strange Suspense Stories)

SUSSEX VAMPIRE, THE (Sherlock Holmes)
Caliber Comics: 1996 ($2.95, 32 pgs., B&W, one-shot)

nn-Adapts Sir Arthur Conan Doyle's story; Warren Ellis scripts 3.00

SUZIE COMICS (Formerly Laugh Comix; see Laugh Comics, Liberty Comics #10, Pep Comics & Top-Notch Comics #28)
Close-Up No. 49,50/MLJ Mag./Archie No. 51 on: No. 49, Spring, 1945 - No. 100, Aug, 1954

49-Ginger begins 60 120 180 381 653 925

Swamp Thing #13 © DC

Swamp Thing V3 #14 © DC

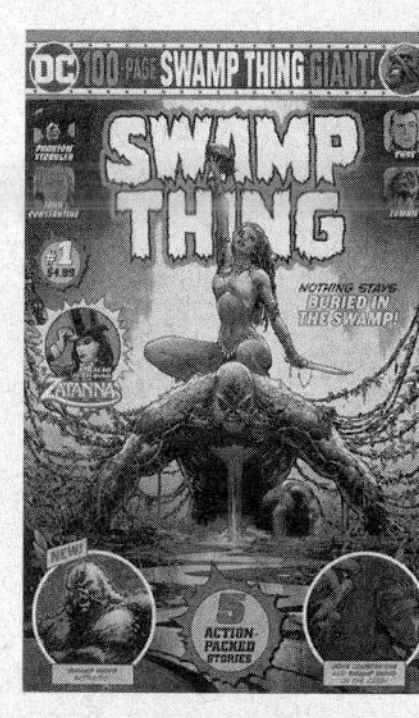

Swamp Thing Giant #1 © DC

	GD 2.0	VG 4.0	FN 6.0	VF 8.0	VF/NM 9.0	NM- 9.2
50-55: 54-Transvestism story. 55-Woggon-a	39	78	117	240	395	550
56-Katy Keene begins by Woggon	55	110	165	352	601	850
57-65	23	46	69	136	223	310
66-80	19	38	57	111	176	240
81-87,89-99	16	32	48	98	154	210
88,100: 88-Used in **POP**, pgs. 76,77; Bill Woggon draws himself in story. 100-Last Katy Keene	18	36	54	108	172	235

NOTE: ***Al Fagaly*** *c-49-67. Katy Keene app. in 53-82, 85-100.*

SWAMP FOX, THE (TV, Disney)(See Walt Disney Presents #2)
Dell Publishing Co.: No. 1179, Dec, 1960

	GD	VG	FN	VF	VF/NM	NM-
Four Color 1179-Leslie Nielsen photo-c	8	16	24	56	108	160

SWAMP THING (See Brave & the Bold, Challengers of the Unknown #82, DC Comics Presents #8 & 85, DC Special Series #2, 14, 17, 20, House of Secrets #92, Limited Collectors' Edition C-59, & Roots of the...)

SWAMP THING
National Per. Publ./DC Comics: Oct-Nov, 1972 - No. 24, Aug-Sept, 1976

	GD	VG	FN	VF	VF/NM	NM-
1-Wrightson-c/a begins; origin	18	36	54	124	275	425
2-1st brief app. Patchwork Man (1 panel)	8	16	24	54	102	150
3-1st full app. Patchwork Man (see House of Secrets #140)	7	14	21	48	89	130
4-6	5	10	15	34	60	85
7-Batman-c/story	6	12	18	41	76	110
8-10: 10-Last Wrightson issue	5	10	15	31	53	75
11-20: 11-19-Redondo-a. 13-Origin retold (1 pg.)	3	6	9	18	28	38
21-24: 22,23-Redondo-a. 23,24-Swamp Thing reverts back to Dr. Holland. 23-New logo	3	6	9	18	28	38
Secret of the Swamp Thing (2005, $9.99, digest) r/#1-10						10.00

NOTE: ***J. Jones*** *a-9i(assist).* ***Kaluta*** *a-9i.* ***Redondo*** *c-11-19, 21.* ***Wrightson*** *issues (#1-10) reprinted in DC Special Series #2, 14, 17, 20 & Roots of the Swamp Thing.*

SWAMP THING (Saga Of The... #1-38,42-45) (See Essential Vertigo:...)
DC Comics (Vertigo imprint #129 on): May, 1982 - No. 171, Oct, 1996
(Direct sales #65 on)

	GD	VG	FN	VF	VF/NM	NM-
1-Origin retold; Phantom Stranger series begins; ends #13; Yeates-c/a begins	2	4	6	11	16	20
2-15: 2-Photo-c from movie. 13-Last Yeates-a						4.00
16-19: Bissette-a.						5.00
20-1st Alan Moore issue	4	8	12	27	44	60
21-New origin	4	8	12	23	37	50
21 Special Editon (5/09, $1.00) reprint with "After Watchmen" cover frame						4.00
22,23	2	4	6	9	12	15
24-JLA x-over; last Yeates-c.	2	4	6	9	13	16
25-John Constantine 1-panel cameo	4	8	12	25	40	55
26-30	1	2	3	5	6	8
31-33,35,36: 33-r/1st app. from House of Secrets #92						6.00
34-Classic-c	2	4	6	9	13	16
37-1st app. John Constantine (Hellblazer) (6/85)	11	22	33	76	163	250
38-40: John Constantine app.	2	4	6	8	11	14
41-52,54-64: 44-Batman cameo. 44-51-John Constantine app. 46-Crisis x-over; Batman cameo. 49-Spectre app. 50-($1.25, 52 pgs.)-Deadman, Dr. Fate, Demon. 52-Arkham Asylum-c/story; Joker-c/cameo. 58-Spectre preview. 64-Last Moore issue						4.00
53-($1.25, 52 pgs.)-Arkham Asylum; Batman-c/story						5.00
65-83,85-99,101-124,126-149,151-153: 65-Direct sales only begins. 66-Batman & Arkham Asylum story. 70,76-John Constantine x-over; 76-X-over w/Hellblazer #9. 79-Superman-c/story. 85-Jonah Hex app. 102-Preview of World Without End. 116-Photo-c. 129-Metallic ink on-c. 140-Millar scripts begin, end #171						4.00
84-Sandman (Morpheus) cameo.						5.00
100,125,150: 100 ($2.50, 52 pgs.). 125-($2.95, 52 pgs.)-20th anniversary issue. 150 (52 pgs.)-Anniversary issue						5.00
154-171: 154-$2.25-c begins. 165-Curt Swan-a(p). 166,169,171-John Constantine & Phantom Stranger app. 168-Arcane returns						4.00
Annual 1,3-6('82-91): 1-Movie Adaptation; painted-c. 3-New format; Bolland-c. 4-Batman-c/story. 5-Batman cameo; re-intro Brother Power (Geek),1st app. since 1968						5.00
Annual 2 (1985)-Moore scripts; Bissette-a(p); Deadman, Spectre app.						7.00
Annual 7(1993, $3.95)-Children's Crusade						5.00
...A Murder of Crows (2001, $19.95)-r/#43-50; Moore-s						20.00
...: Earth To Earth (2002, $17.95)-r/#51-56; Batman app.						18.00
...: Infernal Triangles (2006, $19.99, TPB) r/#77-81 & Annual #3; cover gallery						20.00
...Love and Death (1990, $17.95)-r/#28-34 & Annual #2; Totleben painted-c						18.00
...: Regenesis (2004, $17.95, TPB) r/#65-70; Veitch-s						18.00
...: Reunion (2003, $19.95, TPB) r/#57-64; Moore-s						20.00
...: Roots (1998, $7.95) Jon J Muth-s/painted-a/c						8.00
Saga of the Swamp Thing ('87, '89)-r/#21-27 (1st & 2nd print)						15.00
Saga of the Swamp Thing Book One HC (2009, $24.99, d.j.) r/#20-27; Wein intro.						25.00
Saga of the Swamp Thing Book Two HC (2009, $24.99, d.j.) r/#28-34 & Annual #2						25.00
Saga of the Swamp Thing Book Three HC (2010, $24.99, d.j.) r/#35-42; Bissette intro.						25.00
Saga of the Swamp Thing Book Four HC (2010, $24.99, d.j.) r/#43-50; Gaiman foreword						25.00
Saga of the Swamp Thing Book Five HC (2011, $24.99, d.j.) r/#51-56; Bissette intro.						25.00
...: Spontaneous Generation (2005, $19.99) r/#71-76						20.00
...: The Curse (2000, $19.95, TPB) r/#35-42; Bisley-c						20.00

NOTE: ***Bissette*** *a(p)-16-19, 21-27, 29, 30, 34-36, 39-42, 44, 46, 50, 64; c-17i, 24-32p, 35-37p, 40p, 44p, 46-50p, 51-58, 61, 62, 63p.* ***Kaluta*** *c/a-74.* ***Spiegle*** *a-1-3, 6.* ***Sutton*** *a-98p.* ***Totleben*** *a(i)-10, 16-27, 29, 31, 34-40, 42, 44, 46, 48, 50, 53, 55i; c-25-32i, 33, 35-40i, 42i, 44i, 46-50i, 53, 55i, 59p, 64, 65, 68, 73, 76, 80, 82, 84, 89, 91-100, Annual 4, 5.* ***Vess*** *painted c-121, 129-139, Annual 7.* ***Williamson*** *86i.* ***Wrightson*** *a-18i(r), 33r. John Constantine appears in #37-40, 44-51, 65-67, 70-77, 80-90, 99, 114, 115, 130, 134-138.*

SWAMP THING
DC Comics (Vertigo): May, 2000 - No. 20, Dec, 2001 ($2.50)

	GD	VG	FN	VF	VF/NM	NM-
1-3-Tefé Holland's return; Vaughan-s/Petersen-a; Hale painted-c.						4.00
4-20: 7-9-Bisley-c. 10-John Constantine-c/app. 10-12-Fabry-c. 13-15-Mack-c 18-Swamp Thing app.						3.00
Preview-16 pg. flip book w/Lucifer Preview						3.00

SWAMP THING
DC Comics (Vertigo): May, 2004 - No. 29, Sept, 2006 ($2.95/$2.99)

	GD	VG	FN	VF	VF/NM	NM-
1-29: 1-Diggle-s/Breccia-a; Constantine app. 2-6-Sargon app. 7,8,20-Corben-c/a. 21-29-Eric Powell-c						3.00
...: Bad Seed (2004, $9.95) r/#1-6						10.00
...: Healing the Breach (2006, $17.99) r/#15-20						18.00
...: Love in Vain (2005, $14.99) r/#9-14						15.00

SWAMP THING (DC New 52)
DC Comics: Nov, 2011 - No. 40, May, 2015 ($2.99)

	GD	VG	FN	VF	VF/NM	NM-
1-Snyder-s/Paquette-a; Superman app.						8.00
1-(2nd & 3rd printing)						3.00
2-18: 2-Abigail Arcane returns. 7-Holland transforms. 10-Francavilla-a; Anton Arcane returns. 12-X-over with Animal Man #12. 13-Poison Ivy & Deadman app.; leads into Annual #1						3.00
19-23: 19-Soule-s/Kano-a begin. 19,20-Superman app. 22,23-Constantine app.						3.00
23.1 (11/13, $2.99, regular cover)						3.00
23.1 (11/13, $3.99, 3-D cover) "Arcane #1" on cover; Soule-s/Saiz-a/c; origin of Arcane						5.00
24-39: 24-Leads into Annual #2. 26-Woodrue's origin; Animal Man app. 32-Aquaman app. 39-Constantine app.						3.00
40-($3.99)						4.00
#0-(11/12, $2.99) Kano-a; Arcane app.; Swamp Thing origin re-told						3.00
Annual #1 (12/12, $4.99) Flashback to 1st meeting of Alec & Abby; Cloonan-a						5.00
Annual #2 (12/13, $4.99) Soule-s/Pina-a						5.00
Annual #3 (12/14, $4.99) Soule-s/Pina-a; Etrigan app.						5.00
...: Futures End 1 (11/14, $2.99, regular-c) Five years later; Soule-s/Saiz-a; Arcane app.						3.00
...: Futures End 1 (11/14, $3.99, 3-D cover)						4.00

SWAMP THING
DC Comics: Mar, 2016 - No. 6, Aug, 2016 ($2.99)

	GD	VG	FN	VF	VF/NM	NM-
1-6-Len Wein-s/Kelley Jones-a. 1,2-Phantom Stranger app. 2-Matt Cable returns. 3,4,6-Zatanna app.						3.00
... Winter Special 1 (3/18, $7.99) Wein-s/Jones-a; King-s/Fabok-a; Wein script & tribute						8.00

SWAMP THING GIANT
DC Comics: 2019 - No. 5, 2019 ($4.99, 100 pgs., squarebound, Walmart exclusive)

	GD	VG	FN	VF	VF/NM	NM-
1-5: 1-New story Seeley-s/Perkins-a; reprints from Animal Man ('11), Swamp Thing ('11), and Shadowpact ('06). 2-New story with Joëlle Jones-a plus reprints continue						5.00
Halloween Horror Giant ('18, $4.99) Intro. Briar in new story; Capullo-a; plus reprints						5.00

SWAMP THING GIANT
DC Comics: 2019 - No. 5, 2020 ($4.99, 100 pgs., squarebound, Mass Market & Direct Market editions exist for each issue, with different covers)

	GD	VG	FN	VF	VF/NM	NM-
1-5-New stories Russell-s/Santucci-a & Hester-s/Mandrake-a; plus reprints						5.00

SWASHBUCKLERS: THE SAGA CONTINUES (See Marvel Graphic Novel #14 and Swords of The Swashbucklers)
Dynamite Entertainment: 2018 - No. 5, 2018 ($3.99, limited series)

	GD	VG	FN	VF	VF/NM	NM-
1-5-Marc Guggenheim-s/Andrea Mutti-a						4.00

SWAT MALONE (America's Home Run King)
Swat Malone Enterprises: Sept, 1955

	GD	VG	FN	VF	VF/NM	NM-
V1#1-Hy Fleishman-a	12	24	36	67	94	120

SWEATSHOP
DC Comics: Jun, 2003 - No. 6, Nov, 2003 ($2.95)

	GD	VG	FN	VF	VF/NM	NM-
1-6-Peter Bagge-s/a; Destefano-a						3.00

SWEENEY (Formerly Buz Sawyer)
Standard Comics: No. 4, June, 1949 - No. 5, Sept, 1949

	GD	VG	FN	VF	VF/NM	NM-
4,5: 5-Crane-a	9	18	27	50	65	80

SWEE'PEA (Also see Popeye #46)

Sweetheart Diary V2 #8 © FAW

Sweet Tooth #10 © Jeff Lemire

S.W.O.R.D. #1 © MAR

	GD 2.0	VG 4.0	FN 6.0	VF 8.0	VF/NM 9.0	NM- 9.2

Dell Publishing Co.: No. 219, Mar, 1949

Four Color 219 9 18 27 59 117 175

SWEET CHILDE
Advantage Graphics Press: 1995 - No. 2, 1995 ($2.95, B&W, mature)

1,2 3.00

SWEETHEART DIARY (Cynthia Doyle #66-on)
Fawcett Publications/Charlton Comics No. 32 on: Wint, 1949; #2, Spr, 1950; #3, 6/50 - #5, 10/50; #6, 1951(nd); #7, 9/51 - #14, 1/53; #32, 10/55; #33, 4/56 - #65, 8/62 (#1-14: photo-c)

1 22 44 66 130 213 295
2 14 28 42 80 115 150
3,4-Wood-a 17 34 51 98 154 210
5-10: 8-Bailey-a 10 20 30 56 76 95
11-14: 13-Swayze-a. 14-Last Fawcett issue 9 18 27 47 61 75
32 (10/55; 1st Charlton issue)(Formerly Cowboy Love #31)
9 18 27 52 69 85
33-40: 34-Swayze-a 7 14 21 35 43 50
41-(68 pgs.) 8 16 24 40 50 60
42-60 3 6 9 19 30 40
61-65 3 6 9 17 26 35

SWEETHEARTS (Formerly Captain Midnight)
Fawcett Publications/Charlton No. 122 on: #68, 10/48 - #121, 5/53; #122, 3/54; V2#23, 5/54 - #137, 12/73

68-Photo-c begin 19 38 57 112 179 245
69,70 11 22 33 62 86 110
71-80 9 18 27 52 69 85
81-84,86-93,95-99,105 9 18 27 47 61 75
85,94,103,110,117-George Evans-a 10 20 30 54 72 90
100 9 18 27 52 69 85
101,107-Powell-a 9 18 27 50 65 80
102,104,106,108,109,112-116,118 8 16 24 44 57 70
111-1 pg. Ronald Reagan biography 10 20 30 58 79 100
119-Marilyn Monroe & Richard Widmark photo-c (1/53); also appears in story; part Wood-a 116 232 348 742 1271 1800
120-Atom Bomb story 12 24 36 67 94 120
121-Liz Taylor/Fernanado Lamas photo-c 39 78 117 240 395 550
122-(1st Charlton? 3/54)-Marijuana story 14 28 42 76 108 140
V2#23 (5/54)-28: 28-Last precode issue (2/55) 8 16 24 42 54 65
29-39,41,43,45,47-50 4 8 12 25 40 55
40-Photo-c; Tommy Sands story 4 8 12 27 44 60
42-Ricky Nelson photo-c/story 7 14 21 49 92 135
44-Pat Boone photo-c/story 4 8 12 27 44 60
46-Jimmy Rodgers photo-c/story 4 8 12 27 44 60
51-60 3 6 9 21 33 45
61-80,100 3 6 9 18 28 38
81-99 3 6 9 16 24 32
101-110 2 4 6 13 18 22
111-120,122-124,126-137 2 4 6 10 14 18
121,125-David Cassidy pin-ups 2 4 6 13 18 22

NOTE: *Photo c-68-121(Fawcett), 40, 42, 46(Charlton).* ***Swayze*** *a(Fawcett)-70-118(most).*

SWEETHEART SCANDALS (See Fox Giants)

SWEETIE PIE
Dell Publishing Co.: No. 1185, May-July, 1961 - No. 1241, Nov-Jan, 1961/62

Four Color 1185 (#1) 6 12 18 37 66 95
Four Color 1241 5 10 15 30 50 70

SWEETIE PIE
Ajax-Farrell/Pines (Literary Ent.): Dec, 1955 - No. 15, Fall, 1957

1-By Nadine Seltzer 12 24 36 67 94 120
2 (5/56; last Ajax?) 7 14 21 37 46 55
3-15 6 12 18 31 38 45

SWEET LOVE
Home Comics (Harvey): Sept, 1949 - No. 5, May, 1950 (All photo-c)

1 13 26 39 72 101 130
2 8 16 24 40 50 60
3,4: 3-Powell-a 7 14 21 35 43 50
5-Kamen, Powell-a 9 18 27 50 65 80

SWEET ROMANCE
Charlton Comics: Oct, 1968

1 3 6 9 14 20 25

SWEET SIXTEEN (...Comics and Stories for Girls)
Parents' Magazine Institute: Aug-Sept, 1946 - No. 13, Jan, 1948 (All have movie stars photos on covers)

1-Van Johnson's life story; Dorothy Dare, Queen of Hollywood Stunt Artists begins (in all issues); part photo-c 31 62 93 184 300 415
2-Jane Powell, Roddy McDowall "Holiday in Mexico" photo on-c; Alan Ladd story 20 40 60 115 188 260
3,5,6,8-11: 5-Ann Francis photo on-c; Gregory Peck story. 6-Dick Haymes story. 8-Shirley Jones photo on-c. 10-Jean Simmons photo on-c; James Stewart story 15 30 45 90 140 190
4-Elizabeth Taylor photo on-c 37 74 111 218 354 490
7-Ronald Reagan's life story 30 60 90 177 289 400
12-Bob Cummings, Vic Damone story 15 30 45 92 144 195
13-Robert Mitchum's life story 15 30 45 94 147 200

SWEET XVI
Marvel Comics: May, 1991 - No. 5, Sept, 1991 ($1.00)

1-5: Barbara Slate story & art 4.00

SWEET TOOTH
DC Comics (Vertigo): Nov, 2009 - No. 40, Feb, 2013 ($1.00/$2.99)

1-($1.00) Jeff Lemire-s/a 6 12 18 38 69 100
2 1 2 3 6 8 10
3-39-($2.99) 18,33-Printed sideways. 26-28-Kindt-a 3.00
40-($4.99) Final issue; two covers by Lemire and Truman 5.00
...: Animal Armies TPB (2011, $14.99) r/#12-17 15.00
...: In Captivity TPB (2010, $12.99) r/#6-11 13.00
...: Out of the Deep Woods TPB (2010, $9.99) r/#1-5 10.00

SWEET TOOTH: THE RETURN
DC Comics (Black Label): Jan, 2021 - No. 6 ($3.99, limited series)

1-4-Jeff Lemire-s/a 4.00

SWIFT ARROW (Also see Lone Rider & The Rider)
Ajax/Farrell Publications: Feb-Mar, 1954 - No. 5, Oct-Nov, 1954; Apr, 1957 - No. 3, Sept, 1957

1(1954) (1st Series) 17 34 51 100 158 215
2 10 20 30 58 79 100
3-5: 5-Lone Rider story 9 18 27 50 65 80
1 (2nd Series) (Swift Arrow's Gunfighters #4) 9 18 27 50 65 80
2,3: 2-Lone Rider begins 8 16 24 40 50 60

SWIFT ARROW'S GUNFIGHTERS (Formerly Swift Arrow)
Ajax/Farrell Publ. (Four Star Comic Corp.): No. 4, Nov, 1957

4 8 16 24 40 50 60

SWING WITH SCOOTER
National Periodical Publ.: June-July, 1966 - No. 35, Aug-Sept, 1971; No. 36, Oct-Nov, 1972

1 9 18 27 60 120 180
2,6-10: 9-Alfred E. Newman swipe in last panel 5 10 15 33 57 80
3-5: 3-Batman cameo on-c. 4-Batman cameo inside. 5-JLA cameo 5 10 15 34 60 85
11-13,15-19: 18-Wildcat of JSA 1pg. text. 19-Last 12¢-c 3 6 9 20 31 42
14-Alfred E. Neuman cameo 4 8 12 23 37 50
20 (68 pgs.) 5 10 15 30 50 70
21-23,25-31 3 6 9 17 26 35
24-Frankenstein-c. 4 8 12 23 37 50
32-34 (68 pgs.). 32-Batman cameo. 33-Interview with David Cassidy. 34-Interview with Rick Ely (The Rebels) 4 8 12 28 47 65
35-(52 pgs.). 1 pg. app. Clark Kent and 4 full pgs. of Superman 7 14 21 46 86 125
36-Bat-signal refererence to Batman 3 6 9 21 33 45

NOTE: ***Aragonés*** *a-13 (1pg.), 18(1pg.), 30(2pgs.)* ***Orlando*** *a-1-11; c-1-11, 13. #20, 33, 34: 68 pgs.; #35: 52 pgs.*

SWISS FAMILY ROBINSON (Walt Disney's..; see King Classics & Movie Comics)
Dell Publishing Co.: No. 1156, Dec, 1960

Four Color 1156-Movie-photo-c 8 16 24 51 96 140

SWITCH (Also see Witchblade titles)
Image Comics: Oct, 2015 - No. 4, Jul, 2016 ($3.99)

1-4-Stjepan Sejic-s/a; 3 covers on each 4.00

S.W.O.R.D. (Sentient World Observation and Response Department)
Marvel Comics: Jan, 2010 - No. 5, May, 2010 ($3.99/$2.99)

1-($3.99) Cassaday-c/Gillen-s/Sanders-a; Commander Brand & Henry Gyrich app. 4.00
2-5-($2.99): 2,3-Cassaday-c. 4,5-Del Mundo-c 3.00

S.W.O.R.D. (Sentient World Observation and Response Department)
Marvel Comics: Feb, 2021 - Present ($4.99/$3.99)

1-($4.99) Al Ewing-s/Valerio Schiti-a; Abigail Brand & Magneto app. 5.00
2,3-($3.99) "King in Black" tie-ins 4.00

Sword Daughter #9 © Brian Wood

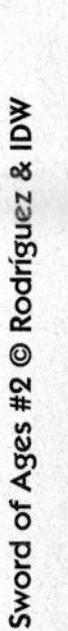
Sword of Ages #2 © Rodríguez & IDW

Symbiote Spider-Man #1 © MAR

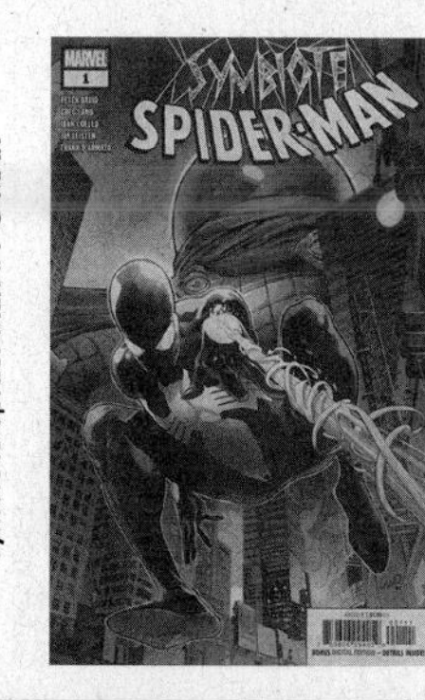

	GD	VG	FN	VF	VF/NM	NM-
	2.0	4.0	6.0	8.0	9.0	9.2

SWORD, THE
Image Comics: Oct, 2007 - No. 24, May, 2010 ($2.99/$4.99)
1-Luna Brothers-s/a 4.00
1-(2nd printing) 3.00
2-23: 12-Zakros killed 3.00
24-($4.99) Final issue 5.00

SWORD & THE DRAGON, THE
Dell Publishing Co.: No. 1118, June, 1960
Four Color 1118-Movie, photo-c 8 16 24 51 96 140

SWORD & THE ROSE, THE (Disney)
Dell Publishing Co.: No. 505, Oct, 1953 - No. 682, Feb, 1956
Four Color 505-Movie, photo-c 8 16 24 55 105 155
Four Color 682-When Knighthood Was in Flower-Movie, reprint of #505; Renamed the Sword & the Rose for the novel; photo-c 6 12 18 40 73 105

SWORD DAUGHTER
Dark Horse Publishing: Jun, 2018 - No. 9, Jan, 2020 ($4.99)
1-9-Brian Wood-s/Mack Chater-a/Greg Smallwood-c 5.00

SWORD IN THE STONE, THE (See March of Comics #258 & Movie Comics & Wart and the Wizard)

SWORD MASTER
Marvel Comics: Sept, 2019 - No. 12, Jan, 2021 ($3.99)
1-12: 1-Shang-Chi & Ares app.; Shuizhu-s/Gunji-a. 5,6-Doctor Strange app. 4.00

SWORD OF AGES
IDW Publishing: Nov, 2017 - No. 4 ($3.99)
1-4-Gabriel Rodríguez-s/a 4.00
1 Special Edition (6/18, $6.99) bonus interview with Gabriel Rodríguez; uncolored art 7.00

SWORD OF DAMOCLES
Image Comics (WildStorm Productions): Mar, 1996 - No. 2, Apr, 1996 ($2.50, limited series)
1,2: Warren Ellis scripts. 1-Prelude to "Fire From Heaven" x-over; 1st app. Sword 3.00

SWORD OF DRACULA
Image Comics: Oct, 2003 - No. 6, Sept, 2004 ($2.95, B&W, limited series)
1-6-Tony Harris-c. 1,2-Greg Scott-a 3.00
TPB (IDW, 2/05, $14.99) r/series 15.00

SWORD OF RED SONJA: DOOM OF THE GODS
Dynamite Entertainment: 2007 - No. 4, 2007 ($3.50, limited series)
1-4-Lui Antonio-a; multiple covers on each 3.50

SWORD OF SORCERY
National Periodical Publications: Feb-Mar, 1973 - No. 5, Nov-Dec, 1973 (20¢)
1-Leiber Fafhrd & The Grey Mouser; Chaykin/Neal Adams (Crusty Bunkers) art; Kaluta-c 3 6 9 17 25 34
2,3: 2-Wrightson-c(i); Adams-a(i). 3-Wrightson-i(5 pgs.) 2 4 6 9 13 16
4,5: 5-Starlin-a(p); Conan cameo 2 4 6 8 10 12
NOTE: *Chaykin a-1-4p; c-2p, 3-5. Kaluta a-3i. Simonson a-3i, 4i, 5p; c-5.*

SWORD OF SORCERY (DC New 52)
DC Comics: No. 0, Nov, 2012 - No. 8, Jun, 2013 ($3.99)
0-8: 0-Origin of Amethyst retold; Lopresti-a; Beowulf back-up; Saiz-a. 4-Stalker back-up 4.00

SWORD OF THE ATOM
DC Comics: Sept, 1983 - No. 4, Dec, 1983 (Limited series)
1-4: Gil Kane-c/a in all 4.00
Special 1-3('84, '85, '88): 1,2-Kane-c/a each 4.00
TPB (2007, $19.99) r/#1-4 and Special #1-3 20.00

SWORDQUEST (Based on the Atari game)
Dynamite Entertainment: No. 0, 2017 - No. 5, 2017 (25¢/$3.99)
0-(25¢) Bowers & Sims-s/Ghostwriter X-a; bonus game history and character art 3.00
1-5-($3.99) Multiple covers on each; George Peréz & others 4.00

SWORDS OF SORROW
Dynamite Entertainment: 2015 - No. 6, 2015 ($3.99, limited series with tie-in series)
1-6-Simone-s/Davila-a; crossover of Vampirella, Red Sonja, Dejah Thoris, Lady Zorro and other female Dynamite characters; multiple covers on each 4.00
...: Black Sparrow & Lady Zorro Special 1 ($3.99, one-shot) Schultz-s/Zamora-a 4.00
...: Chaos! Prequel 1 ($3.99, one-shot) Mairghread Scott-s/Mirka Andolfo-a 4.00
...: Dejah Thoris & Irene Adler 1-3 ($3.99, lim. series) Leah Moore-s/Francesco Manna-a 4.00
...: Masquerade & Kato 1 ($3.99, one-shot) G. Willow Wilson & Erica Schultz-s 4.00
...: Miss Fury & Lady Rawhide 1 ($3.99, one-shot) Mikki Kendall-s/Ronilson Freire-a 4.00
...: Pantha & Jane Porter ($3.99, one-shot) Emma Beeby-s/Rod Rodolfo-a 4.00
...: Red Sonja & Jungle Girl 1-3 ($3.99, lim. series) Bennett-s/Andolfo-a/Anacleto-c 4.00
...: Vampirella & Jennifer Blood 1-4 ($3.99, lim. series) Nancy Collins-s/Dave Acosta-a 4.00

SWORDS OF TEXAS (See Scout #15)
Eclipse Comics: Oct, 1987 - No. 4, Jan, 1988 ($1.75, color, Baxter paper)
1-4: Scout app. 3.00

SWORDS OF THE SWASHBUCKLERS (See Marvel Graphic Novel #14)
Marvel Comics (Epic Comics): May, 1985 - No. 12, Jun, 1987 ($1.50; mature)
1-12-Butch Guice-c/a (cont'd from Marvel G.N. #14) 3.00

SWORN TO PROTECT
Marvel Comics: Sept, 1995 ($1.95) (Based on card game)
nn-Overpower Game Guide; Jubilee story 4.00

SYMBIOTE SPIDER-MAN (Takes place right after acquiring black costume in Secret Wars)
Marvel Comics: Jun, 2019 - No. 5, Oct, 2019 ($4.99/$3.99, limited series)
1-($4.99) Peter David-s/Greg Land-a; Mysterio and Felicia Hardy app. in all 5.00
2-5-($3.99) 3-Kingpin & Electro app. 4.00
...: Marvel Tales 1 (3/21, $7.99) Reprints of notable early Symbiote apps.; Macchio intro. 8.00

SYMBIOTE SPIDER-MAN: ALIEN REALITY
Marvel Comics: Feb, 2020 - No. 5, Sept, 2020 ($4.99/$3.99, limited series)
1-($4.99) Peter David-s/Greg Land-a; Hobgoblin, Doctor Strange & Black Widow app. 5.00
2-5-($3.99) 2-Uncle Ben app. 3-5-Baron Mordo app. 4.00

SYMBIOTE SPIDER-MAN: KING IN BLACK (Tie-in to King in Black crossover)
Marvel Comics: Jan, 2021 - No. 5, May, 2021 ($4.99/$3.99, limited series)
1-($4.99) Peter David-s/Greg Land-a; The Watcher and Kang app. 5.00
2-4-($3.99) 2-Black Knight app. 3,4-Captain Marvel (Monica Rambeau) app. 4.00

SYMMETRY
Image Comics (Top Cow): Dec, 2015 - No. 8, Oct, 2016 ($3.99)
1-8-Hawkins-s/Ienco-a 4.00

SYMPATHY FOR NO DEVILS
AfterShock Comics: Oct, 2020 - No. 5, Feb, 2021 ($3.99)
1-5-Brandon Thomas-s/Lee Ferguson-a 4.00

SYN
Dark Horse Comics: Aug, 2003 - No. 5, Feb, 2004 ($2.99, limited series)
1-5-Giffen-s/Titus-a 3.00

SYNERGY: A HASBRO CREATORS SHOWCASE
IDW Publishing: Mar, 2019 ($7.99, one-shot)
1-Short stories and pin-ups of My Little Pony, Jem, Transformers by women creators 8.00

SYPHONS
Now Comics: V2#1, May, 1994 - V2#3, 1994 ($2.50, limited series)
V2#1-3: 1-Stardancer, Knightfire, Raze & Brigade begin 3.00
TPB (9/04, $15.95) B&W reprints #1-3; intro. by Tony Caputo 16.00

SYSTEM, THE
DC Comics (Vertigo Verite): May, 1996 - No. 3, July, 1996 ($2.95, lim. series)
1-3: Kuper-c/a 3.00
TPB (1997, $12.95) r/#1-3 13.00

TAFFY COMICS (Also see Dotty Dripple)
Rural Home/Orbit Publ.: Mar-Apr, 1945 - No. 12, 1948
1-L.B. Cole-c; origin & 1st app. of Wiggles The Wonderworm plus 7 chapter WWII funny animal adventures 71 142 213 454 777 1100
2-L.B. Cole-c with funny animal Hitler; Wiggles-c/stories in #1-4 48 96 144 302 514 725
3,4,6-12: 6-Perry Como-c/story. 7-Duke Ellington, 2 pgs. 8-Glenn Ford-c/story. 9-Lon McCallister part photo-c & story. 10-Mort Leav-c. 11-Mickey Rooney-c/story 16 32 48 98 154 210
5-L.B. Cole-c; Van Johnson-c/story 24 48 72 144 237 330

TAILGUNNER JO
DC Comics: Sept, 1988 - No. 6, Jan, 1989 ($1.25)
1-6 3.00

TAILS
Archie Publications: Dec, 1995 - No. 3, Feb, 1996 ($1.50, limited series)
1-3: Based on Sonic, the Hedgehog video game 6.00

TAILS OF THE PET AVENGERS (Also see Lockjaw and the Pet Avengers)
Marvel Comics: Apr, 2010 ($3.99, one-shot)
1-Lockjaw, Frog Thor, Zabu, Lockheed and Redwing in short solo stories by various 4.00
...: The Dogs of Summer (9/10, $3.99) Eliopolous-s; see Avengers vs. the Pet Avengers 4.00

TAILSPIN

Takio #2 © Jinxworld

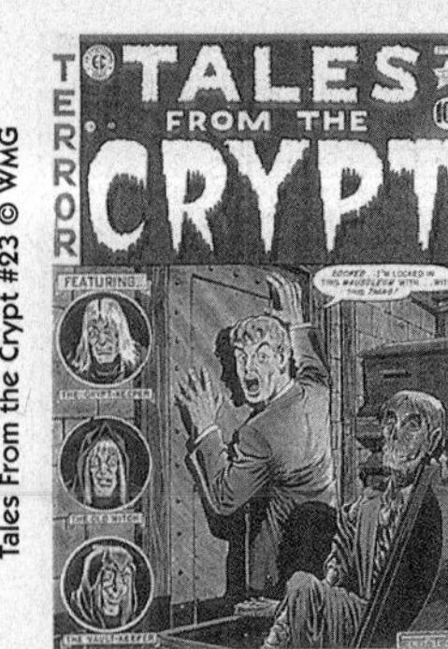

Tales From the Crypt #23 © WMG

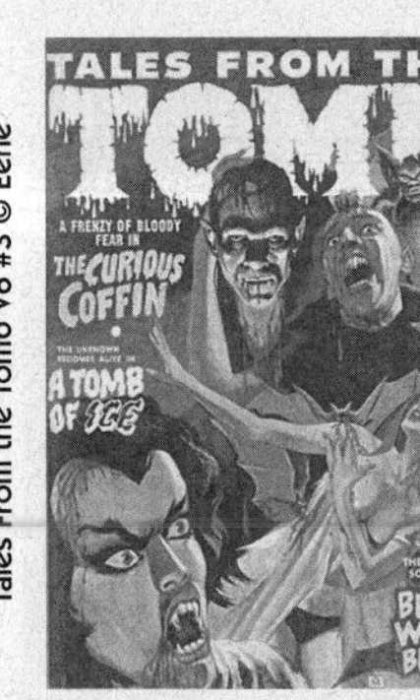

Tales From the Tomb V6 #3 © Eerie

	GD	VG	FN	VF	VF/NM	NM-
	2.0	4.0	6.0	8.0	9.0	9.2

Spotlight Publishers: November, 1944

nn-Firebird app.; L.B. Cole-c	39	78	117	231	378	525

TAILSPIN TOMMY (Also see Popular Comics)
United Features Syndicate/Service Publ. Co.: 1940; 1946

Single Series 23(1940)	47	94	141	296	498	700
1-Best Seller (nd, 1946)-Service Publ. Co.	21	42	63	126	206	285

TAKIO
Marvel Comics (Icon): 2011; May, 2012 - No. 4 ($3.95/$9.95)

HC (2011, $9.95) Bendis-s/Oeming-a/c; Oeming sketch pages 10.00
1-4: 1-(5/12, $3.95) Bendis-s/Oeming-a/c 4.00

TAKION
DC Comics: June, 1996 - No. 7, Dec, 1996 ($1.75)

1-7: Lopresti-c/a(p). 1-Origin; Green Lantern app. 6-Final Night x-over 3.00

TALENT SHOWCASE (See New Talent Showcase)

TALE OF ONE BAD RAT, THE
Dark Horse Comics: Oct, 1994 - No. 4, Jan, 1995 ($2.95, limited series)

1-4: Bryan Talbot-c/a/scripts 3.00
HC ($69.95, signed and numbered) R/#1-4 70.00

TALES CALCULATED TO DRIVE YOU BATS
Archie Publications: Nov, 1961 - No. 7, Nov, 1962; 1966 (Satire)

1-Only 10¢ issue; has cut-out Werewolf mask (price includes mask)	15	30	45	105	233	360
2-Begin 12¢ issues	9	18	27	58	114	170
3-6: 3-UFO cover	7	14	21	49	92	135
7-Storyline change	7	14	21	46	86	125
1(1966, 25¢, 44 pg. Giant)-r/#1; UFO cover	7	14	21	48	89	130

TALES CALCULATED TO DRIVE YOU MAD
E.C. Publications: Summer, 1997 - No. 8, Winter, 1999 ($3.99/$4.99, satire)

1-6-Full color reprints of Mad: 1-(#1-3), 2-(#4-6), 3-(#7-9), 4-(#10-12) 5-(#13-15), 6-(#16-18) 6.00
7,8-($4.99-c): 7-(#19-21), 8-(#22,23) 6.00

TALES FROM HARROW COUNTY (Also see Harrow County)
Dark Horse Comics: Dec, 2019 - No. 4, Mar, 2020 ($3.99, limited series)

1-4-Cullen Bunn-s/Naomi Franquiz-a; set 10 years after the events of Harrow County 4.00

TALES FROM RIVERDALE DIGEST
Archie Publ.: June, 2005 - No. 39, Oct, 2010 ($2.39/$2.49/$2.69, digest-size)

1-39: 1-Sabrina and Josie & the Pussycats app. 11-Begin $2.49-c. 34-Begin $2.69 3.00

TALES FROM THE AGE OF APOCALYPSE
Marvel Comics: 1996 ($5.95, prestige format, one-shots)

1, ...: Sinister Bloodlines (1997, $5.95) 6.00

TALES FROM THE BOG
Aberration Press: Nov, 1995 - No. 7, Nov, 1997 ($2.95/$3.95, B&W)

1-7 4.00
Alternate #1 (Director's Cut) (1998, $2.95) 3.00

TALES FROM THE BULLY PULPIT
Image Comics: Aug, 2004 ($6.95, square-bound)

1-Teddy Roosevelt and Edison's ghost with a time machine; Cereno-s/MacDonald-a 7.00

TALES FROM THE CLERKS (See Jay and Silent Bob, Clerks and Oni Double Feature)
Graphitti Designs, Inc.: 2006 ($29.95, TPB)

nn-Reprints all the Kevin Smith Clerks and Jay and Silent Bob stories; new Clerks II story with Mahfood-a; cover gallery, sketch pages, Mallrats credits covers; Smith intro. 30.00

TALES FROM THE CON
Image Comics: May, 2014 ($3.50, one-shot)

...: Year 1 - Brad Guigar-s/Chris Giarrusso-a/c; comic convention humor strips 3.50

TALES FROM THE CRYPT (Formerly The Crypt Of Terror; see Three Dimensional...)
(Also see EC Archives • Tales From the Crypt)
E.C. Comics: No. 20, Oct-Nov, 1950 - No. 46, Feb-Mar, 1955

20-See Crime Patrol #15 for 1st Crypt Keeper	166	332	498	1328	2114	2900
21-Kurtzman-r/Haunt of Fear #15(#1)	123	246	369	984	1567	2150
22-Moon Girl costume at costume party, one panel	103	206	309	824	1312	1800
23-25: 23-"Reflection of Death" adapted for 1972 TFTC film. 24-E. A. Poe adaptation	83	166	249	664	1057	1450
26-30: 26-Wood's 2nd EC-c	69	138	207	552	876	1200
31-Williamson-a(1st at E.C.); B&W and color illos. in **POP**; Kamen draws himself, Gaines & Feldstein; Ingels, Craig & Davis draw themselves in his story	69	138	207	552	876	1200
32,35-39: 38-Censored-c	60	120	180	480	765	1050
33-Origin The Crypt Keeper	83	166	249	664	1057	1450
34-Used in **POP**, pg. 83; classic Frankenstein Monster, Jack the Ripper-c by Davis; lingerie panels	63	126	189	504	802	1100
40-Used in Senate hearings & in Hartford Courant anti-comics editorials-1954	63	126	189	504	802	1100
41-45: 45-2 pgs. showing E.C. staff; anti-censorship editorial of upcoming Senate hearings	63	126	189	504	802	1000
46-Low distribution; pre-advertised cover for unpublished 4th horror title "Crypt of Terror" used on this book; "Blind Alleys" adapted for 1972 TFTC film; classic werewolf-c by Davis	80	160	240	640	1020	1400

NOTE: ***Ray Bradbury** adaptations-34, 36. **Craig** a-20, 22-24; c-20. **Crandall** a-38, 44. **Davis** a-24-46; c-29-46. **Elder** a-37, 38. **Evans** a-32-34, 36, 40, 41, 43, 46. **Feldstein** a-20-23; c-21-25, 28. Ingels a-in all. **Kamen** a-20, 22, 25, 27-31, 33-36, 39, 41-45. **Krigstein** a-40, 42, 45. **Kurtzman** a-21. **Orlando** a-27-30, 35, 37, 39, 41-45. **Wood** a-21, 24, 25; c-26, 27. Canadian reprints known; see Table of Contents.*

TALES FROM THE CRYPT (Magazine)
Eerie Publications: No. 10, July, 1968 (35¢, B&W)

10-Contains Farrell reprints from 1950s	6	12	18	38	69	100

TALES FROM THE CRYPT
Gladstone Publishing: July, 1990 - No. 6, May, 1991 ($1.95/$2.00, 68 pgs.)

1-r/TFTC #33 & Crime S.S. #17; Davis-c(r) 5.00
2-6: 2,3,5,6-Davis-c(r). 4-Begin $2.00-c; Craig-c(r) 5.00

TALES FROM THE CRYPT
Extra-Large Comics (Russ Cochran)/Gemstone Publishing: Jul, 1991 - No. 6 ($3.95, 10 1/4 x13 1/4", 68 pgs.)

1-6: 1-Davis-c(r); Craig back-c(r); E.C. reprints. 2-6 ($2.00, comic sized) 5.00

TALES FROM THE CRYPT
Russ Cochran: Sept, 1991 - No. 7, July, 1992 ($2.00, 64 pgs.)

1-7 5.00

TALES FROM THE CRYPT (Also see EC Archives • Tales From the Crypt)
Russ Cochran/Gemstone: Sept, 1992 - No. 30, Dec, 1999 ($1.50, quarterly)

1-4-r/Crypt of Terror #17-19, TFTC #20 w/original-c 4.00
5-30: 5-15 ($2.00)-r/TFTC #21-23 w/original-c. 16-30 ($2.50) 4.00
Annual 1-6('93-'99) 1-r/#1-5. 2- r/#6-10. 3- r/#11-15. 4- r/#16-20. 5-r/#21-25. 6- r/#26-30 14.00

TALES FROM THE DARK MULTIVERSE
DC Comics: Dec, 2019 - Feb, 2021 ($5.99, series of one-shots)

...: Batman: Hush 1 (1/21) - Tommy Elliot and Batman The Silenced app.; Soy-a 6.00
...: Batman: Knightfall 1 - What if Jean-Paul Valley remained as Batman; Fernandez-a 6.00
...: Blackest Night 1 - What if Sinestro kept the White Lantern power; Lobo app.; Hotz-a 6.00
...: Crisis on Infinite Earths 1 (2/21) - Justice Society app.; Orlando-s/Perkins-a 6.00
...: Dark Nights Metal 1 (2/21) - What if Barbatos had won; Duke Thomas app. 6.00
...: Flashpoint 1 (2/21) - What if the Flashpoint reality was never undone; Currie-a 6.00
...: Infinite Crisis 1 - What if Blue Beetle killed Max Lord; Tynion IV-s/Lopresti-a 6.00
...: The Death of Superman 1 - What if Lois gained the Eradicator's powers; Brad Walker-a 8.00
...: Teen Titans: The Judas Contract 1 - What if Terra didn't die; Raney-a 6.00
...: Wonder Woman War of the Gods 1 (2/21) - Evil Wonder Woman; Olivetti-a 6.00

TALES FROM THE DARKSIDE
IDW Publishing: Jun, 2016 - No. 4, Sept, 2016 ($3.99, limited series)

1-4-Joe Hill-s/Gabriel Rodriguez-a. 1-Five covers. 2-4-Two covers 4.00

TALES FROM THE GREAT BOOK
Famous Funnies: Feb, 1955 - No. 4, Jan, 1956 (Religious themes)

1-Story of Samson; John Lehti-a in all	12	24	36	67	94	120
2-4: 2-Joshua. 3-Joash the Boy King. 4-David	9	18	27	47	61	75

TALES FROM THE HEART OF AFRICA (The Temporary Natives)
Marvel Comics (Epic Comics): Aug, 1990 ($3.95, 52 pgs.)

1 4.00

TALES FROM THE TOMB (Also see Dell Giants)
Dell Publishing Co.: Oct, 1962 (25¢ giant)

1(02-810-210)-All stories written by John Stanley	16	32	48	110	243	375

TALES FROM THE TOMB (Magazine)
Eerie Publications: V1#6, July, 1969 - V7#3, 1975 (52 pgs.)

V1#6	9	18	27	60	120	180
V1#7,8	6	12	18	42	79	115
V2#1-6: 4-LSD story-r/Weird V3#5. 6-Rulah-r	5	10	15	35	63	90
V3#1-Rulah-r	6	12	18	38	69	100
2-6('71),V4#1-5('72),V5#1-6('73),V6#1-6('74),V7#1-3('75)	5	10	15	33	57	80

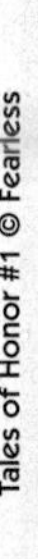
Tales of Honor #1 © Fearless

Tales of Horror #10 © Minoan

Tales of Suspense #57 © MAR

GD VG FN VF VF/NM NM-
2.0 4.0 6.0 8.0 9.0 9.2

TALES OF ASGARD
Marvel Comics Group: Oct, 1968 (25¢, 68 pgs.); Feb, 1984 ($1.25, 52 pgs.)

1-Reprints Tales of Asgard (Thor) back-up stories from Journey into Mystery #97-106;
new Kirby-c; Kirby-a 7 14 21 44 82 120
V2#1 (2/84)-Thor-r; Simonson-c 5.00

TALES OF ARMY OF DARKNESS
Dynamite Entertainment: 2006 ($5.95, one-shot)

1-Short stories by Kuhoric, Kirkman, Bradshaw, Sablik, Ottley, Acs, O'Hare and others 6.00

TALES OF EVIL
Atlas/Seaboard Publ.: Feb, 1975 - No. 3, July, 1975 (All 25¢ issues)

1-3: 1-Werewolf w/Sekowsky-a. 2-Intro. The Bog Beast; Sparling-a.
3-Origin The Man-Monster; Buckler-a(p) 2 4 6 13 18 22

NOTE: ***Grandenetti** a-1, 2. **Lieber** c-1. **Sekowsky** a-1. **Sutton** a-2. **Thorne** c-2.*

TALES OF GHOST CASTLE
National Periodical Publications: May-June, 1975 - No. 3, Sept-Oct, 1975 (All 25¢ issues)

1-Redondo-a; 1st app. Lucien the Librarian from Sandman (1989 series)
3 6 9 18 28 38
2,3: 2-Nino-a. 3-Redondo-a. 2 4 6 10 14 18

TALES OF G.I. JOE
Marvel Comics: Jan, 1988 - No. 15, Mar, 1989

1 ($2.25, 52 pgs.) 5.00
2-15 ($1.50): 1-15-r/G.I. Joe #1-15 4.00

TALES OF HONOR (Based on the David Weber novels)
Image Comics (Top Cow): Mar, 2014 - No. 5, Oct, 2015 ($2.99)

1-5: 1-Matt Hawkins-s/Jung-Geun Yoon-a. 2-5-Sang-il Jeong-a 3.00

TALES OF HONOR VOLUME 2 (Bred to Kill on cover)
Image Comics (Top Cow): No. 0, May, 2015 - No. 4, Dec, 2015 ($3.99)

0-Free Comic Book Day giveaway; Hawkins-s/Linda Sejic-a 3.00
1-4-Hawkins-s/Linda Sejic-a 4.00

TALES OF HORROR
Toby Press/Minoan Publ. Corp.: June, 1952 - No. 13, Oct, 1954

1-"This is Terror-Man" 61 122 183 390 670 950
2-Torture scenes 47 94 141 296 498 700
3-11,13: 9-11-Reprints Purple Claw #1-3 34 68 102 199 325 450
12-Myron Fass-c/a; torture scenes 37 74 111 222 361 500

NOTE: ***Andru** a-5. **Baily** a-5. **Myron Fass** a-2, 3, 12; c-1-3, 12. **Hollingsworth** a-2. **Sparling** a-6, 9; c-9.*

TALES OF JUSTICE
Atlas Comics(MjMC No. 53-66/Male No. 67): No. 53, May, 1955 - No. 67, Aug, 1957

53 20 40 60 118 192 265
54-57: 54-Powell-a 15 30 45 84 127 170
58,59-Krigstein-a 15 30 45 88 137 185
60-63,65: 60-Powell-a 14 28 42 80 115 150
64,66,67: 64,67-Crandall-a. 66-Torres, Orlando-a 14 28 42 81 118 155

NOTE: ***Everett** a-53, 60. **Orlando** a-65, 66. **Severin** a-64; c-58, 60, 65. **Wildey** a-64, 67.*

TALES OF LEONARDO BLIND SIGHT (See Tales of the TMNT Vol. 2 #5)
Mirage Publishing: June, 2006 - No. 4, Sept, 2006 ($3.25, B&W, limited series)

1-Jim Lawson-s/a in all 3 6 9 19 30 40
2-4 2 4 6 9 12 15

TALES OF SOPHISTICATION (Cerebus)
Aardvark-Vanaheim: Aug, 2019 ($4.00, B&W)

1-Cerebus figures with Doré artwork of Hell; cover swipe of Tales of Suspense #39 4.00

TALES OF SUSPENSE (Becomes Captain America #100 on)
Atlas (WPI No. 1,2/Male No. 3-12/VPI No. 13-18)/Marvel No. 19 on:
Jan, 1959 - No. 99, Mar, 1968

1-Williamson-a (5 pgs.); Heck-c; #1-4 have sci/fi-c 483 966 1449 4347 9424 14,500
2-Ditko robot-c 132 264 396 1056 2378 3700
3-Flying saucer-c/story 114 228 342 923 2062 3200
4-Williamson-a (4 pgs.); Kirby/Everett-c/a 107 214 321 856 1928 3000
5-Kirby monster-c begin 86 172 258 688 1544 2400
6,8,10 66 132 198 528 1189 1850
7-Prototype ish. (Lava Man); 1 panel app. Aunt May (see Str. Tales #97)
68 136 204 544 1222 1900
9-Prototype ish. (Iron Man) 62 124 186 502 1126 1750
11,12,15,17-19: 12-Crandall-a. 50 100 150 400 900 1400
13-Elektro-c/story 54 108 162 432 966 1500
14-Intro/1st app. Colossus-c/sty 62 124 186 502 1126 1750
16-1st Metallo-c/story (4/61, Iron Man prototype) 61 122 183 488 1094 1700
20-Colossus-c/story (2nd app.) 53 106 159 424 950 1475

GD VG FN VF VF/NM NM-
2.0 4.0 6.0 8.0 9.0 9.2

21-25: 25-Last 10¢ issue 44 88 132 326 738 1150
26,27,29,30,31,33,34,36-38: 33-(9/62)-Hulk 1st x-over cameo (picture on wall)
38 76 114 285 641 1000
28-Prototype ish. (Stone Men) 42 84 126 311 706 1100
31-Prototype ish. (Doctor Doom) 46 92 138 359 805 1250
32-Prototype ish. (Dr. Strange)(8/62)-Sazzik The Sorcerer app.; "The Man and the Beehive"
story, 1 month before TTA #35 (2nd Antman), came out after "The Man in the Ant Hill" in
TTA #27 (1/62) (1st Antman)-Characters from both stories were tested to see which got
best fan response 66 132 198 528 1189 1850
35-Prototype issue (The Watcher) 42 84 126 311 706 1100
39 (3/63)-Origin/1st app. Iron Man & begin series; 1st Iron Man story has Kirby layouts
2050 4100 7175 14,300 36,150 58,000
40-2nd app. Iron Man (in new armor) 207 414 621 1708 3854 6000
41-3rd app. Iron Man; Dr. Strange (villain) app. 132 264 396 1056 2378 3700
42-45: 45-Intro. & 1st app. Happy & Pepper 91 182 273 737 1644 2550
46,47: 46-1st app. Crimson Dynamo 62 124 186 502 1126 1750
48-New Iron Man red & gold armor by Ditko 68 136 204 544 1222 1900
49-1st X-Men x-over (same date as X-Men #3, 1/64); also 1st Avengers x-over
(w/o Captain America); 1st Tales of the Watcher back-up story & begins
(2nd app. Watcher; see F.F. #13) 84 168 252 672 1511 2350
50-1st app. Mandarin 71 142 213 568 1284 2000
51-1st Scarecrow 34 68 102 245 548 850
52-1st app. The Black Widow (4/64) 193 386 579 1592 3596 5600
53-Origin The Watcher; 2nd Black Widow app. 38 76 114 285 641 1000
54,55-2nd & 3rd Mandarin app. 26 52 78 182 404 625
56-1st app. Unicorn 27 54 81 189 420 650
57-Origin/1st app. Hawkeye (9/64) 155 310 465 1279 2890 4500
58-Captain America battles Iron Man (10/64)-Classic-c; 2nd Kraven app.
(Cap's 1st app. in this title) 59 118 177 472 1061 1650
59-Iron Man plus Captain America double feature begins (11/64); 1st S.A. Captain America
solo story; intro Jarvis, Avenger's butler; classic-c 44 88 132 326 738 1150
60-2nd app. Hawkeye (#64 is 3rd app.) 27 54 81 189 420 650
61,62,64: 62-Origin Mandarin (2/65). 64-1st Black Widow in costume
15 30 45 105 233 360
63-1st Silver Age origin Captain America (3/65) 30 60 90 216 483 750
65-G.A. Red Skull in WWII stories (also in #66-68);-1st Silver-Age Red Skull (5/65); Iron Man
wears old yellow armor 232 64 96 230 515 800
66-Origin Red Skull 18 36 54 124 275 425
67,68,70: 70-Begin alternating-c features w/Capt. America (even #'s)
& Iron Man (odd #'s) 9 18 27 61 123 185
69-1st app. Titanium Man 11 22 33 75 160 245
71-74,78: 78-Col. Nick Fury app. 7 14 21 46 86 125
75-1st app. Agent 13 later named Sharon Carter; intro Batroc
16 32 48 110 243 375
76-2nd app. Batroc & 1st cover app. 9 18 27 57 111 165
77-1st app. Peggy Carter (unnamed) in WW2 flashback (see Captain America #161 & 162)
8 16 24 56 108 160
79-Begin 3 part Iron Man Sub-Mariner battle story; Sub-Mariner-c & cameo;
1st app. Cosmic Cube; 1st modern Red Skull 11 22 33 75 160 245
80-Iron Man battles Sub-Mariner story cont'd in Tales to Astonish #82; classic Red Skull-c
10 20 30 69 147 225
81-93,95,96: 82-Intro the Adaptoid by Kirby (also in #83,84). 88-Mole Man app. in Iron Man
story. 92-1st Nick Fury x-over (cameo, as Agent of S.H.I.E.L.D., 8/67).
95-Capt. America's i.d. revealed 6 12 18 40 73 105
94-Intro Modok 21 42 63 147 324 500
97-1st Whiplash 9 18 27 60 120 180
98-Black Panther-c/s; 1st brief app. new Zemo (son?); #99 is 1st full app.
10 20 30 67 141 215
99-Captain America story cont'd in Captain America #100; Iron Man story cont'd in
Iron Man & Sub-Mariner #1 8 16 24 56 108 160
... No. 39 Facsimile Edition (11/20, $3.99) Reprints #39 with original ads 4.00
Onmibus (See Iron Man Omnibus for reprints of #39-83)

NOTE: ***Abel** a-73-81i(as Gary Michaels), **J. Buscema** a-1; c-3. **Colan** a-39, 73-99p; c(p)-73, 75, 77, 79, 81, 83, 85-87, 89, 91, 93, 95, 97, 99. **Crandall** a-12. **Davis** a-38. **Ditko** a-1-15, 17-44, 46, 47-49p; c-2, 10i, 13i, 23i. **Kirby/Ditko** a-7; c-10, 13, 22, 28, 34. **Everett** a-8. **Forte** a-5, 9. **Giacoia** a-82. **Heath** a-2, 10. **Gil Kane** a-88p, 89-91; c-88, 89-91p. **Kirby** a(p)-2-4, 6-35, 40, 41, 43, 59-75, 77-86, 92-99; layouts-69-75, 77; c(p)4-28(most), 29-56, 58-72, 74, 76, 78, 80, 82, 84, 86, 92, 94, 96, 98. **Leiber/Fox** a-42, 43, 45, 51. **Reinman** a-13, 25, 26, 44i, 49i, 52i, 53i. **Tuska** a-58, 70-74. **Wood** c/a-71i.*

TALES OF SUSPENSE
Marvel Comics: V2#1, Jan, 1995 ($6.95, one-shot)

V2#1-James Robinson script; acetate-c. 1 2 3 5 6 8

TALES OF SUSPENSE (Marvel Legacy)
Marvel Comics: No. 100, Feb, 2018 - No. 104, Jun, 2018 ($3.99)

100-104-Hawkeye & Winter Soldier team-up; Black Widow app.; Foreman-a 4.00

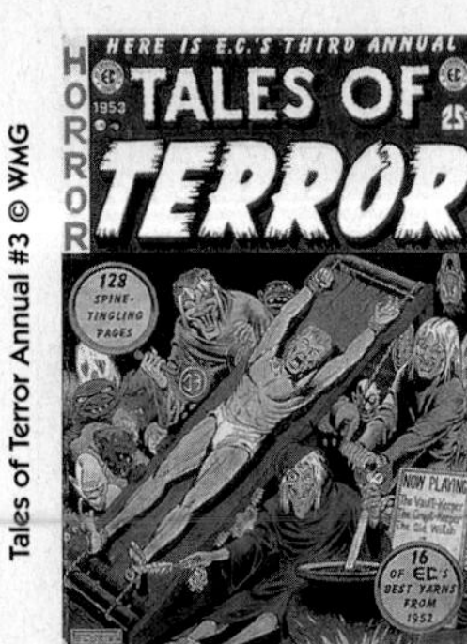

Tales of Terror Annual #3 © WMG

Tales of the Legion of Super-Heroes #325 © DC

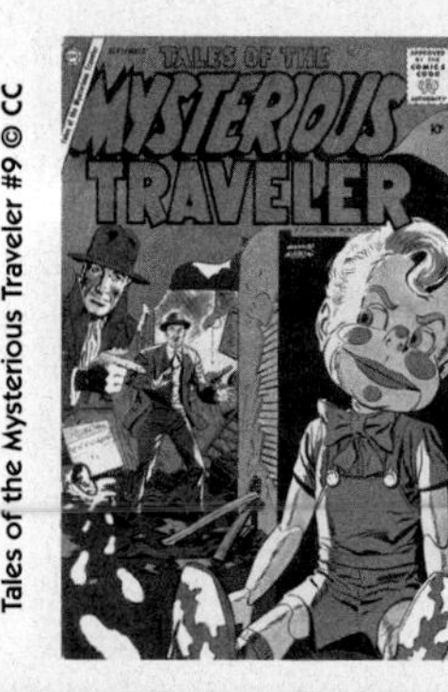

Tales of the Mysterious Traveler #9 © CC

	GD	VG	FN	VF	VF/NM	NM-
	2.0	4.0	6.0	8.0	9.0	9.2

TALES OF SUSPENSE: CAPTAIN AMERICA & IRON MAN #1 COMMEMORATIVE EDITION
Marvel Comics: 2004 ($3.99, one-shot)

nn-Reprints Captain America (2004) #1 and Iron Man (2004) #1 — 5.00

TALES OF SWORD & SORCERY (See Dagar)

TALES OF TELLOS (See Tellos)
Image Comics: Oct, 2004 - No. 3, ($3.50, anthology)

1-3: 1-Dezago-s; art by Yates & Rousseau; Wieringo-c. 3-Porter-a — 3.50

TALES OF TERROR
Toby Press Publications: 1952 (no month)

	GD 2.0	VG 4.0	FN 6.0	VF 8.0	VF/NM 9.0	NM- 9.2
1-Fawcette-c; Ravielli-a	55	110	165	352	601	850

NOTE: *This title was cancelled due to similarity to the E.C. title.*

TALES OF TERROR (See Movie Classics)

TALES OF TERROR (Magazine)
Eerie Publications: Summer, 1964

	GD 2.0	VG 4.0	FN 6.0	VF 8.0	VF/NM 9.0	NM- 9.2
1	6	12	18	42	79	115

TALES OF TERROR
Eclipse Comics: July, 1985 - No. 13, July, 1987 ($2.00, Baxter paper, mature)

1-13: 5-1st Lee Weeks-a. 7-Sam Kieth-a. 10-Snyder-a. 12-Vampire story — 4.00

TALES OF TERROR (IDW's...)
IDW Publishing: Sept, 2004 ($16.99, hardcover)

1-Anthology of short graphic stories and text stories; incl. 30 Days of Night — 17.00

TALES OF TERROR ANNUAL
E.C. Comics: 1951 - No. 3, 1953 (25¢, 132 pgs., 16 stories each)

	GD 2.0	VG 4.0	FN 6.0	VF 8.0	VF/NM 9.0	NM- 9.2
nn(1951)(Scarce)-Feldstein infinity-c	2400	4800	7200	13,000	--	--
2(1952)-Feldstein-c	300	600	900	2070	3635	5200
3(1953)-Feldstein bondage/torture-c	258	516	774	1651	2826	4000

NOTE: *No. 1 contains three horror and one science fiction comic which came out in 1950. No. 2 contains a horror, crime, and science fiction book which generally had cover dates in 1951, and No. 3 had horror, crime, and shock books that generally appeared in 1952. All E.C. annuals contain four complete books that did not sell on the stands which were rebound in the annual format, minus the covers, and sold from the E.C. office and on the stands in key cities. The contents of each annual may vary in the same year. Crypt Keeper, Vault Keeper, Old Witch app. on all-c.*

TALES OF TERROR ILLUSTRATED (See Terror Illustrated)

TALES OF TEXAS JOHN SLAUGHTER (See Walt Disney Presents, 4-Color #997)

TALES OF THE BEANWORLD
Beanworld Press/Eclipse Comics: Feb, 1985 - No. 19, 1991; No. 20, 1993 - No. 21, 1993 ($1.50/$2.00, B&W)

1-21 — 3.00

TALES OF THE BIZARRO WORLD
DC Comics: 2000 ($14.95, TPB)

nn-Reprints early Bizarro stories; new Jaime Hernandez-c — 15.00

TALES OF THE DARKNESS
Image Comics (Top Cow): Apr, 1998 - No. 4, Dec, 1998 ($2.95)

1-4: 1,2-Portacio-c/a(p). 3,4-Lansing & Nocon-a(p) — 3.00
1-American Entertainment Ed. — 3.00
#1/2 (1/01, $2.95) — 3.00

TALES OF THE DRAGON GUARD (English version of French comic title)
Marvel Comics (Soleil): Apr, 2010 - No. 3, Jun, 2010 ($5.99, limited series)

1-3: 1-Ange-s/Varanda-a. 2-Briones-a. 3-Guinebaud-a — 6.00
...: Into the Veil 1-3 (11/10 - No. 3, 1/11) 1-Briones-a. 2-Paty-a. 3-Sieurac-a — 6.00

TALES OF THE GREEN BERET
Dell Publishing Co.: Jan, 1967 - No. 5, Oct, 1969

	GD 2.0	VG 4.0	FN 6.0	VF 8.0	VF/NM 9.0	NM- 9.2
1-Glanzman-a in 1-4 & 5r	4	8	12	23	37	50
2-5: 5-Reprints #1	3	6	9	16	24	32

TALES OF THE GREEN HORNET
Now Comics: Sept, 1990 - No. 2, 1990; V2#1, Jan, 1992 - No.4, Apr, 1992; V3#1, Sept, 1992 - No. 3, Nov, 1992

1,2 — 3.00
V2#1-4 ($1.95) — 3.00
V3#1 ($2.75)-Polybagged w/hologram trading card — 4.00
V3#2,3 ($2.50) — 3.00

TALES OF THE GREEN LANTERN CORPS (See Green Lantern #107)
DC Comics: May, 1981 - No. 3, July, 1981 (Limited series)

	GD 2.0	VG 4.0	FN 6.0	VF 8.0	VF/NM 9.0	NM- 9.2
1-Origin of G.L. & the Guardians	2	4	6	10	14	18
2-1st app. Nekron	2	4	6	10	14	18
3	1	3	4	6	8	10
Annual 1 (1/85)-Gil Kane-c/a	1	2	3	5	6	8

TPB (2009, $19.99) r/#1-3 & stories from G.L. #148-151-154,161,162,164-167 ('82-'83) — 20.00
Volume 2 TPB (2010, $19.99) r/Annual #1 and stories from G.L. ('83-'85) — 20.00
Volume 3 TPB (2010, $19.99) r/Green Lantern #201-206 ('86) — 20.00

TALES OF THE INVISIBLE SCARLET O'NEIL (See Harvey Comics Hits #59)

TALES OF THE KILLERS (Magazine)
World Famous Periodicals: V1#10, Dec, 1970 - V1#11, Feb, 1971 (B&W, 52 pg)

	GD 2.0	VG 4.0	FN 6.0	VF 8.0	VF/NM 9.0	NM- 9.2
V1#10-One pg. Frazetta; r/Crime Does Not Pay	5	10	15	31	53	75
11-similar-c to Crime Does Not Pay #47; contains r/Crime Does Not Pay	4	8	12	28	47	65

TALES OF THE LEGION (Formerly Legion of Super-Heroes)
DC Comics: No. 314, Aug, 1984 - No. 354, Dec, 1987

314-354: 326-r-begin — 4.00
Annual 4,5 (1986, 1987)-Formerly LSH Annual — 5.00

TALES OF THE MARINES (Formerly Devil-Dog Dugan #1-3)
Atlas Comics (OPI): No. 4, Feb, 1957 (Marines At War #5 on)

	GD 2.0	VG 4.0	FN 6.0	VF 8.0	VF/NM 9.0	NM- 9.2
4-Powell-a; grey tone-c by Severin	15	30	45	94	147	200

TALES OF THE MARVELS
Marvel Comics: 1995/1996 (all acetate, painted-c)

...Blockbuster 1 (1995, $5.95, one-shot), ...Inner Demons 1 (1996, $5.95, one shot), ...Wonder Years 1,2 (1995, $4.95, limited series) — 6.00

TALES OF THE MARVEL UNIVERSE
Marvel Comics: Feb, 1997 ($2.95, one-shot)

1-Anthology; wraparound-c; Thunderbolts, Ka-Zar app. — 4.00

TALES OF THE MYSTERIOUS TRAVELER (See Mysterious...)
Charlton Comics: Aug, 1956 - No. 13, June, 1959; V2#14, Oct, 1985 - No. 15, Dec, 1985

	GD 2.0	VG 4.0	FN 6.0	VF 8.0	VF/NM 9.0	NM- 9.2
1-No Ditko-a; Giordano/Alascia-c	52	104	156	328	552	775
2-Ditko-a(1)	41	82	123	256	428	600
3-Ditko-c/a(1)	42	84	126	265	445	625
4-7-Ditko-c/a(3-4 stories each)	48	96	144	302	514	725
8,9-Ditko-a(1-3 each). 8-Rocke-c	41	82	123	250	418	585
10,11-Ditko-c/a(3-4 each)	44	88	132	277	469	660
12	18	36	54	105	165	225
13-Baker-a (r?)	19	38	57	111	176	240
V2#14,15 (1985)-Ditko-c/a-low print run	2	3	4	6	8	10

TALES OF THE NEW GODS
DC Comics: 2008 ($19.99, TPB)

SC-Reprints from Jack Kirby's Fourth World, Orion and Mister Miracle Special; includes previously unpublished story by Millar-s/Ditko-a — 20.00

TALES OF THE NEW TEEN TITANS
DC Comics: June, 1982 - No. 4, Sept, 1982 (Limited series)

	GD 2.0	VG 4.0	FN 6.0	VF 8.0	VF/NM 9.0	NM- 9.2
1	3	6	9	14	20	25
2-4	1	3	4	6	8	10

TALES OF THE PONY EXPRESS (TV)
Dell Publishing Co.: No. 829, Aug, 1957 - No. 942, Oct, 1958

	GD 2.0	VG 4.0	FN 6.0	VF 8.0	VF/NM 9.0	NM- 9.2
Four Color 829 (#1) -Painted-c	5	10	15	35	63	90
Four Color 942-Title -Pony Express	5	10	15	31	53	75

TALES OF THE REALM
CrossGen Comics/MVCreations #4-on: Oct, 2003 - No. 5, May, 2004 ($2.95, limited series)

1-5-Robert Kirkman-s/Matt Tyree-a — 3.00
Volume 1 HC (8/04, $39.95, dust jacket) r/#1-5; sketch pages and concept art — 40.00

TALES OF THE SINESTRO CORPS (See Green Lantern and Green Lantern Corps x-over)
DC Comics: Nov, 2007 - Jan, 2008 ($2.99/$3.99, one-shots)

...: Cyborg-Superman (12/07, $2.99) Burnett-s/Blaine-a/VanSciver-c; JLA app. — 3.00
...: Ion (1/08, $2.99) Marz-s/Lacombe-a/Benes-c; Sodam Yat app. — 3.00
...: Parallax (11/07, $2.99) Marz-s/Melo-a; Kyle Rayner vs. Parallax — 3.00
...: Superman-Prime (12/07, $3.99) Johns-s/VanSciver-c; origin re-told w/Ordway-a — 4.00

TALES OF THE TEENAGE MUTANT NINJA TURTLES (See Teenage Mutant...)
Mirage Studios: May, 1987 - No. 7, Aug (Apr-c), 1989 (B&W, $1.50)

	GD 2.0	VG 4.0	FN 6.0	VF 8.0	VF/NM 9.0	NM- 9.2
1	3	6	9	19	30	40
2-Title merges w/Teenage Mutant Ninja...	2	4	6	9	13	16
3-7	1	3	4	6	8	10

TALES OF THE TEEN TITANS (Formerly The New Teen Titans)
DC Comics: No. 41, Apr, 1984 - No. 91, July, 1988 (75¢)

41,45-49: 46-Aqualad & Aquagirl join — 4.00
42,43: The Judas Contract parts 1&2 with Deathstroke the Terminator; concludes with part 4 in Annual #3. — 6.00

Tales of the Unexpected #30 © DC

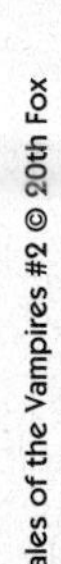
Tales of the Vampires #2 © 20th Fox

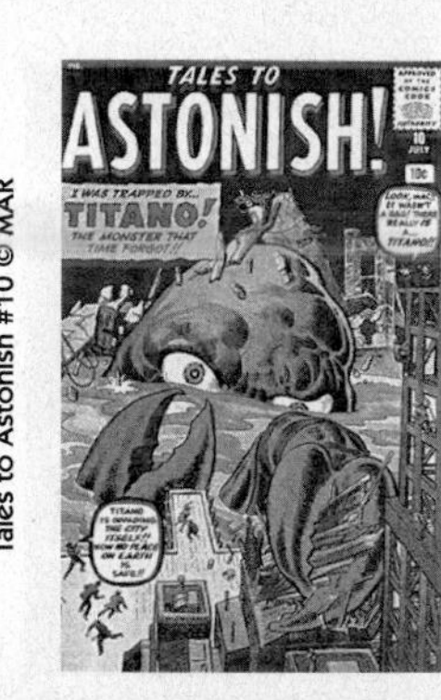

Tales to Astonish #10 © MAR

GD VG FN VF VF/NM NM-
2.0 4.0 6.0 8.0 9.0 9.2

44-Dick Grayson becomes Nightwing (3rd to be Nightwing) & joins Titans; Judas Contract part 3; Jericho (Deathstroke's son) joins; origin Deathstroke 6 12 18 37 66 95
50-Double size; app. Betty Kane (Bat-Girl) out of costume 6.00
51,52,56-91: 52-1st brief app. Azrael (not same as newer character). 56-Intro Jinx. 57-Neutron app. 59-r/DC Comics Presents #26. 60-91-r/New Teen Titans Baxter series. 68-B. Smith-c. 70-Origin Kole 3.00
53-55: 53-1st full app. Azrael; Deathstroke cameo. 54,55-Deathstroke-c/stories 4.00
Annual 3(1984, $1.25)-Part 4 of The Judas Contract; Deathstroke-c/story; Death of Terra; indicia says Teen Titans Annual; previous annuals listed as New Teen Titans Annual #1,2 1 3 4 6 8 10
Annual 4-(1986, $1.25) 4.00

TALES OF THE TEXAS RANGERS (See Jace Pearson...)

TALES OF THE THING (Fantastic Four)
Marvel Comics: May, 2005 - No. 3, July, 2005 ($2.50, limited series)
1-3-Dr. Strange app; Randy Green-c 3.00

TALES OF THE TMNT (Also see Teenage Mutant Ninja Turtles)
Mirage Studios: Jan, 2004 - No. 70, May, 2010 ($2.95/$3.25, B&W)
1-7: 1-Brizuela-a 5.00
8-70: 8-Begin $3.25-c. 47-Origin of the Super Turtles 4.00

TALES OF THE UNEXPECTED (Becomes The Unexpected #105 on)(See Adventure #75, Super DC Giant)
National Periodical Publications: Feb-Mar, 1956 - No. 104, Dec-Jan, 1967-68
1 141 282 423 1142 2571 4000
2 52 104 156 421 936 1450
3-5 37 74 111 274 612 950
6-10: 6-1st Silver Age issue 30 60 90 216 483 750
11,14,19,20 23 46 69 156 346 540
12,13,16,18,21-24: All have Kirby-a. 16-Characters named 'Thor' (with a magic hammer) and Loki by Kirby (8/57, characters do not look like Marvel's Thor & Loki) 26 52 78 182 404 625
15,17-Grey tone-c; Kirby-a 28 56 84 202 451 700
25-30 18 36 54 122 271 420
31-39 16 32 48 108 239 370
40-Space Ranger begins (8/59, 3rd ap.), ends #82 121 242 363 968 2184 3400
41,42-Space Ranger stories 41 82 123 303 689 1075
43-1st Space Ranger-c this title; grey tone-c 71 142 213 568 1284 2000
44-46 30 60 90 216 483 750
47-50 25 50 75 175 388 600
51-60: 54-Dinosaur-c/story 21 42 63 147 324 500
61-67: 67-Last 10¢ issue 17 34 51 117 259 400
68-82: 82-Last Space Ranger 10 20 30 66 138 210
83-90,92-99 6 12 18 40 73 105
91,100: 91-1st Automan (also in #94,97) 6 12 18 41 76 110
101-104 6 12 18 37 66 95
NOTE: ***Neal Adams** c-104. **Anderson** a-50. **Brown** a-50-82(Space Ranger); c-19, 40, & many Space Ranger-c. **Cameron** a-24, 27, 29; c-24. **Heath** a-49. **Bob Kane** a-24, 48. **Kirby** a-12, 13, 15-18, 21-24; c-13, 18, 22. **Meskin** a-15, 18, 26, 27, 35, 66. **Moreira** a-16, 20, 29, 38, 44, 62, 71; c-38. **Roussos** c-10. **Wildey** a-31.*

TALES OF THE UNEXPECTED (See Crisis Aftermath: The Spectre)
DC Comics: Dec, 2006 - No. 8, Jul, 2007 ($3.99, limited series)
1-8-The Spectre, Lapham-s/Battle-a; Dr. 13, Azzarello-s/Chiang-a. 4-Wrightson-c 4.00
1-Variant Spectre cover by Neal Adams 5.00
The Spectre: Tales of the Unexpected TPB (2007, $14.99) r/#4-8 15.00

TALES OF THE VAMPIRES (Also see Buffy the Vampire Slayer and related titles)
Dark Horse Comics: 2003 - No. 5, Apr, 2004 ($2.99, limited series)
1-Short stories by Joss Whedon and others. 1-Totleben-c. 3-Powell-c. 4-Edlund-c 3.00
TPB (11/04, $15.95) r/#1-5; afterword by Marv Wolfman 16.00

TALES OF THE WEST (See 3-D...)

TALES OF THE WITCHBLADE
Image Comics (Top Cow Productions): Nov, 1996 - No. 9 ($2.95)
1/2 1 2 3 5 7 9
1/2 Gold 2 4 6 9 12 15
1-Daniel-c/a(p) 1 3 4 6 8 10
1-Variant-c by Turner 2 4 6 9 12 15
1-Platinum Edition 3 6 9 16 23 30
2,3 6.00
4-6: 6-Green-c 5.00
7-9: 9-Lara Croft-c 4.00
7-Variant-c by Turner 1 2 3 5 6 8
Witchblade: Distinctions (4/01, $14.95, TPB) r/#1-6; Green-c 15.00

TALES OF THE WITCHBLADE COLLECTED EDITION
Image Comics (Top Cow): May, 1998 - No. 2 ($4.95/$5.95, square-bound)
1,2: 1-r/#1,2. 2-($5.95) r/#3,4 6.00

TALES OF THE WIZARD OF OZ (See Wizard of OZ, 4-Color #1308)

TALES OF THE ZOMBIE (Magazine)
Marvel Comics Group: Aug, 1973 - No. 10, Mar, 1975 (75¢, B&W)
V1#1-Reprint/Menace #5; origin Simon Garth 7 14 21 46 86 125
2,3: 2-2nd app. of Brother Voodoo; Everett biog. & memorial 4 8 12 25 40 55
V2#1(#4)-Photos & text of James Bond movie "Live & Let Die" 3 6 9 20 31 42
5-10: 8-Kaluta-a 3 6 9 18 28 38
Annual 1(Summer,'75)(#11)-B&W; Everett, Buscema-a 3 6 9 20 31 42
NOTE: *Brother Voodoo app. 2, 5, 6, 10. **Alcala** a-7-9. **Boris** c-1-4. **Colan** a-2r, 6. **Heath** a-5r. **Reese** a-2. **Tuska** a-2r.*

TALES OF VOODOO
Eerie Publications: V1#11, Nov, 1968 - V7#6, Nov, 1974 (Magazine)
V1#11 8 16 24 54 102 150
V2#1(3/69)-V2#4(9/69) 5 10 15 35 63 90
V3#1-6('70): 4- "Claws of the Cat" redrawn from Climax #1 5 10 15 30 50 70
V4#1-6('71), V5#1-7('72), V6#1-6('73), V7#1-6('74) 5 10 15 30 50 70
Annual 1 5 10 15 31 53 75
NOTE: *Bondage-c-V1#10, V2#4, V3#4.*

TALES OF WELLS FARGO (TV)(See Western Roundup under Dell Giants)
Dell Publishing Co.: No. 876, Feb, 1958 - No. 1215, Oct-Dec, 1961
Four Color 876 (#1)-Photo-c 8 16 24 52 99 145
Four Color 968 (2/59), 1023, 1075 (3/60), 1113 (7-9/60)-All photo-c. 1075,1113-Both have variant edition, back-c comic strip 7 14 21 48 89 130
Four Color 1167 (3-5/61), 1215-Photo-c 7 14 21 44 82 120

TALESPIN (Also see Cartoon Tales & Disney's Talespin Limited Series)
Disney Comics: June, 1991 - No. 7, Dec, 1991 ($1.50)
1-7 3.00

TALES TO ASTONISH (Becomes The Incredible Hulk #102 on)
Atlas (MAP No. 1/ZPC No. 2-14/VPI No. 15-21/Marvel No. 22 on: Jan, 1959 - No. 101, Mar, 1968
1-Jack Davis-a; monster-c. 480 960 1440 4100 9300 14,500
2-Ditko flying saucer-c (Martians); #2-4 have sci/fi-c. 121 242 363 972 2697 3450
3,4 104 208 312 832 1866 2900
5-Prototype issue (Stone Men); Williamson-a (4 pgs.); Kirby monster-c begin 89 178 267 712 1606 2500
6-Prototype issue (Stone Men) 66 132 198 462 1156 1850
7-Prototype issue (Toad Men) 66 132 198 462 1156 1850
8-10 62 124 186 502 1126 1750
11,12,14,17-20 50 100 150 400 900 1400
13-(11/60) 1st app. Groot (Guardians of the Galaxy) by Kirby-cvr/sty; swipes story from Menace #8 700 1400 2100 5100 9550 13,000
15-Prototype issue (Electro) 57 114 171 456 1028 1600
16-Prototype issue (Stone Men) named "Thorr" 52 104 156 421 936 1450
21-(7/61)-Hulk prototype 57 114 171 456 1028 1600
22-26,28-31,33,34 39 78 117 289 657 1025
27-1st Ant-Man app. (1/62); last 10¢ issue (see Strange Tales #73,78 & Tales of Suspense #32) 1070 2140 4280 13,100 33,550 54,000
32-Sandman prototype 42 54 126 311 706 1100
35-(9/62)-2nd app. Ant-Man, 1st in costume; begin series & Ant-Man-c 350 700 1050 3000 8000 13,000
36-3rd app. Ant-Man 93 186 279 744 1672 2600
37,39,40 52 104 156 411 918 1425
38-1st app. Egghead 54 108 162 432 966 1500
41-43 46 92 138 340 770 1200
44-Origin & 1st app. The Wasp (6/63) 295 590 885 1888 3244 4600
45-47 29 58 87 209 467 725
48-Origin & 1st app. The Porcupine 32 64 96 230 515 800
49-Ant-Man becomes Giant Man (11/63) 56 112 168 448 979 1550
50,51,53-56,58: 50-Origin/1st app. Human Top (alias Whirlwind). 58-Origin Colossus 19 38 57 131 291 450
52-Origin/1st app. Black Knight (2/64) 25 50 75 175 388 600
57-Early Spider-Man app. (7/64) 38 76 114 285 641 1000
59-Giant Man vs. Hulk feature story (9/64); Hulk's 1st app. this title; 1st mention that anger triggers his transformation 37 74 111 274 612 750
60-Giant Man & Hulk double feature begins 28 56 84 202 451 700
61,64-69: 61-All Ditko issue; 1st app. of Glenn Talbot; 1st mailbag. 65-New Giant Man

Talon #12 © DC

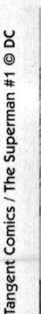

Tangent Comics / The Superman #1 © DC

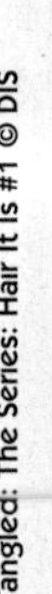

Tangled: The Series: Hair It Is #1 © DIS

	GD	VG	FN	VF	VF/NM	NM-
	2.0	4.0	6.0	8.0	9.0	9.2

costume. 68-New Human Top costume. 69-Last Giant Man 13 26 39 89 195 300
62-1st app./origin The Leader; new Wasp costume; Hulk pin-up page missing from many copies 23 46 69 161 356 550
63-Origin Leader continues 18 36 54 121 268 415
70-Sub-Mariner & Incredible Hulk begins (8/65) 15 30 45 101 223 345
71-81: 72-Begin alternating-c features w/Sub-Mariner (even #'s) & Hulk (odd #'s). 79-Hulk vs. Hercules-c/story. 81-1st app. Boomerang 7 14 21 44 82 120
82-Iron Man battles Sub-Mariner (1st Iron Man x-over outside The Avengers & TOS); story cont'd from Tales of Suspense #80 9 18 27 57 111 165
83-89,94-99: 97-X-Men cameo (brief) 6 12 18 37 66 95
90-1st app. The Abomination 11 22 33 75 160 245
91-The Abomination debut continues & 1st cover 9 18 27 63 129 195
92-1st Silver Surfer x-over (outside of Fantastic Four, 6/67); 1 panel cameo only 8 16 24 52 99 145
93-Hulk battles Silver Surfer-c/story (1st full x-over) 29 58 87 209 467 725
100-Hulk battles Sub-Mariner full-length story 8 16 24 52 99 145
101-Hulk story cont'd in Incredible Hulk #102; Sub-Mariner story continued in Iron Man & Sub-Mariner #1 9 18 27 59 117 175

NOTE: ***Ayers** c(i)-9-12, 16, 18, 19. **Berg** a-1. **Burgos** a-62-64p. **Buscema** a-85-87p. **Colan** a(p)-70-76, 78-82, 84, 85, 101; c(p)-71-76, 78, 80, 82, 84, 86, 88, 90. **Ditko** a-1, 3-48, 50i, 60-67p; c-2, 7i, 8i, 14i, 17i. **Everett** a-78, 79i, 80-84, 85-90i, 94i, 95, 96; c(i)-79-81, 83, 86, 88. **Forte** a-6. **Kane** a-76, 88-91; c-89, 91. **Kirby** a(p)-1, 5-34-40, 44, 49-51, 68-70, 82, 83; layouts-71-84; c(p)-1, 3-48, 50-70, 72, 73, 75, 77, 78, 79, 81, 85, 90. **Kirby/Ditko** a-7, 8, 12, 13, 50; c-7, 8, 10, 13. **Leiber/Fox** a-47, 48, 50, 51. **Powell** a-65-69p, 73, 74. **Reinman** a-6, 36, 45, 46, 54i, 56-60i.*

TALES TO ASTONISH (2nd Series)
Marvel Comics Group: Dec, 1979 - No. 14, Jan, 1981

V1#1-Reprints Sub-Mariner #1 by Buscema 3 6 9 14 20 26
2-14: Reprints Sub-Mariner #2-14 1 3 4 6 8 10

TALES TO ASTONISH
Marvel Comics: V3#1, Oct, 1994 ($6.95, one-shot)

V3#1-Peter David scripts; acetate, painted-c 7.00

TALES TO HOLD YOU SPELLBOUND (See Spellbound)

TALES TO OFFEND
Dark Horse Comics: July, 1997 ($2.95, one-shot)

1-Frank Miller-s/a, EC-style cover 4.00

TALES TOO TERRIBLE TO TELL (Becomes Terrology #10, 11)
New England Comics: Wint, 1989-90 - No. 11, Nov-Dec.1993 ($2.95/$3.50, B&W with cardstock covers)

1-($2.95) Reprints of non-EC pre-code horror; EC-style cover by Bissette 5.00
1-($3.50, 5-6/93) Second printing with alternate cover not by Bissette 4.00
2-8-($3.50) Story reprints, history of the pre-code titles and creators; cover galleries (B&W) inside & on back-c (color) 4.00
9-11-($2.95) 10,11-"Terrology" on cover 4.00

TALKING KOMICS
Belda Record & Publ. Co.: 1947 (20 pgs, slick-c)

Each comic contained a record that followed the story - much like the Golden Record sets. Known titles: Chirpy Cricket, Lonesome Octopus, Sleepy Santa, Grumpy Shark, Flying Turtle, Happy Grasshopper
with records... 4 8 12 25 40 55

TALLY-HO COMICS
Swappers Quarterly (Baily Publ. Co.): Dec, 1944

nn-Frazetta's 1st work as Giunta's assistant; Man in Black horror story; violence; Giunta-c 65 130 195 416 708 1000

TALULLAH (See Comic Books Series I)

TALON (From Batman Court of Owls crossover)
DC Comics: No. 0, Nov, 2012 - No. 17, May, 2014 ($2.99)

0-17: 0-Origin of Calvin Rose; March-a. 7-11-Bane app. 3.00

TAMMY, TELL ME TRUE
Dell Publishing Co.: No. 1233, 1961

Four Color 1233-Movie 7 14 21 44 82 120

TANGENT COMICS
.../ THE ATOM, DC Comics: Dec, 1997 ($2.95, one-shot)
1-Dan Jurgens-s/Jurgens & Paul Ryan-a 4.00

.../ THE BATMAN, DC Comics: Sept, 1998 ($1.95, one-shot)
1-Dan Jurgens-s/Klaus Janson-a 4.00

.../ DOOM PATROL, DC Comics: Dec, 1997 ($2.95, one-shot)
1- Dan Jurgens-s/Sean Chen & Kevin Conrad-a 4.00

.../ THE FLASH, DC Comics: Dec, 1997 ($2.95, one-shot)
1-Todd Dezago-s/Gary Frank & Cam Smith-a 4.00

.../ GREEN LANTERN, DC Comics: Dec, '97 ($2.95, one-shot)
1-James Robinson-s/J.H. Williams III & Mick Gray-a 4.00

.../ JLA, DC Comics: Sept, 1998 ($1.95, one-shot)
1-Dan Jurgens-s/Banks & Rapmund-a 4.00

.../ THE JOKER, DC Comics: Dec, 1997 ($2.95, one-shot)
1-Karl Kesel-s/Matt Haley & Tom Simmons-a 4.00

.../ THE JOKER'S WILD, DC Comics: Sept, 1998 ($1.95, one-shot)
1-Kesel & Simmons-s/Phillips & Rodriguez-a 4.00

.../ METAL MEN, DC Comics: Dec, 1997 ($2.95, one-shot)
1-Ron Marz-s/Mike McKone & Mark McKenna-a 4.00

.../ NIGHTWING, DC Comics: Dec, 1997 ($2.95, one-shot)
1-John Ostrander-s/Jan Duursema-a 4.00

.../ NIGHTWING: NIGHTFORCE, DC Comics: Sept, 1998 ($1.95, one-shot)
1-John Ostrander-s/Jan Duursema-a 4.00

.../ POWERGIRL, DC Comics: Sept, 1998 ($1.95, one-shot)
1-Marz-s/Abell & Vines-a 4.00

.../ SEA DEVILS, DC Comics: Dec, 1997 ($2.95, one-shot)
1-Kurt Busiek-s/Vince Giarrano & Tom Palmer-a 4.00

.../ SECRET SIX, DC Comics: Dec, 1997 ($2.95, one-shot)
1-Chuck Dixon-s/Tom Grummett & Lary Stucker-a 4.00

.../ THE SUPERMAN, DC Comics: Sept, 1998 ($1.95, one-shot)
1-Millar-s/Guice-a 4.00

.../ TALES OF THE GREEN LANTERN, DC Comics: Sept, 1998 ($1.95, one-shot)
1-Story & art by various 4.00

.../ THE TRIALS OF THE FLASH, DC Comics: Sept, 1998 ($1.95, one-shot)
1-Dezago-s/Pelletier & Lanning-a 4.00

.../ WONDER WOMAN DC Comics: Sept, 1998 ($1.95, one-shot),
1-Peter David-s/Unzueta & Mendoza-a 4.00
... Volume One TPB (2007, $19.99) r/The Atom, Metal Men, Green Lantern, The Flash, Sea Devils one-shots; intro and new cover by Jurgens 20.00
... Volume Two TPB (2008, $19.99) r/Batman, Doom Patrol, Joker, Nightwing and Secret Six one-shots; new cover by Jurgens 20.00
... Volume Three TPB (2008, $19.99) r/The Superman, Wonder Woman, Nightwing: Nightforce, The Joker's Wild, The Trials of the Flash, Tales of the Green Lantern, Powergirl, and JLA one-shots; new cover by Jurgens 20.00

TANGENT: SUPERMAN'S REIGN
DC Comics: May, 2008 - No. 12, Apr, 2009 ($2.99, limited series)

1-12-Jurgens-s; Flash & Green Lantern app.; back-up histories of Tangent heroes 3.00
Volume 1 TPB (2009, $19.99) r/#1-6 & Justice League of America #16 20.00
Volume 2 TPB (2009, $19.99) r/#7-12 20.00

TANGLED (Disney movie)
IDW Publishing: Jan, 2018 - No. 3, Mar, 2018 ($3.99)

1-3: 1-Three covers. 2,3-Two covers 4.00
...: The Series: Hair and Now 1-3 (3/19 - 5/19, $3.99) Katie Cook-s 4.00
...: The Series: Hair It Is (8/19, $4.99, one-shot) Short stories by various 5.00
...: The Series: Hair-Raising Adventures 1-3 (9/18 - 11/18, $3.99) 1-Katie Cook-s 4.00

TANGLED WEB (See Spider-Man's Tangled Web)

TANK GIRL
Dark Horse Comics: May, 1991 - No. 4, Aug, 1991 ($2.25, B&W, mini-series)

1-Contains Dark Horse trading cards 6.00
2-4 4.00
...: Dark Nuggets (Image Comics, 12/09, $3.99) Martin-s/Dayglo-a 4.00
...: Dirty Helmets (Image Comics, 4/10, $3.99) Martin-s/Dayglo-a 4.00
...: Hairy Heroes (Image Comics, 8/10, $3.99) Martin-s/Dayglo-a 4.00

TANK GIRL ALL STARS
Titan Comics: Jul, 2018 - No. 4, Oct, 2018 ($3.99, limited series)

1-4: Alan Martin-s; art by Hewlett, Bond, Mahfood, Parson & others; bonus pin-ups 4.00

TANK GIRL: APOCALYPSE
DC Comics: Nov, 1995 - No. 4, Feb, 1996 ($2.25, limited series)

1-4 4.00

TANK GIRL FULL COLOUR CLASSICS
Titan Comics: Jun, 2018 - Present ($6.99, limited series)

1-3.1-Newly colored reprints of original stories from Deadline Magazine; bonus photos 7.00

TANK GIRL: MOVIE ADAPTATION
DC Comics: 1995 ($5.95, 68 pgs., one-shot)

nn-Peter Milligan scripts 6.00

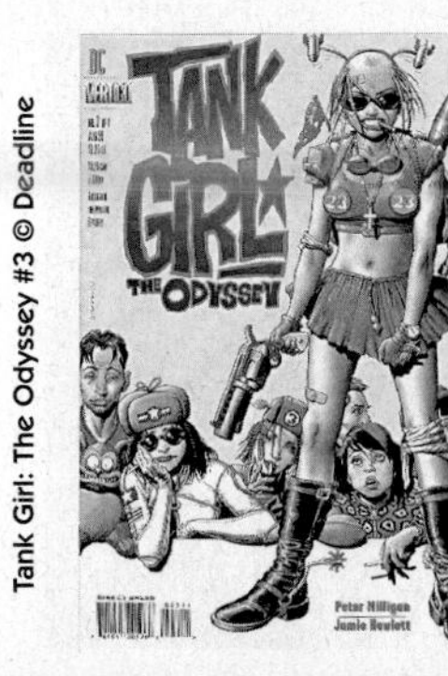

Tank Girl: The Odyssey #3 © Deadline

Target Comics V9 #6 © NOVP

Tarot #1 © MAR

GD VG FN VF VF/NM NM-
2.0 4.0 6.0 8.0 9.0 9.2

TANK GIRL ONGOING
Titan Comics: Jan, 2019 - No. 8, Dec, 2019 ($3.99, limited series)

1-4-Action Alley - Martin-s/Parson-a; multiple covers and centerfold poster on each 4.00
5-8-Forever - Martin-s/Parson-a; multiple covers and centerfold poster on each 4.00

TANK GIRL: TANK GIRL GOLD
Titan Comics: Sept, 2016 - No. 4, Mar, 2017 ($3.99, limited series)

1-4: Alan Martin-s/Brett Parson-a. 2-MAD spoof 4.00

TANK GIRL: THE GIFTING
IDW Publishing: May, 2007 - No. 4, Aug, 2007 ($3.99, limited series)

1-4: 1-Ashley Wood-a/c; Alan Martin-s; 3 covers 4.00

TANK GIRL: THE ODYSSEY
DC Comics: May, 1995 - No. 4, Oct, 1995 ($2.25, limited series)

1-4: Peter Milligan scripts; Hewlett-a 4.00

TANK GIRL: THE ROYAL ESCAPE
IDW Publishing: Mar, 2010 - No. 4, Jun, 2010 ($3.99, limited series)

1-4: Alan Martin-s/Rufus Dayglo-a/c 4.00

TANK GIRL: 21ST CENTURY TANK GIRL
Titan Comics: Jul, 2015 - No. 3, Sept, 2015 ($3.99, limited series)

1-3: Alan Martin-s; art by Hewlett, Bond, Mahfood, Parson & others 4.00

TANK GIRL 2
Dark Horse Comics: June, 1993 - No. 4, Sept, 1993 ($2.50, lim. series, mature)

1-4: Jamie Hewlett & Alan Martin-s/a 4.00
TPB (2/95, $17.95) r/#1-4 18.00

TANK GIRL: TWO GIRLS, ONE TANK
Titan Comics: Jun, 2016 - No. 4, Sept, 2016 ($3.99, limited series)

1-4: Alan Martin-s/Brett Parson-a 4.00

TAPPAN'S BURRO (See Zane Grey & 4-Color #449)

TAPPING THE VEIN (Clive Barker's...)
Eclipse Comics: 1989 - No. 5, 1992 ($6.95, squarebound, mature, 68 pgs.)

Book 1-5: 1-Russell-a, Bolton-c. 2-Bolton-a. 4-Die-cut-c 7.00
TPB (2002, $24.95, Checker Book Publ. Group) r/#1-5 25.00

TARANTULA (See Weird Suspense)

TARGET: AIRBOY
Eclipse Comics: Mar, 1988 ($1.95)

1 4.00

TARGET COMICS (...Western Romances #106 on)
Funnies, Inc./Novelty Publications/Star Publ.: Feb, 1940 - V10#3 (#105), Aug-Sept, 1949

V1#1-Origin & 1st app. Manowar, The White Streak by Burgos, & Bulls-Eye Bill by Everett; City Editor (ends #5), High Grass Twins by Jack Cole (ends #4), T-Men by Joe Simon (ends #9), Rip Rory (ends #4), Fantastic Feature Films by Tarpe Mills (ends #39), & Calling 2-R (ends #14) begin; marijuana use story 459 918 1377 3350 5925 8500
2-Everett-c/a 258 516 774 1651 2826 4000
3,4-Everett, Jack Cole-a 177 354 531 1133 1942 2750
5-Origin The White Streak in text; Space Hawk by Wolverton begins (6/40) (see Blue Bolt & Circus) 465 930 1395 3395 5998 8600
6-The Chameleon by Everett begins (7/40, 1st app.); White Streak origin cont'd. in text; early mention of comic collecting in letter column; 1st letter column in comics? (7/40) 265 530 795 1694 2897 4100
7-Wolverton Spacehawk-c/story (scarce) 1300 2600 3900 9600 18,300 27,000
8-Classic sci-fi cover (scarce) 371 742 1113 2600 4550 6500
9-White Streak-c 200 400 600 1280 2190 3100
10-Intro/1st app. The Target (11/40); Simon-c; Spacehawk-s; text piece by Wolverton 300 600 900 2040 3570 5100
11-Origin The Target & The Targeteers 200 400 600 1280 2190 3100
12-(1/41) Target & The Targeteers-c 148 296 444 947 1624 2300
V2#1-Target by Bob Wood; Uncle Sam flag-c 106 212 318 678 1164 1650
2-Ten part Treasure Island serial begins; Harold Delay-a; reprinted in Catholic Comics V3#1-10 (see Key Comics #5) 71 142 213 454 777 1100
3-5: 4-Kit Carter, The Cadet begins 68 136 204 435 743 1050
6-9: Red Seal with White Streak in #6-10 63 126 189 403 689 975
10-Classic-c 123 246 369 767 1344 1900
11,12: 12-10-part Last of the Mohicans serial begins; Delay-a 60 120 180 381 653 925
V3#1-3,5-7,9,10: 10-Last Wolverton issue 48 96 144 302 514 725
4-V for Victory-c 77 154 231 493 847 1200
8-Hitler, Tojo, Flag-c; 6-part Gulliver Travels serial begins; Delay-a. 113 226 339 723 1237 1750
11,12 21 42 63 122 199 275
V4#1-4,7-12: 8-X-Mas-c 15 30 45 86 133 180
5-Classic Statue of Liberty-c 30 60 90 177 289 400
6-Targetoons by Wolverton 19 38 57 111 176 240
V5#1-8 14 28 42 80 115 150
V6#1-4,6-10 14 28 42 76 108 140
5-Classic Tojo hanging/Buy War Bonds WWII-c 84 168 252 538 919 1300
V7#1-12 12 24 36 67 94 120
V8#1,3-5,8,9,11,12 11 22 33 60 83 105
2,6,7-Krigstein-a 12 24 36 67 94 120
10-L.B. Cole-c 25 50 75 150 245 340
V9#1,4,6,8,10-L.B. Cole-c 25 50 75 150 245 340
2,3,5,7,9,11, V10#1 11 22 33 60 83 105
12-Classic L.B. Cole-c 43 86 129 271 461 650
V10#2,3-L.B. Cole-c 27 54 81 158 259 360

NOTE: ***Certa** c-V8#9, 11, 12, V9#5, 9, 11, V10#1. **Jack Cole** a-1-8. **Everett** a-1-9; c(signed Blake)-1, 2. **Al Fago** c-V6#8. **Sid Greene** c-V2#9, 12, V3#3. **Walter Johnson** c-V5#6, V6#4. **Tarpe Mills** a-1-4, 6, 8, 11, V3#1. **Rico** a-V7#4, 10, V8#5, 6, V9#3; c-V7#6, 8, 10, V8#2, 4, 6, 7. **Simon** a-1, 2. **Bob Wood** c-V2#2, 3, 5, 6.*

GD VG FN VF VF/NM NM-
2.0 4.0 6.0 8.0 9.0 9.2

TARGET: THE CORRUPTORS (TV)
Dell Publishing Co.: No. 1306, Mar-May, 1962 - No. 3, Oct-Dec, 1962 (All have photo-c)

Four Color 1306(#1), #2,3 5 10 15 33 57 80

TARGET WESTERN ROMANCES (Formerly Target Comics; becomes Flaming Western Romances #3)
Star Publications: No. 106, Oct-Nov, 1949 - No. 107, Dec-Jan, 1949-50

106(#1)-Silhouette nudity panel; L.B. Cole-c 30 60 90 177 289 400
107(#2)-L.B. Cole-c; lingerie panels 25 50 75 150 245 340

TARGITT
Atlas/Seaboard Publ.: March, 1975 - No. 3, July, 1975

1-3: 1-Origin; Nostrand-a in all. 2-1st in costume. 3-Becomes Man-Stalker 2 4 6 10 14 18

TAROT
Marvel Comics: Mar, 2020 - No. 4, May, 2020 ($4.99, limited series)

1-4-Alan Davis-s/Paul Renaud-a; Defenders & Avengers vs. Diablo 5.00

TAROT: WITCH OF THE BLACK ROSE
Broadsword Comics: Mar, 2000 - Present ($2.95, mature)

1-Jim Balent-s/c/a; at least two covers on all issues 4 8 12 27 44 60
1-Second printing (10/00) 6.00
2 2 4 6 13 18 22
3-20 1 2 3 5 6 8
21-40 5.00
41-121: 84,113-The Krampus app. 90-Crossover with School Bites characters 3.00
122/Alternate Paths: Raven Hex #1 - Raven Hex as the Swordmaiden 3.00
123/Alternate Paths: Raven Hex #2 ($12.50, only sold online) 12.50
124,125/Alternate Paths: Boo-Cat #1,2 ($3.99)1- Boo-Cat on vacation. 2-Krampus app. 4.00
126-($3.99) 4.00

TARZAN (See Aurora, Comics on Parade, Crackajack, DC 100-Page Super Spec., Edgar Rice Burroughs'..., Famous Feature Stories #1, Golden Comics Digest #4, 9, Jeep Comics, Jungle Tales of..., Limited Collectors' Edition, Popular, Sparkler, Sport Stars #1, Tip Top & Top Comics)

TARZAN
Dell Publishing Co./United Features Synd.: No. 5, 1939 - No. 161, Aug, 1947

Large Feature Comic 5 ('39)-(Scarce)-By Hal Foster; reprints 1st dailies from 1929 252 504 756 1613 2757 3900
Single Series 20 ('40)-By Hal Foster 190 380 570 1216 2083 2950
Four Color 134 (2/47)-Marsh-c/a 57 114 171 456 1028 1600
Four Color 161 (8/47)-Marsh-c/a 46 92 138 359 805 1250

TARZAN (...of the Apes #138 on)
Dell Publishing Co./Gold Key No. 132 on: 1-2/48 - No. 131, 7-8/62; No. 132, 11/62 - No. 206, 2/72

1-Jesse Marsh-a begins 105 210 315 844 1897 2950
2 43 86 129 318 722 1125
3-5 31 62 93 223 499 775
6-10: 6-1st Tantor the Elephant. 7-1st Valley of the Monsters 26 52 78 182 404 625
11-15: 11-Two Against the Jungle begins, ends #24. 13-Lex Barker photo-c begin 19 38 57 131 291 450
16-20 15 30 45 105 233 360
21-24,26-30 13 26 39 86 188 290
25-1st "Brothers of the Spear" episode; series ends #156,160,161,196-206 14 28 42 98 217 335
31-40 10 20 30 66 138 210
41-54: Last Barker photo-c 8 16 24 56 108 160

Tarzan #219 © ERB

Tarzan #2 © ERB

Taskmaster (2020 series) #1 © MAR

	GD 2.0	VG 4.0	FN 6.0	VF 8.0	VF/NM 9.0	NM- 9.2
55-60: 56-Eight pg. Boy story	7	14	21	49	92	135
61,62,64-70	6	12	18	41	76	110
63-Two Tarzan stories, 1 by Manning	6	12	18	42	79	115
71-79	6	12	18	37	66	95
80-99: 80-Gordon Scott photo-c begin	5	10	15	34	60	85
100	6	12	18	37	66	95
101-109	5	10	15	33	57	80
110 (Scarce)-Last photo-c	6	12	18	37	66	95
111-120	5	10	15	31	53	75
121-131: Last Dell issue	5	10	15	30	50	70
132-1st Gold Key issue	5	10	15	31	53	75
133-138,140-154	4	8	12	25	40	55
139-(12/63)-1st app. Korak (Boy); leaves Tarzan & gets own book (1/64)	6	12	18	40	73	105
155-Origin Tarzan; text article on Tarzana, CA	5	10	15	30	50	70
156-161: 157-Banlu, Dog of the Arande begins, ends #159, 195. 169-Leopard Girl app.	3	6	9	21	33	45
162,165,168,171 (TV)-Ron Ely photo covers	4	8	12	22	35	48
163,164,166,167,169,170: 169-Leopard Girl app.	3	6	9	20	31	42
172-199,201-206: 178-Tarzan origin-r/#155; Leopard Girl app., also in #179, 190-193	3	6	9	18	28	38
200	3	6	9	21	33	45
Story Digest 1-(6/70, G.K., 148pp.)(scarce)	6	12	18	41	76	110

NOTE: *#162, 165, 168, 171 are TV issues. #1-153 all have* **Marsh** *art on Tarzan. #154-161, 163, 164, 166, 167, 172-177 all have* **Manning** *art on Tarzan. #178, 202 have* **Manning** *Tarzan reprints. No "Brothers of the Spear" in #1-24, 157-159, 162-195. #39-126, 128-156 all have* **Russ Manning** *art on "Brothers of the Spear". #196-201, 203-205 all have* **Manning** *B.O.T.S. reprints; #25-38, 127 all have Jesse* **Marsh** *art on B.O.T.S. #206 has a Marsh B.O.T.S. reprint.* **Gollub** *c-8-12.* **Marsh** *c-1-7.* **Doug Wildey** *a-162, 179-187. Many issues have front and back photo covers.*

TARZAN (Continuation of Gold Key series)
National Periodical Publications: No. 207, Apr, 1972 - No. 258, Feb, 1977

	GD 2.0	VG 4.0	FN 6.0	VF 8.0	VF/NM 9.0	NM- 9.2
207-Origin Tarzan by Joe Kubert, part 1; John Carter begins (origin); 52 pg. issues thru #209	5	10	15	35	63	90
208,209-(52 pgs.): 208-210-Parts 2-4 of origin. 209-Last John Carter	3	6	9	21	33	45
210-220: 210-Kubert-a. 211-Hogarth, Kubert-a. 212-214: Adaptations from "Jungle Tales of Tarzan". 213-Beyond the Farthest Star begins, ends #218. 215-218,224,225-All by Kubert. 215-part Foster-r. 219-223: Adapts "The Return of Tarzan" by Kubert	3	6	9	14	20	25
221-229: 221-223-Continues adaptation of "The Return of Tarzan". 226-Manning-a	2	4	6	10	14	18
230-DC 100 Page Super Spectacular; Kubert, Kaluta-a(p); Korak begins, ends #234; Carson of Venus app.	4	8	12	25	40	55
231-235-New Kubert-a.: 231-234-(All 100 pgs.)-Adapts "Tarzan and the Lion Man"; Rex, the Wonder Dog r-#232, 233. 235-(100 pgs.)-Last Kubert issue.	4	8	12	23	37	50
236,237,239-258: 240-243 adapts "Tarzan & the Castaways". 250-256 adapts "Tarzan the Untamed." 252,253-r/#213	2	4	6	8	10	12
238-(68 pgs.)	2	4	6	13	18	22
Digest 1-(Fall, 1972, 50¢, 164 pgs.)(DC)-Digest size; Kubert-c; Manning-a	4	8	12	25	40	55
Edgar Rice Burroughs' Tarzan The Joe Kubert Years - Volume One HC (Dark Horse Books, 10/05, $49.95, dust jacket) recolored r/#207-214; intro. by Joe Kubert						50.00
Edgar Rice Burroughs' Tarzan The Joe Kubert Years - Volume Two HC (Dark Horse Books, 2/06, $49.95, dust jacket) recolored r/#215-224; intro. by Joe Kubert						50.00
Edgar Rice Burroughs' Tarzan The Joe Kubert Years - Volume Three HC (Dark Horse Books, 6/06, $49.95, dust jacket) recolored r/#225,227-235; Kubert intro. and sketch pages						50.00

NOTE: **Anderson** *a-207, 209, 217, 218.* **Chaykin** *a-216.* **Finlay** *a(r)-212.* **Foster** *strip-r #207-209, 211, 212, 221.* **Heath** *a-230i.* **G. Kane** *a(r)-232p, 233p.* **Kubert** *a-207-225, 227-235, 257r, 258r; c-207-249, 253.* **Lopez** *a-250-255p; c-250p, 251, 252, 254.* **Manning** *strip-r 230-235, 238.* **Morrow** *a-208.* **Nino** *a-231-234.* **Sparling** *a-230, 231.* **Starr** *a-233r.*

TARZAN (Lord of the Jungle)
Marvel Comics Group: June, 1977 - No. 29, Oct, 1979

	GD 2.0	VG 4.0	FN 6.0	VF 8.0	VF/NM 9.0	NM- 9.2
1-New adaptions of Burroughs stories; Buscema-a	3	6	9	14	19	24
1-(35¢-c variant, limited distribution)(6/77)	6	12	18	42	79	115
2-29: 2-Origin by John Buscema. 9-Young Tarzan. 12-14-Jungle Tales of Tarzan. 25-29-New stories	1	3	4	6	8	10
2-5-(35¢-c variants, limited distribution)(7-10/77)	5	10	15	31	53	75
Annual 1-3: 1-(1977). 2-(1978). 3-(1979)	1	3	4	6	8	10

NOTE: **N. Adams** *c-11i, 12i.* **Alcala** *a-9i, 10i; c-8i, 9i.* **Buckler** *c-25-27p, Annual 3p.* **John Buscema** *a-1-3, 4-18p, Annual 1; c-1-7, 8p, 9p, 10, 11p, 12p, 13, 14-19p, 21p, 22, 23p, 24p, 28p, Annual 1.* **Mooney** *a-22i.* **Nebres** *a-22i.* **Russell** *a-29i.*

TARZAN
Dark Horse Comics: July, 1996 - No. 20, Mar, 1998 ($2.95)

1-20: 1-6-Suydam-c 4.00

TARZAN / CARSON OF VENUS
Dark Horse Comics: May, 1998 - No. 4, Aug, 1998 ($2.95, limited series)

1-4-Darko Macan-s/Igor Korday-a 4.00

TARZAN FAMILY, THE (Formerly Korak, Son of Tarzan)
National Periodical Publications: No. 60, Nov-Dec, 1975 - No. 66, Nov-Dec, 1976

	GD 2.0	VG 4.0	FN 6.0	VF 8.0	VF/NM 9.0	NM- 9.2
60-62-(68 pgs.): 60-Korak begins; Kaluta-r	2	4	6	11	16	20
63-66 (52 pgs.)	2	4	6	9	12	15

NOTE: *Carson of Venus-r 60-65. New John Carter-62-64, 65r, 66r. New Korak-60-66. Pellucidar feature-66. Foster strip r-60(9/4/32-10/16/32), 62(6/29/32-7/31/32), 63(10/11/31-12/13/31).* **Kaluta** *Carson of Venus-60-65.* **Kubert** *a-61, 64; c-60-64.* **Manning** *strip-r 60-62, 64.* **Morrow** *a-66r.*

TARZAN/JOHN CARTER: WARLORDS OF MARS
Dark Horse Comics: Jan, 1996 - No. 4, June, 1996 ($2.50, limited series)

1-4: Bruce Jones scripts in all. 1,2,4-Bret Blevins-c/a. 2-(4/96)-Indicia reads #3 4.00

TARZAN KING OF THE JUNGLE (See Dell Giant #37, 51)

TARZAN, LORD OF THE JUNGLE
Gold Key: Sept, 1965 (Giant) (25¢, soft paper-c)

	GD 2.0	VG 4.0	FN 6.0	VF 8.0	VF/NM 9.0	NM- 9.2
1-Marsh-r	7	14	21	48	89	130

TARZAN: LOVE, LIES AND THE LOST CITY (See Tarzan the Warrior)
Malibu Comics: Aug. 10, 1992 - No. 3, Sept, 1992 ($2.50, limited series)

1-($3.95, 68 pgs.)-Flip book format; Simonson & Wagner scripts 5.00
2,3-No Simonson or Wagner scripts 4.00

TARZAN MARCH OF COMICS (See March of Comics #82, 98, 114, 125, 144, 155, 172, 185, 204, 223, 240, 252, 262, 272, 286, 300, 332, 342, 354, 366)

TARZAN OF THE APES
Metropolitan Newspaper Service: 1934? (Hardcover, 4x12", 68 pgs.)

	GD 2.0	VG 4.0	FN 6.0	VF 8.0	VF/NM 9.0	NM- 9.2
1-Strip reprints	27	54	81	162	266	370

TARZAN OF THE APES
Marvel Comics Group: July, 1984 - No. 2, Aug, 1984 (Movie adaptation)

1,2: Origin-r/Marvel Super Spec. 4.00

TARZAN ON THE PLANET OF THE APES
Dark Horse Comics: Sept, 2016 - No. 5, Jan, 2017 ($3.99, limited series)

1-5-Seeley & Walker-s/Dagnino-a. 1-Cornelius & Zira adopt young Tarzan on Earth 4.00

TARZAN'S JUNGLE ANNUAL (See Dell Giants)

TARZAN'S JUNGLE WORLD (See Dell Giant #25)

TARZAN: THE BECKONING
Malibu Comics: 1992 - No. 7, 1993 ($2.50, limited series)

1-7 4.00

TARZAN: THE LOST ADVENTURE (See Edgar Rice Burroughs' ...)

TARZAN-THE RIVERS OF BLOOD
Dark Horse Comics: Nov, 1999 - No. 8 ($2.95, limited series)

1-4: Korday-c/a 4.00

TARZAN THE SAVAGE HEART
Dark Horse Comics: Apr, 1999 - No. 4, July, 1999 ($2.95, limited series)

1-4: Grell-c/a 4.00

TARZAN THE WARRIOR (Also see Tarzan: Love, Lies and the Lost City)
Malibu Comics: Mar, 19, 1992 - No. 5, 1992 ($2.50, limited series)

1-5: 1-Bisley painted pack-c (flip book format-c) 4.00
1-2nd printing w/o flip-c by Bisley 4.00

TARZAN VS. PREDATOR AT THE EARTH'S CORE
Dark Horse Comics: Jan, 1996 - No. 4, June, 1996 ($2.50, limited series)

1-4: Lee Weeks-c/a; Walt Simonson scripts 4.00

TASKMASTER
Marvel Comics: Apr, 2002 - No. 4, July, 2002 ($2.99, limited series)

1-4-Udon Studio-s/a. 1-Iron Man app. 3.00

TASKMASTER
Marvel Comics: Nov, 2010 - No. 4, Feb, 2011 ($3.99, limited series)

1-4-Van Lente-s/Palo-a; Hydra & A.I.M. app. 4.00

TASKMASTER
Marvel Comics: Jun, 2010 - No. 4, ($3.99, limited series)

1-3-MacKay-s/Vitti-a; Nick Fury and Black Widow app. 2-Hyperion app. 3-White Fox app. 4.00

TASMANIAN DEVIL & HIS TASTY FRIENDS
Gold Key: Nov, 1962 (12¢)

1-Bugs Bunny, Elmer Fudd, Sylvester, Yosemite Sam, Road Runner & Wile E. Coyote x-over

Team America #5 © MAR

Tech Jacket #6 © Kirkman & Su

Teen-Age Diary Secrets #6 © STJ

	GD	VG	FN	VF	VF/NM	NM-
	2.0	4.0	6.0	8.0	9.0	9.2
	17	34	51	114	252	390

TATTERED BANNERS
DC Comics (Vertigo): Nov, 1998 - No. 4, Feb, 1999 ($2.95, limited series)
1-4-Grant & Giffen-s/McMahon-a 3.00

TATTERED MAN
Image Comics: May 2011 ($4.99, one-shot)
1-Justin Gray & Jimmy Palmiotti-s/Norberto Fernandez-a; covers by Fernandez & Conner 5.00

TEAM AMERICA (See Captain America #269)
Marvel Comics Group: June, 1982 - No. 12, May, 1983
1,12: 1-Origin; Ideal Toy motorcycle characters. 12-Double size 5.00
2-11: 9-Iron Man app. 11-Ghost Rider app. 4.00
NOTE: *There are 16 pg. variants known for most issues, possibly all. The only ad is on the inside front cover.*

TEAM HELIX
Marvel Comics: Jan, 1993 - No. 4, Apr, 1993 ($1.75, limited series)
1-4: Teen Super Group. 1,2-Wolverine app. 3.00

TEAM ONE: STORMWATCH (Also see StormWatch)
Image Comics (WildStorm Productions): June, 1995 - No. 2, Aug, 1995 ($2.50, lim. series)
1,2: Steven T. Seagle scripts 3.00

TEAM ONE: WILDC.A.T.S (Also see WildC.A.T.S)
Image Comics (WildStorm Productions): July, 1995 - No. 2, Aug, 1995 ($2.50, lim. series)
1,2: James Robinson scripts 3.00

TEAM 7
Image Comics (WildStorm): Oct, 1994 - No.4, Feb, 1995 ($2.50, limited series)
1-4: Dixon scripts in all, 1-Portacio variant-c 3.00

TEAM 7 (DC New 52)
DC Comics: No. 0, Nov, 2012 - No. 8, Jul, 2013 ($2.99)
0-8: 0-Merino-a/Lashley-c; Slade Wilson, John Lynch, Grifter and others assemble team. 3,4-Eclipso returns. 7-Pandora & Majestic app. 3.00

TEAM 7-DEAD RECKONING
Image Comics (WildStorm): Jan, 1996 - No. 4, Apr, 1996 ($2.50, limited series)
1-4: Dixon scripts in all 3.00

TEAM 7-OBJECTIVE HELL
Image Comics (WildStorm): May, 1995 - No. 3, July, 1995 ($1.95/$2.50, limited series)
1-($1.95)-Newstand; Dixon scripts in all; Barry Smith-c 3.00
1-3: 1-($2.50)-Direct Market; Barry Smith-c, bound-in card 3.00

TEAM SONIC RACING
IDW Publishing: Oct, 2018; May, 2019 ($4.99/$5.99, one-shots)
1-Caleb Goellner-s/Adam Bryce Thomas-a; videogame tie-in 5.00
... Deluxe Turbo Championship Edition (5/19, $5.99) Goellner-s/Thomas-a 6.00

TEAM SUPERMAN
DC Comics: July, 1999 ($2.95, one-shot)
1-Jeanty-a/Stelfreeze-c 4.00
...Secret Files 1 (5/98, $4.95)Origin-s and pin-ups of Superboy, Supergirl and Steel 5.00

TEAM TITANS (See Deathstroke & New Titans Annual #7)
DC Comics: Sept, 1992 - No. 24, Sept, 1994 ($1.75/$1.95)
1-Five different #1s exist w/origins in 1st half & the same 2nd story in each: Kilowat, Mirage, Nightrider w/Netzer/Pérez-a, Redwing, & Terra w/part Pérez-p; Total Chaos Pt. 3 5.00
2-24: 2-Total Chaos Pt 6. 11-Metallik app. 24-Zero Hour x-over 4.00
Annual 1,2 ('93, '94, $3.50, 68 pgs.): 2-Elseworlds tory 5.00

TEAM X/TEAM 7
Marvel Comics: Nov, 1996 ($4.95, one-shot)
1 5.00

TEAM X 2000
Marvel Comics: Feb, 1999 ($3.50, one-shot)
1-Kevin Lau-a; Bishop vs. Shi'ar Empire 4.00

TEAM YOUNGBLOOD (Also see Youngblood)
Image Comics (Extreme Studios): Sept, 1993 - No. 22, Sept, 1995 ($1.95/$2.50)
1-22: 1-9-Liefeld scripts in all: 1,2,4-6,8-Thibert-c(i). 1-1st app. Dutch & Masada. 3-Spawn cameo. 5-1st app. Lynx. 7,8-Coupons 1 & 4 for Extreme Prejudice #0; Black and White Pt. 4 & 8 by Thibert. 8-Coupon #4 for E. P. #0. 9-Liefeld wraparound-c &(p)/a(p) on Pt. I. 16,17-Bagged w/trading card. 21-Angela & Glory-app. 3.00

TEAM ZERO
DC Comics (WildStorm Productions): Feb, 2006 - No. 6, Jul, 2006 ($2.99, limited series)
1-6-Dixon-s/Mahnke-a 3.00

GD VG FN VF VF/NM NM-
2.0 4.0 6.0 8.0 9.0 9.2

TPB (2008, $17.99) r/#1-6 18.00

TECH JACKET
Image Comics: Nov, 2002 - No. 6, Apr, 2003 ($2.95)
1-6-Kirkman-s/Su-a 3.00
Vol. 1: Lost and Found TPB (7/03, $12.95, 7-3/4" x 5-1/4") B&W r/#1-6; Valentino intro. 13.00

TECH JACKET (2nd series)
Image Comics: Jul, 2014 - No. 12, Dec, 2015 ($2.99)
1-12-Keatinge-s/Randolph-a 3.00

TEDDY ROOSEVELT & HIS ROUGH RIDERS (See Real Heroes #1)
Avon Periodicals: 1950

	GD	VG	FN	VF	VF/NM	NM-
1-Kinstler-c; Palais-a; Flag-c	22	44	66	128	209	290

TEDDY ROOSEVELT ROUGH RIDER (See Battlefield #22 & Classics Illustrated Special Issue)

TED MCKEEVER'S METROPOL (See Transit)
Marvel Comics (Epic Comics): Mar, 1991 - No. 12, Mar, 1992 ($2.95, limited series)
V1#1-12: Ted McKeever-c/a/scripts 4.00

TED MCKEEVER'S METROPOL A.D.
Marvel Comics (Epic Comics): Oct, 1992 - No. 3, Dec, 1992 ($3.50, limited series)
V2#1-3: Ted McKeever-c/a/scripts 4.00

TEENA
Magazine Enterprises/Standard Comics No. 20 on: No. 11, 1948 - No. 15, 1948; No. 20, Aug, 1949 - No. 22, Oct, 1950

	GD	VG	FN	VF	VF/NM	NM-
A-1 #11-Teen-age; Ogden Whitney-c	15	30	45	88	137	185
A-1 #12, 15	14	28	42	81	118	155
20-22 (Standard)	11	22	33	62	86	110

TEEN-AGE BRIDES (True Bride's Experiences #8 on)
Harvey/Home Comics: Aug, 1953 - No. 7, Aug, 1954

	GD	VG	FN	VF	VF/NM	NM-
1-Powell-a	13	26	39	72	101	130
2-Powell-a	9	18	27	50	65	80
3-7: 3,6-Powell-a	8	16	24	44	57	70

TEEN-AGE CONFESSIONS (See Teen Confessions)

TEEN-AGE CONFIDENTIAL CONFESSIONS
Charlton Comics: July, 1960 - No. 22, 1964

	GD	VG	FN	VF	VF/NM	NM-
1	5	10	15	30	50	70
2-10	3	6	9	19	30	40
11-22	3	6	9	14	20	26

TEEN-AGE DIARY SECRETS (Formerly Blue Ribbon Comics; becomes Diary Secrets #10 on)
St. John Publishing Co.: No. 4, 9/49; nn (#5), 9/49 - No. 7, 11/49; No. 8, 2/50; No. 9, 8/50

	GD	VG	FN	VF	VF/NM	NM-
4(9/49)-Oversized; part mag., part comic	58	116	174	371	636	900
nn(#5)(no indicia)-Oversized, all comics; contains sty "I Gave Boys the Green Light."	58	116	174	371	636	900
6-(Reg. size) pre-fame Marilyn Monroe photo-c; Baker-a(2-3)	68	136	204	435	743	1050
7-Digest size (Pocket Comics); Baker-a(5); same contents as #9; diff.-c	87	174	261	553	952	1350
8-(Reg. size) Photo-c; Baker-a(2-3)	63	126	189	403	689	975
9-Digest size (Pocket Comics); Baker-a(5); same contents as #7; diff.-c by Baker	142	284	426	909	1555	2200

TEEN-AGE DOPE SLAVES (See Harvey Comics Library #1)

TEENAGE HOTRODDERS (Top Eliminator #25 on; see Blue Bird)
Charlton Comics: Apr, 1963 - No. 24, July, 1967

	GD	VG	FN	VF	VF/NM	NM-
1	6	12	18	37	66	95
2-10	3	6	9	19	30	40
11-24	3	6	9	16	24	32

TEEN-AGE LOVE (See Fox Giants)

TEEN-AGE LOVE (Formerly Intimate)
Charlton Comics: V2#4, July, 1958 - No. 96, Dec, 1973

	GD	VG	FN	VF	VF/NM	NM-
V2#4	5	10	15	30	50	70
5-9	4	8	12	23	37	50
10(9/59)-20	3	6	9	17	26	35
21-35	3	6	9	16	23	30
36-70	3	6	9	14	19	24
71-79,81,82,85-87,90-96: 61&62-Jonnie Love begins (origin)	2	4	6	10	14	18
80,84,88-David Cassidy pin-ups	3	6	9	14	19	24
83,89: 83-Bobby Sherman pin-up. 89-Danny Bonaduce pin-up	3	6	9	14	19	24

Teenage Mutant Ninja Turtles #14 © Mirage

Teenage Mutant Ninja Turtles (2011 series) #109 © Viacom

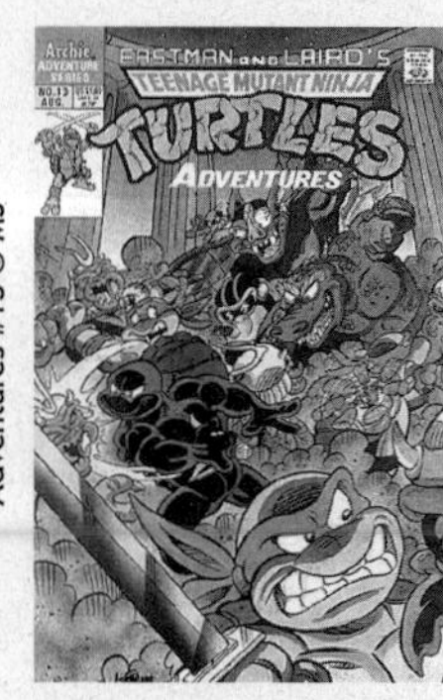

Teenage Mutant Ninja Turtles Adventures #13 © MS

	GD	VG	FN	VF	VF/NM	NM-
	2.0	4.0	6.0	8.0	9.0	9.2

TEENAGE MUTANT NINJA CEREBI (Reprints from Cerebus in Hell)
Aardvark-Vanaheim: 2018 ($4.00, B&W)

1-Cerebus figures placed over original Gustave Doré artwork of Hell; TMNT #1-c swipe 4.00

TEENAGE MUTANT NINJA TURTLES (Also see Anything Goes, Donatello, First Comics Graphic Novel, Gobbledygook, Grimjack #26, Leonardo, Michaelangelo, Raphael & Tales Of The...)
Mirage Studios: 1984 - No. 62, Aug, 1993 ($1.50/$1.75, B&W; all 44-52 pgs.)

1-1st printing (3000 copies)-Origin and 1st app. of the Turtles and Splinter. Only printing to have ad for Gobbledygook #1 & 2; Shredder app. (#1-4: 7-1/2x11") 1800 3600 5400 9000 12,750 16,500
1-2nd printing (6/84)(6,000 copies) 71 142 213 568 1284 2000
1-3rd printing (2/85)(36,000 copies) 36 72 108 259 580 900
1-4th printing, new-c (50,000 copies) 6 12 18 38 69 100
1-5th printing, new-c (8/88-c, 11/88 inside) 6 12 18 38 69 100
1-Counterfeit. **Note**: Most counterfeit copies have a half inch wide white streak or scratch marks across the center of back cover. Black part of cover is a bluish black instead of a deep black. Inside paper is very white & inside cover is bright white (no value)
2-1st printing (1984; 15,000 copies) 21 42 63 147 324 500
2-2nd printing 7 14 21 44 82 120
2-3rd printing; new Corben-c/a (2/85) 4 8 12 23 37 50
2-Counterfeit with glossy cover stock (no value).
3-1st printing (1985, 44 pgs.) 10 20 30 64 132 200
3-Variant, 500 copies, cover printed at different plant, has 'Laird's Photo' in white rather than light blue 54 108 162 432 966 1500
3-2nd printing; contains new back-up story 5 10 15 33 57 80
4-1st printing (1985, 44 pgs.) 10 20 30 67 141 215
4-2nd printing (5/87) all have manufacturing error 13 26 39 89 195 300
5-Fugitoid begins, ends #7; 1st full color-c (1985) 5 10 15 35 63 90
5-2nd printing (11/87) 3 6 9 16 23 30
6-1st printing (1986) 4 8 12 27 44 60
6-2nd printing (4/88-c, 5/88 inside) 2 4 6 9 12 15
7-Four pg. Eastman/Corben color insert; 1st color TMNT (1986, $1.75-c); Bade Biker back-up story 4 8 12 23 37 50
7-2nd printing (1/89) w/o color insert 4 8 12 27 44 60
8-Cerebus-c/story with Dave Sim-a (1986) 4 8 12 23 37 50
9,10: 9-(9/86)-Rip In Time by Corben 3 6 9 17 26 35
11-15 3 6 9 14 20 25
16-18: 18-Mark Bodé-a 2 4 6 10 14 18
18-2nd printing ($2.25, color, 44 pgs.)-New-c 1 2 3 5 6 8
19-34: 19-Begin $1.75-c. 24-26-Veitch-c/a. 1 3 4 6 8 10
32-2nd printing ($2.75, 52 pgs., full color) 6.00
35-49,51: 35-Begin $2.00-c. 1 3 4 6 8 10
50-Features pin-ups by Larsen, McFarlane, Simonson, etc. 2 4 6 9 12 15
52-62: 52-Begin $2.25-c 1 2 3 5 6 8
nn (1990, $5.95, B&W)-Movie adaptation 2 4 6 11 16 20
Book 1,2($1.50, B&W): 2-Corben-c 2 4 6 9 12 15
...Christmas Special 1 (12/90, $1.75, B&W, 52 pgs.)-Cover title: Michaelangelo Christmas Special; r/Michaelangelo one-shot plus new Raphael story 2 4 6 11 16 20
... Color Special (11/09, $3.25) full color reprint of issue #1 2 4 6 11 16 20
...Special: The Haunted Pizza nn (10/92, $2.25, B&W, 32 pgs.) Howarth-s/a 2 4 6 9 12 15
...Special (The Maltese Turtle) nn (1/93, $2.95, color, 44 pgs.) 2 4 6 9 12 15
...Special: "Times" Pipeline nn (9/92, $2.95, color, 44 pgs.)-Mark Bodé-c/a 2 4 6 9 12 15
Hardcover ($100)-r/#1-10 plus one-shots w/dust jackets - limited to 1000 w/letter of authenticity 250.00
Softcover ($40)-r/#1-10 45.00

TEENAGE MUTANT NINJA TURTLES
Mirage Studios: V2#1, Oct, 1993 - V2#13, Oct, 1995 ($2.75)

V2#1-Wraparound-c 2 4 6 11 16 20
2-13 6.00

TEENAGE MUTANT NINJA TURTLES (Volume 3)
Image Comics (Highbrow Ent.): June, 1996 - No. 23, Oct, 1999 ($1.95-$2.95)

1-Erik Larsen-c(i) 2 4 6 11 16 20
2-23: 2-8-Erik Larsen-c(i) on all. 10-Savage Dragon-c/app. 6.00

TEENAGE MUTANT NINJA TURTLES
Mirage Publishing: V4#1, Dec, 2001 - No. 28, Jun, 2006 ($2.95, B&W)

V4#1-Laird-s/a(i)/Lawson-a(p) 2 4 6 11 16 20
V4#2-9,11-28-Laird-s/a(i)/Lawson-a(p). 6.00
10-($3.95) Splinter dies 1 3 4 6 8 10

TEENAGE MUTANT NINJA TURTLES
Dreamwave Productions: June 2003 - No. 7 ($2.95, color)

1-7-Animated style; Peter David-s/Lesean-a 6.00

TEENAGE MUTANT NINJA TURTLES
IDW Publishing: Aug, 2011 - Present ($3.99)

1-Kevin Eastman-s & layouts; four covers by Duncan (each turtle); origin flashback 4 8 12 27 44 60
1-Variant-c by Eastman 6 12 18 38 69 100
1-Halloween Edition (10/12, no cover price) Reprints #1 1 3 4 6 8 10
2-43,45-49,52-74,76-92-Multiple variant covers on each 6.00
44-Donatello killed 20.00
50-(9/15, $7.99) Multiple variant covers; Turtles & Splinter vs. Shredder; Santolouco-a 1 3 4 6 8 10
51-First appearance of Jennika (mutated into Ninja Turtle in #95) 3 6 9 19 30 40
75-(10/17, $7.99) Multiple variant covers; Trial of Krang pt. 3; Santolouco-a 1 3 4 6 8 10
93,94,96-98-City at War. 97-Jennika dons the yellow mask 6.00
95-Jennika mutated into a Ninja Turtle 3 6 9 19 30 40
99,100-($7.99) Conclusion to City at War. 100-Splinter killed 1 3 4 6 8 10
101-114: 101-105-Mutanimals app. 6.00
Annual 2012 (10/12, $8.99) Eastman-s/a; wraparound-c 1 3 4 6 8 10
Annual 2014 (8/14, $7.99) Eastman-s/a; Renet app. 8.00
...: Deviations (3/16, $4.99) What If... the Turtles joined Shredder; Waltz-s/Howard-a 5.00
... FCBD (3/15, giveaway) Santolouco-a 3.00
...: Free Comic Book Day 2019 (5/19, giveaway) Wachter-a; prelude to #94; Jennika app. 3.00
... Funko Universe One Shot (5/17, $4.99) Character rendered in Funko Pop figure style 5.00
Greatest Hits - Teenage Mutant Ninja Turtles #1 (2/16, $1.00) r/#1 3.00
... Kevin Eastman Cover Gallery (12/13, $3.99) Collection of recent Eastman covers 4.00
... Microseries 1-8 (11/11 - No. 8, 9/12) 1-Raphael. 2-Michelangelo. 3-Donatello. 4-Leonardo. 5-Splinter. 6-Casey Jones. 7-April. 8-Fugitoid 4.00
...100 Page Spectacular (4/12, $7.99) r/TMNT Adventures (1988) mini-series #1-3 8.00
...: Road to 100 (11/19, free) Story summary leading to issue #100 3.00
... Samurai Special (7/17, no price, B&W) Stan Sakai-s/a; reprints Usagi Yojimbo x-overs 3.00
... 30th Anniversary Special (5/14, $7.99) History and reprints from all eras; pin-ups by various; multiple covers 8.00
... 20/20 1 (1/19, $4.99) Takes place 20 years in the future; Paul Allor-s/Nelson Daniel-a 5.00
.../ Usagi Yojimbo (7/17, $7.99) Stan Sakai-s/a; multiple covers 8.00
... Villains Microseries 1-8 (4/13 - No. 8, 11/13, $3.99) 1-Krang. 2-Baxter. 8-Shredder 4.00

TEENAGE MUTANT NINJA TURTLES (Adventures)
Archie Publications: Jan, 1996 - No. 3, Mar, 1996 ($1.50, limited series)

1 3 6 9 14 20 26
2,3 1 3 4 6 8 10

TEENAGE MUTANT NINJA TURTLES ADVENTURES (TV)
Archie Comics: Oct, 1988 - No. 3, Dec, 1988; Mar, 1989 - No. 72, Oct, 1995 ($1.00-$1.75)

1-Adapts TV cartoon; not by Eastman/Laird 6 12 18 41 76 110
2,3 (Mini-series) 3 6 9 16 23 30
1 (2nd on-going series) 4 8 12 27 44 60
1-2nd printing 2 4 6 8 10 12
2 2 4 6 11 16 20
2-11: 2nd printings 4.00
3-5: 5-Begins original stories not based on TV 2 4 6 9 12 15
6-18,20-30: 14-Simpson-a(p). 22-Colan-c/a 6.00
19-1st Mighty Mutanimals (also in #20, 51-54) 3 6 9 14 20 25
20,51-54 2 4 6 9 12 15
31-49 5.00
50-Poster by Eastman/Laird 1 2 3 5 7 9
55-60 1 2 3 4 5 7
61-70: 62-w/poster 2 3 4 6 8 10
71 2 4 6 8 10 12
72- Last issue 2 4 6 9 13 16
nn (1990, $2.50)-Movie adaptation 1 3 4 6 8 10
nn (Spring, 1991, $2.50, 68 pgs.)-(Meet Archie) 1 3 4 6 8 10
nn (Sum, 1991, $2.50, 68 pgs.)-(Movie II)-Adapts movie sequel 1 3 4 6 8 10
...Meet the Conservation Corps 1 (1992, $2.50, 68 pgs.) 6.00
...III The Movie: The Turtles are Back...In Time (1993, $2.50, 68 pgs.) 1 3 4 6 8 10

Teenage Mutant Ninja Turtles Amazing Adventures #9 © MS

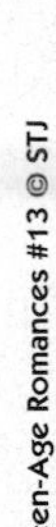
Teen-Age Romances #13 © STJ

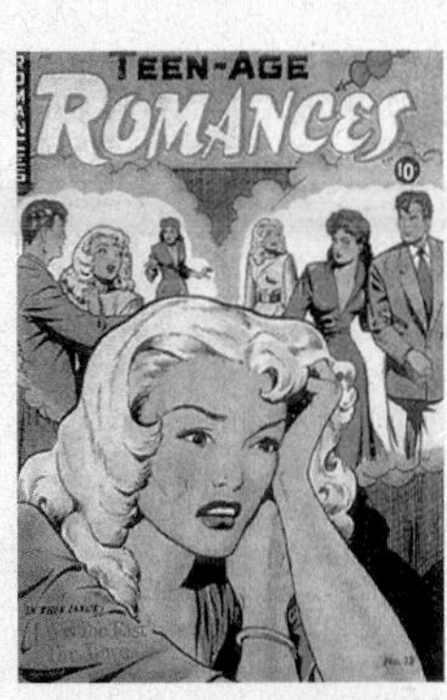

Teen-Age Temptations #1 © STJ

GD VG FN VF VF/NM NM-
2.0 4.0 6.0 8.0 9.0 9.2

GD VG FN VF VF/NM NM-
2.0 4.0 6.0 8.0 9.0 9.2

Special 1,4,5 (Sum/92, Spr/93, Sum/93, 68 pgs.)-1-Bill Wray-c 6.00
Giant Size Special 6 (Fall/93, $1.95, 52 pgs.) 6.00
Special 7-10 (Win/93-Fall//94, 52 pgs.): 9-Jeff Smith-c 5.00
NOTE: *There are 2nd printings of #1-11 w/B&W inside covers. Originals are color.*

TEENAGE MUTANT NINJA TURTLES AMAZING ADVENTURES
IDW Publishing: Aug, 2015 - No. 14, Sept, 2016 ($3.99)

1-14-All-ages animated-style stories; two covers 4.00
... Carmelo Anthony Special One-Shot (5/16, $5.99) Turtles meet the NBA player 6.00

TEENAGE MUTANT NINJA TURTLES AMAZING ADVENTURES: ROBOTANIMALS
IDW Publishing: Jun, 2017 - No. 3, Sept, 2017 ($3.99, limited series)

1-3-All-ages animated-style stories; three covers on each; Goellner-s/Thomas-a 4.00

TEENAGE MUTANT NINJA TURTLES BEBOP & ROCKSTEADY DESTROY EVERYTHING
IDW Publishing: Jun, 2016 - No. 5, Jun, 2016 ($3.99, weekly limited series)

1-5-Dustin Weaver-s; art by various; interlocking covers 4.00

TEENAGE MUTANT NINJA TURTLES BEBOP & ROCKSTEADY HIT THE ROAD
IDW Publishing: Aug, 2018 - No. 5, Aug, 2018 ($3.99, weekly limited series)

1-5-Dustin Weaver & Ben Bates-s/a; interlocking covers 4.00

TEENAGE MUTANT NINJA TURTLES: CASEY AND APRIL
IDW Publishing: Jun, 2015 - No. 4, Sept, 2015 ($3.99, limited series)

1-4-Mariko Tamaki-s/Irene Koh-a; two covers on each 4.00

TEENAGE MUTANT NINJA TURTLES CLASSICS DIGEST (TV)
Archie Comics: Aug, 1993 - No. 8, Mar, 1995? ($1.75)

1-8: Reprints TMNT Advs. 1 3 4 6 8 10

TEENAGE MUTANT NINJA TURTLES COLOR CLASSICS
IDW Publishing: May, 2012 - Mar, 2016 ($3.99)

1-11-Colored reprints of the original 1984 B&W series 4.00
...: Donatello Micro-Series One-Shot (3/13, $3.99) r/Donatello, TMNT #1 (1986) 5.00
...: Leonardo Micro-Series One-Shot (4/13, $3.99) r/Leonardo, TMNT #1 5.00
...: Michaelangelo Micro-Series One-Shot (12/12, $3.99) r/Michaelangelo, TMNT #1 5.00
...: Raphael Micro-Series One-Shot (8/12, $3.99) r/Raphael #1 (1985) 5.00
... Volume 2 (11/13 - No. 7, 5/14, $3.99) 1-7: 1-Reprints TMNT #12 (1987) 4.00
... Volume 3 (1/15 - No. 15, 3/16, $3.99) 1-15: 1-Reprints TMNT #48 (1992) 4.00

TEENAGE MUTANT NINJA TURTLES: DIMENSION X
IDW Publishing: Aug, 2017 - No. 5, Aug, 2017 ($3.99, weekly limited series)

1-5-Takes place during the Trial of Krang (between TMNT #73 & 74); multiple-c on each 4.00

TEENAGE MUTANT NINJA TURTLES/FLAMING CARROT CROSSOVER
Mirage Publishing: Nov, 1993 - No. 4, Feb, 1994 ($2.75, limited series)

1-4: Bob Burden story 1 2 3 5 6 8

TEENAGE MUTANT NINJA TURTLES / GHOSTBUSTERS
IDW Publishing: Oct, 2014 - No. 4, Jan, 2015 ($3.99, limited series)

1-4-Burnham & Waltz-s/Schoening-a; multiple covers on each 4.00
... #1 Director's Cut (5/15, $5.99) r/#1 with creator commentary; bonus script pages 6.00

TEENAGE MUTANT NINJA TURTLES / GHOSTBUSTERS 2
IDW Publishing: Nov, 2017 - No. 5, Nov, 2017 ($3.99, limited series)

1-5-Burnham & Waltz-s/Schoening-a; multiple covers on each 4.00

TEENAGE MUTANT NINJA TURTLES MACRO-SERIES
IDW Publishing: Sept, 2018 - Dec, 2018 ($7.99, limited series)

... #1 Donatello; Paul Allor-s/Brahm Revel-a; four covers; Metalhead app. 8.00
... #2 Michelangelo; Ian Flynn-s/Michael Dialynas-a; four covers 8.00
... #3 Leonardo; Sophie Campbell-s/a; four covers 8.00
... #4 Raphael; Kevin Eastman-s/Eastman and Ben Bishop-a; four covers 8.00

TEENAGE MUTANT NINJA TURTLES: MUTANIMALS
IDW Publishing: Feb, 2015 - No. 4, May, 2015 ($3.99, limited series)

1-4-Paul Allor-s/Andy Kuhn-a; two covers 4.00

TEENAGE MUTANT NINJA TURTLES NEW ANIMATED ADVENTURES
IDW Publishing: Jul, 2013 - No. 24, Jun, 2015 ($3.99)

1-24-Multiple covers on each 4.00
... Free Comic Book Day (5/13) Burnham-s/Brizuela-a 3.00

TEENAGE MUTANT NINJA TURTLES PRESENTS: APRIL O'NEIL
Archie Comics: Mar, 1993 - No. 3, June, 1993 ($1.25, limited series)

1-3 6.00

TEENAGE MUTANT NINJA TURTLES PRESENTS: DONATELLO AND LEATHERHEAD
Archie Comics: July, 1993 - No. 3, Sept, 1993 ($1.25, limited series)

1-3 6.00

TEENAGE MUTANT NINJA TURTLES PRESENTS: MERDUDE
Archie Comics: Oct, 1993 - No. 3, Dec, 1993 ($1.25, limited series)

1-3-See Mighty Mutanimals #7 for 1st app. Merdude 6.00

TEENAGE MUTANT NINJA TURTLES/SAVAGE DRAGON CROSSOVER
Mirage Studios: Aug, 1995 ($2.75, one-shot)

1 6.00

TEENAGE MUTANT NINJA TURTLES: SHREDDER IN HELL
IDW Publishing: Jan, 2019 - No. 5, Jun, 2019 ($3.99, limited series)

1-5-Mateus Santolouco-s/a; 3 covers 4.00
1-Director's Cut (4/19, $4.99) Reprints #1 with uncolored art and commentary 5.00

TEENAGE MUTANT NINJA TURTLES: THE SECRET HISTORY OF THE FOOT CLAN
IDW Publishing: Dec, 2012 - No. 4, Mar, 2013 ($3.99, limited series)

1-4-Santolouco-a/Santolouco & Burnham-s 4.00

TEENAGE MUTANT NINJA TURTLES: TURTLES IN TIME
IDW Publishing: Jun, 2014 - No. 4, Sept, 2014 ($3.99, limited series)

1-4: 1-Paul Allor-s/Ross Campbell-a; Renet app.; three covers. 2-4-Two covers each 4.00

TEENAGE MUTANT NINJA TURTLES UNIVERSE
IDW Publishing: Aug, 2016 - No. 25, Aug, 2018($4.99)

1-25: 1-Allor-s/Couceiro-a; Eastman & Sienkiewicz-a; multiple covers on each 4.00

TEENAGE MUTANT NINJA TURTLES: URBAN LEGENDS
IDW Publishing: May, 2018 - Present ($3.99)

1-22-Reprints the 1996 B&W series in color; multiple covers on each 4.00

TEENAGE MUTANT NINJA TURTLES UTROM EMPIRE
IDW Publishing: Jan, 2014 - No. 3, Mar, 2014 ($3.99, limited series)

1-3-Paul Allor-s/Andy Kuhn-a; two covers on each 4.00

TEEN-AGE ROMANCE (Formerly My Own Romance)
Marvel Comics (ZPC): No. 77, Sept, 1960 - No. 86, Mar, 1962

77-83 7 14 21 46 86 125
84-86-Kirby-c. 84-Kirby-a(2 pgs.). 85,86-(3 pgs.) 8 16 24 51 96 140

TEEN-AGE ROMANCES
St. John Publ. Co. (Approved Comics): Jan, 1949 - No. 45, Dec, 1955 (#3,7,10-18,21 are 1/2 inch taller than other issues)

1-Baker-c/a(1) 161 322 483 1030 1765 2500
2,3: 2-Baker-c/a. 3-Baker-c/a(3) 84 168 252 538 919 1300
4,5,7,8-Photo-c; Baker-a(2-3) each 47 94 141 296 498 700
6-Photo-c; part magazine; Baker-a (10/49) 50 100 150 315 533 750
9-Baker-c/a; Kubert-a 290 580 870 1856 3178 4500
10-12,20-Baker-c/a(2-3) each 142 284 426 909 1555 2200
13-19,21,22-Complete issues by Baker 148 296 444 947 1624 2300
23-25-Baker-c/a(2-3) each 129 258 387 826 1413 2000
26,27,33,34,36,37,39,40,42: Baker-c/a. 33,40-Signed story by Estrada. 42-r/Cinderella
Love #9; last pre-code (3/55) 65 130 195 416 708 1000
28-30-No Baker-a. 28-Estrada-a; painted-c 20 40 60 114 182 250
31,32-Baker-c. 31-Estrada-s 65 130 195 416 708 1000
35-Baker-c/a (16 pgs.) 71 142 213 454 777 1100
38-Baker-c/a; suggestive-c 123 246 369 787 1344 1900
41-Baker-c; Infantino-a(r); all stories are Ziff-Davis-r 65 130 195 416 708 1000
43-45-Baker-c/a 70 142 213 454 777 1100

TEEN-AGE TALK
I.W. Enterprises: 1964

Reprint #1 2 4 6 10 14 18
Reprint #5,8,9: 5-r/Hector #? 9-Punch Comics #?; L.B. Cole-c reprint from School Day
Romances #1 2 4 6 9 13 16

TEEN-AGE TEMPTATIONS (Going Steady #10 on)(See True Love Pictorial)
St. John Publishing Co.: Oct, 1952 - No. 9, Aug, 1954

1-Baker-c/a; has story "Reform School Girl" by Estrada
187 374 561 1197 2049 2900
2,4-Baker-c 103 206 309 659 1130 1600
3,5-7,9-Baker-c/a 110 220 330 704 1202 1700
8-Teenagers smoke reefer; Baker-c/a 123 246 369 787 1344 1900
NOTE: ***Estrada** a-1, 3-5.*

TEEN BEAM (Formerly Teen Beat #1)
National Periodical Publications: No. 2, Jan-Feb, 1968

2-Superman cameo; Herman's Hermits, Yardbirds, Simon & Garfunkel, Lovin Spoonful,
Young Rascals app.; Orlando, Drucker-a(r); Monkees photo-c;
16 32 48 112 249 385

TEEN BEAT (Becomes Teen Beam #2)

Teenie Weenines #11 © Z-D

Teen Titans #17 © DC

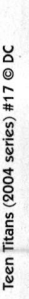

Teen Titans (2004 series) #17 © DC

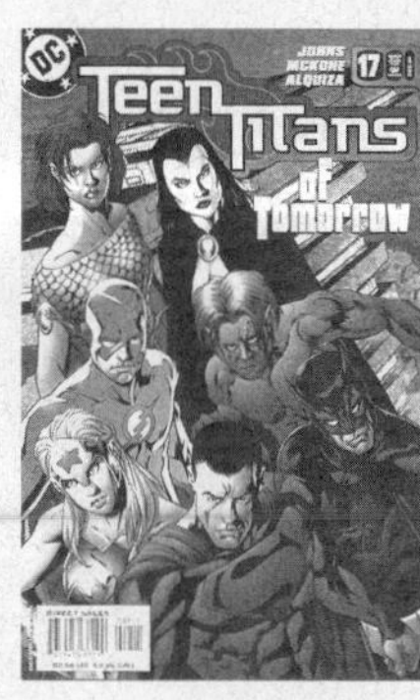

GD VG FN VF VF/NM NM-
2.0 4.0 6.0 8.0 9.0 9.2

GD VG FN VF VF/NM NM-
2.0 4.0 6.0 8.0 9.0 9.2

National Periodical Publications: Nov-Dec, 1967
1-Photos & text only; Monkees photo-c; Beatles, Herman's Hermits, Animals, Supremes, Byrds app. 17 34 51 119 265 410

TEEN COMICS (Formerly All Teen; Journey Into Unknown Worlds #36 on)
Marvel Comics (WFP): No. 21, Apr, 1947 - No. 35, May, 1950
21-Kurtzman's "Hey Look"; Patsy Walker, Cindy (1st app.?), Georgie, Margie app.; Syd Shores-a begins, end #23 34 68 102 204 332 450
22,23,25,27,29,31-35: 22-(6/47)-Becomes Hedy Devine #22 (8/47) on? 24 48 72 140 230 320
24,26,28,30-Kurtzman's "Hey Look". 30-Has anti-Wertham editorial 24 48 72 142 234 325

TEEN CONFESSIONS
Charlton Comics: Aug, 1959 - No. 97, Nov, 1976
1 8 16 24 55 105 155
2 5 10 15 30 50 70
3-10 4 8 12 23 37 50
11-30 3 6 9 19 30 40
31-Beatles-c 11 22 33 75 160 245
32-36,38-55 3 6 9 15 21 26
37 (1/66)-Beatles Fan Club story; Beatles-c 10 20 30 70 150 230
56-58,60-76,78-97: 89,90-Newton-c 2 4 6 10 14 18
59-Kaluta's 1st pro work? (12/69) 3 6 9 19 30 40
77-Partridge Family poster 3 6 9 14 20 24

TEENIE WEENIES, THE (America's Favorite Kiddie Comic)
Ziff-Davis Publishing Co.: No. 10, 1950 - No. 11, Apr-May, 1951 (Newspaper reprints)
10,11-Painted-c 21 42 63 124 202 280

TEEN-IN (Tippy Teen)
Tower Comics: Summer, 1968 - No. 4, Fall, 1969
nn(#1, Summer, 1968)(25¢) Has 3 full pg. B&W photos of Sonny & Cher, Donovan and Herman's Hermits; interviews and photos of Eric Clapton, Jim Morrison and others 9 18 27 62 126 190
nn(#2, Spring, 1969),3,4 6 12 18 37 66 95

TEEN LIFE (Formerly Young Life)
New Age/Quality Comics Group: No. 3, Winter, 1945 - No. 5, Fall, 1945 (Teenage magazine)
3-June Allyson photo on-c & story 15 30 45 84 127 170
4-Duke Ellington photo on-c & story 14 28 42 78 112 145
5-Van Johnson, Woody Herman & Jackie Robinson articles; Van Johnson & Woody Herman photos on-c 15 30 45 84 127 170

TEEN LOVE STORIES (Magazine)
Warren Publ. Co.: Sept, 1969 - No. 3, Jan, 1970 (68 pgs., photo covers, B&W)
1-Photos & articles plus 36-42 pgs. new comic stories in all; Frazetta-a 8 16 24 52 99 145
2,3: 2-Anti-marijuana story 5 10 15 35 63 90

TEEN ROMANCES
Super Comics: 1964
10,11,15-17-Reprints 2 4 6 8 11 14

TEEN SECRET DIARY (Nurse Betsy Crane #12 on)
Charlton Comics: Oct, 1959 - No. 11, June, 1961
1 5 10 15 34 60 85
2 3 6 9 21 33 45
3-11 3 6 9 18 28 38

TEEN TALK (See Teen)

TEEN TITANS (See Brave & the Bold #54,60, DC Super-Stars #1, Marvel & DC Present, New Teen Titans, New Titans, Official...Index and Showcase #59)
National Periodical Publ./DC Comics: 1-2/66 - No. 43, 1-2/73; No. 44, 11/76 - No. 53, 2/78
1-(1-2/66)-Titans join Peace Corps; Batman, Flash, Aquaman, Wonder Woman cameos 40 80 120 296 673 1050
2 14 28 42 96 211 325
3-5: 4-Speedy app. 9 18 27 62 126 190
6-10: 6-Doom Patrol app.; Beast Boy x-over; readers polled on him joining Titans 7 14 21 49 92 135
11-18: 11-Speedy app. 13-X-Mas-c 6 12 18 40 73 105
19-Wood-i; Speedy begins as regular 6 12 18 42 79 115
20-22: All Neal Adams-a. 21-Hawk & Dove app.; last 12¢ issue. 22-Origin Wonder Girl 8 16 24 56 108 160
23-Wonder Girl dons new costume 8 16 24 54 102 150
24-31: 25-Flash, Aquaman, Batman, Green Arrow, Green Lantern, Superman, & Hawk & Dove guests; 1st app. Lilith who joins T.T. West in #50. 29-Hawk & Dove & Ocean Master app. 30-Aquagirl app. 31-Hawk & Dove app. 5 10 15 30 50 70
32-34,40-43: 34-Last 15¢ issue 3 6 9 19 30 40
35-39-(52 pgs.): 36,37-Superboy-r. 38-Green Arrow/Speedy-r; Aquaman/Aqualad story. 39-Hawk & Dove-r. 4 8 12 22 35 48
44-(11/76) Dr. Light app.; Mal becomes the Guardian 3 6 9 14 20 26
45,47,49,51,52 3 6 9 14 19 24
46,48: 46-Joker's daughter begins (see Batman Family). 48-Intro Bumblebee; Joker's daughter becomes Harlequin 3 6 9 21 33 45
50-1st revival original Bat-Girl; intro. Teen Titans West (Bat-Girl, Golden Eagle, Hawk & Dove, Lilith and Beast Boy) 4 8 12 23 37 50
53-Origin retold 3 6 9 15 22 28
... Lost Annual 1 (3/08, $4.99) Sixties-era story by Bob Haney; Jay Stephens & Mike Allred-a; President Kennedy app.; Nick Cardy-c and sketch pages 5.00
NOTE: *Aparo a-36.* ***Buckler*** *c-46-53.* ***Cardy*** *a(p)-1-5, 7, 13, 14, 16, 17, 25, 26, 28-30, 32, c-1-43.* ***Kane*** *a(p)-19, 22-24, 39r.* ***Tuska*** *a(p)-31, 36, 38, 39. DC Super-Stars #1 (3/76) was released before #44.*

TEEN TITANS (Also see Titans Beat for series preview)
DC Comics: Oct, 1996 - No. 24, Sept, 1998 ($1.95)
1-Dan Jurgens-c/a(p)/scripts & George Pérez-c/a(i) begin; Atom forms new team (Risk, Argent, Prysm, & Joto); 1st app. Loren Jupiter & Omen; no indicia. 1-3-Origin. 5.00
2-24: 4,5-Robin, Nightwing, Supergirl, Capt. Marvel Jr. app. 12-"Then and Now" begins w/original Teen Titans-c/app. 15-Death of Joto. 17-Capt. Marvel Jr. and Fringe join. 19-Millennium Giants x-over. 23,24-Superman app. 4.00
Annual 1 (1997, $3.95)-Pulp Heroes story 5.00

TEEN TITANS (Also see Titans/Young Justice: Graduation Day)
DC Comics: Sept, 2003 - No. 100, Late Oct, 2011 ($2.50/$2.99/$3.99)
1-McKone-c/a;Johns-s 5.00
1-Variant-c by Michael Turner 6.00
1-2nd and 3rd printings 3.00
2-Deathstroke app. 5.00
2-2nd printing 3.00
3-15: 4-Impulse becomes Kid Flash. 5-Raven returns. 6-JLA app. 4.00
16-33: 16-Titans go to 31st Century; Legion and Fatal Five app. 17-19-Future Titans app. 21-23-Dr. Light. 24,25-Outsiders #24,25 x-over. 27,28-Liefeld-a. 32,33-Infinite Crisis 3.00
34-49,51-71: 34-One Year Later begins; two covers by Daniel and Benes. 36-Begin $2.99-c. 40-Jericho returns. 42-Kid Devil origin; Snejbjerg-a. 43-Titans East. 48,49-Amazons Attack x-over; Supergirl app. 51-54-Future Titans app. 3.00
50-($3.99) Art by Pérez (4 pgs.), McKone (6 pgs.), Nauck and Green; future Titans app. 4.00
72-88: 72-Begin $3.99-c; Ravager back-up features. 77,78-Blackest Night. 83-87-Coven of Three back-up; Naifeh-a. 88-Nicola Scott-a begins 4.00
89-99-($2.99) 89-Robin (Damian) joins. 93-Solstice app. 98 Superboy-Prime returns 3.00
100-($4.99) Nicola Scott-a; pin-ups by various 5.00
Annual 1 (4/06, $4.99) Infinite Crisis x-over; Benes-c 5.00
Annual 2009 (6/09, $4.99) Deathtrap x-over prelude; McKeever-s 5.00
... And Outsiders Secret Files and Origins 2005 (10/05, $4.99) Daniel-c 5.00
...: Cold Case (2/11, $4.99) Captain Cold and the Rogues app.; Sean Murphy-a 6.00
.../Legion Special (11/04, $3.50) (cont'd from #16) Reis-a; leads into 2005 Legion of Super-Heroes series; LSH preview by Waid & Kitson 4.00
#1/2 (Wizard mail offer) origin of Ravager; Reis-a 8.00
.../Outsiders Secret Files 2003 (12/03, $5.95) Reis & Jimenez-a; pin-ups by various 6.00
...: A Kid's Game TPB (2004, $9.95) r/#1-7; Turner-c from #1; McKone sketch pages 10.00
...: Beast Boys and Girls TPB (2005, $9.99) r/#13-15 and Beast Boy #1-4 10.00
...: Changing of the Guard TPB (2009, $14.99) r/#62-69 15.00
...: Child's Play TPB (2010, $14.99) r/#71-78 15.00
...: Deathtrap TPB (2009, $14.99) r/#70, Annual #1, Titans #12,13, Vigilante #4-6 15.00
...: Family Lost TPB (2004, $9.95) r/#8-12 & #1/2 10.00
...: Life and Death TPB (2006, $14.99) r/#29-33 and pages from Infinite Crisis x-over 15.00
...: On the Clock TPB (2008, $14.99) r/#55-61 15.00
.../ Outsiders: The Death and Return of Donna Troy (2006, $14.99) r/Titans/Young Justice: Graduation Day #1-3, Teen Titans/Outsiders Secret Files 2003 and DC Special: The Return of Donna Troy #1-4; cover gallery 15.00
.../ Outsiders: The Insiders (2006, $14.99) r/Teen Titans/ #24-26 & Outsiders #24,25,28 15.00
...: Ravager - Fresh Hell TPB (2010, $14.99) r/#71-76,79-82 & Faces of Evil: Deathstroke 15.00
... Spotlight: Cyborg TPB (2009, $19.99) r/DC Special: Cyborg #1-6 20.00
... Spotlight: Raven TPB (2008, $14.99) r/DC Special: Raven #1-5 15.00
...: The Future is Now (2005, $9.99) r/#15-23 & Teen Titans/Legion Special 10.00
...: The Hunt For Raven (2011, $17.99) r/#79-87 18.00
...: Titans Around the World TPB (2007, $14.99) r/#34-41 15.00
...: Titans of Tomorrow TPB (2008, $14.99) r/#50-54 15.00

TEEN TITANS (DC New 52)
DC Comics: Nov, 2011 - No. 30, Jun, 2014 ($2.99)
1-14,17-23: 1-Lobdell-s/Booth-a/c; Red Robin assembles a team; Kid Flash, Wonder Girl app. 5-Superboy app. 9-The Culling conclusion. 13,14-Wonder Girl origin; Garza-a 3.00
15,16-"Death of the Family" tie-in. 15-Die-cut Joker mask cover. 16-Red Hood app. 5.00

Teen Titans (2011 series) #21 © DC

Teen Titans Go! #47 © DC

Tellos #2 © Dezago & Wieringo

	GD 2.0	VG 4.0	FN 6.0	VF 8.0	VF/NM 9.0	NM- 9.2

23.1, 23.2 (11/13, $2.99, regular covers) 3.00
23.1 (11/13, $3.99, 3-D cover) "Trigon #1" on cover; origin; Wolfman-s/Cafu-a 5.00
23.2 (11/13, $3.99, 3-D cover) "Deathstroke #1" on cover; flashback; Deathblow app.
1 2 3 5 6 8
24-29: 24-Leads into Annual #2. 25,26-Origin of Kid Flash 3.00
30-($3.99) Last issue; origin of Skitter; Kirkham-a 4.00
#0 (11/12, $2.99) Origin of Red Robin; Kirkham-a 3.00
Annual 1 (7/12, $4.99) The Culling x-over part 1; Legion Lost members app. 5.00
Annual 2 (12/13, $4.99) Future Teen Titans; Lobdell-s/Kitson-a 5.00
Annual 3 (7/14, $4.99) Follows #30; Harvest app. 5.00
... Earth One Volume One HC (2014, $22.99) Lemire-s/Dodson-a/c; new origin story 23.00

TEEN TITANS (DC New 52)
DC Comics: Sept, 2014 - No. 24, Nov, 2016 ($2.99)

1-24: 1-Pfeifer-s/Rocafort-a/c; Manchester Black app. 5-Hepburn-a; new Power Girl app. 15-Robin War tie-in; Professor Pyg app. 18,19-Wonder Woman app. 3.00
Annual 1 (6/15, $4.99) Superboy returns; Borges & St. Claire-a; March-c 5.00
Annual 2 (8/16, $4.99) Lobdell-s/Cory Smith-a/Jonboy Meyers-c; Sister Blood app. 5.00
...: Futures End 1 (11/14, $2.99, regular-c) Five years later; Andy Smith-a 3.00
...: Futures End 1 (11/14, $3.99, 3-D cover) 4.00

TEEN TITANS (DC Rebirth)
DC Comics: Nov, 2016 - No. 47, Jan, 2021 ($2.99/$3.99)

1-6: 1-Percy-s/Meyers-a; Ra's al Ghul app. 3-6-Pham-a. 6-Intro. Aqualad (Jackson Hyde) 3.00
7-11,13-24-($3.99) 7-Aqualad joins; Black Manta cameo. 8-Lazarus Contact x-over; Titans & Deathstroke app. 9-11-Black Manta app. 15-Future adult Superboy (Conner), Wonder Girl (Cassie) and Kid Flash (Bart) app. 20-New team with Crush, Roundhouse, Djinn 4.00
12-Dark Nights: Metal tie-in; 1st full app. The Batman Who Laughs, Harley Quinn app. 24.00
25-($4.99) Origin of Crush; Rocha-a; Roundhouse back-up story 5.00
26-47: 26-32-Chang-a. 28-30-Crossover with Deathstroke #42-44. 31-33,35-37-Lobo app. 4.00
Annual 1 (7/17, $4.99) Conclusion of Lazarus Contact x-over; Titans & Deathstroke app. 5.00
Annual 1 (3/19, $4.99) Red Hood app.; intro. Joystick 5.00
Annual 2 (10/20, $4.99) Batman app.; leads into #45; Crush becomes leader; Fernandez-a 5.00
... : Endless Winter Special 1 (2/21, $3.99) Part 6 of crossover event; Merino-a 5.00
...: Rebirth 1 (11/16, $2.99) Meyers-a; Robin, Raven, Starfire, Beast Boy, Kid Flash app. 3.00
...: Special 1 (8/18, $4.99) Glass-s/Rocha-a; Harley Quinn & Black Mask app. 5.00

TEEN TITANS GIANT (Continues in Titans Giant #1)
DC Comics: 2018 - No. 7, 2019 ($4.99, 100 pgs., squarebound, Walmart exclusive)

1-New story Jurgens-s/Eaton-a; reprints from Teen Titans ('03), Super Sons #1 ('17), and Sideways ('18) 8.00
2-7-New story Jurgens-s/Eaton-a plus reprints continue 5.00

TEEN TITANS GO! (Based on Cartoon Network series)
DC Comics: Jan, 2004 - No. 55, Jul, 2008 ($2.25)

1-12,14-55: 1,2-Nauck-a/Bullock-c/J. Torres-s. 8-Mad Mod app. 14-Speedy-c. 28-Doom Patrol app. 31-Nightwing app. 36-Wonder Girl. 38-Mad Mod app.; Clugston-a 3.00
1-(9/04, Free Comic Book Day giveaway) r/#1; 2 bound-in Wacky Packages stickers 4.00
13-($2.95) Bonus pages with Shazam! reprint 4.00
Jam Packed Action (2005, $7.99, digest) adaptations of two TV episodes 8.00
... Vol 1: Truth, Justice, Pizza! (2004, $6.95, digest-size) r/#1-5 7.00
... Vol 2: Heroes on Patrol (2005, $6.99, digest-size) r/#6-10 7.00
... Vol 3: Bring It On! (2005, $6.99, digest-size) r/#11-15 7.00
... Vol 4: Ready For Action! (2006, $6.99, digest-size) r/#16-20 7.00
... Vol 5: On The Move! (2006, $6.99, digest-size) r/#21-25 7.00
... Titans Together TPB (2007, $12.99) r/#26-32 13.00

TEEN TITANS GO! (Based on the 2013 Cartoon Network series)
DC Comics: Feb, 2014 - Present ($2.99)

1-36: 1-Fisch-s. 2-Brotherhood of Evil app. 4-HIVE Five app. 13-Aqualad app. 3.00
... FCBD Special Edition 1 (6/14, giveaway) r/#1 3.00
... FCBD Special Edition 1 (6/15, giveaway) flipbook with Scooby-Doo! Team Up 3.00
... Giant 1 (2019, $4.99) Two new stories plus reprints 5.00

TEEN TITANS SPOTLIGHT
DC Comics: Aug, 1986 - No. 21, Apr, 1988

1-21: 7-Guice's 1st work at DC. 14-Nightwing; Batman app. 15-Austin-c(i). 18,19-Millennium x-over. 21-($1.00-c)-Original Teen Titans; Spiegle-a 4.00
*Note: **Guice** a-7p, 8p; c-7,8. **Orlando** c/a-11p. **Perez** c-1, 17i, 19. **Sienkiewicz** c-10*

TEEN TITANS YEAR ONE
DC Comics: Mar, 2008 - No. 6, Aug, 2008 ($2.99, limited series)

1-6-The original five form a team; Wolfram-s/Kerschl-a 3.00
TPB (2008, $14.99) r/#1-6; bonus pin-up 15.00

TEEN WOLF: BITE ME (Based on the MTV series)
Image Comics (Top Cow): Sept, 2011 - No. 3, Nov, 2011 ($3.99, limited series)

1-3: 1-Tischman-s/Mooney-a/c 4.00

TEEPEE TIM (...Heap Funny Indian Boy)(Formerly Ha Ha Comics)(Also see "Cookie")
American Comics Group: No. 100, Feb-Mar, 1955 - No. 102, June-July, 1955

100-102 7 14 21 37 46 55

TEGRA JUNGLE EMPRESS (Zegra Jungle Empress #2 on)
Fox Feature Syndicate: August, 1948

1-Blue Beetle, Rocket Kelly app.; used in **SOTI**, pg. 31
90 180 270 576 988 1400

TEK JANSEN (See Stephen Colbert's...)

TEKKEN: BLOOD FEUD (Based on the Bandai Namco video game)
Titan Comics: Jun, 2017 - No. 4, Sept, 2017 ($3.99, limited series)

1-4-Cavan Scott-s/Andie Tong-a; multiple covers on each 4.00

TEKNO COMIX HANDBOOK
Tekno Comix: May, 1996 ($3.95, one-shot)

1-Guide to the Tekno Universe 4.00

TEKNOPHAGE (See Neil Gaiman's...)

TEKNOPHAGE VERSUS ZEERUS
BIG Entertainment: July, 1996 ($3.25, one-shot)

1-Paul Jenkins script 3.25

TEKWORLD (William Shatner's... on-c only)
Epic Comics (Marvel): Sept, 1992 - Aug, 1994 ($1.75)

1-Based on Shatner's novel, TekWar, set in L.A. in the year 2120 4.00
2-24 3.00

TELARA CHRONICLES (Based on the videogame Rift: Planes of Telara)
DC Comics (WildStorm): Jan, 2010; Nov, 2010 - No. 4, Feb, 2011 ($3.99, limited series)

0-(1/10, free) Preview of series 3.00
1-4-Pop Mhan-a/Drew Johnson-c 4.00
TPB (2011, $17.99) r/#0-4; background info on Telara 18.00

TELEVISION (See TV)

TELEVISION COMICS (Early TV comic)
Standard Comics (Animated Cartoons): No. 5, Feb, 1950 - No. 8, Nov, 1950

5-1st app. Willy Nilly 13 26 39 72 101 130
6-8: #6 on inside has #2 on cover 10 20 30 54 72 90

TELEVISION PUPPET SHOW (Early TV comic) (See Spotty the Pup)
Avon Periodicals: 1950 - No. 2, Nov, 1950

1-1st app. Speedy Rabbit, Spotty The Pup 26 52 78 154 252 350
2 17 34 51 105 165 225

TELEVISION TEENS MOPSY (See TV Teens)

TELL IT TO THE MARINES
Toby Press Publications: Mar, 1952 - No. 15, July, 1955

1-Lover O'Leary and His Liberty Belles (with pin-ups), ends #6; Spike & Bat begin, end #6 37 74 111 222 361 500
2-Madame Cobra-c/story; headlights-c 37 74 111 222 361 500
3,5 20 40 60 115 188 260
4-Headlights-c 47 94 141 296 498 700
6-12,14,15: 7-9,14,15-Photo-c 15 30 45 94 147 200
13-John Wayne photo-c 23 46 69 136 223 310
I.W. Reprint #9-r/#1 above 3 6 9 14 20 25
Super Reprint #16(1964)-r/#4 above 2 4 6 9 13 16

TELLOS
Image Comics: May, 1999 - No. 10, Nov, 2000 ($2.50)

1-Dezago-s/Wieringo-a 3.00
1-Variant-c ($7.95) 8.00
2-10: 4-Four covers 3.00
...: Maiden Voyage (3/01, $5.95) Didier Crispeels-a/c 6.00
...: Sons & Moons (2002, $5.95) Nick Cardy-c 6.00
...: The Last Heist (2001, $5.95) Rousseau-a/c 6.00
Prelude ($5.00, AnotherUniverse.com) 5.00
Prologue ($3.95, Dynamic Forces) 4.00
...Collected Edition 1 (12/99, $8.95) r/#1-3 9.00
... Colossal, Vol. 1 TPB (2008, $17.99) r/#1-10, Prelude, Prologue, Scatterjack-s from Section Zero #1, cover gallery, Wieringo sketch pages; Dezago afterword 18.00
...: Kindred Spirits (2/01, $17.95) r/#6-10, Section Zero #1 (Scatterjack-s) 18.00
...: Reluctant Heroes (2/01, $17.95) r/#1-5, Prelude, Prologue; sketchbook 18.00

TELOS (See Convergence)
DC Comics: Dec, 2015 - No. 6, May, 2016 ($2.99)

1-6: 1,2-King-s/Pagulayan-a. 1-Brainiac app. 2-Arak, Son of Thunder and Validus app.

Ten Grand #10 © Studio JMS

The Tenth V2 #8 © Tony Daniel

The Terminator: Hunters and Killers #3 © DH

	GD 2.0	VG 4.0	FN 6.0	VF 8.0	VF/NM 9.0	NM- 9.2

3-6-Hal Jordan Parallax app. 3.00

TEMPEST (See Aquaman, 3rd Series)
DC Comics: Nov, 1996 - No. 4, Feb, 1997 ($1.75, limited series)

1-4: Formerly Aqualad; Phil Jimenez-c/a/scripts in all 4.00

TEMPLARS (Assassin's Creed)
Titan Comics: Apr, 2016 - No. 9, Feb, 2017 ($3.99)

1-9-Black Cross; set in 1927; Van Lente-s/Calero-a 4.00

TEMPUS FUGITIVE
DC Comics: 1990 - No. 4, 1991 ($4.95, squarebound, 52 pgs.)

Book 1,2: Ken Steacy painted-c/a & scripts 6.00
Book 3,4-($5.95-c) 6.00
TPB (Dark Horse Comics, 1/97, $17.95) 18.00

TEN COMMANDMENTS (See Moses & the... and Classics Illustrated Special)

TENDER LOVE STORIES
Skywald Publ. Corp.: Feb, 1971 - No. 4, July, 1971 (Pre-code reprints and new stories)

	GD	VG	FN	VF	VF/NM	NM-
1 (All 25¢, 52 pgs.)	8	16	24	54	102	150
2-4	5	10	15	35	63	90

TENDER ROMANCE (Ideal Romance #3 on)
Key Publications (Gilmour Magazines): Dec, 1953 - No. 2, Feb, 1954

	GD	VG	FN	VF	VF/NM	NM-
1-Headlight & lingerie panels; B. Baily-c	32	64	96	188	307	425
2-Bernard Baily-c	17	34	51	105	165	225

TEN GRAND
Image Comics (Joe's Comics): May, 2013 - No. 12, Jan, 2015 ($2.99)

1-12: 1-4-Straczynski-s/Templesmith-a. 1-Multiple variant covers. 2-Two covers 3.00

TENSE SUSPENSE
Fago Publications: Dec, 1958 - No. 2, Feb, 1959

	GD	VG	FN	VF	VF/NM	NM-
1	14	28	42	80	115	150
2	10	20	30	56	76	95

TEN STORY LOVE (Formerly a pulp magazine with same title)
Ace Periodicals: V29#3, June-July, 1951 - V36#5(#209), Sept, 1956 (#3-6: 52 pgs.)

	GD	VG	FN	VF	VF/NM	NM-
V29#3(#177)-Part comic, part text; painted-c	20	40	60	118	192	265
4-6(1/52)	14	28	42	80	115	150
V30#1(3/52)-6(1/53)	14	28	42	76	108	140
V31#1(2/53),V32#2(4/53)-6(12/53)	13	26	39	74	105	135
V33#1(1/54)-3(5#54, #195), V34#4(7/54, #196)-6(10/54, #198)	13	26	39	72	101	130
V35#1(12/54, #199)-3(4/55, #201)-Last precode	12	24	36	69	97	125
V35#4-6(9/55, #201-204), V36#1(11/55, #205)-3, 5(9/56, #210)	12	24	36	57	94	120
V36#4-L.B. Cole-a	14	28	42	76	108	140

TENTH, THE
Image Comics: Jan, 1997 - No. 4, June, 1997 ($2.50, limited series)

1-4-Tony Daniel-c/a, Beau Smith-s 5.00
Abuse of Humanity TPB ($10.95) r/#1-4 12.00
Abuse of Humanity TPB (10/98, $11.95) r/#1-4 & 0(8/97) 12.00

TENTH, THE
Image Comics: Sept, 1997 - No. 14, Jan, 1999 ($2.50)

0-(8/97, $5.00) American Ent. Ed. 6.00
1-Tony Daniel-c/a, Beau Smith-s 6.00
2-9: 3,7-Variant-c 4.00
10-14 3.00
...Configuration (8/98) Re-cap and pin-ups 3.00
...Collected Edition 1 ('98, $4.95, square-bound) r/#1,2 5.00
...Special (4/00, $2.95) r/#0 and Wizard #1/2 3.00
Wizard #1/2-Daniel-s/Steve Scott-a 10.00

TENTH, THE (Volume 3) (The Black Embrace)
Image Comics: Mar, 1999 - No. 4, June, 1999 ($2.95)

1-4-Daniel-c/a 3.00
TPB (1/00, $12.95) r/#1-4 13.00

TENTH, THE (Volume 4) (Evil's Child)
Image Comics: Sept, 1999 - No. 4, Mar, 2000 ($2.95, limited series)

1-4-Daniel-c/a 3.00

TENTH, THE (Darkk Dawn)
Image Comics: July, 2005 ($4.99, one-shot)

1-Kirkham-a/Bonny-s 5.00

TENTH, THE : RESURRECTED
Dark Horse Comics: July, 2001 - No. 4, Feb, 2002 ($2.99, limited series)

1-4: 1-Two covers; Daniel-s/c; Romano-a 3.00

10th MUSE
Image Comics (TidalWave Studios): Nov, 2000 - No. 9, Jan, 2002 ($2.95)

1-Character based on wrestling's Rena Mero; regular & photo covers 3.00
2-9: 2-Photo and 2 Lashley covers; flip book Dollz preview. 5-Savage Dragon app.; 2 covers by Lashley and Larsen. 6-Tellos x-over 3.00

TEN WHO DARED (Disney)
Dell Publishing Co.: No. 1178, Dec, 1960

	GD	VG	FN	VF	VF/NM	NM-
Four Color 1178-Movie, painted-c; cast member photo on back-c	7	14	21	46	86	125

TERMINAL CITY
DC Comics (Vertigo): July, 1996 - No. 9, Mar, 1997 ($2.50, limited series)

1-9: Dean Motter scripts, 7,8-Matt Wagner-c 3.00
TPB ('97, $19.95) r/series 20.00

TERMINAL CITY: AERIAL GRAFFITI
DC Comics (Vertigo): Nov, 1997 - No. 5, Mar, 1998 ($2.50, limited series)

1-5: Dean Motter-s/Lark-a/Chiarello-c 3.00

TERMINAL HERO
Dynamite Entertainment: 2014 - No. 6, 2015 ($2.99, limited series)

1-6-Milligan-s/Kowalski-a/Jae Lee-c 3.00

TERMINATOR, THE (See Robocop vs. ... & Rust #12 for 1st app.)
Now Comics: Sept, 1988 - No. 17, 1989 ($1.75, Baxter paper)

	GD	VG	FN	VF	VF/NM	NM-
1-Based on movie	2	4	6	9	13	16
2-5						6.00
6-11,13-17						4.00
12-($2.95, 52 pgs.)-Intro. John Connor						5.00
Trade paperback (1989, $9.95)						15.00

TERMINATOR, THE
Dark Horse Comics: Aug, 1990 - No. 4, Nov, 1990 ($2.50, limited series)

	GD	VG	FN	VF	VF/NM	NM-
1-Set 39 years later than the movie	1	2	3	5	6	8
2-4						4.00

TERMINATOR, THE
Dark Horse Comics: 1998 - No. 4, Dec, 1998 ($2.95, limited series)

1-4-Alan Grant-s/Steve Pugh-a/c 4.00
...Special (1998, $2.95) Darrow-c/Grant-s 4.00

TERMINATOR, THE: ALL MY FUTURES PAST
Now Comics: V3#1, Aug, 1990 - V3#2, Sept, 1990 ($1.75, limited series)

V3#1,2 4.00

TERMINATOR, THE: ENDGAME
Dark Horse Comics: Sept, 1992 - No. 3, Nov, 1992 ($2.50, limited series)

1-3: Guice-a(p); painted-c 4.00

TERMINATOR, THE: ENEMY OF MY ENEMY
Dark Horse Comics: Feb, 2014 - No. 6, Oct, 2014 ($3.99, limited series)

1-6-Jolley-s/Igle-a; set in 1985 4.00

TERMINATOR, THE: HUNTERS AND KILLERS
Dark Horse Comics: Mar, 1992 - No. 3, May, 1992 ($2.50, limited series)

1-3 4.00

TERMINATOR, THE: 1984
Dark Horse Comics: Sept, 2010 - No. 3, Nov, 2010 ($3.50, limited series)

1-3: Takes place during and after the 1st movie; Zack Whedon-s/Andy MacDonald-a 3.50

TERMINATOR, THE: ONE SHOT
Dark Horse Comics: July, 1991 ($5.95, 56 pgs.)

nn-Matt Wagner-a; contains stiff pop-up inside 6.00

TERMINATOR: REVOLUTION (Follows Terminator 2: Infinity series)
Dynamite Entertainment: 2008 - No. 5, 2009 ($3.50, limited series)

1-5-Furman-s/Antonio-a. 1-3-Two covers 3.50

TERMINATOR / ROBOCOP: KILL HUMAN
Dynamite Entertainment: 2011 - No. 4, 2011 ($3.99, limited series)

1-4: 1-Covers by Simonson, Lau & Feister. 2-4-Three covers on each 4.00

TERMINATOR: SALVATION MOVIE PREQUEL
IDW Publishing: Jan, 2009 - No. 4, Apr, 2009 ($3.99, limited series)

1-4: Alan Robinson-a/Dara Naraghi-s 4.00

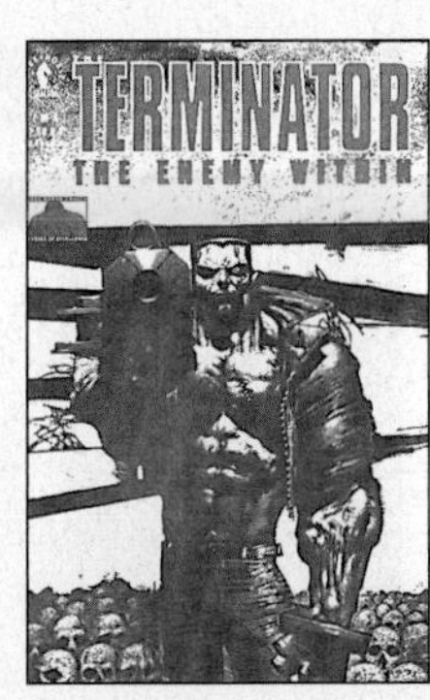

The Terminator: The Enemy Within #3 © DH

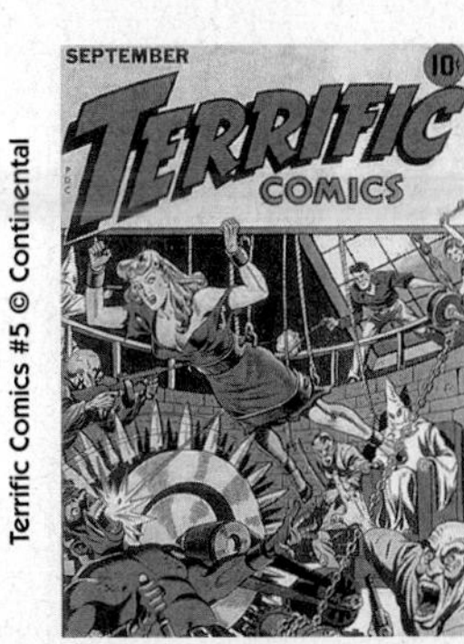

Terrific Comics #5 © Continental

The Terrifics #22 © DC

GD VG FN VF VF/NM NM-
2.0 4.0 6.0 8.0 9.0 9.2

0-Salvation Movie Preview (4/09) Mariotte-s/Figueroa-a 4.00

TERMINATOR SALVATION: THE FINAL BATTLE
Dark Horse Comics: Dec, 2013 - No. 12, Dec, 2014 ($3.99, limited series)
1-12-Straczynski-s/Woods-a 4.00

TERMINATOR, THE: SECONDARY OBJECTIVES
Dark Horse Comics: July, 1991 - No. 4, Oct, 1991 ($2.50, limited series)
1-4: Gulacy-c/a(p) in all 4.00

TERMINATOR SECTOR WAR
Dark Horse Comics: Aug, 2018 - No. 4 ($3.99, limited series)
1-3-Brian Wood-s/Jeff Stokely-a; a different Terminator in 1984 New York City 4.00

TERMINATOR, THE: THE BURNING EARTH
Now Comics: V2#1, Mar, 1990 - V2#5, July, 1990 ($1.75, limited series)
V2#1: Alex Ross painted art (1st published work) 3 6 9 14 19 24
2-5: Ross-c/a in all 1 3 4 6 8 10
Trade paperback (1990, $9.95)-Reprints V2#1-5 18.00
Trade paperback (ibooks, 2003, $17.95)-Digitally remastered reprint 18.00

TERMINATOR, THE: THE DARK YEARS
Dark Horse Comics: Aug, 1999 - No. 4, Dec, 1999 ($2.95, limited series)
1-4-Alan Grant-s/Mel Rubi-a; Jae Lee-c 4.00

TERMINATOR, THE: THE ENEMY FROM WITHIN
Dark Horse Comics: Nov, 1991 - No. 4, Feb, 1992 ($2.50, limited series)
1-4: All have Simon Bisley painted-c 4.00

TERMINATOR, THE: 2029
Dark Horse Comics: Mar, 2010 - No. 3, May, 2010 ($3.50, limited series)
1-3: Kyle Reese before his time-jump to 1984; Zack Whedon-s/Andy MacDonald-a 3.50

TERMINATOR 2: CYBERNETIC DAWN
Malibu: Nov, 1995 - No.4, Feb, 1996; No. 0. Apr, 1996 ($2.50, lim. series)
0 (4/96, $2.95)-Erskine-c/a; flip book w/Terminator 2: Nuclear Twilight 4.00
1-4: Continuation of film. 4.00

TERMINATOR 2: INFINITY
Dynamite Entertainment: 2007 - No. 7 ($3.50)
1-7: 1-Furman-s/Raynor-a; 3 covers. 6,7-Painkiller Jane x-over 3.50

TERMINATOR 2: JUDGEMENT DAY
Marvel Comics: Early Sept, 1991 - No. 3, Early Oct, 1991 ($1.00, lim. series)
1-3: Based on movie sequel; 1-3-Same as nn issues 4.00
nn (1991, $4.95, squarebound, 68 pgs.)-Photo-c 6.00
nn (1991, $2.25, B&W, magazine, 68 pgs.) 4.00

TERMINATOR 2: NUCLEAR TWILIGHT
Malibu: Nov, 1995 - No.4, Feb, 1996; No. 0, Apr, 1996 ($2.50, lim. series)
0 (4/96, $2.95)-Erskine-c/a; flip book w/Terminator 2: Cybernetic Dawn 4.00
1-4:Continuation of film. 4.00

TERMINATOR 3: RISE OF THE MACHINES (... BEFORE THE RISE on cover)
Beckett Comics: July, 2003 - No. 6, Jan, 2004 ($5.95, limited series)
1-6: 1,2-Leads into movie; 2 covers on each. 3-6-Movie adaptation 6.00

TERM LIFE
Image Comics (Shadowline): Jan, 2011 ($16.99, graphic novel)
SC-Lieberman-s/Thornborrow-a/DeStefano-l 17.00

TERRA (See Supergirl {2005 series} #12)
DC Comics: Jan, 2009 - No. 4, Feb, 2009 ($2.99, limited series)
1-4-Conner-a/c. 1,2,4-Power Girl app. 2-4-Geo-Force app. 4.00
TPB (2009, $14.99) r/#1-4 & Supergirl #12 15.00

TERRAFORMERS
Wonder Color Comics: April, 1987 - No. 2, 1987 ($1.95, limited series)
1,2-Kelley Jones-a 3.00

TERRA OBSCURA (See Tom Strong)
America's Best Comics: Aug, 2003 - No. 6, Feb, 2004 ($2.95)
1-6-Alan Moore & Peter Hogan-s/Paquette-a 3.00
TPB (2004, $14.95) r/#1-6 15.00

TERRA OBSCURA VOLUME 2 (See Tom Strong)
America's Best Comics: Oct, 2004 - No. 6, May, 2005 ($2.95)
1-6-Alan Moore & Peter Hogan-s/Paquette-a; Tom Strange app. 3.00
TPB (2005, $14.99) r/#1-6 15.00

TERRARISTS
Marvel Comics (Epic): Nov, 1993 - No. 4, Feb, 1994 ($2.50, limited series)
1-4-Bound-in trading cards in all 3.00

TERRIFIC COMICS (Also see Suspense Comics)
Continental Magazines: Jan, 1944 - No. 6, Nov, 1944
1-Kid Terrific; opium story 360 720 1080 2520 4410 6300
2-1st app. The Boomerang by L.B. Cole & Ed Wheelan's "Comics" McCormick, called the world's #1 comic book fan begins 300 600 900 1950 3375 4800
3-Diana becomes Boomerang's costumed aide; L.B. Cole-c 265 530 795 1694 2897 4100
4-Classic war-c (Scarce) 492 984 1476 3592 6346 9100
5-The Reckoner begins; Boomerang & Diana by L.B. Cole; Classic Schomburg bondage & hooded vigilante-c (Scarce) 1950 3900 5850 11,700 23,100 40,000
6-L.B. Cole-c/a 252 504 756 1613 2757 3900
NOTE: ***L.B. Cole** a-1, 2(2), 3-6. **Fuje** a-5, 6. **Rico** a-2; c-1. **Schomburg** c-2, 5.*

TERRIFIC COMICS (Formerly Horrific; Wonder Boy #17 on)
Mystery Publ.(Comic Media)/(Ajax/Farrell): No. 14, Dec, 1954; No. 16, Mar, 1955 (No #15)
14-Art swipe/Advs. into the Unknown #37; injury-to-eye-c; pg. 2, panel 5 swiped from Phantom Stranger #4; surrealistic Palais-a; Human Cross story; classic-c 106 212 318 659 1130 1600
16-Wonder Boy-c/story (last pre-code) 34 68 102 199 325 450

TERRIFICS, THE
DC Comics: Apr, 2018 - No. 27, Jun, 2020 ($2.99/$3.99)
1-13: 1-Mr. Terrific, Metamorpho, Phantom Girl & Plastic Man team; Lemire-s/Reis-a. 7-10-Tom Strong app. 8,9-Swamp Thing app. 3.00
14-24,26-29-($3.99) 18-23-Bizarro & The Terribles app. 27-Simon Stagg dies 4.00
25-($4.99) Choose Your Adventure; Harley Quinn & Poison Ivy cameo; Yang-s/Mora-a 5.00
Annual 1 (12/18, $4.99) Yang-s/Bennett-a; Tom Strong back-up story 5.00

TERRIFYING TALES (Formerly Startling Terror Tales #10)
Star Publications: No. 11, Jan, 1953 - No. 15, Apr, 1954
11-Used in **POP**, pgs. 99,100; all Jo-Jo-r 77 154 231 493 847 1200
12-Reprints Jo-Jo #19 entirely; L.B. Cole splash 65 130 195 416 708 1000
13-All Rulah-r; classic devil-c 90 180 270 576 988 1400
14-All Rulah reprints 57 114 171 362 619 875
15-Rulah, Zago-r; used in **SOTI**-r/Rulah #22 55 110 165 352 601 850
NOTE: *All issues have **L.B. Cole** covers; bondage covers-No. 12-14.*

TERROR ILLUSTRATED (Adult Tales of...)
E.C. Comics: Nov-Dec, 1955 - No. 2, Spring (April on-c), 1956 (Magazine, 25¢)
1-Adult Entertainment on-c 28 56 84 165 270 375
2-Charles Sultan-a 19 38 57 112 179 245
NOTE: ***Craig, Evans, Ingels, Orlando** art in each. **Crandall** c-1, 2.*

TERROR INC. (See A Shadowline Saga #3)
Marvel Comics: July, 1992 - No. 13, July, 1993 ($1.75)
1-8,11-13: 6,7-Punisher-c/story. 13-Ghost Rider app. 3.00
9,10-Wolverine-c/story 4.00

TERROR INC.
Marvel Comics (MAX): Oct, 2007 - No. 5, Apr, 2008 ($3.99, limited series)
1-5: 1-Lapham-s/Zircher-a; origin of Mr. Terror retold 4.00

TERROR INC. - APOCALYPSE SOON
Marvel Comics (MAX): July, 2009 - No. 4, Sept, 2009 ($3.99, limited series)
1-4: 1-Lapham-s/Turnbull-a 4.00

TERRORS OF DRACULA (Magazine)
Modern Day Periodical/Eerie Publ.: Vol. 1 #3, May, 1979 - Vol. 3 #2, Sept, 1981 (B&W)
Vol. 1 #3 (5/79, 1st issue) 4 8 12 27 44 60
#4(8/79), #5(11/79) 3 6 9 20 31 42
Vol. 2 #1-3: 1-(2/80). 2-(5/80). 3-(8/80) 3 6 9 17 25 34
Vol. 3 #1 (5/81), #2 (9/81) 3 6 9 19 30 40

TERRORS OF THE JUNGLE (Formerly Jungle Thrills)
Star Publications: No. 17, 5/52 - No. 21, 2/53; No. 4, 4/53 - No. 10, 9/54
17-Reprints Rulah #21, used in **SOTI**; L.B. Cole bondage-c 77 154 231 493 847 1200
18-Jo-Jo-r 55 110 165 352 601 850
19,20(1952)-Jo-Jo-r; Disbrow-a 53 106 159 334 567 800
21-Jungle Jo, Tangi-r; used in **POP**, pg. 100 & color illos. 55 110 165 352 601 850
4-10: All Disbrow-a. 5-Jo-Jo-r. 8-Rulah, Jo-Jo-r. 9-Jo-Jo-r; Disbrow-a; Tangi by Orlando10-Rulah-r 55 110 165 352 601 850
NOTE: ***L.B. Cole** c-all; bondage c-17, 19, 21, 5, 7.*

TERROR TALES (See Beware Terror Tales)

Terry and the Pirates #5 © NYNS

Tessie the Typist #7 © MAR

Texas Kid #7 © MAR

TERROR TALES (Magazine)
Eerie Publications: V1#7, 1969 - V6#6, Dec, 1974; V7#1, Apr, 1976 - V10, 1979? (V1-V6: 52 pgs.; V7 on: 68 pgs.)

	GD 2.0	VG 4.0	FN 6.0	VF 8.0	VF/NM 9.0	NM- 9.2
V1#7	8	16	24	56	108	160
V1#8-11('69): 9-Bondage-c	6	12	18	38	69	100
V2#1-6('70), V3#1-6('71), V4#1-7('72), V5#1-6('73), V6#1-6('74), V7#1,4('76) (no V7#2), V8#1-3('77)	5	10	15	34	60	85
V7#3-(7/76) LSD story-r/Weird V3#5	5	10	15	34	60	85
V9#2-4, V10#1(1/79)	5	10	15	35	63	90

TERROR TITANS
DC Comics: Dec, 2008 - No. 6, May, 2009 ($2.99, limited series)

	GD 2.0	VG 4.0	FN 6.0	VF 8.0	VF/NM 9.0	NM- 9.2
1-6: 1-Ravager and Clock King at the Dark Side Club; Bennett-a. 3-Static app.						3.00
TPB (2009, $17.99) r/#1-6						18.00

TERRY AND THE PIRATES (See Famous Feature Stories, Merry Christmas From Sears Toyland, Popular Comics, Super Book #3,5,9,16,28, & Super Comics)

TERRY AND THE PIRATES
Dell Publishing Co.: 1939 - 1953 (By Milton Caniff)

	GD 2.0	VG 4.0	FN 6.0	VF 8.0	VF/NM 9.0	NM- 9.2
Large Feature Comic 2(1939)	119	238	357	762	1306	1850
Large Feature Comic 6(1938)-r/1936 dailies	84	168	252	538	919	1300
Four Color 9(1940)	81	162	243	518	884	1250
Large Feature Comic 27('41), 6('42)	71	142	213	454	777	1100
Four Color 44('43)	31	62	93	223	499	775
Four Color 101('45)	20	40	60	135	.300	465
Family Album(1942)	20	40	60	118	192	265

TERRY AND THE PIRATES (Formerly Boy Explorers; Long John Silver & the Pirates #30 on) (Daily strip-r) (Two #26's)
Harvey Publications/Charlton No. 26-28: No. 3, 4/47 - No. 26, 4/51; No. 26, 6/55 - No. 28, 10/55

	GD 2.0	VG 4.0	FN 6.0	VF 8.0	VF/NM 9.0	NM- 9.2
3(#1)-Boy Explorers by S&K; Terry & the Pirates begin by Caniff; 1st app. The Dragon Lady	40	80	120	246	411	575
4-S&K Boy Explorers	22	44	66	132	216	300
5-11: 11-Man in Black app. by Powell	13	26	39	72	101	130
12-20: 16-Girl threatened with red hot poker	10	20	30	56	76	95
21-26(4/51)-Last Caniff issue & last pre-code issue	10	20	30	54	72	90
26-28('55)(Formerly This Is Suspense)-No Caniff-a	9	18	27	47	61	75

NOTE: *Powell a (Tommy Tween)-5-10, 12, 14; 15-17(1/2 to 2 pgs. each).*

TERRY BEARS COMICS (TerryToons, The... #4)
St. John Publishing Co.: June, 1952 - No. 3, Mar, 1953

	GD 2.0	VG 4.0	FN 6.0	VF 8.0	VF/NM 9.0	NM- 9.2
1-By Paul Terry	14	28	42	78	112	145
2,3	9	18	27	50	65	80

TERRY-TOONS ALBUM (See Giant Comics Edition)

TERRY-TOONS COMICS (1st Series) (Becomes Paul Terry's Comics #85 on; later issues titled "Paul Terry's...")
Timely/Marvel No. 1-59 (8/47)(Becomes Best Western No. 58 on?, Marvel)/ St. John No. 60 (9/47) on: Oct, 1942 - No. 86, May, 1951

	GD 2.0	VG 4.0	FN 6.0	VF 8.0	VF/NM 9.0	NM- 9.2
1 (Scarce)-Features characters that 1st app. on movie screen; Gandy Goose & Sourpuss begin; war-c; Gandy Goose c-1-37	271	542	813	1734	2967	4200
2	97	194	291	621	1061	1500
3-5	63	126	189	403	689	975
6,8-10: 9,10-World War II gag-c	48	96	144	302	514	725
7-Hitler, Hirohito, Mussolini-c	258	516	774	1651	2826	4000
11-20	34	68	102	196	321	445
21-37	24	48	72	140	230	320
38-Mighty Mouse begins (1st app., 11/45); Mighty Mouse-c begin, end #86; Gandy, Sourpuss welcome Mighty Mouse on-c	239	478	717	1530	2615	3700
39-2nd app. Mighty Mouse	68	136	204	435	743	1050
40-49: 43-Infinity-c	37	74	111	222	361	500
50-1st app. Heckle & Jeckle (11/46)	73	146	219	461	796	1125
51-60: 55-Infinity-c. 60-(9/47)-Atomic explosion panel; 1st St. John issue	20	40	60	114	182	250
61-86: 85,86-Same book as Paul Terry's Comics #85,86 with only a title change; published at same time?	15	30	45	88	137	185

TERRY-TOONS COMICS (2nd Series)
St. John Publishing Co./Pines: June, 1952 - No. 9, Nov, 1953; 1957; 1958

	GD 2.0	VG 4.0	FN 6.0	VF 8.0	VF/NM 9.0	NM- 9.2
1-Gandy Goose & Sourpuss begin by Paul Terry	19	38	57	112	179	245
2	10	20	30	58	79	100
3-9	9	18	27	52	69	85
Giant Summer Fun Book 101,102-(Sum, 1957, Sum, 1958, 25¢, Pines)(TV) CBS Television Presents...; Tom Terrific, Mighty Mouse, Heckle & Jeckle Gandy Goose app.	14	28	42	80	115	150

TERRYTOONS, THE TERRY BEARS (Formerly Terry Bears Comics)
Pines Comics: No. 4, Summer, 1958 (CBS Television Presents...)

	GD 2.0	VG 4.0	FN 6.0	VF 8.0	VF/NM 9.0	NM- 9.2
4	8	16	24	44	57	70

TESSIE THE TYPIST (Tiny Tessie #24; see Comedy Comics, Gay Comics & Joker Comics)
Timely/Marvel Comics (20CC): Summer, 1944 - No. 23, Aug, 1949

	GD 2.0	VG 4.0	FN 6.0	VF 8.0	VF/NM 9.0	NM- 9.2
1-Doc Rockblock & others by Wolverton	200	400	600	1280	2190	3100
2-Wolverton's Powerhouse Pepper	77	154	231	493	847	1200
3-(3/45)-No Wolverton	43	84	126	265	445	625
4,5,7,8-Wolverton-a. 4-(Fall/45)	48	96	114	302	514	725
6-Kurtzman's "Hey Look", 2 pgs. Wolverton-a	50	100	150	315	533	750
9-Wolverton's Powerhouse Pepper (8 pgs.) & 1 pg. Kurtzman's "Hey Look"	48	96	144	302	514	725
10-Wolverton's Powerhouse Pepper (4 pgs.)	48	96	144	302	514	725
11-Wolverton's Powerhouse Pepper (8 pgs.)	50	100	150	315	533	750
12-Wolverton's Powerhouse Pepper (4 pgs.) & 1 pg. Kurtzman's "Hey Look"	48	96	144	302	514	725
13-Wolverton's Powerhouse Pepper (4 pgs.)	48	96	144	302	514	725
14,15: 14-Wolverton's Dr. Whackyhack (1 pg.); 1-1/2 pgs. Kurtzman's "Hey Look". 15-Kurtzman's "Hey Look" (3 pgs.) & 3 pgs. Giggles 'n' Grins	37	74	111	218	354	490
16-18-Kurtzman's "Hey Look" (?, 2 & 1 pg.)	30	60	90	177	289	400
19-Annie Oakley story (8 pgs.)	24	48	72	140	230	320
20-23: 20-Anti-Wertham editorial (2/49)	22	44	66	132	216	300

NOTE: *Lana app.-21. Millie The Model app.-13, 15, 17, 21. Rusty app.-10, 11, 13, 15, 17.*

TESTAMENT
DC Comics (Vertigo): Feb, 2006 - No. 22, Mar, 2008 ($2.99)

	GD 2.0	VG 4.0	FN 6.0	VF 8.0	VF/NM 9.0	NM- 9.2
1-22: 1-5-Rushkoff-s/Sharp-a. 6,7-Gross & Erskine-a						3.00

TEXAN, THE (Fightin' Marines #15 on; Fightin' Texan #16 on)
St. John Publishing Co.: Aug, 1948 - No. 15, Oct, 1951

	GD 2.0	VG 4.0	FN 6.0	VF 8.0	VF/NM 9.0	NM- 9.2
1-Buckskin Belle	22	44	66	132	216	300
2	14	28	42	80	115	150
3,10: 10-Oversized issue	14	28	42	82	121	160
4,5,7,15-Baker-c/a	34	68	102	204	332	460
6,9-Baker-c	29	58	87	170	278	385
8,11,13,14-Baker-c/a(2-3) each	39	78	117	231	378	525
12-All Matt Baker-c/a; Peyote story	42	84	126	265	445	625

NOTE: ***Matt Baker** c-4-9, 11-15. **Larsen** a-4-6, 8-10, 15. **Tuska** a-1, 2, 7-9.*

TEXAN, THE (TV)
Dell Publishing Co.: No. 1027, Sept-Nov, 1959 - No. 1096, May-July, 1960

	GD 2.0	VG 4.0	FN 6.0	VF 8.0	VF/NM 9.0	NM- 9.2
Four Color 1027 (#1)-Photo-c	8	16	24	55	105	155
Four Color 1096-Rory Calhoun photo-c	7	14	21	46	86	125

TEXAS CHAINSAW MASSACRE
DC Comics (WildStorm): Jan, 2007 - No. 6, Jun, 2007 ($2.99, limited series)

	GD 2.0	VG 4.0	FN 6.0	VF 8.0	VF/NM 9.0	NM- 9.2
1-6: 1-Two covers by Bermejo & Bradstreet; Abnett & Lanning-s						3.00
...: About a Boy #1 (9/07, $2.99) Abnett & Lanning-s/Gomez-a/Robertson-c						3.00
...: Book Two TPB (2009, $14.99) r/one shots & New Line Cinema's Tales of Horror story						15.00
...: By Himself #1 (10/07, $2.99) Abnett & Lanning-s/Craig-a/Robertson-c						3.00
...: Cut! #1 (8/07, $2.99) Pfeiffer-s/Raffaele-a/Robertson-c						3.00
...: Raising Cain 1-3 (7/08 - No. 3, 9/08, $3.50) Bruce Jones-s/Chris Gugliotti-a						3.50

TEXAS JOHN SLAUGHTER (See Walt Disney Presents, 4-Color #997, 1181 & #2)

TEXAS KID (See Two-Gun Western, Wild Western)
Marvel/Atlas Comics (LMC): Jan, 1951 - No. 10, July, 1952

	GD 2.0	VG 4.0	FN 6.0	VF 8.0	VF/NM 9.0	NM- 9.2
1-Origin; Texas Kid (alias Lance Temple) & his horse Thunder begin; Tuska-a	31	62	93	184	300	415
2	15	30	45	92	144	195
3-10	14	28	42	78	112	145

NOTE: ***Maneely** a-1-4; c-1, 3, 5-10.*

TEXAS RANGERS, THE (See Jace Pearson of... and Superior Stories #4)

TEXAS RANGERS IN ACTION (Formerly Captain Gallant or Scotland Yard?)
Charlton Comics: No. 5, Jul, 1956 - No. 79, Aug, 1970 (See Blue Bird Comics)

	GD 2.0	VG 4.0	FN 6.0	VF 8.0	VF/NM 9.0	NM- 9.2
5	9	18	27	47	61	75
6,7,9,10	6	12	18	31	38	45
8-Ditko-a (signed)	10	20	30	54	72	90
11-(68 pg. Giant) Williamson-a (5&8 pgs.); Torres/Williamson-a (5 pgs.)	10	20	30	54	72	90
12-(68 pg. Giant, 6/58)	6	12	18	28	34	40
13-Williamson-a (5 pgs); Torres, Morisi-a	8	16	24	42	54	65
14-20	5	10	15	23	28	32
21-30	3	6	9	15	22	28
31-59: 32-Both 10¢-c & 15¢-c exist	2	4	6	13	18	22

Tex Ritter Western #3 © FAW

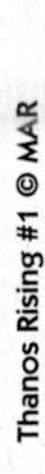
Thanos Rising #1 © MAR

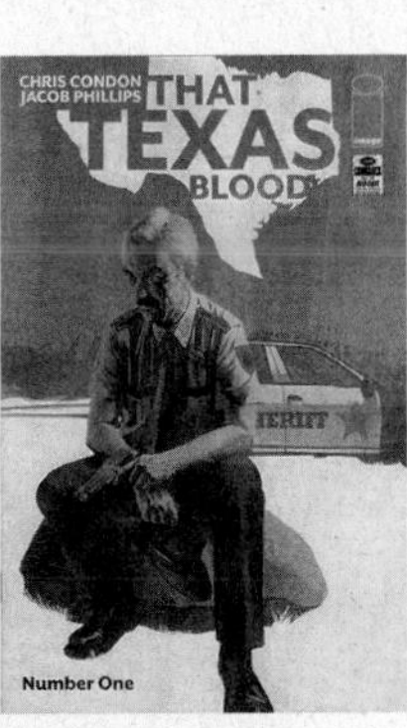

That Texas Blood #1 © Condon & Phillips

	GD 2.0	VG 4.0	FN 6.0	VF 8.0	VF/NM 9.0	NM- 9.2

60-Riley's Rangers begin 3 6 9 14 19 24
61-65,68-70 2 4 6 8 11 14
66,67: 66-1st app. The Man Called Loco. 67-Origin 2 4 6 9 13 16
71-79: 77-(4/70) Ditko-c & a (8 pgs.) 1 3 4 6 8 10
76 (Modern Comics-r, 1977) 6.00

TEXAS SLIM (See A-1 Comics)

TEX DAWSON, GUN-SLINGER (Gunslinger #2 on)
Marvel Comics Group: Jan, 1973 (20¢)(Also see Western Kid, 1st series)

1-Steranko-c; Williamson-r (4 pgs.); Tex Dawson-r by Romita(3) from 1955; Tuska-r 3 6 9 21 33 45

TEX FARNUM (See Wisco)

TEX FARRELL (...Pride of the Wild West)
D. S. Publishing Co.: Mar-Apr, 1948

1-Tex Farrell & his horse Lightning; Shelly-c 16 32 48 98 154 210

TEX GRANGER (Formerly Calling All Boys; see True Comics)
Parents' Magazine Inst./Commended: No. 18, Jun, 1948 - No. 24, Sept, 1949

18-Tex Granger & his horse Bullet begin 14 28 42 80 115 150
19 11 22 33 62 86 110
20-24: 22-Wild Bill Hickok story. 23-Vs. Billy the Kid; Tim Holt app. 9 18 27 50 65 80

TEX MORGAN (See Blaze Carson and Wild Western)
Marvel Comics (CCC): Aug, 1948 - No. 9, Feb, 1950

1-Tex Morgan, his horse Lightning & sidekick Lobo begin 31 62 93 186 303 420
2 20 40 60 118 192 255
3-6: 3,4-Arizona Annie app. 5-Blaze Carson app. 14 28 42 76 108 140
7-9: All photo-c. 7-Captain Tootsie by Beck. 8-18 pg. story "The Terror of Rimrock Valley"; Diablo app. 18 36 54 105 165 225

NOTE: *Tex Taylor app. 2-6, 7, 9.* ***Brodsky*** *c-6.* ***Syd Shores*** *c-2, 5.*

TEX RITTER WESTERN (Movie star; singing cowboy; see Six-Gun Heroes and Western Hero)
Fawcett No. 1-20 (1/54)/Charlton No. 21 on: Oct, 1950 - No. 46, May, 1959 (Photo-c: 1-21)

1-Tex Ritter, his stallion White Flash & dog Fury begin; photo front/back-c begin 43 86 129 271 461 650
2 21 42 63 124 202 280
3-5: 5-Last photo back-c 16 32 48 94 147 200
6-10 14 28 42 80 115 150
11-19 10 20 30 58 79 100
20-Last Fawcett issue (1/54) 11 22 33 62 86 110
21-1st Charlton issue; photo-c (3/54) 14 28 42 80 115 150
22-B&W photo back-c begin, end #32 9 18 27 52 69 85
23-30: 23-25-Young Falcon app. 9 18 27 47 61 75
31-38,40-45 8 16 24 42 54 65
39-Williamson-a; Whitman-c (1/58) 9 18 27 47 61 75
46-Last issue 8 16 24 44 57 70

TEX TAYLOR (...The Fighting Cowboy on-c #1, 2)(See Blaze Carson, Kid Colt, Tex Morgan, Wild West, Wild Western, & Wisco)
Marvel Comics (HPC): Sept, 1948 - No. 9, March, 1950

1-Tex Taylor & his horse Fury begin; Blaze Carson app. 32 64 96 192 314 435
2-Blaze Carson app. 16 32 48 98 154 210
3-Arizona Annie app. 15 30 45 90 140 190
4-6: All photo-c; Blaze Carson app. 4-Anti-Wertham editorial 17 34 51 103 162 220
7-9: 7-Photo-c;18 pg. Movie-Length Thriller "Trapped in Time's Lost Land!" with sabretoothed tigers, dinosaurs; Diablo app. 8-Photo-c; 18 pg. Movie-Length Thriller "The Mystery of Devil-Tree Plateau!" with dwarf horses, dwarf people & a lost miniature Inca type village; Diablo app. 9-Photo-c; 18 pg. Movie-Length Thriller "Guns Along the Border!" Captain Tootsie by Schreiber; Nimo the Mountain Lion app.; Heth-a 20 40 60 115 188 260

NOTE: ***Syd Shores*** *c-1-3.*

THANE OF BAGARTH (Also see Hercules, 1967 series)
Charlton Comics: No. 24, Oct, 1985 - No. 25, Dec, 1985

24,25-Low print run 6.00

THANOS
Marvel Comics: Dec, 2003 - No. 12, Sept, 2004 ($2.99)

1-12: 1-6-Starlin-s/a(p)/Milgrom-i; Galactus app. 7-12-Giffen-s/Lim-a 5.00
Annual 1 (7/14, $4.99) Starlin-s/Lim-a/Keown-c 5.00
...: The Final Threat (11/12, $4.99) r/Avengers Ann. #7 & Marvel Two-In-One Ann. #2 5.00
Vol. 4: Epiphany TPB (2004, $14.99) r/#1-6 15.00
Vol. 5: Samaritan TPB (2004, $14.99) r/#7-12 15.00

THANOS (Also see Cosmic Ghost Rider series)
Marvel Comics: Jan, 2017 - No. 18, Jun, 2018 ($3.99)

1-12: 1-6-Lemire-s/Deodato-a. 1-Starfox & Thane app. 2-Nebula app. 3-Imperial Guard app. 7-12-Peralta-a 4.00
13-1st app. Cosmic Ghost Rider 30.00
14-Cosmic Ghost Rider app. 10.00
15-Cosmic Ghost Rider revealed as Frank Castle 30.00
16-18: 16-Origin Cosmic Ghost Rider. 17,18-Death app. 5.00
Annual 1 (6/18, $4.99) Short stories by various; hosted by Cosmic Ghost Rider 5.00
... Legacy 1 (11/18, $4.99) Cates & Duggan-s; Cosmic Ghost Rider app. 5.00

THANOS
Marvel Comics: Jun, 2019 - No. 6, Nov, 2019 ($3.99, limited series)

1-($4.99) Tini Howard-s/Ariel Olivetti-a; retells Thanos' first meeting with Gamora 5.00
2-6-($3.99) 4.00

THANOS: A GOD UP THERE LISTENING
Marvel Comics: Dec, 2014 - No. 4, Dec, 2014 ($3.99, weekly limited series)

1-4-Thane and Ego The Living Planet app. 4.00

THANOS IMPERATIVE, THE
Marvel Comics: Aug, 2010 - No. 6, Jan, 2011 ($3.99, limited series)

1-6-Abnett & Lanning-s/Sepulveda-a; Vision and Silver Surfer app. 4.00
...: Devastation (3/11, $3.99) Sepulveda-a; leads into The Annihilators #1 4.00
...: Ignition (7/10, $3.99) Walker-a; prequel to series 4.00
Thanos Sourcebook (8/10, $3.99) profiles/history of Thanos and Nova Corps members 4.00

THANOS QUEST, THE (See Capt. Marvel #25, Infinity Gauntlet, Iron Man #55, Logan's Run, Marvel Feature #12, Marvel Universe: The End, Silver Surfer #34 & Warlock #9)
Marvel Comics: 1990 - No. 2, 1990 ($4.95, squarebound, 52 pgs.)

1,2-Both have Starlin scripts & covers (both printings) 3 6 9 17 25 34
1-(3/2000, $3.99) r/material from #1&2 5.00
1-(11/12, $7,99) r/#1&2, new cover by Andy Park 8.00

THANOS: THE INFINITY FINALE (Conclusion to The Infinity Entity series)
Marvel Comics: 2016 ($24.99, HC original graphic novel)

HC - Jim Starlin-s/Ron Lim-a; Adam Warlock & Annihilus app. 25.00

THANOS: THE INFINITY REVELATION (Prelude to The Infinity Entity series)
Marvel Comics: 2014 ($24.99, HC original graphic novel)

HC - Jim Starlin-s/a; Adam Warlock & Silver Surfer app. 25.00

THANOS VS. HULK
Marvel Comics: Feb, 2015 - No. 4, May, 2015 ($3.99, limited series)

1-4-Jim Starlin-s/a/c; Annihilus, Pip the Troll and Iron Man app. 4.00

THAT DARN CAT (See Movie Comics & Walt Disney Showcase #19)

THAT'S MY POP! GOES NUTS FOR FAIR
Bystander Press: 1939 (76 pgs., B&W)

nn-by Milt Gross 39 78 117 240 395 550

THAT TEXAS BLOOD
Image Comics: Jun, 2020 - Present ($3.99)

1-6-Chris Condon-s/Jacob Phillips-a 4.00

THAT WILKIN BOY (Meet Bingo...)
Archie Publications: Jan, 1969 - No. 52, Oct, 1982

1-1st app. Bingo's Band, Samantha & Tough Teddy 5 10 15 31 53 75
2-5 3 6 9 16 23 30
6-11 2 4 6 13 18 22
12-26-Giants. 12-No # on-c 3 6 9 14 20 26
27-40(1/77) 2 4 6 8 10 12
41-49 1 2 3 4 5 7
50-52 (low print) 2 4 6 8 10 12

THB
Horse Press: Oct, 1994 - 2002 ($5.50/$2.50/$2.95, B&W)

1 ($5.50) Paul Pope-s/a in all 3 6 9 21 33 45
1 (2nd Printing)-r/#1 w/new material 6.00
2 ($2.50) 3 6 9 14 20 26
3-5 2 4 6 8 10 12
69 (1995, no price, low distribution, 12 pgs.)-story reprinted in #1 (2nd Printing) 4.00
Giant THB-($4.95) 5.00
Giant THB 1 V2-(2003, $6.95) 7.00
...M3/THB: Mars' Mightiest Mek #1 (2000, $3.95) 4.00
...6A: Mek-Power #1, 6B: Mek-Power #2, 6C: Mek-Power #3 (2000, $3.95) 4.00
... 6D: Mek-Power #4 (2002, $4.95) 5.00

Thief of Thieves #39 © Skybound

The Thing! #2 © CC

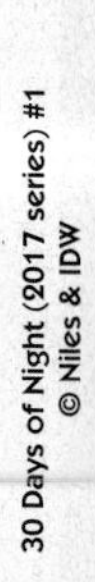
30 Days of Night (2017 series) #1 © Niles & IDW

T.H.E. CAT (TV)
Dell Publishing Co.: Mar, 1967 - No. 4, Oct, 1967 (All have photo-c)

	GD 2.0	VG 4.0	FN 6.0	VF 8.0	VF/NM 9.0	NM- 9.2
1	4	8	12	22	35	48
2-4	3	6	9	16	24	32

THERE'S A NEW WORLD COMING
Spire Christian Comics/Fleming H. Revell Co.: 1973 (35/49¢)

	GD 2.0	VG 4.0	FN 6.0	VF 8.0	VF/NM 9.0	NM- 9.2
nn	2	4	6	10	14	18

THEY ALL KISSED THE BRIDE (See Cinema Comics Herald)

THEY'RE NOT LIKE US
Image Comics: Dec, 2014 - No. 16, Oct, 2017 ($2.99)

	NM- 9.2
1-16-Stephenson-s/Gane-a/c	3.00

THIEF OF BAGHDAD
Dell Publishing Co.: No. 1229, Oct-Dec, 1961 (one-shot)

	GD 2.0	VG 4.0	FN 6.0	VF 8.0	VF/NM 9.0	NM- 9.2
Four Color 1229-Movie, Crandall/Evans-a, photo-c	6	12	18	41	76	110

THIEF OF THIEVES
Image Comics: Feb, 2012 - No. 43, Jul, 2019 ($2.99/$3.99)

	NM- 9.2
1-Kirkman & Spencer-s/Martinbrough-a/c	30.00
1-Second printing	8.00
2	10.00
3,4	8.00
5-37: 8-13-Asmus-s	3.00
38-43-($3.99)	4.00

THIMK (Magazine) (Satire)
Counterpoint: May, 1958 - No. 6, May, 1959

	GD 2.0	VG 4.0	FN 6.0	VF 8.0	VF/NM 9.0	NM- 9.2
1	12	24	36	69	97	125
2-6	9	18	27	47	61	75

THING!, THE (Blue Beetle #18 on)
Song Hits No. 1,2/Capitol Stories/Charlton: Feb, 1952 - No. 17, Nov, 1954

	GD 2.0	VG 4.0	FN 6.0	VF 8.0	VF/NM 9.0	NM- 9.2
1-Weird/horror stories in all; shrunken head-c	129	258	387	826	1413	2000
2,3	81	162	243	518	884	1250
4,6,8,10: 6-Classic decapitation story	74	148	222	470	810	1150
5-Severed head-c; headlights	81	162	243	518	884	1250
7-Injury to eye-c & inside panel	110	220	330	704	1202	1700
9-Used in **SOTI**, pg. 388 & illo "Stomping on the face is a form of brutality which modern children learn early"	123	246	369	787	1344	1900
11-Necronomicon story; Hansel & Gretel parody; Injury-to-eye panel; Check-a	97	194	291	621	1061	1500
12-1st published Ditko-c; "Cinderella" parody; lingerie panels. Ditko-a	168	336	504	1075	1838	2600
13,15-Ditko-c/a(3 & 5)	142	284	426	909	1555	2200
14-Extreme violence/torture; Rumpelstiltskin story; Ditko-c/a(4)	138	276	414	883	1517	2150
16-Injury to eye panel	39	78	117	231	378	525
17-Ditko-c; classic parody "Through the Looking Glass"; Powell-r/Beware Terror Tales #1 & recolored	100	200	300	640	1095	1550

NOTE: *Excessive violence, severed heads, injury to eye are common No. 5 on.* ***Al Fago*** *c-4.* ***Forgione*** *c-1i, 2, 6, 8, 9. All* ***Ditko*** *issues #14, 15.* ***Giordano*** *a-6.*

THING, THE (See Fantastic Four, Marvel Fanfare, Marvel Feature #11,12, Marvel Two-In-One and Startling Stories:...- Night Falls on Yancy Street)
Marvel Comics Group: July, 1983 - No. 36, June, 1986

	GD 2.0	VG 4.0	FN 6.0	VF 8.0	VF/NM 9.0	NM- 9.2
1-Life story of Ben Grimm; Byrne scripts begin	3	6	9	16	24	32
2-5: 5-Spider-Man, She-Hulk and Wonder-Man app.						6.00
6-10: 7-1st app. Goody Two-Shoes. 8-She-Hulk app. 10-Secret Wars tie-in						5.00
11-36						4.00

NOTE: ***Byrne*** *a-2i, 7; c-1, 7, 36i; scripts-1-13, 19-22.* ***Sienkiewicz*** *c-13i.*

THING, THE (Fantastic Four)
Marvel Comics: Jan, 2006 - No. 8, Aug, 2006 ($2.99)

	NM- 9.2
1-8: 1-DiVito-a/Slott-s. 4-Lockjaw app. 6-Spider-Man app. 8-Super-Hero poker game	3.00
...: Idol of Millions TPB (2006, $20.99) r/#1-8; Divito sketch page	21.00

THING & SHE-HULK: THE LONG NIGHT (Fantastic Four)
Marvel Comics: May, 2002 ($2.99, one-shot)

	NM- 9.2
1-Hitch-c/a(pg. 1-25); Reis-a(pg. 26-39); Dezago-s	3.00

THING, THE (From Another World)
Dark Horse Comics: 1991 - No. 2, 1992 ($2.95, mini-series, stiff-c)

	NM- 9.2
1,2-Based on Universal movie; painted-c/a	5.00

THING, THE: FREAKSHOW (Fantastic Four)
Marvel Comics: Aug, 2002 - No. 4, Nov, 2002 ($2.99, limited series)

	NM- 9.2
1-4-Geoff Johns-s/Scott Kolins-a	3.00
TPB (2005, $17.99) r/#1-4 & Thing & She-Hulk: The Long Night one-shot	18.00

THING FROM ANOTHER WORLD: CLIMATE OF FEAR, THE
Dark Horse Comics: July, 1992 - No. 4, Dec, 1992 ($2.50, mini-series)

	NM- 9.2
1-4: Painted-c	4.00

THING FROM ANOTHER WORLD: ETERNAL VOWS
Dark Horse Comics: Dec, 1993 - No. 4, 1994 ($2.50, mini-series)

	NM- 9.2
1-4-Gulacy-c/a	4.00

THINK TANK (Also see Eden's Fall)
Image Comics (Top Cow): Aug, 2012 - No. 12, Feb, 2014 ($3.99)

	NM- 9.2
1-12-Hawkins-s/Ekedal-a	4.00

THINK TANK: ANIMAL
Image Comics (Top Cow): Mar, 2017 - No. 3 ($3.99)

	NM- 9.2
1-3-Hawkins-s/Ekedal-a	4.00

THINK TANK: CREATIVE DESTRUCTION
Image Comics (Top Cow): Apr, 2016 - No. 4, Jul, 2016 ($3.99, limited series)

	NM- 9.2
1-4-Hawkins-s/Ekedal-a	4.00

THIRTEEN (...Going on 18)
Dell Publishing Co.: 11-1/61-62 - No. 25, 12/67; No. 26, 7/69 - No. 29, 1/71

	GD 2.0	VG 4.0	FN 6.0	VF 8.0	VF/NM 9.0	NM- 9.2
1	5	10	15	35	63	90
2-10	4	8	12	28	47	65
11-25	4	8	12	23	37	50
26-29-r	3	6	9	17	26	35

NOTE: ***John Stanley*** *script-No. 3-29; art?*

13: ASSASSIN
TSR, Inc.: 1990 - No. 8, 1991 ($2.95, 44 pgs.)

	NM- 9.2
1-8: Agent 13; Alcala-a(i); Springer back-up-a	4.00

13th ARTIFACT, THE
Image Comics (Top Cow): Mar, 2016 ($3.99, one-shot)

	NM- 9.2
1-Amit Chauhan-s/Eli Powell-a	4.00

13th SON, THE
Dark Horse Comics: Nov, 2005 - No. 4, Feb, 2006 ($2.99, limited series)

	NM- 9.2
1-4-Kelley Jones-s/a/c	3.00

30 DAYS OF NIGHT
Idea + Design Works: June, 2002 - No. 3, Oct, 2002 ($3.99, limited series)

	NM- 9.2
1-Vampires in Alaska; Steve Niles-s/Ben Templesmith-a/Ashley Wood-c	80.00
1-2nd printing	10.00
2	26.00
3	12.00
Annual 2004 (1/04, $4.99) Niles-s/art by Templesmith and others	5.00
Annual 2005 (12/05, $7.49) Niles-s/art by Nat Jones	7.50
... 5th Anniversary (10/07 - No. 3, $2.99) reprints original series	3.00
... Sourcebook (10/07, $7.49) Illustrated guide to the 30 Days world	7.50
... Three Tales TPB (7/06, $19.99) r/Annual 2005, ...: Dead Space #1-3, and short story from Tales of Terror (IDW's...)	20.00
Hundred Penny Press: 30 Days of Night #1 (5/11, $1.00) r/#1	3.00
... 100-Page Giant (3/19, $4.99) r/30 Days of Night: Eben & Stella #1-3	5.00
TPB (2003, $17.99) r/#1-3, foreward by Clive Barker; script for #1	18.00
The Complete 30 Days of Night (2004, $75.00, oversized hardcover with slipcase) r/#1-3; prequel; script pages for #1-3; original cover and promotional materials	75.00

30 DAYS OF NIGHT
IDW Publishing: July, 2004 (Free Comic Book Day edition)

	NM- 9.2
Previews CSI: Bad Rap; The Shield: Spotlight; 24: One Shot; and 30 Days of Night	3.00

30 DAYS OF NIGHT (Ongoing series)
IDW Publishing: Oct, 2011 - No. 12, Nov, 2012 ($3.99)

	NM- 9.2
1-12: 1-4-Niles-s/Kieth-a; covers by Kieth and Furno. 5-12-Niles-s	4.00

30 DAYS OF NIGHT (2017 reimagining of original series)
IDW Publishing: Dec, 2017 - No. 6, May, 2018 ($3.99, limited series)

	NM- 9.2
1-6-Niles-s/Kowalski-a; covers by Kowalski, Wood and Templesmith	4.00

30 DAYS OF NIGHT: BEYOND BARROW
IDW Publishing: Sept, 2007 - No. 3, Dec, 2007 ($3.99, limited series)

	NM- 9.2
1-3-Niles-s/Sienkiewicz-a/c	4.00

30 DAYS OF NIGHT: BLOODSUCKER TALES
IDW Publishing: Oct, 2004 - No. 8, May, 2005 ($3.99, limited series)

	NM- 9.2
1-8-Niles-s/Chamberlain-a; Fraction-s/Templesmith-a/c	4.00
HC (8/05, $49.99) r/#1-8; cover gallery	50.00

This is War #7 © STD

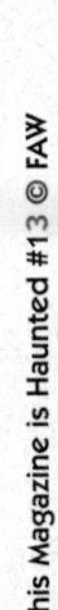

This Magazine is Haunted #13 © FAW

Thor #171 © MAR

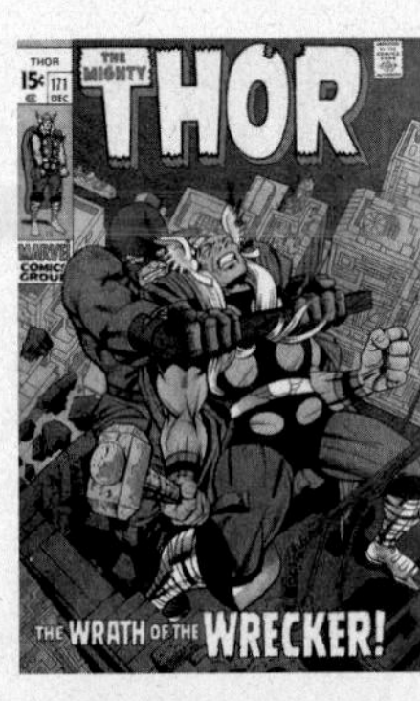

	GD	VG	FN	VF	VF/NM	NM-
	2.0	4.0	6.0	8.0	9.0	9.2

SC (8/05, $24.99) r/#1-8; cover gallery 25.00

30 DAYS OF NIGHT: DEAD SPACE
IDW Publishing: Jan, 2006 - No. 3, Mar, 2006 ($3.99, limited series)
1-3-Niles and Wickline-s/Milx-a/c 4.00

30 DAYS OF NIGHT: EBEN & STELLA
IDW Publishing: May, 2007 - No. 3, July, 2007 ($3.99, limited series)
1-3-Niles and DeConnick-s/Randall-a/c 4.00

30 DAYS OF NIGHT: NIGHT, AGAIN
IDW Publishing: May, 2011 - No. 4, Aug, 2011 ($3.99, limited series)
1-4-Lansdale-s/Kieth-a/c 4.00

30 DAYS OF NIGHT: RED SNOW
IDW Publishing: Aug, 2007 - No. 3, Oct, 2007 ($3.99, limited series)
1-3-Ben Templesmith-s/a/c 4.00

30 DAYS OF NIGHT: RETURN TO BARROW
IDW Publishing: Mar, 2004 - No. 6, Aug, 2004 ($3.99, limited series)
1-6-Steve Niles-s/Ben Templesmith-a/c 4.00
TPB (2004, $19.99) r/#1-6; cover gallery 20.00

30 DAYS OF NIGHT: SPREADING THE DISEASE
IDW Publishing: Dec, 2006 - No. 5, Apr, 2007 ($3.99, limited series)
1-5: 1-Wickline-s/Sanchez-a. 3-5-Sandoval-a 4.00

30 DAYS OF NIGHT: 30 DAYS 'TIL DEATH
IDW Publishing: Dec, 2008 - No. 4, Mar, 2009 ($3.99, limited series)
1-4-David Lapham-s/a; covers by Lapham and Templesmith 4.00

THIRTY SECONDS OVER TOKYO (See American Library)

THIS DAMNED BAND
Dark Horse Comics: Aug, 2016 - No. 6, Jan, 2016 ($3.99, limited series)
1-6-Paul Cornell-s/Tony Parker-a 4.00

THIS IS SUSPENSE! (Formerly Strange Suspense Stories; Strange Suspense Stories #27 on)
Charlton Comics: No. 23, Feb, 1955 - No. 26, Aug, 1955
23-Wood-a(r)/A Star Presentation #3 "Dr. Jekyll & Mr. Hyde"; last pre-code issue
27 54 81 158 259 360
24-Censored Fawcett-r; Evans-a (r/Suspense Detective #1)
15 30 45 86 133 180
25,26: 26-Marcus Swayze-a 12 24 36 67 94 120

THIS IS THE PAYOFF (See Pay-Off)

THIS IS WAR
Standard Comics: No. 5, July, 1952 - No. 9, May, 1953
5-Toth-a 20 40 60 114 182 250
6,9-Toth-a 15 30 45 85 130 175
7,8: 8-Ross Andru-c 13 26 39 72 101 130

THIS IS YOUR LIFE, DONALD DUCK (See Donald Duck..., Four Color #1109)

THIS MAGAZINE IS CRAZY (Crazy #? on)
Charlton Publ. (Humor Magazines): V3#2, July, 1957 - V4#8, Feb, 1959 (25¢, magazine, 68 pgs.)
V3#2-V4#7: V4#5-Russian Sputnik-c parody 11 22 33 64 90 115
V4#8-Davis-a (8 pgs.) 12 24 36 69 97 125

THIS MAGAZINE IS HAUNTED (Danger and Adventure #22 on)
Fawcett Publications/Charlton No. 15(2/54) on: Oct, 1951 - No. 14, 12/53; No. 15, 2/54 - V3#21, Nov, 1954
1-Evans-a; Dr. Death as host begins 87 174 261 553 952 1350
2,5-Evans-a 54 108 162 343 574 825
3,4: 3-Vampire-c/story 47 94 141 296 498 700
6-9,12 39 78 117 240 395 550
10-Severed head-c 87 174 261 553 952 1350
11-Classic skeleton-c 43 86 129 271 461 650
13-Severed head-c/story 73 146 219 467 796 1125
14-Classic burning skull-c 55 110 165 352 601 850
15,20: 15-Dick Giordano-c. 20-Cover is swiped from panel in The Thing #16
31 62 93 182 296 410
16,19-Ditko-c. 19-Injury-to-eye panel; story-r/#1 54 108 162 343 574 825
17-Ditko-c/a(4); blood drainage story 68 136 204 435 743 1050
18-Ditko-c/a(1 story); E.C. swipe/Haunt of Fear #5; injury-to-eye panel; reprints "Caretaker of the Dead" from Beware Terror Tales & recolored
60 120 180 381 653 925
21-Ditko-c, Evans-r/This Magazine Is Haunted #1 48 96 144 302 514 725
NOTE: *Baily a-1, 3, 4, 21r/#1. Moldoff c/a-1-13. Powell a-3-5, 11, 12, 17. Shuster a-18-20. Issues 19-21 have reprints which have been recolored from This Magazine is Haunted #1.*

THIS MAGAZINE IS HAUNTED (2nd Series) (Formerly Zaza the Mystic; Outer Space #17 on)
Charlton Comics: V2#12, July, 1957 - V2#16, May, 1958
V2#12-14-Ditko-c/a in all 53 106 159 334 567 800
15-No Ditko-c/a 20 40 60 115 188 260
16-Ditko-a(4). 39 78 117 240 395 550

THIS MAGAZINE IS WILD (See Wild)

THIS WAS YOUR LIFE (Religious)
Jack T. Chick Publ.: 1964 (3 1/2 x 5 1/2", 40 pgs., B&W and red)
nn, Another version (5x2 3/4", 26 pgs.) 2 4 6 10 14 18

THOR (See Avengers #1, Giant-Size..., Marvel Collectors Item Classics, Marvel Graphic Novel #33, Marvel Preview, Marvel Spectacular, Marvel Treasury Edition, Special Marvel Edition & Tales of Asgard)

THOR (Journey Into Mystery #1-125, 503-on)(The Mighty Thor #413-490)
Marvel Comics Group: No. 126, Mar, 1966 - No. 502, Sept, 1996
126-Thor continues (#125-130 Thor vs. Hercules); Tales of Asgard back-up stories continue through issue #145 38 76 114 285 641 1000
127-130: 127-1st app. Pluto. 129-1st Ares Olympian God of War & Tana Nile of the Rigillian Colonizers 10 20 30 70 150 230
131,135,137-140: 135-Origin of the High Evolutionary. 137-1st Ulik the Troll. 138-139-Thor vs. Ulik. 140-Kang app; 1st Growing Man 9 18 27 59 117 175
132-1st app. Ego the Living Planet 10 20 30 66 138 210
133-Thor vs. Ego 13 26 39 86 188 290
134-Intro High Evolutionary and Man-Beast 32 64 96 230 515 800
136-(1/67) Re-intro. Sif 9 18 27 60 120 180
141-145: 142-Thor vs. Super-Skrull. 143,144-Thor vs. the Enchanters
7 14 21 49 92 135
146,147: 146-Inhumans origin; begin (early app.) in back-up stories, end #152 (see Fantastic Four #45 for 1st app.). 147-Origin continues 8 16 24 54 102 150
148,149-Origin Black Bolt in each. 148-1st app. Wrecker. 149-Origin Medusa, Crystal, Maximus, Gorgon, Karnak 9 18 27 62 126 190
150-152: Inhumans app. 150-Hela app. 151,152-Destroyer and Ulik app.
8 16 24 52 99 145
153-157,159: 154-1st Mangog. 155-157-Thor vs Mangog. 159-Origin Dr. Blake (Thor) concl.
6 12 18 42 79 115
158-Origin-r/#83; origin Dr. Blake 9 18 27 57 111 165
160-162-Galactus app. 7 14 21 49 92 135
163,164-2nd & 3th brief app. Warlock (Him) 5 10 15 35 63 90
165-1st full app. Warlock (Him) (6/69, see Fantastic Four #67); last 12¢ issue; Kirby-a
57 114 171 456 1028 1600
166-2nd full app. Warlock (Him); battles Thor; see Marvel Premiere #1
12 24 36 79 170 260
167,170-179: 170-1st Thermal Man. 171-Thor vs. the Wrecker. 173-Circus of Crime app. 174-1st Crypto-Man. 176-177-Surtur app. 178-1st Buscema-a on Thor; vs the Abomination. 179-Last Kirby issue 5 10 15 35 63 90
168,169-Origin Galactus; Kirby-a 10 20 30 64 132 200
180,181-Neal Adams-a; Mephisto & Loki app. 6 12 18 37 66 95
182,183-Thor vs. Doctor Doom. 182-Buscema-a begins (11/70)
5 10 15 34 60 85
184-192: 184-1st Infinity & the Silent One. 187-Thor vs Odin. 188-Origin of Infinity. 189,190-Thor vs. Hela. 191-1st Durok the Demolisher. 192-Last 15¢ issue; Thor vs. Durok
4 8 12 28 47 65
193-(25¢, 52 pgs.); Silver Surfer x-over; Thor vs. Durok; last Stan Lee story as regular writer
11 22 33 72 154 235
194-199: 194-Gerry Conway stories begin (ends #238). 195-Mangog returns. 196-198-Thor vs. Mangog. 199-1st Ego-Prime; Pluto app. 4 8 12 23 37 50
200-Special Ragnarok issue by Stan Lee 5 10 15 31 53 75
201-206,208-220,222-224; 201-Pluto & Hela app; origin of Ego-Prime. 202-vs Ego-Prime. 203-1st Young Gods. 204-Thor exiled on Earth; Mephisto app. 205-vs Mephisto; Hitler app. 206-vs. the Absorbing Man. 208-1st Mercurio the 4th Dimensional Man. 210-211-vs. Ulik. 214-Mercurio the 4-D Man app; 1st Xorr the God-Jewel. 215-Origin of Xorr; Mecurio the 4-D Man app. 216-Xorr & Mecurio app. 217-Thor vs Odin-c. 218-220-Saga of the Black Stars. 222,223-vs Pluto. 224-The Destroyer app. 3 6 9 15 22 28
207-Rutland, Vermont Halloween x-over; leads into Avengers/Defenders war
3 6 9 20 31 44
221-Thor vs. Hercules; Hercules guest stars through issue #232,234-239
3 6 9 16 24 32
225-Intro. Firelord 10 20 30 64 132 200
226-Galactus and Firelord app. 3 6 9 15 22 28
227-231: 227-228-Thor, Firelord & Galactus vs Ego the Living Planet. 228-Origin of Ego
2 4 6 11 16 20
229 Facsimile Edition (5/20, $3.99) Reprints 1974 issue with original ads & letter column 4.00
232,233: 232-Firelord app. 233-Numerous guest stars; Asgard invades Earth
3 6 9 14 20 25

Thor #333 © MAR

Thor #500 © MAR

Thor V2 #5 © MAR

GD VG FN VF VF/NM NM-
2.0 4.0 6.0 8.0 9.0 9.2

234-245: 234-Iron Man & Firelord app. 235-1st Kamo Tharnn, Elder of the Universe. 236-Thor vs. Absorbing Man. 237-239-Thor vs. Ulik. 240-1st Egyptian Gods; Osiris & Horus; 1st Seth-Egyptian God of Death. 241-Thor vs. Seth. 242-Len Wein scripts begin; ends #271. 242-245-Thor vs. Time-Twisters; Zarko the Tomorrow Man app. 2 4 6 11 16 20
246-250-(Regular 25¢ editions)(4-8/76): 246-247-Firelord app. 249-250-Thor vs. Mangog 2 4 6 11 16 20
246-250-(30¢-c variants, limited distribution) 5 10 15 31 53 75
251-280: 251-Thor vs. Hela. 252,253-Thor vs. Ulik. 255-Re-intro Stone Men of Saturn. 257-259-Thor vs. Grey Gargoyle. 260-Thor vs. Enchantress & Executioner. 261-272-Simonson-a. 264-266-Thor vs. Loki. 265,266-The Destroyer app. 269-Thor vs. Stilt-Man. 270-Thor vs. Blastaar. 271-Iron Man x-over. 272-Roy Thomas scripts begin. 274-Death of Balder the Brave. 276-Thor vs. Red Norvell Thor. 280-Thor vs. Hyperion 2 4 6 8 10 12
260-264-(35¢-c variants, limited distribution)(6-10/77) 9 18 27 58 114 170
281-299: 281-Space Phantom app. 282-Immortus app. 283,284-Celestials app. 284-286-Eternals app. 287-288-Thor vs. the Forgotten one. 291,292-Asgard vs Olympus. 292-1st Eye of Odin (as sentient being). 294-Origin Asgard & Odin 1 3 4 6 8 10
300-(12/80)-End of Asgard; origin of Odin & The Destroyer; double-size 2 4 6 11 16 20
301-Numerous pantheons (skyfathers) app. 1 3 4 6 8 10
302-304 1 2 3 5 6 8
305-306: 305-Airwalker app. 306-Firelord 1 3 4 6 8 10
307-331,334-336: 310-Thor vs. Mephisto. 314-Moondragon and Drax app. 315,316-Bi-Beast & Man-Beast app. 316-Iron Man x-over. 325-Mephisto app. 331-1st Crusader 6.00
332,333-Dracula app. 1 2 3 5 6 8
337-Simonson-c/a begins, ends #382; 1st app. of Beta Ray Bill who becomes the new Thor; intro Lorelei 8 16 24 54 102 150
338-Beta Ray Bill vs. Thor; origin Beta Ray Bill 3 6 9 16 23 30
339,340: 339-Beta Ray Bill gains Thor's powers. 340-Donald Blake returns as Thor; Beta Ray Bill app.; more facts revealed about origin 1 2 3 5 6 8
341-343,345-373,375-381,383,386: 341-Clark Kent & Lois Lane cameo. 345-349-Malekith the Accursed app. 350-352-Avengers app. 353-'Death' of Odin. 356-Hercules app. 363-Secret Wars II crossover. 364-366-Thor as a frog. 367-Malekith app. 373-X-Factor tie-in. 383-Secret Wars flashback 5.00
344-(6/84) 1st app. of Malekith the Accursed (Ruler of the Dark Elves)(villain in the 2013 movie Thor: The Dark World); Simonson-c/a 3 6 9 14 20 25
374-Mutant Massacre; X-Factor app. 1 2 3 5 6 8
382-($1.25)-Anniversary issue; last Simonson-a 6.00
384-Intro. Thor of the 26th century (Dargo Ktor) 6.00
385-Thor vs. Hulk by Stan Lee and Erik Larsen 1 3 4 6 8 10
387-399: Thor vs. the Celestials. 389- 'Alone against the Celestials' climax. 390-Avengers app.; Captain America lifts Mjolnir. 391-Spider-Man x-over; 1st Eric Masterson. 393-395-Daredevil app. 395-Intro. Earth Force. 396-399-Black Knight app. 5.00
400-($1.75, 68 pgs.)-Origin Loki 6.00
401-410: 404,405-Annihilus app. 409-410-Dr. Doom app. 4.00
411-Intro New Warriors (appear in costume in last panel); Juggernaut-c/story 3 6 9 17 26 35
412-1st full app. New Warriors (Marvel Boy, Kid Nova, Namorita, Night Thrasher, Firestar & Speedball) 3 6 9 17 26 35
413-428: 413-Dr. Strange app. 419-425-Black Galaxy saga; origin Celestials 427-428-Excalibur app. 428-Ghost Rider app. 5.00
429-431: 429-Thor vs Juggernaut; Ghost Rider app. 430-Ghost Rider app. 4.00
432-(52 pgs.) Thor's 350th issue (vs. Loki) reprints origin and 1st app. from Journey into Mystery #83 5.00
433-449,451-467: 433-Intro. Eric Masterson as Thor. 434,435-Annihilus app. 437-Quasar app.; Tales of Asgard back-up stories begin. 438-441-Thor War; Beta Ray Bill app. 443-Dr. Strange & Silver Surfer x-over; last $1.00-c. 445,446-Operation Galactic Storm. 445-Thor vs. Gladiator. 448-Spider-Man app. 451,452-Bloodaxe app. 457-Original Thor returns. 458-Thor vs. Thor. 459-Intro Thunderstrike. 460-Starlin scripts begin. 461-Thor vs. Beta Ray Bill. 463-467-Infinity Crusade x-over. 466-Drax app. 4.00
450-($2.50, 68 pgs.)-Flip-book format; r/story JIM #85 (1st Loki) plus-c plus a gallery of past-c; gatefold-c 5.00
468,469-Blood and Thunder x-over. 468-Thor vs. Silver Surfer. 469-Infinity Watch app. 6.00
470,471-Blood and Thunder x-over. 470-Thanos and the Infinity Watch app. 471-Blood and Thunder story conclusion; Infinity Watch and Silver Surfer app. 6.00
472-474: 472-Intro the Godlings. 474-Begin $1.50-c; bound-in trading cards 4.00
475 ($2.00, 52 pgs.)-Regular edition; High Evolutionary and Man-Beast app. 5.00
475 ($2.50, 52 pgs.)-Collectors edition w/foil embossed-c 6.00
476-481, 483,486,487,488: 476-Destroyer app. 477-Thunderstrike app. 478-Return of Red Norvell Thor. 479-Detailed Origin of Thor. 486-Kurse app. 4.00
482 ($2.95, 84 pgs.)-400th Thor issue 5.00
484,485,490: 484-War Machine app. 485-Thing app. 490-Absorbing Man app.; Buscema-a 5.00
489-Hulk app. 6.00

GD VG FN VF VF/NM NM-
2.0 4.0 6.0 8.0 9.0 9.2

491-Warren Ellis scripts begins, ends #494; Worldengine pt.1; Deodato-c/a begins 6.00
492-494: Worldengine pt. 2-4. 492-Reintro The Enchantress; Beta Ray Bill dies 5.00
495-499: 495-Messner-Loebs scripts begin; Isherwood-c/a. 496-Captain America app. 4.00
500 ($2.50)-Double-size; wraparound-c; Deodato-c/a; Dr. Strange app. 5.00
501-Reintro Red Norvell 4.00
502-(9/96) Onslaught tie-in; Red Norvell, Jane Foster & Hela app. 5.00
NOTE: *Numbering continues with Journey Into Mystery #503 (11/96)*
600-up (See Thor 2007 series)
Special 2(9/66)-(See Journey Into Mystery for 1st annual) Destroyer app. 10 20 30 69 147 225
Special 2 (2nd printing, 1994) 2 4 6 8 10 12
King Size Special 3 (1/71) 5 10 15 30 50 70
Special 4 (12/71)-r/Thor #131,132 & JIM #113 3 6 9 19 30 40
Annual 5 (11/76)-Asgard vs Olympus; Hercules app. 2 4 6 11 16 20
Annual 6 (10/77)-Guardians of the Galaxy app. 4 8 12 27 44 60
Annual 7,8: 7 (1978)-Eternals app. 8 (1979)-Thor vs. Zeus-c/story 2 4 6 8 11 14
Annual 9-13: 9 ('81)-Dormammu app. 10 ('82)-1st Demogorge-the God Eater. 11 ('83)-Origin of Thor expanded. 12 ('84)-Intro Vidar (Thor's brother). 13 ('85)-Mephisto app. 6.00
Annual 14-19 ('86-'94, 68 pgs.): 14-Atlantis Attacks. 15 ('90)-Terminus factor Pt. 3. 16-3 pg. origin; Guardians of the Galaxy x-over. 17 ('92)-Citizen Kang Pt. 2. 18-Polybagged w/card; intro the Flame. 19 ('94) vs. Pluto 5.00
...Alone Against the Celestials nn (6/92, $5.95)-r/Thor #387-389 6.00
...Legends Vol. 2: Walter Simonson Book 2 TPB (2003, $24.99) r/#349-355,357-359 25.00
...Legends Vol. 3: Walter Simonson Book 3 TPB (2004, $24.99) r/#360-369 25.00
...: The Eternals Saga TPB (2006, $24.99) r/#283-291 & Annual #7; profile pages 25.00
...: The Eternals Saga Vol. 2 TPB ('07, $24.99) r/#292-301; Thomas & Gruenwald essays 25.00
... Visionaries: Mike Deodato Jr. TPB (2004, $19.99) r/#491-494,498-500 20.00
... Visionaries: Walter Simonson (Vol. 1) TPB (5/01, $24.95) r/#337-348 25.00
... Visionaries: Walter Simonson Vol. 4 TPB (2007, $24.99) r/#371-373 & Balder the Brave #1-4 25.00
... Visionaries: Walter Simonson Vol. 5 TPB (2008, $24.95) r/#375-382 25.00
...: Worldengine (8/96, $9.95)-r/#491-494; Deodato-c/a; story & new intermission by Warren Ellis 10.00
NOTE: ***Neal Adams** a-180,181; c-179-181. **Austin** a-342i, 346i; c-312i. **Buscema** a(p)-178, 182-213, 215-226, 231-238, 241-253, 254r, 256-259, 272-278, 283-285, 370, Annual 6, 8, 11i; c(p)-175, 178, 182-196, 198-200, 202-204, 206, 211, 212, 215, 219, 221, 226, 256, 259, 261, 262, 272-278, 283, 289, 370, Annual 6. **Everett** a(i)-143, 170-175; c(i)-171, 172, 174, 176, 241. **Gil Kane** a-318p; c(p)-201, 205, 207-210, 216, 220, 222, 223, 231, 233-240, 242, 243, 318. **Kirby** a(p)-126-177, 179, 194r, 254r; c(p)-126-169, 171-174, 176, 177, 249-253, 255, 257, 258, Annual 5, Special 2-4. **Mooney** a(i)-201, 204, 214-216, 218, 322i, 324i, 325i, 327i. **Sienkiewicz** c-332, 333, 335. **Simonson** a-260-271p, 337-354, 357-367, 380, Annual 7p; c-260, 263-271, 337-355, 357-369, 371, 373-382, Annual 7. **Starlin** c-213.*

THOR (Volume 2)
Marvel Comics: July, 1998 - No. 85, Dec, 2004 ($2.99/$1.99/$2.25)

1-($2.99)-Follows Heroes Return; Jurgens-s/Romita Jr. & Janson-a; wraparound-c; battles the Destroyer 1 2 3 5 6 8
1-Variant-c 1 3 4 6 8 10
1-Rough Cut-($2.99) Features original script and pencil pages 4.00
1-Sketch cover 28.00
2-($1.99) Two covers; Avengers app. 5.00
3-11,13-23: 3-Assumes Jake Olson ID. 4-Namor-c/app. 8-Spider-Man-c/app. 14-Iron Man c/app. 17-Juggernaut-c 4.00
12-($2.99) Wraparound-c; Hercules appears 5.00
12-($10.00) Variant-c by Jusko 10.00
24,26-31,33,34: 24-Begin $2.25-c. 26-Mignola-c/Larsen-a. 29-Andy Kubert-a. 30-Maximum Security x-over; Beta Ray Bill-c/app. 33-Intro. Thor Girl 4.00
25-($2.99) Regular edition 5.00
25-($3.99) Gold foil enhanced cover 6.00
32-($3.50, 100 pgs.) new story plus reprints w/Kirby-a; Simonson-a 6.00
35-($2.99) Thor battles The Gladiator; Andy Kubert-a 5.00
36-49,51-61: 37-Starlin-a. 38,39-BWS-c. 38-42-Immonen-a. 40-Odin killed. 41-Orbik-c. 44-'Nuff Said silent issue. 51-Spider-Man app. 57-Art by various. 58-Davis-a; x-over with Iron Man #64. 60-Brereton-c 4.00
50-($4.95) Raney-c/a; back-ups w/Nuckols-a & Armenta-s/Bennett-a 5.00
62-84: 62-Begin $2.99-c. 64-Loki-c/app. 80-Oeming-s begins; Avengers app. 4.00
85-Last issue; Thor dies; Oeming-s/DiVito-a/Epting-c 5.00
...1999 Annual ($3.50) Jurgens-s/a(p) 5.00
...2000 Annual ($3.50) Jurgens-s/Ordway-a(p); back-up stories 5.00
...2001 Annual ($3.50) Jurgens-s/Grummett-a(p); Lightle-c 5.00
...Across All Worlds (9/01, $19.95, TPB) r/#28-35 20.00
Avengers Disassembled: Thor TPB (2004, $16.99) r/#80-85; afterword by Oeming 17.00
...Resurrection ($5.99, TPB) r/#1,2 6.00
...: The Dark Gods (7/00, $15.95, TPB) r/#9-13 16.00
...Vol. 1: The Death of Odin (7/02, $12.99, TPB) r/#39-44 13.00
...Vol. 2: Lord of Asgard (9/02, $15.99, TPB) r/#45-50 16.00
...Vol. 3: Gods on Earth (2003, $21.99, TPB) r/#51-58, Avengers #63, Iron Man #64,

Thor (2008 series) #7 © MAR

Thor (2020 series) #9 © MAR

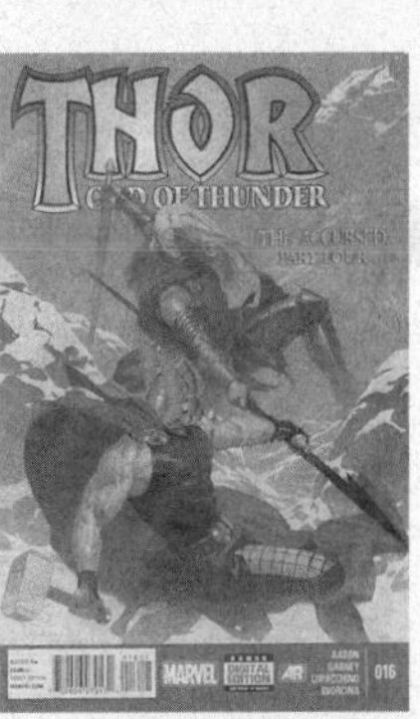

Thor: God of Thunder #16 © MAR

GD VG FN VF VF/NM NM-
2.0 4.0 6.0 8.0 9.0 9.2

Marvel Double-Shot #1; Beck-c 22.00
...Vol. 4: Spiral (2003, $19.99, TPB) r/#59-67; Brereton-c 20.00
...Vol. 5: The Reigning (2004, $17.99, TPB) r/#68-74 18.00
...Vol. 6: Gods and Men (2004, $13.99, TPB) r/#75-79 14.00

THOR (Also see Fantastic Four #538)(Resumes original numbering with #600)
Marvel Comics: Sept, 2007 - No. 12, Mar, 2009; No. 600, Apr, 2009 - No. 621, May, 2011 ($2.99/$3.99) (Continues numbering as Journey Into Mystery #622) (Also see Mighty Thor #1)

1-Straczynski-s/Coipel-a/c 4.00
1-Variant-c by Michael Turner 5.00
1-Zombie variant-c by Suydam 5.00
1-Non-zombie variant-c by Suydam 5.00
1-"Marvel's Greatest Comics" edition (5/10, $1.00) r/#1 3.00
2-12: 2-Two covers by Dell'Otto and Coipel. 3-Iron Man app.; McGuinness var-c. 4-Bermejo var-c. 5-Campbell var-c. 6-Art Adams var-c. 7,8-Djurdjevic-a/c; Coipel var-c 3.00
2-Second printing with wraparound-c 3.00
7-"Marvel's Greatest Comics" edition (6/11, $1.00) r/#7 3.00

(After #12 [Mar, 2009] numbering reverted back to original Journey Into Mystery/Thor numbering with #600, Apr, 2009)

600 (4/09, $4.99) Two wraparound-c by Coipel & Djurdjevic; Coipel, Djurdjevic & Aja-a; r/Tales of Asgard from Journey Into Mystery #106,107,112,113,115; Kirby-a 5.00
601-603,611-621-($3.99) 601-603-Djurdjevic-a. 602-Sif returns. 617-Loki returns 4.00
604-610-($2.99) Tan-a. 607-609-Siege x-over. 610-Braithwaite-a; Ragnarok app. 3.00
620.1 (5/11, $2.99) Brooks-a; Grey Gargoyle app. 3.00
Annual 1 (11/09, $3.99) Suayan, Grindberg, Gaudiano-a; Djurdjevic-c 4.00
...: Ages of Thunder (6/08, $3.99) Fraction-s/Zircher-a/Djurdjevic-c 4.00
... & Hercules: Encyclopaedia Mythologica (2009, $4.99) profile pages of the Pantheons 5.00
... Asgard's Avenger 1 (6/11, $4.99) profile pages of Thor characters 5.00
... By Simonson Halloween Comic Fest 2017 1 (12/17, giveaway) r/#354 & JIM #102 3.00
... Crown of Fools 1 (12/13, $3.99) Di Vito & Simonson-a 4.00
... Giant-Size Finale 1 (1/01, $3.99) Dr. Doom app.; r/origin from JIM #83 4.00
... God-Size Special (2/09, $3.99) story of Skurge the Executioner re-told; art by Brereton, Braithwaite, Allred and Sepulveda; plus reprint of Thor #362 (1985) 4.00
... Goes Hollywood 1 ('11, $3.99) Collection of movie-themed variant Thor covers 4.00
...: Man of War (1/09, $3.99) Fraction-s/Mann & Zircher-a/Djurdjevic-c 4.00
...: Reign of Blood (8/08, $3.99) Fraction-s/Evans & Zircher-a/Djurdjevic-c 4.00
...: Spotlight (5/11, $3.99) movie photo-c; movie preview; creator interviews 4.00
...: The Rage of Thor (10/10, $3.99) Milligan-s/Suayan-c/a 4.00
...: The Trial of Thor (8/09, $3.99) Milligan-s/Nord-c/a 4.00
...: Truth of History (12/08, $3.99) Thor and crew in ancient Egypt; Alan Davis-s/a/c 4.00
...: Where Walk the Frost Giants 1 (12/17, $3.99) Macchio-s/Nauck-a; plus r/JIM #112 4.00
...: Whosoever Wields This Hammer 1 (6/11, $4.99) recolored r/J.I.M. #83,84,88 5.00
...: Wolves of the North (2/11, $3.99) Carey-s/Perkins-a 4.00
... By J. Michael Straczynski Vol. 1 HC (2008, $19.99) r/#1-6; variant cover gallery 20.00

THOR (Female Thor)
Marvel Comics: Dec, 2014 - No. 8, Jul, 2015 ($3.99)

1-Aaron-s/Dauterman-a/c; Thor, Odin and Malekith app. 10.00
2-8 2-4-Malekith app. 4-Thor vs. Thor. 5-Molina-a. 8-Identity revealed 4.00
Annual 1 (4/15, $4.99) Female Thor, King Thor stories; Young Thor by CM Punk-s 5.00

THOR (Odinson back as Thor)(Leads into King Thor series)
Marvel Comics: Aug, 2018 - No. 16, Oct, 2019 ($5.99/$3.99)

1-($5.99) Aaron-s/Del Mundo-a/c; Juggernaut and Loki app. 6.00
2-16-($3.99) 2-4-Skurge & Hela app. 5,6-Ward-a; future Doctor Doom app. 7-Tony Moore-a. 8-10,12,13,15,16-Del Mundo-a. 12-14-War of the Realms tie-ins. 16-Wraparound-c 4.00

THOR (Odinson as King Thor)
Marvel Comics: Mar, 2020 - Present ($4.99/$3.99)

1-($4.99) Cates-s/Klein-a; Galactus, Silver Surfer and Loki app. 5.00
2-8: 2-6-($3.99) Thor as the Herald to Galactus; Beta Ray Bill app. 4,5-Sif app. 7,8-Kuder-a; intro. Adam Aziz 4.00
9-Donald Blake returns 4.00
10,11-Beta Ray Bill & Sif app. 11-Frog Thor app. 4.00
...: The Worthy 1 (2/20, $4.99) Short stories with Beta Ray Bill, Thunderstrike, Sif 5.00

THOR ADAPTATION (MARVEL'S...)
Marvel Comics: Mar, 2012 - No. 2, Apr, 2012 ($2.99, limited series)

1,2-Adaptation of 2012 movie; Gage-s/Medina-a; photo-c 3.00

THOR AND THE WARRIORS FOUR
Marvel Comics: Jun, 2010 - No. 4, Sept, 2010 ($2.99, limited series)

1-4-Thor and Power Pack team-up; Gurihiru-a; back-up with Coover-s/a 3.00

THOR: BLOOD OATH
Marvel Comics: Nov, 2005 - No. 6, Feb, 2006 ($2.99, limited series)

1-6-Oeming-s/Kolins-a/c 3.00

GD VG FN VF VF/NM NM-
2.0 4.0 6.0 8.0 9.0 9.2

HC (2006, $19.99, dust jacket) r/series; afterword by Oeming 20.00
SC (2006, $14.99) r/series; afterword by Oeming 15.00

THOR CORPS
Marvel Comics: Sept, 1993 - No. 4, Jan, 1994 ($1.75, limited series)

1-4: 1-Invaders cameo. 2-Invaders app. 3-Spider-Man 2099, Rawhide Kid, Two-Gun Kid & Kid Colt app. 4-Painted-c 4.00

THOR: FIRST THUNDER
Marvel Comics: Nov, 2010 - No. 5, Mar, 2011 ($3.99, limited series)

1-5: 1-Huat-a; new retelling of origin; reprint of debut in JIM #83 4.00

THOR: FOR ASGARD
Marvel Comics: Nov, 2010 - No. 6, Apr, 2011 ($3.99, limited series)

1-6-Bianchi-a/c. 1-Frost Giants app. 4.00

THOR: GOD OF THUNDER (Marvel NOW!)
Marvel Comics: Jan, 2013 - No. 25, Nov, 2014 ($3.99)

1,3-24: 1-5-Aaron-s/Ribic-a. 6-Guice-a. 13-17-Malekith app. 19-23-Galactus app. 21-1st app. S.H.I.E.L.D. Agent Roz Solomon 4.00
2-1st Gorr the God Butcher 10 20 30 66 138 210
3-2nd app. Gorr 2 4 6 9 12 15
25-($4.99) Art by Guera, Bisley, and Ribic; Malekith app.; new female Thor cameo 5.00

THOR: GODSTORM
Marvel Comics: Nov, 2001 - No. 3, Jan, 2002 ($3.50, limited series)

1-3-Steve Rude-c/a; Busiek-s. 1-Avengers app. 4.00

THOR: HEAVEN & EARTH
Marvel Comics: Sept, 2011 - No. 4, Nov, 2011 ($2.99, limited series)

1-4: 1-Jenkins-s/Olivetti-a/c; Loki app. 2-Texeira-a/c. 3-Alixe-a. 4-Medina-a 3.00

THORION OF THE NEW ASGODS
Marvel Comics (Amalgam): June, 1997 ($1.95, one-shot)

1-Keith Giffen-s/John Romita Jr.-c/a 4.00

THORS (Secret Wars Battleworld tie-in)
Marvel Comics: Aug, 2015 - No. 4, Jan, 2016 ($3.99, limited series)

1-4: Police squad of Thors on Doomworld; Aaron-s/Sprouse-a. 2,3-Sudzuka-a 4.00

THOR: SON OF ASGARD
Marvel Comics: May, 2004 - No. 12, Mar, 2005 ($2.99, limited series)

1-12: Teenaged Thor, Sif, and Balder; Tocchini-a. 1-6-Granov-c. 7-12-Jo Chen-c 3.00
... Vol. 1: The Warriors Teen (2004, $7.99, digest) r/#1-6 8.00
... Vol. 2: Worthy (2005, $7.99, digest) r/#7-12 8.00

THOR: TALES OF ASGARD BY STAN LEE & JACK KIRBY
Marvel Comics: 2009 - No. 6, 2009 ($3.99, limited series)

1-6-Reprints back-up stories from Journey Into Mystery #97-120; new covers by Coipel 4.00

THOR: THE DEVIANTS SAGA
Marvel Comics: Jan, 2012 - No. 5, May, 2012 ($3.99, limited series)

1-5-Rodi-s/Segovia-a; Ereshkigal app. 4.00

THOR: THE DARK WORLD PRELUDE (MARVEL'S...)
Marvel Comics: Aug, 2013 - No. 2, Aug, 2013 ($2.99, limited series)

1,2-Prelude to 2013 movie; Eaton-a; photo-c 3.00

THOR: THE LEGEND
Marvel Comics: Sept, 1996 ($3.95, one-shot)

nn-Tribute issue 4.00

THOR THE MIGHTY AVENGER
Marvel Comics: Sept, 2010 - No. 8, Mar, 2011 ($2.99, limited series)

1-8-Re-imagining of Thor's origin; Langridge-s/Samnee-a. 1-Mr. Hyde app. 3.00
Free Comic Book Day 2011 (giveaway) Captain America app. 3.00

THOR: VIKINGS
Marvel Comics (MAX): Sept, 2003 - No. 5, Jan, 2004 ($3.50, limited series)

1-5-Garth Ennis-s/Glenn Fabry-a/c 3.50
TPB (2004, $13.99) r/series 14.00

THOSE MAGNIFICENT MEN IN THEIR FLYING MACHINES (See Movie Comics)

THREE
Image Comics: Oct, 2013 - No. 5, Feb, 2014 ($2.99)

1-5-Spartans 100 years after the Battle of Thermopylae; Ryan Kelly-a/Kieron Gillen-s 3.00

THREE CABALLEROS (Walt Disney's...)
Dell Publishing Co.: No. 71, 1945

Four Color 71-by Walt Kelly, c/a 64 128 192 512 1156 1800

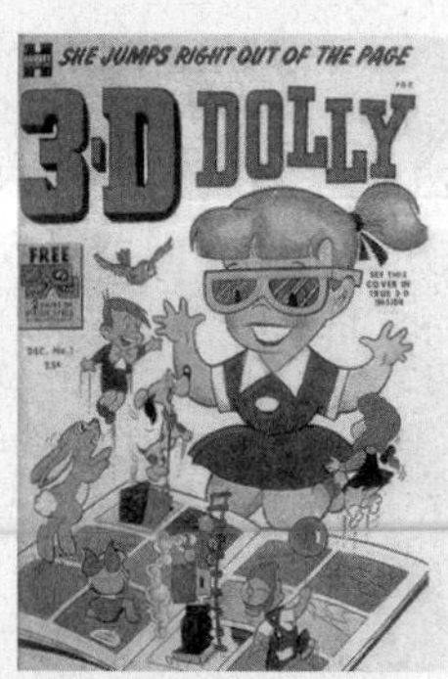
3-D Dolly #1 © HARV

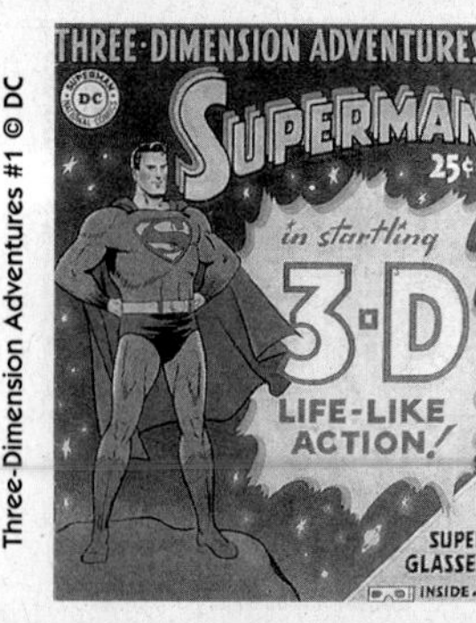

Three-Dimension Adventures #1 © DC

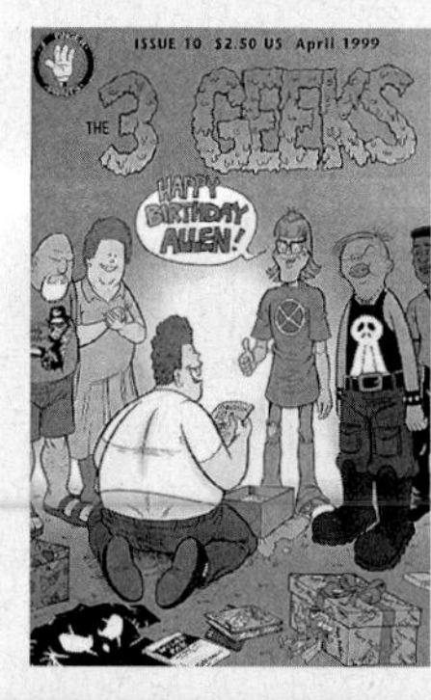

The 3 Geeks #10 © 3 Finger Prints

	GD	VG	FN	VF	VF/NM	NM-
	2.0	4.0	6.0	8.0	9.0	9.2

THREE CHIPMUNKS, THE (TV) (Also see Alvin)
Dell Publishing Co.: No. 1042, Oct-Dec, 1959

Four Color 1042 (#1)-(Alvin, Simon & Theodore) 9 18 27 62 126 190

THREE COMICS (Also see Spiritman)
The Penny King Co.: 1944 (10¢, 52 pgs.) (2 different covers exist)

1,3,4-Lady Luck, Mr. Mystic, The Spirit app. (3 Spirit sections bound together); Lou Fine-a 34 68 102 204 332 460

NOTE: *No. 1 contains Spirit Sections 4/9/44 - 4/23/44, and No. 4 is also from 4/44.*

3-D (NOTE: The prices of all the 3-D comics listed include glasses. Deduct 40-50 percent if glasses are missing, and reduce slightly if glasses are loose.)

3-D ACTION
Atlas Comics (ACI): Jan, 1954 (Oversized, 15¢)(2 pairs of glasses included)

1-Battle Brady; Sol Brodsky-c 54 108 162 343 574 825

3-D ALIEN TERROR
Eclipse Comics: June, 1986 ($2.50)

1-Old Witch, Crypt-Keeper, Vault Keeper cameo; Morrow, John Pound-a, Yeates-c 1 2 3 5 6 8
...in 2-D: 100 copies signed, numbered(B&W) 3 6 9 15 22 28

3-D ANIMAL FUN (See Animal Fun)

3-D BATMAN (Also see Batman 3-D)
National Periodical Publications: 1953 (Reprinted in 1966)

1953-(25¢)-Reprints Batman #42 & 48 (Penguin-c/story); Tommy Tomorrow story; came with pair of 3-D Bat glasses 113 226 339 723 1237 1750
1966-Reprints 1953 issue; new cover by Infantino/Anderson; has inside-c photos of Batman & Robin from TV show (50¢) 20 40 60 141 313 485

3-D CIRCUS
Fiction House Magazines (Real Adventures Publ.): 1953 (25¢, w/glasses)

1 30 60 90 177 289 400

3-D COMICS (See Mighty Mouse, Tor and Western Fighters)

3-D DOLLY
Harvey Publications: December, 1953 (25¢, came with 2 pairs of glasses)

1-Richie Rich story redrawn from his 1st app. in Little Dot #1; shows cover in 3-D on inside 27 54 81 158 259 360

3-D-ELL
Dell Publishing Co.: No. 1, 1953; No. 3, 1953 (3-D comics) (25¢, came w/glasses)

1-Rootie Kazootie (#2 does not exist) 26 52 78 154 252 350
3-Flukey Luke 24 48 72 142 234 325

3 DEVILS
IDW Publishing: Mar, 2016 - No. 4, Jun, 2016 ($3.99, limited series)

1-4-Bo Hampton-s/a/c 4.00

3-D EXOTIC BEAUTIES
The 3-D Zone: Nov, 1990 ($2.95, 28 pgs.)

1-L.B. Cole-c 2 4 6 8 10 12

3-D FEATURES PRESENTS JET PUP
Dimensions Publications: Oct-Dec (Winter on-c), 1953 (25¢, came w/glasses)

1-Irving Spector-a(2) 31 62 93 182 296 410

3-D FUNNY MOVIES
Comic Media: 1953 (25¢, came w/glasses)

1-Bugsey Bear & Paddy Pelican 34 68 102 204 332 460

THREE-DIMENSION ADVENTURES (Superman)
National Periodical Publications: 1953 (25¢, large size, came w/glasses)

nn-Origin Superman (new art) 110 220 330 704 1202 1700

THREE DIMENSIONAL ALIEN WORLDS (See Alien Worlds)
Pacific Comics: July, 1984 (1st Ray Zone 3-D book)(one-shot)

1-Bolton-a(p); Stevens-a(i); Art Adams 1st published-a(p) 1 2 3 5 6 8

THREE DIMENSIONAL DNAGENTS (See New DNAgents)

THREE DIMENSIONAL E. C. CLASSICS (Three Dimensional Tales From the Crypt No. 2)
E. C. Comics: Spring, 1954 (Prices include glasses; came with 2 pair)

1-Stories by Wood (Mad #3), Krigstein (W.S. #7), Evans (F.C. #13), & Ingels (CSS #5); Kurtzman-c (rare in high grade due to unstable paper) 110 220 330 704 1202 1700

NOTE: *Stories redrawn to 3-D format. Original stories not necessarily by artists listed. CSS: Crime SuspenStories; F.C.: Frontline Combat; W.S.: Weird Science.*

	GD	VG	FN	VF	VF/NM	NM-
	2.0	4.0	6.0	8.0	9.0	9.2

THREE DIMENSIONAL TALES FROM THE CRYPT (Formerly Three Dimensional E. C. Classics)(Cover title: ...From the Crypt of Terror)
E. C. Comics: No. 2, Spring, 1954 (Prices include glasses; came with 2 pair)

2-Davis (TFTC #25), Elder (VOH #14), Craig (TFTC #24), & Orlando (TFTC #22) stories; Feldstein-c (rare in high grade) 113 226 339 723 1237 1750

NOTE: *Stories redrawn to 3-D format. Original stories not necessarily by artists listed. TFTC: Tales From the Crypt; VOH: Vault of Horror.*

3-D LOVE
Steriographic Publ. (Mikeross Publ.): Dec, 1953 (25¢, came w/glasses)

1 39 78 117 231 378 525

3-D NOODNICK (See Noodnick)

3-D ROMANCE
Steriographic Publ. (Mikeross Publ.): Jan, 1954 (25¢, came w/glasses)

1 35 70 105 208 339 470

3-D SHEENA, JUNGLE QUEEN (Also see Sheena 3-D)
Fiction House Magazines: 1953 (25¢, came w/glasses)

1-Maurice Whitman-c 74 148 222 470 810 1150

3-D SUBSTANCE
The 3-D Zone: July, 1990 ($2.95, 28 pgs.)

1-Ditko-c/a(r) 5.00

3-D TALES OF THE WEST
Atlas Comics (CPS): Jan, 1954 (Oversized) (15¢, came with 2 pair of glasses)

1 (3-D)-Sol Brodsky-c 48 96 144 302 514 725

3-D THREE STOOGES (Also see Three Stooges)
Eclipse Comics: Sept, 1986 - No. 2, Nov, 1986; No. 3, Oct, 1987; No. 4, 1989 ($2.50)

1-4: 3-Maurer-r. 4-r-/"Three Missing Links" 5.00
1-3 (2-D) 5.00

3-D WHACK (See Whack)

3-D ZONE, THE
The 3-D Zone (Renegade Press)/Ray Zone: Feb, 1987 - No. 20, 1989 ($2.50)

1,3,4,7-9,11,12,14,15,17,19,20: 1-r/A Star Presentation. 3-Picture Scope Jungle Advs. 4-Electric Fear. 7-Hollywood 3-D Jayne Mansfield photo-c. 8-High Seas 3-D, 9-Redmask-r. 11-Danse Macabre; Matt Fox c/a(r). 12-3-D Presidents. 14-Tyranostar. 15-3-Dementia Comics; Kurtzman-c, Kubert, Maurer-a. 17-Thrilling Love. 19-Cracked Classics. 20-Commander Battle and His Atomic Submarine 1 2 3 5 6 8
2,5,6,10,13,18: 2-Wolverton-r. 5-Krazy Kat-r. 6-Ratfink. 10-Jet 3-D; Powell & Williamson-r. 13-Flash Gordon. 18-Spacehawk; Wolverton-r 1 3 4 6 8 10
16-Space Vixens; Dave Stevens-c/a 4 8 12 23 37 50

NOTE: ***Davis** r-19. **Ditko** r-19. **Elder** r-19. **Everett** r-19. **Feldstein** r-17. **Frazetta** r-17. **Heath** r-19. **Kamen** r-17. **Severin** r-19. **Ward** r-17,19. **Wolverton** r-2,18,19. **Wood** r-1,17. Photo c-12*

3 GEEKS, THE (Also see Geeksville)
3 Finger Prints: 1996 - No. 11, Jun, 1999 (B&W)

1,2 -Rich Koslowski-s/a in all 1 2 3 5 6 8
1-(2nd printing) 3.00
3-7, 9-11 3.00
8-(48 pgs.) 4.00
10-Variant-c 3.50
...48 Page Super-Sized Summer Spectacular (7/04, $4.95) 5.00
...Full Circle (7/03, $4.95) Origin story of the 3 Geeks; "Buck Rodinski" app. 5.00
How to Pick Up Girls If You're a Comic Book Geek (color)(7/97) 4.00
When the Hammer Fallls TPB (2001, $14.95) r/#8-11 15.00

3 GEEKS: SLAB MADNESS!
3 Finger Prints: Sept, 2008 - No. 3, Mar, 2009 ($2.99, B&W, limited series)

1-3-Rich Koslowski-s/a; intro. The Cee-Gee-Cee 3.00

3 GUNS
BOOM! Studios: Aug, 2013 - No. 6, Jan, 2014 ($3.99)

1-6-Steven Grant-s/Emilio Laiso-a 4.00

300 (Adapted for 2007 movie)
Dark Horse Comics: May, 1998 - No. 5, Sept, 1998 ($2.95/$3.95, limited series)

1-Frank Miller-s/c/a; Spartans vs. Persians war 3 6 9 16 24 32
1-Second printing 5.00
2-4 2 4 6 8 10 12
5-($3.95-c) 2 4 6 8 10 12
HC ($30.00) -oversized reprint of series 30.00

3 LITTLE KITTENS
BroadSword Comics: Aug, 2002 - No. 3, Dec, 2002 ($2.95, limited series)

1-3-Jim Balent-s/a; two covers 3.00

The Three Mouseketeers #4 © DC

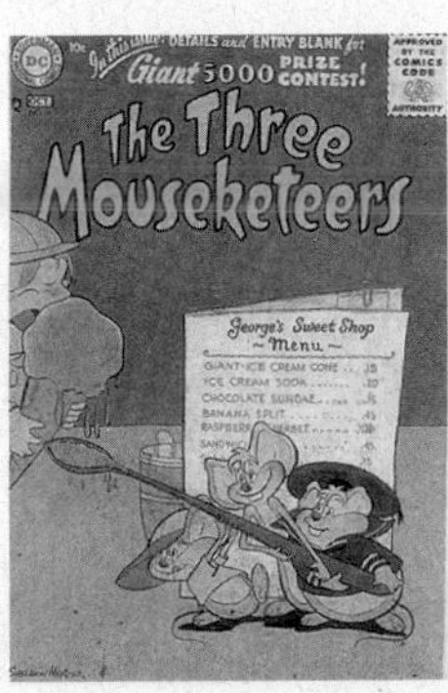

Three Stooges #1 © Norman Mauer

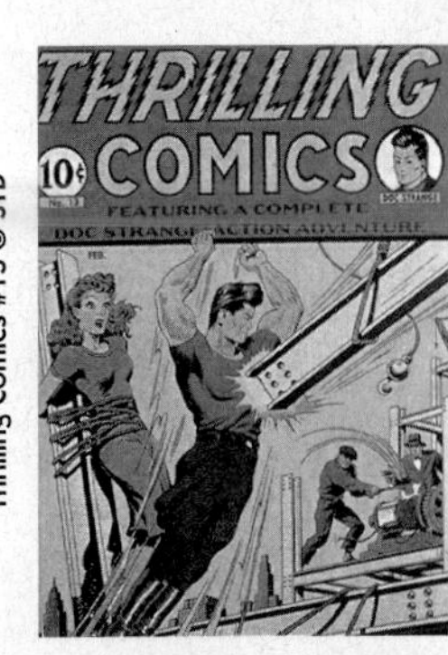

Thrilling Comics #13 © STD

	GD 2.0	VG 4.0	FN 6.0	VF 8.0	VF/NM 9.0	NM- 9.2

3 LITTLE PIGS (Disney)(...and the Wonderful Magic Lamp)
Dell Publishing Co.: No. 218, Mar, 1949

	GD	VG	FN	VF	VF/NM	NM-
Four Color 218 (#1)	10	20	30	68	144	220

3 LITTLE PIGS, THE (See Walt Disney Showcase #15 & 21)
Gold Key: May, 1964; No. 2, Sept, 1968 (Walt Disney)

	GD	VG	FN	VF	VF/NM	NM-
1-Reprints Four Color #218	3	6	9	19	30	40
2	3	6	9	15	21	26

THREE MOUSEKETEERS, THE (1st Series)(See Funny Stuff #1)
National Per. Publ.: 3-4/56 - No. 24, 9-10/59; No. 25, 8-9/60 - No. 26, 10-12/60

	GD	VG	FN	VF	VF/NM	NM-
1	23	46	69	164	362	560
2	11	22	33	73	157	240
3-5,7,9,10	8	16	24	56	108	160
6,8-Grey tone-c	10	20	30	66	138	210
11-26: 24-Cover says 11/59, inside says 9-10/59	7	14	21	49	92	135

NOTE: *Rube Grossman a-1-26. **Sheldon Mayer** a-1-8; c-1-7.*

THREE MOUSEKETEERS, THE (2nd Series) (See Super DC Giant)
National Periodical Publications: May-June, 1970 - No. 7, May-June, 1971 (#5-7: 68 pgs.)

	GD	VG	FN	VF	VF/NM	NM-
1-Mayer-r in all	6	12	18	40	73	105
2-4: 4-Doodles Duck begins (1st app.)	4	8	12	25	40	55
5-7:(68 pgs.). 5-Dodo & the Frog, Bo Bunny begin	5	10	15	31	53	75

THREE MUSKETEERS, THE (Also see Disney's The Three Musketeers)
Gemstone Publishing: 2004 ($3.95, squarebound, one-shot)

nn-Adaptation of the 2004 DVD movie; Petrossi-c/a 4.00

THREE NURSES (Confidential Diary #12-17; Career Girl Romances #24 on)
Charlton Comics: V3#18, May, 1963 - V3#23, Mar, 1964

	GD	VG	FN	VF	VF/NM	NM-
V3#18-23	4	8	12	25	40	55

THREE RASCALS
I. W. Enterprises: 1958; 1963

	GD	VG	FN	VF	VF/NM	NM-
I.W. Reprint #1,2,10: 1-(Says Super Comics on inside)-(M.E.'s Clubhouse Rascals) DeCarlo-a. #2-(1958). 10-(1963)-r/#1	2	4	6	9	13	16

THREE RING COMICS
Spotlight Publishers: March, 1945

	GD	VG	FN	VF	VF/NM	NM-
1-Funny animal	21	42	63	124	202	280

THREE RING COMICS (Also see Captain Wizard & Meteor Comics)
Century Publications: April, 1946

	GD	VG	FN	VF	VF/NM	NM-
1-Prankster-c; Captain Wizard, Impossible Man, Race Wilkins, King O'Leary, & Dr. Mercy app.	41	82	123	256	428	600

THREE ROCKETEERS (See Blast-Off)

THREE STOOGES (See Comic Album #18, Top Comics, The Little Stooges, March of Comics #232, 248, 268, 280, 292, 304, 316, 336, 373, Movie Classics & Comics & 3-D Three Stooges)

THREE STOOGES
Jubilee No. 1/St. John No. 1 (9/53) on: Feb, 1949 - No. 2, May, 1949; Sept, 1953 - No. 7, Oct, 1954

	GD	VG	FN	VF	VF/NM	NM-
1-(Scarce, 1949)-Kubert-a; infinity-c	177	354	531	1133	1942	2750
2-(Scarce)-Kubert, Maurer-a	106	212	318	678	1164	1650
1(9/53)-Hollywood Stunt Girl by Kubert (7 pgs.)	90	180	270	576	988	1400
2(3-D, 10/53, 25¢)-Came w/glasses; Stunt Girl story by Kubert	45	90	135	284	480	675
3(3-D, 10/53, 25¢)-Came w/glasses; has 3-D-c	41	82	123	256	428	600
4(3/54)-7(10/54): 4-1st app. Li'l Stooge?	41	82	123	256	428	600

NOTE: *All issues have **Kubert-Maurer** art & **Maurer** covers. 6, 7-Partial photo-c.*

THREE STOOGES
Dell Publishing Co./Gold Key No. 10 (10/62) on: No. 1043, Oct-Dec, 1959 - No. 55, June, 1972

	GD	VG	FN	VF	VF/NM	NM-
Four Color 1043 (#1)	23	46	69	161	356	550
Four Color 1078,1127,1170,1187	11	22	33	76	163	250
6(9-11/61) - 10: 6-Professor Putter begins; ends #16	9	18	27	58	114	170
11-14,16,18-20	7	14	21	48	89	130
15-Go Around the World in a Daze (movie scenes)	8	16	24	51	96	140
17-The Little Monsters begin (5/64)(1st app.?)	8	16	24	51	96	140
21,23-30	6	12	18	38	69	100
22-Movie scenes from "The Outlaws Is Coming"	6	12	18	41	76	110
31-55	5	10	15	31	53	75

NOTE: *All Four Colors, 6-50, 52-55 have photo-c.*

THREE STOOGES IN 3-D, THE
Eternity Comics: 1991 ($3.95, high quality paper, w/glasses)

1-Reprints Three Stooges by Gold Key; photo-c 5.00

THREE STOOGES
American Mythology Prods.: 2016 - Present (series of one-shots)

...: April Fools' Day Special (2017, $3.99) Check-s/Fraim brothers-a; 5 covers 4.00
...: Astro-Nuts 1 (2019, $3.99, B&W) Check-s/Fraim brothers-a; reprint from FC #1078 4.00
...: Curse of the Frankenstooge (2016, $4.99) New stories and reprint from #24; 5 covers 5.00
...: Dell 1959 Edition 1 (2019, $3.99) Reprints Four Color #1043 from 1959 4.00
...: Halloween Hullabaloo (2016, giveaway) New stories by various; Ropp-c 3.00
...: Halloween Stoogetacular (2017, $3.99) Check-s/Fraim brothers-a; 4 covers 4.00
...: Matinee Madness (2018, $3.99, B&W) New stories; Wolfer-s/Shanover-a 4.00
...: Merry Stoogemas (2016, $3.99) New stories and reprint from #7; 5 covers 4.00
...: Monsters & Mayhem (2018, $3.99, B&W) Check-s/Fraim brothers-a; reprint from #2 4.00
...: Red, White, & Stooge (2016, $3.99) New story and reprint from #44; 4 covers 4.00
...: Shemptastic Shemptacular (2018, $3.99) New story and reprint from #1; 4 covers 4.00
...: Slaptastic Special (2018, $3.99) Check-s/Fraim brothers-a; reprint from #7 4.00
...: Stooge-A-Palooza 1 (2016, $4.99) New stories and reprint from FC #1170; 3 covers 5.00
...: The Boys are Back (2016, $3.99) New stories and reprint from FC #1170; 4 covers 4.00
...: Thru the Ages (2021, $3.99) Check-s/Fraim brothers-a; 2 covers 4.00
...: TV Time Special (2017, $3.99) Check-s/Fraim brothers-a; 4 covers 4.00

3 WORLDS OF GULLIVER
Dell Publishing Co.: No. 1158, July, 1961 (2 issues exist with diff. covers)

	GD	VG	FN	VF	VF/NM	NM-
Four Color 1158-Movie, photo-c	6	12	18	42	79	115

THRESHOLD
DC Comics: Mar, 2013 - No. 8 ($3.99)

1-8-Anthology. 1-5-Back-up Larfleeze stories. 5,6-Brainiac app. 4.00

THRILL COMICS (See Flash Comics, Fawcett)

THRILLER
DC Comics: Nov, 1983 - No. 12, Nov, 1984 ($1.25, Baxter paper)

1-12: 1-Intro Seven Seconds; Von Eeden-c/a begins. 2-Origin. 5,6-Elvis satire 4.00

THRILLING ADVENTURE HOUR, THE
BOOM! Studios: Jul, 2018 - No. 4, Oct, 2018 ($3.99, limited series)

1-4-Acker & Blacker-s/Erickson-a/Case-c 4.00

THRILLING ADVENTURE HOUR PRESENTS:...
Image Comics: ($3.50)

... Beyond Belief 1-3 (4/15 - No. 3, 3/16) Acker & Blacker-s/Hester-a 3.50
... Sparks Nevada: Marshal on Mars 1-4 (2/15 - No. 4, 7/15) Acker & Blacker-s/Bone-a 3.50

THRILLING ADVENTURES IN STAMPS COMICS (Formerly Stamp Comics)
Stamp Comics, Inc. (Very Rare): V1#8, Jan, 1953 (25¢, 100 pgs.)

	GD	VG	FN	VF	VF/NM	NM-
V1#8-Harrison, Wildey, Kiefer, Napoli-a	81	162	243	518	884	1250

THRILLING ADVENTURE STORIES (See Tigerman)
Atlas/Seaboard Publ.: Feb, 1975 - No. 2, Aug, 1975 (B&W, 68 pgs.)

	GD	VG	FN	VF	VF/NM	NM-
1-Tigerman, Kromag the Killer begin; Heath, Thorne-a; Doc Savage movie photos of Ron Ely	3	6	9	21	33	45
2-Heath, Toth, Severin, Simonson-a; Adams-c	4	8	12	25	40	55

THRILLING COMICS
Better Publ./Nedor/Standard Comics: Feb, 1940 - No. 80, April, 1951

	GD	VG	FN	VF	VF/NM	NM-
1-Origin & 1st app. Dr. Strange (37 pgs.), ends #?; Nickie Norton of the Secret Service begins	415	830	1245	2905	5103	7300
2-The Rio Kid, The Woman in Red, Pinocchio begins	232	464	696	1485	2543	3600
3-The Ghost & Lone Eagle begin	194	388	582	1242	2121	3000
4-6,8,9: 5-Dr. Strange changed to Doc Strange	171	342	513	1094	1872	2650
7-Classic-c	371	742	1113	2600	4550	6500
10-1st WWII-c (Nazi)(11/40)	181	362	543	1158	1979	2800
11-18,20: 17-WWII-Nazi-c	164	328	492	1050	1800	2550
19-Origin & 1st app. The American Crusader (8/41), ends #39,41; Schomburg Nazi WWII-c	219	438	657	1402	2401	3400
21-26,28-30: 24-Intro. Mike, Doc Strange's sidekick (1/42). 29-Last Rio Kid	126	252	378	806	1378	1950
27-Robot-c	158	316	474	1011	1731	2450
31-35,37,39,40: 39-Nazi WWII-c. 40-Japan WWII-c	106	212	318	678	1164	1650
36-Commando Cubs begin (7/43, 1st app.)	116	232	348	742	1271	1800
38-Classic Nazi bondage-c	245	490	735	1568	2684	3800
41-Classic Hitler & Mussolini WWII-c	465	930	1395	3395	5998	8600
42-Classic Schomburg Japanese WWII-c	158	316	474	1011	1731	2450
43,46-51: 51(12/45)-Last WWII-c (Japanese)	94	188	282	597	1025	1450
44-Hitler WWII-c by Schomburg	354	708	1062	2478	4339	6200
45-Hitler pict. on-c	123	246	369	787	1344	1900
52-Classic Schomburg hooded bondage-c; the Ghost ends	100	200	300	640	1095	1550

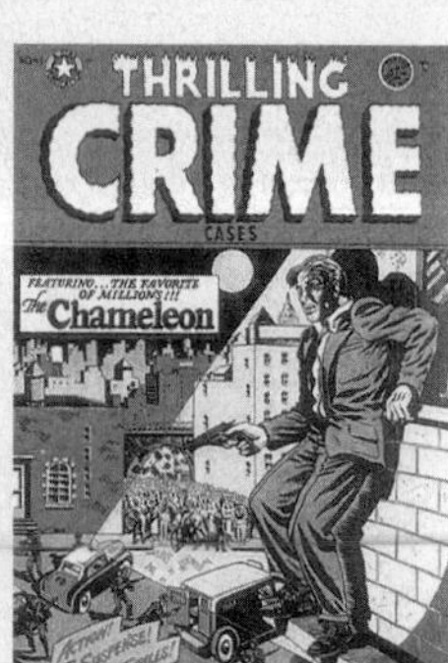

Thrilling Crime Cases #43 © STAR

Thrillkiller #1 © DC

Thun'da #5 © DYN

	GD 2.0	VG 4.0	FN 6.0	VF 8.0	VF/NM 9.0	NM- 9.2
53,54: 53-The Phantom Detective begins. The Cavalier app. in both; no Commando Cubs in either	63	126	189	403	689	975
55-The Lone Eagle ends	52	104	156	328	552	775
56 (10/46)-Princess Pantha begins (not on-c), 1st app.	68	136	204	435	743	1050
57-Doc Strange-c; 2nd Princess Pantha	57	114	171	362	619	875
58-66: All Princess Pantha jungle-c, w/Doc Strange #59, his last-c. 61-Ingels-a; The Lone Eagle app. 65-Last Phantom Detective & Commando Cubs. 66-Frazetta text illo	55	110	165	352	601	850
67,70,71-Last jungle-c; Frazetta-a(5-7 pgs.) in each	60	120	180	381	653	925
68,69-Frazetta-a(2), 8 & 6 pgs.; 9 & 7 pgs.	65	130	195	416	705	1000
72,73: 72-Buck Ranger, Cowboy Detective c/stys begin (western theme), end #80; Frazetta-a(5-7 ps.) in each	43	86	129	271	461	650
74-Last Princess Pantha; Tara app.	32	64	96	192	314	435
75-78: 75-All western format begins	18	36	54	107	169	230
79-Krigstein-a	19	38	57	111	176	240
80-Severin & Elder, Celardo, Moreira-a	19	38	57	111	176	240

NOTE: *Bondage c-5, 9, 13, 20, 22, 27-30, 38, 41, 52, 54, 70.* ***Kinstler*** *a-45.* ***Leo Morey*** *a-7.* ***Schomburg*** *(sometimes signed as* ***Xela****) c-7, 9-19, 36-80 (airbrush 62-71).* ***Tuska*** *a-62, 63. Woman in Red not in #19, 23, 31-33, 39-45. No. 45 exists as a Canadian reprint but numbered #48. No. 72 exists as a Canadian reprint with no* ***Frazetta*** *story. American Crusader c-20-24. Buck Ranger c-72-80. Commando Cubs c-37, 39, 41, 43, 45, 47, 49, 51. Doc Strange c-1-19, 25-36, 38, 40, 42, 44, 46, 48, 50, 52-57, 59. Princess Pantha c-58, 60-71.*

THRILLING COMICS (Also see All Star Comics 1999 crossover titles)
DC Comics: May, 1999 ($1.99, one-shot)

1-Golden Age Hawkman and Wildcat; Russ Heath-a 3.00

THRILLING CRIME CASES (Formerly 4Most; becomes Shocking Mystery Cases #50 on)
Star Publications: No. 41, June-July, 1950 - No. 49, July, 1952

	GD	VG	FN	VF	VF/NM	NM-
41	40	80	120	246	411	575
42-45: 42-L. B. Cole-c/a (1); Chameleon story (Fox-r)	36	72	108	214	347	480
46-48: 47-Used in **POP**, pg. 84	34	68	102	204	332	460
49-(7/52)-Classic L. B. Cole-c	300	600	900	2070	3635	5200

NOTE: ***L. B. Cole*** *c-all; a-43p, 45p, 46p, 49(2 pgs.).* ***Disbrow*** *a-48.* ***Hollingsworth*** *a-48.*

THRILLING ROMANCES
Standard Comics: No. 5, Dec, 1949 - No. 26, June, 1954

	GD	VG	FN	VF	VF/NM	NM-
5	24	48	72	140	230	320
6,8	15	30	45	86	133	180
7-Severin/Elder-a (7 pgs.)	15	30	45	94	147	200
9,10-Severin/Elder-a; photo-c	15	30	45	90	140	190
11,14-21,26: 14-Gene Tierney & Danny Kaye photo-c from movie "On the Riviera". 15-Tony Martin/Janet Leigh photo-c	14	28	42	82	121	160
12-Wood-a (2 pgs.); Tyrone Power/ Susan Hayward photo-c	16	32	48	98	154	210
13-Severin-a	15	30	45	84	127	170
22-25-Toth-a	15	30	45	88	137	185

NOTE: *All photo-c.* ***Celardo*** *a-9, 16.* ***Colletta*** *a-23, 24(2).* ***Toth*** *text illos-19.* ***Tuska*** *a-9.*

THRILLING SCIENCE TALES
AC Comics: 1989 - No. 2 ($3.50, 2/3 color, 52 pgs.)

1,2: 1-r/Bob Colt #6(saucer); Frazetta, Guardineer (Space Ace), Wood, Krenkel, Orlando, WIlliamson-r; Kaluta-c. 2-Capt. Video-r by Evans, Capt. Science-r by Wood, Star Pirate-r by Whitman & Mysta of the Moon-r by Moreira 4.00

THRILLING TRUE STORY OF THE BASEBALL...
Fawcett Publications: 1952 (Photo-c, each)

	GD	VG	FN	VF	VF/NM	NM-
...Giants-photo-c; has Willie Mays rookie photo-biography; Willie Mays, Eddie Stanky & others photos on-c	69	138	207	442	759	1075
...Yankees-photo-c; Yogi Berra, Joe DiMaggio, Mickey Mantle & others photos on-c	68	136	204	435	743	1050

THRILLING WONDER TALES
AC Comics : 1991 ($2.95, B&W)

1-Includes a Bob Powell Thun'da story 4.00

THRILLKILLER
DC Comics : Jan, 1997 - No. 3, Mar, 1997($2.50, limited series)

1-3-Elseworlds Robin & Batgirl; Chaykin-s/Brereton-c/a 4.00
...'62 ('98, $4.95, one-shot) Sequel; Chaykin-s/Brereton-c/a 5.00
TPB-(See Batman: Thrillkiller)

THRILLOGY
Pacific Comics: Jan, 1984 (One-shot, color)

1-Conrad-c/a 4.00

THRILL-O-RAMA
Harvey Publications (Fun Films): Oct, 1965 - No. 3, Dec, 1966

	GD	VG	FN	VF	VF/NM	NM-
1-Fate (Man in Black) by Powell app.; Doug Wildey-a(2); Simon-c	5	10	15	31	53	75
2-Pirana begins (see Phantom #46); Williamson 2 pgs.; Fate (Man in Black) app.; Tuska/Simon-c	3	6	9	21	33	45
3-Fate (Man in Black) app.; Sparling-c	3	6	9	18	28	38

THRILLS OF TOMORROW (Formerly Tomb of Terror)
Harvey Publications: No. 17, Oct, 1954 - No. 20, April, 1955

	GD	VG	FN	VF	VF/NM	NM-
17-Powell-a (horror); r/Witches Tales #7	15	30	45	94	147	200
18-Powell-a (horror); r/Tomb of Terror #1	15	30	45	85	130	175
19,20-Stuntman-c/stories by S&K (r/from Stuntman #1 & 2); 19 has origin & is last pre-code (2/55)	31	62	93	186	303	420

NOTE: ***Kirby*** *c-19, 20.* ***Palais*** *a-17.* ***Simon*** *c-18?*

THROBBING LOVE (See Fox Giants)

THROUGH GATES OF SPLENDOR
Spire Christian Comics (Flemming H. Revell Co.): 1973, 1974 (36 pages) (39-49 cents)

	GD	VG	FN	VF	VF/NM	NM-
nn-1973 Edition	3	6	9	14	19	24
nn-1974 Edition	2	4	6	9	13	16

THULSA DOOM (Robert E. Howard character)
Dynamite Entertainment: 2009 - No. 4, 2009 ($3.50, limited series)

1-4-Alex Ross-c/Lui Antonio-a 3.50

THUMBS
Image Comics: Jun, 2019 - No. 5, Oct, 2019 ($4.99, limited series)

1-5-Sean Lewis-s/Hayden Sherman-a 5.00

THUMPER (Disney)
Dell Publishing Co.: No, 19, 1942 - No. 243, Sept, 1949

	GD	VG	FN	VF	VF/NM	NM-
Four Color 19-Walt Disney's...Meets the Seven Dwarfs; reprinted in Silly Symphonies	46	92	138	359	805	1250
Four Color 243-...Follows His Nose	12	24	36	80	173	265

THUN'DA (...King of the Congo)
Magazine Enterprises: 1952 - No. 6, 1953

	GD	VG	FN	VF	VF/NM	NM-
1(A-1 #47)-Origin; Frazetta c/a; only comic done entirely by Frazetta; all Thun'da stories, no Cave Girl	252	504	756	1613	2757	3900
2(A-1 #56)-Powell-c/a begins, ends #6; Intro/1st app. Cave Girl in filler strip (also app. in 3-6)	35	70	105	208	339	470
3(A-1 #73), 4(A-1 #78)	23	46	69	138	227	315
5(A-1 #83), 6(A-1 #86)	23	46	69	136	223	310

THUN'DA
Dynamite Entertainment: 2012 - No. 5, 2012 ($3.99, limited series)

1-5-Napton-s/Richards-a/Jae Lee-c. 1-4-Bonus reprints of Thun'da #1 (1952) Frazetta-a 4.00

THUN'DA TALES (See Frank Frazetta's...)

THUNDER AGENTS (See Dynamo, Noman & Tales Of Thunder)
Tower Comics: 11/65 - No. 17, 12/67; No. 18, 9/68, No. 19, 11/68, No. 20, 11/69 (No. 1-16: 68 pgs.; No. 17 on: 52 pgs.)(All are 25¢)

	GD	VG	FN	VF	VF/NM	NM-
1-Origin & 1st app. Dynamo, Noman, Menthor, & The Thunder Squad; 1st app. The Iron Maiden	18	36	54	122	271	420
2-Death of Egghead; A-bomb blast panel	9	18	27	63	129	195
3-5: 4-Guy Gilbert becomes Lightning who joins Thunder Squad; Iron Maiden app.	7	14	21	49	92	135
6-10: 7-Death of Menthor. 8-Origin & 1st app. The Raven	6	12	18	38	69	100
11-15: 13-Undersea Agent app.; no Raven story	5	10	15	35	63	90
16-19	5	10	15	34	60	85
20-Special Collectors Edition; all reprints	4	8	12	27	44	60

...Archives Vol. 1 (DC Comics, 2003, $49.95, HC) r/#1-4, restored and recolored 50.00
...Archives Vol. 2 (DC Comics, 2003, $49.95, HC) r/#5-7, Dynamo #1 50.00
...Archives Vol. 3 (DC Comics, 2003, $49.95, HC) r/#8-10, Dynamo #2 50.00
...Archives Vol. 4 (DC Comics, 2004, $49.95, HC) r/#11, Noman #1,2 & Dynamo #3 50.00

NOTE: ***Crandall*** *a-1, 4p, 5p, 18, 20r; c-18.* ***Ditko*** *a-6, 7p, 12p, 13?, 14p, 16, 18.* ***Giunta*** *a-6.* ***Kane*** *a-1, 5p, 6p?, 14, 16p; c-14, 15.* ***Reinman*** *a-13.* ***Sekowsky*** *a-6.* ***Tuska*** *a-1p, 7, 8, 10, 13-17, 19.* ***Whitney*** *a-9p, 10, 13, 15, 17, 18; c-17.* ***Wood*** *a-1-11, 15(w/****Ditko****-12, 18), (inks-#9, 13, 14, 16, 17), 19i, 20r; c-1-8, 9i, 10-13(#10 w/* ***Williamson****(p)), 16.*

T.H.U.N.D.E.R. AGENTS (See Blue Ribbon Comics, Hall of Fame Featuring the..., JCP Features & Wally Wood's...)
JC Comics (Archie Publications): May, 1983 - No. 2, Jan, 1984

1,2: 1-New Manna/Blyberg-c/a. 2-Blyberg-c 6.00

T.H.U.N.D.E.R. AGENTS
DC Comics: Jan, 2011 - No. 10, Oct, 2011 ($3.99/$2.99)

1-3-($3.99): 1-Spencer-s/Cafu-a/Quitely-c. 3-Chaykin-a (5 pgs.) 4.00
4-10-($2.99): 4-Pérez-a (5 pgs.). 7-10-Grell & Dragotta-a 3.00

T.H.U.N.D.E.R. Agents (2013 series) #2 © Radiant

Thunderbolts #65 © MAR

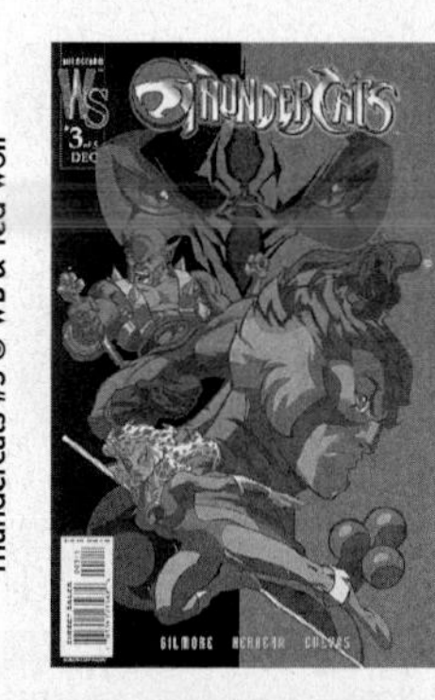

Thundercats #3 © WB & Ted Wolf

	GD	VG	FN	VF	VF/NM	NM-
	2.0	4.0	6.0	8.0	9.0	9.2

1-Variant-c by Darwyn Cooke 8.00

T.H.U.N.D.E.R. AGENTS
DC Comics: Jan, 2012 - No. 6, Jun, 2012 ($2.99, limited series)

1-6-Spencer-s/Craig-a. 1-Andy Kubert-c. 3-Craig & Simonson-a 3.00

T.H.U.N.D.E.R. AGENTS
IDW Publishing: Aug, 2013 - No. 8, Apr, 2014 ($3.99)

1-8: 1-4-Hester-s/Di Vito-a. 1-Four interlocking covers by Di Vito. 5-8-Roger Robinson-a 4.00

THUNDER BIRDS (See Cinema Comics Herald)

THUNDERBOLT (See The Atomic...)

THUNDERBOLT (Peter Cannon...; see Crisis on Infinite Earths, Peter Cannon, Captain Atom and Judomaster)
Charlton Comics: Jan, 1966; No. 51, Mar-Apr, 1966 - No. 60, Nov, 1967

	GD	VG	FN	VF	VF/NM	NM-
1-Origin & 1st app. Thunderbolt	5	10	15	35	63	90
51-(Formerly Son of Vulcan #50)	3	6	9	21	33	45
52-Judomaster story	3	6	9	16	23	30
53-Captain Atom story, 2 pgs.	3	6	9	16	23	30
54-59: 54-Sentinels begin. 59-Last Thunderbolt & Sentinels (back-up story)	3	6	9	14	19	24
60-Prankster only app.	3	6	9	15	21	26
57,58 ('77)-Modern Comics-r	1	3	4	6	8	10

NOTE: *Aparo a-60. Morisi a-1, 51-56, 58; c-1, 51-56, 58, 59.*

THUNDERBOLT JAXON (Revival of 1940s British comics character)
DC Comics (WildStorm): Apr, 2006 - No. 5, Sept, 2006 ($2.99, limited series)

1-5-Dave Gibbons-s/John Higgins-a 3.00
TPB (2007, $19.99) r/#1-5; intro. by Gibbons; cover gallery 20.00

THUNDERBOLTS (Title re-named Dark Avengers with #175)(Also see New Thunderbolts and Incredible Hulk #449)
Marvel Comics: Apr, 1997 - No. 81, Sept, 2003; No. 100, May, 2006 - No. 174, Jul, 2012 ($1.95-$2.99)

	GD	VG	FN	VF	VF/NM	NM-
1-($2.99)-Busiek-s/Bagley-c/a	2	4	6	8	10	12

1-2nd printing; new cover colors 3.00
2-4: 2-Two covers. 4-Intro. Jolt 6.00
5-11: 9-Avengers app. 3.50
12-($2.99)-Avengers and Fantastic Four-c/app. 4.00
13-24: 14-Thunderbolts return to Earth. 21-Hawkeye app. 3.00
25-($2.99) Wraparound-c 4.00
26-38: 26-Manco-a 3.00
39-($2.99) 100 Page Monster; Iron Man reprints 4.00
40-49: 40-Begin $2.25-c; Sandman-c/app. 44-Avengers app. 47-Captain Marvel app. 49-Zircher-a 3.00
50-($2.99) Last Bagley-a; Captain America becomes leader 4.00
51-74,76,77,80,81: 51,52-Zircher-a; Dr. Doom app. 80,81-Spider-Man app. 3.00
75-($3.50) Hawkeye leaves the team; Garcia-a 4.00
78,79-($2.99-c) Velasco-a begins 3.00
(See New Thunderbolts for #82-99)
100 (5/06, $3.99) resumes from New Thunderbolts #18; back-up origin stories 4.00
101-109: 103-105-Civil War x-over 3.00
110-New team begins including Bullseye, Venom and Norman Osborn; Ellis-s/Deodato-a 5.00
111-136,138-149: 111-121-Ellis-s/Deodato-a. 112-Stan Lee cameo. 123-125-Secret Invasion x-over. 128-Dark Reign begins. 130,131-X-over with Deadpool #8,9. 141-143-Siege 3.00
137-(12/09, $3.99) Iron Fist and Luke Cage app. 4.00
150-(1/11, $4.99) Thunderbolts vs. Avengers; r/#1; storyline synopses of #1-150 5.00
151-158,160-163, 163.1, 164-174-($2.99) 151-153-Land-c. 155-Satana joins. 158-162-Fear Itself tie-in. 163-165-Thunderbolts in WWII; Invaders app. 3.00
159-($4.99) Fear Itelf tie-in; Juggernaut app.; short stories of escape from The Raft 5.00
Annual '97 ($2.99)-Wraparound-c 4.00
Annual 2000 ($3.50) Breyfogle-a 4.00
...: Breaking Point (1/08, $2.99, one-shot) Gage-s/Denham-a/Djurdjevic-c 3.00
... By Warren Ellis Vol. 1 HC (2007, $24.99, dustjacket) r/#150-154, ...: Desperate Measures and stories from Civil War: Choosing Sides and The Initiative 25.00
... By Warren Ellis Vol. 1: Faith in Monsters SC (2008, $19.99) same contents as HC 20.00
Civil War: Thunderbolts TPB (2007, $13.99) r/#101-105 14.00
...: Desperate Measures (9/07, $2.99, one-shot) Jenkins-s/Steve Lieber-a 3.00
...: Distant Rumblings (#-1) (7/97, $1.95) Busiek-s 5.00
First Strikes (1997, $4.99,TPB) r/#1,2 5.00
...: From the Marvel Vault (6/11, $3.99) Jack Monroe app.; Nicieza-s/Aucoin-a 4.00
...: Guardian Protocols (2007, $10.99) r/#106-109 11.00
...: International Incident (4/08, $2.99, one-shot) Gage-s/Oliver-a/Djurdjevic-c 3.00
...: Life Sentences (7/01, $3.50) Adlard-a 4.00
...: Marvel's Most Wanted TPB ('98, $16.99) r/origin stories of original Masters of Evil 17.00
...: Reason in Madness (7/08, $2.99, one-shot) Gage-s/Oliver-a/Djurdjevic-c 3.00
Wizard #0 (bagged with Wizard #89) 3.00

THUNDERBOLTS (Marvel NOW!)
Marvel Comics: Feb, 2013 - No. 32, Dec, 2014 ($2.99)

1-32: 1-Punisher, Red Hulk, Elektra, Venom & Deadpool team; Dillon-a. 7-11-Noto-a. 14-18-Infinity tie-ins; Soule-s/Palo-a. 20-Ghost Rider joins 3.00
Annual 1 (2/14, $4.99) Dr. Strange & Elsa Bloodstone app.; Lolli-a 5.00

THUNDERBOLTS
Marvel Comics: Jul, 2016 - No. 12, Jun, 2017 ($3.99)

1-9,11,12: 1-Bucky Barnes leads the team of Kobik, Atlas, Fixer, Moonstone, & Mach-X. 4-Squadron Supreme app. 5-Spider-Man (Miles) app. 11,12-Secret Empire tie-ins 4.00
10-($4.99) 20th Anniversary Special; prologue by Busiek-s/Bagley-a; Jolt returns 5.00

THUNDERBOLTS PRESENTS: ZEMO - BORN BETTER
Marvel Comics: Apr, 2007 - No. 4, July, 2007 ($2.99, limited series)

1-4-History of Baron Zemo; Nicieza-s/Grummett-a/c 3.00
TPB (2007, $10.99) r/#1-4 11.00

THUNDERBUNNY (See Blue Ribbon Comics #13, Charlton Bullseye & Pep Comics #393)
Red Circle Comics: Jan, 1984 (Direct sale only)
WaRP Graphics: Second series No. 1, 1985 - No. 6, 1985
Apple Comics: No. 7, 1986 - No. 12, 1987

1-Humor/parody; origin Thunderbunny; 2 page pin-up by Anderson 5.00
(2nd series) 1,2-Magazine size 4.00
3-12-Comic size 4.00

THUNDERCATS (TV)
Marvel Comics (Star Comics)/Marvel #22 on: Dec, 1985 - No. 24, June, 1988 (75¢)

	GD	VG	FN	VF	VF/NM	NM-
1-Mooney-c/a begins	8	16	24	54	102	150
2-20: 2-(65¢ & 75¢ cover exists). 12-Begin $1.00-c. 18-20-Williamson-i	2	4	6	8	10	12
21-24: 23-Williamson-c(i)	2	4	6	8	11	14

THUNDERCATS (TV)
DC Comics (WildStorm): No. 0, Oct, 2002 - No. 5, Feb, 2003 ($2.50/$2.95, limited series)

0-($2.50) J. Scott Campbell-c/a 4.00
1-5-($2.95) 1-McGuinness-a/c; variant cover by Art Adams; rebirth of Mumm-Ra 4.00
.../ Battle of the Planets (7/03, $4.95) Kaare Andrews-s/a; 2 covers by Campbell & Ross 5.00
...: Origins-Heroes & Villains (2/04, $3.50) short stories by various 3.50
...Reclaiming Thundera TPB (2003, $12.95) r/#0-5 13.00
... Sourcebook (1/03, $2.95) pin-ups and info on characters; art by various; A. Adams-c 4.00

THUNDERCATS: DOGS OF WAR
DC Comics (WildStorm): Aug, 2003 - No. 5, Dec, 2003 ($2.95, limited series)

1-5: 1-Two covers by Booth & Pearson; Booth-a/Layman-s. 2-4-Two covers 3.00
TPB (2004, $14.95) r/#1-5 15.00

THUNDERCATS: ENEMY'S PRIDE
DC Comics (WildStorm): Aug, 2004 - No. 5 ($2.95, limited series)

1-5-Vriens-a/Layman-s 3.00
TPB (2005, $14.99) r/#1-5 15.00

THUNDERCATS: HAMMERHAND'S REVENGE
DC Comics (WildStorm): Dec, 2003 - No. 5, Apr, 2004 ($2.95, limited series)

1-5-Avery-s/D'Anda-a. 2-Variant-c by Warren 3.00
TPB (2004, $14.95) r/#1-5 15.00

THUNDERCATS: THE RETURN
DC Comics (WildStorm): Apr, 2003 - No. 5, Aug, 2003 ($2.95, limited series)

1-5: 1-Two covers by Benes & Cassaday; Gilmore-s 3.00
TPB (2004, $12.95) r/series 13.00

THUNDER MOUNTAIN (See Zane Grey, Four Color #246)

THUNDERSTRIKE (See Thor #459)
Marvel Comics: June, 1993 - No. 24, July, 1995 ($1.25)

1-($2.95, 52 pgs.)-Holo-grafx lightning patterned foil-c; Bloodaxe returns 4.00
2-24: 2-Juggernaut-c/s. 4-Capt. America app. 4-6-Spider-Man app. 8-bound-in trading card sheet. 18-Bloodaxe app. 24-Death of Thunderstrike 3.00
Marvel Double Feature...Thunderstrike/Code Blue #13 ($2.50)-Same as Thunderstrike #13 w/Code Blue flip book 4.00

THUNDERSTRIKE
Marvel Comics: Jan, 2011 - No. 5, Jun, 2011 ($3.99, limited series)

1-5-DeFalco-s/Frenz-a. 1-Back-up origin retold; Nauck-a 4.00

TICK, THE (Also see The Chroma-Tick)
New England Comics Press: Jun, 1988 - No. 12, May, 1993 ($1.75/$1.95/$2.25; B&W, over-sized)

The Tick #1 © Ben Edlund

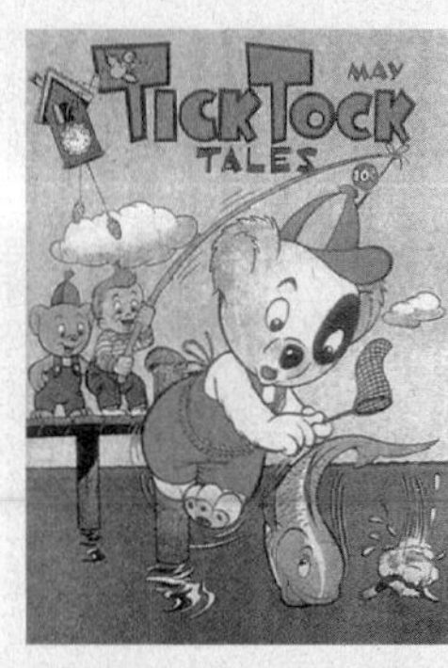

Tick-Tock Tales #5 © ME

Tiger Girl #1 © GK

	GD	VG	FN	VF	VF/NM	NM-
	2.0	4.0	6.0	8.0	9.0	9.2

GD VG FN VF VF/NM NM-
2.0 4.0 6.0 8.0 9.0 9.2

Special Edition 1-1st comic book app. serially numbered & limited to 5,000 copies
10 20 30 69 147 225
Special Edition 1-(5/96, $5.95)-Double-c; foil-c; serially numbered (5,001 thru 14,000)
& limited to 9,000 copies 3 6 9 15 22 28
Special Edition 2-Serially numbered and limited to 3000 copies
5 10 15 35 63 90
Special Edition 2-(8/96, $5.95)-Double-c; foil-c; serially numbered (5,001 thru 14,000)
& limited to 9,000 copies 1 2 3 5 6 8
1-Regular Edition 1st printing; reprints Special Ed. 1 w/minor changes
6 12 18 37 66 95
1-2nd printing 6.00
1-3rd-5th printing 4.00
2-Reprints Special Ed. 2 w/minor changes 3 6 9 14 20 26
2-8-All reprints 4.00
3-5: 4-1st app. Paul the Samurai 1 3 4 6 8 10
6,8 ($2.25) 6.00
7-1st app. Man-Eating Cow 1 2 3 5 6 8
8-Variant with no logo, price, issue number or company logos.
3 6 9 16 24 32
9-12 ($2.75) 5.00
12-Special Edition; card-stock, virgin foil-c; numbered edition
2 4 6 13 18 22
100: The Tick Meets Invincible (6/12, $6.99) Invincible travels to Tick's universe 7.00
101: The Tick Meets Madman (11/12, $6.99) Bonus publishing history of the Tick 7.00
Pseudo-Tick #13 (11/00, $3.50) Continues story from #12 (1993) 5.00
Promo Sampler-(1990)-Tick-c/story 1 2 3 5 6 8

TICK, THE (One shots)
... Big Back to School Special 1-(10/98, $3.50, B&W) Tick & Arthur undercover in H.S. 4.00
... Big Cruise Ship Vacation Special 1-(9/00, $3.50, B&W) 4.00
... Big Father's Day Special 1-(6/00, $3.50, B&W) 4.00
... Big Halloween Special 1-(10/99, $3.50, B&W) 4.00
... Big Halloween Special 2000 (10/00, $3.50) 4.00
... Big Halloween Special 2001 (9/01, $3.95) 4.00
... Big Mother's Day Special 1-(4/00, $3.50, B&W) 4.00
... Big Red-N-Green Christmas Spectacle 1-(12/01, $3.95) 4.00
... Big Romantic Adventure 1-(2/98, $2.95, B&W) Candy box-c with candy map on back 4.00
... Big Summer Annual 1-(7/99, $3.50, B&W) Chainsaw Vigilante vs. Barry 4.00
... Big Summer Fun Special 1-(8/98, $3.50, B&W) Tick and Arthur at summer camp 4.00
... Big Tax Time Terror 1-(4/00, $3.50, B&W) 4.00
... Big Year 2000 Spectacle 1-(3/00, $3.50, B&W) 4.00
FCBD Special Edition (5/10) - reprints debut from 1988; Ben Edlund-s/a 3.00
Free Comic Book Day 2013 (6/13) - New stories; McClelland-s/Redhead-a 3.00
Free Comic Book Day 2014 (6/14) - New stories; McClelland-s/Redhead-a 3.00
Free Comic Book Day 2015 (6/15) - New stories; McClelland-s/Redhead-a 3.00
Free Comic Book Day 2016 (6/16) - New stories; McClelland-s/Redhead-a; Nichols-a 3.00
Free Comic Book Day 2017 (6/17) - New stories; McClelland-s/Redhead-a 3.00
Free Comic Book Day 2018 (6/18) - New stories; McClelland-s/Nichols-a 3.00
Free Comic Book Day 2019 (6/19) - New stories; Nichols-s/a 3.00
...: Halloween Comicfest 2017 (11/17, giveaway) r/#1 (1988) in color 3.00
... Incredible Internet Comic 1-(7/01, $3.95, color) r/New England Comics website story 4.00
Introducing the Tick 1-(4/02, $3.95, color) summary of Tick's life and adventures 4.00
The Tick's Back #0 -(8/97, $2.95, B&W) 4.00
The Tick's Comic Con Extravaganza -(6/07, $3.95, color) Wang-c 4.00
The Tick's 20th Anniversary Special Edition #1 (5/07, $5.95) short stories by various;
history of the character; creator profiles; 2 covers by Suydam & Bisley 6.00

--MASSIVE SUMMER DOUBLE SPECTACLE
1,2-(7,8/00, $3.50, B&W) 5.00

TICK & ARTIE
1-(6/02, $3.50, color) prints strips from Internet comic 4.00
2-(10/02, $3.95) 4.00

TICK AND ARTHUR, THE
New England Comics: Feb, 1999 - No. 6 ($3.50, B&W)
1-6-Sean Wang-s/a 4.00

TICK BIG BLUE DESTINY, THE
New England Comics: Oct, 1997 - No. 9 ($2.95)
1-4: 1-"Keen" Ed. 2-Two covers 4.00
1-($4.95) "Wicked Keen" Ed. w/die cut-c 5.00
5-($3.50) 4.00
6-Luny Bin Trilogy Preview #0 (7/98, $1.50) 4.00
7-9: 7-Luny Bin Trilogy begins 4.00

TICK BIG BLUE YULE LOG SPECIAL, THE
New England Comics: Dec, 1997; 1999 ($2.95, B&W)
1-"Jolly" and "Traditional" covers; flip book w/"Arthur Teaches the Tick About Hanukkah" 4.00
...1999 ($3.50) 4.00
Tick Big Yule Log Special 2001-(12/00, $3.50, B&W) 4.00

TICK, THE : CIRCUS MAXIMUS
New England Comics: Mar, 2000 - No. 4, Jun, 2000 ($3.50, B&W)
1-4-Encyclopedia of characters from Tick comics 4.00
Giant No. 1 (8/03, $14.95) r/#1-4, Redux 15.00
Redux No. 1 (4/01, $3.50) 4.00

TICK, THE - COLOR
New England Comics: Jan, 2001 - No. 6 ($3.95)
1-6: 1-Marc Sandroni-a 4.00

TICK, THE : DAYS OF DRAMA
New England Comics: July, 2005 - No. 6, June, 2006 ($4.95/$3.95, limited series)
1-($4.95) Dave Garcia-a; has a mini-comic attached to cover 5.00
2-6-($3.95) 4.00

TICK, THE - HEROES OF THE CITY
New England Comics: Feb, 1999 - No. 6 ($3.50, B&W)
1-6-Short stories by various 4.00

TICK KARMA TORNADO (The...)
New England Comics Press: Oct, 1993 - No. 9, Mar, 1995 ($2.75, B&W)
1-($3.25) 5.00
2-9: 2-$2.75-c begins 4.00

TICK NEW SERIES (The...)
New England Comics: Dec, 2009 - No. 8 ($4.95)
1-8 5.00

TICK'S BIG XMAS TRILOGY, THE
New England Comics: Dec, 2002 - No. 3, Dec, 2002 ($3.95, limited series)
1-3 4.00

TICK'S GOLDEN AGE COMIC, THE
New England Comics: May, 2002 - No. 3, Feb, 2003 ($4.95, Golden Age size)
1-3-Facsimile 1940s-style Tick issue; 2 covers 5.00
Giant Edition TPB (9/03, $12.95) r/#1-3 13.00

TICK'S GIANT CIRCUS OF THE MIGHTY, THE
New England Comics: Summer, 1992 - No. 3, Fall, 1993 ($2.75, B&W, magazine size)
1-(A-O). 2-(P-Z). 3-1993 Update 5.00

TICK 2017, THE
New England Comics: Sept, 2017 - No. 4, Jun, 2018 ($3.99)
1-4: 1-Bunn & JimmyZ-s/Paszkiewicz-a 4.00

TICKLE COMICS (Also see Gay, Smile, & Whee Comics)
Modern Store Publ.: 1955 (7¢, 5x7-1/4", 52 pgs)
1 9 18 27 50 65 80

TICK TOCK TALES
Magazine Enterprises: Jan, 1946 - V3#33, Jan-Feb, 1951
1-Koko & Kola begin 24 48 72 140 230 320
2 14 28 42 82 121 160
3-10 13 26 39 72 101 130
11-33: 19-Flag-c. 23-Muggsy Mouse, The Pixies & Tom-Tom the Jungle Boy app.
24-X-mas-c. 25-The Pixies & Tom-Tom app. 11 22 33 64 90 115

TIGER (Also see Comics Reading Libraries in the Promotional Comics section)
Charlton Press (King Features): Mar, 1970 - No. 6, Jan, 1971 (15¢)
1 3 6 9 14 20 26
2-6: 3-Ad for life-size inflatable doll 2 4 6 8 11 14

TIGER BOY (See Unearthly Spectaculars)

TIGER GIRL
Gold Key: Sept, 1968 (15¢)
1(10227-809)-Sparling-c/a; Jerry Siegel scripts; advertising on back-c
4 8 12 28 47 65
1-Variant edition with pin-up on back cover 5 10 15 34 60 85

TIGERMAN (Also see Thrilling Adventure Stories)
Seaboard Periodicals (Atlas): Apr, 1975 - No. 3, Sept, 1975 (All 25¢ issues)
1-3: 1-Origin; Colan-c. 2,3-Ditko-p in each 2 4 6 11 16 20

TIGER WALKS, A (See Movie Comics)

TIGRA (The Avengers)
Marvel Comics: May, 2002 - No. 4, Aug, 2002 ($2.99, limited series)

Tillie the Toiler FC #55 © KFS

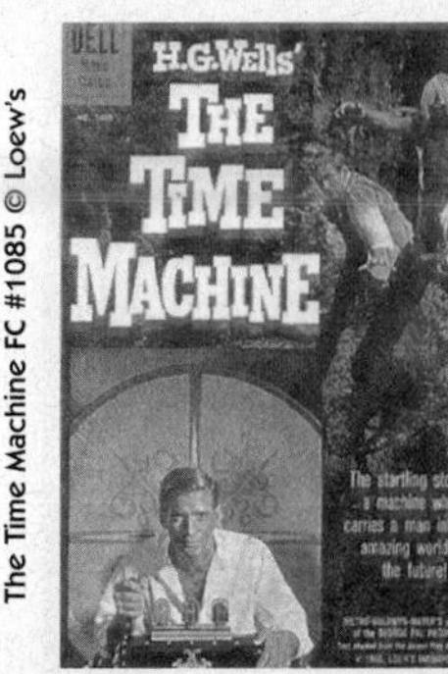

The Time Machine FC #1085 © Loew's

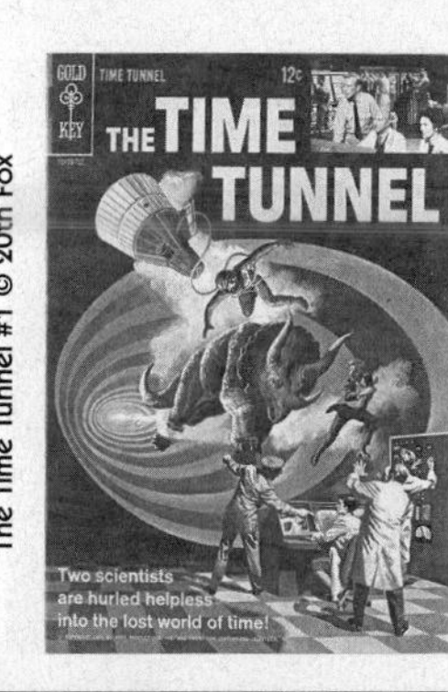

The Time Tunnel #1 © 20th Fox

	GD 2.0	VG 4.0	FN 6.0	VF 8.0	VF/NM 9.0	NM- 9.2
1-4-Christina Z-s/Deodato-c/a						3.00

TIGRESS, THE
Hero Graphics: Aug, 1992 - No. 6?, June, 1993 ($3.95/$2.95, B&W)

	GD	VG	FN	VF	VF/NM	NM-
1,6: 1-Tigress vs. Flare. 6-44 pgs.						4.00
2-5: 2-$2.95-c begins						3.00

TILLIE THE TOILER (See Comic Monthly)
Dell Publishing Co.: No. 15, 1941 - No. 237, July, 1949

	GD	VG	FN	VF	VF/NM	NM-
Four Color 15(1941)	61	122	183	390	670	950
Large Feature Comic 30(1941)	41	82	123	256	428	600
Four Color 8(1942)	25	50	75	182	404	625
Four Color 22(1943)	18	36	54	121	268	415
Four Color 55(1944), 89(1945)	13	26	39	87	191	295
Four Color 106('45),132('46): 132-New stories begin	10	20	30	65	135	205
Four Color 150,176,184	9	18	27	61	123	185
Four Color 195,213,237	8	16	24	52	99	145

TIMBER WOLF (See Action Comics #372, & Legion of Super-Heroes)
DC Comics: Nov, 1992 - No. 5, Mar, 1993 ($1.25, limited series)

1-5 — 3.00

TIME AND WINE
IDW Publishing: Jul, 2017 - No. 4, Oct, 2017 ($4.99, limited series)

1-4-Thomas Zahler-s/a — 5.00

TIME BANDITS
Marvel Comics Group: Feb, 1982 (one-shot, Giant)

1-Movie adaptation — 4.00

TIME BEAVERS (See First Comics Graphic Novel #2)

TIME BOMB
Radical Comics: Jul, 2010 - No. 3, Dec, 2010 ($4.99, limited series)

1-3-Palmiotti & Gray-s/Gulacy-a/c — 5.00

TIMECOP (Movie)
Dark Horse Comics: Sept, 1994 - No. 2, Nov, 1994 ($2.50, limited series)

1,2-Adaptation of film — 3.00

TIME FOR LOVE (Formerly Romantic Secrets)
Charlton Comics: V2#53, Oct, 1966; Oct, 1967 - No. 47, May, 1976

	GD	VG	FN	VF	VF/NM	NM-
V2#53(10/66) Herman-s Hermits app.	3	6	9	21	33	45
1-(10/67)	4	8	12	23	37	50
2-(12/67) -10	3	6	9	15	21	26
11,12,14-20	2	4	6	11	16	20
13-(11/69) Ditko-a (7 pgs.)	3	6	9	16	23	30
21-27	2	4	6	9	13	16
28,29,31: 28-Shirley Jones poster. 29-Bobby Sherman pin-up. 31-Bobby Sherman pin-up	2	4	6	11	16	20
30-(10/72)-David Cassidy full page poster	3	6	9	16	24	32
32-47	2	4	6	8	11	14

TIMELESS TOPIX (See Topix)

TIMELY COMICS... (Reprints of recent Marvel issues)
Marvel Comics: Aug, 2016 ($3.00)

	NM-
...: All-New, All-Different Avengers (8/16) r/#1-3; Alex Ross-c	3.00
...: All-New Inhumans (8/16) r/#1-3; Caselli-c	3.00
...: Carnage (8/16) r/#1-3; Del Mundo-c	3.00
...: Daredevil (8/16) r/#1-3; Garney-c	3.00
...: Doctor Strange (8/16) r/#1-3; Bachalo-c	3.00
...: Drax (8/16) r/#1-3; Hepburn-c	3.00
...: Invincible Iron Man (8/16) r/#1-3; Marquez-c	3.00
...: Moon Girl and Devil Dinosaur (8/16) r/#1-3; Reeder-c	3.00
...: New Avengers (8/16) r/#1-3; Sandoval-c	3.00
...: Scarlet Witch (8/16) r/#1-3; Aja-c	3.00
...: Squadron Supreme (8/16) r/#1-3; Alex Ross-c	3.00
...: The Totally Awesome Hulk (8/16) r/#1-3; Cho-c	3.00
...: Ultimates (8/16) r/#1-3; Rocafort-c	3.00
...: Uncanny Inhumans (8/16) r/#1-3; McNiven-c	3.00
...: Venom: Space Knight (8/16) r/#1-3; Olivetti-c	3.00
...: Web Warriors (8/16) r/#1-3; Tedesco-c	3.00

TIMELY PRESENTS: ALL WINNERS
Marvel Comics: Dec, 1999 ($3.99)

1-Reprints All Winners Comics #19 (Fall 1946); new Lago-c — 5.00

TIMELY PRESENTS: HUMAN TORCH
Marvel Comics: Feb, 1999 ($3.99)

1-Reprints Human Torch Comics #5 (Fall 1941); new Lago-c — 5.00

TIME MACHINE, THE
Dell Publishing Co.: No. 1085, Mar, 1960 (H.G. Wells)

	GD	VG	FN	VF	VF/NM	NM-
Four Color 1085-Movie, Alex Toth-a; Rod Taylor photo-c	14	28	42	94	207	320

TIME MASTERS
DC Comics: Feb, 1990 - No. 8, Sept, 1990 ($1.75, mini-series)

	NM-
1-8: New Rip Hunter series. 5-Cave Carson, Viking Prince app. 6-Dr. Fate app.	3.00
TPB (2008, $19.99) r/#1-8 and Secret Origins #43; intro. by Geoff Johns	20.00

TIME MASTERS: VANISHING POINT (Tie-in to Batman: The Return of Bruce Wayne)
DC Comics: Sept, 2010 - No. 6, Feb, 2011 ($3.99, limited series)

	NM-
1-6-Jurgens-s/a/c; Rip Hunter, Superman, Green Lantern & Booster Gold app.	4.00
TPB (2011, $14.99) r/#1-6	15.00

TIMESLIP COLLECTION
Marvel Comics: Nov, 1998 ($2.99, one-shot)

1-Pin-ups reprinted from Marvel Vision magazine — 3.00

TIMESLIP SPECIAL (The Coming of the Avengers)
Marvel Comics: Oct, 1998 ($5.99, one-shot)

1-Alternate world Avengers vs. Odin — 6.00

TIMESTORM 2009/2099
Marvel Comics: June, 2009 - No. 4, Oct, 2009 ($3.99, limited series)

	NM-
1-4-Punisher 2099 transports Spider-Man to 2099; Wolverine app.; Battle-a	4.00
...: Spider-Man One Shot (8/09, $3.99) Reed-s/Craig-a/Renaud-c	4.00
...: X-Men One Shot (8/09, $3.99) Reed-s/Irving-a/Renaud-c	4.00

TIME TO RUN (Based on 1973 Billy Graham movie)
Spire Christian Comics (Fleming H. Revell Co.): 1975 (39¢)

	GD	VG	FN	VF	VF/NM	NM-
nn-By Al Hartley	2	4	6	13	18	22

TIME TUNNEL, THE (TV)
Gold Key: Feb, 1967 - No. 2, July, 1967 (12¢)

	GD	VG	FN	VF	VF/NM	NM-
1-Photo back-c on both issues	6	12	18	42	79	115
2	5	10	15	31	53	75

TIME TWISTERS
Quality Comics: Sept, 1987 - No. 21, 1989 ($1.25/$1.50)

1-21: Alan Moore scripts in 1-4, 6-9, 14 (2 pg.). 14-Bolland-a (2 pg.). 15,16-Guice-c — 4.00

TIME 2: THE EPIPHANY (See First Comics Graphic Novel #9)

TIMEWALKER (Also see Archer & Armstrong)
Valiant: Jan, 1994 - No. 15, Oct, 1995 ($2.50)

	NM-
1-15,0(3/96): 2-"JAN" on-c, February, 1995 in indicia.	3.00
Yearbook 1 (5/95, $2.95)	3.00

TIME WARP (See The Unexpected #210)
DC Comics, Inc.: Oct-Nov, 1979 - No. 5, June-July, 1980 ($1.00, 68 pgs.)

	GD	VG	FN	VF	VF/NM	NM-
1	2	4	6	13	18	22
2-5	2	4	6	8	11	14

NOTE: *Aparo* a-1. *Buckler* a-1p. *Chaykin* a-2. *Ditko* a-1-4. *Kaluta* c-1-5. *G. Kane* a-2. *Nasser* a-4. *Newton* a-1-5p. *Orlando* a-2. *Sutton* a-1-3.

TIME WARP
DC Comics (Vertigo): May, 2013 ($7.99, one-shot)

1-Short story anthology by various incl. Lindelof, Simone; covers by Risso & Jae Lee — 8.00

TIME WARRIORS: THE BEGINNING
Fantasy General Comics: 1986 (Aug) - No. 2, 1986? ($1.50)

1,2-Alpha Track/Skellon Empire — 3.00

TIM HOLT (Movie star) (Becomes Red Mask #42 on; also see Crack Western #72, & Great Western)
Magazine Enterprises: 1948 - No. 41, April-May, 1954 (All 36 pgs.)

	GD	VG	FN	VF	VF/NM	NM-
1-(A-1 #14)-Line drawn-c w/Tim Holt photo on-c; Tim Holt, His horse Lightning & sidekick Chito begin	55	110	165	352	601	850
2-(A-1 #17)(9-10/48)-Photo-c begin, end #18	27	54	81	158	259	360
3-(A-1 #19)-Photo back-c	20	40	60	117	189	260
4(1-2/49),5: 5-Photo front/back-c	15	30	45	85	130	175
6-(5/49)-1st app. The Calico Kid (alias Rex Fury), his horse Ebony & Sidekick Sing-Song (begin series); photo back-c	23	46	69	138	227	315
7-10: 7-Calico Kid by Ayers. 8-Calico Kid by Guardineer (r-in/Great Western #10). 9-Map of Tim's Home Range	15	30	45	83	124	165
11-The Calico Kid becomes The Ghost Rider (origin & 1st app.) by Dick Ayers (r-in/Great Western I.W. #8); his horse Spectre & sidekick Sing-Song begin series	87	174	261	553	952	1350

Tim Holt #30 © ME

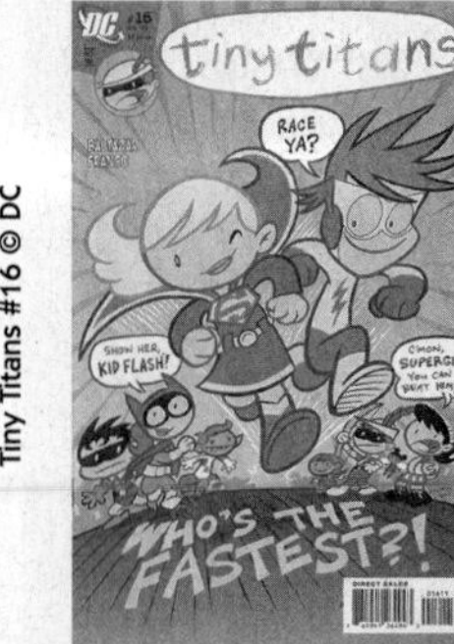

Tiny Titans #16 © DC

Tip Top Comics #34 © UFS

	GD 2.0	VG 4.0	FN 6.0	VF 8.0	VF/NM 9.0	NM- 9.2
12-16,18-Last photo-c	13	26	39	74	105	135
17-Frazetta Ghost Rider-c	77	154	231	493	847	1200
19,22,24: 19-Last Tim Holt-c; Bolle line-drawn-c begin; Tim Holt photo on covers #19-28, 30-41. 22-interior photo-c	11	22	33	62	86	110
20-Tim Holt becomes Redmask (origin); begin series; Redmask-c #20-on	16	32	48	92	144	195
21-Frazetta Ghost Rider/Redmask-c	41	82	123	256	428	600
23-Frazetta Redmask-c	34	68	102	204	332	450
25-1st app. Black Phantom	20	40	60	118	192	265
26-30: 28-Wild Bill Hickok, Bat Masterson team up with Redmask. 29-B&W photo-c	11	22	33	62	86	110
31-33-Ghost Rider ends	10	20	30	56	76	95
34-Tales of the Ghost Rider begins (horror)-Classic "The Flower Women" & "Hard Boiled Harry!"	15	30	45	84	127	170
35-Last Tales of the Ghost Rider	12	24	36	67	94	120
36-The Ghost Rider returns, ends #41; liquid hallucinogenic drug story	14	28	42	82	121	160
37-Ghost Rider classic "To Touch Is to Die!", about Inca treasure	14	28	42	82	121	160
38-The Black Phantom begins (not in #39); classic Ghost Rider "The Phantom Guns of Feather Gap!"	14	28	42	82	121	160
39-41: All 3-D effect c/stories	15	30	45	86	133	180

NOTE: ***Dick Ayers** a-7, 9-41. **Bolle** a-1-41; c-19, 20, 22, 24-28, 30-41.*

TIM McCOY (Formerly Zoo Funnies; Pictorial Love Stories #22 on)
Charlton Comics: No. 16, Oct, 1948 - No. 21, Aug, 1949 (Western Movie Stories)

	GD 2.0	VG 4.0	FN 6.0	VF 8.0	VF/NM 9.0	NM- 9.2
16-John Wayne, Montgomery Clift app. in "Red River"; photo back-c	37	74	111	218	354	490
17-21: 17-Allan "Rocky" Lane guest stars. 18-Rod Cameron guest stars. 19-Whip Wilson, Andy Clyde guest star; Jesse James story. 20-Jimmy Wakely guest stars. 21-Johnny Mack Brown guest stars	27	54	81	160	263	365

TIMMY
Dell Publishing Co.: No. 715, Aug, 1956 - No. 1022, Aug-Oct, 1959

	GD 2.0	VG 4.0	FN 6.0	VF 8.0	VF/NM 9.0	NM- 9.2
Four Color 715 (#1)	6	12	18	37	66	95
Four Color 823 (8/57), 923 (8/58), 1022	5	10	15	33	57	80

TIMMY THE TIMID GHOST (Formerly Win-A-Prize?; see Blue Bird)
Charlton Comics: No. 3, 2/56 - No. 44, 10/64; No. 45, 9/66; 10/67 - No. 23, 7/71; V4#24, 9/85 - No. 26, 1/86

	GD 2.0	VG 4.0	FN 6.0	VF 8.0	VF/NM 9.0	NM- 9.2
3(1956) (1st Series)	14	28	42	82	121	160
4,5	9	18	27	47	61	75
6-10	3	6	9	19	30	40
11,12(4/58,10/58)-(100 pgs.)	6	12	18	37	66	95
13-20	3	6	9	17	26	35
21-45(1966): 27-Nazi story	3	6	9	14	19	24
1(10/67, 2nd series)	3	6	9	15	22	28
2-10	2	4	6	10	14	18
11-23: 23 (7/71)	1	3	4	8	10	12
24-26 (1985-86): Fago-r (low print run)						6.00

TIM TYLER (See Harvey Comics Hits #54)

TIM TYLER (Also see Comics Reading Libraries in the Promotional Comics section)
Better Publications: 1942

	GD 2.0	VG 4.0	FN 6.0	VF 8.0	VF/NM 9.0	NM- 9.2
1	16	32	48	98	154	210

TIM TYLER COWBOY
Standard Comics (King Features Synd.): No. 11, Nov, 1948 - No. 18, Aug, 1950

	GD 2.0	VG 4.0	FN 6.0	VF 8.0	VF/NM 9.0	NM- 9.2
11-By Lyman Young	10	20	30	58	79	100
12-18: 13-15-Full length western adventures	8	16	24	42	54	65

TINKER BELL (Disney, TV)(See Walt Disney Showcase #37)
Dell Publishing Co.: No. 896, Mar, 1958 - No. 982, Apr-June, 1959

	GD 2.0	VG 4.0	FN 6.0	VF 8.0	VF/NM 9.0	NM- 9.2
Four Color 896 (#1)-The Adventures of...	10	20	30	66	138	210
Four Color 982-The New Advs. of...	9	18	27	58	114	170

TINY FOLKS FUNNIES
Dell Publishing Co.: No. 60, 1944

	GD 2.0	VG 4.0	FN 6.0	VF 8.0	VF/NM 9.0	NM- 9.2
Four Color 60	15	30	45	103	227	350

TINY TESSIE (Tessie #1-23; Real Experiences #25)
Marvel Comics (20CC): No. 24, Oct, 1949 (52 pgs.)

	GD 2.0	VG 4.0	FN 6.0	VF 8.0	VF/NM 9.0	NM- 9.2
24	19	38	57	112	179	245

TINY TIM (Also see Super Comics)
Dell Publishing Co.: No. 4, 1941 - No. 235, July, 1949

	GD 2.0	VG 4.0	FN 6.0	VF 8.0	VF/NM 9.0	NM- 9.2
Large Feature Comic 4('41)	50	100	150	315	533	750
Four Color 20(1941)	43	86	129	271	461	650
Four Color 42(1943)	17	34	51	117	259	400
Four Color 235	6	12	18	42	79	115

TINY TITANS (Teen Titans)
DC Comics: Apr, 2008 - No. 50, May, 2012 ($2.25/$2.50/$2.99)

	GD 2.0	VG 4.0	FN 6.0	VF 8.0	VF/NM 9.0	NM- 9.2
1-29-All ages stories of Teen Titans in Elementary school; Baltazar & Franco-s/a						3.00
1-(6/08, Free Comic Book Day giveaway) r/#1; Baltazar & Franco-s/a						3.00
30-50: 30-Begin $2.99-c. 37-Marvel Family app. 44-Doom Patrol app.						3.00

TINY TITANS / LITTLE ARCHIE (Teen Titans) (Digest-size reprint in World of Archie Double Digest Magazine #5)
DC Comics: Dec, 2010 - No. 3, Feb, 2011 ($2.99, limited series)

	GD 2.0	VG 4.0	FN 6.0	VF 8.0	VF/NM 9.0	NM- 9.2
1-3-Character crossover; Baltazar & Franco-s/a. 2-Josie and the Pussycats app.						3.00

TINY TITANS: RETURN TO THE TREEHOUSE
DC Comics: Aug, 2014 - No. 6, Jan, 2015 ($2.99, limited series)

	GD 2.0	VG 4.0	FN 6.0	VF 8.0	VF/NM 9.0	NM- 9.2
1-Baltazar & Franco-s/a in all; Brainiac app.						6.00
2-6: 3-Marvel Family app.						4.00

TINY TOT COMICS
E. C. Comics: Mar, 1946 - No. 10, Nov-Dec, 1947 (For younger readers)

	GD 2.0	VG 4.0	FN 6.0	VF 8.0	VF/NM 9.0	NM- 9.2
1(nn)-52 pg. issues begin, end #4	52	104	156	328	552	775
2 (5/46)	31	62	93	186	303	420
3-10: 10-Christmas-c	27	54	81	160	263	365

TINY TOT FUNNIES (Formerly Family Funnies; becomes Junior Funnies)
Harvey Publ. (King Features Synd.): No. 9, June, 1951

	GD 2.0	VG 4.0	FN 6.0	VF 8.0	VF/NM 9.0	NM- 9.2
9-Flash Gordon, Mandrake, Dagwood, Daisy, etc.	9	18	27	47	61	75

TINY TOTS COMICS
Dell Publishing Co.: 1943 (Not reprints)

	GD 2.0	VG 4.0	FN 6.0	VF 8.0	VF/NM 9.0	NM- 9.2
1-Kelly-a(2); fairy tales	41	82	123	256	428	600

TIPPY & CAP STUBBS (See Popular Comics)
Dell Publishing Co.: No. 210, Jan, 1949 - No. 242, Aug, 1949

	GD 2.0	VG 4.0	FN 6.0	VF 8.0	VF/NM 9.0	NM- 9.2
Four Color 210 (#1)	7	14	21	48	89	130
Four Color 242	5	10	15	31	53	75

TIPPY'S FRIENDS GO-GO & ANIMAL
Tower Comics: July, 1966 - No. 15, Oct, 1969 (25¢)

	GD 2.0	VG 4.0	FN 6.0	VF 8.0	VF/NM 9.0	NM- 9.2
1	9	18	27	63	129	195
2-5,7,9-15: 12-15 titled "Tippy's Friend Go-Go"	6	12	18	37	66	95
6-The Monkees photo-c	8	16	24	56	108	160
8-Beatles app. on front/back-c	10	20	30	68	144	220

TIPPY TEEN (See Vicki)
Tower Comics: Nov, 1965 - No. 25, Oct, 1969 (25¢)

	GD 2.0	VG 4.0	FN 6.0	VF 8.0	VF/NM 9.0	NM- 9.2
1	11	22	33	73	157	240
2-4,6-10	6	12	18	40	73	105
5-1 pg. Beatles pin-up	8	16	24	51	96	140
11-20: 16-Twiggy photo-c	6	12	18	37	66	95
21-25	5	10	15	34	60	85
Special Collectors' Editions nn-(1969, 25¢)	6	12	18	37	66	95

TIPPY TERRY
Super/I. W. Enterprises: 1963

	GD 2.0	VG 4.0	FN 6.0	VF 8.0	VF/NM 9.0	NM- 9.2
Super Reprint #14('63)-r/Little Groucho #1	2	4	6	8	10	14
I.W. Reprint #1 (nd)-r/Little Groucho #1	2	4	6	8	10	14

TIP TOP COMICS
United Features #1-188/St. John #189-210/Dell Publishing Co. #211 on:
4/36 - No. 210, 1957; No. 211, 11-1/57-58 - No. 225, 5-7/61

	GD 2.0	VG 4.0	FN 6.0	VF 8.0	VF/NM 9.0	NM- 9.2
1-Tarzan by Hal Foster, Li'l Abner, Broncho Bill, Fritzi Ritz, Ella Cinders, Capt. & The Kids begin; strip-r (1st comic book app. of each)	950	1900	2850	5800	10,900	16,000
2-Tarzan-c (6/36)	209	418	627	1338	2294	3250
3-Tarzan-c (7/36)	194	388	582	1242	2121	3000
4-(8/36)	106	212	318	678	1164	1650
5-8,10: 7-Photo & biography of Edgar Rice Burroughs. 8-Christmas-c	77	154	231	493	847	1200
9-Tarzan-c (1/37)	103	206	309	659	1130	1600
11,13,16,18-Tarzan-c: 11-Has Tarzan pin-up	77	154	309	493	847	1200
12,14,15,17,19,20: 20-Christmas-c	55	110	165	352	601	850
21,24,27,30-(10/38)-Tarzan-c	61	122	183	390	670	950
22,23,25,26,28,29	39	78	117	240	395	550
31,35,38,40	39	78	117	231	378	525
32,36-Tarzan-c: 32-1st published Jack Davis-a (cartoon). 36-Kurtzman panel (1st published comic work)	60	120	180	381	653	925
33,34,37,39-Tarzan-c	55	110	165	352	601	850
41-Reprints 1st Tarzan Sunday; Tarzan-c	60	120	180	381	653	925

Titan A.E. #1 © 20th Fox

Titans Hunt #8 © DC

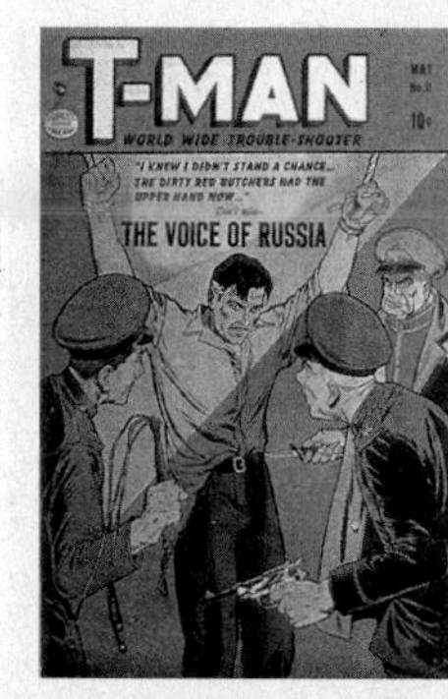

T-Man #11 © QUA

	GD 2.0	VG 4.0	FN 6.0	VF 8.0	VF/NM 9.0	NM- 9.2
42,44,46,48,49	32	64	96	190	310	430
43,45,47,50,52-Tarzan-c. 43-Mort Walker panel	42	84	126	265	445	625
51,53	31	62	93	182	296	410
54-Origin Mirror Man & Triple Terror, also featured on cover	39	78	117	231	378	525
55,56,58: Last Tarzan by Foster	26	52	78	152	249	345
57,59-62-Tarzan by Hogarth	32	64	96	190	310	430
63-80: 65,67-70,72-74,77,78-No Tarzan	16	32	48	98	154	210
81-90	15	30	45	84	127	170
91-99	14	28	42	78	112	145
100	14	28	42	81	118	155
101-140: 110-Gordo story. 111-Li'l Abner app. 118, 132-No Tarzan. 137-Sadie Hawkins Day story	10	20	30	58	79	100
141-170: 145,151-Gordo stories. 153-Fritzi Ritz lingerie panels. 157-Last Li'l Abner; lingerie panels	9	18	27	50	65	80
171,172,174-183: 171-Tarzan reprints by B. Lubbers begin; end #188	9	18	27	52	69	85
173-(3/52) Ties with United Comics #21 for first app. of Peanuts in comics; reprints Peanuts dailies 2/06/51 & 3/05/51 (also see Tip Topper Comics)	306	612	918	2198	3849	5500
184-Peanuts app. (1-2/54)	25	50	75	147	241	335
185-188-Peanuts stories with Charlie Brown & Snoopy on the covers. 185-(3-4/54)	240	480	720	1440	1745	2050
189,191-225-Peanuts apps.(4 pg. to 8 pg stories) in most						
Issues with Peanuts	15	30	45	85	130	175
Issues without Peanuts	8	16	24	42	54	65
190-Peanuts with Charlie Brown & Snoopy partial-c (comic strip at bottom of cover)	36	72	108	211	343	475
Bound Volumes (Very Rare) sold at 1939 World's Fair; bound by publisher in pictorial comic boards (also see Comics on Parade)						
Bound issues 1-12 (Rare)	389	778	1167	2723	4762	6800
Bound issues 13-24	184	368	552	1178	2014	2850
Bound issues 25-36	158	316	474	1011	1731	2450

NOTE: *Tarzan by* ***Foster****-#1-40, 44-50; by* ***Rex Maxon****-#41-43; by* ***Burne Hogarth****-#57, 59, 62.*

TIP TOPPER COMICS
United Features Syndicate: Oct-Nov, 1949 - No. 28, 1954

	GD 2.0	VG 4.0	FN 6.0	VF 8.0	VF/NM 9.0	NM- 9.2
1-Li'l Abner, Abbie & Slats	22	44	66	132	216	300
2	11	22	33	62	86	110
3-5: 5-Fearless Fosdick app.	10	20	30	56	76	95
6-10: 6-Fearless Fosdick app.	9	18	27	52	69	85
11-15	9	18	27	47	61	75
16(4-5/52)-2nd app. of Peanuts (2 pgs.) by Schulz in comics (See United Comics #21 for 1st app. & #22 for 5-6/52 app.)(Also see Tip Top Comics #173)	103	206	309	659	1130	1600
17(6-7/52)-4th app. of Peanuts by Schulz, 2 pgs.	47	94	141	296	498	700
18-28: 18-24,26-28-Early Peanuts (2 pgs.). 25-Early Peanuts (3 pgs.) 26-28-Twin Earths	15	30	45	88	137	200

NOTE: *Many lingerie panels in Fritzi Ritz stories.*

TITAN A.E.
Dark Horse Comics: May, 2000 - No. 3, July, 2000 ($2.95, limited series)

1-3-Movie prequel; Al Rio-a 3.00

TITANS (Also see Teen Titans, New Teen Titans and New Titans)
DC Comics: Mar, 1999 - No. 50, Apr, 2003 ($2.50/$2.75)

1-Titans re-form; Grayson-s; 2 covers 4.00
2-11,13-24,26-50: 2-Superman-c/app. 9,10,21,22-Deathstroke app. 24-Titans from "Kingdom Come" app. 32-36-Asamiya-c. 44-Begin $2.75-c 3.00
12-($3.50, 48 pages) 4.00
25-($3.95) Titans from "Kingdom Come" app.; Wolfman & Faerber-s; art by Pérez, Cardy, Grumment, Jimenez, Dodson, Pelletier 4.00
Annual 1 ('00, $3.50) Planet DC; intro Bushido 4.00
... East Special 1 (1/08, $3.99) Winick-s/Churchill-a; continues in Titans #1 (2008) 4.00
...Secret Files 1,2 (3/99, 10/00; $4.95) Profile pages & short stories 5.00

TITANS (Also see Teen Titans)
DC Comics: Jun, 2008 - No. 38, Oct, 2011 ($3.50/$2.99)

1-($3.50) Titans re-form again; Winick-s/Churchill-a; covers by Churchill & Van Sciver 4.00
2-38: 2-4-Trigon returns. 6-10-Jericho app. 24-Deathstroke & Luthor app. 3.00
Annual 1 (9/11, $4.99) Justice League app.; Jericho returns; Richards-a 5.00
...: Villains For Hire Special 1 (7/10, $4.99) Deathstroke's team; Atom (Ryan Choi) killed 5.00
...: Fractured TPB (2010, $17.99) r/#14,16-22 18.00
...: Lockdown TPB (2009, $14.99) r/#7-11 15.00
...: Old Friends HC (2008, $24.99) r/#1-6 & Titans East Special 25.00
...: Villains For Hire TPB (2011, $14.99) r/#24-27 & Villains For Hire Special 1 15.00

TITANS (DC Rebirth)(Follows Titans Hunt series)
DC Comics: Aug, 2016 - No. 36, Jun, 2019 ($2.99/$3.99)

1-9: 1-Abnett-s/Booth-a; Abra Kadabra returns. 7-Superman app. 3.00
10-24,26-36-($3.99) 10-Fearsome Five app. 11-Lazarus Contract x-over; Teen Titans & Deathstroke app. 12-Rocafort-a. 28-"Drowned Earth" tie-in. 30-34-Kyle Rayner app. 4.00
25-($4.99) Peterson, March & Medri-a 5.00
Annual 1 (5/17, $4.99) Justice League and The Key app.; Abnett-s/Jung-a 5.00
Annual 2 (6/18, $4.99) Abnett-s/Grummett & Derenick-a; Monsieur Mallah & the Brain app. 5.00
...: Rebirth 1 (8/16, $2.99) Abnett-s/Booth-a; Wally West reunites with the Titans 3.00
...: Special 1 (8/18, $4.99) Abnett-s/art by various; Justice League app. 5.00

TITANS BEAT (Teen Titans)
DC Comics: Aug, 1996 (16 pgs., paper-c)

1-Intro./preview new Teen Titans members; Pérez-a 4.00

TITANS: BURNING RAGE (Teen Titans)(Reprints new story from Walmart exclusive)
DC Comics: Oct, 2019 - No. 7, Apr, 2020 ($4.99, limited series)

1-7-Jurgens-s/Eaton-a. 6-Mento app. 7-Blackfire and Mongul app. 4.00

TITANS GIANT (Continued from Teen Titans Giant #7)
DC Comics: 2019 - No. 7, 2019 ($4.99, 100 pgs., squarebound, Walmart exclusive)

1-7: 1-New story Jurgens-s/Eaton-a; reprints from Teen Titans ('03), Super Sons #1 ('17), and Sideways ('18) continue (Issues #8-on) 8.00

TITANS GIANT
DC Comics: 2020 - No. 2, 2020 ($4.99, 100 pgs., squarebound, Mass Market & Direct Market editions exist for each issue, with different covers)

1,2-New stories plus 1st series Teen Titans, Starfire & Super Sons reprints 5.00

TITANS HUNT (Also see DC Universe: Rebirth)
DC Comics: Dec, 2015 - No. 8, Jun, 2016 ($3.99, limited series)

1-7: 1-Abnett-s/Siqueira-a; 1970s-era Titans app. incl. Lilith & Gnarrk. 2,4-Segovia-a 4.00
8-Titans vs. Mr. Twister 4.00

TITANS/ LEGION OF SUPER-HEROES: UNIVERSE ABLAZE
DC Comics: 2000 - No. 4, 2000 ($4.95, prestige format, limited series)

1-4-Jurgens-s/a; P. Jimenez-a; teams battle Universo 5.00

TITAN SPECIAL
Dark Horse Comics: June, 1994 ($3.95, one-shot)

1-($3.95, 52 pgs.) 4.00

TITANS: SCISSORS, PAPER, STONE
DC Comics: 1997 ($4.95, one-shot)

1-Manga style Elseworlds; Adam Warren-s/a(p) 5.00

TITANS SELL-OUT SPECIAL
DC Comics: Nov, 1992 ($3.50, 52 pgs., one-shot)

1-Fold-out Nightwing poster; 1st Teeny Titans 4.00

TITANS/ YOUNG JUSTICE: GRADUATION DAY
DC Comics: Early July, 2003 - No. 3, Aug, 2003 ($2.50, limited series)

1,2-Winick-s/Garza-a; leads into Teen Titans and The Outsiders series. 2-Lilith dies 3.00
3-Death of Donna Troy (Wonder Girl) 3.00
TPB (2003, $6.95) r/#1-3; plus previews of Teen Titans and The Outsiders series 7.00

TITHE, THE (Also see Eden's Fall)
Image Comics (Top Cow): Apr, 2015 - No. 8 ($3.99, limited series)

1-7-Hawkins-s/Ekedal-a; multiple covers on each. 5-7-Sevy-a 4.00

T-MAN (Also see Police Comics #103)
Quality Comics Group: Sept, 1951 - No. 38, Dec, 1956

	GD 2.0	VG 4.0	FN 6.0	VF 8.0	VF/NM 9.0	NM- 9.2
1-Pete Trask, T-Man begins; Jack Cole-a	55	110	165	352	601	850
2-Crandall-c	31	62	93	186	303	420
3,7,8: All Crandall-c	28	56	84	158	274	380
4,5-Crandall-c/a each	30	60	90	177	289	400
6-"The Man Who Could Be Hitler" c/story; Crandall-c.	44	88	132	273	467	660
9,10-Crandall-c	25	50	75	150	245	340
11-Used in **POP**, pg. 95 & color illo.	22	44	66	128	209	290
12,13,15-19,22-26: 23-H-Bomb panel. 24-Last pre-code issue (4/55). 25-Not Crandall-a	17	34	51	105	165	225
14-Hitler-c	33	66	99	194	317	440
20-H-Bomb explosion-c/story	21	42	63	126	206	285
21- "The Return of Mussolini" c/story	21	42	63	126	206	285
27-33,35-38	16	32	48	96	151	205
34-Hitler-c	32	64	96	192	314	435

NOTE: *Anti-communist stories common.* ***Crandall*** *c-2-10p.* ***Cuidera*** *c(i)-1-38. Bondage c-15.*

TMNT: The Last Ronin #1 © Viacom

Toka #1 © DELL

Tomahawk #3 © DC

	GD 2.0	VG 4.0	FN 6.0	VF 8.0	VF/NM 9.0	NM- 9.2

TMNT... (Also see Teenage Mutant Ninja Turtles and related titles)
Mirage Publishing: March 2007 ($3.25/$4.95, B&W, one-shots)

...: Raphael Movie Prequel 1; ...: Michelangelo Movie Prequel 2; ...: Donatello Movie Prequel 3; ...: April Movie Prequel 4; ...: Leonardo Movie Prequel 5; back-story for movie 5.00
...: The Official Movie Adaptation ($4.95) adapts 2007 movie; Munroe-c 5.00

TMNT: BEST OF...
IDW Publishing: Sept, 2020 - Present ($5.99)

... Donatello (11/20) Reprints Donatello #1 (1986), Micro-Series #3 ('11) Macro-Series #1 6.00
... Leonardo (1/21) Reprints Leonardo #1 (1986), Micro-Series #4 ('11) Macro-Series #3 6.00
... Raphael (9/20) Reprints Raphael #1 (1985), Micro-Series #1 ('11) Macro-Series #4 6.00

TMNT: JENNIKA
IDW Publishing: Feb, 2020 - No. 3, Apr, 2020 ($4.99, limited series)

1-3-Brahm Revel-s/a 5.00

TMNT: JENNIKA II
IDW Publishing: Nov, 2020 - Present ($4.99)

1-4: 1-3-Brahm Revel-s/a. 4-Ronda Pattison-s/Jodi Nishijima-a 5.00

TMNT MUTANT UNIVERSE SOURCEBOOK
Archie Comics: 1992 - No. 3, 1992? ($1.95, 52 pgs.)(Lists characters from A-Z)

1-3: 3-New characters; fold-out poster 1 3 4 6 8 10

TMNT: THE LAST RONIN
IDW Publishing: Oct, 2020 - Present ($8.99, oversized 7" x 10-7/8", squarebound)

1-One Turtle in the future; Waltz & Eastman-s/Eastman & Esau-a; Oroku Hiroto app.
3 6 9 19 30 40
2-April O'Neil app.; intro. Casey Marie Jones 2 4 6 9 12 15

TNT COMICS
Charles Publishing Co.: Feb, 1946 (36 pgs.)

1-Yellowjacket app. 41 82 123 256 428 600

TOBY TYLER (Disney, see Movie Comics)
Dell Publishing Co.: No. 1092, Apr-June, 1960

Four Color 1092-Movie, photo-c 6 12 18 38 69 100

TODAY'S BRIDES
Ajax/Farrell Publishing Co.: Nov, 1955; No. 2, Feb, 1956; No. 3, Sept, 1956; No. 4, Nov, 1956

1 14 28 42 76 108 140
2-4 10 20 30 54 72 90

TODAY'S ROMANCE
Standard Comics: No. 5, March, 1952 - No. 8, Sept, 1952 (All photo-c?)

5-Photo-c 15 30 45 85 130 175
6-Photo-c; Toth-a 15 30 45 85 133 180
7,8 14 28 42 76 108 140

TODD, THE UGLIEST KID ON EARTH
Image Comics: Jan, 2013 - No. 8, Jan, 2014 ($2.99)

1-8-Perker-a/Kristensen-s 3.00

TOE TAGS FEATURING GEORGE A. ROMERO
DC Comics: Dec, 2004 - No. 6, May, 2005 ($2.95/$2.99)

1-6-Zombie story by George Romero; Wrightson-c/Castillo-a 3.00

TOIL AND TROUBLE
BOOM! Studios (Archaia): Sept, 2015 - No. 6 ($3.99)

1-6-Mairghread Scott-s/Kelly & Nicole Matthews-a 4.00

TOKA (Jungle King)
Dell Publishing Co.: Aug-Oct, 1964 - No. 10, Jan, 1967 (Painted-c #1,2)

1 4 8 12 28 47 65
2 3 6 9 17 26 35
3-10 3 6 9 15 22 28

TOKYO GHOST
Image Comics: Sept, 2015 - No. 10, Aug, 2016 ($3.99)

1-10-Rick Remender-s/Sean Murphy-a 4.00

TOKYO STORM WARNING (See Red/Tokyo Storm Warning for TPB)
DC Comics (Cliffhanger): Aug, 2003 - No. 3, Dec, 2003 ($2.95, limited series)

1-3-Warren Ellis-s/James Raiz-a 3.00

TOMAHAWK (Son of... on-c of #131-140; see Star Spangled Comics #69 & World's Finest Comics #65)
National Periodical Publications: Sept-Oct, 1950 - No. 140, May-June, 1972

1-Tomahawk & boy sidekick Dan Hunter begin by Fred Ray
187 374 561 1197 2049 2900
2-Frazetta/Williamson-a (4 pgs.) 71 142 213 454 777 1100
3-5 41 82 123 256 428 600
6-10: 7-Last 52 pg. issue 36 72 108 211 343 475
11-20 24 48 72 142 234 325
21-27,30: 30-Last precode (2/55) 21 42 63 126 206 285
28-1st app. Lord Shilling (arch-foe) 22 44 66 132 216 300
29-Frazetta-r/Jimmy Wakely #3 (3 pgs.) 26 52 78 154 252 350
31-40 18 36 54 107 169 230
41-50 10 20 30 64 132 200
51-56,58-60 9 18 27 58 114 170
57-Frazetta-r/Jimmy Wakely #6 (3 pgs.) 10 20 30 64 132 200
61-77: 77-Last 10¢ issue 8 16 24 54 102 150
78-85: 81-1st app. Miss Liberty. 83-Origin Tomahawk's Rangers
7 14 21 46 86 125
86-99: 96-Origin/1st app. The Hood, alias Lady Shilling
5 10 15 35 63 90
100 6 12 18 37 66 95
101-110: 107-Origin/1st app. Thunder-Man 5 10 15 30 50 70
111-115,120,122: 122-Last 12¢ issue 4 8 12 28 47 65
116-1st Neal Adams cover 23 46 69 161 356 550
117-119,121,123-130-Neal Adams-c. 118-Origin of the Rangers
6 12 18 38 69 100
131-Frazetta-r/Jimmy Wakely #7 (3 pgs.); origin Firehair retold
3 6 9 21 33 45
132-135: 135-Last 15¢ issue 3 6 9 16 24 32
136-138,140 (52 pg. Giants) 3 6 9 19 30 40
139-Frazetta-r/Star Spangled #113 3 6 9 21 33 45

NOTE: *Fred Ray c-1, 2, 8, 11, 30, 34, 35, 40-43, 45, 46, 82. Firehair by Kubert-131-134, 136. Maurer a-138. Severin a-135. Starr a-5. Thorne a-137, 140.*

TOM AND JERRY (See Comic Album #4, 8, 12, Dell Giant #21, Dell Giants, Golden Comics Digest #1, 5, 8, 13, 15, 18, 22, 25, 28, 35, Kite fun Book & March of Comics #21, 46, 61, 70, 88, 103, 119, 128, 145, 154, 173, 190, 207, 224, 281, 295, 305, 321,333, 345, 361, 365, 388, 400, 444, 451, 463, 480)

TOM AND JERRY (...Comics, early issues) (M.G.M.)
(Formerly Our Gang No. 1-59) (See Dell Giants for annuals)
Dell Publishing Co./Gold Key No. 213-327/Whitman No. 328 on: No. 193, 6/48; No. 60, 7/49 - No. 212, 7-9/62; No. 213, 11/62 - No. 291, 2/75; No. 292, 3/77 - No. 342, 5/82 - No. 344, 6/84

Four Color 193 (#1)-Titled "M.G.M. Presents..." 26 52 78 182 404 625
60-Barney Bear, Benny Burro cont. from Our Gang; Droopy begins
12 24 36 84 185 285
61 9 18 27 61 123 185
62-70: 66-X-Mas-c 7 14 21 49 92 135
71-80: 77,90-X-Mas-c. 79-Spike & Tyke begin 6 12 18 40 73 105
81-99 5 10 15 35 63 90
100 6 12 18 37 66 95
101-120 5 10 15 31 53 75
121-140: 126-X-Mas-c 4 8 12 28 47 65
141-160 4 8 12 25 40 55
161-200 4 8 12 23 37 50
201-212(7-9/62)(Last Dell issue) 3 6 9 21 33 45
213,214-(84 pgs.)-Titled "...Funhouse" 5 10 15 35 63 90
215-240: 215-Titled "...Funhouse" 3 6 9 16 24 32
241-270 2 4 6 11 16 20
271-300: 286- "Tom & Jerry" 2 4 6 8 11 14
301-327 (Gold Key) 1 3 4 6 8 10
328,329 (Whitman) 2 4 6 8 11 14
330(8/80),331(10/80), 332-(3-pack only) 4 8 12 27 44 60
333-341: 339(2/82), 340(2-3/82), 341(4/82) 2 4 6 8 10 12
342-344 (All #90058, no date, date code, 3-pack): 342(6/83), 343(8/83), 344(6/84)
3 6 9 16 24 32
Mouse From T.R.A.P. 1(7/66)-Giant, G. K. 4 8 12 28 47 65
Summer Fun 1(7/67, 68 pgs.)(Gold Key)-Reprints Barks' Droopy from Summer Fun #1
4 8 12 28 47 65

NOTE: *#60-87, 98-121, 268, 277, 289, 302 are 52 pgs.. Reprints-#225, 241, 245, 247, 252, 254, 266, 268, 270, 292-327, 329-342, 344.*

TOM & JERRY
Harvey Comics: Sept, 1991 - No. 18, Aug, 1994 ($1.25)

1-18: 1-Tom & Jerry, Barney Bear-r by Carl Barks 4.00
50th Anniversary Special 1 (10/91, $2.50, 68 pgs.)-Benny the Lonesome Burro-r by Barks (story/a)/Our Gang #9 5.00

TOMB OF DARKNESS (Formerly Beware)
Marvel Comics Group: No. 9, July, 1974 - No. 23, Nov, 1976

9 4 8 12 23 37 50
10-23: 11,16,18-21-Kirby-a. 15,19-Ditko-r. 17-Woodbridge-r/Astonishing #62; Powell-r.

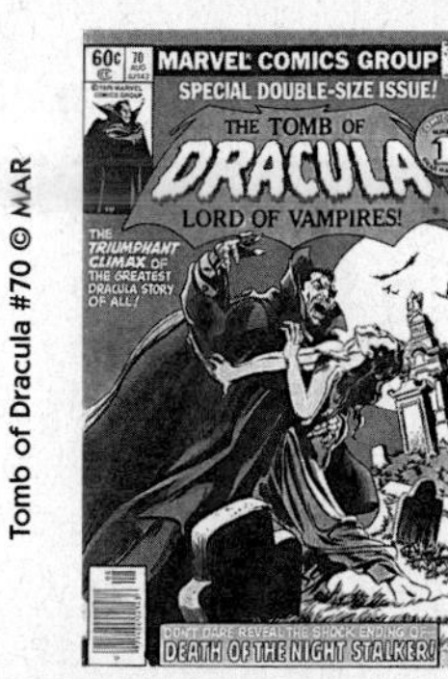

Tomb of Dracula #70 © MAR

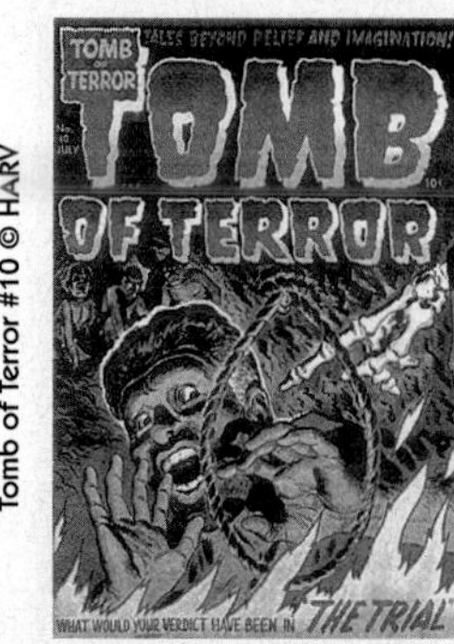

Tomb of Terror #10 © HARV

Tomb Raider (2016 series) #4 © Square Enix

	GD 2.0	VG 4.0	FN 6.0	VF 8.0	VF/NM 9.0	NM- 9.2
20-Everett Venus-r/Venus #19. 23-Everett-r	3	6	9	16	23	30
20,21-(30¢-c variants, limited distribution)(5,7/76)	9	18	27	63	129	195

TOMB OF DRACULA (See Giant-Size Dracula, Dracula Lives, Nightstalkers, Power Record Comics & Requiem for Dracula)
Marvel Comics Group: Apr, 1972 - No. 70, Aug, 1979

	GD 2.0	VG 4.0	FN 6.0	VF 8.0	VF/NM 9.0	NM- 9.2
1-1st app. Dracula & Frank Drake; Colan-p in all; Neal Adams-c	25	50	75	175	388	600
2	8	16	24	52	99	145
3-6: 3-Intro. Dr. Rachel Van Helsing & Inspector Chelm. 6-Neal Adams-c	6	12	18	40	73	105
7-9	5	10	15	35	63	90
10-1st app. Blade the Vampire Slayer (who app. in 1998, 2002 and 2004 movies)	59	118	177	472	1061	1650
10-Facsimile Edition (1/20, $3.99) Reprints #10 with original ads						4.00
11,14-16,20:	5	10	15	30	50	70
12-2nd app. Blade; Brunner-c(p)	9	18	27	57	111	165
13-Origin Blade	10	20	30	69	147	225
17,19: 17-Blade bitten by Dracula. 19-Blade discovers he is immune to vampire's bite. 1st mention of Blade having vampire blood in him	6	12	18	40	73	105
18-Two-part x-over cont'd in Werewolf by Night #15	6	12	18	37	66	95
21,24-Blade app.	5	10	15	30	50	70
22,23,26,27,29	3	6	9	19	30	40
25-1st app. & origin Hannibal King	6	12	18	40	73	105
25-2nd printing (1994)	2	4	6	8	10	12
28-Blade app. on-c & inside as an illusion	5	10	15	30	50	70
30,41,42,44,45-Blade app. 45-Intro. Deacon Frost, the vampire who bit Blade's mother	4	8	12	25	40	55
31-40	3	6	9	17	26	35
43-Blade-c by Wrightson	4	8	12	28	47	65
43-45-(30¢-c variants, limited distribution)	8	16	24	52	99	145
46,47-(Regular 25¢ editions)(4-8/76)	3	6	9	14	20	25
46,47-(30¢-c variants, limited distribution)	7	14	21	44	82	120
48,49,51-57,59,60: 57,59,60-(30¢-c)	3	6	9	14	20	25
50-Silver Surfer app.	4	8	12	25	40	55
57,59,60-(35¢-c variants)(6-9/77)	11	22	33	72	154	235
58-All Blade issue (Regular 30¢ edition)	4	8	12	28	47	65
58-(35¢-c variant)(7/77)	11	22	33	76	163	250
61-69	3	6	9	14	20	25
70-Double size	4	8	12	23	37	50

NOTE: ***N. Adams** c-1, 6. **Colan** a-1-70p; c(p)-8, 38-42, 44-56, 58-70. **Wrightson** c-43.*

TOMB OF DRACULA, THE (Magazine)
Marvel Comics Group: Oct, 1979 - No. 6, Aug, 1980 (B&W)

	GD 2.0	VG 4.0	FN 6.0	VF 8.0	VF/NM 9.0	NM- 9.2
1,3: 1-Colan-a; features on movies "Dracula" and "Love at First Bite" w/photos. 3-Good girl cover-a; Miller-a (2 pg. sketch)	2	4	6	11	16	20
2,6: 2-Ditko-a (36 pgs.); Nosferatu movie feature. 6-Lilith story w/Sienkiewicz-a	2	4	6	8	11	14
4,5: Stephen King interview	2	4	6	13	18	22

NOTE: ***Buscema** a-4p, 5p. **Chaykin** c-5, 6. **Colan** a(p)-1, 3-6. **Miller** a-3. **Romita** a-2p.*

TOMB OF DRACULA
Marvel Comics (Epic Comics): 1991 - No. 4, 1992 ($4.95, 52 pgs., squarebound, mini-series)

Book 1-4: Colan/Williamson-a; Colan painted-c 5.00

TOMB OF DRACULA
Marvel Comics: Dec, 2004 - No. 4, Mar, 2005 ($2.99, limited series)

1-4-Blade app.; Tolagson-a/Sienkiewicz-c 3.00

TOMB OF DRACULA PRESENTS: THRONE OF BLOOD
Marvel Comics: Jun, 2011 ($3.99, one-shot)

1-Story of Raizo Kodo in 1585 Japan; Parlov-a; Hitch-c 4.00

TOMB OF LEGEIA (See Movie Classics)

TOMB OF TERROR (Thrills of Tomorrow #17 on)
Harvey Publications: June, 1952 - No. 16, July, 1954

	GD 2.0	VG 4.0	FN 6.0	VF 8.0	VF/NM 9.0	NM- 9.2
1	61	122	183	390	670	950
2	43	86	129	271	461	650
3-Bondage-c; atomic disaster story	41	82	123	256	428	600
4-12: 4-Heart ripped out. 8-12-Nostrand-a	41	82	123	256	428	600
13-Special S/F issue (1/54) White letter shadow-c	58	116	174	371	636	900
13-Logo variant-c (striped letter shadow)	65	130	195	416	708	1000
14-Classic S/F-c; Check-a	77	154	231	493	847	1200
15-S/F issue; c-shows face exploding	432	864	1296	3154	5577	8000
16-Special S/F issue; horror-c; Nostrand-a	61	122	183	390	670	950

NOTE: ***Edd Cartier** a-13? **Elias** c-3, 5-16. **Kremer** a-1, 7; c-1. **Nostrand** a-8-12, 15r 16. **Palais** a-2, 3, 5-7. **Powell** a-1, 3, 5, 9-16. **Sparling** a-12, 13, 15.*

TOMB OF TERROR
Marvel Comics: Dec, 2010 ($3.99, B&W, one-shot)

1-Short stories of Man-Thing, Son of Satan, Werewolf By Night & The Living Mummy 4.00

TOMB RAIDER (Also see Lara Croft And The Frozen Omen)
Dark Horse Comics: Feb, 2014 - No. 18, Jul, 2015 ($3.50/$3.99)

1-18: 1-6-Gail Simone-s/Nicolás Daniel Selma-a. 13-Begin $3.99-c 4.00

TOMB RAIDER
Dark Horse Comics: Feb, 2016 - No. 12, Jan, 2017 ($3.99)

1-12-Mariko Tamaki-s/Phillip Sevy-a 4.00

TOMB RAIDER (one-shots)
Image Comics (Top Cow Prod.)

...: Arabian Nights (8/04, $5.99) Avery-s/Tan-a/c	6.00
... Cover Gallery 2006 (4/06, $2.99) artist galleries and series gallery; pin-ups	3.00
.../The Darkness Special 1 (2001, TopCowStore.com)-Wohl-s/Tan-a	3.00
Epiphany 1 (8/03, $4.99)-Jurgens-s/Banks-a/Haley-c; preview of Witchblade Animated	5.00
Takeover 1 (1/04, $2.99)-Benefiel-a/Daniel-c	3.00
... Vs. The Wolf-Men: Monster War 2005 (7/05, $2.99) 2nd part of Monster War x-over	3.00
.../Witchblade/Magdalena/Vampirella #1 (8/05, $2.99, B&W) three covers; Chin-a	3.00

TOMB RAIDER: INFERNO
Dark Horse Comics: Jun, 2018 - No. 4, Oct, 2018 ($3.99, limited series)

1-4-Lanzing & Kelly-s/Sevy-a 4.00

TOMB RAIDER: JOURNEYS
Image Comics (Top Cow Prod.): Jan, 2002 - No. 12, May, 2003 ($2.50/$2.99)

1-12: 1-Avery-s/Drew Johnson-a. 1-Two covers by Johnson & Hughes 3.00

TOMB RAIDER: SURVIVOR'S CRUSADE
Dark Horse Comics: Nov, 2017 - No. 4, Apr, 2018 ($3.99, limited series)

1-4-Lanzing & Kelly-s/Ashley Woods-a 4.00

TOMB RAIDER: THE GREATEST TREASURE OF ALL
Image Comics (Top Cow Prod.): 2002; Oct, 2005 ($6.99)

Prelude (2002, 16 pgs., no cover price) Jusko-c/a	3.00
1-(10/05, $6.99) Jusko-a/Jurgens-s; sketch pages, reference photos, art in progress	7.00

TOMB RAIDER: THE SERIES (Also see Witchblade/Tomb Raider)
Image Comics (Top Cow Prod.): Dec, 1999 - No. 50, Mar, 2005 ($2.50/$2.99)

1-Jurgens-s/Park-a; 3 covers by Park, Finch, Turner	5.00
2-24,26-29,31-50: 21-Black-c w/foil. 31-Mhan-a. 37-Flip book preview of Stryke Force	3.00
25-Michael Turner-c/a; Witchblade app.; Endgame x-over with Witchblade #60 & Evo #1	4.00
30-($4.99) Tony Daniel-a	5.00
#0 (6/01, $2.50) Avery-s/Ching-a/c	3.00
#1/2 (10/01, $2.95) Early days of Lara Croft; Jurgens-s/Lopez-a	3.00
...: Chasing Shangri-La (2002, $12.95, TPB) r/#11-15	13.00
Free Comic Book Day giveaway - (5/02) r/#1 with "Free Comic Book Day" banner on-c	3.00
... Gallery (12/00, $2.95) Pin-ups & previous covers by various	3.00
... Magazine (6/01, $4.95) Hughes-c; r/#1,2; Jurgens interview	5.00
...: Mystic Artifacts (2001, $14.95, TPB) r/#5-10	15.00
...: Saga of the Medusa Mask (9/00, $9.95, TPB) r/#1-4; new Park-c	10.00
... Vol. 1 Compendium (11/06, $59.99) r/#1-50; variant covers and pin-up art	60.00

TOMB RAIDER/WITCHBLADE SPECIAL (Also see Witchblade/Tomb Raider)
Top Cow Prod.: Dec, 1997 (mail-in offer, one-shot)

	GD 2.0	VG 4.0	FN 6.0	VF 8.0	VF/NM 9.0	NM- 9.2
1-Turner-s/a(p); green background cover	1	3	4	6	8	10
1-Variant-c with orange sun background	2	4	6	8	10	12
1-Variant-c with black sides	2	4	6	9	12	15
1-Revisited (12/98, $2.95) reprints #1, Turner-c						3.00
...: Trouble Seekers TPB (2002, $7.95) rep. T.R./W & W/T.R. & W/T.R. 1/2; new Turner-c						8.00

TOMBSTONE TERRITORY
Dell Publishing Co.: No. 1123, Aug, 1960

	GD 2.0	VG 4.0	FN 6.0	VF 8.0	VF/NM 9.0	NM- 9.2
Four Color 1123	7	14	21	49	92	135

TOM CAT (Formerly Bo; Atom The Cat #9 on)
Charlton Comics: No. 4, Apr, 1956 - No. 8, July, 1957

	GD 2.0	VG 4.0	FN 6.0	VF 8.0	VF/NM 9.0	NM- 9.2
4-Al Fago-c/a	8	16	24	44	57	70
5-8	6	12	18	31	38	45

TOM CLANCY'S SPLINTER CELL: ECHOES
Dynamite Entertainment: 2014 - No. 4, 2014 ($3.99)

1-4-Nathan Edmonson-s/Marc Laming-a 4.00

TOM CLANCY'S THE DIVISION: EXTREMIS MALIS
Dark Horse Comics: Jan, 2019 - No. 3, Apr, 2019 ($3.99, limited series)

1-3-Christofer Emgard-s/Fernando Baldó-a 4.00

Tom Mix Western #3 © FAW

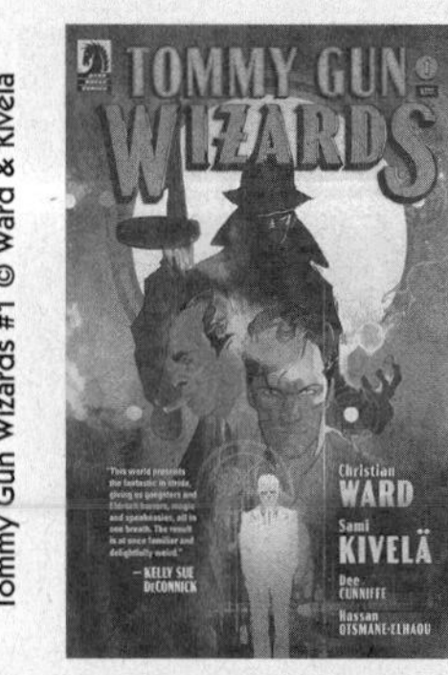

Tommy Gun Wizards #1 © Ward & Kivelä

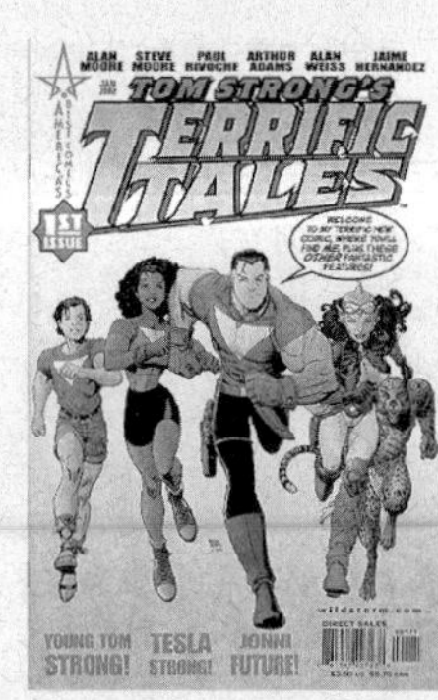

Tom Strong's Terrific Tales #1 © ABC

TOM CORBETT, SPACE CADET (TV)
Dell Publishing Co.: No. 378, Jan-Feb, 1952 - No. 11, Sept-Nov, 1954 (All painted covers)

	GD 2.0	VG 4.0	FN 6.0	VF 8.0	VF/NM 9.0	NM- 9.2
Four Color 378 (#1)-McWilliams-a	17	34	51	117	259	400
Four Color 400,421-McWilliams-a	10	20	30	66	138	210
4(11-1/53) - 11	7	14	21	46	86	125

TOM CORBETT SPACE CADET (See March of Comics #102)

TOM CORBETT SPACE CADET (TV)
Prize Publications: V2#1, May-June, 1955 - V2#3, Sept-Oct, 1955

	GD 2.0	VG 4.0	FN 6.0	VF 8.0	VF/NM 9.0	NM- 9.2
V2#1-Robot-c	37	74	111	222	361	500
2,3-Meskin-c	27	54	81	162	266	370

TOM, DICK & HARRIET (See Gold Key Spotlight)

TOM LANDRY AND THE DALLAS COWBOYS
Spire Christian Comics/Fleming H. Revell Co.: 1973 (35/49¢)

	GD 2.0	VG 4.0	FN 6.0	VF 8.0	VF/NM 9.0	NM- 9.2
nn-35¢ edition	3	6	9	16	23	30
nn-49¢ edition	2	4	6	10	16	20

TOM MIX WESTERN (Movie, radio star) (Also see The Comics, Crackajack Funnies, Master Comics, 100 Pages Of Comics, Popular Comics, Real Western Hero, Six Gun Heroes, Western Hero & XMas Comics)
Fawcett Publications: Jan, 1948 - No. 61, May, 1953 (1-17: 52 pgs.)

	GD 2.0	VG 4.0	FN 6.0	VF 8.0	VF/NM 9.0	NM- 9.2
1 (Photo-c, 52 pgs.)-Tom Mix & his horse Tony begin; Tumbleweed Jr. begins, ends #52,54,55	54	108	162	343	574	825
2 (Photo-c)	25	50	75	150	245	340
3-5 (Painted/photo-c): 5-Billy the Kid & Oscar app.	19	38	57	111	176	240
6-8: 6,7 (Painted/photo-c). 8-Kinstler tempera-c	16	32	48	94	147	200
9,10 (Paint/photo-c) 9-Used in **SOTI**, pgs. 323-325	15	30	45	90	140	190
11-Kinstler oil-c	14	28	42	82	121	160
12 (Painted/photo-c)	14	28	42	78	112	145
13-17 (Painted-c, 52 pgs.)	14	28	42	78	112	145
18,22 (Painted-c, 36 pgs.)	12	24	36	69	97	125
19 (Photo-c, 52 pgs.)	13	26	39	74	105	135
20,21,23 (Painted-c, 52 pgs.)	12	24	36	69	97	125
24,25,27-29 (52 pgs.): 24-Photo-c begin, end #61. 29-Slim Pickens app.	11	22	33	60	83	105
26,30 (36 pgs.)	10	20	30	56	76	95
31-33,35-37,39,40,42 (52 pgs.): 39-Red Eagle app.	10	20	30	56	76	95
34,38 (36 pgs. begin)	9	18	27	52	69	85
41,43-60: 57-(9/52)-Dope smuggling story	8	16	24	40	50	60
61-Last issue	9	18	27	47	61	75

NOTE: *Photo-c from 1930s Tom Mix movies (he died in 1940). Many issues contain ads for Tom Mix, Rocky Lane, Space Patrol and other premiums. Captain Tootsie by* **C.C. Beck** *in #6-11, 20.*

TOM MIX WESTERN
AC Comics: 1988 - No. 2, 1989? ($2.95, B&W w/16 pgs. color, 44 pgs.)

	NM- 9.2
1-Tom Mix-r/Master #124,128,131,102 plus Billy the Kid-r by Severin; photo front/back/inside-c	4.00
2-($2.50, B&W)-Gabby Hayes-r; photo covers	4.00
...Holiday Album 1 (1990, $3.50, B&W, one-shot, 44 pgs.)-Contains photos & 1950s Tom Mix-r; photo inside-c	4.00

TOMMY GUN WIZARDS (Titled Machine Gun Wizards for #4)
Dark Horse Comics: Aug, 2019 - No. 4, Nov, 2019 ($3.99, limited series)

	NM- 9.2
1-4-Christian Ward-s/Sami Kivelä-a; Prohibition era magicians in 1931 Chicago	4.00

TOMMY OF THE BIG TOP (Thrilling Circus Adventures)
King Features Synd./Standard Comics: No. 10, Sep, 1948 - No. 12, Mar, 1949

	GD 2.0	VG 4.0	FN 6.0	VF 8.0	VF/NM 9.0	NM- 9.2
10-By John Lehti	14	28	42	76	108	140
11,12	10	20	30	54	72	90

TOMMY TOMORROW (See Action Comics #127, Real Fact #6, Showcase #41,42,44,46,47 & World's Finest #102)

TOMOE (Also see Shi: The Way Of the Warrior #6)
Crusade Comics: July, 1995 - No. 3, June, 1996($2.95)

	GD 2.0	VG 4.0	FN 6.0	VF 8.0	VF/NM 9.0	NM- 9.2
0-3: 2-B&W Dogs o' War preview. 3-B&W Demon Gun preview						3.00
0 (3/96, $2.95)-variant-c.						3.00
0-Commemorative edition (5,000)	2	4	6	8	10	12
1-Commemorative edition (5,000)	2	4	6	9	12	15
1-($2.95)-FAN Appreciation edition						3.00
TPB (1997, $14.95) r/#0-3						15.00

TOMOE: UNFORGETTABLE FIRE
Crusade Comics: June, 1997 ($2.95, one-shot)

	NM- 9.2
1-Prequel to Shi: The Series	3.00

TOMOE-WITCHBLADE/FIRE SERMON
Crusade Comics: Sept, 1996 ($3.95, one-shot)

	NM- 9.2
1-Tucci-c	5.00
1-($9.95)-Avalon Ed. w/gold foil-c	10.00

TOMOE-WITCHBLADE/MANGA SHI PREVIEW EDITION
Crusade Comics: July, 1996 ($5.00, B&W)

	NM- 9.2
nn-San Diego Preview Edition	5.00

TOMORROW
Dark Horse Comics (Berger Books): Feb, 2020 - No. 5 ($3.99, limited series)

	NM- 9.2
1,2-Peter Milligan-s/Jesús Hervás-a	4.00

TOMORROW KNIGHTS
Marvel Comics (Epic Comics): June, 1990 - No. 6, Mar, 1991 ($1.50)

	NM- 9.2
1-($1.95, 52 pgs.)	4.00
2-6	3.00

TOMORROW STORIES
America's Best Comics: Oct, 1999 - No. 12, Aug, 2002 ($3.50/$2.95)

	NM- 9.2
1-Two covers by Ross and Nowlan; Moore-s	4.00
2-12-($2.95) 6-1st app. Splash Brannigan	3.00
... Special (1/06, $6.99) Nowlan-c; Moore-s; Greyshirt tribute to Will Eisner	7.00
... Special 2 (5/06, $6.99) Gene Ha-c; Moore-s; Promethea app.	7.00
Book 1 Hardcover (2002, $24.95) r/#1-6	25.00
Book 1 TPB (2003, $17.95) r/#1-6	18.00
Book 2 Hardcover (2004, $24.95) r/#7-12	25.00
Book 2 TPB (2005, $17.99) r/#7-12	18.00

TOM SAWYER (See Adventures of... & Famous Stories)

TOM SKINNER-UP FROM HARLEM (See Up From Harlem)

TOM STRONG (Also see Many Worlds of Tesla Strong)
America's Best Comics: June, 1999 - No. 36, May, 2006 ($3.50/$2.95/$2.99)

	NM- 9.2
1-Two covers by Ross and Sprouse; Moore-s/Sprouse-a	4.00
1-Special Edition (9/09, $1.00) reprint with "After Watchmen" cover frame	3.00
2-36: 4-Art Adams-a (8 pgs.) 13-Fawcett homage w/art by Sprouse, Baker, Heath 20-Origin of Tom Stone. 22-Ordway-a. 31,32-Moorcock-s	3.00
...: Book One HC ('00, $24.95) r/#1-7, cover gallery and sketchbook	25.00
...: Book One TPB ('01, $14.95) r/#1-7, cover gallery and sketchbook	15.00
...: Book Two HC ('02, $24.95) r/#8-14, sketchbook	25.00
...: Book Two TPB ('03, $14.95) r/#8-14, sketchbook	15.00
...: Book Three HC ('04, $24.95) r/#15-19, sketchbook	25.00
...: Book Three TPB ('04, $17.95) r/#15-19, sketchbook	18.00
...: Book Four HC ('04, $24.95) r/#20-25, sketch pages	25.00
...: Book Four TPB ('05, $17.99) r/#20-25, sketch pages	18.00
...: Book Five HC ('05, $24.99) r/#26-30, sketch pages	25.00
...: Book Five TPB ('06, $17.99) r/#26-30, sketch pages	18.00
...: Book Six HC ('06, $24.99) r/#31-36	25.00
...: Book Six TPB ('08, $17.99) r/#31-36	18.00
...: The Deluxe Edition Book One (2009, $39.99, d.j.) r/#1-12; Moore intro.; sketch-a	40.00
...: The Deluxe Edition Book Two (2010, $39.99, d.j.) r/#13-24; sketch-a	40.00

TOM STRONG AND THE PLANET OF PERIL
DC Comics (Vertigo): Sept, 2013 - No. 6, Feb, 2014 ($2.99, limited series)

	NM- 9.2
1-6-Hogan-s/Sprouse-a/c. 2-Travel to Terra Obscura	3.00

TOM STRONG AND THE ROBOTS OF DOOM
DC Comics (WildStorm): Aug, 2010 - No. 6, Jan, 2011 ($3.99, limited series)

	NM- 9.2
1-6-Hogan-s/Sprouse-a. 1-Covers by Sprouse & Williams	4.00
TPB (2011, $17.99) r/#1-6	18.00

TOM STRONG'S TERRIFIC TALES
America's Best Comics: Jan, 2002 - No. 12 ($3.50/$2.95)

	NM- 9.2
1-Short stories; Moore-s; art by Art Adams, Rivoche, Hernandez, Weiss	3.50
2-12-($2.95) 2-Adams, Ordway, Weiss-a; Adams-c. 4-Rivoche-a. 5-Pearson, Aragonés-a 11-Timm-a	3.00
...: Book One HC ('04, $24.95) r/#1-6, cover gallery and sketch pages	25.00
...: Book One SC ('05, $17.99) r/#1-6, cover gallery and sketch pages	18.00
...: Book Two HC ('05, $24.95) r/#7-12, covers	25.00

TOM TERRIFIC! (TV)(See Mighty Mouse Fun Club Magazine #1)
Pines Comics (Paul Terry): Summer, 1957 - No. 6, Fall, 1958
(See Terry Toons Giant Summer Fun Book)

	GD 2.0	VG 4.0	FN 6.0	VF 8.0	VF/NM 9.0	NM- 9.2
1-1st app.?; CBS Television Presents...	23	46	69	138	227	315
2-6-(scarce)	17	34	51	103	162	220

TOM THUMB
Dell Publishing Co.: No. 972, Jan, 1959

	GD 2.0	VG 4.0	FN 6.0	VF 8.0	VF/NM 9.0	NM- 9.2
Four Color 972-Movie, George Pal	8	16	24	52	99	145

Tony Stark: Iron Man #14 © MAR

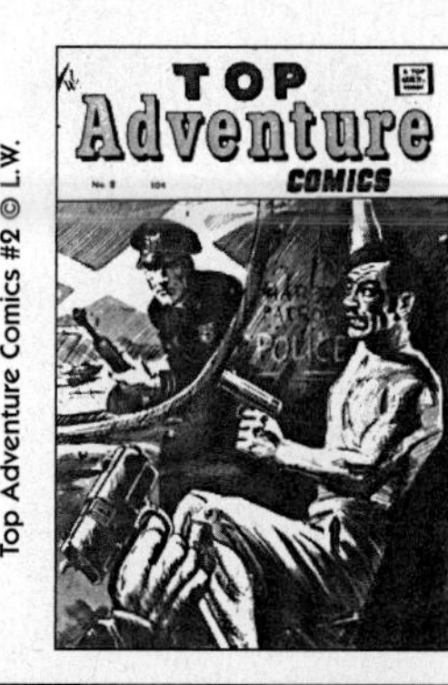

Top Adventure Comics #2 © L.W.

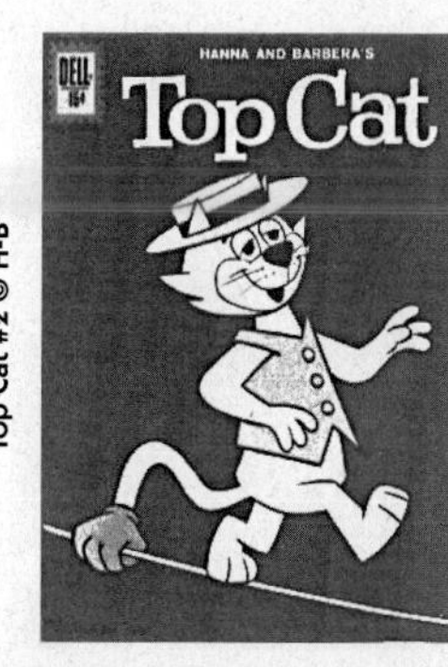

Top Cat #2 © H-B

	GD 2.0	VG 4.0	FN 6.0	VF 8.0	VF/NM 9.0	NM- 9.2

TOM-TOM, THE JUNGLE BOY (See A-1 Comics & Tick Tock Tales)
Magazine Enterprises: 1947 - No. 3, 1947; Nov, 1957 - No. 3, Mar, 1958

1-Funny animal 15 30 45 85 130 175
2,3(1947): 3-Christmas issue 11 22 33 62 86 110
Tom-Tom & Itchi the Monk 1(11/57) - 3(3/58) 6 12 18 31 38 45
I.W. Reprint No. 1,2,8,10: 1,2,8-r/Koko & Kola #? 2 4 6 8 11 14

TONGUE LASH
Dark Horse Comics: Aug, 1996 - No. 2, Sept, 1996 ($2.95, lim. series, mature)

1,2: Taylor-c/a 3.00

TONGUE LASH II
Dark Horse Comics: Feb, 1999 - No. 2, Mar, 1999 ($2.95, lim. series, mature)

1,2: Taylor-c/a 3.00

TONKA (Disney)
Dell Publishing Co.: No. 966, Jan, 1959

Four Color 966-Movie (Starring Sal Mineo)-photo-c 8 16 24 54 102 150

TONTO (See The Lone Ranger's Companion...)

TONY STARK: IRON MAN (Leads into Iron Man 2020 #1)
Marvel Comics: Aug, 2018 - No. 19, Feb, 2020 ($4.99/$3.99)

1-($4.99) Slott-s/Schiti-a; Fin Fang Foom & The Controller app. 5.00
2-19-($3.99) 3-Machine Man app. 4,6-8-Janet Van Dyne app. 5-Arno Stark app.
12,13-War of the Realms tie-ins; Simone-s. 14-Capt. Marvel app. 16-19 Ultron app. 4.00

TONY TRENT (The Face #1,2)
Big Shot/Columbia Comics Group: No. 3, 1948 - No. 4, 1949

3,4: 3-The Face app. by Mart Bailey 20 40 60 115 188 260

TOODLES, THE (The Toodle Twins with #1)
Ziff-Davis (Approved Comics)/Argo: No. 10, July-Aug, 1951; Mar, 1956 (Newspaper-r)

10-Painted-c, some newspaper-r by The Baers 15 30 45 84 127 170
...Twins 1(Argo, 3/56)-Reprints by The Baers 8 16 24 44 57 70

TOO MUCH COFFEE MAN
Adhesive Comics: July, 1993 - No. 10, Dec, 2000 ($2.50, B&W)

1-Shannon Wheeler story & art 2 4 6 9 12 15
2,3 1 2 3 5 7 9
4,5 6.00
6-10 4.00
Full Color Special-nn($2.95),2-(7/97, $3.95) 4.00

TOO MUCH COFFEE MAN SPECIAL
Dark Horse Comics: July, 1997 ($2.95, B&W)

nn-Reprints Dark Horse Presents #92-95 4.00

TOO MUCH HOPELESS SAVAGES
Oni Press: June, 2003 - No. 4, Apr, 2004 ($2.99, B&W, limited series)

1-4-Van Meter-s/Norrie-a 3.00
TPB (8/04, $11.95, digest-size) r/series 12.00

TOOTH & CLAW (See Autumnlands: Tooth & Claw)

TOOTS AND CASPER
Dell Publishing Co.: No. 5, 1942

Large Feature Comic 5 24 48 72 140 230 320

TOP ADVENTURE COMICS
I. W. Enterprises: 1964 (Reprints)

1-r/High Adv. (Explorer Joe #2); Krigstein-r 2 4 6 11 16 20
2-Black Dwarf-r/Red Seal #22; Kinstler-c 2 4 6 13 18 22

TOP CAT (TV) (Hanna-Barbera)(See Kite Fun Book)
Dell Publ.Co./Gold Key No. 4 on: 12-2/61-62 - No. 3, 6-8/62; No. 4, 10/62 - No. 31, 9/70

1 (TV show debuted 9/27/61) 14 28 42 94 207 320
2-Augie Doggie back-ups in #1-4 8 16 24 54 102 150
3-5: 3-Last 15¢ issue. 4-Begin 12¢ issues; Yakky Doodle app. in 1 pg. strip.
5-Touché Turtle app. 6 12 18 37 66 95
6-10 5 10 15 30 50 70
11-20 4 8 12 23 37 50
21-31-Reprints 3 6 9 18 28 38

TOP CAT (TV) (Hanna-Barbera)(See TV Stars #4)
Charlton Comics: Nov, 1970 - No. 20, Nov, 1973

1 6 12 18 41 76 110
2-10 3 6 9 19 30 40
11-20 3 6 9 16 24 32

NOTE: *#8 (1/72) went on sale late in 1972 between #14 and #15 with the 1/73 issues.*

TOP COMICS
K. K. Publications/Gold Key: July, 1967 (All reprints)

nn-The Gnome-Mobile (Disney-movie) 2 4 6 13 18 22
1-Beagle Boys (#7), Beep Beep the Road Runner (#5), Bugs Bunny, Chip 'n' Dale, Daffy Duck (#50), Flipper, Huey, Dewey & Louie, Junior Woodchucks, Lassie, The Little Monsters (#71), Moby Duck, Porky Pig (has Gold Key label - says Top Comics on inside), Scamp, Super Goof, Tom & Jerry, Top Cat (#21), Tweety & Sylvester (#7), Walt Disney C&S (#322), Woody Woodpecker known issues; each character given own book 2 4 6 9 13 16
1-Donald Duck (not Barks), Mickey Mouse 2 4 6 13 18 22
1-Flintstones 3 6 9 21 33 45
1-Huckleberry Hound, Yogi Bear (#30) 3 6 9 14 19 24
1-The Jetsons 4 8 12 28 47 65
1-Tarzan of the Apes (#169) 3 6 9 15 22 28
1-Three Stooges (#35) 3 6 9 17 26 35
1-Uncle Scrooge (#70) 3 6 9 16 23 30
1-Zorro (r/G.K. Zorro #7 w/Toth-a; says 2nd printing) 3 6 9 14 19 24
2-Bugs Bunny, Daffy Duck, Mickey Mouse (#114), Porky Pig, Super Goof, Tom & Jerry, Tweety & Sylvester, Walt Disney's C&S (r/#325), Woody Woodpecker 2 4 6 9 12 15
2-Donald Duck (not Barks), Three Stooges, Uncle Scrooge (#71)-Barks-c, Yogi Bear (#30), Zorro (r/#8; Toth-a) 2 4 6 11 16 20
2-Snow White & 7 Dwarfs(6/67)(1944-r) 2 4 6 10 14 18
3-Donald Duck 2 4 6 11 16 20
3-Uncle Scrooge (#72) 2 4 6 13 18 22
3,4-The Flintstones 3 6 9 21 33 45
3,4: 3-Mickey Mouse (r/#115), Tom & Jerry, Woody Woodpecker, Yogi Bear.
4-Mickey Mouse, Woody Woodpecker 2 4 6 9 12 15

NOTE: *Each book in this series is identical to its counterpart except for cover, and came out at same time. The number in parentheses is the original issue it contains.*

TOP COW (Company one-shots)
Image Comics (Top Cow Productions)

... Book of Revelations (7/03, $3.99)-Pin-ups and info; art by various; Gossett-c 4.00
... Convention Sketchbook 2004 (4/04, $3.00, B&W) art by various 3.00
... Holiday Special Vol. 1 (12/10, $12.99) Flip book with Jingle Belle 13.00
... Preview Book 2005 (3/05, 99¢) Preview pages of Tomb Raider, Darkness, Rising Stars 3.00
... Productions, Inc./Ballistic Studios Swimsuit Special (5/95, $2.95) 3.00
...'s Best of: Dave Finch Vol. 1 TPB (8/06, $19.99) r/issues of Cyberforce, Aphrodite IX, Ascension and The Darkness; art & cover gallery 20.00
...'s Best of: Michael Turner Vol. 1 TPB (12/05, $24.99) r/Witchblade #1,10,12,18,19,25 & Witchblade/Tomb Raider chapters 1&3; Tomb Raider #25; art & cover gallery 25.00
... Secrets: Special Winter Lingerie Edition 1 (1/96, $2.95) Pin-ups 3.00
... 2001 Preview (no cover price) Preview pages of Tomb Raider; Jusko-a; flip cover & pages of Inferno 3.00

TOP COW CLASSICS IN BLACK AND WHITE
Image Comics (Top Cow): Feb, 2000 - Jan, 2003 ($2.95, B&W reprints)

...: Aphrodite IX #1(9/00) B&W reprint 3.00
...: Ascension #1(4/00) B&W reprint plus time-line of series 3.00
...: Battle of the Planets #1(1/03) B&W reprint plus script and cover gallery 3.00
...: Darkness #1(3/00) B&W reprint plus time-line of series 3.00
...: Fathom #1(5/00) B&W reprint 3.00
...: Magdalena #1(10/02) B&W reprint plus time-line of series 3.00
...: Midnight Nation #1(9/00) B&W preview 3.00
...: Rising Stars #1(7/00) B&W reprint plus cover gallery 3.00
...: Tomb Raider #1(12/00) B&W reprint plus back-story 3.00
...: Witchblade #1(2/00) B&W reprint plus back-story 3.00
...: Witchblade #25(5/01) B&W reprint plus interview with Wohl & Haberlin 3.00

TOP DETECTIVE COMICS
I. W. Enterprises: 1964 (Reprints)

9-r/Young King Cole #14; Dr. Drew (not Grandenetti) 2 4 6 10 14 18

TOP DOG (See Star Comics Magazine, 75¢)
Star Comics (Marvel): Apr, 1985 - No. 14, June, 1987 (Children's book)

1-14: 10-Peter Parker & J. Jonah Jameson cameo 5.00

TOP ELIMINATOR (Teenage Hotrodders #1-24; Drag 'n' Wheels #30 on)
Charlton Comics: No. 25, Sept, 1967 - No. 29, July, 1968

25-29 3 6 9 16 23 30

TOP FLIGHT COMICS: Four Star Publ.: 1947 (Advertised, not published)

TOP FLIGHT COMICS
St. John Publishing Co.: July, 1949

1(7/49, St. John)-Hector the Inspector; funny animal 12 24 36 67 94 120

Top Love Stories #14 © STAR

Top-Notch Comics #6 © ACP

Top Ten #9 © ABC

	GD 2.0	VG 4.0	FN 6.0	VF 8.0	VF/NM 9.0	NM- 9.2

TOP GUN (See Luke Short, 4-Color #927 & Showcase #72)

TOP GUNS OF THE WEST (See Super DC Giant)

TOPIX (...Comics) (Timeless Topix-early issues) (Also see Men of Battle, Men of Courage & Treasure Chest)(V1-V5#1,V7 on-paper-c)
Catechetical Guild Educational Society: 11/42 - V10#15, 1/28/52
(Weekly - later issues)

	GD	VG	FN	VF	VF/NM	NM-
V1#1(8 pgs.,8x11")	24	48	72	140	230	320
2,3(8 pgs.,8x11")	14	28	42	80	115	150
4-8(16 pgs.,8x11")	11	22	33	64	90	115
V2#1-10(16 pgs.,8x11"): V2#8-Pope Pius XII	10	20	30	56	76	95
V3#1-10(16 pgs.,8x11"): V3#1-(9/44)	10	20	30	54	72	90
V4#1-10: V4#1-(9/45)	9	18	27	47	61	75
V5#1(10/46,52 pgs.,2(11/46),no #3),4(1/47)-9(6/47),10(7/47), no #13,4(10/47), 14(11/47),15(12/47)	8	16	24	40	50	60
11(8/47),12(9/47)-Life of Christ editions	10	20	30	54	72	90
V6#4(1/48),5(2/48),7(3/48),8(4/48),9(5/48),10(6/48),11(7/48)-14 (no #1-3,6)	7	14	21	35	43	50
V7#1(9/1/48)-20(6/15/49), 36 pgs.	6	12	18	29	36	42
V8#1(9/19/49)-3,5-11,13-30(5/15/50) 30-Hitler app.	6	12	18	28	34	40
4-Dagwood Splits the Atom(10/10/49)-Magazine format	8	16	24	42	54	65
12-Ingels-a	10	20	30	54	72	90
V9#1(9/25/50)-11,13-30(5/14/51)	6	12	18	27	33	38
12-Special 36 pg. Xmas issue, text illos format	6	12	18	28	34	40
V10#1(10/1/51)-15: 14-Hollingsworth-a	6	12	18	27	33	38

TOP JUNGLE COMICS
I. W. Enterprises: 1964 (Reprint)

	GD	VG	FN	VF	VF/NM	NM-
1(nd)-Reprints White Princess of the Jungle #3, minus cover; Kintsler-a	3	6	9	16	23	30

TOP LOVE STORIES (Formerly Gasoline Alley #2)
Star Publications: No. 3, 5/51 - No. 19, 3/54

	GD	VG	FN	VF	VF/NM	NM-
3(#1)	30	60	90	177	289	400
4,5,7-9: 8-Wood story	24	48	72	142	234	325
6-Wood-a	29	58	87	172	281	390
10-16,18,19-Disbrow-a	23	46	69	136	223	310
17-Wood art (Fox-r)	24	48	72	140	230	320

NOTE: *All have* **L. B. Cole** *covers.*

TOP-NOTCH COMICS (...Laugh #28-45; Laugh Comix #46 on)
MLJ Magazines: Dec, 1939 - No. 45, June, 1944

	GD	VG	FN	VF	VF/NM	NM-
1-Origin/1st app. The Wizard; Kardak the Mystic Magician, Swift of the Secret Service (ends #3), Air Patrol, The Westpointer, Manhunters (by J. Cole), Mystic (ends #2) & Scott Rand (ends #3) begin; Wizard covers begin, end #8	535	1070	1605	3906	6903	9900
2-(1/40)-Dick Storm (ends #8), Stacy Knight M.D. (ends #4) begin; Jack Cole-a; 1st app. Nazis swastika on-c	284	568	852	1818	3109	4400
3-Bob Phantom, Scott Rand on Mars begin; J. Cole-a	194	388	582	1242	2121	3000
4-Origin/1st app. Streak Chandler on Mars; Moore of the Mounted only app.; J. Cole-a	177	354	531	1133	1942	2750
5-Flag-c; origin/1st app. Galahad; Shanghai Sheridan begins (ends #8); Shield cameo; Novick-a; classic-c	213	426	639	1363	2332	3300
6-Meskin-a	135	270	405	864	1482	2100
7-The Shield x-over in Wizard; The Wizard dons new costume	164	328	492	1050	1800	2550
8-Origin/1st app. The Firefly & Roy, the Super Boy (9/40, 2nd costumed boy hero after Robin?; also see Toro in Human Torch #1 (Fall/40)	171	342	513	1094	1872	2650
9-Origin & 1st app. The Black Hood; 1st Black Hood-c & logo (10/40); Fran Frazier begins (Scarce)	676	1352	2028	4935	8718	12,500
10-2nd app. Black Hood	239	478	717	1530	2615	3700
11-3rd Black Hood	164	328	492	1050	1800	2550
12-15	135	270	405	864	1482	2100
16-18,20	123	246	369	787	1344	1900
19-Classic bondage-c	138	276	414	883	1517	2150
21-30: 23-26-Roy app. 24-No Wizard. 25-Last Bob Phantom. 27-Last Firefly; Nazi war-c. 28-1st app. Suzie; Pokey Oakey begins. 29-Last Kardak	94	188	282	597	1025	1450
31-44: 33-Dotty & Ditto by Woggon begins (2/43, 1st app.). 44-Black Hood series ends	50	100	150	315	533	750
45-Last issue	57	114	171	362	619	875

NOTE: **J. Binder** *a-1-3.* **Meskin** *a-2, 3, 6, 15.* **Bob Montana** *a-30; c-28-31.* **Harry Sahle** *c-42-45.* **Woggon** *a-33-40, 42. Bondage c-17, 19. Black Hood also appeared on radio in 1944. Black Hood app. on c-9-34, 41-44. Roy the Super Boy app. on c-8, 9, 11-27. The Wizard app. on c-1-8, 11-13, 15-22, 24, 25, 27. Pokey Oakey app. on c-28-43. Suzie app. on c-44-on.*

TOPPER & NEIL (TV)
Dell Publishing Co.: No. 859, Nov, 1957

	GD	VG	FN	VF	VF/NM	NM-
Four Color 859	6	12	18	38	69	100

TOPPS COMICS: Four Star Publications: 1947 (Advertised, not published)

TOPS
July, 1949 - No. 2, Sept, 1949 (25¢, 10-1/4x13-1/4", 68 pgs.)
Tops Magazine, Inc. (Lev Gleason): (Large size-magazine format; for the adult reader)

	GD	VG	FN	VF	VF/NM	NM-
1 (Rare)-Story by Dashiell Hammett; Crandall/Lubbers, Tuska, Dan Barry, Fuje-a; Biro painted-c	300	600	900	1950	3375	4800
2 (Rare)-Crandall/Lubbers, Biro, Kida, Fuje, Guardineer-a	265	530	795	1694	2897	4100

TOPS COMICS
Consolidated Book Publishers: 1944 (10¢, 132 pgs.)

	GD	VG	FN	VF	VF/NM	NM-
2000-(Color-c, inside in red shade & some in full color)-Ace Kelly by Rick Yager, Black Orchid, Don on the Farm, Dinky Dinkerton (Rare)	53	106	159	334	567	800

NOTE: *This book is printed in such a way that when the staple is removed, the strips on the left side of the book correspond with the same strips on the right side. Therefore, if strips are removed from the book, each strip can be folded into a complete comic section of its own.*

TOPS COMICS
Consolidated Book Publs. (Lev Gleason): 1944 (7-1/4x5" digest-size, 32 pgs.)

	GD	VG	FN	VF	VF/NM	NM-
2001-Origin The Jack of Spades (costumed hero)	32	64	96	192	314	435
2002-Rip Raider	20	40	60	120	195	270
2003-Red Birch (gag cartoons)	12	24	36	69	97	125
2004-"Don't Bother to Dry Off" (gag cartoons)	20	40	60	115	188	260

TOP SECRET
Hillman Publ.: Jan, 1952

	GD	VG	FN	VF	VF/NM	NM-
1	27	54	81	158	259	360

TOP SECRET ADVENTURES (See Spyman)

TOP SECRETS (...of the F.B.I.)
Street & Smith Publications: Nov, 1947 - No. 10, July-Aug, 1949

	GD	VG	FN	VF	VF/NM	NM-
1-Powell-c/a	39	78	117	231	378	525
2-Powell-c/a	27	54	81	160	263	365
3-6,8,10-Powell-a	24	48	72	140	230	320
9-Powell-c/a	24	48	72	142	234	325
7-Used in **SOTI**, pg. 90 & illo. "How to hurt people"; used by N.Y. Legis. Comm.; Powell-c/a	39	78	117	231	378	525

NOTE: **Powell** *c-1-3, 5-10.*

TOPS IN ADVENTURE
Ziff-Davis Publishing Co.: Fall, 1952 (25¢, 132 pgs.)

	GD	VG	FN	VF	VF/NM	NM-
1-Crusader from Mars, The Hawk, Football Thrills, He-Man; Powell-a; painted-c	53	106	159	334	567	800

TOPS IN HUMOR
Remington Morse Publ. (Harry A. Chesler, Jr.): No date (1944) (7-1/4x5" digest size, 64 pgs., 10¢)

	GD	VG	FN	VF	VF/NM	NM-
1-WWII serviceman humor (scarce)	27	54	81	158	259	360
2-(Wise Publ.) WWII serviceman humor	15	30	45	94	147	200

TOP SPOT COMICS
Top Spot Publ. Co.: 1945

	GD	VG	FN	VF	VF/NM	NM-
1-The Menace, Duke of Darkness app.	52	104	156	328	552	775

TOPSY-TURVY (Teenage)
R. B. Leffingwell Publ.: Apr, 1945

	GD	VG	FN	VF	VF/NM	NM-
1-1st app. Cookie	34	68	102	199	325	450

TOP TEN
America's Best Comics: Sept, 1999 - No. 12, Oct, 2001 ($3.50/$2.95)

	NM-
1-Two covers by Ross and Ha/Cannon; Alan Moore-s/Gene Ha-a	3.50
2-11-($2.95)	3.00
12-($3.50)	3.50
Hardcover ('00, $24.95) Dust jacket with Gene Ha-a; r/#1-7	25.00
Softcover ('00, $14.95) new Gene Ha-c; r/#1-7	15.00
Book 2 HC ('02, $24.95) Dust jacket with Gene Ha-a; r/#8-12	25.00
Book 2 SC ('03, $14.95) new Gene Ha-c; r/#8-12	15.00
...: The Forty-Niners HC (2005, $24.99, dust jacket) prequel set in 1949; Moore-s/Ha-a	25.00

TOP TEN: BEYOND THE FARTHEST PRECINCT
America's Best Comics: Oct, 2005 - No. 5, Feb, 2006 ($2.99, limited series)

	NM-
1-5-Jerry Ordway-a/Paul DiFilippo-s	3.00
TPB (2006, $14.99) r/series; cover sketch pages	15.00

Torchwood #1 © BBC

Totally Awesome Hulk #6 © MAR

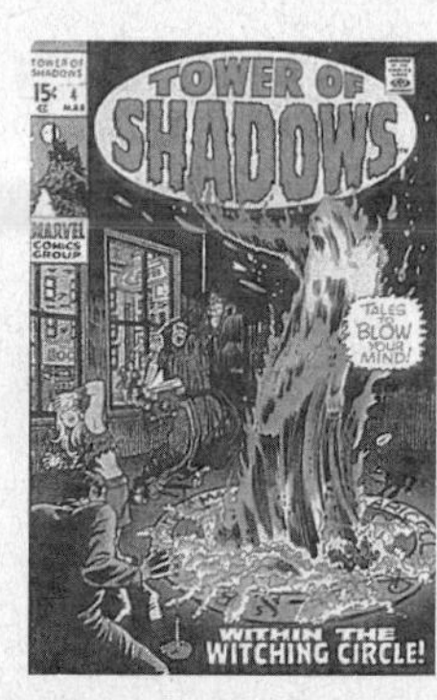

Tower of Shadows #4 © MAR

	GD 2.0	VG 4.0	FN 6.0	VF 8.0	VF/NM 9.0	NM- 9.2

TOP TEN SEASON TWO
America's Best Comics: Dec, 2008 - No. 4, Mar, 2009 ($2.99, limited series)

1-4-Cannon-s/Ha-a 3.00
... Special (5/09, $2.99) Cannon-s/Daxiong-a/Ha-c 3.00

TOR (Prehistoric Life on Earth) (Formerly One Million Years Ago)
St. John Publ. Co.: No. 2, Oct, 1953; No. 3, May, 1954 - No. 5, Oct, 1954

	GD	VG	FN	VF	VF/NM	NM-
3-D 2(10/53)-Kubert-c/a	15	30	45	86	133	180
3-D 2(10/53)-Oversized, otherwise same contents	14	28	42	81	118	155
3-D 2(11/53)-Kubert-c/a; has 3-D cover	14	28	42	81	118	155
3-5-Kubert-c/a: 3-Danny Dreams by Toth; Kubert 1 pg. story (w/self portrait)	20	40	60	115	188	260

NOTE: *The two October 3-D's have same contents and* **Powell** *art; the October & November issues are titled 3-D Comics. All 3-D issues are 25¢ and came with 3-D glasses.*

TOR (See Sojourn)
National Periodical Publications: May-June, 1975 - No. 6, Mar-Apr, 1976

	GD	VG	FN	VF	VF/NM	NM-
1-New origin by Kubert	2	4	6	11	16	20
2-6: 2-Origin-r/St. John #1	1	2	3	5	6	8

NOTE: **Kubert** *a-1, 2-6r; c-1-6.* **Toth** *a(p)-3r.*

TOR (3-D)
Eclipse Comics: July, 1986 - No. 2, Aug, 1987 ($2.50)

	GD	VG	FN	VF	VF/NM	NM-
1,2: 1-r/One Million Years Ago. 2-r/Tor 3-D #2						5.00
...2-D: 1,2-Limited signed & numbered editions	2	4	6	11	16	20

TOR
Marvel Comics (Epic Comics/Heavy Hitters): June, 1993 - No. 4, 1993 ($5.95, lim. series)

1-4: Joe Kubert-c/a/scripts 6.00

TOR (Joe Kubert's...)
DC Comics: Jul, 2008 - No. 6, Dec, 2008 ($2.99, limited series)

1-6-New story; Joe Kubert-c/a/scripts 3.00
...: A Prehistoric Odyssey HC (2009, $24.99, DJ) r/#1-6; Roy Thomas intro.; sketch-a 25.00
...: A Prehistoric Odyssey SC (2010, $14.99) r/#1-6; Roy Thomas intro.; sketch-a 15.00

TOR BY JOE KUBERT
DC Comics: 2001 - 2003 ($49.95, hardcovers with dust jacket)

Volume 1 (2001) r/One Million Years Ago #1 & 3-D Comics #1&2 in flat color; script pages, sketch pages, proposals for TV and newspapers strips; intro. by Roy Thomas 50.00
Volume 2 (2002) r/Tor (St. John) #3-5; Danny Dreams; portfolio section 50.00
Volume 3 (2003) r/Tor (DC '75) #1; (Marvel '93) #1-4; portfolio section 50.00

TORCH, THE
Marvel Comics (with Dynamite Ent.): Nov, 2009 - No. 8, Jul, 2010 ($3.99, limited series)

1-8-Thinker resurrects the Golden Age Human Torch; Toro app; Alex Ross-c on all; Berkenkotter-a. 3-5-Namor app. 4.00

TORCH OF LIBERTY SPECIAL
Dark Horse Comics (Legend): Jan, 1995 ($2.50, one-shot)

1-Byrne scripts 3.00

TORCHWOOD (Based on the BBC TV series)
Titan Comics: Sept, 2010 - No. 6, Jan, 2011 ($3.99)

1-6: 1-Barrowman-s/Edwards-a; Churchill & photo-c. 2-Art by Yeowell & Grist 4.00

TORCHWOOD (Based on the BBC TV series)
Titan Comics: Aug, 2016 - No. 4, Jan, 2017; Vol. 2: Mar, 2017 - No. 4, Jun, 2017; Vol. 3: Nov, 2017 - No. 4, Mar, 2018 ($3.99)

1-4-John & Carole Barrowman-s/Fuso & Qualano-a; multiple covers 4.00
Vol. 2 1-4-John & Carole Barrowman-s/Edwards-a; multiple covers 4.00
Vol. 3 1-4-John & Carole Barrowman-s/Edwards-a; multiple covers; Capt. John Hart app. 4.00

TORCHY (...Blonde Bombshell) (See Dollman, Military, & Modern)
Quality Comics Group: Nov, 1949 - No. 6, Sept, 1950

	GD	VG	FN	VF	VF/NM	NM-
1-Bill Ward-c, Gil Fox-a	239	478	717	1530	2615	3700
2,3-Fox-c/a	97	194	291	621	1061	1500
4-Fox-c/a(3), Ward-a (9 pgs.)	126	252	378	806	1378	1950
5,6-Ward-c/a, 9 pgs; Fox-a(3) each	132	264	396	845	1448	2050
Super Reprint #16(1964)-r/#4 with new-c	8	16	24	54	102	150

TO RIVERDALE AND BACK AGAIN (Archie Comics Presents...)
Archie Comics: 1990 ($2.50, 68 pgs.)

	GD	VG	FN	VF	VF/NM	NM-
nn-Byrne-c, Colan-a(p); adapts NBC TV movie	2	4	6	8	10	12

TORMENTED, THE (Becomes Surprise Adventures #3 on)
Sterling Comics: July, 1954 - No. 2, Sept, 1954

	GD	VG	FN	VF	VF/NM	NM-
1-Good Girl torture-c	129	258	387	826	1413	2000
2-Devil's circus-c	53	106	159	334	567	800

TORNADO TOM (See Mighty Midget Comics)

TORSO (See Jinx: Torso)

TOTAL ECLIPSE
Eclipse Comics: May, 1988 - No. 5, Apr, 1989 ($3.95, 52 pgs., deluxe size)

Book 1-5: 3-Intro/1st app. new Black Terror. 4-Many copies have upside down pages and are mis-cut 5.00

TOTAL ECLIPSE
Image Comics: July, 1998 (one-shot)

1-McFarlane-c; Eclipse Comics character pin-ups by Image artists 3.00

TOTAL ECLIPSE: THE SERAPHIM OBJECTIVE
Eclipse Comics: Nov, 1988 ($1.95, one-shot, Baxter paper)

1-Airboy, Valkyrie, The Heap app. 3.00

TOTAL JUSTICE
DC Comics: Oct, 1996 - No. 3, Nov, 1996 ($2.25, bi-weekly limited series) (Based on toyline)

1-3 3.00

TOTALLY AWESOME HULK, THE (Amadeus Cho as The Hulk)(Continues in Inc. Hulk #709)
Marvel Comics: Feb, 2016 - No. 23, Nov, 2017 ($4.99/$3.99)

1-($4.99) Frank Cho-a/Greg Pak-s; She-Hulk and Spider-Man (Miles) app. 5.00
2-23-($3.99) 2,3-Fin Fang Foom and Lady Hellbender app. 5,6-Mike Choi-a. 7,8-Alan Davis-a. 9-11-Civil War II tie-in. 9-Del Mundo-a. 10-12-Black Panther app. 13-15-Jeremy Lin app. 19-22-Crossover with Weapon X #5,6 and Weapons of Mutant Destruction: Alpha #1; Old Man Logan & Sabretooth app. 23-Frank Cho-c 4.00
#1.MU (5/17, $4.99) Monsters Unleashed tie-in; art by Templeton, Ortiz, Lindsay 5.00

TOTAL RECALL (Movie)
DC Comics: 1990 ($2.95, 68 pgs., movie adaptation, one-shot)

1-Arnold Schwarzenegger photo-c 4.00

TOTAL RECALL (Continuation of movie)
Dynamite Entertainment: 2011 - No. 4, 2011 ($3.99, limited series)

1-4-Quaid and Melina on Mars following the movie; Razek-a/Robertson-c 4.00

TOTAL WAR (M.A.R.S. Patrol #3 on)
Gold Key: July, 1965 - No. 2, Oct, 1965 (Painted-c)

	GD	VG	FN	VF	VF/NM	NM-
1-Wood-a in both issues	6	12	18	41	76	110
2	5	10	15	33	57	80

TOTEMS (Vertigo V2K)
DC Comics (Vertigo): Feb, 2000 ($5.95, one-shot)

1-Swamp Thing, Animal Man, Zatanna, Shade app.; Fegredo-c 6.00

TO THE HEART OF THE STORM
Kitchen Sink Press: 1991 (B&W, graphic novel)

Softcover-Will Eisner-s/a/c 20.00
Hardcover ($24.95) 30.00
TPB-(DC Comics, 9/00, $14.95) reprints 1991 edition 15.00

TO THE LAST MAN (See Zane Grey Four Color #616)

TOUCH OF SILVER, A
Image Comics: Jan, 1997 - No. 6, Nov, 1997 ($2.95, B&W, bi-monthly)

1-6-Valentino-s/a; photo-c: 5-color pgs. w/Round Table 3.00
TPB ($12.95) r/#1-6 13.00

TOUGH KID SQUAD COMICS
Timely Comics (TCI): Mar, 1942

	GD	VG	FN	VF	VF/NM	NM-
1-(Scarce)-Origin & 1st app.The Human Top & The Tough Kid Squad; The Flying Flame app.	920	1840	2760	6700	12,600	18,500

TOWER OF SHADOWS (Creatures on the Loose #10 on)
Marvel Comics Group: Sept, 1969 - No. 9, Jan, 1971

	GD	VG	FN	VF	VF/NM	NM-
1-Romita-c, classic Steranko-a; Craig-a(p)	8	16	24	52	99	145
2,3: 2-Neal Adams-a. 3-Barry Smith, Tuska-a	5	10	15	31	53	75
4,6: 4-Marie Severin-c. 6-Wood-a	4	8	12	28	47	65
5-B. Smith-a(p), Wood-a; Wood draws himself (1st pg., 1st panel)	5	10	15	30	50	70
7-9: 7-B. Smith-a(p), Wood-a. 8-Wood-a; Wrightson-c. 9-Wrightson-c; Roy Thomas app.	5	10	15	31	53	75
Special 1(12/71, 52 pgs.)-Neal Adams-a; Romita-c	4	8	12	28	47	65

NOTE: **J. Buscema** *a-1p, 2p, Special 1r.* **Colan** *a-3p, 6p, Special 1.* **J. Craig** *a(r)-1p.* **Ditko** *a-6, 8, 9r, Special 1.* **Everett** *a-9(i)r; c-5i.* **Kirby** *a-9(p)r.* **Severin** *c-5p, 6.* **Steranko** *a-1p.* **Tuska** *a-3.* **Wood** *a-5-8. Issues 1-9 contain new stories with some pre-Marvel age reprints in 6-9.* **H. P. Lovecraft** *adaptation-9.*

TOXIC AVENGER (Movie)
Marvel Comics: Apr, 1991 - No. 11, Feb, 1992 ($1.50)

1-11: Based on movie character. 3,10-Photo-c 4.00

Toy Story (2012 series) #1 © DIS & Pixar

Trailblazer GN © Palmiotti & Gray

Transformers #63 © Hasbro

GD VG FN VF VF/NM NM-
2.0 4.0 6.0 8.0 9.0 9.2

TOXIC CRUSADERS (TV)
Marvel Comics: May, 1992 - No. 8, Dec, 1992 ($1.25)
1-8: 1-3,8-Sam Kieth-c; based on USA Network cartoon 4.00

TOXIN (Son of Carnage)
Marvel Comics: June, 2005 - No. 6, Nov, 2005 ($2.99, limited series)
1-Milligan-s/Robertson-a in all; Spider-Man app. 2 4 6 10 14 18
2-6 1 2 3 5 6 8
...: The Devil You Know TPB (2006, $17.99) r/#1-6 18.00

TOYBOY
Continuity Comics: Oct, 1986 - No. 7, Mar, 1989 ($2.00, Baxter paper)
1-7 4.00
*NOTE: **N. Adams** a-1; c-1, 2,5. **Golden** a-7p; c-6,7. **Nebres** a(i)-1,2.*

TOYLAND COMICS
Fiction House Magazines: Jan, 1947 - No. 2, Mar, 1947; No. 3, July, 1947
1-Wizard of the Moon begins 31 62 93 186 303 420
2,3-Bob Lubbers-c. 3-Tuska-a 18 36 54 107 169 230
NOTE: *All above contain strips by **Al Walker.***

TOY STORY (Disney/Pixar movies)
BOOM! Entertainment (BOOM! KIDS): No. 0, Nov, 2009 - No. 7, Sept, 2010 ($2.99)
0-7: 0,1-Three covers. 2-7-Two covers 3.00
Free Comic Book Day Edition (5/10, giveaway) r/#0 The Return of Buzz Lightyear 3.00
...: The Return of Buzz Lightyear (10/10, Halloween giveaway, 8-1/2" x 5-1/4") 3.00

TOY STORY (Disney/Pixar movies)
Marvel Comics: May, 2012 - No. 4, 2012 ($2.99, limited series)
1-4: 1-Master Woody. 2-A Scary Night. 3-To The Attic. 4-Water Rescue 3.00

TOY STORY: MYSTERIOUS STRANGER (Disney/Pixar movies)
BOOM! Entertainment (BOOM! KIDS): May, 2009 - No. 4, July, 2009 ($2.99)
1-4-Jolley-s/Moreno-a. 1-Three covers. 2-4-Two covers 3.00

TOY STORY: TALES FROM THE TOY CHEST (Disney/Pixar movies)
BOOM! Entertainment (BOOM! KIDS): July, 2010 - No. 4, Oct, 2010 ($2.99)
1-4-Snider-s/Luthi-a. 1-Two covers. 2-4-One cover 3.00

TOY TOWN COMICS
Toytown/Orbit Publ./B. Antin/Swapper Quarterly: 1945 - No. 7, May, 1947
1-Mertie Mouse; L. B. Cole-c/a; funny animal 41 82 123 256 428 600
2-L. B. Cole-a 24 48 72 140 230 320
3-7-L. B. Cole-a. 5-Wiggles the Wonderworm-c 20 40 60 117 189 260

TRAGG AND THE SKY GODS (See Gold Key Spotlight, Mystery Comics Digest #3,9 & Spine Tingling Tales)
Gold Key/Whitman No. 9: June, 1975 - No. 8, Feb, 1977; No. 9, May, 1982 (Painted-c #3-8)
1-Origin 3 6 9 14 19 24
2-8: 4-Sabre-Fang app. 8-Ostellon app. 2 4 6 8 11 14
9-(Whitman, 5/82) r/#1 1 2 3 5 7 9
NOTE: ***Santos** a-1, 2, 9r; c-3-7. **Spiegel** a-3-8.*

TRAILBLAZER
Image Comics: June 2011 ($5.99, one shot, graphic novel)
nn-Gray & Palmiotti-s/Daly-a; covers by Johnson and Conner 6.00

TRAIL BLAZERS (Red Dragon #5 on)
Street & Smith Publications: 1941; No. 2, Apr, 1942 - No. 4, Oct, 1942
(True stories of American heroes)
1-Life story of Jack Dempsey & Wright Brothers 42 84 126 265 445 625
2-Brooklyn Dodgers-c/story; Ben Franklin story 25 50 75 147 241 335
3,4: 3-Fred Allen, Red Barber, Yankees stories 22 44 66 130 213 295

TRAIL COLT (Also see Extra Comics, Manhunt! & Undercover Girl)
Magazine Enterprises: 1949 - No. 2, 1949
nn(A-1 #24)-7 pg. Frazetta-a r-in Manhunt #13; Undercover Girl app.; The Red Fox by L. B. Cole; Ingels-c; Whitney-a (Scarce)(Republished as Manhunt #12 with a different-c)
42 84 126 265 445 625
2(A-1 #26)-Undercover Girl; Ingels-c; L. B. Cole-a (6 pgs.)
33 66 99 194 317 440

TRAIN CALLED LOVE, A
Dynamite Entertainment: 2015 - No. 10, 2016 ($3.99)
1-9-Garth Ennis-s/Mark Dos Santos-a 4.00
10-($5.99) Last issue 6.00

TRANSFORMERS, THE (TV)(See G.I. Joe and...)
(Continues in Transformers: Regeneration)
Marvel Comics Group: Sept, 1984 - No. 80, July, 1991 (75¢/$1.00)

GD VG FN VF VF/NM NM-
2.0 4.0 6.0 8.0 9.0 9.2

1-Based on Hasbro Toys 7 14 21 49 92 135
1-2nd & 3rd printing 3 6 9 14 19 24
2-5: 2-Golden-c. 3-(1/85) Spider-Man (black costume)-c/app. 4-Texeira-c; brief app. of Dinobots 3 6 9 15 22 28
2-10: 2nd & 3rd prints 4.00
6,7,9: 6-1st Josie Beller. 9-Circuit Breaker 1st full app.
2 4 6 9 13 16
8-Dinobots 1st full app. 3 6 9 19 30 40
10-Intro. Constructicons 3 6 9 16 24 32
11,14: 11-1st app. Jetfire. 14-Jetfire becomes an Autobot; 1st app. of Grapple, Hoist, Smokescreen, Skids, and Tracks 2 4 6 8 11 14
12,13,15,17,18,20-24,26-49: 17-1st app. of Blaster, Powerglide, Cosmos, Seaspray, Warpath, Beachcomber, Preceptor, Straxus, Kickback, Bombshell, Shrapnel, Dirge, and Ramjet. 21-1st app. of Aerialbots; 1st Slingshot; Circuit Breaker app. 22-Retells origin of Circuit Breaker, 1st Stunticons. 23-Battle at Statue of Liberty. 24-1st app. Protectobots, Combaticons; Optimus Prime killed. 26-Intro The Mechanic, Prime's Funeral. 27-Grimlock named new Autobot leader. 28-The Mechanic app. 29-Intro Scraplets, 1st app. of Triple Changers 1 2 3 5 6 8
16-Plight of the Bumblebee 2 4 6 10 14 18
19-1st Omega Supreme 2 4 6 8 10 12
25-1st Predacons 2 4 6 8 11 14
50-60: 53-Jim Lee-c. 54-Intro Micromasters. 60-Brief 1st app. of Primus
2 4 6 8 10 12
61-70: 61-Origin of Cybertron and the Transformers, Unicron app.; app. of Primus, creator of the Transformers. 62-66 Matrix Quest 5-part series. 67-Jim Lee-c
2 4 6 10 14 18
71-77: 75-($1.50, 52 pgs.) (Low print run) 3 6 9 17 26 35
78,79 (Low print run) 4 8 12 23 37 50
80-Last issue 5 10 15 33 57 80
*NOTE: Second and third printings of most early issues (1-9?) exist and are worth less than originals. Was originally planned as a four issue mini-series. **Wrightson** a-64i(4 pgs.).*

TRANSFORMERS
IDW Publishing: No. 0, Oct, 2005 (99¢, one-shot)
0-Prelude to Transformers: Infiltration series; Furman-s/Su-a; 4 covers 3.00

TRANSFORMERS
IDW Publishing: Nov, 2009 - No. 31, Dec, 2011 ($3.99)
1-31: Multple covers on each, 21-Chaos arc begins 4.00
...: Continuum (11/09, $3.99) Plot synopses of recent Transformers storylines 4.00
...: Death of Optimus Prime (12/11, $3.99) Roche-a 4.00
Hundred Penny Press: Transformers Classics #1 (6/11, $1.00) r/#1 (1984 Marvel series) 3.00
Hundred Penny Press (3/14, $1.00) r/#1 (1984 Marvel series) 3.00

TRANSFORMERS (See Transformers: Robots in Disguise for #1-34)
IDW Publishing: No. 34, Nov, 2014 - No. 57, Sept, 2016 ($3.99)
35-49: 39-42-Combiner Wars x-over 4.00
50-($7.99, squarebound) Barber-s/Griffith-a 8.00
51-57: 51-55-All Hail Optimus. 56-Revolution tie-in 4.00
Annual 2017 (2/17, $7.99) Barber-s/Tramontano-a; bonus character profile pages 8.00
...: Deviations (3/16, $4.99) What If... Optimus Prime never died; Easton-s; 2 covers 5.00
... First Strike 1 (10/17, $3.99) Part of Hasbro character crossover 4.00
... Historia (12/18, $5.99) Text history of the Transformers with comic panels 6.00
... Holiday Special (12/15, $5.99) Covers by Coller & Garbowska 6.00
...: Requiem of the Wreckers Annual (5/18, $7.99) Roche-s/a 8.00
...: Revolution 1 (10/16, $3.99) Revolution tie-in; Barber-s/Griffith-a; multiple covers 4.00
...: Salvation One Shot (6/17, $7.99) Barber-s/Ramondelli-a; 2 covers 8.00
...: Titans Return (7/16, $4.99) Road to Revolution; Ramondelli-a 5.00

TRANSFORMERS (Rise of the Decepticons on cover #19-24; War World on cover #25-27)
IDW Publishing: Mar, 2019 - Present ($3.99)
1-24,26,27: 1-Intro Rubble; Ruckley-s. 7,8-Polybagged w/Transformers card game pack 4.00
25-($7.99) Ruckley-s/Malkova-a; Orion Pax becomes Optimus Prime 8.00
... '84 Issue #0 (8/19, $4.99) New story in art style of 1984 comics; Furman-s/Guidi-a 5.00
... 100-Page Giant: Power of the Predacons (1/20, $5.99) Reprints from UK & US comics 6.00
... Valentine's Day Special (2/20, $3.99) Story of Glyph & Tap-Out 4.00

TRANSFORMERS (Free Comic Book Day Editions)
Dreamwave Productions/IDW Publishing
... Animated (IDW, 5/08) Free Comic Book Day Edition; from the Cartoon Network series 3.00
... Armada (Dreamwave Prods., 5/03) Free Comic Book Day Edition 3.00
.../Beast Wars Special (IDW, 2006) Free Comic Book Day Edition; flip book 3.00
.../G.I. Joe (IDW, 2009) Free Comic Book Day Edition; flip book 3.00
... Movie Prequel (IDW, 5/07) Free Comic Book Day Edition; Figueroa-c 3.00

TRANSFORMERS: ALL HAIL MEGATRON
IDW Publishing: Jul, 2008 - No. 16, Oct, 2009 ($3.99, limited series)

Transformers: Devastation #1 © Hasbro

Transformers Energon #20 © Hasbro

Transformers: Generation 1 #3 © Hasbro

GD 2.0 | VG 4.0 | FN 6.0 | VF 8.0 | VF/NM 9.0 | NM- 9.2

1-16: 1-8,10-12-McCarthy-s/Guidi-a; 2 covers 4.00

TRANSFORMERS: ALLIANCE (Prequel to 2009 Transformers 2 movie)
IDW Publishing: Dec, 2008 - No. 4, Mar, 2009 ($3.99, limited series)

1-4-Milne-a; 2 covers 4.00

TRANSFORMERS ANIMATED: THE ARRIVAL
IDW Publishing: Sept, 2008 - No. 5, Dec, 2008 ($3.99, limited series)

1-5-Brizuela-a; 2 covers 4.00

TRANSFORMERS ARMADA (Continues as Transformers Energon with #19)
Dreamwave Productions: July, 2002 - No. 18, Dec, 2003 ($2.95)

1-Sarracini-s/Raiz-a; wraparound gatefold-c 6.00
2-18 4.00
Vol. 1 TPB (2003, $13.95) r/#1-5 14.00
Vol. 2 TPB (2003, $15.95) r/#6-11 16.00

TRANSFORMERS ARMADA: MORE THAN MEETS THE EYE
Dreamwave Productions: Mar, 2004 - No. 3, May, 2004 ($4.95, limited series)

1-3-Pin-ups with tech info; art by Pat Lee & various 5.00

TRANSFORMERS / BACK TO THE FUTURE
IDW Publishing: Oct, 2020 - Present ($3.99, limited series)

1,2-Cavan Scott-s/Juan Samu-a; multiple covers on all 4.00

TRANSFORMERS: BEAST WARS
IDW Publishing: Feb, 2021 - Present ($5.99/$3.99, limited series)

1-($5.99) Maximals and Predacons app.; Erik Burnham-s/Josh Burcham-a 6.00
2-($3.99) 4.00

TRANSFORMERS, BEAST WARS: THE ASCENDING
IDW Publishing: Aug, 2007 - No. 4, Nov, 2007 ($3.99, limited series)

1-4-Furman-s/Figueroa-a; multiple covers on all 4.00

TRANSFORMERS, BEAST WARS: THE GATHERING
IDW Publishing: Feb, 2006 - No. 4, May, 2006 ($2.99, limited series)

1-4-Furman-s/Figueroa-a; multiple covers on all 4.00
TPB (8/06, $17.99) r/series; sketch pages & gallery of covers and variants 18.00

TRANSFORMERS: BUMBLEBEE
IDW Publishing: Dec, 2009 - No. 4, Mar, 2010 ($3.99, limited series)

1-4: Zander Cannon-s; multiple covers on all 4.00
... – Go For the Gold (12/18, $3.99) Asmus-s/Ferreira-a 4.00

TRANSFORMERS: BUMBLEBEE MOVIE PREQUEL
IDW Publishing: Jun, 2018 - No. 4, Sept, 2018 ($3.99, limited series)

1-4: Bumblebee assisting a British spy in 1964; Barber-s/Griffith-a; multiple covers 4.00

TRANSFORMERS COMICS MAGAZINE (Digest)
Marvel Comics: Jan, 1987 - No. 10, July, 1988

1,2-Spider-Man-c/s 2 4 6 11 16 20
3-10 2 4 6 8 11 14

TRANSFORMERS: DARK CYBERTRON
IDW Publishing: Nov, 2013 ($3.99)

1-Part 1 of a 12-part crossover with Transformers: More Than Meets the Eye #23-27 and Transformers: Robots in Disguise #23-27; multiple covers 4.00
1-Deluxe Edition ($7.99, squarebound) r/#1 with bonus script and B&W art pages 8.00
... Finale (3/14, $3.99) Three covers 4.00

TRANSFORMERS: DARK OF THE MOON MOVIE ADAPTATION (2011 movie)
IDW Publishing: Jun, 2011 - No. 4, Jun, 2011 ($3.99, weekly limited series)

1-4-Barber-s/Jimenez-a 4.00

TRANSFORMERS: DEFIANCE (Prequel to 2009 Transformers 2 movie)
IDW Publishing: Jan, 2009 - No. 4, Apr, 2009 ($3.99, limited series)

1-4-Mowry-s; 2 covers 4.00

TRANSFORMERS: DEVASTATION
IDW Publishing: Sept, 2007 - No. 6, Feb, 2008 ($3.99, limited series)

1-6-Furman-s/Su-a; multiple covers on all 4.00

TRANSFORMERS: DRIFT
IDW Publishing: Sept, 2010 - No. 4, Oct, 2010 ($3.99, limited series)

1-4-McCarthy-s/Milne-a; multiple covers on all 4.00

TRANSFORMERS: DRIFT – EMPIRE OF STONE
IDW Publishing: Nov, 2014 - No. 4, Feb, 2015 ($3.99, limited series)

1-4-McCarthy-s/Guidi & Ferreira-a; multiple covers on all 4.00

TRANSFORMERS ENERGON (Continued from Transformers Armada #18)
Dreamwave Productions: No. 19, Jan, 2004 - No. 30, Dec, 2004 ($2.95)

19-30-Furman-s 4.00

TRANSFORMERS: ESCALATION
IDW Publishing: Nov, 2006 - No. 6, Apr, 2007 ($3.99, limited series)

1-6-Furman-s/Su-a; multiple covers 4.00

TRANSFORMERS ESCAPE
IDW Publishing: Dec, 2020 - Present ($3.99, limited series)

1,2-Brian Ruckley-s/Beth McGuire-Smith; multiple covers on all 4.00

TRANSFORMERS: EVOLUTIONS - HEARTS OF STEEL
IDW Publishing: June, 2006 - No. 4, Sept, 2006 ($2.99, limited series)

1-4-Bumblebee meets John Henry in 1880s railroad times 4.00

TRANSFORMERS: FOUNDATION (Prequel to 2011 Transformers: Dark of the Moon movie)
IDW Publishing: Feb, 2011 - No. 4, May, 2011 ($3.99, limited series)

1-4-Barber-s/Griffith-a; 2 covers 4.00

TRANSFORMERS: GALAXIES
IDW Publishing: Sept, 2019 - No. 12, Oct, 2020 ($3.99)

1-12: 1-Tyler Bleszinski-s/Livio Ramondelli-a; Constructicons app. 4.00

TRANSFORMERS: GENERATION 1
Dreamwave Productions: Apr, 2002 - No. 6, Oct, 2002 ($2.95)

Preview- 6 pg. story; robot sketch pages; Pat Lee-a 3.00
1-Pat Lee-a; 2 wraparound covers by Lee 5.00
2-6: 2-Optimus Prime reactivated; 2 covers by Pat Lee 4.00
...Vol. 1 HC (2003, $49.95) r/#1-6; black hardcover with red foil lettering and art 50.00
...Vol. 1 TPB (2002, $17.95) r/#1-6 plus six page preview; 8 pg. preview of future issues 18.00

TRANSFORMERS: GENERATION 1 (Volume 2)
Dreamwave Productions: Apr, 2003 - No. 6, Sept, 2003 ($2.95)

1-6: 1-Pat Lee-a; 2 wraparound gatefold covers by Lee 4.00
1-($5.95) Chrome wraparound variant-c 6.00
...Vol. 2 TPB (IDW Publ., 3/06, $19.99) r/#1-6 plus cover gallery 20.00

TRANSFORMERS: GENERATION 1 (Volume 3)
Dreamwave Productions: No. 0, Dec, 2003 - No. 10, Nov, 2004 ($2.95)

0-10: 0-Pat Lee-a. 1-Figueroa-a; wrapaound-c 4.00

TRANSFORMERS: GENERATION 2
Marvel Comics: Nov, 1993 - No. 12, Oct, 1994 ($1.75)

1-($2.95, 68 pgs.)-Collector's ed. w/bi-fold metallic-c 2 4 6 8 11 14
1-11: 1-Newsstand edition (68 pgs.). 2-G.I. Joe app., Snake-Eyes, Scarlett, Cobra Commander app. 5-Red Alert killed, Optimus Prime gives Grimlock leadership of Autobots. 6-G.I. Joe app. 1 2 3 4 5 7
12-($2.25, 52 pgs.) 1 3 4 6 8 10

TRANSFORMERS: GENERATIONS
IDW Publishing: Mar, 2006 - No. 12, Mar, 2007 ($1.99/$2.49/$3.99)

1,2: 1-R/Transformers #7 (1985); preview of Transformers, Beast Wars. 2-R/#13 4.00
3-10-($2.49) 3-R/Transformers #14 (1986). 4-6-Reprint #16-18. 7-R/#24 4.00
11,12-($3.99) 4.00
Volume 1 (12/06, $19.99) r/#1-6; cover gallery 20.00

TRANSFORMERS / GHOSTBUSTERS
IDW Publishing: Jun, 2019 - No. 5, Oct, 2019 ($3.99, limited series)

1-5-Burnham-s/Schoening-a; Ghostbusters vs. ghost of Starscream 4.00

TRANSFORMERS/G.I. JOE
Dreamwave Productions: Aug, 2003 - No. 6, Mar, 2004 ($2.95/$5.25)

1-Art & gatefold wraparound-c by Jae Lee; Ney Rieber-s; variant-c by Pat Lee 4.00
1-($5.95) Holofoil wraparound-c by Norton 6.00
2-6-Jae Lee-a/c 4.00
TPB (8/04, $17.95) r/#1-6; cover gallery and sketch pages 18.00

TRANSFORMERS/G.I. JOE: DIVIDED FRONT
Dreamwave Productions: Oct, 2004 ($2.95)

1-Art & gatefold wraparound-c by Pat Lee 4.00

TRANSFORMERS: HEADMASTERS
Marvel Comics Group: July, 1987 - No. 4, Jan, 1988 ($1.00, limited series)

1-Springer, Akin, Garvey-a 2 4 6 8 10 12
2-4-Springer-c on all 6.00

TRANSFORMERS: HEART OF DARKNESS
IDW Publishing: Mar, 2011 - No. 4, Jun, 2011 ($3.99, limited series)

1-4-Abnett & Lanning-s/Farinas-a 4.00

Transformers: More Than Meets the Eye #10 © Hasbro

Transformers: Nefarious #5 © Hasbro

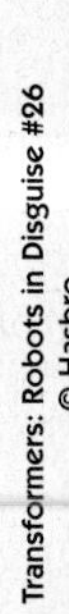
Transformers: Robots in Disguise #26 © Hasbro

	GD	VG	FN	VF	VF/NM	NM-
	2.0	4.0	6.0	8.0	9.0	9.2

GD VG FN VF VF/NM NM-
2.0 4.0 6.0 8.0 9.0 9.2

TRANSFORMERS: INFESTATION (Crossover with Star Trek, Ghostbusters & G.I. Joe)
IDW Publishing: Feb, 2011 - No. 2, Feb, 2011 ($3.99, limited series)
1,2-Abnett & Lanning-s/Roche-a; covers by Roche & Snyder III 4.00

TRANSFORMERS: INFILTRATION
IDW Publishing: Jan, 2006 - No. 6, June, 2006 ($2.99, limited series)
1-6-Furman-s/Su-a; multiple covers on all 4.00
... Cover Gallery (8/06, $5.99) 6.00

TRANSFORMERS: IRONHIDE
IDW Publishing: May, 2010 - No. 4, Aug, 2010 ($3.99, limited series)
1-4: Mike Costa-s; multiple covers on all 4.00

TRANSFORMERS: LAST STAND OF THE WRECKERS
IDW Publishing: Jan, 2010 - No. 5, May, 2010 ($3.99, limited series)
1-5-Nick Roche-s/a; two covers 4.00

TRANSFORMERS: LOST LIGHT
IDW Publishing: Dec, 2016 - No. 25, Oct, 2018 ($3.99)
1-15: 1-7-Roberts-s/Lawrence-a; multiple covers on each. 8,9-Tramontano-a 4.00

TRANSFORMERS: MAXIMUM DINOBOTS
IDW Publishing: Dec, 2008 - No. 5, Apr, 2009 ($3.99, limited series)
1-5-Furman-s/Roche-a; 2 covers for each 4.00

TRANSFORMERS: MEGATRON ORIGIN
IDW Publishing: May, 2007 - No. 4, Sept, 2008 ($3.99, limited series)
1-4-Alex Milne-a; 2 covers 4.00

TRANSFORMERS: MICROMASTERS
Dreamwave Productions: June, 2004 - No. 4 ($2.95, limited series)
1-4-Ruffolo-a; Pat Lee-c 4.00

TRANSFORMERS: MONSTROSITY
IDW Publishing: Jun, 2013 - No. 4, Sept, 2013 ($3.99)
1-4: 1-Three covers; Ramondelli-a 4.00

TRANSFORMERS: MORE THAN MEETS THE EYE
Dreamwave Productions: Apr, 2003 - No. 8, Nov, 2003 ($5.25)
1-8-Pin-ups with tech info on Autobots and Decepticons; art by Pat Lee & various 5.25
Vol. 1,2 (2004, $24.95, TPB) 1-r/#1-4. 2-r/#5-8 25.00

TRANSFORMERS: MORE THAN MEETS THE EYE
IDW Publishing: Jan, 2012 - No. 57, Sept, 2016 ($3.99)
1-49: 1-Five covers; Roche-a. 2-Three covers; Milne-a. 23-27-Dark Cybertron x-over. 26-1st app. of Windblade 4.00
50-(2/16, $7.99) "The Dying of the Light" begins; five covers 8.00
51-57: 51-55-The Dying of the Light. 56,57-Titans Return 4.00
Annual 2012 (8/12, $7.99) Salgado & Cabaltierra-a; three covers 8.00
...: Revolution 1 (11/16, $3.99) Revolution tie-in; Roche-s/Roberts-a; multiple covers 4.00

TRANSFORMERS: MOVIE ADAPTATION (For the 2007 live action movie)
IDW Publishing: June, 2007 - No. 4, June, 2007 ($3.99, weekly limited series)
1-4: Wraparound covers on each; Milne-a 4.00

TRANSFORMERS: MOVIE PREQUEL (For the 2007 live action movie)
IDW Publishing: Feb, 2007 - No. 4, May, 2007 ($3.99, limited series)
1-4: 1-Origin of the Transformers on Cybertron; multiple covers on each 4.00
Special (6/08, $3.99) 2 covers 4.00
TPB (6/07, $19.99) r/series; gallery of covers and variants 20.00

TRANSFORMERS: NEFARIOUS (Sequel to Transformers: Revenge of the Fallen movie)
IDW Publishing: Mar, 2010 - No. 6, Aug, 2010 ($3.99, limited series)
1-6: Furman-s; multiple covers on all 4.00

TRANSFORMERS: PRIMACY
IDW Publishing: Aug, 2014 - No. 4, Nov, 2014 ($3.99, limited series)
1-4-Metzen & Dille-s/Ramondelli-a; Omega Supreme app.; multiple covers on each 4.00

TRANSFORMERS: PRIME
IDW Publishing: Jan, 2011 - No. 4, Jan, 2011 ($3.99, weekly limited series)
1-4: 1-Mike Johnson-s/E.J. Su-a 4.00

TRANSFORMERS PRIME: BEAST HUNTERS
IDW Publishing: May, 2013 - No. 8, Dec, 2013($3.99, limited series)
1-8-Agustin Padilla-a 4.00

TRANSFORMERS PRIME: RAGE OF THE DINOBOTS
IDW Publishing: Nov, 2012 - No. 4, Feb, 2013 ($3.99, limited series)
1-4: 1-Mike Johnson-s/Agustin Padilla-a 4.00

TRANSFORMERS: PUNISHMENT
IDW Publishing: Jan, 2015 ($5.99, squarebound, one-shot)
1-Windblade app.; Barber-s/Ramondelli-a 6.00

TRANSFORMERS: REDEMPTION
IDW Publishing: Oct, 2015 ($7.99, squarebound, one-shot)
1-Dinobots app.; John Barber-s/Livio Ramondelli-a 8.00

TRANSFORMERS: REGENERATION ONE (Continues story from Transformers #80 (1991))
IDW Publishing: No. 80.5, May, 2012 - No. 100, Mar, 2014 ($3.99)
80.5 (5/12, Free Comic Book Day giveaway) Furman-s/Wildman-a 3.00
81-99 ($3.99) 81-92-Furman-s/Wildman-a; multiple covers on all 4.00
100-($5.99) Six covers; Furman-s/Wildman, Senior & Guidi-a; bonus cover gallery 6.00
#0 (9/13, $3.99) Hot Rod in the timestream; various artists; 4 covers 4.00
... 100-Page Spectacular (7/12, $7.99) Reprints Transformers #76-80 (1991) 8.00

TRANSFORMERS: REVENGE OF THE FALLEN OFFICIAL MOVIE ADAPTATION
(For the 2009 live action movie sequel)
IDW Publishing: May, 2009 - No. 4, June, 2009 ($3.99, weekly limited series)
1-4: Furman-s; 2 covers on each 4.00

TRANSFORMERS: RISING STORM (Prequel to 2011 Transformers: Dark of the Moon movie)
IDW Publishing: Feb, 2011 - No. 4, May, 2011 ($3.99, limited series)
1-3-Barber-s/Magno-a; 2 covers 4.00

TRANSFORMERS: ROBOTS IN DISGUISE (Re-titled Transformers #35-on)
IDW Publishing: Jan, 2012 - No. 34, Oct, 2014 ($3.99)
1-34: 1-Five covers; Griffith-a. 2-27-Three covers. 23-27-Dark Cybertron x-over 4.00

TRANSFORMERS: ROBOTS IN DISGUISE (Based on the animated series)
IDW Publishing: No. 0, May, 2015 - No. 5, Dec, 2015 ($3.99)
0-Free Comic Book Day Edition; Barber-s/Tramontano-a; Bumblebee & Strongarm app. 3.00
1-5: 1-Georgia Ball-s/Priscilla Tramontano-a 4.00

TRANSFORMERS: SAGA OF THE ALLSPARK (From the 2007 live action movie)
IDW Publishing: Jul, 2008 - No. 4, Oct, 2008 ($3.99, limited series)
1-4-Launch of the Allspark into outer space; Furman-s/Roche-c 4.00

TRANSFORMERS: SECTOR 7 (From the 2007 live action movie)
IDW Publishing: Sept, 2010 - No. 5, Jan, 2011 ($3.99, limited series)
1-5-Barber-s 4.00

TRANSFORMERS: SINS OF THE WRECKERS
IDW Publishing: Nov, 2015 - No. 5, May, 2016 ($3.99, limited series)
1-5-Roche-s/Burcham-a 4.00

TRANSFORMERS: SPOTLIGHT
IDW Publishing: Sept, 2006 - May, 2013 ($3.99, multiple covers on each)
... Arcee (2/08); ... Blaster (1/08); ... Blurr (11/08); ... Bumblebee (3/13); ... Cliffjumper (6/09); ... Cyclonus (6/08); ...Doubledealer (8/08); ...Drift (4/09); ...Galvatron (7/07);...Grimlock (3/08);
...Hardhead (7/08); ... Hoist (5/13); ... Hot Rod (11/06); ... Jazz (3/09); ... Kup (4/07); ... Megatron (2/13); ... Metroplex (7/09); ... Mirage (3/08); ... Nightbeat (10/06); ... Orion Pax (12/12); ... Prowl (4/10);... Ramjet (11/07); ... Shockwave (9/06); ... Sideswipe (9/08); ... Sixshot (12/06); ... Soundwave (3/07); Thundercracker (1/13); ... Trailcutter (4/13); ... Ultra Magnus (1/07) 4.00
... Optimus Prime: 3-D (11/08, $5.99, with glasses) Furman-s/Figueroa-a 6.00

TRANSFORMERS: STORMBRINGER
IDW Publishing: Jul, 2006 - No. 4, Oct, 2006 ($2.99, limited series)
1-4-Furman-s/Figueroa-a; multiple covers on all 4.00
TPB (2/07, $17.99) r/series; cover gallery and sketch pages 18.00

TRANSFORMERS SUMMER SPECIAL
Dreamwave Productions: May, 2004 ($4.95)
1-Pat Lee-a; Figueroa-a 5.00

TRANSFORMERS: TALES OF THE FALLEN
IDW Publishing: Aug, 2009 - No. 6 ($3.99, limited series)
1-6: 2,4-Furman-s mulitple covers on all 4.00

TRANSFORMERS: TARGET 2006
IDW Publishing: Apr, 2007 - No. 5, Aug, 2007 ($3.99, limited series)
1-5-Reprints from 1980s series; multiple covers on all 4.00

TRANSFORMERS: THE ANIMATED MOVIE
IDW Publishing: Oct, 2006 - No. 4, Jan, 2007 ($3.99, limited series)
1-4-Adapts animated movie; Don Figueroa-a 4.00

TRANSFORMERS, THE MOVIE

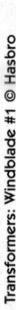

Transformers: Windblade #1 © Hasbro

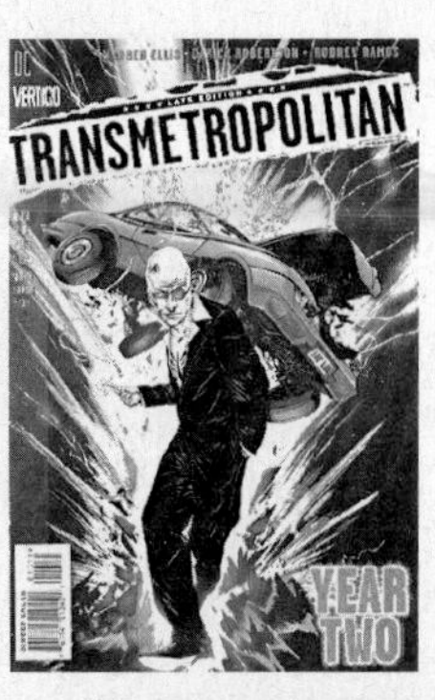

Transmetropolitan #13 © Ellis & Robertson

Treasure Chest V3 #9 © G. Pflaum

	GD 2.0	VG 4.0	FN 6.0	VF 8.0	VF/NM 9.0	NM- 9.2

Marvel Comics Group: Dec, 1986 - No. 3, Feb, 1987 (75¢, limited series)
1-3-Adapts animated movie 2 4 6 10 14 18

TRANSFORMERS: THE REIGN OF STARSCREAM
IDW Publishing: Apr, 2008 - No. 5, Aug, 2008 ($3.99, limited series)
1-5-Continuation of the 2007 movie; Milne-a; multiple covers 4.00

TRANSFORMERS: THE WAR WITHIN
Dreamwave Productions: Oct, 2002 - No. 6, Mar, 2003 ($2.95)
1-6-Furman-s/Figueroa-a. 1-Wraparound gatefold-c 4.00
TPB (2003, $15.95) r/#1-6; plus cover gallery 16.00

TRANSFORMERS: TILL ALL ARE ONE
IDW Publishing: Jun, 2016 - No. 12, Jul, 2017 ($3.99)
1-12-Road to Revolution; Mairghread Scott-s; multiple covers on all 4.00
Annual 2017 (12/17, $7.99) Mairghread Scott-s/Pitre-Durocher-a
...: Revolution 1 (10/16, $3.99) Revolution tie-in; Windblade app.; multiple covers 4.00

TRANSFORMERS: UNICRON (Crossover with Optimus Prime & Transformers: Lost Light)
IDW Publishing: Jul, 2018 - No. 6, Oct, 2018 ($4.99)
1-6-Barber-s/Milne-a; multiple covers on all; Rom app. 5.00
#0 (5/18, FCBD giveaway) Barber-s/Milne-a; Rom app. 3.00

TRANSFORMERS UNIVERSE
Marvel Comics Group: Dec, 1986 - No. 4, Mar, 1987 ($1.25, limited series)
1-4-A guide to all characters 2 4 6 8 11 14
TPB-r/#1-4 15.00

TRANSFORMERS VS. G.I. JOE
IDW Publishing: No. 0, May, 2014 - No. 13, Jun, 2016 ($3.99)
Free Comic Book Day #0 (5/14, giveaway) Tom Scioli-a; Scioli & John Barber-s 3.00
1-12-Tom Scioli-a; Scioli & John Barber-s; multiple covers on each; creator commentary 4.00
13-($7.99, squarebound) Last issue; bonus commentary; 3 covers 8.00
...: The Movie Adaptation (3/17, $4.99) Tom Scioli-s/a; 4 covers; bonus sketch-a 5.00

TRANSFORMERS VS. VISIONARIES
IDW Publishing: Dec, 2017 - No. 5, Apr, 2018 ($3.99, limited series)
1-5-Vissagio-s/Ossio-a 4.00

TRANSFORMERS WAR WITHIN: THE AGE OF WRATH
Dreamwave Productions: Sept, 2004 - No. 6 ($2.95, limited series)
1-3-Furman-s/Ng-a 4.00

TRANSFORMERS WAR WITHIN: THE DARK AGES
Dreamwave Productions: Oct, 2003 - No. 6 ($2.95)
1-6: 1-Furman-s/Wildman-a; two covers by Pat Lee & Figueroa 4.00
TPB (2004, $17.95) r/#1-6; plus cover gallery and design sketches 18.00

TRANSFORMERS: WINDBLADE (See Transformers More Than Meets the Eye #26)
IDW Publishing: Apr, 2014 - No. 4, Jul, 2014 ($3.99, limited series)
1-4-Mairghread Scott-s/Sarah Stone-a; three covers on each 4.00
Vol. 2 (3/15 - No. 7, 9/15, $3.99) 1-7-Scott-s; multiple covers on each. 1-Stone-a 4.00

TRANSIT
Vortex Publ.: March, 1987 - No. 5, Nov, 1987 (B&W)
1-5-Ted McKeever-s/a 1 2 3 5 6 8

TRANSLUCID
BOOM! Studios: Apr, 2014 - No. 6, Sept, 2014 ($3.99)
1-6-Sanchez & Echert-s/Bayliss-a; multiple covers on each 4.00

TRANSMETROPOLITAN
DC Comics (Helix/Vertigo): Sept, 1997 - No. 60, Nov, 2002 ($2.50)
1-Warren Ellis-s/Darick Robertson-a(p) 5 10 15 31 53 75
1-Special Edition (5/09, $1.00) r/#1 with "After Watchmen" cover frame 3.00
2,3 2 4 6 8 10 12
4-8 5.00
9-60: 15-Jae Lee-c. 25-27-Jim Lee-c. 37-39-Bradstreet-c 3.00
Back on the Street ('97, $7.95) r/#1-3 10.00
Back on the Street ('09, $14.99) r/#1-6; intro. by Garth Ennis 15.00
Dirge ('03/'10, $14.95/$14.95) r/#43-48 15.00
Filth of the City ('01, $5.95) Spider's columns with pin-up art by various 6.00
Gouge Away ('02/'09, $14.95/$14.99) r/#31-36 15.00
I Hate It Here ('00, $5.95) Spider's columns with pin-up art by various 6.00
Lonely City ('01/'09, $14.95/$14.99) r/#25-30; intro. by Patrick Stewart 15.00
Lust For Life ('98, $14.95) r/#4-12 20.00
Lust For Life ('09, $14.99) r/#7-12 15.00
One More Time ('04, $14.95) r/#55-60 15.00
One More Time ('11, $19.99) r/#55-60 & Filth of the City & I Hate It Here one-shots 20.00
Spider's Thrash ('02/'10, $14.95/$14.99) r/#37-42; intro. by Darren Aronofsky 15.00
Tales of Human Waste ('04, $9.95) r/Filth of the City, I Hate It Here & story from Vertigo Winter's Edge 2 10.00
The Cure ('03/'11, $14.95/$14.99) r/#49-54 15.00
The New Scum ('00, $12.95) r/#19-24 & Vertigo: Winter's Edge #3 15.00
The New Scum ('09, $14.99) r/#19-24 & Vertigo: Winter's Edge #3 15.00
Year of the Bastard ('99, $12.95)('09, $12.99) r/#13-18 13.00

TRANSMUTATION OF IKE GARUDA, THE
Marvel Comics (Epic Comics): July, 1991 - No. 2, 1991 ($3.95, 52 pgs.)
1,2 4.00

TRAPPED!
Periodical House Magazines (Ace): Oct, 1954 - No. 4, April, 1955
1 (All reprints) 11 22 33 62 86 110
2-4: 4-r/Men Against Crime #4 in its entirety 8 16 24 42 54 65
NOTE: *Colan a-1, 4. Sekowsky a-1.*

TRASH
Trash Publ. Co.: Mar, 1978 - No. 4, Oct, 1978 (B&W, magazine, 52 pgs.)
1,2: 1-Star Wars parody. 2-UFO-c 2 4 6 13 18 22
3-Parodies of KISS, the Beatles, and monsters 3 6 9 14 20 26
4-(84 pgs.)-Parodies of Happy Days, Rocky movies 3 6 9 15 22 28

TRAVELER, THE (Developed by Stan Lee)
BOOM! Studios: Nov, 2010 - No. 12, Oct, 2011 ($3.99)
1-12-Waid-s/Hardin-a; three covers on each 4.00

TRAVELS OF JAIMIE McPHEETERS, THE (TV)
Gold Key: Dec, 1963
1-Kurt Russell photo on-c plus photo back-c 4 8 12 25 40 55

TREASURE CHEST (Catholic Guild; also see Topix)
George A. Pflaum: 3/12/46 - V27#8, July, 1972 (Educational comics)
(Not published during Summer)
V1#1 32 64 96 190 310 430
2-6 (5/21/46): 5-Dr. Styx app. by Baily 15 30 45 85 130 175
V2#1-20 (9/3/46-5/27/47) 11 22 33 60 83 105
V3#1-5,7-20 (1st slick cover) 10 20 30 54 72 90
V3#6-Jules Verne's "Voyage to the Moon" 13 26 39 72 101 130
V4#1-20 (9/9/48-5/31/49) 9 18 27 47 61 75
V5#1-20 (9/6/49-5/31/50) 8 16 24 44 57 70
V6#1-20 (9/14/50-5/31/51) 8 16 24 42 54 65
V7#1-20 (9/13/51-6/5/52) 8 16 24 40 50 60
V8#1-20 (9/11/52-6/4/53) 7 14 21 37 46 55
V9#1-20 ('53-'54), V10#1-20 ('54-'55) 7 14 21 35 43 50
V11('55-'56), V12('56-'57) 6 12 18 29 36 42
V13#1,3-5,7,9-20-V17#1 ('57-'63) 6 12 18 27 33 38
V13#2,6,8-Ingels-a 5 10 15 35 63 90
V17#2- "This Godless Communism" series begins(not in odd #'d issues); cover shows hammer & sickle over Statue of Liberty; 8 pg. Crandall-a of family life under communism (9/28/61) 17 34 51 119 265 410
V17#3,5,7,9,11,13,15,17,19 3 6 9 16 24 32
V17#4,6,14- "This Godless Communism" stories 13 26 39 91 201 310
V17#8-Shows red octopus encompassing Earth, firing squad; 8 pgs. Crandall-a (12/21/61) 16 32 48 111 246 380
V17#10- "This Godless Communism" - how Stalin came to power, part I; Crandall-a 14 28 42 94 207 320
V17#12-Stalin in WWII, forced labor, death by exhaustion; Crandall-a 14 28 42 94 207 320
V17#16-Kruschev takes over; de-Stalinization 14 28 42 94 207 320
V17#18-Kruschev's control; murder of revolters, brainwash, space race by Crandall 14 28 42 94 207 320
V17#20-End of series; Kruschev-people are puppets, firing squads hammer & sickle over Statue of Liberty, snake around communist manifesto by Crandall 17 34 51 119 265 410
V18#1,3,4,6-10,12-20, V19#11-20, V20#1-20(1964-65): V20#6-JFK photo-c & story. V20#16-Babe Ruth-c & story by Sinnott 3 6 9 16 23 30
V18#2-Kruschev on-c (9/27/62) 3 6 9 19 30 40
V18#5- "What About Red China?" - describes how communists took over China 8 16 24 54 102 150
V18#11-Crandall draws himself & 13 other artists on cover (1/31/63) 3 6 9 21 33 45
V19#1-10- "Red Victim" anti-communist series in all 8 16 24 54 102 150
V21, V22 #1-16,18-20,V23-V25(1965-70)-(two V24#5's 11/7/68 & 11/21/68) (no V24#6): 3 6 9 14 19 24
V22#17-Flying saucer wraparound-c 3 6 9 16 24 32

Treasury of Comics #4 © STJ

Treehouse of Horror #6 © Bongo

Triage #5 © Phillip Sevy

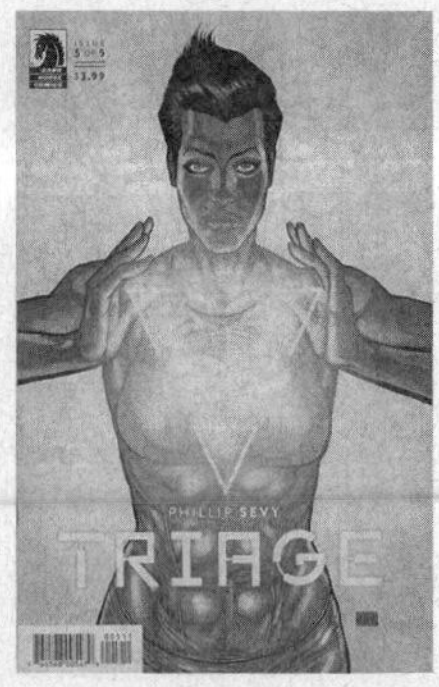

GD VG FN VF VF/NM NM-
2.0 4.0 6.0 8.0 9.0 9.2

V26, V27#1-8 (V26,27-68 pgs.) 3 6 9 15 22 28
Summer Edition V1#1-6('66), V2#1-6('67) 3 6 9 16 23 30
NOTE: ***Anderson** a-V18#13. **Borth** a-V7#10-19 (serial), V8#8-17 (serial), V9#1-10 (serial), V13#2, 6, 11, V14-V25 (except V22#1-3, 11-13), Summer Ed. V1#3-6. **Crandall** a-V16#7, 9, 12, 14, 16-18, 20; V17#1, 2, 4-6, 10, 12, 14, 16-18, 20; V18#1, 2, 3(2 pg.), 7, 9-20; V19#4, 11, 13, 16, 19, 20; V20#1, 2, 4, 6, 8-10, 12, 14-16, 18, 20; V21#1-5, 8-11, 13, 16-18; V22#3, 7, 9-11, 14; V23#3, 6, 9, 16, 18; V24#7, 8, 10, 13, 16; V25#8, 16; V27#1-7r, 8r(2 pg.), Summer Ed. V1#3-5, V2#3; c-V16#7, V18#2(part), 7, 11, V19#4, 19, 20, V20#15, V21#5, 9, V22#3, 7, 9, 11, V23#9, 16, V24#13, 16, V25#8, Summer Ed. V1#2 (back c-V1#2-5). **Powell** a-V10#11. V19#11, 15, V10#13, V13#6, 8 all have wraparound covers.*

TREASURE CHEST OF THE WORLD'S BEST COMICS
Superior, Toronto, Canada: 1945 (500 pgs., hard-c)
Contains Blue Beetle, Captain Combat, John Wayne, Dynamic Man, Nemo, Li'l Abner; contents can vary - represents random binding of extra books; Captain America on-c 158 316 474 1011 1731 2450

TREASURE COMICS
Prize Publications? (no publisher listed): No date (1943) (50¢, 324 pgs., cardboard-c)
1-(Rare)-Contains rebound Prize Comics #7-11 from 1942 (blank inside-c) 394 788 1182 2758 4829 6900

TREASURE COMICS
Prize Publ. (American Boys' Comics): June-July, 1945 - No. 12, Fall, 1947
1-Paul Bunyan & Marco Polo begin; Highwayman & Carrot Topp only app.; Kiefer-a 57 114 171 362 619 875
2-Arabian Knight, Gorilla King, Dr. Styx begin 34 68 102 204 332 460
3,4,9,12: 9-Kiefer-a 27 54 81 158 259 360
5-Marco Polo-c; Krigstein-a 34 68 102 199 325 450
6,11-Krigstein-a; 11-Krigstein-c 33 66 99 194 317 440
7,8-Frazetta-a (5 pgs. each). 7-Capt. Kidd Jr. app. 43 86 129 271 461 650
10-Simon & Kirby-c/a 43 86 129 271 461 650
NOTE: ***Barry** a-9-11; c-12. **Kiefer** a-3, 5, 7; c-2, 6, 7. **Roussos** a-11.*

TREASURE ISLAND (See Classics Illustrated #64, Doc Savage Comics #1, King Classics, Movie Classics & Movie Comics)
Dell Publishing Co.: No. 624, Apr, 1955 (Disney)
Four Color 624-Movie, photo-c 8 16 24 51 96 140

TREASURY OF COMICS
St. John Publishing Co.: 1947; No. 2, July, 1947 - No. 4, Sept, 1947; No. 5, Jan, 1948
nn(#1)-Abbie an' Slats (nn on-c, #1 on inside) 15 30 45 88 137 185
2-Jim Hardy Comics; featuring Windy & Paddles 12 24 36 69 97 125
3-Bill Bumlin 10 20 30 58 79 100
4-Abbie an' Slats 12 24 36 69 97 125
5-Jim Hardy Comics #1 12 24 36 69 97 125

TREASURY OF COMICS
St. John Publishing Co.: Mar, 1948 - No. 5, 1948 (Reg. size); 1948-1950 (Over 500 pgs., $1.00)
1 20 40 60 115 188 260
2(#2 on-c, #1 on inside) 13 26 39 74 105 135
3-5 11 22 33 62 86 110
1-(1948, 500 pgs., hard-c)-Abbie & Slats, Abbott & Costello, Casper, Little Annie Rooney, Little Audrey, Jim Hardy, Ella Cinders (16 books bound together) (Rare) 209 418 627 1338 2294 3250
1(1949, 500 pgs.)-Same format as above 164 328 492 1050 1800 2550
1(1950, 500 pgs.)-Same format as above; different-c; (also see Little Audrey Yearbook) (Rare) 164 328 492 1050 1800 2550

TREASURY OF DOGS, A (See Dell Giants)

TREASURY OF HORSES, A (See Dell Giants)

TREEHOUSE OF HORROR (Bart Simpson's...)
Bongo Comics: 1995 - 2017 ($2.95/$2.50/$3.50/$4.50/$4.99, annual)
1-(1995, $2.95)-Groening-c; Allred, Robinson & Smith stories 3 6 9 15 22 28
2-(1996, $2.50)-Stories by Dini & Bagge; infinity-c by Groening 2 4 6 8 11 14
3-(1997, $2.50)-Dorkin-s/Groening-c 2 4 6 8 10 12
4-(1998, $2.50)-Lash & Dixon-s/Groening-c 2 4 6 8 10 12
5-(1999, $3.50)-Thompson-s; Shaw & Aragonés-s/a; TenNapel-s/a 2 4 6 8 10 12
6-(2000, $4.50)-Mahfood-s/a; DeCarlo-a; Morse-s/a; Kuper-s/a 8.00
7-(2001, $4.50)-Hamill-s/Morrison-a; Ennis-s/McCrea-a; Sakai-s/a; Nixey-s/a; Brereton back-c 8.00
8-(2002, $3.50)-Templeton, Shaw, Barta, Simone, Thompson-s/a 8.00
9-(2003, $4.99)-Lord of the Rings-Brereton-a; Dini, Naifeh, Millidge, Boothby, Noto-s/a 8.00
10-(2004, $4.99)-Monsters of Rock w/Alice Cooper, Gene Simmons, Rob Zombie and Pat Boone; art by Rodriguez, Morrison, Morse, Templeton 15.00
11-(2005, $4.99)-EC style w/art by John Severin, Angelo Torres & Al Williamson and flip book with Dracula by Wolfman/Colan and Squish Thing by Wein/Wrightson 8.00
12-(2006, $4.99)-Terry Moore, Kyle Baker, Eric Powell-s/a 8.00
13-(2007, $4.99)-Oswalt, Posehn, Lennon-s; Guerra, Austin, Barta, Rodriguez-a 8.00
14-(2008, $4.99)-s/a by Niles & Fabry; Boothby & Matsumoto; Gilbert Hernandez 8.00
15-(2009, $4.99)-s/a by Jeffrey Brown, Tim Hensley, Ben Jones and others 8.00
16-(2010, $4.99)-s/a by Kelley Jones, Evan Dorkin and others; Mars Attacks homage 15.00
17-(2011, $4.99)-s/a by Gene Ha, Jane Wiedlin and others; Nosferatu homage 12.00
18-(2012, $4.99)-s/a by Jim Valentino, Phil Noto and others; Rosemary's Baby spoof 8.00
19-(2013, $4.99)-s/a by Len Wein, Dan Brereton and others; Cthulhu spoof 8.00
20-(2014, $4.99)-All Zombie issue, including The Walking Ned 8.00
21-(2015, $4.99)-Gremlins & Metropolis spoofs 8.00
22-(2016, $4.99)-Ghostbusters & Gossamer spoofs 8.00
23-(2017, $4.99)-Spoofs of Stephen King stories: It, Dreamcatcher and Thinner 12.00

GD VG FN VF VF/NM NM-
2.0 4.0 6.0 8.0 9.0 9.2

TREES
Image Comics: May, 2014 - No. 14, Aug, 2016 ($2.99)
1-14-Warren Ellis-s/Jason Howard-a 3.00

TREES: THREE FATES
Image Comics: Sept, 2019 - No. 5, Jan, 2020 ($3.99, limited series)
1-5-Warren Ellis-s/Jason Howard-a 4.00

TREKKER (See Dark Horse Presents #6)
Dark Horse Comics: May, 1987 - No. 6, Mar, 1988 ($1.50, B&W)
1-6: Sci/Fi stories 3.00
Color Special 1 (1989, $2.95, 52 pgs.) 4.00
Collection ($5.95, B&W) 6.00
Special 1 (6/99, $2.95, color) 3.00

TRENCHCOAT BRIGADE, THE
DC Comics (Vertigo): Mar, 1999 - No. 4, Jun, 1999 ($2.50, limited series)
1-4: Hellblazer, Phantom Stranger, Mister E, Dr. Occult app. 3.00

TRENCHER (See Blackball Comics)
Image Comics: May, 1993 - No. 4, Oct, 1993 ($1.95, unfinished limited series)
1-4: Keith Giffen-c/a/scripts. 3-Supreme-c/story 3.00

TRIAGE
Dark Horse Comics: Sept, 2019 - No. 5, Jan, 2020 ($3.99, limited series)
1-5-Phillip Sevy-s/a/c; variant covers for each 4.00

TRIALS OF SHAZAM!
DC Comics: Oct, 2006 - No. 12, May, 2008 ($2.99)
1-12: 1-8-Winick-s/Porter-a. 9-11-Cascioli-a. 10-Shadowpact app. 12-JLA app. 3.00
... Volume 1 TPB (2007, $14.99) r/#1-6 and story from DCU Brave New World #1 15.00
... Volume 2 TPB (2008, $14.99) r/#7-12 15.00

TRIB COMIC BOOK, THE
Winnipeg Tribune: Sept. 24, 1977 - Vol. 4, #36, 1980 (8-1/2"x11", 24 pgs., weekly) (155 total issues)
V1# 1-Color pages (Sunday strips)-Spiderman, Asterix, Disney's Scamp, Wizard of Id, Doonesbury, Inside Woody Allen, Mary Worth, & others (similar to Spirit sections) 2 4 6 10 14 18
V1#2-15, V2#1-52, V3#1-52, V4#1-33 1 3 4 6 8 10
V4#34-36 (not distributed) 2 4 6 11 16 20
NOTE: *All issues have Spider-Man. Later issues contain Star Trek and Star Wars. 20 strips in ea. The first newspaper to put Sunday pages into a comic book format.*

TRIBE (See WildC.A.T.S #4)
Image Comics/Axis Comics No. 2 on: Apr, 1993; No. 2, Sept, 1993 - No. 3, 1994 ($2.50/$1.95)
1-By Johnson & Stroman; gold foil & embossed on black-c 4.00
1-($2.50)-Ivory Edition; gold foil & embossed on white-c; available only through the creators 4.00
2,3: 2-1st Axis Comics issue. 3-Savage Dragon app. 3.00

TRIBUTE TO STEVEN HUGHES, A
Chaos! Comics: Sept, 2000 ($6.95)
1-Lady Death & Evil Ernie pin-ups by various artists; testimonials 7.00

TRICK 'R TREAT
DC Comics (WildStorm): 2009 ($19.95,SC)
nn-Short Halloween-themed story anthology; Andreyko-s; art by Huddleston & others 20.00

TRIGGER (See Roy Rogers'...)

TRIGGER
DC Comics (Vertigo): Feb, 2005 - No. 8, Sept, 2005 ($2.95/$2.99)
1-8-Jason Hall-s/John Watkiss-a/c 3.00

TRIGGER TWINS

Trinity #2 © DC

Trinity of Sin #6 © DC

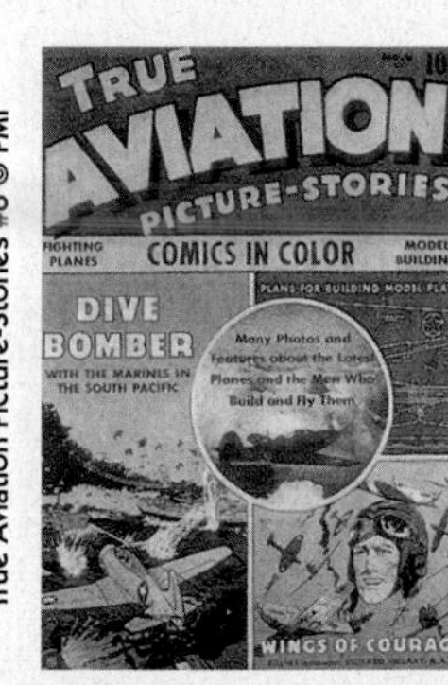

True Aviation Picture-Stories #6 © PMI

GD 2.0 | VG 4.0 | FN 6.0 | VF 8.0 | VF/NM 9.0 | NM- 9.2

National Periodical Publications: Mar-Apr, 1973 (20¢, one-shot)

1-Trigger Twins & Pow Wow Smith-r/All-Star Western #94,103 & Western Comics #81; Infantino-r(p) 2 4 6 13 18 22

TRILLIUM
DC Comics (Vertigo): Oct, 2013 - No. 8, Jun, 2014 ($2.99)

1-8-Jeff Lemire-s/a. 1-Flip-book 3.00

TRINITY (See DC Universe: Trinity)

TRINITY
DC Comics: Aug, 2008 - No. 52, July, 2009 ($2.99, weekly series)

1-52-Superman, Batman & Wonder Woman star; Busiek-s/Bagley-a. 52-Wraparound-c 3.00
Vol. 1 TPB (2009, $29.99) r/#1-17 30.00
Vol. 2 TPB (2009, $29.99) r/#18-35 30.00
Vol. 3 TPB (2009, $29.99) r/#36-52 30.00

TRINITY (DC Rebirth)
DC Comics: Nov, 2016 - No. 22, ($2.99/$3.99)

1-7: 1-Superman, Batman & Wonder Woman; Manapul-s/a. 3-Mann-a. 4-6-Mongul app. 3.00
8-22-($3.99): 9-11-Manapul-s/a; Justice League app. 12-15-Zatanna, Constantine & Deadman app.; Marion-a. 16-Deadshot app. 17-19,21,22-Warlord of Skartaris app. 4.00
Annual 1 (7/17, $4.99) Ra's al Ghul, Circe and Etrigan app.; Guillem March-a/c 5.00

TRINITY ANGELS
Acclaim Comics (Valiant Heroes): July, 1997 - No. 12, June, 1998 ($2.50)

1-12-Maguire-s/a(p). 4-Copycat-c 3.00

TRINITY: BLOOD ON THE SANDS
Image Comics (Top Cow): July, 2009 ($2.99, one-shot)

1-Witchblade, The Darkness and Angelus in the 14th century Arabian desert 3.00

TRINITY OF SIN (DC New 52)
DC Comics: Dec, 2014 - No. 6, May, 2015 ($2.99)

1-6-Pandora, The Question and Phantom Stranger; Guichet-a 3.00

TRINITY OF SIN: PANDORA (DC New 52)
DC Comics: Aug, 2013 - No. 14, Oct, 2014 ($2.99)

1-14: 1-Fawkes-s; origin re-told. 1-3-Trinity War tie-ins. 4-9-Forever Evil tie-ins 3.00
...: Futures End 1 (11/14, $2.99, regular-c) Five years later; Pandora vs. 7 Deadly Sins 3.00
...: Futures End 1 (11/14, $3.99, 3-D cover) 4.00

TRINITY OF SIN: THE PHANTOM STRANGER (See Phantom Stranger 2012 series)

TRIO (Continues in Triple Helix #1)
IDW Publishing: May, 2012 - No. 4, Aug, 2012 ($3.99, limited series)

1-4-John Byrne-s/a/c 4.00

TRIPLE GIANT COMICS (See Archie All-Star Specials under Archie Comics)

TRIPLE HELIX (Also see Trio)
IDW Publishing: Oct, 2013 - No. 4, Jan, 2014 ($3.99, limited series)

1-4-John Byrne-s/a/c; The Trio app. 4.00

TRIPLE THREAT
Special Action/Holyoke/Gerona Publ.: Winter, 1945

1-Duke of Darkness, King O'Leary 39 78 117 231 378 525

TRISH OUT OF WATER
Aspen MLT: Oct, 2013 - No. 5, Mar, 2014 ($1.00/$3.99)

1-($1.00) Vince Hernandez-s/Giuseppe Cafaro-a; multiple covers 3.00
2-5-($3.99) Multiple covers on each 4.00

TRIUMPH (Also see JLA #28-30, Justice League Task Force & Zero Hour)
DC Comics: June, 1995 - No. 4, Sept, 1995 ($1.75, limited series)

1-4: 3-Hourman, JLA app. 3.00

TRIUMPHANT UNLEASHED
Triumphant Comics: No. 0, Nov, 1993 - No. 1, Nov, 1993 ($2.50, lim. series)

0-Serially numbered, 0-Red logo, 0-White logo (no cover price; giveaway), 1-Cover is negative & reverse of #0-c 3.00

TROJAN WAR (Adaptation of Trojan war histories from ancient Greek and Roman sources)
Marvel Comics: July, 2009 - No. 5, Nov, 2009 ($3.99, limited series)

1-5-Roy Thomas-s/Miguel Sepulveda-a/Dennis Calero-c 4.00

TROLL (Also see Brigade)
Image Comics (Extreme Studios): Dec, 1993 ($2.50, one-shot, 44 pgs.)

1-1st app. Troll; Liefeld scripts; Matsuda-c/a(p) 4.00
Halloween Special (1994, $2.95)-Maxx app. 4.00
...Once A Hero (8/94, $2.50) 4.00

GD 2.0 | VG 4.0 | FN 6.0 | VF 8.0 | VF/NM 9.0 | NM- 9.2

TROLLORDS
Tru Studios/Comico V2#1 on: 2/86 - No. 15, 1988; V2#1, 11/88 - V2#4, 1989 (1-15: $1.50, B&W)

1-First printing 5.00
1-Second printing, 2-15: 6-Christmas issue; silver logo 3.00
V2#1-4 ($1.75, color, Comico) 3.00
Special 1 ($1.75, 2/87, color)-Jerry's Big Fun Bk. 3.00

TROLLORDS
Apple Comics: July, 1989 - No. 6, 1990 ($2.25, B&W, limited series)

1-6: 1-"The Big Batman Movie Parody" 3.00

TROLL PATROL
Harvey Comics: Jan, 1993 ($1.95, 52 pgs.)

1 4.00

TROLL II (Also see Brigade)
Image Comics (Extreme Studios): July, 1994 ($3.95, one-shot)

1 4.00

TRON (Based on the video game and film)
Slave Labor Graphics: Apr, 2006 - No. 6 ($3.50/$3.95)

1-4: 1-DeMartinis-a/Walker & Jones-s 4.00
5,6-($3.95) 4.00

TRON: BETRAYAL
Marvel Comics: Nov, 2010 - No. 2, Dec, 2010 ($3.99, limited series)

1,2-Prequel to Tron Legacy movie; Larroca-c 4.00

TRON: ORIGINAL MOVIE ADAPTATION
Marvel Comics: Jan, 2011 - No. 2, Feb, 2011 ($3.99, limited series)

1,2-Peter David-s/Mirco Pierfederici-a/Greg Land-c 4.00

TROUBLE
Marvel Comics (Epic): Sept, 2003 - No. 5, Jan, 2004 ($2.99, limited series)

1-5-Photo-c; Richard and Ben meet Mary and May; Millar-s/Dodson-a 3.00
1-2nd printing with variant Frank Cho-c 5.00

TROUBLED SOULS
Fleetway: 1990 ($9.95, trade paperback)

nn-Garth Ennis scripts & John McCrea painted-c/a. 10.00

TROUBLEMAKERS
Acclaim Comics (Valiant Heroes): Apr, 1997 - No. 19, June, 1998 ($2.50)

1-19: Fabian Nicieza scripts in all. 1-1st app. XL, Rebound & Blur; 2 covers. 8-Copycat-c. 12-Shooting of Parker 3.00

TROUBLE SHOOTERS, THE (TV)
Dell Publishing Co.: No. 1108, Jun-Aug, 1960

Four Color 1108-Keenan Wynn photo-c 6 12 18 40 73 105

TROUBLE WITH GIRLS, THE
Malibu Comics (Eternity Comics) #7-14/Comico V2#1-4/Eternity V2#5 on: 8/87 - #14, 1988; V2#1, 2/89 - V2#23, 1991? ($1.95, B&W/color)

1-14 ($1.95, B&W, Eternity)-Gerard Jones scripts & Tim Hamilton-c/a in all 3.00
V2#1-23-Jones scripts, Hamilton-c/a. 3.00
Annual 1 (1988, $2.95) 4.00
Christmas Special 1 (12/91, $2.95, B&W, Eternity)-Jones scripts, Hamilton-c/a 4.00
Graphic Novel 1,2 (7/88, B&W)-r/#1-3 & #4-6 8.00

TROUBLE WITH GIRLS, THE: NIGHT OF THE LIZARD
Marvel Comics (Epic Comics/Heavy Hitters): 1993 - No. 4, 1993 ($2.50/$1.95, lim. series)

1-Embossed-c; Gerard Jones scripts & Bret Blevins-c/a in all 4.00
2-4: 2-Begin $1.95-c. 3.00

TRUE ADVENTURES (Formerly True Western)(Men's Adventures #4 on)
Marvel Comics (CCC): No. 3, May, 1950 (52 pgs.)

3-Powell, Sekowsky, Maneely-a; Brodsky-c 26 52 78 154 252 350

TRUE ANIMAL PICTURE STORIES
True Comics Press: Winter, 1947 - No. 2, Spring-Summer, 1947

1 14 28 42 82 121 160
2 13 26 39 74 105 135

TRUE AVIATION PICTURE STORIES (Becomes Aviation Adventures & Model Building #16 on)
Parents' Mag. Institute: 1942; No. 2, Jan-Feb, 1943 - No. 15, Sept-Oct, 1946

1-(#1 & 2 titled ...Aviation Comics Digest)(not digest size) 19 38 57 111 176 240
2 12 24 36 69 97 125
3-14: 3-10-Plane photos on-c. 11,13-Photo-c 10 20 30 58 79 100
15-(Titled "True Aviation Adventures & Model Building")

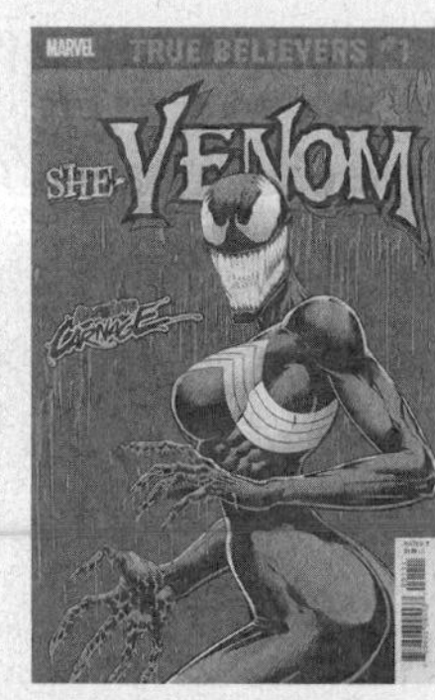

True Believers: Absolute Carnage - She-Venom #1 © MAR

True Believers: Black Widow - Darkstar #1 © MAR

True Believers: Empyre - Mar-Vell #1 © MAR

	GD	VG	FN	VF	VF/NM	NM-
	2.0	4.0	6.0	8.0	9.0	9.2
	10	20	30	54	72	90

TRUE BELIEVERS
Marvel Comics: Sept, 2008 - No. 5, Jan, 2009 ($2.99, limited series)
1-5-Cary Bates-s/Paul Gulacy-a. 1,2-Reed Richards app. 3-Luke Cage app. 3.00

TRUE BELIEVERS...
Marvel Comics: Jun, 2015 - Present ($1.00, series of one-shot reprints)
...: Absolute Carnage – Carnage 1 - Reprints Amazing Spider-Man #361; Bagley-a 3.00
...: Absolute Carnage – Carnage, U.S.A. 1 - Reprints Carnage, U.S.A. #1; Crain-a 3.00
...: Absolute Carnage – Mania 1 - Reprints Venom #1 (2003); Herrera-a 3.00
...: Absolute Carnage – Maximum Carnage 1 - Reprints Spider-Man Unlimited #1 3.00
...: Absolute Carnage – Mind Bomb 1 - Reprints Carnage: Mind Bomb #1; Hotz-a 3.00
...: Absolute Carnage – Planet of the Symbiotes 1 - R/ Amaz. Spider-Man Super Special 3.00
...: Absolute Carnage – Savage Rebirth 1 - Reprints Amazing Spider-Man #430 3.00
...: Absolute Carnage – Separation Anxiety 1 - Reprints Venom: Separation Anxiety #1 3.00
...: Absolute Carnage – She-Venom 1 - Reprints Venom: Sinner Takes All #3 3.00
...: Absolute Carnage – Venom vs. Carnage 1 - Reprints Venom vs. Carnage #1 3.00
...: Age of Apocalypse 1 - Reprints X-Men: Alpha #1; Cruz & Epting-a; wraparound-c 3.00
...: Age of Ultron 1 - Reprints Age of Ultron #1; Bendis-s/Hitch-a 3.00
...: All-New, All-Different Avengers - Cyclone 1 - Reprints issue #4; Waid-s/Asrar-a 3.00
...: All-New Wolverine 1 - Reprints issue #1; Taylor-s/Lopez-a 3.00
...: Amazing Spider-Man 1 - Reprints Amazing Spider-Man #1 3.00
...: Amazing Spider-Man - The Dark Kingdom 1 - Reprints Amazing Spider-Man #6 3.00
...: Annihilation – Annihilus 1 - Reprints Fantastic Four #140 3.00
...: Annihilation – Mantis 1 - Reprints Avengers #112; Heck-a 3.00
...: Annihilation – Man-Wolf in Space 1 - Reprints Marvel Premiere #45 3.00
...: Annihilation – Moondragon 1 - Reprints Iron Man #54; Sub-Mariner app. 3.00
...: Annihilation – Nova 1 - Reprints Nova #1; John Buscema-a 3.00
...: Annihilation – Odinpower 1 - Reprints Thor #349; Simonson-s/a 3.00
...: Annihilation – Omega the Unknown 1 - Reprints Omega the Unknown #1 3.00
...: Annihilation – Quasar 1 - Reprints Incredible Hulk #234; Sal Buscema-a 3.00
...: Annihilation – Super-Adaptoid 1 - Reprints Tales of Suspense #82 & 84; Kirby-a 3.00
...: Annihilation – Super-Skrull 1 - Reprints Thor #142; Kirby-a 3.00
...: Ant-Man and Hawkeye - Avengers Assemble 1 - Reprints Avengers #223 3.00
...: Ant-Man and the Wasp - On the Trail of Spider-Man 1 - Reprints Tales to Astonish #57 3.00
...: Ant-Man and the Wasp - The Birth of Giant-Man 1 - Rep. Tales to Astonish #35 & 49 3.00
...: Ant-Man and the Wasp - 'Til Death Do Us Part 1 - Reprints Avengers #60 3.00
...: Ant-Man Presents Iron Man - The Ghost and the Machine 1 - Reprints Iron Man #219 3.00
...: Ant-Man - The Incredible Shrinking Doom 1 - Reprints Marvel Feature #4 3.00
...: Armor Wars 1 - Reprints Iron Man #225; Michelinie-s/Bright & Layton-a 3.00
...: Astonishing X-Men 1 - Reprints Astonishing X-Men #1 (2004); Whedon-s/Cassaday-a 3.00
...: Avengers – Endgame 1 - Reprints Avengers #71; Sal Buscema-a 3.00
...: Avengers Forever 1 - Reprints Avengers Forever #1; Busiek-s/Pacheco-a 3.00
...: Avengers – Nebula 1 - Reprints Avengers #260; John Buscema-a 3.00
...: Avengers – Rocket Raccoon 1 - Reprints Rocket Raccoon #1; Mignola-a 3.00
...: Avengers – Ronin 1 - Reprints New Avengers #30; Bendis-s/Yu-a 3.00
...: Avengers – Stormbreaker 1 - Reprints Thor #339; Simonson-s/a 3.00
...: Avengers – Thanos & Gamora 1 - Reprints Warlock and the Infinity Watch #9 3.00
...: Avengers – Thanos: The Final Battle 1 - Reprints Infinity Gauntlet #6; Starlin-s/Lim-a 3.00
...: Avengers – Thanos vs. The Marvel Universe 1 - Reprints Infinity Gauntlet #4 3.00
...: Avengers – The Gatherers Saga 1 - Reprints Avengers #343; Epting-a 3.00
...: Avengers vs. Thanos 1 - Reprints Avengers #125; Buscema & Cockrum-a 3.00
...: Black Widow 1 - Reprints Black Widow #1 (2014); Edmondson-s/Noto-a 3.00
...: Black Widow – Amazing Adventures 1 - Reprints stories from Amazing Advs. #1,2 3.00
...: Black Widow & Daredevil 1 - Reprints Daredevil #81 (1971); Conway-s/Colan-a 3.00
...: Black Widow & The Avengers 1 - Reprints Avengers #111 (1973); Magneto app. 3.00
...: Black Widow & The Thing 1 - Reprints Marvel Two-In-One #10 (1975); Brown-a 3.00
...: Black Widow – Darkstar 1 - Reprints Champions #7 (1976); Tuska-a 3.00
...: Black Widow, Introducing The... 1 - Reprints Tales of Suspense #52-53 (1964) 3.00
...: Black Widow – Red Guardian 1 - Reprints Avengers #43 (1967); John Buscema-a 3.00
...: Black Widow – Taskmaster 1 - Reprints Avengers #196 (1980); origin; Pérez-a 3.00
...: Black Widow – Yelena Belova 1 - Reprints Black Widow #1 (1999); J.G. Jones-a 3.00
...: Cable & The New Mutants 1 - Reprints New Mutants #87; L. Simonson-s/Liefeld-a 3.00
...: Captain Marvel 1 - Reprints Captain Marvel #1 (2014); DeConnick-s/Lopez-a 3.00
...: Captain Marvel - Avenger 1 - Reprints Avengers #183; Michelinie-s/Byrne-a 3.00
...: Captain Marvel - Betrayed! 1 - Reprints Avengers Annual #10; Claremont-s/Golden-a 3.00
...: Captain Marvel - Binary 1 - Reprints (Uncanny) X-Men #164; Claremont-s/Cockrum-a 3.00
...: Captain Marvel - Earth's Mightiest Hero 1 - Reprints Captain Marvel #1 (2012) 3.00
...: Captain Mar-vell 1 - Reprints Marvel Super-Heroes #12 & Marvel Fanfare #24 3.00
...: Captain Marvel - Ms. Marvel 1 - Reprints Ms. Marvel #1 (1977); Buscema-a 3.00
...: Captain Marvel - Spider-Man and Ms. Marvel 1 - Reprints Marvel Team-Up #62 3.00
...: Captain Marvel - The Kree/Skrull War 1 - Reprints Avengers #89; Rick Jones app. 3.00
...: Captain Marvel - The New Ms. Marvel 1 - Reprints Ms. Marvel #20 (1978); Cockrum-a 3.00
...: Captain Marvel vs. Ronan 1 - Reprints Captain Marvel #41 (1975); Milgrom-a 3.00
...: Carol Danvers 1 - Reprints Marvel Super-Heroes #13; 1st app. Carol Danvers 3.00
...: Chewbacca 1 - Reprints Chewbacca #1; Duggan-s/Noto-a 3.00
...: Civil War 1 - Reprints Civil War #1; Millar-s/McNiven-a 3.00
...: Conan - Curse of the Golden Skull! 1 - Reps Conan the Barbarian #37; Neal Adams-a 3.00
...: Conan - Queen of the Black Coast! 1 - Reps Conan the Barbarian #58; Bêlit app. 3.00
...: Conan - Resurrection 1 - Reprints Conan the Barbarian #187; Buscema-a 3.00
...: Conan: Serpent War #0 – The Valley of the Worm - Reprints Supernatural Thrillers #3 3.00
...: Conan - Swords in the Night! 1 - Reprints Conan the Barbarian #23; Barry Smith-a 3.00
...: Conan the Barbarian 1 - Reprints Conan the Barbarian #1; Barry Smith-a 3.00
...: Conan - The Devil-God of Bal-Sagoth! 1 - Reprints Conan the Barbarian #17; Kane-a 3.00
...: Conan - The Secret of Skull River 1 - Reprints Savage Tales #5; Starlin-a 3.00
...: Conan - The Tower of the Elephant 1 - Reprints Conan the Barbarian #4; B. Smith-a 3.00
...: Daredevil - Practice to Deceive 1 - Reprints Daredevil #6 (2016); Soule-s/Buffagni-a 3.00
...: Darth Vader 1 - Reprints Darth Vader #1; Gillen-s/Larroca-a 3.00
...: Deadpool 1 - Reprints 1st app. from New Mutants #98 (1991); Liefeld-a 3.00
...: Deadpool - Deadpool vs. Sabretooth 1 - Reprints Deadpool #8 (2016) 3.00
...: Deadpool Origins 1 - Reprints Wolverine Origins #25; Dillon-a 3.00
...: Deadpool The Musical 1 - Reprints Deadpool #49.1; McCrea-a 3.00
...: Deadpool Variants 1 - Gallery of variant covers 3.00
...: Death of Phoenix 1 - Reprints New X-Men #150 3.00
...: Detective Deadpool 1 - Reprints Cable & Deadpool #13; Nicieza-s/Zircher-a 3.00
...: Doctor Strange - The Last Days of Magic 1 - Reprints Doctor Strange #6 (2015) 3.00
...: Droids 1 - Reprints Droids #1; Star Wars C-3PO & R2-D2 app.; John Romita-a 3.00
...: Empyre – Anelle 1 - Reprints Fantastic Four #37 (1965) intro Princess Anelle 3.00
...: Empyre – Galactus 1 - Reprints Fantastic Four #257 (1983) Byrne-s/a 3.00
...: Empyre – Hulkling 1 - Reprints Young Avengers #11 (2006) Cheung-a 3.00
...: Empyre – Lyja 1 - Reprints Fantastic Four #357 (1991) Paul Ryan-a 3.00
...: Empyre – Mantis 1 - Reprints Avengers #133 (1975) origin of Mantis; Sal Buscema-a 3.00
...: Empyre – Mar-Vell 1 - Reprints Avengers #89 (1971) Kree/Skrull war begins 3.00
...: Empyre – Quoi 1 - Reprints Avengers Celestial Quest #3 (12003) Englehart-s 3.00
...: Empyre – She-Hulk 1 - Reprints Savage She-Hulk #1 (1980) John Buscema-a 3.00
...: Empyre – Swordsman 1 - Reprints Avengers #19 (1965) Swordsman's debut; Heck-a 3.00
...: Empyre – Vision 1 - Reprints Giant-Size Avengers #4 (1974) Dormammu app. 3.00
...: Enter – The Phoenix 1 - Reprints X-Men #100-101 (1976) Cockrum-a 3.00
...: Evil Deadpool 1 - Reprints Deadpool #45; Espin-a 3.00
...: Exiles 1 - Reprints Exiles #1 (2001); Winick-s/McKone-a 3.00
...: Extraordinary X-Men - The Burning Man 1 - Reprints issue #6; Ibañez-a 3.00
...: Fantastic Four - Blastaar 1 - Reprints Fantastic Four #62; Kirby-a; Inhumans app. 3.00
...: Fantastic Four By John Byrne 1 - Reprints Fantastic Four #232; Diablo app. 3.00
...: Fantastic Four By Walter Simonson 1 - Reprints Fantastic Four #337 3.00
...: Fantastic Four - Dragon Man 1 - Reprints Fantastic Four #35; Kirby-a 3.00
...: Fantastic Four - Frightful Four 1 - Reprints Fantastic Four #36; Kirby-a 3.00
...: Fantastic Four - Galactus Hungers 1 - Reprints Fantastic Four #175; Buscema-a 3.00
...: Fantastic Four - Hulk vs. Thing 1 - Reprints Fantastic Four #112; Buscema-a 3.00
...: Fantastic Four - Klaw 1 - Reprints Fantastic Four #53; Kirby-a; Black Panther app. 3.00
...: Fantastic Four - Mad Thinker & Awesome Android 1 - Reprints Fantastic Four #15 3.00
...: Fantastic Four - Molecule Man 1 - Reprints Fantastic Four #20; Kirby-a; Watcher app. 3.00
...: Fantastic Four - Puppet Master 1 - Reprints Fantastic Four #8; Kirby-a; intro. Alicia 3.00
...: Fantastic Four - Ronan & The Kree 1 - Reprints Fantastic Four #65; Kirby-a 3.00
...: Fantastic Four - Skrulls 1 - Reprints Fantastic Four #2; Kirby-a 3.00
...: Fantastic Four - Super-Skrull 1 - Reprints Fantastic Four #18; Kirby-a 3.00
...: Fantastic Four - The Birth of Valeria 1 - Reprints Fantastic Four #54 (2002) 3.00
...: Fantastic Four - The Coming of Galactus 1 - Reprints Fantastic Four #48 3.00
...: Fantastic Four - The Coming of H.E.R.B.I.E. 1 - Reprints Fantastic Four #209 3.00
...: Fantastic Four - The Wedding of Reed & Sue 1 - Reprints Fantastic Four Annual #3 3.00
...: Fantastic Four vs. Doctor Doom 1 - Reprints 1st app. in Fantastic Four #5 3.00
...: Fantastic Four vs. The New Fantastic Four 1 - Reprints Fantastic Four #374 3.00
...: Generation X 1 - Reprints Generation X #1; Lobdell-s/Bachalo-a 3.00
...: Giant-Size X-Men 1 - Reprints Giant-Size X-Men #1; Wein-s/Cockrum-a 5.00
...: Guardians of the Galaxy - Galaxy's Most Wanted 1 - Reprints GOTG #6 (2015) 3.00
...: House of M 1 - Reprints House of M #1; Bendis-s/Coipel-a 3.00
...: Hulk - Devil Hulk 1 - Reprints Incredible Hulk #13 (2000); Jenkins-s/Garney-a 3.00
...: Hulk - Grey Hulk Returns 1 - Reprints Incredible Hulk #324; Milgrom-s/a 3.00
...: Hulk - Head of Banner 1 - Reprints Incredible Hulk #6; Stan Lee-s/Steve Ditko-a 3.00
...: Hulk - Intelligent 1 - Reprints Incredible Hulk #272; Mantlo-s/Sal Buscema-a 3.00
...: Hulk - Joe Fixit 1 - Reprints Incredible Hulk #347; David-s/Purves-a 3.00
...: Hulk - Mindless Hulk 1 - Reprints Incredible Hulk #299; Mantlo-s/Sal Buscema-a 3.00
...: Hulk - Professor Hulk 1 - Reprints Incredible Hulk #377; David-s/Keown-a 3.00
...: Hulk - Red Hulk 1 - Reprints Hulk #1 (2008); Loeb-s/McGuinness-a 3.00
...: Hulk - The Other Hulks 1 - r/Journey Into Mystery #62 (Xemnu) & Strange Tales #75 3.00
...: Infinity Gauntlet 1 - Reprints Infinity Gauntlet #1; Starlin-s/Pérez-a 3.00
...: Infinity Incoming! 1 - Reprints Avengers #1 (2013); Hickman-s/Opeña-a 3.00
...: Infinity War 1 - Reprints Infinity War #1; Starlin-s/Lim-a 3.00
...: Invincible Iron Man - The War Machines 1 - Reprints Invincible Iron Man #6 3.00
...: Iron Man 2020 - Albert & Elsie-Dee 1 - Reprints Wolverine #37 (1988); Silvestri-a 3.00
...: Iron Man 2020 - Arno Stark 1 - Reprints Machine Man #2 (1984); Trimpe-a 3.00

True Believers: King In Black - Black Panther #1 © MAR

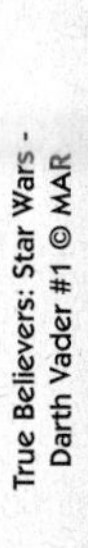
True Believers: Star Wars - Darth Vader #1 © MAR

True Believers: X-Men Blue #1 © MAR

	GD 2.0	VG 4.0	FN 6.0	VF 8.0	VF/NM 9.0	NM- 9.2
...: Iron Man 2020 - Jocasta 1 - Reprints Avengers #162; Ultron app.; Perez-a						3.00
...: Iron Man 2020 - Pepper Potts 1 - Reprints Tales of Suspense #45; Heck-a						3.00
...: Iron Man 2020 - War Machine 1 - Reprints Iron Man #118 (1979); Byrne-a						3.00
...: Kanan 1 - Reprints Kanan #1; Star Wars; Weisman-s/Larraz-a	2	4	6	9	12	15
...: King Conan 1 - Reprints King Conan #1; Buscema-a						3.00
...: King in Black – Beta Ray Bill 1 - Reprints Thor #337; 1st app. Bill; Simonson-s/a						3.00
...: King in Black – Black Cat 1 - Reprints 1st app. in Amazing Spider-Man #194						3.00
...: King in Black – Black Knight 1 - Reprints Avengers #48 (1968); 1st app.; Tuska-a						3.00
...: King in Black – Black Panther 1 - Reprints Fantastic Four #52 (1966); 1st app.						3.00
...: King in Black – Franklin Richards 1 - Reprints Fantastic Four #245; Byrne-s/a						3.00
...: King in Black – Gamma Flight's Doc Samson 1 - Reprints Incredible Hulk #141; origin						3.00
...: King in Black – Iron Man/Doctor Doom 1 - Reprints Iron Man #149; Romita Jr.-a						3.00
...: King in Black – Monsterworld 1 - Reprints Venom Super Special #1 (1995); Hotz-a						3.00
...: King in Black – Thunderbolts 1 - Reprints Incredible Hulk #449; Deodato Jr.-a						3.00
...: King in Black – Valkyrie 1 - Reprints Avengers #83 (1970); origin.; Buscema-a						3.00
...: Kitty Pryde and Wolverine 1 - Reprints Kitty Pryde and Wolverine #1; Milgrom-a						3.00
...: Lando 1 - Reprints Lando #1; Star Wars; Soule-s/Maleev-a						3.00
...: Marvel Knights 20th Anniversary – Black Widow By Grayson & Jones 1 - r/#1('99)						3.00
...: Marvel Knights 20th Anniversary – Daredevil and the Defenders 1 - r/Daredevil #80						3.00
...: Marvel Knights 20th Anniversary – Daredevil By Bendis & Maleev 1 - r/Daredevil #26						3.00
...: Marvel Knights 20th Anniversary – Daredevil By Lee & Everett 1 - r/Daredevil #1 ('64)						3.00
...: Marvel Knights 20th Anniversary – Daredevil By Smith, Quesada & Palmiotti 1 - r/#1 ('98)						3.00
...: Marvel Knights 20th Anniversary – Hellcat: The First Appearance 1 - r/Avengers #144						3.00
...: Marvel Knights 20th Anniversary – Iron Fist By Thomas & Kane 1 - r/Marvel Prem. #15						3.00
...: Marvel Knights 20th Anniversary – Jessica Jones: Alias By Bendis & Gaydos 1 - r/Alias #1						3.00
...: Marvel Knights 20th Anniversary – Luke Cage, Hero For Hire 1 - r/Hero For Hire #1						3.00
...: Marvel Knights 20th Anniversary – Power Man and Iron Fist 1 - r/Power Man #48						3.00
...: Marvel Knights 20th Anniversary – Punisher: The First Appearance 1 - r/AS-M #129						3.00
...: Marvel Knights 20th Anniversary – Punisher By Ennis, Dillon & Palmiotti 1 - r/#1 ('00)						3.00
...: Marvel Knights 20th Anniversary – Punisher By Grant & Zeck 1 - r/Punisher #1 ('86)						3.00
...: Marvel Knights 20th Anniversary – Punisher War Journal By Potts & Lee 1 - r/#1 ('88)						3.00
...: Marvel Tails Starring Peter Porker, The Spectacular Spider-Ham 1 - Reprints #1						3.00
...: Marvel Zombies 1 - Reprints Marvel Zombies #1; Bendis-s/Phillips-a						3.00
...: Mighty Thor - The Strongest Viking There Is 1 - Reprints Mighty Thor #6						3.00
...: Miles Morales 1 - Reprints Ultimate Comics Spider-Man #1; Bendis-s/Pichelli-a						3.00
...: Ms. Marvel 1 - Reprints Ms. Marvel #1 (2014); Wilson-s/Alphona-a						3.00
...: New Mutants 1 - Reprints New Mutants #1; Claremont-s/McLeod-a						3.00
...: Old Man Logan 1 - Reprints Wolverine #66 (2008); Millar-s/McNiven-a; wraparound-c						5.00
...: Phoenix – Bizarre Adventures 1 - Reprints Bizarre Adventures #27; Buscema-a						3.00
...: Phoenix Classic 1 - Reprints Classic X-Men #13 & 18; Bolton-a						3.00
...: Phoenix Origins 1 - Reprints X-Men Origins: Jean Grey; Mayhew-a						3.00
...: Phoenix Presents Cyclops & Marvel Girl 1 - Reprints X-Men #48 & 57 (1968,1969)						3.00
...: Phoenix Presents Jean Grey vs. Sabretooth 1 - Reprints X-Men #28 (1994)						3.00
...: Phoenix Presents The Wedding of Scott Summers & Jean Grey 1 - Reprints X-Men #30						3.00
...: Phoenix Returns 1 - Reprints Fantastic Four #286; Byrne-s/a						3.00
...: Phoenix – What If? 1 - Reprints What If? #27 (Phoenix Had Not Died?)						3.00
...: Planet Hulk 1 - Reprints Incredible Hulk #92 (2006); Pak-s/Pagulayan-a						3.00
...: Princess Leia 1 - Reprints Princess Leia #1; Waid-s/Dodson-a						3.00
...: Rebirth of Thanos 1 - Reprints Silver Surfer #34 (1990); Starlin-s/Lim-a						3.00
...: Scott Lang, The Astonishing Ant-Man 1 - Reprints Marvel Premiere #47; Byrne-a						3.00
...: Shattered Empire 1 - Reprints Journey to Star Wars: The Force Awakens – Shattered Empire #1; Rucka-s/Checchetto-a						3.00
...: She-Hulk 1 - Reprints She-Hulk #1 (2014); Soule-s/Pulido-a						3.00
...: Silk 1 - Reprints Silk #1 (2015); Thompson-a/Stacey Lee-a; Spider-Man app.						3.00
...: Spider-Gwen 1 - Reprints Spider-Gwen #1 (2015); Latour-s/Robbi Rodriguez-a						3.00
...: Spider-Man – Morbius 1 - Reprints Amazing Spider-Man #101; Gil Kane-a						3.00
...: Spider-Man – Spider-Armor 1 - Reprints Web of Spider-Man #100; Saviuk-a						3.00
...: Spider-Man – Spidey Fights in London 1 - Reprints Amazing Spider-Man #95						3.00
...: Spider-Man – The New Spider-Man 1 - Reprints Marvel Team-Up #141						3.00
...: Spider-Man – The Wedding of Aunt May & Doc Ock 1 - Reprints ASM #131						3.00
...: Spider-Man vs. Hulk 1 - Reprints Amazing Spider-Man #328; McFarlane-a						3.00
...: Spider-Man vs. Mysterio 1 - Reprints debut in Amazing Spider-Man #13						3.00
...: Spider-Woman 1 - Reprints Spider-Woman #5 (2015); Hopeless-s/Javier Rodriguez-a						3.00
...: Star Wars 1 - Reprints Star Wars #1 (2015); Aaron-s/Cassaday-a						3.00
...: Star Wars – According to the Droids 1 - Reprints Droids #6						3.00
...: Star Wars Classic 1 - Reprints Star Wars #1 (1977); Roy Thomas-s/Howard Chaykin-a						3.00
...: Star Wars Covers 1 - Gallery of variant covers for Star Wars #1 (2015)						3.00
...: Star Wars – Darth Maul 1 - Reprints Star Wars: Darth Maul – Son of Dathomir #1	1	3	4	6	8	10
...: Star Wars – Darth Vader 1 - Reprints Darth Vader #1						3.00
...: Star Wars – Dead Probe 1 - Reprints Star Wars #45 (1977); Infantino-a						3.00
...: Star Wars – Ewoks 1 - Reprints Ewoks #1; Kremer-a						3.00
...: Star Wars – Hutt Run 1 - Reprints Star Wars #35 (2015); Larroca-a						3.00
...: Star Wars – Rebel Jail 1 - Reprints Star Wars #16 (2015); Doctor Aphra app.; Yu-a						3.00
...: Star Wars – Skywalker Strikes - Reprints Star Wars #1 (2015); Aaron-s/Cassaday-a						3.00
...: Star Wars – The Ashes of Jedha 1 - Reprints Star Wars #38 (2015); Larroca-a						3.00
...: Star Wars – The Hunter 1 - Reprints Star Wars #16 (1977); Simonson-a						3.00
...: Star Wars – The Original Marvel Years No. 107 - Reprints Star Wars #107 (1986)						3.00
...: Star Wars – Thrawn 1 - Reprints Star Wars: Thrawn #1; Luke Ross-a						3.00
...: Star Wars – Vader vs. Leia 1 - Reprints Star Wars #48 (1977); Infantino-a						3.00
...: Thanos the First 1 - Reprints Iron Man #55 (1973); 1st app. Thanos & Drax						3.00
...: Thanos Rising 1 - Reprints Thanos Rising #1; Aaron-s/Bianchi-a						3.00
...: The Criminally Insane – Absorbing Man 1 - Reprints Journey Into Mystery #114						3.00
...: The Criminally Insane – Bullseye 1 - Reprints debut in Daredevil #131						3.00
...: The Criminally Insane – Bushman 1 - Reprints Moon Knight #1 (1980)						3.00
...: The Criminally Insane – Dracula 1 - Reprints Tomb of Dracula #24; Colan-a						3.00
...: The Criminally Insane – Green Goblin 1 - Reprints debut in Amazing Spider-Man #14						3.00
...: The Criminally Insane – Gypsy Moth 1 - Reprints Spider-Woman #10; Infantino-a						3.00
...: The Criminally Insane – Klaw 1 - Reprints Black Panther #14 (1977)						3.00
...: The Criminally Insane – Mandarin 1 - Reprints Tales of Suspense #50 & 55						3.00
...: The Criminally Insane – Masters of Evil 1 - Reprints Avengers #6 (1963)						3.00
...: The Criminally Insane – Purple Man 1 - Reprints Daredevil #4 (1964)						3.00
...: The Groovy Deadpool 1 - Reprints Deadpool #13 (2013) 1970s art style						3.00
...: The Meaty Deadpool 1 - Reprints Deadpool #11 (2008) Bullseye (as Hawkeye) app.						3.00
...: The Sinister Secret of Spider-Man's New Costume 1 - Rep. Amaz. Spider-Man #258						3.00
...: The Unbeatable Squirrel Girl 1 - Reprints The Unbeatable Squirrel Girl #1 (2015)						3.00
...: The Wedding of Deadpool 1 - Reprints Deadpool #27 (2013) wraparound-c						3.00
...: Thor 1 - Reprints Thor #1 (2014); debut of female Thor; Aaron-s/Dauterman-a						3.00
...: Uncanny Avengers - The Bagalia Job 1 - Reprints Uncanny Avengers #5						3.00
...: Uncanny Deadpool 1 - Reprints Cable & Deadpool #38; Nicieza-s/Brown-a						3.00
...: Vader Down 1 - Reprints Star Wars: Vader Down #1; Aaron-s/Deodato-a						3.00
...: Venom - Agent Venom 1 - Reprints Venom #1 (2011) Remender-s/Moore-a						3.00
...: Venom - Carnage 1 - Reprints Amazing Spider-Man #363 (1992) Bagley-a						3.00
...: Venom - Dark Origin 1 - Reprints Venom: Dark Origin #3 (2008) Wells-s/Medina-a						3.00
...: Venom - Flashpoint 1 - Reprints Amazing Spider-Man #654.1 (2011) Ramos-a						3.00
...: Venom - Homecoming 1 - Reprints Venom #6 (2017) Costa-s/Sandoval-a						3.00
...: Venom - Lethal Protector 1 - Reprints Venom: Lethal Protector #1; Bagley-a						5.00
...: Venom - Shiver 1 - Reprints Venom #1 (2003) Way-s/Herrera-a						3.00
...: Venom - Symbiosis 1 - Reprints Web of Spider-Man #1 (1985) Larocque-a						3.00
...: Venom - Toxin 1 - Reprints Venom #17 (2011) Remender & Bunn-s/Walker-a						3.00
...: Venom vs. Spider-Man 1 - Reprints Amazing Spider-Man #300 (1988) McFarlane-a						6.00
...: What If Conan the Barbarian Walked the Earth Today? 1 - Reprints What If? #13						3.00
...: What If Doctor Doom Had Become a Hero? 1 - Reprints What If? #22						3.00
...: What If Jane Foster Had Found the Hammer of Thor? 1 - Reprints What If? #10						3.00
...: What If Kraven the Hunter Had Killed Spider-Man? 1 - Reprints What If? #17						3.00
...: What If Legion Had Killed Magneto? 1 - Reprints What If? #77; Gomez-a						3.00
...: What If Spider-Man Had Rescued Gwen Stacy? 1 - Reprints What If? #24; Kane-a						3.00
...: What If Spider-Man Joined the Fantastic Four? 1 - Reprints What If? #1						3.00
...: What If The Alien Costume Had Possessed Spider-Man? 1 - Reprints What If? #4						3.00
...: What If The Avengers Had Fought Evil During the 1950s? 1 - Reprints What If? #9						3.00
...: What If The Fantastic Four Had Different Super-Powers? 1 - r/What If? #6						3.00
...: What If The Fantastic Four Had Not Gained Their Super-Powers? 1 - r/What If? #36						3.00
...: What If The Silver Surfer Possessed the Infinity Gauntlet? 1 - Reprints What If? #49						3.00
...: Wolverine 1 - Reprints #1 (1982) Claremont-s/Miller-a						3.00
...: Wolverine and the X-Men 1 - Reprints #1; Aaron-s/Bachalo-a						3.00
...: Wolverine – Blood Hungry 1 - Reprints Marvel Comics Presents #85-87; Kieth-a						3.00
...: Wolverine – Enemy of the State 1 - Reprints Wolverine #20 (2003); Millar-s/Romita Jr.-a						3.00
...: Wolverine – Evolution 1 - Reprints Wolverine #50 (2007); Loeb-s/Bianchi-a						3.00
...: Wolverine – Fatal Attractions 1 - Reprints X-Men #25 (1993); Nicieza-s/Andy Kubert-a						3.00
...: Wolverine – Old Man Logan 1 - Reprints Old Man Logan #1; Bendis-s/Sorrentino-a						3.00
...: Wolverine – Origin 1 - Reprints Wolverine: The Origin #1; Andy Kubert-a						3.00
...: Wolverine – Save the Tiger 1 - Reprints Marvel Comics Presents #1-3; Buscema-a						3.00
...: Wolverine – Sword Quest 1 - Reprints Wolverine #1 (1988); Claremont-s/Buscema-a						3.00
...: Wolverine – The Brothers 1 - Reprints Wolverine #1 (2003); Rucka-s/Robertson-a						3.00
...: Wolverine – The Dying Game 1 - Reprints Wolverine #90 (1995); Adam Kubert-a						3.00
...: Wolverine vs. Hulk 1 - Reprints Incredible Hulk #181; Wein-s/Trimpe-a						5.00
...: Wolverine vs. Sabretooth 1 - Reprints Wolverine #10 (1989); Buscema-a						3.00
...: Wolverine vs. Venom 1 - Reprints Venom: Tooth and Claw #1; Hama-s/St. Pierre-a						3.00
...: Wolverine – Weapon X 1 - Reprints Marvel Comics Presents #72-74						3.00
...: Wolverine – X-23 1 - Reprints X-23 #1; Craig Kyle-s/Billy Tan-a						3.00
...: X-Factor - Mutant Genesis 1 - Reprints X-Factor #71; David-s/Stroman-a						3.00
...: X-Force 1 – Reprints X-Force #1; Liefeld-s/a; Nicieza-s						3.00
...: X-Men 1 – Reprints X-Men #1 (1963); Stan Lee-s/Jack Kirby-a						3.00
...: X-Men – Apocalypse 1 - Reprints X-Factor #6; Louise Simonson-s/Jackson Guice-a						3.00
...: X-Men – Betsy Braddock 1 - Reprints from Captain Britain #8-10						3.00
...: X-Men – Bishop 1 - Reprints debut in Uncanny X-Men #282; Portacio-a						3.00
...: X-Men Blue 1 – Reprints X-Men #1 (1991); Chris Claremont-s/Jim Lee-a						3.00
...: X-Men – Cypher - Reprints New Mutants #13; Chris Claremont-s/Sal Buscema-a						3.00
...: X-Men – Empath - Reprints New Mutants #16; Chris Claremont-s/Sal Buscema-a						3.00

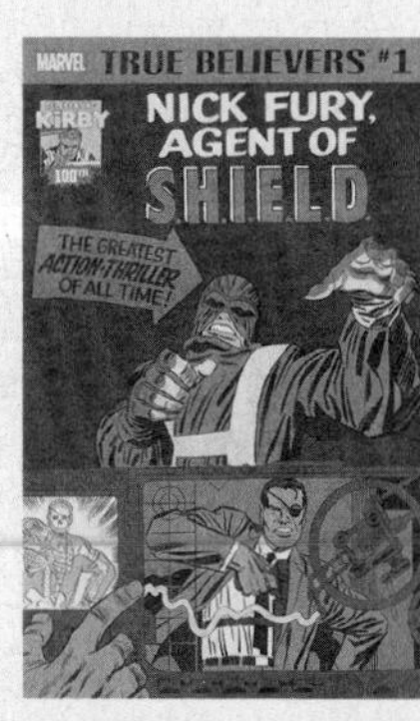

True Believers: Kirby 100th - Nick Fury #1 © MAR

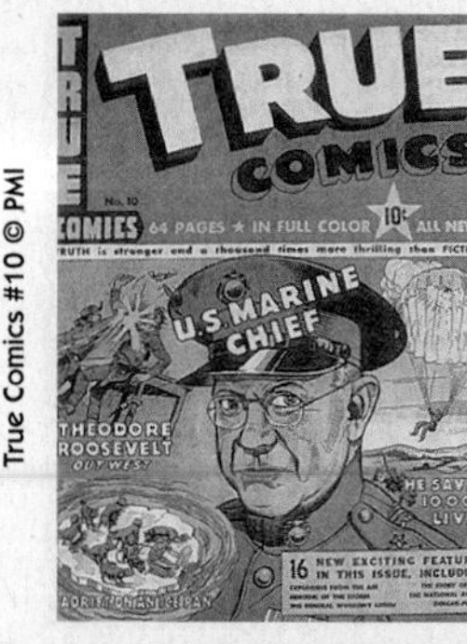

True Comics #10 © PMI

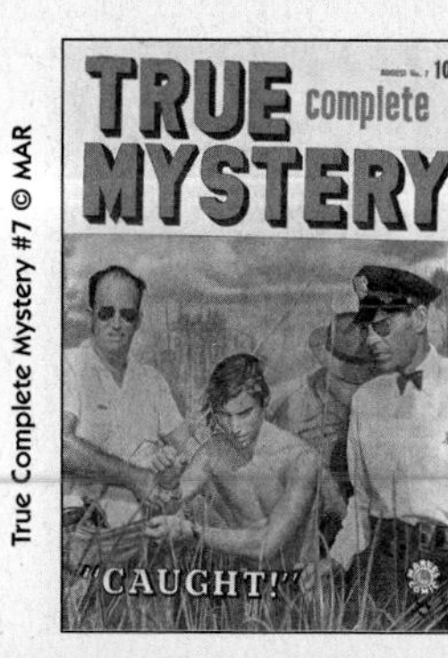

True Complete Mystery #7 © MAR

GD VG FN VF VF/NM NM-
2.0 4.0 6.0 8.0 9.0 9.2

...: X-Men Gold 1 – Reprints Uncanny X-Men #281; Byrne-s/Portacio-a 3.00
...: X-Men – Greycrow - Reprints Uncanny X-Men #211; Claremont-s/Romita Jr.-a 3.00
...: X-Men – Jubilee 1 - Reprints debut in Uncanny X-Men #244; Silvestri-a 3.00
...: X-Men – Havok - Reprints X-Men #58; Roy Thomas-s/Neal Adams-a 3.00
...: X-Men – Karima Shapandar, Omega Sentinel 1 - Reprints X-Men Unlimited #27 3.00
...: X-Men – Kitty Pryde & Emma Frost 1 - Reprints debuts in X-Men #129; Byrne-a 3.00
...: X-Men – Kwannon 1 - Reprints debut in X-Men #17 (1992); Andy Kubert-a 3.00
...: X-Men – Magik - Reprints Magik #1; Chris Claremont-s/John Buscema-a 3.00
...: X-Men – Mister Sinister - Reprints Uncanny X-Men #221; Claremont-s/Silvestri-a 3.00
...: X-Men – Moira MacTaggert 1 - Reprints debut in X-Men #96 3.00
...: X-Men – Nanny & Orphan Maker - Reprints X-Factor #35; Louise Simonson-s 3.00
...: X-Men – Pyro 1 - Reprints debut in Uncanny X-Men #141; Byrne-a 3.00
...: X-Men – Rictor 1 - Reprints debut in X-Factor #17; Simonson-a 3.00
...: X-Men – Saturnyne - Reprints Marvel Super Heroes UK #380-383; Captain Britain 3.00
...: X-Men – Soulsword - Reprints Uncanny X-Men #171; Claremont-s/Simonson-a 3.00
...: X-Men – Wild Child - Reprints Alpha Flight #11 & Marvel Comics Presents #51 3.00

TRUE BELIEVERS: KIRBY 100TH
Marvel Comics: Oct, 2017 ($1.00, one-shot reprints celebrating Jack Kirby's 100th birthday)

... – Ant-Man and The Wasp #1 - Reprints Tales to Astonish #27 & #44 3.00
... – Avengers: Captain America Lives Again! #1 - Reprints Avengers #4; bonus pin-ups 3.00
... – Black Panther #1 - Reprints Black Panther #1 3.00
... – Captain America #1 - Reprints Captain America Comics #1 & Tales of Suspense #63 3.00
... – Devil Dinosaur #1 - Reprints Devil Dinosaur #1; cover gallery & letter columns 3.00
... – Eternals #1 - Reprints Eternals #1; pin-ups & letter columns 3.00
... – Groot #1 - Reprints Tales to Astonish #13 & Journey Into Mystery #62 (Hulk/Xemnu) 3.00
... – Inhumans #1 - Reprints Amazing Adventures #1,2; bonus pin-ups 3.00
... – Introducing... The Mighty Thor #1 - Reprints Journey Into Mystery #83,85 3.00
... – Iron Man #1 - Reprints Tales of Suspense #40,41 3.00
... – Nick Fury #1 - Reprints Strange Tales #135,141 3.00
... – Thor vs. Hulk #1 - Reprints Journey Into Mystery #112 3.00

TRUE BLOOD (Based on the HBO vampire series)
IDW Publishing: Aug, 2010 - No. 6, Dec, 2010 ($3.99)

1-Messina-a; 4 covers by Messina, Campbell, Currie and Corroney 5.00
2-6-Multiple covers on each 4.00
...: Legacy Edition (1/11, $4.99) r/#1, cover gallery; full script 5.00

TRUE BLOOD (2nd series)(Based on the HBO vampire series)
IDW Publishing: May, 2012 - No. 14, Jun, 2013 ($3.99)

1-14-Gaydos-a in most; 2 covers (photo & Bradstreet-c) on each. 5-Manfredi-a 4.00

TRUE BLOOD: TAINTED LOVE (Based on the HBO vampire series)
IDW Publishing: Feb, 2011 - No. 6, Jul, 2011 ($3.99, limited series)

1-4: 1,2,4,5-Corroney-a; multiple covers. 3-Molnar-a 4.00
... Legacy Edition 1 (7/11, $4.99) r/#1 with full script and cover gallery 5.00

TRUE BLOOD: THE FRENCH QUARTER (Based on the HBO vampire series)
IDW Publishing: Aug, 2011 - No. 6, Jan, 2012 ($3.99, limited series)

1-6-Huehner & Tischman-s; multiple covers. 3-Molnar-a 4.00

TRUE BLOOD: THE GREAT REVELATION (Prequel to the 2008 HBO vampire series)
HBO/Top Cow: July, 2008 (no cover price, one shot continued on HBO website)

1-David Wohl-s/Jason Badower-a/c 4.00

TRUE BRIDE'S EXPERIENCES (Formerly Teen-Age Brides)
(True Bride-To-Be Romances No. 17 on)
True Love (Harvey Publications): No. 8, Oct, 1954 - No. 16, Feb, 1956

8-"I Married a Farmer" 11 22 33 62 86 110
9,10: 10-Last pre-code (2/55) 8 16 24 42 54 65
11-15 7 14 21 35 43 50
16-Last issue 8 16 24 42 54 65

NOTE: *Powell a-8-10, 12, 13.*

TRUE BRIDE-TO-BE ROMANCES (Formerly True Bride's Experiences)
Home Comics/True Love (Harvey): No. 17, Apr, 1956 - No. 30, Nov, 1958

17-S&K-c, Powell-a 11 22 33 62 86 110
18-20,22,25-28,30 7 14 21 35 43 50
21,23,24,29-Powell-a. 29-Baker-a (1 pg.) 7 14 21 37 46 55

TRUE COMICS (Also see Outstanding American War Heroes)
True Comics/Parents' Magazine Press: April, 1941 - No. 84, Aug, 1950

1-Marathon run story; life story Winston Churchill 39 78 117 231 378 525
2-Red Cross story; Everett-a 17 34 51 105 165 225
3-Baseball Hall of Fame story; Chiang Kai-Shek-c/s 18 36 54 109 172 235
4,5: 4-Story of American flag "Old Glory". 5-Life story of Joe Louis
15 30 45 84 127 170
6-Baseball World Series story 16 32 48 98 154 210
7-10: 7-Buffalo Bill story. 10,11-Teddy Roosevelt 13 26 39 72 101 130
11-14,16,18-20: 11-Thomas Edison, Douglas MacArthur stories. 13-Harry Houdini story. 14-Charlie McCarthy story. 18-Story of America begins, ends #26. 19-Eisenhower-c/s
11 22 33 62 86 110
15-Flag-c; Bob Feller story 12 24 36 67 94 120
17-Brooklyn Dodgers story 13 26 39 74 105 135
21-30: 24-Marco Polo story. 28-Origin of Uncle Sam. 29-Beethoven story. 30-Cooper Brothers baseball story 9 18 27 52 69 85
31-Red Grange "Galloping Ghost" story 8 16 24 44 57 70
32-46: 33-Origin/1st app. Steve Saunders, Special Agent of the FBI, series begins. 35-Mark Twain story. 38-General Bradley-c/s. 39-FDR story. 44-Truman story. 46-George Gershwin story 8 16 24 42 54 65
47-Atomic bomb issue (c/story, 3/46) 12 24 36 69 97 125
48-(4/46) "Hero Without a Gun" Desmond Doss story; inspired 2016 movie Hacksaw Ridge
9 18 27 50 65 80
49-54,56-65: 49-1st app. Secret Warriors. 53-Bobby Riggs story. 58-Jim Jeffries (boxer) story; Harry Houdini story. 59-Bob Hope story; pirates-c/s. 60-Speedway Speed Demon-c/story.
8 16 24 40 50 60
55-(12/46)-1st app. Sad Sack by Baker (1/2 pg.) 40 80 120 244 402 560
66-Will Rogers-c/story 8 16 24 42 54 65
67-1st oversized issue (12/47); Steve Saunders, Special Agent begins
9 18 27 50 65 80
68-70,74-77,79: 68-70,74-77-Features Steve Sanders True FBI advs. 68-Oversized; Admiral Byrd-c/s. 69-Jack Benny story. 74-Amos 'n' Andy story
8 16 24 40 50 60
71-Joe DiMaggio-c/story. 10 20 30 54 72 90
72-Jackie Robinson story; True FBI advs. 9 18 27 47 61 75
73-Walt Disney's life story 10 20 30 54 72 90
78-Stan Musial-c/story; True FBI advs. 9 18 27 47 61 75
80-84 (Scarce)-All distr. to subscribers through mail only; paper-c. 80-Rocket trip to the moon story. 81-Red Grange story. 84-Wyatt Earp app. (1st app. in comics?); Rube Marquard story
20 40 60 115 188 260
(Prices vary widely on issues 80-84)

NOTE: ***Bob Kane** a-7. **Palais** a-80. **Powell** c/a-80. #80-84 have soft covers and combined with Tex Granger, Jack Armstrong, and Calling All Kids. #68-78 featured true FBI adventures.*

TRUE COMICS AND ADVENTURE STORIES
Parents' Magazine Institute: 1965 (Giant) (25¢)

1,2: 1-Fighting Hero of Viet Nam; LBJ on-c 3 6 9 19 30 40

TRUE COMPLETE MYSTERY (Formerly Complete Mystery)
Marvel Comics (PrPl): No. 5, Apr, 1949 - No. 8, Oct, 1949

5-Criminal career of Rico Mancini 32 64 96 188 307 425
6-8: 6-8-Photo-c 23 46 69 136 223 310

TRUE CONFIDENCES
Fawcett Publications: 1949 (Fall) - No. 4, June, 1950 (All photo-c)

1-Has ad for Fawcett Love Adventures #1, but publ. as Love Memoirs #1 as Marvel published the title first; Swayze-a 18 36 54 109 172 235
2-4: 3-Swayze-a. 4-Powell-a 13 26 39 72 101 130

TRUE CRIME CASES (...From Official Police Files)
St. John Publishing Co.: 1951 (25¢, 100 pg. Giant)

nn-Matt Baker-c 90 180 270 576 988 1400

TRUE CRIME COMICS (Also see Complete Book of...)
Magazine Village: No. 2, May, 1947; No. 3, July-Aug, 1948 - No. 6, June-July, 1949; V2#1, Aug-Sept, 1949 (52 pgs.)

2-Jack Cole-c/a; used in **SOTI**, pgs. 81,82 plus illo. "A sample of the injury-to-eye motif" & illo. "Dragging living people to death"; used in **POP**, pg. 105; "Murder, Morphine and Me" classic drug propaganda story used by N.Y. Legis. Comm.
255 510 765 1632 2791 3950
3-Classic Cole-c/a; drug story with hypo, opium den & with drawing addict
187 374 561 1197 2049 2900
4-Jack Cole-c/a; c-taken from a story panel in #3 (r-(2) **SOTI** & **POP** stories/#2?) 123 246 369 787 1344 1900
5-Jack Cole-c, Marijuana racket story (Canadian ed. w/cover similar to #3 exists w/out drug story) 87 174 261 553 952 1350
6-Not a reprint, original story (Canadian ed. reprints #4 w/different coloring on-c)
74 148 222 470 810 1150
V2#1-Used in **SOTI**, pgs. 81,82 & illo. "Dragging living people to death"; Toth, Wood (3 pgs.), Roussos-a; Cole-r from #2 119 238 357 762 1306 1850

NOTE: *V2#1 was reprinted in Canada as V2#9 (12/49); same-c & contents minus Wood-a.*

TRUE FAITH
Fleetway: 1990 ($9.95, graphic novel)

nn-Garth Ennis scripts 2 4 6 12 16 20
Reprinted by DC/Vertigo ('97, $12.95) 13.00

True Love Pictorial #5 © STJ

True Sport Picture Stories V2 #7 © S&S

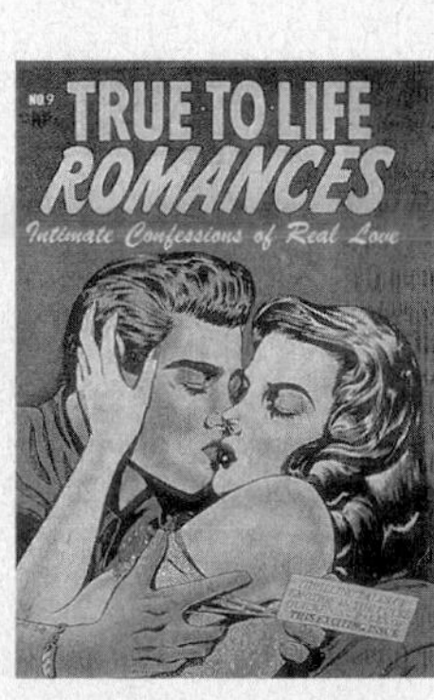

True-To-Life Romances #9 © STAR

TRUE GHOST STORIES (See Ripley's...)

TRUE LIFE ROMANCES (...Romance on cover)
Ajax/Farrell Publications: Dec, 1955 - No. 3, Aug, 1956

	GD 2.0	VG 4.0	FN 6.0	VF 8.0	VF/NM 9.0	NM- 9.2
1	15	30	45	88	137	185
2	11	22	33	62	86	110
3-Disbrow-a	12	24	36	69	97	125

TRUE LIFE SECRETS
Romantic Love Stories/Charlton: Mar-April, 1951 - No. 28, Sept, 1955; No. 29, Jan, 1956

	GD 2.0	VG 4.0	FN 6.0	VF 8.0	VF/NM 9.0	NM- 9.2
1-Photo-c begin, end #3?	22	44	66	128	209	290
2	14	28	42	81	118	155
3-11,13-19:	13	26	39	72	101	130
12-"I Was An Escort Girl" story	20	40	60	114	182	250
20-22,24-29: 25-Last precode (3/55)	12	24	36	67	94	120
23-Classic-c	37	74	111	222	361	500

TRUE LIFE TALES (Formerly Mitzi's Romances #8?)
Marvel Comics (CCC): No. 8, Oct, 1949 - No. 2, Jan, 1950 (52 pgs.)

	GD 2.0	VG 4.0	FN 6.0	VF 8.0	VF/NM 9.0	NM- 9.2
8(#1, 10/49), 2-Both have photo-c	15	30	45	94	147	200

TRUE LIVES OF THE FABULOUS KILLJOYS
Dark Horse Comics: Jun, 2013 - No. 6, Jan, 2014 ($3.99)

	GD 2.0	VG 4.0	FN 6.0	VF 8.0	VF/NM 9.0	NM- 9.2
1-6-Gerald Way & Shaun Simon-s/Becky Cloonan-a; covers by Cloonan & Bá						4.00

TRUE LIVES OF THE FABULOUS KILLJOYS: NATIONAL ANTHEM
Dark Horse Comics: Oct, 2020 - No. 6, Mar, 2021 ($3.99, limited series)

	GD 2.0	VG 4.0	FN 6.0	VF 8.0	VF/NM 9.0	NM- 9.2
1-5-Gerald Way & Shaun Simon-s/Leonardo Romero-a						4.00

TRUE LOVE
Eclipse Comics: Jan, 1986 - No. 2, Jan, 1986 ($2.00, Baxter paper)

	GD 2.0	VG 4.0	FN 6.0	VF 8.0	VF/NM 9.0	NM- 9.2
1-Love stories reprinted from pre-code Standard Comics; Toth-a(p); Dave Stevens-c	1	3	4	6	8	10
2-Toth-a; Mayo-a						4.00

TRUE LOVE CONFESSIONS
Premier Magazines: May, 1954 - No. 11, Jan, 1956

	GD 2.0	VG 4.0	FN 6.0	VF 8.0	VF/NM 9.0	NM- 9.2
1-Marijuana story	22	44	66	128	209	290
2	14	28	42	81	118	155
3-11	14	28	42	76	108	140

TRUE LOVE PICTORIAL
St. John Publishing Co.: Dec, 1952 - No. 11, Aug, 1954

	GD 2.0	VG 4.0	FN 6.0	VF 8.0	VF/NM 9.0	NM- 9.2
1-Only photo-c	37	74	111	222	361	500
2-Baker-c/a	100	200	300	640	1095	1550
3-5(All 25¢, 100 pgs.): 4-Signed story by Estrada. 5-(4/53)-Formerly Teen-Age Temptations; Kubert-a in #3; Baker-c/a in #3-5	129	258	387	826	1413	2000
6,7: Baker-c/a; signed stories by Estrada	81	162	243	518	884	1250
8,10,11-Baker-c/a	81	162	243	518	884	1250
9-Baker-c	71	142	213	454	777	1100

TRUE LOVE PROBLEMS AND ADVICE ILLUSTRATED (Becomes Romance Stories of True Love No. 45 on)
McCombs/Harvey Publ./Home Comics: June, 1949 - No. 6, Apr, 1950; No. 7, Jan, 1951 - No. 44, Mar, 1957

	GD 2.0	VG 4.0	FN 6.0	VF 8.0	VF/NM 9.0	NM- 9.2
V1#1	16	32	48	98	154	210
2-Elias-c	11	22	33	62	86	110
3-10: 3,4,7-9-Elias-c	8	16	24	44	57	70
11-13,15-23,25-31: 31-Last pre-code (1/55)	7	14	21	37	46	55
14,24-Rape scene	8	16	24	44	57	70
32-37,39-44	6	12	18	31	38	45
38-S&K-c	10	20	30	54	72	90

NOTE: ***Powell** a-1, 2, 7-14, 17-25, 28, 29, 33, 40, 41. #3 has True Love... on inside.*

TRUE MOVIE AND TELEVISION (Part teenage magazine)
Toby Press: Aug, 1950 - No. 3, Nov, 1950; No. 4, Mar, 1951 (52 pgs.)(1-3: 10¢)

	GD 2.0	VG 4.0	FN 6.0	VF 8.0	VF/NM 9.0	NM- 9.2
1-Elizabeth Taylor photo-c; Gene Autry, Shirley Temple app.	77	154	231	493	847	1200
2-(9/50)-Janet Leigh/Liz Taylor/Ava Gardner & others photo-c; Frazetta John Wayne illo from J.Wayne Adv. Comics #2 (4/50)	54	108	162	343	574	825
3-June Allyson photo-c; Montgomery Cliff, Esther Williams, Andrews Sisters app; Li'l Abner featured; Sadie Hawkins' Day	36	72	108	214	347	480
4-Jane Powell photo-c (15¢)	23	46	69	138	227	315

NOTE: *16 pgs. in color, rest movie material in black & white.*

TRUE SECRETS (Formerly Our Love?)
Marvel (IPS)/Atlas Comics (MPI) #4 on: No. 3, Mar, 1950; No. 4, Feb, 1951 - No. 40, Sept, 1956

	GD 2.0	VG 4.0	FN 6.0	VF 8.0	VF/NM 9.0	NM- 9.2
3 (52 pgs.)(IPS one-shot)	23	46	69	136	223	310
4,5,7-10	15	30	45	88	137	185
6,22-Everett-a	16	32	48	98	154	210
11-20	15	30	45	83	124	165
21,23-28: 24-Colletta-c. 28-Last pre-code (2/55)	14	28	42	81	118	155
29-40: 34,36-Colletta-a	14	28	42	78	112	145

TRUE SPORT PICTURE STORIES (Formerly Sport Comics)
Street & Smith Publications: V1#5, Feb, 1942 - V5#2, July-Aug, 1949

	GD 2.0	VG 4.0	FN 6.0	VF 8.0	VF/NM 9.0	NM- 9.2
V1#5-Joe DiMaggio-c/story	37	74	111	218	354	490
6-12 (1942-43): 12-Jack Dempsey story	21	42	63	122	199	275
V2#1-12 (1943-45): 7-Stan Musial-c/story; photo story of the New York Yankees	20	40	60	115	185	255
V3#1-12 (1946-47): 7-Joe DiMaggio, Stan Musial, Bob Feller & others back from the armed service story. 8-Billy Conn vs. Joe Louis-c/story	19	38	57	111	176	240
V4#1-12 (1947-49), V5#1,2: v4#8-Joe Louis on-c	18	36	54	105	165	225

NOTE: ***Powell** a-V3#10, V4#1-4, 6-8, 10-12; V5#1, 2; c-V3#10-12, V4#2-7, 9-12. **Ravielli** c-V5#2.*

TRUE STORIES OF ROMANCE
Fawcett Publications: Jan, 1950 - No. 3, May, 1950 (All photo-c)

	GD 2.0	VG 4.0	FN 6.0	VF 8.0	VF/NM 9.0	NM- 9.2
1	15	30	45	92	144	195
2,3: 3-Marcus Swayze-a	13	26	39	72	101	130

TRUE STORY OF JESSE JAMES, THE (See Jesse James, Four Color 757)

TRUE SWEETHEART SECRETS
Fawcett Publs.: 5/50; No. 2, 7/50; No. 3, 1951(nd); No. 4, 9/51 - No. 11, 1/53 (All photo-c)

	GD 2.0	VG 4.0	FN 6.0	VF 8.0	VF/NM 9.0	NM- 9.2
1-Photo-c; Debbie Reynolds?	18	36	54	109	172	235
2-Wood-a (11 pgs.)	21	42	63	124	202	280
3-11: 4,5-Powell-a. 8-Marcus Swayze-a. 11-Evans-a	14	28	42	81	118	155

TRUE TALES OF LOVE (Formerly Secret Story Romances)
Atlas Comics (TCI): No. 22, April, 1956 - No. 31, Sept, 1957

	GD 2.0	VG 4.0	FN 6.0	VF 8.0	VF/NM 9.0	NM- 9.2
22	15	30	45	84	127	170
23-24,26-31-Colletta-a in most:	11	22	33	62	86	110
25-Everett-a; Colletta-a	12	24	36	67	94	120

TRUE TALES OF ROMANCE
Fawcett Publications: No. 4, June, 1950

	GD 2.0	VG 4.0	FN 6.0	VF 8.0	VF/NM 9.0	NM- 9.2
4-Photo-c	12	24	36	69	97	125

TRUE 3-D
Harvey Publications: Dec, 1953 - No. 2, Feb, 1954 (25¢)(Both came with 2 pair of glasses)

	GD 2.0	VG 4.0	FN 6.0	VF 8.0	VF/NM 9.0	NM- 9.2
1-Nostrand, Powell-a	5	10	15	33	57	80
2-Powell-a	5	10	15	34	60	85

NOTE: *Many copies of #1 surfaced in 1984.*

TRUE-TO-LIFE ROMANCES (Formerly Guns Against Gangsters)
Star Publ.: #8, 11-12/49; #9, 1-2/50; #3, 4/50 - #5, 9/50; #6, 1/51 - #23, 10/54

	GD 2.0	VG 4.0	FN 6.0	VF 8.0	VF/NM 9.0	NM- 9.2
8(#1, 1949)	36	72	108	211	343	475
9(#2),4-10	25	50	75	150	245	340
3-Janet Leigh/Glenn Ford photo on-c plus true life story of each	27	54	81	158	259	360
11,22,23	22	44	66	132	216	300
12-14,17-21-Disbrow-a	24	48	72	144	237	330
15,16-Wood & Disbrow-a in each	27	54	81	158	259	360

NOTE: ***Kamen** a-13. **Kamen/Feldstein** a-14. All have **L.B. Cole** covers.*

TRUE WAR EXPERIENCES
Harvey Publications: Aug, 1952 - No. 4, Dec, 1952

	GD 2.0	VG 4.0	FN 6.0	VF 8.0	VF/NM 9.0	NM- 9.2
1-Korean War	8	16	24	56	108	160
2-4	5	10	15	33	57	80

TRUE WAR ROMANCES (Becomes Exotic Romances #22 on)
Quality Comics Group: Sept, 1952 - No. 21, June, 1955

	GD 2.0	VG 4.0	FN 6.0	VF 8.0	VF/NM 9.0	NM- 9.2
1-Photo-c	19	38	57	111	176	240
2-(10/52)	12	24	36	69	97	125
3-10: 3-(12/52). 8,9-Whitney-a	11	22	33	62	86	110
11-21: 20-Last precode (4/55). 14-Whitney-a	10	20	30	56	76	95

TRUE WAR STORIES (See Ripley's...)

TRUE WESTERN (True Adventures #3)
Marvel Comics (MMC): Dec, 1949 - No. 2, March, 1950

	GD 2.0	VG 4.0	FN 6.0	VF 8.0	VF/NM 9.0	NM- 9.2
1-Photo-c; Billy The Kid story	20	40	60	114	182	250
2-Alan Ladd photo-c	22	44	66	128	209	290

TRUMP
HMH Publishing Co.: Jan, 1957 - No. 2, Mar, 1957 (50¢, magazine)

	GD 2.0	VG 4.0	FN 6.0	VF 8.0	VF/NM 9.0	NM- 9.2
1-Harvey Kurtzman satire	28	56	84	168	274	380
2-Harvey Kurtzman satire	22	44	66	130	213	295

NOTE: ***Davis, Elder, Heath, Jaffee** art-#1,2; **Wood** a-1. Article by Mel Brooks in #2.*

Truth: Red, White & Black #1 © MAR

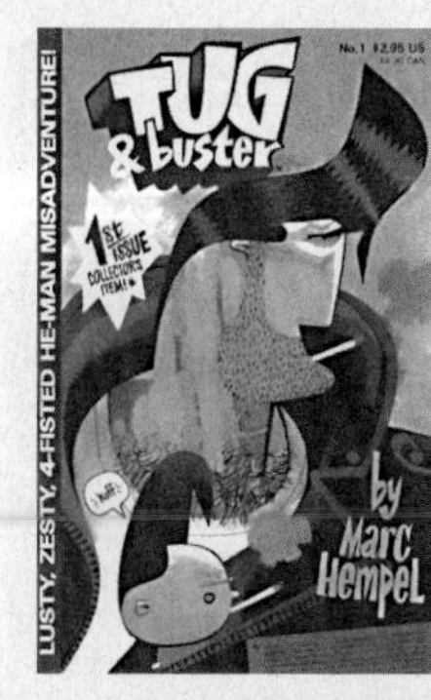

Tug & Buster #1 © Marc Hempel

Turok, Son of Stone #4 © DELL

GD VG FN VF VF/NM NM-
2.0 4.0 6.0 8.0 9.0 9.2

GD VG FN VF VF/NM NM-
2.0 4.0 6.0 8.0 9.0 9.2

TRUMPETS WEST (See Luke Short, Four Color #875)

TRUTH ABOUT CRIME (See Fox Giants)

TRUTH ABOUT MOTHER GOOSE (See Mother Goose, Four Color #862)

TRUTH & JUSTICE
DC Comics: Apr, 2021 - Present ($4.99, printing of digital first anthology series)

1-Vixen teams with Dr. Mist and Impala; Thorne-s/Tarragona-a 5.00

TRUTH BEHIND THE TRIAL OF CARDINAL MINDSZENTY, THE (See Cardinal Mindszenty in the Promotional Comics section))

TRUTHFUL LOVE (Formerly Youthful Love)
Youthful Magazines: No. 2, July, 1950

2-Ingrid Bergman's true life story 15 30 45 94 147 200

TRUTH RED, WHITE & BLACK
Marvel Comics: Jan, 2003 - No. 7, Jul, 2003 ($3.50, limited series)

1-Kyle Baker-a/Robert Morales-s; the testing of Captain America's super-soldier serum
3 6 9 19 30 40
2-7: 3-Isaiah Bradley 1st dons the Captain America costume
1 3 4 6 8 10
TPB (2004, $17.99) r/series 18.00

TRY-OUT WINNER BOOK
Marvel Comics: Mar, 1988

1-Spider-Man vs. Doc Octopus 3 6 9 21 33 45

TSR WORLD (...Annual on cover only)
DC Comics: 1990 ($3.95, 84 pgs.)

1-Advanced D&D, ForgottenRealms, Dragonlance & 1st app. Spelljammer 4.00

TSUNAMI GIRL
Image Comics: 1999 - No. 3, 1999 ($2.95)

1-3-Sorayama-c/Paniccia-s/a 3.00

TUBBY (See Marge's...)

TUFF GHOSTS STARRING SPOOKY
Harvey Publications: July, 1962 - No. 39, Nov, 1970; No. 40, Sept, 1971 - No. 43, Oct, 1972

1-12¢ issues begin 13 26 39 89 195 300
2-5 7 14 21 44 82 120
6-10 5 10 15 31 53 75
11-20 4 8 12 23 37 50
21-30: 29-Hot Stuff/Spooky team-up story 3 6 9 16 23 30
31-39,43 2 4 6 13 18 22
40-42: 52 pg. Giants 3 6 9 14 20 25

TUFFY
Standard Comics: No. 5, July, 1949 - No. 9, Oct, 1950

5-All by Sid Hoff 10 20 30 54 72 90
6-9 8 16 24 40 50 60

TUFFY TURTLE
I. W. Enterprises: No date

1-Reprint 2 4 6 9 13 16

TUG & BUSTER
Art & Soul Comics: Nov, 1995 - No. 7, Feb, 1998 ($2.95, B&W, bi-monthly)

1-7: Marc Hempel-c/a/scripts 3.00
1-(Image Comics, 8/98, $2.95, B&W) 3.00

TUKI
Cartoon Books: Jul, 2014 - No. 4, Jan, 2016 ($3.99)

1-4-Jeff Smith-s/a/c; story reads sideways 4.00

TURF
Image Comics: Apr, 2010 - No. 2 ($2.99, limited series)

1,2-Jonathan Ross-s/Tommy Lee Edwards-a 3.00

TUROK
Acclaim Comics: Mar, 1998 - No. 4, Jun, 1998 ($2.50)

1-4-Nicieza-s/Kayanan-a 4.00
..., Child of Blood 1 (1/98, $3.95) Nicieza-s/Kayanan-a 4.00
... Evolution 1 (8/02, $2.50) Nicieza-s/Kayanan-a 3.00
..., Redpath 1 (10/97, $3.95) Nicieza-s/Kayanan-a 4.00
... / Shadowman 1 (2/99, $3.95) Priest-s/Broome & Jimenez-a 4.00
...: Spring Break in the Lost Land 1 (7/97, $3.95) Nicieza-s/Kayanan-a 4.00
...: Tales of the Lost Land 1 (4/98, $3.95) 4.00
...: The Empty Souls 1 (4/97, $3.95) Nicieza-s/Kayanan-a; variant-c 4.00

TUROK (Volume 1) (Also see Sovereigns and Magnus)
Dynamite Entertainment: 2017 - No. 5, 2017 ($3.99)

1-5: 1-Wendig-s/Sarraseca-a; Doctor Spektor back-up serial with other Sovereigns titles 4.00

TUROK, DINOSAUR HUNTER (See Magnus Robot Fighter #12 & Archer & Armstrong #2)
Valiant/Acclaim Comics: June, 1993 - No. 47, Aug, 1996 ($2.50)

1-($3.50)-Chromium & foil-c 4.00
1-Gold foil-c variant 15.00
0, 2-47: 4-Andar app. 5-Death of Andar. 7-9-Truman/Glanzman-a. 11-Bound-in trading card.
16-Chaos Effect 3.00
Yearbook 1 (1994, $3.95, 52 pgs.) 4.00

TUROK: DINOSAUR HUNTER
Dynamite Entertainment: 2014 - No. 12, 2015 ($3.99)

1-12: 1-5-New version; Greg Pak-s/Mirko Colak-a; Sears-c. 6-8-Miyazawa-a 4.00
1-12-Variant-c by Jae Lee 4.00

TUROK, SON OF STONE (See Dan Curtis, Golden Comics Digest #31, Space Western #45 & March of Comics #378, 399, 408)
Dell Publ. Co. #1-29(9/62)/Gold Key #30(12/62)-85(7/73)/Gold Key or Whitman #86(9/73)-125(1/80)/Whitman #126(3/81) on: No. 596, 12/54 - No. 29, 9/62; No. 30, 12/62 - No. 91, 7/74; No. 92, 9/74 - No. 125, 1/80; No. 126, 3/81 - No. 130, 4/82

Four Color 596 (12/54)(#1)-1st app./origin Turok & Andar; dinosaur-c. Created by
Matthew H. Murphy; written by Alberto Giolitti 89 178 267 712 1606 2500
Four Color 656 (10/55)(#2)-1st mention of Lanok 37 74 111 274 612 950
3(3-5/56)-5: 3-Cave men 21 42 63 147 324 500
6-10: 8-Dinosaur of the deep; Turok enters Lost Valley; series begins.
9-Paul S. Newman-s (most issues thru end) 15 30 45 103 227 350
11-20: 17-Prehistoric Pygmies 11 22 33 76 163 250
21-29 9 18 27 58 114 170
30-1st Gold Key. 30-33-Painted back-c. 9 18 27 60 120 180
31-Drug use story 9 18 27 58 114 170
32-40 7 14 21 46 86 125
41-50 6 12 18 37 66 95
51-57,59,60 5 10 15 34 60 85
58-Flying Saucer c/story 5 10 15 35 63 90
61-70: 62-12¢ & 15¢ covers. 63,68-Line drawn-c 5 10 15 30 50 70
71-84: 84-Origin & 1st app. Hutec 4 8 12 27 44 60
85-99: 93-r-c/#19 w/changes. 94-r-c/#28 w/changes. 97-r-c/#31 w/changes.
98-r/#58 w/o spaceship & spacemen on-c. 99-r-c/#52 w/changes.
4 8 12 23 37 50
100 4 8 12 28 47 65
101-129: 114,115-(52 pgs.). 129(2/82) 4 8 12 23 37 50
130(4/82)-Last issue 5 10 15 35 63 90
Giant 1(30031-611) (11/66)-Slick-c; r/#10-12 & 16 plus cover to #11
10 20 30 64 132 200
Giant 1-Same as above but with paper-c 10 20 30 68 144 220

NOTE: *Most painted-c; line-drawn #63 & 130.* ***Alberto Gioletti*** *a-24-27, 30-119, 123; painted-c No. 30-129.* ***Sparling*** *a-117, 120-130. Reprints-#36, 54, 57, 75, 112, 114(1/3), 115(1/3), 118, 121, 125, 127(1/3), 128, 129(1/3), 130(1/3), Giant 1. Cover r-93, 94, 97-99, 126(all different from original covers.*

TUROK, SON OF STONE
Dark Horse Comics: Oct, 2010 - No. 4, Oct, 2011 ($3.50)

1-4: 1-Shooter-s/Francisco-a/Swanland-c; back-up reprint of debut in Four Color 596 3.50
1-Variant-c by Francisco 3.50

TUROK THE HUNTED
Valiant/Acclaim Comics: Mar, 1995 - No. 2, Apr, 1995 ($2.50, limited series)

1,2-Mike Deodato-a(p); price omitted on #1 4.00

TUROK THE HUNTED
Acclaim Comics (Valiant): Feb, 1996 - No. 2, Mar, 1996 ($2.50, limited series)

1,2-Mike Grell story 4.00

TUROK, TIMEWALKER
Acclaim Comics (Valiant): Aug, 1997 - No. 2, Sept, 1997 ($2.50, limited series)

1,2-Nicieza story 4.00

TUROK 2 (Magazine)
Acclaim Comics: Oct, 1998 ($4.99, magazine size)

...Seeds of Evil - Nicieza-s/Broome & Benjamin-a; origin back-up story 5.00
#2 Adon's Curse - Mack painted-c/Broome & Benjamin-a; origin pt. 2 5.00

TUROK 3: SHADOW OF OBLIVION
Acclaim Comics: Sept, 2000 ($4.95, one-shot)

1-Includes pin-up gallery 5.00

TUROK VOLUME 4
Dynamite Entertainment: 2019 - No. 5, 2019 ($3.99)

1-5-Ron Marz-s/Roberto Castro-a 4.00

TV Stars #4 © H-B

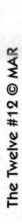

The Twelve #12 © MAR

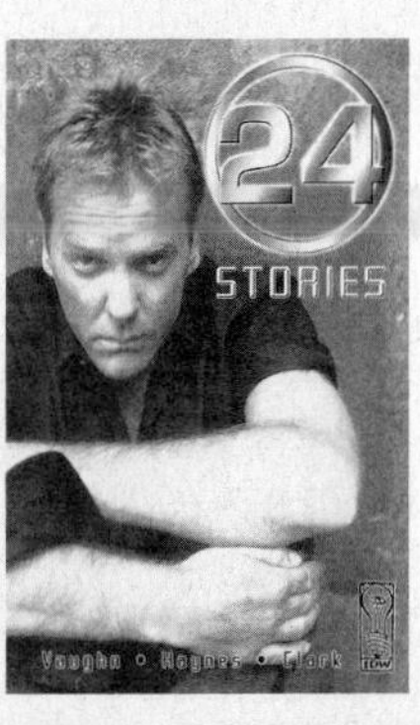

24: Stories © 20th Fox

	GD 2.0	VG 4.0	FN 6.0	VF 8.0	VF/NM 9.0	NM- 9.2
TURTLE SOUP **Mirage Studios:** Sept, 1987 ($2.00, 76 pgs., B&W, one-shot)						
1-Featuring Teenage Mutant Ninja Turtles	2	4	6	9	12	15
TURTLE SOUP **Mirage Studios:** Nov, 1991 - No. 4, 1992 ($2.50, limited series, coated paper)						
1-4: Features the Teenage Mutant Ninja Turtles						5.00
TV CASPER & COMPANY **Harvey Publications:** Aug, 1963 - No. 46, April, 1974 (25¢ Giants)						
1- 68 pg. Giants begin; Casper, Little Audrey, Baby Huey, Herman & Catnip, Buzzy the Crow begin	10	20	30	66	138	210
2-5	6	12	18	37	66	95
6-10	4	8	12	28	47	65
11-20	4	8	12	23	37	50
21-31: 31-Last 68 pg. issue	3	6	9	17	26	35
32-46: All 52 pgs.	3	6	9	16	23	30
NOTE: *Many issues contain reprints.*						
TV FUNDAY FUNNIES (See Famous TV...)						
TV FUNNIES (See New Funnies)						
TV FUNTIME (See Little Audrey)						
TV LAUGHOUT (See Archie's...)						
TV SCREEN CARTOONS (Formerly Real Screen) **National Periodical Publ.:** No. 129, July-Aug, 1959 - No. 138, Jan-Feb, 1961						
129-138 (Scarce) Fox and the Crow	6	12	18	37	66	95
TV STARS (TV) (Newsstand sales only) **Marvel Comics Group:** Aug, 1978 - No. 4, Feb, 1979 (Hanna-Barbera)						
1-Great Grape Ape app.	3	6	9	18	28	38
2,4: 4-Top Cat app.	3	6	9	15	22	28
3-Toth-c/a; Dave Stevens inks	3	6	9	16	24	32
TV TEENS (Formerly Ozzie & Babs; Rock and Rollo #14 on) **Charlton Comics:** V1#14, Feb, 1954 - V2#13, July, 1956						
V1#14 (#1)-Ozzie & Babs	13	26	39	74	105	135
15 (#2)	9	18	27	47	61	75
V2#3(6/54),4, 6-Don Winslow	8	16	24	44	57	70
5(10-11/54) Headlight/groping-c by Chic Stone	15	30	45	94	149	200
7-13-Mopsy. 8(7/55). 9-Paper dolls	8	16	24	42	54	65
TWEETY AND SYLVESTER (1st Series) (TV) (Also see Looney Tunes and Merrie Melodies) **Dell Publishing Co.:** No. 406, June, 1952 - No. 37, June-Aug, 1962						
Four Color 406 (#1)	13	26	39	89	195	300
Four Color 489,524	8	16	24	54	102	150
4 (3-5/54) - 20	5	10	15	35	63	90
21-37	5	10	15	31	53	75
(See March of Comics #421, 433, 445, 457, 469, 481)						
TWEETY AND SYLVESTER (2nd Series)(See Kite Fun Book) **Gold Key No. 1-102/Whitman No. 103 on:** Nov, 1963; No. 2, Nov, 1965 - No. 121, Jun, 1984						
1	7	14	21	46	86	125
2-10	4	8	12	23	37	50
11-30	3	6	9	14	20	25
31-50	2	4	6	9	12	15
51-70	1	3	4	6	8	10
71-102	1	2	3	5	6	8
103,104 (Whitman)	1	3	4	6	8	10
105(9/80),106(10/80),107(12/80) 3-pack only	4	8	12	28	47	65
108-116: 113(2/82),114(2-3/82),115(3/82),116(4/82)	2	4	6	8	10	12
117-121 (All # 90094 on-c; nd, nd code): 117(6/83). 118(7/83). 119(2/84)-r(1/3). 120(5/84). 121(6/84)	3	6	9	17	26	35
Digest nn (Charlton/Xerox Pub., 1974) (low print run)	3	6	9	16	23	30
Mini Comic No. 1(1976, 3-1/4x6-1/2")	1	3	4	6	8	10
TWELVE, THE (Golden Age Timely heroes) **Marvel Comics:** No. 0; 2008; No. 1, Mar, 2008 - No. 12, Jun, 2012 ($2.99, limited series)						
0-Rockman, Laughing Mask & Phantom Reporter intro. stories (1940s); series preview						4.00
1/2 (2008, $3.99) r/early app. of Fiery Mask, Mister E and Rockman; Weston-c						5.00
1-12-Straczynski-s/Weston-a; Timely heroes re-surface in the present						4.00
... Must Have 1 (4/12, $3.99) r/#7,8						4.00
...: Spearhead 1 (5/10, $3.99) Weston-s/a; Phantom Reporter in WW2; Invaders app.						5.00
12 O'CLOCK HIGH (TV) **Dell Publishing Co.:** Jan-Mar, 1965 - No. 2, Apr-June, 1965 (Photo-c)						
1- Sinnott-a	5	10	15	34	60	85
2	4	8	12	28	47	65

	GD 2.0	VG 4.0	FN 6.0	VF 8.0	VF/NM 9.0	NM- 9.2
TWELVE REASONS TO DIE **Black Mask Studios:** 2013 - No. 6, 2014 ($3.50)						
1-6: 1-Five covers; created by Ghostface Killah						3.50
2099 **Marvel Comics:** Jan, 2020 - Feb, 2020 ($4.99, bookends for series of one-shots)						
... Alpha 1 (1/20) Spencer-s/Bogdanovic-a; Miguel O'Hara and Herbie app.						5.00
... Omega 1 (2/20) Spencer-s/Sandoval-a; Doom and the Watcher app.						5.00
2099 A.D. **Marvel Comics:** May, 1995 ($3.95, one-shot)						
1-Acetate-c by Quesada & Palmiotti						4.00
2099 APOCALYPSE **Marvel Comics:** Dec, 1995 ($4.95, one-shot)						
1-Chromium wraparound-c; Ellis script						5.00
2099 GENESIS **Marvel Comics:** Jan, 1996 ($4.95, one-shot)						
1-Chromium wraparound-c; Ellis script						5.00
2099 MANIFEST DESTINY **Marvel Comics:** Mar, 1998 ($5.99, one-shot)						
1-Origin of Fantastic Four 2099; intro Moon Knight 2099	3	6	9	19	30	40
2099 UNLIMITED **Marvel Comics:** Sept, 1993 - No. 10, 1996 ($3.95, 68 pgs.)						
1-10: 1-1st app. Hulk 2099 & begins. 1-3-Spider-Man 2099 app. 9-Joe Kubert-c; Len Wein & Nancy Collins scripts						4.00
2099 WORLD OF DOOM SPECIAL **Marvel Comics:** May, 1995 ($2.25, one-shot)						
1-Doom's "Contract w/America"						4.00
2099 WORLD OF TOMORROW **Marvel Comics:** Sept, 1996 - No. 8, Apr, 1997 ($2.50) (Replaces 2099 titles)						
1-8: 1-Wraparound-c. 2-w/bound-in card. 4,5-Phalanx						3.00
20XX **Image Comics:** Dec, 2019 - Present ($3.99, B&W)						
1-6-Jonathan Luna-s/a; Lauren Keely-s						4.00
21 **Image Comics (Top Cow Productions):** Feb, 1996 - No. 3, Apr, 1996 ($2.50)						
1-3: Len Wein scripts						3.00
1-Variant-c						3.00
21 DOWN **DC Comics (WildStorm):** Nov, 2002 - No. 12, Nov, 2003 ($2.95)						
1-12: 1-Palmiotti & Gray-s/Saiz-a/Jusko-c						3.00
...: The Conduit (2003, $19.95, TPB) r/#1-7; intro. by Garth Ennis						20.00
24 (Based on TV series) **IDW Publishing:** Apr, 2014 - No. 5, Aug, 2014 ($3.99, limited series)						
1-5-Brisson-s/Gaydos-a; multiple covers on each						4.00
24 (Based on TV series) **IDW Publishing:** July, 2004 - July, 2005 ($6.99/$7.49, square-bound, one-shots)						
...: Midnight Sun (7/05, $7.49) J.C. Vaughn & Mark Haynes-s; Renato Guedes-a						7.50
...: One Shot (7/04, $6.99)-Jack Bauer's first day on the job at CTU; Vaughn & Haynes-s; Guedes-a						7.50
...: Stories (1/05, $7.49) Manny Clark-a; Vaughn & Haynes-s						7.50
24: LEGACY – RULES OF ENGAGEMENT (Based on TV series) **IDW Publishing:** Apr, 2017 - No. 5, Aug, 2017 ($3.99, limited series)						
1-5-Early days of Eric Carter in DC & Iraq; Farnsworth-s/Fuso-a; art and photo-c						4.00
24: NIGHTFALL (Based on TV series) **IDW Publishing:** Nov, 2006 - No. 5, Mar, 2007 ($3.99, limited series)						
1-5-Two years before Season One; Vaughn & Haynes-s; Diaz-a; two covers						4.00
28 DAYS LATER (Based on the 2002 movie) **Boom! Studios:** July, 2009 - No. 24, Jun, 2011 ($3.99)						
1-24: 1-Covers by Bradstreet and Phillips						4.00
2020 FORCE WORKS **Marvel Comics:** Apr, 2020 - No. 3, Oct, 2020 ($3.99, limited series)						
1-3-Rosenberg-s/Ramírez-a; War Machine and Mockingbird app.						4.00
2020 IRON AGE						

2020 iWolverine #1 © MAR

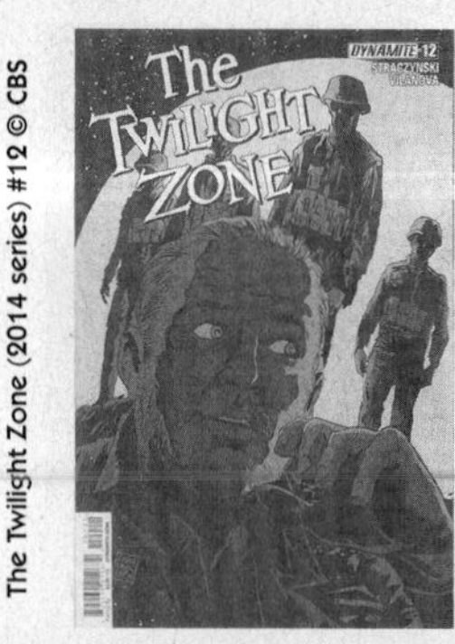

The Twilight Zone (2014 series) #12 © CBS

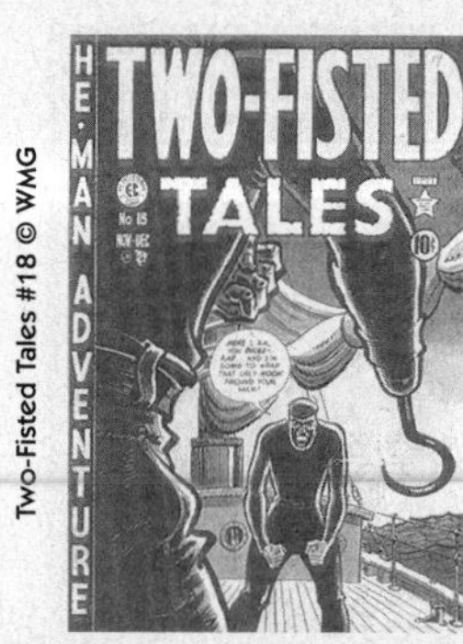

Two-Fisted Tales #18 © WMG

GD VG FN VF VF/NM NM-
2.0 4.0 6.0 8.0 9.0 9.2

GD VG FN VF VF/NM NM-
2.0 4.0 6.0 8.0 9.0 9.2

Marvel Comics: May, 2020 ($4.99, one-shot)
1-Machine Man, Alkhema, & Doctor Shapiro in short stories by various 5.00

2020 iWOLVERINE
Marvel Comics: Sept, 2020 - No. 2, Oct, 2020 ($3.99, limited series)
1,2-Larry Hama-s/Roland Boschi-a; Wolverine android copy; Tyger Tiger app. 4.00

2020 MACHINE MAN
Marvel Comics: Apr, 2020 - No. 2, May, 2020 ($4.99, limited series)
1,2-Ties in with Iron Man 2020 series; Jocasta & X-52 app. 5.00

2020 RESCUE
Marvel Comics: Apr, 2020 - No. 2, Jun, 2020 ($3.99, limited series)
1,2-Schwartz-s/Burrows-a; Pepper Potts in the Rescue armor 4.00

2020 VISIONS
DC Comics (Vertigo): May, 1997 - No. 12, Apr, 1998 ($2.25, limited series)
1-12-Delano-s: 1-3-Quitely-a. 4-"la tormenta"-Pleece-a 3.00

20,000 LEAGUES UNDER THE SEA (Movie)(See King Classics, Movie Comics & Power Record Comics)
Dell Publishing Co.: No. 614, Feb, 1955 (Disney)
Four Color 614-Movie, painted-c 9 18 27 59 117 175

TWICE TOLD TALES (See Movie Classics)

TWILIGHT
DC Comics: 1990 - No. 3, 1991 ($4.95, 52 pgs, lim. series, squarebound, mature)
1-3: Tommy Tomorrow app; Chaykin scripts, Garcia-Lopez-c/a 5.00

TWILIGHT CHILDREN, THE
DC Comics (Vertigo): Dec, 2015 - No. 4, Mar, 2016 ($4.99, limited series)
1-4-Gilbert Hernandez-s/Darwyn Cooke-a/c 5.00

TWILIGHT EXPERIMENT
DC Comics (WildStorm): Apr, 2004 - No. 6, Sept, 2005 ($2.95, limited series)
1-6-Gray & Palmiotti-s/Santacruz-a 3.00
TPB (2011, $17.99) r/#1-6 18.00

TWILIGHT GUARDIAN (Also see Pilot Season: Twilight Guardian)
Image Comics (Top Cow): Jan, 2011 - No. 4, Apr, 2011 ($3.99, limited series)
1-4-Hickman-s/Kotean-a 4.00

TWILIGHT MAN
First Publishing: June, 1989 - No. 4, Sept, 1989 ($2.75, limited series)
1-4 3.00

TWILIGHT ZONE, THE (TV) (See Dan Curtis & Stories From...)
Dell Publishing Co./Gold Key/Whitman No. 92: No. 1173, 3-5/61 - No. 91, 4/79; No. 92, 5/82
Four Color 1173 (#1)-Crandall-c/a 20 40 60 138 307 475
Four Color 1288-Crandall/Evans-c/a 11 22 33 72 154 235
01-860-207 (5-7/62-Dell, 15¢) 9 18 27 61 123 185
12-860-210 on-c; 01-860-210 on inside(8-10/62-Dell)-Evans-c/a (3 stories); art by Frazetta & Crandall 9 18 27 58 114 170
1(11/62-Gold Key)-Crandall/Frazetta-a (10 & 11 pgs.); Evans-a 15 30 45 105 233 360
2 7 14 21 49 92 135
3-11: 3(11 pgs.),4(10 pgs.),9-Toth-a 6 12 18 37 66 95
12-15: 12-Williamson-a. 13,15-Crandall-a. 14-Orlando/Crandall/Torres-a 5 10 15 31 53 75
16-20 4 8 12 25 40 55
21-25: 21-Crandall-a(r). 25-Evans/Crandall-a(r); Toth-r/#4; last 12¢ issue 3 6 9 19 30 40
26,27: 26-Flying Saucer-c/story; Crandall, Evans-a(r). 27-Evans-r(2) 3 6 9 18 28 38
28-32: 32-Evans-a(r) 3 6 9 16 24 32
33-51: 43-Celardo-a. 51-Williamson-a 2 4 6 13 18 22
52-70 2 4 6 10 14 18
71-82,86-91: 71-Reprint 2 4 6 8 11 14
83-(52 pgs.) 3 6 9 14 20 25
84-(52 pgs.) Frank Miller's 1st comic book work 11 22 33 77 166 255
85-Frank Miller-a (2nd) 5 10 15 35 63 90
92-(Whitman, 5/82) Last issue; r/#1. 2 4 6 9 13 16
Mini Comic #1(1976, 3-1/4x6-1/2") 2 4 6 8 10 12
NOTE: ***Bolle*** *a-13(w/**McWilliams**), 50, 55, 57, 59, 77, 78, 80, 83, 84.* ***McWilliams*** *a-59, 78, 80, 82, 84.* ***Miller*** *a-84, 85.* ***Orlando*** *a-15, 19, 20, 22, 23.* ***Sekowsky*** *a-3.* ***Simonson*** *a-50, 54, 55, 83r.* ***Weiss*** *a-39, 79r(#39). (See Mystery Comics Digest 3, 6, 9, 12, 15, 18, 21, 24). Reprints-26(1/3), 71, 73, 79, 83, 84, 86, 92. Painted c-1-91.*

TWILIGHT ZONE, THE (TV)
Now Comics: Nov, 1990 ($2.95); Oct, 1991; V2#1, Nov, 1991 - No. 11, Oct, 1992 ($1.95); V3#1, 1993 - No. 4, 1993 ($2.50)
1-(11/90, $2.95, 52 pgs.)-Direct sale edition; Neal Adams-a, Sienkiewicz-c; Harlan Ellison scripts 6.00
1-(11/90, $1.75)-Newsstand ed. w/N. Adams-c 5.00
1-Prestige Format (10/91, $4.95)-Reprints above with extra Harlan Ellison short story 5.00
1-Collector's Edition (10/91, $2.50)-Non-code approved and polybagged; reprints 11/90 issue; gold logo, 1-Reprint ($2.50)-r/direct sale 11/90 version, 1-Reprint ($2.50)-r/newsstand 11/90 version each... 5.00
V2#1-Direct sale & newsstand ed. w/different-c 4.00
V2#2-8,10-11 4.00
V2#9-($2.95)-3-D Special; polybagged w/glasses & hologram on-c 5.00
V2#9-($4.95)-Prestige Edition; contains 2 extra stories & a different hologram on-c; polybagged w/glasses 5.00
V3#1-4, Anniversary Special 1 (1992, $2.50) 4.00
Annual 1 (4/93, $2.50)-No ads 5.00
...Science Fiction Special (3/93, $3.50) 5.00

TWILIGHT ZONE, THE (TV)
Dynamite Entertainment: 2014 - No. 12, 2015 ($3.99)
1-12-Straczynski-s/Vilanova-a/Francavilla-c 4.00
#1959 (2016, $5.99) Short stories set in 1959; Valiente & Worley-a; Lau-c 6.00
Annual 2014 ($7.99) Three short stories; Rahner-s/Valiente, Malaga, Menna-a 8.00

TWILIGHT ZONE THE SHADOW (TV)
Dynamite Entertainment: 2016 - No. 4, 2016 ($3.99, limited series)
1-4-Avallone-s/Acosta-a/Francavilla-c; Shiwwan Khan app. 4.00

TWILIGHT ZONE, THE: SHADOW & SUBSTANCE (TV)
Dynamite Entertainment: 2015 - No. 4, 2015 ($3.99)
1-4-Rahner-s/Menna-a; multiple covers on each 4.00

TWINKLE COMICS
Spotlight Publishers: May, 1945
1 29 58 87 174 285 395

TWIST, THE
Dell Publishing Co.: July-Sept, 1962
01-864-209-Painted-c 10 20 30 68 144 220

TWISTED TALES (See Eclipse Graphic Album Series #15)
Pacific Comics/Independent Comics Group (Eclipse) #9,10: 11/82 - No. 8, 5/84; No. 9, 11/84; No. 10, 12/84 (Baxter paper)
1-9: 1-B. Jones/Corben-c; Alcala-a; nudity/violence in al. 2-Wrightson-c; Ploog-a 5.00
10-Wrightson painted art; Morrow-a 1 2 3 4 5 7
NOTE: ***Bolton*** *painted c-4, 6, 7; a-7.* ***Conrad*** *a-1, 3, 5; c-1i, 3, 5.* ***Guice*** *a-8.* ***Wildey*** *a-3.*

TWO BIT THE WACKY WOODPECKER (See Wacky...)
Toby Press: 1951 - No. 3, May, 1953
1 14 28 42 78 112 145
2,3 8 16 24 44 57 70

TWO FACE: YEAR ONE
DC Comics: 2008 - No. 2, 2008 ($5.99, squarebound, limited series)
1,2-Origin re-told; Sable-s/Saiz & Haun-a 6.00

TWO-FISTED TALES (Formerly Haunt of Fear #15-17)
(Also see EC Archives • Two-Fisted Tales)
E. C. Comics: No. 18, Nov-Dec, 1950 - No. 41, Feb-Mar, 1955
18(#1)-Kurtzman-c 123 246 369 984 1567 2150
19-Kurtzman-c 77 154 231 616 983 1350
20-Kurtzman-c 53 106 159 424 675 925
21,22-Kurtzman-c 43 86 129 344 547 750
23-25-Kurtzman-c 33 66 99 264 420 575
26-29,31-Kurtzman-c. 31-Civil War issue 25 50 75 200 320 440
30-Classic Davis-c 33 66 99 164 420 575
32-34: 33- "Atom Bomb" by Wood 25 50 75 200 320 440
35-Classic Davis Civil War-c/s 34 68 102 272 436 600
36-41: 41-Contains "In Memoriam" editorial about the ending of EC War titles 20 40 60 160 255 350
Two-Fisted Annual (1952, 25¢, 132 pgs.) 135 270 405 864 1482 2100
Two-Fisted Annual (1953, 25¢, 132 pgs.) 103 206 309 659 1130 1500
NOTE: ***Berg*** *a-29.* ***Colan*** *a-30,39p.* ***Craig*** *a-18, 19, 32.* ***Crandall*** *a-35, 36.* ***Davis*** *a-20-36, 40; c-30, 34, 35, 41, Annual 2.* ***Estrada*** *a-30.* ***Evans*** *a-34, 40, 41; c-40.* ***Feldstein*** *a-18.* ***Krigstein*** *a-41.* ***Kubert*** *a-32, 33.* ***Kurtzman*** *a-18-25; c-18-29, 31, Annual 1.* ***Severin*** *a-26, 28, 29, 31, 34-41 (No. 37-39 are all-**Severin** issues); c-36-39.* ***Severin/Elder*** *a-19-29, 31, 33, 36.* ***Wood*** *a-18-28, 30-35, 41; c-32, 33. Special issues: #26 (ChanJin Reservoir), 31 (Civil War), 35 (Civil War). Canadian reprints known; see Table of Contents. #25-Davis biog. #27-Wood biog. #28-Kurtzman biog.*

TWO-FISTED TALES
Russ Cochran/Gemstone Publishing: Oct, 1992 - No. 24, May, 1998 ($1.50/$2.00/$2.50)

Two-Gun Kid #62 © MAR

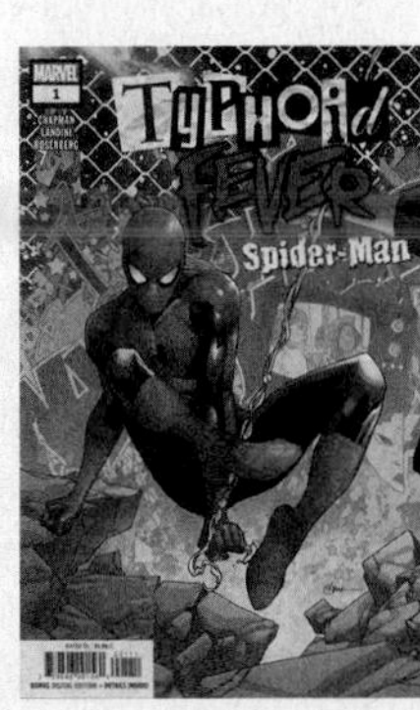

Typhoid Fever: Spider-Man #1 © MAR

Über #3 © Avatar

	GD 2.0	VG 4.0	FN 6.0	VF 8.0	VF/NM 9.0	NM- 9.2
1-24: 1-4r/Two-Fisted Tales #18-21 w/original-c						4.00

TWO-GUN KID (Also see All Western Winners, Best Western, Black Rider, Blaze Carson, Kid Colt, Western Winners, Wild West, & Wild Western)
Marvel/Atlas (MCI No. 1-10/HPC No. 11-59/Marvel No. 60 on): 3/48(No mo.) - No. 10, 11/49; No. 11, 12/53 - No. 59, 4/61; No. 60, 11/62 - No. 92, 3/68; No. 93, 7/70 - No. 136, 4/77

	GD 2.0	VG 4.0	FN 6.0	VF 8.0	VF/NM 9.0	NM- 9.2
1-Two-Gun Kid & his horse Cyclone begin; The Sheriff begins	158	316	474	1011	1731	2450
2	60	120	180	381	653	925
3,4: 3-Annie Oakley app.	43	86	129	271	461	650
5-Pre-Black Rider app. (Wint. 48/49); Anti-Wertham editorial (1st?)	45	90	135	284	480	675
6-10(11/49): 8-Blaze Carson app. 9-Black Rider app.	39	78	117	231	378	525
11(12/53)-Black Rider app.; 1st to have Atlas globe on-c; explains how Kid Colt became an outlaw	34	68	102	199	325	450
12-Black Rider app.	28	56	84	168	274	380
13-20: 14-Opium story	23	46	69	136	223	310
21-24,26-29	21	42	63	126	206	285
25,30: 25-Williamson-a (5 pgs.). 30-Williamson/Torres-a (4 pgs.)	22	44	66	132	216	300
31-33,35,37-40	12	24	36	79	170	260
34-Crandall-a	12	24	36	80	173	265
36,41,42,48-Origin in all	12	24	36	82	179	275
43,44,47	11	22	33	73	157	240
45,46-Davis-a	11	22	33	76	163	250
49,50,52,53-Severin-a(2/3) in each	10	20	30	70	150	230
51-Williamson-a (5 pgs.)	11	22	33	76	163	250
54,55,57,59-Severin-a(3) in each. 59-Kirby-a; last 10¢ issue (4/61)	11	22	33	75	160	245
56	11	22	33	73	157	240
58-New origin; Kirby/Ayers-c/a "The Monster of Hidden Valley" cover/story (Kirby monster-c)	31	62	93	223	499	775
60-New origin	66	132	198	535	1193	1850
60-Edition w/handwritten issue number on cover	69	138	207	559	1255	1950
61,62-Kirby-a	14	28	42	96	211	325
63-74: 64-Intro. Boom-Boom	8	16	24	55	105	155
75,76-Kirby-a (reprint)	9	18	27	57	111	165
77-Kirby-a (reprint); Black Panther-esque villain	13	26	39	89	195	300
78-89	5	10	15	33	57	80
90,95-Kirby-a	5	10	15	33	57	80
91,92: 92-Last new story; last 12¢ issue	4	8	12	28	47	65
93,94,96-99	3	6	9	16	23	30
100-Last 15¢-c	3	6	9	16	24	32
101-Origin retold/#58; Kirby-a	3	6	9	16	24	32
102-120-reprints	2	4	6	11	16	20
121-136-reprints. 129-131-(Regular 25¢ editions)	2	4	6	11	16	20
129-131-(30¢-c variants, limited distribution)(4-8/76)	7	14	21	49	92	135

NOTE: ***Ayers** a-13, 24, 26, 27, 63, 66. **Davis** c-45-47. **Drucker** a-23. **Everett** a-82, 91. **Fuje** a-13. **Heath** a-3(2), 4(3), 5(2), 7; c-13, 21, 23, 53. **Keller** a-16, 19, 28, 42. **Kirby** a-54, 55, 57-62, 75-77, 90, 95, 101, 119, 120, 129; c-10, 52, 54-65, 67-72, 74-76, 116. **Maneely** a-20; c-11, 12, 16, 19, 20, 24-28, 30, 35, 41, 42, 49. **Powell** a-38, 102, 104. **Severin** a-9, 29, 51, 55, 57, 99r(3); c-9, 39, 51. **Shores** c-1-8, 11. **Trimpe** c-99. **Tuska** a-11, 12. **Whitney** a-87, 89-92, 98-113, 124, 129; c-87, 89, 91, 113. **Wildey** a-21. **Williamson** a-110r. Kid Colt in #13, 14, 16-21.*

TWO GUN KID: SUNSET RIDERS
Marvel Comics: Nov, 1995 - No. 2, Dec, 1995 ($6.95, squarebound, lim. series)

1,2: Fabian Nicieza scripts in all. 1-Painted-c. 7.00

TWO GUN WESTERN (1st Series) (Formerly Casey Crime Photographer #1-4? or My Love #1-4?)
Marvel/Atlas Comics (MPC): No. 5, Nov, 1950 - No. 14, June, 1952

	GD 2.0	VG 4.0	FN 6.0	VF 8.0	VF/NM 9.0	NM- 9.2
5-The Apache Kid (Intro & origin) & his horse Nightwind begin by Buscema	34	68	102	199	325	450
6-10: 8-Kid Colt, The Texas Kid & his horse Thunder begin?	23	46	69	136	223	310
11-14: 13-Black Rider app.	17	34	51	100	158	215

NOTE: ***Maneely** a-6, 7, 9; c-6, 11-13. **Morrow** a-9. **Romita** a-8. **Wildey** a-8.*

2-GUN WESTERN (2nd Series) (Formerly Billy Buckskin #1-3; Two-Gun Western #5 on)
Atlas Comics (MgPC): No. 4, May, 1956

	GD 2.0	VG 4.0	FN 6.0	VF 8.0	VF/NM 9.0	NM- 9.2
4-Colan, Ditko, Severin, Sinnott-a; Maneely-c	20	40	60	115	185	255

TWO-GUN WESTERN (Formerly 2-Gun Western)
Atlas Comics (MgPC): No. 5, July, 1956 - No. 12, Sept, 1957

	GD 2.0	VG 4.0	FN 6.0	VF 8.0	VF/NM 9.0	NM- 9.2
5-Return of the Gun-Hawk-c/story; Black Rider app.	20	40	60	114	182	250
6,7	15	30	45	90	140	190
8,10,12-Crandall-a	15	30	45	94	147	200
9,11-Williamson-a in both (5 pgs. each)	16	32	48	98	154	210

NOTE: ***Ayers** a-9. **Colan** a-5. **Everett** c-12. **Forgione** a-5, 6. **Kirby** a-12. **Maneely** a-6, 8, 12; c-5, 6, 8, 11. **Morrow** a-9, 10. **Powell** a-7, 11. **Severin** c-10. **Sinnott** a-5. **Wildey** a-9.*

TWO MINUTE WARNING
Ultimate Sports Ent.: 2000 - No. 2 ($3.95, cardstock covers)

1,2-NFL players & Teddy Roosevelt battle evil 4.00

TWO MOONS
Image Comics: Feb, 2021 - Present ($3.99)

1-Arcudi-s/Giangiordano-a; set during the Civil War 4.00

TWO MOUSEKETEERS, THE (See 4-Color #475, 603, 642 under M.G.M.'s...;

TWO ON A GUILLOTINE (See Movie Classics)

TWO-STEP
DC Comics (Cliffhanger): Dec, 2003 - No. 3, Jul, 2004 ($2.95, limited series)

1-3-Warren Ellis-s/Amanda Conner-a 3.00
TPB (2010, $19.99) r/#1-3; sketch pages; script for #1 with B&W art 20.00

2000 A.D. MONTHLY/PRESENTS (Showcase #25 on)
Eagle Comics/Quality Comics No. 5 on: 4/85 - #6, 9/85; 4/86 - #54, 1991 ($1.25-$1.50, Mando paper)

1-6,1-25:1-4 r/British series featuring Judge Dredd; Alan Moore scripts begin. 1-25 ($1.25)-Reprints from British 2000 AD 4.00
26,27/28, 29/30, 31-54: 27/28, 29/30,31-Guice-c 3.00

2001, A SPACE ODYSSEY (Movie) (See adaptation in Treasury edition)
Marvel Comics Group: Dec, 1976 - No. 10, Sept, 1977 (30¢)

	GD 2.0	VG 4.0	FN 6.0	VF 8.0	VF/NM 9.0	NM- 9.2
1-Kirby-c/a in all	3	6	9	21	33	45
2-7,9,10	2	4	6	9	12	15
7,9,10-(35¢-c variants, limited distribution)(6-9/77)	9	18	27	58	114	170
8-Origin/1st app. Machine Man (called Mr. Machine)	5	10	15	35	63	90
8-(35¢-c variant, limited distribution)(6,8/77)	18	36	54	128	284	440
...Treasury 1 ('76, 84 pgs.)-All new Kirby-a	3	6	9	16	23	30

2010 (Movie)
Marvel Comics Group: Apr, 1985 - No. 2, May, 1985

1,2-r/Marvel Super Special movie adaptation. 4.00

TYPHOID (Also see Daredevil)
Marvel Comics: Nov, 1995 - No. 4, Feb, 1996 ($3.95, squarebound, lim. series)

1-4: Typhoid Mary; Van Fleet-c/a 4.00

TYPHOID FEVER
Marvel Comics: Dec, 2018 - Feb, 2019 ($4.99, limited series)

....: Iron Fist 1 (2/19, $4.99) Typhoid Mary conclusion; Chapman-s/Villanelli-a 5.00
....: Spider-Man 1 (12/18, $4.99) Typhoid Mary returns; Chapman-s/Landini-a 5.00
....: X-Men 1 (1/19, $4.99) Spider-Man app.; Chapman-s/Robson & Beyruth-a 5.00

ÜBER
Avatar Press: No. 0, Mar, 2013 - No. 27, Jul, 2015 ($3.99)

0-27: 0-11-Kieron Gillen-s/Caanan White-a. 12-14-Andrade-a 4.00
... FCBD 2014 (2/14, Free Comic Book Day giveaway) Text synopsis of early storyline 3.00
... Special 1 (3/14, $5.99) Andrade-a 6.00

UFO & ALIEN COMIX
Warren Publishing Co.: Jan, 1978 (B&W magazine, 84 pgs., one-shot)

	GD 2.0	VG 4.0	FN 6.0	VF 8.0	VF/NM 9.0	NM- 9.2
nn-Toth-a, J. Severin-a(r); Pie-s	2	4	6	13	18	22

UFO & OUTER SPACE (Formerly UFO Flying Saucers)
Gold Key: No. 14, June, 1978 - No. 25, Feb, 1980 (All painted covers)

	GD 2.0	VG 4.0	FN 6.0	VF 8.0	VF/NM 9.0	NM- 9.2
14-Reprints UFO Flying Saucers #3	1	3	4	6	8	10
15,16-Reprints	1	3	4	6	8	10
17-25: 17-20-New material. 23-McWilliams-a. 24-(3 pg.-r). 25-Reprints UFO Flying Saucers #2 w/cover	1	3	4	6	8	10

UFO ENCOUNTERS
Western Publishing Co.: May, 1978 ($1.95, 228 pgs.)

	GD 2.0	VG 4.0	FN 6.0	VF 8.0	VF/NM 9.0	NM- 9.2
11192-Reprints UFO Flying Saucers	4	8	12	28	47	65
11404-Vol.1 (128 pgs.)-See UFO Mysteries for Vol. 2	4	8	12	25	40	55

UFO FLYING SAUCERS (UFO & Outer Space #14 on)
Gold Key: Oct, 1968 - No. 13, Jan, 1977 (No. 2 on, 36 pgs.)

	GD 2.0	VG 4.0	FN 6.0	VF 8.0	VF/NM 9.0	NM- 9.2
1(30035-810) (68 pgs.)	6	12	18	37	66	95
2(11/70), 3(11/72), 4(11/74)	3	6	9	19	30	40
5(2/75)-13: Bolle-a #4 on	3	6	9	14	20	25

UFOLOGY
BOOM! Studios: Apr, 2015 - No. 6, Nov, 2015 ($3.99, limited series)

1-6-James Tynion IV & Noah J. Yuenkel-s/Matthew Fox-a 4.00

Ultimate Armor Wars #1 © MAR

Ultimate Fallout #4 © MAR

Ultimate Hawkeye #1 © MAR

GD	VG	FN	VF	VF/NM	NM-
2.0	4.0	6.0	8.0	9.0	9.2

UFO MYSTERIES
Western Publishing Co.: 1978 ($1.00, reprints, 96 pgs.)

11400-(Vol.2)-Cont'd from UFO Encounters, pgs. 129-224 4 8 12 27 44 60

ULTIMAN GIANT ANNUAL (See Big Bang Comics)
Image Comics: Nov, 2001 ($4.95, B&W, one-shot)

1-Homage to DC 1960's annuals 5.00

ULTIMATE... (Collects 4-issue alternate titles from X-Men Age of Apocalypse crossovers)
Marvel Comics: May, 1995 ($8.95, trade paperbacks, gold foil covers)

Amazing X-Men, Astonishing X-Men, Factor-X, Gambit & the X-Ternals, Generation Next, X-Calibre, X-Man 9.00
Weapon X 10.00

ULTIMATE ADVENTURES
Marvel Comics: Nov, 2002 - No. 6, Dec, 2003 ($2.25)

1-6: 1-Intro. Hawk-Owl; Zimmerman-s/Fegredo-a. 3-Ultimates app. 3.00
One Tin Soldier TPB (2005, $12.99) r/#1-6 13.00

ULTIMATE ANNUALS
Marvel Comics: 2006; 2007 ($13.99, SC)

Vol. 1 (2006, $13.99) r/Ult. FF Ann. #1, Ult. X-Men Ann. #1, Ult S-M #1, Ultimates Ann #1 14.00
Vol. 2 (2007, $13.99) r/Ult. FF Ann. #2, Ult. X-Men Ann. #2, Ult S-M #2, Ultimates Ann #2 14.00

ULTIMATE ARMOR WARS (Follows Ultimatum x-over)
Marvel Comics: Nov, 2009 - No. 4, Apr, 2010 ($3.99, limited series)

1-4-Warren Ellis-s/Steve Kurth-a/Brandon Peterson-c. 1-Variant-c by Kurth 4.00

ULTIMATE AVENGERS (Follows Ultimatum x-over)
Marvel Comics: Oct, 2009 - No. 18 ($3.99)

1-6-Mark Millar-s/Carlos Pacheco-a/c; Red Skull app. 4.00
1-Variant Red Skull-c by Leinil Yu 8.00
7-12-(Ultimate Avengers 2 #1-6 on cover) Yu-a; Punisher joins. 10-Origin Ghost Rider 4.00
7-Variant Ghost Rider-c by Silvestri 8.00
13-18-(Ultimate Avengers 3 #1-6 on cover) Dillon-a; Blade and a new Daredevil app. 4.00

ULTIMATE AVENGERS VS. NEW ULTIMATES (Death of Spider-Man tie-in)
Marvel Comics: Apr, 2011 - No. 6, Sept, 2011 ($3.99, limited series)

1-6: 1-Millar-s/Yu-a/c; variant covers by Cho & Hitch. 3-6-Punisher app. 4.00

ULTIMATE CAPTAIN AMERICA
Marvel Comics: Mar, 2011 - No. 4, Jun, 2011 ($3.99)

1-4: 1-Aaron-s/Garney-a; 2 covers by Garney & McGuinness 4.00
Annual 1 (12/08, $3.99, one-shot) Origin of the Black Panther; Djurdjevic-a 4.00

ULTIMATE CIVIL WAR: SPIDER-HAM (See Civil War and related titles)
Marvel Comics: March, 2007 ($2.99, one-shot)

1-Spoof of Civil War series featuring Spider-Ham; art by various incl. Olivetti, Severin 3.00

ULTIMATE COMICS IRON MAN
Marvel Comics: Dec, 2012 - No. 4, Mar, 2013 ($3.99, limited series)

1-4-Edmonson-s/Buffagni-a/Stockton-c 4.00

ULTIMATE COMICS SPIDER-MAN (See Ultimate Spider-Man 2011 series)

ULTIMATE COMICS ULTIMATES (See Ultimates 2011 series)

ULTIMATE COMICS WOLVERINE
Marvel Comics: May, 2013 - No. 4, Jul, 2013 ($3.99, limited series)

1-4: 1-Bunn-s/Messina-a/Art Adams-c; Wolverine app. in flashback 4.00

ULTIMATE COMICS X-MEN (See Ultimate X-Men 2011 series)

ULTIMATE DAREDEVIL AND ELEKTRA
Marvel Comics: Jan, 2003 - No. 4, Mar, 2003 ($2.25, limited series)

1-4-Rucka-s/Larroca-c/a; 1st meeting of Elektra and Matt Murdock 3.00
... Vol.1 TPB (2003, $11.99) r/#1-4, Daredevil Vol. 2 #9; Larroca sketch pages 12.00

ULTIMATE DOOM (Follows Ultimate Mystery mini-series)
Marvel Comics: Feb, 2011 - No. 4, May, 2011 ($3.99, limited series)

1-4-Bendis-s/Sandoval-a; Fantastic Four, Spider-Man, Jessica Drew & Nick Fury app. 4.00

ULTIMATE ELEKTRA
Marvel Comics: Oct, 2004 - No. 5, Feb, 2005 ($2.25, limited series)

1-5-Carey-s/Larroca-c/a. 2-Bullseye app. 3.00
... : Devil's Due TPB (2005, $11.99) r/#1-5 12.00

ULTIMATE END (Secret Wars Battleworld tie-in)
Marvel Comics: Jul, 2015 - No. 5, Feb, 2016 ($3.99, limited series)

1-5-Bendis-s/Bagley-a; Spider-Man & Earth-616 Avengers & Ultimate Universe app. 4.00

GD	VG	FN	VF	VF/NM	NM-
2.0	4.0	6.0	8.0	9.0	9.2

ULTIMATE ENEMY (Follows Ultimatum x-over)(Leads into Ultimate Mystery)
Marvel Comics: Mar, 2010 - No. 4, July, 2010 ($3.99, limited series)

1-4-Bendis-s/Sandoval-a 1-Covers by McGuinness and Pearson 4.00

ULTIMATE EXTINCTION (See Ultimate Nightmare and Ultimate Secret limited series)
Marvel Comics: Mar, 2006 - No. 5, July, 2006 ($2.99, limited series)

1-5-The coming of Gah Lak Tus; Ellis-s/Peterson-a 3.00
TPB (2006, $12.99) r/#1-5 13.00

ULTIMATE FALLOUT (Follows Death of Spider-Man in Ultimate Spider-Man #160)
Marvel Comics: Sept, 2011 - No. 6, Oct, 2011 ($3.99, weekly limited series)

1-3,5,6: 1-Bendis-s/Bagley-a/c. 2,6-Hitch-c. 3,5-Andy Kubert-c 4.00
4-Debut of Miles Morales as the new Spider-Man; polybagged 15 30 45 103 227 350

ULTIMATE FANTASTIC FOUR (Continues in Ultimatum mini-series)
Marvel Comics: Feb, 2004 - No. 60, Apr, 2009 ($2.25/$2.50/$2.99)

1-Bendis & Millar-s/Adam Kubert-a/Hitch-c 5.00
2-20: 2-Adam Kubert-a/c; intro. Moleman 7-Ellis-s/Immonen-a begin; Dr. Doom app. 13-18-Kubert-a. 19,20-Jae Lee-a. 20-Begin $2.50-c 3.50
21-Marvel Zombies; begin Greg Land-c/a; Mark Millar-s; variant-c by Land 5.00
22-29,33-59: 24-26-Namor app. 28-President Thor. 33-38-Ferry-a. 42-46-Silver Surfer 3.00
30-32-Marvel Zombies; Millar-s/Land-a; Dr. Doom app. 5.00
30-32-Zombie variant-c by Suydam 6.00
50-White variant-c by Kirkham 5.00
60-($3.99) Ultimatum crossover; Kirkham-a 4.00
Annual 1 (10/05, $3.99) The Inhumans app.; Jae Lee-a/Mark Millar-s/Greg Land-c 4.00
Annual 2 (10/06, $3.99) Mole Man app.; Immonen & Irving-a/Carey-s 4.00
... MGC #1 (6/11, $1.00) r/#1 with "Marvel's Greatest Comics" logo on cover 3.00
.../Ult. X-Men Annual 1 (11/08, $3.99) Continued from Ult. X-Men/Ult. F.F. Annual #1 4.00
.../X-Men 1 (3/06, $2.99) Carey-s/Ferry-a; continued from Ult. X-Men/Fantastic Four #1 3.00
... Vol. 1: The Fantastic (2004, $12.99, TPB) r/#1-6; cover gallery 13.00
... Vol. 2: Doom (2004, $12.99, TPB) r/#7-12 13.00
... Vol. 3: N-Zone (2005, $12.99, TPB) r/#13-18 13.00
... Vol. 4: Inhuman (2005, $12.99, TPB) r/#19,20 & Annual #1 13.00
... Vol. 5: Crossover (2006, $12.99, TPB) r/#21-26 13.00
... Vol. 6: Frightful (2006, $14.99, TPB) r/#27-32; gallery of cover sketches & variants 15.00
... Vol. 7: God War (2007, $16.99, TPB) r/#33-38 17.00
... Vol. 8: Devils (2007, $12.99, TPB) r/#39-41 & Annual #2 13.00
... Vol. 9: Silver Surfer (2007, $13.99, TPB) r/#42-46 14.00
Volume 1 HC (2005, $29.99, 7x11", dust jacket) r/#1-12; introduction, proposals and scripts by Millar and Bendis; character design pages by Hitch 30.00
Volume 2 HC (2006, $29.99, 7x11", dust jacket) r/#13-20; Jae Lee sketch page 30.00
Volume 3 HC (2007, $29.99, 7x11", dust jacket) r/#21-32; Greg Land sketch pages 30.00
Volume 4 HC (2007, $29.99, 7x11", dust jacket) r/#33-41, Annual #2, Ultimate FF/X-Men and Ultimate X-Men/FF; character design pages 30.00
Volume 5 HC (2008, $34.99, 7x11", dust jacket) r/#42-53 35.00

ULTIMATE FF
Marvel Comics: Jun, 2014 - No. 6, Oct, 2014 ($3.99)

1-6: 1-Team of Sue Storm, Iron Man, Falcon, Machine Man. 4,5-Spider-Ham app. 4.00

ULTIMATE GALACTUS TRILOGY
Marvel Comics: 2007 ($34.99, hardcover, dustjacket)

HC-Oversized reprint of Ultimate Nightmare #1-5, Ultimate Secret #1-4, Ultimate Vision #0, and Ultimate Extinction #1-5; sketch pages and cover galery 35.00

ULTIMATE HAWKEYE (Ultimate Comics)
Marvel Comics: Oct, 2011 - No. 4, Jan, 2012 ($3.99, limited series)

1-4: 1-Hickman-s/Sandoval-a/Andrews-c; polybagged. 2-4-Hulk app. 4.00
1-Variant-c by Neal Adams 6.00
1-Variant-c by Adam Kubert 8.00

ULTIMATE HULK
Marvel Comics: Dec, 2008 ($3.99, one-shot)

Annual 1 (12/08, $3.99) Zarda battles Hulk; McGuinness & Djurdjevic-a/Loeb-s 4.00

ULTIMATE HUMAN
Marvel Comics: Mar, 2008 - No. 4, Jun, 2008 ($2.99, limited series)

1-4-Iron Man vs. The Hulk; The Leader app.; Ellis-s/Nord-a 3.00
HC (2008, $19.99) r/#1-4 20.00

ULTIMATE IRON MAN
Marvel Comics: May, 2005 - No. 5, Feb, 2006 ($2.99, limited series)

1-Origin of Iron Man; Orson Scott Card-s/Andy Kubert-a; two covers 4.00
1-2nd & 3rd printings; each with B&W variant-c 3.00
2-5-Kubert-c 3.00
Volume 1 HC (2006, $19.99, dust jacket) r/#1-5; rough cut of script for #1, cover sketches 20.00

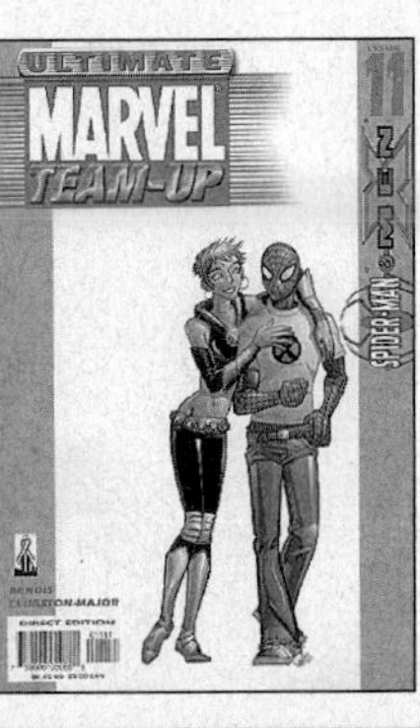

Ultimate Marvel Team-Up #11 © MAR

The Ultimates #7 © MAR

Ultimate Spider-Man #60 © MAR

	GD	VG	FN	VF	VF/NM	NM-
	2.0	4.0	6.0	8.0	9.0	9.2

Volume 1 SC (2006, $14.99) r/#1-5; rough cut of script for #1, cover sketches 15.00

ULTIMATE IRON MAN II
Marvel Comics: Feb, 2008 - No. 5, July, 2008 ($2.99, limited series)

1-5-Early days of the Iron Man prototype; Orson Scott Card-s/Pasqual Ferry-a/c 3.00

ULTIMATE MARVEL FLIP MAGAZINE
Marvel Comics: July, 2005 - No. 26, Aug, 2007 ($3.99/$4.99)

1-11-Reprints Ultimate Fantastic Four and Ultimate X-Men in flip format 4.00
12-26-($4.99) 5.00

ULTIMATE MARVEL MAGAZINE
Marvel Comics: Feb, 2001 - No. 11, 2002 ($3.99, magazine size)

1-11: Reprints of recent stories from the Ultimate titles plus Marvel news and features. 1-Reprints Ultimate Spider-Man #1&2. 11-Lord of the Rings-c 4.00

ULTIMATE MARVEL SAMPLER
Marvel Comics: 2007 (no cover price, limited series)

1-Previews of 2008 Ultimate Marvel story arcs; Finch-c 3.00

ULTIMATE MARVEL TEAM-UP (Spider-Man Team-up)
Marvel Comics: Apr, 2001 - No. 16, July, 2002 ($2.99/$2.25)

1-Spider-Man & Wolverine; Bendis-s in all; Matt Wagner-a/c 5.00
2,3-Hulk; Hester-a 3.50
4,5,9-16: 4,5-Iron Man; Allred-a. 9-Fantastic Four; Mahfood-a. 10-Man-Thing; Totleben-a. 11-X-Men; Clugston-Major-a. 12,13-Dr. Strange; McKeever-a.14-Black Widow; Terry Moore-a. 15,16-Shang-Chi; Mays-a 3.00
6-8-Punisher; Sienkiewicz-a. 7,8-Daredevil app. 4.00
TPB (11/01, $14.95) r/#1-5 15.00
... Ultimate Collection TPB ('06, $29.99) r/#1-16 & Ult. Spider-Man Spec.; sketch pages 30.00
HC (8/02, $39.99) r/#1-16 & Ult. Spider-Man Special; Bendis afterword 40.00
...: Vol. 2 TPB (2003, $11.99) r/#9-13; Mahfood-c 12.00
...: Vol. 3 TPB (2003, $12.99) r/#14-16 & Ultimate Spider-Man Super Special; Moore-c 13.00

ULTIMATE MYSTERY (Follows Ultimate Enemy)(Leads into Ultimate Doom)
Marvel Comics: Sept, 2010 - No. 4, Dec, 2010 ($3.99, limited series)

1-4-Bendis-s/Sandoval-a; Rick Jones returns; Captain Marvel app. 1-3-Campbell-c 4.00

ULTIMATE NEW ULTIMATES (Follows Ultimatum x-over)
Marvel Comics: May, 2010 - No. 5, Mar, 2011 ($3.99)

1-5: 1-Jeph Loeb-s/Frank Cho-a; 6-page wraparound-c by Cho; Defenders app. 4.00
1-Villains variant-c by Yu 8.00

ULTIMATE NIGHTMARE (Leads into Ultimate Secret limited series)
Marvel Comics: Oct, 2004 - No. 5, Feb, 2005 ($2.25, limited series)

1-5: Ellis-s; Ultimates, X-Men, Nick Fury app. 1,2,4,5-Hairsine-a/c. 3-Epting-a 3.00
Ultimate Galactus Book 1: Nightmare TPB (2005, $12.99) r/Ultimate Nightmare #1-5 13.00

ULTIMATE ORIGINS
Marvel Comics: Aug, 2008 - No. 5, Dec, 2008 ($2.99, limited series)

1-5-Bendis-s/Guice-a. 1-Nick Fury origin in the 1940s. 2-Capt. America origin 3.00

ULTIMATE POWER
Marvel Comics: Dec, 2006 - No. 9, Feb, 2008 ($2.99, limited series)

1-9: 1-Ultimate FF meets the Squadron Supreme; Bendis-s; Land-a/c. 2-Spider-Man, X-Men and the Ultimates app. 6-Doom app. 3.00
1-Variant sketch-c 5.00
1-Director's Cut (2007, $3.99) r/#1 and B&W pencil and ink pages; covers to #2,3 4.00
HC (2008, $34.99) oversized r/series; profile pages; B&W sketch art 35.00

ULTIMATES, THE (Avengers of the Ultimate line)
Marvel Comics: Mar, 2002 - No. 13, Apr, 2004 ($2.25)

1-Intro. Capt. America; Millar-s/Hitch-a & wraparound-c 6.00
2-Intro. Giant-Man and the Wasp 4.00
3-12: 3-1st Capt. America in new costume. 4-Intro. Thor. 5-Ultimates vs. The Hulk. 8-Intro. Hawkeye 3.00
13-($3.50) 4.00
... MGC #1 (5/11, $1.00) r/#1 with "Marvel's Greatest Comics" logo on cover 3.00
... Saga (2007, $3.99) Re-caps 1st 2 Ultimates series; new framing art by Charest; prelude to Ultimates 3 series; Brooks-c 4.00
... Volume 1 HC (2004, $29.99) oversized r/series; commentary pages with Millar & Hitch; cover gallery and character design pages; intro. by Joss Whedon 30.00
... Volume 1: Super-Human TPB (8/02, $12.99) r/#1-6 13.00
... Volume 2: Homeland Security TPB (2004, $17.99) r/#7-13 18.00

ULTIMATES (Ultimate Comics) (Continues in Hunger)
Marvel Comics: Oct, 2011 - No. 30, Nov, 2013 ($3.99)

1-30: 1-Hickman-s/Ribic-a/Andrews-c; polybagged. 4-Reed Richards returns 4.00
1-Variant-c by Esad Ribic 6.00
#18.1 (2/13, $2.99) Eaglesham-a; Stark gets the Iron Patriot armor 3.00
Ultimate Comics Ultimates Must Have 1 (2/12, $4.99) r/#1-3 5.00

ULTIMATES (Follows Secret War event)
Marvel Comics: Jan, 2016 - No. 12, Dec, 2016 ($3.99)

1-12: 1-Ewing-s/Rocafort-a; team of Capt. Marvel, Blue Marvel, Black Panther, Spectrum, and Ms. America; Galactus app. 5,7-11-Thanos app. 6,12-Christian Ward-a. 8-12-Civil War II tie-ins 4.00

ULTIMATES 2
Marvel Comics: Feb, 2005 - No. 13, Feb, 2007 ($2.99/$3.99)

1-Millar-s/Hitch-a; Giant-Man becomes Ant-Man 4.00
2-11: 6-Intro. The Defenders. 7-Hawkeye shot. 8-Intro The Liberators 3.00
12,13-($3.99) Wraparound-c; X-Men, Fantastic Four, Spider-Man app. 4.00
13-Variant white cover featuring The Wasp 15.00
Annual 1 (10/05, $3.99) Millar-s/Dillon-a/Hitch-c; Defenders app. 4.00
Annual 2 (10/06, $3.99) Deodato-a; flashback to WWII with Sook-a; Falcon app. 4.00
HC (2007, $34.99) oversized r/series; commentary pages with Millar & Hitch; cover gallery, sketch and script pages; intro. by Jonathan Ross 35.00
... Volume 1: Gods & Monsters TPB (2005, $15.99) r/#1-6 16.00
... Volume 2: Grand Theft America TPB (2007, $19.99) r/#7-13; cover gallery w/sketches 20.00

ULTIMATES 2
Marvel Comics: Jan, 2017 - No. 9, Sept, 2017; No. 100, Oct, 2017 ($3.99)

1-9: 1-Ewing-s/Foreman-a; team of Capt. Marvel, Blue Marvel, Black Panther, Spectrum, and Ms. America. 7,8-Secret Empire tie-ins; Koch-a. 8,9-Ego the Living Planet app. 4.00
100-(10/17, $4.99) The original Ultimates app. 5.00

ULTIMATES 3
Marvel Comics: Feb, 2008 - No. 5, Nov, 2008 ($2.99)

1-Loeb-s/Madureira-a; two gatefold wraparound covers by Madureira; Scarlet Witch shot 4.00
1,2-Second printings: 1-Wraparound cover by Madureira. 2-Madureira-c 3.00
2-5: 2-Spider-Man app. 3-Wolverine app. 5-Two gatefold wraparound-c (Heroes & Ultron) 3.00
2-Variant Thor cover by Turner 8.00
3-Variant Scarlet Witch cover by Cho 8.00
4-Variant Valkyrie cover by Finch 4.00

ULTIMATE SECRET (See Ultimate Nightmare limited series)
Marvel Comics: May, 2005 - No. 4, Dec, 2005 ($2.99, limited series)

1-4-Ellis-s; Captain Marvel app. 1,2-McNiven-a. 2,3-Ultimates & FF app. 3.00
Ultimate Galactus Book 2: Secret TPB (2006, $12.99) r/#1-4 13.00

ULTIMATE SECRETS
Marvel Comics: 2008 ($3.99, one-shot)

1-Handbook-styled profiles of secondary teams and characters from Ultimate universe 4.00

ULTIMATE SIX (Reprinted in Ultimate Spider-Man Vol. 5 hardcover)
Marvel Comics: Nov, 2003 - No. 7, June, 2004 ($2.25) (See Ultimate Spider-Man for TPB)

1-The Ultimates & Spider-Man team-up; Bendis-s/Quesada & Hairsine-a; Cassaday-c 5.00
2-7-Hairsine-a; Cassaday-c 3.00

ULTIMATE SPIDER-MAN
Marvel Comics: Oct, 2000 - No. 133, June, 2009 ($2.99/$2.25/$2.99/$3.99)

	GD	VG	FN	VF	VF/NM	NM-
1-Bendis-s/Bagley & Thibert-a; cardstock-c; introduces revised origin and cast separate from regular Spider-continuity	6	12	18	41	76	110
1-Variant white-c (Retailer incentive)	9	18	27	62	126	190
1-Dynamic Forces Edition	5	10	15	35	63	90
1-Kay Bee Toys variant edition	2	4	6	9	12	15
2-Cover with Spider-Man on car	3	6	9	18	27	35
2-Cover with Spider-Man swinging past building	3	6	9	18	27	35
3,4: 4-Uncle Ben killed	2	4	6	10	14	18
5-7: 6,7-Green Goblin app.	2	4	6	9	12	15
8-13: 13-Reveals secret to MJ	1	3	4	6	8	10

14-21: 14-Intro. Gwen Stacy & Dr. Octopus 5.00
22-($3.50) Green Goblin returns 6.00
23-32 4.00
33-1st Ultimate Venom-c; intro. Eddie Brock 5.00
34-38-Ultimate Venom 4.00
39-49,51-59: 39-Nick Fury app. 43,44-X-Men app. 46-Prelude to Ultimate Six; Sandman app. 51-53-Elektra app. 54-59-Doctor Octopus app. 3.00
50-($2.99) Intro. Black Cat 4.00
60-Intro. Ultimate Carnage on cover 4.00
61-Intro Ben Reilly; Punisher app. 3.00
62-Gwen Stacy killed by Carnage 4.00
63-92: 63,64-Carnage app. 66,67-Wolverine app. 68,69-Johnny Storm app. 78-Begin $2.50-c. 79-Debut Moon Knight. 81-85-Black Cat app. 90-Vulture app. 91-94-Deadpool 3.00
93-99: 93-Begin $2.99-c. 95-Morbius & Blade app. 97-99-Clone Saga 3.00
100-($3.99) Wraparound-c; Clone Saga; re-cap of previous issues 4.00

Ultimate Spider-Man #160 © MAR

Ultimate Vision #1 © MAR

Ultimate X-Men #34 © MAR

GD VG FN VF VF/NM NM-
2.0 4.0 6.0 8.0 9.0 9.2

101-103-Clone Saga continues; Fantastic Four app. 102-Spider-Woman origin 3.00
104-($3.99) Clone Saga concludes; Fantastic Four and Dr. Octopus app. 4.00
105-132: 106-110-Daredevil app. 111-Last Bagley art; Immonen-a (6 pgs.) 112-Immonen-a; Norman Osborn app. 118-Liz Allen ignites. 123,128-Venom app. 129-132-Ultimatum 3.00
133-($3.99) Ultimatum crossover; Spider-Woman app. 4.00
(Issues #150-up, see second series)
Annual 1 (10/05, $3.99) Kitty Pryde app.; Bendis-s/Brooks-a/Bagley-c 4.00
Annual 2 (10/06, $3.99) Punisher, Moon Knight and Daredevil app.; Bendis-s/Brooks-a 4.00
Annual 3 (12/08, $3.99) Mysterio app.; Bendis-s/Lafuente-a 4.00
Collected Edition (1/01, $3.99) r/#1-3 4.00
Free Comic Book Day giveaway (5/02) - r/#1 with "Free Comic Book Day" banner on-c 3.00
... MGC #1 (5/11, $1.00) r/#1 with "Marvel's Greatest Comics" logo on cover 3.00
...Special (7/02, $3.50) art by Bagley and various incl. Romita, Sr., Brereton, Cho, Mack, Sienkiewicz, Phillips, Pearson, Oeming, Mahfood, Russell 4.00
Ultimate Spider-Man 100 Project (2007, $10.00, SC, charity book for the HERO Initiative) collection of 100 variant covers by Romita Sr. & Jr., Cho, Bagley, Quesada and more 10.00
...: Venom HC (2007, $19.99) r/#33-39 20.00
...(Vol. 1): Power and Responsibility TPB (4/01, $14.95) r/#1-7 15.00
...(Vol. 2): Learning Curve TPB (12/01, $14.95) r/#8-13 15.00
...(Vol. 3): Double Trouble TPB (6/02, $17.95) r/#14-21 18.00
Vol. 4: Legacy TPB (2002, $14.99) r/#22-27 15.00
Vol. 5: Public Scrutiny TPB (2003, $11.99) r/#28-32 12.00
Vol. 6: Venom TPB (2003, $15.99) r/#33-39 16.00
Vol. 7: Irresponsible TPB (2003, $12.99) r/#40-45 13.00
Vol. 8: Cats & Kings TPB (2004, $17.99) r/#47-53 18.00
Vol. 9: Ultimate Six TPB (2004, $17.99) r/#46 & Ultimate Six #1-7 18.00
Vol. 10: Hollywood TPB (2004, $12.99) r/#54-59 13.00
Vol. 11: Carnage TPB (2004, $12.99) r/#60-65 13.00
Vol. 12: Superstars TPB (2005, $12.99) r/#66-71 13.00
Vol. 13: Hobgoblin TPB (2005, $15.99) r/#72-78 16.00
Vol. 14: Warriors TPB (2005, $17.99) r/#79-85 18.00
Vol. 15: Silver Sable TPB (2006, $15.99) r/#86-90 & Annual #1 16.00
Vol. 16: Deadpool TPB (2006, $19.99) r/#91-96 & Annual #2 20.00
Vol. 17: Clone Saga TPB (2007, $24.99) r/#97-105 25.00
Vol. 18: Ultimate Knights TPB (2007, $13.99) r/#106-111 14.00
Vol. 19: Death of a Goblin TPB (2008, $14.99) r/#112-117 15.00
Hardcover (3/02, $34.95, 7x11", dust jacket) r/#1-13 & Amazing Fantasy #15; sketch pages and Bill Jemas' initial plot and character outlines 35.00
Volume 2 HC (2003, $29.99, 7x11", dust jacket) r/#14-27; pin-ups & sketch pages 30.00
Volume 3 HC (2003, $29.99, 7x11", dust jacket) r/#28-39 & #1/2; script pages 30.00
Volume 4 HC (2004, $29.99, 7x11", dust jacket) r/#40-45, 47-53; sketch pages 30.00
Volume 5 HC (2004, $29.99, 7x11", dust jacket) r/#46,54-59, Ultimate Six #1-7 30.00
Volume 6 HC (2005, $29.99, 7x11", dust jacket) r/#60-71; sketch page 30.00
Volume 7 HC (2006, $29.99, 7x11", dust jacket) r/#72-85; sketch & profile pages 30.00
Volume 8 HC (2007, $29.99, 7x11", dust jacket) r/#86-96 & Annual #1&2; sketch page 30.00
Volume 9 HC (2008, $39.99, 7x11", dust jacket) r/#97-111; sketch pages 40.00
Volume 10 HC (2009, $39.99, 7x11", dust jacket) r/#112-122; sketch pages 40.00
Wizard #1/2 1 3 4 6 8 10

ULTIMATE SPIDER-MAN (2nd series)(Follows Ultimatum x-over)
Marvel Comics: Oct, 2009 - No. 15, Dec, 2010; No. 150, Jan, 2011 - No. 160, Aug, 2011 ($3.99)

1-15: 1-Bendis-s/Lafuente-a/c; new Mysterio. 1-Variant-c by Djurdjevic. 7,8-Miyazawa-a. 9-Spider-Woman app. 4.00
150-(1/11, $5.99) Resumes original numbering; wraparound-c by Lafuente; Bendis-s with art by Lafuente, Pichelli, Joëlle Jones, McKelvie & Young; r/Ult. S-M Special #1 6.00
150-Variant wraparound-c by Bagley 10.00
151-159: 151-154-Black Cat & Mysterio app. 157-Spider-Man shot by Punisher 4.00
153-159-Variant covers. 153-155-Pichelli. 157-McGuinness. 158-McNiven. 159-Cho 8.00
160-Black Polybagged; Bagley cover inside; Death of Spider-Man part 5 4.00
160-Red Polybagged variant; Kaluta cover inside; Death of Spider-Man part 5 20.00

ULTIMATE SPIDER-MAN (3rd series, with Miles Morales)(See Ultimate Fallout #4 for debut)
Marvel Comics: Nov, 2011 - No. 28, Dec, 2013 ($3.99)

1-Polybagged, with Kaare Andrews-c; Bendis-s/Pichelli-a; origin 6 12 18 38 69 100
1-Variant Pichelli-c with unmasked Spider-Man 13 26 39 89 195 300
1-Variant Pichelli-c with Spider-Man & city bkgrd 13 26 39 89 195 300
2 3 6 9 16 23 30
3-28: 4,5-Spider-Woman app. 5-Nick Fury & Ultimates app. 6-Samnee-a. 19-22-Venom War; Pichelli-a. 23-Cloak and Dagger app. 28-Leads into Cataclysm 4.00
#16.1 (12/12, $2.99) Marquez-a; Venom returns 3.00
200-(6/14, $4.99) Art by Marquez and others; 2 interlocking covers by Bagley & Marquez 5.00
Ultimate Comics Spider-Man Must Have 1 (2/12, $4.99) r/#1-3 5.00

ULTIMATE SPIDER-MAN (Based on the animated series)(See Marvel Universe...)

ULTIMATE TALES FLIP MAGAZINE

GD VG FN VF VF/NM NM-
2.0 4.0 6.0 8.0 9.0 9.2

Marvel Comics: July, 2005 - No. 26, Aug, 2007 ($3.99/$4.99)

1-11-Each reprints 2 issues of Ultimate Spider-Man in flip format 4.00
12-26-($4.99) 5.00

ULTIMATE THOR
Marvel Comics: Dec, 2010 - No. 4, Apr, 2011 ($3.99, limited series)

1-4: 1-Hickman-s/Pacheco-a; two covers by Pacheco & Choi; origin story 4.00

ULTIMATE VISION
Marvel Comics: No. 0, Jan, 2007 - No. 5, Jan, 2008 ($2.99, limited series)

0-Reprints back-up serial from Ultimate Extinction and related series; pin-ups 3.00
1-5: 1-(2/07) Carey-s/Peterson-a/c 3.00
TPB (2007, $14.99) r/#0-5; design pages and cover gallery 15.00

ULTIMATE WAR
Marvel Comics: Feb, 2003 - No. 4, Apr, 2003 ($2.25, limited series)

1-4-Millar-s/Bachalo-c/a; The Ultimates vs. Ultimate X-Men 3.00
Ultimate X-Men Vol. 5: Ultimate War TPB (2003, $10.99) r/#1-4 11.00

ULTIMATE WOLVERINE VS. HULK
Marvel Comics: Feb, 2006 - No. 6, July, 2009 ($2.99, limited series)

1,2-Leinil Yu-a/c; Damon Lindelof-s. 2-(4/06) 4.00
1,2-(2009) New printings 3.00
3-6: 3-(5/09) Intro. She-Hulk. 4-Origin She-Hulk 3.00

ULTIMATE X (Follows Ultimatum x-over)
Marvel Comics: Apr, 2010 - No. 5, Aug, 2011 ($3.99)

1-5: 1-Jeph Loeb-s/Art Adams-a; two covers by Adams. 5-Hulk app. 4.00

ULTIMATE X-MEN
Marvel Comics: Feb, 2001 - No. 100, Apr, 2009 ($2.99/$2.25/$2.50)

1-Millar-s/Adam Kubert & Thibert-a; cardstock-c; introduces revised origin and cast separate from regular X-Men continuity 2 4 6 10 16 20
1-DF Edition 3 6 9 14 19 24
1-DF Sketch Cover Edition 3 6 9 16 23 30
1-Free Comic Book Day Edition (7/03) r/#1 with "Free Comic Book Day" banner on-c 3.00
2 2 4 6 9 12 15
3-6 1 3 4 6 8 10
7-10 6.00
11-24,26-33: 13-Intro. Gambit. 18,19-Bachalo-a. 23,24-Andrews-a 4.00
25-($3.50) leads into the Ultimate War mini-series; Kubert-a 5.00
34-Spider-Man-c/app.; Bendis-s begin; Finch-a 5.00
35-74: 35-Spider-Man app. 36,37-Daredevil-c/app. 40-Intro. Angel. 42-Intro. Dazzler. 44-Beast dies. 46-Intro. Mr. Sinister. 50-53-Kubert-a; Gambit app. 54-57,59-63-Immonen-a. 60-Begin $2.50-c. 61-Variant Coipel-c. 66-Kirkman-s begin. 69-Begin $2.99-c 3.00
61-Retailer Edition with variant Coipel B&W sketch-c 10.00
75-($3.99) Turner-c; intro. Cable; back-up story with Emma Frost's students 4.00
76-99: 76-Intro. Bishop. 91-Fantastic Four app. 92-96-Phoenix app. 96-Spider-Man app. 99-Ultimatum x-over 3.00
100-($3.99) Ultimatum x-over; Brooks-a 4.00
Annual 1 (10/05, $3.99) Vaughan-s/Raney-a; Gambit & Rogue in Vegas 4.00
Annual 2 (10/06, $3.99) Kirkman-s/Larroca-a; Nightcrawler & Dazzler 4.00
.../Fantastic Four 1 (2/06, $2.99) Carey-s/Ferry-a; concluded in Ult. Fantastic Four/X-Men 3.00
... MGC #1 (6/11, $1.00) r/#1 with "Marvel's Greatest Comics" logo on cover 3.00
.../Ult. Fantastic Four Ann. 1 (11/08, $3.99) Continues in Ult. F.F./Ult. X-Men Annual #1 4.00
.../Fantastic Four TPB (2006, $12.99) reprints Ult X-Men/Ult. FF x-over and Official Handbook of the Ultimate Marvel Universe #1-2 13.00
... Ultimate Collection Vol. 1 (2006, $24.99) r/#1-12 & #1/2; unused Bendis script for #1 25.00
... Ultimate Collection Vol. 2 (2007, $24.99) r/#13-25; Kubert cover sketch pages 25.00
...: (Vol. 1) The Tomorrow People TPB (7/01, $14.95) r/#1-6 15.00
...: (Vol. 2) Return to Weapon X TPB (4/02, $14.95) r/#7-12 15.00
Vol. 3: World Tour TPB (2002, $17.99) r/#13-20 18.00
Vol. 4: Hellfire and Brimstone TPB (2003, $12.99) r/#21-25 13.00
Vol. 5 (See Ultimate War)
Vol. 6: Return of the King TPB (2003, $16.99) r/#26-33 17.00
Vol. 7: Blockbuster TPB (2004, $12.99) r/#34-39 13.00
Vol. 8: New Mutants TPB (2004, $12.99) r/#40-45 13.00
Vol. 9: The Tempest TPB (2004, $10.99) r/#46-49 11.00
Vol. 10: Cry Wolf TPB (2005, $8.99) r/#50-53 9.00
Vol. 11: The Most Dangerous Game TPB (2005, $9.99) r/#54-57 10.00
Vol. 12: Hard Lessons TPB (2005, $12.99) r/#58-60 & Annual #1 13.00
Vol. 13: Magnetic North TPB (2006, $12.99) r/#61-65 13.00
Vol. 14: Phoenix? TPB (2006, $14.99) r/#66-71 15.00
Vol. 15: Magical TPB (2007, $11.99) r/#72-74 & Annual #2 12.00
Vol. 16: Cable TPB (2007, $14.99) r/#75-80; sketch pages 15.00
Vol. 17: Sentinels TPB (2008, $17.99) r/#81-88 18.00
Volume 1 HC (8/02, $34.99, 7x11", dust jacket) r/#1-12 & Giant-Size X-Men #1;

Ultimate X-Men (2011 series) #1 © MAR

Ultraman Tiga #1 © Tsuburaya Prods.

The Umbrella Academy: Dallas #6 © Gerald Way

GD	VG	FN	VF	VF/NM	NM-
2.0	4.0	6.0	8.0	9.0	9.2

sketch pages and Millar and Bendis' initial plot and character outlines 35.00
Volume 2 HC (2003, $29.99, 7x11", dust jacket) r/#13-25; script for #20 30.00
Volume 3 HC (2003, $29.99, 7x11", dust jacket) r/#26-33 & Ultimate War #1-4 30.00
Volume 4 HC (2005, $29.99, 7x11", dust jacket) r/#34-45 30.00
Volume 5 HC (2006, $29.99, 7x11", dust jacket) r/#46-57; Vaughan intro.; sketch pages 30.00
Volume 6 HC (2006, $29.99, 7x11", dust jacket) r/#58-65, Annual #1 & Wizard #1/2 30.00
Volume 7 HC (2007, $29.99, 7x11", dust jacket) r/#66-74, Annual #2 30.00
Wizard #1/2 2 4 6 9 12 15

ULTIMATE X-MEN (Ultimate Comics X-Men) (See Cataclysm)
Marvel Comics: Nov, 2011 - No. 33, Dec, 2013 ($3.99)

1-Spencer-s/Medina-a/Andrews-c; polybagged 4.00
1-Variant-c by Mark Bagley 6.00
2-33: 2-Rogue returns. 6-Prof. X returns. 21-Iron Patriot app. 4.00
#18.1 (1/13, $2.99) Andrade-a/Pichelli-c 3.00
Ultimate Comics X-Men Must Have 1 (2/12, $4.99) r/#1-3 5.00

ULTIMATUM
Marvel Comics: Jan, 2009 - No. 5, July, 2009 ($3.99, limited series)

1-5-Loeb-s/Finch-a; cover by Finch & ; Ultimate heroes vs. Magneto 4.00
1-5-Variant covers by McGuinness 8.00
5-Double gatefold variant-c by Finch 4.00
March on Ultimatum Saga ('08, giveaway) text and art panel history of Ultimate universe 3.00
...: Fantastic Four Requiem 1 (9/09,$3.99) Pokaski-s/Atkins-a; Dr. Strange app. 4.00
...: Spider-Man Requiem 1,2 (8/09, 9/09,$3.99) Bendis-s/Bagley & Immonen-a 4.00
...: X-Men Requiem 1 (9/09,$3.99) Coleite-s/Oliver-a/Brooks-c 4.00
NOTE: *Numerous variant covers and 2nd & 3rd printings exist.*

ULTRA
Image Comics: Aug, 2004 - No. 8, Mar, 2005 ($2.95, limited series)

1-8: 1-Intro. Ultra/Pearl Penalosa; Luna Brothers-s/a 3.00
Vol. 1: Seven Days TPB (4/05, $17.95) r/#1-8; sketch pages 18.00

ULTRAFORCE (1st Series) (Also see Avengers/Ultraforce #1)
Malibu Comics (Ultraverse): Aug, 1994 - No. 10, Aug, 1995 ($1.95/$2.50)

0 (9/94, $2.50)-Perez-c/a. 4.00
1-($2.50, 44 pgs.)-Bound-in trading card; team consisting of Prime, Prototype, Hardcase, Pixx, Ghoul, Contrary & Topaz; Gerard Jones scripts begin, ends #6; Pérez-c/a begins 4.00
1-Ultra 5000 Limited Silver Foil Edition 1 2 3 5 6 8
1-Holographic-c, no price 1 2 3 6 8 10
2-5: Perez-c/a in all. 2 (10/94, $1.95)-Prime quits, Strangers cameo. 3-Origin of Topaz; Prime rejoins. 5-Pixx dies. 3.00
2 ($2.50)-Florescent logo; limited edition stamp on-c 4.00
6-10: 6-Begin $2.50-c, Perez-c/a. 7-Ghoul story, Steve Erwin-a. 8-Marvel's Black Knight enters the Ultraverse (last seen in Avengers #375); Perez-c/a. 9,10-Black Knight app.; Perez-c. 10-Leads into Ultraforce/Avengers Prelude 3.00
Malibu "Ashcan ": Ultraforce #0A (6/94) 3.00
.../Avengers Prelude 1 (8/95, $2.50)-Perez-c. 3.00
.../Avengers 1 (8/95, $3.95)-Warren Ellis script; Perez-c/a; foil-c 4.00

ULTRAFORCE (2nd Series)(Also see Black September)
Malibu Comics (Ultraverse): Infinity, Sept, 1995 - V2#15, Dec, 1996 ($1.50)

Infinity, V2#1-15: Infinity-Team consists of Marvel's Black Knight, Ghoul, Topaz, Prime & redesigned Prototype; Warren Ellis scripts begin, ends #3; variant-c exists. 1-1st app.Cromwell, Lament & Wreckage. 2-Contains free encore presentation of Ultraforce #1; flip book "Phoenix Resurrection" Pt. 7. 7-Darick Robertson, Jeff Johnson & others-a. 8,9-Intro. Future Ultraforce (Prime, Hellblade, Angel of Destruction, Painkiller & Whipslash); Gary Erskine-c/a. 9-Foxfire app. 10-Len Wein scripts & Deodato Studios-c/a begin. 10-Lament back-up story. 11-Ghoul back-up story by Pander Bros. 12-Ultraforce vs. Maxis (cont'd in Ultraverse Unlimited #2); Exiles & Iron Clad app. 13-Prime leaves; Hardcase returns 3.00
Infinity (2000 signed) 4.00
.../Spider-Man ($3.95)-Marv Wolfman script; Green Goblin app; 2 covers exist. 4.00

ULTRAGIRL
Marvel Comics: Nov, 1996 - No. 3 Mar, 1997 ($1.50, limited series)

1-1st app.; Barbara Kesel-s/Leonard Kirk-a 6.00
2,3-New Warriors app. 3.00

ULTRA KLUTZ
Onward Comics: 1981; 6/86 - #27, 1/89, #28, 4/90 - #31, 1990? ($1.50/$1.75/$2.00, B&W)

1 (1981)-Re-released after 2nd #1 3.00
1-30: 1-(6/86). 27-Photo back-c 3.00
31-($2.95, 52 pgs.) 4.00

ULTRAMAN
Nemesis Comics: Mar, 1994 - No. 4, Sept, 1994 ($1.75/$1.95)

1-($2.25)-Collector's edition; foil-c; special 3/4 wraparound-c 4.00
1-($1.75)-Newsstand edition 3.00
2-4: 3-$1.95-c begins 3.00
#(-1) (3/93) 3.00

ULTRAMAN TIGA
Dark Horse Comics: Aug, 2003 - No. 10, June, 2004 ($3.99)

1-10-Khoo Fuk Lung-a/Tony Wong-s 4.00

ULTRAVERSE DOUBLE FEATURE
Malibu Comics (Ultraverse): Jan, 1995 ($3.95, one-shot, 68 pgs.)

1-Flip-c featuring Prime & Solitaire. 4.00

ULTRAVERSE ORIGINS
Malibu Comics (Ultraverse): Jan, 1994 (99¢, one-shot)

1-Gatefold-c; 2 pg. origins all characters 3.00
1-Newsstand edition; different-c, no gatefold 3.00

ULTRAVERSE PREMIERE
Malibu Comics (Ultraverse): 1994 (one-shot)

0-Ordered thru mail w/coupons 5.00

ULTRAVERSE UNLIMITED
Malibu Comics (Ultraverse): June, 1996; No. 2, Sept, 1996 ($2.50)

1,2: 1-Adam Warlock returns to the Marvel Universe; Rune-c/app. 2-Black Knight, Reaper & Sierra Blaze return to the Marvel Universe 3.00

ULTRAVERSE YEAR ONE
Malibu Comics (Ultraverse): 1994 ($4.95, one-shot)

nn-In-depth synopsis of the first year's titles & stories. 5.00

ULTRAVERSE YEAR TWO
Malibu Comics (Ultraverse): Aug, 1995 ($4.95, one-shot)

nn-In-depth synopsis of second year's titles & stories 5.00

ULTRAVERSE YEAR ZERO: THE DEATH OF THE SQUAD
Malibu Comics (Ultraverse): Apr, 1995 - No. 4, July, 1995 ($2.95, lim. series)

1-4: 3-Codename: Firearm back-up story. 3.00

ULTRON (See Age of Ultron series)
Marvel Comics: Jun, 2013 ($3.99, one-shot)

1AU-Victor Mancha from the Runaways (son of Ultron); K. Immonen-s/Pinna-a 4.00

UMBRAL
Image Comics: Nov, 2013 - No. 12, Jan, 2015 ($2.99)

1-12-Johnston-s/Mitten-a 3.00

UMBRELLA ACADEMY (Also see Hazel & Cha Cha Save Christmas)
Dark Horse Comics: Apr, 2007

1-Free Comic Book Day Edition - previews of the upcoming series; James Jean-c; Zero Killer & Pantheon City on back-c 5 10 15 33 57 80

UMBRELLA ACADEMY: APOCALYPSE SUITE
Dark Horse Comics: Sept, 2007 - No. 6, Feb, 2008 ($2.99, limited series)

1-Origin of the Umbrella Academy; Gerald Way-s/Gabriel Bá-a/James Jean-c 4 8 12 27 44 60
1-White variant-c by Bá 5 10 15 34 60 85
1-Variant-c by Gerald Way 6 12 18 42 79 115
1-2nd printing with variant-c by Bá 1 3 4 6 8 10
2-6 2 4 6 8 10 12
...: One for One (9/10, $1.00) r/#1 with red cover frame 2 4 6 9 12 15
Vol.1: Apocalypse Suite TPB (7/08, $17.95) r/#1-6, FCBD story and web shorts; design art; Grant Morrison intro.; cover gallery 3 6 9 18 24 32

UMBRELLA ACADEMY: DALLAS
Dark Horse Comics: Nov, 2008 - No. 6, May, 2009 ($2.99, limited series)

1-6-Gerald Way-s/Gabriel Bá-a/c 2 4 6 8 10 12
1-Wraparound variant-c by Jim Lee 3 6 9 19 30 40

UMBRELLA ACADEMY: HOTEL OBLIVION
Dark Horse Comics: Oct, 2018 - No. 7, Jun, 2019 ($3.99, limited series)

1-Gerald Way-s/Gabriel Bá-a/c in all 1 3 4 6 8 10
2-7 4.00

UNBEATABLE SQUIRREL GIRL, THE
Marvel Comics: Mar, 2015 - No. 8, Oct, 2015 ($3.99)

1-8: 1-Doreen Green and Tippy-Toe at college; North-s/Henderson-a. 1-Kraven app. 3,4-Galactus app. 7-Avengers cameo. 8-Lady Thor, Odinson & Loki app. 4.00

UNBEATABLE SQUIRREL GIRL, THE
Marvel Comics: Dec, 2015 - No. 50, Jan, 2020 ($3.99)

The Unbelievable Gwenpool #4 © MAR

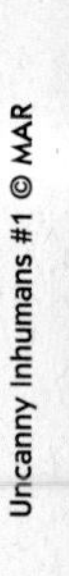

Uncanny Inhumans #1 © MAR

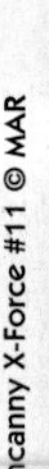

Uncanny X-Force #11 © MAR

GD	VG	FN	VF	VF/NM	NM-
2.0	4.0	6.0	8.0	9.0	9.2

1-25,27-50: 1-North-s/Henderson-a. 2-Doreen goes to the 1960s; Doctor Doom app. 6-Crossover with Howard the Duck #6. 10-Mole Man app. 13,14-Scott Lang app. 16-25th Anniversary issue; origin re-told; Hulk app. 23-25-Dinosaur Ultron app. 43-46-War of the Realms tie-ins. 43-Intro. Ratatoskr. 48-50-Iron Man app. 4.00
26-"Zine" issue; includes Silver Surfer/Galactus by Garfield's Jim Davis (2 pgs.) 4.00
... Beats Up The Marvel Universe (2016, $24.99, HC) original graphic novel; North-s; Henderson-a; Spider-Man & Avengers app.; bonus game pages and design art 25.00
...: You Choose the Story No. 1 Halloween Comic Fest 2016 (giveaway, 12/16) r/#7 3.00

UN-BEDABLE VARK, THE (Reprints from Cerebus in Hell)
Aardvark-Vanaheim: Jun, 2018 ($4.00, B&W)

1-Cerebus figures over original Gustave Doré artwork of Hell; Inc. Hulk #1-c swipe 4.00

UNBELIEVABLE GWENPOOL, THE (Also see Gwenpool Special)
Marvel Comics: Jun, 2016 - No. 25, Apr, 2018 ($3.99)

1-($4.99) Hastings-s/Gurihiru-a; MODOK app. 2 4 6 9 12 15
2-25-($3.99) 2-Thor (Jane) app. 3-Doctor Strange app. 5,6,19,20-Spider-Man (Miles) app. 13-Deadpool app. 14,15-Hawkeye & Ghost Rider app. 22,23-Doctor Doom app. 4.00
#0-(7/16, $4.99) Reprints apps. in Howard the Duck #1-3 & Gwenpool Special #1 2 4 6 9 12 15

UNBIRTHDAY PARTY WITH ALICE IN WONDERLAND (See Alice In Wonderland, Four Color #341)

UNCANNY
Dynamite Entertainment: 2013 - No. 6, 2014 ($3.99)

1-6-Andy Diggle-s/Aaron Campbell-a 4.00

UNCANNY, (SEASON TWO)
Dynamite Entertainment: 2015 - No. 6, 2015 ($3.99)

1-6-Andy Diggle-s/Aaron Campbell-a 4.00

UNCANNY AVENGERS (Marvel NOW!)
Marvel Comics: Dec, 2012 - No. 25, Dec, 2014 ($3.99)

1-25: 1-Capt. America, Thor, Scarlet Witch, Wolverine, Havok & Rogue team; Remender-s/Cassaday-a; Red Skull app. 5-Coipel-a. 14-Rogue & Scarlet Witch die. 24,25-Axis 4.00
8AU-(7/13, $3.99) Age of Ultron tie-in; Adam Kubert-a 4.00
Annual 1 (6/14, $4.99) Remender-s/Renaud-a/Art Adams-c; Mojo app. 5.00

UNCANNY AVENGERS
Marvel Comics: Mar, 2015 - No. 5, Aug, 2015 ($3.99)

1-5: 1-Capt. America (Sam Wilson), Vision, Scarlet Witch, Quicksilver, Sabretooth, Rogue & Doctor Voodoo team; Remender-s/Acuna-a 4.00

UNCANNY AVENGERS
Marvel Comics: Dec, 2015 - No. 30, Feb, 2018 ($3.99)

1-($4.99) Steve Rogers, Spider-Man, Deadpool, Human Torch, Quicksilver, Rogue, Synapse & Doctor Voodoo team; Duggan-s/Stegman-a 5.00
2-20,26-30-($3.99) 2-5-Cable app. 5,6-Pacheco-a. 7,8-Pleasant Hill Standoff tie-ins. 13,14-Civil War II tie-in. 16,17-Hulk returns. 24-Secret Empire tie-in. 26-Scarlet Witch joins. 29-Juggernaut app. 4.00
25-($4.99) Secret Empire tie-in; Shocker & Scorpina app.; Zub-s/Jacinto-a 5.00
Annual 1 (1/16, $4.99) Robinson-s/Laming & Giles-a/Deodato-c; Emerald Warlock app. 5.00

UNCANNY AVENGERS: ULTRON FOREVER
Marvel Comics: Jul, 2015 ($4.99)(Continued from New Avengers: Ultron Forever)

1-Part 3 of 3-part crossover with Avengers and New Avengers; Ewing-s/Alan Davis-a; team-up of past, present and future Avengers vs. Ultron 5.00

UNCANNY INHUMANS
Marvel Comics: No. 0, Jun, 2015; No. 1, Dec, 2015 - No. 20, May, 2017 ($4.99/$3.99)

0-Soule-s/McNiven-a/c; Black Bolt, Medusa & Kang the Conqueror app. 5.00
1-($4.99) Johnny Storm, Beast & Kang the Conqueror app. 5.00
2-19-($3.99) 2-4-Kang app. 5-Mad Thinker and The Leader app. 11-14-Civil War II tie-in 4.00
20-($4.99) Leads into Inhumans Prime #1 5.00
#1.MU (4/17, $4.99) Monsters Unleashed tie-in; Allor-s/Level-a 5.00
Annual 1 (10/16, $4.99) Soule-s/Kev Walker-a 5.00

UNCANNY ORIGINS
Marvel Comics: Sept, 1996 - No. 14, Oct, 1997 (99¢)

1-14: 1-Cyclops. 2-Quicksilver. 3-Archangel. 4-Firelord. 5-Hulk. 6-Beast. 7-Venom. 8-Nightcrawler. 9-Storm. 10-Black Cat. 11-Black Knight. 12-Dr. Strange. 13-Daredevil. 14-Iron Fist 3.00

UNCANNY SKULLKICKERS (See Skullkickers #19)

UNCANNY TALES
Atlas Comics (PrPl/PPI): June, 1952 - No. 56, Sept, 1957

1-Heath-a; horror / weird stories begin 151 302 453 966 1658 2350
2 73 146 219 467 796 1125
3-5 66 132 198 419 722 1025
6-Wolvertonish-a by Matt Fox 69 138 207 442 759 1075
7-10: 8-Atom bomb story; Tothish-a (by Sekowsky?). 9-Crandall-a 58 116 174 371 636 900
11-20: 17-Atom bomb panels; anti-communist story; Hitler story. 19-Krenkel-a. 20-Robert Q. Sale-c 50 100 150 315 533 750
21-25,27: 25-Nostrand-a? 43 86 129 271 461 650
26-Spider-Man prototype c/story 77 154 231 493 847 1200
28-Last precode issue (1/55); Kubert-a; #1-28 contain 2-3 sci/fi stories each 42 84 126 265 445 625
29-41,43-49,51: 29-Variant-c exists with Feb. blanked out and Mar. printed on. Regular version just has Mar. 32 64 96 190 310 430
42,54,56-Krigstein-a 33 66 99 194 317 440
50,53,55-Torres-a 32 64 96 190 310 430
52-Oldest Iron Man prototype (2/57) 40 80 120 244 402 560

NOTE: ***Andru** a-15, 27. **Ayers** a-14, 22, 28, 37. **Bailey** a-51. **Briefer** a-19, 20. **Brodsky** c-1, 3, 4, 6, 8, 12-16, 19. **Brodsky/Everett** c-9. **Cameron** a-47. **Colan** a-11, 16, 17, 49, 52. **Drucker** a-37, 42, 45. **Everett** a-2, 9, 12, 32, 36, 39, 48; c-7, 11, 17, 39, 41, 50, 52, 53. **Fass** a-9, 10, 15, 24. **Forte** a-18, 27, 33-35, 52, 53. **Heath** a-13, 14; c-5, 10, 18. **Keller** a-3. **Lawrence** a-14, 17, 19, 23, 27, 28, 35. **Maneely** a-4, 8, 10, 16, 29, 35; c-2, 22, 26, 33, 38. **Moldoff** a-23. **Morisi** a-48, 52. **Morrow** a-46, 51. **Orlando** a-49, 50, 53. **Powell** a-12, 18, 34, 36, 38, 43, 50, 56. **Robinson** a-3, 13. **Reinman** a-12, 36. **Romita** a-10. **Roussos** a-8. **Sale** a-34, 47, 53; c-20. **Sekowsky** a-25. **Sinnott** a-14, 15, 38, 52. **Torres** a-53. **Tothish**-a by **Andru**-27. **Wildey** a-22, 48.*

UNCANNY TALES
Marvel Comics Group: Dec, 1973 - No. 12, Oct, 1975

1-Crandall-r/Uncanny Tales #9('50s) 4 8 12 27 44 60
2-12: 7,12-Kirby-a 3 6 9 17 26 35

NOTE: ***Ditko** reprints-#4, 6-8, 10-12.*

UNCANNY X-FORCE
Marvel Comics: Dec, 2010 - No. 35, Feb, 2013 ($3.99)

1-17: 1-Wolverine, Psylocke, Archangel, Fantomex & Deadpool team; Opeña-a; Ribic-c 4.00
1-Variant-c by Clayton Crain 10.00
5.1 (5/11, $2.99) Albuquerque-a/Bianchi-c; Lady Deathstrike app. 3.00
18-Polybagged; Dark Angel Saga conclusion 4.00
19-35: 19-Grampa-c. 20-Yu-c 4.00
19.1 (3/12, $2.99) Remender-s/Tan-a; other-dimension X-Men vs. Apocalypse 3.00
...: The Apocalypse Solution 1 (5/11, $4.99) r/#1-3 5.00

UNCANNY X-FORCE (Marvel NOW!)
Marvel Comics: Mar, 2013 - No. 17, Mar, 2014 ($3.99)

1-17: 1-Storm, Psylocke, Spiral, Fantomex & Puck team; Bishop app.; Garney-a 4.00

UNCANNY X-MEN, THE (See **X-Men, The**, 1st series, #142-on)

UNCANNY X-MEN (2nd series) (X-Men Regenesis)
Marvel Comics: Dec, 2010 - No. 20, Dec, 2012 ($3.99)

1-10: 1-3-Gillen-s/Pacheco-a/c; Mr. Sinister app. 4-Peterson-a. 5-8-Land-a 4.00
1-Variant-c by Keown 6.00
11-20: 11-19-Avengers vs. X-Men x-over 4.00

UNCANNY X-MEN (3rd series) (Marvel NOW!)
Marvel Comics: Apr, 2013 - No. 35, Sept, 2015 ($3.99)

1-24,26-35: 1-Cyclops, Emma Frost, Magneto, Magik team; Bendis-s/Bachalo-a. 2,3-Avengers app. 5-7,10,11-Irving-a. 8,9,12,13,16,17,19,20-22,25,27-32-Bachalo-a. 12,13-Battle of the Atom. 23,24-Original Sin tie-in 4.00
25-($4.99) Original Sin tie-in 5.00
#600-(1/16, $5.99) Stories by various incl. Bendis, Pichelli, Immonen; Bachalo-c 6.00
Annual 1 (2/15, $4.99) Story of Eva Bell; Bendis-s/Sorrentino-a 5.00
Special 1 (8/14, $4.99) Death's Head & Iron Man app.; Ackins-a 5.00

UNCANNY X-MEN (4th series) (After Secret Wars)
Marvel Comics: Mar, 2016 - No. 19, May, 2017 ($3.99)

1-5: 1-Bunn-s/Land-a; Magneto, Psylocke, Sabretooth, M, and Archangel team 4.00
6-($4.99) Apocalypse Wars x-over; Lashley-a 5.00
7-19: 7-10-Apocalypse Wars x-over; Lashley-a. 11-14-Land-a; Hellfire Club app. 4.00
Annual 1 (1/17, $4.99) Bunn-s/Lashley-a; Elixir returns 5.00

UNCANNY X-MEN (5th series)
Marvel Comics: Jan, 2019 - No. 22, Sept, 2019 ($7.99/$3.99)

1-($7.99) Asrar-a; Apocalypse app. 8.00
2-9,12-22-($3.99) 2-Silva-a; Legion returns. 4-Nate Grey returns. 12-16,20-22-Larroca-a 4.00
10-($4.99) Leads into Uncanny X-Men Annual #1 5.00
11-($7.99) Cyclops returns; Captain America app.; Wolverine returns; McCrea-a 8.00
22-($4.99) Leads into X-Men #1 (2019 series); Larrocca-a 5.00
Annual 1 (3/19, $4.99) Cyclops saved by Cable; leads into #11; Carlos Gomez-a 5.00
...: Winter's End 1 (5/19, $4.99) Grace-s/Stockman-a; future Iceman app. 5.00

UNCANNY X-MEN AND THE NEW TEEN TITANS (See Marvel and DC Present...)

UNCANNY X-MEN: FIRST CLASS

Uncle Grandpa #1 © CN

Uncle Sam and the Freedom Fighters #2 © DC

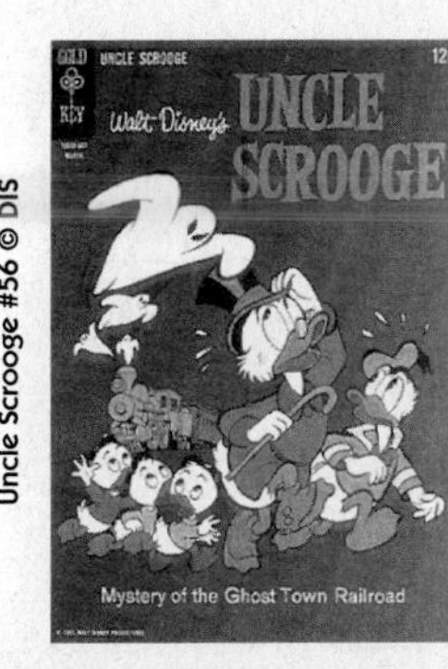

Uncle Scrooge #56 © DIS

	GD	VG	FN	VF	VF/NM	NM-
	2.0	4.0	6.0	8.0	9.0	9.2

Marvel Comics: Sept, 2009 - No. 8, Apr, 2010 ($2.99)

1-8: 1-The X-Men #94 (1975) team; Cruz-a; Inhumans app. 3.00
... Giant-Size Special (8/09, $3.99) short stories by various; Scottie Young-c 4.00

UNCENSORED MOUSE, THE
Eternity Comics: Apr, 1989 - No. 2, Apr, 1989 ($1.95, B&W)(Came sealed in plastic bag) (Both contain racial stereotyping & violence)

1,2-Early Gottfredson strip-r in each 2 4 6 11 16 20
NOTE: *Both issues contain unauthorized reprints. Series was cancelled.* ***Win Smith*** *r-1, 2.*

UNCHARTED (Based on the video game)
DC Comics: Jan, 2012 - No. 6, Jun, 2012 ($2.99, limited series)

1-6-Williamson-s/Sandoval-a. 1-3-Harris-c 3.00

UNCLE CHARLIE'S FABLES (Also see Adventures in Wonderland)
Lev Gleason Publ.: Jan, 1952 - No. 5, Sept, 1952 (All have Biro painted-c)

1-Peter Pester by Hy Mankin begins, ends #5. Michael the Misfit by Kida, Janice & the Lazy Giant by Maurer, Lawrence the Fortune Teller app.; has photo of Biro 19 38 57 111 176 240
2-Fuje-a; Biro photo 11 22 33 64 90 115
3-5: 5-Two Who Built a Dream, The Blacksmith & The Gypsies by Maurer, The Sleepy King by Hubbel; has photo of Biro 10 20 30 56 76 95
NOTE: ***Kida*** *a-1.* ***Hubbell*** *a-5.* ***Hy Mankin*** *a-1-5.* ***Norman Maurer*** *a-1, 5.* ***Dick Rockwell*** *a-5.*

UNCLE DONALD & HIS NEPHEWS DUDE RANCH (See Dell Giant #52)

UNCLE DONALD & HIS NEPHEWS FAMILY FUN (See Dell Giant #38)

UNCLE GRANDPA (Based on the Cartoon Network series)
BOOM! Studios (kaboom!): Oct, 2014 - No. 4, Jan, 2015 ($3.99)

1-4-Short stories and gag pages; multiple covers on each 4.00
...: Good Morning Special 1 (4/16, $4.99) Short stories and gag pages; back-c mask 5.00
...: Pizza Steve Special 1 (6/15, $4.99) Short stories and gag pages 5.00

UNCLE JOE'S FUNNIES
Centaur Publications: 1938 (B&W)

1-Games, puzzles & magic tricks, some interior art; Bill Everett-c 168 336 504 1075 1838 2600

UNCLE MILTY (TV)
Victoria Publications/True Cross: Dec, 1950 - No. 4, July, 1951 (52 pgs.)(Early TV comic)

1-Milton Berle photo on-c of #1,2 55 110 165 352 601 850
2 36 72 108 214 347 480
3,4 30 60 90 177 289 400

UNCLE REMUS & HIS TALES OF BRER RABBIT (See Brer Rabbit, 4-Color #129, 208, 693)

UNCLE SAM
DC Comics (Vertigo): 1997 - No. 2, 1997 ($4.95, limited series)

1,2-Alex Ross painted c/a. Story by Ross and Steve Darnell 5.00
Hardcover (1998, $17.95) 18.00
Softcover (2000, $9.95) 10.00

UNCLE SAM AND THE FREEDOM FIGHTERS
DC Comics: Sept, 2006 - No. 8, Apr, 2007 ($2.99, limited series)

1-8-Acuña-a/c; Gray & Palmiotti-s. 3-Intro. Black Condor 3.00
TPB (2007, $14.99) r/#1-8 and story from DCU Brave New World #1 15.00

UNCLE SAM AND THE FREEDOM FIGHTERS
DC Comics: Nov, 2007 - No. 8, Jun, 2008 ($2.99, limited series)

1-8-Gray & Palmiotti-s/Arlem-a/Johnson-c 3.00
...: Brave New World TPB (2008, $14.99) r/#1-8 15.00

UNCLE SAM QUARTERLY (Blackhawk #9 on)(See Freedom Fighters)
Quality Comics Group: Autumn, 1941 - No. 8, Autumn, 1943 (see National Comics)

1-Origin Uncle Sam; Fine/Eisner-c, chapter headings, 2 pgs. by Eisner; (2 versions: dark cover, no price; light cover with price sticker); Jack Cole-a 377 754 1131 2639 4620 6600
2-Cameos by The Ray, Black Condor, Quicksilver, The Red Bee, Alias the Spider, Hercules & Neon the Unknown; Eisner, Fine-c/a 155 310 465 992 1696 2400
3-Tuska-c/a; Eisner-a(2) 123 246 369 787 1344 1900
4-Hitler app. 116 232 348 742 1271 1800
5,7-Hitler, Mussolini & Tojo-c 161 322 483 1030 1765 2500
6,8 77 154 231 493 847 1200
NOTE: ***Kotzky*** *(or* ***Tuska****) a-3-8.*

UNCLE SCROOGE (Disney) (Becomes Walt Disney's... #210 on) (See Cartoon Tales, Dell Giants #33, 55, Disney Comic Album, Donald and Scrooge, Dynabrite, Four Color #178, Gladstone Comic Album, Walt Disney's Comics & Stories #98, Walt Disney's ...)
Dell #1-39/Gold Key #40-173/Whitman #174-209: No. 386, 3/52 - No. 39, 8-10/62; No. 40, 12/62 - No. 209, 7/84

	GD	VG	FN	VF	VF/NM	NM-
	2.0	4.0	6.0	8.0	9.0	9.2

Four Color 386(#1)-in "Only a Poor Old Man" by Carl Barks; r-in Uncle Scrooge & Donald Duck #1('65) & The Best of Walt Disney Comics ('74). The 2nd cover app. of Uncle Scrooge (see Dell Giant Vacation Parade #2 (7/51) for 1st-c) 185 370 555 1500 4000 6500
1-(1986)-Reprints F.C. #386; given away with lithograph "Dam Disaster at Money Lake" & as a subscription offer giveaway to Gladstone subscribers 3 6 9 15 20 24
Four Color 456(#2)-in "Back to the Klondike" by Carl Barks; r-in Best of U.S. & D.D. #1('66) & Gladstone C.A. #4 90 180 270 720 1860 3000
Four Color 495(#3)-r-in #105 60 120 180 480 1240 2000
4(12-2/53-54)-r-in Gladstone Comic Album #11 46 92 138 340 770 1200
5-r-in Gladstone Special #2 & Walt Disney Digest #1 37 74 111 274 612 950
6-r-in U.S. #106,165,233 & Best of U.S. & D.D. #1('66) 34 68 102 245 548 850
7-The Seven Cities of Cibola by Barks; r-in #217 & Best of D.D. & U.S. #2 ('67) 30 60 90 216 483 750
8-10: 8-r-in #111,222. 9-r-in #104,214. 10-r-in #67 26 52 78 182 404 625
11-20: 11-r-in #237. 17-r-in #215. 19-r-in Gladstone C.A. #1. 20-r-in #213 21 42 63 147 324 500
21-30: 24-X-Mas-c. 26-r-in #211 16 32 48 112 249 385
31-35,37-40: 34-r-in #228. 40-X-Mas-c 15 30 45 103 227 350
36-1st app. Magica De Spell; Number one dime 1st identified by name 15 30 45 100 220 340
41-60: 48-Magica De Spell-c/story (3/64). 49-Sci/fi-c. 51-Beagle Boys-c/story (8/64) 11 22 33 73 157 240
61-63,65,66,68-71:71-Last Barks issue w/original story (#71-he only storyboarded the script) 10 20 30 66 138 210
64-(7/66) Barks Vietnam War story "Treasure of Marco Polo" banned for reprints by Disney from 1977-1989 because of its Third World revolutionary war theme. It later appeared in the hardcover Carl Barks Library set (4/89) and Walt Disney's Uncle Scrooge Adventures #42 (1/97) 15 30 45 103 227 350
67,72,73: 67,72,73-Barks-r 9 18 27 60 120 180
74-84: 74-Barks-r(1pg.). 75-81,83-Not by Barks. 82,84-Barks-r begin 7 14 21 44 82 120
85-100 6 12 18 38 69 100
101-110 5 10 15 33 57 80
111-120 4 8 12 27 44 60
121-141,143-152,154-157 3 6 9 21 33 45
142-Reprints Four Color #456 with-c 4 8 12 22 35 48
153,158,162-164,166,168-170,178,180: No Barks 3 6 9 15 22 28
155-Whitman edition 3 6 9 17 26 35
159-160,165,167 3 6 9 16 23 30
161(r/#14), 171(r/#11), 177(r/#16),183(r/#6)-Barks-r 3 6 9 16 23 30
172(1/80),173(2/80)-Gold Key. Barks-a 3 6 9 17 26 35
174(3/80),175(4/80),176(5/80)-Whitman. Barks-a 4 8 12 22 35 48
177(6/80),178(7/80) 4 8 12 23 37 50
179(9/80)(r/#9)-(Very low distribution) 37 74 111 274 612 950
180(11/80),181(12/80, r/4-Color #495), pre-pack? 8 16 24 51 96 140
182-195: 182-(50¢-c). 184,185,187,188-Barks-a. 182,186,191-194-No Barks. 189(r/#5), 190(r/#4), 195(r/4-Color #386) 3 6 9 16 23 30
182(1/81, 40¢-c) Cover price error variant 4 8 12 22 35 48
196(4/82),197(5/82): 196(r/#13) 3 6 9 17 26 35
198-209 (All #90038 on-c; pre-pack; no date or date code): 198(4/83), 199(5/83), 200(6/83), 201(6/83), 202(7/83), 203(7/83), 204(8/83), 205(8/83), 206(4/84), 207(5/83), 208(6/84), 209(7/84). 198-202,204-206: No Barks. 203(r/#12), 207(r/#93,92), 208(r/U.S. #18), 209(r/U.S. #21)-Barks-r 4 8 12 25 40 55
Uncle Scrooge & Money(G.K.)-Barks-r/from WDC&S #130 (3/67) 5 10 15 31 53 75
Mini Comic #1(1976)(3-1/4x6-1/2")-r/U.S. #115; Barks-c 2 4 6 8 10 12
NOTE: ***Barks*** *c-Four Color 386, 456, 495, #4-37, 39, 40, 43-71.*

UNCLE SCROOGE (See Walt Disney's Uncle Scrooge for previous issues)
Boom Entertainment (BOOM! Kids): No. 384, Oct, 2009 - No. 404, Jun, 2011 ($2.99/$3.99)

384-399: 384-Magica de Spell app.; 2 covers. 392-399-Duck Tales 3.00
400-(2/11, $3.99) "Carl Barks" apps. as Scrooge story-teller; Rosa wraparound-c 4.00
400-$6.99) Deluxe Edition with Barks painted cover of Four Color #386 cover image 7.00
401-404: 401-($3.99)-Rosa-s/a 4.00
...: The Mysterious Stone Ray and Cash Flow (5/11, $6.99) reprints; Barks-s/a; Rosa-s/a 7.00

UNCLE SCROOGE
IDW Publishing: Apr, 2015 - Present ($3.99/$4.99)

1-Legacy numbered #405; art by Scarpa and others; multiple covers 4.00
2-43-English translations of Dutch, Norwegian & Italian stories; multiple covers on each 4.00
44-49,51-54 ($4.99) 5.00
50-($5.99) Magica de Spell app. 6.00

Undercover Girl #6 © ME

Underwinter #4 © Fawkes & Piper Snow

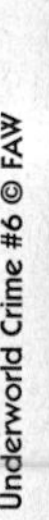
Underworld Crime #6 © FAW

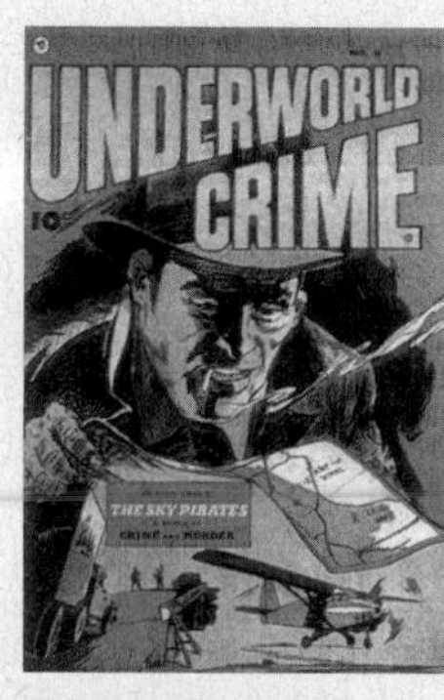

	GD 2.0	VG 4.0	FN 6.0	VF 8.0	VF/NM 9.0	NM- 9.2

UNCLE SCROOGE AND DONALD DUCK
Gold Key: June, 1965 (25¢, paper cover)

1-Reprint of Four Color #386(#1) & lead story from Four Color #29	8	16	24	51	96	140

UNCLE SCROOGE COMICS DIGEST
Gladstone Publishing: Dec, 1986 - No. 5, Aug, 1987 ($1.25, Digest-size)

1,3	1	2	3	5	6	8
2,4						6.00
5 (low print run)	1	2	3	5	7	9

UNCLE SCROOGE GOES TO DISNEYLAND (See Dell Giants)
Gladstone Publishing Ltd.: Aug, 1985 ($2.50)

1-Reprints Dell Giant w/new-c by Mel Crawford, based on old cover	2	4	6	8	10	12
...Comics Digest 1 ($1.50, digest size)	2	4	6	8	11	14

UNCLE SCROOGE IN COLOR
Gladstone Publishing: 1987 ($29.95, Hardcover, 9-1/4"X12-1/4", 96 pgs.)

nn-Reprints "Christmas on Bear Mountain" from Four Color 178 by Barks; Uncle Scrooge's Christmas Carol (published as Donald Duck & the Christmas Carol, A Little Golden Book), reproduced from the original art as adapted by Norman McGary from pencils by Barks; and Uncle Scrooge the Lemonade King, reproduced from the original art, plus Barks' original pencils	4	8	12	25	40	55
nn-Slipcase edition of 750, signed by Barks, issued at $79.95						300.00

UNCLE SCROOGE: MY FIRST MILLIONS
IDW Publishing: Sept, 2018 - No. 4, Dec, 2018 ($3.99, limited series)

1-4-English version of Italian comics; Vitaliano-s; multiple covers						4.00

UNCLE SCROOGE THE LEMONADE KING
Whitman Publishing Co.: 1960 (A Top Top Tales Book, 6-3/8"x7-5/8", 32 pgs.)

2465-Storybook pencilled by Carl Barks, finished art adapted by Norman McGary	33	66	99	238	532	825

UNCLE WIGGILY (See March of Comics #19) (Also see Animal Comics)
Dell Publishing Co.: No. 179, Dec, 1947 - No. 543, Mar, 1954

Four Color 179 (#1)-Walt Kelly-c	14	28	42	97	214	330
Four Color 221 (3/49)-Part Kelly-c	9	18	27	60	120	180
Four Color 276 (5/50), 320 (#1, 3/51)	7	14	21	49	92	135
Four Color 349 (9-10/51), 391 (4-5/52)	6	12	18	41	76	110
Four Color 428 (10/52), 503 (10/53), 543	5	10	15	34	63	90

UNDATEABLE VARK, THE (Reprints from Cerebus in Hell)
Aardvark-Vanaheim: May, 2018 ($4.00, B&W)

1-Cerebus figures over Gustave Doré artwork of Hell; Uncanny X-Men #141-c swipe						4.00

UNDEAD, THE
Chaos! Comics (Black Label): Feb, 2002 ($4.99, B&W)

1-Pulido-s/Denham-a						5.00

UNDERCOVER GIRL (Starr Flagg) (See Extra Comics, Manhunt! & Trail Colt)
Magazine Enterprises: No. 5, 1952 - No. 7, 1954

5(#1)(A-1 #62)-Fallon of the F.B.I. in all	40	80	120	244	402	560
6(A-1 #98), 7(A-1 #118)-All have Starr Flagg	39	78	117	236	388	540

NOTE: *Powell c-6, 7. Whitney a-5-7.*

UNDERDOG (TV)(See Kite Fun Book, March of Comics #426, 438, 467, 479)
Charlton Comics/Gold Key: July, 1970 - No. 10, Jan, 1972; Mar, 1975 - No. 23, Feb, 1979

1 (1st series, Charlton)-1st app. Underdog	11	22	33	75	160	245
2-10	6	12	18	38	69	100
1 (2nd series, Gold Key)	6	12	18	41	76	110
2-10	4	8	12	23	37	50
11-20: 13-1st app. Shack of Solitude	3	6	9	18	28	38
21-23	3	6	9	19	30	40

UNDERDOG
Spotlight Comics: 1987 - No. 3?, 1987 ($1.50)

1-3						4.00

UNDERDOG (Volume 2)
Harvey Comics: Nov, 1993 - No. 5, July, 1994 ($2.25)

1-5						4.00
Summer Special (10/93, $2.25, 68 pgs.)						4.00

UNDERDOG
American Mythology Productions: Apr, 2017 - No. 3, 2018 ($3.99)

1-3: 1-New stories and reprint #1 (1970); multiple covers incl. Action #1 swipe						4.00
...and Pals 1-3 (2019, $3.99) New stories and reprint; 2 covers on each						4.00
... 1975 #1 (2017, $3.99) Reprints stories from #23 (1979) and unpublished #24						4.00

UNDERSEA AGENT
Tower Comics: Jan, 1966 - No. 6, Mar, 1967 (25¢, 68 pgs.)

1-Davy Jones, Undersea Agent begins	8	16	24	51	96	140
2-6: 2-Jones gains magnetic powers. 5-Origin & 1st app. of Merman. 6-Kane/Wood-c(r)	5	10	15	34	60	85

NOTE: *Gil Kane a-3-6; c-4, 5. Moldoff a-2i.*

UNDERSEA FIGHTING COMMANDOS (See Fighting Undersea...)
I.W. Enterprises: 1964

I.W. Reprint #1,2('64): 1-r/#? 2-r/#1; Severin-c	2	4	6	9	13	16

UNDERTAKER (World Wrestling Federation)(Also see WWE Undertaker)
Chaos! Comics: Feb, 1999 - No. 10, Jan, 2000 ($2.50/$2.95)

Preview (2/99)						3.00
1-10: Reg. and photo covers for each. 1-(4/99)						3.00
1-($6.95) DF Ed.; Brereton painted-c						7.00
...Halloween Special (10/99, $2.95) Reg. & photo-c						3.00
Wizard #0						3.00

UNDERWATER CITY, THE
Dell Publishing Co.: No. 1328, 1961

Four Color 1328-Movie, Evans-a	7	14	21	46	86	125

UNDERWINTER
Image Comics: Mar, 2017 - No. 6, Aug, 2017 ($3.99)

1-6-Ray Fawkes-s/a/c. 1-Lemire var-c. 2-Nguyen var-c. 3-Zdarsky var-c						4.00

UNDERWINTER: A FIELD OF FEATHERS
Image Comics: Oct, 2017 - No. 5, Feb, 2018 ($3.99)

1-4-Ray Fawkes-s/a/c. 1-Fawkes var-c						4.00

UNDERWORLD (...True Crime Stories)
D. S. Publishing Co.: Feb-Mar, 1948 - No. 9, June-July, 1949 (52 pgs.)

1-Moldoff (Shelly)-c; excessive violence	55	110	165	352	601	850
2-Moldoff (Shelly)-c; Ma Barker story used in **SOTI**, pg. 95; female electrocution panel; lingerie art	48	96	144	302	514	725
3-McWilliams-c/a; extreme violence, mutilation	43	86	129	271	461	650
4-Used in Love and Death by Legman; Ingels-a	45	90	135	284	480	675
5-Ingels-a	26	52	78	156	256	355
6-9: 8-Ravielli-a. 9-R.Q. Sale-a	21	42	63	124	202	280

UNDERWORLD
DC Comics: Dec, 1987 - No. 4, Mar, 1988 ($1.00, limited series, mature)

1-4						3.00

UNDERWORLD (Movie)
IDW Publishing: Sept, 2003; Dec, 2005 ($6.99)

1-Movie adaptation; photo-c						7.00
... Evolution (12/05, $7.49) adaptation of movie sequel; Vazquez-a						7.50
TPB (7/04, $19.99) r/#1 and Underworld:Red in Tooth and Claw #1-3						20.00

UNDERWORLD
Marvel Comics: Apr, 2006 - No. 5, Aug, 2006 ($2.99, limited series)

1-5: Staz Johnson-a. 2-Spider-Man app. 3,4-Punisher app.						3.00

UNDERWORLD CRIME
Fawcett Publications: June, 1952 - No. 7, Sept, 1953

1	36	72	108	216	351	485
2	23	46	69	136	223	310
3-6	20	40	60	120	195	270
7-(9/53)-Red hot poker/bondage/torture-c	295	590	885	1888	3244	4600

UNDERWORLD: RED IN TOOTH AND CLAW (Movie)
IDW Publishing: Feb, 2004 - No. 3, Apr, 2004 ($3.99, limited series)

1-3-The early days of the Vampire and Lycan war; Postic & Marinkovich-a						4.00

UNDERWORLD: RISE OF THE LYCANS (Movie)
IDW Publishing: Nov, 2008 - No. 2, Nov, 2008 ($3.99, limited series)

1,2-Grevioux-s/Huerta-a						4.00

UNDERWORLD STORY, THE (Movie)
Avon Periodicals: 1950

nn-(Scarce)-Ravielli-c	37	74	111	222	361	500

UNDERWORLD UNLEASHED
DC Comics: Nov, 1995 - No. 3, Jan, 1996 ($2.95, limited series)

1-3: Mark Waid scripts & Howard Porter-c/a(p)						4.00
...: Abyss: Hell's Sentinel 1-($2.95)-Alan Scott, Phantom Stranger, Zatanna app.						3.00

The Unexpected #186 © DC

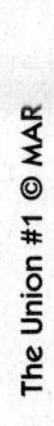
The Union #1 © MAR

Union Jack #1 © MAR

GD 2.0 | VG 4.0 | FN 6.0 | VF 8.0 | VF/NM 9.0 | NM- 9.2

...: Apokolips-Dark Uprising 1 ($1.95) 3.00
...: Batman-Devil's Asylum 1-($2.95)-Batman app. 3.00
...: Patterns of Fear-($2.95) 3.00
TPB (1998, $17.95) r/#1-3 & Abyss-Hell's Sentinel 18.00

UNDISCOVERED COUNTRY
Image Comics: Nov, 2019 - Present ($3.99)

1-12-Snyder & Soule-s/Camuncoli-a 4.00

UNEARTH
Image Comics: Jul, 2019 - Present ($3.99)

1-9-Bunn & Strahm-s/Rivas-a 4.00

UNEARTHLY SPECTACULARS
Harvey Publications: Oct, 1965 - No. 3, Mar, 1967

1-(12¢)-Tiger Boy; Simon-c 4 8 12 27 44 60
2-(25¢ giants)-Jack Q. Frost, Tiger Boy & Three Rocketeers app.; Williamson, Wood, Kane-a; r-1 story/Thrill-O-Rama #2 5 10 15 30 50 70
3-(25¢ giants)-Jack Q. Frost app.; Williamson/Crandall-a; r-from Alarming Advs. #1,1962 5 10 15 30 50 70

NOTE: ***Crandall** a-3r. **G. Kane** a-2. **Orlando** a-3. **Simon, Sparling, Wood** c-2. **Simon/Kirby** a-3r. **Torres** a-1?. **Wildey** a-1(3). **Williamson** a-2, 3r. **Wood** a-2(2).*

UNEXPECTED, THE (Formerly Tales of the...)
National Per. Publ./DC Comics: No. 105, Feb-Mar, 1968 - No. 222, May, 1982

105-Begin 12¢ cover price 6 12 18 40 73 105
106-113: 113-Last 12¢ issue (6-7/69) 5 10 15 30 50 70
114,115,117,118,120-125 4 8 12 22 35 48
116 (36 pgs.)-Wrightson-a 4 8 12 23 37 50
119-Wrightson-a, 8pgs.(36 pgs.) 5 10 15 31 53 75
126,127,129-136-(52 pgs.) 4 8 12 22 35 48
128(52 pgs.)-Wrightson-a 5 10 15 31 53 75
137-156 3 6 9 15 22 28
157-162-(100 pgs.) 4 8 12 28 47 65
163-188: 187,188-(44 pgs.) 2 4 6 11 16 20
189,190,192-195 ($1.00, 68 pgs.): 189 on are combined with House of Secrets & The Witching Hour 2 4 6 13 18 22
191-Rogers-a(p) ($1.00, 68 pgs.) 3 6 9 14 19 24
196-222: 200-Return of Johhny Peril by Tuska. 205-213-Johnny Peril app. 210-Time Warp story. 222-Giffen-a 2 4 6 8 10 12

NOTE: ***Neal Adams** c-110, 112-115, 118, 121, 124. **J. Craig** a-195. **Ditko** a-189, 221p, 222p; c-222. **Drucker** a-107r, 132r. **Giffen** a-219, 222. **Kaluta** c-203, 212. **Kirby** a-127r, 162. **Kubert** c-204, 214-216, 219-221. **Mayer** a-217p, 220, 221p. **Moldoff** a-136r. **Moreira** a-133. **Mortimer** a-212p. **Newton** a-204p. **Orlando** a-202; c-191. **Perez** a-217p. **Redondo** a-155, 166, 195. **Reese** a-145. **Sparling** a-107, 205-209p, 212p. **Spiegle** a-217. **Starlin** c-198. **Toth** a-126r, 127r. **Tuska** a-127, 132, 134, 136, 139, 152, 180, 200p. **Wildey** a-128r, 193. **Wood** a-122i, 133i, 137i, 138i. **Wrightson** a-161r(2 pgs.). Johnny Peril in #106-114, 116, 117, 200, 205-213.*

UNEXPECTED, THE
DC Comics: Dec, 2011 ($7.99, one-shot)

1-Short horror stories by various incl. Gibbons, Thompson, Lapham, Fialkov; 2 covers 8.00

UNEXPECTED, THE (Follows events of Dark Nights: Metal)
DC Comics: Aug, 2018 - No. 8, Mar, 2019 ($2.99)

1-8: 1-Orlando-s/Sook & Nord-a; intro. Firebrand, Bad Samaritan & Neon the Unknown. 4-Huntress app. 4-8-Hawkman app. 3.00

UNEXPECTED ANNUAL, THE (See DC Special Series #4)

UNFOLLOW
DC Comics (Vertigo): Jan, 2016 - No 18, Jun, 2017 ($3.99)

1-18: 1-Rob Williams-s/Mike Dowling-a. 6-R.M. Guéra-a. 7-Marguerite Sauvage-a 4.00
... Special Edition 1 (3/16, $4.99) r/#1&2 5.00

UNHOLY BASTARDS (Characters from The Goon)
Albatross Funnybooks: 2020 ($3.99, one-shot)

1-Eric Powell-c/Sniegoski-s/Mannion & Brown-a; The Goon and Franky app. 4.00

UNHOLY GRAIL
AfterShock Comics: July, 2017 - No. 5, Dec, 2017 ($3.99)

1-5-Cullen Bunn-s/Mirko Colak-a. 1-Multiple covers. 2-Covers by Colak & Francavillla 4.00

UNHOLY UNION
Image Comics (Top Cow): July, 2007 ($3.99, one-shot)

1-Witchblade & The Darkness meet Hulk, Ghost Rider & Doctor Strange; Silvestri-c 4.00

UNIDENTIFIED FLYING ODDBALL (See Walt Disney Showcase #52)

UNION
Image Comics (WildStorm Productions): June, 1993 - No. 0, July, 1994 ($1.95, lim. series)

0-(7/94, $2.50) 3.00
0-Alternate Portacio-c (See Deathblow #5) 5.00
1-($2.50)-Embossed foil-c; Texeira-c/a in all 4.00
1-($1.95)-Newsstand edition w/o foil-c 3.00
2-4: 4-(7/94) 3.00

UNION
Image Comics (WildStorm Prod.): Feb, 1995 - No. 9, Dec, 1995 ($2.50)

1-3,5-9: 3-Savage Dragon app. 6-Fairchild from Gen 13 app. 3.00
4-($1.95, Newsstand)-WildStorm Rising Pt. 3 3.00
4-($2.50, Direct Market)-WildStorm Rising Pt. 3, bound-in card 3.00

UNION, THE (Tie-in series to The King in Black crossover event)
Marvel Comics: Feb, 2021 - Present ($3.99)

1-3-Grist-s/Di Vito-a; team of Britannia, Snakes, Kelpie and The Choir; Union Jack app. 4.00

UNION: FINAL VENGEANCE
Image Comics (WildStorm Productions): Oct, 1997 ($2.50)

1-Golden-c/Heisler-s 3.00

UNION JACK
Marvel Comics: Dec, 1998 - No. 3, Feb, 1999 ($2.99, limited series)

1-3-Raab-s/Cassaday-s/a 3.00

UNION JACK
Marvel Comics: Nov, 2006 - No. 4, Feb, 2007 ($2.99, limited series)

1-4-Gage-s/Perkins-c/a 3.00
...: London Falling TPB (2007, $10.99) r/#1-4; Perkins sketch page 11.00

UNITED COMICS (Formerly Fritzi Ritz #7; has Fritzi Ritz logo)
United Features Syndicate: Aug, 1940; No. 8, 1950 - No. 26, Jan-Feb, 1953

1(68 pgs.)-Fritzi Ritz & Phil Fumble 32 64 96 188 307 425
8-Fritzi Ritz, Abbie & Slats 14 28 42 80 115 150
9-20: 20-Strange As It Seems; Russell Patterson Cheesecake-a 12 24 36 67 94 120
21-(3-4/52) 2 pg. early Peanuts by Schulz; ties with Tip Top Comics #173 for 1st app. of Peanuts in comics. (Also see Tip Topper Comics) 300 600 900 1920 3310 4700
22-(5-6/52) 2 pgs. early Peanuts by Schulz (3rd app.) 52 104 156 328 552 775
23-26: 23-(7-8/52). 24-(9-10/52). 25-(11-12/52). 26-(1-2/53). All have 2 pgs. early Peanuts by Schulz 27 54 81 162 266 370

NOTE: *Abbie & Slats reprinted from Tip Top.*

UNITED NATIONS, THE (See Classics Illustrated Special Issue)

UNITED STATES AIR FORCE PRESENTS: THE HIDDEN CREW
U.S. Air Force: 1964 (36 pgs.)

nn-Schaffenberger-a 2 4 6 13 18 22

UNITED STATES FIGHTING AIR FORCE (Also see U.S. Fighting Air Force)
Superior Comics Ltd.: Sept, 1952 - No. 29, Oct, 1956

1 19 38 57 111 176 240
2 12 24 36 67 94 120
3-10 10 20 30 56 76 95
11-29 9 18 27 52 69 85

UNITED STATES MARINES
William H. Wise/Life's Romances Publ. Co./Magazine Ent. #5-8/Toby Press #7-11: 1943 - No. 4, 1944; No. 5, 1952 - No. 8, 1952; No. 7 - No. 11, 1953

nn-Mart Bailey-c/a; Marines in the Pacific theater 37 74 111 222 361 500
2-Bailey-a; Tojo classic-c 129 258 387 826 1413 2000
3-Classic WWII Tojo-c 119 238 357 762 1306 1850
4-WWII photos; Tony DiPreta-a; grey-tone-c 21 42 63 122 199 275
5(A-1 #55)-Bailey-a, 6(A-1 #60), 8(A-1 #72) 14 28 42 81 118 155
7(A-1 #68) Flamethrower with burning bodies-c 107 214 321 856 1928 3000
7-11 (Toby) 14 28 42 80 115 150

NOTE: ***Powell** a-5-7.*

UNITED STATES OF MURDER INC., THE
Marvel Comics (Icon): May, 2014 - No. 6, Feb, 2015 ($3.99)

1-6-Bendis-s/Oeming-a 4.00

UNITED STATES OF MURDER INC.
DC Comics (Jinxworld): Nov, 2018 - No. 6, Apr, 2019 ($3.99)

1-6-Bendis-s/Oeming-a; second story arc 4.00

UNITY
Valiant: No. 0, Aug, 1992 - No. 1, 1992 (Free comics w/limited dist., 20 pgs.)

0 (Blue)-Prequel to Unity x-overs in all Valiant titles; B. Smith-c/a. (Free to everyone that bought all 8 titles that month.) 1 3 4 6 8 10
0 (Red)-Same as above, but w/red logo (5,000) 4 8 12 28 47 65
1-Epilogue to Unity x-overs; B. Smith-c/a. (1 copy available for every 8 Valiant books

Unity (2013 series) #1 © VAL

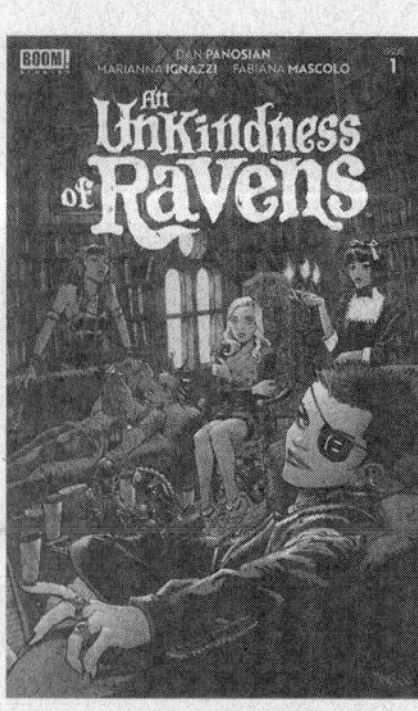

An Unkindness of Ravens #1 © Dan Panosian

Unknown Soldier (2008 series) #25 © DC

GD VG FN VF VF/NM NM-
2.0 4.0 6.0 8.0 9.0 9.2

ordered by dealers.) 5.00
1 (Gold), 1-(Platinum)-Promotional copy. 2 4 6 8 10 12
...: The Lost Chapter 1 (Yearbook) (2/95, $3.95)-"1994" in indicia 4.00

UNITY
Valiant Entertainment: Nov, 2013 - No. 25, Dec, 2015 ($3.99)

1-24: Multiple covers on each. 1-Kindt-s/Braithwaite-a. 5,6-Cafu-a 4.00
25-($4.99) Short stories by various incl. Kindt, Asmus, Kano, Jordan, Schkade 5.00
#0 (10/14, $3.99) Kindt-s/Nord-a; the story of Unit Y in WW One 4.00

UNITY 2000 (See preludes in Shadowman #3,4 flipbooks)
Acclaim Comics: Nov, 1999 - No. 3, Jan, 2000 ($2.50, unfinished limited series planned for 6 issues)

Preview -B&W plot preview and cover art; paper cover 3.00
1-3-Starlin-a/Shooter-s 3.00

UNIVERSAL MONSTERS
Dark Horse Comics: 1993 ($4.95/$5.95, 52 pgs.)(All adapt original movies)

Creature From the Black Lagoon nn-($4.95)-Art Adams/Austin-c/a
2 4 6 9 12 15
Dracula nn-($4.95), Frankenstein nn-($3.95)-Painted-c/a, The Mummy nn-($4.95)-Painted-c
1 2 3 4 5 7
...: Cavalcade of Horror TPB (1/06, $19.95) r/one-shots; Eric Powell intro. & cover 20.00

UNIVERSAL PICTURES PRESENTS DRACULA-THE MUMMY& OTHER STORIES
Dell Publishing Co.: Sept-Nov, 1963 (one-shot, 84 pgs.) (Also see Dell Giants)

02-530-311-r/Dracula 12-231-212, The Mummy 12-437-211 & part of Ghost Stories No. 1
15 30 45 100 220 340

UNIVERSAL SOLDIER (Movie)
Now Comics: Sept, 1992 - No. 3, Nov, 1992 (Limited series, polybagged, mature)

1-3 ($2.50, Direct Sales) 1-Movie adapatation; hologram on-c (all direct sales editions have painted-c) 4.00
1-3 ($1.95, Newsstand)-Rewritten & redrawn code approved version; all newsstand editions have photo-c 3.00

UNIVERSAL WAR ONE
Marvel Comics (Soleil): 2008 - No. 3, 2008 ($5.99, limited series)

1-3-Denis Bajram-s/a; English version of French comic. 1-Bajram interview 6.00
...: Revelations 1-3 (2009 - No. 3, 2009, $5.99) Bajram-s/a 6.00

UNIVERSE
Image Comics (Top Cow): Sept, 2001 - No. 8, July, 2002 ($2.50)

1-7-Jenkins-s 3.00
8-($4.95) extra short-s by Jenkins; pin-up pages 5.00

UNIVERSE X (See Earth X)
Marvel Comics: Sept, 2000 - No. 12, Sept, 2001 ($3.99/$3.50, limited series)

0-Ross-c/Braithwaite-a/Ross & Krueger-s 4.00
1-12: 5-Funeral of Captain America 4.00
... Beasts (6/00, $3.99) Yeates-a/Ross-c 4.00
... Cap (Capt. America) (2/01, $3.99) Yeates & Totleben-a/Ross-c; Cap dies 4.00
... 4 (Fantastic 4) (10/00, $3.99) Brent Anderson-a/Ross-c 4.00
... Iron Men (9/01, $3.99) Anderson-a/Ross-c; leads into #12 4.00
... Omnibus (6/01, $3.99) Ross B&W sketchbook and character bios 4.00
Sketchbook- Wizard supplement; B&W character sketches and bios 3.00
...Spidey (1/01, $3.99) Romita Sr. flashback-a/Guice-a/Ross-c 4.00
...X (11/01, $3.99) Series conclusion; Braithwaith-a/Ross wraparound-c 4.00
Volume 1 TPB (1/02, $24.95) r/#0-7 & Spidey, 4, & Cap; new Ross-c 25.00
Volume 2 TPB (6/02, $24.95) r/#8-12 &X, Beasts, Iron Men and Omnibus 25.00

UNKINDNESS OF RAVENS, AN
BOOM! Studios: Sept, 2020 - No. 5, Jan, 2021 ($3.99, limited series)

1-5-Dan Panosian-s/Marianna Ignazzi-a 4.00

UNKNOWN, THE
BOOM! Studios: May, 2009 - No. 4, Aug, 2009 ($3.99)

1-4-Mark Waid-s/Minck Oosterveer-a; two covers on each 4.00
...: The Devil Made Flesh 1-4 (9/09 - No. 4, 12/09, $3.99) Waid-s/Oosterveer-a 4.00

UNKNOWN MAN, THE (Movie)
Avon Periodicals: 1951

nn-Kinstler-c 36 72 108 216 351 485

UNKNOWN SOLDIER (Formerly Star-Spangled War Stories)
National Periodical Publications/DC Comics: No. 205, Apr-May, 1977 - No. 268, Oct, 1982 (See Our Army at War #168 for 1st app.)

205 3 6 9 17 26 35
206-210,220,221,251: 220,221 (44pgs.). 251-Enemy Ace begins
3 6 9 14 19 24
211-218,222-247,250,252-264 2 4 6 11 16 20
219-Miller-a (44 pgs.) 3 6 9 16 23 30
248,249,265-267: 248,249-Origin. 265-267-Enemy Ace vs. Balloon Buster.
2 4 6 11 16 20
268-Death of Unknown Soldier 3 6 9 19 30 40
NOTE: ***Chaykin** a-234. **Evans** a-265-267; c-235. **Kubert** c-Most. **Miller** a-219p. **Severin** a-251-253, 260, 261, 265-267. **Simonson** a-254-256. **Spiegle** a-258, 259, 262-264.*

UNKNOWN SOLDIER, THE (Also see Brave &the Bold #146)
DC Comics: Winter, 1988-'89 - No. 12, Dec, 1989 ($1.50, maxi-series, mature)

1-12: 8-Begin $1.75-c 5.00

UNKNOWN SOLDIER
DC Comics (Vertigo): Apr, 1997 - No 4, July, 1997 ($2.50, mini-series)

1-Ennis-s/Plunkett-a/Bradstreet-c in all 6.00
2-4 4.00
TPB (1998, $12.95) r/#1-4 13.00

UNKNOWN SOLDIER
DC Comics (Vertigo): Dec, 2008 - No. 25, Dec, 2010 ($2.99)

1-25: 1-Dysart-s/Ponticelli-a; intro. Lwanga Moses; two covers by Kordey and Corben. 2-20,22-25-Ponticelli-a. 21-Veitch-a 3.00
...: Beautiful World TPB (2011, $14.99) r/#21-25; Dysart afterword; sketch/design art 15.00
...: Dry Season TPB (2010, $14.99) r/#15-20; war history 15.00
...: Easy Kill TPB (2010, $17.99) r/#7-14; war history 18.00
...: Haunted House TPB (2009, $9.99) r/#1-6; glossary 10.00

UNKNOWN WORLD (Strange Stories From Another World #2 on)
Fawcett Publications: June, 1952

1-Norman Saunders painted-c 63 126 189 403 689 975

UNKNOWN WORLDS (See Journey Into...)

UNKNOWN WORLDS
American Comics Group/Best Synd. Features: Aug, 1960 - No. 57, Aug, 1967

1-Schaffenberger-c 23 46 69 161 356 550
2-Dinosaur-c/story 10 20 30 68 144 220
3-5 8 16 24 56 108 160
6-11: 9-Dinosaur-c/story. 11-Last 10¢ issue 7 14 21 46 86 125
12-19: 12-Begin 12¢ issues?; ends #57 6 12 18 37 66 95
20-Herbie cameo (12-1/62-63) 6 12 18 41 76 110
21-35: 27-Devil on-c. 31-Herbie one pagers thru #39 5 10 15 30 50 70
36- "The People vs. Hendricks" by Craig; most popular ACG story ever
5 10 15 33 57 80
37-46 4 8 12 27 44 60
47-Williamson-a r-from Adventures Into the Unknown #96, 3 pgs.; Craig-a
4 8 12 28 47 65
48-57: 53-Frankenstein app. 4 8 12 25 40 55
NOTE: ***Ditko** a-49, 50p, 54. **Forte** a-3, 6, 11. **Landau** a-56(2). **Reinman** a-3, 9, 13, 20, 22, 23, 36, 38, 54. **Whitney** c/a-most issues. John Force, Magic Agent app.-35, 36, 48, 50, 52, 54, 56.*

UNKNOWN WORLDS OF FRANK BRUNNER
Eclipse Comics: Aug, 1985 - No. 2, Aug, 1985 ($1.75)

1,2-B&W-r in color 4.00

UNKNOWN WORLDS OF SCIENCE FICTION
Marvel Comics: Jan, 1975 - No. 6, Nov, 1975; 1976 ($1.00, B&W Magazine)

1-Williamson/Krenkel/Torres/Frazetta-r/Witzend #1, Neal Adams-r/Phase 1; Brunner & Kaluta-r; Freas/Romita-c 3 6 9 17 26 35
2-6: 5-Kaluta text illos 3 6 9 14 20 26
Special 1(1976,100 pgs.)-Newton painted-c 3 6 9 16 23 30
NOTE: ***Brunner** a-2; c-4, 6. **Buscema** a-Special 1p. **Chaykin** a-5. **Colan** a(p)-1, 3, 5, 6. **Corben** a-4. **Kaluta** a-2, Special 1(ext illos); c-2. **Morrow** a-3, 5. **Nino** a-3, 6, Special 1. **Perez** a-2, 3. Ray Bradbury interview in #1.*

UNLIMITED ACCESS (Also see Marvel Vs. DC))
Marvel Comics: Dec, 1997 - No. 4, Mar, 1998 ($2.99/$1.99, limited series)

1-Spider-Man, Wonder Woman, Green Lantern & Hulk app. 4.00
2,3-($1.99): 2-X-Men, Legion of Super-Heroes app. 3-Original Avengers vs. original Justice League 3.00
4-($2.99) Amalgam Legion vs. Darkseid & Magneto 4.00

UN-MEN, THE
DC Comics (Vertigo): Oct, 2007 - No. 13, Oct, 2008 ($2.99)

1-13-Whalen-s/Hawthorne-a/Hanuka-c 3.00
...: Children of Paradox TPB (2008, $19.99) r/#6-13 20.00
...: Get Your Freak On! TPB (2008, $9.99) r/#1-5; cover gallery 10.00

UNNATURAL
Image Comics: Jul, 2018 - No. 12, Aug, 2019 ($3.99)

The Unstoppable Wasp (2018 series) #2 © MAR

Untold Tales of Spider-Man #6 © MAR

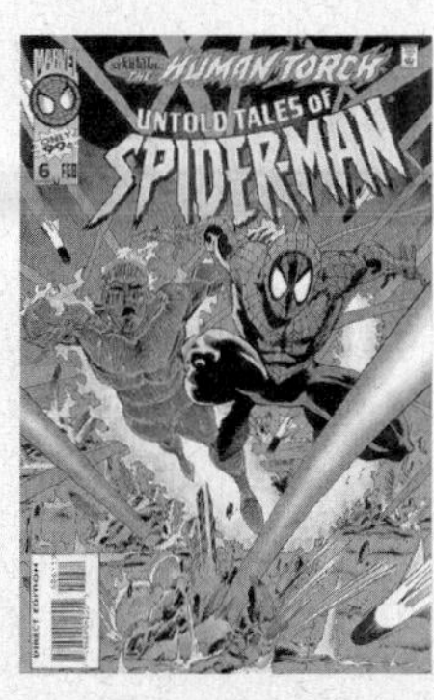

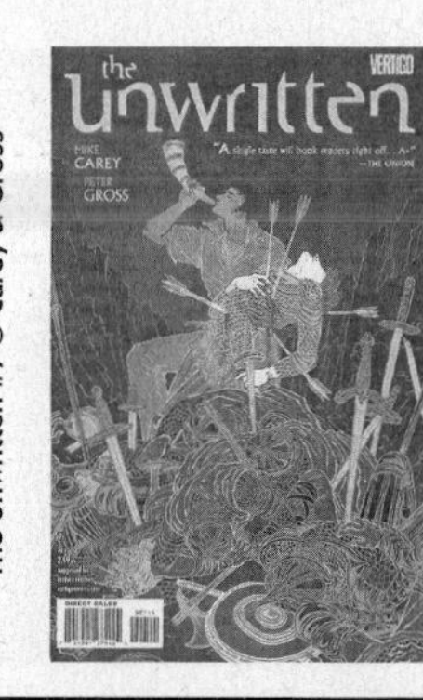

The Unwritten #7 © Carey & Gross

	GD 2.0	VG 4.0	FN 6.0	VF 8.0	VF/NM 9.0	NM- 9.2
1-12-Mirka Andolfo-s/a; English version of a 2016 Italian comic series						4.00

UN/SACRED
Ablaze Publishing: 2019 - No. 7, 2020 ($3.99)

	GD 2.0	VG 4.0	FN 6.0	VF 8.0	VF/NM 9.0	NM- 9.2
1-7-Mirka Andolfo-s/a; multiple covers on each						4.00
Vol. 2 (2020 - Present) 1-4-Mirka Andolfo-s/a						4.00

UNSANE (Formerly Mighty Bear #13, 14? or The Outlaws #10-14?)(Satire)
Star Publications: No. 15, June, 1954

	GD 2.0	VG 4.0	FN 6.0	VF 8.0	VF/NM 9.0	NM- 9.2
15-Disbrow-a(2); L. B. Cole-c	39	78	117	231	378	525

UNSEEN, THE
Visual Editions/Standard Comics: No. 5, 1952 - No. 15, July, 1954

	GD 2.0	VG 4.0	FN 6.0	VF 8.0	VF/NM 9.0	NM- 9.2
5-Horror stories in all; Toth-a	55	110	165	352	601	850
6,7,9,10-Jack Katz-a	43	86	129	271	461	650
8,11,13,14	40	80	120	244	402	550
12,15-Toth-a. 12-Tuska-a	45	90	135	284	480	675

NOTE: ***Nick Cardy** c-12. **Fawcette** a-13, 14. **Sekowsky** a-7, 8(2), 10, 13, 15.*

UNSTOPPABLE WASP, THE
Marvel Comics: Mar, 2017 - No. 8, Oct, 2017 ($3.99)

	GD 2.0	VG 4.0	FN 6.0	VF 8.0	VF/NM 9.0	NM- 9.2
1-8: 1-6-Whitley-s/Charretier-a. 1-Ms. Marvel & Mockingbird app. 2,3-Moon Girl app.						4.00

UNSTOPPABLE WASP, THE
Marvel Comics: Dec, 2018 - No. 10, Sept, 2019 ($3.99)

	GD 2.0	VG 4.0	FN 6.0	VF 8.0	VF/NM 9.0	NM- 9.2
1-10: Whitley-s. 1-5,8-10-Gurihiru-a. 7-Winter Soldier and Young Avengers app.						4.00

UNTAMED
Marvel Comics (Epic Comics/Heavy Hitters): June, 1993 - No. 3, Aug, 1993 ($1.95, lim. series)

	GD 2.0	VG 4.0	FN 6.0	VF 8.0	VF/NM 9.0	NM- 9.2
1-($2.50)-Embossed-c						4.00
2,3						3.00

UNTAMED LOVE (Also see Frank Frazetta's Untamed Love)
Quality Comics Group (Comic Magazines): Jan, 1950 - No. 5, Sept, 1950

	GD 2.0	VG 4.0	FN 6.0	VF 8.0	VF/NM 9.0	NM- 9.2
1-Ward-c, Gustavson-a	39	78	117	240	395	550
2,4: 2-5-Photo-c	24	48	72	140	230	320
3,5-Gustavson-a	32	64	96	188	307	425

UNTOLD LEGEND OF CAPTAIN MARVEL, THE
Marvel Comics: Apr, 1997 - No. 3, June, 1997 ($2.50, limited series)

	GD 2.0	VG 4.0	FN 6.0	VF 8.0	VF/NM 9.0	NM- 9.2
1-3						5.00

UNTOLD LEGEND OF THE BATMAN, THE (Also see Promotional section)
DC Comics: July, 1980 - No. 3, Sept, 1980 (Limited series)

	GD 2.0	VG 4.0	FN 6.0	VF 8.0	VF/NM 9.0	NM- 9.2
1-Origin; Joker-c; Byrne's 1st work at DC	2	4	6	8	10	12
2,3	1	2	3	5	6	8

NOTE: ***Aparo** a-1i, 2, 3. **Byrne** a-1p.*

UNTOLD ORIGIN OF THE FEMFORCE, THE (Also see Femforce)
AC Comics: 1989 ($4.95, 68 pgs.)

	GD 2.0	VG 4.0	FN 6.0	VF 8.0	VF/NM 9.0	NM- 9.2
1-Origin Femforce; Bill Black-a(i) & scripts						6.00

UNTOLD TALES OF BLACKEST NIGHT (Also see Blackest Night crossover titles)
DC Comics: Dec, 2010 ($4.99, one-shot)

	GD 2.0	VG 4.0	FN 6.0	VF 8.0	VF/NM 9.0	NM- 9.2
1-Short stories by various incl. Johns, Benes, Booth; 2 covers by Kirkham & Van Sciver						5.00

UNTOLD TALES OF CHASTITY
Chaos! Comics: Nov, 2000 ($2.95, one-shot)

	GD 2.0	VG 4.0	FN 6.0	VF 8.0	VF/NM 9.0	NM- 9.2
1-Origin; Steven Grant-s/Peter Vale-c/a						3.00
1-Premium Edition with glow in the dark cover						10.00

UNTOLD TALES OF LADY DEATH
Chaos! Comics: Nov, 2000 ($2.95, one-shot)

	GD 2.0	VG 4.0	FN 6.0	VF 8.0	VF/NM 9.0	NM- 9.2
1-Origin of Lady Death; Cremator app.; Kaminski-s						3.00
1-Premium Edition with glow in the dark cover by Steven Hughes						10.00

UNTOLD TALES OF PUNISHER MAX
Marvel Comics: Aug, 2012 - No. 5, Dec, 2012 ($4.99/$3.99, limited series)

	GD 2.0	VG 4.0	FN 6.0	VF 8.0	VF/NM 9.0	NM- 9.2
1-($4.99) Anthology; Starr-s/Boschi-a/c						5.00
2-5-($3.99) 2-Andrews-c. 3-Ribic-c. 5-Skottie Young-s/Del Mundo-c						4.00

UNTOLD TALES OF PURGATORI
Chaos! Comics: Nov, 2000 ($2.95, one-shot)

	GD 2.0	VG 4.0	FN 6.0	VF 8.0	VF/NM 9.0	NM- 9.2
1-Purgatori in 57 B.C.; Rio-a/Grant-s						3.00
1-Premium Edition with glow in the dark cover						10.00

UNTOLD TALES OF SPIDER-MAN (Also see Amazing Fantasy #16-18)
Marvel Comics: Sept, 1995 - No. 25, Sept, 1997 (99¢)

	GD 2.0	VG 4.0	FN 6.0	VF 8.0	VF/NM 9.0	NM- 9.2
1-Kurt Busiek scripts begin; Pat Olliffe-c/a in all (except #9).						4.00
2-22, -1(7/97), 23-25: 2-1st app. Batwing. 4-1st app. The Spacemen (Gantry, Orbit, Satellite & Vacuum). 8-1st app. The Headsman; The Enforcers (The Big Man, Montana, The Ox & Fancy Dan) app. 9-Ron Frenz-a. 10-1st app. Commanda. 16-Reintro Mary Jane Watson. 21-X-Men-c/app. 25-Green Goblin						3.00
...'96-(1996, $1.95, 46 pgs.)-Kurt Busiek scripts; Mike Allred-c/a; Kurt Busiek & Pat Olliffe app. in back-up story; contains pin-ups						4.00
...'97-(1997, $1.95)-Wraparound-c						4.00
...: Strange Encounters ('98, $5.99) Dr. Strange app.						6.00

UNTOLD TALES OF THE NEW UNIVERSE (Based on Marvel's 1986 New Universe titles)
Marvel Comics: May, 2006 ($2.99, series of one-shots)

	GD 2.0	VG 4.0	FN 6.0	VF 8.0	VF/NM 9.0	NM- 9.2
...: D. P. 7 - Takes place between issues #4 & 5 of D. P. 7 series; Bright-a/Cebulski-s						3.00
...: Justice - Peter David-s/Carmine Di Giandomenico-a						3.00
...: Nightmask - Takes place between issues #4 & 5 of Nightmask series; The Gnome app.						3.00
...: Psi-Force - Tony Bedard-s/Russ Braun-a						3.00
...: Star Brand - Romita & Romita Jr.-c/Pulido-a						3.00
TPB (2006, $15.99) r/one-shots & stories from Amaz. Fantasy #18,19 & New Avengers #16						16.00

UNTOUCHABLES, THE (TV)
Dell Publishing Co.: No. 1237, 10-12/61 - No. 4, 8-10/62 (All have Robert Stack photo-c)

	GD 2.0	VG 4.0	FN 6.0	VF 8.0	VF/NM 9.0	NM- 9.2
Four Color 1237(#1)	17	34	51	117	259	400
Four Color 1286	12	24	36	82	179	275
01-879-207, 12-879-210(01879-210 on inside)	8	16	24	54	102	150

UNTOUCHABLES
Caliber Comics: Aug, 1997 - No. 4 ($2.95, B&W)

	GD 2.0	VG 4.0	FN 6.0	VF 8.0	VF/NM 9.0	NM- 9.2
1-4: 1-Pruett-s; variant covers by Kaluta & Showman						3.00

UNUSUAL COMICS
Bell Features: No date (1940s)(10¢)

8-Zago Jungle Princess (a VG copy sold in 2018 for $185)

UNUSUAL TALES (Blue Beetle & Shadows From Beyond #50 on)
Charlton Comics: Nov, 1955 - No. 49, Mar-Apr, 1965

	GD 2.0	VG 4.0	FN 6.0	VF 8.0	VF/NM 9.0	NM- 9.2
1-Horror stories	34	68	102	204	332	460
2	18	36	54	109	172	235
3-5	15	30	45	86	133	180
6-Ditko-c only	21	42	63	124	202	280
7,8-Ditko-c/a. 8-Robot-c	32	64	96	190	310	430
9-Ditko-c/a (20 pgs.)	34	68	102	204	332	460
10-Ditko-c/a(4)	35	70	105	208	339	470
11-(3/58, 68 pgs.)-Ditko-a(4)	34	68	102	204	332	460
12,14-Ditko-a	21	42	63	122	199	275
13,16-20	7	14	21	48	89	130
15-Ditko-c/a	28	56	84	165	270	375
21,24,28	6	12	18	38	69	100
22,23,25-27,29-Ditko-a	10	20	30	64	132	200
30-49	5	10	15	33	57	80

NOTE: ***Colan** a-11. **Ditko** c-22, 23, 25-27, 31(part).*

UNWORTHY THOR, THE (See Original Sin)
Marvel Comics: Jan, 2017 - No. 5, May, 2017 ($3.99)

	GD 2.0	VG 4.0	FN 6.0	VF 8.0	VF/NM 9.0	NM- 9.2
1-5-Aaron-s/Coipel-a; multiple covers; Beta Ray Bill app. 2-Thanos app.						4.00

UNWRITTEN, THE
DC Comics (Vertigo): July, 2009 - No. 54, Dec, 2013 ($1.00/$2.99)

	GD 2.0	VG 4.0	FN 6.0	VF 8.0	VF/NM 9.0	NM- 9.2
1-($1.00) Intro. Tommy Taylor; Mike Carey-s/Peter Gross-a; two covers (white & black)						3.00
2-16,18-31,(31.5), 32, (32.5), 33, (33.5), 34, (34.5), (35.5), 36-49-($2.99): 31.5-Art by Gross, Kaluta, Geary & Talbot. 37-Series re-cap						3.00
17-($3.99) Story printed sideways; Pick-a-Story format						4.00
35-($4.99)						5.00
50-(8/13, $4.99) Fables characters app.; Carey & Willingham-s; Gross & Buckingham-a						5.00
51-54-Fables characters app.						3.00
...: Dead Man's Knock TPB (2011, $14.99) r/#13-18; intro. by novelist Steven Hall						15.00
...: Inside Man TPB (2010, $12.99) r/#6-12; intro. by Paul Cornell						13.00
...: Tommy Taylor and the Bogus Identity TPB (2010, $9.99) r/#1-5; sketch art; prose						10.00

UNWRITTEN, THE: APOCALYPSE
DC Comics (Vertigo): Mar, 2014 - No. 12, Mar, 2015 ($3.99)

	GD 2.0	VG 4.0	FN 6.0	VF 8.0	VF/NM 9.0	NM- 9.2
1-11-Mike Carey-s/Peter Gross-a						4.00
12-($4.99) Mike Carey-s/Peter Gross-a						5.00

UP FROM HARLEM (Tom Skinner...)
Spire Christian Comics (Fleming H. Revell Co.): 1973 (35/49¢)

	GD 2.0	VG 4.0	FN 6.0	VF 8.0	VF/NM 9.0	NM- 9.2
nn-(35¢ cover)	3	6	9	14	20	26
nn-(49¢ cover)	2	4	6	10	14	18

UP-TO-DATE COMICS
King Features Syndicate: No date (1938) (36 pgs.; B&W cover) (10¢)

nn-Popeye & Henry cover; The Phantom, Jungle Jim & Flash Gordon by Raymond, The Katzenjammer Kids, Curley Harper & others. Note: Variations in content exist.

USA Comics #11 © MAR

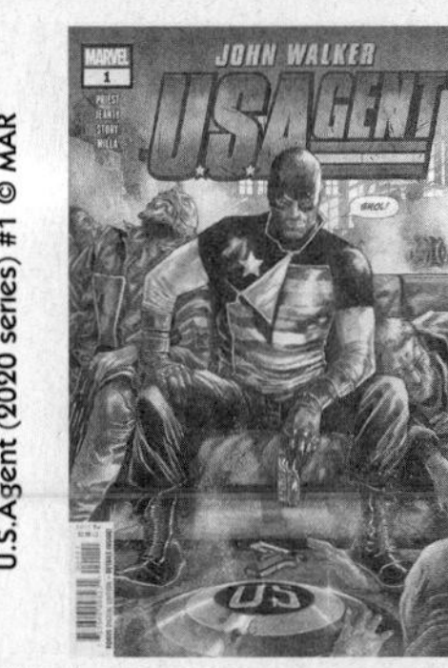

U.S.Agent (2020 series) #1 © MAR

Usagi Yojimbo (2019 series) #6 © Stan Sakai

	34	68	102	206	336	465

UP YOUR NOSE AND OUT YOUR EAR (Satire)
Klevart Enterprises: Apr, 1972 - No. 2, June, 1972 (52 pgs., magazine)

V1#1,2 — 2 4 6 11 16 20

URTH 4 (Also see Earth 4)
Continuity Comics: May, 1989 - No. 4, Dec, 1990 ($2.00, deluxe format)

1-4: Ms. Mystic characters. 2-Neal Adams-c(i) — 3.00

URZA-MISHRA WAR ON THE WORLD OF MAGIC THE GATHERING
Acclaim Comics (Armada): 1996 - No. 2, 1996 ($5.95, limited series)

1,2 — 6.00

U.S. (See Uncle Sam)

USA COMICS
Timely Comics (USA): Aug, 1941 - No. 17, Fall, 1945

1-Origin Major Liberty (called Mr. Liberty #1), Rockman by Wolverton; 1st app. The Whizzer by Avison; The Defender with sidekick Rusty & Jack Frost begin; The Young Avenger only app.; S&K-c plus 1 pg. art — 1050 2100 3150 7350 14,425 21,500
2-Origin Captain Terror & The Vagabond; last Wolverton Rockman; Hitler-c — 492 984 1476 3592 6346 9100
3-No Whizzer — 382 764 1146 2674 4687 6700
4-Last Rockman, Major Liberty, Defender, Jack Frost, & Capt. Terror; Corporal Dix app.; "Remember Pearl Harbor" small cover logo — 354 708 1062 2478 4339 6200
5-Origin American Avenger & Roko the Amazing; The Blue Blade, The Black Widow & Victory Boys, Gypo the Gypsy Giant & Hills of Horror only app.; Sergeant Dix begins; no Whizzer; Hitler, Mussolini & Tojo-c — 524 1048 1572 3825 6763 9700
6-Captain America (ends #17), The Destroyer, Jap Buster Johnson, Jeep Jones begin; Terror Squad only app. — 1000 2000 3000 7400 13,200 19,000
7-Captain Daring, Disk-Eyes the Detective by Wolverton app.; origin & only app. Marvel Boy (3/43); Secret Stamp begins; no Whizzer, Sergeant Dix; classic Schomburg-c — 1500 3000 4500 11,400 20,700 30,000
8-Classic Japanese WWII bondage/torture-c — 946 1892 2838 6906 12,203 17,500
9-Last Secret Stamp; Hitler-c; classic-c — 1000 2000 3000 7300 12,900 18,500
10-The Thunderbird only app.; Schomburg Japanese WWII-c — 838 1676 2514 6119 10,809 15,500
11-13: 11-No Jeep Jones. 13-No Whizzer; Jeep Jones ends; Schomburg Japanese WWII-c — 476 952 1428 3475 6138 8800
14-17: 15-No Destroyer; Jap Buster Johnson ends — 239 478 717 1530 2615 3700

NOTE: ***Brodsky** c-14. **Gabrielle** c-4. **Schomburg** c-6, 7, 10, 12, 13, 15-17. **Shores** a-1, 4; c-9, 11. **Ed Win** a-4. Cover features: 1-The Defender; 2, 3-Captain Terror; 4-Major Liberty; 5-Victory Boys; 6-17-Captain America & Bucky.*

USA COMICS 70TH ANNIVERSARY SPECIAL
Marvel Comics: Sept, 2009 ($3.99, one-shot)

1-New story of The Destroyer; Arcudi-s/Ellis-a; r/All Winners #3; two covers — 5.00

U.S. AGENT (See Jeff Jordan...)

U.S. AGENT (See Captain America #354)
Marvel Comics: June, 1993 - No. 4, Sept, 1993 ($1.75, limited series)

1-4 — 4.00

U.S. AGENT
Marvel Comics: Aug, 2001 - No. 3, Oct, 2001 ($2.99, limited series)

1-3: Ordway-s/a(p)/c. 2,3-Captain America app. — 3.00

U.S.AGENT (John Walker)(See Captain America #354 for 1st app.)
Marvel Comics: Jan, 2021 - Present ($3.99)

1-3-Priest-s/Jeanty-a — 4.00

USAGI YOJIMBO (See Albedo, Doomsday Squad #3 & Space Usagi)
Fantagraphics Books: July, 1987 - No. 38 ($2.00/$2.25, B&W)

1 — 10 20 30 64 132 200
1,8,10-2nd printings — 4.00
2-9 — 1 3 4 6 8 10
10,11: 10-Leonardo app. (TMNT). 11-Aragonés-a — 2 4 6 11 16 20
12-29 — 4.00
30-38: 30-Begin $2.25-c — 6.00
Color Special 1 (11/89, $2.95, 68 pgs.)-new & r — 1 3 4 6 8 10
Color Special 2 (10/91, $3.50) — 1 3 4 6 8 10
Color Special #3 (10/92, $3.50)-Jeff Smith's Bone promo on inside-c — 1 3 4 6 8 10
Summer Special 1 (1986, B&W, $2.75)-r/early Albedo issues — 1 3 4 6 8 10

USAGI YOJIMBO (Volume 2)
Mirage Studios: V2#1, Mar, 1993 - No. 16, 1994 ($2.75)

V2#1-Teenage Mutant Ninja Turtles app. — 2 4 6 9 12 15
2-16 — 4.00

USAGI YOJIMBO (Volume 3)
Dark Horse Comics: Apr, 1996 - No. 165, Jan, 2018 ($2.95/$2.99/$3.50, B&W)

V3#1-Stan Sakai-c/a in all — 2 4 6 8 10 12
2-10 — 6.00
11-99,101-116: Stan Sakai-c/a — 3.50
100-(1/07, $3.50) Stan Sakai roast by various incl. Aragonés, Wagner, Miller, Geary — 1 3 4 6 8 10
117-150-($3.50) 136-Variant-c. 141-"200th issue" — 3.50
151-165-($3.99) 152-The River Rising — 4.00
...: One For One (8/10, $1.00) Reprints #1 — 3.00
Color Special #4 (7/97, $2.95) "Green Persimmon" — 3.00
Color Special #5: The Artist (7/14, $3.99) Bonus preview of Usagi Yojimbo: Senso — 4.00
Daisho TPB ('98, $14.95) r/Mirage series #7-14 — 15.00
Demon Mask TPB ('01, $15.95) — 16.00
Glimpses of Death TPB (7/06, $15.95) r/#76-82 — 16.00
Grasscutter TPB ('99, $16.95) r/#13-22 — 17.00
Gray Shadows TPB ('00, $14.95) r/#23-30 — 15.00
Seasons TPB ('99, $14.95) r/#7-12 — 15.00
Shades of Death TPB ('97, $14.95) r/Mirage series #1-6 — 15.00
The Brink of Life and Death TPB ('98, $14.95) r/Mirage series #13,15,16 & Dark Horse series #1-6 — 15.00
The Shrouded Moon TPB (1/03, $15.95) r/#46-52 — 16.00

USAGI YOJIMBO (Volume 4)
IDW Publishing: Jun, 2019 - Present ($3.99, color)

1-16-Stan Sakai-c/a in all — 4.00

USAGI YOJIMBO: COLOR CLASSICS
IDW Publishing: Jan, 2020 - No. 7, Sept, 2020 ($3.99, color)

1-7-Reprints early Fantagraphics B&W issues with added color; Stan Sakai-c/a in all — 4.00

USAGI YOJIMBO: SENSO
Dark Horse Comics: Aug, 2014 - No. 6, Jan, 2015 ($3.99, B&W)

1-6-Stan Sakai-s/c/a; Martian invasion set 20 years later; wraparound-c on each — 4.00

USAGI YOJIMBO: THE HIDDEN (Doubles as issues #166-172 for Volume 3)
Dark Horse Comics: Mar, 2018 - No. 7, Oct, 2018 ($3.99, B&W)

1-7-Stan Sakai-s/c/a — 4.00

USAGI YOJIMBO: WANDERER'S ROAD
IDW Publishing: Nov, 2020 - No. 6 ($3.99, color)

1-3: 1-Reprints #7 (3/88) with new color; Stan Sakai-c/a. 2,3-Reprint #8,#9 — 4.00

U.S. AIR FORCE COMICS (Army Attack #38 on)
Charlton Comics: Oct, 1958 - No. 37, Mar-Apr, 1965

1 — 7 14 21 48 89 130
2 — 4 8 12 28 47 65
3-10 — 4 8 12 23 37 50
11-20 — 3 6 9 21 33 45
21-37 — 3 6 9 17 26 35

NOTE: ***Glanzman** c/a-9, 10, 12. **Montes/Bache** a-33.*

USA IS READY
Dell Publishing Co.: 1941 (68 pgs., one-shot)

1-War propaganda — 58 116 174 371 636 900

U.S.AVENGERS (Also see Avengers #675 -678)
Marvel Comics: Mar, 2017 - No. 12, Jan, 2017 ($3.99)

1-3-Ewing-s/Medina-a; team of Squirrel Girl, Cannonball, Iron Patriot, Enigma, Red Hulk. 5-9-Secret Empire tie-ins. 11,12-Archie Riverdale spoof; Skrulls app. — 4.00

U.S. BORDER PATROL COMICS (Sgt. Dick Carter of the...) (See Holyoke One Shot)

USER
DC Comics (Vertigo): 2001 - No. 3, 2001 ($5.95, limited series)

1-3-Devin Grayson-s; Sean Phillips & John Bolton-a — 6.00

U.S. FIGHTING AIR FORCE (Also see United States Fighting Air Force)
I. W. Enterprises: No date (1960s?)

1,9(nd): 1-r/United States Fighting...#?. 9-r/#1 — 2 4 6 9 13 16

U.S. FIGHTING MEN
Super Comics: 1963 - 1964 (Reprints)

10-r/With the U.S. Paratroops #4(Avon) — 2 4 6 9 13 16
11,12,15-18: 11-r/Monty Hall #10. 12,16,17,18-r/U.S. Fighting Air Force #10,3,?&? 15-r/Man Comics #11 — 2 4 6 9 13 16

U.S. JONES (Also see Wonderworld Comics #28)

U.S. War Machine #12 © MAR

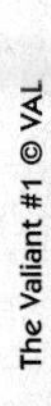

The Valiant #1 © VAL

Valkyrie: Jane Foster #6 © MAR

	GD 2.0	VG 4.0	FN 6.0	VF 8.0	VF/NM 9.0	NM- 9.2

Fox Feature Syndicate: Nov, 1941 - No. 2, Jan, 1942

1-U.S. Jones & The Topper begin; Nazi-c	258	516	774	1651	2826	4000
2-Nazi-c	252	504	756	1613	2757	3900

U.S. MARINES
Charlton Comics: Fall, 1964 (12¢, one-shot)

1-1st app. Capt. Dude; Glanzman-a	5	10	15	31	53	75

U.S. MARINES IN ACTION
Avon Periodicals: Aug, 1952 - No. 3, Dec, 1952

1-Louis Ravielli-c/a	15	30	45	88	137	185
2,3: 3-Kinstler-c	12	24	36	67	94	120

U.S. 1
Marvel Comics Group: May, 1983 - No. 12, Oct, 1984 (7,8: painted-c)

1-12: 2-Sienkiewicz-c. 3-12-Michael Golden-c 4.00

U.S. PARATROOPS (See With the...)

U.S. PARATROOPS
I. W. Enterprises: 1964?

1,8: 1-r/With the U.S. Paratroops #1; Wood-c. 8-r/With the U.S. Paratroops #6; Kinstler-c	2	4	6	10	14	18

U.S. TANK COMMANDOS
Avon Periodicals: June, 1952 - No. 4, Mar, 1953

1-Kinstler-c	15	30	45	88	137	185
2-4: Kinstler-c	13	26	39	74	105	135
I.W. Reprint #1,8: 1-r/#1. 8-r/#3	2	4	6	10	14	18

NOTE: ***Kinstler** a-I.W. #1; c-1-4, I.W. #1, 8.*

U.S. WAR MACHINE (Also see Iron Man and War Machine)
Marvel Comics (MAX): Nov, 2001 - No. 12, Jan, 2002 ($1.50, B&W, weekly limited series)

1-12-Chuck Austen-s/a/c 3.00
TPB (12/01, $14.95) r/#1-12 15.00

U.S. WAR MACHINE 2.0
Marvel Comics (MAX): Sept, 2003 - No. 3, Sept, 2003 ($2.99, weekly, limited series)

1-3-Austen-s/Christian Moore-CGI art 3.00

"V" (TV)
DC Comics: Feb, 1985 - No. 18, July, 1986

1-Based on TV movie & series (Sci/Fi) 5.00
2-18: 17,18-Denys Cowan-c/a 4.00

VACATION COMICS (Also see A-1 Comics)
Magazine Enterprises: No. 16, 1948 (one-shot)

A-1 16-The Pixies, Tom Tom, Flying Fredd & Koko & Kola	11	22	33	60	83	105

VACATION DIGEST
Harvey Comics: Sept, 1987 ($1.25, digest size)

1	1	2	3	5	6	8

VACATION IN DISNEYLAND (Also see Dell Giants)
Dell Publishing Co./Gold Key (1965): Aug-Oct, 1959; May, 1965 (Walt Disney)

Four Color 1025-Barks-a	14	28	42	93	204	315
1(30024-508)(G.K., 5/65, 25¢)-r/Dell Giant #30 & cover to #1 ('58); celebrates Disneyland's 10th anniversary	5	10	15	31	53	75

VACATION PARADE (See Dell Giants)

VALEN THE OUTCAST
BOOM! Studios: Dec, 2011 - No. 8, Jul, 2012 ($1.00/$3.99)

1-($1.00) Nelson-s/Scalera-a; eight covers 3.00
2-8-($3.99) 2-4-Six covers on each. 5-8-Five covers on each 4.00

VALERIA THE SHE BAT
Continuity Comics: May, 1993 - No. 5, Nov, 1993

1-Premium; acetate-c; N. Adams-a/scripts; given as gift to retailers	1	3	4	6	8	10

5 (11/93)-Embossed-c; N. Adams-a/scripts 5.00
NOTE: *Due to lack of continuity, #2-4 do not exist.*

VALERIA THE SHE BAT
Acclaim Comics (Windjammer): Sept, 1995 - No.2, Oct, 1995 ($2.50, limited series)

1,2 4.00

VALHALLA MAD
Image Comics: May, 2015 - No. 4, Aug, 2015 ($3.50, limited series)

1-4-Joe Casey-s/Paul Maybury-a 3.50

VALIANT, THE (Leads into Bloodshot Reborn series)
Valiant Entertainment: Dec, 2014 - No. 4, Mar, 2015 ($3.99, limited series)

1-4-Lemire & Kindt-s/Rivera-a; Eternal Warrior & Bloodshot app. 4.00

VALIANT...
Valiant Entertainment: May, 2012 - Present (giveaways)

... Bloodshot FCBD 2019 Special (5/19) Previews Bloodshot & Fallen World; Brereton-c 3.00
... Comics FCBD 2012 Special 1 (5/12) Previews X-O Manowar, Harbinger and other Valiant 2012 titles; creator interviews 3.00
... FCBD 2013 Special #1 (5/13) Previews Harbinger Wars, X-O Manowar and others 3.00
... FCBD 2014 Armor Hunters Special #1 (5/14) Previews Armor Hunters and others 3.00
... FCBD 2014 Valiant Universe Handbook #1 (5/14) Character profiles 3.00
... FCBD 2015 Valiant 25th Anniversary Special (5/15) Previews Bloodshot and Ninjak 3.00
... : 4001 A.D. FCBD Special (5/16) Prelude to the 4001 A.D. series; Crain-c 3.00
... Masters: 2013 Showcase Edition #1 (5/13) Samples of hardcover volume offerings 3.00
... : Shadowman FCBD 2018 Special (5/18) Short stories of Shadowman, X-O Manowar, Harbinger Wars 3.00
... Universe Handbook 2015 Edition #1 (5/15, $2.99) Character profiles 3.00
... Universe Handbook 2016 Edition #1 (8/16, $2.99) Character profiles 3.00
... Universe Handbook 2019 Edition #1 (6/19, $3.99) Character profiles; Massafera-c 4.00
... : X-O Manowar 2017 FCBD Special (5/17) Short stories of X-O Manowar, Secret Weapons, Bloodshot Salvation 3.00

VALIANT HIGH
Valiant Entertainment: May, 2018 - No. 4, Aug, 2018 ($3.99, limited series)

1-4-Valiant heroes as high-schoolers; Kibblesmith-s/Charm-a 4.00

VALKYRIE (See Airboy)
Eclipse Comics: May, 1987 - No. 3, July, 1987 ($1.75, limited series)

1-3: 2-Holly becomes new Black Angel 4.00

VALKYRIE
Marvel Comics: Jan, 1997; Nov, 2010 ($2.95/$3.99, one-shots)

1-(1/97, $2.95) w/pin-ups 4.00
1-(11/10, $3.99) Origin re-told; Winslade-a/Glass-s; Anacleto-c 4.00

VALKYRIE!
Eclipse Comics: July, 1988 - No. 3, Sept, 1988 ($1.95, limited series)

1-3 4.00

VALKYRIE: JANE FOSTER (See the 2016 Mighty Thor series and War of the Realms Omega)
Marvel Comics: Sept, 2019 - No. 10, Oct, 2020 ($3.99)

1-10: 1,2-Aaron & Ewing-s/Cafu-a; Bullseye & Heimdall app. 4-7-Dr. Strange app. 4.00

VALLEY OF THE DINOSAURS (TV)
Charlton Comics: Apr, 1975 - No. 11, Dec, 1976 (Hanna-Barbera)

1-W. Howard-i	3	6	9	15	20	26
2,4-11: 2-W. Howard-i	2	4	6	8	11	14
3-Byrne text illos (early work, 7/75)	2	4	6	10	14	18

VALLEY OF THE DINOSAURS (Volume 2)
Harvey Comics: Oct, 1993 ($1.50, giant-sized)

1-Reprints 5.00

VALLEY OF GWANGI (See Movie Classics)

VALOR
E. C. Comics: Mar-Apr, 1955 - No. 5, Nov-Dec, 1955

1-Williamson/Torres-a; Wood-c/a	31	62	93	248	399	550
2-Williamson-c/a; Wood-a	26	52	78	208	329	450
3,4: 3-Williamson, Crandall-a. 4-Wood-c	21	42	63	168	264	360
5-Wood-c/a; Williamson/Evans-a	19	38	57	152	246	340

NOTE: ***Crandall** a-3, 4. **Ingels** a-1, 2, 4, 5. **Krigstein** a-1-5. **Orlando** a-3, 4; c-3. **Wood** a-1, 2, 5; c-1, 4, 5.*

VALOR
Gemstone Publishing: Oct, 1998 - No. 5, Feb, 1999 ($2.50)

1-5-Reprints 4.00

VALOR (Also see Legion of Super-Heroes & Legionnaires)
DC Comics: Nov, 1992 - No. 23, Sept, 1994 ($1.25/$1.50)

1-22: 1-Eclipso The Darkness Within aftermath. 2-Vs. Supergirl. 4-Vs. Lobo. 12-Lobo cameo. 14-Legionnaires, JLA app. 17-Austin-c(i); death of Valor. 18-22-Build-up to Zero Hour 3.00
23-Zero Hour tie-in 3.00

VAMPI (Vampirella's...)
Harris Publications (Anarchy Studios): Aug, 2000 - No. 25, Feb, 2003 ($2.95/$2.99)

Limited Edition Preview Book (5/00) Preview pages & sketchbook 4.00
1-(8/00, $2.95) Lau-a(p)/Conway-s 6.00
1-Platinum Edition 20.00
2-25: 17-Barberi-a 4.00

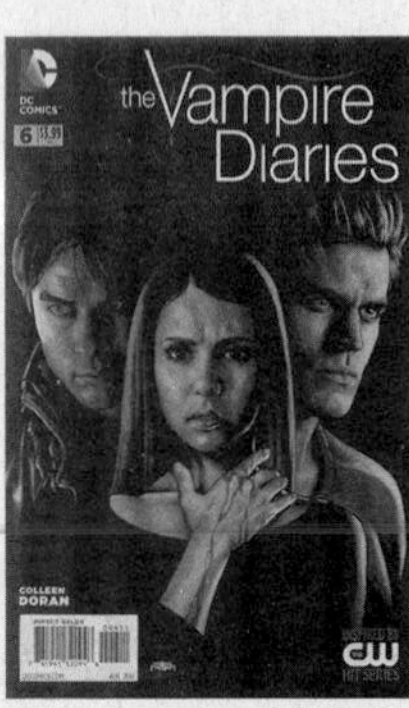

The Vampire Diaries #6 © WB

Vampirella #28 © WP

Vampirella (2001 series) #3 © Harris

GD VG FN VF VF/NM NM-
2.0 4.0 6.0 8.0 9.0 9.2

2-25-Deluxe Edition variants ($9.95): 4-Finch-c. 5-Wieringo-c. 6-Cha-c 10.00
...Digital 1 (11/01, $2.95) CGI art; Haberlin-s 4.00
...Digital Preview (Anarchy Studios, 7/01, $2.95) preview of CGI art 4.00
Switchblade Kiss HC (2001, $24.95) r/#1-6 25.00
Vicious Preview Ed. (Apr, 2003, $1.99) Flip book w/ Xin: Journey of the Monkey King Preview Ed. 4.00
Wizard #1/2 (mail order, $9.95) includes sketch pages 10.00

VAMPIRE BITES
Brainstorm Comics: May, 1995 - No. 2, Sept, 1996 ($2.95, B&W)

1,2:1-Color pin-up 4.00

VAMPIRE DIARIES, THE (Based on the CW television series)
DC Comics: Mar, 2014 - No. 6, Aug, 2014 ($3.99, printings of online comics)

1-6: 1,3-Doran-s/Shasteen-a. 5-Calero-a. 6-Doran-s/a 4.00

VAMPIRE LESTAT, THE
Innovation Publishing: Jan, 1990 - No. 12, 1991 ($2.50, painted limited series)

1-Adapts novel; Bolton painted-c on all 2 4 6 10 14 18
1-2nd printing (has UPC code, 1st prints don't) 3.00
1-3rd & 4th printings 3.00
2-1st printing 1 2 3 5 6 8
2-2nd & 3rd printings 3.00
3-5 5.00
3-6,9-2nd printings 3.00
6-12 4.00

VAMPIRELLA (Magazine)(See Warren Presents)(Also see Heidi Saha)
Warren Publishing Co./Harris Publications #113: Sept, 1969 - No. 112, Feb, 1983; No. 113, Jan, 1988? (B&W)

1-Intro. Vampirella in original costume & wings; Frazetta-c/intro. page; Adams-a; Crandall-a 61 122 183 488 1094 1700
2-1st app. Vampirella's cousin Evily-c/s; 1st/only app. Draculina, Vampirella's blonde twin sister 12 24 36 81 176 270
3 (Low distribution) 19 38 57 131 291 450
4,6 8 16 24 54 102 150
5,7,9: 5,7-Frazetta-c. 9-Barry Smith-a; Boris/Wood-c 9 18 27 57 111 165
8-Vampirella begins by Tom Sutton as serious strip (early issues-gag line) 9 18 27 60 120 180
10-No Vampi story; Brunner, Adams, Wood-a 6 12 18 40 73 105
11-Origin & 1st app. Pendragon; Frazetta-c 7 14 21 46 86 125
12-Vampi by Gonzales begins 7 14 21 46 86 125
13-15: 14-1st Maroto-a; Ploog-a 6 12 18 42 79 115
16,22,25: 16-1st full Dracula-c/app. 22-Color insert preview of Maroto's Dracula. 25-Vampi on cocaine-s 6 12 18 41 76 110
17,18,20,21,23,24: 17-Tomb of the Gods begins by Maroto, ends #22. 18-22-Dracula-s 6 12 18 38 69 100
19 (1973 Annual) Creation of Vampi text bio 7 14 21 44 82 120
26-35,38-40,45: 26,28,34,35,39,40-All have 8 pg. color inserts. 27-(1974 Annual) New color Vampi-s; mostly-r. 28-Board game inside covers. 30-Intro. Pantha; Corben-a(color). 31-Origin Luana, the Beast Girl. 32-Jones-a. 33-Wrightson-a; Pantha ends. 34,35-1st Fleur the Witch Woman. 38-2nd Vampi as Cleopatra/Blood Red Queen of Hearts; 1st Mayo-a. 39,40-Color Dracula-s. 40-Wrightson bio 5 10 15 31 53 75
36,37: 36-1st Vampi as Cleopatra/Blood Red Queen of Hearts; issue has 8 pg. color insert. 37-(1975 Annual) 5 10 15 34 60 85
41-44,47,48: 41-Dracula-s 4 8 12 28 47 65
46-(10/75) Origin-r from Annual 1 5 10 15 30 50 70
49-1st Blind Priestess; The Blood Red Queen of Hearts storyline begins; Poe-s 4 8 12 28 47 65
50-Spirit cameo by Eisner; 40 pg. Vampi-s; Pantha & Fleur app.; Jones-a 4 8 12 28 47 65
51-57,59-63,65,66,68,75,79-89: 54-Vampi-s (42 pgs.); 8 pg. color Corben-a. 55-All Gonzales-a(r). 60-62,65,66-The Blood Red Queen of Hearts app. 60-1st Blind Priestess-c. 63-10 pgs. Wrightson-a 4 8 12 23 37 50
58,70,72: 58-(92 pgs.) 70-Rook app. 4 8 12 27 44 60
64,73: 64-(100 pg. Giant) All Mayo-a; 70 pg. Vampi-s. 73-69 pg. Vampi-s; Mayo-a 4 8 12 28 47 65
67,69,71,74,76-78-All Barbara Leigh photo-c 4 8 12 27 44 60
90-99: 90-Toth-a. 91-All-r; Gonzales-a. 93-Cassandra St. Knight begins, ends #103; new Pantha series begins, ends #108 4 8 12 23 37 50
100 (96 pg. r-special)-Origin reprinted from Ann. 1; mostly reprints; Vampirella appears topless in new 21 pg. story 6 12 18 41 76 110
101-104,106,107: All lower print run. 101,102-The Blood Red Queen of Hearts app. 107-All Maroto reprint-a issue 5 10 15 34 60 85
105,108-110: 108-Torpedo series by Toth begins; Vampi nudity splash page. 110-(100 pg. Summer Spectacular) 5 10 15 34 60 85
111,112: Low print run. 111-Giant Collector's Edition ($2.50) 112-(84 pgs.) last Warren issue 7 14 21 49 92 135
113 (1988)-1st Harris Issue; very low print run 24 48 72 168 372 575
Annual 1(1972)-New definitive origin of Vampirella by Gonzales; reprints by Neal Adams (from #1), Wood (from #9) 19 38 57 133 297 460
Special 1 (1977) Softcover (color, large-square bound)-Only available thru mail order 15 30 45 100 220 340
Special 1 (1977) Hardcover (color, large-square bound)-Only available through mail order (scarce)(500 produced, signed & #'d) 30 60 90 216 483 750
#1 1969 Commemorative Edition (2001, $4.95) reprints entire #1 5.00
#30 (1974) Facsimile Edition (2020, $6.99) reprints entire #30 7.00
...Crimson Chronicles Vol. 1 (2004, $19.95, TPB) reprints stories from #1-10 20.00
...Crimson Chronicles Vol. 2 (2005, $19.95, TPB) reprints stories from #11-18 20.00
...Crimson Chronicles Vol. 3 (2005, $19.95, TPB) reprints stories from #19-28 20.00
...Crimson Chronicles Vol. 4 (2006, $19.95, TPB) reprints stories from #29-41 20.00

NOTE: ***Ackerman** s-1-3. **Neal Adams** a-1, 10p, 19p(r/#10), 44(1 pg.), Annual 1. **Alcala** a-78, 90, 93i. **Bodé/Todd** c-3. **Bodé/Jones** c-4. **Boris/Wood** c-9. **Brunner** a-10, 12(1 pg.). **Corben** a-30, 31, 33, 36, 54; c-30, 31, 33, 54. **Crandall** a-1, 19(r/#1). **Frazetta** c-1, 5, 7, 11, 31. **Heath** a-58, 61, 67, 76-78, 83. **Infantino** a-57-62. **Jones** a-5, 9, 12, 27, 32 (color), 33(2 pg.), 34, 50i, 83r. **Ken Kelly** c-6, 38, 39, 40(back-c), 46, 70, 95. **Nebres** a-84, 88-90, 92-96. **Nino** a-59i, 61i, 67, 76, 85, 90. **Ploog** a-14. **Barry Smith** a-9. **Starlin** a-78. **Sutton** a-1-5, 7-11, Annual 1. **Toth** a-90i, 108, 110. **Wood** a-9, 10, 12, 19(r/#12), 27r, Annual 1; c-9(partial). **Wrightson** a-33(w/**Jones**), 40(Bio cameo) 63r. All reprint issues-19, 74, 83, 91, 105, 107, 109, 111. Annuals from 1973 on are included in regular numbering. Later annuals are same format as regular issues. Color inserts (8 pgs.) in 22, 25-28, 30-35, 39, 40, 45, 46, 49, 54, 55, 67, 72. 16 pg color insert in #36.*

VAMPIRELLA (Also see Cain/... & Vengeance of...)
Harris Publications: Nov, 1992 - No. 5, Nov, 1993 ($2.95)

0-Bagged 1 2 3 5 6 8
0-Gold 3 6 9 17 25 34
1-Jim Balent inks in #1-3; Adam Hughes c-1-3 3 6 9 14 20 25
1-2nd printing 5.00
1-(11/97) Commemorative Edition 4.00
2 2 4 6 9 13 16
3-5: 4-Snyder III-c. 5-Brereton painted-c 1 2 3 5 6 8
Trade paperback nn (10/93, $5.95)-r/#1-4; Jusko-c 1 3 4 6 8 10

NOTE: *Issues 1-5 contain certificates for free **Dave Stevens** Vampirella poster.*

VAMPIRELLA (THE NEW MONTHLY)
Harris Publications: Nov, 1997 - No. 26, Apr, 2000 ($2.95)

1-3-"Ascending Evil" -Morrison & Millar-s/Conner & Palmiotti-a. 1-Three covers by Quesada/Palmiotti, Conner, and Conner/Palmiotti 5.00
1-3-($9.95) Jae Lee variant covers 10.00
1-($24.95) Platinum Ed.w/Quesada-c 25.00
4-6-"Holy War"-Small & Stull-a, 4-Linsner variant-c 4.00
7-9-"Queen's Gambit"-Shi app. 7-Two covers. 8-Pantha-c/app. 4.00
7-($9.95) Conner variant-c 10.00
10-12-"Hell on Earth"; Small-a/Coney-s. 12-New costume 4.00
10-Jae Lee variant-c 1 3 4 6 8 10
13-15-"World's End" Zircher-p; Pantha back-up, Texeira-a 4.00
16,17: 16-Pantha-c;Texeira-a; Vampi back-up story. 17-(Pantha #2) 4.00
18-20-"Rebirth": Jae Lee-c on all. 18-Loeb-s/Sale-a. 19-Alan Davis-a. 20-Bruce Timm-a 4.00
18-20-($9.95) Variant covers: 18-Sale. 19-Davis. 20-Timm 12.00
21-26: 21,22-Dangerous Games; Small-a. 23-Lady Death-c/app.; Cleavenger-a. 24,25-Lau-a. 26-Lady Death & Pantha-c/app.; Cleavenger-a. 4.00
0-(1/99) also variant-c with Pantha #0; same contents 4.00
TPB ($7.50) r/#1-3 "Ascending Evil" 8.00
Ascending Evil Ashcan (8/97, $1.00) 3.00
...: Grant Morrison/Mark Millar Collection TPB (2006, $24.95) r/#1-6; interviews 25.00
Hell on Earth Ashcan (7/98, $1.00) 3.00
... Presents: Tales of Pantha TPB (2006, $19.95) r/stories from #13-17 & one-shots 20.00
The End Ashcan (3/00, $6.00) 6.00
...30th Anniversary Celebration Preview (7/99) B&W preview of #18-20 10.00

VAMPIRELLA
Harris Publications: June, 2001 - No. 22, Aug, 2003 ($2.95/$2.99)

1-Four covers (Mayhew w/foil logo, Campbell, Anacleto, Jae Lee) Mayhew-a; Mark Millar-s 5.00
2-22: 2-Two covers (Mayhew & Chiodo). 3-Timm var-c. 4-Horn var-c. 7-10-Dawn Brown-a; Pantha back-up w/Texeira-a. 15-22-Conner-c 4.00
Giant-Size Ashcan (5/01, $5.95) B&W preview art and Mayhew interview 6.00
...: Halloween Trick & Treat (10/04, $4.95) stories & art by various; three covers 5.00
... : Nowheresville Preview Edition (3/01, $2.95)- previews Mayhew art and photo models 4.00
...Nowheresville TPB (1/02, $12.95) r/#1-3 with cover gallery 13.00
... Summer Special #1 (2005, $5.95) Batman Begins photo-c and 2 variant-c 6.00
...: 2006 Halloween Special (2006, $2.95) Conner-c; Hester-s/Segovia-a; 4 covers 4.00

VAMPIRELLA
Dynamite Entertainment: 2010 - No. 38, 2014 ($3.99)

Vampirella (2014 series) #8 © DYN

Vampirella Classic #5 © Harris

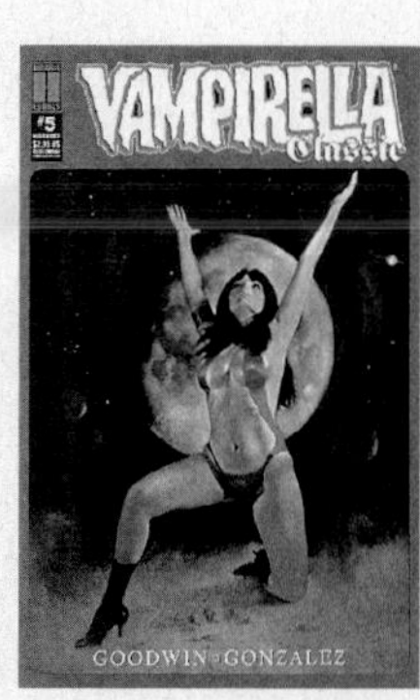

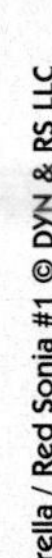
Vampirella / Red Sonja #1 © DYN & RS LLC

	GD	VG	FN	VF	VF/NM	NM-
	2.0	4.0	6.0	8.0	9.0	9.2

1-Four covers (Campbell, Madureira, J. Djurdjevic, Alex Ross swipe of Frazetta's #1) 4.00
1-Variant-c of blood-soaked Vampirella by Alex Ross 8.00
2-37: 2-6-Trautmann-s/Wagner Reis-a; four covers. 7-Geovani-a 4.00
38-($4.99, 40 pgs.) Pantha and Dracula app. 5.00
Annual 1 (2011, $4.99) Jerwa-s/Casalos-a; reprint with Alan Davis-a 5.00
Annual 2 (2012, $4.99) Rahner-s/Kyriazis-a; reprint with Pantha app.; Linsner-c 5.00
Annual 2013 ($4.99) Rahner-s/Valiente-a/Bolson-c 5.00
...: NuBlood (2013, $4.99) Spoof of True Blood; Rahner-s/Razek-a/c; back-up w/Timm-a 5.00
... Vs. Fluffy (2012, $4.99) Spoof of Buffy the Vampire Slayer; Bradshaw-c 5.00

VAMPIRELLA (Volume 2)
Dynamite Entertainment: 2014 - No. 13, 2015 ($3.99)

1-12: Multiple covers on each. 1-Nancy Collins-s/Berkenkotter-a 4.00
13-($4.99) Lord Drago app.; Collins-s/Berkenkotter-a; 3 covers 5.00
#100 (2015, $7.99) Short stories by various incl. Tim Seeley; multiple covers 8.00
#1969 (2015, $7.99) Short stories by various incl. Hester & Worley; 2 covers 8.00
Annual 2015 ($5.99) Collins-s/Aneke-a/Anacleto-c 6.00
...: Prelude to Shadows (2014, $7.99) Collins-s/Zamora-a; r/Vampirella #13 w/new color 8.00

VAMPIRELLA (Volume 3)
Dynamite Entertainment: 2016 - No. 6, 2016 ($3.99)

1-6: Multiple covers on each. 1-Kate Leth-s/Eman Casallos-a; new costume 4.00

VAMPIRELLA (Volume 4)
Dynamite Entertainment: 2017 - No. 11, 2018 ($3.99)

#0-(25¢) Multiple covers; Cornell-s/Broxton-a 3.00
1-11-($3.99) Vampirella in the far future. 1-5-Cornell-s/Broxton-a. 6-10-Belanger-a 4.00
... Halloween Special One-Shot (2018, $4.99) Reilly Brown-c 5.00
... Valentine's Day Special (2019, $4.99) Williams-s/Sanapo-a 5.00

VAMPIRELLA (Volume 5)
Dynamite Entertainment: 2019 - Present ($3.99)

0-(2019 Free Comic Book Day giveaway) Priest-s/Gündüz-a; reprint with Art Adams-a 3.00
1-17-Vampirella's mother Lilith app.; Priest-s/Gündüz-a; multiple covers on each 4.00
...: Trial of the Soul (2020, $4.99) Intro. Prester John; Willingham-s/Cafaro-a 5.00
...: Valentine's Day Special (2021, $4.99) Marcos Ramos-a; Dracula app. 5.00

VAMPIRELLA / ALIENS
Dynamite Entertainment: 2015 - No. 6, 2016 ($3.99, limited series)

1-6-Corinna Bechko-s/Javier Garcia-Miranda-a; multiple covers on each 4.00

VAMPIRELLA & PANTHA SHOWCASE
Harris Publications: Jan, 1997 ($1.50, one-shot)

1-Millar-s/Texeira-c/a; flip book w/"Blood Lust"; Robinson-s/Jusko-c/a 4.00

VAMPIRELLA & THE BLOOD RED QUEEN OF HEARTS
Harris Publications: Sept, 1996 ($9.95, 96 pgs., B&W, squarebound, one-shot)

nn-r/Vampirella #49,60-62,65,66,101,102; John Bolton-c; Michael Bair back-c 1 3 4 6 8 10

VAMPIRELLA AND THE SCARLET LEGION
Dynamite Entertainment: 2011 - No. 5 ($3.99)

1-5: 1-Three covers (Campbell, Chen and Tucci); Malaga-a 4.00

VAMPIRELLA / ARMY OF DARKNESS
Dynamite Entertainment: 2015 - No. 4, 2015 ($3.99, limited series)

1-4-Ash meets Vampirella in 1300 AD; Mark Rahner-s/Jeff Morales-a 4.00

VAMPIRELLA: BLOODLUST
Harris Publications: July, 1997 - No. 2, Aug, 1997 ($4.95, limited series)

1,2-Robinson-s/Jusko-painted c/a 6.00

VAMPIRELLA CLASSIC
Harris Publications: Feb, 1995 - No. 5, Nov, 1995 ($2.95, limited series)

1-5: Reprints Archie Goodwin stories. 4.00

VAMPIRELLA COMICS MAGAZINE
Harris Publications: Oct, 2003 - No. 9 ($3.95/$9.95, magazine-sized)

1-9-($3.95) 1-Texiera-c; b&w and color stories, Alan Moore interview; reviews. 2-KISS interview. 4-Chiodo-c. 6-Brereton-c 4.00
1-9-($9.95) 1-Three covers (Model Photo cover, Palmiotti-c, Wheatley Frankenstein-c) 10.00

VAMPIRELLA: CROSSOVER GALLERY
Harris Publications: Sept, 1997 ($2.95, one-shot)

1-Wraparound-c by Campbell, pinups by Jae Lee, Mack, Allred, Art Adams, Quesada & Palmiotti and others 1 3 4 6 8 10

VAMPIRELLA: DEATH & DESTRUCTION
Harris Publications: July, 1996 - No. 3, Sept, 1996 ($2.95, limited series)

1-3: Amanda Conner-a(p) in all. 1-Tucci-c. 2-Hughes-c. 3-Jusko-c 4.00

1-($9.95)-Limited Edition; Beachum-c 10.00

VAMPIRELLA / DEJAH THORIS
Dynamite Entertainment: 2018 - No. 5, 2019 ($3.99, limited series)

1-5-Erik Burnham-s/Ediano Silva-a; multiple covers on each; Vampirella on Barsoom 4.00

VAMPIRELLA/DRACULA & PANTHA SHOWCASE
Harris Publications: Aug, 1997 ($1.50, one-shot)

1-Ellis, Robinson, and Moore-s; flip book w/"Pantha" 4.00

VAMPIRELLA/DRACULA: THE CENTENNIAL
Harris Publications: Oct, 1997 ($5.95, one-shot)

1-Ellis, Robinson, and Moore-s; Beachum, Frank/Smith, and Mack/Mays-a Bolton-painted-c 6.00

VAMPIRELLA: FEARY TALES
Dynamite Entertainment: 2014 - No. 5, 2015 ($3.99, limited series)

1-5: Anthology of short stories by various; multiple covers on each 4.00

VAMPIRELLA: INTIMATE VISIONS
Harris Publications: 2006 ($3.95, one-shots)

..., Amanda Conner 1 - r/Vampirella Monthly #1 with commentary; interview; 2 covers 4.00
..., Joe Jusko 1 - r/Vampirella; Blood Lust #1 with commentary; interview; 2 covers 4.00

VAMPIRELLA: JULIE STRAIN SPECIAL
Harris Publications: Sept, 2000 ($3.95, one-shot)

1-Photo-c w/yellow background; interview and photo gallery 4.00
1-Limited Edition ($9.95); cover photo w/black background 10.00

VAMPIRELLA/LADY DEATH (Also see Lady Death/Vampirella)
Harris Publications: Feb, 1999 ($3.50, one-shot)

1-Small-a/Nelson painted-c 6.00
1-Valentine Edition ($9.95); pencil-c by Small 10.00

VAMPIRELLA: LEGENDARY TALES
Harris Publications: May, 2000 - No. 2, June, 2000 ($2.95, B&W)

1,2-Reprints from magazine; Cleavenger painted-c 4.00
1,2-($9.95) Variant painted-c by Mike Mayhew 10.00

VAMPIRELLA LIVES
Harris Publications: Dec, 1996 - No. 3, Feb, 1997 ($3.50/$2.95, limited series)

1-Die cut-c; Quesada & Palmiotti-c, Ellis-s/Conner-a 6.00
1-Deluxe Ed.-photo-c 6.00
2,3-($2.95)-Two editions (1 photo-c): 3-J. Scott Campbell-c 5.00

VAMPIRELLA: MORNING IN AMERICA
Harris Publications/Dark Horse Comics: 1991 - No. 4, 1992 ($3.95, B&W, lim. series, 52 pgs.)

1,2-All have Kaluta painted-c 2 4 6 8 10 12
3,4 2 4 6 8 10 12

VAMPIRELLA OF DRAKULON
Harris Publications: Jan, 1996 - No. 5, Sept, 1996 ($2.95)

0-5: All reprints. 0-Jim Silke-c. 3-Polybagged w/card. 4-Texeira-c 4.00

VAMPIRELLA/PAINKILLER JANE
Harris Publications: May, 1998 ($3.50, one-shot)

1-Waid & Augustyn-s/Leonardi & Palmiotti-a 4.00
1-($9.95) Variant-c 10.00

VAMPIRELLA PIN-UP SPECIAL
Harris Publications: Oct, 1995 ($2.95, one-shot)

1-Hughes-c, pin-ups by various 5.00
1-Variant-c 5.00

VAMPIRELLA QUARTERLY
Harris Publications: Spring, 2007 - Summer, 2008 ($4.95/$4.99, quarterly)

Spring, 2007 - Summer, 2008-New stories and re-colored reprints; five or six covers 5.00

VAMPIRELLA / RED SONJA
Dynamite Entertainment: 2019 - No. 12, 2020 ($3.99, limited series)

1-12: 1-Set in 1969; Jordie Bellaire-s/Drew Moss-a; multiple-c on each. 7,8-1920s NY 4.00

VAMPIRELLA: RETRO
Harris Publications: Mar, 1998 - No. 3, May, 1998 ($2.50, B&W, limited series)

1-3: Reprints; Silke painted covers 4.00

VAMPIRELLA: REVELATIONS
Harris Publications: No. 0, Oct, 2005 - No. 3, Feb, 2006 ($2.99, limited series)

0-3-Vampirella's origin retold, Lilith app.; Carey-s/Lilly-a; two covers on each 4.00
... Book 1 TPB (2006, $12.95) r/series; Carey interview, script for #1, Lilly sketch pages 13.00

Vampirella: Roses For the Dead #1 © DYN

Vampironica: New Blood #1 © ACP

Vamps #3 © Lee & Simpson

GD VG FN VF VF/NM NM-
2.0 4.0 6.0 8.0 9.0 9.2

GD VG FN VF VF/NM NM-
2.0 4.0 6.0 8.0 9.0 9.2

VAMPIRELLA: ROSES FOR THE DEAD
Dynamite Entertainment: 2018 - No. 4, 2019 ($3.99, limited series)
1-4-Kristina Deak-Linsner-s/Joseph Linsner-a; covers by Linsner & Tucci; Evily app. 4.00

VAMPIRELLA: SAD WINGS OF DESTINY
Harris Publications: Sept, 1996 ($3.95, one-shot)
1-Jusko-c 6.00

VAMPIRELLA: SECOND COMING
Harris Publications: 2009 - No. 4 ($1.99, limited series)
1-4: 1-Hester-s/Sampere-a; multiple covers on each. 3,4-Rio-a 4.00

VAMPIRELLA/SHADOWHAWK: CREATURES OF THE NIGHT (Also see Shadowhawk)
Harris Publications: 1995 ($4.95, one-shot)
1 5.00

VAMPIRELLA/SHI (See Shi/Vampirella)
Harris Publications: Oct, 1997 ($2.95, one-shot)
1-Ellis-s 6.00
1-Chromium-c 1 2 3 5 6 8

VAMPIRELLA: SILVER ANNIVERSARY COLLECTION
Harris Publications: Jan, 1997 - No. 4 Apr, 1997 ($2.50, limited series)
1-4: Two editions: Bad Girl by Beachum, Good Girl by Silke 5.00

VAMPIRELLA: SOUTHERN GOTHIC
Dynamite Entertainment: 2013 - No. 5, 2014 ($3.99)
1-5-Nate Cosby-s/José Luis-a; regular & photo-c on each 4.00

VAMPIRELLA'S SUMMER NIGHTS
Harris Publications: 1992 (one-shot)
1-Art Adams infinity cover; centerfold by Stelfreeze 2 4 6 10 14 18

VAMPIRELLA STRIKES
Harris Publications: Sept, 1995 - No. 8, Dec, 1996 ($2.95, limited series)
1-8: 1-Photo-c. 2-Deodato-c; polybagged w/card. 5-Eudaemon-c/app; wraparound-c; alternate-c exists. 6-(6/96)-Mark Millar script; Texeira-c; alternate-c exists. 7-Flip book 4.00
1-Newsstand Edition; diff. photo-c., 1-Limited Ed.; diff. photo-c 4.00
Annual 1-(12/96, $2.95) Delano-s; two covers 4.00

VAMPIRELLA STRIKES
Dynamite Entertainment: 2013 - No. 6, 2013 ($3.99)
1-6: 1-Five covers (Turner, Finch, Manara, Desjardins & photo); Desjardins-a 4.00

VAMPIRELLA: THE DARK POWERS
Dynamite Entertainment: 2020 - Present ($3.99)
1-3-Vampirella joins Project Superpowers team; Abnett-s/Davidson-a. 3-The Flame app. 4.00

VAMPIRELLA THE RED ROOM
Dynamite Entertainment: 2012 - No. 4, 2012 ($3.99)
1-4-Three covers on each; Brereton-s/Diaz-a 4.00

VAMPIRELLA: 25TH ANNIVERSARY SPECIAL
Harris Publications: Oct, 1996 ($5.95, squarebound, one-shot)
nn-Reintro The Blood Red Queen of Hearts; James Robinson, Grant Morrison & Warren Ellis scripts; Mark Texeira, Michael Bair & Amanda Conner-a(p); Frank Frazetta-c 1 2 3 5 6 8
nn-($6.95)-Silver Edition 1 3 4 6 8 10

VAMPIRELLA VS. DRACULA
Dynamite Entertainment: 2012 - No. 6, 2012 ($3.99, limited series)
1-6-Harris-s/Rodriguez-a/Linsner-c 4.00

VAMPIRELLA VS. HEMORRHAGE
Harris Publications: Apr, 1997 ($3.50)
1 6.00

VAMPIRELLA VS. PANTHA
Harris Publications: Mar, 1997 ($3.50)
1-Two covers; Millar-s/Texeira-c/a 4.00

VAMPIRELLA VS. REANIMATOR
Dynamite Entertainment: 2018 - No. 4, 2019 ($3.99, limited series)
1-4-Herbert West app.; Cullen Bunn-s/Blacky Shepherd-a; multiple covers on each 4.00

VAMPIRELLA/WETWORKS (See Wetworks/Vampirella)
Harris Publications: June, 1997 ($2.95, one-shot)
1 4.00
1-($9.95) Alternate Edition; cardstock-c 10.00

VAMPIRELLA/WITCHBLADE
Harris Publications: 2003; Oct, 2004; Oct, 2005 ($2.99, one-shots)
1-Brian Wood-s/Steve Pugh-a; 3 covers by Texeira, Conner and Pugh 4.00
...: The Feast (10/05, $2.99) Joyce Chin-a; covers by Chin, Conner, Rodriguez 4.00
...: Union of the Damned (10/04, $2.99, one-shot) Sharp-a; three covers 4.00
Trilogy TPB (2006, $12.95) r/one-shots; art gallery and gallery of multiple covers 13.00

VAMPIRE, PA
Moonstone: 2010 - No. 3, Oct, 2010 ($3.99)
1-3: 1-Intro. Vampire Hunter Dean; J.C. Vaughn-s/Brendon & Brian Fraim-a; three covers. 3-Zombie Proof back-up; Spencer-a 4.00
...: Bite Out of Crime (American Mythology, 7/19, $3.99) Vaughn-s/Fraims-a; six covers 4.00

VAMPIRE'S CHRISTMAS, THE (Also see Dark Ivory)
Image Comics: Oct, 2003 ($5.95, over-sized graphic novel)
nn-Linsner-s/a; Dubisch-painted-a 6.00

VAMPIRE STATE BUILDING
Ablaze Publishing: 2019 - Present ($3.99)
1-3-Charlie Adlard-a; Ange & Renault-s 4.00

VAMPIRES: THE MARVEL UNDEAD
Marvel Comics: Dec, 2011 ($3.99, one-shot)
1-Handbook-style profiles of vampire characters in the Marvel Universe; Seeley-c 4.00

VAMPIRE TALES
Marvel Comics Group: Aug, 1973 - No. 11, June, 1975 (75¢, B&W, magazine)
1-Morbius, the Living Vampire begins by Pablo Marcos (1st solo Morbius series & 5th Morbius app.) 9 18 27 59 117 175
2-Intro. Satana; Steranko-r 19 38 57 133 297 460
3,5,6: 3-Satana app. 5-Origin Morbius. 6-1st full Lilith app. in this title (continued from Giant-Size Chillers #1) 5 10 15 33 57 80
4,7: 4-1st Lilith cameo app. on inside back-c 5 10 15 30 50 70
8-1st solo Blade story (see Tomb of Dracula) 7 14 21 46 86 125
9-Blade app. 5 10 15 33 57 80
10,11 4 8 12 23 37 50
Annual 1(10/75)-Heath-r/#9 4 8 12 25 40 55
NOTE: ***Alcala** a-6, 8, 9i. **Boris** c-4, 6. **Chaykin** a-7. **Everett** a-1r. **Gulacy** a-7p. **Heath** a-9. **Infantino** a-3r. **Gil Kane** a-4, 5r.*

VAMPIRE VERSES, THE
CFD Productions: Aug, 1995 - No. 4, 1995 ($2.95, B&W, mature)
1-4 3.00

VAMPIRONICA (Archie Comics' Veronica)(Continues in Jughead The Hunger vs Vampironica)
Archie Comic Publications: May, 2018 - No. 5, Feb, 2019 ($3.99, limited series)
1-5: 1-Veronica becomes a vampire; Greg & Meg Smallwood-s/Greg S.-a; multiple covers. 4,5-Greg Scott-a 4.00

VAMPIRONICA: NEW BLOOD (Archie Comics' Veronica)
Archie Comic Publications: Jan, 2020 - No. 4, Aug, 2020 ($3.99, limited series)
1-4: 1-Tieri & Moreci-s/Mok-a; multiple covers. 3-Story of Sir Francis Lodge 4.00

VAMPI VICIOUS
Harris Publications (Anarchy Studios): Aug, 2003 - No. 3, Nov, 2003 ($2.99)
1-3: 1-McKeever-s/Dogan-a; 3 covers by Dogan, Lau & Noto. 3-Kau-a 4.00

VAMPI VICIOUS CIRCLE
Harris Publications (Anarchy Studios): Jun, 2004 - No. 3, Sept, 2004 ($2.99/$9.95)
1-3: B. Clay Moore-s 4.00
1-3-($9.95) Limited Edition w/variant-c. 1-Noto-c. 2-Norton-c. 3-Lucas-c 10.00

VAMPI VICIOUS RAMPAGE
Harris Publications (Anarchy Studios): Feb, 2005 - No. 2, Apr, 2005 ($2.99)
1,2: Raab-s/Lau-a; two covers on each 4.00

VAMPI VS. XIN
Harris Publications (Anarchy Studios): Oct, 2004 - No. 2, Jan, 2005 ($2.99)
1,2-Faerber-s/Lau-a; two covers 4.00

VAMPS
DC Comics (Vertigo): Aug, 1994 - No. 6, Jan, 1995 ($1.95, lim. series, mature)
1-6-Bolland-c 3.00
Trade paperback ($9.95)-r/#1-6 10.00

VAMPS: HOLLYWOOD & VEIN
DC Comics (Vertigo): Feb, 1996 - No. 6, July, 1996 ($2.25, lim. series, mature)
1-6: Winslade-c 3.00

VAMPS: PUMPKIN TIME
DC Comics (Vertigo): Dec, 1998 - No. 3, Feb, 1999 ($2.50, lim. series, mature)

Vandroid #5 © Vandroid Ltd.

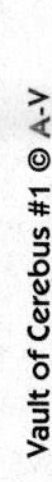

Vault of Cerebus #1 © A-V

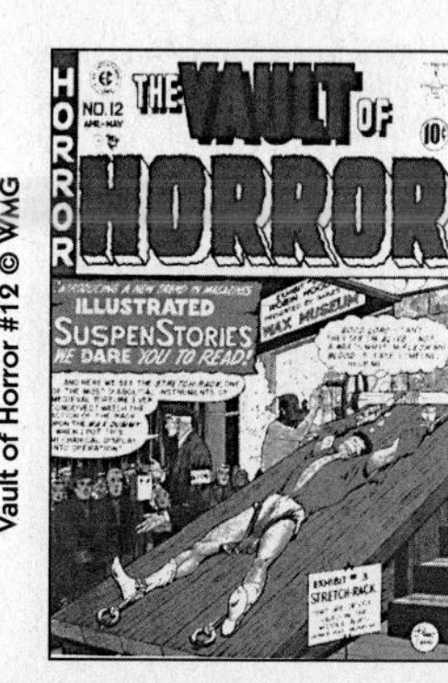

Vault of Horror #12 © WMG

GD VG FN VF VF/NM NM-
2.0 4.0 6.0 8.0 9.0 9.2

1-3: Quitely-c 3.00

VANDROID
Dark Horse Comics: Feb, 2014 - No. 5, Jun, 2014 ($3.99, limited series)

1-5-Tommy Lee Edwards & Noah Smith-s/Dan McDaid-a/Edwards-c 4.00

VANGUARD (...Outpost: Earth) (See Megaton)
Megaton Comics: 1987 ($1.50)

1-Erik Larsen-c(p) 4.00

VANGUARD (See Savage Dragon #2)
Image Comics (Highbrow Entertainment): Oct, 1993 - No. 6, 1994 ($1.95)

1-6: 1-Wraparound gatefold-c; Erik Larsen back-up-a; Supreme x-over. 3-(12/93)-Indicia says December 1994. 4-Berzerker back-up. 5-Angel Medina-a(p) 3.00

VANGUARD (See Savage Dragon #2)
Image Comics: Aug, 1996 - No. 4, Feb, 1997 ($2.95, B&W, limited series)

1-4 3.00

VANGUARD: ETHEREAL WARRIORS
Image Comics: Aug, 2000 ($5.95, B&W)

1-Fosco & Larsen-a 6.00

VANGUARD ILLUSTRATED
Pacific Comics: Nov, 1983 - No. 11, Oct, 1984 (Baxter paper)(Direct sales only)

1,3-6,8-11: 1-Nudity scenes 5.00
2-1st app. Stargrazers (see Legends of the Stargrazers; Dave Stevens-c
2 4 6 9 12 15
7-1st app. Mr. Monster (r-in Mr. Monster #1); nudity scenes 6.00
NOTE: ***Evans*** *a-7.* ***Kaluta*** *c-5, 7p.* ***Perez*** *a-6; c-6.* ***Rude*** *a-1-4; c-4.* ***Williamson*** *c-3.*

VANGUARD: STRANGE VISITORS
Image Comics: Oct, 1996 - No.4, Feb, 1997 ($2.95, B&W, limited series)

1-4: 3-Supreme-c/app. 3.00

VAN HELSING: FROM BENEATH THE RUE MORGUE (Based on the 2004 movie)
Dark Horse Comics: Apr, 2004 ($2.99, one-shot)

1-Hugh Jackman photo-c; Dysart-s/Alexander-a 3.00

VANITY (See Pacific Presents #3)
Pacific Comics: Jun, 1984 - No. 2, Aug, 1984 ($1.50, direct sales)

1,2: Origin 3.00

VARIETY COMICS (The Spice of Comics)
Rural Home Publ./Croyden Publ. Co.: 1944 - No. 2, 1945; No. 3, 1946

	GD 2.0	VG 4.0	FN 6.0	VF 8.0	VF/NM 9.0	NM- 9.2
1-Origin Captain Valiant	29	58	87	170	278	385
2-Captain Valiant	17	34	51	100	158	215
3(1946-Croyden)-Captain Valiant	15	30	45	88	137	185

VARIETY COMICS (See Fox Giants)

VARKING DEAD (Cerebus)
Aardvark-Vanaheim: Mar, 2020 ($4.00, B&W)

1-Walking Dead homage; Cerebus figures placed over original Doré artwork of Hell 4.00

VARK THING (Cerebus)
Aardvark-Vanaheim: Dec, 2019 ($4.00, B&W)

1-Swamp Thing homage figures placed over original Gustave Doré artwork of Hell 4.00

VARK WARS (Cerebus)
Aardvark-Vanaheim: Nov, 2019 ($4.00, B&W)

1-Cerebus figures placed over original Gustave Doré artwork of Hell 4.00

VARSITY
Parents' Magazine Institute: 1945

	GD 2.0	VG 4.0	FN 6.0	VF 8.0	VF/NM 9.0	NM- 9.2
1	12	24	36	69	97	125

VAULT OF CEREBUS (Imagery from Glamourpuss & Cerebus in Hell)
Aardvark-Vanaheim: Oct, 2020 ($4.00, B&W)

1-Cerebus figures placed over Doré artwork and zombies; Vault of Horror #19-c swipe 4.00

VAULT OF EVIL
Marvel Comics Group: Feb, 1973 - No. 23, Nov, 1975

	GD 2.0	VG 4.0	FN 6.0	VF 8.0	VF/NM 9.0	NM- 9.2
1 (1950s reprints begin)	5	10	15	31	53	75
2-23: 3,4-Brunner-c. 11-Kirby-a	3	6	9	17	26	35

NOTE: ***Ditko*** *a-14r, 15r, 20-22r.* ***Drucker*** *a-10r(Mystic #52), 13r(Uncanny Tales #42).* ***Everett*** *a-11r(Menace #2), 13r(Menace #4); c-10.* ***Heath*** *a-5r.* ***Gil Kane*** *c-1, 6.* ***Kirby*** *a-11.* ***Krigstein*** *a-20r(Uncanny Tales #54).* ***Reinman*** *r-1.* ***Tuska*** *a-6r.*

VAULT OF HORROR (Formerly War Against Crime #1-11) (Also see EC Archives)
E. C. Comics: No. 12, Apr-May, 1950 - No. 40, Dec-Jan, 1954-55

	GD 2.0	VG 4.0	FN 6.0	VF 8.0	VF/NM 9.0	NM- 9.2
12 (Scarce)-ties w/Crypt Of Terror as 1st horror comic; classic horror story "Terror Train" reprinted by popular demand in Haunt of Fear #20	686	1372	2058	5488	8744	12,000
13-Morphine story	143	286	429	1144	1822	2500
14-Classic horror story "The Strong Couple" redrawn in 3-D Tales of Terror #2	103	206	309	824	1312	1800
15- "Terror in the Swamp" is same story w/minor changes as "The Thing in the Swamp" from Haunt of Fear #15	94	188	282	752	1201	1650
16	74	148	222	592	946	1300
17-Classic werewolf-c	86	172	258	688	1094	1500
18,19	63	126	189	504	802	1100
20-25: 22-Frankenstein-c & adaptation. 23-Used in **POP**, pg. 84; Davis-a(2); Ingels bio. 24-Craig bio.	54	108	162	432	691	950
26-B&W & color illos in **POP**	63	126	189	504	802	1100
27-29,31,33,34,36: 31-Ray Bradbury bio. 36- "Pipe Dream" classic opium addict story by Krigstein; "Twin Bill" cited in articles by T.E. Murphy, Wertham	50	100	150	400	638	875
30-Classic severed arm-c	97	194	291	776	1238	1700
32-Censored-c	74	148	222	592	946	1300
35-X-Mas-c; "And All Through the House" adapted for 1972 Tales From The Crypt film	143	286	429	1144	1822	2500
37-1st app. Drusilla, a Vampirella look alike; Williamson-a	63	126	189	504	802	1100
38	50	100	150	400	638	875
39-Classic Craig woman in bondage/torture-c	80	160	240	640	1020	1400
40-Low distribution	57	114	171	456	728	1000

NOTE: ***Craig*** *art in all but No. 13 & 33; c-12-40.* ***Crandall*** *a-33, 34, 39.* ***Davis*** *a-17-38.* ***Evans*** *a-27, 28, 30, 32, 33.* ***Feldstein*** *a-12-16.* ***Ingels*** *a-13-20, 22-40.* ***Kamen*** *a-15-22, 25, 29, 35.* ***Krigstein*** *a-36, 38-40.* ***Kurtzman*** *a-12, 13.* ***Orlando*** *a-24, 31, 40.* ***Wood*** *a-12-14. #22, 29 & 31 have Ray Bradbury adaptations. #16 & 17 have H. P. Lovecraft adaptations.*

VAULT OF HORROR, THE
Gladstone Publ.: Aug, 1990 - No. 6, June, 1991 ($1.95, 68 pgs.)(#4 on: $2.00)

1-Craig-c(r); all contain EC reprints 6.00
2-6: 2,4-6-Craig-c(r). 3-Ingels-c(r) 5.00

VAULT OF HORROR
Russ Cochran/Gemstone Publishing: Sept, 1991 - No. 5, May, 1992 ($2.00); Oct, 1992 - No. 29, Oct, 1999 ($1.50/$2.00/$2.50)

1-29: E.C reprints. 1-4r/VOH #12-15 w/original-c 4.00

VAULT OF SPIDERS (Tie-ins to the Spider-Geddon x-over)
Marvel Comics: Dec, 2018 - No. 2, Jan, 2019 ($4.99)

1,2-Short stories of alternate Spider-Verse Spider-heroes; s/a by various 5.00

V...-COMICS (Morse code for "V" - 3 dots, 1 dash)
Fox Feature Syndicate: Jan, 1942 - No. 2, Mar-Apr, 1942

	GD 2.0	VG 4.0	FN 6.0	VF 8.0	VF/NM 9.0	NM- 9.2
1-Origin V-Man & the Boys; The Banshee & The Black Fury, The Queen of Evil, & V-Agents begin; Nazi-c	290	580	870	1856	3178	4500
2-Nazi bondage/torture-c	284	568	852	1818	3109	4400

VECTOR
Now Comics: 1986 - No. 4, 1986? ($1.50, 1st color comic by Now Comics)

1-4: Computer-generated art 3.00

VEIL
Dark Horse Comics: Mar, 2014 - No. 5, Oct, 2014 ($3.50)

1-5-Greg Rucka-s/Toni Fejzula-a/c 3.50

VEILS
DC Comics (Vertigo): 1999 ($24.95, one-shot)

Hardcover-($24.95) Painted art and photography; McGreal-s 25.00
Softcover ($14.95) 15.00

VELOCITY (Also see Cyberforce)
Image Comics (Top Cow Productions): Nov, 1995 - No. 3, Jan, 1996 ($2.50, limited series)

1-3: Kurt Busiek scripts in all. 2-Savage Dragon-c/app. 4.00
...: Pilot Season 1 (10/07, $2.99) Casey-s/Maguire-a 4.00
Vol. 2 #1-4 (6/10 - No. 4, 4/11, $3.99) Rocafort-a/Marz-s; multiple covers 4.00

VELVET
Image Comics: Oct, 2013 - No. 15, Jul, 2016 ($3.50/$3.99)

1-14-Brubaker-s/Epting-a/c. 5-$2.99-c 3.50
15-($3.99) 4.00

VENGEANCE
Marvel Comics: Sept, 2011 - No. 6, Feb, 2012 ($3.99, limited series)

1-6-Casey-s/Dragotta-a. 1-Magneto and Red Skull app. 4-Loki cover 4.00

VENGEANCE OF THE MOON KNIGHT
Marvel Comics: Nov, 2009 - No. 10, Sept, 2010 ($3.99/$2.99)

Vengeance of Vampirella (2019 series) #9 © DYN

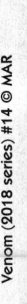

Venom (2011 series) #32 © MAR

Venom (2018 series) #14 © MAR

	GD	VG	FN	VF	VF/NM	NM-
	2.0	4.0	6.0	8.0	9.0	9.2

1,9: 1-($3.99) Hurwitz-s/Opeña-a; covers by Yu, Ross & Finch; back-up r/Moon Knight #1 ('80) 9-Spider-Man & Sandman app.; Campbell-c 4.00
2-8,10: 2-Sentry app. 5-Spider-Man app. 7,8-Deadpool app. 10-Secret Avengers app. 3.00

VENGEANCE OF VAMPIRELLA (Becomes Vampirella: Death & Destruction)
Harris Comics: Apr, 1994 - No. 25, Apr, 1996 ($2.95)

1-($3.50)-Quesada/Palmiotti "bloodfoil" wraparound-c 1 3 4 6 8 10
1-2nd printing; blue foil-c 4.00
1-Gold 20.00
2-8: 8-Polybagged w/trading card 5.00
9-25: 10-w/coupon for Hyde -25 poster. 11,19-Polybagged w/ trading card. 25-Quesada & Palmiotti red foil-c 4.00
...: Bloodshed (1995, $6.95) 7.00

VENGEANCE OF VAMPIRELLA (Volume 2)
Dynamite Entertainment: 2019 - Present ($3.99)

1-15-Set 25 years in the future; Sniegoski-s/Sta. Maria-a; multiple covers on each 4.00

VENGEANCE OF VAMPIRELLA: THE MYSTERY WALK
Harris Comics: Nov, 1995 ($2.95, one-shot)

0 4.00

VENGEANCE SQUAD
Charlton Comics: July, 1975 - No. 6, May, 1976 (#1-3 are 25¢ issues)

1-Mike Mauser, Private Eye begins by Staton 2 4 6 11 16 20
2-6: Morisi-a in all 1 3 4 6 8 10
5,6 (Modern Comics-r, 1977) 1 2 3 5 6 8

VENOM
Marvel Comics: June, 2003 - No. 18, Nov, 2004 ($2.25/$2.99)

1-Herrera-a/Way-s 1 3 4 6 8 10
2-15: 2-7-Herrera-a/Way-s. 6,7-Wolverine app. 8-10-Wolverine-c/app.; Kieth-c. 11-Fantastic Four app. 5.00
16-18 1 2 3 5 6 8
... Vol. 1: Shiver (2004, $13.99, TPB) r/#1-5 14.00
... Vol. 2: Run (2004, $19.99, TPB) r/#6-13 20.00
... Vol. 3: Twist (2004, $13.99, TPB) r/#14-18 14.00

VENOM (See Amazing Spider-Man #654 & 654.1)(Also see Secret Avengers)
Marvel Comics: May, 2011 - No. 42, Dec, 2013 ($3.99/$2.99)

1-Flash Thompson with the symbiote; Remender-s/Tony Moore-a/Quesada-c 2 4 6 13 18 22
2-Cover swipe of ASM #300; Kraven app. 3 6 9 16 23 30
3-12-($2.99) 3-Deodato-c. 6-8-Spider Island 4.00
13-($3.99) Circle of Four; Red Hulk, X-23, and Ghost Rider app. 4.00
13.1, 13.2, 13.3, 13.4, 14-($2.99) Circle of Four parts 2-6 3.00
15-27, 27.1, 28-42: 15-Secret Avengers app. 16,17-Toxin app. 26,27-Minimum Carnage. 38-1st app. Mania. 42-Mephisto app. 4.00
...: Flashpoint 1 (2011, $4.99) r/Amazing Spider-Man #654, 654.1 and Venom #1 2 4 6 10 14 18

VENOM (Also see Amazing Spider-Man: Venom Inc.)
Marvel Comics: Jan, 2017 - No. 6, Jun, 2017; No. 150, Jul, 2017 - No. 165, Jun, 2018 ($3.99)

1-Mike Costa-s/Gerardo Sandoval-a; intro. Lee Price; Mac Gargan app. 1 2 3 5 6 8
2-6 4.00

[Title switches to legacy numbering after #6 (6/17)]

150-($5.99) Eddie Brock as Venom; Spider-Man app.; Tradd Moore-a; cover gallery 6.00
151-165: 152,153-Moon Girl and Devil Dinosaur app. 155-158-Kraven app.; Bagley-a. 159-Venom Inc. part 3; Sandoval-a. 160-Venom Inc. part 5 4.00

VENOM (Follows Venomized series)
Marvel Comics: Jul, 2018 - Present ($4.99/$3.99)

1-($4.99) Cates-s/Stegman-a; Eddie Brock with the symbiote; intro. Rex Strickland 1 3 4 6 8 10
2,4-24,26-33 ($3.99) 2-5-Spider-Man (Miles Morales) app. 4-Origin of Knull. 13-15-War of the Realms tie-ins. 17-20-Absolute Carnage tie-ins. 21-24-Venom Island; Bagley-a. 31-33-King In Black 4.00
3-1st app. Knull 6 12 18 38 69 100
25-($5.99) 1st app. Virus; Cates-s/Bagley-a; Carnage app.; back-up w/Michelinie-s/Lim-a 6.00
Annual 1 (12/18, $4.99) Short stories by various incl. Cates, Michelinie, Lim, Stokoe 5.00
Annual 1 (9/19, $4.99) Cady-s/Di Meo-a; Lady Hellbender app.; back-up origin; Ibáñez-a 5.00
...: The End 1 (3/20, $4.99) Warren-s/Cruz-a; Venom's last story in the far future 5.00
... 2099 #1 (2/20, $4.99) Tie-in to 2099 x-over; Venom's new host; Houser-s 5.00

VENOMIZED
Marvel Comics: Jun, 2018 - No. 5, Jul, 2018 ($4.99/$3.99, weekly limited series)

1-($4.99) Bunn-s/Coello-a; X-Men vs. The Poisons 5.00
2-5-($3.99) 2,3,5-Bunn-s/Coello-a. 4-Libranda-a 4.00

VENOM: LETHAL PROTECTOR
Marvel Comics: Feb, 1993 - No. 6, July, 1993 ($2.95, limited series)

1-Red holo-grafx foil-c; Bagley-c/a in all 3 6 9 19 30 40
1-Gold variant sold to retailers 12 24 36 81 176 270
1-Black-c 46 92 138 340 770 1200
NOTE: Counterfeit copies of the black-c exist and are valueless
2,4-6: Spider-Man app. in all 2 4 6 9 12 15
5-1st app. Phage, Lasher, Riot & Agony 3 6 9 14 20 26

VENOM: SPACE KNIGHT
Marvel Comics: Jan, 2016 - No. 13, Dec, 2016 ($3.99)

1-13: 1-Robbie Thompson-s/Ariel Olivetti-a. 8-10-Jacinto-a. 11,12-Civil War II tie-in 4.00

VENOM: Marvel Comics (Also see Amazing Spider-Man #298-300)
... ALONG CAME A SPIDER, 1/96 - No. 4, 4/96 ($2.95)-Spider-Man & Carnage app. 2 4 6 9 12 15
... CARNAGE UNLEASHED, 4/95 - No. 4, 7/95 ($2.95) 1 3 4 6 8 10
... DARK ORIGIN, 10/08 - No. 5, 2/09 ($2.99) 1-5-Medina-a 6.00
... /DEADPOOL: WHAT IF?, 4/11 ($2.99) Remender-s/Moll-a/Young-c; Galactus app. 10 20 30 65 135 205
... DEATHTRAP: THE VAULT, 3/93 ($6.95) r/Avengers: Deathtrap: The Vault 2 4 6 8 10 12
... FIRST HOST, 10/18 - No. 5, 11/18 ($3.99) 1-5-Costa-s/Bagley & Lim-a 4.00
... FUNERAL PYRE, 8/93- No. 3, 10/93 ($2.95)-#1-Holo-grafx foil-c; Punisher app. in all 1 3 4 6 8 10
... LICENSE TO KILL, 6/97 - No. 3, 8/97 ($1.95) 1 3 4 6 8 10
... NIGHTS OF VENGEANCE, 8/94 - No. 4, 11/94 ($2.95), #1-Red foil-c 1 3 4 6 8 10
... ON TRIAL, 3/97 - No. 3, 5/97 ($1.95) 1 3 4 6 8 10
... SEED OF DARKNESS, 7/97 ($1.95) #(-1) Flashback 1 3 4 6 8 10
... SEPARATION ANXIETY, 12/94- No. 4, 3/95 ($2.95) #1-Embossed-c 1 3 4 6 8 10
... SIGN OF THE BOSS, 3/97 - No. 2, 10/97 ($1.99) 1 3 4 6 8 10
... SINNER TAKES ALL, 8/95 - No. 5, 10/95 ($2.95) 1,2,4,5 1 3 4 6 8 10
3-1st time Ann Weying app. as female Venom 5 10 15 34 60 85
... SUPER SPECIAL, 8/95($3.95) #1-Flip book 2 4 6 10 14 18
... THE ENEMY WITHIN, 2/94 - No. 3, 4/94 ($2.95)-Demogoblin & Morbius app. 1-Glow-in-the-dark-c 1 3 4 6 8 10
... THE FINALE, 11/97 - No. 3, 1/98 ($1.99) 1 3 4 6 8 10
... THE HUNGER, 8/96- No. 4, 11/96 ($1.95) 1 3 4 6 8 10
... THE HUNTED, 5/96-No. 3, 7/96 ($2.95) 1 3 4 6 8 10
... THE MACE, 5/94 - No. 3, 7/94 ($2.95)-#1-Embossed-c 1 3 4 6 8 10
... THE MADNESS, 11/93- No. 3, 1/94 ($2.95)-Kelley Jones-c/a(p). 1-Embossed-c; Juggernaut app. 1 3 4 6 8 10
... TOOTH AND CLAW, 12/96 - No. 3, 2/97 ($1.95)-Wolverine-c/app. 1 3 4 6 8 10
... VS. CARNAGE, 9/04 - No. 4, 12/04 ($2.99)-Milligan-s/Crain-a; Spider-Man app. 1 3 4 6 8 10
TPB (2004, $9.99) r/#1-4 10.00

VENOMVERSE
Marvel Comics: Nov, 2017 - No. 5, Dec, 2017 ($4.99/$3.99, weekly limited series)

1-($4.99) Bunn-s/Coello-a; Venoms vs. The Poisons 5.00
2-5-($3.99) Bunn-s/Coello-a 4.00
...: War Stories 1 (11/17, $4.99) Multiverse of Venoms; short stories by various 5.00

VENTURE
AC Comics (Americomics): Aug, 1986 - No. 3, 1986? ($1.75)

1-3: 1-3-Bolt. 1-Astron. 2-Femforce. 3-Fazers 3.00

VENTURE
Image Comics: Jan, 2003 - No. 4, Sept, 2003 ($2.95)

1-4-Faerber-s/Igle-a 3.00

VENUS (See Agents of Atlas, Marvel Spotlight #2 & Weird Wonder Tales)

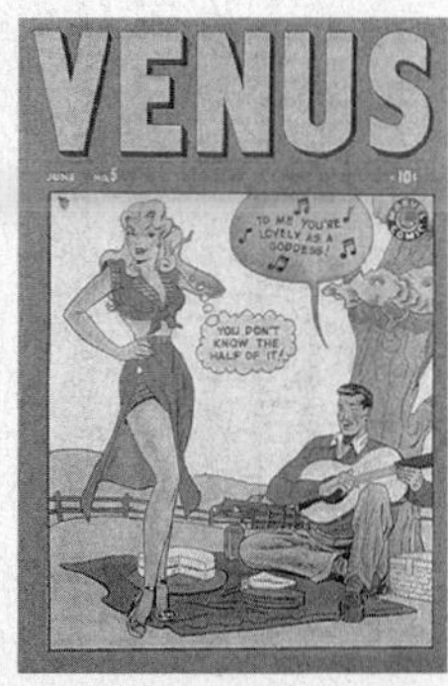

Venus #5 © MAR

Veronica #49 © ACP

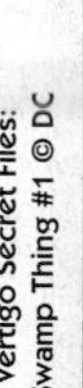

Vertigo Secret Files: Swamp Thing #1 © DC

	GD 2.0	VG 4.0	FN 6.0	VF 8.0	VF/NM 9.0	NM- 9.2

Marvel/Atlas Comics (CMC 1-9/LCC 10-19): Aug, 1948 - No. 19, Apr, 1952 (Also see Marvel Mystery #91)

	GD	VG	FN	VF	VF/NM	NM-
1-Venus & Hedy Devine begin; 1st app. Venus; Kurtzman's "Hey Look"	295	590	885	1888	3244	4600
2	148	296	444	947	1624	2300
3,5	97	194	291	621	1061	1500
4-Kurtzman's "Hey Look"	100	200	300	640	1095	1550
6-9: 6-Loki app. 7,8-Painted-c. 9-Begin 52 pgs.; book-length feature "Whom the Gods Destroy!"	84	168	252	538	919	1300
10-S/F-horror issues begin (7/50)	116	232	348	742	1271	1800
11-S/F end of the world (11/50)	129	258	387	826	1413	2000
12-Colan-a	81	162	243	518	884	1250
13-16-Venus by Everett, 2-3 stories each; covers-#13,15,16; 14-Everett part cover (Venus).	145	290	435	928	1589	2250
17-Classic Everett horror & skeleton/bondage-c (scarce)	459	918	1377	3350	5925	8500
18-Classic Everett horror-c	343	686	1029	2400	4200	6000
19-Classic Everett skeleton Good Girl-c	541	1082	1623	3950	6975	10,000

NOTE: ***Berg** s/f story-13. **Everett** c-13, 14(part; Venus only), 15-19. **Heath** s/f story-11. **Maneely** s/f story 10(3pg.), 16. **Morisi** a-19. **Syd Shores** c-6.*

VENUS
BOOM! Studios: Dec, 2015 - No. 4, Mar, 2016 ($3.99)

1-4-Loverd-s/Danlan-a 4.00

VERI BEST SURE FIRE COMICS
Holyoke Publishing Co.: No date (circa 1945) (Reprints Holyoke one-shots)

	GD	VG	FN	VF	VF/NM	NM-
1-Captain Aero, Alias X, Miss Victory, Commandos of the Devil Dogs, Red Cross, Hammerhead Hawley, Capt. Aero's Sky Scouts, Flagman app.; same-c as Veri Best Sure Shot #1	52	104	156	328	552	775

VERI BEST SURE SHOT COMICS
Holyoke Publishing Co.: No date (circa 1945) (Reprints Holyoke one-shots)

	GD	VG	FN	VF	VF/NM	NM-
1-Capt. Aero, Miss Victory by Quinlan, Alias X, The Red Cross, Flagman, Commandos of the Devil Dogs, Hammerhead Hawley, Capt. Aero's Sky Scouts; same-c as Veri Best Sure Fire #1	52	104	156	328	552	775

VERMILLION
DC Comics (Helix): Oct, 1996 - No. 12, Sept, 1997 ($2.25/$2.50)

1-12: 1-4: Lucius Shepard scripts. 4,12-Kaluta-c 3.00

VERONICA (Also see Archie's Girls, Betty &...)
Archie Comics: Apr, 1989 - No. 210, Feb, 2012

	GD	VG	FN	VF	VF/NM	NM-
1-(75¢-c)	2	4	6	10	14	18
2-10: 2-(75¢-c)						5.00
11-38						4.00
39-Love Showdown pt. 4, Cheryl Blossom						6.00
40-70: 34-Neon ink-c						3.00
71-201,203-206: 134-Begin $2.19-c. 152,155-Cheryl Blossom app. 163-Begin $2.25-c						3.00
202-Intro. Kevin Keller, 1st openly gay Archie character; cover has blue background	2	4	6	9	12	15
202-Second printing; cover has black background	1	3	4	6	8	10
207-210-Kevin Keller mini-series						3.00

VERONICA'S PASSPORT DIGEST MAGAZINE (Becomes Veronica's Digest Magazine #3 on)
Archie Comics: Nov, 1992 - No. 6 ($1.50/$1.79, digest size)

1 5.00
2-6 3.00

VERONICA'S SUMMER SPECIAL (See Archie Giant Series Magazine #615, 625)

VERTICAL
DC Comics (Vertigo): 2003 ($4.95, 3-1/4" wide pages, one-shot)

1-Seagle-s/Allred & Bond-a; odd format 1/2 width pages with some 20" long spreads 5.00

VERTIGO DOUBLE SHOT
DC Comics (Vertigo): 2008 ($2.99)

1-Reprints House of Mystery (2008) #1 and Young Liars #1 in flip-book format 3.00

VERTIGO ESSENTIALS
DC Comics (Vertigo): Dec, 2013 - Feb, 2014 ($1.00, Flip book reprints with DC & Vertigo Essential Graphics novels catalog)

...: American Vampire 1 (2/14) Reprints #1; flip-c by Ryan Sook 3.00
...: Fables 1 (1/14) Reprints #1; flip-c by Ryan Sook 3.00
...: 100 Bullets 1 (2/14) Reprints #1; flip-c by Ryan Sook 3.00
...: The Sandman #1 (12/13, $1.00) Reprints Sandman #1 (1989) with flipbook 3.00
...: V For Vendetta 1 (12/13) Reprints first chapter; flip-c by Ryan Sook 3.00
...: Y: The Last Man 1 (1/14) Reprints #1; flip-c by Ryan Sook 3.00

VERTIGO: FIRST BLOOD
DC Comics (Vertigo): Feb, 2012 ($7.99, squarebound)

TPB-Reprints first issues of American Vampire, I Zombie, The Unwritten & Sweet Tooth 8.00

VERTIGO: FIRST CUT
DC Comics (Vertigo): 2008 ($4.99, TPB)

TPB-Reprints first issues of DMZ, Army@Love, Jack of Fables, Exterminators, Scalped, Crossing Midnight, and Loveless; preview of Air 5.00

VERTIGO: FIRST OFFENSES
DC Comics (Vertigo): 2005 ($4.99, TPB)

TPB-Reprints first issues of The Invisibles, Preacher, Fables, Sandman Mystery Theater, and Lucifer 5.00

VERTIGO: FIRST TASTE
DC Comics (Vertigo): 2005 ($4.99, TPB)

TPB-Reprints first issues of Y: The Last Man, 100 Bullets, Transmetropolitan, Books of Magick: Life During Wartime, Death: The High Cost of Living, and Saga of the Swamp Thing #21 (Alan Moore's first story on that title) 5.00

VERTIGO GALLERY, THE: DREAMS AND NIGHTMARES
DC Comics (Vertigo): 1995 ($3.50, one-shot)

1-Pin-ups of Vertigo characters by Sienkiewicz, Toth, Van Fleet & others; McKean-c 4.00

VERTIGO JAM
DC Comics (Vertigo): Aug, 1993 ($3.95, one-shot, 68 pgs.)(Painted-c by Fabry)

1-Sandman by Neil Gaiman, Hellblazer, Animal Man, Doom Patrol, Swamp Thing, Kid Eternity & Shade the Changing Man 5.00

VERTIGO POP! BANGKOK
DC Comics (Vertigo): July, 2003 - No. 4, Oct, 2003 ($2.95, limited series)

1-4-Camuncoli-c/a; Jonathan Vankin-s 3.00

VERTIGO POP! LONDON
DC Comics (Vertigo): Jan, 2003 - No. 4, Apr, 2003 ($2.95, limited series)

1-4-Philip Bond-c/a; Peter Milligan-s 3.00

VERTIGO POP! TOKYO
DC Comics (Vertigo): Sept, 2002 - No. 4, Dec, 2002 ($2.95, limited series)

1-4-Seth Fisher-c/a; Jonathan Vankin-s 3.00
Tokyo Days, Bangkok Nights TPB (2009, $19.99) r/#1-4 & Vertogo Pop! Bangkok #1-4 20.00

VERTIGO PREVIEW
DC Comics (Vertigo): 1992 (75¢, one-shot, 36 pgs.)

1-Vertigo previews; Sandman story by Neil Gaiman 3.00

VERTIGO QUARTERLY CMYK
DC Comics (Vertigo): Jun, 2014 - No. 4, Mar, 2015 ($7.99, limited series)

1-4-Color themed short story anthology. 1-Cyan. 2-Magenta. 3-Yellow. 4-Black 8.00

VERTIGO QUARTERLY SFX
DC Comics (Vertigo): Jun, 2015 - No. 4, Mar, 2016 ($7.99, limited series)

1-4-Sound effect-themed short story anthology. 1-"Pop!". 2-"Slam!". 3-"Krak!". 4-"Bang" 8.00

VERTIGO RAVE
DC Comics (Vertigo): Fall, 1994 (99¢, one-shot)

1-Vertigo previews 3.00

VERTIGO RESURRECTED: ...
DC Comics (Vertigo): Dec, 2010 - Feb, 2012 ($7.99, squarebound, reprints)

The Extremist 1 (1/11, 12/13) r/The Extremist #1-4 8.00
Finals 1 (5/11) r/Finals #1-4; Jill Thompson-a 8.00
Hellblazer 1 (2/11) r/Hellblazer #57,58,245,246 8.00
Hellblazer - Bad Blood 1 (6/11) r/Hellblazer Special: Bad Blood #1-4 8.00
Jonny Double 1 (10/11) r/Jonny Double #1-4; Azzarello-s/Risso-a 8.00
My Faith in Frankie 1 (1/12) r/My Faith in Frankie #1-4; Carey-s 8.00
Sandman Presents - Petrefax 1 (8/11) r/Sandman Presents: Petrefax #1-4 8.00
Sgt. Rock: Between Hell and a Hard Place 1,2 (1/12, 2/12) r/the 2003 HC 8.00
Shoot 1 (12/10) r/short stories by various incl. Quitely, Sale, Bolland, Risso, Jim Lee 8.00
The Eaters 1 (12/11) r/Vertigo Visions - The Eaters and other short stories 8.00
Winter's Edge 1 (2/11) r/Vertigo's Winter Edge #1-3; Bermejo-c 8.00

VERTIGO SECRET FILES
DC Comics (Vertigo): Aug, 2000 ($4.95)

...: Hellblazer 1 (8/00, $4.95) Background info and story summaries 5.00
...: Swamp Thing 1 (11/00, $4.95) Backstories and origins; Hale-c 5.00

VERTIGO VERITE: THE UNSEEN HAND
DC Comics (Vertigo): Sept, 1996 - No. 4, Dec, 1996 ($2.50, limited series)

1-4: Terry LaBan scripts in all 3.00

Vertigo Visions: Prez #1 © DC

The Victories #15 © Michael Oeming

Vigilante #17 © DC

	GD	VG	FN	VF	VF/NM	NM-
	2.0	4.0	6.0	8.0	9.0	9.2

VERTIGO VISIONS
DC Comics (Vertigo): June, 1993 - Sept, 1998 (one-shots)
Dr. Occult 1 (7/94, $3.95) 4.00
Dr. Thirteen 1 (9/98, $5.95) Howarth-s 6.00
Prez 1 (7/95, $3.95) 4.00
The Geek 1 (6/93, $3.95) 4.00
The Eaters ($4.95, 1995)-Milligan story. 5.00
The Phantom Stranger 1 (10/93, $3.50) 4.00
Tomahawk 1 (7/98, $4.95) Pollack-s 5.00

VERTIGO WINTER'S EDGE
DC Comics (Vertigo): 1998, 1999 ($7.95/$6.95, square-bound, annual)
1-Winter stories by Vertigo creators; Desire story by Gaiman/Bolton; Bolland wraparound-c 8.00
2,3-($6.95)-Winter stories: 2-Allred-c. 3-Bond-c; Desire by Gaiman/Zulli 7.00

VERTIGO X ANNIVERSARY PREVIEW
DC Comics (Vertigo): 2003 (99¢, one-shot, 48 pgs.)
1-Previews of upcoming titles and interviews; Endless Nights, Shade, The Originals 4.00

VERY BEST OF DENNIS THE MENACE, THE
Fawcett Publ.: July, 1979 - No. 2, Apr, 1980 (95¢/$1.00, digest-size, 132 pgs.)
1,2-Reprints 2 4 6 8 10 12

VERY BEST OF DENNIS THE MENACE, THE
Marvel Comics Group: Apr, 1982 - No. 3, Aug, 1982 ($1.25, digest-size)
1-3: Reprints 2 3 4 6 8 10
1,2-Mistakenly printed with DC logo on cover 2 4 6 9 12 15
NOTE: ***Hank Ketcham** c-all. A few thousand of #1 & 2 were printed with DC emblem.*

VERY VICKY
Meet Danny Ocean: 1993? - No. 8, 1995 ($2.50, B&W)
1-8, ...: Calling All Hillbillies (1995, $2.50) 4.00

VERY WEIRD TALES (Also see Slithiss Attacks!)
Oceanspray Comics Group: Aug, 2002 - No. 2, Oct, 2002 ($4.00)
1-Mutant revenge, methamphetamine, corporate greed horror stories 3 6 9 16 23 30
2-Weird fantasy and horror stories 2 4 6 9 12 15
NOTE: *Created in prevention classes taught by Jon McClure at the Oceanspray Family Center in Newport, Oregon, and paid for by the Housing Authority of Lincoln County. All books are b&w with color covers. Issues #1-2 penciled and inked by various artists. All comics feature characters created by students and are signed and numbered by Jon McClure. Issues #1-2 have print runs of 100 each.*

VEXT
DC Comics: Mar, 1999 - No. 6, Aug, 1999 ($2.50, limited series)
1-6-Giffen-s. 1-Superman app. 3.00

V FOR VENDETTA
DC Comics: Sept, 1988 - No. 10, May, 1989 ($2.00, maxi-series)
1-Alan Moore scripts in all; David Lloyd-a 4 8 12 25 40 55
2-10 1 3 4 6 8 10
HC (1990) Limited edition 60.00
HC (2005, $29.99, dustjacket) r/series; foreward by Lloyd; promo art and sketches 30.00
Trade paperback (1990, $14.95) 20.00

VICE
Image Comics (Top Cow): Nov, 2005 - No. 5 ($2.99)
1-5-Coleite-s/Kirkham-a. 1-Three covers 3.00
1-Code Red Edition; variant Benitez-c 3.00

VIC FLINT (Crime Buster...)(See Authentic Police Cases #10-14 & Fugitives From Justice #2)
St. John Publ. Co.: Aug, 1948 - No. 5, Apr, 1949 (Newspaper reprints; NEA Service)
1 23 46 69 138 227 315
2 15 30 45 85 130 175
3-5 14 28 42 78 112 145

VIC FLINT (Crime Buster...)
Argo Publ.: Feb, 1956 - No. 2, May, 1956 (Newspaper reprints)
1,2 10 20 30 54 72 90

VIC JORDAN (Also see Big Shot Comics #32)
Civil Service Publ.: April, 1945
1-1944 daily newspaper-r; WWII-c 20 40 60 118 192 265

VICKI (Humor)
Atlas/Seaboard Publ.: Feb, 1975 - No. 4, Aug, 1975 (No. 1,2: 68 pgs.)
1,2-(68 pgs.)-Reprints Tippy Teen; Good Girl art 5 10 15 33 57 80
3,4 (Low print) 5 10 15 34 60 85

VICKI VALENTINE (...Summer Special #1)
Renegade Press: July, 1985 - No. 4, July, 1986 ($1.70, B&W)
1-4: Woggon, Rausch-a; all have paper dolls. 2-Christmas issue 4.00

VICKY
Ace Magazine: Oct, 1948 - No. 5, June, 1949
nn(10/48)-Teenage humor 14 28 42 82 121 160
4(12/48), nn(2/49), 4(4/49), 5(6/49): 5-Dotty app. 11 22 33 64 90 115

VICTOR CROWLEY'S HATCHET HALLOWEEN TALES (Based on the 2007 movie)
American Mythology Productions: 2019, 2020 ($3.99)
1-Short stories by Pell-s/Mesarcia-a, Check-s/Bonk-a, Kuhoric-s/Calzada-a; 4 covers 4.00
... II (2020) Short stories by Kuhoric-s/Cantada-a, Pell-s/Miracolo-a, Green-s/Hoey-a 4.00

VICTORIAN UNDEAD
DC Comics (WildStorm): Jan, 2010 - No. 6, Jun, 2010 ($2.99)
1-6-Sherlock Holmes vs. Zombies; Edginton-s/Fabbri-a. 1-Two covers (Moore, Coleby) 3.00
...: Sherlock Holmes vs. Jekyll and Hyde (12/10, $4.99) Domingues-a/Van Sciver-c 5.00
...: Sherlock Holmes vs. Zombies TPB (2010, $17.99) r/#1-6; character design sketch art 18.00
... Volume 2 (1/11 - No. 5, 5/11) 1-3-($3.99) "Sherlock Holmes vs. Dracula" on-c; Fabbri-a 4.00
... Volume 2 - 4,5-($2.99) "Sherlock Holmes vs. Dracula" on-c; Fabbri-a 3.00

VICTORIES, THE
Dark Horse Comics: Aug, 2012 - No. 5, Dec, 2012 ($3.99 limited series)
1-5-Michael Avon Oeming-s/a/c 4.00
...Volume 2: Transhuman 1-15 (6/13 - No. 15, 9/14) Oeming-s/a/c. 11-15 Metahuman 4.00

VIC TORRY & HIS FLYING SAUCER (Also see Mr. Monster's...#5)
Fawcett Publications: 1950 (one-shot)
nn-Book-length saucer story by Powell; photo/painted-c 74 148 222 470 810 1150

VICTORY
Topps Comics: June, 1994 ($2.50, unfinished limited series)
1-Kurt Busiek script; Giffen-c/a; Rob Liefeld variant-c exists 3.00

VICTORY COMICS
Hillman Periodicals: Aug, 1941 - No. 4, Dec, 1941 (#1 by Funnies, Inc.)
1-The Conqueror by Bill Everett, The Crusader, & Bomber Burns begin; Conqueror's origin in text; Everett-c 364 728 1092 2548 4474 6400
2-Everett-c/a 194 388 582 1242 2121 3000
3,4: 4-WWII Japanese-c 161 322 483 1030 1765 2500

VIC VERITY MAGAZINE
Vic Verity Publ: 1945; No. 2, Jan?, 1946 - No. 7, Sept, 1946 (A comic book)
1-C. C. Beck-c/a 45 90 135 284 480 675
2-Beck-c 31 62 93 182 296 410
3-7: 6-Beck-a. 7-Beck-c 28 56 84 168 274 380

VIDEO JACK
Marvel Comics (Epic Comics): Nov, 1987 - No. 6, Nov, 1988 ($1.25)
1-5 3.00
6-Neal Adams, Keith Giffen, Wrightson, others-a 5.00

VIETNAM JOURNAL
Apple Comics: Nov, 1987 - No. 16, Apr, 1991 ($1.75/$1.95, B&W)
1-16: Don Lomax-c/a/scripts in all, 1-2nd print 4.00
...: Indian Country Vol. 1 (1990, $12.95)-r/#1-4 plus one new story 13.00

VIETNAM JOURNAL: VALLEY OF DEATH
Apple Comics: June, 1994 - No. 2, Aug, 1994 ($2.75, B&W, limited series)
1,2: By Don Lomax 4.00

VIGILANTE, THE (Also see New Teen Titans #23 & Annual V2#2)
DC Comics: Oct, 1983 - No. 50, Feb, 1988 ($1.25, Baxter paper)
1-Origin 1 2 3 5 6 8
2-16,19-49: 3-Cyborg app. 4-1st app. The Exterminator; Newton-a(p). 6,7-Origin. 20,21-Nightwing app. 35-Origin Mad Bomber. 47-Batman-c/s 4.00
17,18-Alan Moore scripts 5.00
50-Ken Steacy painted-c 5.00
Annual nn, 2 ('85, '86) 5.00

VIGILANTE
DC Comics: Nov, 2005 - No. 6, Apr, 2006 ($2.99, limited series)
1-6-Bruce Jones-s. 1,2,4-6-Ben Oliver-a 3.00

VIGILANTE
DC Comics: Feb, 2009 - No. 12, Jan, 2010 ($2.99)
1-12: 1-Wolfman-s/Leonardi-a. 3-Nightwing app. 5-X-over with Titans and Teen Titans 3.00

VIGILANTE: CITY LIGHTS, PRAIRIE JUSTICE (Also see Action Comics #42,

The Viking Prince HC © DC

Violator #1 © TMP

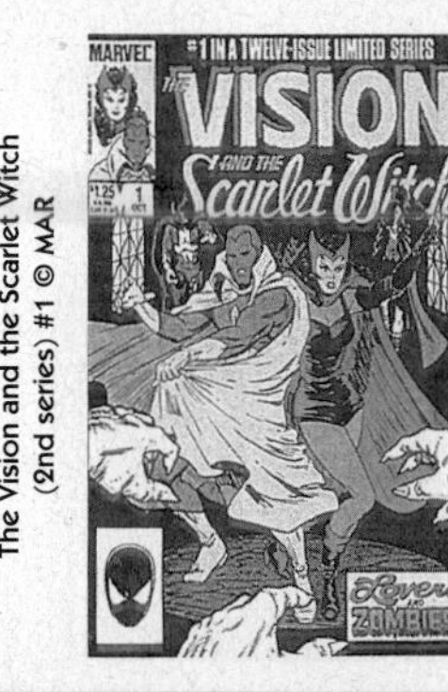

The Vision and the Scarlet Witch (2nd series) #1 © MAR

GD VG FN VF VF/NM NM-
2.0 4.0 6.0 8.0 9.0 9.2

Justice League of America #78, Leading Comics & World's Finest #244)
DC Comics: Nov, 1995 - No. 4, Feb, 1996 ($2.50, limited series)

1-4: James Robinson scripts/Tony Salmons-a/Mark Chiarello-c 3.00
TPB (2009, $19.99) r/#1-4 20.00

VIGILANTE 8: SECOND OFFENSE
Chaos! Comics: Dec, 1999 ($2.95, one-shot)

1-Based on video game 3.00

VIGILANTES, THE
Dell Publishing Co.: No. 839, Sept, 1957

Four Color 839-Movie 8 16 24 51 96 140

VIGILANTE: SOUTHLAND
DC Comics: Dec, 2016 - No. 3, Feb, 2017 ($3.99, unfinished series originally set for 6 issues)

1-3-Phillips-s/Casagrande-a; intro. Donny Fairchild 4.00

VIKING PRINCE, THE
DC Comics: 2010 ($39.99, hardcover with dustjacket)

HC-Recolored reprints of apps. in Brave and the Bold #1-5, 7-24 & team-up with Sgt. Rock in Our Army at War #162,163; new intro. by Joe Kubert 40.00

VIKINGS, THE (Movie)
Dell Publishing Co.: No. 910, May, 1958

Four Color 910-Buscema-a, Kirk Douglas photo-c 8 16 24 56 108 160

VIKINGS: GODHEAD (Based on the History Channel series)
Titan Comics: May, 2016 - No. 4, Sept, 2016 ($3.99)

1-4: 1-Cavan Scott-s/Staz Johnson-a; 3 covers 4.00

VIKINGS: UPRISING (Based on the History Channel series)
Titan Comics: Oct, 2016 - No. 4, Jan, 2017 ($3.99)

1-4: 1-Cavan Scott-s/Daniel Indro-a. 1-Five covers. 2-4-Three covers 4.00

VILLAINS AND VIGILANTES
Eclipse Comics: Dec, 1986 - No. 4, May, 1987 ($1.50/$1.75, limited series, Baxter paper)

1-4: Based on role-playing game. 2-4 ($1.75-c) 3.00

VILLAINS FOR HIRE
Marvel Comics: No. 0.1, Jan, 2012; No. 1, Feb, 2012 - No. 4, May, 2012 ($2.99)

0.1-Misty Knight, Silver Sable, Black Panther app.; Arlem-a 3.00
1-4-Abnett & Lanning-s/Arlem-a; Misty Knight app. 3.00

VILLAINS GIANT
DC Comics: 2019 ($4.99, 100 pgs., square-bound)

1-Three new short stories and three reprints; Joker, Harley, Deathstroke, Darkseid app. 5.00

VILLAINS UNITED (Leads into Infinite Crisis)
DC Comics: July, 2005 - No. 6, Dec, 2005 ($2.95/$2.50, limited series)

1-6-Simone-s/JG Jones-c. 1-The Secret Six and the "Society" form 3.00
...: Infinite Crisis Special 1 (6/06, $4.99) Simone-s/Eaglesham-a 5.00

VILLAINY OF DOCTOR DOOM, THE
Marvel Comics: 1999 ($17.95, TPB)

nn-Reprints early battle with the Fantastic Four 18.00

VIMANARAMA
DC Comics (Vertigo): Apr, 2005 - No. 3, June, 2005 ($2.95, limited series)

1-3-Grant Morrison-s/Philip Bond-a 3.00
TPB (2005, $12.99) r/#1-3 13.00

VINDICATION
Image Comics: Feb, 2019 - No. 4, May, 2019 ($3.99, limited series)

1-4-MD Marie-s/Carlos Miko-a 4.00

VINTAGE MAGNUS (...Robot Fighter)
Valiant: Jan, 1992 - No. 4, Apr, 1992 ($2.25, limited series)

1-4: 1-Layton-c; r/origin from Magnus R.F. #22 3.00

VINYL UNDERGROUND
DC Comics (Vertigo): Dec, 2007 - No. 12, Nov, 2008 ($2.99)

1-12: 1-Spencer-s/Gane & Stewart-a/Phillips-c 3.00
...: Pretty Dead Things TPB ('08, $17.99) r/#6-12 18.00
...: Watching the Detectives TPB ('08, $9.99) r/#1-5; David Laphan intro. 10.00

VIOLATOR (Also see Spawn #2)
Image Comics (Todd McFarlane Prods.): May, 1994 - No. 3, Aug, 1994 ($1.95, lim. series)

1-Alan Moore scripts in all 5.00
2,3: Bart Sears-c(p)/a(p) 4.00

VIOLATOR VS. BADROCK

GD VG FN VF VF/NM NM-
2.0 4.0 6.0 8.0 9.0 9.2

Image Comics (Extreme Studios): May, 1995 - No. 4, Aug, 1995 ($2.50, limited series)

1-4: Alan Moore scripts in all. 1-1st app Celestine; variant-c (3?) 3.00

VIOLENT, THE
Image Comics: Dec, 2015 - No. 5, Jul, 2016 ($2.99)

1-5-Brisson-s/Gorham-a 3.00

VIOLENT LOVE
Image Comics: Nov, 2016 - No. 10, Dec, 2017 ($3.99)

1-10-Frank Barbiere-s/Victor Santos-a/c 4.00

VIOLENT MESSIAHS (...: Lamenting Pain on cover for #9-12, numbered as #1-4)
Image Comics: June, 2000 - No. 12 ($2.95)

1-Two covers by Travis Smith and Medina 4.00
1-Tower Records variant edition 5.00
2-8: 5-Flip book sketchbook 3.00
9-12-Lamenting Pain; 2 covers on each 3.00
...: Genesis (12/01, $5.95) r/'97 B&W issue, Wizard 1/2 prologue 6.00
...: The Book of Job TPB (7/02, $24.95) r/#1-8; Foreward by Gossett 25.00

VIP (TV)
TV Comics: 2000 ($2.95, unfinished series)

1-Based on the Pamela Lee (Anderson) TV show; photo-c 3.00

VIPER (TV)
DC Comics: Aug, 1994 - No. 4, Nov, 1994 ($1.95, limited series)

1-4-Adaptation of television show 3.00

VIRGINIAN, THE (TV)
Gold Key: June, 1963

1(10060-306)-Part photo-c of James Drury plus photo back-c
4 8 12 27 44 60

VIRTUA FIGHTER (Video Game)
Marvel Comics: Aug, 1995 (2.95, one-shot)

1-Sega Saturn game 3.00

VIRUS
Dark Horse Comics: 1993 - No. 4, 1993 ($2.50, limited series)

1-4: Ploog-c 4.00

VISION, THE
Marvel Comics: Nov, 1994 - No. 4, Feb, 1995 ($1.75, limited series)

1-4 4.00

VISION, THE (AVENGERS ICONS: ...)
Marvel Comics: Oct, 2002 - No. 4, Jan, 2003 ($2.99, limited series)

1-4-Geoff Johns-s/Ivan Reis-a 4.00
...: Yesterday and Tomorrow TPB (2005, $14.99) r/#1-4 & Avengers #57 (1st app.) 15.00

VISION (From the Avengers)
Marvel Comics: Jan, 2016 - No. 12, Dec, 2016 ($3.99)

1-Tom King-s/Gabriel Walta-a; the Vison and his new synthezoid family
3 6 9 16 23 30
2-5,7-12 4.00
6-1st Sparky the Dog 2 4 6 9 12 15
... Director's Cut 1-6 (8/17 - No. 6, 1/18, $6.99) r/2 issues each with script and bonus art 7.00

VISION AND THE SCARLET WITCH, THE (See Marvel Fanfare)
Marvel Comics Group: Nov, 1982 - No. 4, Feb, 1983 (Limited series)

1-Mantlo-s/Leonardi-a 1 3 4 6 8 10
2-4: 2-Nuklo & Future Man app. 5.00

VISION AND THE SCARLET WITCH, THE
Marvel Comics Group: Oct, 1985 - No. 12, Sept, 1986 (Maxi-series)

V2#1-Retells origin; 1st app. in Avengers #57 1 3 4 6 8 10
2-12: 2-West Coast Avengers x-over 5.00

VISIONS
Vision Publications: 1979 - No. 5, 1983 (B&W, fanzine)

1-Flaming Carrot begins (1st app?); N. Adams-c 7 14 21 44 82 120
2-N. Adams, Rogers-a; Gulacy back-c; signed & numbered to 2000
5 10 15 35 63 90
3-Williamson-c(p); Steranko back-c 4 8 12 23 37 50
4-Flaming Carrot-c & info. 4 8 12 25 40 55
5-1 pg. Flaming Carrot 3 6 9 19 30 40

NOTE: ***Eisner*** *a-4.* ***Miller*** *a-4.* ***Starlin*** *a-3.* ***Williamson*** *a-5. After #4, Visions became an annual publication of The Atlanta Fantasy Fair.*

VISITOR, THE

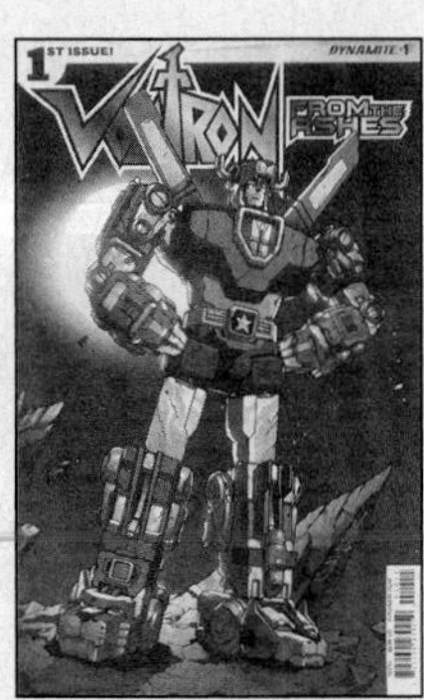

Voltron: From the Ashes #1 © DYN

Voodoo #9 © AJAX

Voodoo (2011 series) #1 © DC

	GD	VG	FN	VF	VF/NM	NM-
	2.0	4.0	6.0	8.0	9.0	9.2

Valiant/Acclaim Comics (Valiant): Apr, 1995 - No. 13, Nov, 1995 ($2.50)

1-13: 8-Harbinger revealed. 13-Visitor revealed to be Sting from Harbinger 3.00

VISITOR, THE
Valiant Entertainment: Dec, 2019 - No. 6 ($3.99)

1-4-Paul Levitz-s/MJ Kim-a 4.00

VISITOR: HOW AND WHY HE STAYED, THE (Character from Hellboy)
Dark Horse Comics: Feb, 2017 - No. 5, Jul, 2017 ($3.99, limited series)

1-5-Mignola & Roberson-s/Grist-a/c; Hellboy app. 4.00

VISITOR VS. THE VALIANT UNIVERSE, THE
Valiant: Feb, 1995 - No. 2, Mar, 1995 ($2.95, limited series)

1,2 3.00

VIXEN: RETURN OF THE LION (From Justice League of America)
DC Comics: Dec, 2008 - No. 5, Apr, 2009 ($2.99, limited series)

1-5-G. Willow Wilson-s/Cafu-a; Justice League app. 3.00
TPB (2009, $17.99) r/#1-5 18.00

VOGUE (Also see Youngblood)
Image Comics (Extreme Studios): Oct, 1995 - No.3, Jan, 1996 ($2.50, limited series)

1-3: 1-Liefeld-c, 1-Variant-c 3.00

VOID INDIGO (Also see Marvel Graphic Novel)
Marvel Comics (Epic Comics): 11/84 - No. 2, 3/85 ($1.50, direct sales, unfinished series, mature)

1,2: Cont'd from Marvel G.N.; graphic sex & violence 3.00

VOLCANIC REVOLVER
Oni Press: Dec, 1998 - No. 3, Mar, 1999 ($2.95, B&W, limited series)

1-3: Scott Morse-s/a 3.00
TPB (12/99, $9.95, digest size) r/#1-3 and Oni Double Feature #7 prologue 10.00

VOLITION
AfterShock Comics: Aug, 2018 - No. 6, Jun, 2019 ($3.99)

1-6: 1-Ryan Parrott-s/Omar Francia-a 4.00

VOLTRON (TV)
Modern Publishing: 1985 - No. 3, 1985 (75¢, limited series)

1-Ayers-a in all; Jim Fry-c 3 6 9 21 33 45
2,3 2 4 6 10 14 18

VOLTRON (Volume 1)
Dynamite Entertainment: 2011 - No. 12, 2013 ($3.99)

1-12: 1-Padilla-a; covers by Alex Ross, Sean Chen & Wagner Reis. 2-5-Two covers 4.00

VOLTRON: A LEGEND FORGED (TV)
Devils Due Publishing: Jul, 2008 - No. 5, Apr, 2009 ($3.50)

1-5-Blaylock-s/Bear-a; 4 covers 3.50

VOLTRON: DEFENDER OF THE UNIVERSE (TV)
Image Comics: No. 0, May, 2003 - No. 5, Sept, 2003 ($2.50)

0-Jolley-s/Brooks-a; character pin-ups with background info 3.00
1-5-($2.95) 1-Three covers by Norton, Brooks and Andrews; Norton-a 3.00
...: Revelations TPB (2004, $11.95, digest-sized) r/#1-5; cover gallery 12.00

VOLTRON: DEFENDER OF THE UNIVERSE (TV)
Image Comics: Jan, 2004 - No. 11, Dec, 2004 ($2.95)

1-11: 1-Jolley-s; wraparound-c 3.00

VOLTRON: FROM THE ASHES
Dynamite Entertainment: 2015 - No. 6, 2016 ($3.99)

1-6: 1-Cullen Bunn-s/Blacky Shepherd-a 4.00

VOLTRON: YEAR ONE
Dynamite Entertainment: 2012 - No. 6, 2012 ($3.99, limited series)

1-6: 1-Two covers; Brandon Thomas-s/Craig Cermak-a 4.00

VOODA (Jungle Princess) (Formerly Voodoo) (See Crown Comics)
Ajax-Farrell (Four Star Publications): No. 20, April, 1955 - No. 22, Aug, 1955

20-Baker-c/a (r/Seven Seas #6) 60 120 180 381 653 925
21,22-Baker-a plus Kamen/Baker story, Kimbo Boy of Jungle, & Baker-c(p) in all.
22-Censored Jo-Jo-r (name Powaa) 54 108 162 343 574 825

NOTE: *#20-22 each contain one heavily censored-r of South Sea Girl by* ***Baker*** *from Seven Seas Comics with name changed to Vooda. #20-r/Seven Seas #6; #21-r/#4; #22-r/#3.*

VOODOO (Weird Fantastic Tales) (Vooda #20 on)
Ajax-Farrell (Four Star Publ.): May, 1952 - No. 19, Jan-Feb, 1955

1-South Sea Girl-r by Baker 100 200 300 640 1095 1550
2-Rulah story-r plus South Sea Girl from Seven Seas #2 by Baker (name changed from Alani to El'nee) 84 168 252 538 919 1300
3-Bakerish-a; man stabbed in face 65 130 195 416 708 1000
4,8-Baker-r. 8-Severed head panels 65 130 195 416 708 1000
5-Nazi death camp story (flaying alive) 66 132 198 419 722 1025
6,7,9,10: 6-Severed head panels 57 114 171 362 619 875
11-18: 14-Zombies take over America. 15-Opium drug story-r/Ellery Queen #3. 16-Post nuclear world story.17-Electric chair panels 54 108 162 343 574 825
19-Bondage-c; Baker-r(2)/Seven Seas #5 w/minor changes & #1, heavily modified; last pre-code; contents & covers change to jungle theme 60 120 180 381 653 925
Annual 1(1952, 25¢, 100 pgs.)-Baker-a (scarce) 206 412 618 1318 2259 3200

VOODOO
Image Comics (WildStorm): Nov, 1997 - No. 4, Mar, 1998 ($2.50, lim. series)

1-4: Alan Moore-s in all; Hughes-c. 2-4-Rio-a 4.00
1-Platinum Ed 10.00
Dancing on the Dark TPB ('99, $9.95) r/#1-4 10.00
...-Zealot: Skin Trade (8/95, $4.95) 5.00

VOODOO (DC New 52) (Also see Grifter)
DC Comics: Nov, 2011 - No. 12, Oct, 2012; No. 0, Nov, 2012 ($2.99)

1-12: 1-Marz-s/Basri-a/c. 3-Green Lantern (Kyle) app. 3.00
#0 (11/12, $2.99) Origin of Voodoo; Basri-a/c 3.00

VOODOO (See Tales of...)

VOODOO CHILD (Weston Cage & Nicolas Cage's...)
Virgin Comics: July, 2007 - No. 6, Dec, 2007 ($2.99)

1-6: 1-Mike Carey-s/Dean Hyrapiet-a; covers by Hyrapiet & Templesmith 3.00
Vol. 1 TPB (1/08, $14.99) r/#1-6; variant covers; intro by Weston Cage & Nicolas Cage 15.00

VOODOOM
Oni Press: June, 2000 ($4.95, B&W)

1-Scott Morse-s/Jim Mahfood-a 5.00

VORTEX
Vortex Publs.: Nov, 1982 - No. 15, 1988 (No month) ($1.50/$1.75, B&W)

1 ($1.95)-Peter Hsu-a; Ken Steacy-c; nudity 1 3 4 6 8 10
2,12: 2-1st app. Mister X (on-c only). 12-Sam Kieth-a 6.00
3-11,13-15 4.00

VORTEX
Comico: 1991 - No. 2? ($2.50, limited series)

1,2: Heroes from The Elementals 4.00

VOTE LOKI
Marvel Comics: Aug, 2016 - No. 4, Nov, 2016 ($3.99, limited series)

1-4: 1-Loki runs for President; Hastings-s/Foss-a. 2-McCaffrey-a 4.00

VOYAGE TO THE BOTTOM OF THE SEA (Movie, TV)
Dell Publishing Co./Gold Key: No. 1230, Sept-Nov, 1961; Dec, 1964 - #16, Apr, 1970 (Painted-c)

Four Color 1230 (1961) 10 20 30 70 150 230
10133-412(#1, 12/64)(Gold Key) 8 16 24 54 102 150
2(7/65) - 5: Photo back-c, 1-5 5 10 15 35 63 90
6-14 4 8 12 28 47 65
15,16-Reprints 3 6 9 18 27 36

VOYAGE TO THE DEEP
Dell Publishing Co.: Sept-Nov, 1962 - No. 4, Nov-Jan, 1964 (Painted-c)

1 5 10 15 31 53 75
2-4 4 8 12 23 37 50

VS
Image Comics: Feb, 2018 - No. 5, Jul, 2018 ($3.99)

1-5-Ivan Brandon-s/Esad Ribic-a 4.00

V-WARS
IDW Publishing: Apr, 2014 - No. 11, Mar, 2015 ($3.99)

1-11: 1-Vampire epidemic; Jonathan Maberry-s/Alan Robinson-a 4.00
...: God of Death One-Shot (4/19, $4.99) Maberry-s/Milne-a 5.00

WACKO
Ideal Publ. Corp.: Sept, 1980 - No. 3, Oct, 1981 (84 pgs., B&W, magazine)

1-3 2 4 6 9 13 16

WACKY ADVENTURES OF CRACKY (Also see Gold Key Spotlight)
Gold Key: Dec, 1972 - No. 12, Sept, 1975

1 3 6 9 14 20 26

Wacky Witch #3 © GK

The Wake #10 © Snyder & Murphy

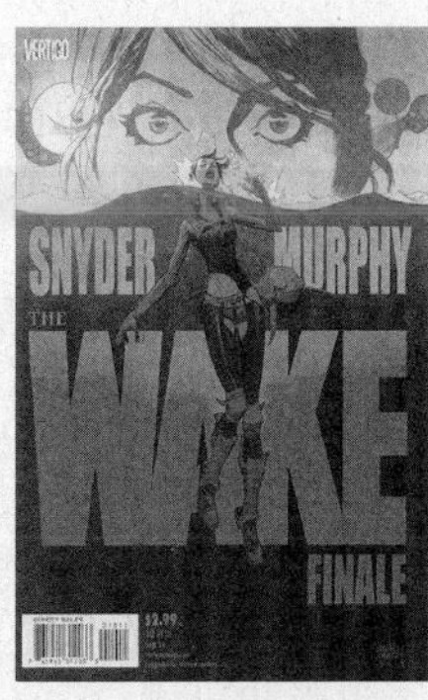

The Walking Dead #40 © R. Kirkman

	GD	VG	FN	VF	VF/NM	NM-
	2.0	4.0	6.0	8.0	9.0	9.2

2 — 2 4 6 10 14 18
3-12 — 2 4 6 8 10 12
(See March of Comics #405, 424, 436, 448)

WACKY DUCK (...Comics #3-6; formerly Dopey Duck; Justice Comics #7 on)(See Film Funnies)
Marvel Comics (NPP): No. 3, Fall, 1946 - No. 6, Summer, 1947; Aug, 1948 - No. 2, Oct, 1948

3 — 34 68 102 204 332 460
4-Infinity-c — 26 52 78 156 256 355
5,6(1947)-Becomes Justice comics — 23 46 69 136 223 310
1(1948) — 24 48 72 144 237 330
2(1948) — 18 36 54 107 169 230
I.W. Reprint #1,2,7('58): 1-r/Wacky Duck #6 — 2 4 6 11 16 20
Super Reprint #10(I.W. on-c, Super-inside) — 2 4 6 10 14 18

WACKY QUACKY (See Wisco)

WACKY RACELAND (Update of Hanna-Barbera's Wacky Races)
DC Comics: Aug, 2016 - No. 6, Jan, 2017 ($3.99)

1-6: 1-Pontac-s/Manco-a; multiple covers; Penelope Pitstop & Dick Dastardly app. — 4.00

WACKY RACES (TV)
Gold Key: Aug, 1969 - No. 7, Apr, 1972 (Hanna-Barbera)

1 — 5 10 15 31 53 75
2-7 — 3 6 9 21 33 45

WACKY SQUIRREL (Also see Dark Horse Presents)
Dark Horse Comics: Oct, 1987 - No. 4, 1988 ($1.75, B&W)

1-4: 4-Superman parody — 3.00
Halloween Adventure Special 1 (1987, $2.00) — 3.00
Summer Fun Special 1 (1988, $2.00) — 3.00

WACKY WITCH (Also see Gold Key Spotlight)
Gold Key: March, 1971 - No. 21, Dec, 1975

1 — 4 8 12 25 40 55
2 — 3 6 9 14 20 26
3-10 — 2 4 6 10 14 18
11-21 — 2 4 6 8 10 12
(See March of Comics #374, 398, 410, 422, 434, 446, 458, 470, 482)

WACKY WOODPECKER (See Two Bit the...)
I. W. Enterprises/Super Comics: 1958; 1963

I.W. Reprint #1,2,7 (nd-reprints Two Bit...): 7-r/Two-Bit, the Wacky Woodpecker #1. — 2 4 6 10 14 18
Super Reprint #10('63): 10-r/Two-Bit, The Wacky Woodpecker #? — 2 4 6 9 13 16

WAGON TRAIN (1st Series) (TV) (See Western Roundup under Dell Giants)
Dell Publishing Co.: No. 895, Mar, 1958 - No. 13, Apr-June, 1962 (All photo-c)

Four Color 895 (#1) — 9 18 27 62 126 190
Four Color 971(#2),1019(#3) — 6 12 18 41 76 110
4(1-3/60),6-13 — 5 10 15 34 60 85
5-Toth-a — 6 12 18 37 66 95

WAGON TRAIN (2nd Series)(TV)
Gold Key: Jan, 1964 - No. 4, Oct, 1964 (All front & back photo-c)

1-Tufts-a in all — 5 10 15 30 50 70
2-4 — 4 8 12 23 37 50

WAITING PLACE, THE
Slave Labor Graphics: Apr, 1997 - No. 6, Sept, 1997 ($2.95)

1-6-Sean McKeever-s — 3.00
Vol. 2 - 1(11/99), 2-11 — 3.00
12-($4.95) — 5.00

WAITING ROOM WILLIE (See Sad Case of...)

WAKANDA FOREVER (See Amazing Spider-Man: Wakanda Forever for part 1)
Marvel Comics: Sept, 2018 - Oct, 2018 ($4.99, limited series)

... Avengers (10/18) Part 3; Capt. America, She-Hulk, Black Panther, Storm, Rogue app. — 5.00
... X-Men (9/18) Part 2; Storm, Rogue, Nightcrawler app. — 5.00

WAKE, THE
DC Comics (Vertigo): Jul, 2013 - No. 10, Sept, 2014 ($2.99)

1-Scott Snyder-s/Sean Murphy-a/c — 5.00
1-Variant-c by Andy Kubert — 8.00
1-Director's Cut (10/13, $4.99) B&W version, behind-the-scenes production content — 5.00
2-10: 6-Story jumps 200 years ahead; Leeward app. — 3.00
... Part One TPB (2/14, $9.99) r/#1-5 — 10.00

WAKE THE DEAD
IDW Publishing: Sept, 2003 - No. 5, Mar, 2004 ($3.99, limited series)

1-5-Steve Niles-s/Chee-a — 4.00
TPB (6/04, $19.99) r/series; intro. by Michael Dougherty; embossed die cut cover — 20.00

WALK IN (Dave Stewart's ...)
Virgin Comics: Dec, 2006 - No. 6, May, 2007 ($2.99)

1-6: 1-5-Parker-s/Padlekar-a. 6-Parker-a — 3.00

WALKING DEAD, THE (Inspired the 2010 AMC television series)(Also see Negan Lives!)
Image Comics: Oct, 2003 - No. 193, Jul, 2019 ($2.95/$2.99, B&W)

1-Robert Kirkman-s in all/Tony Moore-a; 1st app. Rick Grimes, Shane, Morgan & Duane — 48 96 138 350 788 1225
1 Special Edition (5/08, $3.99) r/#1; Kirkman afterword; original script and proposal — 3 6 9 16 23 30
2-Tony Moore-a through #6 — 16 32 48 111 246 380
3 — 9 18 27 61 123 185
4 — 8 16 24 52 99 145
5,6: 6-Shane killed — 6 12 18 41 76 110
7-Charlie Adlard-a begins; 1st app. Tyreese — 6 12 18 38 69 100
8-10 — 4 8 12 25 40 55
11-18,20: 13-Prison arc begins — 3 6 9 16 23 30
19-1st app. Michonne — 11 22 33 76 163 250
21-26,28-47,49,50: 25-Adlard covers begin. 28-Rick loses his hand. 46-Tyreese killed. — 2 4 6 9 12 15
27-1st app of The Governor — 8 16 24 54 102 150
48-Lori, Herschel, others killed — 4 8 12 25 40 55
50-Variant wraparound superhero-style cover by Erik Larsen — 5 10 15 34 60 85
51,52,54-60: 58-Morgan returns — 2 4 6 8 10 12
53-1st app. Abraham & Rosita — 5 10 15 33 57 80
61-Preview of Chew; 1st app. Gabriel — 4 8 12 25 40 55
62,64-74: 66-Dale dies. 70-1st Douglas Monroe — 1 3 4 6 8 10
63-Flip book with B&W reprint of Chew #1 — 3 6 9 16 24 32
75-(7/10, $3.99) Orange background-c; back-up alien/sci-fi "fantasy" in color; TV series preview with cast photos — 2 4 6 9 12 15
75-Variant-c homage to issue #1 — 3 6 9 21 33 45
76-91: 85-Flip book w/Witch Doctor #0. 86-Flip book w/Elephantmen — 1 3 4 6 8 10
92-Intro. Paul Monroe (Jesus) — 3 6 9 17 26 35
93-96 — 6.00
97-99,101-114: 97-"Something to Fear" pt. 1. 98-Abraham killed. 107-Intro Ezekiel — 5.00
100-(7/12, $3.99) 1st app. Negan; Glen killed; multiple covers by Adlard, Silvestri, Quitely, McFarlane, Phillips, Hitch, & Ottley — 3 6 9 16 23 30
100-Wraparound-c by Adlard — 2 4 6 9 12 15
106-Variant wraparound-c by Adlard for his 100th issue — 2 4 6 10 16 20
115-"All Out War" begins; 10 connecting covers by Adlard — 1 2 3 5 6 8
116-126-"All Out War" — 4.00
127-(5/14) Intro. Magna; bonus preview of Outcast — 2 4 6 8 10 12
128-174: 132-1st Whisperers attack. 135-Intro. Lydia. 138-Intro. Alpha. 139-Michonne returns 144-Death of Ezekiel and Rosita and others. 150-Six covers. 156-Death of Alpha. 157-162-Whisperer War; 2 covers (Adlard & Art Adams). 163-(25¢-c). 167-Death of Andrea. 171-Intro Princess — 4.00
175-191-($3.99) 175-1st app. The Commonwealth. 185-Flip book with Outpost Zero #14.00
192-Death of Rick Grimes — 5.00
193-($3.99, 84 pgs.) Final issue; afterword by Kirkman; fake cover art for #194-196 — 4.00
193-2nd printing ($3.99, 84 pgs.) — 4.00
... FCBD 2013 Special (5/13, giveaway) reprints bonus stories from Michonne Special and The Governor Special; new Tyreese background story — 3.00
Image Firsts: The Walking Dead #1 (3/10, $1.00) reprints #1 — 2 4 6 13 18 22
...: Michonne Special (10/12, $2.99) Reprints debut from #19 and story from Playboy — 1 3 4 6 8 10
...: Michonne Special - 2nd printing (3/13, $2.99) — 3.00
... #1 Tenth Anniversary Special (10/13, $5.99) reprints #1 with color; Kirkman's original series proposal; Kirkman interview — 2 4 6 8 11 14
... "The Alien" (2020, $19.99, HC) New story taking place in Barcelona; Brian K. Vaughan-s/ Marcos Martin-a; bonus character sketches, page layouts and cover concepts — 20.00
...: The Governor Special (2/13, $2.99) Reprints debut from #27 and story from CBLDF Liberty Annual 2012 — 6.00
...: Tyreese Special (10/13, $2.99) Reprints debut from #7 and story from FCBD 2013 — 4.00
... Book 1 HC (2006, $29.99) r/#1-12; sketch pages, cover gallery; Kirkman afterword — 45.00
... Book 2 HC (2006, $29.99) r/#13-24; sketch pages, cover gallery — 40.00
... Book 3 HC (2007, $29.99) r/#25-36; sketch pages, cover gallery — 35.00
... Book 4 HC (2008, $29.99) r/#37-48; sketch pages, cover gallery — 35.00
... Book 5 HC (2010, $29.99) r/#49-60; sketch pages, cover gallery — 35.00

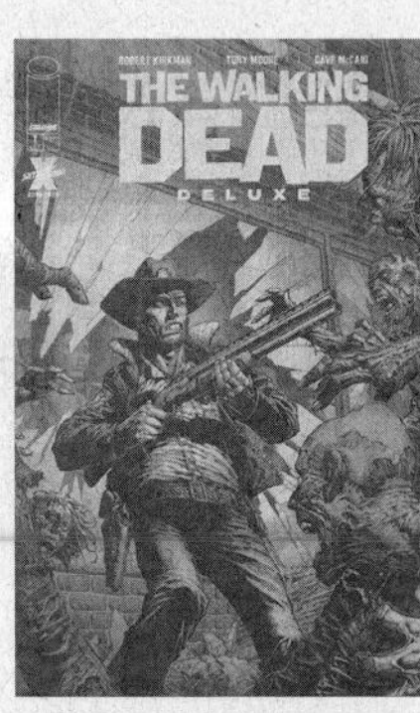

The Walking Dead Deluxe #1 © R. Kirkman

Walt Disney Comic Digest #22 © DIS

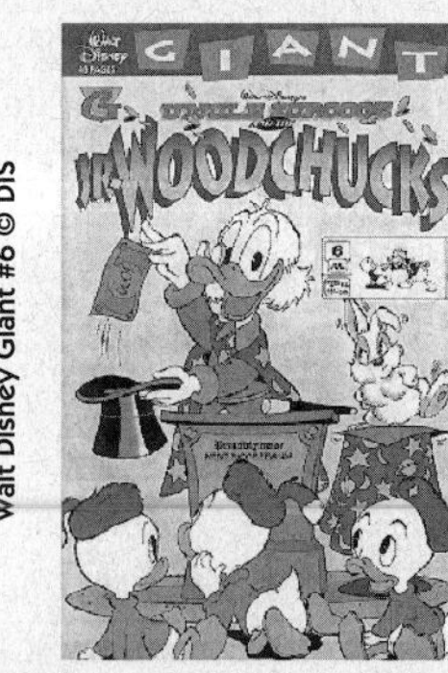

Walt Disney Giant #6 © DIS

	GD	VG	FN	VF	VF/NM	NM-
	2.0	4.0	6.0	8.0	9.0	9.2

... Book 6 HC (2010, $34.99) r/#61-72; sketch pages, cover gallery 35.00
... Book 7 HC (2011, $34.99) r/#73-84; sketch pages, cover gallery 35.00
... Book 8 HC (2012, $34.99) r/#85-96; sketch pages, cover gallery 35.00
... Book 9 HC (2013, $34.99) r/#97-108; sketch pages, cover gallery 35.00
... Book 10 HC (2014, $34.99) r/#109-120; sketch pages, cover gallery 35.00
... Book 11 HC (2015, $34.99) r/#121-132; sketch pages, cover gallery 35.00
...Vol. 1: Days Gone Bye (5/04, $9.95, TPB) r/#1-4 20.00
...Vol. 2: Miles Behind Us (10/04, $12.95, TPB) r/#7-12 18.00
...Vol. 3: Safety Behind Bars (2005, $12.95, TPB) r/#13-18 18.00
...Vol. 4: The Heart's Desire (2005, $12.99, TPB) r/#19-24 18.00
...Vol. 5: The Best Defense (2006, $12.99, TPB) r/#25-30 18.00
...Vol. 6: This Sorrowful Life (2007, $12.99, TPB) r/#31-36 15.00
...Vol. 7: The Calm Before (2007, $12.99, TPB) r/#37-42 15.00
...Vol. 8: Made to Suffer (2008, $14.99, TPB) r/#43-48 15.00
...Vol. 9: Here We Remain (2009, $14.99, TPB) r/#49-54 15.00
...Vol. 10: The Road Ahead (2009, $14.99, TPB) r/#55-60 15.00
...Vol. 11: Fear the Hunters (2010, $14.99, TPB) r/#61-66 15.00
...Vol. 12: Life Among Them (2010, $14.99, TPB) r/#67-72 15.00
...Vol. 13: Too Far Gone (2010, $14.99, TPB) r/#73-78 15.00
...Vol. 14: No Way Out (2011, $14.99, TPB) r/#79-84 15.00
...Vol. 15: We Find Ourselves (2011, $14.99, TPB) r/#85-90 15.00
...Vol. 16: A Larger World (2012, $14.99, TPB) r/#91-96 15.00
...Vol. 17: Something to Fear (2012, $14.99, TPB) r/#97-102 15.00
...Vol. 18: What Comes After (2013, $14.99, TPB) r/#103-108 15.00
...Vol. 19: March To War (2013, $14.99, TPB) r/#109-114 15.00
...Vol. 20: All Out War Part 1 (2014, $14.99, TPB) r/#115-120 15.00
...Vol. 21: All Out War Part 2 (2014, $14.99, TPB) r/#121-126 15.00
...Vol. 22: A New Beginning (2014, $14.99, TPB) r/#127-132 15.00
...Vol. 23: Whispers Into Screams (2015, $14.99, TPB) r/#133-138 15.00
...Vol. 24: Life and Death (2015, $14.99, TPB) r/#139-144 15.00
...Vol. 25: No Turning Back (2016, $14.99, TPB) r/#145-150 15.00
...Vol. 26: Call to Arms (2016, $14.99, TPB) r/#151-156 15.00
...Vol. 27: The Whisperer War (2017, $14.99, TPB) r/#157-162 15.00
...Vol. 28: A Certain Doom (2017, $16.99, TPB) r/#163-168 17.00
...Vol. 29: Lines We Cross (2018, $16.99, TPB) r/#169-174 17.00
...Vol. 30: New World Order (2018, $16.99, TPB) r/#175-180 17.00
...Vol. 31: The Rotten Core (2018, $16.99, TPB) r/#181-186 17.00
...Vol. 32: Rest in Peace (2019, $16.99, TPB) r/#187-193 17.00

WALKING DEAD DELUXE, THE
Image Comics: Oct, 2020 - Present ($3.99)

1-9-Newly colored reprints of original issues with Kirkman commentary and bonus "cutting room floor" content; multiple variant covers on each 4.00

WALKING DEAD SURVIVORS' GUIDE, THE
Image Comics: Apr, 2011 - No. 4 ($2.99, B&W)

1,2-Alphabetical listings of character profiles, first (and last) apps. and current status
2 4 6 11 16 20
3,4 1 3 4 6 8 10

WALKING DEAD WEEKLY, THE (Reprints)
Image Comics: Jan, 2011 - No. 52, Dec, 2011 ($2.99, B&W, weekly)

1-Reprints issues with original letter columns; new Kirkman afterword
3 6 9 21 33 45
1-Arizona Comic Con variant-c 3 6 9 16 23 30
2-4,7 2 4 6 9 12 15
5-Death of Amy 4 8 12 27 44 60
6-Death of Shane 3 6 9 19 30 40
8-18,20-26,28-52 1 2 3 5 6 8
19-r/1st Michonne 6 12 18 38 69 100
27-r/1st app. The Governor 3 6 9 16 23 30

WALK THROUGH HELL, A
AfterShock Comics: May, 2018 - No. 12, Jul, 2019 ($3.99)

1-12-Garth Ennis-s/Goran Sudzuka-a 4.00

WALL·E (Based on the Disney/Pixar movie)
BOOM! Studios: No. 0, Nov, 2009 - No. 7, Jun, 2010 ($2.99)

0-7: 0-Prequel; J. Torres-s 3.00

WALLY (Teen-age)
Gold Key: Dec, 1962 - No. 4, Sept, 1963

1 3 6 9 20 31 42
2-4 3 6 9 16 24 32

WALLY THE WIZARD
Marvel Comics (Star Comics): Apr, 1985 - No. 12, Mar, 1986 (Children's comic)

1-12: Bob Bolling a-1,3; c-1,9,11,12 5.00
1-Variant with "Star Chase" game on last page and inside back-c
2 4 6 9 12 15

WALLY WOOD'S T.H.U.N.D.E.R. AGENTS (See Thunder Agents)
Deluxe Comics: Nov, 1984 - No. 5, Oct, 1986 ($2.00, 52 pgs.)

1-5: 5-Jerry Ordway-c/a in Wood style 6.00

NOTE: ***Anderson** a-2i, 3i. **Buckler** a-4. **Ditko** a-3, 4. **Giffen** a-1p-4p. **Perez** a-1p, 2, 4; c-1-4.*

WALT DISNEY CHRISTMAS PARADE (Also see Christmas Parade)
Whitman Publ. Co. (Golden Press): Wint, 1977 ($1.95, cardboard-c, 224 pgs.)

11191-Barks-r/Christmas in Disneyland #1, Dell Christmas Parade #9 & Dell Giant #53
4 8 12 27 44 60

WALT DISNEY COMICS DIGEST
Gold Key: June, 1968 - No. 57, Feb, 1976 (50¢, digest size)

1-Reprints Uncle Scrooge #5; 192 pgs. 6 12 18 42 79 115
2-4-Barks-r 5 10 15 31 53 75
5-Daisy Duck by Barks (8 pgs.); last published story by Barks (art only) plus 21 pg. Scrooge-r by Barks 7 14 21 44 82 120
6-13-All Barks-r 3 6 9 21 33 45
14,15 3 6 9 16 23 30
16-Reprints Donald Duck #26 by Barks 3 6 9 20 31 42
17-20-Barks-r 3 6 9 17 26 35
21-31,33,35-37-Barks-r; 24-Toth Zorro 3 6 9 16 23 30
32,41,45,47-49 2 4 6 11 16 20
34,38,39: 34-Reprints 4-Color #318. 38-Reprints Christmas in Disneyland #1. 39-Two Barks-r/WDC&S #272, 4-Color #1073 plus Toth Zorro-r
3 6 9 16 23 30
40-Mickey Mouse-r by Gottfredson 2 4 6 13 18 22
42,43-Barks-r 2 4 6 13 18 22
44-(Has Gold Key emblem, 50¢)-Reprints 1st story of 4-Color #29,256,275,282
5 10 15 30 50 70
44-Republished in 1976 by Whitman; not identical to original; a bit smaller, blank back-c, 69¢
3 6 9 16 23 30
46,50,52-Barks-r. 52-Barks-r/WDC&S #161,132 2 4 6 11 16 20
51-Reprints 4-Color #71 3 6 9 16 23 30
53-55: 53-Reprints Dell Giant #30. 54-Reprints Donald Duck Beach Party #2. 55-Reprints Dell Giant #49 2 4 6 10 14 18
56-r/Uncle Scrooge #32 (Barks) 2 4 6 13 18 22
57-r/Mickey Mouse Almanac('57) & two Barks stories 2 4 6 11 16 20

NOTE: ***Toth** a-52r. #1-10, 196 pgs.; #11-41, 164 pgs.; #42 on, 132 pgs. Old issues were being reprinted & distributed by Whitman in 1976.*

WALT DISNEY GIANT (Disney)
Bruce Hamilton Co. (Gladstone): Sept, 1995 - No. 7, Sept, 1996 ($2.25, bi-monthly, 48 pgs.)

1-7: 1-Scrooge McDuck in "Hearts of the Yukon"; Rosa-c/a/scripts plus r/F.C. #218; Scrooge & Glittering Goldie-c. 2-Uncle Scrooge-r by Barks plus 17 pg. text story. 3-Donald the Mighty Duck; Rosa-c; Barks & Rosa-r. 4-Mickey and Goofy; new-a (story actually stars Goofy. Mickey Mouse by Caesar Ferioli; Donald Duck by Giorgio Cavazzano (1st in U.S.). 6-Uncle Scrooge & the Jr. Woodchucks; new-a and Barks-r. 7-Uncle Scrooge-r by Barks plus new-a 4.00

NOTE: *Series was initially solicited as Uncle Walt's Collectory. Issue #8 was advertised, but later cancelled.*

WALT DISNEY PAINT BOOK SERIES
Whitman Publ. Co.: No dates; circa 1975 (Beware! Has 1930s copyright dates) (79¢-c, 52 pgs. B&W, treasury-sized) (Coloring books, text stories & comics-r)

#2052 (Whitman #886-r) Mickey Mouse & Donald Duck Gag Book
3 6 9 20 31 42
#2053 (Whitman #677-r) 3 6 9 20 31 42
#2054 (Whitman #670-r) Donald-c 4 8 12 22 35 48
#2055 (Whitman #627-r) Mickey-c 3 6 9 20 31 42
#2056 (Whitman #660-r) Buckey Bug-c 3 6 9 18 28 38
#2057 (Whitman #887-r) Mickey & Donald-c 3 6 9 20 31 42

WALT DISNEY PRESENTS (TV)(Disney)
Dell Publishing Co.: No. 997, 6-8/59 - No. 6, 12-2/1960-61; No. 1181, 4-5/61 (All photo-c)

Four Color 997 (#1) 6 12 18 42 79 115
2(12-2/60)-The Swamp Fox(origin), Elfego Baca, Texas John Slaughter (Disney TV show) begin 5 10 15 30 50 70
3-6: 5-Swamp Fox by Warren Tufts 4 8 12 28 47 65
Four Color 1181-Texas John Slaughter 5 10 15 35 63 90

WALT DISNEY'S CHRISTMAS PARADE (Also see Christmas Parade)
Gladstone: Winter, 1988; No. 2, Winter, 1989 ($2.95, 100 pgs.)

1-Barks-r/painted-c 2 4 6 8 10 12
2-Barks-r 1 2 3 5 7 9

WALT DISNEY'S CHRISTMAS PARADE

Walt Disney's Comics and Stories #6 © DIS

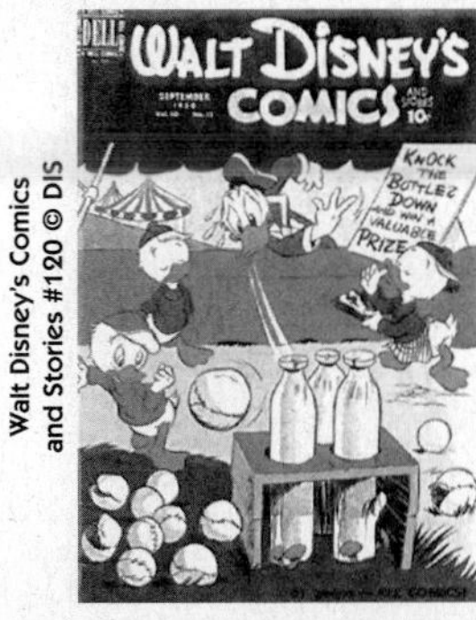

Walt Disney's Comics and Stories #120 © DIS

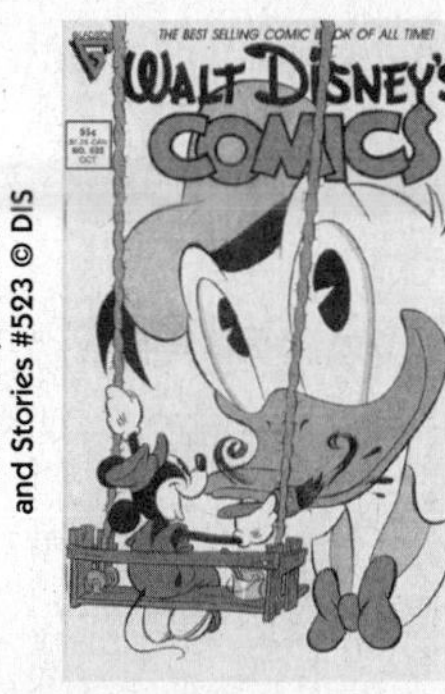

Walt Disney's Comics and Stories #523 © DIS

	GD 2.0	VG 4.0	FN 6.0	VF 8.0	VF/NM 9.0	NM- 9.2
Gemstone Publishing: Dec, 2003; 2004, 2005, 2006, 2008 ($8.95/$9.50, prestige format)						
1-4: 1-Reprints and 3 new European holiday stories. 2-All reprints. 3-Reprints and 2 new stories, 4-Reprints and 5 new stories						9.00
5-($9.50) R/Uncle Scrooge #47 and European stories						9.50

WALT DISNEY'S COMICS AND STORIES (Cont. of Mickey Mouse Magazine)
(#1-30 contain Donald Duck newspaper reprints) (Titled "Comics And Stories" #264 to #?; titled "Walt Disney's Comics And Stories" #511 on)
Dell Publishing Co./Gold Key #264-473/Whitman #474-510/Gladstone #511-547/ Disney Comics #548-585/Gladstone #586-633/Gemstone Publishing #634-698/ Boom! Kids #699-720/IDW Publishing #721-on: 10/40 - #263, 8/62; #264, 10/62 - #510, 7/84; #511, 10/86 - #633, 2/99; #634, 7/03 - #698, 11/08; #699, 10/09 - #720, 6/11; #721, 7/15 - No. 743, 7/18

NOTE: The whole number can always be found at the bottom of the title page in the lower left-hand or right hand panel.

	GD 2.0	VG 4.0	FN 6.0	VF 8.0	VF/NM 9.0	NM- 9.2
1(V1#1-c; V2#1-indicia)-Donald Duck strip-r by Al Taliaferro & Gottfredson's Mickey Mouse begin	2300	4600	6900	16,000	34,500	53,000
2	848	1696	2544	5936	12,718	19,500
3	383	766	1149	2681	5741	8800
4-Christmas-c; 1st Huey, Dewey & Louie-c this title (See Mickey Mouse Magazine V4#2 for 1st-c ever)	326	652	978	2282	4891	7500
4-Special promotional, complimentary issue; cover same except one corner was blanked out & boxed in to identify the giveaway (not a paste-over). This special pressing was probably sent out to former subscribers to Mickey Mouse Mag. whose subscriptions had expired. (Very rare-5 known copies)	480	960	1440	3360	7930	12,500
5-Goofy-c	260	520	780	1820	3510	5200
6-10: 8-Only Clarabelle Cow-c. 9-Taliaferro-c (1st)	218	436	654	1395	2823	4250
11-14: 11-Huey, Dewey & Louie-c/app.	167	334	501	1069	2160	3250
15-17: 15-The 3 Little Kittens (17 pgs.). 16-The 3 Little Pigs (29 pgs.); Christmas-c. 17-The Ugly Duckling (4 pgs.)	138	276	414	883	1792	2700
18-21	128	256	384	819	1660	2500
22-30: 22-Flag-c. 24-The Flying Gauchito (1st original comic book story done for WDC&S). 27-Jose Carioca by Carl Buettner (2nd original story in WDC&S)	108	216	324	691	1396	2100
31-New Donald Duck stories by Carl Barks begin (See F.C. #9 for 1st Barks Donald Duck)	400	800	1200	2560	5180	7800
32-Barks-a	232	464	696	1485	2543	3600
33-Barks-a; Gremlins app. (Vivie Risto-s/a); infinity-c	166	332	498	1062	1856	2650
34-Gremlins by Walt Kelly begin, end #41; Barks-a	141	282	423	902	1576	2250
35,36-Barks-a	138	276	414	883	1542	2200
37-Donald Duck by Jack Hannah	81	162	243	518	909	1300
38-40-Barks-a. 39-X-Mas-c. 40,41-Gremlins by Kelly	88	176	264	563	982	1400
41-50-Barks-a. 43-Seven Dwarfs-c app. (4/44). 45-50-Nazis in Gottfredson's Mickey Mouse Stories. 46-War Bonds-c	78	156	234	499	875	1250
51-60-Barks-a. 51-X-Mas-c. 52-Li'l Bad Wolf begins, ends #203 (not in #55). 58-Kelly flag-c	32	64	96	230	515	800
61-70: Barks-a. 61-Dumbo story. 63,64-Pinocchio stories. 63-Cover swipe from New Funnies #94. 64-X-Mas-c. 65-Pluto story. 66-Infinity-c. 67,68-Mickey Mouse Sunday-r by Bill Wright	28	56	84	202	451	700
71-80: Barks-a. 75-77-Brer Rabbit stories, no Mickey Mouse. 76-X-Mas-c. 78-"Bark's" name on wooden box shown on cover	25	50	75	175	388	600
81-87,89,90: Barks-a. 82-Goofy-c. 82-84-Bongo stories. 86-90-Goofy & Agnes app. 89-Chip 'n' Dale story	20	40	60	138	307	475
88-1st app. Gladstone Gander by Barks (1/48)	25	50	75	175	388	600
91-97,99: Barks-a. 95-1st WDC&S Barks-c. 96-No Mickey Mouse; Little Toot begins, ends #97. 99-X-Mas-c	18	36	54	126	281	435
98-1st Uncle Scrooge app. in WDC&S (11/48)	31	62	93	223	499	775
100-(1/49)-Barks-a	21	42	63	147	324	500
101-110-Barks-a. 107-Taliaferro-c; Donald acquires super powers	16	32	48	107	236	365
111,114,117-All Barks-a	13	26	39	89	195	300
112-Drug (ether) issue (Donald Duck)	19	38	57	131	291	450
113,115,116,118-123: No Barks. 116-Dumbo x-over. 121-Grandma Duck begins, ends #168; not in #135,142,146,155	10	20	30	64	132	200
124,126-130-All Barks-a. 124-X-Mas-c	10	20	30	70	150	230
125-1st app. Junior Woodchucks (2/51); Barks-a	17	34	51	119	265	410
131,133,135-137,139-All Barks-a	10	20	30	67	141	215
132-Barks-a(2) (D. Duck & Grandma Duck)	10	20	30	69	147	225
134-Intro. & 1st app. The Beagle Boys (11/51)	21	42	63	147	324	500
138-Classic Scrooge money story	15	30	45	100	220	340
140-(5/52)-1st app. Gyro Gearloose by Barks; 2nd Barks Uncle Scrooge-c; 3rd Uncle Scrooge cover app.	20	40	60	141	313	485
141-150-All Barks-a. 143-Little Hiawatha begins, ends #151,159	9	18	27	58	114	170
151-170-All Barks-a	8	16	24	51	96	140
171-199-All Barks-a	7	14	21	46	86	125
200	7	14	21	49	92	135
201-240: All Barks-a. 204-Chip 'n' Dale & Scamp begin	6	12	18	40	73	105
241-283: Barks-a. 241-Dumbo x-over. 247-Gyro Gearloose begins, ends #274. 256-Ludwig Von Drake begins, ends #274	5	10	15	35	63	90
284,285,287,290,295,296,309-311-Not by Barks	3	6	9	19	30	40
286,288,291-294,297,298,308-All Barks stories; 293-Grandma Duck's Farm Friends. 297-Gyro Gearloose. 298-Daisy Duck's Diary-r	4	8	12	23	37	50
289-Annette-c & back-c & story; Barks-s	4	8	12	27	44	60
299-307-All contain early Barks-r (#43-117). 305-Gyro Gearloose	4	8	12	25	40	55
312-Last Barks issue with original story	4	8	12	25	40	55
313-315,317-327,329-334,336-341	3	6	9	15	22	28
316-Last issue published during life of Walt Disney	3	6	9	15	22	28
328,335,342-350-Barks-r	3	6	9	15	22	28
351-360-With posters inside; Barks reprints (2 versions of each with & without posters)	4	8	12	25	40	55
351-360-Without posters...	3	6	9	14	19	24
361-400-Barks-r	3	6	9	14	20	26
401-429-Barks-r	3	6	9	14	19	24
430,433,437,438,441,444,445,466-No Barks	2	4	6	8	11	14
431,432,434-436,439,440,442,443-Barks-r	2	4	6	10	14	18
440-Whitman edition	3	6	9	14	19	24
446-465,467-473-Barks-r	2	4	6	9	13	16
474(3/80),475-478 (Whitman)	3	6	9	14	19	24
479(8/80),481(10/80)-484(1/81) pre-pack only	5	10	15	30	50	70
480 (8-12/80)-(Very low distribution)	12	24	36	84	185	285
484 (1/81, 40¢-c) Cover price error variant (scarce)	6	12	18	38	69	100
484 (1/81) Regular 50¢ cover price; not pre-pack	3	6	9	19	30	40
485-499: 494-r/WDC&S #98	2	4	6	11	16	20
500-510 (All #90011 on-c; pre-packs): 500(4/83), 501(5/83), 502&503(7/83), 504-506(all 8/83), 507(4/84), 508(5/84), 509(6/84), 510(7/84). 506-No Barks	2	4	6	13	18	22
511-Donald Duck by Daan Jippes (1st in U.S.; in all through #518); Gyro Gearloose Barks-r begins (in most through #547); Wuzzles by Disney Studio (1st by Gladstone)	3	6	9	16	24	32
512,513	2	4	6	10	14	18
514-516,520	2	4	6	8	10	12
517-519,521,522,525,527,529,530,532-546: 518-Infinity-c. 522-r/1st app. Huey, Dewey & Louie from D. Duck Sunday. 535-546-Barks-r. 537-1st Donald Duck by William Van Horn in WDC&S. 541-545-52 pgs. 546,547-68 pgs. 546-Kelly-r. 547-Rosa-a						6.00
523,524,526,528,531,547: Rosa-s/a in all. 523-1st Rosa 10 pager	2	4	6	9	12	15
548-($1.50, 6/90)-1st Disney issue; new-a; no M. Mouse	1	2	3	4	5	7
549,551-570,572,573,577-579,581,584 ($1.50): 549-Barks-r begin, ends #585, not in #555, 556, & 564. 551-r/1 story from F.C. #29. 556,578-r/Mickey Mouse Cheerios Premium by Dick Moores. 562,563,568-570, 572, 581-Gottfredson strip-r. 570-Valentine issue; has Mickey/Minnie centerfold. 584-Taliaferro strip-r						4.00
550 ($2.25, 52 pgs.)-Donald Duck by Barks; previously printed only in The Netherlands (1st time in U.S.); r/Chip 'n Dale & Scamp from #204						5.00
571-($2.95, 68 pgs)-r/Donald Duck's Atom Bomb by Barks from 1947 Cheerios premium						6.00
574-576,580,582,583 ($2.95, 68 pgs.): 574-r/1st Pinocchio Sunday strip (1939-40). 575-Gottfredson-r, Pinocchio-r/WDC&S #64. 580-r/Donald Duck's 1st app. from Silly Symphony strip 12/16/34 by Taliaferro; Gottfredson strip-r begin; not in #584 & 600. 582,583-r/Mickey Mouse on Sky Island from WDC&S #1,2						5.00
585 ($2.50, 52 pgs.)-r/#140; Barks-r/WDC&S #140						5.00
586,587: 586-Gladstone issues begin again; begin $1.50-c; Gottfredson-r begins (not in #600). 587-Donald Duck by William Van Horn begins						4.00
588-597: 588,591-599-Donald Duck by William Van Horn						3.00
598,599 ($1.95, 36 pgs.): 598-r/1st drawings of Mickey Mouse by Ub Iwerks						3.00
600 ($2.95, 48 pgs.)-L.B. Cole-c(r)/WDC&S #1; Barks-r/WDC&S #32 plus Rosa, Jippes, Van Horn-r and new Rosa centerspread						4.00
601-611 ($5.95, 64 pgs., squarebound, bi-monthly): 601-Barks-c, r/Mickey Mouse V1#1, Rosa-a/scripts. 602-Rosa-c. 604-Taliaferro strip-r/1st Silly Symphony Sundays from 1932. 604,605-Jippes-a. 605-Walt Kelly-c; Gottfredson "Mickey Mouse Outwits the Phantom Blot" r/F.C. #16						6.00
612-633 ($6.95): 633-(2/99) Last Gladstone issue						7.00
634-675: 634-(7/03) First Gemstone issue; William Van Horn-c. 666-Mickey's Inferno						7.00
676-681: 676-Begin $7.50-c. 677-Bucky Bug's 75th Anniversary						7.50
682-698-($7.99)						8.00
699-714: 699-(9/09, $2.99) First BOOM! Kids issue. 700-Back-up story w/Van Horn-a						3.00

Walt Disney's Donald and Mickey #21 © DIS

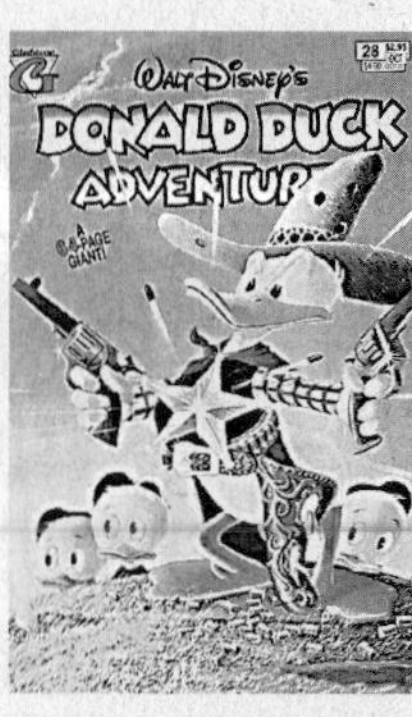

Walt Disney's Donald Duck Adventures #28 © DIS

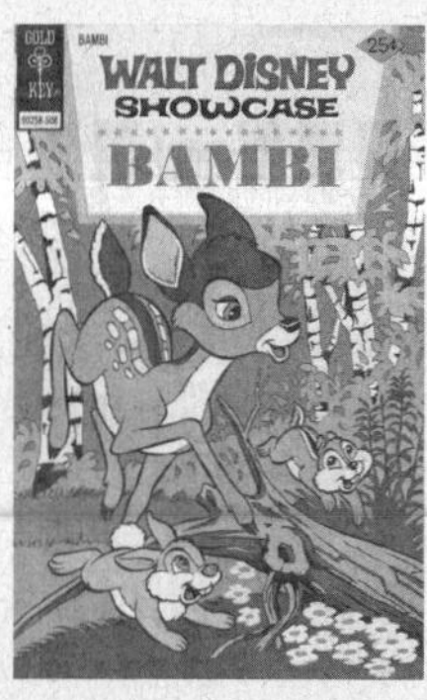

Walt Disney Showcase #31 © DIS

	GD 2.0	VG 4.0	FN 6.0	VF 8.0	VF/NM 9.0	NM- 9.2

715-720: 715-(1/11, $3.99) 70th Anniversary issue; cover swipe of #1 by Van Horn; Jippes, Rosa-a. 716-Barks reprints 4.00
721-738: 721-(7/15, $3.99) First IDW issue; Italian, Dutch & classic reprints 4.00
739-743-($5.99): 741-Eurasia Toft app. 743-(7/18) 6.00
... 75th Anniversary Special (10/15, $5.99) Classic short story reprints by various 6.00

NOTE: *(#1-38, 68 pgs.; #39-42, 60 pgs.; #43-57, 61-134, 143-168, 446, 447, 52 pgs.; #58-60, 135-142, 169-540, 36 pgs.)*

NOTE: ***Barks** art in all issues #31 on, except where noted; c-95, 96, 104, 108, 109, 130-172, 174-178, 183, 198-200, 204, 206-209, 212-216, 218, 220, 226, 228-233, 235-238, 240-243, 247, 250, 253, 256, 260, 261, 276-283, 288-292, 295-298, 301, 303, 304, 306, 307, 309, 310, 313-316, 319, 321, 322, 324, 326, 328, 329, 331, 332, 334, 341, 342, 350, 351, 527r, 530r, 540(never before published), 546r, 557-586r(most), 596p, 601p. **Kelly** a-24p, 34-41, 43; r-522-524, 546, 547, 582, 583; covers(most)-34-118, 531r, 537r, 541r-543r, 562r, 571r, 605r. Walt Disney's Comics & Stories featured Mickey Mouse serials which were in practically every issue from #1 through #394 and #511 to date. The titles of the serials, along with the issues they are in, are listed in previous editions of this price guide. **Floyd Gottfredson** Mickey Mouse serials in issues #1-14, 18-66, 69-74, 78-100, 128, 562, 563, 568-572, 582, 583, 586-599 , 601-603 , 605-present , plus "Service with a Smile" in #13; "Mickey Mouse in a Warplant" (3 pgs.), and "Pluto Catches a Nazi Spy" (4 pgs.) in #62; "Mystery Next Door", #93; "Sunken Treasure", #94; "Aunt Marissa", #95 (r in #575); "Gangland", #98 (r in #562); "Thanksgiving Dinner", #99 (r in #567); and "The Talking Dog", #100 (r in #563); "Morty's Escapade," #128. "The Brave Little Tailor", #580; "Introducing Mickey Mouse Movies ", #581; Circus Roustabout, #585; "Rumplewatt the Giant", #604. Mickey Mouse by **Paul Murry** #152-547 except 155-57 (**Dick Moore**), 327-29 (**Tony Strobl**), 348-50 (**Jack Manning**), 533 (**Bill Wright**). **Don Rosa** story/a-523, 524, 526, 528, 531, 547, 601-present. **Al Taliaferro** Silly Symphonies in #5-"Three Little Pigs"; #13-"Birds of a Feather"; #14-"The Boarding School Mystery"; #15-"Cookieland" and "Three Little Kittens"; #16-"The Practical Pig"; #17-"The Ugly Duckling"; "The Wise Little Hen" in #580; and "Ambrose the Robber Kitten"; #19-"Penguin Isle"; and "Bucky Bug" in #20-23, 25, 26, 28 (one continuous story from 1932-34; first 2 pgs. not Taliaferro). **Gottfredson** strip r-562, 563, 568-572, 581, 585, 586, 590. **Taliaferro** strip r-584, 580. **Van Horn** a-537, 545, 561, 574, 587, 588, 591-on.*

WALT DISNEY'S COMICS DIGEST
Gladstone: Dec, 1986 - No. 7, Sept, 1987

1 1 2 3 5 6 8
2-7 6.00

WALT DISNEY'S COMICS PENNY PINCHER
Gladstone: May, 1997 - No. 4, Aug, 1997 (99¢, limited series)

1-4 4.00

WALT DISNEY'S DONALD AND MICKEY (Formerly Walt Disney's Mickey and Donald)
Gladstone (Bruce Hamilton Co.): No. 19, Sept, 1993 - No. 30, 1995 ($1.50, 36 & 68 pgs.)

19,21-24,26-30: New & reprints. 19,21,23,24-Barks-r. 19,26-Murry-r. 22-Barks "Omelet" story r/WDC&S #146. 27-Mickey Mouse story by Caesar Ferioli (1st U.S work). 29-Rosa-c; Mickey Mouse story actually starring Goofy (does not include Mickey except on title page.) 4.00
20,25-($2.95, 68 pgs.): 20-Barks, Gottfredson-r 5.00
NOTE: *Donald Duck stories were all reprints.*

WALT DISNEY'S DONALD DUCK
Gemstone Publishing: 2006, 2008

... Free Comic Book Day (5/06) r/WDC&S #531; Rosa-s/a; P&S. Block-s/a; Van Horn-s/a 3.00
nn-(8-1/2"x 5-1/2", Halloween giveaway) r/"A Prank Above" -Barks-s/a; Rosa-s/a 3.00
nn-(2008, 8-1/2"x 5-1/2", Halloween giveaway) "The Halloween Huckster"; Rota-s/a 3.00

WALT DISNEY'S DONALD DUCK ADVENTURES (D.D. Adv. #1-3)
Gladstone: 11/87-No. 20, 4/90 (1st Series); No. 21,8/93-No. 48, 2/98(3rd Series)

1 1 2 3 5 6 8
2-r/F.C. #308 4.00
3,4,6,7,9-11,13,15-18: 3-r/F.C. #223. 4-r/F.C. #62. 9-r/F.C. #159, "Ghost of the Grotto". 11-r/F.C. #159, "Adventure Down Under." 16-r/F.C. #291; Rosa-c. 18-r/FC #318; Rosa-c 4.00
5,8: 5-Don Rosa-c/a. 8-Rosa-a 5.00
12($1.50, 52pgs)-Rosa-c/s/a; "Return to Plain Awful" story; sequel to Four Color #223 (square egg story); Barks centerfold poster 6.00
14-r/F.C. #29, "Mummy's Ring" 4.00
19($1.95, 68 pgs.)-Barks-r/F.C. #199 (1 pg.) 4.00
20($1.95, 68 pgs.)-Barks-r/F.C. #189 & cover-r; William Van Horn-a 4.00
21,22: 21-r/D.D. #46. 22-r/F.C. #282 3.00
23-25,27,29,31,32-($1.50, 36 pgs.): 21,23,29-Rosa-c. 23-Intro/1st app. Andold Wild Duck by Marco Rota. 24-Van Horn-a. 27-1st Pat Block-a, "Mystery of Widow's Gap." 31,32-Block-c 3.00
26,28($2.95, 68 pgs.): 26-Barks-r/F.C. #108, "Terror of the River". 28-Barks-r/F.C. #199, "Sheriff of Bullet Valley" 4.00
30($2.95, 68 pgs.)-r/F.C. #367, Barks' "Christmas for Shacktown" 4.00
33($1.95, 68 pgs.)-r/F.C. #408, Barks' "The Golden Helmet;"Van Horn-c 4.00
34-43: 34-Resume $1.50-c. 34,35,37-Block-a/scripts. 38-Van Horn-c/a 3.00
44-48-($1.95-c) 3.00
NOTE: ***Barks** a-1-22r, 26r, 28r, 33r, 36r; c-3r, 8r, 10r, 14r, 20r. **Block** a-27, 30, 34, 35, 37; c-27, 30-32, 34, 35, 37; c-27, 30, 31, 32, 34, 35, 37. **Rosa** a-5, 8, 12, 43; c-13, 16, 18, 21, 23, 43.*

WALT DISNEY'S DONALD DUCK ADVENTURES (2nd Series)
Disney Comics: June, 1990 - No. 38, July, 1993 ($1.50)

1-Rosa-a & scripts 5.00
2-21,23,25,27-33,35,36,38: 2-Barks-r/WDC&S #35; William Van Horn-a begins, ends #20. 9-Barks-r/F.C. #178. 9,11,14,17-No Van Horn-a. 11-Mad #1 cover parody. 14-Barks-r. 17-Barks-r. 21-r/FC #203 by Barks. 29-r/MOC #20 by Barks 3.00
22,24,26,34,37: 22-Rosa-a (10 pgs.) & scripts. 24-Rosa-a & scripts. 26-r/March of Comics #41 by Barks. 34-Rosa-c/a. 37-Rosa-a; Barks-r 4.00
NOTE: ***Barks** r-2, 4, 9(F.C. #178), 14(D.D. #45), 17, 21, 26, 27, 29 , 35, 36(D.D #60)-38. **Taliaferro** a-34r, 36r.*

WALT DISNEY'S DONALD DUCK ADVENTURES
Gemstone Publishing: May, 2003 (giveaway promoting 2003 return of Disney Comics)

...Free Comic Book Day Edition - cover logo on red background; reprints "Maharajah Donald" & "The Peaceful Hills" from March of Comics #4; Barks-s/a; Kelly original-c on back-c 3.00
...San Diego Comic-Con 2003 Edition - cover logo on gold background 3.00
...ANA World's Fair of Money Baltimore Edition - cover logo on green background 3.00
...WizardWorld Chicago 2003 Edition - cover logo on blue background 3.00

WALT DISNEY'S DONALD DUCK ADVENTURES (Take-Along Comic)
Gemstone Publishing: July, 2003 - No. 21, Nov, 2006 ($7.95, 5" x 7-1/2")

1-21-Mickey Mouse & Uncle Scrooge app. 9-Christmas-c 8.00
... , The Barks/Rosa Collection Vol. 2 (3/08, $8.99) reprints Donald Duck's Atom Bomb, Super Snooper & The Trouble With Dimes by Barks; The Duck Who Fell to Earth, Super Snooper Strikes Again & The Money Pit by Rosa 9.00
... , The Barks/Rosa Collection Vol. 3 (9/08, $8.99) r/FC #408 "The Golden Helmet" by Barks & DDA #43 "The Lost Charts of Columbus" by Rosa; cover gallery and bonus art 9.00

WALT DISNEY'S DONALD DUCK AND FRIENDS (Continues as Donald Duck and Friends)
Gemstone Publishing: No. 308, Oct, 2003 - No. 346, Dec, 2006 ($2.95)

308-346: 308-Numbering resumes from Gladstone Donald Duck series; Halloween-c. 332-Halloween-c; r/#26 by Carl Barks 3.00

WALT DISNEY'S DONALD DUCK AND MICKEY MOUSE (Formerly Walt Disney's Donald and Mickey)
Gladstone (Bruce Hamilton Company): Sept, 1995 - No. 7, Sept, 1996 ($1.50, 32 pgs.)

1-7: 1-Barks-r and new Mickey Mouse stories in all. 5,6-Mickey Mouse stories by Caesar Ferioli. 7-New Donald Duck and Mickey Mouse x-over story; Barks-r/WDC&S #51 3.00
NOTE: *Issue #8 was advertised, but cancelled.*

WALT DISNEY'S DONALD DUCK AND UNCLE SCROOGE
Gemstone Publishing: Nov, 2005 ($6.95, square-bound one-shot)

nn-New story by John Lustig and Pat Block and r/Uncle Scrooge #59 7.00

WALT DISNEY'S DONALD DUCK FAMILY
Gemstone Publishing: Jun, 2008 ($8.99, square-bound)

... The Daan Jippes Collection Vol. 1 - R/Barks-s re-drawn by Jippes for Dutch comics 9.00

WALT DISNEY'S DONALD DUCK IN THE CASE OF THE MISSING MUMMY
Gemstone Publishing: Oct, 2007 ($8.99, square-bound one-shot)

nn-New story by Shelley and Pat Block and r/Donald Duck FC #29 9.00

WALT DISNEY'S GYRO GEARLOOSE
Gemstone Publishing: May, 2008

... Free Comic Book Day (5/08) short stories by Barks, Rosa, Van Horn, Gerstein 3.00

WALT DISNEY SHOWCASE
Gold Key: Oct, 1970 - No. 54, Jan, 1980 (No. 44-48: 68pgs., 49-54: 52pgs.)

	GD 2.0	VG 4.0	FN 6.0	VF 8.0	VF/NM 9.0	NM- 9.2
1-Boatniks (Movie)-Photo-c	3	6	9	17	26	35
2-Moby Duck	3	6	9	14	19	24
3,4,7: 3-Bongo & Lumpjaw-r. 4,7-Pluto-r	2	4	6	10	14	18
5-$1,000,000 Duck (Movie)-Photo-c	3	6	9	15	22	28
6-Bedknobs & Broomsticks (Movie)	3	6	9	15	22	28
8-Daisy & Donald	2	4	6	11	16	20
9- 101 Dalmatians (cartoon feat.); r/F.C. #1183	3	6	9	16	24	32
10-Napoleon & Samantha (Movie)-Photo-c	3	6	9	15	22	28
11-Moby Duck-r	2	4	6	10	14	18
12-Dumbo-r/Four Color #668	2	4	6	11	16	20
13-Pluto-r	2	4	6	10	14	18
14-World's Greatest Athlete (Movie)-Photo-c	3	6	9	15	22	28
15- 3 Little Pigs-r	2	4	6	11	16	20
16-Aristocats (cartoon feature); r/Aristocats #1	3	6	9	15	22	28
17-Mary Poppins; r/M.P. #10136-501-Photo-c	3	6	9	15	22	28
18-Gyro Gearloose; Barks-r/F.C. #1047,1184	3	6	9	17	26	35
19-That Darn Cat; r/That Darn Cat #10171-602-Hayley Mills photo-c	3	6	9	15	22	28
20,23-Pluto-r	2	4	6	11	16	20
21-Li'l Bad Wolf & The Three Little Pigs	2	4	6	10	14	18
22-Unbirthday Party with Alice in Wonderland; r/Four Color #341	3	6	9	14	19	24
24-26: 24-Herbie Rides Again (Movie); sequel to "The Love Bug"; photo-c. 25-Old Yeller (Movie); r/F.C. #869; Photo-c. 26-Lt. Robin Crusoe USN (Movie); r/Lt. Robin Crusoe USN #10191-601; photo-c	2	4	6	11	16	20

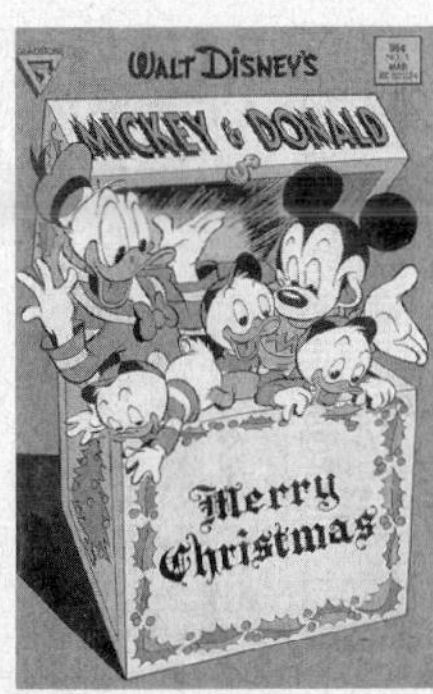

Walt Disney's Mickey and Donald #1 © DIS

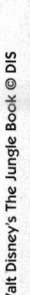

Walt Disney's The Jungle Book © DIS

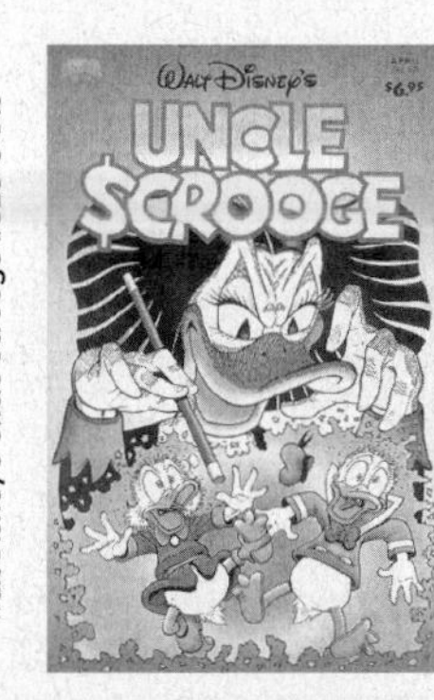

Walt Disney's Uncle Scrooge #328 © DIS

	GD	VG	FN	VF	VF/NM	NM-
	2.0	4.0	6.0	8.0	9.0	9.2

27-Island at the Top of the World (Movie)-Photo-c 3 6 9 14 19 24
28-Brer Rabbit, Bucky Bug-r/WDC&S #58 2 4 6 11 16 20
29-Escape to Witch Mountain (Movie)-Photo-c 3 6 9 14 19 24
30-Magica De Spell; Barks-r/Uncle Scrooge #36 & WDC&S #258
3 6 9 20 31 42
31-Bambi (cartoon feature); r/Four Color #186 2 4 6 13 18 22
32-Spin & Marty-r/F.C. #1026; Mickey Mouse Club (TV)-Photo-c
3 6 9 14 19 24
33-40: 33-Pluto-r/F.C. #1143. 34-Paul Revere's Ride with Johnny Tremain (TV); r/F.C. #822. 35-Goofy-r/F.C. #952. 36-Peter Pan-r/F.C. #442. 37-Tinker Bell & Jiminy Cricket-r/F.C. #982,989. 38,39-Mickey & the Sleuth, Parts 1 & 2. 40-The Rescuers (cartoon feature)
2 4 6 9 13 16
41-Herbie Goes to Monte Carlo (Movie); sequel to "Herbie Rides Again"; photo-c
2 4 6 10 14 18
42-Mickey & the Sleuth 2 4 6 9 13 16
43-Pete's Dragon (Movie)-Photo-c 2 4 6 13 18 22
44-Return From Witch Mountain (new) & In Search of the Castaways-r (Movies)-Photo-c; 68 pg. giants begin 3 6 9 14 19 24
45-The Jungle Book (Movie); r/#30033-803 3 6 9 16 24 32
46-48: 46-The Cat From Outer Space (Movie)(new), & The Shaggy Dog (Movie)-r/F.C. #985; photo-c. 47-Mickey Mouse Surprise Party-r. 48-The Wonderful Advs. of Pinocchio-r/F.C. #1203; last 68 pg. issue 2 4 6 10 14 18
49-54: 49-North Avenue Irregulars (Movie); Zorro-r/Zorro #11; 52 pgs. begin; photo-c. 50-Bedknobs & Broomsticks-r/#6; Mooncussers-r/World of Adv. #1; photo-c. 51-101 Dalmatians-r. 52-Unidentified Flying Oddball (Movie); r/Picnic Party #8; photo-c. 53-The Scarecrow-r (TV). 54-The Black Hole (Movie)-Photo-c (predates Black Hole #1)
2 4 6 9 13 16

WALT DISNEY SHOWCASE
IDW Publishing: Jan, 2018 - No. 6, Jun, 2018 ($3.99)
1-6-English versions of Italian Disney stories; 3 covers 4.00

WALT DISNEY'S MAGAZINE (TV)(Formerly Walt Disney's Mickey Mouse Club Magazine) (50¢, bi-monthly)
Western Publishing Co.: V2#4, June, 1957 - V4#6, Oct, 1959
V2#4-Stories & articles on the Mouseketeers, Zorro, & Goofy and other Disney characters & people 6 12 18 38 69 100
V2#5, V2#6(10/57) 5 10 15 35 63 90
V3#1(12/57), V3#3-5 5 10 15 33 57 80
V3#2-Annette Funicello photo-c 10 20 30 68 144 220
V3#6(10/58)-TV Zorro photo-c 7 14 21 48 89 130
V4#1(12/58) - V4#2-4,6(10/59) 5 10 15 33 57 80
V4#5-Annette Funicello photo-c, w/ 2-photo articles 10 20 30 68 144 220
NOTE: *V2#4-V3#6 were 11-1/2x8-1/2", 48 pgs.; V4#1 on were 10x8", 52 pgs. (Peak circulation of 400,000).*

WALT DISNEY'S MERRY CHRISTMAS (See Dell Giant #39)

WALT DISNEY'S MICKEY AND DONALD (M & D #1,2)(Becomes Walt Disney's Donald & Mickey #19 on)
Gladstone: Mar, 1988 - No. 18, May, 1990 (95¢)
1-Don Rosa-a; r/1949 Firestone giveaway 6.00
2-8: 3-Infinity-c. 4-8-Barks-r 4.00
9-15: 9-r/1948 Firestone giveaway; X-Mas-c 3.00
16($1.50, 52 pgs.)-r/FC #157 5.00
17-(68 pgs.) Barks M.M.-r/FC #79 plus Barks D.D.-r; Rosa-a; x-mas-c 6.00
18($1.95, 68 pgs.)-Gottfredson-r/WDC&S #13,72-74; Kelly-c(r); Barks-r 5.00
NOTE: ***Barks** reprints in 1-15, 17, 18. **Kelly** c-13r, 14 (r/Walt Disney's C&S #58), 18r.*

WALT DISNEY'S MICKEY MOUSE
Gemstone Publishing: May, 2007
... Free Comic Book Day (5/07) Floyd Gottfredson-s/a 3.00

WALT DISNEY'S MICKEY MOUSE ADVENTURES (Take-Along Comic)
Gemstone Publishing: Aug, 2004 - No. 12 ($7.95, 5" x 7-1/2")
1-12-Goofy, Donald Duck & Uncle Scrooge app. 8.00

WALT DISNEY'S MICKEY MOUSE AND BLOTMAN IN BLOTMAN RETURNS
Gemstone Publishing: Dec, 2006 ($5.99, squarebound, one-shot)
nn-Wraparound-c by Noel Van Horn; Super Goof back-up story 6.00

WALT DISNEY'S MICKEY MOUSE AND FRIENDS (See Mickey Mouse and Friends for #296)
Gemstone Publishing: No. 257, Oct, 2003 - No. 295, Dec, 2006 ($2.95)
257-295: 257-Numbering resumes from Gladstone Mickey Mouse series; Halloween-c. 285-Return of the Phantom Blot 3.00

WALT DISNEY'S MICKEY MOUSE AND UNCLE SCROOGE
Gemstone Publishing: June, 2004 (Free Comic Book Day giveaway)
nn-Flip book with r/Uncle Scrooge #15 and r/Mickey Mouse Four Color #79 (only Barks drawn Mickey Mouse story) 3.00

WALT DISNEY'S MICKEY MOUSE CLUB MAGAZINE (TV)(Becomes Walt Disney's Magazine)
Western Publishing Co.: Winter, 1956 - V2#3, Apr, 1957 (11-1/2x8-1/2", quarterly, 48 pgs.)
V1#1 13 26 39 89 195 300
2-4 8 16 24 54 102 150
V2#1,2 7 14 21 44 82 120
3-Annette photo-c 12 24 36 81 176 270
Annual(1956)-Two different issues; ($1.50-Whitman); 120 pgs., cardboard covers, 11-3/4x8-3/4"; reprints 13 26 39 86 188 290
Annual(1957)-Same as above 11 22 33 72 154 235

WALT DISNEY'S MICKEY MOUSE MEETS BLOTMAN
Gemstone Publishing: Aug, 2005 ($5.99, squarebound, one-shot)
nn-Wraparound-c by Noel Van Horn; Super Goof back-up story 6.00

WALT DISNEY'S PINOCCHIO SPECIAL
Gladstone: Spring, 1990 ($1.00)
1-50th anniversary edition; Kelly-r/F.C. #92 3.00

WALT DISNEY'S SEBASTIAN
Disney Comics, Inc.: 1992
1-(36 pgs.) 3.00

WALT DISNEY'S SPRING FEVER
Gemstone Publishing: Apr, 2007; Apr, 2008 ($9.50, squarebound)
1,2: 1-New stories and reprints incl. "Mystery of the Swamp" by Carl Barks 9.50

WALT DISNEY'S THE ADVENTUROUS UNCLE SCROOGE MCDUCK
Gladstone: Jan, 1998 - No. 2, Mar, 1998 ($1.95)
1,2: 1-Barks-a(r). 2-Rosa-a(r) 3.00

WALT DISNEY'S THE JUNGLE BOOK
W.D. Publications (Disney Comics): 1990 ($5.95, graphic novel, 68 pgs.)
nn-Movie adaptation; movie rereleased in 1990 6.00
nn-($2.95, 68 pgs.)-Comic edition; wraparound-c 4.00

WALT DISNEY'S UNCLE SCROOGE (Formerly Uncle Scrooge #1-209)
Gladstone #210-242/Disney Comics #243-280/Gladstone #281-318/Gemstone #319 on: No. 210, 10/86 - No. 242, 4/90; No. 243, 6/90 - No. 318, 2/99; No. 319, 7/03 - No. 383, 11/08
210-1st Gladstone issue; r/WDC&S #134 (1st Beagle Boys)
2 4 6 9 13 16
211-218: 216-New story ("Go Slowly Sands of Time") plotted and partly scripted by Barks. 217-r/U.S. #7, "Seven Cities of Cibola" 2 4 6 9 12 15
219-"Son Of The Sun" by Rosa (his 1st pro work) 3 6 9 14 20 25
220-Don Rosa-a/scripts 1 2 3 5 6 8
221-223,225,228-234,236-240 4.00
224,226,227,235: 224-Rosa-c/a. 226,227-Rosa-a. 235-Rosa-a/scripts 5.00
241-($1.95, 68 pgs.)-Rosa finishes over Barks-r 6.00
242-($1.95, 68 pgs.)-Barks-r; Rosa-a(1 pg.) 6.00
243-249,251-260,264-275,277-280,282-284-($1.50): 243-1st by Disney Comics. 274-All Barks issue. 275-Contains centerspread by Rosa. 279-All Barks issue; Rosa-c. 283-r/WDC&S #98 3.00
250-($2.25, 52 pgs.)-Barks-r; wraparound-c 4.00
261-263,276-Don Rosa-c/a 5.00
281-Gladstone issues start again; Rosa-c 6.00
285-The Life and Times of Scrooge McDuck Pt. 1; Rosa-c/a/scripts
1 3 4 6 8 10
286-293: The Life and Times of Scrooge McDuck Pt. 2-9; Rosa-c/a/scripts. 292-Scrooge & Glittering Goldie & Goose Egg Nugget on-c 6.00
294-299, 301-308-($1.50, 32 pgs.): 294-296-The Life and Times of Scrooge McDuck Pt. 10-12. 295-Titanic on-c. 296-Beagle Boys & Christmas-c. 297-The Life and Times of Uncle Scrooge Pt. 0; Rosa-c/a/scripts 3.00
300-($2.25, 48 pgs.)-Rosa-c; Barks-r/WDC&S #104 and U.S. #216; r/U.S. #220; includes new centerfold. 4.00
309-($6.95) Low print run 3 6 9 14 20 25
310-($6.95) Low print run 4 8 12 27 44 60
311-320-($6.95) 318-(2/99) Last Gladstone issue. 319-(7/03) First Gemstone issue; The Dutchman's Secret by Don Rosa 2 4 6 8 10 12
321-360 7.00
361-366: 361-Begin $7.50-c 7.50
367-383-($7.99) 8.00
... Adventures, The Barks/Rosa Collection Vol. 1 (Gemstone, 7/07, $8.50) reprints Pygmy Indians appearances in U.S. #18 by Barks and WDC&S #633 by Rosa 8.50
Walt Disney's The Life and Times of Scrooge McDuck by Don Rosa TPB (Gemstone, 2005, $16.99) Reprints #285-296, with foreword, commentaries & sketch pages by Rosa 17.00
Walt Disney's The Life and Times of Scrooge McDuck Companion by Don Rosa TPB (Gemstone, 2006, $16.99) additional chapters, with foreword & commentaries 17.00
NOTE: ***Barks** r-210-218, 220-223, 224(2pg.), 225-234, 236-242, 245, 246, 250-253, 255, 256, 258, 261(2 pg.),*

Walt Disney's Uncle Scrooge Adventures #28 © DIS

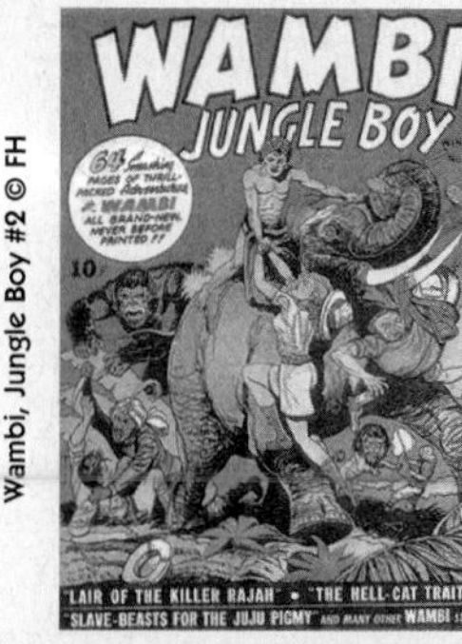

Wambi, Jungle Boy #2 © FH

Wanted Comics #34 © Toytown

GD VG FN VF VF/NM NM-
2.0 4.0 6.0 8.0 9.0 9.2

*265, 267, 268, 270(2), 272-284, 299-present; c(r)-210, 212, 221, 228, 229, 232, 233, 284. scripts-287, 293. **Rosa** a-219, 220, 224, 226, 227, 235, 261-263, 268, 275-277, 285-297; c-219, 224, 231, 261-263, 276, 278-281, 285-296; scripts-219, 220, 224, 235, 261-263, 268, 276, 285-296.*

WALT DISNEY'S UNCLE SCROOGE
Gemstone Publishing

nn-(5/05, FCBD) Reprints Uncle Scrooge's debut in Four Color Comics #386; Barks-s/a 3.00
nn-(2007, 8-1/2"x 5-1/2", Halloween giveaway) Hound of the Whiskevilles; Barks-s/a 3.00

WALT DISNEY'S UNCLE SCROOGE ADVENTURES (U. Scrooge Advs. #1-3)
Gladstone Publishing: Nov, 1987 - No. 21, May, 1990; No. 22, Sept, 1993 - No. 54, Feb, 1998

1-Barks-r begin, ends #26 2 4 6 8 10 12
2-4 4.00
5,9,14: 5-Rosa-c/a; no Barks-r. 9,14-Rosa-a 5.00
6-8,10-13,15-19: 10-r/U.S. #18(all Barks) 3.00
20,21 ($1.95, 68 pgs.) 20-Rosa-c/a. 21-Rosa-a 5.00
22 ($1.50)-Rosa-c; r/U.S. #26 5.00
23-($2.95, 68 pgs.)-Vs. The Phantom Blot-r/P.B. #3; Barks-r 4.00
24-26,29,31,32,34-36: 24,25,29,31,32-Rosa-c. 25-r/U.S. #21 3.00
27-Guardians of the Lost Library - Rosa-c/a/story; origin of Junior Woodchuck Guidebook 4.00
28-($2.95, 68 pgs.)-r/U.S. #13 w/restored missing panels 4.00
30-($2.95, 68 pgs.)-r/U.S. #12; Rosa-c 4.00
33-($2.95, 64 pgs.)-New Barks story 4.00
37-54 3.00

NOTE: ***Barks** r-1-4, 6-8, 10-13, 15-21, 23, 22, 24; c(r)-15, 16, 17, 21. **Rosa** a-5, 9, 14, 20, 21, 27, 51; c-5, 13, 14, 17(finishes), 20, 22, 24, 25, 27, 28, 51; scripts-5, 9, 14, 27.*

WALT DISNEY'S UNCLE SCROOGE AND DONALD DUCK
Gladstone: Jan, 1998 - No. 2, Mar, 1998 ($1.95)

1,2: 1-Rosa-a(r) 3.00

WALT DISNEY'S UNCLE SCROOGE ADVENTURES IN COLOR
Gladstone Publ.: Dec, 1995 - No. 56 ($8.95/$9.95, squarebound, 56 issue limited series) (Polybagged w/card) (Series chronologically reprints all the stories written & drawn by Carl Barks)

1-56: 1-(12/95)-r/FC #386. 15-(12/96)-r/US #15. 16-(12/96)-r/US #16. 18-(1/97)-r/US #18 10.00

WALT DISNEY'S VACATION PARADE
Gemstone Publishing: 2004 - No. 5, July, 2008 ($8.95/$9.95, squarebound, annual)

1-3: 1-Reprints stories from Dell Giant Comics Vacation Parade 1 (July 1950) 10.00
4,5-($9.95): 4-(5/07). 5-(7/08) 10.00

WALT DISNEY'S WHEATIES PREMIUMS (See Wheaties in the Promotional section)

WALT DISNEY'S WORLD OF THE DRAGONLORDS
Gemstone Publishing: 2005 ($12.99, squarebound, graphic novel)

SC-Uncle Scrooge, Donald & nephews app.; Byron Erickson-s/Giorgio Cavazzano-a 13.00

WALT DISNEY TREASURES - DISNEY COMICS: 75 YEARS OF INNOVATION
Gemstone Publishing: 2006 ($12.99, TPB)

SC-Reprints from 1930-2004, including debut of Mickey Mouse newspaper strip 13.00

WALT DISNEY TREASURES - UNCLE SCROOGE: A LITTLE SOMETHING SPECIAL
Gemstone Publishing: 2008 ($16.99, TPB)

SC-Uncle Scrooge classics from 1954-2006, including "The Seven Cities of Cibola" 17.00

WALT DISNEY UNCLE SCROOGE AND DONALD DUCK
Fantagraphic Books: 2014 (giveaway)

Free Comic Book Day - A Matter of Some Gravity; Don Rosa-s/a 3.00

WALTER LANTZ ANDY PANDA (Also see Andy Panda)
Gold Key: Aug, 1973 - No. 23, Jan, 1978 (Walter Lantz)

1-Reprints 3 6 9 14 19 24
2-10-All reprints 2 4 6 9 12 15
11-23: 15,17-19,22-Reprints 1 2 3 5 7 9

WALT KELLY'S...
Eclipse Comics: Dec, 1987; Apr, 1988 ($1.75/$2.50, Baxter paper)

...Christmas Classics 1 (12/87)-Kelly-r/Peter Wheat & Santa Claus Funnies,
...Springtime Tales 1 (4/88, $2.50)-Kelly-r 4.00

WALTONS, THE (See Kite Fun Book)

WALT SCOTT (See Little People)

WALT SCOTT'S CHRISTMAS STORIES (See Little People, 4-Color #959, 1062)

WAMBI, JUNGLE BOY (See Jungle Comics)
Fiction House Magazines: Spr, 1942; No. 2, Win, 1942-43; No. 3, Spr, 1943; No. 4, Fall, 1948; No. 5, Sum, 1949; No. 6, Spr, 1950; No. 7-10, 1950(nd); No. 11, Spr, 1951 - No. 18, Win, 1952-53 (#1-3: 68 pgs.)

GD VG FN VF VF/NM NM-
2.0 4.0 6.0 8.0 9.0 9.2

1-Wambi, the Jungle Boy begins 113 226 339 723 1237 1750
2 (1942)-Kiefer-c 47 94 141 296 498 700
3 (1943)-Kiefer-c/a 41 82 123 256 428 600
4 (1948)-Origin in text 32 64 96 192 314 435
5 (Fall, 1949, 36 pgs.)-Kiefer-c/a 21 42 63 126 206 285
6-10: 7-(52 pgs.)-New logo 17 34 51 100 158 215
11-18 15 30 45 83 124 165
I.W. Reprint #8('64)-r/#12 with new-c 3 6 9 14 20 25

NOTE: ***Alex Blum** c-8. **Kiefer** c-1-5. **Whitman** c-11-18.*

WANDERERS (See Adventure Comics #375, 376)
DC Comics: June, 1988 - No. 13, Apr, 1989 ($1.25) (Legion of Super-Heroes spin off)

1-13: 1,2-Steacy-c. 3-Legion app. 4.00

WANDERING STAR
Pen & Ink Comics/Sirius Entertainment No. 12 on: 1993 - No. 21, Mar, 1997 ($2.50/$2.75, B&W)

1-1st printing; Teri Sue Wood c/a/scripts in all 1 2 3 5 6 8
1-2nd and 3rd printings 3.00
2-1st printing. 4.00
2-21: 2-2nd printing. 12-(1/96)-1st Sirius issue 3.00
Trade paperback ($11.95)-r/1-7; 1st printing of 1000, signed and #'d 18.00
Trade paperback-2nd printing, 2000 signed 15.00
TPB Volume 2,3 (11/98, 12/98, $14.95) 2-r/#8-14, 3-r/#15-21 15.00

WANTED
Image Comics (Top Cow): Dec, 2003 - No. 6, Feb, 2004 ($2.99)

1-Three covers; Mark Millar-s/J.G. Jones-a; intro Wesley Gibson 4.00
1-4-Death Row Edition; r/#1-4 with extra sketch pages and deleted panels 3.00
2-6: 2-Cameos of DC villains. 6-Giordano-a in flashback scenes 3.00
...Dossier (5/04, $2.99) Pin-ups and character info; art by Jones, Romita Jr. & others 3.00
Image Firsts: Wanted #1 (9/10, $1.00) reprints #1 3.00
... Movie Edition Vol. 1 TPB (2008, $19.99) r/#1-6 & Dossier; movie photo-c; sketch pages & cover gallery; interviews with movie cast and director 20.00
HC (2005, $29.99) r/#1-6 & Dossier; intro by Vaughan, sketch pages & cover gallery 30.00

WANTED COMICS
Toytown Publications/Patches/Orbit Publ.: No. 9, Sept-Oct, 1947 - No. 53, April, 1953 (#9-33: 52 pgs.)

9-True crime cases; radio's Mr. D. A. app. 40 80 120 244 402 560
10,11: 10-Giunta-a; radio's Mr. D. A. app. 25 50 75 147 241 335
12-Used in **SOTI**, pg. 277 27 54 81 160 263 365
13-Heroin drug propaganda story 25 50 75 150 245 340
14-Marijuana drug mention story (2 pgs.) 23 46 69 136 223 310
15-17,19,20 20 40 60 115 185 255
18-Marijuana story, "Satan's Cigarettes"; r-in #45 & retitled 41 82 123 256 428 600
21,22: 21-Krigstein-a. 22-Extreme violence 20 40 60 115 185 255
23,25-32,34,36-38,40-44,46-48,53 17 34 51 103 162 220
24-Krigstein-a; "The Dope King", marijuana mention story 23 46 69 136 223 310
33-Spider web-c 26 52 78 154 252 350
35-Used in **SOTI**, pg. 160 23 46 69 136 223 310
39-Drug propaganda story "The Horror Weed" 34 68 102 199 325 450
45-Marijuana story from #18 20 40 60 120 195 270
49-Has unstable pink-c that fades easily; rare in mint condition 29 58 87 170 278 385
50-Has unstable pink-c like #49; surrealist-c by Buscema; horror stories 37 74 111 218 354 490
51- "Holiday of Horror" junkie story; drug-c 34 68 102 204 332 460
52-Classic "Cult of Killers" opium use story 58 116 174 371 636 900

NOTE: ***Buscema** c-50, 51. **Lawrence** and **Leav** c/a most issues. **Syd Shores** c/a-48; c-37. Issues 9-46 have wanted criminals with their descriptions & drawn picture on cover.*

WANTED: DEAD OR ALIVE (TV)
Dell Publishing Co.: No. 1102, May-July, 1960 - No. 1164, Mar-May, 1961

Four Color 1102 (#1)-Steve McQueen photo-c 11 22 33 76 163 250
Four Color 1164-Steve McQueen photo-c 9 18 27 58 114 170

WANTED, THE WORLD'S MOST DANGEROUS VILLAINS (See DC Special)
National Periodical Publ.: July-Aug, 1972 - No. 9, Aug-Sept, 1973 (All reprints & 20¢ issues)

1-Batman, Green Lantern (story r-from G.L. #1), & Green Arrow 4 8 12 23 37 50
2-Batman/Joker/Penguin-c/story r-from Batman #25; plus Flash story (r-from Flash #121) 3 6 9 17 25 34
3-9: 3-Dr. Fate(r/More Fun #65), Hawkman(r/Flash #100), & Vigilante(r/Action #69). 4-Green Lantern(r/All-American #61) & Kid Eternity(r/Kid Eternity #15). 5-Dollman/Green

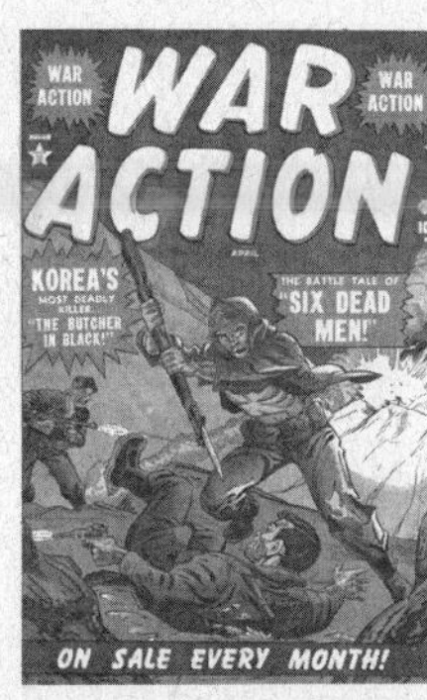

War Action #1 © MAR

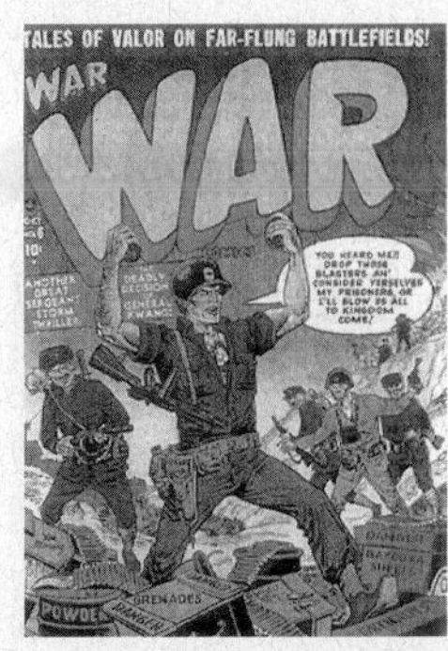

War Comics #6 © MAR

Warfront #1 © HARV

	GD 2.0	VG 4.0	FN 6.0	VF 8.0	VF/NM 9.0	NM- 9.2
Lantern. 6-Burnley Starman; Wildcat/Sargon. 7-Johnny Quick(r/More Fun #76), Hawkman(r/Flash #90), Hourman by Baily(r/Adv. #72). 8-Dr. Fate/Flash(r/Flash #114). 9-S&K Sandman/Superman	3	6	9	15	22	28

NOTE: ***B. Bailey** a-7r. **Infantino** a-2r. **Kane** r-1, 5. **Kubert** r-3i, 6, 7. **Meskin** r-3, 7. **Reinman** r-4, 6.*

WAR (See Fightin' Marines #122)
Charlton Comics: Jul, 1975 - No. 9, Nov, 1976; No. 10, Sept, 1978 - No. 47, 1984

	GD 2.0	VG 4.0	FN 6.0	VF 8.0	VF/NM 9.0	NM- 9.2
1-Boyette painted-c	3	6	9	14	19	24
2-10: 3-Sutton painted-c	2	4	6	8	10	12
11-20	1	2	3	5	6	8
21-40	1	2	3	4	5	7
41,42,44-47 (lower print run): 47-Reprints	1	2	3	5	6	8
43 (2/84) (lower print run) Ditko-a (7 pgs.)	2	4	6	8	10	12
7,9 (Modern Comics-r, 1977)						6.00

WAR, THE (See The Draft & The Pitt)
Marvel Comics: 1989 - No. 4, 1990 ($3.50, squarebound, 52 pgs.)

	GD 2.0	VG 4.0	FN 6.0	VF 8.0	VF/NM 9.0	NM- 9.2
1-4: Characters from New Universe						5.00

WAR ACTION (Korean War)
Atlas Comics (CPS): April, 1952 - No. 14, June, 1953

	GD 2.0	VG 4.0	FN 6.0	VF 8.0	VF/NM 9.0	NM- 9.2
1	39	78	117	231	378	525
2-Hartley-a	20	40	60	115	188	260
3-10,14: 7-Pakula-a/Heath-c. 14-Colan-a	17	34	51	103	162	220
11-13-Krigstein-a. 11-Romita-a	18	36	54	107	189	230

NOTE: ***Berg** c-11. **Brodsky** a-2; c-1-4. **Heath** a-1; c-7, 14. **Keller** a-6. **Maneely** a-1; c-12. **Sale** a-7.**Tuska** a-2, 8.*

WAR ADVENTURES (Korean War)
Atlas Comics (HPC): Jan, 1952 - No. 13, Feb, 1953

	GD 2.0	VG 4.0	FN 6.0	VF 8.0	VF/NM 9.0	NM- 9.2
1-Tuska-a	37	74	111	222	361	500
2	20	40	60	115	188	260
3-7,9-11,13: 3-Pakula-a. 7-Maneely-c. 9-Romita-a	17	34	51	103	162	220
8-Krigstein-a	18	36	54	107	169	230
12-Grey tone-c	21	42	63	124	202	280

NOTE: ***Brodsky** c-1-3, 6, 8, 11, 12. **Heath** a-2, 5, 7, 10; c-4, 5, 9, 13. **Reinman** a-13. **Robinson** a-3; c-10.*

WAR ADVENTURES ON THE BATTLEFIELD (See Battlefield)

WAR AGAINST CRIME! (Becomes Vault of Horror #12 on)
E. C. Comics: Spring, 1948 - No. 11, Feb-Mar, 1950

	GD 2.0	VG 4.0	FN 6.0	VF 8.0	VF/NM 9.0	NM- 9.2
1-Real Stories From Police Records on-c #1-9	135	270	405	864	1482	2100
2,3	71	142	213	454	777	1100
4-9	58	116	174	371	636	900
10-1st Vault Keeper app. & 1st Vault of Horror	232	464	696	1485	2543	3600
11-2nd Vault Keeper app.; 1st EC horror-c	213	426	639	1363	2332	3300

NOTE: *All have **Johnny Craig** covers. **Feldstein** a-4, 7-9. **Harrison/Wood** a-11. **Ingels** a-1, 2, 8. **Palais** a-8. Changes to horror with #10.*

WAR AGAINST CRIME
Gemstone Publishing: Apr, 2000 - No. 11, Feb, 2001 ($2.50)

	GD 2.0	VG 4.0	FN 6.0	VF 8.0	VF/NM 9.0	NM- 9.2
1-11: E.C. reprints						4.00

WAR AND ATTACK (Also see Special War Series #3)
Charlton Comics: Fall, 1964; V2#54, June, 1966 - V2#63, Dec, 1967

	GD 2.0	VG 4.0	FN 6.0	VF 8.0	VF/NM 9.0	NM- 9.2
1-Wood-a (25 pgs.)	6	12	18	40	73	105
V2#54(6/66)-#63 (Formerly Fightin' Air Force)	3	6	9	16	23	30

NOTE: ***Montes/Bache** a-55, 56, 60, 63.*

WAR AT SEA (Formerly Space Adventures)
Charlton Comics: No. 22, Nov, 1957 - No. 42, June, 1961

	GD 2.0	VG 4.0	FN 6.0	VF 8.0	VF/NM 9.0	NM- 9.2
22	8	16	24	44	57	70
23-30: 26-Pearl Harbor, FDR app.	6	12	18	31	38	45
31-42: 42-Cuba's Fidel Castro story	3	6	9	19	30	40

WAR BATTLES
Harvey Publications: Feb, 1952 - No. 9, Dec, 1953

	GD 2.0	VG 4.0	FN 6.0	VF 8.0	VF/NM 9.0	NM- 9.2
1-Powell-a; Elias-c	10	20	30	70	150	230
2-Powell-a	5	10	15	35	63	90
3,4,7-9: 3,7-Powell-a	5	10	15	34	60	85
5-Flamethrower cover	10	20	30	64	132	200
6-Nostrand-a	6	12	18	38	69	100

WAR BEARS
Dark Horse Comics: Sept, 2018 - No. 3, Dec, 2018 ($4.99, limited series)

	GD 2.0	VG 4.0	FN 6.0	VF 8.0	VF/NM 9.0	NM- 9.2
1-3-Margaret Atwood-s/Ken Steacy-a; creators of Canadian Whites comics in 1943						5.00

WAR BIRDS
Fiction House Magazines: 1952(nd) - No. 3, Winter, 1952-53

	GD 2.0	VG 4.0	FN 6.0	VF 8.0	VF/NM 9.0	NM- 9.2
1	23	46	69	136	223	310
2,3	15	30	45	84	127	170

WARBLADE: ENDANGERED SPECIES (Also see WildC.A.T.S: Covert Action Teams)
Image Comics (WildStorm Productions): Jan, 1995 - No. 4, Apr, 1995 ($2.50, limited series)

	GD 2.0	VG 4.0	FN 6.0	VF 8.0	VF/NM 9.0	NM- 9.2
1-4: 1-Gatefold wraparound-c						3.00

WAR COMBAT (Becomes Combat Casey #6 on)
Atlas Comics (LBI No. 1/SAI No. 2-5): March, 1952 - No. 5, Nov, 1952

	GD 2.0	VG 4.0	FN 6.0	VF 8.0	VF/NM 9.0	NM- 9.2
1	36	72	108	211	343	475
2	20	40	60	114	182	250
3-5	17	34	51	103	162	220

NOTE: ***Berg** a-2, 4, 5. **Brodsky** c-1, 2, 4. **Henkel** a-5. **Maneely** a-1, 4; c-3. **Reinman** a-2. **Sale** a-5; c-5.*

WAR COMICS (War Stories #5 on)(See Key Ring Comics)
Dell Publishing Co.: May, 1940 (No month given) - No. 4, Sept, 1941

	GD 2.0	VG 4.0	FN 6.0	VF 8.0	VF/NM 9.0	NM- 9.2
1-Sikandur the Robot Master, Sky Hawk, Scoop Mason, War Correspondent begin; McWilliams-c; 1st war comic	119	238	357	762	1306	1850
2-Origin Greg Gilday (5/41)	47	94	141	296	498	700
3-Joan becomes Greg Gilday's aide	37	74	111	222	361	500
4-Origin Night Devils	39	78	117	231	378	525

WAR COMICS
Marvel/Atlas (USA No. 1-41/JPI No. 42-49): Dec, 1950 - No. 49, Sept, 1957

	GD 2.0	VG 4.0	FN 6.0	VF 8.0	VF/NM 9.0	NM- 9.2
1-1st Atlas War comic	55	110	165	352	601	850
2	27	54	81	162	266	370
3-10	23	46	69	138	227	315
11-Flame thrower w/burning bodies on-c	77	154	231	493	847	1200
12-20: 16-Romita-a	21	42	63	124	202	280
21,23-32: 26-Valley Forge story. 32-Last pre-code issue (2/55)	20	40	60	115	188	260
22-Krigstein-a	20	40	60	120	195	270
33-37,39-42,44,45,47,48: 40-Romita-a	19	38	57	111	176	240
38-Kubert/Moskowitz-a	20	40	60	114	182	250
43,49-Torres-a. 43-Severin/Elder E.C. swipe from Two-Fisted Tales #31	20	40	60	114	182	250
46-Crandall-a	20	40	60	114	182	250

NOTE: ***Ayers** a-17, 32. **Berg** a-13. **Colan** a-4, 28, 34, 36, 48, 49; c-17. **Drucker** a-37, 43, 48. **Everett** a-17. **Heath** a-6-9, 16, 19, 25, 36; c-11, 16, 19, 23, 25, 26, 29-32, 36. **G. Kane** a-19. **Katz** a-34. **Lawrence** a-36. **Maneely** a-7, 9, 13, 14, 20, 23, 28; c-6, 27, 37. **Orlando** a-42, 48. **Pakula** a-26, 40. **Ravielli** a-27. **Reinman** a-11, 16, 26. **Robinson** a-15; c-13. **Sale** c-28. **Severin** a-26, 27; c-48. **Shores** a-13. **Sinnott** a-37.*

WAR DANCER (Also see Charlemagne, Doctor Chaos #2 & Warriors of Plasm)
Defiant: Feb, 1994 - No. 6, July, 1994 ($2.50)

	GD 2.0	VG 4.0	FN 6.0	VF 8.0	VF/NM 9.0	NM- 9.2
1-3,5,6: 1-Intro War Dancer; Weiss-c/a begins. 1-3-Weiss-a(p). 6-Pre-Schism issue						3.00
4-($3.25, 52 pgs.)-Charlemagne app.; Billy Ballistic gains quantum powers						4.00

WAR DOGS OF THE U.S. ARMY
Avon Periodicals: 1952

	GD 2.0	VG 4.0	FN 6.0	VF 8.0	VF/NM 9.0	NM- 9.2
1-Kinstler-c/a	20	40	60	114	182	250

WAREHOUSE 13 (Based on the Syfy TV series)
Dynamite Entertainment: 2011 - No. 5, 2012 ($3.99)

	GD 2.0	VG 4.0	FN 6.0	VF 8.0	VF/NM 9.0	NM- 9.2
1-5: 1-Raab & Hughes-s/Morse-a						4.00

WAR FOR THE PLANET OF THE APES (Prequel to the 2017 movie)
BOOM! Studios: Jul, 2017 - No. 4, Oct, 2017 ($3.99, limited series)

	GD 2.0	VG 4.0	FN 6.0	VF 8.0	VF/NM 9.0	NM- 9.2
1-4-David F. Walker-s/Jonas Scharf-a						4.00

WARFRAME: GHOULS (Based on the video game)
Image Comics (Top Cow): Oct, 2017 - No. 5, May, 2018 ($3.99)

	GD 2.0	VG 4.0	FN 6.0	VF 8.0	VF/NM 9.0	NM- 9.2
1-5-Matt Hawkins & Ryan Cady-s/Studio Hive-a						4.00

WARFRONT
Harvey Publications: 9/51 - #35, 11/58; #36, 10/65; #39, 2/67

	GD 2.0	VG 4.0	FN 6.0	VF 8.0	VF/NM 9.0	NM- 9.2
1-Korean War	10	20	30	68	144	220
2	6	12	18	40	73	105
3-10	5	10	15	33	57	80
11,12,14,16-20	4	8	12	28	47	65
13,15,22-Nostrand-a	5	10	15	35	63	90
21,23-27,31-33,35	4	8	12	28	47	65
28-30,34-Kirby-c	6	12	18	37	66	95
36-(12/66)-Dynamite Joe begins, ends #39; Williamson-a	5	10	15	31	53	75
37-Wood-a (17 pgs.)	5	10	15	31	53	75
38,39-Wood-a, 2-3 pgs.; Lone Tiger app.	4	8	12	28	47	65

NOTE: ***Powell** a-1-6, 9-11, 14, 17, 20, 23, 25-28, 30, 31, 34, 36. **Powell/Nostrand** a-12, 13, 15. **Simon** c-36?, 38.*

WAR FURY
Comic Media/Harwell (Allen Hardy Assoc.): Sept, 1952 - No. 4, Mar, 1953

	GD 2.0	VG 4.0	FN 6.0	VF 8.0	VF/NM 9.0	NM- 9.2
1-Heck-c/a in all; Palais-a; bullet hole in forehead-c; all issues are very violent; soldier using flame thrower on enemy	300	600	900	2010	3505	5000

War is Hell #9 © MAR

Warlock (1982 series) #6 © MAR

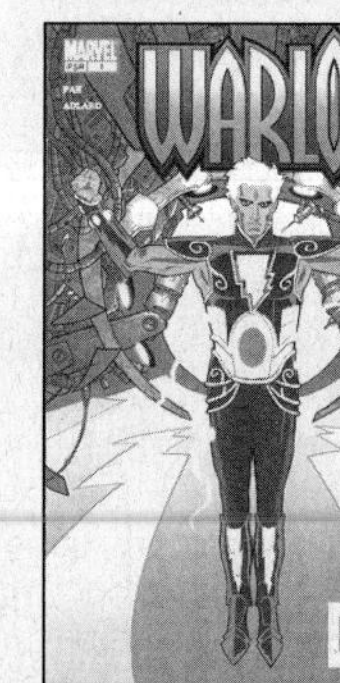

Warlock (2004 series) #1 © MAR

	GD 2.0	VG 4.0	FN 6.0	VF 8.0	VF/NM 9.0	NM- 9.2

2-4: 4-Morisi-a 41 82 123 256 428 600

WAR GODS OF THE DEEP (See Movie Classics)

WARHAMMER 40,000: MARNEUS CALGAR (Based on the game)
Marvel Comics: Dec, 2020 - No. 5, Apr, 2021 ($4.99, limited series)

1-5-Kieron Gillen-s/Jacen Burrows-a 5.00

WARHAWKS
TSR, Inc.: 1990 - No. 10, 1991 ($2.95, 44 pgs.)

1-10-Based on TSR game, Spiegle a-1-6 4.00

WARHEADS
Marvel Comics UK: June, 1992 - No. 14, Aug, 1993 ($1.75)

1-Wolverine-c/story; indicia says #2 by mistake 4.00
2-14: 2-Nick Fury app. 3-Iron Man-c/story. 4,5-X-Force. 5-Liger vs. Cable. 6,7-Death's Head II app. (#6 is cameo) 3.00

WAR HEROES (See Marine War Heroes)

WAR HEROES
Dell Publishing Co.: 7-9/42 (no month); No. 2, 10-12/42 - No. 10, 10-12/44 (Quarterly)

1-General Douglas MacArthur-c 34 68 102 199 325 450
2-James Doolittle and other officers-c 18 36 54 107 169 230
3,5: 3-Pro-Russian back-c; grey-tone-c. 5-General Patton-c 15 30 45 90 140 190
4-Disney's Gremlins app.; grey-tone-c 22 44 66 128 209 290
6-10: 6-Tothish-a by Discount. 6,9-Grey-tone-c 14 28 42 76 108 140
NOTE: *No. 1 was to be released in July, but was delayed. Painted c-4, 6-9.*

WAR HEROES
Ace Magazines: May, 1952 - No. 8, Apr, 1953

1 16 32 48 98 154 210
2-Lou Cameron-a 13 26 39 72 101 130
3-8: 6,7-Cameron-a 11 22 33 62 86 110

WAR HEROES (Also see Blue Bird Comics)
Charlton Comics: Feb, 1963 - No. 27, Nov, 1967

1,2: 2-John F. Kennedy story 4 8 12 28 47 65
3-10 3 6 9 18 28 38
11-26: 22-True story about plot to kill Hitler 3 6 9 15 22 28
27-1st Devils Brigade by Glanzman 3 6 9 18 28 38
NOTE: ***Montes/Bache** a-3-7, 21, 25, 27; c-3-7.*

WAR HEROES
Image Comics: July, 2008 - No. 6 ($2.99, limited series)

1-3-Soldiers given super powers; Mark Millar-s/Tony Harris-a/c; four covers 3.00

WAR IS HELL
Marvel Comics Group: Jan, 1973 - No. 15, Oct, 1975

1-Williamson-a(r), 5 pgs.; Ayers-a 4 8 12 25 40 55
2-8-Reprints. 6-(11/73). 7-(6/74). 7,8-Kirby-a 2 4 6 11 16 20
9-Intro Death 8 16 24 51 96 140
10-15-Death app. 3 6 9 18 28 38
NOTE: ***Bolle** a-3r. **Powell** a-1. **Woodbridge** a-1. Sgt. Fury reprints-7, 8.*

WAR IS HELL (Marvel 80th Anniversary salute to War comics)
Marvel Comics: Mar, 2019 ($3.99, one-shot)

1-Howard Chaykin-s/a; P.K. Johnson-s/Alberto Alburquerque-a; Panosian-c 4.00

WAR IS HELL: THE FIRST FLIGHT OF THE PHANTOM EAGLE
Marvel Comics (MAX): May, 2008 - No. 5, Sept, 2008 ($3.99, limited series)

1-5-World War I fighter pilots; Ennis-s/Chaykin-a/Cassaday-c 4.00

WARLANDS
Image Comics: Aug, 1999 - No. 12, Feb, 2001 ($2.50)

1-9,11,12-Pat Lee-a(p)/Adrian Tsang-s 3.00
10-($2.95) Flip book w/Shidima preview 4.00
... Chronicles 1,2 (2/00, 7/00; $7.95) 1-r/#1-3. 2-r/#4-6 8.00
...Darklyte TPB (8/01, $14.95) r/#0,1/2,1-6 w/cover gallery; new Lee-c 15.00
...Epilogue: Three Stories (3/01, $5.95) includes r/Wizard #1/2 & AE #0 6.00
Another Universe #0 3.00
Wizard #1/2 5.00

WARLANDS: THE AGE OF ICE (Volume 2)
Image Comics: July, 2001 - No. 9, Nov, 2002 ($2.95)

#0-(2/02, $2.25) 3.00
#1/2 (4/02, $2.25) 3.00
1-9: 2-Flip book preview of Banished Knights 3.00
TPB (2003, $15.95) r/#1-9 16.00

WARLANDS: DARK TIDE RISING (Volume 3)
Image Comics: Dec, 2002 - No. 6, May, 2003 ($2.95)

1-6: 1-Wraparound gatefold-c 3.00

WARLOCK (The Power of...)(Also see Avengers Annual #7, Fantastic Four #66, 67, Incredible Hulk #178, Infinity Crusade, Infinity Gauntlet, Infinity War, Marvel Premiere #1, Marvel Two-In-One Annual #2, Silver Surfer V3#46, Strange Tales #178-181 & Thor #165)
Marvel Comics Group: Aug, 1972 - No. 8, Oct, 1973; No. 9, Oct, 1975 - No. 15, Nov, 1976

1-Origin by Gil Kane 10 20 30 64 132 200
2,3 5 10 15 30 50 70
4-8: 4-Death of Eddie Roberts 3 6 9 18 28 38
9-Starlin's 2nd Thanos saga begins, ends #15; new costume Warlock; Thanos cameo only; story cont'd from Strange Tales #178-181; Starlin-c/a in #9-15 5 10 15 33 57 80
10-Origin Thanos & Gamora; recaps events from Capt. Marvel #25-34. Thanos vs.The Magus-c/story 5 10 15 33 57 80
11-Thanos app.; Warlock dies 4 8 12 25 40 55
12-14: (Regular 25¢ edition) 14-Origin Star Thief; last 25¢ issue 3 6 9 18 28 38
12-14-(30¢-c, limited distribution) 5 10 15 33 57 80
15-Thanos-c/story 5 10 15 30 50 70
NOTE: ***Buscema** a-2p; c-8p. **G. Kane** a-1p, 3-5p; c-1p, 2, 3, 4p, 5p, 7p. **Starlin** a-9-14p, 15; c-9, 10, 11p, 12p, 13-15. **Sutton** a-1-8i.*

WARLOCK (...Special Edition on-c)
Marvel Comics Group: Dec, 1982 - No. 6, May, 1983 ($2.00, slick paper, 52 pgs.)

1-Warlock-r/Strange Tales #178-180. 1 3 4 6 8 10
2-6: 2-r/Str. Tales #180,181 & Warlock #9. 3-r/Warlock #10-12(Thanos origin recap). 4-r/Warlock #12-15. 5-r/Warlock #15, Marvel Team-Up #55 & Avengers Ann. #7. 6-r/2nd half Avengers Annual #7 & Marvel Two-in-One Annual #2 5.00
Special Edition #1(12/83) 5.00
NOTE: ***Byrne** a-5r. **Starlin** a-1-6r; c-1-6(new). Direct sale only.*

WARLOCK
Marvel Comics: V2#1, May, 1992 - No. 6, Oct, 1992 ($2.50, limited series)

V2#1-6: 1-Reprints 1982 reprint series w/Thanos 4.00

WARLOCK
Marvel Comics: Nov, 1998 - No. 4, Feb, 1999 ($2.99, limited series)

1-4-Warlock vs. Drax 4.00

WARLOCK (M-Tech)
Marvel Comics: Oct, 1999 - No. 9, June, 2000 ($1.99/$2.50)

1-5: 1-Quesada-c. 2-Two covers 4.00
6-9: 6-Begin $2.50-c. 8-Avengers app. 4.00

WARLOCK
Marvel Comics: Nov, 2004 - No. 4, Feb, 2005 ($2.99, limited series)

1-4-Adlard-a/Williams-c 3.00

WARLOCK AND THE INFINITY WATCH (Also see Infinity Gauntlet)
Marvel Comics: Feb, 1992 - No. 42, July, 1995 ($1.75) (Sequel to Infinity Gauntlet)

1-Starlin-s begin; continued from Infinity Gauntlet #6; brief origin recap; Living Tribunal app. 2 4 6 9 13 16
2-7: 2-1st app. Infinity Watch: Infinity Gauntlet broken up; Warlock (Soul gem), Gamora (Time gem), Drax (Power gem), Moondragon (Mind gem) & Pip (Space gem). 3,4-High Evolutionary app. 5,6-Man-Beast app. 7-Re-intro Magus (dream sequence); brief Thanos app; leads into Infinity War #1. Tom Raney-a begins 4.00
8-10: 8-Thanos teams up w/Infinity Watch; Magus app; X-Men, Avengers, Alpha Flight & Fantastic Four cameo; leads into Infinity War #4. 9-Origin Gamora; Galactus, Eternity, Thanos & Infinity app; leads into Infinity War #5. 10-Thanos vs. his doppelganger; Magus app.; continues in Infinity War #6 4.00
11-22: 11-Eternity & Living Tribunal app.; origins of the Watch. 12-1st app Maxam (brief cameo); Hulk cameo. 13-Drax vs Hulk; last Raney-a. 14-1st app. Count Abyss. 15-Eternity app. 16-1st full app. Maxam; Count Abyss app. 17-Maxam joins the Watch. 18-22-Infinity Crusade tie-ins; 18-Goddess & Reed Richards app; continued in Infinity Crusade #2. 19-X-Men, Avengers, Fantastic Four, Thanos app.; continued in Infinity Crusade #3. 20-Pip becomes master of reality; Goddess app; continued in Infinity Crusade #4. 21-Drax vs. Thor; continued in Infinity Crusade #5. 22-Goddess app; continued in Infinity Crusade #6 4.00
23,24-Blood and Thunder Pts. 4 & 8; continued from Warlock Chronicles #6; Silver Surfer & Warlock vs. Thor; continued in Thor #469. 24-Continued from Warlock Chronicles #7; Silver Surfer app.; continued in Thor #470 5.00
25-($2.95, 52 pgs.)-Die-cut & embossed double-c; Blood & Thunder Pt.12; continued from Warlock Chronicles #8; Thor, Dr. Strange, Beta Ray Bill & Silver Surfer app.; Thanos vs. Odin 2 4 6 9 12 15
26-32: 26-Avengers & Count Abyss app. 27-vs. the Avengers. 28-Avengers, Man-Beast & Count Abyss app. 29,30-Count Abyss app. 31-Origin Count Abyss; last Starlin-s. 32-Count Abyss defeats the Watch 4.00

Warlord #49 © DC

Warlord of Mars #32 © DYN

War Machine #4 © MAR

	GD 2.0	VG 4.0	FN 6.0	VF 8.0	VF/NM 9.0	NM- 9.2

33-35: 33-vs. Count Abyss. 34-Mole Man app.; Tyrannus cameo. 35-Mole Man & Tyrannus app. 4.00
36-Dr. Strange app; as 'Strange' 7.00
37-39: 37-1st app. Zakaius; Firelord app. 38-1st app. Domitan; Zakaius app. 39-Zakaius, Domitan & Firelord app. 6.00
40,41: 40-Thanos app.; Gamora leaves the Watch; Maxam receives the Time gem. 41-Origin Maxam; Gamora joins Thanos 1 2 3 5 6 8
42-Last issue; the Watch breaks up; the Infinity Gems disappear (see Rune/Silver Surfer #1); Thanos app. 2 4 6 10 14 18
NOTE: *Austin c/a-1-4i, 7i. Leonardi a(p)-3, 4. Medina c/a(p)-1, 2, 5; 6, 9, 10, 14, 15, 20. Williams a(i)-8, 12, 13, 16-19.*

WARLOCK CHRONICLES
Marvel Comics: June, 1993 - No. 8, Feb, 1994 ($2.00, limited series)
1-($2.95)-Holo-grafx foil & embossed-c; Starlin/Raney-s/a; Infinity Crusade tie-in; 1st app. Darklore; origin of Warlock & the Infinity Gems; cont'd in Warlock & the Infinity Watch #18 5.00
2-5-Infinity Crusade x-overs; 2-Cont'd from Infinity Crusade #2; Lord Order, Master Chaos, Eternity & Thanos app.; cont'd in Warlock & the Infinity Watch #19. 3-Cont'd from Infinity Crusade #3; Mephisto teams up w/Warlock & Thanos; cont'd in Warlock & the Infinity Watch #20. 4-Magus app.; cont'd in Warlock & the Infinity Watch #21. 5-Cont'd from Infinity Crusade #5; Goddess & Magus app.; cont'd in Warlock & the Infinity Watch #22 4.00
6-Blood & Thunder Pt. 3; cont'd from Silver Surfer #86; insane Thor cameo; brief Silver Surfer app.; cont'd in Warlock & the Infinity Watch #23 5.00
7-Blood & Thunder Pt. 7; cont'd from Silver Surfer #87; Dr. Strange, Beta Ray Bill & Silver Surfer app.; cont'd in Warlock & the Infinity Watch #24 6.00
8-Blood & Thunder Pt. 11; cont'd from Silver Surfer #88; Thanos, Silver Surfer, Dr. Strange app.; cont'd in Warlock & the Infinity Watch #25 1 2 3 5 6 8

WARLOCK 5
Aircel Pub.: 11/86 - No. 22, 5/89; V2#1, June, 1989 - V2#5, 1989 ($1.70, B&W)
1-5,7-11-Gordon Derry-s/Denis Beauvais-a thru #11. 5-Green Cyborg on-c. 5-Misnumbered as #6 (no #6); Blue Girl on-c. 4.00
12-22-Barry Blair-s/a. 18-$1.95-c begins 4.00
V2#1-5 ($2.00, B&W)-All issues by Barry Blair 4.00
Compilation 1,2: 1-r/#1-5 (1988, $5.95); 2-r/#6-9 6.00

WARLORD (See 1st Issue Special #8) (B&W reprints in Showcase Presents: Warlord)
National Periodical Publications/DC Comics #123 on: 1-2/76; No.2, 3-4/76; No.3, 10-11/76 - No. 133, Win, 1988-89
1-Story cont'd. from 1st Issue Special #8 4 8 12 25 40 55
2-Intro. Machiste 3 6 9 14 20 25
3-5 2 4 6 9 12 15
6-10: 6-Intro Mariah. 7-Origin Machiste. 9-Dons new costume 1 3 4 6 8 10
11-20: 11-Origin-r. 12-Intro Aton. 15-Tara returns; Warlord has son 6.00
21-36,40,41: 27-New facts about origin. 28-1st app. Wizard World. 32-Intro Shakira. 40-Warlord gets new costume 5.00
22-Whitman variant edition 3 6 9 15 22 28
37-39: 37,38-Origin Omac by Starlin; cont'd from Kamandi #59. 38-Intro Jennifer Morgan, Warlord's daughter. 39-Omac ends. 6.00
42-48: 42-47-Omac back-up series. 48-(52 pgs.)-1st app. Arak; contains free 14 pg. Arak Son of Thunder; Claw The Unconquered app. 5.00
49-62,64-99,101-132: 49-Claw The Unconquered app. 50-Death of Aton. 51-Reprints #1. 55-Arion Lord of Atlantis begins, ends #62. 91-Origin w/new facts. 114,115-Legends x-over. 125-Death of Tara. 131-1st DC work by Rob Liefeld (9/88) 4.00
63-The Barren Earth begins; free 16pg. Masters of the Universe preview 5.00
100-($1.25, 52 pgs.) 5.00
133-($1.50, 52 pgs.) 5.00
Annual 1-6 ('82-'87): 1-Grell-c,/a(p). 6-New Gods app. 5.00
The Savage Empire TPB (1991, $19.95) r/#1-10,12 & First Issue Special #8; Grell intro. 25.00
NOTE: *Grell a-1-15, 16-50p, 51r, 52p, 59p, Annual 1p; c-1-70, 100-104, 112, 116, 117, Annual 1, 5. Wayne Howard a-64i. Starlin a-37-39p.*

WARLORD
DC Comics: Jan, 1992 - No. 6, June, 1992 ($1.75, limited series)
1-6: Grell-c & scripts in all 3.00

WARLORD
DC Comics: Apr, 2006 - No. 10, Jan, 2007 ($2.99)
1-10: 1-Bruce Jones-s/Bart Sears-a. 10-Winslade-a 3.00

WARLORD
DC Comics: Jun, 2009 - No. 16, Sept, 2010 ($2.99)
1-16: 1-Grell-s/Prado-a/Grell-c. 7-9,11,12,15,16-Grell-s/a/c. 10-Hardin-a 3.00
...: The Saga SC (2010, $17.99) r/#1-6; cover gallery 18.00

WARLORD OF MARS
Dynamite Entertainment: 2010 - No. 35, 2014 ($1.00/$3.99)
1-($1.00) John Carter on Earth; Sadowski-a; covers by Ross, Campbell, Jusko. Parrillo 3.00
2-35-($3.99) Multiple covers on each. 3-Carter arrives on Mars. 4-Dejah Thoris intro. 4.00
100-($7.99, squarebound) Short stories; art by Antonio, Malaga, Luis; multiple covers 8.00
#0 (2014, $3.99) Brady-s/Jadson-a; John Carter back on Earth 4.00
... Annual 1 (2012, $4.99) Sadowski-a/Parrillo-c 5.00

WARLORD OF MARS ATTACKS
Dynamite Entertainment: 2019 - No. 5, 2019 ($3.99, limited series)
1-5-John Carter battles the Topps card Martians; Jeff Parker-s/Dean Kotz-a 4.00

WARLORD OF MARS: DEJAH THORIS
Dynamite Entertainment: 2011 - No. 37, 2014 ($3.99/$4.99)
1-36: 1-Five covers; Nelson-s/Rafael-a. 2-5-Four covers. 6-31-Multiple covers on all 4.00
37-($4.99) Napton-s/Carita-a; Neves & Anacleto-c 5.00

WARLORD OF MARS: FALL OF BARSOOM
Dynamite Entertainment: 2011 - No. 5, 2012 ($3.99, limited series)
1-5-Napton-s/Castro-a/Jusko-c 4.00

WARLORDS (See DC Graphic Novel #2)

WARLORDS OF APPALACHIA
BOOM! Studios: Oct, 2016 - No. 4 ($3.99)
1,2-Phillip Kennedy Johnson-s/Jonas Scharf-a 4.00

WAR MACHINE (Also see Iron Man #281,282 & Marvel Comics Presents #152)
Marvel Comics: Apr, 1994 - No. 25, Apr, 1996 ($1.50)
"Ashcan" edition (nd, 75¢, B&W, 16 pgs.) 4.00
1-($2.00, 52 pgs.)-Newsstand edition; Cable app. 5.00
1-($2.95, 52 pgs.)-Collectors ed.; embossed foil-c 1 2 3 5 6 8
2-14, 16-25: 2-Bound-in trading card sheet; Cable app. 2,3-Deathlok app. 8-red logo 3.00
8-($2.95)-Polybagged w/16 pg. Marvel Action Hour preview & acetate print; yellow logo 4.00
15 ($2.50)-Flip book 4.00

WAR MACHINE (Also see Dark Reign and Secret Invasion crossovers)
Marvel Comics: Feb, 2009 - No. 12, Feb, 2010 ($2.99)
1-12: 1-5-Pak-s/Manco-a/c; cyborg Jim Rhodes. 10-12-Dark Reign 3.00
1-Variant Titanium Man cover by Deodato 6.00

WAR MAN
Marvel Comics (Epic Comics): Nov, 1993 - No. 2, Dec, 1993 ($2.50, limited series)
1,2-Chuck Dixon-s 4.00

WAR MOTHER
Valiant Entertainment: Aug, 2017 - No. 4, Nov, 2017 ($3.99, limited series)
1-4-Van Lente-s/Segovia-a; multiple covers; Ana in 4001 AD 4.00

WAR OF KINGS
Marvel Comics: May, 2009 - No. 6, Oct, 2009 ($3.99, limited series)
1-6-Pelletier-a/Abnett & Lanning-s; Inhumans vs. the Shi'Ar 4.00
... Saga (2009, giveaway) synopsies of stories involving Kree, Shi'Ar, Inhumans, etc. 3.00
...: Savage World of Skaar 1 (8/09, $3.99) Gorgon & Starbolt land on Sakaar 4.00
...: Who Will Rule? 1 (11/09, $3.99) Pelletier-a; profile pages 4.00

WAR OF KINGS: ASCENSION
Marvel Comics: June, 2009 - No. 4, Sept, 2009 ($3.99, limited series)
1-4-Alves-a/Abnett & Lanning-s; Darkhawk app. 4.00

WAR OF KINGS: DARKHAWK (Leads into War Of Kings: Ascension limited series)
Marvel Comics: Apr, 2009 - No. 2, May, 2009 ($3.99, limited series)
1,2-Cebulski-s/Tolibao & Dazo-a/Peterson-c; r/Darkhawk #1,2 (1991) origin 4.00

WAR OF KINGS: WARRIORS
Marvel Comics: Sept, 2009 - No. 2, Oct, 2009 ($3.99, limited series)
1,2-Prequel to x-over; Gage-s/Asrar & Magno-a 4.00

WAR OF THE GODS
DC Comics: Sept, 1991 - No. 4, Dec, 1991 ($1.75, limited series)
1-4: Perez layouts, scripts & covers. 1-Contains free mini posters (Robin, Deathstroke). 2-4-Direct sale versions include 4 pin-ups printed on cover stock plus different-c 4.00

WAR OF THE GREEN LANTERNS: AFTERMATH
DC Comics: Sept, 2011 - No. 2, Oct, 2011 ($3.99, limited series)
1,2: 1-Bedard-s/Sepulveda & Kirkham-a. 2-Getty & Smith-a 4.00

WAR OF THE REALMS (Tie-in issues exist in many 2019 Marvel titles)
Marvel Comics: Jun, 2019 - No. 6, Aug, 2019 ($5.99/$4.99, limited series)
1,6-($5.99): 1-Aaron-s/Dauterman-a; Malekith attacks Earth; Loki eaten. 6-Jane Thor app. 6.00
2-5-($4.99) 2-Avengers, Punisher, Jane Foster app. 4-Venom app. 5.00

War of the Realms #4 © MAR

War Report #1 © AJAX

War Story: Johann's Tiger © Ennis & Weston

GD VG FN VF VF/NM NM-
2.0 4.0 6.0 8.0 9.0 9.2

GD VG FN VF VF/NM NM-
2.0 4.0 6.0 8.0 9.0 9.2

... Omega 1 (9/19, $4.99) Short stories; Jane Foster becomes Valkyrie; Punisher app. 5.00

WAR OF THE REALMS: JOURNEY INTO MYSTERY
Marvel Comics: Jun, 2019 - No. 5, Aug, 2019 ($3.99, limited series)

1-5-Spider-Man (Miles), Hawkeye (Kate), Wonder Man, Ares app. 4.00

WAR OF THE REALMS: NEW AGENTS OF ATLAS
Marvel Comics: Jul, 2019 - No. 4, Aug, 2019 ($3.99, limited series)

1-4-Greg Pak-s/Gang Hyuk Lim-a; Ms. Marvel, Silk, Shang-Chi & Amedeus Cho app. 4.00

WAR OF THE REALMS STRIKEFORCE:...
Marvel Comics: Jul, 2019 ($4.99, series of one-shots)

... The Dark Elf Realm 1 - Bryan Hill-s/Yu-a; Punisher, She-Hulk, Blade, Ghost Rider 5.00
... The Land of Giants 1 - Taylor-s/Molina-a; Wolverine, Capt. America, Luke Cage app. 5.00
... The War Avengers 1 - Anindito-a; Deadpool, Namor, Capt. Marvel, Sif, Venom app. 5.00

WAR OF THE REALMS: THE PUNISHER
Marvel Comics: Jun, 2019 - No. 3, Aug, 2019 ($3.99, limited series)

1-3-Duggan-s/Ferreira-a 4.00

WAR OF THE REALMS: UNCANNY X-MEN
Marvel Comics: Jun, 2019 - No. 3, Aug, 2019 ($3.99, limited series)

1-3-Rosenberg-s/Pere Pérez-a; Cyclops, Dani Moonstar app. 2-Sabretooth app. 4.00

WAR OF THE REALMS: WAR SCROLLS
Marvel Comics: Jun, 2019 - No. 3, Aug, 2019 ($4.99, limited series)

1-3-Short stories by various; Daredevil serial in all w/Sorrentino-a; Alan Davis-c 5.00

WAR OF THE UNDEAD
IDW Publishing: Jan, 2007 - No. 3, Apr, 2007 ($3.99, limited series)

1-3-Bryan Johnson-s/Walter Flanagan-a 4.00

WAR OF THE WORLDS, THE
Caliber: 1996 - No. 5 ($2.95, B&W, 32 pgs.)(Based on H. G. Wells novel)

1-5: 1-Randy Zimmerman scripts begin 4.00

WARP
First Comics: Mar, 1983 - No. 19, Feb, 1985 ($1.00/$1.25, Mando paper)

1-Sargon-Mistress of War app.; Brunner-c/a thru #9 4.00
2-19: 2-Faceless Ones begin. 10-New Warp advs., & Outrider begin 3.00
Special 1-3: 1(7/83, 36 pgs.)-Origin Chaos-Prince of Madness; origin of Warp Universe begins, ends #3; Chaykin-c/a. 2,3-Silvestri-c/a. 2(1/84)-Lord Cumulus vs. Sargon Mistress of War ($1.00). 3(6/84)-Chaos-Prince of Madness 3.00

WARPATH (Indians on the...)
Key Publications/Stanmor: Nov, 1954 - No. 3, Apr, 1955

	GD 2.0	VG 4.0	FN 6.0	VF 8.0	VF/NM 9.0	NM- 9.2
1	12	24	36	69	97	125
2,3	8	16	24	44	57	70

WARP GRAPHICS ANNUAL
WaRP Graphics: Dec, 1985; 1988 ($2.50)

1-Elfquest, Blood of the Innocent, Thunderbunny & Myth Adventures 5.00
1 (1988) 4.00

WARREN PRESENTS
Warren Publications: Jan, 1979 - No. 14, Nov, 1981(B&W magazine)

	GD 2.0	VG 4.0	FN 6.0	VF 8.0	VF/NM 9.0	NM- 9.2
1-Eerie, Creepy, & Vampirella-r; Ring of the Warlords; Merlin-s; Dax-s; Sanjulian-c	3	6	9	15	22	28
2-6(10/79): 2-The Rook. 3-Alien Invasions Comix. 4-Movie Aliens. 5-Dracula '79. 6-Strange Stories of Vampires Comix	2	4	6	10	14	18
8(10/80)-r/1st app. Pantha from Vamp. #30	2	4	6	13	18	22
9(11/80) Empire Encounters Comix	2	4	6	11	16	20
13(10/81),14(11/81):13-Sword and Sorcery Comix	3	6	9	14	19	24

(#7,10,11,12 may not exist, or may be a Special below)

	GD 2.0	VG 4.0	FN 6.0	VF 8.0	VF/NM 9.0	NM- 9.2
Special-Alien Collectors Edition (1979)	3	6	9	14	20	26
Special-Close Encounters of the Third Kind (1978)	2	4	6	10	14	18
Special-Lord of the Rings (6/79)	3	6	9	19	30	40
Special-Meteor (1/80)	2	4	6	10	14	18
Special-Moonraker/James Bond (10/79)	2	4	6	10	14	18
Special-Star Wars (1977)	3	6	9	21	33	45

WAR REPORT
Ajax/Farrell Publications (Excellent Publ.): Sept, 1952 - No. 5, May, 1953

	GD 2.0	VG 4.0	FN 6.0	VF 8.0	VF/NM 9.0	NM- 9.2
1	19	38	57	112	179	245
2-Flame thrower w/burning bodies on-c	29	58	87	170	278	385
3,5	13	26	39	72	101	130
4-Used in **POP**, pg. 94	14	28	42	76	108	140

WARRIOR (Wrestling star)
Ultimate Creations: May, 1996 - No. 4, 1997 ($2.95)

1-4: Warrior scripts; Callahan-c/a. 3-Wraparound-c. 4-Warrior #3 in indicia; pin-ups 4.00

	GD 2.0	VG 4.0	FN 6.0	VF 8.0	VF/NM 9.0	NM- 9.2
1-Variant-c	1	3	4	6	8	10

X-Mas (11/96, $3.50) listed as "No. 3" in indicia; pin-ups by various; Quesada-c 4.00

WARRIOR COMICS
H.C. Blackerby: 1945 (1930s DC reprints)

	GD 2.0	VG 4.0	FN 6.0	VF 8.0	VF/NM 9.0	NM- 9.2
1-Wing Brady, The Iron Man, Mark Markon	26	52	78	154	252	350

WARRIOR OF WAVERLY STREET, THE
Dark Horse Comics: Nov, 1996 - No. 2, Dec, 1996 ($2.95, mini-series)

1,2-Darrow-c 4.00

WARRIORS
CFD Productions: 1993 (B&W, one-shot)

	GD 2.0	VG 4.0	FN 6.0	VF 8.0	VF/NM 9.0	NM- 9.2
1-Linsner, Dark One-a	2	4	6	11	16	20

WARRIORS, THE: OFFICIAL MOVIE ADAPTATION (Based on the 1979 movie)
Dabel Brothers Publishing/Dynamite Ent.: Feb, 2009 - No. 5, 2010 ($3.99, limited series)

1-5: 1-Three covers plus wraparound photo-c; Dibari-a. 3-Eric Powell-c 4.00
...: Jailbreak 1 (7/09, $3.99) Apon & Herman-a 4.00

WARRIORS OF MARS (Also see Warlord of Mars titles)
Dynamite Entertainment: 2012 - No. 5, 2012 ($3.99, limited series)

1-5-Gullivar Jones visits Barsoom; Jusko-c 4.00

WARRIORS OF PLASM (Also see Plasm and Dogs of War #5)
Defiant: Aug, 1993 - No. 13, Aug, 1995 ($2.95/$2.50)

1-4: Shooter-scripts; Lapham-c/a: 1-1st app. Glory. 4-Bound-in fold-out poster 4.00
5-7,10-13: 5-Begin $2.50-c. 13-Schism issue; last Defiant comic published 3.00
8,9-($2.75, 44 pgs.) 4.00
...Graphic Novel #1 (Home for the Holidays)(11/93, $5.95) Len Wein story; Cockrum-a; Christmas issue; story takes place between Warriors of Plasm #4 and #5 6.00
The Collected Edition (2/94, $9.95)-r/Plasm #0, WOP #1-4 & Splatterball 10.00

WARRIORS THREE (Fandral, Volstagg, and Hogun from Thor)
Marvel Comics: Jan, 2011 - No. 4, Apr, 2011 ($3.99, limited series)

1-4-Bill Willingham-s/Neil Edwards-a. 2,4-Conner-c 4.00

WAR ROMANCES (See True...)

WAR SHIPS
Dell Publishing Co.: 1942 (36 pgs.)(Similar to Large Feature Comics)

	GD 2.0	VG 4.0	FN 6.0	VF 8.0	VF/NM 9.0	NM- 9.2
nn-Cover by McWilliams; contains photos & drawings of U.S. war ships	22	44	66	128	209	290

WAR STORIES (Formerly War Comics)
Dell Publ. Co.: No. 5, 1942(nd); No. 6, Aug-Oct, 1942 - No. 8, Feb-Apr, 1943

	GD 2.0	VG 4.0	FN 6.0	VF 8.0	VF/NM 9.0	NM- 9.2
5-Origin The Whistler	35	70	105	208	339	470
6-8: 6-8-Night Devils app. 8-Painted-c	27	54	81	162	266	370

WAR STORIES (Korea)
Ajax/Farrell Publications (Excellent Publ.): Sept, 1952 - No. 5, May, 1953

	GD 2.0	VG 4.0	FN 6.0	VF 8.0	VF/NM 9.0	NM- 9.2
1	20	40	60	114	182	250
2	13	26	39	72	101	130
3-5	12	24	36	69	97	125

WAR STORIES
Avatar Press: Sept, 2014 - No. 26, Jan, 2018 ($3.99)

1-26: Garth Ennis-s in all; multiple covers on all. 1-Matt Martin-a 4.00

WAR STORIES (See Star Spangled...)

WAR STORY
DC Comics (Vertigo): Nov, 2001 - Apr, 2003 ($4.95, series of World War II one-shots)

...: Archangel (4/03) Ennis-s/Erskine-a 5.00
...: Condors (3/03) Ennis-s/Ezquerra-a 5.00
...: D-Day Dodgers (12/01) Ennis-s/Higgins-a 5.00
...: J For Jenny (2/03) Ennis-s/Lloyd-a 5.00
...: Johann's Tiger (11/01) Ennis-s/Weston-a 5.00
...: Nightingale (2/02) Ennis-s/Lloyd-a 5.00
...: Screaming Eagles (1/02) Ennis-s/Gibbons-a 5.00
...: The Reivers (1/03) Ennis-s/Kennedy-a 5.00
Vol. 1 (2004, $19.95) r/Johann's Tiger, D-Day Dodgers, Screaming Eagles, Nightingale 20.00
Vol. 2 (2006, $19.99) r/J For Jenny, The Reivers, Condors, Archangel; Ennis afterword 20.00

WARSTRIKE
Malibu Comics (Ultraverse): May, 1994 - No. 7, Nov, 1995 ($1.95)

1-7: 1-Simonson-c 3.00
1-Ultra 5000 Limited silver foil 6.00
Giant Size 1 (12/94, $2.50, 44pgs.)-Prelude to Godwheel 4.00

Wartime Romances #18 © STJ

Watchmen #3 © DC

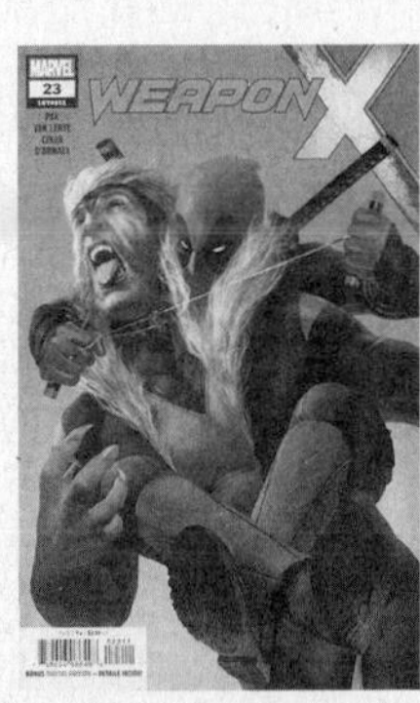

Weapon X (2017 series) #23 © MAR

GD VG FN VF VF/NM NM-
2.0 4.0 6.0 8.0 9.0 9.2

WART AND THE WIZARD (See The Sword & the Stone under Movie Comics)
Gold Key: Feb, 1964 (Walt Disney)(Characters from Sword in the Stone movie)
1 (10102-402) 4 8 12 28 47 65

WAR THAT TIME FORGOT, THE
DC Comics: Jul, 2008 - No. 12, Jun, 2009 ($2.99, limited series)
1-12: 1-Bruce Jones-s/Al Barrionuevo-a/Neal Adams-c; Enemy Ace app. 3.00

WARTIME ROMANCES
St. John Publishing Co.: July, 1951 - No. 18, Nov, 1953
1-All Baker-c/a 135 270 405 864 1482 2100
2-All Baker-c/a 77 154 231 493 847 1200
3,4-All Baker-c/a 81 162 243 518 884 1250
5-8-Baker-c/a(2-3) each 65 130 195 416 708 1000
9,11,12,16,18: Baker-c/a each. 9-Two signed stories by Estrada
60 120 180 381 653 925
10,13-15,17-Baker-c only 55 110 165 352 601 850

WAR VICTORY ADVENTURES (#1 titled War Victory Comics)
U.S. Treasury Dept./War Victory/Harvey Publ.: Sum, 1942 - No. 3, Wint, 1943-44 (5¢/10¢)
1-(5¢)(Promotion of Savings Bonds)-Featuring America's greatest comic art by top syndicated cartoonists; Blondie, Joe Palooka, Green Hornet, Dick Tracy, Superman, Gumps, etc.; (36 pgs.); all profits were contributed to U.S.O. & Army/Navy relief funds
65 130 195 416 708 1000
2-(10¢) Battle of Stalingrad story; Powell-a (8/43); flag & WWII Japanese-c
100 200 300 640 1095 1550
3-(10¢) Capt. Red Cross-c & text only; WWII Nazi-c; Powell-a
87 174 261 553 952 1350

WAR WAGON, THE (See Movie Classics)

WAR WINGS
Charlton Comics: Oct, 1968
1 3 6 9 14 20 26

WARWORLD!
Dark Horse Comics: Feb, 1989 ($1.75, B&W, one-shot)
1-Gary Davis sci/fi art in Moebius style 4.00

WASHABLE JONES AND THE SHMOO (Also see Al Capp's Shmoo)
Toby Press: June, 1953
1- "Super-Shmoo" 20 40 60 115 188 260

WASH TUBBS (See The Comics, Crackajack Funnies)
Dell Publishing Co.: No. 11, 1942 - No. 53, 1944
Four Color 11 (#1) 27 514 81 189 420 650
Four Color 28 (1943) 17 34 51 119 265 410
Four Color 53 13 26 39 91 201 310

WASP (See Unstoppable Wasp)

WASTELAND
DC Comics: Dec, 1987 - No. 18, May, 1989 ($1.75-$2.00 #13 on, mature)
1-5(4/88), 5(5/88), 6(5/88)-18: 13,15-Orlando-a 4.00
NOTE: *Orlando a-12, 13, 15. Truman a-10; c-13.*

WATCHMEN (Also see 2012-2013 Before Watchmen prequel titles)
DC Comics: Sept, 1986 - No. 12, Oct, 1987 (maxi-series)
1-Alan Moore scripts & Dave Gibbons-c/a in all 5 10 15 33 57 80
1-(2009, $1.50) Second printing 3.00
2-12 2 4 6 11 16 20
Hardcover Collection-Slip-cased-r/#1-12 w/new material; produced by Graphitti Designs 100.00
HC (2008, $39.99) recolored r/#1-12; design & promotional art; Moore & Gibbons intros 40.00
Trade paperback (1987, $14.95)-r/#1-12 25.00

WATCHVARK COMICS (Reprints from Cerebus in Hell)(Also see Aardvark Comics)
Aardvark-Vanaheim: Jan, 2018 ($4.00, B&W)
1-Cerebus figures placed over original Doré artwork of Hell; Watchmen #6-c swipe 4.00

WATER BIRDS AND THE OLYMPIC ELK (Disney)
Dell Publishing Co.: No. 700, Apr, 1956
Four Color 700-Movie 5 10 15 33 57 80

WATERWORLD: CHILDREN OF LEVIATHAN
Acclaim Comics: Aug, 1997 - No. 4, Nov, 1997 ($2.50, mini-series)
1-4 3.00

WAY OF THE RAT
CrossGeneration Comics: Jun, 2002 - No. 24, June, 2004 ($2.95)
1-24: 1-Dixon-s/ Jeff Johnson-a. 5-Whigham-a. 9,14-Luke Ross-a 3.00
Free Comic Book Day Special (6/03) reprints #1 w/features, interviews, CrossGen info 3.00
...: The Walls of Zhumar Vol. 1 (1/03, $15.95) r/#1-6 16.00
Vol. 2: The Dragon's Wake (2003, $15.95) r/#7-12 16.00

WAYWARD
Image Comics: Aug, 2014 - No. 30, Oct, 2018 ($3.50/$3.99)
1-29: 1-Jim Zub-s/Cummings-a; multiple covers. 16-Begin $3.99-c 4.00
30-($4.99) Last issue; bonus pin-up gallery 5.00

WEAPON H (See Weapon X [2017 series] #6 for debut)(See Hulkverines #1)
Marvel Comics: May, 2018 - No. 12, Mar, 2019 ($4.99/$3.99)
1-($4.99) Greg Pak-s/Cory Smith-a; Wendigo app. 5.00
2-12-($3.99) 2-Doctor Strange app. 3-7-Man-Thing app. 6,7-Captain America app. 4.00

WEAPON PLUS: WORLD WAR IV
Marvel Comics: Mar, 2020 ($4.99, one-shot)
1-Percy-s/Jeanty-a; Weapon IV app. (Man-Thing-like soldier) 5.00

WEAPONS OF MUTANT DESTRUCTION: ALPHA
Marvel Comics: Aug, 2017 ($4.99, one-shot)
1-Crossover with Weapon X #4-6 and Totally Awesome Hulk #19-22; Stryker app. 4.00

WEAPON X
Marvel Comics: Apr, 1994 ($12.95, one-shot)
nn-r/Marvel Comics Presents #72-84 2 4 6 10 14 18

WEAPON X
Marvel Comics: Mar, 1995 - No. 4, June, 1995 ($1.95)
1-Age of Apocalypse 4.00
2-4 3.00

WEAPON X
Marvel Comics: Nov, 2002 - No. 28, Nov, 2004 ($2.25/$2.99)
1-7: 1-Sabretooth-c/app.; Tieri-s/Jeanty-a 3.00
8-28: 8-Begin $2.99-c. 14-Invaders app. 15-Chamber joins. 16-18,21-25-Wolverine app. 3.00
Vol. 1: The Draft TPB (2003, $21.99) r/#1-5, #1/2 & The Draft one-shots 22.00
Vol. 2: The Underground TPB (2003, $19.99) r/#6-13 20.00
Wizard #1/2 (2002) 5.00

WEAPON X
Marvel Comics: Jun, 2017 - No. 27, Feb, 2019 ($3.99)
1-27: 1-Pak-s/Land-a; Old Man Logan & Sabretooth. 4-6-Crossover with Totally Awesome Hulk #19-22. 6-Intro. Weapon H. 17-19-Omega Red app. 23-27-Deadpool app. 4.00

WEAPON X: DAYS OF FUTURE NOW
Marvel Comics: Sept, 2005 - No. 5, Jan, 2006 ($2.99, limited series)
1-5-Tieri-s/Sears-a; Chamber, Sauron & Fantomex app. 3.00
TPB (2006, $13.99) r/#1-5 14.00

WEAPON X: FIRST CLASS
Marvel Comics: Jan, 2009 - No. 3, Mar, 2009 ($3.99, limited series)
1-3:1-Sabretooth-c/app. 2-Deadpool-c/app. 4.00

WEAPON X NOIR
Marvel Comics: May, 2010 ($3.99, one-shot)
1-Dennis Calero-s/a; C.P. Smith-c 4.00

WEAPON X: THE DRAFT (Leads into 2002 Weapon X series)
Marvel Comics: Oct, 2002 ($2.25, one-shots)
...Kane 1- JH Williams-c/Raimondi-a 3.00
...Marrow 1- JH Williams-c/Badeaux-a 3.00
...Sauron 1- JH Williams-c/Kerschl-a; Emma Frost app. 3.00
...Wild Child 1- JH Williams-c/Van Sciver-a; Aurora (Alpha Flight) app. 3.00
...Zero 1- JH Williams-c/Plunkett-a; Wolverine app. 3.00

WEAPON ZERO
Image Comics (Top Cow Productions): No. T-4(#1), June, 1995 - No. T-0(#5), Dec, 1995 ($2.50, limited series)
T-4(#1): Walt Simonson scripts in all. 5.00
T-3(#2) - T-1(#4) 4.00
T-0(#5) 3.00

WEAPON ZERO
Image Comics (Top Cow Productions): V2#1, Mar, 1996 - No. 15, Dec, 1997 ($2.50)
V2#1-Walt Simonson scripts. 4.00
2-14: 8-Begin Top Cow. 10-Devil's Reign 3.00
15-($3.50) Benitez-a 4.00

WEAPON ZERO/SILVER SURFER
Image Comics/Marvel Comics: Jan, 1997 ($2.95, one-shot)

The Weatherman V2 #1 © Brutal Noodles

Web of Evil #7 © QUA

Web of Spider-Man #114 © MAR

	GD	VG	FN	VF	VF/NM	NM-
	2.0	4.0	6.0	8.0	9.0	9.2

1-Devil's Reign Pt. 1 3.00

WE ARE ROBIN (Also see Batman: Rebirth #1)
DC Comics: Aug, 2015 - No. 12, Jul, 2016 ($3.99)
1-12: 1-Bermejo-s/c; Corona-a. 3-Batman (Gordon) app. 4-Batgirl app.; Harvey-a 4.00

WEASELGUY: ROAD TRIP
Image Comics: Sept, 1999 - No. 2 ($3.50, limited series)
1,2-Steve Buccellato-s/a 3.50
1-Variant-c by Bachalo 5.00

WEASELGUY/WITCHBLADE
Hyperwerks: July, 1998 ($2.95, one-shot)
1-Steve Buccellato-s/a; covers by Matsuda and Altstaetter 4.00

WEASEL PATROL SPECIAL, THE (Also see Fusion #17)
Eclipse Comics: Apr, 1989 ($2.00, B&W, one-shot)
1-Funny animal 4.00

WEATHERMAN, THE
Image Comics: Jun, 2018 - No. 6, Nov, 2018 ($3.99)
1-6-Jody LeHeup-s/Nathan Fox-a 4.00

WEATHERMAN, THE (Volume 2)
Image Comics: Jun, 2019 - Present ($3.99)
1-6-Jody LeHeup-s/Nathan Fox-a 4.00

WEAVEWORLD
Marvel Comics (Epic): Dec, 1991 - No. 3, 1992 ($4.95, lim. series, 68 pgs.)
1-3: Clive Barker adaptation 5.00

WEB, THE (Also see Mighty Comics & Mighty Crusaders)
DC Comics (Impact Comics): Sept, 1991 - No. 14, Oct, 1992 ($1.00)
1-14: 5-The Fly x-over 9-Trading card inside 5.00
Annual 1 (1992, $2.50, 68 pgs.)-With Trading card 5.00
NOTE: ***Gil Kane** c-5, 9, 10, 12-14. **Bill Wray** a(i)-1-9, 10(part).*

WEB, THE (Continued from The Red Circle)
DC Comics: Nov, 2009 - No. 10, Aug, 2010 ($3.99)
1-10: 1-Roger Robinson-a; The Hangman back-up feature. 3-Batgirl app. 5-Caldwell-a 4.00

WEB OF BLACK WIDOW, THE
Marvel Comics: Nov, 2019 - No. 5, Mar, 2020 ($3.99, limited series)
1-5-Jody Houser-s/Stephen Mooney-a. 1,5-Iron Man app. 2-Winter Soldier app. 4.00

WEB OF EVIL
Comic Magazines/Quality Comics Group: Nov, 1952 - No. 21, Dec, 1954
1-Used in **SOTI**, pg. 388. Jack Cole-a; morphine use story
94 188 282 597 1025 1450
2-4,6,7: 2,3-Jack Cole-a. 4,6,7-Jack Cole-c/a 52 104 156 328 552 775
5-Electrocution-c/story; Jack Cole-c/a 161 322 483 1030 1765 2500
8-11-Jack Cole-a 47 94 141 296 498 700
12,13,15,16,19-21 34 68 102 204 332 460
14-Part Crandall-c; Old Witch swipe 40 80 120 246 411 575
17-Opium drug propaganda story 39 78 117 231 378 525
18-Acid-in-face story 45 90 135 284 480 675
NOTE: ***Jack Cole** a(2 each)-2, 6, 8, 9. **Cuidera** c-1-21i. **Ravielli** a-13.*

WEB OF HORROR
Major Magazines: Dec, 1969 - No. 3, Apr, 1970 (Magazine)
1-Jeff Jones painted-c; Wrightson-a, Kaluta-a 10 20 30 64 132 200
2-Jones painted-c; Wrightson-a(2), Kaluta-a 8 16 24 55 105 155
3-Wrightson-c/a (1st published-c); Brunner, Kaluta, Bruce Jones-a
10 20 30 54 132 200

WEB OF MYSTERY
Ace Magazines (A. A. Wyn): Feb, 1951 - No. 29, Sept, 1955
1 87 174 261 553 952 1350
2-Bakerish-a 43 86 129 271 461 650
3-10: 4-Colan-a 40 80 120 246 411 575
11-18,20-26: 12-John Chilly's 1st cover art. 13-Surrealistic-c. 20-r/The Beyond #1
39 78 117 231 378 525
19-Reprints Challenge of the Unknown #6 used in N.Y. Legislative Committee
39 78 117 231 378 525
27-Bakerish-a(r/The Beyond #2); last pre-code ish 34 68 102 204 332 460
28,29: 28-All-r 27 54 81 158 259 360
NOTE: *This series was to appear as "Creepy Stories", but title was changed before publication. **Cameron** a-6, 8, 11-13, 17-20, 22, 24, 25, 27; c-8, 13, 17. **Palais** a-28r. **Sekowsky** a-1-3, 7, 8, 11, 14, 21, 29. **Tothish** a-by **Bill Discount** #16. 29-all-r, 19-28-partial-r.*

WEB OF SCARLET SPIDER
Marvel Comics: Oct, 1995 - No. 4, Jan, 1996 ($1.95, limited series)
1-4: Replaces "Web of Spider-Man" 4.00

WEB OF SPIDER-MAN (Replaces Marvel Team-Up)
Marvel Comics Group: Apr, 1985 - No. 129, Sept, 1995
1-Painted-c by Charles Vess (black costume app.) 3 6 9 19 30 40
2,3 1 3 4 6 8 10
4-8: 7-Hulk x-over; Wolverine splash 6.00
9-13: 10-Dominic Fortune guest stars; painted-c 5.00
14-17,19-28: 19-Intro Humbug & Solo 5.00
18-1st app. Venom (behind the scenes, 9/86) 3 6 9 15 22 28
29-Wolverine, new Hobgoblin (Macendale) app. 2 4 6 8 11 14
30-Origin recap The Rose & Hobgoblin I (entire book is flashback story);
Punisher & Wolverine cameo 6.00
31,32-Six part Kraven storyline begins 2 4 6 9 12 15
33-35,37,39-47,49 4.00
36-1st app. Tombstone 3 6 9 19 30 40
38-Hobgoblin app.; begin $1.00-c 5.00
48-Origin Hobgoblin II(Demogoblin) cont'd from Spectacular Spider-Man #147;
Kingpin app. 2 4 6 8 10 12
50-($1.50, 52 pgs.) 5.00
51-58 4.00
59-Cosmic Spidey cont'd from Spect. Spider-Man 5.00
60-89,91-99,101-106: 66,67-Green Goblin (Norman Osborn) app. as a super-hero. 69,70-Hulk x-over. 74-76-Austin-c(i). 76-Fantastic Four x-over. 78-Cloak & Dagger app. 81-Origin/1st app. Bloodshed. 84-Begin 6 part Rose & Hobgoblin II storyline; last $1.00-c. 86-Demon leaves Hobgoblin; 1st Demogoblin. 93-Gives brief history of Hobgoblin. 93,94-Hobgoblin (Macendale) Reborn-c/story, parts 1,2; MoonKnight app. 94-Venom cameo. 95-Begin 4 part x-over w/Spirits of Venom w/Ghost Rider/Blaze/Spidey vs. Venom & Demogoblin (cont'd in Ghost Rider/Blaze #5,6). 96-Spirits of Venom part 3; painted-c. 101,103-Maximum Carnage x-over. 103-Venom & Carnage app. 104-Infinity Crusade tie-in. 104-106-Nightwatch back-up stories 4.00
90-($2.95, 52 pgs.)-Polybagged w/silver hologram-c, gatefold poster showing
Spider-Man & Spider-Man 2099 (Williamson-i) 2 4 6 8 11 14
90-2nd printing; gold hologram-c 4.00
100-($2.95, 52 pgs.)-Holo-grafx foil-c; intro new Spider-Armor 5.00
107-111: 107-Intro Sandstorm; Sand & Quicksand app. 4.00
112-116,121-124, 126-128: 112-Begin $1.50-c; bound-in trading card sheet.
113-Regular Ed.; Gambit & Black Cat app. 4.00
113-($2.95)-Collector's ed. polybagged w/foil-c; 16 pg. preview of Spider-Man cartoon & animation cel 5.00
117-($1.50)-Flip book; Power & Responsibility Pt.1 4.00
117-($2.95)-Collector's edition; foil-c; flip book 5.00
118-1st solo Scarlet Spider story; Venom app. 5 10 15 35 63 90
119-Regular edition 6.00
119-($6.45)-Direct market edition; polybagged w/ Marvel Milestone Amazing Spider-Man #150 & coupon for Amazing Spider-Man #396, Spider-Man #53, & Spectacular Spider-Man #219.
2 4 6 10 14 18
120 ($2.25)-Flip book w/ preview of the Ultimate Spider-Man 4.00
125 ($3.95)-Holodisk-c; Gwen Stacy clone 5.00
125,129: 125 ($2.95)-Newsstand. 129-Last issue 5.00
#129.1, #129.2 (both 10/12, $2.99) Brooklyn Avengers app.; Damion Scott-a 4.00
Annual 1 (1985) 1 3 4 6 8 10
Annual 2 (1986)-New Mutants; Art Adams-a 2 4 6 8 10 12
Annual 3-10 ('87-'94, 68 pgs.): 4-Evolutionary War x-over. 5-Atlantis Attacks; Captain Universe by Ditko (p) & Silver Sable stories; F.F. app. 6-Punisher back-up plus Capt. Universe by Ditko; G. Kane-a. 7-Origins of Hobgoblin I, Hobgoblin II, Green Goblin I & II & Venom; Larsen/Austin-c. 9-Bagged w/card 5.00
Super Special 1 (1995, $3.95)-flip book 5.00
NOTE: ***Art Adams** a-Annual 2. **Byrne** c-3-6. **Chaykin** c-10. **Mignola** a-Annual 2. **Vess** c-1, 8, Annual 1, 2. **Zeck** a-6i, 31, 32; c-31, 32.*

WEB OF SPIDER-MAN (Anthology)
Marvel Comics: Dec, 2009 - No. 12, Nov, 2010 ($3.99)
1-12: 1-Spider-Girl app. thru #7; Ben Reilly app. 2-6-Origins of villains retold. 7-Kraven origin; Paper Doll app.; Mahfood-a. 9-11-Jackpot back-up; Takeda-a. 11,12-Black Cat app. 4.00

WEB OF VENOM...
Marvel Comics: Oct, 2018 - Jan, 2021 ($4.99, one-shots)
...: Carnage Born 1 (1/19) Story of Cletus Kasady; Cates-s/Beyruth-a 5.00
...: Cult of Carnage 1 (6/19) Misty Knight & John Jameson app.; Tieri-s/Beyruth-a 5.00
...: Empyre's End 1 (1/21) Knull app.; Chapman-s/Vilanova-a 5.00
...: Funeral Pyre 1 (9/19) Story of Andi Benton (Mania); Carnage app. 5.00
...: The Good Son 1 (3/20) Story of Eddie Brock's son Dylan and Normie Osborn 5.00
...: Ve'Nam 1 (10/18) The first symbiote & Rex Strickland app.; Cates-s/Ramírez-a 5.00
...: Venom Unleashed 1 (3/19) Venom Dog and Carnage app.; Cates-s/Hotz & Gedeon-a 5.00

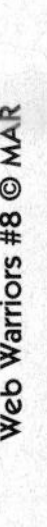
Web Warriors #8 © MAR

Weird Comics #16 © FOX

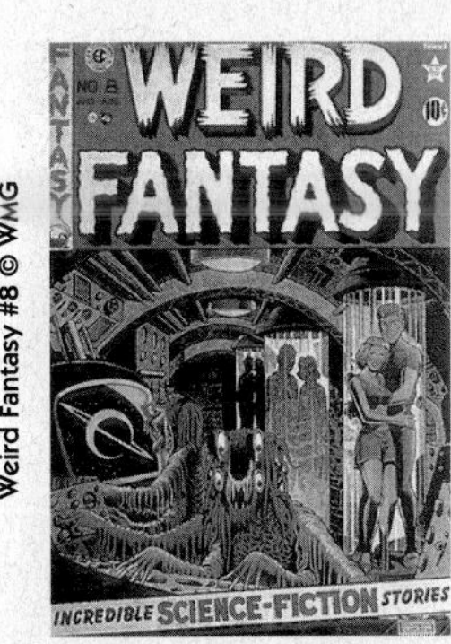

Weird Fantasy #8 © WMG

GD VG FN VF VF/NM NM-
2.0 4.0 6.0 8.0 9.0 9.2

...: Wraith 1 (11/20) Origin of Wraith re-told; Cates-s/Vilanova-a 5.00

WEBSPINNERS: TALES OF SPIDER-MAN
Marvel Comics: Jan, 1999 - No. 18, Jun, 2000 ($2.99/$2.50)

1-DeMatteis-s/Zulli-a; back-up story w/Romita Sr. art 6.00
1-($6.95) DF Edition 1 2 3 5 6 8
2,3: 2-Two covers 4.00
4-11,13-18: 4,5-Giffen-a; Silver Surfer-c/app. 7-9-Kelly-s/Sears and Smith-a. 10,11-Jenkins-s/Sean Phillips-a 4.00
12-($3.50) J.G. Jones-c/a; Jenkins-s 5.00

WEB WARRIORS
Marvel Comics: Jan, 2016 - No. 11, Nov, 2016 ($4.99/$3.99)

1-($4.99) Spider-verse characters team-up; Mike Costa-s/David Baldeon-a; alternate Black Cat app. 5.00
2-11-($3.99) 2-5-Multiple Spider-Mans vs. multiple Electros 4.00

WEDDING BELLS
Quality Comics Group: Feb, 1954 - No. 19, Nov, 1956

1-Whitney-a 22 44 66 132 216 300
2 14 28 42 81 118 155
3-9: 8-Last precode (4/55) 12 24 36 69 97 125
10-Ward-a (9 pgs.) 17 34 51 100 158 215
11-14,17 11 22 33 64 90 115
15-Baker-c 20 40 60 114 182 250
16-Baker-c/a 22 44 66 132 216 300
18,19-Baker-a each 15 30 45 90 140 190

WEDDING OF DRACULA
Marvel Comics: Jan, 1993 ($2.00, 52 pgs.)

1-Reprints Tomb of Dracula #30,45,46 4.00

WEDNESDAY COMICS (Newspaper-style, twice folded pages on 20" x 14" newsprint)
DC Comics: Sept, 2009 - No. 12, Nov, 2009 ($3.99, weekly limited series)

1-12-Superman, Batman, Kamandi, Hawkman, Deadman, Green Lantern, Flash, Teen Titans, Metamorpho, Adam Strange, Supergirl, Metal Men, Wonder Woman, The Demon with Catwoman, Sgt. Rock; s-a/ by various incl. Ryan Sook, Joe Kubert, Gaiman, Allred, Risso, Kyle Baker, Paul Pope, Conner, Simonson, Garcia-Lopez, Stelfreeze, Bermejo 4.00
HC (2010, $49.99, 17-3/4"x11-1/4") r/#1-12 plus new 1 pg. stories of Plastic Man by Dorkin-s/DeStefano-a and Beware the Creeper by Giffen-s/Canete-a; bonus sketch art 50.00

WEEKENDER, THE (Illustrated...)
Rucker Pub. Co.: V1#1, Sept, 1945? - V1#4, Nov, 1945; V2#1, Jan, 1946 - V2#3, Aug, 1946 (52 pgs.)

V#1-Same-c as Zip Comics #45 (nurse in peril), inside-c and back-c blank; Steel Sterling, Senor Banana, Red Rube and Ginger 53 106 159 334 567 800
V1#2-4: 2-Capt. Victory on-c. 3-Super hero-c; Mr. E, Dan Hastings, Sky Chief and the Echo. 4-Same-c as Punch Comics #10 (9/44); r/Hale the Magician (7 pgs.) & r/Mr. E (8 pgs.-Lou Fine? or Gustavson?) plus 3 humor strips & many B&W photos & r/newspaper articles plus cheesecake photos of Hollywood stars 47 94 141 296 498 700
V2#1-Same-c as Dynamic Comics #11; 36 pgs. comics, 16 in newspaper format with photos; partial Dynamic Comics reprints; 4 pgs. of cels from the Disney film Pinocchio; Little Nemo story by Winsor McCay, Jr.; Jack Cole-a 65 130 195 416 708 1000
V2#2,3: 2-Same-c as Dynamic Comics #9 by Raboy; Dan Hastings (Tuska), Rocket Boy, The Echo, Lucky Coyne. 3-Humor-c by Boddington?; Dynamic Man, Ima Slooth, Master Key, Dynamic Boy, Captain Glory 41 82 123 256 428 600

WEEKND PRESENTS, THE: STARBOY
Marvel Comics: Aug, 2018 ($3.99, one-shot)

1-Abel Tesfaye, La Mar Taylor & Christos Gage-s/Eric Nguyen-a/c 4.00

WEIRD
Eerie Publications: V1#10, 1/66 - V8#6, 12/74; V9#1, 1/75 - V14#3, Nov, 1981 (Magazine) (V1-V8: 52 pgs.; V9 on: 68 pgs.)

V1#10(#1)-Intro. Morris the Caretaker of Weird (ends V2#10); Burgos-a
9 18 27 58 114 170
11,12 6 12 18 38 69 100
V2#1-4(10/67), V3#1(1/68), V2#6(4/68)-V2#7,9,10(12/68)
6 12 18 38 69 100
V2#8-r/Ditko's 1st story/Fantastic Fears #5 7 14 21 44 82 120
V3#1(2/69)-V3#4 5 10 15 35 63 90
V3#5(12/69)-Rulah reprint; "Rulah" changed to "Pulah", LSD story reprinted in Horror Tales V4#4, Tales From the Tomb V2#4, & 20 5 10 15 35 63 90
V4#1-6('70), V5#1-6('71), V6#1-7('72), V7#1-7('73), V8#1-3, V8#4(8/74), V8#4(10/74), (V8#5 does not exist), V8#6('74), V9#1-4(1/75-'76), V10#1-3('77), V11#1-4('78), V12#1(2/79)-V14#3(11/81) 5 10 15 34 60 85

NOTE: *There are two V8#4 issues (8/74 & 10/74). V9#4 (12/76) has a cover swipe from Horror Tales V5#1 (2/73). There are two V13#3 issues (6/80 & 9/80).*

WEIRD
DC Comics (Paradox Press): Sum, 1997 - No. 4 ($2.99, B&W, magazine)

1-4: 4-Mike Tyson-c 3.00

WEIRD, THE
DC Comics: Apr, 1988 - No. 4, July, 1988 ($1.50, limited series)

1-4: Wrightson-c/a in all 5.00

WEIRD ADVENTURES
P. L. Publishing Co. (Canada): May-June, 1951 - No. 3, Sept-Oct, 1951

1- "The She-Wolf Killer" by Matt Baker (6 pgs.) 71 142 213 454 777 1100
2-Bondage/hypodermic panel 55 110 165 352 601 850
3-Male bondage/torture-c; severed head story 50 100 150 315 533 750

WEIRD ADVENTURES
Ziff-Davis Publishing Co.: No. 10, July-Aug, 1951

10-Painted-c 48 96 144 302 514 725

WEIRD CHILLS
Key Publications: July, 1954 - No. 3, Nov, 1954

1-Wolverton-r/Weird Mysteries No. 4; blood transfusion-c by Baily
194 388 582 1242 2121 3000
2-Extremely violent injury to eye-c by Baily; Hitler story
194 388 582 1242 2121 3000
3-Bondage E.C. swipe-c by Baily 148 296 444 947 1624 2300

WEIRD COMICS
Fox Feature Syndicate: Apr, 1940 - No. 20, Jan, 1942

1-The Birdman, Thor, God of Thunder (ends #5), The Sorceress of Zoom, Blast Bennett, Typhon, Voodoo Man, & Dr. Mortal begin; George Tuska bondage-c
1000 2000 3000 7400 13,200 19,000
2-Lou Fine-c 486 972 1458 3550 6275 9000
3,4: 3-Simon-c. 4-Torture-c 300 600 900 1920 3310 4700
5-Intro. Dart & sidekick Ace (8/40) (ends #20); bondage/hypo-c
300 600 900 1920 3310 4700
6-Dynamite Thor app.; super hero covers begin 171 342 513 1094 1872 2650
7-Dynamite Thor app. 239 478 717 1530 2615 3700
8-Dynamo, the Eagle (11/40, early app.; see Science #1) & sidekick Buddy & Marga, the Panther Woman begin 187 374 531 1197 2049 2900
9,10: 10-Navy Jones app. 151 302 453 966 1658 2350
11-19: 16-The Eagle vs. Nazi battle-c/flag-c. 17-Origin The Black Rider; WWII Nazi-c
138 276 414 883 1517 2150
20-Origin The Rapier; Swoop Curtis app; Churchill & Hitler-c
975 1950 2919 7100 12,550 18,000

NOTE *Cover features: Sorceress of Zoom-4; Dr. Mortal-5; Dart & Ace-6-13, 15; Eagle-14, 16-20.*

WEIRD DETECTIVE
Dark Horse Comics: Jun, 2016 - No. 5, Oct, 2016 ($3.99)

1-5-Van Lente-s/Vilanova-a 4.00

WEIRD FANTASY (Formerly A Moon, A Girl, Romance; becomes Weird Science-Fantasy #23 on)
E. C. Comics: No. 13, May-June, 1950 - No. 22, Nov-Dec, 1953

13(#1) (1950) 229 458 687 1832 2916 4000
14-Necronomicon story; Cosmic Ray Bomb explosion-c/story by Feldstein; Feldstein & Gaines star 123 246 369 984 1567 2150
15,16: 16-Used in **SOTI**, pg. 144 91 182 273 728 1164 1600
17 (1951) 69 138 207 552 876 1200
6-Robot-c 61 122 183 488 782 1075
7-10 57 114 171 456 728 1000
11-13 (1952): 11-Cover inspired by Chesley Bonstell painting "The End of the World" from Coronet magazine (July 1947); Feldstein bio. 12-E.C. artists cameo; Orlando bio. 13-Anti-Wertham "Cosmic Correspondence" 47 94 141 376 601 825
14-Frazetta/Williamson(1st team-up at E.C.)/Krenkel-a (7 pgs.); Orlando draws E.C. staff
60 120 180 480 765 1050
15-Williamson/Evans-a(3), 4,3,&7 pgs. 50 100 150 400 638 875
16-19-Williamson/Krenkel-a in all. 17-Feldstein dinosaur-c; classic sci-fi story "The Aliens". 18-Williamson/Feldstein-c; classic anti-prejudice story "Judgment Day". 19-Williamson bio.
46 92 138 368 584 800
20-Frazetta/Williamson-a (7 pgs.); contains house ad for original, uncensored cover to Vault of Horror #32 (meat cleaver in forehead) 53 106 159 424 675 925
21-Frazetta/Williamson-c & Williamson/Krenkel-a 81 162 243 648 1038 1425
22-Bradbury adaptation 41 82 123 328 527 725

NOTE: ***Crandall** a-22. **Elder** a-17. **Feldstein** a-13(#1)-8; c-13(#1)-18 (#18 w/**Williamson**), 20. **Harrison/Wood** a-13. **Kamen** a-13(#1)-16, 18-22. **Krigstein** a-22. **Kurtzman** a-13(#1)-17(#5), 6. **Orlando** a-9-22 (2 stories in #16); c-19, 22. **Severin/Elder** a-18-21. **Wood** a-13(#1)-14, 17(2 stories ea. in #10-13). Ray Bradbury adaptations in #13,17-22. Canadian reprints exist; see Table of Contents.*

WEIRD FANTASY
Russ Cochran/Gemstone Publ.: Oct, 1992 - No. 22, Jan, 1998 ($1.50/$2.00/$2.50)

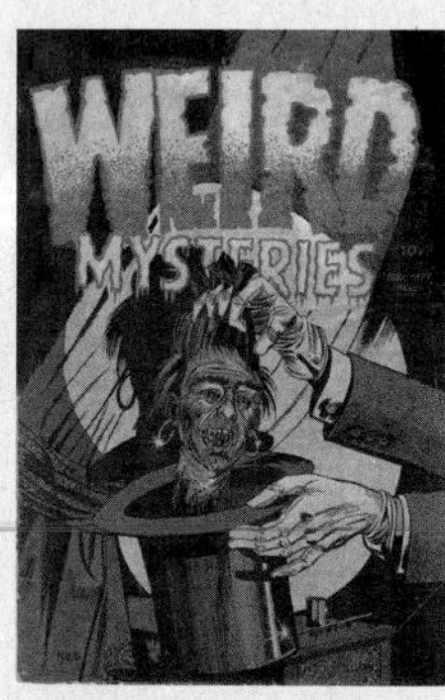

Weird Mysteries #6 © GIL

Weird Science #7 © WMG

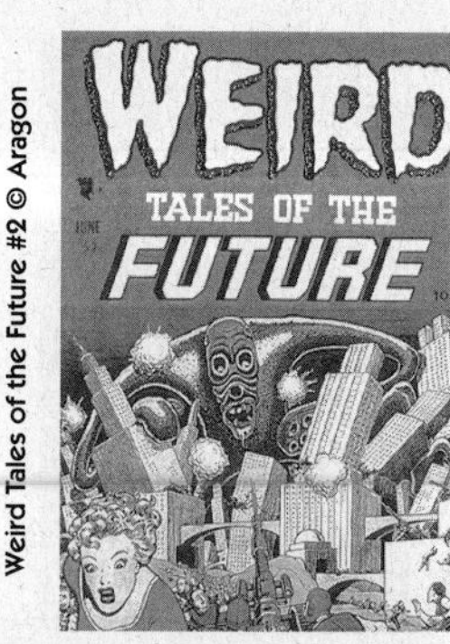

Weird Tales of the Future #2 © Aragon

	GD	VG	FN	VF	VF/NM	NM-
	2.0	4.0	6.0	8.0	9.0	9.2

1-22: 1,2: 1,2-r/Weird Fantasy #13,14; Feldstein-c. 3-5-r/Weird Fantasy #15-17 4.00

WEIRD HORRORS (Nightmare #10 on)
St. John Publishing Co.: June, 1952 - No. 9, Oct, 1953

1-Tuska-a 84 168 252 538 919 1300
2,3: 3-Hashish story 47 94 141 296 498 700
4,5 42 84 126 265 445 625
6-Ekgren-c; atomic bomb story 94 188 282 597 1025 1450
7-Ekgren-c; Kubert, Cameron-a 100 200 300 640 1095 1550
8,9-Kubert-c/a 54 108 162 343 574 825
NOTE: ***Cameron** a-7, 9. **Finesque** a-1-5. **Forgione** a-6. **Morisi** a-3. Bondage c-8.*

WEIRD MYSTERIES
Gillmor Publications: Oct, 1952 - No. 12, Sept, 1954

1-Partial Wolverton-c swiped from splash page "Flight to the Future" in Weird Tales of the Future #2; "Eternity" has an Ingels swipe 168 336 504 1075 1838 2600
2- "Robot Woman" by Wolverton; Bernard Baily-c reprinted in Mister Mystery #18; acid in face panel 229 458 687 1466 2508 3550
3,6: Both have decapitation-c 119 238 357 762 1306 1850
4- "The Man Who Never Smiled" (3 pgs.) by Wolverton; Classic B. Baily skull-c
649 1298 1947 4738 8369 12,000
5-Wolverton story "Swamp Monster" (6 pgs.). Classic exposed brain-c
1000 2000 3000 7400 13,200 19,000
7-Used in **SOTI**, illo "Indeed", illo "Sex and blood" 158 316 474 1011 1731 2450
8-Wolverton-c panel-r/#5; used in a '54 Readers Digest anti-comics article by T. E. Murphy entitled "For the Kiddies to Read" 100 200 300 640 1095 1550
9-Excessive violence, gore & torture 87 174 261 553 952 1350
10-Silhouetted nudity panel 81 162 243 518 884 1250
11,12: 12-r/Mr. Mystery #8(2), Weird Mysteries #3 & Weird Tales of the Future #6
81 162 243 518 884 1250
NOTE: ***Baily** c-2-12. Anti-Wertham column in #5. #1-12 all have 'The Ghoul Teacher' (host).*

WEIRD MYSTERIES (Magazine)
Pastime Publications: Mar-Apr, 1959 (35¢, B&W, 68 pgs.)

1-Torres-a; E. C. swipe from Tales From the Crypt #46 by Tuska "The Ragman"
15 30 45 90 140 190

WEIRD MYSTERY TALES (See DC 100 Page Super Spectacular)

WEIRD MYSTERY TALES (See Cancelled Comic Cavalcade)
National Periodical Publications: July-Aug, 1972 - No. 24, Nov, 1975

1-Kirby-a; Wrightson splash pg. 5 10 15 35 63 90
2-Titanic-c/s 3 6 9 21 33 45
3,21: 21-Wrightson-c 3 6 9 17 26 35
4-10 3 6 9 14 19 24
11-20,22-24 2 4 6 11 16 20
NOTE: ***Alcala** a-5, 10, 13, 14. **Aparo** c-4. **Bailey** a-8. **Bolle** a-8?. **Howard** a-4. **Kaluta** a-4, 24; c-1. **G. Kane** a-10. **Kirby** a-1, 2p, 3p. **Nino** a-5, 6, 9, 13, 16, 21. **Redondo** a-9, 17. **Sparling** c-6. **Starlin** a-3?, 4. **Wood** a-23.*

WEIRD ROMANCE (Seduction of the Innocent #9)
Eclipse Comics: Feb, 1988 ($2.00, B&W)

1-Pre-code horror-r; Lou Cameron-r(2) 4.00

WEIRD SCIENCE (Formerly Saddle Romances) (Becomes Weird Science-Fantasy #23 on) (Also see EC Archives • Weird Science)
E. C. Comics: No. 12, May-June, 1950 - No. 22, Nov-Dec, 1953

12(#1) (1950)-"Lost in the Microcosm" classic-c/story by Kurtzman; "Dream of Doom" stars Gaines & E.C. artists 309 618 927 2472 3936 5400
13-Flying saucers over Washington-c/story, 2 years before supposed UFO sighting
129 258 387 1032 1641 2250
14-Robot, End of the World-c/story by Feldstein 111 222 333 888 1419 1950
15-War of Worlds-c/story (1950) 100 200 300 800 1275 1750
5-Atomic explosion-c 73 146 219 584 930 1275
6-8,10 64 128 192 512 819 1125
9-Wood's 1st EC-c 79 158 237 632 1004 1375
11-14 (1952) 11-Kamen bio. 12-Wood bio 50 100 150 400 638 875
15-18-Williamson/Krenkel-a in each; 15-Williamson-a. 17-Used in **POP**, pgs. 81,82. 18-Bill Gaines doll app. in story 51 102 153 408 654 900
19,20-Williamson/Frazetta-a (7 pgs. each). 19-Used in **SOTI**, illo "A young girl on her wedding night stabs her sleeping husband to death with a hatpin..." 19-Bradbury bio.
64 128 192 512 819 1125
21-Williamson/Frazetta-a (6 pgs.); Wood draws E.C. staff; Gaines & Feldstein app. in story
64 128 192 512 819 1125
22-Williamson/Frazetta/Krenkel-a (8 pgs.); Wood draws himself in his story (last pg. & panel) 67 134 201 536 856 1175
NOTE: ***Elder** a-14, 19. **Evans** a-22. **Feldstein** a-12(#1)-8; c-12(#1)-8, 11. **Ingels** a-15. **Kamen** a-12(#1)-13, 15-18, 20, 21. **Kurtzman** a-12(#1)-7. **Orlando** a-10-22. **Wood** a-12(#1), 13(#2), 5-22 (#9, 10, 12, 13 all have 2 **Wood** stories); c-9, 10, 12-22. Canadian reprints exist; see Table of Contents. Ray Bradbury adaptations in #17-22.*

WEIRD SCIENCE
Gladstone Publishing: Sept, 1990 - No. 4, Mar, 1991 ($1.95/$2.00, 68 pgs.)

1-4: Wood-c(r); all reprints in each 5.00

WEIRD SCIENCE (Also see EC Archives • Weird Science)
Russ Cochran/Gemstone Publishing: Sept, 1992 - No. 22, Dec, 1997 ($1.50/$2.00/$2.50)

1-22: 1,2: r/Weird Science #12,13 w/original-c. ,4-r/#14,15. 5-7-w/original-c 4.00

WEIRD SCIENCE-FANTASY (Formerly Weird Science & Weird Fantasy) (Becomes Incredible Science Fiction #30)
E. C. Comics: No. 23 Mar, 1954 - No. 29, May-June, 1955 (#23,24: 15¢)

23-Williamson, Wood-a; Bradbury adaptation 47 94 141 376 601 825
24-Williamson & Wood-a; Harlan Ellison's 1st professional story, "Upheaval!", later adapted into a short story as "Mealtime", and then into a TV episode of Voyage to the Bottom of the Sea as "The Price of Doom" 47 94 141 376 601 825
25-Williamson dinosaur-c; Williamson/Torres/Krenkel-a plus Wood-a; Bradbury adaptation and fan letter; cover price back to 10¢ 53 106 159 424 675 925
26-Flying Saucer Report; Wood, Crandall-a; A-bomb panels
49 98 147 392 621 850
27-Adam Link/I Robot series begins 46 92 138 368 584 800
28-Williamson/Krenkel/Torres-a; Wood-a 47 94 141 376 601 825
29-Classic Frazetta-c; Williamson/Krenkel & Wood-a; Adam Link/I Robot series concludes; last pre-code issue; new logo 197 394 591 1576 2513 3450
NOTE: ***Crandall** a-26, 27, 29. **Evans** a-26. **Feldstein** c-24, 26, 28. **Kamen** a-27, 28. **Krigstein** a-23-25. **Orlando** a-in all. **Wood** a-in all; c-23, 27. The cover to #29 was originally intended for Famous Funnies #217 (Buck Rogers), but was rejected for being "too violent."*

WEIRD SCIENCE-FANTASY
Russ Cochran/Gemstone Publishing: Nov, 1992 - No. 7, May , 1994 ($1.50/$2.00/$2.50)

1-7: 1,2: r/Weird Science-Fantasy #23,24. 3-7 r/#25-29 4.00

WEIRD SCIENCE-FANTASY ANNUAL
E. C. Comics: 1952, 1953 (Sold thru the E. C. office & on the stands in some major cities) (25¢, 132 pgs.)

1952-Feldstein-c 335 670 1005 2513 3857 5200
1953-Feldstein-c 187 374 561 1403 2152 2900
NOTE: *The 1952 annual contains books cover-dated in 1951 & 1952, and the 1953 annual from 1952 & 1953. Contents of each annual may vary in same year.*

WEIRD SECRET ORIGINS
DC Comics: Oct, 2004 ($5.95, square-bound, one-shot)

nn-Reprints origins of Dr. Fate, Spectre, Congorilla, Metamorpho, Animal Man & others 6.00

WEIRD SUSPENSE
Atlas/Seaboard Publ.: Feb, 1975 - No. 3, July, 1975

1-3: 1-Tarantula begins. 3-Freidrich-s 2 4 6 11 16 20
NOTE: ***Boyette** a-1-3. **Buckler** c-1, 3.*

WEIRD SUSPENSTORIES
Superior Comics (Canada): Oct, 1951 - No. 3, Dec, 1951; No. 3, no date (EC reprints)

1-3,3(no date)-(Rare): Reprints Crime SuspenStories #1-3, covers & contents w/Canadian ads replacing U.S. ads 1000 2000 300 - - -
NOTE: *Canada passed a law against importing crime comic books between 1949-1953, thus Crime Suspenstories became Weird Suspenstories in Canada creating a new EC title. The word "crime" was not allowed on comic books in Canada during this time.*

WEIRD TALES ILLUSTRATED
Millennium Publications: 1992 - No. 2, 1992 ($2.95, high quality paper)

1,2-Bolton painted-c. 1-Adapts E.A. Poe & Harlan Ellison stories. 2-E.A. Poe & H.P. Lovecraft adaptations 4.00
1-($4.95, 52 pgs.)-Deluxe edition w/Tim Vigil-a not in regular #1; stiff-c; Bolton painted-c 6.00

WEIRD TALES OF THE FUTURE
S.P.M. Publ. No. 1-4/Aragon Publ. No. 5-8: Mar, 1952 - No. 8, July-Aug, 1953

1-Andru-a(2); Wolverton partial-c 174 348 522 1114 1907 2700
2,3-Wolverton-c/a(3) each. 2- "Jumpin Jupiter" satire by Wolverton begins, ends #5
300 600 900 2040 3570 5100
4-(11/52) Wolverton-c from three panels of Wolverton's "Nightmare World" from issue #3 (9/52) and the girl on the cover from Mister Mystery #6 (7/52) "The Fatal Chord" by Ed Robbins, pg. 4, which was cut apart, pasted up to form the cover and partially redrawn by Harry Kantor, the editor; "Jumpin Jupiter" satire by Wolverton
168 336 504 1075 1838 2600
5-Wolverton-c/a(2); "Jumpin Jupiter" satire 423 846 1269 3000 5250 7500
6-Bernard Baily-c 100 200 300 640 1095 1550
7- "The Mind Movers" from the art to Wolverton's "Brain Bats of Venus" from Mr. Mystery #7 which was cut apart, pasted up, partially redrawn, and rewritten by Harry Kantor, the editor; Baily-c 300 600 900 2010 3505 5000
8-Reprints Weird Mysteries #1(10/52) minus cover; gory cover showing heart ripped out, by B. Baily 300 600 900 2010 3505 5000

WEIRD TALES OF THE MACABRE (Magazine)

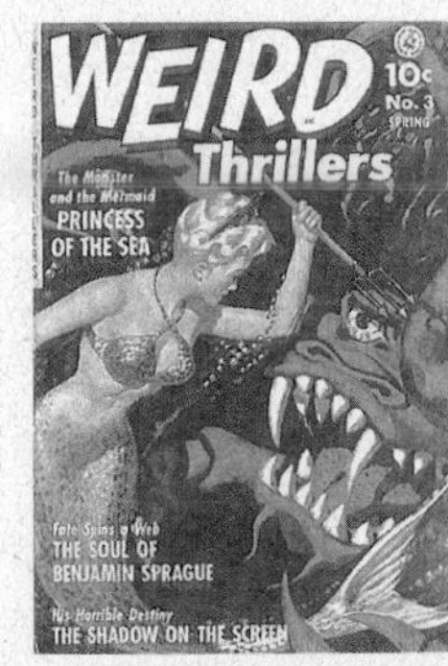

Weird Thrillers #3 © Z-D

Weird War Tales #102 © DC

Weird Wonder Tales #17 © MAR

	GD 2.0	VG 4.0	FN 6.0	VF 8.0	VF/NM 9.0	NM- 9.2

Atlas/Seaboard Publ.: Jan, 1975 - No. 2, Mar, 1975 (75¢, B&W)

	GD	VG	FN	VF	VF/NM	NM-
1-Jeff Jones painted-c; Boyette-a	5	10	15	33	57	80
2-Boris Vallejo painted-c; Severin-a	5	10	15	34	60	85

WEIRD TERROR (Also see Horrific)
Allen Hardy Associates (Comic Media): Sept, 1952 - No. 13, Sept, 1954

	GD	VG	FN	VF	VF/NM	NM-
1- "Portrait of Death", adapted from Lovecraft's "Pickman's Model"; lingerie panels, Hitler story	90	180	270	576	988	1400
2,3: 2-Text on Marquis DeSade, Torture, Demonology, & St. Elmo's Fire. 3-Extreme violence, whipping, torture; article on sin eating, dowsing	65	130	195	416	708	1000
4-Dismemberment, decapitation, article on human flesh for sale, Devil, whipping	71	142	213	454	777	1100
5-Article on body snatching, mutilation; cannibalism story	58	116	174	371	636	900
6-Dismemberment, decapitation, man hit by lightning	65	130	195	416	708	1000
7-Body burning in fireplace-c	77	154	231	493	847	1200
8,11: 8-Decapitation story; Ambrose Bierce adapt. 11-End of the world story w/atomic blast panels; Tothish-a by Bill Discount	58	116	174	371	636	900
9,10,13: 13-Severed head panels	50	100	150	315	533	750
12-Discount-a	50	100	150	315	533	750

NOTE: *Don Heck a-most issues; c-1-13. Landau a-6. Morisi a-2-5, 7, 9, 12. Palais a-1, 5, 6, 8(2), 10, 12. Powell a-10. Ravielli a-11.*

WEIRD THRILLERS
Ziff-Davis Publ. Co. (Approved Comics): Sept-Oct, 1951 - No. 5, Oct-Nov, 1952 (#2-5: painted-c)

	GD	VG	FN	VF	VF/NM	NM-
1-Rondo Hatton photo-c	113	226	339	723	1237	1750
2-Toth, Anderson, Colan-a	77	154	231	493	847	1200
3-Two Powell, Tuska-a; classic-c; Everett-a	106	212	318	678	1164	1650
4-Kubert, Tuska-a	71	142	213	454	777	1100
5-Powell-a	68	136	204	435	743	1050

NOTE: *M. Anderson a-2, 3. Roussos a-4. #2, 3 reprinted in Nightmare #10 & 13; #4, 5 reprinted in Amazing Ghost Stories #16 & #15.*

WEIRD VAMPIRE TALES (Comic magazine)
Modern Day Periodical Pub.: V3 #1, Apr, 1979 - V5 #3, Mar, 1982 (B&W)

	GD	VG	FN	VF	VF/NM	NM-
V3 #1 (4/79) First issue, no V1 or V2	4	8	12	27	44	60
V3 #2-4	3	6	9	19	30	40
V4 #2 (4/80), V4 #3 (7/80) (no V4 #1)	3	6	9	17	26	35
V5 #1 (1/81), V5 #2 (two issues, 4/81 & 8/81)	3	6	9	17	26	35
V5 #3 (3/82) Last issue; low print	3	6	9	21	33	45

WEIRD WAR TALES
National Periodical Publ./DC Comics: Sept-Oct, 1971 - No. 124, June, 1983 (#1-5: 52 pgs.)

	GD	VG	FN	VF	VF/NM	NM-
1-Kubert-a in #1-4,7; c-1-7	21	42	63	147	324	500
2,3-Drucker-a: 2-Crandall-a. 3-Heath-a	10	20	30	64	132	200
4,5: 5-Toth-a; Heath-a	8	16	24	54	102	150
6,7,9,10: 6,10-Toth-a. 7-Heath-a	6	12	18	37	66	95
8-Neal Adams-c/a(i)	6	12	18	41	76	110
11-20	4	8	12	22	35	48
21-35	3	6	9	16	24	32
36-(68 pgs.)-Crandall & Kubert-r/#2; Heath-r/#3; Kubert-c	3	6	9	18	28	38
37-50: 38,39-Kubert-c	2	4	6	10	14	18
51-63: 58-Hitler-c/app. 60-Hindenburg-c/s	2	4	6	9	13	16
64-Frank Miller-a (1st DC work)	6	12	18	38	69	100
65-67,69-89,91,92: 89-Nazi Apes-c/s.	2	4	6	8	10	12
68-Frank Miller-a (2nd DC work)	3	6	9	21	33	45
90-Hitler app.	2	4	6	8	11	14
93-Intro/origin Creature Commandos	2	4	6	8	11	14
94-Return of War that Time Forgot; dinosaur-c/s	2	4	6	10	14	18
95,96,98,102-123: 98-Sphinx-c. 102-Creature Commandos battle Hitler. 110-Origin/1st app. Medusa. 123-1st app. Captain Spaceman	2	4	6	8	10	12
97,99,100,101,124: 99-War that Time Forgot. 100-Creature Commandos in War that Time Forgot. 101-Intro/origin G.I. Robot	2	4	6	8	11	14

NOTE: *Chaykin a-76, 82. Ditko a-95, 99, 104-106. Evans c-73, 74, 83, 85. Kane c-116, 118. Kubert c-55, 58, 60, 62, 72, 75-81, 87, 88, 90-96, 100, 103, 104, 106, 107. Newton a-122. Starlin c-89. Sutton a-91, 92, 103. Creature Commandos -93, 97, 100, 102, 105, 108-112, 114, 116-119, 121, 124. G.I. Robot - 101, 108, 111, 113, 116-118, 120, 122. War That Time Forgot - 94, 99, 100, 103, 106, 109, 120.*

WEIRD WAR TALES
DC Comics (Vertigo): June, 1997 - No. 4, Sept, 1997 ($2.50)

	GD	VG	FN	VF	VF/NM	NM-
1-4-Anthology by various						4.00

WEIRD WAR TALES
DC Comics (Vertigo): April, 2000 ($4.95, one-shot)

	GD	VG	FN	VF	VF/NM	NM-
1-Anthology by various; last Biukovic-a						5.00

WEIRD WAR TALES
DC Comics: Nov, 2010 ($3.99, one-shot)

	GD	VG	FN	VF	VF/NM	NM-
1-Anthology by various incl. Cooke, Strnad, Pugh; Cooke-c						4.00

WEIRD WESTERN TALES (Formerly All-Star Western)
National Per. Publ./DC Comics: No. 12, June-July, 1972 - No. 70, Aug, 1980

	GD	VG	FN	VF	VF/NM	NM-
12-(52 pgs.)-3rd app. Jonah Hex; Bat Lash, Pow Wow Smith reprints; El Diablo by Neal Adams/Wrightson	10	20	30	64	132	200
13-Jonah Hex-c & 4th app.; Neal Adams-a	7	14	21	48	89	130
14-Toth-a	5	10	15	35	63	90
15-Adams-c/a; no Jonah Hex	4	8	12	28	47	65
16,17,19,20	4	8	12	28	47	65
18,29: 18-1st all Jonah Hex issue (7-8/73) & begins. 29-Origin Jonah Hex; 1st full app. of Quentin Turnbull	6	12	18	37	66	95
21-28,30: Jonah Hex in all	4	8	12	23	37	50
31-38: Jonah Hex in all. 38-Last Jonah Hex	3	6	9	18	28	38
39-Origin/1st app. Scalphunter & begins	2	4	6	13	18	22
40-47,50-69: 64-Bat Lash-c/story	2	4	6	8	10	12
48,49: (44 pgs.)-1st & 2nd app. Cinnamon	2	4	6	8	11	14
70-Last issue	2	4	6	9	13	16

NOTE: *Alcala a-16, 17. Evans inks-39-48; c-39i, 40, 47. G. Kane a-15, 20. Kubert c-12, 33. Starlin c-44, 45. Wildey a-26. 48 & 49 are 44 pgs..*

WEIRD WESTERN TALES (Blackest Night crossover)
DC Comics: No. 71, March, 2010 ($2.99, one-shot)

	GD	VG	FN	VF	VF/NM	NM-
71-Jonah Hex, Scalphunter, Super-Chief, Firehair and Bat Lash rise as Black Lanterns						3.00

WEIRD WESTERN TALES
DC Comics (Vertigo): Apr, 2001 - No. 4, Jul, 2001 ($2.50, limited series)

	GD	VG	FN	VF	VF/NM	NM-
1-4-Anthology by various						3.00

WEIRD WONDER TALES
Marvel Comics Group: Dec, 1973 - No. 22, May, 1977

	GD	VG	FN	VF	VF/NM	NM-
1-Wolverton-r/Mystic #6 (Eye of Doom)	4	8	12	27	44	60
2-10	3	6	9	17	26	35
11-22: 16-18-Venus-r by Everett from Venus #19,18 & 17. 19-22-r/Dr. Droom (re-named Dr. Druid) by Kirby. 22-New art by Byrne	3	6	9	16	23	30
15-17-(30¢-c variants, limited distribution)(4-8/76)	5	10	15	34	60	85

NOTE: *All 1950s & early 1960s reprints. Check r-1. Colan r-17. Ditko r-4, 5, 10-13, 19-21. Drucker r-12, 20. Everett r-3(Spellbound #16), 6(Astonishing #10), 9(Adv. Into Mystery #5). Heath a-13r. Heck a-10r, 14r. Gil Kane c-1, 2, 10. Kirby r-4, 6, 10, 11, 13, 15-22; c-17, 19, 20. Krigstein r-19. Kubert r-22. Maneely r-8. Mooney r-7p. Powell r-3, 7. Torres r-7. Wildey r-2, 7.*

WEIRDWORLD (Secret Wars tie-in)
Marvel Comics: Aug, 2015 - No. 5, Dec, 2015 ($3.99, limited series)

	GD	VG	FN	VF	VF/NM	NM-
1-5-Aaron-s/Del Mundo-a; Arkon, Morgan Le Fay, and Skull the Slayer app.						4.00

WEIRDWORLD (After Secret Wars)
Marvel Comics: Feb, 2016 - No. 6, Jul, 2016 ($3.99)

	GD	VG	FN	VF	VF/NM	NM-
1-6-Humphries-s/Del Mundo-a; Goleta the Wizardslayer & Morgan Le Fay app.						4.00

WEIRD WORLD OF JACK STAFF (See Jack Staff)
Image Comics: Feb, 2010 - No. 6, Apr, 2011 ($3.50)

	GD	VG	FN	VF	VF/NM	NM-
1-6-Paul Grist-s/a. 2-Ian Churchill-c						3.50

WEIRD WORLDS (See Adventures Into...)

WEIRD WORLDS (Magazine)
Eerie Publications: V1#10(12/70), V2#1(2/71) - No. 4, Aug, 1971 (52 pgs.)

	GD	VG	FN	VF	VF/NM	NM-
V1#10-Sci-fi/horror	5	10	15	35	63	90
V2#1-4	5	10	15	33	57	80

WEIRD WORLDS (Also see Ironwolf: Fires of the Revolution)
National Periodical Publications: Aug-Sept, 1972 - No. 9, Jan-Feb, 1974; No. 10, Oct-Nov, 1974 (All 20¢ issues)

	GD	VG	FN	VF	VF/NM	NM-
1-Edgar Rice Burrough's John Carter Warlord of Mars & David Innes begin (1st DC app.); Kubert-c	3	6	9	19	30	40
2-4: 2-Infantino/Orlando-c. 3-Murphy Anderson-c. 4-Kaluta-a	2	4	6	10	14	18
5-7: 5-Kaluta-c. 7-Last John Carter.	2	4	6	8	11	14
8-10: 8-Iron Wolf begins by Chaykin (1st app.)	2	4	6	8	11	14

NOTE: *Neal Adams a-2i, 3i. John Carter by Andersonin #1-3. Chaykin c-7, 8. Kaluta a-4; c-4-6, 10. Orlando a-4i; c-2, 3, 4i. Wrightson a-2i, 4i.*

WEIRD WORLDS
DC Comics: Mar, 2011 - No. 6, Aug, 2011 ($3.99, limited series)

	GD	VG	FN	VF	VF/NM	NM-
1-6-Short stories of Lobo, Garbage Man and Tanga; Ordway-a; Maguire-s/a; Lopresti-s/a						4.00

WELCOME BACK, KOTTER (TV) (See Limited Collectors' Edition #57 for unpublished #11)

We Live #4 © Miranda Brothers

Werewolf By Night (2020 series) #1 © MAR

West Coast Avengers #45 © MAR

	GD 2.0	VG 4.0	FN 6.0	VF 8.0	VF/NM 9.0	NM- 9.2

National Periodical Publ./DC Comics: Nov, 1976 - No. 10, Mar-Apr, 1978

1-Sparling-a(p)	3	6	9	18	28	38
2-10: 3-Estrada-a	2	4	6	11	16	20

WELCOME SANTA (See March of Comics #63,183)

WELCOME TO THE LITTLE SHOP OF HORRORS
Roger Corman's Cosmic Comics: May, 1995 -No. 3, July, 1995 ($2.50, limited series)

1-3						5.00

WELCOME TO TRANQUILITY
DC Comics (WildStorm): Feb, 2007 - No. 12, Jan, 2008 ($2.99)

1-12: 1-Simone-s/Googe-a; two covers by Googe and Campbell. 8-Pearson-a						3.00
...: Armageddon 1 (1/08, $2.99) Gage-s/Googe-a						3.00
...: One Foot in the Grave 1-6 (7/10 - No. 6, 2/11, $3.99) Simone-s/Domingues-a						4.00
...: One Foot in the Grave TPB (2011, $17.99) r/mini-series #1-6						18.00
... Book One TPB (2008, $19.99) r/#1-6 and variant cover gallery						20.00
... Book Two TPB (2008, $19.99) r/#7-12; sketch pages						20.00

WE LIVE
AfterShock Comics: Oct, 2020 - Present ($4.99, limited series)

1-5-Inaki Miranda-s/a; Roy Miranda-s						5.00

WELLS FARGO (See Tales of...)

WELLINGTON
IDW Publishing: Dec, 2019 - Present ($3.99)

1-3-Aaron Mahnke & Delilah S. Dawson-s/Piotr Kowalski-a; 2 covers on each						4.00

WENDY AND THE NEW KIDS ON THE BLOCK
Harvey Comics: Mar, 1991 - No. 3, July, 1991 ($1.25)

1-3						5.00

WENDY DIGEST
Harvey Comics: Oct, 1990 - No. 5, Mar, 1992 ($1.75, digest size)

1-5						4.00

WENDY PARKER COMICS
Atlas Comics (OMC): July, 1953 - No. 8, July, 1954

1	37	74	111	222	361	500
2	28	56	84	165	270	375
3-8	22	44	66	132	216	300

WENDY, THE GOOD LITTLE WITCH (TV)
Harvey Publ.: 8/60 - #82, 11/73; #83, 8/74 - #93, 4/76; #94, 9/90 - #97, 12/90

1-Wendy & Casper the Friendly Ghost begin	37	74	111	274	612	1000
2	12	24	36	84	185	285
3-5	9	18	27	62	126	190
6-10	7	14	21	44	82	120
11-20	5	10	15	34	60	85
21-30	4	8	12	27	44	60
31-50	3	6	9	17	26	35
51-64,66-69	2	4	6	13	18	22
65 (2/71)-Wendy origin.	3	6	9	16	24	32
70-74: All 52 pg. Giants	3	6	9	16	23	30
75-93	2	4	6	9	13	16
94-97 (1990, $1.00-c): 94-Has #194 on-c						5.00

(See Casper the Friendly Ghost #20 & Harvey Hits #7, 16, 21, 23, 27, 30, 33)

WENDY THE GOOD LITTLE WITCH (2nd Series)
Harvey Comics: Apr, 1991 - No. 15, Aug, 1994 ($1.00/$1.25 #7-11/$1.50 #12-15)

1-15-Reprints Wendy & Casper stories. 12-Bunny app.						3.00

WENDY WITCH WORLD
Harvey Publications: 10/61; No. 2, 9/62 - No. 52, 12/73; No. 53, 9/74

1-(25¢, 68 pg. Giants begin)	12	24	36	84	185	285
2-5	7	14	21	44	82	120
6-10	5	10	15	33	57	80
11-20	4	8	12	27	44	60
21-30	3	6	9	21	33	45
31-39: 39-Last 68 pg. issue	3	6	9	16	24	32
40-45: 52 pg. issues	2	4	6	13	18	22
46-53	2	4	6	9	13	16

WE ONLY FIND THEM WHEN THEY'RE DEAD
BOOM! Studios: Sept, 2020 - Present ($3.99)

1-5-Al Ewing-s/Simone Di Meo-a						4.00

WEREWOLF (Super Hero) (Also see Dracula & Frankenstein)
Dell Publishing Co.: Dec, 1966 - No. 3, April, 1967

1-1st app.	4	8	12	23	37	50
2,3	3	6	9	16	23	30

WEREWOLF BY NIGHT (See Giant-Size..., Marvel Spotlight #2-4 & Power Record Comics)
Marvel Comics Group: Sept, 1972 - No. 43, Mar, 1977

1-Ploog-a cont'd. from Marvel Spotlight #4	17	34	51	117	259	400
2	7	14	21	44	82	120
3-5	5	10	15	33	57	80
6-10	4	8	12	27	44	60
11-14,16-20	3	6	9	19	30	40
15-New origin Werewolf; Dracula-c/story cont'd from Tomb of Dracula #18; classic Ploog-c	6	12	18	37	66	95
21-31	3	6	9	15	22	28
32-Origin & 1st app. Moon Knight (8/75)	190	380	570	1140	1870	2600
33-2nd app. Moon Knight	14	28	42	96	211	325
34,36,38-43	3	6	9	14	20	26
35-Starlin/Wrightson-c	3	6	9	19	30	40
37-Moon Knight app; part Wrightson-c	7	14	21	46	86	125
38,39-(30¢-c variants, limited distribution)(5,7/76)	5	10	15	31	53	75

NOTE: ***Bolle** a-6i. **G. Kane** a-11p, 12p; c-21, 22, 24-30, 34p. **Mooney** a-7i. **Ploog** 1-4p, 5, 6p, 7p, 13-16p; c-5-8, 13-16. **Reinman** a-8i. **Sutton** a(i)-9, 11, 16, 35.*

WEREWOLF BY NIGHT (Vol. 2, continues in Strange Tales #1 (9/98))
Marvel Comics Group: Feb, 1998 - No. 6, July, 1998 ($2.99)

1-6-Manco-a: 2-Two covers. 6-Ghost Rider-c/app.						3.00

WEREWOLF BY NIGHT
Marvel Comics: Dec, 2020 - No. 4, Mar, 2021 ($3.99)

1-4: 1-Intro. Jake Gomez; Scot Eaton-a						4.00

WEREWOLVES & VAMPIRES (Magazine)
Charlton Comics: 1962 (One Shot)

1	9	18	27	60	120	180

WEREWOLVES ON THE MOON: VERSUS VAMPIRES
Dark Horse Comics: June, 2009 - No. 3 ($3.50, limited series)

1,2-Dave Land-s & Fillbach Brothers-s/a						3.50

WE STAND ON GUARD
Image Comics: Jul, 2015 - No. 6, Dec, 2015 ($2.99, limited series)

1-U.S. invasion of Canada; Vaughan-s/Skroce-a						5.00
2-6						3.00

WEST COAST AVENGERS
Marvel Comics Group: Sept, 1984 - No. 4, Dec, 1984 (lim. series, Mando paper)

1-Origin & 1st app. W.C. Avengers (Hawkeye, Iron Man, Mockingbird & Tigra)	2	4	6	10	14	18
2-4						6.00

WEST COAST AVENGERS (Becomes Avengers West Coast #48 on)
Marvel Comics Group: Oct, 1985 - No. 47, Aug, 1989

V2#1	2	4	6	10	14	18
2-41						4.00
42-44,46,47: 42-Byrne-a(p)/scripts begin. 46-Byrne-c; 1st app. Great Lakes Avengers						4.00
45-(6/89) 1st app. Vision in all-white exterior; cover swipe of Avengers #57	6	12	18	41	76	110
Annual 1-3 (1986-1988): 3-Evolutionary War app.						5.00
Annual 4 (1989, $2.00)-Atlantis Attacks; Byrne/Austin-a						5.00

WEST COAST AVENGERS
Marvel Comics: Oct, 2018 - No. 10, Jun, 2019 ($4.99/$3.99)

1-($4.99) Hawkeye, Kate Bishop, Gwenpool, America, Kid Omega, Fuse team						5.00
2-10-($3.99) 2-4-Tigra app. 4-M.O.D.O.K. app. 6-Marvel Boy returns						4.00

WESTERN ACTION
I. W. Enterprises: No. 7, 1964

7-Reprints Cow Puncher #? by Avon	2	4	6	9	13	16

WESTERN ACTION
Atlas/Seaboard Publ.: Feb, 1975

1-Kid Cody by Wildey & The Comanche Kid stories; intro. The Renegade	2	4	6	11	16	20

WESTERN ACTION THRILLERS
Dell Publishers: Apr, 1937 (10¢, square binding; 100 pgs.)

1-Buffalo Bill, The Texas Kid, Laramie Joe, Two-Gun Thompson, & Wild West Bill app.	132	264	396	845	1448	2050

WESTERN ADVENTURES COMICS (Western Love Trails #7 on)
Ace Magazines: Oct, 1948 - No. 6, Aug, 1949

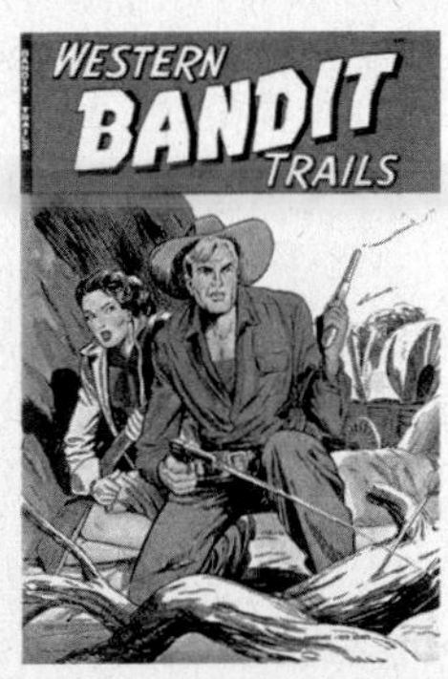

Western Bandit Trails #1 © STJ

Western Fighters #4 © HILL

Western Hearts #1 © STD

GD VG FN VF VF/NM NM-
2.0 4.0 6.0 8.0 9.0 9.2

nn(#1)-Sheriff Sal, The Cross-Draw Kid, Sam Bass begin
24 48 72 142 234 325

nn(#2)(12/48) 14 28 42 82 121 160

nn(#3)(2/49)-Used in **SOTI**, pgs. 30,31 15 30 45 83 124 165

4-6 13 26 39 74 105 135

WESTERN BANDITS
Avon Periodicals: 1952 (Painted-c)

1-Butch Cassidy, The Daltons by Larsen; Kinstler-a; c-part-r/paperback Avon Western Novel #1 21 42 63 126 206 285

WESTERN BANDIT TRAILS (See Approved Comics)
St. John Publishing Co.: Jan, 1949 - No. 3, July, 1949

1-Tuska-a; Baker-c; Blue Monk, Ventrilo app. 39 78 117 231 378 525

2-Baker-c 34 68 102 199 325 450

3-Baker-c/a; Tuska-a 39 78 117 231 378 525

WESTERN COMICS (See Super DC Giant #15)
National Per. Publ: Jan-Feb, 1948 - No. 85, Jan-Feb, 1961 (1-27: 52pgs.)

1-Wyoming Kid & his horse Racer, The Vigilante in "Jesse James Rides Again" (Meskin-a), Cowboy Marshal, Rodeo Rick begin 81 162 243 518 884 1250

2 36 72 108 216 351 485

3,4-Last Vigilante 33 66 99 194 317 440

5-Nighthawk & his horse Nightwind begin (not in #6); Captain Tootsie by Beck
29 58 87 170 278 385

6,7,9,10 21 42 63 126 206 285

8-Origin Wyoming Kid; 2 pg. pin-ups of rodeo queens
34 68 102 204 332 460

11-20 18 36 54 107 169 230

21-40: 24-Starr-a. 27-Last 52 pgs. 28-Flag-c 15 30 45 84 127 170

41,42,44-49: 49-Last precode issue (2/55) 14 28 42 82 121 160

43-Pow Wow Smith begins, ends #85 15 30 45 83 124 165

50-60 13 26 39 72 101 130

61-85-Last Wyoming Kid. 77-Origin Matt Savage Trail Boss. 82-1st app. Fleetfoot, Pow Wow's girlfriend 10 20 30 58 79 100

NOTE: ***G. Kane, Infantino** art in most. **Meskin** a-1-4. **Moreira** a-28-39. **Post** a-3-5.*

WESTERN CRIME BUSTERS
Trojan Magazines: Sept, 1950 - No. 10, Mar-Apr, 1952

1-Six-Gun Smith, Wilma West, K-Bar-Kate, & Fighting Bob Dale begin; headlight-a
39 78 117 231 378 525

2 20 40 60 115 188 260

3-5: 3-Myron Fass-c 18 36 54 109 172 235

6-Wood-a 33 66 99 194 317 440

7-Six-Gun Smith by Wood 33 66 99 194 317 440

8 18 36 54 109 172 235

9-Tex Gordon & Wilma West by Wood; Lariat Lucy app.
33 66 99 194 317 440

10-Wood-a 30 60 90 177 289 400

WESTERN CRIME CASES (Formerly Indian Warriors #7,8; becomes The Outlaws #10 on)
Star Publications: No. 9, Dec, 1951

9-White Rider & Super Horse; L. B. Cole-c 24 48 72 142 234 325

WESTERNER, THE (Wild Bill Pecos)
"Wanted" Comic Group/Toytown/Patches: No. 14, June, 1948 - No. 41, Dec, 1951 (#14-31: 52 pgs.)

14 15 30 45 88 137 185

15-17,19-21: 19-Meskin-a 10 20 30 54 72 90

18,22-25-Krigstein-a 11 22 33 60 83 105

26(4/50)-Origin & 1st app. Calamity Kate, series ends #32; Krigstein-a
14 28 42 78 112 145

27-Krigstein-a(2) 13 26 39 74 105 135

28-41: 33-Quest app. 37-Lobo, the Wolf Boy begins 8 16 24 40 50 60

NOTE: ***Mort Lawrence** a-20-27, 29, 37, 39; c-19, 22-24, 26, 27. **Leav** c-14-18, 20, 31. **Syd Shores** a-39; c-34, 35, 37-41.*

WESTERNER, THE
Super Comics: 1964

Super Reprint 15-17: 15-r/Oklahoma Kid #? 16-r/Crack West. #65; Severin-c; Crandall-r. 17-r/Blazing Western #2; Severin-c 2 4 6 8 11 14

WESTERN FIGHTERS
Hillman Periodicals/Star Publ.: Apr-May, 1948 - V4#7, Mar-Apr, 1953 (#1-V3#2: 52 pgs.)

V1#1-Simon & Kirby-c 39 78 117 231 378 525

2-Not Kirby-a 15 30 45 84 127 170

3-Fuje-c 14 28 42 76 108 140

GD VG FN VF VF/NM NM-
2.0 4.0 6.0 8.0 9.0 9.2

4-Krigstein, Ingels, Fuje-a 14 28 42 81 118 155

5,6,8,9,12 11 22 33 62 86 110

7,10-Krigstein-a 13 26 39 72 101 130

11-Williamson/Frazetta-a 31 62 93 186 303 420

V2#1-Krigstein-a 13 26 39 72 101 130

2-12: 4-Berg-a 9 18 27 50 65 80

V3#1-11,V4#1,4-7 9 18 27 47 61 75

12,V4#2,3-Krigstein-a 13 26 39 72 101 130

3-D 1(12/53, 25¢, Star Publ.)-Came w/glasses; L. B. Cole-c
37 74 111 222 361 500

NOTE: ***Kinstlerish** a-V2#6, 8, 9, 12; V3#2, 5-7, 11, 12; V4#1(plus cover). **McWilliams** a-11. **Powell** a-V2#2. **Reinman** a-1-12, V4#3. **Rowich** c-5, 6i. **Starr** a-5.*

WESTERN FRONTIER
P. L. Publishers: Apr-May, 1951 - No. 7, 1952

1 15 30 45 90 140 190

2 10 20 30 56 76 95

3-7 9 18 27 50 65 80

WESTERN GUNFIGHTERS (1st Series) (Apache Kid #11-19)
Atlas Comics (CPS): No. 20, June, 1956 - No. 27, Aug, 1957

20 16 32 48 98 154 210

21-Crandall-a 16 32 48 98 154 210

22-Wood & Powell-a 22 44 66 132 216 300

23,24: 23-Williamson-a. 24-Toth-a 16 32 48 98 154 210

25-27 14 28 42 81 118 155

NOTE: ***Berg** a-20. **Colan** a-20, 26, 27. **Crandall** a-21. **Heath** a-25. **Maneely** a-24, 25; c-22, 23, 25. **Morisi** a-24. **Morrow** a-26. **Pakula** a-23. **Severin** c-20, 27. **Torres** a-26. **Woodbridge** a-27.*

WESTERN GUNFIGHTERS (2nd Series)
Marvel Comics Group: Aug, 1970 - No. 33, Nov, 1975 (#1-6: 25¢, 68 pgs.)

1-Ghost Rider begins; Fort Rango, Renegades & Gunhawk app.
6 12 18 41 76 110

2,3,5,6: 2-Origin Nightwind (Apache Kid's horse) 3 6 9 21 33 45

4-Barry Smith-a 4 8 12 23 37 50

7-(52 pgs) Origin Ghost Rider retold 3 6 9 19 30 40

8-13: 10-Origin Black Rider. 12-Origin Matt Slade 3 6 9 14 20 25

14-Steranko-c 3 6 9 16 24 32

15-20 2 4 6 10 14 18

21-33 2 4 6 9 13 16

NOTE: ***Baker** r-2, 3. **Colan** r-2. **Drucker** r-3. **Everett** a-6i. **G. Kane** c-29, 31. **Kirby** a-1p(r), 5, 10-12; c-19, 21. **Kubert** r-2. **Maneely** r-2, 10. **Morrow** r-29. **Severin** c-10. **Shores** a-3, 4. **Barry Smith** a-4. **Steranko** c-14. **Sutton** a-1, 2i, 5, 4. **Torres** r-26('57). **Wildey** r-8, 9. **Williamson** r-2, 18. **Woodbridge** r-27('57). Renegades in #4, 5; Ghost Rider in #1-7.*

WESTERN HEARTS
Standard Comics: Dec, 1949 - No. 10, Mar, 1952 (All photo-c)

1-Severin-a; Whip Wilson & Reno Browne photo-c 24 48 72 144 237 330

2-Beverly Tyler & Jerome Courtland photo-c from movie "Palomino"; Williamson/Frazetta-a (2 pgs.) 24 48 72 144 237 330

3-Rex Allen photo-c 15 30 45 84 127 170

4-7,10: 4-Severin & Elder, Al Carreno-a. 5-Ray Milland & Hedy Lamarr photo-c from movie "Copper Canyon". 6-Fred MacMurray & Irene Dunn photo-c from movie "Never a Dull Moment". 7-Jock Mahoney photo-c. 10-Bill Williams & Jane Nigh photo-c
14 28 42 81 118 155

8-Randolph Scott & Janis Carter photo-c from "Santa Fe"; Severin & Elder-a
14 28 42 82 121 160

9-Whip Wilson & Reno Browne photo-c; Severin & Elder-a
15 30 45 85 130 175

WESTERN HERO (Wow Comics #1-69; Real Western Hero #70-75)
Fawcett Publications: No. 76, Mar, 1949 - No. 112, Mar, 1952

76(#1, 52 pgs.)-Tom Mix, Hopalong Cassidy, Monte Hale, Gabby Hayes, Young Falcon (ends #78,80), & Big Bow and Little Arrow (ends #102,105) begin; painted-c begin
16 32 48 94 147 200

77 (52 pgs.) 11 22 33 64 90 115

78,80-82 (52 pgs.): 81-Capt. Tootsie by Beck 11 22 33 60 83 105

79,83 (36 pgs.): 83-Last painted-c 10 20 30 54 72 90

84-86,88-90 (52 pgs.): 84-Photo-c begin, end #112. 86-Last Hopalong Cassidy
10 20 30 53 76 95

87,91,95,99 (36 pgs.): 87-Bill Boyd begins, ends #95
9 18 27 50 65 80

92-94,96-98,101 (52 pgs.): 96-Tex Ritter begins. 101-Red Eagle app.
9 18 27 52 69 85

100 (52 pgs.) 10 20 30 56 76 95

102-111: 102-Begin 36 pg. issues 9 18 27 50 65 80

112-Last issue 9 18 27 52 69 85

NOTE: *1/2 to 1 pg. Rocky Lane (Carnation) in 80-83, 86, 88, 97. Photo covers feature Hopalong Cassidy #84, 86,*

Western Love #2 © Prize

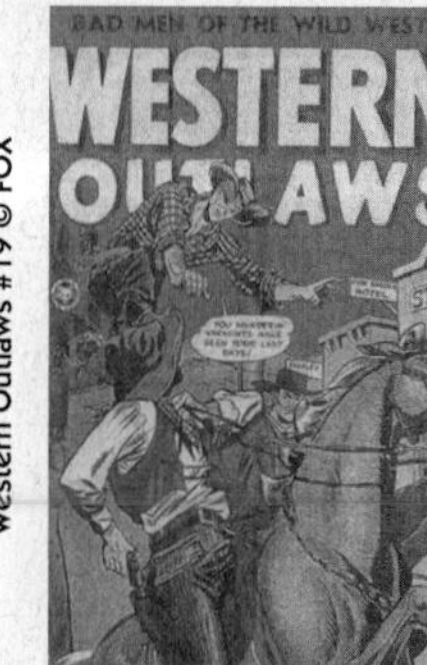

Western Outlaws #19 © FOX

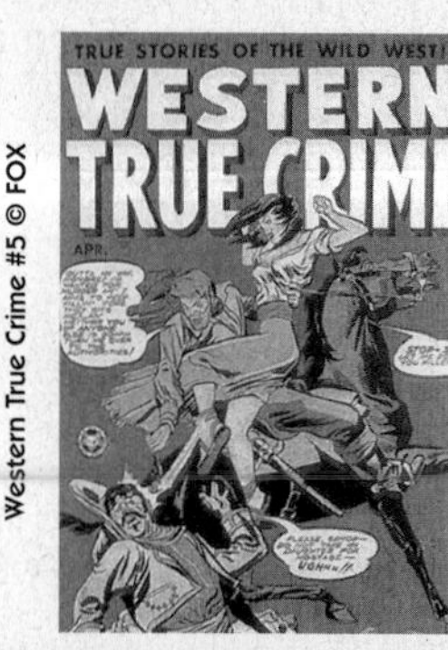

Western True Crime #5 © FOX

	GD	VG	FN	VF	VF/NM	NM-
	2.0	4.0	6.0	8.0	9.0	9.2

89; Tom Mix #85, 87, 90, 92, 94, 97; Monte Hale #88, 91, 93, 95, 98, 100, 104, 107, 110; Tex Ritter #96, 99, 101, 105, 108, 111; Gabby Hayes #103.

WESTERN KID (1st Series)
Atlas Comics (CPC): Dec, 1954 - No. 17, Aug, 1957

1-Origin; The Western Kid (Tex Dawson), his stallion Whirlwind & dog Lightning begin
24 48 72 140 230 320
2 (2/55)-Last pre-code 15 30 45 84 127 170
3-8 14 48 42 76 108 140
9,10-Williamson-a in both (4 pgs. each) 14 28 42 78 112 145
11-17 12 24 36 67 94 120

NOTE: *Ayers a-6, 7. Heck a-3. Maneely c-2-7, 10, 13-15. Romita a-1-17; c-1, 12. Severin c-11, 16, 17.*

WESTERN KID, THE (2nd Series)
Marvel Comics Group: Dec, 1971 - No. 5, Aug, 1972 (All 20¢ issues)

1-Reprints; Romita-c/a(3) 3 6 9 19 30 40
2,4,5: 2-Romita-a; Severin-c. 4-Everett-r 3 6 9 14 20 25
3-Williamson-a 3 6 9 15 22 28

WESTERN KILLERS
Fox Feature Syndicate: nn, July?, 1948; No. 60, Sept, 1948 - No. 64, May, 1949; No. 6, July, 1949

nn(#59?)(nd, F&J Trading Co.)-Range Busters; formerly Blue Beetle #57?
28 56 84 165 270 375
60 (#1, 9/48)-Extreme violence; lingerie panel 29 58 87 172 281 390
61-Jack Cole, Starr-a 23 46 69 136 223 310
62-64, 6 (#6-exist?) 21 42 63 122 199 275

WESTERN LIFE ROMANCES (My Friend Irma #3 on?)
Marvel Comics (IPP): Dec, 1949 - No. 2, Mar, 1950 (52 pgs.)

1-Whip Wilson & Reno Browne photo-c 22 44 66 132 216 300
2-Audie Murphy & Gale Storm photo-c 19 38 57 111 176 240

WESTERN LOVE
Prize Publ.: July-Aug, 1949 - No. 5, Mar-Apr, 1950 (All photo-c & 52 pgs.)

1-S&K-a; Randolph Scott photo-c from movie "Canadian Pacific" (see Prize Comics #76)
32 64 96 192 314 435
2,5-S&K-a: 2-Whip Wilson & Reno Browne photo-c. 5-Dale Robertson photo-c 25 50 75 150 245 340
3,4: 3-Pat Williams photo-c 15 30 45 92 144 195

NOTE: *Meskin & Severin/Elder a-2-5.*

WESTERN LOVE TRAILS (Formerly Western Adventures)
Ace Magazines (A. A. Wyn): No. 7, Nov, 1949 - No. 9, Mar, 1950

7 13 26 39 72 101 130
8,9 10 20 30 54 72 90

WESTERN MARSHAL (See Steve Donovan...)
Dell Publishing Co.: No. 534, 2-4/54 - No. 640, 7/55 (Based on Ernest Haycox's "Trailtown")

Four Color 534 (#1)-Kinstler-a 6 12 18 41 76 110
Four Color 591 (10/54), 613 (2/55), 640-All Kinstler-a 5 10 15 34 60 85

WESTERN OUTLAWS (Junior Comics #9-16; My Secret Life #22 on)
Fox Feature Syndicate: No. 17, Sept, 1948 - No. 21, May, 1949

17-Kamen-a; Iger shop-a in all; 1 pg. "Death and the Devil Pills" r-in Ghostly Weird #122
35 70 105 208 339 470
18-21 20 40 60 115 188 260

WESTERN OUTLAWS
Atlas Comics (ACI No. 1-14/WPI No. 15-21): Feb, 1954 - No. 21, Aug, 1957

1-Heath, Powell-a; Maneely hanging-c 29 58 87 172 281 390
2 15 30 45 88 137 185
3-10: 7-Violent-a by R.Q. Sale 14 28 42 78 112 145
11,14-Williamson-a in both (6 pgs. each) 14 28 42 82 121 160
12,18,20,21: Severin covers 13 26 39 74 105 135
13,15: 13-Baker-a. 15-Torres-a 14 28 42 78 112 145
16-Williamson text illo 13 26 39 74 105 135
17,19-Crandall-a. 17-Williamson text illo 14 28 42 80 115 150

NOTE: *Ayers a-7, 10, 18, 20. Bolle a-21. Colan a-5, 10, 11, 17. Drucker a-11. Everett a-9, 10. Heath a-1; c-3, 4, 8, 16. Kubert a-9p. Maneely a-13, 16, 17, 19; c-1, 5, 7, 9, 10, 12, 13. Morisi a-18. Powell a-3, 16. Romita a-7, 13. Severin a-8, 16, 19; c-17, 18, 20, 21. Tuska a-6, 15.*

WESTERN OUTLAWS & SHERIFFS (Formerly Best Western)
Marvel/Atlas Comics (IPC): No. 60, Dec, 1949 - No. 73, June, 1952

60 (52 pgs.) Photo-c; first Maneely Atlas work 25 50 75 150 245 340
61-65: 61-Photo-c 20 40 60 114 182 250
66-Story contains 5 hangings 20 40 60 115 188 260
67-Cannibalism story 20 40 60 115 188 260
68-72 15 30 45 88 137 185
73-Black Rider story; Everett-c 17 34 51 103 162 220

NOTE: *Maneely a-60-62, 67; c-62, 69-73. Robinson a-68. Sinnott a-70. Tuska a-69-71.*

WESTERN PICTURE STORIES (1st Western comic)
Comics Magazine Company: Feb, 1937 - No. 4, June, 1937

1-Will Eisner-a 258 516 774 1651 2826 4000
2-Will Eisner-a 142 284 426 909 1555 2200
3,4: 3-Eisner-a. 4-Caveman Cowboy story 123 246 369 787 1344 1900

WESTERN PICTURE STORIES (See Giant Comics Edition #6, 11)

WESTERN ROMANCES (See Target...)

WESTERN ROUGH RIDERS
Gillmor Magazines No. 1,4 (Stanmor Publ.): Nov, 1954 - No. 4, May, 1955

1 10 20 30 58 79 100
2-4 8 16 24 42 54 65

WESTERN ROUNDUP (See Dell Giants & Fox Giants)

WESTERN SERENADE
DC Comics: May/June, 1949

nn - Ashcan comic, not distributed to newsstands, only for in-house use (no known sales)

WESTERN TALES (Formerly Witches...)
Harvey Publications: No. 31, Oct, 1955 - No. 33, July-Sept, 1956

31,32-All S&K-a; Davy Crockett app. in each 15 30 45 90 140 190
33-S&K-a; Jim Bowie app. 15 30 45 86 133 180

NOTE: *#32 & 33 contain Boy's Ranch reprints. Kirby c-31.*

WESTERN TALES OF BLACK RIDER (Formerly Black Rider; Gunsmoke Western #32 on)
Atlas Comics (CPS): No. 28, May, 1955 - No. 31, Nov, 1955

28 (#1): The Spider (a villain) dies 24 48 72 140 230 320
29-31 17 34 51 103 162 220

NOTE: *Lawrence a-30. Maneely c-28-30. Severin a-28. Shores c-31.*

WESTERN TEAM-UP
Marvel Comics Group: Nov, 1973 (20¢)

1-Origin & 1st app. The Dakota Kid; Rawhide Kid-r; Gunsmoke Kid-r by Jack Davis
3 6 9 21 33 45

WESTERN THRILLERS (My Past Confessions #7 on)
Fox Feature Syndicate/M.S. Distr. No. 52: Aug, 1948 - No. 6, June, 1949; No. 52, 1954?

1- "Velvet Rose" (Kamenish-a); "Two-Gun Sal", "Striker Sisters" (all women outlaws issue); Brodsky-c 61 122 183 390 670 950
2 29 58 87 170 278 385
3-6: 4,5-Bakerish-a; 5-Butch Cassidy app. 22 44 66 128 209 290
52-(Reprint, M.S. Dist.)-1954? No date given (becomes My Love Secret #53)
11 22 33 62 86 110

WESTERN THRILLERS (Cowboy Action #5 on)
Atlas Comics (ACI): Nov, 1954 - No. 4, Feb, 1955 (All-r/Western Outlaws & Sheriffs)

1 21 42 63 122 199 275
2-4 14 28 42 78 112 145

NOTE: *Heath c-3. Maneely a-1; c-2. Powell a-4. Robinson a-4. Romita c-4. Tuska a-2.*

WESTERN TRAILS (Ringo Kid Starring in...)
Atlas Comics (SAI): May, 1957 - No. 2, July, 1957

1-Ringo Kid app.; Severin-c 17 34 51 100 158 215
2-Severin-c 12 24 36 69 97 125

NOTE: *Bolle a-1, 2. Maneely a-1, 2. Severin c-1, 2.*

WESTERN TRUE CRIME (Becomes My Confessions)
Fox Feature Syndicate: No. 15, Aug, 1948 - No. 6, June, 1949

15(#1)-Kamen-a; formerly Zoot #14 (5/48)? 36 72 108 211 343 475
16(#2)-Kamenish-a; headlight panels, violence 25 50 75 150 245 340
3-Kamen-a 27 54 81 160 263 365
4-6: 4-Johnny Craig-a 16 32 48 98 154 210

WESTERN WINNERS (Formerly All-Western Winners; becomes Black Rider #8 on & Romance Tales #7 on?)
Marvel Comics (CDS): No. 5, June, 1949 - No. 7, Dec, 1949

5-Two-Gun Kid, Kid Colt, Black Rider; Shores-c 34 68 102 199 325 450
6-Two-Gun Kid, Black Rider, Heath Kid Colt story; Captain Tootsie by C.C. Beck
27 54 81 162 266 370
7-Randolph Scott Photo-c w/true stories about the West
27 54 81 162 266 370

WEST OF THE PECOS (See Zane Grey, 4-Color #222)

WESTWARD HO, THE WAGONS (Disney)(Also see Classic Comics #14)
Dell Publishing Co.: No. 738, Sept, 1956 (Movie)

Four Color 738-Fess Parker photo-c 8 16 24 54 102 150

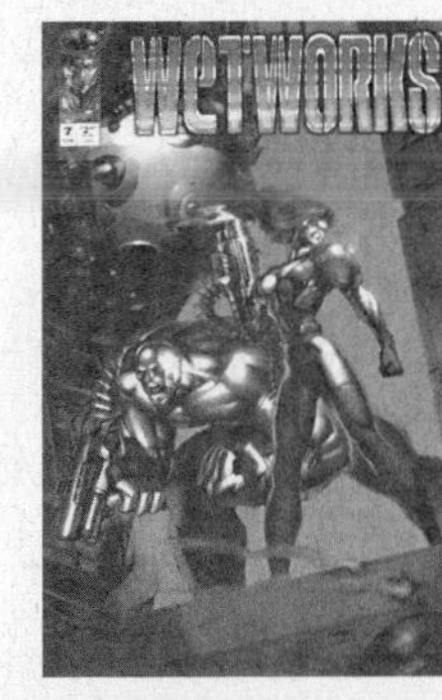

Wetworks #7 © WSP

What If? #65 © MAR

What If...? #105 © MAR

	GD	VG	FN	VF	VF/NM	NM-
	2.0	4.0	6.0	8.0	9.0	9.2

WET HOT AMERICAN SUMMER (Based on the 2001 movie and Netflix series)
BOOM! Studios: Nov, 2018 ($19.99, squarebound graphic novel)

nn-Christopher Hastings-s/Noah Hayes-a; takes place after the 1st week of camp 20.00

WE3
DC Comics (Vertigo): Oct, 2004 - No. 3, May, 2005 ($2.95, limited series)

1-3-Domestic animal cyborgs: Grant Morrison-s/Frank Quitely-a 3.00
TPB (2005, $12.99) r/series 13.00

WETWORKS (See WildC.A.T.S: Covert Action Teams #2)
Image Comics (WildStorm): June, 1994 - No. 43, Aug, 1998 ($1.95/$2.50)

1-"July" on-c; gatefold wraparound-c; Portacio/Williams-c/a 4.00
1-Chicago Comicon edition 6.00
1-(2/98, $4.95) "3-D Edition" w/glasses 5.00
2-4 3.00
2-Alternate Portacio-c, see Deathblow #5 6.00
5-7,9-24: 5-($2.50). 13-Portacio-c. 16,17-Fire From Heaven Pts. 4 & 11 3.00
8 ($1.95)-Newstand, Wildstorm Rising Pt. 7 3.00
8 ($2.50)-Direct Market, Wildstorm Rising Pt. 7 3.00
25-($3.95) 4.00
26-43: 32-Variant-c by Pat Lee & Charest. 39,40-Stormwatch app. 42-Gen 13 app. 3.00
Sourcebook 1 (10/94, $2.50)-Text & illustrations (no comics) 3.00
Voyager Pack (8/97, $3.50)- #32 w/Phantom Guard preview 4.00

WETWORKS
DC Comics (WildStorm): Nov, 2006 - No. 15, Jan, 2008 ($2.99)

1-15: 1-Carey-s/Portacio-a; two covers by Portacio and Van Sciver. 2-Golden var-c
3-Pearson var-c. 4-Powell var-c 3.00
...: Armageddon 1 (1/08, $2.99) Gage-s/Badeaux-a 3.00
... Book One (2007, $14.99) r/#1-5 and stories from Eye of the storm Annual and
Coup D'Etat Afterword 15.00
... Book Two (2008, $14.99) r/#6-9,13-15 15.00
...: Mutations 1 (11/10, $3.99) Grevioux & Long-s/Gopez-a 4.00

WETWORKS/VAMPIRELLA (See Vampirella/Wetworks)
Image Comics (WildStorm Productions): July, 1997 ($2.95, one-shot)

1-Gil Kane-c 4.00

WHACK (Satire)
St. John Publishing Co. (Jubilee Publ.): Oct, 1953 - No. 3, May, 1954

1-(3-D, 25¢)-Kubert-a; Maurer-c; came w/glasses 28 56 84 165 270 375
2,3-Kubert-a in each. 2-Bing Crosby on-c; Mighty Mouse & Steve Canyon parodies.
3-Li'l Orphan Annie parody; Maurer-c 16 32 48 98 154 210

WHACKY (See Wacky)

WHA...HUH?
Marvel Comics: 2005 ($3.99, one-shot)

1-Humor spoofs of Marvel characters; Mahfood-a/c; Bendis, Stan Lee and others-s 4.00

WHAM COMICS (See Super Spy)
Centaur Publications: Nov, 1940 - No. 2, Dec, 1940

1-The Sparkler, The Phantom Rider, Craig Carter and his Magic Ring, Detecto, Copper Slug,
Speed Silvers by Gustavson, Speed Centaur & Jon Linton (s/f) begin
206 412 618 1318 2259 3200
2-Origin Blue Fire & Solarman; The Buzzard app. 168 336 504 1075 1838 2600

WHAM-O GIANT COMICS
Wham-O Mfg. Co. : April, 1967 (98¢, newspaper size, one-shot)(Six issue subscription was advertised)

1-Radian & Goody Bumpkin by Wood; 1 pg. Stanley-a; Fine, Tufts-a; flying saucer reports;
wraparound-c 10 20 30 66 138 210

WHATEVER HAPPENED TO BARON VON SHOCK?
Image Comics: May, 2010 - No. 4, Nov, 2010 ($3.99, unfinished limited series)

1-4-Rob Zombie-s/Donny Hadiwidjaja-a 4.00

WHAT IF? (1st Series) (What If? Featuring... #13 & #?-33) (Also see Hero Initiative)
Marvel Comics Group: Feb, 1977 - No. 47, Oct, 1984; June, 1988 (All 52 pgs.)

1-Brief origin Spider-Man, Fantastic Four 5 10 15 31 53 75
2-Origin The Hulk retold 3 6 9 14 20 25
3-5: 3-Avengers. 4-Invaders. 5-Capt. America 2 4 6 9 13 16
6-9,13,17: 7-Betty Brant as Spider-Girl. 8-Daredevil; Spidey parody. 9-Origins Venus,
Marvel Boy, Human Robot, 3-D Man. 13-Conan app.; John Buscema-c/a(p).
17-Ghost Rider & Son of Satan app. 2 4 6 8 10 12
10-(8/78) What if Jane Foster was Thor 8 16 24 54 102 150
11,12,14-16: 11-Marvel Bullpen as F.F. 1 3 4 6 8 10
18-26,29: 18-Dr. Strange. 19-Spider-Man. 22-Origin Dr. Doom retold
1 2 3 5 6 8
27-X-Men app.; Miller-c 3 6 9 14 20 26
28-Daredevil by Miller; Ghost Rider app. 2 4 6 13 18 22
30-"What If...Spider-Man's Clone Had Lived?" 2 4 6 9 13 16
31-Begin $1.00-c; featuring Wolverine & the Hulk; X-Men app.; death of Hulk, Wolverine &
Magneto 4 8 12 25 40 55
32-34,36-47: 32,36-Byrne-a. 34-Marvel crew each draw themselves. 37-Old X-Men &
Silver Surfer app. 39-Thor battles Conan 6.00
35-What if Elektra had lived?; Miller/Austin-a. 2 4 6 8 11 14
Special 1 ($1.50, 6/88)-Iron Man, F.F., Thor app. 6.00
... Classic Vol. 1 TPB (2004, $24.99) r/#1-6; checklist 25.00
... Classic Vol. 2 TPB (2005, $24.99) r/#7-12 25.00
... Classic Vol. 3 TPB (2006, $24.99) r/#14,15,17-20 25.00
... Classic Vol. 4 TPB (2007, $24.99) r/#21-26; checklist of all What If? series/issues 25.00

NOTE: ***Austin** a-27p, 32i, 34, 35i; c-35i, 36i. **J. Buscema** a-13p, 15p; c-10, 13p, 23p. **Byrne** a-32i, 36; c-36p. **Colan** a-21p; c-17p, 18p, 21p. **Ditko** a-35, Special 1. **Golden** c-29, 40-42. **Guice** a-40p. **Gil Kane** a-3p, 24p; c(p)-2-4, 7, 8. **Kirby** a-11p; c-9p, 11p. **Layton** a-32i, 33i; c-30, 32p, 33i, 34. **Mignola** c-39i. **Miller** a-28p, 32i, 34(1), 35p; c-27, 28p. **Mooney** a-8i, 30i. **Perez** a-15p. **Robbins** a-4p. **Sienkiewicz** c-43-46. **Simonson** a-15p, 32i. **Starlin** a-32i. **Stevens** a-8, 16i(part). **Sutton** a-2i, 18p, 28. **Tuska** a-5p. **Weiss** a-37p.*

WHAT IF...? (2nd Series)
Marvel Comics: V2#1, July, 1989 - No. 114, Nov, 1998 ($1.25/$1.50)

V2#1-...The Avengers Had Lost the Evolutionary War 6.00
2-5: 2-Daredevil, Punisher app. 4.00
6-X-Men app. 5.00
7-Wolverine app.; Liefeld-c/a(1st on Wolvie?) 6.00
8,10,11,13-15,17-30: 10-Punisher app. 11-Fantastic Four app.; McFarlane-c(i).13-Prof. X;
Jim Lee-c. 14-Capt. Marvel; Lim/Austin-c.15-F.F.; Capullo-c/a(p). 17-Spider-Man/Kraven.
18-F.F. 19-Vision. 20,21-Spider-Man. 22-Silver Surfer by Lim/Austin-c/a 23-X-Men.
24-Wolverine; Punisher app. 25-(52 pgs.)-Wolverine app. 26-Punisher app. 27-Namor/F.F.
28,29-Capt. America. 29-Swipes cover to Avengers #4. 30-(52 pgs.)-F.F. 4.00
9,12-X-Men 5.00
16-Wolverine battles Conan; Red Sonja app.; X-Men cameo 5.00
31-40,42-48: 31-Cosmic Spider-Man & Venom app.; Hobgoblin cameo. 32,33-Phoenix;
X-Men app. 35-Fantastic Five (w/Spidey). 36-Avengers vs. Guardians of the Galaxy.
37-Wolverine; Thibert-c(i). 38-Thor; Rogers-p(part). 40-Storm; X-Men app. 42-Spider-Man.
43-Wolverine. 44-Venom/Punisher. 45-Ghost Rider. 46-Cable. 47-Magneto 3.00
41,50: 41-(52 pgs.)-Avengers vs. Galactus. 50-(52 pgs.)-Foil embossed-c; "What If Hulk Had
Killed Wolverine" 2 4 6 8 10 12
49-Infinity Gauntlet w/Silver Surfer & Thanos 3 6 9 19 30 40
51-(7/93) "What If the Punisher Became Captain America" (see it happen in 2007's Punisher
War Journal #6-10) 6.00
52-99,101-103: 52-Dr. Doom. 54-Death's Head. 57-Punisher as Shield. 58-"What if Punisher
Had Killed Spider-Man" w/cover similar to Amazing S-M #129. 59-...Wolverine led Alpha
Flight. 60-X-Men Wedding Album. 61-Bound-in card sheet. 61,86,88-Spider-Man.
74,77,81,84,85-X-Men. 76-Last app. Watcher in title. 78-Bisley-c. 80-Hulk. 87-Sabretooth.
89-Fantastic Four. 90-Cyclops & Havok. 91-The Hulk. 93-Wolverine. 94-Juggernaut.
95-Ghost Rider 3.00
100-($2.99, double-sized) Gambit and Rogue, Fantastic Four
1 2 3 5 6 8
104-Silver Surfer, Thanos vs. Impossible Man 1 2 3 5 6 8
105-Spider-Girl (Peter Parker's daughter) debut; Sienkiewicz-a; (Betty Brant also app. as
a Spider-Girl in What If? (1st series) #7) 5 10 15 31 53 75
106,107,109-114: 106-Gambit. 111-Wolverine. 114-Secret Wars 3.00
108-Avengers vs. Carnage 2 4 6 9 14 18
#(-1) Flashback (7/97) 3.00

WHAT IF...? (one-shots)
Marvel Comics: Feb, 2005 ($2.99)

... Aunt May Had Died Instead of Uncle Ben? - Brubaker-s/DiVito-a/Brase-c 3.00
... Dr. Doom Had Become The Thing? - Karl Kesel-s/Paul Smith-a/c 3.00
... General Ross Had Become The Hulk? - Peter David-s/Pat Olliffe-a/Gary Frank-c 3.00
... Jessica Jones Had Joined The Avengers? - Bendis-s/Gaydos-a/McNiven-c 3.00
... Karen Page Had Lived? - Bendis-s/Lark-a/c 3.00
... Magneto and Professor X Had Formed The X-Men Together? - Claremont-s/Raney-a 3.00
What If...: Why Not? TPB (2005, $16.99) r/one-shots 17.00

WHAT IF... (one-shots)
Marvel Comics: Feb, 2006 ($2.99)

... : Captain America - Fought in the Civil War?; Bedard-s/Di Giandomenico-a 3.00
... : Daredevil - The Devil Who Dares; Daredevil in feudal Japan; Veitch-s/Edwards-a 3.00
... : Fantastic Four - Were Cosmonauts?; Marshall Rogers-a/c; Mike Carey-s 3.00
... : Submariner - Grew Up on Land?; Pak-s/Lopez-a 3.00
... : Thor - Was the Herald of Galactus?; Kirkman-s/Oeming-a/c 3.00
... : Wolverine - In the Prohibition Era; Way-s/Proctor-a/Harris-c 3.00
What If: Mirror Mirror TPB (2006, $16.99) r/one-shots; design pages and Rogers sketches 17.00

WHAT IF ?... (one-shots altering recent Marvel "event" series)
Marvel Comics: Jan, 2007 - Feb, 2007 ($3.99)

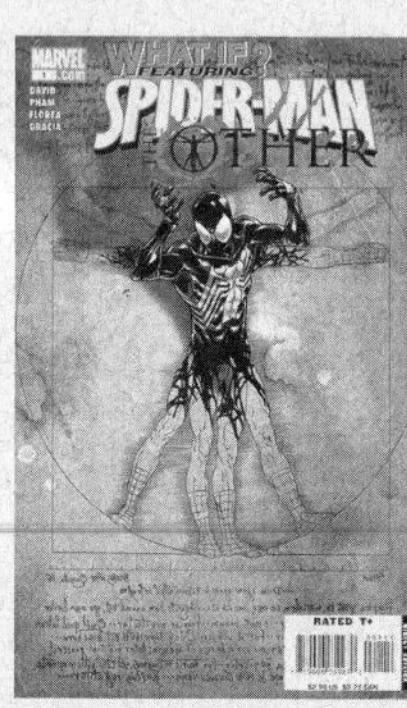

What If?... Spider-Man The Other #1 © MAR

Where Creatures Roam #3 © MAR

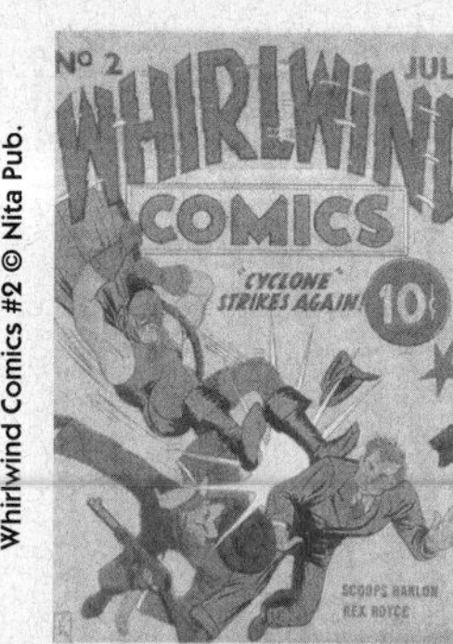

Whirlwind Comics #2 © Nita Pub.

	GD	VG	FN	VF	VF/NM	NM-
	2.0	4.0	6.0	8.0	9.0	9.2

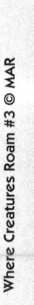

... Avengers Disassembled; Parker-s/Lopresti-a/c 4.00
... Spider-Man The Other; Peter David-s/Khoi Pham-a; Venom app. 4.00
... Wolverine Enemy of the State; Robinson-s/DiGiandomenico-a/Alexander-c 4.00
... X-Men Age of Apocalypse; Remender-s/Wilkins-a/Djurdjevic-c 4.00
... X-Men Deadly Genesis; Hine-s/Yardin-a/c 4.00
What If?: Event Horizon TPB (2007, $16.99) r/one-shots; design pages and cover sketches 17.00

WHAT IF ?... (one-shots altering recent Marvel "event" series)
Marvel Comics: Dec, 2007 - Feb, 2008 ($3.99)

... Annihilation; Nova, Iron Man, Captain America app. 2 4 6 9 12 15
... Civil War; 2 covers by Silvestri & Djurdjevic 1 3 4 6 8 10
... Planet Hulk; Pagulayan-c; Kirk, Sandoval & Hembeck-a 10.00
... Spider-Man vs. Wolverine; Romita Jr.-c; Henry-a; Nick Fury app. 6.00
... X-Men - Rise and Fall of the Shi'ar Empire; Coipel-c 4.00
What If?: Civil War TPB (2008, $16.99) r/one-shots; design pages and cover sketches 17.00

WHAT IF ?... (one-shots altering recent Marvel "event" series)
Marvel Comics: Feb, 2009 ($3.99) (Serialized back-up Runaways story in each issue)

... Fallen Son; if Iron Man had died instead of Capt. America; McGuinness-c 4.00
... House of M; if the Scarlet Witch had said "No more powers" instead; Cheung-c 4.00
... Newer Fantastic Four; team of Spider-Man, Hulk, Iron Man and Wolverine 4.00
... Secret Wars; if Doctor Doom had kept the Beyonder's power; origin re-told 4.00
... Spider-Man Back in Black; if Mary Jane had been shot instead of Aunt May 4.00

WHAT IF ?... (one-shots)
Marvel Comics: Feb, 2010 ($3.99)

... Astonishing X-Men; if Ord resurrected Jean Grey; Campbell-c 4.00
... Daredevil vs. Elektra; Kayanan-a; Klaus Janson-c swipe of Daredevil #168 4.00
... Secret Invasion; if the Skrulls succeeded; Yu-c 4.00
... Spider-Man: House of M; if Gwen Stacy survived the House of M; Dodson-c 4.00
... World War Hulk; if the heroes lost the war; Romita Jr.-c 4.00

WHAT IF ?... (one-shots) (4 part Deadpool back-up story in all but #200)
(Also see Venom/Deadpool: What If?)
Marvel Comics: Feb, 2011 ($3.99)

... #200 ($4.99) Siege on cover; if Osborn won the Siege of Asgard; Stan Lee back-up 5.00
... Dark Reign; if Norman Osborn was killed; Tanaka-a/Deodato-c 4.00
... Iron Man: Demon in an Armor; if Tony Stark became Dr. Doom; Nolan-a 4.00
... Spider-Man; if Spider-Man killed Kraven; Jimenez-c 4.00
... Wolverine: Father; if Wolverine raised Daken; Tocchini-a; Yu-a 4.00

WHAT IF ?... (one-shots)
Marvel Comics: Dec, 2018 ($3.99)

... Ghost Rider 1; Girner-s/Wijngaard-a; heavy metal band becomes the Ghost Rider 4.00
... Majik 1; if Majik became Sorceror Supreme; Belasco app.; Williams-s/Andrade-a 4.00
... Spider-Man 1; if Flash Thompson became Spider-Man; Conway-s/Olortegui-a 4.00
... The Punisher 1; if Peter Parker became The Punisher; Potts-s/Ramírez-a 4.00
... Thor 1; if Thor was raised by the Frost Giants; Sacks-s/Bandini-a 4.00
... X-Men 1; X-Men in cyberspace; Hill-s/Milonogiannis & Edwards-a 4.00

WHAT IF ? AGE OF ULTRON
Marvel Comics: Jun, 2014 - No. 5, Jun, 2014 ($3.99, weekly limited series)

1-5: 1-Hank Pym's story. 2-Wolverine, Hulk, Spider-Man, Ghost Rider app. 4.00

WHAT IF ? AVX (Avengers vs. X-Men)
Marvel Comics: Sept, 2013 - No. 4, Sept, 2013 ($3.99, weekly limited series)

1-4-Palmiotti-s/Molina-a; Hope merges with the Phoenix force 4.00

WHAT IF ? INFINITY - ... (one-shots)
Marvel Comics: Dec, 2015 ($3.99)

... Dark Reign; if The Green Goblin stole the Infinity Gauntlet; Williamson-s/Sudzuka-a 4.00
... Guardians of the Galaxy; if The Guardians tried to free Thanos; Copland-a 4.00
... Inhumans; if Black Bolt betrayed Earth; Rossmo-a 4.00
... Thanos; if Thanos joined the Avengers; Henderson-a 4.00
... X-Men; if the X-Men were the sole survivors of Infinity; Norton-a 4.00

'WHAT'S NEW? - THE COLLECTED ADVENTURES OF PHIL & DIXIE'
Palliard Press: Oct, 1991 - No. 2, 1991 ($5.95, mostly color, sq.-bound, 52 pgs.)

1,2-By Phil Foglio 6.00

WHAT THE- -?!
Marvel Comics: Aug, 1988 - No. 26, 1993 ($1.25/$1.50/$2.50, semi-annual #5 on)

1-All contain parodies 6.00
2-24: 3-X-Men parody; Todd McFarlane-a. 5-Punisher/Wolverine parody; Jim Lee-a. 6-Punisher, Wolverine, Alpha Flight. 9-Wolverine. 16-EC back-c parody. 17-Wolverine/Punisher parody. 18-Star Trek parody w/Wolverine. 19-Punisher, Wolverine, Ghost Rider. 21-Weapon X parody. 22-Punisher/Wolverine parody 4.00
25-Summer Special 1 (1993, $2.50)-X-Men parody 5.00

	GD	VG	FN	VF	VF/NM	NM-
	2.0	4.0	6.0	8.0	9.0	9.2

26-Fall Special ($2.50, 68 pgs.)-Spider-Ham 2099-c/story; origin Silver Surfer; Hulk & Doomsday parody; indica reads "Winter Special." 5.00
NOTE: ***Austin*** *a-6i.* ***Byrne*** *a-2, 6, 10; c-2, 6-8, 10, 12, 13.* ***Golden*** *a-22.* ***Dale Keown*** *a-8p(8 pgs.).* ***McFarlane*** *a-3.* ***Rogers*** *c-15i, 16p.* ***Severin*** *a-2.* ***Staton*** *a-21p.* ***Williamson*** *a-2i.*

WHEDON THREE WAY, THE
Dark Horse Comics: Sept, 2014 ($1.00, one-shot)

1-Reprints Buffy Season 10 #1, Angel & Faith Season 10 #1, Serenity: Leaves #1 3.00

WHEE COMICS (Also see Gay, Smile & Tickle Comics)
Modern Store Publications: 1955 (7¢, 5x7-1/4", 52 pgs.)

1-Funny animal 9 18 27 50 65 80

WHEEDIES (See Panic #11 -EC Comics)

WHEELIE AND THE CHOPPER BUNCH (TV)
Charlton Comics: July, 1975 - No. 7, July, 1976 (Hanna-Barbera)

1-3: 1-Byrne text illo (see Nightmare for 1st art); Staton-a. 2-Byrne-a. 2,3-Mike Zeck text illos. 3-Staton-a; Byrne-c/a 3 6 9 17 26 35
4-7-Staton-a 2 4 6 12 16 20

WHEN KNIGHTHOOD WAS IN FLOWER (See The Sword & the Rose, 4-Color #505, 682)

WHEN SCHOOL IS OUT (See Wisco in Promotional Comics section)

WHERE CREATURES ROAM
Marvel Comics Group: July, 1970 - No. 8, Sept, 1971

1-Kirby/Ayers-c/a(r) 6 12 18 37 66 95
2-8: 2-5,7,8-Kirby-c/a(r). 6-Kirby-a(r) 4 8 12 22 35 48
NOTE: ***Ditko*** *r-1-6, 7.* ***Heck*** *r-2, 5. All contain pre super-hero reprints.*

WHERE IN THE WORLD IS CARMEN SANDIEGO (TV)
DC Comics: June, 1996 - No. 4, Dec, 1996 ($1.75)

1-4: Adaptation of TV show 3.00

WHERE MONSTERS DWELL
Marvel Comics Group: Jan, 1970 - No. 38, Oct, 1975

1-Kirby/Ditko-r; all contain pre super-hero-r 6 12 18 38 69 100
2-5,7-10: 4-Crandall-a(r) 4 8 12 23 37 50
6-(11/70) Reprints Groot's 1st app. in Tales to Astonish #13 7 14 21 44 82 120
11,13-20: 11-Last 15¢ issue. 18,20-Starlin-c 3 6 9 19 30 40
12-Giant issue (52 pgs.) 4 8 12 25 40 55
21-Reprints 1st Fin Fang Foom app. 4 8 12 23 37 50
22-37 3 6 9 16 24 32
38-Williamson-r/World of Suspense #3 3 6 9 17 26 35
NOTE: ***Colan*** *r-12.* ***Ditko*** *a(r)-4, 6, 8, 10, 12, 17-19, 23-25, 37.* ***Kirby*** *r-1-3, 5-16, 18-27, 30-32, 34-36, 38; c-12?* ***Reinman*** *a-3r, 4r, 12r.* ***Severin*** *c-15.*

WHERE MONSTERS DWELL (Secret Wars tie-in)
Marvel Comics: Jul, 2015 - No. 5, Dec, 2015 ($3.99, limited series)

1-5-Garth Ennis-s/Russ Braun-a/Frank Cho-c; The Phantom Eagle app. 4.00

WHERE'S HUDDLES? (TV) (See Fun-In #9)
Gold Key: Jan, 1971 - No. 3, Dec, 1971 (Hanna-Barbera)

1 3 6 9 18 28 38
2,3: 3-r/most #1 2 4 6 11 16 20

WHIP WILSON (Movie star) (Formerly Rex Hart; Gunhawk #12 on; see Western Hearts, Western Life Romances, Western Love)
Marvel Comics: No. 9, April, 1950 - No. 11, Sept, 1950 (#9,10: 52 pgs.)

9-Photo-c; Whip Wilson & his horse Bullet begin; origin Bullet; issue #23 listed on splash page; cover changed to #9; Maneely-a 52 104 156 328 552 775
10,11: Both have photo-c. 11-36 pgs.; Maneely-a 29 58 87 172 281 390
I.W. Reprint #1(1964)-Kinstler-c; r-Marvel #11 3 6 9 16 23 30

WHIRLWIND COMICS (Also see Cyclone Comics)
Nita Publication: June, 1940 - No. 3, Sept, 1940

1-Origin & 1st app. Cyclone; Cyclone-c 309 618 927 2198 3849 5500
2,3: Cyclone-c 194 388 582 1242 2121 3000

WHIRLYBIRDS (TV)
Dell Publishing Co.: No. 1124, Aug, 1960 - No. 1216, Oct-Dec, 1961

Four Color 1124 (#1)-Photo-c 7 14 21 49 92 135
Four Color 1216-Photo-c 7 14 21 46 86 125

WHISKEY DICKEL, INTERNATIONAL COWGIRL
Image Comics: Aug, 2003 ($12.95, softcover, B&W)

nn-Mark Ricketts-s/Mike Hawthorne-a; pin-up by various incl. Oeming, Thompson, Mack 13.00

WHISPER (Female Ninja)
Capital Comics: Dec, 1983 - No. 2, 1984 ($1.75, Baxter paper)

Whisper #1 © BOOM & Grant

White Tiger #5 © MAR

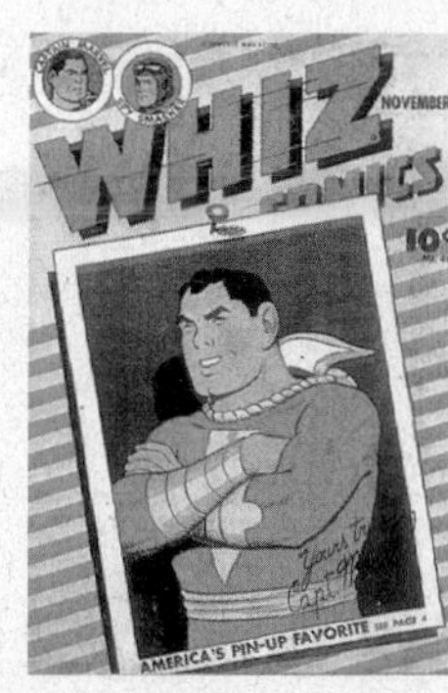

Whiz Comics #48 © FAW

GD VG FN VF VF/NM NM-
2.0 4.0 6.0 8.0 9.0 9.2

1,2: 1-Origin; Golden-c, Special (11/85, $2.50) 4.00

WHISPER (Vol. 2)
First Comics: Jun, 1986 - No. 37, June, 1990 ($1.25/$1.75/$1.95)

1-37 3.00

WHISPER
BOOM! Studios: Nov, 2006 ($3.99)

1-Grant-s/Dzialowski-a 4.00

WHISPERING DARK, THE
Dark Horse Comics: Oct, 2018 - No. 4, Feb, 2019 ($3.99)

1-4-Christopher Emgård-s/Tomás Aira-a 4.00

WHISPERS
Image Comics: Jan, 2012 - No. 6, Oct, 2013 ($2.99)

1-6-Joshua Luna-s/a 3.00

WHITE CHIEF OF THE PAWNEE INDIANS
Avon Periodicals: 1951

nn-Kit West app.; Kinstler-c 21 42 63 122 199 275

WHITE EAGLE INDIAN CHIEF (See Indian Chief)

WHITE FANG
Disney Comics: 1990 ($5.95, 68 pgs.)

nn-Graphic novel adapting new Disney movie 6.00

WHITE INDIAN
Magazine Enterprises: No. 11, July, 1953 - No. 15, 1954

11(A-1 94), 12(A-1 101), 13(A-1 104)-Frazetta-r(Dan Brand) in all from Durango Kid.
11-Powell-c 22 44 66 132 216 300
14(A-1 117), 15(A-1 135)-Check-a; Torres-a-#15 15 30 45 84 127 170
NOTE: *#11 contains reprints from Durango Kid #1-4; #12 from #5, 9, 10, 11; #13 from #7, 12, 13, 16. #14 & 15 contain all new stories.*

WHITEOUT (Also see Queen & Country)
Oni Press: July, 1998 - No. 4, Nov, 1998 ($2.95, B&W, limited series)

1-4: 1-Matt Wagner-c. 2-Mignola-c. 3-Gibbons-c 3.00
TPB (5/99, $10.95) r/#1-4; Miller-c 11.00

WHITEOUT: MELT
Oni Press: Sept, 1999 - No. 4, Feb, 2000 ($2.95, B&W, limited series)

1-4-Greg Rucka-s/Steve Lieber-a 3.00
Whiteout: Melt, The Definitive Edition TPB (9/07, $13.95) r/#1-4; Rucka afterword 14.00

WHITE PRINCESS OF THE JUNGLE (Also see Jungle Adventures & Top Jungle Comics)
Avon Periodicals: July, 1951 - No. 5, Nov, 1952

1-Origin of White Princess (Taanda) & Capt'n Courage (r); Kinstler-c
77 154 231 493 847 1200
2-Reprints origin of Malu, Slave Girl Princess from Avon's Slave Girl Comics #1 w/Malu changed to Zora; Kinstler-c/a(2) 52 104 156 328 552 775
3-Origin Blue Gorilla; Kinstler-c/a 47 94 141 296 498 700
4-Jack Barnum, White Hunter app.; r/Sheena #9 41 82 123 256 428 600
5-Blue Gorilla by McCann?; Kinstler inside-c; Fawcette/Alascia-a(3)
42 84 126 265 445 625

WHITE RIDER AND SUPER HORSE (Formerly Humdinger V2#2; Indian Warriors #7 on; also see Blue Bolt #1, 4Most & Western Crime Cases)
Novelty-Star Publications/Accepted Publ.: No. 4, 9/50 - No. 6, 3/51

4-6-Adapts "The Last of the Mohicans". 4(#1)-(9/50)-Says #11 on inside
18 36 54 107 169 230
Accepted Reprint #5(r/#5),6 (nd); L.B. Cole-c 10 20 30 54 72 90
NOTE: *All have* ***L. B. Cole*** *covers.*

WHITE TIGER
Marvel Comics: Jan, 2007 - No. 6, Nov, 2007 ($2.99, limited series)

1-David Mack-c; Pierce & Liebe-s/Briones-a; Spider-Man & Black Widow app.
1 3 4 6 8 10
2-6 4.00
...: A Hero's Compulsion SC (2007,$14.99) r/#1-6; re-cap art and profile page 15.00

WHITE TREES: A BLACKSAND TALE
Image Comics: Aug, 2019 - No. 2, Sept, 2019 ($4.99, limited series)

1,2-Chip Zdarsky-s/Kris Anka-a/c 5.00

WHITE WILDERNESS (Disney)
Dell Publishing Co.: No. 943, Oct, 1958

Four Color 943-Movie 6 12 18 37 66 95

WHITMAN COMIC BOOK, A
Whitman Publishing Co.: Sept., 1962 (136 pgs.; 7-3/4x5-3/4; hardcover) (B&W)

1-3,5,7: 1-Yogi Bear. 2-Huckleberry Hound. 3-Mr. Jinks and Pixie & Dixie. 5-Augie Doggie & Loopy de Loop. 7-Bugs Bunny-r from #47,51,53,54 & 55
6 12 18 41 76 110
4,6: 4-The Flintstones. 6-Snooper & Blabber Fearless Detectives/Quick Draw McGraw of the Wild West 7 14 21 44 82 120
8-Donald Duck-reprints most of WDC&S #209-213. Includes 5 Barks stories, 1 complete Mickey Mouse serial by Paul Murry & 1 Mickey Mouse serial missing the 1st episode
7 14 21 49 92 135
NOTE: *Hanna-Barbera #1-6(TV), reprints of British tabloid comics. Dell reprints-#7,8.*

WHIZ COMICS (Formerly Flash & Thrill Comics #1)(See 5 Cent Comics)
Fawcett Publications: No. 2, Feb, 1940 - No. 155, June, 1953

1-(nn on cover, #2 inside)-Origin & 1st newsstand app. Captain Marvel (formerly Captain Thunder) by C. C. Beck (created by Bill Parker), Spy Smasher, Golden Arrow, Ibis the Invincible, Dan Dare, Scoop Smith, Sivana, & Lance O'Casey begin
31,200 62,400 93,600 187,200 281,100 375,000
(The only Mint copy sold in 1995 for $176,000 cash)

1-Reprint, oversize 13-1/2x10". **WARNING**: This comic is an exact duplicate reprint (except for dropping "Gangway for Captain Marvel" from-c) of the original except for its size. DC published it in 1974 with a second cover titling it as a Famous First Edition. There have been many reported cases of the outer cover being removed and the interior sold as the original edition. The reprint with the new outer cover removed is practically worthless. See Famous First Edition for value.

2-(3/40, nn on cover, #3 inside); cover to Flash #1 redrawn, pg. 12, panel 4; Spy Smasher reveals I.D. to Eve 975 1950 2919 7100 12,550 18,000
3-(4/40, #3 on-c, #4 inside)-1st app. Beautia 488 976 1458 3550 6275 9000
4-(5/40, #4 on cover, #5 inside)-Brief origin Capt. Marvel retold
405 810 1215 2835 4968 7100
5-Captain Marvel wears button-down flap on splash page only
348 696 1044 2436 4268 6100
6-10: 7-Dr. Voodoo begins (by Raboy-#9-22) 275 550 825 1760 3030 4300
11-14: 12-Capt. Marvel does not wear cape 203 406 609 1299 2225 3150
15-Origin Sivana; Dr. Voodoo by Raboy 203 406 609 1299 2225 3150
16-18-Spy Smasher battles Captain Marvel 226 452 678 1446 2413 3500
19-Classic shark-c 209 418 627 1338 2294 3250
20 126 252 378 806 1378 1950
21-(9/41)-Origin & 1st cover app. Lt. Marvels, the 1st team in Fawcett comics. In this issue, Capt. Death similar to Ditko's later Dr. Strange 129 258 387 826 1413 2000
22-24: 23-Only Dr. Voodoo by Tuska 100 200 300 640 1095 1550
25-(12/41)-Captain Nazi jumps from Master Comics #21 to take on Capt. Marvel solo after being beaten by Capt. Marvel/Bulletman team, causing the creation of Capt. Marvel Jr.; 1st app./origin of Capt. Marvel Jr. (part II of trilogy origin by CC. Beck & Mac Raboy); Captain Marvel sends Jr. back to Master #22 to aid Bulletman against Capt. Nazi; origin Old Shazam in text 730 1460 2190 5329 9415 13,500
26-30 69 138 207 442 759 1075
31,32: 32-1st app. The Trolls; Hitler/Mussolini satire by Beck
60 120 180 381 653 925
33-Spy Smasher, Captain Marvel x-over on cover and inside
77 154 231 493 847 1200
34,36-40: 37-The Trolls app. by Swayze 47 94 141 296 498 700
35-Captain Marvel & Spy Smasher-c 68 136 204 435 743 1050
41-50: 42-Classic time travel-c. 43-Spy Smasher, Ibis, Golden Arrow x-over in Capt. Marvel. 44-Flag-c. 47-Origin recap (1 pg.) 40 80 120 246 411 575
51-60: 52-Capt. Marvel x-over in Ibis. 57-Spy Smasher, Golden Arrow, Ibis cameo
33 66 99 194 317 440
61-70 31 62 93 182 296 410
71,77-80 29 58 87 170 278 385
72-76-Two Captain Marvel stories in each; 76-Spy Smasher becomes Crime Smasher
29 58 87 172 281 390
81-85,87-99: 91-Infinity-c 29 58 87 170 278 385
86-Captain Marvel battles Sivana Family; robot-c 34 68 102 204 332 460
100-(8/48)-Anniversary issue 39 78 117 240 395 550
101-106: 102-Commando Yank app. 106-Bulletman app.
31 62 93 182 296 410
107-149: 107-Capitol Building photo-c. 108-Brooklyn Bridge photo-c. 112-Photo-c. 139-Infinity-c. 140-Flag-c. 142-Used in **POP**, pg. 89 31 62 93 186 303 420
150-152-(Low dist.) 39 78 117 240 395 550
153-155-(Scarce):154,155-1st/2nd Dr. Death stories 55 110 165 352 601 850
NOTE: ***C.C. Beck*** *Captain Marvel-No. 25(part).* ***Krigstein*** *Golden Arrow-No. 75, 78, 91, 95, 96, 98-100.* ***Mac Raboy*** *Dr. Voodoo-No. 9-22. Captain Marvel-No. 25(part).* ***M.Swayze*** *a-37, 38, 59; c-38.* ***Schaffenberger*** *c-138-155(most).* ***Wolverton*** *1/2 pg. "Culture Corner"-No. 65-67, 68(2 1/2 pgs), 70-85, 87-96, 98-100, 102-109, 112-121, 123, 125, 126, 128-131, 133, 134, 136, 142, 143, 146.*

WHIZ KIDS (Also see Big Bang Comics)
Image Comics: Apr, 2003 ($4.95, B&W, one-shot)

1-Galahad, Cyclone, Thunder Girl and Moray app.; Jeff Austin-a 5.00

WHOA, NELLIE (Also see Love & Rockets)

Whodunnit? #3 © ECL

The Wicked + The Divine #45 © Gillen

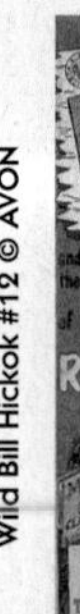

Wild Bill Hickok #12 © AVON

Fantagraphics Books: July, 1996 - No. 3, Sept, 1996 ($2.95, B&W, lim. series)

	GD 2.0	VG 4.0	FN 6.0	VF 8.0	VF/NM 9.0	NM- 9.2
1-3: Jamie Hernandez-c/a/scripts						4.00

WHODUNIT
D.S. Publishing Co.: Aug-Sept, 1948 - No. 3, Dec-Jan, 1948-49 (#1,2: 52 pgs.)

	GD 2.0	VG 4.0	FN 6.0	VF 8.0	VF/NM 9.0	NM- 9.2
1-Baker-a (7 pgs.)	34	68	102	204	332	460
2,3-Detective mysteries	15	30	45	94	147	200

WHODUNNIT?
Eclipse Comics: June, 1986 - No. 3, Apr, 1987 ($2.00, limited series)

	GD 2.0	VG 4.0	FN 6.0	VF 8.0	VF/NM 9.0	NM- 9.2
1-3: Spiegle-a. 2-Gulacy-c						4.00

WHO FRAMED ROGER RABBIT (See Marvel Graphic Novel)

WHO IS NEXT?
Standard Comics: No. 5, Jan, 1953

	GD 2.0	VG 4.0	FN 6.0	VF 8.0	VF/NM 9.0	NM- 9.2
5-Toth, Sekowsky, Andru-a; crime stories; Strangler on the Loose-c	71	142	213	454	777	1100

WHO'S MINDING THE MINT? (See Movie Classics)

WHO'S WHO IN STAR TREK
DC Comics: Mar, 1987 - #2, Apr, 1987 ($1.50, limited series)

	GD 2.0	VG 4.0	FN 6.0	VF 8.0	VF/NM 9.0	NM- 9.2
1,2	1	2	3	5	6	8

NOTE: ***Byrne** a-1, 2. **Chaykin** c-1, 2. **Morrow** a-1, 2. **McFarlane** a-2. **Perez** a-1, 2. **Sutton** a-1, 2.*

WHO'S WHO IN THE LEGION OF SUPER-HEROES
DC Comics: Apr, 1987 - No. 7, Nov, 1988 ($1.25, limited series)

	GD 2.0	VG 4.0	FN 6.0	VF 8.0	VF/NM 9.0	NM- 9.2
1-7						4.00

WHO'S WHO: THE DEFINITIVE DIRECTORY OF THE DC UNIVERSE
DC Comics: Mar, 1985 - No. 26, Apr, 1987 (Maxi-series, no ads)

	GD 2.0	VG 4.0	FN 6.0	VF 8.0	VF/NM 9.0	NM- 9.2
1-DC heroes from A-Z						4.00
2-26: All have 1-2 pgs-a by most DC artists						4.00

NOTE: ***Art Adams** a-4, 11, 18, 20. **Anderson** a-1-5, 7-12, 14, 15, 19, 21, 23-25. **Aparo** a-2, 3, 9, 10, 12, 13, 14, 15, 17, 18, 21, 23. **Byrne** a-4, 7, 14, 16, 18i, 19, 22i, 24; c-22. **Cowan** a-3-5, 8, 10-13, 16-18, 22-25. **Ditko** a-19-22. **Evans** a-20. **Giffen** a-1, 3,-6, 8, 13, 15, 17, 18, 23. **Grell** a-6, 9, 14, 20, 23, 25, 26. **Infantino** a-1-10, 12, 15, 17-22, 24, 25. **Kaluta** a-14, 21. **Gil Kane** a-1-11, 13, 14, 16, 19, 21-23, 25. **Kirby** a-2-6, 8-18, 20, 22, 25. **Kubert** a-2, 3, 7-11, 19, 20, 25. **Erik Larsen** a-24. **McFarlane** a-10-12, 17, 19, 25, 26. **Morrow** a-4, 7, 25, 26. **Orlando** a-1, 4, 10, 11, 21i. **Perez** a-1-5, 8-19, 22-26; c-1-4, 13-18. **Rogers** a-1, 2, 5-7, 11, 12, 15, 24. **Starlin** a-13, 14, 16. **Stevens** a-4, 7, 18.*

WHO'S WHO UPDATE '87
DC Comics: Aug, 1987 - No. 5, Dec, 1987 ($1.25, limited series)

	GD 2.0	VG 4.0	FN 6.0	VF 8.0	VF/NM 9.0	NM- 9.2
1-5: Contains art by most DC artists						4.00

NOTE: ***Giffen** a-1. **McFarlane** a-1-4; c-4. **Perez** a-1-4.*

WHO'S WHO UPDATE '88
DC Comics: Aug, 1988 - No. 4, Nov, 1988 ($1.25, limited series)

	GD 2.0	VG 4.0	FN 6.0	VF 8.0	VF/NM 9.0	NM- 9.2
1-4: Contains art by most DC artists						4.00

NOTE: ***Giffen** a-1. **Erik Larsen** a-1.*

WICKED, THE
Avalon Studios: Dec, 1999 - No. 7, Aug, 2000 ($2.95)

	GD 2.0	VG 4.0	FN 6.0	VF 8.0	VF/NM 9.0	NM- 9.2
Preview-(7/99, $5.00, B&W)						5.00
1-7-Anacleto-c/Martinez-a						4.00
...: Medusa's Tale (11/00, $3.95, one shot) story plus pin-up gallery						4.00
...: Vol. 1: Omnibus (2003, $19.95) r/#0-8; Drew-c						20.00

WICKED + THE DIVINE, THE
Image Comics: Jun, 2014 - No. 45, Sept, 2019 ($3.50/$3.99)

	GD 2.0	VG 4.0	FN 6.0	VF 8.0	VF/NM 9.0	NM- 9.2
1-25: 1-Gillen-s/McKelvie-a. 12-Kate Brown-a. 13-Lotay-a. 15-Hans-a. 23-Wada-a						3.50
26-45-($3.99)						4.00
... Christmas Annual (12/17, $3.99) Art by Anka, Clugston, McNeil						4.00
455 One-Shot (5/17, $3.99) Set in 455 AD Rome; André Araújo-a						4.00
1373 One-Shot (9/18, $3.99) Set in 1373; Ryan Kelly-a; Lucifer during the Black Death						4.00
1831 One-Shot (9/16, $3.99) Set in 1831; Stephanie Hans-a						4.00
1923 One-Shot (2/18, $4.99) Set in 1923; Aud Koch-a						5.00
...: The Funnies 1 (11/18, $3.99) Short humor stories by various incl. Zdarsky						5.00

WICKED THINGS
BOOM! Studios: Mar, 2020 - Present ($3.99)

	GD 2.0	VG 4.0	FN 6.0	VF 8.0	VF/NM 9.0	NM- 9.2
1-5-John Allison-s/Max Sarin-a; intro. Charlotte Grote						4.00

WIDOWMAKER
Marvel Comics: Feb, 2011 - No. 4, Apr, 2011 ($3.99, limited series)

	GD 2.0	VG 4.0	FN 6.0	VF 8.0	VF/NM 9.0	NM- 9.2
1-4-Black Widow, Hawkeye & Mockingbird app. 1,2-Jae Lee-c. 3,4-Noto-c						4.00

WIDOWMAKERS: RED GUARDIAN AND YELENA BELOVA
Marvel Comics: Jan, 2021 - Present ($3.99, limited series)

	GD 2.0	VG 4.0	FN 6.0	VF 8.0	VF/NM 9.0	NM- 9.2
1-Devin Grayson-s/Michele Bandini-a						4.00

WIDOW WARRIORS
Dynamite Entertainment: 2010 - No. 4, 2010 ($3.99, limited series)

	GD 2.0	VG 4.0	FN 6.0	VF 8.0	VF/NM 9.0	NM- 9.2
1-4-Pat Lee-a/c						4.00

WILBUR COMICS (Teen-age) (Also see Laugh Comics, Laugh Comix, Liberty Comics #10 & Zip Comics)
MLJ Magazines/Archie Publ. No. 8, Spring, 1946 on: Sum', 1944 - No. 87, 11/59; No. 88, 9/63; No. 89, 10/64; No. 90, 10/65 (No. 1-46: 52 pgs.) (#1-11 are quarterly)

	GD 2.0	VG 4.0	FN 6.0	VF 8.0	VF/NM 9.0	NM- 9.2
1	76	152	228	486	831	1175
2(Fall, 1944)	40	80	120	246	411	575
3,4(Wint, '44-45; Spr, '45)	29	58	87	172	281	390
5-1st app. Katy Keene (Sum, '45) & begin series; Wilbur story same as Archie story in Archie #1 except Wilbur replaces Archie	295	580	885	1888	3244	4600
6-10: 10-(Fall, 1946)	34	68	102	199	325	450
11-20	18	36	54	109	172	235
21-30: 30-(4/50)	14	28	42	78	112	145
31-50	11	22	33	62	86	110
51-70	10	20	30	54	72	90
71-90: 88-Last 10¢ issue (9/63)	5	10	15	31	53	75

NOTE: *Katy Keene in No. 5-56, 58-61, 63-69. **Al Fagaly** c-6-9, 12-24 at least. **Vigoda** c-2.*

WILD
Atlas Comics (IPC): Feb, 1954 - No. 5, Aug, 1954

	GD 2.0	VG 4.0	FN 6.0	VF 8.0	VF/NM 9.0	NM- 9.2
1	39	78	117	240	395	550
2	23	46	69	136	223	310
3-5	20	40	60	120	195	270

NOTE: ***Berg** a-5; c-4. **Burgos** a-5, c-2,3. **Colan** a-4. **Everett** a-1-3. **Heath** a-2, 3, 5. **Maneely** a-1-3, 5; c-1, 5. **Post** a-2, 5. **Ed Win** a-1, 3.*

WILD! (This Magazine Is...) (Satire)
Dell Publishing Co.: Jan, 1968 - No. 3, 1968 (35¢, magazine, 52 pgs.)

	GD 2.0	VG 4.0	FN 6.0	VF 8.0	VF/NM 9.0	NM- 9.2
1-3: Hogan's Heroes, The Rat Patrol & Mission Impossible TV spoofs	3	6	9	16	23	30

WILD ANIMALS
Pacific Comics: Dec, 1982 ($1.00, one-shot, direct sales)

	GD 2.0	VG 4.0	FN 6.0	VF 8.0	VF/NM 9.0	NM- 9.2
1-Funny animal; Sergio Aragonés-a; Shaw-c/a						4.00

WILD BILL ELLIOTT (Also see Western Roundup under Dell Giants)
Dell Publishing Co.: No. 278, 5/50 - No. 643, 7/55 (No #11,12) (All photo-c)

	GD 2.0	VG 4.0	FN 6.0	VF 8.0	VF/NM 9.0	NM- 9.2
Four Color 278 (#1, 52 pgs.)-Titled "Bill Elliott"; Bill & his horse Stormy begin; photo front/back-c begin	12	24	36	82	179	275
2 (11/50), 3 (52 pgs.)	7	14	21	44	82	120
4-10 (10-12/52)	5	10	15	35	63	90
Four Color 472 (6/53), 520(12/53)-Last photo back-c	5	10	15	35	63	90
13 (4-6/54) - 17 (4-6/55)	5	10	15	30	50	70
Four Color 643 (7/55)	5	10	15	33	57	80

WILD BILL HICKOK (Also see Blazing Sixguns)
Avon Periodicals: Sept-Oct, 1949 - No. 28, May-June, 1956

	GD 2.0	VG 4.0	FN 6.0	VF 8.0	VF/NM 9.0	NM- 9.2
1-Ingels-c	32	64	96	188	307	425
2-Painted-c; Kit West app.	15	30	45	92	144	195
3-5-Painted-c (4-Cover by Howard Winfield)	14	28	42	78	112	145
6-10,12: 8-10-Painted-c. 12-Kinsler-c?	14	28	42	76	108	140
11,13,14-Kinstler-c/a (#11-c & inside-f/c art only)	14	28	42	80	115	150
15,17,18,20: 18-Kit West story. 20-Kit West by Larsen	12	24	36	69	97	125
16-Kamen-a; r-3 stories/King of the Badmen of Deadwood	13	26	39	72	101	130
19-Meskin-a	12	24	36	69	97	125
21-Reprints 2 stories/Chief Crazy Horse	11	22	33	62	86	110
22-McCann-a?; r/Sheriff Bob Dixon's...	11	22	33	62	86	110
23-27: 23-Kinstler-c. 24-27-Kinstler-c/a(r) (24,25-r?)	11	22	33	62	86	110
28-Kinstler-c/a (new); r-/Last of the Comanches	11	22	33	64	90	115
I.W. Reprint #1-r/#2; Kinstler-c	2	4	6	9	13	16
Super Reprint #10-12: 10-r/#18. 11-r/#?. 12-r/#8	2	4	6	9	13	16

NOTE: *#23, 25 contain numerous editing deletions in both art and script due to code. **Kinstler** c-6, 7, 11-14, 17, 18, 20-22, 24-28. **Howard Larsen** a-1, 2, 4, 5, 6(3), 7-9, 11, 12, 17, 18, 20-24, 26. **Meskin** a-7. **Reinman** a-6, 17.*

WILD BILL HICKOK AND JINGLES (TV)(Formerly Cowboy Western) (Also see Blue Bird)
Charlton Comics: No. 68, Aug, 1958 - No. 75, Dec, 1959

	GD 2.0	VG 4.0	FN 6.0	VF 8.0	VF/NM 9.0	NM- 9.2
68,69-Williamson-a (all are 10¢ issues)	11	22	33	60	83	105
70-Two pgs. Williamson-a	8	16	24	42	54	65
71-75 (#76, exist?)	6	12	18	28	34	40

WILD BILL PECOS WESTERN (Also see The Westerner)
AC Comics: 1989 ($3.50, 1/2 color, 1/2 B&W, 52 pgs.)

	GD 2.0	VG 4.0	FN 6.0	VF 8.0	VF/NM 9.0	NM- 9.2
1-Syd Shores-c/a(r)/Westerner; photo back-c						4.00

WILD BOY OF THE CONGO (Also see Approved Comics)

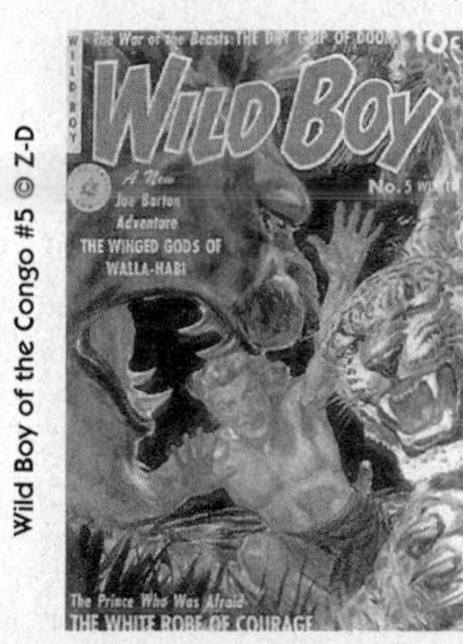

Wild Boy of the Congo #5 © Z-D

WildC.A.T.s #18 © WSP

Wild Core #2 © WSP

	GD 2.0	VG 4.0	FN 6.0	VF 8.0	VF/NM 9.0	NM- 9.2

Ziff-Davis No. 10-12,4-8/St. John No. 9,11 on: No. 10, 2-3/51 - No. 12, 8-9/51; No. 4, 10-11/51 - No. 9, 10/53; No. 11-#15,6/55 (No #10, 1953)

	GD 2.0	VG 4.0	FN 6.0	VF 8.0	VF/NM 9.0	NM- 9.2
10(#1)(2-3/51)-Origin; bondage-c by Saunders (painted); used in **SOTI**, pg. 189; painted-c begin thru #9 (except #7)	36	72	108	211	343	475
11(4-5/51),12(8-9/51)-Norman Saunders painted-c	18	36	54	109	172	235
4(10-11/51)-Saunders painted bondage-c	17	34	51	105	165	225
5(Winter,'51)-Saunders painted-c	15	30	45	90	140	190
6,8,9(10/53): Painted-c. 6-Saunders-c	15	30	45	90	140	190
7(8-9/52)-Kinstler-a	17	34	51	100	158	215
11-13-Baker-c. 11-r/#7 w/new Baker-c; Kinstler-a (2 pgs.)	77	154	231	493	847	1200
14(4/55)-Baker-c; r-#12('51)	77	154	231	493	847	1200
15(6/55)-Baker-c	41	82	123	256	428	600

WILDCAT (See Sensation Comics #1)

WILDC.A.T.S ADVENTURES (TV cartoon)
Image Comics (WildStorm): Sept, 1994 - No. 10, June, 1995 ($1.95/$2.50)

1-10: 1,2-Templeton-c. 2,3-Templeton-a. 4,5-Joe Phillips-a. 7,9-Wieringo-c 4.00
Sourcebook 1 (1/95, $2.95) Jeff Smith-c; art by Hamner, Phillips, Staton, Stelfreeze 4.00

WILDC.A.T.S: COVERT ACTION TEAMS (Also see Alan Moore's... for TPB reprints)
Image Comics (WildStorm Productions): Aug, 1992 - No. 4, Mar, 1993; No. 5, Nov, 1993 - No. 50, June, 1998 ($1.95/$2.50)

1-1st app; Jim Lee/Williams-c/a & Lee scripts begin; contains 2 trading cards (Two diff versions of cards inside); 1st WildStorm Productions title 6.00
1-All gold foil signed edition 24.00
1-All gold foil unsigned edition 12.00
1-Newsstand edition w/o cards 4.00
1-"3-D Special"(8/97, $4.95) w/3-D glasses; variant-c by Jim Lee. 5.00
2-($2.50)-Prism foil stamped-c; contains coupon for Image Comics #0 & 4 pg. preview to Portacio's Wetworks (back-up) 5.00
2-With coupon missing 2.00
2-Direct sale misprint w/o foil-c 5.00
2-Newsstand ed., no prism or coupon 3.00
3-Lee/Liefeld-c (1/93-c, 12/92 inside) 4.00
4-($2.50)-Polybagged w/Topps trading card; 1st app. Tribe by Johnson & Stroman; Youngblood cameo 4.00
4-Variant w/red card 6.00
5-7-Jim Lee/Williams-c/a; Lee script 3.00
8-X-Men's Jean Grey & Scott Summers cameo 4.00
9-12: 10-1st app. Huntsman & Soldier; Claremont scripts begin, ends #13. 11-1st app. Savant, Tapestry & Mr. Majestic. 3.00
11-Alternate Portacio-c, see Deathblow #5 5.00
13-19,21-24: 15-James Robinson scripts begin, ends #20. 15,16-Black Razor story. 21-Alan Moore scripts begin, end #34; intro Tao & Ladytron; new WildC.A.T.S team forms (Mr. Majestic, Savant, Condition Red (Max Cash), Tao & Ladytron). 22-Maguire-a 3.00
20-($2.50)-Direct Market, WildStorm Rising Pt. 2 w/bound-in card 4.00
20-($1.95)-Newsstand, WildStorm Rising Part 2 3.00
25-($4.95)-Alan Moore script; wraparound foil-c. 5.00
26-49: 29-(5/96)-Fire From Heaven Pt 7; reads Apr on-c. 30-(6/96)-Fire From Heaven Pt. 13; Spartan revealed to have transplanted personality of John Colt (from Team One: WildC.A.T.s). 31-(9/96)-Grifter rejoins team; Ladytron dies 3.00
40-($3.50)Voyager Pack bagged w/Divine Right preview 5.00
50-($3.50) Stories by Robinson/Lee, Choi & Peterson/Benes, and Moore/Charest; Charest sketchbook; Lee wraparound-c 4.00
50-Chromium cover 6.00
Annual 1 (2/98, $2.95) Robinson-s 4.00
Compendium (1993, $9.95)-r/#1-4; bagged w/#0 15.00
Sourcebook 1 (9/93, $2.50)-Foil embossed-c 3.00
Sourcebook 1-($1.95)-Newsstand ed. w/o foil embossed-c 3.00
Sourcebook 2 (11/94, $2.50)-wraparound-c 3.00
Special 1 (11/93, $3.50, 52 pgs.)-1st Travis Charest WildC.A.T.S-a 4.00
...A Gathering of Eagles (5/97, $9.95, TPB) r/#10-12 10.00
.../ Cyberforce: Killer Instinct TPB (2004, $14.95) r/#5-7 & Cyberforce V2 #1-3 15.00
...Gang War ('98, $16.95, TPB) r/#28-34 17.00
...Homecoming (8/98, $19.95, TPB) r/#21-27 20.00
James Robinson's Complete Wildc.a.t.s TPB (2009, $24.99) r/#15-20,50; Annual 1, WildStorm Rising #1, Team One Wildc.a.t.s #1,2; cover and pin-up gallery 25.00

WILDCATS (3rd series)
DC Comics (WildStorm): Mar, 1999 - No. 28, Dec, 2001 ($2.50)

1-Charest-a; six covers by Lee, Adams, Bisley, Campbell, Madureira and Ramos; Lobdell-s 4.00
1-($6.95) DF Edition; variant cover by Ramos 7.00
2-28: 2-Voodoo cover. 3-Bachalo variant-c. 5-Hitch-a/variant-c. 7-Meglia-a. 8-Phillips-a begins. 17-J.G. Jones-c. 18,19-Jim Lee-c. 20,21-Dillon-a 3.00
Annual 2000 (12/00, $3.50) Bermejo-a; Devil's Night x-over 4.00
...: Battery Park ('03, $17.95, TPB) r/#20-28; Phillips-c 18.00
... Ladytron (10/00, $5.95) Origin; Casey-s/Canete-a 6.00
... Mosaic (2/00, $3.95) Tuska-a (10 pg. back-up story) 4.00
...: Serial Boxes ('01, $14.95, TPB) r/#14-19; Phillips-c 15.00
...: Street Smart ('00, $24.95, HC) r/#1-6; Charest-c 25.00
...: Street Smart ('02, $14.95, SC) r/#1-6; Charest-c 15.00
...: Vicious Circles ('00, $14.95, TPB) r/#8-13; Phillips-c 15.00

WILDCATS (Volume 4)
DC Comics (WildStorm): Dec, 2006 ($2.99)

1-Grant Morrison-s/Jim Lee-a; Jim Lee-c 3.00
1-Variant-c by Todd McFarlane/Jim Lee 6.00
...: Armageddon 1 (2/08, $2.99) Gage-s/Caldwell-a 3.00

WILDCATS (Volume 5) (World's End on cover for #1,2)
DC Comics (WildStorm): Sept, 2008 - No. 30, Feb, 2011 ($2.99)

1-30: 1-Christos Gage-s/Neil Googe-a. 5-Woods-a 3.00
...: Family Secrets TPB (2010, $17.99) r/#8-12 18.00
...: World's End TPB (2009, $17.99) r/#1-7 18.00

WILDC.A.T.S/ ALIENS
Image Comics/Dark Horse: Aug, 1998 ($4.95, one-shot)

	GD 2.0	VG 4.0	FN 6.0	VF 8.0	VF/NM 9.0	NM- 9.2
1-Ellis-s/Sprouse-a/c; Aliens invade Skywatch; Stormwatch app.; death of Winter; destruction of Skywatch	1	2	3	5	6	8
1-Variant-c by Gil Kane	1	3	4	6	8	10

WILDCATS: NEMESIS
DC Comics (WildStorm): Nov, 2005 - No. 9, July, 2006 ($2.99, limited series)

1-9: 1-Robbie Morrison-s/Talent Caldwell & Horacio Domingues-a/Caldwell-c 3.00
TPB (2006, $19.99) r/#1-9; cover gallery 20.00

WILDC.A.T.S: SAVANT GARDE FAN EDITION
Image Comics/WildStorm Productions: Feb, 1997 - No. 3, Apr, 1997 (Giveaway, 8 pgs.) (Polybagged w/Overstreet's FAN)

1-3: Barbara Kesel-s/Christian Uche-a(p) 4.00
1-3-(Gold): All retailer incentives 10.00

WILDC.A.T.S TRILOGY
Image Comics (WildStorm Productions): June, 1993 - No. 3, Dec, 1993 ($1.95, lim. series)

1-($2.50)-1st app. Gen 13 (Fairchild, Burnout, Grunge, Freefall) Multi-color foil-c; Jae Lee-c/a in all 6.00
1-($1.95)-Newsstand ed. w/o foil-c 4.00
2,3-($1.95)-Jae Lee-c/a 4.00

WILDCATS VERSION 3.0
DC Comics (WildStorm): Oct, 2002 - No. 24, Oct, 2004 ($2.95)

1-24: 1-Casey-s/Nguyen-a; two covers by Nguyen and Rian Hughes and Nguyen. 8-Back-up preview of The Authority: High Stakes pt. 3 3.00
...: Brand Building TPB (2003, $14.95) r/#1-6 15.00
...: Full Disclosure TPB (2004, $14.95) r/#7-12 15.00
...: Year One TPB (2010, $24.99) r/#1-12 25.00
...: Year Two TPB (2011, $24.99) r/#13-24 25.00

WILDC.A.T.S/ X-MEN: THE GOLDEN AGE (See also X-Men/WildC.A.T.S.: The Dark Age)
Image Comics (WildStorm Productions): Feb, 1997 ($4.50, one-shot)

1-Lobdell-s/Charest-a; Two covers (Charest, Jim Lee) 5.00
1-"3-D" Edition ($6.50) w/glasses 7.00

WILDC.A.T.S/ X-MEN: THE MODERN AGE
Image Comics (WildStorm Productions): Aug, 1997 ($4.50, one-shot)

1-Robinson-s/Hughes-a; Two covers (Hughes, Paul Smith) 5.00
1-"3-D" Edition ($6.50) w/glasses 7.00

WILDC.A.T.S/ X-MEN: THE SILVER AGE
Image Comics (WildStorm Productions): June, 1997 ($4.50, one-shot)

1-Lobdell-s/Jim Lee-a; Two covers(Neal Adams, Jim Lee) 5.00
1-"3-D" Edition ($6.50) w/glasses 7.00

WILDCORE
Image Comics (WildStorm Prods.): Nov, 1997 - No. 10, Dec, 1998 ($2.50)

1-10: 1-Two covers (Booth/McWeeney, Charest) 3.00
1-($3.50)-Voyager Pack w/DV8 preview 4.00
1-Chromium-c 5.00

WILD DOG
DC Comics: Sept, 1987 - No. 4, Dec, 1987 (75¢, limited series)

1-4 3.00

Wildsiderz #1 © J.S. Campbell

The Wild Storm #19 © DC

Wild Thing #1 © MAR

	GD 2.0	VG 4.0	FN 6.0	VF 8.0	VF/NM 9.0	NM- 9.2

Special 1 (1989, $2.50, 52 pgs.) 4.00

WILDERNESS TREK (See Zane Grey, Four Color 333)

WILDFIRE (See Zane Grey, FourColor 433)

WILDFIRE
Image Comics (Top Cow): Jun, 2014 - No. 4, Oct, 2014 ($3.99, limited series)

1-4-Matt Hawkins-s/Linda Sejic-a 4.00

WILD FRONTIER (Cheyenne Kid #8 on)
Charlton Comics: Oct, 1955 - No. 7, Apr, 1957

	GD	VG	FN	VF	VF/NM	NM-
1-Davy Crockett	10	20	30	56	76	95
2-6-Davy Crockett in all	8	16	24	40	50	60
7-Origin & 1st app. Cheyenne Kid	9	18	27	50	65	80

WILD GIRL
DC Comics (WildStorm): Jan, 2005 - No. 6, Jun, 2005 ($2.95/$2.99)

1-6-Leah Moore & John Reppion-s/Shawn McManus-a/c 3.00

WILDGUARD: CASTING CALL
Image Comics: Sept, 2003 - No. 6, Feb, 2004 ($2.95)

1-6: 1-Nauck-s/a; two covers by Nauck and McGuinness. 2-Wieringo var-c. 6-Noto var-c 3.00
... Vol. 1: Casting Call (1/05, $17.95, TPB) r/#1-6; cover gallery; Todd Nauck bio 18.00
Wildguard: Fire Power 1 (12/04, $3.50) Nauck-a; two covers 3.50
Wildguard: Fool's Gold (7/05 - No. 2, 7/05, $3.50) 1,2-Todd Nauck-s/a 3.50
Wildguard: Insider (5/08 - No. 3, 7/08, $3.50) 1-3-Todd Nauck-s/a 3.50

WILD'S END
BOOM! Studios: Sept, 2014 - No. 6, Feb, 2015 ($3.99, limited series)

1-6-Dan Abnett-s/I.N.J. Culbard-a/c 4.00

WILD'S END: THE ENEMY WITHIN
BOOM! Studios: Sept, 2015 - No. 6, Feb, 2016 ($3.99, limited series)

1-6-Dan Abnett-s/I.N.J. Culbard-a/c 4.00

WILDSIDERZ
DC Comics (WildStorm): No. 0, Aug, 2005 - No. 2, Jan, 2006 ($1.99/$3.50)

0-(8/05, $1.99) Series preview & character profiles; J. Scott Campbell-a 3.00
1,2: 1-(10/05, $3.50) J. Scott Campbell-s/a; Andy Hartnell-s 3.50

WILDSTAR (Also see The Dragon & The Savage Dragon)
Image Comics (Highbrow Entertainment): Sept, 1995 - No. 3, Jan, 1996 ($2.50, lim. series)

1-3: Al Gordon scripts; Jerry Ordway-c/a 3.00

WILDSTAR: SKY ZERO
Image Comics (Highbrow Entertainment): Mar, 1993 - No. 4, Nov, 1993 ($1.95, lim. series)

1-4: 1-($2.50)-Embossed-c w/silver ink; Ordway-c/a in all 3.00
1-($1.95)-Newsstand ed. w/silver ink-c, not embossed 3.00
1-Gold variant 6.00

WILD STARS
Collector's Edition/Little Rocket Productions: Summer, 1984 - Present (B&W)

Vol. 1 #1 (Summer 1984, $1.50) 5.00
Vol. 2 #1 (Winter 1988, $1.95) Foil-c; die-cut front & back-c 5.00
Vol. 3: #1-6-Brunner-c; Tierney-s. 1,2-Brewer-a. 3-6-Simons-a 3.00
7-($5.95) Simons-a 6.00
TPB (2004, $17.95) r/Vol. 1-3 18.00

WILDSTORM
Image Comics/DC Comics (WildStorm Publishing): 1994 - 2009 (one-shots, TPBs)

... After the Fall TPB (2009, $19.99) r/back-up stories from Wildcats V5 #1-11, The Authority V5 #1-11; Gen 13 V4 #21-28, and Stormwatch: PHD #13-20 20.00
...Annual 2000 (12/00, $3.50) Devil's Night x-over; Moy-a 4.00
...: Armageddon TPB (2008, $17.99) r/Armageddon one-shots in Midnighter, Welcome To Tranquility, Wetworks, Gen13, Stormwatch PHD, and Wildcats titles 18.00
...Chamber of Horrors (10/95, $3.50)-Bisley-c 4.00
...Fine Arts: Spotlight on Gen13 (2/08, $3.50) art and covers with commentary 3.50
...Fine Arts: Spotlight on Jim Lee (2/07, $3.50) art and covers by Lee with commentary 3.50
...Fine Arts: Spotlight on J. Scott Campbell (5/07, $3.50) art and covers with commentary 3.50
...Fine Arts: Spotlight on The Authority (1/08, $3.50) art and covers with commentary 3.50
...Fine Arts: Spotlight on WildCATs (3/08, $3.50) art and covers with commentary 3.50
...Fine Arts: The Gallery Collection (12/98, $19.95) Lee-c 20.00
...Halloween 1 (10/97, $2.50) Warner-c 3.00
...Rarities 1(12/94, $4.95, 52 pgs.)-r/Gen 13 1/2 & other stories 5.00
...Summer Special 1 (2001, $5.95) Short stories by various; Hughes-c 6.00
...Swimsuit Special 1 (12/94, $2.95), ...Swimsuit Special 2 (1995, $2.50) 3.00
...Swimsuit Special '97 #1 (7/97, $2.50) 3.00
...Thunderbook 1 (10/00, $6.95) Short stories by various incl. Hughes, Moy 7.00
...Ultimate Sports 1 (8/97, $2.50) 3.00
...Universe Sourcebook (5/95, $2.50) 3.00
...Universe 2008 Convention Exclusive ('08, no cover price) preview of World's End x-over 3.00

WILDSTORM!
Image Comics (WildStorm): Aug, 1995 - No. 4, Nov, 1995 ($2.50, B&W/color, anthology)

1-4: 1-Simonson-a 3.00

WILD STORM, THE
DC Comics (WildStorm): Apr, 2017 - No. 24, Sept, 2019 ($3.99)

1-24-Warren Ellis-s/Jon Davis-Hunt-a; Zealot and the Engineer app. 19-New Apollo & Midnighter 4.00

WILD STORM: MICHAEL CRAY, THE
DC Comics (WildStorm): Dec, 2017 - No. 12, Dec. 2018 ($3.99)

1-12: 1-Bryan Hill-s/N. Steven Harris-a; Oliver Queen app. 8-10,12-Constantine app. 4.00

WILDSTORM PRESENTS: ...
DC Comics (WildStorm): Jan, 2011 - Feb, 2011 ($7.99, squarebound, reprints)

1-(1/11) r/short stories by various incl. Pearson, Conner, Corben, Jeanty, Mahnke 8.00
Planetary: Lost Worlds (2/11) r/Planetary/Authority & Planetary/JLA: Terra Occulta 8.00

WILDSTORM REVELATIONS
DC Comics (WildStorm): Mar, 2008 - No. 6, May, 2008 ($2.99, limited series)

1-6-Beatty & Gage-s/Craig-a. 2-The Authority app. 3.00
TPB (2008, $17.99) r/#1-6; cover sketches 18.00

WILDSTORM RISING
Image Comics (WildStorm Publishing): May, 1995 - No.2, June, 1995 ($1.95/$2.50)

1-($2.50)-Direct Market, WildStorm Rising Pt. 1 w/bound-in card 3.00
1-($1.95)-Newstand, WildStorm Rising Pt. 1 3.00
2-($2.50)-Direct Market, WildStorm Rising Pt. 10 w/bound-in card; continues in WildC.A.T.S #21. 3.00
2-($1.95)-Newstand, WildStorm Rising Pt. 10 3.00
Trade paperback (1996, $19.95)-Collects x-over; B. Smith-c 20.00

WILDSTORM SPOTLIGHT
Image Comics (WildStorm Publishing): Feb, 1997 - No. 4 ($2.50)

1-4: 1-Alan Moore-s 3.00

WILDSTORM UNIVERSE '97
Image Comics (WildStorm Publishing): Dec, 1996 - No. 3 ($2.50, limited series)

1-3: 1-Wraparound-c. 3-Gary Frank-c 3.00

WILDTHING
Marvel Comics UK: Apr, 1993 - No. 7, Oct, 1993 ($1.75)

1-($2.50)-Embossed-c; Venom & Carnage cameo 5.00
2-7: 2-Spider-Man & Venom. 6-Mysterio app. 4.00

WILD THING (Wolverine's daughter in the M2 universe)
Marvel Comics: Oct, 1999 - No. 5, Feb, 2000 ($1.99)

1-5: 1-Lim-a in all. 2-Two covers 3.00
Wizard #0 supplement; battles the Hulk 3.00
Spider-Girl Presents Wild Thing. Crash Course (2007, $7.99, digest) r/#0-5 8.00

WILDTIMES
DC Comics (WildStorm Productions): Aug, 1999 ($2.50, one-shots)

...Deathblow #1 -set in 1899; Edwards-a; Jonah Hex app., ...DV8 #1 -set in 1944; Altieri-s/p; Sgt. Rock app., ...Gen13 #1 -set in 1969; Casey-s/Johnson-a; Teen Titans app., ...Grifter #1 -set in 1923; Paul Smith-a, ...Wetworks #1 -Waid-s/Lopresti-a; Superman app. 3.00
...WildC.A.T.s #0 -Wizard supplement; Charest-c 3.00

WILD WEST (Wild Western #3 on)
Marvel Comics (WFP): Spring, 1948 - No. 2, July, 1948

	GD	VG	FN	VF	VF/NM	NM-
1-Two-Gun Kid, Arizona Annie, & Tex Taylor begin; Shores-c	39	78	117	240	395	550
2-Captain Tootsie by Beck; Shores-c	27	54	81	158	259	360

WILD WEST (Black Fury #1-57)
Charlton Comics: V2#58, Nov, 1966

	GD	VG	FN	VF	VF/NM	NM-
V2#58	2	4	6	11	16	20

WILD WEST C.O.W.-BOYS OF MOO MESA (TV)
Archie Comics: Dec, 1992 - No. 3, Feb, 1993 (limited series)
V2#1, Mar, 1993 - No. 3, July, 1993 ($1.25)

1-3,V2#1-3 3.00

WILD WESTERN (Formerly Wild West #1,2)
Marvel/Atlas (WFP): No. 3, 9/48 - No. 57, 9/57 (3-11: 52 pgs, 12-on: 36 pgs)

3(#1)-Tex Morgan begins; Two-Gun Kid, Tex Taylor, & Arizona Annie continue from Wild West

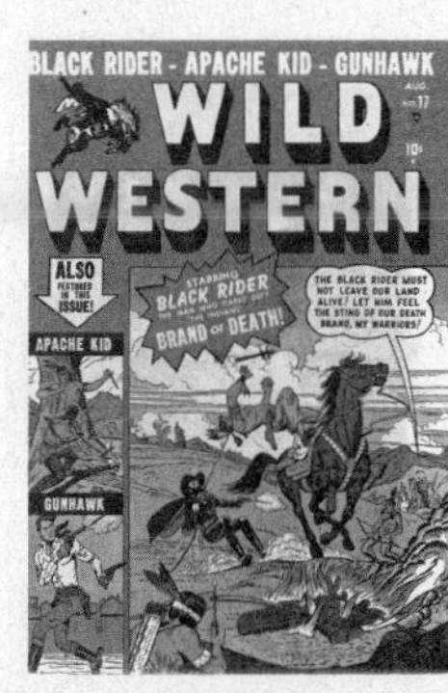

Wild Western #17 © MAR

Will to Power #6 © DH

Wings Comics #79 © FH

	GD	VG	FN	VF	VF/NM	NM-
	2.0	4.0	6.0	8.0	9.0	9.2

32 64 96 188 307 425
4-Last Arizona Annie; Captain Tootsie by Beck; Kid Colt app.
22 44 66 130 213 295
5-2nd app. Black Rider (1/49); Blaze Carson, Captain Tootsie (by Beck) app.
27 54 81 158 259 360
6-8: 6-Blaze Carson app; anti-Wertham editorial 17 34 51 98 154 210
9-Photo-c; Black Rider app., also in #11-19 20 40 60 120 195 270
10-Charles Starrett photo-c 24 48 72 140 230 320
11-(Last 52 pg. issue) The Prairie Kid app. 18 36 54 103 162 220
12-14,16-19: All Black Rider-c/stories. 12-14-The Prairie Kid & his horse Fury app.
20 40 60 117 189 260
15-Red Larabee, Gunhawk (origin), his horse Blaze, & Apache Kid begin, end #22;
Black Rider-c/story 20 40 60 120 195 270
20-30: 20-Kid Colt-c begin. 24-Has 2 Kid Colt stories. 26-1st app. The Ringo Kid? (2/53);
4 pg. story. 30-Katz-a 14 28 42 82 121 160
31-40 11 22 33 67 94 120
41-47,49-51,53,57 11 22 33 60 83 105
48-Williamson/Torres-a (4 pgs); Drucker-a 13 26 39 72 101 130
52-Crandall-a 13 26 39 72 101 130
54,55-Williamson-a in both (5 & 4 pgs.), #54 with Mayo plus 2 text illos
14 28 42 76 108 140
56-Baker-a? 11 22 33 62 86 110

NOTE: *Annie Oakley in #46, 47. Apache Kid in #15-22, 39. Arizona Kid in #21, 23. Arrowhead in #34-39. Black Rider in #5, 8-19, 33-44. Fighting Texan in #17. Kid Colt in #4-6, 8-11, 20-47, 51, 52, 54-56. Outlaw Kid in #43. Red Hawkins in #13, 14. Ringo Kid in #26, 39, 41, 43, 44, 46, 47, 50-56. Tex Morgan in #3, 4, 6, 9, 11. Tex Taylor in #3-6, 9, 11. Texas Kid in #23-25. Two-Gun Kid in #3-6, 8, 9, 11, 12, 33-39, 41. Wyatt Earp in #47.* ***Ayers*** *a-41, 42, 53, 54.* ***Berg*** *a-26; c-24.* ***Colan*** *a-49.* ***Forte*** *a-28, 30.* ***Al Hartley*** *a-16, 51.* ***Heath*** *a-4, 5, 8; c-34, 44.* ***Keller*** *a-24, 26(2), 29-40, 44-46, 48, 51, 52.* ***Maneely*** *a-10, 12, 15, 16, 28, 35, 38, 40-45; c-11, 18-22, 33, 35, 36, 38-42, 45, 51, 53, 54, 56, 57.* ***Morisi*** *a-23, 52.* ***Pakula*** *a-42, 52.* ***Powell*** *a-51.* ***Romita*** *a-24(2).* ***Severin*** *a-46, 47; c-48.* ***Shores*** *a-3, 5, 30, 31, 33, 35, 36, 38, 41; c-3-5.* ***Sinnott*** *a-34-39.* ***Wildey*** *a-43. Bondage c-19.*

WILD WESTERN ACTION (Also see The Bravados)
Skywald Publ. Corp.: Mar, 1971 - No. 3, June, 1971 (25¢, reprints, 52 pgs.)

1-Durango Kid, Straight Arrow-r; with all references to "Straight" in story relettered to
"Swift"; Bravados begin; Shores-a (new) 3 6 9 16 24 32
2,3: 2-Billy Nevada, Durango Kid. 3-Red Mask, Durango Kid
2 4 6 13 18 22

WILD WESTERN ROUNDUP
Red Top/Decker Publications/I. W. Enterprises: Oct, 1957; 1960-'61

1(1957)-Kid Cowboy-r 5 10 15 22 26 30
I.W. Reprint #1('60-61)-r/#1 by Red Top 2 4 6 8 11 14

WILD WEST RODEO
Star Publications: 1953 (15¢)

1-A comic book coloring book with regular full color cover & B&W inside
10 20 30 56 76 95

WILD WILD WEST, THE (TV)
Gold Key: June, 1966 - No. 7, Oct, 1969 (All have Robert Conrad photo-c)

1-McWilliams-a 11 22 33 73 157 240
1-Variant edition with photo back-c (scarce) 12 24 36 79 170 260
2-Robert Conrad photo-c; McWilliams-a 8 16 24 52 99 145
2-Variant edition with Conrad photo back-c (scarce) 9 18 27 59 117 175
3-7 6 12 18 42 79 115
3-Variant edition with photo back-c (scarce) 8 16 24 56 108 160

WILD, WILD WEST, THE (TV)
Millennium Publications: Oct, 1990 - No. 4, Jan?, 1991 ($2.95, limited series)

1-4-Based on TV show 3.00

WILKIN BOY (See That...)

WILL EISNER READER
Kitchen Sink Press: 1991 ($9.95, B&W, 8 1/2" x 11", TPB)

nn-Reprints stories from Will Eisner's Quarterly; Eisner-s/a/c 15.00
nn-(DC Comics, 10/00, $9.95) 10.00

WILL EISNER'S JOHN LAW: ANGELS AND ASHES, DEVILS AND DUST
IDW Publ.: Apr, 2006 - No. 4 ($3.99, B&W, limited series)

1-New stories with Will Eisner's characters; Gary Chaloner-s/a 4.00

WILLIE COMICS (Formerly Ideal #1-4; Crime Cases #24 on; Li'l Willie #20 & 21)
(See Gay Comics, Laugh, Millie The Model & Wisco)
Marvel Comics (MgPC): #5, Fall, 1946 - #19, 4/49; #22, 1/50 - #23, 5/50 (No #20 & 21)

5(#1)-George, Margie, Nellie the Nurse & Willie begin
42 84 126 265 445 625
6,8,9 24 48 72 144 237 330
7(1),10,11-Kurtzman's "Hey Look" 25 50 75 150 245 340
12,14-18,22,23 23 46 69 136 223 310
13,19-Kurtzman's "Hey Look" (#19-last by Kurtzman?)
24 48 72 140 230 320

NOTE: *Cindy app. in #17. Jeanie app. in #17. Little Lizzie app. in #22.*

WILLIE MAYS (See The Amazing...)

WILLIE THE PENGUIN
Standard Comics: Apr, 1951 - No. 6, Apr, 1952

1-Funny animal 12 24 36 67 94 120
2-6 8 16 24 40 50 60

WILLIE THE WISE-GUY (Also see Cartoon Kids)
Atlas Comics (NPP): Sept, 1957

1-Kida, Maneely-a 17 34 51 105 165 225

WILLOW
Marvel Comics: Aug, 1988 - No. 3, Oct, 1988 ($1.00)

1-R/Marvel Graphic Novel #36 (movie adaptation) 1 3 4 6 8 10
2,3 6.00

WILLOW (From Buffy the Vampire Slayer)
Dark Horse Comics: Nov, 2012 - No. 5, Mar, 2013 ($2.99, limited series)

1-5-Jeff Parker-s/Brian Ching-a; covers by David Mack & Megan Lara; Aluwyn app. 3.00

WILL ROGERS WESTERN (Formerly My Great Love #1-4; see Blazing & True Comics #66)
Fox Feature Syndicate: No. 5, June, 1950 - No. 2, Aug, 1950

5(#1) Photo-c 31 62 93 186 303 420
2: Photo-c 26 52 78 154 252 350

WILL TO POWER (Also see Comic's Greatest World)
Dark Horse Comics: June, 1994 - No. 12, Aug, 1994 ($1.00, weekly limited series, 20 pgs.)

1-12: 12-Vortex kills Titan. 3.00

NOTE: ***Mignola*** *c-10-12.* ***Sears*** *c-1-3.*

WILL-YUM!
Dell Publishing Co.: No. 676, Feb, 1956 - No. 902, May, 1958

Four Color 676 (#1), 765 (1/57), 902 4 8 12 28 47 65

WIN A PRIZE COMICS (Timmy The Timid Ghost #3 on?)
Charlton Comics: Feb, 1955 - No. 2, Apr, 1955

V1#1-S&K-a; Poe adapt; E.C. War swipe 74 148 222 470 810 1150
2-S&K-a 54 108 162 343 574 825

WINDY & WILLY (Also see Showcase #81)
National Periodical Publications: May-June, 1969 - No. 4, Nov-Dec, 1969

1- r/Dobie Gillis with some art changes begin 5 10 15 33 57 80
2-4 3 6 9 21 33 45

WINGS COMICS
Fiction House Mag.: 9/40 - No. 109, 9/49; No. 110, Wint, 1949-50; No. 111, Spring, 1950; No. 112, 1950(nd); No. 113 - No. 115, 1950(nd); No. 116, 1952(nd); No. 117, Fall, 1952 - No. 122, Wint, 1953-54; No. 123 - No. 124, 1954(nd)

1-Skull Squad, Clipper Kirk, Suicide Smith, Jane Martin, War Nurse, Phantom Falcons,
Greasemonkey Griffin, Parachute Patrol & Powder Burns begin; grey-tone-c
300 600 900 1965 3408 4850
2 132 264 396 845 1448 2050
3-5 87 174 261 553 952 1350
6-10: 8-Indicia shows #7 (#8 on cover) 68 136 204 435 743 1050
11-15 63 126 189 403 689 975
16-Origin & 1st app. Captain Wings & begin series 68 136 204 435 743 1050
17-20: 20-(4/42) 1st Japanese WWII-c 54 108 162 343 574 825
21-25,27-30 49 98 147 309 522 735
26-1st Good Girl WWII-c for this title 84 168 252 538 919 1300
31-34,36-40 41 82 123 256 428 600
35-Classic Nazi WWII-c 52 104 156 328 552 775
41-50 36 72 108 211 343 475
51-60: 60-Last Skull Squad 32 64 96 192 314 435
61-67: 66-Ghost Patrol begins (becomes Ghost Squadron #71 on), ends #112?
30 60 90 177 289 400
68,69: 68-Clipper Kirk becomes The Phantom Falcon-origin, Part 1; part 2 in #69
30 60 90 177 289 400
70-72: 70-1st app. The Phantom Falcon in costume, origin-Part 3; Capt. Wings battles
Col. Kamikaze in all 29 58 87 170 278 385
73-85,87,88,92,93,95-99: 80-Phantom Falcon by Larsen. 99-King of the Congo begins?
29 58 87 170 278 385
86-Graphic decapitation panel 31 62 93 182 296 410
89-91,94-Classic Good Girl covers 90 180 270 576 988 1400
100-(12/48) 31 62 93 182 296 410
101-124: 111-Last Jane Martin. 112-Flying Saucer-c (1950). 115-Used in **POP**, pg. 89.

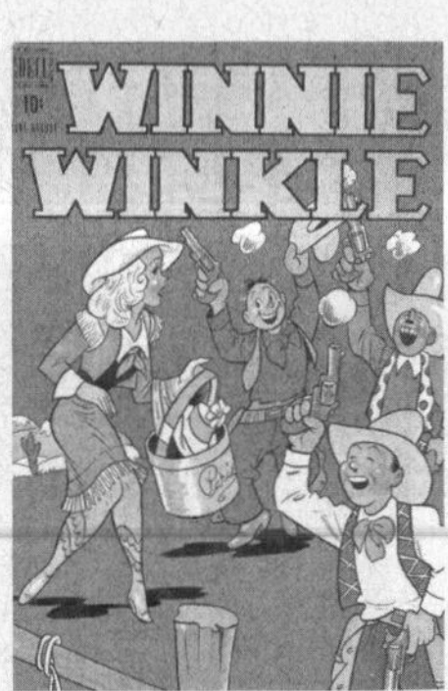

Winnie Winkle #6 © NYNS

Winter Soldier: The Bitter March #1 © MAR

Witchblade #24 © TCOW

GD VG FN VF VF/NM NM-
2.0 4.0 6.0 8.0 9.0 9.2

121-Atomic Explosion-c. 122-Korean War 22 44 66 130 213 295

NOTE: *World War II covers (Nazi or Japanese) on #1-17, 19-67. Bondage covers are common. Captain Wings battles Sky Hag-#75, 76; ...Mr. Atlantis-#85-92; ...Mr. Pupin(Red Agent)-#98-103. Capt. Wings by* **Elias**-*#52-64, 68, 69; by* **Lubbers**-*#29-32, 70-111; by* **Renee**-*#33-46.* **Evans** *a-85-106, 108-111(Jane Martin); text illos-72-84.* **Larsen** *a-52, 59, 64, 73-77. Jane Martin by* **Fran Hopper**-*#68-84; Suicide Smith by* **John Celardo**-*#72, 74, 76, 80-104; by* **Hollingsworth**-*#68-70, 105-109, 111; Ghost Squadron by* **Astarita**-*#67-79; by* **Maurice Whitman**-*#80-111. King of the Congo by* **Moreira**-*#99, 100. Skull Squad by* **M. Baker**-*#52-60; Clipper Kirk by* **Baker**-*#60, 61; by* **Colan**-*#53; by* **Ingels**-*(some issues?). Phantom Falcon by* **Larsen**-*#73-84.* **Elias** *c-58-72.* **Fawcette** *c-3-12, 16, 17, 19, 22-33.* **Lubbers** *c-74-109.* **Tuska** *a-5.* **Whitman** *c-110-124.* **Zolnerwich** *c-15, 21.*

WINGS OF THE EAGLES, THE
Dell Publishing Co.: No. 790, Apr, 1957 (10¢ & 15¢ editions exist)

Four Color 790-Movie; John Wayne photo-c; Toth-a 13 26 39 89 195 300

WINKY DINK (Adventures of...)
Pines Comics: No. 75, Mar, 1957 (one-shot)

75-Marv Levy-c/a 7 14 21 35 43 50

WINKY DINK (TV)
Dell Publishing Co.: No. 663, Nov, 1955

Four Color 663 (#1) 8 16 24 54 102 150

WINNEBAGO GRAVEYARD
Image Comics: Jun, 2017 - No. 4, Sept, 2017 ($3.99)

1-4-Steve Niles-s/Alison Sampson-a 4.00

WINNIE-THE-POOH (Also see Dynabrite Comics)
Gold Key No. 1-17/Whitman No. 18 on: January, 1977 - No. 33, July, 1984
(Walt Disney) (Winnie-The-Pooh began as Edward Bear in 1926 by Milne)

1-New art 5 10 15 30 50 70
2-5: 5-New material 3 6 9 14 20 26
6-17: 12-up-New material 2 4 6 9 13 16
18,19(Whitman) 2 4 6 13 18 22
20,21('80) pre-pack only 5 10 15 31 53 75
22('80) (scarcer) pre-pack only 8 16 24 55 105 155
23-28: 27(2/82), 28(4/82) 3 6 9 14 19 24
29-33 (#90299 on-c, no date or date code; pre-pack): 29(4/82), 30(5/83), 31(8/83), 32(4/84), 33(7/84) 3 6 9 21 33 45

WINNIE WINKLE (See Popular Comics & Super Comics)
Dell Publishing Co.: 1941 - No. 7, Sept-Nov, 1949

Large Feature Comic 2 (1941) 34 68 102 199 325 450
Four Color 94 (1945) 12 24 36 81 176 270
Four Color 174 8 16 24 56 108 160
1(3-5/48)-Contains daily & Sunday newspaper-r from 1939-1941
8 16 24 51 96 140
2 (6-8/48) 5 10 15 33 57 80
3-7 4 8 12 27 44 60

WINTER MEN, THE
DC Comics (WildStorm): Oct, 2005 - No. 5, Nov, 2006 ($2.99, limited series)

1-5-Brett Lewis-s/John Paul Leon-a 3.00
... Winter Special (2/09, $3.99) Lewis-s/Leon-a 4.00

WINTER SOLDIER (See Captain America 2005 series)
Marvel Comics: Apr, 2012 - No. 19, Aug, 2013 ($2.99)

1-Black Widow app.; Brubaker-s/Guice-a/Bermejo-c 1 3 4 6 8 10
2 6.00
3-19: 3-5-Dr. Doom app. 4.00

WINTER SOLDIER (See Captain America 2005 series)
Marvel Comics: Feb, 2019 - No. 5, Jun, 2019 ($3.99)

1-5-Kyle Higgins-s/Rod Reis-a; origin re-cap; intro RJ. 3-New robot arm 4.00

WINTER SOLDIER: THE BITTER MARCH
Marvel Comics: Apr, 2014 - No. 5, Sept, 2014 ($3.99, limited series)

1-5: 1-Remender-s/Boschi-a/Robinson-c; set in 1966; Nick Fury app. 4.00

WINTER SOLDIER: WINTER KILLS
Marvel Comics: Feb, 2007 ($3.99, one-shot)

1-Flashback to Christmas Eve 1944; Toro & Sub-Mariner app.; Brubaker-s/Weeks-a 5.00

WINTERWORLD
Eclipse Comics: Sept, 1987 - No. 3, Mar, 1988 ($1.75, limited series)

1-3 3.00

WINTERWORLD
IDW Publishing: Jun, 2014 - No. 7, Jan, 2015 ($3.99)

1-7: 1-Chuck Dixon-s/Butch Guice-a; three covers. 5-7-Giorello-a 4.00
#0-(3/15, $3.99) Origin of Wynn; Dixon-s/Edwards-a; covers by Edwards & Guice 4.00

GD VG FN VF VF/NM NM-
2.0 4.0 6.0 8.0 9.0 9.2

WINTERWORLD: FROZEN FLEET
IDW Publishing: May, 2015 - No. 3, Jul, 2015 ($3.99, limited series)

1-3: 1-Chuck Dixon-s/Esteve Polls-a; three covers. 2,3-Two covers 4.00

WISDOM
Marvel Comics (MAX): Jan, 2007 - No. 6, July, 2007 ($3.99, limited series)

1-6: 1-Hairsine-a/c; Cornell-s. 3-6-Manuel Garcia-a 4.00
...: Rudiments of Wisdom TPB (2007, $21.99) r/#1-6; series pitch and sketch page 22.00

WISE GUYS (See Harvey...)

WISE LITTLE HEN, THE
David McKay Publ./Whitman: 1934 ,1935(48 pgs.); 1937 (Story book)

nn-(1934 edition w/dust jacket)(48 pgs. with color, 8-3/4x9-3/4") -Debut of Donald Duck (see Advs. of Mickey Mouse); Donald app. on cover with Wise Little Hen & Practical Pig; painted cover; same artist as the B&W's from Silly Symphony Cartoon, The Wise Little Hen (1934) (McKay)
Book w/dust jacket 265 530 795 1694 2897 4100
Dust jacket only 63 126 189 403 689 975
nn-(1935 edition w/dust jacket), same as 1934 ed. 152 304 456 965 1658 2350
888 (1937)(9-1/2x13", 12 pgs.)(Whitman) Donald Duck app.
39 78 117 231 378 525

WISE SON: THE WHITE WOLF
DC Comics (Milestone): Nov, 1996 - No. 4, Feb, 1997 ($2.50, limited series)

1-4: Ho Che Anderson-c/a 3.00

WIT AND WISDOM OF WATERGATE (Humor magazine)
Marvel Comics: 1973, 76 pgs., squarebound

1-Low print run 5 10 15 33 57 80

WITCHBLADE (Also see Cyblade/Shi, Tales Of The..., & Top Cow Classics)
Image Comics (Top Cow Productions): Nov, 1995 - No. 185, Nov, 2015 ($2.50/$2.99)

0 1 2 3 5 6 8
1/2-Mike Turner/Marc Silvestri-c. 3 6 9 19 30 40
1/2 Gold Ed., 1/2 Chromium-c 3 6 9 19 30 40
1/2-(Vol. 2, 11/02, $2.99) Wohl-s/Ching-a/c 3.00
1-Mike Turner-a(p) 4 8 12 19 30 45
1-Anniversary Edition (7/20, $4.99) r/#1 with creator interviews and character history 5.00
1,2-American Ent. Encore Ed. 1 2 3 4 5 7
2,3 2 4 6 11 16 20
4,5 2 4 6 8 10 12
6-9: 8-Wraparound-c. 9-Tony Daniel-a(p) 1 2 3 5 6 8
9-Sunset variant-c 2 4 6 8 10 12
9-DF variant-c 2 4 6 9 12 15
10-Flip book w/Darkness #0, 1st app. the Darkness 1 3 4 6 8 10
10-Variant-c 2 4 6 8 10 12
10-Gold logo 3 6 9 14 20 25
10-($3.95) Dynamic Forces alternate-c 1 2 3 5 6 8
11-15 5.00
16-19: 18,19-"Family Ties" Darkness x-over pt. 1,4 4.00
18-Face to face variant-c, 18-American Ent. Ed., 19-AE Gold Ed.
1 2 3 5 6 8
20-25: 24-Pearson, Green-a. 25-($2.95) Turner-a(p) 4.00
25 (Prism variant) 25.00
25 (Special) 10.00
26-39: 26-Green-a begins 3.00
27 (Variant) 6.00
40-49,51-53: 40-Begin Jenkins & Veitch-s/Keu Cha-a. 47-Zulli-c/a 3.00
40-Pittsburgh Convention Preview edition; B&W preview of #40 3.00
49-Gold logo 5.00
50-($4.95) Darkness app.; Ching-a; B&W preview of Universe 5.00
54-59: 54-Black outer-c with gold foil logo; Wohl-s/Manapul-a 3.00
60-74,76-91,93-99: 60-($2.99) Endgame x-over with Tomb Raider #25 & Evo #1. 64,65-Magdalena app. 71-Kirk-a. 77,81-85-Land-c. 80-Four covers. 87-Bachalo-a 3.00
75-($4.99) Manapul-a 5.00
92-($4.99) Origin of the Witchblade; art by various incl. Bachalo, Perez, Linsner, Cooke 5.00
100-($4.99) Five covers incl. Turner, Silvestri, Linsner; art by various; Jake dies 5.00
101-124,126-143: 103-Danielle Baptiste gets the Witchblade; Linsner variant-c. 116-124,140,141-Sejic-a. 126-128-War of the Witchblades. 134-136-Aphrodite IV app. 139-Gaydos-a. 143-Matt Dow Smith-a 3.00
125-($3.99) War of the Witchblades begins; 3 covers; Sejic-a 4.00
144-($4.99) Origin retold; wraparound-c; Sejic-a; back-up w/Sablik-s; pin-up gallery 5.00
145-149-($3.99) Sejic-a/c. 149-Angelus app. 4.00
150-($4.99) Four covers; last Marz-s; Sejic-a; cover gallery & series timeline 5.00
151-174-($2.99) Altered reality after Artifacts #13; Seeley-s; multiple covers 3.00
175-($5.99) Three covers; Marz-s; Laura Braga-a; Temple of Shadows back-up 6.00

Witchblade (2017 series) #3 © TCOW

The Witcher #1 © CD Projekt

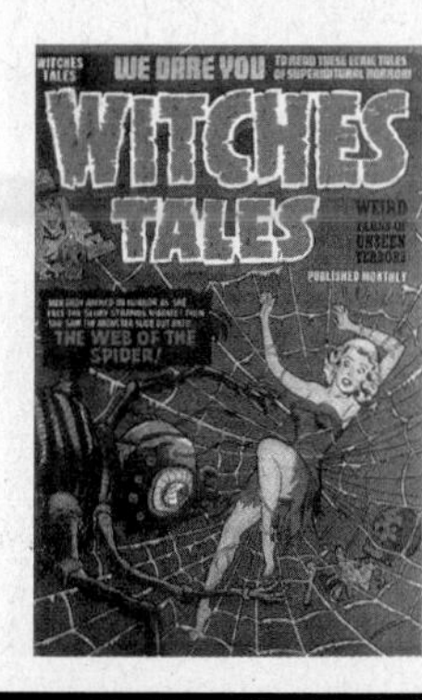

Witches Tales #12 © HARV

	GD	VG	FN	VF	VF/NM	NM-
	2.0	4.0	6.0	8.0	9.0	9.2

176-184-($3.99) 180-Hine-s/Rearte-a 4.00
185-($5.99)-Last issue; Marz & Hawkins-s; art by various; bonus preview of Switch #1 6.00
... and Tomb Raider (4/05, $2.99) Jae Lee-c; art by Lee and Texiera 3.00
...: Animated (8/03, $2.99) Magdalena & Darkness app.; Dini-s/Bone, Bullock, Cooke-a/c 3.00
... Annual 2009 (4/09, $3.99) Basaldua-a 4.00
... Annual #1 (12/10, $4.99) the Witchblade in Stalingrad 1942, Shasteen-a; Haley-a 5.00
...: Art of the Witchblade (7/06, $2.99) pin-ups by various incl. Turner, Land, Linsner 3.00
...: Bearers of the Blade (7/06, $2.99) pin-up/profiles of bearers of the Witchblade 3.00
...: Blood Oath (8/04, $4.99) Sara teams with Phenix & Sibilla; Roux-a 5.00
...: Blood Relations TPB (2003, $12.99) r/#54-58 13.00
... Case Files 1 (10/14, $3.99) Character profiles and story summaries 4.00
... Compendium Vol. 1 (2006, $59.99) r/#1-50; gallery of variant covers and art 60.00
... Compendium Vol. 2 (2007, $59.99) r/#51-100; gallery of variant covers and art 60.00
... Cover Gallery Vol. 1 (12/05, $2.99) intro. by Stan Lee 3.00
.../Darkchylde (7/00, $2.50) Green-s/a(p) 3.00
.../Dark Minds (6/04, $9.99) new story plus r/Dark Minds/Witchblade #1 10.00
.../Darkness: Family Ties Collected Edition (10/98, $9.95) r/#18,19 and Darkness #9,10 10.00
.../Darkness Special (12/99, $3.95) Green-c/a 4.00
... Day of the Outlaws (4/13, $3.99) Fialkov-s/Blake-a; Witchblade in 1878 Colorado 4.00
...: Demon 1 (2003, $6.99) Mark Millar-s/Jae Lee-c/a 7.00
.../Devi (4/08, $3.99) Basaldua-a/Land-c; continues in Devi/Witchblade 4.00
...: Distinctions (See Tales of the Witchblade)
...: Due Process (8/10, $3.99) Alina Urusov-a/c; Phil Smith-s 4.00
.../Elektra (3/97, $2.95) Devil's Reign Pt. 6 4.00
... Gallery (11/00, $2.95) Profile pages and pin-ups by various; Turner-c 3.00
Image Firsts: Witchblade #1 (4/10, $1.00) reprints #1 3.00
Infinity (5/99, $3.50) Lobdell-s/Pollina-c/a 4.00
.../Lady Death (11/01, $4.95) Manapul-c/a 5.00
...: Prevailing TPB (2000, $14.95) r/#20-25; new Turner-c 15.00
...: Revelations TPB (2000, $24.95) r/#9-17; new Turner-c 25.00
.../The Punisher (6/07, $3.99) Marz-s/Melo-a/Linsner-c 4.00
.../Tomb Raider #1/2 (7/00, $2.95) Covers by Turner and Cha 4.00
... Unbalanced Pieces FCBD Edition (5/12, giveaway) Christopher-c 3.00
...: Vol. 1 TPB (1/08, $4.99) r/#80-85; Marz intro.; cover gallery 5.00
...: Vol. 2 TPB (2/08, $14.99) r/#86-92; cover gallery 15.00
...: Vol. 3 TPB (3/08, $14.99) r/#93-100; Edgington intro.; cover gallery 15.00
... vs. Frankenstein: Monster War 2005 (8/05, $2.99) pt. 3 of x-over 3.00
...: Witch Hunt Vol. 1 TPB (2/06, $14.99) r/#80-85; Marz intro.; Choi afterward; cover gallery 15.00
Wizard #500 10.00
.../Wolverine (6/04, $2.99) Basaldua-c/a; Claremont-s 3.00

WITCHBLADE
Image Comics (Top Cow): Dec, 2017 - Present ($3.99)

1-18: 1-Kittredge-s/Ingranata-a; intro. Alex Underwood 4.00

WITCHBLADE/ALIENS/THE DARKNESS/PREDATOR
Dark Horse Comics/Top Cow Productions: Nov, 2000 ($2.99)

1-3-Mel Rubi-a 4.00

WITCHBLADE COLLECTED EDITION
Image Comics (Top Cow Productions): July, 1996 - No. 8 ($4.95/$6.95, squarebound, limited series)

1-7-($4.95): Two issues reprinted in each 5.00
8-($6.95) r/#15-17 7.00
...Slipcase (10/96, $10.95)-Packaged w/ Coll. Ed. #1-4 11.00

WITCHBLADE: DEMON REBORN
Dynamite Entertainment: 2012 - No. 4, 2012 ($3.99, limited series)

1-4-Ande Parks-s/Jose Luis-a; covers by Calero & Jae Lee 4.00

WITCHBLADE: DESTINY'S CHILD
Image Comics (Top Cow): Jun, 2000 - No. 3, Sept, 2000 ($2.95, limited series)

1-3: 1-Boller-a/Keu Cha-c 3.00

WITCHBLADE: MANGA (Takeru Manga)
Image Comics (Top Cow): Feb, 2007 - No. 12, Mar, 2008 ($2.99/$3.99)

1-4-Colored reprints of Japanese Witchblade manga. 1-Three covers. 2-Two covers 3.00
5-12-($3.99) 4.00

WITCHBLADE: OBAKEMONO
Image Comics (Top Cow Productions): 2002 ($9.95, one-shot graphic novel)

1-Fiona Avery-s/Billy Tan-a; forward by Straczynski 10.00

WITCHBLADE/ RED SONJA
Dynamite Ent./Top Cow: 2012 - No. 5, 2012 ($3.99, limited series)

1-5-Doug Wagner-s/Cezar Razek-a/Alé Garza-c 4.00

WITCHBLADE: SHADES OF GRAY
Dynamite Ent./Top Cow: 2007 - No. 4, 2007 ($3.50, lim. series)

1,2: 1-Sara Pezzini meets Dorian Gray; Segovia-a; multiple covers 3.50

WITCHBLADE/ TOMB RAIDER SPECIAL (Also see Tomb Raider/...)
Image Comics (Top Cow Productions): Dec, 1998 ($2.95)

1-Based on video game character; Turner-a(p) 4.00
1-Silvestri variant-c 6.00
1-Turner bikini variant-c 10.00
1-Prism-c 12.00
Wizard 1/2 -Turner-s 10.00

WITCHCRAFT (See Strange Mysteries, Super Reprint #18)
Avon Periodicals: Mar-Apr, 1952 - No. 6, Mar, 1953

	GD	VG	FN	VF	VF/NM	NM-
1-Kubert-a; 1 pg. Check-a	110	220	330	704	1202	1700
2-Kubert & Check-a; classic skull-c	161	322	483	1030	1765	2500
3,6: 3-Lawrence-a; Kinstler inside-c	61	122	183	390	670	950
4-People cooked alive c/story	129	258	387	826	1413	2000
5-Kelly Freas painted-c	129	258	387	826	1413	2000

NOTE: *Hollingsworth a-4-6; c-4, 6.* **McCann** *a-3?*

WITCHCRAFT
DC Comics (Vertigo): June, 1994 - No. 3, Aug, 1994 ($2.95, limited series)

1-3: James Robinson scripts & Kaluta-c in all 4.00
1-Platinum Edition 15.00
Trade paperback-(1996, $14.95)-r/#1-3; Kaluta-c 15.00

WITCHCRAFT: LA TERREUR
DC Comics (Vertigo): Apr, 1998 - No. 3, Jun, 1998 ($2.50, limited series)

1-3: Robinson-s/Zulli & Locke-a; interlocking cover images 3.00

WITCH DOCTOR (See Walking Dead #85 flip book for preview)
Image Comics: Jun, 2011 - No. 4, Nov, 2011 ($2.99, limited series)

1-4-Seifert-s/Ketner-a/c 3.00
...: Mal Practice 1-6 (11/12 - No. 6, 4/13, $2.99) Seifert-s/Ketner-a/c 3.00
...: The Resuscitation (12/11, $2.99) Seifert-s/Ketner-a/c 3.00

WITCHER, THE
Dark Horse Comics: Mar, 2014 - No. 5, Jul, 2014 ($3.99, limited series)

1-5-Tobin-s/Querio-a 4.00

WITCHER, THE: FADING MEMORIES
Dark Horse Comics: Nov, 2020 - No. 4 ($3.99, limited series)

1-3-Bartosz Sztybor-s/Amad Mir-a 4.00

WITCHER, THE: FOX CHILDREN
Dark Horse Comics: Apr, 2015 - No. 5, Aug, 2015 ($3.99, limited series)

1-5-Tobin-s/Querio-a 4.00

WITCHER, THE: OF FLESH AND FLAME
Dark Horse Comics: Dec, 2018 - No. 4, Mar, 2019 ($3.99, limited series)

1-4-Motyka-s/Strychowska-a 4.00

WITCHES
Marvel Comics: Aug, 2004 - No. 4, Sept, 2004 ($2.99, limited series)

1-4: 1,2-Deodato, Jr-a; Dr. Strange app. 3,4-Conrad-a 3.00
... Vol. 1: The Gathering (2004, $9.99) r/series 10.00

WITCHES TALES (Witches Western Tales #29,30)
Witches Tales/Harvey Publications: Jan, 1951 - No. 28, Dec, 1954 (date misprinted as 4/55)

	GD	VG	FN	VF	VF/NM	NM-
1-Powell-a (1 pg.)	77	154	231	493	847	1200
2-Eye injury panel	42	84	126	265	445	625
3-7,9,10	39	78	117	231	378	525
8-Eye injury panels	40	80	120	246	411	575
11-13,15,16: 12-Acid in face story	36	72	108	214	347	480
14,17-Powell/Nostrand-a. 17-Atomic disaster story	37	74	111	218	354	490
18-Nostrand-a; E.C. swipe/Shock S.S.	37	74	111	218	354	490
19-Nostrand-a; E.C. swipe/ "Glutton"; Devil-c	53	106	159	334	567	800
20-24-Nostrand-a. 21-E.C. swipe; rape story. 23-Wood E.C. swipes/Two-Fisted Tales #34	37	74	111	222	361	500
25-Nostrand-a; E.C. swipe/Mad Barber; decapitation-c	432	864	1296	3154	5577	8000
26-28: 27-r/#6 with diff.-c. 28-r/#8 with diff.-c	26	52	78	154	252	350

NOTE: **Check** *a-24.* **Elias** *c-8, 10, 16-27.* **Kremer** *a-18; c-25.* **Nostrand** *a-17-25; 14, 17(w/Powell).* **Palais** *a-1, 2, 4(2), 5(2), 7-9, 12, 14, 15, 17.* **Powell** *a-3-7, 10, 11, 19-27. Bondage-c 1, 3, 5, 6, 8, 9.*

WITCHES TALES (Magazine)
Eerie Publications: V1#7, July, 1969 - V7#1, Feb, 1975 (B&W, 52 pgs.)

	GD	VG	FN	VF	VF/NM	NM-
V1#7(7/69)	8	16	24	54	102	150
V1#8(9/69), 9(11/69)	6	12	18	41	76	110

The Witching Hour #84 © DC

Witness #1 © MAR

Wolf Moon #1 © Bunn & Haun

	GD 2.0	VG 4.0	FN 6.0	VF 8.0	VF/NM 9.0	NM- 9.2
V2#1-6('70), V3#1-6('71)	5	10	15	33	57	80
V4#1-6('72), V5#1-6('73), V6#1-6('74), V7#1	5	10	15	30	50	70

NOTE: *Ajax/Farrell reprints in early issues.*

WITCHES' WESTERN TALES (Formerly Witches Tales)(Western Tales #31 on)
Harvey Publications: No. 29, Feb, 1955 - No. 30, Apr, 1955

	GD 2.0	VG 4.0	FN 6.0	VF 8.0	VF/NM 9.0	NM- 9.2
29,30-Featuring Clay Duncan & Boys' Ranch; S&K-r/from Boys' Ranch including-c. 29-Last pre-code	15	30	45	94	147	200

WITCHFINDER, THE
Image Comics (Liar): Sept, 1999 - No. 3, Jan, 2000 ($2.95)

	GD 2.0	VG 4.0	FN 6.0	VF 8.0	VF/NM 9.0	NM- 9.2
1-3-Romano-a/Sharon & Matthew Scott-plot						3.00

WITCHFINDER: CITY OF THE DEAD
Dark Horse Comics: Aug, 2016 - No. 5, Dec, 2016 ($3.99, limited series)

	GD 2.0	VG 4.0	FN 6.0	VF 8.0	VF/NM 9.0	NM- 9.2
1-5-Mignola & Roberson-s/Stenbeck-a/Tedesco-c						4.00

WITCHFINDER: LOST AND GONE FOREVER
Dark Horse Comics: Feb, 2011 - No. 5, Jun, 2011 ($3.50, limited series)

	GD 2.0	VG 4.0	FN 6.0	VF 8.0	VF/NM 9.0	NM- 9.2
1-5-John Severin-a; Mignola & Arcudi-s. 1-Two covers by Mignola & Severin						3.50

WITCHFINDER: THE GATES OF HEAVEN
Dark Horse Comics: May, 2018 - No. 5, Sept, 2018 ($3.99, limited series)

	GD 2.0	VG 4.0	FN 6.0	VF 8.0	VF/NM 9.0	NM- 9.2
1-5-Mignola & Roberson-s/D'Israeli-c/a						4.00

WITCHFINDER: THE REIGN OF DARKNESS
Dark Horse Comics: Nov, 2019 - No. 5, Mar, 2020 ($3.99, limited series)

	GD 2.0	VG 4.0	FN 6.0	VF 8.0	VF/NM 9.0	NM- 9.2
1-5-Mignola & Roberson-s/Mitten-a/c						4.00

WITCH HUNTER
Malibu Comics (Ultraverse): Apr, 1996 ($2.50, one-shot)

	GD 2.0	VG 4.0	FN 6.0	VF 8.0	VF/NM 9.0	NM- 9.2
1						3.00

WITCHING, THE
DC Comics (Vertigo): Aug, 2004 - No. 10, May, 2005 ($2.95/$2.99)

	GD 2.0	VG 4.0	FN 6.0	VF 8.0	VF/NM 9.0	NM- 9.2
1-10-Vankin-s/Gallagher-a/McPherson-c. 1,2-Lucifer app.						3.00

WITCHING HOUR ("The ..." in later issues)
National Periodical Publ./DC Comics: Feb-Mar, 1969 - No. 85, Oct, 1978

	GD 2.0	VG 4.0	FN 6.0	VF 8.0	VF/NM 9.0	NM- 9.2
1-Toth-a, plus Neal Adams-a (2 pgs.)	16	32	48	110	243	375
2,6: 6-Toth-a	7	14	21	48	89	130
3,5-Wrightson-a; Toth-p. 3-Last 12¢ issue	7	14	21	49	92	135
4,12-Toth-a	5	10	15	33	57	80
7-11-Adams-c; Toth-a in all. 8-Adams-a	6	12	18	41	76	110
13-Neal Adams-c/a, 2pgs.	7	14	21	46	86	125
14-Williamson/Garzon, Jones-a; N. Adams-c	7	14	21	44	82	120
15	3	6	9	19	30	40
16-21-(52 pg. Giants)	4	8	12	23	37	50
22-37,39,40	3	6	9	14	19	24
38-(100 pgs.)	5	10	15	31	53	75
41-60	2	4	6	10	14	18
61-83,85	2	4	6	8	11	14
84-(44 pgs.)	2	4	6	9	13	16

NOTE: *Combined with The Unexpected with #189.* ***Neal Adams*** *c-7-11, 13, 14.* ***Alcala*** *a-24, 27, 33, 41, 43.* ***Anderson*** *a-9, 38.* ***Cardy*** *c-4, 5.* ***Kaluta*** *a-7.* ***Kane*** *a-12p.* ***Morrow*** *a-10, 13, 15, 16.* ***Nino*** *a-31, 40, 45, 47.* ***Redondo*** *a-20, 23, 24, 34, 65; c-53.* ***Reese*** *a-23.* ***Sparling*** *a-1.* ***Toth*** *a-1, 3-12, 38r.* ***Tuska*** *a-11, 12.* ***Wood*** *a-15.*

WITCHING HOUR, THE
DC Comics (Vertigo): 1999 - No. 3, 2000 ($5.95, limited series)

	GD 2.0	VG 4.0	FN 6.0	VF 8.0	VF/NM 9.0	NM- 9.2
1-3-Bachalo & Thibert-c/a; Loeb & Bachalo-s						6.00
Hardcover (2000, $29.95) r/#1-3; embossed cover						30.00
Softcover (2003, $19.95), (2009, $19.99) r/#1-3						20.00

WITCHING HOUR, THE
DC Comics (Vertigo): Dec, 2013 ($7.99, one-shot)

	GD 2.0	VG 4.0	FN 6.0	VF 8.0	VF/NM 9.0	NM- 9.2
1-Short story anthology by various incl. DeConnick, Doyle, Buckingham; Frison-c						8.00

WITHIN OUR REACH
Star Reach Productions: 1991 ($7.95, 84 pgs.)

	GD 2.0	VG 4.0	FN 6.0	VF 8.0	VF/NM 9.0	NM- 9.2
nn-Spider-Man, Concrete by Chadwick, Gift of the Magi by Russell; Christmas stories; Chadwick-c; Spidey back-c						8.00

WITH THE MARINES ON THE BATTLEFRONTS OF THE WORLD
Toby Press: 1953 (no month) - No. 2, Mar, 1954 (Photo covers)

	GD 2.0	VG 4.0	FN 6.0	VF 8.0	VF/NM 9.0	NM- 9.2
1-John Wayne story	34	68	102	199	325	450
2-Monty Hall in #1,2	14	28	42	76	108	140

WITH THE U.S. PARATROOPS BEHIND ENEMY LINES (Also see U.S. Paratroops...; #2-6 titled U.S. Paratroops...)
Avon Periodicals: 1951 - No. 6, Dec, 1952

	GD 2.0	VG 4.0	FN 6.0	VF 8.0	VF/NM 9.0	NM- 9.2
1-Wood-c & inside f/c	22	44	66	128	209	290
2-Kinstler-c & inside f/c only	14	28	42	81	118	155
3-6: 5-Extreme violence. 6-Kinstler-c & inside f/c only	13	26	39	74	105	135

NOTE: ***Kinstler*** *c-2, 4-6.*

WITNESS, THE (Also see Amazing Mysteries, Captain America #71, Ideal #4, Marvel Mystery #92 & Mystic #7)
Marvel Comics (MjMe): Sept, 1948

	GD 2.0	VG 4.0	FN 6.0	VF 8.0	VF/NM 9.0	NM- 9.2
1(Scarce)-Rico-c?	300	600	900	2070	3635	5200

WITTY COMICS
Irwin H. Rubin Publ./Chicago Nite Life News No. 2: 1945 - No. 2, 1945

	GD 2.0	VG 4.0	FN 6.0	VF 8.0	VF/NM 9.0	NM- 9.2
1-The Pioneer, Junior Patrol; Japanese war-c	39	78	117	240	395	550
2-The Pioneer, Junior Patrol	18	36	54	109	172	235

WIZARD BEACH
BOOM! Studios: Dec, 2018 - No. 5, Apr, 2019 ($3.99, limited series)

	GD 2.0	VG 4.0	FN 6.0	VF 8.0	VF/NM 9.0	NM- 9.2
1-5-Shaun Simon-s/Conor Nolan-a						4.00

WIZARD OF FOURTH STREET, THE
Dark Horse Comics: Dec, 1987 - No. 2, 1988 ($1.75, B&W, limited series)

	GD 2.0	VG 4.0	FN 6.0	VF 8.0	VF/NM 9.0	NM- 9.2
1,2: Adapts novel by S/F author Simon Hawke						3.00

WIZARD OF OZ (See Classics Illustrated Jr. 535, Dell Jr. Treasury No. 5, First Comics Graphic Novel, Marvel Treasury of Oz, and MGM's Marvelous...)
Dell Publishing Co.: No. 1308, Mar-May, 1962 (TV)

	GD 2.0	VG 4.0	FN 6.0	VF 8.0	VF/NM 9.0	NM- 9.2
Four Color 1308	12	24	36	83	182	280

WIZARDS OF MICKEY (Mickey Mouse)
BOOM! Studios: Jan, 2010 - No. 8, Aug, 2010 ($2.99)

	GD 2.0	VG 4.0	FN 6.0	VF 8.0	VF/NM 9.0	NM- 9.2
1-8: 1,2-Ambrosio-s; 3 covers on each. 3-8-Two covers						3.00

WIZARD'S TALE, THE
Image Comics (Homage Comics): 1997 ($19.95, squarebound, one-shot)

	GD 2.0	VG 4.0	FN 6.0	VF 8.0	VF/NM 9.0	NM- 9.2
nn-Kurt Busiek-s/David Wenzel-painted-a/c						20.00

WOLF & RED
Dark Horse Comics: Apr, 1995 - No. 3, June, 1995 ($2.50, limited series)

	GD 2.0	VG 4.0	FN 6.0	VF 8.0	VF/NM 9.0	NM- 9.2
1-Characters created by Tex Avery	2	4	6	9	12	15
2,3						6.00

WOLF COP
Dynamite Entertainment: 2016 - No. 3, 2016 ($3.99)

	GD 2.0	VG 4.0	FN 6.0	VF 8.0	VF/NM 9.0	NM- 9.2
1-3-Max Marks-s/Arcana Studios-a						4.00

WOLFF & BYRD, COUNSELORS OF THE MACABRE (Becomes Supernatural Law with issue #24)
Exhibit A Press: May, 1994 - No. 23, Aug, 1999 ($2.50, B&W)

	GD 2.0	VG 4.0	FN 6.0	VF 8.0	VF/NM 9.0	NM- 9.2
1-23-Batton Lash-s/a						3.00

WOLF GAL (See Al Capp's...)

WOLFMAN, THE (See Movie Classics)

WOLF MOON
DC Comics (Vertigo): Feb, 2015 - No. 6, Jul, 2015 ($3.99, limited series)

	GD 2.0	VG 4.0	FN 6.0	VF 8.0	VF/NM 9.0	NM- 9.2
1-6-Bunn-s/Haun-a. 1-Covers by Jae Lee and Jeremy Haun						4.00

WOLFPACK
Marvel Comics: Feb, 1988 ($7.95); Aug, 1988 - No. 12, July, 1989 (Lim. series)

	GD 2.0	VG 4.0	FN 6.0	VF 8.0	VF/NM 9.0	NM- 9.2
1-(2/88) 1st app./origin (Marvel Graphic Novel #31)	2	4	6	8	10	12
1-12: 1-(8/88) Hama-s						4.00

WOLVERINE (See Alpha Flight, Daredevil #196, 249, Ghost Rider; Wolverine; Punisher, Havok &..., Incredible Hulk #180, Incredible Hulk &..., Kitty Pryde And..., Marvel Comics Presents, New Avengers, Power Pack, Punisher and..., Rampaging ..., Spider-Man vs... & X-Men #94)

WOLVERINE (See Incredible Hulk #180 for 1st app.)
Marvel Comics Group: Sept, 1982 - No. 4, Dec, 1982 (limited series)

	GD 2.0	VG 4.0	FN 6.0	VF 8.0	VF/NM 9.0	NM- 9.2
1-Frank Miller-c/a(p) in all; Claremont-s	7	14	21	46	86	125
2-4	4	8	12	28	47	65
... By Claremont & Miller No. 1 Facsimile Edition (4/20, $3.99) r/#1 with original ads						4.00
... By Claremont & Miller HC (2006, $19.99) r/#1-4 & Uncanny X-Men #172-173						20.00
TPB 1(7/87, $4.95)-Reprints #1-4 with new Miller-c	2	4	6	11	16	20
TPB nn (2nd printing, $9.95)-r/#1-4	2	4	6	8	10	12

WOLVERINE
Marvel Comics: Nov, 1988 - No. 189, June, 2003 ($1.50/$1.75/$1.95/$1.99/$2.25)

	GD 2.0	VG 4.0	FN 6.0	VF 8.0	VF/NM 9.0	NM- 9.2
1-Claremont-s/Buscema-a/c	5	10	15	30	50	70
2	3	6	9	16	23	30
3-5: 4-BWS back-c	2	4	6	11	16	20

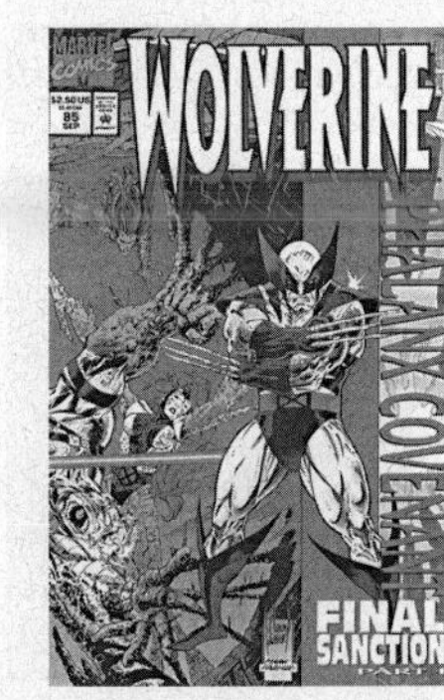

Wolverine #85 © MAR

Wolverine #186 © MAR

Wolverine V3 #42 © MAR

	GD 2.0	VG 4.0	FN 6.0	VF 8.0	VF/NM 9.0	NM- 9.2
6,7,9: 6-McFarlane back-c. 7-Hulk app.	2	4	6	8	10	12
8-Classic Grey Hulk-c; Hulk app.	5	10	15	30	50	70
10-1st battle with Sabretooth (before Wolverine had his claws)	4	8	12	23	37	50
11-16: 11-New costume	1	3	4	6	8	10
17-20: 17-Byrne-c/a(p) begins, ends #23	1	2	3	5	6	8
21-30: 24,25,27-Jim Lee-c. 26-Begin $1.75-c						6.00
31-40,44,47						5.00
41-Sabretooth claims to be Wolverine's father; Cable cameo	2	4	6	9	12	15
41-Gold 2nd printing ($1.75)	2	4	6	9	12	15
42-Sabretooth, Cable & Nick Fury app.; Sabretooth proven not to be Wolverine's father	2	4	6	8	10	12
42-Gold ink 2nd printing ($1.75)	2	4	6	8	10	12
43-Sabretooth cameo (2 panels); saga ends						6.00
45,46-Sabretooth-c/stories						6.00
48,49,51-Sabretooth app. 48-Begin 3 part Weapon X sequel. 51-Sabretooth-c & app.						6.00
50-(64 pgs.)-Die cut-c; Wolverine back to old yellow costume; Forge, Cyclops, Jubilee, Jean Grey & Nick Fury app.	2	4	6	9	12	15
52-74,76-80: 54-Shatterstar (from X-Force) app. 55-Gambit, Jubilee, Sunfire-c/story. 55-57,73-Gambit app. 57-Mariko Yashida dies (Late 7/92). 58,59-Terror, Inc. x-over. 60-64-Sabretooth storyline (60,62,64-c)						5.00
75-($3.95, 68 pgs.)-Wolverine hologram on-c	1	2	3	5	6	8
81-84,86: 81-bound-in card sheet						5.00
85-($2.50)-Newsstand edition						5.00
85-($3.50)-Collectors edition						6.00
87-90 ($1.95)-Deluxe edition						5.00
87-90 ($1.50)-Regular edition						4.00
91-99,101-114: 91-Return from "Age of Apocalypse," 93-Juggernaut app. 94-Gen X app. 101-104-Elektra app. 104-Origin of Onslaught. 105-Onslaught x-over. 110-Shaman-c/app. 114-Alternate-c						4.00
100 ($3.95)-Hologram-c; Wolverine loses humanity	2	4	6	9	13	16
100 ($2.95)-Regular-c.	1	3	4	6	8	10
102.5 (1996 Wizard mail-away)-Deadpool app.; Vallejo-c/Buckingham-a						110.00
115-124: 115- Operation Zero Tolerance						4.00
125-($2.99) Wraparound-c; Viper secret						5.00
125-($6.95) Jae Lee variant-c						8.00
126-144: 126,127-Sabretooth-c/app. 128-Sabretooth & Shadowcat app.; Platt-a. 129-Wendigo-c/app. 131-Initial printing contained lettering error. 133-Begin Larsen-s/ Matsuda-a. 138-Galactus-c/app. 139-Cable app.; Yu-a. 142,143-Alpha Flight app.						3.00
145-($2.99) 25th Anniversary issue; Hulk and Sabretooth app.						4.00
145-($3.99) Foil enhanced cover (also see Promotional section for Nabisco mail-in ed.)						5.00
146,147-Apocalypse: The Twelve; Angel-c/app.	1	2	3	5	6	8
148,149: 149-Nova-c/app.						3.00
150-($2.99) Steve Skroce-s/a						4.00
151-153,156-174,176-182,184-189: 151-Begin $2.25-c. 156-Churchill-a. 159-Chen-a begins. 160-Sabretooth app. 163-Texeira-a(p). 167-BWS-c. 172,173-Alpha Flight app. 176-Colossus app. 185,186-Punisher app.						3.00
154,155-Deadpool app.; Liefeld-s/a.	3	6	9	14	20	26
175,183-($3.50) 175-Sabretooth app.						4.00
#(-1) Flashback (7/97) Logan meets Col. Fury; Nord-a						3.00
Annual nn (1990, $4.50, squarebound, 52 pgs.)-The Jungle Adventure; Simonson scripts; Mignola-c/a						6.00
Annual 2 (12/90, $4.95, squarebound, 52 pgs.)-Bloodlust						6.00
Annual nn (#3, 8/91, $5.95, 68 pgs.)-Rahne of Terror; Cable & The New Mutants app.; Andy Kubert-c/a (2nd print exists)						6.00
Annual '95 (1995, $3.95)						5.00
Annual '96 (1996, $2.95)- Wraparound-c; Silver Samurai, Yukio, and Red Ronin app.						5.00
Annual '97 ($2.99) - Wraparound-c						5.00
Annual 1999, 2000 ($3.50) : 1999-Deadpool app.						5.00
Annual 2001 ($2.99) - Tieri-s; JH Williams-c						5.00
...Battles The Incredible Hulk nn (1989, $4.95, squarebound, 52 pg.) r/Incr. Hulk #180,181	2	4	6	9	13	16
Best of Wolverine Vol. 1 HC (2004, $29.99) oversized reprints of Hulk #181, mini-series #1-4, Capt. America Ann, #8, Uncanny X-Men #205 & Marvel Comics Presents #72-84						30.00
...Black Rio (11/98, $5.99)-Casey-s/Oscar Jimenez-a						6.00
...Blood Debt TPB (7/01, $12.95)-r/#150-153; Skroce-c						13.00
...Blood Hungry nn (1993, $6.95, 68 pgs.)-Kieth-r/Marvel Comics Presents #85-92 w/ new Kieth-c						7.00
...: Bloody Choices nn (1993, $7.95, 68 pgs.)-r/Graphic Novel; Nick Fury app.						8.00
... By Claremont & Buscema No. 1 Facsimile Edition (4/20, $3.99) r/#1 with original ads						4.00
... Cable Guts and Glory (10/99, $5.99) Platt-a						6.00
... Classic Vol. 1 TPB (2005, $12.99) r/#1-5						15.00
... Classic Vol. 2 TPB (2005, $12.99) r/#6-10						15.00
... Classic Vol. 3 TPB (2006, $14.99) r/#11-16; The Gehenna Stone Affair						15.00

	GD 2.0	VG 4.0	FN 6.0	VF 8.0	VF/NM 9.0	NM- 9.2
... Classic Vol. 4 TPB (2006, $14.99) r/#17-23						15.00
... Classic Vol. 5 TPB (2007, $14.99) r/#24-30						15.00
.../Deadpool: Weapon X TPB (7/02, $21.99)-r/#162-166 & Deadpool #57-60						22.00
... Doombringer (11/97, $5.99)-Silver Samurai-c/app.						6.00
... Evilution (9/94, $5.95)						6.00
... Exit Wounds 1 (8/19, $4.99) Short stories by Hama/Eaton; Claremont/Larroca; Kieth						5.00
...: Global Jeopardy 1 (12/93, $2.95, one-shot)-Embossed-c; Sub-Mariner, Zabu, Ka-Zar, Shanna & Wolverine app.; produced in cooperation with World Wildlife Fund						5.00
...:Inner Fury nn (1992, $5.95, 52 pgs.)-Sienkiewicz-c/a						6.00
...: Judgment Night (2000, $3.99) Shi app.; Battlebook						4.00
...: Killing (9/93)-Kent Williams-a						6.00
...: Knight of Terra (1995, $6.95)-Ostrander script						7.00
... Legends Vol. 2: Meltdown (2003, $19.99) r/Havok & Wolverine: Meltdown #1-4						20.00
... Legends Vol. 3 (2003, $12.99) r/#181-186						13.00
... Legends Vol. 4,5: 4-(See Wolverine: Xisle). 5-(See Wolverine: Snikt!)						
... Legends Vol. 6: Marc Silvestri Book 1 (2004, $19.99) r/#31-34, 41-42, 48-50						20.00
.../ Nick Fury: The Scorpio Connection Hardcover (1989, $16.95)						25.00
.../ Nick Fury: The Scorpio Connection Softcover(1990, $12.95)						15.00
...: Not Dead Yet (12/98, $14.95, TPB)-r/#119-122						15.00
...: Save The Tiger 1 (7/92, $2.95, 84 pgs.)-Reprints Wolverine stories from Marvel Comics Presents #1-10 w/new Kieth-c						4.00
...Scorpio Rising ($5.95, prestige format, one-shot)						6.00
.../Shi: Dark Night of Judgment (Crusade Comics, 2000, $2.99) Tucci-a						4.00
...Triumphs And Tragedies-(1995, $16.95, trade paperback)-r/Uncanny X-Men #109,172,173, Wolverine limited series #4, & Wolverine #41,42,75						17.00
...Typhoid's Kiss (6/94, $6.95)-r/Wolverine stories from Marvel Comics Presents #109-116						7.00
...Vs. Sabretooth 3D 1 (3/20, $7.99) -r/Wolverine #10; bagged with 3D glasses						8.00
...Vs. Spider-Man 1 (3/95, $2.50) -r/Marvel Comics Presents #48-50						5.00
.../Witchblade 1 (3/97, $2.95) Devil's Reign Pt. 5						4.00
Wizard #1/2 (1997) Joe Phillips-a(p)						10.00

NOTE: ***Austin*** *c-3i.* ***Bolton*** *c(back)-5.* ***Buscema*** *a-1-16,25,27p; c-1-10.* ***Byrne*** *a-17-22p, 23; c-1(back), 17-22, 23p.* ***Colan*** *a-24.* ***Andy Kubert*** *c/a-51.* ***Jim Lee*** *c-24, 25, 27.* ***Silvestri*** *a(p)-31-43, 45, 46, 48-50, 52, 53, 55-57; c-31-42p, 43, 45p, 46p, 48, 49p, 50p, 52p, 53p, 55-57p.* ***Stroman*** *a-44p; c-60p.* ***Williamson*** *a-1i, 3-8i; c(i)-1, 3-6.*

WOLVERINE (Volume 3) (Titled Dark Wolverine from #75-90)(See Daken: Dark Wolverine)
Marvel Comics: July, 2003 - No. 90, Oct, 2010 ($2.25/$2.50/$2.99)

	GD 2.0	VG 4.0	FN 6.0	VF 8.0	VF/NM 9.0	NM- 9.2
1-Rucka-s/Robertson-a	1	3	4	6	8	10
2-19: 6-Nightcrawler app. 13-16-Sabretooth app.						3.00
20-Millar-s/Romita, Jr.-a begin, Elektra app.						4.00
20-B&W variant-c	1	3	4	6	8	10
21-39: 21-Elektra-c/app. 23,24-Daredevil app. 26-28-Land-c. 29-Quesada-c; begin $2.50-c. 33-35-House of M. 36,37-Decimation. 36-Quesada-c. 39-Winter Soldier app.						3.00
40,43-48: 40-Begin $2.99-c; Winter Soldier app.; Texeira-a. 43-46-Civil War; Ramos-a. 45-Sub-Mariner app.						3.00
41,49-($3.99) 41-C.P. Smith-a/Stuart Moore-s						4.00
42-Civil War						5.00
50-($3.99) Sabretooth app.; Bianchi-a/c & Loeb-s begin; wraparound-c; McGuinness-a						4.00
50-($3.99) Variant Edition; uncolored art and cover; Bianchi pencil art page						4.00
51-55-(Regular and variant uncolored editions) Bianchi-a/Loeb-s; Sabretooth app.						3.00
55-EC-style variant-c by Greg Land						5.00
56-($3.99) Howard Chaykin-a/c						4.00
57-65: 57-61-Suydam Zombie-c; Chaykin-a. 62-65-Mystique app.						3.00
66-Old Man Logan begins; Millar-s/McNiven-a; McNiven wraparound-c	3	6	9	21	33	45
66-Variant-c by Michael Turner	6	12	18	38	69	100
66-Variant sketch-c by Michael Turner						140.00
66-2nd printing with McNiven variant-c of Logan and Hulk gang member	3	6	9	17	26	34
66-(5/10, $1.00) Reprint with "Marvel's Greatest Comics" on cover						3.00
67-70,72-Old Man Logan (concludes in Wolverine: Old Man Logan Giant-Sized Special). 67-Intro. Ashley, Spider-Man's granddaughter. 72-Red Skull app.	1	3	4	6	8	10
71-Old Man Logan; Venom-ized T-Rex app.	2	4	6	11	16	20
73,74-Andy Kubert-a						4.00
75-($3.99) Dark Reign, Daken as Wolverine on Osborn's team; Camuncoli-a						5.00
76-90: 76-86-Multiple covers for each. 76-Dark Reign; Yu-c. 82-84-Siege. 88,89-Franken-Castle x-over; Punisher app.						3.00
#900 (7/10, $4.99) Short stories by various incl. Finch, Rivera, Segovia, McGuinness						5.00
Annual 1 (12/07, $3.99) Hurwitz-s/Frusin-a						4.00
Annual 2 (11/08, $3.99) Swierczynski-s/Deodato-a/c						4.00
...: Blood & Sorrow TPB (2007, $13.99) r/#41,49, stories from Giant-Size Wolverine #1 and X-Men Unlimited #12						14.00
...: Chop Shop 1 (1/09, $2.99) Benson-s/Boschi-a/Hanuka-c						3.00
Civil War: Wolverine TPB (2007, $17.99) r/#42-48; gallery of B&W cover inks						18.00
... Dangerous Games 1 (8/08, $3.99) Spurrier-s/Oliver-a; Remender-s/Opena-a						4.00
...Enemy of the State HC Vol. 1 (2005, $19.99) r/#20-25; Ennis intro.; variant covers						20.00

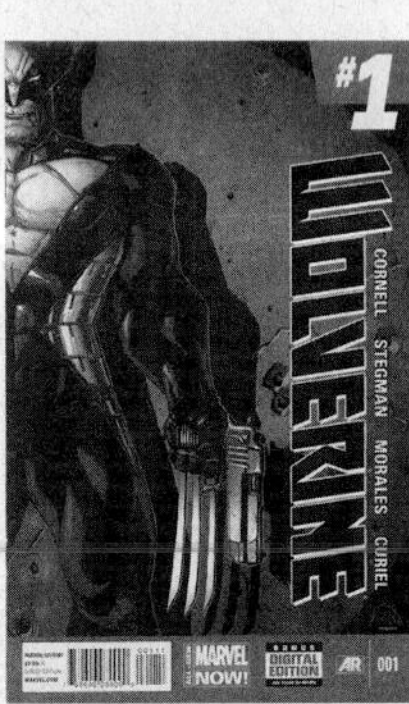

Wolverine (2014 series) #1 © MAR

Wolverine & Black Cat: Claws 2 #3 © MAR

Wolverine MAX #4 © MAR

GD 2.0 | VG 4.0 | FN 6.0 | VF 8.0 | VF/NM 9.0 | NM- 9.2

...Enemy of the State HC Vol. 2 (2005, $19.99) r/#26-32 20.00
...Enemy of the State SC Vol. 1 (2005, $14.99) r/#20-25; Ennis intro.; variant covers 15.00
...Enemy of the State SC Vol. 2 (2006, $16.99) r/#26-32 17.00
...Enemy of the State - The Complete Edition (2006, $34.99) r/#20-32; Ennis intro.; sketch pages, variant covers and pin-up art 35.00
...: Evolution SC (2008, $14.99) r/#50-55 15.00
...: Flies to a Spider (2/09, $3.99) Bradstreet-c/Hurwitz-s/Opena-a 4.00
...: Killing Made Simple (10/08, $3.99) Yost-s/Turnbull-a 4.00
...: Enemy of the State MGC #20 (7/11, $1.00) r/#20 with "Marvel's Greatest Comics" logo 3.00
...: Japan's Most Wanted HC (2014, $34.99) printing of material that debuted online 35.00
...: Mr. X (5/10, $3.99) Tieri-s/Diaz-a/Mattina-c 4.00
...: Old Man Logan Giant-Sized Special (11/09, $4.99) Continued from #72; cover gallery 5.00
...Origins & Endings HC (2006, $19.99) r/#36-40 20.00
...Origins & Endings SC (2006, $13.99) r/#36-40 14.00
...: Origin of an X-Man Free Comic Book Day 2009 (5/09) Gurihiru-a/McGuinness-c 3.00
...: Revolver (8/09, $3.99) Gischler-s/Pastoras-a 4.00
... Saga (2009, giveaway) history of the character in text and comic panels 3.00
...: Saudade (2008, $4.99) English adaptation of Wolverine story from French comic 5.00
...: Savage (4/10, $3.99) J. Scott Campbell-c; The Lizard app. 4.00
...Special: Firebreak (2/08, $3.99) Carey-s/Kolins-a; Lolos-a 4.00
...: Switchback 1 (3/09, $3.99) short stories; art by Pastoras & Doe 4.00
...: The Amazing Immortal Man & Other Bloody Tales (7/08, $3.99) Lapham short stories 4.00
...: The Anniversary (6/09, $3.99) Mariko flashback short stories; art by various 4.00
...: The Death of Wolverine HC (2008, $19.99) r/#56-61 20.00
...: The Road to Hell (11/10, $3.99) Previews new Wolverine titles and Generation Hope 4.00
...: Under the Boardwalk (2/10, $3.99) Coker-a 4.00
...Vol. 1: The Brotherhood (2003, $12.99) r/#1-6 13.00
...Vol. 2: Coyote Crossing (2004, $11.99) r/#7-11 12.00
... Weapon X Files (2009, $4.99) Handbook-style pages of Wolverine characters 5.00
...: Wendigo! 1 (3/10, $3.99) Gulacy-a; back-up with Thor 4.00

WOLVERINE (Volume 4) (Also see Savage Wolverine)
Marvel Comics: Nov, 2010 - No. 20, Feb, 2012; No. 300, Mar, 2012 - No. 317, Feb, 2013 ($3.99/$4.99)

1-5-Jae Lee-c/Guedes-a; Wolverine Goes to Hell. 1-Back-up with Silver Samurai 4.00
5.1-(4/11, $2.99) Aaron-s/Palo-a/Rivera-c 3.00
6-20: 6-Jae Lee-c/Acuña-a; X-Men & Magneto app. 20-Kingpin & Sabretooth app. 4.00
300-(3/12, $4.99) Adam Kubert-c; Sabretooth & new Silver Samurai app. 5.00
301-308,310-317: 301-304-Aaron-s. 302-Art Adams-c. 310-313-Bianchi-a/c 4.00
309-($4.99) Elixir with X-Force; Albuquerque-a; Ribic-c 5.00
#1000 (4/11, $4.99) Short stories by various incl. Palmiotti, Green, Luke Ross; Segovia-c 5.00
Annual 1 (10/12, $4.99) Alan Davis-s/a/c; the Clan Destine app. (see Daredevil Ann. #1) 5.00
...: Debt of Death 1 (11/11, $3.99) Lapham-s/Aja-a/c; Nick Fury app. 4.00
.../Deadpool: The Decoy 1 (9/11, $3.99) prints online story from Marvel.com; Young-c 4.00

WOLVERINE (5th series)
Marvel Comics: May, 2013 - No. 13, Mar, 2014 ($3.99)

1-13: 1-4-Cornell-s/Alan Davis-a/c; Nick Fury II app. 5-7-Pierfederici-a. 8-13-Killable 4.00
... In the Flesh (9/13, $3.99) Cosentino-s/Talajic-a 4.00

WOLVERINE (6th series)
Marvel Comics: Apr, 2014 - No. 12, Oct, 2014 ($3.99)

1-11: 1-Cornell-s/Stegman-a. 2-Superior Spider-Man app. 8,9-Iron Fist app. 4.00
12-($5.99) "1 Month To Die"; Cornell-s/Woods-a; Thor & Sabretooth app. 6.00
Annual 1 (10/14, $4.99) Jubilee app; Nguyen-c/Kalan-s/Marks-a 5.00

WOLVERINE (7th series)
Marvel Comics: Apr, 2020 - Present ($7.99/$3.99)

1-($7.99) Percy-s/Adam Kubert-a; multiple covers; Dracula app. 8.00
2-7,9-($3.99) 2,3-Percy-s/Adam Kubert-a. 4-6-Bogdanovic-a. 6,7-"X of Swords" tie-in 4.00
8-($4.99) 350th Wolverine issue; short stories; Kubert, Bogdanovic-a; Patch returns 5.00
Annual 1 (11/19, $4.99) "Acts of Evil" tie-in; Houser-s/Borges-a; Morgan Le Fay app. 5.00
... vs. Blade Special (9/19, $5.99) Guggenheim-s/Wilkins-a/c; Doctor Strange app. 6.00

WOLVERINE & BLACK CAT: CLAWS 2 (See Claws for 1st series)
Marvel Comics: Aug, 2011 - No. 3, Nov, 2011 ($3.99, limited series)

1-3-Linsner-a/c; Palmiotti & Gray-s; Killraven app. 4.00

WOLVERINE & CAPTAIN AMERICA: WEAPON PLUS
Marvel Comics: Sept, 2019 ($4.99, one-shot)

1-Sacks-s/Neves-a 5.00

WOLVERINE AND JUBILEE
Marvel Comics: Mar, 2011 - No. 4, Jun, 2011 ($2.99, limited series)

1-4: 1-Vampire Jubilee; Kathryn Immonen-s/Phil Noto-a; Coipel-c
1 2 3 5 6 8

WOLVERINE AND POWER PACK
Marvel Comics: Jan, 2009 - No. 4, Apr, 2009 ($2.99, limited series)

1-4-Sumerak-s. 1,2-GuriHiru-a. 1-Sauron app. 3-Meet Wolverine as a child; Koblish-a 3.00

WOLVERINE AND THE PUNISHER: DAMAGING EVIDENCE
Marvel Comics: Oct, 1993 - No. 3, Dec, 1993 ($2.00, limited series)

1-3: 2,3-Indicia says "The Punisher and Wolverine..." 5.00

WOLVERINE & THE X-MEN (Regenesis)(See X-Men: Schism)
Marvel Comics: Dec, 2011 - No. 42, Apr, 2014 ($3.99)

1-8: 1-3-Aaron-s/Bachalo-a/c. 3-Sabretooth app. 4-Bradshaw-a; Deathlok app. 4.00
9-27: 9-16,18-Avengers vs. X-Men tie-in. 17-Allred-a 4.00
27AU (6/13, $3.99) Age of Ultron tie-in; continues in Age of Ultron #6 4.00
28-41: 30-35-Hellfire Saga. 36,37-Battle of the Atom 4.00
42-($4.99) Cover swipe of X-Men #141 (1981) Graduation Day 5.00
Annual 1 (1/14, $4.99) Aaron-s/Bradshaw-a; Gladiator app. 5.00

WOLVERINE & THE X-MEN (2nd series)
Marvel Comics: May, 2014 - No. 12, Jan, 2015 ($3.99)

1-9,11,12: 1-Latour-s/Asrar-a; Fantomex app. 7-Daredevil app. 11-Spider-Man app. 4.00
10-($4.99) Follows Wolverine's death; art by various incl. Anka, Bertram, Rugg, Shalvey 5.00

WOLVERINE AND THE X-MEN: ALPHA & OMEGA
Marvel Comics: Dec, 2011 - No. 5, Jul, 2012 ($3.99, limited series)

1-5-Brooks-c/Boschi & Brooks-a; Quentin Quire vs. Wolverine 4.00

WOLVERINE: BLACK, WHITE & BLOOD
Marvel Comics: Jan, 2021 - Present ($4.99, limited series, B&W&Red)

1-3-Short story anthology by various. 1-Duggan-s/Adam Kubert-a; Shalvey-s/a 5.00

WOLVERINE/CAPTAIN AMERICA
Marvel Comics: Apr, 2004 - No. 4, Apr, 2004 ($2.99, limited series)

1-4-Derenick-a/c 3.00

WOLVERINE: DAYS OF FUTURE PAST
Marvel Comics: Dec, 1997 - No. 3, Feb, 1998 ($2.50, limited series)

1-3: J.F. Moore-s/Bennett-a 4.00

WOLVERINE/DOOP (Also see X-Force and X-Statix)(Reprinted in X-Statix Vol. 2)
Marvel Comics: July, 2003 - No. 2, July, 2003 ($2.99, limited series)

1,2-Peter Milligan-s/Darwyn Cooke & J. Bone-a 3.00

WOLVERINE: FIRST CLASS
Marvel Comics: May, 2008 - No. 21, Jan, 2010 ($2.99)

1-21: 1-Wolverine and Kitty Pryde's first mission; DiVito-a. 2,9-Sabretooth app. 3.00

WOLVERINE/GAMBIT: VICTIMS
Marvel Comics: Sept, 1995 - No. 4, Dec, 1995 ($2.95, limited series)

1-4: Jeph Loeb scripts & Tim Sale-a; foil-c 5.00

WOLVERINE/HERCULES: MYTHS, MONSTERS & MUTANTS
Marvel Comics: May, 2011 - No. 4, Aug, 2011 ($2.99, limited series)

1-4-Tieri-s/Santacruz-a/Jusko-c 3.00

WOLVERINE/HULK
Marvel Comics: Apr, 2002 - No. 4, July, 2002 ($3.50, limited series)

1-4-Sam Kieth-s/a/c 4.00
Wolverine Legends Vol. 1: Wolverine/Hulk (2003, $9.99, TPB) r/#1-4 10.00

WOLVERINE: INFINITY WATCH
Marvel Comics: Apr, 2019 - No. 5, Aug, 2019 ($3.99, limited series)

1-5-Duggan-s/MacDonald-a; Loki app. 4.00

WOLVERINE: MANIFEST DESTINY
Marvel Comics: Dec, 2008 - No. 4, Mar, 2009 ($2.99, limited series)

1-4-Aaron-s/Segovia-a 3.00

WOLVERINE MAX
Marvel Comics: Dec, 2012 - No. 15, Mar, 2014 ($3.99)

1-15: 1-5-Starr-s/Boschi-a/Jock-c; Victor Creed app. 4.00

WOLVERINE: NETSUKE
Marvel Comics: Nov, 2002 - No. 4, Feb, 2003 ($3.99, limited series)

1-4-George Pratt-s/painted-a 4.00

WOLVERINE: NOIR (1930s Pulp-style)
Marvel Comics: Apr, 2009 - No. 4, Sept, 2009 ($3.99, limited series)

1-4-C.P. Smith-a/Stuart Moore; covers by Smith & Calero; alternate Logan as detective 4.00

WOLVERINE: ORIGINS
Marvel Comics: June, 2006 - No. 50, Sept, 2010 ($2.99)

1-15: 1-Daniel Way-s/Steve Dillon-a/Quesada-c 3.00

Wolverine: Soultaker #1 © MAR

Wolverine: The Origin #1 © MAR

Women Outlaws #3 © FOX

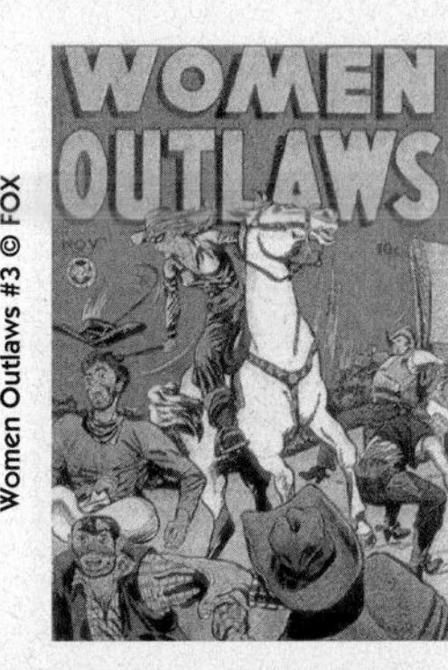

GD 2.0 | VG 4.0 | FN 6.0 | VF 8.0 | VF/NM 9.0 | NM- 9.2

1-10-Variant covers. 1-Turner. 2-Quesada & Hitch. 3-Bianchi. 4-Dell'Otto. 7-Deodato 4.00
16-($3.99) Captain America WW2 app.; preview of Wolverine #56; r/X-Men #268 4.00
16-Variant-c by McGuinness 4.00
17-24: 17-20-Capt. America & Bucky app. 21-24-Deadpool app.; Bianchi-c 3.00
25-($3.99) Deadpool app.; Bianchi-c; r/Deadpool's 1st app. in New Mutants #98 5.00
26-49: 26-Origin of Dakan; Way-s/Segovia-a/Land-c. 28-Hulk & Wendigo app. 3.00
50-($3.99) Last issue; Nick Fury app. 4.00
Annual 1 (9/07, $3.99) Way-s/Andrews-a; flashback to 1932 4.00
... Vol. 1 - Born in Blood HC (2006, $19.99, dustjacket) r/#1-5; variant covers 20.00
... Vol. 1 - Born in Blood SC (2007, $13.99) r/#1-5; variant covers 14.00
... Vol. 2 - Savior HC (2007, $19.99, dustjacket) r/#6-10; variant covers 20.00
... Vol. 2 - Savior SC (2007, $13.99) r/#6-10; variant covers 14.00
... Vol. 3 - Swift & Terrible HC (2007, $19.99, dustjacket) r/#11-15 20.00
... Vol. 3 - Swift & Terrible SC (2007, $13.99) r/#11-15 14.00
... Vol. 4 - Our War HC (2008, $19.99, dustjacket) r/#16-20 & Annual #1 20.00
... Vol. 4 - Our War SC (2008, $14.99) r/#16-20 & Annual #1 15.00

WOLVERINE/PUNISHER
Marvel Comics: May, 2004 - No. 5, Sept, 2004 ($2.99, limited series)

1-5: Milligan-s/Weeks-a 3.00
... Vol. 1 TPB (2004, $13.99) r/series 14.00

WOLVERINE, PUNISHER & GHOST RIDER: OFFICIAL INDEX TO THE MARVEL UNIVERSE
Marvel Comics: Oct, 2011 - No. 8, May, 2012 ($3.99)

1-8-Each issue has chronological synopsies, creator credits, character lists for 30-40 issues of their own titles and headlining mini-series 4.00

WOLVERINE/PUNISHER REVELATIONS (Marvel Knights)
Marvel Comics: Jun, 1999 - No. 4, Sept, 1999 ($2.95, limited series)

1-4: Pat Lee-a(p) 4.00
...: Revelation (4/00, $14.95, TPB) r/#1-4 15.00

WOLVERINES (Follows Death of Wolverine)
Marvel Comics: Mar, 2015 - No. 20, Aug, 2015 ($3.99, weekly series)

1-20: 1-Soule-s/Bradshaw-a; Sabretooth, Daken, Mystique, X-23 app. 13-Deadpool app. 4.00

WOLVERINE SAGA
Marvel Comics: Sept, 1989 - No. 4, Mid-Dec, 1989 ($3.95, lim. series, 52 pgs.)

1-Gives history; Liefeld/Austin-c (front & back) 6.00
2-4: 2-Romita, Jr./Austin-c. 4-Kaluta-c 6.00

WOLVERINE: SNIKT!
Marvel Comics: July, 2003 - No. 5, Nov, 2003 ($2.99, limited series)

1-5-Manga-style; Tsutomu Nihei-s/a 3.00
Wolverine Legends Vol. 5: Snikt! TPB (2003, $13.99) r/#1-5 14.00

WOLVERINE: SOULTAKER
Marvel Comics: May, 2005 - No. 5, Aug, 2005 ($2.99, limited series)

1-5-Yoshida-s/Nagasawa-a/Terada-c; Yukio app. 3.00
TPB (2005, $13.99) r/#1-5 14.00

WOLVERINE: THE BEST THERE IS
Marvel Comics: Feb, 2011 - No. 12, Jan, 2012 ($3.99)

1-12: 1,2-Huston-s/Ryp-a; covers by Hitch and Djurdjevic. 3-12-Hitch-c 4.00
... - Contagion 1 (6/11, $4.99) r/#1-3, cover gallery 5.00

WOLVERINE: THE END
Marvel Comics: Jan, 2004 - No. 6, Dec, 2004 ($2.99, limited series)

1-5-Jenkins-s/Castellini-a 3.00
1-Wizard World Texas variant-c 20.00
TPB (2005, $14.99) r/#1-5 15.00

WOLVERINE: THE LONG NIGHT ADAPTATION (Based on the 2018 10-part podcast)
Marvel Comics: Mar, 2019 - No. 5, Jul, 2019 ($4.99/$3.99, limited series)

1-($4.99) Benjamin Percy-s/Marcio Takara-a; Wolverine in Alaska 5.00
2-5-($3.99) 4.00

WOLVERINE: THE ORIGIN
Marvel Comics: Nov, 2001 - No. 6, July, 2002 ($3.50, limited series)

1-Origin of Logan; Jenkins-s/Andy Kubert-a; Quesada-c 35.00
1-DF edition 25.00
2 10.00
3-6 6.00
HC (3/02, $34.95, 11" x 7-1/2") r/#1-6; dust jacket; sketch pages and treatments 35.00
HC (2006, $19.99) r/#1-6; dust jacket; sketch pages and treatments 20.00
SC (2002, $14.95) r/#1-6; afterwords by Jemas and Quesada 15.00

WOLVERINE WEAPON X
Marvel Comics: June, 2009 - No. 16, Oct, 2010 ($3.99)

1-16: 1-5,11-Aaron-s/Garney-a. 1-Four covers. 2,3-Two covers. 11-15-Deathlok app. 4.00

WOLVERINE: XISLE
Marvel Comics: June, 2003 - No. 5, June, 2003 ($2.50, weekly limited series)

1-5-Bruce Jones-s/Jorge Lucas-a 3.00
Wolverine Legends Vol. 4 TPB (2003, $13.99) r/ #1-5 14.00

WOMANTHOLOGY: SPACE
IDW Publishing: Sept, 2012 - No. 5, Feb, 2013 ($3.99)

1-5-Anthology of short stories by women creators 4.00

WOMEN IN LOVE (A Feature Presentation #5)
Fox Feature Synd./Hero Books: Aug, 1949 - No. 4, Feb, 1950

	GD	VG	FN	VF	VF/NM	NM-
1	48	96	144	302	514	725
2-Kamen/Feldstein-c	41	82	123	256	428	600
3	32	64	96	190	310	430
4-Wood-a	39	78	117	231	378	525

WOMEN IN LOVE (Thrilling Romances for Adults)
Ziff-Davis Publishing Co.: Winter, 1952 (25¢, 100 pgs.)

	GD	VG	FN	VF	VF/NM	NM-
nn-(Scarce)-Kinstler-a; painted-c	90	180	270	576	988	1400

WOMEN OF MARVEL
Marvel Comics: 2006, 2007 ($24.99, TPB)

SC-Reprints 1st apps. of Dazzler, Ms. Marvel, Shanna, The Cat plus notable stories of other female Marvel characters; Mayhew-c 25.00
Vol. 2 (2007) More stories of female Marvel characters; Mayhew-c; cover process art 25.00

WOMEN OF MARVEL
Marvel Comics: Jan, 2011 - No. 2, Feb, 2011 ($3.99, limited series)

1,2-Short stories of female Marvel characters. 1-Pichelli-c. 2-Land-c 4.00

WOMEN OUTLAWS (My Love Memories #9 on)(Also see Red Circle)
Fox Feature Syndicate: July, 1948 - No. 8, Sept, 1949

	GD	VG	FN	VF	VF/NM	NM-
1-Used in **SOTI**, illo "Giving children an image of American womanhood"; negligee panels	100	200	300	640	1095	1550
2,3: 3-Kamenish-a	73	146	219	467	796	1125
4-8	58	116	174	371	636	900
nn(nd)-Contains Cody of the Pony Express; same cover as #7	31	62	93	182	296	410

WOMEN TO LOVE
Realistic: No date (1953)

	GD	VG	FN	VF	VF/NM	NM-
nn-(Scarce)-Reprints Complete Romance #1; c-/Avon paperback #165	54	108	162	343	574	825

WONDER BOY (Formerly Terrific Comics) (See Blue Bolt, Bomber Comics & Samson)
Ajax/Farrell Publ.: No. 17, May, 1955 - No. 18, July, 1955 (Code approved)

	GD	VG	FN	VF	VF/NM	NM-
17-Phantom Lady app. Bakerish-c/a	55	110	165	352	601	850
18-Phantom Lady app.	47	94	141	296	498	700

NOTE: *Phantom Lady not by Matt Baker.*

WONDER COMICS (Wonderworld #3 on)
Fox Feature Syndicate: May, 1939 - No. 2, June, 1939 (68 pgs.)

	GD	VG	FN	VF	VF/NM	NM-
1-(Scarce)-Wonder Man only app. by Will Eisner; Dr. Fung (by Powell), K-5 begins; Bob Kane-a; Eisner-c	2850	5700	8550	20,000	35,000	50,000
2-(Scarce)-Yarko the Great, Master Magician (see Samson) by Eisner begins; 'Spark' Stevens by Bob Kane, Patty O'Day, Tex Mason app. Lou Fine's 1st-c; Fine-a (2 pgs.); Yarko-c (Wonder Man-c #1)	975	1950	2919	7100	12,550	18,000

WONDER COMICS
Great/Nedor/Better Publications: May, 1944 - No. 20, Oct, 1948

	GD	VG	FN	VF	VF/NM	NM-
1-The Grim Reaper & Spectro, the Mind Reader begin; Hitler/Hirohito bondage-c	389	778	1167	2723	4762	6800
2-Origin The Grim Reaper; Super Sleuths begin, end #8,17; Schomburg Nazi WWII-c	209	418	627	1338	2294	3250
3-5: All Schomburg Nazi WWII-c. 3-Indicia reads "Vol. 1, #2"	194	388	582	1242	2121	3000
6-Japanese WWII Flag-c	138	276	414	883	1517	2150
7-10: 8-Last Spectro. 9-Wonderman begins	97	194	291	621	1061	1500
11-13: 11-Dick Devens, King of Futuria begins, ends #14. 11,12-Ingels-c & splash pg. 12-Bondage/headlight-c by Ingels	116	232	348	742	1271	1800
14-Classic Schomburg sci-fi good girl bondage-c	151	302	453	966	1658	2350
15-Tara begins (origin), ends #20; classic Schomburg bondage/torture-c	245	490	735	1568	2684	3800
16,18: 16-Spectro app.; last Grim Reaper. 18-The Silver Knight begins	87	174	261	553	952	1350
17-Wonderman with Frazetta panels; Jill Trent with all Frazetta inks	100	200	300	640	1095	1550

Wonder Man #17 © MAR

Wonder Twins #7 © DC

Wonder Woman #178 © DC

GD VG FN VF VF/NM NM-
2.0 4.0 6.0 8.0 9.0 9.2

GD VG FN VF VF/NM NM-
2.0 4.0 6.0 8.0 9.0 9.2

19-Frazetta panels 94 188 282 597 1025 1450
20-Most of Silver Knight by Frazetta 110 220 330 704 1202 1700

NOTE: ***Ingels** c-11, 12. **Roussos** a-19. **Schomburg (Xela)** c-1-10; (airbrush)-13-20. Bondage c-12, 13, 15. Cover features: Grim Reaper #1-8; Wonder Man #9-15; Tara #16-20.*

WONDER DUCK (See Wisco)
Marvel Comics (CDS): Sept, 1949 - No. 3, Mar, 1950

1-Funny animal 25 50 75 150 245 340
2,3 16 32 48 98 154 210

WONDERFUL ADVENTURES OF PINOCCHIO, THE (See Movie Comics & Walt Disney Showcase #48)
Whitman Publishing Co.: April, 1982 (Walt Disney)

nn-(#3 Continuation of Movie Comics?); r/FC #92 6.00

WONDERFUL WIZARD OF OZ (Adaptation of the original 1900 L. Frank Baum book)
(Also see the sequels Marvelous Land of Oz, Ozma of Oz, and Dorothy & The Wizard in Oz)
Marvel Comics: Feb, 2009 - No. 8, Sept, 2009 ($3.99, limited series)

1-8-Eric Shanower-a/Skottie Young-a/c 4.00
1-Variant Good Witch & Dorothy wraparound cover by J. Scott Campbell 8.00
1-Variant Scarecrow & Dorothy cover by Eric Shanower 10.00
1-(4/10, $1.00) Reprint with "Marvel's Greatest Comics" on cover 3.00
... Sketchbook (2008, giveaway) Young character design sketches; Shanower intro. 3.00
HC (2009, $29.99, dustjacket) r/#1-8; Shanower intro.; cover gallery; sketch art 30.00

WONDERFUL WORLD FOR BOYS AND GIRLS
DC Comics: May, 1964

nn - Ashcan comic, not distributed to newsstands, only for in-house use (no known sales)

WONDERFUL WORLD OF DISNEY, THE (Walt Disney)
Whitman Publishing Co.: 1978 (Digest, 116 pgs.)

1-Barks-a (reprints) 3 6 9 16 23 30
2 (no date) 2 4 6 11 16 20

WONDERFUL WORLD OF TANK GIRL
Titan Comics: Nov, 2017 - No. 4, May, 2018 ($3.99, limited series)

1-4: 1-Tank Girl Strikes Again; Martin-s/Parson-a; multiple covers 4.00

WONDERFUL WORLD OF THE BROTHERS GRIMM (See Movie Comics)

WONDER GIRL (Cassandra Sandsmark from Teen Titans)
DC Comics: Nov, 2007 - No. 6, Apr, 2008 ($2.99, limited series)

1-6-Torres-s/Greene-a; Hercules app. 2-6-Female Furies app. 5,6-Wonder Woman app. 3.00
Teen Titans Spotlight: Wonder Girl TPB (2008, $17.99) r/#1-6 18.00
1-(3/11, $2.99, one-shot) Nicola Scott-c; intro. Solstice 3.00

WONDERLAND (See Grimm Fairy Tales Presents Wonderland)

WONDERLAND COMICS
Feature Publications/Prize: Summer, 1945 - No. 9, Feb-Mar, 1947

1-Alex in Wonderland begins; Howard Post-c 37 74 111 222 361 500
2-Howard Post-c/a(2) 20 40 60 115 188 260
3-9: 3,4-Post-c 17 34 51 105 165 225

WONDER MAN (See The Avengers #9, 151)
Marvel Comics Group: Mar, 1986 ($1.25, one-shot, 52 pgs.)

1 6.00

WONDER MAN
Marvel Comics Group: Sept, 1991 - No. 29, Jan, 1994 ($1.00)

1-29: 1-Free fold out poster by Johnson/Austin. 1-3-Johnson/Austin-c/a. 2-Avengers West Coast x-over. 4 Austin-c(i) 3.00
Annual 1 (1992, $2.25)-Immonen-a (10 pgs.) 4.00
Annual 2 (1993, $2.95)-Bagged w/trading card 4.00

WONDER MAN
Marvel Comics: Feb, 2007 - No. 5, June, 2007 ($2.99, limited series)

1-5: 1-Peter David-s/Andrew Currie-a; Beast app. 4-Nauck-a 3.00
...: My Fair Super Hero TPB (2007, $13.99) r/#1-5; Currie sketch page 14.00

WONDERS OF ALADDIN, THE
Dell Publishing Co.: No. 1255, Feb-Apr, 1962

Four Color 1255-Movie 6 12 18 40 73 105

WONDER TWINS (From Superfriends)
DC Comics (Wonder Comics): Apr, 2019 - No. 12, Apr, 2020 ($3.99)

1-12: 1-Mark Russell-s/Stephen Byrne-a; Justice League and Mr. Mxyzptlk app. 3-Intro Gleek 4.00

WONDER WOMAN (See Adventure Comics #459, All-Star Comics, Brave & the Bold, DC Comics Presents, JLA, Justice League of America, Legend of..., Power Record Comics, Sensation Comics, Super Friends and World's Finest Comics #244)

WONDER WOMAN
DC Comics: Jan 1942

1-Ashcan comic, not distributed to newsstands, only for in-house use. Cover art is Sensation Comics #1 with interior being Sensation Comics #2. A CGC certified 8.5 copy sold for $17,250 in 2002. A CGC certified 8.5 copy sold for $57,668 in 2018.

WONDER WOMAN
National Periodical Publications/All-American Publ./DC Comics: Summer, 1942 - No. 329, Feb, 1986

1-Origin Wonder Woman retold (more detailed than All Star #8); H. G. Peter-c/a begins 12,400 24,800 37,200 82,700 151,350 220,000
1-Reprint, Oversize 13-1/2x10". **WARNING:** This comic is an exact reprint of the original except for its size. DC published it in 1974 with a second cover titling it as a Famous First Edition. There have been many reported cases of the outer cover being removed and the interior sold as the original edition. The reprint with the new outer cover removed is practically worthless. See Famous First Edition for value.

2-Origin/1st app. Mars; Duke of Deception app. 811 1622 2433 5920 10,460 15,000
3 360 720 1080 2520 4410 6300
4,5: 5-1st Dr. Psycho app. 300 600 900 2040 3570 5100
6-1st Cheetah app. 919 1838 2757 6709 11,855 17,000
7-Wonder Woman for President-c/sty 919 1838 2757 6709 11,855 17,000
8,9: 9-1st app. Giganta (Sum/44) 236 472 708 1510 2580 3650
10-Invasion from Saturn classic sci-fi-c/s 239 478 717 1530 2615 3700
11-20 145 290 435 928 1589 2250
21-30: 23-Story from Wonder Woman's childhood. 28-Cheetah and Giganta-c/app. 123 246 369 787 1344 1900
31-33,35-40: 37-1st app. Circe. 38-Last H.G. Peter-c 113 226 339 723 1237 1750
34-Robot-c 116 232 348 742 1271 1800
41-44,46-48 106 212 318 678 1164 1650
45-Origin retold 226 452 678 1446 2473 3500
49-Used in **SOTI**, pgs. 234,236; last 52 pg. issue 110 220 330 704 1202 1700
50-(44 pgs.)-Used in **POP**, pg. 97 110 220 330 704 1202 1700
51-60: 60-New logo 100 200 300 640 1095 1550
61-72: 62-Origin of W.W. i.d. 64-Story about 3-D movies. 70-1st Angle Man app. 72-Last pre-code (2/55) 95 190 285 608 1042 1475
73-90: 80-Origin The Invisible Plane. 89-Flying saucer-c/story 86 172 258 546 936 1325
91-94,96,97: 97-Last H. G. Peter-a 73 146 219 467 796 1125
95-A-Bomb-c 77 154 231 493 847 1200
98-(5/58) 1st Silver Age Wonder Woman; new origin & new art team (Andru & Esposito) begin; Kanigher-s; 1st meets Steve Trevor 541 1082 1623 3950 6975 10,000
99-New origin continues; origin Diana Prince i.d. 94 188 282 597 1025 1450
100-(8/58) 87 174 261 553 952 1350
101-104,106,108-110 54 108 162 343 574 825
105-(Scarce, 4/59)-Wonder Woman's origin (part 3); she appears as a girl (no costume yet) (called Wonder Girl - see DC Super-Stars #1) 284 568 852 1818 3109 4400
107-1st advs. of Wonder Girl; 1st Merboy; tells how Wonder Woman won her costume 61 122 183 390 670 950
111-120 40 80 120 246 411 575
121-126: 121-1st app. Wonder Woman Family. 122-1st app. Wonder Tot. 124-Wonder Woman Family app. 126-Last 10¢ issue 34 68 102 204 332 460
127-130: 128-Origin The Invisible Plane retold. 129-3rd app. Wonder Woman Family (#133 is 4th app.) 15 30 45 105 233 360
131-150: 132-Flying saucer-c 13 26 39 86 188 290
151-155,157,158,161-170 (1967): 151-Wonder Girl solo issue. 10 20 30 65 135 205
156-(8/65)-Early mention of a comic book shop & comic collecting; mentions DCs selling for $100 a copy 10 20 30 67 141 215
159-Origin retold (1/66); 1st S.A. origin? 12 24 36 81 176 270
160-1st S.A. Cheetah app. 30 60 90 216 483 750
171-176 8 16 24 52 99 145
177-W. Woman/Supergirl battle 10 20 30 66 138 210
178-(10/68) 1st new Wonder Woman on-c only; appears in old costume w/powers inside 11 22 33 76 163 250
179-Classic-c; wears no costume to issue #203 11 22 33 76 163 250
180-195: 180-Death of Steve Trevor. 182-Last 12¢ issue. 195-Wood inks 6 12 18 38 69 100
196 (52 pgs.)-Origin-r/All Star #8 (6 out of 9 pgs.) 7 14 21 48 89 130
197,198 (52 pgs.)-Reprints 6 12 18 41 76 110
199-Jeff Jones painted-c; 52 pgs. 9 18 27 61 123 185
200 (5-6/72)-Jeff Jones-c; 52 pgs. 9 18 27 60 120 180
201,202-Catwoman app. 202-Fafhrd & The Grey Mouser debut. 5 10 15 35 57 80
203,205-210,212: 212-The Cavalier app. 3 6 9 21 33 45
204-(2/73) Return to old costume; death of I Ching; intro. Nubia

Wonder Woman (2nd series) #88 © DC

Wonder Woman (2nd series) #219 © DC

Wonder Woman (2006 series) #611 © DC

	GD	VG	FN	VF	VF/NM	NM-
	2.0	4.0	6.0	8.0	9.0	9.2

25 50 75 175 388 600
211,214-(100 pgs.) 7 14 21 48 89 130
213,215,216,218-220: 220-N. Adams assist 3 6 9 18 28 38
217: (68 pgs.) 4 8 12 25 40 55
221,222,224-227,229,230,233-236,238-240: 227-Judy Garland tribute 3 6 9 14 19 24
223,228,231,232,237,241,248: 223-Steve Trevor revived as Steve Howard & learns W.W.'s I.D. 228-Both Wonder Women team up & new World War II stories begin, end #243. 231,232: JSA app. 237-Origin retold. 240-G.A. Flash app. 241-Intro Bouncer; Spectre app. 248-Steve Trevor Howard dies (44 pgs.) 3 6 9 14 20 26
242-246,252-266,269,270: 243-Both W. Women team-up again. 269-Last Wood a(i) for DC? (7/80) 2 4 6 8 11 14
247,249,250,271: 247,249 (44 pgs.). 249-Hawkgirl app. 250-Origin/1st app. Orana, the new Wonder Woman. 271-Huntress & 3rd Life of Steve Trevor begin 2 4 6 9 12 15
250-252,255-262-264-(Whitman variants, low print run, no issue # on cover) 3 6 9 14 20 26
251-Orana dies 3 6 9 14 19 24
267,268-Re-intro Animal Man (5/80 & 6/80) 2 4 6 9 13 16
272-280,284-286,289,290,294-299,301-325 1 3 4 6 8 10
281-283: Joker-c/stories in Huntress back-ups 2 4 6 8 11 14
287,288,291-293: 287-New Teen Titans x-over. 288-New costume & logo. 291-293-Three part epic with Super-Heroines 1 2 3 5 7 9
300-($1.50, 76 pgs.)-Anniv. issue; Giffen-a; New Teen Titans, Bronze Age Sandman, JLA & G.A. Wonder Woman app.; 1st app. Lyta Trevor who becomes Fury in All-Star Squadron #25; G.A. Wonder Woman & Steve Trevor revealed as married 2 4 6 10 14 18
326-328 1 2 3 5 7 9
329 (Double size)-S.A. W.W. & Steve Trevor wed 2 4 6 13 18 22
...: Chronicles Vol. 1 TPB (2010, $17.99) reprints debut in All Star Comics #8, apps. in Sensation Comics #1-9 and Wonder Woman #1 18.00
Diana Prince: Wonder Woman Vol. 1 TPB (2008, $19.99) r/#178-183 20.00
Diana Prince: Wonder Woman Vol. 2 TPB (2008, $19.99) r/#185-189, Brave and the Bold #87, and Superman's Girl Friend, Lois Lane #93 20.00
Diana Prince: Wonder Woman Vol. 3 TPB ('08, $19.99) r/#190-198, World's Finest #204 20.00
Diana Prince: Wonder Woman Vol. 4 TPB ('09, $19.99) r/#199-204, Brave & Bold #105 20.00
...: The Greatest Stories Ever Told TPB (2007, $19.99) intro. by Lynda Carter; Ross-c 20.00

NOTE: ***Andru/Esposito** c-66-160(most). **Buckler** a-300. **Colan** a-288-305p; c-288-290p. **Giffen** a-300p. **Grell** c-217. **Kaluta** c-297. **Gil Kane** c-294p, 303-305, 307, 312, 314. **Miller** c-298p. **Morrow** c-233. **Nasser** a-232p; c-231p, 232p. **Bob Oskner** c(i)-39-65(most). **Perez** c-283p, 284p. **Spiegle** a-312. **Staton** a(p)-241, 271-287, 289, 290, 294-299; c(p)-241, 245, 246. Huntress back-up stories 271-287, 289, 290, 294-299, 301-321.*

WONDER WOMAN
DC Comics: Feb, 1987 - No. 226, Apr, 2006 (75¢/$1.00/$1.25/$1.95/$1.99/$2.25/$2.50)

0-(10/94) Zero Hour; released between #90 & #91 2 4 6 8 10 12
1-New origin; Perez-c/a begins 3 6 9 21 33 45
1 (Facsimile Edition) (12/20, $3.99) Reprints #1 with original ads 4.00
2-5 1 2 3 5 6 8
6-20: 9-Origin Cheetah. 12,13-Millennium x-over. 18,26-Free 16 pg. story 5.00
21-49: 24-Last Perez-a; scripts continue thru #62 4.00
50-($1.50, 52 pgs.)-New Titans, Justice League 5.00
51-62: Perez scripts. 60-Vs. Lobo; last Perez-c. 62-Last $1.00-c 4.00
63-New direction & Bolland-c begin; Deathstroke story continued from W. W. Special #1 5.00
64-84 4.00
85-1st Deodato-a; ends #100 2 4 6 9 13 16
86-88: 88-Superman-c & app. 6.00
89-97: 90-(9/94)-1st Artemis. 91-(11/94). 93-Hawkman app. 96-Joker-c 5.00
98,99 4.00
100 ($2.95, Newsstand)-Death of Artemis; Bolland-c ends. 5.00
100 ($3.95, Direct Market)-Death of Artemis; foil-c 1 2 3 5 6 8
101-119, 121-125: 101-Begin $1.95-c; Byrne-c/a/scripts begin. 101-104-Darkseid app. 105-Phantom Stranger cameo. 106-108-Phantom Stranger & Demon app. 107,108-Arion app. 111-1st app. new Wonder Girl. 111,112-Vs. Doomsday. 112-Superman app. 113-Wonder Girl-c/app; Sugar & Spike app. 3.00
120 ($2.95)-Perez-c 4.00
126-149: 128-Hippolyta becomes new W.W. 130-133-Flash (Jay Garrick) & JSA app. 136-Diana returns to W.W. role; last Byrne issue. 137-Priest-s. 139-Luke-s/Paquette-a begin; Hughes-c thru #146 3.00
150-($2.95) Hughes-c/Clark-a; Zauriel app. 4.00
151-158-Hughes-c. 153-Superboy app. 3.00
159-163: 159-Begin $2.25-c. 160,161-Clayface app. 162,163-Aquaman app. 3.00
164-171: Phil Jimenez-s/a begin; Hughes-c; Batman app. 168,169-Pérez co-plot 169-Wraparound-c.170-Lois Lane-c/app. 3.00
172-Our Worlds at War; Hippolyta killed 4.00
173,174: 173-Our Worlds at War; Darkseid app. 174-Every DC heroine app. 3.00
175-($3.50) Joker: Last Laugh; JLA app.; Jim Lee-c 4.00
176-199: 177-Paradise Island returns. 179-Jimenez-c. 184,185-Hippolyta-c/app.; Hughes-c 186-Cheetah app. 189-Simonson-s/Ordway-a begin. 190-Diana's new look. 195-Rucka-s/Drew Johnson-a begin. 197-Flash-c/app. 198,199-Noto-c 3.00
200-($3.95) back-up stories in 1940s and 1960s styles; pin-ups by various 4.00
201-218,220-225: 203,204-Batman-c/app. 204-Matt Wagner-c. 212-JLA app. 214-Flash app. 215-Morales-a begins. 218-Begin $2.50-c. 220-Batman app. 3.00
219-Omac tie-in/Sacrifice pt. 4; Wonder Woman kills Max Lord; Superman app. 4.00
219-(2nd printing) Altered cover with red background 3.00
226-Last issue; flashbacks to meetings with Superman; Rucka-s/Richards-a 4.00
#1,000,000 (11/98) 853rd Century x-over; Deodato-c 3.00
Annual 1,2: 1 ('88, $1.50)-Art Adams-a. 2 ('89, $2.00, 68 pgs.)-All women artists issue; Perez-c(i)/a. 5.00
Annual 3 (1992, $2.50, 68 pgs.)-Quesada-c(p) 4.00
Annual 4 (1995, $3.50)-Year One 4.00
Annual 5 (1996, $2.95)-Legends of the Dead Earth story; Byrne scripts; Cockrum-a 4.00
Annual 6 (1997, $3.95)-Pulp Heroes 4.00
Annual 7,8 ('98,'99, $2.95)-7-Ghosts; Wrightson-c. 8-JLApe, A.Adams-c 4.00
...: Beauty and the Beasts TPB (2005, $19.95) r/#15-19 & Action Comics #600 20.00
...: Bitter Rivals TPB (2004, $13.95) r/#200-205; Jones-c 14.00
...: Challenge of the Gods TPB ('04, $19.95) r/#8-14; Pérez-s/a 20.00
...: Destiny Calling TPB (2006, $19.99) r/#20-24 & Annual #1; Pérez-c & pin-up gallery 20.00
...Donna Troy (6/98, $1.95) Girlfrenzy; Jimenez-a 3.00
...: Down To Earth TPB (2004, $14.95) r/#195-200; Greg Land-c 15.00
... 80-Page Giant 1 (2002, $4.95) reprints in format of 1960s' 80-Page Giants 5.00
...: Eyes of the Gorgon TPB ('05, $19.99) r/#206-213 20.00
Gallery (1996, $3.50)-Bolland-c; pin-ups by various 4.00
...: Gods and Mortals TPB ('04, $19.95) r/#1-7; Pérez-a 20.00
...: Gods of Gotham TPB ('01, $5.95) r/#164-167; Jimenez-s/a 6.00
...: Land of the Dead TPB ('06, $12.99) r/#214-217 & Flash #219 13.00
Lifelines TPB ('98, $9.95) r/#106-112; Byrne-c/a 10.00
...: Mission's End TPB ('06, $19.99) r/#218-226; cover gallery 20.00
...: Our Worlds at War (10/01, $2.95) History of the Amazons; Jae Lee-c 3.00
...: Paradise Found TPB ('03, $14.95) r/#171-177, Secret Files #3; Jimenez-s/a 15.00
...: Paradise Lost TPB ('02, $14.95) r/#164-170; Jimenez-s/a 15.00
Plus 1 (1/97, $2.95)-Jesse Quick-c/app. 4.00
Second Genesis TPB (1997, $9.95)-r/#101-105 10.00
Secret Files 1-3 (3/98, 7/99, 5/02; $4.95) 5.00
Special 1 (1992, $1.75, 52 pgs.)-Deathstroke-c/story continued in Wonder Woman #63 5.00
...: The Blue Amazon (2003, $6.95) Elseworlds; McKeever-a 7.00
The Challenge Of Artemis TPB (1996, $9.95)-r/#94-100; Deodato-c/a 10.00
...: The Once and Future Story (1998, $4.95) Trina Robbins-s/Doran & Guice-a 5.00

NOTE: ***Art Adams** a-Annual 1. **Byrne** c/a 101-107. **Bolton** a-Annual 1. **Deodato** a-85-100. **Perez** a-Annual 1; c-Annual 1(i). **Quesada** c(p)-Annual 3.*

WONDER WOMAN (Also see Amazons Attack mini-series)
DC Comics: Aug, 2006 - No. 44, Jul, 2010; No. 600, Aug, 2010 - No. 614, Oct, 2011 ($2.99)

1-Donna Troy as Wonder Woman after Infinite Crisis; Heinberg-s/Dodson-a/c 5.00
1-Variant-c by Adam Kubert 6.00
2-44: 2-4-Giganta & Hercules app. 6-Jodi Picoult-s begins. 8-Hippolyta returns. 9-12-Amazons Attack tie-in; JLA app. 14-17-Simone-s/Dodson-a/c. 20-23-Stalker app. 26-33-Rise of the Olympian. 40,41-Power Girl app. 3.00
14-DC Nation Convention giveaway edition 6.00
(Title re-numbered after #44, July 2010 to cumilative numbering of #600)
600-(8/10, $4.99) Short stories and pin-ups by various incl. Pérez, Conner, Kramer, Jim Lee; intro. by Lynda Carter; debut of new costume; cover by Pérez 5.00
600-Variant cover by Adam Hughes 8.00
600-2nd printing with new costume cover by Don Kramer 5.00
601-614: 601-606-Kramer-a; two covers by Kramer and Garner. 608-Borges-a 3.00
... Annual 1 (11/07, $3.99) Story cont'd from #4; Heinberg-s/Dodson-a/c; back-up Frank-a 4.00
...: Contagion SC (2010, $14.99) r/#40-44 15.00
...: Ends of the Earth HC (2009, $24.99) r/#20-25 25.00
...: Ends of the Earth SC (2010, $14.99) r/#20-25 15.00
...: Love and Murder HC (2007, $19.99) r/#6-10 20.00
...: Odyssey Volume One HC (2011, $22.99) r/#600-606; afterwords by Jim Lee & JMS 23.00
...: Rise of the Olympian HC (2009, $24.99) r/#26-33 & pages from DC Universe #0 25.00
...: Rise of the Olympian SC (2009, $14.99) r/#26-33 & pages from DC Universe #0 15.00
...: The Circle HC (2008, $24.99) r/#14-19; Mercedes Lackey intro.; Dodson sketch pages 25.00
...: The Circle SC (2009, $14.99) r/#14-19; Mercedes Lackey intro.; Dodson sketch pages 15.00
...: Warkiller SC (2010, $14.99) r/#34-39 15.00
...: Who is Wonder Woman? HC (2007, $19.99) r/#1-4 & Annual #1; Vaughan intro. 20.00
...: Who is Wonder Woman? SC (2009, $14.99) r/#1-4 & Annual #1; Vaughan intro. 15.00

WONDER WOMAN (DC New 52)
DC Comics: Nov, 2011 - No. 52, Jul, 2016 ($2.99/$3.99)

1-Azzarello-s/Chiang-a/c 2 4 6 11 16 20
2-23: 2-4-Azzarello-s/Chiang-a/c. 5,6,9,10,13,14,17-Akins-a. 14-19,21-23-Orion app. 3.00

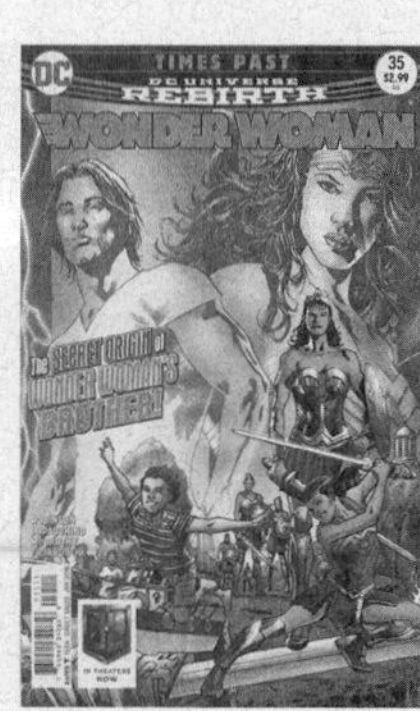

Wonder Woman (2016 series) #35 © DC

Wonder Woman / Conan #1 © DC & CPI

Wonderworld Comics #3 © FOX

	GD 2.0	VG 4.0	FN 6.0	VF 8.0	VF/NM 9.0	NM- 9.2

23.1, 23.2 (11/13, $2.99, regular covers) 3.00
23.1 (11/13, $3.99, 3-D cover) "Cheetah #1" on cover; origin; Ostrander-s/Ibanez-a 5.00
23.2 (11/13, $3.99, 3-D cover) "First Born #1" on cover; origin; Azzarello-s/Aco-a 5.00
24-35: 25-Orion app. 29-Diana becomes God of War. 35-Last Azzarello-s/Chiang-a/c 3.00
36-40: 36-Meredith Finch-s/David Finch-a begins. 37-Donna Troy returns 3.00
41-49,51,52: 41-New costume; begin $3.99-c. 43-Churchill-a 4.00
50-($4.99) Finch & Desjardins-a; Ares app.; back-up Donna Troy story 5.00
#0 (11/12, $2.99) 12 year-old Princess Diana's training; Azzarello-s/Chiang-a/c 3.00
Annual 1 (8/15, $4.99) Concludes "War Torn" arc from #36-40; David Finch-a 5.00
...: Futures End 1 (11/14, $2.99, regular-c) Five years later; Soule-s/Morales-a 3.00
...: Futures End 1 (11/14, $3.99, 3-D cover) 4.00

WONDER WOMAN (DC Rebirth)(Reverts to legacy numbering with #750)
DC Comics: Aug, 2016 - No. 83, Late Feb, 2020; No. 750, Late March, 2020 - Present ($2.99/$3.99)

1-24: 1,3,5,7-Rucka-s/Sharp-a; Cheetah app. 2,4,6,10,12,14-Year One; Nicola Scott-a 3.00
25-($3.99) Justice League and Shaggy Man app. 4.00
26-49: 26-Andolfo-a. 31,33-Grail & baby Darkseid app. 35-Intro. Jason. 37-Zeus vs. Darkseid. 38-40-Silver Swan app. 42-45-Darkseid app. 47-Supergirl app.; leads into Annual 2 3.00
50-74-($3.99): 50-Justice League app. 52,53-Aztek app. 56,57-The Witching Hour tie-in 4.00
75-($4.99) Amazons vs. Grail; Wilson-s/Xermanico & Merino-a 5.00
76-83-Cheetah app. (Year of the Villain) 4.00
750-($9.99, 96 pages) Conclusion vs. Cheetah; short stories and pin-ups by various incl. Simone-s/Doran-a, Rucka-s/Scott-a, Snyder-s/Hitch-a; multiple covers 10.00
751-769-($3.99) 751-Intro. Valda, The Iron Maiden. 758-Phantom Stranger app. 760-767-Max Lord app. 762-Intro. Liar Liar. 768-Deathstroke app. 4.00
Annual 1 (7/17, $4.99) Retells 1st meeting with Superman & Batman; Scott-a 5.00
Annual 2 (8/18, $4.99) The Star Sapphires app.; Putri-c/Laming, Calafiore, & Irving-a 5.00
Annual 3 (12/19, $4.99) Gorilla Grodd app.; Orlando-s/Marion-a 5.00
Annual 4 (10/20, $4.99) Orlando-s/Herbert-a 5.00
... and Justice League Dark: The Witching Hour 1 (12/18, $4.99) Part 1 of x-over 5.00
... 1984 (11/20, $3.99) Movie tie-in; art by Blevins & Sauvage; Steve Trevor app. 4.00
... #1 FCBD 2017 Special Edition (5/17, giveaway) r/#2; Year One; Nicola Scott-a 3.00
...: Rebirth 1 (8/16, $2.99) Rucka-s; multiples origins; new costume 3.00
... 75th Anniversary Special 1 (12/16, $7.99) short stories and pin-ups by various incl. Sharp, Moon, Bolland, DeLiz, Frison, Albuquerque, Larson, Jimenez, Sauvage; Jim Lee-c 8.00
...: Steve Trevor 1 (8/17, $3.99) Seeley-s/Duce-a 4.00
... / Tasmanian Devil Special 1 (8/17, $4.99) Bedard-s/Kitson-a; Circe app.; cartoon-style back-up with Caldwell-a; Daffy Duck & Wile E. Coyote app. 5.00

WONDER WOMAN: AMAZONIA
DC Comics: 1997 ($7.95, Graphic Album format, one shot)

	GD	VG	FN	VF	VF/NM	NM-
1-Elseworlds; Messner-Loebs-s/Winslade-a	2	4	6	8	10	12

WONDER WOMAN: COME BACK TO ME
DC Comics: Sept, 2019 - No. 6, Feb, 2020 ($4.99, limited series)

1-6: 1-Reprints serialized story from Walmart exclusive Justice League Giant #3,4 5.00

WONDER WOMAN / CONAN
DC Comics: Nov, 2017 - No. 6, Apr, 2018 ($3.99, limited series)

1-6-Simone-s/Lopresti-a; meet-up in Conan's time; the Corvidae app. 4.00

WONDER WOMAN: DEAD EARTH
DC Comics (Black Label): Feb, 2020 - No. 4, Oct, 2020 ($6.99, 10-7/8" x 8-1/2", lim. series)

1-4-Wonder Woman in post-apocalyptic future; Daniel Warren Johnson-s/a; 2 covers 7.00

WONDER WOMAN: EARTH ONE
DC Comics: 2016; 2018 ($22.99/$24.99, HC Graphic Novel)

Volume 1 ($22.99) - Morrison-s/Paquette-a; alternate retelling of origin; bonus art 23.00
Volume 2 ($24.99) - Morrison-s/Paquette-a; Dr. Psycho app.; bonus art 25.00

WONDER WOMAN GIANT (See reprint of new stories in Wonder Woman: Come Back to Me) (See Justice League Giant #1-7 for previous JL & Aquaman reprints)
DC Comics: 2019 - No. 7, 2019 ($4.99, 100 pgs., squarebound, Walmart exclusive)

1-7-New Wonder Woman story Conner & Palmiotti-s/Derenick-a; Jonah Hex app. plus reprints Justice League ('11), Wonder Woman ('06), and Aquaman ('11) in all 5.00

WONDER WOMAN GIANT
DC Comics: 2019 - No. 4, 2020 ($4.99, 100 pgs., squarebound, Mass Market & Direct Market editions exist for each issue, with different covers)

1-4: 1-New story with Harley Quinn and reprints. 2-4-New stories and reprints 5.00

WONDER WOMAN '77
DC Comics: Jun, 2015 - No. 4, Nov, 2016 ($7.99, square-bound, printing of digital-first stories)

1-4-Stories based on the Lynda Carter series. 1-Covers by Nicola Scott & Phil Jimenez; Dr. Psycho app.; bonus sketch design art; afterword by Mangels. 2-(11/15) Scott-c; The Cheetah, Celsia & Solomon Grundy app. 3-Clayface app. 8.00

WONDER WOMAN '77 MEETS THE BIONIC WOMAN (TV)
Dynamite Entertainment: 2016 - No. 6, 2017 ($3.99, limited series)

1-6-Andy Mangels-s/Judit Tondora-a; multiple covers 4.00

WONDER WOMAN SPECTACULAR (See DC Special Series #9)

WONDER WOMAN: SPIRIT OF TRUTH
DC Comics: Nov, 2001 ($9.95, treasury size, one-shot)

nn-Painted art by Alex Ross; story by Alex Ross and Paul Dini 10.00

WONDER WOMAN: THE HIKETEIA
DC Comics: 2002 ($24.95, hardcover, one-shot)

nn-Wonder Woman battles Batman; Greg Rucka-s/J.G. Jones-a 25.00
Softcover (2003, $17.95) 18.00

WONDER WOMAN: THE TRUE AMAZON
DC Comics: 2016 ($22.99, HC Graphic Novel)

HC-Retelling of childhood & origin; Jill Thompson-s/painted-a; bonus design pages 23.00

WONDERWORLD COMICS (Formerly Wonder Comics)
Fox Feature Syndicate: No. 3, July, 1939 - No. 33, Jan, 1942

	GD	VG	FN	VF	VF/NM	NM-
3-Intro The Flame by Fine; Dr. Fung (Powell-a), K-51 (Powell-a?), & Yarko the Great, Master Magician (Eisner-a) continues; Eisner/Fine-c	1250	2500	3750	9500	17,250	21,125
4-Lou Fine-c	423	846	1269	3088	5444	7800
5,6,9,10: Lou Fine-c	300	600	900	2010	3505	5000
7-Classic Lou Fine-c	1000	2000	3000	7600	13,800	20,000
8-Classic Lou Fine-c	495	990	1785	4350	7675	11,000
11-Origin The Flame	300	600	900	2010	3505	5000
12-15: 13-Dr. Fung ends; last Fine-c(p)	219	438	657	1402	2401	3400
16-20	155	310	465	992	1696	2400
21-Origin The Black Lion & Cub	158	316	474	1011	1731	2450
22-27: 22,25-Dr. Fung app.	129	258	387	826	1413	2000
28-Origin & 1st app. U.S. Jones (8/41); Lu-Nar, the Moon Man begins	290	580	870	1856	3178	4500
29,31: 29-Torture-c	116	232	348	742	1271	1800
30-Intro & Origin Flame Girl	155	310	465	992	1696	2400
32-Hitler-c	306	612	918	2198	3849	5500
33-Last issue	284	568	852	1818	3109	4400

NOTE: *Spies at War by* **Eisner** *in #13, 17. Yarko by* **Eisner** *in #3-11.* **Eisner** *text illos-3.* **Lou Fine** *a-3-11; c-3-13, 15(i); text illos-4.* **Nordling** *a-4-14.* **Powell** *a-3-12.* **Tuska** *a-5-9. Bondage-c 14, 15, 28, 31, 32. Cover features: The Flame-#3, 5-31; U.S. Jones-#32, 33.*

WONDERWORLDS
Innovation Publishing: 1992 ($3.50, squarebound, 100 pgs.)

1-Rebound super-hero comics, contents may vary; Hero Alliance, Terraformers, etc. 5.00

WOODS, THE
BOOM! Studios: May, 2014 - No. 36, Oct, 2017 ($3.99)

1-36: 1-Tynion-s/Dialynas-a; multiple covers 4.00

WOODSY OWL (See March of Comics #395)
Gold Key: Nov, 1973 - No. 10, Feb, 1976 (Some Whitman printings exist)

	GD	VG	FN	VF	VF/NM	NM-
1	2	4	6	13	18	22
1-Whitman variant	3	6	9	14	20	25
2-10	2	4	6	8	10	12

WOODY WOODPECKER (Walter Lantz... #73 on?)(See Dell Giants for annuals) (Also see The Funnies, Jolly Jingles, Kite Fun Book, New Funnies)
Dell Publishing Co./Gold Key No. 73-187/Whitman No. 188 on:
No. 169, 10/47 - No. 72, 5-7/62; No. 73, 10/62 - No. 201, 3/84 (nn 192)

	GD	VG	FN	VF	VF/NM	NM-
Four Color 169(#1)-Drug turns Woody into a Mr. Hyde	19	38	57	131	291	450
Four Color 188	11	22	33	76	163	250
Four Color 202,232,249,264,288	8	16	24	56	108	160
Four Color 305,336,350	6	12	18	41	76	110
Four Color 364,374,390,405,416,431('52)	6	12	18	37	66	95
16 (12-1/52-53) - 30('55)	4	8	12	27	44	60
31-50	3	6	9	21	33	45
51-72 (Last Dell)	3	6	9	17	26	35
73-75 (Giants, 84 pgs., Gold Key)	5	10	15	30	50	70
76-80	3	6	9	15	22	28
81-103: 103-Last 12¢ issue	3	6	9	14	19	24
104-120	2	4	6	11	16	20
121-140	2	4	6	9	12	15
141-160: 141-UFO-c	1	3	4	6	8	10
161-187	1	2	3	5	7	9
188,189 (Whitman)	2	4	6	9	13	16
190(9/80),191(11/80)-pre-pack only	6	12	18	38	69	100

(No #192)

The World Around Us #1 © GIL

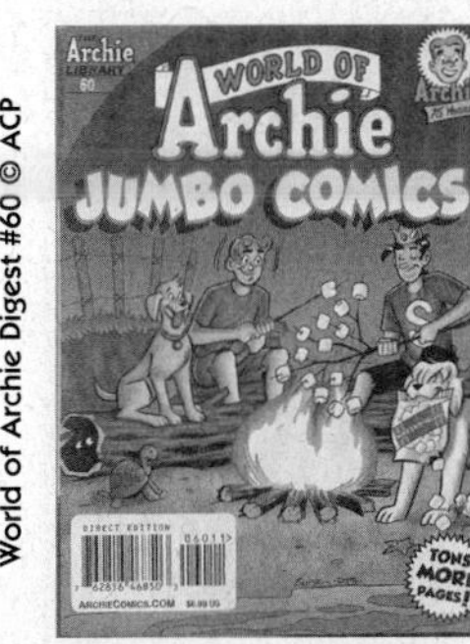

World of Archie Digest #60 © ACP

World of Fantasy #2 © MAR

GD VG FN VF VF/NM NM-
2.0 4.0 6.0 8.0 9.0 9.2

193-197: 196(2/82), 197(4/82) 2 4 6 11 16 20
198-201 (All #90062 on-c, no date or date code, pre-pack): 198(6/83), 199(7/83), 200(8/83), 201(3/84) 3 6 9 16 24 32
Christmas Parade 1(11/68-Giant)(G.K.) 4 8 12 25 40 55
Summer Fun 1(6/66-G.K.)(84 pgs.) 4 8 12 28 47 65
nn (1971, 60¢, 100 pgs. digest) B&W one page gags 3 6 9 16 24 32
NOTE: *15¢ Canadian editions of the 12¢ issues exist. Reprints-No. 92, 102, 103, 105, 106, 124, 125, 152, 153, 157, 162, 165, 194(1/3)-200(1/3).*

WOODY WOODPECKER (See Comic Album #5,9,13, Dell Giant #24, 40, 54, Dell Giants, The Funnies, Golden Comics Digest #1, 3, 5, 8, 15, 16, 20, 24, 32, 37, 44, March of Comics #16, 34, 85, 93, 109, 124, 139, 158, 177, 184, 203, 222, 239, 249, 261, 420, 454, 466, 478, New Funnies & Super Book #12, 24)

WOODY WOODPECKER
Harvey Comics: Sept, 1991 - No. 15, Aug, 1994 ($1.25)
1-15: 1-r/W.W. #53 4.00
50th Anniversary Special 1 (10/91, $2.50, 68 pgs.) 5.00

WOODY WOODPECKER AND FRIENDS
Harvey Comics: Dec, 1991 - No. 4, 1992 ($1.25)
1-4 4.00

WOOL (Hugh Howey's...)
Cryptozoic Entertainment: Jul, 2014 - No. 6, Nov, 2014 ($3.99)
1-6-Palmiotti & Gray-s/Broxton-a/Darwyn Cooke-c 4.00

WORD WARRIORS (Also see Quest for Dreams Lost)
Literacy Volunteers of Chicago: 1987 ($1.50, B&W)(Proceeds donated to help literacy)
1-Jon Sable by Grell, Ms. Tree, Streetwolf; Chaykin-c 3.00

WORLD AROUND US, THE (Illustrated Story of...)
Gilberton Publishers (Classics Illustrated): Sep, 1958 -No. 36, Oct, 1961 (25¢)
1-Dogs; Evans-a 9 18 27 52 69 85
2-4: 2-Indians; Check-a. 3-Horses; L. B. Cole-c. 4-Railroads; L. B. Cole-a (5 pgs.) 9 18 27 47 61 75
5-Space; Ingels-a 10 20 30 56 76 95
6-The F.B.I.; Disbrow, Evans, Ingels-a 10 20 30 56 76 95
7-Pirates; Disbrow, Ingels, Kinstler-a 9 18 27 52 69 85
8-Flight; Evans, Ingels, Crandall-a 9 18 27 52 69 85
9-Army; Disbrow, Ingels, Orlando-a 9 18 27 47 61 75
10-13: 10-Navy; Disbrow, Kinstler-a. 11-Marine Corps. 12-Coast Guard; Ingels-a (9 pgs.). 13-Air Force; L.B. Cole-c 9 18 27 47 61 75
14-French Revolution; Crandall, Evans, Kinstler-a 10 20 30 56 76 95
15-Prehistoric Animals; Al Williamson-a, 6 & 10 pgs. plus Morrow-a 10 20 30 58 79 100
16-18: 16-Crusades; Kinstler-a. 17-Festivals; Evans, Crandall-a. 18-Great Scientists; Crandall, Evans, Torres, Williamson, Morrow-a 9 18 27 52 69 85
19-Jungle; Crandall, Williamson, Morrow-a 10 20 30 58 79 100
20-Communications; Crandall, Evans, Torres-a 10 20 30 56 76 95
21-American Presidents; Crandall/Evans, Morrow-a 10 20 30 56 76 95
22-Boating; Morrow-a 8 16 24 44 57 70
23-Great Explorers; Crandall, Evans-a 9 18 27 52 69 85
24-Ghosts; Morrow, Evans-a 10 20 30 56 76 95
25-Magic; Evans, Morrow-a 10 20 30 56 76 95
26-The Civil War 11 22 33 62 86 110
27-Mountains (High Advs.); Crandall/Evans, Morrow, Torres-a 9 18 27 52 69 85
28-Whaling; Crandall, Evans, Morrow, Torres, Wildey-a; L.B. Cole-c 9 18 27 52 69 85
29-Vikings; Crandall, Evans, Torres, Morrow-a 10 20 30 58 79 100
30-Undersea Adventure; Crandall/Evans, Kirby, Morrow, Torres-a 10 20 30 56 76 95
31-Hunting; Crandall/Evans, Ingels, Kinstler, Kirby-a 9 18 27 52 69 85
32,33: 32-For Gold & Glory; Morrow, Kirby, Crandall, Evans-a. 33-Famous Teens; Torres, Crandall, Evans-a 9 18 27 52 69 85
34-36: 34-Fishing; Crandall/Evans-a. 35-Spies; Kirby, Morrow?, Evans-a. 36-Fight for Life (Medicine); Kirby-a 9 18 27 52 69 85
NOTE: See Classics Illustrated Special Edition. Another *World Around Us* issue entitled *The Sea* had been prepared in 1962 but was never published in the U.S. It was published in the British/European *World Around Us* series. Those series then continued with seven additional WAU titles not in the U.S. series.

WORLD BELOW, THE
Dark Horse Comics: Mar, 1999 - No. 4, Jun, 1999 ($2.50, limited series)
1-4-Paul Chadwick-s/c/a 3.00
TPB (1/07, $12.95) r/#1-4; intro. by Chadwick; gallery of sketches and covers 13.00

WORLD BELOW, THE: DEEPER AND STRANGER
Dark Horse Comics: Dec, 1999 - No. 4, Mar, 2000 ($2.95, B&W)
1-4-Paul Chadwick-s/c/a 3.00

GD VG FN VF VF/NM NM-
2.0 4.0 6.0 8.0 9.0 9.2

WORLD FAMOUS HEROES MAGAZINE
Comic Corp. of America (Centaur): Oct, 1941 - No. 4, Apr, 1942 (comic book)
1-Gustavson-c; Lubbers, Glanzman-a; Davy Crockett, Paul Revere, Lewis & Clark, John Paul Jones stories; Flag-c 129 258 387 826 1413 2000
2-Lou Gehrig life story; Lubbers-a 63 126 189 403 689 975
3,4-Lubbers-a. 4-Wild Bill Hickok story; 2 pg. Marlene Dietrich story 60 120 180 381 653 925

WORLD FAMOUS STORIES
Croyden Publishers: 1945
1-Ali Baba, Hansel & Gretel, Rip Van Winkle, Mid-Summer Night's Dream 15 30 45 83 124 165

WORLD IS HIS PARISH, THE
George A. Pflaum: 1953 (15¢)
nn-The story of Pope Pius XII 7 14 21 35 43 50

WORLD OF ADVENTURE (Walt Disney's...)(TV)
Gold Key: Apr, 1963 - No. 3, Oct, 1963 (12¢)
1-Disney TV characters; Savage Sam, Johnny Shiloh, Capt. Nemo, The Mooncussers 3 6 9 20 31 42
2,3 3 6 9 15 21 26

WORLD OF ANIMOSITY (See Animosity)
AfterShock Comics: Sept, 2017 ($3.99, one-shot)
nn-Character profiles and series summary 4.00

WORLD OF ARCHIE, THE (See Archie Giant Series Mag. #148, 151, 156, 160, 165, 171, 177, 182, 188, 193, 200, 208, 213, 225, 232, 237, 244, 249, 456, 461, 468, 473, 480, 485, 492, 497, 504, 509, 516, 521, 532, 543, 554, 565, 574, 587, 599, 612, 627)

WORLD OF ARCHIE
Archie Comics: Aug, 1992 - No. 22 ($1.25/$1.50)
1 6.00
2-15: 9-Neon ink-c 3.00
16-22 3.00

WORLD OF ARCHIE DOUBLE DIGEST MAGAZINE (World of Archie Comics Digest #41-on)
Archie Comics: Dec, 2010 - Present ($3.99/$4.99/$5.99/$6.99/$7.99)
1-29,31-37,39,40: 5-r/Tiny Titans/Little Archie #1-3 with sketch-a. 17-Archie babies 4.00
30-($5.99) Double Double Digest 6.00
38-$4.99-c 5.00
41,46,51,55,60,63,67,71,73,75-91-($6.99) 41-World of Archie Double Double Digest 7.00
42-45,47-50,52,54,57,58,61,64,65,68-($4.99) Titled World of Archie Comics Digest 5.00
53,56,59,62,66,70,72,74-($5.99): 56-Winter Annual. 59,70-Summer Annual 6.00
92-106-($7.99): 100-Time Police app. 103-Halloween-c. 104,105-Christmas-c 8.00
World of Archie Digest, Free Comic Book Day Edition (6-7/13, giveaway) Reprints 3.00

WORLD OF BETTY AND VERONICA JUMBO COMICS DIGEST
Archie Comics: Feb, 2021 - Present ($7.99)
1,2-New story and reprints 8.00

WORLD OF BLACK HAMMER ENCYCLOPEDIA, THE (See Black Hammer)
Dark Horse Comics: Jul, 2019 ($3.99, one-shot)
nn-Character profiles with art by various and series timeline; Sorrentino-c 4.00

WORLD OF FANTASY
Atlas Comics (CPC No. 1-15/ZPC No. 16-19): May, 1956 - No. 19, Aug, 1959
1 84 168 252 538 919 1300
2-Williamson-a (4 pgs.) 47 94 141 296 498 700
3-Sid Check, Roussos-a 42 84 126 265 445 625
4-7 39 78 117 231 378 525
8-Matt Fox, Orlando, Berg-a 40 80 120 246 411 575
9-Krigstein-a 39 78 117 231 378 525
10-15: 10-Colan-a. 11-Torres-a 36 72 108 211 343 475
16-Williamson-a (4 pgs.); Ditko, Kirby-a 52 104 156 328 552 775
17-19-Ditko, Kirby-a 50 100 150 315 533 750
NOTE: ***Ayers** a-3. **B. Baily** a-4. **Berg** a-5, 6, 8. **Brodsky** c-3. **Check** a-3. **Ditko** a-17, 19. **Everett** a-2; c-4-7, 9, 12, 13. **Forte** a-4, 8, 18. **Heck** a-18. **Infantino** a-14. **Kirby** c-15, 17-19. **Krigstein** a-9. **Maneely** c-2, 14. **Mooney** a-14. **Morrow** a-7. **Orlando** a-8, 13, 14. **Pakula** a-9. **Powell** a-4, 6. **Reinman** a-8, 10. **R.Q. Sale** a-3, 7, 9, 10. **Severin** c-1. **Sinnott** a-16,18.*

WORLD OF GIANT COMICS, THE (See Archie All-Star Specials under Archie Comics)

WORLD OF GINGER FOX, THE (Also see Ginger Fox)
Comico: Nov, 1986 ($6.95, 8 1/2 x 11", 68 pgs., mature)
Graphic Novel ($6.95) 10.00
Hardcover ($27.95) 30.00

WORLD OF JUGHEAD, THE (See Archie Giant Series Mag. #9, 14, 19, 24, 30, 136, 143, 149, 152, 157, 161, 166, 172, 178, 183, 189, 194, 202, 209, 215, 227, 233, 239, 245, 251, 457, 463, 469, 475, 481, 487, 493, 499,

World of Mystery #6 © MAR

World of Warcraft #1 © Blizzard

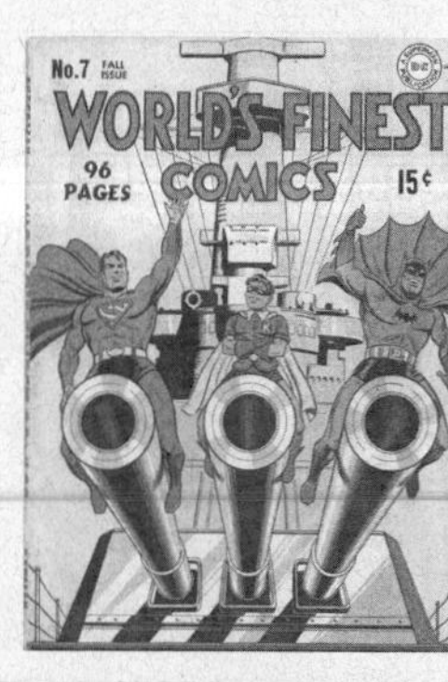

World's Finest Comics #7 © DC

	GD 2.0	VG 4.0	FN 6.0	VF 8.0	VF/NM 9.0	NM- 9.2

505, 511, 517, 523, 531, 542, 553, 564, 577, 590, 602)

WORLD OF KRYPTON, THE (World of...#3) (See Superman #248)
DC Comics, Inc.: 7/79 - No. 3, 9/79; 12/87 - No. 4, 3/88 (Both are lim. series)

1-3 (1979, 40¢; 1st comic book mini-series): 1-Jor-El marries Lara. 3-Baby Superman sent to Earth; Krypton explodes; Mon-El app. 1 3 4 6 8 10
1-4 (75¢)-Byrne scripts; Byrne/Simonson-c 4.00

WORLD OF METROPOLIS, THE
DC Comics: Aug, 1988 - No. 4, July, 1988 ($1.00, limited series)

1-4: Byrne scripts 4.00

WORLD OF MYSTERY
Atlas Comics (GPI): June, 1956 - No. 7, July, 1957

	GD	VG	FN	VF	VF/NM	NM-
1-Torres, Orlando-a; Powell-a?	61	122	183	390	670	950
2-Woodish-a	28	56	84	168	274	380
3-Torres, Davis, Ditko-a	32	64	96	190	310	430
4-Pakula, Powell-a	32	64	96	190	310	430
5,7: 5-Orlando-a	27	54	81	162	266	370
6-Williamson/Mayo-a (4 pgs.); Ditko-a; Colan-a; Crandall text illo	32	64	96	192	310	430

NOTE: ***Ayers** a-4. **Brodsky** c-2, 5, 6. **Colan** a-6, 7. **Everett** c-1, 3. **Pakula** a-4, 6. **Romita** a-2. **Severin** c-7.*

WORLD OF SMALLVILLE
DC Comics: Apr, 1988 - No. 4, July, 1988 (75¢, limited series)

1-4: Byrne scripts. 3-Baby torture-c 5.00

WORLD OF SUSPENSE
Atlas News Co.: Apr, 1956 - No. 8, July, 1957

	GD	VG	FN	VF	VF/NM	NM-
1	58	116	174	371	636	900
2-Ditko-a (4 pgs.)	35	70	105	208	339	470
3,7-Williamson-a in both (4 pgs.); #7-with Mayo	31	62	93	186	303	420
4-6,8	27	54	81	158	259	360

NOTE: ***Berg** a-6. **Cameron** a-2. **Ditko** a-2. **Drucker** a-1. **Everett** a-1, 5; c-6. **Heck** a-5. **Maneely** a-1; c-1-3. **Orlando** a-5. **Powell** a-6. **Reinman** a-4. **Roussos** a-6. **Sale** a-4. **Shores** a-1.*

WORLD OF TANKS
Dark Horse Comics: Aug, 2016 - No. 5, Feb, 2017 ($3.99)

1-5-Ennis-s/Ezquerra-a; set in 1944 Normandy 4.00

WORLD OF TANKS II: CITADEL
Dark Horse Comics: May, 2018 - No. 5, Sept, 2018 ($3.99)

1-5-Ennis-s/Holden-a; set in 1943 Russia during the Battle of Kursk 4.00

WORLD OF WARCRAFT (Based on the Blizzard Entertainment video game)
DC Comics (WildStorm): Jan, 2008 - No. 25, Jan, 2010 ($2.99)

1-Walt Simonson-s/Lullabi-a; cover by Samwise Didier 8.00
1-Variant cover by Jim Lee 12.00
1,2-Second printing with Jim Lee sketch cover 5.00
2-Two covers by Jim Lee and Samwise Didier 5.00
3-24: 3-14-Two covers on each 3.00
25-($3.99) Walt & Louise Simonson-s 4.00
... Special 1 (2/10, $3.99) Costa-s/Mhan-a/c 4.00
... Book One HC (2008, $19.99, dustjacket) r/#1-7; intro. by Chris Metzen of Blizzard 20.00
... Book One SC (2009, $14.99) r/#1-7; intro. by Chris Metzen of Blizzard 15.00
... Book Two HC (2009, $19.99, dustjacket) r/#8-14 20.00
... Book Two SC (2010, $14.99) r/#8-14 15.00
... Book Three HC (2010, $19.99, dustjacket) r/#15-21 20.00
... Book Three SC (2011, $17.99) r/#15-21 18.00

WORLD OF WARCRAFT: ASHBRINGER
DC Comics (WildStorm): Nov, 2008 - No. 4, Feb, 2009 ($3.99)

1-4-Neilson-s/Lullabi & Washington-a; 2 covers by Robinson & Lullabi 4.00
TPB (2010, $14.99) r/#1-4 15.00

WORLD OF WARCRAFT: CURSE OF THE WORGEN
DC Comics (WildStorm #1,2): Jan, 2011 - No. 5, May, 2011 ($3.99/$2.99)

1,2-($3.99) Neilson & Waugh-s/Lullabi & Washington-a; Polidora-c 4.00
3-5-($2.99) 3.00

WORLD OF WHEELS (Formerly Dragstrip Hotrodders)
Charlton Comics: No. 17, Oct, 1967 - No. 32, June, 1970

	GD	VG	FN	VF	VF/NM	NM-
17-20-Features Ken King	3	6	9	17	26	35
21-32-Features Ken King	3	6	9	15	22	28
Modern Comics Reprint 23(1978)						6.00

WORLD OF WOOD
Eclipse Comics: 1986 - No. 4, 1987; No. 5, 2/89 ($1.75, limited series)

	GD	VG	FN	VF	VF/NM	NM-
1,2: 1-Dave Stevens-c. 2-Wood/Stevens-c	2	4	6	8	11	14
3-5: 5-($2.00, B&W)-r/Avon's Flying Saucers						5.00

WORLD READER
AfterShock Comics: Apr, 2017 - No. 6, Sept, 2017 ($3.99, limited series)

1-6-Jeff Loveness-s/Juan Doe-a 4.00

WORLD'S BEST COMICS
DC Comics: Feb 1940

nn - Ashcan comic, not distributed to newsstands, only for in-house use. Cover art is Action Comics #29 with interior being Action Comics #24. One copy sold for $21,000 in 2000.

WORLD'S BEST COMICS (World's Finest Comics #2 on)
National Per. Publications (100 pgs.): Spring, 1941 (Cardboard-c)(DC's 6th annual format comic)

1-The Batman, Superman, Crimson Avenger, Johnny Thunder, The King, Young Dr. Davis, Zatara, Lando, Man of Magic, & Red, White & Blue begin; Superman, Batman & Robin covers begin (inside-c is blank); Fred Ray-c; 15¢ cover price 1600 3200 4800 12,400 27,700 31,000

WORLD'S BEST COMICS: GOLDEN AGE SAMPLER
DC Comics: 2003 (99¢, one-shot, samples from DC Archive editions)

1-Golden Age reprints from Superman #6, Batman #5, Sensation #11, Police #11 3.00

WORLD'S BEST COMICS: SILVER AGE SAMPLER
DC Comics: 2004 (99¢, one-shot, samples from DC Archive editions)

1-Silver Age reprints from Justice League #4, Adventure #247, Our Army at War #81 3.00

WORLDS BEYOND (Stories of Weird Adventure)(Worlds of Fear #2 on)
Fawcett Publications: Nov, 1951

1-Powell, Bailey-a; Moldoff-c 65 130 195 416 708 1000

WORLDS COLLIDE
DC Comics: July, 1994 ($2.50, one-shot)

1-($2.50, 52 pgs.)-Milestone & Superman titles x-over 4.00
1-($3.95, 52 pgs.)-Polybagged w/vinyl clings 5.00

WORLD'S FAIR COMICS (See New York...)

WORLD'S FINEST (Also see Legends of The World's Finest)
DC Comics: 1990 - No. 3, 1990 ($3.95, squarebound, limited series, 52 pgs.)

1-3: Batman & Superman team-up against The Joker and Lex Luthor; Dave Gibbons scripts & Steve Rude-c/a. 2,3-Joker/Luthor painted-c by Steve Rude 5.00
TPB-(1992, $19.95) r/#1-3; Gibbons intro. 20.00
...: The Deluxe Edition HC (2008, $29.99) r/#1-3; Gibbons intro. from 1992; Gibbons story outline and sketches; Rude sketch pages and notes 30.00

WORLD'S FINEST
DC Comics: Dec, 2009 - No. 4, Mar, 2010 ($2.99, limited series)

1-4: Gates-s/two covers by Noto on each. 3-Supergirl/Batgirl team up. 4-Noto-a 3.00
TPB (2010, $14.99) r/#1-4, Action Comics #865 & DC Comics Presents #31 15.00

WORLDS' FINEST (Also see Earth 2 series)
DC Comics: Jul, 2012 - No. 32, May, 2015 ($2.99)

1-32: 1-Huntress and Power Girl; Levitz-s/art by Pérez & Maguire. 6,7-Damian app. 19-Huntress meets Batman. 20,21-X-over with Batman/Superman #8,9. 25-Return to Earth-2. 27-29-Secret History of Earth 2. 32-Death of Lois 3.00
1-Variant-c by Maguire 5.00
#0-(11/12, $2.99) Flashback to Robin's and Supergirl's training 3.00
Annual 1 (3/14, $4.99) Earth 2 flashback; Wonder Woman & Fury app. 5.00
...: Futures End 1 (11/14, $2.99, regular-c) Five years later; Cinar-a; Deathstroke app. 3.00
...: Futures End 1 (11/14, $3.99, 3-D cover) 4.00

WORLD'S FINEST COMICS (Formerly World's Best Comics #1)
National Periodical Publ./DC Comics: No. 2, Sum, 1941 - No. 323, Jan, 1986 (#1-17 have cardboard covers) (#2-9 have 100 pgs.)

	GD	VG	FN	VF	VF/NM	NM-
2 (100 pgs.)-Superman, Batman & Robin covers continue from World's Best; (cover price 15¢ #2-70)	437	874	1311	3190	5645	8100
3-The Sandman begins; last Johnny Thunder; origin & 1st app. The Scarecrow	432	864	1296	3154	5577	8000
4-Hop Harrigan app.; last Young Dr. Davis	275	550	825	1760	3030	4300
5-Intro. TNT & Dan the Dyna-Mite; last King & Crimson Avenger	273	546	819	1747	2999	4250
6-Star Spangled Kid begins (Sum/42); Aquaman app.; S&K Sandman with Sandy in new costume begins, ends #7	203	406	609	1299	2225	3150
7-Green Arrow begins (Fall/42); last Lando & Red, White & Blue; S&K art	226	452	678	1446	2473	3500
8-Boy Commandos begin (by Simon(p) #12); last The King; includes "Minute Man Answers the Call" promo	194	388	582	1242	2121	3000
9-Batman cameo in Star Spangled Kid; S&K-a; last 100 pg. issue; Hitler, Mussolini, Tojo-c	271	542	813	1734	2967	4200
10-S&K-a; 76 pg. issues begin	171	342	513	1094	1872	2650

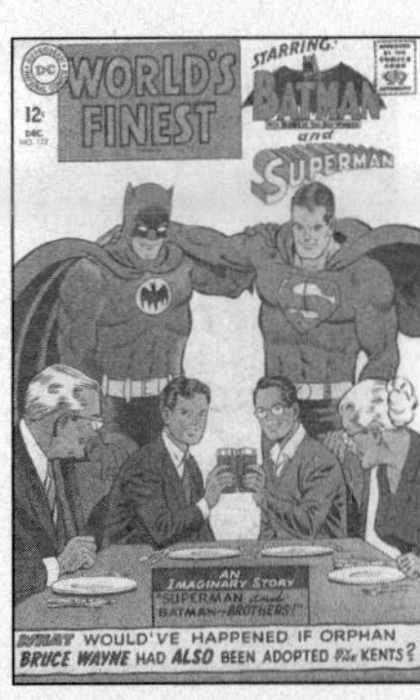

World's Finest Comics #172 © DC

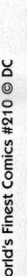

World's Finest Comics #210 © DC

World's Finest: Our Worlds at War #1 © DC

	GD 2.0	VG 4.0	FN 6.0	VF 8.0	VF/NM 9.0	NM- 9.2
11-17: 17-Last cardboard cover issue	164	328	492	1050	1800	2550
18-20: 18-Paper covers begin; last Star Spangled Kid. 19-Joker story. 20-Last quarterly issue	158	316	474	1011	1731	2450
21-30: 21-Begin bi-monthly. 30-Johnny Everyman app.	110	220	330	704	1202	1700
31-40: 33-35-Tomahawk app. 35-Penguin app.	106	212	318	678	1164	1650
41-43,45-50: 41-Boy Commandos end. 42-The Wyoming Kid begins (9-10/49), ends #63. 43-Full Steam Foley begins, ends #48. 48-Last square binding. 49-Tom Sparks, Boy Inventor begins; robot-c	103	206	309	659	1130	1600
44-Used in SOTI, ref. to Batman & Robin being gay, and a cop being shot in the face	119	238	357	762	1306	1850
51-60: 51-Zatara ends. 54-Last 76 pg. issue. 59-Manhunters Around the World begins (7-8/52), ends #62	100	200	300	640	1095	1550
61-64: 61-Joker story. 63-Capt. Compass app.	97	194	291	621	1061	1500
65-Origin Superman; Tomahawk begins (7-8/53), ends #101	148	296	444	947	1624	2300
66-70-(15¢ issues, scarce)-Last 15¢, 68pg. issue	103	206	309	659	1130	1600
71-(10¢ issue, scarce)-Superman & Batman begin as team (7-8/54); were in separate stories until now; Superman & Batman exchange identities; 10¢ issues begin	303	606	909	2121	3711	5300
72,73-(10¢ issue, scarce)	129	258	387	826	1413	2000
74-Last pre-code issue	97	194	291	621	1061	1500
75-(1st code approved, 3-4/55)	94	188	282	597	1024	1450
76-80: 77-Superman loses powers & Batman obtains them	68	136	204	435	743	1050
81-87,89: 84-1st S.A. issue. 89-2nd Batmen of All Nations (aka Club of Heroes)	32	64	96	230	515	800
88-1st Joker/Luthor team-up	63	126	189	403	689	975
90-Batwoman's 1st app. in World's Finest (10/57, 3rd app. anywhere) plus-c app.	77	154	231	493	847	1200
91-93,95-99: 96-99-Kirby Green Arrow. 99-Robot-c	25	50	75	175	388	600
94-Origin Superman/Batman team retold	62	124	186	502	1126	1750
100 (3/59)	36	72	108	266	596	925
101-110: 102-Tommy Tomorrow begins, ends #124	15	30	45	105	233	360
111-121: 111-1st app. The Clock King. 113-Intro. Miss Arrowette in Green Arrow; 1st Bat-Mite/Mr. Mxyzptlk team-up (11/60). 117-Batwoman-c. 121-Last 10¢ issue	12	24	36	79	170	260
122-128: 123-2nd Bat-Mite/Mr. Mxyzptlk team-up (2/62). 125-Aquaman begins (5/62), ends #139 (Aquaman #1 is dated 1-2/62)	10	20	30	64	132	200
129-Joker/Luthor team-up-c/story	12	24	36	82	179	275
130-142: 135-Last Dick Sprang story. 140-Last Green Arrow. 142-Origin The Composite Superman (villain); Legion app.	8	16	24	51	96	140
143-150: 143-1st Mailbag. 144-Clayface/Brainiac team-up. 148-Clayface/Luthor team-up; last Clayface until Action #443	6	12	18	42	79	115
151-153,155,157-160: 157-2nd Super Sons story; last app. Kathy Kane (Bat-Woman) until Batman Family #10; 1st Bat-Mite Jr.	5	10	15	35	63	90
154-1st Super Sons story; last Bat-Woman in costume until Batman Family #10.	6	12	18	42	79	115
156-1st Bizarro Batman; Joker-c/story	13	26	39	91	201	310
161,170 (80-Pg. Giants G-28,G-40)	6	12	18	40	73	105
162-165,167,168,171,172: 168,172-Adult Legion app.	5	10	15	31	53	75
166-Joker-c/story	7	14	21	44	82	120
169-3rd app. new Batgirl(9/67)(cover and 1 panel cameo); 3rd Bat-Mite/Mr. Mxyzptlk team-up	9	18	27	62	126	190
173-('68)-1st S.A. app. Two-Face as Batman becomes Two-Face in story	9	18	27	59	117	175
174-Adams-c	5	10	15	33	57	80
175,176-Neal Adams-c/a; both reprint J'onn J'onzz origin/Detective #225,226	6	12	18	40	73	105
177-Joker/Luthor team-up-c/story	6	12	18	41	76	110
178-(9/68) Intro. of Super Nova (revived in "52" weekly series); Adams-c	6	12	18	37	66	95
179-(80 Page Giant G-52) -Adams-c; r/#94	6	12	18	37	66	95
180,182,183,185,186: Adams-c on all. 182-Silent Knight-r/Brave & Bold #6. 185-Last 12¢ issue. 186-Johnny Quick-r	4	8	12	27	44	60
181,184,187: 187-Green Arrow origin-r by Kirby (Adv. #256)	4	8	12	23	37	50
188,197:(Giants G-64,G-76; 64 pages)	5	10	15	34	60	85
189-196: 190-193-Robin-r	3	6	9	20	31	42
198,199-3rd Superman/Flash race (see Flash #175 & Superman #199). 199-Adams-c	10	20	30	66	138	210
200-Adams-c	4	8	12	25	40	55
201-203: 203-Last 15¢ issue.	3	6	9	18	38	38
204,205-(52 pgs.) Adams-c: 204-Wonder Woman app. 205-Shining Knight-r (6 pgs.) by Frazetta/Adv. #153; Teen Titans x-over	3	6	9	21	33	45
206 (Giant G-88, 64 pgs.)	5	10	15	31	53	75
207,212-(52 pgs.)	3	6	9	20	31	42
208-211(25¢-c) Adams-c: 208-(52 pgs.) Origin Robotman-r/Det. #138. 209-211-(52 pgs.)	3	6	9	21	33	45
213,214,216-222,229: 217-Metamorpho begins, ends #220; Batman/Superman team-ups resume. 229-r/origin Superman-Batman team	2	4	6	13	18	22
215-(12/72-1/73) Intro. Batman Jr. & Superman Jr. (see Superman/Batman: Saga of the Super Sons TPB for all the Super Sons stories)	3	6	9	18	28	38
223-228-(100 pgs.). 223-N. Adams-r. 223-Deadman origin. 226-N. Adams, S&K, Toth-r; Manhunter part origin-r/Det. #225,226. 227-Deadman app.	5	10	15	30	50	70
230-(68 pgs.)	3	6	9	17	26	35
231-243: 231, 233, 238, 242-Super Sons	2	4	6	9	13	16
244-246-Adams-c: 244-$1.00, 84 pg. issues begin; Green Arrow, Black Canary, Wonder Woman, Vigilante begin; 246-Death of Stuff in Vigilante; origin Vigilante retold	3	6	9	14	20	26
247-252 (84 pgs.): 248-Last Vigilante. 249-The Creeper begins by Ditko, 84 pgs. 250-The Creeper origin retold by Ditko. 251-1st app. Count Vertigo. 252-Last 84 pg. issue	2	4	6	13	18	22
253-257,259-265: 253-Capt. Marvel begins; 68 pgs. begin, end #265. 255-Last Creeper. 256-Hawkman begins. 257-Black Lightning begins. 263-Super Sons. 264-Clay Face app.	2	4	6	8	11	14
258-Adams-c	2	4	6	11	1	20
266-270,272-282-(52 pgs.). 267-Challengers of the Unknown app.; 3 Lt. Marvels return. 268-Capt. Marvel Jr. origin retold. 274-Zatanna begins. 279, 280-Capt. Marvel Jr. & Kid Eternity learn they are brothers	1	3	4	6	8	10
271-(52pgs.) Origin Superman/Batman team retold	2	4	6	8	10	12
283-299: 284-Legion app.	1	2	3	4	5	7
300-($1.25, 52pgs.)-Justice League of America, New Teen Titans & The Outsiders app.; Perez-a (4 pgs.)	1	2	3	5	7	9
301-322: 304-Origin Null and Void. 309,319-Free 16 pg. story in each (309-Flash Force 2000, 319-Mask preview)						5.00
323-Last issue						6.00

NOTE: ***Neal Adams*** *a-230ir; c-174-176, 178-180, 182, 183, 185, 186, 199-205, 208-211, 244-246, 258.* ***Austin*** *a-244-246i.* ***Burnley*** *a-8, 10; c-7-9, 11-14, 15p?, 16-18p, 20-31p.* ***Colan*** *a-274p, 297, 299.* ***Ditko*** *a-249-255.* ***Giffen*** *a-322; c-284p, 322.* ***G. Kane*** *a-38, 174r, 282, 283; c-281, 282, 289.* ***Kirby*** *a-187.* ***Kubert*** *Zatara-40-44.* ***Miller*** *c-285p.* ***Mooney*** *c-134.* ***Morrow*** *a-245-248.* ***Mortimer*** *c-16-21, 26-71.* ***Nasser*** *a(p)-244-246, 259, 260.* ***Newton*** *a-253-281p.* ***Orlando*** *a-224r.* ***Perez*** *a-300i; c-271, 276, 277p, 278p.* ***Fred Ray*** *c-1-5.* ***Fred Ray/Robinson*** *c-13-16.* ***Robinson*** *a-5, 6, 9-11, 13?, 14-16; c-6.* ***Rogers*** *a-259p.* ***Roussos*** *a-212r.* ***Simonson*** *c-291.* ***Spiegle*** *a-275-278, 284.* ***Staton*** *a-262p, 273p.* ***Swan/Moldoff*** *c-126.* ***Swan/Mortimer*** *c-79-82.* ***Toth*** *a-228r.* ***Tuska*** *a-230r, 250p, 252p, 254p, 257p, 283p, 284p, 308p. Boy Commandos by* ***Infantino*** *#39-41.*

WORLD'S FINEST COMICS DIGEST (See DC Special Series #23)

WORLD'S FINEST: OUR WORLDS AT WAR
DC Comics: Oct, 2001 ($2.95, one-shot)

1-Concludes the Our Worlds at War x-over; Jae Lee-c; art by various 3.00

WORLD'S FINITE CEREBUS(Reprints from Cerebus in Hell)
Aardvark-Vanaheim: Mar, 2018 ($4.00, B&W)

1-Cerebus figures with original Gustave Doré artwork of Hell; World's Finest #7-c swipe 4.00

WORLD'S GREATEST ATHLETE (See Walt Disney Showcase #14)

WORLD'S GREATEST SONGS
Atlas Comics (Male): Sept, 1954

	GD	VG	FN	VF	VF/NM	NM-
1-(Scarce)-Heath & Harry Anderson-a; Eddie Fisher life story plus-c; gives lyrics to Frank Sinatra song "Young at Heart"	50	100	150	315	533	750

WORLD'S GREATEST STORIES
Jubilee Publications: Jan, 1949 - No. 2, May, 1949

	GD	VG	FN	VF	VF/NM	NM-
1-Alice in Wonderland; Lewis Carroll adapt.	37	74	111	218	354	490
2-Pinocchio	34	68	102	204	332	460

WORLD'S GREATEST SUPER-HEROES HOLIDAY SPECIAL
DC Comics: 2018 ($4.99, 100 pgs., squarebound, Walmart exclusive)

1-New Flash story Lobdell-s/Booth-a; plus holiday-themed reprints; Andy Kubert-c 5.00

WORLDS OF ASPEN
Aspen MLT, Inc.: 2006 - Present (Free Comic Book Day giveaways)

....: FCBD 2006, 2007, #3, #4 Editions; Fathom, Soulfire, Shrugged short stories; Turner-c 3.00
... 2010 (5/10) Previews Fathom, Mindfield, Soulfire, Executive Assistant: Iris and Dellec 3.00
... 2011 (5/11) Previews Fathom, Soulfire, Charismagic, Lady Mechanika & others 3.00
... 2012 (5/12) Previews Fathom, Homecoming, Idolized, Shrugged & others 3.00
... 2013 (5/13) Flip book; previews Fathom, Zoohunters & others 3.00
... 2014 (5/14) Flip book; previews Damsels in Excess & Zoohunters; pin-ups 3.00
... 2015 (5/15) Flip book; previews Eternal Soulfire & Fathom Blue; pin-ups 3.00
... 2016 (5/16) Prelude to Aspen Universe: Revelations; character profile pages 3.00
... 2018 (5/18) Dimension: War Eternal; Nu Way 3.00

World War Hulk #4 © MAR

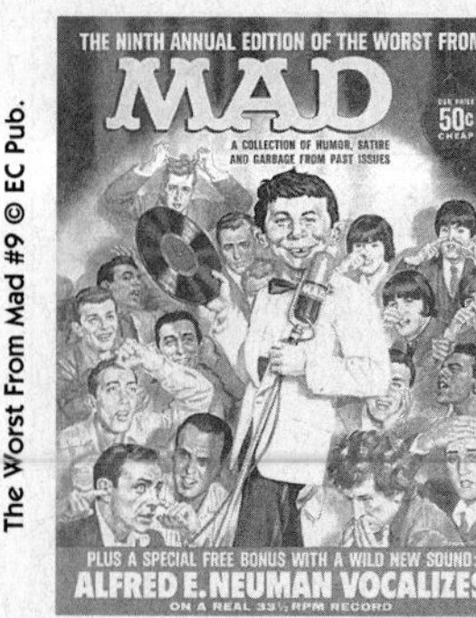

The Worst From Mad #9 © EC Pub.

Wow Comics #10 © FAW

	GD 2.0	VG 4.0	FN 6.0	VF 8.0	VF/NM 9.0	NM- 9.2

WORLDS OF FEAR (Stories of Weird Adventure)(Formerly Worlds Beyond #1)
Fawcett Publications: V1#2, Jan, 1952 - V2#10, June, 1953

V1#2 61 122 183 390 670 950
3-Evans-a 52 104 156 328 552 775
4-6(9/52) 44 90 135 284 480 675
V2#7,8 42 84 126 265 445 625
9-Classic drowning-c (4/53) 65 130 195 416 708 1000
10-Saunders painted-c; man with no eyes surrounded by eyeballs-c plus eyes ripped out story 258 516 774 1651 2826 4000
NOTE: ***Moldoff** c-2-8. **Powell** a-2, 4, 5. **Sekowsky** a-4, 5.*

WORLDSTORM
DC Comics (WildStorm): Nov, 2006 (Dec on cover) - No. 2, May, 2007 ($2.99)

1,2-Previews and pin-ups for re-launched WildStorm titles.1-Art Adams-c 3.00

WORLDS UNKNOWN
Marvel Comics Group: May, 1973 - No. 8, Aug, 1974

1-r/from Astonishing #54; Torres, Reese-a 3 6 9 21 33 45
2-8 3 6 9 14 20 26
NOTE: ***Adkins/Mooney** a-5. **Buscema** c/a-4p. W. **Howard** c/a-3i. **Kane** a(p)-1,2; c(p)-5, 6, 8. **Sutton** a-2. **Tuska** a(p)-7, 8; c-7p. No. 7, 8 has Golden Voyage of Sinbad movie adaptation.*

WORLD WAR HULK (See Incredible Hulk #106)
Marvel Comics: Aug, 2007 - No. 5, Jan, 2008 ($3.99, limited series)

1-Hulk returns to Earth; Iron Man and Avengers app.; Romita Jr.-a/Pak-s/Finch-c 4.00
1-Variant cover by Romita Jr. 6.00
2-5: 2-Hulk battles The Avengers and FF; Finch-c. 3,4-Dr. Strange app. 5-Sentry app. 4.00
2-5-Variant cover by Romita Jr. 6.00
...: Aftersmash 1 (1/08, $3.99) Sandoval-a/Land-c; Hercules, Iron Man app. 4.00
...: Gamma Files (2007, $3.99) profile pages of Hulk characters 4.00
...Prologue: World Breaker 1 (7/07, one-shot) Rio, Weeks, Phillips, Miyazawa-a 4.00
TPB (2008, $19.99) r/#1-5 20.00

WORLD WAR HULK AFTERSMASH: DAMAGE CONTROL
Marvel Comics: Mar, 2008 - No. 3, May, 2008 ($2.99, limited series)

1-3-The clean-up; McDuffie-s. 2-Romita- Jr.-c. 3-Romita Sr.-c 3.00

WORLD WAR HULK AFTERSMASH: WARBOUND
Marvel Comics: Feb, 2008 - No. 5, Jun, 2008 ($2.99, limited series)

1-5-Kirk & Sandoval-a/Cheung-c 3.00

WORLD WAR HULK: FRONT LINE (See Incredible Hulk #106)
Marvel Comics: Aug, 2007 - No. 6, Dec, 2007 ($2.99, limited series)

1-6-Ben Urich & Sally Floyd report World War Hulk; Jenkins-s/Bachs-a 3.00
TPB (2008, $16.99) r/#1-5 & WWH Prologue: World Breaker 17.00

WORLD WAR HULK: GAMMA CORPS
Marvel Comics: Sept, 2007 - No. 4, Jan, 2008 ($2.99, limited series)

1-4-Tieri-s/Ferreira-a/Roux-c 3.00
TPB (2008, $10.99) r/#1-4 11.00

WORLD WAR HULKS
Marvel Comics: Jun, 2010; Sept, 2010 ($3.99, one-shot & limited series)

1-Short stories by various; Deadpool app.; Romita Jr.-c 4.00
...: Spider-Man vs. Thor 1,2 (9/10 - No. 2, 9/10) Gillen-s/Molina-a 4.00
...: Wolverine vs. Captain America 1,2 (9/10 - No. 2, 9/10) "Capt America vs Wolv." on-c 4.00

WORLD WAR HULK: X-MEN (See New Avengers: Illuminati and Incredible Hulk #92)
Marvel Comics: Aug, 2007 - No. 3, Oct, 2007 ($2.99, limited series)

1-3-Gage-s/DiVito-a/McGuinness-c; Hulk invades the Xavier Institute 3.00
TPB (2008, $24.99) r/#1-3, Avengers: The Initiative #4-5, Irredeemable Ant-Man #10, Iron Man #19-20, and Ghost Rider #12-13 25.00

WORLD WAR STORIES
Dell Publishing Co.: Apr-June, 1965 - No. 3, Dec, 1965

1-Glanzman-a in all 4 8 12 25 40 55
2,3 3 6 9 16 24 32

WORLD WAR TANK GIRL
Titan Comics: May, 2017 - No. 4, Sept, 2017 ($3.99, limited series)

1-4-Tank Girl and crew in 1944 Germany; Alan Martin-s/Brett Parson-a; multiple covers 4.00

WORLD WAR II (See Classics Illustrated Special Issue)

WORLD WAR III
Ace Periodicals: Mar, 1953 - No. 2, May, 1953

1-(Scarce)-Atomic bomb blast-c; Cameron-a 194 388 582 1242 2121 3000
2-Used in **POP**, pg. 78 & B&W & color illos; Cameron-a 94 188 282 597 1025 1450

WORLD WAR X
Titan Comics: Jan, 2017 - No. 6, Jun, 2017 ($3.99, English version of French comic series)

1-6-Jerry Frissen-s/Peter Snejbjerg-a; multiple covers on each 4.00

WORLD WITHOUT END
DC Comics: 1990 - No. 6, 1991 ($2.50, limited series, mature, stiff-c)

1-6: Horror/fantasy; all painted-c/a 3.00

WORLD WRESTLING FEDERATION BATTLEMANIA
Valiant: 1991 - No. 5?, 1991 ($2.50, magazine size, 68 pgs.)

1-5: 5-Includes 2 free pull-out posters 4.00

WORST FROM MAD, THE (Annual)
E. C. Comics: 1958 - No. 12, 1969 (Each annual cover is reprinted from the cover of the Mad issues being reprinted)(Value is 1/2 if bonus is missing)

nn(1958)-Bonus; record labels & travel stickers; 1st Mad annual; r/Mad #29-34 47 94 141 296 498 700
2(1959)-Bonus is small 33 1/3 rpm record entitled "Meet the Staff of Mad"; r/Mad #35-40 45 90 135 284 480 675
3(1960)-Has 20x30" campaign poster "Alfred E. Neuman for President"; r/Mad #41-46 15 30 45 103 227 350
4(1961)-Sunday comics section; r/Mad #47-54 14 28 42 97 214 330
5(1962)-Has 33-1/3 record; r/Mad #55-62 20 40 60 138 307 475
6(1963)-Has 33-1/3 record; r/Mad #63-70 20 40 60 138 307 475
7(1964)-Mad protest signs; r/Mad #71-76 9 18 27 61 123 185
8(1965)-Build a Mad Zeppelin 10 20 30 66 138 210
9(1966)-33-1/3 rpm record; Beatles on-c 14 28 42 97 214 330
10(1967)-Mad bumper sticker 6 12 18 40 73 105
11(1968)-Mad cover window stickers 6 12 18 37 66 95
12(1969)-Mad picture postcards; Orlando-a 6 12 18 37 66 95
NOTE: *Covers: **Bob Clarke**-#8. **Mingo**-#7, 9-12.*

WOTALIFE COMICS (Formerly Nutty Life #2; Phantom Lady #13 on)
Fox Feature Syndicate/Norlen Mag.: No. 3, Aug-Sept, 1946 - No. 12, July, 1947; 1959

3-Cosmo Cat, Li'l Pan, others begin 15 30 45 84 127 170
4-12-Cosmo Cat, Li'l Pan in all 11 22 33 62 86 110
1(1959-Norlen)-Atomic Rabbit, Atomic Mouse; reprints cover to #6; reprints entire book? 8 16 24 42 54 65

WOTALIFE COMICS
Green Publications: 1959 - No. 5, 1959

1-Funny animal; Li'l Pan & Tamale app. 7 14 21 35 43 50
2-5 5 10 15 22 26 30

WOW COMICS ("Wow, What A Magazine!" on cover of first issue)
Henle Publishing Co.: July, 1936 - No. 4, Nov, 1936 (52 pgs., magazine size)

1-Buck Jones in "The Phantom Rider" (1st app. in comics), Fu Manchu; Capt. Scott Dalton begins; Will Eisner-a (1st in comics); Baily-a(1); Briefer-c 423 846 1269 3046 5323 7600
2-Ken Maynard, Fu Manchu, Popeye by Segar plus article on Popeye; Eisner-a 300 600 900 1965 3408 4850
3-Eisner-c/a(3); Popeye by Segar, Fu Manchu, Hiram Hick by Bob Kane, Space Limited app.; Jimmy Dempsey talks about Popeye's punch; Bob Ripley Believe it or Not begins; Briefer-a 300 600 900 1904 3277 4650
4-Flash Gordon by Raymond, Mandrake, Popeye by Segar, Tillie The Toiler, Fu Manchu, Hiram Hick by Bob Kane; Eisner-a(3); Briefer-c/a 320 640 960 2240 3920 5600

WOW COMICS (Real Western Hero #70 on)(See XMas Comics)
Fawcett Publ.: Winter, 1940-41; No. 2, Summer, 1941 - No. 69, Fall, 1948

nn(#1)-Origin Mr. Scarlet by S&K; Atom Blake, Boy Wizard, Jim Dolan, & Rick O'Shay begin; Diamond Jack, The White Rajah, & Shipwreck Roberts, only app.; 1st mention of Gotham City in comics; the cover was printed on unstable paper stock and is rarely found in fine or mint condition; blank inside-c; bondage-c by Beck 1475 2950 4425 11,400 20,450 29,500
2 (Scarce)-The Hunchback begins 187 374 561 1197 2049 2900
3 (Fall, 1941) 110 220 330 704 1202 1700
4-Origin & 1st app. Pinky 113 226 339 723 1237 1750
5 68 136 204 435 743 1050
6-Origin & 1st app. The Phantom Eagle (7/15/42); Commando Yank begins 71 142 213 454 777 1100
7,8 58 116 174 371 636 900
9-(1/6/43)-Capt. Marvel, Capt. Marvel Jr., Shazam app.; Scarlet & Pinky x-over; Mary Marvel-c/stories begin 300 600 900 1965 3408 4850
10-Swayze-c/a on Mary Marvel 97 194 291 621 1061 1500
11-17,19,20: 15-Flag-c 57 114 171 362 619 875
18-1st app. Uncle Marvel (10/43); infinity-c 66 132 198 419 722 1025
21-30: 23-Robot-c. 28-Pinky x-over in Mary Marvel 39 78 117 240 395 550

Wraith #1 © IDW

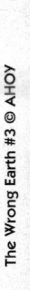

The Wrong Earth #3 © AHOY

Wynonna Earp #5 © Beau Smith

	GD	VG	FN	VF	VF/NM	NM-
	2.0	4.0	6.0	8.0	9.0	9.2
31-40: 32-68-Phantom Eagle by Swayze	29	58	87	170	278	385
41-50	26	52	78	154	252	350
51-58: Last Mary Marvel	23	46	69	136	223	310
59-69: 59-Ozzie (teenage) begins. 62-Flying Saucer gag-c (1/48). 65-69-Tom Mix stories (cont'd in Real Western Hero)	20	40	60	115	188	260

NOTE: *Cover features: Mr. Scarlet-#1-5; Commando Yank-#6, 7, (w/Mr. Scarlet #8); Mary Marvel-#9-56, (w/ Commando Yank-#46-50), (w/Mr. Scarlet & Commando Yank-#51), (w/Mr. Scarlet & Pinky #53), (w/Phantom Eagle #54, 56), (w/Commando Yank & Phantom Eagle #58); Ozzie-#59-69.*

WRAITH (Prequel to the novel NOS4A2)
IDW Publishing: Nov, 2013 (incorrect Nov, 2012 in indicia) - No. 7, May, 2014 ($3.99)

1-7: Joe Hill-s/C.P. Wilson III-a. 5-(incorrect #4 in indicia) 4.00
1-Director's Cut (7/14, $4.99) Includes full script 5.00

WRAITHBORN
DC Comics (WildStorm): Nov, 2005 - No. 6, July, 2006 ($2.99, limited series)

1-6-Marcia Chen & Joe Benitez-s/a 3.00
TPB (2007, $19.99) r/series; sketch pages and unused cover sketches 20.00

WRAITHBORN REDUX
Benitez Productions: Feb, 2016 - No. 6, Aug, 2016 ($3.99)

1-6-Remastered printing of the 2005 series; Chen & Benitez-s/a; multiple covers 4.00
... HCF 2016 #1 (10/16, Halloween giveaway) r/#1 3.00

WRATH (Also see Prototype #4)
Malibu Comics: Jan, 1994 - No. 9, Nov, 1995 ($1.95)

1-9: 2-Mantra x-over. 3-Intro/1st app. Slayer. 4,5-Freex app. 8-Mantra & Warstrike app. 9-Prime app. 3.00
1-Ultra 5000 Limited silver foil 6.00
Giant Size 1 (2.50, 44 pgs.) 4.00

WRATH OF THE ETERNAL WARRIOR
Valiant Entertainment: Nov, 2015 - No. 14, Dec, 2016 ($3.99)

1-14: 1-Venditti-s/Allén-a 4.00

WRATH OF THE SPECTRE, THE
DC Comics: May, 1988 - No. 4, Aug, 1988 ($2.50, limited series)

1-3: Aparo-r/Adventure #431-440 5.00
4-Three scripts intended for Adventure #441-on, but not drawn by Aparo until 1988 1 2 3 5 6 8
TPB (2005, $19.99) r/series; Peter Sanderson intro. 20.00

WRECK OF GROSVENOR (See Superior Stories #3)

WRETCH, THE
Caliber: 1996 ($2.95, B&W)

1-Phillip Hester-a/scripts 3.00

WRETCH, THE
Amaze Ink: 1997 - No. 4, 1998 ($2.95, B&W)

1-4-Phillip Hester-a/scripts 3.00
... Vol. 1: Everyday Doomsday (4/03, $13.95) 14.00

WRINGLE WRANGLE (Disney)
Dell Publishing Co.: No. 821, July, 1957

Four Color 821-Based on movie "Westward Ho, the Wagons"; Marsh-a; Fess Parker photo-c 7 14 21 46 86 125

WRONG EARTH, THE (Also see "Dragonfly & Dragonflyman")
AHOY Comics: 2018 - No. 6, 2019 ($3.99)

1-6-Tom Peyer-s/Jamal Igle-a; intro. Dragonfly & Dragonflyman 4.00

WRONG EARTH, THE : NIGHT & DAY
AHOY Comics: 2020 - Present ($3.99)

1,2-Dragonfly & Dragonflyman meet; Tom Peyer-s/Jamal Igle-a; Lady Dragonflyman app. 4.00

WULF
Ardden Entertainment: Mar, 2011 - No. 6, Sept, 2012 ($2.99)

1-6-Steve Niles-s/Nat Jones-a/c; Lomax app. 3-6-Iron Jaw app. 3.00

WULF THE BARBARIAN
Atlas/Seaboard Publ.: Feb, 1975 - No. 4, Sept, 1975

1,2: 1-Origin; Janson-a. 2-Intro. Berithe the Swordswoman; Janson-a w/Neal Adams, Wood, Reese-a assists 3 6 9 14 19 24
3,4: 3-Skeates-s. 4-Friedrich-s 2 4 6 10 14 18

WWE (WWE Wrestling)
BOOM! Studios: Jan, 2017 - No. 25, Feb, 2019 ($3.99)

1-24: 1-4-Seth Rollins & Triple H app.; Serg Acuña-a; multiple covers. 1-Back-up w/Guillory-a. 13-Raw 25 Years. 14-17-Spotlight on the Four Horsewomen 4.00
25-($4.99) Hopeless-s/Serg Acuña-a; AJ Styles and Samoa Joe app. 5.00
... Attitude Era 2018 Special 1 (8/18, $7.99) Mick Foley & Steve Austin app. 8.00
...: Forever 1 (1/19, $7.99) Short stories by various; multiple covers 8.00
... Royal Rumble 2018 Special 1 (1/18, $7.99) Ric Flair & Randy Savage app. 8.00
...: SmackDown 1 (10/19, $4.99) Short stories by various; multiple covers 5.00
...: Summerslam 2017 Special 1 (8/17, $7.99) Art by Guillory and others 8.00
... Survivor Series 2017 Special 1 (11/17, $7.99) Shawn Michaels & Kurt Angle app. 8.00
...Then. Now. Forever. 1 (11/16, $3.99) Short stories by various; multiple covers 4.00
...: Wrestlemania 2017 Special 1 (8/17, $7.99) Art by Guillory, Corona, Mora and others 8.00
...: Wrestlemania 2018 Special 1 (4/18, $7.99) Art by Goode, Lorenzo and others 8.00
...: Wrestlemania 2019 Special 1 (3/19, $7.99) Art by Goode, Acuña and others 8.00

WWE HEROES (WWE Wrestling) (#7,8 titled WWE Undertaker)
Titan Comics: Apr, 2010 - No. 8 ($3.99)

1-6: 1-Two covers by Andy Smith and Liam Sharp. 5-Covers by Smith and Mayhew 4.00
7,8-"Undertaker" on cover; Rey Mysterio app. 4.00

WWE: NXT TAKEOVER (WWE Wrestling)
BOOM! Studios: Sept, 2018 ($3.99, weekly series of one-shots)

... – Into the Fire 1; Dennis Hopeless-s/Hyoenjin Kim-a; the rise of Asuka 4.00
... – Proving Ground 1; Dennis Hopeless-s/Kendall Goode-a; Finn Balor vs. Samoa Joe 4.00
... – Redemption 1; Hopeless-s/Lorenzo-a; Johnny Gargano & Shayna Baszler app. 4.00
... – The Blueprint 1; Hopeless-s/Elphick-a; Triple H & Dusty Rhodes app. 4.00

WWE SUPERSTARS (WWE Wrestling)
Papercutz (Super Genius): Dec, 2013 - No. 12, Feb, 2015 ($2.99/$3.99)

1-($2.99)-Mick Foley-s; John Cena, Randy Orton & CM Punk app. 3.00
2-12: 2-($3.99) Mick Foley-s. 9-Hulk Hogan cover by Jusko 4.00

WYATT EARP
Atlas Comics/Marvel No. 23 on (IPC): Nov, 1955 - #29, Jun, 1960; #30, Oct, 1972 - #34, Jun, 1973

	GD	VG	FN	VF	VF/NM	NM-
1	27	54	81	158	259	360
2-Williamson-a (4 pgs.)	15	30	45	88	137	185
3-6,8-11: 3-Black Bart app. 8-Wild Bill Hickok app.	12	24	36	69	97	125
7,12-Williamson-a, 4 pgs. ea.; #12 with Mayo	13	26	39	74	105	135
13-20: 17-1st app. Wyatt's deputy, Grizzly Grant	11	22	33	62	86	110
21-Davis-c	10	20	30	58	79	100
22-24,26-29: 22-Ringo Kid app. 23-Kid From Texas app. 29-Last 10¢ issue	9	18	27	52	69	85
25-Davis-a	10	20	30	54	72	90
30-Williamson-r (1972)	2	4	6	13	18	22
31-34-Reprints. 32-Torres-a(r)	2	4	6	9	13	16

NOTE: ***Ayers** a-8, 10(2), 16(4), 17, 20(4), 26(5), 27(3), 29(3). **Berg** a-9. **Everett** c-6. **Kirby** c-22, 24-26, 29. **Maneely** a-1; c-1-4, 8, 12, 17, 20. **Maurer** a-2(2), 3(4), 4(4), 8(4). **Severin** a-4, 9(4), 10; c-2, 9, 10, 14. **Wildey** a-5, 17, 24, 27, 28.*

WYATT EARP (TV) (Hugh O'Brian Famous Marshal)
Dell Publishing Co.: No. 860, Nov, 1957 - No. 13, Dec-Feb, 1960-61 (Hugh O'Brian photo-c)

	GD	VG	FN	VF	VF/NM	NM-
Four Color 860 (#1)-Manning-a	10	20	30	65	135	205
Four Color 890,921(6/58)-All Manning-a	7	14	21	46	86	125
4 (9-11/58) - 12-Manning-a. 4-Variant edition exists with back-c comic strip; Russ Manning-a. 5-Photo back-c	5	10	15	33	57	80
13-Toth-a	5	10	15	34	60	85

WYATT EARP FRONTIER MARSHAL (Formerly Range Busters) (Also see Blue Bird)
Charlton Comics: No. 12, Jan, 1956 - No. 72, Dec, 1967

	GD	VG	FN	VF	VF/NM	NM-
12	9	18	27	47	61	75
13-19	6	12	18	31	38	45
20-(68 pgs.)-Williamson-a(4), 8,5,5,& 7 pgs.	10	20	30	54	72	90
21-(100 pgs.) Mastroserio, Maneely, Severin-a (signed LePoer)	5	10	15	30	50	70
22-30	3	6	9	16	23	30
31-50	2	4	6	12	16	20
51-72 (1967)	2	4	6	9	11	14

WYNONNA EARP
Image Comics (WildStorm Productions): Dec, 1996 - No. 5, Apr, 1997 ($2.50)

1-5-Beau Smith-s/Joyce Chin-a/c 3.00

WYNONNA EARP
IDW Publishing: Feb, 2016 - No. 8, Sept, 2016 ($3.99)

1-8: 1-Beau Smith-s/Lora Innes-a; multiple covers; bonus look at the SyFy TV series 4.00
...: Greatest Hits 1 (7/18, $1.00) Reprints #1 3.00

WYNONNA EARP: HOME ON THE STRANGE
IDW Publishing: Dec, 2003 - No. 3, Feb, 2004 ($3.99)

1-3-Beau Smith-s/Ferreira-a 4.00

WYNONNA EARP LEGENDS: DOC HOLLIDAY
IDW Publishing: Nov, 2016 - No. 2, Dec, 2016 ($3.99)

Wytches #1 © Snyder & Jock

X-Campus #1 © MAR

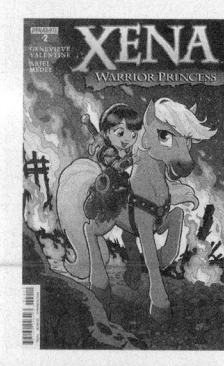

Xena: Warrior Princess V2 #2 © Universal

	GD 2.0	VG 4.0	FN 6.0	VF 8.0	VF/NM 9.0	NM- 9.2

1,2: 1-Beau Smith & Tim Rozon-s/Chris Evenhuis-a; multiple covers; 4.00

WYNONNA EARP LEGENDS: THE EARP SISTERS
IDW Publishing: No. 3, Jan, 2017 - No. 4, Feb, 2017 ($3.99)

3,4-Beau Smith & Melanie Scrofano-s/Chris Evenhuis-a; multiple covers; 4.00

WYNONNA EARP SEASON ZERO
IDW Publishing: Jun, 2017 - No. 5, Oct, 2017 ($3.99)

1-5-Beau Smith & Tim Rozon-s/Angel Hernandez-a; multiple covers; 4.00

WYNONNA EARP: THE YETI WARS
IDW Publishing: May, 2011 - No. 4, Aug, 2011 ($3.99)

1-4-Beau Smith-s/Enrique Villagran-a 4.00

WYRD
Dark Horse Comics: Jan, 2019 - No. 4, Sept, 2019 ($3.99, limited series)

1-4-Curt Pires-s/Antonio Fuso-a 4.00

WYRMS
Marvel Comics (Dabel Brothers): Feb, 2007 - No. 6, Jan, 2008 ($2.99)

1-6-Orson Scott Card & Jake Black-s. 1-3-Batista-a 3.00
TPB (2008, $14.99) r/#1-6 15.00

WYTCHES
Image Comics: Oct, 2014 - No. 6, May, 2015 ($2.99/$3.99)

1-Scott Snyder-s/Jock-a 5.00
2-5 3.00
6-($3.99) Bonus production art and Snyder afterword 4.00
...: Bad Egg Halloween Special 1 (10/18, $7.99) reprints serial from Image+ magazine 8.00
Image Firsts: Wytches (12/14, $1.00) r/#1 3.00

X (Comics' Greatest World: X #1 only) (Also see Comics' Greatest World & Dark Horse Comics #8)
Dark Horse Comics: Feb, 1994 - No. 25, Apr, 1996 ($2.00/$2.50)

1-25: 3-Pit Bulls x-over. 8-Ghost-c & app. 18-Miller-c.; Predator app. 19-22-Miller-c. 3.00
Hero Illustrated Special #1,2 (1994, $1.00, 20 pgs.) 3.00
One Shot to the Head (1994, $2.50, 36 pgs.)-Miller-c. 3.00
NOTE: *Miller c-18-22. Quesada c-6. Russell a-6.*

X (Comics' Greatest World)
Dark Horse Comics: No. 0, Apr, 2013 - No. 24, Apr, 2015 ($2.99)

0-24: 0-Swierczynski-s/Eric Nguyen-a. 13,14-Atkins-a 3.00
One For One (1/14, $1.00) r/#1 3.00

XANADU COLOR SPECIAL
Eclipse Comics: Dec, 1988 ($2.00, one-shot)

1-Continued from Thoughts & Images 4.00

XAVIER INSTITUTE ALUMNI YEARBOOK (See X-Men titles)
Marvel Comics: Dec, 1996 ($5.95, square-bound, one-shot)

1-Text w/art by various 6.00

X-BABIES
Marvel Comics: Dec, 2009 - No. 4, Mar, 2010 ($3.99, limited series)

1-4-Schigiel-s/Chabot-a; Skottie Young-c 4.00
...: Murderama (8/98, $2.95) J.J. Kirby-a 4.00
...: Reborn (1/00, $3.50) J.J. Kirby-a 4.00

X-CALIBRE
Marvel Comics: Mar, 1995 - No. 4, July, 1995 ($1.95, limited series)

1-4-Age of Apocalypse 4.00

X-CAMPUS
Marvel Comics: July, 2010 - No. 4, Nov, 2010 ($4.99, limited series)

1-4-Alternate version of X-Men; stories by European creators; Nauck-c 5.00

X-CLUB
Marvel Comics: Feb, 2012 - No. 5, Jun, 2012 ($2.99, limited series)

1-5-X-Men scientist team; Dr. Nemesis & Danger app. 1-Bradshaw-c. 2-5-Esquejo-c 3.00

XENA (TV)
Dynamite Entertainment: 2006 - 2007 ($3.50)

1-4-Three covers on each; Neves-a/Layman-s 3.50
Vol. 2 #1-4-(Dark Xena) Four covers; Salonga-a/Layman-s 3.50
Annual 1 (2007, $4.95) Three covers; Salonga-a/Champagne-s 5.00
... Vol. 2: Dark Xena TPB (2007, $14.99) r/Vol. 2 #1-4; variant cover gallery 15.00

XENA (Volume 4) (TV)
Dynamite Entertainment: 2018 - No. 10, 2018 ($3.99)

1-10: 1-Meredith Finch-s/Vicente Cifuentes-a; main covers by Cifuentes & David Finch 4.00

XENA / ARMY OF DARKNESS: WHAT...AGAIN?!
Dynamite Entertainment: 2008 - No. 4, 2009 ($3.50, limited series)

1-4-Xena, Gabrielle, & Autolycus team up with Ash; Montenegro-a; two covers on each 3.50

XENA: WARRIOR PRINCESS (TV)
Topps Comics: Aug, 1997 - No. 0, Oct, 1997 ($2.95)

	GD	VG	FN	VF	VF/NM	NM-
1-Two stories by various; J. Scott Campbell-c	1	3	4	6	8	10
1,2-Photo-c	1	3	4	6	8	10
2-Stevens-c	1	3	4	6	8	10
0-(10/97)-Lopresti-c, 0-(10/97)-Photo-c	1	2	3	5	6	8

...First Appearance Collection ('97, $9.95) r/Hercules the Legendary Journeys #3-5 and 5-page story from TV Guide 10.00

XENA: WARRIOR PRINCESS (TV)
Dark Horse Comics: Sept, 1999 - No. 14, Oct, 2000 ($2.95/$2.99)

1-14: 1-Mignola-c and photo-c. 2,3-Bradstreet-c & photo-c 4.00

XENA: WARRIOR PRINCESS (Volume 2) (TV)
Dynamite Entertainment: 2016 - No. 6, 2016 ($3.99)

1-6: 1-Valentine-s/Medel-a; main covers by Land & Frison 4.00

XENA: WARRIOR PRINCESS (Volume 3) (TV)
Dynamite Entertainment: 2018 - No. 6, 2019 ($3.99)

1-6: Vita Ayala-s; covers by David Mack and others. 1,2-Sweetman-a 4.00

XENA: WARRIOR PRINCESS AND THE ORIGINAL OLYMPICS (TV)
Topps Comics: Jun, 1998 - No. 3, Aug, 1998 ($2.95, limited series)

1-3-Regular and Photo-c; Lim-a/T&M Bierbaum-s 3.50

XENA: WARRIOR PRINCESS-BLOODLINES (TV)
Topps Comics: May, 1998 - No. 2, June, 1998 ($2.95, limited series)

1,2-Lopresti-s/c/a. 2-Reg. and photo-c 3.50
1-Bath photo-c, 1-American Ent. Ed. 4.50

XENA: WARRIOR PRINCESS / JOXER: WARRIOR PRINCE (TV)
Topps Comics: Nov, 1997 - No. 3, Jan, 1998 ($2.95, limited series)

1-3-Regular and Photo-c; Lim-a/T&M Bierbaum-s 3.50

XENA: WARRIOR PRINCESS-THE DRAGON'S TEETH (TV)
Topps Comics: Dec, 1997 - No. 3, Feb, 1998 ($2.95, limited series)

1-3-Regular and Photo-c; Teranishi-a/Thomas-s 3.50

XENA: WARRIOR PRINCESS-THE ORPHEUS TRILOGY (TV)
Topps Comics: Mar, 1998 - No. 3, May, 1998 ($2.95, limited series)

1-3-Regular and Photo-c; Teranishi-a/T&M Bierbaum-s 3.50

XENA: WARRIOR PRINCESS VS. CALLISTO (TV)
Topps Comics: Feb, 1998 - No. 3, Apr, 1998 ($2.95, limited series)

1-3-Regular and Photo-c; Morgan-a/Thomas-s 3.50

XENOBROOD
DC Comics: No. 0, Oct, 1994 - No. 6, Apr, 1995 ($1.50, limited series)

0-6: 0-Indicia says "Xenobroods" 3.00

XENOZOIC TALES (Also see Cadillacs & Dinosaurs, Death Rattle #8)
Kitchen Sink Press: Feb, 1986 - No. 14, Oct, 1996

	GD	VG	FN	VF	VF/NM	NM-
1-Mark Schultz-s/a in all	2	4	6	9	12	15

1(2nd printing)(1/89) 4.00
2-14 6.00
Volume 1 ($14.95) r/#1-6 & Death Rattle #8 15.00
Volume 2 (5/03, $14.95, TPB) B&W r/#7-14; intro by Frank Cho 15.00

XENYA
Sanctuary Press: Apr, 1994 - No. 3 ($2.95)

1-3: 1-Hildebrandt-c; intro Xenya 3.00

XERO
DC Comics: May, 1997 - No. 12, Apr, 1998 ($1.75)

1-7 3.00
8-12 3.00

XERXES: THE FALL OF THE HOUSE OF DARIUS AND THE RISE OF ALEXANDER
Dark Horse Comics: Apr, 2018 - No. 5, Aug, 2018 ($4.99, limited series)

1-5-Prequel to 300; Frank Miller-s/a 5.00

X-FACTOR (Also see The Avengers #263, Fantastic Four #286 and Mutant X)
Marvel Comics Group: Feb, 1986 - No. 149, Sept, 1998

	GD	VG	FN	VF	VF/NM	NM-
1-($1.25, 52 pgs)-Story recaps 1st app. from Avengers #263; story cont'd from F.F. #286; return of original X-Men (now X-Factor); Guice/Layton-a; Baby Nathan app. (2nd after X-Men #201)	3	6	9	16	23	30
2-4	1	2	3	5	6	8

X-Factor #127 © MAR

X-Factor (2006 series) #32 © MAR

The X-Files (2008 series) #1 © 20th Fox

GD VG FN VF VF/NM NM-
2.0 4.0 6.0 8.0 9.0 9.2

5-1st brief app. Apocalypse (1 page) 3 6 9 16 24 32
6-1st full app. Apocalypse 6 12 18 37 66 95
7-10: 10-Sabretooth app. (11/86, 3 pgs.) cont'd in X-Men #212; 1st app. in an X-Men comic book 6.00
11-18,20-22: 13-Baby Nathan app. in flashback. 14-Cyclops vs. The Master Mold. 15-Intro wingless Angel 4.00
19-Apocalypse-c/app. 2 4 6 11 16 20
23-1st brief app. Archangel (2 pages) 2 4 6 9 13 16
24-1st full app. Archangel (now in Uncanny X-Men); Fall Of The Mutants begins; origin Apocalypse 4 8 12 25 40 55
25,26: Fall Of The Mutants; 26-New outfits 6.00
27-37,39,41-49,51-59,63-70,72-83,87-91,93-99,101: 35-Origin Cyclops. 51-53-Sabretooth app. 52-Liefeld-c(p). 54-Intro Crimson; Silvestri-c/a(p). 63-Portacio/Thibert-c/a(p) begins, ends #69. 65-68-Lee co-plots. 65-The Apocalypse Files begins, ends #68. 66,67-Baby Nathan app. 67-Inhumans app. 68-Baby Nathan is sent into future to save his life. 69,70-X-Men(w/Wolverine) x-over. 77-Cannonball (of X-Force) app. 87-Quesada-c/a(p) in monthly comic begins, ends #92. 88-1st app. Random 4.00
38,50,60-62,71,75: 38,50-(52 pgs.): 50-Liefeld/McFarlane-c. 60-X-Tinction Agenda x-over; New Mutants (w/Cable) x-over in #60-62; Wolverine in #62. 61,62-X-Tinction Agenda. 62-Jim Lee-c. 71-New team begins (Havok, Polaris, Strong Guy, Wolfsbane & Madrox); Stroman-c/a begins. 75-(52 pgs.) 5.00
40-Rob Liefeld-c/a (4/89, 1st at Marvel?) 5.00
60,71-2nd printings. 60-Gold ink 2nd printing. 71-2nd printing ($1.25) 3.00
84-86 -Jae Lee a(p); 85,86-Jae Lee-c. Polybagged with trading card in each; X-Cutioner's Song x-overs. 4.00
87-Facsimile Edition (10/19, $3.99) Reprints #87 with original ads and letter column 4.00
92-($3.50, 68 pgs.)-Wraparound-c by Quesada w/Havok hologram on-c; begin X-Men 30th anniversary issues; Quesada-a. 6.00
92-2nd printing 4.00
100-($2.95, 52 pgs.)-Embossed foil-c; Multiple Man dies. 6.00
100-($1.75, 52 pgs.)-Regular edition 4.00
102-105,107: 102-bound-in card sheet 3.00
106-($2.00)-Newsstand edition 3.00
106-($2.95)-Collectors edition 4.00
108-124,126-148: 112-Return from Age of Apocalypse. 115-card insert. 119-123-Sabretooth app. 123-Hound app. 124-w/Onslaught Update. 126-Onslaught x-over; Beast vs. Dark Beast. 128-w/card insert; return of Multiple Man. 130-Assassination of Grayson Creed. 146,148-Moder-a 3.00
125-($2.95)-"Onslaught"; Post app.; return of Havok 4.00
149-Last issue 5.00
#(-1) Flashback (7/97) Matsuda-a 4.00
Annual 1-9: 1-(10/86-'94, 68 pgs.) 3-Evolutionary War x-over. 4-Atlantis Attacks; Byrne/Simonson-a;Byrne-c. 5-Fantastic Four, New Mutants x-over; Keown 2 pg. pin-up. 6-New Warriors app.; 5th app. X-Force cont'd from X-Men Annual #15. 7-1st Quesada-a(p) on X-Factor plus-c(p). 8-Bagged w/trading card. 9-Austin-a(i) 5.00
...Prisoner of Love (1990, $4.95, 52 pgs.)-Starlin scripts; Guice-a 5.00
... Visionaries: Peter David Vol. 1 TPB (2005, $15.99) r/#71-75 16.00
... Visionaries: Peter David Vol. 2 TPB (2007, $15.99) r/#76-78 & Incr. Hulk #390-392 16.00
... Visionaries: Peter David Vol. 3 TPB (2007, $15.99) r/#79-83 & Annual #7 16.00

NOTE: ***Art Adams*** *a-41p, 42p.* ***Buckler*** *a-50p.* ***Liefeld*** *a-40; c-40, 50i, 52p.* ***McFarlane*** *c-50i.* ***Mignola*** *c-70.* ***Brandon Peterson*** *a-78p(part).* ***Whilce Portacio*** *c/a(p)-63-69.* ***Quesada*** *a(p)-87-92, Annual 7. c(p)-78, 79, 82, Annual 7.* ***Simonson*** *c/a-10, 11, 13-15, 17-19, 21, 23-31, 33, 34, 36-39; c-12, 16.* ***Paul Smith*** *a-44-48; c-43.* ***Stroman*** *a(p)-71-75, 77, 78(part), 80, 81; c(p)-71-77, 80, 81, 84.* ***Zeck*** *c-2.*

X-FACTOR (Volume 2)
Marvel Comics: June, 2002 - No. 4, Oct, 2002 ($2.50)

1-4: Jensen-s/Ranson-a. 1-Phillips-c. 2,3-Edwards-c 3.00

X-FACTOR (Volume 3) (Also see All-New X-Factor)
Marvel Comics: Jan, 2006 - No. 262, Nov, 2013 ($2.99)

1-24: 1-Peter David-s/Ryan Sook-a. 8,9-Civil War. 21-24-Endangered Species back-up 3.00
25-49: 25-27-Messiah Complex x-over; Finch-c. 26-2nd printing with new Eaton-c 3.00
50-(12/09, $3.99) Madrox in the future; DeLandro-a/Yardin-c 4.00
200-(2/10, $4.99) Resumes original series numbering; 3 covers; Fantastic Four app. 5.00
201-224,224.1, 225-262 ($2.99) 201,202-Dr. Doom & Fant. Four app. 211,212-Thor app. 230-Wolverine app.; Havok & Polaris return 3.00
... Special: Layla Miller (10/08, $3.99) David-s/DeLandro-a 4.00
...: The Quick and the Dead (7/08, $2.99) Raimondi-a; Quicksilver regains powers 3.00
...: The Longest Night HC (2006, $19.99, dust jacket) r/#1-6; sketch pages by Sook 20.00
...: The Longest Night SC (2007, $14.99) r/#1-6; sketch pages by Sook 15.00
...: Life and Death Matters HC (2007, $19.99, dust jacket) r/#7-12 20.00
...: Life and Death Matters SC (2007, $14.99) r/#7-12 15.00
...: The Many Lives of Madrox SC (2007, $14.99) r/#13-17 15.00
...: Heart of Ice HC (2007, $19.99, dust jacket) r/#18-24 20.00
...: Heart of Ice SC (2008, $17.99, dust jacket) r/#18-24 18.00

X-FACTOR (4th series)
Marvel Comics: Sept, 2020 - Present ($4.99/$3.99)

1-($4.99) Leah Williams-s/David Baldeon-a; Northstar, Polaris, Daken app. 5.00
2,3,5,6-($3.99) 3-Shatterstar app. 4.00
4-($4.99) "X of Swords" tie-in; Carlos Gomez-a 5.00

X-FACTOR FOREVER
Marvel Comics: May, 2010 - No. 5, Sept, 2010 ($3.99, limited series)

1-5-Louise Simonson-s/Dan Panosian-a; back-up origin of Apocalypse 4.00

X-51 (Machine Man)
Marvel Comics: Sept, 1999 - No. 12, Jul, 2000 ($1.99/$2.50)

1-7: 1-Joe Bennett-a. 2-Two covers 3.00
8-12: 8-Begin $2.50-c 3.00
Wizard #0 3.00

X-FILES, THE (TV)
Topps Comics: Jan, 1995 - No. 41, July, 1998 ($2.50)

-2(9/96)-Black-c; r/X-Files Magazine #1&2 5.00
-1(9/96)-Silver-c; r/Hero Illustrated Giveaway 5.00
0-($3.95)-Adapts pilot episode 4.00
0-"Mulder" variant-c 1 2 3 5 6 8
0-"Scully" variant-c 1 2 3 5 6 8
1/2-W/certificate 1 2 3 5 6 8
1-New stories based on the TV show; direct market & newsstand editions; Miran Kim-c on all 3 6 9 15 22 28
2 1 2 3 6 8 10
3,4 6.00
5-10: 6-Begin $2.95-c 5.00
11-41: 21-W/bound-in card. 40,41-Reg. & photo-c 4.00
Annual 1,2 ($3.95) 4.00
Afterflight TPB ($5.95) Art by Thompson, Saviuk, Kim 6.00
Classics #1: Hundred Penny Press Edition (12/13 $1.00) r/#1 3.00
Collection 1 TPB ($19.95)-r/#1-6. 20.00
Collection 2 TPB ($19.95)-r/#7-12, Annual #1. 20.00
...Fight the Future ('98, $5.95) Movie adaptation 6.00
Hero Illustrated Giveaway (3/95) 1 2 3 5 6 8
Special Edition 1-5 ($3.95/$4.95)-r/#1-3, 4-6, 7-9, 10-12, 13, Annual 1 5.00
Star Wars Galaxy Magazine Giveaway (B&W) 1 3 4 6 8 10
Trade paperback ($19.95) 20.00
Volume 1 TPB (Checker Books, 2005, $19.95) r/#13-17, #0, Season One: Squeeze 20.00
Volume 2 TPB (Checker Books, 2005, $19.95) r/#18-24, #1/2, Comics Digest #1 20.00
Volume 3 TPB (Checker Books, 2006, $19.95) r/#23-26, Fire, Ice, Hero Ill. Giveaway 20.00

X-FILES, THE (TV)
DC Comics (WildStorm): No. 0, Sept, 2008 - No. 6, Jun, 2009 ($3.99/$3.50)

0-($3.99) Spotnitz-s/Denham-a; photo-c 4.00
1-6-($3.50) 1-Spotnitz-s/Denham-a; 2 covers. 4-Wolfman-s 3.50
TPB (2009, $19.99) r/#0-6 20.00

X-FILES, THE (TV)
IDW Publishing: Apr, 2016 - Present ($3.99)

1-17: 1-Joe Harris-s/Matthew Dow Smith-a. 12,13-Flashback to Skinner in Viet Nam 4.00
... Annual 2014 (4/14, $7.99) Back-up story with Dave Sim-s/Currie-a; 2 covers 8.00
... Annual 2016 (7/16, $7.99) Greg Scott-a; Valenzuela & photo-c 8.00
...: Art Gallery (5/14, $3.99) Gallery of sketch card art by various incl. Kim & Staggs 4.00
...: Deviations (3/16, $4.99) What If... young Fox Mulder was abducted by aliens 5.00
...: Deviations 2017 (3/17, $4.99) Samantha Mulder and Scully team; Califano-a 5.00
... Funko Universe One Shot (5/17, $4.99) Short stories with Funko Pop-styled characters 5.00
... X-Mas Special (12/14, $7.99) Joe Harris-s/Matt Smith-a; Kesel-s/Southworth-a 8.00
... X-Mas Special 2016 (12/16, $7.99) Joe Harris-s/Wayne Nichols-a 8.00

X-FILES, THE: CASE FILES
IDW Publishing: 2018 ($3.99, limited series)

... - Florida Man 1,2 (4/18 - No. 2, 5/18) Dawson-s/Casagrande-a 4.00
... - Hoot Goes There? 1,2 (7/18 - No. 2, 8/18) Joe & Keith Lansdale-s/Califano-a 4.00

X-FILES COMICS DIGEST, THE
Topps Comics: Dec, 1995 - No. 3 ($3.50, quarterly, digest-size)

1-3: 1,2: New X-Files stories w/Ray Bradbury Comics-r. 1-Reg. & photo-c 4.00

NOTE: ***Adlard*** *a-1, 2.* ***Jack Davis*** *a-2r.* ***Russell*** *a-1r.*

X-FILES, THE: CONSPIRACY
IDW Publishing: Jan, 2014 - No. 2, Mar, 2014 ($3.99, limited series)

1,2-Bookends for 6-part Lone Gunmen series; Crilley-s/Stanisci-a; Kim & Corroney-c 4.00
X-Files/Ghostbusters: Conspiracy (1/14, $3.99) Part 2; Navarro-a 4.00
X-Files/Teenage Mutant Ninja Turtles: Conspiracy (2/14, $3.99) Part 3; Walsh-a 4.00
X-Files/Transformers: Conspiracy (2/14, $3.99) Part 4; Verma-a 4.00
X-Files/The Crow: Conspiracy (3/14, $3.99) Part 5; Malhotra-a 4.00

The X-Files: Season 10 #9 © 20th Fox

X-Force (2019 series) #5 © MAR

X-Man #1 © MAR

	GD	VG	FN	VF	VF/NM	NM-
	2.0	4.0	6.0	8.0	9.0	9.2

X-FILES, THE: GROUND ZERO (TV)
Topps Comics: Nov, 1997 - No. 4, March, 1998 ($2.95, limited series)

1-4-Adaptation of the Kevin J. Anderson novel 4.00

X-FILES, THE: JFK DISCLOSURE (TV)
IDW Publishing: Oct, 2017 - No. 2, Nov, 2017 ($4.99)

1,2-Tipton-s/Menton3-a 5.00

X-FILES, THE: ORIGINS (TV)
IDW Publishing: Aug, 2016 - No. 4, Nov, 2016 ($4.99)

1-4-Flipbooks with teenage Mulder and Scully 5.00

X-FILES, THE: ORIGINS – DOG DAYS OF SUMMER (TV)
IDW Publishing: Jun, 2017 - No. 4, Sept, 2017 ($3.99)

1-4-Flipbooks with teenage Mulder in 1974 and Scully in 1977 4.00

X-FILES, THE: SEASON ONE (TV)
Topps Comics: July, 1997 - July, 1998 ($4.95, adaptations of TV episodes)

1-(Pilot Episode, r/X-Files #0), 2-(Deep Throat), Squeeze, Conduit, Ice, Space, Fire, Beyond the Sea, Shadows 1 2 3 5 6 8

X-FILES, THE: SEASON 10 (TV)
IDW Publishing: Jun, 2013 - No. 25, Jun, 2015 ($3.99)

1-25: 1-5-Co-written by Chris Carter; multiple covers on each. 6,7-Flukeman returns. 17-Frank Black app. 18-Doggett & Reyes app. 4.00
... #1: IDW's Greatest Hits (4/16, $1.00) r/#1 3.00

X-FILES, THE: SEASON 11 (TV)
IDW Publishing: Aug, 2015 - No. 8, Mar, 2016 ($3.99)

1-8: 1-Joe Harris-s/Matthew Smith-a 4.00

X-FILES, THE / 30 DAYS OF NIGHT
DC Comics (WildStorm)/IDW: Sept, 2010 - No. 6, Feb, 2011 ($3.99, limited series)

1-6-Steve Niles & Adam Jones-s/Tom Mandrake-a. 1-Three covers 4.00
TPB (2011, $17.99) r/#1-6; cover gallery 18.00

X-FILES, THE: YEAR ZERO (TV)
IDW Publishing: Jul, 2014 - No. 5, Nov, 2014 ($3.99)

1-5: 1-Karl Kesel-s; Greg Scott & Vic Malhotra-a; flashback to 1946 4.00

X-FORCE (Becomes X-Statix) (Also see The New Mutants #100)
Marvel Comics: Aug, 1991 - No. 129, Aug, 2002 ($1.00-$2.25)

1-($1.50, 52 pgs.)-Polybagged with 1 of 5 diff. Marvel Universe trading cards inside (1 each); 6th app. of X-Force; Liefeld-c/a begins 6.00
1-1st printing with Cable trading card inside 2 4 6 11 16 20
1-1st printing with Deadpool trading card inside 2 4 6 11 16 20
1-2nd printing; metallic ink-c (no bag or card) 6.00
2-Deadpool-c/story (2nd app.) 3 6 9 14 20 26
3,4: 3-New Brotherhood of Evil Mutants app. 4-Spider-Man x-over; cont'd from Spider-Man #16; reads sideways; 2-pg pin-up by Mignola 5.00
5-10: 6-Last $1.00-c. 7,9-Weapon X back-ups. 8-Intro The Wild Pack (Cable, Kane, Domino (not Copycat), Hammer, G.W. Bridge, & Grizzly); Liefeld-c/a (4); Mignola-a. 10-Weapon X full-length story (part 3). 5.00
11-2nd app. the real Domino (not Copycat); Deadpool-c/story (3rd app.) 3 6 9 16 24 32
12-14,20-22,24,26-33 3.00
15-Cable leaves X-Force; Deadpool-c/app. 2 4 6 10 14 18
16-18-Polybagged w/trading card in each; X-Cutioner's Song x-overs 4.00
19-1st Copycat 2 4 6 10 14 18
23-Deadpool-c/app. 6.00
25-($3.50, 52 pgs.)-Wraparound-c w/Cable hologram on-c; Cable returns 5.00
34-37,39-45: 34-bound-in card sheet 3.00
38,40-43: 38-($2.00)-Newsstand edition. 40-43 ($1.95)-Deluxe edition 3.00
38-($2.95)-Collectors edition (prismatic) 5.00
44-49,51-74: 44-Return from Age of Apocalypse. 45-Sabretooth app. 49-Sebastian Shaw app. 52-Blob app., Onslaught cameo. 55-Vs. S.H.I.E.L.D. 56-Deadpool app. 57-Mr. Sinister & X-Man-c/app. 57,58-Onslaught x-over. 59-W/card insert; return of Longshot. 60-Dr. Strange 68-Operation Zero Tolerance 3.00
50 ($3.95)-Gatefold wrap-around foil-c 4.00
50 ($3.95)-Liefeld variant-c 5.00
75,100-($2.99): 75-Cannonball-c/app. 4.00
76-99,101,102: 81-Pollina poster. 95-Magneto-c. 102-Ellis-s/Portacio-a 3.00
103-115: 103-Begin $2.25-c; Portacio-a thru #106. 115-Death of old team 3.00
116-New team debuts; Allred-c/a; Milligan-s; no Comics Code stamp on-c 4.00
117-129: 117-Intro. Mr. Sensitive. 120-Wolverine-c/app. 123-'Nuff Said issue. 124-Darwyn Cooke-a/c. 128-Death of U-Go Girl. 129-Fegredo-a 3.00
#(-1) Flashback (7/97) story of John Proudstar; Pollina-a 3.00
Annual 1-3 ('92-'94, 68 pgs.) 1-1st Greg Capullo-a(p) on X-Force. 2-Polybagged w/trading card; intro X-Treme & Neurtap 4.00
...And Cable '95 (12/95, $3.95)-Impossible Man app. 4.00
...And Cable '96, ...'97 ('96, 7/97) -'96-Wraparound-c 4.00
...And Spider-Man: Sabotage nn (11/92, $6.95)-Reprints X-Force #3,4 & Spider-Man #16 7.00
.../ Champions '98 ($3.50) 4.00
Annual 99 ($3.50) 4.00
...: Famous, Mutant & Mortal HC (2003, $29.99) oversized r/#116-129; foreward by Milligan; gallery of covers and pin-ups; script for #123 30.00
...New Beginnings TPB (10/01, $14.95) r/#116-120 15.00
...Rough Cut ($2.99) Pencil pages and script for #102 3.00
...Youngblood (8/96, $4.95)-Platt-c 5.00
NOTE: ***Capullo** a(p)-15-25, Annual 1; c(p)-14-27. **Rob Liefeld** a-1-7, 9p; c-1-9, 11p; plots-1-12. **Mignola** a-8p.*

X-FORCE
Marvel Comics: Oct, 2004 - No. 6, Mar, 2005 ($2.99, limited series)

1-6-Liefeld-c/a; Nicieza-s. 5,6-Wolverine & The Thing app. 3.00
X-Force & Cable Vol. 1: The Legend Returns (2005, $14.99) r/#1-6 15.00

X-FORCE (Also see Uncanny X-Force)
Marvel Comics: Apr, 2008 - No. 28, Sept, 2010 ($2.99)

1-Crain-a; Wolverine & X-23 app.; two covers (regular and bloody) by Crain on #1-5 4.00
2-21,23-28: 2,3-Bastion app. 4-6-Archangel app. 7-10-Choi-a. 9-11-Ghost Rider app. 26-28-Second Coming x-over; Granov-c. 26-Nightcrawler killed 3.00
22-($3.99) Necrosha x-over; Crain-a 4.00
...: Angels and Demons MGC #1 (5/11, $1.00) r/#1 with "Marvel's Greatest Comics" on-c 3.00
... Annual 1 (2/10, $3.99) Kirkman-s/Pearson-a/c; Deadpool back-up w/Barberi-a 4.00
... /Cable: Messiah War 1 (5/09, $3.99) Choi-a; covers by Andrews and Choi 4.00
... Special: Ain't No Dog (8/08, $3.99) Huston-s/Palo-a; Dell'Edera-a; Hitch-c 4.00

X-FORCE
Marvel Comics: Apr, 2014 - No. 15, Apr, 2015 ($3.99)

1-15: 1-Team of Cable, Fantomex, Psylocke & Marrow; Rock-He Kim-a. 4-6-Molina-a 4.00

X-FORCE
Marvel Comics: Feb, 2019 - No. 10, Sept, 2019 ($3.99)

1-10: 1-Team of Cable, Domino, Shatterstar, Warpath, Cannonball, Deathlok; Brisson-s 4.00

X-FORCE
Marvel Comics: Jan, 2020 - Present ($3.99)

1-($4.99) Team of Jean Grey, Wolverine, Domino, Beast, Colossus; Percy-s/Cassara-a 5.00
2-17-($3.99) 2-Kid Omega app. 6-Segovia-a. 7,8-Bazaldua-a. 13,14-"X of Swords" tie-in 4.00

X-FORCE MEGAZINE
Marvel Comics: Nov, 1996 ($3.95, one-shot)

1-Reprints 4.00

X-FORCE: SEX AND VIOLENCE
Marvel Comics: Sept, 2010 - No. 3, Nov, 2010 ($3.99, limited series)

1-3-Dell'Otto-a/Kyle & Yost-s; Domino & Wolverine vs. The Hand & The Assassins Guild 4.00

X-FORCE: SHATTERSTAR
Marvel Comics: Apr, 2005 - No. 4, July, 2005 ($2.99, limited series)

1-4-Liefeld-c/s; Michaels-a 3.00
TPB (2005, $15.99) r/#1-4 & New Mutants #99,100 16.00

X-INFERNUS
Marvel Comics: Feb, 2009 - No. 4, May, 2009 ($3.99, limited series)

1-4-Illyana Rasputin in Limbo; Cebulski-s/Camuncoli-a/Finch-c 4.00

XIN: JOURNEY OF THE MONKEY KING
Anarchy Studios: May, 2003 - No. 3, July, 2003 ($2.99)

Preview Edition (Apr, 2003, $1.99) Flip book w/ Vampi Vicious Preview Edition 3.00
1-3-Kevin Lau-a. 1-Three covers by Lau, Park and Nauck. 2-Three covers 3.00

XIN: LEGEND OF THE MONKEY KING
Anarchy Studios: Nov, 2002 - No. 3, Jan, 2003 ($2.99)

Preview Edition (Summer 2002, Diamond Dateline supplement) 3.00
1-3-Kevin Lau-a. 1-Two covers by Lau & Madureira. 2-Two covers by Lau & Oeming 3.00
TPB (10/03, $12.95) r/#1-3; cover gallery and sketch pages 13.00

X-MAN (Also see X-Men Omega & X-Men Prime)
Marvel Comics: Mar, 1995 - No. 75, May, 2001 ($1.95/$1.99/$2.25)

1-Age of Apocalypse 5.00
1-2nd print 3.00
2-4,25: 25-($2.99)-Wraparound-c 4.00
5-24, 26-28: 5-Post Age of Apocalypse stories begin. 5-7-Madelyne Pryor app. 10-Professor X app. 12-vs. Excalibur. 13-Marauders, Cable app. 14-Vs. Cable; Onslaught app. 15-17-Vs. Holocaust. 17-w/Onslaught Update. 18-Onslaught x-over; X-Force-c/app; Marauders app. 19-Onslaught x-over. 20-Abomination-c/app.; w/card insert. 23-Bishop app.

X-Men #7 © MAR

X-Men #48 © MAR

X-Men #135 © MAR

GD VG FN VF VF/NM NM-
2.0 4.0 6.0 8.0 9.0 9.2

24-Spider-Man, Morbius-c/app. 27-Re-appearance of Aurora(Alpha Flight) 3.00
29-49,51-62: 29-Operation Zero Tolerance. 37,38-Spider-Man-c/app. 56-Spider-Man app. 3.00
50-($2.99) Crossover with Generation X #50 4.00
63-74: 63-Ellis & Grant-s/Olivetti-a begins. 64-Begin $2.25-c 3.00
75 ($2.99) Final issue; Alcatena-a 4.00
#(-1) Flashback (7/97) 3.00
...'96, ...'97-($2.95)-Wraparound-c; '96-Age of Apocalypse 4.00
...: All Saints' Day ('97, $5.99) Dodson-a 6.00
.../Hulk '98 ($2.99) Wraparound-c; Thanos app. 4.00

XMAS COMICS
Fawcett Publications: 12?/1941 - No. 2, 12?/1942; (50¢, 324 pgs.)
No. 7, 12?/1947 (25¢, 132 pgs.)(#3-6 do not exist for this series, see 1949-1952 series)

1-Contains Whiz #21, Capt. Marvel #3, Bulletman #2, Wow #3, & Master #18; front & back-c by Raboy. Not rebound, remaindered comics; printed at same time as originals 486 972 1458 3550 6275 9000
2-Capt. Marvel, Bulletman, Spy Smasher 219 438 657 1402 2401 3400
7-Funny animals (Hoppy, Billy the Kid & Oscar) 90 180 270 576 988 1400

XMAS COMICS
Fawcett Publications: No. 4, Dec, 1949 - No. 7, Dec, 1952 (50¢, 196 pgs.)

4-Contains Whiz, Master, Tom Mix, Captain Marvel, Nyoka, Capt. Video, Bob Colt, Monte Hale, Hot Rod Comics, & Battle Stories. Not rebound, remaindered comics; printed at the same time as originals. Title logo and Santa's suit on cover are topped by red felt 123 246 369 787 1344 1900
5-7: 5-Green felt tree on-c. 6-Cover has red felt like #4. 7-Bill Boyd app.; stocking on cover is made of green felt (novelty cover) 100 200 300 640 1095 1550

X-MEN, THE (See Adventures of Cyclops and Phoenix, Amazing Adventures, Archangel, Brotherhood, Capt. America #172, Classic X-Men, Exiles, Further Adventures of Cyclops & Phoenix, Gambit, Giant-Size..., Heroes For Hope..., Kitty Pryde & Wolverine, Marvel & DC Present, Marvel Collector's Edition:..., Marvel Fanfare, Marvel Graphic Novel, Marvel Super Heroes, Marvel Team-Up, Marvel Triple Action, The Marvel X-Men Collection, New Mutants, Nightcrawler, Official Marvel Index To..., Rogue, Special Edition..., Ultimate..., Uncanny..., Wolverine, X-Factor, X-Force, X-Terminators)

X-MEN, THE (1st series)(Becomes Uncanny X-Men at #142)(The X-Men #1-93; X-Men #94-141) (The Uncanny X-Men on-c only #114-141)
Marvel Comics Group: Sept, 1963 - No. 66, Mar, 1970; No. 67, Dec, 1970 - No. 141, Jan, 1981; Uncanny X-Men No. 142, Feb, 1981 - No. 544, Dec, 2011

1-Origin/1st app. X-Men (Angel, Beast, Cyclops, Iceman & Marvel Girl); 1st app. Magneto & Professor X 1900 3800 7600 17,600 43,800 70,000
2-1st app. The Vanisher 169 338 507 1394 3147 4900
3-1st app. The Blob (1/64) 107 214 321 856 1928 3000
4-1st Quicksilver & Scarlet Witch & Brotherhood of the Evil Mutants (3/64); 1st app. Toad; 2nd app. Magneto 259 518 777 2137 4819 7500
5-Magneto & Evil Mutants-c/story 86 172 258 688 1544 2400
6-Sub-Mariner app. 62 124 186 502 1126 1750
7-Magneto app. 56 112 168 448 979 1550
8,9,11: 8-1st Unus the Untouchable. 9-Early Avengers app. (1/65); 1st Lucifer. 11-1st app. The Stranger. 46 92 138 359 805 1250
10-1st S.A. app. Ka-Zar & Zabu the sabertooth (3/65) 49 98 147 382 866 1350
12-Origin Prof. X; Origin/1st app. Juggernaut 125 250 375 1000 2250 3500
13-Juggernaut and Human Torch app. 38 76 114 285 641 1000
14,15: 14-1st app. Sentinels. 15-Origin Beast 35 70 105 252 564 875
16-20: 19-1st app. The Mimic (4/66) 19 38 57 133 297 460
21-27,29,30: 27-Re-enter The Mimic (r-in #75); Spider-Man cameo 13 26 39 91 201 310
28-1st app. The Banshee (1/67)(r-in #76) 25 50 75 175 388 600
28-2nd printing (1994) 2 4 6 9 12 15
31-34,36,37,39: 34-Adkins-c/a. 39-New costumes 11 22 33 72 154 235
35-Spider-Man x-over (8/67)(r-in #83); 1st app. Changeling 28 56 84 202 451 700
38,40: 38-Origins of the X-Men series begins, ends #57. 40-(1/68) 1st app. Frankenstein's monster at Marvel 11 22 33 76 163 250
41-48: 42-Death of Prof. X (Changeling disguised as). 44-1st S.A. app. G.A. Red Raven. 10 20 30 66 138 210
49-Steranko-c; 1st Polaris 25 50 75 175 388 600
50,51-Steranko-c/a 10 20 30 70 150 230
52 9 18 27 63 129 195
53-Barry Smith-c/a (his 1st comic book work) 10 20 30 68 144 220
54,55-B. Smith-c. 54-1st app. Alex Summers who later becomes Havok. 55-Summers discovers he has mutant powers 10 20 30 69 147 225
56,57,59-63,65-Neal Adams-a(p). 56-Intro Havok w/o costume. 60-1st Sauron. 65-Return of Professor X. 11 22 33 76 163 250
58-1st app. Havok in costume; N. Adams-a(p) 25 50 75 175 388 600
62,63-2nd printings (1994) 2 4 6 8 10 12
64-1st app. Sunfire 19 38 57 131 291 450
66-Last new story w/original X-Men; battles Hulk 12 24 36 81 176 270
67-70: 67-Reprints begin, end #93. 67-70: (52 pgs.) 9 18 27 61 123 185
71-93: 71-Last 15¢ issue. 72: (52 pgs.). 73-86-r/#25-38 w/new-c. 83-Spider-Man-c/story. 87-93-r/#39-45 with covers 8 16 24 54 102 150
94 (8/75)-New X-Men begin (see Giant-Size X-Men for 1st app.); Colossus, Nightcrawler, Thunderbird, Storm, Wolverine, & Banshee join; Angel, Marvel Girl & Iceman resign 100 200 300 700 1350 2000
95-Death of Thunderbird 16 32 48 110 243 375
96,97 10 20 30 66 138 210
98,99-(Regular 25¢ edition)(4,6/76) 10 20 30 65 135 205
98,99-(30¢-c variants, limited distribution) 26 52 78 182 404 625
100-Old vs. New X-Men; part origin Phoenix; last 25¢ issue (8/76) 11 22 33 76 163 250
100-(30¢-c variant, limited distribution) 30 60 90 216 483 750
101-Phoenix origin concludes 25 50 75 175 388 600
102-104: 102-Origin Storm. 104-1st brief app. Starjammers; Magneto-c/story 8 16 24 52 99 145
105-107-(Regular 30¢ editions). 106-(8/77)Old vs. New X-Men. 107-1st full app. Starjammers; last 30¢ issue 7 14 21 49 92 135
105-107-(35¢-c variants, limited distribution) 33 66 99 238 532 825
108-Byrne-a begins (see Marvel Team-Up #53) 8 16 24 52 99 145
109-1st app. Weapon Alpha (becomes Vindicator) 8 16 24 52 99 145
110,111: 110-Phoenix joins 6 12 18 40 73 105
112-116 6 12 18 40 73 105
117-119: 117-Origin Professor X 5 10 15 35 63 90
120-1st app. Alpha Flight, story line begins (4/79); 1st app. Vindicator (formerly Weapon Alpha); last 35¢ issue 10 20 30 66 138 210
121-1st full Alpha Flight story 8 16 24 56 108 160
122-128: 123-Spider-Man x-over. 124-Colossus becomes Proletarian 5 10 15 31 53 75
129-Intro Kitty Pryde (1/80); last Banshee; Dark Phoenix saga begins; intro. Emma Frost (White Queen) 12 24 36 82 179 275
130-1st app. The Dazzler by Byrne (2/80) 8 16 24 54 102 150
131-133: 131-Dazzler app.; 1st White Queen-c. 133-1st Wolverine solo-c 5 10 15 33 57 80
134-Phoenix becomes Dark Phoenix 7 14 21 44 82 120
135-1st Dark Phoenix-c 5 10 15 31 53 75
136,138: 138-History of the X-Men recounted; Dazzler app.; Cyclops leaves 5 10 15 30 50 70
137-Giant; death of Phoenix 6 12 18 41 76 110
139-Alpha Flight app.; Kitty Pryde joins; new costume for Wolverine 5 10 15 31 53 75
140-Alpha Flight app. 5 10 15 31 53 75
141-"Days of Future Past" part 1; intro Future X-Men & The New Brotherhood of Evil Mutants; 1st app. Rachel (Phoenix II); Death of alt. future Franklin Richards; classic cover 8 16 24 51 96 140

X-MEN: Titled THE UNCANNY X-MEN No. 142, Feb, 1981 - No. 544, Dec, 2011

142-"Days of Future Past" part 2; Rachel app.; deaths of alt. future Wolverine, Storm & Colossus 6 12 18 38 69 100
143-Last Byrne issue 4 8 12 25 40 55
144-150: 144-Man-Thing app. 145-Old X-Men app. 148-1st app. Caliban; Spider-Woman, Dazzler app. 150-Double size 2 4 6 10 14 18
151-157,159-161,163,164: 161-Origin Magneto. 163-Origin Binary. 164-1st app. Binary as Carol Danvers 2 4 6 8 11 14
158-1st app. Rogue in X-Men (6/82, see Avengers Annual #10) 4 8 12 23 37 50
162-Wolverine solo story 3 6 9 14 20 25
165-Paul Smith-c/a begins, ends #175 2 4 6 10 14 18
166-170: 166-Double size; Paul Smith-a. 167-New Mutants app. (3/83); same date as New Mutants #1; 1st meeting w/X-Men; ties into N.M. #3,4; Starjammers app.; contains skin "Tattooz" decals. 168-1st brief app. Madelyne Pryor (last page) in X-Men (see Avengers Annual #10) 2 4 6 8 10 12
171-Rogue joins X-Men; Simonson-c/a 3 6 9 16 23 30
172-174: 172,173-Two part Wolverine solo story. 173-Two cover variations, blue & black. 174-Phoenix cameo 2 4 6 8 10 12
175-(52 pgs.)-Anniversary issue; Phoenix returns 2 4 6 9 13 16
176-185,187-192,194-199: 181-Sunfire app. 182-Rogue solo story. 184-1st app. Forge (8/84). 190,191-Spider-Man & Avengers x-over. 195-Power Pack x-over 1 3 4 6 8 10
186,193: 186-Double-size; Barry Smith/Austin-a. 193-Double size; 100th app. New X-Men; 1st app. Warpath in costume (see New Mutants #16) 2 4 6 8 10 12
200-(12/85, $1.25, 52 pgs.) 3 6 9 14 19 24
201-(1/86)-1st app. Cable? (as baby Nathan; see X-Factor #1); 1st Whilce Portacio-c/a(i) on X-Men (guest artist) 3 6 9 19 30 40

Uncanny X-Men #257 © MAR

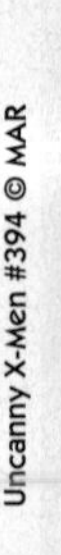

Uncanny X-Men #394 © MAR

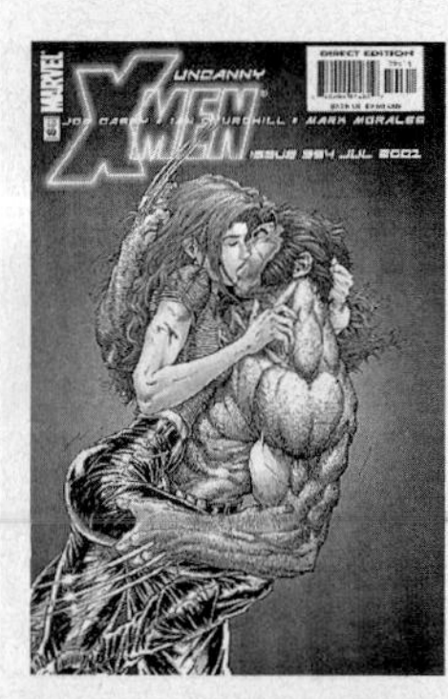

Uncanny X-Men #505 © MAR

	GD 2.0	VG 4.0	FN 6.0	VF 8.0	VF/NM 9.0	NM- 9.2
202-204,206-209: 204-Nightcrawler solo story; 2nd Portacio-a(i) on X-Men. 207-Wolverine/Phoenix story	2	4	6	8	10	12
205-Wolverine solo story by Barry Smith	3	6	9	14	19	24
210,211-Mutant Massacre begins	3	6	9	15	22	28
212,213-Wolverine vs. Sabretooth (Mutant Mass.)	3	6	9	17	25	34
214-220,223,224: 219-Havok joins (7/87); brief app. Sabretooth.	1	3	4	6	8	10
221-1st app. Mr. Sinister	5	10	15	31	53	75
222-Wolverine battles Sabretooth-c/story	3	6	9	16	23	30
225-242: 225-227: Fall Of The Mutants. 226-Double size. 240-Sabretooth app. 242-Double size, X-Factor app., Inferno tie-in	1	3	4	6	8	10
243,245-247: 245-Rob Liefeld-a(p)	1	3	4	6	8	10
244-1st app. Jubilee	4	8	12	23	37	50
248-1st Jim Lee art on X-Men (1989)	3	6	9	16	23	30
248-2nd printing (1992, $1.25)	1	3	4	6	8	10
249-252: 252-Lee-c	1	2	3	5	6	8
253-255: 253-All new X-Men begin. 254-Lee-c	1	2	3	5	6	8
256-Betsy Braddock (Psylocke) 1st app. as purple-haired Asian in ninja costume; Jim Lee-c/a	3	6	9	16	23	30
257-Jim Lee-c/a; Psylocke as Lady Mandarin	2	4	6	8	11	14
258-Wolverine solo story; Lee-c/a	2	4	6	8	11	14
259-Silvestri-c/a; no Lee-a	1	2	3	5	6	8
260-265-No Lee-a. 260,261,264-Lee-c	1	2	3	5	6	8
266-(8/90) 1st full app. Gambit (see Annual #14)-No Lee-a	8	16	24	55	105	155
267-Jim Lee-c/a resumes; 2nd full Gambit app.	3	6	9	14	20	25
268-Capt. America, Black Widow & Wolverine team-up; Lee-c/a	3	6	9	16	23	30
268,270: 268-2nd printing. 270-Gold 2nd printing	2	4	6	8	10	12
269,273,274: 269-Lee-a. 273-New Mutants (Cable) & X-Factor x-over; Golden, Byrne & Lee part pencils	1	2	3	5	6	8
270-X-Tinction Agenda begins	1	3	4	6	8	10
271,272-X-Tinction Agenda	1	3	4	6	8	10
275-(52 pgs.)-Tri-fold-c by Jim Lee (p); Prof. X	1	3	4	6	8	10
275-Gold 2nd printing						5.00
276-280: 277-Last Lee-c/a. 280-X-Factor x-over	1	2	3	5	6	8
281-(10/91)-New team begins (Storm, Archangel, Colossus, Iceman & Marvel Girl); Whilce Portacio-c/a begins; Byrne scripts begin; wraparound-c (white logo)	2	4	6	9	12	15
281-2nd printing with red metallic ink logo w/o UPC box ($1.00-c); does not say 2nd printing inside						5.00
282-1st brief app. Bishop (cover & 1 page)	3	6	9	16	24	32
282-Gold ink 2nd printing ($1.00-c)	1	3	4	6	8	10
283-1st full app. Bishop (12/91)	2	4	6	9	13	16
284-299: 284-Last $1.00-c. 286,287-Lee plots. 287-Bishop joins team. 288-Lee/Portacio plots. 290-Last Portacio-c/a. 294-Peterson-a(p) begins (#292 is 1st Peterson-c). 294-296 ($1.50)-Bagged w/trading card in each; X-Cutioner's Song x-overs; Peterson/Austin-c/a on all						6.00
297-Gold Edition	13	26	39	86	188	290
300-($3.95, 68 pgs.)-Holo-grafx foil-c; Magneto app.	1	3	4	6	8	10
301-303,305-309,311						4.00
303,307-Gold Edition	6	12	18	38	69	100
304-($3.95, 68 pgs.)-Wraparound-c with Magneto hologram on-c; 30th anniversary issue; Jae Lee-a (4 pgs.)	2	4	6	8	10	12
310-($1.95)-Bound-in trading card sheet						4.00
312-$1.50-c begins; bound-in card sheet; 1st Madureira						5.00
313-321: 318-1st app. Generation X						4.00
316,317-($2.95)-Foil enhanced editions						5.00
318-321-($1.95)-Deluxe editions						5.00
322-Onslaught						5.00
323,324,326-346: 323-Return from Age of Apocalypse. 328-Sabretooth-c. 329,330-Dr. Strange app. 331-White Queen-c/app. 334-Juggernaut app.; w/Onslaught Update. 335-Onslaught, Avengers, Apocalypse, & X-Man app. 336-Onslaught. 338-Archangel's wings return to normal. 339-Havok vs. Cyclops; Spider-Man app. 341-Gladiator-c/app. 342-Deathbird cameo; two covers. 343,344-Phalanx						4.00
325-($3.95)-Anniversary issue; gatefold-c						6.00
342-Variant-c	2	4	6	9	13	16
347-349:347-Begin $1.99-c. 349-"Operation Zero Tolerance"						4.00
350-Newsstand version	2	4	6	10	14	18
350-($3.99, 48 pgs.) Prismatic etched foil gatefold wraparound-c; Trial of Gambit; Seagle-s begin	2	4	6	11	16	20
351-359: 353-Bachalo-a begins. 354-Regular-c. 355-Alpha Flight-c/app. 356-Original X-Men-c						4.00
354-Dark Phoenix variant-c	2	4	6	8	10	12
360-($2.99) 35th Anniv. issue; Pacheco-c						5.00
360-($3.99) Etched Holo-foil enhanced-c						6.00
360-($6.95) DF Edition with Jae Lee variant-c	2	4	6	8	10	12
361-374,378,379: 361-Gambit returns; Skroce-a. 362-Hunt for Xavier pt. 1; Bachelo-a. 364-Yu-a. 366-Magneto-c. 369-Juggernaut-c						4.00
375-($2.99) Autopsy of Wolverine						6.00
376,377-Apocalypse: The Twelve	1	3	4	6	8	10
380-($2.99) Polybagged with X-Men Revolution Genesis Edition preview						5.00
381,382,384-389,391-393: 381-Begin $2.25-c; Claremont-s. 387-Maximum Security						4.00
383-($2.99)						5.00
390-Colossus dies to cure the Legacy Virus	2	4	6	8	11	14
394-New look X-Men begins; Casey-s/Churchill-c/a						5.00
395-399-Poptopia. 398-Phillips & Wood-a						4.00
400-($3.50) Art by Ashley Wood, Eddie Campbell, Hamner, Phillips, Pulido and Matt Smith; wraparound-c by Wood						6.00
401-421: 401-'Nuff Said issue; Garney-a. 404,405,407-409,413-415-Phillips-a. 416-Asamiya-a begins. 421-Garney-a						4.00
422-($3.50) Alpha Flight app.; Garney-a						5.00
423-(25¢-c) Holy War pt. 1; Garney-a/Philip Tan-c						4.00
424-449,452-454: 425,426,429,430-Tan-a. 428-Birth of Nightcrawler. 437-Larroca-a begins. 444-New team, new costumes; Claremont-s/Davis-a begins. 448,449-Coipel-a						4.00
450-X-23 app.; Davis-a	2	4	6	9	13	16
451-X-23 app.; Davis-a	2	4	6	11	16	20
455-459-X-23 app.; Davis-a						6.00
460-471: 460-Begin $2.50-c; Raney-a. 462-465-House of M. 464-468-Bachalo-a						4.00
472-499: 472-Begin $2.99-c; Bachalo-a. 475-Wraparound-c. 492-494-Messiah Complex						4.00
500-($3.99) X-Men new HQ in San Francisco; Magneto app.; Land & Dodson-a; wraparound covers by Alex Ross and Greg Land						6.00
500-Classic X-Men Dynamic Forces var.-c by Ross	2	4	6	9	12	15
500-X-Men variant-c by Michael Turner	4	8	12	22	32	40
500-X-Men sketch variant-c by Michael Turner	12	24	36	82	179	275
500-X-Women variant-c by Dodson	3	6	9	14	20	25
500-X-Women sketch variant-c by Dodson	10	20	30	69	147	225
501-511,515-521,523-525: 501-Brubaker & Fraction-s/Land-a. 523-525-Second Coming						4.00
512-514,522-($3.99). 513,514-Utopia x-over. 522-Kitty Pryde returns to Earth; Portacio-a						5.00
526-543-($3.99) 526-The Heroic Age; aftermath of Second Coming. 530-534-Land-a 540-543-Fear Itself tie-in, Juggernaut attacks; Land-a. 542-Colossus becomes the Juggernaut						5.00
534.1 (6/11, $2.99) Pacheco-a/c						4.00
544-(12/11, $3.99) Final issue; Land-a/c; Mr. Sinister app.	2	4	6	8	10	12
#(-1) Flashback (7/97) Ladronn-c/Hitch & Neary-a						4.00
... No. 1 Facsimile Edition (9/19, $3.99) Reprints #1 with original ads						4.00
... No. 4 Facsimile Edition (1/21, $3.99) Reprints #4 with original ads						4.00
... No. 137 Facsimile Edition (9/19, $3.99) Reprints #137 with original ads						4.00
... No. 266 Facsimile Edition (1/20, $3.99) Reprints #266 with original ads and letters						4.00
Special 1(12/70)-Kirby-c/a; origin The Stranger	10	20	30	68	144	220
Special 2(11/71, 52 pgs.)	8	16	24	51	96	140
Annual 3(1979, 52 pgs.)-New story; Miller/Austin-c; Wolverine still in old yellow costume	5	10	15	30	48	65
Annual 4(1980, 52 pgs.)-Dr. Strange guest stars	3	6	9	14	20	25
Annual 5(1981, 52 pgs.)	2	4	6	8	10	12
Annual 6-8('82-'84 52 pgs.)-6-Dracula app.	1	2	3	5	6	8
Annual 9,10('85, '86)-9-New Mutants x-over cont'd from New Mutants Special Ed. #1; Art Adams-a. 10-Art Adams-a	2	4	6	8	10	12
Annual 11-13:('87-'89, 68 pgs.): 12-Evolutionary War; A.Adams-a(p). 13-Atlantis Attacks						5.00
Annual 14(1990, $2.00, 68 pgs.)-1st app. Gambit (minor app., 5 pgs.); Fantastic Four, New Mutants (Cable) & X-Factor x-over; Art Adams-c/a(p)	4	8	12	27	44	60
Annual 15 (1991, $2.00, 68 pgs.)-4 pg. origin; New Mutants x-over; 4 pg. Wolverine solo back-up story; 4th app. X-Force cont'd from New Warriors Annual #1						5.00
Annual 16-18 ('92-'94, 68 pgs.)-16-Jae Lee-c/a(p). 17-Bagged w/card						5.00
Annual '95-(11/95, $3.95)-Wraparound-c						5.00
Annual '96,'97-Wraparound-c						5.00
.../Fantastic Four Annual '98 ($2.99) Casey-s						5.00
Annual '99 ($3.50) Jubilee app.						5.00
Annual 2000 ($3.50) Cable app.; Ribic-a						5.00
Annual 2001 ($3.50, printed wide-ways) Ashley Wood-c/a; Casey-s						5.00
Annual (Vol. 2) #1 (8/06, $3.99) Storm & Black Panther wedding prelude						5.00
Annual (Vol. 2) #2 (3/09, $3.99) Dark Reign; flashback to Sub-Mariner/Emma Frost						5.00
Annual (Vol. 2) #3 (5/11, $3.99) Escape From the Negative Zone; Bradshaw-a						4.00
....At The State Fair of Texas (1983, 36 pgs., one-shot); Supplement to the Dallas Times Herald	2	4	6	9	12	15
...: The Dark Phoenix Saga TPB 1st printing (1984, $12.95)						40.00
...: The Dark Phoenix Saga TPB 2nd-5th printings						25.00
...: The Dark Phoenix Saga TPB 6th-10th printings						20.00
... Days of Future Past TPB (2004, $19.99) r/#138-143 & Annual #4						20.00

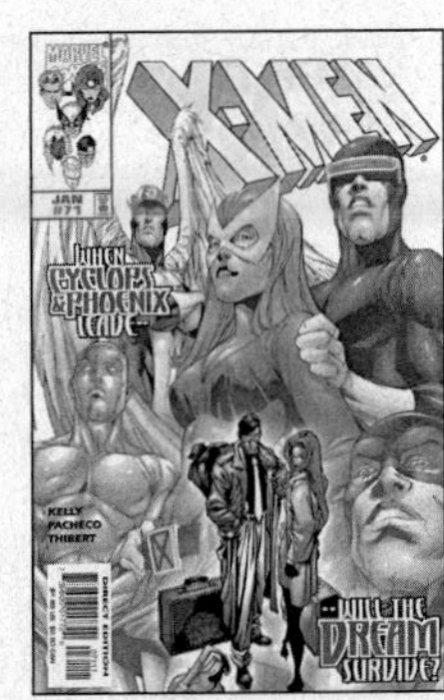

X-Men (2nd series) #71 © MAR

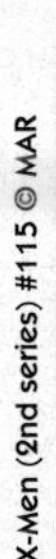
X-Men (2nd series) #115 © MAR

X-Men (2nd series) #209 © MAR

GD VG FN VF VF/NM NM-
2.0 4.0 6.0 8.0 9.0 9.2

... Eve of Destruction TPB (2005, $14.99) r/#391-393 & X-Men #111-113; Churchill-c 15.00
...:Dream's End (2004, $17.99)-r/Death of Colossus story arc from Uncanny X-Men #388-390, Cable #87, Bishop #16 and X-Men #108,110; debut pages from Giant-Size X-Men #1 18.00
... From The Ashes TPB (1990, $14.95) r/#168-176 15.00
... Future History - The Messiah War Sourcebook (2009, $3.99) Cable's files on X-Men 4.00
...: God Loves, Man Kills ($6.95)-r/Marvel Graphic Novel #5 7.00
...: God Loves, Man Kills Extended Cut (6/20 - No. 2 10/20, $4.99) 1-Reprint with 5 new opening pages by Claremont & Anderson; creator interviews. 2-New 5-page epilogue 5.00
...: God Loves, Man Kills - Special Edition (2003, $4.99)-reprint with new Hughes-c 5.00
...: God Loves, Man Kills HC (2007, $19.99) reprint with Claremont & Anderson interviews; original artist Neal Adams' six sketch pages and interview 20.00
...: Hope (5/10, $2.99) Collects Cable and Hope back-ups; Dillon-a 3.00
House of M: Uncanny X-Men TPB (2006, $13.99) r/#462-465 and selections from Secrets Of The House of M one-shot 14.00
...In The Days of Future Past TPB (1989, $3.95, 52 pgs.) 10.00
...: No More Humans HC (2014, $24.99) Carey-s/Larroca-a 25.00
...Old Soldiers TPB (2004, $19.99) r/#213,215 & Ann. #11; New Mutants Ann. #2&3 20.00
...Poptopia TPB (10/01, $15.95) r/#394-399 16.00
...: Rise & Fall of the Shi'Ar Empire HC (2007, $34.99, dustjacket) r/#475-486; bonus art 35.00
...: Rise & Fall of the Shi'Ar Empire SC (2008, $29.99) r/#475-486; bonus art 30.00
...: Season One HC (2012, $24.99) Origin re-told; Hopeless-s/McKelvie-a 25.00
...: Sword of the Braddocks (5/09, $3.99) Psylocke vs. Slaymaster; Claremont-s 4.00
...: The Complete Onslaught Epic Book 1 TPB (2007, $29.99) r/X-Men #53-54, Uncanny X-Men #334-335, Fantastic Four #414-415, Avengers #400-401, Onslaught: X-Men, Cable #34 and Incredible Hulk #444 30.00
...: The Complete Onslaught Epic Book 2 TPB ('08, $29.99) r/Excalibur #100, Wolverine #104, X-Factor #125-126, Amazing Spider-Man #415, Green Goblin #12, Spider-Man #72, Punisher #11, X-Man #18 & X-Force #57 30.00
...: The Extremists TPB (2007, $13.99) r/#487-491 14.00
...: The Heroic Age (9/10, $3.99) Beast, Steve Rogers and Princess Powerful app. 4.00
Uncanny X-Men Omnibus Vol. 1 HC (2006, $99.99, dust jacket) r/Giant-Size X-Men #1, (Uncanny) X-Men #94-131 & Annual #3; cover gallery, promo and sketch art 140.00
Uncanny X-Men 3D #1 (3/19, $7.99) Reprints #268 polybagged with 3-D glasses 8.00
Vignettes TPB (9/01, $17.95) r/Claremont & Bolton Classic X-Men #1-13 18.00
Vignettes Vol. 2 TPB (2005, $17.99) r/Claremont & Bolton Classic X-Men #14-25 18.00
... Vol. 1: Hope TPB (2003, $12.99) r/#410-415; Harris-c 13.00
... Vol. 2: Dominant Species TPB (2003, $11.99) r/#416-420; Asamiya-c 12.00
... Vol. 3: Holy War TPB (2003, $17.99) r/#421-427 18.00
... Vol. 4: The Draco TPB (2004, $15.99) r/#428-434 16.00
... Vol. 5: She Lies with Angels TPB (2004, $11.99) r/#437-441 12.00
... Vol. 6: Bright New Mourning TPB (2004, $14.99) r/#435,436,442,443 & (New) X-Men #155,156; Larroca sketch covers 15.00
...Vs. Apocalypse Vol. 1: The Twelve TPB (2008, $29.99) r/#376-377, Cable #73-76, X-Men #96,97 and Wolverine #145-147 30.00
... - The New Age Vol. 1: The End of History (2004, $12.99) r/#444-449 13.00
... - The New Age Vol. 2: The Cruelest Cut (2005, $11.99) r/#450-454 12.00
... - The New Age Vol. 3: On Ice (2006, $15.99) r/#455-461 16.00
... - The New Age Vol. 4: End of Greys (2006, $14.99) r/#466-471 15.00
... - The New Age Vol. 5: First Foursaken (2006, $11.99) r/#472-474 & Annual #1 12.00

NOTE: **Art Adams** *a-Annual 9, 10p, 12p, 14p; c-218p.* **Neal Adams** *a-56-63p, 65p; c-56-63.* **Adkins** *a-34, 35p; c-31, 34, 35.* **Austin** *a-108i, 109i, 111-117i, 119-143i, 186i, 204i, 228i, 294-297i, Annual 3i, 7i, 9i, 13; c-109-111i, 114-122i, 123, 124-141i, 142, 143, 196i, 204i, 228i, 294-297i, Annual 3i.* **J. Buscema** *c-42, 43, 45.* **Buscema/Tuska** *a-45.* **Byrne** *a(p)-108, 109, 111-143, 273; c(p)-113-116, 127, 129, 131-141.* **Capullo** *c-14.* **Ditko** *r-86, 89-91, 93.* **Everett** *c-73.* **Golden** *a-273, Annual 7p.* **Guice** *a-216p, 217p.* **G. Kane** *c(p)-33, 74-76, 79, 80, 94, 95.* **Kirby** *a(p)-1-17 (#12-17, 67r-layouts); c(p)-1-17, 25, 30 (18, 26-parts).* **Layton** *a-105i; c-112i, 113i.* **Jim Lee** *a(p)-248, 256-258, 267-277; c(p)-252, 254, 256-261, 264, 267, 268 ,270, 275-277, 286.* **Perez** *a-Annual 3p; c(p)-112, 128, Annual 3.* **Peterson** *a(p)-294-300, 304(part); c(p)-294-299.* **Whilce Portacio** *a(p)-281-286, 289, 290; a(i)-267; c-281-285p, 289p, 290; c(i)-267.* **Romita, Jr.** *a-300; c-300.* **Roussos** *a-84i.* **Simonson** *a-171p; c-171, 217.* **B. Smith** *a-53, 186p, 198p, 205, 214; c-53-55, 186p, 198, 205, 212, 214, 216.* **Paul Smith** *a(p)-165-170, 172-175, 278; c-165-170, 172-175, 278.* **Sparling** *a-78p.* **Steranko** *a-50p, 51p; c-49-51.* **Sutton** *a-106i.* **Art Thibert** *a(i)-281-286; c(i)-281, 282, 284, 285.* **Toth** *a-12p, 67p(r).* **Tuska** *a-40-42i, 43-46p, 88i(r); c-39-41, 77p, 78p.* **Williamson** *a-202i, 203i, 211i; c-202i, 203i, 206i.* **Wood** *c-14i.*

UNCANNY X-MEN AND THE NEW TEEN TITANS (See Marvel and DC Present...)

X-MEN (2nd Series)(Titled New X-Men with #114) (Titled X-Men Legacy with #210)
Marvel Comics: Oct, 1991 - No. 275, Dec, 2012 ($1.00-$2.99)

1 a-d (four different covers, $1.50, 52 pgs.)-Jim Lee-c/a begins, ends #11; new team begins (Cyclops, Beast, Wolverine, Gambit, Psylocke & Rogue); new Uncanny X-Men & Magneto app.; 3 6 9 14 20 25
1 e ($3.95)-Double gate-fold-c consisting of all four covers from 1a-d by Jim Lee; contains all pin-ups from #1a-d plus inside-c foldout poster; no ads; printed on coated stock 3 6 9 14 20 25
1-20th Anniversary Edition-(12/11, $3.99) r/#1 with double gatefold-c; Jim Lee pin-ups5.00
2,3,5-7: 5-Byrne scripts. 6-Sabretooth-c/story 6.00
4-1st app. Omega Red; Wolverine back to old yellow costume (same date as Wolverine #50); last $1.00-c 4 8 12 23 37 50
8-10: 8-Gambit vs. Bishop-c/story; last Lee-a; Ghost Rider cameo cont'd in Ghost Rider #26. 9-Wolverine vs. Ghost Rider; cont'd/G.R. #26. 10-Return of Longshot 6.00
11-Regular edition; X-Men vs. Mojo 2 4 6 8 10 12
11-Silver ink 2nd printing; came with X-Men board game 4 8 12 23 37 50
12,13,17-24,26-29,31: 12,13-Art Thibert-c/a. 28,29-Sabretooth app. 5.00
14-16-($1.50)-Polybagged with trading card in each; X-Cutioner's Song x-overs; 14-Andy Kubert-c/a begins 6.00
25-($3.50, 52 pgs.)-Wraparound-c with Gambit hologram on-c; Professor X erases Magneto's mind 3 6 9 14 20 25
25-30th anniversary issue w/B&W-c with Magneto in color & Magneto hologram & no price on-c 4 8 12 28 47 65
25-Gold 4 8 12 27 44 60
30-($1.95)-Wedding issue w/bound-in trading card sheet 1 2 3 5 6 8
32-37: 32-Begin $1.50-c; bound-in card sheet. 33-Gambit & Sabretooth-c/story 5.00
36,37-($2.95)-Collectors editions (foil-c) 6.00
38-44,46-49,51-65: 42,43- Paul Smith-a. 46,49,53-56-Onslaught app. 51-Waid scripts begin, end #56. 54-(Reg. edition)-Onslaught revealed as Professor X. 55,56-Onslaught x-over; Avengers, FF & Sentinels app. 56-Dr. Doom app. 57-Xavier taken into custody; Byrne-c/swipe (X-Men,1st Series #138). 59-Hercules-c/app. 61-Juggernaut-c/app. 62-Re-intro. Shang Chi; two covers. 63-Kingpin cameo. 64- Kingpin app. 5.00
45-($3.95)-Annual issue; gatefold-c 6.00
50-($2.95)-Vs. Onslaught, wraparound-c. 6.00
50-($3.95)-Vs. Onslaught, wraparound foil-c. 6.00
50-($2.95)-Variant gold-c. 4 8 12 23 37 50
50-($2.95)-Variant silver-c. 2 4 6 10 14 18
54-(Limited edition)-Embossed variant-c; Onslaught revealed as Professor X 3 6 9 21 33 45
66-69,71-74,76-79: 66-Operation Zero Tolerance. 76-Origin of Maggott 4.00
70-($2.99, 48 pgs.)-Joe Kelly-s begin, new members join 5.00
75-($2.99, 48 pgs.) vs. N'Garai; wraparound-c 5.00
80-($3.99) 35th Anniv. issue; holo-foil-c 6.00
80-($2.99) Regular-c 5.00
80-($6.95) Dynamic Forces Ed.; Quesada-c 7.00
81-93,95,98,99: 82-Hunt for Xavier pt. 2. 85-Davis-a. 86-Origin of Joseph. 87-Magneto War ends. 88-Juggernaut app. 4.00
94-($2.99) Contains preview of X-Men: Hidden Years 5.00
96,97-Apocalypse: The Twelve 1 2 3 5 6 8
100-($2.99) Art Adams-c; begin Claremont-s/Yu-a 4.00
100-DF alternate-c 2 4 6 8 10 12
101-105,107,108,110-114: 101-Begin $2.25-c. 107-Maximum Security x-over; Bishop-c/app. 108-Moira MacTaggart dies; Senator Kelly shot. 111-Magneto-c. 112,113-Eve of Destruction 4.00
106-($2.99) X-Men battle Domina 5.00
109-($3.50, 100 pgs.) new and reprinted Christmas-themed stories 5.00
114-(7/01) Title change to "New X-Men," Morrison-s/Quitely-c/a begins 4.00
114-(8/10, $1.00) "Marvel's Greatest Comics" reprint 3.00
115-Two covers (Quitely & BWS) 5.00
116-125,127,129-149: 116-Emma Frost joins. 117,118-Van Sciver-a. 121,122,135-Quitely-a. 127-Leon & Sienkiewicz-a. 132,139-141-Jimenez-a. 136-138-Quitely-a. 142-Sabretooth app.; Bachalo-c/a thru #145. 146-Magneto returns; Jimenez-a 3.00
126-($3.25) Quitely-a; defeat of Cassanova 4.00
128-1st app. Fantomex; Kordey-a 3 6 9 17 26 45
150-($3.50) Jean Grey dies again; last Jimenez-a 4.00
151-156: 151-154-Silvestri-c/a 3.00
157-169: 157-X-Men Reload begins 3.00
170-184: 171- Begin $2.50-c. 175,176-Crossover with Black Panther #8,9. 181-184-Apocalypse returns 3.00
185-199,201-229,231-249,251-261: 185-Begin $2.99-c. 188-190,192-194,197-199-Bachalo-a. 195,196,201-203-Ramos-a. 201-204-Endangered Species back-up. 205-207-Messiah Complex x-over. 208-Romita Jr.-a. 210-Starts X-Men: Legacy. 228,229-Acuña-a. 235-237-Second Coming x-over. 238-The Heroic Age. 245-Age of X begins 3.00
200-($3.99) Two wraparound covers by Bachalo & Finch; Bachalo & Ramos-a 4.00
230-($3.99) Acuña-a; Rogue vs. Emplate 4.00
250-($4.99) Suayan-c/Pham-a; back-up r/New Mutants #27 5.00
261.1-(3/12, $2.99) The N'Garai app.; Brooks-c 3.00
262-275-Brooks-c. 266-270-Avengers vs. X-Men tie-in 3.00
#(-1) Flashback (7/97); origin of Magneto 4.00
Annual 1-3 ('92-'94, $2.25-$2.95, 68 pgs.) 1-Lee-c & layouts; #2-Bagged w/card 5.00
Special '95 ($3.95) 5.00
... '96,...'97-Wraparound-c 5.00
.../ Dr. Doom '98 Annual ($2.99) Lopresti-a 5.00
... Annual '99 ($3.50) Adam Kubert-c 5.00
Annual 2000 ($3.50) Art Adams-c/Claremont-s/Eaton-a 4.00
...2001 Annual ($3.50) Morrison-s/Yu-a; issue printed sideways 4.00

GD VG FN VF VF/NM NM-
2.0 4.0 6.0 8.0 9.0 9.2

X-Men (2010 series) #37 © MAR

X-Men (2019 series) #10 © MAR

X-Men / Alpha Flight #2 © MAR

GD VG FN VF VF/NM NM-
2.0 4.0 6.0 8.0 9.0 9.2

...2007 Annual #1 (3/07, $3.99) Casey-s/Brooks-a; Cable and Mystique app. 4.00
...Legacy Annual 1 (11/09, $3.99) Acuña-a; Emplate returns 4.00
Animation Special Graphic Novel (12/90, $10.95) adapts animated series 12.00
Ashcan #1 (1994, 75¢) Introduces new team members 4.00
... Archives Sketchbook (12/00, $2.99) Early B&W character design sketches by various incl. Lee, Davis, Yu, Pacheco, BWS, Art Adams, Liefeld 4.00
...: Bizarre Love Triangle TPB (2005, $9.99)-r/X-Men #171-174 10.00
.../ Black Panther TPB (2006, $11.99)-r/X-Men #175,176 & Black Panther (2005) #8,9 12.00
...: Blinded By the Light (2007, $14.99)-r/X-Men #200-204 15.00
...: Blind Science (7/10, $3.99) Second Coming x-over; Parel-c 4.00
...: Blood of Apocalypse (2006, $17.99)-r/X-Men #182-187 18.00
...: Day of the Atom (2005, $19.99)-r/X-Men #157-165 20.00
Decimation: X-Men - The Day After TPB (2006, $15.99) r/#177-181 & Decimation: House of M - The Day After 16.00
...: Declassified (10/00, $3.50) Profile pin-ups by various; Jae Lee-c 4.00
...: Earth's Mutant Heroes (7/11, $4.99) Handbook-style profiles of mutants 5.00
...: Endangered Species (8/07, $3.99) prologue to 17-part back-up series in X-Men titles 4.00
...: Endangered Species HC (2008, $24.99, d.j.) over-sized r/prologue and 17-part series 25.00
...: Evolutions 1 (12/11, $3.99) Collection of variant covers from May 2011 Marvel titles 4.00
...: Fatal Attractions ('94, $17.95)-r/x-Factor #92, X-Force #25, Uncanny X-Men #304, X-Men #25, Wolverine #75, & Excalibur #71 18.00
...: Golgotha (2005, $12.99)-r/X-Men #166-170 13.00
... Millennial Visions (8/00, $3.99) Various artists interpret future X-Men 4.00
... Millennial Visions 2 (1/02, $3.50) Various artists interpret future X-Men 4.00
...: Mutant Genesis (2006, $19.99)-r/X-Men #1-7; sketch pages and extra art 20.00
New X-Men: E is for Extinction TPB (11/01, $12.95) r/#114-117 13.00
New X-Men: Imperial TPB (7/02, $19.99) r/#118-126; Quitely-c 20.00
New X-Men: New Worlds TPB (2002, $14.99) r/#127-133; Quitely-c 15.00
New X-Men: Riot at Xavier's TPB (2003, $11.99) r/#134-138; Quitely-c 12.00
New X-Men: Vol. 5: Assault on Weapon Plus TPB (2003, $14.99) r/#139-145 15.00
New X-Men: Vol. 6: Planet X TPB (2004, $12.99) r/#146-150 13.00
New X-Men: Vol. 7: Here Comes Tomorrow TPB (2004, $10.99) r/#151-154 11.00
New X-Men: Volume 1 HC (2002, $29.99) oversized r/#114-126 & 2001 Annual 30.00
New X-Men: Volume 2 HC (2003, $29.99) oversized r/#127-141; sketch & script pages 30.00
New X-Men: Volume 3 HC (2004, $29.99) oversized r/#142-154; sketch & script pages 30.00
New X-Men Omnibus HC (2006, $99.99) oversized r/#114-154 & Annual 2001; Morrison's original pitch; sketch & script pages; variant covers & promo art; Carey intro. 140.00
...: Odd Men Out (2008, $3.99) Two unpublished stories with Dave Cockrum-a 4.00
... Original Sin 1 (12/08, $3.99) Wolverine and Daken; Deodato & Eaton-a 4.00
... Origin: Colossus (7/08, $3.99) Yost-s/Hairsine-a; Piotr Rasputin before joining X-Men 4.00
... Phoenix Force Handbook (9/10, $4.99) bios of those related to the Phoenix; Raney-c 5.00
...: Pixies and Demons Director's Cut (2008, $3.99) r/FCBD 2008 story with script 4.00
... Pizza Hut Mini-comics-(See Marvel Collector's Edition: X-Men in Promotional Comics section)
... Premium Edition #1 (1993)-Cover says "Toys 'R' Us Limited Edition X-Men" 4.00
...: Rarities (1995, $5.95)-Reprints 6.00
...: Return of Magik Must Have (2008, $3.99) r/X-Men Unlimited #14, New X-Men #37 and X-Men: Divided We Stand #2; Coipel-c 4.00
...: Road Trippin' ('99, $24.95, TPB) r/X-Men road trips 25.00
...: Supernovas ('07, $34.99, oversized HC w/d.j.) r/X-Men 188-199 & Annual #1 35.00
...: Supernovas ('08, $29.99, SC) r/X-Men 188-199 & Annual #1 30.00
...: The Coming of Bishop ('95, $12.95)-r/Uncanny X-Men #282-285, 287,288 13.00
...: The Magneto War (3/99, $2.99) Davis-a 4.00
...: The Rise of Apocalypse ('98, $16.99)-r/Rise Of Apocalypse #1-4, X-Factor #5,6 17.00
... Visionaries: Chris Claremont ('98, $24.95)-r/Claremont-s; art by Byrne, BWS, Jim Lee 25.00
... Visionaries: Jim Lee ('02, $29.99)-r/Jim Lee-a from various issues between Uncanny X-Men #248 & 286; r/Classic X-Men #39 and X-Men Annual #1 30.00
... Visionaries: Joe Madureira (7/00, $17.95)-r/Uncanny X-Men #325,326,329,330,341-343; new Madureira-c 18.00
... Vs. Hulk (3/09, $3.99) Claremont-s/Raapack-a; r/X-Men #66 4.00
...: Zero Tolerance ('00, $24.95, TPB) r/crossover series 25.00

NOTE: ***Jim Lee** a-1-11p; c-1-6p, 7, 8, 9p, 10, 11p.* ***Art Thibert** a-6-9i, 12, 13; c-6i, 12, 13.*

X-MEN (3rd series)
Marvel Comics: Sept, 2010 - No. 41, Apr, 2013 ($3.99)

1-41: 1-6-"Curse of the Mutants" x-over; Medina-a. 7-10-Spider-Man app.; Bachalo-a. 12-Continued from X-Men Giant-Size #1. 16-19-FF & Skull the Slayer app. 20-23-War Machine app. 16-Deadpool app. 28-FF & Spider-Man app. 38,39-Domino & Daredevil team-up 4.00
15.1 ($2.99) Pearson-c/Conrad-a; Ghost Rider app. 3.00
...: Curse of the Mutants - Blade 1 (10/10, $3.99) Tim Green-a 4.00
...: Curse of the Mutants - Smoke and Blood 1 (11/10, $3.99) Crain-c 4.00
...: Curse of the Mutants Spotlight 1 (1/11, $3.99) creator profiles and interviews 4.00
...: Curse of the Mutants - Storm and Gambit 1 (11/10, $3.99) Bachalo-a; 2 covers 4.00
...: Curse of the Mutants - X-Men vs. Vampires 1,2 (11/10 - No. 2, 12/10, $3.99) Bradshaw-c 4.00
... Giant-Size 1 (7/11, $4.99) Medina & Talajic-a; cover swipe of Giant-Size X-Men #1 5.00
...: Regenesis 1 (12/11, $3.99) Splits X-Men into 2 teams; Tan-a/Bachalo-c 4.00
... Spotlight 1 (7/11, $3.99) Character profiles and creator interviews 4.00
...: With Great Power 1 (2011, $4.99) r/#7-9 5.00

X-MEN (4th series)
Marvel Comics: Jul, 2013 - No. 26, Jun, 2015 ($3.99)

1-26: 1-All-female team; Brian Wood-s/Olivier Coipel-a. 5,6-Battle of the Atom 4.00
100th Anniversary Special: X-Men (9/14, $3.99) Takes place in 2061; Furth-s/Masters-a 4.00

X-MEN (5th series)
Marvel Comics: Dec, 2019 - Present ($4.99/$3.99)

1-($4.99) Hickman-s/Yu-a; follows House of X and Powers of X series; intro Serafina 5.00
2-17-($3.99) 5-Serafina app.; Silva-a. 6-Mystique app.; Buffagni-a. 9-The Brood app. 10,11-Empyre tie-in. 13-15-"X of Swords" tie-in. 17-Booth-a 4.00
...: Marvels Snapshots 1 (11/20, $4.99) Flashback to Cyclops' childhood; Alex Ross-c 5.00

X-MEN (Free Comic Book Day giveaways)
Marvel Comics: 2006; May, 2008

FCBD 2008 Edition #1-(5/08) Features Pixie; Carey-s/Land-a/c 3.00
.../Runaways: FCBD 2006 Edition; new x-over story; Mighty Avengers preview; Chen-c 3.00

X-MEN ADVENTURES (TV)
Marvel Comics: Nov, 1992 - No. 15, Jan, 1994 ($1.25)(Based on animated series)

1,15: 1-Wolverine, Cyclops, Jubilee, Rogue, Gambit. 15-($1.75, 52 pgs.) 5.00
2-14: 3-Magneto-c/story. 6-Sabretooth-c/story. 7-Cable-c/story. 10-Archangel guest star. 11-Cable-c/story. 4.00

X-MEN ADVENTURES II (TV)
Marvel Comics: Feb, 1994 - No. 13, Feb, 1995 ($1.25/$1.50)(Based on 2nd TV season)

1-13: 4-Bound-in trading card sheet. 5-Alpha Flight app. 4.00
...Captive Hearts/Slave Island (TPB, $4.95)-r/X-Men Adventures #5-8 5.00
...The Irresistible Force, The Muir Island Saga ($5.95, 10/94, TPB) r/X-Men Advs. #9-12 6.00

X-MEN ADVENTURES III (TV)(See Adventures of the X-Men)
Marvel Comics: Mar, 1995 - No. 13, Mar, 1996 ($1.50) (Based on 3rd TV season)

1-13 4.00

X-MEN: AGE OF APOCALYPSE
Marvel Comics: May, 2005 - No. 6, June, 2005 ($2.99, weekly limited series)

1-6-Bachalo-c/a; Yoshida-s; follows events in the "Age of Apocalypse" storyline 4.00
... One Shot (5/05, $3.99) prequel to series; Hitch wraparound-c; pin-ups by various 4.00
X-Men: The New Age of Apocalypse TPB (2005, $20.99) r/#1-6 & one-shot 21.00

X-MEN ALPHA
Marvel Comics: 1994 ($3.95, one-shot)

	GD 2.0	VG 4.0	FN 6.0	VF 8.0	VF/NM 9.0	NM- 9.2
nn-Age of Apocalypse; wraparound chromium-c	2	4	6	9	12	15
nn ($49.95)-Gold logo						55.00

X-MEN/ALPHA FLIGHT
Marvel Comics Group: Dec, 1985 - No. 2, Dec, 1985 ($1.50, limited series)

1,2: 1-Intro The Berserkers; Paul Smith-a 5.00

X-MEN/ALPHA FLIGHT
Marvel Comics Group: May, 1998 - No. 2, June, 1998 ($2.99, limited series)

1,2-Flashback to early meeting; Raab-s/Cassaday-s/a 4.00

X-MEN AND POWER PACK
Marvel Comics: Dec, 2005 - No. 4, Mar, 2006 ($2.99, limited series)

1-4-Sumerak-s/Gurihiru-a. 1-Wolverine & Sabretooth app. 3.00
...: The Power of X (2006, $6.99, digest size) r/#1-4 7.00

X-MEN AND THE MICRONAUTS, THE
Marvel Comics Group: Jan, 1984 - No. 4, Apr, 1984 (Limited series)

1-4: Guice-c/a(p) in all 5.00

X-MEN: APOCALYPSE/DRACULA
Marvel Comics: Apr, 2006 - No. 4, July, 2006 ($2.99, limited series)

1-4-Tieri-s/Henry-a/Jae Lee-c 3.00
TPB (2006, $10.99) r/series; cover gallery 11.00

X-MEN ARCHIVES
Marvel Comics: Jan, 1995 - No. 4, Apr, 1995 ($2.25, limited series)

1-4: Reprints Legion stories from New Mutants. 4-Magneto app. 4.00

X-MEN ARCHIVES FEATURING CAPTAIN BRITAIN
Marvel Comics: July, 1995 - No. 7, 1996 ($2.95, limited series)

1-7: Reprints early Capt. Britain stories 4.00

X-MEN: BATTLE OF THE ATOM
Marvel Comics: Nov, 2013 - No. 2, Dec, 2013 ($3.99, bookends for X-Men title crossover)

X-Men: Blue #1 © MAR

X-Men: Evolution #1 © MAR

X-Men Forever 2 #1 © MAR

GD 2.0 VG 4.0 FN 6.0 VF 8.0 VF/NM 9.0 NM- 9.2

1,2: 1-Bendis-s/Cho-a/Art Adams-c; bonus pin-ups of the various X-teams 4.00

X-MEN: BLACK
Marvel Comics: Dec, 2018 ($4.99, series of one-shots, back-up Apocalypse story in each)
...: Emma Frost 1 - Williams-s/Bachalo-a; Sebastian Shaw app.; Apocalypse part 5 5.00
...: Juggernaut 1 - Thompson-s/Crystal-a; Apocalypse part 4 5.00
...: Magneto 1 - Claremont-s/Talajic-a; Apocalypse part 1 5.00
...: Mojo 1 - Aukerman-s/Bradshaw-a; Apocalypse part 2 5.00
...: Mystique 1 - McGuire-s/Failla-a; Apocalypse part 3 5.00

X-MEN BLACK SUN (See Black Sun:...)

X-MEN: BLUE (Continued from All-New X-Men)
Marvel Comics: Jun, 2017 - No. 36, Nov, 2018 ($4.99/$3.99)
1-($4.99) Bunn-s/Molina-a; Juggernaut & Black Tom Cassidy app. 5.00
2-24,26-36-($3.99): 4-Jimmy Hudson joins. 7-9-Secret Empire tie-ins. 13-15-"Mojo Worldwide." 18-Generation X app. 21,22-Venom app. 4.00
25-($4.99) Bunn-s/Molina-a; Sebastian Shaw & Bastion app. 5.00
Annual 1 (3/18, $4.99) Poison-X part 1; Venom app.; Bunn-s/Salazar-a 5.00

X-MEN BOOKS OF ASKANI
Marvel Comics: 1995 ($2.95, one-shot)
1-Painted pin-ups w/text 4.00

X-MEN: CHILDREN OF THE ATOM
Marvel Comics: Nov, 1999 - No. 6 ($2.99, limited series)
1-6-Casey-s; X-Men before issue #1. 1-3-Rude-c/a. 4-Paul Smith-a/Rude-c. 5,6-Essad Ribic-c/a 4.00
TPB (11/01, $16.95) r/series; sketch pages; Casey intro. 17.00

X-MEN CHRONICLES
Marvel Comics: Mar, 1995 - No. 2, June, 1995 ($3.95, limited series)
1,2: Age of Apocalypse x-over. 1-wraparound-c 5.00

X-MEN: CLANDESTINE
Marvel Comics: Oct, 1996 - No. 2, Nov, 1996 ($2.95, limited series, 48 pgs.)
1,2: Alan Davis-c(p)/a(p)/scripts & Mark Farmer-c(i)/a(i) in all; wraparound-c 4.00

X-MEN CLASSIC (Formerly Classic X-Men)
Marvel Comics: No. 46, Apr, 1990 - No. 110, Aug, 1995 ($1.25/$1.50)
46-110: Reprints from X-Men. 54-(52 pgs.). 57,60-63,65-Russell-c(i); 62-r/X-Men #158 (Rogue). 66-r/#162 (Wolverine). 69-Begins-r of Paul Smith issues (#165 on). 70,79,90,97 (52 pgs.). 70-r/X-Men #166. 90-r/#186. 100-($1.50). 104-r/X-Men #200 4.00

X-MEN CLASSICS
Marvel Comics Group: Dec, 1983 - No. 3, Feb, 1984 ($2.00, Baxter paper)
1-3: X-Men-r by Neal Adams 6.00
NOTE: *Zeck c-1-3.*

X-MEN: COLOSSUS BLOODLIINE
Marvel Comics: Nov, 2005 - No. 5, Mar, 2006 ($2.99, limited series)
1-5-Colossus returns to Russia; David Hine-s/Jorge Lucas-a; Bachalo-c 3.00
TPB (2006, $13.99) r/#1-5 14.00

X-MEN: DEADLY GENESIS (See Uncanny X-Men #475)
Marvel Comics: Jan, 2006 - No. 6, July, 2006 ($3.99/$3.50, limited series)
1-($3.99) Silvestri-c swipe of Giant-Size X-Men #1; Hairsine-a/Brubaker-s 4.00
2-6-($3.50) 2-Silvestri-c; Banshee killed. 4-Intro Kid Vulcan 3.50
HC (2006, $24.99, dust jacket) r/#1-6 25.00
SC (2006, $19.99) r/#1-6 20.00

X-MEN: DIE BY THE SWORD
Marvel Comics: Dec, 2007 - No. 5, Feb, 2008 ($2.99, limited series)
1-5-Excalibur and The Exiles app.; Claremont-s/Santacruz-a 3.00
TPB (2008, $13.99) r/#1-5; handbook pages of Merlyn, Roma and Saturne 14.00

X-MEN: DIVIDED WE STAND
Marvel Comics: June, 2008 - No. 2, July, 2008 ($3.99, limited series)
1,2-Short stories by various; Peterson-c 4.00

X-MEN: EARTHFALL
Marvel Comics: Sept, 1996 ($2.95, one-shot)
1-r/Uncanny X-Men #232-234; wraparound-c 4.00

X-MEN: EMPEROR VULCAN
Marvel Comics: Nov, 2007 - No. 5, Mar, 2008 ($2.99, limited series)
1-5: 1-Starjammers app.; Yost-s/Diaz-a/Tan-c 3.00
TPB (2008, $13.99) r/#1-5 14.00

X-MEN: EVOLUTION (Based on the animated series)
Marvel Comics: Feb, 2002 - No. 9, Sept, 2002 ($2.25)
1-9: 1-8-Grayson-s/Udon-a. 9-Farber-s/J.J.Kirby-a 3.00
TPB (7/02, $8.99) r/#1-4 9.00
Vol. 2 TPB (2003, $11.99) r/#5-9; Asamiya-c 12.00

X-MEN FAIRY TALES
Marvel Comics: July, 2006 - No. 4, Oct, 2006 ($2.99, limited series)
1-4-Re-imagining of classic stories; Cebulski-s. 2-Baker-a. 3-Sienkiewicz-a. 4-Kobayashi-a 3.00
TPB (2006, $10.99) r/#1-4 11.00

X-MEN/ FANTASTIC FOUR
Marvel Comics: Feb, 2005 - No. 5, June, 2005 ($3.50, limited series)
1-5-Pat Lee-a/c; Yoshida-s; the Brood app. 3.50
HC (2005, $19.99, 7 1/2" x 11", dustjacket) oversized r/#1-5; cover gallery 20.00

X-MEN/ FANTASTIC FOUR
Marvel Comics: Apr, 2020 - No. 4, Sept, 2020 ($4.99, limited series)
1-4-Zdarsky-s/Dodson-a; Franklin recruited by X-Men; Doctor Doom app. 5.00

X-MEN FIRST CLASS
Marvel Comics: Nov, 2006 - No. 8, Jun, 2007 ($2.99, limited series)
1-8-Xavier's first class of X-Men; Cruz-a/Parker-s. 5-Thor app. 7-Scarlet Witch app. 3.00
... Special 1 (7/07, $3.99) Nowlan-c; Nowlan, Paul Smith, Coover, Dragotta & Allred-a 4.00
... - Tomorrow's Brightest HC (2007, $24.99, d.j) r/#1-8; cover & character design art 25.00
... - Tomorrow's Brightest SC (2007, $19.99) r/#1-8; cover & character design art 20.00

X-MEN FIRST CLASS (2nd series)
Marvel Comics: Aug, 2007 - No. 16, Nov, 2008 ($2.99)
1-16: 1-Cruz-a/Parker-s; Fantastic Four app. 8-Man-Thing app. 10-Romita Jr.-c 3.00
... Giant-Size Special 1 (12/08, $3.99) 5 new short stories; Haspiel-a; r/X-Men #40 4.00
... - Mutant Mayhem TPB (2008, $13.99) r/#1-5 & X-Men First Class Special 14.00

X-MEN FIRST CLASS FINALS
Marvel Comics: Apr, 2009 - No. 4, July, 2009 ($3.99, limited series)
1-4-Cruz-a/Parker-s. 1-3-Coover-a 4.00

X-MEN FIRSTS
Marvel Comics: Feb, 1996 ($4.95, one-shot)
1-r/Avengers Annual #10, Uncanny X-Men #266, #221; Incredible Hulk #181 5.00

X-MEN FOREVER
Marvel Comics: Jan, 2001 - No. 6, June, 2001 ($3.50, limited series)
1-6-Jean Grey, Iceman, Mystique, Toad, Juggernaut app.; Maguire-a 4.00

X-MEN FOREVER
Marvel Comics: Aug, 2009 - No. 24, July, 2010 ($3.99)
1-24: 1-Claremont-s/Grummett-a/c. 7-Nick Fury app. 4.00
... Alpha 1 (2009, $4.99) r/X-Men (1991) #1-3; 8 page preview of X-Men Forever #1 5.00
... Annual 1 (6/10, $4.99) Wolverine & Jean Grey romance; Sana Takeda-a/c 5.00
... Giant-Size 1 (7/10, $3.99) Grell-a/c; Lilandra & Gladiator app.; r/(Uncanny)X-Men #108 4.00

X-MEN FOREVER 2
Marvel Comics: Aug, 2010 - No. 16, Mar, 2011 ($3.99)
1-16: 1-Claremont-s/Grummett-a/c. 2,3-Spider-Man app. 9,10-Grell-a 4.00

X-MEN: GOLD
Marvel Comics: Jan, 2014 ($5.99, one-shot)
1-50th Anniversary anthology; short stories by various incl. Stan Lee, Simonson, Claremont, Thomas, Olliffe, Wein, Molina, McLeod, Larroca; Coipel-c 6.00

X-MEN: GOLD
Marvel Comics: Jun, 2017 - No. 36, Nov, 2018 ($4.99/$3.99)
1-($4.99) Syaf-a; Storm, Nightcrawler, Old Man Logan, Colossus, Kitty Pryde team 5.00
2-24-($3.99): 4-6-Silva-a. 7,8-Secret Empire tie-ins; Lashley-a. 13-15-"Mojo Worldwide" 4.00
25-($4.99) Guggenheim-s/Siqueira-a; Captain Britain app. 5.00
26-29,31-36: 26-29-Til Death Do Us Part; prelude to wedding of Kitty Pryde & Colossus 4.00
30-($4.99) Wedding of Rogue and Gambit; leads into Mr. & Mrs. X series; Marquez-a 5.00
Annual 1 (3/18, $4.99) Excalibur reunion; Capt. Britain app.; Martinez-a 5.00
Annual 2 (10/18, $4.99) McGuire-s/Failla-a; 14-year-old Kitty Pryde at summer camp 5.00

X-MEN: GRAND DESIGN
Marvel Comics: Feb, 2018 - No. 2, Mar, 2018 ($5.99, limited series)
1,2-Origins and early days of the X-Men re-told; Ed Piskor-s/a/c 6.00

X-MEN: GRAND DESIGN - SECOND GENESIS
Marvel Comics: Sept, 2018 - No. 2, Oct, 2018 ($5.99, limited series)
1,2-Days of the X-Men from #94 (1975) to #186 (1984) re-told; Ed Piskor-s/a/c 6.00

X-MEN: GRAND DESIGN - X-TINCTION
Marvel Comics: Jul, 2019 - No. 2, Aug, 2019 ($5.99, limited series)
1,2-Days of the X-Men from mid-'80s to early '90s re-told; Ed Piskor-s/a/c 6.00

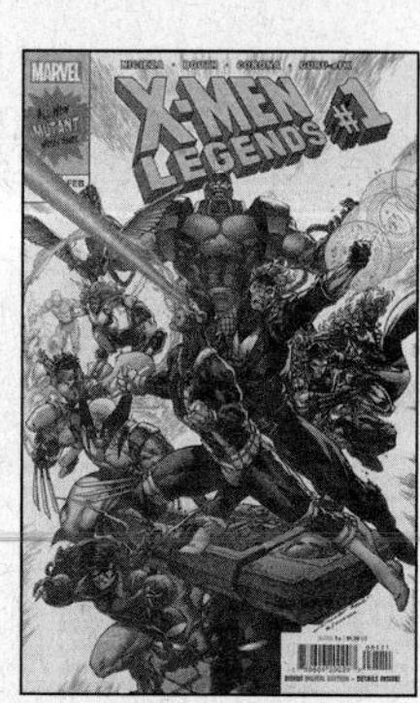

X-Men Legends #1 © MAR

X-Men: Origins: Jean Grey #1 © MAR

X-Men: Red #8 © MAR

	GD	VG	FN	VF	VF/NM	NM-
	2.0	4.0	6.0	8.0	9.0	9.2

X-MEN: HELLBOUND
Marvel Comics: July, 2010 - No. 3, Sept, 2010 ($3.99, limited series)
1-3-Second Coming x-over; Tolibao-a/Djurdjevic-c; Majik rescued from Limbo 4.00

X-MEN: HELLFIRE CLUB
Marvel Comics: Jan, 2000 - No. 4, Apr, 2000 ($2.50, limited series)
1-4-Origin of the Hellfire Club 3.00

X-MEN: HIDDEN YEARS
Marvel Comics: Dec, 1999 - No. 22, Sept. 2001 ($3.50/$2.50)
1-New adventures from pre-#94 era; Byrne-s/a(p) 4.00
2-4,6-11,13-22-($2.50): 2-Two covers. 3-Ka-Zar app. 8,9-FF-c/app. 3.00
5-($2.75) 3.00
12-($3.50) Magneto-c/app. 4.00

X-MEN: KING BREAKER
Marvel Comics: Feb, 2009 - No. 4, May, 2009 ($3.99, limited series)
1-4-Emperor Vulcan and a Shi'ar invasion; Havok, Rachel Grey and Polaris app. 4.00

X-MEN: KITTY PRYDE - SHADOW & FLAME
Marvel Comics: Aug, 2005 - No. 5, Dec, 2005 ($2.99, limited series)
1-5-Akira Yoshida-s/Paul Smith-a/c; Kitty & Lockheed go to Japan 3.00
TPB (2006, $14.99) r/#1-5 15.00

X-MEN LEGACY (See X-Men 2nd series)

X-MEN LEGACY (Marvel NOW!)
Marvel Comics: Jan, 2013 - No. 24, Apr, 2014; No. 300, May, 2014 ($2.99)
1-24: 1-Legion (Professor X's son); Spurrier-s/Huat-a. 2-X-Men app. 5,6-Molina-a 3.00
300-(5/14, $4.99) Spurrier, Carey & Gage-s/Huat, Kurth & Sandoval-a; Mann-c 5.00

X-MEN LEGENDS
Marvel Comics: Apr, 2021 - Present ($4.99)
1-Nicieza-s/Booth-a; the 1990s version of the X-Men & Cable app. 5.00

X-MEN: LIBERATORS
Marvel Comics: Nov, 1998 - No. 4, Feb, 1999 ($2.99, limited series)
1-4-Wolverine, Nightcrawler & Colossus; P. Jimenez 4.00

X-MEN LOST TALES
Marvel Comics: 1997 ($2.99)
1,2-r/Classic X-Men back-up stories 4.00

X-MEN: MAGNETO TESTAMENT
Marvel Comics: Nov, 2008 - No. 5, Mar, 2009 ($3.99, limited series)
1-5-Max Eisenhardt in 1930s Nazi-occupied Poland; Pak-s/DiGiandomenico-a. 5-Back-up story of artist Dina Babbitt with Neal Adams-a 4.00

X-MEN: MANIFEST DESTINY
Marvel Comics: Nov, 2008 - No. 5, Mar, 2009 ($3.99, limited series)
1-5-Short stories of X-Men re-location to San Francisco; s/a by various 4.00
... Nightcrawler 1 (5/09, $3.99) Molina & Syaf-a; Mephisto app. 4.00

X-MEN: MESSIAH COMPLEX
Marvel Comics: Dec, 2007 ($3.99)
1-Part 1 of x-over with X-Men, Uncanny X-Men, X-Factor and New X-Men; 2 covers 4.00
... - Mutant Files (2007, $3.99) Handbook pages of x-over participants; Kolins-c 4.00
HC (2008, $39.99, oversized) r/#1, Uncanny X-Men #492-494, X-Men #205-207, New X-Men #44-46 and X-Factor #25-27 40.00

X-MEN '92 (Secret Wars tie-in)
Marvel Comics: Aug, 2015 - No. 4, Nov, 2015 ($4.99, limited series)
1-4-Koblish-a; Cassandra Nova app. 2-4-X-Force app. 4-Apocalypse cameo 5.00

X-MEN '92 (Follows Secret Wars)
Marvel Comics: May, 2016 - No. 10, Feb, 2017 ($3.99)
1-10: 1-Firmansyah-a; Omega Red & Alpha Red app. 2-U-Go Girl joins. 3,4-Dracula app. 9,10-New Mutants app. 4.00

X-MEN NOIR
Marvel Comics: Nov, 2008 - No. 4, May, 2009 ($3.99, limited series)
1-4-Pulp-style story set in 1930s NY; Van Lente-s/Calero-a 4.00
...: Mark of Cain (2/10 - No. 4, 5/10, $3.99) Van Lente-s/Calero-a 4.00

X-MEN OMEGA
Marvel Comics: June, 1995 ($3.95, one-shot)
nn-Age of Apocalypse finale 2 4 6 8 10 12
nn-($49.95)-Gold edition 55.00

X-MEN: ORIGINS
Marvel Comics: Oct, 2008 - Sept, 2010 ($3.99, series of one-shots)
...: Beast (11/08) High school years; Carey-s; painted-a/c by Woodward 5.00
...: Cyclops (3/10) Magneto app.; Delperdang-a/Granov-c 1 2 3 5 6 8
...: Deadpool (9/10) Fernandez-a/Swierczynski-s 4 8 12 23 37 50
...: Emma Frost (7/10) Moline-a; r/excerpt from 1st app. in Uncanny X-Men #129 5.00
...: Gambit (8/09) Mr. Sinister, Sabretooth and the Marauders app.; Yardin-a 2 4 6 12 18 22
...: Iceman (1/10) Noto-a 5.00
...: Jean Grey (10/08) Childhood & early X-days; McKeever-s; Mayhew painted-a/c 5.00
...: Nightcrawler (5/10) Cary Nord-a; r/excerpt from 1st app. in Giant-Size X-Men #1 5.00
...: Sabretooth (4/09) Childhood and early meetings with Wolverine; Panosian-a/c 1 2 3 5 6 8
...: Wolverine (6/09) Pre-X-Men days and first meeting with Xavier; Texeira-a/c 5.00

X-MEN: PHOENIX
Marvel Comics: Dec, 1999 - No. 3, Mar, 2000 ($2.50, limited series)
1-3: 1-Apocalypse app. 4.00

X-MEN: PHOENIX - ENDSONG
Marvel Comics: Mar, 2005 - No. 5, June, 2005 ($2.99, limited series)
1-5-The Phoenix Force returns to Earth; Greg Land-c/a; Greg Pak-s 3.00
HC (2005, $19.99, dust jacket) r/#1-5; Land sketch pages 20.00
SC (2006, $14.99) 15.00

X-MEN: PHOENIX - LEGACY OF FIRE
Marvel Comics: July, 2003 - No. 3, Sep, 2003 ($2.99, limited series)
1-3-Manga-style; Ryan Kinnard-s/a/c; intro page art by Adam Warren 3.00

X-MEN: PHOENIX - WARSONG
Marvel Comics: Nov, 2006 - No. 5, Mar, 2007 ($2.99, limited series)
1-5-Tyler Kirkham-a/Greg Pak-s/Marc Silvestri-c 3.00
HC (2007, $19.99, dustjacket) r/#1-5; variant cover gallery and Handbook pages 20.00
SC (2007, $14.99) r/#1-5; variant cover gallery and Handbook pages 15.00

X-MEN: PIXIE STRIKES BACK
Marvel Comics: Apr, 2010 - No. 4, July, 2010 ($3.99, limited series)
1-4-Kathryn Immonen-s/Sara Pichelli-a/Stuart Immonen-c 4.00

X-MEN: PRELUDE TO SCHISM
Marvel Comics: Jul, 2011 - No. 4, Aug, 2011 ($2.99, limited series)
1-4-Jenkins-s/Camuncoli-c. 1-De La Torre-a. 2-Magneto childhood. 3-Conrad-a 3.00

X-MEN PRIME
Marvel Comics: July, 1995 ($4.95, one-shot)
nn-Post Age of Apocalyse begins 2 4 6 8 10 12

X-MEN PRIME
Marvel Comics: May, 2017 ($4.99, one-shot)
1-Preludes to X-Men: Blue #1, X-Men: Gold #1 and Weapon X #1 5.00

X-MEN RARITIES
Marvel Comics: 1995 ($5.95, one-shot)
nn-Reprints hard-to-find stories 6.00

X-MEN: RED
Marvel Comics: Apr, 2018 - No. 11, Feb, 2019 ($4.99/$3.99)
1-($4.99) Asrar-a; Jean Grey, Nightcrawler, Namor, Wolverine (X-23) team 5.00
2-11-($3.99) 4-Black Panther app. 4.00
Annual 1 (7/18, $4.99) Taylor-s/Alixe-a; Black Bolt app. 5.00

X-MEN ROAD TO ONSLAUGHT
Marvel Comics: Oct, 1996 ($2.50, one-shot)
nn-Retells Onslaught Saga 4.00

X-MEN: RONIN
Marvel Comics: May, 2003 - No. 5, July, 2003 ($2.99, limited series)
1-5-Manga-style X-Men; Torres-s/Nakatsuka-a 3.00

X-MEN: SCHISM
Marvel Comics: Sept, 2011 - No. 5, Dec, 2011 ($4.99/$3.99, limited series)
1-($4.99) Aaron-s/Pacheco-a/c 5.00
2-5-($3.99) 2-Cho-a/c. 3-Acuña-a/c. 4-Alan Davis-a/c. 5-Adam Kubert-a 4.00

X-MEN: SEARCH FOR CYCLOPS
Marvel Comics: Oct, 2000 - No. 4, Mar, 2001 ($2.99, limited series)
1-4-Two covers (Raney, Pollina); Raney-a 4.00

X-MEN: SECOND COMING
Marvel Comics: May, 2010 - No. 2, Sept, 2010 ($3.99)
1-Cable & Hope return to the present; Bastion app.; Finch-a; covers by Granov & Finch 4.00

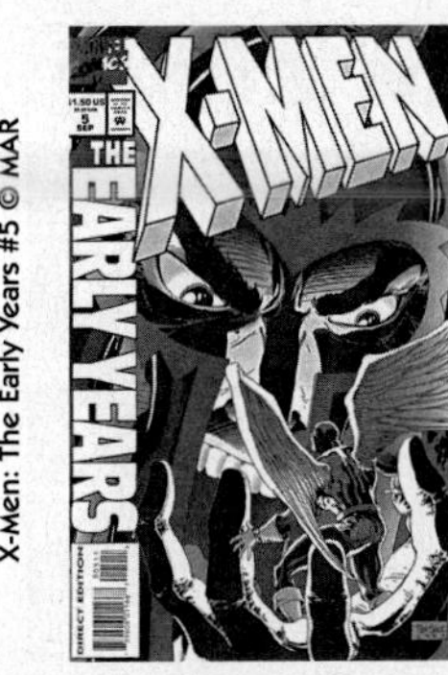

X-Men: The Early Years #5 © MAR

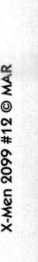

X-Men 2099 #12 © MAR

X-Men Unlimited #3 © MAR

	GD 2.0	VG 4.0	FN 6.0	VF 8.0	VF/NM 9.0	NM- 9.2

2-Conclusion to x-over; covers by Granov & Finch 4.00
...: Prepare (4/10, free) previews x-over; short story w/Immonen-a; cover sketch art 3.00

X-MEN / SPIDER-MAN ("X-Men and Spider-Man" on cover)
Marvel Comics: Jan, 2009 - No. 4, Apr, 2009 ($3.99, limited series)
1-4: 1-Team-up from pre-blue Beast days; Kraven app.; Gage-s/Alberti-a 4.00

X-MEN SPOTLIGHT ON... STARJAMMERS (Also see X-Men #104)
Marvel Comics: 1990 - No. 2, 1990 ($4.50, 52 pgs.)
1,2: Features Starjammers 5.00

X-MEN SURVIVAL GUIDE TO THE MANSION
Marvel Comics: Aug, 1993 ($6.95, spiralbound)
1 7.00

X-MEN: THE COMPLETE AGE OF APOCALYPSE EPIC
Marvel Comics: 2005 - Vol. 4, 2006 ($29.99, TPB)
Book 1-4: Chronological reprintings of the crossover 30.00

X-MEN: THE EARLY YEARS
Marvel Comics: May, 1994 - No. 17, Sept, 1995 ($1.50/$2.50)
1-16: r/X-Men #1-8 w/new-c 4.00
17-$2.50-c; r/X-Men #17,18 5.00

X-MEN: THE END
Marvel Comics: Oct, 2004 - No. 6, Feb, 2005 ($2.99, limited series)
1-6-Claremont-s/Chen-a/Land-c 3.00
... Book One: Dreamers and Demons TPB (2005, $14.99) r/#1-6 15.00

X-MEN: THE END - HEROES AND MARTYRS (Volume 2)
Marvel Comics: May, 2005 - No. 6, Oct, 2005 ($2.99, limited series)
1-6-Claremont-s/Chen-a/Land-c; continued from X-Men: The End 3.00
... Vol. 2 TPB (2006, $14.99) r/#1-6 15.00

X-MEN: THE END (MEN & X-MEN) (Volume 3)
Marvel Comics: Mar, 2006 - No. 6, Aug, 2006 ($2.99, limited series)
1-6-Claremont-s/Chen-a. 1-Land-c. 2-6-Gene Ha-c 3.00
... Vol. 3 TPB (2006, $14.99) r/#1-6 15.00

X-MEN: THE EXTERMINATED
Marvel Comics: Feb, 2019 ($4.99, one-shot)
1-Prelude to Uncanny X-Men #1 (2019); Hope and Jean Grey story; Deadpool app. 5.00

X-MEN: THE MANGA
Marvel Comics: Mar, 1998 - No. 26, June, 1999 ($2.99, B&W)
1-26-English version of Japanese X-Men comics: 23,24-Randy Green-c 4.00

X-MEN: THE MOVIE
Marvel Comics: Aug, 2000; Sept, 2000
Adaptation (9/00, $5.95) Macchio-s/Williams & Lanning-a 6.00
Adaptation TPB (9/00, $14.95) Movie adaptation and key reprints of main characters; four photo covers (movie X, Magneto, Rogue, Wolverine) 15.00
Prequel: Magneto (8/00, $5.95) Texeira & Palmiotti-a; art & photo covers 6.00
Prequel: Rogue (8/00, $5.95) Evans & Nikolakakis-a; art & photo covers 6.00
Prequel: Wolverine (8/00, $5.95) Waller & McKenna-a; art & photo covers 6.00
TPB X-Men: Beginnings (8/00, $14.95) reprints 3 prequels w/photo-c 15.00

X-MEN 2: THE MOVIE
Marvel Comics: 2003
Adaptation (6/03, $3.50) Movie adaptation; photo-c; Austen-s/Zircher-a 4.00
Adaptation TPB (2003, $12.99) Movie adaptation & r/Prequels Nightcrawler & Wolverine 13.00
Prequel: Nightcrawler (5/03, $3.50) Kerschl-a; photo cover 4.00
Prequel: Wolverine (5/03, $3.50) Mandrake-a; photo cover; Sabretooth app. 4.00

X-MEN: THE 198 (See House of M)
Marvel Comics: Mar, 2006 - No. 5, July, 2006 ($2.99, limited series)
1-5-Hine-s/Muniz-a 3.00
... Files (2006, $3.99) profiles of the 198 mutants who kept their powers after House of M 4.00
Decimation: The 198 (2006, $15.99, TPB) r/#1-5 & X-Men: The 198 Files 16.00

X-MEN: THE TIMES AND LIFE OF LUCAS BISHOP
Marvel Comics: Apr, 2009 - No. 3, June, 2009 ($3.99, limited series)
1-3-Swierczynski-s/Stroman-a. 1-Bishop's birth and childhood 4.00

X-MEN: THE ULTRA COLLECTION
Marvel Comics: Dec, 1994 - No. 5, Apr, 1995 ($2.95, limited series)
1-5: Pin-ups; no scripts 4.00

X-MEN: THE WEDDING ALBUM
Marvel Comics: 1994 ($2.95, magazine size, one-shot)
1-Wedding of Scott Summers & Jean Grey 4.00

X-MEN: THE WEDDING SPECIAL
Marvel Comics: Jul, 2018 ($4.99, one-shot)
1-Prelude to wedding of Kitty Pryde & Colossus; art by Nauck, Land & Cresta 5.00

X-MEN: TO SERVE AND PROTECT
Marvel Comics: Jan, 2011 - No. 4, Apr, 2011 ($3.99, limited series)
1-4-Short story anthology by various.1-Bradshaw-c. 2-Camuncoli-c 4.00

X-MEN TRUE FRIENDS
Marvel Comics: Sept, 1999 - No. 3, Nov, 1999 ($2.99, limited series)
1-3-Claremont-s/Leonardi-a 4.00

X-MEN 2099 (Also see 2099: World of Tomorrow)
Marvel Comics: Oct, 1993 - No. 35, Aug, 1996 ($1.25/$1.50/$1.95)
1-($1.75)-Foil-c; Ron Lim/Adam Kubert-a begins 1 2 3 5 6 8
1-2nd printing ($1.75) 3.00
1-Gold edition (15,000 made); sold thru Diamond for $19.40 20.00
2-24,26-35: 3-Death of Tina; Lim-c/a(p) in #1-8. 8-Bound-in trading card sheet. 35-Nostromo (from X-Nation) app; storyline cont'd in 2099: World of Tomorrow 4.00
25-($2.50)-Double sized 4.00
Special 1 ($3.95) 4.00
...: Oasis ($5.95, one-shot) -Hildebrandt Bros.-c/a 6.00

X-MEN ULTRA III PREVIEW
Marvel Comics: 1995 ($2.95)
nn-Kubert-a 4.00

X-MEN UNIVERSE
Marvel Comics: Dec, 1999 - No. 15, Feb, 2001 ($4.99/$3.99)
1-8-Reprints stories from recent X-Men titles 5.00
9-15-($3.99) 4.00

X-MEN UNIVERSE: PAST, PRESENT AND FUTURE
Marvel Comics: Feb, 1999 ($2.99, one-shot)
1-Previews 1999 X-Men events; background info 1 2 3 5 6 8

X-MEN UNLIMITED
Marvel Comics: 1993 - No. 50, Sept, 2003 ($3.95/$2.99, 68 pgs.)
1-Chris Bachalo-c/a; Quesada-a. 1 3 4 6 8 10
2-11: 2-Origin of Magneto script. 3-Sabretooth-c/story. 10-Dark Beast vs. Beast; Mark Waid script. 11-Magneto & Rogue 6.00
12-33: 12-Begin $2.99-c; Onslaught x-over; Juggernaut-c/app. 19-Caliafore-a. 20-Generation X app. 27-Origin Thunderbird. 29-Maximum Security x-over; Bishop-c/app. 30-Mahfood-a. 31-Stelfreeze-c/a. 32-Dazzler; Thompson-c/a 33-Kaluta-c 5.00
34-37,39,40-42-($3.50) 34-Von Eeden-a. 35-Finch, Conner, Maguire-a. 36-Chiodo-c/a; Larroca, Totleben-a. 39-Bachalo-c; Pearson-a. 41-Bachalo-c; X-Statix app. 5.00
38-($2.25) Kitty Pryde; Robertson-a 4.00
43-50-($2.50) 43-Sienkiewicz-c/a; Paul Smith-a. 45-Noto-c. 46-Bisley-a. 47-Warren-s/Mays-a. 48-Wolverine story w/Isanove painted-a 4.00
X-Men Legends Vol. 4: Hated and Feared TPB (2003, $19.99) r/stories by various 20.00
NOTE: ***Bachalo** c/a-1. **Quesada** a-1. **Waid** scripts-10*

X-MEN UNLIMITED
Marvel Comics: Apr, 2004 - No. 14, Jun, 2006 ($2.99)
1-14: 1-6-Pat Lee-c; short stories by various. 2-District X preview; Granov-a 3.00

X-MEN VS. AGENTS OF ATLAS
Marvel Comics: Dec, 2009 - No. 2, Jan, 2010 ($3.99, limited series)
1,2-Pagulayan-a. 1-McGuinness-c. 2-Granov-c 4.00

X-MEN VS. DRACULA
Marvel Comics: Dec, 1993 ($1.75)
1-r/X-Men Annual #6; Austin-c(i) 1 2 3 5 6 8

X-MEN VS. THE AVENGERS, THE
Marvel Comics Group: Apr, 1987 - No. 4, July, 1987 ($1.50, limited series, Baxter paper)
1-Silvestri-a/c 1 3 4 6 8 10
2-4: 2,3-Silvestri-a/c. 4-Pollard-a/c 5.00

X-MEN VS. THE BROOD, THE
Marvel Comics Group: Sept, 1996 - No. 2, Oct, 1996 ($2.95, limited series)
1,2-Wraparound-c; Ostrander-s/Hitch-a(p) 4.00
TPB('97, $16.99) reprints X-Men/Brood: Day of Wrath #1,2 & Uncanny X-Men #232-234 17.00

X-MEN VISIONARIES
Marvel Comics: 1995,1996,2000 (trade paperbacks)
nn-($8.95) Reprints X-Men stories; Adam & Andy Kubert-a 9.00
...2: The Neal Adams Collection (1996) r/X-Men #56-63,65 30.00

X of Swords: Creation #1 © MAR

X-O Manowar (2017 series) #18 © VAL

X-Statix #21 © MAR

GD VG FN VF VF/NM NM-
2.0 4.0 6.0 8.0 9.0 9.2

...2: The Neal Adams Col. (2nd printing, 2000, $24.95) new Adams-c 25.00

X-MEN/WILDC.A.T.S.: THE DARK AGE (See also WildC.A.T.S./X-Men...)
Marvel Comics: 1998 ($4.50, one-shot)

1-Two covers (Broome & Golden); Ellis-s 5.00

X-MEN: WORLDS APART
Marvel Comics: Dec, 2008 - No. 4, Mar, 2009 ($3.99, limited series)

1-4-Storm and the Black Panther vs. the Shadow King. 1-Campbell-c 4.00

X-MEN: WORST X-MAN EVER
Marvel Comics: Apr, 2016 - No. 5, Aug, 2016 ($3.99, limited series)

1-5: 1-Intro. Bailey Hoskins; Max Bemis-s/Michael Walsh-a. 3,4-Magneto app. 4.00

X-NATION 2099
Marvel Comics: Mar, 1996 - No. 6, Aug, 1996 ($1.95)

1-($3.95)-Humberto Ramos-a(p); wraparound, foil-c 5.00
2-6: 2,3-Ramos-a. 4-Exodus-c/app. 6-Reed Richards app 3.00

X NECROSIA
Marvel Comics: Dec, 2009 ($3.99)

1-Beginning of X-Force/X-Men/New Mutants x-over; Crain-a; Selene returns 4.00
...: The Gathering (2/10, $3.99) Wither, Blink, Senyaka, Mortis & Eliphas short stories 4.00

X OF SWORDS (Marvel Event crossing over Wolverine, Cable, and the X-Men titles)
Marvel Comics: Nov, 2020 - Jan, 2021 ($6.99/$4.99)

...: Creation (11/20, $6.99) Part 1 of crossover; Hickman & Howard-s/Larraz-a 7.00
...: Destruction (1/21, $4.99) Part 22 conclusion; Hickman & Howard-s/Larraz & Gracia-a 5.00
...: Handbook (11/20, $4.99) Profile pages of the mutants of Krakoa 5.00
...: Stasis (12/20, $4.99) Part 11 of crossover; Hickman & Howard-s/Larraz & Asrar-a 5.00

X-O MANOWAR (1st Series)
Valiant/Acclaim Comics (Valiant) No. 43 on: Feb, 1992 - No. 68, Sept, 1996 ($1.95/$2.25/$2.50, high quality)

0-(8/93, $3.50)-Wraparound embossed chromium-c by Quesada; Solar app.; origin Aric (X-O Manowar) 6.00
0-Gold variant 2 4 6 13 18 22
1-Intro/1st app. & partial origin of Aric (X-O Manowar); Barry Smith/Layton-a; Shooter & Englehart-s 3 6 9 19 30 40
2,3: 2-B. Smith/Layton-c. 3-Layton-c(i) 1 3 4 6 8 10
4-1st app. Shadowman; Harbinger app. 3 6 9 21 33 45
5,6: 5-B. Smith-c. 6-Begin $2.25-c; Ditko-a(p) 1 2 3 5 6 8
7-15: 7,8-Unity x-overs. 7-Miller-c. 8-Simonson-c. 12-1st app. Randy Calder. 14,15-Turok-c/stories 4.00
15-Hot pink logo variant; came with Ultra Pro Rigid Comic Sleeves box; no price on-c 1 2 3 5 6 8
16-24,26-43: 20-Serial number contest insert. 27-29-Turok x-over. 28-Bound-in trading card. 30-1st app. new "good skin"; Solar app. 33-Chaos Effect Delta Pt. 3. 42-Shadowman app.; includes X-O Manowar Birthquake! Prequel 3.00
25-($3.50)-Has 16 pg. Armorines #0 bound-in w/origin 4.00
44-66: 44-Begin $2.50-c. 50-X, 50-O, 51, 52, 63-Bart Sears-c/a/scripts.
67 1 2 3 5 6 8
68-Revealed that Aric's past stories were premonitions of his future 2 4 6 11 16 20
...: Birth HC (2008, $24.95) recolored reprints #0-6; script and breakdowns for #0; cover gallery; new "The Rise of Lydia" story by Layton and Leeke 25.00
Trade paperback nn (1993, $9.95)-Polybagged with copy of X-O Database #1 inside 15.00
Yearbook 1 (4/95, $2.95) 4.00

NOTE: *Layton a-1i, 2i(part); c-1, 2i, 3i, 6i, 21i.* ***Reese*** *a-4i(part); c-26i.*

X-O MANOWAR (2nd Series)(Also see Iron Man/X-O Manowar: Heavy Metal)
Acclaim Comics (Valiant Heroes): V2#1, Oct, 1996 - No. 21, Jun, 1998 ($2.50)

V2#1-21: 1-Mark Waid & Brian Augustyn scripts begin; 1st app. Donavon Wylie; Rand Banion dies; painted variant-c exists. 2-Donavon Wylie becomes new X-O Manowar. 7-9-Augustyn-s. 10-Copycat-c 3.00

X-O MANOWAR (3rd series)
Valiant Entertainment: May, 2012 - No. 50, Sept, 2016 ($3.99)

1-Robert Venditti-s/Cary Nord-a/Esad Ribic-c; origin re-told 4.00
1-Pullbox variant-c by Nord 5.00
1-Variant-c by David Aja 10.00
1-QR Voice variant-c by Jelena Kevic-Djurdjevic 25.00
2-24: 2-Origin continues. 2,3-Kevic-Djurdjevic-c. 5-8-Ninjak app.; Garbett-a. 9,10-Hairsine-a 11-14-Planet Death; Nord-a. 19-21-Unity tie-in 4.00
2-5,8-14-Pullbox variant covers. 2-Lozzi. 3-Suayan. 4-Kramer. 5-Tan. 14-Eight-bit art 5.00
25-($4.99) Hitch-a; Armor Hunters app., Owly & Wormy short story by Runton 5.00
26-37,39-49: 26-29-Armor Hunters tie-in. 30-32-Armorines app. 34-37-Dead Hand. 47-49-Polybagged with micro-print 4.00
38-(7/15, $4.99) Wedding of Aric and Saana; Doctor Mirage app.; flashbacks 5.00
50-(9/16, $4.99) Polybagged; wraparound-c by 50 artists; art by various 5.00
#0 (10/14, $3.99) Flashback to Aric before his kidnapping; Clay Mann-a 4.00
Annual 2016 #1 (5/16, $5.99) Art by JG Jones, Perez, McKone, Gorham, De La Torre 6.00
...: Commander Trill #0 (12/15, $3.99) Origin of Trill; Venditti-s/Portela-a 4.00
...: Valiant 25th Anniversary Special (6/15, $3.99) Origin of Shanhara; Venditti-s/Cafu-a 4.00

X-O MANOWAR (2017) (4th series)
Valiant Entertainment: Mar, 2017 - No. 26, Apr, 2019 ($3.99)

1-26: 1-Kindt-s/Giorello-a; Aric on planet Gorin. 4-6 Braithwaite-a. 7-9-Crain-a 4.00

X-O MANOWAR (5th series)
Valiant Entertainment: Mar, 2020 - Present ($3.99)

1-4-Hallum-s/Laiso-a. 1-Bonus preview of Final Witness #1 4.00

X-O MANOWAR FAN EDITION
Acclaim Comics (Valiant Heroes): Feb, 1997 (Overstreet's FAN giveaway)

1-Reintro the Armorines & the Hard Corps; 1st app. Citadel; Augustyn scripts; McKone-c/a 4.00

X-O MANOWAR/IRON MAN: IN HEAVY METAL (See Iron Man/X-O Manowar: Heavy Metal)
Acclaim Comics (Valiant Heroes): Sept, 1996 ($2.50, one-shot)
(1st Marvel/Valiant x-over)

1-Pt 1 of X-O Manowar/Iron Man x-over; Arnim Zola app.; Nicieza scripts; Andy Smith-a 5.00

XOMBI
DC Comics (Milestone): Jan, 1994 - No. 21, Feb, 1996 ($1.75/$2.50)

0-($1.95)-Shadow War x-over; Simonson silver ink varnish-c 3.00
1-21: 1-John Byrne-c 3.00
1-Platinum 8.00

XOMBI
DC Comics: May, 2011 - No. 6, Oct, 2011 ($2.99)

1-6-Rozum-s/Irving-a/c 3.00

X-PATROL
Marvel Comics (Amalgam): Apr, 1996 ($1.95, one-shot)

1-Cruz-a(p) 3.00

X-RAY ROBOT
Dark Horse Comics: Mar, 2020 - No. 4, Nov, 2020 ($3.99)

1-4-Mike Allred-s/a. 4-Madman app. 4.00

XSE
Marvel Comics: Nov, 1996 - No. 4, Feb, 1997 ($1.95, limited series)

1-4: 1-Bishop & Shard app. 3.00
1-Variant-c 4.00

X-STATIX
Marvel Comics: Sept, 2002 - No. 26, Oct, 2004 ($2.99/$2.25)

1-($2.99) Allred-a/c; intro. Venus Dee Milo; back-up w/Cooke-a 4.00
2-9-($2.25) 4-Quitely-c. 5-Pope-c/a 3.00
10-26: 10-Begin $2.99-c; Bond-a; U-Go Girl flashback. 13,14-Spider-Man app. 21-25-Avengers app. 26-Team dies 3.00
... Vol. 1: Good Omens TPB (2003, $11.99) r/#1-5 12.00
... Vol. 2: Good Guys & Bad Guys TPB (2003, $15.99) r/#6-10 & Wolverine/Doop #1&2 16.00
... Vol. 3: Back From the Dead TPB (2004, $19.99) r/#11-18 20.00
... Vol. 4: X-Statix Vs. the Avengers TPB (2004, $19.99) r/#19-26; pin-ups 20.00

X-STATIX PRESENTS: DEAD GIRL
Marvel Comics: Mar, 2006 - No. 5, July, 2006 ($2.99, limited series)

1-5-Dr. Strange, Dead Girl, Miss America, Tike app. Milligan-s/Dragotta & Allred-a 3.00
TPB (2006, $13.99) r/series 14.00

X-TERMINATION (Crossover with Astonishing X-Men and X-Treme X-Men)
Marvel Comics: May, 2013 - No. 2, Jun, 2013 ($3.99)

1,2-Lapham-s/David Lopez-a 4.00

X-TERMINATORS
Marvel Comics: Oct, 1988 - No. 4, Jan, 1989 ($1.00, limited series)

1-1st app.; X-Men/X-Factor tie-in; Williamson-i 5.00
2-4 4.00

X, THE MAN WITH THE X-RAY EYES (See Movie Comics)

X-TINCTION AGENDA (Secret Wars tie-in)
Marvel Comics: Aug, 2015 - No. 4, Nov, 2015 ($3.99, limited series)

1-4-Guggenheim-s/Di Giandomenico-a; Havok & Wolfsbane app. 4.00

X-TREME X-MEN (Also see Mekanix)
Marvel Comics: July, 2001 - No. 46, Jun, 2004 ($2.99/$3.50)

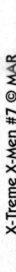

X-Treme X-Men #7 © MAR

X-23 (2018 series) #1 © MAR

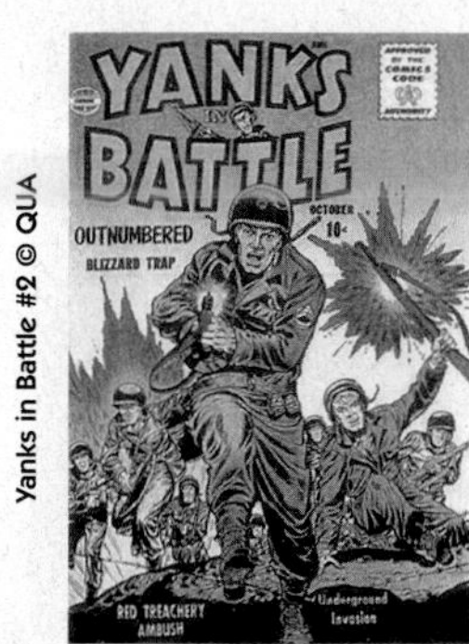
Yanks in Battle #2 © QUA

	GD	VG	FN	VF	VF/NM	NM-
	2.0	4.0	6.0	8.0	9.0	9.2

1-Claremont-s/Larroca-c/a 4.00
2-24: 2-Two covers (Larroca & Pacheco); Psylocke killed 3.00
25-35, 40-46: 25-30-God Loves, Man Kills II; Stryker app.; Kordey-a 3.00
36-39-($3.50) 3.50
Annual 2001 ($4.95) issue opens longways 5.00
... Vol. 1: Destiny TPB (2002, $19.95) r/#1-9 20.00
... Vol. 2: Invasion TPB (2003, $19.99) r/#10-18 20.00
... Vol. 3: Schism TPB (2003, $16.99) r/#19-23; X-Treme X-Posé #1&2 17.00
... Vol. 4: Mekanix TPB (2003, $16.99) r/Mekanix #1-6 17.00
... Vol. 5: God Loves Man Kills TPB (2003, $19.99) r/#25-30 20.00
... Vol. 6: Intifada TPB (2004, $16.99) r/#24,31-35 17.00
... Vol. 7: Storm the Arena TPB (2004, $16.99) r/#36-39 17.00
... Vol. 8: Prisoner of Fire TPB (2004, $19.99) r/#40-46 and Annual 2001 20.00

X-TREME X-MEN
Marvel Comics: Sept, 2012 - No. 13, Jun, 2013 ($2.99)

1-13: 1-Pak-s/Segovia-a; Dazzler with alternate reality Wolverine, Nightcrawler, Emma 3.00
7.1-(2/12) Cyclops & The Brood app. 3.00

X-TREME X-MEN: SAVAGE LAND
Marvel Comics: Nov, 2001 - No. 4, Feb, 2002 ($2.99, limited series)

1-4-Claremont-s/Sharpe-c/a; Beast app. 3.00

X-TREME X-POSE
Marvel Comics: Jan, 2003 - No. 2, Feb, 2003 ($2.99, limited series)

1,2-Claremont-s/Ranson-a/Migliari-c 3.00

X-23 (See debut in NYX #3)(See NYX X-23 HC for reprint)
Marvel Comics: Mar, 2005 - No. 6, July, 2005 ($2.99, limited series)

1-Origin of the Wolverine clone girl; Tan-a 3 6 9 14 20 26
1-Variant Billy Tan-c with red background 3 6 9 15 22 28
2-6-Origin continues 1 3 4 6 8 10
2-Variant B&W sketch-c 2 4 6 9 12 15
One shot 1 (5/10, $3.99) Urasov-c/Liu-s; Wolverine & Jubilee app.
3 6 9 18 27 36
...: Innocence Lost MGC 1 (5/11, $1.00) r/#1 with "Marvel's Greatest Comics" cover logo 3.00
...: Innocence Lost TPB (2006, $15.99) r/#1-6 20.00

X-23
Marvel Comics: Nov, 2010 - No. 21, May, 2012 ($3.99/$2.99)

1-Marjorie Liu-s/Will Conrad-a; origin retold; Luo-c 3 6 9 16 23 30
1-Djurdjevic variant-c 3 6 9 16 23 30
1-Dell'Otto variant-c 23 46 69 168 382 560
2-Luo-c 2 4 6 8 10 12
2-Mayhew variant-c 6 12 18 42 79 115
3-21: 3,10-12,17-19-Takeda-a. 8,9-Daken app. 13-16-Spider-Man app.; Noto-a. 20-Jubilee app.; Noto-a. 21-Silent issue; Noto-a 4.00

X-23
Marvel Comics: Sept, 2018 - No. 12, Jul, 2019 ($4.99/$3.99)

1-($4.99) Tamaki-s/Cabal-a; Honey Badger and the Stepford Cuckoos app. 5.00
2-12-($3.99) 7-Intro X-Assassin 4.00

X-23: TARGET X
Marvel Comics: Feb, 2007 - No. 6, July, 2007 ($2.99, limited series)

1-Kyle & Yost-s/Choi & Oback-a 3 6 9 14 20 26
2-6: 6-Gallery of variant covers and sketches 6.00
TPB (2007, $15.99) r/#1-6; gallery of variant covers and sketches 16.00

X-UNIVERSE
Marvel Comics: May, 1995 - No. 2, June, 1995 ($3.50, limited series)

1,2: Age of Apocalypse 5.00

X-VENTURE (Super Heroes)
Victory Magazines Corp.: July, 1947 - No. 2, Nov, 1947

1-Atom Wizard, Mystery Shadow, Lester Trumble begin
132 264 396 845 1448 2050
2 61 122 183 390 670 950

X-WOMEN
Marvel Comics: 2010 ($4.99, one-shot)

1-Milo Manara-a/Chris Claremont-s; a female X-Men adventure; Quesada afterword 5.00

XYR (See Eclipse Graphic Album Series #21)

YAK YAK
Dell Publishing Co.: No. 1186, May-July, 1961 - No. 1348, Apr-June, 1962

Four Color 1186 (#1)- Jack Davis-c/a; 2 versions, one minus 3 pgs.
8 16 24 54 102 150
Four Color 1348 (#2)-Davis c/a 7 14 21 46 86 125

YAKKY DOODLE & CHOPPER (TV) (See Dell Giant #44)
Gold Key: Dec, 1962 (Hanna-Barbera)

1 8 16 24 51 96 140

YANG (See House of Yang)
Charlton Comics: Nov, 1973 - No. 13, May, 1976; V14#15, Sept, 1985 - No. 17, Jan, 1986 (No V14#14, series resumes with #15)

1-Origin; Sattler-a begins; slavery-s 2 4 6 13 18 22
2-13(1976) 1 2 3 6 9 10
15-17(1986): 15-Reprints #1 (Low print run) 6.00
3,10,11(Modern Comics-r, 1977) 6.00

YANKEE COMICS
Harry 'A' Chesler: Sept, 1941 - No. 7, 1942?

1-Origin The Echo, The Enchanted Dagger, Yankee Doodle Jones, The Firebrand, & The Scarlet Sentry; Black Satan app.; Yankee Doodle Jones app. on all covers
242 484 726 1549 2650 3750
2-Origin Johnny Rebel; Major Victory app.; Barry Kuda begins
110 220 330 704 1202 1700
3,4: 4-(3/42) 90 180 270 576 988 1400
4 (nd, 1940s; 7-1/4x5", 68 pgs, distr. to the service)-Foxy Grandpa, Tom, Dick & Harry, Impy, Ace & Deuce, Dot & Dash, Ima Slooth by Jack Cole (Remington Morse publ.)
20 40 60 114 182 250
5-7 (nd; 10¢, 7-1/4x5", 68 pgs.)(Remington Morse publ.)-urges readers to send their copies to servicemen. 15 30 45 94 147 200

YANKEE DOODLE THE SPIRIT OF LIBERTY
Spire Publications: 1984 (no price, 36 pgs)

nn-Al Hartley-s/c/a 2 4 6 9 13 16

YANKS IN BATTLE
Quality Comics Group: Sept, 1956 - No. 4, Dec, 1956

1-Cuidera-c(i) 15 30 45 86 133 180
2-4: Cuidera-c(i) 10 20 30 56 76 95

YARDBIRDS, THE (G. I. Joe's Sidekicks)
Ziff-Davis Publishing Co.: Summer, 1952

1-By Bob Oskner 20 40 60 138 307 475

YARNS OF YELLOWSTONE
World Color Press: 1972 (50¢, 36 pgs.)

nn-Illustrated by Bill Chapman 2 4 6 9 12 15

YEAH!
DC Comics (Homage): Oct, 1999 - No. 9, Jun, 2000 ($2.95)

1-Bagge-s/Hernandez-a 3.00
2-9: 2-Editorial page contains adult language 3.00

YEAR OF MARVELS, A
Marvel Comics: ($4.99)

...: The Amazing (6/16) Spider-Man vs. The Vulture; Ant-Man 5.00
...: The Incredible (8/16) Spider-Man & D-Man story; Wolverine (X-23) & She-Hulk story 5.00
...: The Unbeatable (12/16) Nick Fury story; Rocket Raccoon & Tippy-Toe story 5.00
...: The Uncanny (2/17) Hawkeye (Kate Bishop) story; Punisher story 5.00
...: The Unstoppable (10/16) Nova & Iron Man story; Winter Soldier story 5.00

YEAR OF THE VILLAIN: HELL ARISEN
DC Comics: Feb, 2020 - No. 4, May, 2020 ($4.99, limited series)

1,2-Apex Lex vs. The Batman Who Laughs; Tynion IV-s/Epting-a. 1-Crime Syndicate app. 5.00
3-First full app. of Punchline; Joker app. 6 12 18 38 69 100
4-Perpertua app.; leads into the Death Metal series 5.00

YEAR ONE: BATMAN/RA'S AL GHUL
DC Comics: 2005 - No. 2, 2005 ($5.99, squarebound, limited series)

1-Devin Grayson-s/Paul Gulacy-a 6.00
TPB (2006, $9.99) r/#1,2 10.00

YEAR ONE: BATMAN SCARECROW
DC Comics: 2005 - No. 2, 2005 ($5.99, squarebound, limited series)

1-Scarecrow's origin; Bruce Jones-s/Sean Murphy-a 6.00

YEARS OF FUTURE PAST (Secret Wars Battleworld tie-in)
Marvel Comics: Aug, 2015 - No. 5, Nov, 2015 ($4.99/$3.99, limited series)

1-($4.99) Bennett-s/Norton-a; Art Adams-c; Kitty Pryde, Wolverine, Colossus app. 5.00
2-5-($3.99) Storm, Magneto, Mystique, Blob, Sentinels app. 4.00

YEAR ZERO
AWA Studios: Apr, 2020 - No. 5, Sept, 2020; Nov, 2020 - No. 5 ($3.99)

Yellowjacket Comics #3 © Frank Comunale

Yondu #3 © MAR

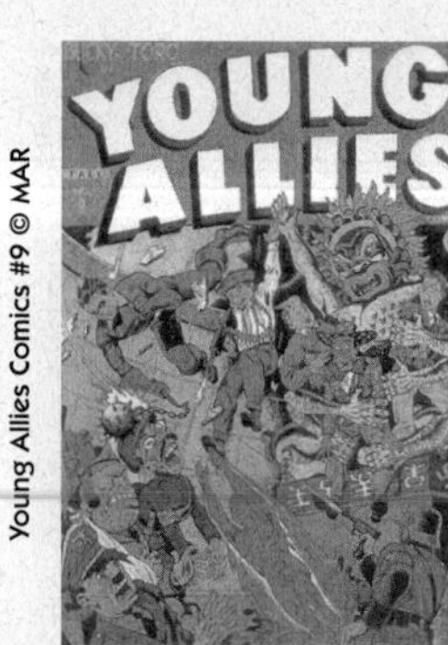

Young Allies Comics #9 © MAR

	GD	VG	FN	VF	VF/NM	NM-
	2.0	4.0	6.0	8.0	9.0	9.2

1-5-Benjamin Percy-s/Ramon Rosanas-a 4.00
Vol. 2 (11/20 - No. 5) 1-4-Percy-s/Ryp-a 4.00

YELLOW CLAW (Also see Giant Size Master of Kung Fu)
Atlas Comics (MjMC): Oct, 1956 - No. 4, Apr, 1957

1-Origin by Joe Maneely 168 336 504 1075 1838 2600
2-Kirby-a 135 270 405 864 1482 2100
3-Kirby-a 119 238 357 762 1306 1850
4-Kirby/Severin-a 126 252 378 808 1378 1950
NOTE: *Everett c-3. **Maneely** c-1. **Reinman** a-2i, 3. **Severin** c-2, 4.*

YELLOWJACKET COMICS (Jack in the Box #11 on)(See TNT Comics)
E. Levy/Frank Comunale/Charlton: Sept, 1944 - No. 5. Jan, 1945; No. 6, Dec, 1945 - No. 10, June, 1946

1-Intro & origin Yellowjacket; Diana, the Huntress begins; "Famous Tales of Terror" begins with E.A. Poe's "The Black Cat" adaptation 84 168 252 538 919 1300
2-Yellowjacket-c begin, end #10; no "Famous Tales of Terror" 53 106 159 334 567 800
3,5: 3-"Famous Tales of Terror" with Poe's "The Pit and the Pendulum" adaptation. 5-No "Famous Tales of Terror" 52 104 156 328 552 775
4-"Famous Tales of Terror" with Poe's "Fall of the House Of Usher" adaptation; Palais-a 53 106 159 334 567 800
6-Last "Famous Tales of Terror", with Poe's "The Tell Tale Heart" adaptation 48 96 144 302 514 725
7-Classic Skull-c; "Tales of Terror" begins by Alan Mandel-narrated by the Ancient Witch, wearing a red cloak, stirring her bubbling cauldron at beginning and end of story just like E.C.'s Old Witch 5 years later; tells story "The Avenging Hand!" similar to "The Maestro's Hand!" in Crypt of Terror #18. (1st horror series?) Toth-a (1 pg. gag feature) 71 142 213 454 777 1100
8-"Tales of Terror" narrated by the Old Witch; classic splash & end panel with skull & bones; early "return from the grave story" 42 84 126 265 445 625
9,10-"Tales of Terror" in each, narrated by the Old Witch in a red cloak, w/classic splash and end panels 42 84 126 265 445 625
NOTE: *The Old Witch in #7-10 above may have inspired creation of E.C.'s Old Witch. Her costume, dialogue, use of bubbling cauldron, skull and bones and even the title "Tales of Terror" were possibly used.*

YELLOWSTONE KELLY (Movie)
Dell Publishing Co.: No. 1056, Nov-Jan, 1959/60

Four Color 1056-Clint Walker photo-c 6 12 18 37 66 95

YELLOW SUBMARINE (See Movie Comics)

YOGA HOSERS: A SUNDANCE SUPER SPECIAL
Dynamite Entertainment: 2016 ($10.00, one-shot)

1-Prologue to the Kevin Smith movie; Smith-s/Jeff Quigley-a 10.00
1-Third printing (2017, $3.99) 4.00

YOGI BEAR (See Dell Giant #41, Golden Comics Digest, Kite Fun Book, March of Comics #253, 265, 279, 291, 309, 319, 337, 344, Movie Comics under "Hey There It's..." & Whitman Comic Books)

YOGI BEAR (TV) (Hanna-Barbera) (See Four Color #990)
Dell Publishing Co./Gold Key No. 10 on: No. 1067, 12-2/59-60 - No. 9, 7-9/62; No. 10, 10/62 - No. 42, 10/70

Four Color 1067 (#1)-TV show debuted 1/30/61 12 24 36 84 185 285
Four Color 1104,1162 (5-7/61) 8 16 24 56 108 160
4(8-9/61) - 6(12-1/61-62) 5 10 15 33 57 80
Four Color 1271(11/61) 6 12 18 40 73 105
Four Color 1349(1/62)-Photo-c 8 16 24 54 102 150
7(2-3/62) - 9(7-9/62)-Last Dell 5 10 15 33 57 80
10(10/62-G.K.), 11(1/63)-titled "Yogi Bear Jellystone Jollies" (80 pgs.); 11-X-Mas-c 6 12 18 41 76 110
12(4/63), 14-20 4 8 12 28 47 65
13(7/63, 68 pgs.)-Surprise Party 6 12 18 40 73 105
21-30 3 6 9 19 30 40
31-42 3 6 9 16 24 32

YOGI BEAR (TV)
Charlton Comics: Nov, 1970 - No. 35, Jan, 1976 (Hanna-Barbera)

1 5 10 15 31 53 75
2-6,8-10 3 6 9 16 24 32
7-Summer Fun (Giant, 52 pgs.) 4 8 12 27 44 60
11-20 3 6 9 15 22 28
21-35: 28-31-partial-r 2 4 6 11 16 20
Digest (nn, 1972, 75¢-c, B&W, 100 pgs.) (scarce) 3 6 9 18 28 38

YOGI BEAR (TV)(See The Flintstones, 3rd series & Spotlight #1)
Marvel Comics Group: Nov, 1977 - No. 9, Mar, 1979 (Hanna-Barbera)

1,7-9: 1-Flintstones begin (Newsstand sales only) 3 6 9 16 23 30
2-6 2 4 6 11 16 20

YOGI BEAR (TV)
Harvey Comics: Sept, 1992 - No. 6, Mar, 1994 ($1.25/$1.50) (Hanna-Barbera)

V2#1-6 3.00
...Big Book V2#1,2 ($1.95, 52 pgs): 1-(11/92). 2-(3/93) 4.00
...Giant Size V2#1,2 ($2.25, 68 pgs.): 1-(10/92). 2-(4/93) 4.00

YOGI BEAR (TV)
Archie Publ.: May, 1997

1 3.00

YOGI BEAR'S EASTER PARADE (See The Funtastic World of Hanna-Barbera #2)

YOGI BERRA (Baseball hero)
Fawcett Publications: 1951 (Yankee catcher)

nn-Photo-c (scarce) 79 158 237 502 864 1225

YONDU (Guardians of the Galaxy)
Marvel Comics: Jan, 2020 - No. 5, Apr, 2020 ($3.99, limited series)

1-5-Zac Thompson & Lonnie Nadler-s/John McCrea-a; future Yondu app. 4.00

YOSEMITE SAM (...& Bugs Bunny) (TV)
Gold Key/Whitman: Dec, 1970 - No. 81, Feb, 1984

1 5 10 15 31 53 75
2-10 3 6 9 16 23 30
11-20 2 4 6 11 16 20
21-30 2 4 6 9 13 16
31-50 2 4 6 8 10 12
51-65 (Gold Key) 1 2 3 5 7 9
66,67 (Whitman) 2 4 6 8 10 12
68(9/80), 69(10/80), 70(12/80) 3-pack only 5 10 15 30 50 70
71-78: 76(2/82), 77(3/82), 78(4/82) 2 4 6 9 13 16
79-81 (All #90263 on-c, no date or date code; 3-pack): 79(7/83). 80(8/83). 81(2/84)-(1/3-r) 3 6 9 16 24 32
(See March of Comics #363, 380, 392)

YOSSEL
DC Comics: 2003/2011 ($14.99, B&W graphic novel)

SC-Joe Kubert-s/a/c; Nazi-occupied Poland during World War II 15.00

YOU ARE DEADPOOL
Marvel Comics: Jul, 2018 - No. 5, Jul, 2018 ($3.99, weekly limited series)

1-5-Ewing-s; interactive role-playing adventure. 3-Man-Thing app. 4-Bullseye app. 4.00

YOU ARE OBSOLETE
AfterShock Comics: Sept, 2019 - No. 5, Jan, 2020 ($3.99)

1-5-Matthew Klickstein-s/Evgeniy Bornyakov-a/Andy Clarke-c 4.00

YOU LOOK LIKE DEATH: TALES FROM THE UMBRELLA ACADEMY
Dark Horse Comics: Sept, 2020 - No. 6, Feb, 2021 ($3.99, limited series)

1-6-Gerald Way & Shaun Simon-s/I.N.J. Culbard-a; spotlight on Klaus 4.00

YOUNG ALLIES
Marvel Comics: Aug, 2010 - No. 6, Jan, 2011 ($3.99/$2.99)

1-($3.99) Wraparound-c; Nomad, Araña, Firestar, Gravity, Toro team-up; origin pages 5.00
2-6-($2.99) 2-Lafuente-c/McKeever-s/Baldeon-a. 6-Miyazawa-c; Emma Frost app. 4.00

YOUNG ALLIES COMICS (All-Winners #21; see Kid Komics #2)
Timely Comics (USA 1-7/NPI 8,9/YAI 10-20): Sum, 1941 - No. 20, Oct, 1946

1-Origin/1st app. The Young Allies (Bucky, Toro, others); 1st meeting of Captain America & Human Torch; Red Skull-c & app.; S&K-c/splash; Hitler-c; Note: the cover was altered after its preview in Human Torch #5. Stalin was shown with Hitler but was removed due to Russia becoming an ally 1350 2700 4050 9450 17,213 27,500
2-(Winter, 1941)-Captain America & Human Torch app.; Simon & Kirby-c 443 886 1329 3234 5717 8200
3-Remember Pearl Harbor issue (Spring, 1942); Stan Lee scripts; Vs. Japanese-c/full-length story; Captain America & Human Torch app.; Father Time story by Alderman 411 822 1233 2877 5039 7200
4-The Vagabond & Red Skull, Capt. America, Human Torch app. Classic Red Skull-c 524 1048 1572 3825 6763 9700
5-Captain America & Human Torch app. 275 550 825 1760 3030 4300
6,7: 6-Japanese/Nazi war-c 200 400 600 1280 2190 3100
8-Classic Schomburg WWII Japanese bondage-c 219 438 657 1402 2401 3400
9-Hitler, Tojo, Mussolini-c. 306 612 918 2198 3849 5500
10-Classic Schomburg Hooded Villain bondage-c; origin Tommy Tyme & Clock of Ages; ends #19 187 374 561 1197 2049 2900
11-16: 12-Classic decapitation story; Japanese war-c. 16-Last Schomburg WWII-c 161 322 483 1030 1765 2500
17-20 123 246 369 787 1344 1900
NOTE: ***Brodsky** c-15. **Ferstadt** a-3. **Gabriele** a-3; c-3, 4. **S&K** c-1, 2. **Schomburg** c-5-13, 16-19. **Shores** c-20.*

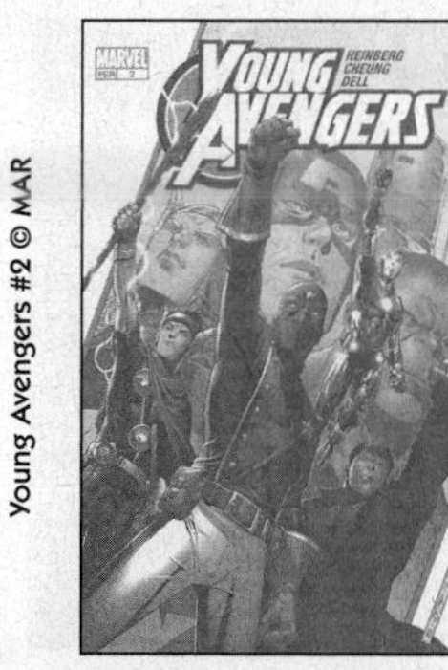
Young Avengers #2 © MAR

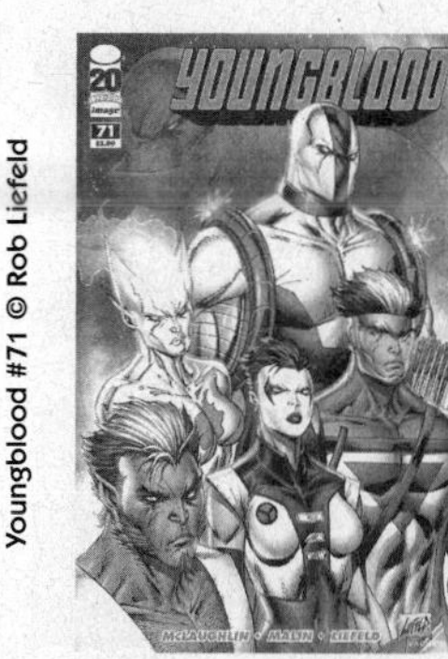
Youngblood #71 © Rob Liefeld

Young Eagle #6 © FAW

	GD 2.0	VG 4.0	FN 6.0	VF 8.0	VF/NM 9.0	NM- 9.2

YOUNG ALLIES 70TH ANNIVERSARY SPECIAL
Marvel Comics: Aug, 2009 ($3.99, one-shot)

1-Bucky & Young Allies app.; Stern-s/Rivera-a; Terry Vance rep. from Marvel Myst. #14 5.00

YOUNG ALL-STARS
DC Comics: June, 1987 - No. 31, Nov, 1989 ($1.00, deluxe format)

1-31: 1-1st app. Iron Munro & The Flying Fox. 8,9-Millennium tie-ins 4.00
Annual 1 (1988, $2.00) 4.00

YOUNG AVENGERS
Marvel Comics: Apr, 2005 - No. 12, Aug, 2006 ($2.99)

	GD	VG	FN	VF	VF/NM	NM-
1-1st app Kate Bishop; intro. Iron Lad, Patriot, Hulkling, Asgardian; Heinberg-s/Cheung-a	10	20	30	69	147	225
1-Director's Cut (2005, $3.99) r/#1 plus character sketches; original script	4	8	12	27	44	60
2-8,10,11: 3-6-Kang app. 7-DiVito-a. 9-Skrulls app.						3.00
9-1st Kate Bishop-c	2	4	6	11	16	20
12-1st Kate Bishop as Hawkeye	3	6	9	16	23	30

... Special 1 (2/06, $3.99) origins of the heroes; art by various incl. Neal Adams, Jae Lee, Bill Sienkiewicz, Gene Ha, Michael Gaydos and Pasqual Ferry 4.00
... Vol. 1: Sidekicks HC (2005, $19.99, dustjacket) r/#1-6; character design sketches 20.00
... Vol. 1: Sidekicks TPB (2006, $14.99) r/#1-6; character design sketches 15.00
... Vol. 2: Family Matters HC (2006, $22.99, dustjacket) r/#7-12 & YA Special #1 23.00
... Vol. 2: Family Matters SC (2007, $17.99) r/#7-12 & YA Special #1 18.00
HC (2008, $29.99, d.j.) oversized reprint of #1-12 and Special #1; script & sketch pages 30.00

YOUNG AVENGERS (Marvel NOW!)
Marvel Comics: Mar, 2013 - No. 15, Mar, 2014 ($2.99)

1-15: 1-Loki assembles team; Marvel Boy, Miss America app.; Gillen-s/McKelvie-a/c. 11-Loki ages back to adult. 14,15-Multiple artists 3.00
1-Variant-c by Bryan Lee O'Malley 6.00
1-Variant-c by Skottie Young 6.00

YOUNG AVENGERS PRESENTS
Marvel Comics: Mar, 2008 - No. 6, Aug, 2008 ($2.99, limited series)

1-6: 1-Patriot; Bucky app. 2-Hulkling; Captain Marvel app. 3-Wiccan & Speed. 4-Vision. 5-Stature. 6-Hawkeye; Clint Barton app.; Alan Davis-a 3.00

YOUNGBLOOD (See Brigade #4, Megaton Explosion & Team Youngblood)
Image Comics (Extreme Studios): Apr, 1992 - No. 4, Feb, 1993 ($2.50, lim. series); No. 5-(Flip book w/Brigade #4); No. 6, June, 1994 - No. 10, Dec, 1994 ($1.95/$2.50)

1-Liefeld-c/a/scripts in all; flip book format with 2 trading cards; 1st Image/Extreme Studios title. 5.00
1,2-2nd printing 3.00
2-(JUN-c, July 1992 indicia)-1st app. Shadowhawk in solo back-up story; 2 trading cards inside; flip book format; 1st app. Prophet, Kirby, Berzerkers, Darkthorn 4.00
3,0,4,5: 3-(OCT-c, August 1992 indicia)-Contains 2 trading cards inside (flip book); 1st app. Supreme in back-up story; 1st app. Showdown. 0-(12/92, $1.95)-Contains 2 trading cards; 2 cover variations exist, green or beige logo; w/Image #0 coupon. 4-(2/93)-Glow-in-the-dark cover w/2 trading cards; 2nd app. Dale Keown's The Pitt; Bloodstrike app. 5-Flip book w/Brigade #4 3.00
6-($3.50, 52 pgs.)-Wraparound-c 4.00
7-10: 7, 8-Liefeld-c(p)/a(p)/story. 8,9-(9/94) 9-Valentino story & art 3.00
Battlezone 1 (May-c, 4/93 inside, $1.95)-Arsenal book; Liefeld-c(p) 3.00
Battlezone 2 (7/94, $2.95)-Wraparound-c 4.00
Image Firsts: Youngblood #1 (3/10, $1.00) reprints #1 3.00
...Super Special (Winter '97, $2.99) Sprouse -a 4.00
Yearbook 1 (7/93, $2.50)-Fold out panel; 1st app. Tyrax & Kanan 4.00
Vol. 1 HC (2008, $34.99) oversized r/#1-5, recolored and remastered; sketch art and cover gallery; Mark Millar intro. 35.00
TPB (1996, $16.95)-r/Team Youngblood #8-10 & Youngblood #6-8,10 17.00

YOUNGBLOOD
Image Comics (Extreme Studios)/Maximum Press No. 14: V2#1, Sept, 1995 - No. 14, Dec, 1996 ($2.50)

V2#1-10,14: Roger Cruz-a in all. 4-Extreme Destroyer Pt. 4 w/gaming card. 5-Variant-c exists. 6-Angela & Glory. 7-Shadowhunt Pt. 3; Shadowhawk app. 8,10-Thor (from Supreme) app. 10-(7/96). 14-(12/96)-1st Maximum Press issue 3.00

YOUNGBLOOD (Volume 3)
Awesome/ Awesome-Hyperwerks #2: Feb, 1998 - No. 2, Aug, 1998 ($2.50)

1-Alan Moore-s/Skroce & Stucker-a; 12 diff. covers 3.00
2-(8/98) Skroce & Liefeld covers 3.00
...Imperial 1 (Arcade Comics, 6/04, $2.99) Kirkman-sMychaels-a 3.00

YOUNGBLOOD (Volume 4)
Image Comics: Jan, 2008 - No. 9, Sept, 2009; No. 71, May, 2012 - No. 78, Jul, 2013 ($2.99/$3.99)

1-7-Casey-s/Donovan-a; two covers by Donovan & Liefeld on each 3.00
8-Obama flip cover by Liefeld; Obama app. in story 3.00
9-(9/09, $3.99) Obama flip cover by Liefeld; Free Agent rejoins; Obama app. in story 4.00
71-74: 71-(5/12, $2.99) Liefeld & Malin-a; three covers 3.00
75-(1/13, $4.99) Five covers; Malin-a 5.00
76-78-($3.99) Malin-a 4.00

YOUNGBLOOD (Volume 5)
Image Comics: May, 2017 - No. 11, May, 2018 ($3.99)

1-11-Bowers-s/Towe-a; multiple covers on each. 1-Back-up story w/Liefeld-s/a. 4,5-Bloodstrike flip book; Liefeld-s/a 4.00

YOUNGBLOOD: STRIKEFILE
Image Comics (Extreme Studios): Apr, 1993 - No. 11, Feb, 1995 ($1.95/$2.50/$2.95)

1-10: 1-($1.95)-Flip book w/Jae Lee-c/a & Liefeld-c/a in #1-3; 1st app. The Allies,Giger, & Glory. 3-Thibert-i asisst. 4-Liefeld-c(p); no Lee-a. 5-Liefeld-c(p). 8-Platt-c 3.00
NOTE: *Youngblood: Strikefile began as a four issue limited series.*

YOUNGBLOOD/X-FORCE
Image Comics (Extreme Studios): July, 1996 ($4.95, one-shot)

1-Cruz-a(p); two covers exist 5.00

YOUNG BRIDES (True Love Secrets)
Feature/Prize Publ.: Sept-Oct, 1952 - No. 30, Nov-Dec, 1956 (Photo-c: V1 #1-6, V2 #1,2)

	GD	VG	FN	VF	VF/NM	NM-
V1#1-Simon & Kirby-a	50	100	150	315	533	750
2-S&K-a	28	56	84	168	274	380
3-6-S&K-a	24	48	72	144	237	330
V2#1-7,10-12 (#7-18)-S&K-a	21	42	63	126	206	285
8,9-No S&K-a	13	26	39	74	105	135
V3#1-3(#19-21)-Last precode (3-4/55)	12	24	36	67	94	120
4,6(#22,24), V4#1,3(#25,27)	11	22	33	62	86	110
V3#5(#23)-Meskin-c	11	22	33	64	90	115
V4#2(#26)-All S&K issue	20	40	60	120	195	270
V4#4(#28)-S&K-a	17	34	51	103	162	220
V4#5,6(#29,30)	12	24	36	67	94	120

YOUNG DR. MASTERS (See The Adventures of Young Dr. Masters)

YOUNG DOCTORS, THE
Charlton Comics: Jan, 1963 - No. 6, Nov, 1963

	GD	VG	FN	VF	VF/NM	NM-
V1#1	4	8	12	23	37	50
2-6	3	6	9	14	20	26

YOUNG EAGLE
Fawcett Publications/Charlton: 12/50 - No. 10, 6/52; No. 3, 7/56 - No. 5, 4/57 (Photo-c: 1-10)

	GD	VG	FN	VF	VF/NM	NM-
1-Intro Young Eagle	19	38	57	111	176	240
2-Complete picture novelette "The Mystery of Thunder Canyon"	12	24	36	67	94	120
3-9	9	18	27	52	69	85
10-Origin Thunder, Young Eagle's Horse	9	18	27	47	61	75
3-5(Charlton)-Formerly Sherlock Holmes?	7	14	21	37	46	55

YOUNG GUNS SKETCHBOOK
Marvel Comics: Feb, 2005 ($3.99, one-shot)

1-Sketch pages from 2005 Marvel projects by Coipel, Granov, McNiven, Land & others 4.00

YOUNG HEARTS
Marvel Comics (SPC): Nov, 1949 - No. 2, Feb, 1950

	GD	VG	FN	VF	VF/NM	NM-
1-Photo-c	23	46	69	136	223	310
2-Colleen Townsend photo-c from movie	15	30	45	90	140	190

YOUNG HEARTS IN LOVE
Super Comics: 1964

	GD	VG	FN	VF	VF/NM	NM-
17,18: 17-r/Young Love V5#6 (4-5/62)	2	4	6	9	13	16

YOUNG HELLBOY: THE HIDDEN LAND
Dark Horse Comics: Feb, 2021 - No. 4 ($3.99, limited series)

1-Mignola & Sniegoski-s/Rousseau-a; Prof. Bruttenholm app. 4.00

YOUNG HEROES (Formerly Forbidden Worlds #34)
American Comics Group (Titan): No. 35, Feb-Mar, 1955 - No. 37, Jun-Jul, 1955

	GD	VG	FN	VF	VF/NM	NM-
35-37-Frontier Scout	10	20	30	58	79	100

YOUNG HEROES IN LOVE
DC Comics: June, 1997 - No. 17; #1,000,000, Nov, 1998 ($1.75/$1.95/$2.50)

1-1st app. Young Heroes; Madan-a 4.00
2-17: 3-Superman-c/app. 7-Begin $1.95-c 3.00
#1,000,000 (11/98, $2.50) 853 Century x-over 3.00

YOUNG INDIANA JONES CHRONICLES, THE
Dark Horse Comics: Feb, 1992 - No. 12, Feb, 1993 ($2.50)

1-12: Dan Barry scripts in all 3.00

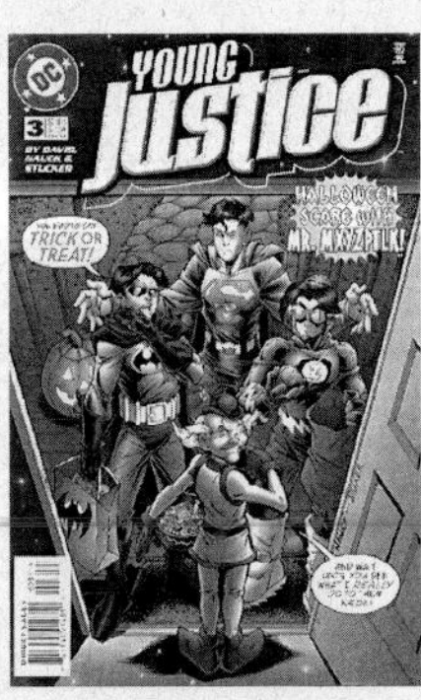

Young Justice #3 © DC

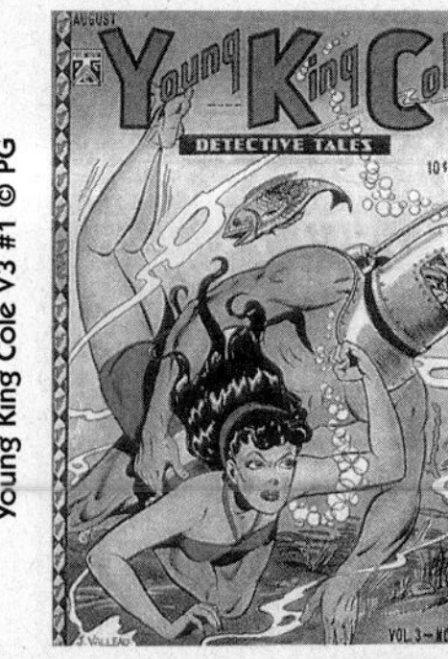

Young King Cole V3 #1 © PG

Young Love #3 © Prize

GD 2.0 | VG 4.0 | FN 6.0 | VF 8.0 | VF/NM 9.0 | NM- 9.2

GD 2.0 | VG 4.0 | FN 6.0 | VF 8.0 | VF/NM 9.0 | NM- 9.2

NOTE: *Dan Barry a(p)-1, 2, 5, 6, 10; c-1-10.* ***Morrow*** *a-3, 4, 5p, 6p.* ***Springer*** *a-1i, 2i.*

YOUNG INDIANA JONES CHRONICLES, THE
Hollywood Comics (Disney): 1992 ($3.95, squarebound, 68 pgs.)
1-3: 1-r/YIJC #1,2 by D. Horse. 2-r/#3,4. 3-r/#5,6 — 4.00

YOUNG JUSTICE (Also see Teen Titans, Titans/Young Justice and DC Comics Presents: ...)
DC Comics: Sept, 1998 - No. 55, May, 2003 ($2.50/$2.75)
1-Robin, Superboy & Impulse team-up; David-s/Nauck-a — 4.00
2,3: 3-Mxyzptlk app. — 3.00
4-20: 4-Wonder Girl, Arrowette and the Secret join. 6-JLA app. 13-Supergirl x-over. 20-Sins of Youth aftermath — 3.00
21-49: 25-Empress ID revealed. 28,29-Forever People app. 32-Empress origin. 35,36-Our Worlds at War x-over. 38-Joker: Last Laugh. 41-The Ray joins. 42-Spectre-c/app. 44,45-World Without YJ x-over pt. 1,5; Ramos-c. 48-Begin $2.75-c — 3.00
50-($3.95) Wonder Twins, CM3 and other various DC teen heroes app. — 4.00
51-55: 53,54-Darkseid app. 55-Last issue; leads into Titans/Young Justice mini-series — 3.00
#1,000,000 (11/98) 853 Century x-over — 3.00
...: A League of Their Own (2000, $14.95, TPB) r/#1-7, Secret Files #1 — 15.00
...: 80-Page Giant (5/99, $4.95) Ramos-c; stories and art by various — 5.00
...: In No Man's Land (7/99, $3.95) McDaniel-c — 4.00
...: Our Worlds at War (8/01, $2.95) Jae Lee-c; Linear Men app. — 3.00
...: Secret Files (1/99, $4.95) Origin-s & pin-ups — 5.00
...: The Secret (6/98, $1.95) Girlfrenzy; Nauck-a — 3.00

YOUNG JUSTICE (Based on the 2011 Cartoon Network series)
DC Comics: No. 0, Mar, 2011 - No. 25, Apr, 2013 ($2.99)
0-19: 1-Miss Martian joins; Joker app. 2-Joker-c/app. 5-Kid Flash & Aqualad origins — 3.00
20-25: 20-(11/12) Starts Invasion; 5 years later — 3.00
FCBD 2011 Young Justice Batman BB Super Sampler (7/11) Flash app. — 3.00

YOUNG JUSTICE
DC Comics (Wonder Comics): Mar, 2019 - No. 20, Jan, 2021 ($4.99/$3.99)
1-($4.99) Robin, Wonder Girl & Impulse team; intro Jinny Hex & Teen Lantern; Bendis-s — 5.00
2-20-($3.99): 2-Gleason & Lupacchino-a. 3-Gleason & Bogdanovic-a. 7-Capt. Carrot and the Kingdom Come Justice League app. 8-10-Earth-3 counterparts app. 13-Warlord app.; art by Grell (5 pages). 20-Red Tornado app. — 4.00

YOUNG JUSTICE: SINS OF YOUTH (Also see Sins of Youth x-over issues and Sins of Youth: Secret Files)
DC Comics: May, 2000 - No. 2, May, 2000 ($3.95, limited series)
1,2-Young Justice, JLA & JSA swap ages; David-s/Nauck-a — 4.00
TPB (2000, $19.95) r/#1,2 & all x-over issues) — 20.00

YOUNG KING COLE (...Detective Tales)(Becomes Criminals on the Run)
Premium Group/Novelty Press: Fall, 1945 - V3#12, July, 1948

	GD	VG	FN	VF	VF/NM	NM-
V1#1-Toni Gayle begins	40	80	120	244	402	560
2	20	40	60	115	188	260
3-4	18	36	54	107	169	230
V2#1-7(8-9/46-7/47): 6,7-Certa-c	15	30	45	83	124	165
V3#1,3-6,8,9,12: 3-Certa-c. 5-McWilliams-c/a. 8,9-Harmon-c	14	28	42	81	118	155
2-L.B. Cole-a; Certa-c	19	38	57	112	179	245
7-L.B. Cole-c/a	24	48	72	142	234	325
10,11-L.B. Cole-c	28	56	84	165	270	375

YOUNG LAWYERS, THE (TV)
Dell Publishing Co.: Jan, 1971 - No. 2, Apr, 1971 (photo-c)

	GD	VG	FN	VF	VF/NM	NM-
1	3	6	9	16	23	30
2	2	4	6	11	16	20

YOUNG LIARS (David Lapham's...)(See Vertigo Double Shot for reprint of #1)
DC Comics (Vertigo): May, 2008 - No. 18, Oct, 2009 ($2.99)
1-18: 1-Intro. Sadie Dawkins; David Lapham-s/a/c in all — 3.00
...: Daydream Believer TPB (2008, $9.99) r/#1-6; Gerald Way intro. — 10.00
...: Maestro TPB (2009, $14.99) r/#7-12; Peter Milligan intro. — 15.00
...: Rock Life TPB (2010, $14.99) r/#13-18; Brian Azzarello intro. — 15.00

YOUNG LIFE (Teen Life #3 on)
New Age Publ./Quality Comics Group: Summer, 1945 - No. 2, Fall, 1945

	GD	VG	FN	VF	VF/NM	NM-
1-Skip Homeier, Louis Prima stories	21	42	63	124	202	280
2-Frank Sinatra photo on-c plus story	23	46	69	138	227	315

YOUNG LOVE (Sister title to Young Romance)
Prize(Feature)Publ.(Crestwood): 2-3/49 - No. 73, 12-1/56-57; V3#5, 2-3/60 - V7#1, 6-7/63

	GD	VG	FN	VF	VF/NM	NM-
V1#1-S&K-c/a(2)	77	154	231	493	847	1200
2-Photo-c begin; S&K-a	39	78	117	240	395	550
3-S&K-a	26	52	78	154	252	350
4-6-Minor S&K-a	18	36	54	107	169	230
V2#1(#7)-S&K-a(2)	24	48	72	144	237	330
2-5(#8-11)-Minor S&K-a	15	30	45	88	137	185
6,8(#12,14)-S&K-c only. 14-S&K 1 pg. art	18	36	54	109	172	235
7,9-12(#13,15-18)-S&K-c/a	24	48	72	140	230	320
V3#1-4(#19-22)-S&K-c/a	21	42	63	126	206	285
5-7,9-12(#23-25,27-30)-Photo-c resume; S&K-a	17	34	51	105	165	225
8(#26)-No S&K-a	12	24	36	67	94	120
V4#1,6(#31,36)-S&K-a	15	30	45	94	147	200
2-5,7-12(#32-35,37-42)-Minor S&K-a	14	28	42	82	121	160
V5#1-12(#43-54), V6#3,7,9(#57,61,63)-Last precode	11	22	33	62	86	110
V6#1,2,4-6,8(#55,56,58-60,62) S&K-a	13	26	39	72	101	130
V6#10-12(#64-66)	5	10	15	35	63	90
V7#1-7(#67-73)	5	10	15	33	57	80
V3#5(2-3/60),6(4-5/60)(Formerly All For Love)	5	10	15	30	50	70
V4#1(6-7/60)-6(4-5/61)	4	8	12	28	47	65
V5#1(6-7/61)-6(4-5/62)	4	8	12	28	47	65
V6#1(6-7/62)-6(4-5/63), V7#1	4	8	12	27	44	60

NOTE: ***Meskin*** *a-14(2), 27, 42.* ***Powell*** *a-V4#6.* ***Severin/Elder*** *a-V1#3. S&K art not in #53, 57, 61, 63-65. Photo-c most V1 #1-6, V2 #3, V3#5-V5#11.*

YOUNG LOVE
National Periodical Publ.(Arleigh Publ. Corp #49-61)/DC Comics:
#39, 9-10/63 - #120, Wint./75-76; #121, 10/76 - #126, 7/77

	GD	VG	FN	VF	VF/NM	NM-
39	6	12	18	41	76	110
40-50	4	8	12	28	47	65
51-68,70	4	8	12	25	40	55
69-(68 pg. Giant)(8-9/68)	7	14	21	44	82	120
71,72,75-77,80	3	6	9	20	31	42
73,74,78,79-Toth-a	3	6	9	21	33	45
81-99: 88-96-(52 pg. Giants)	3	6	9	19	30	40
100	3	6	9	20	31	42
101-106,115-120	3	6	9	16	24	32
107 (100 pgs.)	8	16	24	52	99	145
108-114 (100 pgs.)	7	14	21	48	89	130
121-126 (52 pgs.)	4	8	12	27	44	60

NOTE: ***Bolle*** *a-117.* ***Colan*** *a-107r.* ***Nasser*** *a-123, 124.* ***Orlando*** *a-122.* ***Simonson*** *c-125.* ***Toth*** *a-73, 78, 79, 122-125r.* ***Wood*** *a-109r(4 pgs.).*

YOUNG LOVER ROMANCES (Formerly & becomes Great Lover...)
Toby Press: No. 4, June, 1952 - No. 5, Aug, 1952

	GD	VG	FN	VF	VF/NM	NM-
4,5-Photo-c	14	28	42	81	118	155

YOUNG LOVERS (My Secret Life #19 on)(Formerly Brenda Starr?)
Charlton Comics: No. 16, July, 1956 - No. 18, May, 1957

	GD	VG	FN	VF	VF/NM	NM-
16,17('56): 16-Marcus Swayze-a	15	30	45	84	127	170
18-Elvis Presley picture-c, text story (biography)(Scarce)	100	200	300	640	1095	1550

YOUNG MARRIAGE
Fawcett Publications: June, 1950

	GD	VG	FN	VF	VF/NM	NM-
1-Powell-a; photo-c	15	30	45	92	144	195

YOUNG MEN (Formerly Cowboy Romances)(...on the Battlefield #12-20(4/53); ...In Action #21)
Marvel/Atlas Comics (IPC): No. 4, 6/50 - No. 11, 10/51; No. 12, 12/51 - No. 28, 6/54

	GD	VG	FN	VF	VF/NM	NM-
4-(52 pgs.)	31	62	93	182	296	410
5-11	20	40	60	114	182	250
12-23: 12-20-War format. 21-23-Hot Rod issues starring Flash Foster	20	40	60	118	192	265
24-(12/53)-Origin Captain America, Human Torch, & Sub-Mariner which are revived thru #28; Red Skull app.	423	846	1269	3000	5250	7500
25-28: 25-Romita-c/a (see Men's Advs.). 27-Death of Golden Age Red Skull	177	354	531	1133	1942	2750
25-2nd printing (1994)	2	4	6	8	11	14

NOTE: ***Berg*** *a-7, 14, 17, 18, 20; c-17?* ***Brodsky*** *c-4-9, 13, 14, 16, 17, 21-25.* ***Burgos*** *c-26-28.* ***Colan*** *a-14, 15, 20.* ***Everett*** *a-18-20.* ***Heath*** *a-13, 14.* ***Maneely*** *c-10-12, 15.* ***Pakula*** *a-14, 15.* ***Robinson*** *c-18. Captain America by* ***Romita****-#24?, 25, 26?, 27, 28. Human Torch by* ***Burgos****-#25, 27, 28. Sub-Mariner by* ***Everett****-#24-28.*

YOUNG MONSTERS IN LOVE
DC Comics: Apr, 2018 ($9.99, 80 pages, one-shot)
1-Horror short stories by various; Swamp Thing, Raven, Deadman app.; Kelley Jones-c — 10.00

YOUNG REBELS, THE (TV)
Dell Publishing Co.: Jan, 1971

	GD	VG	FN	VF	VF/NM	NM-
1-Photo-c	3	6	9	14	19	24

YOUNG ROMANCE COMICS (The 1st romance comic)
Prize/Headline (Feature Publ.) (Crestwood): Sept-Oct, 1947 - V16#4, June-July, 1963 (#1-33: 52 pgs.)

	GD	VG	FN	VF	VF/NM	NM-
V1#1-S&K-c/a(2)	90	180	270	576	988	1400

Young Romance Comics #1 © DC

Your Pal Archie #4 © ACP

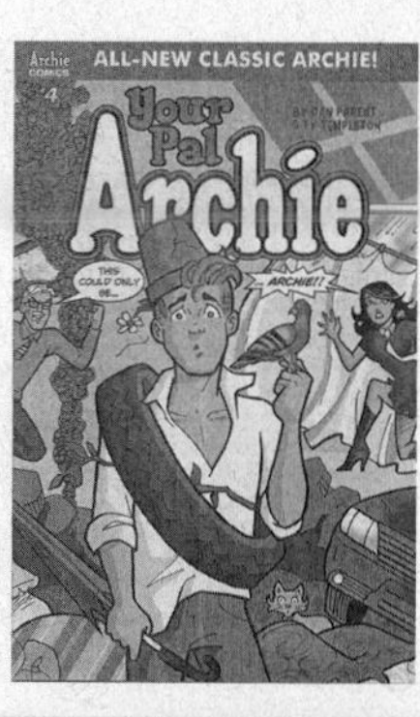

Y: The Last Man #55 © DC

	GD 2.0	VG 4.0	FN 6.0	VF 8.0	VF/NM 9.0	NM- 9.2
2-S&K-c/a(2-3)	45	90	135	284	480	675
3-6-S&K-c/a(2-3) each	39	78	117	236	388	540
V2#1-6(#7-12)-S&K-c/a(2-3) each	34	68	102	204	332	460
V3#1-3(#13-15): V3#1-Photo-c begin; S&K-a	22	44	66	130	213	295
4-12(#16-24)-Photo-c; S&K-a	22	44	66	130	213	295
V4#1-11(#25-35)-S&K-a	21	42	63	124	202	280
12(#36)-S&K, Toth-a	22	44	66	130	213	295
V5#1-12(#37-48), V6#4-12(#52-60)-S&K-a	21	42	63	124	202	280
V6#1-3(#49-51)-No S&K-a	13	26	39	72	101	130
V7#1-11(#61-71)-S&K-a in most	16	32	48	96	151	205
V7#12(#72), V8#1-3(#73-75)-Last precode (12-1/54-55)-No S&K-a	11	22	33	64	90	115
V8#4(#76, 4-5/55), 5(#77)-No S&K-a	10	20	30	58	79	100
V8#6-8(#78-80, 12-1/55-56)-S&K-a	15	30	45	83	124	165
V9#3,5,6(#81, 2-3/56, 83,84)-S&K-a	15	30	45	83	124	165
4, V10#1(#82,85)-All S&K-a	15	30	45	86	133	180
V10#2-6(#86-90, 10-11/57)-S&K-a	9	18	27	57	111	165
V11#1,2,5,6(#91,92,95,96)-S&K-a	9	18	27	57	111	165
3,4(#93,94), V12#2,4,5(#98,100,101)-No S&K	5	10	15	35	63	90
V12#1,3,6(#97,99,102)-S&K-a	9	18	27	57	111	165
V13#1(#103)-Powell-a; S&K's last-a for Crestwood	9	18	27	57	111	165
2,4-6(#104-108)	5	10	15	33	57	80
V13#3(#105, 4-5/60)-Elvis Presley-c app. only	9	18	27	58	114	170
V14#1-6, V15#1-6, V16#1-4(#109-124)	5	10	15	31	53	75

*NOTE: **Meskin** a-16, 24(2), 33, 47, 50. **Robinson/Meskin** a-6. **Leonard Starr** a-11. Photo c-13-32, 34-65. Issues 1-3 say "Designed for the More **Adult** Readers of **Comics**" on cover.*

YOUNG ROMANCE COMICS (Continued from Prize series)
National Periodical Publ.(Arleigh Publ. Corp. No. 127): No. 125, Aug-Sept, 1963 - No. 208, Nov-Dec, 1975

	GD	VG	FN	VF	VF/NM	NM-
125	8	16	24	52	99	145
126-140	5	10	15	31	53	75
141-153,156-162,165-169	4	8	12	25	40	55
154-Neal Adams-c	5	10	15	31	53	75
155-1st publ. Aragonés-s (no art)	5	10	15	30	50	70
163,164-Toth-a	4	8	12	27	44	60
170-172 (68 pg. Giants): 170-Michell from Young Love ends; Lily Martin, the Swinger begins	5	10	15	30	50	70
173-183 (52 pgs.)	4	8	12	23	37	50
184-196	3	6	9	17	26	35
197-204-(100 pgs.)	7	14	21	45	89	130
205-208	3	6	9	16	24	32

YOUNG ROMANCE: THE NEW 52 VALENTINE'S DAY SPECIAL
DC Comics: Apr, 2013 ($7.99, one-shot)

1-Short stories by various; Superman/Wonder Woman-c by Rocafort; bonus valentines 8.00

YOUNG X-MEN
Marvel Comics: May, 2008 - No. 12, May, 2009 ($2.99)

1-12: 1-Cyclops forms new team; Guggenheim-s/Paquette-a/Dodson-c. 11,12-Acuña-a 3.00

YOUR DREAMS (See Strange World of...)

YOUR HIGHNESS
Dark Horse Comics: 2011 ($7.99, one-shot)

nn-Prequel to 2011 movie; Danny McBride & Jeff Fradley-s/Phillips-a/c 8.00

YOUR PAL ARCHIE
Archie Comic Publications: Sept, 2017 - No. 5, Feb, 2018 ($3.99)

1-5-New stories with classic-style Archie gang, plus back-up reprints in #1-4 4.00

YOUR UNITED STATES
Lloyd Jacquet Studios: 1946

	GD	VG	FN	VF	VF/NM	NM-
nn-Used in **SOTI**, pg. 309,310; Sid Greene-a	29	58	87	170	278	385

YOUTHFUL HEARTS (Daring Confessions #4 on)
Youthful Magazines: May, 1952 - No. 3, Sept, 1952

	GD	VG	FN	VF	VF/NM	NM-
1- "Monkey on Her Back" swipes E.C. drug story/Shock SuspenStories #12; Frankie Laine photo on-c; Doug Wildey-a in al	43	86	129	271	461	650
2,3: 2-Vic Damone photo on-c. 3-Johnny Raye photo on-c	26	52	78	154	252	350

YOUTHFUL LOVE (Truthful Love #2)
Youthful Magazines: May, 1950

	GD	VG	FN	VF	VF/NM	NM-
1	37	74	111	222	361	500

YOUTHFUL ROMANCES
Pix-Parade #1-14/Ribage #15 on: 8-9/49 - No. 5, 4/50; No. 6, 2/51; No. 7, 5/51 - #14, 10/52; #15, 1/53 - #18, 7/53; No. 5, 9/53 - No. 9, 8/54

	GD 2.0	VG 4.0	FN 6.0	VF 8.0	VF/NM 9.0	NM- 9.2
1-(1st series)-Titled Youthful Love-Romances	39	78	117	231	378	525
2-Walter Johnson c-1-4	23	46	69	136	223	310
3-5	20	40	60	115	188	260
6,7,9-14(10/52, Pix-Parade; becomes Daring Love #15). 10(1/52)-Mel Torme photo-c/story. 12-Tony Bennett photo-c, 8pg. story & text bio.13-Richard Hayes (singer) photo-c/story; Bob & Ray photo/text story. 14-Doris Day photo/text story	18	36	54	109	172	235
8-Frank Sinatra photo/text story; Wood-c/a	27	54	81	162	266	370
15-18 (Ribage)-All have photos on-c. 15-Spike Jones photo-c/story. 16-Tony Bavaar photo-c	17	34	51	103	162	220
5(9/53, Ribage)-Les Paul & Mary Ford photo-c/story; Charlton Heston photo/text story	16	32	48	98	154	210
6-9: 6-Bobby Wayne (singer) photo-c/story; Debbie Reynolds photo/text story. 7(2/54)-Tony Martin photo-c/story; Cyd Charise photo/text story. 8(5/54)-Gordon McCrae photo-c/story. (8/54)-Ralph Flanagan (band leader) photo-c/story; Audrey Hepburn photo/text story	15	30	45	94	147	200

YTHAQ: NO ESCAPE
Marvel Comics (Soleil): 2009 - No. 3, 2009 ($5.99, limited series)

1-3-English language version of French comic; Arleston-s/Floch-a 6.00

YTHAQ: THE FORSAKEN WORLD
Marvel Comics (Soleil): 2008 - No. 3, 2009 ($5.99, limited series)

1-3-English language version of French comic; Arleston-s/Floch-a 6.00

Y: THE LAST MAN
DC Comics (Vertigo): Sept, 2002 - No. 60, Mar, 2008 ($2.95/$2.99)

	GD	VG	FN	VF	VF/NM	NM-
1-Intro. Yorick Brown; Brian K. Vaughan-s/Pia Guerra-a/J.G. Jones-c	10	20	30	69	147	225
2	3	6	9	18	27	36
3-5	1	2	3	5	6	8
6-10						5.00
11-59: 16,17-Chadwick-a. 21,22-Parlov-a. 32,39-41,48,53,54-Sudzuka-a.						3.00
60-($4.99) Final issue; sixty years in the future						6.00
... Double Feature Edition (2002, $5.95) r/#1,2	2	4	6	9	12	15
... Special Edition (2009, $1.00) r/#1, "After Watchmen" trade dress on cover						3.00
... - Cycles TPB (2003, $12.95) r/#6-10; sketch pages by Guerra						13.00
... - Girl on Girl TPB (2005, $12.99) r/#32-36						13.00
... - Kimono Dragons TPB (2006, $14.99) r/#43-48						15.00
... - Motherland TPB (2007, $14.99) r/#49-54						15.00
... - One Small Step TPB (2004, $12.95) r/#11-17						13.00
... - Paper Dolls TPB (2006, $14.99) r/#37-42						15.00
... - Ring of Truth TPB (2005, $14.99) r/#24-31						15.00
... - Safeword TPB (2004, $12.95) r/#18-23						13.00
... - Unmanned TPB (2002, $12.95) r/#1-5						15.00
... - Whys and Wherefores TPB (2008, $14.99) r/#55-60						15.00
... - The Deluxe Edition Book One HC (2008, $29.99, dustjacket) oversized r/#1-10; Guerra sketch pages						30.00
... - The Deluxe Edition Book Two HC (2009, $29.99, dustjacket) oversized r/#11-23; full script to #18						30.00
... - The Deluxe Edition Book Three HC (2010, $29.99, dustjacket) oversized r/#24-36; full script to #36						30.00
... - The Deluxe Edition Book Four HC (2010, $29.99, dustjacket) oversized r/#37-48; full script to #42						30.00
... - The Deluxe Edition Book Five HC (2011, $29.99, dustjacket) oversized r/#49-60; full script to #60						30.00

Y2K: THE COMIC
New England Comics Press: Oct, 1999 ($3.95, one-shot)

1-Y2K scenarios and survival tips 4.00

YUPPIES FROM HELL (Also see Son of...)
Marvel Comics: 1989 ($2.95, B&W, one-shot, direct sales, 52 pgs.)

1-Satire 4.00

ZAGO (..., Jungle Prince) (My Story #5 on)(See Unusual Comics)
Fox Feature Syndicate: Sept, 1948 - No. 4, Mar, 1949

	GD	VG	FN	VF	VF/NM	NM-
1-Blue Beetle app.; partial-r/Atomic #4 (Toni Luck)	79	158	237	502	864	1225
2,3-Kamen-a	65	130	195	416	708	1000
4-Baker-c	63	126	189	403	689	975

ZANE GREY'S STORIES OF THE WEST
Dell Publishing Co./Gold Key 11/64: No. 197, 9/48 - No. 996, 5-7/59; 11/64 (All painted-c)

	GD	VG	FN	VF	VF/NM	NM-
Four Color 197(#1)(9/48)	11	22	33	76	163	250
Four Color 222,230,236('49)	7	14	21	49	92	135
Four Color 246,255,270,301,314,333,346	6	12	18	37	66	95
Four Color 357,372,395,412,433,449,467,484	5	10	15	33	57	80
Four Color 511-Kinstler-a; Kubert-a	5	10	15	35	63	90

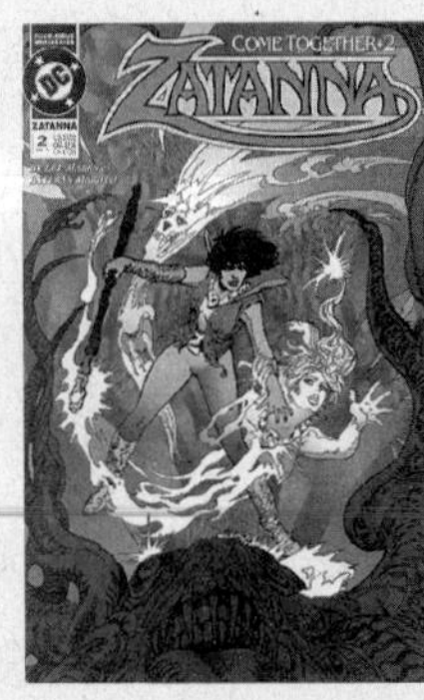

Zatanna #2 © DC

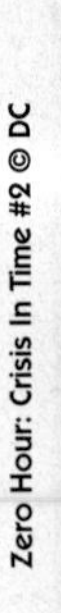

Zero Hour: Crisis In Time #2 © DC

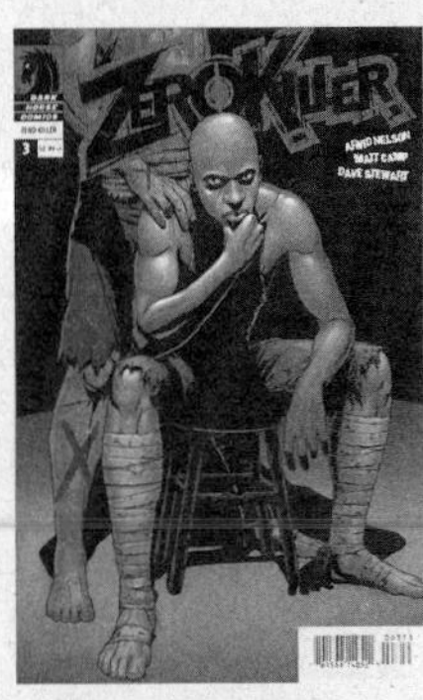

Zero Killer #3 © Arvid Nelson

	GD 2.0	VG 4.0	FN 6.0	VF 8.0	VF/NM 9.0	NM- 9.2
Four Color 532,555,583,604,616,632(5/55)	5	10	15	33	57	80
27(9-11/55) - 39(9-11/58)	4	8	12	28	47	65
Four Color 996(5-7/59)	5	10	15	33	57	80
10131-411-(11/64-G.K.)-Nevada; r/4-Color #996	3	6	9	21	33	45

ZANY (Magazine)(Satire)(See Frantic & Ratfink)
Candor Publ. Co.: Sept, 1958 - No. 4, May, 1959

1-Bill Everett-c	16	32	48	94	147	205
2-4: 4-Everett-c	12	24	36	69	97	125

ZATANNA (See Adv. Comics #413, JLA #161, Supergirl #1, World's Finest Comics #274)
DC Comics: July, 1993 - No. 4, Oct, 1993 ($1.95, limited series)

1-4						6.00
...: Everyday Magic (2003, $5.95, one-shot) Dini-s/Mays-a/Bolland-c; Constantine app.	3	6	9	19	30	40
Special 1(1987, $2.00)-Gray Morrow-c/a	1	3	4	6	8	10

ZATANNA
DC Comics: Jul, 2010 - No. 16, Oct, 2011 ($2.99)

1-Dini-s/Roux-a/c	2	4	6	8	10	12
1-Variant-c by Bolland	3	6	9	17	26	35
2-6-Variant-c by Bolland	2	4	6	10	14	18
2-10,12: 4,5,7-Hardin-a. 7-Beechen-s. 8-Chang-a						6.00
11,13,14-Hughes-c	2	4	6	10	14	18
15-Hughes-c	4	8	12	27	44	60
16-Hughes-c	5	10	15	31	53	75
...: Shades of the Past TPB (2011, $19.99) r/#7-16; cover gallery						20.00
...: The Mistress of Magic TPB (2011, $17.99) r/#1-6; variant cover gallery						18.00

ZAZA, THE MYSTIC (Formerly Charlie Chan; This Magazine Is Haunted V2#12 on)
Charlton Comics: No. 10, Apr, 1956 - No. 11, Sept, 1956

10,11	15	30	45	85	130	175

ZEALOT (Also see WildC.A.T.S: Covert Action Teams)
Image Comics: Aug, 1995 - No. 3, Nov, 1995 ($2.50, limited series)

1-3						3.00

ZEGRA (Jungle Empress) (Formerly Tegra)(My Love Life #6 on)
Fox Feature Syndicate: No. 2, Oct, 1948 - No. 5, April, 1949

2	77	154	231	493	847	1200
3-5	57	114	171	362	619	875

ZEN INTERGALACTIC NINJA
No Publisher: 1987 -1993 ($1.75/$2.00, B&W)

1	6	12	18	41	76	110
2-Copyright-Stern & Cote	3	6	9	19	30	40
3-6: Copyright-Stern & Cote	2	4	6	8	10	12
V2#1-4-($2.00)						4.00
V3#1-5-($2.95)						4.00
... :Christmas Special 1 (1992, $2.95)						4.00
... :Earth Day Special 1 (1993, $2.95)						4.00

ZEN (Intergalactic Ninja)
Zen Comics Publishing: No. 0, Apr, 2003 - No. 4, Aug, 2003 ($2.95)

0-4-Bill Maus-a/Steve Stern-s. 0-Wraparound-c						3.00

ZEN, INTERGALACTIC NINJA (mini-series)
Zen Comics/Archie Comics: Sept, 1992 - No. 3, 1992 ($1.25)(Formerly a B&W comic by Zen Comics)

1-3: 1-Origin Zen; contains mini-poster						4.00

ZEN INTERGALACTIC NINJA
Entity Comics: No. 0, June-July, 1993 - No. 3, 1994 ($2.95, B&W, limited series)

0-Gold foil stamped-c; photo-c of Zen model						5.00
1-3: Gold foil stamped-c; Bill Maus-c/a						5.00
0-(1993, $3.50, color)-Chromium-c by Jae Lee						4.00
...Sourcebook 1-(1993, $3.50)						4.00
...Sourcebook '94-(1994, $3.50)						4.00
... Spring Spectacular 1 (1994, $2.95, B&W) Gold foil logo						4.00

ZEN INTERGALACTIC NINJA: APRIL FOOL'S SPECIAL
Parody Press: 1994 ($2.50, B&W)

1-w/flip story of Renn Intergalactic Chihuahua						5.00

ZEN INTERGALACTIC NINJA COLOR
Entity Comics: 1994 - No. 7, 1995 ($2.25)

1-($3.95)-Chromium die cut-c						5.00
1, 0-($2.25)-Newsstand; Jae Lee-c; r/...All New Color Special #0						4.00
2-($2.50)-Flip book						4.00
2-($3.50)-Flip book, polybagged w/chromium trading card						5.00
3-7						4.00
Summer Special (1994, $2.95)						4.00
Yearbook: Hazardous Duty 1 (1995)						4.00
Zen-isms 1 (1995, 2.95)						4.00
Ashcan-Tour of the Universe-(no price) w/flip cover						4.00

ZEN INTERGALACTIC NINJA COMMEMORATIVE EDITION
Zen Comics Publishing: 1997 ($5.95, color)

1-Stern-s/Cote-a						6.00

ZEN INTERGALACTIC NINJA: HARD BOUNTY
1First Comics: 2015 - No. 6 ($3.99, limited series)

1-Stern-s/Mychaels-a						4.00

ZEN INTERGALACTIC NINJA MILESTONE
Entity Comics: 1994 - No. 3, 1994 ($2.95, limited series)

1-3: Gold foil logo; r/Defend the Earth						4.00

ZEN INTERGALACTIC NINJA STARQUEST
Entity Comics: 1994 - No. 6, 1995 ($2.95, B&W)

1-6: Gold foil logo						4.00

ZEN, INTERGALACTIC NINJA: THE HUNTED
Entity Comics: 1993 - No. 3, 1994 ($2.95, B&W, limited series)

1-3: Newsstand Edition; foil logo						4.00
1-($3.50)-Polybagged w/chromium card by Kieth; foil logo						5.00

ZERO GIRL
DC Comics (Homage): Feb, 2001 - No. 5, Jun, 2001 ($2.95, limited series)

1-5-Sam Kieth-s/a						3.00
TPB (2001, $14.95) r/#1-5; intro. by Alan Moore						15.00

ZERO GIRL: FULL CIRCLE
DC Comics (Homage): Jan, 2003 - No. 5, May, 2003 ($2.95, limited series)

1-5-Sam Kieth-s/a						3.00
TPB (2003, $17.95) r/#1-5						18.00

ZERO HOUR: CRISIS IN TIME (Also see Showcase '94 #8-10)
DC Comics: No. 4(#1), Sept, 1994 - No. 0(#5), Oct, 1994 ($1.50, limited series)

4(#1)-0(#5)						4.00
"Ashcan"-(1994, free, B&W, 8 pgs.) several versions exist						3.00
TPB ('94, $9.95)						10.00

ZERO KILLER
Dark Horse Comics: Jul, 2007 - No.6, Oct, 2009 ($2.99)

1-6-Arvid Nelson-s/Matt Camp-a						3.00

ZERO PATROL, THE
Continuity Comics: Nov, 1984 - No. 2 ($1.50); 1987 - No. 5, May, 1989 ($2.00)

1,2: Neal Adams-c/a; Megalith begins						5.00
1-5 (#1,2-reprints above, 1987)						4.00

ZERO TOLERANCE
First Comics: Oct, 1990 - No. 4, Jan, 1991 ($2.25, limited series)

1-4: Tim Vigil-c/a(p) (his 1st color limited series)						3.00

ZIGGY PIG – SILLY SEAL COMICS (See Animal Fun, Animated Movie-Tunes, Comic Capers, Krazy Komics, Silly Tunes & Super Rabbit)
Timely Comics (CmPL): Fall, 1944 - No. 4, Summer, 1945; No. 5, Summer, 1946; No. 6, Sept, 1946

1-Vs. the Japanese	40	80	120	246	411	575
2-(Spring, 1945)	25	50	75	150	245	340
3-5	20	40	60	117	189	260
6-Infinity-c	22	44	66	130	213	295
I.W. Reprint #1(1958)-r/Krazy Komics	2	4	6	11	16	20
I.W. Reprint #2,7,8	2	4	6	11	16	20

ZIGGY PIG – SILLY SEAL COMICS (Marvel 80th Anniversary salute)
Marvel Comics: May, 2019 ($3.99, one-shot)

1-Tieri & Cerilli-s/Chabot-a; Doctor Doom app.; Deadpool cameo						4.00

ZIP COMICS
MLJ Magazines: Feb, 1940 - No. 47, Summer, 1944 (#1-7?: 68 pgs.)

1-Origin Kalathar the Giant Man, The Scarlet Avenger, & Steel Sterling; Mr. Satan (by Edd Ashe), Nevada Jones (masked hero) & Zambini, the Miracle Man, War Eagle, Captain Valor begins	465	930	1395	3395	5998	8600
2-Nevada Jones adds mask & horse Blaze	274	548	822	1754	3002	4250
3-Biro robot-c	300	600	900	1980	3440	4900
4,5-Biro WWII-c	209	418	627	1338	2294	3250

Zip Comics #7 © MLJ

Zombie Proof #3 © Vaughn & Spencer

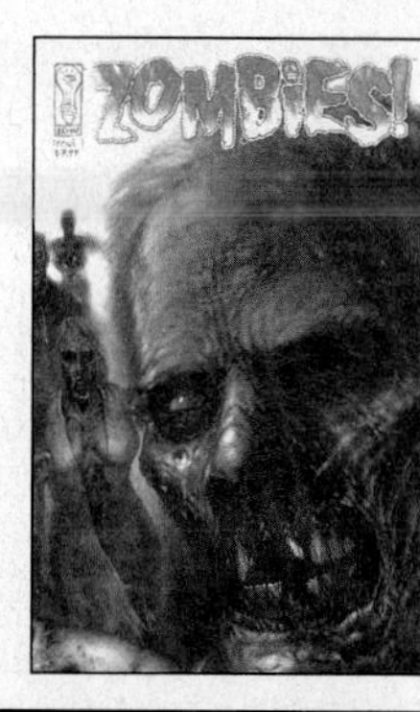

Zombies!: Feast #1 © IDW

	GD 2.0	VG 4.0	FN 6.0	VF 8.0	VF/NM 9.0	NM- 9.2
6-8-Biro-c	197	394	591	1261	2156	3050
9-Last Kalathar & Mr. Satan; classic-c	284	568	852	1818	3100	4400
10-Inferno, the Flame Breather begins, ends #13	213	426	639	1363	2332	3300
11-Inferno without costume	168	336	504	1075	1838	2600
12-Biro bondage/torture-c with dwarf ghouls	200	400	600	1280	2190	3100
13-Electrocution-c	232	464	696	1485	2543	3600
14-Biro bondage/torture guillotine-c	187	374	561	1197	2049	2900
15-Classic spider-c	229	458	687	1466	2508	3550
16-Female hanging execution-c by Biro (Rare)	239	478	717	1530	2615	3700
17-Last Scarlet Avenger; women in bondage being cooked alive-c by Biro	252	504	758	1613	2757	3900
18-Wilbur begins (9/41, 1st app.); sci-fi-c	258	516	774	1651	2826	4000
19	177	354	531	1133	1942	2750
20-Origin & 1st app. Black Jack (11/41); Hitler-c	300	600	900	2010	3505	5000
21-Sinister Nazi using lethal chemical weapons on the General-c	206	412	618	1318	2259	3200
22-Classic Nazi Grim Reaper w/sickle, V for Victory-c	459	918	1377	3350	5925	8500
23-Nazi WWII-c	155	310	465	992	1696	2400
24,25: 25-Last Nevada Jones	138	276	414	883	1517	2150
26-Classic Nazi/Japanese "Remember Pearl Harbor!" WWII cover; Black Witch begins; last Captain Valor (scarce)	290	580	870	1856	3178	4500
27-Intro. Web (7/42) plus-c app.; Japanese WWII-c	300	600	900	1920	3310	4700
28-Origin Web; classic Baron Gastapo Nazi WWII-c	271	542	813	1734	2967	4200
29-The Hyena app. (scarce); Nazi WWII-c	222	444	666	1421	2436	3450
30-WWII-c	181	362	543	1158	1979	2800
31,35-WWII-c. 35-Last Zambini, Black Jack	151	302	453	966	1658	2350
32-Classic skeleton Nazi WWII-c	284	568	852	1818	3109	4400
33-Japanese war-c showing nurses bound, blindfolded, lined up at a firing squad	177	354	531	1133	1942	2750
34-Japanese WWII bondage & hanging-c; 1st Applejack app.	245	490	735	1568	2684	3800
36-38: 38-Last Web issue	69	138	207	442	759	1075
39-Red Rube begins (origin, 8/43)	71	142	213	454	777	1100
40-43	60	120	180	381	653	925
44-46: WWII covers. 45-Wilbur ends	69	138	207	442	759	1075
47-Last issue; scarce	73	146	219	467	796	1125

NOTE: *Biro a-5, 9, 17; c-3-17.* ***Meskin*** *a-1-3, 5-7, 9, 10, 12, 13, 15, 16 at least.* ***Montana*** *c-29, 30, 32-35.* ***Novick*** *c-18-28, 31.* ***Sahle*** *c-37, 38, 40-46. Bondage c-8, 9, 33, 34. Cover features: Steel Sterling-1-43, 47; (w/ Blackjack-20-27 & Web-27-35), 28-39; (w/Red Rube-40-43); Red Rube-44-47.*

ZIP-JET (Hero)
St. John Publishing Co.: Feb, 1953 - No. 2, Apr-May, 1953

	GD 2.0	VG 4.0	FN 6.0	VF 8.0	VF/NM 9.0	NM- 9.2
1-Rocketman-r from Punch Comics; #1-c from splash in Punch #10	119	238	357	752	1306	1850
2	60	120	180	381	653	925

ZIPPY THE CHIMP (CBS TV Presents...)
Pines (Literary Ent.): No. 50, March, 1957; No. 51, Aug, 1957

	GD 2.0	VG 4.0	FN 6.0	VF 8.0	VF/NM 9.0	NM- 9.2
50,51	8	16	24	42	54	65

Z NATION (Based on the 2014 TV series on Syfy)
Dynamite Entertainment: 2017 - No. 6, 2017 ($3.99)

1-6: 1-Engler & Van Lente-s/Menna-a; multiple covers 4.00

ZODIAC STARFORCE
Dark Horse Comics: Aug, 2015 - No. 4, Feb, 2016 ($3.99, limited series)

1-4-Kevin Panetta-s/Paulina Ganucheau-a. 2-Wada-c. 4-Babs Tarr-c 4.00

ZODIAC STARFORCE: CRIES OF THE FIRE PRINCE
Dark Horse Comics: Jul, 2017 - No. 4, May, 2018 ($3.99, limited series)

1-4-Kevin Panetta-s/Paulina Ganucheau-a 4.00

ZODY, THE MOD ROB
Gold Key: July, 1970

	GD 2.0	VG 4.0	FN 6.0	VF 8.0	VF/NM 9.0	NM- 9.2
1	3	6	9	16	23	30

ZOMBIE
Marvel Comics: Nov, 2006 - No. 4, Feb, 2007 ($3.99, limited series)

1-4-Kyle Hotz-a/c; Mike Raicht-s 4.00
...: Simon Garth (1/08 - No. 4, 4/08) Hotz-s/a/c 4.00

ZOMBIE BOY
Timbuktu Graphics/Antarctic Press: Mar, 1988 - Nov, 1996 ($1.50/$2.50/$2.95, B&W)

1-Mark Stokes-s/a 4.00
...'s Hoodoo Tales (11/89, $1.50) 4.00
... Rises Again (1/94, $2.50) r/#1 and Hoodoo Tales 4.00
1-(Antarctic Press, 11/96, $2.95) new story 4.00

ZOMBIE KING
Image Comics: No. 0, June, 2005 ($2.95, B&W, one-shot)

0-Frank Cho-s/a 5.00

ZOMBIE PROOF
Moonstone: 2007 - Present ($3.50)

1-3: 1-J.C. Vaughn-s/Vincent Spencer-a; two covers by Spencer and Neil Vokes 4.00
1-Baltimore Comic-Con 2007 variant-c by Vokes (ltd. ed. of 500) 6.00
2-Big Apple 2008 Convention Edition; Tucci-c (ltd. ed. of 250) 6.00
3-Convention Edition; Beck-c (ltd. ed. of 100) 6.00
...: Zombie Zoo #1 Virginia Comicon Exclusive Edition (2012, ed. of 150) 10.00
...: Zombie Zoo - WVPOP Exclusive Edition (2012) 10.00

ZOMBIES ASSEMBLE
Marvel Comics: Jul, 2017 - No. 3, Aug, 2017 ($4.99, B&W, manga style back to front)

1-3-English translation of Avengers Japanese manga; Komiyama-s/a 5.00
#0-(9/17) Follows Tony Stark after Avengers: Age of Ultron; Komiyama-s/a 5.00

ZOMBIES ASSEMBLE 2
Marvel Comics: Oct, 2017 - No. 4, Jan, 2018 ($4.99, B&W, manga style back to front)

1-4-Continuation of story from Zombies Assemble #1-3; Komiyama-s/a 5.00

ZOMBIES CHRISTMAS CAROL (See Marvel Zombies Christmas Carol)

ZOMBIES!: ECLIPSE OF THE UNDEAD
IDW Publ.: Nov, 2006 - No. 4, Feb, 2007 ($3.99, limited series)

1-4-Torres-s/Herrera-a; two covers 4.00

ZOMBIES!: FEAST
IDW Publ.: May, 2006 - No. 5, Oct, 2006 ($3.99, limited series)

1-5: 1-Chris Bolton-a/Shane McCarthy-s. 3-Lorenzana-a 4.00

ZOMBIES!: HUNTERS
IDW Publ.: May, 2008 ($3.99)

1-Don Figueroa-a/c; Dara Naraghi-s 4.00

ZOMBIES VS. ROBOTS
IDW Publ.: Oct, 2006 - No. 2, Dec, 2006 ($3.99, limited series)

1-Chris Ryall-s/Ashley Wood-a; two covers by Wood 18.00
2 12.00

ZOMBIES VS. ROBOTS
IDW Publ.: Jan, 2015 - No. 10, Oct, 2015 ($3.99/$4.99)

1-8-Short stories by Chris Ryall-s/Ashley Wood-a and others 5.00
9,10-($4.99) Two covers on each 6.00

ZOMBIES VS. ROBOTS AVENTURE
IDW Publ.: Feb, 2010 - No. 4, May, 2010 ($3.99, limited series)

1-4-Short stories; Ryall-s; art by Matthews III, McCaffrey, & Hernandez; Wood-c 5.00

ZOMBIES VS. ROBOTS: UNDERCITY
IDW Publ.: Apr, 2011 - No. 3, Jun, 2011 ($3.99, limited series)

1-3-Chris Ryall-s/Mark Torres; two covers on each by Torres and Garry Brown 5.00

ZOMBIES VS. ROBOTS VS. AMAZONS
IDW Publ.: Sept, 2007 - No. 3, Feb, 2008 ($3.99, limited series)

1-3-Chris Ryall-s/Ashley Wood-a; two covers by Wood on each 6.00

ZOMBIE TALES THE SERIES
BOOM! Studios: Apr, 2008 - No. 12, Mar, 2009 ($3.99)

1-Niles-s; Lansdale-s/Barreto-a; two covers on each 5.00

ZOMBIE WAR
IDW Publishing: Oct, 2013 - No. 2, Nov, 2013 ($3.99, limited series)

1,2-Kevin Eastman & Tom Skulan-s/Eastman & Eric Talbot-a; 2 covers on each 4.00

ZOMBIE WORLD (one-shots)
Dark Horse Comics

... :Eat Your Heart Out (4/98, $2.95) Kelley Jones-c/s/a 4.00
... :Home For The Holidays (12/97, $2.95) 4.00

ZOMBIE WORLD: CHAMPION OF THE WORMS
Dark Horse Comics: Sept, 1997 - No. 3, Nov, 1997 ($2.95, limited series)

1-3-Mignola & McEown-c/s/a 4.00

ZOMBIE WORLD: DEAD END
Dark Horse Comics: Jan, 1998 - No. 2, Feb, 1998 ($2.95, limited series)

1,2-Stephen Blue-c/s/a 4.00

ZOMBIE WORLD: TREE OF DEATH
Dark Horse Comics: Jun, 1999 - No. 4, Oct, 1999 ($2.95, limited series)

Zoohunters #1 © Aspen MLT

Zorro: Galleon of the Dead #1 © Zorro Prods.

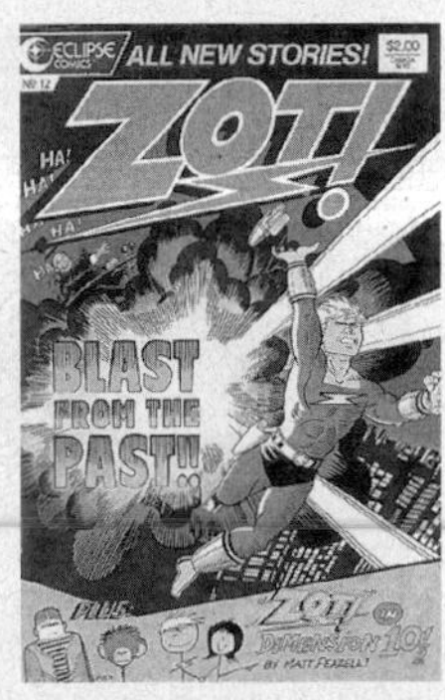

Zot! #12 © Scott McCloud

GD 2.0 | VG 4.0 | FN 6.0 | VF 8.0 | VF/NM 9.0 | NM- 9.2

1-4-Mills-s/Deadstock-a 4.00

ZOMBIE WORLD: WINTER'S DREGS
Dark Horse Comics: May, 1998 - No. 4, Aug, 1998 ($2.95, limited series)

1-4-Fingerman-s/Edwards-a 4.00

ZOO ANIMALS
Star Publications: No. 8, 1954 (15¢, 36 pgs.)

8-(B&W for coloring) 9 18 27 50 65 80

ZOO FUNNIES (Tim McCoy #16 on)
Charlton Comics/Children Comics Publ.: Nov, 1945 - No. 15, 1947

101(#1)(11/45, 1st Charlton comic book)-Funny animal; Al Fago-c 24 48 72 142 234 325
2(12/45, 52 pgs.) Classic-c 15 30 45 86 133 180
3-5 12 24 36 69 97 125
6-15: 8-Diana the Huntress app. 10 20 30 56 76 95

ZOO FUNNIES (Becomes Nyoka, The Jungle Girl #14 on?)
Capitol Stories/Charlton Comics: July, 1953 - No. 13, Sept, 1955; Dec, 1984

1-1st app.? Timothy The Ghost; Fago-c/a 13 26 39 74 105 135
2 8 16 24 44 57 70
3-7 8 16 24 40 50 60
8-13-Nyoka app. 10 20 30 54 72 90
1(1984) (Low print run) 1 2 3 4 5 7

ZOOHUNTERS, THE
Aspen MLT: Nov, 2014 - No. 4 ($3.99, limited series)

1-4-Peter Stiegerwald-s/a; five covers on each 4.00

ZOONIVERSE
Eclipse Comics: 8/86 - No. 6, 6/87 ($1.25/$1.75, limited series, Mando paper)

1-6 3.00

ZOO PARADE (TV)
Dell Publishing Co.: #662, 1955 (Marlin Perkins)

Four Color 662 5 10 15 34 60 85

ZOOM COMICS
Carlton Publishing Co.: Dec, 1945 (one-shot)

nn-Dr. Mercy, Satannas, from Red Band Comics; Capt. Milksop origin retold 48 96 144 302 514 725

ZOOT (Rulah Jungle Goddess #17 on)
Fox Feature Syndicate: nd (1946) - No. 16, July, 1948 (Two #13s & 14s)

nn-Funny animal only 30 60 90 177 289 400
2-The Jaguar app. 23 46 69 136 223 310
3(Fall, 1946) - 6-Funny animals & teen-age 15 30 45 90 140 190
7-(6/47)-Rulah, Jungle Goddess (origin/1st app.) 138 276 414 883 1517 2150
8-10 82 164 246 528 902 1275
11-Kamen bondage-c 102 204 306 653 1114 1575
12-Injury-to-eye panels, torture scene 71 142 213 454 777 1100
13(2/48) 66 132 198 419 722 1025
14(3/48)-Used in **SOTI**, pg. 104, "One picture showing a girl nailed by her wrists to trees with blood flowing from the wounds, might be taken straight from an ill. ed. of the Marquis deSade" 100 200 300 640 1095 1550
13(4/48),14(5/48)-Western True Crime #15 on? 65 130 195 416 708 1000
15,16 65 130 195 416 708 1000

ZORRO (Walt Disney with #882)(TV)(See Eclipse Graphic Album)
Dell Publishing Co.: May, 1949 - No. 15, Sept-Nov, 1961 (Photo-c 882 on)
(Zorro first appeared in a pulp story Aug 19, 1919)

Four Color 228 (#1) 21 42 63 147 324 500
Four Color 425,617,732 11 22 33 75 160 245
Four Color 497,538,574-Kinstler-a 12 24 36 79 170 260
Four Color 882-Photo-c begin;1st TV Disney; Toth-a 13 26 39 91 201 310
Four Color 920,933,960,976-Toth-a in all 10 20 30 66 138 210
Four Color 1003('59)-Toth-a 10 20 30 66 138 210
Four Color 1037-Annette Funicello photo-c 12 24 36 81 176 270
8(12-2/59-60) 7 14 21 48 89 130
9-Toth-a 8 16 24 51 96 140
10,11,13-15-Last photo-c 7 14 21 46 86 125
12-Toth-a; last 10¢ issue 8 16 24 51 96 140

NOTE: *Warren Tufts a-4-Color 1037, 8, 9, 10, 13.*

ZORRO (Walt Disney)(TV)
Gold Key: Jan, 1966 - No. 9, Mar, 1968 (All photo-c)

1-Toth-a 7 14 21 44 82 120
2,4,5,7-9-Toth-a. 5-r/F.C. #1003 by Toth 4 8 12 28 47 65
3,6-Tufts-a 4 8 12 27 44 60

NOTE: *#1-9 are reprinted from Dell issues.* ***Tufts*** *a-3, 4. #1-r/F.C. #882. #2-r/F.C. #960. #3-r/#12-c & #8 inside. #4-r/#9-c & insides. #6-r/#11(all); #7-r/#14-c. #8-r/F.C. #933 inside & back-c & #976-c. #9-r/F.C. #920.*

ZORRO (TV)
Marvel Comics: Dec, 1990 - No. 12, Nov, 1991 ($1.00)

1-12: Based on TV show. 12-Toth-c 4.00

ZORRO (Also see Mask of Zorro)
Topps Comics: Nov, 1993 - No. 11, Nov, 1994 ($2.50/$2.95)

0-(11/93, $1.00, 20 pgs.)-Painted-c; collector's ed. 3.00
1,4,6-9,11: 1-Miller-c. 4-Mike Grell-c. 6-Mignola-c. 7-Lady Rawhide-c by Gulacy. 8-Perez-c. 10-Julie Bell-c. 11-Lady Rawhide-c 4.00
2-Lady Rawhide-app. (not in costume) 5.00
3-1st app. Lady Rawhide in costume, 3-Lady Rawhide-c by Adam Hughes 2 4 6 9 12 15
5-Lady Rawhide app. 4.00
10-($2.95)-Lady Rawhide-c/app. 4.00
The Lady Wears Red (12/98, $12.95, TPB) r/#1-3 13.00
Zorro's Renegades (2/99, $14.95, TPB) r/#4-8 15.00

ZORRO
Dynamite Entertainment: 2008 - No. 20, 2010 ($3.50)

1-Origin retold; Wagner-s; three covers 3.50
2-20-Two covers on all 3.50

ZORRO: GALLEON OF THE DEAD
American Mythology Prods.: 2020 - No. 4, ($3.99, limited series)

1-3-Mike Wolfer-s/Alessandro Miracolo-a 4.00

ZORRO IN THE LAND THAT TIME FORGOT
American Mythology Prods.: 2020 - No. 4, ($3.99, limited series)

1,2-Mike Wolfer-s/Alessandro Ranaldi-a 4.00

ZORRO: LEGENDARY ADVENTURES
American Mythology Prods.: 2018 - Present ($3.99)

1-4-English reprints of French Zorro comics from 1975-1976; Robert Rigot-a 4.00
... Book 2 (2019 - No. 4, 2019, $3.99) 1-4-Art by Marcello & Rigot 4.00

ZORRO MASTERS
American Mythology Prods.: 2019 ($3.99)

1-Reprints Four Color #1003; art by Alex Toth 4.00

ZORRO MATANZAS
Dynamite Entertainment: 2010 - No. 4, 2010 ($3.99, limited series)

1-4-Mayhew-a/McGregor-s 4.00

ZORRO RIDES AGAIN
Dynamite Entertainment: 2011 - No. 12, 2012 ($3.99)

1-12: 1-6-Wagner-s/Polls-a. 7-12-Snyder III-a. 10-Lady Zorro on cover 4.00

ZORRO: RISE OF THE OLD GODS
American Mythology Prods.: 2019 - No. 4, 2019 ($3.99, limited series)

1-4-Jason Pell-s/Puis Calzada-a. 1-Main cover by Kaluta 4.00

ZORRO: SACRILEGE
American Mythology Prods.: 2019 - No. 4 ($3.99, limited series)

1-4: 1,2-Mike Wolfer-s/Mauricio Melo-a. 1-Main cover by Kaluta. 3,4-Miracolo-a 4.00

ZORRO: SWORDS OF HELL
American Mythology Prods.: 2018 - No. 4, 2019 ($3.99, limited series)

1-4-David Avallone-s/Roy Allan Martinez-a 4.00

ZORRO TIMELESS TALES
American Mythology Prods.: 2020 ($3.99, limited series)

1,2-Nadaud-s/Marcello-a; art in the style of the Toth stories 4.00

ZOT!
Eclipse Comics: 4/84 - No. 10, 7/85; No. 11, 1/87 - No. 36 7/91 ($1.50, Baxter-p)

1 5.00
2,3 4.00
4-10: 4-Origin. 10-Last color issue 3.00
10½ (6/86, 25¢, Not Available Comics) Ashcan; art by Feazell & Scott McCloud 4.00
11-14,15-35-($2.00-c) B&W issues 3.00
14½ (Adventures of Zot! in Dimension 10½)(7/87) Antisocialman app. 3.00
36-($2.95-c) B&W 5.00
... The Complete Black and White Collection TPB (2008, $24.95) r/#11-36 with commentary, interviews and bonus artwork 25.00

Z-2 COMICS (Secret Agent...)(See Holyoke One-Shot #7)

ZULU (See Movie Classics)

Bill Hughes
Paid You How Much?

972-539-9190

CALL NOW FOR IMMEDIATE PAYMENT!!

ALWAYS SEEKING:

Golden-Age, Silver-Age, & Bronze-Age Comics
Vintage Original Comic & Collector Card Art
Vintage Baseball Cards & Uncut Sheets
Movie Posters & Stills
Western, Sci-Fi, and Comedy Collectibles
Vintage Toys in Original Boxes
Vintage Disneyana & Other Animation
Original Comic Art

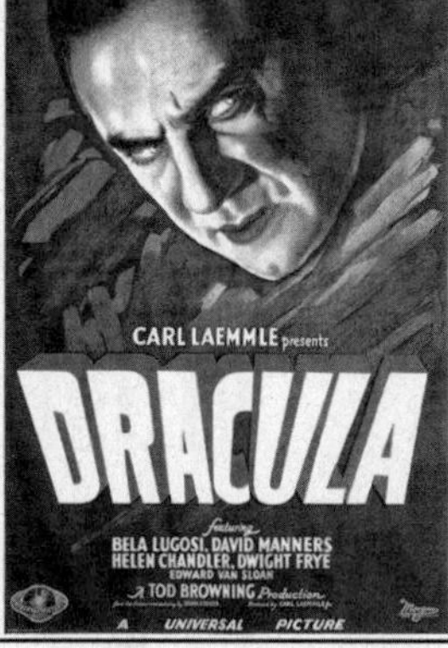

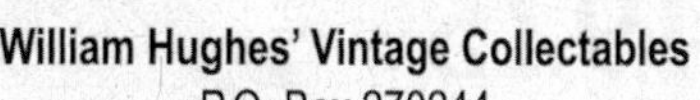

William Hughes' Vintage Collectables
P.O. Box 270244
Flower Mound, Texas 75027
Office: 972-539-9190
Mobile: 973-432-4070

CGC
Comics Guaranty, LLC
CHARTER MEMBER DEALER

Senior Advisor Overstreet Price Guide

www.VintageCollectables.net
Email: whughes199@yahoo.com
eBay User: comic-warehouse

FANTASY
ILLUSTRATED

THE DOMINO LADY'S DOUBLE
Mystery Adventure Magazine
Mysterious Island
RICHARD B. SALE
SAUCY MOVIE
"Shark!"
Mystery Adventure Magazine
A Zenith Rand Story by Richard Tooker
THE SPIDER
MASTER OF MEN!
BLACK MASK
"THE TENTH CLUE"

SPICY MYSTERY STORIES
BATMAN
by Lew Merrill
THE SECRET 6
THE GOLDEN ALLIGATOR
WEIRD TALES
THE UNIQUE MAGAZINE
"OOZE"
The Tale of A Thousand Thrills

GEMSTONE
PUBLISHING

World's Greatest Comics

Celebrating
10 YEARS!

5974 Westerville Rd, Westerville, OH 43081

Just minutes from downtown Columbus

(614) 891-3000 * www.wgcomics.com

If you are looking to sell your collection, call us first! We will work with you, and make you a competitive offer that is fair to both of us.

We buy comics of all types and all ages, from the 1930's to Present day! We won't cherry pick your collection. If you have books we need, we'll buy it all, so you're not stuck with the leftovers!

Call us before you sell to the big used bookstore chain! Comic books are what we do, and *not* just a sideline! In addition, our staff has *over 80 years* combined experience in the comic book retail field.

Worried about answering an anonymous ad and meeting up with a stranger in a parking lot? We're an established, full-time place of business, and we'll gladly look at your collection in-store, or travel to your location, in or out of Ohio, to view quality collections. For a fast response, message us on Faceboook, or **call Jeff or Keith at (614) 891-3000**.

BUSINESS CARD ADS

To have your ads seen here in future editions, contact our Advertising Dept. Gemstone Publishing, Inc. 10150 York Rd., Suite 300 Hunt Valley, MD 21030 or e-mail feedback@gemstonepub.com.

ALWAYS BUYING COMICS .COM

Top Five Selection on the Web!

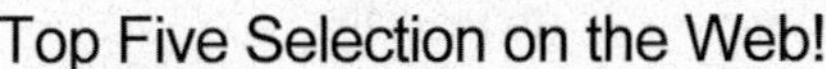

NEW COLLECTIONS in the House!
EASY-TO-USE, secure WEBSITE!
FREE SHIPPING w/ $75 order!

info@houseofcomics.com Call us at (510) 847-3376

www.HouseofComics.com

30% OFF ALL COMIC BOOKS WITH MEMBERSHIP

BEST COMICS INTERNATIONAL
(Est.1991)

•COMIC BOOKS•BACK ISSUES
•GRAPHIC NOVELS•TOYS•STATUES
•SPORTS MEMORABILIA

1300 JERICHO TURNPIKE NEW HYDE PARK, NY 11040
Phone: 516-328-1900 WWW.BESTCOMICS.COM

COMIC BOOKS*STAMPS*MAGAZINES*ART
BUYING & SELLING

EBAY ID: CLASSICBOOKS 646.408.5365
CLBKSCOM@GMAIL.COM

BATMAN WONDER WOMAN COLLECTORS

E-mail: batt90@aol.com
wwali@aol.com

COLLECTORS
P.O. Box 604925
Flushing, NY 11360-4925

The lowest prices in Kentucky and Tennessee on New & Back Issue Comic Books, Graphic Novels, Trade Paperbacks & more!

Since 1977

SPECIALIZING IN BUYING LARGE COLLECTIONS!
(At our place our yours; we travel for large acquisitions)

Largest selection of Back Issue Comic Books in Kentucky or Tennessee (100,000+)

ALL NEW COMICS, GRAPHIC NOVELS & TRADE PAPERBACKS DISCOUNTED

FREE SUBSCRIPTION SERVICE
(No minimum or advance deposit required.)

2 Store Locations in Kentucky: Louisville * Bowling Green
3 Stores in Middle Tennessee: Nashville * Madison * Murfreesboro

Call individual store locations or check online for our hours.
www.TheGreatEscapeOnLine.com

DIRECTORY LISTINGS

(PAID ADVERTISING - STORE LISTINGS)

You can have your store listed here for very reasonable rates. Send for details for next year's Guide. The following list of stores have paid to be included in this list. We cannot assume any responsibility in your dealings with these shops. This list is provided for your information only. When planning trips, it would be advisable to make appointments in advance. Remember, to get your shop included in the next edition, contact us for rates.

Gemstone Publishing, Inc.
10150 York Rd., Suite 300
Hunt Valley, MD 21030
E-MAIL: feedback@gemstonepub.com

Items stocked by these shops are noted at the end of each listing and are coded as follows:

(1) Golden Age Comics
(2) Silver Age Comics
(3) Bronze Age Comics
(4) New Comics & Magazines
(5) Back Issue magazines
(6) Comic Supplies
(7) Collectible Card Games
(8) Role Playing Games
(9) Gaming Supplies
(10) Manga
(11) Anime
(12) Underground Comics
(13) Original Comic Art
(14) Pulps
(15) Big Little Books
(16) Books - Used
(17) Books - New
(18) Comic Related Posters
(19) Movie Posters
(20) Trading Cards
(21) Statues/Mini-busts, etc.
(22) Premiums (Rings, Decoders)
(23) Action Figures
(24) Other Toys
(25) Records/CDs
(26) DVDs/VHS
(A) Doctor Who Items
(B) Simpsons Items
(C) Star Trek Items
(D) Star Wars Items
(E) HeroClix

ALABAMA

Collector's Corner
700 C East Glenn Avenue
Auburn, AL 36830
(334) 821-1772
aucomics1@gmail.com
(2-4, 6, 7)

Bob's Comics
979 Gadsden Highway
Birmingham, AL 35235
(205) 833-6914
comicbkbob@aol.com
(1-6)

Sanctum Tattoos and Comics
4410 4th Avenue S #B
Birmingham, AL 35222
(205) 201-6862
sanctumtattoosandcomics@gmail.com
www.sanctumtattoosandcomics.com
(2-6, 10, 12)

Camelot Books and Comics
207 3rd Street SW
Cullman, AL 35055
(256)736-2622
camelotbooksandcomics@gmail.com
www.camelotbooksandcomics.com
(2-10, 14, 16-18, 20, 21, 23, D, E)

Dragon Quills
506 Broad Street
Gadsden, AL 35901
(256) 549-1979
farfirecomics@gmail.com
(1-8, 10, 12, 18, 21)

The Deep, Comics & Games
2310 Memorial Pkwy SW
Huntsville, AL 35801
(256) 532-1292
e.walls@deepcomics.com
www.deepcomics.com
(1-4, 6-10, 18, 20-24, A, C-E)

Haven Comics
1871 Slaughter Rd, Suite F
Madison, AL 35758
(256) 430-0505
havencomicsetc@gmail.com
www.havencomics.com
(1-4, 6, 8, 9, 13, 21, D)

ALASKA

Aegis Comics of Alaska
500 E Swanson Avenue, Suite 2
Wasilla, AK 99654
(907) 376-3400
admin@aegisofalaska.com
https://aegiscomicsalaska.com
(1-6, 10, 12-18, 20, 21, 23, 24, D, E)

ARKANSAS

Arkham Comics
514 W Main Street
Blytheville, AR 72315
(870) 776-1021
arkham_comics@yahoo.com
arkhamcomics.weebly.com
(3, 4, 6, 10, 16, 18, 21, 23, 24, A, C-E)

ARIZONA

Samurai Comics Chandler
1994 N Alma School Rd
Chandler, AZ 85224
(480) 855-2919
samuraicomicschandler@gmail.com
www.samuraicomics.com
1-15, 17-21, 23-26, A-E

Samurai Comics West
6808 N. Dysart Rd.
Glendale, AZ 85307
(623) 872-8886
glendale@samuraicomics.com
www.samuraicomics.com
(1-12, 15, 17-21, 23, 24, A-E)

Limited Edition Comics
2156 McCulloch Blvd. N. 7
Lake Havasu City, AZ 86403
(928) 486-7843
limitededitioncomics@hotmail.com
www.LimitedEditionComics.com
(1-4, 6, 10, 15, 23, 24, E)

Gotham City Comics and Collectibles
46 West Main Street
Mesa, AZ 85201
(480) 649-3065
batcavecomic.com
(1-26, A-E)

Samurai Comics East
1120 S. Country Club Drive
Mesa, AZ 85210
(480) 962-1123
mesa@samuraicomics.com
www.samuraicomics.com
(1-2, 18-21, 23, 24, A-E)

Samurai Comics
1602 E. Indian School Rd.
Phoenix, AZ 85016
(602) 265-8886
phoenix@samuraicomics.com
www.samuraicomics.com
(1-15, 17-21, 23, 24, A-E)

Fantastic Worlds Comics
9393 N 90th Street, Suite 119
Scottsdale, AZ 85258
(480) 256-1454
bill@fantasticworldscomics.com
www.fantasticworldscomics.com
1-7, 10-16, 18, 20-24, A-E)

Brandon's Comics
1833 E Southern Avenue
Tempe, AZ 85282
(480) 438-4779
brandonscomics@gmail.com
www.brandonscomics.com
(1-4, 6, 18)

CALIFORNIA

The Comic Cellar
135 W. Main Street
Alhambra, CA 91801
(626) 570-8743
comiccellar@comiccellar.com
www.comiccellar.com
(1-6, 10, 12-15, 18, D, E)

Atomic Comics
11414 Artesia Blvd, Suite B
Artesia, CA 90701
(562) 319-7572
atomiccomics18@gmail.com
(2-4, 6-11, 18, 20, 21, 23, 24, D, E)

Worlds of Wonder
4005 Manzanita Ave.
Ste. 6 #219
Carmichael, CA 95608
(480) 310-1172
worldsofwondercomics
@yahoo.com
worldsofwondercomics.com
(1-5, 12-14, 16, 23, 24)

Crush Comics
2869 Castro Valley Blvd
Castro Valley, CA 94546
(510) 581-4779
crush@crushcomics.com
crushcomics.com
(2-10, 18, 20, 21, 23, 24, E)

Bat Comics & Games
218 Broadway Street
Chico, CA 95928
(530) 898-0550
bat@batcomics.com
www.batcomics.com
(2-4, 6-10, 13, 18,-21, 23, 24, A, C-E)

Collectors Ink
2593 State Hwy 32
Chico, CA 95973
(530) 345-0958
collectorsink@ymail.com
(1-10, 12-24, A-E)

Flying Colors Comics & Other Cool Stuff
2980 Treat Blvd
Concord, CA 94518
(925) 825-5410
coolstuff@flyingcolorscomics.com
FlyingColorsComics.com
(1-6, 10, 17, 18, E)

Metahumans Comics
444 North Imperial Avenue
El Centro, CA 92243
(949) 444-9955
metahumanshq@gmail.com
www.metahumanscomics.com
(1-24, 26, B, D, E)

Treasure Island Comics
37244 Fremont Blvd
Fremont, CA 94536
(510) 744-9287
alex@treasureislandcomics.com
treasureislandcomics.com
(2, 4, 6)

Heroes Comics
110 E Shaw Avenue
Fresno, CA 93710
(559) 229-4376
heroes@pacbell.net
heroes-comics.com
(1-7, 10, 12, 18, 21, 23, E)

Legacy Comics and Cards
123 W. Wilson Ave.
Glendale, CA 91203
PH: (818) 247-8803
FAX: (818) 247-2328
LegacyComics@hotmail.com
www.LegacyComics.com
(1-10, 12, 18, 20, 21, 23, D, E)

Comic Cult HD
9594 I Avenue, Suite F
Hesperia, CA 92345
(760) 998-2730
comicculthd@gmail.com
(1-4, 6, 7, 21, 23, D, E)

Horizon Comics and Collectibles
42156 10th Street West, Unit K
Lancaster, CA 93534
(661) 206-7168
horizoncomicsllc@gmail.com
www.horizoncomics.com
(2-7, 9-12, 18, 20, 21, 23, 24, D, E)

Alternate Universe
1498 W Sunset Blvd, Suite 1
Los Angeles, CA 90026
(213) 537-0992
altversela@gmail.com
facebook.com/altversela
(2-10, 15-17, 20, 21, 23, 24, A-E)

Golden Apple Comics
7018 Melrose Avenue
Los Angeles, CA 90038
(323) 658-6047
goldenappleonine@gmail.com
www.goldenapplecomics.com
(1-24, A-E)

Comics Plus
547 I Street
Los Banos, CA 93635
(209) 827-8847
lb.comicsplus@att.net
(2-4, 6-11, 18-21, 23-26, D, E)

Terry's Comics
P.O. Box 2065
Orange, CA 92859
PH: (714) 288-8993
FAX: (714) 288-8992
info@TerrysComics.com
www.TerrysComics.com
(1-3,5,6,12-16,18,19)

ArchAngels
4629 Cass Street #9
Pacific Beach, CA 92109
PH: (310) 480-8105
rhughes@archangels.com
www.archangels.com

Funny Business
896 N. Garey Avenue
Pomona, CA 91768
(909) 868-1974
samanieg@verizon.net
fbcomicshop.com
(2-6, 10, 12, 18, 23)

Now Or Never Comics
1055 F Street
San Diego, CA 92101
(619) 892-7310
aaron@nowornevercomics.com
nowornevercomics.com
(1-6, 8, 10, 12, 16, 20, 21, 23, 24, A-E)

Amazing Fantasy
650 Irving Street
San Francisco, CA 94122
(415) 681-4344
amazingfantasy00@aol.com
amazingfantasy.com
(1-7, 12-14, 17, 18, 20, 21, 23, 24, A-E)

SpaceCat
1415 West San Carlos Street
San Jose, CA 95126
(408) 280-7257
Sales@SuperSpaceCat.com
www.SuperSpaceCat.com
(1-19, 21-26, A-E)

Captain Nemo Comics
563 Higuera Street
San Luis Obispo, CA 93401
(805) 503-9400
captainnemo@captainnemo.biz
www.facebook.com/
CaptainNemoGames
(1-12, 18, 21, 23, 25, 26, C, D)

Knowhere Games and Comics
744 Grand Avenue, Suite 102
San Marcos, CA 92078
(760) 891-8333
www.
KnowhereGamesAndComics.
com
(2-14, 16-18, 20,-24, A-E)

Atlantis Fantasyworld
1020 Cedar Street
Santa Cruz, CA 95060
(831) 426-0158
joe@atlantisfantasyworld.com
(1-10, 18, 21, 23, 24, A-E)

Waterfront Comics
609 Main Street
Suisun City, CA 94585
(707) 425-6308
(3-6, 9, 12, 21, 23, A-E)

The Boys of Summer
490 Merchant Street #103
Vacaville, CA 95688
(707) 448-0833
kmbrown62.kb@gmail.com
(4, 6, 20, 23, C-E)

Undercity Comics
12920 Philadelphia Street
Whittier, CA 90603
(562) 696-1718
contactundercity@gmail.com
www.undercitycomics.com
(4, 6, 8-10, 17, 20, 21, 23, 24, A-E)

COLORADO

All C's Collectibles
1250 S Abilene Street
Aurora, CO 80012
(303) 751-6882
allcs@comcast.net
allcscollectibles.com
(1-10, 12, 18-21, 23-25, B-E)

Time Warp Comics
3105 28th Street
Boulder, CO 80301
(303) 443-4500
timewarp1@time-warp.com
time-warp.com
(2-10, 12, 18, 20, 21, 23, A-E)

Heroes and Dragons
4408 Austin Bluffs Parkway
Colorado Springs, CO 80918
(719) 388-9524
heroesanddragons@q.com
http://heroesanddragonscom-
ics.com
(4, 6, 7-9, 12, 17, 18, 23, A, C, E)

KaPow Comics & Coffee
4239 N. Nevada Avenue
Suite 100
Colorado Springs, CO 80907
(719) 896-4376
contact@
kapowcomicsandcoffee.com
kapowcomicsandcoffee.com
(1-6, 10, 15-17, 21, 23, 24, A, C-E)

Muse Comics + Games
1338 N Academy Blvd
Colorado Springs, CO 80909
(719) 573-7096
musecomicsco@gmail.com
www.musecomicscolorado.com
(1-4, 6-10, 16, 17, 21-24, A-E)

Beeda's Thingamajigits
153 N College Avenue
Fort Collins, CO 80524
(970) 443-1493
info@beedasthingamajigits.com
BeedasThingamajigits.com
(1-4, 6-10, 12, 21, 23, 24, D, E)

Tesseract Comics & Games
809 Grand Avenue, Suite 1
Glenwood Springs, CO 81601
(970) 945-9017
tesseractcomicsandgames@
gmail.com
www.tesseractcomicsandgames.
com
(2-4, 6-8, 9, 12, 13, 21, 24, D, E)

RTS Unlimited, Inc.
P. O. Box 150412
Lakewood, CO 80215-0412
PH: (303) 403-1840
FAX: (303) 403-1837
RTSUnlimitedinc@gmail.com
www.RTSUnlimited.com
(1-3, 5, 6, 12, 13, 18, 19)

Aamazing Fantasy Comics
6721 W Ken Caryl Avenue
Littleton, CO 80128
(303) 933-4604
shawno01@aol.com
AamazingFantasyComics.com
(2-7, 10, 12)

Eagle Valley Music & Comics
211 Main Street
PO Box 69
Minturn, CO 81645-0069
(970) 476-1713
tom122863@aol.com
https://www.facebook.com/vinylcomicscdsandmore
(2-5, 10, 23, 25, 26, E)

Hall of Justice Comics
10136 Parkglenn Way #115
Parker, CO 80134
(303) 484-9103
hojcomics@gmail.com
www.hallofjusticecomics.com
(1-6, 12, 13, 23, 24, D, E)

Hero Headquarters
8757 Sheridan Blvd
Westminster, CO 80003
(303) 426-0768
herohq@comcast.net
(1-12, 16-21, 23, 24, A-E)

Heroes and Horrors Games
1215 Main Street, Unit B
Windsor, CO 80550
(970) 833-5128
hnhgames@gmail.com
(4, 6, 10, 21, E)

CONNECTICUT

Matt's Sportscards and Comics
348 Hazard Avenue
Enfield, CT 06082
(860) 803-1965
campanime@ymail.com
cardandcomicshop.com
(1-13, 15, 18, 20, 21, 23, 24, A-E)

Heroes Comics & Cards
194 Main Street, Suite 1
Norwalk, CT 06851-3502
(203) 750-0505
heroescomics95@gmail.com
www.heroescomicsandcards.com
(1-7, 9, 12, 13, 18, 20, 21, 23, 24, A-E)

Heroes & Hitters
1845 Silas Deane Hwy
Rocky Hill, CT 06067
(860) 529-8824
Fax: (860) 760-8044
waynehorgan@gmail.com
www.facebook.com/heroescomics
(2-6, 18, C, D,)

Boom Tube Comics, LLC
1475 Meriden Waterbury Turnpike
Southington, CT 06479
(203) 537-2755
requests@boomtubecomics.com
boomtubecomics.com
(1-7, 17, 18, 20, 21, 23, 24, E)

DJ's Comics
116 North Plains Industrial Road
Wallingford, CT 06492
(203) 294-1576
djscomics@snet.net
(2-4, 6, 21, 23, 26, E)

Richie's Comic Cabana
96 Store Avenue
Waterbury, CT 06705-1429
(203) 597-1952
cabanaman40@comcast.net
richies-comic-cabana.com
(1-4, 6, 7, 12, 20, 21, 23, D, E)

DELAWARE

Ogre's Grove
129 Union Street
Milton, DE 19968
(302) 643-2125
Ogresgrove@gmail.com
www.OgresGrove.com
(2-6, 10-12, 19-24, 26, C-E)

Comicmania
4381 Kirkwood Highway
Wilmington, DE 19808
(302) 995-1971
mycomicmania@gmail.com
www.mycomicmania.com
(1-4, 6, 7, 9, 21, 23, E)

FLORIDA

Emerald City
4902 113th Ave. N
Clearwater, FL 33760
(727) 398-2665
email@emeraldcitycomics.com
emeraldcitycomics.com
(1-13, 15, 17, 18, 20-24, A-E)

Wonder Water Cards & Comics
29113 US Highway 19 N
Clearwater, FL 33761-2408
(727) 799-4855
roberto.wonderwater@gmail.com
(4, 6, 7, 9, 20, 21, E)

Windu's Comics & Collectibles, LLC
194 N. Highway 27
Suite A
Clermont, FL 34711
(352) 404-6452
winducomicworld@aol.com
(1-13, 15-19, 21, 23, 24, A-E)

Docking Bay 94 Comics and Games
7710 NW 56th Way
Suite 100
Coconut Creek, FL 33073
(954) 427-1694
comicsandgames@comcast.net
www.comicsandgames.com
(2, 4, 6-10, 18, 19, 21, 23, D, E)

Cliff's Books
209 N Woodland Boulevard
Deland, FL 32720
cliffsbooksdeland@gmail.com
Cliffsbooks.net
(1-6, 8, 9, 12, 14-16, 19, 24-26, D)

All Star Sportscards & Comics
7241 NW 4th Boulevard
Gainesville, FL 32607
(352) 372-2700
comicartfiend@yahoo.com
www.facebook.com/allstar-sportscardsandcomics
(1-5, 7, 8, 12, 20, 21, 23, D)

Mythical Mountain
11570 San Jose Boulevard
Suite 13
Jacksonville, FL 32223
(904) 680-1308
kathy@mythicalmountain.com
mythicalmountain.com
(1-11, 13, 17-24, A-E)

Phil's Comic Shoppe
6950 NW 14 Place
Margate, FL 33063
(954) 977-6947
philscomix@att.net
www.ebay.com/usr/philscomicshop
(2-7, 10, 12, 13, 20)

Kingdom of Comics
4320 S. Babcock Street #104
Melbourne, FL 32904
(321) 600-4567
info@kingdomofcomics.com
www.kingdomofcomics.com
(1-13, 16-18, 21, 23, 24, D, E)

The Book Exchange & Comic Book Shop
807 Northlake Boulevard
North Palm Beach, FL 33401
(561) 863-1555
bookexchange2001@hotmail.com
www.facebook.com/TheBookExchangeAndComicShop
(1-6, 10, 12, 14-21, 23-26, A-E)

Epic Comics, LLC
570 N Alafaya Trail
Suite 106C
Orlando, FL 32828
(407) 730-3742
epic.comics.orlando0@gmail.com
www.epiccomicsonline.com
(2-4, 6, 7, 10, 18, 21, 23, A, C-E)

Gods & Monsters
5421 International Drive
Orlando, FL 32819
(407) 270-6273
info@godmonsters.com
www.godmonsters.com
(1-4, 6-13, 17-19, 21-24, 26, A-E)

Cloak & Dagger Comics and Games
729 South Nova Road
Ormond Beach, FL 32174
(386) 672-4980
TheIrishJP@yahoo.com
Cloakanddaggercomicsonline.com
(1-9, 12, 14, 18, 20, 21, 23, 24, A-E)

Yancy Street Comics
9409 US Highway 19, 381-A
Port Richey, FL 34668
(727) 817-0888
yancystreetllc@gmail.com
www.yancystreetcomics.com
(1-6, 10, 11, 13, 15, 18-21, 23, 24, A-E)

Comic Central
1425 WP Ball Boulevard
Sanford, FL 32771
(407) 321-5111
www.comic-central.com
(2-4, 6-10, 18, 19, 21, 23, D, E)

Classic Collectible Services
P.O. Box 4738
Sarasota, FL 34230
PH: (855) CCS-1711
CCSpaper.com

CGC
P.O. Box 4738
Sarasota, FL 34230
PH: (877) NM-COMIC
FAX: (941) 360-2558
www.CGCcomics.com

The Dark Side
935 N Beneva Road
Suite 902
Sarasota, FL 34232
(941) 360-0840
contact@darksidecomics.com
www.darksidecomics.com
(1-12, 15, 17-19, 21, 23, 24, A-E)

World of Comics
2133 South Ridgewood Avenue
South Daytona, FL 32119-3015
(386) 760-0555
slawsonm@att.net
(1-6, 8-12, 16, 18, 20-23, 25, 26, A, C, D)

Cosmic Cat Comics
625 Industrial Drive
Tallahassee, FL 32310
(850) 224-5554
cosmiccatcomics@gmail.com
www.facebook.com/CosmicCatComics
(1-6, 10-13, 16, 17, 21, 23, 24, A, C-E)

David T. Alexander Collectibles
P.O. Box 273086
Tampa, FL 33618
PH: (813) 968-1805
davidt@cultureandthrills.com
www.dtacollectibles.com
(1-3, 5, 12-15, 18-20, 22, 24, C, D)

Yancy Street Comics South
13944 West Hillsborough Avenue
Tampa, FL 33635
(813) 336-4974
yancystsouth@yahoo.com
www.facebook.com/YancyStComicsSouth
(1-6, 8, 10, 12, 21, 23, 24, D, E)

Pedigree Comics, Inc.
12541 Equine Lane
Wellington, FL 33414
PH/FAX: (561) 422-1120
CELL: (561) 596-9111
E-Mail: DougSchmell@pedigreecomics.com
www.pedigreecomics.com

Famous Faces and Funnies
3020 W New Haven Avenue
West Melbourne, FL 32904
(321) 259-3575
FFFcomics@gmail.com
FFFComics.Com
(2-4, 6, 10, 11, 21, 23, 24, A, C-E)

Doombrowski Games & Comics
6260 Cypress Gardens Boulevard
Winter Haven, FL 33884
(863) 324-1323
owner@doombrowski.com
www.doombrowski.com
(2-10, 16, 17, 20, 21, 24, A, C-E)

GEORGIA

Top Dog Comics LLC
3309 Washington Road
Augusta, GA 30907
(706) 650-5737
topdogcomicsllc@gmail.com
www.topdogcomics.com
(1-11, 15, 20, 21, 23, 24, C-E)

Galactic Quest
4264 Sudderth Road
Buford, GA 30518
(770) 614-4804
kyle@galacticquest.com
www.galacticquest.com
(1-10, 13, 18-21, 23, 24, D, E)

Dragons Eye Game & Hobby
116 Riverstone Parkway
Canton, GA 30114
(770) 213-8120
dragonseyegames2033@gmail.com
www.facebook.com/profile.php?id=100057834811860
(4, 7-11, 16, 17, 20, 21, 25, 26)

Quest Comic Shop
225 Lovvorn Road
Carrollton, GA 30117
(770) 832-0172
greg@questcomicshop.com
questcomicshop.com
(6-10, 17-19, 21)

Galactic Quest
116 East Crogan Street
Lawrenceville, GA 30046
(770) 339-3001
galacticquestcomics@gmail.com
www.galacticquest.com
(1-4, 6-10, 13, 18, 19, 21, 23, 24, D, E)

Dr. No's Comics & Games SuperStore
3372 Canton Road
Suite 104
Marietta, GA 30066
(770) 422-4642
manager@drnos.com
www.drnos.com
(1-11, 16-19, 21, 22-24, A, C-E)

Great Escape Comics and Games
1050 East Piedmont Road
Suite 106
Marietta, GA 30114
(770) 973-2253
greatescapecomics@gmail.com
www.greatescapecomics.com
(2-10, 20, 21, 23, D)

Neighborhood Comics
1205 Bull Street
Savannah, GA 31401
(912) 349-3095
team@neighborhoodcomics.com
neighborhoodcomics.com
(1-6, 10, 12, 13, 18, 21-24, B, D)

Galactic Comics & Games
21 E Vine Street
Statesboro, GA 30458
(912) 489-3123
galacticcg@gmail.com
galacticcg.com
(2-10, 18-21, 23, 24, A-E)

Infinite Realities Comics
5007 Lavista Road
Tucker, GA 30084-3512
(470) 359-5988
infiniterealitiescomics@gmail.com
(1-10, 12, 15)

Fantasy Factory
257 North Hamilton Street
Dalton, GA 30720
orders@fantasyfactory.com
www.fantasyfactory.com
(1-6, 8, 24, C, D)

Fanboy Collectibles & Comics
5854 Columbus Road, Suite 4
Macon, GA 31206
(478) 216-7820
fanboycollectiblescomics@gmail.com
www.fanboycollectiblescomics.com
(1-9, 20, 21, 23, 24, 26, A, C-E)

Origin Story Comics
569 Jonesboro Road
McDonough, GA 30253
(678) 565-4886
originstorycomics@gmail.com
(2-4, 6, 10, 18, 21)

HAWAII

Enjoy Comics
111 E. Puainako Street
#612
Hilo, HI 96720
(808) 494-8047
enjoycomicshilo@gmail.com
www.facebook.com/EnjoyComicsHilo
(1-13, 15, 18-24, A-E)

IDAHO

Safari Pearl
660 W Pullman Road
Moscow, ID 83843
(208) 882-9499
safaripearl@moscow.com
www.safaripearl.com
(2-4, 6-10)

Cosmic Comics, Games & Collectibles
132 W Main Street
Belleville, IL 62220
(618) 416-3115
cosmiccomicsbelleville@gmail.com
cosmiccomicsbelleville.com
(1-10, 12-18, 20, 21, 23-25, A, C-E)

ILLINOIS

Alternate Reality Inc.
3149 West 111th Street
Chicago, IL 60655
(773) 881-4376
arcomics@msn.com
myalternatereality.com
(2-10, 12, 17-19, 23, A-E)

Atlas Comics, Inc.
5251 N. Harlem Avenue
Chicago, IL 60656
(708) 453-2110
atlas@acomics.com
atlas@acomics.com
(1-6, 12, 21-24, C)

First Aid Comics
1617 E. 55th Street
Chicago, IL 60615
(773) 752-6642
firstaidchicago@gmail.com
www.firstaidcomics.com
(2-10, 12, 23, 24)

Amazing Fantasy Comics
20505 S. LaGrange Road
Frankfort, IL 60423
(815) 469-5092
www.afbooks.com
(2, 4, 6-10, 17, 21, 23, 24, E)

Amazing Fantasy Comics
113 E 9th Street
Lockport, IL 60441
(815) 834-1658
contact_us@moonstonebookscom
www.afbooks.com
(2, 4, 6-10, 14, 17, 21, 23, E)

Fox Comics & Games
108 E. Paradise Alley
Marion, IL 62959
(618) 364-0800
foxcomicsandgames@hotmail.com
(1-4, 6-10, 12, 13, 16-18, 20-24, A, C-E)

One Stop Comics
111 South Ridgeland
Oak Park, IL 60302
(708) 524-2287
onestopcomics@sbcglobal.net
onestopcomics.net
(1-21, 23, 24, A-E)

Beyond Tomorrow Comics & Cards
327 N. Northwest Highway
Palatine, IL 60067
(847) 705-6633
beyondtomcomics@sbcglobal.net
(2-6, 12, 16-18, 20, 21, 23, 24, 26, A-E)

Batcave Treasures LLC
10 East Main Street
Plano, IL 60545
(815) 514-6104
batcavetreasures@sbcglobal.net
batcave-treasures.com
(4, 6-9, 11-13, 17-21, 23, 24, 26, A-E)

Mellow Blue Planet Comics & Collectibles
2212 5th Avenue
Rock Island, IL 61201
(309) 788-1653
mellowblueplanet@hotmail.com
mellowblueplanet.com
(1-6, 9, 10, 12, 15, 18-21, 23, 24, A-E)

Clyde's Comics & Fantasy Shop
1528 Broadway
Rockford, IL 61104
(815) 964-0101
newnajar@gmail.com
(3-6, 10, 12, A-C)

Amazing Fantasy Comics
16649 Oak Park Avenue
Tinley Park, IL 60477
(708) 633-0837
http://www.afbooks.com
(4, 6, 7, 10, 21, 23)

INDIANA

Reader Copies
1610 S Scatterfield Road
Anderson, IN 46016
(765) 649-5767
readercopies@aol.com
readercopies.com
(2-4, 6-10, 20)

Khahan's Americana
522 S. Main Street
Elkhart, IN 46516
(574) 322-4173
accounts@khahan.com
(3, 4, 6-10, E)

Comic Quest
2260 East Morgan Avenue
Evansville, IN 47711
(812) 477-1133
sales@comicquest.com
www.comicquest.com
(1-9, 11, 17, 18, 20, 21, 23, 24, A-E)

Comics Ina Flash
P.O. Box 3611
Evansville, IN 47735-3611
PH/FAX: (812) 401-6127
comicflash@aol.com
www.comicsinaflash.com

The Book Broker, Inc.
2717 Covert Avenue
Evansville, IN 47714-3950
(812) 479-5647
bbtas56@aol.com
www.bookbrokercollectibles.com
(2-4, 6-9, 16, 20, 23, 25, 26, E)

Summit Comics & Games
4240 W Jefferson Boulevard
Suite M-8
Fort Wayne, IN 46804
(260) 436-2719
pilgrimboy14@yahoo.com
www.summitfortwayne.com
(1-10, 21, 23, D, E)

Circle City Comics
5303 W 86th Street
Indianapolis, IN 46268
(317) 280-7530
jnellis@circlecitycomics.com
www.circlecitycomics.com
(1-4, 6-10, 13, 21-24, A, C-E)

Collector's Paradise
5618 E Washington Street
Indianapolis, IN 46219
(317) 357-2291
dianaduncan@msn.com
(2, 3, 6, 7, 18, 21, 23, 24, E)

Comic Carnival
7235 N. Keystone Avenue
Suite E
Indianapolis, IN 46240
(317) 253-8882
comiccarnival@yahoo.com
www.comiccarnival.com
(1-10, 12, 13, 15, 17, 18, 20, 21, 23, 24, 26, A-E)

Downtown Comics
11 East Market Street
Indianapolis, IN 46204
(317) 237-0397
circle@downtowncomics.com
www.downtowncomics.com
(2-4, 6-8, 10, 18, 20, 21, 23, D, E)

Downtown Comics North
5767 East 86th Street
Indianapolis, IN 46250
(317) 845-9991
north@downtowncomics.com
www.downtowncomics.com
(2-4, 6-10, 18, 21, 23, E)

Downtown Comics West
7301 West 10th Street
Indianapolis, IN 46214
(317) 271-7610
west@downtowncomics.com
www.downtowncomics.com
(3, 4, 6-8, 10, 18, 21, 23, E)

Comics Cubed
1139 South Ohio Street
Kokomo, IN 46902
(765) 271-7256
Shawn@kokomocon.com
(2-4, 6, 8, A, D, E)

Mancave Comics & Collectables LLC
1310 South Miller Avenue
Shelbyville, IN 46176
(812) 614-8253
tmc304@tds.net
(1-4, 6, 7, 9, 13, 18, 20, 21, 23, 24, 26, A, C-E)

Galactic Greg's
1407 Lincoln Way
Valparaiso, IN 46383
(219) 669-6933
info@galacticgregs.com
www.galacticgregs.com
(1-10, 13, 15, 21, D, E)

IOWA

Mayhem Collectibles
2532 Lincoln Vay
Ames, IA 50014
(515) 292-3510
shop@mayhem.com
mayhemcomics.com
(2-11, 18, 20, 21, 23, 24, A-E)

The CORE Comics & Games
1926 Valley Park Drive
Cedar Falls, IA 50613
(319) 277-1835
thecore@cfu.net
thecoreonline.com
(2-4, 6-10, 21, 23, E)

Superstars and Superheroes
1527 Harrison Street
Davenport, IA 52803
(563) 323-4392
suzlarr@yahoo.com
larryssuperstars.com
(2-4, 6, 7, 18, 20, 23)

Dungeons & Dodgers
1018 Central Avenue
Fort Dodge, IA 50501
(515) 302-8670
dungeonsanddodgers@gmail.com
(1-4, 6-11, 16-18, 21, 23, 24, D, E)

Alter Ego Comics
331 7th Avenue
Marion, IA 52302
(319) 373-8935
erin@alteregoia.com
www.alteregoia.com
(2, 4, 6, 23, E)

Oak Leaf Comics & Collectibles
221 North Federal Avenue
Mason City, IA 50401
(641) 424-0333
miket@dustcatchers.com
oakleafcomics.com
(1-13, 15, 16, 18-21, 23-26, A-E)

KANSAS

B•Bop Comics South
A Division of Friendly Frank's
5336 W. 95th St.
Prairie Village, KS 66207
PH/FAX: (913) 383-1777
bbop@swbell.net
(1-21, 23, 24, A-E)

Lunatix Comix LLC
4035 SW 10th Avenue
Topeka, KS 66604
(785) 271-0771
ryan@lunatixcomix.com
www.lunatixcomix.com
(2-6, 18, 21, 23, 24, A, C-E)

Prairie Dog Comics
4800 West Maple Street
Suite 122
Wichita, KS 67209
(316) 942-3456
pdogcomics@gmail.com
(1-10, 12-24, A-E)

Wizards Asylum ICT
1309 W 31st Street S
Wichita, KS 67217
(316) 262-6642
wizardsasylumict@yahoo.com
www.wizardsict.com
(1-4, 6-12, 16, 21, 23, 24, A, C-E)

KENTUCKY

The Great Escape
2945 Scottsville Road
Suites B17 & B18
Bowling Green, KY 42104
PH: (270) 782-8092
FAX: (270) 843-3090
thegreatescapebg@gmail.com
www.TheGreatEscapeOnLine.com
(1-26, A-E)

Comic Book World, Inc.
7130 Turfway Road
Burlington, KY 41005
(859) 371-9562
(859) 371-6925
priscilla@comicbookworld.com
www.comicbookworld.com
(1-10, 12, 13, 15, 18, 23, D, E)

Comics2Games
8470 US Highway 42
Suite D
Florence, KY 41042
(859) 647-7568
info@Comics2Games.com
www.comics2games.com
(1-9, 15, 21, 23, 24, C-E)

Comic Book World Louisville
6905 Shepherdsville Road
Louisville, KY 40219
(502) 964-5500
Louisville@comicbookworld.com
stores.comichub.com/comic-bookworldlouisville
(1-10, 18, E)

Comic Book World, Inc.
6905 Shepherdsville Road
Louisville, KY 40219
(502) 964-5500
jacob@comicbookworld.com
www.comicbookworld.com
(1-10, 23, E)

The Great Escape
2433 Bardstown Road
Louisville, KY 40205
PH: (502) 456-2216
FAX: (502) 456-5964
thegreatescapelouisville@gmail.com
www.TheGreatEscapeOnLine.com
(1-26, A-E)

Heroes Comics & Gaming
361 Baxter Avenue
Louisville, KY 40204
(502) 589-2601
heroeslouisville@gmail.com
http://www.heroescg.com
(1-9, 12, 15, 24, D, E)

Big Bang
4786 Frederica Street
Owensboro, KY 42301
(270) 688-5800
contact@buybigbang.com
buybigbang.com
(2-10, 15, 18-21, 23, 24, 26, C-E)

Leroy Harper
P.O. Box 212
West Paducah, KY 42086
PH: (270) 748-9364
LHCOMICS@hotmail.com

LOUISIANA

Louisiana Double Play
2834 S. Sherwood Forest Boulevard
Suite C-5
Baton Rouge, LA 70816
(225) 296-5812
ladp@cox.net
www.facebook.com/LADoublePlay
(1-7, 9, 10, 13, 18-24, A-E)

Excalibur Comics, Cards & Games
937 E. 70th Street
Shreveport, LA 71106
(318) 868-4389
(318) 868-4369
excaliburccg@gmail.com
www.excaliburccg.com
(1-10, 20, 21, 23, 24, A, C-E)

MAINE

Top Shelf Comics
115 Main Street
Bangor, ME 04401
(207) 947-4939
topshelf@tcomics.com
tcomics.com
(1-6, 12, 15, 18)

MARYLAND

Amazing Spiral Comics & Games
5851 York Road
Baltimore, MD 21212
(410) 889-6005
info@amazingspiral.com
(1, 4-10, 18, 19, 21, 23, 24, A, C-E)

E. Gerber
1720 Belmont Ave.; Suite C
Baltimore, MD 21244

Esquire Comics.com
Mark S. Zaid, ESQ.
P.O. Box 3422492
Bethesda, MD 20827
PH: (202) 498-0011
esquirecomics@aol.com
www.esquirecomics.com
(2-11, 18, 21, 23, D, E)

Comics to Astonish, Inc.
9400 Snowden River Parkway
Suite 112
Columbia, MD 21045
(410) 381-2732
comics2u@aol.com
www.comicstoastonish.com
(1-11, 18, 21, 23, D, E)

Portals Games & Comics
415A E Dover Street
Easton, MD 21601
(410) 800-8787
contact@portalsshop.com
www.portalsshop.com
(1-11, 17, 20, 21, 23, 24, A-E)

Comics To Astonish Inc
1312 Londontown Boulevard
Suite 110
Eldersburg, MD 21784
(301) 829-1017
comics2u@aol.com
www.comicstoastonish.com
(1-11, 18, 21, 23, B, D, E)

KC's Comics
2807 Belair Road
Fallston, MD 21047
(410) 877-3152
kcscomics@gmail.com
(1-4, 6, 18, 21, 23, 24, D, E)

Beyond Comics
5632 Buckeystown Pike
Frederick, MD 21704
(301) 668-8202
beyondcomics@beyondcomics.com
www.beyondcomics.com
(1-10, 12, 18, 20, 21, 23, 24, D)

Beyond Comics
18749 B North Frederick Road
Gaithersburg, MD 20879
(301) 216-0007
gaithersburg@beyondcomics.com
www.beyondcomics.com
(2-4, 6-10, 12, 20, 21, 23, 24, D)

Diamond Comic Distributors
10150 York Road, Suite 300
Hunt Valley, MD 21030
PH: (443) 318-8001

Diamond International Galleries
10720 Gilroy Rd., Suite 300
Hunt Valley, MD 21030
Contact: pokevin@DiamondGalleries.com
www.DiamondGalleries.com

Reece's Rare Comics
11028 Graymarsh Pl.
Ijamsville, MD 21754
PH: (240) 575-8600
greg@gregreececomics.com
www.reececomics.com
(1, 2, 3, 5, 6)

Collectors Corner Inc.
7911 Harford Road
Parkville, MD 21234
(410) 668-3353
collectorscornermd@comcast.net
www.collectorscornermd.com
(1-14, 16-21, 23-26, A-E)

Cards Comics and Collectibles
51 Main St.
Reisterstown, MD 21136
PH: (410) 526-7410
FAX: (410) 526-4006
cardscomicscollectibles@yahoo.com
www.cardscomicscollectibles.com
(1-4, 6, 7, 10, 20, 23, 5)

Alliance Comics
8317 Fenton Street
Silver Spring, MD 20910
(301) 588-2546
myalliancecomics@gmailcom
alliancecomicsonline.com
(2-4, 6-10, 12, 17-21, 23, 24, A-E)

Gotham Comics
15 East Main Street
Suite B-1
Westminster, MD 21157
(410) 848-7447
gothamcomics2003@gmail.com
www.gotham-comics.com
(2-10, 21, 23, C-E)

Barbarian Comics
11242 Triangle Lane
Wheaton, MD 20902
(301) 946-4184
barbariancomics@yahoo.com
barbariancomics.com
(1-4, 6, 7, 10, 18, 21, 23, A-E)

MASSACHUSETTS

The One Stop Shop
1175 Main Street
Clinton, MA 01510
(978) 733-4737
owner@tosscomics.com
tosscomics.com
(1-4, 6, 10, 20, 21, 23, 24, D, E)

Gary Dolgoff Comics
116 Pleasant St.
Easthampton, MA 01027
PH: (413) 529-0326
FAX: (413) 529-9824
gary@gdcomics.com
www.gdcomics.com

Federation Comics
Fulfilling orders for
Bill Cole Enterprises Inc.
3065 Cranberry Highway
Suite B17
East Wareham, MA 02538
PH: (781) 986-2653
sales@bcemylar.com
www.bcemylar.com

Blast From The Past
315 Main Street
Falmouth, MA 02540
(508) 548-1918
Krjuaire@comcast.net
blastfromthepastma.com
(2, 3, 23-25, C-E)

That's Entertainment
56 John Fitch Highway
Fitchburg, MA 01420
PH: (978) 342-8607
fitch@thatse.com
www.ThatsE.com
(1-26, A-E)

SuperworldComics.com
456 Main St., Suite F
Holden, MA 01520
PH: (508) 829-2259
PH: (508) UB-WACKY
Ted@Superworldcomics.com
www.Superworldcomics.com
(1-3, 13)

TJ Cafe & Games
146 South Main Street
Unit 2
Milford, MA 01757
(508) 473-5874
tjcafeandgames@yahoo.com
(4, 6-10)

Harrison's Comics
252 Essex Street
Salem, MA 01970
(978) 741-0786
harrisonscomics@hotmail.com
(1-26, A-E)

The Outer Limits
437 Moody Street
Waltham, MA 02453
PH: (781) 891-0444
askouterlimits@aol.com
www.eouterlimits.com
(1-26, A-E)

Silver Moon Comics
1 E. India Square Mall, #131
Witch City Mall
Salem, MA 01970
(978) 594-8641
silvermooncomics@yahoo.com
www.silvermooncomics.com
(2-6, 8, 15-19, 21, 23, 24, A-E)

That's Entertainment
244 Park Avenue
(At the corner of Lois Lane)
Worcester, MA 01609
PH: (508) 755-4207
Ken@thatse.com
www.ThatsE.com
(1-26, A-E)

MICHIGAN

Vault of Midnight
219 S Main Street
Ann Arbor, MI 48104
(734) 998-1413
annarbor@vaultofmidnight.com
www.vaultofmidnight.com
(2, 4, 6-10, 12, 21, 24, D)

Cashman's Comics
1018 South Madison Avenue
Bay City, MI 48708
(989) 895-1113
cashmanscomics@aol.com
www.cashmanscomics.com
(1-7, 10, 12, 21, 23, 24, B-E)

Secret Crisis Comics
1165 S Main Street
Chelsea, MI 48118
(734) 593-7110
chief@secretcrisiscomics.com
www.secretcrisiscomics.com
(2-4, 6-10, 23, E)

Vault of Midnight
2857 E Grand Boulevard
Detroit, MI 48202
(313) 481-2165
detroit@vaultofmidnight.com
www.vaultofmidnight.com
(2, 4, 6-10, 12, 23, 24, D)

Goldmine Comics & Cards
65 54th Street SW
Grand Rapids, MI 49548-5682
(616) 534-7227
toymaniac@comcast.net
www.goldminecomics.com
(3, 4, 6-9, 18-24, D)

Tardy's Collectors Corner
2009 Eastern Avenue SE
Grand Rapids, MI 49507
(616) 247-7828
tccorner@att.net
www.tardys.com
(1-6, 10-15, 18-24, A-E)

Vault of Midnight
95 Monroe Center NW
Grand Rapids, MI 49503
(616) 776-9013
grandrapids@vaultofmidnight.com
(2, 4, 6-10, 12, 21, 23, 24, D)

Nostalgia, Ink
139 S. Mechanic Street
Jackson, MI 49201
(517) 784-8955
nostalgiaink2.0@gmail.com
nostalgia-ink.net
(1-10, 12, 18, 21, 23, 24, C-E)

Fanfare
4415 S Westnedge Avenue
Kalamazoo, MI 49008-3209
(269) 349-8866
comics@fanfareland.com
fanfareland.com
(1-10, 14, 18, 20-24, A, C-E)

Summit Comics & Games
216 Washington Square
Lansing, MI 48933
(517) 485-2369
summitlansing@gmail.com
www.summitlansing.com
(1-10, 21, 23, 24, C-E)

Comic Explosion
216 E. Nepessing Street
Lapeer, MI 48446
(810) 667-3972
comic.explosion@gmail.com
(1-4, 6, 11, 18, 21, 24, A, C-E)

Harley Yee Comics
P.O. Box 51758
Livonia, MI 48151-5758
PH: (800) 731-1029
FAX: (734) 421-7928
HarleyComx@aol.com
www.HarleyYeeComics.com

Rebel's Sanctuary
135 Washington Street
Manistee, MI 49660
(231) 887-4274
www.Facebook.com/Rebelssanc
(2-4, 6-8, 10)

Collector's Corner, Inc.
2750 S Homer Road
Midland, MI 48640
(989) 750-7130
info@ccornermi.com
ccornermi.com
(2-10, 20-24, A-E)

Modern Explorers Guild
4011 Jefferson Avenue
Midland, MI 48640
(989) 865-0505
support@meguild.com
modernexplorersguild.com
(3, 4, 6-10, 23, 24)

Sanctum Sanctorum Comics & Oddities
15071 Northville Road
Plymouth, MI 48170
www.sanctumsanctorumcomics.com
(1-4, 6, 10, 11, 13, 16-18, 21, 23)

State of Comics, LLC
575 Forest Avenue
Plymouth, MI 48170
(734) 392-7905
Ryan@stateofcomics.com
www.stateofcomics.com
(2-4, 6-12, 15-17, 21, 23, 24, B, D, E)

Coy's Comics
3220 Bay Road
Suite B
Saginaw, MI 48603
(989) 401-0007
admin@coyscomics.com
www.coyscomics.com
(1-7, 9, 10, 13, 18, 20, 21, 23, 24, D, E)

Galaxy Comics
2616 State Street
Saginaw, MI 48602
(989) 799-6334
Scott@GalaxyComicsOnline.com
www.GalaxyComicsOnline.com
(2-6, 20, 23, 24, D)

Back to the Past Collectibles
50420 Dennis Court
Wixom, MI 48393
(313) 533-3130
sales@gobacktothepast.com
gobacktothepast.com
(1-8, 12-26, A-E)

The Outer Limits
1120 Burton SW
Wyoming, MI 49509
(616) 204-6716
www.theouterlimitscomics.com
(1, 2, 4, 6-9, 17, 20, 21, 23, E)

MINNESOTA

Mind's Eye Comics
200 E Travelers Trail
Suite 105
Burnsville, MN 55337
(952) 492-9350
info@mindseyecomics.com
www.mindseyecomics.com
(1-12, 14, 16-18, 20, 21, 23, 24, 26, A, B-D)

Highlander Games MN
3015 Coon Rapids Boulevard
Coon Rapids, MN 55433
(763) 301-4236
highlandergames@live.com
www.highlandergamesmn.com
(4-11, 21-24, E)

Collector's Connection
2220 Mountain Shadow Drive
Duluth, MN 55811
(218) 726-1360
collconn@gmail.com
CollectorsConnectionDuluth.com
(1-4, 6-9, 20, 23, 26)

DreamHaven Books & Comics
2301 E. 38th Street
Minneapolis, MN 55406
(612) 823-6161
dream@dreamhavenbooks.com
dreamhavenbooks.com
(1-3, 5, 6, 12-19, 22, 24)

Book Review
1618 Highway 52 N
Rochester, MN 55901
(507) 285-1600
bookreviewmn@yahoo.com
www.bookreviewmn.com
(1-4, 6-11, 16-18, 20, 21, 23, 24, 26, E)

Midway Book
1579 University Avenue W
St. Paul, MN 55104
(651) 644-7605
orders@midwaybook.com
www.midwaybook.com
(1-6, 12, 14-16)

MISSISSIPPI

3 Alarm Comics
15210 Lemoyne Boulevard
Biloxi, MS 39532-5207
(228) 547-7376
3alarmcomics@gmail.com
www.threealarmcomics.com
(1-6, 10, 12, 13, 15, 18, 20-24, A-E)

MISSOURI

B•Bop Comics North
A Division of Friendly Frank's
6320 NW Barry Rd.
Kansas City, MO 64154
PH/FAX: (816) 746-4569
bbop@swbell.net
(1-21, 23, 24, A-E)

Clint's Books & Comics
3941 Main Street
Kansas City, MO 64111-1916
(816) 561-2848
clintsbooks@gmail.com
clintscomics.com
(1-6, 17-19, 21, 23, 24, B-E)

Not Just Comix
339 W. Main Street
Park Hills, MO 63601
(573) 431-4587
notjustcomix@gmail.com
(2-10, 18, 23, 24)

Nameless City Board Games & Comics
2244 S. Campbell Avenue
Springfield, MO 65807
(417) 882-2990
namelesscitygames@gmail.com
(1-4, 6-9, 12, 14, 17, 21)

Comic Relief
2300 N 3rd Street
St. Charles, MO 63301-0962
(636) 940-1244
info@comicbookrelief.com
www.comicbookrelief.com
(1-4, 6, 10, 11, 16, 17, 21-24, A-E)

Justin's Comics
500 South 5th Street
St. Charles, MO 63301
(636) 493-1267
jburnette@justinscomics.shop
www.JustinsComics.Shop
(1-7, 10-24, A-E)

MONTANA

Kelly's Comics
1201 10th Avenue South
Suite 100
Great Falls, MT 59406
(406) 453-0588
kellyskomix@gmail.com
(1-4, 6, 8-10, 21, 23, 24, A-E)

NEBRASKA

Game On
2108 Lawrence Lane
Grand Island, NE 68803
(308) 675-3444
gameon@gameongames.com
www.gameongames.com
(2, 4, 6-11, 17, 20, 21, 23, 24, 26, A-E)

Game On
5012 3rd Avenue
Suite 140
Kearney, NE 68845
(308) 455-1080
gameon@gameongames.com
www.gameongames.com
(2, 4, 6-11, 13, 17, 20, 21, 23, 24, 26, A-E)

Trade A Tape Comic Center
145 S 9th Street
Lincoln, NE 68508
(402) 435-6063
tradeatape@neb.rr.com
tradeatapecomiccenter.com
(1-4, 6, 10, 12, 18)

Game On
220 Westview Plaza
McCook, NE 69001
(308) 345-8888
gameon@gameongames.com
www.gameongames.com
(2, 4, 6-11, 13, 17, 20, 21, 23, 24, 26, A-E)

Game On
517 South Dewey Street
North Platte, NE 69101
(308) 221-6966
gameon@gameongames.com
www.gameongames.com
(2, 4, 6-11, 17, 20, 21, 23, 24, 26, A-E)

NEVADA

Frank-N-Fred's Comics & Cards
1910 Idaho Street
Unit 103
Elko, NV 89801
(775) 777-1325
franknfreds@aol.com
(1-16, 18-26, A-E)

Cosmic Comics!
3830 E. Flamingo Rd.; Ste F-2
Las Vegas, NV 89121
PH: (702) 451-6611
info@CosmicComicsLV.com
CosmicComics.vegas
(1-10, 17-19, 21, 23, C-E)

Fandomverse Comics
3250 N. Tenaya Way
Suite 106
Las Vegas, NV 89129
(702) 677-7245
fandomverse@gmail.com
www.fandomverse.com
(2-4, 6, 7, 10, 11, 17, 21, 23, 24, E)

Torpedo Comics
7300 Arroyo Crossing Pkwy
Unit 105
Las Vegas, NV 89113
PH: (702) 444-4432
BMarvelman@aol.com
(1-6, 10-15, 21, 23, A-D)

NEW HAMPSHIRE

Rare Books & Comics
James F. Payette
P.O. Box 750
Bethlehem, NH 03574
PH: (603) 869-2097
FAX: (603) 869-3475
JimPayette@msn.com
www.JamesPayetteComics.com
(1-3, 5, 14-16)

Enterprize Comics, Etc.
109B Key Road
Keene, NH 03431
(603) 352-2624
info@ecomicsetc.com
www.ecomicsetc.com
(1-10, 12, 16-18, 21, 23, 24, A, C-E)

Double Midnight Comics & Collectibles LLC
245 Maple Street
Unit 11
Manchester, NH 03103
(603) 669-9636
chris@dmcomics.com
www.dmcomics.com
(2-4, 6-10, 21, 23)

Jetpack Comics, LLC
37 North Main Street
Rochester NH 03867
(603) 330-9636
jetpackcomics@gmail.com
www.jetpackcomics.com
(1-10, 12, 13, 17, 18, 20, 21, 23, 24, A-E)

NEW JERSEY

Conquest Comics
659 Route 9
Bayville, NJ 08721
(732) 551-2164
conquestcomics@yahoo.com
conquestcomics.com
(1-10, 12, 21, 23, 24, A-E)

Gotham Comics
79 Bloomfield Avenue
Caldwell, NJ 07006
(973) 226-3900
www.gothamcomicsnj.com
(1-9, 12, 13, 21, 23, 24, B-E)

Nationwide Comics
Buying All 10¢ & 12¢ original priced comics
Derek Woywood
Clementon, NJ 08021
PH: (856) 217-5737 or
Hotline: (800) 938-0325
FAX: (714) 288-8992
dwoywood@yahoo.com
www.philadelphiacomic-con.com
(1, 2, 4-8, 13, 14, 17)

Secret Origins Comics & More
554 Haddon Avenue
Collingswood, NJ 08108
(856) 448-5496
secretoriginscomics@gmail.com
www.secretoriginscomics.com
(2-4, 6, 7, 10, 23, B, E)

The Comic Crypt
73 Highway 35
Eatontown, NJ 07724
(732) 747-8686
amazingstoriesnj@aol.com
(1-10, 12, 21, 23-25, C-E)

Expired Robot
25 Kinnelon Road
Kinnelon, NJ 07405
(973) 750-1377
expiredrobot@gmail.com
expiredrobot.com
(3, 4, 6, 7, 9, 10, 20, 23, 24, D, E)

Comic Relief
4120 Quakerbridge Road
Lawrenceville, NJ 08648
(609) 452-7548
idiaftn55@aol.com
(1-12, 16-18, 20, 21, 23-26, A-E)

Main Street Comics & Toys
74 N Main Street
Milltown, NJ 08850
(732) 744-4642
mainstreetcomics@gmail.com
mainstreetcomicsnj.com
(1-7, 9, 12, 20, 23, 24, D, E)

East Side Mags
7 South Fullerton Avenue
Montclair, NJ 07042
(862) 333-4961
(862) 333-4964
jeff@eastsidemags.com
www.eastsidemags.com
(1-10, 13, 16-24, 26, D, E)

Comic Lair
1606 S Broad Street
Trenton, NJ 08610
(609) 695-8855
comic-lair@comic-lair.com
comic-lair.com
(1-4, 6-9, 20, 23, 24)

Pyramid Comics and Cards
24 Main Street
Sparta, NJ 07871
(973) 729-5343
Fax: (973) 729-4307
pyramidcomics@embarqmail.com
http://www.pyramidcomics.com
(4, 6, 12)

JHV Associates
(By Appointment Only)
P. O. Box 317
Woodbury Heights, NJ 08097
PH: (856) 845-4010
FAX: (856) 845-3977
JHVassoc@hotmail.com
(1,2,14,19)

NEW MEXICO

Astro-Zombies
3100 Central Avenue SE
Albuquerque, NM 87106
(505) 232-7800
info@astrozombies.com
www.astrozombies.com
(1-13, 18, 21-26, A-E)

Comic Warehouse
9617 Menaul Boulevard NE
Albuquerque, NM 87112-2216
(505) 293-3065, (505) 237-1000
comics@c-warehouse.com
www.c-warehouse.com
(1-7, 10, 12, 18, 20, 21, 23)

Red Planet Books & Comics
1002 Park Avenue SW
Albuquerque, NM 87102
(505) 361-1182
shopkeep@redplanetbnc.com
www.redplanetbooksncomics.com
(4, 8, 12, 13, 16, 17, D, E)

Zia Comics LLC
125 North Main Street
Las Cruces, NM 88001
(575) 222-4347
ziacomics@gmail.com
www.ziacomics.com
(1-4, 6-10, 12, 18, 20-24, A, C-E)

NEW YORK

Earthworld Comics
537 Central Avenue
Albany, NY 12206
(518) 459-2400
earthwrld1@aol.com
www.earthworldcomics.com
(1-4, 6, 10, 18, 21, 23, E)

Silver Age Comics
22-55 31st Street
Astoria, NY 11105
(718) 721-9691
gus@silveragecomics.com
silveragecomics.com
(1-26, A-E)

Babylon Collectibles LLC
225 Deer Park Avenue
Babylon, NY 11702
(631) 579-9490
babyloncollectibles@gmail.com
babyloncollectibles.com
(1-7, 10-13, 17, 18, 20, 21, 23-25, D, E)

Excellent Adventures Comics
110 Milton Avenue (Rt #50)
Ballston Spa, NY 12020
(518) 884-9498, (518) 884-9498
jbelskis37@aol.com
www.excellentadventurescomics.com
(1-6, 12-16, 18-23, A-D)

Lost Planet Comics
65 E Main Street
Bay Shore, NY 11706
(631) 647-9777
lostplanetcomics1@gmail.com
https://lpcomics.com
(4, 6-8, 10-12, 15, 17, 20, 21, 23, 24, A-E)

Pulp Nouveau Comix
217 South Main Street
Canandaigua, NY 14424
(585) 394-8250
pulpnouveaucomix@gmail.com
https://www.facebook.com/PulpNouveau
(1-6, 12, 13, 25)

HighGradeComics.com
17 Bethany Drive
Commack, NY 11725
PH: (631) 543-1917
FAX: (631) 864-1921
BobStorms@HighGradeComics.com
www.HighGradeComics.com
(1-3, 5)

Superhero Comics Express
146 Jericho Turnpike
Floral Park, NY 11001
(516) 328-9290
rbrindisi@nyc.rr.com
(1-7, 10, 12, 18, 20-24, B-E)

Phoenix Comics & Collectibles
107 Stewart Avenue
Hicksville, NY 11801
(516) 939-9129
ph.rebirth@gmail.com
(1-6, 10, 12, 14, 16-18, 21, 23, 24, A, C-E)

Tor Comics
997 Waverly Avenue
Holtsville, NY 11742
(631) 758-4772
dnkoch@optonline.net
tor_comics.com
(1-6, 21)

Bailey's Comics
282 North Wellwood Ave.
Lindenhurst, NY 11757
(631) 225-5085
baileyscomics@gmail.com
www.baileyscomics.com
(1-4, 6, 7, 10-13, 15, 17, 20, 23, 24, D, E)

The Comic Box
840B North Broadway
Massapequa, NY 11758
(516) 795-2528
thecomicboxny@gmail.com
instagram.com/thecomicboxny
(1-4, 6, 10, 12, 23, 24, D, E)

Ravenswood Inc.
8451 Seneca Turnpike
New Hartford, NY 13413
(315) 735-3699
info@ravenswoodcomics.com
(1, 2, 4-9, 16-18, 21, 23, A)

Best Comics
1300 Jericho Turnpike
New Hyde Park, NY 11040
PH: (516) 328-1900
FAX: (516) 328-1909
TommyBest@aol.com
www.bestcomics.com
(1, 2, 4, 6, 13, 20, 21, 23, C, D)

ComicConnect.com
36 West 37th St.; 6th Floor
New York, NY 10018
PH: (212) 895-3999
FAX: (212) 260-4304
support@comicconnect.com
www.comicconnect.com
(1-3, 13, 14, 19, 22)

Metropolis Collectibles
36 West 37th St.; 6th Floor
New York, NY 10018
PH: (800) 229-6387
FAX: (212) 260-4304
E-Mail: buying@metropoliscomics.com
www.metropoliscomics.com

Comix Zone
628 South Main Street
North Syracuse, NY 13212
(315) 452-1037
info@comixzone.com
www.comixzone.com
(1-4, 6-10, 17, 20, 21, 23, 24, D, E)

Funny Business
130 Main Street
Nyack, NY 10960
(845) 348-4747
info@funnybiz.com
(2-7, 10, 20, 23, 24, D)

Red Shirt Comics
322 Main Street
Port Jefferson, NY 11777
(631) 474-1701
josh@redshirtcomics.com
www.redshirtcomics.com
(2-4, 6-12, 20-24, C-E)

13th Verse Comics
3200 West Ridge Road
Rochester, NY 14626
(585) 663-2377
michael@13thversecomics.com
www.13thversecomics.com
(1-6, 8, 10, 17, 21, 23, A-E)

All Heroes Comics
4410 Lake Avenue
Rochester, NY 14612
(585) 865-9113
chwhallheroes@aol.com
www.allheroescomics.com
(1-6, 10, 18, 20, 21, 23, 24, B, D, E)

Comics Etc.
1115 East Main Street
Unit 81
Rochester, NY 14609
(585) 473-7150
comicsetc1@gmail.com
comicsetc.biz
(4, 6-8, 10, 12, 20, 23, 24, A, C-E)

Wonderland Comics
1620 Penfield Road
Rochester, NY 14625
(585) 248-0450
wonderlandcomicsny@gmail.com
wonderlandcomicsny.com
(1-6, 7, 9, 15, 17)

Androids Comics
61 Railroad Avenue
Sayville, NY 11782
(631) 567-8069
Androidsamazingcomics@gmail.com
Androidscomics.com
(1-6, 7, 9, 17, 18, 20, 21, 23, 24, D, E)

Golden Memories Comics
235 Middle Country Road
Selden, NY 11784
(631) 696-6991
GoMemSel@gmail.com
www.GoldenMemoriesComics.com
(1-6, 7, 9-12, 15-24, A-E)

Hypno-Tronic Comics
156 Stuyvesant Place
Staten Island, NY 10301
(718) 720-0001
hypnotroniccomics@gmail.com
hypnotroniccomics.com
(1-6, 10, 12, 13, 16-18, 21, 23, 24, 26, A-E)

Play The Game Read The Story
689 N Clinton Street
Syracuse, NY 13204
(315) 472-4263
info@playthegamereadthestory.com
www.playthegaemreadthestory.com
(1-12, 16, 17, 21, 23, 24, A-E)

Play The Game Read The Story
1 Destiny USA Drive
Destiny USA Mall
Syracuse, NY 13290
(315) 472-4263
info@playthegamereadthestory.com
www.playthegamereadtehstory.com
(4, 6-10, 17, 18, 20-24, A-E)

Dave and Adam's
55 Oriskany Dr.
Tonawanda, NY 14150
PH: (888) 440-9787
FAX: (716) 838-9896
service@dacardworld.com
www.dacardworld.com
(1-9, 13, 18, 20, 23, 24, A-E)

Dave and Adam's
2217 Sheridan Dr.
Tonawanda, NY 14223
PH: (716) 837-4920
sheridan-store@dacardworld.com
www.dacwstore.com
(1-3, 6-9, 13, 20, 23, 24, A-E)

Aquilonia Comics, Cards & More
412 Fulton Street
Troy, NY 12180
(518) 271-1069
lupir@aol.com
(2-4, 6-9, 23)

Sanctuary Comics
24764 Route 12 N Outer Bradley Street
Watertown, NY 13601
(315) 779-9636
sanctuarycomics@hotmail.com
www.sanctuarycomics.biz
(2-4, 6-9, 11)

Long Island Comics
276 Little East Neck Road
West Babylon, NY 11704
(631) 321-4822
frank@licomics.com
licomics.com
(2-6, 26)

Freakopolis Geekery
120 Main Street
Whitehall, NY 12887
(518) 294-5551
geekery@freakopolis.com
https://freakopolis.com
(4, 6-10, 17, 18, 21, 23, C-E)

Dan Gallo
White Plains, NY
PH: (954) 547-9063
DGallo1291@aol.com
eBay ID: DGallo1291
(1-3, 13)

Dave and Adam's
8075 Sheridan Dr.
Williamsville, NY 14221
PH: (716) 626-0000
Transit-store@dacardworld.com
www.dacwstore.com
(1-4, 6-9, 13, 18, 20, 23, 24, A-E)

Grasshopper's Comics
76 Hillside Avenue
Williston Park, NY 11596
(516) 741-5724
grasshopperscomics@gmail.com
grasshopperscomics.com
(2-4, 6-9, 15)

NORTH CAROLINA

Bad Dog Comics
405W Main Street
Albemarle, NC 28001
(704) 982-4708
emyers@baddogcomics.com
(2-7, 9, 12, 14, 16-18, 20, 21, 23, 24, D, E)

Pastimes
175 Weaverville Highway
Suite Y
Asheville, NC 28804
(828) 658-0588
pastimes.comics.games@gmail.com
comicshopasheville.com
(1-8, 10-12, 15, 17-24, A-E)

Appalachian State University Bookstore
219 College Street
Boone, NC 28608
(828) 262-3072
scholarsbookshop@appstate.edu
https://bookstore.appstate.edu
(4, 6, 8-10, 17-20, D)

Heroes Aren't Hard to Find
417 Pecan Avenue.
Charlotte, NC 28204
PH: (704) 375-7462
www.heroesonline.com

Atomic Empire
3400 Westgate Drive
Suite 14B
Durham, NC 27707
(919) 490-7900
support@atomicempire.com
www.atomicempire.com
(4-10, 12, 14, 17-24, A-E)

Books Do Furnish a Room
1809 W. Markham Avenue
Durham, NC 27705
(919) 286-1076
booksdofurnisharoom@frontier.com
www.booksdofurnisharom.com
(4, 6, 16, 25, 26)

Enterprise Comics
The Raleigh Flea Market NC Fairgrounds
4285 Trinity Road
Raleigh, NC 27607
(919) 444-9910
r_thumith@yahoo.com
(4-7, 10, 17, 18, 20, 21, 23-26, A-D)

Foundation's Edge
2526 Hillsborough Street
Raleigh, NC 27607
(919) 832-0044
foundationsedgecomics@gmail.com
(2-6, 8, 10, 12, 21)

Collectivity The Comic Shoppe
308 North Salisbury GQ Avenue
Salisbury, NC 28146
(704) 433-5231
collectivity@att.net
(1-4, 10, 16, 18, 20, 21, 23, 25, 26, A, D)

DreamDaze Comics Fun & Games
2801-1B Ward Boulevard
Wilson, NC 27893
(252) 281-5586
ddcfg@dreamdazecfg.com
https://stores.comichub.com/dreamdazecfg
(2, 4, 6-10, 17-19, 21, 23, 24, A, C-E)

NORTH DAKOTA

Comic Realms
106 N Mandan Street
Bismarck, ND 58501
(701) 751-4540
info@comicrealms.com
www.comicrealms.com
(1-4, 6, 8, 10, 17, 18, 21, D, E)

Comic Junction
1621 So. University Drive
Suite 203
Fargo, ND 58103
(701) 232-7121
kip@comic-junction.com
Comic-Junction.com
(1-6, 10, 11, 16, 18, 21, 23, 24, A, C, D)

Grand Cities Games
120 N Washington Street
Grand Forks, ND 58203
(701) 775-8602
Grandcitiesgames@yahoo.com
(2-10, 16-21, 23, 24, 26, A, C-E)

OHIO

Kidforce Collectibles
103 Front Street
Berea, OH 44017
(440) 239-7777
(1-10, 15, 18-20, 23, 24, D, E)

Comics, Cards and Collectables
724 Cleveland Avenue SW
Canton, OH 44702
(330) 456-8907
comics5@yahoo.com
https://www.comicscardscollectables.com
(1-6, 12, 20, 21, 23, 26)

Queen City Comic and Card Company
6101 Montgomery Road
Cincinnati, OH 45213
(513) 351-5674
qccomics@aol.com
queencitycomics.com
(1-7, 9, 12, 18-21, 23, 24, D)

Flying Monkey Comics and Games
1778 Columbus Pike
Delaware, OH 43015-2726
(740) 990-1066
flyingmonkeycomicsandgames@gmail.com
flyingmonkeycomics.com
(1-4, 6-10, 13, 21, 23, 24, A-E)

Keith's Comics
394 Broad Street
Elyria, OH 44035
(440) 323-2000
wachowskis@yahoo.com
(3, 4, 6, 10)

Cosmic Comics & Games
17 W. National Road
Englewood, OH 45322
(937) 836-0083
cosmicomicsandgames@gmail.com
https://cosmic-comics-games.com
(1-4, 6-9, 16-21, 23, 24, B-E)

Queen City Comic and Card Company
6600-V Dixie Highway
Fairfield, OH 45014
(513) 860-5805
qccomics@aol.com
queencitycomics.com
(2-7, 9, 18, 20, 23, 24)

Maverick's Cards & Comic
2312 E Dorothy Lane
Kettering, OH 45420
(937) 294-4900
jackmavericks@sbcglobal.net
(1-7, 9, 10, 12, 20, 21, 23, 24, D, E)

Comics and Friends, LLC
7850 Mentor Ave.; Suite 1054
Mentor, OH 44096
PH: (440) 255-4242
comics.and.friends.store@gmail.com
www.comicsandfriends.com
(1-7, 9, 10, 12-14, 18, 20, 21, 23-26, A-E)

Capital City Comics
7530 East Main Street
Reynoldsburg, OH 43068
(614) 577-0220
tonykazlausky@aol.com
capitalcitycomics.net
(1-7, 9-12, 14, 17, 20, 21, 23, 24, D, E)

New Dimension Comics
Ohio Valley Mall
67800 Mall Ring Rd Unit 875
Saint Clairsville, OH 43950
PH: (740) 695-1020
ohiovalley@ndcomics.com
www.ndcomics.com

Freedom Comics
2746 W. Sylvania Avenue
Toledo, OH 43613
(419) 266-8404
freedomcomics@hotmail.com
https://m.facebook.com/FreedomComicsandcollectibles
(1-13, 18, 21, 23, 24, C-E)

JC's Comics N' More: Your Pop Culture Super-Store
6725 W Central Avenue
Toledo, OH 43617
(419) 531-6097
jcscomicsnmore@hotmail.com
jcscomicsnmore.com
(1-6, 12, 18, 20, 21, 23-25, B-E)

Wonder Comics and More
100 N Miami Street
Trenton, OH 45067
(513) 468-4001
wondercomicsmore@gmail.com
https://www.facebook.com/Wonder-Comics-More-628267834313782
(1-13, 16-18, 20, 21, 23-26, A, E)

Jim & Dan Comics and Collectibles
1 East Dayton Street
West Alexandria, OH 45381
(937) 839-7068
jimdancomics@gmail.com
www.jimdancomics.com
(1-25, A-E)

World's Greatest Comics
5974 Westerville Rd.
Westerville, OH 43081
(614) 891-3000
worldsgreatestcomics@gmail.com
www.wgcomics.com
(1-6, 18, 21, 23)

OKLAHOMA

Carolina Comics
305 SW C Avenue
Lawton, OK 73501
(580) 353-5164
carolinacomics@sbcglobal.net
carolinacomics.net
(1-10, 16, 17, 20-24, A, C-E)

All Star Comics
12325 N May Avenue
Suite 113
Oklahoma City, OK 73120
(405) 842-7800
allstarcomicsokc@gmail.com
allstarcomicsokc@gmail.com
(1-4, 6, 10, 12, 13, 21, 23, A, C-E)

Impulse Creations Comics & Collectibles
8228 E 61st Street
Suite 121
Tulsa, OK 74133
(918) 884-7130
staff@impulsecreations.com
impulsecreations.com
(2-10, 17, 21, 23, 24, A, D, E)

Want List Comics
(Appointment Only)
P.O. Box 701932
Tulsa, OK 74170
PH: (918) 299-0440
E-Mail: wlc777@cox.net
(1-3, 13-15, 19, 20, 24, C)

OREGON

Tony's Kingdom of Comics and Collectibles LLC
3856 River Road N
Keizer, OR 97303
(503) 463-1142
sirwag@comcast.net
https://www.facebook.com/TonysKingdom
(1-11, 14, 16-24, A-C, E)

Rogue City Comics
32 N. Central Avenue
Medford, OR 97501
(541) 500-1985
roguecity@usa.com
roguecitycomics.com
(1-4, 6-10, 17, 21, D)

Comics Adventure
15705 SE McLoughlin Boulevard
Suite A
Milwaukie, OR 97267
(503) 305-7946
info@comicsadventure.com
www.comicsadventure.com
(1-6, 9, 10, 12, 16-21, 23, B, D, E)

Comic Cave PDX
1924 N. Kilpatrick Street
Portland, OR 97217
(503) 484-5600
doug@comiccavepdx.com
www.comiccavepdx.com
(2-6, 12)

Cosmic Monkey Comics
5335 NE Sandy Boulevard
Portland, OR 97213
(503) 517-9050
cosmicmonkeymail@gmail.com
www.cosmicmonkeycomics.com
(2-12, 16-21, 23, 24, 26, A-E)

Excalibur Comics
2444 SE Hawthorne Boulevard
Portland, OR 97214
(503) 231-7351
excaliburcomicspdx@gmail.com
www.excaliburcomicspdx.com
(1-6, 10, 12)

Wild Things Games
241 Commercial Street NE
Salem, OR 97301
(503) 364-4263, (503) 485-2957
rush@wild-things.com
WildThingsGames.com
(1-10, 16, 20, 23, C, D)

PENNSYLVANIA

The Encounter
811 Union Boulevard
Allentown, PA 18109
(610) 774-9565
encountercomics@gmail.com
facebook.com/encountercomics
(1-9, 18, 21, 23, 24, D, E)

JAF Comics
224 Nazareth Pike
Bethlehem, PA 18020
(484) 292-1914
info@jafcomics.com
jafcomics.com
(1-11, 13, 17, 18, 20, 21, 23, 24, A-E)

New Dimension Comics
108 South Main Street
Butler, PA 16001
PH: (724) 282-5283
butler@ndcomics.com
www.ndcomics.com
(1-12, 14, 15, 18, 20, 21, 23, 24, A-E)

Comics World
1670 Lincoln Way East
Chambersburg, PA 17202
(717) 264-9918
john@comicsworldonline.com
(1-4, 6, 21, 23, 24, D, E

New Dimension Comics – Cranberry
20550 Route 19
#20 Piazza Plaza
Cranberry Township, PA 16066
(724) 776-0433
cranberry@ndcomics.com
www.ndcomics.com
(1-4, 6-10, 12, 14, 15, 17, 18, 20-24, A-E)

Codex Comics & Collectibles
125 West High Street
Ebensburg, PA 15931
(814) 472-2233
codexcomics@yahoo.com
codexcomicshop.com
(2, 4, 6-10, 18, 21, 23, D, E)

New Dimension Comics
Megastore
516 Lawrence Ave.
Ellwood City, PA 16117
PH: (724) 758-2324
ec@ndcomics.com
www.ndcomics.com
(1-12, 14, 15, 18, 20, 21, 23, 24, A-E)

Comic Collection & Records Too
83 Bustleton Pike
Unit B
Feasterville, PA 19053
(215) 357-3332
www.TheComicCollection.net
(1-12, 17-25, A-E)

Comic Universe LLC
446 MacDade Boulevard
Folsom, PA 19033
(610) 461-7960
comicuniversellc@yahoo.com
comicuniversellc.com
(2-6, 18, 23, 24)

Comix Universe
130 Eisenhower Drive
Suite B-1
Hanover, PA 17331
(717) 637-1637
comixuniverse@yahoo.com
(4, 6-11, 18, 20, 21, 23, 24, 26, C-E)

New Dimension Comics
630 East Waterfront Dr.
Homestead, PA 15120
PH: (412) 655-8661
waterfront@ndcomics.com
www.ndcomics.com
(1-12, 14, 15, 18, 20, 21, 23, 24, A-E)

Comic Zen
301-A W Main Street
Lansdale, PA 19446
(267) 263-4219
comiczenpa@gmail.com
comiczenpa.com
(2-4, 6-8, 10, 18, 21, 23, E)

AA Comics and Cards
610 Cumberland Street
Lebanon, PA 17042-5232
(717) 644-9345
contact@aacomicsandcards.com
(1-4, 6-10, 13, 15, 16, 18, 20, 21, 23, D, E)

Hooked on Comics
600 E Cumberland Street
Lebanon, PA 17042
(717) 628-5171
gamers.realm@yahoo.com
https://www.facebook.com/hookedoncomixworksforme
1-12, 14, 18-22, 24, A-E)

Pittsburgh Comics
113 E. McMurray Road
McMurray, PA 15317
(724) 941-5445
colin@pittsburghcomics.com
www.pittsburghcomics.com
(2-4, 6, 17)

Phantom of the Attic
3766 William Penn Highway
Monroeville, PA 15146
(412) 856-4403
phantomattic@gmail.com
stores.comichub.com/phantom_of_the_attic
(1-6, 10, 15, 21, 23, 25, E)

Comics and Paperbacks Plus
201 E Main Street
Palmyra, PA 17078-1740
(717) 838-4854
Ralph@comicsandpaperbacksplus.com
www.comicsandpaperbacksplus.com
(2-4, 6, 10, 16, 17, 25)

The Ontario Street Comic Book Shop
2235 E Ontario Street
Philadelphia, PA 19134
(215) 288-7338
wfink27240@aol.com
https://www.facebook.com/OntarioComics
(1-4, 6, 7, 10, 20, 21, 23, 24, E)

Eide's Entertainment, LLC
1121 Penn Ave.
Pittsburgh, PA 15222
PH: (412) 261-0900
eBay: Eides_Entertainment
eides@eides.com
www.eides.com
(1-26, A-E)

Duncan Comics, Books, & Accessories
398 Perry Highway
First Floor West View Firemen's Building
Pittsburgh, PA 15229
(412) 635-0886
duncanbooks@aol.com
www.duncancomics.com
(1-6, 14, 16-20, 22-24, A-E)

Phantom Of The Attic
411 S Craig Street
Suite 2
Pittsburgh, PA 15213
(412) 621-1210
comics@pota-oakland.com
www.pota-oakland.com
(1-4, 6, 10, 12, 18, 21, 23, A, C-E)

South Side Comics
4133 Brownsville Road
Pittsburgh, PA 15227
www.southsidecomicspgh.com
(2-4, 6, 10, 21, 23, 24, E)

Krav'n Comics
349 Upland Square
Pottstown, Pa 19464
(610) 323-3868
comics@kravncomics.com
www.kravncomics.com
(4, 6-11, 15, 17, 21, 23, 24, A-E)

Bennie's Comics & Cards
462 Sharpsville Avenue
Sharon, PA 16146
(724) 347-3390
crah@infonline.net
(1-8, 14, 16, 18, 20, 23, 25, C-E)

New Wave Comics & Collectibles
4020 Skippack Pike
Souderton, PA 18964
(610) 222-9200
info@newwavecomics.net
newwavecomics.net
(4, 6-12, 21, 23, 24, A, D)

Isle of Comics
56 West Southern Avenue
South Williamsport, PA 17702
(570) 322-4753
IsleOfComics@hotmail.com
www.IsleOfComics.com
(1-6, 12, 15, 18-24, A-E)

New Dimension Comics
Pittsburgh Mills
590 Pittsburgh Mill Circle
Tarentum, PA 15084
PH: (724) 758-1560
mills@ndcomics.com
www.ndcomics.com
(1-12, 14, 15, 18, 20, 21, 23, 24, A-E)

Rubber Mallet Comics
802 Wyoming Avenue
West Pittston, PA 18643
(570) 655-5522
rubbermalletcomics@gmail.com
rmcomics.com
(4, 6, 23)

ComicMasters Inc.
1978 Whitehall Mall
Whitehall, PA 18052
(610) 366-7670
comicmasters@msn.com
www.ComicMastersOnline.com
(1-7, 21, 23, 26, D)

Toy & Comic Heaven
21 Easton Road
Willow Grove, PA 19090
PH: (215) 643-7000
jgallony@aol.com
www.toyandcomicheaven.com
(1-3, 5-7, 20, 23, 24, B-D)

Comics World LLC
1002 Graham Avenue
Windber, PA 15963
(814) 467-4116
pcomicon@gmail.com
(1-6, 8, 23, B, D)

Hake's Americana & Collectibles
P.O. Box 12001
York, PA 17402
PH: (866) 404-9800
www.hakes.com

RHODE ISLAND

Fantasy Zone Comics
7610 Post Road
North Kingstown, RI 02852
(401) 294-6044
fzcomics@verizon.net
(1-6, 10, 16, 24)

SOUTH CAROLINA

Planet Comics
2704 N Main Street
Anderson, SC 29621
(864) 261-3578
planetcomics@gmail.com
www.planetcomicsdirect.com
(4, 6-10, 18, 20, 21, 23, 24, D, E)

Cosmic Rays
4427 Devine Street
Columbia, SC 29205
(803) 661-8504
cosmicray2013@gmail.com
www.cosmicrays-online.com
(1-6, 10-14, 16-19, 21, 23-26, B-E)

Borderlands Comics and Games
1434 Laurens Road
Greenville, SC 29607
(864) 235-3488
borderlandscomics@gmail.com
(1-10, 13, 14, 18-21, 23, 24, A, C-E)

Noble Nostalgia
33 Market Point Drive
Greenville, SC 29607
(864) 383-8610
nik@noblenostalgia.com
www.noblenostalgia.com
(1-3, 5, 7, 13, 14, 20, D)

Planet Comics
1633 Woodruff Road
Greenville, SC 29607
(864) 509-6850
planetcomics@gmail.com
www.planetcomicsdirect.com
(4-10, 21, 23, E)

Player's Choice
10177 N. Kings Hwy, Unit G4
Myrtle Beach, SC 29572
(843) 272-0268
playerschoicenmb@gmail.com
playerschoicenmb.com
(2-11, 18-21, 23, 24, 26, D)

SOUTH DAKOTA

Storyteller
520 6th Street
Rapid City, SD 57701
(605) 348-7242
(1-11, 17, 18, 20, 21, 24, A, C, D)

Rainbow Comics, Cards & Collectibles
3310 S. Minnesota Avenue
Sioux Falls, SD 57105
(605) 338-9519
mcelroy.dave@gmail.com
rainbowcomicsandcards.com
(1-10, 15, 17-24, A-E)

TENNESSEE

B & M Amusement
5036 Hwy 58
Chattanooga, TN 37416
(423) 605-2913
bandmorders@aol.com
(1-11, 15, 17, 20, D)

Infinity Flux
3643 Hixson Pike, Suite B
Chattanooga, TN 37415
(423) 591-5689
infinityfluxjohn@gmail.com
www.infinityflux.net
(1-10, 12, 18-21, 24, C-E)

Comics Universe
1869 Hwy 45 Bypass
Jackson, TN 38305
(731) 664-9131
rethelmiller@gmail.com
(1, 2, 4, 24)

Dewayne's World - Comics & Games
457 E Sullivan Street
Kingsport, TN 37660
(423) 247-8997
dewayne@dewaynes-world.com
www.dewaynes-world.com
(4, 6-10, 21, 23, D, E)

The Great Escape
105 Gallatin Road North
Madison, TN 37115
PH: (615) 865-8052
FAX: (615) 865-8779
thegreatescapemadison@gmail.com
www.TheGreatEscapeOnLine.com
(1-26, A-E)

Everscape
104 East Fort Street
Manchester, TN 37355
(931) 954-1520
everscape.enterprises@gmail.com
www.everscapeonline.com
(4, 6, 7, 8, 9, 10, 17, 20, 23, 24, E)

The Golden Age, 1942
316 Court Street
Maryville, TN 37804
(865) 980-8330
Davidlaney@thegoldenage1942.com
Thegoldenage1942.com
(1-18, 20-24, A-E)

Outer Limits Boro
1244 NW Broad Street
Murfreesboro, TN 37129
(615) 804-3775
info@outerlimitsboro.org
theouterlimitsboro.com
(1-4, 6-11, 13, 18-21, 23, 24, A, C-E)

The Great Escape
810 NW Broad St., Suite 202
Murfreesboro, TN 37129
PH: (615) 900-1937
FAX: (615) 962-9562
thegreatescapemurfreesboro@gmail.com
www.TheGreatEscapeOnLine.com
(1-26, A-E)

The Great Escape
5400 Charlotte Avenue
Nashville, TN 37209
PH: (615) 385-2116
FAX: (615) 297-6588
contactus@thegreatescapeonline.com
www.TheGreatEscapeOnLine.com
(1-26, A-E)

Dragonfly Comics & Collectibles
111 Hwy 76
White House, TN 37188
(615) 334-1259
pulls@dragonflycomics.com
www.dragonflycomics.com
(2, 4, 6, 8, 9, 21, E)

TEXAS

Wild West Comics and Games
400 E Division Street, Suite 110
Arlington, TX 76015
(817) 265-0491
elaine@wildwestcomics.com
wildwestcomics.com
(4, 6-10, 18, 20, 22, 23, C-E)

Comic Heaven
P.O. Box 900
Big Sandy, TX 75755
PH: (903) 539-8875
www.ComicHeaven.net

Nostalgia Video Games & Comics
1474 W Price Road, Suite 2
Brownsville, TX 78520
(956) 459-8232
zhaoyunfan@live.com
www.facebook.com/nostalgiavideogamesandcomics
(4, 6-11, 20, 23, D, E)

Space Cadets Collection
27326 Robinson Road #117
Conroe, TX 77385
(281) 298-1111
ming4king@yahoo.com
www.spacecadetscollection.com
(1-4, 6, 13, 18, 19, 22-25, A-E)

Comic Book Certification Service (CBCS)
4635 McEwen Road
Dallas, TX 75244
PH: (727) 803-6822
PH: (844) 870-CBCS
www.CBCScomics.com

Heritage Auction Galleries
2801 W. Airport Freeway
Dallas, TX 75261-4127
PH: (877) 437-4827
www.HA.com

Keith's Comics
5400 E. Mockingbird #120
Dallas, TX 75206
(214) 827-3060
info@keithscomics.com
www.keithscomics.com
(1-10, 16-18, 23, D, E)

Keith's Comics North Dallas
17610 Midway Road #136
Dallas, TX 75287
(972) 735-8333
k4ndallas@gmail.com
www.keithscomics.com
(4-9, 16, 17, 21, 23, D, E)

Titan Comics
3128 Forest Lane, Suite 250
Dallas, TX 75234
(214) 350-4420
info@titancomics.com
www.titancomics.com
(2-6, 10, 12, 18, 21, 24, E)

Asylum Comics
5360 N Mesa
El Paso, TX 79912
(915) 875-8600
comics63@aol.com
(2-4, 6, 12, 13, 15, 18-21, 23, 24, D, E)

Black Sheep Comics
1491 N Lee Trevino, Suite L
El Paso, TX 79936
(915) 235-7872
blacksheepcomicsep@gmail.com
(2-7, 10, 11, 13, 18, 19, 23, 24, D, E)

Worldwide Comics
29369 Raintree Ridge
Fair Oaks Ranch, TX 78015
PH: (830) 368-4103
stephen@wwcomics.com
wwcomics.com

Twenty Eleven Comics
2230 Morriss Road
Flower Mound, TX 75028
(214) 285-2011
twentyelevencomics@gmail.com
www.twentyelevencomics.com
1-14, 18, 21, 23, D)

William Hughes' Vintage Collectables
P.O. Box 270244
Flower Mound, TX 75027
PH: (972) 539-9190
PH: (973) 432-4070
Whughes199@yahoo.com
www.VintageCollectables.net

Keith's Comics Firewheel
345 Coneflower
Garland, TX 75040
(972) 640-8484
teamcomics@gmail.com
www.keithscomics.com
(2-4, 6-10, 17, 18, 21, 23, D, E)

The Multiverse
931 Melbourne Road
Hurst, TX 76053
(817) 616-3052
staff@multiverse.shop
multiverse.shop
(1-4, 6-11, 18, 19, 21-24, D, E)

Lewisville Comics
2417 South Stemmons Fwy. #106
Lewisville, TX 75067
(972) 315-3664
info@lewisvillecomics.com
www. lewisvillecomics.com

Urban Legends Comics
3501 Gus Thomasson Road #51
Mesquite, TX 75150
(972) 681-2040
urbanlegendscomicshop@gmail.com
www.urbanlegendscomicshop.com
(4, 6, 8-10, 18, 21, 23, D, E)

All-Star Comics
3520 Hwy 365
Nederland, TX 77627
(409) 724-6077
allstar.comics@gmail.com
(2-4, 6-10, 18, 20-24, D, E)

Madness Games & Comics
3000 Custer Road, Suite 310
Plano, TX 75075
(972) 943-8135
mgc@madnessgames.com
www.madnessgames.com
(4, 6-11, 17-24, A-E)

Outer Rim Collective
1608 West Beauregard Avenue
San Angelo, TX 76901
(325) 227-0403
outerrimco@gmail.com
www.outerrimcollective.com
(1-4, 6, 10, 15, 17-19, 21, 23, 24, E)

Collectors Authority
1534 SE Military Drive #107
San Antonio, TX 78214
(210) 977-8818
punisher@collectorsauthority.com
collectorsauthority.com
(1-4, 6)

Dragon's Lair Comics & Fantasy
7959 Fredericksburg Road, Suite 129
San Antonio, TX 78229
(210) 615-1229
kappamoollc@yahoo.com
www.dlair.net/medicalcenter
(4-11, 17, 20, 21, 23, 24, 26, A, C-E)

UTAH

Black Cat Comics
2261 Highland Drive
Salt Lake City, UT 84106
(801) 467-4228
cybergage817@gmail.com
www.blackcat-comics.com
(1-6, 10, 12, 18, 20, 21, 23, 24, A-E)

VERMONT

Wonder Cards & Comics
445 US Route 302
Berlin, VT 05641
(802) 476-4706
roydatema3@gmail.com
wondercardsandcomics.com
(1-16, 18-21, 23-26, C-E)

VIRGINIA

Zeno's Books
1112 Sparrow Road
Chesapeake, VA 23325
(757) 420-2344
zenosbooks@yahoo.com
www.facebook.com/zenos-books
(1-4, 6, 12-16, 20, 21, C, D)

Trade Cave
10960 Forest Trace Lane
Glen Allen, VA 23059
(804) 869-0742
cadoodoo@yahoo.com
www.facebook.com/tradecave
(4, 6, 7, 17-21, 23, 24, 26, A, B, D, E)

Richmond Comix
14249 Midlothian Turnpike
Midlothian, VA 23113
(804) 594-2845
richmix@richmondcomix.com
richmondcomix.com
(1-6, 8, 10, 16-18, 21, D)

B & D Comic Shop
802 Elm Avenue SW
Roanoke, VA 24016-3824
(540) 342-6642
bdcomics1@verizon.net
www.banddcomics.com
(2-6, 16, 23, 24, D)

WASHINGTON

Tectonic Comics
601 S Boone Street, Suite 3
Aberdeen, WA 98520
(360) 637-9285
tectoniccomics@gmail.com
tectoniccomic.com
(1-4, 6-11, 16, 18-24, 26, A-E)

Mighty Moose Comics
4015 Factoria Mall SE, Unit C7
Bellevue, WA 98006
(425) 643-9924
fatmoose97@aol.com
mightymoosecomics@gmail.com
(2-4, 6-10, 21, 23, E)

Mill Geek Comics
17624 15th Avenue SE, Suite #105a
Bothell, WA 98012
(206) 427-9663
millgeekcomics@gmail.com
millgeekcomics.com
(1-4, 6)

The Comics Keep
5060 State Hwy 303 NW, Suite 120
Bremerton, WA 98311
(360) 479-6421
contact@thecomicskeep.com
www.thecomicskeep.com
(2-4, 6-9, 21, 23, E)

A World of Collections
22611 76th Avenue West #101
Edmonds, WA 98026
(425) 778-2678
jdgoldy@yahoo.com
worldofcollections.com
(1-10, 12, 20, 21, A-E)

Everett Comics
2831 Wetmore Avenue
Everett, WA 98201
(425) 252-8181
everettcomics@aol.com
(2-7, 9, 10, 12, 18, 21, 23, D, E)

Pristine Comics
2008 South 314th Street
Federal Way, WA 98003
PH: (253) 941-1986
www.PristineComics.com

Danger Room Comics
201 4th Avenue W
Olympia, WA 98501
(360) 705-3050
Info@DangerRoomOly.com
www.DangerRoomOly.com
(1-10, 12, 20, 23)

Dreamstrands Comics
115 N 85th Street, Suite 106
Seattle, WA 98103
(206) 297-3737
delanor@dreamstrands.com
www.dreamstrands.com
(1-10, 18, 21, 23, D)

Golden Age Collectables
1501 Pike Place
#401 Lower Level
Seattle, WA 98101
(206) 622-9799
gacollect@gmail.com
www.goldenagecollectables.com
(1-4, 6-10, 15, 18, 19, 22-24, A-E)

Grumpy Old Man's Comics, Art & Collectibles
1732 NW Market Street
Seattle, WA 98107
(206) 257-0557
grumpyoldmanscomics@gmail.com
grumpyoldmanscomicsartcollectibles.com
(1-6, 12, 13, 16-18, 21, 24, E)

Arcane Comics, LLC
15202 Aurora Avenue N, Suite A
Shoreline, WA 98133
(206) 781-4875
info@arcanecomicbooks.com
arcanecomicbooks.com
(4, 6, 8-10, 12, 21, 23, 24, A-E)

Avalon Comics
10315 Silverdale Way D09
Silverdale, WA 98383
(360) 698-1501
leozak@hotmail.com
(2-9, 20-24, D, E)

Merlyn's Comics and Games
15 W Main
Spokane, WA 99201
(509) 624-0957
goribob@gmail.com
https://www.merlyns.biz
(3, 4, 6-10, 16, 17, E)

Monkey Biz, LLC
2928 N Nevada Street
Spokane, WA 99207
(509) 242-3500
monkeybizspokane@gmail.com
www.monkeybizspokane.com
(1-11, 15, 17, 18, 21, 23, A, C-E)

Atomic Comics
4020 S. Steele Street
Tacoma, WA 98409
(253) 472-1908
atomiccomics@comcast.net
www.facebook.com/atomic-comics
(1-4, 6, 10, 12, 16, 18, 21, 23, 24, A-E)

Phantom Zone Comics
1057 Southcenter Mall
Tukwila, WA 98188
(206) 695-2611
phantomzoneonline.com
(4, 10, 11, 21, 23, 24, A-E)

Digital Heroes
120 E. Alder St.
Walla Walla, WA 99362
PH: (509) 525-0380
info@digitalheroes.com
www.digitalheroes.com
(2-4, 6-10, 20, 21, 23, A, C-E)

WEST VIRGINIA

Comic Paradise Plus
401 Walnut Avenue
Fairmont, WV 26554
(304) 366-2228
comics@comicparadiseplus.com
www.comicparadiseplus.com
(1-5, 7-9, 18, 21-24, A-E)

Comic World
1204 4th Avenue
Huntington, WV 25701
(304) 522-3923
(1-6, 18, 20, 23, E)

Engage!
149 N Queen Street
Martinsburg, WV 25401
(681) 260-6691
engagebooksmartinsburg@gmail.com
engagebooksmartinsburg.com
(1-11, 16-18, 20, 21, 23-25, C-E)

Comic Paradise Plus 2
183 Holland Avenue
Morgantown, WV 26501
(304) 291-9576
comics@comicparadiseplus.com
www.comicparadiseplus.com
(4, 6-9, 21-24, A-E)

WISCONSIN

Inner Child Collectibles and Comics
5921 Sixth Avenue "A"
Kenosha, WI 53140
PH: (262) 653-0400
StevenKahn@sbcglobal.net
innerchildcomics.com
(1-6, 12-16, 18, 19, 21-24, A-D)

Galaxy Comics, Games & More
925 Clark Street
Stevens Point, WI 54481
(715) 544-0857
galaxycomicsstevenspoint@gmail.com
(4, 6, 8)

CANADA

ALBERTA

Beat Box Comics & Collectibles
5205 B Duncan Ave.
Box 720
Blackfalds, AB T0M 0J0
4038966777
beatboxcomics@gmail.com
(1-4, 6, 13, 18, 20, 23, 24, D, E)

Another Dimension
424 B - 10th Street NW
Calgary, AB T2N 1V9
(403) 283-7078
comics@another-dimension.com
www.another-dimension.com
(1-10, 12, 13, 18, 21, 23, 24, A-E)

Redd Skull Comics
720A Edmonton Trail NE
Calgary, AB T2E 3J4
(403) 230-2716
reddskullcomicscalgary@gmail.com
www.reddskull.com
(1-7, 10, 12, 18, 21-24, A, C-E)

BRITISH COLUMBIA

Heroes For Sale
33780 George Ferguson Way
Abbotsford, BC V2S 2M6
(604) 853-3790
heroesforsale@shaw.ca
www.heroesforsale.ca
(1-6, 18, 20, 21, 23, C-E)

Curious Comics
844 Goldstream Ave
Langford, BC V9B 2X7
(250) 592-1656
curiouscomics2@shaw.ca
curiouscomics.com
(2-10, 17-24, A-E)

Curious Comics
8c - 3200 North Island Hwy
Country Club Centre
Nanaimo, BC V9T 1W1
(250) 756-2157
curiouscomics3@shaw.ca
curiouscomics.com
(2, 4, 6-10, 17-24, A-E)

Curious Comics
631 Johnson St
Victoria, BC V8W 1M7
(250) 384-1656
curiousinfo@shaw.ca
curiouscomics.com
(1-10, 12, 17-24, A-E)

Legends Comics & Books
633 Johnson St
Victoria, BC V8R 5T4
(250) 388-3696
legendscomics@shaw.ca
legendscomics.ca
(1-6, 8, 10, 12, 13, 14, 17)

MANITOBA

Doug Sulipa's Comic World
Box 21986
Steinbach, MB., R5G 1B5
PH: (204) 346-3674
FAX: (204) 346-1632
dsulipa@gmail.com
www.dougcomicworld.com
(1-5, 8, 12, 14-20, 25, 26, C, D)

Book Fair Winnipeg, Inc.
340 Portage Ave
Winnipeg, MB R3C 0C3
(204) 957-0142
info@bookfaircomics.com
bookfaircomics.com
(1-6, 8-10, 12, 15-18, 20, 23, A-D)

Cover to Cover Bookshelf
3737B Portage Ave
Winnipeg, MB R3K 2A8
(204) 275-5700
tonyhazzardsbookshelf@hotmail.com
www.covertocoverbookshelf.com
(1-6, 10-12, 15, 16, 18, 21, 23-25, E)

NEW BRUNSWICK

Comic Hunter Fredericton
98 Regent St
Fredericton, NB E3B 3W4
(506) 206-2200
comichunterfton@gmail.com
https://comichunter.crystalcommerce.com
(1-10, 16, 17, 20, 21, 23, 24, A, C-E)

The Comic Hunter
467 Main St, Unit 300
Moncton, NB E1C 6T7
(506) 855-4950
thecomichunter@gmail.com
www.comichunter.net
(1-10, 21, 23, 24, D, E)

Heroes' Beacon Comics & Games
25 Charlotte Street
Saint John, NB E2L 2H3
(506) 214-5755
heroes@heroesbeacon.com
heroesbeacon.com
(1-4, 6-10, 21, 23, 24, A, C-E)

NOVA SCOTIA

Monster Comic Lounge
2089 Gottingen St.
Halifax, NS B3K 3B2
(902) 429-2398
mcrossman@ns.sympstico.ca
www.facebook.com/MonsterComicLounge
(1-10, 12, 16, 17, 21, 23, 24, A-E)

Strange Adventures Comix & Curiosities
5110 Prince St
Halifax, NS B3J 1L3
(902) 425-2140
shop@strangeadventures.com
www.strangeadventures.com
(1-14, 16-18, 20-24, A-E)

ONTARIO

Alternate Icons
156 Market Street
Brantford, ON N3T 3A4
(519) 865-7992
info@alternateicons.com
www.alternateicons.com
(2, 4, 6, 9, 10, 21, 23)

CaptCan Comics, Inc.
466 Elgin St
Brantford, ON N3S 7P8
(519) 770-2770
warren@captcancomics.ca
www.captcancomics.ca
(1-4, 6, 18, 21, 23, D, E)

Aardvark Comics
516 Plains Rd, Unit 4
Burlington, ON L7T 2E1
(905) 639-2161
aardvarkcomics@outlook.com
aardvarkcomics.com
(1-6, 12, 14, 15, 23)

Fantasy Realm
227 Pitt Street
Cornwall, ON K6J 3P8
(613) 933-7997
fantasyrealm@cogeco.ca
(2-4, 6, 23, E)

Big B Comics
1045 Upper James St.
Hamilton, ON L9C 3A6
PH: (905) 318-9636
mailbox@bigbcomics.com
www.bigbcomics.com
(1-7, 9, 10, 12, 13, 21-24, A-E)

Kingston Gaming Nexus / Kingston Nexus Hobbie
270 Bagot Street
Kingston, ON K7L 3G5
(613) 546-2565
kingstonnexus@gmail.com
www.kingstonnexus.ca
(1-10, 12, 20-24, A, C-E)

Heroes Comics
186 Dundas St
London, ON N6A 1G7
(519) 439-4955
heroes@heroescomics.ca
heroescomics.ca
(1-7, 9, 10, 12-15, 18, 20, 21, 23, 24, A-E)

AOD Collectables
3136 Cambourne Crescent
Mississauga, ON L5N 5E7
(416) 809-7067
aodcollectables@gmail.com
www.ebay.ca/str/aodcollectables
(1-21, 23-26, A-E)

Image Collections
181A Queen St. South
Mississauga, ON L5M 1L1
(905) 542-8307
comics@iprimus.ca
www.imagecollections.ca
(1-12, 14, 17, 18, 20, 23-26, B-E)

Fourth Dimension
237 Main Street South
Newmarket, ON L3Y 3Z4
(905) 715-7091
fourthdimensioncomics@gmail.com
(4, 6, 7, 12, 21, 23, E)

Worlds Collide
80 Simcoe St N
Oshawa, ON L1G 4S2
(905) 436-8999
comics@worldscollide.ca
www.worldscollide.ca
(1-4, 6-10, 21)

Myths, Legends & Heroes
240 Bank Street Unit #103
Ottawa, ON K2P 1X4
(613) 746-5772
mythslegendsandheroes@rogers.com
www.mythslegendsandheroes.com
(1-6, 10, 18, 21-24, A-E)

Comics North and Hidden Level Games
106 Elm Street
Sudbury, ON P3C 1T5
(705) 674-1015
comicsnorth@gmail.com
(2-4, 6, 21, 23, 24, D,

Comix Plus / Music Exchange
186 S. Algoma Street
Thunder Bay, ON P7B 3B9
(807) 345-5700
comixplusmusic@shaw.ca
www.comixplusmusic.com
(1-7, 10, 11, 16-21, 23-26, (A, C-E)

BMV Books
471 Bloor St West
Toronto, ON M5S 1X9
(416) 967-5757
bmvbooksannex@gmail.com
www.bmvbooks.com
(1-6, 8, 10-12, 16, 23-26, A-E)

Pendragon Comics and Cards
Cloverdale Mall
181-250 The East Mall
Toronto, ON M9B 3Y8
(416) 253-6974
pendragoncomics@gmail.com
pendragoncomics.com
(1-7, 12, 14, 16, 20-24, B-E)

The Beguiling Books and Art
319 College St
Toronto, ON M5T 1S2
(416) 533-9168
mail@beguiling.ca
www.beguiling.com
(1-6, 10, 12, 13, 15-17)

PRINCE EDWARD ISL.

The Comic Hunter
183 Queen Street
Charlottetown, PEI C1A 4B4
(902) 566-2926
jeff.comichunter@gmail.com
www.comichunter.net
(1-9)

QUEBEC

Multinational Comics & Cards
Montreal, QC
PH: (514) 891-6666
Larry.mcd1985@gmail.com
www.multinationalcomics.com
(1-9, 16-24, 26, C, D)

Librairie Première Issue
27A Rue d'Auteuil
Québec, PQ G1R 4B9
(418) 692-3985
lib.premiere.issue@gmail.com
www.facebook.com/librairiepremiereissue
(2, 4, 10, 12, 17, D)

SASKATCHEWAN

ComicReaders, Inc.
4603 Albert Stree
Regina, SK S4S 6B6
(306) 586-1414
contact@comicreaders.com
www.comicreaders.com
(4, 6-11, 23, 24, A-E)

Amazing Stories
2508A 8th Street E
Saskatoon, SK S7H OV6
(306) 242-8996
amazingstoriessk@gmail.com
amazingstoriescomics.com
(2-4, 6-10, 20, 21, 23, 24, B-E)

ITALY

La Borsa del Fumetto
Via Panfilo Castaldi 23
Milano 20124
Italy
info@borsadelfumetto.com
www.borsadelfumetto.com
(3, 4, 6, 8, 10, 13, 18)

THE NETHERLANDS

Henk Comics and Manga Store
Zeedijk 101
Amsterdam 1012 AV
Netherlands
+31-20-4213688
henk@comics.nl
www.comics.nl
(2-10, 12, 18-21, 23, 24, A-E)

SWEDEN

Comics Heaven
Stora Nygatan 23
Stockholm 11127
Sweden
info@comicsheaven.se
www.comicsheaven.se
(2, 4-6, 10, 12, 21, 23)

INTERNET

ComicLink Auctions & Exchange
PH: (617) 517-0062
buysell@ComicLink.com
www.ComicLink.com

Get Cash For Comics
PH: (888) 440-9787; ext. 117
buying@getcashforcomics.com

Multinational Comics & Cards
PH: (514) 891-6666
Larry.mcd1985@gmail.com
www.multinationalcomics.com
(1-9, 16-24, 26, C, D)

MyComicShop.com
PH: (817) 860-7827
buytrade@mycomicshop.com
www.mycomicshop.com

ITEM CODES
(1) Golden Age Comics
(2) Silver Age Comics
(3) Bronze Age Comics
(4) New Comics & Magazines
(5) Back Issue magazines
(6) Comic Supplies
(7) Collectible Card Games
(8) Role Playing Games
(9) Gaming Supplies
(10) Manga
(11) Anime
(12) Underground Comics
(13) Original Comic Art
(14) Pulps
(15) Big Little Books
(16) Books - Used
(17) Books - New
(18) Comic Related Posters
(19) Movie Posters
(20) Trading Cards
(21) Statues/Mini-busts, etc.
(22) Premiums (Rings, Decoders)
(23) Action Figures
(24) Other Toys
(25) Records/CDs
(26) DVDs/VHS
(A) Doctor Who Items
(B) Simpsons Items
(C) Star Trek Items
(D) Star Wars Items
(E) HeroClix

GLOSSARY

a - Story art; **a(i)** - Story art inks; **a(p)** - Story art pencils; **a(r)** - Story art reprint.

ADULT MATERIAL - Contains story and/or art for "mature" readers. Re: sex, violence, strong language.

ADZINE - A magazine primarily devoted to the advertising of comic books and collectibles as its first publishing priority as opposed to written articles.

ALLENTOWN COLLECTION - A collection discovered in 1987-88 just outside Allentown, Pennsylvania. The Allentown collection consisted of 135 Golden Age comics, characterized by high grade and superior paper quality.

ANNUAL - (1) A book that is published yearly; (2) Can also refer to some square bound comics.

ARRIVAL DATE - The date written (often in pencil) or stamped on the cover of comics by either the local wholesaler, newsstand owner, or distributor. The date precedes the cover date by approximately 15 to 75 days, and may vary considerably from one locale to another or from one year to another.

ASHCAN - A publisher's in-house facsimile of a proposed new title. Most ashcans have black and white covers stapled to an existing coverless comic on the inside; other ashcans are totally black and white. In modern parlance, it can also refer to promotional or sold comics, often smaller than standard comic size and usually in black and white, released by publishers to advertise the forthcoming arrival of a new title or story.

ATOM AGE - Comics published from 1946-1956.

B&W - Black and white art.

BACK-UP FEATURE - A story or character that usually appears after the main feature in a comic book; often not featured on the cover.

BAD GIRL ART - A term popularized in the early '90s to describe an attitude as well as a style of art that portrays women in a sexual and often action-oriented way.

BAXTER PAPER - A high quality, heavy, white paper used in the printing of some comics.

BC - Abbreviation for Back Cover.

BI-MONTHLY - Published every two months.

BI-WEEKLY - Published every two weeks.

BONDAGE COVER - Usually denotes a female in bondage.

BOUND COPY - A comic that has been bound into a book. The process requires that the spine be trimmed and sometimes sewn into a book-like binding.

BRITISH ISSUE - A comic printed for distribution in Great Britain; these copies sometimes have the price listed in pence or pounds instead of cents or dollars.

BRITTLENESS - A severe condition of paper deterioration where paper loses its flexibility and thus chips and/or flakes easily.

BRONZE AGE - Comics published from 1970 to 1984.

BROWNING - (1) The aging of paper characterized by the ever-increasing level of oxidation characterized by darkening; (2) The level of paper deterioration one step more severe than tanning and one step before brittleness.

c - Cover art; **c(i)** - Cover inks; **c(p)** - Cover pencils; **c(r)** - Cover reprint.

CAMEO - The brief appearance of one character in the strip of another.

CANADIAN ISSUE - A comic printed for distribution in Canada; these copies sometimes have no advertising.

CCA - Abbreviation for **Comics Code Authority**.

CCA SEAL - An emblem that was placed on the cover of all CCA approved comics beginning in April-May, 1955.

CENTER CREASE - See Subscription Copy.

CENTERFOLD or CENTER SPREAD - The two folded pages in the center of a comic book at the terminal end of the staples.

CERTIFIED GRADING - A process provided by a professional grading service that certifies a given grade for a comic and seals the book in a protective **Slab**.

CF - Abbreviation for Centerfold.

CFO - Abbreviation for Centerfold Out.

CGC - Abbreviation for the certified comic book grading company, Comics Guaranty, LLC.

CIRCULATION COPY - See Subscription Copy.

CIRCULATION FOLD - See Subscription Fold.

CLASSIC COVER - A cover considered by collectors to be highly desirable because of its subject matter, artwork, historical importance, etc.

CLEANING - A process in which dirt and dust is removed.

COLOR TOUCH - A restoration process by which colored ink is used to hide color flecks, color flakes, and larger areas of missing color. Short for Color Touch-Up.

COLORIST - An artist who paints the color guides for comics. Many modern colorists use computer technology.

COMIC BOOK DEALER - (1) A seller of comic books; (2) One who makes a living buying and selling comic books.

COMIC BOOK REPAIR - When a tear, loose staple or centerfold has been mended without changing or adding to the original finish of the book. Repair may involve tape, glue or nylon gossamer, and is easily detected; it is considered a defect.

COMICS CODE AUTHORITY - A voluntary organization comprised of comic book publishers formed in 1954 to review (and possibly censor) comic books before they were printed and distributed. The emblem of the CCA is a white stamp in the upper right hand corner of comics dated after February 1955. The term "post-Code" refers to the time after this practice started, or approximately 1955 to the present.

COMPLETE RUN - All issues of a given title.

CON - A convention or public gathering of fans.

CONDITION - The state of preservation of a comic book, often inaccurately used interchangeably with Grade.

CONSERVATION - The European Confederation of Conservator-Restorers' Organizations (ECCO) in its professional guidelines, defines conservation as follows: "Conservation consists mainly of direct action carried out on cultural heritage with the aim of stabilizing condition and retarding further deterioration."

COPPER AGE - Comics published from 1984 to 1992.

COSMIC AEROPLANE COLLECTION - A collection from Salt Lake City, Utah discovered by Cosmic Aeroplane Books, characterized by the moderate to high grade copies of 1930s-40s comics with pencil check marks in the margins of inside pages. It is thought that these comics were kept by a commercial illustration school and the check marks were placed beside panels that instructors wanted students to draw.

COSTUMED HERO - A costumed crime fighter with "developed" human powers instead of super powers.

COUPON CUT or COUPON MISSING - A coupon has been neatly removed with scissors or razor blade from the interior or exterior of the comic as opposed to having been ripped out.

COVER GLOSS - The reflective quality of the cover inks.

COVER TRIMMED - Cover has been reduced in size by neatly cutting away rough or damaged edges.

COVERLESS - A comic with no cover attached. There is a niche demand for coverless comics, particularly in the case of hard-to-find key books otherwise impossible to locate intact.

C/P - Abbreviation for **Cleaned and Pressed**. See **Cleaning**.

CREASE - A fold which causes ink removal, usually resulting in a white line. See **Reading Crease**.

CROSSOVER - A story where one character appears prominently in the story of another character. See **X-Over**.

CVR - Abbreviation for Cover.

DEALER - See **Comic Book Dealer**.

DEACIDIFICATION - Several different processes that reduce acidity in paper.

DEBUT - The first time that a character appears anywhere.

DEFECT - Any fault or flaw that detracts from perfection.

DENVER COLLECTION - A collection consisting primarily of early 1940s high grade number one issues bought at auction in Pennsylvania by a Denver, Colorado dealer.

DIE-CUT COVER - A comic book cover with areas or edges precut by a printer to a special shape or to create a desired effect.

DISTRIBUTOR STRIPES - Color brushed or sprayed on the edges of comic book stacks by the distributor/wholesaler to code them for expedient exchange at the sales racks. Typical colors are red, orange, yellow, green, blue, and purple. Distributor stripes are not a defect.

DOUBLE - A duplicate copy of the same comic book.

DOUBLE COVER - When two covers are stapled to the comic interior instead of the usual one; the exterior cover often protects the interior cover from wear and damage. This is considered a desirable situation by some collectors and may increase collector value; this is not considered a defect.

DRUG PROPAGANDA STORY - A comic that makes an editorial stand about drug use.

DRUG USE STORY - A comic that shows the actual use of drugs: needle use, tripping, harmful effects, etc.

DRY CLEANING - A process in which dirt and dust is removed.

DUOTONE - Printed with black and one other color of ink. This process was common in comics printed in the 1930s.

DUST SHADOW - Darker, usually linear area at the edge of some comics stored in stacks. Some portion of the cover was not covered by the comic immediately above it and it was exposed to settling dust particles. Also see **Oxidation Shadow** and **Sun Shadow**.

EDGAR CHURCH COLLECTION - See **Mile High Collection**.

EMBOSSED COVER - A comic book cover with a pattern, shape or image pressed into the cover from

the inside, creating a raised area.
ENCAPSULATION - Refers to the process of sealing certified comics in a protective plastic enclosure. Also see **Slabbing**.
EYE APPEAL - A term which refers to the overall look of a comic book when held at approximately arm's length. A comic may have nice eye appeal yet still possess defects which reduce grade.
FANZINE - An amateur fan publication.
FC - Abbreviation for Front Cover.
FILE COPY - A high grade comic originating from the publisher's file; contrary to what some might believe, not all file copies are in Gem Mint condition. An arrival date on the cover of a comic does not indicate that it is a file copy, though a copyright date may.
FIRST APPEARANCE - See **Debut**.
FLASHBACK - When a previous story is recalled.
FOIL COVER - A comic book cover that has had a thin metallic foil hot stamped on it. Many of these "gimmick" covers date from the early '90s, and might include chromium, prism and hologram covers as well.
FOUR COLOR - Series of comics produced by Dell, characterized by hundreds of different features; named after the four color process of printing. See **One Shot**.
FOUR COLOR PROCESS - The process of printing with the three primary colors (red, yellow, and blue) plus black.
FUMETTI - Illustration system in which individual frames of a film are colored and used for individual panels to make a comic book story. The most famous example is DC's *Movie Comics* #1-6 from 1939.
GATEFOLD COVER - A double-width fold-out cover.
GENRE - Categories of comic book subject matter; e.g. Science Fiction, Super-Hero, Romance, Funny Animal, Teenage Humor, Crime, War, Western, Mystery, Horror, etc.
GIVEAWAY - Type of comic book intended to be given away as a premium or promotional device instead of being sold.
GLASSES ATTACHED - In 3-D comics, the special blue and red cellophane and cardboard glasses are still attached to the comic.
GLASSES DETACHED - In 3-D comics, the special blue and red cellophane and cardboard glasses are not still attached to the comic; obviously less desirable than Glasses Attached.
GOLDEN AGE - Comics published from 1938 (*Action Comics* #1) to 1945.
GOOD GIRL ART - Refers to a style of art, usually from the 1930s-50s, that portrays women in a sexually implicit way.
GREY-TONE COVER - A cover art style in which pencil or charcoal underlies the normal line drawing, used to enhance the effects of light and shadow, thus producing a richer quality. These covers, prized by most collectors, are sometimes referred to as **Painted Covers** but are not actually painted.
HC - Abbreviation for Hardcover.
HEADLIGHTS - Forward illumation devices installed on all automobiles and many other vehicles... OK, OK, it's a euphemism for a comic book cover prominently featuring a woman's breasts in a provocative way. Also see **Bondage Cover** for another collecting euphemism that has long since outlived its appropriateness in these politically correct times.
HOT STAMPING - The process of pressing foil, prism paper and/or inks on cover stock.
HRN - Abbreviation for Highest Reorder Number. This refers to a method used by collectors of Gilberton's *Classic Comics* and *Classics Illustrated* series to distinguish first editions from later printings.
ILLO - Abbreviation for Illustration.
IMPAINT - Another term for **Color Touch**.
INDICIA - Publishing and title information usually located at the bottom of the first page or the bottom of the inside front cover. In some pre-1938 comics and many modern comics, it is located on internal pages.
INFINITY COVER - Shows a scene that repeats itself to infinity.
INKER - Artist that does the inking.
INTRO - Same as **Debut**.
INVESTMENT GRADE COPY - (1) Comic of sufficiently high grade and demand to be viewed by collectors as instantly liquid should the need arise to sell; (2) A comic in VF or better condition; (3) A comic purchased primarily to realize a profit.
ISSUE NUMBER - The actual edition number of a given title.
ISH - Short for Issue.
JLA - Abbreviation for Justice League of America.
JSA - Abbreviation for Justice Society of America.
KEY, KEY BOOK or KEY ISSUE - An issue that contains a first appearance, origin, or other historically or artistically important feature considered especially desirable by collectors.
LAMONT LARSON - Pedigreed collection of high grade 1940s comics with the initials or name of its original owner, Lamont Larson.
LENTICULAR COVERS or "FLICKER" COVERS - A comic book cover overlayed with a ridged plastic sheet such that the special artwork underneath appears to move when the cover is tilted at different angles perpendicular to the ridges.
LETTER COL or LETTER COLUMN - A feature in a comic book that

prints and sometimes responds to letters written by its readers.

LINE DRAWN COVER - A cover published in the traditional way where pencil sketches are over-drawn with india ink and then colored. See also **Grey-Tone Cover**, **Photo Cover**, and **Painted Cover**.

LOGO - The title of a strip or comic book as it appears on the cover or title page.

LSH - Abbreviation for Legion of Super-Heroes.

MAGIC LIGHTNING COLLECTION - A collection of high grade 1950s comics from the San Francisco area.

MARVEL CHIPPING - A bindery (trimming/cutting) defect that results in a series of chips and tears at the top, bottom, and right edges of the cover, caused when the cutting blade of an industrial paper trimmer becomes dull. It was dubbed Marvel Chipping because it can be found quite often on Marvel comics from the late '50s and early '60s but can also occur with any company's comic books from the late 1940s through the middle 1960s.

MILE HIGH COLLECTION - High grade collection of over 22,000 comics discovered in Denver, Colorado in 1977, originally owned by Mr. Edgar Church. Comics from this collection are now famous for extremely white pages, fresh smell, and beautiful cover ink reflectivity.

MODERN AGE - A catch-all term applied to comics published since 1992.

MYLAR™ - An inert, very hard, space-age plastic used to make high quality protective bags and sleeves for comic book storage. "Mylar" is a trademark of the DuPont Co.

ND - Abbreviation for **No Date**.

NN - Abbreviation for **No Number**.

NO DATE - When there is no date given on the cover or indicia page.

NO NUMBER - No issue number is given on the cover or indicia page; these are usually first issues or one-shots.

N.Y. LEGIS. COMM. - New York Legislative Committee to Study the Publication of Comics (1951).

ONE-SHOT - When only one issue is published of a title, or when a series is published where each issue is a different title (e.g. Dell's *Four Color Comics*).

ORIGIN - When the story of a character's creation is given.

over guide - When a comic book is priced at a value over *Guide* list.

OXIDATION SHADOW - Darker, usually linear area at the edge of some comics stored in stacks. Some portion of the cover was not covered by the comic immediately above it, and it was exposed to the air. Also see **Dust Shadow** and **Sun Shadow**.

p - Art pencils.

PAINTED COVER - (1) Cover taken from an actual painting instead of a line drawing; (2) Inaccurate name for a grey-toned cover.

PANELOLOGIST - One who researches comic books and/or comic strips.

PANNAPICTAGRAPHIST - One possible term for someone who collects comic books; can you figure out why it hasn't exactly taken off in common parlance?

PAPER COVER - Comic book cover made from the same newsprint as the interior pages. These books are extremely rare in high grade.

PARADE OF PLEASURE - A book about the censorship of comics.

PB - Abbreviation for Paperback.

PEDIGREE - A book from a famous and usually high grade collection - e.g. Allentown, Lamont Larson, Edgar Church/Mile High, Denver, San Francisco, Cosmic Aeroplane, etc. Beware of non-pedigree collections being promoted as pedigree books; only outstanding high grade collections similar to those listed qualify.

PENCILER - Artist that does the pencils...you're figuring out some of these definitions without us by now, aren't you?

PERFECT BINDING - Pages are glued to the cover as opposed to being stapled to the cover, resulting in a flat binded side. Also known as **Square Back or Square Bound**.

PG - Abbreviation for Page.

PHOTO COVER - Comic book cover featuring a photographic image instead of a line drawing or painting.

PIECE REPLACEMENT - A process by which pieces are added to replace areas of missing paper.

PIONEER AGE - Comics published from the 1500s to 1828.

PLATINUM AGE - Comics published from 1883 to 1938.

POLYPROPYLENE - A type of plastic used in the manufacture of comic book bags; now considered harmful to paper and not recommended for long term storage of comics.

POP - Abbreviation for the anti-comic book volume, *Parade of Pleasure*.

POST-CODE - Describes comics published after February 1955 and usually displaying the CCA stamp in the upper right-hand corner.

POUGHKEEPSIE - Refers to a large collection of Dell Comics file copies believed to have originated from the warehouse of Western Publishing in Poughkeepsie, NY.

PP - Abbreviation for Pages.

PRE-CODE - Describes comics published before the **Comics Code Authority** seal began appearing on covers in 1955.

PRE-HERO DC - A term used to describe *More Fun* #1-51

(pre-Spectre), *Adventure* #1-39 (pre-Sandman), and *Detective* #1-26 (pre-Batman). The term is actually inaccurate because technically there were "heroes" in the above books.

PRE-HERO MARVEL - A term used to describe *Strange Tales* #1-100 (pre-Human Torch), *Journey Into Mystery* #1-82 (pre-Thor), *Tales To Astonish* #1-35 (pre-Ant-Man), and *Tales Of Suspense* #1-38 (pre-Iron Man).

PRESERVATION - Another term for **Conservation**.

PRESSING - A term used to describe a variety of processes or procedures, professional and amateur, under which an issue is pressed to eliminate wrinkles, bends, dimples and/or other perceived defects and thus improve its appearance. Some types of pressing involve disassembling the book and performing other work on it prior to its pressing and reassembly. Some methods are generally easily discerned by professionals and amateurs. Other types of pressing, however, can pose difficulty for even experienced professionals to detect. In all cases, readers are cautioned that unintended damage can occur in some instances. Related defects will diminish an issue's grade correspondingly rather than improve it.

PROVENANCE - When the owner of a book is known and is stated for the purpose of authenticating and documenting the history of the book. Example: A book from the Stan Lee or Forrest Ackerman collection would be an example of a value-adding provenance.

PULP - Cheaply produced magazine made from low grade newsprint. The term comes from the wood pulp that was used in the paper manufacturing process.

QUARTERLY - Published every three months (four times a year).

R - Abbreviation for Reprint.

RARE - 10-20 copies estimated to exist.

RAT CHEW - Damage caused by the gnawing of rats and mice.

RBCC - Abbreviation for Rockets Blast Comic Collector, one of the first and most prominent adzines instrumental in developing the early comic book market.

READING COPY - A comic that is in FAIR to GOOD condition and is often used for research; the condition has been sufficiently reduced to the point where general handling will not degrade it further.

READING CREASE - Book-length, vertical front cover crease at staples, caused by bending the cover over the staples. Square-bounds receive these creases just by opening the cover too far to the left.

REILLY, TOM - A large high grade collection of 1939-1945 comics with 5000+ books.

REINFORCEMENT - A process by which a weak or split page or cover is reinforced with adhesive and reinforcement paper.

REPRINT COMICS - In earlier decades, comic books that contained newspaper strip reprints; modern reprint comics usually contain stories originally featured in older comic books.

RESTORATION - Any attempt, whether professional or amateur, to enhance the appearance of an aging or damaged comic book using additive procedures. These procedures may include any or all of the following techniques: recoloring, adding missing paper, trimming, re-glossing, reinforcement, glue, etc. Amateur work can lower the value of a book, and even professional restoration has now gained a negative aura in the modern marketplace from some quarters. In all cases a restored book can never be worth the same as an unrestored book in the same condition. There is no consensus on the inclusion of pressing, non-aqueous cleaning, tape removal and in some cases staple replacement in this definition. Until such time as there is consensus, we encourage continued debate and interaction among all interested parties and reflection upon the standards in other hobbies and art forms.

REVIVAL - An issue that begins republishing a comic book character after a period of dormancy.

ROCKFORD - A high grade collection of 1940s comics with 2000+ books from Rockford, IL.

ROLLED SPINE - A condition where the left edge of a comic book curves toward the front or back; a defect caused by folding back each page as the comic was read.

ROUND BOUND - Standard saddle stitch binding typical of most comics.

RUN - A group of comics of one title where most or all of the issues are present. See **Complete Run**.

S&K - Abbreviation for the legendary creative team of Joe Simon and Jack Kirby, creators of Marvel Comics' Captain America.

SADDLE STITCH - The staple binding of magazines and comic books.

san francisco collection - (see **Reilly, Tom**)

SCARCE - 20-100 copies estimated to exist.

SEDUCTION OF THE INNOCENT - An inflammatory book written by Dr. Frederic Wertham and published in 1953; Wertham asserted that comics were responsible for rampant juvenile deliquency in American youth.

SET - (1) A complete run of a given title; (2) A grouping of comics for sale.

SEMI-MONTHLY - Published twice a month, but not necessarily **Bi-Weekly**.
SEWN SPINE - A comic with many spine perforations where binders' thread held it into a bound volume. This is considered a defect.
SF - Abbreviation for Science Fiction (the other commonly used term, "sci-fi," is often considered derogatory or indicative of more "low-brow" rather than "literary" science fiction, i.e. "sci-fi television."
SILVER AGE - Comics published from 1956 to 1970.
SILVER PROOF - A black and white actual size print on thick glossy paper hand-painted by an artist to indicate colors to the engraver.
SLAB - Colloquial term for the plastic enclosure used by grading certification companies to seal in certified comics.
SLABBING - Colloquial term for the process of encapsulating certified comics in a plastic enclosure.
SOTI - Abbreviation for **Seduction of the Innocent**.
SPINE - The left-hand edge of the comic that has been folded and stapled.
SPINE ROLL - A condition where the left edge of the comic book curves toward the front or back, caused by folding back each page as the comic was read.
SPINE SPLIT SEALED - A process by which a spine split is sealed using an adhesive.
SPLASH PAGE - A **Splash Panel** that takes up the entire page.
SPLASH PANEL - (1) The first panel of a comic book story, usually larger than other panels and usually containing the title and credits of the story; (2) An oversized interior panel.
SQUARE BACK or SQUARE BOUND - See **Perfect Binding**.
STORE STAMP - Store name (and sometimes address and telephone number) stamped in ink via rubber stamp and stamp pad.
SUBSCRIPTION COPY - A comic sent through the mail directly from the publisher or publisher's agent. Most are folded in half, causing a subscription crease or fold running down the center of the comic from top to bottom; this is considered a defect.
SUBSCRIPTION CREASE - See **Subscription Copy**.
SUBSCRIPTION FOLD - See **Subscription Copy**. Differs from a **Subscription Crease** in that no ink is missing as a result of the fold.
SUN SHADOW - Darker, usually linear area at the edge of some comics stored in stacks. Some portion of the cover was not covered by the comic immediately above it, and it suffered prolonged exposure to light. A serious defect, unlike a **Dust Shadow**, which can sometimes be removed. Also see **Oxidation Shadow**.
SUPER-HERO - A costumed crime fighter with powers beyond those of mortal man.
SUPER-VILLAIN - A costumed criminal with powers beyond those of mortal man; the antithesis of **Super-Hero**.
SWIPE - A panel, sequence, or story obviously borrowed from previously published material.
TEAR SEALS - A process by which a tear is sealed using an adhesive.
TEXT ILLO. - A drawing or small panel in a text story that almost never has a dialogue balloon.
TEXT PAGE - A page with no panels or drawings.
TEXT STORY - A story with few if any illustrations commonly used as filler material during the first three decades of comics.
3-D COMIC - Comic art that is drawn and printed in two color layers, producing a 3-D effect when viewed through special glasses.
3-D EFFECT COMIC - Comic art that is drawn to appear as if in 3-D but isn't.
TITLE - The name of the comic book.
TITLE PAGE - First page of a story showing the title of the story and possibly the creative credits and indicia.
TRIMMED - (1) A bindery process which separates top, right, and bottom of pages and cuts comic books to the proper size; (2) A repair process in which defects along the edges of a comic book are removed with the use of scissors, razor blades, and/or paper cutters. Comic books which have been repaired in this fashion are considered defectives.
TTA - Abbreviation for *Tales to Astonish*.
UK - Abbreviation for British edition (United Kingdom).
UNDER GUIDE - When a comic book is priced at a value less than Guide list.
UPGRADE - To obtain another copy of the same comic book in a higher grade.
VARIANT COVER - A different cover image used on the same issue.
VERY RARE - 1 to 10 copies estimated to exist.
VICTORIAN AGE - Comics published from 1828 to 1883.
WANT LIST - A listing of comics needed by a collector, or a list of comics that a collector is interested in purchasing.
WAREHOUSE COPY - Originating from a publisher's warehouse; similar to file copy.
WHITE MOUNTAIN COLLECTION - A collection of high grade 1950s and 1960s comics which originated in New England.
X-OVER - Short for **Crossover**.
ZINE - Short for **Fanzine**.

CGC

How the Company Has Grown and How It Works

By the CGC Grading Team

The world of comic book collecting has grown and matured considerably since the 2000 introduction of CGC (Certified Guaranty Company). Before the founding of CGC comic book transactions required sellers to grade their own comic books, a practice that often lacked consistency and impartiality. They also had to check their books for restoration, which was limited to each sellers' skills at detection. During the first decades of fandom most sales took place through mail order, as well as local comic shops or the occasional convention. The advent of the internet changed all that, allowing global buying and selling, regardless of a person's location or experience. While this greatly expanded the comic book market, it also greatly increased the potential for inaccurate grading and restoration detection.

CGC was created to help bring order and stability to comic book sales, and to put an end to the risk and the chaos that accompanied online sales. CGC is the first and largest independent, impartial, third-party comic book grading service. A proven and respected commitment to integrity, accuracy, consistency, and impartiality has made CGC the leader in its field, becoming a tool to help people with their buying and selling decisions. The universally accepted grading scale ensures consistency and gives both dealers and collectors a sense of dependability when making purchasing decisions. With CGC certification, a collector knows what he or she is getting based on an accurate and comprehensive description that can be found on the CGC certification label.

If you've ever wondered about how it's done, here's a look at how CGC came together and how a book is certified.

The Formation of the Company

In January of 2000, CGC was launched under the umbrella of the Certified Collectibles Group, which includes Numismatic Guaranty Corporation (NGC), the largest third-party coin grading company in the world, Numismatic Conservation Services (NCS), the leading authority in numismatic conservation, Paper Money Guaranty (PMG), the world's leading currency certification company, and Classic Collectible Services (CCS), the world's premier comic book restoration, restoration removal and pressing company.

The Collectibles Group sought out talented and ethical individuals to grade comic books. Experts needed a history of comics as well as necessary skills to verify a comic book's authenticity and to detect restoration that can affect its value. To identify these individuals, many of the most respected individuals in the hobby were consulted, and, based on their recommendations a core grading team was selected.

The members of the CGC grading team come from diverse backgrounds, and many were comic book dealers at some time in their careers. Experience in the commercial sector can be an essential ingredient in becoming familiar with market standards.

When it was time to develop a uniform grading standard, the hobby's leaders were once again called upon. Everyone agreed that *The Overstreet Comic Book Price Guide* was the foundation of this standard, but there were a number of subjective interpretations of its published definitions. It was critical to understand how these guidelines were being applied to the everyday buying and selling of comics. To accomplish this, approximately 50 of the hobby's top experts took part in an extensive grading test. Their grades were averaged and an accurate grading standard reflecting the collective experience of the hobby's most prominent individuals was thus developed. CGC now had the best standard and the best team to apply it.

With the graders in place and the grading scale established, the next step was to develop a tamper-evident holder for the long-term storage and display of certified comics. This proved to be a technical challenge. Exhaustive material tests were conducted to determine that the holders were archival safe. To create a true first line of defense, it was determined that the comic book should be sealed in a soft inner well, then sealed again inside a tamper evident hard plastic case with interlocking ridges to enable compact storage. The CGC certified grade appears on a label sealed inside the holder for an additional level of security.

Submitting Books

Comic books may be submitted for certification in two ways - they can be submitted by authorized dealers or by Collectors Society members. The Collectors Society is an online community with direct access to certification service from CGC, and submissions can be prepared using the online submission form. Both dealers and Collectors Society members typically send their comics to CGC's offices by registered mail or through an insured express company. Submissions are also accepted at many of the comic cons that occur around the country throughout the year. CGC will grade on-site at selected shows.

Receiving the Books

Every day, CGC's Receiving Department opens arrived packages and immediately verifies that the number of books in each package matches the number shown on the submitted invoice and checks the submission for any damage sustained in shipping. Once this is done, a more detailed comparison is made to ensure that their invoice descriptions correspond to the actual comics. This information is entered into a computer, and from this time forth, the comics will be traceable at all stages of the grading process by their invoice number and their line number within that invoice. Each book is checked to see that it is properly prepared for grading in an appropriately sized comic bag with backing board and then is labeled with a numbered barcode containing the pertinent data of invoice number and line-item information for quick reading by the computer.

The Grading Begins

The book is then passed on to the graders. The grading process begins by having the book's pages counted and entering into the computer any peculiarities or flaws that may affect a book's grade. Some examples of this would be "Spine Stress Lines Break Color," "Right Top Front Cover Small Crease Breaks Color," "Top Back Cover Tear with Crease" and "Staple Rusted with Rust Stained Interior." This information is entered into the "Graders Notes" field and a grade is assigned. The book is also examined for restoration; if any form of restoration work is detected, this information is entered into the computer, broken down by each form of restoration found.

When other graders examine the comic, they do not see any previous assigned grades, so as to not influence their evaluation. Graders are able to view previous Graders Notes while determining their own grade. The Grader may then add to the existing commentary if he or she believes more remarks are in order. The Grading Finalizer is the last person to examine the book. He or she makes a final restoration check before determining their own grade, at which time the grades and notes entered by the previous graders are reviewed. If all grades match or are very close, they will assign the book's final grade. The book is then forwarded to the Encapsulation Department for sealing. If there is disagreement among the graders, a discussion will ensue until a final determination is made and the book forwarded.

Each comic book receives a restoration check and the results appear on the label.

CGC RESTORED GRADE
X-Men #1
Marvel Comics, 9/63
Restoration includes: color touch, pieces added, tear seals, cover cleaned, interior lightened, reinforced.
OFF-WHITE Pages

Encapsulating the Comics

After each comic has been graded and the necessary numbers and text entered into their respective data fields, all the comics on a particular invoice are taken from the Grading Department into the Encapsulation Department. Here, appropriately color-coded labels are printed bearing the proper descriptive text, including each book's grade and identification number. This is critical, as it serves to make each certified comic unique and is also a significant deterrent to counterfeiting CGC's valued product. All of the above information is duplicated in a barcode, which also appears on the comic's label.

The newly printed labels are stacked in the same sequence as the comics to be encapsulated with them, ensuring that each book and its label match one another. The comic is now ready to be fitted inside an archival-quality interior well, which is then sealed within a transparent capsule, along with the book's color-coded label. This is accomplished through a combination of compression and ultrasonic vibration.

The Comics are Shipped

After encapsulation, all comics are sent briefly to the Quality Control for inspection. Here, they are examined to make certain that their labels are correct for both the grade and its accompanying descriptive information. Quality control also inspects each book for any flaws in its holder, such as scuffs or nicks. While these are quite rare, CGC is careful to make certain that the comics it certifies are not only accurately graded, but attractively presented as well. When all the comics have been inspected, they are delivered to our Shipping Department for packaging. The comics are counted, and their labels checked against the original invoice to make certain that no mistakes have occurred. A Shipping Department employee then verifies the method of transport as selected by the submitter on the invoice and prepares the comics for delivery or they are held in CGC's vault for in-person pick-up by the submitter.

No matter whether the US Postal Service or a private carrier is used, the method of packaging is essentially the same. The encapsulated comics are placed inside sturdy cardboard boxes. CGC has developed a custom shipping box to enable the highest level of stability during shipping. A copy of the submitter's invoice is included before the box is sealed and heavy tape is used to prevent accidental or unauthorized opening of the box while it is in transit.

The barcode of every comic book is scanned before it is placed into its shipping box. The status of the book is changed to "shipped" in our tracking system, and we retain a record of what books were shipped in which box. This is the final crucial step of our detailed internal tracking system.

The CGC Label

Comic books certified by CGC bear color-coded labels that have different meanings. Whenever purchasing a CGC-certified comic, be certain to note not only the book's grade but also its label category. A Universal label is denoted by the color blue and indicates that a book was not found to have any qualifying defects or signs of restoration. There is one exception to this policy: At CGC's discretion, comics having a very minor amount of color touch or glue may still qualify for a Universal label provided such restoration is noted underneath the assigned grade.

As its name implies, the Restored label, identified by its purple color, is used for books found to have restoration work performed on them. The grade assigned is based on the book's appearance, with the restoration noted. The Restoration scale determines the quality (A, B, or C) and quantity (between 1 and 5) of any restoration present, and is as follows: **Quality (Aesthetic) Scale** – (Determined by materials used and visual quality of work)

A (Excellent)

- Material used: rice paper, wheat paste, acrylic or water color, leaf casting
- Color match near perfect, no bleed through
- Piece fill seamless and correct thickness
- No fading, excessive whiteness, ripples, cockling, or ink smudges from cover or interior cleaning
- Book feels natural
- Near perfect staple alignment, or replaced exactly as they were
- Filled edges cut to look natural and even
- Cleaned staples or staples replaced with vintage staples
- Married cover/pages match in size and page quality. Professionally attached

B (Fine)

- Material used: pencil, crayon, chalk, re-glossing agent, piece fill from cadavers
- Piece fill obvious upon close inspection, obvious to the touch
- Color touch obvious upon close inspection, or done with materials listed above
- Cover cleaning resulting in slight color fading or excessively white
- Interior cleaning resulting in slight puffiness, cockling, excessively white
- Enlarged staple holes, obviously crooked staples, or backwards staple insertion
- Replaced staples not vintage
- Married cover/pages do not match in size and/or page quality. Professionally attached

C (Poor)

- Material used: glue, pen, marker, white out, white paper to fill missing pieces
- Piece fill obvious at arm's length
- Bad color matching, use of pen or marker. Bleed through evident
- Cover cleaning resulting in washed out/speckled colors, moderate cockling and/or ripples
- New staple holes created upon reinsertion, or non-comic book staples used
- Married cover/pages poorly attached with non-professional materials

Quantity Scale – *(Determined primarily by extent of piece fill and color touch)*

1 (Slight)

Re-glossing, interior lightening, piece fill no more than size of two bindery chips, light color touch in small areas like spine stress, corner crease or bindery chip fill. Married cover or interior pages/wraps (if other work is present)

2 (Slight/Moderate)

Piece fill up to the ½" x ½" and/or color touch covering up to 1" x 1". Interior piece fill up to 1" x 1"

3 (Moderate)

Piece fill up to the size of 1" x 1" and/or color touch covering up to 2" x 2". Interior piece fill up to 2" x 2"

4 (Moderate/Extensive)

Piece fill up to the size of 2" x 2" and/or color touch covering up to 4" x 4". Interior piece fill up to 4" x 4"

5 (Extensive)

Any piece fill over 2" x 2" and/or color touch over 4" x 4". Recreated interior pages or cover

The presence of trimming on a comic book will receive a CGC purple restored label. But if only trimming is present, it will not garner a quality or quantity rating, only displaying the word "apparent." If restoration is present in addition to trimming, the trimming will have no bearing on the quality or quantity assigned to the restoration.

The Conserved Label is similar to the blue Universal label but is differentiated by a silver bar across the top. Conservation is noted in a similar fashion on the label as on the purple CGC Restored Label. This label is applied to any comic book with specific, professional repairs done to improve the structural integrity and long-term preservation. These repairs include tear seals, support, staple replacement, piece reattachment, leafcasting, and certain kinds of cleaning:

Conservation Repairs

- Tear seals
- Spine split seals
- Reinforcement
- Piece reattachment
- Some cover or interior cleaning (water or solvent)
- Staples cleaned or replaced
- Leaf casting

Materials Used for Conservation Repairs:

- Rice paper
- Wheat glue
- Vintage staples
- Archival tape

The Qualified label is green, indicating one qualifying defect is present on a book, and includes detachments, missing parts, and unverified signatures. An example of such a qualifying feature would be a Marvel Value Stamp missing from an interior page that does not affect the story. If such a book appears 9.6 otherwise but would downgrade to 3.5 due to the missing stamp, assigning a grade of 3.5 does not fully represent the appearance of the comic to a collector. Through use of the green Qualified label, a comic buyer is able to make an informed decision as to what he is purchasing in terms of its overall desirability. Because of the complexity involved, green labels are seldomly assigned. In addition, high grade comic books that have an unwitnessed signature, and therefore are not eligible for the Signature Series label (see below), get the Qualified label. This is the most common use for the Qualified label, and shows what the grade of the book would have been if the signature was not present. Qualified labels are always used for married parts; if no restoration is present, a comic book with a married cover, wrap, or page will always receive a Qualified label.

CGC's Signature Series label is yellow, and this is used when a comic book has been signed or been sketched on by a creator in the presence of a CGC representative, assuring the signature's or sketch's authenticity. Only books that meet CGC's strict criteria for authenticity are eligible for the Signature Series label. In addition to the certified grade, the yellow label includes who signed it and when it was signed. If appropriate, a Signature Series label may state where a book was signed. In 2007, CGC introduced a Signature Series Restored label. Similar to the CGC Signature Series label in color, it is differentiated by a purple bar across the top. In 2016, CGC also introduced a Signature Series Conserved label (silver bar across the top) and Qualified label (green bar across the top). Restoration, conservation and qualifying defects are noted in the same fashion as on the CGC Restored, Conserved and Qualified label, and, as with the regular Signature Series label, these books must be signed in the presence of CGC representatives in order to be eligible for signature authentication.

In 2019 CGC launched its Pedigree label, which indicates that the certified comic book hails from one of 60 pedigreed collections recognized by CGC. These famous collections, which include Larson, San Francisco, White Mountain, Twin Cities, and the most famous of all, Edgar Church/Mile High, contain many of the best-known examples of rare, high value comics in existence. A breakdown of each collection can be found on CGC's website, which includes their backstory and examples of markings if present.

The Evolution of CGC and CCG

In October of 2003, CGC began to certify comic book related magazines. The certification process and label system for magazines is exactly the same as for comic books. Some examples of comic book related magazines CGC certifies are *MAD Magazine*, *Vampirella*, *Creepy*, *Eerie* and *Famous Monsters of Filmland*.

More recently CGC introduced grading and encapsulation for *Sports Illustrated* and *Playboy* magazines, movie lobby cards, photographs, and concert posters. In 2016, CGC launched a redesign of their holder with enhanced strength, design, clarity, and tamper-proof features. CGC has graded over 5 million collectibles to date.

In a move intended to strengthen CGC's commitment to promoting the comic collecting hobby and enhance the collecting experience, CGC's parent company Certified Collectibles Group acquired Classics Incorporated, the world's premier comic book restoration, restoration removal and pressing company, in 2012. Previously located in Dallas, TX, Classics Incorporated relocated to Sarasota, FL to become an independent member of the Certified Collectibles Group under the new name Classic Collectible Services (CCS). Customers who wish to send books in for pressing, restoration or restoration removal are able to send them to CCS and have them transfer directly to CGC for grading — creating a synergistic relationship that saves customers time, shipping and insurance expenses.

For more information on comic book certification, pressing, restoration, and CGC's many other services, please visit our website at www.CGCcomics.com

HEROISM DEFEATS ADVERSITY:

SUPERHEROES WITH DISABILITIES

By Amanda Sheriff

As a medium, comic books have long been ahead of the curve in promoting tolerance, acceptance, and understanding of people with different abilities. While far from having a perfect record, a number of successful characters over the generations have shined in the effort to showcase characters with disabilities.

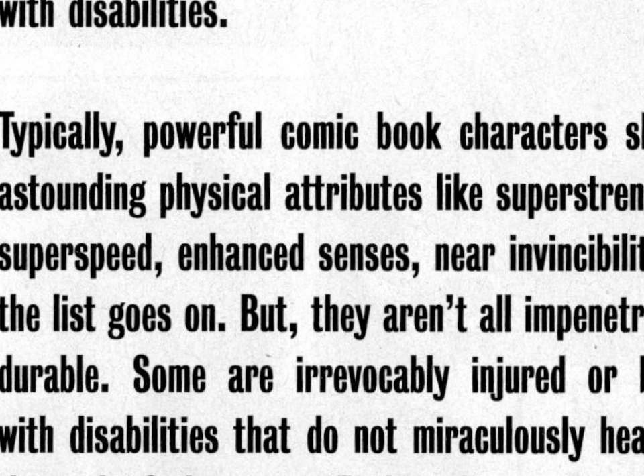

Typically, powerful comic book characters share astounding physical attributes like superstrength, superspeed, enhanced senses, near invincibility – the list goes on. But, they aren't all impenetrably durable. Some are irrevocably injured or born with disabilities that do not miraculously heal by the end of the story. Rather than ending their superhero journey (or quitting before it even began), these characters adjust and innovate to continue the good fight.

The following are some of the more high-profile characters, although there are certainly others.

Daredevil

Matt Murdock didn't lose his sight in a battle, but rather during childhood when radioactive material hit his eyes. If that wasn't shocking enough for the boy, he gained superhuman senses that compensated for his loss of vision. Matt can track people by their scent, can hear a person's heartbeat from over 20 feet away, and hear cries for help from across city blocks. What is perhaps his greatest ally is the radar sense he uses to perceive the distance and location of objects around him. Not only does this aid Matt in everyday situations, it is also indispensable during fights.

As his origin was expanded later, Matt was trained by Stick, a martial arts expert who is also blind, who taught him combat skills and how to use his newly acquired heightened senses. Mastering the martial arts disciplines also gave him incredible reflexes, agility, endurance, and strength.

The disadvantage of these extremely acute senses is that the magnitude of input can overwhelm Daredevil. It takes a great deal of concentration and self-control to protect himself from sensory overload – all while battling powerful villains and seedy criminals. Still, the Man without Fear skips across rooftops, jumps off edifices, and dodges attacks in his unwavering determination to protect his home and community of Hell's Kitchen.

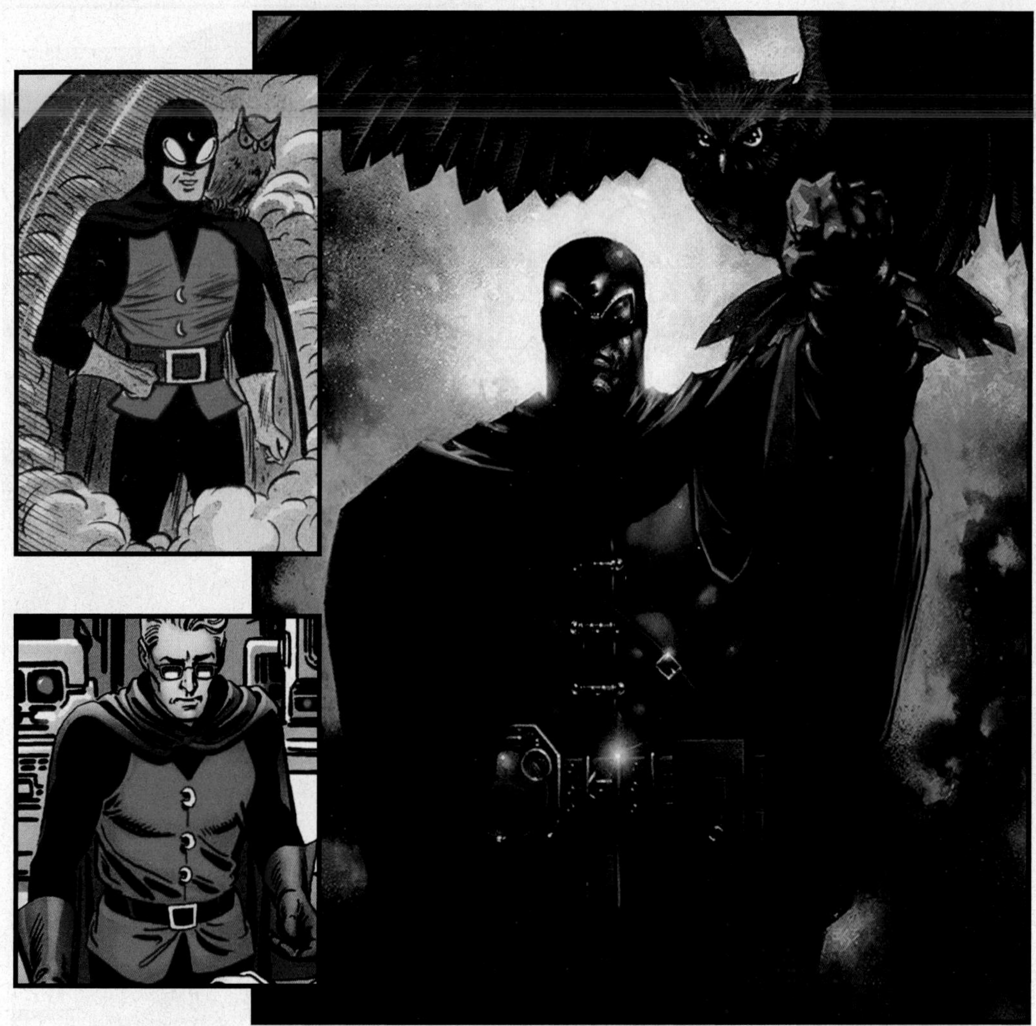

Doctor Mid-Nite

When Doctor Mid-Nite's sight was damaged, he turned to science and technology. Before Doctor Mid-Nite became a member of the Justice Society of America, he was Dr. Charles McNider, one of Keystone City's best surgeons. In a bizarre attack, Charles was blinded when a grenade was thrown into an operating room to kill the patient, who happened to be a witness against mafia boss Maroni.

Needing to rely on his body in new ways, Charles spent his recovery time exercising to improve his physical condition. His life changed again when he removed his bandages one night and discovered that he could see in the dark. Charles kept this revelation a secret and became Doctor Mid-Nite to bring Maroni to justice.

It was then that he created the cowl with infrared, then ultrasonic, lenses to see in the daylight. He also developed blackout bombs to blanket areas in darkness, which gives him a sizeable advantage, and he trains owls for reconnaissance. Once Maroni was brought to justice, he continued as a crime-fighter and eventually joined the JSA.

Using his skills as a surgeon, Dr. Mid-Nite also helps fellow heroes when they need medical attention. By doing this, they can avoid endangering their secret identities by not seeking help in hospitals.

Echo

There are a few characters, like Echo, who do not use technological assistance or have superhuman abilities. Echo is Maya Lopez, a Native American woman and one of the few prominent characters who is deaf. When she was a child, her father was a criminal who was killed by his partner in crime, Kingpin. As he died, Maya's father asked Kingpin to make sure she would be raised well.

Kingpin honored the request, and when her many talents surfaced, he sent her to schools for prodigies. Just by watching others, Maya can mimic and learn their skills. She used this talent to become a concert level pianist, a skilled gymnast, and talented ballerina. By watching videos of Daredevil and Bullseye, she learned the former's acrobatic skills and the latter's precise aim.

Echo was pulled into the Kingpin-Daredevil feud, falling in love with Matt while also fighting Daredevil when Fisk convinced her that Daredevil was the villain. After nearly killing Daredevil and learning that Fisk had been manipulating her, Echo sought the Chief, her father's old friend, for guidance. He sent her on a vision quest where she met and befriended Wolverine. Echo returned to performing arts, but has since been a Ronin, helping the Avengers defeat Hydra.

Professor X and the Original X-Men

When it comes to adapting to immense physical changes, the X-Men are experts. The X-Men are led by Charles Xavier/ Professor X, a very powerful telepath and extremely smart man who has spent much of his life using a wheelchair. He traveled the world meeting other mutants, many of whom were overwhelmed, even traumatized by their mutations.

Three years after his introduction, the story of how Professor X lost the use of his legs was told. He had encountered the alien scout Lucifer who dropped a huge rock on Charles, severely damaging his legs. Charles used his telepathic powers to call out for help from a fellow mutant and was rushed to a hospital.

For nearly all of his time in comics he has used a chair of some kind, including a standard wheelchair and a highly technologically advanced hoverchair. The latter featured a direct network to Cerebro and the team's jet, communications, and other devices.

While helping Jean Grey with her new abilities, he decided to open a school for young mutants, which initially included Jean (as Marvel Girl), Cyclops, Iceman, Angel, and Beast. For most of these kids, their abilities also came with physical differences. Cyclops must wear special goggles at all times to harness the energy that shoots from his eyes, Iceman physically looks like he's made of ice and snow, Angel has large wings, and Beast is covered in fur. Racism, bigotry, and ableism are themes often explored in the *X-Men* books stemming from what these characters endure and how it shapes their experiences. Despite facing prejudice, the X-Men consistently fight to help people – whether they have mutations or not.

Oracle

Barbara Gordon has had two superheroine roles: boots on the ground as Batgirl and eyes in the sky as Oracle. As Batgirl, she does not possess special powers, though she is a skilled fighter, a whiz at technology, and has a didactic memory.

After 20 years of crimefighting, Barbara was shot and paralyzed by the Joker in an attempt to break her father, Commissioner Gordon. Rather than give up after sustaining her injuries, Barbara reinvented herself. Now using a wheelchair, Barbara traded hand to hand combat for disseminating valuable information as Oracle.

Reintroduced as Oracle, Barbara focused on her hacking skills, providing important intel and technical support to her allies. These skills gave Barbara the ability to reach beyond the city limits of Gotham to help heroes all over the world. She was given a meatier role, collaborating with most other heroes and law enforcement agencies.

Barbara and Dinah Lance formed a partnership, adding Huntress and Lady Blackhawk to become the Birds of Prey. When Barbara met Cassandra Cain, she started training the young woman to be Batgirl, making her the first character to take the mantle since Barbara was shot.

Cyborg

In the list of comic characters who have lost appendages, few, if any, can compare to the extreme case of Cyborg. Victor Stone was an intelligent teenager and star athlete who aspired to compete in the Olympics. But fate stepped in when his parents, both scientists, did an experiment that summoned a creature from another dimension. It killed Victor's mother and destroyed most of his body.

Consumed by guilt and loss, his father saved Victor by replacing much of his body and half of his face with cybernetic material. Vic, now Cyborg, woke up horrified by what had become of his body. Cyborg's new body features cybernetic systems that gave him superstrength, speed, flight, and protection from most harm. He can hack into computer systems, has a self-repair system, can shoot lasers, and a sound cannon.

Misty Knight

Misty Knight was already heroic, but when she lost her arm, she found a way to enhance her abilities to help more people. A decorated New York City police officer, Misty was an exceptional detective, skilled hand to hand fighter, and impressive markswoman. After she lost her right arm during a terrorist bombing, Tony Stark created a bionic replacement and her friend Colleen Wing encouraged Misty to continue helping people.

The cybernetic arm is wired into her nervous system, giving her full control over it. Now she has superstrength, and can generate an antigravity repulsor field, cryogenic energy, an energy shield, and other features. Its many technological advancements are updated periodically by Tony and Reed Richards.

With her new abilities, Misty has broadened the scope of people she can help as a part of Knightwing Restorations, the Daughters of the Dragon, Heroes for Hire, and the Defenders. Through her associations as a police officer and crimefighter, Misty has allied with the most impressive/prominent superheroes in Marvel.

Life as he knew it was over, leaving Vic lonely and depressed. His situation did improve once Raven found him and asked Cyborg to join the New Teen Titans. Now feeling a sense of purpose and connection with teammates, Vic's life became much better. He has used his enhanced abilities in countless battles as a member of the Titans and Justice League.

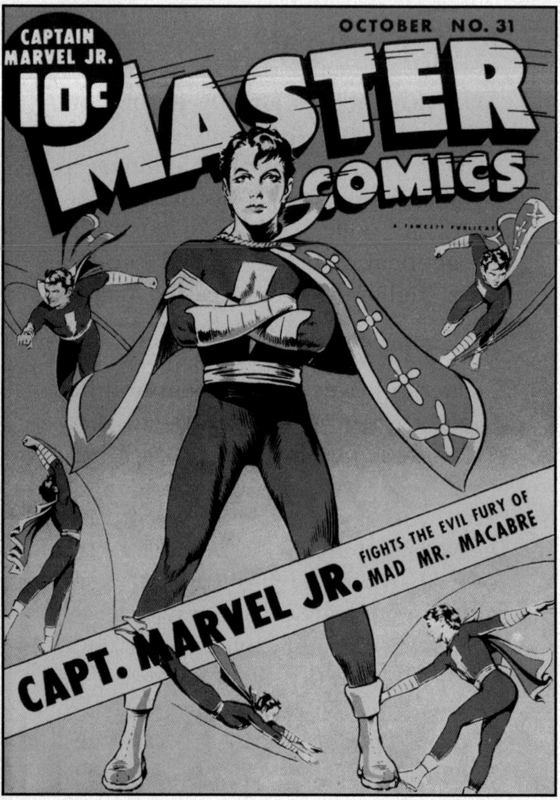

Captain Marvel Jr.

Freddy Freeman was one of the earliest comic characters whose injury sparked his superhero journey. Freddy was nearly killed during a battle between Captain Marvel and Captain Nazi, so after subduing the villain, Captain Marvel took the injured boy to Shazam's secret throne room.

The Wizard declared that he could save Freddy, but couldn't reverse the damage that had been done. This was achieved when the Wizard passed some of his powers on to Freddy, which in addition to saving his life gave him superpowers. Freddy turned into Captain Marvel Jr., gaining the Shazam powers of wisdom, superstrength, stamina, power, courage, and speed.

Billy warned Freddy that he couldn't stay in his Captain Marvel Jr. form because he must allow his human form to heal. When he changed back into his regular body, Freddy discovered that his left leg had been permanently injured in the accident and he must now walk with a crutch.

He maintained anonymity and protected his identity as Freddy by wearing shabby clothes and living in rundown accommodations. Despite having nearly limitless powers as a superhero, Freddy always returned to his human body to heal and preserve his powers so that he could continue helping others as a superhero. Throughout the Golden Age, Freddy would engage in adventures alongside Captain Marvel, the Shazam family, and in Master Comics and his own self-titled *Captain Marvel Jr.* comic.

These and many other heroes in comics haven't given up because of a disability. They have persevered and, in many cases, became even more powerful. It is a hopeful message for readers with disabilities who can find inspiration in these heroes.

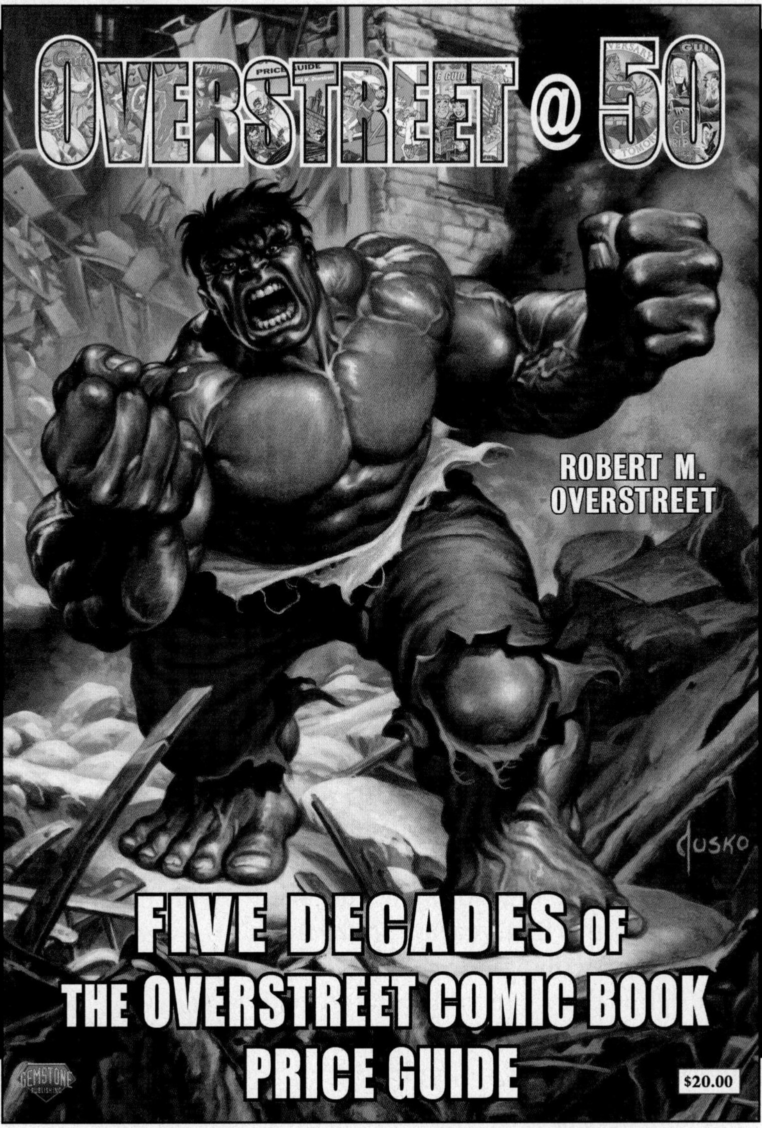

In Memoriam:

John Paul Leon

Artist John Paul Leon passed away May 1, 2021 at the age of 49 after a 14-year battle with cancer.

Born on April 26, 1972 in New York City, at 16 years old he sold illustrations to *Dragon and Dungeon* magazines. After attending the School of Visual Arts and being taught by instructors including Will Eisner and Walter Simonson, he made his comic book debut with *Robocop* at Dark Horse in 1992.

Leon's first big splash came with his run on the first year of *Static* from Milestone Media, one of the company's debut titles. He collaborated with Dwayne McDuffie and Robert Washington III on it beginning in 1993.

The early days of *Static* have often been compared favorably in tone to the early Stan Lee-Steve Ditko issues of *Amazing Spider-Man*, and that comparison is apt. Simply put, there is the same kind of character- and world-building magic going on in these pages. Teenage life and struggles, bullies, popular people, romance, would-be romance, true friends, and plenty of jerks. And a witty, brainy kid with newly acquired powers, just brimming with possibilities.

Leon's work on the series crackles with the energy you'd expect with a character who has electricity-based powers. And it was just a taste of what was to come.

He later returned to the character with the miniseries *Static Shock: Rebirth of the Cool* in 2001. He had followed his initial run on *Static* with a stint on Milestone's *Shadow Cabinet*.

"Inking John never felt like work," artist Shawn Martinbrough, who inked Leon at Milestone, wrote. "Sure, there would be a page with an insane amount of detail but it was always fun to decipher his lines and a true master class in draftsmanship. For someone so unbelievably talented, John was one of the most understated and humble persons I've ever known."

Over the span of his career, his work included *The Winter Men*, *Logan: Path Of The Warlord*, *The Further Adventures Of Cyclops And Phoenix*, and *Challengers Of The Unknown*. He served as cover artist for *DMZ*, and his most recent efforts included *Batman: Creature of the Night*.

Perhaps his highest profile work came in the form of *Earth X*, the Marvel miniseries on which he collaborated with Jim Krueger, Alex Ross, and Bill Reinhold.

"He drew some of my very favorite comics before he and I got to work together. The way he drew the shadow a figure cast instead of just the figure made him a master of the craft even the first time I saw his work," Krueger wrote.

–J.C. Vaughn

EARTH X #5 PAGES 4 - 5. IMAGE COURTESY OF HERITAGE AUCTIONS.

OVERSTREET ADVISORS

DARREN ADAMS
Pristine Comics
Seattle, WA

WELDON ADAMS
Heritage Auctions
Fort Worth, TX

GRANT ADEY
Halo Certification
Brisbane, QLD, Australia

BILL ALEXANDER
Collector
Sacramento, CA

DAVID T. ALEXANDER
David Alexander Comics
Tampa, FL

TYLER ALEXANDER
David Alexander Comics
Tampa, FL

LON ALLEN
Heritage Auctions
Dallas, TX

DAVE ANDERSON
Want List Comics
Tulsa, OK

L.E. BECKER
Comic*Pop Collectibles
Wixom, MI

JIM BERRY
Collector
Portland, OR

PETER BILELIS, ESQ.
Collector
South Windsor, CT

MIKE BOLLINGER
Hake's Auctions
York, PA

STEVE BOROCK
CBCS
Dallas, TX

SCOTT BRADEN
Comics Historian
Red Lion, PA

RUSS BRIGHT
Mill Geek Comics
Marysville, WA

RICHARD BROWN
Collector
Detroit, MI

SHAWN CAFFREY
Finalizer/Modern Age Specialist
CGC

MICHAEL CARBONARO
Dave & Adam's
New York

BRETT CARRERAS
VA Comicon
Richmond, VA

GARY CARTER
Collector
Coronado, CA

CHARLES CERRITO
Hotflips
Farmingdale, NY

JEFF CERRITO
Hotflips
Farmingdale, NY

JOHN CHRUSCINSKI
Tropic Comics
Lyndora, PA

PAUL CLAIRMONT
PNJ Comics
Winnipeg, MB
Canada

ART CLOOS
Collector/Historian
Flushing, NY

GARY COLABUONO
Dealer/Collector
Arlington Heights, IL

BILL COLE
Bill Cole Enterprises, Inc.
South Dartmouth, MA

TIM COLLINS
RTS Unlimited, Inc.
Lakewood, CO

JON B. COOKE
Editor - Comic Book Artist Magazine
West Kingston, RI

JACK COPLEY
Coliseum of Comics
Florida

ASHLEY COTTER-CAIRNS
SellMyComicBooks.com
Montreal, Canada

JESSE JAMES CRISCIONE
Jesse James Comics
Glendale, AZ

JAIME ADRIANO DAEZ
Collector/Dealer
Metro Manilla, Philippines

BROCK DICKINSON
Collector
St. Catharines, ONT Canada

GARY DOLGOFF
Gary Dolgoff Comics
Easthampton, MA

JOHN DOLMAYAN
Torpedo Comics
Las Vegas, NV

SHELTON DRUM
Heroes Aren't Hard to Find
Charlotte, NC

WALTER DURAJLIJA
Big B Comics
Hamilton, ONT Canada

KEN DYBER
Cloud 9 Comics
Portland, OR

DANIEL ERTLE
Modern Age Specialist
CBCS
Dallas, TX

MICHAEL EURY
Author
Concord, NC

D'ARCY FARRELL
Pendragon Comics
Toronto, ONT Canada

BILL FIDYK
Collector
Annapolis, MD

PAUL FIGURA
Quality Control Specialist
CBCS
Dallas, TX

JOSEPH FIORE
ComicWiz.com
Toronto, ONT Canada

STEPHEN FISHLER
Metropolis Collectibles, Inc.
New York, NY

DAN FOGEL
Hippy Comix, Inc.
Cleveland, OH

JOHN FOSTER
Ontario Street Comics
Philadelphia, PA

ERIC FOURNIER
Guardian Comics
Pickering, ON, Canada

KEIF A. FROMM
Collector/Historian
Hillsborough, NJ

DAN GALLO
Dealer/Comic Art Con
Westchester Co., NY

JAMES GALLO
Toy & Comic Heaven
Willow Grove, PA

STEPHEN H. GENTNER
Golden Age Specialist
Portland, OR

JOSH GEPPI
Diamond Int. Galleries
Sapphire Studios
Hunt Valley, MD

STEVE GEPPI
Diamond Int. Galleries
Hunt Valley, MD

DOUG GILLOCK
ComicLink
Portland, ME

SEAN GOODRICH
SellMyComicBooks.com
Maine, USA

TOM GORDON III
Monumental Holdings LLC
Westminster, MD

JAMIE GRAHAM
Graham Crackers
Chicago, IL

ANDY GREENHAM
Forest City Coins
London, ON Canada

ERIC J. GROVES
Dealer/Collector
Oklahoma City, OK

GARY GUZZO
Atomic Studios
Boothbay Harbor, ME

JOHN HAINES
Dealer/Collector
Kirtland, OH

JIM HALPERIN
Heritage Auctions
Dallas, TX

JAY HALSTEAD
International Comic Exchange
Hamilton, ON Canada

MARK HASPEL
Finalizer/
Pedigree Specialist
CGC

JEF HINDS
Jef Hinds Comics
Madison, WI

TERRY HOKNES
Hoknes Comics
Saskatoon, SK
Canada

GREG HOLLAND, Ph.D.
Collector
Alexander, AR

JOHN HONE
Collector
Silver Spring, MD

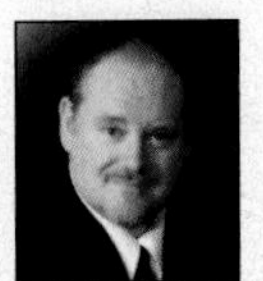

STEVEN HOUSTON
Torpedo Comics
Las Vegas, NV

BILL HUGHES
Dealer/Collector
Flower Mound, TX

ROB HUGHES
Arch Angels
Pacific Beach, CA

ROBERT ISAAC
Red Hood Comics
Las Vegas, NV

JEFF ITKIN
Elite Comic Source
Portland, OR

ED JASTER
Heritage Auctions
Dallas, TX

DR. STEVEN KAHN
Inner Child Comics
& Collectibles
Kenosha, WI

NICK KATRADIS
Collector
Tenafly, NJ

DENNIS KEUM
Fantasy Comics
Goldens Bridge, NY

IVAN KOCMAREK
Comics Historian
Hamilton, ON
Canada

ROBERT KRAUSE
Primo Comics
Venice, FL

TIMOTHY KUPIN
Koop's Comics
Tucson, AZ

BENJAMIN LABONOG
Primetime Comics
Stockton, CA

BEN LICHTENSTEIN
Zapp Comics
Wayne, NJ

STEPHEN LIPSON
Comics Historian
Mississauga, ON

PAUL LITCH
Primary Grader
CGC

DOUG MABRY
The Great Escape
Madison, TN

JOE MANNARINO
Heritage Auctions
Ridgewood, NJ

NADIA MANNARINO
Heritage Auctions
Ridgewood, NJ

BRIAN MARCUS
Cavalier Comics
Wise, VA

WILL MASON
Dave & Adam's
New York

HARRY MATETSKY
Collector
Middletown, NJ

JIM McCALLUM
Guardian Comics
Pickering, ON Canada

KELLY McCLAIN
Hake's Auctions
York, PA

JON McCLURE
Comics Historian,
Writer
Astoria, OR

TODD McDEVITT
New Dimension Comics
Cranberry Township,
PA

PETER MEROLO
Collector
Sedona, AZ

JOHN JACKSON MILLER
Historian, Writer
Scandinavia, WI

BRENT MOESHLIN
Quality Comix
Montgomery, AL

STEVE MORTENSEN
Miracle Comics
Santa Clara, CA

MARC NATHAN
Cards, Comics &
Collectibles
Reisterstown, MD

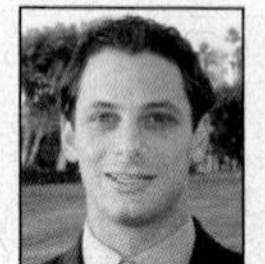

JOSHUA NATHANSON
ComicLink
Portland, ME

MATT NELSON
Primary Grader
CGC

TOM NELSON
Top Notch Comics
Yankton, SD

JAMIE NEWBOLD
Southern California
Comics
San Diego, CA

CHARLIE NOVINSKIE
Silver Age Specialist
Lake Havasu City, AZ

KAREN O'BRIEN
Comics Journalist
Dyer, IN

VINCE OLIVA
Grader
CGC

RICHARD OLSON
Collector/Academician
Poplarville, MS

TERRY O'NEILL
Terry's Comics
Orange, CA

MICHAEL PAVLIC
Purple Gorilla Comics
Calgary, AB Canada

JIM PAYETTE
Golden Age Specialist
Bethlehem, NH

BILL PONSETI
Fantastic Worlds
Comics
Scottsdale, AZ

RON PUSSELL
Redbeard's Book Den
Crystal Bay, NV

JEFF RADER
Offbeat Archives
Comics & Collectibles
Gilroy, CA

ALEX REECE
Reece's Rare Comics
Ijamsville, MD

GREG REECE
Reece's Rare Comics
Ijamsville, MD

ROB REYNOLDS
ComicConnect
New York, NY

STEVE RICKETTS
CBCS Pressing
Dallas, TX

STEPHEN RITTER
Worldwide Comics
Fair Oaks Ranch, TX

CHUCK ROZANSKI
Mile High Comics
Denver, CO

SEAN RUTAN
Hake's Auctions
York, PA

BEN SAMUELS
Golden Age/Foreign
Comics Specialist
Shanghai, China

BARRY SANDOVAL
Heritage Auctions
Dallas, TX

BUDDY SAUNDERS
MyComicShop.com
Arlington, TX

CONAN SAUNDERS
MyComicShop.com
Arlington, TX

MATT SCHIFFMAN
Bronze Age Specialist
Bend, OR

PHIL SCHLAEFER
CPRS
Champion Comics
Sunnyvale, CA

DOUG SCHMELL
Pedigree Comics, Inc.
Wellington, FL

BRIAN SCHUTZER
Sparkle City Comics
Neat Stuff Collectibles
North Bergen, NJ

ALIKA SEKI
Maui Comics and
Collectibles
Waiehu, HI

TODD SHEFFER
Hake's Auctions
York, PA

FRANK SIMMONS
Coast to Coast Comics
Rocklin, CA

MARC SIMS
Big B Comics
Barrie, ONT

LAUREN SISSELMAN
Comics Journalist
Baltimore, MD

MARK SQUIREK
Collector/Historian
Baltimore, MD

TONY STARKS
Silver Age Specialist
Evansville, IN

WEST STEPHAN
CBCS
Dallas, TX

MIKE STEVENS
Hake's Auctions
York, PA

AL STOLTZ
Basement Comics
Havre de Grace, MD

DOUG SULIPA
"Everything 1960-1996"
Manitoba, Canada

MAGGIE THOMPSON
Collector/Historian
Iola, WI

MICHAEL TIERNEY
The Comic Book Store
Little Rock, AR

TED VAN LIEW
Superworld Comics
Worcester, MA

JOE VERENEAULT
JHV Associates
Woodbury Heights, NJ

JASON VERSAGGI
Collector
Brooklyn, NY

FRANK VERZYL
Long Island Comics
West Babylon, NY

TODD WARREN
Collector
Fort Washington, PA

BOB WAYNE
Collector
Fairfield, CT

JEFF WEAVER
Victory Comics
Falls Church, VA

LON WEBB
Dark Adventure
Comics
Norcross, GA

RICK WHITELOCK
New Force Comics
Lynn Haven, FL

MIKE WILBUR
Diamond Int.
Galleries
Hunt Valley, MD

ALEX WINTER
Hake's Auctions
York, PA

HARLEY YEE
Dealer/Collector
Detroit, MI

MARK ZAID
EsquireComics.com
Bethesda, MD

VINCENT ZURZOLO, JR.
Metropolis
Collectibles, Inc.
New York, NY

OVERSTREET PRICE GUIDE BACK ISSUES

The Overstreet® Comic Book Price Guide has held the record for being the longest running annual comic book publication. We are now celebrating our 51st anniversary, and the demand for the Overstreet® price guides is very strong. Collectors have created a legitimate market for them, and they continue to bring record prices each year. Collectors also have a record of comic book prices going back further than any other source in comic fandom. The prices listed below are for NM condition only, with GD-25% and FN-50% of the NM value. Canadian editions exist for a couple of the early issues. Abbreviations: SC-softcover, HC-hardcover, L-leather bound.

1970
#1 White SC
$1950.00

1970
#1 Blue SC
(2nd Printing)
$1600.00

1972
#2 SC $650.00
#2 HC $1100.00

1973
#3 SC $325.00
#3 HC $950.00

1974
#4 SC $165.00
#4 HC $475.00

1975
#5 SC $155.00
#5 HC $260.00

1976
#6 SC $105.00
#6 HC $155.00

1977
#7 SC $155.00
#7 HC $230.00

1978
#8 SC $130.00
#8 HC $180.00

1979
#9 SC $130.00
#9 HC $180.00

1980
#10 SC $140.00
#10 HC $190.00

1981
#11 SC $85.00
#11 HC $115.00

1982

#12 SC $85.00
#12 HC $115.00

1983

#13 SC $85.00
#13 HC $115.00

1984

#14 SC $55.00
#14 HC $110.00
#14 L $190.00

1985

#15 SC $55.00
#15 HC $80.00
#15 L $170.00

1986

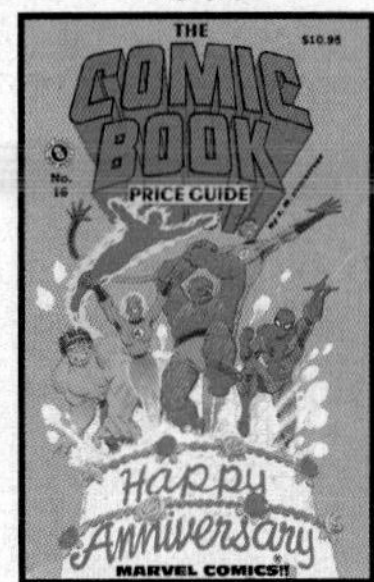

#16 SC $60.00
#16 HC $85.00
#16 L $180.00

1987

#17 SC $55.00
#17 HC $110.00
#17 L $170.00

1988

#18 SC $45.00
#18 HC $65.00
#18 L $170.00

1989

#19 SC $50.00
#19 HC $60.00
#19 L $190.00

1990

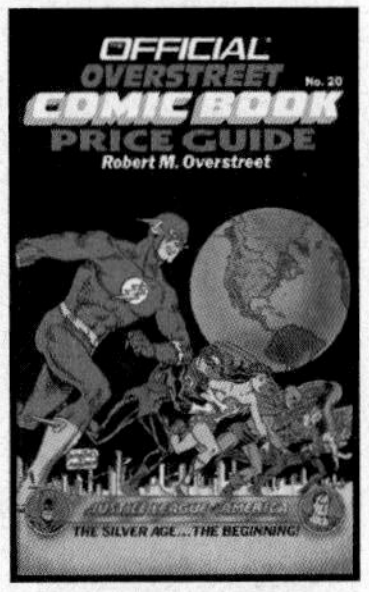

#20 SC $32.00
#20 HC $50.00
#20 L $150.00

1991

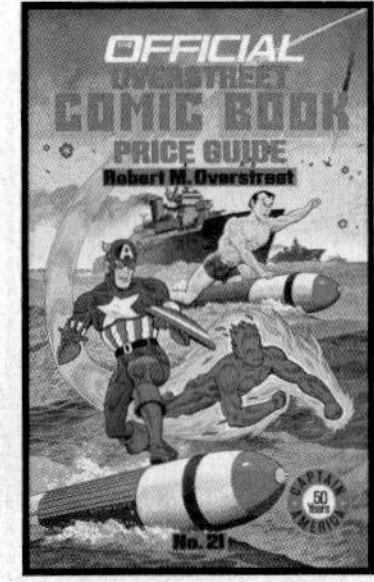

#21 SC $40.00
#21 HC $60.00
#21 L $160.00

1992

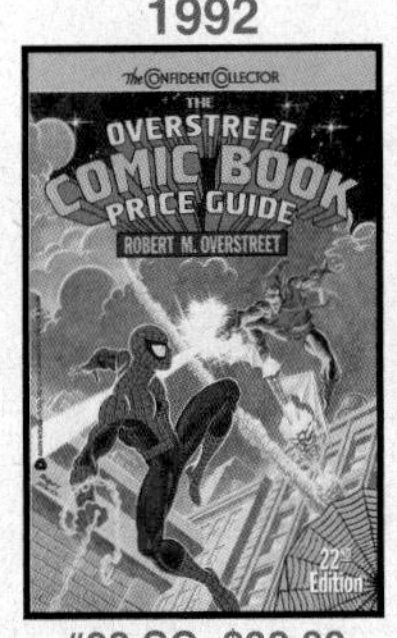

#22 SC $32.00
#22 HC $50.00

1993

#23 SC $32.00
#23 HC $50.00

1994

#24 SC $26.00
#24 HC $36.00

1995

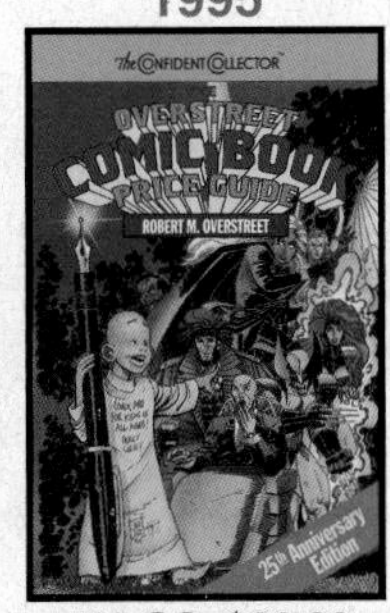

#25 SC $26.00
#25 HC $36.00
#25 L $110.00

1996

#26 SC $20.00
#26 HC $30.00
#26 L $100.00

1997

#27 SC $22.00
#27 HC $38.00
#27 L $125.00

1997

#27 SC $22.00
#27 HC $38.00
#27 L $125.00

1998

#28 SC $20.00
#28 HC $35.00

1998

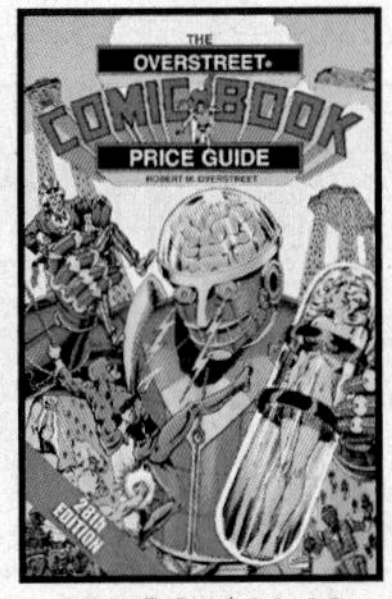

#28 SC $20.00
#28 HC $35.00

1999

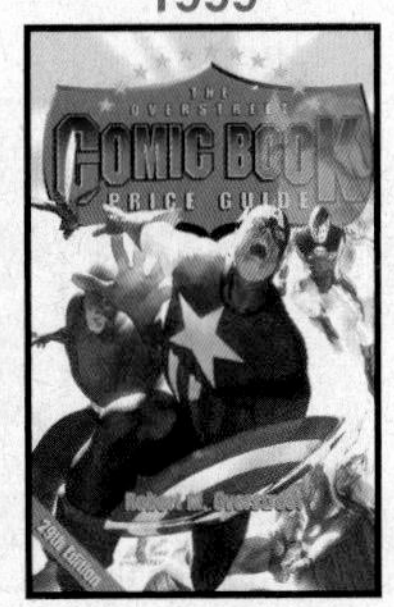

#29 SC $25.00
#29 HC $40.00

1999

#29 SC $20.00
#29 HC $37.00

2000

#30 SC $22.00
#30 HC $32.00

2000

#30 SC $22.00
#30 HC $32.00

2001

#31 SC $22.00
#31 HC $32.00

2001

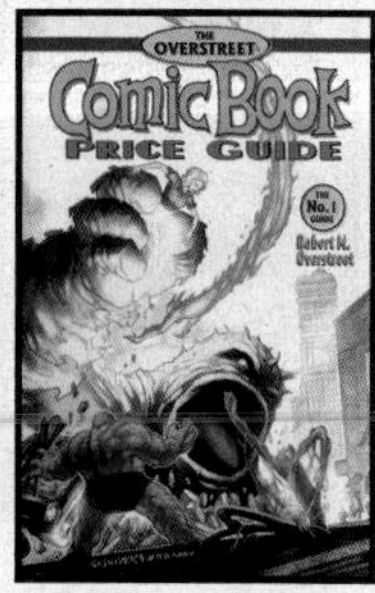

#31 SC $22.00
#31 HC $32.00

2001

#31 Bookstore Ed.
SC only $22.00

2002

#32 SC $22.00
#32 HC $32.00

2002

#32 SC $22.00
#32 HC $32.00

2002

#32 Bookstore Ed.
SC only $22.00

2003

#33 SC $25.00
#33 HC $32.00

2003

#33 SC $25.00
#33 HC $32.00

2003

#33 Bookstore Ed.
SC only $25.00

2004

#34 SC $25.00
#34 HC $32.00

2004

#34 SC $25.00
#34 HC $32.00

2004

#34 Bookstore Ed.
SC only $25.00

2005

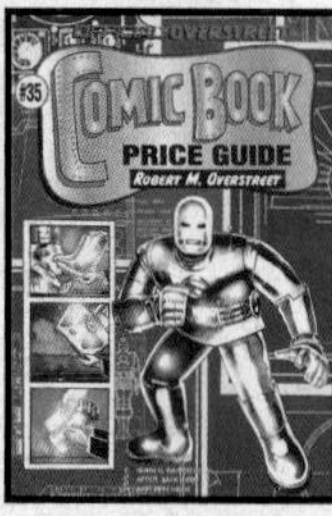

#35 SC $25.00
#35 HC $32.00

2005

#35 SC $25.00
#35 HC $32.00

2005

#35 Bookstore Ed.
SC only $25.00

2006

#36 SC $25.00
#36 HC $32.00

2006

#36 SC $25.00
#36 HC $32.00

2006

#36 Bookstore Ed.
SC only $25.00

2007

#37 SC $25.00
#37 HC $32.00

2007

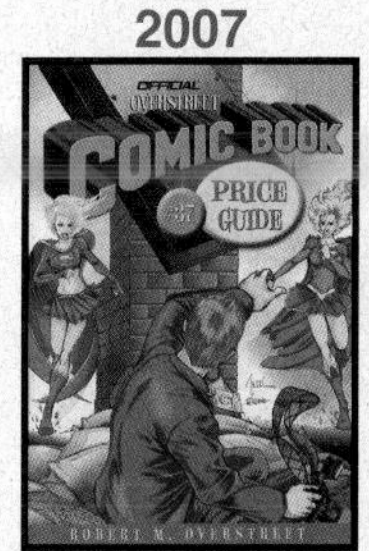

#37 SC $30.00
#37 HC $35.00

2007

#37 Bookstore Ed.
SC only $30.00

2008

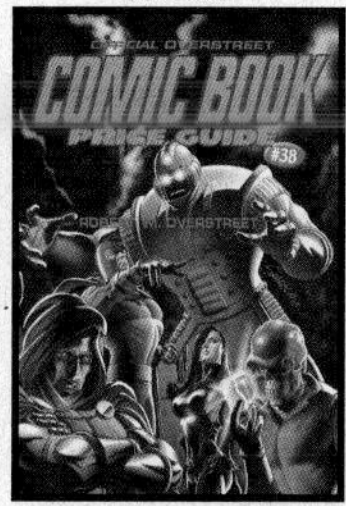

#38 SC $30.00
#38 HC $35.00

2008

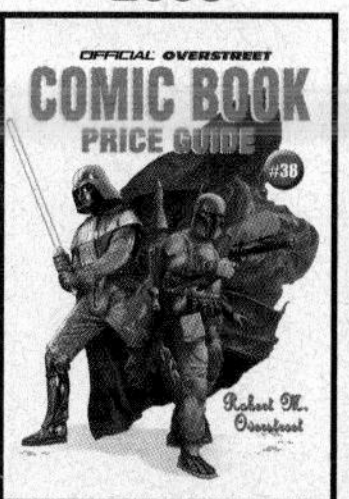

#38 SC $30.00
#38 HC $35.00

2008

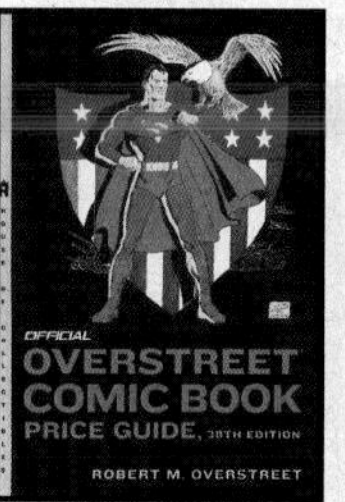

#38 Bookstore Ed.
SC only $30.00

2009

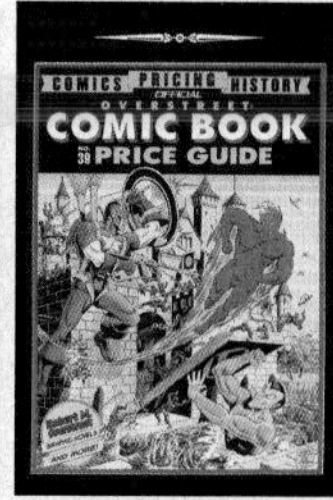

#39 SC $30.00
#39 HC $35.00

2009

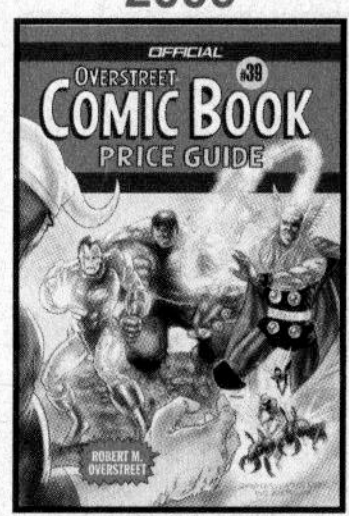

#39 SC $30.00
#39 HC $35.00

2009

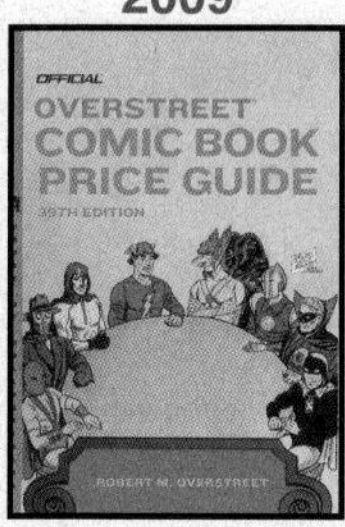

#39 Bookstore Ed.
SC only $30.00

2010

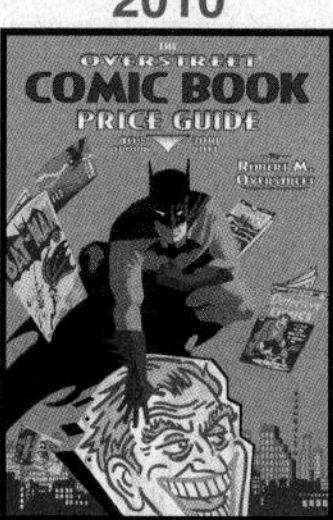

#40 SC $30.00
#40 HC $35.00

2010

#40 SC $30.00
#40 HC $35.00

2010

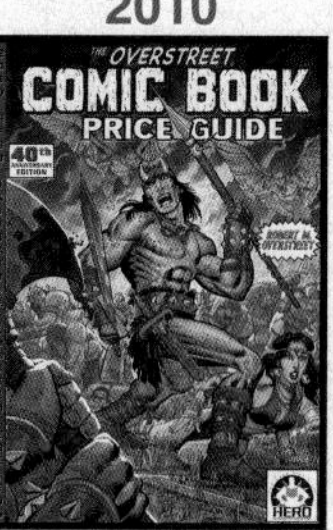

#40 HERO Ed.
HC only $35.00

2011

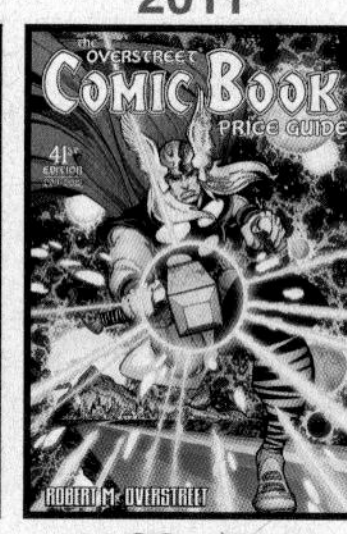

#41 SC $30.00
#41 HC $35.00

2011

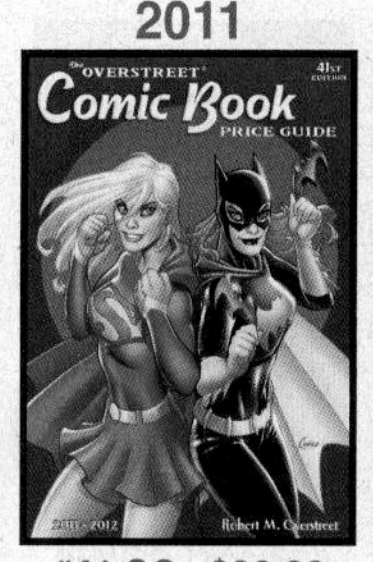

#41 SC $30.00
#41 HC $35.00

2011

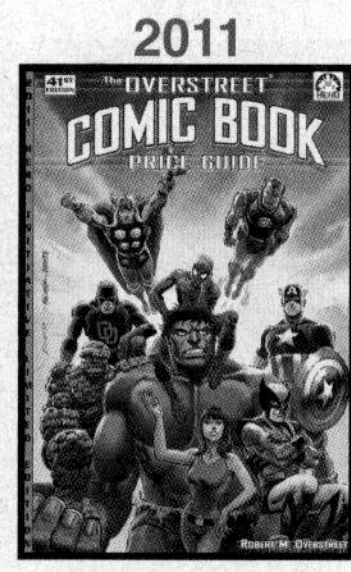

#41 HERO Ed.
HC only $35.00

2012

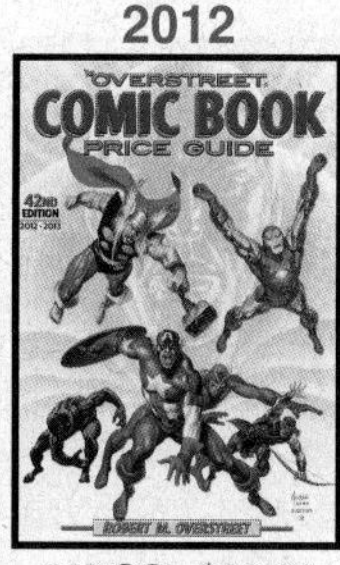

#42 SC $30.00
#42 HC $35.00

2012

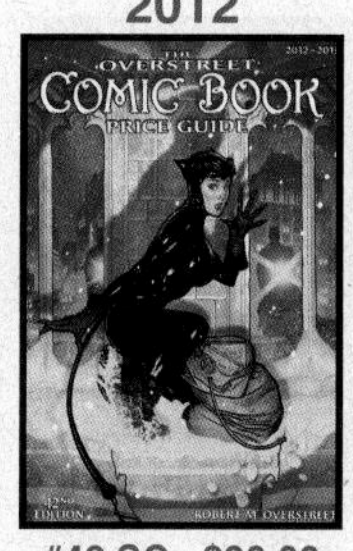

#42 SC $30.00
#42 HC $35.00

2012

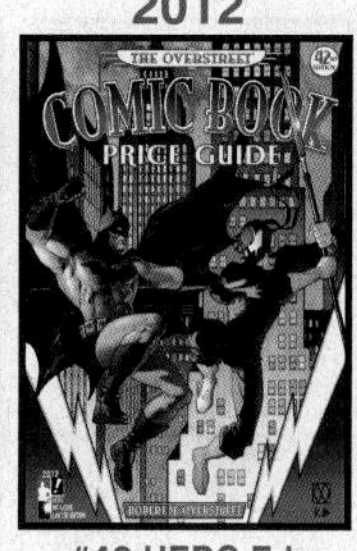

#42 HERO Ed.
HC only $35.00

2013

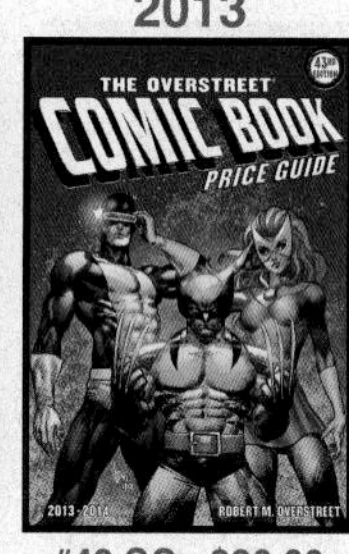

#43 SC $30.00
#43 HC $35.00

2013

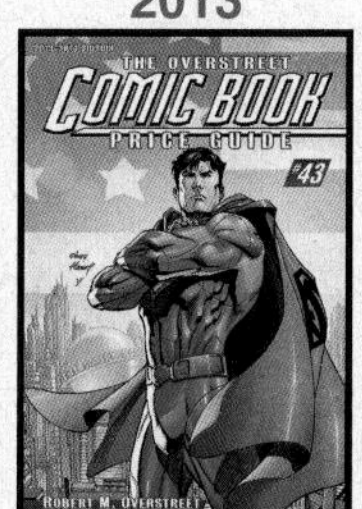

#43 SC $30.00
#43 HC $35.00

2013

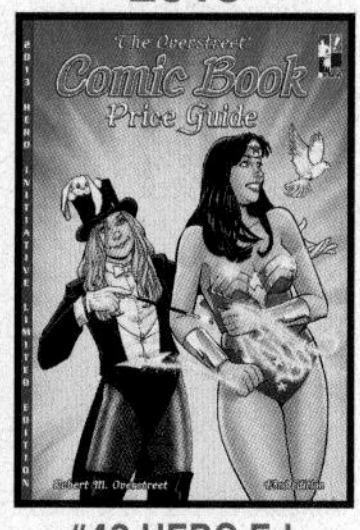

#43 HERO Ed.
HC only $35.00

2014

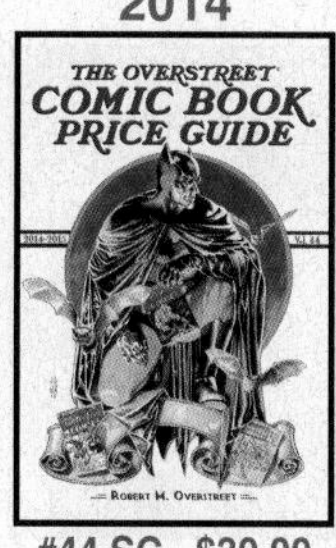

#44 SC $30.00
#44 HC $35.00

2014

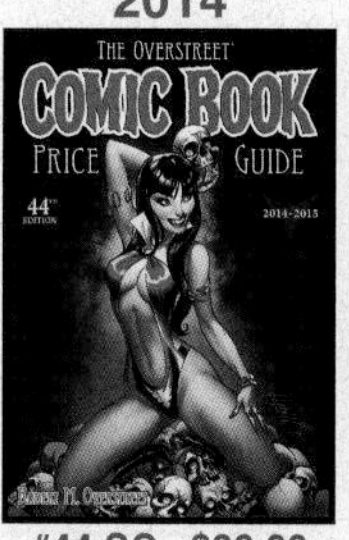

#44 SC $30.00
#44 HC $35.00

2014

#44 HERO Ed.
HC only $35.00

2015

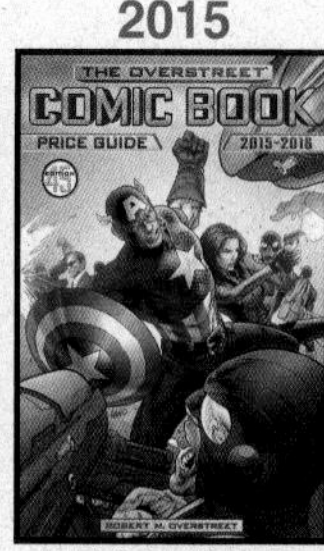

#45 SC $30.00
#45 HC $35.00

2015

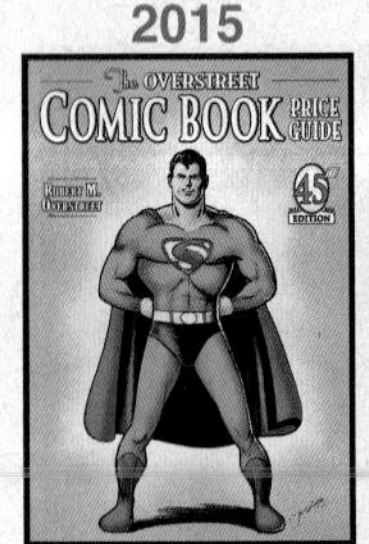

#45 SC $30.00
#45 HC $35.00

2015

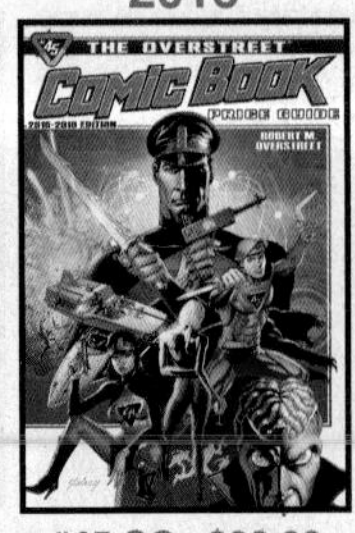

#45 SC $30.00
#45 HC $35.00

2015

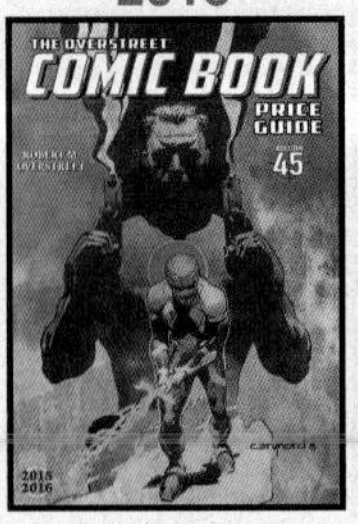

#45 SC $30.00
#45 HC $35.00

2015

#45 HERO Ed.
HC only $35.00

2016

#46 SC $30.00
#46 HC $35.00

2016

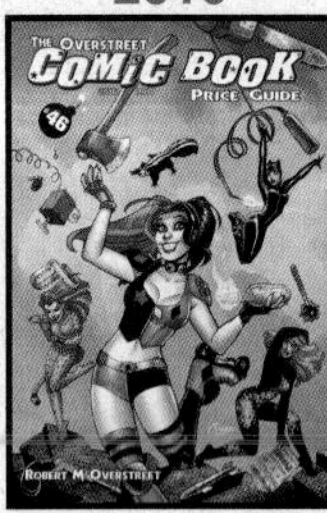

#46 SC $30.00
#46 HC $35.00

2016

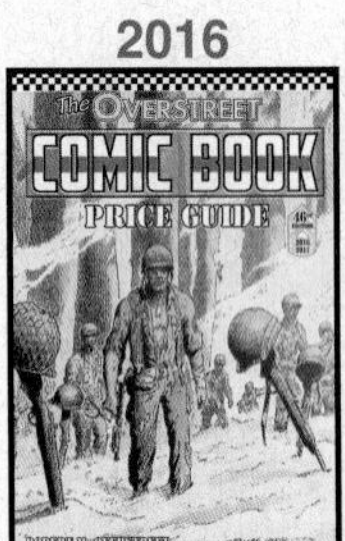

#46 SC $30.00
#46 HC $35.00

2016

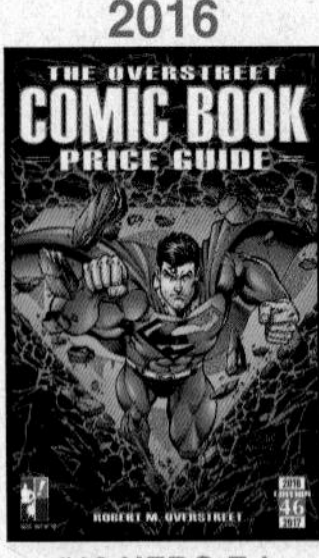

#46 HERO Ed.
HC only $35.00

2017

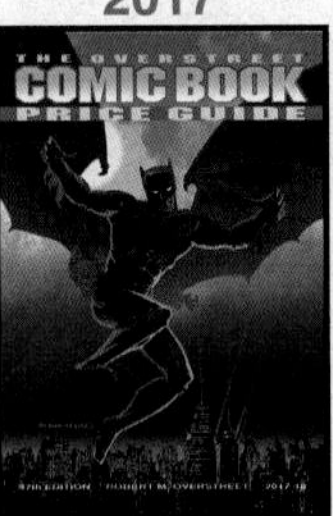

#47 SC $30.00
#47 HC $35.00

2017

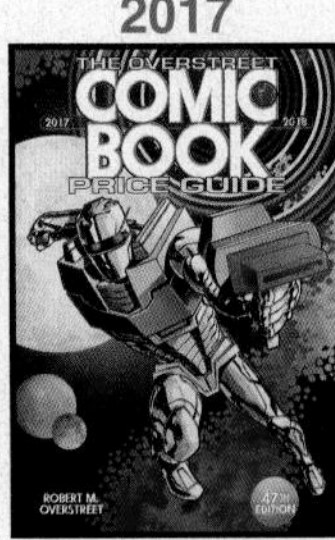

#47 SC $30.00
#47 HC $35.00

2017

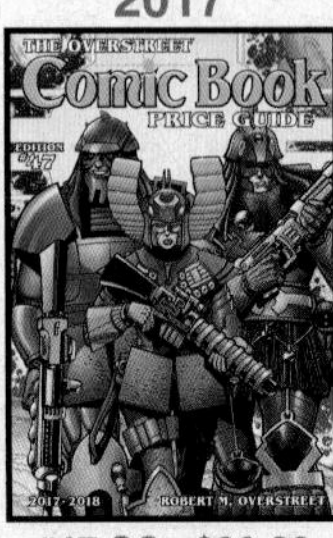

#47 SC $30.00
#47 HC $35.00

2017

#47 HERO Ed.
HC only $35.00

2018

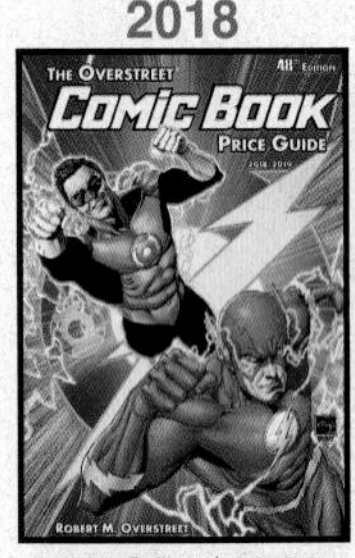

#48 SC $30.00
#48 HC $35.00

2018

#48 SC $30.00
#48 HC $35.00

2018

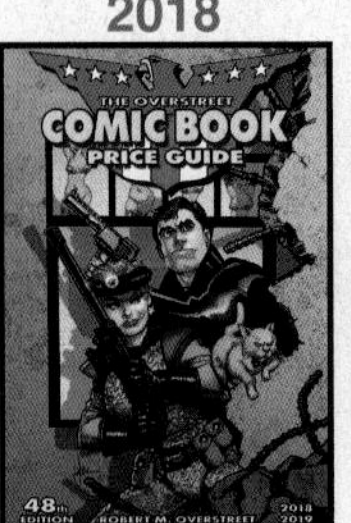

#48 SC $30.00
#48 HC $35.00

2018

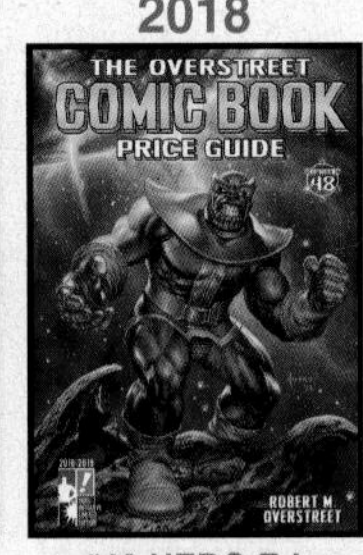

#48 HERO Ed.
HC only $35.00

2019

#49 SC $30.00
#49 HC $35.00

2019

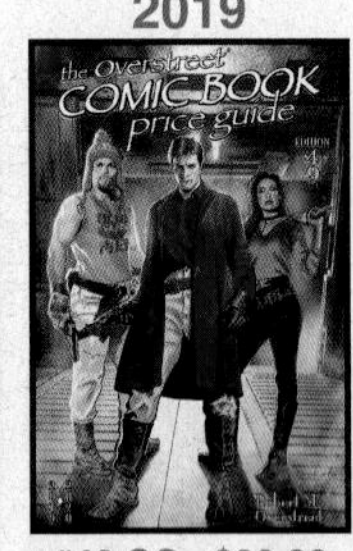

#49 SC $30.00
#49 HC $35.00

2019

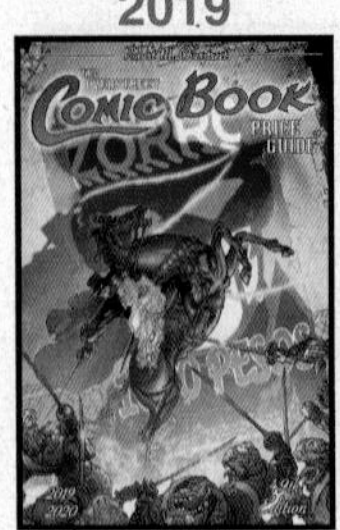

#49 SC $30.00
#49 HC $35.00

2019

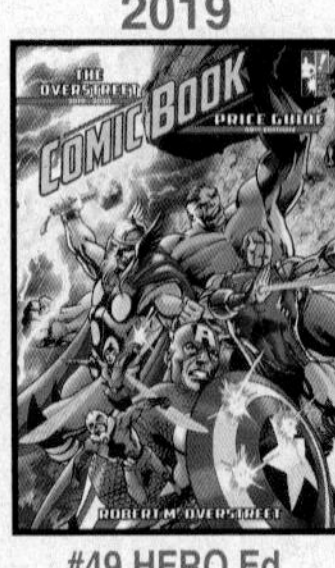

#49 HERO Ed.
HC only $35.00

2020

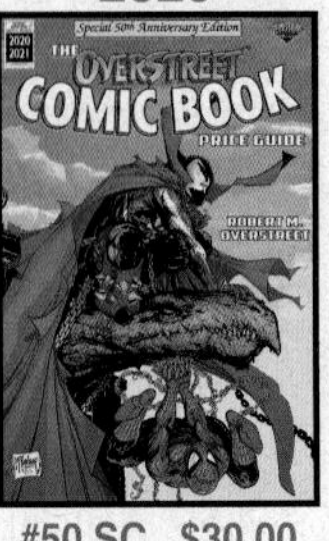

#50 SC $30.00
#50 HC $37.50

2020

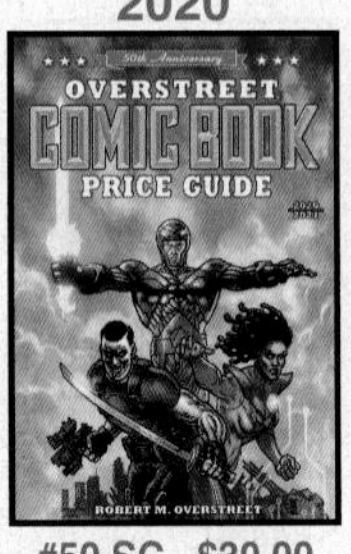

#50 SC $30.00
#50 HC $37.50

2020

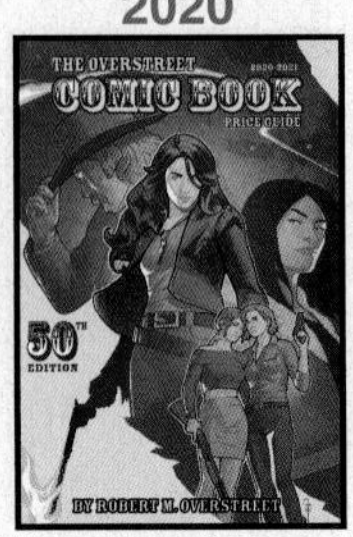

#50 SC $30.00
#50 HC $37.50

2020

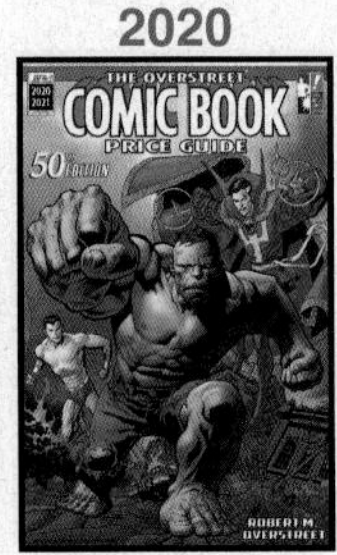

#50 HERO Ed.
HC only $37.50

2001

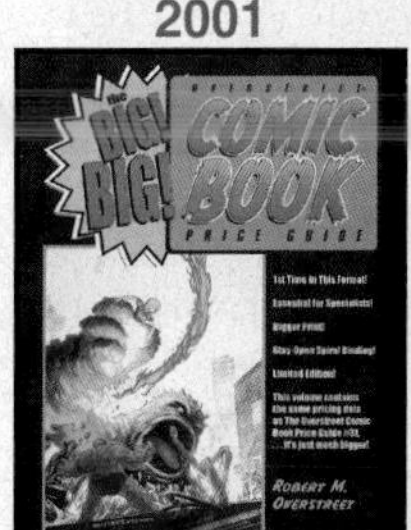

#31 Big Big CBPG
$35.00

2002

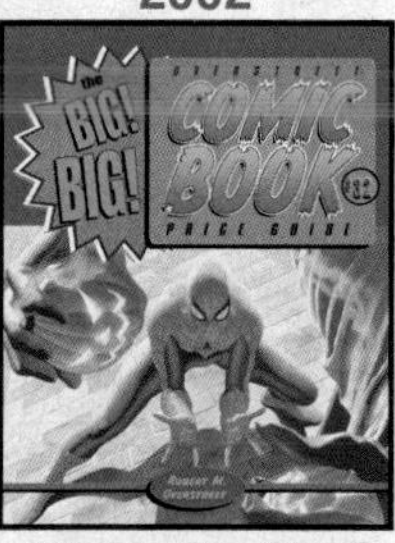

#32 Big Big CBPG
$35.00

2003

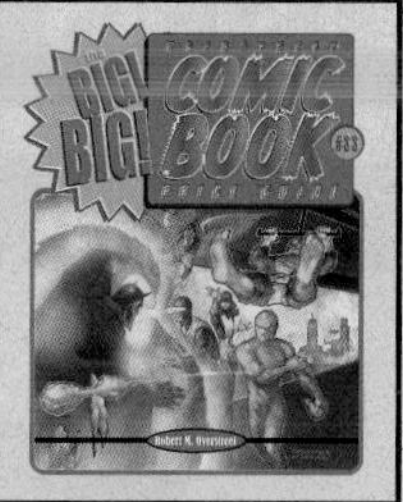

#33 Big Big CBPG
$37.00

2004

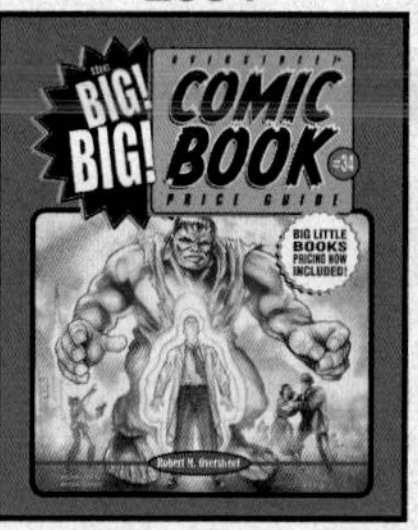

#34 Big Big CBPG
$37.00

2005

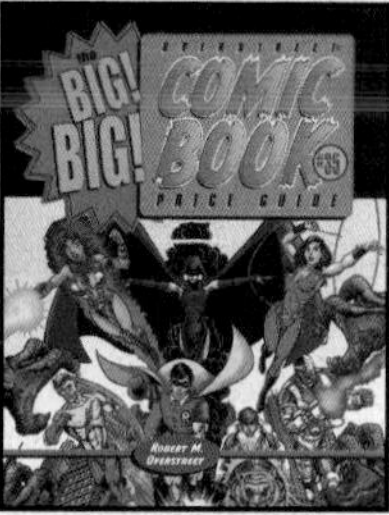

#35 Big Big CBPG
$37.00

2006

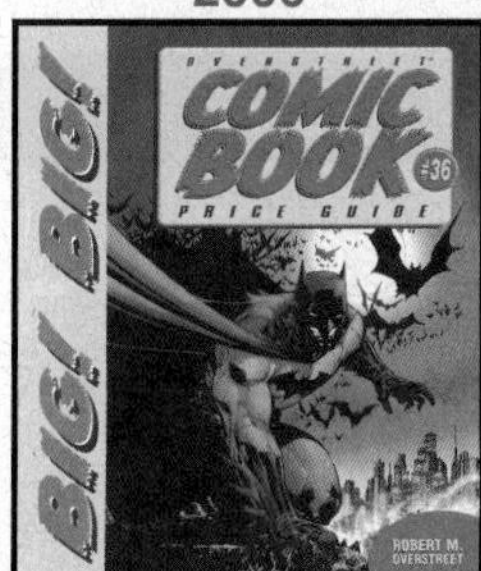

#36 Big Big CBPG
$37.00

2007

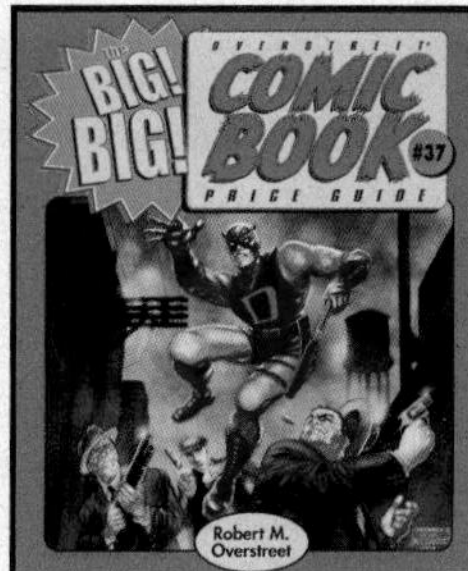

#37 Big Big CBPG
$37.00

2008

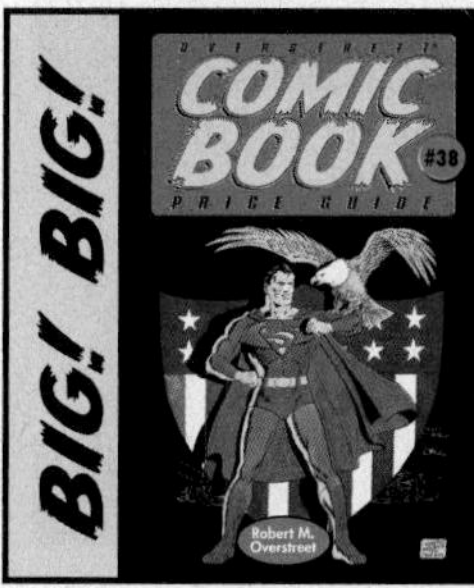

#38 Big Big CBPG
$37.00

2012

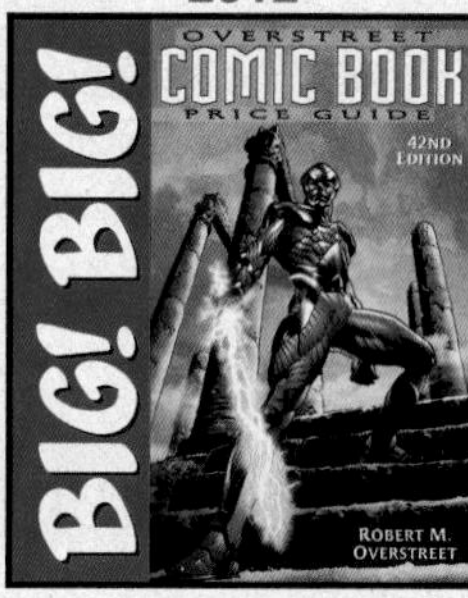

#42 Big Big CBPG
$45.00

2013

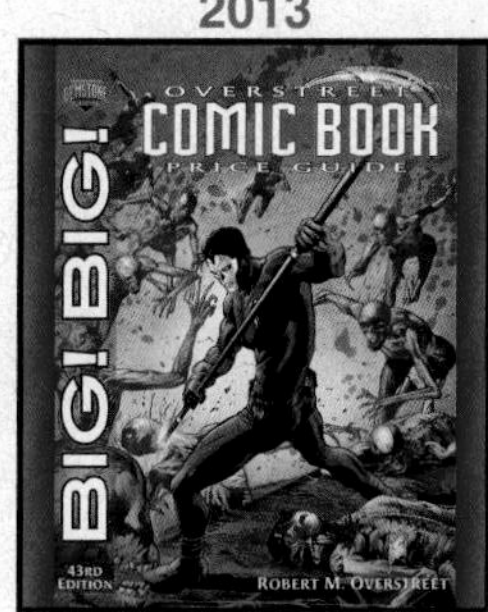

#43 Big Big CBPG
$45.00

2014

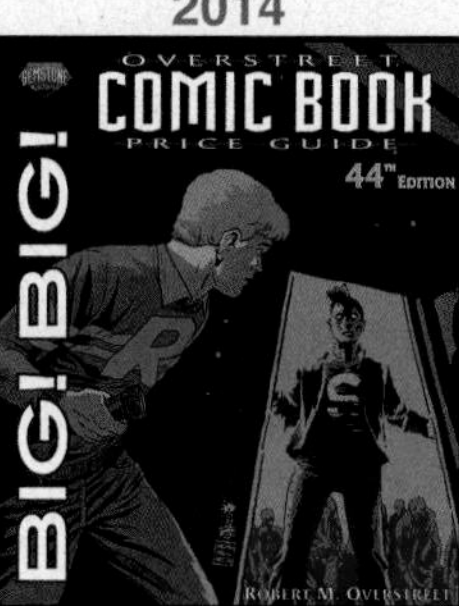

#44 Big Big CBPG
$45.00

2015

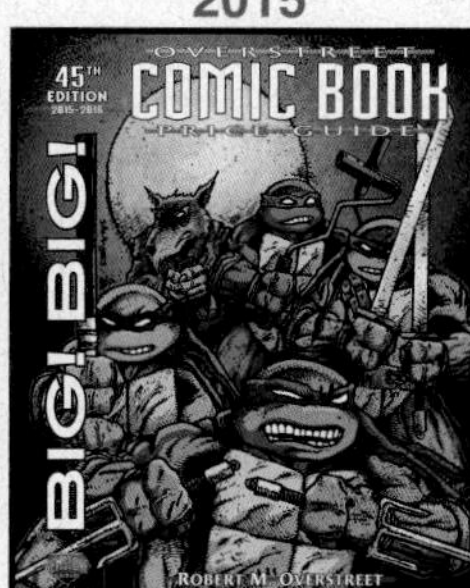

#45 Big Big CBPG
$47.50

2016

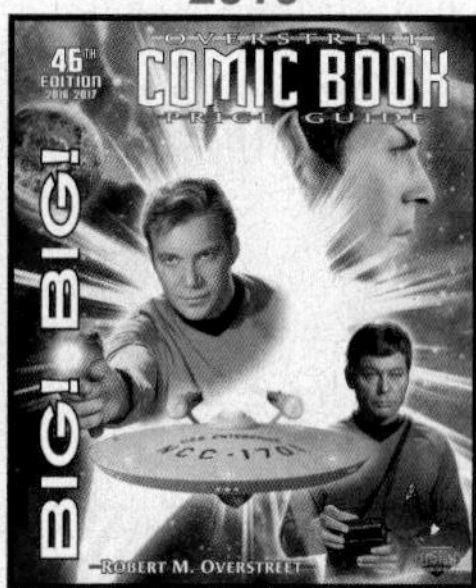

#46 Big Big CBPG
$47.50

2017

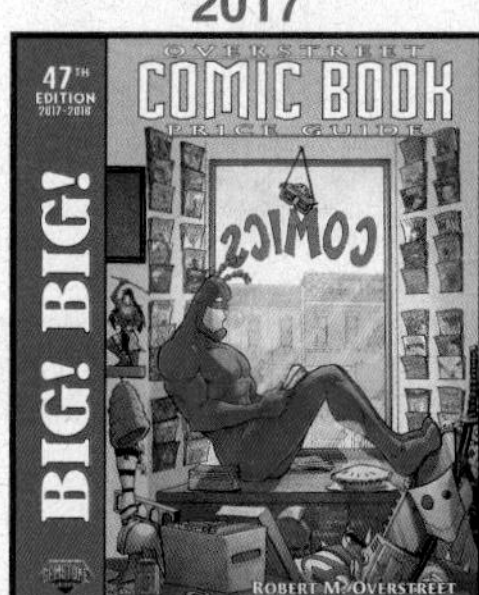

#47 Big Big CBPG
$47.50

2018

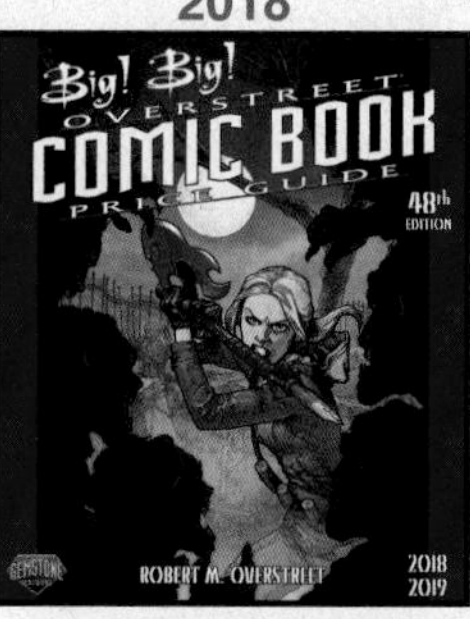

#48 Big Big CBPG
$47.50

2019

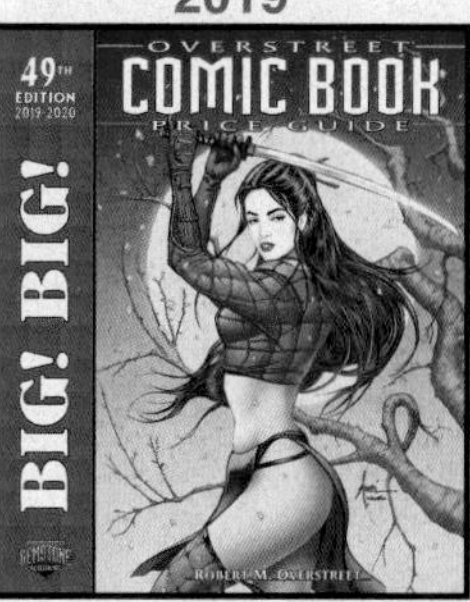

#49 Big Big CBPG
$49.50

2020

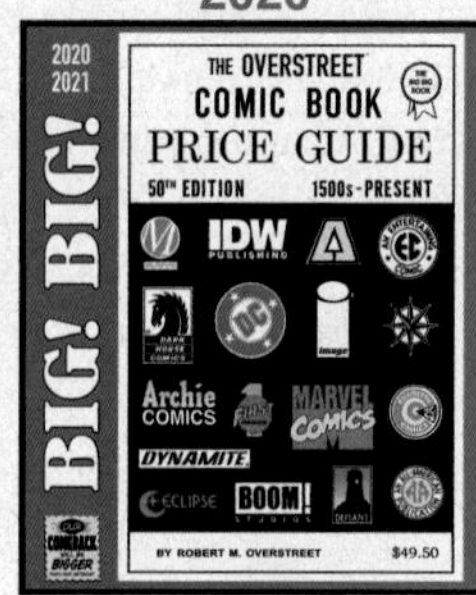

#50 Big Big CBPG
$49.50

ADVERTISERS' INDEX

A

B

C

D

E

F

G

H

J

HERITAGE®

COMICS & COMIC ART AUCTIONS

WHEN IT'S TIME TO SELL, CONSIGN TO HERITAGE

THE WORLD'S LARGEST COLLECTIBLES AUCTIONEER

1.25 Million+ Online Bidder-Members

We have provided cash advances as high as $10 million against individual comic consignments

2.33 Million+ different people visit our website each month on average (source: SimilarWeb.com, January 2021), no other comic dealer even comes close.

SOLD FOR $600,000! 11/2019

SOLD FOR $132,000! 1/2021

SOLD FOR $1,260,000! 11/2019

To discuss selling your comics or art at auction, call or email us today!

TO LEARN HOW HERITAGE GETS YOU MORE MONEY, SEE OUR ADS ON PAGES 6 & 7, 71, AND 1214!

DALLAS | NEW YORK | BEVERLY HILLS | SAN FRANCISCO | CHICAGO | PALM BEACH
LONDON | PARIS | GENEVA | AMSTERDAM | HONG KONG

Always Accepting Quality Consignments in 40+ Categories
Immediate Cash Advances Available

HERITAGE AUCTIONS
THE WORLD'S LARGEST COLLECTIBLES AUCTIONEER